AF575213

Who's Who Among American High School Students®

Honoring Tomorrow's Leaders Today®

1995|1996

Thirtieth Annual Edition

Volume XI

Educational Communications, Inc.®

Students are listed alphabetically within the state where they attend school. Students featured in this volume attended school in the following states:

Arkansas, Kansas, Oklahoma

Who's Who Among American High School Students® is a publication of Educational Communications, Inc. of Lake Forest, Illinois and has no connection with "Who's Who in America" and its publisher, Marquis Who's Who, Inc.

Educational Communications, Inc.
721 N. McKinley Road
Lake Forest, IL 60045

Printed in U.S.A.

Vol. I ISBN 1-56244-118-3
Vol. II ISBN 1-56244-119-1
Vol. III ISBN 1-56244-120-5
Vol. IV ISBN 1-56244-121-3
Vol. V ISBN 1-56244-122-1
Vol. VI ISBN 1-56244-123-X
Vol. VII ISBN 1-56244-124-8
Vol. VIII ISBN 1-56244-125-6
Vol. IX ISBN 1-56244-126-4
Vol. X ISBN 1-56244-127-2
Vol. XI ISBN 1-56244-128-0
Vol. XII ISBN 1-56244-129-9
Vol. XIII ISBN 1-56244-130-2
Vol. XIV ISBN 1-56244-131-0
Vol. XV ISBN 1-56244-132-9
Vol. XVI ISBN 1-56244-133-7
Vol. XVII ISBN 1-56244-134-5
Vol. XVIII ISBN 1-56244-135-3
18 Volume Set ISBN 1-56244-117-5

Library of Congress Catalog Card Number 68-43796

Table of Contents

Summon the Heroes*

Summon the heroes. The community heroes. The 10,000 American heroes who were part of the 1996 Olympic Torch Relay. They started the 15,000 mile trek across the United States in Los Angeles and ended 84 days later in Atlanta at the opening ceremonies of the 26th Olympiad.

Heroes. Community heroes. Ten thousand American heroes nominated and selected to carry the flame symbolizing the continuity between the ancient and modern Games. They weren't star athletes. They weren't celebrities. They weren't connected to corporations that paid hefty fees to participate. No, they were regular people who, because of their goodwill, their spirit of volunteerism, and their contributions to their communities have added more light to the world than the Olympic flame itself.

It isn't surprising that many of the participants in the Olympic torch relay are students and teachers who are included in *The National Dean's List, Who's Who Among American High School Students* and *Who's Who Among America's Teachers.* Educational·Communications, Inc. salutes these heroes and is proud to honor them in our publications. Their lives exemplify the Olympic Creed:

> *The most important thing . . . is not to win but to take part, just as the most important thing in life is not the triumph but the struggle. The essential thing is not to have conquered but to have fought well.*

Jennifer Kurdy, a Junior at Bishop Kelly High School in Boise, Idaho is one of the students included in *Who's Who Among American High School Students* who was selected to be a participant in the 1996 Olympic Torch Relay. Featured on NBC's Coca-Cola Presents the Olympic Torch Relay, Jennifer is a Congressional Award Winner, a state tennis champion, plays the violin and counsels children. Her academic, personal and community accomplishments earned her this "opportunity of a lifetime". We salute Jennifer's achievements and all of the student and teacher participants who represented the educational community.

*"Summon the Heroes" is the title of John Williams' dramatic theme music featured in the television coverage of the 1996 Olympic Games.

PAUL C. KROUSE
Publisher

Publisher's Corner

Waving the Flag — Then & Now

As I was driving to my office on the morning of June 3, 1996, I saw a large crowd of people of all ages gathering around the railroad station and town square. Many of the little children were waving miniature American flags and lots of adults were toting cameras. Scattered throughout the throng were a number of American Legion members wearing their distinctive caps. I parked my car and walked across the street to find out what was going on. It seems that I was the only person in town who didn't know (or forgot) that the Olympic train carrying the torch was going to be passing through and making a short stop in Lake Forest.

As I was wandering through the crowd waiting for the train, it occurred to me that 30 years ago my wife and I created *Who's Who Among American High School Students.*[1] In 1966 most teenagers, particularly upperclassmen in high school and most college students were being characterized in a negative manner due to their demonstrations against the escalating war in Vietnam. *Who's Who* was created to balance the coverage. Flags were part of the scene 30 years ago too, except kids were burning them, not waving them.

As the train appeared in the distance, the chattering of the crowd diminished and we all stood quietly listening as the familiar train sounds approached closer and closer. When the train slowed to a stop at our depot, which was decorated with red, white and blue bunting, the crowd began clapping and cheering in unison, without any prompting whatsoever. The little children, some perched on their fathers' shoulders waved their flags proudly. It was such a warm and thrilling feeling. With all due respect to the political convictions of the young people who were burning flags 30 years ago, I must admit I enjoyed this demonstration much more.

Today as we debate the relevance of values education, whether they should be taught in the home or school or both, I can't help wonder where patriotism fits into the mix since it is so rarely discussed and even more rarely experienced. When I go to a ball game and the Star Spangled Banner is played, I notice that only a few people seem to know the words. I understand the controversy about school prayer, but I don't understand why our national anthem isn't taught or sung in all schools today.

In my youth, virtually all young men had to fulfill a military obligation and the cold war was a constant threat to world peace. Most of my peers had a parent or relative who served in World War II or Korea so patriotism was part and parcel of the "growing up" process. How do we instill a feeling of patriotism in our youth when there is no compulsory military training, no obligation to give something back to our country (not just taking what it has to offer), and a global economy where our business partners may work across an ocean, not just across the street? Is patriotism passé? If it is, what's next for the junk heap?

I never considered myself a super patriot or a left or right wing radical. In fact, I have often referred to myself as "a flaming moderate". Yet, the scene at the train station made me feel good and proud to be an American. Maybe I'm just a dinosaur, but I don't want anyone to miss the feelings I experienced. Let's all think about what we may miss and what we all stand to lose if patriotism becomes passé.

1. *The National Dean's List* was first published in 1978. *Who's Who Among America's Teachers* was first published in 1990.

Who's Who Review

A Summary of Objectives, Policies and Programs

Since 1967, *Who's Who Among American High School Students*® has been committed to honoring outstanding students for their achievements in academics, athletics, school and community service. Our first edition recognized 13,000 students from 4,000 high schools; the current, 30th edition, published in eighteen regional volumes, honors 751,929 high school students representing approximately 18,000 of the 22,000 public, private and parochial high schools nationwide.

The growth, acceptance and preeminence of *Who's Who Among American High School Students* as the leading student recognition publication in the nation can be attributed to the involvement of educators in the policy-making areas of our programs.

Specifically, we must acknowledge the contributions of our Committee on Ethics, Standards and Practices, a group of distinguished educators representing secondary and post-secondary education.

The standards developed by the committee have been used as a model by several education associations who have created their own guidelines for evaluating student recognition programs on a uniform basis. *Who's Who* is proud of its well-documented leadership role in promoting standards and ethics for all student recognition programs.

The *Who's Who* standards are distributed to 80,000 high school principals, guidance counselors and other faculty members each year. The committee meets regularly and brings a perspective to the company which assures students and school administrators that *Who's Who* policies and programs are compatible with the objectives of the educational community.

WHO'S WHO annually sponsors scholarships for American Legion Auxiliary Girls Nation. President Clinton greets one of the winners, Amy Bice of Idaho.

Who's Who Standards

Our company's adherence to the standards listed below has been attested to by an independent public accounting firm. A copy of their report is available upon request. Copies of the standards/guidelines adopted by other education associations are also available upon request.

1. Nominations will be from established organizations that work with and for the benefit of high school aged youth. Under no circumstances will recommendations be accepted from students, their parents or solicited from standard commercial lists.
2. Criteria for students to be selected will be clearly defined and reflect high personal achievement.
3. Listing in *Who's Who* will not require purchase of any items or payments of any fees.
4. Additional programs and services which are available to those listed in *Who's Who* at cost to the students, will be clearly described in the literature provided.
5. A refund policy will be clearly stated in all literature.
6. Nominators will be able to recommend students without releasing confidential data or fear of having confidential data released by program sponsors.
7. Student information will be confidential and will not be released except where authorized by the student.
8. Home addresses will not be published in the book or made public in any way.
9. Under no circumstances will *Who's Who* sell student information or lists.
10. The publisher will describe, disseminate and verify the methods employed to assure national/regional recognition to students listed.
11. The publisher will respond to all inquiries, complaints and requests for relevant background information.
12. The basis of the scholarship program competition will be defined. Number and amount of awards will be stated, lists of previous winners will be available. Finalist selection process and funding method will be clearly defined. Employees or their relatives will not be eligible for scholarships.
13. There will be an advisory council (external to the organization) to review and make recommendations regarding the policies, procedures and evaluation process of the *Who's Who* programs.
14. The publisher will set forth in writing and make publicly known the policies and procedures it follows in the implementation of these standards.

Former President Reagan greeted MissTeenage America, Amy Sue Brenkacz. WHO'S WHO sponsored a $5,000 scholarship for Miss Teenage America and listed Amy Sue in the publication.

Programs and Benefits for Students

Scholarship Awards:
From $4,000 in 1968 to over $210,000 annually

The Educational Communications Scholarship Foundation®, a not-for-profit organization funded by the publishing company, sponsors two scholarship award programs which award over $210,000 in scholarships each year. More than $1,947,000 has been funded to date.

The Educational Communications Scholarship Foundation's program represents one of the ten largest scholarship programs funded by a single private sector organization. The Foundation is listed in numerous directories on financial aid and scholarships.

The College Referral Service® (CRS):
Links students with colleges

Who's Who students receive a catalog listing 1,800 four-year colleges and universities. They may complete a form indicating which institutions they wish us to notify of their honorary award. This service links interested students with colleges and universities.

Several hundred colleges have indicated that the CRS and the publication are valuable reference sources in their recruitment programs. (Surveys from colleges available for inspection.)

Grants-in-Aid:
Financial support for organizations who work with or for students

Since 1975, we have funded grants to youth and educational organizations to support their student programs and scholarships. A partial listing of grants issued or committed to date of over $600,000 appears in this review.

Local Newspaper Publicity:
Additional recognition for honor students

Over 2,000 newspapers nationwide receive rosters of their local students featured in the publication with appropriate background information. (Home addresses are not included in these releases.)

News anchor Morton Dean reports WHO'S WHO survey findings on ABC's Good Morning America.

Annual Survey of High Achievers®:
The views of student leaders are as important as their achievements

Since 1969, we have polled the attitudes and opinions of *Who's Who* students on timely issues. This study provides students with a collective voice otherwise not available to them. A summary of the poll is sent to leaders in government, education and the press.

College-Bound Digest®:
What students need to know

A compilation of articles written by prominent educators covering topics of interest to college-bound students. The Digest appears in the introductory section of *Who's Who* and is made available to school guidance offices and students.

Dan Rather discusses the results of the WHO'S WHO survey on the CBS Evening News.

Teachers Nomination Program:
The Best Teachers in America Selected by the Best Students®

All students listed in *Who's Who* may nominate one of their former teachers for recognition in *Who's Who Among America's Teachers®*. Thus, students acknowledge those teachers, counselors and coaches who have contributed significantly to their success and growth.

Memberships:

American Association for Higher Education
American Association of School Administrators
American Library Association
American School Counselors Association
Better Business Bureau of Chicago & Northern Illinois, Inc.
Distributive Education Clubs of America, National Advisory Board
Educational Press Association
National Association of Student Financial Aid Administrators
National FFA Foundation, Executive Sponsor
National School Public Relations Association

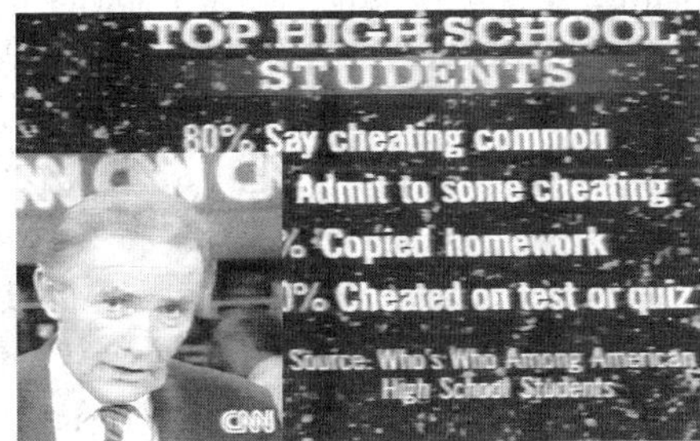

CNN's Bob Kain reviews the data from the WHO'S WHO student poll.

Major Policies and Procedures

Free Book Program:
Guarantees extensive recognition through wide circulation

Who's Who sponsors the largest Free Book Program of any publisher in any field. The book is sent free to all participating high schools and youth organizations and offered free to all 7,500 libraries and to all four-year colleges and universities.

This extensive distribution system provides meaningful, national recognition for listed students among institutions traditionally concerned with student achievement, and makes it convenient for students to view their published biography without purchasing the book.

The recognition and reference purpose(s) of *Who's Who Among American High School Students* have been acknowledged in the favorable review of the publication by the Reference and Subscription Books Reviews Committee of the American Library Association.

Financial Policies:
Legitimate honors do not cost the recipient money

There are no financial requirements whatsoever contingent upon recognition in *Who's Who Among American High School Students.*

For students who do purchase the publication or any related award insignia, satisfaction is guaranteed. Refunds are always issued on request.

Nominating Procedures:
Representation from all areas of student achievement

Each year, all 22,000 public, private and parochial high schools are invited to nominate students who have achieved a "B" grade point average or better and demonstrated leadership in academics, athletics or extracurricular activities.

Approximately 15,000 high schools participate in our program by nominating students. An additional 3,000 to 5,000 schools are represented by their outstanding students as a result of nominations received from bona fide youth organizations, churches with organized youth activities, scholarship agencies and civic and service groups. Many of our nation's major youth groups participate in our program by nominating their student leaders.

Editing:
Maintains the integrity of the honor

When biography forms are submitted for publication, they are all reviewed to monitor compliance with our high standards. In the past 20 years, 441,041 students were disqualified by our editors because they did not meet our standards, including over 103,500 students who ordered the publication. More than $3,019,100 in orders was returned to these students. Our standards are never compromised by the profit motive. (Auditor's verification available upon request.)

Verification of Data:
To monitor the accuracy of self reported data

A nationally respected accounting firm conducts regular, independent audits of published biographical data. Previous audits reveal that up to 94.5 percent of the data published was substantially accurate. (Complete studies available upon request.)

Who's Who Student Profile

Statistics from 1996 Edition

General Listing
Total Number of Students • 751,929
Seniors • 173,900
Juniors • 278,694
Sophomores • 211,586
Freshmen • 87,749
Who's Who Students as Percentage of 14,000,000 High School Students Enrolled Nationwide • 5%
Females • 65%
Males • 35%

Academics
Grade Point Average (% rounded)
"A+/A" • 64%
"B+/B" • 36%
Honor Roll • 584,874
National Honor Society • 182,210
Valedictorian/Salutatorian • 10,947

Leadership Activities
Student Council • 97,609
Senior Class Officers • 29,202
Junior Class Officers • 52,164
Sophomore Class Officers • 61,014
Freshman Class Officers • 59,534

Major Vocational Organizations
4-H • 42,122
National FFA Organization • 27,049
Distributive Education Clubs of America • 7,923
Business Professionals of America • 9,905

Athletics
Basketball • 139,182
Track • 107,895
Cheerleading/Pom Pon • 73,672
Volleyball • 69,482
Football • 66,908
Soccer • 61,338
Baseball • 47,660
Tennis • 46,245
Cross Country • 44,050
Wrestling • 17,514

Music/Performing Arts
Orchestra/Band • 186,273
Chorus • 127,633
Drama • 73,717
School Play/Stage Crew • 112,993

Miscellaneous
Church/Temple Activities • 299,955
Yearbook • 84,043
School Paper • 61,824
Students Against Driving Drunk • 69,435

Grants to Youth and Educational Organizations*

The Grants program funded by *Who's Who* was inaugurated in 1975 to support educational programs and activities committed to assisting our nation's youth. Following is a partial list of grant recipients to date:

American Association for Gifted Children - $2,000, 1 Grant
American Children's Television Festival - $2,000, 1 Grant
American Council on the Teaching of Foreign Language - $500, 1 Grant
American Indian College Fund - $2,600, 2 Grants
American Legion Auxiliary Girls Nation - $39,500, 18 Grants
American Legion Boys Nation - $51,500, 19 Grants
Animal Welfare Institute - $1,582, 2 Grants
Black United Fund - $5,000, 1 Grant
Business Professionals of America - $56,000, 18 Grants
The Chicago Youth Success Foundation - $3,000, 2 Grants
Civil Air Patrol - $3,000, 3 Grants
The College Board - $10,500, 1 Grant
Colorado Forum of Educational Leaders - $1,000, 1 Grant
Contemporary-Family Life Curriculum - $1,500, 1 Grant
Dale Boatright Memorial Fund - $1,000, 1 Grant
Distributive Education Clubs of America (DECA) - $56,000, 22 Grants
Earthwatch - $3,000, 3 Grants
Education Roundtable - $5,000, 1 Grant
Fellowship of Christian Athletes - $12,800, 5 Grants
Hugh O'Brian Youth Foundation - $4,000, 2 Grants
Joint Council on Economic Education - $10,000, 3 Grants
Junior Achievement - $13,000, 8 Grants
Junior Classical League - $6,000, 6 Grants
Junior Engineering Technical Society - $23,000, 12 Grants
Key Club International - $11,000, 11 Grants
Law and Economic Center, University of Miami Law School - $4,500, 1 Grant
LEAD or LEAVE Education Fund - $2,000, 1 Grant
Lester Benz Memorial Fund - $1,000, 1 Grant
Miss American Co-Ed - $10,500, 13 Grants
Miss Teenage America Scholarship Program - $33,000, 8 Grants
Modern Miss - $2,500, 5 Grants
Modern Music Masters - $4,500, 2 Grants
Mu Alpha Theta - $28,700, 10 Grants
National Cheerleaders Association - $14,100, 15 Grants
National Exchange Club - $3,500, 2 Grants
National Federation for Catholic Youth Ministry - $1,500, 1 Grant
National Forensic League - $11,000, 6 Grants
National Foundation for Advancement in the Arts - $13,000, 13 Grants
National 4-H Council - $20,000, 8 Grants
National FFA Foundation - $40,900, 20 Grants
National Scholastic Press Association - $2,000, 2 Grants
National Society of Professional Engineers - $1,000, 1 Grant
Performing & Visual Arts Society (PAVAS) - $4,000, 2 Grants
The President's Committee on Employment of People with Disabilities - $6,000, 6 Grants
Quill and Scroll Society - $19,000, 15 Grants
Soroptimist International of the Americas, Inc. - $3,000, 3 Grants
Special Olympics, Inc. - $1,000, 1 Grant

**As of September 30, 1996*

▲ Peter Jennings, anchorman on ABC's World News Tonight, introduces correspondent Michelle Norris who interviewed high school students and WHO'S WHO publisher Paul Krouse about the recent study, "A Portrait Of A Generation: 25 Years of Teen Behavior and Attitudes".

◀ NBC Today Show newsmen, Matt Lauer and Bob Kur, report on the findings of the WHO's WHO student surveys.

Also from Educational Communications, Inc.

The National Dean's List

The eighteenth edition of *The National Dean's List* recognizes 125,000 outstanding college students from 2,500 colleges and universities. Each year $35,000 in scholarships are awarded.

Who's Who Among America's Teachers

The fourth edition of *Who's Who Among America's Teachers*, published in 1996, lists 120,000 teachers from grades K-12, colleges and graduate schools.

Who's Who Committee on Ethics, Standards and Practices

Dr. Wesley L. Apker
President
The Wescat Corporation
Sacramento, CA

Dr. Adrienne Y. Bailey
Senior Consultant to the Council of the Great City Schools
Washington, DC

Dr. James T. Barry
Vice President for Advancement
Avila College
Kansas City, MO

Dr. S. Norman Feingold
President
National Career & Counseling Services
Washington, DC

Edward B. Fiske
Author
The Fiske Guide To Colleges and Smart Schools, Smart Kids
Alstead, NH

Charles R. Hilston
Executive Director Emeritus
Association of Wisconsin School Administrators
Madison, WI

Dr. John R. Lucy
Superintendent of Schools
District 171
Lansing, IL

Dr. Paul W. Masem
Superintendent
Cleveland Heights-University Heights City School District
University Heights, OH

Robert G. McLendon
Vice President and Dean for Admissions and Financial Aid
Brevard College
Brevard, NC

Dr. Vincent Reed
Vice President for Communications
The Washington Post
Washington, DC

Dr. Neill Sanders
Dean of Undergraduate Enrollment Policy & Management
University of Rochester
Rochester, NY

The Educational Communications Scholarship Foundation

From a pool of such extremely capable students, it is always difficult to select winners for these scholarships. Our dedicated committee of educators reviews several thousand applications and evaluates each with attention to grade point average, aptitude test scores, extra-curricular activities and/or work experience and general background information. Semi-finalists were required to write an essay which was an additional criterion in selecting the winners. Some consideration was also given to financial need.

In 1968, the first year scholarships were awarded, a total of $4,000 was distributed to qualified students. This year $150,000 was awarded with 150 students each receiving $1,000. For the 1996-97 academic year, 175 scholarships will be awarded.

Educational Communications Scholarship Foundation Committee members meet to select scholarship winners. Each winner receives a $1,000 award.

The 1995-96 Scholarship Winners

Billy R. Abercrombie
Bauxite High School
Benton, AR
University of Arkansas at Little Rock
Little Rock, AR

Melissa K. Adam
Lincolnview High School
Fort Jennings, OH
University of Toledo
Toledo, OH

Chinweze N. Ahaghotu
Calvin Coolidge Senior High School
Washington, DC
Harvard University
Cambridge, MA

Amanda Leigh Albrecht
William Horlick High School
Racine, WI
University of Wisconsin
Kenosha, WI

Jaclyn Allen
Moore High School
Norman, OK
University of Oklahoma
Norman, OK

Anthony Arguez
Miami Southridge Senior High School
Miami, FL
Florida State University
Tallahasse, FL

Sabrina A. Artale
Grover Cleveland High School
Ridgewood, NY
Columbia University
New York, NY

Teodoro Arvizo, III
Oklahoma School of Science and Math
Stillwater, OK
Massachusetts Institute of Technology
Cambridge, MA

Erik Y. Assadourian
Avon Old Farms School
Avon, CT
Dartmouth College
Hanover, NH

Sally Anne Bachman
Roosevelt High School
Portland, OR
Montana State University at Bozeman
Bozeman, MT

Brian D. Bank
Joseph Case High School
Swansea, MA
Duke University
Durham, NC

Sarah J. Bates
Sisseton High School
Sisseton, SD
University of Notre Dame
Notre Dame, IN

Erin Elizabeth Baugh
Cookeville High School
Cookeville, TN
University of Tennessee
Knoxville, TN

Samuel T. Bishop
Lewis and Clark High School
Spokane, WA
University of Washington
Seattle, WA

Jeffrey D. Brown
Cypress Falls High School
Houston, TX
Baylor University
Waco, TX

Ann M. Bruegger
Minnesota Valley Lutheran High School
North Mankato, MN
University of Minnesota
Minneapolis, MN

David A. Bruns
Aspermont High School
Old Glory, TX
Texas Lutheran University
Seguin, TX

Kent A. Carmichael
Blair High School
Blair, NE
University of Nebraska at Lincoln
Lincoln, NE

Jerry Chu
George Washington High School
San Bruno, CA
University of California at Berkeley
Berkeley, CA

Erin Elizabeth Conlan
Duke Ellington School of the Arts
Ormond Beach, FL
University of Florida
Gainesville, FL

Joseph D. Crawfis
Pandora-Gilboa High School
Ottawa, OH
Kent State University
Kent, OH

Jennifer Lynn Custard
Elmwood-Murdock High School
Elmwood, NE
Nebraska Wesleyan University
Lincoln, NE

Mary Therese Dahling
Cathedral High School
Apple Valley, MN
Vanderbilt University
Nashville, TN

Lan Bao-Thanh Dang
James A. Garfield High School
Los Angeles, CA
Harvard University
Cambridge, MA

Roger Da Silva
Seton Hall Prep
Elizabeth, NJ
University of Pennsylvania
Philadelphia, PA

Dakota A. Derr
Hillside Academy
Burlington Junction, MO
Northwest Missouri State University
Maryville, MO

Gina Di Canio
Sachem High School
Lake Grove, NY
University of Virginia
Charlottesville, VA

Marisa Pamela Dolled
Freehold Borough High School
Englishtown, NJ
Cornell University
Ithaca, NY

Katherine B. Dougherty
Aquinas Institute
Rochester, NY
Siena College
Loudonville, NY

William J. Doyle
Newaygo High School
Grant, MI
Alma College
Alma, MI

The 1995-96 Scholarship Winners

Steven Edward Driver
Hudson High School
Hudson, OH
Case Western Reserve University
Cleveland, OH

Amber A. Dufseth
Austin E. Lathrop High School
Fairbanks, AK
Reed College
Portland, OR

Robert G. Dvorak
Grand Forks Central High
Grand Forks, ND
University of North Dakota
Grand Forks, ND

Laura K. Ediger
Aurora High School
Aurora, NE
Galvin College
Grand Rapids, MI

Jeremy Daniel Ellis
Spruce Creek High School
Ormond Beach, FL
Duke University
Durham, NC

Sheri Engebretsen
Mineral County High School
Hawthorne, NV
St. Stephens University
Calais, ME

Daniel Floyd
Westminster Christian Academy
Madison, AL
Mississippi State University
Mississippi State, MS

Marie J. Frehulfer
Broadalbin-Perth High School
Galway, NY
Hudson Valley Community College
Troy, NY

Timothy J. Fuller
Chicago Christian High School
Crete, IL
University of Chicago
Chicago, IL

Shana K. Galeon
Baldwin High School
Baldwin Harbor, NY
New York University
New York, NY

Michelle Marie Galvez
Chester W. Nimitz High School
Houston, TX
Columbia University
New York, NY

Brad Garret
Dickson County High School
Dickson, TN
Washington University
St. Louis, MO

Heather Lynne Garten
Pine Ridge High School
Deltona, FL
Stetson University
Deland, FL

Karen R. Gertz
Estero High School
Fort Myers, FL
Maryville College
Maryville, TN

Zola Marie Gibson
Burns High School
Burns, OR
Eastern Oregon State College
La Grande, OR

Christopher K. Gotberg
University City High School
San Diego, CA
University of California at San Diego
La Jolla, CA

Rodney Gray
Claiborne County High School
New Tazewell, TN
University of Florida
Gainesville, FL

Jessica Groathouse
Weeping Water High School
Weeping Water, NE
University of Nebraska at Lincoln
Lincoln, NE

Edin Hajdarpasic
Gulf High School
New Port Richey, FL
New College of University of South Florida
Sarasota, FL

Melissa Jo Hamilton
IN Academy for Sci, Math & Humanities
Crown Point, IN
Northwestern University
Evanston, IL

Allysa Hampton
Martin Luther King Magnet High School
Nashville, TN
Free Will Baptist Bible College
Nashville, TN

Chris Hardee
J H Rose High School
Greenville, NC
North Carolina State University
Raleigh, NC

Cynthia A. Harmon
Bandys High School
Claremont, NC
Wake Forest University
Winston-Salem, NC

Christina L. Hayes
Ashe Central High School
Crumpler, NC
Appalachian State University
Boone, NC

Joshua Daniel Hays
Fort Dodge Senior High School
Fort Dodge, IA
Iowa State University
Ames, IA

Steven R. Henderson
Cambridge High School
Isanti, MN
University of St. Thomas
St. Paul, MN

Maria Hollendonner
Boardman High School
Youngstown, OH
Northwestern University
Evanston, IL

George Hsu
Midlothian High School
Midlothian, VA
University of Virginia
Charlottesville, VA

Arlie S. Huff
Phillips Academy
Collegeville, PA
Northwestern University
Evanston, IL

Anna Jan
Mt. Lebanon Senior High School
Pittsburgh, PA
Washington University
St. Louis, MO

The 1995-96 Scholarship Winners

Yusuf Johnson
Amphitheater High School
Tucson, AZ
University of Arizona
Tucson, AZ

Amos Nathanael Jones
P.L. Dunbar High School
Lexington, KY
Emory University
Atlanta, GA

Kristine J. Kalanges
Gresham High School
Gresham, OR
University of Puget Sound
Tacoma, WA

Whitney Lyn Kalin
Northeast High School
Clarksville, TN
Vanderbilt University
Nashville, TN

Moronai K. Kanekoa
Maui High School
Kahului, HI
University of Hawaii at Manoa
Honolulu, HI

Charles A. Keyes, Jr.
Binghamton High School
Binghamton, NY
Harvard University
Cambridge, MA

Kathy Kim
Whitney High School
Cerritos, CA
University of California at Berkeley
Berkeley, CA

Jordanna M. King
Hunter-Tannersville Central School
Elka Park, NY
Vassar College
Poughkeepsie, NY

John M. King, IV
Spruce Creek High School
Port Orange, FL
Johns Hopkins University
Baltimore, MD

Nathan Boyd Kitchen
Uintah High School
Vernal, UT
Brigham Young University
Provo, UT

Nathan I. Kleinschmit
Canton High School
Canton, SD
South Dakota School of Mines & Technology
Rapid City, SD

Boris Kozinsky
Bellaire High School
Houston, TX
Massachusetts Institute of Technology
Cambridge, MA

SreyRam Kuy
Crescent Valley High School
Corvallis, OR
Oregon State University
Corvallis, OR

Jeremy C. La Valva
Delaware Valley Regional High School
Milford, NJ
University of Virginia
Charlottesville, VA

Long Phi Le
Tri-Cities High School
Hapeville, GA
Massachusetts Institute of Technology
Cambridge, MA

Janet Lee
Thomas S. Wootton High School
North Potomac, MD
University of Virginia
Charlottesville, VA

Adam Lefebvre
Weymouth High School
Weymouth, MA
Duquesne University
Pittsburgh, PA

Young-Soo Lim
Northern Valley Regional High School
Harrington Park, NJ
Harvard University
Cambridge, MA

Gamon Cole Long
Charlotte Country Day School
Charlotte, NC
Cornell University
Ithaca, NY

Joshua N. Long
Ashtabula High School
Ashtabula, OH
Grove City College
Grove City, PA

Gary Look
Franklin High School
Seattle, WA
University of Washington
Seattle, WA

Janine Lopez-Soto
Jose Felipe Zayas High School
Coamo, PR
University of Puerto Rico at Mayaguez
Mayaguez, PR

Christin Lundblad
Jefferson Senior High School
Alexandria, MN
Bethel College
St. Paul, MN

Berta J. Lyles
Rancho Buena Vista High School
Vista, CA
University of California at San Diego
La Jolla, CA

Curtis J. Mahoney
Russell High School
Russell, KS
Harvard University
Cambridge, MA

Robert Curtis Malkovich, Jr.
Duluth East High School
Duluth, MN
University of Wisconsin at Madison
Madison, WI

Randy G. Mangelsen
Siren High School
Shell Lake, WI
Lawrence University
Appleton, WI

Jason Martin
Centennial High School
Boise, ID
Bard College
Annandale-on-Hudson, NY

Kory Martin
Seymour High School
Seymour, TX
Rice University
Houston, TX

Lisa M. Mathena
Park High School
Cottage Grove, MN
North Central Bible College
Minneapolis, MN

The 1995-96 Scholarship Winners

Benjamin R. Mc Daniel
Newton High School
Newton, KS
Hutchinson Community College
Hutchinson, KS

Michael B. Mc Donald
Kirkwood High School
Kirkwood, MO
University of Missouri
Columbia, MO

Adrienne Messenger
Morgantown High School
Morgantown, WV
Carnegie Mellon University
Pittsburgh, PA

Ryan B. Meyer
Mazama High School
Klamath Falls, OR
Vassar College
Poughkeepsie, NY

Alexandria Miller
Juniata High School
Mifflintown, PA
Eastern Mennonite University
Harrisonburg, VA

Kristie Moses
Rolling Meadows High School
Rolling Meadows, IL
Indiana University
Bloomington, IN

Matthew Niva
Memorial High School
Madison, WI
Cornell University
Ithaca, NY

David John Nothnagle
New Hampton School
Center Harbor, NH
University of Rochester
Rochester, NY

Malgorzata J. Ochocinska
City High School
Grand Rapids, MI
University of Michigan
Ann Arbor, MI

Ryan P. O'Donnell
O'Dea High School
Seattle, WA
University of New Hampshire
Durham, NH

Michelle Oliveira
Portsmouth High School
Portsmouth, RI
University of New Hampshire
Durham, NH

Jill Olthouse
Clay Senior High School
Findlay, OH
Bowling Green State University
Bowling Green, OH

Sean O'Neill
St. Louis University High School
St. Louis, MO
University of Chicago
Chicago, IL

Michael Ryan Osterman
Redmond High School
Redmond, WA
Northwestern University
Evanston, IL

Martin Luther Owens
George Washington High School
South Bend, IN
Harvard University
Cambridge, MA

Alexa Panagoulis
Plymouth Regional High School
Plymouth, NH
Duke University
Durham, NC

Lora Eukyung Park
Federal Way High School
Federal Way, WA
University of Washington
Seattle, WA

Nancy E. Pieper
North Knox High School
Edwardsport, IN
Vincennes University
Vincennes, IN

Jaime S. Puderer
St. Mary's Dominican High School
Terrytown, LA
Texas A & M University
College Station, TX

Justin P. Radick
Thornton Fractional South High School
Lansing, IL
Harvey Mudd College
Claremont, CA

Kimberly N. Reagans
Crockett High School
Crockett, TX
Spelman College
Atlanta, GA

Meredith L. Reaves
Liberty High School
Coleman Falls, VA
The College of William and Mary
Williamsburg, VA

Amber Reinker
Goodrich High School
Grand Blanc, MI
University of Nebraska at Lincoln
Lincoln, NE

Louise Rew
Mountain Crest High School
Providence, UT
Brigham Young University
Provo, UT

Rebecca L. Riggs
Greensburg Community High School
Greensburg, IN
Taylor University
Upland, IN

Jennifer M. Rupnow
Lake Catholic High School
Willoughby, OH
Ohio State University
Columbus, OH

Andrew Rymer
Suffern High School
Suffern, NY
Dartmouth College
Hanover, NH

Alexandria Victoria Sams
DuPont Manual High School
Louisville, KY
Yale University
New Haven, CT

David A. Schaefer
Benton High School
Benton, AR
University of Southern California
Los Angeles, CA

Lee R. Schnee
Washburn Rural High School
Topeka, KS
University of Kansas
Lawrence, KS

The 1995-96 Scholarship Winners

Mark A. Seidl
Kuemper Catholic
High School
Coon Rapids, IA
Iowa State University
Ames, IA

A. Noel Shanks
Burlington Christian
School
Niota, IL
Greenville College
Greenville, IL

James Pat Simmons, III
Bellarmine College
Preparatory
San Jose, CA
Princeton University
Princeton, NJ

Barbara Sit
Whitney M. Young
Magnet High School
Chicago, IL
Cornell University
Ithaca, NY

Jessica Elaine Smith
Union-Endicott High
School
Endicott, NY
Bucknell University
Lewisburg, PA

Stephen Son
Norco High School
Corona, CA
University of
California at Berkeley
Berkeley, CA

Melissa Alice Sparr
Andrew High School
Tinley Park, IL
University of Illinois at
Urbana-Champaign
Champaign, IL

Laela Sturdy
Cooper City High
School
Cooper City, FL
Harvard University
Cambridge, MA

Andrea K. Suh
Lexington Christian
Academy
Belmont, MA
Stanford University
Stanford, CA

Kate A. Szajkowski
Tunkhannock Area
High School
Dalton, PA
Johns Hopkins
University
Baltimore, MD

Olivette Grace Talbert
St. Paul's Episcopal
School
Theodore, AL
University of South
Alabama
Mobile, AL

Edward Wang Tamiso
Valdosta High School
Valdosta, GA
Georgia Institute of
Technology
Atlanta, GA

Elizabeth O'Toole
Tegins
St. Anthony's High
School
Great River, NY
Boston College
Chestnut Hill, MA

Jacqui Marie Terrill
Western Mennonite
School
Amity, OR
George Fox University
Newberg, OR

Pyper Marie Thaller
Judge Memorial High
School
Salt Lake City, UT
Lake Forest College
Lake Forest, IL

Colin Theriot
South Lafourche High
School
Larose, LA
Louisiana State
University
Baton Rouge, LA

Christina Tolman
Lafayette High School
Lexington, KY
University of Kentucky
Lexington, KY

Sarah B. Tomsyck
Divine Savior Holy
Angels High School
Milwaukee, WI
Knox College
Galesburg, IL

Elizabeth Uyen Tran
Louisiana School for
Math,Science & Arts
Alexandria, LA
Bryn Mawr College
Bryn Mawr, PA

Daniel A. Turner
Benson Polytechnic
High School
Portland, OR
Wheaton College
Wheaton, IL

Linda Marie Van
Bruggen
Litchville-Marion High
School
Marion, ND
North Dakota State
University
Fargo, ND

Jayson Charles Vantuyl
Central Computers
Unlimited High School
Claycomo, MO
Southwest Missouri
State University
Springfield, MO

Michelle S. Vernick
El Toro High School
Lake Forest, CA
Stanford University
Stanford, CA

Jackie R. Watters, Jr.
Washington High
School
Washington, NC
University of North
Carolina at Chapel Hill
Chapel Hill, NC

Melissa A. Weaver
Oxford Area High
School
Oxford, PA
Washington College
Chestertown, MD

Beth Wells
Poway High School
Poway, CA
Point Loma Nazarene
College
San Diego, CA

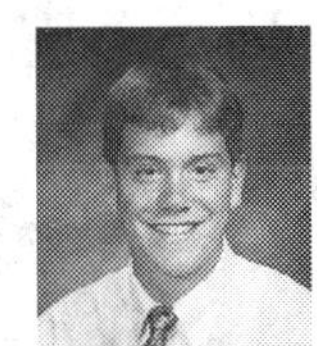
Liam M. West
Wahconah Regional
High School
Dalton, MA
Hamilton College
Clinton, NY

Amanda Whitney
Brighton High School
Commerce City, CO
Colorado State
University
Fort Collins, CO

Tiffany L. Williams
Thomas Jefferson High
School
Denver, CO
North Carolina A & T
State University
Greensboro, NC

Melissa Lynn
Woodvine
George Washington
High School
Commerce City, CO
University of Colorado
Boulder, CO

The 1995-96 Scholarship Winners

Lulu-Zhe Xu
Taylor Allderdice High School
Pittsburgh, PA
University of Pennsylvania
Philadelphia, PA

Scholarships From Grants

WHO'S WHO funds a grants program to support educational programs and activities (see page ix). Many of the grant recipients choose to award scholarships with their grant money. We are proud to feature a few of these scholarship winners below.

American Legion Auxiliary Girls Nation

Angela Aman
South Dakota

Katherine Franklin
West Virginia

American Legion Boys Nation

Rick Lam, Jr.
Oklahoma

James Wong
New Jersey

Business Professionals of America

Elesha Allen
Kansas

Hugh O'Brian Youth Foundation

Lauren Temmermand
New Jersey

Kathryn Barenberg
Arkansas

National FFA Foundation

Michael Boehm
Ohio

Ryan Isom
Idaho

Quill and Scroll Society

Laura Oppenheimer
Iowa

College-Bound Digest

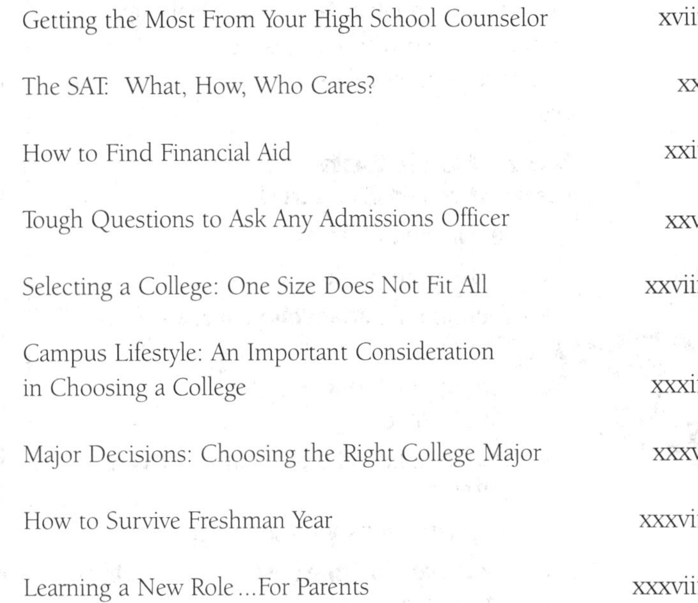

We wish to acknowledge the special contribution of Robert G. McLendon, Vice President and Dean for Admissions and Financial Aid, Brevard College, Brevard, North Carolina who was instrumental in selecting appropriate topics and authors for this publication

Getting the Most From Your High School Counselor

By James Warfield

Your high school counselor's job is to help you. Your job is to get to know your counselor so that he/she can help you in an effective manner. Helping your counselor help you requires open and frank discussions regarding your goals and personal plans.

Your High School Counselor Should:

- **know your abilities**
- **know your goals**
- **recommend academic course selections**
- **recommend which college entrance test to take**
- **recommend colleges that meet your criteria**
- **help you focus your ideas and goals**
- **assist you in applying for scholarships and financial aid**
- **most importantly, make you think**

Recommendations should be based upon your academic abilities and goals. This is a critical issue because the appropriateness of this advice is determined by the consistency between your aspirations and aptitudes. Verifying the accuracy of your self-perceptions is important in order to avoid sudden surprises caused by false hopes or unrealistic expectations or under-estimating your abilities and aiming too low. Your counselor exists to help you become everything you are capable of within a realistic framework.

College Entrance Exams

For many students, the college selection process begins with the PSAT, taken in the fall of the junior year. Your counselor should advise you which of the college entrance tests to take, SAT I, SAT II, ACT and AP, and when to take them. The type and location of college you apply to will determine which tests to take. The quality of the college, the quality of your own academic program, and whether or not you plan to apply Early Decision, will determine when you should take such tests. Many juniors don't know to which schools they'd like to apply, so advance planning is necessary in order to maintain open options.

Questions You Need to Know

Finding the right college will require you to know yourself, your likes and dislikes. In what kind of environment do you see yourself being most comfortable? Can you picture yourself at a small college or a mid-size or large university setting? Do you want a college to be in a rural community, a suburb or to be in an urban environment? Do you want to be in a different geographic part of the country, or is being close to home important to you? What are some of your academic areas of interest? What kind of extracurricular offering do you want to participate in? As you answer these questions, the attributes of your ideal college will become more clear. Through discussion with your counselor you'll be able to assess your needs, and more clearly focus

your perceptions of yourself and of the schools you will be researching.

College Selection

Your counselor should help generate a list of colleges that meet your requirements by drawing upon his/her own wealth of knowledge or utilizing the many reference materials available.

Campus visits are the most effective means to determine if the college is right for you. When to visit is a matter of individual taste or need. Keep in mind that as you visit more schools your observational skills will become more sophisticated and your reflections of each will be altered. It may be more prudent to visit only those schools to which you have been accepted, after you have received all your admissions decisions.

As you narrow your choice of colleges, your counselor should review with you the possibilities of acceptance or rejection at each. At least one of your choices should be a safety choice, one in which you are almost guaranteed of being admitted.

Applications

After the list of colleges to which you are going to apply has been determined, it is your responsibility to obtain the application and meet deadline dates. Many colleges require a counselor's recommendation or a Secondary School Reference. Some require additional recommendations from specific teachers. Establish application procedures with your counselor so that he/she, the teacher, and school have adequate time to do their part in order to meet your deadline dates. If you are required to write an essay or personal statement, discuss this with your counselor and English teacher. These discussions serve several purposes: help you generate ideas and narrow topics that you wish to write about; provide you with suggestions that will enhance your applications; and provide the counselor with insights that will compliment your application.

It is your responsibility to file your applications on time, see that your test scores are sent to the admissions office, and file the financial aid applications. Your counselor will help you determine which scores to send, which financial aid form is required and how to fulfill these requirements.

Finding, selecting and applying to the colleges that are right for you is a long and studied process. It involves a lot of letter-writing, telephoning, research, weighing alternatives, and just plain old thinking. It's a decision-making process that requires questioning, information gathering, evaluation of the information and more questioning. This cycle is often repeated in order to make effective decisions. The better the decision-making process the more likely your college experience will be successful.

James Warfield is Director of Pupil Personnel at Lake Forest High School, Lake Forest, Illinois.

The SAT: What, How, Who Cares?

It's time to take the SAT. Your best strategy is to learn as much as you can about the test:

SAT I: *Reasoning Test.* This first part of the SAT is composed of both a verbal and a math section.

Verbal — half of the questions assess your ability to read and think critically. Through analogies, defining vocabulary words in the context of a passage and sentence completion questions, your reasoning abilities will be assessed.

Math — math problems are presented, some of which require you to produce your own answers instead of all multiple choice questions (calculators are encouraged).

SAT II: *Subject Tests.* This second part is optional; you take one or more tests if requested by the colleges to which you are applying. These are one-hour tests in subjects such as writing, literature, history, science, foreign languages, etc.

Can you prepare for the SAT? YES!

Whether you prepare on your own, with friends or through a formal SAT review course, the key is PRACTICE!

Practice taking the test in your sophomore or junior year by taking the PSAT/NMSQT. You can take the SAT multiple times. Score reports tell you how you compared to other state and national test takers. In addition, the reports give you customized answers to questions about your particular score that will help you analyze your performance and prepare for more testing.

The Student Answer Service will provide a computer-produced report telling you how you answered the questions on the SAT by type (e.g., sentence completion, analogy) and difficulty. You can assess your strengths and weaknesses, plan and take additional course work, then retake the tests and score higher.

Your guidance counselor, public library and local bookstore are sources for practice tests and test preparation materials. You can also write to: College Board Promotional Services Office, 45 Columbus Avenue, New York, NY 10023.

If you feel the need for a structured preparation program for the SAT, investigate school-sponsored and commercial preparation programs by comparing:

- **number of sessions over a period of time (more is better)**
- **class size (10-15 students is ideal)**
- **opportunity to make up missed classes**
- **experience of previous enrollees**

How will your SAT scores be used?

How important, really, are your scores and how will college admissions committees interpret them?

Very few colleges use arbitrary cut-off scores to determine acceptance. College admissions staffs know that, for a variety of reasons, your scores may not match your high school achievement level. Your test scores are reviewed along with your:

- **class rank**
- **course selection and grades**
- **extracurricular activities**
- **recommendations**
- **relationship with alumni**
- **success of other graduates from your school at the institution**

Every selective college or university attempts to admit students who they can predict will do well. Admissions staff experience suggests that certain levels of achievement can be predicted with a fair degree of accuracy when used in conjunction with the high school record.

Colleges and universities publish their average SAT. Their average SAT is just that; there have been many applicants whose scores are under the average but who have the proven achievement to be admitted. Likewise, there may be applicants with higher than the average test scores who are rejected.

Test scores do not show the desire to learn, the ambition to succeed or the perseverance necessary for academic excellence. College admissions officers are aware of these facts and they will read your entire application with an awareness that you are more than a score on a computer printout.

Prepared from articles by: Dr. Judith T. Bainbridge, Director of Educational Services, Furman University; Lisa K. Bartl, Associate Director, New SAT Project, College Board; Stanley H. Kaplan, Chairman, Stanley H. Kaplan Educational Center Ltd.

How to Find Financial Aid

By Debra M. Kirby

Did you know that approximately 24 billion dollars in education-related financial aid are awarded each year? This aid comes in many forms, including scholarships, fellowships, grants, loans, awards, work study, and internships. These awards are given through a variety of public and private sources, from federal and state government organizations to local associations. In addition, colleges and universities offer many forms of aid for their students.

The key to increasing the likelihood of meeting your aid-related financial goals is to plan ahead. This means allowing enough time to carefully assess your particular needs and preferences, consider any special circumstances or conditions that might qualify you for aid, and thoroughly research available aid programs.

Following are some guidelines to help you maximize your chances of finding financial aid.

✎ Start Your Research Early

Allow enough time to complete all of the necessary steps and you will be more likely to identify and meet application deadlines for a wide variety of awards for which you may qualify.

Begin this process as early as possible preferably at least two years before you think you will need financial assistance. Many awards are given on a first-come, first-served basis, which means if you don't file your application early enough, the aid will already have been distributed. An early start may also allow you to identify organizations that offer scholarships to members or participants, such as scouting groups or 4-H clubs, in time to establish membership or otherwise meet their qualifying criteria.

Along with widely varying eligibility criteria, many awards carry application deadlines that come up throughout the year. Even if you miss the deadline for a particular award, you may still be eligible for the same award the following year. In fact, many awards are specifically designed for undergraduate students at the sophomore, junior, and/or senior levels.

✎ Assess Your Needs and Goals

The intended recipients for financial aid programs, and the purposes for which these awards were established, can vary greatly. Some programs are open to almost anyone; others are restricted to very specific categories of recipients. The majority of awards fall somewhere in between.

Your first step in seeking financial aid should be to establish your basic qualifications as a potential recipient. To help you do this, ask yourself these general questions to help define your educational and financial needs and goals:

- **What kinds of colleges or universities interest me?**
- **What careers or fields of study interest me?**

- **Do I plan to earn a degree?**
- **Am I willing to consider a loan or part-time work?**
- **In what parts of the country am I willing to live and study?**

✎ Compile a List of Potential Qualifying Factors

Once you have defined your goals, the next step is to identify any special factors that would qualify you for aid programs that are offered only to a restricted group. Examine this area carefully, and remember that even slight or unlikely connections may be worth checking out.

The most common qualifications involve:

- gender
- race or ethnic heritage
- place of residence
- citizenship
- employer
- membership in an organization (such as a union, association, or a fraternal group)
- religious affiliation
- military or veteran status
- financial need
- athletic ability
- merit or academic achievement
- creative or professional accomplishment
- community involvement or volunteer work

Some of these qualifiers may also apply to your parents, step-parents, guardians and/or spouse. If your parents are divorced, you should be aware of both parents' affiliations — even if you don't live with one (or both) of them. If your parents are deceased, you may be eligible for some awards based on their status or affiliations. And given enough lead time, it may be possible for you (or your parents) to join a particular organization, or establish residence, in time for you to be eligible for certain funds. You should contact any organization with which you or your parent may be affiliated for financial aid information, since some associations, unions, and employers do not make this information available to the public.

✎ Contact the Financial Aid Office of the Schools and Other Educational Institutions That You Are Considering

Most colleges and universities, and other educational institutions offer their own institution-specific financial aid programs. Their financial aid offices may also have information on privately sponsored awards that are specifically designated for students at those institutions. Contact the financial aid offices at all institutions in which you have an interest and request applications and detailed information on all aid programs that they sponsor.

✎ Use Every Available Resource

Thoroughly search the various directories and guides available through high school counseling offices and career resource centers, college financial aid offices, and libraries. These references provide a wealth of information on all types of financial aid and are generally the best source for privately-funded programs.

Some directories contain information on federal and state-administered aid. In addition, you may contact the U.S. Department of Education at 400 Maryland Ave., S.W.,

Washington, DC 20202, for up-to-date information on U.S. government award programs. Similarly, you should contact your state department of education for details on what is offered in your particular state. Your high school counselor, public or school librarian should be able to provide you with contact information for various government organizations.

Keep in mind that a large number of financial aid programs are sponsored by small or local organizations. High school counselors are often aware of local programs, and can usually tell you how to get in touch with the sponsoring or administrating organizations. Local newspapers are also a rich source of information on financial aid programs.

✎ Allow Enough Time for the Application Process

The amount of time needed to complete the application process for individual awards can vary, so pay close attention to application details and deadlines. Some awards have deadlines that require you to apply more than a year before study will actually begin. In general, allow plenty of time to write for official applications (you won't be considered for some awards unless you apply using the correct forms.)

Carefully read and follow all instructions when you fill out the application forms. If you fail to answer certain questions, you may be disqualified even though you are a worthy candidate. Be sure to accurately and completely file all required supporting material, such as essays and resumés. Additionally, you will need to give your references enough time to submit their recommendations. Teachers, in particular, get many requests for letters of recommendation and should be given as much advance notice as possible.

✎ Don't Apply Unless You Are Sure You Qualify

Finally, don't submerge yourself under needless paperwork. If you find you don't qualify for a particular award, don't apply for it. Instead, use your time and energy to unearth and apply for more likely sources of aid.

A Word of Encouragement

By doing your homework, you'll greatly increase your chances of finding funding for your education. The personal labor involved in securing financial support for school is much like the resumé shuffling and door knocking that occurs during a job hunt. Success is likely to come to those who make themselves aware of the opportunities available, and who pursue those opportunities in a dedicated, continuous, and organized manner. And last, but not least, don't get discouraged. Frustration is part of the game and should not bring your financial aid search to a halt.

Debra M. Kirby is editor of Scholarships, Fellowships and Loans, and Fund Your Way Through College published by Gale Research, Inc.

Tough Questions to Ask Any Admissions Officer

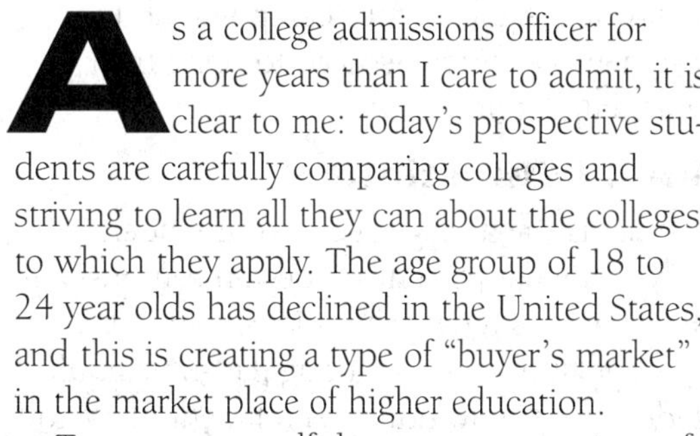

By Robert G. McLendon

As a college admissions officer for more years than I care to admit, it is clear to me: today's prospective students are carefully comparing colleges and striving to learn all they can about the colleges to which they apply. The age group of 18 to 24 year olds has declined in the United States, and this is creating a type of "buyer's market" in the market place of higher education.

To assure yourself that your expectations of a college are met, you, the student consumer, need not hesitate to ask admissions officers some "tough questions." Here are a few suggestions of tough questions that could help you make the right choice when selecting a college.

Academic Questions

1. How many students in last year's freshman class returned for their sophomore year?

2. What percent of the freshman class obtained a 2.00 (C) average or above last year?

3. If accepted, will you tell me my predicted freshman grade point average? Many colleges use a mathematical formula based on studies of currently enrolled students to predict an applicant's freshman grade point average.

4. What is the college's procedure for class placement? This is especially important in the areas of English and mathematics because freshmen often vary significantly in their ability to handle these important academic skills.

5. What procedure is used to assign a faculty advisor? This is especially important if the student is undecided as to their major area of study.

6. What type of additional academic services does your college offer at no additional cost to the student (e.g., tutoring, career or personal counseling, study-skill workshops, improving reading speed, etc.)?

7. How effective is your college's honor code? What is the penalty for cheating?

8. How accessible is your computer lab to freshmen? Do students need to bring their own computers?

Social Questions

1. What is the average age of your student body and what percent resides on campus? Many colleges today have a large and increasing population of commuting part-time adult students and a dwindling enrollment of 17 to 18 year old full-time, degree-seeking students residing on campus.

2. Is your college a "suitcase college" on the weekends? If not, what are some typical weekend activities for students on your campus?

3. What procedure is used to select roommates if no preference is listed?

4. What are some of the causes of students being suspended or dismissed from your college? Is there a system of appeal for those who have been dismissed?

5. How can a prospective student arrange a campus visit? Can a prospecive student stay overnight on campus? Clearly the best possible way to evaluate a college socially is to plan a visit to the campus. When you visit, try not to be shy. After your talk and tour with the admissions officer, walk around by yourself and informally ask students their opinions. A good place to chat with students is in the college's student center or at the dining hall.

6. What are some of the rules and regulations that govern residence hall life? Are there coeducational residence halls?

7. What is the college's policy concerning alchohol on campus?

8. Ask for statistics on the crime rate on campus. Colleges are required to have this information available to the public. Also ask about the crime rate in the community surrounding the college.

Financial Questions

1. What percent of your students received financial aid based on financial need?

2. What percent of your students received scholarships based on academic ability?

3. What percent of a typical financial aid offer is in the form of a loan?

4. How much did your college increase cost (room, board, tuition, and fees) from last year to current year?

5. If an accepted student must submit a room deposit, when is the deposit due, and when is it refundable? The deposit should be refundable in full up to May 1, if the college or university is a member of the National Association of College Admissions Counselors.

6. If my family demonstrates a financial need on the federal financial aid forms, what percent of the established need will typically be awarded? When can I expect to receive an official financial aid award letter?

Knowing what questions to ask an admissions officer is an important part of the decision-making process. Most admissions officers want you to ask "tough questions" because if you make the wrong choice we, too, have failed in our job.

Robert G. McLendon is Vice President and Dean for Admissions and Financial Aid at Brevard College, Brevard, North Carolina.

- Be prompt.
- Don't pretend to be someone you're not.
- Try to schedule the interview after you have toured the campus so you will know more about the college.
- You cannot overdress, but you can underdress for an interview, so dress up, not down.
- Speak clearly and use good non-verbal communications, such as good posture, facial expression and eye contact.
- Answer questions to the best of your knowledge and ability; don't be afraid to admit you don't know something.
- After the interview, ask about your chance for being admitted (or in receiving a scholarship).
- Get a business card of the interviewer.
- Send a courtesy thank you note after the interview simply stating you enjoyed the conversation. This is polite and a good way to be remembered.

Remember, this is a chance to showcase your accomplishments and help the interviewer see you as a thinking, feeling individual instead of just another statistic like an SAT score. It's your chance to show your maturity; to display your sensitivity and to convey your outlook on what a college education should do for you. The interview is not an obstacle—it is an opportunity.

—Robert G. McLendon

Selecting a College: One Size Does Not Fit All

Colleges and universities come in different sizes and types with different emphasis and opportunities. Your needs and priorities will determine how you select from such a wide range of choices (public/private, large/small, 4 year/2 year, urban/rural, secular/religious ...) and find an institution that is appropriate for you.

Choose a LARGE UNIVERSITY (enrollment greater than 10,000) if you want:

- a large number of academic majors. At a large university available academic majors often number in the hundreds, not dozens. If you change your major or career choice, a large university is more able to accommodate that change

- more sophisticated laboratory equipment and libraries of considerable size available for undergraduate use
- a multiplicity of services designed to help students identify and pursue career options
- more student activities and more varied opportunities to associate with other students
- a variety of opportunities for student involvement — organizations which cater to a wide range of interests, religious denominations, political involvement, etc.
- student services staffs — personal counseling and other opportunities to improve social awareness and skills as well as improved opportunities for career identification and job seeking
- to meet students whose backgrounds present a wide variety of experiences, values and perspectives. A large university is an excellent place to gain experience in being able to live and work with a wide variety of persons

Choose a MID-SIZE STATE UNIVERSITY if you want:

- a less expensive institution compared to a private institution
- the option of living at home while pursuing your degree
- to take advantage of state scholarship programs
- to use a system that is supported by your tax dollars
- proximity to parents, friends and your home community
- an integrated educational program with easy transfer from campuses as well as two-year institutions
- cooperative extension, continuing education or satellite program because you cannot

attend classes full-time on campus

- opportunities to establish long-lasting relationships as a source of friendship and professional contacts for a lifetime in your home state

Choose a TWO-YEAR COLLEGE (designed to prepare you for continuation at a four-year institution) if you want:

- a good start at the essential foundations of undergraduate training
- access to the faculty. Typically faculty members choose to teach at two-year institutions because they are dedicated to teaching. You often get to know professors on a one-to-one basis in the classroom and socially at extracurricular events.
- less expense (especially if you plan on commuting)
- more opportunities for leadership and participation in the first two years of your college career

Ensure a Successful Campus Visit

Making the Appointment

- Make your appointment to visit a campus by telephone, not mail. (You can find out immediately if you need to pick an alternate date.)
- Try to schedule your visit when college classes are in session.
- Plan for a minimum half a day visit.
- Ask for travel directions and parking assignments.
- Request that a campus map, catalog, and student newspaper be mailed to you.
- Ask for an appointment to speak with someone in your special interest (athletics, fine arts) areas during your campus visit.
- Make an appointment to talk with the financial aid administrator. Ask if it is helpful to the financial aid staff if you bring a copy of you and your parents' last tax return.
- If an interview is required for admissions, request time for the interview.
- You can also request to visit with a professor, attend a class, and stay overnight in a college dorm.

Prepare Yourself

- List questions to ask and places you want to see.
- Talk with your guidance counselor for more suggestions on how to prepare.
- Ask for the names of students from your high school enrolled at the college(s) you plan to visit.
- Read the catalog and other college materials before you visit.

The Visit

- If your tour guide is a student, ask "what attracted you to this college?"
- Take notes during your campus visit and tour.
- Write down the name and address of your tour guide and other people you meet.
- Make sure the housing you see is typical freshman housing.
- Check out information on the campus bulletin boards.
- Ask for campus crime statistics and about the type of security system on campus.
- Have a meal on campus.

Don't be bashful, ask a lot of questions, college is expensive and you are the customer. Relax and have a good time.

–Robert G. McLendon

- an entire institution's budget spent on the first two undergraduate years
- emphasis on the basics — reading, writing and math
- to transfer to a four-year institution better prepared and with a greater possibility of being accepted than if you were right out of high school

Choose an INDEPENDENT RESEARCH UNIVERSITY if you want:

- a school with an extraordinary reputation in academic circles boasting an outstanding faculty
- to learn as much from your gifted fellow students as from your professors
- informal associations between yourself and your professors
- seminar classes with leaders in public affairs, the arts and sciences
- a diverse student body (deliberately created by the admissions office)
- a smaller size school which provides a critical mass for a wide variety of activities and sense of community

Choose a CHURCH-RELATED COLLEGE or UNIVERSITY if you want:

- a values-based education. A church-related institution offers the opportunity to explore the values inherent in the ideas and behaviors presented in the curriculum
- spiritual growth opportunities. A church-related institution operates on the notion of educating the whole person spiritually and intellectually.
- a broader view of the role of ethics in society. You will be encouraged to develop and maintain a personal perspective as a moral being in the workplace and at home.

Choose a COLLEGE FOR WOMEN if you want:

- to develop your leadership skills. Women hold all the leadership positions in a women's college. This leadership extends into the working world — 40% of female members of Congress and a third of the women board members of Fortune 1000 companies are graduates of women's colleges.

- to attend graduate or professional school after graduation. Graduates of women's colleges are more than twice as likely as graduates of coeducational colleges to receive doctorate degrees. Furthermore, women's colleges produce a higher percentage of graduates who go on to medical school and study in the sciences.
- to study science, math or economics. Women's colleges produce a disproportionate share of women who enroll in fields such as science, math and economics.
- to pursue a career which is nontraditional for women. About 50% of the working women who graduate from women's colleges are in nontraditional jobs, for example, law, medicine, business management and computer science.

Choose an HISTORICALLY BLACK COLLEGE if you want:

- excellent scholarship opportunities
- typically small class sizes allowing interaction and personal attention from the faculty
- a "family atmosphere" where strong friendships are easily formed with a wide range of extra-curricular acitivities
- an excellent alumni network, strong job placement and career counseling

Prepared from articles by: James C. Blackburn, Director of Admissions and Records, California State University at Fullerton; Stanley Z. Koplik, Executive Director, Kansas Board of Regents; Dr. Jacob C. Martinson, Jr., President, High Point University; F. Gregory Campbell, President, Carthage College; Neil K. Clark, Director of College Counseling and Guidance, The Walker School; Dr. Anita M. Pampusch, President, College of St. Catherine; Robert G. McLendon, Vice President and Dean for Admissions and Financial Aid, Brevard College, Brevard, North Carolina.

Getting the Most Out of a College Fair Program

- **Be well prepared.** Read catalogs and college materials and have specific questions ready.
- **General questions you want answered** include: location, typical class size, religious affiliations, admissions requirements, fees and timetables, your major offered, expenses to budget beyond room, board, tuition, and fees, financial aid deadlines and percent receiving financial aid, housing availability and requirements, recreational facilities, activities of interest to you, and when and how to arrange a campus visit.
- **Be organized.** Most college fairs arrange colleges in alphabetical order. Have an alphabetical list of colleges you want to see.
- **Take a notebook** so you can write down notes and names of college representatives you meet.
- **Meet with your guidance counselor** prior to the college fair for suggestions of colleges that fit your interest and abilities.
- **Bring a copy of your high school transcript** to the college fair; this will help admissions officers give you a better answer concerning your chances for admission.
- **Leave time to "shop around"** and discover colleges that might not be on your advanced list.

–Robert G. McLendon

Campus Lifestyle: an Important Consideration in Choosing a College

By Dr. Neill Sanders

What do meal plans, student organizations, fraternities and sororities, and residence halls have to do with choosing a college? A great deal. From late August through May the campus is a student's home and typically three-quarters of your time will be spent outside of the classroom. Therefore, campus lifestyle, the sum of what you can expect to experience when not in class, is a very important component of college life worthy of careful attention.

A few tips when trying to determine a campus lifestyle: **Don't believe everything you hear about a college!** For instance, some may have a party school reputation while others might be known for a student body that cares about nothing but studying. The truth about all campuses lies somewhere in between.

Draw up a list of lifestyle characteristics you think are the most important. What do you want in a dormitory environment? Does the university have the student organizations that interest you? What about security?

Ask questions! Colleges make a sincere effort to inform prospective students about campus lifestyle, but neither brochures nor campus videos can address all the topics that are important to you. Ask your friends or recent alumni who attend a certain college about their impressions; call or write the admissions office of a particular institution to get answers to key questions; and carefully review the literature and videos sent to you. Whenever possible, visit the colleges that are highest on your list because there is no better way to learn about an institution than actually being there.

There are several lifestyle features that you should investigate.

Residence Halls: If you elect to live in a residence hall, you will spend more time there (studying, talking with friends, sleeping) than any other place on campus, so it is important to know the facts about university housing policies. • Does the college require all freshmen to live on campus? • Can you move off campus after the freshman year? • Are the resident halls co-ed and, if so, are men and women distributed throughout the halls? (Some colleges have men and women on the same floors while others reserve certain floors or wings for each sex.) • If you are to share a room, how is your roommate chosen?

Regulations: Most colleges have strict regulations regarding alcohol, regardless of the student's age. Many also have "quiet time" policies when stereos, televisions, and radios must be turned down or off. Universities do vary greatly on such issues as allowing freshmen to bring their car to campus, how much furniture (if

any) the college provides for your dormitory room, and if you can bring your pet to campus.

Greek Life: At many campuses fraternities and sororities play a big role in campus life. "Greek" life has many rewards for those who join. It provides members with social and cultural opportunities beyond what the campus typically offers. But keep in mind that not all Greek houses are residential. In some cases only the officers or upperclassmen can live in the house. If "going Greek" fits your lifestyle, you'll need to learn about "rush" and "pledging." Because not all who want to join are permitted to do so, how do you think you would fit into a campus if you could not (or elected not to) join a fraternity or sorority? Keep in mind too that Greek membership will add to your overall college costs.

Food: Does the college have a meal plan where you purchase in advance so many meals per week each semester and pay for them whether or not you eat in the dining halls? A few colleges let you pay for each meal. Others issue collegiate credit cards that can be used for meals and other services (such as at sports events or at the bookstore). What about special dietary needs, such as kosher or vegetarian meals? When visiting a college, plan to have a meal on campus.

Security: College campuses are safe, but don't take security for granted. While the door to your dorm room can be locked anytime you want, what about the resident hall's outside doors? Think of a residence hall as a large hotel: is there a worker (often a student working part-time) located in the lobby to monitor when guests come in and when they leave? What are the school's policies regarding guests in the room, especially overnight guests? Most college campuses are large, encompassing hundreds of acres. They can be pretty lonely places if you are walking alone from the library to your dormitory at night. Women should check and see if the college has student volunteers who will escort you to your campus destination during certain evening hours.

Extracurricular: For many students a very important part of college life is participation in campus clubs and organizations as well as attending the social, cultural, and athletic events sponsored by the school. Virtually every

college has a student government organization, a campus newspaper and yearbook. Campus-based radio and television stations are not uncommon.

Student centered clubs and intramural sports activities are great ways to meet new friends and develop new skills. But do the universities high on your selection list have the activities that interest you the most? Can anyone try out for a varsity team? Can you be part of campus musical or drama productions without being a fine arts major? Does the student recreation center have facilities where you can jog, exercise, swim, or shoot a few baskets on a schedule convenient to you?

Attending a concert offered by the college's music faculty, going to a lecture given by a well known guest lecturer, or cheering on the football team at homecoming are all part of the college experience. But make sure to find out in advance if tickets to such events routinely are made available to students and if the tickets are part of the "student fees" most colleges charge all students. If not, you will need to plan ahead and budget for those events of greatest interest to you.

As a college student, you may want to participate in organizations designed to celebrate your religious or ethnic heritage. Do the colleges of your choice have such clubs? What activities do they provide? Unlike your high school environment, you might find fewer students at a college who share your religious beliefs or cultural heritage. Do students currently enrolled at the college with backgrounds similar to yours feel accepted in the college's environment?

Service Activities: Campus lifestyle should not be restricted simply to the events which take place at the college. Perhaps as a high school student you tutor middle school children with math deficiencies, work with the homeless, or are involved with ecology issues in your community. Such volunteer activities do not have to end once you enroll in college. Will your college encourage such activities; do they have an office that can assist you in locating ways to express your willingness to help others? Does the local community in which your final college choice is located offer the amenities of interest to you?

The choice of the college that best meets your needs is seldom easy, often time consuming, frequently requires family participation, and always should be exciting. As you explore your options, remember that a campus lifestyle is an important feature that makes for a rewarding college experience!

Dr. Neill Sanders is Enrollment Manager at University of Rochester in Rochester, New York.

Major Decisions: Choosing the Right College Major

By Dr. Donald Quirk

Under the best of circumstances, choosing a college major is not easy, and a number of conditions often complicate the task. First of all, most freshmen are surprised to learn that college is significantly different from their previous school experience and that the nature of most major fields differ considerably from courses offered in high school. So, to major in history because you are good at memorizing dates, names and battles or to choose accountancy because you enjoyed a high school bookkeeping or "accounting" course is likely to lead to dissatisfaction. Secondly, well-intentioned but naive "advisors," often as not, ignore your interests, skills or ambitions. Blindly following Dad's suggestion to "study law so you can get rich like Uncle Zeke" nearly guarantees a mismatch. Finally, many young people find themselves in the midst of personal change and discovery. Making a commitment that may affect the rest of your life at a time when your dreams change more often than the blue-light special at Kmart can leave the hardiest person paralyzed by fear.

Adding to the pressure felt by many students are the expectations of those around them that everyone beginning college should have already decided what he or she intends to study. Even colleges — often unintentionally — add to the pressure; applications usually require a student to select from a list of intended majors. Typically, a college will list 30 to 100 major choices; in the list — usually appearing last — comes the choice, "undecided." It comes as little surprise that many students feel that they are somehow defective if they have not yet made up their minds.

Now, there are some students who "always wanted to study medicine" and a good number of others who have given a great deal of time to their selection of a major, but the hard truth of the matter is that many students — including those who have declared a major — really don't know what they want to study. This is evidenced by a national statistic showing that nearly four out of five college students eventually change their major at least once. So what's a person to do?

Don't Worry

If you're beginning college and you're unsure about what you want to study, you probably don't have to make a choice quite yet. While a few technical and scientific fields have highly structured curricula that require beginning courses be taken immediately, most students can delay major decisions for one or even two years without disastrous consequences. For colleges — unlike vocational schools — require students to study subjects that provide a breadth of knowledge outside the major. Usually described as general education courses, these courses include selections in the arts, the natural and social sciences and the humanities. Typically, they represent a third to a half of the total course requirement for graduation and they provide an opportunity to experiment, to get a taste of a range of fields.

"Know Thyself"

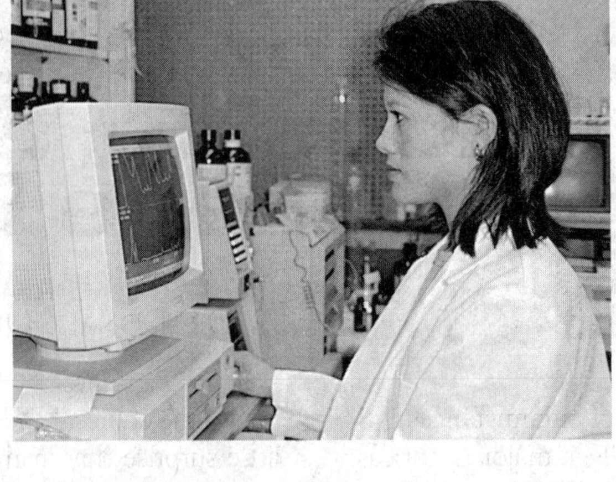

Get to know more about what fits you. Remember, you are not choosing a major for Uncle Zeke; you're choosing one for yourself, so the place to begin is with yourself, your personality, your interests, your abilities, your values and your goals. Choosing a major — like any significant personal decision — requires you to think through some important questions about yourself. What has my previous experience prepared me to do? How can I connect the knowledge and skills that I've already developed with a course of study? What areas that I've studied in the past were interesting to me? What college majors capitalize on that interest? How do my personal and career goals connect with my selection of a major?

Avoid Career Planning "Tunnel Vision"

Be broad-minded when thinking about a major that matches your career plan. Many students recognize that choosing a major is closely linked to choosing a career but are confused into believing that only management majors can hope to become business executives or only "pre-law" students can hope to become lawyers. The fact of the matter is that there are many majors that lead to these or a number of other career goals. Increasingly, firms have shown that they value the analytical thinking, communication and research skills developed by students in the liberal arts by hiring graduates from philosophy, English, sociology and a variety of other non-vocational majors.

Find Help

There are a large number of tools — books, interest inventories, aptitude tests, values and goal assessments — that can help you find a major that fits. A number of self-help books, like Richard Bolles' *What Color is Your Parachute,* provide a guided tour through the process of choosing a field of study and a career. Interest inventories, like the Kuder or the Strong-Campbell, help you match your interests with those of people in a variety of professions. Computerized self-assessments like Discover, developed by ACT, or SIGI, from the College Board, lead you through a systematic process of self-exploration that leads to some potential matches. High school counselors or college advising or career planning offices can help you put these and a number of other resources to work for you.

In addition, a growing number of colleges have programs and services to help students develop an academic plan. Some of these include academic advising programs, special courses for undecided students, and career planning workshops and counseling services to name a few. In recent years, more and more colleges have also developed freshman seminars. Designed to help new students make the transition to college life, these seminars often include the related topics of choosing a major field and choosing a career.

But probably the most effective resources are people. Find someone you can trust — a good high school guidance counselor, a sympathetic college advisor, an accessible faculty member, or a knowledgeable career planning counselor in your college. They can help you begin the process. With a little help and some persistence, you'll find that major decisions do not have to be major problems.

Donald Quirk, Ph.D., is Director of Assessment at Northeastern Illinois University.

How to Survive Freshman Year

1. Go to class. Students who attend class rarely fail.

2. Work hard. Work harder than you did in high school. Spend two to three hours out of class studying for every hour of the week you spend in class. For a fifteen hour class schedule, spend 30 hours a week studying and 15 in class.

3. Play hard. College is not meant to be all work. Relax and have some kind of balance in your life.

4. Participation. Participate in all the orientation activities that your college offers. Students who participate in these elective courses have a higher probability of becoming sophomores.

5. Live on campus. Students who live on campus have a higher survival rate, especially during your first two years of college.

6. Choose your friends wisely. You are likely to become just like them. Winners select winners. Losers select losers.

7. Get help early. Don't wait until late in the semester. There is no stigma to seeking assistance. Remember, you're paying the salaries of the college employees and you have a right to ask them for help.

8. Develop a relationship with your academic advisor. If you don't have one initially who seems to show an interest in you and whom you feel you can relate to comfortably, ask for another one.

9. Find a significant adult during the semester. College students who find at least one special adult during the freshman year are much more likely to survive.

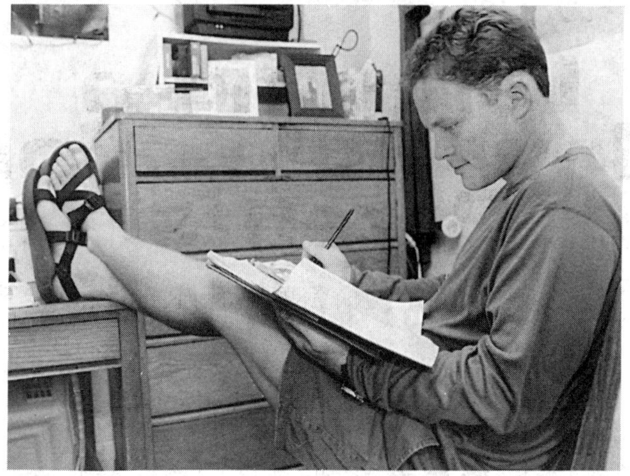

10. Identify outstanding upper class students after whose behaviors you can pattern your own behaviors.

11. Join a group sponsored by the college. Students who join groups have much higher survival rates.

12. Get involved. Attend plays, concerts, lectures, sports activities, etc. The more time you invest in activities on campus other than simply going to class, the more likely you are to survive the freshman year.

13. Get career planning early. Visit your campus career planning center; take a battery of vocational aptitude tests; sign up for computer assisted interactive guidance and career planning; and most importantly, see a career planning specialist to discuss your individual needs and characteristics.

14. Use helping services and resources offered. There is no stigma to accepting assistance. For example, use a personal counseling center. Many colleges offer academic support services, especially in the areas of math and writing skills.

15. Learn college study skills. Most high school students have not learned the kind of study skills they need to do well in college. Use study skills centers; ask your professors what study skills are particularly useful and appropriate.

Prepared from the research and experience of John Gardner, Associate Vice Provost for Regional Campuses and Continuing Education, University of South Carolina.

Learning a New Role...For Parents

BY ANN AND PAUL KROUSE

Most literature directed to parents of college-bound students focuses on financial matters, an area of great interest and concern to most of us. Yet there are other roles besides bankrolls which require attention and involvement. Some are obvious and others more subtle. Having completed the college admissions process four times with our own children, my wife and I would like to share our experiences and views.

Be involved.

Selecting a college is just one more experience in the parenting process with the usual mixture of risks, rewards, joys, and uncertainties. You will find yourself poring over directories, college catalogs, counselor recommendations, applications, and financial aid forms. The more you do together, the less tedious the tasks and the more enlightening the process becomes. We found ourselves engaged in a very productive cycle which started with counselor/student meetings. From this counselor-to-parent shuttle which was repeated several times over a period of a few weeks, our daughter developed a list of six or seven college choices. We visited several of her college choices on a 4-day car trip and ultimately she selected a college which happily accepted her. Waiting for the acceptance letter was agonizing, receiving it was joyous. The family celebration which followed was memorable.

Our experiences were undoubtedly quite common. The subtleties merit equal awareness.

Listen to your child.

Most of us have our own preferences of where we would like our children to go to school, but we've had our chance(s) and now it's their turn. Certainly your guidance, opinions, and views are important. You may have some inflexible requirements which your child must be responsive to such as financial limitations. Nevertheless, it is imperative that you listen to your child's preferences and to the best of your ability and with your best judgement encourage your child to fulfill his or her dreams, not yours.

Be patient and "tune-in."

The separation between child and family is beginning and it impacts on everyone involved in different ways and at different times. So much of the college admissions process requires that the children initiate action which will cause separation that there is frequently a reluctance to complete a task which can easily be misinterpreted as laziness or irresponsibility. An application may remain untouched, an essay delayed, a conference postponed. You must "tune-in" to your child's emotions and try to determine when he or she is being lax and when normal anxieties are rising to the surface, slowing down progress. Try to be patient, guide instead of push, and acknowledge your mutual feelings instead of hiding them. The closer the family is, the more pronounced these experiences may be.

Respect your child's privacy.

Social gatherings will undoubtedly bring you into contact with other parents of college-bound students and the plans and experiences of your children will become timely topics of conversation. Sharing experiences with other parents can be mutually beneficial. But, revealing your child's exact SAT scores, GPA, class rank and similar information is an invasion of privacy. If your child wants to announce this information to friends, relatives or other parents, that's his or her business and choice — not yours. Certainly you wouldn't want your child publicizing your income or other personal information to outsiders. Similarly, your child probably would prefer that some aspect of this process remain within the family. You will be amazed at what remarkably bad taste some parents exhibit in discussing their children's experiences.

Shop carefully.

As adults, you are undoubtedly a more experienced and sophisticated shopper than your child and your experience can be significant as your child shops for a college. Most colleges are very ethical and professional in their recruitment practices, but remember they are "selling." At college fairs, admissions officers can be persuasive, which is not to their discredit. College catalogs can be slick and attractive, which is also understandable and acceptable. But remember, most colleges are selling a package that can cost $5,000 to $15,000 per year or $20,000 to $60,000 over four years. They need from 100 to 1,000 new students each year to keep their doors open. That's not an indictment of their motives, but simply a representation of their realities. Read between the lines and beyond the pretty pictures. Don't hesitate to confer with your child's counselors about the choices and options available — counselors are generally objective and committed to service the student, not a particular institution.

When you visit campuses, allow enough time to wander on your own after your formal tour, usually conducted by the admissions office. Walk into the library, dormitories, student union and even classrooms, if possible. Talk to students around the campus and observe as much as you can. Virtually all college admissions officials will encourage such "investigations" on your part since they don't want your child to make a mistake and stay for one year or less any more than you do.

Naturally, each family's experiences will be a little different. The process is not very scientific, in spite of computerbanks, search services, video presentations, etc. Like looking for a house, there is more emotion in the process than some are ready to acknowledge. Nevertheless, as we look back, it was another enjoyable family experience where the rewards far outweigh the risks.

Ann and Paul Krouse are the publishers of Who's Who Among American High School Students and the parents of four children: Amy, entered the freshman class at Tufts University class of 1987. Beth followed at the University of Illinois, class of 1989; Joe at the University of Michigan, class of 1993; and Katie at Indiana University, class of 1994. WHEW!

Glossary of Abbreviations

Acad Academic
Acpl Chr Acappella Choir
AFS American Field Service
Am Leg Boys St American Legion Boys State
Am Leg Aux Girls St American Legion Auxiliary Girls State
Assoc Association
Aud/Vis Audio-Visual
Awd Award

Badmtn Badminton
Bsbl Baseball
Bsktbl Basketball
Bus Business
Bwlng Bowling

C of C Awd Chamber of Commerce Award
Camp Fr Inc Camp Fire, Inc.
CAP Civil Air Patrol
Capt Captain
Cheerldng Cheerleading
Chrmn Chairman
Cit Awd Citizenship Award
Clb Club
Cmnty Wkr Community Worker
Co-Capt Co-Captain
Co-Ed Co-Editor
Coach Actv Coaching Activities
Crs Cntry Cross Country

DAR Awd Daughters of the American Revolution Award
DECA Distributive Education Clubs of America
Dnfth Awd Danforth (I Dare You) Award
Drm & Bgl Drum and Bugle Corps
Drm Mjr(t) Drum Major(ette)

Ed Editor
Ed-Chief Editor-in-Chief

FBLA Future Business Leaders of America
FCA Fellowship of Christian Athletes
FFA National FFA Organization
FHA Future Homemakers of America
Fit Fitness
Fld Hcky Field Hockey
FNA Future Nurses of America
FTA Future Teachers of America
Ftbl Football

GAA Girls Athletic Association
Gov Hon Prg Awd Governors Honor Program Award
Gym Gymnastics

Hist Historian
Hon Honor
Hosp Aide Hospital Aide

Ice Hcky Ice Hockey
Indus Industrial
Intnl Clb International Club
Intrml Intramural

JA Junior Achievement
JC Awd Jaycees Award
JCL Junior Classical League
JETS Awd Junior Engineering Technical Society Award
JP Sousa Awd John Philip Sousa Award
Jr NHS Junior National Honor Society
JV Junior Varsity

L Letter
Lbrn Librarian
Lcrss Lacrosse
Lion Award Lions Club Award
Lit Mag Literary Magazine

Mgr(s) Manager(s)
Mrchg Band Marching Band

NCTE Awd National Council of Teachers of English Award
NEDT National Educational Development Test Award
NFL National Forensic League
NHS National Honor Society
Ntl National
Nwsp Newspaper

Off Officer
Opt Clb Awd Optimist Club Award
Orch Orchestra

PAVAS Performing and Visual Arts Society
Phtg Photographer
Pres President
Prfct Atten Awd Perfect Attendance Award
Profs Professionals

Rep Representative
Rptr Reporter
ROTC Reserve Officer Training Corps

S.A.D.D. Students Against Driving Drunk
Sal Salutatorian
SAR Awd Sons of the American Revolution Award
Schol Scholarship
Scrkpr Scorekeeper
Sec Secretary
SF Semifinalist
Sftbl Softball
Socr Soccer
Sprt Ed Sports Editor
Stat Statistician
St Schlr State Scholar
Stf Staff
Stu Cncl Student Council
Swmmng Swimming
Symp Band Symphonic Band

Tm Team
Thesps Thespians
Trea, Treas Treasurer
Trk Track
Twrlr Twirler

V, Var Varsity
Val Valedictorian
VICA Vocational Industrial Clubs of America
Vllybl Volleyball
Voice Dem Awd Voice of Democracy Award
VP Vice President

Wrstlng Wrestling
Wt Lftg Weight Lifting

Yrbk Yearbook

Sample Biographical Sketch

This sample is presented to familiarize the reader with the format of the biographical listings. Students are identified by name, school, home city and state. In order to protect the privacy and integrity of all students, home addresses are not published.

Key

1 Name
2 High School
3 Home, City and State
4 Year in School*
5 Class Rank (when given)
6 Accomplishments
7 Future Plans

1 WOLK, BARNET D.; **2** Normandy Isle H.S.; **3**Miami, FL; **4** (4); **5** 10-350; **6** Pres Stu Cncl; VP Sr Cls; Ftbl; 4-H; NHS; Cit Awd; Am Leg Awd; **7** Harvard University; Biochemist

* 1 = Freshman 2 = Sophomore 3 = Junior 4 = Senior

STUDENT BIOGRAPHIES

ARKANSAS

AARON, ALLEN A; El Dorado Sr HS; El Dorado, AR; (2); Church Yth Grp; Drama Clb; 4-H; Church Choir; Ftbl; Trk; Hon Roll; Scholar Ath; UALR; Psych/Sociology.

AARON, STACEY A; El Dorado Sr HS; El Dorado, AR; (1); Church Yth Grp; FBLA; Band; Church Choir; Color Guard; Flag Corp; Mrchg Band; Hon Roll.

AARON, TABITHA M; Spring Hill HS; Hope, AR; (3); Am Leg Aux Girls St; Church Yth Grp; French Clb; FBLA; FHA; Quiz Bowl; SADD; Rptr Nwsp; Ed Yrbk; VP Jr Cls; Girl St; Rice; Geneticist; Lawyer.

ABBOTT, BRIAN A; Fayetteville Sr HS; Fayetteville, AR; (4); Sec Frsh Cls; Var Socr; Tennis; Pres Acad Fit Awd; UCA; Phy Thrpst.

ABBOTT, EMILY; Sparkman Jr Sr HS; Sparkman, AR; (4); 2/23; Sec 4-H; VP Natl Beta Clb; Spanish Clb; Chorus; Ed Yrbk; Sec Soph Cls; Sec Jr Cls; VP Sr Cls; Pres Stu Cncl; Sal; U Of Cntrl AR; Jrnlsm.

ABBOTT, JESSICCA L; Mena HS; Mena, AR; (2); Church Yth Grp; French Clb; FBLA; FHA; Science Clb; Band; Mrchg Band; Bearcats Against Drgs; Flwshp Chrstn Stdnts.

ABERCROMBIE, BILLY; Bauxite Jr Sr HS; Benton, AR; (4); 1/38; Am Leg Boys St; Church Yth Grp; Capt Quiz Bowl; SADD; Ed Yrbk; Rep Stu Cncl; L Bsktbl; Pres NHS; Pres Schlr; Val; U Of AR; Bio.

ABLES, DANIEL; Norphlet HS; Calion, AR; (2); Art Clb; Church Yth Grp; Cmnty Wkr; FBLA; Capt Quiz Bowl; Spanish Clb; Band; Church Choir; Jazz Band; Mrchg Band; 5 Yr Natl Mem Natl Piano Playing Auditions W/Superor Ratings Natl Guild Of Piano Tchrs.

ABLES, TIM; Humphrey Schl; Humphrey, AR; (1); Church Yth Grp; Natl FFA Org; Rptr Nwsp; Hon Roll.

ABNEY, CANDI; Drew Central Jr Sr HS; Monticello, AR; (3); 5/60; Am Leg Aux Girls St; Drama Clb; Pres FBLA; Science Clb; Speech Tm; Band; School Play; NHS; Pres Acad Fit Awd; U Of AR Monticello; BSN.

ABNEY, CASEY C; Drew Central Jr Sr HS; Tillar, AR; (2); CAP; 4-H; Natl FFA Org; Teachers Aide; Chorus; Cit Awd; Stu Pilot/A&P Lic.

ABNEY, MEGHANN K; Parkview Arts-Science HS; Roland, AR; (3); Art Clb; Pres Church Yth Grp; Key Clb; Natl Beta Clb; School Play; Yrbk; Cit Awd; High Hon Roll; Jr NHS; NHS.

ABRAHAM, EDWIN JOHN; Ozark Adventist Acad; Pine Bluff, AR; (3); Art Clb; Church Yth Grp; Cmnty Wkr; FCA; Hosp Aide; Office Aide; Teachers Aide; Orch; School Musical; School Play; Southwestern Adv Coll; Med.

ABRAHAM, SARA J; White Co Central Schl; Searcy, AR; (2); 3/40; Art Clb; Church Yth Grp; FBLA; FHA; Band; Flag Corp; Mrchg Band; Tennis; Cit Awd; High Hon Roll; Miss Cntrl Jr High; Sci Awd; Eng II Schlrshp Awd; FHA Banqt Queen; Art II Awd; Lyon Coll; Corp Law.

ABRAHAM, SELWIN J; Ozark Adventist Acad; Pine Bluff, AR; (2); Church Yth Grp; Cmnty Wkr; Hosp Aide; Quiz Bowl; Orch; Treas Soph Cls; Cit Awd; High Hon Roll; Prfct Atten Awd; Southwestern Adventist Coll.

ABRAMS, MICAH; Morrilton Sr HS; Morrilton, AR; (4); 7/150; Rep Am Leg Boys St; Math Clb; Natl Beta Clb; Quiz Bowl; Pres Science Clb; Thesps; Sec Sr Cls; High Hon Roll; Pres Acad Fit Awd; UCA; Chem.

ABRAMS, MICHELLE; Dumas HS; Winchester, AR; (3); 13/138; Am Leg Aux Girls St; Church Yth Grp; Drama Clb; FBLA; Math Clb; Natl Beta Clb; Science Clb; Spanish Clb; Band; Drm Mjr(t); All Stars; U Of AR Fayetteville.

ABSON, ALISON L; Parkview Arts-Science HS; Mabelvale, AR; (3); Cmnty Wkr; FBLA; Spanish Clb; Band; Church Choir; Rep Frsh Cls; Var Vllybl; Cit Awd; Hon Roll; NHS; Career Awrness; Sftbl By YWCA; Ladies Club; Sprts Med.

ACORD, KERRY L; Ozark HS; Ozark, AR; (3); Church Yth Grp; Natl Beta Clb; Rep Sr Cls; Rep Stu Cncl; Bsktbl; Capt Chrldng; Hon Roll; Westark CC.

ADAMS, AMANDA R; Dardanelle HS; Dardanelle, AR; (2); 1/119; Church Yth Grp; FCA; FBLA; Natl Beta Clb; Varsity Clb; Mrchg Band; Chrldng; Sftbl; High Hon Roll; Pres Acad Fit Awd; Med.

ADAMS, AMBER; Cutter Morning Star HS; Hot Springs, AR; (3); 1/42; Church Yth Grp; VP FCA; HOBY; Natl Beta Clb; Quiz Bowl; Pres Science Clb; Yrbk; Pres Soph Cls; Bsktbl; Sftbl; Stu Bible Study; Med.

ADAMS, AMBER D; Greene Co Tech HS; Walcott, AR; (4); 64/164; Drama Clb; FBLA; Acpl Chr; Band; Chorus; Color Guard; Flag Corp; Mrchg Band; Pep Band; Stage Crew; All Amer & All St Prfmr; AR St Univ.

ADAMS, ASHLEY; Dumas HS; Dumas, AR; (3); #10 in class; Am Leg Aux Girls St; Church Yth Grp; FBLA; FTA; Math Clb; Natl Beta Clb; Science Clb; Spanish Clb; Band; Mrchg Band; Majorette; U Of AR Fayetteville; Pre Med.

ADAMS, ASHLEY L; Bryant Sr HS; Alexander, AR; (2); Pres Church Yth Grp; FBLA; Teachers Aide; Church Choir; Hon Roll; Chrstn Cncl; Riding Horses; Sftbl; Cnslr.

ADAMS, BEN; England HS; Tucker, AR; (3); Church Yth Grp; FCA; FHA; Ofcr Bsbl; Ftbl; Hon Roll; Acad Excl Awd; Admin Awd; Horizon Awd Ftbl; Beta Clb; Lion Heart Awd; Ath Awd; Ftbl Ltr 94-96; U Of Monticello.

ADAMS, BRYANT F; Dewitt HS; De Witt, AR; (1); 17/120; FCA; French Clb; Science Clb; Rptr Frsh Cls; JV L Bsktbl; JV L Ftbl; JV L Trk; Hon Roll; PRIDE.

ADAMS, CHRISTOPHER L; Bauxite Jr Sr HS; Bauxite, AR; (2); SADD; Band; JV Var Ftbl; Var Mgr(s); Var Trk; Var Wt Lftg; Hon Roll; Big Bros/Big Str; Champs; CONSTR.

ADAMS, EDWARD S; Harrisburg HS; Harrisburg, AR; (2); Church Yth Grp; FCA; Library Aide; Office Aide; Quiz Bowl; Science Clb; Spanish Clb; Bsktbl; Ftbl; Prfct Atten Awd; ASU.

ADAMS, EMILY; Hamburg Jr HS; Hamburg, AR; (1); Church Yth Grp; Bsktbl; Chrldng; Sftbl; Hon Roll; Capt Jr NHS.

ADAMS, ISAAC E; Arkansas Sr HS; Texarkana, AR; (3); 8/4; Am Leg Boys St; Church Yth Grp; Mu Alpha Theta; Quiz Bowl; ROTC; Spanish Clb; Band; Crs Cntry; NHS; Pres Acad Fit Awd; US Air Force Acad; Pilot.

ADAMS, JENNIFER; Ozark Adventist Acad; Gentry, AR; (4); Church Yth Grp; Band; Chorus; Church Choir; Orch; Sec Frsh Cls; Intrml Bsktbl; Capt Ftbl; Intrml Socr; Intrml Sftbl; Southern Advntst Acad; Scl Wrk.

ADAMS, JEREMY C; Cabot HS; Cabot, AR; (3); Boy Scts; Church Yth Grp; Debate Tm; NFL; Hon Roll; Stdnt Congress; NASAR; Contmpry Hist Awd; Pre-Pharm.

ADAMS, KATRINA R; Nettleton HS; Jonesboro, AR; (2); Science Clb; Chorus; Rep Stu Cncl; Lee Coll; Psych.

ADAMS, KEITH; Central HS; Mississippi State, MS; (4); Am Leg Aux Girls St; Bus Profs of Am; Church Yth Grp; FCA; FBLA; German Clb; Letterman Clb; Natl FFA Org; Science Clb; Band; M L King Jr Comm Of AR; Del Chrch Yth Sum Camp 90-92; Miss ST; Ag.

ADAMS, NATHAN; Bentonville Sr HS; Bentonville, AR; (3); Church Yth Grp; FCA; Spanish Clb; L Ftbl; Var Trk; Var Wt Lftg; Hon Roll; NHS; Pres Acad Fit Awd; Multi-Yr Listee; Pre-Med; Dr.

ADAMS, RACHEL D; St Joe Public Schl; Saint Joe, AR; (2); Church Yth Grp; FBLA; Natl FFA Org; Capt Quiz Bowl; Pres Frsh Cls; Rptr Soph Cls; Var Capt Bsktbl; Sftbl; Hon Roll; Prfct Atten Awd; PT.

ADAMS, ROTESHIA D; Lonoke Jr HS; Scott, AR; (1); #27 in class; FHA; Science Clb; Teachers Aide; Ed Nwsp; Hon Roll; Pulaski Tech Coll; Comp Data.

ADAMS, RYAN H; Russellville Sr HS; Russellville, AR; (3); French Clb; Science Clb; Teachers Aide; Varsity Clb; Chorus; Ofcr Bsbl; Bsktbl; AR Tech Univ.

ADAMS, SARA R; Mt St Mary Acad; Little Rock, AR; (4); 1/125; VP JCL; Latin Clb; Model UN; Treas Mu Alpha Theta; Ed Yrbk; Crs Cntry; Pom Pon; Trk; NHS; Val; Govs Schl; Prjct Arise & Camp For Handicapped Kids Vlntr.

ADAMS, SARAH; Brinkley HS; Brinkley, AR; (3); Drama Clb; French Clb; Pres FBLA; Quiz Bowl; Rep Church Choir; Sec Jr Cls; Sec Stu Cncl; NHS; Actns Pres; Jr Hmcmng Md; Ouachita Bapt U; Bus Adm.

ADAMS, SEAN; Kirby HS; Amity, AR; (2); 4/40; Chess Clb; FBLA; Natl Beta Clb; Natl FFA Org; Church Choir; Mgr Bsbl; Mgr Bsktbl; Mgr(s); Hon Roll; Henderson; Mech Or Elec Engr.

ADAMS, TAWNY S; England HS; England, AR; (2); Church Yth Grp; Drama Clb; Natl Beta Clb; Spanish Clb; Band; Color Guard; Flag Corp; Mrchg Band; Stage Crew; Band Plaque For 1st Div Percussion; Cert For Natl Sci Olympiad; Fire Marshall; LOYAL; U Of AR Little Rock; Soc Stud.

ADAMS, TAYLOR; Dumas HS; Dumas, AR; (2); 12/170; Church Yth Grp; FCA; FBLA; Math Clb; Natl Beta Clb; Quiz Bowl; Science Clb; Spanish Clb; Rep Stu Cncl; Ftbl; Beta Club Pres; U Of AR Fayettevl; Pre Med.

ADAMSKI, JULIE; Gosnell Jr Sr HS; Blytheville, AR; (2); Church Yth Grp; Cmnty Wkr; FHA; Science Clb; Band; Church Choir; Flag Corp; Mrchg Band; Pep Band; Hon Roll.

ADAMSON, DEVON; Northside HS; Fort Smith, AR; (1); Church Yth Grp; FCA; Chorus; Co-Capt Chrldng; Hon Roll; Jr NHS; Cmnty Wkr; Dance Clb; Teachers Aide; School Musical; Valentine Queen; Dirs Awd 95-96; Mixed Chorus; N Stepper Drill Team; West AR; Vet.

ADAMSON, NICOLE M; Bryant Sr HS; Mabelvale, AR; (3); Church Yth Grp; French Clb; Hon Roll; Hosp Explrs Pgm; U Of NE Lincoln; Med.

ADAMSON, VERONICA K; Springdale Sr HS; Springdale, AR; (3); Church Yth Grp; FCA; FBLA; Natl FFA Org; Phtg Co-Ed Yrbk; Intrml Powder Puff Ftbl; Hon Roll; NHS; Natl Svc & Ldrshp Awd Wnnr; All-Maer Schlr; Can Do Ctr & Mission NW AR Vol; Ouachita Bapt Univ; Chrstn Mins.

ADAWAY, CHANDRA L; West Memphis Sr HS; West Memphis, AR; (3); Natl Beta Clb; ROTC; Spanish Clb; Band; Drill Tm; Yrbk; Sec Stu Cncl; Trk; High Hon Roll; Prfct Atten Awd; Grand Princess Matron Royal Grand Chptr Yth Frat; Med.

ADCOCK, JEREMY S; Horatio HS; De Queen, AR; (2); Library Aide; Natl FFA Org; Office Aide; Hon Roll; Prfct Atten Awd.

ADCOCK, LAURA; Drew Central Jr Sr HS; Monticello, AR; (3); FBLA; Natl FFA Org; Socr; Hon Roll; Jr Sci Project Relating Stress Differences Between Sexes; Won 1st Pl At Schl & Went To Dist; Vet.

ADDINGTON, ELLEN MARIE; Rogers HS; Rogers, AR; (3); Church Yth Grp; FCA; FBLA; Model UN; Science Clb; Teachers Aide; Orch; Sec Soph Cls; VP Jr Cls; Sec VP Stu Cncl; Rogers Chamber Of Commerce Awd; AR Gov Schl; Multi-Cultural Clb; PACE Clb; REACH Clb.

ADDISON, BRANDI; Hazen Jr Sr HS; Hazen, AR; (1); Church Yth Grp; FHA; GAA; Church Choir; Ofcr Stu Cncl; JV Bsktbl; JV Co-Capt Chrldng; JV Trk; Hon Roll.

ADELOWO, SOLA; Arkansas Schl Math & Science; Blytheville, AR; (4); 4-H; FBLA; Mu Alpha Theta; Natl Beta Clb; Yrbk; Hist Stu Cncl; Var Bsktbl; L Vllybl; NHS; Spanish NHS; Sahkarov Rdngs; Wellesley Coll; Chem.

ADKINS, MICHAEL L; Yellville Summit HS; Yellville, AR; (3); 14/72; Church Yth Grp; Drama Clb; Quiz Bowl; Teachers Aide; Band; Mrchg Band; Pep Band; Ofcr Stu Cncl; High Hon Roll; Hon Roll; All-Region Band; Univ Of AR; Criminal Law.

ADKINS, SARAH; Central Sr HS; Little Rock, AR; (4); 4/420; Church Yth Grp; Cmnty Wkr; Pres French Clb; Natl Beta Clb; Ed Nwsp; Yrbk; Rep Sr Cls; Sec Jr NHS; NHS; Ntl Merit SF; 1st St Natl Frnch Exam 2 Yrs.

ADKINS, SHAWNA; Pea Ridge HS; Pea Ridge, AR; (4); 5/40; Art Clb; Church Yth Grp; FBLA; Office Aide; Yrbk; Cit Awd; Hon Roll; Kiwanis Awd; NHS; Pres Acad Fit Awd; 2nd Runner Up Ms Conginiality; Tchrs Aide; Kiwanis Youth Excl Awd; John Brown U; Elem Spec Ed.

ADWAY, CHRISTY; Star City HS; Star City, AR; (3); 30/100; Drama Clb; Spanish Clb; Band; Mrchg Band; School Play; Ntl Merit Ltr; Gftd & Tlntd; Stu Congress; Congressional Yth Ldrshp Cncl Nom; Comp Sci; Nrsng.

AGDEPPA, ROBERT M; Bergman Schl; Harrison, AR; (4); Natl Beta Clb; Natl FFA Org; Pep Clb; Spanish Clb; Ofcr Bsbl; Bsktbl; Hon Roll; U Of AR Fayetteville; Arch.

AGEE, JESSICA; Abundant Life Schools; Jacksonville, AR; (3); Church Yth Grp; Spanish Clb; Chorus; School Musical; School Play; Chrldng; Hon Roll; NHS; Arch/Dsgn.

AGEE, MARY; Prairie Grove HS; Prairie Grove, AR; (2); Acpl Chr; Chorus; High Hon Roll; VP Jr NHS; Mascot; Ftr Ctzns Of Hvn Treas; ACE Team; Eng Tchr.

AHART, ERIC A; Bryant Sr HS; Alexander, AR; (2); Hon Roll; Pres Acad Fit Awd; Play Guitar; UCA Conway.

AHMED, MEHREEN J; Waldron HS; Waldron, AR; (4); 2/91; Drama Clb; French Clb; FBLA; HOBY; Rep Natl Beta Clb; Office Aide; Spanish Clb; Teachers Aide; Band; Mrchg Band; Navy Hnrs/Tandy Awd; Mdlln Schlr; Hendrix Coll; Pre-Med.

AHNE, ANGELA D; Greenwood Sr HS; Greenwood, AR; (3); 19/215; FBLA; FHA; Natl Beta Clb; Spanish Clb; Teachers Aide; Rep Stu Cncl; Hon Roll; NHS; Ntl Merit Ltr; U Of AR; Phy Thrpy.

AITKEN, TARA; Lake Hamilton Sr HS; Hot Springs, AR; (4); 24/279; Church Yth Grp; FCA; Natl Beta Clb; Rptr Stu Cncl; Capt Bsktbl; Capt Chrldng; Hon Roll; NHS; Ntl Merit Ltr; Pres Acad Fit Awd; Garland Cty CC; Nrsng.

AJAYI, CHRIS; Dollarway HS; Pine Bluff, AR; (2); ROTC; Ofcr Jr Cls; Ftbl; Engrng.

AKBAR, NADEEM A; Russellville Sr HS; Russellville, AR; (2); #1 in class; Spanish Clb; Band; Mrchg Band; Rep Soph Cls; Rep Stu Cncl; JV Socr; Rptr Jr NHS; NHS; Pres Acad Fit Awd; Harvard; Genetic Engrng.

AKBAR, SAFDAR; Arkansas Schl Math & Science; Russellville, AR; (4); Am Leg Boys St; Church Yth Grp; Hosp Aide; Treas Mu Alpha Theta; Band; Rep Stu Cncl; Socr; Pres NHS; French Clb; FBLA; AR Govs Schl 95; Intnl Sci/Engrng Fair Fnlst; Lyon Coll; Chem/Med Dctr.

AKERS, AMBER R; Cabot HS; Cabot, AR; (3); #70 in class; Church Yth Grp; JA; Natl FFA Org; Spanish Clb; Teachers Aide; Hon Roll; Jr NHS; Kiwanis Awd; NHS; Prjct PALS; Schl Ltr; Med.

AKIN, KENDRA; Danville HS; Danville, AR; (4); 3/43; Am Leg Aux Girls St; Church Yth Grp; Pres FBLA; SADD; Band; Bsktbl; Hon Roll; Pres Acad Fit Awd; Pres Schlr; Sal; Atten Natl Yth Ldrshp Forum On Med In Boston; U Of Ozarks; Bio; Pre-Med.

AKINS, EMILY S; Foreman Jr Sr HS; Foreman, AR; (3); 4-H; FTA; Office Aide; SADD; Teachers Aide; Band; Mrchg Band; Hon Roll; Attnd AR Schl For Math & Sci; Occptnl Thrpst.

AKINS, JENNIFER D; Ozark HS; Ozark, AR; (3); 23/98; Church Yth Grp; FCA; FBLA; FHA; GAA; Natl Beta Clb; Red Cross Aide; Varsity Clb; Rep Frsh Cls; Rep Soph Cls; Frosh Hmcmng Maid/Soph Ftbl Hmcmn Maid/Jr Hmcmng Maid; Franklin Cnty Fair Queen Soph 95; U Cntrl AR; PT.

AKINS, RHONDA J; Yellville Summit HS; Pyatt, AR; (3); 11/72; FCA; FBLA; Office Aide; Ofcr Stu Cncl; Capt Bsktbl; High Hon Roll; Hon Roll; NHS; All-Conf, All-Regn Bsktbl; Finance.

AKKAD, REEM; Southside HS; Fort Smith, AR; (2); Debate Tm; French Clb; VP Q&S; Ed Yrbk; Pres French Hon Soc; High Hon Roll; NHS; Intnl Stud.

ALBERTSON JR, JAMES R; Jessieville HS; Hot Springs Villa, AR; (1); CAP; Red Cross Aide; Spanish Clb; Capt Color Guard; Capt Drill Tm; JV Var Bsbl; JV Var Bsktbl; JV Ftbl; Var Golf; Hon Roll; Air Force Acad; Aviation Sci.

ALBERTSON, MYRRIAH L; Jessieville HS; Hot Springs Natio, AR; (2); 24/54; Church Yth Grp; FCA; FHA; HOBY; Natl Beta Clb; Bsktbl; Mgr(s); Sftbl; Trk; Hero Amer Lung Assn Against Smoking; LSU; Vet.

ALBRIGHT, JESSICA J; Oden Schl; Sims, AR; (4); 4/16; VP FBLA; Natl Beta Clb; Natl FFA Org; Yrbk; Sec Stu Cncl; Capt Bsktbl; Capt Chrldng; Var Sftbl; Trk; Hon Roll; Bud/Katie Sampley Schlrshp; AR Chlng Schlrshp; U Of AR Fayettevl; Sports Med.

ALDRIDGE, MELISSA; Alma HS; Van Buren, AR; (4); 30/148; French Clb; Science Clb; Teachers Aide; Band; Mrchg Band; Hon Roll; NHS; Hnrs Dplma; AR Tech Univ.

ALEX, CHRIS; Gosnell Jr HS; Blytheville, AR; (1); Band; Mrchg Band; Pep Band; Ofcr Bsbl; Var Bsktbl; Cit Awd; High Hon Roll; Prfct Atten Awd; U Of MI; Engrng.

ALEXANDER, ANGELA R; Eudora HS; Eudora, AR; (2); 4/60; FHA; ROTC; SADD; Band; Church Choir; Cit Awd; High Hon Roll; Jr NHS; NHS; Prfct Atten Awd; Prins List; Lib Clb; U Of AR Fayetteville; Soc Work.

ALEXANDER, BECKAH; Bentonville Sr HS; Bentonville, AR; (4); 13/250; Am Leg Aux Girls St; Church Yth Grp; FCA; FBLA; HOBY; SADD; Pres Stu Cncl; Var JV Bsktbl; NHS; Pres Acad Fit Awd; AR Athtlcs Assn Interschlstc Achvt Awd; Homcmng Maid 93-94 & 94-95, Qn 95-96.

ALEXANDER, BRAD W; Springdale Sr HS; Springdale, AR; (1); Church Yth Grp; FCA; Chorus; Rep Frsh Cls; Treas Stu Cncl; Ftbl; Trk; Hon Roll; Jr NHS; Pres Acad Fit Awd; SPRTS Med.

ALEXANDER, CELESTE; Pine Bluff HS; Pine Bluff, AR; (2); French Clb; Natl Beta Clb; Teachers Aide; Acpl Chr; Band; Drm Mjr(t); Lit Mag; VP Frsh Cls; Rep Jr Cls; Capt JV Chrldng; Odyssey Of The Mind; A Team Mem; Chrch Pianist; Pine Bluff Yth Cncl Mem; NCA All Amer Chrldr Nom.

ALEXANDER, CHRIS M; Southside HS; Batesville, AR; (3); 20/90; Key Clb; Sec Soph Cls; Sec Jr Cls; Rep Stu Cncl; Hon Roll.

ALEXANDER, CODY R; Midland HS; Bradford, AR; (2); Church Yth Grp; Library Aide; Quiz Bowl; Spanish Clb; Ofcr Bsbl; Bsktbl; Ftbl; Score Keeper; Wt Lftg; Hon Roll; Dnstry.

ALEXANDER, JASON W; North Little Rock Hs-West; North Little Rock, AR; (3); Am Leg Boys St; Boy Scts; Computer Clb; Quiz Bowl; VICA; Band; Hon Roll; 1st Place ST Cmptr Comptn For VICA In AR; Attnd Natl Comptns; Cmptr Anlyst/Prgrmr.

ALEXANDER, PAIGE; Arkansas Sr HS; Texarkana, AR; (3); 30/342; Art Clb; Church Yth Grp; Dance Clb; Drama Clb; Mu Alpha Theta; Drill Tm; Variety Show; Ofcr Stu Cncl; Jr NHS; NHS; SAU At Mgnla; Bus Mgmt.

ALEXANDER, SHANNDOAN S; Leslie Schl; Leslie, AR; (2); FBLA; FHA; Key Clb; Natl Beta Clb; Teachers Aide; Treas Soph Cls; Bsktbl; High Hon Roll; Hon Roll; Homcmng Royalty; Key Clb Treas; Coll Of Ozarks; Marine Bio.

ALEXANDER, STEVEN J; Black Rock Jr Sr HS; Powhatan, AR; (2); Boy Scts; Church Yth Grp; Natl Beta Clb; Natl FFA Org; School Play; Ofcr Frsh Cls; Bsktbl; Hon Roll.

ALEXANDER, TRUSTAN T M; Magnolia HS; Waldo, AR; (3); Am Leg Boys St; Science Clb; Nwsp; Hon Roll.

ALFORD, BRANDY M; White Hall Sr HS; Pine Bluff, AR; (2); 46/214; Church Yth Grp; Drama Clb; FHA; JA; Natl Beta Clb; Spanish Clb; Teachers Aide; Chorus; Variety Show; Yrbk; FHA STAR Events Speech Cont 4th Pl; All-Region Cchoir 14th Chair; Marine Bio; Photo.

ALFORD, JAMES M; Oden Schl; Pencil Bluff, AR; (3); Cmnty Wkr; Natl Beta Clb; Natl FFA Org; Bsktbl; High Hon Roll; Hon Roll; Val; Rodeos Bare Back Riding; Show Cattle At Fairs; Southern AR Univ.

ALFORD, RACHEL; Cabot HS; Cabot, AR; (4); Church Yth Grp; FCA; HOBY; Key Clb; Ofcr Church Choir; JV Stat Bsktbl; Sftbl; Var Tennis; Hon Roll; Chrstn JUST Clb Pres; Cmmrcl Music.

ALFORD, TRAVIS D; Mc Crory Jr Sr HS; Mc Crory, AR; (3); Church Yth Grp; Teachers Aide; Varsity Clb; Church Choir; Ofcr Bsbl; Bsktbl; Ftbl; Trk; Wt Lftg; FL St Univ; Arch.

ALGEE, CARRIE; Lakeside HS; Hot Springs, AR; (4); 25/129; Am Leg Aux Girls St; Church Yth Grp; French Clb; FBLA; Natl Beta Clb; Thesps; Drill Tm; School Musical; Hon Roll; Jr NHS; AR ST U.

ALGOOD, JENNIFER E; Riverview HS; Kensett, AR; (2); Church Yth Grp; Library Aide; Natl Beta Clb; Office Aide; Pep Clb; Spanish Clb; Teachers Aide; Yrbk; Hon Roll.

ALI, SHAHRYAR; Highland HS; Hardy, AR; (2); Art Clb; Boy Scts; Computer Clb; FBLA; Key Clb; Library Aide; Math Clb; Science Clb; Teachers Aide; Yrbk; Harvard.

ALKINE, KALEB; Mountain Pine Jr Sr HS; Hot Springs, AR; (3); 1/50; French Clb; HOBY; Quiz Bowl; School Play; Hon Roll; Ntl Merit Ltr; Gfted And Tlnted; Env Clb; GCCC.

ALLABY, ERIC J; Bryant Sr HS; Alexander, AR; (2); Church Yth Grp; FBLA; L Bsktbl; Var L Crs Cntry; L Ftbl; Var Socr; Var L Trk; Spec Olympics Hlpr; U Of AR; PT/SPRTS Med.

ALLABY, NATALIE; Bryant Sr HS; Alexander, AR; (1); Church Yth Grp; Capt Chrldng.

ALLBAUGH, ERIN L; Mena HS; Mena, AR; (2); 27/159; Church Yth Grp; FBLA; Girl Scts; SADD; Band; Mrchg Band; Nwsp; Tennis; French Hon Soc; Hon Roll; Eastern OK ST; Ped Nurse.

ALLBRIGHT, BENJAMIN B; Lonoke Jr HS; Scott, AR; (1); Church Yth Grp; CAP; Church Choir; Trk; Hon Roll; Ecology Clb; Univ Of AR; Law Enfrcmnt.

ALLEN, ADAM D; Greenwood Sr HS; Greenwood, AR; (2); Church Yth Grp; Letterman Clb; Band; Jazz Band; Mrchg Band; Pep Band; Hon Roll; Pres Acad Fit Awd; Tae Kwon Do Red Belt; Ozark Chrstn Coll; Yth Mnstr.

ALLEN, ALONZA; Ashdown Jr HS; Ashdown, AR; (1); Church Yth Grp; Cmnty Wkr; Drama Clb; Spanish Clb; Teachers Aide; Church Choir; School Play; Chrldng; Vllybl; NHS; Miss Essence; Miss Ashdown Talent Cmptn Wnnr; Howard Univ; Lawyer.

ALLEN, ANTHONY J; Riverview HS; Judsonia, AR; (2); Natl Beta Clb; Spanish Clb; Hon Roll; Guitar Plyng; Psych.

ALLEN, ASHLEY L; Greenwood Sr HS; Greenwood, AR; (2); Church Yth Grp; High Hon Roll; Hon Roll; Jr NHS; U Of AR; Nurse.

ALLEN, BRYAN O; Blytheville Sr HS; Blytheville, AR; (4); Art Clb; Cmnty Wkr; DECA; Drama Clb; FBLA; FHA; Natl Beta Clb; Spanish Clb; Hon Roll; Pres Acad Fit Awd; ATA Tae Kwondo Assn Red Blt; Yth Amer Bwlng Assn; SE MO ST U; Crmnl Jstc.

ALLEN, CODI C; Rogers HS; Rogers, AR; (3); Church Yth Grp; FCA; 4-H; Pep Clb; Drill Tm; Nwsp; Pom Pon; Hon Roll; Jr NHS; NHS; Regnl Graphic Art Awd 3rd Pl; Capt Drill Team 96-97; UCA; Vet.

ALLEN, ELISABET; Rogers HS; Rogers, AR; (4); Cmnty Wkr; FBLA; Library Aide; Science Clb; SADD; Orch; Mgr Yrbk; Rptr Stu Cncl; Gov Hon Prg Awd; High Hon Roll; FBLA Parlmntrn; Govs Schl Natural Sci; Baylor U; Genetics Cnslr.

ALLEN, ERIN; Batesville Sr HS; Batesville, AR; (4); 2/150; Am Leg Aux Girls St; HOBY; School Play; Stage Crew; Pres Stu Cncl; Chrldng; Gov Hon Prg Awd; Ntl Merit SF; Vlntr NE AR Reg AIDS Ntwrk; AR Yth Cmmssn Epscpl Diocese Of AR; U Of South; Pltcl Sci.

ALLEN, EVELYN; Hughes Jr-Sr HS; Hughes, AR; (3); Church Yth Grp; Math Clb; Mu Alpha Theta; Quiz Bowl; Science Clb; VP Spanish Clb; Band; Jazz Band; Mrchg Band; Pep Band; GT; Beta Clb; AR ST U; Comp Sci.

ALLEN, JANIS L; Sheridan Sr HS; Sheridan, AR; (4); Sec Church Yth Grp; Drama Clb; Chorus; Church Choir; Sec Soph Cls; Hon Roll; GCECA; S AR Univ; Busmktg.

ALLEN, JENNIFER L; Southside HS; Fort Smith, AR; (4); 228/459; FBLA; FHA; JA; Latin Clb; Service Clb; SADD; Band; Drill Tm; Flag Corp; Hon Roll.

ALLEN, LAURA; Dewitt HS; Gillett, AR; (4); 4/80; Am Leg Aux Girls St; Church Yth Grp; FBLA; FTA; HOBY; Natl Beta Clb; Q&S; School Play; Nwsp; Yrbk; U Of AR; Acctng.

ALLEN, MELISSA A; Hope HS; Hope, AR; (4); 23/195; French Clb; Natl Beta Clb; Natl FFA Org; Nwsp; Hon Roll; Red River Coll; Bus.

ALLEN, SHANIKA T; Nevada Schl; Rosston, AR; (2); 5/70; French Clb; FBLA; FHA; FTA; Library Aide; Natl Beta Clb; Natl FFA Org; Office Aide; Quiz Bowl; Teachers Aide; Hmcmng Ct; Cmptr Prgrmr.

ALLEN, SHEILA M; Lakeside HS; Portland, AR; (3); 26/89; Drama Clb; FHA; School Play; Stage Crew; Powder Puff Ftbl; Hon Roll; Prfct Atten Awd; Stu Of Mnth; Pre Optom.

ALLEN, SHELLY; Bradley Jr Sr HS; Bradley, AR; (1); 3/35; Church Yth Grp; FHA; Quiz Bowl; Band; VP Frsh Cls; Rep Stu Cncl; Capt Chrldng; Sftbl; Piano; Smmr Sftbl; Henderson ST U; Med.

ALLEN, SHIQUENA; Crawfordsville HS; Crawfordsville, AR; (1); 4/24; Cmnty Wkr; French Clb; FTA; Natl Beta Clb; Sec Sr Cls; Pres Stu Cncl; Cit Awd; Hon Roll; Ntl Merit Schol; FHA; Gftd & Tlntd Pgm; POWER Clb; UAPB; Producer.

ALLEN, TAMLA M; Nevada Schl; Rosston, AR; (2); 1/73; FBLA; FHA; FTA; HOBY; Natl Beta Clb; Quiz Bowl; VP Frsh Cls; Pres Soph Cls; Stat Bsktbl; Var Chrldng; Pediatrician.

ALLEN, WILL R; Fordyce HS; Fordyce, AR; (4); Am Leg Boys St; Church Yth Grp; Cmnty Wkr; FBLA; Office Aide; Science Clb; Chorus; Yrbk; Ofcr Jr Cls; Ofcr Sr Cls; All St Track; Athl Of Yr; Decathalon; AR ST U.

ALLENDER, LETA C; Midland HS; Floral, AR; (3); Drama Clb; School Play; Treas Frsh Cls; Bsktbl; Hon Roll; Poem Pub In Nation Wide Bk Poetry In The Schls.

ALLEY, ROBYN D; Springdale Sr HS; Springdale, AR; (3); FBLA; Key Clb; Q&S; Teachers Aide; Ed Yrbk; Hon Roll; Jr NHS; PAL Pgm; Jrnlsm/Bus.

ALLINDER, MELISSA D; Conway Sr HS; Conway, AR; (2); Art Clb; Church Yth Grp; Drama Clb; FBLA; German Clb; Hosp Aide; Rptr Nwsp; Yrbk; Hon Roll; All Stars; Renaissance Fndtn; Harding Univ; Tchr; Psycht.

ALLISON, AMBER; Hackett Schl; Hackett, AR; (4); 8/40; Church Yth Grp; FBLA; Pep Clb; Spanish Clb; Teachers Aide; Drill Tm; Sec Frsh Cls; Sec Soph Cls; VP Jr Cls; Bsktbl; Chrldng Capt & Co-Capt; All-Star Chrldr; Westark JC; Dntl.

ALLISON, JAROD; Delaplaine Schl; Beech Grove, AR; (1); Church Yth Grp; Cmnty Wkr; Debate Tm; FCA; Ofcr Frsh Cls; Quiz Bowl; Teachers Aide; Chorus; Bsktbl; Score Keeper; Clss King.

ALLISON, JENNIFER; Morrilton Sr HS; Morrilton, AR; (3); Church Yth Grp; Library Aide; Math Clb; Natl Beta Clb; Science Clb; Spanish Clb; Thesps; Band; Church Choir; Mrchg Band; Bst Mscn Awd; AR Tech Rssllvlle; Law.

ALLISON, JENNIFER L; Searcy HS; Searcy, AR; (2); 32/256; Art Clb; Church Yth Grp; Dance Clb; French Clb; FTA; Natl Beta Clb; Yrbk; Sec Frsh Cls; Ofcr Stu Cncl; Chrldng; City Sftbl; All-Star Dnc Tm; Stanford Univ; Med Prfssn/Obgyn.

ALLISON, JOSHUA G; John L Mcclellan Magnet HS; Little Rock, AR; (3); Boy Scts; Church Yth Grp; Letterman Clb; Natl Beta Clb; Mgr Bsbl; Mgr Ftbl; High Hon Roll; Hon Roll; AR Governors Schl Alt.

ALLISON, MISTY; Harrisburg HS; Cherry Valley, AR; (2); Sec Church Yth Grp; FCA; Hist FBLA; Quiz Bowl; Science Clb; Spanish Clb; Co-Ed JV Chrldng; Hon Roll; NHS; Acpl Chr; Intgeract Clb; Madrigals Choir; Gftd & Tlntd Mem.

ALLISON III, ROBERT M; Cabot HS; Cabot, AR; (3); 44/398; CAP; ROTC; Color Guard; Hon Roll; Jr NHS; Kiwanis Awd; NHS; Sons Of Maer Revltn Awd; Natl Sojourners Awd; Air Frc Assoc Awd; U Of AR; Aero Eng.

ALLISON, STACEY R; Fountain Hill Schl; Hamburg, AR; (3); 3/19; Am Leg Aux Girls St; Church Yth Grp; Drama Clb; FBLA; Chorus; Church Choir; Var JV Bsktbl; Var Sftbl; Cit Awd; Hon Roll; Hmcmng Maid; Premed.

ALLMON, JOHN; Brinkley HS; Brinkley, AR; (2); Quiz Bowl; VICA; VP Stu Cncl; Var L Bsbl; Hon Roll; Jr NHS; NHS; Gftd & Tlntd; St Page; Engl, Auto Mech, Civics & Phys Sci Hghst GPA Gold Mdl; Bus/Commnctns.

ALLRED, JESSICA; Morrilton Sr HS; Morrilton, AR; (4); 17/150; VP French Clb; Rptr Library Aide; Natl Beta Clb; Thesps; Band; School Play; Stage Crew; Ed Nwsp; Hon Roll; Mjrtt Cap & Co Cap; U Of Ozarks; Thtr.

ALLRED, KIMBERLY D; Dollarway HS; Pine Bluff, AR; (2); 11/300; Art Clb; Teachers Aide; Chorus; Cit Awd; Hon Roll; Pres Acad Fit Awd; Pines Tech Coll; Nrsng.

ALLRED, LANA J; Des Arc Jr Sr HS; Griffithville, AR; (3); 10/37; FTA; Library Aide; Natl Beta Clb; Office Aide; Science Clb; Spanish Clb; Teachers Aide; Ed Yrbk; Hon Roll; Psych.

ALLRED, MELISSA L; Green Forest Jr Sr HS; Green Forest, AR; (2); Girl Scts; Band; Flag Corp; Mrchg Band; Pep Band; Ed Yrbk; High Hon Roll; Jr NHS; Girl Scout Ldrshp Awd/Silver Awd; Coll Of Ozarks; Pharm Chem.

ALLSPACH, STEVEN D; Mansfield Jr Sr HS; Booneville, AR; (1); Art Clb; Debate Tm; Drama Clb; FCA; JV Bsbl; JV Bsktbl; JV Ftbl; JV Trk; Hon Roll.

ALMAND, ANDY; Prescott HS; Prescott, AR; (2); #1 in class; Church Yth Grp; FBLA; Band; Jazz Band; Mrchg Band; Pres Soph Cls; Pres Rep Stu Cncl; Hon Roll; Kiwanis Awd; NHS; Piano.

ALMAND, MELISSA; Nevada Schl; Prescott, AR; (3); 1/50; Church Yth Grp; Phtg FBLA; HOBY; Treas Natl Beta Clb; Quiz Bowl; Treas Band; High Hon Roll; Drug Free Tm; Gftd/Tlntd; U Cntrl AR; Phrmcy.

ALMOND, AMBER; Mountain Home HS; Mountain Home, AR; (4); Church Yth Grp; FCA; Treas Key Clb; Natl Beta Clb; Spanish Clb; Ed Nwsp; Sec Stu Cncl; Capt Chrldng; Sftbl; AR Acad Challenge Schlsp; Top 10 Fnlst In Mr & Mrs Mtn Home HS Cont; AR ST U; Sci Of Nrsng.

ALRED, JONI N; Quitman Jr Sr HS; Quitman, AR; (2); Church Yth Grp; FBLA; FHA; SADD; Teachers Aide; Yrbk; Hon Roll; JR Beta Club; Aprntc Vet; BETA Club; Vet.

ALTOM, BRANDY; Bradford Jr Sr HS; Bradford, AR; (3); 2/50; French Clb; VP FBLA; Pres FHA; Girl Scts; Band; Yrbk; Pres Jr Cls; Hist Stu Cncl; Bsktbl; Hon Roll; Lyons Coll; Pre-Med.

ALTON, AMANDA; Harding Acad; Searcy, AR; (2); Church Yth Grp; Key Clb; Natl Beta Clb; Pep Clb; Spanish Clb; Chorus; School Musical; Sec Frsh Cls; Rep Soph Cls; Var Bsktbl; Harding Univ.

ALTON, TONI M; West Fork HS; West Fork, AR; (1); Band; Color Guard; West Fork HS Band Letterman Awd; U Of AR; Chem.

ALVARADO, ANGELICA L; Benton Cty Christian School; Springdale, AR; (1); Church Yth Grp; Chorus; School Play; VP Frsh Cls; High Hon Roll; Stdnt Mnth Awd; Certf Achvmt Wrlg Geography; Harding; Acctng.

ALVARADO, MELISSA R; Poyen Schl; Poyen, AR; (2); FCA; FHA; Natl Beta Clb; Spanish Clb; Treas Soph Cls; Sftbl; High Hon Roll; Hon Roll; Medcl.

ALVERSON, ZACK; Humphrey Schl; Humphrey, AR; (1); Church Yth Grp; Natl FFA Org; Quiz Bowl; Nwsp; Bsktbl; Hon Roll; Gftd/Tlntd Pgm.

ALVIS, HARRY G; Southside HS; Batesville, AR; (4); Art Clb; Key Clb; Library Aide; Spanish Clb; Stage Crew; Hon Roll; St Schlr; Hnr Awd 96; AR Acad Challenge Schlsp; Acad Distinction Schlsp AR ST Univ; AR Tech Univ; Medicine.

AMAN, GAYLA D; Decatur HS; Decatur, AR; (4); Art Clb; Rptr Nwsp; Yrbk; High Hon Roll; Hon Roll; Eng Awd; Span Awd; NWACC; Acctng.

AMBRO, AMBER; Augusta HS; Augusta, AR; (1); Church Yth Grp; Phtg 4-H; VP Natl Beta Clb; Science Clb; Church Choir; Flag Corp; VP Frsh Cls; JV Bsktbl; High Hon Roll; Pres Acad Fit Awd; KS U; Pedtrcn.

AMBROSE, APRIL; Searcy HS; Searcy, AR; (3); Church Yth Grp; FCA; 4-H; FTA; HOBY; Natl Beta Clb; Spanish Clb; Teachers Aide; Band; Church Choir; Tae Kwon Do; Shclrshp Pgm Fndr; Hndrsn ST U; Tchng.

AMBROSE, CAROL; Harmony Grove Jr Sr HS; Camden, AR; (1); 1/70; Church Yth Grp; Pres Natl Beta Clb; Quiz Bowl; Spanish Clb; Band; Chrmn Chrldng; High Hon Roll; USAF Acad CS; Math.

AMBROSE, KELLEY; Central HS; West Helena, AR; (4); 4/200; Am Leg Aux Girls St; Church Yth Grp; Teachers Aide; Acpl Chr; High Hon Roll; Jr NHS; NHS; Pres Of Natl Hnr Soc; Sr Hmcmng Ct; Phillips Coll Of U Of AK; Nrs.

AMERSON, GREG; Mt Ida Jr Sr HS; Mount Ida, AR; (3); 1/45; Rep Am Leg Boys St; Church Yth Grp; Cmnty Wkr; Pres Natl Beta Clb; Quiz Bowl; Band; Jazz Band; Mrchg Band; Ftbl; High Hon Roll; Trig Awd 11th Grd; Wld His Awd 10th Grd; Univ Of AR; Engrng.

AMIN, MANISH J; Goza Jr HS; Arkadelphia, AR; (1); Bsktbl; Hon Roll; Jr NHS; NHS; Choir; Knowledge Mstrs Open; Rice; Med.

AMIS, KARIN L; Parkers Chapel Schl; El Dorado, AR; (3); 1/55; Am Leg Aux Girls St; Church Yth Grp; French Clb; FBLA; Natl Beta Clb; Quiz Bowl; Teachers Aide; School Play; Yrbk; High Hon Roll; Best All Around Sr HS Of Parkers Chapel Schl 95-96; Evangel Coll; Pediatrician; Med.

AMMONS, KRISTI; Gosnell Jr Sr HS; Blytheville, AR; (2); #1 in class; VP French Clb; FHA; Key Clb; Natl Beta Clb; SADD; Capt Chrldng; Powder Puff Ftbl; High Hon Roll; Pres Acad Fit Awd; Concert Choir; MS U; Med.

AMONETTE, JAMIE; Clarendon Jr Sr HS; Clarendon, AR; (3); Church Yth Grp; Cmnty Wkr; FCA; VP FBLA; FHA; HOBY; Natl Beta Clb; Pep Clb; Chorus; Church Choir; OM; Yth Action Cncl; AR ST U Jonesboro; Commnctns.

ANDERS, CATHY; Jacksonville HS; Jacksonville, AR; (2); 12/360; Church Yth Grp; Drama Clb; FCA; Natl Beta Clb; Spanish Clb; Yrbk; VP Stu Cncl; Capt Chrldng; Hon Roll; Wildlife Rehabilitation Vlntr.

ANDERSO, HILLARY S; Central Sr HS; Little Rock, AR; (2); FBLA; Band; Drill Tm; Var Capt Bsktbl; Var Capt Vllybl; Hon Roll; U Of Houston.

ANDERSON, AMANDA K; Lake Hamilton Sr HS; Pearcy, AR; (3); Church Yth Grp; FBLA; Library Aide; Spanish Clb; Teachers Aide; Band; Color Guard; Mrchg Band; Orch; School Musical; EMT Explr; Henderson; Med Rdlgy.

ANDERSON, AMY; Van Buren Sr HS; Fort Smith, AR; (3); FBLA; FHA; Mu Alpha Theta; Quiz Bowl; Spanish Clb; Band; Mrchg Band; High Hon Roll; Jr NHS; NHS; Erth Club Treas; Dartmouth; Neonatology.

ANDERSON, ANDREA; Greenwood Sr HS; Greenwood, AR; (3); French Clb; Teachers Aide; NHS; Ntl Merit Ltr; Westark CC; Elem Ed.

ANDERSON, BLYTHE E; Southside HS; Batesville, AR; (3); Treas Am Leg Aux Girls St; Church Yth Grp; GAA; Hosp Aide; Key Clb; Natl Beta Clb; Band; Rep Stu Cncl; Hon Roll; Bsktbl; PRIDE.

ANDERSON, BROOKE E; Jessieville HS; Mountain Pine, AR; (2); 4/50; Church Yth Grp; Natl Beta Clb; Teachers Aide; Band; Mrchg Band; Pep Band; Hon Roll; Prfct Atten Awd.

ANDERSON, CARLA L; John L Mcclellan Magnet HS; Little Rock, AR; (2); FBLA; FHA; Mu Alpha Theta; Spanish Clb; Cit Awd; Hon Roll; NHS; U Of AR Little Rock; Nrsng.

ANDERSON, CHRISTINA D; Northside HS; Fort Smith, AR; (3); Teachers Aide; Rptr Nwsp; Rptr Yrbk; Hon Roll.

ANDERSON, CHRISTINE M; Springdale Sr HS; Springdale, AR; (3); Am Leg Aux Girls St; Church Yth Grp; Cmnty Wkr; Key Clb; SADD; Acpl Chr; VP Soph Cls; Rep Jr Cls; VP Stu Cncl; Stat Bsktbl; Piano 4 Yrs; Pre-Med/Orthpdc Srgn.

ANDERSON, CHRYSTIE R; Central HS; West Helena, AR; (2); French Clb; Office Aide; Teachers Aide; Acpl Chr; Chorus; Lit Mag; Ofcr Soph Cls; Trk; Hon Roll; GA Tech; Electrcl Engr.

ANDERSON, CINDY; Genoa Central HS; Texarkana, AR; (4); Church Yth Grp; Cmnty Wkr; FCA; Bsktbl; Crs Cntry; Trk; Cit Awd; Hon Roll; NHS; Prfct Atten Awd; Schl Play Role; Texarkana Coll.

ANDERSON II, DENNIS L; Lake Hamilton Sr HS; Pearcy, AR; (2); 1/230; Church Yth Grp; Natl Beta Clb; Capt Quiz Bowl; Spanish Clb; Church Choir; High Hon Roll; NHS; Pres Acad Fit Awd; Chrch Bible Quiz Tm Capt; PTSA Rprtr; Chrch Drmmr; Gateway Coll Evnglsm; Theolgy.

ANDERSON, IVAN A; Forrest City HS; Forrest City, AR; (3); Drama Clb; FTA; Science Clb; Thesps; Chorus; Church Choir; School Play; High Hon Roll; Hon Roll; Ntl Yth Forum Med; PT.

ANDERSON, JESSICA; Rogers HS; Rogers, AR; (4); 1/550; Church Yth Grp; FCA; Science Clb; Spanish Clb; Acpl Chr; Trk; Vllybl; DAR Awd; Pres Schlr; Val; Hendrix Coll; Bio.

ANDERSON, JOSHUA; Southside HS; Fort Smith, AR; (3); 79/502; Ofcr FBLA; Math Clb; Mu Alpha Theta; Spanish Clb; JV Bsktbl; Hon Roll; Jr NHS; NHS; Pres Acad Fit Awd; Spanish NHS; Pub Kudos 90-91; Acctng.

ANDERSON, JULIA R; Blytheville Sr HS; Blytheville, AR; (4); 15/221; FBLA; Math Clb; Natl Beta Clb; ROTC; Spanish Clb; Band; Drill Tm; Drm Mjr(t); Pres Jr Cls; Rep Sr Cls; Young Ladies Clb; Hampton Univ; Acctng.

ANDERSON, JULIE E; Central Sr HS; Little Rock, AR; (2); Church Yth Grp; French Clb; Natl Beta Clb; Band; Powder Puff Ftbl; Socr; Flwshp Of Chrstn Stdnts; VP Of Chrch Yth Group; V-Teens Mem.

ANDERSON, KIM; Delta Special Schl; Arkansas City, AR; (3); 10/20; Church Yth Grp; Girl Scts; Quiz Bowl; Spanish Clb; Church Choir; Variety Show; Rptr Nwsp; Rptr Yrbk; Hist Frsh Cls; Stat Chrldng; Reg Hist Day Cont 3rd Pl; Beta Clb; Tchr.

ANDERSON, MADALYN; Mills HS; Little Rock, AR; (4); 9/173; Sec Church Yth Grp; Mu Alpha Theta; Church Choir; VP Soph Cls; Var L Bsktbl; High Hon Roll; NHS; Natl Beta Clb; Science Clb; Pres Acad Excl Awd; Army Rsrv Schlr Ath Awd; U Of Cntrl AR; Nrsng.

ANDERSON, MARK; Central Ark Christian Schl; Little Rock, AR; (3); Church Yth Grp; Science Clb; Spanish Clb; Pres Jr Cls; Stat Bsbl; Var L Ftbl; Var L Trk; Histry Clb; U Of Cntrl AR; Chem Eng.

ANDERSON, MICHELLE D; Rose Bud Jr Sr HS; Romance, AR; (1); Drama Clb; FHA; Natl FFA Org; Band; School Play; Ofcr Frsh Cls; Mgr(s); Score Keeper; Sftbl; High Hon Roll; Natl FFA Org Greenhand Awd; ASU; Ag Dr/Med.

ANDERSON, MILLICENT D; Mills HS; Little Rock, AR; (2); 17/449; VP Church Yth Grp; Cmnty Wkr; Mu Alpha Theta; Spanish Clb; Church Choir; Drill Tm; Variety Show; Pres Soph Cls; Hon Roll; NHS; Homcmng Qn 94; Natl Sci Olympiad For Bio; Law; Span.

ANDERSON, RICKY; El Dorado Sr HS; Lawrenceville, GA; (3); 10/300; Boy Scts; Church Yth Grp; Key Clb; Library Aide; Natl Beta Clb; Band; Mrchg Band; Socr; Swmmng; Hon Roll; Basic Club.

ANDERSON, RYAN COLLIN; Monticello HS; Monticello, AR; (3); Boy Scts; Church Yth Grp; FCA; Math Clb; Natl Beta Clb; Science Clb; SADD; Var L Trk; NHS; JV Ftbl; Mascot; HOSA Prlmntrn.

ANDERSON, SABRINA; Camden-Fairview HS; Camden, AR; (4); 62/265; SADD; Band; High Hon Roll; Hon Roll; NHS; US Army Rsrv; Southern AK U Tech; Elec Engr.

ANDERSON, SHELLY N; Van Buren Sr HS; Alma, AR; (2); FCA; SADD; Drill Tm; Ofcr Stu Cncl; Bsktbl; Vllybl; Hon Roll; Jr NHS; Church Yth Grp; GAA; Soph Bsktbl Hmcmng Crt; Soph Cls Fvrt; Scl Wrkr.

ANDERSON, TAMEKA C; Palestine-Wheatley HS; Palestine, AR; (3); 17/54; Church Yth Grp; 4-H; FHA; Chorus; Church Choir; Yth Opportunities Unltd U Of AR; U Of AR Pine Bluff; Gen Math.

ANDERSON, TOREZ L; Hope HS; Hope, AR; (3); Church Yth Grp; FHA; Natl Beta Clb; Chorus; Church Choir; Hon Roll; Church Pianist 5 Yrs; Henderson; Pdtrcs.

ANDERSON, VICKI; Rogers HS; Rogers, AR; (4); 52/468; Church Yth Grp; Cmnty Wkr; Pres VP FTA; Church Choir; Hon Roll; NHS; Pres Acad Fit Awd; FBLA; Girl Scts; Office Aide; Immanuel Bapt Portable Players Dir; U AR; Scndry Hstry Tchr.

ANDERSON, WESLEY; Pine Bluff HS; Pine Bluff, AR; (3); 19/485; Am Leg Boys St; JA; Varsity Clb; Var Bsbl; Var Bsktbl; High Hon Roll; Jr NHS; NHS; Pres Acad Fit Awd; Pres Schlr; Amer Lgn Boys St.

ANDREAS, LALONI L; Van Buren Sr HS; Van Buren, AR; (2); FBLA; Pep Clb; Chorus; Drill Tm; Pom Pon; Hon Roll; Tchg/Athltcs.

ANDREPONT, VERONICA; Greenwood Sr HS; Greenwood, AR; (2); Var JV Chrldng; JV Trk; Cit Awd; High Hon Roll; Hon Roll; Jr NHS; Prfct Atten Awd; Engrng.

ANDREWS, BENJAMIN L; Conway Sr HS; Conway, AR; (3); Church Yth Grp; Acpl Chr; Band; Chorus; Church Choir; Mrchg Band; School Musical.

ANDREWS, BRYAN; Forrest City HS; Colt, AR; (3); Am Leg Boys St; Natl Beta Clb; Q&S; Quiz Bowl; Spanish Clb; Band; Sprt Ed Nwsp; Var L Ftbl; High Hon Roll; Delta Sigma Natl Frat Beta Zeta Chptr Mem.

ANDREWS, CHARLOTTE D; Sacred Heart Schl; Morrilton, AR; (3); Art Clb; Drama Clb; German Clb; GAA; Key Clb; Natl Beta Clb; SADD; Stage Crew; Rptr Yrbk; Treas Soph Cls; Univ Of Cntrl AR; PT.

ANDREWS, JAMIE; Mc Gehee HS; Mc Gehee, AR; (4); 5/104; Am Leg Aux Girls St; Drama Clb; FTA; Mu Alpha Theta; Natl Beta Clb; Band; Drm Mjr(t); Rep Sr Cls; Rep Stu Cncl; Hon Roll; AR St Univ; Spch Path.

ANDREWS, SAMANTHA; Ozark HS; Ozark, AR; (4); 4/91; Pres French Clb; Pres Rep FHA; Intnl Clb; Math Clb; Model UN; Mu Alpha Theta; Natl Beta Clb; Quiz Bowl; SADD; Band; Oxford Brookes U; Peds Oncolgst.

ANGELETTI, NIKKI; West Memphis Christian Schl; Crawfordsville, AR; (2); Church Yth Grp; FCA; Natl Beta Clb; Quiz Bowl; Pres Frsh Cls; Pres Soph Cls; JV Var Bsktbl; JV Chrldng; Var Trk; High Hon Roll; Bsktbl Hmcmng Ct; Cls Fvrt For 9/10 Grds; Med.

ANGLES, MELISSA A; Northside HS; Barling, AR; (4); Church Yth Grp; 4-H; FHA; Band; Mrchg Band; Nwsp; 4-H Awd; Medcl Image.

ANGLIN, DONNA M; Booneville Jr Sr HS; Booneville, AR; (3); Art Clb; Fshn Dsgnr.

ANGLIN, TRENTON C; Dollarway HS; Pine Bluff, AR; (4); 23/96; Boy Scts; Church Yth Grp; ROTC; L Ftbl; Trk; Distngd Cadet 2 Yrs; Hnr Cadet 1 Yr; Amer Legion Acad Awd; Nashville Auto & Diesel Schl.

ANGTUACO, MICHAEL J; Catholic HS; Little Rock, AR; (3); 7/172; Church Yth Grp; Cmnty Wkr; Hosp Aide; Library Aide; Math Tm; ROTC; Service Clb; Chorus; Stage Crew; Phtg Rptr Yrbk; Princeton; Med.

ANHALT, DUSTIN P; Russellville Sr HS; Russellville, AR; (3); Church Yth Grp; High Hon Roll; Jr NHS; Bosy & Girls Clb Bsktbl; HS All-Stars; U Of AR; Engr.

ANSCHUTZ, JESSICA; Cabot HS; Cabot, AR; (4); Am Leg Aux Girls St; Pres Sec Art Clb; Pres Church Yth Grp; Capt Debate Tm; Key Clb; Sec Spanish Clb; Stage Crew; VP NHS; Pres Acad Fit Awd; Spanish NHS; Dist Cncl & Conf Cncl On Yth Ministry; Rhodes Coll.

ANTHONY, ALISHA L; Forrest City HS; Forrest City, AR; (3); FHA; Office Aide; Hon Roll; U Of Cntrl AR; Psych.

ANTHONY, ASHLEE N; Goza Jr HS; Arkadelphia, AR; (1); 20/180; Church Yth Grp; Office Aide; Rptr Nwsp; Phtg Yrbk; Capt Bsktbl; Sftbl; Hon Roll; Homecmng Royalty; Frosh Class Most Ath/All Around Favorite; U Of AR Fayetteville.

ANTHONY, CHRISTY; Bearden HS; Bearden, AR; (2); Church Yth Grp; 4-H; FBLA; Model UN; Natl Beta Clb; Church Choir; Chrldng; Score Keeper; Hon Roll; Pres Acad Fit Awd; U Of AR Fayetteville.

ANTHONY, KRYSTAL J; Hampton Jr Sr HS; Hampton, AR; (3); Church Yth Grp; 4-H; Teachers Aide; Acpl Chr; Chorus; Church Choir; Trk; 4-H Awd; Hon Roll; Band; Math Awd; PRIDE; RN.

ANTHONY, LA TONYA L; Trumann HS; Trumann, AR; (3); Church Yth Grp; Cmnty Wkr; Science Clb; Spanish Clb; Acpl Chr; Chorus; Church Choir; Yrbk; Vllybl; NHS; Var Choir Pres; Cert Of Achvmt; AR ST Univ; Medicine.

APPLE, BRANDON L; Southside HS; Batesville, AR; (2); High Hon Roll; Violin In My Band; Restore Cars.

APPLEBERRY, RUSTY; Dumas Jr HS; Dumas, AR; (1); Church Yth Grp; FBLA; Natl Beta Clb; Science Clb; Spanish Clb; Var Gym; High Hon Roll; Gymnast Of Yr.

APPLEGATE, JERRI M; Spring Hill HS; Hope, AR; (3); Church Yth Grp; French Clb; FBLA; FHA; Natl Beta Clb; Quiz Bowl; SADD; Church Choir; Ofcr Stu Cncl; Bsktbl.

APPLETON, EMILY; Pulaski Acad; Little Rock, AR; (3); Church Yth Grp; FCA; French Clb; Natl Beta Clb; Chorus; Treas Jr Cls; Chrldng; Powder Puff Ftbl; Socr; High Hon Roll; Bus.

ARCENEAUX, KIMBERLY D; Rose Bud Jr Sr HS; Rose Bud, AR; (3); Drama Clb; French Clb; FHA; Library Aide; Stage Crew; Work People; Work Animals; U Cntrl AR; Bus/Cmptrs.

ARCHER, JENNIFER L; Springdale Sr HS; Springdale, AR; (2); Church Yth Grp; French Clb; FBLA; Hosp Aide; Math Clb; Red Cross Aide; Band; Color Guard; Mrchg Band; Orch; Piano; All Region Band; U Of AR; Med; Criminal Path.

ARCHER, LAURA L; Bryant Sr HS; Bryant, AR; (2); Church Yth Grp; Hosp Aide; Office Aide; Teachers Aide; Band; Chorus; Church Choir; Color Guard; Mrchg Band; School Musical; Most Imprvd Band Stdnt; Band 1st Yr Letter; Pediatrition.

ARENSMAN, WILLIAM L; Hamburg HS; Portland, AR; (4); Am Leg Boys St; Quiz Bowl; School Play; Nwsp; Tennis; Hon Roll; NHS; Ntl Merit SF; Drama Clb; Yrbk; Govs Schl; Physics Clb; Hendrix Coll.

ARIVETT, BROCK A; Dequeen HS; De Queen, AR; (2); Church Yth Grp; Natl FFA Org; JV Bsbl; Var Bsktbl; Cit Awd; Hon Roll; Pres Acad Fit Awd; U Of AR.

ARMER, LACY; Alpena Schl; Harrison, AR; (3); 8/48; Church Yth Grp; FCA; Pres Rptr FBLA; Library Aide; Rptr Natl Beta Clb; Pres Spanish Clb; Chorus; Church Choir; Capt Chrldng; Hon Roll; U Of AR; Phys Thpy.

ARMOUR, MYRON L; Lakeside HS; Lake Village, AR; (2); #15 in class; Church Yth Grp; Drama Clb; FBLA; Band; Church Choir; Mrchg Band; School Play; Rep Stu Cncl; L Var Trk; Jr NHS; US Ar Frc Acad; Elctrcl Engrng.

ARMSTRONG, ADRIAN C; Conway Sr HS; Conway, AR; (3); Church Yth Grp; FBLA; Spanish Clb; Band; Church Choir; Mrchg Band; Intrml Bsktbl; Intrml Ftbl; Spanish NHS; Conway All-Stars Staff; Henderson ST Univ; Pre-Dental.

ARMSTRONG, DORA L; Harrison Sr HS; Harrison, AR; (4); Teachers Aide; Hon Roll; North AR Comm Tech Coll; RN.

ARMSTRONG, IRIS L; Lake Hamilton Sr HS; Hot Springs Natio, AR; (3); 32/224; Church Yth Grp; Cmnty Wkr; Library Aide; School Musical; School Play; Stage Crew; Variety Show; JV Var Bsktbl; Intrml JV Sftbl; JV Var Vllybl; Geometry Awd; Bus.

ARMSTRONG, MANDIE; Rogers HS; Rogers, AR; (4); FBLA; Model UN; Rep Frsh Cls; Rep Stu Cncl; Capt Chrldng; Socr; Trk; Hon Roll; Jr NHS; NHS; Chmbr Cmmrce Awd; Renssnce Awd Gld, Slvr; PACE Clb; U AR Fyttvlle; Art.

ARMSTRONG, TOWONDA M; J A Fair Sr HS; Little Rock, AR; (2); FBLA; FHA; Vllybl; Cit Awd; Hon Roll; Ntl Merit Schol; Bus.

ARMSTRONG, YAKIMA V; Fairview HS; Camden, AR; (3); Church Yth Grp; Dance Clb; Drama Clb; Natl Beta Clb; Science Clb; Spanish Clb; Mrchg Band; School Play; Hon Roll; U Of AR Fayetteville; Nrsng.

ARNETT, JODI E; Vilonia HS; Vilonia, AR; (4); Art Clb; FBLA; VP FHA; Mu Alpha Theta; Natl Beta Clb; Spanish Clb; High Hon Roll; U Of Cntrl AR; Pharm.

ARNOLD, AMANDA B; Trumann HS; Harrisburg, AR; (2); 1/126; Spanish Clb; Yrbk; Bsktbl; Trk; Vllybl; High Hon Roll; NHS; Pres Acad Fit Awd; Vlybl All Conf/All Tournament 9; Vlybl Miss Hustle Awd 10; Excl In Ed 9-10; U Of AR; PT.

ARNOLD, BROOKE; Jonesboro HS; Jonesboro, AR; (3); Art Clb; Church Yth Grp; French Clb; FBLA; Key Clb; Mu Alpha Theta; Ofcr Stu Cncl; L Chrldng; L Pom Pon; Hon Roll; Psych.

ARNOLD, CRISSA; Fayetteville Sr HS; Fayetteville, AR; (4); 16/386; Am Leg Aux Girls St; Church Yth Grp; FCA; Key Clb; SADD; JV Var Bsktbl; Var Trk; High Hon Roll; NHS; Letterman Clb; Ath Schlr Awd; Chmbr/Commerce; U Of AR; Tchr.

ARNOLD, DANIEL; Cabot HS; Austin, AR; (3); German Clb; ROTC; Color Guard; Drill Tm; Hon Roll; Kiwanis Awd; Doedolier Awd; Air Force Acad; Elec Eng.

ARNOLD, LANDIS; Harrisburg HS; Harrisburg, AR; (3); Church Yth Grp; HOBY; Science Clb; Spanish Clb; Chorus; Church Choir; Yrbk; VP Jr Cls; Prfct Atten Awd; Dir Televised Announcement Pgm; AR ST U; Bus.

ARNOLD, SARA; Bentonville Sr HS; Bentonville, AR; (4); 3/242; Pres Key Clb; Model UN; SADD; Ed Nwsp; Ed Yrbk; Treas Jr Cls; Treas Sr Cls; High Hon Roll; NHS; Pres Acad Fit Awd; Upward Bd 9-12; Acad Comp 11-12; Hendrix Coll; Eng/Coll Prof.

ARNOLD, THOMAS J; Pine Bluff HS; Pine Bluff, AR; (4); 77/367; Church Yth Grp; French Clb; FBLA; FTA; Acpl Chr; Church Choir; Jr NHS; U Of AR; Comp Sci.

ARNOLD, TYNESHIA; Gould HS; Gould, AR; (4); 1/26; 4-H; Sec FBLA; Sec FHA; Pres Math Clb; Pres Science Clb; VP Spanish Clb; Ed Yrbk; Capt Chrldng; Hon Roll; Val; U Of AR; Bio.

ARONHALT, KEVIN E; Russellville Sr HS; Russellville, AR; (2); German Clb; Math Clb; Natl Beta Clb; Band; School Play; Rep Frsh Cls; Var Bsbl; Var Ftbl; Var Trk; Var Wrstlng; U Of KY; Aviatn/Chem.

ARRINGTON, DOROTHY E; Cabot HS; Lonoke, AR; (3); 41/398; Church Yth Grp; Ed Lit Mag; Kiwanis Awd; Acad Ltr & Gold Bar; Hendrix; Chemist.

ARRINGTON, JOHN B; Catholic HS; Little Rock, AR; (3); 35/206; Church Yth Grp; Band; Jazz Band; Orch; Pep Band; Var L Bsktbl; High Hon Roll; Hon Roll; All St Bnd; All Reg Bnd; Amrcn Lgn Baseball; Med.

ARTERBURY, MARK W; Hope HS; Hope, AR; (3); 11/238; VP Church Yth Grp; Band; Mrchg Band; JV Var Bsbl; High Hon Roll.

ARTHUR, JULIEANA; St Joe Public Schl; Saint Joe, AR; (2); VP FBLA; FHA; Natl FFA Org; VP Frsh Cls; Pres Soph Cls; Bsktbl; Hon Roll; Ntl Merit Ltr; Prfct Atten Awd; Ms St Joe Beauty Pageant Wnnr; Fr I Highest Grd; Project WET; U Of Ar; Surveillance Expert.

ASBURY, SIRIA; Green Forest Jr Sr HS; Oak Grove, AR; (3); Church Yth Grp; French Clb; FHA; Intnl Clb; Natl Beta Clb; SADD; Teachers Aide; Co-Ed Yrbk; Chrldng; Hon Roll; Coll Of Ozarks; Elem Ed.

ASFAHL, ERICA R; Fayetteville Sr HS; Fayetteville, AR; (4); 18/382; Art Clb; Church Yth Grp; FBLA; Mu Alpha Theta; Band; Drm Mjr(t); Jazz Band; Mrchg Band; Pep Band; Lit Mag; Band All Reg; Rep Wrtng Cont 1st Pl; Frgn Lang Clb; Stdnt Ambass; Karate; U Of AR; Arch.

ASH, MARY K; Russellville Sr HS; London, AR; (2); Church Yth Grp; Band; Flag Corp; Crs Cntry; Diving; Swmmng; Trk; NHS; FCA; French Clb; All Stars; CSU; USAF Acad; Aerody/Aeront Engr.

ASHABRANNER, MICHAEL W; Manila HS; Manila, AR; (1); Church Yth Grp; Library Aide; Natl Beta Clb; Natl FFA Org; Chorus; Church Choir; Variety Show; Hon Roll; Prfct Atten Awd; Saturday Schlrs; MASH Pgm; Gen Surgeon.

ASHBY, LAURA; Augusta HS; Augusta, AR; (1); Art Clb; Church Yth Grp; Girl Scts; Natl Beta Clb; Science Clb; Flag Corp; Mrchg Band; Cit Awd; Hon Roll; Prfct Atten Awd; Tchr.

ASHCRAFT, ANDREA L; Dumas HS; Dumas, AR; (2); Natl Beta Clb; High Hon Roll; Hon Roll; NHS.

ASHCRAFT, ANNETTE; Lead Hill Schl; Lead Hill, AR; (3); 6/23; Treas Church Yth Grp; FCA; FHA; Teachers Aide; Sec VP Band; Phtg Yrbk; JV Var Chrldng; Hon Roll; FBLA; High Hon Roll; ATAD; Kds Tchng Kds Drg Prvntn Prgm; U Of AR; Med Fld.

ASHCRAFT, CECILIA; White Hall Sr HS; Pine Bluff, AR; (4); Drama Clb; FCA; Sec FBLA; VP Key Clb; Mu Alpha Theta; Natl Beta Clb; L Trk; Hon Roll; Art Clb; Hosp Aide; Pine Bluff Yth Cncl; Natl Chrldng Assn Cmp Mst Sprtd Msct; AR ST U; Poltcl Sci.

ASHCRAFT, DAVY W; Mena HS; Mena, AR; (1); 52/156; Church Yth Grp; FCA; Quiz Bowl; SADD; Church Choir; School Play; Variety Show; Ofcr Bsbl; Bsktbl; Ftbl; Glf; OSU; Bsbl.

ASHCRAFT, SARAH A; Arkansas Bapt Schl; Little Rock, AR; (4); 1/34; Church Yth Grp; Pres French Clb; VP FBLA; Natl Beta Clb; Chorus; School Play; Ed Nwsp; Phtg Yrbk; JV Var Chrldng; Frgn Missions Clb; Poltcl Awrnss Clb; AR 4th Assocs Interschlstc Star; U Of AR Fayettevl; Intr Dsgn.

ASHCRAFT, TYSON; Warren Sr HS; New Edinburg, AR; (3); 1/145; Am Leg Boys St; Church Yth Grp; Drama Clb; French Clb; Natl Beta Clb; VICA; Band; Jazz Band; Mrchg Band; High Hon Roll.

ASHLEY, E JENNIFER; Lee Acad; Aubrey, AR; (1); Church Yth Grp; Church Choir; Rep Yrbk; High Hon Roll; Hon Roll.

ASMAR, SUZETTE M; Searcy HS; Searcy, AR; (3); 8/260; Art Clb; FCA; French Clb; FHA; Natl Beta Clb; Var Golf; Var Sftbl; French Hon Soc; High Hon Roll; NHS; Natl Eng Merit Awd; Natl His/Govt Awd; Alumn Recgn Prgm For Congrsnl Yth Ldrshp Cncl; U Of CO Boulder; Mktg/Acctnt.

ATCHISON, JODY E; Mills HS; North Little Rock, AR; (3); Am Leg Boys St; Church Yth Grp; FCA; Church Choir; Var Bsbl; Var Ftbl; High Hon Roll; NHS; Pres Schlr; Spanish Clb; Natl Young Ldrshp Conf Alumni.

ATCHLEY, MARYANNE A; Bentonville Sr HS; Bentonville, AR; (3); Church Yth Grp; Office Aide; Hon Roll.

ATCHLEY, PAUL W; Osceola HS; Wilson, AR; (3); French Clb; Science Clb; Band; Ofcr Bsbl; Ftbl; Hon Roll; NHS.

ATES, LEAH N; Arkansas Sr HS; Texarkana, AR; (2); Church Yth Grp; Cmnty Wkr; Hosp Aide; HOBY; Math Clb; Mu Alpha Theta; Spanish Clb; Church Choir; High Hon Roll; Jr NHS; Almni Achvmnt Awd.

ATKINS, HENRY J; Mc Crory Jr Sr HS; Mc Crory, AR; (4); Church Yth Grp; Am Leg Boys St; Teachers Aide; Yrbk; Rep Stu Cncl; Ftbl; Wt Lftg; U Of Cntrl AR; Automatic Engr.

ATKINS, LAURA J; Hall Sr HS; Little Rock, AR; (3); 8/350; Church Yth Grp; French Clb; Natl Beta Clb; Band; French Hon Soc; Jr NHS; NHS; Drama Clb; Pep Clb; Quiz Bowl; AGS; AEGIS Laureate Intnl Stud; Explrr Scouts; Ofcr Assn Pres & Sec; Post 8 VP & Pres; Post 589 Treas; Pre-Vet; Environmental Scis.

ATKINS, LESLIE M; Parkview Arts-Science HS; Little Rock, AR; (4); 99/261; Church Yth Grp; FBLA; FHA; Girl Scts; Spanish Clb; Teachers Aide; Church Choir; Cit Awd; Hon Roll; NHS; Dillard U; Phys Thrp.

ATKINS, SAMMY; Augusta HS; Augusta, AR; (2); Art Clb; Boy Scts; Church Yth Grp; Bsktbl; Ftbl; Trk; Wt Lftg; Gov Hon Prg Awd; Hon Roll; U Of AR; Pharmcy.

ATKINSON, CHRISTINA; Conway Sr HS; Conway, AR; (4); Drama Clb; FHA; Natl Beta Clb; Science Clb; Stage Crew; High Hon Roll; Pres Schlr; Natl Vo-Tech Hnr Soc; Renaissance Pgm; Hnr Grad.

ATKINSON, JASON W; Hot Springs HS; Hot Springs, AR; (4); 5/155; Am Leg Boys St; Church Yth Grp; Drama Clb; FBLA; Math Clb; Mu Alpha Theta; Ftbl; Wt Lftg; High Hon Roll; NHS; U Of Central AR; Mechncl Engr.

ATKINSON, SHANE; Morrilton Sr HS; Morrilton, AR; (2); 4-H; French Clb; Quiz Bowl; Science Clb; 4-H Awd; Hon Roll.

ATKINSON, STEVE L; Deer Jr Sr HS; Deer, AR; (3); Church Yth Grp; FBLA; Capt Quiz Bowl; Chorus; Nwsp; Pres Frsh Cls; Ofcr Stu Cncl; Var L Bsbl; Var Bsktbl; Pres Acad Fit Awd; Odyssey Of The Mind; U Of AR.

ATNIP, KASSIE J; Waldron HS; Waldron, AR; (2); 4-H; Natl Beta Clb; Natl FFA Org; JV Bsktbl; Hon Roll; Prfct Atten Awd; 2nd Pl Natl FFA Pltry Team; 1st Pl AR ST Poultry Team; FFA Rprtr; Univ Of AR; Pharm.

AUBREY, AARON; Emerson HS; Emerson, AR; (3); 4/28; Church Yth Grp; 4-H; FBLA; HOBY; Natl Beta Clb; Natl FFA Org; Spanish Clb; Rep Stu Cncl; Hon Roll; Prfct Atten Awd; 4 Sts HS Rodeo Assn Bll Rdng; U AR; Agri Bus.

AUD, SHANAE S; Rison HS; Rison, AR; (1); 10/50; Church Yth Grp; FHA; Cls Favorite.

AUKES, JOSH H; Lonoke Jr HS; Lonoke, AR; (1); Boy Scts; Church Yth Grp; Cmnty Wkr; Letterman Clb; Science Clb; Ftbl; Trk; Hon Roll; Pres NHS; Eclgy Clb; U Of AR; Pilot.

AUNER, AMELIA; Central Ark Christian Schl; North Little Rock, AR; (3); 3/75; Hosp Aide; Science Clb; Spanish Clb; Chorus; Hon Roll; Jr NHS; NHS; Piano; Hist Clb.

AUSBURN, WILLIAM J; Bryant HS; Benton, AR; (4); 34/354; Church Yth Grp; FBLA; Math Tm; Teachers Aide; Hon Roll; Pres Acad Fit Awd; Chrch Bsktbl & Sftbl; U Of Cntrl AR; Phy Thrpst.

AUSTIN, AMBER L; El Dorado Sr HS; El Dorado, AR; (3); 24/303; Cmnty Wkr; Key Clb; Library Aide; Natl Beta Clb; Teachers Aide; Rep Soph Cls; Rep Jr Cls; Hon Roll; NHS; Pres Acad Fit Awd; Navy Hnrs Prgm Awd; Natl Yth Svc Day Little Rock; Treas SEACER; Pre-Vet.

AUSTIN, JUSTIN D; Springdale Sr HS; Springdale, AR; (3); Church Yth Grp; VP Computer Clb; FCA; FBLA; Library Aide; Science Clb; Var Tennis; Hon Roll; NHS; Pres Acad Fit Awd; MIT; Cmptr Engrng/Math.

AUSTIN, KELLY; Devalls Bluff Jr Sr HS; Ulm, AR; (2); Drama Clb; FBLA; Natl Beta Clb; Chorus; School Play; Entertainment Field.

AUSTIN, MELINDA L; Fourche Valley Schl; Harvey, AR; (3); 2/14; FBLA; FHA; Library Aide; Church Choir; Yrbk; Crowned Hnr Star; Esther Awd; Westark CC; Lab Tech.

AUSTIN, RONDA L; Gravette HS; Gravette, AR; (3); #3 in class; Art Clb; FCA; FBLA; FHA; Letterman Clb; Library Aide; Natl FFA Org; Office Aide; Ski Clb; Spanish Clb; Tae Kwon Do; U Of AR; Phy Ther.

AUSTIN, SHANE M; Star City HS; Star City, AR; (1); English Clb; Quiz Bowl; Science Clb; Rep Stu Cncl; JV Bsktbl; Hon Roll; Gftd/Tlntd.

AUSTIN, STEVEN; North Little Rock Hs-East; North Little Rock, AR; (3); Bus Profs of Am; FCA; FBLA; Mu Alpha Theta; Ofcr Stu Cncl; Bsktbl; Ftbl; Trk; Gov Hon Prg Awd; Hon Roll; Phi Beta Zigma Awd; AR Govnrs Schl; All Conf Ftbll; Comp Prog.

AUSTIN, WILLIAM; Crossett Sr HS; Crossett, AR; (4); 19/160; Church Yth Grp; Cmnty Wkr; Mu Alpha Theta; Natl Beta Clb; Varsity Clb; Church Choir; Bsktbl; Swmmng; Cit Awd; NHS; Stdnts For Chrst; Sfty Sqd Aids Awrnss Club; Sr Of Dstnctn; Ouachita Bapt Univ.

AVANCE, VISA L; Central HS; West Helena, AR; (4); 13/192; SADD; Acpl Chr; Drill Tm; Mrchg Band; Gov Hon Prg Awd; Hon Roll; Jr NHS; Kiwanis Awd; Prfct Atten Awd; TONE/TCK; AR St Univ; Spch Path.

AVANTS, AMBER R; Carlisle Jr Sr HS; Carlisle, AR; (4); 13/48; Drama Clb; FBLA; Spanish Clb; Pres Band; Mrchg Band; School Play; Hon Roll; NHS; PRIDE Rptr & Historian; AR ST Univ; Music.

AVERETT, CHRISTY M; Oak Grove HS; Maumelle, AR; (2); Church Yth Grp; Drama Clb; Mu Alpha Theta; Natl Beta Clb; Spanish Clb; Band; Church Choir; Mrchg Band; Pep Band; School Play; Music/Drama.

AVERITT, HANNAH E; North Little Rock Hs-East; Jacksonville, AR; (3); Church Yth Grp; Hon Roll; Vet.

AVERY, JERED L; Valley Springs Schl; Harrison, AR; (3); 7/60; Art Clb; Church Yth Grp; French Clb; Key Clb; Natl FFA Org; Church Choir; School Play; Var L Bsbl; Var L Bsktbl; Cit Awd; 96 Cls A Bsktbl Champions Team; AR HS Boys All-Star Mgr; OK ST Univ; Arch.

AVILEZ, GERSHUN; Mills HS; Jacksonville, AR; (2); 1/260; Church Yth Grp; FTA; Mu Alpha Theta; Natl Beta Clb; Quiz Bowl; Science Clb; Spanish Clb; High Hon Roll; Jr NHS; NHS; Vanderbilt U; Eng Lit/Span.

AVRA, JAKE D; Conway Sr HS; Conway, AR; (2); Church Yth Grp; FBLA; Spanish Clb; Hon Roll; Bible Study; Prtcpt Actvts K-Life Mnstrs; Snow Ski.

AYECOCK, JESSICA; Dumas HS; Tillar, AR; (2); Church Yth Grp; Rptr FBLA; FTA; Math Clb; Natl Beta Clb; Band; Mrchg Band; Yrbk; Treas Jr Cls; Tennis; Dumas HS Majorette; House Of Repspage; Roads Col; Premed.

AYRES, MONTE C; Leslie Schl; Leslie, AR; (2); Ofcr Frsh Cls; Ofcr Soph Cls; JV Bsktbl; Hon Roll; Tlnt Srch; Comp Grphc.

BABCOCK, RAVEN M; Bentonville Sr HS; Bentonville, AR; (3); 3/389; Am Leg Aux Girls St; Church Yth Grp; Cmnty Wkr; Pres FBLA; JA; Letterman Clb; Pep Clb; SADD; Teachers Aide; Acpl Chr; RYLA; Jr Bank Bd; Pre Med.

BACK, SAMANTHA; Hot Springs HS; Hot Springs, AR; (2); Church Yth Grp; SADD; Stage Crew; Nwsp; Crs Cntry; Score Keeper; Socr; Trk; Cit Awd; Hon Roll; Decorating; Univ Of M; Psych.

BACKERMAN, JIMMY; Prairie Grove HS; Prairie Grove, AR; (3); 4/94; FCA; Letterman Clb; Natl FFA Org; Quiz Bowl; Scholastic Bowl; Teachers Aide; L Bsbl; L Ftbl; L Wt Lftg; High Hon Roll; U Of AR; Comp Engr.

BACON, COREY A; Conway Sr HS; Conway, AR; (2); Church Yth Grp; FBLA; Var Socr; Hon Roll; Ozark Mission Proj 3 Yrs; Soccer; Art Skills/Comptns; Hendrix Coll; Grphc Arts/MLS.

BADER, AMBER N; Yellville Summit HS; Yellville, AR; (2); 15/78; Church Yth Grp; Cmnty Wkr; FBLA; Natl Beta Clb; Pep Clb; SADD; Teachers Aide; Band; Church Choir; Mrchg Band; Prins Awd; Best Chrstn Character; Best All Aroung Camper; Quachita Bapt.

BADER, MICHAEL S; Yellville Summit HS; Yellville, AR; (3); Church Yth Grp; FCA; FBLA; Math Clb; Sec Jr Cls; Var Bsktbl; Trk; High Hon Roll; Hon Roll; NHS; AR Schl Math/Sci Finalist; Ouachita Bapt Univ; Bus Mngmt.

BAGGETT, JACY; Charleston HS; Charleston, AR; (1); Church Yth Grp; FCA; FBLA; FHA; Teachers Aide; Hon Roll; Westark CC; Phrmcy.

BAGGETT, JHERI D; North Little Rock Hs-East; North Little Rock, AR; (1); 209/646; Church Yth Grp; Cmnty Wkr; Drama Clb; FBLA; Math Clb; Band; Mrchg Band; School Play; Ofcr Stu Cncl; Pom Pon; United Way Pulaski Cty 3 Yrs; Sylvan Hills Sftbl Team; Stu Cncl 96-97; Drill Team 96-97; Spellman; Lawyer; Civil Rights.

BAGGETT, KRYSTAL D; Russellville Sr HS; Russellville, AR; (2); GAA; Band; Drm Mjr(t); Mrchg Band; Pep Band; Var JV Bsktbl; Var Trk; Var JV Vllybl.

BAHUS, HOLLY N; Nettleton HS; Jonesboro, AR; (2); Church Yth Grp; GAA; Letterman Clb; Natl Beta Clb; Office Aide; Science Clb; Spanish Clb; Varsity Clb; Bsktbl; Hon Roll; Vtd Mst Schl Spirited By Class; Lady Raider Bsktbl Awd Sprtmnshp/Grd/Ablty/Attd; Crowley's Ridge Coll.

BAILEY, ALLISON L; Clarendon Jr Sr HS; Holly Grove, AR; (4); Am Leg Aux Girls St; Pres Computer Clb; Quiz Bowl; Rep Jr Cls; Pres Sr Cls; VP Stu Cncl; Var Bsktbl; Sftbl; Trk; Hon Roll; Sr Homcmng Maid; Mst Outgoing Sr; Phillips Cty CC.

BAILEY, AMY M; Fayetteville Sr HS; Fayetteville, AR; (2); Church Yth Grp; French Clb; Hosp Aide; Office Aide; Chorus; Church Choir; Hon Roll; Chldrns Chrch Sun Vol; Bystng; Chrch Vol Rstr Hse; WA Univ St Louis; Pediatrician.

BAILEY, ANDREA L; Clarendon Jr Sr HS; Holly Grove, AR; (4); Am Leg Aux Girls St; Church Yth Grp; Computer Clb; 4-H; FBLA; FHA; Chorus; Nwsp; Yrbk; Bsktbl; All Sports Awd; Best Trk Sprinter & Rnnr; Best Offensive Player In Sftbl; UCA; PE.

BAILEY, ANTHONY E; Horatio HS; Horatio, AR; (2); Church Yth Grp; Pep Clb; Quiz Bowl; Band; Chorus; Rptr Yrbk; JV Var Ftbl; Trk; Hon Roll; Cmptrs; Gftd/Tlntd; Marine Bio/Astrnt.

BAILEY, CHRISTIE A; Fountain Lake Jr Sr HS; Hot Springs, AR; (3); 2/87; Art Clb; FBLA; FHA; Key Clb; Natl Beta Clb; Quiz Bowl; Spanish Clb; Acpl Chr; Rep Stu Cncl; Environmental Clb; Henderson ST U; Pre-Med.

BAILEY, JEANNIE; Hot Springs HS; Hot Springs, AR; (4); 15/164; Cmnty Wkr; FBLA; Spanish Clb; Thesps; Co-Capt Chrldng; Gym; High Hon Roll; Hon Roll; VP NHS; Prfct Atten Awd; Beta Clb; PRIDE; Homcmng Maid; AR ST Univ; Acctng.

BAILEY, JENNI M; Ozark Adv Acad; Albuquerque, NM; (3); Church Yth Grp; Band; Rptr Nwsp; Var Bsktbl; Intrml Ftbl; Gym; High Hon Roll; NHS; Intrml Socr; Intrml Vllybl; Missionary; Camp Cnslr; Scndry Ed.

BAILEY, KRISTY; Swifton Schl; Swifton, AR; (3); 3/21; Pres FBLA; Girl Scts; Library Aide; Natl Beta Clb; Natl FFA Org; Office Aide; Pep Clb; Teachers Aide; Ed Nwsp; Yrbk; ASU; Phys Thrpy.

BAILEY, MARY A; Lake Hamilton Sr HS; Hot Springs, AR; (3); Natl Beta Clb; Quiz Bowl; Spanish Clb; Thesps; Drill Tm; School Musical; Chrldng; DAR Awd; Gov Hon Prg Awd; NHS; Eng.

BAILEY, MICHA C; Hall Sr HS; Little Rock, AR; (2); Boy Scts; Chess Clb; Church Yth Grp; FBLA; Math Clb; Church Choir; Socr; Eagle Scout Awd.

BAILEY, SARA; Farmington Jr Sr HS; Farmington, AR; (3); Girl Scts; Natl FFA Org; School Play; Cit Awd; Hon Roll; Jr NHS; NHS; Ntl Merit Ltr; Prfct Atten Awd; Pres Acad Fit Awd.

BAILEY, SHERRHONDA; John L Mcclellan Magnet HS; Little Rock, AR; (2); Church Yth Grp; Dance Clb; FBLA; FTA; Mu Alpha Theta; Sec Natl Beta Clb; Spanish Clb; Church Choir; Drill Tm; Rep Frsh Cls; Sunday Schl Sec; Spellman; Pedtrcn.

BAILEY, STEPHANIE R; C V White Jr Sr HS; Helena, AR; (3); 3/16; FHA; Natl FFA Org; Office Aide; ROTC; Teachers Aide; Sec Jr Cls; Chrldng; Cit Awd; UAPB; Child & Family Dev.

BAIN, TWYLA D; Hughes Jr-Sr HS; Hughes, AR; (2); 15/73; JA; Math Clb; Natl Beta Clb; Science Clb; Spanish Clb; JV Bsktbl; Cit Awd; Hon Roll; NHS; Pres Acad Fit Awd; Med.

BAIR, JANET; Fountain Lake Jr Sr HS; Lonsdale, AR; (2); Pep Clb; Prfct Atten Awd.

BAIRD, HEATHER A; Evening Shade Schl; Sidney, AR; (2); Teachers Aide; Bus Awd.

BAIRD, KATHY L; Dover HS; Dover, AR; (2); 24/99; Church Yth Grp; Library Aide; Teachers Aide; Chorus; Church Choir; Hon Roll; PRIDE; STEP; Chrch Drama Grp; Nrsing.

BAKER, ALICIA; Morrilton Sr HS; Morrilton, AR; (3); Hosp Aide; Spanish Clb; Nwsp; Hon Roll; Psych.

BAKER, ANDREA; J A Fair Sr HS; Mabelvale, AR; (3); 7/241; Church Yth Grp; Cmnty Wkr; FBLA; Natl Beta Clb; Spanish Clb; Teachers Aide; Thesps; Church Choir; School Play; Yrbk; Mdrgls; Chrch Hndblls; Law.

BAKER, BRIAN; Arkansas Schl Math & Science; Witts Springs, AR; (3); FBLA; HOBY; Library Aide; Natl Beta Clb; Quiz Bowl; Science Clb; Rep Soph Cls; Bsktbl; Crs Cntry; High Hon Roll; Engrng.

BAKER, CAMERON C; Bald Knob HS; Bald Knob, AR; (3); FHA; Natl Beta Clb; Spanish Clb; Pres Chorus; Swing Chorus; Ed Yrbk; Ofcr Frsh Cls; Ofcr Soph Cls; Ofcr Jr Cls; Pres Stu Cncl; Ouachita Bapt Univ.

BAKER, DONNIE G; Bentonville Sr HS; Bentonville, AR; (3); Church Yth Grp; FCA; JV Var Bsbl; LA ST U; Law.

BAKER, DORRIE L; Rose Bud Jr Sr HS; Mount Vernon, AR; (3); Dance Clb; Drama Clb; FBLA; Girl Scts; Library Aide; Spanish Clb; Teachers Aide; School Play; Stage Crew; Hon Roll; Upward Bound Math & Sci; Math; Marine Bio.

BAKER, EDWIN L; Blytheville Sr HS; Blytheville, AR; (4); Office Aide; Bsktbl; Ftbl; Hon Roll; Prfct Atten Awd; U Of AZ; Mus.

BAKER, HOLLIE D; Arkansas Sr HS; Texarkana, AR; (3); 2/331; Am Leg Aux Girls St; Church Yth Grp; FTA; Mu Alpha Theta; Drm Mjr(t); Rep Jr Cls; NHS; Pres Acad Fit Awd; Art Clb; French Clb; All-St Hnr Band; 4 Sts Hnr Band; Fllwshp Chrstn Stus; Scndry Ed.

BAKER, JERI A; Mountain Home HS; Mountain Home, AR; (3); 6/257; Am Leg Aux Girls St; Church Yth Grp; Pres 4-H; Sec Natl Beta Clb; Natl FFA Org; Rptr Stu Cncl; 4-H Awd; High Hon Roll; Pep Clb; Spanish Clb; 4-H ST Rcrd Bk Wnr/Ambsdr; U Of AL Fayetteville; Food Sci.

BAKER, JOSH D; Marion HS; Marion, AR; (3); VICA; Ofcr Bsbl; Ftbl; Trk; Wt Lftg; U Of AR; Race Car Drvr.

BAKER, KIMBERLY M; Sylvan Hills HS; Sherwood, AR; (2); 7/362; Church Yth Grp; Cmnty Wkr; French Clb; Mu Alpha Theta; Natl Beta Clb; Chorus; Yrbk; High Hon Roll; Jr NHS; NHS.

BAKER, KRATINA N; John L Mcclellan Magnet HS; Little Rock, AR; (3); Church Yth Grp; FBLA; FHA; Library Aide; Rptr Nwsp; Cit Awd; Prfct Atten Awd; Vol AR Chldrns Hosp; Brdcst Jrnlst.

BAKER, MINDY; Searcy HS; Searcy, AR; (4); 42/201; Am Leg Aux Girls St; Art Clb; FCA; Natl Beta Clb; Spanish Clb; Sec Treas Soph Cls; Sec Treas Jr Cls; Var L Bsktbl; NHS; Spanish NHS; Harding Univ.

BAKER, RACHEL B; Pine Bluff HS; Pine Bluff, AR; (2); Church Yth Grp; DECA; Teachers Aide; Church Choir; School Play; High Hon Roll; Hon Roll; Jr NHS; Pres Schlr; Acctng.

BAKER, ROBERT; Hughes Jr-Sr HS; Hughes, AR; (2); 1/73; Math Clb; Math Tm; Natl Beta Clb; Quiz Bowl; Science Clb; Band; Rep Frsh Cls; Rep Soph Cls; Bsktbl; Trk; Prof Theatre; All Region Band; Actor.

BAKER, TAMARA K; Arkansas Sr HS; Texarkana, AR; (4); 1/374; Art Clb; Church Yth Grp; Hosp Aide; Mu Alpha Theta; Spanish Clb; Band; Drm Mjr(t); Rep Stu Cncl; Pres NHS; All St Band; Barrett Hamilton Yng AR Artists Cmptn, Exhbtn; North Heights Alumni Awd; Ouachita Bapt U; Engrng.

BAKER, WHITNEY L; Mc Crory Jr Sr HS; Mc Crory, AR; (2); 6/65; Church Yth Grp; GAA; Letterman Clb; Pep Clb; Teachers Aide; Band; Church Choir; Jazz Band; Mrchg Band; Pep Band; U Of AR Fayettville; Pre-Med.

BALDRIDGE, KRISTIE L; Rose Bud Jr Sr HS; Rose Bud, AR; (1); Drama Clb; 4-H; Natl FFA Org; Office Aide; Band; Score Keeper; Hon Roll.

BALDRIDGE, LISA ANJININ; Rose Bud Jr Sr HS; Rose Bud, AR; (3); 14/38; Church Yth Grp; FBLA; FHA; Math Tm; Natl Beta Clb; Natl FFA Org; Spanish Clb; Teachers Aide; Church Choir; Sftbl; Proj PALS; FFA Wrk Hrs Aed; Gftd & Tlntd; Nrsng.

BALDWIN, AMANDA; Hatfield Schl; Hatfield, AR; (1); Natl FFA Org; Bsktbl; Trk; Church Yth Grp; Chrldr 94-96; U Of AR; Military.

BALDWIN, CHRISTIAN; Magnolia HS; Magnolia, AR; (4); 1/1205; Boy Scts; Church Yth Grp; FCA; FBLA; HOBY; Mu Alpha Theta; Mrchg Band; Pres Stu Cncl; NHS; Val.

BALDWIN, JANA L; Devalls Bluff Jr Sr HS; Hazen, AR; (3); French Clb; FBLA; Key Clb; Natl Beta Clb; Chorus; School Musical; School Play; Rep Frsh Cls; Rep Soph Cls; Rep Jr Cls; Pre-Law.

BALDWIN, JON; Hatfield Schl; Hatfield, AR; (4); 3/14; FCA; FBLA; Natl Beta Clb; Natl FFA Org; Yrbk; VP Sr Cls; Ofcr Stu Cncl; Bsktbl; Hon Roll; Pres Acad Fit Awd; Monticello; Forestry.

BALDWIN, TONY; Heber Springs HS; Heber Springs, AR; (2); 20/90; Church Yth Grp; 4-H; Quiz Bowl; Teachers Aide; Band; Var Bsbl; JV Bsktbl; Var Ftbl; JV Trk; AR; Sprts.

BALENTINE, RACHEL A; Mt Pleasant Jr Sr HS; Sidney, AR; (3); Art Clb; FBLA; FHA; Teachers Aide; Yrbk; Rep Frsh Cls; Rep Soph Cls; Rep Jr Cls; Rep Stu Cncl; Chrldng; Spec Olym Bsktbl Coach; Psych.

BALL, BETHANY; Horace Mann HS; Little Rock, AR; (1); Church Yth Grp; FCA; Natl Beta Clb; Band; Church Choir; School Musical; School Play; Rptr Nwsp; Chrldng; Cit Awd; U Of Cntrl AR; Elem Ed.

BALL, DANIEL L; Delaplaine Schl; O Kean, AR; (3); FBLA; Natl FFA Org; Spanish Clb; High Hon Roll; Hon Roll; Jr NHS; Project Pals; Wet Project.

BALL, JONATHAN; Mt Pleasant Jr Sr HS; Mount Pleasant, AR; (2); Church Yth Grp; FBLA; Natl Beta Clb; Sec Frsh Cls; Hon Roll.

BALL, SHANNA M; Mc Gehee HS; Mc Gehee, AR; (2); Church Yth Grp; Drama Clb; FTA; HOBY; Natl Beta Clb; Spanish Clb; Ed Phtg Nwsp; Rep Stu Cncl; Soph Srvr; Page At AR ST Cptl; Jrnlsm.

BALL, STACY; Norphlet HS; El Dorado, AR; (2); 1/57; Art Clb; FBLA; Spanish Clb; Band; Color Guard; Mrchg Band; Pep Band; Treas Frsh Cls; Var Chrldng; High Hon Roll; Schlstc Awd.

BALL, STEPHANIE; Bradford Jr Sr HS; Bradford, AR; (4); 7/36; Church Yth Grp; French Clb; FBLA; FHA; Natl Beta Clb; Chorus; Church Choir; Ed Nwsp; Co-Ed Yrbk; Hon Roll; Chrch Pianist; AR ST Univ; Bus/Ed.

BALL, THOMAS N; Mc Crory Jr Sr HS; Mc Crory, AR; (2); Church Yth Grp; Ftbl; Trk.

BALLARD, BRANDON; Alpena Schl; Alpena, AR; (3); Natl Beta Clb; Natl FFA Org; Quiz Bowl; Spanish Clb; School Play; Lit Mag; Bsktbl; High Hon Roll; Hon Roll; Med.

BALLARD, LORI; Murfreesboro HS; Murfreesboro, AR; (3); Church Yth Grp; 4-H; FBLA; FHA; GAA; Natl Beta Clb; Science Clb; Spanish Clb; Chorus; Pres Jr Cls; Ortho/Dentist.

BALLARD, MARCUS D; Parkers Chapel Schl; El Dorado, AR; (3); Natl Beta Clb; Quiz Bowl; Spanish Clb; Band; Jazz Band; Mrchg Band; Pep Band; School Play; Hon Roll; Pres Acad Fit Awd.

BALLARD, SWINTON W; Tuckerman HS; Tuckerman, AR; (2); Art Clb; Boy Scts; Church Yth Grp; Cmnty Wkr; Dance Clb; FBLA; FHA; Letterman Clb; Natl Beta Clb; Spanish Clb; Pro Rock Band; U Of WA St Louis; Pro Musician.

BALLARD, TASHA L; Cabot HS; Austin, AR; (3); Church Yth Grp; Cmnty Wkr; FBLA; Natl FFA Org; Office Aide; Red Cross Aide; Spanish Clb; Teachers Aide; Drill Tm; Sftbl; UALR; Comp Tech.

BALLEW, AMANDA F; Horatio HS; Horatio, AR; (2); FHA; Chorus; Hon Roll; Henderson ST Univ; Phy Thrpst.

BALSTERS, SARA B; Siloam Springs Sr HS; Siloam Springs, AR; (3); Church Yth Grp; FCA; FBLA; Natl Beta Clb; Natl FFA Org; Spanish Clb; Band; Sec Jr Cls; NHS; Voice Of Democracy Awd 3rd Pl; Brooks Coll Long Beach.

BALTZ, ANDREA; Walnut Ridge HS; Walnut Ridge, AR; (4); 14/66; Art Clb; Church Yth Grp; French Clb; FBLA; Library Aide; Science Clb; Rptr Nwsp; Co-Capt Chrldng; Tennis; Hon Roll; Lfegrd 3 Yrs; Tght Swmmng Lssns; GATE; Ambssdr; AR ST Univ.

BALTZ, ELIZABETH; Pocahontas HS; Pocahontas, AR; (2); 37/133; Hist Rep Church Yth Grp; FBLA; Treas FHA; Math Tm; Office Aide; Red Cross Aide; Spanish Clb; Band; Chrldng; PRIDE; AR ST U; Bus Admin; Comps.

BALTZ, TONYA; Paris HS; Paris, AR; (4); 3/80; Am Leg Aux Girls St; Sec Church Yth Grp; FCA; FBLA; School Play; Ofcr Stu Cncl; Bsktbl; Trk; Vllybl; NHS; U Of Cntrl AR; Comp Sci.

BANDI, JUSTIN C; Siloam Springs Sr HS; Siloam Springs, AR; (2); Church Yth Grp; FCA; Natl Beta Clb; Teachers Aide; Band; Church Choir; Jazz Band; Mrchg Band; Orch; Pep Band; U Of Tulsa.

BANE, MOLLIE A; Southside HS; Fort Smith, AR; (2); Church Yth Grp; FCA; Church Choir; Orch; Bsktbl; Vllybl; Hon Roll; SAIL CREW; Bsktbl St Champs 33-1; Sport Comentater; Coach.

BANISTER, JASON P; Blevins HS; Blevins, AR; (3); Church Yth Grp; Rep Stu Cncl; Var Bsbl; Var Bsktbl; All-Dist Bsbl 95-.

BANKS, HEATHER; Mills HS; Little Rock, AR; (2); 5/439; Pres Church Yth Grp; VP Mu Alpha Theta; Pres Natl Beta Clb; Rep Soph Cls; Ofcr Stu Cncl; Capt Pom Pon; Hon Roll; Jr NHS; NHS; Pres Acad Fit Awd; Duke Univ TIPF Qlfr; Ch Yth Choir Dir; Pianist; Northwestern U; Med/Pediatrics.

BANKS, MELISSA; North Little Rock Hs-West; North Little Rock, AR; (3); 5/654; Am Leg Aux Girls St; Church Yth Grp; Key Clb; Model UN; Mrchg Band; School Musical; Rep Sr Cls; Capt Chrldng; High Hon Roll; Renaissnce Outstndg Stu Awd; NLR Chmbr Of Commrce Jr Ldrshp Clss.

BANKS, MIESHA S; Stephens Jr Sr HS; Stephens, AR; (2); 1/45; FBLA; Church Choir; Variety Show; Yrbk; Bsktbl; Cit Awd; High Hon Roll; Pres Acad Fit Awd; GT; Soil Consvtn; U Of AR.

BARBER, JIMMY G; Fouke Jr Sr HS; Fouke, AR; (3); 1/90; Sec Chess Clb; Natl FFA Org; Quiz Bowl; Ofcr Stu Cncl; Hon Roll; NHS; Pres Acad Fit Awd; Gifted/Talented Prgm Sec; Eng.

BARBER, MELISSA L; Nettleton HS; Jonesboro, AR; (2); #13 in class; FBLA; Math Clb; Science Clb; Spanish Clb; Chorus; School Play; Sec Stu Cncl; Bsktbl; Vllybl; AR ST Univ; Med.

BARDSLEY, AMANDA M; Van Buren Sr HS; Van Buren, AR; (2); Cmnty Wkr; Computer Clb; Debate Tm; Drama Clb; FBLA; HOBY; Mu Alpha Theta; Science Clb; Speech Tm; SADD; Earth Clb VP; Frst Pl Applause Wrtng Cnts Westark CC; Stndt Of Mnth; UC At Berkeley; Psychlgy.

BARENBERG, KATHRYN; El Dorado Sr HS; El Dorado, AR; (4); 1/260; HOBY; Pres Natl Beta Clb; VP Service Clb; Rep Frsh Cls; Rep Jr Cls; Rep Sr Cls; Rep Stu Cncl; Var L Tennis; NHS; Ntl Merit SF.

BARFIELD, MELISSA; Cabot HS; Austin, AR; (4); 82/299; French Clb; Lit Mag; Cit Awd; Hon Roll; Pres Acad Fit Awd; UCA Acad Schlrshp; U Of Cntrl AR; Law.

BARHAM, ASHLEY M; Oak Grove HS; Maumelle, AR; (1); Church Yth Grp; FCA; FTA; Pres Natl Beta Clb; Band; Church Choir; Capt Drill Tm; Mrchg Band; Capt Chrldng.

BARHAM, TEAH J; Southside HS; Desha, AR; (1); Church Yth Grp; Key Clb; Natl Beta Clb; Science Clb; Teachers Aide; Band; Chorus; Church Choir; Rep Stu Cncl; Hon Roll; Voice Lssn; Piano.

BARIBEAU, CHRIS M; Dequeen HS; De Queen, AR; (3); 1/150; Church Yth Grp; FBLA; SADD; Chorus; Nwsp; Bsktbl; Hon Roll; NHS; Pres Acad Fit Awd; FCS Pres; U Of AR; Arch.

BARKER, ASHLEY R; Corning HS; Corning, AR; (1); Church Yth Grp; Drama Clb; Rptr Library Aide; Spanish Clb; School Play; Stage Crew; JV Var Chrldng; Hon Roll; Anesthslgst.

BARKER, MARCO; Osceola HS; Osceola, AR; (4); 8/111; Pres FBLA; Pres Key Clb; Quiz Bowl; Spanish Clb; Mrchg Band; Yrbk; VP Soph Cls; Pres Jr Cls; Rep Stu Cncl; VP NHS; U Of AR Fytvl; Indstrl ENGRNG.

BARKER, RAUN M; Manila HS; Manila, AR; (1); Church Yth Grp; Library Aide; Natl FFA Org; Chorus; Church Choir; Variety Show; Hon Roll; Lib Clb; Madrigals Select Chorus.

BARKHIMER, JOSH; Harmony Grove Jr Sr HS; Camden, AR; (4); Church Yth Grp; FCA; 4-H; FBLA; Natl FFA Org; Ftbl; Hon Roll; NHS; U Of AR Monticello; Forestry.

BARKLEY, HEATHER; Harrison Sr HS; Harrison, AR; (2); Church Yth Grp; Drama Clb; French Clb; Chorus; School Musical; Hon Roll; Top Stu Awds In Wrld Hist; Geom; Bio And Engl; Col Of Ozarks; Tchr.

BARLOW, SHAUNA L; Rose Bud Jr Sr HS; Rose Bud, AR; (2); Art Clb; Church Yth Grp; FCA; FBLA; FHA; GAA; Spanish Clb; Ofcr Frsh Cls; Ofcr Soph Cls; Bsktbl; Interior Dsgn.

BARLOW, TONI D; Des Arc Jr Sr HS; Des Arc, AR; (4); Church Yth Grp; 4-H; FHA; FTA; Library Aide; Office Aide; Science Clb; Spanish Clb; Teachers Aide; Band; FHA Dist Conv Gld Wnnr, St Conv Slvr Mdl; Nrsng.

BARNARD, CARRIE; Springdale Sr HS; Hindsville, AR; (4); 7/486; FCA; French Clb; FBLA; Key Clb; Acpl Chr; Chorus; Ofcr Soph Cls; Ofcr Jr Cls; Ofcr Sr Cls; Var Bsktbl; Vice Chrmn Btmns Jr Bnk Bd; Chmbr Of Cmrc Awd; U Of Cntrl AR; Phys Thrpy.

BARNARD, HILLARY; Taylor HS; Taylor, AR; (2); 5/25; Church Yth Grp; FHA; Natl FFA Org; Church Choir; VP Soph Cls; L Bsktbl; L Sftbl; Hon Roll; Cntrl Bapt Coll; Music Prof.

BARNARD, SPENCER R; Valley Springs Schl; Harrison, AR; (4); 25/53; Art Clb; Church Yth Grp; FBLA; Sec Key Clb; Letterman Clb; Church Choir; VP Stu Cncl; Var Capt Bsktbl; Var Golf; Hon Roll; Sr Schlrs; Sr Hall Of Fame; Mr VSHS; 1a St Champions Bsktbl; Ouachita Bapt U; Rel; Yth Minstr.

BARNES, AMANDA M; Magnolia HS; Magnolia, AR; (2); Church Yth Grp; FBLA; Hon Roll; Southern AR U.

BARNES, ASHLEA L; Fairview HS; Camden, AR; (3); 23/309; Church Yth Grp; Drama Clb; French Clb; Rep Natl FFA Org; Sec Natl FFA Org; Service Clb; SADD; Chorus; Church Choir; School Musical; Hofstra Univ; Drama.

BARNES, BECKIE L; Valley Springs Schl; Harrison, AR; (2); FBLA; FHA; Library Aide; Teachers Aide; Yrbk; Bus; Acctng.

BARNES, MELISSA M; Yellville Summit HS; Yellville, AR; (2); FCA; Teachers Aide; Bsktbl; Sftbl; Trk; Cit Awd; High Hon Roll; Hon Roll; Prfct Atten Awd; Reg Nrs.

BARNES, MICHAEL B; Valley Springs Schl; Harrison, AR; (3); French Clb; FBLA; Teachers Aide; School Play; VP Jr Cls; French Hon Soc; Pres Schlr; Natl Congrssnl Schlr; U Of AR At Fayetteville; Ed.

BARNES, TIFFANY; Hot Springs HS; Hot Springs, AR; (4); 9/154; Am Leg Aux Girls St; FBLA; Mu Alpha Theta; Natl Beta Clb; Science Clb; Yrbk; VP Soph Cls; Var Chrldng; High Hon Roll; NHS; Henderson ST Univ; Pre-Vet.

BARNES, TONDA M; Mc Gehee HS; Mc Gehee, AR; (4); 29/101; FBLA; FTA; Mu Alpha Theta; Band; Co-Capt Flag Corp; Rep Stu Cncl; Chrldng; FHA; Library Aide; Office Aide; Peer Cnslr; Prd Awd 3 Yrs; Cmptr Aplctns Awd; U Of AR Pine Bluff; Cmptr Sci.

BARNETT, ANGELA D; J A Fair Sr HS; Little Rock, AR; (3); 31/288; Am Leg Aux Girls St; FBLA; FHA; Treas Natl Beta Clb; Sprt Ed Yrbk; Hon Roll; Prfct Atten Awd; Law Explrs Club; Ladies Club; Comm Svc; Pol Sci/DA.

BARNETT, BRANDY E; Van Buren Sr HS; Van Buren, AR; (2); Church Yth Grp; FCA; SADD; Teachers Aide; Church Choir; Hon Roll.

BARNETT, JONATHON B; Cave City HS; Batesville, AR; (2); 1/95; Church Yth Grp; French Clb; Science Clb; Band; Pep Band; High Hon Roll; Prfct Atten Awd; Ofcr Frsh Cls; Ofcr Soph Cls; Sr Beta; Lyon Coll; Biologist.

BARNETT, JOSHUA H; Cabot HS; Cabot, AR; (3); 18/398; Co-Capt Debate Tm; FBLA; Stage Crew; Ftbl; Tennis; Trk; Kiwanis Awd; Spanish NHS; Henderson Tourn 1st Pl Sprkr; Stu Congress; Pre-Law.

BARNETT, MATTHEW W; Van Buren Sr HS; Van Buren, AR; (2); Church Yth Grp; FCA; French Clb; Mu Alpha Theta; Band; Jazz Band; Mrchg Band; High Hon Roll; Jr NHS; U Of AR; Doctor.

BARNETT, MICHELLE K; Cedarville Jr Sr HS; Cedarville, AR; (4); FBLA; FHA; Quiz Bowl; SADD; Teachers Aide; Chorus; Bsktbl; High Hon Roll; Hon Roll; NHS; Woodsmen Of The Wrld Awd For Wrldhistry; FHA Hgst Avg Awd; Westark CC.

BARNETT, NATALIE; West Memphis Christian Schl; West Memphis, AR; (2); 3/25; Natl Beta Clb; Var Bsktbl; Var Chrldng; Var Sftbl; Var Trk; Var Vllybl; High Hon Roll; NHS; Pres Acad Fit Awd.

BARNETT, RAMONA J; Cave City Jr-Sr HS; Cave City, AR; (4); 2/69; Church Yth Grp; French Clb; Natl Beta Clb; Quiz Bowl; Science Clb; SADD; Phtg Yrbk; High Hon Roll; Pres Acad Fit Awd; Sal; Radio & TV Awd Schl Station; Acctng Awd; Lyon Coll Trustee Schlsp; Lyon Coll; Bus Mgmt; Acctng.

BARNETT, REBEKAH; Waldron HS; Waldron, AR; (4); 2/91; Natl Beta Clb; Chrmn Spanish Clb; Bsktbl; Chrldng; Gov Hon Prg Awd; High Hon Roll; NHS; Pres Acad Fit Awd; Pres Schlr; Sal; Natl Schlr Ath Awd; Navy Math/Sci Awd; Active Schlr Awd; AR Tech Univ; Pre-Phrmcy.

BARNHART, DERRICK D; Augusta HS; Augusta, AR; (4); 18/42; Am Leg Boys St; Church Yth Grp; Cmnty Wkr; English Clb; 4-H; FBLA; FHA; FTA; Mu Alpha Theta; Natl Beta Clb; U Of Cntrl AR; Chldhd Educ.

BARNHILL, AMANDA L; Weiner HS; Weiner, AR; (2); Church Yth Grp; FBLA; FHA; Natl FFA Org; Science Clb; Ofcr Frsh Cls; Tennis; Cit Awd; Hon Roll; NHS; UCA; Human Svcs; Phy Thrpsy.

BAROCCO, REBECCA L; Springdale Sr HS; Springdale, AR; (1); Chorus; Hon Roll; Jr NHS; U Of CA; Drama; Archaelogy.

BARR, PAM; Malvern Sr HS; Malvern, AR; (3); FBLA; Natl Beta Clb; Office Aide; Teachers Aide; Band; Drm Mjr(t); Mrchg Band; Hon Roll; Jr NHS; NHS; Frgn Lang Clb; Peer Cnslr; U Of AR Fayettevl; Med.

BARRETT, BRANDI; Hamburg Jr HS; Hamburg, AR; (1); Church Yth Grp; Dance Clb; Chorus; School Play; Pres Stu Cncl; Bsktbl; Capt Chrldng; Sftbl; High Hon Roll; Jr NHS; U Of MS; Orthdntst.

BARRETT, CHRISSY M; Cabot HS; Cabot, AR; (3); 22/400; Dance Clb; Key Clb; Spanish Clb; Band; Hon Roll; Kiwanis Awd; NHS; Spanish NHS; Govnr Schl; Histr Clb.

BARRETT, JOLENE; Bergman Schl; Harrison, AR; (3); 4/52; Church Yth Grp; FBLA; FHA; Model UN; Natl Beta Clb; Natl FFA Org; Quiz Bowl; Spanish Clb; School Play; JV Var Bsktbl; Phys Sci & Geometry Hnr Awd; Marine Biologist.

BARRETT, RAEGAN B; Mc Gehee HS; Mc Gehee, AR; (2); 5/109; FBLA; FTA; Library Aide; Natl Beta Clb; Science Clb; Spanish Clb; Yrbk; Var Chrldng; Hon Roll; NHS; Pride Awd; Bio Awd; Oral Commnctns Awd; Phy Thrpst.

BARRINGTON, KRISTY D; Sylvan Hills HS; Sherwood, AR; (2); 13/400; Drama Clb; French Clb; Mu Alpha Theta; Natl Beta Clb; Speech Tm; Acpl Chr; Sec Stu Cncl; Chrldng; Pres Jr NHS; Named To All-Region Choir; 1st Chair Sec; Dist 150 Rotry Oratory Wnnr-St Schlsp Wnnr; Speech Competitor; Juillard; Theater; Music.

BARROW, MICHAEL A; Ridgecrest HS; Paragould, AR; (2); 71/256; Ntl Merit Ltr; ROTC.

BARROW, TIFFANY P; Ridgecrest HS; Paragould, AR; (2); Church Yth Grp; FBLA; Rptr FHA; Natl FFA Org; Chorus; Bsktbl; Hon Roll; Pres Schlr; TV/MEDIA Clb Awds; U Of AR; Law.

BARRY, CANDICE; Southside HS; Fort Smith, AR; (4); 40/459; Art Clb; Church Yth Grp; FBLA; Mu Alpha Theta; Science Clb; Spanish Clb; Ed Nwsp; Pres Frsh Cls; Pres Soph Cls; Rep Jr Cls; Ping Pong Clb Ofcr; OK ST Univ.

BARRY, HELEN; Mt St Mary Acad; Sherwood, AR; (3); 18/125; Ofcr Church Yth Grp; Model UN; Mu Alpha Theta; Q&S; Spanish Clb; Ed Nwsp; Bsktbl; Var Trk; Hon Roll; NHS.

BARTHOLOMEW, SAMANTHA L; Russellville Sr HS; Russellville, AR; (3); 100/340; Am Leg Aux Girls St; Church Yth Grp; Cmnty Wkr; Hosp Aide; Band; Mrchg Band; Pep Band; JV Bsktbl; L Var Crs Cntry; Mgr(s); Math.

BARTLETT, BRAD D; Mayflower HS; Mayflower, AR; (3); Am Leg Boys St; Church Yth Grp; FCA; German Clb; School Musical; School Play; Stage Crew; Powder Puff Ftbl; Trk; Hon Roll; Chiropractor.

BARTLETT, JESSICA R; Marvell Acad; Marvell, AR; (2); Spanish Clb; JV Var Bsktbl; JV Var Trk; Hon Roll; Capt Jr NHS; NHS; MS ST; Sports Medicine.

BARTON, JEFF B; Crossett Sr HS; Crossett, AR; (2); Church Yth Grp; Natl Beta Clb; Ofcr Bsbl; Hon Roll.

BARTON, JERI E; Alma HS; Alma, AR; (4); 9/139; Sec Pres Church Yth Grp; French Clb; FBLA; Sec Pres FHA; Library Aide; Church Choir; Rep Stu Cncl; High Hon Roll; NHS; St Schlr; Jr Exec Trng Team; Chief Fin Ofcr; 2nd Pl St Team Biennial Report; Plcd 3rd In Bus Procedures FBLA; AR Tech Univ; Acctng.

BARTON, MICHELLE; Mineral Springs Schl; Mineral Springs, AR; (2); 12/60; Church Yth Grp; 4-H; FBLA; FHA; Natl Beta Clb; Yrbk; Ofcr Frsh Cls; Ofcr Jr Cls; Ofcr Stu Cncl; Score Keeper; U Of Cntrl AR; Phys Therapy.

BARTSCH, BECKY E; Southside HS; Fort Smith, AR; (2); Church Yth Grp; Cmnty Wkr; FCA; Treas Service Clb; Band; Drm Mjr(t); Mrchg Band; Pep Band; School Play; Stage Crew; Schlrshp Intl Rotary Clb; OT/PT.

BASE, AMY E; Watson Chapel Sr HS; Pine Bluff, AR; (3); 14/215; Church Yth Grp; Drama Clb; Model UN; Natl Beta Clb; Science Clb; Spanish Clb; Band; Church Choir; Flag Corp; Mrchg Band.

BASFORD, MANDY J; Pangburn Jr Sr HS; Pangburn, AR; (4); FCA; French Clb; FHA; SADD; Teachers Aide; Chorus; Yrbk; Mgr(s); Hon Roll; AR ST U; Psych.

BASKIN, DAWNYA M; Rogers HS; Rogers, AR; (2); 27/460; Church Yth Grp; Model UN; Office Aide; Quiz Bowl; Teachers Aide; Drill Tm; Mgr Yrbk; Crs Cntry; High Hon Roll; Pres Acad Fit Awd; Brigham Yng Univ; Tchng.

BASS, KIMBERLY; Abundant Life Schools; North Little Rock, AR; (4); 1/18; Church Yth Grp; School Musical; School Play; Sec Jr Cls; Sec Sr Cls; Capt Chrldng; Vllybl; High Hon Roll; NHS; Val; AR ST U Jonesboro.

BASS, MANDY; Eureka Springs Jr Sr HS; Eureka Springs, AR; (3); 1/64; Church Yth Grp; Cmnty Wkr; FHA; GAA; HOBY; Letterman Clb; Natl Beta Clb; Quiz Bowl; SADD; Teachers Aide; Prom Cmmtte; Jr Bnk Brd Fundraisng Chrprsn; Med.

BASS, RACHEL N; Robinson HS; Little Rock, AR; (2); 5/100; Church Yth Grp; FCA; French Clb; FBLA; FHA; Chorus; Drill Tm; Hon Roll; NHS; Drill Team Let; Univ Of AR Conway.

BASS, STEPHANIE; J A Fair Sr HS; Little Rock, AR; (3); 18/350; Am Leg Aux Girls St; FBLA; Quiz Bowl; Science Clb; Spanish Clb; Band; Drill Tm; Yrbk; Sec Stu Cncl; NHS; Piano; Rdng; Fisk U; Brdcstng.

BATEMAN, KENNETH W; Ridgecrest HS; Paragould, AR; (2); 29/207; ROTC; Band; Color Guard; Drill Tm; Jazz Band; Mrchg Band; Pep Band; School Musical; Hon Roll; Prfct Atten Awd; Band Dir Awd; Sons Of The Amer Revolution; AR ST Univ.

BATES, AMY L; Fountain Lake Jr Sr HS; Hot Springs, AR; (1); FCA; VP Natl Beta Clb; Spanish Clb; Band; Mrchg Band; JV Capt Bsktbl; JV Tennis; Cit Awd; High Hon Roll; Envrnmntl Clb; AR Coll; Bus.

BATES, ASHLEY S; Star City HS; Star City, AR; (3); 13/120; Church Yth Grp; Cmnty Wkr; FCA; Church Choir; Mrchg Band; Hon Roll; NHS; French Clb; FBLA; FHA; Feature Majrt; Church Sftbl Tm; Most Imprvd Band; Henderson ST U Clinic Most Outstndng Majrt; UAM; Med.

BATES, HALEY M; Conway Sr HS; Conway, AR; (2); Church Yth Grp; Band; Church Choir; Mrchg Band.

BATES, JESSICA; Barton HS; Lexa, AR; (3); Church Yth Grp; FCA; FBLA; FHA; Natl Beta Clb; Spanish Clb; Pres Frsh Cls; Pres Soph Cls; VP Jr Cls; Capt Bsktbl; Zoolgy.

BATES, JILL; Robinson HS; Little Rock, AR; (3); 16/113; Church Yth Grp; Dance Clb; French Clb; FBLA; FHA; Math Tm; Natl Beta Clb; Office Aide; School Play; Phtg Yrbk; Unted Meth Chrchs Dist Pres; Ouchita Bapt Univ; Pre-Med.

BATES, MEREDITH R; Star City HS; Star City, AR; (3); 29/99; Art Clb; Church Yth Grp; Drama Clb; French Clb; FBLA; Natl Beta Clb; Science Clb; Church Choir; NHS; Perfect Attendance Awd; U Of Ozarks; RN.

BATES, MICHELLE R; Lake Hamilton Sr HS; Pearcy, AR; (3); Church Yth Grp; Cmnty Wkr; FCA; FBLA; FHA; Natl Beta Clb; Office Aide; Pep Clb; Science Clb; Teachers Aide; Garland Cty Jvnle Advy Bd; Acctng/Rl Est.

BATES, RENATA R; Central HS; Helena, AR; (3); ROTC; Cit Awd; Hon Roll; Jr NHS; Pres Acad Fit Awd; Grambling ST Univ; Social Wrkr.

BATH, LACEY; Lake Hamilton Jr HS; Hot Springs, AR; (1); Church Yth Grp; Natl Beta Clb; Natl FFA Org; Band; Mrchg Band; Cit Awd; Hon Roll; Jr NHS; PRIDE Dance Team; SAU Magnolia; Crimnlgy.

BATTISTO, ALYCIA A; Sheridan Sr HS; Mabelvale, AR; (4); #2 in class; Church Yth Grp; Cmnty Wkr; FBLA; Hosp Aide; Service Clb; Var Sftbl; Gov Hon Prg Awd; High Hon Roll; NHS; Sal; VALR.

BATTLES, CARLETTER; Sylvan Hills Jr HS; North Little Rock, AR; (2); Church Yth Grp; FCA; FHA; Office Aide; Spanish Clb; Ofcr Stu Cncl; Trk; Cit Awd; Hon Roll; Prfct Atten Awd; Tchrs Of Tomorrow; Care Bears; Fire Marshal.

BAUER, CHRIS; Lake Hamilton Jr HS; Hot Springs, AR; (1); Church Yth Grp; 4-H; Natl Beta Clb; Natl FFA Org; Quiz Bowl; Pres Band; Hon Roll; All-Regn 1st Chr 1st Bnd Fr Horn; Wolf Pride; Duke U; Med.

BAUER, TODD; Southside HS; Fort Smith, AR; (3); 8/450; Am Leg Boys St; Church Yth Grp; FCA; Ofcr Sr Cls; Var Capt Socr; High Hon Roll; NHS; Ntl Merit Ltr; Mu Alpha Theta; Capt Quiz Bowl; SAIL Crew; Med Mssn Trip.

BAUGH, PHYLLIS MARLENE; Russellville Sr HS; Russellville, AR; (4); Am Leg Aux Girls St; Art Clb; Church Yth Grp; Cmnty Wkr; Drama Clb; French Clb; Chorus; School Play; Lit Mag; Cit Awd; Emory And Henry Col.

BAUMGARDNER, JOSH K; Junction City HS; El Dorado, AR; (1); FBLA; Quiz Bowl; Spanish Clb; Comp Tech.

BAUMGARDNER, MELANIE D; Junction City HS; El Dorado, AR; (4); 17/60; Office Aide; Science Clb; Spanish Clb; Teachers Aide; Mgr(s); High Hon Roll; Hon Roll; NHS; South AR U; Med Lab.

BAXLEY, KELLY E; Sheridan Sr HS; Sheridan, AR; (2); 32/286; Church Yth Grp; FCA; 4-H; FBLA; Hosp Aide; Office Aide; Teachers Aide; Ofcr Stu Cncl; Bsktbl; Mgr(s); Frosh Speech Awd; Schl Broadcast News Team Mem; St 4-H Champion Rep AR In Natl Cont; U Of AR-FAYETTEVILLE; Broadcst.

BAXTER, AARON A; Watson Chapel Sr HS; Pine Bluff, AR; (4); 4/230; Drama Clb; FCA; French Clb; Natl Beta Clb; School Play; Var L Bsbl; Capt L Ftbl; High Hon Roll; Hon Roll; Prfct Atten Awd; Just Of Peace Bys St; Wendy Heisman Nom; US Army Rsrv Natl Schlr Awd; UCA; Med.

BAXTER, HALEY E; Russellville Sr HS; Russellville, AR; (3); Q&S; Yrbk; NHS; U Of AR; Psychiatrist.

BAXTER, KATIE; Vilonia HS; Conway, AR; (2); FBLA; Mu Alpha Theta; Natl Beta Clb; Sec Frsh Cls; Ofcr Stu Cncl; L Bsktbl; Var Trk; JV Vllybl; Cit Awd; High Hon Roll; A E Bio Stdnt Of Semester; Microbio/Math.

BAXTER, KEVIN R; Valley View HS; Jonesboro, AR; (2); Church Yth Grp; FCA; Natl FFA Org; ROTC; Spanish Clb; Ofcr Bsbl; Stat Bsktbl; Hon Roll; Rotary Intrct Clb; AR ST Univ.

BAXTER, KRISTY M; Dumas HS; Watson, AR; (2); Church Yth Grp; Natl Beta Clb; Church Choir; Hon Roll; UAMS; PT.

BAXTER, SHAWNA; Dumas HS; Watson, AR; (2); Church Yth Grp; Drama Clb; Chrldng; Soph Homecoming Maid 95; Fayetteville; Flight Attndnt.

BAXTER, STACI; Crossett Sr HS; Crossett, AR; (3); 13/201; VP Art Clb; Church Yth Grp; HOBY; Mu Alpha Theta; Natl Beta Clb; Ed Nwsp; Phtg Yrbk; Ed Lit Mag; Rep Soph Cls; Pres Acad Fit Awd; Stus For Christ VP; Missnry Wrk Mexico, Ghana & Haiti; Photojrnlsm.

BAY, KEVIN D; Catholic HS; Sherwood, AR; (2); #69 in class; Church Yth Grp; Latin Clb; Band; Jazz Band; Orch; Pep Band; School Musical; Intrml Socr; Hon Roll; Prcsn Ensmbl; Bnd Wrk Crew; Music.

BEAL, BETHENY D; Clay Co Central Jr Sr HS; Rector, AR; (3); Art Clb; Church Yth Grp; Drama Clb; 4-H; FBLA; FTA; German Clb; Natl FFA Org; Science Clb; Thesps; Medcl.

BEALE, LATOYA S; Wynne HS; Wynne, AR; (2); Cmnty Wkr; Key Clb; Spanish Clb; Chorus; Flag Corp; Mrchg Band; Hon Roll; Spanish NHS; AEGIS Pgrm Project LAND; Attnd Schlrshp Banquet; IMAG; AR ST Univ; Bus Admin.

BEALER, NICOLE M; Bauxite Jr Sr HS; Benton, AR; (3); 3/70; Treas FBLA; Quiz Bowl; Spanish Clb; SADD; Drill Tm; Phtg Yrbk; VP Sec Stu Cncl; High Hon Roll; Hon Roll; NHS; Big Bros/Big Sisters.

BEALLY, MARTIN; Arkansas Schl Math & Science; North Little Rock, AR; (4); HOBY; Mu Alpha Theta; Spanish Clb; School Play; Rep Sr Cls; Rep Stu Cncl; NHS; Ntl Merit SF; Tae Kwon Do Clb Pres; Rcrtrs Asst; Princeton U.

BEAM, AMANDA; Van Buren Sr HS; Van Buren, AR; (3); 3/350; French Clb; Mu Alpha Theta; Band; Mrchg Band; Bsktbl; Trk; High Hon Roll; Jr NHS; NHS; Earth Clb; U Of AR Fayetteville; Med.

BEAM, RAYMOND; Dewitt HS; De Witt, AR; (3); Am Leg Boys St; Church Yth Grp; 4-H; French Clb; FBLA; FTA; Library Aide; Natl Beta Clb; Science Clb; Var Ftbl; ASU; Ed.

BEAM, SARA N; Southside HS; Fort Smith, AR; (2); Art Clb; French Clb; Key Clb; Mu Alpha Theta; Ed Nwsp; Var Gym; French Hon Soc; Hon Roll; Jr NHS; NHS; 12th ST Natl Frnch Exm; Rice; Peds.

BEAN, ASHLEY; Atkins Schl; Russellville, AR; (3); 2/52; Am Leg Aux Girls St; Drama Clb; VP FBLA; Natl Beta Clb; Pres Jr Cls; Rep Stu Cncl; Capt Chrldng; Sftbl; High Hon Roll; Pres Acad Fit Awd; Tch Chldrn Undr 5 Chrch; Univ Of AR; Advrtsng/Archt.

BEAN, ZACK I; Mills HS; Roland, AR; (3); 6/298; Natl Beta Clb; School Play; Var Bsbl; Mr Monopoly.

BEARD, AMY N; Mansfield Jr Sr HS; Huntington, AR; (3); 6/60; FHA; Model UN; Natl Beta Clb; Quiz Bowl; Speech Tm; Band; Church Choir; Mrchg Band; Nwsp; Var Cit Awd; Yth Pres Chrch; U Of AR; Eng.

BEARD, LAWANDA Y; West Memphis Sr HS; West Memphis, AR; (4); FHA; Mrchg Band; MSCC.

BEARD, MEGHAN; Arkansas Bapt Schl; Little Rock, AR; (3); Church Yth Grp; FCA; FBLA; Natl Beta Clb; Spanish Clb; Varsity Clb; Chorus; Church Choir; Sec Jr Cls; Chrldng; Homcmng Court; Chrstn Cmptn Sports Ldr; Patients Pals Vol; Excel Modeling; Stu Ath Trainer; Phy Thrpst.

BEARD, MIN K; Sheridan Sr HS; Prattsville, AR; (3); Art Clb; Cmnty Wkr; 4-H; Hosp Aide; Quiz Bowl; Teachers Aide; School Play; Rep Frsh Cls; Rep Stu Cncl; Intrml Bsktbl; AR Schl For Math & Scis; U Of AR Fayetteville; Med.

BEARD, SHAWNN; Monticello HS; Monticello, AR; (4); 54/134; FHA; Library Aide; Natl Beta Clb; Office Aide; Mrchg Band; Hon Roll; U Of AR Monticello; Ed.

BEARD, WENDY D; Marion HS; Clarkedale, AR; (4); #15 in class; Church Yth Grp; FCA; French Clb; Mu Alpha Theta; Church Choir; Chrldng; Trk; French Hon Soc; Hon Roll; NHS; AR ST U.

BEARDEN, CLAIRE E; Mississippi Co Christian Acad; Osceola, AR; (2); 4/13; Church Yth Grp; Drama Clb; French Clb; FBLA; Key Clb; Math Clb; Science Clb; Band; Pres Soph Cls; Bsktbl; All Star Chrldr; Fayetville; Child Psycht.

BEARDEN, LANA S; Marvell Acad; Aubrey, AR; (3); 6/30; Am Leg Aux Girls St; Church Yth Grp; FBLA; Spanish Clb; Teachers Aide; Rptr Yrbk; Hon Roll; Jr NHS; NHS; Stu Of Mnth; AR St Univ; Bus.

BEASLEY, AMBER; Foreman Jr Sr HS; Foreman, AR; (2); Church Yth Grp; Cmnty Wkr; Chrldng; Gym; Sftbl; High Hon Roll; Sftbl 2 Yrs, All Stars 2 Yrs; SAU; Elem Ed.

BEASLEY, ANDREW D; Rogers HS; Rogers, AR; (3); Church Yth Grp; Cmnty Wkr; FCA; Math Clb; Science Clb; Band; Mrchg Band; Pep Band; Var Crs Cntry; Socr; Toxiclgy; Bio Chem.

BEASLEY, J KYLE; Springdale Sr HS; Springdale, AR; (1); Church Yth Grp; Intrml Bsktbl; L Ftbl; Babe Ruth Bsbl; Intnl Yth Missions Participant; U Of AR-FAYETTEVILLE; Attorney.

BEASLEY, SHAWNA B; Genoa Central HS; Genoa, AR; (3); Church Yth Grp; Office Aide; Spanish Clb; Band; Nwsp; High Hon Roll; Hon Roll; Prfct Atten Awd; Band/Solo Ensmbl 1st Pl; Flwshp Of Chrstn Stdnts; Nrs Clb; Med Sci/Radiology.

BEAUDRE, SARAH A; Springdale Sr HS; Springdale, AR; (3); Church Yth Grp; French Clb; Office Aide; Teachers Aide; Band; Color Guard; Mrchg Band; Orch; Hon Roll; SW Bapt U; Elem Ed.

BEAUMONT, SHANNON E; Conway Sr HS; Conway, AR; (3); Church Yth Grp; French Clb; Office Aide; Q&S; VICA; Chorus; Drill Tm; Pom Pon; Delta Beta Signa Sorority Custodian & Historian; Dance.

BEAVER, CARLYNN R; Mills HS; Jacksonville, AR; (3); DECA; French Clb; ROTC; Spanish Clb; Nwsp; Yrbk; Rep Stu Cncl; Var Chrldng; Gym; Hon Roll; FADDS Mem; IN Univ Of PA; Bus.

BEAVER, CHRISTY M; Fairview HS; Camden, AR; (2); Church Yth Grp; Drama Clb; Natl Beta Clb; Drm Mjr(t); Mrchg Band; Yrbk; Mgr Gym; Var Socr; Cit Awd; Hon Roll; Swim Team; Lifeguard; UCA; Animal Sci.

BEAVER, CRYSTAL; Kingston Jr Sr HS; Compton, AR; (4); 2/17; Church Yth Grp; Sec Treas FBLA; German Clb; GAA; Library Aide; Office Aide; Quiz Bowl; Teachers Aide; Yrbk; Var Bsktbl; N AR Tech Univ; Bus.

BEAVER, MISTY; Marion Co Rural Schl; Everton, AR; (2); 1/28; Church Yth Grp; 4-H; FHA; Pres Soph Cls; Bsktbl; Sftbl; Hon Roll; U Of AR; Coach.

BEAVERS, JAROD; Harding Acad; Searcy, AR; (4); French Clb; Natl Beta Clb; Office Aide; Acpl Chr; Chorus; School Musical; Var L Bsktbl; Var Capt Ftbl; Wt Lftg; Cit Awd; All-Conf Team Ftbl 10-12th Grd; All-Cntry Team Ftbl 11-12th Grd; Chmbr Of Cmmrc Schlsp; Hnr Choir 9th; Harding Univ; PT.

BEAVERS, JERROLD; Ozark Adventist Acad; Pine Bluff, AR; (3); Art Clb; Church Yth Grp; Cmnty Wkr; School Play; Phtg Nwsp; Phtg Yrbk; Prfct Atten Awd; Comm Young & Elderly Vol; RN.

BECK, BRANDI E; Lake Hamilton Sr HS; Royal, AR; (3); FCA; Sftbl; Vllybl; Pres Acad Fit Awd.

BECK, BRANDI V; Jessieville HS; Mountain Pine, AR; (2); FCA; FHA; Key Clb; Teachers Aide; Sec Soph Cls; Var Bsktbl; Var Tennis; Var Trk; Hon Roll; All Dist Bsktbl Soph Yr.

BECK, DIMITY D; Glen Rose HS; Traskwood, AR; (1); Spanish Clb; Church Choir; Variety Show; Cit Awd; Ouachita Bapt Univ.

BECKER, AMY M; Southside HS; Fort Smith, AR; (2); Rep FHA; Chorus; Variety Show; Chrldng; Trk; Hon Roll; Jr NHS; NHS; Prfct Atten Awd; Pres Schlr; Girls Clb Drill Team Instr; Interior Decorating.

BECKHAM, JON REGAN; Hope HS; Hope, AR; (3); 1/220; VP Church Yth Grp; FBLA; Pres Natl Beta Clb; Pres Spanish Clb; Church Choir; Bsktbl; Ftbl; Golf; Wt Lftg; High Hon Roll; Natl Eng Merit Awd; DARE; A Hope For Teens; Indstrl Engrng.

BEDONE, JESSICA G; Mills HS; Sweet Home, AR; (3); 42/298; Cmnty Wkr; FTA; Natl Beta Clb; Spanish Clb; SADD; Band; Mrchg Band; Hon Roll; Majorette; Upward Bound Philander Smith Coll; Bus, Mrktng, Spnsh III Achvt Awdsfhnr Roll; Hendrix Coll; Acctng.

BEEKS, CAMILLE D; Farmington Jr Sr HS; Fayetteville, AR; (3); 23/93; Church Yth Grp; Drama Clb; 4-H; FBLA; Band; Church Choir; Mrchg Band; Orch; School Play; Hon Roll; U Of AR; Perf Arts.

BEEKS, WILLIAM M; Farmington Jr Sr HS; Fayetteville, AR; (4); 23/78; Art Clb; Church Yth Grp; FCA; FBLA; Natl FFA Org; VP Soph Cls; Var Ftbl; Cit Awd; Hon Roll; Jr NHS; Northwest AR CC.

BEEN, MELISSA; Greenwood Sr HS; Greenwood, AR; (3); 99/199; Art Clb; Teachers Aide; Chrldng; Hon Roll; Natl Eng Mrt Awd.

BEENE, AMY S; Magnolia HS; Magnolia, AR; (2); Art Clb; Church Yth Grp; Cmnty Wkr; FBLA; Pep Clb; Science Clb; Spanish Clb; Band; Church Choir; Mrchg Band.

BEENE, BECKY L; Arkadelphia Sr HS; Gurdon, AR; (3); Treas FHA; Natl Beta Clb; Spanish Clb; Capt Band; Capt Flag Corp; Mrchg Band; Sftbl; High Hon Roll; Jr NHS; NHS; Bdgr Schlr 2 Yrs; Outstdng Fmly/Cnsmr Awd; Intrschlstc Stars Invlvmnt In Schls/Comm; Henderson ST U; Spch Thrpy.

BEENE, NATASHA R; Vilonia HS; Vilonia, AR; (2); FHA; Natl Beta Clb; Office Aide; Bsktbl; Hon Roll; All Stars; Harding Coll Searcy; Marine Bio.

BEENE, TIFFANY N; Quitman Jr Sr HS; Quitman, AR; (3); FBLA; VP FHA; Natl Beta Clb; Natl FFA Org; Teachers Aide; Bsktbl; Sftbl; Hon Roll.

BEERMAN, ANGELA M; Clarksville HS; Clarksville, AR; (2); 10/140; DECA; Treas FBLA; Model UN; Natl Beta Clb; Quiz Bowl; Rptr Spanish Clb; Band; Hon Roll; Pres Acad Fit Awd; Pride Tm Drug Free Pgm; PAWS; CPA.

BEERY, BRIGITTE M; Springdale Sr HS; Springdale, AR; (1); Cmnty Wkr; Drama Clb; French Clb; FBLA; FHA; SADD; Teachers Aide; Chorus; Hon Roll; All Reg Choir 2nd Chair; SW Jr HS S Awd; YFC; Quiachita Bapt Univ; Pdtrcn/Vet.

BEGLEY, MARCUS H; Bald Knob HS; Bald Knob, AR; (1); Chess Clb; Church Yth Grp; Natl Beta Clb; Quiz Bowl; Band; Jazz Band; Mrchg Band; Hon Roll; Pres Acad Fit Awd; 1st Band 2nd Chair All Reg; AR ST U; Med.

BEI, SHIHONG; Arkansas Schl Math & Science; Rego Park, NY; (4); Chess Clb; FBLA; Math Tm; VP Mu Alpha Theta; Science Clb; Speech Tm; Teachers Aide; School Play; VP Jr Cls; Gov Hon Prg Awd; 5th Sakharovs Rdng; Intnl HS Sci Conf Russia Physics Awd; Edison/Mc Graw 2nd Pl Awd; Jr Acad Sci Pres; Columbia Univ; Ec.

BEISTLINE, JOHN A; Southside HS; Fort Smith, AR; (2); Church Yth Grp; FCA; German Clb; Acpl Chr; Chorus; Church Choir; School Musical; Stage Crew; Ofcr Stu Cncl; Ftbl; Penn ST Univ; Scndry Ed.

BELAND, BRITTNEY SARA; Greenwood Sr HS; Fort Smith, AR; (4); 41/187; Church Yth Grp; Mu Alpha Theta; Natl Beta Clb; Spanish Clb; Pres Band; Mrchg Band; School Play; High Hon Roll; NHS; French Clb; Chrch Drama Team; Sunday Schl Tchr; Evangel Coll; Missions; Span.

BELCHER, AMY D; Oden Schl; Oden, AR; (3); Church Yth Grp; Key Clb; Rep Natl Beta Clb; Band; Church Choir; Ed Nwsp; Pres FCA; Sec FBLA; Pres FHA; Rep Frsh Cls; Band & Outstdng Stu Awds; Henderson.

BELCHER, STEFFANY D; Marvell Acad; Brinkley, AR; (2); 1/35; Spanish Clb; Teachers Aide; VP Soph Cls; Cit Awd; High Hon Roll; Hon Roll; Jr NHS; NHS; Prfct Atten Awd; Schlr At Natl Young Ldrs Conf Nom; Math Tutor Soph Yr; Horseshows Participiant; OK ST Univ; Vet.

BELEW, BRANDON D; Jacksonville HS; Jacksonville, AR; (2); Church Yth Grp; Cmnty Wkr; FCA; Yrbk; JV Var Bsbl; JV Bsktbl; JV Ftbl; Hon Roll; Prfct Atten Awd; Ath Spec O/Lympics Unified Sports Vol.

BELIN, CHARLIE; Mc Gehee HS; Mc Gehee, AR; (3); 1/109; VP Church Yth Grp; Pres Drama Clb; French Clb; FTA; Mu Alpha Theta; Natl Beta Clb; Science Clb; VP Stu Cncl; NHS; Phtg Yrbk; Chem Engrng.

BELL, AMANDA; Ft Smith Christian Schl; Van Buren, AR; (1); Church Yth Grp; Cmnty Wkr; FCA; GAA; Band; Mrchg Band; Sec Frsh Cls; Ofcr Stu Cncl; Capt L Bsktbl; Capt L Chrldng; Vndrblt; Pre-Med.

BELL, AMANDA K; Conway Sr HS; Conway, AR; (3); Church Yth Grp; French Clb; FBLA; VP JA; Natl Beta Clb; Science Clb; French Hon Soc; High Hon Roll; Hon Roll; Delta Beta Sigma HS Sorority VP; U Of AR; Bio; Pre-Med.

BELL, ANGELIA D; Pangburn Jr Sr HS; Pangburn, AR; (3); Art Clb; 4-H; French Clb; FBLA; Natl Beta Clb; French Hon Soc; Hon Roll; Loan Ofcr.

BELL, ANGIE; Sparkman Jr Sr HS; Sparkman, AR; (4); 3/20; 4-H; Natl Beta Clb; Spanish Clb; Yrbk; Treas Frsh Cls; Treas Soph Cls; Treas Jr Cls; Treas Sr Cls; VP Stu Cncl; Bsktbl; Chrldr; Henderson ST U; Hum.

BELL, CANDI M; Mc Gehee HS; Tillar, AR; (2); Church Yth Grp; GAA; Natl FFA Org; Church Choir; Ofcr Soph Cls; FFA Greenhand Cert; Upward Bound Pgm.

BELL, CHRIS D; Batesville Sr HS; Batesville, AR; (4); 9/155; Church Yth Grp; Drama Clb; FBLA; Natl Beta Clb; Teachers Aide; School Play; Rptr Nwsp; Bsktbl; Golf; High Hon Roll; U AR; Med.

BELL, CRISTY; Alpena Schl; Green Forest, AR; (3); FBLA; Natl Beta Clb; Spanish Clb; Hon Roll; NACC Harrison.

BELL II, EDWARD BECTON; Rivercrest HS; Wilson, AR; (2); 30/125; Church Yth Grp; FBLA; Letterman Clb; Teachers Aide; Varsity Clb; Ftbl; Pres Acad Fit Awd; Hunting & Fishing; Cooking; U Of AR; Ag Bus; Farmer.

BELL, JENNIFER; Delight HS; Delight, AR; (1); 4-H; FHA; Quiz Bowl; Pres Nwsp; Chrldng; Hon Roll; NEMA; All Amer Scholar; Fros Class Favorite.

BELL, JENNIFER M; Van Cove HS; Cove, AR; (2); 1/40; Church Yth Grp; FCA; FBLA; FHA; Natl FFA Org; SADD; Sec Frsh Cls; Var Bsktbl; Stat Sftbl; Trk; Kids Baking For Kids; U Of AR Fayetteville; Elem Ed.

BELL, JOSHUA; Ft Smith Christian Schl; Van Buren, AR; (2); Church Yth Grp; Cmnty Wkr; FCA; FBLA; Chorus; Treas Stu Cncl; L Bsktbl; L Trk; Wt Lftg; Cit Awd; U ARZ; Pedtrc Orthdntst.

BELL, LATOYA; Sylvan Hills Jr HS; Little Rock, AR; (1); FCA; FHA; Spanish Clb; Teachers Aide; Cit Awd; Hon Roll; TOT; Designing Clothes; Henderson Coll; Clothes Dsgn.

BELL, LORI; Delight HS; Murfreesboro, AR; (3); 4-H; FBLA; VP FHA; Natl Beta Clb; Quiz Bowl; School Play; Nwsp; Sftbl; Hon Roll; JETS Awd; Int Dsgn.

BELL, MEGAN E; Batesville Sr HS; Batesville, AR; (3); 1/150; Am Leg Aux Girls St; Key Clb; Natl Beta Clb; Spanish Clb; Bsktbl; Golf; High Hon Roll; Ntl Merit SF; St Schlr.

BELL, NICOLE; Carlisle Jr Sr HS; Carlisle, AR; (2); 7/60; FBLA; Office Aide; Spanish Clb; Yrbk; VP Soph Cls; VP Jr Cls; Bsktbl; Chrldng; Sftbl; Trk; Med.

BELL, ROXIE; Victory Christian Schl; Camden, AR; (2); #1 in class; Church Yth Grp; Debate Tm; Speech Tm; Rptr Yrbk; Rep Stu Cncl; Bsktbl; Chrldng; Vllybl; Wt Lftg; High Hon Roll; NASA Jr Wrld Chmpn Pwrlftr Jr Wrld Hnr; NASA Teenage Athl Yr 94.

BELL, TONYA; Morrilton Sr HS; Perry, AR; (2); French Clb; Natl Beta Clb; Science Clb; Mgr Rptr Nwsp; 4-H Awd; Hon Roll; Natl Hstry/Govt Awd; Natl Hnr Rll; Wrtr.

BELL, WHITNEY; Southside HS; Fort Smith, AR; (3); Church Yth Grp; FCA; Key Clb; Orch; Sec Jr Cls; VP Stu Cncl; Var JV Chrldng; Var JV Gym; Jr NHS; NHS; Mnt Tp Soc Rck Clmbng Hkng; Latn Natl Hnr Soc; Baylor; Bio Sci.

BELLNGER, JESSICA L; Fouke Jr Sr HS; Texarkana, AR; (3); 46/84; FHA; SADD; Cit Awd; TX Coll; Pre-Med.

BELOTE, CRYSTAL D; Piggott HS; Piggott, AR; (4); 1/70; Church Yth Grp; Sec FBLA; Letterman Clb; Natl Beta Clb; Rptr Natl FFA Org; Church Choir; Yrbk; Rep Frsh Cls; Rep Soph Cls; Rep Jr Cls; AK St Univ; Accty.

BELOTTI, LEAH M; Central Sr HS; North Little Rock, AR; (3); 45/540; Am Leg Aux Girls St; Mu Alpha Theta; Q&S; Yrbk; High Hon Roll; Hon Roll; NHS; Pres Acad Fit Awd; Church Yth Grp; French Clb; AR Gov Schl; L R Jr Cotillon Helper; Capitol City Ballet Co; Lauerate Intl Stds Pgm.

BELVEDRESI, LORI R; Star City HS; Pine Bluff, AR; (4); 18/105; FBLA; Math Clb; NHS; Univ Of AR.

BENDER, CHERYL L; Northside HS; Fort Smith, AR; (3); 7/300; Art Clb; Church Yth Grp; Math Tm; Mu Alpha Theta; Pom Pon; Tennis; High Hon Roll; NHS; Pres Acad Fit Awd; Spanish NHS; Grand Prz Cty Art Awd; St Art Awd 2nd Pl; 2nd Pl Regional Math Cmptn; Medicine.

BENDER, JOHN; Cedarville Jr Sr HS; Cedarville, AR; (4); 5/64; Natl FFA Org; Quiz Bowl; Science Clb; SADD; Band; Drm Mjr(t); Mrchg Band; Ftbl; Hon Roll; NHS; Univ Schlsp; U Of AR; Chem Engrng.

BENDER, JOSHUA; Lake Hamilton Jr HS; Hot Springs, AR; (1); Church Yth Grp; Drama Clb; FCA; Natl Beta Clb; Ski Clb; Spanish Clb; School Play; Rep Frsh Cls; Rep Stu Cncl; Var Golf; CO U; Pro Golf.

BENEFIELD, JENNIFER A; Monticello HS; Monticello, AR; (3); Bus Profs of Am; 4-H; FBLA; FHA; Library Aide; Spanish Clb; Speech Tm; Gym; ULAR; Speech Thrpy.

BENEFIELD, SABRINA; Cross Co Jr Sr HS; Hickory Ridge, AR; (4); 3/43; Sec FBLA; FHA; Library Aide; Math Tm; Natl Beta Clb; Office Aide; Spanish Clb; SADD; Chorus; Church Choir; Crowleys Ridge Tech; Bus Ed.

BENISH, DEANNA; Farmington Jr Sr HS; Farmington, AR; (2); 4-H; French Clb; FBLA; Model UN; Band; Hon Roll; NHS.

BENNETT, ANDREA; Rivercrest HS; Joiner, AR; (4); 1/106; Pres FHA; Capt Quiz Bowl; Pres Frsh Cls; Pres Soph Cls; Pres Jr Cls; Pres Stu Cncl; Val; Church Yth Grp; French Clb; Treas FBLA; Rivercrest HS Dist Stu Awd; Universl Chrldrs Assoc All Star; Principles Ldhp Awd; AR St Univ; Chem.

BENNETT, BRANDY N; Dierks HS; Langley, AR; (1); FHA; Varsity Clb; Pres Frsh Cls; Rep Frsh Cls; Rep Stu Cncl; Chrldng; High Hon Roll; PRIDE Team.

BENNETT, BRIDGET D; Van Buren Sr HS; Van Buren, AR; (2); Church Yth Grp; Drama Clb; FCA; FBLA; Speech Tm; SADD; Teachers Aide; Lit Mag; High Hon Roll; Hon Roll.

BENNETT, DENA A; Dewitt HS; De Witt, AR; (2); 5/84; FCA; French Clb; FBLA; Natl Beta Clb; Science Clb; Stage Crew; Rep Stu Cncl; Hon Roll.

BENNETT, GABRIEL A; Russellville Sr HS; Russellville, AR; (3); Church Yth Grp; FCA; SADD; Band; Mrchg Band; Pep Band; High Hon Roll; Hon Roll; Jr NHS; Prfct Atten Awd; 1st Pl Natl Obsrvd Trials; Chrch Yth Band; Chrch Drama Tm.

BENNETT, GEORGE R; Nettleton HS; Jonesboro, AR; (2); Debate Tm; Natl Beta Clb; Rptr Science Clb; Band; Chorus; Jazz Band; Mrchg Band; Orch; Pep Band; School Musical; Msc.

BENNETT, J R; Mammoth Spring HS; Thayer, MO; (3); 8/40; Am Leg Boys St; Pres FBLA; Library Aide; Natl Beta Clb; Pep Clb; Quiz Bowl; Red Cross Aide; SADD; Teachers Aide; Yrbk; Pre-Law.

BENNETT, JACKIE L; Wynne HS; Wynne, AR; (3); Church Yth Grp; Natl Beta Clb; Spanish Clb; SADD; Band; Cit Awd; High Hon Roll; Hon Roll; NHS; Spanish NHS; E AR CC; Med Records Tech.

BENNETT, JAMES C; Emmet Schl; Emmet, AR; (2); Art Clb; Natl FFA Org; Nwsp; Ftbl; Wt Lftg; High Hon Roll; Hon Roll; Rodeo; Span Awd; U Of Cntrl AR; Rodeo; Radiolgst.

BENNETT, JASON C; Star City HS; Star City, AR; (3); FCA; Natl Beta Clb; Natl FFA Org; Spanish Clb; Yrbk; VP Frsh Cls; VP Soph Cls; Rep Stu Cncl; Ofcr Bsbl; Ftbl.

BENNETT, JILL K; Bryant Sr HS; Alexander, AR; (3); Church Yth Grp; Cmnty Wkr; Am Leg Aux Girls St; FBLA; Hosp Aide; Speech Tm; SADD; Teachers Aide; Church Choir; Drill Tm; UCA Conway; Sprts Med.

BENNETT, KAREN L; Rogers HS; Garfield, AR; (2); Cmnty Wkr; SADD; Teachers Aide; Drill Tm; Pom Pon; Gov Hon Prg Awd; Hon Roll; Pres Acad Fit Awd; Rogers Chmbr Cmmrc Cert Acad Achvmt; U Of AR; Ed.

BENNETT, KEVIN D; Rivercrest HS; Dyess, AR; (3); VICA; Band; Jazz Band; Mrchg Band; Hon Roll; Duke Tlnt Srch Pgm Part; Duke Univ; Oeronautics.

BENNETT, MASON; Carlisle Jr Sr HS; Carlisle, AR; (3); Am Leg Boys St; Church Yth Grp; Cmnty Wkr; FBLA; Spanish Clb; Varsity Clb; Pres Jr Cls; Pres Jr Cls; Pres Stu Cncl; L Bsbl; Attnd AR Bus Acad; U Of AR.

BENNETT, STEPHANIE L; Arkansas Sr HS; Texarkana, AR; (4); 40/379; Church Yth Grp; Drama Clb; FBLA; FHA; Mu Alpha Theta; Natl FFA Org; Spanish Clb; School Play; NHS; Phys Thrpy.

BENNETT, SUMMER M; Quitman Jr Sr HS; Quitman, AR; (2); FBLA; FHA; HOBY; Treas Natl Beta Clb; Ofcr Stu Cncl; High Hon Roll; Hon Roll; Jr NHS; NHS; Pres Acad Fit Awd; U Of AR; Sports Med.

BENNETT, SUSAN C; Cushman Schl; Batesville, AR; (2); Sec Pres FBLA; Library Aide; Rep Natl Beta Clb; Chorus; Rep Nwsp; Cit Awd; Hon Roll; Prfct Atten Awd; ASU; Jrnlsm.

BENNETT, WILLIAM K; Fountain Lake Jr Sr HS; Hot Springs, AR; (3); 12/85; Boy Scts; Church Yth Grp; FCA; Key Clb; Natl Beta Clb; Spanish Clb; Ftbl; Hon Roll; Natl Ftbl Fnd/Coll Hl Of Fame Nom; U Of AR; Law.

BENOIT, RASHAD; Forrest City HS; Fullerton, CA; (2); Office Aide; Church Choir; JV Bsktbl; Washington U.

BENTLEY, DAWN BETH; Magnolia HS; Magnolia, AR; (4); 3/200; Mu Alpha Theta; Band; Ed Yrbk; Sec Stu Cncl; Powder Puff Ftbl; Gov Hon Prg Awd; High Hon Roll; NHS; Pres Schlr; Church Yth Grp; Vc Demcrcy Spch Cntst Schl, Dist Wnnr; Whos Who Mst Lkly Succeed; Grad Spkr; LA Tech U; Consumer Affrs.

BENTLEY, MICHELLE A; Parkview Arts-Science HS; Little Rock, AR; (3); 96/270; Church Yth Grp; FCA; Band; Mrchg Band; School Musical; Co-Capt Chrldng; Early Chldhd Ed.

BENTON, ANDREA; Norphlet HS; El Dorado, AR; (2); Church Yth Grp; FHA; Spanish Clb; Church Choir; Pres Frsh Cls; VP Soph Cls; Rep Jr Cls; Bsktbl; Chrldng; Sftbl.

BENTON, JEFF E; Booneville Jr Sr HS; Booneville, AR; (2); Church Yth Grp; FCA; Natl Beta Clb; Science Clb; Spanish Clb; Bsktbl; Tennis; Cit Awd; Prfct Atten Awd; Nrs.

BENTON, JOYCELIN L; North Little Rock Hs-East; North Little Rock, AR; (1); 87/646; Church Yth Grp; Cmnty Wkr; FCA; Girl Scts; Key Clb; VP Stu Cncl; JV Bsktbl; Powder Puff Ftbl; Hon Roll; Child Psych.

BENTON, KIM; El Dorado Sr HS; El Dorado, AR; (2); Church Yth Grp; Cmnty Wkr; Dance Clb; 4-H; FHA; Girl Scts; Pep Clb; Acpl Chr; Church Choir; Drill Tm; Shorter Coll; Rdlgst Tech.

BENTON, MINDY K; Fountain Lake Jr Sr HS; Hot Springs Natio, AR; (3); 20/78; Art Clb; FHA; Key Clb; Sec Natl Beta Clb; Pep Clb; Spanish Clb; Chorus; School Play; Hon Roll; SCA; UCA; PT/INTER Dec Phtgrphr.

BENZING, AARON; Jonesboro HS; Jonesboro, AR; (4); 52/297; Church Yth Grp; FCA; FBLA; German Clb; Quiz Bowl; Science Clb; Band; Church Choir; Drm Mjr(t); Jazz Band; Physics Awd; AR ST; Engrng.

BERCHER, COURTNEY; Northside HS; Barling, AR; (2); Spanish Clb; Chorus; Chrldng; Pom Pon; Hon Roll; Comm Work Vol; Coach Little League Chrldrs; OSU; Phys Therapy.

BERG, LARA; Southside HS; Fort Smith, AR; (3); Church Yth Grp; German Clb; Pep Clb; Pres Q&S; Ed Nwsp; Yrbk; Hon Roll; NHS; U Of MO At Columbia; Law.

BERGER, ALLISON M; Jacksonville HS; Sherwood, AR; (2); Art Clb; Cmnty Wkr; FBLA; Drill Tm; FOZ Mem; Chrstn Clb; U Of Cntrl AR; Child Psych.

BERGER, LISA J; Corning HS; Corning, AR; (3); Church Yth Grp; Drama Clb; Library Aide; Spanish Clb; Church Choir; School Play; Bsktbl; Trk; High Hon Roll; Jr NHS; RN.

BERGMAN, DIANA L; North Little Rock Hs-East; North Little Rock, AR; (2); Dance Clb; Drama Clb; German Clb; Hosp Aide; ROTC; School Play; Variety Show; Cit Awd; Hon Roll; Rfl Tm.

BERNARD, STEVEN; Mills HS; North Little Rock, AR; (2); 25/435; Drama Clb; FBLA; Math Clb; Mu Alpha Theta; Natl Beta Clb; Quiz Bowl; Science Clb; Sec Spanish Clb; School Play; Hon Roll; Invtd To Attnd AR JR Sci & Hum Sympsm; Cntrl AR Regnl JR Acd 2nd Pl; Comptd In St Levl Cmptn; Law; Med.

BERNER, JENNIFER M; Beebe Sr HS; Beebe, AR; (4); 20/94; FCA; FBLA; Math Clb; Natl Beta Clb; Science Clb; Spanish Clb; Treas Stu Cncl; Var L Crs Cntry; Var L Trk; Hon Roll; Henderson ST Univ; Bio.

BERNER, KEITH M; Russellville Sr HS; Russellville, AR; (2); Church Yth Grp; HOBY; Band; Mrchg Band; Pep Band; Treas Var Soph Cls; JV Var Socr; Jr NHS; NHS.

BERRY, AMBER; Bradford Jr Sr HS; Bradford, AR; (2); GAA; Natl Beta Clb; Natl FFA Org; Bsktbl; Sftbl; Trk; Hon Roll; Bio.

BERRY, BELINDA; Holly Grove HS; Holly Grove, AR; (3); 6/38; FHA; German Clb; HOBY; Rptr Nwsp; Var Crs Cntry; Child Dev.

BERRY, BRANDY M; Fordyce HS; Fordyce, AR; (4); 43/85; Chess Clb; FBLA; Hosp Aide; Science Clb; Spanish Clb; Teachers Aide; Band; Chorus; Flag Corp; Mrchg Band; Eng Awd; Chld Dev Awd; Band Awd; US Army; Commnctns-Fibre Optcs.

BERRY, BRETT W; Carlisle Jr Sr HS; Carlisle, AR; (3); 4/40; Am Leg Boys St; Church Yth Grp; FBLA; Office Aide; Quiz Bowl; Spanish Clb; Band; Rep Stu Cncl; Bsktbl; Ftbl; Xerox Awd; Schlrshp/Ldrshp/Comm Svc; PT.

BERRY, ELIZABETH E; Watson Chapel Sr HS; Pine Bluff, AR; (3); Church Yth Grp; FCA; Natl Beta Clb; Co-Capt Pep Clb; Drill Tm; School Play; Phtg Nwsp; Ofcr Stu Cncl; Pom Pon; Hon Roll; Mental Hlth Thrpst.

BERRY, JAMES; Bearden HS; Bearden, AR; (2); Church Yth Grp; Cmnty Wkr; 4-H; FBLA; Ftbl; Trk; Wt Lftg; High Hon Roll; Hon Roll.

BERRY, LORI; Bryant Jr HS; Alexander, AR; (3); Cmnty Wkr; Hosp Aide; VP Science Clb; Ofcr Jr Cls; Pres Sr Cls; VP Stu Cncl; Chrldng; Hon Roll; Pres Jr NHS; Pres NHS; U Of AR-FAYETTVILLE; Ped Med.

BERRY, NATHAN L; Searcy HS; Searcy, AR; (3); FBLA; Natl Beta Clb; Quiz Bowl; Spanish Clb; Hon Roll; Jr NHS; NHS; Spanish NHS; AR Govnrs Schl.

BERRY, TONNISHA; Holly Grove HS; Holly Grove, AR; (4); 3/28; Drama Clb; English Clb; FHA; Natl Beta Clb; Natl FFA Org; Science Clb; Speech Tm; Band; Drill Tm; Pep Band; Hnrs Awd TN ST U; Tougaloo Coll; Chld Psychlgy.

BERTRAM, JUSTIN; Arkansas Bapt Schl; Little Rock, AR; (3); 1/50; Church Yth Grp; FCA; FBLA; Natl Beta Clb; Spanish Clb; Var Socr; High Hon Roll; U Of AR.

BERUMEN, MICHAEL; Southside HS; Fort Smith, AR; (2); Math Tm; Mu Alpha Theta; Band; Mrchg Band; School Play; Stage Crew; Sec Stu Cncl; Var Bsktbl; Var Ftbl; Var Trk; Natl Math Counts.

BESHEA, KERRI; Bradley Jr Sr HS; Bradley, AR; (4); Sec FBLA; Sec FHA; Sec Math Clb; Spanish Clb; Ofcr Frsh Cls; Ofcr Soph Cls; VP Jr Cls; Ofcr Sr Cls; Ofcr Stu Cncl; Sftbl; Homcmng Qn; Maid; Red River Tech Coll; LPN.

BESHEARS, AMY L; Mt Ida Jr Sr HS; Mount Ida, AR; (2); Church Yth Grp; FBLA; FHA; Natl Beta Clb; Sec Soph Cls; Rep Stu Cncl; Bsktbl; Prfct Atten Awd; Faith Tabernacle Mem; UCA; Nuclear Med.

BESHONER, LEE; Scranton HS; Scranton, AR; (4); 3/23; Am Leg Boys St; FBLA; German Clb; Letterman Clb; Natl Beta Clb; Natl FFA Org; Science Clb; Sec Frsh Cls; Sec Soph Cls; Sec Jr Cls; Coll Of Ozarks; Civil Engrng.

BESS, CATHERINE; Malvern Sr HS; Malvern, AR; (4); 4/163; Sec Art Clb; Church Yth Grp; Dance Clb; FCA; FBLA; Math Clb; Natl Beta Clb; Pep Clb; Science Clb; Spanish Clb; U Of AR Fayetteville; Arch.

BEST, LISA L; Tuckerman HS; Newport, AR; (2); Church Yth Grp; Treas FBLA; FHA; Natl Beta Clb; Spanish Clb; Sec Frsh Cls; Rptr Stu Cncl; Var Bsktbl; Sftbl; Trk; Tone Staff; T-BAD; History Club.

BETHANY, ASHLEY; Smackover HS; Smackover, AR; (3); 7/49; VP Drama Clb; HOBY; Spanish Clb; Rep Sec Band; Mgr Yrbk; Rep Soph Cls; VP Jr Cls; Tennis; NHS; Hon Roll; Anchr Clb; Med.

BETHANY, SARA; Taylor HS; Taylor, AR; (3); FCA; Quiz Bowl; Variety Show; Bsktbl; Sftbl; Hon Roll; NHS; Pres Acad Fit Awd; CHAMPS; Frnch Awd; Typing Awd; S AR Univ; Pharm.

BETHEA, ANGELA M; Fouke Jr Sr HS; Fouke, AR; (3); 4/85; Church Yth Grp; FHA; GAA; Natl Beta Clb; Office Aide; Rep Frsh Cls; Rep Soph Cls; Rep Stu Cncl; JV Var Bsktbl; Cit Awd; Barrel Racing; MASH; Northwestern ST Univ; Vet Tech.

BETHEA, DAVID M; Hampton Jr Sr HS; Hampton, AR; (3); 1/65; Am Leg Boys St; Pres Church Yth Grp; FCA; Natl Beta Clb; Natl FFA Org; Var L Bsbl; Var L Ftbl; Var Wt Lftg; Hon Roll; AR Intrschlstc Str; Plmbrs Apprntc; Sthrn AR U; Plmbr.

BETHELL, CRYSTAL; Brinkley HS; Brinkley, AR; (3); Church Yth Grp; Drama Clb; FBLA; FHA; Office Aide; VICA; Church Choir; Tennis; Hon Roll; Jr NHS; Acteens; Handbells; HOSA; Mission Friends; Acteen Activators; U Of Cntrl AR; Reg Nrs.

BETTIS, ALLAN; Lake Hamilton Sr HS; Royal, AR; (2); Hon Roll; Medcl.

BETTIS, AMY; Arkansas Bapt Schl; Little Rock, AR; (3); 18/55; Church Yth Grp; Cmnty Wkr; FCA; Natl Beta Clb; Spanish Clb; Chorus; Church Choir; Stage Crew; Ofcr Stu Cncl; Co-Capt Chrldng; U Of AR Fayetteville; Elem Ed.

BEVEL, APRIL M; Atkins Schl; Atkins, AR; (1); Chorus; Ofcr Frsh Cls; Hon Roll; Obstetrics.

BEVERAGE, GRANT W; Sheridan Sr HS; Sheridan, AR; (2); Church Yth Grp; FCA; Varsity Clb; Intrml Ftbl; Var Trk; High Hon Roll; Jr NHS; Pres Acad Fit Awd; U Of AR; Arch/Tele-Comm.

BEVILL, TODD; Dierks HS; Dierks, AR; (3); 2/40; Church Yth Grp; FBLA; HOBY; Quiz Bowl; School Play; L Bsbl; L Crs Cntry; L Ftbl; L Trk; NHS; PRIDE; Law.

BEWLEY, DANA R; Russellville Sr HS; London, AR; (3); Chorus; High Hon Roll; Jr NHS; Prfct Atten Awd; AR Tech Univ; Cert Med Asst.

BHALEEYA, SWETANGI; Magnolia HS; Magnolia, AR; (2); 1/243; FBLA; Rptr Nwsp; High Hon Roll; Math & Sci Schl Hot Springs.

BIANCA, PHILLIPS N; Nettleton HS; Jonesboro, AR; (2); 1/210; Church Yth Grp; French Clb; Hist FHA; Natl Beta Clb; Science Clb; Band; Mrchg Band; Pep Band; School Musical; School Play; Frnch Top Score Awd; Alg I Top Score Awd; UCLA; Jrnlsm.

BIBBS, TINA; Beebe Sr HS; Beebe, AR; (4); 10/90; Am Leg Aux Girls St; Drama Clb; Natl Beta Clb; Spanish Clb; Band; Chorus; Yrbk; Hon Roll; Prims Spnsr; Hnr Star; ASU; Engl Ed.

BIBLE, CINDY; Bradford Jr Sr HS; Bradford, AR; (4); 3/36; Church Yth Grp; French Clb; FBLA; FHA; Natl Beta Clb; Chorus; School Play; VP Sr Cls; Treas Stu Cncl; Chrldng; ASU; Rdlgy.

BICKLEY, NATALIE; Dequeen HS; De Queen, AR; (3); FCA; 4-H; FBLA; HOBY; Office Aide; SADD; Chorus; Rep Soph Cls; Rep Jr Cls; High Hon Roll; Yng Democrats; Coll Courses; Rice; Bus.

BIERMAN, KENNY J; Cabot HS; Cabot, AR; (2); CAP; ROTC; Band; Color Guard; Drill Tm; NHS; Red Cross Aide; Mrchg Band; Amer Vet Awd; Ldrshp Unlimited; US Air Force Acad; Meteorology.

BIESCHKE, ADAM M; Alpena Schl; Harrison, AR; (2); 2/51; FCA; HOBY; Natl Beta Clb; Natl FFA Org; Bsktbl; High Hon Roll; Hon Roll; U Of AR; Mechanic.

BIGGERS, JAYME M; Russellville Sr HS; Russellville, AR; (2); Church Yth Grp; Hosp Aide; SADD; Band; Drill Tm; Ofcr Jr Cls; Golf; High Hon Roll; Jr NHS; NHS; U Of AR; Dermatologist.

BIGGERS, PHILIP; Morrilton Sr HS; Springfield, AR; (2); Rep Church Yth Grp; Natl Beta Clb; Natl FFA Org; Hon Roll; Tech Stu Assn.

BIGGS, CODY L; England HS; Scott, AR; (2); Ftbl; Wt Lftg; Cit Awd; Medcl.

BIGGS, REBECCA L; Scotland Schl; Scotland, AR; (2); Church Yth Grp; Cmnty Wkr; Drama Clb; FCA; FBLA; FHA; GAA; Quiz Bowl; Church Choir; Yrbk.

BIGHAM, GINGER; Arkansas Sr HS; Texarkana, AR; (4); 78/370; Art Clb; FBLA; VP Spanish Clb; Rep Stu Cncl; L Bsktbl; Capt Chrldng; L Gym; L Vllybl.

BIGHAM, JENNIFER K; Arkansas Sr HS; Texarkana, AR; (4); Art Clb; FBLA; VP Spanish Clb; Rep Sr Cls; L Bsktbl; Var Capt Chrldng; Capt Gym; Var L Vllybl; Cit Awd; Vllybl All-Conf; Gymnastcs All-St, Cls B All-St All-Arond Champn & Aaa St All-Arond Rnnr Up.

BILBO, AUDRA L; Dequeen HS; De Queen, AR; (1); Band; Mrchg Band; Cit Awd; Hon Roll; Pres Acad Fit Awd; Dr.

BILDERBACK, ANGELA L; Springdale Sr HS; Springdale, AR; (3); Chorus; Hon Roll.

BILER, JESSICA L; Conway Sr HS; Conway, AR; (2); Church Yth Grp; FBLA; German Clb; Rptr VICA; Church Choir; Orch; Quiz Bowl; Powder Puff Ftbl; Hon Roll; All Region Orch; All ST 1st Alternae 10 Grd; AR Hnrs Orch; AR Yth Symphony Orch; Arch.

BILES, RYAN; Abundant Life Schools; Sherwood, AR; (1); Church Yth Grp; Rptr Nwsp; Yrbk; Sec Stu Cncl; Hon Roll.

BILEY, MARGARET L; Pine Bluff HS; Pine Bluff, AR; (4); 14/412; Am Leg Aux Girls St; Key Clb; Natl Beta Clb; Mrchg Band; VP Stu Cncl; Bsktbl; NHS; Pres Acad Fit Awd; GAA; Band; Ray A Kroc Yth Achvmt Awd Mc Donalds Corp; Prin Ldrshp Awd; U Of AR; Cmptr Systms Engr.

BILLINGS, ROCKY; Hatfield Schl; Hatfield, AR; (2); #2 in class; FCA; Natl Beta Clb; School Play; Capt Bsktbl; Ntl Merit Ltr; Prfct Atten Awd; U Cntrl AR; Coach.

BILLINGS, SHARON; Sylvan Hills Jr HS; Little Rock, AR; (1); 46/266; Church Yth Grp; FCA; FBLA; FHA; Spanish Clb; Drill Tm; Ofcr Frsh Cls; Trk; Rcvd Awds In Civics/Algebra/Hlth/Spnsh; Drill Team Mbr Of Yr; Brdcstng/Nwsrprtr.

BILLINGSLEY, AMBER V; Horatio HS; Winthrop, AR; (2); Church Yth Grp; FCA; VP FBLA; HOBY; Natl FFA Org; Hon Roll; Sec NHS; Miss Horatio HS; Gftd & Tlntd; Yth Action Cncl.

BILLINGSLEY, KEONA L; Central HS; West Helena, AR; (3); 10/23; Church Yth Grp; Teachers Aide; Band; Church Choir; Flag Corp; Mrchg Band; Chrldng; Hon Roll; Prfct Atten Awd.

BILLINGSLEY, MICHELLE D; Lavaca Jr Sr HS; Lavaca, AR; (2); FCA; FHA; GAA; Ofcr Soph Cls; Bsktbl; Sftbl; Trk; Vllybl; USVBA Vllybl; UCA; Veterinarian.

BILLINGSLEY JR, RICKEY A; Newport HS; Newport, AR; (2); Boy Scts; Church Yth Grp; Library Aide; Office Aide; ROTC; Church Choir; VP Frsh Cls; VP Stu Cncl; Var Bsbl; L Bsktbl; All Star Tm 9-10 Grds; Bsbl; Bsktbl; Track; UCA; Bus Ed/Mgmt.

BINAM, LINDA; Springdale HS; Fayetteville, AR; (4); FBLA; Key Clb; Library Aide; Natl FFA Org; Q&S; Band; Mrchg Band; Yrbk; Hon Roll; Yth For Christ; U Of AR; Acctng.

BINGHAM, CHAD J; Nevada Schl; Rosston, AR; (2); 24/73; Church Yth Grp; FBLA; Natl Beta Clb; Natl FFA Org; Quiz Bowl; Church Choir; Hon Roll; FFA Treas.

BINGHAM, LATOYA; Delta Special Schl; Tillar, AR; (4); Art Clb; FHA; GAA; Math Clb; Natl Beta Clb; Pep Clb; Sec Frsh Cls; Sec Soph Cls; VP Jr Cls; High Hon Roll; Hmcmng Queen; ASU; Med.

BINNS, AMANDA L; Russellville Sr HS; Russellville, AR; (2); 106/420; Art Clb; Church Yth Grp; FBLA; Spanish Clb; Rptr Nwsp; Rptr Yrbk; Hon Roll; Beta Club; Church Sftbl League; Teenage Repblcns ST Treas; UCLA; Jrnlsm.

BINNS, TAMORRISE L; Dumas HS; Dumas, AR; (4); 46/188; Bus Profs of Am; Church Yth Grp; Cmnty Wkr; Computer Clb; FBLA; FHA; FTA; Library Aide; Office Aide; Speech Tm; Stu Cncl Awd; Univ Of AR Fayettville; Acctnt.

BIRCHFIELD, REGINA M; Mc Gehee HS; Mc Gehee, AR; (2); FBLA; Science Clb; Spanish Clb; Hendrix Univ AR; Pediatrician.

BIRD, LATISHA; Pangburn Jr Sr HS; Searcy, AR; (2); 3/60; French Clb; FHA; Natl Beta Clb; Pres Frsh Cls; Sftbl; Hon Roll; NHS; Prfct Atten Awd; UCA; Ed/His Tchr.

BIRMINGHAM, AARON J; Catholic HS; Little Rock, AR; (2); Cmnty Wkr; ROTC; Teachers Aide; Color Guard; School Play; Hon Roll; Bsktbl, Ftbl Team Mgr.

BIRMINGHAM, BRANDON D; Catholic HS; Little Rock, AR; (4); Boy Scts; Cmnty Wkr; Office Aide; Teachers Aide; ITT Tech Inst; Cmptr.

BIRMINGHAM, RYAN N; Cord-Charlotte Schl; Cord, AR; (4); 5/21; Church Yth Grp; Natl Beta Clb; Teachers Aide; Pres Band; Chorus; School Musical; Bsktbl; Trk; Hon Roll; HS Fire Chief; Div I And II Mdlsat Solo Ensmble; Law Enfcmnt.

BISBEE, CHRISTINA; Mayflower HS; Mayflower, AR; (3); Church Yth Grp; Cmnty Wkr; Drama Clb; French Clb; FBLA; FHA; HOBY; Pep Clb; Teachers Aide; Varsity Clb; OBU.

BISBEE, MATTHEW S; Sheridan Sr HS; Hensley, AR; (4); Church Yth Grp; Math Tm; Teachers Aide; Band; Jazz Band; Mrchg Band; Pep Band; School Play; U Of AR; Mus.

BISBEE, TIM A; Robinson HS; Little Rock, AR; (4); Math Tm; Natl Beta Clb; Hon Roll; Pulaski Tech Col; Auto Repair.

BISHOP, CAMERON G; Gravette HS; Maysville, AR; (3); JA; Teachers Aide; Hon Roll; Jr NHS; NHS; Pres Acad Fit Awd; U Of AR; Acctng.

BISHOP JR, GREGORY L; Watson Chapel Sr HS; Pine Bluff, AR; (4); 39/230; Church Yth Grp; 4-H; French Clb; FBLA; Natl Beta Clb; VICA; Bsktbl; Ftbl; Trk; Cit Awd; U Of Cntrl AR; Bus.

BISHOP, JAMIE R; Ridgecrest HS; Paragould, AR; (3); 8/200; Church Yth Grp; French Clb; Natl Beta Clb; Band; Jazz Band; Mrchg Band; Hon Roll; NHS; Prfct Atten Awd; Pres Acad Fit Awd; Sftbl St Champ; Fishing; AR ST Univ; Elem Ed.

BISHOP, JEREMIAH; Brookland Jr Sr HS; Brookland, AR; (4); 3/60; Church Yth Grp; Drama Clb; FBLA; Quiz Bowl; Teachers Aide; Band; Pep Band; Ed Nwsp; Sec Stu Cncl; High Hon Roll; All Region Choir 3 Yrs; All St Choir 1 Yrs; Stu Conductor Band 4 Yrs; Ouachita Bapt U; Music Educ.

BISHOP, JEREMY; Plainview Rover Schl; Plainview, AR; (3); Church Yth Grp; French Clb; HOBY; Natl Beta Clb; Natl FFA Org; Pres Frsh Cls; Rep Jr Cls; Bsktbl; Trk; High Hon Roll.

BISHOP, KEVIN D; Trumann HS; Trumann, AR; (2); 1/100; Church Yth Grp; Treas Science Clb; Pres Spanish Clb; Var Bsbl; Var Bsktbl; Var Ftbl; JV Trk; High Hon Roll; NHS; Stu Cncl; AR ST; Phy Thrpst; Vet.

BISHOP, LISA; Southside HS; Fort Smith, AR; (4); 75/550; Church Yth Grp; Debate Tm; Drama Clb; German Clb; Speech Tm; Thesps; Band; School Musical; School Play; Stage Crew; Westark Coll; Marine Bio.

BISHOP, MISTY M; Trumann HS; Trumann, AR; (3); Computer Clb; Spanish Clb; Band; Chorus; Mrchg Band; Vllybl; Cit Awd; Hon Roll; NHS; Prfct Atten Awd; Adv Eng Class; AR ST Univ; Lawyer.

BISSWANGER, JAMIE E; Dewitt HS; Ethel, AR; (2); 14/90; FCA; 4-H; French Clb; GAA; Natl Beta Clb; Science Clb; Var JV Bsktbl; JV Capt Chrldng; JV Powder Puff Ftbl; Var Sftbl.

BITTLE, ASHLEY; Dermott HS; Dermott, AR; (1); Church Yth Grp; Yrbk.

BITTLE, JENNY M; Cabot HS; Cabot, AR; (2); Church Yth Grp; Key Clb; Spanish Clb; High Hon Roll; Bus & Comp.

BITTLE, MATTHEW; Southside HS; Fort Smith, AR; (3); Church Yth Grp; FCA; Chorus; Church Choir; Ofcr Bsbl; Ftbl; Hon Roll; Jr NHS; NHS; Prfct Atten Awd; Med.

BITTLE, SHAWN; Ola Jr Sr HS; Ola, AR; (3); Natl Beta Clb; Spanish Clb; VP Soph Cls; Rep Jr Cls; L Bsbl; L Bsktbl; High Hon Roll.

BIVENS, JAMIE; J A Fair Sr HS; Little Rock, AR; (3); 4/300; Am Leg Aux Girls St; Art Clb; Church Yth Grp; Dance Clb; FCA; VP FBLA; FHA; Math Clb; Math Tm; Mu Alpha Theta; UALR; Social Work.

BIVENS, RONNIESHA R; Parkview Arts-Science HS; Little Rock, AR; (3); Church Yth Grp; Natl Beta Clb; Chorus; Church Choir; School Play; Yrbk; Sec Stu Cncl; Cit Awd; High Hon Roll; Kiwanis Awd; Psych.

BIVINS, CAROLLYN J; Horatio HS; Winthrop, AR; (2); FHA; Acpl Chr; Chorus; School Musical; Bsktbl.

BIXLER, GARRETT C; Pine Bluff HS; Pine Bluff, AR; (3); 11/427; Boy Scts; Church Yth Grp; CAP; French Clb; Library Aide; ROTC; Orch; Hon Roll; Jr NHS; NHS; USAF Acad; Aviation.

BLACK, BENJAMIN A; Morrilton Sr HS; Plumerville, AR; (3); Art Clb; Church Yth Grp; Cmnty Wkr; Drama Clb; Math Clb; Office Aide; Teachers Aide; Varsity Clb; Bsktbl; Wt Lftg; Bus.

BLACK, BRANDI L; Lake Hamilton Sr HS; Hot Springs, AR; (3); Pres Art Clb; Q&S; Spanish Clb; Co-Ed Nwsp; Yrbk; AR Governors Schl; Upward Bound; Art.

BLACK, CHRISTOPHER; Rogers HS; Rogers, AR; (4); 2/468; Church Yth Grp; FCA; Pres Stu Cncl; Ofcr Bsbl; Bsktbl; Ftbl; Trk; Wt Lftg; High Hon Roll; NHS; Chmbr Cmmrc All As, Renaissance Awds; Med.

BLACK, DANE T; Hot Springs HS; Hot Springs, AR; (2); 10/200; Boy Scts; Chess Clb; Computer Clb; Quiz Bowl; Scholastic Bowl; Spanish Clb; JV Ftbl; Cit Awd; Hon Roll; BSA Patrol Ldr; Knowledge Bowl Capt; Pol Sci; His.

BLACK, EVAN; Lake Hamilton Jr HS; Royal, AR; (3); Pres Natl FFA Org; Spanish Clb; Hon Roll; ST High Indvdl Ag Mech Cntst 96; 2nd Pl Teame St Ag Mech Cntst 96; FFA Schlrshp Awd.

BLACK, HOLLY K; West Memphis Sr HS; West Memphis, AR; (4); 28/286; Cmnty Wkr; French Clb; Pres FBLA; Math Clb; Mu Alpha Theta; Natl Beta Clb; Chorus; Cit Awd; Hon Roll; Pres Acad Fit Awd; U Of Memphis.

BLACK, JOSHUA C; Atkins Schl; Atkins, AR; (1); Art Clb; Ftbl; Trk; Wt Lftg; Hon Roll; Pres Awd Educl Excl; Jr Beta Clb.

BLACK, KRISTI L; Dewitt HS; De Witt, AR; (3); Am Leg Aux Girls St; FCA; French Clb; FBLA; Natl Beta Clb; Science Clb; Ofcr Stu Cncl; Bsktbl; Chrldng; All ST Track.

BLACK, LAURA D; Stuttgart Sr HS; Humphrey, AR; (4); Church Yth Grp; FBLA; Key Clb; Library Aide; Science Clb; Spanish Clb; Teachers Aide; Band; Church Choir; Stage Crew; REACH; U Of AR Little Rock; Bio.

BLACK, MARK; Lake Hamilton Sr HS; Pearcy, AR; (4); 12/279; Church Yth Grp; Computer Clb; FBLA; Natl Beta Clb; Natl FFA Org; Spanish Clb; Band; Church Choir; Mrchg Band; Pep Band; Lake Hmltn Tech Team Ldr; U Of AR-FAYETTEVILLE; Comp Sci.

BLACK, PRISCILLA R; Bearden HS; Bearden, AR; (3); FHA; FTA; Model UN; Natl Beta Clb; VP Soph Cls; Ofcr Stu Cncl; JV Chrldng; Hon Roll; Ntl Merit Ltr; GATE; Baptist Bible Coll.

BLACK, REAGAN; Morrilton Sr HS; Morrilton, AR; (3); Church Yth Grp; Natl Beta Clb; Spanish Clb; Var Bsktbl; Hon Roll; AAU Bsktbl; U Of AR; Bus Admin.

BLACK, WILLIAM; Bearden HS; Bearden, AR; (2); Church Yth Grp; Cmnty Wkr; Model UN; Natl Beta Clb; Quiz Bowl; VP Soph Cls; Hon Roll; GT.

BLACK, WILLIAM C; Southside HS; Fort Smith, AR; (3); Am Leg Boys St; Cmnty Wkr; FCA; German Clb; JV Ftbl; Gov Hon Prg Awd; Hon Roll; Pres Acad Fit Awd.

BLACKBURN, NICHOLE; Springdale Sr HS; Springdale, AR; (4); 60/518; Church Yth Grp; French Clb; Pres Natl FFA Org; Chorus; Powder Puff Ftbl; Trk; High Hon Roll; Jr NHS; NHS; Ntl Merit SF; AR HS Rodeo; Goshen & Springdale Riding Clb; U Of AR; Vet.

BLACKLAW, AARON D; Robinson HS; Little Rock, AR; (2); 5/100; Church Yth Grp; FCA; French Clb; Natl Beta Clb; Ofcr Bsbl; Chrldng; Ftbl; High Hon Roll; NHS; Pres Acad Fit Awd; Mssn Trip One Week W/Chrch Nuevo Laredo.

BLACKLAW, AMY E; Robinson HS; Little Rock, AR; (3); Church Yth Grp; FCA; Natl Beta Clb; Office Aide; Spanish Clb; Yrbk; Var Bsktbl; JV Var Vllybl; Hon Roll; Pres Acad Fit Awd; UALR.

BLACKMAN, BRIDGETTE; Mabelvale Jr HS; Little Rock, AR; (2); Drama Clb; French Clb; FBLA; Drill Tm; Pres Frsh Cls; Pres Soph Cls; Pres Jr Cls; Chrldng; L Trk; Hon Roll; Med.

BLACKMAN, BRYCE; Brookland Jr Sr HS; Brookland, AR; (2); VP FCA; VP 4-H; HOBY; Natl Beta Clb; Chorus; School Play; Treas Soph Cls; Var Bsbl; JV Bsktbl; Hon Roll.

BLACKMON, KENDRA A; El Dorado Sr HS; El Dorado, AR; (4); FBLA; Natl Beta Clb; Rep Sr Cls; Rep Stu Cncl; JV Var Chrldng; Var Crs Cntry; Var Trk; Hon Roll; NHS; U Of Cntrl AR.

BLACKMON, MATT T; Huttig Schl; Huttig, AR; (2); Church Yth Grp; Natl Beta Clb; Science Clb; Ofcr Bsbl; Bsktbl; Prfct Atten Awd; Sr Babe Ruth Assn All-Star Team; U Of AR.

BLACKSHEAR, EMILY K; Ridgecrest HS; Paragould, AR; (2); Church Yth Grp; Office Aide; Hon Roll; Rdgcrst Sr HS Dnc Team Capt 96-; Leo Club Spon Lions Club; Prin Dncr Eastern AR Ballet Co; VALR.

BLACKSTONE, BRETT D; Bryant Sr HS; Alexander, AR; (2); Var Bsbl; U Of AR.

BLACKWEL, DALESHA; Rison HS; Rison, AR; (1); 2/52; Church Choir; JV Bsktbl; Hon Roll; Pres Acad Fit Awd; Jr Beta Clb; U Of AR Pine Bluff; Med.

BLACKWELL, LA QUANDRIA D; Jacksonville HS; Sherwood, AR; (2); Art Clb; FHA; Chorus; Church Choir; Archonettes Zeta Club; Zeta Phi Beta; Tchrs/Tmrw; Med Fld.

BLACKWOOD, CARA; Izard Co Cons Jr Sr HS; Franklin, AR; (3); Church Yth Grp; Treas FBLA; Sec Natl Beta Clb; Office Aide; Pep Clb; Band; Yrbk; Rep Soph Cls; Ofcr Stu Cncl; JV Chrldng; AR ST Univ-Jonesboro; Elem Ed.

BLACKWOOD, EMILY R; Greenwood Sr HS; Greenwood, AR; (3); 5/194; FCA; Math Clb; Pres Natl Beta Clb; Science Clb; Rep Sr Cls; Bsktbl; Sftbl; High Hon Roll; NHS; S Sebastian Cty Yth Umpire; JETS Cmptn; MASH Pgm; OSU.

BLACKWOOD, JEREMY B; Harrisburg HS; Harrisburg, AR; (2); Church Yth Grp; Science Clb; Spanish Clb; Teachers Aide; Chorus; Church Choir; Rep Stu Cncl; Cit Awd; High Hon Roll; All Star Choir; Schlrshp Awd; Great Books Lit Awd; AR ST Univ; Bus/Music/Med.

BLAGRAVE, CHRISTIE M; Emerson HS; Magnolia, AR; (4); 1/18; Church Yth Grp; Treas 4-H; French Clb; Treas FBLA; VP FHA; Treas Natl Beta Clb; Natl FFA Org; Spanish Clb; Band; Church Choir; Southern AR Univ.

BLAHA, DANIEL C; Mt Ida Jr Sr HS; Mount Ida, AR; (2); Natl Beta Clb; Natl FFA Org; Band; Jazz Band; Mrchg Band; Pep Band; Hon Roll; Gftd/Tlntd Prgm; 1st Dgre Blckbl Tae Kwon Do; Class A All Star Bnd/All Rgn Bnd; PT.

BLAIR, JEREMIAH J; Fountain Lake Jr Sr HS; Lonsdale, AR; (1); Ftbl; Hon Roll; PT.

BLAIR, MARIA K; Gravette HS; Gravette, AR; (2); FBLA; Yrbk; Var Chrldng; Hon Roll; NHS; Prfct Atten Awd; Med.

BLAIR, RAMONDA; Crossett Sr HS; Crossett, AR; (3); Am Leg Aux Girls St; Art Clb; Church Yth Grp; FBLA; Natl Beta Clb; Band; Drm Mjr(t); Hon Roll; NHS; Drama Clb; All Amer Schlr; Frgn Lang Hnr Soc Span; Stdnts For Christ; U Of AR Pine Bluff.

BLAKE, LESLIE; Riverside HS; Caraway, AR; (4); 15/40; Art Clb; Church Yth Grp; Pres 4-H; Sec French Clb; FBLA; FTA; Key Clb; Natl Beta Clb; Chorus; Church Choir; Pres Of RAID; Pres Of Rebels With A Cause, Chrstn Clb; Record Bk Wnnr & 4-H Teen Star; 1st Pl Dougles; AR ST Univ; Elem Ed.

BLAKE, MATT J; Bryant Sr HS; Benton, AR; (3); Church Yth Grp.

BLAKE, MELISSA A; Sheridan Sr HS; Hensley, AR; (2); Library Aide; Jr NHS; Cmptr Techncn.

BLAKELY, ASHLEY J; Searcy HS; Searcy, AR; (3); Church Yth Grp; FCA; French Clb; Natl Beta Clb; Office Aide; Nwsp; JV Bsktbl; French Hon Soc; Hon Roll; NHS; U Of AR At Fayetteville.

BLAKELY, MARIO; Elaine Jr Sr HS; Elaine, AR; (1); 4-H; Church Choir; Bsktbl; Memphis ST U; Nursng.

BLAKELY, TIMIKO; Lakeside HS; Montrose, AR; (3); 6/80; Sec Church Yth Grp; Rptr Drama Clb; VP FBLA; HOBY; Rep Jr Cls; Ofcr Stu Cncl; DAR Awd; Hon Roll; Jr NHS; NHS; U Of Conway; Pre-Med.

BLAKNEY, TRAVIS G; Dequeen HS; De Queen, AR; (3); Church Yth Grp; Office Aide; Chorus; Ed Nwsp; Bsktbl; Ftbl; Trk; Hon Roll; NHS; Pres Acad Fit Awd; U Of AR; Comm.

BLANCHARD, CHIP B; Russellville Sr HS; Russellville, AR; (2); 20/440; Church Yth Grp; FCA; Letterman Clb; Lit Mag; Rep Frsh Cls; Rep Soph Cls; Var Bsktbl; Var Ftbl; Var Tennis; Var Trk; All Acad Tennis; Bus.

BLAND, ANGELA; Caddo Hills Jr Sr HS; Norman, AR; (4); 4/37; Art Clb; FBLA; FHA; Spanish Clb; SADD; Chorus; Hon Roll; Navy Hnrs Pgm; Intrprsnl Reltns Awd; Homcmng Princss & Maid 2yrs; Whos Who At Caddo Hills 3 Yrs; UCA.

BLAND, BRANDY M; Russellville Sr HS; Russellville, AR; (2); Art Clb; Natl Beta Clb; SADD; Nwsp; Yrbk; Rep Frsh Cls; Rep Stu Cncl; Hon Roll; Cmpgn Vol; U Of AR-FAYETTEVILLE.

BLAND, DANAE; Ozark Adventist Acad; Jay, OK; (3); Rep Frsh Cls; Gym; High Hon Roll.

BLAND, DEMEDRICK A; Cloverdale Jr HS; Little Rock, AR; (1); Church Yth Grp; FBLA; JA; Quiz Bowl; Yrbk; VP Stu Cncl; Trk; Hon Roll; Jr NHS; FCA; Pres Ed Awds Prgm; Church Musician; Attrny.

BLAND, EBONY E; Parkview Arts-Science HS; Little Rock, AR; (2); FBLA; FHA; Hosp Aide; Teachers Aide; Stage Crew; Powder Puff Ftbl; Cit Awd; Hon Roll.

BLAND, JULIE; Ridgecrest HS; Paragould, AR; (4); 17/185; Am Leg Aux Girls St; Sec Church Yth Grp; Sec FCA; FBLA; HOBY; Key Clb; Model UN; Science Clb; Spanish Clb; Nwsp; Hmcmng Qn; Wrld Yth Smmt Del; Natl Chrldrs Assn-Natl Chmpn; Phys Thrpy.

BLAND, MARK L; Rivercrest HS; Joiner, AR; (2); Bus Profs of Am; Mrchg Band; L Bsktbl; Hon Roll; Prfct Atten Awd; Outstdng Bndsmn Awd 9th Grd; Bsktbl Tm Dist Chmpns/Ltrmn Awd 10th Grd; U Of AR; Vet.

BLANKENSHIP, COURTNEY D; Corning HS; Corning, AR; (1); Art Clb; Drama Clb; Spanish Clb; School Play; Capt Chrldng; Trk; Cit Awd; High Hon Roll; Hon Roll; Jr NHS; Summer Swim Team 8 Yrs; Jr Olympics; Piano 8 Yrs; Psych.

BLANKENSHIP, JAMIE L; Ridgecrest HS; Paragould, AR; (2); 46/207; 4-H; FTA; Hosp Aide; Library Aide; Natl FFA Org; Band; Stage Crew; 4-H Awd; Hon Roll; Schl Bnd/Orch Assn Solo Ensmbl I; AR ST; PT.

BLANKENSOP, HEATHER; West Jr HS; Proctor, AR; (1); Band; Color Guard; Flag Corp; Mrchg Band; Gym; Soc Stds Clb; U Memphis; Nrs.

BLASDEL, LACEY; Mountain Home HS; Mountain Home, AR; (4); 77/280; Cmnty Wkr; Pres FCA; Sec German Clb; Key Clb; Teachers Aide; Treas Soph Cls; Sec Jr Cls; Var Bsktbl; Var Chrldng; Gym; STARS; Fire Mrshll; Hmcmng Qn 95, Ct; Med.

BLASINGAME, ALLYSON M; Hope HS; Hope, AR; (3); Church Yth Grp; FBLA; Natl Beta Clb; Band; Color Guard; Mrchg Band; Rep Stu Cncl; Tennis; Hon Roll; Majorette; UCA; Vet.

BLAYLOCK, DIANNA; Mountainburg Jr Sr HS; Mountainburg, AR; (3); Drama Clb; HOBY; Natl Beta Clb; Office Aide; Spanish Clb; School Play; Mgr Chrldng; High Hon Roll; Pres Acad Fit Awd; Fort Smith Ltl Theatre; Ballet; NY U; Prfrmng Arts.

BLAYLOCK, JOSH A; Catholic HS; Mabelvale, AR; (2); Art Clb; Boy Scts; Chess Clb; French Clb; Math Clb; Intrml Bsbl; Intrml Bsktbl; Ftbl; Intrml Socr; Hon Roll.

BLEAU, NICK R; Russellville Sr HS; Russellville, AR; (3); Boy Scts; Church Yth Grp; Office Aide; Teachers Aide; Band; Mrchg Band; Ftbl.

BLEDSOE, KRISTA E; Fouke Jr Sr HS; Fouke, AR; (3); 25/82; FHA; Natl Beta Clb; Rptr Natl FFA Org; Office Aide; Spanish Clb; Band; Rptr Co-Ed Nwsp; Hon Roll; YoRAD.

BLEDSOE, TRICIA F; Shiloh Christian Schools; Rogers, AR; (2); Church Yth Grp; HOBY; Chorus; Bsktbl; Crs Cntry; Socr; Trk; High Hon Roll; NHS; Cert Lf Grd & Scuba Dvr; Hmcmng Ct; Med.

BLEVINS, JENNY L; Harmony Grove Jr Sr HS; Benton, AR; (2); Art Clb; Natl Beta Clb; Office Aide; DATE; Champs; Peer Cnslrs; Nrsng.

BLEVINS, MANDY; Omaha Schl; Omaha, AR; (2); Church Yth Grp; FCA; Natl Beta Clb; Church Choir; Nwsp; Yrbk; Cit Awd; Hon Roll; Prfct Atten Awd; Law.

BLEVINS, MELISSA; Omaha Schl; Omaha, AR; (1); Church Yth Grp; FBLA; Natl Beta Clb; Bsktbl; Vllybl; Cit Awd; Hon Roll; Prfct Atten Awd; OTAD.

BLEVINS, SARAH R; Lake Hamilton Sr HS; Hot Springs Natio, AR; (2); FCA; FBLA; Natl Beta Clb; Spanish Clb; Hon Roll; Photo Jrnlsm.

BLEVINS, SHANE; Bradford Jr Sr HS; Bradford, AR; (3); Art Clb; Church Yth Grp; FHA; Natl Beta Clb; Quiz Bowl; Yrbk; Sec Frsh Cls; Rep Stu Cncl; Bsktbl; Hon Roll; Harding U; Law Enfrcmt.

BLOCKER, AMANDA L; Northside HS; Fort Smith, AR; (3); French Clb; School Play; High Hon Roll; Westark CC.

BLOCKER, LENARD T; Russellville Sr HS; Russellville, AR; (2); 71/407; Church Yth Grp; Spanish Clb; JV Var Bsktbl; Hon Roll; Jr NHS; NHS; Pres Acad Fit Awd; U Of AR; Mech/Elec Engr.

BLOODWORTH, HILARY L; Brookland Jr Sr HS; Jonesboro, AR; (3); VP Drama Clb; FBLA; Hosp Aide; Model UN; Natl Beta Clb; Sec Spanish Clb; Chorus; School Play; Chrldng; Hon Roll; AR ST Univ; RN.

BLOT, ROBERT; J A Fair Sr HS; Little Rock, AR; (2); Socr; Tennis; High Hon Roll; Hon Roll; Jr NHS; NHS.

BLOUNT II, BENNIE P; Blevins HS; Blevins, AR; (2); Church Yth Grp; Var Cit Awd; Pres Acad Fit Awd; U Of AR; His.

BLOUNT, KRYSTAL L; Maynard Jr Sr HS; Pocahontas, AR; (3); Natl FFA Org; School Play; Hon Roll; Blk Rvr Tech Coll; Paralegal.

BLUE, BETH; Rivercrest HS; Wilson, AR; (3); 1/92; Church Yth Grp; Cmnty Wkr; Treas FBLA; FHA; Math Clb; Teachers Aide; Band; Church Choir; Flag Corp; Mrchg Band; Ouachita Bapt U.

BLY, DAWN T; Harrisburg HS; Harrisburg, AR; (2); FHA; Science Clb; Spanish Clb; Teachers Aide; Chorus; 3-D Clb; Stu Cncl; AR ST Univ; Pharmacist.

BOATMAN, KENNY W; Lavaca Jr Sr HS; Lavaca, AR; (2); Church Yth Grp; FCA; Natl FFA Org; School Play; Rep Stu Cncl; Var Bsbl; Var Ftbl; Var Trk; Hon Roll; Phy Thrpst.

BOBO, BRANDI; White Hall Sr HS; Pine Bluff, AR; (4); 19/161; Church Yth Grp; Sec Mu Alpha Theta; VP Natl Beta Clb; Sec Science Clb; VP Spanish Clb; VP Sr Cls; Rep Stu Cncl; L Chrldng; Powder Puff Ftbl; High Hon Roll; U Of AR; Nrsng.

BOBO, CRYSTAL; Blevins HS; Hope, AR; (1); Church Yth Grp; Natl Beta Clb; Band; Church Choir; Hon Roll.

BOBO, JENNIFER R; Dierks HS; Dierks, AR; (1); 7/57; GAA; JV Var Bsktbl; JV Chrldng; JV Var Tennis; Hon Roll; U Of AR; Vet.

BOBO, KIMBERLY D; Blytheville Sr HS; Blytheville, AR; (2); Church Yth Grp; Dance Clb; Church Choir; Trk; Wt Lftg; Cit Awd; Hon Roll; Pres Acad Fit Awd; Wrtng Poems; Typing; Memphis ST Univ; Med/Tchng.

BODDIE, NATASHA R; Russellville Sr HS; Russellville, AR; (3); French Clb; Church Choir; Mrchg Band; Stage Crew; Phtg Nwsp; Mgr Ftbl; Mgr(s); NHS; Library Aide; Office Aide; AIDS 5k Marathon; Vacation Bible Schl Tchr; Designed Backdrop For Jr Follies; Sports Medicine; Phys Therapy.

BOE, JASON M; Fayetteville Sr HS; Fayetteville, AR; (3); FBLA; Var L Bsbl; Var L Ftbl; High Hon Roll; NHS; Yth Hockey; U Of IL; Intnl Bus.

BOECKMANN, ASHLEY; Wynne HS; Wynne, AR; (3); FBLA; Sec FTA; Q&S; Nwsp; Ed Yrbk; Rep Stu Cncl; Var L Tennis; Hon Roll; VP Sec NHS; Am Leg Aux Girls St; Search Ldrshp Team MOM; Ground Schl In Prep For Pilots License; Psych.

BOERNER, CAREY D; Northside HS; Fort Smith, AR; (4); 40/369; German Clb; Mu Alpha Theta; Capt Drill Tm; School Play; Treas Soph Cls; Pres Stu Cncl; Mgr Trk; Hon Roll; NHS; Pres Acad Fit Awd; Ldrshp Ft Smith Explr Post; German Natl Hnr Soc; Westark CC; Psychiatrist.

BOETTGER, LINDSAY; Lake Hamilton Jr HS; Hot Springs, AR; (1); Church Yth Grp; Dance Clb; FCA; FBLA; GAA; Natl Beta Clb; Drill Tm; Sftbl; Trk; High Hon Roll; FBS; Drll Tm Offcr; Sci Fair Wnnr; All Hnrs Classes; GATE; Ftr Prblm Slvng; Brdcst Jrnlsm.

BOGAN, TIFFANY N; Mills HS; Jacksonville, AR; (2); Church Yth Grp; Cmnty Wkr; Computer Clb; Debate Tm; FBLA; Mu Alpha Theta; Spanish Clb; Band; Church Choir; Flag Corp; Biomed/Clncl Lab Sci.

BOGDON, KATRINA A; Greenwood Sr HS; Greenwood, AR; (2); Church Yth Grp; French Clb; Girl Scts; Hosp Aide; Mu Alpha Theta; Science Clb; Band; Cit Awd; High Hon Roll; Jr NHS; Tae Kwon Do; Sci Fair; Girl Sct Silver Awd; Astrophysics; Space Medicine.

BOGGS, RHONDA L; Black Rock Jr Sr HS; Black Rock, AR; (3); FHA; Girl Scts; Library Aide; Chorus; School Musical; Cit Awd; Prfct Atten Awd.

BOGGS, WILLIAM J; Plainview Rover Schl; Ola, AR; (3); 4/30; Church Yth Grp; French Clb; VP FBLA; Natl Beta Clb; Nwsp; Hon Roll; AR Tech Univ; Comp Sci.

BOGY, NICK; Humphrey Schl; Wabbaseka, AR; (2); 1/32; HOBY; Natl FFA Org; Ed Nwsp; Pres Frsh Cls; Rep Soph Cls; High Hon Roll; Hon Roll; Piano; Gftd Tlntd Pgm; Stu Tutr.

BOHANNAN, DAVID S; Huntsville HS; Huntsville, AR; (3); 20/128; FCA; Science Clb; Var Ftbl; Var Trk; Var Wt Lftg; Hon Roll; DART; MASH; UCA; Phys Thrpy.

BOHANNON, TANESHA L; Forrest City HS; Forrest City, AR; (3); 4-H; FHA; Nrsng.

BOHR, WESLEY A; Clay Co Central Jr Sr HS; Rector, AR; (3); Teachers Aide; Ofcr Bsbl; NHS.

BOLDEN, JAMES G; Clinton HS; Clinton, AR; (1); Hon Roll; UCA.

BOLDEN, LASHANA; Parkin Jr Sr HS; Parkin, AR; (2); 2/30; Cmnty Wkr; FHA; FTA; Natl Beta Clb; Science Clb; School Play; Variety Show; Rep Frsh Cls; Rep Soph Cls; Rep Stu Cncl; Frgn Lang Clb; Achvmts High Scores Algebra I/Srvy Fine Arts/Career Orient/Prctcl Arts; Asu; Med.

BOLDEN, SONJA L; Lake Hamilton Sr HS; Royal, AR; (2); 23/274; Hon Roll; Pres Acad Fit Awd; Reg Eng, Alg I, Phys Sci Awds; Garland Cty CC; Nrsng.

BOLDING, ALLISON BLAKE; Woodlawn Schl; Monticello, AR; (1); Church Yth Grp; Cmnty Wkr; GAA; Natl Beta Clb; Teachers Aide; Acpl Chr; Chorus; Rep Stu Cncl; Var Bsktbl; Var Sftbl; Speech Thrpy.

BOLEN, AMBER L; Star City HS; Pine Bluff, AR; (3); #14 in class; Church Yth Grp; FCA; FBLA; Mu Alpha Theta; Science Clb; Color Guard; Mrchg Band; School Play; Cit Awd; NHS.

BOLEY, HEATHER; Van Buren Sr HS; Van Buren, AR; (4); Pep Clb; Spanish Clb; Band; Drill Tm; Rep Stu Cncl; Cit Awd; Hon Roll; NHS; Pres Acad Fit Awd.

BOLIN, CANDICE M; Trumann HS; Trumann, AR; (2); Var Church Yth Grp; Ofcr Stu Cncl; L Bsktbl; Sftbl; Trk; Vllybl; High Hon Roll; NHS; Prfct Atten Awd; Pres Acad Fit Awd; Jr High Homcmng Qn Frosh Yr; Hlth Awd.

BOLIN, KEVIN L; Trumann HS; Trumann, AR; (2); Church Yth Grp; French Clb; Science Clb; Ofcr Stu Cncl; L Bsbl; L Bsktbl; High Hon Roll; NHS; Cmnty Wkr; Math Clb; Soph Cls Favorite; Fire Marshall Inner Cncl; Eng, Algebra, Phy Sci, Geom & Fr Awds.

BOLING, CHASE; Pea Ridge HS; Pea Ridge, AR; (3); 18/52; Debate Tm; 4-H; FBLA; FHA; Spanish Clb; Speech Tm; Band; Flag Corp; School Play; Rptr Nwsp; Coll Of Ozark; Med.

BOLLINGER, SARA; Re Wells Jr HS; Greenwood, AR; (1); Chrldng; Jr NHS; U Of Sthrn MS Smmr Gftd Stds Prgm; Mrn Bio.

BOLLMAN, MELANIE; Clarksville HS; Clarksville, AR; (3); Am Leg Aux Girls St; Art Clb; Church Yth Grp; Drama Clb; Key Clb; Art Clb; Odyssey Of The Mind.

BOLNER, JENNIFER C; Springdale Sr HS; Springdale, AR; (3); Key Clb; Office Aide; Chorus; Hon Roll; Jr NHS; NHS; Pres Acad Fit Awd; Northwest AR Jr HS All Regn Choir; Env Clb; Sci Fair Frst Pl 94; U Of AR; Fin.

BOLNER, TONYA T; Springdale Sr HS; Springdale, AR; (2); Girl Scts; Chorus; Hon Roll; Jr NHS; Jst Sy No; Fshng Clb; Psychlgst.

BOLTON, CHRISTY; Marion HS; Marion, AR; (3); Art Clb; Drama Clb; FHA; Mu Alpha Theta; Pres Spanish Clb; School Play; Var Chrldng; Hon Roll; Jr NHS; NHS; Stdnts Actvty Bd Sec; AR ST U; Dntl Hygn.

BOMAR, DANA N; Rose Bud Jr Sr HS; Romance, AR; (3); 1/60; Art Clb; Church Yth Grp; FCA; Spanish Clb; Yrbk; VP Jr Cls; Var Bsktbl; High Hon Roll; Mrs Rose Bud Jr HS 9th Grd Acad; All-Conf Jr Girls Ath Frosh; Acctng; Math.

BONACCI, ANGELO R; Catholic HS; Little Rock, AR; (3); 20/197; Latin Clb; Band; Jazz Band; Mrchg Band; Orch; Pep Band; Hon Roll; Architecture.

BOND, APRIL; Lee Sr HS; Marianna, AR; (3); 9/160; French Clb; FTA; Math Clb; Natl Beta Clb; Science Clb; VICA; School Play; Cit Awd; High Hon Roll; NHS; 2nd Pl French Cmptn.

BOND, CHAD A; Emerson HS; Emerson, AR; (3); #9 in class; Boy Scts; Church Yth Grp; Spanish Clb; Jr Patrol Ldr As A Boy Sct; Eagle Sct; Comp.

BOND, CHRISTINA L; Searcy HS; Searcy, AR; (3); 12/230; Am Leg Aux Girls St; Church Yth Grp; FTA; Girl Scts; Acpl Chr; Band; Chorus; Color Guard; NHS; Spanish NHS; Pre-Med.

BONDS, NICOLE E; White Co Central Schl; Judsonia, AR; (2); Church Yth Grp; FHA; HOBY; Office Aide; Red Cross Aide; Teachers Aide; Band; Color Guard; Drm Mjr(t); Mrchg Band; Natl Ldrshp Forum Delegate; Univ Of Cntrl AR; Tchr.

BONEE, BRANDI R; Bradford Jr Sr HS; Bradford, AR; (3); FBLA; FHA; Pep Clb; Quiz Bowl; Band; Chorus; Yrbk; Hon Roll; ASU Newport AR; Elem Ed.

BONET, TERENCE A; Hampton Jr Sr HS; Hampton, AR; (3); Art Clb; Bsktbl; Ftbl; Mgr(s); Trk; Wt Lftg; Frst ST Bk Awd HS Track; All Conf Awd; LA Tech.

BONNEMA, TERESA M; Vilonia HS; Vilonia, AR; (4); 18/120; Church Yth Grp; FBLA; FHA; Model UN; Mu Alpha Theta; Natl Beta Clb; Teachers Aide; Nwsp; Yrbk; Hon Roll; U Central AR; Infomtn Prcssng.

BONNER, BRIDGET L; Searcy HS; Searcy, AR; (2); Church Yth Grp; French Clb; FBLA; Natl Beta Clb; Band; Color Guard; Mrchg Band; Yrbk; French Hon Soc.

BONNER, ROBERT; Murfreesboro HS; Murfreesboro, AR; (2); Church Yth Grp; Natl Beta Clb; Science Clb; Spanish Clb; Band; Mrchg Band; Ofcr Bsbl; Bsktbl; Ftbl; Trk; U Of AR; Ag Sci.

BONSALL, BROOKE; Norphlet HS; Norphlet, AR; (3); 4/40; Sec Art Clb; Church Yth Grp; Pres French Clb; HOBY; Mgr Yrbk; Rep Stu Cncl; Capt Chrldng; Pres Jr NHS; NHS; Cmnty Wkr; Natrl Hlpr; Psych.

BOOHER, KELLY A; Mt St Mary Acad; Memphis, TN; (4); Church Yth Grp; Cmnty Wkr; French Clb; Spanish Clb; Teachers Aide; Band; Drill Tm; Mrchg Band; Variety Show; High Hon Roll; Natl Stdnt Svc Awd; Dance Ballet/Jazz/Tap; U Of Memphis.

BOOK, ANDEE L; Piggott HS; Saint Francis, AR; (2); Sec Treas Church Yth Grp; Natl Beta Clb; Quiz Bowl; Band; Chorus; Jazz Band; Mrchg Band; Ed Nwsp; Ed Yrbk; Pres Acad Fit Awd; All Region Choir; All ST Choir; Optimist Oratorical Contest Schlrshp.

BOOK, KERI; Trinity Christian Acad; Hamburg, AR; (3); 1/4; Church Yth Grp; Church Choir; Var Bsktbl; High Hon Roll; AR ST Univ.

BOOKER, AARON J; Melbourne HS; Melbourne, AR; (3); Band; Pep Band; Acad Achv Awd; Audio Tech.

BOOKER, JOHN RUSSELL; Marvell Acad; Clarendon, AR; (2); Church Yth Grp; Varsity Clb; Pres Frsh Cls; Var Bsktbl; Capt Ftbl; Var Trk; Var Wt Lftg; Hon Roll; NHS; Prfct Atten Awd; Schlr Athlt; Acad Btrmnt Cntst; AR ST Univ; Wldlf Bio.

BOOKER, STEVEN R; Monticello HS; Monticello, AR; (3); 50/175; Church Yth Grp; French Clb; FBLA; Natl Beta Clb; Quiz Bowl; SADD; Acpl Chr; Church Choir; School Play; Hon Roll; Phy Thrpst.

BOONE, MARY E; White Co Central Schl; Judsonia, AR; (2); FHA; Quiz Bowl; Trk; High Hon Roll; NHS; Prfct Atten Awd; Pres Acad Fit Awd.

BOONE, MELISSA A; Searcy HS; Searcy, AR; (3); Girl Scts; Library Aide; Natl Beta Clb; Spanish Clb; Cit Awd; Hon Roll; Jr NHS; NHS; Prfct Atten Awd; Spanish NHS; Acad Achvmts Geog 10th Grd/Span II/ACCTNG I 11th Grd; Jr Review; Harding Univ; Ed/Acct.

BOOTH, BILLYNDA; Little Rock Cntrl HS; Little Rock, AR; (4); 9/420; Am Leg Aux Girls St; Girl Scts; Latin Clb; Mu Alpha Theta; Natl Beta Clb; Band; Ofcr Stu Cncl; Hon Roll; Pres NHS; Ntl Merit SF; Natl Achvt; Govs Schl; Chem.

BOOTH, BRIAN R; Brookland Jr Sr HS; Jonesboro, AR; (3); #1 in class; FBLA; German Clb; Math Clb; Model UN; Natl FFA Org; Pep Clb; Quiz Bowl; Scholastic Bowl; VP Soph Cls; Var Bsktbl; AR ST Univ; Engrng.

BOOTH, ROBERT P; West Side HS; Weiner, AR; (4); Church Yth Grp; FBLA; HOBY; Band; Nwsp; Yrbk; Pres Rep Stu Cncl; Ofcr Bsbl; Bsktbl; Hon Roll; Stu Of Month Awd; AR ST Univ; Ag Bus.

BOQUIN, HENCY L; Dequeen HS; De Queen, AR; (2); Cossalot Tech Coll.

BORCHERDING, AMY M; Stuttgart Sr HS; Stuttgart, AR; (4); 11/133; Pres Church Yth Grp; FBLA; Key Clb; Mu Alpha Theta; Quiz Bowl; Science Clb; Spanish Clb; Band; NHS; Band Cncl Pres; Boston Univ; Intl Bus.

BORDEN, BETH A; Southside HS; Fort Smith, AR; (3); Church Yth Grp; Dance Clb; FBLA; FHA; Science Clb; Spanish Clb; Speech Tm; Drill Tm; School Play; Hon Roll; Sci.

BORDEN, JAIME L; Lonoke Jr HS; Jacksonville, AR; (1); Church Yth Grp; Band; Church Choir; Jazz Band; Mrchg Band; Pep Band; Hon Roll; NHS; All Region Band; Dirs Awd; Ecology Clb; Lyon Coll.

BORDERS, TRACEY; Arkansas Schl Math & Science; North Little Rock, AR; (3); Church Yth Grp; Drama Clb; Mu Alpha Theta; Natl Beta Clb; Chorus; School Musical; Powder Puff Ftbl; Vllybl; Gov Hon Prg Awd; NHS; Chemist.

BOREN, JAMES D; Goza Jr HS; Arkadelphia, AR; (1); Church Yth Grp; Golf; Hon Roll.

BORGMAN, BEN L; Pine Bluff HS; Pine Bluff, AR; (2); Boy Scts; Spanish Clb; Chorus; Yrbk; Ftbl; LA Tech; Wildlife Mngmnt/Bio.

BORGOGNONI, SHEILA; Monticello HS; Monticello, AR; (3); #1 in class; Treas Debate Tm; Treas Drama Clb; FBLA; VP FHA; Rep HOBY; Natl Beta Clb; VP Spanish Clb; SADD; Band; NHS; All Amer Schlr; Natl Yng Ldrs Conf Wshngtn DC; Med.

BORLAND, BRYAN; Monticello HS; Monticello, AR; (3); 28/160; Library Aide; Natl Beta Clb; Quiz Bowl; Spanish Clb; SADD; Band; Ed Yrbk; Hon Roll; NHS; All Amer Schol; Natl Yng Ldrs Confyth Ldshp Awd; AR HS Press Assocyrbk Edtr Of Yr; Psych.

BORRESON, ANDREA S; Oak Ridge Central Schl; Ravenden Springs, AR; (3); Band; Jazz Band; Mrchg Band; Pep Band; Hon Roll; Math & Sci Clb; Army.

BOSCH, CHRIS L; Mena HS; Mena, AR; (1); Church Yth Grp; Cmnty Wkr; French Clb; FBLA; Church Choir; Var Bsbl; Hon Roll; Pres Acad Fit Awd; Bsbl St Trnmt 96; Southern Nazarene Univ Extravaganza; Southern Nazarene U; Arch.

BOSCHETT, LISSA; Pulaski Acad; Roland, AR; (2); Church Yth Grp; Cmnty Wkr; FCA; Natl Beta Clb; Spanish Clb; NHS; All Stars Chrldng; Interact Clb; U Of AR Fayetteville.

BOSLEY, HANNAH; Caddo Hills Jr Sr HS; Caddo Gap, AR; (4); 3/40; FCA; FBLA; HOBY; Model UN; Quiz Bowl; Ed Nwsp; Ed Yrbk; VP Sr Cls; Hon Roll; Beta Club; Gftd/Tlntd; AR ST U; Jrnlsm.

BOSSONG, JENNIFER E; Cabot HS; Cabot, AR; (1); FBLA; Hosp Aide; Hon Roll; Nrs.

BOST, AARON A; Salem HS; Salem, AR; (4); Church Yth Grp; Quiz Bowl; Nwsp; Yrbk; Crs Cntry; Var L Ftbl; Powder Puff Ftbl; Trk; Hon Roll; Ftbl Awd Most Imprvd 95-96; AR Army Natl Guard Mem 95; AR ST U; Psych.

BOTTOMS, HEATHER J; Cty Line HS; Ratcliff, AR; (4); 4/38; Church Yth Grp; FCA; VP FBLA; VP FHA; Sec Natl Beta Clb; Spanish Clb; Ofcr Stu Cncl; Var Capt Bsktbl; Var Sftbl; Hon Roll; Miss Cty Line 96; 95-96 Homcmng Qn; Carl Albert ST Coll; Comp Sci.

BOTTS, JASON B; Nettleton HS; Jonesboro, AR; (3); 1/116; Math Clb; Science Clb; Spanish Clb; Chorus; School Play; Ftbl; High Hon Roll; Beta Clb; Hendrix; Pre-Med.

BOUGHTON, TANJLISA M; Jacksonville HS; Jacksonville, AR; (2); Cmnty Wkr; Dance Clb; Drama Clb; VP FBLA; Band; Ed Nwsp; Bsktbl; Cit Awd; Hon Roll; Prfct Atten Awd; Jrnlsm Awd; Cert Of Apprctn In Math And Sci; UALR; Engl.

BOULDIN, ERIC A; Greene Co Tech HS; Paragould, AR; (4); VP Frsh Cls; VP Jr Cls; VP Sr Cls; Var Bsbl; Var Ftbl; Hon Roll.

BOURDO, SHAWN E; Cabot HS; Cabot, AR; (3); 41/400; Debate Tm; Key Clb; NFL; Spanish Clb; Var Tennis; Jr NHS; Kiwanis Awd; NHS; Spanish NHS; 1st Pl AAAA E Conf Tns Trnmnt ; 3rd Pl AAAA ST Tns Trnmnt; 2nd Pl Ovrl ST Tns Trnmnt; Bio Chem/Med Schl/Law Schl.

BOUSQUET, MIKIA; Central Sr HS; Little Rock, AR; (4); 161/410; Am Leg Aux Girls St; FBLA; FTA; Acpl Chr; Drill Tm; Yrbk; VP Sr Cls; Hon Roll; Sr Homcmng Maid; Schl Dist Acad Achvmt Awd Madrigals; U Of AR Pine Bluff; Nrsng.

BOWARD, TRAVIS J; Weiner HS; Weiner, AR; (2); Art Clb; Natl FFA Org; Science Clb; Hon Roll; Jr NHS; NHS; Prfct Atten Awd; Pres Acad Fit Awd; GATE; Electrician.

BOWDLER, JENNIFER A; Rivercrest HS; Luxora, AR; (2); Church Yth Grp; French Clb; Treas Key Clb; Band; Flag Corp; Mrchg Band; Pep Band; High Hon Roll; Hon Roll; Jr NHS; Acctng.

BOWDLER, STEVEN; Rivercrest HS; Luxora, AR; (4); 13/106; French Clb; VP FBLA; FHA; Key Clb; Math Clb; Quiz Bowl; Teachers Aide; Var L Bsbl; Var Bsktbl; High Hon Roll; Teens Agnst Drugs; AR ST Univ; Mech Eng.

BOWEN, JESSICA J; Huntsville HS; Wesley, AR; (4); 10/120; Art Clb; Teachers Aide; Ofcr Soph Cls; Ofcr Jr Cls; Hon Roll; Frosh Clr Days Maid; NA; Art, Alg, Soc Stud, Prntng & Fmly Dynmcs Awds; Bapt Schl Of Nursing; Nursing.

BOWEN, JULIE A; Mena HS; Mena, AR; (2); 1/160; Church Yth Grp; French Clb; Rptr FBLA; Science Clb; Band; Church Choir; Drm Mjr(t); Mrchg Band; Pep Band; Nwsp; Bearcats Against Drugs VP/PRES; Flwshp Chrstn Stdnts; Ouachita Baptist U; Msc/Spch.

BOWEN, KEVIN; Van Buren Sr HS; Van Buren, AR; (3); Church Yth Grp; FCA; Math Clb; Mu Alpha Theta; Q&S; SADD; Ofcr Bsbl; Bsktbl; Cit Awd; High Hon Roll.

BOWEN, OLIVIA; Harding Acad; Augusta, AR; (3); Church Yth Grp; FBLA; HOBY; Pres Key Clb; Natl Beta Clb; Sec Chorus; School Musical; Rptr Yrbk; Intrml Var Chrldng; High Hon Roll; AEGIS Pre Med Pgm; MASH; Sigma Tau Alpha Rho STAR Scl Clb; U AR; Med.

BOWER, ARETHA L; Leslie Schl; Clinton, AR; (3); Drama Clb; 4-H; FBLA; FHA; Key Clb; Teachers Aide; Chorus; School Play; Ed Nwsp; VP Frsh Cls; Coll Of Ozarks.

BOWERS, ERIC; Arkansas Schl Math & Science; Kirby, AR; (3); Chess Clb; Computer Clb; 4-H; FBLA; Hist Library Aide; Natl Beta Clb; Natl FFA Org; Quiz Bowl; Band; Pep Band; Mst Tlntd 11th Grd; Engl Awd 94; Geomtry Awd 95; MIT; Cmptr Sci.

BOWERS, SHILOH; Springdale Sr HS; Springdale, AR; (4); Cmnty Wkr; FBLA; Sec FHA; Office Aide; Band; Chorus; Color Guard; Mrchg Band; Pep Band; Sftbl; Multi Yr Listee; NW AR CC; Elem Ed/Chldcr.

BOWERS, TREY R; Corning HS; Corning, AR; (3); Church Yth Grp; Ofcr Bsbl; Bsktbl; Ftbl; Wt Lftg; Hon Roll; Pride Teaqm; AR ST Univ; Ag Bus.

BOWLES, ELIZABETH; St Paul Schl; Witter, AR; (1); 1/30; Church Yth Grp; FHA; Quiz Bowl; SADD; Rep Stu Cncl; Capt Bsktbl; Stat Score Keeper; Intrml Trk; High Hon Roll; Ntl Merit Ltr; U Of AR; Tchr.

BOWLES, JAMES R; Morrilton Sr HS; Morrilton, AR; (2); Church Yth Grp; Drama Clb; FBLA; Math Clb; Natl Beta Clb; Spanish Clb; Thesps; School Musical; School Play; Rptr Nwsp.

BOWLING, LANCE D; Clinton HS; Clinton, AR; (2); FBLA; Bsktbl; Hon Roll.

BOWMAN, ALLYSON K; Mc Gehee HS; Mcgehee, AR; (2); #1 in class; FTA; Mu Alpha Theta; Natl Beta Clb; Science Clb; Spanish Clb; Band; Bsktbl; Tennis; Trk; NHS; PT.

BOWMAN, EMILY; Mc Gehee HS; Mc Gehee, AR; (3); 10/140; Am Leg Aux Girls St; Art Clb; Church Yth Grp; Drama Clb; FCA; FBLA; FTA; Mu Alpha Theta; Natl Beta Clb; Office Aide; U AR.

BOWSER, HAILEY M; Ridgecrest HS; Paragould, AR; (4); 47/185; Church Yth Grp; French Clb; Science Clb; Chorus; Church Choir; JV Vllybl; Cit Awd; Hon Roll; Leo Clb; World Chngrs Savannah GA 95; Natl Ldrshp Forum Med; Acteens Encore Ensemble Natl Cnvntn; Ouachita Bapt U; Elem Ed/Psych.

BOX, AMBER R; Gillett Jr Sr HS; Dumas, AR; (2); Art Clb; FBLA; Spanish Clb; Ed Nwsp; Sftbl; High Hon Roll; Hon Roll; Jr NHS; NHS; ASU.

BOX, DAVID; Trumann HS; Trumann, AR; (3); Am Leg Boys St; Church Yth Grp; French Clb; Natl FFA Org; Science Clb; Church Choir; Pres Jr Cls; Var L Bsbl; High Hon Roll; NHS; U Of MS; Phy Thrpst.

BOX, GINGER; Abundant Life Schls; Jacksonville, AR; (4); Church Yth Grp; Hon Roll.

BOX, TRISH L; Abundant Life Schools; Jacksonville, AR; (2); Church Yth Grp; Church Choir; NHS; UCA; Elem Tchr.

BOXNICK, STEPHEN S; Russellville Sr HS; London, AR; (2); Teachers Aide; Band; Mrchg Band; Pep Band; JV Bsktbl; Hon Roll; NHS; Cmptr Animation.

BOYCE, MARY M; Russellville Sr HS; Russellville, AR; (3); 21/350; Church Yth Grp; Cmnty Wkr; Treas Frsh Cls; Treas Soph Cls; Var Chrldng; Var Trk; Jr NHS; NHS; High Hon Roll; Hmcmng Qn Jr HS 9th Grd; Hmcmng Maid 10-11th Grd; Rnssnc Ldrshp; U Of AR; Acctng.

BOYD, HOLLIE I; Mountainburg Jr Sr HS; Mountainburg, AR; (3); 2/75; Am Leg Aux Girls St; Church Yth Grp; Cmnty Wkr; Debate Tm; FCA; GAA; Natl Beta Clb; Quiz Bowl; SADD; Ed Yrbk; U Of The Ozarks.

BOYD, JASON; Rison HS; Rison, AR; (1); Church Yth Grp; Natl Beta Clb; Natl FFA Org; U Of AR Monticello.

BOYD, KIMBERLEE T; Riverview HS; Kensett, AR; (3); Pres Drama Clb; FBLA; FHA; Natl Beta Clb; Spanish Clb; Pres Frsh Cls; L Bsktbl; L Trk; St Ofcr Intnl Order Of The Rainbow For Girls.

BOYD, STEPHANIE M; Magnolia HS; Magnolia, AR; (4); 18/240; Dance Clb; FBLA; Mu Alpha Theta; Science Clb; Band; Color Guard; Mrchg Band; Pep Band; Nwsp; Yrbk; Panther Pride; Mst Pretty; Majorette Co Captain Cap; SAU; Phy Thrpst; Nurse.

BOYD, STEPHEN; Hoxie Schl; Hoxie, AR; (3); 1/61; Natl Beta Clb; Spanish Clb; Teachers Aide; L Ftbl; Trk; Wt Lftg; Cit Awd; High Hon Roll; Ftbl All Conf; Med.

BOYETT, VICKIE M; Rogers HS; Rogers, AR; (3); Church Yth Grp; Hosp Aide; Spanish Clb; Teachers Aide; Church Choir; Co-Capt Pom Pon; Cit Awd; Hon Roll; NHS; Spelling Bee Fnslt.

BOYETTE, JENNINGS R; Lonoke Jr HS; Lonoke, AR; (1); 1/130; Boy Scts; Church Yth Grp; Hosp Aide; Science Clb; Nwsp; Bsktbl; Ftbl; Socr; High Hon Roll; NHS; Eng/Cmptr Ltrcy Highest Grd Awds.

BOYKIN, VICKIE; Crawfordsville HS; Crawfordsville, AR; (4); 3/24; Church Yth Grp; 4-H; FBLA; FHA; Natl Beta Clb; Natl FFA Org; Church Choir; Treas Sr Cls; Cit Awd; High Hon Roll; Acctng Career Awrnss Prog 95; Chrch Sec; Mid-South CC; Bus.

BOYT, JOY L; Mena HS; Mena, AR; (1); Church Yth Grp; French Clb; FBLA; SADD; U AR.

BOZYNSKI, RACHEL A; Central Sr HS; Little Rock, AR; (4); 24/401; Church Yth Grp; Cmnty Wkr; French Clb; Sec Treas Intnl Clb; Treas Natl Beta Clb; Church Choir; High Hon Roll; Jr NHS; Kiwanis Awd; Treas NHS; Yth Serv Awrd; Psych Awrd; Rhodes Coll; Psych.

BRACELY, NAKIA; Parkview Arts-Science HS; North Little Rock, AR; (2); Church Yth Grp; GAA; Hosp Aide; Natl Beta Clb; Spanish Clb; Band; Church Choir; Bsktbl; Trk; Vllybl; Peer Helpers; Ladys Clb; Pediatrics; Med Scis.

BRACKETT, MONTANA L; Concord Jr Sr HS; Drasco, AR; (3); 3/34; Am Leg Aux Girls St; VP Art Clb; FCA; Sec Natl Beta Clb; Science Clb; Rep Band; Stat Bsktbl; Sftbl; High Hon Roll; MASH; Chem/Sports Med.

BRACKMAN, REBEKAH; Butterfield Jr HS; Van Buren, AR; (1); Church Yth Grp; HOBY; Office Aide; Pep Clb; Nwsp; Ed Rptr Lit Mag; High Hon Roll; Jr NHS; Prfct Atten Awd; Vet.

BRADBERRY, ASHLEY; Concord Jr Sr HS; Concord, AR; (4); 4/27; Am Leg Aux Girls St; FCA; FBLA; Natl Beta Clb; Quiz Bowl; Scholastic Bowl; Treas Yrbk; VP Sr Cls; Pres Stu Cncl; Mgr(s); Speech Cont Wnnr AR Rural Elec Coop WADC Trip; U Cntrl AR; Math.

BRADBURY, ARMENDA; Arkansas Schl Math & Science; Mabelvale, AR; (4); Church Yth Grp; Drama Clb; Mu Alpha Theta; Natl Beta Clb; Church Choir; School Musical; Chrldng; Sftbl; NHS; Cmnty Wkr; All Region Choir; Univ Of Cntrl AR; Marine Maml.

BRADEN, ASHLEY D; Crowleys Ridge Acad; Paragould, AR; (1); Church Yth Grp; FBLA; Pep Clb; Science Clb; Spanish Clb; VP Frsh Cls; JV Bsktbl; JV Socr; JV Trk; Bsktbl All Conf; FACES Pgm; AAU Bsktbl; Sprts Med.

BRADFORD, ARTHUR; Magnolia HS; Magnolia, AR; (2); 48/217; Church Yth Grp; Church Choir; JV Ftbl; JV Trk; Schlrs Banquet; Grambling ST U; Chemical Engr.

BRADFORD, JAMES CASEY; Springdale Sr HS; Springdale, AR; (1); Chess Clb; Church Yth Grp; FCA; Letterman Clb; Math Tm; Var L Bsktbl; Hon Roll; Babe Ruth All-Star Bsbl Team 15 Yr Old 0-0, 14 Yr Old Won Dist; AANBC Bsbl All-Star 4th In World Srs; LSU; Pre-Law; Bsbl.

BRADFORD, JENNIFER; Forrest City HS; Forrest City, AR; (2); Church Yth Grp; Mu Alpha Theta; Natl Beta Clb; Office Aide; Yrbk; Tennis; Hon Roll; Pres Acad Fit Awd; Law.

BRADLEY, AMBER L; Dewitt HS; Altheimer, AR; (4); 23/78; Pres 4-H; FBLA; FTA; Natl Beta Clb; Office Aide; 4-H Awd; Hon Roll; Prfct Atten Awd; Wnnr Geo Sclgy Awd; AR St Univ; Vet Med.

BRADLEY, CORTNEY; Augusta HS; Augusta, AR; (2); 1/46; Church Yth Grp; Girl Scts; Hosp Aide; HOBY; Pres Stu Cncl; Var L Bsktbl; Capt Chrldng; NHS; Art Clb; Sec FBLA; Hln E Dvs Awd; Gov Yth Conf Del; Soph Hmcmng Maid; U Central AR; Phys Ther.

BRADLEY, CYNTHIA A; Dumas HS; Dumas, AR; (4); 39/127; Church Yth Grp; FBLA; Library Aide; Spanish Clb; Chorus; Rep Stu Cncl; Ventures In Ed; Span Honor Soc; Lib Clb; U Of AR Pine Bluff; Acctng.

BRADLEY, HEATHER; Morrilton Sr HS; Morrilton, AR; (2); Natl Beta Clb; Natl FFA Org; Science Clb; Spanish Clb; Band; Hon Roll; Grand Champ Heifer Cnty Fair; Shwd Steer State Fair; FFA State Band; U Of Cntrl AR; Lawyr.

BRADLEY, JASON; Mineral Springs Schl; Lockesburg, AR; (3); 1/48; FHA; Natl Beta Clb; Quiz Bowl.

BRADLEY, JASON; Rison HS; Rison, AR; (2); 8/345; FCA; French Clb; FBLA; Natl Beta Clb; Science Clb; Band; Mrchg Band; High Hon Roll; Hon Roll; Pyrotech.

BRADLEY, KATRINA; Perryville Jr Sr HS; Perryville, AR; (3); Church Yth Grp; FBLA; Girl Scts; HOBY; Pres Sec Library Aide; Pep Clb; Spanish Clb; Band; Pep Band; Jr NHS; AEGIS Lrt Intl Stdys; Media Clb Pres; VITA Vol; AR Tech U; Erly Chldhd Educ.

BRADLEY, KAWIA; Evening Shade Schl; Sidney, AR; (2); FCA; FBLA; Natl Beta Clb; Natl FFA Org; School Play; Bsktbl; Hon Roll; Stu Cncl Rptr; TAD.

BRADLEY, LEIGH E; Searcy HS; Searcy, AR; (3); Church Yth Grp; FCA; Natl Beta Clb; Thesps; Band; Chorus; Church Choir; Orch; School Musical; School Play; 1st Chair, 1st Soprano, All Rgn Choir; All St Choir; Musical; Belmont U; Vocal Perfrmnce.

BRADLEY, PHILLIP S; Clarksville HS; Clarksville, AR; (2); Var Ftbl.

BRADLEY, SARA M; Trumann HS; Trumann, AR; (2); Church Yth Grp; French Clb; GAA; Library Aide; Science Clb; Chorus; L Bsktbl; High Hon Roll; Hon Roll; NHS; Phy Thrpst.

BRADLEY, TIFFANY L; Mills HS; Mabelvale, AR; (3); Key Clb; Mu Alpha Theta; Natl Beta Clb; Quiz Bowl; Science Clb; Spanish Clb; Band; Flag Corp; Rep Stu Cncl; Hon Roll; Pre-Med.

BRADLEY, TOLINA K; Russellville Sr HS; Russellville, AR; (4); Church Yth Grp; Drama Clb; VICA; Chorus; Church Choir; School Play; Hon Roll; Cyclone Achiver; Best Attitude Awd.

BRADOW, CHRIS; Hazen Jr Sr HS; Hazen, AR; (4); 6/29; Am Leg Boys St; Church Yth Grp; FTA; Natl Beta Clb; Science Clb; Jazz Band; Ed Nwsp; Mgr Yrbk; Capt Bsbl; NHS; MS ST; Sprts Med.

BRADSHAW, JODY A; Ozark HS; Ozark, AR; (2); 5/104; Church Yth Grp; Letterman Clb; Quiz Bowl; Church Choir; Var L Bsbl; Var L Ftbl; Var L Trk; Var L Wt Lftg; High Hon Roll; Ntl Merit Ltr; Med Field.

BRADSHAW, ZANE L; Magnolia HS; Magnolia, AR; (3); Church Yth Grp; Natl FFA Org; Golf; Hon Roll; S AR Univ.

BRADY, ALI; Hot Springs HS; Hot Springs, AR; (1); Natl Beta Clb; Chrldng; Hon Roll; Future Problem Solving; Chrstns On Campus.

BRADY, ALISON M; Russellville Sr HS; Russellville, AR; (2); Church Yth Grp; FCA; GAA; Hosp Aide; Natl Beta Clb; Yrbk; Var Crs Cntry; Var Trk; Tchr/Pedtrcn.

BRADY, GINGER D; North Little Rock Hs-West; North Little Rock, AR; (3); 191/654; Church Yth Grp; Cmnty Wkr; Dance Clb; FCA; Q&S; Spanish Clb; Drill Tm; Rptr Yrbk; Rep Stu Cncl; Intrml JV Chrldng; Octagon Clb; U Of Cntrl AR; Occptnl Therapy.

BRADY, NICOLE M; Russellville Sr HS; Russellville, AR; (3); 30/320; Church Yth Grp; Band; Church Choir; Mrchg Band; High Hon Roll; Jr NHS; NHS; ATU; Bus; Fin; Acctng.

BRAFFORD, EVERETT E; Russellville Sr HS; Russellville, AR; (2); 85/444; JV Socr; Hon Roll; Jr NHS; Lawyer.

BRAGG, NATALYA G; Fairview HS; Camden, AR; (2); Church Yth Grp; Drama Clb; GAA; Natl Beta Clb; Band; Church Choir; Flag Corp; Mrchg Band; School Musical; L Crs Cntry; Trk & Crss Cntry Letterman; Talent Search; Fayetteville; Med Researcher.

BRAIN, SARAH D; Mt St Mary Acad; Little Rock, AR; (4); Church Yth Grp; Spanish Clb; Chorus; Church Choir; Hon Roll; Bacclrte Cmmtte Chrprsn; Litrgy Planning Team; AR ST U.

BRAMLETT, ADRIENNE; Fayetteville Sr HS; Fayetteville, AR; (4); 1/372; Am Leg Aux Girls St; FCA; FBLA; Mu Alpha Theta; SADD; Drm Mjr(t); Lit Mag; Ofcr Stu Cncl; Chrldng; NHS; Girls Nation; UCA All Star London Del; AP Schlr; Georgetown Univ; His/Pre-Law.

BRAMLETT, EDNA D; Mc Rae Schl; Mc Rae, AR; (3); FHA; Stdnt Month; BETA; Russion Club; U Of Central AR; Pre-Schl.

BRAMLETT, HEATHER R; Russellville Sr HS; Russellville, AR; (3); 37/400; French Clb; Band; Color Guard; Mrchg Band; Pep Band; High Hon Roll; Jr NHS; NHS; Hon Roll; Al Region Band; All ST Band; AR Tech Univ; Acctnt.

BRAMLETT, JUSTIN A; Benton Sr HS; Benton, AR; (3); 15/250; Am Leg Boys St; FCA; Gov Hon Prg Awd; High Hon Roll; Hon Roll; Jr NHS; Kiwanis Awd; NHS; Pres Acad Fit Awd; Church Yth Grp.

BRAMLETT, PATRICIA; Mc Rae Schl; Mc Rae, AR; (1); FHA; Mgr(s); Hon Roll; Beta; U Central AR; Elem Ed.

BRANCH, BILLY L; Marked Tree Jr Sr HS; Marked Tree, AR; (1); Natl FFA Org; ROTC; Spanish Clb; Wt Lftg; Cit Awd; HS Rodeo; ASU; Farm Mgmt.

BRANCH, CHASEY; Jessieville HS; Hot Springs, AR; (3); Art Clb; Church Yth Grp; FCA; Natl Beta Clb; Band; Color Guard; Sec Jr Cls; Chrldng; Lifegrd; Bus Mgmt.

BRANCH, TEMEKA; Dermott HS; Dermott, AR; (2); FBLA; Math Clb; Natl Beta Clb; Science Clb; Spanish Clb; Band; Ofcr Stu Cncl; Cit Awd; Hon Roll; Ntl Merit Ltr; Flagline; U AR; Speech Pathology.

BRAND, JOHN; Newport HS; Newport, AR; (3); 13/134; Church Yth Grp; HOBY; Letterman Clb; Spanish Clb; Teachers Aide; Ofcr Stu Cncl; Ftbl; Golf; High Hon Roll; Hon Roll.

BRAND, K ALICIA; Rogers HS; Rogers, AR; (3); 19/537; Pres Church Yth Grp; Cmnty Wkr; Science Clb; Drill Tm; Rep Stu Cncl; JV Socr; Cit Awd; NHS; Rcptnst; Peer Hlprs; PTSA Bd; Pre-Med.

BRAND, STACY; North Little Rock Hs-West; North Little Rock, AR; (3); Q&S; Lit Mag; Var Bsktbl; Var Sftbl; Interschltc Star Awd.

BRAND, TONYA R; North Little Rock Hs-East; North Little Rock, AR; (3); Drama Clb; Math Clb; Mu Alpha Theta; Spanish Clb; Stage Crew; High Hon Roll; Hon Roll; Peer Ldrshp; Octagon Clb; UALR; Nrsng.

BRANDEBURA, MATTHEW E; Southside HS; Fort Smith, AR; (2); Church Yth Grp; Drama Clb; FBLA; Band; Mrchg Band; School Musical; School Play; Hon Roll; WASA; TARE; Intrct; Hendrix Coll; Vet.

BRANDON, KATIE; Wynne HS; Wynne, AR; (4); 3/170; Church Yth Grp; Cmnty Wkr; Drama Clb; FBLA; FTA; HOBY; Office Aide; Quiz Bowl; Spanish Clb; Rep Stu Cncl; Govs Schl; Natl Rrl Elect Cprtv Assn Yth Cncl Bd; MS ST U; Mech Engrng.

BRANDT, JAMIE; Prairie Grove HS; Prairie Grove, AR; (2); 1/95; Church Yth Grp; French Clb; VP FBLA; VP Library Aide; Scholastic Bowl; SADD; Acpl Chr; Rptr Soph Cls; Pres Jr NHS; Chorus; Odyssey; Merit Awd; U Of AR; Law.

BRANNAN, JACKIE; Hackett Schl; Fort Smith, AR; (3); Art Clb; Church Yth Grp; FHA; Hosp Aide; Scholastic Bowl; Band; Pres Frsh Cls; Hon Roll.

BRANNAN, SHALLAN; Coleman Jr HS; Van Buren, AR; (1); FBLA; VP FHA; Capt Drill Tm; Vllybl; High Hon Roll; VP Jr NHS.

BRANNON, HALLIE N; Bradford Jr Sr HS; Bradford, AR; (3); 10/50; Art Clb; Drama Clb; French Clb; FBLA; FHA; GAA; Bsktbl; Sftbl; Swmmng; High Hon Roll; Homecmg Princess 10th Grd 94; Whos Who Most Talntd 9th/11th Grd/Mst Ath 9th/11th Grd; ASU; PT.

BRANNON, LORI A; Mayflower HS; Mayflower, AR; (3); 2/40; Am Leg Aux Girls St; FHA; Natl Beta Clb; Teachers Aide; High Hon Roll; Hon Roll; AR Stu Forum; Highest Grd In Cls Awd; Hendrix; Phy Thrpst.

BRANNON, RICK D; Brookland Jr Sr HS; Jonesboro, AR; (3).

BRANSCOMB, LA CHER; John L Mcclellan Magnet HS; Little Rock, AR; (3); 3/288; Church Yth Grp; FBLA; Natl Beta Clb; Spanish Clb; Band; Cit Awd; High Hon Roll; Hon Roll; NHS; Ntl Merit Ltr; Hendrix; Math.

BRANSCOMB, LACHER D; John L Mcclellan Magnet HS; Little Rock, AR; (3); 3/288; Am Leg Aux Girls St; Church Yth Grp; FBLA; Mu Alpha Theta; Natl Beta Clb; Spanish Clb; Band; High Hon Roll; NHS; Ntl Merit Ltr; Hendrix; Pediatrician.

BRANSCUM, BRYAN J; Southside HS; Batesville, AR; (2); Art Clb; Key Clb; Natl Beta Clb; Natl FFA Org; Science Clb; Teachers Aide; Treas Soph Cls; Ofcr Bsbl; Bsktbl; Vllybl; Elec Engrng.

BRANSCUM, DEVAN R; North Pulaski HS; Jacksonville, AR; (4); 47/296; Church Yth Grp; Cmnty Wkr; JV Bsktbl; JV Fld Hcky; Cit Awd; High Hon Roll; Jr NHS; NHS; Prfct Atten Awd; FL ST U; Marn Bio; Envrnmt Sci.

BRANSCUM, MIRANDA; Calico Rock HS; Pineville, AR; (3); 5/50; Church Yth Grp; FCA; FBLA; GAA; Letterman Clb; Natl Beta Clb; Science Clb; Spanish Clb; SADD; Sec Frsh Cls; Woodman Of World Hist Awd; Svc & Achvmt Awd Miss Teen AR; U Of Cntrl AR.

BRANSON, BEN M; Lake Hamilton Sr HS; Hot Springs Natio, AR; (2); Church Yth Grp; Bsktbl; Golf; Hon Roll.

BRANSON, NAARON E; Southside HS; Fort Smith, AR; (2); Church Yth Grp; Dance Clb; FCA; GAA; Capt Drill Tm; Bsktbl; Trk; Vllybl; Hon Roll; Prfct Atten Awd; US Rep For Yth For Undrstdng Vlybl Tm Australia; Math/Sci.

BRANTLEY, DREW P; Catholic HS; England, AR; (4); 70/153; Boy Scts; FCA; French Clb; FBLA; Natl Beta Clb; Ofcr Frsh Cls; Ofcr Soph Cls; Ofcr Stu Cncl; L Bsbl; L Bsktbl; Yth Grp FUMC England; U Of AR; Bus Adm.

BRANTLEY, KAIESHA S; Central HS; West Helena, AR; (2); FBLA; JA; Library Aide; Natl Beta Clb; Office Aide; Pep Clb; Quiz Bowl; Teachers Aide; Acpl Chr; Band; PRIDE; TCK; Spelman; Engrng.

BRANTON, CHRISTY R; Mills HS; Jacksonville, AR; (2); 20/496; Art Clb; Church Yth Grp; Drama Clb; Mu Alpha Theta; Science Clb; Spanish Clb; Band; Church Choir; Mrchg Band; School Play; Music Ed.

BRANTON, MARY K; Mills HS; Jacksonville, AR; (3); 4/298; Mu Alpha Theta; Pres Natl Beta Clb; Q&S; Band; Ed Nwsp; Pres Jr Cls; Treas Stu Cncl; Var L Sftbl; NHS; Pres Acad Fit Awd; AR Governors Schl; Chem Eng.

BRASHEARS, JOE H; Ozark HS; Ozark, AR; (3); 15/110; Church Yth Grp; Natl Beta Clb; Quiz Bowl; Mrchg Band; Pep Band; Bsktbl; Golf; Hon Roll; U Of AR.

BRASSFIELD, ADAM H; Gosnell Jr Sr HS; Blytheville, AR; (1); Church Yth Grp; Ftbl; Offensive Player Of Yr-Ftbl; Fire Marshall; Notre Dame; PE.

BRASWELL, JASON; Valley View HS; Jonesboro, AR; (4); 1/64; Rep Am Leg Boys St; Church Yth Grp; HOBY; Spanish Clb; Pres Jr Cls; Pres Stu Cncl; Capt Socr; High Hon Roll; NHS; Val; U Cntrl AR; Phys Thrpy.

BRATTON, ELIZABETH A; Cabot HS; Austin, AR; (4); 88/287; Church Yth Grp; 4-H; FBLA; Key Clb; Office Aide; Red Cross Aide; Spanish Clb; 4-H Awd; Harding Univ; Pre Law.

BRATTON, KACHERA; Cutter Morning Star HS; Hot Springs, AR; (2); FBLA; FHA; Library Aide; Office Aide; Ofcr Soph Cls; High Hon Roll; Hon Roll; Algebra Awd; Nrs.

BRAWLEY, JOHN R; Bismarck Jr-Sr HS; Bismarck, AR; (2); FCA; Yrbk; Ofcr Bsbl; Bsktbl; Ftbl; AR Of Fayetteville; Coach.

BRAWNER, BEGINA; Wynne HS; Wynne, AR; (3); Am Leg Aux Girls St; Church Yth Grp; Drama Clb; FBLA; FTA; Q&S; Sec Spanish Clb; SADD; Nwsp; Yrbk; Schlsp Banquet; AR Bus Acad 96; U Of AR Fayetteville.

BRAY, KEONDRA N; Northside HS; Fort Smith, AR; (3); Church Yth Grp; Spanish Clb; Teachers Aide; School Play; Stage Crew; Ofcr Soph Cls; Ofcr Jr Cls; L Pom Pon; Hon Roll; Grizzly Pride Perf Group; U Of Cntrl AR; Bus Admin.

BRAY, MICHAEL; West Memphis Christian Schl; West Memphis, AR; (4); 5/30; Am Leg Boys St; Art Clb; Church Yth Grp; Cmnty Wkr; Pres FCA; French Clb; Natl Beta Clb; Office Aide; Rptr Nwsp; VP Jr Cls; Ftbl/Bsktbl/Bsbl All Conf; Bsktbl All Trn Tm; Mst Chrstn/Mst Lkly Scd/Mr WMCS; Vet Apprn Prgm; MS ST Univ; Pre Vet.

BRAZILE, KRISTI M; Sylvan Hills HS; Sherwood, AR; (3); 15/240; Church Yth Grp; FBLA; FHA; Mu Alpha Theta; Natl Beta Clb; Science Clb; Hon Roll; Jr NHS; NHS; Psychlgy.

BREASHEARS, ROBERT; Arkansas Schl Math & Science; Danville, AR; (4); Cmnty Wkr; FBLA; Mu Alpha Theta; Natl Beta Clb; Quiz Bowl; Spanish Clb; Teachers Aide; Nwsp; Yrbk; Rep Jr Cls; Civil Engr.

BRECH, ANDREA; Maynard Jr Sr HS; Pocahontas, AR; (4); 1/27; French Clb; VP FBLA; GAA; Natl Beta Clb; Red Cross Aide; Teachers Aide; Nwsp; Sec Frsh Cls; VP Soph Cls; VP Jr Cls; U S Presdntl Natl Schlr Athl Awd; ASU; Acctng.

BRECH, STEPHANIE L; Maynard Jr Sr HS; Pocahontas, AR; (3); Chess Clb; Rptr French Clb; FBLA; Rptr Soph Cls; Rptr Jr Cls; Bsktbl; Sftbl; ASU; Cmptr Tech.

BRECHEISEN, DAVID J; Dequeen HS; De Queen, AR; (3); Speech Tm; SADD; Yrbk; Rep Frsh Cls; Ofcr Stu Cncl; Bsktbl; Ftbl; Trk; Wt Lftg; Lcl Hosp Med Explrs Clb; Cvl War; Henderson ST U; Ansthslgy Dr.

BREE, BRIAN P; Searcy HS; Searcy, AR; (4); 13/207; Am Leg Boys St; Natl Beta Clb; Band; Mrchg Band; Yrbk; French Hon Soc; High Hon Roll; Jr NHS; NHS; Ntl Merit SF; Rgnl & St Sci Fair; 2nd Pl Rgnl Hmn Antmy & Phslgy Cntst; Hmn Antmy & Phslgy Dept Awds; Med.

BREEDEN, DANIEL B; Mulberry HS; Mulberry, AR; (2); Natl FFA Org; Teachers Aide; Var Bsbl; Var Bsktbl; Horseback Riding.

BREEDING, CARRIE; Central Ark Christian Schl; Little Rock, AR; (3); 8/76; Church Yth Grp; Sec Stu Cncl; Var Bsktbl; Var Chrldng; Var Crs Cntry; Hon Roll; Pres Jr NHS; NHS; Capt Drill Tm; Sec Soph Cls; Natl Sci Mrt Awd; Natl Stu Cncl Awd.

BRENT, CODY; Genoa Cntrl HS; Fouke, AR; (4); Art Clb; FBLA; Spanish Clb; Intrml JV Bsktbl; Intrml JV Trk; Cit Awd; Hon Roll; NHS; Prfct Atten Awd; Pres Acad Fit Awd; Mst Ath In Trk & Bsktbl; Whos Who In Sports; Cls Favorite & Mst Fashionable; St Awd In 800m Run; Texarkana Coll.

BRESHEARS, CARRIE A; Star City HS; Star City, AR; (4); 1/105; French Clb; Mu Alpha Theta; Quiz Bowl; Pres Band; Drm Mjr(t); Sec Jazz Band; Mrchg Band; Ed Nwsp; Phtg Yrbk; Ed Lit Mag; All-Region Band; Fr, Chem, Amer His & Advanced Math Awds; Henderson ST U; Music Ed.

BRESHEARS, JARROD D; Fountain Lake Jr Sr HS; Hot Springs Natio, AR; (3); 3/80; Natl Beta Clb; Quiz Bowl; Spanish Clb; Teachers Aide; Rep Stu Cncl; Cit Awd; DAR Awd; Hon Roll; NHS; Med.

BRESHEARS, STEVEN E; Star City HS; Star City, AR; (2); 4/119; Church Yth Grp; Mu Alpha Theta; Natl FFA Org; Church Choir; Var Ftbl; Cit Awd; Hon Roll; Prfct Atten Awd; Alg II Awd; Outstdng Oral Cmnctns Stdnt; S Awd.

BRESSLER, AMY J; West Fork HS; West Fork, AR; (3); Church Yth Grp; Cmnty Wkr; FHA; Hosp Aide; Library Aide; Spanish Clb; Chorus; Church Choir; Cit Awd; Hon Roll; Sunday Schl Tchr; Concordia Col; Psych.

BREWER, AMANDA N; El Dorado Sr HS; El Dorado, AR; (2); Church Yth Grp; English Clb; FHA; Library Aide; Service Clb; Teachers Aide; Acpl Chr; Chorus; Hon Roll; Harding Univ; Law.

BREWER, AUDREY D; Van Buren Sr HS; Van Buren, AR; (2); Church Yth Grp; HOBY; Band; Church Choir; Mrchg Band; Orch; High Hon Roll; Hon Roll; Mst Imprvd Prcnst; Play Pinao Chrch; Piano.

BREWER, BRANDY S; Jacksonville HS; Jacksonville, AR; (3); Art Clb; Cmnty Wkr; Computer Clb; FBLA; FHA; Math Tm; Spanish Clb; SADD; COE; Choctaw Tribe Indian Rl; AR ST Univ; Pediatrcn.

BREWER, DENISE; Rural Special Schl; Mountain View, AR; (4); 5/26; Church Yth Grp; FBLA; FHA; Spanish Clb; School Play; Ofcr Jr Cls; High Hon Roll; Hon Roll; Jr Beta Clb; Sr Beta Clb VP; Choir; AR ST U; Bus.

BREWER, DUSTIN D; Stamps HS; Stamps, AR; (4); Church Yth Grp; Cmnty Wkr; FHA; Natl FFA Org; Science Clb; Band; Jazz Band; Mrchg Band; Orch; Pep Band; Agri Achvmt Awds; Solo/Ensmble Bnd Achvmt Awds; Otstdng Brass Plyr; Bnd Booster Schlrsp; Otstdng Sr; Southern AR Univ; Radiologist.

BREWER, HEATHER A; Van Buren Sr HS; Van Buren, AR; (2); Art Clb; FHA; GAA; Library Aide; Spanish Clb; Vllybl; Hon Roll; Stu Of The Week; Adv Bd Mem Parent Ed Pgm; Westark Comm Coll; Dntl.

BREWER, JERUSHA A; Mena HS; Mena, AR; (1); Church Yth Grp; Cmnty Wkr; Band; Mrchg Band; Orch; Hon Roll; Flwshp Of Chrstn Stdnts; TX A&M; Psych.

BREWER, KATHRYN; Parkview Arts-Science HS; North Little Rock, AR; (2); Church Yth Grp; Drama Clb; FBLA; German Clb; Church Choir; Cit Awd; High Hon Roll; Hon Roll; Jr NHS; Tae Kwon Do; Child Care.

BREWER, KINDRA D; North Little Rock Hs-West; North Little Rock, AR; (3); Am Leg Aux Girls St; Girl Scts; Key Clb; VP Natl Beta Clb; Band; Orch; Rep Stu Cncl; Hon Roll; Cmnty Wkr; FCA; Dance Team; Tri M; Interact Clb VP; Comp Engrng.

BREWER, LAURA; Bright Star Schl; Fouke, AR; (1); 3/30; Church Yth Grp; 4-H; Hosp Aide; Natl FFA Org; Office Aide; Rep Frsh Cls; Chrldng; Crs Cntry; Trk; 4-H Awd; Babist Coll; Rsrch Phy.

BREWER, RICKY S; Glenwood Jr Sr HS; Amity, AR; (3); Chess Clb; Natl FFA Org; Intrml Ftbl; Henderson ST Univ; Avionics.

BREWER, SHERRY M; Lake Hamilton Sr HS; Pearcy, AR; (3); Church Yth Grp; Drama Clb; FCA; FBLA; FHA; Library Aide; Pep Clb; Spanish Clb; Stage Crew; Trk; Wolf Pride; Henderson ST U.

BREWSTER, CAROL; Scranton HS; Scranton, AR; (3); 1/33; Pres Church Yth Grp; Pres Sec 4-H; Sec Treas FBLA; FHA; German Clb; HOBY; Letterman Clb; Sec Natl Beta Clb; Capt Quiz Bowl; Science Clb; U Of Cntrl AR; Speech Pthlgy.

BRIDGES, AMY; Arkadelphia Sr HS; Arkadelphia, AR; (4); 11/170; Am Leg Aux Girls St; Church Yth Grp; FCA; Natl Beta Clb; Spanish Clb; Church Choir; Yrbk; Powder Puff Ftbl; Sftbl; NHS; Quachita Bapt Univ; Pharmacy.

BRIDGES, BRADLEY; Elaine Jr Sr HS; Elaine, AR; (1); Church Yth Grp; Quiz Bowl; Church Choir; Var Bsbl; Var Bsktbl; Var Ftbl; Hon Roll; Jr NHS.

BRIDGES, HEATHER R; Northside HS; Fort Smith, AR; (3); 31/418; Am Leg Aux Girls St; Church Yth Grp; French Clb; Drill Tm; Rep Jr Cls; Vllybl; French Hon Soc; Hon Roll; NHS; Pres Acad Fit Awd; Sports Med/PT.

BRIDGES, MICHAEL A; Lonoke Jr HS; Lonoke, AR; (1); Boy Scts; Church Yth Grp; Science Clb; Pres Stu Cncl; Ftbl; Trk; High Hon Roll; NHS; Prfct Atten Awd.

BRIDGES, SARA A; Goza Jr HS; Arkadelphia, AR; (1); Church Yth Grp; FCA; Chorus; Church Choir; Nwsp; Yrbk; Pres Frsh Cls; Capt Chrldng; Vllybl; Jr NHS; Chrch Yth Drama Team.

BRIGGS, GESULA A; Mountain Pine Jr Sr HS; Mountain Pine, AR; (4); 5/33; Cmnty Wkr; French Clb; Girl Scts; VP Key Clb; Natl Beta Clb; Science Clb; Color Guard; Jr NHS; Hosp Aide; Teachers Aide; Cls Up Clb Sec/VP/WASHINGTON D C; Wtr Ed Tm Data Entry; J C Penny Gldn Rl Awd; Hendrix Coll; Veterinarian.

BRIGGS, KATIE J; West Memphis Christian Schl; Crawfordsville, AR; (1); Church Yth Grp; Hosp Aide; Rptr Nwsp; Rep Soph Cls; JV Bsktbl; Var Sftbl; JV Trk; Hon Roll; Cmnty Wkr; DAR Awd; JV Girls Bsktbl MVP Defense; Natl Sci Merit Awd; AR ST Univ; OBGYN.

BRIGGS, LA SHAUNDA; Mineral Springs Schl; Mineral Springs, AR; (1); Quiz Bowl; Band; Church Choir; Drm Mjr(t); School Play; Rep Frsh Cls; Ofcr Stu Cncl; Bsktbl; Chrldng; Hon Roll; Odyssy Mnd.

BRIGHT, PAMELA; Bradford Jr Sr HS; Bradford, AR; (2); French Clb; FBLA; Treas FHA; GAA; Math Tm; Bsktbl; Crs Cntry; Score Keeper; Sftbl; Trk; Jr & Sr Beta Clb; ASU Beebe; Phys Thpry.

BRIGHT, ZACHARY M; Oak Grove HS; Maumelle, AR; (1); Art Clb; Church Yth Grp; FCA; Natl Beta Clb; Hon Roll; Pres Acad Fit Awd; GATE; U Of AR; Cmptr Animation Art.

BRILL, CHRISTIAN H; Fayetteville Sr HS; Fayetteville, AR; (4); 1/400; Church Yth Grp; Quiz Bowl; Orch; Ed Lit Mag; Intrml Bsktbl; Var L Tennis; NHS; Ntl Merit Schol; Sal; AP Schlr W/Dstnctn; 2 Yr Natl Ctzn Bee Fnlst, 6th Pl Nation 94; All St Orch 2xs; U VA; Amer Stds.

BRILL, ELIZABETH C; Fayetteville Sr HS; Fayetteville, AR; (3); 1/450; Church Yth Grp; FCA; French Clb; Key Clb; VP Pres Mu Alpha Theta; Acpl Chr; Church Choir; Gov Hon Prg Awd; High Hon Roll; NHS; All Reg Choir; All Reg Orch.

BRIM, ANGIE C; Mountain Home HS; Mountain Home, AR; (3); Church Yth Grp; Cmnty Wkr; FBLA; FHA; Office Aide; ROTC; Chorus.

BRIMLEY, JAMIE; Forrest City HS; Colt, AR; (1); Band; Mrchg Band; U AR.

BRINEGAR, JENNIFER; Lake Hamilton Sr HS; Hot Springs, AR; (2); Church Yth Grp; Natl Beta Clb; Spanish Clb; Pres Chorus; Var Crs Cntry; Var Trk; Cit Awd; High Hon Roll; NHS; Stu Chrstn Life Clb; Optmst Clb Stu Yr.

BRINGHAM, KRISTY; Southside HS; Fort Smith, AR; (4); Church Yth Grp; FCA; FBLA; Mu Alpha Theta; Spanish Clb; Chorus; Var Gym; Var Trk; NHS; Spanish NHS; Long Beach Cc.

BRINKER, JANNA D; Pottsville Schl; Pottsville, AR; (4); 1/54; Drama Clb; Model UN; Natl Beta Clb; Office Aide; Quiz Bowl; Band; Church Choir; Pep Band; School Play; Val; AR Tech Univ; Chem.

BRINKLEY, HOLLY A; Crowleys Ridge Acad; Paragould, AR; (4); Church Yth Grp; Cmnty Wkr; Drama Clb; FBLA; Pep Clb; Science Clb; Spanish Clb; Chorus; School Play; Variety Show; Bible Bowl; Best Suptng Actress Awd; Overall Sci Fair Winner; Crowleys Ridge Coll; Spec Ed.

BRINKLEY, MICHAEL L; Midland HS; Pleasant Plains, AR; (2); Church Yth Grp; Cmnty Wkr; FBLA; Natl Beta Clb; Pep Clb; Spanish Clb; Ofcr Bsbl; Bsktbl; Crs Cntry; Trk; Spts Med.

BRINKLEY, WENDI R; Mt St Mary Acad; North Little Rock, AR; (2); Prfct Atten Awd.

BRINKMEYER, LAURA L; St Joe Public Schl; Saint Joe, AR; (2); 1/16; FBLA; FHA; HOBY; Ed Yrbk; Treas Soph Cls; JV Bsktbl; Hon Roll; CAVES; LAND; WET N WILD; Project WET; AR Schl Of Math & Sci; Scripps; Marine Bio.

BRISCOE JR, SHAWN; Augusta HS; Augusta, AR; (2); Natl Beta Clb; Spanish Clb; Band; Ofcr Soph Cls; Bsktbl; Ftbl; Trk; Hon Roll; NHS; Prfct Atten Awd; Rgn Bnd; Helen E Davis Awd; Memphis ST; Art.

BRISCOE, TIFFINEY; Augusta HS; Augusta, AR; (1); 4-H; Natl Beta Clb; Bsktbl; Mgr(s); Hon Roll; Memphis ST.

BRISIEL, RYAN D; Fayetteville Sr HS; Fayetteville, AR; (2); FCA; Letterman Clb; Var Bsbl; Var Bsktbl; Var Ftbl; L Trk.

BRITT, AYRELLE; Nashville HS; Nashville, AR; (4); 13/106; Church Yth Grp; 4-H; FBLA; FHA; Model UN; Q&S; Quiz Bowl; Spanish Clb; Teachers Aide; Mrchg Band; U Of AR; Psych.

BRITT, JASON W; Nettleton HS; Jonesboro, AR; (2); Boy Scts; French Clb; Teachers Aide; Nwsp; Law Enforcement.

BRITTAIN, TARA; Brinkley HS; Brinkley, AR; (3); Church Yth Grp; Drama Clb; French Clb; FBLA; Band; Church Choir; Drm Mjr(t); Mrchg Band; Orch; Tennis; Lib Clb; Acteens; Handbells; Southwest MO ST; Finance Admn.

BRITTING, STUART M; Greenwood Sr HS; Fort Smith, AR; (2); Cmnty Wkr; FBLA; Quiz Bowl; Science Clb; Spanish Clb; Teachers Aide; Band; Jazz Band; Mrchg Band; Orch; All Rgn Bnd 1st Chair/1st Bnd; All Rgn Solo/Ensmble 5 1st Pl Mdls; Mst Otstndng Musician; AZ ST Univ; Instrmntl Music.

BRIXEY, ANGELA; Morrilton Sr HS; Perry, AR; (4); Art Clb; Church Yth Grp; FBLA; Math Clb; Natl Beta Clb; Office Aide; Science Clb; Spanish Clb; Thesps; Sec Jr Cls; Phys Thrp.

BROADWAY, AMY K; Piggott HS; Piggott, AR; (2); Church Yth Grp; French Clb; Natl Beta Clb; Band; Mrchg Band; Hon Roll; Prfct Atten Awd; Psych.

BROADWAY, CHASTITY L; North Little Rock Hs-West; North Little Rock, AR; (3); Am Leg Aux Girls St; FCA; FBLA; Mu Alpha Theta; Ofcr Stu Cncl; Bsktbl; Hon Roll; Var Danz Team; Drill Team Lieutenant; Co-Capt Keystone; Engr.

BROADWAY, JAYME; Black Rock Jr Sr HS; Portia, AR; (3); 3/20; VP FBLA; Sec FHA; Treas Natl Beta Clb; Chorus; School Musical; Sec Soph Cls; Sec Jr Cls; Rep Stu Cncl; Stat Bsktbl; Intrml Sftbl; Bio & Hlth Hnr Awds; Bus; Comp; Tchr.

BROADWAY, JENNIFER; Brinkley HS; Brinkley, AR; (3); Drama Clb; VP French Clb; FBLA; Yrbk; VP Stu Cncl; Chrldng; Tennis; High Hon Roll; Pres Jr NHS; NHS; Conway; Bus Mgmt.

BROCK, BRITNEY M; Southside HS; Batesville, AR; (4); Church Yth Grp; FCA; FHA; Key Clb; Natl Beta Clb; Office Aide; Science Clb; Spanish Clb; Band; Church Choir; AR ST U.

BROCK, JASON A; Judsonia Jr Sr HS Riverview; Judsonia, AR; (4); 15/65; Church Yth Grp; French Clb; GCE; ASU Bebee.

BROCK, KELLY; Atkins Schl; Atkins, AR; (4); 17/81; Natl Beta Clb; Science Clb; Spanish Clb; Band; Chorus; Drm Mjr(t); Mrchg Band; Hon Roll; Pres Acad Fit Awd; Sftbl; AR Tech Univ; Mrkt Mngmt.

BROCK, TARA; J A Fair Sr HS; Little Rock, AR; (4); 2/350; Church Yth Grp; FBLA; Mu Alpha Theta; Spanish Clb; High Hon Roll; NHS; Pres Acad Fit Awd; Sal; Piano 10 Yrs; Ouachita Bapt Univ.

BROGDON, TRACY L; Crowleys Ridge Acad; Paragould, AR; (3); Art Clb; Church Yth Grp; Drama Clb; FHA; Quiz Bowl; Band; Color Guard; Jazz Band; Hon Roll; NHS; GATE Pgm; Elem Ed.

BROOKS, BENJAMIN D; Crossett Sr HS; Crossett, AR; (2); Boy Scts; Church Yth Grp; SADD; Ftbl; Swimming League High Point Dist Champ; Navy Seals.

BROOKS, BRIAN W; Maynard Jr Sr HS; Maynard, AR; (3); Chess Clb; French Clb; FBLA; Natl Beta Clb; Band; School Play; Hon Roll; Pres Acad Fit Awd; IM Roller Hockey; Bus.

BROOKS, CHRISTY L; Trumann HS; Trumann, AR; (4); 14/85; Art Clb; Church Yth Grp; FHA; Math Clb; Natl FFA Org; Teachers Aide; Yrbk; Hon Roll; NHS; Hnr Stu; AR Acad Challenge Schlsp; AR ST Univ; Early Chldhd Ed.

BROOKS, CRYSTAL; Bryant Sr HS; Benton, AR; (2); Church Yth Grp; Cmnty Wkr; FBLA; Science Clb; Hon Roll; NHS; Pres Acad Fit Awd; Chrch Vol & Lfgrd; Chrldr All Star; Gymnstcs Tchr; Med.

BROOKS, EDMUND D; Dollarway HS; Pine Bluff, AR; (2); Boy Scts; Church Yth Grp; Band; Chorus; Church Choir; Ofcr Stu Cncl; Ftbl; Trk; Ladies/Gntlmn Club; U Of AR; Engrng Elctrnc/Law.

BROOKS, JACQUELINE L; North Little Rock Hs-East; North Little Rock, AR; (4); Dance Clb; FBLA; GAA; Pep Clb; Band; Yrbk; Ofcr Frsh Cls; Bsktbl; Swmmng; Cit Awd; Future 500; Crm Stpr; Police Acad; Officer.

BROOKS, JEFF; Southside HS; Fort Smith, AR; (3); Church Yth Grp; FCA; Spanish Clb; Rep Frsh Cls; Rep Soph Cls; JV Bsbl; JV Bsktbl; Var L Ftbl; Var L Trk; Hon Roll; Spec Olympcs & Boys Clb Vol; OK ST U; Phys Ed.

BROOKS, JENNIFER; Hamburg HS; Hamburg, AR; (2); Drama Clb; HOBY; Natl FFA Org; Quiz Bowl; Chorus; Rep Stu Cncl; Capt Co-Capt Chrldng; Ntl Merit Ltr; Church Yth Grp; Church Choir; UCA All St Chrldr; NCA All Amer Chrldr; Law Clb; Vet Med.

BROOKS, MATT; Abundant Life Schools; Jacksonville, AR; (1); Church Yth Grp; Debate Tm; Drama Clb; Speech Tm; School Play; Hon Roll; Ntl Merit SF; Pres Acad Fit Awd.

BROOKS, STEPHANIE N; Central Sr HS; Little Rock, AR; (3); 107/540; Church Yth Grp; Cmnty Wkr; FBLA; Natl Beta Clb; Office Aide; Band; Church Choir; Mrchg Band; Pep Band; Rptr Nwsp; Upward Bnd Pgm; Yth Ldrshp Inst; U Of Memphis; Jrnlsm.

BROOKS, WHITNEY; North Little Rock Hs-West; North Little Rock, AR; (3); Church Yth Grp; Cmnty Wkr; FCA; German Clb; GAA; Key Clb; Mu Alpha Theta; Mu Alpha Theta; Natl Beta Clb; High Hon Roll; Boys & Girls Clb Tutor; U AR Fyttvlle; Phys Thrpy.

BROOKS, YOLANDA P; Maynard Jr Sr HS; Maynard, AR; (3); 7/37; Am Leg Aux Girls St; French Clb; FBLA; Natl Beta Clb; School Play; Bsktbl; Sftbl; Hon Roll; Prfct Atten Awd; Westlark CC; Nrsng Tech.

BROWN, ALISON D; Trumann HS; Trumann, AR; (2); Church Yth Grp; Chorus; Church Choir; AR ST Univ; Dr.

BROWN, AMANDA; Charleston HS; Charleston, AR; (1); Church Yth Grp; FCA; FBLA; FHA; Nwsp; Yrbk; JV Var Bsktbl; Var Sftbl; JV Trk; Hon Roll; U Of A; Pdtrcn Nrs.

BROWN, AMANDA D; Crowleys Ridge Acad; Powhatan, AR; (2); 3/21; Church Yth Grp; FBLA; Pep Clb; Science Clb; Spanish Clb; Band; Chorus; Sec Soph Cls; High Hon Roll; NHS; Freed Hardemanuniv; Bus.

BROWN, AMY; Mt Pleasant Jr Sr HS; Mount Pleasant, AR; (1); Art Clb; Church Yth Grp; FBLA; FHA; Natl Beta Clb; Quiz Bowl; Yrbk; VP Frsh Cls; High Hon Roll; G/T; Cartoonist.

BROWN, ASHLEY G; St Joe Public Schl; Saint Joe, AR; (2); FBLA; FHA; School Musical; School Play; Rep Frsh Cls; Hon Roll; NHS; Pres Acad Fit Awd; Pres Ed Awds Pgm; Certs Of Awd; Coll Of Ozarks; Math Tchr.

BROWN, BILLY D; Mills HS; Little Rock, AR; (4); 13/173; Am Leg Boys St; Art Clb; Church Yth Grp; Cmnty Wkr; FCA; French Clb; Letterman Clb; Natl Beta Clb; Office Aide; Ofcr Jr Cls; Natl Yth Ldrshp Frm On Law/Constitution; Odessey Of The Mind; Stu Advy Comm; U Of Cntrl AR; Ecs.

BROWN, BRAD; Hartford Schl; Hartford, AR; (3); Church Yth Grp; FBLA; Band; Jazz Band; Mrchg Band; Pep Band; JV Bsktbl; Stat Mgr(s); JV Trk; High Hon Roll; Frgn Lang Awd; FBLA Pres; Rnnr Up For Mr FBLA.

BROWN, BRANDON C; Arkansas Sr HS; Texarkana, AR; (2); Art Clb; Church Yth Grp; Cmnty Wkr; Key Clb; Ftbl; Socr; Trk; Wt Lftg; Hon Roll; Txrkna Sccr Assn 95.

BROWN, BRANDY N; Spring Hill HS; Hope, AR; (3); Art Clb; Bus Profs of Am; French Clb; FBLA; GAA; Library Aide; Office Aide; SADD; Church Choir; School Musical.

BROWN, BRIAN L; Lake Hamilton Sr HS; Hot Springs, AR; (2); 1/250; Church Yth Grp; FCA; Pres 4-H; Natl Beta Clb; Spanish Clb; Ftbl; Trk; High Hon Roll; Hon Roll; NHS; Wolfpride; Teen Ctr Bd; CO Sprngs; Med.

BROWN, BRIDGET A; Central Sr HS; Little Rock, AR; (3); 108/563; FBLA; Natl Beta Clb; Church Choir; Drill Tm; Cit Awd; Hon Roll; U Of Cntrl AR; Jrnlst.

BROWN, BROOKE; Glen Rose HS; Malvern, AR; (3); Church Yth Grp; FCA; FBLA; Spanish Clb; Church Choir; Mrchg Band; VP Soph Cls; Bsktbl; Chrldng; Sftbl; Interschlstc Star Stdnt Recogtn Awd; Majorette; Frgn Lang Awd; Henderson ST U; RN/SPORTS Med.

BROWN, CARLA; Evening Shade Schl; Evening Shade, AR; (2); Math Clb; Natl Beta Clb; Science Clb; School Play; Bsktbl; Hon Roll; Vet.

BROWN, CARLA; Evening Shade Schl; Sidney, AR; (2); Church Yth Grp; Math Clb; Natl FFA Org; Science Clb; Temple Yth Grp; Ofcr Frsh Cls; Bsktbl; Sftbl; Hon Roll; Beauty Schl; Vet/Csmtlgst.

BROWN, CARLETON H; Forrest City HS; Forrest City, AR; (4); Church Yth Grp; DECA; FBLA; FHA; FTA; Mu Alpha Theta; Natl Beta Clb; Church Choir; Kiwanis Awd; NAACP, AME Church Mem; Deans List; All Amer Schlr; Stu Of Wk & Sr Of Wk; U Cntrl AR; Bus Mgmt.

BROWN, CHAD A; Hartford Schl; Hartford, AR; (3); Church Yth Grp; FBLA; Natl FFA Org; Band; Church Choir; Jazz Band; Mrchg Band; Pep Band; Rep Frsh Cls; Sec Soph Cls; Sci & Math Awds; Challenger Congress Pub Speaking Champion.

BROWN, CHASITY D; Bentonville Sr HS; Bentonville, AR; (4); 20/274; Model UN; Band; Flag Corp; Mrchg Band; High Hon Roll; Hon Roll; VP NHS; Prfct Atten Awd; Pres Acad Fit Awd; Library Aide; Peer Hlprs Sec; Fire Marshall; Life Svr.

BROWN, CHRIS L; Rogers HS; Rogers, AR; (3); 20/600; FCA; FHA; Letterman Clb; Intrml Bsbl; Var Bsktbl; Var L Tennis; Intrml L Trk; High Hon Roll; Prfct Atten Awd; UCA; PT.

BROWN, CRYSTAL J; Cutter Morning Star HS; Hot Springs, AR; (2); FCA; Spanish Clb; SADD; Drill Tm; Bsktbl; Sftbl; Hon Roll; Radiologist.

BROWN JR, CURTIS; Altheimer-Sherrill HS; Tucker, AR; (3); 1/60; Drama Clb; HOBY; Teachers Aide; School Musical; Ofcr Frsh Cls; Ofcr Soph Cls; Ofcr Jr Cls; Bsktbl; Trk; Cit Awd.

BROWN, DANIEL; Rogers HS; Rogers, AR; (4); Church Yth Grp; Cmnty Wkr; FCA; Trk; High Hon Roll; NHS; Prfct Atten Awd; Pres Acad Fit Awd; Hendrix Coll; Rsrch Biolgst.

BROWN, DAVID; Dumas HS; Grady, AR; (3); Math Clb; Natl Beta Clb; Science Clb; Spanish Clb; Band; Yrbk; Tennis; Cit Awd; Hon Roll; NHS.

BROWN, DIANA S; Huntsville HS; Huntsville, AR; (4); 19/118; Church Yth Grp; FCA; Band; Church Choir; Jazz Band; Mrchg Band; Pep Band; Sftbl; Trk; Hon Roll; U Of AR; Nrsng.

BROWN, DONALD M; Harding Acad; Augusta, AR; (3); Am Leg Boys St; Key Clb; Quiz Bowl; Spanish Clb; Hon Roll; Harding Univ Hnr Symposium; Indctd Circle Acad Excllnc; Harding Univ; Law.

BROWN, ERICA L; Parkview Arts-Science HS; Little Rock, AR; (3); Trk; Church Yth Grp; FCA; Pres FBLA; Math Tm; Natl Beta Clb; Capt Drill Tm; School Musical; Stage Crew; Pom Pon; Rice; Phy Thrpst.

BROWN, ERIN; Charleston HS; Charleston, AR; (1); 13/82; Church Yth Grp; FCA; FBLA; Bsktbl; Co-Capt Chrldng; Powder Puff Ftbl; Sftbl; Hon Roll; U Of AR; Med.

BROWN, HELEN M; Mc Gehee HS; Mcgehee, AR; (2); FHA; Band; Church Choir; Flag Corp; Rep Stu Cncl; Prfct Atten Awd; Pride Awd; Majrtt; Visions; Spelman Coll; Prodctn.

BROWN, HOLLY E; Junction City HS; El Dorado, AR; (1); FBLA; Quiz Bowl; Science Clb; Spanish Clb; Yrbk; Powder Puff Ftbl; High Hon Roll; Univ AR; Med.

BROWN, JACKIE T; Bearden HS; Bearden, AR; (3); 7/57; Am Leg Aux Girls St; Treas 4-H; Natl Beta Clb; Band; Mrchg Band; Bsktbl; Trk; 4-H Awd; Hon Roll; Majorette Feature & Capt; U Of AR Monticello; Animal Sci.

BROWN, JAMESIA R; El Dorado Sr HS; El Dorado, AR; (3); 30/303; Am Leg Aux Girls St; Cmnty Wkr; FBLA; Natl Beta Clb; Rep Stu Cncl; Cit Awd; Hon Roll; NHS; Spanish Clb; Teachers Aide; Upward Bound Pres; Amer Natl Teenager Fnlst; Howard Univ; Psychiatrist.

BROWN, JASON; Parkview Arts-Science HS; Little Rock, AR; (3); Am Leg Boys St; Drama Clb; FBLA; FTA; Mu Alpha Theta; Natl Beta Clb; Rep Jr Cls; JV Var Bsktbl; Var Ftbl; High Hon Roll.

BROWN, JENNIFER M; Augusta HS; Augusta, AR; (2); Church Yth Grp; FHA; Natl FFA Org; Band; ASU Beebe; Pediatrics.

BROWN, JENNIFER R; Mena HS; Mena, AR; (4); French Clb; Treas FBLA; Science Clb; School Play; Stage Crew; Mgr Yrbk; Hon Roll; Pres NHS; Ntl Merit Ltr; Helped At Ctzn Promoting Recycling; Participated As Stage Crew In 2 Ouachita Little Theater Prod; U Of Cntrl AR-CONWAY; Adv.

BROWN, JEREMY L; Clarendon Jr Sr HS; Roe, AR; (1); Natl Beta Clb; Ofcr Frsh Cls; Ftbl; Trk.

BROWN, JEREMY M; J A Fair Sr HS; Mabelvale, AR; (4); 41/344; Church Yth Grp; FCA; Math Clb; Mu Alpha Theta; Natl Beta Clb; Science Clb; Varsity Clb; Church Choir; Var L Bsbl; Var Bsktbl; All ST/ALL Conf Coachs Bsbl Team; Coll; Scndry Ed.

BROWN, JESSE L; Bright Star Schl; Doddridge, AR; (2); Natl FFA Org; Office Aide; VP Soph Cls; Hon Roll; High Hnrs Awd Ag Engine Repair/Wldng; Texarkana Coll.

BROWN, JESSICA N; Mena HS; Mena, AR; (2); French Clb; FBLA; FHA; Stat Ftbl; French Hon Soc; High Hon Roll; NHS; Ntl Merit Ltr; Schl Choir; BAD; Bus Admin.

BROWN, JODY D; Crossett Sr HS; Crossett, AR; (3); Church Yth Grp; GAA; Chorus; Drill Tm; Pom Pon; Tennis; Cit Awd; Modeling; Lifeguarding.

BROWN, JOHN L; Russellville Sr HS; Russellville, AR; (3); 1/340; Am Leg Boys St; Church Yth Grp; Model UN; SADD; Band; Ofcr Jr Cls; Ofcr Stu Cncl; Socr; High Hon Roll; Jr NHS; NHS Pres; World Affairs Smnr Participant.

BROWN, JOSH L; Greenwood Sr HS; Greenwood, AR; (3); 29/199; Am Leg Boys St; Church Yth Grp; Model UN; Natl Beta Clb; Band; Drm Mjr(t); Jazz Band; Mrchg Band; Hon Roll; NHS; 1st Chair French Horn; Chldrns Chrch Vol; Mst Outstdng Musician; Henderson ST Univ; Music Ed.

BROWN, JOSHUA B; Booneville Jr Sr HS; Booneville, AR; (2); 21/106; Church Yth Grp; Library Aide; Natl Beta Clb; Band; Mrchg Band; Rep Stu Cncl; Hon Roll; Prfct Atten Awd; Ouachita Bapt Univ; Theology.

BROWN, KARY L; Alma HS; Mountainburg, AR; (4); 20/150; Church Yth Grp; Cmnty Wkr; FBLA; Math Clb; Mu Alpha Theta; Spanish Clb; Band; Mrchg Band; Orch; Pep Band; Westark CC; Scndry Ed.

BROWN, KEN; Eudora HS; Eudora, AR; (4); 3/62; FBLA; FHA; Quiz Bowl; School Play; Yrbk; Ofcr Sr Cls; Ofcr Stu Cncl; Capt Bsbl; Bsktbl; High Hon Roll; UA; Fin.

BROWN, KENNY E; Ashdown Sr HS; Ashdown, AR; (3); FCA; French Clb; Ftbl; Wt Lftg; French Hon Soc; Comp Sci.

BROWN, KRIS; White Hall Sr HS; Redfield, AR; (4); Church Yth Grp; Cmnty Wkr; Debate Tm; Math Clb; Math Tm; Natl Beta Clb; ROTC; Science Clb; Spanish Clb; Ftbl; U Of AR Fayetteville; Engrng.

BROWN, KRISTY R; Yellville Summit HS; Summit, AR; (3); 17/82; Church Yth Grp; Drama Clb; Natl Beta Clb; Teachers Aide; Band; Mrchg Band; Cit Awd; Hon Roll; NHS; Prfct Atten Awd; Oral Roberts Univ; Nrsng.

BROWN, LATONYA S; Central Sr HS; Little Rock, AR; (2); Church Yth Grp; Debate Tm; Drama Clb; GAA; Band; JV Vllybl; Cit Awd; Hon Roll; Prfct Atten Awd; Lewis St Church Of Christ Yth Grp; Harding; Psychtry.

BROWN, LE ANN; Rural Special Schl; Fox, AR; (4); #1 in class; Church Yth Grp; Library Aide; Natl Beta Clb; Office Aide; Quiz Bowl; Science Clb; Spanish Clb; Teachers Aide; Hon Roll; Jr NHS; Engrng.

BROWN, LISA R; Charleston HS; Charleston, AR; (3); 9/54; Church Yth Grp; Cmnty Wkr; FCA; FBLA; FHA; GAA; Natl Beta Clb; Office Aide; Spanish Clb; Teachers Aide; Rdlgy X-Rays.

BROWN, LORA S; Arkansas Sr HS; Texarkana, AR; (4); Church Yth Grp; Drama Clb; French Clb; Service Clb; Church Choir; Drill Tm; Rep Stu Cncl; Teenage Rpblcns; Hosp Explrs Club; Flwsp Chrstn Stdnts Sec; Ouachita Bapt Univ; Bio/Nrsg.

BROWN, MARCUS; Dollarway HS; Pine Bluff, AR; (3); Church Yth Grp; FCA; FHA; Church Choir; JV Bsktbl; Var Ftbl; Trk; Wt Lftg; Cit Awd; Prfct Atten Awd; Aut Mech; Athl Trng; MS ST U; Bus.

BROWN, MATTHEW; Conway Sr HS; Conway, AR; (3); FBLA; HOBY; Sec Natl Beta Clb; Pres SADD; Sec Frsh Cls; Hist Rep Stu Cncl; Var L Bsktbl; Var L Diving; Var L Swmmng; Ntl Merit SF; FBLA St Cmptns 94-95 & 93-94; Multi Yr Listing; U Of TN Knoxville; Med.

BROWN, MEGAN; East Poinsett Sr HS; Lepanto, AR; (2); 10/75; Church Yth Grp; Treas VP FBLA; Nwsp; Yrbk; High Hon Roll; Hon Roll; Jr NHS; NHS; U Of AR; Eng Ed.

BROWN, MELISSA; Jonesboro HS; Jonesboro, AR; (3); Art Clb; Church Yth Grp; Key Clb; Natl Beta Clb; Science Clb; Spanish Clb; Chorus; VP Frsh Cls; VP Jr Cls; Capt Var Chrldng; Mss Tn NE AR; Shwstpprs Reg Dance Cmptn Wnnr.

BROWN, MICHAEL; Mammoth Spring HS; Mammoth Spring, AR; (1); Church Yth Grp; FHA; Natl Beta Clb; Pep Clb; Band; Mrchg Band; Bsktbl; Golf; Cit Awd; Hon Roll; Stu Of Mnth; Law.

BROWN, MISTI L; Marked Tree Jr Sr HS; Marked Tree, AR; (3); FBLA; FHA; FTA; Natl Beta Clb; Spanish Clb; Sec Treas Soph Cls; NHS; Church Yth Grp; Cmnty Wkr; JA; GT; Hmcmng Rylty; AR ST Univ; Nrsng/Bus.

BROWN, MONICA R; John L Mcclellan Magnet HS; Little Rock, AR; (2); Beta Clb; Phys.

BROWN, NATASHA R; Northside HS; Fort Smith, AR; (2); Church Yth Grp; Drama Clb; FCA; GAA; Church Choir; Orch; School Play; L Var Bsktbl; L Capt Chrldng; L Trk; 1st Pl MLK Ortrcl Spch Cntst; Prin Awd; N AR All Reg Orch; Univ Of AR; Msc/Comm.

BROWN, NATASHA T; Magnolia HS; Magnolia, AR; (2); Bsktbl; Powder Puff Ftbl; Vllybl; Cit Awd; Hon Roll; Southern AR Univ; Tchr.

BROWN, NATHAN; Lake Hamilton Jr HS; Pearcy, AR; (1); 1/280; Pres FCA; Pres 4-H; Math Clb; Natl Beta Clb; Spanish Clb; Pres Soph Cls; Rep Stu Cncl; Trk; Pres 4-H Awd; High Hon Roll.

BROWN, NICHOLAS A; Catholic HS; Little Rock, AR; (2); 47/159; Hon Roll; Cmptrs; Jrnlsm; Math; Tulane; Engr/Jrnlsm.

BROWN, NICOLE; Greenwood Sr HS; Greenwood, AR; (3); FCA; French Clb; Natl Beta Clb; Nwsp; Yrbk; Bsktbl; Var Chrldng; Gym; Var Sftbl; Hon Roll; U Of AR; Psych.

BROWN, NIKKI D; Springdale Sr HS; Springdale, AR; (2); Church Yth Grp; FCA; Hosp Aide; Acpl Chr; School Musical; Sec Soph Cls; Chrldng; Hon Roll; Sec Jr NHS; NHS; Harding Univ; RN; Sec.

BROWN, SAMANTHA A; Russellville Sr HS; Russellville, AR; (2); Church Yth Grp; Band; Drm Mjr(t); Mrchg Band; Treas Frsh Cls; Var L Swmmng; Hon Roll; NHS; Celbrtn Excl; Mar Bio.

BROWN, SCOTT; Woodlawn Schl; Star City, AR; (2); 1/47; Church Yth Grp; FCA; HOBY; Natl Beta Clb; Quiz Bowl; JV Bsbl; L Bsktbl; L Crs Cntry; L Ftbl; L Trk; Ldrshp Conf HOBY 96; High Point Track 93; Beta Clb Quiz Bowl Team 96; U Of AR Monticello; Mech Engr.

BROWN, TABITHA; Bearden HS; Bearden, AR; (3); 7/57; Treas 4-H; Natl Beta Clb; Varsity Clb; Color Guard; Mrchg Band; School Musical; Var JV Bsktbl; Var JV Trk; 4-H Awd; Hon Roll; Natl Schlr Natl Yough Ldrshp Conf; U Of AR Fayetteville; Biologi.

BROWN, TAMARA L; Russellville Sr HS; Russellville, AR; (2); Church Yth Grp; Teachers Aide; Band; Mrchg Band; High Hon Roll; Hon Roll; Jr NHS; Flag Line Co-Capt 9th Grd; Band All Region Flute 9th Grd; AR Tech Univ; Jrnlsm.

BROWN, TAMARA M; Marked Tree Jr Sr HS; Marked Tree, AR; (4); 9/403; Computer Clb; FBLA; FHA; Library Aide; Spanish Clb; Teachers Aide; Chorus; Church Choir; Ofcr Sr Cls; Hon Roll; U Of AR Little Rock; Nrsng.

BROWN, TAMRA L; Decatur HS; Decatur, AR; (2); 4/45; Church Yth Grp; Pres FHA; Spanish Clb; Ofcr Stu Cncl; Sftbl; Hon Roll; Kiwanis Awd; NHS; Pres Acad Fit Awd; ACE Team.

BROWN, TARA G; Scotland Schl; Clinton, AR; (3); FBLA; Spanish Clb; Treas Chorus; High Hon Roll; Hon Roll; Woodman Of Wrld Life Ins Soc Awd Outstndng Prfcncy In Amer His; Petit Jean Tech Coll; Ofc Admin.

BROWN, TERESA L; Central HS; Helena, AR; (2); ROTC; SADD; Color Guard; Drill Tm; Ofcr Soph Cls; Cit Awd; Prfct Atten Awd; Cert Of Color Guard; U Of Pine Bluff.

BROWN, TERRIE; Gurdon HS; Gurdon, AR; (3); 1/55; Church Yth Grp; FBLA; Natl Beta Clb; Natl FFA Org; Spanish Clb; High Hon Roll; Nursng.

BROWN, TIFFANY K; Forrest City HS; Forrest City, AR; (1); Hon Roll; Archt Schl; Archt Engrng.

BROWN, TOBY R; Hartford Schl; Hackett, AR; (2); Cit Awd; Hon Roll; FFA; Duke Univ; Cmptr Prgrmr.

BROWNFIELD, BRANDI J; Greenwood Sr HS; Greenwood, AR; (2); Church Yth Grp; French Clb; Drill Tm; School Play; Stage Crew; Hon Roll; Ntl Merit SF; Westark; Med Doc.

BROWNFIELD, BRODY A; Greenwood Sr HS; Greenwood, AR; (2); FCA; FBLA; Natl FFA Org; Teachers Aide; Var Bsbl; Var Bsktbl; Var Wt Lftg; Cit Awd; Hon Roll; Prfct Atten Awd.

BROWNING, FAITH E; Clarendon Jr Sr HS; Roe, AR; (2); FBLA; Chorus; Church Choir; Rep Frsh Cls; Beebe AR.

BROWNING, JARROD; Augusta HS; Augusta, AR; (2); 9/46; FBLA; FTA; Natl Beta Clb; Science Clb; Spanish Clb; Band; Mrchg Band; Pep Band; Rep Soph Cls; Rep Stu Cncl; Pride Team; Medcl Sci Camp; U Of AR; Scndry Educ.

BROWNING, KATHY; Kingsland Schl; Kingsland, AR; (3); 2/30; FBLA; FHA; Hosp Aide; HOBY; Natl Beta Clb; Quiz Bowl; Band; Pep Band; VP Jr Cls; Hon Roll; Beauty Pgnts; MASH Pgm; Phys Fitness.

BROWNLEE, LEAH G; Booneville Jr Sr HS; Booneville, AR; (2); 4-H; Quiz Bowl; Teachers Aide; Band; Mrchg Band; Pep Band; Var Bsktbl; Var L Trk; JV Vllybl; High Hon Roll; Hlpd Paint Mural Booneville Cmmnty Hosp; CO Schl Of Mines; Engrng.

BROWNLEE, YAVANNA M; Booneville Jr Sr HS; Booneville, AR; (3); Drama Clb; 4-H; Quiz Bowl; Chorus; School Play; Var L Chrldng; JV Tennis; Wt Lftg; Prfct Atten Awd; Comm Svc At Booneville Hosp; Westark CC; Scndry Ed.

BROWNMILLER, SCOTT; Southside HS; Fort Smith, AR; (3); 57/510; Boy Scts; Treas Church Yth Grp; Mu Alpha Theta; Socr; Hon Roll; Jr NHS; NHS; Spanish NHS.

BROYLES, AMANDA; Newport HS; Newport, AR; (4); 1/143; Am Leg Aux Girls St; Q&S; Yrbk; Ofcr Stu Cncl; High Hon Roll; Sec Treas NHS; Val; Church Yth Grp; French Clb; FBLA; AR Governors Schl; Bible Clb Treas; 3rd Place St Math Cont; Ouachita Bapt U; Math.

BRUCE, BONNIE; Southside HS; Fort Smith, AR; (3); Mu Alpha Theta; Service Clb; Band; Drill Tm; Drm Mjr(t); Flag Corp; Mrchg Band; Hon Roll; Jr NHS; NHS; Elem Ed.

BRUCE, CHRIS D; Dierks HS; Dierks, AR; (2); Letterman Clb; Varsity Clb; Var L Bsbl; Var L Ftbl; Var Wt Lftg; Hon Roll.

BRUCKER, ALLISON T; Russellville Sr HS; Russellville, AR; (2); Church Yth Grp; Drama Clb; Band; Mrchg Band; Hon Roll; Jr NHS; NHS; Coll Theater; Oddesy Of The Mind; Genetics.

BRUCKER, COLE B; Jessieville HS; Hot Springs Natio, AR; (2); 1/51; Church Yth Grp; FCA; VP Key Clb; Natl Beta Clb; Band; VP Frsh Cls; Var Bsktbl; Var Golf; Var Tennis; High Hon Roll; Med.

BRUMFIELD, JANIS A; Russellville Sr HS; Russellville, AR; (3); Church Yth Grp; FHA; Office Aide; Spanish Clb; Chorus; All-Star Prgm; Soc Studies Club; Psych.

BRUMLEY, JESSICA L; El Dorado Sr HS; El Dorado, AR; (4); FBLA; Sec FHA; Office Aide; Spanish Clb; Hon Roll; DECA; Elem Tchr.

BRUNE, TRISHA D; Bryant Sr HS; Alexander, AR; (2); 1/450; English Clb; Science Clb; Acpl Chr; Band; Chorus; Mrchg Band; High Hon Roll; Jr NHS; NHS; Hon Roll; 7th Pl Class Natl Sci Olympd Test; 2nd Chair All Region Choir/Alto/SATB Choir; Metrlgy.

BRUNER, VALERIE; Fayetteville Sr HS; Fayetteville, AR; (2); Spanish Clb; JV Bsktbl; JV Crs Cntry; JV Trk; Cit Awd; 4-H Awd; Gov Hon Prg Awd; Jr NHS; Kiwanis Awd; NHS; OK ST U; Vet Med.

BRUNO, RICHARD A; Parkview Arts-Science HS; Little Rock, AR; (2); Drama Clb; Key Clb; Mu Alpha Theta; Natl Beta Clb; School Musical; Treas Frsh Cls; Pres Soph Cls; Pres Jr Cls; Jr NHS; Sal; 1st Pl Dist Optimist Ortrcl Contest Schlrshp; Kodak Yng Ldr Awd; Dist Acdmc Achvmnt Awd In Comm; WA Univ; Pre-Med/Rdlgst.

BRUNS, JOSH; Central Ark Christian Schl; North Little Rock, AR; (1); 1/100; Church Yth Grp; Spanish Clb; Capt Bsktbl; Socr; High Hon Roll; Pres Jr NHS.

BRYAN, BRANDY; Wonderview HS; Jerusalem, AR; (1); FHA; Band; Sprt Ed Nwsp; VP Frsh Cls; JV Capt Bsktbl; Trk; Hon Roll; Prfct Atten Awd; U Of MI; Phys Educ.

BRYAN, EMILY; Crossett Sr HS; Crossett, AR; (4); 7/165; Chess Clb; Drama Clb; Mu Alpha Theta; Q&S; Band; Flag Corp; Ed Yrbk; Pres Soph Cls; Hon Roll; NHS; U Of Central AR.

BRYANT, AUGUST D; Yellville Summit HS; Yellville, AR; (3); 1/85; Church Yth Grp; Teachers Aide; Band; Jazz Band; Mrchg Band; Pep Band; Pres Frsh Cls; Pres Soph Cls; Rep Stu Cncl; Cit Awd; Natl Hon Soc; Bnd Awds Mrchr Of Wk; Best All-Around Plyr; Best All-Aroung Stdnt Awd; Middle TN ST Univ; Music.

BRYANT, BELINDA A; Mills HS; Jacksonville, AR; (3); 13/298; Am Leg Aux Girls St; Pres FTA; Latin Clb; Natl Beta Clb; Science Clb; Orch; School Play; Ofcr Soph Cls; Ofcr Jr Cls; Ofcr Stu Cncl; NSF Mole Bio Enchmnt Yths; UAMS Antl Inst Hlth Apprntcshp Prog.

BRYANT, CARL; Cloverdale Jr HS; Little Rock, AR; (1); FBLA; Natl Beta Clb; Office Aide; Band; Chorus; Cit Awd; Hon Roll; Jr NHS; NHS; Mst Outstdng Stdnt Gftd/Tlntd Eng/Sci.

BRYANT, CINDY D; Nemo Vista Jr Sr HS; Bee Branch, AR; (2); FBLA; Sec FHA; Girl Scts; Natl Beta Clb; Spanish Clb; Acpl Chr; Hon Roll; Cosmetology.

BRYANT, CLINT D; Fountain Lake Jr Sr HS; Hot Springs Natio, AR; (3); Pres FCA; VP Key Clb; Natl Beta Clb; Treas Natl FFA Org; VP Frsh Cls; Pres Soph Cls; Var Bsbl; Var Bsktbl; Var Ftbl; Sthrn Nazarene Univ; Coach/Tchr.

BRYANT, CRYSTAL G; Piggott HS; Piggott, AR; (3); 12/71; Church Yth Grp; French Clb; Natl Beta Clb; Science Clb; Teachers Aide; Chorus; Church Choir; School Musical; School Play; High Hon Roll; AR Schl Band/Orch Piano Solo/Ensmbl No 1 Ratgs 94-; Jr Eng Awd; Choir Awd 95-; Nrsng.

BRYANT, DARRIN R; Fayetteville Sr HS; Fayetteville, AR; (2); Band; Mrchg Band; Bus Law.

BRYANT, JACOB Q; Amity Jr Sr HS; Amity, AR; (4); Art Clb; Church Yth Grp; Computer Clb; Nwsp; Yrbk; Henderson St Univ.

BRYANT, JACQUE; Crossett Sr HS; N Crossett, AR; (4); 16/176; Am Leg Aux Girls St; Church Yth Grp; Drama Clb; French Clb; FTA; Math Clb; Mu Alpha Theta; Natl Beta Clb; Science Clb; Capt L Bsktbl; Hnr Grad; Ath Schlsp Bsktbl, Sftbl To MDCC; MDCC; Pre-Nrsng.

BRYANT, JASON; Valley Springs Schl; Harrison, AR; (4); 7/51; Art Clb; Key Clb; Natl FFA Org; Speech Tm; School Play; Ofcr Sr Cls; Var Bsbl; Var Bsktbl; Hon Roll; NHS; Ldrshp Awd Sr Yr; Schlr/Ath Awd; Dklb Awd; OK ST U; Ag Ed.

BRYANT, JENNIFER L; Lonoke Sr HS; England, AR; (3); #5 in class; Cmnty Wkr; FCA; FBLA; HOBY; Yrbk; VP Jr Cls; Rep Sec Stu Cncl; Cit Awd; High Hon Roll; NHS; U Of AR Little Rock; Bus.

BRYANT, JIM E; De Soto Schl; Helena, AR; (1); Church Yth Grp; Stage Crew; Var Bsbl; JV L Bsktbl; JV L Ftbl; JV L Trk; High Hon Roll; Hon Roll; MASH; U Of AR; :bio; Med Dr.

BRYANT, KEVIN A; Arkansas Sr HS; Texarkana, AR; (3); 54/343; Boy Scts; Church Yth Grp; Cmnty Wkr; Drama Clb; Key Clb; Mu Alpha Theta; Spanish Clb; Pres Soph Cls; Ofcr Stu Cncl; Pres Acad Fit Awd.

BRYANT, LAURA; Lonoke Sr HS; England, AR; (3); 5/111; Cmnty Wkr; FCA; FBLA; HOBY; Math Clb; Science Clb; Spanish Clb; Band; Mrchg Band; Nwsp; Afro Amer Hist Clb Qn; Big Sis Pgm; Annual Qn 1st Fnlst; U Of AR; Cmptr Info Systms.

BRYANT, MELISSA; Arkansas City Schl; Arkansas City, AR; (2); Church Yth Grp; French Clb; Math Clb; Science Clb; Speech Tm; Nwsp; Yrbk; Rep Soph Cls; Treas Stu Cncl; Cit Awd; Church Yth Cncl; Animal Care.

BRYANT, MICAH A; Southside HS; Batesville, AR; (1); Church Yth Grp; Band; Mrchg Band; Pep Band; Stage Crew; Hon Roll; FFA.

BRYANT, RENATA D; Palestine-Wheatley HS; Wheatley, AR; (2); 3/55; FCA; 4-H; FHA; Natl Beta Clb; Science Clb; Church Choir; Rptr Nwsp; Bsktbl; Chrldng; Trk; Drug-Free Clb; Parlimentarty Procedure Team; Pre-Law.

BRYANT, YOHN C; Harmony Grove Jr Sr HS; Alexander, AR; (3); Church Yth Grp; French Clb; FHA; Church Choir; Var Bsktbl; Law Enfrcmnt.

BRYNIARSKI, THEODORE; Mountain Home HS; Fayetteville, AR; (4); 21/211; Church Yth Grp; Computer Clb; FCA; German Clb; Quiz Bowl; Band; Jazz Band; Mrchg Band; Orch; Pep Band; U Of AR; Acctng.

BRYSON, CASEY; Bentonville Sr HS; Bentonville, AR; (4); 41/242; Church Yth Grp; Cmnty Wkr; Office Aide; SADD; Color Guard; Flag Corp; Yrbk; Hon Roll; Jr NHS; NHS; U Of AR; Elem Ed.

BRYSON, ERIN L; Russellville Sr HS; London, AR; (2); GAA; Teachers Aide; Bsktbl; Score Keeper; Sftbl; Trk; Vllybl; Hon Roll; Prfct Atten Awd; Pres Acad Fit Awd; Ar Tech; PT/CNSLNG.

BUCCELLA, VANESA; Northside HS; Fort Smith, AR; (4); 15/320; Drama Clb; French Clb; Mu Alpha Theta; Q&S; Speech Tm; School Play; Stage Crew; Variety Show; Var Socr; French Hon Soc; Environmental Clb; U Of AR; Film; His.

BUCHANAN, LORI; Southside HS; Fort Smith, AR; (3); 51/520; FCA; HOBY; Key Clb; Natl Beta Clb; Sec Jr Cls; VP Frsh Cls; VP Soph Cls; Treas Stu Cncl; Bsktbl; Trk; Red Cross Crtfd Lfgrd; U Of AR; Brdcst Jrnlsm.

BUCHER, CRAIG; Catholic HS; Sherwood, AR; (4); Var Crs Cntry; Var Socr; Hon Roll; VA Tech; Mech Engrng.

BUCHER, ROSE; Ozark Adventist Acad; Gentry, AR; (3); 1/70; Church Yth Grp; Office Aide; Teachers Aide; Cit Awd; High Hon Roll; NHS; Prfct Atten Awd; Royal Aires; Adopt-A-Grandparent; Adopt-A-Kid; Loma Linda; Occptnl Thrpst.

BUCK, CAROL; Sylvan Hills HS; Sherwood, AR; (3); 39/300; Am Leg Aux Girls St; FCA; Pres French Clb; Key Clb; Mu Alpha Theta; Science Clb; Teachers Aide; Ofcr Stu Cncl; Hon Roll; NHS; Jr Exec Comm Mem.

BUCK, JOHN; Rogers HS; Rogers, AR; (1); Church Yth Grp; Cmnty Wkr; FCA; Pres FBLA; Ftbl; High Hon Roll; Hon Roll; Univ Of AR; Bus.

BUCK, MICHAEL; Caddo Hills Jr Sr HS; Glenwood, AR; (4); 1/40; FBLA; Model UN; Pres Natl Beta Clb; Capt Quiz Bowl; Spanish Clb; Rep Stu Cncl; Hon Roll; Pres Schlr; Val; Art Clb; Amateur Radio; AR ST U; Elect Engrng.

BUCKINGHAM, ELIZABETH; Butterfield Jr HS; Van Buren, AR; (1); Church Yth Grp; Speech Tm; Chrldng; Jr NHS; Pres Acad Fit Awd.

BUCKLEY, AMANDA E; Fairview HS; Camden, AR; (2); Church Yth Grp; Drama Clb; 4-H; French Clb; Science Clb; Teachers Aide; Chorus; Church Choir; School Musical; School Play; High Scores Natl Fr Exam; U Of AR; RN.

BUCKMASTER, SONJE ANNE; Clarksville HS; Clarksville, AR; (2); French Clb; Key Clb; Natl Beta Clb; SADD; High Hon Roll; Model UN; Quiz Bowl; Hon Roll; OM Regnl Judge; Bay View Music Assn Vesper Choir; Pres Ed Awds Pgm; MI Tech Univ; Assn Women In Math; Pre-Law.

BUCKNER, TRINTIY M; Crossett Sr HS; Crossett, AR; (2); 36/207; Church Yth Grp; Band; Mrchg Band; Pep Band; Hon Roll; Eagle High Flyer; Rensnce Prgm; Elem Schl Tchr.

BUDY, BROOKE; Mountain View Jr Sr HS; Mountain View, AR; (4); 1/90; Art Clb; Girl Scts; Library Aide; Natl Beta Clb; Quiz Bowl; Science Clb; School Play; Pom Pon; High Hon Roll; Val; Beta, Fine Arts Clb Variety Shw Mstr Ceremonies; Vassar Coll; Art Hist.

BUEHLER, JENNIFER M; Magnolia HS; Magnolia, AR; (4); 29/300; French Clb; Math Clb; Mu Alpha Theta; Band; Mrchg Band; Pep Band; Nwsp; Hon Roll; NHS; Southern AR Univ; Bus.

BUFORD, KENDRA; Lee Sr HS; Lexa, AR; (2); 3/188; Church Yth Grp; Cmnty Wkr; French Clb; FTA; Natl Beta Clb; Band; Flag Corp; Ofcr Soph Cls; High Hon Roll; Prfct Atten Awd; Ftr Wmn Tmrrw; PHD; TIE; Howard U; Law.

BUFORD, MARY T; Russellville Sr HS; London, AR; (2); Church Yth Grp; FCA; French Clb; Hosp Aide; Bsktbl; Mgr(s); Score Keeper; Vllybl; Hon Roll; Jr NHS; AR Tech U; Plastic Surgeon; Med.

BUFORD, THOMAS; Marion HS; Marion, AR; (3); Boy Scts; Church Yth Grp; Drama Clb; HOBY; Mu Alpha Theta; Ed Yrbk; Rep Frsh Cls; French Hon Soc; High Hon Roll; NHS; Hendrix Coll.

BUI, BEN; Southside HS; Fort Smith, AR; (3); 51/502; French Clb; Mu Alpha Theta; Bsktbl; JV Ftbl; Trk; Hon Roll; NHS; Stu Of Mnth 94.

BUIE, AMY R; Russellville Sr HS; Russellville, AR; (3); Church Yth Grp; French Clb; Teachers Aide; Band; Church Choir; Mrchg Band; High Hon Roll; Jr NHS; NHS; Chrch Yth Group Pres.

BUIE, SHAWNDA R; Malvern Sr HS; Malvern, AR; (3); Church Yth Grp; FBLA; Natl Beta Clb; Spanish Clb; SADD; Chorus; Rptr Nwsp; Hon Roll; NHS; Pres Acad Fit Awd; Tutor; Henderson St Univ.

BUIRTS, TIFFANY M; Augusta HS; Augusta, AR; (2); Art Clb; Church Yth Grp; FTA; Spanish Clb; Chorus; Church Choir; Flag Corp; Sec Soph Cls; Bsktbl; Bsktbl; AR ST; Nrsng.

BULGER, AMANDA L; Southside HS; Batesville, AR; (3); Church Yth Grp; Dance Clb; Key Clb; Natl Beta Clb; Office Aide; Science Clb; Spanish Clb; Teachers Aide; Chorus; Church Choir; ASU; Phy Thrpst.

BULICE, CHRISTOPHER M; Cabot HS; Cabot, AR; (2); JV Bsbl; Ftbl; Bsbl 9 Yrs, All-Stars 6 Yrs; LSU; Soil Engrng.

BULICE, JONATHAN R; Rose Bud Jr Sr HS; Rose Bud, AR; (3); Art Clb; Boy Scts; Church Yth Grp; FBLA; Hosp Aide; Math Clb; Model UN; Natl Beta Clb; Spanish Clb; Ofcr Bsbl; Comp Graphics.

BULL, AMBER; Genoa Central HS; Fouke, AR; (3); FBLA; Spanish Clb; Yrbk; Ofcr Jr Cls; Bsktbl; Crs Cntry; Trk; Cit Awd; Hon Roll; NHS.

BULL, AMY R; Conway Sr HS; Conway, AR; (3); Church Yth Grp; FBLA; Natl Beta Clb; Q&S; Spanish Clb; Church Choir; Yrbk; Cit Awd; High Hon Roll; Hon Roll; All Stars; Placed In Top 10 Percentile In Natl Span Exam; Ouachita Bapt Univ.

BULLARD, KELLY D; Springdale Sr HS; Springdale, AR; (4); 112/546; DECA; School Play; Rep Frsh Cls; Rep Soph Cls; Rep Stu Cncl; Hon Roll; Pres Acad Fit Awd; Peer Hlprs Grp; Vol Church Grp; U Of AR Fayetteville; Phrmcy.

BULLARD, TIMOTHY J; Arkansas Sr HS; Texarkana, AR; (3); FBLA; Band; 2nd Dist IV Of AR FBLA Accntng II; E TX; Accntng.

BULLINGTON, JENNIFER L; Southside HS; Fort Smith, AR; (4); 29/459; Church Yth Grp; Cmnty Wkr; Drama Clb; FCA; German Clb; GAA; Pep Clb; Q&S; Teachers Aide; Church Choir; Frst Prsbytrn Bible Study Mbr/Strtr; U Of AR Schlsp; Schlr Awd; AR HS Press Assn Awd; U Of AR; Psych.

BULLINGTON, JONATHAN; Southside HS; Fort Smith, AR; (4); 98/432; Church Yth Grp; FCA; FHA; Mu Alpha Theta; Spanish Clb; Var Bsbl; Var Bsktbl; Trk; Hon Roll; Jr NHS; Sthnr Achv Awd; Elks Lodge Stu Of Mnth; U Of AR; Ath Trng.

BULLMAN, CRYSTAL; Stephens Jr Sr HS; Camden, AR; (3); Art Clb; Pres Church Yth Grp; Pres FBLA; Sec FHA; Library Aide; Church Choir; Yrbk; Hon Roll; VP NHS; SAAR; Prncpls Awd; Gftd & Tlntd; Sthrn AR U; Soc.

BULLOCH, CHRIS; Central Sr HS; Little Rock, AR; (3); Church Yth Grp; FCA; Natl Beta Clb; Red Cross Aide; Spanish Clb; Ofcr Stu Cncl; Ofcr Bsbl; Ftbl; Socr; Hon Roll.

BULLOCK, JASON; Hazen Jr Sr HS; Hazen, AR; (3); 2/53; Bus Profs of Am; Church Yth Grp; French Clb; FBLA; FHA; FTA; Natl Beta Clb; Rep Frsh Cls; VP Soph Cls; VP Jr Cls.

BULLOCK, LINDA; Rison HS; Rison, AR; (4); 4/53; Am Leg Aux Girls St; FCA; HOBY; Nwsp; Sec Jr Cls; Rep Stu Cncl; Capt Bsktbl; Trk; Hon Roll; Prfct Atten Awd; Gov Schl.

BULLOCK, SCOTT D; Dewitt HS; Crocketts Bluff, AR; (3); 6/102; Am Leg Boys St; Natl Beta Clb; VP Science Clb; School Play; VP Frsh Cls; Pres Soph Cls; VP Jr Cls; Ofcr Stu Cncl; Ofcr Bsbl; Bsktbl.

BUMGARDNER, CARRIE; Bryant Sr HS; Benton, AR; (3); Church Yth Grp; Cmnty Wkr; Hosp Aide; Teachers Aide; Mgr Bsktbl; Mgr(s); Score Keeper; Hon Roll; Ntl Merit SF; Pres Acad Fit Awd; Voice Dmcrcy Spch Hnrbl Mntn; U Of Central AR; Pre Med.

BUMGARNER, MELINDA S; Highland HS; Hardy, AR; (3); Hosp Aide; Teachers Aide; Hon Roll; NHS; NM ST Univ; Nrsng.

BUMP, BART O; Lake Hamilton Sr HS; Royal, AR; (3); Boy Scts; Natl Beta Clb; VP Natl FFA Org; School Musical; School Play; High Hon Roll; Hon Roll; NHS; Rodeo; TX A&M; Vet.

BUMPAS, CARRIE; Beebe Sr HS; Beebe, AR; (4); 10/93; Am Leg Aux Girls St; Rptr Drama Clb; FCA; Rptr FBLA; Pres FHA; HOBY; Thesps; Pres Band; Ed Yrbk; Chrldng; All St Bnd; U Cntrl AR; Phrmcy.

BUMPERS, ANNE; Conway Sr HS; Conway, AR; (4); 11/500; Church Yth Grp; FBLA; Natl Beta Clb; Orch; School Musical; Yrbk; Rep Stu Cncl; French Hon Soc; High Hon Roll; Hon Roll; All St Orch; AR Gov Schl; U Of AR; Acctng.

BUMPERS, MELODIE P; Mc Crory Jr Sr HS; Mc Crory, AR; (2); Teachers Aide; Band; Church Choir; Mrchg Band; Pep Band.

BUNCH, DARREN S; Gravette HS; Maysville, AR; (4); 3/57; FBLA; Natl FFA Org; Rep Frsh Cls; Treas Jr Cls; VP Sr Cls; Rep Stu Cncl; Var Bsbl; Var Golf; Hon Roll; Pres NHS; U AR; Corp Law.

BUNCH, KELLY L; Alpena Schl; Harrison, AR; (2); 10/50; Church Yth Grp; FBLA; FHA; Natl Beta Clb; Natl FFA Org; Pep Clb; Mgr Bsktbl; Mgr(s); Trk; Hon Roll; Comp.

BUNDREN, CAREY E; Clarendon Jr Sr HS; Clarendon, AR; (3); FBLA; FHA; Library Aide; Teachers Aide; Chorus; Rep Stu Cncl; JV Var Chrldng; Hon Roll.

BUNN, WINDY; Searcy HS; Searcy, AR; (4); 1/201; Art Clb; French Clb; Natl Beta Clb; Var L Bsktbl; Capt Socr; Cit Awd; VP French Hon Soc; NHS; Val; Jr NHS; AR Governors Schl; WA Univ St Louis; Bus.

BUNTING, ANGELA K; Nettleton HS; Jonesboro, AR; (3); Church Yth Grp; Teachers Aide; Band; Chorus; Jazz Band; Mrchg Band; Pep Band; School Play; Hon Roll; Band All Reg & St; Music.

BUNTING, CASSONDRA K; Jonesboro HS; Jonesboro, AR; (3); 42/372; Cmnty Wkr; French Clb; Natl Beta Clb; Office Aide; Band; Mrchg Band; High Hon Roll; Hon Roll; NHS; Math Clb VP; AR ST Univ; Elem Ed.

BUONO, REGINA M; Fayetteville East HS; Fayetteville, AR; (4); 1/400; Mu Alpha Theta; Thesps; Stage Crew; Lit Mag; Var Bsktbl; Mgr Trk; Vllybl; Hon Roll; Treas NHS; Pres Acad Fit Awd; Governors Schl Del; Natl Merit Commende Dschlr; U Of AR.

BURANAWATANACHOKE, BOONJONG; Pine Bluff HS; Pine Bluff, AR; (4); Boy Scts; Church Yth Grp; English Clb; Intnl Clb; Math Tm; Natl Beta Clb; Acpl Chr; Church Choir; School Musical; School Play; Ping Pong; Math Cmptn; Spkr For Pub; MIT; Engrng.

BURCH, DONALD G; Southside HS; Batesville, AR; (1); Church Yth Grp; Teachers Aide; Acpl Chr; Chorus; Church Choir; School Musical; School Play; Nwsp; Yrbk; Ofcr Frsh Cls; All Rgn Chor; Top 10% Of Frosh Clss; Famly Gspl Grp Touched By Master.

BURCH, NICHOLE D; Alma HS; Alma, AR; (3); Church Yth Grp; Cmnty Wkr; FCA; FBLA; FHA; Model UN; VP Pres SADD; Chrldng; Cit Awd; Hon Roll; Jr Exec Trnng; Med.

BURCHETTE, NEKEAII; Mineral Springs Schl; Mineral Springs, AR; (1); Church Yth Grp; FBLA; FHA; Natl FFA Org; Red Cross Aide; Band; Ofcr Frsh Cls; Ofcr Bsbl; Cit Awd; Hon Roll; Inrichment Pool; GATE; Battle Of Bks; Mineral Sprngs Drug Tm; Princeton U; Law.

BURDEN, MATTHEW SCOTT; Pulaski Acad; Little Rock, AR; (4); Church Yth Grp; Cmnty Wkr; FCA; Library Aide; Mu Alpha Theta; Natl Beta Clb; Teachers Aide; Band; Chorus; Church Choir; Natl Mrchntl Bnk Stdnt Ldrshp Bd; All Reg/St Choir; Apostles; Abilene Chrstn U; Mnstry.

BURDEN, MEREDITH; Prairie Grove HS; Prairie Grove, AR; (2); 11/87; Church Yth Grp; FHA; Spanish Clb; SADD; Chorus; Hon Roll; Jr NHS; U AR.

BURGENER, CHRIS; Wonderview HS; Hattieville, AR; (1); Natl FFA Org; Quiz Bowl; Band; Pep Band; Ofcr Bsbl; Bsktbl; Hon Roll.

BURGER, COLE; Greenwood Sr HS; Greenwood, AR; (3); 2/200; Am Leg Boys St; Church Yth Grp; FBLA; Mu Alpha Theta; Natl Beta Clb; Quiz Bowl; Church Choir; Var Golf; High Hon Roll; NHS; 3 1st Pl Solo Piano Cmptn; Comp Sci; Math.

BURGER, JENNIFER D; Mena HS; Mena, AR; (3); Church Yth Grp; French Clb; FBLA; Science Clb; Rep Frsh Cls; Rep Soph Cls; Var Chrldng; Intrml Sftbl; Var Vllybl; High Hon Roll.

BURGESS, CLAIRE E; Pulaski Acad; Little Rock, AR; (2); Church Yth Grp; Cmnty Wkr; German Clb; Hosp Aide; VP Model UN; Natl Beta Clb; Service Clb; Varsity Clb; Ed Lit Mag; High Hon Roll; Piano.

BURGESS, HEATHER B; Bentonville Sr HS; Bentonville, AR; (3); 11/350; Am Leg Aux Girls St; Art Clb; Key Clb; Acpl Chr; School Musical; Lit Mag; Var Gym; High Hon Roll; NHS; Ntl Merit Ltr; Pre-Law/FBI.

BURGESS, LASHONDA; Forrest City HS; Forrest City, AR; (2); FHA; Girl Scts; Church Choir; Bsktbl; Hon Roll; FTAD VP; ASU; Bus.

BURGESS, LESLIE; Hermitage Jr Sr HS; Hermitage, AR; (2); #1 in class; Natl Beta Clb; Natl FFA Org; Sec Frsh Cls; Bsktbl; Chrldng; Sftbl; Pres Acad Fit Awd; U Of AR.

BURGHART, DANIEL; Arkansas Bapt Schl; Little Rock, AR; (2); Church Yth Grp; Quiz Bowl; Hon Roll; Med.

BURGIE, JOCELYN; El Dorado Sr HS; El Dorado, AR; (3); 64/310; Natl Beta Clb; Spanish Clb; Band; Mrchg Band; Ftrstc Otlks; Reach; Jr Strng Comm; U Of AR At Fayetteville; Acctg.

BURK, CRYSTAL D; Corning HS; Corning, AR; (3); FHA; Office Aide; Var Bsktbl; Hon Roll.

BURKE, ANGELA; Ola Jr Sr HS; Danville, AR; (3); HOBY; Natl Beta Clb; Quiz Bowl; Spanish Clb; Rep Soph Cls; Bsktbl; Chrldng; High Hon Roll; Prfct Atten Awd; Girls St; AR Tech U; Med.

BURKE, CASEY L; Westside HS; Coal Hill, AR; (2); 4/36; FBLA; Natl Beta Clb; Chorus; Bsktbl; Sftbl; Hon Roll; Jr NHS; PRIDE Alcohol-Drugs-Tobacco Free Stdnts; Interview Awd Miss Teen AR Pageant; Westark CC; Pub Relations Spec.

BURKE, JARED T; Emmet Schl; Hope, AR; (4); 6/11; Speech Tm; Yrbk; Pres Frsh Cls; Pres Soph Cls; Pres Jr Cls; VP Sr Cls; High Hon Roll; Hon Roll; Red River; Cmptrs.

BURKE, JENNIFER; Bearden HS; Thornton, AR; (3); 4-H; FBLA; FHA; Natl Beta Clb; School Play; Rptr Nwsp; Rptr Yrbk; Rep Stu Cncl; Hon Roll; Ntl Merit Ltr; All Amer Schlr; Elem Ed.

BURKES, ANDREA L; Southside HS; Fort Smith, AR; (2); Cmnty Wkr; Drama Clb; Hosp Aide; Speech Tm; SADD; Stage Crew; Rptr Yrbk; Ofcr Soph Cls; High Hon Roll; Hon Roll; Poetry Pub Antlgy Yng Amers; Stu Of Month 94-95; Soc Work.

BURKHART, AMY L; Alma HS; Rudy, AR; (3); Science Clb; Band; Chorus; Hon Roll; Most Imprvd Musician 93-94 9th Grd Band; Westark Univ Ctr; Cmptr.

BURKHART, KRISTEN R; Alma HS; Alma, AR; (3); Church Yth Grp; FCA; FBLA; GAA; Mu Alpha Theta; Church Choir; Var Capt Chrldng; Cit Awd; Hon Roll; NHS; Chrldng Capt 12th Grd; U Of AR; Bus.

BURKHEAD, SUSAN L; Lake Hamilton Sr HS; Hot Springs, AR; (3); 3/225; Church Yth Grp; French Clb; Q&S; Spanish Clb; Church Choir; Yrbk; Hon Roll; Jr NHS; NHS.

BURKHEART, CANDICE L; Corning Jr Sr HS; Corning, AR; (2); Church Yth Grp; FBLA; FHA; Girl Scts; Spanish Clb; Church Choir; Drm Mjr(t); Co-Capt Chrldng; Hon Roll; Grl Sct Slvr Awd; Univ Of AR; Phy Thrpst.

BURKHEART, DERICK A; Corning HS; Corning, AR; (3); Art Clb; Boy Scts; Pres Drama Clb; Thesps; School Play; Ftbl; Tennis; Pres Acad Fit Awd; AR ST U; Elec Engr.

BURKS, BRITTANY K; Lonoke Jr HS; Lonoke, AR; (1); #4 in class; Church Yth Grp; GAA; Science Clb; JV Var Bsktbl; Var Chrldng; High Hon Roll; NHS; Pres Acad Fit Awd; Sftbl; Vanderbilt; Pre Med.

BURKS, CHAROLETTE D; Lonoke Sr HS; Lonoke, AR; (3); 12/100; Church Yth Grp; Spanish Clb; Church Choir; Hon Roll; NHS; Oddsey Of The Mind; U Central AR; Radiology.

BURKS, JAIME L; Magnet Cove HS; Malvern, AR; (3); 10/55; FHA; Hosp Aide; Math Clb; Natl Beta Clb; Science Clb; Spanish Clb; School Play; Hon Roll; Outsdng Appld Bio I/II Stdnt.

BURKS, JEREMY L; Hampton Jr Sr HS; Hampton, AR; (2); 26/59; 4-H; Mgr Ftbl; 4-H Awd; Math Awd Acad Excl; Radiology.

BURKS, MELVIN L; North Little Rock Hs-West; North Little Rock, AR; (3); Art Clb; VICA; Gov Hon Prg Awd; Hon Roll; Arch.

BURKS, MINDIE; Manila HS; Manila, AR; (4); 4/42; Natl Beta Clb; Chorus; School Play; Yrbk; Pres Frsh Cls; Sec Jr Cls; Pres Stu Cncl; Capt Chrldng; Hon Roll; Miss Manila HS; All Region Choir 3rd Chr; Homcmng Maid; AR ST U; Medcl.

BURLESON, JENNIFER L; Midland HS; Marcella, AR; (2); FBLA; FHA; Natl Beta Clb; Pres Spanish Clb; Mgr Yrbk; Treas Soph Cls; Hon Roll; U Of Cntrl AR; Phys Thrpst.

BURNETT, BRANDT J; Mills HS; North Little Rock, AR; (3); 6/280; Church Yth Grp; Mu Alpha Theta; Natl Beta Clb; Band; Sec VP Stu Cncl; Var L Ftbl; Var L Trk; Var Wt Lftg; Gov Hon Prg Awd; NHS; U Of AR; Scndry Ed/Coaching.

BURNETT, CHRISTIE; West Side HS; Higden, AR; (3); 1/40; Am Leg Aux Girls St; Pres FHA; School Play; Phtg Yrbk; Var Capt Chrldng; Var Capt Pom Pon; Cit Awd; Gov Hon Prg Awd; NHS; Cmnty Wkr; Air Force Math/Sci Awrd; Premed.

BURNETT, CHRISTY R; Harrisburg HS; Harrisburg, AR; (1); Sec Church Yth Grp; Sec Treas FHA; Spanish Clb; Cit Awd; Hon Roll; NHS; Sat Schlrs Pgm ASU Jonesboro AR 96; ARK Yth Bible Drl Cmptn/Dist; Clct Pz Dspnsrs/Clwns; ASU; PT.

BURNETT, DINAH F; Eureka Springs Jr Sr HS; Eureka Springs, AR; (4); 3/52; Church Yth Grp; Drama Clb; Hosp Aide; Library Aide; Natl Beta Clb; Ofcr Soph Cls; Pres Sr Cls; Sec Stu Cncl; High Hon Roll; Ldrshp Awd; Walmart & Oxford Schlsps; John Brown U; Scndry Ed Eng.

BURNETT, JESSICA; Dermott HS; Dermott, AR; (2); Church Yth Grp; Dance Clb; HOBY; Natl Beta Clb; Band; Jazz Band; Mrchg Band; Rep Soph Cls; Sftbl; Ntl Merit Ltr.

BURNETT, KATRINA D; Central Sr HS; Little Rock, AR; (3); Church Yth Grp; Natl Beta Clb; Pep Clb; Band; Mrchg Band; Pep Band; Cit Awd; Hon Roll; Ladies Clb; Natl Yth Ldrshp Forum; All-Region 2nd Band; Dermatology; Psycht.

BURNETT, REALATY M; Dumas HS; Dumas, AR; (2); Church Yth Grp; FBLA; Office Aide; Band; Church Choir; Jazz Band; Mrchg Band; Pep Band; School Play; Hon Roll; U Of Monticello; Bus; Acctng.

BURNETT, STEVE A; Huntsville HS; Huntsville, AR; (4); 12/123; Art Clb; Library Aide; L Bsbl; High Hon Roll; U Ozarks; Cmptr Sci.

BURNETTE, LA TISHA; Rivercrest HS; Luxora, AR; (2); 11/179; Church Yth Grp; French Clb; FBLA; Band; Church Choir; School Play; Var Bsktbl; Var Sftbl; Jr NHS; Ballet 8 Yrs; WA ST Univ; Psychlgst.

BURNHAM, BROCK; Danville HS; Danville, AR; (3); Am Leg Boys St; FCA; FBLA; Natl FFA Org; Quiz Bowl; SADD; Band; Ofcr Bsbl; Ftbl; Wt Lftg; Multi Yr Listee; Natl Young Ldrs Conf Schlr; Boys ST; Law.

BURNS, AMY L; Corning HS; Corning, AR; (3); 1/81; FBLA; Quiz Bowl; Spanish Clb; Chorus; Tennis; High Hon Roll; Ntl Merit SF; Drama Clb; Bausch/Lomb Sci Awd; Hghst GPA Clss; AHSME Cmptn Scrd 96% 95; Engrng.

BURNS, BRANDON; Foreman Jr Sr HS; Foreman, AR; (4); 7/50; Boy Scts; Chess Clb; Quiz Bowl; Varsity Clb; Rep Soph Cls; Var Capt Ftbl; Var L Trk; Var L Wt Lftg; High Hon Roll; U AL-FAYETTEVILLE; Dentistry.

BURNS, KRYSTAL; Dewitt HS; De Witt, AR; (2); Church Yth Grp; 4-H; French Clb; FHA; Science Clb; Sec Treas Band; Church Choir; Mrchg Band; Pep Band; School Play; Majorette; 2nd Pl ST Sci Fair Behavorial Sci; Won Several Majorette Awrds; U Of AR.

BURNS, LARRY J; Mena HS; Mena, AR; (1); Church Yth Grp; Cmnty Wkr; French Clb; Hosp Aide; Band; Mrchg Band; Sec Frsh Cls; Cit Awd; Hon Roll; 250 Hrs Vol Awd Phoenix Hosp; Optmtry/Bus Adm.

BURNS, LATOYA L; Dumas HS; Dumas, AR; (2); Church Yth Grp; FBLA; Church Choir; Hon Roll; NHS; Ar ST Univ; Cmptr Tech.

BURNS, MARIE D; Russellville Sr HS; Russellville, AR; (2); Church Yth Grp; Computer Clb; GAA; Office Aide; Band; Color Guard; Mrchg Band; JV Gym; JV Var Socr; Hon Roll; Soccer Soph Ldrshp Awd.

BURNS, MELISSA L; Harrison Sr HS; Harrison, AR; (4); 2/207; Church Yth Grp; Drama Clb; FBLA; Office Aide; Science Clb; Spanish Clb; Teachers Aide; Thesps; Band; Church Choir; U Of Cntrl AR; Phrmcy.

BURNS, SHARI E; Russellville Sr HS; Russellville, AR; (3); Church Yth Grp; Debate Tm; Drama Clb; Office Aide; Spanish Clb; Acpl Chr; Band; Chorus; Church Choir; Jazz Band.

BURNS, STEVEN A; Corning HS; Lafe, AR; (1); Art Clb; Bsktbl; Agri-FFA; Hnrs Engl; MI ST Univ; Ag.

BURNWORTH, BRANDI M; Malvern Sr HS; Malvern, AR; (3); Church Yth Grp; FBLA; Natl Beta Clb; Teachers Aide; Band; Mrchg Band; High Hon Roll; Hon Roll; Jr NHS; Pres Schlr.

BURRELL, TERESA L; Eudora HS; Eudora, AR; (2); 2/102; Natl Beta Clb; Quiz Bowl; ROTC; Band; Color Guard; Drill Tm; Flag Corp; Mrchg Band; Sec Stu Cncl; Cit Awd; Jackson ST Univ; Eng Ed.

BURREUGHS, HUNTER M; Lake Hamilton Sr HS; Hot Springs Natio, AR; (2); Boy Scts; Church Yth Grp; Cmnty Wkr; Drama Clb; FCA; FBLA; Letterman Clb; Library Aide; Natl Beta Clb; Office Aide; Southern Assn Stdnt Cncl Pres; Reg 6 Rep Natls; Ldrshp Hot Spring; Pol/Gov.

BURRIS, CHARLES R; Mills HS; Mabelvale, AR; (3); 20/291; Natl Beta Clb; Science Clb; Spanish Clb; Var Ftbl; Var L Trk; 4-H Awd; NHS; Mt Biking; Scuba Diving; Camping; USAF Acad; Pilot.

BURRIS, DAVID K; Morrilton Sr HS; Morrilton, AR; (4); Art Clb; Church Yth Grp; Computer Clb; French Clb; FBLA; FHA; Science Clb; Crs Cntry; Trk.

BURRIS, ERIN; Malvern Jr HS; Malvern, AR; (2); Church Yth Grp; FCA; FBLA; Natl Beta Clb; Drill Tm; Co-Ed Yrbk; Ofcr Stu Cncl; Chrldng; High Hon Roll; Jr NHS; Peer Cnslr.

BURRIS, HOLLY; Ouachita Jr Sr HS; Malvern, AR; (4); 1/30; Am Leg Aux Girls St; Church Yth Grp; FBLA; FHA; HOBY; Math Clb; Natl Beta Clb; Science Clb; Spanish Clb; Val; DAR; High Hnr Roll; Presdntl Acad Ftnss Awd; Ouachita Bapt U; Chem.

BURROUGHS, JENNIFER A; Hot Springs HS; Hot Springs, AR; (2); #7 in class; Church Yth Grp; FBLA; HOBY; Key Clb; Natl Beta Clb; Q&S; Spanish Clb; Thesps; Chrldng; High Hon Roll; PRICE Natl Trnr; AR ST PRIDE Tm; Univ Chrldrs Assoc All ST; U Of AR; Med.

BURROW, JAMES; Searcy HS; Augusta, AR; (3); 1/230; Church Yth Grp; HOBY; Natl Beta Clb; Acpl Chr; Band; Mrchg Band; Pep Band; Phtg Yrbk; NHS; Cntrl Rgn Solo/Ensm 1st Pl Soloist; Med.

BURROW, SARAH L; Greene Co Tech HS; Paragould, AR; (4); 8/167; Church Yth Grp; FBLA; Pep Clb; Red Cross Aide; Spanish Clb; Band; Chorus; Drm Mjr(t); Mrchg Band; Rptr Yrbk; AR ST U; Bio.

BURROW, TARA; Calico Rock HS; Calico Rock, AR; (1); Math Clb; Natl Beta Clb; Pep Clb; Science Clb; Bsktbl; Sftbl; Prfct Atten Awd; SADD; U Of TN; Bsktbl Coach.

BURROWS, DARYL R; Rogers HS; Rogers, AR; (3); Boy Scts; Church Yth Grp; Latin Clb; Band; Church Choir; Jazz Band; Mrchg Band; Orch; Pep Band; High Hon Roll; Pre-Med/Srgn.

BURROWS, MISTY D; Bryant Sr HS; Bryant, AR; (2); Church Yth Grp; FCA; FBLA; Church Choir; Bsktbl; Trk; Hon Roll; U Of AR; Elem Ed.

BURROWS, TENNILL; Hughes Jr-Sr HS; Hughes, AR; (3); Office Aide; Science Clb; Spanish Clb; Church Choir; Sec Frsh Cls; Bus; Nrsng.

BURSE, COURTNEY S; Dewitt HS; De Witt, AR; (2); Church Yth Grp; Cmnty Wkr; Dance Clb; FCA; 4-H; FBLA; FHA; GAA; Girl Scts; Pep Clb; UAPB; Comp; Cosmetology.

BURT, RHONDA; Ft Smith Christian Schl; Fort Smith, AR; (2); 6/30; FCA; Bsktbl; Trk; High Hon Roll; NHS; Vet.

BURTON, BRENT G; Cabot HS; Cabot, AR; (4); Quiz Bowl; Spanish Clb; Jr NHS; Kiwanis Awd; NHS; Ntl Merit SF; AP Schlr; Ctzn Bee St Champ; Knwldg Mstr; Hist Clb; Multi Yr Lstng.

BURTON, BRIAN D; Abundant Life Schools; Jacksonville, AR; (2); Church Yth Grp; Drama Clb; Spanish Clb; Church Choir; U Of AR; Pre-Med.

BURTON, GREG; Bradley Jr Sr HS; Bradley, AR; (2); 4-H; FHA; Math Clb; Natl FFA Org; Quiz Bowl; Spanish Clb; Band; Rep Frsh Cls; Rep Soph Cls; Rep Stu Cncl.

BURTON, MARY BETH; Bryant Sr HS; Alexander, AR; (2); Pep Clb; Drill Tm; Ofcr Stu Cncl; Chrldng; High Hon Roll; Hon Roll; Phy Thrpst.

BURTON, SANDRA L; Heber Springs HS; Hope, AR; (3); 22/88; FCA; FBLA; Natl Beta Clb; Science Clb; Spanish Clb; Stat Bsktbl; Sftbl; Cit Awd; Hon Roll; Pres Acad Fit Awd; Sprt Awd 94; U Of A; Bus Admin.

BUSBEA, ERIN; John L Mcclellan Magnet HS; Little Rock, AR; (2); French Clb; FBLA; GAA; Girl Scts; Natl Beta Clb; Var Bsktbl; Var Chrldng; Var Crs Cntry; Var Sftbl; Var Trk; Lib, Grdn, PRIDE, Career & Intrct Clbs.

BUSHEY, LEAH; Arkansas Bapt Schl; Little Rock, AR; (3); Church Yth Grp; Cmnty Wkr; Natl Beta Clb; Church Choir; Mgr Socr; Hon Roll; Frgn Mssn Clb.

BUSHONG, MINDA V; Oak Ridge Central Schl; Imboden, AR; (2); FBLA; VP German Clb; Math Clb; Natl Beta Clb; Science Clb; Band; Sftbl; Hon Roll; Eng Mrt Awd; All Schl Ltr Awd; MADD Wrtng Cont 1st Pl 95; Scndry Ed.

BUSSELL, NICHOLAS; Brinkley HS; Brinkley, AR; (1); Church Yth Grp; Ofcr Frsh Cls; JV Bsktbl; JV Ftbl; High Hon Roll; Jr NHS.

BUSSEY, MEREDITH L; Arkansas Sr HS; Texarkana, TX; (4); 12/388; Church Yth Grp; Key Clb; Mu Alpha Theta; Q&S; Drill Tm; Ed Yrbk; Rep Stu Cncl; Vllybl; Hon Roll; NHS; Soc Stds Stu Of Yr; Stephen F Austin ST U; Med.

BUSSEY, SHANNAN H; Berryville HS; Berryville, AR; (2); Church Yth Grp; FHA; Flag Corp; Hon Roll; NHS; FHA Otstndng Sr Awd 95-; FHA Rec Ldr/Sec Yth Actv Chrstn Club 96-; Cmptrs/Acctng.

BUSTER, MONICA; Raymond E Wells Schl; Greenwood, AR; (1); Church Yth Grp; Cmnty Wkr; FCA; GAA; Office Aide; Rptr Frsh Cls; Ofcr Stu Cncl; Bsktbl; Chrldng; Var Sftbl; OK Univ; Entrnl Med.

BUTCHER, JUSTIN; Lake Hamilton Jr HS; Hot Springs, AR; (1); Church Yth Grp; FCA; FBLA; Natl Beta Clb; Natl FFA Org; Ofcr Frsh Cls; Crs Cntry; Trk; DAR Awd; Hon Roll; Cmptr Pgrmmr.

BUTLER, ARTHUR L; Rison HS; Rison, AR; (2); Art Clb; Church Yth Grp; Cmnty Wkr; FCA; FHA; Library Aide; Natl FFA Org; Science Clb; Band; Church Choir; Hlpng Elderly In Chrch Org; U Little Rock; Law Schl.

BUTLER, AUTUMN; North Little Rock HS West; North Little Rock, AR; (4); 120/427; Church Yth Grp; FCA; Q&S; Drill Tm; Stage Crew; Rep Stu Cncl; City Owned TV Station Operated HS TV Classes; Schl Musical Crew; Acad Dstnctn Tuition AR ST Univ; AR ST Univ.

BUTLER, AYANA K; Hot Springs HS; Hot Springs, AR; (2); 2/207; Natl Beta Clb; Church Choir; Sec Frsh Cls; Var Bsktbl; Chrldng; High Hon Roll; Homcmng Maid; Bio-Med Engrng.

BUTLER, BENJAMIN R; Rogers HS; Rogers, AR; (3); Boy Scts; Church Yth Grp; Science Clb; Band; Mrchg Band; Co-Ed Nwsp; Trk; High Hon Roll; Yth & Chrch League Bsktbl; Participation In Art Cmptns.

BUTLER, BEVERLY G; Fairview HS; Camden, AR; (3); 23/250; Church Yth Grp; Mu Alpha Theta; Office Aide; Band; Church Choir; Mrchg Band; French Hon Soc; Hon Roll; NHS; Region Band 95-96; SAU Magnolia; Nuclear Med Tech.

BUTLER, BRENT D; Stuttgart Sr HS; Stuttgart, AR; (3); Am Leg Boys St; Church Yth Grp; Spanish Clb; Church Choir; Cit Awd; All Region Chair; HOSA; REACH; Bio; Pre-Med.

BUTLER, BRIAN A; Benton Sr HS; Benton, AR; (3); 50/320; Church Yth Grp; Cmnty Wkr; FBLA; Key Clb; Math Clb; Teachers Aide; Church Choir; High Hon Roll; Hon Roll; Jr NHS; Chrch Yth Cncl Pres; PT.

BUTLER, DON L; North Little Rock Hs-West; North Little Rock, AR; (3); Church Yth Grp; Cmnty Wkr; Dance Clb; Drama Clb; 4-H; Speech Tm; Church Choir; School Musical; School Play; Gov Hon Prg Awd; Won Numerous Trophies In ST Tournmnts; Juilierd; Thtr.

BUTLER, ERIKA L; Sheridan Sr HS; Pine Bluff, AR; (3); Church Yth Grp; FHA; Teachers Aide; Chorus; Church Choir; Hon Roll; Jr NHS; NHS; OT.

BUTLER, GARY; John L Mcclellan Magnet HS; Little Rock, AR; (2); Church Yth Grp; Natl Beta Clb; Church Choir; Cit Awd; High Hon Roll; Hon Roll; NHS; U Of AR; Bus.

BUTLER, JAMES F; Fayetteville Christian Schl; Fayetteville, AR; (2); Church Yth Grp; Science Clb; Bsktbl; Hon Roll.

BUTLER, JENNIFER M; Waldron HS; Waldron, AR; (2); Church Yth Grp; Drama Clb; HOBY; Natl Beta Clb; Color Guard; School Play; Stage Crew; Phtg Yrbk; Hon Roll; Quachita; Psychtrst.

BUTLER, JENNIFER M; Springdale Sr HS; Springdale, AR; (1); Band; Mrchg Band; High Hon Roll; Jr NHS; U Of AR.

BUTLER, KRISTI L; Oak Grove HS; North Little Rock, AR; (3); Art Clb; Church Yth Grp; FHA; Spanish Clb; High Hon Roll; Hon Roll; Spanish NHS; Hosp Vol; UCA; OB/GYN.

BUTLER, LAVON L; Pocahontas HS; Pocahontas, AR; (3); 70/147; Church Yth Grp; FBLA; Spanish Clb; AR ST Univ; Anesthesiology.

BUTLER, MARTY; Lincoln HS; Lincoln, AR; (2); FBLA; Natl FFA Org; JV Bsbl; Var Ftbl; Wt Lftg; Cit Awd; Hon Roll; Ntl Merit Ltr; Coach.

BUTLER, NINA J; Arkadelphia Sr HS; Arkadelphia, AR; (4); VP Church Yth Grp; Dance Clb; VP FCA; FBLA; Spanish Clb; Band; Gym; Powder Puff Ftbl; Gov Hon Prg Awd; High Hon Roll; AR Governors Schl; AR Enrichment For Gftd Summer Camp 3 Yrs; U Of AR.

BUTLER, TONIKKA S; Arkansas Sr HS; Texarkana, AR; (3); DECA; FHA; Math Clb; Mu Alpha Theta; VICA; Pres Acad Fit Awd; Giftd & Tlnted; U Of AR; Acctng.

BUTLER, VERONICA; Huntsville HS; Hindsville, AR; (4); 16/120; Treas Church Yth Grp; FBLA; German Clb; Chorus; Church Choir; High Hon Roll; Hon Roll; U AR; Bus Finance.

BUTNER, MARIA; Central Ark Christian Schl; Alexander, AR; (3); 1/75; Church Yth Grp; Office Aide; Science Clb; Spanish Clb; Teachers Aide; JV Bsktbl; High Hon Roll; Jr NHS; NHS; Acpl Chr; Hist Clb.

BUTTERFIELD, CHRISTIE; Norphlet HS; El Dorado, AR; (2); 1/53; Art Clb; FBLA; Spanish Clb; Band; Sec Frsh Cls; Ofcr Stu Cncl; Hon Roll; Jr NHS; NHS; Church Yth Grp; Schltc Awd.

BUTTERFIELD, LORI J; Yellville Summit HS; Yellville, AR; (2); 3/78; Service Clb; Band; Rptr Nwsp; Crs Cntry; Sftbl; Trk; Vllybl; High Hon Roll; NHS; Prfct Atten Awd; LEO Clb Pres; Med.

BUTTRUM, KIMBERLY M; Mountain Pine Jr Sr HS; Mountain Pine, AR; (2); Phtg Yrbk; Capt Chrldng; Cit Awd; High Hon Roll; NHS; Ntl Merit Ltr; Pres Acad Fit Awd; Pres Schlr; Church Yth Grp; Hmcmng Crt; OBU; Pre Ntl/Neontl Nrsng.

BUZBEE, BARBARA R; Central Sr HS; Little Rock, AR; (3); Church Yth Grp; Drama Clb; German Clb; Mu Alpha Theta; Natl Beta Clb; JV Var Chrldng; Hon Roll; NHS; Piano; Ballet; Jazz; Tap Dance.

BUZIK, ALEX; Rogers HS; Rogers, AR; (4); 1/468; Cmnty Wkr; FBLA; HOBY; Rep Jr Cls; Rep Sr Cls; Var Socr; JV Trk; Var NHS; Ntl Merit SF; Prfct Atten Awd; Dartmouth Coll; Med.

BUZZARD, JEREMY; Caddo Hills Jr Sr HS; Glenwood, AR; (4); 4/40; Art Clb; Church Yth Grp; FBLA; Natl Beta Clb; Natl FFA Org; Red Cross Aide; Spanish Clb; Church Choir; Rptr Rep Yrbk; Rep Stu Cncl; Envglst.

BYERLY, AMANDA M; Star City HS; Monticello, AR; (4); 17/105; Church Yth Grp; French Clb; FBLA; FHA; Hosp Aide; Mu Alpha Theta; Natl Beta Clb; Office Aide; Science Clb; SADD; Jefferson Schl Of Nursing.

BYERLY, KATRINIA L; Star City HS; Monticello, AR; (2); 6/115; Church Yth Grp; Drama Clb; Mu Alpha Theta; Spanish Clb; Band; Chorus; School Musical; School Play; High Hon Roll; Jr NHS; Talent Shows, Telethons & Beauty Pageant Singer; X-Ray Tech.

BYERS, AMANDA K; Hope HS; Hope, AR; (3); 1/260; Am Leg Aux Girls St; Church Yth Grp; Hist FBLA; Natl Beta Clb; Natl FFA Org; Spanish Clb; Church Choir; Chrmn Jr Cls; Bsktbl; Sftbl; Hnry Bausch/Lomb Sci Awd From Sci Tchrs 11th Grd; Navy Natl Awd; Played Piano 10 Yrs; UCA Of Conway; Nrsng.

BYFORD, SAMANTHA E; Waldron HS; Waldron, AR; (2); Art Clb; GAA; Spanish Clb; VP Soph Cls; Trk; Vllybl; Hon Roll; Keyboarding Awd; AR Tech; Crmnl Psych.

BYINGTON, CRYSTAL D; Bryant Sr HS; Bryant, AR; (2); Church Yth Grp; Cmnty Wkr; FBLA; Chorus; Church Choir; Nwsp; Yrbk; Hon Roll; Widelife Tech; Jrnlsm.

BYNDOM, TALISHA L; John L Mcclellan Magnet HS; Little Rock, AR; (4); 26/255; Drama Clb; FHA; Math Clb; Mu Alpha Theta; Office Aide; SADD; Church Choir; Drill Tm; School Play; Yrbk; DECA Sec; SECME; Univ Of AR; Bus Admin.

BYRD, JASON R; Bald Knob HS; Judsonia, AR; (1); Natl Beta Clb; Band; Mrchg Band; Pep Band; High Hon Roll; Hon Roll; AR ST Univ.

BYRD, MARK; Nettleton HS; Jonesboro, AR; (3); Natl Beta Clb; Science Clb; Chorus; School Play; Ofcr Bsbl; Bsktbl; Golf; Wt Lftg; Hon Roll; AR ST Univ; Bus Mgmt.

BYRNE, LENA; Farmington Jr Sr HS; Farmington, AR; (2); FBLA; Natl FFA Org; VP Pres Frsh Cls; Rep Soph Cls; Rep Stu Cncl; Hon Roll; Jr NHS; NHS; Equine Sci.

CAAGBAY, DON E; Ozark Adventist Acad; Oklahoma City, OK; (3); Church Yth Grp; Band; Chorus; Treas Jr Cls; VP Stu Cncl; JV Bsktbl; Capt Vllybl; Hon Roll; NHS; Prfct Atten Awd; Sthrn Adventist Col; Bus Mktng.

CAGLE, AMBER D; Crowleys Ridge Acad; Paragould, AR; (1); Church Yth Grp; Spanish Clb; Rep Stu Cncl; Bsktbl; Vllybl.

CAGLE, BRITTANY; Camden Fairview HS; Camden, AR; (2); Church Yth Grp; Drama Clb; Natl Beta Clb; Science Clb; Acpl Chr; Sec Frsh Cls; Intrml JV Chrldng; Intrml Gym; Hon Roll; Anchor Club; U Of AR Monticello; Phys Thrpy.

CAGLE, DARIUS Z; Bryant Sr HS; Alexander, AR; (2).

CAGLE, HILARY J; West Memphis Sr HS; West Memphis, AR; (4); 6/265; Am Leg Aux Girls St; FBLA; Mu Alpha Theta; VP Natl Beta Clb; Chorus; Stage Crew; Ed Yrbk; High Hon Roll; Hon Roll; Pres Acad Fit Awd; U Central AR; Occptnl Thrpy.

CAGLE, MONICA A; Clarksville HS; Clarksville, AR; (2); Drama Clb; Hosp Aide; Spanish Clb; Rptr Nwsp; Hon Roll; Bldrs Club.

CAHOON, MICHAEL W; Nettleton HS; Jonesboro, AR; (2); Boy Scts; Church Yth Grp; FBLA; Spanish Clb; Chorus; School Play; Ftbl; Powder Puff Ftbl; Tennis; Stdnt Glider Pilot; Mock Law Tm.

CAINS, CHRISTINE E; Russellville Sr HS; Russellville, AR; (2); Church Yth Grp; Spanish Clb; Band; Mrchg Band; Pep Band; Socr; High Hon Roll; Hon Roll; Jr NHS; NHS.

CALAMESE, DARREN; Parkview Arts Sciences Magnet; Little Rock, AR; (4); 27/261; German Clb; Library Aide; Math Clb; Math Tm; Mu Alpha Theta; Natl Beta Clb; Quiz Bowl; Band; Yrbk.

CALDWELL, ASHLEY; Parkin Jr Sr HS; Parkin, AR; (4); 3/33; Church Yth Grp; FHA; Hosp Aide; JA; Natl Beta Clb; Science Clb; Teachers Aide; Sec Frsh Cls; Sec Soph Cls; Rep Jr Cls; Gama Beta Phi; EACE ASU; PT.

CALDWELL, JAKE A; Junction City HS; Junction City, AR; (3); Church Yth Grp; Science Clb; VP Jr Cls; Ftbl; Hon Roll; NHS; LA Tech.

CALDWELL, JENNIFER A; Southside HS; Fort Smith, AR; (3); 15/502; Church Yth Grp; Hosp Aide; Mu Alpha Theta; Vllybl; Hon Roll; NHS; Ntl Merit Ltr.

CALDWELL, JENNIFER L; Mt St Mary Acad; Little Rock, AR; (3); French Clb; Acpl Chr; Chorus; School Play; French Hon Soc; Hon Roll; Alternate AR Governors Schl 96; AR Close-Up Prtcpnt 95; Natl Yth Svc Day Prtcpnt 96.

CALDWELL, KORIE; Yerger Jr HS; Hope, AR; (1); Church Yth Grp; Dance Clb; Natl Beta Clb; Variety Show; Rep Stu Cncl; JV Chrldng; Gym; Hon Roll; Pres Acad Fit Awd; Duke.

CALDWELL, TANYA M; Poyen Schl; Leola, AR; (2); Church Yth Grp; FCA; Spanish Clb; Teachers Aide; Sec Frsh Cls; Chrldng; Hon Roll; Henderson ST Univ; Cmptr Tech.

CALDWELL, TREVER; Hackett Schl; Fort Smith, AR; (1); 2/50; Church Yth Grp; FBLA; FHA; Spanish Clb; Band; Church Choir; Ofcr Stu Cncl; Jr NHS; Prof Mdl; Bwlng; Med.

CALHOUN, BRAD D; Lake Hamilton Sr HS; Pearcy, AR; (3); Church Yth Grp; FBLA; Natl Beta Clb; Natl FFA Org; Science Clb; Spanish Clb; Yrbk; Ftbl; Trk; Cit Awd.

CALHOUN, LESLIE A; Jonesboro HS; Jonesboro, AR; (2); French Clb; Key Clb; Chorus; Var L Bsktbl; Var L Vllybl.

CALLAHAN, AMBER L; Searcy HS; Searcy, AR; (2); Church Yth Grp; Cmnty Wkr; French Clb; Hosp Aide; Office Aide; SADD; Chorus; Ed Yrbk; Tennis; Cit Awd; Yth To Yth; White Cty Sheriffs Office Vol; Del To Natl Ldrshp Forum Spnsrd By Optimist Clb Of Searcy; Quachita Bapt U; Law Enforcmnt.

CALLAHAN, JEFF A; Clarksville HS; Clarksville, AR; (3); FBLA; Natl Beta Clb; Chorus; Hon Roll; Prfct Atten Awd; Tutoring; Ftbl; Bsbl; Swim; Play Pool; AR Tech Univ; Electrncs.

CALLAHAN, SAMANTHA S; Black Rock Jr Sr HS; Black Rock, AR; (1); 1/50; Church Yth Grp; FBLA; FHA; Model UN; Natl Beta Clb; Church Choir; Ofcr Stu Cncl; Bsktbl; Sftbl; High Hon Roll; U Of AR; Med.

CALLAWAY, SUSAN G; Dierks HS; Dierks, AR; (1); 3/56; FHA; Quiz Bowl; Yrbk; Rep Stu Cncl; Bsktbl; Sftbl; Trk; Hon Roll; Amers Pride; Marine Bio.

CALLOWAY, RASHENDA L; Arkansas Sr HS; Texarkana, AR; (4); 57/374; Am Leg Aux Girls St; Girl Scts; Hosp Aide; Math Clb; Mu Alpha Theta; Office Aide; Quiz Bowl; Spanish Clb; Band; Church Choir; U Of Central AR; Psych.

CALVERT, JENNIFER; Prairie Grove HS; Prairie Grove, AR; (3); Quiz Bowl; Spanish Clb; Speech Tm; Band; Color Guard; Drill Tm; Chrldng; Sftbl; High Hon Roll; NHS; U Of AR; Pediatrician.

CALVIN, TERENATA; Morrilton Sr HS; Plumerville, AR; (2); French Clb; FHA; GAA; Natl Beta Clb; Rep Frsh Cls; Bsktbl; Sftbl; Hon Roll; Memphis ST U; Exec Acntng.

CAMARILLO, DIANA E; Dequeen HS; De Queen, AR; (1); Church Yth Grp; Trk; U Of TX.

CAMERON, CHRISTINA R; Ozark HS; Ozark, AR; (3); Church Yth Grp; Drama Clb; FBLA; FHA; Intnl Clb; Natl Beta Clb; Office Aide; Acpl Chr; Chorus; Church Choir; Psych.

CAMERON, CHRISTOPHER M; Yellville Summit HS; Yellville, AR; (2); English Clb; FCA; Math Clb; School Play; Var L Bsbl; Var L Ftbl; Socr; Trk; Wt Lftg; Hon Roll; Stu Of Month; Ftbl.

CAMERON, DEVON K; Springdale Sr HS; Springdale, AR; (1); Church Yth Grp; Band; Church Choir; Color Guard; Mrchg Band; Hon Roll; Jr NHS; Stu Ministry Team; Yth For Christ; John Brown Univ.

CAMET, CORYN; Southside HS; Fort Smith, AR; (3); 26/502; Mu Alpha Theta; Band; Pom Pon; High Hon Roll; NHS; Pres Acad Fit Awd; 7th Pl ST Natl Span Exam; SAIL; Pre Law.

CAMP, CHARISSE A; Oak Grove HS; Little Rock, AR; (3); Am Leg Aux Girls St; Church Yth Grp; FBLA; FHA; Science Clb; Spanish Clb; Church Choir; Hon Roll; Dist Champs Mock Trial; Pediatrics.

CAMP, KATHLEEN J; Mountain Home HS; Mountain Home, AR; (3); Church Yth Grp; FCA; FTA; Spanish Clb; Teachers Aide; Capt Chrldng.

CAMP, KELLI M; Star City HS; Star City, AR; (2); Church Yth Grp; Mu Alpha Theta; Natl Beta Clb; Teachers Aide; Band; Church Choir; Jazz Band; Mrchg Band; Mgr(s); Hon Roll; Comm Sftbl; FL ST Univ; Phy Thrpst.

CAMP, MEGAN; Weiner HS; Weiner, AR; (4); 12/28; Church Yth Grp; FBLA; FHA; FTA; Natl FFA Org; Pep Clb; Spanish Clb; Drm Mjr(t); Phtg Yrbk; VP Frsh Cls; Wakeup Clb; FHA Pres; Horticulture Jdng Team 4 Yrs; UCA; Early Chldhd Dev.

CAMPBELL, ANNETTE M; Benton Sr HS; Benton, AR; (3); French Clb; Key Clb; Math Clb; Spanish Clb; Rep Stu Cncl; JV Var Chrldng; High Hon Roll; Jr NHS; Kiwanis Awd; Pres Acad Fit Awd; Reg Sci Fiar 3rd Plc Hlth/Med Div; 1st Plc Schl Sci Fair; Baylor Univ; Pol Sci/Chem Engr.

CAMPBELL, BRIAN L; Springdale Sr HS; Springdale, AR; (1); FBLA; Chorus; Gov Hon Prg Awd; High Hon Roll; Hon Roll; Jr NHS; Pres Schlr; Yth For Christ; Med Dr; Surgeon.

CAMPBELL, CRYSTAL D; Lake Hamilton Sr HS; Pearcy, AR; (2); Chorus; Bsktbl; RN.

CAMPBELL, ERICA; Beebe Sr HS; Beebe, AR; (2); Church Yth Grp; Natl Beta Clb; Band; Mrchg Band; Pharmacist.

CAMPBELL, JENNIFER; Bismarck Jr-Sr HS; Bismarck, AR; (4); 5/67; Art Clb; Bus Profs of Am; FCA; Sec FBLA; Sec FHA; FTA; Math Clb; Natl Beta Clb; Quiz Bowl; Teachers Aide; Vol Work; Henderson ST U; Nrsng.

CAMPBELL, JORDAN T; Fountain Lake Jr Sr HS; Hot Springs Natl, AR; (2); Art Clb; Church Yth Grp; Quiz Bowl; Spanish Clb; Hon Roll; Pres Schlr; VP Expl Post 7; Future Prob Slvrs Regnl Finlst; Raising Capuchin Mnky For Helping Hands; Rhodes; Pharm.

CAMPBELL, JULIE; Sylvan Hills HS; Sherwood, AR; (1); Church Yth Grp; Chorus; Church Choir; Ofcr Stu Cncl; Chrldng; Hon Roll; Jr NHS; Care Bears Sec; Univ Of Cntrl AR; PT.

CAMPBELL, LA SHANNA D; Central HS; West Helena, AR; (2); Church Yth Grp; ROTC; Varsity Clb; Chorus; Color Guard; Drill Tm; Vllybl; Chrch Choir Pres; RN; LPN.

CAMPBELL, MOLLY S; Magnolia HS; Magnolia, AR; (2); 4-H; Teachers Aide; Sftbl; Vllybl; Tae Kwon Do; Southern AR Univ; Med.

CAMPBELL, RANDI; Delight HS; Delight, AR; (4); 4/23; Cmnty Wkr; FBLA; Quiz Bowl; School Play; Sec Frsh Cls; Sec Soph Cls; Sec Jr Cls; Sec Sr Cls; Rep Stu Cncl; Chrldng; FFA; Adv Math Awd; Adv Eng Awd; Hendrix Coll; Marine Bio.

CAMPBELL, ROBBY; Bergman Schl; Harrison, AR; (3); Rptr FBLA; Natl Beta Clb; Spanish Clb; Teachers Aide; Ed Yrbk; Tennis; Hon Roll; Jr NHS; NHS; Prfct Atten Awd; MO Southern ST Coll; Eng; His.

CAMPBELL, ROY D; Conway Sr HS; Conway, AR; (3); Art Clb; Church Yth Grp; Socr; Awd Algebra Stu Of The Yr; U Of AR; Photo; Drafting.

CAMPBELL, STEPHANIE; Dumas HS; Dumas, AR; (2); FBLA; Girl Scts; Band; Yrbk; Cit Awd; High Hon Roll; Hon Roll; NHS; Pres Acad Fit Awd.

CAMPBELL, TITUS P; Valley Springs Schl; Harrison, AR; (4); 3/51; Boy Scts; Church Yth Grp; French Clb; Teachers Aide; Band; Pep Band; School Play; Ofcr Soph Cls; 4-H Awd; High Hon Roll.

CAMPER, NATHANIEL; Brinkley HS; Brinkley, AR; (4); Am Leg Boys St; Church Yth Grp; Cmnty Wkr; Debate Tm; Drama Clb; French Clb; Science Clb; SADD; Church Choir; School Play; Mech Engrng.

CANADA, JON; Southside HS; Fort Smith, AR; (2); Church Yth Grp; Key Clb; Math Clb; Mu Alpha Theta; Quiz Bowl; Jr NHS; NHS; Pres Acad Fit Awd; Stu Of Yr 95; Pre-Med.

CANADA, MONICA R; Dumas HS; Little Rock, AR; (4); 48/158; FBLA; FHA; FTA; Church Choir; Hon Roll; ITT Tech Col; Elec Eng Tech.

CANADA, TASHANDA; Pine Bluff HS; Pine Bluff, AR; (3); 73/481; Art Clb; Church Yth Grp; Cmnty Wkr; Debate Tm; FHA; Hosp Aide; Office Aide; Spanish Clb; Teachers Aide; Band; Cncrt Band; Med.

CANADY, LORI A; Huttig Schl; Huttig, AR; (3); FHA; FTA; Natl Beta Clb; High Hon Roll; Pharmacy; Nrsng.

CANADY, TRATINA R; Morrilton Sr HS; Morrilton, AR; (2); Church Yth Grp; GAA; Church Choir; JV Vllybl; Natl Hnr Rl.

CANALICHIO, LAURA J; Bryant Sr HS; Alexander, AR; (2); Church Yth Grp; Dance Clb; Teachers Aide; Sftbl; Cit Awd; Hon Roll; Jr NHS; CHAMPS; FBI Spcl Agent.

CANANT, NICK; Perryville Jr Sr HS; Perryville, AR; (3); 1/80; Am Leg Boys St; FCA; JA; Quiz Bowl; Band; Mrchg Band; Sec Soph Cls; Var L Bsbl; Var L Ftbl; Var L Wt Lftg; Ftbl Coaches Awd.

CANARD, NATALIE; Mtn View HS; Mountain View, AR; (3); 10/60; Am Leg Aux Girls St; Church Yth Grp; Natl Beta Clb; Spanish Clb; Band; Mrchg Band; Pep Band; Var Chrldng; High Hon Roll; Pres Acad Fit Awd; UCA; Marine Bio.

CANGIALOSI, MICHELE L; Beebe Sr HS; Beebe, AR; (2); Church Yth Grp; Drama Clb; FBLA; Pep Clb; Spanish Clb; Chorus; School Play; Yth Psycht.

CANITZ, JENIFER M; Dardanelle HS; Dardanelle, AR; (3); 7/100; Drama Clb; FBLA; Natl Beta Clb; Drill Tm; School Play; Ed Nwsp; Tennis; Trk; High Hon Roll; Church Yth Grp; Vc Dmcrcy Essay Cont 1st Pl; Brdcst Jrnlsm.

CANNADY, ELIZABETH N; Corning HS; Corning, AR; (3); Church Yth Grp; FCA; FBLA; Pres Frsh Cls; Pres Soph Cls; Pres Jr Cls; Pres Stu Cncl; Bsktbl; Chrldng; Trk; PRIDE Group Against Drugs; First Bapt Chrch Yth Group; Ambassador.

CANNON, ASHLEY; Murfreesboro HS; Murfreesboro, AR; (4); 6/39; Am Leg Aux Girls St; Church Yth Grp; Cmnty Wkr; Ed Phtg Yrbk; Pres Sr Cls; Hon Roll; FBLA; Pres FHA; Pep Clb; Red Cross Aide; 95-96 Homcmng Qn; FHA Dist Pres, St Prlmntrn; U Cntrl AR; Vet.

CANNON, KRISTEN; Bradley Jr Sr HS; Bradley, AR; (2); Pres FHA; Rptr Math Clb; Quiz Bowl; Spanish Clb; Band; Sec Soph Cls; Sftbl; Cit Awd; High Hon Roll; Pres Acad Fit Awd.

CANODE, EMILY A; Rogers HS; Rogers, AR; (3); FBLA; Color Guard; Mrchg Band; Orch; Nwsp; VP Sr Cls; Pom Pon; Var Sftbl; High Hon Roll; NHS; GEO Clb; Medicine.

CANTRELL, JOSH; Amity Jr Sr HS; Amity, AR; (1); 1/12; Sec Church Yth Grp; FHA; Pres Natl Beta Clb; Natl FFA Org; Quiz Bowl; Nwsp; Pres Frsh Cls; Rptr Stu Cncl; Ofcr Bsbl; Bsktbl; Ram Schlr Prgm; Henderson ST U.

CANTRELL, JUSTIN; Amity Jr Sr HS; Amity, AR; (4); 7/15; Church Yth Grp; FBLA; FHA; Natl Beta Clb; Pres Natl FFA Org; School Play; VP Jr Cls; Pres Sr Cls; Pres Stu Cncl; Var Capt Bsbl; FFA Grnhnd Awd; Amity FFA Vol Sr Ctzn Prgm; Henderson ST U; Bus Mgmt.

CANTRELL, LEAH; Arkansas Schl Math & Science; Rison, AR; (4); Am Leg Aux Girls St; Church Yth Grp; FCA; Mu Alpha Theta; Natl Beta Clb; Yrbk; Treas Stu Cncl; Capt Chrldng; Hon Roll; NHS; U Of Central AR; Dentistry.

CANTRELL, MICHAEL; Morrilton Sr HS; Plumerville, AR; (2); Church Yth Grp; Math Clb; Natl Beta Clb; Office Aide; Science Clb; Spanish Clb; Ftbl; DAR Awd; High Hon Roll; Pres Acad Fit Awd; Polysci.

CAPANESCU, CRISTINA; Jonesboro HS; Jonesboro, AR; (4); 1/292; FBLA; Hosp Aide; Pres Math Clb; Mu Alpha Theta; Treas Natl Beta Clb; Capt Quiz Bowl; Tennis; High Hon Roll; Hon Roll; Pres Acad Fit Awd; Intl Optimist Clb Awd Svc, Lifeguard; Rotary Clb Outstndng Schlr Awd; Brd Of Educ Outstndng Schlr Awd; Phy.

CAPERTON, JENNIFER L; Southside HS; Fort Smith, AR; (2); Church Yth Grp; Chorus; Hon Roll; Jr NHS; NHS; Pres Awd 95; OK ST Univ; Arch.

CAPLE, JENNIFER; Glen Rose HS; Benton, AR; (2); FCA; FBLA; Math Clb; Natl Beta Clb; Science Clb; Spanish Clb; Sec Stu Cncl; Chrldng; High Hon Roll; Pres Acad Fit Awd; Elem Chrldng Coach; Elem Ed.

CAPPER, REBECCA; Farmington Jr Sr HS; Fayetteville, AR; (1); Church Yth Grp; FHA; Band; Mrchg Band; Pep Band; High Hon Roll; Hon Roll; Jr NHS; All-Rgn Bnd; Lrmntry Proc Tm.

CAPPS, SHAWNA M; Riverview HS; Griffithville, AR; (2); Church Yth Grp; Drama Clb; French Clb; FHA; VP Pres Natl Beta Clb; Natl FFA Org; Chorus; Ed Yrbk; Hon Roll; Radier Clb Cncl; U Of Cntrl AR Conway.

CARBONARO, NATALIE A; Parkview Arts-Science HS; Little Rock, AR; (2); Church Yth Grp; Dance Clb; FBLA; German Clb; Hosp Aide; Natl Beta Clb; Rptr Nwsp; Var Chrldng; High Hon Roll; Jr NHS.

CARBONERO, LOUIS M; Monticello HS; Monticello, AR; (3); Church Yth Grp; French Clb; FBLA; Natl Beta Clb; Office Aide; Science Clb; Church Choir; Hon Roll; AR Army Natl Guard; Ouachita Bapt Univ; Cmptr Sci.

CARD, ROBIN E; Berryville HS; Berryville, AR; (2); Girl Scts; Science Clb; Spanish Clb; Band; Mrchg Band; Pep Band; Rep Frsh Cls; Cit Awd; High Hon Roll; Hon Roll; Piano; Flute; Region Band; Dance; John Philip Sousa Awd; Young Democrats Clb; Bio.

CARDEN, DE WAYNE; East End Jr Sr HS; Bigelow, AR; (1); 4/50; Church Yth Grp; Cmnty Wkr; Natl Beta Clb; Bsktbl; Ftbl; Wt Lftg; High Hon Roll.

CARDEN, WHITNEY C; Fayetteville Sr HS; Fayetteville, AR; (3); 119/480; Boy Scts; Cmnty Wkr; Science Clb; SADD; Ftbl; Var L Socr; Trk; Hon Roll; Eagle Scout; Order Arrow; Explr Scout; Soccer Tm ST Champs; Hike; Rockclimb; Marine Bio/Var Coll Soccer.

CARDWELL, LAUREN A; Southside HS; Fort Smith, AR; (2); Church Yth Grp; FHA; Key Clb; Latin Clb; Drill Tm; Hon Roll; Phys Therapy.

CAREY, NICOLE J; Mills HS; Little Rock, AR; (3); 78/28; Cmnty Wkr; Debate Tm; French Clb; FHA; Teachers Aide; Chorus; JV Var Vllybl; Hon Roll; TAG Prgm; 1st Pl Cem 95- Sci Fair; 2nd Pl Chem 94-95 Sci Fair; Henderson ST Univ; Tchr.

CARGILE, JAMIE; Nashville HS; Nashville, AR; (3); 11/145; Church Yth Grp; Sec FBLA; Office Aide; Quiz Bowl; VP Spanish Clb; Church Choir; School Play; Nwsp; Yrbk; Hon Roll; Natl Guild Auditions Piano; Del Girls ST AR 96; U Of Cntrl AR Conway; Pre Med.

CARLE, LAURA T; El Dorado Sr HS; El Dorado, AR; (4); Cmnty Wkr; Drama Clb; FBLA; FHA; Teachers Aide; Thesps; School Musical; School Play; Stage Crew; Variety Show; Thespian Exec Bd; Hnr Thespian; LA Tech Univ; Theater.

CARLISLE, CHRIS; Bryant Sr HS; Mabelvale, AR; (3); Am Leg Boys St; Boy Scts; Office Aide; Pep Clb; Science Clb; Jazz Band; Pep Band; Jr NHS; Ntl Merit SF; Drama Clb; HS Heroes; U Of AR.

CARMAN, CYNDI; Northside HS; Fort Smith, AR; (2); Church Yth Grp; FCA; Girl Scts; Red Cross Aide; Spanish Clb; Band; Chorus; Mrchg Band; School Play; Rptr Nwsp; Lifeguard; All Star Chrldng Squad Flame Gymnstcs/Gymnstcs; U AR; Phyclgy.

CARNES, MISTY L; Sheridan Sr HS; Sheridan, AR; (4); 5/285; Church Yth Grp; Cmnty Wkr; FCA; 4-H; GAA; Natl FFA Org; SADD; L Bsktbl; L Trk; L Vllybl; Pres AR HS Rodeo Assoc; Pres Natl Hnr Soc; Pres FFA; TX A&M Univ; Molecular Bio.

CARNEY, PENNY; Hermitage Jr Sr HS; Warren, AR; (2); Church Yth Grp; Dance Clb; HOBY; Natl FFA Org; Band; Church Choir; Flag Corp; Mrchg Band; Variety Show; Yrbk; Human Dev Ctr Rec Actvts Vlntr; Local Bueaty Conts; Barrel Racng & Pole Bending; Light House Church; U Of AR Monticello.

CARNICE, TELISHA A; England HS; England, AR; (3); Art Clb; FHA; Spanish Clb; Hon Roll; Eng Awd; Nrs.

CARPENTER, ANNA; Arkansas Schl Math & Science; Hot Springs, AR; (3); Church Yth Grp; Cmnty Wkr; FBLA; HOBY; Model UN; Natl Beta Clb; Church Choir; Flag Corp; Mrchg Band; Rptr Nwsp.

CARPENTER, KRISTY; Delight HS; Delight, AR; (3); Church Yth Grp; FBLA; Natl Beta Clb; Natl FFA Org; Rep Stu Cncl; FFA Dairy Foods St Wnnr.

CARPENTER, MATTHEW L; Southside HS; Batesville, AR; (1); Art Clb; Quiz Bowl; Science Clb; Teachers Aide; Ofcr Stu Cncl; Chrldng; Golf; Tennis; Hon Roll; St Schlr; Comp; Art; Comp.

CARPENTER, SHERYL E; Huntsville HS; Huntsville, AR; (4); 13/120; VP Sec Chorus; Rptr Frsh Cls; Rptr Soph Cls; Rptr Jr Cls; Rptr Sr Cls; Rptr Stu Cncl; High Hon Roll; Hon Roll; NHS; Prfct Atten Awd; St Choir Cmptn; United Campus Chrstn Minstries Sec; Northwest Tech Inst; Bus.

CARR, CALLIE A; Monticello HS; Monticello, AR; (3); Church Yth Grp; 4-H; FHA; Natl Beta Clb; Office Aide; Spanish Clb; SADD; Acpl Chr; Chorus; 4-H Awd; Rodeo Clb Sec/Pres; Minds In Motion Awd; U Of AR; Agri Bus.

CARR, CINDY; Gosnell Jr HS; Blytheville, AR; (1); Chrldng.

CARRELL, JENNIFER; Horatio HS; Winthrop, AR; (2); Art Clb; Church Yth Grp; 4-H; French Clb; FHA; Natl FFA Org; Office Aide; Acpl Chr; Cit Awd; Hon Roll; FIN Trnsctns.

CARRIGAN, RELISSA M; Cave City HS; Cave City, AR; (2); Church Yth Grp; Cmnty Wkr; Computer Clb; English Clb; 4-H; FBLA; FHA; FTA; JA; Natl Beta Clb; AR ST Univ; Elem Ed.

CARROLL, ALINDRIA; Pine Bluff HS; Pine Bluff, AR; (3); Hosp Aide; Band; Orch; Sec Jr Cls; Var Chrldng; NHS; Pres Acad Fit Awd; Pres Schlr; Church Yth Grp; French Clb; AR Governors Schl; Girls ST Del; Xavier Univ; Bio; Pre-Med.

CARROLL, ANGEL C; Dewitt HS; De Witt, AR; (3); Church Yth Grp; FCA; FBLA; FTA; GAA; Natl Beta Clb; Science Clb; Church Choir; Bsktbl; Hon Roll; Chrch Pptrs; Law.

CARROLL, ASHLEY; Ft Smith Christian Schl; Fort Smith, AR; (3); Church Yth Grp; FCA; Church Choir; Sec Frsh Cls; Sec Soph Cls; Var L Bsktbl; Var L Chrldng; Var L Trk; High Hon Roll; NHS.

CARROLL, GINA; Murfreesboro HS; Murfreesboro, AR; (4); 2/39; Am Leg Aux Girls St; VP Church Yth Grp; FBLA; VP FHA; Natl Beta Clb; Science Clb; Spanish Clb; Co-Ed Yrbk; VP Stu Cncl; Capt Chrldng; Cty Yth Brd; Peer Ldrshp Tm.

CARROLL, JASON C; Bright Star Schl; Doddridge, AR; (4); Church Yth Grp; Cmnty Wkr; English Clb; FBLA; Spanish Clb; Church Choir; Yrbk; Ofcr Jr Cls; Crs Cntry; Mgr(s); Sthrn AR U; Phy Ther.

CARROLL, JENNIFER; Maynard Jr Sr HS; Maynard, AR; (4); 7/29; Am Leg Aux Girls St; Pres French Clb; FBLA; HOBY; Natl Beta Clb; Rptr Sr Cls; Pres Stu Cncl; Var Capt Bsktbl; Chess Clb; Church Yth Grp; Ldrs Only Grp; Bsktbl All Conf; UCA; Cmmnctns.

CARROLL, JOSH L; Bright Star Schl; Doddridge, AR; (3); Church Yth Grp; FBLA; Natl FFA Org; Church Choir; Ofcr Soph Cls; Rep Stu Cncl; Bsktbl; Mgr(s); Score Keeper; Sftbl; Hosp Admin.

CARRUTH, FELICIA Y; J A Fair Sr HS; Little Rock, AR; (2); Church Yth Grp; Drama Clb; French Clb; Band; Church Choir; Drill Tm; Bsktbl; Chrldng; SECME; Ladys Clb; FL ST Univ; Rec Phy Thrpst.

CARSON, BRANDI; Gosnell Jr Sr HS; Blytheville, AR; (3); Church Yth Grp; Drama Clb; FHA; Key Clb; Natl Beta Clb; Science Clb; Spanish Clb; SADD; Band; Chorus; Psych.

CARSON, CHRISTINA L; North Little Rock Hs-West; North Little Rock, AR; (3); Debate Tm; FCA; Acpl Chr; Ofcr Stu Cncl; Chrldng; Powder Puff Ftbl; Sftbl; Hon Roll; Jr NHS; NHS; PT/OT.

CARSON, JAMES; Little Rock Cntrl HS; Sherwood, AR; (3); 34/540; German Clb; Natl Beta Clb; Quiz Bowl; Ofcr Frsh Cls; Golf; Socr; High Hon Roll; Jr NHS; NHS; Pres Acad Fit Awd; Scnd Dgr Blcblt Taekwondo Asst Instr.

CARSON, JEREMY L; Junction City HS; El Dorado, AR; (1); Church Yth Grp; FBLA; Quiz Bowl; Band; JV Bsktbl; High Hon Roll; BASIC; Dr.

CARSON, KEITH A; Junction City HS; El Dorado, AR; (3); 2/54; Treas FBLA; Capt Quiz Bowl; Science Clb; Spanish Clb; School Play; Co-Ed Yrbk; Var Trk; High Hon Roll; NHS; Ntl Merit Ltr; BASIL; Woodmen Of The World Awd; Comp Engr.

CARSON, TERESA L; Huntsville HS; Witter, AR; (2); 20/154; Church Yth Grp; FCA; FBLA; FTA; Science Clb; Treas Soph Cls; Rep Stu Cncl; Bsktbl; High Hon Roll; United Chrstn Campus Ministry; ATU; Elem Educ.

CARTER, ALMEITA KIMBERLY; Searcy HS; Searcy, AR; (3); Church Yth Grp; Natl Beta Clb; Science Clb; Thesps; Band; Mrchg Band; School Musical; NHS; Spanish NHS; All Reg Band 2 Yrs; All ST Band 1 Yr; Engrng/Meterlgy.

CARTER, AMY A; Crossett Sr HS; Crossett, AR; (3); Art Clb; Church Yth Grp; Spanish Clb; Stdnts For Christ; Future Edctrs Of Amer; Mem Of Pleasant Lane Bapt Chrch; U Of AR Monticello.

CARTER, BETH ANNELLE; Rogers HS; Rogers, AR; (3); 3/600; Am Leg Aux Girls St; Church Yth Grp; FCA; Band; Drm Mjr(t); Mgr(s); Hon Roll; NHS; Hosp Aide; Intnl Clb; Chrstns In Actn; Piano; Baylor Univ; Elem Ed.

CARTER, BRENT D; Mulberry HS; Mulberry, AR; (3); 3/32; FCA; Office Aide; Science Clb; Rep Sr Cls; Ofcr Bsbl; Bsktbl; Golf; Score Keeper; Tennis; Trk; Bsktbl All-Dist Best Defensive Player; Bsbl Stolen Base Ldr; Tnns Mst Outstdng Singles; Westark; Bus.

CARTER, DAVID W; Springdale Sr HS; Springdale, AR; (3); FCA; 4-H; VICA; Ofcr Bsbl; Bsktbl; Ftbl; Golf; Wt Lftg; Hon Roll; Prfct Atten Awd; Hunting; Taxidermy; Restoring Old Cars; Abilene Chstn Univ; Coach.

CARTER, HEATHER L; De Soto Schl; West Helena, AR; (3); Church Yth Grp; Drama Clb; GAA; Spanish Clb; Thesps; Varsity Clb; Sec Soph Cls; Sec Jr Cls; JV Bsktbl; Var Chrldng; U Of MS; Pre-Med; Phy.

CARTER, HILLARY D; Russellville Sr HS; Russellville, AR; (2); Church Yth Grp; Hosp Aide; Band; Mrchg Band; High Hon Roll; Hon Roll; Jr NHS; NHS; Pres Acad Fit Awd; Psych.

CARTER, JANNA L; Lee Acad; Marianna, AR; (3); SADD; Yrbk; Bsktbl; Sftbl; Hon Roll; NHS; Outstndng Stu; Chcm Awd; Sftbl All Conf; AR ST U.

CARTER, JEFFERSON C; Russellville Sr HS; Russellville, AR; (2); 131/405; Church Yth Grp; Natl Beta Clb; Var Bsktbl; Var Ftbl; NW AR Jr HS Reg Bsktbl All Trnmnt Tm 95; Bus Ownr.

CARTER, JENNIFER; Perryville Jr Sr HS; Perryville, AR; (3); Cmnty Wkr; FCA; FBLA; Spanish Clb; Teachers Aide; Var Bsktbl; DAR Awd; High Hon Roll; Jr NHS; NHS; U MS; Math.

CARTER, JILL A; Fouke Jr Sr HS; Fouke, AR; (3); 8/90; Rptr FBLA; Library Aide; Natl Beta Clb; Natl FFA Org; Spanish Clb; Ed Nwsp; JV Chrldng; High Hon Roll; Hon Roll; Amer Schlr; Mock Trial.

CARTER, KARA D; Robinson HS; Little Rock, AR; (3); Art Clb; French Clb; VICA; French Hon Soc; Gov Hon Prg Awd; High Hon Roll; NHS; Pres Acad Fit Awd.

CARTER, KELLI L; Des Arc Jr Sr HS; Des Arc, AR; (2); Natl Beta Clb; Science Clb; Rep Frsh Cls; Pres Soph Cls; JV Bsktbl; JV Chrldng; JV Trk; Hon Roll; Miss DAHS; Miss Prairie Co; Miss Steamboat Days; ASU.

CARTER, KIMBERLY S; Parkview Arts-Science HS; North Little Rock, AR; (3); Art Clb; Church Yth Grp; FBLA; German Clb; Natl Beta Clb; Science Clb; Church Choir; Cit Awd; High Hon Roll; Jr NHS; U Of Washington; Marine Bio.

CARTER, KRISTY; North Little Rock Hs-West; North Little Rock, AR; (3); 141/650; Drama Clb; FCA; Key Clb; Spanish Clb; School Play; Rep Stu Cncl; Capt Chrldng; JV Powder Puff Ftbl; JV Sftbl; Hon Roll; All Amer Chrldr 95, All Star Chrldr 92-94; U AR Fayetteville; Interior Ds.

CARTER, MICHAEL C; Mountain Home HS; Lakeview, AR; (3); Church Yth Grp; FBLA; FHA; Key Clb; Office Aide; Spanish Clb; Band; Church Choir; School Musical; School Play; UCA; Psych/Soc Wrk.

CARTER, MYESHIA J; North Little Rock Hs-West; North Little Rock, AR; (4); 131/439; Church Yth Grp; Debate Tm; FCA; Natl Beta Clb; Speech Tm; Band; School Musical; School Play; Trk; Vllybl; Tri-M; U Of Cntrl AR.

CARTER, NICOLE; Dumas Jr HS; Dumas, AR; (1); 8/160; Church Yth Grp; FBLA; Band; Mrchg Band; U Of AR Monticello; Elem Tchr.

CARTER, TARA; Fairview HS; Camden, AR; (2); FTA; Spanish Clb; Nwsp; Rep Frsh Cls; Rep Stu Cncl; JV Chrldng; Var Gym; Hon Roll; Honors & Sports Banquets; Child Care.

CARTER, TROY A; Fairview HS; Camden, AR; (4); Church Yth Grp; Natl FFA Org; Am Leg Aux Girls St; Chorus; Church Choir; School Musical; Socr; Cit Awd; Prfct Atten Awd; Stu For Christ; SAU Tech; Elem Ed.

CARTHRON, JENNIFER; North Little Rock Hs-East; North Little Rock, AR; (3); FBLA; FHA; Spanish Clb; Band; Flag Corp; Mrchg Band; Orch; School Play; Sftbl; Hon Roll; UCA; Comp Analysis.

CASE, JAMIE S; Cty Line HS; Ozark, AR; (2); Computer Clb; FBLA; FHA; Library Aide; Natl Beta Clb; Office Aide; Quiz Bowl; Teachers Aide; Band; Bsktbl; Typing Awd; Stdnt Of Month; Hnr Rl Awd; U Of A; Cmptr Engr/Tech.

CASE, KATHERINE; J A Fair Sr HS; Little Rock, AR; (2); FBLA; FHA; Spanish Clb; Chorus; Cit Awd; High Hon Roll; Hon Roll; Jr NHS; NHS; ASU.

CASEY, CRYSTAL; Jacksonville HS; Sherwood, AR; (3); 1/301; Church Yth Grp; Cmnty Wkr; Capt Debate Tm; Sec Drama Clb; Pres FTA; Natl Beta Clb; Sec Spanish Clb; Pres Jr Cls; NHS; Chem Engr.

CASEY, JUSTIN R; Parkview Magnet HS; Little Rock, AR; (2); Church Yth Grp; FCA; FBLA; FHA; FTA; Natl Beta Clb; Office Aide; Science Clb; Ofcr Frsh Cls; Ofcr Soph Cls; Gentlemens Clb; FBLA; Pharmacy.

CASH, MICHELE; Leslie Schl; Leslie, AR; (1); Church Yth Grp; VP Frsh Cls; Bsktbl; High Hon Roll; Hon Roll; Pres Acad Fit Awd; Teachers Aide; Band; Sftbl; All-Amer Schlr; Med.

CASH, MIKE D; Lake Hamilton Sr HS; Hot Springs, AR; (3); 61/258; Science Clb; Spanish Clb; Ofcr Stu Cncl; Crs Cntry; Ftbl.

CASHION, SCOTT A; Lakeside HS; Lake Village, AR; (2); 1/100; Church Yth Grp; Cmnty Wkr; Drama Clb; 4-H; Treas FBLA; Letterman Clb; Capt Quiz Bowl; Speech Tm; Church Choir; School Play; Lang Arts, World His, Word Processing & Civics Ltrs; Mst Outstdng St Bio; Stu Of Month; U Of AR Fayetteville; Med.

CASTAGNA, MICHAEL B; Benton Cty Christian School; Rogers, AR; (2); 1/13; Church Yth Grp; Var Bsktbl; High Hon Roll; John Brown Univ; Engr.

CASTALDI, NATHAN J; Lake Hamilton Sr HS; Hot Springs Natio, AR; (2); Church Yth Grp; FCA; Spanish Clb; Var Bsbl; Var Bsktbl; Reflections Cont Wnnr.

CASTEEL, AMIE L; Huntsville HS; Huntsville, AR; (3); Church Yth Grp; FCA; Letterman Clb; Office Aide; Spanish Clb; Varsity Clb; Ofcr Stu Cncl; JV Var Bsktbl; Sftbl; Var Trk; Renaissnce Crd Hldr; PRIDE.

CASTEEL, ANGELA; Bentonville Sr HS; Bentonville, AR; (4); 8/247; Church Yth Grp; CAP; Hosp Aide; Model UN; Treas Sec SADD; Band; Drm Mjr(t); Jazz Band; Mrchg Band; Pep Band; Peerhlprs; Kndgtn Tutor; Proj WET; Bnd Lttr; Hnrs Banquet; Acad Lttr; Strght A 7 Smstr Awd; OK Bapt Univ; Pre-Med/Bio.

CASTEEL, BRANDI; Bauxite Jr Sr HS; Bauxite, AR; (3); 5/70; Dance Clb; FBLA; Natl Beta Clb; Spanish Clb; SADD; Yrbk; Var Chrldng; Var Sftbl; NHS; All Amer Schlr; UCA; CPA.

CASTEEL, CASEY D; Arkansas Sr HS; Texarkana, AR; (3); Dance Clb; Drama Clb; French Clb; Library Aide; Drill Tm; Variety Show; Rep Stu Cncl; Chrldng; NIKE; Anchr For HOG TV; Pg For Rep Barbhorn In AR Legsltr; U Of AR; Brdcstng.

CASTEEL, J TYLER; Huntsville HS; Huntsville, AR; (4); 1/126; Pres VP FTA; Quiz Bowl; Rep Sr Cls; Ofcr Stu Cncl; Var L Ftbl; NHS; Val; Ftbl 2nd Tm All Dist; Acad All St 93-94, 94-95; Elks Ldge Stu Mnth; U AR; Mech Engr.

CASTEEL, KEISHA; Lee Acad; Marianna, AR; (2); Yrbk; Trk; High Hon Roll; Hon Roll; Natl Sci Mrt Awd; UT Martin; Stable Mngng.

CASTLEMAN, AMANDA; Stuttgart Sr HS; Stuttgart, AR; (3); 17/150; Am Leg Aux Girls St; FBLA; Natl Beta Clb; Natl FFA Org; Spanish Clb; Band; Drm Mjr(t); Church Yth Grp; Key Clb; Science Clb; Dlta Bta Sgma; Coop Offc Ed; Vntrs Ed; U Of Central AR; Elem Ed.

CASTSTEEL, JOHNNY; Cotter Jr Sr HS; Gassville, AR; (4); 2/29; Am Leg Boys St; 4-H; FBLA; Library Aide; Natl Beta Clb; Quiz Bowl; Spanish Clb; Band; Mrchg Band; Pep Band; AR Tech Univ; His Tchr.

CATE, SARAH A; Marion HS; Marion, AR; (3); 1/180; Am Leg Aux Girls St; Church Yth Grp; Mu Alpha Theta; Quiz Bowl; Spanish Clb; Ed Nwsp; NHS; Ntl Merit SF; Band; Church Choir; AR Governors Schl; Hattie Carraway Conf; TEAM-ATES; Lawyer; Pol Sci.

CATER, KATHLEEN E; Siloam Springs Sr HS; Siloam Springs, AR; (3); Church Yth Grp; Key Clb; Natl Beta Clb; Church Choir; School Play; Pres Soph Cls; Cit Awd; Hon Roll; NHS; Comm Theatre; AEGIS Camp Steps To The Stage; His.

CATER, WILLIAM S; Mc Gehee HS; Mc Gehee, AR; (3); Am Leg Boys St; Boy Scts; Church Yth Grp; Drama Clb; FCA; VP FTA; Mu Alpha Theta; Natl Beta Clb; Science Clb; Spanish Clb; UAM; Acctng/Law.

CATES, CHARLES C; Southside HS; Fort Smith, AR; (3); Band; Hon Roll.

CATES, HEATHER L; Bergman Schl; Harrison, AR; (4); Church Yth Grp; FBLA; FHA; GAA; Natl Beta Clb; Pep Clb; Spanish Clb; JV Bsktbl; JV Tennis; Cit Awd; Bus/Law.

CATHCART, NANCY G; Greenwood Sr HS; Greenwood, AR; (3); Church Yth Grp; FCA; French Clb; FBLA; FHA; GAA; Letterman Clb; L Var Bsktbl; L Var Sftbl; L Var Trk; Multi-Yr Listee; Williams Bapt Coll; Dentistry.

CATHCART, SARAH; Greenwood Sr HS; Greenwood, AR; (1); 32/250; Church Yth Grp; FCA; FBLA; Bsktbl; Chrldng; Vllybl; Hon Roll; Jr NHS.

CATHEY, JASON D; Newport HS; Newport, AR; (2); Church Yth Grp; JCL; Latin Clb; Letterman Clb; Math Tm; Varsity Clb; Ftbl; Trk; Hon Roll; Med.

CATHEY, MICHELLE; Warren Jr HS; Warren, AR; (1); 4/130; Sec Natl Beta Clb; Church Choir; Phtg Yrbk; High Hon Roll; Pres Schlr; Jr High Choir Pres; Outstdng Alto Ensemble.

CATLETT, BRANDY L; Booneville Jr Sr HS; Booneville, AR; (4); FBLA; Science Clb; Spanish Clb; Westark CC.

CATO, LARA; Harrison Jr HS; Harrison, AR; (2); #1 in class; Church Yth Grp; Cmnty Wkr; Drama Clb; FBLA; Key Clb; Quiz Bowl; Spanish Clb; Thesps; Chorus; Stage Crew.

CATT, ADAM; Prairie Grove HS; Prairie Grove, AR; (4); 1/89; Pres Spanish Clb; Teachers Aide; Band; Jazz Band; NHS; U Of AR; Music.

CAUDILL, DONALD J; Hot Springs HS; Hot Springs Natio, AR; (2); 48/190; Quiz Bowl; ROTC; Color Guard; Drill Tm; Hon Roll; U Of MI; Air Force.

CAUDLE, ADAM L; Pottsville Schl; Russellville, AR; (3); 4/45; Am Leg Boys St; Church Yth Grp; FBLA; Natl Beta Clb; Rep Frsh Cls; Pres Jr Cls; Rep Stu Cncl; Var Bsbl; Var Bsktbl; Var Crs Cntry; AR Tech U.

CAUDLE, CARRIE; Arkansas Sr HS; Texarkana, AR; (4); Drama Clb; FTA; Mu Alpha Theta; Drill Tm; School Play; Yrbk; Rep Sr Cls; Var Chrldng; Gym; Pres Acad Fit Awd; Schltc Star Achvt Awd; Gftd, Tlntd; Fllwshp Chrstn Stu; Henderson ST U; Elem Educ.

CAUDLE, KACEY L; Arkansas Sr HS; Texarkana, AR; (2); Church Yth Grp; Drama Clb; Church Choir; Drill Tm; Ofcr Stu Cncl; JV Bsktbl; Trk; Fllwshp Chrstn Schls; Fshn Dsgn.

CAUDLE, MELISSA; Benton Sr HS; Benton, AR; (4); 23/123; Art Clb; Church Yth Grp; FBLA; Key Clb; Math Clb; Spanish Clb; Hon Roll; Jr NHS; Kiwanis Awd; NHS; Jr Rotarian; Harding Univ; Bus Mgmt.

CAULDWELL, CORBIN; Rogers HS; Rogers, AR; (4); 4/468; Church Yth Grp; FCA; Pres Rep Stu Cncl; Var L Bsbl; L Capt Bsktbl; L Capt Ftbl; High Hon Roll; NHS; Pres Acad Fit Awd; Jr Bnk Brd; Engrng.

CAUTHEN, KEVIN; Vilonia HS; Conway, AR; (3); Art Clb; FHA; Math Clb; Mu Alpha Theta; Natl Beta Clb; Spanish Clb; Band; Church Choir; Jazz Band; Mrchg Band; All-Stars; AR Tech Univ; Ftbl Coach.

CAVETTE, JACK L; Marvell Acad; Marvell, AR; (3); 10/32; Am Leg Boys St; Boy Scts; Church Yth Grp; Computer Clb; Spanish Clb; School Musical; School Play; Stage Crew; Stat Bsbl; Bsktbl; AR State Univ; Jrnlsm.

CAVINESS, PATRICIA L; Parkview HS; Little Rock, AR; (2); Key Clb; Natl Beta Clb; Spanish Clb; Band; Yrbk; Rep Jr Cls; Hon Roll; Jr NHS; Y-Teens; Med.

CAZZELL, JEFF; Ft Smith Christian Schl; Fort Smith, AR; (3); 2/32; Church Yth Grp; FCA; Spanish Clb; VP Frsh Cls; Var L Bsbl; Var L Bsktbl; Var L Trk; High Hon Roll; NHS; Chrch Wrshp Team; Schl Wrshp Team Ldr.

CEARLEY, GLENDA R; Charleston HS; Charleston, AR; (3); 11/45; Church Yth Grp; Cmnty Wkr; Spanish Clb; Hon Roll; Westkart 6 Credit Hrs; Pub Church Bulletin; Westark; Dental Hygenist.

CENTER, RANDAN L; Fayetteville Chrstn Acad; West Fork, AR; (4); Church Yth Grp; FBLA; FHA; Library Aide; Natl Beta Clb; Office Aide; Church Choir; Yrbk; Vllybl; Cit Awd.

CESSOR, JODY I; Dumas HS; Dumas, AR; (3); Library Aide; Bsktbl; Hunting; AR-MONTICELLO; Comp.

CHADWICK, HOLLIE; Hoxie Schl; Portia, AR; (3); Church Yth Grp; FHA; HOBY; Natl Beta Clb; Natl FFA Org; Office Aide; Spanish Clb; Teachers Aide; VP Sec Stu Cncl; Bsktbl; Natl Ldshp Soc.

CHADWICK, HOLLIE; Hoxie Schl; Pocahontas, AR; (3); 9/47; FHA; HOBY; Natl Beta Clb; Spanish Clb; Sec VP Stu Cncl; L Bsktbl; L Trk; L Vllybl; Cit Awd; Hon Roll; Best All Around; I Dare You Awd; Advanced Eng Awd; Bus Fin.

CHADWICK, STEFANIE B; Black Rock Jr Sr HS; Black Rock, AR; (1); Church Yth Grp; FBLA; FHA; Natl Beta Clb; School Musical; Ofcr Stu Cncl; JV Bsktbl; Hon Roll.

CHAFFEY, TRAVIS P; Southside HS; Fort Smith, AR; (2); FCA; Var Bsktbl; Cit Awd; Hon Roll; Jet Skiing; Water Skiing; Invstr.

CHAFFIN, JOSHUA K; Van Buren Sr HS; Van Buren, AR; (2); Art Clb; Boy Scts; Mu Alpha Theta; Cit Awd; High Hon Roll; NHS; Ntl Merit Ltr; Egl Sct; Jr Asst Sctmstr; Explr Sct; Wrk Sct Cmp; Tch Yng Scts.

CHAFFIN, ROBIN G; Magnolia HS; Magnolia, AR; (3); Church Yth Grp; Cmnty Wkr; FCA; French Clb; FBLA; Mu Alpha Theta; Science Clb; Band; Mrchg Band; Chrldng; Panther Pride Tm; AR ST Pride Tm; Yth Of Month Awd; Med.

CHAMBERLAIN, SASHA N; Southside HS; Fort Smith, AR; (2); Drill Tm; Co-Ed Nwsp; Hon Roll; Jr NHS; Radiologist.

CHAMBERLIN, JAMES A; Mena HS; Mena, AR; (3); Church Yth Grp; FCA; Spanish Clb; Ed Yrbk; VP Frsh Cls; JV Bsktbl; Var Capt Ftbl; Pres Acad Fit Awd; Pol Sci; Govt.

CHAMBERLIN, KRISTEN L; Mena HS; Mena, AR; (2); Church Yth Grp; French Clb; GAA; Science Clb; Church Choir; JV Bsktbl; JV Mgr(s); JV Vllybl; AR Tech; Tch.

CHAMBERS, CHAD; Murfreesboro HS; Murfreesboro, AR; (4); 3/37; Art Clb; FBLA; Quiz Bowl; Science Clb; Ftbl; Wt Lftg; Hon Roll; Pres Acad Fit Awd; Henderson ST U.

CHAMBERS, DEREK A; Springdale Sr HS; Springdale, AR; (2); Church Yth Grp; 4-H; Office Aide; Band; Church Choir; Mrchg Band; Pep Band; School Play; Ed Yrbk; Cit Awd; Police; Law Enfrcmnt.

CHAMBERS, HEATHER; Kirby HS; Kirby, AR; (1); 4/36; FCA; FHA; Girl Scts; Sec Natl Beta Clb; Hist Frsh Cls; L Bsktbl; Trk; Wt Lftg; Hon Roll; U Of AR Fayetteville.

CHAMBERS, JENNIFER; Brookland Jr Sr HS; Brookland, AR; (4); 11/51; Church Yth Grp; Cmnty Wkr; 4-H; Pres Natl Beta Clb; VP Natl FFA Org; Yrbk; Rep Stu Cncl; Chrldng; Hon Roll; Prfct Atten Awd; Elec Team; Natl Engl Mrt Awd; Natl FFA Conv; AR ST U; Radiational Thrpst.

CHAMBERS, MICAH; Harmony Grove Jr Sr HS; Camden, AR; (1); Chess Clb; Church Yth Grp; Drama Clb; FCA; Natl Beta Clb; Quiz Bowl; Band; Mrchg Band; Ofcr Stu Cncl; Ftbl; Stanford 8 Tests High Scores; US Naval Acad; Surgeon.

CHAMBERS, PHYLLIS L; Mills HS; Jacksonville, AR; (2); 18/449; Debate Tm; FBLA; Spanish Clb; Band; Co-Capt Flag Corp; Mrchg Band; Nwsp; Powder Puff Ftbl; Hon Roll; AEGIS 96; All Regn Band 95-; Natl Macy Schlr 96; Biomdcl Engrng.

CHAMBERS, RACHEL D; Searcy HS; Searcy, AR; (3); Art Clb; Church Yth Grp; FCA; French Clb; Natl Beta Clb; Office Aide; Quiz Bowl; JV Bsktbl; Socr; JV Trk.

CHAMBERS, ROBERT L; Kingsland Schl; New Edinburg, AR; (3); 6/26; Am Leg Boys St; Var Bsbl; Var Bsktbl; Beta Club 2yrs.

CHAMBLISS, JAMES; Bearden HS; Bearden, AR; (4); 4/58; Am Leg Boys St; Church Yth Grp; Cmnty Wkr; FBLA; FHA; FTA; Model UN; Natl Beta Clb; Quiz Bowl; Pres Sr Cls; U Of AR; Acctng.

CHAMBLISS, LAUREN; Pine Bluff HS; Pine Bluff, AR; (2); Church Yth Grp; Dance Clb; French Clb; Office Aide; Acpl Chr; Church Choir; Yrbk; Chrldng; Tennis; Hon Roll; Homecoming Court; U Of AR At Fayetville.

CHAMERS, AMBER; Dumas HS; Dumas, AR; (2); FBLA; Natl Beta Clb; Science Clb; Color Guard; School Play; Yrbk; Tennis; High Hon Roll; NHS; Pres Acad Fit Awd; Amer Legion Awd; Outstdng Stdnt Awd; Outstdng Womens Tennis Awd.

CHAMPION, CARTERSIA M; Strong Jr Sr HS; Strong, AR; (4); 4/54; Drama Clb; French Clb; Sec FHA; Natl Beta Clb; Science Clb; Nwsp; Hon Roll; De Vry Inst Tech; Cmptr Info Sy.

CHANCELLOR, ADA M; Hot Springs HS; Hot Springs, AR; (1); Natl Beta Clb; Chorus; High Hon Roll; Hon Roll; Child Facilities.

CHANCELLOR, BLAKE; Bismarck Jr-Sr HS; Bismarck, AR; (4); 3/60; FCA; HOBY; Natl Beta Clb; Capt Quiz Bowl; Science Clb; Teachers Aide; Yrbk; Var Capt Bsktbl; Ftbl; Hon Roll; U Of AR; Bio.

CHANCEY, KERRI S; Russellville Sr HS; Russellville, AR; (2); Art Clb; Natl Beta Clb; Church Choir; Yth Grp; Mst Faithful Teen Awd; OK Bapt Coll; Vet.

CHANDLER, ADRIENNE; Bryant Sr HS; Bryant, AR; (2); Church Yth Grp; English Clb; FBLA; Church Choir; Var Chrldng; Var L Trk; Hon Roll; Chrstn Cncl.

CHANDLER, D J; Bryant Sr HS; Mabelvale, AR; (2); Church Yth Grp; FBLA; Office Aide; L Ftbl; L Socr; Hon Roll; Pres Acad Fit Awd.

CHANDLER, HOLLY R; Horatio HS; Horatio, AR; (2); 12/68; FCA; Sec Jr Cls; Var Bsktbl; Hon Roll; Henderson; Pdtrcn.

CHANEY, CHARITY A; Horatio HS; Horatio, AR; (2); JA; Library Aide; Office Aide; Teachers Aide; Chorus; School Musical; Phtg Rptr Yrbk; Hon Roll; Prfct Atten Awd; Pres Acad Fit Awd; Show Choir; Law; Music.

CHANEY, NATHAN P; Arkadelphia Sr HS; Arkadelphia, AR; (3); 1/168; Am Leg Boys St; Boy Scts; Church Yth Grp; Natl Beta Clb; Spanish Clb; Band; Jazz Band; Mrchg Band; Yrbk; Treas Jr Cls; Eagle Sct; Future Problem Solvers; Knowledge Masters; Hendrix Coll; Lawyer.

CHANEY, QUENTIN E; Fountain Hill Schl; Fountain Hill, AR; (2); Church Yth Grp; French Clb; Var Bsktbl; PE Awd; Gftd & Tlntd Pgm.

CHANG, MICHAEL; Arkansas Schl Math & Science; De Queen, AR; (4); Art Clb; Mu Alpha Theta; Natl Beta Clb; Band; VP Frsh Cls; Hon Roll; JETS Awd; NHS; 1st Pl ST Sci Fair/Engr; 6th Sakharovs Rdng St Ptrsbrg/Russia; Vndrblt U; Chem Engr.

CHAPA, ORLANDA E; El Dorado Sr HS; El Dorado, AR; (4); 10/266; Am Leg Aux Girls St; Church Yth Grp; Cmnty Wkr; FBLA; Natl Beta Clb; Nwsp; Yrbk; Treas Soph Cls; Ofcr Sr Cls; Ofcr Stu Cncl; U Of AR; Cmmnctn.

CHAPARRO, ELIASER R; Pulaski Acad; Little Rock, AR; (2); Natl Beta Clb; Spanish Clb; Band; Jazz Band; Stage Crew; Treas Stu Cncl; Cit Awd; High Hon Roll; NHS; Natl Macy Schlr; Med.

CHAPMAN, AMANDA; Greenbrier HS; Greenbrier, AR; (4); 1/132; Am Leg Aux Girls St; Church Yth Grp; Drama Clb; HOBY; Natl Beta Clb; Teachers Aide; School Play; Yrbk; High Hon Roll; Ntl Merit SF.

CHAPMAN, AMBER; Siloam Springs Sr HS; Siloam Springs, AR; (2); Church Yth Grp; FCA; Key Clb; Natl Beta Clb; Band; Church Choir; Mrchg Band; Rep Stu Cncl; Chrldng; Hon Roll; U Of AR; Frgn Lang.

CHAPMAN, AUDREY A; Oak Grove HS; N Little Rock, AR; (3); #5 in class; Church Yth Grp; FCA; Hosp Aide; Chorus; School Musical; Swmmng; Jr NHS; NHS; Band; Mrchg Band; Red Cross Jr Vol Of Yr 95; Church Drama Tm; HS Heroes; Nursing.

CHAPMAN, NICHOLAS D; Arkansas Sr HS; Texarkana, AR; (2); #6 in class; Boy Scts; Cmnty Wkr; French Clb; DAR Awd; Hon Roll; Arch.

CHAPMAN, STEPHEN Z; Oak Grove HS; North Little Rock, AR; (1); Natl FFA Org; Med.

CHAPPEL, ELIZABETH A; Nettleton HS; State University, AR; (3); Church Yth Grp; French Clb; FBLA; Math Clb; Natl Beta Clb; Science Clb; Teachers Aide; Acpl Chr; Band; Chorus; Majorette; Stus Who Care; AR ST U; Vet.

CHAPPELL, APRIL L; Black Rock Jr Sr HS; Portia, AR; (2); FHA; Chorus; Church Choir; School Musical; Bsktbl; Hon Roll; Ftr Hmemkrs Of Amer Pres; Ftr Hmemkrs Of Amer VP Pub Rltns; Lib Club; Black River Votech; Lab Tech.

CHAPPELL, SARAH L; Clarksville HS; Clarksville, AR; (4); 3/96; Am Leg Aux Girls St; Church Yth Grp; FCA; Natl Beta Clb; Chorus; Flag Corp; Pres Frsh Cls; Sec Jr Cls; FBLA; Band; Ms Clarksville HS; Stu Of Yr; AR Tech Univ; Vocal Mus.

CHARLES, ANTONIO C; Dumas HS; Dumas, AR; (3); Church Yth Grp; Cmnty Wkr; FCA; JA; Library Aide; Chorus; Church Choir; JV Bsktbl; Var L Ftbl; Var L Trk; Hon Mntn All-Conf Ftbl; Otstndng Off Lnmn; Bus.

CHARLESTON, ANGELA L; Beebe Sr HS; Beebe, AR; (4); Hist Drama Clb; FBLA; FHA; Math Clb; Natl Beta Clb; Science Clb; Spanish Clb; Thesps; School Play; Stage Crew; AR ST Univ; Gen Sci.

CHARLTON, JASON K; Greenwood Sr HS; Greenwood, AR; (3); 32/210; Art Clb; Natl Beta Clb; VICA; Hon Roll; NHS; Natl Sci Merit Awd Wnnr; Natl Ldshp Svc Awd Wnnr; U Of AR; Eng.

CHARTON, DANIEL SCOTT; Morrilton Sr HS; Morrilton, AR; (4); 47/150; Math Clb; Office Aide; Spanish Clb; Thesps; Band; Jazz Band; Mrchg Band; Pep Band; Stage Crew; Yrbk; Natl Hnr Rll; AR Tech.

CHARTON, JUSTIN; Morrilton Sr HS; Morrilton, AR; (3); Church Yth Grp; French Clb; Natl Beta Clb; Office Aide; Science Clb; Nwsp; Yrbk; Var Bsbl; Gov Hon Prg Awd; Hon Roll; Vet.

CHASE, ERIK R; Booneville Jr Sr HS; Magazine, AR; (3); Church Yth Grp; Cmnty Wkr; FCA; Natl Beta Clb; Science Clb; Spanish Clb; Bsktbl; Ftbl; Trk; Wt Lftg; U Of AR; Gen Engrng.

CHASE, SHAWNA M; Lake Hamilton Sr HS; Hot Springs, AR; (2); 1/320; FCA; FBLA; German Clb; Natl Beta Clb; Teachers Aide; Cit Awd; High Hon Roll; NHS; Optmst Clb Stu Yr; Aikido Prple Blt.

CHASTAIN, JEFF D; Stuttgart Sr HS; Stuttgart, AR; (3); Am Leg Boys St; FBLA; Mu Alpha Theta; Spanish Clb; Chorus; Rptr Nwsp; Cit Awd; High Hon Roll; Hon Roll; NHS; Commnctn; Bus.

CHATHAM, EMILY R; Greenwood Sr HS; Fort Smith, AR; (4); 26/200; Church Yth Grp; Model UN; Mu Alpha Theta; Natl Beta Clb; Speech Tm; Sec Band; High Hon Roll; Sec NHS; Pres Acad Fit Awd; Partners In Chris VP; U Of AR; Engrng.

CHATHAM, JEREMY; Dumas HS; Tillar, AR; (4); Natl Beta Clb; Yrbk; Cit Awd; Hon Roll; NHS; Pres Acad Fit Awd; Pharmacy.

CHATMAN, ALEX; Guy Perkins Schl; Guy, AR; (2); 8/30; Church Yth Grp; Drama Clb; FBLA; FHA; HOBY; Natl Beta Clb; Office Aide; Teachers Aide; Church Choir; School Play; Creative Presentations, Publ Spkg; U Of AR; TV Prod.

CHATMAN, KIMBERLY; Dumas Jr HS; Dumas, AR; (1); FBLA; GAA; Spanish Clb; Capt Bsktbl; Hon Roll; Law.

CHAVARRIA, TRISHA C; Fountain Lake Jr Sr HS; Hot Springs Natio, AR; (3); 3/60; FCA; Sec FHA; Key Clb; Varsity Clb; Chorus; Church Choir; School Musical; School Play; Bsktbl; Chrldng; Choir; Math/Sci/Eng Awds; Psychp.

CHAVEZ, AMBER C; Piggott HS; Piggott, AR; (3); Church Yth Grp; Cmnty Wkr; 4-H; Teachers Aide; Band; Chorus; Church Choir; Jazz Band; Mrchg Band; School Musical; Tlnt Show Blue Ribbon Wnnr; Solo Ensemble 1st Pl Medals; Coll Of Ozarks; Choir; Band Dir.

CHEATAM, EBONY M; Central Sr HS; Little Rock, AR; (3); Sec Church Yth Grp; Cmnty Wkr; Pres FHA; Capt Pep Clb; Church Choir; Drill Tm; Variety Show; Rep Frsh Cls; Vllybl; Hon Roll; Philander Smith Coll.

CHEATHAM, DUSTIN A; Dardanelle HS; Dardanelle, AR; (3); Chess Clb; Church Yth Grp; FCA; Letterman Clb; Natl Beta Clb; Quiz Bowl; JV Bsktbl; Var Tennis; High Hon Roll; NHS; AR St Univ; Acctnt.

CHEATHAM, LISA M; Lincoln HS; Canehill, AR; (3); 2/75; Church Yth Grp; FBLA; Model UN; Natl Beta Clb; Quiz Bowl; Science Clb; Spanish Clb; Rptr Ed Lit Mag; Var JV Chrldng; High Hon Roll; Prm Comm; Hmcmng Ct; U Of AR; Pre-Med.

CHEATHAM, LYNSI; Hope HS; Hope, AR; (1); Church Yth Grp; Dance Clb; FBLA; Natl Beta Clb; Office Aide; Church Choir; Variety Show; Chrldng; Gym; Trk; U AR; Interior Dsgnr.

CHEEK, LESLEE T; Dewitt HS; De Witt, AR; (1); Art Clb; Church Yth Grp; Cmnty Wkr; FBLA; Natl Beta Clb; Science Clb; 3rd Pl Sci Fair Project.

CHEEKS, KRISTI; Ozark Adventist Acad; Denham Springs, LA; (4); Church Yth Grp; Cmnty Wkr; Natl Beta Clb; Chorus; School Musical; School Play; Stage Crew; Variety Show; Rep Soph Cls; VP Sr Cls; SW Adventist Col; Dent Hyg.

CHENEY, ANNA; Pulaski Acad; Little Rock, AR; (2); Church Yth Grp; FCA; Natl Beta Clb; Spanish Clb; School Play; Chrldng; Socr; Wt Lftg; Hon Roll; Jr NHS; Beta Clb; Bus.

CHERRY, ALAN; Woodlawn Schl; Star City, AR; (4); 2/26; Am Leg Boys St; Church Yth Grp; 4-H; HOBY; Natl Beta Clb; High Hon Roll; Pres Acad Fit Awd; Medcl.

CHERRY, BRENT A; Southside HS; Fort Smith, AR; (3); Drama Clb; Latin Clb; Spanish Clb; Acpl Chr; Chorus; Church Choir; School Musical; School Play; Stage Crew; Hon Roll; Lorri Weller Art Achvmt Awd 94; 1st Deg Blk Blt KKF; AR HS Rodeo Assn; Comm Art/Advrtsng.

CHERRY, CARLLA K; Crossett Sr HS; Crossett, AR; (3); Drama Clb; Spanish Clb; Band; Drill Tm; High Hon Roll; Hon Roll; Pres Acad Fit Awd; All Regn Band; Solo Ensmbl Band 1st Pl; UCA.

CHERRY, JENNIFER D; Mc Gehee HS; Tillar, AR; (2); FBLA; FTA; Natl Beta Clb; Office Aide; Science Clb; Spanish Clb; Rep Soph Cls.

CHERRY, KELLY S; Arkansas Sr HS; Texarkana, AR; (2); Drama Clb; FCA; Hosp Aide; Mu Alpha Theta; Spanish Clb; Drill Tm; Yrbk; Rep Stu Cncl; Var Bsktbl; Pom Pon; U Of TX Austin; Chld Psycht.

CHERRY, MICHAEL; Woodlawn Schl; Star City, AR; (4); 2/26; Am Leg Boys St; Church Yth Grp; 4-H; HOBY; Natl Beta Clb; SAU; Hlth.

CHESHIRE, BROOKE; Southside HS; Fort Smith, AR; (2); FCA; French Clb; Key Clb; Chorus; Nwsp; Ofcr Frsh Cls; Ofcr Soph Cls; Chrldng; Gym; Hon Roll; U Of AR; Jrnlsm.

CHESSER, DREW S; Mc Gehee HS; Mcgehee, AR; (2); Art Clb; Church Yth Grp; FTA; Math Clb; Mu Alpha Theta; Natl Beta Clb; Science Clb; Spanish Clb; Golf; Natl Yng Ldrs Conf; ASU; Engr.

CHIA, ANNE M; Piggott HS; Piggott, AR; (4); Art Clb; Church Yth Grp; Drama Clb; 4-H; French Clb; Natl Beta Clb; Science Clb; Teachers Aide; Band; Chorus; Majorette Capt 2 Yrs; Three Rivers CC; Spch Thrpst.

CHIDAMBARAM, VINITHA; Central Sr HS; Little Rock, AR; (3); 47/540; Cmnty Wkr; Mu Alpha Theta; Natl Beta Clb; Hist Spanish Clb; Stage Crew; Rptr Nwsp; Cit Awd; Gov Hon Prg Awd; Hon Roll; NHS; Sci Fair Awd At Schl; Accept No Boundaries; Premed.

CHILCOAT, JASON D; Ashdown Sr HS; Ashdown, AR; (4); Church Yth Grp; Drama Clb; French Clb; Thesps; School Play; Stage Crew; Ftbl; Trk; Wt Lftg; Hon Roll; Body Bldng; Hackey Sack.

CHILDERS, DEREK D; Greenwood Sr HS; Greenwood, AR; (2); Church Yth Grp; Band; Jazz Band; Mrchg Band; Pep Band; Hon Roll; OK Univ; Dentist.

CHILDERS, ELIZABETH; Greenwood Sr HS; Greenwood, AR; (2); Church Yth Grp; FCA; Pres FBLA; Letterman Clb; Model UN; Varsity Clb; Sec Treas Frsh Cls; Treas Soph Cls; Chrldng; Hon Roll; Med.

CHILDERS, GARRETT; North Little Rock Hs-East; North Little Rock, AR; (2); Church Yth Grp; FCA; Stage Crew; Bsktbl; Ftbl; Socr; Hon Roll; Pres Acad Fit Awd; Peer Ldrshp; Univ Of AR Fayetteville; Sport.

CHILDERS, WENDY; Mountain Home HS; Calico Rock, AR; (4); 37/226; Am Leg Aux Girls St; Church Yth Grp; FCA; 4-H; FBLA; Natl Beta Clb; Natl FFA Org; Science Clb; School Play; Var Bsktbl; AR ST Univ Mtn Home; Vet.

CHILDRESS, CHRIS; Marion HS; Marion, AR; (2); Church Yth Grp; CAP; Color Guard; High Hon Roll; Hon Roll; U Of ND; Pilot.

CHILDRESS, JENNIFER K; Glen Rose HS; Malvern, AR; (4); Art Clb; Church Yth Grp; Cmnty Wkr; FBLA; FHA; Office Aide; Spanish Clb; SADD; Teachers Aide; Church Choir; Tutoring/Offering Advice Lower Classmen; Henderson ST Univ; Med Tech.

CHILDRESS, ROCKY A; Fouke Jr Sr HS; Fouke, AR; (3); 10/90; Chess Clb; Natl Beta Clb; Natl FFA Org; Spanish Clb; Hon Roll; Pres Schlr; GATE Prgm; Odyssey Mind.

CHILDRESS, SUMER; Ridgecrest HS; Paragould, AR; (4); 5/160; Am Leg Aux Girls St; Art Clb; Church Yth Grp; Treas French Clb; Key Clb; Model UN; Rptr Nwsp; VP Jr Cls; Ofcr Stu Cncl; NHS; Hnr Stdnt; AP Amer His Awd; Actv Schlr Awd; FL Southern Coll; Crmnlgy.

CHIN, HENRY; Lee Sr HS; Marianna, AR; (1); 1/139; Natl Beta Clb; Quiz Bowl; Science Clb; Rep Frsh Cls; U Of CO Boulder; Comp Prgrmmr.

CHIN, STACY J; West Memphis Sr HS; West Memphis, AR; (3); 1/350; Church Yth Grp; French Clb; Mu Alpha Theta; Natl Beta Clb; Chorus; School Musical; Yrbk; French Hon Soc; Gov Hon Prg Awd; High Hon Roll; Natl Frnch Exam AR 1st Lvl II &III-7TH Nation; All Reg Chr 3 Yrs.

CHISM, DANIEL; Gosnell Jr Sr HS; Blytheville, AR; (3); Drama Clb; FHA; Math Clb; Science Clb; Ftbl; Trk; Hon Roll; Pres Acad Fit Awd.

CHITWOOD, CAROLYN; Russellville Sr HS; Russellville, AR; (3); Am Leg Aux Girls St; Rep Church Yth Grp; Cmnty Wkr; Model UN; Band; Church Choir; Drm Mjr(t); NHS; Mrchg Band; Variety Show; Odyssey Of Mind Wrld Fnlst; All Reg Band 3 Yrs; All ST Band 2 Yrs.

CHITWOOD, JASON; Perryville Jr Sr HS; Perryville, AR; (2); 5/74; Church Yth Grp; FCA; HOBY; Model UN; Office Aide; Pep Clb; Quiz Bowl; Spanish Clb; Teachers Aide; Treas Sec Stu Cncl; Coalition Of Essential Schls Ntl Conf Roundtable Presener 94-95; St Stu Forum Rep 95.

CHOATE, AMY M; Southside HS; Clarksville, AR; (3); CAP; Natl Beta Clb; Quiz Bowl; Spanish Clb; VICA; Mgr Stage Crew; Rptr Nwsp; JV Sftbl; High Hon Roll; Pres Acad Fit Awd; USAF.

CHOI, SAM Y; North Little Rock Hs-West; North Little Rock, AR; (3); Church Yth Grp; Cmnty Wkr; Drama Clb; FCA; FBLA; Mu Alpha Theta; Natl Beta Clb; School Musical; School Play; Stage Crew; Bldg Mdls; 1st Pl Cllctng Money Leukiemia Soc; Top 10% Of Cls; U Of TX Austin; Engr.

CHON, CHAE YONG; Parkview Arts-Science HS; Sherwood, AR; (4); 13/261; FTA; Natl Beta Clb; Orch; School Musical; 4-H Awd; Gov Hon Prg Awd; High Hon Roll; NHS; Prfct Atten Awd; Pres Acad Fit Awd; Pianist At Chrch; U Of AR.

CHON, KA YONG; Parkview Arts-Science HS; Sherwood, AR; (4); 21/261; Church Yth Grp; Cmnty Wkr; Math Tm; Natl Beta Clb; Orch; School Musical; High Hon Roll; Hon Roll; NHS; Prfct Atten Awd; Church Pianist; HS Orchestra Cncrt Master; Ar Yth Symphony Orchestra; Univ Of Cntrl AR; Music Ed.

CHRISP, RANDY R; Rogers HS; Rogers, AR; (2); JV Var Ftbl; JV Var Wt Lftg; Prfct Atten Awd; U Of AR; Accntng/Bus.

CHRISTENSEN, ALICIA; Lake Hamilton Sr HS; Hot Springs, AR; (2); Church Yth Grp; FCA; 4-H; Hosp Aide; Natl Beta Clb; School Musical; Lit Mag; Hon Roll; NHS; Ntl Merit Ltr; Gov Yth Conf; Medcl.

CHRISTENSEN, KAMEESHA; Hatfield Schl; Hatfield, AR; (1); Church Yth Grp; 4-H; FBLA; Natl Beta Clb; Natl FFA Org; Quiz Bowl; JV Bsktbl; JV Chrldng; JV Trk; Cit Awd; Ozark; Music/Acting.

CHRISTENSON, JENNIFER; Harrison Sr HS; Harrison, AR; (3); Church Yth Grp; FBLA; HOBY; Rep Key Clb; VP Spanish Clb; Band; Ntl Merit Ltr; Spanish NHS; Cmnty Wkr; Drama Clb; NYLC Delg; Ntl Engl Mrt Awd; 9 Yrs Piano; Intl Lang.

CHRISTIAN, JESSICA L; Southside HS; Fort Smith, AR; (2); 105/540; Church Yth Grp; Latin Clb; Service Clb; Drill Tm; Var L Golf; Hon Roll; Jr NHS; Pres Schlr; Natl Fed Music Clbs Piano Guild; All ST Hnrs Glf 2 Yrs.

CHRISTIANSEN, MELISSA; Hackett Schl; Hackett, AR; (3); 8/40; Band; Color Guard; Drill Tm; Rep Stu Cncl; Chrldng; Sftbl; High Hon Roll; Jr NHS; NHS; Prfct Atten Awd; Westark; Dntl.

CHRISTIE, SARA J; Booneville Jr Sr HS; Booneville, AR; (4); Church Yth Grp; FBLA; Key Clb; Sec Natl Beta Clb; Office Aide; Q&S; Science Clb; Spanish Clb; Teachers Aide; Band; Mntr Pgm Big Sis; U Of Cntrl AR; Pharm.

CHRISTMAS, LORA BETH; Dermott HS; Dermott, AR; (3); 1/75; Church Yth Grp; Dance Clb; FBLA; Natl Beta Clb; Spanish Clb; Rep Frsh Cls; Rep Soph Cls; Sec Jr Cls; VP Stu Cncl; Chrldng; U Of AR; Nrsng.

CHRISTOPHER, AARON; Cabot HS; Ward, AR; (4); 30/285; Boy Scts; Church Yth Grp; Cmnty Wkr; L VP Computer Clb; English Clb; French Clb; Pres FBLA; Key Clb; Latin Clb; Hendrix Coll; Bus.

CHRISTOPHER, BRONICA L; John L Mcclellan Magnet HS; Little Rock, AR; (4); 12/246; VP FBLA; Hist Mu Alpha Theta; VP Natl Beta Clb; Teachers Aide; Church Choir; Drill Tm; Capt Vllybl; High Hon Roll; Hon Roll; NHS; SECME Pres; Pres Ed Awd; Navy Hnrs Awd; U Of Cntrl AR; Engrng.

CHRISTY, NATHAN D; Springdale Sr HS; Springdale, AR; (3); Computer Clb; Teachers Aide; Hon Roll; Cmptr Prgmng/Art.

CHRONISTER, MEGEN; Southside HS; Fort Smith, AR; (2); Church Yth Grp; Key Clb; Mu Alpha Theta; Chorus; Church Choir; Co-Ed Nwsp; Hon Roll; Jr NHS; Pres Acad Fit Awd; Piano; Delta Beta Sigma; All Rgn Choir 94; Music.

CHUDY, AMANDA; Carlisle Jr Sr HS; Carlisle, AR; (2); Church Yth Grp; Cmnty Wkr; FBLA; Church Choir; Rep Soph Cls; Ofcr Stu Cncl; Bsktbl; Chrldng; Trk; Cit Awd.

CHUNG, HON Q; Northside HS; Fort Smith, AR; (4); 1/360; Church Yth Grp; Intnl Clb; Math Clb; Mu Alpha Theta; Quiz Bowl; Science Clb; VP Spanish Clb; L Band; Mrchg Band; Ofcr Frsh Cls; Century III Ldrshp; Natl Acad Bowl Team; TANO Chem Clb Pres; Escape Clb Treas; Harvard U; Bio Chem.

CHUNG, LEE I; Lincoln HS; Lincoln, AR; (3); 1/72; Capt Debate Tm; FBLA; HOBY; Key Clb; Pres Natl Beta Clb; Quiz Bowl; VP Science Clb; Spanish Clb; Variety Show; High Hon Roll; AR St Debate 1st Pl Spkr, Chmpnshp Debate, Undftd Chmpns; HOBY Wrld Yth Fndtn Alt.

CHUNN, JOY L; Greene Co Tech HS; Paragould, AR; (4); Drama Clb; French Clb; FTA; Teachers Aide; Band; Jazz Band; Mrchg Band; Pep Band; All Regn Band; Eagle Schlr Ctzn; AR ST Univ; Music Ed.

CHUNN, KANIKA; Brinkley HS; Brinkley, AR; (3); French Clb; FHA; Band; Mrchg Band; Bsktbl; Hon Roll; Jr NHS; NHS; Reg Nrs.

CHUTE, MATTHEW R; Highland HS; Hardy, AR; (3); Am Leg Boys St; Church Yth Grp; Cmnty Wkr; FHA; Natl Beta Clb; Office Aide; Teachers Aide; Chorus; High Hon Roll; Prfct Atten Awd; HIGHGATE; Bes Moines Area CC; Rtl Mrchnd.

CIECIWA, BECKY J; Eureka Springs Jr Sr HS; Eureka Springs, AR; (4); 5/55; Dance Clb; Natl Beta Clb; Bsktbl; Chrldng; Hon Roll; U Of Cntrl AR; Bio.

CIGANEK JR, TERRY L; Hazen Jr Sr HS; Hazen, AR; (3); Am Leg Boys St; Church Yth Grp; FBLA; Sec FHA; FTA; Treas Natl Beta Clb; Rptr Stu Cncl; Var JV Bsbl; Var JV Bsktbl; Var JV Ftbl; U AR Fayetteville.

CINGOLANI, BROOKE; Mc Gehee HS; Mc Gehee, AR; (3); 15/108; Art Clb; Church Yth Grp; Drama Clb; FCA; FTA; Jazz Band; Quiz Bowl; Science Clb; Spanish Clb; L Tennis; Dist Grls Dbls Tennis Chmpnshp 95; Natl Cngrssnl Ldrshp Conf; LSU; Psych.

CINGOLANI, ELIZABETH A; Mc Gehee HS; Mc Gehee, AR; (4); 8/100; Church Yth Grp; FBLA; FTA; Mu Alpha Theta; Natl Beta Clb; Science Clb; Spanish Clb; Cit Awd; NHS; Var Co-Capt Chrldng; AR ST U; Accnt/Law.

CINGOLANI, MISTY M; Mc Gehee HS; Mcgehee, AR; (2); FBLA; FTA; GAA; Natl Beta Clb; Science Clb; Sec Spanish Clb; Varsity Clb; Chrldng; Pres Acad Fit Awd; LSU; Med.

CISNEROZ, ANGELA M; Capital City Christian Acad; Benton, AR; (4); Church Yth Grp; Hosp Aide; Spanish Clb; Teachers Aide; Rptr Nwsp; Hon Roll; Church Drama/Puppet Tm; Flwshp Chrstn Stdnts; Biling Studies.

CLACK, CHRISTI; Harmony Grove Jr Sr HS; Bearden, AR; (2); FCA; Pres 4-H; FBLA; Natl FFA Org; Science Clb; Church Choir; JV Var Bsktbl; JV Chrldng; 4-H Awd; Var Trk; St 4-H Record Book Wnnr Pet Care; LA ST U; Vet.

CLAIRDAY, CHARLES M; Mc Rae Schl; Searcy, AR; (2); 2/23; Church Yth Grp; FBLA; Natl FFA Org; Spanish Clb; Yrbk; Var L Bsbl; Var L Bsktbl; Var L Crs Cntry; Var L Trk; Hon Roll.

CLAMPIT, JASON K; Elkins Jr Sr HS; Elkins, AR; (2); Church Yth Grp; Cmnty Wkr; Computer Clb; Band; Mrchg Band; Pep Band; High Hon Roll; Hon Roll; Habitat For Humanity In Dallas TX Vol; U Of AR; Comp Engr; Prgmr; Music.

CLANTON, JEFF; Conway Sr HS; Conway, AR; (4); Art Clb; Church Yth Grp; FBLA; Office Aide; JV Bsbl; Intrml Ftbl; Hon Roll; Hendrix Coll; His.

CLANTON, MISTY; Warren Sr HS; Warren, AR; (4); #14 in class; Art Clb; Drama Clb; French Clb; Natl Beta Clb; Band; NHS; Pres Acad Fit Awd; Jr Rtrn; Head Wtrs Prom; Sr Maid Hmcmng Crt; Univ Of Central AR.

CLAPP, WENDI; Ozark Adventist Acad; Decatur, AR; (3); Drama Clb; Band; Ofcr Soph Cls; Intrml Bsktbl; Intrml Ftbl; Co-Capt Gym; Intrml Socr; Intrml Sftbl; Cit Awd; High Hon Roll; S A Olympcs Wmns MPV 3xs; Hndblls; Mssn Trp Mexico; Sthwstrn Adv Coll; Phys Thrpy.

CLARDY, ALISHA C; Glen Rose HS; Malvern, AR; (1); 4/62; Spanish Clb; Band; Flag Corp; Mrchg Band; Ofcr Stu Cncl; High Hon Roll; Prfct Atten Awd; Pres Acad Fit Awd; Spanish NHS; All Regn Band 2 Yrs; Gift/Tlntd Prgm; Acdmc Awd Span/Hlth; Intnl Frgn Lang Awd Span; Hendrix Coll; Eng/Span.

CLARDY, TASHA N; Glen Rose HS; Malvern, AR; (1); Church Yth Grp; Office Aide; Spanish Clb; Teachers Aide; Varsity Clb; Church Choir; Chrldng; Hon Roll; Pres Acad Fit Awd.

CLARDY, TOYA; Nashville HS; Nashville, AR; (3); 27/144; Church Yth Grp; 4-H; FHA; Spanish Clb; Stage Crew; Cit Awd; Hon Roll; NHS; Pres Acad Fit Awd; FHA Sec; U Of AR Fayetteville; Bus Mgmt.

CLARDY, VANESSA R; Glen Rose HS; Malvern, AR; (3); 6/60; Art Clb; FBLA; Math Clb; Spanish Clb; Band; Jazz Band; Mrchg Band; Pep Band; Hon Roll; Pres Acad Fit Awd; U Of AR Monticello; Pre-Med.

CLARE, NATHAN E; Booneville Jr Sr HS; Magazine, AR; (3); Church Yth Grp; FCA; FBLA; FHA; Natl Beta Clb; Spanish Clb; Var Bsbl; Var Bsktbl; High Hon Roll; Hon Roll; AEGIS Pgms; Essay For Elec Co-Op Trip To Washington DC; All Star Summer League Bsbl; U Of AR; Pilot.

CLARE, SARAH E; Heber Springs HS; Heber Springs, AR; (3); 28/105; Am Leg Aux Girls St; Chess Clb; Church Yth Grp; Drama Clb; Natl Beta Clb; Science Clb; Spanish Clb; Band; Co-Capt Flag Corp; Mrchg Band; Jrnlsm.

CLARET, ROGER A; Sheridan Sr HS; Pine Bluff, AR; (2); Church Yth Grp; ROTC; Band; Church Choir; Color Guard; Drill Tm; Mrchg Band; School Play; ROTC Amer Lgn Mltry Excl Awd.

CLARK, AMANDA R; Hackett Schl; Hackett, AR; (3); 5/41; Sec Pres FBLA; Spanish Clb; Band; Color Guard; Co-Capt Capt Flag Corp; Mrchg Band; Rep Stu Cncl; Chrldng; Hon Roll; NHS.

CLARK, AMY; Newport HS; Newport, AR; (4); 8/149; Church Yth Grp; Spanish Clb; High Hon Roll; NHS; Pres Acad Fit Awd; Outstdng Achvmt Awd; Univ Of Cntrl AR; Occ Thpy.

CLARK, ANGELA F; Hope HS; Hope, AR; (3); 1/230; French Clb; FBLA; Natl Beta Clb; High Hon Roll; Stu Of Month; Navy Hnrs Pgm Achvmnt Awd.

CLARK, ANTHONY R; Heber Springs HS; Tumbling Shoals, AR; (3); 4/100; Am Leg Boys St; Church Yth Grp; FBLA; Natl Beta Clb; Church Choir; Treas Frsh Cls; Treas Soph Cls; Treas Jr Cls; Rep Stu Cncl; Hon Roll.

CLARK, APRIL M; Newport HS; Newport, AR; (3); Chorus; Ofcr Jr Cls; Auto Axles Awd; ASU Beebe; Bus.

CLARK, ASHLEY; Walnut Ridge HS; Walnut Ridge, AR; (4); 22/60; Am Leg Aux Girls St; Church Yth Grp; Cmnty Wkr; Pres 4-H; Treas FBLA; GAA; Library Aide; Office Aide; Pep Clb; Quiz Bowl; U Of AK; Hosptlty/Restrnt Mgmt.

CLARK, BOBBY; Lewisville HS; Hope, AR; (2); 2/37; Church Yth Grp; HOBY; VP Frsh Cls; Capt Bsbl; L Bsktbl; L Ftbl; L Trk; Hon Roll; Jr NHS; NHS; U Of AR; Mjr Leag Bsbl Plyr.

CLARK, BRANDY; Pea Ridge HS; Pea Ridge, AR; (2); 4/71; Drama Clb; Sec FHA; GAA; Spanish Clb; Stage Crew; Nwsp; Rep Stu Cncl; JV Bsktbl; Hon Roll; NHS; Town Sftbl; Bsktbl Ltr; NW AR CC; Elem Tchr.

CLARK, BRITNEY; Tuckerman HS; Tuckerman, AR; (3); FHA; Natl Beta Clb; Office Aide; Chorus; Treas Frsh Cls; Bsktbl; High Hon Roll; Hstry Clb-Hstry Day Dist, St Wnnr; AR ST U Jnsboro; Nrsng.

CLARK, CANDACE L; Mansfield Jr Sr HS; Booneville, AR; (2); Church Yth Grp; FCA; Intnl Clb; Speech Tm; Cit Awd; High Hon Roll; Prfct Atten Awd; Space Sci.

CLARK, CHARLEY M; Hartford Schl; Hackett, AR; (2); 1/42; FBLA; Band; Mrchg Band; Pep Band; Rep Soph Cls; VP Stu Cncl; Var Bsbl; Var Bsktbl; High Hon Roll; NHS; Bsktbl Referee & Asst Coach.

CLARK, DUSTY D; Sheridan Sr HS; Sheridan, AR; (2); Church Yth Grp; Chorus; Church Choir; Chrldng; Hon Roll; Jr NHS.

CLARK, ERIKA P; Nettleton HS; Jonesboro, AR; (4); 11/140; Drama Clb; Hosp Aide; Math Clb; Teachers Aide; School Play; Stage Crew; High Hon Roll; Stdnts Who Care; AR ST U; Zoology; Radiologist.

CLARK, GAYLYNN; Fayetteville Sr HS; Fayetteville, AR; (4); French Clb; SADD; Acpl Chr; Chorus; Stage Crew; Variety Show; High Hon Roll; U Of AR; Glgy.

CLARK, HEATHER; Hackett Schl; Hackett, AR; (3); 15/37; Teachers Aide; Band; Chorus; Color Guard; Flag Corp; Mrchg Band; Chrldng; High Hon Roll; Hon Roll; NHS; U Of AR; Math.

CLARK, JEB S; Clarksville HS; Clarksville, AR; (2); Boy Scts; Church Yth Grp; FBLA; Red Cross Aide; Spanish Clb; Ofcr Bsbl; Crs Cntry; Cit Awd; High Hon Roll; Pres Schlr.

CLARK, JUSTIN R; Southside HS; Batesville, AR; (2); 1/120; Boy Scts; Church Yth Grp; CAP; Key Clb; Natl Beta Clb; Quiz Bowl; Spanish Clb; Band; Church Choir; Pep Band.

CLARK, KADRE; Gurdon HS; Gurdon, AR; (3); 2/65; Natl Beta Clb; Rptr Natl FFA Org; Spanish Clb; School Musical; Pres Soph Cls; Capt Chrldng; Tennis; High Hon Roll; NHS; Pres Acad Fit Awd; LA Tech; Pharmcy.

CLARK, KISHA S; Arkansas Sr HS; Texarkana, AR; (2); 4-H; FHA; Chorus; Church Choir; Drill Tm; Mgr(s); Sftbl; Howard Univ; Law.

CLARK, KORY E; Harrison Sr HS; Harrison, AR; (4); 4-H; Natl FFA Org; JV Ftbl; JV Var Socr; JV Trk; Var Wt Lftg.

CLARK, KRISTEN L; Arkadelphia Sr HS; Arkadelphia, AR; (4); 19/152; Am Leg Aux Girls St; Church Yth Grp; Drama Clb; FCA; FBLA; Natl Beta Clb; Pres Speech Tm; Chorus; Rep Stu Cncl; NHS; Govs Schl Dlgte Choir; All Rgn Choir 1st Chr; Ouachita Bapt Univ; Acctng.

CLARK, KRISTY; Hackett Schl; Hackett, AR; (4); 1/45; Cmnty Wkr; Debate Tm; Drama Clb; FBLA; Ofcr Soph Cls; Ofcr Jr Cls; Ofcr Sr Cls; Ofcr Stu Cncl; NHS; Val; UAR Fayetteville; Soc Sci.

CLARK, LA JOAN N; North Little Rock Hs-West; Little Rock, AR; (3); 90/554; Church Yth Grp; FCA; FBLA; Hosp Aide; Math Clb; Mu Alpha Theta; Natl Beta Clb; Quiz Bowl; Drill Tm; School Musical; U Of AR; Bus.

CLARK, LEAH; Nashville HS; Nashville, AR; (3); Church Yth Grp; 4-H; Spanish Clb; Nwsp; Yrbk; Bsktbl; Tennis; Hon Roll; NHS; Sec FBLA; Showing Brangus Cattle 4-H; TAG; Harding Univ.

CLARK, MANDY M; Rogers HS; Rogers, AR; (4); 124/442; Church Yth Grp; Cmnty Wkr; FBLA; Drill Tm; VP Frsh Cls; Pres Soph Cls; Pres Jr Cls; Pres Sr Cls; Rep Stu Cncl; Chrldng; Renaissance; Rotary Stdnt Of Mnth; U Of AR; Mktng Mgmnt.

CLARK, MANLEY T; Morrilton Sr HS; Springfield, AR; (3); Church Yth Grp; French Clb; Math Clb; Science Clb; Thesps; School Musical; School Play; Yrbk; Var Crs Cntry; Var Ftbl; MI Univ; Cmptr Sci.

CLARK, MICAHLENE C; Tuckerman HS; Newport, AR; (2); Church Yth Grp; FBLA; FHA; GAA; Natl Beta Clb; Science Clb; Spanish Clb; Church Choir; Sec Frsh Cls; VP Soph Cls; AR ST Univ.

CLARK, MICHAEL J; Nettleton HS; Jonesboro, AR; (2); 21/140; Spanish Clb; RAD; AR ST Univ; Wrtng.

CLARK, MISTY; Trumann HS; Harrisburg, AR; (3); Church Yth Grp; Science Clb; Band; Chorus; Church Choir; Mrchg Band; Pep Band; Rep Jr Cls; Hon Roll; NHS; All Region Choir; All Region Band Alt 95-96; Choir Ltr 93-94; Band Ltr 93-96; Solo-Ensemble Div I; Pediatric Medicine.

CLARK, NIKYIA; Jonesboro HS; Jonesboro, AR; (3); Church Yth Grp; FCA; FBLA; Spanish Clb; Church Choir; Bsktbl; Trk; PRIDE; TOP VP; U Of MO; Soc Wk.

CLARK, ROBERT A; Springdale Sr HS; Springdale, AR; (2); Acpl Chr; Band; Church Choir; Mrchg Band; Pep Band; Hon Roll; Jr NHS.

CLARK, SARA; Crowleys Ridge Acad; Paragould, AR; (4); 4/25; Art Clb; Church Yth Grp; FBLA; Hosp Aide; Pep Clb; Science Clb; Spanish Clb; Chorus; School Play; VP Jr Cls; ASU; Dntl Hygienist.

CLARK, SHANNON; Sulphur Rock Schl; Batesville, AR; (4); Church Yth Grp; FBLA; Natl Beta Clb; Rptr Nwsp; Rep Stu Cncl; Bsktbl; Trk; Hon Roll; Ntl Merit Ltr; St Schlr.

CLARK, SHANNON N; Central Sr HS; Sherwood, AR; (2); Church Yth Grp; Cmnty Wkr; Mu Alpha Theta; Natl Beta Clb; SADD; Yrbk; Rep Stu Cncl; Chrldng; DAR Awd; High Hon Roll; AR Schl Math/Sci; Duke Univ; Pre-Med.

CLARK, SHAWNA; Jasper HS; Jasper, AR; (4); 6/44; Cmnty Wkr; Pres FBLA; FHA; Math Clb; Natl Beta Clb; Treas Natl Beta Clb; Science Clb; Spanish Clb; Rptr Stu Cncl; Hon Roll; AR Tech U; Bus Mrktng.

CLARK, SUMMER; Paron Schl; Paron, AR; (3); 2/30; FBLA; FHA; Math Clb; Quiz Bowl; Science Clb; School Play; Capt Bsktbl; Hon Roll; Jr NHS; Prfct Atten Awd; Chosen Del Girls St; All Dist Bsktbl; Marine Bio.

CLARK, TAMMY D; Mena HS; Mena, AR; (2); 18/300; French Clb; FBLA; FHA; Chorus; French Hon Soc; Hon Roll; Fr II Awd; Acad Letter; Med.

CLARK, TIFFANY; Berryville HS; Berryville, AR; (1); Spanish Clb; Chrldng; Sftbl; Hon Roll; Prfct Atten Awd; U Of AR; Optometry.

CLARK, TIFFANY L; Jacksonville HS; North Little Rock, AR; (2); Church Yth Grp; Teachers Aide; Church Choir; Bsktbl; Trk; Vllybl; Hon Roll; Prfct Atten Awd; FCS; Lib Asst; Bus/Mngmt.

CLARK, TOMMY L; Hartford Schl; Hackett, AR; (3); 1/36; FBLA; Office Aide; Band; Mrchg Band; Pep Band; Rptr Soph Cls; Pres Stu Cncl; Var Bsbl; Var Bsktbl; High Hon Roll; Interfaith Comm Ctr Vol; Bsktbl Referee.

CLARK, VIRGINIA B; West Memphis Sr HS; West Memphis, AR; (4); 3/265; French Clb; Library Aide; Math Clb; Mu Alpha Theta; Natl Beta Clb; Science Clb; Band; Color Guard; Mrchg Band; Pep Band; U Of Memphis; Engl.

CLARY, LUKE; Bradley Jr Sr HS; Bradley, AR; (1); Church Yth Grp; 4-H; FHA; Band; Rep Frsh Cls; JV Bsbl; JV Bsktbl; JV Ftbl; 4-H Awd; High Hon Roll; U AR; Med.

CLASH, YOLANDA D; Elaine Jr Sr HS; Elaine, AR; (3); 3/30; 4-H; Girl Scts; Spanish Clb; Speech Tm; Drill Tm; Rep Stu Cncl; Bsktbl; Gov Hon Prg Awd; Hon Roll; NHS; Global Studies Clb/Choir; U Of Cntrl AR; Cmptr Sci.

CLAUSEN, KAREN LYNN; Fayetteville Sr HS; Fayetteville, AR; (3); 1/431; Church Yth Grp; Cmnty Wkr; Key Clb; Mu Alpha Theta; SADD; Church Choir; NHS; Ntl Merit Ltr; Co-Capt Drill Tm; Hist Stu Cncl; AR Governors Schl Participant; Stdnts For Wellness; Chem Engrng.

CLAUSING, CAMERON P; Rogers HS; Rogers, AR; (3); Am Leg Boys St; Boy Scts; CAP; Debate Tm; Model UN; NFL; Science Clb; Speech Tm; Rep Stu Cncl; High Hon Roll; Tae Kwon Do; Flying Lessons; Westpoint; Pol Sci.

CLAWSON, CHARLOTTE L; Magnolia HS; Magnolia, AR; (2); 54/226; Pep Clb; Hon Roll.

CLAWSON, DANA L; Gillett Jr Sr HS; Tichnor, AR; (3); 8/25; Art Clb; FBLA; FHA; Pep Clb; Spanish Clb; School Play; Yrbk; Bsktbl; Chrldng; Score Keeper; Phy Thrpst.

CLAY, BILLY J; Bryant Sr HS; Benton, AR; (2); Jr NHS; NHS; 4th Pl Natl Sci Olympiad; U Of CO; Biologist/FBI.

CLAY, KARA D; Searcy HS; Searcy, AR; (2); Church Yth Grp; Natl Beta Clb; Spanish Clb; Band; Church Choir; Drm Mjr(t); Mrchg Band; L Var Bsktbl; NHS; Spanish NHS; Ouachita Bapt Univ; Yth Mnstry.

CLAY, LAURIE A; Jonesboro HS; Jonesboro, AR; (2); VICA; High Hon Roll; Hon Roll; Pres Acad Fit Awd; Washington Univ.

CLAY, LISA M; Bright Star Schl; Doddridge, AR; (2); Church Yth Grp; Drama Clb; Speech Tm; Band; Chorus; Mrchg Band; Ofcr Soph Cls; Ofcr Bsbl; Sftbl; Prfct Atten Awd; Texarkana; Data Retrieval.

CLAY, RENALDO; West Memphis Sr HS; Proctor, AR; (2); Church Yth Grp; Cmnty Wkr; FCA; Varsity Clb; Church Choir; Var Capt Bsktbl; Hon Roll; Beta Clb; Fire Marshall; U Of AR Fayetteville; Comp Sci.

CLAY, SHAVONDA M; North Little Rock Hs-East; Little Rock, AR; (1); Church Yth Grp; FTA; Lit Mag; High Hon Roll; Hon Roll; Wrtng Poetry; Hnr Stdnt; Jrnlsm.

CLAYBORN, LETA G; Lamar HS; Lamar, AR; (2); Church Yth Grp; FCA; FBLA; Church Choir; JV Sftbl; Hon Roll; Ntl Merit Ltr.

CLAYTON, ANGELA L; Russellville Sr HS; Russellville, AR; (2); 74/408; Church Yth Grp; Office Aide; Church Choir; Hon Roll; Work With Children; AR Tech Univ; Day Care Owner.

CLAYTON, CHRISTINA; Sparkman Jr Sr HS; Sparkman, AR; (4); FBLA; FHA; Library Aide; Office Aide; Spanish Clb; Teachers Aide; Ed Yrbk; Hist Jr Cls; Hon Roll; Henderson St Univ.

CLEAVER, ERIC; Dermott HS; Dermott, AR; (1); 3/75; Church Yth Grp; FCA; Natl Beta Clb; Ftbl; Trk; Hon Roll; NHS.

CLEGG, APRIL M; Sheridan Sr HS; Prattsville, AR; (2); 98/250; Church Yth Grp; FCA; Quiz Bowl; Chorus; Church Choir; School Play; Ofcr Frsh Cls; Ofcr Stu Cncl; Bsktbl; Sftbl; Law.

CLEGG, PRESTON O; Lee Acad; Colt, AR; (1); 3/30; Church Yth Grp; JV Bsktbl; JV Ftbl; JV Trk; Hon Roll.

CLEGG, TRAVIS; Ozark Adventist Acad; Gentry, AR; (2); Bsktbl.

CLEGHORN, BRIDGETT L; Horatio HS; Eagletown, OK; (2); Church Yth Grp; English Clb; Letterman Clb; Quiz Bowl; Spanish Clb; Acpl Chr; Chorus; Church Choir; Rptr Nwsp; Ed Yrbk; Close-Up AR; Yth Action Cncl; Quiz Bowl Alt; OK ST Univ; Zoology.

CLEGHORN, TROY S; Ridgecrest HS; Paragould, AR; (3); 49/200; Spcl Awd-Outstdng Art Work For RAM Channel 48.

CLEMENT, CASEY; Rogers HS; Rogers, AR; (4); Church Yth Grp; High Hon Roll; Hon Roll; Pres Acad Fit Awd; Bible Stud; Ernd 23 Coll Crdt Hrs CC; SW Bapt Bus.

CLEMENT, ERIN N; Jacksonville HS; Cabot, AR; (3); 62/323; 4-H; French Clb; FBLA; Natl Beta Clb; Capt Drill Tm; School Musical; School Play; Powder Puff Ftbl; High Hon Roll; Hon Roll; NHRA Bracket Racing; Homcmng; Miss Red Devil; Bus.

CLEMENT, MATT S; Lake Hamilton Sr HS; Pearcy, AR; (2); 30/274; FCA; Letterman Clb; Natl Beta Clb; Spanish Clb; Varsity Clb; Ofcr Stu Cncl; Ftbl; Trk; NHS; Pres Acad Fit Awd; Stu Chrstn Life; Eng & Prsdntl Acad Awds; Acad Lttrmn; Wolf Prd; U Of AR; Med.

CLEMENT, MEGHAN J; Russellville Sr HS; Dardanelle, AR; (3); 60/400; Church Yth Grp; FCA; French Clb; Bsktbl; Sftbl; High Hon Roll; NHS; Pres Acad Fit Awd; U Of AR; Hotel Restaurant Mgmt.

CLEMENTS, JEFFERSON; Lake Hamilton Jr HS; Pearcy, AR; (1); Church Yth Grp; Natl Beta Clb; Teachers Aide; Bsktbl; Tennis; High Hon Roll; Hon Roll; Pres Acad Fit Awd; Pres Schlr.

CLEMENTS, JULIE A; Nevada Schl; Emmet, AR; (3); Church Yth Grp; FBLA; Natl Beta Clb; Band; Church Choir; High Hon Roll.

CLEMENTS, KATHY L; Leslie Schl; Conway, AR; (4); 6/32; Art Clb; Church Yth Grp; Cmnty Wkr; Computer Clb; Drama Clb; 4-H; FBLA; FTA; Girl Scts; Key Clb; U Of Cntrl AR; Tchr.

CLEMENTS, LAURA B; Conway Sr HS; Conway, AR; (3); FBLA; GAA; Natl Beta Clb; Spanish Clb; Varsity Clb; Ofcr Soph Cls; Bsktbl; Sftbl; Vllybl.

CLEMENTS, MARK; Central Ark Christian Schl; Sherwood, AR; (3); 11/75; Church Yth Grp; Chorus; Variety Show; High Hon Roll; NHS; Southern Magic; SWACDA Hnr Choir.

CLEMMER, CRYSTAL R; Ridgecrest HS; Paragould, AR; (2); Church Yth Grp; HOBY; Library Aide; Church Choir; High Hon Roll; Hon Roll; Prfct Atten Awd; Psych.

CLEMONS, ANDY C; Hope HS; Hope, AR; (3); Natl Beta Clb; Bsktbl; Tennis; High Hon Roll; Pre-Medicine.

CLEVELAND, JOHN T; Rogers HS; Rogers, AR; (3); Boy Scts; Intnl Clb; Rptr Nwsp; Rptr Yrbk; High Hon Roll; Hon Roll; NHS; Ntl Merit Ltr; BSA Eagle Scout; Military Ofcr.

CLEVELAND, KIZZIE; Holly Grove HS; Holly Grove, AR; (2); 4/27; Church Yth Grp; FHA; Girl Scts; Natl FFA Org; Church Choir; Drill Tm; Var Chrldng; Hon Roll; Nrsng.

CLEVELAND, SYLVIA M; Holly Grove HS; Holly Grove, AR; (3); 15/40; Church Yth Grp; English Clb; JA; SADD; Nwsp; Ofcr Sr Cls; Vllybl; Specl Recgn Wrld His; Food Nutrtn; UAPB; Nrsing.

CLICK, NED S; Horatio HS; Winthrop, AR; (2); FCA; Natl FFA Org; Quiz Bowl; Bsktbl; Ftbl; Hon Roll.

CLIFT, AMANDA; Emmet Schl; Emmet, AR; (2); Sec Frsh Cls; Hon Roll; Prfct Atten Awd; Pres Acad Fit Awd.

CLIFT, JARED R; Harmony Grove Jr Sr HS; Benton, AR; (2); Model UN; Natl Beta Clb; Band; Mrchg Band; Ofcr Bsbl; Bsktbl; Cit Awd.

CLIFTON, ANNIE; Farmington Jr Sr HS; Farmington, AR; (3); Church Yth Grp; FCA; Natl FFA Org; Sec Frsh Cls; Sec Jr Cls; Rep Stu Cncl; Bsktbl; Chrldng; Powder Puff Ftbl; Trk; Ozark Jr Rodeo Assn; CFC; U AR; Jrnlsm.

CLINE, BRIAN K; Southside HS; Fort Smith, AR; (4); 156/482; Church Yth Grp; Cmnty Wkr; FCA; FBLA; Key Clb; Letterman Clb; Office Aide; Teachers Aide; Varsity Clb; Variety Show; U Of AR; Phy Thrpy.

CLINKINGBEARD, AMBER; Calico Rock HS; Calico Rock, AR; (1); Art Clb; Church Yth Grp; FCA; FHA; Math Clb; Pres Natl Beta Clb; Pep Clb; Science Clb; SADD; Church Choir; Homcmng Maid; Math Tchr.

CLINKINGBEARD, TAMI M; Russellville Sr HS; Russellville, AR; (2); 1/500; Church Yth Grp; Cmnty Wkr; Spanish Clb; Band; Capt Color Guard; Mrchg Band; Pep Band; School Play; Rep Stu Cncl; Golf; All Stars; AR Ambassadors Of Music; Teen Age Repblcns Sec; Pol Sci.

CLINTON, ROBERT; Walnut Ridge HS; Walnut Ridge, AR; (3); Am Leg Boys St; Art Clb; 4-H; French Clb; FBLA; Science Clb; Band; Jazz Band; Mrchg Band; Pep Band.

CLOND, LORA B; Siloam Springs Sr HS; Siloam Springs, AR; (3); 1/160; Church Yth Grp; FCA; Natl Beta Clb; Band; Church Choir; Rep Stu Cncl; Var Swmmng; High Hon Roll; Pres NHS; Treas FBLA; Wheaton Col; Physcs.

CLOSSON, JESSICA R; Dewitt HS; Crocketts Bluff, AR; (1); FCA; Science Clb; JV Powder Puff Ftbl; JV Sftbl; JV Trk; Church Yth Grp; FBLA; FHA; Cit Awd; NLSA; All Amer Schlr; Ath Ltr Awd; FL ST Univ.

CLOUD, BRANDY L; Harmony Grove Jr Sr HS; Benton, AR; (4); Church Yth Grp; French Clb; FBLA; FHA; Girl Scts; Chorus; VFW Schlsp; U Of AR; Med.

CLOUGH, RAYMOND; Gravette HS; Sulphur Springs, AR; (3); HOBY; Litry Clb.

CLOUSE, MIKE W; Jessieville HS; Jessieville, AR; (2); 10/60; Natl Beta Clb; Bsktbl.

CLUPNY, BRIANA L; Rogers HS; Rogers, AR; (3); Church Yth Grp; Office Aide; Drill Tm; Mgr(s); Green Earth Optimists Clb; Chamber Of Commerce Acad Achvmt Awd; Elem Ed.

COAD, JASON A; West Memphis Sr HS; West Memphis, AR; (3); Mu Alpha Theta; Natl Beta Clb; Ofcr Stu Cncl; Ftbl; High Hon Roll; Zoology; Prof Pre-Med.

COATS, ADAM T; North Little Rock Hs-West; North Little Rock, AR; (3); 12/554; Boy Scts; Mu Alpha Theta; Natl Beta Clb; Band; Church Choir; Jazz Band; Mrchg Band; Ofcr Stu Cncl; High Hon Roll; Hon Roll; Beta Clb; All Rgn, All St Jz Bnd Gtr; All Rgn Cncrt Bnd Tnr Sax; Msc Prfrmnc.

COATS, JENNIFER; White Hall Sr HS; Pine Bluff, AR; (4); 10/163; Church Yth Grp; Cmnty Wkr; Dance Clb; English Clb; HOBY; Key Clb; Letterman Clb; Mu Alpha Theta; Natl Beta Clb; Science Clb; Miss White Hall 95; Miss Teen AR 1st Rnnr Up; WHHS Homcmng Maid Of Hnr 95; U Of AR Fayetteville; Educ.

COBB, CHARLOTTE; Mc Gehee HS; Mc Gehee, AR; (3); Art Clb; Church Yth Grp; FBLA; FTA; Mu Alpha Theta; Natl Beta Clb; Science Clb; Sec Spanish Clb; NHS; Acctng.

COBB, LESLIE; North Little Rock HS; N Little Rock, AR; (3); 3/654; HOBY; Key Clb; Math Clb; Mu Alpha Theta; Natl Beta Clb; School Musical; School Play; Rep Stu Cncl; Chrldng; Powder Puff Ftbl; Dance.

COBBS, ALISHA D; Holly Grove HS; Brinkley, AR; (2); 3/26; Church Yth Grp; 4-H; FBLA; FHA; Natl Beta Clb; Quiz Bowl; Church Choir; Rep Frsh Cls; Hon Roll; Reading Clb.

COBBS, SHAMEEKA R; Holly Grove HS; Brinkley, AR; (3); 1/38; FBLA; FHA; German Clb; Office Aide; Red Cross Aide; Band; Nwsp; Sec Jr Cls; Hon Roll; Church Yth Grp; Operation Enterprise Schlsp; FBLA Dist VII Treas & Sec; U Of AR Little Rock; Sociology.

COBLE, AARON K; Springdale Sr HS; Springdale, AR; (1); FCA; Letterman Clb; Office Aide; Science Clb; Teachers Aide; Ofcr Bsbl; Bsktbl; L Capt Ftbl; Trk; Wt Lftg; Dr Vet Sci.

COBURN, BLAIR; Rivercrest HS; Osceola, AR; (1); 1/140; Church Yth Grp; 4-H; GAA; Girl Scts; Band; Pres Frsh Cls; L Bsktbl; L Trk; Hon Roll; Jr NHS; Ole Miss; Pre-Med.

COBURN, DENZIL C; Arkansas Sr HS; Texarkana, AR; (3); VICA; Texarkana Coll; Auto Mechncs.

COBURN, SHANNON R; Mc Crory Jr Sr HS; Mc Crory, AR; (2); Church Yth Grp; Spanish Clb; Teachers Aide; Mrchg Band; Yrbk; Rptr Frsh Cls; Chrldng; Hon Roll; Jr NHS; Freed-Hardmans; Lit/Crtve Wrtng.

COCHRAN, AMBER LEANN; Bryant Sr HS; Benton, AR; (3); Church Yth Grp; Drama Clb; English Clb; FBLA; HOBY; Science Clb; Spanish Clb; Chorus; Drill Tm; Hon Roll; FMP; REACH; The A-Tm; UCA; Athletic Trnr.

COCHRAN, ASHLEA M; Russellville Sr HS; Russellville, AR; (3); Church Yth Grp; Office Aide; Ski Clb; SADD; Chorus; Marine Bio.

COCHRAN, CARLA; Forrest City HS; Colt, AR; (3); FBLA; High Hon Roll; Hon Roll; Stdnt Mo; ASU; Acctng.

COCHRAN, LIEGH A; Russellville Sr HS; Russellville, AR; (2); Church Yth Grp; Natl Beta Clb; Spanish Clb; Band; Mrchg Band; Ofcr Frsh Cls; Rep Stu Cncl; Var L Socr; High Hon Roll; Lady Cycline Soccer Ldrshp Awd 95-96; AR Tech Univ; Psychiatrist.

COCKMAN, CARLOS; Fountain Lake Jr Sr HS; Hot Springs, AR; (4); 10/65; Am Leg Boys St; FCA; Pres FBLA; Natl FFA Org; Quiz Bowl; Spanish Clb; Band; Church Choir; Ftbl; Hon Roll; Henderson ST U; Phrmcy.

COCKRILL, ELIZABETH D; Norfork Jr Sr HS; Calico Rock, AR; (3); Art Clb; FCA; FBLA; Pep Clb; Co-Capt Chrldng; Cit Awd; Hon Roll; Jr NHS; Excl Spch Cls Awd; U Of Cntrl AR; Crim Law.

CODEY, PAIGE; Nashville HS; Nashville, AR; (1); 1/130; FBLA; Quiz Bowl; Church Choir; Nwsp; Yrbk; Pres Stu Cncl; Bsktbl; Chrldng; High Hon Roll; VP Jr NHS.

CODY, RAMANDA F; Valley Springs Schl; Harrison, AR; (3); 8/57; Church Yth Grp; Cmnty Wkr; French Clb; FBLA; Key Clb; Teachers Aide; Church Choir; Var Sftbl; High Hon Roll; NHS; BASIC Sec; Lee Coll; Bus Mgmt.

COE, LINDSAY; Newport HS; Newport, AR; (1); 2/431; Church Yth Grp; Math Tm; Church Choir; Var Chrldng; Var Pom Pon; Cit Awd; Hon Roll; Pres Acad Fit Awd; Pres Schlr; Math.

COE, NICHOLAS C; Cave City HS; Batesville, AR; (2); 8/75; French Clb; Math Clb; Natl Beta Clb; Science Clb; Teachers Aide; Band; Jazz Band; Mrchg Band; Pep Band; Cit Awd; Lyon Coll Comm Bnd; Part Time Employee Krogers; Collector Antique Adv.

COFFEE, JASON D; Arkansas Sr HS; Texarkana, AR; (2); Boy Scts; Church Yth Grp; French Clb; Phtg Yrbk; JV Bsktbl; JV Ftbl; JV Mgr(s); JV Score Keeper; High Hon Roll; Hon Roll; Vet.

COFFMAN, DERICK G; Harrison Sr HS; Harrison, AR; (3); #2 in class; Art Clb; Drama Clb; Hon Roll; NACTC; Arch.

COFFMAN, MEGAN N; Glenwood Jr Sr HS; Glenwood, AR; (2); Church Yth Grp; FCA; FBLA; FHA; GAA; Natl FFA Org; Church Choir; Drill Tm; Ofcr Frsh Cls; Ofcr Soph Cls.

COFFMAN, THURMAN T; Hector Jr Sr HS; Hector, AR; (3); 1/59; Am Leg Boys St; Church Yth Grp; FCA; FHA; Natl Beta Clb; Spanish Clb; SADD; VP Jr Cls; Var Bsbl; Var Bsktbl; U AR Fyttvlle; Med.

COGAN, MONICA B; Clarksville HS; Clarksville, AR; (2); Pres Church Yth Grp; FBLA; Natl Beta Clb; Chorus; Hon Roll.

COGBURN, CASSI S; Dierks HS; Dierks, AR; (2); 3/45; Church Yth Grp; FBLA; Rep Frsh Cls; VP Soph Cls; Rep Jr Cls; Rep Stu Cncl; Var L Bsktbl; Var L Crs Cntry; Var L Trk; High Hon Roll; Dntl Hyg.

COGBURN, GLEN A; Mt Ida Jr Sr HS; Mount Ida, AR; (2); 1/46; Church Yth Grp; Natl Beta Clb; Natl FFA Org; Band; Jazz Band; Mrchg Band; Pep Band; Var Bsbl; Var Bsktbl; Var Ftbl.

COGBURN, KATIE; Kirby HS; Amity, AR; (1); 12/36; FHA; Sec Frsh Cls; Bsktbl; Pres Acad Fit Awd.

COGBURN, MISTY; Amity Jr Sr HS; Amity, AR; (4); Church Yth Grp; FBLA; FHA; Natl Beta Clb; School Play; Rep Jr Cls; Sec Sr Cls; L Bsktbl; Sftbl; Trk; All-Dist; Fshng; Hntng; Bus.

COGBURN, SAMANTHA C; Kirby HS; Glenwood, AR; (4); 8/35; FBLA; FHA; Natl Beta Clb; Spanish Clb; Band; Pep Band; Ed Nwsp; Yrbk; Hon Roll; Garland Cnty CC; Chld Ed.

COGGINS, JEREMY D; El Dorado Sr HS; El Dorado, AR; (3); Cmnty Wkr; Natl Beta Clb; Office Aide; ROTC; Chorus; Church Choir; Rep Sr Cls; Rep Stu Cncl; Var L Bsbl; JV Ftbl; All-Region & All-St Choirs; Governors Yth Conf On Alcohol & Drugs Yth Ldr; Southern Univ; Broadcast Jrnlsm.

COGSHELL, KIMBERLY J; J A Fair Sr HS; Little Rock, AR; (2); Church Yth Grp; Drama Clb; FBLA; FHA; FTA; School Play; Yrbk; Bsktbl; Mgr(s); Score Keeper; Ladies Clb; RN.

COIN, ADAM T; Trumann HS; Trumann, AR; (2); Natl FFA Org; Band; Mrchg Band; Hon Roll; AR ST Univ.

COKER, JAMIE B; Dequeen HS; De Queen, AR; (2); 1/160; Church Yth Grp; HOBY; Office Aide; SADD; Band; Chorus; Church Choir; Pres Jr Cls; High Hon Roll; FCS.

COKER, SHELLIE L; St Joe Public Schl; Saint Joe, AR; (2); Church Yth Grp; Cmnty Wkr; FBLA; Church Choir; Rptr Nwsp; Phtg Yrbk; Sec Soph Cls; Coll Of Ozarks; Vet.

COKER, TRACY; Pocahontas HS; Pocahontas, AR; (4); Church Yth Grp; Cmnty Wkr; Rptr FBLA; Library Aide; Office Aide; Spanish Clb; Band; Church Choir; Flag Corp; Mrchg Band; Grad As Honor Grad With Distinction; 2 Bus Awds; U Of AR Fytvl; Bus Admin.

COLBERT, JENNIFER R; Searcy HS; Searcy, AR; (2); Art Clb; French Clb; JA; Hon Roll; Art Work Pub; Art Awds; Natl Fr Contest ST Div 8th Pl; Fr I Awd; Fine Arts.

COLDIRON, DONALD R; Horatio HS; Horatio, AR; (2); FCA; Natl FFA Org; JV Bsbl; JV Bsktbl; Var Ftbl; JV Trk; JV Hon Roll; NHS; TX A&M; Arch.

COLE, ALAN W; Fayetteville Sr HS; Fayetteville, AR; (2); Church Yth Grp; Cmnty Wkr; Var Bsbl; Ftbl; Trk; High Hon Roll; Hiking Clb.

COLE, ALARIC; Southside HS; Fort Smith, AR; (3); Boy Scts; JCL; Latin Clb; Mu Alpha Theta; Band; Jazz Band; Hon Roll; NHS; Summa Cum Laude Natl Latin Exam; All Region Band; Soc Sci.

COLE, ANGELIQUE; Southside HS; Fort Smith, AR; (3); 53/460; Church Yth Grp; VP Sec Drama Clb; JCL; Latin Clb; Mu Alpha Theta; Service Clb; Speech Tm; Thesps; Chorus; School Musical; All Region Chair 93, 95; Natl Latin Exam Summa Cum Laude 96; Latin Natl Hnr Soc; Harding Univ; Theatre Ed.

COLE, CARRIE; Cty Line HS; Branch, AR; (2); Church Yth Grp; Cmnty Wkr; FCA; FBLA; HOBY; Natl Beta Clb; Natl FFA Org; Quiz Bowl; Spanish Clb; Bsktbl; Hmcmng Maid; Ms CLHS; Stu Mnth; Sprts Med.

COLE, DANIEL L; Valley Springs Schl; Harrison, AR; (3); Art Clb; Church Yth Grp; French Clb; Natl FFA Org; Teachers Aide; School Play; Stage Crew; Ofcr Bsbl; Bsktbl; Golf; Area Classic Soccer Team Mem; U Of AR; Landscape Arch.

COLE, J MICHAEL; Springdale Sr HS; Springdale, AR; (2); Church Yth Grp; FBLA; Band; Church Choir; Mrchg Band; Orch; Pep Band; Hon Roll; Jr NHS; NHS; U Of AR; Law/Fine Arts.

COLE, JENNIFER; Southside HS; Fort Smith, AR; (4); Drama Clb; German Clb; Key Clb; Math Clb; Mu Alpha Theta; Pep Clb; Science Clb; Speech Tm; Rep Sr Cls; Var Chrldng; U Of Cntrl AK; Bio.

COLE, JYME B; Cty Line HS; Branch, AR; (4); 3/36; FCA; FBLA; Pres Natl Beta Clb; Pres Natl FFA Org; Pres Spanish Clb; School Play; VP Sr Cls; Pres Stu Cncl; L Bsktbl; 4-H Awd; Cath Yth Ministries; AR HS RODEO Assn; AR Tech U; Agribus.

COLE, LA TONYA; Brinkley HS; Brinkley, AR; (4); Am Leg Aux Girls St; Church Yth Grp; 4-H; French Clb; FBLA; GAA; Church Choir; Sec Frsh Cls; Sec Soph Cls; Sec Jr Cls; Sci, Engl, Amer Hstry Awds; UCN; Bus.

COLE, NATASHA L; Lonoke Sr HS; Lonoke, AR; (3); 3/104; FCA; Sec FBLA; Spanish Clb; Ed Yrbk; Rep Soph Cls; Treas Jr Cls; Pres Stu Cncl; Trk; VP NHS; Prelaw.

COLE, NATHAN A; Hartford Schl; Hartford, AR; (2); Natl FFA Org; Var Bsktbl; Hon Roll.

COLEMAN, AMANDA D; Prairie Grove HS; Prairie Grove, AR; (3); FHA; Natl FFA Org; Spanish Clb; Hon Roll; Jr NHS; U Of A; Nrsng.

COLEMAN, AXXIS; Lee Sr HS; Marianna, AR; (2); Church Yth Grp; FTA; Girl Scts; Math Tm; Science Clb; Spanish Clb; Band; Chorus; Church Choir; Mrchg Band; Cert Of Participation, Recognition & Citizenship; Jackson ST Univ; Phys Thrpst.

COLEMAN, COSTINA C; Rivercrest HS; Luxora, AR; (3); 15/92; FBLA; Office Aide; Teachers Aide; High Hon Roll; Hon Roll; NHS; Prfct Atten Awd; ST Tech Inst; Bus/Cmptr Tech.

COLEMAN, JENNIFER; Mountainburg Jr Sr HS; Mountainburg, AR; (3); Church Yth Grp; Cmnty Wkr; Pres FCA; Pres 4-H; Sec FHA; GAA; Natl Beta Clb; Natl FFA Org; Spanish Clb; SADD; U Of AR Fayetteville.

COLEMAN, LATONYA M; Parkview Arts-Science HS; Little Rock, AR; (2); Church Yth Grp; Drama Clb; FBLA; Girl Scts; Natl Beta Clb; Rep Stu Cncl; Bsktbl; Cit Awd; High Hon Roll; Hon Roll; Y Teen; Peer Medtr; Fut 500; Accnt.

COLLIE, CHRIS; Bismarck Jr-Sr HS; Donaldson, AR; (2); Church Yth Grp; Natl FFA Org; Band; Drm Mjr(t); Jazz Band; Mrchg Band; Pep Band; School Musical; Var Bsbl; Hon Roll; Bsbl.

COLLIE, STEPHANIE L; Malvern Sr HS; Malvern, AR; (4); Church Yth Grp; FBLA; FHA; Science Clb; Spanish Clb; SADD; Acpl Chr; Chorus; Church Choir; School Play; Gracenotes, Peer Cnslrs; OTC; Psych.

COLLIER, ANGEL A; Abundant Life Schools; Little Rock, AR; (2); Drama Clb; Spanish Clb; Bsktbl; NHS; Criminal Law.

COLLIER, KEVIN; Taylor HS; Stamps, AR; (2); 1/25; Church Yth Grp; FCA; VP 4-H; Treas Natl FFA Org; Church Choir; VP Frsh Cls; Pres Soph Cls; Ofcr Bsbl; Bsktbl; Cit Awd; Bst All Arnd Boy; FFA #1 Frt Sllr, Dist Lvstck Jdgr; SAU; Vet.

COLLIER, TEAKQWANDA S; Norphlet HS; Calion, AR; (2); Art Clb; Church Yth Grp; FBLA; FTA; Library Aide; Office Aide; Science Clb; Spanish Clb; Teachers Aide; Band; Black Stu Assn; Anchor Clb; U Of AR; Psych; Pediatrics.

COLLINS, ALISSA; Hall Sr HS; Little Rock, AR; (3); 3/230; Church Yth Grp; FCA; FHA; Natl Beta Clb; Quiz Bowl; Hist Spanish Clb; Band; Ofcr Sr Cls; Ofcr Stu Cncl; Bsktbl; Chrldng; Y Teens ICC Prjct Coord, VP; Bausch & Lomb Outstndng Sci Stu; Med.

COLLINS, AMANDA; Leslie Schl; Leslie, AR; (4); 2/19; Church Yth Grp; Cmnty Wkr; 4-H; Girl Scts; VP Key Clb; Natl Beta Clb; Teachers Aide; Band; Church Choir; High Hon Roll; Singing Group Travel; Talent Awds; Coll Of Ozarks; Music.

COLLINS, BRENT; North Little Rock Hs-East; North Little Rock, AR; (4); Debate Tm; Mu Alpha Theta; ROTC; Science Clb; Color Guard; Drill Tm; High Hon Roll; US Air Frce Acad.

COLLINS, DANA; Gosnell Jr Sr HS; Blytheville, AR; (2); Library Aide; Natl Beta Clb; Hon Roll; Ntl Merit Ltr.

COLLINS, EVAN T; Sylvan Hills HS; Sherwood, AR; (2); 31/342; Church Yth Grp; FCA; Mu Alpha Theta; Natl Beta Clb; Science Clb; Var Ftbl; High Hon Roll; Hon Roll; Jr NHS; NHS; 9th Grd SAT Duke Univ Talent Id Prgm; 10th Grd Attnd LSU Ftbl Camp.

COLLINS, JENNIFER L; Star City HS; Star City, AR; (3); 1/110; Church Yth Grp; FBLA; Mu Alpha Theta; Band; Mrchg Band; Nwsp; Yrbk; High Hon Roll; NHS; Prfct Atten Awd; Electric Cooperative Washington DC Tour Wnnr.

COLLINS, JESSICA L; Southside HS; Fort Smith, AR; (2); FCA; Band; Mrchg Band; Pep Band; NHS; Ntl Merit Ltr; Dir Awd; Bio Med Eng.

COLLINS, JULIA G; Fayetteville Sr HS; Fayetteville, AR; (3); Church Yth Grp; FCA; Hosp Aide; Letterman Clb; Mu Alpha Theta; SADD; Swing Chorus; Var Bsktbl; Var Trk; High Hon Roll; Pre-Med.

COLLINS, KEVIN W; Star City HS; Star City, AR; (2); Church Yth Grp; Math Tm; Intrml Bsktbl; Intrml Vllybl; High Hon Roll; Hon Roll; U Of AR Monticello; Cmptr Engr.

COLLINS, LARRY S; Jacksonville HS; Jacksonville, AR; (3); Art Clb; Drama Clb; Office Aide; Band; School Musical; School Play; Stage Crew; Hon Roll; Harding Univ; Bio.

COLLINS, NIKKI; Lake Hamilton Sr HS; Royal, AR; (3); Church Yth Grp; FCA; Treas FHA; Natl Beta Clb; Spanish Clb; Band; Rep Treas Stu Cncl; Co-Capt Chrldng; All Reg 1st Bnd, 1st Chr; NCA All Amer Cheerldr 3 Yrs; Nurse.

COLLINS, REBECCA A; Bald Knob HS; Judsonia, AR; (1); Natl Beta Clb; Band; Mrchg Band; Pep Band; JV Bsktbl; Var Sftbl; JV Trk; Hon Roll; Pres Acad Fit Awd.

COLLINS, SCOTT T; Bauxite Jr Sr HS; Bauxite, AR; (2); 16/83; Spanish Clb; Teachers Aide; Treas Soph Cls; Var L Bsbl; Var L Ftbl; Var L Trk; Cit Awd; Hon Roll; Acctng.

COLLINS, TIMOTHY S; Lake Hamilton Jr HS; Royal, AR; (1); Church Yth Grp; FCA; Band; Pres Stu Cncl; Ouachita Bapt U; Mnstry.

COLSTON, DORI L; Northside HS; Fort Smith, AR; (3); Art Clb; Chess Clb; Drama Clb; Latin Clb; Speech Tm; Teachers Aide; Thesps; Stage Crew; Bsktbl; Trk; Art; Washington Univ; Arch Dsgn.

COLTRAIN, CHRISTOPHER R; Southside HS; Batesville, AR; (1); CAP; Office Aide; Quiz Bowl; Science Clb; Golf; Cit Awd; Hon Roll; Prfct Atten Awd; GATE; Civics Awd 95-; Quiz Bowl Awd 95-; Cmptr Prgmng.

COLTRANE JR, RONALD DOUGLAS; Cabot HS; Ward, AR; (1); Church Yth Grp; JV Ftbl; Hon Roll; Jr NHS; Play Non Schl Bsbl Babe Ruth League; William & Mary Coll; Bus.

COLVILLE, LACRESHA A; Gravette HS; Gravette, AR; (1); 1/106; Library Aide; Teachers Aide; Hon Roll; Jr NHS.

COLVIN, CONNIE N; Monticello HS; Monticello, AR; (3); Church Yth Grp; Drama Clb; 4-H; French Clb; Natl Beta Clb; SADD; Band; Mrchg Band; NHS; Harding Univ; Music Ed.

COMBS, COURTNEY; Mc Rae Schl; Searcy, AR; (4); 1/30; FBLA; VP FHA; Hosp Aide; Natl Beta Clb; Sec Stu Cncl; Bsktbl; Ntl Merit Ltr; Pres Acad Fit Awd; Val; Trck; Sci Clb Sec; Rssn Clb; ASU Beebe; Occup Thrp.

COMBS, JENNIFER L; Southside HS; Fort Smith, AR; (4); Church Yth Grp; FCA; FBLA; GAA; Key Clb; Office Aide; Pep Clb; Speech Tm; Rep Jr Cls; Rep Sr Cls; U Of Central AR.

COMBS, JERAMY; Bismarck Jr-Sr HS; Bismarck, AR; (4); 12/60; Natl Beta Clb; Quiz Bowl; Science Clb; Phtg Rptr Yrbk; Chorus; Pres Stu Cncl; L Bsktbl; Swmmng; Trk; Hon Roll; Ouachita Bapt Univ; Jrnlsm.

COMBS, KENNETH A; Osceola HS; Osceola, AR; (3); Cmnty Wkr; Letterman Clb; Library Aide; Ofcr Soph Cls; Ftbl; Trk; Wt Lftg; Hon Roll; St Chmpnshp; AR Actvts Assn; Hnrs All Conf Tm; U Of AR; Bus.

COMBS, ROBYN N; Russellville Sr HS; Russellville, AR; (3); 89/320; Am Leg Aux Girls St; Church Yth Grp; Natl Beta Clb; Office Aide; Spanish Clb; SADD; Chorus; Church Choir; Hon Roll; UCA; PT.

COMBS, RYAN; Nashville HS; Nashville, AR; (4); 10/106; Spanish Clb; Hon Roll; NHS; Pres Acad Fit Awd; Jehovahs Wittnesses; Won Regnl AR Cncl Of Tchrs Of Math Calculus Cmptn; Henderson ST Univ; Comp Sci.

COMPTON, CHRYSTAL; Dover HS; Dover, AR; (4); 24/84; GAA; Office Aide; Spanish Clb; Ed Nwsp; Bsktbl; Chrldng; Sftbl; Trk; Hon Roll; Treas Jr NHS; AAU Bsktbl; Pride Team; AR Tech Univ; Hlth Info Mngmt.

CONATSER, JOSEPH H; Horatio HS; Horatio, AR; (2); 4-H; Natl FFA Org; ROTC; School Play; Yrbk; Var Bsbl; Var Bsktbl; Var Ftbl; Var Trk; 4-H Awd; Draw; Air Force/Cmptr.

CONDRA, CASEY; Dewitt HS; De Witt, AR; (3); 6/120; FCA; HOBY; Natl Beta Clb; Sec Frsh Cls; Sec Soph Cls; Sec Jr Cls; VP Stu Cncl; JV Capt Chrldng; Sftbl; Clss Fav.

CONDREY, RACHEL A; John L Mcclellan Magnet HS; Little Rock, AR; (3); Art Clb; Drama Clb; FBLA; Spanish Clb; School Musical; L Var Chrldng; JV Capt Sftbl; Gov Hon Prg Awd; High Hon Roll; Hon Awds Word Prcsng I/Kybrdng I/Advrtsng; Pulaski Tech; Psych.

CONLEY, SHAUN P; England HS; Scott, AR; (4); 19/64; Church Yth Grp; Drama Clb; French Clb; FBLA; Natl Beta Clb; Mrchg Band; School Play; Yrbk; Hon Roll; Henderson ST U; Pre-Pharmacy.

CONNALLY, CISSY; Greenwood Sr HS; Greenwood, AR; (1); Church Yth Grp; Pres FCA; GAA; Chrldng; Gym; Trk; Wt Lftg; Hon Roll; Prfct Atten Awd.

CONNELL, CASEY; Batesville Sr HS; Batesville, AR; (4); 4-H; FBLA; Natl Beta Clb; Office Aide; Q&S; Spanish Clb; Yrbk; 4-H Awd; Hon Roll; Earth Clb; Builders Clb; Bus Mgmt.

CONNELLY, SIOBHAN E; Ashdown Sr HS; Ashdown, AR; (4); 9/134; Cmnty Wkr; FBLA; Natl Beta Clb; Cit Awd; French Hon Soc; NHS; Acad Achvt Awds Wrld His, Comp Tech, Fr III; Tae Kwon Do 2nd Degr Black Blt, Co Instr; Piano-Hymn Fst; U Of AR Fayetteville; Bus.

CONNELY, JAMIE N; Gillett Jr Sr HS; Gillett, AR; (2); Church Yth Grp; FBLA; FHA; Pep Clb; Spanish Clb; Rptr Nwsp; Rep Frsh Cls; JV Var Chrldng; MASH Prgm; Lib Club Sec; Art Club; Medical Prof.

CONNER, SAMANTHA A; Mt Ida Jr Sr HS; Mount Ida, AR; (2); Church Yth Grp; Natl Beta Clb; Band; Mrchg Band; Pep Band; Hon Roll; Pride.

CONRAD, AMBER L; Watson Chapel Sr HS; Pine Bluff, AR; (3); 12/220; Art Clb; Sec Church Yth Grp; JA; Science Clb; Spanish Clb; Band; Church Choir; Flag Corp; Mrchg Band; School Play; All-Amer Schlr Awd; Pre-Med.

CONTRATTO, CHRISTY; Magnolia HS; Magnolia, AR; (3); 1/185; FBLA; Mu Alpha Theta; Science Clb; Band; Color Guard; Powder Puff Ftbl; Hon Roll; 1st Plc Sci Fair; Ind Pl Regnl Sci Fair; All Rgn Band; Acctng.

CONWAY, KIMBERLY L; White Hall Sr HS; Pine Bluff, AR; (3); 27/171; VP Art Clb; Church Yth Grp; Key Clb; Mu Alpha Theta; Natl Beta Clb; ROTC; Band; Color Guard; Drill Tm; Trk; Sons Amer Rev Awd For Ldrshp; Soldry Bearing/Excl; Mltry Order Wrld War Awd Of Merit; Natl Sojrn Awd; Baylor Univ; Psych.

COOK, ANNE NOEL; Northside HS; Fort Smith, AR; (3); Church Yth Grp; Cmnty Wkr; Intnl Clb; Spanish Clb; Acpl Chr; Band; Chorus; Church Choir; Jazz Band; Mrchg Band; Play Piano; Cultural Ambassadors; West Ark Comm Coll; Phy Thrpst.

COOK, BRANDY; Nashville HS; Nashville, AR; (3); 2/152; Church Yth Grp; 4-H; FBLA; Natl FFA Org; Spanish Clb; Band; Drill Tm; Flag Corp; Mrchg Band; Yrbk; Cossatot; Bus.

COOK, BRANDY; Butterfield Jr HS; Van Buren, AR; (1); HOBY; Teachers Aide; Band; Drm Mjr(t); Jazz Band; Mrchg Band; High Hon Roll; Jr NHS; Prfct Atten Awd; Dirs Awd Band; Acad Lttr; Coll; Nrlgst.

COOK, DAVID; Rogers HS; Conway, MO; (4); 13/468; Office Aide; Teachers Aide; Band; Jazz Band; High Hon Roll; Jr NHS; Pres Acad Fit Awd; Rnssnc; Chmbr Of Cmmrc Cert Of Acad Achvt; Comp Sci.

COOK, DE ANN; Casa Schl; Casa, AR; (4); 1/14; FHA; Natl Beta Clb; Spanish Clb; Yrbk; Sec Frsh Cls; VP Soph Cls; Pres Jr Cls; Pres Sr Cls; Bsktbl; Val; ACT Schol To U Of Cent AR; U Of Cent AR; Mass Comm.

COOK, DIANNA M; Mena HS; Mena, AR; (4); 50/118; Cmnty Wkr; Office Aide; Hon Roll; Prfct Atten Awd; Poem Pub; Air Force; Cmptr Tech.

COOK, J R; Perryville Jr Sr HS; Perryville, AR; (3); Chess Clb; Cmnty Wkr; FCA; FBLA; Library Aide; Model UN; Red Cross Aide; Sec Soph Cls; Ofcr Bsbl; Ftbl; Hendrix-Conway; Radiology.

COOK, JAMES R; Perryville Jr Sr HS; Perryville, AR; (3); Chess Clb; Debate Tm; FCA; FBLA; Library Aide; Model UN; Teachers Aide; Var JV Bsbl; Var JV Ftbl; DAR Awd; Hendrix; Radiologist.

COOK, JESSICA; Danville HS; Danville, AR; (2); 7/37; Church Yth Grp; Drama Clb; FCA; Pres 4-H; FBLA; VP FHA; SADD; Band; Church Choir; Color Guard; Color Grd Co-Capt; AR Tech; Crimnlgy.

COOK, JONATHAN A; Brookland Jr Sr HS; Jonesboro, AR; (3); Treas Art Clb; FBLA; Natl Beta Clb; Natl FFA Org; Quiz Bowl; Sec VICA; Hon Roll; Pres Acad Fit Awd; Art Club Treas; SERVISTAR Coast To Coast All-Amer Voc Stu Awd 95-96; ASU; Arch Drftng.

COOK, KATRINA A; Oak Grove HS; North Little Rock, AR; (3); Church Yth Grp; Drama Clb; FHA; Chorus; Hon Roll; Psych.

COOK, KYLE L; Valley View HS; Jonesboro, AR; (4); Church Yth Grp; Capt Quiz Bowl; Spanish Clb; Band; Chorus; Capt Fld Hcky; Hon Roll; ASU; Arch.

COOK, MARCUS L; Ashdown Sr HS; Ashdown, AR; (3); French Clb; Ofcr Bsbl; Bsktbl; Vllybl; Hsu; Bus; Acctng.

COOK, MISTY; Southside HS; Fort Smith, AR; (3); FCA; Spanish Clb; Church Choir; Capt Chrldng; Trk; Vllybl; Hon Roll; NHS; Pres Acad Fit Awd; Church Yth Grp; Girls Clb Vol; Psych.

COOK, MYNEEKA; Arkansas Schl Math & Science; Fayetteville, AR; (4); 4-H; Mu Alpha Theta; NHS; Lead 94 UPENN; AR Schl For Math/Scis; PBS; Fisk; Chem Eng.

COOK, NATHAN; Bryant Jr HS; Benton, AR; (2); Church Yth Grp; Cmnty Wkr; Ftbl; Wt Lftg; Hon Roll; FL ST; Engrng.

COOK, PAMELA W; Mc Rae Schl; Mc Rae, AR; (3); FBLA; FHA; Natl Beta Clb; Bsktbl; Sftbl; High Hon Roll; Hon Roll; Church Yth Grp; 4-H; Crs Cntry; Russian Clb; All Dist Bsktbll; Wendys HS Heisman Sftbll.

COOK, RACHEL B; Sylvan Hills HS; Sherwood, AR; (2); 9/265; Mu Alpha Theta; Natl Beta Clb; Spanish Clb; Band; Jazz Band; Mrchg Band; Var Tennis; High Hon Roll; Jr NHS; NHS.

COOK, REASON I; Russellville Sr HS; Russellville, AR; (3); Band; Jazz Band; Mrchg Band; NHS.

COOK, ROBERT R; Harrisburg HS; Harrisburg, AR; (2); Church Yth Grp; Prfct Atten Awd; Pub Speaking; FFA Mem; Intense Bible Stud; U Of Tulsa; Botanist.

COOK, RUSELL E; Arkansas Sr HS; Texarkana, AR; (2); Boy Scts; Ftbl; Wt Lftg; Hon Roll; U Of AR; Ortho Srgn.

COOK, SAMANTHA C; John L Mcclellan Magnet HS; Little Rock, AR; (4); 20/250; French Clb; FBLA; Library Aide; Mu Alpha Theta; Yrbk; Sftbl; High Hon Roll; Hon Roll; NHS; ST Cmptn Exec Bus Games; Pres Ed Awd Prgm Otsdng Acad; Stdnt Of WK/EXECUTIVE Of Wk; U Of Cntrl AR; Nrsg.

COOK, SONYA; Delight HS; Delight, AR; (2); 2/25; 4-H; FBLA; FHA; Natl Beta Clb; Quiz Bowl; Church Choir; Rep Stu Cncl; Var Bsktbl; Hon Roll; Ntl Merit Ltr; Gftd/Tlntd; U AR Fayetteville; Pedtrcn.

COOK, STEPHANIE; Sylvan Hills HS; Sherwood, AR; (4); 48/233; Church Yth Grp; Q&S; Teachers Aide; Acpl Chr; Yrbk; Ofcr Jr Cls; Treas Sr Cls; Ofcr Stu Cncl; Hon Roll; All-Region Choir; AR ST Univ.

COOK, TAMMY L; Lavaca Jr Sr HS; Lavaca, AR; (2); FHA; Hon Roll; Working With Animals; Westark CC; Sci; Bio.

COOK, WESLEY M; Magnolia HS; Fouke, AR; (3); 49/259; Bus Profs of Am; Church Yth Grp; FBLA; Teachers Aide; Band; Chorus; Church Choir; Mrchg Band; Pep Band; Stage Crew; All Region Band; 1st Div On Solo; Henderson ST Univ; Band Dir.

COOKE, KATHERINE E; Prairie Grove HS; Prairie Grove, AR; (3); Drama Clb; FBLA; FHA; Quiz Bowl; Spanish Clb; SADD; Chorus; School Play; Powder Puff Ftbl; High Hon Roll; U AR; Commcntns.

COOKSEY, ERIKA N; Sylvan Hills HS; North Little Rock, AR; (4); Church Yth Grp; FHA; FTA; Girl Scts; High Hon Roll; Hon Roll; Tchrs Of Tomorrow; Tot Club; Erly Grad; SAACCLUB; Stdy Afrcn Amer Cltrs; Future 500; Sci Club; AR Tech Univ; Elem Ed/Adm.

COOKSEY, SAMANTHA E; Springdale Sr HS; Springdale, AR; (2); Church Yth Grp; FBLA; Band; Church Choir; Drm Mjr(t); Mrchg Band; Orch; Pep Band; High Hon Roll; Hon Roll; Slctd Best 9th Grd GATE Eng Stdnt; All-Rgn 1st Bnd 3 Yrs; 2nd Plc ST Media Fstvl 9th Grd Yr; U Of Cntrl AR; OT/PT.

COOLEY, SHONEY L; Scotland Schl; Scotland, AR; (1); Church Yth Grp; Pres Frsh Cls; Hon Roll; Frosh Clss Beauty.

COOLIDGE, THOMAS; Oark HS; Clarksville, AR; (2); 2/20; Cmnty Wkr; Math Clb; Acpl Chr; Hon Roll; Comp Sci.

COOMBE, TRAVIS M; Bald Knob HS; Bald Knob, AR; (3); 33/121; Am Leg Boys St; Natl Beta Clb; Quiz Bowl; Spanish Clb; Teachers Aide; Rep Band; Jazz Band; Mrchg Band; Pep Band; Hon Roll; Phi Beta Mu Outstdng Stu Awd; U Of AR Fayetteville; Comp Sci.

COON, AMBER; Northside HS; Fort Smith, AR; (2); Church Yth Grp; Chorus; Church Choir; Ed Rptr Nwsp; Chrldng; Cit Awd; High Hon Roll; Hon Roll; Jr NHS; NHS; Jr Optimist; TAPS; Partners In Christ; Kimmons Jr HS Choral Dirctorsawd; Crch Yth Ensemble; Ouachita Baptist Univ; Mus Ed.

COONFIELD, MARY A; Bentonville Sr HS; Bentonville, AR; (4); Church Yth Grp; FCA; Acpl Chr; Crs Cntry; Hon Roll; All Reg Choir; C Cntry MIP; Oral Comm.

COONTS, CYNTHIA N; Valley Springs Schl; Harrison, AR; (2); Church Yth Grp; Varsity Clb; Band; Mrchg Band; Pep Band; School Play; Chrldng; High Hon Roll; Hon Roll; Harding Univ; El Ed.

COOPER, ALISHA L; Van Buren Sr HS; Van Buren, AR; (2); Church Yth Grp; FBLA; Mu Alpha Theta; Pep Clb; Speech Tm; SADD; Capt Chrldng; Trk; High Hon Roll; Jr NHS; All Amer Chrldr; Power Tumbling; Dancing; U AR; Med.

COOPER, ANDREA; Evening Shade Schl; Evening Shade, AR; (3); VP FCA; Rep FBLA; Math Clb; Science Clb; Variety Show; Var Bsktbl; Capt Var Sftbl; Hon Roll; Chrch Yth Cls Ldr; Gifted & Talented; Harding; Law.

COOPER, BRANDON; Bay Jr Sr HS; Jonesboro, AR; (4); 1/35; Church Yth Grp; Pres FBLA; HOBY; Pres Natl Beta Clb; Capt Quiz Bowl; Science Clb; Chorus; Ed Nwsp; Pres Frsh Cls; Pres Soph Cls; Optimist Clb Yth Apprctn Awd; Phrmcy.

COOPER, BRETT A; Southside HS; Fort Smith, AR; (3); 129/502; Church Yth Grp; FCA; Key Clb; Mu Alpha Theta; Spanish Clb; Teachers Aide; Ftbl; Hon Roll; Jr NHS; NHS; Citadel; Law.

COOPER, CAMELIA; Gurdon HS; Gurdon, AR; (1); 1/80; Church Yth Grp; Letterman Clb; Church Choir; Pres Frsh Cls; Bsktbl; Chrldng; Trk; Cit Awd; Hon Roll; Pres Acad Fit Awd.

COOPER, CARON; Brinkley HS; Brinkley, AR; (1); Church Yth Grp; Band; Church Choir; Drm Mjr(t); Mrchg Band; Sec Frsh Cls; Hon Roll; Pres Jr NHS; 4-H Awd; 4-H; Drg-Fr Schl Pgm TOPS; 1st Bapt Chrch Actns, Yth Hndbls; Ouachita Bapt U.

COOPER, ERICA L; Dollarway HS; Pine Bluff, AR; (2); 3/190; Rptr FBLA; ROTC; Sec Science Clb; Chorus; Flag Corp; Mrchg Band; Pep Band; Rep Soph Cls; Pres Stu Cncl; Teachers Aide; Achvmt Awds In Sci, Eng & Soc Stud; Awd Of Dedication Ladies-Gentlemens Clb Sec; AR ST; Law.

COOPER, HALEY; White Hall Sr HS; Pine Bluff, AR; (3); Church Yth Grp; Science Clb; Spanish Clb; Rep Frsh Cls; Rep Soph Cls; Rep Jr Cls; Rep Sr Cls; Rep Stu Cncl; Var Chrldng; Hon Roll; Teens For Christ; Merit List.

COOPER, JONATHON D; Ridgecrest HS; Paragould, AR; (2); 12/210; Church Yth Grp; Band; Jazz Band; Mrchg Band; Cit Awd; Hon Roll; Prfct Atten Awd.

COOPER, JORDAN; Central Ark Christian Schl; Jacksonville, AR; (2); Church Yth Grp; Pres Soph Cls; Ofcr Stu Cncl; High Hon Roll; Hon Roll; Jr NHS.

COOPER, JULIE A; Russellville Sr HS; Russellville, AR; (4); 23/220; Church Yth Grp; Cmnty Wkr; FHA; Library Aide; Spanish Clb; Rptr Nwsp; Var Gym; Trk; Hon Roll; Drama Clb; All Stars; CSU; AR ST Univ; Comp Pgmng.

COOPER, LISA A; Springdale Sr HS; Springdale, AR; (3); Acpl Chr; Band; Chorus; Drill Tm; Ofcr Soph Cls; Ofcr Stu Cncl; Pom Pon; High Hon Roll; Hon Roll; NHS; Drill Tm Capt 9th Grd; U Of AR; Arch.

COOPER, NICHOLAS L; Van Buren Sr HS; Van Buren, AR; (3); FCA; Letterman Clb; Office Aide; Teachers Aide; Varsity Clb; Chorus; Var Ftbl; Var Trk.

COOPER, SARAH; Rogers HS; Rogers, AR; (4); 11/457; Am Leg Aux Girls St; Church Yth Grp; Cmnty Wkr; HOBY; Acpl Chr; Band; Chorus; Church Choir; Jazz Band; Mrchg Band; UT Knoxville; Med.

COOPER, SCOTTY E; Siloam Springs Sr HS; Siloam Springs, AR; (2); Natl FFA Org; Var L Ftbl; Trk; Hon Roll; Mrtl Arts Gld Mdl Jr Olympcs 94-95.

COOPER, TERROY D; Sheridan Sr HS; Prattsville, AR; (2); Church Yth Grp; FCA; Bsktbl; Hon Roll; Prfct Atten Awd; U Of AR.

COPAS, MICHAEL; Cabot HS; Cabot, AR; (1); Church Yth Grp; Bsktbl; Hon Roll; U Of AR; Arch.

COPE, LEAH R; Bergman Schl; Bergman, AR; (1); Church Yth Grp; Natl FFA Org; Pep Clb; JV Var Chrldng; Trk; Prfct Atten Awd; Jr BETA; Coll Of The Ozarks; Cnslr.

COPE, TABBY J; Southside HS; Fort Smith, AR; (2); Drama Clb; Orch; School Musical; School Play; Stage Crew; Hon Roll; Jr NHS; NHS; Pres Acad Fit Awd.

COPELAND, ANGIE; Prairie Grove HS; Prairie Grove, AR; (4); French Clb; Math Clb; Science Clb; Spanish Clb; Teachers Aide; Varsity Clb.

COPELAND, BRITNEY; Central Ark Christian Schl; North Little Rock, AR; (2); Church Yth Grp; Cmnty Wkr; Spanish Clb; Chorus; Rep Stu Cncl; Var Crs Cntry; Var Trk; Hon Roll; Histry Clb; All St All Str In CC; Multi Yr Listee; Harding Univ.

COPELAND JR, JERRY D; Osceola HS; Osceola, AR; (3); Art Clb; Drama Clb; French Clb; Sec FBLA; Model UN; Natl Beta Clb; Science Clb; Rptr Nwsp; Tennis; Hon Roll.

COPELAND, JODIE; Pea Ridge HS; Bentonville, AR; (2); 15/70; Drama Clb; Rptr 4-H; Rptr FBLA; FHA; HOBY; Spanish Clb; Band; Flag Corp; Mrchg Band; School Play; Teen Crt; Ed Tlnt Srch; Law; Lwyr.

COPELAND, KAREN L; Magnolia HS; Magnolia, AR; (3); 43/215; Church Yth Grp; FBLA; Mu Alpha Theta; Science Clb; Band; Flag Corp; Nwsp; Powder Puff Ftbl; Trk; Hon Roll; Sci Fair Grnd Prz; LA Tech Univ; Elem Ed.

COPELAND, SHAUNA; Danville HS; Danville, AR; (2); Pres 4-H; HOBY; Quiz Bowl; VP Soph Cls; Rep Stu Cncl; JV Bsktbl; JV Chrldng; Cit Awd; 4-H Awd; NHS.

COPELAND, SUSANN; Danville HS; Danville, AR; (4); 1/44; Rep Am Leg Aux Girls St; VP FHA; HOBY; Sec SADD; VP Sr Cls; Sec Stu Cncl; Capt Chrldng; 4-H Awd; Pres NHS; Val; AR Ofc Chld Spprt Enfrcmnt Essy Wnnr; Frshman Sr Hmcmng Maid; 95 Pope Co Rodeo Qun; UAR; Psych.

COPELAND, SUSANN M; Danville HS; Belleville, AR; (4); 1/44; Rep Am Leg Aux Girls St; 4-H; Treas FBLA; VP FHA; HOBY; Spanish Clb; Sec SADD; VP Jr Cls; VP Sr Cls; Sec Stu Cncl; Mst Congenial Miss Yell Co Pageant; ARK Dept Of Human Svcs Essay Cont Wnnr; Yell Cty Rodeo Qn; U Of AR Fayetteville; Psych.

COPELIN, PRISCILLA G; Dumas HS; Dumas, AR; (2); Church Yth Grp; English Clb; FBLA; GAA; Girl Scts; Library Aide; Math Clb; Science Clb; Spanish Clb; Band; US Achvmnt Acad 95; U Of AR.

COPENING, ERIKA; Greenwood Sr HS; Greenwood, AR; (4); 1/179; Church Yth Grp; FCA; Mu Alpha Theta; Natl Beta Clb; Pres Jr Cls; VP Sr Cls; Capt Vllybl; NHS; Val; Bsch Lmb Sci Awd Excllnc; Ouachita Baptist U; Psych.

COPLEY, AMANDA W; Southside HS; Fort Smith, AR; (3); UCA; Vet.

COPPAGE, PRECIOUS A; Forrest City HS; Forrest City, AR; (3); Dance Clb; DECA; Drama Clb; FHA; Library Aide; Office Aide; School Musical; School Play; High Hon Roll; Hon Roll; U Of Memphis; Cmptr Sci.

CORBELL, MICHAEL S; Ashdown Sr HS; Ben Lomond, AR; (3); Library Aide; Natl FFA Org; Fire Marshall 3 Yrs; Elec.

CORBETT, AMANDA J; Mountain Home HS; Mountain Home, AR; (4); French Clb; Natl Beta Clb; Nwsp; Pres Soph Cls; Pres Jr Cls; Fr Exch Stu; AR Governors Schl Attendee; Interact; U Of Cntrl AR; Mrktng.

CORBIN, CARA; St Paul Schl; Combs, AR; (4); 3/26; Art Clb; Church Yth Grp; Drama Clb; FBLA; FHA; Natl Beta Clb; Quiz Bowl; Science Clb; SADD; Nwsp; U Of AR; Tchr.

CORBIN, KYRONE; Watson Chapel Sr HS; Pine Bluff, AR; (4); 53/240; Art Clb; Key Clb; Natl Beta Clb; Ofcr Stu Cncl; Ftbl; Wt Lftg; Hon Roll; Prfct Atten Awd; Engrng Tem Tld For 1st In St; Selctd As Delta Gentlmn For Delta Sigma Theta Sorrty; Henderson ST U; Comp Sci; Bus.

CORBIN, TANYA C; Little Rock Cntrl HS; Little Rock, AR; (2); Church Yth Grp; Drama Clb; Natl Beta Clb; Quiz Bowl; Spanish Clb; Drill Tm; Rep Soph Cls; Rep Jr Cls; Hon Roll; Jr NHS; Polysci.

CORCORAN, JARED; Mulberry HS; Mulberry, AR; (3); 2/38; Church Yth Grp; 4-H; HOBY; VP Natl FFA Org; Science Clb; VP Jr Cls; Var Bsbl; Mgr Bsktbl; Hon Roll; NHS; U Of AR.

CORDELL, JONATHAN D; Corning HS; Corning, AR; (1); Art Clb; Church Yth Grp; Tennis; Hon Roll; GT OM Team.

CORDELL, STACIE L; Lake Hamilton Sr HS; Hot Springs, AR; (2); Church Yth Grp; FBLA; Pep Clb; Teachers Aide; Chorus; Hon Roll; Gftd/Tlntd Prgm; 5 Yr Old Sndy Schl Tchr.

CORDER, DAMON; Bryant HS; Benton, AR; (4); Church Yth Grp; Cmnty Wkr; FCA; Spanish Clb; Band; Pep Band; Ftbl; Wt Lftg; Cit Awd; Gov Awd For Volunte; U Of Cntrl AR; PT/SPORTS Med.

CORE, JON; Charleston HS; Charleston, AR; (3); 2/40; Church Yth Grp; FCA; FBLA; Natl Beta Clb; Quiz Bowl; Spanish Clb; High Hon Roll; Prfct Atten Awd.

CORE, STEPHANIE; Berryville HS; Berryville, AR; (2); Art Clb; French Clb; Key Clb; Office Aide; Science Clb; Rep Frsh Cls; Rep Jr Cls; Rep Stu Cncl; JV Capt Chrldng; Sftbl.

CORLEY, JIMMY; Poyen Schl; Malvern, AR; (4); 1/34; FCA; Quiz Bowl; Treas Frsh Cls; VP Jr Cls; VP Sr Cls; Sec Stu Cncl; Var Bsbl; Var Bsktbl; Val; U Of Cntrl AR.

CORLEY, WAYLON T; Glen Rose HS; Malvern, AR; (1); Natl Beta Clb; Spanish Clb; JV Ftbl; Mgr(s); High Hon Roll; Tae Kwon Do; Future Prblm Slvng.

CORMACK, BRIAN; North Little Rock Hs-West; North Little Rock, AR; (3); 191/554; Art Clb; Library Aide; Spanish Clb; Phtg Yrbk; U Of AR Fayetteville; Jrnlsm.

CORNELIOUS, FELICHA R; Mc Crory Jr Sr HS; Mc Crory, AR; (4); FBLA; GAA; Bsktbl; Powder Puff Ftbl; Trk; Henderson Coll; Engrng.

CORNELIUS, MISTY C; Arkansas Sr HS; Texarkana, AR; (2); Church Yth Grp; Band; Drill Tm; Flag Corp; Mrchg Band; Pom Pon; Cit Awd; Hon Roll; Sec Jr NHS; Pres Acad Fit Awd; Prd Drg Fre Clb; Tn Crt Tn Lwyrs Fr Tns; TX A&M; Rdlgst.

CORNETT, AMY; Bentonville Sr HS; Bentonville, AR; (3); #3 in class; FBLA; SADD; Band; Capt Drm Mjr(t); Mrchg Band; Pep Band; High Hon Roll; NHS; Pres Acad Fit Awd; Homecoming Maid; U Of AR; Bus.

CORNISH, CRYSTAL R; Nashville HS; Nashville, AR; (4); 8/106; FBLA; FHA; Spanish Clb; Band; School Play; Hon Roll; Jr NHS; NHS; All Amer Schlr; Hnr Grad; Univ Of AR/FAYTVL; Poultry Sci.

CORRY, NICOLAS E; Marion HS; Marion, AR; (4); 18/184; Cmnty Wkr; FCA; FBLA; Math Clb; Mu Alpha Theta; Quiz Bowl; Spanish Clb; Band; Yrbk; Rep Frsh Cls; Millikin U.

COSH, JAN S; Arkadelphia Sr HS; Arkadelphia, AR; (4); 1/131; Am Leg Aux Girls St; FCA; French Clb; Natl Beta Clb; Drill Tm; Sec Sr Cls; Ofcr Stu Cncl; Swmmng; Trk; NHS; Ouachita Bapt Univ; Bio; Orthod.

COSSEY, AMANDA L; Sheridan Sr HS; Hensley, AR; (2); Teachers Aide; Chorus; Hon Roll; Jr NHS; Pres Schlr; Prod Stinger 1 News.

COSSEY, BRIAN; Bradford Jr Sr HS; Bradford, AR; (4); 1/36; Boy Scts; French Clb; FBLA; FHA; Treas Natl FFA Org; Quiz Bowl; Varsity Clb; School Musical; School Play; Treas Sr Cls; Sr Beta Pres; PRIDE.

COSSEY, CHASSITY; Hamburg HS; Wilmot, AR; (3); Church Yth Grp; Natl FFA Org; School Play; Rep Soph Cls; Pres Jr Cls; Rep VP Stu Cncl; Capt Chrldng; Var Sftbl; Pres Jr NHS; NHS.

COSTIGAN, NICOLE; Mansfield Jr Sr HS; Mansfield, AR; (1); Art Clb; Church Yth Grp; Drama Clb; FCA; Speech Tm; Chorus; School Play; Chrldng; Trk; Vllybl; Frst Plc 9th Grd Poetry KUAF Wrtng Cntst; Westark CC; Rec Therapist.

COSTNER, KACI; Manila HS; Manila, AR; (2); 1/75; Natl Beta Clb; Chorus; Church Choir; Chrldng; Hon Roll.

COSTNER, MATT; Southside HS; Fort Smith, AR; (3); Boy Scts; Church Yth Grp; Library Aide; Spanish Clb; Band; Church Choir; Hon Roll; Jr NHS; NHS; Pres Acad Fit Awd; Quachita Bapt U.

COSTON, NICHOLAS; Lake Hamilton Sr HS; Royal, AR; (4); 8/279; Am Leg Boys St; Computer Clb; 4-H; Pres FBLA; Natl Beta Clb; Pres Natl Beta Clb; Science Clb; Spanish Clb; Tennis; NHS; Natl FFA Ag Mech Cont 13th Pl Hgh Ind; Adv Cmptr Tech Tm Ldr; Optmst Yth Awd; U AR; Vet.

COTTA, JOE D; Alma HS; Alma, AR; (2); Teachers Aide; Rep Soph Cls; U AR.

COTTEN, STEPHANIE D; Dewitt HS; De Witt, AR; (3); FCA; French Clb; FBLA; FTA; Natl Beta Clb; Science Clb; Teachers Aide; Rep Stu Cncl; Var L Bsktbl; JV Chrldng; Art Awd; Interior Dsgn.

COTTON, BRANDY L; Ozark HS; Ozark, AR; (3); FCA; FHA; Natl Beta Clb; Chorus; Cit Awd; Hon Roll; West AR; Receptionist.

COTTON, CHARITY; Fordyce HS; Fordyce, AR; (3); 8/84; Am Leg Aux Girls St; Pres Church Yth Grp; Pres FHA; HOBY; Natl Beta Clb; ROTC; Church Choir; Rptr Nwsp; Pres Soph Cls; High Hon Roll; FHA St Offcr Sec; Chrch Asst Sec; Star Events; U Of Little Rock; Pharm.

COTTON, JAMIE B; Southside HS; Fort Smith, AR; (3); Boy Scts; FCA; Socr; Hon Roll; U Of AR; Bus; Fin.

COTTON, JOSEPH A; Arkansas Sr HS; Texarkana, AR; (4); 24/374; Drama Clb; Key Clb; Mu Alpha Theta; Q&S; Quiz Bowl; Spanish Clb; Yrbk; Ofcr Stu Cncl; Hon Roll; U Of AR Fayetteville; Engrng.

COTTON, JULIE; Fayetteville Christian Schl; Fayetteville, AR; (3); Art Clb; Church Yth Grp; Cmnty Wkr; FCA; HOBY; Key Clb; Mu Alpha Theta; Co-Ed Yrbk; Hon Roll; NHS; John Brown U.

COTTRELL, ANGELA; Bergman Schl; Harrison, AR; (4); 7/54; Church Yth Grp; Sec FBLA; Natl Beta Clb; Natl FFA Org; Church Choir; Chrldng; Hon Roll; Pres Acad Fit Awd; Oral Roberts Univ; Radio Brdcst.

COUCH, JASON; Van Buren Sr HS; Van Buren, AR; (2); Art Clb; Science Clb; Teachers Aide; Band; Jazz Band; Mrchg Band; School Play; Stage Crew; Hon Roll; Ntl Merit Ltr; All Amer Schlr 95; Natl Ldrshp & Svc Awd 95.

COUCH, PORTIA L; Brookland Jr Sr HS; Jonesboro, AR; (3); Debate Tm; FHA; Hosp Aide; VP Natl FFA Org; Quiz Bowl; Hist Band; Jazz Band; Pep Band; Phtg Yrbk; JV Var Chrldng; Ffa Animal Sci Awd; Band Awd; Eng Merit Awd; ASU; Animal Sci/Vet.

COULSON, AMANDA B; North Little Rock Hs-West; North Little Rock, AR; (3); 145/554; FBLA; Pep Clb; Teachers Aide; Band; Mrchg Band; Pep Band; Cit Awd; Hon Roll; ASU Jonesborro; Lawyer.

COULSON, MELISSA; Pea Ridge HS; Pea Ridge, AR; (2); FBLA; FHA; Spanish Clb; Hon Roll; NHS; Pres Acad Fit Awd; Sftbll Rec.

COULTER, AMANDA; Blevins HS; Ozan, AR; (2); Church Yth Grp; GAA; Church Choir; Bsktbl; Hon Roll; Nal Yth Ldrshp Forum; Lawyer.

COULTER, BENJAMIN L; Montrose Acad; Montrose, AR; (2); 3/5; Church Yth Grp; Natl Beta Clb; Spanish Clb; School Musical; Pres Frsh Cls; Sec Soph Cls; Ofcr Stu Cncl; Ofcr Bsbl; Bsktbl; Ftbl; U Of AR At Monticello.

COULTER, KRISTE L; Crowleys Ridge Acad; Paragould, AR; (1); 13/27; GAA; Pep Clb; Science Clb; Spanish Clb; Chorus; Ofcr Soph Cls; Ofcr Stu Cncl; Bsktbl; Socr; Trk; Freed Hardiman Univ; Eng Tchr.

COUNCIL, SARAH D; Cty Line HS; Charleston, AR; (2); FCA; 4-H; Natl Beta Clb; Natl FFA Org; Quiz Bowl; Spanish Clb; Bsktbl; Trk; Hon Roll; Natl Jr Holstein Assn.

COUNTS, AMY; Benton Sr HS; Benton, AR; (2); 1/350; Cmnty Wkr; Acpl Chr; School Musical; Rptr Nwsp; Yrbk; Rep Soph Cls; Ofcr Stu Cncl; Church Yth Grp; French Clb; Dance Machn-Sr Line Cmptn Team; Benton Main St Stu Advy Bd; Mst Entertnng Dance Routn At Applaus Natls; Jungian Analyst.

COUNTS, BO R; Springdale Sr HS; Springdale, AR; (1); Teachers Aide; Hon Roll; Golf; Cmptrs; U Of AR.

COURSON, AMANDA R; Crossett Sr HS; Crossett, AR; (2); Church Yth Grp; FTA; Natl Beta Clb; Hon Roll; LA Tech; Orthodontist.

COURSON, CHRIS P; Mc Gehee HS; Mc Gehee, AR; (2); Church Yth Grp; FCA; FTA; Mu Alpha Theta; Natl Beta Clb; Natl FFA Org; Spanish Clb; L Bsbl; Hon Roll; VP NHS; U Of AR.

COURSON, JILL D; Magnolia HS; Magnolia, AR; (4); 7/207; Mu Alpha Theta; Pep Clb; Science Clb; Teachers Aide; Band; Nwsp; Var Chrldng; Powder Puff Ftbl; High Hon Roll; NHS; Stdnt Rotarian; U Of MS.

COURSON, JOSH; Mc Gehee HS; Mc Gehee, AR; (3); Boy Scts; Church Yth Grp; FCA; FTA; Letterman Clb; Mu Alpha Theta; Natl Beta Clb; Spanish Clb; VP Soph Cls; VP Jr Cls; St Bible Drill Awd.

COURTNEY, DEWANE; Weiner HS; Fisher, AR; (3); Art Clb; Church Yth Grp; Drama Clb; FHA; FTA; Teachers Aide; Chorus; Stat Bsbl; Stat Bsktbl; Hon Roll; Outstdng Stdnt Awd; HS Wrtng Cmptn; Cmptr Tech.

COURTNEY, GRETCHEN D; Warren Sr HS; Warren, AR; (4); Library Aide; Teachers Aide; School Musical; Stage Crew; Yrbk; Score Keeper; High Hon Roll; IM Bsktbl; Summe Cumme Laude; U Of AR; Pre-Med/Pdtrc Onclgst.

COUSAR, MICHAEL I; Russellville Sr HS; Russellville, AR; (2); Church Yth Grp; Natl Beta Clb; Neural Surgeon.

COVINGTON, CATHERINE; Mt St Mary Acad; Little Rock, AR; (1); FBLA; SADD; Var Chrldng; Cit Awd; DAR Awd; French Hon Soc; Hon Roll; Diamond All Star Chrldng Squad NCA.

COVINGTON, JEREMY; Mc Rae Schl; Vilonia, AR; (2); FHA; Rptr Frsh Cls; Rptr Soph Cls; Ofcr Bsbl; Bsktbl; Hon Roll; U Of Central AR.

COVINGTON, KADE; Ft Smith Christian Schl; Fort Smith, AR; (3); 2/35; Church Yth Grp; FCA; HOBY; Spanish Clb; Band; Church Choir; VP Jr Cls; Gov Hon Prg Awd; NHS; Prfct Atten Awd; OSU.

COVINGTON, KATHERINE M; Cabot HS; Ward, AR; (2); Church Yth Grp; German Clb; Office Aide; Band; Church Choir; Mrchg Band; Pep Band; Natl Discovery Awds Wnnr; Criminal Analyst.

COVINGTON, MATTHEW D; Fayetteville Sr HS; Fayetteville, AR; (2); Boy Scts; Church Yth Grp; Math Tm; Band; Church Choir; Jazz Band; Stage Crew; Hon Roll; Vlntr Caretaker; Backpacking.

COWAN, CARISSA L; Flippin Jr Sr HS; Bull Shoals, AR; (4); 4/42; Cmnty Wkr; FBLA; German Clb; Key Clb; Service Clb; SADD; Treas Sr Cls; High Hon Roll; NHS; Intract; U Of AZ; Intl Bus.

COWAN, FREDRECA D; Palestine-Wheatley HS; Palestine, AR; (4); 4-H; FHA; Girl Scts; Natl Beta Clb; Office Aide; Church Choir; School Musical; Yrbk; Lit Mag; High Hon Roll; Drug Free Clb; Rdng; AR ST U; Nrsng.

COWAN, JEREME MICHAEL; Southside HS; Fort Smith, AR; (2); Church Yth Grp; Cmnty Wkr; FCA; Teachers Aide; Rep Stu Cncl; JV Bsktbl; Ftbl; Gov Hon Prg Awd; High Hon Roll; Hon Roll; Southern Nazarene U; Evnglst.

COWAN, KRISTIE L; Russellville Sr HS; Russellville, AR; (2); 201/405; Chorus.

COWAN, SHIRRELL; Lamar HS; Lamar, AR; (3); FCA; Math Clb; Var Capt Chrldng; Mgr(s); Hon Roll; Ntl Merit SF; GATE; Ar Tech U.

COWART, KELLY D; Fountain Lake Jr Sr HS; Hot Springs, AR; (3); 9/87; FCA; FHA; Key Clb; Pep Clb; Quiz Bowl; Spanish Clb; Church Choir; Bsktbl; Vllybl; Hon Roll; U Of Cntrl AR; Med.

COWDERY, JOSH; Sylvan Hills HS; Sherwood, AR; (3); Boy Scts; Church Yth Grp; Drama Clb; FCA; French Clb; Mu Alpha Theta; Treas Natl Beta Clb; School Musical; Variety Show; Ftbl; Eagle Scout Boy Scouts.

COWELL, JARED; Lamar HS; Lamar, AR; (4); 8/64; Am Leg Boys St; Church Yth Grp; FCA; Math Clb; Quiz Bowl; Science Clb; Ed Nwsp; Ed Yrbk; Rep Stu Cncl; L Bsktbl; FCA Ldrshp Team; AR ST Univ; Commnctn.

COWGER, SCARLET L; Russellville Sr HS; Russellville, AR; (3); Art Clb; Church Yth Grp; Cmnty Wkr; GAA; Hosp Aide; Var Bsktbl; Var Vllybl; Hon Roll; AR Tech Univ.

COWLEY, JASON B; Fouke Jr Sr HS; Fouke, AR; (2); Natl FFA Org; Ofcr Soph Cls; Hon Roll; Motorcycle & Car Racing.

COWSERY, JOSHUA W; Sylvan Hills HS; Sherwood, AR; (3); Boy Scts; Church Yth Grp; Drama Clb; FCA; Mu Alpha Theta; Natl Beta Clb; School Musical; Variety Show; Ftbl; NHS; Attained Rank Of Eagle Sct 94.

COX, AMANDA B; Mt St Mary Acad; Maumelle, AR; (2); 1/160; FCA; Hosp Aide; JCL; Latin Clb; Mu Alpha Theta; Natl Beta Clb; Intrml Bsktbl; Var Sftbl; JV Vllybl; High Hon Roll; Jr Olympic Vllybl; CO Outward Bound; Natl Svc Awd; Sports Med.

COX, AMY R; Bald Knob HS; Bald Knob, AR; (2); Church Yth Grp; Cmnty Wkr; Drama Clb; Spanish Clb; Acpl Chr; VP Church Choir; School Musical; School Play; Swing Chorus; FHA; PRIDE Clb; Play Piano; ASU; Music Dir/Elem Tchr.

COX, BLAIR; Walnut Ridge HS; Walnut Ridge, AR; (4); 25/66; Art Clb; Church Yth Grp; FCA; Library Aide; Quiz Bowl; Science Clb; Spanish Clb; Teachers Aide; Band; Chorus; Miss WRAS; Algebra II Awd Highest Avrg End Yr; 3 Art Awds 1st Pl Schl Shows/NEA Fair Show 94; AR ST U At Jonesboro; Art.

COX, BRITTNEY; Murfreesboro HS; Murfreesboro, AR; (1); Church Yth Grp; FHA; Bsktbl; Cit Awd; Hon Roll; Prfct Atten Awd; Pres Acad Fit Awd.

COX, BRYEN G; Beebe Sr HS; Mc Rae, AR; (2); Boy Scts; Church Yth Grp; Band; Church Choir; Mrchg Band; Hon Roll; UALR; Hrptlgy.

COX, CHRISTY C; Russellville Sr HS; Russellville, AR; (3); 72/400; Cmnty Wkr; 4-H; FBLA; Chorus; Capt Mgr(s); Cit Awd; 4-H Awd; High Hon Roll; NHS; Pres Acad Fit Awd; All Stars; Farm Bureau Sweepstakes Wnnr; AR Tech Univ; Bus; Psych.

COX, COURTNEY S; Dumas HS; Tillar, AR; (3); Sec FBLA; Math Clb; Natl Beta Clb; Science Clb; Spanish Clb; Band; Co-Capt Flag Corp; Yrbk; Hon Roll; NHS; PT.

COX, JOLEE R; Bald Knob HS; Bald Knob, AR; (2); Church Yth Grp; FCA; FHA; Spanish Clb; Teachers Aide; Chorus; Variety Show; Cit Awd; Hon Roll; Pres Acad Fit Awd; FHA Dist ST STAR Evnts 2(d ST; All Rgn Choir; Vctn Bible Schl Vol; Univ Cnrtl AR; Bus Mngmt.

COX, JUSTIN M; Crowleys Ridge Acad; Paragould, AR; (1); 2/30; Church Yth Grp; Cmnty Wkr; Bsktbl; Socr; Trk; High Hon Roll; Hon Roll; Jr High Bible Awd 96; Hnr Stu Awd 96.

COX, KATHY J; Corning HS; Corning, AR; (1); Library Aide; Chorus.

COX, KRISTIE; Delight HS; Antoine, AR; (1); FHA; Quiz Bowl; Hon Roll; All Amer Schlr; S Plains Coll; Perf Arts Tech.

COX, KRISTOPHER M; Alma HS; Alma, AR; (4); Rep Am Leg Boys St; Church Yth Grp; Cmnty Wkr; VP Science Clb; Drm Mjr(t); Jazz Band; School Play; Pres Stu Cncl; Cit Awd; NHS; 2nd Pl St Sci Fair; Westark CC; Music.

COX, KYLA JO; Mt Vernon-Enola HS; Enola, AR; (3); 5/30; Drama Clb; FHA; Library Aide; Office Aide; Spanish Clb; School Play; Stage Crew; Variety Show; Cit Awd; Hon Roll; Petit Jean Tech Coll; LPN.

COX, MELISSA S; Hughes Jr-Sr HS; Heth, AR; (2); 12/73; Art Clb; Math Clb; Natl Beta Clb; Quiz Bowl; Science Clb; Band; Jazz Band; Mrchg Band; Sec Stu Cncl; Pres Acad Fit Awd; U Of Memphis; Law.

COX, MICKI; Murfreesboro HS; Murfreesboro, AR; (2); #1 in class; Church Yth Grp; FHA; Natl Beta Clb; Quiz Bowl; Spanish Clb; Band; Mrchg Band; Yrbk; Var Sftbl; Hon Roll.

COX, NANCY; Beebe Sr HS; Beebe, AR; (4); Am Leg Aux Girls St; Drama Clb; FBLA; FHA; Math Clb; Science Clb; Spanish Clb; Thesps; School Play; Yrbk; FBLA Sec; ASU Beebe; Acctng.

COX, PEPPER J; Cabot HS; Cabot, AR; (4); 30/300; Church Yth Grp; French Clb; FHA; Pep Clb; Chorus; Mrchg Band; School Musical; School Play; Lit Mag; Chrldng; Hnr Grad; Pres Schol To U Of Centrark; Sing With Natl Yth Hnr Choir Crngie Hall; U Of Centr AR; Premed.

COX, SARA; Murfreesboro HS; Nashville, AR; (3); Art Clb; Church Yth Grp; FBLA; FHA; Natl Beta Clb; Science Clb; Spanish Clb; Band; Mrchg Band; High Hon Roll; Bus.

COX, SARAH G; Rogers HS; Rogers, AR; (2); 60/698; SADD; Teachers Aide; Vllybl; High Hon Roll; Hon Roll; PE Awd; Civic Awd; Vet.

COX, STEPHANIE D; Bald Knob HS; Bald Knob, AR; (3); Band; Color Guard; Drm Mjr(t); Mrchg Band; Yrbk; Hon Roll; Prfct Atten Awd; ASU Jonesboro; Tchr.

COX, STEPHANIE J; North Little Rock Hs-East; North Little Rock, AR; (2); Drama Clb; 4-H; Girl Scts; Key Clb; School Play; Variety Show; Gld Awd; Slvr Awd; Vol At Museum Ofsci And Histr; U Of AR; Drama.

COX, STEVE M; Conway Sr HS; Conway, AR; (3); Art Clb; FBLA; Hon Roll.

COX, TERESEA; Delight HS; Lexington, SC; (1); 4-H; FHA; Natl FFA Org; Quiz Bowl; Chorus; School Musical; Hon Roll; GATE; Gold Medal Star Evnts FHA; Ouachita Bapt Univ Upwrd Bnd Prgm; Sci Tchr; Arch Prof.

COX, TIFFANY D; Lake Hamilton Sr HS; Pearcy, AR; (2); 52/269; Art Clb; FCA; Sec FHA; Natl Beta Clb; Office Aide; Teachers Aide; Q&S; Lit Mag; Mgr(s); Cit Awd; Spcl Olympcs Vlntr; Wrtng Poetry; U Of AR; Child Psych.

COX, TRISHA L; Fountain Lake Jr Sr HS; Benton, AR; (1); Church Yth Grp; Cmnty Wkr; FCA; Sec 4-H; Hosp Aide; Key Clb; Treas Natl Beta Clb; Spanish Clb; Band; Church Choir; Church Sftbl Tm; U Of Cntrl AR; Spch Pathlgy.

COYLE, CAMISTA D; Piggott HS; Piggott, AR; (3); Church Yth Grp; 4-H; Natl Beta Clb; Natl FFA Org; Science Clb; School Musical; Stage Crew; Chrldng; Tennis; Hon Roll; Pageants Church Camp 5 Yrs; VFW Voice Of Democracy Audio Essay Contest 1st Pl Winner; ASUI.

CRABB, AMY E; Harrison Sr HS; Harrison, AR; (4); 1/187; Drama Clb; FBLA; Key Clb; Office Aide; Thesps; Chorus; Stage Crew; Nwsp; Yrbk; Hon Roll; Med Sci Rsrch Clb; Govs Schlr; AR ST U; Chem.

CRABB, CANDY J; Bauxite Jr Sr HS; Bauxite, AR; (3); 8/65; Cmnty Wkr; FBLA; Spanish Clb; SADD; Teachers Aide; Chorus; Hon Roll; NHS; CHAMPS; Big Bro/Sis; TX A&M Kingsville; Vet.

CRABB, DEREK; Warren Sr HS; Warren, AR; (3); Nwsp; Var Bsbl; Ftbl.

CRABILL, TRISHA L; Searcy HS; Searcy, AR; (4); 19/190; Pres Church Yth Grp; FBLA; Natl Beta Clb; Spanish Clb; Yrbk; Var Golf; Jr NHS; NHS; Ntl Merit SF; Spanish NHS; Harding U; Chem Engrng.

CRABTREE, DANNY R; Fouke Jr Sr HS; Fouke, AR; (3); 1/85; Church Yth Grp; FCA; FBLA; FHA; Natl Beta Clb; Natl FFA Org; Pres Frsh Cls; VP Soph Cls; VP Jr Cls; VP Sr Cls; U Of AR Little Rock; Med/An.

CRABTREE, R K; Ridgecrest HS; Paragould, AR; (3); 21/210; Am Leg Boys St; Boy Scts; FCA; Quiz Bowl; Ftbl; Pres Acad Fit Awd; Tutor; U Of AR; Sprts Med.

CRAFT, CASEY; Glenwood Jr Sr HS; Glenwood, AR; (4); 11/27; Church Yth Grp; FCA; FBLA; Natl FFA Org; JV Bsktbl; JV Crs Cntry; JV Var Ftbl; Golf; JV Var Trk; Hon Roll; FFA Pres; Beef Profcncy 94-; Dvrsfd Lvstck; Star Chptr Frmr; Southern AR Univ; Ag Bus.

CRAIG, AMANDA; Gentry HS; Gentry, AR; (4); Church Yth Grp; FCA; VP FBLA; Key Clb; Spanish Clb; Ofcr Stu Cncl; Bsktbl; Capt Chrldng; Golf; Hon Roll; Miss Benton Cty 95; Miss Gentry 95; Miss Teen Lake Dordanell 95; Yng Miss Dogwood 95; AR ST U; Commnctns.

CRAIG, BRET T; Southside HS; Batesville, AR; (2); Church Yth Grp; FBLA; Natl Beta Clb; Quiz Bowl; High Hon Roll; Hon Roll; Prfct Atten Awd; Gftd & Tlntd Prgm; Arch.

CRAIG, CASSADY B; Southside HS; Fort Smith, AR; (2); Church Yth Grp; Cmnty Wkr; Dance Clb; FCA; FBLA; Key Clb; Pep Clb; Spanish Clb; Teachers Aide; Band; Washington U.

CRAIG, JASON E; Trumann HS; Trumann, AR; (3); Church Yth Grp; French Clb; Natl FFA Org; Var Bsbl; Hon Roll; NHS; AR St AA Bsbll Champ; AR St Univ; Bus.

CRAIG, REBECCA; Rison HS; Rison, AR; (4); 6/56; Church Yth Grp; FCA; French Clb; FBLA; FHA; Natl Beta Clb; Office Aide; Science Clb; Teachers Aide; JV Bsktbl; U Monticello; CPA.

CRAIN, BENJAMIN J; Rogers HS; Rogers, AR; (3); 16/566; Church Yth Grp; Cmnty Wkr; FCA; FBLA; Scholastic Bowl; Band; Var Bsktbl; High Hon Roll; NHS; Pres Acad Fit Awd; Abilene Chrstn U.

CRAIN, KATHERINE; Camden Fairview HS; Camden, AR; (3); Church Yth Grp; Drama Clb; French Clb; FBLA; Natl Beta Clb; Science Clb; SADD; Acpl Chr; Church Choir; School Musical; Anchor Clb; Spanish Clb VP; U Of AR; Speech Pthlgy.

CRAIN, LESLIE M; Southside HS; Fort Smith, AR; (2); Drama Clb; FCA; FBLA; Key Clb; Speech Tm; Phtg Nwsp; Hon Roll; Jr NHS; NHS; Pres Acad Fit Awd; Law; Psych.

CRAIN, ROSALYN M; El Dorado Sr HS; El Dorado, AR; (3); Church Yth Grp; Cmnty Wkr; FBLA; Hosp Aide; Natl Beta Clb; Teachers Aide; Church Choir; Orch; School Musical; Rptr Nwsp; All Region, All South Orch; Gftd/Tlntd; Rotary Clb Mntr Pgm; Hosp Vlntr; Anchor Clb; REACH; Futrstc Outlk; Biochem.

CRAMER, AMANDA L; Lake Hamilton Sr HS; Hot Springs Natio, AR; (3); Computer Clb; FCA; GAA; Office Aide; Spanish Clb; Teachers Aide; Band; Mrchg Band; Bsktbl; Sftbl; Wolf Pride Stdnts Against Drugs; Ouachita Bapt Univ; Ed.

CRANDELL, JENNY; Pleasant View Schl; Mulberry, AR; (1); Church Yth Grp; GAA; Natl Beta Clb; Nwsp; Bsktbl; Trk; Hon Roll.

CRANE, AUTUMN L; Hope HS; Hope, AR; (4); 52/193; Am Leg Aux Girls St; Church Yth Grp; FBLA; FHA; Natl Beta Clb; Office Aide; Band; Jazz Band; Mrchg Band; Hon Roll; Grl Sct Cnslr; Red River CC; Nrsng.

CRANE, REBECCA I; Southside HS; Fort Smith, AR; (3); 304/502; Church Yth Grp; Pep Clb; Teachers Aide; Radio Installation; Pool; St Edwards Mercy Med Ctr; Xray.

CRANFILL, RACHEL S; Cushman Schl; Batesville, AR; (2); Church Yth Grp; FHA; Library Aide; Office Aide; Quiz Bowl; Chorus; Rptr Co-Ed Nwsp; Hon Roll; Ntl Merit Ltr; AR Schlr; Law.

CRANFORD, KATIE E; Southside HS; Batesville, AR; (3); #1 in class; Am Leg Aux Girls St; Treas FBLA; Key Clb; Natl Beta Clb; Pres Treas Science Clb; Drill Tm; Yrbk; High Hon Roll; Spanish Clb; Natl Yong Ldrs Conf; Outstdng Key Clb Mem In MO & AR; PRIDE; Outstdng Soph Key Clb Mem; Acad Awds.

CRANFORD, PRISCILA G; Horatio HS; Horatio, AR; (3); Church Yth Grp; FHA; Hosp Aide; Speech Tm; Acpl Chr; Chorus; Church Choir; High Hon Roll; Hon Roll; Prfct Atten Awd; U Of AR Little Rock; Doctor.

CRAVEY, ANGIE L; Hartford Schl; Hackett, AR; (3); Church Yth Grp; FBLA; FHA; GAA; Chorus; VP Frsh Cls; Capt Var Bsktbl; Var Chrldng; Var Powder Puff Ftbl; Var Sftbl; Westark Univ.

CRAWFORD, BRADLEY K; Bradford Jr Sr HS; Bradford, AR; (2); Hon Roll; Jr Beta Club; Mst Imprvd Awd Alg I; Cmptr Tech.

CRAWFORD, CINDY; Eureke Springs HS; Eureka Springs, AR; (4); Natl Beta Clb; Hon Roll; Pres Schlr; St Schlr; High Hnr Grad; Art Awds & Hnrb Mntns; Participated In Numerous Art Act; U Of A; Comp Graphc-Fshn Dsgnr.

CRAWFORD, COZETTE; Blytheville Sr HS; Blytheville, AR; (2); FHA; Hon Roll; Grambling St Univ; Psych.

CRAWFORD, JENNIFER; Ft Smith Christian Schl; Van Buren, AR; (2); Church Yth Grp; FBLA; VP Soph Cls; Co-Capt Chrldng; NHS; U AR; Law.

CRAWFORD, JOHN A; Lakeside HS; Hot Springs Natio, AR; (3); Church Yth Grp; FCA; FBLA; JV Var Bsktbl; Ftbl; Hon Roll; Jr NHS; Hunting; Fishing; Engrng/Wldlfe Mngmnt.

CRAWFORD, JOSHUA; Fayetteville Christian Schl; Lincoln, AR; (2); Church Yth Grp; Computer Clb; 4-H; Yrbk; Sec Frsh Cls; 4-H Awd; High Hon Roll; Hon Roll; NHS.

CRAWFORD, MELISSA; Carlisle Jr Sr HS; Lonoke, AR; (2); 3/52; FHA; Library Aide; Spanish Clb; Teachers Aide; School Play; Sec Jr Cls; Ofcr Stu Cncl; Chrldng; High Hon Roll; Prins Clb.

CRAWFORD, ROBERT; Mc Rae Schl; Mc Rae, AR; (3); 1/26; Church Yth Grp; HOBY; Math Tm; Quiz Bowl; Teachers Aide; VICA; Church Choir; Bsktbl; High Hon Roll; Hon Roll; Collective Assn Chrstns Fndr; Cntrl Bible Coll; Preacher.

CREACY, TONYA A; Watson Chapel Sr HS; Pine Bluff, AR; (3); Church Yth Grp; English Clb; Natl Beta Clb; Office Aide; Church Choir; Lit Mag; Cit Awd; Hon Roll; Pres Acad Fit Awd; Intl Frgn Lang Awd.

CREAMER, AMANDA; Bergman Schl; Harrison, AR; (4); 6/58; Church Yth Grp; VP FBLA; FHA; Treas Natl Beta Clb; Natl FFA Org; Pep Clb; Mgr Bsktbl; Mgr(s); Score Keeper; Sftbl; AR Times All-Star Tm; Cntrl Bapt Coll; Bus Admin.

CREASMAN, MATT D; Central Ark Christian Schl; Maumelle, AR; (2); Church Yth Grp; Spanish Clb; Rep Frsh Cls; Treas Soph Cls; Var Bsktbl; Var Crs Cntry; Var Tennis; High Hon Roll; Hon Roll; Jr NHS; All St Tennis; HS Art Awd; Var Bsktbll Cmmtmnt Awd.

CREDEUR, BRANDY N; Arkansas Sr HS; Texarkana, AR; (3); Church Yth Grp; 4-H; Band; Mrchg Band; Trk; Pres Acad Fit Awd; Explrs Grp St Michaels Hosp; Hazels Dinner Vol; TN Coll; Med Field.

CREED, PHILLIP; West Side Christian Schl; Magnolia, AR; (3); Mu Alpha Theta; Chorus; Co-Ed Yrbk; Pres Jr Cls; VP Stu Cncl; Var Bsktbl; Var Socr; Var Trk; High Hon Roll; Hon Roll; Reflections Awd Bsktbl; Musical Composition.

CREEKMORE, JAMIE C; Southside HS; Fort Smith, AR; (2); Church Yth Grp; Key Clb; Chorus; Drill Tm; Rep Soph Cls; Treas Stu Cncl; Hon Roll; NHS; Pres Acad Fit Awd; Spec Olympics Vol; U Of Ar; Psych/Sociology.

CRENSHAW, ANGELA D; Parkview Arts-Science HS; Little Rock, AR; (2); Church Yth Grp; Dance Clb; FBLA; FHA; FTA; Natl Beta Clb; Science Clb; Spanish Clb; Band; Church Choir; Soc Stud Club; Howard Univ; Appld Arts.

CRENSHAW, JEFF D; Booneville Jr Sr HS; Magazine, AR; (2); Band; Westark CC; Bus Admin.

CREWS, REGINA; Brinkley HS; Brinkley, AR; (1); Church Yth Grp; Band; Church Choir; Mrchg Band; Hon Roll; Jr NHS; Jr Stdnt Cncl; U Of AR; Psych.

CRIGGER, CATHERINE; Blytheville Sr HS; Blytheville, AR; (2); Church Yth Grp; Dance Clb; French Clb; GAA; Key Clb; Red Cross Aide; Varsity Clb; Bsktbl; Chrldng; Gym; AR Univ; Law.

CRILL, MORRIS; Humphrey Schl; Humphrey, AR; (1); Church Yth Grp; Natl FFA Org; Quiz Bowl; Church Choir; Lbrn Nwsp; Hon Roll; Cdt Tchng; Awana; Yth Mssn; OBU; Dr.

CRISEL, JEFFERY C; Des Arc Jr Sr HS; Des Arc, AR; (2); Nvlst.

CRISWELL, ANTHONY J; Harmony Grove Jr Sr HS; Benton, AR; (2); Science Clb; Acpl Chr; Band; Mrchg Band; Nwsp; Yrbk; Ftbl; Wt Lftg; Wrstlng; Prfct Atten Awd; 1st Pl St Sci Fair; 1st Pl St Wrestling Cmptns In IN; Sci Tchr; Nrs.

CRISWELL, CANDICE M; Stuttgart Sr HS; Stuttgart, AR; (4); 2/143; Am Leg Aux Girls St; Hist FBLA; Key Clb; VP Mu Alpha Theta; Quiz Bowl; Spanish Clb; Band; Rep Stu Cncl; Treas NHS; Sal; AR Govrs Schl; Girls ST Cnslr 96; Westminster Coll; Bus Admin.

CRITES, JOSHUA M; Mt Ida Jr Sr HS; Mount Ida, AR; (1); Church Yth Grp; Natl FFA Org; Bsktbl; Ftbl; Ag.

CRITTENDEN, PRENTISS L; Morrilton Sr HS; Morrilton, AR; (3); Church Yth Grp; Drama Clb; French Clb; FBLA; Thesps; Band; Church Choir; Drm Mjr(t); Jazz Band; Mrchg Band; Wkshps In Washington DC; Outstdng Band Mem; AR Tech; Bus.

CRITTON, MYRA; Magnolia HS; Magnolia, AR; (3); Church Yth Grp; FBLA; Library Aide; Office Aide; Church Choir; Yrbk; Mrt List; U Of AR; Lawyer.

CROCKER, AMY B; Beebe Sr HS; Beebe, AR; (3); 29/126; Church Yth Grp; 4-H; FBLA; Treas Sec FHA; Treas FTA; GAA; Pep Clb; Science Clb; Spanish Clb; Teachers Aide; ASU; Mrktng.

CROCKER, CASEY H; Fayetteville Sr HS; Fayetteville, AR; (2); Science Clb; Tae Kwon Do; Arch; Comp Animation; Drama.

CRODDY, KENDRA; Huntsville HS; Huntsville, AR; (4); Girl Scts; Quiz Bowl; Science Clb; Teachers Aide; Thesps; Band; Mrchg Band; School Musical; School Play; Stage Crew; Ptry Cont; Svr Hrlm Plnt Vrts; Spec Int-Mdvl Lfe Brtsh Isles; Wrtr.

CROMEANS, CHRIS; Hughes Jr-Sr HS; Hughes, AR; (2); 3/74; HOBY; Math Tm; Natl Beta Clb; Quiz Bowl; Science Clb; Spanish Clb; Band; Jazz Band; Mrchg Band; Rep Soph Cls; Meteorology.

CROSBY, CHRISTOPHER J; Arkansas Schl For The Blind; Stuttgart, AR; (3); 1/15; FHA; HOBY; VP Key Clb; Pep Clb; Co-Capt Quiz Bowl; Band; Chorus; Mrchg Band; Pep Band; School Musical; ASB Best All Around Stu Awd 95; MO-AR Dist Of Key Clubs Div Lt Govrnr 94-95; Class B St Track Champ; U Of Memphis; Corp Bus.

CROSBY, LATASHA L; J A Fair Sr HS; Little Rock, AR; (3); Church Yth Grp; Computer Clb; FBLA; FHA; Science Clb; Spanish Clb; Church Choir; Powder Puff Ftbl; Score Keeper; Cit Awd; Future 500 Club.

CROSS, CASEY; Pulaski Acad; Little Rock, AR; (2); Church Yth Grp; FCA; Natl Beta Clb; Spanish Clb; Band; Mrchg Band; Var Pom Pon; Powder Puff Ftbl; High Hon Roll; NHS; 4-H Excel Pgrm; Comm Svce Hnrd Vol; NCA DANC Supr Awd; Sprts Med.

CROSS, CHRISTOPHER B; Southside HS; Fort Smith, AR; (3); 39/500; Church Yth Grp; FCA; French Clb; Church Choir; Nwsp; Bsktbl; Golf; French Hon Soc; Hon Roll; Jr NHS; Pre-Med.

CROSS, JARRETT A; Forrest City HS; Forrest City, AR; (1); 4-H; FBLA; FHA; Hon Roll; U Of Pine Bluff AR; Elec Engr.

CROSS, RICHIE; Southside HS; Fort Smith, AR; (4); Am Leg Boys St; Church Yth Grp; Pres FBLA; Key Clb; Nwsp; Pres Sr Cls; Ofcr Stu Cncl; Church Choir; Variety Show; Ftbl; Coach Of Pee Wee Bsbl Team For Boys Clb; Lead Role In Chrch Musical Damn Yankees; Westark CC.

CROSSEN, APRIL D; Corning Jr Sr HS; Corning, AR; (4); 3/62; Band; JV Bsktbl; High Hon Roll; Pres Jr NHS; Sec NHS; Pres Schlr; Mentor Clb Pres; Pride Tm; U Cntrl AR; Phy Thrpy.

CROSSETT, JOSEPH M; Monticello HS; Monticello, AR; (3); Am Leg Boys St; Art Clb; Church Yth Grp; Natl Beta Clb; Var L Bsbl; Var L Ftbl; Wt Lftg; Hon Roll; NHS; Fllwshp Chrstn Ath; Art.

CROSSLAND, GINGER; Junction City HS; El Dorado, AR; (1); Church Yth Grp; Pres 4-H; Science Clb; Spanish Clb; 4-H Awd; High Hon Roll; U Of AR Fayetteville; Med.

CROUCH, ELIZABETH C; Springdale Sr HS; Springdale, AR; (3); 33/500; Church Yth Grp; Cmnty Wkr; Drama Clb; French Clb; FBLA; Key Clb; Model UN; Acpl Chr; Chorus; Church Choir; Comm Theatre; Jones Ctr For Families Newscaster; Video CAP Pgm Spokesperson; Perf Arts.

CROUSE-MC FALLS, TABITHA M; Magnolia HS; Magnolia, AR; (3); French Clb; Band; Color Guard; Drill Tm; Mrchg Band; Rep Frsh Cls; Var Pom Pon; Var Powder Puff Ftbl; High Hon Roll; Hon Roll; LA Tech; Acctng.

CROW, BILLY D; Clinton HS; Clinton, AR; (2); Boy Scts; Church Yth Grp; Natl Beta Clb; Natl FFA Org; Quiz Bowl; Science Clb; Church Choir; Rep Soph Cls; Rep Stu Cncl; Mgr Bsktbl; Tchr Of Chrch Yth Group; Williams Bapt Coll; Minister.

CROW, CANDIE S; Casa Schl; Casa, AR; (2); FBLA; FHA; Natl FFA Org; Spanish Clb; Pres Soph Cls; Var Bsktbl; Hon Roll.

CROW, MARTHA; Newark Jr Sr HS; Bradford, AR; (4); 5/41; Church Yth Grp; FBLA; Library Aide; Math Clb; Natl Beta Clb; Pep Clb; Quiz Bowl; Spanish Clb; Band; Mrchg Band; AR ST U.

CROW, MONICA N; Sloan Hendrix HS; Pocahontas, AR; (2); 1/54; FBLA; FHA; FTA; Hosp Aide; Natl Beta Clb; Band; Rptr Nwsp; High Hon Roll; Bio/Phys Sci Metals; Algebra II Metal; Lamp Learning Plaques 9th-10th Grds Lions Clb; Pre Med/Pre Law.

CROWDER, LYNDSEY R; Oak Grove HS; Maumelle, AR; (2); FCA; Hosp Aide; Mu Alpha Theta; Spanish Clb; Teachers Aide; Hon Roll; U Of Central AR; PT.

CROWELL, CASEY M; Van Buren Sr HS; Van Buren, AR; (2); Drama Clb; FBLA; Pep Clb; Speech Tm; SADD; Drill Tm; Pom Pon; Gov Hon Prg Awd; Hon Roll; NHS; Gldn Poet Awd; USA Pgm Ambssdr; Sci Mrt Awd; Hendrix.

CROWLEY, CHARITY S; Cedarville Jr Sr HS; Chester, AR; (3); 12/60; Church Yth Grp; Rptr FBLA; Ofcr FHA; Spanish Clb; Sec Soph Cls; Sec Jr Cls; Sec Sr Cls; Var Chrldng; Var Sftbl; Var Trk; U Of AR Fayettville; Comps.

CROWLEY, ELIZA D; Cabot HS; Cabot, AR; (1); Church Yth Grp; Key Clb; Band; Church Choir; Mrchg Band; Pep Band; Cit Awd; Jr NHS; Prfct Atten Awd; Dancing; People To People Stu Ambassador; Tchr.

CRUCE, JERRY; Drew Central Jr Sr HS; Hamburg, AR; (4); 19/58; Church Yth Grp; Cmnty Wkr; Natl FFA Org; Chorus; Cit Awd; Hon Roll; Won Local/Dist Welding Cmptn; Attnd/Cert OK Horseshoeing Schl; UAM At Monticello; Ag.

CRUGER, JACOB D; Junction City HS; El Dorado, AR; (3); Church Yth Grp; 4-H; Sec Science Clb; Thesps; Band; Chorus; School Musical; School Play; BASIC; S AR U; Educ.

CRUMLEY, CASANDRA; Forrest City HS; Forrest City, AR; (3); Pres 4-H; FBLA; Math Clb; Science Clb; 4-H Awd; Hon Roll; 4-H Ambass; Delta Beta Simga Omega Pres; U Of AR; Poultry Sci.

CRUMPTON, KRISTINA M; Hot Springs HS; Hot Springs Natio, AR; (2); Chorus; Cit Awd; Hon Roll; Cert Acad Achvt; Choir Awd; Hand Bell Awd; U Of AR Little Rock; Med.

CRUZ, EDWIN J; Mills HS; Little Rock, AR; (2); Cmnty Wkr; FCA; FBLA; HOBY; Math Clb; Spanish Clb; Band; Church Choir; Mrchg Band; Pep Band; PT.

CUE, JOSEPH D; Beebe Sr HS; Beebe, AR; (3); 17/120; FBLA; Science Clb; Band; Jazz Band; Mrchg Band; Pep Band; Rptr Nwsp; Var Capt Crs Cntry; Var Trk; Hon Roll; POP.

CULLBREATH, HOLLI; Brinkley HS; Brinkley, AR; (3); Church Yth Grp; Cmnty Wkr; Drama Clb; FBLA; Q&S; Quiz Bowl; Ed Nwsp; Yrbk; Hon Roll; NHS; ASU; Med Tech.

CULLBREATH, JENNIFER; Brinkley HS; Hunter, AR; (2); Drama Clb; 4-H; Quiz Bowl; Band; Mrchg Band; Orch; Pep Band; School Musical; School Play; Stage Crew; AHA; Vol CPR Acrs AR; Beekpng; Vet.

CULLEN, MIKE J; Flippin Jr Sr HS; Flippin, AR; (2); FBLA; Library Aide; Science Clb; Ofcr Bsbl; Hon Roll; NHS; Physics; Internet; Fshng; U Of AR; Cmptr Engr.

CULLINS, JANE C; Jonesboro HS; Jonesboro, AR; (4); 32/279; Cmnty Wkr; FBLA; Key Clb; Mu Alpha Theta; Natl Beta Clb; Spanish Clb; Chorus; Hon Roll; NHS; Pres Acad Fit Awd; Interact Clb; PRIDE Clb; AR ST Univ; Bus.

CULLIPHER, CASEY L; Dewitt HS; De Witt, AR; (2); 1/95; Church Yth Grp; FCA; Natl Beta Clb; Pres VP Natl FFA Org; VP Frsh Cls; Rptr Soph Cls; Ofcr Stu Cncl; JV L Bsktbl; Var L Ftbl; Hon Roll; Parlmntry Team 2 Yrs, VP 2 Yrs, Dist Wnnrs 2 Yrs, Reg Wnnr 1 Yr.

CULLUM, BRYANT W; Bald Knob HS; Bald Knob, AR; (3); 12/120; Am Leg Boys St; FBLA; Natl Beta Clb; Quiz Bowl; Spanish Clb; VICA; Powder Puff Ftbl; Hon Roll; Connie Mack Bsbl; Lyons Coll; Dntl.

CULLUM, CANDICE M; Morrilton Sr HS; Morrilton, AR; (3); Church Yth Grp; Math Clb; Math Tm; Natl Beta Clb; Quiz Bowl; Spanish Clb; Thesps; School Musical; School Play.

CULP, THOMAS; Southside HS; Fort Smith, AR; (3); Am Leg Boys St; Jazz Band; JETS Awd; Pres Acad Fit Awd; German Clb; Mu Alpha Theta; Service Clb; Band; Mrchg Band; School Musical; Sailing.

CULPEPPER, AUTUMN; Lake Hamilton Jr HS; Hot Springs, AR; (1); 2/264; Church Yth Grp; Cmnty Wkr; FBLA; Natl Beta Clb; Natl FFA Org; Quiz Bowl; SADD; Teachers Aide; Band; Church Choir; Natl Eng Mert Awd 95; Stdnt Yr Awd 94-95; Optmst Stdnt Yr; All Reg Band; Grphc Art.

CULPEPPER, DANIEL A; Arkansas Schl Math & Science; Alexander, AR; (3); English Clb; German Clb; Natl Beta Clb; Quiz Bowl; Science Clb; Band; Mrchg Band; Pep Band; Var L Crs Cntry; Var L Trk; W Cntrl Rgn/AR ST Sci Fair 1st Pl Zoology; St Petersburg/Russia/Sci Cmptn Sakharovs Rdngs; TX A&M; Marine Bio.

CULPEPPER, JASON A; North Little Rock HS; Sherwood, AR; (2); 5/567; Church Yth Grp; Cmnty Wkr; Drama Clb; FCA; Key Clb; Math Clb; Mu Alpha Theta; Natl Beta Clb; Science Clb; Rep Jr Cls; Schlr Ath 2 Yrs; Cert Of Excl Chem; Trk MVP.

CULSHAW, SHELLI R; Rogers HS; Rogers, AR; (3); 68/562; Pep Clb; Teachers Aide; Chorus; High Hon Roll; Hon Roll; Renaissnc Awd; Rogers Chmbr Of Commrc Awd 2 Yrs; Jrnlsm Advrtsmt Awd; NW AR CC; Restrnt/Bus Mngmt.

CULVER, BRAD D; Ozark HS; Ozark, AR; (3); Boy Scts; FCA; FHA; Var Bsktbl; Most Imprvd Jr; U Of AR.

CULVER, RHEADAWN; Black Rock Jr Sr HS; Portia, AR; (2); 2/44; Church Yth Grp; Cmnty Wkr; FBLA; VP Treas FHA; Model UN; Sec Natl Beta Clb; Quiz Bowl; Chorus; School Musical; Hon Roll; Gftd & Tlntd; USAA; Amer Natl Teenager Fnlst; ASU; Lawyer.

CULVERHOUSE, EDDIE R; Booneville Jr Sr HS; Booneville, AR; (3); Art Clb; Boy Scts; Bus Profs of Am; Cmnty Wkr; 4-H; FBLA; FTA; Chorus; Yrbk; Cit Awd.

CUMMINGS, AMANDA C; Nevada Schl; Emmet, AR; (2); FBLA; Natl Beta Clb; Quiz Bowl; Band; JV Co-Capt Chrldng; JV Pom Pon; Hon Roll; 1st Plc Word Proc Cmptn Dist IV FBLA 95-; Best Cls Word Proc I/II; Drug Tm; Southern AR Univ; Bus.

CUMMINGS, CANDICE A; Harmony Grove Jr Sr HS; Benton, AR; (2); Art Clb; Church Yth Grp; French Clb; Girl Scts; Natl Beta Clb; Quiz Bowl; Science Clb; Color Guard; Var Bsktbl; JV Score Keeper; ST Sci Fair; Hnrbl Mntn Biochem; Regnl Sci Fair Twice; 3rd Pl Paper; 2nd Pl Proj Biochem; Coaching Bsktbl.

CUMMINGS, DA MARV A; J A Fair Sr HS; Little Rock, AR; (2); French Clb; FBLA; Natl Beta Clb; SECME; Acctng.

CUMMINGS, KCRISTII; Rison HS; Rison, AR; (4); 6/54; FBLA; FHA; Library Aide; Natl Beta Clb; Cit Awd; High Hon Roll; Hon Roll; NHS; Prfct Atten Awd; Lib Clb Pres; FHA Treas; Drg Awrnss Grp; U Of Cntrl AR; Lib Media Tech.

CUMMINGS, TREY; North Little Rock Hs-East; North Little Rock, AR; (2); 16/567; Cmnty Wkr; FCA; Key Clb; Math Clb; Mu Alpha Theta; Natl Beta Clb; Stage Crew; Var L Bsbl; High Hon Roll; Jr NHS; ST Champn Bsbl Tm Soph 2nd Bsmn 96; Sprts Med/Physcn.

CUMMINS, CRYSTAL; Beebe Jr HS; Beebe, AR; (1); FBLA; FHA; GAA; Natl Beta Clb; Pep Clb; Band; Mrchg Band; Pep Band; JV Chrldng; JV Trk; Cmpttv Swmmng; Med.

CUNNINGHAM, ASHLEY N; Hamburg HS; Hamburg, AR; (3); Spanish Clb; U Of AR.

CUNNINGHAM, CASEY; Perryville Jr Sr HS; Clinton, AR; (2); 4/72; Church Yth Grp; Natl Beta Clb; Spanish Clb; SADD; Teachers Aide; Varsity Clb; Bsktbl; Trk; Cit Awd; High Hon Roll; Coach/Ed.

CUNNINGHAM, KARA S; Mulberry HS; Mulberry, AR; (2); Art Clb; Natl FFA Org; VP Frsh Cls; VP Soph Cls; VP Jr Cls; Var Bsktbl; Var Sftbl; Var Tennis; JV Vllybl; High Hon Roll.

CUNNINGHAM, KELLY; J A Fair Sr HS; Little Rock, AR; (4); 30/290; French Clb; FBLA; Rptr Yrbk; Capt Chrldng; Var Capt Sftbl; Var Capt Vllybl; Hon Roll; NHS; Ntl Merit SF; U Of AR Little Rock; Sports.

CUNNINGHAM, KRISTYN N; Yellville Summit HS; Yellville, AR; (2); Church Yth Grp; FCA; FBLA; Yrbk; JV Bsktbl; Var Chrldng; Hon Roll; Oauchita Bapt U.

CUNNINGHAM, MICHAEL R; Beebe Sr HS; Beebe, AR; (3); 25/100; Church Yth Grp; Natl Beta Clb; SADD; Chorus; Church Choir; Stage Crew; Hon Roll; Construction; Marines.

CUNNINGHAM, TRACY J; Mena HS; Mena, AR; (1); Church Yth Grp; French Clb; FBLA; Band; Church Choir; Drm Mjr(t); Mrchg Band; Var Chrldng; Hon Roll; Henderson; Tchr.

CUPIT, BEN; Fayetteville Sr HS; Fayetteville, AR; (2); 73/617; Band; Mrchg Band; High Hon Roll.

CURBO, JAMES R; Mc Crory Jr Sr HS; Mc Crory, AR; (2); 7/60; Capt Quiz Bowl; Band; Jazz Band; Mrchg Band; Orch; Pep Band; Ed Yrbk; Rep Stu Cncl; High Hon Roll; Hon Roll; Slctd All Rgn Band 2 Yrs; Nmrs Solo Ensmbl Cntst Awd; U Of AR; Chem/Physcs.

ARKANSAS

CURNE, MELISSA D; Hughes Jr-Sr HS; Hughes, AR; (1); Math Clb; Spanish Clb; Church Choir; High Hon Roll; Hon Roll; Prfct Atten Awd; Church Yth Grp; Acpl Chr; Chorus; Nwsp; Drug Free Clb; Marion Symposium; GYC; ASU; Pediatrcn.

CURRAN, ALICIA G; Mayflower HS; Mayflower, AR; (3); 3/50; Church Yth Grp; Drama Clb; FHA; GAA; Natl Beta Clb; Chorus; Church Choir; School Play; Stage Crew; Variety Show; Congressional Yth Ldrshp Cncl To Washington Jrnlsm Conf; Henderson 100 Pgm; Foulkner Cty Ldrsh Inst; Commnctn.

CURRIE, DAVID M; Stuttgart Sr HS; Stuttgart, AR; (3); Church Yth Grp; FBLA; Mu Alpha Theta; Natl Beta Clb; Spanish Clb; Chorus; Golf; Mgr(s); Tennis; Hon Roll; Cmptr Tech.

CURRY, JERRY L; Hermitage Jr Sr HS; Warren, AR; (1); Church Yth Grp; Letterman Clb; Natl FFA Org; Band; Mrchg Band; Ofcr Bsbl; Ftbl; Trk; Wt Lftg.

CURSH, KEISHA; Arkansas Sr HS; Texarkana, AR; (2); Church Yth Grp; 4-H; FBLA; Band; Church Choir; Drill Tm; Flag Corp; Mrchg Band; Conway; Phy Thrpst.

CURTIS, AMBER R; Lee Acad; Marianna, AR; (2); 8/36; Church Yth Grp; Cmnty Wkr; Church Choir; JV Var Bsktbl; Var Sftbl; JV Trk; High Hon Roll; Hon Roll; NHS; Awd Mrt Poetry; Schl Mascott; U Of AR; Pre-Law/Govt/Pol Sci.

CURTIS, CASEY C; Nevada Schl; Rosston, AR; (2); 2/76; Church Yth Grp; FBLA; Natl Beta Clb; Quiz Bowl; Church Choir; Var Bsktbl; Cit Awd; High Hon Roll; Hon Roll; Pres Acad Fit Awd; Algebra II Awd.

CURTIS, CHRIS; Paron Schl; Paron, AR; (3); 1/17; Am Leg Boys St; Church Yth Grp; FBLA; FHA; Hosp Aide; Math Clb; Office Aide; Quiz Bowl; Science Clb; Spanish Clb; Piano 3 Yrs; Pediatrician.

CURTIS, SUSAN R; Atkins Schl; Atkins, AR; (4); 4/80; Am Leg Aux Girls St; Natl Beta Clb; Quiz Bowl; Spanish Clb; Nwsp; Ed Yrbk; Stat Bsktbl; L Tennis; Pres Clssrm Yng Amer; HS Svc Awd; AR Tech Univ; Ed.

CURTON, LINDSAY; Central Ark Christian Schl; Maumelle, AR; (3); Church Yth Grp; Sec French Clb; Ed Yrbk; Hist Jr Cls; Treas Sr Cls; Sec Stu Cncl; Var Crs Cntry; Var Trk; Hon Roll; Jr NHS.

CUTHBERTSON, JILL; Warren Sr HS; Warren, AR; (4); 1/115; French Clb; FBLA; Pres Natl Beta Clb; Quiz Bowl; L Bsktbl; NHS; Val; Pres Acad Fit Awd; AR Govs Schl; Natl Vo-Tech Hnr Soc; Akpalachia Svc Proj; Soutern Methodist U.

CUZICK, GREG R; Springdale Sr HS; Springdale, AR; (1); Church Yth Grp; FCA; FBLA; Teachers Aide; Var L Bsktbl; Hon Roll; Jr NHS; Pres Acad Fit Awd; Yth For Christ; Builders Clb; All-Star Bsbl.

CWENAR, JENNIFER; Jacksonville Christian Acad; Jacksonville, AR; (3); 2/7; Church Yth Grp; Yrbk; VP Frsh Cls; VP Soph Cls; VP Jr Cls; Var Vllybl; Cit Awd; High Hon Roll; Hon Roll; Sal; Ouchita Bptst Univ; Med.

CYPHERS, BROOKE; Pulaski Acad; Little Rock, AR; (2); Art Clb; Church Yth Grp; Cmnty Wkr; FCA; Spanish Clb; Chrldng; Hon Roll; NHS; Med.

CYPRET, KAMALA; Hoxie Schl; Walnut Ridge, AR; (2); 1/70; Church Yth Grp; Model UN; Natl Beta Clb; Spanish Clb; Band; Cit Awd; High Hon Roll; Hosp Aide; Quiz Bowl; Mrchg Band; PRIDE Team; Peer Cnslrs; Band Dirs Awd; Harding U.

DACHS, JOSHUA A; Ridgecrest HS; Paragould, AR; (3); Natl FFA Org; Chorus; ASU; Wildlife Mgmt.

DAGGETT, MARY BETH; Lee Acad; Marianna, AR; (3); 1/22; Yrbk; Rep Jr Cls; Var Bsktbl; Var Chrldng; JV Trk; High Hon Roll; NHS.

DAGOSTINO, CHERIE A; Arkansas Sr HS; Texarkana, AR; (3); Art Clb; Office Aide; Spanish Clb.

DAHL, DUSTY B; Lead Hill Schl; Wyoming, IL; (1); School Play; JV Bsktbl; Hon Roll; Zoologist.

DAI, ANNIE; Southside HS; Fort Smith, AR; (2); Key Clb; Rep Frsh Cls; Sec Soph Cls; Pres Jr Cls; Rep Stu Cncl; Cit Awd; Hon Roll; Jr NHS; NHS; Pres Acad Fit Awd; Natl Jr Hnr Soc 2nd VP.

DAILEY, AMY; Morrilton Sr HS; Morrilton, AR; (3); Church Yth Grp; French Clb; Library Aide; Math Clb; Thesps; Band; Church Choir; Flag Corp; School Musical; School Play; Library Clb; UCA; Rdlgst.

DAILEY, J PATRICK; Marked Tree Jr Sr HS; Marked Tree, AR; (2); 4/60; Boy Scts; HOBY; Natl Beta Clb; Natl FFA Org; Quiz Bowl; Band; Chorus; Jazz Band; Mrchg Band; Ed Nwsp; Eagle Sct; Concert Choir Accompanist; Order Of The Arrow Vice Chief; Civil Ware Re Enactor Vol; Exch Stu; Juliard; Actor; Writer; Dir.

DAILEY, STEPHAINE N; Harmony Grove Jr Sr HS; Malvern, AR; (3); 1/45; Church Yth Grp; Debate Tm; French Clb; FBLA; FHA; Natl Beta Clb; Quiz Bowl; Red Cross Aide; Science Clb; Chorus; Modern Woodmen Of Amer; ASU-MEDICINE.

DALE, AMANDA L; Jessieville HS; Jessieville, AR; (2); Church Yth Grp; FCA; Key Clb; Natl Beta Clb; Band; Bsktbl; Crs Cntry; Trk; High Hon Roll; Hon Roll.

DALE, ANTHURL L; Forrest City HS; Forrest City, AR; (4); Art Clb; ITT Tech Inst; Cmptr Engr.

DALE, JACLYN B; Weiner HS; Fisher, AR; (2); FBLA; FHA; Pres Natl FFA Org; Boy Scts; Spanish Clb; Teachers Aide; Chorus; Variety Show; Nwsp; Yrbk; Ag.

DALMUT, MEGHAN; Mansfield Jr Sr HS; Mansfield, AR; (1); Church Yth Grp; FCA; JV L Bsktbl; L Capt Chrldng; JV L Vllybl; Hon Roll; Bsbl Scorekeeper; Tchr.

DAMON, JAMES; Sloan Hendrix HS; Imboden, AR; (4); 5/32; Church Yth Grp; 4-H; FTA; Var Rptr Natl FFA Org; Science Clb; Varsity Clb; Band; Jazz Band; VP Frsh Cls; Ofcr Bsbl; AR ST Univ; Ag Extsn Agent.

DAMRON, GERALD A; Booneville Jr Sr HS; Booneville, AR; (4); Art Clb; Boy Scts; Church Yth Grp; Band; Mrchg Band; Yrbk; 3 Yrs Mrtl Arts 2nd Natl Coll; Mrtl Arts 96; Rcvd Acad Hnrs Schlsp; Westark CC; Acctg.

DANG, KHUONG T; Southside HS; Barling, AR; (2); Drill Tm; Nwsp; Yrbk; Hon Roll; NHS; Dietician.

DANG, MINH D; Northside HS; Fort Smith, AR; (2); FBLA; Spanish Clb; Rep Frsh Cls; Hon Roll; Jr NHS; Prfct Atten Awd; Spanish NHS.

DANIEL, ALLISON; West Memphis Christian Schl; West Memphis, AR; (4); Church Yth Grp; Cmnty Wkr; FCA; Natl Beta Clb; Ed Nwsp; Sec Ed Yrbk; Rep Soph Cls; Rep Jr Cls; Rep Sr Cls; Rep Stu Cncl; NCA All-Amer; Natl Beta Clb Pres; Hnr Grad; All-Dist Sftbl; Fighting Heart Sftbl & Vllybl; U Of MS; Dentistry.

DANIEL, AN DY; Booneville Jr Sr HS; Booneville, AR; (4); 5/85; Am Leg Boys St; Boy Scts; Church Yth Grp; Cmnty Wkr; FCA; FBLA; FTA; Key Clb; Letterman Clb; Model UN; Univ Of AR; Engrg.

DANIEL, BRIAN A; Trumann HS; Trumann, AR; (2); Math Clb; Science Clb; Spanish Clb; Yrbk; NHS; ASU; Automotive Engr.

DANIEL, DE JAUN; Arkansas City Schl; Arkansas City, AR; (4); 2/6; Am Leg Boys St; Art Clb; Church Yth Grp; Cmnty Wkr; FCA; 4-H; French Clb; HOBY; Letterman Clb; Pres Science Clb; AAU Bsktbl; All Dist Bsktbl; AR ST U; Sports Med.

DANIEL, DEJUAN; Arkansas City Schls; Arkansas City, AR; (4); 2/6; Am Leg Boys St; Art Clb; Church Yth Grp; Cmnty Wkr; FCA; 4-H; French Clb; HOBY; Letterman Clb; Pres Science Clb; AAU Bsktbl; All Dist Bsktbl; AR ST U; Sports Med.

DANIEL, EDWIN E; Pine Bluff HS; Pine Bluff, AR; (4); Church Yth Grp; FBLA; FHA; Office Aide; Spanish Clb; VICA; Band; Mrchg Band; Pep Band; Hon Roll; Yng Gentlemns Club; U Of AR Pine Bluff.

DANIEL, LUKE; Fairview HS; Camden, AR; (4); 54/248; Church Yth Grp; Natl FFA Org; Teachers Aide; Band; Church Choir; Mrchg Band; JV Var Ftbl; Hon Roll; NHS; Prfct Atten Awd; FFA Pres Local; FFA Wrld Ldrshp Conf; Stdnts Christ; Sthrn AR U; Agri Educ.

DANIEL, STEPHANIE; Cave City HS; Cave City, AR; (3); French Clb; Key Clb; Math Clb; Sec Natl FFA Org; Quiz Bowl; Science Clb; Cit Awd; Hon Roll; Kiwanis Awd; Hlth, Geom, Cvcs, Eng Awds; AR Tech U; Wldlf Bio.

DANIELS, ANGELA Q; Parkview Arts/Sci Magnet HS; Little Rock, AR; (3); Pres Church Yth Grp; FBLA; Mu Alpha Theta; Natl Beta Clb; Church Choir; AR Governors Schl 96; Pre-Law.

DANIELS, DARAH L; Cutter Morning Star HS; Hot Springs, AR; (3); FBLA; FHA; Natl Beta Clb; Spanish Clb; Church Choir; Yrbk; Capt Chrldng; Cit Awd; DAR Awd; Hon Roll; Tlnt Srch.

DANIELS, JARED T; Fairview HS; Camden, AR; (2); Church Yth Grp; French Clb; Natl Beta Clb; Science Clb; JV Ftbl; High Hon Roll; Hon Roll; Jr NHS.

DANIELS, KAMESHA; Lee Sr HS; Marianna, AR; (1); 3/297; Chess Clb; Cmnty Wkr; English Clb; French Clb; FBLA; Hosp Aide; Math Clb; Math Tm; Natl Beta Clb; Science Clb; Chrch Yth Dept Pres; Nrsng Hm Vol Asstnt; Med.

DANIELS, LA TOYA L; Mc Gehee HS; Mc Gehee, AR; (4); 11/96; Treas Art Clb; French Clb; FBLA; Mu Alpha Theta; Natl Beta Clb; SADD; Pres Jr Cls; Pres Stu Cncl; Trk; Pride Awd; AR ST Univ; Spch Pthlgy.

DANIELS, LATOYA; Mc Gehee HS; Mc Gehee, AR; (4); 11/96; Treas Art Clb; French Clb; FBLA; Pres Mu Alpha Theta; SADD; Rep Yrbk; Pres Jr Cls; Pres Stu Cncl; Trk; AR ST Univ; Acctng.

DANIELS, LINDSEY E; Pulaski Acad; Little Rock, AR; (2); Art Clb; FCA; Natl Beta Clb; Spanish Clb; Sec Jr Cls; Var Pom Pon; Hon Roll; NHS; Stdnt Cncl Rep; Baylor; Acctng.

DANIELS, MATT L; Harrison Sr HS; Harrison, AR; (3); 1/197; Thesps; L Var Bsbl; L Var Crs Cntry; High Hon Roll; NHS; Pres Acad Fit Awd; Spanish NHS; Drama Clb; Natl FFA Org; Science Clb; Hnr Awd Acc Bio/Eng II; 1st Pl AFLTA Frgn Lang Fstvl; Engrng.

DANIELS, NICOLA; Jacksonville HS; Jacksonville, AR; (2); 28/435; Drama Clb; FBLA; Band; Chorus; Mrchg Band; Pep Band; Cit Awd; U Of AR; Med.

DANLEY, SARAH I; Lakeside HS; Hot Springs, AR; (3); Church Yth Grp; Drama Clb; VP FBLA; Math Clb; Pres Natl Beta Clb; Pep Clb; Pres Science Clb; Spanish Clb; Thesps; Church Choir; Yth Advy Comm AR Caths; AR Governors Schl; Search Team; Pre-Med; Intnl Stud.

DANNER, DUSTIN; Dewitt HS; De Witt, AR; (4); 28/76; FCA; FBLA; FTA; Office Aide; Science Clb; Teachers Aide; L Bsbl; L Bsktbl; L Ftbl; Hon Roll; U Of A Monticello; Forestry.

DARBY, JAMIE; Arkansas City Schl; Arkansas City, AR; (4); 1/6; Church Yth Grp; Quiz Bowl; VP Science Clb; Nwsp; Yrbk; Sec Sr Cls; Pres Stu Cncl; Var Bsktbl; Var Socr; NHS; Hmcmng Qn; LA Tech U; Spch Pthlgy.

DARBY, JIMMY R; Mt Ida Jr Sr HS; Mount Ida, AR; (3); #1 in class; Church Yth Grp; Natl Beta Clb; Natl FFA Org; Quiz Bowl; School Play; Phtg Yrbk; Ofcr Soph Cls; Treas Jr Cls; Pres Stu Cncl; Hon Roll; Xerox Awd Hum & Soc Stud; U Of AR Fayetteville; Lawyer.

DARDENNE, MATTHEW RICHARD; Stuttgart Sr HS; Stuttgart, AR; (2); Boy Scts; Drama Clb; FBLA; Quiz Bowl; Church Choir; VP Soph Cls; Rep Stu Cncl; High Hon Roll; Pres Acad Fit Awd; Art Clb; Pony League Bsbl; Page To ST Lgsltr; Ar Schl Math/Sci; Air Force Acad.

DARLING, COURTNEY B; Ozark HS; Ozark, AR; (3); Church Yth Grp; FBLA; Natl Beta Clb; Chorus; Church Choir; Rep Frsh Cls; Rep Sr Cls; Rep Stu Cncl; Var Bsktbl; High Hon Roll.

DARNELL, SCOTT K; Central Sr HS; Little Rock, AR; (2); Church Yth Grp; Natl Beta Clb; Spanish Clb; Socr; High Hon Roll; Hon Roll; Jr NHS; Cntrl AR Regnl Sci/Engrng Fair 1st Pl Zoolgy; AR ST Sci Fair 2nd Pl Zoolgy; Med/Physician.

DARR, CLADEECA M; Jonesboro HS; Jonesboro, AR; (3); FBLA; FHA; Key Clb; Spanish Clb.

DART, RYAN G; Booneville Jr Sr HS; Booneville, AR; (4); 23/81; FHA; FTA; Natl FFA Org; Strings; Art Awd; Westark CC; Arts.

DAUGHERTY, JASON D; Lincoln HS; Morrow, AR; (4); 3/59; Am Leg Boys St; Church Yth Grp; FBLA; Key Clb; Math Clb; Natl Beta Clb; Science Clb; Spanish Clb; Teachers Aide; Cit Awd; Odyssey Of Mind; Knwldg Mstr; Bio.

DAVENPORT, DENA; Dewitt HS; De Witt, AR; (3); 2/90; Am Leg Aux Girls St; FCA; French Clb; FBLA; FTA; HOBY; Natl Beta Clb; Office Aide; Science Clb; Chorus.

DAVENPORT, MEGAN; Arkansas Schl Math & Science; Violet Hill, AR; (3); Treas Church Yth Grp; HOBY; Natl Beta Clb; Chorus; Nwsp; Ed Yrbk; Cmnty Wkr; FHA; Key Clb; St Chmpnshp Quiz Bwl; 4th Pl FBLA; Regis Frnch Cmp; WA U; Arch.

DAVID, CORI; Pea Ridge HS; Pea Ridge, AR; (2); Sec Frsh Cls; NHS; Educl Tlnt Srch; Art.

DAVID, KEEGAN N; Vilonia HS; Vilonia, AR; (3); Am Leg Aux Girls St; Math Clb; Model UN; Mu Alpha Theta; Natl Beta Clb; Office Aide; Treas Spanish Clb; Speech Tm; SADD; Teachers Aide; All-Stars; Vol; Mst Likely To Succees Jr Cls; UCA; Lawyer.

DAVIDSON, AMANDA; Westside HS; Bono, AR; (4); FBLA; FHA; Office Aide; Nwsp; Yrbk; Trk; Hon Roll; Prfct Atten Awd; ASU.

DAVIDSON, ANDY; Harmony Grove Jr Sr HS; Camden, AR; (4); 1/49; Am Leg Boys St; Art Clb; Church Yth Grp; Natl Beta Clb; Band; Ofcr Jr Cls; Ofcr Stu Cncl; Cit Awd; Hon Roll; NHS; Woodmen Of World Amer Hstry Awd; Deptmntl Awds Engl, Sci, Art; Ouachita Bapt U; Engl.

DAVIDSON, ANGELA C; North Little Rock Hs-West; North Little Rock, AR; (3); Art Clb; Cmnty Wkr; Drama Clb; Math Clb; ROTC; Yrbk; Hon Roll; Hendrix; Bus.

DAVIDSON, COREY M; Conway Sr HS; Conway, AR; (2); Var Trk; AR; Pre-Med.

DAVIDSON, ELIZABETH; Marvell Acad; Marvell, AR; (2); 4/34; Treas Church Yth Grp; Spanish Clb; VP Frsh Cls; Var Chrldng; Trk; High Hon Roll; Hon Roll; Jr NHS; VP NHS; Prfct Atten Awd; U Of AR; Med Fld.

DAVIDSON, MELODY; Morrilton Sr HS; Morrilton, AR; (2); Church Yth Grp; Natl Beta Clb; Thesps; Drill Tm; Co-Ed Yrbk; Rep Soph Cls; Vllybl; Hon Roll; NHS; Ntl Merit Ltr; AR Tech; Scndry Ed.

DAVIDSON, NATHAN J; Trumann HS; Harrisburg, AR; (2); Church Yth Grp; Library Aide; Natl FFA Org; JV Var Bsbl; JV Var Ftbl; JV Trk; JV Var Wt Lftg; Hon Roll; Auto Mech; AZ ST Univ; Mech Eng.

DAVIDSON, VANESSA L; Northside HS; Fort Smith, AR; (3); Church Yth Grp; Cmnty Wkr; Spanish Clb; Drill Tm; L Trk; Hon Roll; NHS; FBI.

DAVIDSON, WILLIAM S; Southside HS; Fort Smith, AR; (4); 14/459; Boy Scts; VP Chess Clb; Church Yth Grp; CAP; Cmnty Wkr; Treas Latin Clb; Mu Alpha Theta; Quiz Bowl; School Musical; Stage Crew; Physics Clb Co Fndr & Pres; MA Inst Tech; Comp Engr.

DAVIES, ADAM H; Oak Grove HS; Maumelle, AR; (1); Boy Scts; Hon Roll.

DAVIES, CRYSTAL; Eudora HS; Eudora, AR; (3); FBLA; Sec Natl Beta Clb; ROTC; Drm Mjr(t); Mrchg Band; School Play; Yrbk; Sec Frsh Cls; Pres Jr Cls; Sec Stu Cncl; U Of AR; Poli Sci.

DAVIES, LACEY; Lakeside Jr HS; North Little Rock, AR; (1); Church Yth Grp; Drama Clb; FCA; FBLA; Chrldng; Hon Roll; NCA All Amrcn Awd 95; UCA All Str 94.

DAVIS, ALISA B; Pangburn Jr Sr HS; Pangburn, AR; (3); FBLA; FHA; School Play; Chrldng; Mgr(s); Sftbl; Upward Bound; U Of Cntrl AR; Hstry Tchr.

DAVIS, ALISHA N; Mountain Pine Jr Sr HS; Mountain Pine, AR; (2); 6/70; FCA; 4-H; Treas FHA; Teachers Aide; Band; Chorus; Mrchg Band; VP Frsh Cls; Chrldng; Ntl Merit Ltr; Harding Univ; Acctng; Math Tchr.

DAVIS, ALLYSON D; Stuttgart Sr HS; Stuttgart, AR; (3); Am Leg Aux Girls St; Church Yth Grp; FCA; FBLA; Key Clb; Mu Alpha Theta; School Play; Chrldng; NHS; Office Aide; Alpha Beta Chptr Of Delta Beta Sigma.

DAVIS, AMANDA; Dollarway HS; Pine Bluff, AR; (3); Natl Beta Clb; Band; VP Stu Cncl; Chrldng; Var L Socr; NHS; Pres Acad Fit Awd; Jags Peer Cnslng; Chargers Soccer Club.

DAVIS, AMY; Beebe Jr HS; Searcy, AR; (1); Church Yth Grp; FBLA; FHA; Natl Beta Clb; Pep Clb; Trk; Vllybl; Wt Lftg; Hon Roll; Med.

DAVIS, ANGELA; West Memphis Sr HS; West Memphis, AR; (3); Math Clb; Treas Mu Alpha Theta; VP Natl Beta Clb; Band; Mrchg Band; Nwsp; Ofcr Stu Cncl; High Hon Roll; Pres Acad Fit Awd; Nbhbrhd Action Cncl; Crimestoppers VP; Very Imprtnt Peers Orientn VP; AR ST U; Pre-Med.

DAVIS, ANGELA; Poyen Schl; Poyen, AR; (2); FHA; Natl Beta Clb; Spanish Clb; Teachers Aide; Yrbk; Lit Mag; Hon Roll; Poetry Publshd Ntl Libry Of Poetry; U Cntrl AR; Psycht.

DAVIS, BETTINA; Dumas HS; Dumas, AR; (4); 3/126; Am Leg Aux Girls St; FBLA; Spanish Clb; Band; Jazz Band; Mrchg Band; School Play; Rptr Yrbk; Var Soph Cls; Pres Sr Cls; AR ST U Jonesboro; Med; Hlth.

DAVIS, BILLY D; Blytheville Sr HS; Blytheville, AR; (3); Church Yth Grp; Cmnty Wkr; 4-H; JA; Natl FFA Org; Office Aide; ROTC; Acpl Chr; Drill Tm; Trk; Gentlemens Clb; Grambling ST U; Pediatrician.

DAVIS, BRANDY L; Arkansas Schl Math & Science; Higden, AR; (3); Pres Art Clb; Cmnty Wkr; Hosp Aide; Library Aide; Capt Quiz Bowl; Teachers Aide; School Musical; Stage Crew; Ed Nwsp; Pres Frsh Cls; LSU; Microbio.

DAVIS, CHARLES J; Rogers HS; Rogers, AR; (3); FBLA; Quiz Bowl; Spanish Clb; SADD; Socr; High Hon Roll; Hon Roll; Pres Acad Fit Awd; Spring Hill Coll.

DAVIS, CODI NICOLE; Mc Gehee HS; Mc Gehee, AR; (3); Art Clb; Church Yth Grp; Cmnty Wkr; Drama Clb; French Clb; FTA; Mu Alpha Theta; Natl Beta Clb; Ed Nwsp; Tennis; Vp Of Drama Clb; Cnslrs Aid; Jrnlsmawd; U Of AR; Med.

DAVIS, CORNEAL; Crawfordsville HS; West Memphis, AR; (4); 10/24; French Clb; FBLA; FHA; Natl Beta Clb; Chrldng; Hon Roll; Mid-South CC; Cmptr Sci.

DAVIS, CRYSTAL; Sylvan Hills HS; Mabelvale, AR; (4); 17/233; Mu Alpha Theta; Natl Beta Clb; Q&S; Spanish Clb; Ed Nwsp; Mgr Yrbk; NHS; Pres Acad Fit Awd; Tchrs Of Tomorrow Acad & Clb VP; Henderson ST Univ; Ed.

DAVIS, DANIEL C; Arkansas Sr HS; Texarkana, AR; (4); Church Yth Grp; Band; Church Choir; Mrchg Band; Sthrn Bapt Cnvntn Yth Spkrs Trnmt, Yth Bible Drill; FCS; East TX Bapt U; Yth Mnstry.

DAVIS, DAVID A; Black Rock Jr Sr HS; Black Rock, AR; (2); FHA; Quiz Bowl; Murray ST Univ; Psychtry.

DAVIS, DEEDRA; Dumas Jr HS; Dumas, AR; (1); 2/21; Girl Scts; SADD; Acpl Chr; Chorus; Church Choir; School Musical; Ofcr Frsh Cls; Hon Roll; UAPB; Sngr/Actrss/Nrse/Dr.

DAVIS, DEMARCHE D; Dumas HS; Dumas, AR; (3); Church Yth Grp; FCA; FBLA; Yrbk; VP Sr Cls; Capt Bsktbl; Wt Lftg; Hon Roll; Kiwanis Awd; NHS.

DAVIS, DIDI; Pangburn Jr Sr HS; Searcy, AR; (2); Church Yth Grp; French Clb; Phtg FBLA; Phtg FHA; Natl Beta Clb; Church Choir; Ofcr Soph Cls; Bsktbl; Hon Roll; NHS; U Of AR; Photo.

DAVIS, ELECIA D; Poyen Schl; Leola, AR; (2); Church Yth Grp; FCA; FHA; Library Aide; Natl Beta Clb; Teachers Aide; Chorus; Chrldng; Sftbl; Indians Against Drugs; Pediatrician.

DAVIS, ELIZABETH A; Southside HS; Fort Smith, AR; (3); Church Yth Grp; French Clb; Girl Scts; Key Clb; Mu Alpha Theta; Band; Chorus; French Hon Soc; NHS; SAIL; Psych; Phy Therapy.

DAVIS, EMILY; Gosnell Jr Sr HS; Blytheville, AR; (2); 1/86; Church Yth Grp; French Clb; FHA; Key Clb; Mu Alpha Theta; Natl Beta Clb; Band; Mrchg Band; Pep Band; High Hon Roll.

DAVIS, ERIN M; West Memphis Christian Schl; Memphis, TN; (1); Church Yth Grp; Hon Roll; Pres Acad Fit Awd.

DAVIS, GARY; Gosnell Jr HS; Blytheville, AR; (1); Church Yth Grp; Church Choir; Bsktbl; Ftbl; Cit Awd; High Hon Roll.

DAVIS, GWENYTH B; Mayflower HS; Little Rock, AR; (2); 3/70; FBLA; Natl Beta Clb; Chorus; High Hon Roll; His/Algebra/Eng Hghst Grds Awds; Phycologist.

DAVIS, HEATHER M; Timbo Schl; Big Flat, AR; (1); Church Yth Grp; Natl Beta Clb; Church Choir; Rep Frsh Cls; French Hon Soc; High Hon Roll; Hon Roll; Mrt Awd In St Art Cmptn; Mrt Awd In Cntry Art Cmptn; Certs Of Achvmt For Highest In Fr & Geom Classes.

DAVIS, JACQUELINE A; Nettleton HS; Jonesboro, AR; (2); Natl Beta Clb; Science Clb; School Musical; School Play; High Hon Roll; Ftbl Hmcmng Ct 95-; AR ST Univ; Rdlgst/PT.

DAVIS, JACQUELYN S; Russellville Sr HS; Dover, AR; (2); 1/400; Drama Clb; French Clb; Band; Orch; Crs Cntry; Swmmng; Trk; High Hon Roll; Jr NHS; NHS; Fr Clb VP; All Reg Band; Sci.

DAVIS, JAMES O; Batesville Sr HS; Batesville, AR; (4); 6/155; Am Leg Boys St; Key Clb; Natl Beta Clb; Band; Yrbk; Ofcr Stu Cncl; Var L Bsktbl; Var L Tennis; High Hon Roll; Ntl Merit SF; U Of AR; Pre-Med.

DAVIS, JASON; Nashville HS; Nashville, AR; (3); 4/150; Quiz Bowl; Var Bsbl; Var L Ftbl; Var Score Keeper; Var Trk; Var Wt Lftg; High Hon Roll; Hon Roll; Jr NHS; NHS; Math Awd; Scl Sci Awd; Stdnt Cncl Sci Awd; Eng.

DAVIS, JASON E; Hamburg HS; Hamburg, AR; (4); 20/119; Am Leg Boys St; Drama Clb; Science Clb; Spanish Clb; Band; Jazz Band; Mrchg Band; Pep Band; School Play; Co-Ed Nwsp; Percussion Ldr; Hendeson ST Univ; Bio.

DAVIS, JED; Beebe Jr HS; Beebe, AR; (1); Church Yth Grp; FBLA; FHA; Natl Beta Clb; Natl FFA Org; Church Choir; Capt Ftbl; Trk; Wt Lftg; JETS Awd; FFA Pres.

DAVIS, JENIFER; Pleasant View Schl; Ozark, AR; (1); Church Yth Grp; Drama Clb; FBLA; Natl Beta Clb; JV Bsktbl; Hon Roll; Cls VP; Gifted & Talented; Harding U.

DAVIS, JEREMY; Gosnell Jr Sr HS; Blytheville, AR; (4); 1/66; Church Yth Grp; Key Clb; Natl Beta Clb; Chorus; Church Choir; Variety Show; Ftbl; High Hon Roll; NHS; Val.

DAVIS, JERRI G; Bearden HS; Bearden, AR; (3); FBLA; FHA; School Play; Hon Roll; Henderson St Univ; Tchng.

DAVIS, JOE; Hatfield Schl; Hatfield, AR; (3); Art Clb; FBLA; Math Clb; Natl FFA Org; Hon Roll; NHS; Prfct Atten Awd; Rich Mtn CC; Rdlgst.

DAVIS, JONATHAN J; Southside HS; Fort Smith, AR; (4); Boy Scts; Church Yth Grp; French Clb; Mu Alpha Theta; Science Clb; Band; Church Choir; Mrchg Band; Ofcr Stu Cncl; Trk; Mission Trps Church Youth Group; Musical Trs Church Youth Choir; Pre-Med.

DAVIS, JONI M; Gravette HS; Gravette, AR; (3); Chorus; Hon Roll.

DAVIS, JOSH; Pangburn Jr Sr HS; Pangburn, AR; (3); FBLA; Library Aide; Natl Beta Clb; Band; Church Choir; Hon Roll; NHS; Chrch Music Bass Guitar; U Of Cntrl FL; Cmptr Graphics.

DAVIS, JOSH; Southside HS; Fort Smith, AR; (4); 111/459; Boy Scts; Church Yth Grp; French Clb; Mu Alpha Theta; Science Clb; Band; Church Choir; Mrchg Band; Ofcr Stu Cncl; Crs Cntry; Church Mssns Trips; U Of AR Fayetteville; Chem Eng.

DAVIS, JUSTIN S; Rose Bud Jr Sr HS; Rose Bud, AR; (2); 3/58; Church Yth Grp; FCA; Natl Beta Clb; Natl FFA Org; Spanish Clb; Speech Tm; Ofcr Bsbl; Bsktbl; Golf; Vllybl; Golf Awd; Offensive & 3 Point Awd Bsktbl; All Conf Sr Boys Bsktbl Awd; PE.

DAVIS, K WESLEY; Paris HS; Paris, AR; (4); Am Leg Boys St; Boy Scts; Pres Church Yth Grp; Pres Drama Clb; FCA; FBLA; Pres Speech Tm; School Musical; School Play, Nwsp, Odyssy Mnd Wrld Fnlst; Westminster; Psych.

DAVIS, KALVIN L; Watson Chapel Sr HS; Pine Bluff, AR; (3); Boy Scts; Church Yth Grp; Key Clb; Natl Beta Clb; Chorus; Ftbl; Trk; St Trk Comps 3 Yrs; Clark U; Cmptr Progrmng.

DAVIS, KARA; Ft Smith Christian Schl; Fort Smith, AR; (1); 2/36; Church Yth Grp; Band; Church Choir; VP Frsh Cls; Mgr Bsktbl; Var Mgr(s); High Hon Roll; Natl Fed Msc Clb; Jr Festvl Piano Supr; Natl Guild Audtn Piano.

DAVIS, KARA A; El Dorado Sr HS; El Dorado, AR; (4); 35/266; Church Yth Grp; Cmnty Wkr; FBLA; Library Aide; Natl Beta Clb; Office Aide; Red Cross Aide; Rep Stu Cncl; Trk; Hon Roll; Peer Ldrshp; Drug & AIDS Awareness; U Of A; Pre-Pharmacy.

DAVIS, KEITH L; Gravette HS; Gravette, AR; (4); 31/57; Teachers Aide; JV Var Bsbl; JV Var Ftbl; Intrml Trk; Var Wt Lftg; Hon Roll; Pop Alum Schlrshp; Yng Life; NW Tech Schl; Htng/Air/Plmbng.

DAVIS, KELLIE C; Deer Jr Sr HS; Pelsor, AR; (3); 3/27; VP FBLA; JA; Latin Clb; Letterman Clb; Natl FFA Org; Varsity Clb; Ofcr Stu Cncl; Bsktbl; High Hon Roll; Univ AR; Accntng.

DAVIS, KERI N; Crowleys Ridge Acad; Walnut Ridge, AR; (1); Church Yth Grp; FBLA; Pep Clb; Science Clb; Spanish Clb; Hon Roll; Med.

DAVIS, KRISTIN L; Gosnell Jr Sr HS; Blytheville, AR; (1); Church Yth Grp; Bsktbl; Powder Puff Ftbl; Chrch Soloist; Nrsng Home Vol Through Chrch; Horse Show Cmptn; U Of TN-MARTIN; Vet.

DAVIS, LA TASHA N; White Co Central Schl; Judsonia, AR; (4); 1/28; Am Leg Aux Girls St; Sec Treas FBLA; FHA; Sec Treas Sr Cls; Var Capt Bsktbl; Var Capt Sftbl; High Hon Roll; NHS; Pres Acad Fit Awd; Val; Sftbl League; Trigonometry Awd; AR Acad Challenge Schlsp; Tuition Schlsp; ASU-BEEBE; Acctng; Bus.

DAVIS, LAKETRA L; Crossett Sr HS; Crossett, AR; (2); Drill Tm; Hon Roll; Stu Of Month; Miss Essence; Eagle Action Pride; Nrsng.

DAVIS, LANA; Hall Sr HS; Little Rock, AR; (4); 2/270; FBLA; Service Clb; Church Choir; School Play; VP Stu Cncl; NHS; Sal; Am Leg Aux Girls St; Church Yth Grp; Drama Clb; Handbell Choir 9 Yrs; Stephens Awd; Govs Schlr Schlsp; Hendrix Coll; Acctng.

DAVIS, LATOSHA L; Central HS; West Helena, AR; (4); 58/208; Church Yth Grp; ROTC; Teachers Aide; Church Choir; Color Guard; Drill Tm; Trk; High Hon Roll; Hon Roll; ASU; Cmptr Engr.

DAVIS, MACKENZIE L; Ridgecrest HS; Paragould, AR; (3); Art Clb; Treas Drama Clb; VP Pres FBLA; Library Aide; Office Aide; Science Clb; Pres Spanish Clb; Teachers Aide; Thesps; School Musical; Dist II Rptr Of FBLA; AR ST Univ.

DAVIS, MEREDITH; Pulaski Acad; Little Rock, AR; (4); Church Yth Grp; Cmnty Wkr; FCA; French Clb; Natl Beta Clb; Science Clb; Teachers Aide; Chorus; Church Choir; School Musical; Y-Teens City ICC; U Of AR Fayettville; BSN.

DAVIS, MICHELLE; Bradley Jr Sr HS; Taylor, AR; (2); Art Clb; Church Yth Grp; 4-H; Spanish Clb; Nwsp; Ofcr Soph Cls; Ofcr Stu Cncl; Bsktbl; Chrldng; Sftbl; Med.

DAVIS, MINDY; Gosnell Jr Sr HS; Blytheville, AR; (1); Church Yth Grp; Church Choir; Bsktbl; Powder Puff Ftbl; Sftbl; Cit Awd; Hon Roll.

DAVIS, MISTY R; Mt Ida Jr Sr HS; Mount Ida, AR; (3); Church Yth Grp; Library Aide; Natl FFA Org; VP Frsh Cls; Ofcr Stu Cncl; Chrldng; Prfct Atten Awd; Stu Cncl Membr Of Yr; UALR; Intr Desgnt.

DAVIS, NANCY J; Dewitt HS; De Witt, AR; (3); 8/90; Church Yth Grp; 4-H; French Clb; Natl Beta Clb; Science Clb; Band; Flag Corp; Hon Roll.

DAVIS, RACHEL; North Little Rock Hs-East; North Little Rock, AR; (2); 12/567; Church Yth Grp; FCA; Key Clb; Pres Math Clb; Mu Alpha Theta; Natl Beta Clb; Spanish Clb; Band; Church Choir; Flag Corp; Outstdng 10th Grd Musician Of The Yr; Soph Chrldr Of The Yr; Biochem.

DAVIS, REGINALD L; Dollarway HS; Pine Bluff, AR; (3); Band; Church Choir; Mrchg Band; TN St Univ; Comp Tech.

DAVIS, ROBBYE E; Searcy HS; Higginson, AR; (2); 48/250; Church Yth Grp; Natl Beta Clb; Chorus; Church Choir; Mgr(s); Trk; Hon Roll; NHS; CBC; Music; Cnslng.

DAVIS, RYAN D; Central Sr HS; Little Rock, AR; (4); Am Leg Boys St; Cmnty Wkr; Debate Tm; Q&S; Quiz Bowl; Rptr Nwsp; Tennis; NHS; French Clb; Church Choir; JC Penneys Gldn Rl Awd; Olympc Trch Bearer; Lake Forest Coll; Polysci.

DAVIS, SAMANTHA; Central Ark Christian Schl; North Little Rock, AR; (4); #11 in class; Church Yth Grp; FHA; Science Clb; Spanish Clb; Teachers Aide; Vllybl; High Hon Roll; Jr NHS; NHS; Pres Acad Fit Awd; U Central AR.

DAVIS, SAMANTHA L; Lamar HS; Lamar, AR; (3); FCA; Math Clb; Quiz Bowl; VP Sr Cls; Var Bsktbl; Var Sftbl; Hon Roll.

DAVIS, SARA; St Paul Schl; Pettigrew, AR; (1); 5/30; FHA; SADD; Treas Frsh Cls; Rep Stu Cncl; L Bsktbl; L Trk; Hon Roll; Ntl Merit Ltr; U AR; Tchr.

DAVIS, SHANNON; Sulphur Rock Schl; Newark, AR; (4); 4/21; VP FHA; Key Clb; Natl Beta Clb; Natl FFA Org; Teachers Aide; Chorus; Ofcr Stu Cncl; Bsktbl; Hon Roll; Ag.

DAVIS, SHARONDA D; Mc Gehee HS; Tillar, AR; (3); Cmnty Wkr; FTA; GAA; Natl FFA Org; Spanish Clb; Church Choir; L Bsktbl; L Trk; AR ST Univ Jonesboro; PE.

DAVIS, STEPHANIE; Newark Jr Sr HS; Newark, AR; (3); 15/65; Church Yth Grp; FBLA; Natl Beta Clb; Church Choir; Ofcr Frsh Cls; Pres Stu Cncl; Bsktbl; Sftbl; Tennis; Hon Roll; U Of AR.

DAVIS, STEPHANIE; Crowleys Ridge Acad; Walnut Ridge, AR; (3); 5/25; Art Clb; FBLA; Pep Clb; Science Clb; Pres Spanish Clb; High Hon Roll; NHS; Chrstn Wmn's Club; AR ST Univ; Bus.

DAVIS, TAMMY; Mayflower HS; Mayflower, AR; (3); 10/45; Church Yth Grp; Drama Clb; Pres FHA; Girl Scts; Hosp Aide; Science Clb; Teachers Aide; Church Choir; School Play; Hon Roll; U Of Cntrl AR; Ped.

DAVIS, TODD R; Ozark Adventist Acad; Gentry, AR; (2); Cmnty Wkr; Band; Phtg Yrbk; Treas Stu Cncl; Intrml Bsktbl; Intrml Sftbl; Cit Awd; Hon Roll; Prfct Atten Awd; Videogrphr; Off Rd Vehicles; Walla Walla Coll; Aviation.

DAVIS, TOMEKA L; Dollarway HS; Pine Bluff, AR; (3); #10 in class; Drama Clb; French Clb; FBLA; FHA; Key Clb; Quiz Bowl; Spanish Clb; Teachers Aide; Band; Church Choir; Fayetteville; Nrsng/Ed/Pre-Law.

DAVIS, TOR L; Springdale Sr HS; Springdale, AR; (2); Church Yth Grp; Chorus; Powder Puff Ftbl; Socr; Hon Roll; Environmental Clb; Yth For Christ; U Cntrl AR; Vet.

DAVIS, TROY G; Newport HS; Newport, AR; (2); Cit Awd; Hon Roll; Prfct Atten Awd; ASU Beebe Newport; Cmptr Tech.

DAVIS, TYKISHIA; Hughes Jr-Sr HS; Hughes, AR; (2); 6/72; Church Yth Grp; HOBY; Natl Beta Clb; VP Frsh Cls; VP Soph Cls; Bsktbl; Trk; Wt Lftg; High Hon Roll; Hon Roll; Alpha Beta; Rec Wrkr; U Of AR At Fayetteville; Psych.

DAVIS, WESLEY; Wynne HS; Wynne, AR; (3); Boy Scts; Church Yth Grp; Pres Drama Clb; HOBY; Church Choir; School Musical; School Play; Rep Stu Cncl; Hon Roll; NHS; Poltcl Sci.

DAVISON, KRISTY C; Sheridan Sr HS; Sheridan, AR; (2); Church Yth Grp; Teachers Aide; Church Choir; Yrbk; High Hon Roll; Hon Roll; Jr NHS; Bapt Nrsng Schl; RN.

DAWSON, GINA M; Fountain Lake Jr Sr HS; Benton, AR; (2); 12/86; Church Yth Grp; FCA; FHA; Key Clb; Acpl Chr; Chorus; Church Choir; School Musical; School Play; Stage Crew; Champs Clb Treas; Bus; Drama; Broadcasting.

DAWSON, JEANELLE L; Gravette HS; Gravette, AR; (4); 1/58; Church Yth Grp; Office Aide; Chorus; High Hon Roll; Hon Roll; NHS; Val; AR Acad Challenge Schlsp; Tandy Tech Schlr; Harding Univ.

DAWSON, KATRINA A; Mills HS; North Little Rock, AR; (3); 23/298; Am Leg Aux Girls St; Church Yth Grp; Natl Beta Clb; Band; Church Choir; Drm Mjr(t); Mrchg Band; Rptr Frsh Cls; Rptr Soph Cls; Sec Jr Cls; Bus Admin.

DAWSON, MIKI D; Mississippi Co Christian Acad; Osceola, AR; (4); 3/15; Church Yth Grp; 4-H; French Clb; FBLA; GAA; JA; Key Clb; Math Clb; Natl Beta Clb; Pep Clb; John Philip Sousa Awd; Rotry Clb Schlsp; Parent Eagle Assn Schlsp; MS Cty CC; Nrs.

DAWSON, NATHALIA E; North Pulaski HS; Jacksonville, AR; (4); 4/296; Church Yth Grp; Sec FTA; Spanish Clb; Drill Tm; Yrbk; Treas Sr Cls; VP NHS; Drama Clb; Math Clb; Science Clb; Nrth Pulaski Miss 95 Mis Congeniality; Jesus Uniting Stu Tgthr Pres; Tandy Tech Schol; AR St Univ; Elem Ed.

DAWSON, TARA M; Osceola HS; Burdette, AR; (3); Cmnty Wkr; French Clb; FHA; Pep Clb; Acpl Chr; High Hon Roll; Hon Roll; NHS; U Of AR; RN.

DAY, ALICIA; Perryville Jr Sr HS; Perryville, AR; (2); 13/74; Chess Clb; Church Yth Grp; FCA; Pep Clb; Spanish Clb; Teachers Aide; Var Bsktbl; Var Powder Puff Ftbl; Var Trk; Prfct Atten Awd.

DAY, CHRIS L; Magnet Cove HS; Malvern, AR; (2); Church Yth Grp; Teachers Aide; Band; Church Choir; Mrchg Band; Orch; Pep Band; School Play; Stage Crew; Class A All Star Band 96; Chess Club; AR Tech Univ; Band/Prfmg Arts.

DAY, DANIELLE E; Springdale Sr HS; Springdale, AR; (3); 12/400; Church Yth Grp; Cmnty Wkr; FCA; Key Clb; Model UN; Teachers Aide; Acpl Chr; Church Choir; School Musical; Variety Show; Ath Of Yr; 3 Yrs All Region Choir Mem; U Of KS Lawrence; Phy Therapy.

DAYANANDA, NILU; Little Rock Cntrl HS; Little Rock, AR; (2); Church Yth Grp; Debate Tm; JCL; Latin Clb; Science Clb; Speech Tm; Cmnty Wkr; FBLA; Intnl Clb; Natl Latn Exm Slvr Medl Maxima Cum Laude; Stu Congrss; US Natl Math Awd; Washington Univ.

DAYBERRY, JENN; Springdale Sr HS; Springdale, AR; (4); Church Yth Grp; Library Aide; NFL; Q&S; Quiz Bowl; Science Clb; Chorus; Ed Lit Mag; Hon Roll; Jr NHS; Educl Talent Search; Upward Bound; U Of AR; Zoology.

DEACON, JENNIFER L; West Memphis Sr HS; West Memphis, AR; (3); 22/286; Am Leg Aux Girls St; Church Yth Grp; Cmnty Wkr; French Clb; Mu Alpha Theta; Natl Beta Clb; Mgr Yrbk; Ofcr Stu Cncl; French Hon Soc; High Hon Roll; Rotry Frgn Exch Stu To France; Nrsng Home Vol; Delta Beta Sigma Comm Svc Org; U Of AR Fayetteville.

DEAL, CARRIE D; Southside HS; Van Buren, AR; (3); 97/507; Church Yth Grp; FCA; Mu Alpha Theta; Office Aide; Science Clb; Spanish Clb; Teachers Aide; Var Bsktbl; Var Trk; Var Vllybl; All ST Vlybl 95-; Bsktbl ST Champs 95-; 4-A West All Region Plyr Bsktbl; PT.

DEAN, CASSIE A; Waldron HS; Parks, AR; (2); Drama Clb; 4-H; Natl FFA Org; Bsktbl; Trk; Vllybl; Cit Awd; Prfct Atten Awd; School Play; Stage Crew; Chrch Yth Grp; Southern AR Univ Tech; Pol Ofc.

DEAN, CHASITY; Hughes Jr-Sr HS; Hughes, AR; (4); 5/47; Am Leg Aux Girls St; Church Yth Grp; Cmnty Wkr; 4-H; Girl Scts; Natl FFA Org; Office Aide; Science Clb; Spanish Clb; Band; Henderson ST Univ; Scndry Ed.

DEAN, ISASHA N; West Memphis Sr HS; West Memphis, AR; (3); Church Yth Grp; Cmnty Wkr; French Clb; FHA; Mu Alpha Theta; Natl Beta Clb; Pep Clb; Quiz Bowl; Science Clb; Chorus; Henderson ST Univ; Pdtrcn.

DEAN, JASMIN J; Mc Crory Jr Sr HS; Mc Crory, AR; (2); Church Yth Grp; 4-H; GAA; SADD; Teachers Aide; Band; Church Choir; Flag Corp; Mrchg Band; School Play; Non-Schl Sftbl; UCA; Pediatrc Nrsng.

DEAN, JEFF S; Alma HS; Alma, AR; (4); Math Clb; Mu Alpha Theta; Science Clb; Band; Church Choir; Jazz Band; Mrchg Band; Orch; Pep Band; Hon Roll; AR Tech Univ; Engr.

DEAN, ZACHARY W; Alma HS; Alma, AR; (3); Church Yth Grp; Pres FCA; Spanish Clb; Teachers Aide; Ofcr Stu Cncl; Var Bsbl; Var Bsktbl; Var Ftbl; Var Golf; Hon Roll; Danforth I Darey You Awd 11th Grd; U Of Ozarks.

DEASE, SHARALEIGH R; Southside HS; Pleasant Plains, AR; (4); Key Clb; Natl Beta Clb; Teachers Aide; Chorus; School Musical; Stage Crew; Hon Roll; Kiwanis Awd; Madrigal Choir; STOP; UCA; Bus Law/Music.

DEATON, AMY M; Dierks HS; Newhope, AR; (1); Church Yth Grp; 4-H; FHA; Natl FFA Org; PRIDE; Pediatrics/Psyclgy.

DEATON, JENNIFER; Morrilton Sr HS; Morrilton, AR; (2); Art Clb; Church Yth Grp; 4-H; Math Clb; Natl Beta Clb; Science Clb; Spanish Clb; Thesps; Band; Hon Roll; Harding.

DEATON, JOE W; Rivercrest HS; Keiser, AR; (2); 4/139; Church Yth Grp; Scholastic Bowl; Band; Church Choir; Jazz Band; VP Mrchg Band; Pep Band; Ofcr Soph Cls; High Hon Roll; Hon Roll; World Schlr Athl Game 97; Natl Yng Ldrs Conf 96; Musician Trumpet/Piano.

DEATON, MICAH; Delight HS; Delight, AR; (1); 1/32; Church Yth Grp; Cmnty Wkr; 4-H; Natl FFA Org; Capt Quiz Bowl; Intrml Bsktbl; 4-H Awd; High Hon Roll; Hon Roll.

DE CHAINE, JACOB A; Siloam Springs Sr HS; Siloam Springs, AR; (4); Debate Tm; FCA; Teachers Aide; School Play; JV Var Bsbl; Var Chrldng; Var L Ftbl; Var L Trk; Var Wt Lftg; Pres Acad Fit Awd; US Marine Corps; Aviation Elec.

DECKARD, SARAH; Lake Hamilton Jr HS; Pearcy, AR; (1); Church Yth Grp; FCA; FBLA; Natl Beta Clb; Chorus; Drill Tm; Sec Treas Stu Cncl; Hon Roll; Wolf Pride; LH Sngrs; Ouachita Bptst U; Acctng.

DECKER, MARY; Yellville Summit HS; Yellville, AR; (2); Church Yth Grp; Teachers Aide; Band; Mrchg Band; Pep Band; Bsktbl; Chrldng; Trk; Cit Awd; Hon Roll; UCA All Star Chrldr.

DECKER, NATHAN; Mammoth Spring HS; Mammoth Spring, AR; (4); 2/44; Church Yth Grp; FBLA; FHA; Natl Beta Clb; Natl FFA Org; Office Aide; Quiz Bowl; SADD; Band; Jazz Band; J C Penney AZ Schlrsp Our Area; Rtry Club Lit Awd; Elks Schlrsp/Most Vlbl Stdnt; Averett; His/Eng.

DECKER, VIKKIE R; Riverview HS; Kensett, AR; (2); FHA; GAA; Girl Scts; Pep Clb; Spanish Clb; Teachers Aide; Yrbk; Bsktbl; Crs Cntry; Sftbl; Beebe; Bus.

DE CLERK, SHEA; Pocahontas HS; Pocahontas, AR; (3); 1/160; Am Leg Aux Girls St; Church Yth Grp; Key Clb; Natl Beta Clb; VP Sr Cls; VP Pres Stu Cncl; Capt Var Chrldng; High Hon Roll; NHS; Gym; 95 Overall & AA St Chrldng Champion Team; Acad Awds; U Of AR; Pre-Law.

DEDMON, NIKKI; R E Wells Jr HS; Greenwood, AR; (1); FCA; Varsity Clb; Nwsp; Yrbk; L Chrldng; JV Sftbl; High Hon Roll; Jr NHS; Med.

DEERE, MOLLY M; Central Sr HS; Little Rock, AR; (3); 58/540; Church Yth Grp; German Clb; VP Pres Natl Beta Clb; Acpl Chr; School Musical; Lit Mag; Capt Var Vllybl; Gov Hon Prg Awd; High Hon Roll; NHS; Fnlst Rgnl NATS AR/MS/LA; 2nd Place SR Jr Acad Of Sci; 5 Yrs Dance; Voice.

DE FOOR, JESSICA G; Searcy HS; Searcy, AR; (3); 20/230; Church Yth Grp; FCA; FTA; Natl Beta Clb; Spanish Clb; SADD; Band; Chorus; Church Choir; Color Guard; Vocal Music; Pharmacology.

DE FREECE, JUSTIN R; Siloam Springs Sr HS; Siloam Springs, AR; (3); HOBY; Key Clb; Natl Beta Clb; Teachers Aide; School Play; Stage Crew; Rep Stu Cncl; Var L Bsbl; Var Bsktbl; Var Trk; Psych.

DEGUNION, CARMEN; Brinkley HS; Brinkley, AR; (4); Drama Clb; French Clb; School Play; Nwsp; Yrbk; VP Frsh Cls; Treas Stu Cncl; Hon Roll; Jr NHS; NHS; All Amer Schlr; Csmtlgy.

DE HAAN, RAYMOND P; Manila HS; Manila, AR; (1); Church Yth Grp; Cmnty Wkr; Natl Beta Clb; Natl FFA Org; Var Bsbl; Mgr(s); Cit Awd; High Hon Roll; Hon Roll; AR ST; Engrng.

DE HAN, LAURA; Arkansas Bapt Schl; Maumelle, AR; (2); Church Yth Grp; FCA; FBLA; JA; Natl Beta Clb; Chorus; Church Choir; Rep Stu Cncl; Var Chrldng; High Hon Roll; Frgn Mission Clb.

DE HEM, SCOTT M; Southside HS; Fort Smith, AR; (4); 11/459; FBLA; Mu Alpha Theta; Spanish Clb; Teachers Aide; High Hon Roll; Hon Roll; Jr NHS; NHS; Pres Acad Fit Awd; Spanish NHS; Northwood Univ; Intl Bus.

DEISLINGER, REBECCA A; Flippin Jr Sr HS; Flippin, AR; (2); FBLA; German Clb; GAA; Key Clb; Rep Stu Cncl; Bsktbl; Hon Roll; Homcmng Royalty; Sci Fair Hnrb Mntn.

DELANEY, KIM M; Huttig Schl; Huttig, AR; (2); FBLA; FHA; GAA; Library Aide; Natl Beta Clb; Pres Science Clb; Ed Yrbk; Rep Stu Cncl; Var Sftbl; Hon Roll; Water Ski, Vlybl; LA Tech Univ; RN.

DE LAUGHTER, TRINITY K; Parkview Arts-Science HS; Jacksonville, AR; (2); Art Clb; Church Yth Grp; Cmnty Wkr; Drama Clb; Drill Tm; School Play; Rep Frsh Cls; Rep Soph Cls; High Hon Roll; Hon Roll; Alpha Omega Chrstn Clb; BASIC; Modlng; Actng.

DELEE, ADAM N; Lake Hamilton Sr HS; Hot Springs, AR; (2); Church Yth Grp; FCA; Natl Beta Clb; Spanish Clb; L Bsbl; L Bsktbl; High Hon Roll; NHS; Duke U TIP St Fnlst Math; Govs Yth Conf Alcohol/Tobacco Prvntn; Med.

DELGUDO WACLAW, JACOB R; North Little Rock Hs-West; North Little Rock, AR; (4); 14/554; Computer Clb; Drama Clb; FCA; Key Clb; Math Clb; Mu Alpha Theta; Natl Beta Clb; Spanish Clb; School Musical; School Play; U Of AR; Arch.

DE LONEY, DUSTIN; Mineral Springs Schl; Mineral Springs, AR; (2); Boy Scts; FBLA; Letterman Clb; Natl Beta Clb; SADD; Band; Mrchg Band; High Hon Roll; Hon Roll; Pres Schlr.

DE LONEY, RENAY; Mineral Springs Schl; Mineral Springs, AR; (3); 1/51; HOBY; Natl Beta Clb; Quiz Bowl; Drm Mjr(t); Mrchg Band; Rep Jr Cls; Ofcr Stu Cncl; Var Chrldng; Cit Awd; High Hon Roll; Med.

DE LONEY, RITA; Mineral Springs Schl; Mineral Springs, AR; (2); Church Yth Grp; Quiz Bowl; Rep Soph Cls; Rep Stu Cncl; Chrldng; High Hon Roll; Beta Clb; OM; Med.

DELPH, DEVERICK; Morrilton Sr HS; Menifee, AR; (4); Am Leg Boys St; Art Clb; Church Yth Grp; Cmnty Wkr; FCA; French Clb; Library Aide; Math Clb; Science Clb; Bsktbl; All St Ftbl Tm; Bus.

DELROSE, SABREENA A; Mountain Home HS; Mountain Home, AR; (3); 37/135; Art Clb; Quiz Bowl; Hon Roll; Pastel Yng AR Art Comp/Exb; 1st Pl Dist/ST Wtrclr Div GFWCA Conv; AR ST Univ; Drftng.

DE MENT, SCOTT; Abundant Life Schools; Sherwood, AR; (1); Boy Scts; Church Yth Grp; Hosp Aide; Chorus; Rep Stu Cncl; Capt Bsktbl; Hon Roll; Awana.

DE MENT, SHELLEY; Abundant Life Schools; Sherwood, AR; (3); 1/20; Church Yth Grp; Cmnty Wkr; Hosp Aide; Chorus; VP Jr Cls; VP Stu Cncl; Var L Bsktbl; Var L Vllybl; High Hon Roll; Treas NHS; Coutstndng Chrstn Awd; Awana Clb; UCA; Reg Nrs.

DENGER, FOREST; Jessieville HS; Hot Springs Natio, AR; (2); 5/55; Church Yth Grp; Key Clb; Natl Beta Clb; Spanish Clb; Hon Roll; Local PTA Rflctns Visual Arts 2nd Pl; ST PTA Rflctns Visual Arts Hnrbl Mntn.

DENHAM, DEANNA M; Searcy HS; Searcy, AR; (3); Church Yth Grp; FTA; Girl Scts; Key Clb; Quiz Bowl; Church Choir; Yrbk; Var Tennis; French Hon Soc; NHS.

DENHAM, KIMBERLY A; Searcy HS; Searcy, AR; (2); Church Yth Grp; French Clb; FBLA; Girl Scts; Natl Beta Clb; SADD; Chorus; Church Choir; School Play; Hon Roll.

DENHAM, MIA; Robinson HS; Little Rock, AR; (2); 13/165; Church Yth Grp; FTA; Natl Beta Clb; Band; Jazz Band; Bsktbl; High Hon Roll; Jr NHS; NHS; Pres Schlr; UCA; Med.

DENMAN, MONICA; Little Rock Cntrl HS; Little Rock, AR; (2); Church Yth Grp; Cmnty Wkr; French Clb; Natl Beta Clb; Office Aide; Band; Chorus; Jazz Band; School Play; Rptr Nwsp; Sci Fair 3rd Pl Prjct, To Regnls; Y-Teens Ofcr; All-Star Chrldng; U Of TX Austin; Advertsng.

DENMON, STEPHANIE E; Taylor HS; Taylor, AR; (2); Church Yth Grp; FBLA; VP FHA; Yrbk; Rep Stu Cncl; Stat Score Keeper; Hon Roll; CYC; SAU; Pediatrics.

DENNINGTON, JOY; Genoa Central HS; Texarkana, AR; (3); 1/60; Church Yth Grp; FBLA; GAA; Quiz Bowl; Spanish Clb; Sec Jr Cls; Bsktbl; Chrldng; Trk; Hon Roll; ULAR; Med.

DENNIS, CHAD; Central Ark Christian Schl; North Little Rock, AR; (2); Church Yth Grp; Chorus; Var L Socr; L Trk; High Hon Roll; Jr NHS; NHS; Prfct Atten Awd; Natl Mrt Sci Awd.

DENT, ANGELA; Jonesboro HS; Jonesboro, AR; (3); Art Clb; Church Yth Grp; FBLA; Key Clb; Spanish Clb; Rep Frsh Cls; Rep Stu Cncl; Var L Chrldng; Powder Puff Ftbl; Hon Roll; Natl Cmptn 9th Pl Chrldng Awd; Homcmng Ct; Cls Favorite; U Of ARFAYETTEVILLE; Dntl Hygn.

DENTON, AMANDA L; Clarksville HS; Clarksville, AR; (2); Church Yth Grp; FCA; FBLA; Key Clb; Natl Beta Clb; Spanish Clb; Var Sftbl; Var Trk; Hon Roll; Model UN; PRIDE; LEAD; Sign Lang Intrprtr/Psych.

DENTON, BARRY; Hatfield Schl; Hatfield, AR; (4); 1/16; Church Yth Grp; FBLA; Pres Natl Beta Clb; Pres Natl FFA Org; Co-Ed Nwsp; Pres Sr Cls; Pres Stu Cncl; Var Capt Bsktbl; High Hon Roll; Val; UAR; Ag Ed.

DENTON, EMILY C; Russellville Sr HS; Russellville, AR; (2); Church Yth Grp; Cmnty Wkr; Model UN; Teachers Aide; Drill Tm; Variety Show; High Hon Roll; Hon Roll; Jr NHS; Pres Schlr; U Of AR.

DENTON, REGINA A; Bentonville Sr HS; Bentonville, AR; (3); 121/350; CAP; DECA; FBLA; Spanish Clb; Hon Roll; Rep DECA; U Of AR Fayetteville; Bus.

DE PRIEST, DAVID A; Mena HS; Mena, AR; (2); 1/175; Church Yth Grp; FCA; French Clb; Var L Bsbl; Var L Bsktbl; Var L Ftbl; High Hon Roll; Pres Acad Fit Awd; Science Clb; BAD; Pee Wee Bsktbl Coach; Rice Univ.

DERDEN, J ANDREW; Conway Sr HS; Conway, AR; (3); Church Yth Grp; FBLA; Office Aide; Teachers Aide; VICA; TX A&M Univ; Vet Med.

DERICKSON, L M; Leslie Schl; Leslie, AR; (3); 3/20; Church Yth Grp; FCA; FBLA; FHA; GAA; Natl Beta Clb; Teachers Aide; VP Jr Cls; Bsktbl; Trk; Handicapped Yth Camp Cnslr; U Of Cntrl AR; Med.

DE SHIELDS, JENNIFER L; Bentonville Sr HS; Bentonville, AR; (3); Cmnty Wkr; Ed Nwsp; Yrbk; Ed Lit Mag; High Hon Roll; NHS; Pres Acad Fit Awd; ACE; Acad Excl Awrds Soph/Jr Yrs; Pietry/Shrt Stry Wrtng 1st Pl NW AR Poetry Cmptn; Psych.

DESMOND, JASON R; Gosnell Jr Sr HS; Dell, AR; (1); 42/160; Art Clb; Church Yth Grp; Natl Beta Clb; Natl FFA Org; Spanish Clb; Variety Show; Ofcr Bsbl; Trk; U Of AR.

DETERS, CADE M; Monticello HS; Monticello, AR; (4); Church Yth Grp; FCA; FBLA; Letterman Clb; Math Clb; Natl Beta Clb; Science Clb; SADD; Var Ftbl; Intrml Socr; U Of MO Rolla; Chem Engr.

DETERS, JEREMY S; Monticello HS; Monticello, AR; (2); Math Clb; Science Clb; Spanish Clb; Hon Roll; SADD; Anesthesiology; Dr.

DEVAULT, JENNY M; Junction City HS; Junction City, AR; (3); 3/56; Church Yth Grp; Quiz Bowl; Science Clb; Band; Jazz Band; Mrchg Band; VP Stu Cncl; High Hon Roll; NHS; Tchng.

DEVER, DEVRON J; Cutter Morning Star Jr Sr HS; Hot Springs, AR; (4); 2/29; Church Yth Grp; Natl Beta Clb; High Hon Roll; Hon Roll; Kiwanis Awd; NHS; Sal; Am Leg Boys St; Art Clb; Cmnty Wkr; Elks Clb Stu Of Month; Physics Awd Top Stu; Chamber Of Commerce Awd; Mech Engrng.

DEVEREUX, AMANDA; Russellville Sr HS; London, AR; (2); Church Yth Grp; Office Aide; Teachers Aide; Band; Mrchg Band; Pep Band; Nwsp; Yrbk; JV Var Gym; High Hon Roll; All Reg Bnd 2 Yrs; Solo; Ensmbl; Boston Coll; Obstrtcn/Nun.

DEVINE, AMBER NICOLE; Benton Sr HS; Benton, AR; (4); 52/233; Church Yth Grp; FCA; 4-H; French Clb; FBLA; Key Clb; Math Clb; Science Clb; Teachers Aide; Ofcr Stu Cncl; Pepsteppers Dnce Tm Squd Ldr; Chrch Yth Choir; U Of Centr AR; Spch Path.

DEWEY, AMANDA G; Farmington Jr Sr HS; Prairie Grove, AR; (2); Church Yth Grp; Cmnty Wkr; Drama Clb; FCA; 4-H; FHA; JA; Natl FFA Org; Office Aide; Teachers Aide; UAR; Nrsng.

DEWEY, JEREMY T; Mountain Home HS; Mountain Home, AR; (4); 4/238; Am Leg Boys St; Church Yth Grp; FCA; FBLA; Scholastic Bowl; Yrbk; Ofcr Bsbl; Bsktbl; High Hon Roll; Sal; U Of AR; Bus.

DEWEY, RUSSELL J; Mountain Home HS; Mountain Home, AR; (3); Natl FFA Org; ROTC; Pres Acad Fit Awd; AR Governors Schl; FFA ST Farmer Deg; Ag Bus Team 1st In NE Dist/4th In ST; Fayetteville Univ; Vet Sci.

DE WITT, ANGELA G; Fayetteville Sr HS; Fayetteville, AR; (4); 32/372; Cmnty Wkr; SADD; Teachers Aide; Drill Tm; Lit Mag; Powder Puff Ftbl; Hon Roll; NHS; 95 AR Govnr Schl; Scl Sci; 26 Clb Sec; U Of AR; Bus.

DEWITT, COURTNEY; Augusta HS; Augusta, AR; (3); Natl Beta Clb; Science Clb; Spanish Clb; Band; Flag Corp; Yrbk; High Hon Roll; NHS; GATE; Devil Pride Team; Sigma Alpha Omega.

DE YAMPERT, ERIC W; Smackover HS; Smackover, AR; (3); Am Leg Boys St; Art Clb; Cmnty Wkr; FBLA; Science Clb; Spanish Clb; Teachers Aide; Ofcr Stu Cncl; Var L Bsktbl; Var L Ftbl; Peer Medtr; Homecmng Escrt; Sr Day Commencemnt Usher; U Of ARK; Bus.

DE ZALIA, MARK; Arkansas Schl Math & Science; Bentonville, AR; (3); Key Clb; Mu Alpha Theta; Natl Beta Clb; Ed Nwsp; Ed Yrbk; Lit Mag; VP Soph Cls; Treas Stu Cncl; NHS; Pres Acad Fit Awd; Arch.

DICKENS, AMANDA; Morrilton Sr HS; Morrilton, AR; (3); 4-H; French Clb; Math Clb; Natl Beta Clb; Office Aide; Quiz Bowl; Science Clb; Thesps; Drill Tm; Nwsp.

DICKENS, CANDICE; Morrilton Sr HS; Morrilton, AR; (2); Church Yth Grp; Drama Clb; Natl Beta Clb; Thesps; Chorus; School Musical; Hon Roll; Schl Choir; UCA; Law.

DICKENSHEETS, MELISSA S; Morrilton Sr HS; Morrilton, AR; (2); Church Yth Grp; Natl Beta Clb; Science Clb; Band; Chorus; Flag Corp; Stage Crew; Hon Roll; Prfct Atten Awd; Central Bapt Coll; Music.

DICKER, SHANDRA L; Central Sr HS; Little Rock, AR; (3); #30 in class; French Clb; Latin Clb; Natl Beta Clb; French Hon Soc; High Hon Roll; Jr NHS; NHS; Pres Acad Fit Awd; Dance Ballet, Tap & Jazz.

DICKERSON, CHRIS; Oark HS; Oark, AR; (2); FBLA; FHA; Natl Beta Clb; Rep Frsh Cls; VP Soph Cls; Ofcr Stu Cncl; Ofcr Bsbl; Bsktbl; High Hon Roll; Hon Roll.

DICKERSON, CRYSTAL; Mulberry HS; Mulberry, AR; (4); 1/28; Rptr French Clb; Pres FBLA; VP FHA; Science Clb; Co-Capt Band; Co-Ed Yrbk; Pres Sr Cls; Vllybl; Pres NHS; Val; Dntstry.

DICKERSON, MAKEBA J; El Dorado Sr HS; El Dorado, AR; (4); 26/275; Pres Church Yth Grp; Cmnty Wkr; Key Clb; Natl Beta Clb; Capt ROTC; Spanish Clb; Band; Drill Tm; NHS; Ntl Merit SF; FL A&M U; Spnsh.

DICKERSON, SARAH; Pangburn Jr Sr HS; Heber Springs, AR; (4); 6/52; French Clb; Pres FBLA; Treas FHA; Teachers Aide; Ed Yrbk; Treas Jr Cls; Treas Sr Cls; JV Chrldng; Hon Roll; NHS; AR St Univ; Intl Bus.

DICKEY, DEVEN; Harmony Grove Jr Sr HS; Camden, AR; (2); FCA; 4-H; FBLA; Natl FFA Org; Spanish Clb; Bsktbl; Cit Awd; Hon Roll; Pres Acad Fit Awd.

DICKEY, ERICA S; El Dorado Sr HS; El Dorado, AR; (4); 41/266; Art Clb; Cmnty Wkr; FBLA; Natl Beta Clb; Office Aide; Chorus; Hon Roll; NHS; Brothers & Sisters In Christ; Anchor Clb; Jr-Sr Steering Comm; Oratorio Choir; Jr Civitan; U Of Memphis.

DICKEY, JILL; Central Ark Christian Schl; North Little Rock, AR; (3); 6/76; Church Yth Grp; FHA; Science Clb; Spanish Clb; Church Choir; High Hon Roll; Jr NHS; NHS; Advnc Opn Wtr Scb Dvr; Chrch Mssn Trps; Marine Bio.

DICKEY, KETRINA; West Memphis Sr HS; West Memphis, AR; (1); Church Yth Grp; Cmnty Wkr; English Clb; French Clb; Math Clb; Science Clb; Church Choir; School Play; Chrldng; Gym; LSU; Ed.

DICKEY, KIMBERLEY D; Highland HS; Ash Flat, AR; (3); 8/96; Natl Beta Clb; Quiz Bowl; Band; Chorus; Jazz Band; School Musical; School Play; Rep Stu Cncl; High Hon Roll; NHS; All Region Band & Choir; Upward Bound Math Sci Pgm; Lyon Coll; Math Ed; Eng.

DICKEY, KINSEY R; Fayetteville Christian Schl; Fayetteville, AR; (2); Church Yth Grp; Phtg Yrbk; Var Chrldng; NHS; Sprindgale Music Clb Piano Clinic Hnrs 96; NCA Camp Spirit Stick Wnnr; HS His Tchr.

DICKSON, DEENA E; Malvern Sr HS; Malvern, AR; (4); 25/178; Church Yth Grp; French Clb; FBLA; FHA; Quiz Bowl; Teachers Aide; Cit Awd; Hon Roll; Jr NHS; Pres Schlr; Prdcr, TV Brdcst; U Of Cntrl AR; Psych.

DICTSON, KHANDRA; Bentonville Sr HS; Bentonville, AR; (4); 8/248; Pres 4-H; Sec Treas Key Clb; Scholastic Bowl; SADD; Rptr Nwsp; Co-Ed Yrbk; 4-H Awd; High Hon Roll; Sec NHS; Pres Acad Fit Awd; Jr Bank Bd; Univ Of Cntrl AR/OT.

DIERKS, AMANDA L; Stuttgart Sr HS; Stuttgart, AR; (3); Treas DECA; FBLA; GAA; JA; Mu Alpha Theta; Natl Beta Clb; Cit Awd; High Hon Roll; NHS; Prfct Atten Awd; Bus.

DIEST, LISA; Kirby HS; Glenwood, AR; (2); Chess Clb; Church Yth Grp; Cmnty Wkr; FCA; FBLA; FHA; Natl Beta Clb; Pep Clb; Bsktbl; Chrldng; Beauty Pgnt Wnnr; Henderson ST; Bnkng.

DIETZ, K AMANDA; Fayetteville Sr HS; Fayetteville, AR; (2); Church Yth Grp; Band; Church Choir; Flag Corp; Mrchg Band; Pep Band; High Hon Roll; Hon Roll; Math.

DIETZ, NICOLE N; Piggott HS; Piggott, AR; (2); Drama Clb; FCA; French Clb; Natl Beta Clb; Chorus; Church Choir; School Musical; Chrldng; Hon Roll; Fr I Awd; Coll Prep Eng II Awd; Drama Awd; Ole Miss.

DIGBY, JEREMY W; Prairie Grove HS; Prairie Grove, AR; (3); Drama Clb; SADD; School Play; Nwsp; Rptr Frsh Cls; Ofcr Stu Cncl; Ftbl; Socr; High Hon Roll; NHS; Perf Arts.

DIGGS, TRINA D; Parkview Arts-Science HS; Little Rock, AR; (3); Dance Clb; German Clb; Office Aide; Varsity Clb; Chorus; School Musical; Bsktbl; Trk; High Hon Roll; Hon Roll; Peer Helper; Ladies Clb; St Champ Trk Trophies; U Of Cntrl AR; Pre-Dentistry.

DILDINE, CASEY M; Genoa Central HS; Texarkana, AR; (4); 5/35; Church Yth Grp; 4-H; FBLA; Quiz Bowl; Spanish Clb; School Play; Yrbk; VP Frsh Cls; Cit Awd; 4-H Awd; Jr Santa Gertrudes Mem; Texarkana Coll; Ag Bus.

DILDINE JR, RICKY; Wynne HS; Wynne, AR; (3); 1/200; Am Leg Boys St; VP Drama Clb; Sec FBLA; VP FTA; Drm Mjr(t); Ofcr Stu Cncl; Var L Tennis; NHS; Church Yth Grp; FCA; Unity Bible Clb Pres; Acting Awd; AR Governors Schl Drama; Actor.

DILES, SCOTT; Central Ark Christian Schl; North Little Rock, AR; (3); Church Yth Grp; FHA; Library Aide; Chorus; Rep Stu Cncl; JV Bsbl; Var Ftbl; Var Trk; Hon Roll; NHS; Harding U.

DILL, JAMES; Benton Sr HS; Benton, AR; (4); Am Leg Boys St; Church Yth Grp; Cmnty Wkr; Science Clb; Varsity Clb; Ftbl; Wt Lftg; Hon Roll; Jr NHS; NHS; Bells Chrch Choir; U Of The Ozarks.

DILL, JENNIFER R; Fountain Lake Jr Sr HS; Hot Springs, AR; (1); FCA; Spanish Clb; JV Bsktbl; High Hon Roll.

DILLARD, DAN C; Pulaski Acad; Little Rock, AR; (2); Cmnty Wkr; Drama Clb; English Clb; Latin Clb; Natl Beta Clb; School Musical; School Play; Crs Cntry; Gym; Trk.

DILLARD, SPARKAL E; Arkansas Sr HS; Texarkana, AR; (3); Var L Dance Clb; Drama Clb; Sec FHA; Pep Clb; Band; Church Choir; L Drill Tm; School Musical; School Play; Stage Crew; U Cntrl AR; Chem.

DILLION, KEVIN L; Dewitt HS; De Witt, AR; (3); 8/98; French Clb; FBLA; Natl Beta Clb; Rptr Science Clb; Teachers Aide; Cit Awd; High Hon Roll; Ntl Merit Ltr; Prfct Atten Awd; Pres Acad Fit Awd; GPA Awd; Cls Day Usher; U Cntrl AR Conway; Elec Engr.

DILLON, SHILOH; Coleman Jr HS; Van Buren, AR; (1); FBLA; Drill Tm; Pres Stu Cncl; High Hon Roll; Jr NHS; Perf Bank Untd Thanksgvng Day Pard As All-Star Dancr; Partcptd In Ft Smith Jr Cotlln; All Amer Schlr; Penn ST; Onocology.

DILLS, JEFF; Izard Co Cons Jr Sr HS; Horseshoe Bend, AR; (3); Am Leg Boys St; Church Yth Grp; FCA; Key Clb; Natl Beta Clb; Pep Clb; Teachers Aide; VP Jr Cls; Var L Bsbl; Var Capt Bsktbl; Bus.

DILWORTH, AMY; Harmony Grove Jr Sr HS; Camden, AR; (4); 6/51; Am Leg Aux Girls St; Church Yth Grp; Treas Natl Beta Clb; Quiz Bowl; Band; Capt Flag Corp; School Play; Yrbk; Rep Stu Cncl; NHS; Henderson ST U.

DI MAGGIO, JOHN M; Arkansas Schl Math & Science; Lake Village, AR; (4); Church Yth Grp; Cmnty Wkr; Drama Clb; Mu Alpha Theta; Natl Beta Clb; Band; Mrchg Band; School Play; Cit Awd; U Of AR; Chem Engr.

DI MICCO, CYNDI A; Jonesboro HS; Jonesboro, AR; (3); Church Yth Grp; FBLA; Key Clb; Natl Beta Clb; Band; Jazz Band; Mrchg Band; Hon Roll; NHS; Pres Acad Fit Awd; Eng/Wrtng.

DINGLER, AUDREY; Ouachita Jr Sr HS; Malvern, AR; (3); 2/35; Church Yth Grp; 4-H; FBLA; FHA; HOBY; Natl Beta Clb; Natl FFA Org; Chorus; Var Bsktbl; Var Sftbl; Hot Spring Co Yth Bd; Gorilla Found; Hmne Soc; Ethlgy.

DINGLER, COURTNEY M; North Little Rock Hs-East; North Little Rock, AR; (2); 55/567; Var Crs Cntry; Var Socr; JV Trk; JV Vllybl; High Hon Roll; Hon Roll; JV Trk MVP.

DINNAN, RA DORA; Morrilton Sr HS; Morrilton, AR; (2); #1 in class; Church Yth Grp; 4-H; FBLA; HOBY; Math Clb; Natl Beta Clb; Science Clb; Spanish Clb; Thesps; Band; Spch Pthlgy.

DISEL, JAMAICA D; Decatur HS; Decatur, AR; (4); Church Yth Grp; FHA; Office Aide; Spanish Clb; Teachers Aide; Bsktbl; Chrldng; Hon Roll; Human Relations.

DISNEY, LIANNA O; Fayetteville Christian Schl; Fayetteville, AR; (2); Church Yth Grp; Acpl Chr; Church Choir; School Musical; Yrbk; Capt Bsktbl; Hon Roll; HS Office Aide; Choir Ldr For 6th Grd Girls; All Dist 95-96; MVP NACA Natl Champ 94-96; Natl All Amer; Bapt Schl Of Nrsng; RN.

DISTERDICK, MINDI; North Little Rock Hs-West; North Little Rock, AR; (3); 215/653; Church Yth Grp; FCA; GAA; Red Cross Aide; Bsktbl; JV Var Chrldng; Gym; Powder Puff Ftbl; Score Keeper; JV Var Sftbl; NCA All-Amer Team Awd Chrldng; MVP Awds Sftbl; U KY-LEXINGTON; Vet.

DITTMAN, DARCY; Ozark Adventist Acad; Killeen, TX; (1); 3/40; Church Yth Grp; Stage Crew; Bsktbl; Score Keeper; Vllybl; High Hon Roll; Prfct Atten Awd; Good Conduct Awd; Top Team In Vlybl & Bsktbl; U Of TX Austin; Law.

DIXON, DENISHA R; Strong Jr Sr HS; Strong, AR; (2); Sec Church Yth Grp; French Clb; FHA; Quiz Bowl; Church Choir; Nwsp; JV Var Chrldng; Hon Roll; Beta Clb; Gftd & Tlntd; Northeast LA Univ; Accountant.

DIXON, DUSTIN MARK; Stuttgart Sr HS; Stuttgart, AR; (3); Am Leg Boys St; FCA; FBLA; Spanish Clb; Ftbl; Hon Roll; U Of AR Fayetteville; Acctng.

DIXON, JUSTIN; Morrilton Sr HS; Springfield, AR; (2); Art Clb; Drama Clb; Natl Beta Clb; Office Aide; Thesps; Stage Crew; Var Bsbl; Var Ftbl; NHS; Ntl Merit Ltr.

DIXON, KIM; Ola Jr Sr HS; Ola, AR; (4); #3 in class; Am Leg Aux Girls St; Pres VP FHA; HOBY; Natl Beta Clb; Spanish Clb; Rep Nwsp; Phtg Yrbk; VP Soph Cls; Sec Jr Cls; Treas Stu Cncl; Annl Qn 95; Mss Yll Cty 94; Hmcmng Qn 95; U Of AR; Phys Thrp.

DIXON, MONICA; Blevins HS; Emmet, AR; (4); 3/36; Pres FBLA; VP Natl Beta Clb; Office Aide; Teachers Aide; Church Choir; Pres Sr Cls; Sec Stu Cncl; Hon Roll; Nrsng.

DIXON, NIHISSA D; Cloverdale Jr HS; Little Rock, AR; (1); Computer Clb; French Clb; FBLA; FHA; JA; Natl Beta Clb; Band; School Play; Trk; Cit Awd; Acad Excl; Outstndng Citizenship; Cert Of Ldrshp; Travel Agent; Soc Svcs.

DIXON, PAISLEY; Cabot HS; Austin, AR; (3); 56/398; VP French Clb; Hosp Aide; Office Aide; Quiz Bowl; Teachers Aide; Drill Tm; Var Pom Pon; French Hon Soc; Hon Roll; Qz Bwl Cap; Knwldg Mstrs; AR Govs Schl Alt; U Of AR Fayetteville; Psych.

DIXON, RACHEL A; Arkansas Schl Math & Science; Morristown, NJ; (4); Am Leg Aux Girls St; FBLA; FHA; Girl Scts; Mu Alpha Theta; Natl Beta Clb; Nwsp; Bsktbl; Hon Roll; NHS; Rutgers Univ.

DIXON, TIMOTHY R; Catholic HS; North Little Rock, AR; (4); 40/153; Boy Scts; Latin Clb; ROTC; Drill Tm; Crs Cntry; Hon Roll; Search/Rescue Tm; Fireman Vol; UALR.

DO, NGA T; Arkansas Sr HS; Texarkana, AR; (4); 8/380; Church Yth Grp; FBLA; Mu Alpha Theta; Treas Spanish Clb; Band; Mrchg Band; Pep Band; High Hon Roll; Jr NHS; NHS; Mst Outstndng Stu Amer Hstry, Spnsh I; All Region, All St Band; U Of Notre Dame; Pre-Med.

DO, STACY; Hot Springs HS; Hot Springs, AR; (1); Church Yth Grp; FBLA; Science Clb; Treas Frsh Cls; Chrldng; High Hon Roll; Hon Roll; FCA; Key Clb; Natl Beta Clb; St PRIDE; Trng PRIDE; Gymnstcs; Frosh Maid; COC; Hosp Candy Strpr; Stanford; Pthlgst.

DOBBINS, MATT F; Mountain View Jr Sr HS; Mountain View, AR; (3); 5/67; Church Yth Grp; FCA; Natl Beta Clb; Quiz Bowl; Rep Stu Cncl; L Capt Chrldng; Pre-Med.

DOBBS, AMY; Woodlawn Schl; Rison, AR; (3); Church Yth Grp; GAA; Natl Beta Clb; School Play; Yrbk; Var Bsktbl; Var Chrldng; Var Crs Cntry; Var Sftbl; Var Trk; UCA; Cmptr Prgmng.

DOBBS, COURTNEY; Central Ark Christian Schl; North Little Rock, AR; (2); Church Yth Grp; Library Aide; Spanish Clb; Chorus; Hon Roll; Jr NHS; Natl Sci Mrt Awd.

DOBBS, MELISSA A; Westside HS; Hartman, AR; (3); FBLA; FHA; Chorus; Powder Puff Ftbl; Natl Eng Mrt Awd.

DOBBS, MICHAEL; Arkansas Bapt Schl; Little Rock, AR; (2); Boy Scts; Church Yth Grp; Natl Beta Clb; Spanish Clb; Church Choir; High Hon Roll.

DOBBS, TRACY; Dumas HS; Dumas, AR; (2); Church Yth Grp; Math Clb; Natl Beta Clb; Science Clb; Color Guard; Ofcr Stu Cncl; Tennis; High Hon Roll; NHS; Pres Acad Fit Awd; Ventures Ed; ASU; Med.

DOBSON, JEANNIE; Humphrey Schl; Humphrey, AR; (4); 2/22; FBLA; FHA; Spanish Clb; Teachers Aide; Co-Ed Yrbk; Ofcr Jr Cls; Ofcr Sr Cls; Bsktbl; Sftbl; Hon Roll; UAM; Soc Wk.

DODD, R ADAM; Southside HS; Fort Smith, AR; (2); Church Yth Grp; FCA; Spanish Clb; JV Ftbl; Hon Roll; Jr NHS; NHS; Pre Med.

DODD, REGINA A; Crossett Sr HS; Crossett, AR; (3); 31/200; Art Clb; Church Yth Grp; Math Clb; Mu Alpha Theta; Natl Beta Clb; Church Choir; JV Bsktbl; JV Trk; Hon Roll; NHS; Hunting; Fishing; Drawing.

DODDRIDGE, JOSH P; Glen Rose HS; Traskwood, AR; (2); Art Clb; FCA; Spanish Clb; Ofcr Bsbl; Bsktbl; Hon Roll; PT.

DODGE, ANGIE C; Hartford Schl; Hartford, AR; (2); Church Yth Grp; Sec FBLA; Teachers Aide; Band; Color Guard; Mrchg Band; Pep Band; Bsktbl; Trk; Hon Roll; PT/CHLD Care.

DODGE, EDWARD C; De Soto Schl; Helena, AR; (2); Spanish Clb; Rep Soph Cls; Hon Roll; NHS; Roller Hockey; Write Short Stories & Poetry; His Tchr.

DODGEN, JODI R; Cabot HS; Cabot, AR; (3); Rep Am Leg Aux Girls St; Art Clb; Church Yth Grp; Key Clb; Math Tm; Spanish Clb; Band; Church Choir; Mrchg Band; Pep Band; Governors Schl; Marion Trivium Quadrivium Symposium; Occptnl Thrpst.

DODSON, KELLEY L; Fouke Jr Sr HS; Fouke, AR; (3); Band; Mrchg Band; Pep Band; Rptr Nwsp; Hon Roll.

DODSON, TARSY L; Springdale Sr HS; Springdale, AR; (3); Church Yth Grp; Cmnty Wkr; FCA; FBLA; Key Clb; Model UN; Office Aide; Chorus; Church Choir; JV Bsktbl; STAND; UCA; Ed.

DOEPEL, HEATHER; Devalls Bluff Jr Sr HS; De Valls Bluff, AR; (2); French Clb; FBLA; Natl Beta Clb; Rptr Rep Stu Cncl; Var Bsktbl; Var Crs Cntry; Var Trk; Hon Roll; All Dist HS Bsktbl.

DOHERTY, MARI K; Salem HS; Salem, AR; (3); Am Leg Aux Girls St; Sec Key Clb; Natl Beta Clb; Spanish Clb; Band; Rep Nwsp; Var Bsktbl; High Hon Roll; Pre-Med.

DOHERTY, RYAN C; Mc Gehee HS; Mcgehee, AR; (2); FTA; Natl Beta Clb; Natl FFA Org; NHS; PRIDE Awd; Hunt & Fish; Engrng.

DOKE, TOBY; Trumann HS; Trumann, AR; (2); Church Yth Grp; FCA; FHA; Spanish Clb; Church Choir; Ofcr Soph Cls; Ofcr Bsbl; Bsktbl; Ftbl; Wt Lftg; FHA Sec, Treas; Hnr Soc.

DOLD, KIMBERLY S; Sacred Heart Schl; Perry, AR; (2); Art Clb; Church Yth Grp; Drama Clb; GAA; Key Clb; Natl Beta Clb; SADD; Church Choir; School Play; Stage Crew; Cmptr Oper Fshn Dsgn.

DOLLAR JR, DOW; Russellville Sr HS; Russellville, AR; (3); 30/375; Church Yth Grp; FBLA; Teachers Aide; High Hon Roll; Hon Roll; Jr NHS; Pres Acad Fit Awd; Span Immrsn Prgm AR Tech Univ; U Of AR; Bus/Law/Acctng.

DOLLAR, JENNIFER L; Conway Sr HS; Conway, AR; (3); Natl Beta Clb; Office Aide; Science Clb; Acpl Chr; Hon Roll; VFW Ladies Auxiliary Post 2259 Mem.

DOLLAR, TRACY; Rison HS; Rison, AR; (2); 1/45; Church Yth Grp; FCA; French Clb; FBLA; Sec FHA; HOBY; Natl Beta Clb; Office Aide; Science Clb; Var Capt Chrldng; Math, Hist, Sci & Hm Econ Ltr R Awds; Eng Mdl; Gftd Tlntd.

DOLLISON, CRYSTAL E; Fouke Jr Sr HS; Fouke, AR; (2); Church Yth Grp; Natl FFA Org; Spanish Clb; Sec Frsh Cls; JV Bsktbl; Capt Chrldng; Hon Roll; Keybrdng/His Awd; Univ Of AR.

DONALDSON, JENNY L; Crossett Sr HS; Crossett, AR; (2); 92/222; Church Yth Grp; FHA; Science Clb; Band; Church Choir; Flag Corp; Mrchg Band; Pom Pon; Sftbl; Tennis; Chrch Act; Law Enforcement.

DONALDSON, SCOTT A; Hope HS; Hope, AR; (3); 18/238; Am Leg Boys St; Church Yth Grp; French Clb; Key Clb; Natl Beta Clb; Band; Tennis; High Hon Roll; Stdnt Of Month 2 Times; U Of AR Henderson; Pre-Med/Eng.

DONELSON, SHAYLAN A; Arkansas Sr HS; Texarkana, AR; (3); Art Clb; Cmnty Wkr; Drama Clb; Service Clb; Rptr Nwsp; Phtg Yrbk; Rep Stu Cncl; Bsktbl; Tennis; Church Yth Grp; Med.

DONHAM, DOUGLAS C; Central Sr HS; North Little Rock, AR; (2); Boy Scts; Church Yth Grp; French Clb; German Clb; Math Clb; Natl Beta Clb; Science Clb; Jazz Band; Rep Soph Cls; Jr NHS; Judo; Eagle Rank Boy Scouts; Suptndts Stdnt Cbnt Litl Rock Schl Dist.

DONLEY, CARISSA; Dumas HS; Winchester, AR; (4); 15/126; Church Yth Grp; FBLA; Natl Beta Clb; Spanish Clb; Chorus; Church Choir; Rep Stu Cncl; Cit Awd; High Hon Roll; Hon Roll; Drama; GCE; All-Stars; U Of AR At Monticello.

DONOVAN, SHAWN M; Searcy HS; Searcy, AR; (2); Church Yth Grp; FCA; Natl Beta Clb; Var Socr; Hon Roll; Math Talent Srsch Geometry Hon Mention 9th Grd; Dfnsve MVP U Of NC Soccer Camp Excl 95; U Of NC Wilmington; Marine Bio.

DOOLEY, HEATHER; Dierks HS; Lockesburg, AR; (4); 2/35; Art Clb; Church Yth Grp; FBLA; Rptr FHA; Church Choir; School Play; Yrbk; Hon Roll; NHS; Quiz Bowl; All Amer Schlr; Ouachita Baptist U.

DOOLEY, HOLLY B; Clay Co Central Jr Sr HS; Rector, AR; (2); 1/45; Church Yth Grp; FBLA; FTA; Quiz Bowl; Band; Church Choir; Flag Corp; VP Soph Cls; Hon Roll; NHS; U Of Cntrl AR.

DOOLEY, LEIGH A; Arkadelphia Sr HS; Arkadelphia, AR; (3); French Clb; Spanish Clb; Sec Soph Cls; Treas Sr Cls; Gov Hon Prg Awd; High Hon Roll; Jr NHS; Kiwanis Awd; NHS; Prfct Atten Awd; Beta Clb VP 95-96; Upward Bound; Pre-Med; Bio.

DOOLEY, RACHEL C; Dierks HS; Lockesburg, AR; (1); Church Yth Grp; 4-H; FHA; Band; Mrchg Band; Sftbl; 4-H Awd; Hon Roll; Pres Acad Fit Awd; Med.

DOOLITTLE, CHRISTOPHER J; Catholic HS; North Little Rock, AR; (3); 25/172; Church Yth Grp; Capt L Bsktbl; Vllybl; High Hon Roll; Bsbl, AAU Natl Trnmnt; U Of AR; Engrng.

DOOLY, KIMBERLY A; Southside HS; Fort Smith, AR; (4); 195/459; Church Yth Grp; DECA; Drama Clb; Girl Scts; Key Clb; Q&S; Spanish Clb; Thesps; School Play; Stage Crew; Photo-Jrnlst Of Yr Hnrbl Mntn; ARHS Press Assoc; Yrbk Future Photoexcel; Nswpr Photo Essay Excel; Westark Univ; Bus.

DORAN, KIMBERLY M; Jacksonville HS; Jacksonville, AR; (3); Art Clb; Spanish Clb; Var Golf; Jr NHS; DODDS Ath Awd; Acad All Conf; Painting I Awd; Art.

DORETHY, KELLY A; Springdale Sr HS; Springdale, AR; (1); Church Yth Grp; Band; Chorus; Flag Corp; Mrchg Band; Hon Roll; U Of A.

DORMAN, CASEY; Prairie Grove HS; Prairie Grove, AR; (4); 1/103; Am Leg Aux Girls St; VP FBLA; Pres SADD; Co-Capt Drill Tm; Treas Stu Cncl; Sec NHS; Val; Math Clb; Science Clb; Jr Bank Bd Chrmn; UDA All-Star; Natl Ldrshp & Svc Awd; U Of AR; Acctng.

DORN, DAVID A; Rogers HS; Rogers, AR; (3); Boy Scts; Church Yth Grp; Natl Beta Clb; Office Aide; Teachers Aide; Band; Mrchg Band; Pep Band; High Hon Roll; Hon Roll; VP Alpha Omega Assn; Aerospace Engrng.

DOROTHY, WILLIAM N; Rogers HS; Rogers, AR; (3); FBLA; Model UN; Office Aide; Orch; Socr; Hon Roll; Rogers Chmbr Comm Acad Awd; Pol Sci.

DORROUGH, SARAH D; Lavaca Jr Sr HS; Lavaca, AR; (2); 4/75; Church Yth Grp; FBLA; FHA; Natl Beta Clb; Church Choir; Treas Frsh Cls; Ofcr Soph Cls; Chrldng; Hon Roll; Tchr.

DORSE, JENNIFER A; North Little Rock Hs-West; North Little Rock, AR; (3); 260/554; French Clb; FHA; ROTC; Color Guard; Drill Tm; Stage Crew; Cit Awd; Hon Roll; BSA Post 630; U Of AR Little Rock; Psycht.

DORSEY, ANDREA S; Lake Hamilton Sr HS; Hot Springs, AR; (2); Church Yth Grp; Dance Clb; FCA; FHA; Library Aide; Natl Beta Clb; Office Aide; Teachers Aide; Drill Tm; Pres Frsh Cls; Brdcst Jrnlsm.

DORSEY, ANGEL; Delta Special Schl; Tillar, AR; (1); 1/22; GAA; Natl Beta Clb; Pres Frsh Cls; Ofcr Stu Cncl; Bsktbl; Mgr(s); Cit Awd; Hon Roll; NHS; Pres Acad Fit Awd; All-Am Schlr; Spellma.

DORSEY, ASHLEY; Berryville HS; Berryville, AR; (3); 1/95; Church Yth Grp; Sec FCA; FBLA; HOBY; Bsktbl; Chrldng; Trk; High Hon Roll; Hon Roll; NHS; Stu Cncl Offcr; Ms Carroll Cty 95; U Of AR; Law.

DORSEY, JESSE; Delta Special Schl; Tillar, AR; (3); 1/29; Math Clb; Natl Beta Clb; Science Clb; Spanish Clb; Yrbk; VP Jr Cls; Ofcr Stu Cncl; Capt Bsktbl; Hon Roll; NHS; Comp Engrng.

DOSS, CALVIN J; Morrilton Sr HS; Springfield, AR; (2); Church Yth Grp; Cmnty Wkr; Drama Clb; French Clb; Thesps; School Musical; School Play; VP Jr Cls; Capt Ftbl; Capt Trk; Boxing; U Of Cntrl AR; Psychlgy.

DOSS, JENNIFER L; Arkansas Bapt Schl; Little Rock, AR; (3); Church Yth Grp; FBLA; Service Clb; Spanish Clb; Band; Chorus; Church Choir; Yrbk; Score Keeper; Hon Roll; Ouachita Bapt Univ; Marine Bio.

DOTSON, CRISTY L; Southside HS; Batesville, AR; (3); Church Yth Grp; FHA; Office Aide; Spanish Clb; Chrldng; Vllybl; Hon Roll; Prfct Atten Awd; ASU; Bus.

DOTY, CHRIS; Fayetteville HS East Campus; Fayetteville, AR; (4); Band; Hon Roll; Odyssey Of Mind Wrld Finlst Twice/Regnl Chmpns 5 Yrs; Univ Of AR; Engrng.

DOUCET, TYSON C; Hot Springs HS; Hot Springs, AR; (2); Church Yth Grp; Crs Cntry; Ftbl; Trk; Hon Roll; Henderson ST Univ; Bus.

DOUCETTE, DAVID A; Arkansas Schl Math & Science; Hot Springs, AR; (3); Library Aide; Natl Beta Clb; Quiz Bowl; Hon Roll; NHS; Ntl Merit Ltr; Comp Sci.

DOUCETTE JR, DAVID A; AR Schl For Math & Scis; Glenwood, AR; (3); Library Aide; Natl Beta Clb; Quiz Bowl; High Hon Roll; Hon Roll; NHS; Ntl Merit Ltr; Cmptr Sci.

DOUGHTY, JOSEPH; Perryville Jr Sr HS; Houston, AR; (4); 2/56; Art Clb; Church Yth Grp; FCA; FBLA; Spanish Clb; Bsktbl; Hon Roll; Jr NHS; NHS; Sal; General Coopertv Eductl Clbs Of AR; Wildlife Clb; Poem Publishd Anthology Of Poetry By Yng Amers 95; AR Tech; Bus Admin.

DOUGLAS, BOBBY E; Lavaca Jr Sr HS; Lavaca, AR; (3); Natl Beta Clb; Natl FFA Org; Pres Science Clb; L Var Bsbl; L Var Bsktbl; L Var Ftbl; Hon Roll; Jr NHS; HOPE Ldr; GYC Ldr; UCA; Coach; Comp Technologist.

DOUGLAS, BRIAN L; Lavaca Jr Sr HS; Lavaca, AR; (2); Science Clb; Spanish Clb; Teachers Aide; JV Var Bsktbl; Hon Roll; His Clb; Jr Babe Ruth Sportsmanship Awd.

DOUGLAS, ERIN E; Mena HS; Mena, AR; (2); 27/160; Church Yth Grp; French Clb; FBLA; GAA; Science Clb; Bsktbl; Vllybl; French Hon Soc; Hon Roll; U Of AR; Phrmclgy.

DOUGLAS, MELANIE; Crowleys Ridge Acad; Paragould, AR; (4); Church Yth Grp; FBLA; Pep Clb; Science Clb; Spanish Clb; Acpl Chr; Chorus; School Play; Bsktbl; Vllybl.

DOUGLAS, WESLEY; Genoa Central HS; Fouke, AR; (3); Church Yth Grp; Computer Clb; English Clb; Math Clb; Science Clb; Bsktbl; Trk; Wt Lftg; Hon Roll; NHS; Orth Srgn.

DOVER, JULIANNA; Jonesboro HS; Jonesboro, AR; (3); Church Yth Grp; French Clb; FBLA; Key Clb; Letterman Clb; Natl Beta Clb; Acpl Chr; L Swmmng; High Hon Roll; Hon Roll; AR St Univ; Law.

DOWDY, GINA; Umpire Schl; Newhope, AR; (3); 1/12; FBLA; Natl Beta Clb; Yrbk; Rep Stu Cncl; Bsktbl; Trk; High Hon Roll; Hon Roll; NHS; U Of AR Fayetteville; Med.

DOWDY, KELLY J; Southside HS; Batesville, AR; (2); 12/115; Church Yth Grp; GAA; Key Clb; Natl Beta Clb; Science Clb; Band; Ofcr Stu Cncl; Bsktbl; Golf; High Hon Roll; GATE Pgm; Hlth, Math & Eng Schl Awds; Harding Univ; Bus Mgmt.

DOWDY, NICOLE L; Southside Schl; Bee Branch, AR; (1); Church Yth Grp; FCA; GAA; Rep Frsh Cls; Rep Stu Cncl; JV Var Bsktbl; JV Var Trk; Hon Roll; AZ ST U; Accntg.

DOWLER, JOSHUA S; Marmaduke HS; Paragould, AR; (3); Church Yth Grp; Drama Clb; FCA; FBLA; Natl Beta Clb; School Play; Var L Bsktbl; Hon Roll; Sprts Msnry Venezuela; BCI Natl Trny; PE.

DOWLING, LAURA K; Central Sr HS; Little Rock, AR; (3); 40/540; Church Yth Grp; Girl Scts; Mu Alpha Theta; Natl Beta Clb; Science Clb; Spanish Clb; Church Choir; Stage Crew; Cit Awd; Hon Roll; OM; Physics.

DOWNES, ROCHELLE M; Cabot HS; Cabot, AR; (2); Band; Mrchg Band; Hon Roll; Jr NHS; Poetry Wrtng; U Of AR; Prof Accnt.

DOWNEY, CYRUS R; Junction City HS; Junction City, AR; (2); Church Yth Grp; Cmnty Wkr; Quiz Bowl; Science Clb; Spanish Clb; VP Soph Cls; High Hon Roll; Hon Roll; NHS; Harding U; Bus.

DOWNING, LANCE W; Watson Chapel Sr HS; Pine Bluff, AR; (3); Am Leg Boys St; Var L Bsbl; Var L Ftbl; Hon Roll.

DRAHEIM, AILIEN M; Southside HS; Little Rock, AR; (3); Cmnty Wkr; Hosp Aide; Teachers Aide; Hon Roll; Write; Msc; Biking; U Of AR Little Rock; His.

DRAIN, HEATHER M; Springdale Sr HS; Springdale, AR; (2); Drama Clb; Chorus; School Play; Springdale Animal Shelter Vol; Sci Fiction Clb Pres; Film Dir; Actor; Writer.

DRAKE, BEN W; Crowleys Ridge Acad; Paragould, AR; (1); 10/30; Church Yth Grp; FBLA; Pep Clb; Science Clb; Acpl Chr; Chorus; Bsktbl; Socr; Trk; Hon Roll.

DRAKE, CHRISLYN; Rogers HS; Rogers, AR; (4); 3/475; Model UN; Mu Alpha Theta; Quiz Bowl; SADD; Ed Yrbk; High Hon Roll; Pres NHS; Grn Erth Optmst VP, Pub Rltns; Wtr Ed Trng; REACH/PACE; SW MO St; Envrnmntl Sci.

DRAKE, DUSTIN C; Star City HS; Star City, AR; (2); Quiz Bowl.

DRAKE, SANDRA LYNN; Mountain Home HS; Mountain Home, AR; (3); 34/285; Am Leg Aux Girls St; Church Yth Grp; Cmnty Wkr; FCA; Pres FBLA; FHA; FTA; GAA; JA; Pres Key Clb; Natl Young Ldrs Conf Schlr; US First Robotics Cmptn Participant; Mr & Miss MHHS Fnlst; Mech Engrng.

DRAPER III, DONALD D; Booneville Jr Sr HS; Booneville, AR; (2); Church Yth Grp; FCA; Natl Beta Clb; Science Clb; Spanish Clb; Band; Ofcr Bsbl; High Hon Roll; Prfct Atten Awd; Pres Acad Fit Awd; LA ST Univ; Vet.

DRAUGHON, MEGHAN; Forest Heights Jr HS; Little Rock, AR; (1); Church Yth Grp; Drama Clb; English Clb; FBLA; Natl Beta Clb; Spanish Clb; Teachers Aide; Church Choir; Chrldng; Powder Puff Ftbl; Universal Chrldng Assn All Star Chldr; US Chrldr Achvt Awd; Phys Thrpy.

DRENNAN, BECKY; Malvern Sr HS; Malvern, AR; (3); Pres FBLA; Natl Beta Clb; Office Aide; Pep Clb; Science Clb; Spanish Clb; SADD; VP Stu Cncl; High Hon Roll; NHS; Malvern Natl Bnk Stu Advy Bd Of Dir Mem; US Achvmt Acad Sci Mrt Awd; Attnd Governors Yth Conf; Hnederson ST Univ.

DRIGGERS, WILLIAM J; Dierks HS; Dierks, AR; (1); 2/40; Church Yth Grp; Natl FFA Org; Varsity Clb; Church Choir; Var Bsbl; Var L Ftbl; Var Trk; Var Wt Lftg; Hon Roll; Engrng.

DRIGGS, BRANDY; Bentonville Sr HS; Bentonville, AR; (4); 59/244; Pres Sec 4-H; Natl FFA Org; Band; Mrchg Band; 4-H Awd; Hon Roll; Sub-Area Pub Spch Wnnr FFA; AR ST Univ; Anml Sci.

DRINKER, LEOMA T; Holly Grove Jr Sr HS; Holly Grove, AR; (3); FBLA; FHA; Hon Roll; U Of AR; Law.

DRIVER, CHRISTOPHER B; West Memphis Christian Schl; West Memphis, AR; (2); Natl Beta Clb; Quiz Bowl; Var L Bsbl; Var L Ftbl; Var L Trk; High Hon Roll; Hon Roll; Pres Acad Fit Awd; Natl Yth Forum Nom; VA Tech; Law.

DROBENA, GINA; Malvern Sr HS; Malvern, AR; (3); Natl Beta Clb; Rptr Nwsp; High Hon Roll; Jr NHS; NHS; Pres Acad Fit Awd.

DROST, ROBERT J; Central Sr HS; Little Rock, AR; (4); #9 in class; Chess Clb; Orch; JV Bsbl; High Hon Roll; Ntl Merit Schol; U Of AR Fayetteville; Engr.

DUBOSE, JASON B; Crossett Sr HS; Crossett, AR; (2); Natl Beta Clb; Science Clb; Cit Awd; High Hon Roll; Hon Roll; Write Shore Stories/Poetry; Active Chrch Mem; Stdnt Of Biblical Prophecy.

DUCHANOY, LEAH; Batesville Sr HS; Batesville, AR; (3); Church Yth Grp; Dance Clb; FCA; FBLA; Key Clb; Letterman Clb; Natl Beta Clb; Pep Clb; Teachers Aide; Chorus; St PRIDE Tm; NCA Danz All Amer Wnnr; Upward Bnd Math And Sci Prog; U Of AR; Chem Eng.

DUCKER, COURTNEY N; Riverview HS; Searcy, AR; (2); Church Yth Grp; HOBY; Natl Beta Clb; Quiz Bowl; Spanish Clb; Thesps; High Hon Roll; Hon Roll; Cmnty Wkr; Drama Clb; Intnl Order Of Rainbow Girls; Raider Club; Sunday Schl Secy; Hendrix Coll; Nurse Anesthesia.

DUCKETT, SARA A; Scotland Schl; Scotland, AR; (2); 5/12; Drama Clb; Speech Tm; School Play; Yrbk; Bsktbl; Hon Roll; Petti Jean Tech; Ob.

DUCKWORTH, MELISSA L; Van Buren Sr HS; Van Buren, AR; (3); FBLA; HOBY; Pep Clb; Chorus; Drill Tm; Hon Roll.

DUCKWORTH, STACI R; Hot Springs HS; Hot Springs Natio, AR; (2); #12 in class; Bus Profs of Am; Drama Clb; FBLA; Girl Scts; Hosp Aide; Key Clb; Mu Alpha Theta; Natl Beta Clb; Office Aide; Q&S; U Of TX; Play Prdctn.

DUDRA, MANDY S; Izard Co Cons Jr Sr HS; Melbourne, AR; (4); 10/40; FBLA; Natl Beta Clb; Pep Clb; Spanish Clb; Yrbk; Mgr(s); Sftbl; High Hon Roll; NHS; Prfct Atten Awd; CHASE; Ozark Tech Coll; Bus.

DUFFEL, JONATHAN SHEA; Clarksville HS; Clarksville, AR; (2); Pres Art Clb; Church Yth Grp; FCA; Letterman Clb; Church Choir; L Bsbl; L Bsktbl; Hon Roll; Pres Acad Fit Awd.

DUFFLE, LUKE; Morrilton Sr HS; Morrilton, AR; (2); Church Yth Grp; Math Clb; Natl Beta Clb; Spanish Clb; Church Choir; Bsktbl; Crs Cntry; Trk; Hon Roll; NHS.

DUGAN, MICHAEL; Hackett Schl; Hackett, AR; (4); Natl FFA Org; Spanish Clb; Pres Frsh Cls; VP Soph Cls; VP Jr Cls; VP Sr Cls; Ofcr Stu Cncl; Var Bsbl; Var Bsktbl; Var Capt Ftbl.

DUGAS, JENNIE B; Fayetteville Sr HS; Fayetteville, AR; (2); Church Yth Grp; FBLA; Spanish Clb; Chorus; Church Choir; Ofcr Stu Cncl; Capt Chrldng; Powder Puff Ftbl; Trk; Hon Roll; 9th Grd Peer Hlpr.

DUGGAN, GERA; Kirby HS; Glenwood, AR; (4); 4/35; Am Leg Aux Girls St; Natl Beta Clb; VP Natl FFA Org; Yrbk; Rep Jr Cls; Rep Sr Cls; Sec Rep Stu Cncl; Capt Chrldng; Var Sftbl; Hon Roll; Med.

DUGGER, LISA; Beebe Sr HS; Beebe, AR; (3); 2/120; Pres Church Yth Grp; Pres Treas FBLA; Pres FHA; FTA; Pres Natl Beta Clb; Pep Clb; Science Clb; Spanish Clb; VP Band; Chorus; GMA; AR Miss GMA 95; Natl Alt Miss GMA 95; Cntrl Bapt Coll; Phys Therapy.

DUGGIN, GENE K; Elkins Jr Sr HS; Fayetteville, AR; (3); Church Yth Grp; Band; School Play; Nwsp; Rep Jr Cls; JV Var Bsktbl; JV Var Trk; Hon Roll; NW AR Yth Symphony; YABA ST Tm Chmpns; Bus Mngmnt.

DUKE, CINDY; Riverview HS; Searcy, AR; (4); 7/70; Church Yth Grp; FBLA; FHA; HOBY; Natl Beta Clb; Spanish Clb; Ed Yrbk; Pres Sr Cls; Pres Stu Cncl; Hon Roll; AR ST U.

DUKE, DAVID L; Harding Acad; Searcy, AR; (4); 4/32; Church Yth Grp; FBLA; Rep Key Clb; Pres Natl Beta Clb; Band; Chorus; VP Stu Cncl; Var L Bsktbl; Var L Ftbl; Ntl Merit SF; Harding U; Math.

DUKE, LOUISA; Harding Acad; Searcy, AR; (2); 2/54; Church Yth Grp; Cmnty Wkr; Key Clb; Natl Beta Clb; Service Clb; Acpl Chr; Chorus; Ofcr Frsh Cls; Sec Jr Cls; Var L Bsktbl; Harding Univ; Phy Thrpy.

DUKE, MATTHEW D; Monticello HS; Monticello, AR; (3); Church Yth Grp; FCA; FBLA; Natl Beta Clb; Spanish Clb; Ofcr Bsbl; Bsktbl; Ftbl; Trk; Wt Lftg; AAA ST Chmpns Ftbl 94; Ldng Tcklr Bst Def AAA 95-; All SW AR Ftbl Tm 95-; U Of Cntrl AR; Bus.

DUKE, RACHEL K; North Little Rock Hs-West; Sherwood, AR; (4); 99/497; Church Yth Grp; Drama Clb; Natl Beta Clb; Speech Tm; Teachers Aide; School Musical; School Play; Swing Chorus; Nwsp; Hon Roll; Schol For Wilhelmina Mdls Inc; U Of Cntrl AR; Mass Comm.

DUKES, TERRA D; Central Sr HS; Little Rock, AR; (4); 90/460; Church Yth Grp; Cmnty Wkr; Dance Clb; FBLA; FHA; FTA; Intnl Clb; Mu Alpha Theta; Natl Beta Clb; Science Clb; Alpha Phi Fraternity Inc Pi Lambda Chptr Debutante; Sunday Schl Tcrh & Usher; Coop Ofc Ed; Peer Faciltr; Lane Coll; Pharmecauticals.

DULANEY, ADRIENE A; Forrest City HS; Forrest City, AR; (2); FBLA; FHA; FTA; Natl Beta Clb; Science Clb; Church Choir; School Musical; Rep Stu Cncl; Vllybl; High Hon Roll; Med Sci Clb; UALR; Acctng; Denistry.

DULING, DOUG; St Paul Schl; Pettigrew, AR; (3); 5/18; Quiz Bowl; SADD; Hon Roll; Beta Clb; SLA; Voc.

DUMAS, KIM; Arkansas Sr HS; Texarkana, AR; (1); Church Yth Grp; GAA; Pep Clb; Church Choir; Rptr Nwsp; Yrbk; Ofcr Stu Cncl; JV Bsktbl; Chrldng; JV Vllybl; Flwshp Of Chrstn Stdnts.

DUMOND, WILLIAM KENNETH; Bismarck Jr-Sr HS; Bismarck, AR; (4); 10/62; Boy Scts; Natl Beta Clb; Natl FFA Org; Teachers Aide; Band; Jazz Band; Mrchg Band; Pep Band; Rptr Nwsp; Hon Roll; Henderson ST U; Music Ed.

DUNAS, RACHIEL A; J A Fair Sr HS; Little Rock, AR; (3); Art Clb; Cmnty Wkr; English Clb; FBLA; Girl Scts; Spanish Clb; SADD; Band; Drm Mjr(t); Mrchg Band; Elem Schl Vol; Brownie Troop Vol; UALR; RN; Bus Mgmt.

DUNAWAY, LANE; Hughes Jr-Sr HS; Forrest City, AR; (1); 5/82; Natl Beta Clb; Quiz Bowl; Band; Mrchg Band; Sec Frsh Cls; JV Var Chrldng; Hon Roll; Pres Acad Fit Awd; Most Improved Band Awd 9th Grd; Solo/Ensmbl Band Awds; Vetrn.

DUNBAR, LONYETTA D; Prescott HS; Prescott, AR; (2); Church Yth Grp; 4-H; FHA; Chorus; Church Choir; Hon Roll; Henderson ST U; Tchng.

DUNBAR, STEPHANIE M; John L Mcclellan Magnet HS; Little Rock, AR; (2); Cmnty Wkr; DECA; FBLA; FHA; Natl Beta Clb; Co-Capt Chrldng; Hon Roll; UCA Ole Miss Jump-Off Wnr-Chrldr 95; NCA All-Amer Chrldg 96; Amer Coll; Fshn Merch.

DUNBAR, STEVEN L; Stamps HS; Buckner, AR; (3); Mu Alpha Theta; Spanish Clb; Church Choir; Rep Stu Cncl; Var Bsbl; Var Bsktbl; Var Trk; NHS; UA Fayetteville; Phy Thrpst.

DUNCAN, ANTHONY W; Jessieville HS; Hot Springs Natio, AR; (2); Church Yth Grp; FCA; FTA; Natl Beta Clb; Spanish Clb; Band; Jazz Band; Mrchg Band; Pep Band; VP Soph Cls; AR Tech/Engr/Music.

DUNCAN, CANDACE L; Pangburn Jr Sr HS; Letona, AR; (3); Art Clb; Drama Clb; French Clb; Hosp Aide; Natl Beta Clb; Quiz Bowl; Chorus; Ofcr Stu Cncl; Hon Roll; ASU; Nrsng.

DUNCAN, CHRIS; Morrilton Sr HS; Morrilton, AR; (2); 28/211; Church Yth Grp; Cmnty Wkr; 4-H; French Clb; Natl Beta Clb; Natl FFA Org; Church Choir; Nwsp; Yrbk; Ofcr Bsbl.

DUNCAN, FAITH E; Lake Hamilton Sr HS; Royal, AR; (2); FHA; Chorus; Lit Mag; Tennis; Wolf Pride Drug Free Partnership For Amer; Henderson; Pediatrician.

DUNCAN, GINGER; Lee Acad; Marianna, AR; (3); 3/22; Church Yth Grp; Yrbk; Treas Frsh Cls; Treas Soph Cls; Treas Jr Cls; Var Sftbl; High Hon Roll; Hon Roll; NHS; MASH; U Of AR-FAYETTEVILLE; Med.

DUNCAN, JENNIFER M; Central HS; Helena, AR; (3); Church Yth Grp; Teachers Aide; Church Choir; Hon Roll; Jackson Coll Of Ministries; Msc.

DUNCAN, MATT; Pulaski Acad; Little Rock, AR; (4); Church Yth Grp; Cmnty Wkr; FCA; Mu Alpha Theta; Natl Beta Clb; L Golf; High Hon Roll; NHS; German Clb; Jr NHS; Cum Laude Scty; Male Stu Ath Of Yr; U Of AR; Bus.

DUNCAN, SCOTT; England HS; England, AR; (3); Am Leg Boys St; Quiz Bowl; Band; Jazz Band; Mrchg Band; Pep Band; High Hon Roll; Jr NHS; Ntl Merit Ltr; Bebee Branch U; Game Warden.

DUNCAN, SHANTA E; Elaine Jr Sr HS; Elaine, AR; (2); Church Yth Grp; Church Choir; Bsktbl; GATE Awd; Stu Of The Month; Criminal Justice; Police Ofcr.

DUNCAN, SUSAN; Lake Hamilton Sr HS; Hot Springs, AR; (2); Church Yth Grp; FCA; FBLA; Natl Beta Clb; Spanish Clb; Teachers Aide; High Hon Roll; Stu Chrstn Life; Oral Cmmnctn Awd 94-95; 1st Pl Optmst Orrtcl Spkr; Wrtr.

DUNHAM, CURTIS W; Scotland Schl; Scotland, AR; (3); FBLA; German Clb; HOBY; Quiz Bowl; Phtg Yrbk; Capt Bsktbl; Hon Roll; Fire Marshal; Gifted And Talented; AR Tech.

DUNIGAN, BRANDY N; Buffalo Island Central HS; Monette, AR; (3); 6/51; Rep Am Leg Aux Girls St; Drama Clb; Hist FBLA; Hist FTA; Quiz Bowl; School Play; Stage Crew; VP Jr Cls; Sec NHS; Buffalo Island Yth Ldrshp Participant; AR ST Univ; Psych.

DUNIGAN, LEAH M; Buffalo Island Central HS; Black Oak, AR; (2); 3/65; FBLA; FTA; Girl Scts; Chorus; Pres Soph Cls; Co-Capt Chrldng; Sftbl; Cit Awd; High Hon Roll; NHS; AR ST Univ; Pre-Med.

DUNKIN, MARK R; Mc Crory Jr Sr HS; Mc Crory, AR; (3); Art Clb; Church Yth Grp; FCA; FTA; Letterman Clb; Spanish Clb; Varsity Clb; Nwsp; Yrbk; Sec Soph Cls; U Of AR Fayetteville; Med.

DUNKLIN, SARAH; Dumas HS; Dumas, AR; (3); Church Yth Grp; Pres Latin Clb; Model UN; Mu Alpha Theta; Ed Yrbk; Ofcr Stu Cncl; Powder Puff Ftbl; Var Tennis; DAR Awd; Hon Roll; Chldrn Amer Rvltn ST Pres/VP/ORG Sec/Soc Pres; Chldrn Confdrcy VP/REC Sec/Ed Gen/Div Pres; Lyon Coll; Bio/Dentist.

DUNKUM, ANGELA C; Pine Bluff HS; Pine Bluff, AR; (3); 39/540; Am Leg Aux Girls St; FHA; Chorus; Yrbk; Hon Roll; Univ Of AR; Art/Arch.

DUNLAP, BRADLEY K; Piggott HS; Pollard, AR; (3); 4-H; Science Clb; Hon Roll; Prfct Atten Awd; Appld Math I And II Awds; Geom Invstgtn Awds; Comp Prog.

DUNLAP, DANIEL W; Westside HS; Coal Hill, AR; (2); FBLA; Model UN; Natl Beta Clb; Quiz Bowl; Church Choir; School Play; Var Bsbl; JV Var Bsktbl; JV Ftbl; AR Tech U.

DUNLAP, HILARI; Sylvan Hills HS; North Little Rock, AR; (3); Church Yth Grp; French Clb; Mu Alpha Theta; Science Clb; Acpl Chr; Swing Chorus; Sec Stu Cncl; Hon Roll; Jr NHS; NHS; Rivercity Workfest; Sweet Adeline Choir Group; Pharmacy.

DUNLAP, VINCENT K; Conway Sr HS; Conway, AR; (3); FBLA; Science Clb; Ftbl; Trk; French Hon Soc; High Hon Roll; Prfct Atten Awd; Jr Beta Clb; Beta Clb; Chem.

DUNN, AMANDA L; North Pulaski HS; Jacksonville, AR; (3); Mu Alpha Theta; Chorus; Church Choir; Rptr Nwsp; JV Capt Vllybl; Stat Wrstlng; High Hon Roll; Hon Roll; Jr NHS; NHS; Duke Edinburgh Awd England; Orange/Silvr Awd; U Of AR Little Rock; Nrs.

DUNN, ASHLEY D; Lavaca Jr Sr HS; Lavaca, AR; (3); Art Clb; Church Yth Grp; VP FHA; Hosp Aide; Science Clb; Speech Tm; Church Choir; Hon Roll; Hmcmng Ct; U Cntrl AR; Elem Ed.

DUNN, AUDRA R; Pleasant View Schl; Mulberry, AR; (3); Church Yth Grp; Pres FBLA; Natl Beta Clb; Rptr Natl FFA Org; Yrbk; Rptr Frsh Cls; Rptr Soph Cls; VP Jr Cls; Var Bsktbl; Hon Roll; Acctng.

DUNN, LA SHONDA D; Star City HS; Star City, AR; (2); Church Yth Grp; FBLA; Office Aide; Teachers Aide; Svc Awd; UCA; Nrsng.

DUNN, LESLIE; Bradford Jr Sr HS; Bradford, AR; (2); 1/44; Art Clb; Church Yth Grp; Dance Clb; French Clb; FBLA; FHA; GAA; Natl Beta Clb; Chorus; Church Choir; ASU; Law.

DUNN, NONA; West Memphis Christian Schl; West Memphis, AR; (2); Art Clb; Church Yth Grp; GAA; Chorus; School Play; Chrldng; Gym; Sftbl; Hon Roll; NHS; Vol Nrsng Hm Asst; AR Univ; Med.

DUNSINO, MARIE S; Alpena Schl; Alpena, AR; (3); Church Yth Grp; Library Aide; Natl Beta Clb; Pep Clb; Spanish Clb; Chorus; Chrldng; Cit Awd; North AR Tech Coll; Engrng.

DUPREE, JONATHAN; Arkadelphia Sr HS; Arkadelphia, AR; (4); 14/161; Church Yth Grp; FCA; Pres Natl Beta Clb; Pres Church Choir; Yrbk; Pres Sr Cls; Ftbl; Gov Hon Prg Awd; NHS; Ntl Merit SF; Stu Christ; Ftr Prblm Slvrs; Badger Schlr; WA U; Arch.

DUPUY, JOSHUA C; Bald Knob HS; Bald Knob, AR; (3); 15/125; FBLA; Natl Beta Clb; Quiz Bowl; Band; Mrchg Band; Var L Bsbl; JV Var Ftbl; Var Wt Lftg; High Hon Roll; Hon Roll; Lyon Coll; Pre-Med.

DUPUY, ROBERT W; Mann Magnet Jr HS; Maumelle, AR; (1); Boy Scts; Band; Var Capt Socr; Cit Awd; High Hon Roll; Jr NHS; Pres Acad Fit Awd.

DUQUETTE, ERIC; Mills HS; Jacksonville, AR; (3); Art Clb; Latin Clb; Sec Mu Alpha Theta; Natl Beta Clb; Science Clb; Orch; JV Var Bsbl; High Hon Roll; Hon Roll; NHS; City Ping-Pong Lg; Geolgy/Paleontology Awd.

DURBY, AVONIA M; Eudora HS; Eudora, AR; (2); 1/6; Rptr FHA; VP Natl Beta Clb; Pep Clb; ROTC; SADD; Band; Church Choir; Mrchg Band; Ofcr Soph Cls; Cit Awd; U Of AR; Criminal Justice; Law.

DURDEN, SHERITA; Arkansas Schl Math & Science; Jonesboro, AR; (4); Church Yth Grp; Treas French Clb; FBLA; FHA; Mu Alpha Theta; VP Natl Beta Clb; Spanish Clb; Band; Church Choir; Flag Corp; Natl Frgn Lang Awd; PRIDE; U Of Cntrl AR; Pre-Med.

DURHAM, DAVID J; Riverview HS; West Point, AR; (2); 6/75; Pres Church Yth Grp; Rep FCA; FBLA; Math Tm; Natl Beta Clb; Quiz Bowl; Spanish Clb; Band; Mrchg Band; Pep Band; Riverview Schlr; Harvard; Law.

DURHAM, DIANA; Bradford Jr Sr HS; Bradford, AR; (3); Art Clb; Church Yth Grp; French Clb; FBLA; FHA; Girl Scts; Quiz Bowl; Band; Chorus; Hon Roll; Twe Kon Do; Choir; Piano; ASU; 6 Yrs Psych/Home Ec.

DURHAM, LORI M; Lake Hamilton Sr HS; Hot Springs, AR; (2); FCA; Drill Tm; Ofcr Stu Cncl; JV Var Tennis; High Hon Roll; NHS; Pres Acad Fit Awd; Jr Beta Clb Pres; Jr High Droll Tm Co Capt; Mardi Gras Qn.

DURHAM, ZACHARY M; Springdale Sr HS; Springdale, AR; (3); Boy Scts; Chess Clb; Church Yth Grp; Cmnty Wkr; Computer Clb; Drama Clb; FCA; FBLA; FHA; Key Clb; All Region Choirs; All Sst Choirs; All Regn Bands; Kiwanis Oratorial Contest 1st Pl; Northwestern; Music Ed/Music Hi.

DURICHEK, MICHAL; Ozark Adventist Acad; Pine Bluff, AR; (2); Church Yth Grp; Cmnty Wkr; Quiz Bowl; Scholastic Bowl; Band; Chorus; School Musical; High Hon Roll; Prfct Atten Awd; Perf Arts Bell Choir; Southern Coll; Med.

DURRETT, KIMBERLY A; Siloam Springs Sr HS; Siloam Springs, AR; (4); 10/162; Church Yth Grp; Cmnty Wkr; Drama Clb; FCA; Natl Beta Clb; Pres Spanish Clb; Church Choir; School Play; Sec VP Stu Cncl; Cit Awd; Hmcmng Maid; Bsktbl Hmcmng Qn; Chrch Drama Muscls; John Brown U.

DUSSEX, ELIZABETH; Sheridan Sr HS; Sheridan, AR; (3); 23/258; Art Clb; Church Yth Grp; Cmnty Wkr; FCA; Library Aide; Service Clb; JV Socr; JV Var Vllybl; High Hon Roll; Treas NHS; Spirit Club; Optmtrst/Vet.

DUTTON, ADRIAN M; Star City HS; Star City, AR; (4); 22/110; FCA; French Clb; Pres FBLA; Mu Alpha Theta; Science Clb; SADD; Hon Roll; Treas NHS; Prfct Atten Awd; Pines Tech Col; Nrsing.

DUVALL, AARON; Sacred Heart Schl; Morrilton, AR; (2); Church Yth Grp; Natl Beta Clb; Quiz Bowl; Rep Stu Cncl; Var Bsbl; Var L Bsktbl; High Hon Roll; NHS; Pres Schlr; Bsktbl Tm All Conf; Prncpls Awd All Around Excllnc; Amer Hist Awd; U Of AR; Law.

DUVALL, CLAYTON M; Jessieville HS; Hot Springs Vlg, AR; (2); 12/55; Church Yth Grp; Cmnty Wkr; FCA; Key Clb; Natl Beta Clb; Service Clb; Band; Mrchg Band; Pep Band; Golf; 2nd Pl Optimist Club Speech; 1st Pl ST DAR Poetry Contest 95-; U Of AR Fayetteville; Law.

DUVALL, STEPHEN; Atkins Schl; Russellville, AR; (4); 9/81; Church Yth Grp; Cmnty Wkr; Computer Clb; Drama Clb; FBLA; FHA; Rep Natl Beta Clb; Science Clb; Spanish Clb; Band; Bsktbl St Champions AA 95; Selected All-Conf Ftbl; Selected All-Region Band; U Of AR Fayetteville; Engrng.

DUZAN, ZEB R; Russellville Sr HS; Russellville, AR; (3); Am Leg Boys St; 4-H; Model UN; Quiz Bowl; Phtg Yrbk; Treas Sr Cls; Rep Stu Cncl; High Hon Roll; NHS; Bys St; Mod UN & Arab Lg Outstndng Dlgt; U Of AR Fayetteville; Engrng.

DWYER, MELODY; Mountain Home HS; Mountain Home, AR; (2); Hon Roll; Theater Cls; Stu Of Week.

DYCUS, JOSEPH L; Mayflower HS; Mayflower, AR; (3); French Clb; Variety Show; Ofcr Bsbl; Ftbl; Hon Roll; U Of Centr AR; Photo.

DYCUS, NINA M; Mayflower HS; Mayflower, AR; (2); 7/70; French Clb; GAA; Var Bsktbl; Var Sftbl; Var Trk; High Hon Roll; Hon Roll; Tchng.

DYE, ANGELA; Mansfield Jr Sr HS; Greenwood, AR; (4); 2/54; Art Clb; Drama Clb; VP FBLA; Intnl Clb; Natl Beta Clb; Pres Natl FFA Org; Rep Stu Cncl; Trk; Cit Awd; High Hon Roll.

DYE, BENJAMIN H; Northside HS; Fort Smith, AR; (3); 6/316; Am Leg Boys St; Church Yth Grp; FCA; Mu Alpha Theta; Teachers Aide; Ofcr Stu Cncl; Ofcr Bsbl; Ftbl; Hon Roll; NHS; Nom For Ldshp Fort Smith; Eleced Assoc Ark Supreme Crt Justce.

DYE, LEANNA E; Wynne HS; Wynne, AR; (3); 7/179; Am Leg Aux Girls St; Church Yth Grp; Drama Clb; Girl Scts; Hosp Aide; Natl Beta Clb; Office Aide; Spanish Clb; Thesps; Chorus; Governors Schl At Hendrix Coll; Natl Yth Ldrshp Forum On Med; Natl Hlth Occupation Stdnts Of Amer Com; Bio.

DYER, ANTANESHA M; Eudora HS; Eudora, AR; (1); #2 in class; 4-H; Band; Mrchg Band; Bsktbl; Chrldng; Trk; Cit Awd; Hon Roll; Jr NHS; U Of AR; Pre-Med.

DYER, KYLE S; Lake Hamilton Sr HS; Pearcy, AR; (3); Pres Church Yth Grp; Cmnty Wkr; Drama Clb; FCA; FBLA; Natl Beta Clb; Quiz Bowl; Science Clb; Pres Spanish Clb; Thesps; Stu Chrstn Lf VP; Natl Span Exm Hnree; Optmst Yth Ctznshp Awd.

DYER, MARY ANN; Riverview HS; Griffithville, AR; (2); Hist FHA; Hosp Aide; Natl Beta Clb; Spanish Clb; Psychiatrist.

DYER, MELINDA S; Arkansas Sr HS; Texarkana, AR; (4); 76/350; Art Clb; FBLA; Math Clb; Mu Alpha Theta; Office Aide; Spanish Clb; Ofcr Stu Cncl; Chrldng; Vllybl; Texarkana Coll.

DYER, SONJA D; Cloverdale Jr HS; Little Rock, AR; (1); FBLA; FHA; Ed Nwsp; Rptr Yrbk; Cit Awd; Hon Roll.

DYKES, ASHLI L; Lake Hamilton Sr HS; Hot Springs, AR; (2); 13/320; Church Yth Grp; FCA; Library Aide; Sec Natl Beta Clb; Spanish Clb; Church Choir; Hon Roll; NHS; Pres Acad Fit Awd; Stu Chrstn Lf; PTSA; Chrstn Educ.

EAGLE, KRYSTAL L; Central Sr HS; Little Rock, AR; (4); Church Yth Grp; Intnl Clb; Mu Alpha Theta; Natl Beta Clb; Q&S; Orch; Ed Yrbk; Hon Roll; NHS; Ntl Merit SF; U Of Southern CA; Filmic Wrtng.

EAGLE, MICHAEL B; Lincoln HS; Prairie Grove, AR; (1); FBLA; Natl Beta Clb; Band; Mrchg Band; Pep Band; School Musical; L Bsbl; L Bsktbl; Capt Ftbl; High Hon Roll.

EARLEYWINE, ASHLEY; Little Rock Cntrl HS; Little Rock, AR; (2); Church Yth Grp; FBLA; Intnl Clb; Mu Alpha Theta; Natl Beta Clb; Quiz Bowl; Science Clb; Spanish Clb; Rep Soph Cls; Ofcr Jr Cls; Young Democrats; AR St Sci Fair 1st Pl Microbiology; RAIN.

EARNHART, CRYSTAL G; Mayflower HS; Mayflower, AR; (2); Hon Roll; Wrte Poetry; UCA; Psych.

EASLEY, AMBER L; Fouke Jr Sr HS; Fouke, AR; (3); 25/89; Church Yth Grp; FBLA; Natl Beta Clb; Natl FFA Org; Church Choir; First Priority Chrch Grp; Texarkan Coll; Zoology.

EASLEY, CHRISTINA A; Fouke Jr Sr HS; Fouke, AR; (2); FBLA; FHA; GAA; JV Var Bsktbl; Var Sftbl; Hon Roll; TC Coll Texarkana.

EASLEY, HEATHER L; Marvell Acad; W Helena, AR; (2); Spanish Clb; JV Var Bsktbl; JV Capt Chrldng; JV Var Trk; Hon Roll; Sec Jr NHS; Rep NHS; Hmcmng Maid; Hnr Bnqt 4 Yrs; ABC Cntst; AR ST Univ; Pre-Med.

EASLEY, TONYA M; Bryant Sr HS; Alexander, AR; (3); Dance Clb; Drama Clb; French Clb; FBLA; Speech Tm; Chorus; Sftbl; Trk; Hon Roll; Prfct Atten Awd; FBLA Creed 1st; ASU; Psych.

EASON, DREW; Walker Schl; Magnolia, AR; (3); Pres Drama Clb; FBLA; HOBY; Natl FFA Org; Quiz Bowl; Band; Chorus; Church Choir; School Play; Pres Stu Cncl; MA Inst Of Tech; Cmptr Sci.

EASON, JEFF; Forrest City HS; Colt, AR; (3); 1/350; Mu Alpha Theta; Natl Beta Clb; Quiz Bowl; Jazz Band; Mrchg Band; Ed Nwsp; Treas Sr Cls; Pres Acad Fit Awd; Church Yth Grp; Regnl, St & Four St Hnr Bands; Natl Conf Of Chrsnts & Jews Del; Prin Clb Pres; U Of AR-FAYETTEVILLE; Engrng.

EASON, LINDSEY R; Magnolia HS; Magnolia, AR; (3); Church Yth Grp; Band; Church Choir; Drill Tm; Flag Corp; Mrchg Band; Chrldng; Hon Roll; All Region Band; Phy Thrpst.

EASON, NIKKI; Central Ark Christian Schl; Little Rock, AR; (3); Church Yth Grp; FBLA; Spanish Clb; Hon Roll; NHS; US Achvt Acad Natl Awd 94; Hstry Clb; Harding U; Med.

EAST, JILL; Collee Hill Jr HS; Texarkana, AR; (1); Church Yth Grp; English Clb; FCA; Rptr Nwsp; Rptr Yrbk; Ofcr Stu Cncl; Bsktbl; Chrldng; Vllybl; Jr NHS; Texarkana Coll; Med.

EAST, SHALA; Cabot HS; Cabot, AR; (2); Church Yth Grp; German Clb; Church Choir; Office Aide; School Play; Hon Roll; FFA; Prjct PALS; German Clb Sweetheart; 1st Pl Poetry Flanfest; Theater.

EAST, TISHA; Cabot HS; Cabot, AR; (3); 1/399; Am Leg Aux Girls St; Church Yth Grp; Cmnty Wkr; FCA; French Clb; Girl Scts; Math Clb; Quiz Bowl; Teachers Aide; Church Choir; Med.

EASTER, BRIANNE L; Rogers HS; Lowell, AR; (4); Church Yth Grp; FBLA; Teachers Aide; JV Bsktbl; JV Sftbl; JV Trk; Hon Roll; Pres Acad Fit Awd; Chmbr Of Commrce Awd; U Of AR; CPA.

EASTER, ERIN; Camden-Fairview HS; Camden, AR; (4); 14/243; Am Leg Aux Girls St; Church Yth Grp; Cmnty Wkr; Drama Clb; French Clb; FBLA; GAA; Mu Alpha Theta; Service Clb; Church Choir; Anchor Clb; TN ST U; Crmnl Jstc.

EASTER, FLOYD J; Bryant Sr HS; Mabelvale, AR; (2); Church Yth Grp; FBLA; Spanish Clb; Teachers Aide; Hon Roll; Chrstn Cncl Prgmr Club; Pleasant Hill Bapt Chrch Yth Cncl.

EASTER, JASON R; Hot Springs HS; Hot Springs, AR; (4); Church Yth Grp; Cmnty Wkr; Computer Clb; Library Aide; Office Aide; Spanish Clb; Teachers Aide; Mrchg Band; Stage Crew; Yrbk; U Of AK; Comp Engr.

EASTERLING, APRIL A; Sparkman Jr Sr HS; Sparkman, AR; (3); Church Yth Grp; 4-H; Spanish Clb; Yrbk; Pres Frsh Cls; Pres Jr Cls; Sec Sr Cls; Pres Treas Stu Cncl; Capt Chrldng; Hon Roll.

EASTERLING, LARAE; Huntsville HS; Huntsville, AR; (3); 11/138; Church Yth Grp; Cmnty Wkr; VP FBLA; FHA; Science Clb; Ofcr Soph Cls; Ofcr Jr Cls; Sftbl; High Hon Roll; Hon Roll; Mash Clb; Hendrix Coll.

EASTERLING, MATTHEW M; Pea Ridge HS; Pea Ridge, AR; (3); Church Yth Grp; Natl FFA Org; Spanish Clb; Sec Soph Cls; L Capt Bsbl; L Bsktbl; L Capt Ftbl; Powder Puff Ftbl; All St Ftbl, Bsbl; 96 Rgnls MVP Bsbl.

EASTIN, STEPHANIE; Harrisburg HS; Harrisburg, AR; (2); Church Yth Grp; FCA; Hosp Aide; HOBY; Yrbk; Ofcr Stu Cncl; Tennis; Hon Roll; NHS; Prfct Atten Awd; 3D Clb; Gfted And Tlnted Prog; Faclted Annual AR Stu Forum; Med.

EATON, ANNESA D; Decatur HS; Decatur, AR; (2); Church Yth Grp; Sec FCA; VP Soph Cls; Sec Stu Cncl; JV Var Bsktbl; High Hon Roll; NHS; Pres Acad Fit Awd; Acad Excl Awd Decatur Schl Bd.

EATON, MICHAEL P; St Paul Schl; Pettigrew, AR; (3); Yrbk; Ofcr Sr Cls.

EATON, PATRICK; North Little Rock Hs-East; North Little Rock, AR; (2); Cit Awd; Hon Roll; Prfct Atten Awd; U Of AR Fayetteville; Arch.

EATON, REBEKAH; Magnet Cove HS; Malvern, AR; (2); Church Yth Grp; FCA; FBLA; FHA; Natl Beta Clb; Spanish Clb; Chorus; Var Capt Chrldng; High Hon Roll; Jr Beta Pres 94-95; Chmps Peer Cnslr; FBLA Sec 95-96; Ouchita Bapt U.

EAVES, JAMEY D; Fouke Jr Sr HS; Fouke, AR; (2); Church Yth Grp; FBLA; Library Aide; SADD; Church Choir; School Musical; Cit Awd; Pres Acad Fit Awd.

ECHLIN, SARA R; Star City HS; Star City, AR; (1); 9/134; Church Yth Grp; GAA; Chorus; Church Choir; School Musical; Mgr(s); Cit Awd; Hon Roll; Non-Schl Sftbl; Govs Yth Conf; Rice Univ; Acctng/Law.

ECHOLS, ALISHA G; Leslie Schl; Leslie, AR; (4); Drama Clb; 4-H; Treas FBLA; Treas FHA; Treas Key Clb; Natl Beta Clb; Teachers Aide; School Play; Rptr Nwsp; Yrbk; Dust Chmp St Track Mt; AR Tech Univ; Rehab Sci.

ECHOLS, CHERISH H; Fountain Lake Jr Sr HS; Hot Springs, AR; (1); Church Yth Grp; FCA; Spanish Clb; Church Choir; Vllybl; High Hon Roll; Kiwanis Awd; TIP Schlr Of Duke Univ; 2 Yrs Prvt Piano Lssns Garland Co CC; Hnrs Classes; Law/Med Fld.

ECHOLS, SUSAN M; Southside HS; Fort Smith, AR; (3); Am Leg Aux Girls St; Church Yth Grp; German Clb; Intnl Clb; Mu Alpha Theta; Service Clb; Band; Jazz Band; Hon Roll; NHS; Top 10 In St On Natl Ger Exam; Intnl Stud.

ECKELS, MARIA A; Springdale Sr HS; Springdale, AR; (3); FHA; Chorus; Ofcr Stu Cncl; Socr; Hon Roll; Jr NHS; NHS; U Of AR; Bus Mngmt.

ECKERT, BRYAN J; Jonesboro HS; Jonesboro, AR; (3); 63/327; Boy Scts; Church Yth Grp; German Clb; Letterman Clb; Band; Mrchg Band; Orch; Pep Band; Nwsp; Dirs Awd; All-ST 1st Band/1st Chr Bassoon; Outstdnt Band Classman; AR ST Univ; Music Perf/Ed.

ECKERT, DEBBIE; Springdale Sr HS; Springdale, AR; (4); Church Yth Grp; Q&S; Thesps; School Play; Lit Mag; Var L Sftbl; JV Vllybl; 4-H Awd; 4-H; JV Bsktbl; AR Acad Chal Schol; PAL Clb; AR Tech Univ; Psych.

ECKERT, SCOTT; Mc Gehee HS; Mc Gehee, AR; (4); Art Clb; Drama Clb; FBLA; FTA; Library Aide; Math Clb; Mu Alpha Theta; Natl Beta Clb; Science Clb; Spanish Clb; U Of Cntrl AR.

EDDINGS, MISTIE; Rivercrest HS; Wilson, AR; (3); Math Clb; Chrldng; Sftbl; Hon Roll; Henderson Univ; Law.

EDDINGS, MISTIE B; Rivercrest HS; Marion, AR; (3); FBLA; Math Clb; Chorus; Rep Soph Cls; Bsktbl; Chrldng; Hon Roll; Jr NHS; Law.

EDDINGTON, KAREN L; Newport HS; Newport, AR; (3); FBLA; Spanish Clb; Drill Tm; Pharm.

EDGE, GREGORY; Ozark Adventist Acad; Cicero, IN; (2); Church Yth Grp; Library Aide; Band; Gym; High Hon Roll; Andrews U; Arch.

EDINGTON, KELLY N; Russellville Sr HS; Russellville, AR; (2); Church Yth Grp; Teachers Aide; Band; Mrchg Band; High Hon Roll; Jr NHS; Rep NHS; Race For The Cure/Susan G Komen Chptr; Majorette Rep.

EDMISON, CAMILLE; Perryville Jr Sr HS; Perryville, AR; (2); 2/75; Chess Clb; Church Yth Grp; Debate Tm; Model UN; Quiz Bowl; Spanish Clb; Teachers Aide; Hon Roll; Jr NHS; Atnd 3 St Spon Gftd Resdntl Cmps; Mdl UN Del For Pst 2 Yrs; Bio.

EDMONDS, JODY A; Star City HS; Star City, AR; (3); 10/110; FCA; Natl FFA Org; Yrbk; Pres Stu Cncl; Ofcr Bsbl; Bsktbl; Ftbl; High Hon Roll; NHS; 13th Pl In Nation Natl HS Finals Rodeo 96; Rodeo Clb Pres; U Of AR; Medicine.

EDMONDSON, JENNY L; Cabot HS; Cabot, AR; (3); 35/398; Church Yth Grp; Hon Roll; Kiwanis Awd; Prfct Atten Awd; Alg II Acad Awd; Harding U; Psych.

EDMUNDSON, KELLY L; Russellville Sr HS; Russellville, AR; (3); Cmnty Wkr; Drama Clb; Speech Tm; Teachers Aide; Chorus; School Play; Stage Crew; Hon Roll; NHS; French Clb; Drama Clb Pres; AR Tech Univ; Spch Ed.

EDSTROM, KRISTIN; Pulaski Acad; Little Rock, AR; (2); Church Yth Grp; Natl Beta Clb; Band; Church Choir; Hon Roll; Majorette; Chrch Handbells.

EDWARDS, ARTIS D; Bradley Jr Sr HS; Bradley, AR; (2); Quiz Bowl; Spanish Clb; Phtg Rptr Yrbk; Pres Soph Cls; Rep Stu Cncl; Var Bsbl; Var Bsktbl; JV Ftbl; Hon Roll; NHS; High Adv Engl; Drug Team; Comp Engrng.

EDWARDS, BRANDIE S; Sylvan Hills HS; Sherwood, AR; (2); 26/363; Church Yth Grp; French Clb; Mu Alpha Theta; Natl Beta Clb; Band; Color Guard; Phtg Yrbk; Socr; Hon Roll; NHS; Basc 10th/11th Srgnt Arms; U Of AR; Pdtrcn.

EDWARDS, BROOKE A; Northside HS; Fort Smith, AR; (3); French Clb; Acpl Chr; Chorus; Church Choir; School Play; Ofcr Stu Cncl; Capt Chrldng; French Hon Soc; High Hon Roll; NHS; Dance Classes; Dance Schlsp; 1st Pl Soloist Dance Caravan 96; OK ST Univ; Dance.

EDWARDS, CRAIG A; Hartford Schl; Hartford, AR; (2); 11/40; Church Yth Grp; Cmnty Wkr; FBLA; Natl FFA Org; Teachers Aide; Church Choir; JV Var Bsbl; Var Bsktbl; High Hon Roll; Hon Roll; Star Green Hand & Forest Mgmt FFA Awds.

EDWARDS, CRANDALL D; Pine Bluff HS; Pine Bluff, AR; (3); #40 in class; Church Yth Grp; 4-H; JA; Spanish Clb; Mrchg Band; Ofcr Stu Cncl; Ftbl; 4-H Awd; Hon Roll; NHS; VP SE Dist AR 4h; Gentlemen Clb; Church Choir; U Of AR; Agronomy.

EDWARDS, CURTIS; Dewitt HS; De Witt, AR; (3); 16/90; Am Leg Boys St; Boy Scts; 4-H; French Clb; FTA; Natl Beta Clb; Science Clb; Hon Roll; Natl Ldrshp & Svc Awd; Cls Day & Grad Usher; All Amer Schlr; AR ST U; Acctng.

EDWARDS, DAVID M; Rogers HS; Rogers, AR; (3); High Hon Roll; Hon Roll; Prfct Atten Awd.

EDWARDS, DORIE; Gentry HS; Gentry, AR; (4); 33/80; Church Yth Grp; Drama Clb; Office Aide; Spanish Clb; Chorus; Powder Puff Ftbl; Hon Roll; MO Southern ST Coll; Dntl Hyg.

EDWARDS, ELIZABETH J; Dumas HS; Dumas, AR; (2); FBLA; School Play; Chrldng; Hon Roll; NHS; All Stars Ambassador; Ouachita Bapt Univ; Commnctn.

EDWARDS, ERIN C; Arkansas Sr HS; Atascadero, CA; (2); Office Aide; Teachers Aide; Chorus; San Luis Obispo Civic Ballet; CA Acad Kids Jazz/Tap; Nrsng/Pediatrics.

EDWARDS, HAYLEY; Union Schl; El Dorado, AR; (4); 1/28; Art Clb; FCA; French Clb; Pres Natl Beta Clb; Science Clb; Chorus; Ed Yrbk; Sec Frsh Cls; Pres Jr Cls; Hon Roll; Cyclone Schlr; Natural Hlprs; U Of Cntrl AR.

EDWARDS, JASON L; Mansfield Jr Sr HS; Mansfield, AR; (3); Church Yth Grp; FCA; FBLA; Intnl Clb; Church Choir; Sec Stu Cncl; Var Bsktbl; Var Ftbl; Var Golf; FBLA Sec; Hnrb Mntn All Dist Ftbl; All Dist Golf; OK Bapt Univ; Wildlife Bio.

EDWARDS, JEMECA D; Pine Bluff HS; Pine Bluff, AR; (3); Am Leg Aux Girls St; Church Yth Grp; Cmnty Wkr; DECA; FTA; Hosp Aide; Red Cross Aide; Science Clb; Spanish Clb; Band; JRMC Cap Team; PRIDE; Eckerd Coll Schlsp; Howard Univ; Bio; Cardiologist.

EDWARDS, JILL; Northside HS; Fort Smith, AR; (1); Church Yth Grp; FCA; FBLA; Bsktbl; Capt Chrldng; Trk; Vllybl; High Hon Roll; Hon Roll; Jr NHS; NCA All Amer Team; 1st Pl St Geom Team; Ouachita Bapt U; Nutritionist.

EDWARDS, JOSEPH M; Benton Cty Christian School; Rogers, AR; (2); Church Yth Grp; Church Choir; Var Bsktbl; Sports Jrnlsm.

EDWARDS, JUSTIN M; Vilonia HS; Conway, AR; (3); Natl Beta Clb; Spanish Clb; Church Choir; High Hon Roll; Jrnlsm.

EDWARDS, KRISTY M; Piggott HS; Piggott, AR; (2); Church Yth Grp; FCA; French Clb; Natl Beta Clb; Science Clb; Band; Chorus; Church Choir; Mrchg Band; Hon Roll; AR ST Univ; Elem Ed; His.

EDWARDS, LAUREN L; Bald Knob HS; Bald Knob, AR; (1); Church Yth Grp; Natl Beta Clb; Band; Church Choir; Mrchg Band; Chrldng; Hon Roll; Prfct Atten Awd; Pres Acad Fit Awd; Pres Schlr; Ctst Whos Who Beethoven Club; Pyng Piano 7 Yrs; Coll Mjr.

EDWARDS, LAVONDA S; Arkansas Sr HS; Texarkana, AR; (4); Church Yth Grp; 4-H; ROTC; Spanish Clb; Band; Flag Corp; Mrchg Band; Pep Band; Ofcr Sr Cls; Deb 95; U Of Conway; Bus.

EDWARDS, MANDI N; Southside Schl; Bee Branch, AR; (1); 1/37; Church Yth Grp; FCA; Pres Natl Beta Clb; Natl FFA Org; Sec Treas Frsh Cls; Rep Stu Cncl; Bsktbl; Stat Trk; High Hon Roll; Prfct Atten Awd; Fall Fstvl Queen; Hmcmng Rep; Won FFA Creed Debate; CBC; Doctor.

EDWARDS, MARCI; Clarksville HS; Clarksville, AR; (1); Church Yth Grp; FCA; FBLA; Natl Beta Clb; Band; Ofcr Frsh Cls; Chrldng; Trk; Hon Roll; Prfct Atten Awd; All Amer Chrldr.

EDWARDS, MICHAEL; Brinkley HS; Brinkley, AR; (3); Church Yth Grp; Drama Clb; Teachers Aide; VICA; Band; Stage Crew; Ftbl; Hon Roll.

EDWARDS, MICHAEL P; Valley Springs Schl; Harrison, AR; (4); 1/53; Debate Tm; FBLA; HOBY; Key Clb; Quiz Bowl; Teachers Aide; Band; School Play; Ofcr Soph Cls; High Hon Roll; Gold, Silvr & Bronze Medl Jr Intnl Tae Kwon Do Champnshps Rome, Italy; BOS Sci Fiar; Mst Studious; U Of AR Fayetteville; Comp Sci.

EDWARDS, RACHEL M; Springdale Sr HS; Springdale, AR; (2); 84/649; Church Yth Grp; Office Aide; Band; Color Guard; Mrchg Band; Sec Frsh Cls; NHS; Yth For Christ; HOSA; U Of AR; Pediatrician.

EDWARDS, RYAN; Beebe Sr HS; El Paso, AR; (4); 11/91; Boy Scts; Church Yth Grp; Drama Clb; FBLA; Math Clb; Natl Beta Clb; Natl FFA Org; Science Clb; Spanish Clb; Band; Lib Clb; Show Chor; All-Reg Chor; St Solo & Ensmbl Band & Chor; Chrch NYI Cncl; NYI Conv Del & Cncl VP; U Of Cntrl AR; HS Tchr.

EDWARDS, SHELLY; Poyen Schl; Poyen, AR; (1); Church Yth Grp; 4-H; FHA; German Clb; GAA; Girl Scts; Natl Beta Clb; Teachers Aide; Band; Church Choir; Teens For Christ; AAU Bsktbl; U Of AR; Elem Ed.

EDWARDS, STAR L; Springdale Sr HS; Springdale, AR; (2); Church Yth Grp; Cmnty Wkr; Office Aide; Band; Color Guard; Mrchg Band; Pep Band; Jr NHS; Pres Acad Fit Awd; Yth Apprenticeship Pgm; All Region Band; SBU; Phy Thrpst.

EDWARDS, TARA L; Jonesboro HS; Jonesboro, AR; (3); Cmnty Wkr; French Clb; Sec FBLA; Mu Alpha Theta; Natl Beta Clb; Chorus; Gov Hon Prg Awd; High Hon Roll; NHS; Pres Acad Fit Awd; Adv Math, Frnch & Chem Awds; Sprts Med.

EDWARDS, TRAVIS J; Morrilton Sr HS; Morrilton, AR; (2); Art Clb; Church Yth Grp; Drama Clb; Natl Beta Clb; Science Clb; Spanish Clb; Thesps; School Play; Ftbl; Hon Roll; Eng.

EFIRD, AARON J; Magnet Cove HS; Malvern, AR; (3); 9/45; Am Leg Boys St; Church Yth Grp; FCA; Natl Beta Clb; Sec Sr Cls; Var Bsbl; Var Ftbl; Var Trk; Hon Roll; All Dist Track & Bsbl; Med.

EFIRD, ALLISON E; Mc Gehee HS; Mc Gehee, AR; (4); Church Yth Grp; Drama Clb; FBLA; FTA; Mu Alpha Theta; Natl Beta Clb; Office Aide; Science Clb; Spanish Clb; Church Choir; Outstdng Achvmnt Jrnlsm 2 Yrs/Keybrdng/Cmptr Aplctns; U Of AR; Jrnlst.

EFURD, STACIE; Magnet Cove HS; Malvern, AR; (4); FCA; FBLA; Sec Treas FHA; FTA; Library Aide; Natl Beta Clb; Pres Spanish Clb; Teachers Aide; Hon Roll; Quachita Tech Coll; Bus.

EGGERT, CHRISTINA M; Mountain Home HS; Mountain Home, AR; (2); Church Yth Grp; French Clb; FBLA; Key Clb; Yrbk; Ofcr Stu Cncl; Mgr(s); Hon Roll; Stdnt Wk; Natl Yng Ldrs Conf; Interact; U Of Nrthrn CO; Bus.

EGLESTON, ASHLEA J; Bauxite Jr Sr HS; Bauxite, AR; (2); Church Yth Grp; Sec Spanish Clb; Ed Nwsp; JV Bsktbl; Var Mgr(s); JV Var Score Keeper; JV Trk; High Hon Roll; Jr NHS; Psych.

EGLOFF, AIMEE; Van Buren Sr HS; Van Buren, AR; (3); Art Clb; Mu Alpha Theta; Q&S; Speech Tm; SADD; School Play; Ed Yrbk; NHS; Pep Clb; Spanish Clb; Commnctn.

EGNER, STEPHANIE M; North Little Rock Hs-West; North Little Rock, AR; (4); 1/445; Key Clb; Mu Alpha Theta; Natl Beta Clb; Service Clb; Band; Drill Tm; Capt Flag Corp; Mrchg Band; Intrml Vllybl; Math Clb; Tri-M Mus Hnr Scty Sec; Tulane Univ; Bio Med Eng.

EHRIG, BECKY L; West Fork HS; West Fork, AR; (1); Chorus; Prfct Atten Awd; U Of AR.

EHRIG, BETH L; West Fork HS; West Fork, AR; (1); Chorus; Tlnt Srch; U Of AR; Nrse To Peace Corps.

EHRLE, PAULA A; Oak Grove HS; Maumelle, AR; (1); Church Yth Grp; Cmnty Wkr; FCA; FTA; Letterman Clb; Drill Tm; Pom Pon; Hon Roll; NHS; Y-Teens; NE LA U; Drug Alc Abuse Cnslg.

EICHELBERGER, MISTY; Lamar HS; Knoxville, AR; (3); Church Yth Grp; FCA; 4-H; FBLA; Chrldng; Sftbl; Hon Roll; Attnd Miss AR Natl Teenager Schlsp Pgm; Bus.

EICHENBERGER, J D; Morrilton Sr HS; Morrilton, AR; (2); Art Clb; Church Yth Grp; Drama Clb; Math Clb; Natl Beta Clb; VP Science Clb; Spanish Clb; Thesps; School Play; Ftbl.

EICHENBERGER, JOHN D; Morrilton Sr HS; Morrilton, AR; (2); Church Yth Grp; Drama Clb; Math Clb; Natl Beta Clb; Science Clb; Spanish Clb; Thesps; Church Choir; School Musical; Ftbl.

EIFERT, KELLY; Fayetteville Sr HS; Tontitown, AR; (4); 96/367; Var Socr; Hon Roll; 2nd Pl PT Aid HOSA ST Comp; CNA; Vol A-Plus Prog; PT/OT.

EILBOTT, LEE E; Pine Bluff HS; Pine Bluff, AR; (4); 5/419; Am Leg Aux Girls St; VP French Clb; Key Clb; Acpl Chr; Ed Yrbk; Hon Roll; VP NHS; Jr Pollyanna Clb Pres; Pine Bluff Sngrs; Amer Fld Svc Treas; Rhodes Coll; Intnl Bus/Fr.

EKART, JULIE; Lead Hill Schl; Lead Hill, AR; (3); Pres FBLA; Natl FFA Org; Quiz Bowl; Capt Varsity Clb; Yrbk; Treas Frsh Cls; Treas Soph Cls; Pres Jr Cls; Capt Bsktbl; Trk.

ELAM, AMANDA; Amity Jr Sr HS; Amity, AR; (2); 2/30; FBLA; Rptr FHA; Sec Natl Beta Clb; Quiz Bowl; Rptr Frsh Cls; Var Bsktbl; Var Trk; Var Wt Lftg; Hon Roll; Hmcmng Ct 4xs; Ram Schlr Acad Pgm; Gftd/Tlntd; Close Up Wshngtn; Natl Lbry Ptry Pblshd Poems; Psych.

ELAM, LISA D; Waldo Jr Sr HS; Waldo, AR; (3); 1/30; Church Yth Grp; FBLA; Office Aide; Quiz Bowl; School Play; Stage Crew; Phtg Nwsp; Yrbk; Hon Roll; NHS; Acad #1 Clb; Southern AR Univ; Acctng.

ELAM, RACHEL M; Mt St Mary Acad; England, AR; (2); FCA; French Clb; Mu Alpha Theta; Natl Beta Clb; Mgr Yrbk; Rep Soph Cls; Swmmng; French Hon Soc; High Hon Roll; Figure Skating; Sports Med.

ELBERT, AMBER; Izard Co Cons Jr Sr HS; Horseshoe Bend, AR; (2); 1/56; Rep FBLA; VP FHA; Quiz Bowl; Chorus; Rptr Nwsp; Ed Yrbk; Treas Soph Cls; Ofcr Stu Cncl; Var Chrldng; Mock Trial; FHA Star Events; Jr Miss Izard Co; U Of AR; Law.

ELDER, GRETCHEN J; Elkins Jr Sr HS; Elkins, AR; (2); Pres Treas Church Yth Grp; Band; Chorus; Church Choir; Capt Flag Corp; Mrchg Band; High Hon Roll; U Of AR; Obstrctn.

ELDERS, DANIELLE M; Corning HS; Corning, AR; (1); 4/91; Drama Clb; FBLA; FHA; Spanish Clb; Flag Corp; School Play; Var Tennis; High Hon Roll; Treas Jr NHS; Odyssey Of Mind Awd; Pediatrician/Pre Med.

ELDRIDGE, CHRISTOPHER; Calico Rock HS; Calico Rock, AR; (2); Natl Beta Clb; Natl FFA Org; Quiz Bowl; Science Clb; Spanish Clb; SADD; School Play; JV Var Bsktbl; Hon Roll.

ELDRIDGE, NIKIA W; Dumas HS; Dumas, AR; (3); FBLA; Band; Pines Tech Coll; Nrsng.

ELDRIED, KENNETH J; Salem HS; Glencoe, AR; (3); Church Yth Grp; FCA; Natl FFA Org; Spanish Clb; Band; Church Choir; Ofcr Soph Cls; Ofcr Jr Cls; Mgr Bsktbl; Mgr Ftbl; FFA Dairy Cattle Judging; Greenhand Degree; Hunting & Fishing.

ELIA, ASHUR E; Mc Clellan HS; Little Rock, AR; (4); 14/255; Art Clb; DECA; French Clb; FBLA; FHA; Intnl Clb; Mu Alpha Theta; Natl Beta Clb; Quiz Bowl; Treas Soph Cls; Nwsp; PRIDE; Garden Clb; Yth Ldrshp Inst; Excel Grad; Yrbk Staff; Jr Opt Clb; U Of AR; Advrtsng; Peace Corps.

ELIJAH, JAMES W; Arkansas Sr HS; Texarkana, AR; (3); Church Yth Grp; Band; Mrchg Band; Intrml Bsbl; JV Bsktbl; JV Ftbl; Var Trk; Hon Roll; Arch Engr.

ELIZANDRO, TRINA C; Bryant Sr HS; Alexander, AR; (2); Church Yth Grp; Office Aide; Teachers Aide; Chorus; School Musical; School Play; Hon Roll.

ELKINS, RENAE L; Clarksville HS; Clarksville, AR; (2); 1/150; FBLA; Natl Beta Clb; Spanish Clb; VP Frsh Cls; Bsktbl; Var Sftbl; Trk; High Hon Roll; Prfct Atten Awd; Pres Acad Fit Awd.

ELLEDGE, CHRIS L; Pulaski Acad; Roland, AR; (2); Rep French Clb; Natl Beta Clb; Band; High Hon Roll; NHS; Gym Team; 2nd Deg Blck Belt Tae-Kwon-Do; Partner Cmptr Sftwr Co; Elec Engrng.

ELLERY, KERRI; Northside HS; Fort Smith, AR; (4); 36/327; Am Leg Aux Girls St; HOBY; Key Clb; Mu Alpha Theta; Pep Clb; Quiz Bowl; Spanish Clb; Chorus; Variety Show; Treas Stu Cncl; Auburn Univ; Psychlgy.

ELLIOTT, CARIE J; Magnolia HS; Magnolia, AR; (3); 1/196; Am Leg Aux Girls St; Church Yth Grp; Sec FBLA; Mu Alpha Theta; Science Clb; Band; Color Guard; Flag Corp; Mrchg Band; Pep Band; Panther PRIDE; Premed.

ELLIOTT, EDDIE T; Mountain Home HS; Mountain Home, AR; (3); Church Yth Grp; FCA; JV Bsbl; Var Ftbl; JV Socr; Blue & Gold Royalty Court King; Ftbl All St Team; Ftbl 4-AAAA Hnrb Mntn All Conf; Schl Mascot Top Gun; His.

ELLIOTT, JENNIFER; Dequeen HS; De Queen, AR; (3); FBLA; FHA; Teachers Aide; Chorus; Var Chrldng.

ELLIOTT, MATT; Farmington Jr Sr HS; Farmington, AR; (3); Rptr FCA; Model UN; Quiz Bowl; Rep Jr Cls; Rep Stu Cncl; Var L Ftbl; Hon Roll; Ntl Merit Ltr; Prfct Atten Awd; Pres Schlr; Nvl Wrtr; Natl Hist, Govt, Intl Frgn Lang Awds; U Of CO-BOULDER; Psycht.

ELLIOTT, RACHEL; Emmet Schl; Emmet, AR; (1); Natl Beta Clb; Ofcr Frsh Cls; Bsktbl; Chrldng; Jr Homcmng Qn; GATE; WA U; Military Sci.

ELLIOTT, WHITNEY E; Marion HS; West Memphis, AR; (4); 15/170; Church Yth Grp; Mu Alpha Theta; Band; Church Choir; Color Guard; Mrchg Band; Orch; French Hon Soc; NHS; Pres Acad Fit Awd; Ouachita Bapt Univ; Bio.

ELLIS, ADAM W; Clarendon Jr Sr HS; Clarendon, AR; (3); 2/31; Am Leg Boys St; Church Yth Grp; FBLA; FHA; Natl Beta Clb; Quiz Bowl; Phtg Yrbk; Rep Frsh Cls; Rep Soph Cls; Rep Sr Cls; Filmed Ftbl Games; Cinematography; Video; Photo.

ELLIS, CHRISTI M; Smackover HS; El Dorado, AR; (1); Church Yth Grp; Q&S; Spanish Clb; Bsktbl; Trk; BASIC.

ELLIS, ERICA; Central Ark Christian Schl; North Little Rock, AR; (4); 13/75; Church Yth Grp; Drama Clb; Mu Alpha Theta; Science Clb; School Play; Nwsp; Ed Yrbk; Chrldng; NHS; Miss Metroplex Teen USA; Miss Little Rock Teen USA; AR ST U; Broadcasting.

ELLIS, KIMBERLY; Maynard Jr Sr HS; Maynard, AR; (3); 1/40; Am Leg Aux Girls St; Chess Clb; VP Church Yth Grp; Drama Clb; French Clb; FBLA; Natl Beta Clb; Red Cross Aide; Church Choir; School Play.

ELLIS, KRETH W; John L Mcclellan Magnet HS; Little Rock, AR; (2); Church Yth Grp; Cmnty Wkr; Computer Clb; Debate Tm; FBLA; VP Jr Cls; Cit Awd; Hon Roll; 1st Plc Wnnr In Big Bud Run; DARE; Bus Admin.

ELLIS, REGAN L; Hall Sr HS; Little Rock, AR; (3); 27/278; Dance Clb; FCA; FBLA; FHA; Natl Beta Clb; Pep Clb; Spanish Clb; Thesps; Yrbk; Rep Stu Cncl; U Of AR Fayetteville; Vet.

ELLIS, TIMMY R; Fairview HS; Camden, AR; (3); 69/289; Hon Roll; Pres Schlr; Natl Hnr Roll; Geom Awd; SAU Tech; Comp Engr.

ELLISON, AUGUSTUS G; Fairview HS; Camden, AR; (2); Church Yth Grp; Drama Clb; Quiz Bowl; Band; Church Choir; Mrchg Band; School Play; Stage Crew; JV Var Bsktbl; Ftbl; Mst Outstdng Male Stdnt; Richard Johnson Ath Awd Outstdng Perfrmnc Ftbl/Bskbl/Trck; Mst Outstdng Bnd; PT/HIS.

ELLISON, PATRICK B; Mansfield Jr Sr HS; Huntington, AR; (3); Church Yth Grp; Debate Tm; Drama Clb; VP FCA; Intnl Clb; Natl Beta Clb; Quiz Bowl; Speech Tm; Band; Mrchg Band; Cls A All-Star Band; All-St Bapt Band; AR Tech Univ.

ELLISON, TEPHANIE L; Jessieville HS; Hot Springs, AR; (3); FHA; Natl Beta Clb; Office Aide; Teachers Aide; Band; Bsktbl; Hon Roll; Garland County CC; Nrsng.

ELLSWORTH, RACHELE L; Russellville Sr HS; Russellville, AR; (3); 116/321; Church Yth Grp; Spanish Clb; Rptr Yrbk; JV Bsktbl; Hon Roll; All-Stars; Chldrns Church; AR Tech Univ.

ELMORE, BRAD C; Mansfield Jr Sr HS; Mansfield, AR; (2); Church Yth Grp; Intnl Clb; Natl FFA Org; Spanish Clb; U Of AR.

ELMORE, JENNIFER L; Southside HS; Fort Smith, AR; (2); FCA; GAA; Letterman Clb; Varsity Clb; Band; Mrchg Band; Var Crs Cntry; Capt Trk; Hon Roll; NHS.

ELMORE, TONYA L; Mansfield Jr Sr HS; Mansfield, AR; (4); 9/58; Church Yth Grp; FBLA; FHA; Intnl Clb; Natl Beta Clb; Office Aide; Rep Stu Cncl; Hon Roll; Prfct Atten Awd; Westark CC; Nrsng.

ELMS, JENNIFER J; North Little Rock Hs-East; North Little Rock, AR; (3); Church Yth Grp; Drama Clb; FTA; Natl Beta Clb; Service Clb; Spanish Clb; Teachers Aide; Church Choir; Stage Crew; Hon Roll; U Of Cntrl AR; Tchr.

ELROD, JOEY K; Northside HS; Barling, AR; (4); Q&S; Teachers Aide; Variety Show; Ed Nwsp; JV Var Bsbl; Hon Roll; 96 Jrnlst Yr; Bleacher Crtr; Westark JC; Poly Sci.

ELROD, NATALIE G; North Little Rock Hs-West; North Little Rock, AR; (3); 57/554; Church Yth Grp; Cmnty Wkr; Natl Beta Clb; Spanish Clb; Stage Crew; Lit Mag; Hon Roll; NHS; FHA; Girl Scts; STARS; Octagon Club; UALR; Elem Ed.

ELSKEN, CHRISTY M; Rogers HS; Lowell, AR; (3); 114/567; Church Yth Grp; Drama Clb; FCA; Band; Drill Tm; Mrchg Band; Var Socr; Hon Roll; NHS; FBLA; Chmbr Comm Awd High GPA; Rogers Rennaisance High GPA; Frgn Lang Clb; Elem Tchr/Pub Rltns.

ELZEY, AMANDA C; West Memphis Christian Schl; West Memphis, AR; (2); Church Yth Grp; Hon Roll; Pediatrcn.

EMBRY, BENJAMIN P; Atkins Schl; Atkins, AR; (1); Church Yth Grp; FBLA; Letterman Clb; Natl Beta Clb; Quiz Bowl; Bsktbl; Ftbl; Trk; Hon Roll; Pres Acad Fit Awd; ASP Sr High Mission Tm Tazewell TN Thru 1st Untd Meth Chrch; GATE Prgm 2nd Thru Present; U Of AR Fayettvl; Cmptr Engr.

EMERSON, AMANDA M; Cabot HS; Ward, AR; (1); Church Yth Grp; Cit Awd; High Hon Roll; Jr NHS; Sbjct Area Awd Intrprsnl Rltnshps 9th Grd; Harding Univ; Pharm.

EMERSON, KELLIE M; Midland HS; Pleasant Plains, AR; (3); 4-H; French Clb; FBLA; Natl Beta Clb; Pep Clb; Science Clb; Spanish Clb; Speech Tm; Yrbk; Ofcr Frsh Cls; Paralegal.

EMERY, AMBER; Newport HS; Newport, AR; (1); Spanish Clb; Ofcr Stu Cncl; Capt JV Chrldng; Gym; Sftbl; Hon Roll; Pres Acad Fit Awd; Hosp Vol Chldrns Hllwn Crnvl.

EMMICK, MICHELLE; Mountain Home HS; Mountain Home, AR; (3); 119/267; Church Yth Grp; Library Aide; ROTC; Band; Flag Corp; Mrchg Band; Pep Band; Nwsp; Pub Afrs Ofcr NJROTC 95-96; Unarmed Drill Team NJROTC 94-96; IL; Tchr/Crmnl Jstc.

ENABNIT, ELISHA A; Star City HS; Star City, AR; (3); Art Clb; Church Yth Grp; Cmnty Wkr; FBLA; Natl Beta Clb; Ofcr Stu Cncl; Bsktbl; Trk; Cit Awd; Prfct Atten Awd; Ozark Chrstn Coll; His Prof.

ENDERS, ROBIN R; Ozark Adventist Acad; Peru, KS; (2); Church Yth Grp; Cmnty Wkr; Office Aide; Cit Awd.

ENDERSON, SHADA M; North Little Rock Hs-West; North Little Rock, AR; (3); 33/550; Art Clb; Church Yth Grp; Math Clb; Mu Alpha Theta; Natl Beta Clb; Spanish Clb; Drill Tm; Cit Awd; Hon Roll; NHS; Psychoway Stu Of Yr Awd; Sci; Math.

ENDSLEY, JENNIFER A; Arkansas Sr HS; Texarkana, AR; (3); Art Clb; Drama Clb; French Clb; FBLA; Drill Tm; Hon Roll; Jr NHS; NHS; Pres Acad Fit Awd; Dance, Piano, Voice 14 Yrs; Amer U Of Paris.

ENGEL, LORI E; Corning Jr Sr HS; Peach Orchard, AR; (3); 3/81; Art Clb; Drama Clb; FHA; Bsktbl; Trk; High Hon Roll; Hon Roll; Jr NHS; Pres Acad Fit Awd; Williams Bapt Coll; Elem Ed.

ENGLAND, KELLIE J; Searcy HS; Searcy, AR; (4); Art Clb; Church Yth Grp; Dance Clb; FCA; FBLA; FTA; Library Aide; Natl Beta Clb; Pep Clb; Spanish Clb; Cmnty Sftbl; Piano; Dance; AR ST U.

ENGLAND, MELANIE; Farmington Jr Sr HS; Fayetteville, AR; (3); 4-H; Rptr FHA; HOBY; Model UN; Band; Rep Stu Cncl; Treas NHS; Mock Trial; Jr City Cncl; Law.

ENGLE, JAMES; Norphlet HS; Norphlet, AR; (1); Band; Mrchg Band; Pep Band; Attrny.

ENGLEDOWL, CHRISTY; Genoa Cntrl HS; Fouke, AR; (2); FHA; HOBY; Spanish Clb; Bsktbl; Var Chrldng; Trk; Hon Roll; Prfct Atten Awd; Hrsbck Rdng, Chrldng; Texarkana Coll; Vet Asst.

ENGLES, AMANDA G; Mt Pleasant Jr Sr HS; Melbourne, AR; (3); Art Clb; Hist FBLA; Rep FHA; Sec Natl Beta Clb; Band; Chorus; Yrbk; Ofcr Stu Cncl; Hon Roll; All-Amer Schlr Awd; Ozarka Tech Coll; RN.

ENGLISH, CHRISTOPHER E; El Dorado Sr HS; El Dorado, AR; (4); Church Yth Grp; FBLA; FHA; Natl Beta Clb; Office Aide; Score Keeper; Trk; Hon Roll; Fire Marshall; Futuristic Outlook; U Of AR Pine Bluff; Pol Sci.

ENGLISH, JASON W; Clarksville HS; Clarksville, AR; (3); FBLA; Speech Tm; Teachers Aide; Ftbl; Trk; Wt Lftg; Cit Awd; Hon Roll; Stu Of 9 Weeks.

ENGLISH, MELISSA; Benton Sr HS; Benton, AR; (3); 2/265; Am Leg Aux Girls St; Church Yth Grp; Model UN; Capt Quiz Bowl; Rep Stu Cncl; Ntl Merit Ltr; Pres Acad Fit Awd; French Clb; Key Clb; Math Clb; FPS Intl Twice; Fllwshp Chrstn Stus VP; Rural Elec Yth Tour 96.

ENGLISH, RANEY; Jonesboro HS; Jonesboro, AR; (4); 21/286; Church Yth Grp; Cmnty Wkr; Dance Clb; Drama Clb; FBLA; HOBY; VP Key Clb; VP Natl Beta Clb; NFL; Office Aide; Choir Sec; U MS; Law.

ENGLISH, SALLY A; Morrilton Sr HS; Morrilton, AR; (3); Bsktbl; Trk; Vllybl; Comps.

ENGLISH, WENDY M; Clarksville HS; Clarksville, AR; (2); Church Yth Grp; FCA; FBLA; GAA; Natl Beta Clb; Office Aide; SADD; Church Choir; Var Bsktbl; Mgr(s); AR Tech U; Phys Thrpy.

ENGSTRAM, JOHN E; Ridgecrest HS; Paragould, AR; (3); Church Yth Grp; FCA; Key Clb; Var Bsktbl; NHS.

ENNIS, AARON R; Springdale Sr HS; Springdale, AR; (3); Church Yth Grp; Acpl Chr; Church Choir; School Musical; Ftbl; JV Var Socr; High Hon Roll; Hon Roll; NHS; Engrng.

ENNIS, BRUCE B; Atkins Schl; Atkins, AR; (3); Yrbk; Ofcr Bsbl; Bsktbl; Cit Awd; Hon Roll; Sportsmanship Awd Bsbl; Ldrshp Awd Bsbl; All-Conf Bsbl; 2 Yr Letterman Bsbl; Vo Tech; Agricultural Farming.

ENNIS, OLIVIA C; Monticello HS; Monticello, AR; (3); Am Leg Aux Girls St; Art Clb; Church Yth Grp; FCA; FHA; GAA; Letterman Clb; Math Clb; Natl Beta Clb; Office Aide; Dntst.

ENOCH, CAROL E; Central Sr HS; Little Rock, AR; (3); 127/600; Dance Clb; Drama Clb; French Clb; NFL; Service Clb; Speech Tm; Thesps; Orch; School Musical; School Play; TAILS Bd Mem; Thtr.

ENOCH, KATIE; Parkview Arts/Sci Magnet; Little Rock, AR; (3); Drama Clb; Pres Key Clb; Pres Natl Beta Clb; Q&S; Spanish Clb; Band; Mrchg Band; School Musical; School Play; Yrbk; VP Y Teens; Peer Fcltrs.

EOFF, ERIN M; Conway Sr HS; Conway, AR; (4); 25/538; Hist FBLA; Natl Beta Clb; Pep Clb; VICA; Phtg Nwsp; Phtg Yrbk; Rep Stu Cncl; High Hon Roll; Spanish NHS; Lyon Col; Tchr.

EOFF, JENNIFER D; Russellville Sr HS; Russellville, AR; (2); 1/450; Church Yth Grp; French Clb; SADD; Band; Mrchg Band; Jr NHS; NHS; Pres Acad Fit Awd; Teenage Repub; Chrstn Stdnt Union; Tchng Sci/Math.

EPHLIN, BETH; Rivercrest HS; Luxora, AR; (2); Church Yth Grp; FBLA; Sec Key Clb; Band; Chorus; Jazz Band; Mrchg Band; Pep Band; High Hon Roll; Hon Roll; Harding Univ; Bio.

EPPERSON, KRISTIN L; John L Mcclellan Magnet HS; Little Rock, AR; (2); FHA; FTA; Natl Beta Clb; Spanish Clb; Band; Drill Tm; Bsktbl; Trk; Vllybl; Cit Awd.

ERB, SARAH M; Greenwood Sr HS; Greenwood, AR; (4); 159/260; Church Yth Grp; Debate Tm; Drama Clb; French Clb; Model UN; NFL; Spanish Clb; Speech Tm; Teachers Aide; Thesps; U Of Cntrl AR; Anthro.

ERICKSON, EDWARD A; Bryant Sr HS; Benton, AR; (2); Band; Jazz Band; Mrchg Band; Orch; Pep Band; Hon Roll; First Luth Yth Of Benton Pres; AR Yth Wind Orch 95-; U Of Central AR.

ERVIN, BRADLEY H; Ridgecrest HS; Paragould, AR; (2); 20/223; Church Yth Grp; FBLA; Library Aide; Science Clb; Band; Church Choir; Mrchg Band; High Hon Roll; Cmptr Prgm.

ERVIN, KAMERON D; Central Sr HS; Little Rock, AR; (4); FHA; Girl Scts; Latin Clb; Natl Beta Clb; Band; Mrchg Band; Hon Roll; NHS; Mltrcl Club Strng Comm; Tails Peer Hlpng Prgm; Natl Conf Chrstn/Jews; U Of AR; Soc Wrk.

ERVIN, MATT; Gosnell Jr Sr HS; Blytheville, AR; (4); 10/66; Am Leg Boys St; Boy Scts; HOBY; VP Science Clb; SADD; Rep Stu Cncl; Var Bsktbl; DAR Awd; High Hon Roll; NHS; Natl Yng Ldrshp Conf WA DC; MCCC; Bus Mgmt.

ERWIN, CANDACE; Morrilton Sr HS; Morrilton, AR; (2); Art Clb; Church Yth Grp; Dance Clb; Drama Clb; FBLA; Office Aide; Science Clb; Spanish Clb; Thesps; Stage Crew; Ayer Bty Qn-Schl Pgnt 96; Ayer Tlnt Wnnr 96; U AR; Phys Thrpy.

ERWIN, MICHELLE; Bergman Schl; Harrison, AR; (1); 10/65; Church Yth Grp; FBLA; GAA; Natl Beta Clb; Pep Clb; Spanish Clb; Rptr Frsh Cls; JV Var Bsbl; JV Var Bsktbl; DAR Awd; U Of AR; Tchr.

ESCUE, LAURA C; Sylvan Hills HS; Sherwood, AR; (1); #1 in class; Mu Alpha Theta; Chorus; Yrbk; High Hon Roll; Jr NHS; Horseback Riding; U Of Miami; Marine Zoologist.

ESSEX, LAURA W; Dewitt HS; De Witt, AR; (1); 25/108; Church Yth Grp; FCA; FBLA; GAA; Science Clb; School Play; Bsktbl; L Trk; Hon Roll; Prfct Atten Awd; Natl Eng Merit Awd; Cooresponding Sec Untd Meth Yth; Pol Sci.

ESTEP, CASEY L; Van Buren Sr HS; Van Buren, AR; (2); FBLA; FHA; Mu Alpha Theta; Science Clb; Golf; Mgr(s); Hon Roll; Prfct Atten Awd; U Of AR; Med.

ESTEP, WENDY C; Westside HS; Hartman, AR; (2); Church Yth Grp; Natl Beta Clb; Pep Clb; SADD; Chorus; Hon Roll; Col Of Ozarks.

ESTES, CHERRIE; Calico Rock HS; Calico Rock, AR; (1); #2 in class; Math Clb; Natl Beta Clb; Science Clb; SADD; Mgr Bsktbl; Mgr(s); High Hon Roll; Jr Beta VP; U Of Cntrl AR; Phrmcy.

ESTES, KELLI D; Oden Schl; Sims, AR; (2); Church Yth Grp; FBLA; Key Clb; Natl FFA Org; Quiz Bowl; Church Choir; Rep Stu Cncl; Stat Bsbl; JV Var Bsktbl; Var Sftbl; Teens As Tchrs; U Of AR; Sprts Med/Brdcstng.

ESTES, SHANNON; Sylvan Hills HS; Jacksonville, AR; (4); 22/233; Church Yth Grp; FBLA; Mu Alpha Theta; Natl Beta Clb; Office Aide; SADD; Band; Rep Stu Cncl; Hon Roll; Jr NHS; Pres Awd Drftng/Dsgn; Merit Awd Bus Law; U Of Cntrl AR; Pre-Law.

ESTES WHITE, TONYA L; Drew Central Jr Sr HS; Wilmar, AR; (4); Art Clb; Library Aide; Teachers Aide; Hon Roll; Lib Club VP/PRES; Rstrnt Ownr.

ESTLINBAUM, CHIP; Leslie Schl; Leslie, AR; (3); 4/25; Church Yth Grp; Cmnty Wkr; Key Clb; Natl Beta Clb; Quiz Bowl; Church Choir; Phtg Yrbk; Sec Jr Cls; JV Bsktbl; High Hon Roll; AR Tech U.

ESTOKER, CHRIS; Sheridan Sr HS; Little Rock, AR; (2); Pres Boy Scts; Church Yth Grp; Cmnty Wkr; Hosp Aide; Intnl Clb; ROTC; Color Guard; Drill Tm; Cit Awd.

ETHRIDGE, BILLY; Bright Star Schl; Doddridge, AR; (3); 3/17; Library Aide; Quiz Bowl; Band; Pres Soph Cls; VP Jr Cls; Cit Awd; Hon Roll; NHS; Pres Acad Fit Awd; U Of AR Fayettevl; Comp Tech.

ETZKORN, ANDREA G; Scranton HS; Subiaco, AR; (3); VP Art Clb; Pres Church Yth Grp; FHA; German Clb; Natl Beta Clb; Science Clb; Teachers Aide; Chorus; Hon Roll; Prfct Atten Awd; Sec Math Ed.

EUBANKS, ANDEE; Hamburg HS; Hamburg, AR; (2); Church Yth Grp; Dance Clb; Drama Clb; Chorus; Yrbk; Sec Jr Cls; Bsktbl; Chrldng; Hon Roll; Jr NHS; Homecoming Court.

EUBANKS, STEPHANIE L; Delaplaine Schl; Delaplaine, AR; (1); FBLA; FHA; Quiz Bowl; Spanish Clb; Chorus; Nwsp; Yrbk; JV Co-Capt Bsktbl; Trk; High Hon Roll; Medicine.

EULER, ASHLEA J; Cabot HS; Cabot, AR; (3); Church Yth Grp; Dance Clb; French Clb; Bsktbl; Chrldng; Speech Pathologist.

EVANS, ADREAN N; Lakeside HS; Lake Village, AR; (3); 8/77; Am Leg Aux Girls St; Church Yth Grp; Drama Clb; FBLA; Church Choir; Mrchg Band; Stage Crew; Rptr Nwsp; VP Stu Cncl; Cit Awd; NE LA Univ; Psych.

EVANS, AMBER; Melbourne HS; Melbourne, AR; (1); FHA; Quiz Bowl; Ofcr Frsh Cls; NHS; Excel Interest Art Survey; Legal Sec.

EVANS, ANGELA K; Siloam Springs Sr HS; Siloam Springs, AR; (3); Church Yth Grp; FCA; Spanish Clb; Teachers Aide; Band; Church Choir; Jazz Band; Mrchg Band; Orch; Pep Band; Outstndng Crs Cntry Prfrmr 94-95; John Brown U; Elem Ed.

EVANS, DEBORAH; Lakeside HS; Hot Springs, AR; (3); Church Yth Grp; FCA; Library Aide; Var Chrldng; Hon Roll; Jr NHS; Yth To Yth; U Of Cntrl AR; Attnry.

EVANS, ELLIE; Prairie Grove HS; Prairie Grove, AR; (3); 1/120; FBLA; School Play; Nwsp; Chrldng; Tennis; High Hon Roll; NHS; Library Aide; Jr NHS; Acad Cmptn In Ed Team; Scott Hi-Q Team; Prom Cmmtte 96.

EVANS, HANNAH; Brookland Jr Sr HS; Brookland, AR; (3); 1/83; Church Yth Grp; FBLA; Natl Beta Clb; Spanish Clb; Pres Soph Cls; Capt Var Bsktbl; Var Sftbl; Var Vllybl; High Hon Roll; Prfct Atten Awd; Acctng I, Bio, Span, Soc Stud Awds; Best Server; Mst Imprvd Awds; AR ST Univ.

EVANS, JANINA M; Piggott HS; Kennett, MO; (4); 21/70; Art Clb; Key Clb; Jazz Band; Mrchg Band; Nwsp; Yrbk; High Hon Roll; Prfct Atten Awd; Church Yth Grp; 4-H; Art Awds; Poetry Hnrble Mntn/Pblctn; Three Rivers CC; Art/Jrnlsm.

EVANS, JULIE; North Little Rock Hs-East; North Little Rock, AR; (3); Art Clb; Drama Clb; French Clb; Mu Alpha Theta; Natl Beta Clb; Band; Jazz Band; Stage Crew; Rptr Jr Cls; Prfct Atten Awd; Music.

EVANS, JUSTIN M; Junction City HS; El Dorado, AR; (2); Church Yth Grp; FCA; 4-H; Quiz Bowl; Spanish Clb; Pres Frsh Cls; Rep Stu Cncl; JV Bsbl; JV Ftbl; Wt Lftg; Cert Of Achvmt Amer Govt; Cert Of Achvmt Eng Lit I; LSU; Vet.

EVANS, LARA E; Southside HS; Fort Smith, AR; (4); 63/459; Mu Alpha Theta; Red Cross Aide; Treas Service Clb; Teachers Aide; Rptr Nwsp; Yrbk; L Swmmng; Hon Roll; NHS; Pres Acad Fit Awd; U Of Tulsa; Pre-Law.

EVANS, SARAH J; Ft Smith Christian Schl; Fort Smith, AR; (3); Church Yth Grp; Cmnty Wkr; FBLA; Pep Clb; Spanish Clb; Teachers Aide; Chorus; Drill Tm; School Play; Nwsp; Hghst Math Scr; Perfrmd Macy Thnksgvng Parade 93; Mssn Trps Mexico & TX.

EVANS, STEVE R; Dollarway HS; Pine Bluff, AR; (4); 1/125; Cmnty Wkr; Ofcr Bsbl; Bsktbl; Cit Awd; High Hon Roll; Jr NHS; NHS; Pres Schlr; Val; U Of AR; Bus.

EVANS, SYARD G; Cty Line HS; Charleston, AR; (2); #2 in class; FCA; Natl Beta Clb; Natl FFA Org; Quiz Bowl; Spanish Clb; Bsktbl; Sftbl; Trk; Hon Roll; NHS; Attnd Churchil Acad.

EVANS, TIMOTHY LLOYD; El Dorado Sr HS; El Dorado, AR; (3); 12/328; Am Leg Boys St; Church Yth Grp; Drama Clb; Pres FBLA; Key Clb; Thesps; Chorus; School Play; Hon Roll; NHS; Odyssey Of The Mind World Fnlst; Comp Engr.

EVANS-MORGAN, RANDY; Southside HS; Fort Smith, AR; (4); 78/467; Church Yth Grp; FBLA; Key Clb; Latin Clb; Mu Alpha Theta; Var Socr; Hon Roll; NHS; Pres Acad Fit Awd; Cmnty Wkr; U Of Tulsa; Bus Admin; Pre-Law.

EVENSON, CHRIS; Ozark Adventist Acad; Gentry, AR; (1); Band; VP Frsh Cls; Intrml Bsktbl; Intrml Ftbl; Intrml Gym; Intrml Socr; Intrml Sftbl; High Hon Roll; Mission Team Pastorisa MX; Little Brother Pgm; Bus.

EVERETT, ERIKA; Ozark Adventist Acad; Owasso, OK; (3); Church Yth Grp; Ofcr Frsh Cls; Ofcr Soph Cls; Ofcr Jr Cls; Ofcr Stu Cncl; High Hon Roll; Prfct Atten Awd; SA Pres; Med.

EVERETT, ROY P; Mena HS; Mena, AR; (1); French Clb; Ftbl; Wt Lftg; French Hon Soc; Hon Roll.

EVERETTS, CHRIS A; Van Buren Sr HS; Van Buren, AR; (3); Westark; Accntng.

EVERITT, CHRISTOPHER T; Searcy HS; Searcy, AR; (4); Church Yth Grp; FCA; Key Clb; SADD; Ofcr Bsbl; Bsktbl; Ftbl; U Of AR; PT/SPTS Med.

EWBANK, CHRISTOPHER P; Rogers HS; Lowell, AR; (3); 46/596; Teachers Aide; Var Ftbl; Var Wt Lftg; Hon Roll; Renaissance Acad Achvmnt Awd 2 Yrs; Chmbr Of Comm Acad Awd 2 Yrs; Def Player Of Yr/MVP Ftbl; Pittsburgh ST; Bus.

EWELL, DARCI; Atkins Schl; Atkins, AR; (4); 16/80; Drama Clb; FHA; GAA; Natl Beta Clb; Science Clb; Spanish Clb; Teachers Aide; School Play; Rep Frsh Cls; Rep Soph Cls; Dist Dbls Tennis Champs 93-95; Dist Single Tennis Champ Rnnr Up ST 96; ST Dbls Tennis Champ 95; AR Tech Univ.

EWIN, KARI; Decatur HS; Decatur, AR; (4); 5/25; Church Yth Grp; FHA; HOBY; Office Aide; School Play; Hon Roll; Kiwanis Awd; Pride Tm; HOBY; FHA Star Events; SW Baptist U; Sec Ed.

EWING, AMANDA; Hazen Jr Sr HS; Hazen, AR; (1); Church Yth Grp; Cmnty Wkr; Dance Clb; FHA; GAA; Letterman Clb; Church Choir; Bsktbl; Chrldng; Trk; AR Star Evnts St Silvr Medalst; Jr Miss Grand Prairie Rice; Psych.

EWING, CAROL B; Sheridan Sr HS; Sheridan, AR; (3); Church Yth Grp; Natl Beta Clb; Chorus; Church Choir; Rep Frsh Cls; Chrldng; Mgr(s); Cantatrice; Dental Hygentist.

EWING, KIMBERLEE; Rogers HS; Rogers, AR; (4); Cmnty Wkr; FCA; Intnl Clb; Science Clb; SADD; Tennis; Hon Roll; NHS; ACE; Drury Coll; Env Sci.

EWING, MARLA; Charleston HS; Charleston, AR; (2); Church Yth Grp; FCA; FBLA; FHA; Natl Beta Clb; Spanish Clb; Church Choir; Yrbk; Pres Frsh Cls; Sec Soph Cls; Westark JC; Elem Educ.

EZELL, DARRIEL L; Searcy HS; Searcy, AR; (3); Art Clb; Church Yth Grp; FBLA; FHA; Natl FFA Org; Quiz Bowl; Science Clb; Stage Crew; Hunting; Started Concord Chrstn Clb; Funeral Dir.

EZELL, DENNY L; Jacksonville HS; Jacksonville, AR; (3); Art Clb; Church Yth Grp; Drama Clb; FCA; Spanish Clb; Speech Tm; School Musical; School Play; Ofcr Bsbl; Bsktbl; Prof Baseball.

EZELL, MICHAEL E; Lake Hamilton Sr HS; Pearcy, AR; (3); Cmnty Wkr; Computer Clb; Letterman Clb; Natl FFA Org; Science Clb; Spanish Clb; Teachers Aide; Varsity Clb; Ofcr Bsbl; Ftbl; Cmptr Tech Netwrkng Cls; Cmptr Sci.

FABER, JERROD C; Greenwood Sr HS; Hackett, AR; (3); 4-H; Band; Mrchg Band; 4-H Awd; Hon Roll; St Record Book Wnnr 4 H; EXCEL Camp 4 H; Parlimentary Procdre Tm 4 Hst; U Of AR.

FAGALA, PHIL; Crowleys Ridge Acad; Jonesboro, AR; (4); 1/18; School Play; Quiz Bowl; Acpl Chr; Nwsp; Yrbk; VP Soph Cls; VP Pres Stu Cncl; Bsktbl; NHS; Val; Harding Univ; Pre-Med.

FAGAN, DARLA D; Alma HS; Alma, AR; (2); French Clb; FHA; SADD; Chorus; Hon Roll; Musician Yr, Best Female Vocalist Awds; PSYCO; Westark CC; Psych.

FAGAN, TALITHA; Heber Springs HS; Drasco, AR; (4); 22/92; Church Yth Grp; FCA; FBLA; FHA; Natl Beta Clb; Science Clb; Spanish Clb; Chorus; Crs Cntry; Tennis; ASU; Psych.

FAGRAS, COY M; Southside HS; Fort Smith, AR; (2); Drama Clb; Speech Tm; Teachers Aide; Thesps; School Musical; School Play; Stage Crew; Variety Show; Nwsp; Yrbk; 1st Pl Schl Sci Fair Chem; Dist 1st Pl Chem; Finals In Duet Acting; U Of AR.

FAHR, SARA; Clay Co Central Jr Sr HS; Rector, AR; (2); 9/51; Church Yth Grp; German Clb; GAA; Science Clb; Band; Flag Corp; Bsktbl; Sftbl; Cit Awd; Hon Roll; AR ST Univ.

FAIRCHILD, JOHN; Nettleton HS; Jonesboro, AR; (4); French Clb; Natl Beta Clb; Natl FFA Org; Hon Roll; Mock Law Team; Voc Stu Of The Yr; AR ST Univ; Pre-Vet.

FAIRLESS, JENNIFER J; Hatfield Schl; Hatfield, AR; (2); FCA; FBLA; Sec FHA; GAA; Natl FFA Org; Sec Soph Cls; Var Bsktbl; Var Sftbl; Var Trk; Hon Roll; All Amer Schol Awd; FFA Show Tm Awds; FFA Hrse Judge Tm Awds; KS St Univ; Crim Law.

FAIRLESS, JODIE L; Mena HS; Hatfield, AR; (4); Cmnty Wkr; Model UN; Spanish Clb; Teachers Aide; Band; Mrchg Band; Chrldng; Trk; Explorer Post; Personal Dev Awd; Embry Riddle; Aerospace Engrng.

FAIRLEY, MARIAH T; El Dorado Sr HS; El Dorado, AR; (2); 58/356; Church Yth Grp; Pres 4-H; Natl Beta Clb; Band; Church Choir; Mrchg Band; Rep Frsh Cls; Ofcr Stu Cncl; Hon Roll; NHS; Yth Apprntcshp Prog; Jackson ST; Phrmcy.

FAIR SLISHER, JENNIFER; Mt Pleasant Jr Sr HS; Batesville, AR; (4); 2/21; FBLA; Library Aide; Teachers Aide; Hist Frsh Cls; Treas Soph Cls; Sec Sr Cls; High Hon Roll; Sal; Poetry Pblshd Natl Beta Clb Jrnl/Local Paper/Mag; All Amer Schlr; AR ST U; Acctng.

FALKNER, MATTHEW A; Fayetteville Sr HS; Fayetteville, AR; (4); 60/388; FBLA; Letterman Clb; SADD; JV Var Bsktbl; High Hon Roll; Hon Roll; Jr NHS; NHS; Pres Acad Fit Awd; U Of AR; Criminal Justice.

FALLIS, MICHELLE; Lake Hamilton Sr HS; Royal, AR; (4); 16/279; Treas FCA; Natl Beta Clb; Co-Capt Drill Tm; Pres Frsh Cls; VP Soph Cls; Pres Jr Cls; VP Stu Cncl; Cit Awd; Hon Roll; NHS; Southern Assn Stu Cncl Co-Sec; Schlr Athl; U Of AR; Pre-Phys Thrpy.

FANNIN, JARROD R; Dierks HS; Dierks, AR; (1); Church Yth Grp; Rep Frsh Cls; L Bsbl; L Bsktbl; L Ftbl; Wt Lftg; Prfct Atten Awd; Chrch Yth Choir, Puppet Team, Drama; Phy Ed.

FANNON, ERIC; Altus Denning HS; Altus, AR; (3); FBLA; VP Stu Cncl; Var L Bsbl; Var L Bsktbl; Var L Trk; Hon Roll; Bsktbl All Dist 93-94; Westark; Cvl Engrng.

FARAR, LORRIE F; Rogers HS; Garfield, AR; (2); Church Yth Grp; Bsktbl; Hon Roll; Bsktbl/Music.

FARLEY, MISTY D; Fouke Jr Sr HS; Fouke, AR; (3); 11/93; FBLA; FHA; GAA; Natl Beta Clb; Pep Clb; Spanish Clb; Sec Frsh Cls; Sec Treas Jr Cls; Ofcr Stu Cncl; L Var Bsktbl; Southern AK Univ; Med.

FARMER, ASHLEY N; England HS; England, AR; (2); CPR Clss; Pulaski Tech Coll; Nrsng.

FARMER, CANDICE R; Valley View HS; Jonesboro, AR; (2); Art Clb; Church Yth Grp; Drama Clb; School Musical; School Play; High Hon Roll; Hon Roll; Jr NHS; NHS; Socr; U Of AR; Law; Art.

FARMER, JAMES P; Pulaski Acad; Little Rock, AR; (3); Boy Scts; Church Yth Grp; Cmnty Wkr; FCA; 4-H; French Clb; Color Guard; Ftbl; Swmmng; Trk; CO Outward Bound Schl Grad; N Amer Outdoor Ldrshp Schl Grad; Vanderbilt; Bus.

FARMER, KELLY J; Booneville Jr Sr HS; Booneville, AR; (2); 10/99; Church Yth Grp; FCA; French Clb; Library Aide; Natl Beta Clb; Office Aide; Science Clb; Service Clb; SADD; Teachers Aide; Poems Publshd; Ouachita Bapt Univ; Tchg Deaf.

FARMER, KIMBERLY A; Cabot HS; Cabot, AR; (3); 27/450; Key Clb; Spanish Clb; Band; Mrchg Band; School Play; Rep Frsh Cls; Rep Soph Cls; Rep Stu Cncl; Var Tennis; NHS; All-Region Band; Acad Letter; Harding Univ; Psych.

FARMER, KIMBERLY DAWN; Booneville Jr Sr HS; Booneville, AR; (4); 33/81; Am Leg Aux Girls St; Church Yth Grp; French Clb; FBLA; FHA; FTA; Key Clb; Office Aide; Science Clb; Band; All ST/ALL Reg/All Str Mjrt; 1st Div Drm Mjr; John Phillips Sousa/Paul Ray Mem Flwshp Outstndg Achvt; West Ark CC; Cmptr Info Systms.

FARMER, SHEREE; Parkin Jr Sr HS; Parkin, AR; (3); #1 in class; Church Yth Grp; FHA; Natl Beta Clb; Science Clb; Chorus; Church Choir; Rep Jr Cls; Var Bsktbl; High Hon Roll; Quiz Bowl; Italian Clb; RN.

FARRAR, SYLVIA R; Clarksville HS; Clarksville, AR; (4); Am Leg Aux Girls St; Church Yth Grp; French Clb; FBLA; Natl Beta Clb; Band; Chorus; Flag Corp; Mrchg Band; High Hon Roll; Amer Legion Schl Awd; Harding Univ; Elem Ed.

FARRELL, ASHLEY D; Gosnell Jr Sr HS; Gosnell, AR; (2); Church Yth Grp; Cmnty Wkr; Drama Clb; Spanish Clb; Church Choir; School Play; Yrbk; Powder Puff Ftbl; Prfct Atten Awd; Vet.

FARRELL, MEREDITH T; Southside HS; Fort Smith, AR; (2); 109/550; Church Yth Grp; Cmnty Wkr; FCA; SADD; Key Clb; Spanish Clb; Teachers Aide; Varsity Clb; School Play; Ofcr Stu Cncl; Duke.

FARRIS, BELINDA A; Beebe Sr HS; Beebe, AR; (3); 6/132; Church Yth Grp; 4-H; FBLA; Natl Beta Clb; Spanish Clb; Teachers Aide; Band; Jazz Band; Mrchg Band; 4-H Awd; MASH Part; All Region Bnd; UNSBA Honoree; ASU; Pharm.

FARRIS, LAUREN A; St Joseph HS; Conway, AR; (1); Church Yth Grp; GAA; Natl Beta Clb; Bsktbl; Trk; Vllybl; High Hon Roll; Hon Roll; Jr NHS; NHS; Jr NHS Soc; Vlybl/Bsktbl Starter; U Of AR; Photo/Fshn/Mdlng.

FAULKNER, RUSH D; North Little Rock Hs-West; North Little Rock, AR; (3); 125/550; Church Yth Grp; FCA; Office Aide; Stage Crew; Ofcr Bsbl; Bsktbl; Ftbl; Hon Roll; Peer Ldrshp; Engr/Arch.

FAVRE, SARAH; Arkansas Bapt Schl; Little Rock, AR; (4); #1 in class; Church Yth Grp; French Clb; Sec FBLA; Band; Church Choir; Ed Yrbk; Score Keeper; Val; Frgn Mssns Clb; TX Chrstn U; Acctng.

FEARN, KIMBER D; Hartford Schl; Hartford, AR; (3); Church Yth Grp; Cmnty Wkr; FBLA; Library Aide; Teachers Aide; Church Choir; Ed Yrbk; Chrldng; Mgr(s); Powder Puff Ftbl; FBLA Natls; Phys Thrpy.

FEEMSTER, BRYAN S; Russellville Sr HS; Russellville, AR; (3); 88/386; Boy Scts; Church Yth Grp; Drama Clb; Spanish Clb; Chorus; Mgr(s); Socr; Hon Roll; USAFA Smmr Sci Smnr; USYSA Ref; Rogers Sct Resvtn Staff; USAF Acad; Navgtn.

FEERICK, MILES; Hatfield Schl; Hatfield, AR; (2); Boy Scts; Church Yth Grp; Office Aide; FFA; Show Steer; Poultry Judging Team; Ag/Bus.

FELDMAN, IRIS JAYNELL; West Side Christian Schl; El Dorado, AR; (4); 5/16; Church Yth Grp; Mu Alpha Theta; Office Aide; Amer Legion Schlsp; South AR CC; Comp Sci.

FELLOWS, HOLLY; Newport HS; Newport, AR; (2); Art Clb; Church Yth Grp; FBLA; Spanish Clb; SADD; Drill Tm; Chrldng; Cit Awd; Hon Roll; Frshmn Clss Sec; Soph Clss Tres; LA ST U.

FELLOWS, RYAN; Bergman Schl; Harrison, AR; (3); 4/55; Church Yth Grp; Cmnty Wkr; FBLA; Natl Beta Clb; Pep Clb; Spanish Clb; Band; Church Choir; Pep Band; Treas Jr Cls; Atten Natl Young Ldrs Conf 96.

FELLS, NATHANIEL; J A Fair Sr HS; Little Rock, AR; (3); FBLA; Science Clb; VP Soph Cls; VP Jr Cls; High Hon Roll; Jr NHS; NHS; Ntl Merit Schol; Pres Acad Fit Awd; Boy Scts; Yth Ldrshp Inst; Duke; Lab Tech.

FELLS, SEAN; Dumas HS; Dumas, AR; (3); FCA; 4-H; FTA; Spanish Clb; Band; Cit Awd; Hon Roll; NHS; Pres Acad Fit Awd.

FELTON, RACHEAL; White Co Central Schl; Judsonia, AR; (3); 1/42; Church Yth Grp; FBLA; FHA; HOBY; Math Tm; Teachers Aide; Co-Ed Yrbk; Bsktbl; Crs Cntry; Score Keeper; Sci, Music & Spnsh Acad Awds; U Of AR; Envrnmntl Sci.

FELTS, AIMEE B; Des Arc Jr Sr HS; Des Arc, AR; (3); 2/35; Church Yth Grp; Natl Beta Clb; Spanish Clb; Jazz Band; Mrchg Band; Ofcr Stu Cncl; Hon Roll; FBLA; FTA; Teachers Aide; Soul Mission-Chrstn Clb; Nrsng Home Vol; U Of AR.

FELTY, KASI; Magnet Cove HS; Malvern, AR; (2); FCA; Math Clb; Natl Beta Clb; Science Clb; Var Bsktbl; Var Sftbl; Var Trk; Var Vllybl; Wt Lftg; Dance Clb; Pediatrician; Medicine; Hlth.

FENDLEY, DARRYL; Bismarck Jr-Sr HS; Bismarck, AR; (3); VP FCA; FBLA; Natl Beta Clb; Pres Frsh Cls; Pres Soph Cls; VP Jr Cls; VP Stu Cncl; Var Bsbl; Var Bsktbl; Var Ftbl.

FENNELL, SUSAN; Rogers HS; Rogers, AR; (4); 66/468; Church Yth Grp; Cmnty Wkr; FCA; FBLA; Spanish Clb; Teachers Aide; Varsity Clb; Rep Jr Cls; Pres Stu Cncl; Var Capt Bsktbl; Hnr Stu Mmth; Chmbr Cmmrce Acad Awd; Natl Ldrshp Frm; Stu Bnk Brd; Prnt, Tchr, Stu Assn; KS U; Bus Cmmnctns.

FENTER, MICHAEL A; Poyen Schl; Traskwood, AR; (3); Church Yth Grp; FCA; 4-H; FHA; Spanish Clb; VICA; Band; School Musical; 4-H Awd; 4-H Frstry Schlrshp; Most Advncd 1st Yr Welder Awd Vo-Tech; Awds/Trophies For Shootng 4-H ST AR; U Of AR Monticello; Frstry.

FERGUS, CHRIS M; Mississippi Co Christian Acad; Osceola, AR; (3); #1 in class; Pres Key Clb; Sec Soph Cls; Pres Jr Cls; VP Stu Cncl; Var Bsktbl; Var Golf; French Hon Soc; High Hon Roll; NHS; Pres Acad Fit Awd.

FERGUSON, BRANDY A; Elkins Jr Sr HS; Fayetteville, AR; (2); Church Yth Grp.

FERGUSON, DEVIN M; Bay Jr Sr HS; Bay, AR; (4); Church Yth Grp; FCA; FBLA; GAA; Library Aide; Pep Clb; Science Clb; Teachers Aide; Church Choir; Rptr Nwsp; All-St Vllybl; BEA, Winnie Holmes & Vllybl Schlsps; Most Ath Awd 95-96; Outstdng Hustle; Outstdng Ath; Crowleys Ridge Coll; Phys Therp.

FERGUSON, GLENDA; Fairview HS; Camden, AR; (4); 1/245; Am Leg Aux Girls St; Quiz Bowl; Capt Mrchg Band; Ed Yrbk; Rep Jr Cls; French Hon Soc; Gov Hon Prg Awd; NHS; Val; Natl Achvmt Fnlst; Washington Univ.

FERGUSON, JOSH; Mena HS; Mena, AR; (3); 54/130; Art Clb; French Clb; FBLA; Golf; U Of AR Little Rock; Graphics.

FERGUSON, KATIE S; Guy Perkins Schl; Greenbrier, AR; (4); 1/26; Church Yth Grp; FCA; FHA; Natl Beta Clb; Spanish Clb; Teachers Aide; Yrbk; VP Jr Cls; Treas Sr Cls; Var Capt Bsktbl; Homecmng Queen; Clss Fav; Bsktbl Schlsp; Trinity Vly JC; Pre-Med/Pedtrc.

FERGUSON, KRISTIN M; Clarksville HS; Clarksville, AR; (2); FBLA; Model UN; Natl Beta Clb; Sec Frsh Cls; Sftbl; Hon Roll; Prfct Atten Awd; Marine Bio.

FERGUSON III, ROBERT L; Booneville Jr Sr HS; Booneville, AR; (3); Church Yth Grp; FCA; Natl Beta Clb; Science Clb; Spanish Clb; Varsity Clb; Bsktbl; Ftbl; Wt Lftg; Hon Roll; Natl Yth League Forum On Medicine; U Of AR; Pre-Med.

FERGUSON, SHANE A; Elkins Jr Sr HS; Fayetteville, AR; (4); Boy Scts; Church Yth Grp; FBLA; Phtg Yrbk; Ftbl; Trk; Hon Roll; Eagle Scout Awd; U Of AR Fay.

FERRARI, BRITTANY R; Ft Smith Christian Schl; Fort Smith, AR; (3); 7/36; Church Yth Grp; FCA; FBLA; Band; Chorus; Chrldng; Hon Roll; NHS; Prfct Atten Awd; Pre-Med.

FERRARI, CONNIE M; Bergman Schl; Harrison, AR; (2); Art Clb; Church Yth Grp; FBLA; FHA; Pep Clb; Teachers Aide; Hon Roll.

FERRELL, ANGIE; Augusta HS; Augusta, AR; (4); 4/42; Treas English Clb; Pres FBLA; FTA; Treas Natl Beta Clb; Office Aide; Science Clb; Spanish Clb; Rptr Yrbk; High Hon Roll; Sec NHS; Girls St Delg; Hnr Grad; AR ST U Jonesboro; Radiology.

FETTE, TANYA; Northside HS; Fort Smith, AR; (2); Cmnty Wkr; Pres FBLA; Orch; Socr; Sec Jr NHS; NHS; Pres Acad Fit Awd; Latin Clb; Math Tm; Quiz Bowl; TAPS; GATE; Cultural Ambassadors; Pre-Med.

FETTE, THERESA A; Northside HS; Fort Smith, AR; (4); 26/350; FBLA; Band; Pres Frsh Cls; Sec Soph Cls; Rep Jr Cls; Rep Sr Cls; High Hon Roll; Pres Acad Fit Awd; St Schlr; Art Clb; AR Govrn Schl Soc Sci; Lyon Coll Upward Bnd; AAA Schlr; U Of AR; Bio-Chem/OB.

FETTERS, DUSTIN C; Clarksville HS; Lamar, AR; (2); Trk; Bus Mgmt.

FETZ, BREIHAN; Sheridan Sr HS; Lewisville, TX; (4); 89/248; Teachers Aide; Color Guard; Drill Tm; Prfct Atten Awd; Pres Acad Fit Awd; ROTC; UT Arlington; Army.

FIELDER, ANDREW H; Guy Perkins Schl; Greenbrier, AR; (4); Pres VP Church Yth Grp; FCA; FBLA; Pres Natl Beta Clb; Natl FFA Org; VP Jr Cls; Pres Sr Cls; Ofcr Bsbl; Hon Roll; NHS.

FIELDS, COURTNEY R; Russellville Sr HS; Russellville, AR; (2); Church Yth Grp; FCA; GAA; Spanish Clb; Teachers Aide; Chorus; Bsktbl; Vllybl; Cit Awd; High Hon Roll; Quachita Bapt U; Math; Span Ed.

FIELDS, JASON B; Springdale Sr HS; Springdale, AR; (3); Church Yth Grp; FCA; Var L Golf; Hon Roll; Made Newspr Sprts Sctn Fr Golf.

FIELDS, LAURA J; Central Sr HS; Little Rock, AR; (3); 8/540; FBLA; German Clb; Hosp Aide; Mu Alpha Theta; Natl Beta Clb; Gov Hon Prg Awd; High Hon Roll; NHS; Pres Acad Fit Awd; Jr Acad Sci Awd; Engr.

FIELDS, LISA; Abundant Life Schools; Sherwood, AR; (4); 6/18; Church Yth Grp; School Play; Ed Nwsp; Pres Jr Cls; Pres Sr Cls; Treas Stu Cncl; Var L Bsktbl; Var Sftbl; Capt L Vllybl; NHS; Bsktbl All-Conf 4 Yrs; Conf MVP 93-94; U Of Central AR.

FIELDS, MIRANDA M; Fayetteville Sr HS; Fayetteville, AR; (2); Church Yth Grp; Chorus; Church Choir; Drill Tm; Nwsp; Powder Puff Ftbl; Animal Hosp Vol; Large Animal Vet; Tchr.

FIFE, CRYSTAL; West Side HS; Greers Ferry, AR; (2); 5/45; Church Yth Grp; Library Aide; Hon Roll; NHS; Prfct Atten Awd; Pres Acad Fit Awd; Wrld His Mdl; Geometry Mdl; Lib Mdl; Lib Clb Rprtr; Vo-Tech; Acctnt.

FIKES, JACLYN; Lake Hamilton Sr HS; Hot Springs, AR; (2); FCA; FBLA; FHA; Natl Beta Clb; Natl FFA Org; Spanish Clb; Rep Stu Cncl; JV Var Chrldng; UALR; Med.

FINCH, LISA R; Beebe Sr HS; Beebe, AR; (3); 12/124; Church Yth Grp; FBLA; FHA; Hosp Aide; Hist Library Aide; Math Clb; Natl Beta Clb; Science Clb; Spanish Clb; Hon Roll; Stu Of Month; Voice Of Democracy Wnnr; Spcl Achvmt Acctng Awd; Ag Bus.

FINCHER, CHRISTIE D; Springdale Sr HS; Springdale, AR; (1); Church Yth Grp; FBLA; Band; Drm Mjr(t); Mrchg Band; School Play; Cit Awd; Hon Roll; Jr NHS; Pres Acad Fit Awd; Yth Chrst, Advncd Math Prgm; Odysy Mnd; 4-Yr Coll; Bus/Cmptr Field.

FINDLEY, JENNIFER R; Lonoke Sr HS; Lonoke, AR; (3); 11/120; FBLA; FHA; Spanish Clb; Drill Tm; Hon Roll; NHS; Odyssey Mind; AZ ST U Beebe; Engr.

FINLEY, CEDRIC; Stamps HS; Stamps, AR; (2); Science Clb; Rep Jr Cls; Var Bsbl; L Ftbl.

FINLEY, ERICA S; Manila HS; Manila, AR; (1); Church Yth Grp; FBLA; FHA; Natl Beta Clb; Quiz Bowl; Chorus; Rep Soph Cls; Rep Stu Cncl; Hon Roll; Piano; Vet.

FINNEY, JESSICA C; Glen Rose HS; Malvern, AR; (1); Art Clb; Church Yth Grp; FCA; GAA; Pep Clb; Spanish Clb; Drill Tm; Bsktbl; Pom Pon; Pres Acad Fit Awd; UCLA; Psyclgy.

FINSTER, CARLA M; Batesville Sr HS; Batesville, AR; (3); Cmnty Wkr; Treas FHA; Chorus; High Hon Roll; Hon Roll; Schlstc Letter 95-; Upward Bound Math/Sci Ctr 95; Soc Wrkr/Dietician.

FIRESTONE, LAURA; Cabot HS; Cabot, AR; (3); #6 in class; FCA; Key Clb; Spanish Clb; Band; Mrchg Band; Bsktbl; Chrldng; Trk; High Hon Roll; NHS; Acad Ltrs 3 Yrs; Prom Cmmtte; PA ST; Psycht.

FISCHER, KIMBERLY A; Sheridan Sr HS; Hensley, AR; (3); #5 in class; Church Yth Grp; Cmnty Wkr; Dance Clb; FCA; Temple Yth Grp; Chorus; Church Choir; Drill Tm; Chrldng; Mgr(s).

FISHER, ALICIA R; El Dorado Sr HS; El Dorado, AR; (3); Key Clb; Natl Beta Clb; Rep Jr Cls; Rep Sr Cls; Var Chrldng; L Tennis; Vllybl; NHS; Campfire; U Of AR Fayetteville; Chem Eng.

FISHER, BETSY; Wynne HS; Wynne, AR; (1); Church Yth Grp; Drama Clb; Co-Capt Chrldng; Hon Roll; Bus Mgmt.

FISHER, CHRISTOPHER M; Pea Ridge HS; Garfield, AR; (1); Natl FFA Org; Office Aide; Elctrnc Engnr.

FISHER, DENA; Ozark Adventist Acad; Bristow, OK; (4); 5/54; Cmnty Wkr; Drama Clb; Ski Clb; Church Choir; Drill Tm; Nwsp; Sec Soph Cls; Treas Jr Cls; Gym; Trk; Pacific Union Coll; Psych.

FISHER, JUSTIN; Spring Hill HS; Hope, AR; (2); Church Yth Grp; French Clb; FBLA; Natl Beta Clb; Quiz Bowl; Pres Frsh Cls; Sec Soph Cls; JV Var Bsktbl; Hon Roll; Ntl Merit Ltr.

FISHER, KRISTIE; East Poinsett Cty JR HS; Tyronza, AR; (3); FBLA; FHA; Bsktbl; Chrldng; Hon Roll; NHS; Med.

FISHER, LORI C; Ozark Adventist Acad; Tulsa, OK; (2); Church Yth Grp; Cmnty Wkr; Drama Clb; Teachers Aide; School Play; Yrbk; Treas Frsh Cls; Sec Stu Cncl; Vllybl; Cit Awd; Pacific Union Coll.

FISHER, TIM A; Goza Jr HS; Arkadelphia, AR; (1); JV Ftbl; Hon Roll; Jr NHS; Prfct Atten Awd.

FISK, HOLLY; Nashville HS; Nashville, AR; (4); Church Yth Grp; FBLA; FHA; Spanish Clb; School Play; Ed Nwsp; Ed Yrbk; Chrldng; U Of AR; Publc Rltns.

FITZ, B MICHELLE; Bryant Sr HS; Bryant, AR; (2); English Clb; French Clb; VP FBLA; Office Aide; Teachers Aide; Nwsp; Mgr Yrbk; High Hon Roll; Hon Roll; Sec Jr NHS; Hendrix; Tech Wrtng/Jrnlsm.

FITZGERALD, CHASIDY A; Lavaca Jr Sr HS; Lavaca, AR; (3); 9/64; Art Clb; Cmnty Wkr; Drama Clb; FCA; 4-H; FHA; Hosp Aide; Library Aide; Natl Beta Clb; Natl FFA Org; AR Tech Univ; RN.

FITZPATRICK, BETHANY; Marion Co Rural Schl; Yellville, AR; (4); Spanish Clb.

FITZPATRICK JR, GARY D; Van Buren Sr HS; Van Buren, AR; (2); Church Yth Grp; Library Aide; Hon Roll.

FITZWATER, VALERIE L; Omaha Schl; Omaha, AR; (2); Church Yth Grp; Natl Beta Clb; Church Choir; Lit Mag; Pres Frsh Cls; Ofcr Stu Cncl; Sftbl; Hon Roll; Pres Acad Fit Awd.

FLAMMANG, ELIZABETH M; Ark Schl For Math And Sci; Little Rock, AR; (3); Am Leg Aux Girls St; Chess Clb; German Clb; Mu Alpha Theta; Natl Beta Clb; Service Clb; Rep Stu Cncl; Chrldng; Mgr(s); High Hon Roll; Sr Co At Ctr For Dansarts; Atten AR Schl For Math & Sci; Oncologist.

FLANAGAN, GABRIEL L; Ft Smith Christian Schl; Fort Smith, AR; (2); Church Yth Grp; Cmnty Wkr; Computer Clb; Band; Mrchg Band; School Musical; Cit Awd; Hon Roll.

FLANNIGAN, AMY M; Manila HS; Manila, AR; (1); Church Yth Grp; Natl Beta Clb; Natl FFA Org; Church Choir; Bsktbl; Sftbl; High Hon Roll; Vet.

FLEHARTY, STEPHANIE M; Decatur HS; Decatur, AR; (2); Art Clb; Church Yth Grp; Natl FFA Org; Spanish Clb; Bsktbl; Hon Roll; Pres Acad Fit Awd; Sntnl FFA Chptr; Prlmntry Prcdr Tm; Crtsy Corp ST Conv; Univ Of AR; Lawyer/Vet.

FLEMENS, ANGELA C; Dierks HS; Newhope, AR; (3); 1/38; Am Leg Aux Girls St; FBLA; Quiz Bowl; VP Sr Cls; Pres Stu Cncl; Chrldng; High Hon Roll; NHS; FHA; Nwsp; Blck Blt Tae Kwon Do; Gftd/Tlntd; Coll Of The Ozarks; Drmtlgy.

FLEMING, ADEANA M; Walker Schl; Magnolia, AR; (2); Church Yth Grp; Band; Color Guard; Ntl Merit Ltr; Stu Cncl; Fire Mrshll; Bus.

FLEMING, ASHLEY D; Star City HS; Star City, AR; (1); Church Yth Grp; SADD; Teachers Aide; Chorus; Church Choir; School Musical; Hon Roll; Gov Yth Conf Of AR; Ouachita Bapt Univ; PT.

FLEMING, CRYSTAL; Prairie Grove HS; Prairie Grove, AR; (4); Church Yth Grp; Drama Clb; FHA; Spanish Clb; Teachers Aide; Ed Nwsp; Yrbk; High Hon Roll; Jr NHS; NHS; Future Citizens Heaven Fndr/Pres.

FLEMING, SHARON D; Pulaski Acad; Maumelle, AR; (2); Drama Clb; French Clb; Girl Scts; Natl Beta Clb; Spanish Clb; Band; Drm Mjr(t); Stage Crew; Variety Show; Hon Roll.

FLEMING, VERONICA; Dardanelle HS; Dardanelle, AR; (4); 9/103; FBLA; HOBY; Natl Beta Clb; Band; Yrbk; Lit Mag; Sftbl; High Hon Roll; Pres Schlr; FHA; Hmcmng Crt; Peer Tutor; AR Tech U; Pre-Physcl Thrpy.

FLETCHER, BRIDGETTE; Westside HS; Bono, AR; (4); 4/81; Church Yth Grp; FCA; FHA; FTA; Hosp Aide; Math Clb; Natl Beta Clb; Science Clb; Spanish Clb; Teachers Aide; All Star Chrldr 95; Sr Miss Warrior 94/96; Maid Of Hon Ftbl Homecoming; AR ST Univ; Bio Ed/Tchr.

FLETCHER, FELICIA; Atkins Schl; Atkins, AR; (2); 8/81; Church Yth Grp; Drama Clb; 4-H; FBLA; Natl Beta Clb; Science Clb; Spanish Clb; Band; Church Choir; Mrchg Band; Neurosurgeon.

FLETCHER, JULIE W; Lonoke Jr HS; Lonoke, AR; (2); Rptr Church Yth Grp; FCA; Hosp Aide; Stat Bsbl; JV Bsktbl; Score Keeper; Hon Roll; Jr NHS; Pres Acad Fit Awd; Spirit Rabbit; Vet.

FLETCHER, KAMI L; Pine Bluff HS; Pine Bluff, AR; (3); Sec Church Yth Grp; FHA; Spanish Clb; Speech Tm; Rptr Yrbk; Sec Frsh Cls; Jr NHS; Ntl Merit Ltr; Sunday Schl Tchr; Sec Sunday Schl; U Of AR; Eng; Pre-Law; Lawyer.

FLETCHER, KATHLEEN E; Mann Magnet Jr HS; North Little Rock, AR; (1); Hosp Aide; Natl Beta Clb; School Play; Rptr Yrbk; Hon Roll; Pres Jr NHS; Piano; Dncng; Invlvmnt In Chldrns Hosp Prgm; Med.

FLETCHER, KEISHA; Fairview HS; Camden, AR; (4); 14/245; Church Yth Grp; French Clb; FBLA; FHA; Mu Alpha Theta; Natl Beta Clb; Ofcr Stu Cncl; Capt Vllybl; French Hon Soc; NHS; U Of Cntrl AR.

FLETCHER, LARRYANNA; Eudora HS; Eudora, AR; (3); 1/60; Rptr FHA; Natl Beta Clb; SADD; School Play; Phtg Yrbk; Trk; High Hon Roll; Hon Roll; NHS; Val; Alg II Excel; AR St Univ; TV Brdcstng.

FLETCHER, YAVONDA; Booneville Jr Sr HS; Booneville, AR; (4); 2/85; FBLA; Key Clb; Rptr Natl Beta Clb; VP Chorus; Ed Nwsp; Yrbk; Rep Stu Cncl; Sal; FTA; Q&S; Natl Eng Mrt Awds; AR Stu Cngrss Bst Bll Hse; Harding U; Eng.

FLINT, JEREMY A; Bearden HS; Bearden, AR; (2); Cmnty Wkr; FHA; Letterman Clb; Varsity Clb; Lbrn Ftbl; Lbrn Trk; Lbrn Wt Lftg; Hon Roll; Prfct Atten Awd.

FLODEN, LORALEI; Morrilton Sr HS; Plumerville, AR; (4); 12/150; French Clb; Math Clb; Natl Beta Clb; Quiz Bowl; Thesps; Band; Stage Crew; Nwsp; Yrbk; Hon Roll; Outstndng Stu Awd; Staff All AR HS Nwsp; U Of Cntrl AR; Engl.

FLORA, KIMBERLY; Springdale Sr HS; Springdale, AR; (4); 1/486; Am Leg Aux Girls St; Key Clb; School Musical; Variety Show; VP Sr Cls; Pom Pon; Hon Roll; NHS; Pres Acad Fit Awd; Miss SHS Rnnr Up; UDA All Star Dancer; U Cntrl AR.

FLORY, TIFFANY L; Russellville Sr HS; Russellville, AR; (3); FCA; GAA; Band; Flag Corp; Mrchg Band; Pep Band; JV Bsktbl; Var L Sftbl; L Trk; JV Var Vllybl; Meals On Whls; U Of AR; Lwyr.

FLOURNOY, TRELONI L; Stuttgart Sr HS; Stuttgart, AR; (3); Am Leg Aux Girls St; DECA; FCA; Mu Alpha Theta; Natl Beta Clb; Spanish Clb; Band; Swing Chorus; High Hon Roll; Hon Roll; UCA.

FLOWERS, ASHLEY D; Nemo Vista Jr Sr HS; Center Ridge, AR; (2); 3/34; FBLA; FHA; Natl Beta Clb; Spanish Clb; Treas Frsh Cls; Ofcr Stu Cncl; Var Bsktbl; Hon Roll; AAU Bsktbl; GATE; Marine Bio.

FLOWERS, SONYA D; Paron Schl; Paron, AR; (2); FBLA; FHA; Math Clb; Science Clb; Teachers Aide; Band; Chorus; VP Frsh Cls; Hon Roll; Med.

FLOYD, AUTUMN; Berryville HS; Berryville, AR; (2); Art Clb; FBLA; Science Clb; Rep Soph Cls; Rep Stu Cncl; Chrldng; Trk; DAR Awd; High Hon Roll; NHS.

FLOYD, CRYSTAL N; Blytheville Sr HS; Blytheville, AR; (2); 23/323; Church Yth Grp; 4-H; Band; Church Choir; Color Guard; Mrchg Band; 4-H Awd; Hon Roll; FBLA; Flwsp Chrstn Stu; Prairie View A&M Univ; Elem Ed.

FLOYD, FARA; Swifton Schl; Swifton, AR; (4); 4/12; 4-H; Natl Beta Clb; Pep Clb; Quiz Bowl; Spanish Clb; Pres Sr Cls; Sftbl; Tennis; NHS; Grls St Dlgt; ASU; Pub Rltns.

FLOYD, MARY E; Russellville Sr HS; Russellville, AR; (3); Church Yth Grp; Pres FCA; FBLA; Office Aide; SADD; School Musical; Var Crs Cntry; Var Trk; High Hon Roll; NHS; Occptnl Therapy.

FLOYD, MELANIE V; Cabot HS; Cabot, AR; (2); Church Yth Grp; Cmnty Wkr; Spanish Clb; Band; Mrchg Band; Pep Band; Hon Roll; Jr NHS; Chrch Actvts; Fayetteville; Archlgy.

FLOYD, ROBERT O; Mena HS; Mena, AR; (3); 3/125; Am Leg Boys St; Boy Scts; Church Yth Grp; French Clb; Bsktbl; High Hon Roll; NHS.

FLOYD, SCOTT A; Southside HS; Fort Smith, AR; (2); Chess Clb; Mu Alpha Theta; Quiz Bowl; Spanish Clb; JV Var Socr; Hon Roll; Jr NHS; NHS; Pres Schlr; Omer & Ranatra Tusca Awds Odyssey Of The Mind; Keyboardist Of Yr.

FLOYD, WILL; Hoxie Schl; Walnut Ridge, AR; (3); #1 in class; Church Yth Grp; FHA; Model UN; Quiz Bowl; JV Var Bsktbl; High Hon Roll; Hon Roll; AR ST U; Bus Finance.

FLUGER, KRIS; J A Fair Sr HS; Little Rock, AR; (3); #3 in class; Am Leg Boys St; Church Yth Grp; FCA; Ofcr Bsbl; Bsktbl; Golf; NHS.

FLUHART, JONATHAN T; West Side Christian Schl; El Dorado, AR; (3); Am Leg Boys St; Church Yth Grp; DECA; FCA; JA; Letterman Clb; Mu Alpha Theta; Natl Beta Clb; Office Aide; School Play; Amer Legion Bsbl; Natl Yth Ldrshp Forum On Law & The Constitution Wash DC Nom; U Of AR; Law; Criminal.

FLYNT, CHRIS N; Decatur HS; Decatur, AR; (2); FCA; Natl FFA Org; Pres Soph Cls; Pres Jr Cls; VP Stu Cncl; Var Bsbl; Var Bsktbl; Var Ftbl; Hon Roll; Pres Acad Fit Awd; Arch/Ag.

FOEOMSDORF, AMANDA L; North Little Rock Hs-West; North Little Rock, AR; (3); Drama Clb; Hosp Aide; Q&S; Spanish Clb; Stage Crew; Yrbk; Lit Mag; High Hon Roll; 96 AR St Govs Schl.

FOGERTY, MARCUS B; Yellville Summit HS; Yellville, AR; (3); Church Yth Grp; FCA; Natl Beta Clb; Office Aide; Pep Clb; Rep Frsh Cls; Pres Soph Cls; Ofcr Stu Cncl; Ofcr Bsbl; Bsktbl; Cmptr Engr.

FOLDS, WESLEY; Malvern Jr HS; Malvern, AR; (2); 17/220; Church Yth Grp; FCA; Natl Beta Clb; Acpl Chr; Pres Stu Cncl; Ofcr Bsbl; Ftbl; Cit Awd; High Hon Roll; Jr NHS; Pr Cnlsrs; CHAMPS; GYC; La Tech; Med.

FOLEY, HEATHER; Gosnell Jr HS; Blytheville, AR; (1); Band; Mrchg Band; Pep Band; Hon Roll; TAP.

FOLEY, KEITH P; Fayetteville Sr HS; Fayetteville, AR; (2); Yrbk; Ofcr Bsbl; Cit Awd; Hon Roll; Pres Acad Fit Awd; 2 Yrs Span; Skate Bdng; Shrtstp Soph HS Bsbl Tm; U Of AR; Ele Engr.

FOLK, MICHAEL A; Bald Knob HS; Bald Knob, AR; (2); 1/126; FBLA; Natl Beta Clb; Quiz Bowl; Band; Jazz Band; Mrchg Band; Orch; Pep Band; Cit Awd; High Hon Roll.

FOLLIS, JEREMY; Blevins HS; Mc Caskill, AR; (1); 7/48; Art Clb; FBLA; Natl Beta Clb; Quiz Bowl; Mgr Bsktbl; Pres Acad Fit Awd; Gftd/Tlntd; Arch Engrng.

FONG, FELICIA; Lee Acad; Marianna, AR; (2); Chrldng; Hon Roll; NHS; Prfct Atten Awd; Typng Awd; U Memphis.

FOOTE, ISAAC; Bright Star Schl; Doddridge, AR; (4); 7/22; Office Aide; Quiz Bowl; Nwsp; Yrbk; NHS; Monticello Coll.

FOOTE, JENNIFER; Winslow Schl; Winslow, AR; (3); 15/15; Church Yth Grp; Cmnty Wkr; Dance Clb; FCA; FBLA; FHA; Library Aide; SADD; Varsity Clb; Church Choir; Ldrsp Awds; AR Cooprtve Essay Cntst Yth Tour; Bus/Psych.

FORBES, MATTHEW L; Farmington Jr Sr HS; Farmington, AR; (3); Art Clb; Drama Clb; FCA; FBLA; FHA; Natl FFA Org; Ofcr Bsbl; Ftbl; Trk; Wt Lftg; U Of AR; PE.

FORBUS, PIPER J; Eureka Springs Jr-Sr HS; Eureka Springs, AR; (4); 4/59; Cmnty Wkr; Capt Dance Clb; VP Natl Beta Clb; Co-Capt Drill Tm; Co-Ed Yrbk; Pres Frsh Cls; Pres Soph Cls; Pres Jr Cls; Pres Stu Cncl; High Hon Roll; HS Recyclng Coord; Randolph-Macon Wmns Coll Ldrshp Conf; Rotary Yth Ldrshp Awd Cmp; Randolph Macon Wmns Coll; Psych.

FORD, BOBBY D; Walker Schl; Magnolia, AR; (2); 5/23; Drama Clb; FHA; Quiz Bowl; Science Clb; Band; Chorus; Church Choir; Bsktbl; Trk; Hon Roll; Plays Drums Chrch Choir; U Of AR Fayetteville; Pre-Med.

FORD, BRANDI A; Russellville Sr HS; Russellville, AR; (2); Art Clb; Church Yth Grp; Cmnty Wkr; French Clb; Chorus; Church Choir; Hon Roll; NHS; Peer Ldr In Chrch Yth Group; Golden Rule Awd Fnlst; Yth Of The Yr Fnlst.

FORD, CODY A; Parkers Chapel Schl; El Dorado, AR; (1); Art Clb; 4-H; FBLA; Golf; Hon Roll; Natl Hstry/Govt Awd; PRIDE; Beta Clb.

FORD, CRAIG D; Siloam Springs Sr HS; Siloam Springs, AR; (3); 1/150; Church Yth Grp; French Clb; Model UN; Natl Beta Clb; Quiz Bowl; Scholastic Bowl; Band; Church Choir; Mrchg Band; Pep Band; J Brown U; Psych.

FORD, DARIAN E; J A Fair Sr HS; Little Rock, AR; (3); Art Clb; French Clb; FBLA; FHA; Math Clb; Science Clb; Cit Awd; French Hon Soc; Jr NHS; Prfct Atten Awd; Gntlmns Club; Med Asstnt.

FORD, HEATHER R; Lake Hamilton Sr HS; Hot Springs, AR; (2); Church Yth Grp; Dance Clb; FCA; FBLA; Library Aide; Natl Beta Clb; Spanish Clb; Drill Tm; Stat Crs Cntry; Stat Trk.

FORD, JEFFERY N; Oak Grove HS; Maumelle, AR; (2); Church Yth Grp; FCA; Letterman Clb; Spanish Clb; Teachers Aide; Rep Frsh Cls; Var Bsktbl; Var Ftbl; Cit Awd; Hon Roll.

FORD, KRISTAL D; Pine Bluff HS; Pine Bluff, AR; (4); 67/410; Church Yth Grp; Cmnty Wkr; Spanish Clb; Band; Drm Mjr(t); Mrchg Band; Pep Band; Rep Jr Cls; Rep Stu Cncl; JV Bsktbl; UAPB; Pol Sci.

FORD, LAURA; Sulphur Rock Schl; Charlotte, AR; (3); JA; Math Clb; Natl FFA Org; Rep Jr Cls; High Hon Roll; Hon Roll; Ntl Merit Ltr; Prfct Atten Awd; FFA VP.

FORD, MORGAN N; Southside HS; Batesville, AR; (2); Church Yth Grp; FCA; Key Clb; Quiz Bowl; Chorus; Church Choir; School Musical; Hon Roll.

FORD, ROBERT; Gosnell Jr Sr HS; Blytheville, AR; (4); 13/65; Church Yth Grp; Letterman Clb; Spanish Clb; Speech Tm; School Musical; L Bsbl; Stat Ftbl; Wt Lftg; Cit Awd; High Hon Roll.

FORD, SUMMER L; Sloan Hendrix HS; Ravenden, AR; (3); FBLA; FHA; FTA; Band; Hon Roll; Engl Awd; Nursng.

FORD, THOMAS R; Clarksville HS; Clarksville, AR; (2); JV Bsktbl; Hon Roll; Prfct Atten Awd; Pride; Auburn U; Bus Mgmt.

FORD, WENDY M; Jacksonville HS; Jacksonville, AR; (2); Pres FBLA; Natl Beta Clb; Spanish Clb; Ed Nwsp; FBLA Pres; Dist FBLA VP; Pres Ed Awds Pgm; ASU Bebee; Law.

FOREMAN, ALICIA R; Central Sr HS; Little Rock, AR; (2); Pres Church Yth Grp; 4-H; FBLA; FHA; Hosp Aide; Chorus; Treas Church Choir; Ofcr Stu Cncl; Co-Capt Chrldng; Hon Roll; TSU; Occptnl Thrpst.

FOREMAN, ANGELA H; Bryant Sr HS; Benton, AR; (2); Church Yth Grp; English Clb; FBLA; Teachers Aide; Band; Church Choir; Color Guard; Mrchg Band; Hon Roll; Jr NHS; U AR Fayetteville; Music; Eng.

FOREMAN, TOWANNA D; Harmony Grove Jr Sr HS; Camden, AR; (2); FCA; FBLA; Natl FFA Org; Stat Bsktbl; Hon Roll; Natl Jr Beta Club; Henderson ST Univ; Cmptr Engr.

FORLINES, JAMES D; Southside HS; Batesville, AR; (2); Church Yth Grp; FBLA; Natl Beta Clb; Quiz Bowl; Band; Church Choir; Mrchg Band; Pep Band; High Hon Roll; Prfct Atten Awd; Chrch Sound Technician.

FORMBY, WINTER D; Magnolia HS; Magnolia, AR; (2); Library Aide; Pep Clb; Church Choir; Chrldng; Powder Puff Ftbl; High Hon Roll; Hon Roll; UCLA.

FORREST, AMANDA J; Valley Springs Schl; Harrison, AR; (3); Art Clb; Hist French Clb; FBLA; Key Clb; Quiz Bowl; Band; Sec Jr Cls; High Hon Roll; Rptr NHS; Prfct Atten Awd; Hmcmng Maid; Prom Cmmtte Head; Sr Schlrs Schlrshp Chllng Tm; U Of AR; Poltcl Sci.

FORREST, DAVID C; Springdale Sr HS; Springdale, AR; (2); Chorus; Hon Roll; Jr NHS.

FORSBERG, CHAILA R; Southside Schl; Damascus, AR; (1); Church Yth Grp; GAA; Natl Beta Clb; Natl FFA Org; Spanish Clb; Capt Bsktbl; Sftbl; Cit Awd; Hon Roll; Ntl Merit Ltr; Fire Marshal; Beta Club Sec; Rcvd Awd Mst Offnsv Plyr Bsktbl 95-; Bus.

FORSE, BRIAN M; Oak Grove HS; North Little Rock, AR; (2); Boy Scts; Church Yth Grp; Cmnty Wkr; FCA; FBLA; Mu Alpha Theta; Natl Beta Clb; High Hon Roll; Hon Roll; Pres Acad Fit Awd; Univ AR Fayettville; Med Field.

FORSYTH, KIM; Cabot HS; Cabot, AR; (3); 9/398; Drama Clb; French Clb; Key Clb; NFL; Quiz Bowl; Speech Tm; Thesps; School Musical; French Hon Soc; Kiwanis Awd; USS Swim Tm; PRIDE Pres; AR Gov Schl Drama; Intr Dsgn.

FORT, BROOKE E; Lonoke Jr HS; Lonoke, AR; (1); 9/133; Church Yth Grp; Science Clb; VP Stu Cncl; Bsktbl; Chrldng; High Hon Roll; NHS; Outstdng 9th Grd Stu.

FORT, HOLLY; Joe T Robinson HS; Warren, AR; (4); 11/103; Art Clb; Church Yth Grp; Cmnty Wkr; Pres DECA; Drama Clb; Treas French Clb; Natl Beta Clb; High Hon Roll; Hon Roll; NHS; Spacers; Caring Cmte; Drwng & Dsgn Awd; U Of AR.

FORTE, REANETTA M; Parkview Arts-Science HS; Little Rock, AR; (2); Church Yth Grp; FBLA; Girl Scts; Natl Beta Clb; ROTC; Spanish Clb; High Hon Roll; Hon Roll; Jr NHS; Vanderbilt; Law.

FORTENBERRY, LEAH D; Tuckerman HS; Tuckerman, AR; (2); #6 in class; Cmnty Wkr; FBLA; FHA; Rep Natl Beta Clb; Spanish Clb; SADD; VP Chorus; Church Choir; School Musical; Phtg Yrbk; AR ST Univ Jonesboro; PT.

FORTENBERRY, MARK E; Springdale Sr HS; Springdale, AR; (1); Boy Scts; Church Yth Grp; Chorus; Rep Stu Cncl; High Hon Roll; Jr NHS; Pres Acad Fit Awd; ESA Outstdng Yth Awd; Odessey Of Mind ST Team; Regnl Sci Fair; U Of Cntrl AR; PT.

FORTNER, APRIL M; Newport HS; Newport, AR; (3); FHA; JCL; Latin Clb; Church Choir; Cit Awd; Hon Roll; Princpls Awd; ABCI Outstndng Accmplshmnt; Path.

FORTNEY, JYLL; North Little Rock Hs-East; North Little Rock, AR; (3); 50/618; Art Clb; Church Yth Grp; FCA; Mu Alpha Theta; Natl Beta Clb; Q&S; Yrbk; Socr; Hon Roll; NHS; FL Southern Col; Prevet.

FORTUNE, JERRY W; Augusta HS; Augusta, AR; (1); Church Yth Grp; SADD; Ofcr Bsbl; Ftbl; Prfct Atten Awd; Beta Clb.

FOSHEE, DARBY D; Cutter Morning Star HS; Hot Springs, AR; (2); Art Clb; Church Yth Grp; FCA; FHA; Natl Beta Clb; Spanish Clb; Ofcr Soph Cls; Ofcr Stu Cncl; Bsktbl; Hon Roll.

FOSHEE, JAYME E; Jessieville HS; Hot Springs Natio, AR; (2); 1/50; Church Yth Grp; FCA; GAA; Key Clb; Natl Beta Clb; Quiz Bowl; Band; Church Choir; Mrchg Band; Pep Band; UCA; OT.

FOSTER, CHARLA; Central Ark Christian Schl; North Little Rock, AR; (4); 2/75; Church Yth Grp; FBLA; Mu Alpha Theta; Science Clb; Spanish Clb; Drill Tm; Var L Tennis; JV L Vllybl; Jr NHS; NHS; Phys Thrpy.

FOSTER, CLINT A; Swifton Schl; Swifton, AR; (3); Church Yth Grp; FBLA; Natl FFA Org; Pep Clb; Spanish Clb; Teachers Aide; Var Bsbl; Var Bsktbl; Hon Roll; Prfct Atten Awd; AR ST.

FOSTER, JOSEPH W; Mena HS; Mena, AR; (4); 32/130; Am Leg Boys St; Art Clb; Church Yth Grp; Cmnty Wkr; French Clb; FBLA; Science Clb; SADD; Varsity Clb; School Play; General Coop Ed Clbs Of Amer Pres; U Of Cntrl AR; Bus; Law.

FOSTER, JOSHUA A; Biggers-Reyno HS; Biggers, AR; (2); Art Clb; FHA; Natl FFA Org; Office Aide; Quiz Bowl; Spanish Clb; Rep Stu Cncl; Ofcr Bsbl; Bsktbl; Prfct Atten Awd; U Of Cntrl AR; PE.

FOSTER, KIM; Hatfield Schl; Mena, AR; (4); 4/25; FCA; Pres FBLA; FHA; Sec Natl Beta Clb; Office Aide; Spanish Clb; Ed Nwsp; VP Jr Cls; Sec Stu Cncl; Capt Bsktbl.

FOSTER, PRISCILLA; Hope HS; Hope, AR; (1); Church Yth Grp; FBLA; Variety Show; JV Chrldng; JV Gym; Hon Roll; U Of AR.

FOSTER, ROSEMARY L; El Dorado Sr HS; El Dorado, AR; (2); Church Yth Grp; Service Clb; Socr; NHS; Anchor Clb.

FOSTER, RUTHIE; Holly Grove HS; Holly Grove, AR; (4); 9/29; Drama Clb; English Clb; FHA; German Clb; Science Clb; Band; School Play; Stage Crew; Chrldng; Hon Roll; Reading Clb; UAPB; Tchr.

FOSTER, STEPHEN; Danville HS; Danville, AR; (1); 1/40; Church Yth Grp; Co-Capt FCA; Natl FFA Org; SADD; VP Frsh Cls; JV L Bsktbl; JV L Ftbl; JV L Trk; Hon Roll; Jr NHS; Greenhand Awd FFA; All Conf Ftbl/Bsktbl/Sr High Trck; Mr Jr; U Of AR; Fshry/Wldlf Bio.

FOSTER, STEVEN; Swifton Schl; Swifton, AR; (3); Church Yth Grp; Natl Beta Clb; Sec Natl FFA Org; Pres Frsh Cls; Rep Soph Cls; Pres Jr Cls; Pres Stu Cncl; Ofcr Bsbl; Bsktbl; Hon Roll; Prlmntry Prcdr Tm; AR ST U; Med.

FOUST, HEATHER S; Delta Special Schl; Watson, AR; (3); Art Clb; Debate Tm; Drama Clb; Math Clb; Speech Tm; Yrbk; Ofcr Jr Cls; Hon Roll; U Of AR Monticello; Scl Svc.

FOUST, SONYA D; Ridgecrest HS; Paragould, AR; (3); 72/182; Church Yth Grp; Hosp Aide; Band; Jazz Band; Mrchg Band; Tennis; Hon Roll; All Regn Band/All ST Band Jr Yr; Sci/Math/RN.

FOWLER, ANTHONY R; Hoxie Schl; Hoxie, AR; (3); 6/48; Boy Scts; Computer Clb; Drama Clb; English Clb; Natl Beta Clb; Natl FFA Org; Office Aide; Spanish Clb; Thesps; Varsity Clb; AR ST; PE.

FOWLER, CHRISTIE; Arkansas Schl Math & Science; Atkins, AR; (3); Cmnty Wkr; FBLA; Mu Alpha Theta; Natl Beta Clb; Science Clb; Ofcr Band; High Hon Roll; NHS; Prfct Atten Awd; Pres Acad Fit Awd; Spirit Of Amer Natl Hnr Bnd 95 Prfrmng Europe Tour; NASA Shrp Plus; QEM Smmr Intrnsp 96; Purdue U; Aeronautical Engrng.

FOWLER, DENNIS E; Southside HS; Fort Smith, AR; (3); 192/502; German Clb; Key Clb; Ed Nwsp; VP Frsh Cls; Hon Roll; Intl Reltns.

FOWLER, JENNIFER; Corning HS; Corning, AR; (4); Sec Church Yth Grp; Hist FBLA; VP FHA; HOBY; Thesps; Ofcr Stu Cncl; Capt Chrldng; Cmnty Wkr; Drama Clb; Sec Girl Scts; Girl Sct Gold Awd; All St Chrldr; PRIDE Tm; AR ST U; Phrmcy.

FOWLER, JON; Beebe Sr HS; Beebe, AR; (2); Natl Beta Clb; JV Ftbl; Hon Roll.

FOX, HOWARD D; Cutter Morning Star HS; Hot Springs, AR; (2); Art Clb; Spanish Clb; Certfd Scuba Diver; CHAMPS Mem; Stu Of Martial Arts; U Of AR Fayettville; Comps.

FOX, JOEL M; Jessieville Jr-Sr HS; Hot Springs, AR; (4); Pres Art Clb; Chess Clb; Church Yth Grp; Sec FCA; Key Clb; Natl Beta Clb; Teachers Aide; School Musical; Stage Crew; Var L Bsktbl; Rotary Schlrshp; Swan Lake Schl Of Taxidermy.

FOX, NATHAN A; Farmington Jr Sr HS; Farmington, AR; (3); Natl FFA Org; Ftbl; Trk; Hon Roll; FFA; Arkansas.

FOX, RONNIE M; Mills HS; Little Rock, AR; (3); Art Clb; Debate Tm; Latin Clb; Natl Beta Clb; Jazz Band; Pres Acad Fit Awd; Odyssey Of The Mind 1st Place Regnls; Painting I & II Cls Awds; UALR.

FOX, SHANE A; Southside HS; Batesville, AR; (1); #1 in class; Church Yth Grp; Natl Beta Clb; Quiz Bowl; Church Choir; Bsktbl; Cit Awd; High Hon Roll; Hon Roll; NHS; St Schlr; Church Drama; Sci Awd; Eng Awd.

FOX, WYLE P; Blevins HS; Mc Caskill, AR; (1); Art Clb; FBLA; Natl Beta Clb; Quiz Bowl; High Hon Roll; Gftd Tlntd.

FRADY, JONATHAN S; Horatio HS; Winthrop, AR; (2); FCA; Quiz Bowl; Rep Frsh Cls; Var Ftbl; JV Trk; High Hon Roll; Hon Roll; NHS; Pres Acad Fit Awd; GATE Pgm; Commercial Arts.

FRAIZE, MORGAN A; Dewitt HS; Saint Charles, AR; (1); 1/109; FBLA; Band; Color Guard; Var Sftbl; Hon Roll; Ntl Merit Ltr; Pres Acad Fit Awd; AR ST Univ; Tchr.

FRAIZE, RONALD L; Dewitt HS; Saint Charles, AR; (2); FCA; 4-H; French Clb; FBLA; Natl FFA Org; Science Clb; L Bsbl.

FRALEY, KANDACE L; Valley Springs Schl; Harrison, AR; (2); 5/66; Office Aide; Band; Mrchg Band; Pep Band; School Musical; VP Soph Cls; Hon Roll; Prfct Atten Awd; BASIC VP & Prayer Coord; Svc Awd; Coll Of The Ozarks; Tchr.

FRANCE, LENA C; Alma HS; Mountainburg, AR; (4); 2/150; French Clb; FBLA; Math Clb; Mu Alpha Theta; Teachers Aide; VP Soph Cls; High Hon Roll; VP NHS; Sal; 1st Pl Bill Of Rights Essay :AR ACLU; OK ST Univ; Vet Med.

FRANCE, LISA M; Alma HS; Mountainburg, AR; (2); Church Yth Grp; FCA; French Clb; FBLA; Quiz Bowl; Teachers Aide; JV Bsktbl; JV Var Vllybl; High Hon Roll; NHS; Pub Poet Fms Poets Soc Amer/Natl Yth Anthlgy Poetry; 17th ST Natl Fr Exm; Jrnlsm/Pre Law.

FRANCIS, ANNA; Danville HS; Danville, AR; (4); Church Yth Grp; 4-H; FBLA; FHA; Spanish Clb; Ed Nwsp; Bsktbl; Capt Chrldng; Trk; Poem Publshd In Rainbows End Anthlgy; U Of Ozarks; Jrnlsm.

FRANCIS, JINGER C; Trumann HS; Trumann, AR; (3); 2/100; Art Clb; French Clb; Intnl Clb; Math Clb; Model UN; Science Clb; Yrbk; Pres Stu Cncl; Bsktbl; Score Keeper; U Of AR; Orthpdc Srgn.

FRANCIS, JULIE; Blytheville Sr HS; Blytheville, AR; (4); 25/195; Am Leg Aux Girls St; Key Clb; Natl Beta Clb; Spanish Clb; Rep Soph Cls; Gym; Vllybl; High Hon Roll; Hon Roll; NHS; Dancing; Swim Team; Berry Coll; Nrsng.

FRANCIS, LESLEA M; Arkadelphia Sr HS; Arkadelphia, AR; (4); 25/154; DECA; FBLA; VP FHA; Natl Beta Clb; Spanish Clb; Chorus; Rep Yrbk; High Hon Roll; NHS; Badger Schlr; Henderson ST Univ.

FRANKENBERGER, LISA M; Mountain Home HS; Mountain Home, AR; (3); Pep Clb; Quiz Bowl; Spanish Clb; Mrchg Band; Pep Band; Lit Mag; JV Socr; Hon Roll; Prfct Atten Awd; U Of AR; Psychiatry.

FRANKHOUSE, AUBREY L; Russellville Sr HS; Russellville, AR; (3); Am Leg Aux Girls St; Pres Church Yth Grp; Hosp Aide; Model UN; Natl Beta Clb; VP Stu Cncl; Capt L Socr; Hon Roll; Spanish Clb; Yrbk; Model League Of Arab Sts; Renaissance Stu Ldrshp; Soc Stud Clb & Teenage Republicans FP; UT ST Univ; Pol Sci.

FRANKLIN, LATONYA; Morrilton Sr HS; Atkins, AR; (2); Church Yth Grp; FBLA; GAA; Girl Scts; Natl Beta Clb; Church Choir; Var Sftbl; Trk; Vllybl; Hon Roll; UALR; Bus Mgmt.

FRANKS, SANDRA N; Vilonia HS; Conway, AR; (2); FBLA; FHA; Spanish Clb; Hon Roll.

FRASER, BRENT D; Searcy HS; Searcy, AR; (3); 11/290; Am Leg Boys St; Church Yth Grp; Natl Beta Clb; Band; Chorus; Drm Mjr(t); Jazz Band; French Hon Soc; Gov Hon Prg Awd; NHS; All St Choir; Att Region Band & Jazz Band; Band Stu Cncl Pres & Rep; U Of AR Fayetteville; Math; Eng.

FRASER, ERIN D; Magnet Cove HS; Hot Springs Natio, AR; (3); Cmnty Wkr; FCA; JA; Office Aide; Red Cross Aide; Service Clb; Teachers Aide; Band; School Musical; Variety Show; UCA; Psych.

FRASHER, STEPHEN KEITH; Hartford Schl; Midland, AR; (3); 6/40; Natl FFA Org; Mgr(s); Hon Roll; FFA Ofcr & Judging Teams.

FRAUENTHAL, JULIE A; Springdale Sr HS; Fayetteville, AR; (1); FCA; FBLA; Chorus; Var Bsktbl; Var Trk; Hon Roll; Jr NHS; Otstndng Stdnt Of Yr; Pres Ed Awd; S Awd For Natl Jr Hnrs; Most Hstl Awd Bsktbl; Dfnsv Plyr Of Yr.

FRAZER, NICHOLAS; Gosnell Jr Sr HS; Blytheville, AR; (2); Science Clb; Teachers Aide; Bsktbl; Psych.

FRAZIER, JACQUELINE D; Fairview HS; Louann, AR; (2); Drama Clb; Spanish Clb; Church Choir; Hon Roll; Prfct Atten Awd; Spanish NHS; Southern AR U; RN.

FRAZIER, JASON C; Southside HS; Fort Smith, AR; (2); Church Yth Grp; Var Socr; High Hon Roll; NHS; Sports Medicine.

FRAZIER, KRISTY L; Mills HS; Jacksonville, AR; (2); 36/449; Drama Clb; Mu Alpha Theta; Spanish Clb; Teachers Aide; Chorus; NHS; Harding Univ.

FRAZIER, RODNEY; Fairview HS; Louann, AR; (2); Art Clb; Bus Profs of Am; Church Yth Grp; Cmnty Wkr; Drama Clb; FCA; FBLA; FTA; Key Clb; Natl FFA Org; U Of AR Pine Bluff; His.

FRAZIER, SHANNON M; Riverview HS; Floral, AR; (2); Drama Clb; FHA; Natl Beta Clb; Pep Clb; Spanish Clb; Band; Mrchg Band; Pep Band; School Play; Hon Roll; St Jude Children Hos Math-A-Thon.

FREDINBERG, DANIEL; Norfork Jr Sr HS; Calico Rock, AR; (1); Art Clb; Computer Clb; FBLA; Math Clb; Quiz Bowl; Science Clb; Var Bsktbl; High Hon Roll; Pres Schlr; Artistic Awd; Comp Dsgn.

FREDINBURG, TRICIA; Norfork Jr Sr HS; Calico Rock, AR; (3); Art Clb; English Clb; FBLA; Pres FHA; Pres Math Clb; Natl Beta Clb; Science Clb; Spanish Clb; Teachers Aide; Band; Law.

FREE, KELLY L; Cabot HS; Cabot, AR; (1); Computer Clb; Vllybl; Cit Awd; High Hon Roll; Jr NHS; Math Achvt Awd; JUST Clb; Med.

FREE, MICHELLE A; Beebe Sr HS; Beebe, AR; (3); 1/120; Am Leg Aux Girls St; Church Yth Grp; Sec VP Drama Clb; Math Clb; Natl Beta Clb; Thesps; Sec Rep Chorus; School Play; Co-Ed Yrbk; Pres Acad Fit Awd.

FREEMAN, APRIL M; Newport HS; Newport, AR; (3); Am Leg Aux Girls St; Girl Scts; Letterman Clb; Spanish Clb; Bsktbl; Mgr Ftbl; Sftbl; Cit Awd; Ntl Merit Ltr; Stu Of Week; U Of Pine Bluff.

FREEMAN, BRANDI D; Oak Grove HS; N Little Rock, AR; (2); Church Yth Grp; Drama Clb; Hosp Aide; Natl Beta Clb; Spanish Clb; Hon Roll; UCA; Bus.

FREEMAN, CATRINA; Sparkman Jr Sr HS; Sparkman, AR; (2); Church Yth Grp; FBLA; Natl Beta Clb; Spanish Clb; Church Choir; Yrbk; Sec Soph Cls; Capt Chrldng; Hon Roll; NHS; Henderson ST.

FREEMAN, EMILY S; Dardanelle HS; Dardanelle, AR; (3); Church Yth Grp; Debate Tm; Drama Clb; FCA; FBLA; Intnl Clb; Library Aide; Natl Beta Clb; Speech Tm; School Play.

FREEMAN, JAMEY A; Dover HS; Dover, AR; (2); Church Yth Grp; Spanish Clb; Bsktbl; Ftbl; Hon Roll; Med Proffe; Phys Thrpst.

FREEMAN, JENNIFER; Clarksville HS; Clarksville, AR; (1); Church Yth Grp; FCA; FBLA; Library Aide; Natl Beta Clb; Capt Chrldng; Hon Roll; PRIDE Clb; All Star Chrldng & Gymnastics; Merle Norman Cosmetics Trng Pgm Cert; U Of Tulsa; Bus Admin.

FREEMAN, JOSHUA D; Hector Jr Sr HS; Russellville, AR; (4); 1/52; Pres FBLA; Treas Natl Beta Clb; Spanish Clb; SADD; School Musical; Yrbk; High Hon Roll; NHS; Pres Acad Fit Awd; Val; Cty Teen Crt; Ar Tech U; Cmptr Sci.

FREEMAN, KARA; Jonesboro HS; Jonesboro, AR; (4); Church Yth Grp; FCA; FBLA; Key Clb; Office Aide; Acpl Chr; Chorus; Sec Frsh Cls; Treas Sec Soph Cls; Treas Jr Cls; David Lipscomb U; Dntl Hyg.

FREEMAN, KATIE; Morrilton Sr HS; Morrilton, AR; (2); Church Yth Grp; Math Clb; Science Clb; Var Bsktbl; Var Socr; Var Sftbl; Hon Roll; Beta Clb.

FREEMAN, MELINDA A; Russellville Sr HS; Russellville, AR; (3); Am Leg Aux Girls St; Church Yth Grp; FHA; Quiz Bowl; Spanish Clb; Band; Mrchg Band; Orch; Pep Band; Prfct Atten Awd; HOSA Pres; All-Stars; PT.

FREEMAN, MICHAEL; Charleston HS; Charleston, AR; (3); 3/43; Church Yth Grp; FBLA; FHA; Natl Beta Clb; Ofcr Bsbl; Bsktbl; High Hon Roll; Hon Roll; NHS; 4a Dist Plyr Of Yr JV Bsktbl; Babe Ruth St Trnmt MVP Awd; Outstndng Pitcher Awd Bsbl.

FREEMAN, NATALIE L; Mc Clellan HS; Little Rock, AR; (3); 18/288; Am Leg Aux Girls St; Cmnty Wkr; FBLA; FHA; Mu Alpha Theta; Pres Natl Beta Clb; Drill Tm; Yrbk; Vllybl; NHS; DARE Vol; HS HERO; Mktg.

FREEMAN, STEPHANIE J; Stuttgart Sr HS; Stuttgart, AR; (3); 1/200; Church Yth Grp; Rptr FBLA; Mu Alpha Theta; Quiz Bowl; Spanish Clb; Band; Mrchg Band; School Play; High Hon Roll; NHS; REACH; First United Meth Church Jubilee Ringers; Acctg.

FREESE, SUMMER; Cross Co Jr Sr HS; Hickory Ridge, AR; (3); 2/45; Church Yth Grp; Natl Beta Clb; Spanish Clb; Yrbk; Pres Frsh Cls; Rep Stu Cncl; Bsktbl; Sftbl; High Hon Roll; Gftd/Tlntd Pgm; Miss Thunderbird 94-95; Fire Marshal.

FREIBOLT, JANNA M; Arkadelphia Sr HS; Arkadelphia, AR; (4); 43/156; Church Yth Grp; Cmnty Wkr; FCA; Natl Beta Clb; Spanish Clb; Rptr Nwsp; Rep Stu Cncl; L Trk; NHS; Band; Cty Fair Qn 95; Ouachita Bapt U; Scl Sci.

FREIN, KRISTINA; Brinkley HS; Brinkley, AR; (4); Am Leg Aux Girls St; Sec Church Yth Grp; Drama Clb; French Clb; Library Aide; Office Aide; Rep Science Clb; Teachers Aide; Band; Chorus; Sweethrt Pagnt Clss Rep 95-96; Homcmng Maid 95; Jrnlsm Edtr In Chief; EACC; Psych.

FRENCH, APRIL; Rison HS; Rison, AR; (2); 1/54; FCA; French Clb; GAA; Letterman Clb; Ofcr Soph Cls; Bsktbl; Crs Cntry; Sftbl; Trk; High Hon Roll; Athltc Trng.

FRENCH, KAWANNACA J; Arkansas Sr HS; Texarkana, AR; (3); Church Yth Grp; Pres 4-H; Mu Alpha Theta; Church Choir; Mgr Bsktbl; Mgr(s); Mgr Trk; Mgr Vllybl; Cit Awd; DAR Awd; Pep Squad Capt; PRIDE; FCS & FHA Acad Awds; Phys Therapy.

FRENCH, LAURI M; Mayflower HS; Mayflower, AR; (2); Church Yth Grp; HOBY; Natl Beta Clb; Yrbk; VP Soph Cls; Var Bsktbl; Var Sftbl; Ath Coach.

FRENCH, NICK R; St Paul Schl; Combs, AR; (1); FHA; Ofcr Bsbl; Bsktbl; Trk; Annapolis; Navy.

FRENCH, TIARA; Walker Schl; Magnolia, AR; (2); 7/22; Sec Drama Clb; FHA; Science Clb; Chorus; Church Choir; Sec Stu Cncl; Capt Chrldng; Trk; Hon Roll; Upward Bound.

FRENCH, TIFFANY M; Arkansas Sr HS; Texarkana, AR; (3); Church Yth Grp; Girl Scts; Library Aide; Band; Mrchg Band; Ofcr Frsh Cls; Ofcr Stu Cncl; U Of AR Conway; Bus Mgmt.

FRETHEIM, AMY; Chaffin Jr HS; Fort Smith, AR; (1); Church Yth Grp; FCA; Chorus; Bsktbl; Co-Capt Chrldng; Vllybl; Hon Roll; Jr NHS; Pres Acad Fit Awd; Mxd Chorus; Grls Quartet; U Of Cntrl AR; Phys Thrp.

FRETHEIM, TODD; Southside HS; Fort Smith, AR; (4); 76/459; Church Yth Grp; FCA; French Clb; Key Clb; Ftbl; Hon Roll; Pres Acad Fit Awd; AR Tech Univ; Bus.

FRIDDLE, CODY; Southside HS; Fort Smith, AR; (2); Church Yth Grp; FCA; Office Aide; SADD; Variety Show; Rep Frsh Cls; Rep Soph Cls; Rep Stu Cncl; L Bsktbl; Var Socr; Mayors Cncl On Yth Crime Convntn; Stu Cncl Pres Elect.

FRIEDLANDER, WHITNEY B; Parkview Arts-Science HS; Little Rock, AR; (2); 13/430; Dance Clb; Debate Tm; Drama Clb; FBLA; Natl Beta Clb; Speech Tm; Hist VP Temple Yth Grp; School Musical; School Play; Rep Frsh Cls; Peer Helpers; UCLA; Theatre.

FRIEND, BENJAMIN A; Flippin Jr Sr HS; Flippin, AR; (3); Boy Scts; Drama Clb; FBLA; German Clb; Natl FFA Org; Teachers Aide; School Play; Rep Frsh Cls; Rep Soph Cls; Rep Jr Cls; Eagle Scout; FL ST.

FRITS, CHRISTY A; Conway Sr HS; Conway, AR; (2); 104/540; Church Yth Grp; FBLA; Natl Beta Clb; Office Aide; Q&S; Yrbk; Hon Roll; Hnr Amer Schlr; Elem Ed.

FRITSCHIE, SETH W; Alma HS; Alma, AR; (2); FCA; Spanish Clb; Rep Soph Cls; Ofcr Stu Cncl; Bsktbl; Tennis; Hon Roll; NHS.

FRITTS, BRIAN D; Bald Knob HS; Bald Knob, AR; (3); 27/121; Natl Beta Clb; Spanish Clb; Band; Jazz Band; Mrchg Band; Pep Band; Yrbk; Hon Roll; Demolays.

FRITTS, LA TEESHA; Bald Knob HS; Bald Knob, AR; (2); Pres Art Clb; FBLA; Natl Beta Clb; Spanish Clb; Sec Frsh Cls; Ofcr Stu Cncl; JV Var Chrldng; Hon Roll; Soph Hmcmng Maid.

FRIX, KATIE M; Russellville Sr HS; Russellville, AR; (3); Church Yth Grp; Cmnty Wkr; Band; Chorus; Church Choir; Mrchg Band; Orch; Hon Roll; Jr NHS; NHS; Nrsng Home Vol; Sunday Schl Tchr; Dntl Hygenist; Phy Thrpst.

FRIZZELL, JEFF D; Clarksville HS; Clarksville, AR; (2); Cmnty Wkr; Letterman Clb; Varsity Clb; Var Bsbl; Var Ftbl; Var Wt Lftg; ATU; Wildlife Bio.

FRIZZELL, JOSALYN D; Dover HS; Vilonia, AR; (4); Church Yth Grp; Cmnty Wkr; FCA; FBLA; FHA; GAA; Library Aide; Natl Beta Clb; Teachers Aide; School Play; Numerous Poetry Awds; Awds For Helping Handicaped Stus; U Of A; Phy Thrpy.

FROEHLICH, CARRIE L; Russellville Sr HS; Russellville, AR; (2); Pres Church Yth Grp; Red Cross Aide; Band; Mrchg Band; Pep Band; Piano; Chrch Daycare; Govt Pol; Music.

FROMAN, JASON J; Mc Crory Jr Sr HS; Mc Crory, AR; (3); FBLA; FTA; Spanish Clb; Ftbl; Golf; Trk; Wt Lftg; Hon Roll; Bus.

FROMM, KEVIN; Little Rock Cntrl HS; Little Rock, AR; (4); Boy Scts; CAP; German Clb; Intnl Clb; Key Clb; Quiz Bowl; Science Clb; Hon Roll; NHS; Eagle Sct; Gen Billy Mitchell Awd & Cadet Ofcr Schl; Fencing & Rifle Shooting; West Point; Military; His.

FRONTERHOUSE, JESSICA D; West Fork HS; West Fork, AR; (3); Chorus; High Hon Roll; Hon Roll; Workplace Readiness, Child Dev, Acad Achvmt, Keyboarding & Geom Awds; Massage Thrpst; Biling Tchr.

FROST, GABE J; Springdale Sr HS; Lowell, AR; (4); 56/512; Art Clb; FCA; FBLA; FHA; Key Clb; JV Var Ftbl; Powder Puff Ftbl; JV Var Trk; Var L Wt Lftg; High Hon Roll; UCA; Bus.

FROST, JOSHUA L; Lee Acad; Marianna, AR; (2); Church Yth Grp; Church Choir; Var L Ftbl; Hon Roll; NHS; Fire Marshall; Evangel Coll.

FROST, PRISCILLA; Hatfield Schl; Mena, AR; (4); 6/14; Sec FBLA; Sec FHA; Natl Beta Clb; Nwsp; Yrbk; Pres Frsh Cls; Pres Soph Cls; VP Jr Cls; VP Sr Cls; Bsktbl; Early Grad; Rich Mountain CC; Bus.

FROST, TIFFANY M; Mena HS; Mena, AR; (3); French Clb; FBLA; SADD; Band; Flag Corp; Mrchg Band; Yrbk; French Hon Soc; Cptn Of Flgln; Cncrt Bnd; U Of AR; Tchng.

FROYCK, JAREN E; Mountain Home HS; Mountain Home, AR; (3); 14/267; Church Yth Grp; Quiz Bowl; Spanish Clb; Teachers Aide; Chorus; Ed Yrbk; Powder Puff Ftbl; High Hon Roll; Pres Acad Fit Awd; Interact Clb; Stu Chrstn Assn; Praise & Worship Band Singer; VBS Ldr; Sunday Schl Tchr; Music; Commnctn.

FRY, BRADLEY; Clay Co Central Jr Sr HS; Greenway, AR; (3); 4/65; Church Yth Grp; FBLA; German Clb; Model UN; Science Clb; Chorus; School Play; Yrbk; VP Frsh Cls; Rep Soph Cls; AR ST U Jonesboro; Acctng.

FRY, KARRIE E; Siloam Springs Sr HS; Siloam Springs, AR; (3); Church Yth Grp; FCA; Key Clb; Natl Beta Clb; Band; Color Guard; L Tennis; Hon Roll; NHS; Prfct Atten Awd; John Brown U; Phys Thrpy.

FRY, KRISTIN L; Nevada Schl; Emmet, AR; (1); FBLA; Band; Hon Roll; Tlnt Srch; Vet Sci.

FRY, MARCUS L; Mountain Pine Jr Sr HS; Hot Springs Natio, AR; (2); French Clb; Ofcr Bsbl; Ftbl; Hon Roll.

FRYAR, AMBER L; Mt Ida Jr Sr HS; Pencil Bluff, AR; (2); Church Yth Grp; Cmnty Wkr; FBLA; FHA; GAA; Natl Beta Clb; Church Choir; School Play; Stage Crew; Bsktbl; Eng Merit Awd; Gratitude/Thanky Ou Awds; Best Seller Fundrsrs Letters/Awds; UCA; PT.

FRYAR, CANDI; Caddo Hills Jr Sr HS; Glenwood, AR; (3); FCA; FBLA; Pres FHA; Natl Beta Clb; Spanish Clb; School Play; Sec Frsh Cls; Sec Jr Cls; Mgr(s); Sftbl; Scndry Tchr.

FRYAR, CHRISTINA M; Rogers HS; Rogers, AR; (3); 10/500; Church Yth Grp; Library Aide; Model UN; Natl FFA Org; Spanish Clb; Teachers Aide; Chorus; Church Choir; High Hon Roll; NHS; Atten Math Modeling Aegis Pgm; Chrch Acteens; Future Problem Solving Cmptns Regnl & St; Acctng; CPA.

FRYAR, HASKELL K; Fountain Lake Jr Sr HS; Hot Springs Natio, AR; (2); Varsity Clb; Ftbl; Hon Roll; Art.

FRYAR, LETHA G; Bauxite Jr Sr HS; Bauxite, AR; (1); Cmnty Wkr; GAA; Drill Tm; Ed Nwsp; Pres Frsh Cls; High Hon Roll; Jr NHS; Pres Acad Fit Awd; Office Aide; Teachers Aide; Miner Herald Ed; Law; Jrnlsm.

FRYAR, MISCHELLE; Lake Hamilton Sr HS; Royal, AR; (4); 2/279; Cmnty Wkr; 4-H; Rptr FBLA; Pres Natl Beta Clb; Sec Natl FFA Org; Q&S; Science Clb; Ed Yrbk; Rep Stu Cncl; Rptr NHS; St FFA Prepared Spkng Wnnr; Natl Semi-Fnlst Extemp Pblc Spkng; U Of AR Fayetteville; Ag Comm.

FRYE, CHRISTINA R; Scotland Schl; Scotland, AR; (2); FBLA; FHA; GAA; Bsktbl; Hon Roll.

FRYE, ERICA J; Cutter Morning Star HS; Hot Springs, AR; (2); Art Clb; FBLA; FHA; Spanish Clb.

FRYER, DAVIN M; Crossett Sr HS; Crossett, AR; (2); Church Yth Grp; Band; Hon Roll; Pres Acad Fit Awd; Beta Clb; Love Cmptr.

FRYER, JERRY D; Ozark HS; Ozark, AR; (3); 8/110; Church Yth Grp; FCA; FBLA; Natl Beta Clb; Quiz Bowl; Chorus; Yrbk; VP Soph Cls; Rep Jr Cls; Rep Stu Cncl; Aviation.

FUENTES, MARIA E; Smackover HS; Camden, AR; (1); 13/69; Dance Clb; Spanish Clb; JV Bsktbl; JV Co-Capt Chrldng; Trk; START Clb; U Of A Fayetteville; RN.

FUGITT, CHERYL D; Nashville Sr HS; Murfreesboro, AR; (3); 8/130; Am Leg Aux Girls St; Church Yth Grp; FBLA; FHA; Spanish Clb; School Play; Nwsp; Yrbk; Ofcr Soph Cls; Ofcr Jr Cls.

FULKERSON, TONYA; Pangburn Jr Sr HS; Heber Springs, AR; (3); Church Yth Grp; Drama Clb; FBLA; Office Aide; ROTC; Color Guard; School Play; Hon Roll; Ed.

FULLER, JARED C; Dewitt HS; De Witt, AR; (2); 1/80; Church Yth Grp; FCA; French Clb; FBLA; Library Aide; Office Aide; Science Clb; Var Bsbl; Var Ftbl; JV Trk.

FULLER, KARONDA R; John L Mcclellan Magnet HS; Little Rock, AR; (2); Church Yth Grp; FBLA; Mu Alpha Theta; Natl Beta Clb; Nwsp; Yrbk; Bsktbl; Cit Awd; Hon Roll; NHS; Howard; Cmptr Sci.

FULLER, MICHELLE; Atkins Schl; Atkins, AR; (4); #10 in class; Church Yth Grp; FBLA; Natl Beta Clb; Flag Corp; Art Clb; Drama Clb; Science Clb; Spanish Clb; Teachers Aide; Band; Reach-Out Pres; 4th AR Future Bus Ldrs Amer Comp Acctng II; Awd Outstndng Bus Stu 95-; AR Tech Univ; Fin Analyst.

FULLER, OCTAVIA S; Mills HS; Maumelle, AR; (3); Am Leg Aux Girls St; Cmnty Wkr; FBLA; Latin Clb; Natl Beta Clb; Science Clb; Orch; FTA; Spanish Clb; Futr 500 Med Clb; Minrty Mntr Clb; Proj WET; Soc Stds Clb Secy; Pre-Law.

FULLER, ROSHUNDA D; Smackover HS; Smackover, AR; (4); 14/45; Pres Church Yth Grp; FBLA; Spanish Clb; Band; Pres Church Choir; Mrchg Band; VP Soph Cls; L Bsktbl; Powder Puff Ftbl; Var Tennis; Anchr Clb; BSA; Ntrl Hlpr; U Of AR Pine Bluff; Law.

FULLER, SHANEIL C; Conway Sr HS; Conway, AR; (4); 30/524; Church Yth Grp; Cmnty Wkr; FBLA; FTA; Hosp Aide; JA; Natl Beta Clb; Spanish Clb; Church Choir; High Hon Roll; Faulkner Cnty Yth Ldshp Inst Grad; All Star Staff; U Of AR; Bus Mgnt.

FULLER, TIFFANY A; Russellville Sr HS; Russellville, AR; (3); Church Yth Grp; Drama Clb; French Clb; Teachers Aide; Chorus; School Musical; Stage Crew; High Hon Roll; Jr NHS; NHS; Cyclone Achv Awd; AR Tech Univ.

FULLERTON, SAMUEL D; Leslie Schl; Leslie, AR; (2); Chess Clb; 4-H; FBLA; Key Clb; Natl Beta Clb; Band; Phtg Yrbk; Pres Frsh Cls; Pres Soph Cls; Cit Awd; Art/Zoology.

FULLMER, MELISSA D; Gravette HS; Gravette, AR; (3); 6/80; FCA; Rep FBLA; GAA; Varsity Clb; Var L Bsktbl; Var Powder Puff Ftbl; Var Sftbl; Var L Trk; Hon Roll; NHS.

FULMER, BRUCE; Charleston HS; Charleston, AR; (1); FBLA; Spanish Clb; Ofcr Bsbl; Ftbl; Trk; Wt Lftg; Hon Roll; U Of AR.

FULMER, MELISSA S; Russellville Sr HS; Russellville, AR; (3); Hosp Aide; VICA; Band; Mrchg Band; Pep Band; Boy/Girls Club Sftbl; Vol AR Dept Hum Svc; AR Muzzle Loading Assc; ITT Tech Inst; Drftng.

FULMER, SAMUEL M; Cabot HS; Cabot, AR; (1); JV Bsktbl; High Hon Roll; Jr NHS; NHS; Prfct Atten Awd; Pres Acad Fit Awd; Ouachita Bapt.

FULMER, TONI; Rose Bud Jr Sr HS; Quitman, AR; (3); 4/37; FBLA; FHA; Natl Beta Clb; Natl FFA Org; Nwsp; Yrbk; Sec Frsh Cls; Pres Soph Cls; Ofcr Stu Cncl; Ortho.

FULTON, VERNA; East Poinsett Sr HS; Rivervale, AR; (4); 12/60; FHA; Teachers Aide; Hon Roll; Jr NHS; NHS; Prfct Atten Awd; Coll Of Ozarks.

FULTS, AMY; Redfield Jr HS; Redfield, AR; (1); Cmnty Wkr; Ed Nwsp; Yrbk; Pres Stu Cncl; Bsktbl; Capt Chrldng; Sftbl; Pres Acad Fit Awd; UCA All-Star 3 Consectve Yrs.

FULWIDER, ANGELA N; Springdale Sr HS; Springdale, AR; (2); Debate Tm; French Clb; Model UN; Science Clb; Band; Color Guard; High Hon Roll; NHS; All Region Band 1st Chair; Contra Clarinet; Shakespeare Festvl; All City Sci Fair 2nd Pl, Regnl Qualfr.

FUNDERBURG, JOHN D; Hughes Jr-Sr HS; Hughes, AR; (2); Spanish Clb; Ftbl; Spnsh Awd; ASU; Engrng.

FUNK, BECKY A; Clarksville HS; Lamar, AR; (2); Church Yth Grp; Ofcr 4-H; FBLA; Natl Beta Clb; Chorus; Yrbk; Var L Crs Cntry; L Trk; 4-H Awd; High Hon Roll.

FUNK, MISTY; Newark Jr Sr HS; Newark, AR; (2); Church Yth Grp; 4-H; HOBY; Speech Tm; Church Choir; Mrchg Band; Pep Band; School Play; Pres Soph Cls; 4-H Awd; Band & Acad Awds; Pre-Law.

FURDGE, HOLLY; Central HS; West Helena, AR; (4); 1/200; French Clb; Math Tm; Office Aide; Teachers Aide; High Hon Roll; Kiwanis Awd; NHS; Prfct Atten Awd; Pres Schlr; Val; US Marine Corps Schol Exc Awd; Tandy Tech Schol; Pres Ed Awds Prog; AR St Univ; Bio Sci.

FUREIGH, AMANDA K; Russellville Sr HS; London, AR; (3); Church Yth Grp; Spanish Clb; Band; Multi-Yr Listee; AZ Tech Univ; Interior Design.

FURGASON, TODD; Siloam Springs Sr HS; Gentry, AR; (4); 1/160; Natl Beta Clb; Band; Church Choir; Mrchg Band; Orch; Pep Band; Gov Hon Prg Awd; High Hon Roll; NHS; Prfct Atten Awd; Jr Exec Bank Bd; U Of AR; Arch.

FURLOW, LINDSAY; Beebe Sr HS; Beebe, AR; (2); 54/139; Church Yth Grp; FBLA; FHA; Spanish Clb; Sec Soph Cls; Chrldng; FBLA Treas; AR ST; Phys Thrpy.

FURMAN, AMANDA R; Northside HS; Fort Smith, AR; (4); Church Yth Grp; Office Aide; Spanish Clb; Teachers Aide; Chorus; Church Choir; Variety Show; Hon Roll; Westark Comm Coll; Oral Roberts.

FURR, BOBBY A; Fountain Lake Jr Sr HS; Lonsdale, AR; (3); Church Yth Grp; Natl Beta Clb; Natl FFA Org; Quiz Bowl; Spanish Clb; Var Bsktbl; Var Ftbl; Var Tennis; Hon Roll; NHS; Henderson ST U; Med.

FURR, JAMI M; Arkansas Sr HS; Texarkana, AR; (3); 83/331; Church Yth Grp; Cmnty Wkr; FTA; Spanish Clb; Teachers Aide; Band; Drm Mjr(t); Mrchg Band; Nwsp; Mst Outstndg Engl Stu 94-95; All-Regn 1st Div 93-94 & 95-96; All-St Band Alt 94-95 & 95-96; Southern AR U; Elem Ed.

FURR, KEYONNA; Parkview Arts-Science HS; Little Rock, AR; (3); Pres Church Yth Grp; Pres 4-H; Pres FBLA; Natl Beta Clb; Teachers Aide; Nwsp; Rep Frsh Cls; Mgr Bsktbl; Mgr(s); Score Keeper; Comp Sci; Bus Admin.

FURR, LINDSEY; Hampton Jr Sr HS; Hampton, AR; (3); 1/68; HOBY; Natl Beta Clb; Natl FFA Org; Yrbk; Tennis; Hon Roll; NHS; Pres Acad Fit Awd; Chrch Yth Grp; Harding U; Psych.

FUSTON, GINA R; Mc Rae Schl; Mc Rae, AR; (3); Prfct Atten Awd; Stu Of Mnth 3 Times; Russian Club; Jrnlsm; Awd For Achv In Abc II; Awd For Achv Clthing; Elem Rsrc Tchr/Kndrgrtn.

GABBARD, KELLYE; Farmington Jr Sr HS; Fayetteville, AR; (1); Band; Jazz Band; Mrchg Band; Hon Roll; All Reg Band; Med.

GABBERT, MELINDA D; Rogers HS; Rogers, AR; (3); 57/585; FCA; Key Clb; Letterman Clb; SADD; Teachers Aide; JV Capt Bsktbl; Var Capt Sftbl; Trk; Hon Roll; Prfct Atten Awd; Bus Mgmt.

GABRIEL, ANTHONY K; Yellville Summit HS; Yellville, AR; (2); Art Clb; Computer Clb; 4-H; Pres Natl FFA Org; Teachers Aide; Band; Jazz Band; Mrchg Band; Pep Band; 4-H Awd; Showing Cattle Overall Grand Champ Red Poll Heifer AR ST Fair; Eng Hons; Northern IL Univ; Drafting/Cad.

GABRIEL, BRANDON J; Sylvan Hills HS; Sherwood, AR; (2); 54/300; FCA; Spanish Clb; Bsktbl; Ftbl; Hon Roll; All Region Choir; Amer Legn Bsbl; Unif Of AR.

GABRIEL, WILLIAM; Parkview Arts-Science HS; North Little Rock, AR; (2); Math Clb; Natl Beta Clb; Teachers Aide; Var Ftbl; Var Trk; Var Wt Lftg; High Hon Roll; Jr NHS.

GACK, BRIAN; Cty Line HS; Ratcliff, AR; (4); 1/35; Am Leg Boys St; VP 4-H; HOBY; Sec Natl Beta Clb; Quiz Bowl; Rptr Band; Pep Band; School Play; Ed Yrbk; Pres Soph Cls; AR Prpl Ccrcl Clb; Westartk CC; Anml Sci.

GADBERRY III, CARROLL E; Forrest City HS; Forrest City, AR; (1); Boy Scts; Church Yth Grp; CAP; Teachers Aide; Band; Hon Roll; Prfct Atten Awd; August 95 Achvd Rank Of Eagle Sct; Pilot.

GAGE, CHRISTY; Harmony Grove Jr Sr HS; Camden, AR; (3); 3/50; Am Leg Aux Girls St; Church Yth Grp; Drama Clb; Natl Beta Clb; Science Clb; Spanish Clb; Band; Chorus; Flag Corp; Mrchg Band; UALR; Pediatrcs.

GAINES, MELISSA; Arkansas City Schl; Arkansas City, AR; (3); Art Clb; French Clb; FHA; Library Aide; Pep Clb; Science Clb; Nwsp; Yrbk; Cit Awd; U Of Little Rock; Pediatrician.

GAIRHAN, THOMAS S; Trumann HS; Trumann, AR; (3); Am Leg Boys St; VP Science Clb; Spanish Clb; VP Stu Cncl; Var L Bsbl; Var L Bsktbl; Var L Ftbl; Hon Roll; NHS; CIA; U Of AR; Pre-Med.

GALDAMEZ, JUAN E; Crossett Sr HS; Crossett, AR; (2); 1/300; Art Clb; Sec French Clb; Mu Alpha Theta; Science Clb; Sec Spanish Clb; French Hon Soc; Hon Roll; Mst Awds Given Hghst Grd Each Individual Cls; Learned Eng Lang 6 Months; Pediatrician.

GALDAMEZ, KENIA L; Crossett Sr HS; Crossett, AR; (2); Art Clb; Church Yth Grp; French Clb; Science Clb; Cit Awd; Hon Roll.

GALGANI, SAMANTHA; Lakeside HS; Hot Springs, AR; (4); Sec Art Clb; FCA; Office Aide; Spanish Clb; Chorus; Hon Roll; Outstdng Achvmnt Awd; Cmptrs/Reading Books; Henderson ST Univ; Psych.

GALLAGHER, RACHEL E; Alma HS; Alma, AR; (3); Debate Tm; Drama Clb; French Clb; FBLA; Nwsp; Lit Mag; High Hon Roll; Hon Roll; Coll Lit Prof.

GALLEGLY, JASON C; North Little Rock Hs-West; North Little Rock, AR; (4); 72/439; Drama Clb; FCA; Mu Alpha Theta; Natl Beta Clb; Service Clb; School Play; Stage Crew; Rptr Nwsp; Var L Socr; Hon Roll; Octagon Club; Hendrix; Pre-Vet/Zllgy.

GALLEGOS, LYDIA; Hall Sr HS; Little Rock, AR; (3); 26/285; Church Yth Grp; Cmnty Wkr; FBLA; Natl Beta Clb; Pep Clb; Spanish Clb; Yrbk; Ofcr Sr Cls; Ofcr Stu Cncl; Var Chrldng; Little Rock Outstdnt Comm Svc Awd; Supt Stdnt Cbnt; Bus Mngmt/Admin.

GALLEGOS, TINA M; Jacksonville HS; Jacksonville, AR; (2); Church Yth Grp; FBLA; FTA; Spanish Clb; Teachers Aide; Band; Church Choir; Mrchg Band; Comm Sftbl; UMAS Med Schl; RN.

GALLOWAY, ANNIE; Southside HS; Fort Smith, AR; (4); 124/442; Church Yth Grp; FBLA; Hosp Aide; Key Clb; Natl Beta Clb; Service Clb; Spanish Clb; Drill Tm; Nwsp; Sftbl; Westark; Comp Sci.

GALLOWAY, ROSEMARY J; Southside HS; Alma, AR; (3); 24/500; Am Leg Aux Girls St; Mu Alpha Theta; Quiz Bowl; Acpl Chr; Chorus; Rep Jr Cls; Chrldng; High Hon Roll; NHS; Spanish NHS; Comm Theater; UCA; Med.

GALLOWAY, WILLIAM R; Texarkana AR Sr High; Texarkana, AR; (3); 2/373; Am Leg Boys St; FCA; FBLA; Key Clb; Math Clb; Spanish Clb; Rep Stu Cncl; JV Bsbl; Bsktbl; Ftbl; AR Schlr Ath Natl Ftbl Fndtn & Coll Hall Of Fame; Wendys Heisman Awd.

GALUCKI, KATHLEEN; Cabot HS; Cabot, AR; (3); 12/398; Art Clb; Church Yth Grp; Teachers Aide; Hon Roll; Jr NHS; NHS; Pres Acad Fit Awd; Marine Bio.

GALYEAN, BRANDY; Piggott HS; Piggott, AR; (4); 24/70; Cmnty Wkr; French Clb; FBLA; FHA; Key Clb; Letterman Clb; Natl FFA Org; Office Aide; Pep Clb; Red Cross Aide; Barlow Schlsp; Black River Tech Coll; Bus.

GAMBILL, BETHANY K; Nettleton HS; Jonesboro, AR; (3); 1/116; Am Leg Aux Girls St; Church Yth Grp; French Clb; Math Clb; Natl Beta Clb; Nwsp; Powder Puff Ftbl; Tennis; Vllybl; Hon Roll.

GAMMAGE, DAMON H; Nevada Schl; Prescott, AR; (3); Art Clb; Boy Scts; Church Yth Grp; FBLA; Teachers Aide; Band; Rep Stu Cncl; Ofcr Bsbl; Capt Bsktbl; Trk; U Of Cntrl AR.

GAMMILL, HELEN; Hazen Jr Sr HS; Hazen, AR; (2); #1 in class; VP Church Yth Grp; FBLA; Rptr FTA; HOBY; Natl Beta Clb; Ofcr Soph Cls; Co-Ed Chrldng; Sftbl; Hon Roll; U Of AR Fayetteville.

GANN, AMANDA; Beebe Sr HS; Beebe, AR; (3); 24/127; Church Yth Grp; Drama Clb; FHA; HOBY; Library Aide; Natl Beta Clb; Pep Clb; Spanish Clb; Teachers Aide; Thesps; U AR Fyttville; Theatre.

GANN, MELISSA A; Williford HS; Mammoth Spring, AR; (2); 2/25; Drama Clb; FBLA; FHA; GAA; Natl Beta Clb; Quiz Bowl; Scholastic Bowl; JV Var Bsktbl; Var Sftbl; JV Trk.

GANNAWAY, AMY; Arkansas Bapt Schl; Little Rock, AR; (2); Church Yth Grp; FBLA; Natl Beta Clb; Bsktbl; High Hon Roll; Pres Acad Fit Awd.

GANNAWAY, LAURA R; Magnolia HS; Magnolia, AR; (3); 1/200; Church Yth Grp; FCA; FBLA; Mu Alpha Theta; Science Clb; Band; Church Choir; Mrchg Band; Pep Band; Bsktbl; PRIDE; U Of Cntrl AR.

GANT, MARQUAN C; Smackover HS; Smackover, AR; (2); FBLA; Office Aide; JV Bsbl; Bsktbl; Ftbl; Bsbl & Bsktbl Card Collector; Electronic Engr.

GARCIA, ANGEL; Rison HS; Rison, AR; (4); 2/54; Church Yth Grp; FCA; Sec FBLA; Sec Natl Beta Clb; Pep Clb; Co-Capt Chrldng; Sftbl; DAR Awd; Gov Hon Prg Awd; Hon Roll; Pines Tech Coll; Bus Mgmt.

GARCIA, JULIE; Lake Hamilton Sr HS; Royal, AR; (4); #29 in class; Treas Church Yth Grp; Cmnty Wkr; Pres 4-H; FBLA; Natl Beta Clb; Spanish Clb; Chorus; Bsktbl; NHS; Pres Acad Fit Awd; Acteens; Wolf Pride Pres; Henderson ST U; RN.

GARCIA, MISSY J; Huttig Schl; Huttig, AR; (1); Church Yth Grp; FTA; GAA; Science Clb; Church Choir; Ofcr Frsh Cls; Bsktbl; Sftbl; Crdt From Southark; Southark; Cmptr Prgrmr.

GARDNER, CLINTON B; Hughes Jr-Sr HS; Hughes, AR; (1); Church Yth Grp; Cmnty Wkr; Band; Mrchg Band; Ofcr Bsbl; Tennis; Hon Roll; Yale.

GARDNER, MISHA; Van Buren Sr HS; Van Buren, AR; (4); Am Leg Aux Girls St; Art Clb; Nwsp; Ed Yrbk; Rep Frsh Cls; VP Soph Cls; Rep Jr Cls; Rep Sr Cls; Ofcr Stu Cncl; Pom Pon; Photo; U Of AR; Photo Jrnlsm.

GARDNER, WENDY M; Hermitage Jr Sr HS; Hermitage, AR; (2); 5/54; Natl Beta Clb; Natl FFA Org; Band; Mrchg Band; School Musical; 4-H Awd; Hon Roll; Prfct Atten Awd; HOBY; HOBY Crew; Sr HS His Aw:aegis Pgm At Lyon Coll; Pediatrician.

GARDNER, WILLIAM T; Hermitage Jr Sr HS; Hermitage, AR; (3); Natl FFA Org; Ofcr Jr Cls; Ofcr Bsbl; Ftbl; Wt Lftg; Hon Roll; Ntl Merit Ltr; Comp Graphics.

GARISON, GENNY; Mc Gehee HS; Mc Gehee, AR; (4); 6/104; Art Clb; Church Yth Grp; VP Pres FBLA; FTA; Mu Alpha Theta; VP Pres Natl Beta Clb; Science Clb; Spanish Clb; Rep Stu Cncl; Capt Chrldng; NE LA Univ; Med.

GARLAND, SARA D; Corning HS; Corning, AR; (1); #1 in class; Sec Drama Clb; Capt Quiz Bowl; Spanish Clb; Band; Jazz Band; Mrchg Band; Pep Band; School Play; High Hon Roll; Sec Jr NHS; Frosh Rep Band/Jr High All Rgn Band/All Rgn Jazz Band; 1st Pl Rgnl Odyssey Of Mind; U Of AR; Radio/TV Brdcstng.

GARMAN, TYLER; Rogers HS; Rogers, AR; (4); FBLA; Ofcr Stu Cncl; Ftbl; Trk; High Hon Roll; NHS; All-Conf, All-St, H M All-Amer Ftbl; Jr Exec Trng Pres; Bank Bd Pres; U Of AR; Bus.

GARNER, ANTHONY R; Newport HS; Bradford, AR; (2); Quiz Bowl; ROTC; Hon Roll; Prfct Atten Awd.

GARNER, CHRISTOPHER L; Fouke Jr Sr HS; Fouke, AR; (2); Chess Clb; Sec Natl FFA Org; Hon Roll; Pres Acad Fit Awd; Rankd 1st Dist Hrs Judgng, 10th Pl St; Sec FFA; Rodeo Tm; Livestck Jdgng Tm; Tm Ropng; Frstry Tm; UAR; Bus Ownr.

GARNER, EMILY A; Booneville Jr Sr HS; Booneville, AR; (2); Church Yth Grp; French Clb; Nwsp; Yrbk; Bsktbl; Tennis.

GARNER, GINA; Cabot HS; Cabot, AR; (3); 10/398; Church Yth Grp; Rptr French Clb; Key Clb; NFL; Chorus; Church Choir; School Musical; French Hon Soc; High Hon Roll; NHS; All Reg Choir; Natl Hnrs Choiir; 1st Plce Duet At St Fornscs Tnmt; Intl Bus.

GARNER, JOCYLIN Y; Kirby HS; Kirby, AR; (4); 6/32; Pres FBLA; FHA; VP Natl Beta Clb; Natl FFA Org; Spanish Clb; Nwsp; Ed Yrbk; Pres Stu Cncl; Bsktbl; Crs Cntry; Garland County CC; Bus.

GARNER, JOHN E; Mc Crory Jr Sr HS; Patterson, AR; (2); Art Clb; Church Yth Grp; Cmnty Wkr; Letterman Clb; Spanish Clb; School Play; Rep Stu Cncl; L Golf; L Trk; L Ftbl; U Of AR.

GARNER, JOHN W; Ft Smith Christian Schl; Fort Smith, AR; (1); Church Yth Grp; FCA; Red Cross Aide; Church Choir; Cit Awd; Hon Roll; Bible Quiz St Champ 94-95.

GARNER, KATE; Lake Hamilton Sr HS; Hot Springs, AR; (3); 53/275; Drama Clb; 4-H; FBLA; German Clb; Natl Beta Clb; VP Natl FFA Org; Thesps; School Musical; School Play; Stage Crew; Washington & Lee Univ; Bus.

GARRARD, BRANDY; Rose Bud Jr Sr HS; Rose Bud, AR; (4); 3/38; Am Leg Aux Girls St; VP Pres FHA; HOBY; Natl Beta Clb; Ed Yrbk; Sec Sr Cls; Var Bsktbl; Var Sftbl; Hmcmng Queen; U Cntrl AR; Occuptnl Thrpy.

GARRETT, ANTHONY D; Alma HS; Alma, AR; (3); Church Yth Grp; Math Clb; Mu Alpha Theta; Science Clb; Teachers Aide; Acpl Chr; Chorus; School Musical; Golf; Hon Roll; Call Of Acceptance For AR Schl Of Math & Sci; Mst Imprvd Male Choir Stu; 3rd Place Schl Sci Fair; Westark; HS Algebra Tchr.

GARRETT, BRITTNEY D; Conway Sr HS; Conway, AR; (3); Church Yth Grp; French Clb; FBLA; Hosp Aide; Natl Beta Clb; French Hon Soc; High Hon Roll; Pre-Med.

GARRETT, CHRISTY; Central Ark Christian Schl; Little Rock, AR; (2); Church Yth Grp; Pres French Clb; FHA; Model UN; Acpl Chr; Chorus; School Play; Rep Stu Cncl; Var Co-Capt Chrldng; Swmmng; Vltne Ct; Clss Idl; Bus.

GARRETT, GRANT W; Siloam Springs Sr HS; Siloam Springs, AR; (4); 27/161; FCA; Model UN; Capt Quiz Bowl; School Play; Ftbl; Hon Roll; Pres Acad Fit Awd; Knwldge Mstrs Open; Beta Clb; Scott Hi-Q; U Of AR; Pre-Law/Attrny.

GARRETT, JENNIFER M; Vilonia HS; Vilonia, AR; (3); Church Yth Grp; Rptr FBLA; Sec Girl Scts; Office Aide; Teachers Aide; Band; Co-Capt Flag Corp; Mrchg Band; Pep Band; Hon Roll; Univ Cntrl AR; Elem Ed.

GARRETT, KRISTIN R; Magnolia HS; Magnolia, AR; (2); Church Yth Grp; Dance Clb; FCA; Pep Clb; Band; Church Choir; Intrml JV Chrldng; Hon Roll; Rep Stu Cncl; CPA.

GARRETT, SANITA K; Riverview HS; Kensett, AR; (2); Art Clb; Church Yth Grp; Cmnty Wkr; Pres Rep FHA; GAA; Pep Clb; Pres Soph Cls; Var Bsktbl; Hon Roll; Ml Univ; Lwyr/Plt.

GARRETT, SARAH M; Parkview Arts-Science HS; Jacksonville, AR; (2); Art Clb; Chess Clb; Church Yth Grp; Debate Tm; Model UN; Natl Beta Clb; Capt Drill Tm; High Hon Roll; Barrett Hamilton Art Cont Mrt Awd 94-95; Pol Sci; Law; Art.

GARRIS, JARED J; Mountain Home HS; Lakeview, AR; (1); Art Clb; Boy Scts; Church Yth Grp; Cmnty Wkr; ROTC; Color Guard; Drill Tm; Cit Awd; Hon Roll; Pres Acad Fit Awd; ARSU; Graphic Arts.

GARRISON, ANDREA; Rogers HS; Rogers, AR; (4); Church Yth Grp; Cmnty Wkr; Dance Clb; FCA; FBLA; GAA; Letterman Clb; Teachers Aide; Drill Tm; Chrldng; U Of AR; Phys Thrpy.

GARRISON, ERIN A; Southside HS; Fort Smith, AR; (3); Church Yth Grp; Drama Clb; Spanish Clb; Teachers Aide; Chorus; Rptr Nwsp; Hon Roll; Eastern OK ST C; Lrg Anml Veu.

GARRISON, JULIE; Lakeside HS; Hot Springs, AR; (1); Church Yth Grp; FCA; FHA; Drill Tm; Chrldng; Gym; Hon Roll; U Of AR; Kndgtn Tchr/Psych.

GARRISON, LIZETTE; Central Ark Christian Schl; North Little Rock, AR; (1); Church Yth Grp; Cmnty Wkr; Church Choir; Yrbk; High Hon Roll; Pres Acad Fit Awd; Dscplshp Prog; True Love Waits; Sdwlk Sun Schl; SW Assemblies Of God U.

GARRISON, NEISHA C; England HS; England, AR; (1); Band; Hon Roll; Horseback Rdng; U Of MT; Law Enforcement.

GARTMAN, AMY D; Trumann HS; Trumann, AR; (4); 21/86; Art Clb; Church Yth Grp; FBLA; Treas FHA; Treas Intnl Clb; Library Aide; Math Clb; Treas Natl FFA Org; Science Clb; Spanish Clb; Excl Ed; Who's Who Best Drssd; Hmdmng Maid 11th Grd; AR ST Univ; Rdlgy.

GARVER, WENDY; Southside HS; Batesville, AR; (3); GAA; Key Clb; Natl Beta Clb; Office Aide; Spanish Clb; Hist Stu Cncl; Bsktbl; Crs Cntry; Sftbl; Trk; St Trck; Reg Bsktbll; St Sftbll; Alldist Sftbll; William Baptist Univ.

GARVIN, ELIZABETH P; Valley Springs Schl; Everton, AR; (2); Church Yth Grp; VP 4-H; Key Clb; Natl FFA Org; Teachers Aide; Band; JV Bsktbl; Trk; Hon Roll; NACTC; Anml Hsbndry.

GARVIN, MELISSA; Cabot HS; Cabot, AR; (4); 72/299; FCA; Math Clb; Spanish Clb; Band; Rep Stu Cncl; Bsktbl; Capt Var Chrldng; Golf; Trk; Hon Roll; All Star Chrldr; U Of AR.

GASAWAY, BRANDON L; Mansfield Jr Sr HS; Huntington, AR; (3); Church Yth Grp; FCA; Intnl Clb; Letterman Clb; Model UN; Natl Beta Clb; Natl FFA Org; Spanish Clb; Varsity Clb; Band; Band Camp; Ftbl Camp; Band Schlsp From HSU; Henderson ST Univ; Engrng.

GASAWAY, CHARLA; Gillett Jr Sr HS; Gould, AR; (3); 1/26; Am Leg Aux Girls St; Art Clb; Church Yth Grp; FBLA; Quiz Bowl; Spanish Clb; School Play; Yrbk; VP Frsh Cls; Treas Jr Cls; Xerox Awd; Univ Of AR; Dntstry.

GASAWAY, DAVID; Warren Sr HS; Warren, AR; (4); 11/121; Am Leg Boys St; Art Clb; Church Yth Grp; FBLA; Latin Clb; Model UN; Natl Beta Clb; Natl FFA Org; Quiz Bowl; Teachers Aide; U Of Central AR; Biology.

GASKINS, AMANDA L; St Joseph HS; Conway, AR; (2); Church Yth Grp; Cmnty Wkr; FBLA; Pep Clb; Spanish Clb; Med Field.

GASKINS, JEAN ANN; Izard Co Cons Jr Sr HS; Horseshoe Bend, AR; (1); Church Yth Grp; FHA; Natl Beta Clb; Pep Clb; Bsktbl; Golf; High Hon Roll; Ntl Merit Ltr; Pres Acad Fit Awd; U Of AR; Coach.

GAST, ROBERT; Sylvan Hills HS; North Little Rock, AR; (3); 1/200; Church Yth Grp; Mu Alpha Theta; Natl Beta Clb; Teachers Aide; Var Bsbl; Var Bsktbl; Var Ftbl; High Hon Roll; NHS; Pres Acad Fit Awd; Eng/Math/Sci Pres Awds.

GASTON, CAMBRIA; Mountain Home HS; Mountain Home, AR; (4); Dance Clb; FCA; FBLA; Ger Club; ASU.

GASTON, ROBERT F; De Soto Schl; Helena, AR; (3); Drama Clb; Phtg Yrbk; VP Frsh Cls; Bsktbl; Golf; High Hon Roll; Treas NHS; Ag Econ.

GATELEY, JESS M; Riverview HS; Searcy, AR; (2); FHA; Natl FFA Org; Spanish Clb; Yrbk; Capt Bsktbl; Hon Roll; Prfct Atten Awd; U Of AR Fayetteville.

GATEWOOD, FELICIA R; Piggott HS; Piggott, AR; (2); Church Yth Grp; French Clb; FHA; Natl Beta Clb; Science Clb; Band; Flag Corp; Hon Roll; Psych.

GATEWOOD, JEANENE; Eudora HS; Eudora, AR; (3); #3 in class; Drama Clb; Natl Beta Clb; ROTC; SADD; Color Guard; Mrchg Band; Rep Jr Cls; Hon Roll; U Of AR Fayettevl; Psych.

GATHRIGHT, JUSTIN W; Buffalo Island Central HS; Monette, AR; (2); 17/57; Natl FFA Org; Rep Soph Cls; Rep Stu Cncl; NHS; Ag.

GATLIN, AMANDA; East Poinsett Sr HS; Lepanto, AR; (4); 4/54; FBLA; FHA; Library Aide; Natl FFA Org; Quiz Bowl; Rptr Soph Cls; L Bsktbl; Intrml Powder Puff Ftbl; L Tennis; Hon Roll; MS U; Phrmcy.

GATLIN, JASON W; Conway Sr HS; Conway, AR; (4); 37/520; Bus Profs of Am; Church Yth Grp; Cmnty Wkr; FCA; FBLA; Letterman Clb; Teachers Aide; Golf; High Hon Roll; Natl HS Math Exam Fnlst; U Of Cntrl AR; Pre-Med; Chem.

GATLIN, LISA G; Conway Sr HS; Conway, AR; (3); Church Yth Grp; FBLA; Q&S; Teachers Aide; VICA; Yrbk; Powder Puff Ftbl; Hon Roll; Delta Beta Sigma; Young Life; U Of Cntrl AR; FBI.

GATTIS, JEFF L; Ozark HS; Ozark, AR; (4); VP Sr Cls; L Bsbl; L Ftbl; Hon Roll; Pres Acad Fit Awd.

GATTIS, JOJO; Gurdon HS; Gurdon, AR; (2); Church Yth Grp; Library Aide; Natl Beta Clb; Spanish Clb; Ed Nwsp; Var L Chrldng; Gym; Hon Roll; Pres Acad Fit Awd; Beta Of Yr.

GATTIS, MORGAN; Cty Line HS; Ratcliff, AR; (2); FCA; Natl Beta Clb; Natl FFA Org; Quiz Bowl; Spanish Clb; Pres Frsh Cls; Cit Awd; High Hon Roll.

GAUB, ALISON M; Beebe Sr HS; Beebe, AR; (2); 9/139; Church Yth Grp; Cmnty Wkr; GAA; Girl Scts; Teachers Aide; JV Stat Bsktbl; Stat Mgr(s); Hon Roll; Girl Scout Silver Awd; Acad Deca Decathalon; Frgn Lang.

GAUSE, LA TASHA D; Central HS; West Helena, AR; (2); Trk; Hon Roll; Tchr Choice Awd; ASU; Med.

GAUW, BETH; Calvary Christian Schl; Forrest City, AR; (2); 3/17; Church Yth Grp; Cmnty Wkr; Chorus; School Musical; School Play; Sec Frsh Cls; VP Soph Cls; Var Bsktbl; Var Vllybl; High Hon Roll; Piano & Violin; Sports Med.

GAVIN, DEMIKA N; Osceola HS; Osceola, AR; (4); #17 in class; Church Yth Grp; Cmnty Wkr; French Clb; FBLA; Key Clb; Church Choir; Rep Stu Cncl; Var Bsktbl; Var Trk; Hon Roll; Natl Schlr Athl & Acad Achvt Awds; U Of AR-FAYETTEVILLE; Acctng.

GAY, NANCY; Southside HS; Fort Smith, AR; (1); Church Yth Grp; FCA; Library Aide; Office Aide; Teachers Aide; Chrldng; Vllybl; High Hon Roll; Jr NHS; Pres Acad Fit Awd; All-Amer Chrldr Capt 95-96.

GAY, TIFFANY N; Midland HS; Floral, AR; (2); 6/58; Treas FBLA; Girl Scts; Natl Beta Clb; Rptr Natl FFA Org; Pep Clb; Science Clb; Spanish Clb; Ed Yrbk; Pres Soph Cls; Sec Stu Cncl; Mash Pgm; U Of Conway; Pharmacist.

GEAN, AMY; East Poinsett Cty HS; Tyronza, AR; (4); 10/80; Am Leg Aux Girls St; Church Yth Grp; FBLA; FHA; GAA; Natl FFA Org; Variety Show; Yrbk; Ofcr Jr Cls; Ofcr Stu Cncl; Hndrsn 100; Ouachita Bptst U; Med Tech.

GEBHART, GENNA; Weiner HS; Waldenburg, AR; (2); Pres FHA; Library Aide; Science Clb; Teachers Aide; Chorus; Variety Show; Chrldng; NHS; Ntl Merit Ltr; U Of AR At Fayetville; Phys Th.

GEE, KRISTYN M; John L Mcclellan Magnet HS; Mabelvale, AR; (2); Church Yth Grp; Cmnty Wkr; Computer Clb; Drama Clb; French Clb; Natl Beta Clb; Office Aide; Spanish Clb; Teachers Aide; Thesps; Choir Camp Schlrshp; U Of Central AR; Child Psych.

GEIER, DONALD W; Russellville Sr HS; Russellville, AR; (3); Church Yth Grp; Red Cross Aide; Spanish Clb; Band; Mrchg Band; L Ftbl; Var Trk; Ntl Merit Ltr; All-Stars; PT.

GEIGER, HANNAH; Hatfield Schl; Mena, AR; (4); #5 in class; Church Yth Grp; FHA; Church Choir; Yrbk; Pres Jr Cls; Rep Stu Cncl; Mgr(s); Hon Roll; NHS; Rich Mountain CC.

GEISLER, AMBER K; Marvell Acad; Brinkley, AR; (2); 9/34; Spanish Clb; School Play; Rep Frsh Cls; Treas Soph Cls; JV Var Bsktbl; Var Chrldng; Var Sftbl; Trk; Jr NHS; NHS; AR ST Univ; PT.

GENTIS, JENNIFER M; Clarendon Jr Sr HS; Clarendon, AR; (2); FBLA; Natl Beta Clb; Quiz Bowl; Bsktbl; Sftbl; Trk; High Hon Roll; Pres Acad Fit Awd; Church Yth Grp; Computer Clb; SERC Japanese I, II; Explorers; U Of AR Fayetteville; Chem.

GENTRY, CRISTIN M; Arkansas Sr HS; Texarkana, AR; (2); Church Yth Grp; Drama Clb; French Clb; FTA; Mu Alpha Theta; Drill Tm; Ed Nwsp; Hon Roll; Jr NHS; Pres Acad Fit Awd; PRIDE; Gifted & Talented; Teen Republicanns; Henderson ST U; Drama.

GENTRY, GABE S; Searcy HS; Searcy, AR; (3); Church Yth Grp; Office Aide; VP Soph Cls; Drama Clb; Thesps; School Play; Stage Crew; Variety Show; Ftbl; Harding Univ; Crmnl Psychlgy.

GENTRY, HANNAH; Coleman Jr HS; Van Buren, AR; (1); Church Yth Grp; Cmnty Wkr; FHA; Teachers Aide; Pres Chorus; Hon Roll; Chrmn Jr NHS; Spcl Olympics Coach; Partners In Christ, Clb Pres; Schl Acad Honoree & TIP; Hillsdale Frawill Bapt; Spcl Ed.

GENTRY, TARAH; Nashville HS; Mc Caskill, AR; (4); Cmnty Wkr; FHA; Stage Crew; Hon Roll; Red River; Elem Ed.

GEORGE, AIMEE; Ola Jr Sr HS; Danville, AR; (1); Church Yth Grp; Spanish Clb; Band; Ofcr Stu Cncl; High Hon Roll; Ntl Merit Ltr.

GEORGE, BRANDON; Butterfield Jr HS; Van Buren, AR; (2); Bsktbl; JETS Awd; NHS.

GEORGE, DENISE P; De Soto Schl; Elaine, AR; (2); Church Yth Grp; Drama Clb; HOBY; School Play; Yrbk; Treas Frsh Cls; Treas Soph Cls; Rep Stu Cncl; Capt Chrldng; High Hon Roll; Amer His High Avg Awd; Hnr Soc; Homcmng Queen; Pre-Law.

GEORGE, LORI; Coleman Jr HS; Van Buren, AR; (1); Church Yth Grp; FBLA; Sec Stu Cncl; Chrldng; Hon Roll; Jr NHS; Ntl Merit Ltr; Prfct Atten Awd; Prtnrs In Chrst; Jazz Dnce; Gymnstcs; UCA At Conway; PT.

GEORGE, MARLA; Warren Sr HS; Warren, AR; (3); 10/145; Am Leg Aux Girls St; Church Yth Grp; Sec Drama Clb; Natl Beta Clb; Drm Mjr(t); School Musical; Pres Jr Cls; VP Stu Cncl; Var Chrldng; All ST Choir; Baylor Univ.

GEORGE, MELODY; Ola Jr Sr HS; Danville, AR; (4); 4/23; Am Leg Aux Girls St; GAA; Pres Natl Beta Clb; Quiz Bowl; Spanish Clb; Rptr Nwsp; Phtg Yrbk; VP Sr Cls; Sec Stu Cncl; Hon Roll; AR Tech U; Geology.

GEORGE, NATHAN; Ola Jr Sr HS; Danville, AR; (1); Chess Clb; Church Yth Grp; JA; Quiz Bowl; Spanish Clb; Band; Mrchg Band; Pep Band; VP Frsh Cls; JV Bsbl; Sports Med.

GERBER, JENNIFER S; Lake Hamilton Sr HS; Hot Springs, AR; (3); Cmnty Wkr; Drama Clb; FCA; GAA; Church Choir; School Musical; School Play; Variety Show; JV Bsktbl; Var Crs Cntry; Prin Schl Spirit Awd 94-95; Asst For Natl Leagur Of Jr Cotillions; Friends Univ; Piano/Dance.

GEREN, JEREMY K; Southside HS; Fort Smith, AR; (2); Church Yth Grp; Cmnty Wkr; FCA; German Clb; Teachers Aide; Chorus; Church Choir; Ofcr Soph Cls; Var Bsktbl; Var Ftbl; Spcl Olympics Vol.

GEREN, WILLIAM J; Northside HS; Fort Smith, AR; (3); Church Yth Grp; FBLA; HOBY; JV Bsbl; High Hon Roll; Jr NHS; FBLA Comp; Hnrs Crses; Tommy Seafood; AR Tech Univ; Bus.

GERMAN, VALANDRA; Crossett Sr HS; Crossett, AR; (3); Art Clb; Church Yth Grp; Dance Clb; Drama Clb; FBLA; FHA; Mu Alpha Theta; Band; L Chrldng; Hon Roll; U Of AR; Crim Just.

GERRALD, AMANDA; Genoa Central HS; Genoa, AR; (3); #1 in class; Dance Clb; 4-H; FBLA; Sec Stu Cncl; Var Bsktbl; Var Chrldng; Var Trk; High Hon Roll; NHS; GAA; AR HS Rodeo; Crmnl Invstgtn.

GERRALD, HOLLY; Genoa Cntrl HS; Genoa, AR; (1); 5/80; Dance Clb; 4-H; GAA; Spanish Clb; Pres Frsh Cls; Capt Chrldng; Crs Cntry; Trk; 4-H Awd; Hon Roll; AR HS Rodeo.

GETCHELL, PAUL J; Ouachita Hills Acad; Pearcy, AR; (4); Cmnty Wkr; Speech Tm; Teachers Aide; Band; Church Choir; Orch; Nwsp; Reader; Math Tutor; Cmptrs; Andrews U; Arch.

GETZ, NATALIE; Morrilton Sr HS; Morrilton, AR; (4); 9/150; Art Clb; Church Yth Grp; Dance Clb; VP Math Clb; Natl Beta Clb; Science Clb; Spanish Clb; Thesps; Var Crs Cntry; Pom Pon; 13 Yrs Dance; U AR Fayetteville.

GEURTZ, JAMES; Southside HS; Fort Smith, AR; (3); Chess Clb; German Clb; AR OK Prsnl Cmptr Usrs Grp, Gamea Spec Intrst Grp Co Ldr; U Of AR; Engrng.

GHENT, WENDY L; Quitman Jr Sr HS; Quitman, AR; (3); Church Yth Grp; FCA; FBLA; FHA; Natl Beta Clb; SADD; Teachers Aide; VP Stu Cncl; L Bsktbl; Hon Roll; Miss QHS Pgnt 95-; Wrd Prcsng Awd 95-; Keyboarding Awd 93-94; ASU; Elem Tchr/Bus Mgnmt.

GHIDOTTI, CHARITY; East End Jr Sr HS; Roland, AR; (4); 6/39; Church Yth Grp; Drama Clb; Rptr FBLA; Natl Beta Clb; Spanish Clb; Teachers Aide; Drill Tm; Yrbk; Stat Bsktbl; Hon Roll; U AR Lttle Rck; Nrsng.

GIANG, AN V; Central Sr HS; Little Rock, AR; (3); 70/540; Chess Clb; Latin Clb; Math Clb; Mu Alpha Theta; Natl Beta Clb; High Hon Roll; Natl Ltn Exm Slvr Mdl; Latin II Awd Excllnc; U Of AR Fayetteville.

GIBBS, HEIDI; Conay Sr HS; Conway, AR; (3); Church Yth Grp; Drama Clb; FBLA; Hosp Aide; Natl Beta Clb; Quiz Bowl; Spanish Clb; Church Choir; Sftbl; Vllybl; All-Stars; Renaissance Gold Card Holder; Nrsng.

GIBBS, JIMDAN F; Black Rock Jr Sr HS; Black Rock, AR; (2); 5/45; Boy Scts; Cmnty Wkr; FBLA; FHA; Model UN; Treas Natl Beta Clb; Capt Quiz Bowl; Color Guard; Nwsp; Yrbk; Top Five 95-; AR ST Univ.

GIBBY, LAKE A; Morrilton Sr HS; Springfield, AR; (2); Art Clb; French Clb; Science Clb; Thesps; Band; Hon Roll; Gymnastics; Waterskiing; Rappeling; Hunting.

GIBBY, TESSICA C; Morrilton Sr HS; Morrilton, AR; (2); Art Clb; Church Yth Grp; Key Clb; Math Clb; Science Clb; SADD; Chorus; Variety Show; Ed Nwsp; Ed Yrbk; Pres Achvmt Awd; U Of AR; Psych.

GIBSON, ALISA K; Waldron HS; Waldron, AR; (2); Drama Clb; Natl Beta Clb; Spanish Clb; Chorus; Hon Roll; AR Tech; Criminal Law.

GIBSON, AMY E; Riverview Jr-Sr HS; Judsonia, AR; (3); Church Yth Grp; FBLA; FHA; GAA; Natl Beta Clb; Spanish Clb; Bsktbl; Sftbl; Trk; Prfct Atten Awd; AR St Univ; Ed.

GIBSON, ANGELA M; Bald Knob HS; Russell, AR; (1); Church Yth Grp; Natl Beta Clb; Band; Jazz Band; Mrchg Band; Pep Band; Capt L Bsktbl; Var Sftbl; High Hon Roll; All Reg Bnd; Psychlgy.

GIBSON, BENJAMIN A; Yellville Summit HS; Yellville, AR; (2); FBLA; Band; Mrchg Band; Pep Band; VP Frsh Cls; Var Bsbl; Var Bsktbl; Var Capt Ftbl; Var Trk; Var Wt Lftg; YEAC; Law.

GIBSON, CARRIE L; West Memphis Christian Schl; Tyronza, AR; (1); Hon Roll; Prfct Atten Awd; Amer His/Algebra I Straight A'Sall Yr; Lamar ST Univ; Cmptr Sci.

GIBSON, CRYSTAL; Dumas HS; Tillar, AR; (3); 3/150; Am Leg Aux Girls St; FTA; Spanish Clb; VP Stu Cncl; L Gym; High Hon Roll; NHS; Pres Acad Fit Awd; U Of AR Fayetteville; Chem Eng.

GIBSON, JENNIFER L; Wynne HS; Wynne, AR; (4); Pres Church Yth Grp; FCA; Q&S; Pres Band; Ed Yrbk; Tennis; Hon Roll; Kiwanis Awd; NHS; Hist Drama Clb; Outstdng Sr; Dist & ST Tnns; Region & ST Band; U Of Cntrl AR; Elem Ed.

GIBSON, JOSHUA A; Rogers HS; Rogers, AR; (3); Teachers Aide; Chorus; Hon Roll; Prfct Atten Awd; Church Yth Grp; Chmbr Commerce Acad Achvmnt Awd; Yth Apprntcshp; Bnkng/Fin/Gerfiatric Hlth.

GIBSON, KELLIE M; Crossett Sr HS; Crossett, AR; (2); Church Yth Grp; French Clb; FTA; Natl Beta Clb; Band; Church Choir; Mrchg Band; Rptr Soph Cls; French Hon Soc; Hon Roll; SFC; Stu Of Month; Bus; Psych.

GIBSON, KERI A; Nevada Schl; Waldo, AR; (2); FHA; Quiz Bowl; Band; Hon Roll; Natl Beta Clb; Creative Wrtng Awd; Eng; Music.

GIBSON, KIMBERLY D; Rogers HS; Rogers, AR; (4); Church Yth Grp; Cmnty Wkr; Debate Tm; FCA; Library Aide; Office Aide; Speech Tm; Orch; Hon Roll; Jr NHS; Wtr Skiing; Taekwondo; Southwest Baptist U; Elem Ed.

GIBSON, PHOEBE E; Yellville Summit HS; Yellville, AR; (3); Art Clb; Cmnty Wkr; Office Aide; Teachers Aide; Band; Sprt Ed Nwsp; Yrbk; Ofcr Soph Cls; Yellville Envrnmntl Awareness Clb; Stu Of Month; Bus Mgmt.

GIBSON, ROBERT B; Monticello HS; Monticello, AR; (3); FCA; French Clb; Natl Beta Clb; SADD; Ofcr Bsbl; Ftbl; Tennis; Wt Lftg; Tnns Dist Chmpnshps Semifnlst, St Chmpnshps; Wght Lftng 5th Pl Div St Chmpnshps 96; Sci.

GIDDEON, TRACE G; Springdale Sr HS; Springdale, AR; (1); Church Yth Grp; Cmnty Wkr; Intrml Ftbl; Golf; L Trk; Wt Lftg; Hon Roll; 100 Meter Dash First Pl NWA Conf.

GIEB, SARA M; Fayetteville Sr HS; Fayetteville, AR; (2); Church Yth Grp; FBLA; Spanish Clb; Chorus; Pom Pon; Powder Puff Ftbl; High Hon Roll; 4 Yr Coll.

GIFFORD, AMBER M; Corning Jr Sr HS; Corning, AR; (2); 7/98; Church Yth Grp; FBLA; FHA; Model UN; Lit Mag; High Hon Roll; Hon Roll; Jr NHS; NHS; Pres Acad Fit Awd; 1st Pl Reg/St OM Cmptn; Close Up WA; Ftr Prblm Slvng; 3rd Pl St Stckmrkt Gm; Jr Natl Hnr Soc VP; Law.

GIFFORD, MARK; Rogers HS; Rogers, AR; (3); 1/577; Am Leg Boys St; Rep Key Clb; Spanish Clb; Pres Frsh Cls; Rep Soph Cls; Rep Jr Cls; Rep Sr Cls; Rep Stu Cncl; JV Bsbl; JV Bsktbl; Altar Server; United Way Vol; Math; Sci; Pre-Med.

GIFFORD, SHAWNA L; Crossett Sr HS; Crossett, AR; (3); Church Yth Grp; French Clb; FTA; Mu Alpha Theta; Natl Beta Clb; Pep Clb; Chorus; Drill Tm; Swmmng; High Hon Roll; Smmr Swim Team; Dance Lessons; Schl Dance Team; U Of Central AR; Phys Thrpy.

GIGLLELLO, JAIME L; Lavaca Jr Sr HS; Lavaca, AR; (2); Drama Clb; FHA; HOBY; Natl Beta Clb; Science Clb; Spanish Clb; Band; Color Guard; Mrchg Band; Stat Trk; Helping Our Peers Excell; Govs Yth Conf Ldr; Med.

GILBERT, AMY; Mills HS; Little Rock, AR; (4); 3/173; Mu Alpha Theta; Natl Beta Clb; Q&S; Yrbk; NHS; Pres Acad Fit Awd; U Of AR At Little Rock.

GILBERT, JASON; Mountain View Jr Sr HS; Mountain View, AR; (2); Church Yth Grp; FCA; Natl Beta Clb; Quiz Bowl; Bsktbl; High Hon Roll; Pres Acad Fit Awd.

GILBERT, KYLA; Bearden HS; Bearden, AR; (4); 7/58; Church Yth Grp; 4-H; Sec FBLA; Pres FTA; Natl Beta Clb; Science Clb; Ed Nwsp; Ed Yrbk; VP Soph Cls; Rep Sr Cls; Hnr Grad; S AR U; Phrmcy.

GILBERT, NIKKI; Wynne HS; Wynne, AR; (4); Drama Clb; FTA; GAA; Q&S; SADD; Ed Yrbk; Crs Cntry; Trk; U Of CO; Dntl Hygiene.

GILBERT, STEPHANIE; Southwest Christian Acad; Mabelvale, AR; (1); Church Yth Grp; Hosp Aide; Chorus; Church Choir; School Musical; Yrbk; Bsktbl; Cit Awd; Hon Roll; Ouchita Bapt Coll.

GILBERT, TROY MASTERS; Rogers HS; Rogers, AR; (3); 34/500; FBLA; Teachers Aide; Orch; Nwsp; Score Keeper; Hon Roll; Ntl Merit SF; WA U; Comp Sci.

GILBREATH, JONATHAN G; Izard Co Cons Jr Sr HS; Violet Hill, AR; (3); Natl Beta Clb; Natl FFA Org; Office Aide; Teachers Aide; Yrbk; Var Bsbl; Var L Bsktbl; Ntl Merit Ltr.

GILCHRIST, PAMELA A; Lake Hamilton Sr HS; Pearcy, AR; (4); 49/229; FBLA; FHA; Natl FFA Org; Yrbk; Hon Roll; Child Care Mgmt-Kndgtn Tchrs Aide; Quapaw Tech Inst; Acctnt.

GILES, CHRIS; Lavaca Jr Sr HS; Lavaca, AR; (3); Church Yth Grp; Ofcr Bsbl; Bsktbl; Hon Roll; Sports Med.

GILL, BOBBY; Bradley Jr Sr HS; Bradley, AR; (3); 2/26; FBLA; Math Clb; Natl FFA Org; Quiz Bowl; Spanish Clb; Rep Frsh Cls; Rep Soph Cls; Rep Jr Cls; Var Bsbl; JV Bsktbl; Ftbl MVP 93-94; ACT Test 23 94-95, 25 95-96; All-Star Team Asst Coach Smmr 95; U Of AR Fayetteville; Arch.

GILL, FERNANDO D; Harmony Grove Jr Sr HS; Camden, AR; (3); FCA; 4-H; FBLA; Letterman Clb; Natl FFA Org; Spanish Clb; Band; Church Choir; Mrchg Band; Pep Band; Comp Prgmr.

GILL, LATASHIA; Harmony Grove Jr Sr HS; Camden, AR; (4); Am Leg Aux Girls St; Art Clb; Church Yth Grp; FHA; Science Clb; Chorus; Stage Crew; Ofcr Jr Cls; Ofcr Stu Cncl; Chrldng; Natl Hlth Occptns Stu Amer Rep; Miss Harmony Grv; South AR CC; RN.

GILLASPIE, ALISON; Abundant Life Schools; Jacksonville, AR; (3); Church Yth Grp; Church Choir; School Play; Rep Jr Cls; Ofcr Stu Cncl; Var Bsktbl; JV Chrldng; High Hon Roll; Hon Roll; NHS; U Of Cntrl AR; Occ Ther.

GILLENWATER, SHAWNA C; Fouke Jr Sr HS; Fouke, AR; (3); Church Yth Grp; Drama Clb; FCA; Math Clb; Spanish Clb; Chorus; Church Choir; School Musical; Nwsp; Yrbk; Ouachita Baptist U; Music.

GILLEY, LORI; Yellville Summit HS; Yellville, AR; (2); 5/78; Church Yth Grp; FCA; FBLA; Teachers Aide; Band; Yrbk; Treas Soph Cls; Capt Chrldng; Mgr Tennis; High Hon Roll; 4th Pl Wrd Prcssng FBLA Dist VI Conf; Harding U; Arch.

GILLHAM, BOBBIE J; Riverview HS; Judsonia, AR; (2); Church Yth Grp; Drama Clb; FBLA; Hosp Aide; Spanish Clb; Band; Jazz Band; Mrchg Band; Pep Band.

GILLIAM, BRANDI; Gosnell Jr HS; Blytheville, AR; (1); Art Clb; Church Yth Grp; Library Aide; Hon Roll; Ntl Merit Ltr; Hrsbck Rdng; Zoology.

GILLIAM, GREG; Drew Central Jr Sr HS; Monticello, AR; (3); 1/70; Am Leg Boys St; Ofcr Frsh Cls; Ofcr Soph Cls; Ofcr Jr Cls; Var Bsktbl; Var Tennis; High Hon Roll; Hon Roll; Jr NHS; NHS; Army Natl Grd Schlr Ath 96; ST AA Dbls Tnns Champ 95-; Adv Monticellean Rep 95-.

GILLIAM, JENNY; Gosnell Jr HS; Blytheville, AR; (1); Church Yth Grp; Band; Pep Band; Powder Puff Ftbl; Trk; Natl Sci Mrt Awd.

GILLION, ANDREA L; Mc Crory Jr Sr HS; Mc Crory, AR; (3); #1 in class; Am Leg Aux Girls St; Church Yth Grp; Cmnty Wkr; FBLA; FTA; GAA; Letterman Clb; Quiz Bowl; SADD; Varsity Clb; All Region Band; Pre-Medicine.

GILLIP, JACOB; Danville HS; Coal Hill, AR; (1); High Hon Roll.

GILLIS, LORI B; Jonesboro HS; Jonesboro, AR; (3); FBLA; Math Clb; Spanish Clb; Band; Chorus; Church Choir; Drm Mjr(t); Mrchg Band; Pep Band; School Musical; Most Outstdng Majorette.

GILLISPIE, JOSH; North Little Rock Hs-East; North Little Rock, AR; (1); 101/646; Var Bsktbl; Hon Roll; Pre AP Bio/Eng; Geometry/Hnrs Civcs.

GILLMAN, JULIE A; Lake Hamilton Sr HS; Hot Springs, AR; (3); 46/258; Library Aide; Office Aide; Spanish Clb; Teachers Aide; Bsktbl; Hon Roll; Prfct Atten Awd; Pres Acad Fit Awd; Mstr Scb Dvr.

GILLMING, DENNIS G; Gravette HS; Gravette, AR; (2); Church Yth Grp; FBLA; Quiz Bowl; Hon Roll; NHS; Acad Cmptn; Rnssnce Pgm; U AR; Phrmcy.

GILLMORE, BOBBY D; Southside HS; Batesville, AR; (1); VP Church Yth Grp; Pres 4-H; Natl Beta Clb; Natl FFA Org; Science Clb; Band; 4-H Awd; Hon Roll; N AR Western Assn Horseshowing; Ag Tchr.

GILLUM, ZEBRULIN J; Lonoke Jr HS; Lonoke, AR; (1); Church Yth Grp; Science Clb; Band; Jazz Band; Mrchg Band; Pep Band; Gftd & Tlntd.

GILMORE, JAMES E; Huttig Schl; Strong, AR; (3); FBLA; FHA; Var Bsbl; Var Bsktbl.

GILMORE, JASON H; Ft Smith Christian Schl; Alma, AR; (2); Church Yth Grp; FCA; FBLA; Spanish Clb; Yrbk; Pres Soph Cls; Pres Jr Cls; Cit Awd; High Hon Roll; NHS; Westark; Occptnl Thrpst.

GILMORE, TRAVIS; Van Buren Sr HS; Van Buren, AR; (2); Church Yth Grp; FCA; FBLA; Mu Alpha Theta; Science Clb; SADD; Ftbl; Jr NHS; NHS.

GILPIN, MIRANDA B; Southside HS; Batesville, AR; (2); Art Clb; Church Yth Grp; Key Clb; Natl Beta Clb; Rep Frsh Cls; Bsktbl; Sftbl; Hon Roll; Savannah Coll; Graphic Dsgn.

GIPSON, APRIL A; Manila HS; Manila, AR; (1); Hon Roll; Gftd & Tlntd; Criminal Prosecuting Attorney.

GIPSON, DALLAS A; Bay Jr Sr HS; Jonesboro, AR; (4); 2/34; Pres VP Church Yth Grp; VP Treas Natl Beta Clb; Pres VP Natl FFA Org; Treas NFL; Yrbk; Treas Sr Cls; Var Bsktbl; JETS Awd; Pres Schlr; Sal; Optmst Clb Yth Awd; Elks Clb Stdnt Mo; ST Frmr Dgr FFA; AR ST Univ; Elect Engrg.

GIPSON, EMILY; Gosnell Jr Sr HS; Blytheville, AR; (2); 1/105; Church Yth Grp; FCA; French Clb; Key Clb; Natl Beta Clb; Science Clb; Chorus; Rep Stu Cncl; Var Chrldng; FHA; Dentist.

GIPSON, KARA; Mc Crory HS; Mc Crory, AR; (2); 3/62; Church Yth Grp; FBLA; Office Aide; Quiz Bowl; SADD; Band; Church Choir; Jazz Band; Mrchg Band; Pep Band; Miss Mc Crory Jr HS; Jr Jaguar & Soph Class Fav; U Of Cntrl AR; Wldlf Bio.

GISON, AMY L; Drew Central Jr Sr HS; Tillar, AR; (2); 1/100; Church Yth Grp; VP Frsh Cls; Rep Sec Stu Cncl; JV Var Bsktbl; High Hon Roll; Jr NHS; NHS; FBLA; Math Tm; Natl FFA Org; Chptr FFA Sec; All-Regnl Bsktbl Team; St FFA Crops Cont 3rd Pl Individual; Agronomy; Soil Scis.

GIURBINO, GINA L; Springdale Sr HS; Springdale, AR; (2); FHA; Chorus; Mgr(s); Score Keeper; Hon Roll; U Of A; Pdtrcn.

GIVENS, EVE L; Sheridan Sr HS; Sheridan, AR; (3); FCA; French Clb; GAA; Pep Clb; Pres Chorus; Church Choir; Drill Tm; School Musical; School Play; JV Var Chrldng; Natl Interpreters For Deaf; Silent Fingers; Pageantry/Tlnt Comps; Prof Interpretor For Deaf.

GIVENS, MCKINLEY L; Mills HS; North Little Rock, AR; (2); Bsktbl; U Of AR; PT.

GIVENS, RENESA A; Jacksonville HS; Jacksonville, AR; (2); Church Yth Grp; French Clb; Hon Roll; Intrst/Chldrn; Sing; Tech Ed Awds; U Of Cntrl AR; Chld Care/Bus.

GIVENS, TRACEY; Hamburg HS; Hamburg, AR; (4); #2 in class; Am Leg Aux Girls St; Church Yth Grp; Drama Clb; HOBY; Natl FFA Org; Capt Flag Corp; Ed Yrbk; Ofcr Stu Cncl; Cit Awd; Pres NHS; Med.

GLADDEN, LORI B; Fouke Jr Sr HS; Fouke, AR; (2); Church Yth Grp; FHA; GAA; JV Bsktbl; JV Crs Cntry; Intrml Sftbl; Odyssey Of Mind; Mortician.

GLADNEY, SHEREE A; Arkansas Schl Math & Science; Newport, AR; (4); 4-H; FBLA; Library Aide; Office Aide; Spanish Clb; SADD; Rptr Nwsp; Hon Roll; NHS; Pres Acad Fit Awd; Natl MACY Schlr; Southwestern Bell Minority Internship Pgm; AR Cncl Tchrs Of Math Hnrbl Mntn; AR ST Univ; Bio; Vet Med.

GLANDON, CHAVAUGHN M; Pangburn Jr Sr HS; Pangburn, AR; (1); 8/45; Church Yth Grp; 4-H; Natl Beta Clb; Natl FFA Org; Pep Clb; Speech Tm; Bsktbl; Sftbl; Hon Roll; Math/Engl Tchr.

GLANDON, JENNIFER; Pangburn Jr Sr HS; Pangburn, AR; (1); 7/45; Church Yth Grp; Pep Clb; Quiz Bowl; Nwsp; Ofcr Frsh Cls; Bsktbl; Chrldng; Powder Puff Ftbl; Sftbl; Natl Hnr Roll; U AR; Vet.

GLASPIE, JACQUELINE C; Marion HS; Marion, AR; (3); School Play; Intrml Bsktbl; U Of Memphis; Comp Tech.

GLASS, CLYDE; Marvell HS; Poplar Grove, AR; (2); French Clb; FHA; FTA; Quiz Bowl; Bsktbl; French Hon Soc; High Hon Roll; Hon Roll; NHS; U Of AR; Eng.

GLASS, SARAH E; Fayetteville Sr HS; Fayetteville, AR; (4); 19/388; Pres 4-H; Sec FBLA; Key Clb; Spanish Clb; Ed Nwsp; High Hon Roll; NHS; Pres Acad Fit Awd; Close Up Sec WA Prtcpnt; AP Schlr; Natl Spnsh Exam Awd; U AR; Hstry Tchr.

GLASS, SUSAN; Mt Holly Schl; El Dorado, AR; (3); 2/21; Church Yth Grp; FBLA; FHA; FTA; Hosp Aide; Natl Beta Clb; Church Choir; JV Bsktbl; Var Chrldng; Sftbl; Wtrskiing; Southern AR U.

GLASSCO, MELISSA A; Sheridan Sr HS; Sheridan, AR; (2); 40/286; Church Yth Grp; Quiz Bowl; Band; Jazz Band; Mrchg Band; Orch; Pep Band; Hon Roll; Jr NHS; Pres Acad Fit Awd; Prtcptd AR Dem Gazette Stck Mrkt Game; Lifeguard Comm Pool; Vol Chrch/Elem Schl; Henderson ST Univ; Orthdntst.

GLEGHORN, SHELIA; Genoa Central HS; Texarkana, AR; (4); 5/40; FBLA; FHA; Hosp Aide; Model UN; Spanish Clb; Band; Hon Roll; NHS; U Of Cntrl AR; Psych.

GLENN, ALISON J; Mc Crory Jr Sr HS; Mc Crory, AR; (2); Church Yth Grp; Natl FFA Org; Spanish Clb; Teachers Aide; Trk; Hon Roll; Jr NHS; Prfct Atten Awd; Tchr.

GLENN, DIANE L; Rogers HS; Rogers, AR; (2); Hosp Aide; Acpl Chr; Cit Awd; High Hon Roll; Hon Roll; Veterans Admin Vol; Vol Svc Awds; U Of AR; Tchr.

GLENN, MEGAN; St Paul Schl; Elkins, AR; (2); FHA; Natl Beta Clb; SADD; Rep Frsh Cls; Sec Soph Cls; Bsktbl; Hon Roll; NHS; Stu Lib Assn; Stu Cncl; AR Tech.

GLENN, STACY; Jonesboro HS; Jonesboro, AR; (4); 27/274; Church Yth Grp; FBLA; Natl Beta Clb; Chorus; VP Stu Cncl; Co-Capt Chrldng; Capt Swmmng; High Hon Roll; VP NHS; Art Clb; Intrct Clb Sec; Spr Srs VP; Optmst Clb Otstndng Stu; David Lipscomb U; Phys Thrpy.

GLIDEWELL, BETHANY; Booneville Jr Sr HS; Booneville, AR; (3); 1/84; Am Leg Aux Girls St; Church Yth Grp; FCA; FBLA; Natl Beta Clb; Science Clb; Spanish Clb; Var Chrldng; Cit Awd; High Hon Roll; Eng.

GLIDEWELL, JULIE A; Marked Tree Jr Sr HS; Tyronza, AR; (3); 22/68; Church Yth Grp; Band; Church Choir; Mrchg Band; VP Jr Cls; Bsktbl; Chrldng; Powder Puff Ftbl; Sftbl; AR St Univ; Dgtl Elec.

GLOVER, DAVID JASON; North Little Rock Hs-East; North Little Rock, AR; (2); 79/567; Church Yth Grp; FCA; Ftbl; Trk; Hon Roll; Ath Acad Excel Awd.

GLOVER, KATHERINE L; Pine Bluff HS; Pine Bluff, AR; (3); Am Leg Aux Girls St; Church Yth Grp; Cmnty Wkr; French Clb; Model UN; Band; Orch; Rep Frsh Cls; NHS; Pres Acad Fit Awd; Obstetrician.

GLOVER, MATTHEW; Catholic HS; Little Rock, AR; (3); 4/172; Church Yth Grp; ROTC; Orch; Var Tennis; High Hon Roll; Weightlftg; Bsebl Trng; Tutor; Notre Dame; Med.

GLOVER, REGAN; Heber Springs HS; Heber Springs, AR; (3); 1/102; Church Yth Grp; FCA; VP FBLA; GAA; HOBY; Natl Beta Clb; Science Clb; Spanish Clb; Band; Flag Corp; U AR; Sprts Med.

GLOVER, SONYA; Stephens Jr Sr HS; Stephens, AR; (3); 6/44; Church Yth Grp; FBLA; FHA; Library Aide; Spanish Clb; Varsity Clb; Var Bsktbl; High Hon Roll; Hon Roll; NHS; U Of AR; Bus Admin.

GOAD, ANGELA; Nettleton HS; Jonesboro, AR; (3); Rptr French Clb; Treas FHA; Natl Beta Clb; Mgr Nwsp; Tennis; Hon Roll; Pres Acad Fit Awd; School Play; PRIDE; 2nd Headline Wrtng At AR ST Univ; Elks Awd; AR ST Univ; Elem Ed.

GOCKE, LEIGHANNE; Bryant Sr HS; Alexander, AR; (2); Church Yth Grp; Teachers Aide; Band; Flag Corp; Mrchg Band; Hon Roll; Henderson; Astrnmy/Meteorlgy.

GODANYOVA, ADRIANA; Smackover HS; Smackover, AR; (3); Art Clb; Drama Clb; Office Aide; School Play; Nwsp; Tennis; Vllybl; Hon Roll; Sign Lang Clb; Applied Bio & Chem Best In Cls; NE LA U; Psych; Photo.

GODDARD, FELICIA; Mansfield Jr Sr HS; Mansfield, AR; (4); 18/53; HOBY; Natl Beta Clb; Speech Tm; Nwsp; VP Soph Cls; Pres Stu Cncl; Var Chrldng; Cit Awd; Hon Roll; Art Clb; Westark CC; Poltcl Sci.

GODDARD, NATHANIEL; Waldron HS; Waldron, AR; (2); Church Yth Grp; FBLA; Natl Beta Clb; Spanish Clb; Var Bsktbl; Var Ftbl; Var Trk; Var Hon Roll.

GODFREY, AARON K; Springdale Sr HS; Springdale, AR; (1); FBLA; Chorus; Var L Socr; Hon Roll; NHS; Pres Acad Fit Awd; Jr High Bsktbl-Var & Ltr; Jr High Soccer Var & Ltr.

GODFREY, TRAVIS L; Sylvan Hills HS; Sherwood, AR; (2); 20/275; Church Yth Grp; Mu Alpha Theta; Natl Beta Clb; Science Clb; Spanish Clb; Acpl Chr; L Var Socr; Hon Roll; Jr NHS; NHS; Med.

GODSEY, LAUREN K; Central Ark Christian Schl; North Little Rock, AR; (4); 12/72; FBLA; Mu Alpha Theta; Natl Beta Clb; VP Science Clb; VP Spanish Clb; Var Bsktbl; Trk; Hon Roll; NHS; Hstry Clb; Harding U; Mrktng.

GODSEY, RYAN D; Arkansas Schl Math & Science; Fayetteville, AR; (3); Church Yth Grp; FBLA; Quiz Bowl; Ftbl; High Hon Roll; Hon Roll; Comm Svc Vol; Hnrb Mntn W Cntrl AR Regnl Sci Fair; Comp Sci.

GODWIN, ALISHA; Mansfield Jr Sr HS; Mansfield, AR; (1); Church Yth Grp; FCA; Rep Frsh Cls; Bsktbl; Chrldng; Vllybl; Hon Roll; Westark; Tchr.

GODWIN, GARY L; Jessieville HS; Jessieville, AR; (2); Library Aide; Natl Beta Clb; Teachers Aide; Var Crs Cntry; Var Trk; Hon Roll; Chlng Aw 10th Grd; Marine Bio.

GODWIN, JAMIE S; Watson Chapel Sr HS; Pine Bluff, AR; (4); #24 in class; Key Clb; ROTC; VICA; Lit Mag; Ofcr Stu Cncl; Hon Roll.

GODWIN, KORY E; Dequeen HS; De Queen, AR; (2); Natl FFA Org; Office Aide; JV Bsbl; L Ftbl; Hon Roll; Fishing; Hunting; Camping; Hiking.

GOFF, BONNIE I; Armorel HS; Armorel, AR; (2); Church Yth Grp; FBLA; FHA; Natl Beta Clb; Natl FFA Org; Spanish Clb; School Play; Nwsp; Rep Frsh Cls; Rep Soph Cls; Span Achvmnt Awd; Bus Mgmnt.

GOFF, JESSICA A; North Little Rock Hs-West; North Little Rock, AR; (3); 97/554; Art Clb; Church Yth Grp; Mu Alpha Theta; VICA; Swmmng; Hon Roll; U Of AR.

GOFF, KERBY A; Robinson HS; Little Rock, AR; (2); #1 in class; Church Yth Grp; French Clb; Math Tm; Natl Beta Clb; Chrldng; Tennis; Hon Roll; 4th In St Tnns.

GOFF, TARA; Central Ark Christian Schl; Jacksonville, AR; (2); Church Yth Grp; Cmnty Wkr; FHA; Spanish Clb; Hon Roll; Jr NHS; Ntl Merit Ltr; Hist Clb.

GOFFENEY, DAVID A; Lake Hamilton Sr HS; Hot Springs Natio, AR; (2); 95/262; Church Yth Grp; VP FCA; VP Science Clb; Sec Spanish Clb; Thesps; Ofcr Stu Cncl; Wrstlng; Hon Roll; Cmnty Wkr; Computer Clb; Aegis Lang Cmp; Pride His; Optomist Oratoracle.

GOFORTH, JUSTIN; Mountain Home HS; Gamaliel, AR; (4); 38/227; German Clb; Natl Beta Clb; Natl FFA Org; Pres Band; Mrchg Band; VP Sr Cls; VP Stu Cncl; Cit Awd; Hon Roll; FFA ST VP 96-; Mr MHHS 1st Rnnr Up; Stdnt Of Yr 96; US Frst Tm 96; AR Amb Music 95 Tour; U Of AR; Ag Bus.

GOINES, SHAWNA; Oak Grove HS; Maumelle, AR; (1); FHA; Letterman Clb; Natl Beta Clb; Bsktbl; Trk; Vllybl; Hon Roll.

GOINS, RANDALL T; Southside HS; Fort Smith, AR; (3); Church Yth Grp; FCA; Key Clb; Teachers Aide; VP Soph Cls; Rep Jr Cls; Pres Sr Cls; Hon Roll; Boys Clb Bsbl & Bsktbl Coach.

GOLDEN, DANNA M; Kingsland Schl; Kingsland, AR; (4); 4/20; Am Leg Aux Girls St; French Clb; FBLA; FHA; Natl Beta Clb; Quiz Bowl; Teachers Aide; Yrbk; Sec Jr Cls; Pres Sr Cls; Henderson St Univ; Elem Ed.

GOLDEN, TARA A; Lake Hamilton Sr HS; Hot Springs Natio, AR; (2); Church Yth Grp; Cmnty Wkr; FBLA; Library Aide; Band; Chorus; Flag Corp; Mrchg Band; Orch; Pep Band; All Regn Band; 2 Yr Ltr; Hnrb Mntn Local Reflections Pgm; Baylor; Law.

GOLETT, SHIAMEKIA; Lee Sr HS; Haynes, AR; (4); #13 in class; Science Clb; Spanish Clb; Varsity Clb; Variety Show; Ofcr Jr Cls; Bsktbl; Cit Awd; Trk; Criminal Justice.

GOLIGHTLY, HOLLY; Norfork Jr Sr HS; Norfork, AR; (3); FHA; Library Aide; VP Math Clb; Science Clb; Yrbk; JV Bsktbl; High Hon Roll; Hon Roll; Prfct Atten Awd; Pres Acad Fit Awd; AR ST U; Bus.

GOLSTON, AVERY; Saratoga Schl; Washington, AR; (2); 3/40; Church Yth Grp; FHA; Natl FFA Org; Spanish Clb; Chorus; Church Choir; School Musical; School Play; Rep Frsh Cls; Trk.

GONZALES, MICHAEL; East Poinsett Sr HS; Lepanto, AR; (4); 1/60; Church Yth Grp; Natl FFA Org; Quiz Bowl; Treas Stu Cncl; Var Ftbl; Hon Roll; NHS; Prfct Atten Awd; Pres Acad Fit Awd; Cmptr Sci.

GONZALES, PAULA; Forrest City HS; Forrest City, AR; (3); Mu Alpha Theta; Natl Beta Clb; Office Aide; Spanish Clb; School Play; Chrldng; Tae Kwon Do Black Belt.

GONZALEZ, GERARDO M; Hamburg HS; Hamburg, AR; (3); Church Yth Grp; Latin Clb; Spanish Clb; Church Choir; Crs Cntry; Golf; Trk; NHS; Attnd Natl Yth Ldrshp Forum On Defense, Intelligence & Diplomacy 96.

GOOCH, MATTHEW; Conway Sr HS; Conway, AR; (4); Boy Scts; Church Yth Grp; FCA; HOBY; Natl Beta Clb; Quiz Bowl; Spanish Clb; Band; Church Choir; Jazz Band; Sci Fr 37th Annl 1st Pl City, 1st Rgn, Army Awd-Engrng, St Fr; Ntl Yth Ldrshp Frm Med; Hgh Advntr Trck; U AR Fyttvlle; Med.

GOOD, KATIE; West Memphis Sr HS; West Memphis, AR; (3); Church Yth Grp; Girl Scts; Math Clb; Science Clb; Acpl Chr; Chorus; Rep Frsh Cls; Rep Stu Cncl; Var Chrldng; Var Gym; Univ Of Memphis; PT.

GOODMAN, COREY R; Gosnell Jr Sr HS; Blytheville, AR; (2); Art Clb; Drama Clb; French Clb; Key Clb; Band; Pep Band; Ofcr Bsbl; Bsktbl; Ftbl; Engineering.

GOODMAN, MARY E; Southside HS; Floral, AR; (3); 17/97; VP FHA; Natl Beta Clb; Science Clb; Spanish Clb; Chrldng; Hon Roll; Prfct Atten Awd; AR ST Hnr Roll.

GOODMAN, MICHAEL W; Lonoke Sr HS; Jacksonville, AR; (4); 5/102; Church Yth Grp; FBLA; Office Aide; Spanish Clb; Teachers Aide; High Hon Roll; NHS; Math Tm; Natl FFA Org; Hon Roll; 1st Plc Cmptr Cncpts/Dist VIII FBLA 3rd Plc ST; Frst ST Bank Advy Bd; 1st Plc Actng II Tech Inst; AR ST U Beebe; Cmpbr Sys.

GOODMAN, REBECCA; Poyen Schl; Prattsville, AR; (4); 1/34; Church Yth Grp; FCA; German Clb; Natl Beta Clb; Church Choir; Rptr Yrbk; Rptr Jr Cls; Sec Sr Cls; Hon Roll; Val; Natl Amer Bptst Assn Yth Sec; Indns Agnst Drgs; Teens For Chrst; Ouachita Bptst U; Acctng.

GOODMAN, REBECCA; Palestine-Wheatley HS; Wheatley, AR; (4); 2/50; Rptr FBLA; FHA; HOBY; Natl Beta Clb; Spanish Clb; Chorus; Rep Stu Cncl; Chrldng; Hon Roll; Sal; Vol Sr Ctzns, Sprng Fst; Hlpd St Jd Bk-A-Thn; AR ST U; Engr.

GOODMAN, SHAWANA; Southwest Jr HS; Little Rock, AR; (4); Church Yth Grp; Cmnty Wkr; FBLA; FHA; Girl Scts; Spanish Clb; SADD; Church Choir; Bsktbl; Sftbl; U Of Cntrl AR.

GOODMAN, TREY; Southside HS; Fort Smith, AR; (3); 52/800; Tennis; High Hon Roll; Hon Roll; Jr NHS; NHS; Pres Acad Fit Awd; Spanish NHS; U Of AR; Radiology.

GOODMAN, W L; Ozark HS; Ozark, AR; (2); Quiz Bowl; Spanish Clb; Band; Pep Band; L Bsktbl; L Ftbl; Hon Roll; Jr NHS; NHS; CODA Band; NW OK Hnr Band; AAU Bsktbl; Duke Univ TIP Prog.

GOODNER, BROOKE L; Oden Schl; Oden, AR; (2); FBLA; FHA; GAA; Natl FFA Org; Drill Tm; Ofcr Frsh Cls; Ofcr Soph Cls; Ofcr Stu Cncl; Ofcr Bsbl; Bsktbl; Sftbl; Fayetteville; Dsgnr.

GOODNER, MELISSA; Mountainburg Jr Sr HS; Mountainburg, AR; (4); 2/42; Am Leg Aux Girls St; Church Yth Grp; FCA; FBLA; FHA; Natl Beta Clb; Natl FFA Org; SADD; Ed Yrbk; Sec Frsh Cls; Ernest Allen Memrl Schlsp; Deans Schlsp; U Of The Ozarks.

GOODNOH, LAURA; Pleasant View Schl; Mulberry, AR; (2); Church Yth Grp; Drama Clb; Rptr FBLA; HOBY; Natl Beta Clb; Quiz Bowl; Spanish Clb; Church Choir; VP Frsh Cls; Rep Soph Cls; Gftd/Tlntd Pgm; Sci By Mail Enrchmnt Pgm; Jrnlsm.

GOODSELL, JANE; Warren Sr HS; Warren, AR; (4); 1/107; U Of AR; Engrng.

GOODSELL, SALLY; Warren Jr HS; Warren, AR; (1); 6/132; Church Yth Grp; Cmnty Wkr; Math Tm; Natl Beta Clb; Band; Flag Corp; Crs Cntry; Trk; Hon Roll; Pres Schlr; AEGIS Math & Sci Pgm 95, Perfmnc Arts Pgm 96; Algebra Regnl Math Cont 3rd Pl 96.

GOODSON, JESSICA A; Highland HS; Ash Flat, AR; (2); FHA; Natl FFA Org; Flag Corp; Ofcr Stu Cncl; Hon Roll; Prfct Atten Awd; Ed.

GOODSON, KELLY L; Robinson HS; Little Rock, AR; (2); 40/150; French Clb; FBLA; Hon Roll; Algebra I Awd; Advncd Wrd Prcsng Awd; FBLA VP; Rdlgc Tech.

GOODSON, MARK O; Russellville Sr HS; Russellville, AR; (2); Church Yth Grp; Cmnty Wkr; Band; Pres Soph Cls; Pres Jr Cls; Rep Stu Cncl; Var Bsktbl; L Ftbl; Var Trk; Pres Jr NHS; Hosp Admin.

GOODWIN, AMANDA; Bradford Jr Sr HS; Newark, AR; (3); Church Yth Grp; French Clb; Natl FFA Org; Chorus; Church Choir; School Play; Chrldng; Mgr(s); Score Keeper; Hon Roll; AR ST Univ; Med.

GOODWIN, AMANDA A; Shirley Jr Sr HS; Fairfield Bay, AR; (3); 2/58; Church Yth Grp; Drama Clb; Natl Beta Clb; Quiz Bowl; School Play; Sec Stu Cncl; Chrldng; Tennis; Gov Hon Prg Awd; Pres Acad Fit Awd; U Of AR Fayetteville; Engl.

GOODWIN, BEN MATTHEW; Conway Sr HS; Conway, AR; (3); 2/600; Am Leg Boys St; Church Yth Grp; Debate Tm; Natl Beta Clb; Quiz Bowl; High Hon Roll; Ntl Merit SF.

GOODWIN, JASON M; Magnolia HS; Magnolia, AR; (2); Church Yth Grp; Acpl Chr; Church Choir; Nwsp; JV Bsbl; JV Bsktbl; JV Ftbl; Hon Roll; Sr Thomas J Lipton Yth Sprtmnshp Awd 96; AWANA Var ST Olympc Chmpn Tm 94-; AR ST Bsbl Chmps 95.

GOODWIN, JOYCE H; Forrest City HS; Forrest City, AR; (3); Church Yth Grp; Drama Clb; French Clb; Library Aide; Mu Alpha Theta; Natl Beta Clb; Spanish Clb; Teachers Aide; High Hon Roll; AR ST U; Nrs Practitioner.

GOODWIN, RAMONICA T; Eudora HS; Eudora, AR; (3); 2/50; Church Yth Grp; FBLA; SADD; Church Choir; Flag Corp; Treas Jr Cls; Rep Stu Cncl; Co-Capt Chrldng; Capt Trk; Cit Awd; UAPB; Nrsng; Child Care.

GOODWIN, RONALD J; North Little Rock Hs-West; Sherwood, AR; (3); 70/554; Cmnty Wkr; FCA; Mu Alpha Theta; Q&S; Stage Crew; Yrbk; L Bsbl; High Hon Roll; Hon Roll; NHS; Bsbl All Conf/All Metro/All 4a ST Ptchr/96 ST Chmpns; U Of AR; Med Field/Prof Bsbl.

GOODWON, WILLIAM J; North Little Rock Hs-West; North Little Rock, AR; (3); Church Yth Grp; Mu Alpha Theta; Teachers Aide; Band; Chorus; Church Choir; Variety Show; High Hon Roll; Hon Roll; NHS; Choir Stu Yr; All Rgn Choir.

GORDON, CANDI; Delight HS; Delight, AR; (4); 1/25; Church Yth Grp; 4-H; VP FBLA; Capt GAA; Pres Natl Beta Clb; Pres Natl FFA Org; Quiz Bowl; Church Choir; School Play; Nwsp; CIA Reprtr 95-96, VP 93-95; FFA Poultry Judgng Team; Peer Cnslr; U Of AR Fayetteville.

GORDON, DARREN R; Bald Knob HS; Bald Knob, AR; (1); Church Yth Grp; Cmnty Wkr; Math Tm; Quiz Bowl; Band; Church Choir; Mrchg Band; Var Bsbl; High Hon Roll; Pres Acad Fit Awd; AR ST Univ; Psych.

GORDON, JOSEPH B; Central Sr HS; Little Rock, AR; (3); 43/540; Church Yth Grp; German Clb; Latin Clb; Natl Beta Clb; Office Aide; Quiz Bowl; Church Choir; Jazz Band; Ed Nwsp; Ofcr Stu Cncl; Chrch Mscl 5 Yrs; Chrch Yth Eldr; Amer Yth Fnd Ldrshp Awd; Odyssey Of Mind ST Wnnr; Pre-Med.

GORDON, LISA; Gosness HS; Blytheville, AR; (3); 15/55; Key Clb; Natl Beta Clb; Chorus; Bsktbl; Var Chrldng; Pom Pon; Sftbl; Trk; Natl Hnrs Choir; All Rgn Choir; Elem Ed.

GORDON, RAYMOND C; Arkansas Sr HS; Texarkana, AR; (2); 82/427; Rep Frsh Cls; Var JV Bsbl; Var JV Ftbl; North Heights Jr HS Bsktbl MVP, Ftbl Ouutstndng Offnsv Plyr & A-B Hnr Roll; Hnr Roll 95-96.

GORDON, TARA R; Bald Knob HS; Bald Knob, AR; (4); 7/80; Pres Church Yth Grp; Sec FBLA; Natl Beta Clb; VP Chorus; Church Choir; School Play; Rep Jr Cls; Rep Sr Cls; Cit Awd; High Hon Roll; ASU; Med.

GORE, AMANDA R; North Little Rock Hs-East; North Little Rock, AR; (2); Church Yth Grp; Debate Tm; Natl Beta Clb; Q&S; Spanish Clb; Band; Rptr Nwsp; Hon Roll; Pharmist.

GORE, BENJAMIN D; Clay Co Central Jr Sr HS; Rector, AR; (4); 7/55; Art Clb; FBLA; German Clb; Natl FFA Org; Science Clb; Ftbl; Hon Roll; Jr NHS; NHS; Pres Acad Fit Awd; AR Gov Schl; AEGTS; AR ST Univ; Cmptr Sci.

GORE, MICHELLE L; Magnolia HS; Magnolia, AR; (3); Church Yth Grp; FBLA; Science Clb; Band; Pep Band; Rep Soph Cls; Sec Jr Cls; Rep Stu Cncl; Powder Puff Ftbl; Hon Roll; Bus.

GORHAM, JILL; Mineral Springs Schl; Mineral Springs, AR; (1); Church Yth Grp; 4-H; FHA; GAA; Quiz Bowl; Band; Drm Mjr(t); Flag Corp; Jazz Band; Mrchg Band.

GOSCH, JESSICA L; Springdale Sr HS; Springdale, AR; (1); Band; Color Guard; Mrchg Band; Orch; Pep Band; School Play; Hon Roll; Jr NHS; Pres Acad Fit Awd; OM; Harvard; Law.

GOSDIN, JONATHAN M; Magnolia HS; Magnolia, AR; (3); 29/210; Am Leg Boys St; Church Yth Grp; VP FCA; FBLA; Quiz Bowl; Rptr Nwsp; Ed Yrbk; VP Frsh Cls; Treas Sr Cls; Ofcr Stu Cncl; Northwestern ST Univ.

GOSLYN, JENNIFER R; Glen Rose HS; Malvern, AR; (1); Spanish Clb; Band; Mrchg Band; Hon Roll; Spanish NHS; Vet Med.

GOSNELL, AMBER P; Russellville Sr HS; Russellville, AR; (2); #1 in class; French Clb; Band; Flag Corp; Mrchg Band; Pep Band; JV Var Sftbl; Jr NHS; NHS; Celebration Excl; All Stars; All Rgn Bnd 3 Yrs; U Of AR Fayetteville; Sci.

GOSNELL, JENNIFER; St Joseph HS; Conway, AR; (4); 1/28; Am Leg Aux Girls St; Ed Yrbk; VP Sr Cls; VP Stu Cncl; Var Bsktbl; Sec NHS; Val; Church Yth Grp; Cmnty Wkr; HOBY; 4th Pl Intl 16 Yr Old Wrld Solo; Miss Mjrtt Of AR; Ftr Twrlr; Vanderbilt; Dntst.

GOSNELL, STEPHANIE N; St Joseph HS; Conway, AR; (1); Church Yth Grp; Ofcr Frsh Cls; Rep Stu Cncl; JV Bsktbl; Var Sftbl; JV Vllybl; High Hon Roll; Jr NHS; Twirling Line; Prosecuting Atty.

GOSNEY, LEONNA M; Woodlawn Schl; Monticello, AR; (2); FHA; Library Aide; Teachers Aide; Chorus; Hon Roll; UAM; Photographer.

GOSS, SAMANTHA A; Mountain Home HS; Mountain Home, AR; (3); Art Clb; Church Yth Grp; Cmnty Wkr; FBLA; Hosp Aide; Spanish Clb; Church Choir; School Play; Lit Mag; JV Var Socr; Raise Horses & Cows; Comp Tech; Vacation Bible Schl Tchr; Univ Of AR; Eng; Art Tchr.

GOTTSPONER, ERIN M; St Joseph HS; North Little Rock, AR; (1); Church Yth Grp; Church Choir; School Play; Bsktbl; Sftbl; Swmmng; Vllybl; Roller Bladeing; Drawing; Bowling.

GOUCHER, ANDREA R; Springdale Sr HS; Springdale, AR; (2); French Clb; FBLA; Hosp Aide; Office Aide; Chorus; School Play; Phtg Yrbk; Var Sftbl; Gov Hon Prg Awd; Hon Roll; Yth For Christ; ST Media Festival; Univ Of FL; Pathlgy.

GOUDE VERA, LISA; Newport HS; Diaz, AR; (2); Church Yth Grp; English Clb; Intnl Clb; Natl Beta Clb; Spanish Clb; Teachers Aide; Hon Roll; AR Tech Univ; Col Prof.

GOVAN, JOY M; Huttig Schl; Huttig, AR; (2); Church Yth Grp; FTA; Natl Beta Clb; Band; Chorus; Church Choir; Ofcr Stu Cncl; Var Bsktbl; Hon Roll; Obstetrician.

GRADDY, ERICA L; Valley Springs Schl; Harrison, AR; (4); French Clb; FBLA; Treas Key Clb; Teachers Aide; Treas Jr Cls; Var Chrldng; Hon Roll.

GRADDY, JOSH B; Valley Springs Schl; Harrison, AR; (2); Key Clb; Natl FFA Org; Ofcr Bsbl; Bsktbl; Prfct Atten Awd; FFA Natl Cnvntn KS City MO 95.

GRADDY, MIRANDA N; Conway Sr HS; Conway, AR; (2); Sec Natl FFA Org; Office Aide; Teachers Aide; Horses; NASCAR Stock Car Races; Ag.

GRADY, JENNIFER; Southside HS; Fort Smith, AR; (4); Church Yth Grp; Mu Alpha Theta; Spanish Clb; Band; Pres Church Choir; Drm Mjr(t); Flag Corp; NHS; Spanish NHS; Interact Svc Clb Brd; AR Tech; Accntng.

GRADY, JULIE; Hazen Jr Sr HS; Hazen, AR; (4); 2/27; Am Leg Aux Girls St; Pres FHA; HOBY; Natl Beta Clb; Yrbk; Pres Frsh Cls; VP Soph Cls; Var Chrldng; Cit Awd; Sal; ASU Jonesboro; Accntng.

GRADY, SCARLETT S; Dierks HS; Dierks, AR; (3); 6/38; Church Yth Grp; FBLA; FHA; Quiz Bowl; VP Frsh Cls; VP Soph Cls; Sec Jr Cls; Sec Sr Cls; Var Bsktbl; Var Chrldng; PRIDE & St PRIDE Teams; Ouachita Bptst U.

GRAGG, ADRIANNA K; Monticello HS; Monticello, AR; (3); 18/160; Sec Debate Tm; Sec Drama Clb; Hosp Aide; Natl Beta Clb; Red Cross Aide; Speech Tm; Church Choir; VP Jr Cls; Var Trk; Hon Roll; Hmcmng Ct 2 Yrs; 1st Pl Nrs Asst ST Comp; HOSA Pres; Pedtrc Cardlgst.

GRAHAM, DENELIA L; El Dorado Sr HS; El Dorado, AR; (1); Church Yth Grp; Cmnty Wkr; FBLA; FHA; Band; Church Choir; Flag Corp; Mrchg Band; Frosh Cls Treas; Chrch Choir Pianist; SAU; Acctng.

GRAHAM, JACQUELYN; Ola Jr Sr HS; Danville, AR; (2); 1/25; FHA; GAA; Natl Beta Clb; Natl FFA Org; Pep Clb; Quiz Bowl; Spanish Clb; VP Soph Cls; Ofcr Stu Cncl; High Hon Roll; U Of AR; Psycht.

GRAHAM, JENNY L; El Dorado Sr HS; El Dorado, AR; (4); Church Yth Grp; Cmnty Wkr; FBLA; FHA; Girl Scts; Key Clb; Library Aide; Office Aide; ROTC; Teachers Aide; Key Clb; Seacers; Teenage Republicans; Jr Civitans; U Of The Ozarks; Kndgtn Tchr.

GRAHAM, LA TOYA; Dermott HS; Dermott, AR; (1); Church Yth Grp; Quiz Bowl; Ofcr Frsh Cls; Bsktbl; Chrldng; Trk; Cit Awd; High Hon Roll; Hon Roll; GA Tech; Actress/Nrsng/Mdlng.

GRAHAM, LASHONDA; Dermott HS; Dermott, AR; (3); FBLA; FHA; Natl Beta Clb; Science Clb; Spanish Clb; Rep Frsh Cls; Cit Awd; Hon Roll; ULAR; Comp Sci.

GRAHAM, TIMOTHY A; England HS; England, AR; (2); Church Yth Grp; FBLA; Spanish Clb; Band; Church Choir; Jazz Band; Mrchg Band; Bandsmn Of Yr 95-96; Natl Sci Olympd 3rd Pl Schl Team; Reg Band Alt 94-95; CBC; Engrng.

GRAHAM, TIMOTHY G; Springdale Sr HS; Springdale, AR; (3); FCA; FBLA; Key Clb; Rep Natl FFA Org; Rep Frsh Cls; Rep Soph Cls; Treas Stu Cncl; JV Bsbl; JV Ftbl; High Hon Roll; U Of AR; Bus.

GRAHAM, WENDY; Hoxie Schl; Alicia, AR; (4); 4/60; Am Leg Aux Girls St; FBLA; FHA; Natl Beta Clb; Science Clb; Teachers Aide; Thesps; L Bsktbl; Art Clb; Church Yth Grp; Prin Ldrshp Awd; I Dare You Awd; Sci Awd 3 Yrs; AEGIS Mem; Williams Bapt Coll; Scndry Sci.

GRAMLICH, NICK; Southside HS; Fort Smith, AR; (4); FCA; German Clb; Letterman Clb; Service Clb; Teachers Aide; Temple Yth Grp; Varsity Clb; Ofcr Soph Cls; Ofcr Jr Cls; Ofcr Sr Cls; Westark CC; Electr.

GRAMLICH, STACEY; Charleston HS; Charleston, AR; (4); 2/58; Am Leg Aux Girls St; FCA; FBLA; Pres Natl Beta Clb; Sec Spanish Clb; Mgr Yrbk; Sec Sr Cls; Sec Stu Cncl; Capt Bsktbl; Sal; Hendrix Coll; Accntng.

GRANBERRY, KANDI A; Newport HS; Newport, AR; (2); VP Soph Cls; Trk; Phy Thrpst.

GRANT, PERRY C; Fairview HS; Camden, AR; (3); 28/330; Church Yth Grp; Mu Alpha Theta; Var L Ftbl; Var L Tennis; Var Wt Lftg; Ntl Merit SF; Spanish NHS.

GRASSE, JOSEPH; Calico Rock HS; Pineville, AR; (2); Church Yth Grp; Pres Natl Beta Clb; Science Clb; Var Bsktbl; High Hon Roll; Prfct Atten Awd; Wkng With Cmptrs; Soccer; Cmptr Field.

GRATTON, ANDREW; Bergman Schl; Harrison, AR; (2); 2/80; Church Yth Grp; Model UN; Natl Beta Clb; Natl FFA Org; Pep Clb; Acpl Chr; Band; Chorus; Church Choir; Jazz Band; Congress Bundestag Yth Exch Schlsp Pgm; Received 3 AEGIS Pgms; Forensics.

GRAVES, AMANDA C; Pine Bluff HS; Pine Bluff, AR; (2); 20/400; Church Yth Grp; French Clb; FHA; Hosp Aide; Hon Roll; Jr NHS; Pres Schlr; 2nd Degree Black Belt; U Of Ozarks; Pediatrician.

GRAVES, BETHANY K; Dewitt HS; De Witt, AR; (2); 8/90; Church Yth Grp; French Clb; FBLA; FTA; HOBY; Science Clb; DAR Awd; Jr NHS; NHS; PRIDE; Univ Of AR; Pharmacy.

GRAVES, CHRISTOPHER G; Sloan Hendrix HS; Black Rock, AR; (2); 5/60; 4-H; FHA; Natl Beta Clb; Natl FFA Org; Quiz Bowl; 4-H Awd; Hon Roll; Showing Cattle Local Dist & St Level; Parliamentary Procedure Team; Livestock Judging; Ag; Comp.

GRAVES, JOSH B; Valley Springs Schl; Harrison, AR; (2); Band; Var Bsbl; Var Bsktbl; Var Golf; Hon Roll; U Of AR.

GRAVES, LINDE D; Sheridan Sr HS; Sheridan, AR; (4); Cmnty Wkr; Q&S; Band; Drm Mjr(t); Flag Corp; Jazz Band; School Play; Mgr Nwsp; Cit Awd; Hon Roll; Yth For Christ VP; Southern AR U; Cmmrcl Art.

GRAVES, MELINDA D; Mc Crory Jr Sr HS; Mc Crory, AR; (3); Church Yth Grp; FBLA; FTA; Letterman Clb; Office Aide; Spanish Clb; Teachers Aide; School Play; JV Var Bsktbl; Var Tennis; GT Prgm; SHADOW; ASU Beebe; Med Lab Tech.

GRAY, AARON D; Malvern Sr HS; Malvern, AR; (4); Church Yth Grp; Cmnty Wkr; Am Leg Aux Girls St; Drama Clb; French Clb; FBLA; FHA; Speech Tm; Temple Yth Grp; Thesps; Mnrgls; Entrtnrs; Ptry Awd; Hndrsn ST U; Msc.

GRAY, AMANDA G; Rogers HS; Rogers, AR; (3); Church Yth Grp; FBLA; Model UN; Science Clb; Band; Drill Tm; Swmmng; Hon Roll; NHS; Odyssey Of The Mind; Bus.

GRAY, AMY M; Alma HS; Alma, AR; (2); FCA; FBLA; SADD; Variety Show; Ofcr Stu Cncl; Var Bsktbl; Hon Roll; Wlmrts Annul Fnd Rsng Cmpagn; Cops For Kids Shpng Prgm; Phys Thrpst.

GRAY, BRAD L; Ridgecrest HS; Paragould, AR; (2); Church Yth Grp; FCA; Natl FFA Org; JV Var Bsktbl; Var Trk; Cit Awd; Hon Roll.

GRAY, BRANDI R; Clinton HS; Lincoln, NE; (4); Drama Clb; FCA; FBLA; Natl Beta Clb; Natl FFA Org; Science Clb; Spanish Clb; JV Chrldng; Hon Roll; Thrd Pl FFA ST Jdgng Crops Cntst; Univ Of NE; Anml Sci.

GRAY, BRANDY M; Cloverdale Jr HS; Little Rock, AR; (1); Church Yth Grp; FBLA; JA; Natl Beta Clb; Hon Roll; Jr NHS; Pres Acad Fit Awd; Pediatrician.

GRAY, CHRISSY M; Alma HS; Alma, AR; (1); Chorus; Hon Roll; All-Region; Super Rating Solo & Trio; Commercial Advertising; Psych.

GRAY, DANIEL A; Arkansas Sr HS; Texarkana, AR; (3); Am Leg Boys St; Boy Scts; Drama Clb; Pres Stu Cncl; Var Bsktbl; Var Ftbl; Var Tennis; High Hon Roll; NHS; Pres Acad Fit Awd.

GRAY, HILARY A; Morrilton Sr HS; Morrilton, AR; (2); Church Yth Grp; French Clb; Science Clb; Chorus.

GRAY, JENNIFER A; Siloam Springs Sr HS; Siloam Springs, AR; (3); Church Yth Grp; Natl Beta Clb; Spanish Clb; Band; Flag Corp; Mrchg Band; Mgr(s); Vllybl; Hon Roll; NHS.

GRAY, JEREMY E; Harrisburg HS; Harrisburg, AR; (2); FCA; 4-H; FBLA; Quiz Bowl; Science Clb; Spanish Clb; Band; Chorus; Mrchg Band; Yrbk; AR ST; Medicine.

GRAY, JULIE D; Ozark HS; Altus, AR; (2); Church Yth Grp; 4-H; FBLA; Natl Beta Clb; Acpl Chr; Band; Church Choir; Mrchg Band; Orch; Pep Band; Piano Fed Cntst; U Of AR; Msc Ed.

GRAY, KAREN B; Southside HS; Batesville, AR; (1); Church Yth Grp; Key Clb; Library Aide; Office Aide; Spanish Clb; Teachers Aide; Chorus; Capt Chrldng; Trk; Hon Roll; 2nd Age Category ST Gymnstcs Meet 96; Wrk With Chldrn Arts Pk; UCA; PT.

GRAY, KIMBERLY A; Riverview HS; Searcy, AR; (3); Am Leg Aux Girls St; Drama Clb; French Clb; Sec FBLA; Rep FHA; Natl Beta Clb; Band; Chorus; Sec Treas Jr Cls; Sec Treas Jr Cls; FBLA Impromptue Speaking Wnnr; Prom & Homcmng Comms; Raider Clb; U Of Cntrl AR; Fshn Merchandsg.

GRAY, MARY BETH E; North Little Rock Hs-East; North Little Rock, AR; (2); Church Yth Grp; Drama Clb; English Clb; Acpl Chr; Chorus; Variety Show; High Hon Roll; Hon Roll; Solo Perfmnc For Civic Orgs; AR All-St Choir; George Mason Univ; Music; Drama.

GRAY, MEGAN M; Stuttgart Sr HS; Roe, AR; (2); Church Yth Grp; FBLA; Key Clb; Natl Beta Clb; Office Aide; Science Clb; Chorus; Bsktbl; Trk; Cit Awd; HOBY; Cmnty Sftbl; AR ST U; Bus.

GRAY, MICHAEL D; Rison HS; Rison, AR; (4); 12/54; Art Clb; French Clb; Natl Beta Clb; Natl FFA Org; Bsktbl; Var L Ftbl; Wt Lftg; Hon Roll; Prfct Atten Awd; All Amer Schlr; ST Chmpnshp Ftbl Tm; Reg Fnlst Elec Tm; U Of AR; Elec Engr.

GRAY, PAULA J; Alpena Schl; Green Forest, AR; (2); 1/50; Church Yth Grp; FCA; Sec FBLA; Sec FHA; Sec Natl Beta Clb; Spanish Clb; Church Choir; Var Bsktbl; Trk; Cit Awd; GATE; Southwest Bapt U; Ministries.

GRAY, ROBERT D; Harrisburg HS; Harrisburg, AR; (2); Treas Chess Clb; Church Yth Grp; FCA; Quiz Bowl; Rptr Science Clb; Spanish Clb; Sec Frsh Cls; Rptr Soph Cls; Rep Stu Cncl; L Bsbl; Acthctc.

GRAY, SALONICA N; Central Sr HS; Little Rock, AR; (3); 67/540; Am Leg Aux Girls St; Natl Beta Clb; Science Clb; Band; Hon Roll; Jr NHS; NHS; AR Govnr Schl; Brdgng Gap Prog Bst Overall Perf; Premed.

GRAY, WILLIAM C; Sloan Hendrix HS; Imboden, AR; (3); Natl Beta Clb; Natl FFA Org; Ofcr Bsbl; Bsktbl; Hon Roll; ASU Jonesboro.

GRAY, WILLIAM F; Bauxite Jr Sr HS; Benton, AR; (2); Church Yth Grp; Quiz Bowl; Teachers Aide; Ofcr Stu Cncl; Mgr(s); Hon Roll.

GRAYSON, JAMIE L; Searcy HS; Searcy, AR; (3); Natl Beta Clb; Quiz Bowl; Thesps; Chorus; School Musical; School Play; Yrbk; Church Yth Grp; Drama Clb; FTA; AR Governors Schl Choral Music; All ST Choir; Madrigals; Theatre.

GRAYSON, JOHN A; Bald Knob HS; Bald Knob, AR; (2); L Ftbl; L Trk; L Wt Lftg; Hon Roll; Outstdng Lifter Awd; Ftbl Rudy Awd 95; U Of AK; Ath/Prsnl Trng.

GRAYSON, KATRINA L; Holly Grove Jr Sr HS; Holly Grove, AR; (3); 3/37; Am Leg Aux Girls St; Church Yth Grp; FBLA; Rptr FHA; Church Choir; Bsktbl; Hon Roll; Drama Clb; German Clb; Natl FFA Org; UCA; Pre-Law.

GRAYSTON, KIM S; Southside HS; Fort Smith, AR; (2); Church Yth Grp; Spanish Clb; Chorus; Drill Tm; School Musical; High Hon Roll; Jr NHS; NHS; Pres Acad Fit Awd; SAIL.

GREEN, AMY; Arkadelphia Sr HS; Arkadelphia, AR; (4); 7/161; Church Yth Grp; Natl Beta Clb; Spanish Clb; Band; Chorus; Church Choir; Drm Mjr(t); CAP; Co-Ed Nwsp; High Hon Roll; U AR Fayetteville; Chrl Msc Pe.

GREEN, ANDREA; Sylvan Hills HS; North Little Rock, AR; (4); 8/233; Pres Church Yth Grp; Drama Clb; FCA; French Clb; Pres Mu Alpha Theta; Natl Beta Clb; SADD; Drill Tm; Ofcr Jr Cls; Pres Acad Fit Awd; Dance; Miss Sylvan Hills HS; Tchrs Ldrsp Awd; Univ AR Fayetville; Commnctn.

GREEN, BRITTANI; Malvern Jr HS; Malvern, AR; (2); Church Yth Grp; Natl Beta Clb; SADD; Teachers Aide; Band; Drm Mjr(t); Mrchg Band; Cit Awd; High Hon Roll; NHS; Mjrte; GFTD/TLNTD Prgm; Univ Of NC; Amer Eng/Lit/Music.

GREEN, ELIZABETH; Maynard Jr Sr HS; Pocahontas, AR; (3); FHA; Library Aide; Teachers Aide; Cit Awd; High Hon Roll; Prfct Atten Awd.

GREEN, FELICIA NACOLE; Gosnell Jr Sr HS; Gosnell, AR; (3); 8/75; FHA; Math Clb; Mu Alpha Theta; Science Clb; SADD; Teachers Aide; Band; Chorus; Mrchg Band; Pep Band; Sci Awd Hghst Grd; Sol & Ensmbl 1st Pl 3 Songs; Music.

GREEN, GREG; Strong Jr Sr HS; Strong, AR; (2); 2/53; French Clb; Quiz Bowl; Science Clb; Bsktbl; Beta Club.

GREEN, HOLLY; Jessieville HS; Hot Springs, AR; (4); 2/38; Church Yth Grp; Cmnty Wkr; Drama Clb; Key Clb; Natl Beta Clb; Office Aide; Speech Tm; School Play; Cit Awd; High Hon Roll; HS Rodeo Assn LA; Outstndng Vol Cmnty; 3rd Pl Optimist Speech; UAM; Nrs.

GREEN, JAIME D; Springdale Sr HS; Springdale, AR; (2); Church Yth Grp; FCA; GAA; Acpl Chr; Chorus; VP Stu Cncl; Var Bsktbl; JV Crs Cntry; Trk; Hon Roll; Coach/Tchr.

GREEN, JASON L; Blytheville Sr HS; Blytheville, AR; (2); French Clb; Chorus; Ofcr Bsbl; Ftbl; Wt Lftg; Hon Roll.

GREEN, JUSTIN A; White Co Central Schl; Judsonia, AR; (2); FHA; VP Soph Cls; Bsktbl; High Hon Roll; Hon Roll; 1st Plc Sci Fair.

GREEN, KATADRA D; Parkview Arts-Science HS; Little Rock, AR; (3); Church Yth Grp; Dance Clb; Drama Clb; FBLA; Natl Beta Clb; Spanish Clb; Drill Tm; Cit Awd; High Hon Roll; Prfct Atten Awd; TN ST Univ; Pharmacy.

GREEN, KELLIE L; Sheridan Sr HS; Sheridan, AR; (3); Church Yth Grp; Cmnty Wkr; FCA; GAA; Office Aide; Spanish Clb; Teachers Aide; Varsity Clb; Ofcr Bsbl; Bsktbl; Bsktbl Capt; Channel 1 Producer; All ST Track; Advrtsng.

GREEN, KENDRA D; Trumann HS; Trumann, AR; (4); 15/82; Church Yth Grp; French Clb; FBLA; VP FHA; Library Aide; Math Clb; Model UN; Chorus; Church Choir; Ed Yrbk; AR St Univ; Comm.

GREEN, KIMBERLY D; Central Sr HS; Little Rock, AR; (3); Church Yth Grp; Natl Beta Clb; Band; Church Choir; Flag Corp; Mrchg Band; Mgr(s); Powder Puff Ftbl; Hon Roll; NHS; Completion Of The Holy Bible; Hendrix; Pediatrics/Mdcn.

GREEN, LA TEESHA R; Camden-Fairview HS; Camden, AR; (4); 12/245; Church Yth Grp; FBLA; Sec Mu Alpha Theta; Var Natl Beta Clb; Spanish Clb; L Chorus; Church Choir; Yrbk; Sec Stu Cncl; L Sftbl; CNA; Attnd Natl Yth Ldrshp Forum On Med In San Francisco; UAR Fayettevll; Nrs Anesthtst.

GREEN, LAYNI D; Star City HS; Star City, AR; (2); Science Clb; Spanish Clb; Band; Jazz Band; Mrchg Band; Sr All Region Band, 1st Chair Clarinet, All St Band 2nd Alt; Solo/Ensemble Medals I & II; Henderson ST Univ; Music Ed.

GREEN, LETITIA; Mineral Springs Schl; Mineral Springs, AR; (3); Church Yth Grp; FBLA; Bsktbl; Stdnt Mnth; Drg Intrvntn Team.

GREEN, LINDA N; Central Sr HS; Little Rock, AR; (3); 93/540; Am Leg Aux Girls St; Drama Clb; Girl Scts; Mu Alpha Theta; Natl Beta Clb; Spanish Clb; Co-Capt Drill Tm; High Hon Roll; Jr NHS; NHS; SECME; Black Cultural Soc; Hampton Univ; Psych.

GREEN, MATTHEW A; Mc Crory Jr Sr HS; Mc Crory, AR; (2); Boy Scts; Ofcr Bsbl; Ftbl; Trk; Wt Lftg; Jr NHS; Phys Thrpy.

GREEN, NAKITA L; Russellville Sr HS; Russellville, AR; (3); Am Leg Aux Girls St; Church Yth Grp; Cmnty Wkr; FCA; Natl Beta Clb; Spanish Clb; Band; Church Choir; Mrchg Band; Pep Band; CSU; Homcmng Royalty 94-95; Colors Day Royalty 95-96; Renaissance Stu Ldrshp Comm; Natl Yth Assembly 94; FL A&M Univ; Bio.

GREEN, NIKKI L; Arkadelphia Sr HS; Arkadelphia, AR; (4); FHA; Letterman Clb; Teachers Aide; Band; Color Guard; Drm Mjr(t); Mrchg Band; High Hon Roll; White Cndl Awd; Cm Ld; Henderson ST U; Rdlgy.

GREEN, REGINALD S; Crossett Sr HS; Crossett, AR; (2); Pres Church Yth Grp; Natl Beta Clb; Church Choir; Bsktbl; JV Trk; Cit Awd; Hon Roll; LA Tech Univ; Cvl Eng.

GREEN, RODERICK N; El Dorado Sr HS; El Dorado, AR; (3); Natl Beta Clb; Ftbl; Schlr Ath Awd; Futuristic Otlk; Grambling ST Univ; Med Field.

GREEN, SHANDA D; Black Rock Jr Sr HS; Black Rock, AR; (2); 5/25; School Musical; Bsktbl; Hon Roll; Math Awd; Sci Awd; PE Awd; Vet.

GREEN, SHANNON; Star City HS; Star City, AR; (3); Art Clb; FCA; HOBY; Sec Spanish Clb; School Play; Sec Frsh Cls; Pres Soph Cls; Pres Jr Cls; Rep Stu Cncl; AP Engl; Stu Congress; Gifted & Talented.

GREEN, SHANNON; Southside HS; Fort Smith, AR; (4); Church Yth Grp; FCA; FBLA; FHA; Pep Clb; Teachers Aide; Drill Tm; Rep Sr Cls; Chrldng; Hon Roll; Bsktbl Homcmng Qn; Westark CC; Mrktg.

GREEN, SHELLY A; Russellville Sr HS; Russellville, AR; (2); Drama Clb; Band; Drill Tm; Mrchg Band; Pep Band; Stage Crew; NHS.

GREEN, SUMMER; Calvary Christian Schl; Marianna, AR; (2); Church Yth Grp; Church Choir; School Musical; School Play; Stage Crew; Var Bsktbl; Var Chrldng; Var Vllybl; High Hon Roll; Dntst.

GREEN, TENE L; Parkview Fine Arts Science HS; Little Rock, AR; (3); 14/270; Am Leg Aux Girls St; Treas Girl Scts; Key Clb; Mu Alpha Theta; Pres Natl Beta Clb; Chorus; School Musical; Treas Sr Cls; NHS; Pres Acad Fit Awd; Wellesley Bk Awd; Lawyer.

GREEN, TENISHA; Stephens Jr Sr HS; Stephens, AR; (3); 11/42; FHA; Hon Roll; NHS; U Of AR Pine Bluff; Psych.

GREEN, TOSHA NICOLE; Clay Co Central Jr Sr HS; Rector, AR; (3); FBLA; German Clb; Hosp Aide; Science Clb; Bsktbl; Sftbl; Vllybl; Cit Awd; Hon Roll; Pres Acad Fit Awd; Stndrzd Tstng Awd Otsdng Prfrmnc; ATA Amer Ty Kwon Do Assn; Smmr Sftbl Natnls; ASU; Paramedic.

GREEN, WHITNEY K; Arkansas Sr HS; Texarkana, AR; (3); Church Yth Grp; Drama Clb; Mu Alpha Theta; Spanish Clb; Rep Stu Cncl; Chrldng; Hon Roll; Jr NHS; NHS; Pres Acad Fit Awd; Drill Team Capt; Nike Clb.

GREENE, CAMILLE; Dequeen HS; De Queen, AR; (3); 7/110; Am Leg Aux Girls St; Church Yth Grp; Pres FHA; Sec Soph Cls; Rptr Jr Cls; Pres Sr Cls; Sec Stu Cncl; Capt Chrldng; Hon Roll; NHS; Tap, Ballet Dnc; Mss Deqn HS Pgnt; Dntstry.

GREENE, CASEY C; Southside HS; Fort Smith, AR; (2); Church Yth Grp; Spanish Clb; Teachers Aide; Band; Church Choir; Flag Corp; Mrchg Band; Orch; Hon Roll.

GREENE, HEATHER M; Arkansas Sr HS; Texarkana, AR; (3); 9/440; Church Yth Grp; Mu Alpha Theta; Natl FFA Org; Quiz Bowl; Band; Drm Mjr(t); Mrchg Band; Ed Yrbk; DAR Awd; Hon Roll; Psych.

GREENE, MICHAEL J; Flippin Jr Sr HS; Flippin, AR; (2); German Clb; Natl FFA Org; Science Clb; SADD; Band; Chorus; JV Var Bsktbl; GATE Pgm; Tchng.

GREENE, RANDALL H; Arkansas Sr HS; Texarkana, AR; (4); 41/372; Art Clb; Church Yth Grp; DECA; French Clb; Treas Pres Natl FFA Org; JV Intrml Bsbl; JV Intrml Ftbl; JV Trk; JV Wt Lftg; Hon Roll; Algebra II Stu Of Yr 94-95; Multi Yr Listing; S AR U; Vet.

GREENE, REBEKAH; Arkansas Bapt Schl; Little Rock, AR; (4); 1/34; FCA; FBLA; Natl Beta Clb; Spanish Clb; Church Choir; School Play; Capt Var Chrldng; High Hon Roll; US Chrldrs Achvt Awd; U Cntrl AR; Phys Thrpy.

GREENFIELD, MICAH R; Abundant Life Schools; Sherwood, AR; (3); Church Yth Grp; Church Choir; Stage Crew; Var Bsktbl; Hon Roll; NHS; Distngd Chrstn HS Stdnt; Interior Dsgn.

GREENFIELD, WENDY; Huttig Schl; Huttig, AR; (3); FBLA; FHA; FTA; Hosp Aide; HOBY; Library Aide; Science Clb; Yrbk; VP Soph Cls; Pres Jr Cls; Elem Ed.

GREENLEE, ANGELINA D; Springdale Sr HS; Springdale, AR; (3); Church Yth Grp; Cmnty Wkr; Office Aide; Teachers Aide; Chorus; Hon Roll; Jr NHS; Pres Acad Fit Awd; Dance Class 8 Yrs; Animal Care.

GREENO, AMBER L; Weiner HS; Fisher, AR; (2); Art Clb; GAA; Natl FFA Org; Science Clb; Varsity Clb; VP Frsh Cls; L Bsktbl; Sftbl; Tennis; Hon Roll; Regnl Sci Fair Wnnr; All-Conf Bsktbl.

GREENSLADE, WALT; Mountain Home HS; Mountain Home, AR; (4); 64/264; Church Yth Grp; French Clb; FBLA; Rptr Nwsp; JV Bsktbl; JV Var Ftbl; L Trk; Hon Roll; SCA VP; Moody Bible Inst; Missionary.

GREENWAY, ADAM J; Catholic HS; Little Rock, AR; (2); 8/200; Church Yth Grp; Cmnty Wkr; ROTC; Socr; High Hon Roll; Hon Roll.

GREENWOOD, GINGER L; West Memphis Christian Schl; Heth, AR; (3); Speech Tm; Thesps; School Play; Ed Nwsp; Rep Stu Cncl; Intrml Mgr Ftbl; Hon Roll; Dist Sci Fair Wnnr; Stu Cncl Rptr; U Of Memphis; Jrnlsm.

GREENWOOD, SARAH; Central Ark Christian Schl; Little Rock, AR; (4); 8/74; Am Leg Aux Girls St; Church Yth Grp; Dance Clb; Ed Yrbk; Bsktbl; Trk; Vllybl; VP Jr NHS; NHS; Dnce; Acad Fair Wnnr 94, 95; Law.

GREER, COURTNEY A; Searcy HS; Searcy, AR; (3); 41/230; FCA; Key Clb; Natl Beta Clb; Spanish Clb; Var JV Bsktbl; Var Sftbl; Spanish NHS; PT.

GREER, ERIN ELISABETH; Star City HS; Star City, AR; (3); #1 in class; FBLA; Mu Alpha Theta; School Play; Nwsp; Ed Yrbk; Co-Capt Chrldng; NHS; Art Clb; Church Yth Grp; FCA; Frndshp MBC Yth Assn Sec; Hnrs Awds Span I, Chem, AP Eng III, & Acad Achvmnt; 1st Pl St Prjct Art.

GREER, JAMIE E; Russellville Sr HS; Russellville, AR; (2); Pres Church Yth Grp; Cmnty Wkr; Debate Tm; Hosp Aide; Office Aide; Spanish Clb; Chorus; Church Choir; Drill Tm; School Musical; UDA Drl Tm All Star 2nd Pl Clogging Cmptn; Brigham Yng U; Musical Theatre.

GREER, JENNIFER; Bismarck Jr-Sr HS; Bismarck, AR; (3); 1/57; Church Yth Grp; Treas FBLA; Library Aide; Natl Beta Clb; Natl FFA Org; Chorus; Church Choir; Variety Show; Bsktbl; Chrldng; Pee Wee Chrldng Coach; Sprts Med.

GREER, KRISTEN M; El Dorado Sr HS; El Dorado, AR; (2); 24/350; Church Yth Grp; Natl Beta Clb; Band; Drm Mjr(t); Mrchg Band; Swmmng; Hon Roll; NHS; Church Choir; Rep Soph Cls; BASIC; REACH-PRIDE; Anchor Clb; All Regn Bands; Vet.

GREER, MECHELLE D; Lakeside HS; Montrose, AR; (3); 33/88; Drama Clb; FHA; Chorus; Stage Crew; Powder Puff Ftbl; Hon Roll; Wrtng Clb; UAM.

GREER, MIRANDA L; Lakeside HS; Lake Village, AR; (3); 3/80; Drama Clb; FHA; School Play; High Hon Roll; Hon Roll; NHS; Ntl Merit Ltr; Art.

GREER, SHERRY R; Searcy HS; Searcy, AR; (3); Church Yth Grp; Cmnty Wkr; Chorus; Socr; Cit Awd; Summer Acad Outstdng Stu Tchr Awd; Outstdng Acvmt Housing Authority Searcy St Clean-Up; Mission Work; Med.

GREESON, FREDRICK L; Arkansas Bapt Schl; Little Rock, AR; (4); Church Yth Grp; FCA; Pres FBLA; JA; Natl Beta Clb; Spanish Clb; Band; Chorus; Church Choir; Mrchg Band; U AR; Mech Engrng.

GREGERSON, JANELLE; Morrilton Sr HS; Springfield, AR; (2); Drama Clb; Math Clb; Science Clb; Spanish Clb; Thesps; Trk; Vllybl; Optmst Oratorcl Speech Cont; Respirtry Thrpy.

GREGORY, AMANDA D; Timbo Schl; Mountain View, AR; (2); Debate Tm; 4-H; French Clb; FHA; Natl Beta Clb; Spanish Clb; Church Choir; Ofcr Stu Cncl; Bsktbl; Chrldng; RN.

GREGORY, BECKY A; Russellville Sr HS; Russellville, AR; (2); Cmnty Wkr; French Clb; Chorus; High Hon Roll; Hon Roll; Jr NHS; NHS; All-Stars; All Region Choir; Natl Fr Test 19th Pl In St; Tulane Unv; Zoology.

GREGORY, BRYAN SCOT; Rogers HS; Rogers, AR; (3); 10/600; Pres Church Yth Grp; Model UN; Science Clb; Orch; Ed Yrbk; Hon Roll; Jr NHS; NHS; CIA Clb; Scuba Dvng; Civil Engr.

GREGORY, JASON; Timbo Schl; Mountain View, AR; (3); Chorus; Bsktbl; Trk; Federal Forest Law Enforcement.

GREGORY, JUANA; Van Buren Sr HS; Van Buren, AR; (4); Church Yth Grp; FBLA; Mu Alpha Theta; Pep Clb; Science Clb; Spanish Clb; SADD; Teachers Aide; Pres Jr Cls; Rep Stu Cncl; U Cntrl AR; Phys Thrpy.

GREGORY, LAURA K; Sylvan Hills HS; Sherwood, AR; (2); 9/341; Church Yth Grp; Mu Alpha Theta; Natl Beta Clb; Drill Tm; JV Var Bsktbl; Capt Socr; High Hon Roll; Jr NHS; NHS; Pres Acad Fit Awd; Stdnt Of Yr; U Of Cntrl AR; Pre-Med/Pdtrcn.

GREGORY, MATTHEW J; Forrest City HS; Forrest City, AR; (1); Church Yth Grp; Cmnty Wkr; Church Choir; High Hon Roll; Hon Roll; Acctng.

GREGORY, PATRICE B; Pine Bluff HS; Pine Bluff, AR; (3); Natl Beta Clb; Treas Science Clb; Sec Spanish Clb; High Hon Roll; Treas Jr NHS; His Clb; Macys Minority In Med; Howard; Engrng.

GREGORY, RUSSELL; Morrilton Sr HS; Plumerville, AR; (3); Art Clb; Drama Clb; Math Clb; Natl Beta Clb; Science Clb; Spanish Clb; JV Var Bsbl; Prfct Atten Awd; AR Tech U.

GREGORY JR, TIMOTHY M; Forrest City HS; Forrest City, AR; (3); Church Yth Grp; FHA; Hon Roll; 2nd Pl Poetry Recitation Cont For Span I Stdnts; Bus Admin.

GREIG, HEATHER A; Brookland Jr Sr HS; Jonesboro, AR; (3); Pres Art Clb; Church Yth Grp; FCA; FBLA; GAA; Office Aide; Var Bsktbl; Var Sftbl; Var Vllybl; All-Conf Bsktbl & Sftbl; Ath Coach.

GREIS, AMY; Lake Hamilton Sr HS; Royal, AR; (4); FCA; Natl Beta Clb; Spanish Clb; Hon Roll; NHS; Prfct Atten Awd; Pres Acad Fit Awd; Home Ec Awd; Henderson ST U; Bio.

GRESHAM, LORA; Clarksville HS; Clarksville, AR; (2); #1 in class; Church Yth Grp; FCA; FBLA; Hosp Aide; HOBY; Pres Spanish Clb; Bsktbl; Chrldng; Crs Cntry; Sftbl.

GRESHAM, NANCY M; Crossett Sr HS; Crossett, AR; (3); Church Yth Grp; Dance Clb; FTA; HOBY; Mu Alpha Theta; Natl Beta Clb; Q&S; Spanish Clb; Band; Phtg Yrbk; Span II/WORLD His/Sci/Algebra II/HLTH/KEYBOARDING Awds.

GRIDER, CAREY; Gosnell Jr Sr HS; Blytheville, AR; (2); 3/125; Church Yth Grp; FCA; Natl Beta Clb; Chorus; Orch; Ofcr Bsbl; Ftbl; High Hon Roll; Jr NHS; Pres Acad Fit Awd; Church Yth Grp Pres; Church Sftbl; Flwshp Of Chrstn Stdnts; Medicine.

GRIESHABER, LILAH C; Jacksonville HS; Jacksonville, AR; (3); 9/242; Pres Church Yth Grp; Drama Clb; French Clb; Acpl Chr; Band; Chorus; Church Choir; Mrchg Band; Variety Show; Hon Roll; Psych.

GRIFFIN, J C; El Dorado Sr HS; El Dorado, AR; (3); 42/318; Church Yth Grp; Cmnty Wkr; Key Clb; Service Clb; Hist Thesps; Acpl Chr; Church Choir; School Play; Rptr Nwsp; High Hon Roll; Alternate Choral Music AR Govrnrs Schl 96; Hendrix Coll; Phlsphy.

GRIFFIN, JESSICA; Leslie Schl; Leslie, AR; (3); 1/20; FBLA; FHA; Quiz Bowl; Nwsp; Yrbk; Treas Jr Cls; High Hon Roll; AR Tech U; Scndry Ed.

GRIFFIN, MELINDA A; Lavaca Jr Sr HS; Lavaca, AR; (2); FCA; FHA; Sprt Ed Nwsp; Var Bsktbl; Var Sftbl; Var Vllybl; Hon Roll; U Of Cntrl AR; Sprts Med/PT.

GRIFFIN, MICHELLE L; Dardanelle HS; Dardanelle, AR; (4); 1/99; Art Clb; Library Aide; Teachers Aide; Chorus; Ed Nwsp; Yrbk; Lit Mag; Vllybl; High Hon Roll; Val; Anchr For KLIZ News; Tandy Tech Schol; 3rd Plc At VFW Art Comp; AR Tech Univ; Grphc Dsgn.

GRIFFIN, STEPHEN S; Catholic HS; Little Rock, AR; (2); Church Yth Grp; Cmnty Wkr; ROTC; Socr; Hon Roll; Bstl; Bsktbl; Ftbl; Univ Of AR; Pre-Phrmcy.

GRIFFIN, TROY V; Taylor HS; Stamps, AR; (2); Art Clb; Church Yth Grp; Natl FFA Org; Sec Frsh Cls; L Bsktbl; Hon Roll; Cls Favorite; Most Outstdng In Bsktbl; Most Handsome; Southern AR U.

GRIFFIS, ERIC; Camden-Fairview HS; Camden, AR; (3); 9/289; Church Yth Grp; Drama Clb; Natl Beta Clb; Teachers Aide; School Musical; School Play; Gov Hon Prg Awd; Hon Roll; NHS; Spanish NHS; Best Supporting Actor CADDY Awds 95; Attnd Mission Trip To Mexico With Chrch Ythgroup; Theater.

GRIFFIS, JOEL ERIC; Fairview HS; Camden, AR; (3); 9/289; Church Yth Grp; Drama Clb; Natl Beta Clb; Quiz Bowl; Teachers Aide; School Musical; School Play; Stage Crew; Gov Hon Prg Awd; Hon Roll; Theatre.

GRIFFIS, LINDSAY L; White Co Central Schl; Judsonia, AR; (3); Letterman Clb; Church Yth Grp; 4-H; FBLA; FHA; Hosp Aide; Office Aide; Band; Mrchg Band; Pep Band; Lion Coll; Pediatrics; Radiolgst.

GRIFFITH, GRIFF M; De Soto Schl; Elaine, AR; (1); 1/30; Church Yth Grp; Natl Beta Clb; Pres Frsh Cls; Rep Stu Cncl; Var L Bsbl; JV L Bsktbl; JV Capt Ftbl; JV Tennis; JV L Trk; Var Wt Lftg; Cert Red Cross Lfgrd/CPR/FIRST Aid; Bible Schl Tchr Elem; ST/DIST Sci Fair Winner; Ole Miss; Engrng/Med.

GRIFFITH, JASON; Highland HS; Cherokee Village, AR; (3); Church Yth Grp; Library Aide; Quiz Bowl; Chorus; Hon Roll; Prfct Atten Awd; Accepted To Governors Schl 95-96; GATE; Black River Tech Coll.

GRIFFITH, MATTHEW K; Southside HS; Fort Smith, AR; (2); Boy Scts; Church Yth Grp; Mu Alpha Theta; Orch; Hon Roll; Jr NHS; NHS; Prfct Atten Awd; Pres Acad Fit Awd; Eagle Sct; St Sci Fair 2nd Pl Medicine & Hlth 95; Regnl ACTM Math Cont 2nd Pl In Algebra II 96.

GRIFFITH, NATALIE N; Heritage Christian Schl; Little Rock, AR; (2); Church Yth Grp; Ofcr Stu Cncl; Var L Bsktbl; L Vllybl; Cit Awd; Hon Roll; Jr NHS; PT.

GRIGGS, BEN W; Siloam Springs Sr HS; Siloam Springs, AR; (2); Chess Clb; Debate Tm; Model UN; Natl Beta Clb; Band; Mrchg Band; Pep Band; Golf; Hon Roll; NW AR Regnl Sci Fair.

GRIGGS, CHARLES A; Fountain Lake Jr Sr HS; Hot Springs, AR; (1); Var Bsktbl; High Hon Roll; Hon Roll; Prfct Atten Awd; St Schlr; Mscn Gtr.

GRIGGS, RACHEL; Cabot HS; Cabot, AR; (4); 45/300; Church Yth Grp; Key Clb; Teachers Aide; Band; Chorus; Mrchg Band; Pep Band; Stage Crew; Cit Awd; Hon Roll; Poetry Awd Wmns Soc; Harding Univ.

GRIGSBY, WEBBER L; Bradley Jr Sr HS; Bradley, AR; (3); Bsktbl; Ice Hcky.

GRIMES, ANNA B; Swifton Schl; Swifton, AR; (3); Church Yth Grp; FHA; Library Aide; Spanish Clb; Teachers Aide; Nwsp; Sec Frsh Cls; JV Chrldng; Hon Roll; AR ST U; Medcl Lab Tech.

GRIMES, JAMES H; Rogers HS; Garfield, AR; (3); Church Yth Grp; Teachers Aide; Hon Roll; Arch Drftsmn.

GRIMM, LAURA B; Cabot HS; Cabot, AR; (3); Pres Church Yth Grp; Teachers Aide; Band; Var Capt Socr; Var Trk; U AR Little Rock; Bus.

GRIMMETT, MEAGAN A; Stamps HS; Buckner, AR; (3); 1/50; Church Yth Grp; FCA; Mu Alpha Theta; Natl FFA Org; Science Clb; Treas Jr Cls; Trk; Hon Roll; Jr NHS; NHS; Chrch Missn Trip To Sula Honduras; 3rd Place Dist Sci Fair; SAU.

GRINDER, CHRISTY; St Joe Public Schl; Pindall, AR; (3); 1/18; Treas FBLA; Sec FHA; Sec Natl FFA Org; Yrbk; Sec Soph Cls; Sec Jr Cls; Bsktbl; Hon Roll; Ntl Merit Ltr; WET.

GRISHAM, ALISHA R; Alpena Schl; Alpena, AR; (2); FBLA; FHA; Natl Beta Clb; Spanish Clb; Teachers Aide; School Play; Bsktbl; Trk; High Hon Roll; Hon Roll; U Of AR; Tchg/Wrkg Cmptrs.

GRIZZLE, BRADLEY T; Ft Smith Christian Schl; Fort Smith, AR; (2); Church Yth Grp; FCA; FBLA; Ski Clb; Chorus; Yrbk; Bsktbl; Cit Awd; Hon Roll; OK ST Univ; Phtgrphy/Bus.

GROGAN, JOHN D; Fouke Jr Sr HS; Fouke, AR; (2); Church Yth Grp; Natl FFA Org; Varsity Clb; JV Var Bsktbl; Var Ftbl; High Hon Roll; U Of AR.

GROSS, KRISTIN; Marion HS; Marion, AR; (2); FCA; French Clb; Band; Color Guard; Mrchg Band; Var Chrldng; Var Sftbl; High Hon Roll; Hon Roll; PRIDE; U Of CA; Marine Bio.

GROSS, ROBERT S; Van Buren Sr HS; Van Buren, AR; (2); Mu Alpha Theta; Ftbl; Hon Roll; Bus Owner.

GROTJOHN, JAMES A; Waldron HS; Waldron, AR; (2); Art Clb; Drama Clb; Natl FFA Org; Hon Roll; Archetechtual Engrng.

GROUNDS, LINDSEY J; Pulaski Acad; North Little Rock, AR; (2); FCA; Spanish Clb; Yrbk; Chrldng; Powder Puff Ftbl; Hon Roll; NHS; Beta Clb; All Star Chrldr 8th Natl; Comm Svc; Ole Miss; Dsgn Archtctrl.

GROVES, REGINA; Omaha Schl; Omaha, AR; (1); Church Yth Grp; Church Choir; VP Frsh Cls; Capt Bsktbl; Hon Roll; Coll Of Ozarks; Tchr.

GROVES, TRACY C; Highland HS; Hardy, AR; (3); Church Yth Grp; FBLA; Band; Mrchg Band; Powder Puff Ftbl; Hon Roll; Cert Of Awds In Sci; Gdnce Asst; Bus; Csmtlgy.

GRUBBS, KRISTEN; Mena HS; Mena, AR; (4); Church Yth Grp; English Clb; 4-H; French Clb; FBLA; Ed Yrbk; Ofcr Stu Cncl; Chrldng; Socr; High Hon Roll; U Of AR; Jrnlsm.

GRUBBS, MARY F; De Soto Schl; West Helena, AR; (1); Church Yth Grp; Yrbk; Hon Roll; Chance; Duke Univ; Pedtrcn.

GRUETZMACHER, PAMELA SUE; Rogers HS; Rogers, AR; (3); 38/596; Church Yth Grp; Cmnty Wkr; FBLA; FHA; Scholastic Bowl; Science Clb; High Hon Roll; Hon Roll; NHS; Prfct Atten Awd; Wet Club 94-; Merit Awd 6 Wks Pre-Prep Coll Schlsp U Of N TX 95; Dscvr Card Yth Schlsp AR Brnz 96; Marin Biologist.

GRUNDY, ALFREDA; Arkansas City Schl; Arkansas City, AR; (3); 2/9; 4-H; French Clb; FBLA; Quiz Bowl; Science Clb; Nwsp; Yrbk; Pres Jr Cls; VP Stu Cncl; Bsktbl; Grambling ST Univ.

GRYKA, BRYAN J; Catholic HS; Little Rock, AR; (2); ROTC; Hist Temple Yth Grp; Stage Crew; Pres Schlr; Tulane; Bus; Law.

GUBANSKI, LAURA A; Oak Grove HS; North Little Rock, AR; (2); Drama Clb; FHA; Natl Beta Clb; Spanish Clb; High Hon Roll; Hon Roll; FCA; Soc Studies Clb; UCA; Gen Hlth Care.

GUDGEON, REBECCA A; Mountainburg Jr Sr HS; Mountainburg, AR; (3); FCA; 4-H; FHA; Natl Beta Clb; Science Clb; SADD; Bsktbl; Sftbl; Hon Roll; Prfct Atten Awd; John Brown Univ; Pediatrician.

GUENTHER, ARLINE; Oark HS; Oark, AR; (2); 1/25; FBLA; FHA; HOBY; Natl Beta Clb; Natl FFA Org; Bsktbl; Chrldng; Hon Roll; Phys Sci Awd; Math.

GUENTHER, ARLINE; Clarksville HS; Hot Springs, AR; (2); FBLA; FHA; HOBY; Natl Beta Clb; Bsktbl; Chrldng; Hon Roll; Phy Sci Awd; Comm Svc Awd.

GUENTHER, SHANNA C; Robinson HS; Roland, AR; (2); Art Clb; Church Yth Grp; Drama Clb; FCA; French Clb; FBLA; Natl Beta Clb; Drill Tm; Hon Roll; NHS; Comm.

GUERRA, ARGENTINA; Rivercrest HS; Osceola, AR; (3); 15/100; Var Bsktbl; Var Mgr(s); Var Trk; High Hon Roll; Hon Roll; Ar ST Univ; Nurse.

GUESS, VERNON T; Sheridan Sr HS; Sheridan, AR; (2); Church Yth Grp; Band; Jazz Band; Mrchg Band; Pep Band; All-Region Band; U Of Cntrl AK; Music Ed.

GUEST, LEE; Marvell HS; Marvell, AR; (4); 11/39; Am Leg Boys St; Church Yth Grp; Cmnty Wkr; French Clb; Natl FFA Org; Office Aide; L Bsbl; L Ftbl; Hon Roll; Amer Leg Bsbll; 11 Yrs Prfct Attndnc Sndy Schl; PCC Ua-Helena; Gm Wrdn.

GUILLORY, DEVAN M; Mills HS; North Little Rock, AR; (2); 8/449; Church Yth Grp; French Clb; VP FTA; JCL; Latin Clb; Science Clb; Sec Stu Cncl; High Hon Roll; Jr NHS; NHS; MUSH TV Anchor.

GUILLORY, JASON C; John L Mcclellan Magnet HS; Little Rock, AR; (2); Church Yth Grp; Cmnty Wkr; Math Clb; Mu Alpha Theta; Science Clb; Service Clb; Spanish Clb; Band; Drill Tm; Mrchg Band; Explr Post 1033; Hunting; Fishing; UALR; Law Enfrcmnt.

GUILLORY, SUSAN M; Hot Springs HS; Hot Springs, AR; (4); 4/156; Pres Art Clb; Natl Beta Clb; Q&S; Thesps; School Musical; School Play; Ed Yrbk; Sec Jr Cls; High Hon Roll; NHS; AR Governors Schl; UCA; Jrnlsm.

GUILLOT, ELIZABETH; Central Ark Christian Schl; Little Rock, AR; (1); Church Yth Grp; Cmnty Wkr; Jr NHS; Valentine Ct 96.

GUIMBELLOT, ERIC W; Mc Gehee HS; Mcgehee, AR; (2); Church Yth Grp; FCA; Mu Alpha Theta; Natl Beta Clb; Science Clb; Band; Church Choir; Mrchg Band; Pep Band; NHS.

GUINN, BRAD A; Arkansas Sr HS; Texarkana, AR; (2); Intrml Tennis; Jr NHS; Vet.

GUINN, MELBA; J A Fair Sr HS; Little Rock, AR; (3); Dance Clb; FBLA; Chorus; Rep Frsh Cls; Rep Stu Cncl; Capt Bsktbl; Chrldng; Trk; Capt Vllybl; Cit Awd; Bsktbl Mst Ddctd; Chrldng NCA All Amer; Vlybl All Conf.

GUIST, JERED M; Prairie Grove HS; Prairie Grove, AR; (4); Math Clb; Science Clb; Spanish Clb; Teachers Aide; Nwsp; JV Bsktbl; Capt Var Socr; Var Trk; High Hon Roll; Hon Roll; St Media Festival Wnnr 95 & 96; U Of AR Fayettville; Comp Sci.

GULLEY, JULIUS L; Nevada Schl; Rosston, AR; (1); FHA; Band; Mrchg Band; School Musical; School Play; Nwsp; Ofcr Stu Cncl; Ofcr Bsbl; Bsktbl; Trk; Mech.

GULLEY, SHEA L; Melbourne HS; Melbourne, AR; (2); 7/53; FCA; 4-H; Natl Beta Clb; Quiz Bowl; SADD; Bsktbl; Cit Awd; 4-H Awd; NHS; ST Talent Wnnr 1st Pl; ST Speech Wnnr 1st Pl; U Of N FL; Tchng/Arts/Drama.

GUMINSKY, JULIE A; North Little Rock Hs-West; North Little Rock, AR; (4); 45/505; Church Yth Grp; Cmnty Wkr; Drama Clb; Math Clb; Mu Alpha Theta; Q&S; Spanish Clb; School Musical; School Play; Variety Show; U Of AR; Bus.

GUNN, PAMELA A; Cave City HS; Cave City, AR; (2); Church Yth Grp; French Clb; Band; Chorus; Church Choir; Pep Band; High Hon Roll; Hon Roll.

GUNN, RACHAEL; Elaine Jr Sr HS; West Helena, AR; (2); 1/30; Art Clb; Church Yth Grp; Office Aide; Quiz Bowl; Spanish Clb; Church Choir; School Play; Cit Awd; High Hon Roll; Hon Roll; Proj Fair; Rcvd Jdgs Awd Proj Fair; GATE Pgm; Harding U; Nrsng.

GUNN, STEVEN P; Forrest City HS; Forrest City, AR; (3); French Clb; Teachers Aide; Hon Roll; Golf; Fishing; Civil Engrng.

GUNNELLS, TOMIKA D; Conway Sr HS; Bigelow, AR; (2); GAA; Letterman Clb; Bsktbl; Trk; Vllybl; Bsktbl All-Stars, All-Trnmt 2 Yr Ltr Awd, All-Conf & 1st Pl Kittenfst; Vllybl 2 Yr Ltr Awd & All-Conf; UAPB; Comp Sci; Comp Pgmng.

GUNNELS, REBECCA J; Cabot HS; Cabot, AR; (4); 60/299; French Clb; Teachers Aide; Acpl Chr; Band; Chorus; Jazz Band; Mrchg Band; Pep Band; School Musical; French Hon Soc; Sr Girls Choir Acad Area Excllnc Awd; AR ST U; Bio.

GUNSOLUS, JONATHAN E; Mountain Home HS; Mountain Home, AR; (3); 112/253; Hon Roll; Rotary Clb; GCECA.

GUNTER, KIMBERLY C; Mayflower HS; Conway, AR; (4); 3/50; French Clb; FBLA; Natl Beta Clb; Teachers Aide; JV Var Bsktbl; Var Capt Chrldng; Sftbl; Hon Roll; U Of Cntrl AR; Pre Med.

GUNTHER, JUDY; Wonderview HS; Hattieville, AR; (4); 2/26; Am Leg Aux Girls St; FBLA; Pres FHA; Intnl Clb; Pres Natl Beta Clb; Natl FFA Org; Yrbk; Ofcr Stu Cncl; DAR Awd; Sal; Woodmen Wrld Amer Hstry Awd; U Cntrl AR.

GUNTHER, RICK C; Catholic HS; Little Rock, AR; (2); Boy Scts; Church Yth Grp; Latin Clb; Stage Crew; Hon Roll.

GUPTA, SUNEEL C; Arkansas Schl Math & Science; Hot Springs, AR; (3); Am Leg Boys St; FBLA; Hosp Aide; Mu Alpha Theta; Capt Quiz Bowl; Band; Yrbk; Golf; NHS; Beta Clb.

GUSBY, MARJORIE A; El Dorado Sr HS; El Dorado, AR; (2); Band; Mrchg Band; Hon Roll; LA Tech; Law.

GUSTIN, CRISTA R; Berryville HS; Berryville, AR; (3); FBLA; Key Clb; Office Aide; Science Clb; Var L Bsktbl; Var Sftbl; Var L Trk; Hon Roll.

GUTHRIE, ELIZABETH A; Parkview Arts-Science HS; Little Rock, AR; (2); FBLA; German Clb; Hosp Aide; Cit Awd; Hon Roll; Jr NHS; Natl Jr Beta Clb; Y-Teens; Nrsng.

GUTHRIE, JASON E; Gosnell Jr Sr HS; Gosnell, AR; (3).

GUTHRIE, JENNIFER; Murfreesboro HS; Nashville, AR; (1); 2/45; Debate Tm; FHA; Natl Beta Clb; Band; Flag Corp; Sec Frsh Cls; Var Bsktbl; Var Chrldng; High Hon Roll; Pres Acad Fit Awd.

GUTIERREZ, FELICIA J; Newport HS; Newport, AR; (2); Church Yth Grp; FBLA; Spanish Clb; Church Choir; School Musical; Hon Roll; LA ST Univ; Law.

GUY, LE KEISHA D; Dumas HS; Dumas, AR; (2); Church Yth Grp; FBLA; Library Aide; Natl Beta Clb; Church Choir; Hon Roll; Ntl Merit Schol; UALA; Rec Thrpst.

GUYOT, CATHERINE; White Co Central Schl; Judsonia, AR; (2); Church Yth Grp; 4-H; FHA; Pep Clb; Quiz Bowl; Band; Mrchg Band; High Hon Roll; Hon Roll; Span Awd 10th Grd; 1st Place Botany Sci Fair 95-; 3rd Place Botany At Rgnls; Hnr Soc 95-; U Of AR; Psych.

GWIN, NATASHA; Fouke Jr Sr HS; Texarkana, AR; (3); 3/84; GAA; HOBY; Natl Beta Clb; Pres Jr Cls; Ofcr Stu Cncl; Var Bsktbl; Var Capt Chrldng; High Hon Roll; Gftd/Tlntd Pres; Ed.

GWIN, TASHA; Fouke Jr Sr HS; Texarkana, AR; (3); 3/85; HOBY; Natl Beta Clb; Pres Jr Cls; Ofcr Stu Cncl; Var Bsktbl; Var Capt Chrldng; Cit Awd; Gov Hon Prg Awd; High Hon Roll; Austin Coll; Psych; Tchr.

HA, ROY R; Osceaola HS; Osceola, AR; (2); 1/155; FBLA; Math Clb; Quiz Bowl; Science Clb; Drm Mjr(t); Nwsp; Hon Roll; NHS.

HA, THU V; Southside HS; Fort Smith, AR; (2); Art Clb; Drama Clb; Hosp Aide; Latin Clb; Math Clb; Math Tm; Mu Alpha Theta; Red Cross Aide; Speech Tm; Thesps; Sail Crew; Juilliard; Theater.

HAAS, EMILY A; Batesville Sr HS; Batesville, AR; (4); 3/155; Am Leg Aux Girls St; Church Yth Grp; Hosp Aide; Pres Key Clb; Mgr Nwsp; Ed Yrbk; Sec Stu Cncl; DAR Awd; Ntl Merit SF; PRIDE Grp Ldr; Harding U; Ed.

HABEGER, SALLY L; Mena HS; Mena, AR; (4); 45/108; Church Yth Grp; Science Clb; Spanish Clb; Chorus; Church Choir; School Play; Lit Mag; Hon Roll; Fllwship Of Chrstn Stu; Slct Choir; Rich Mtn CC; Engl.

HABERER, JOHN P; Ozark HS; Ozark, AR; (3); FCA; Chorus; Ofcr Frsh Cls; Bsktbl; Hon Roll; Pres Acad Fit Awd; Scl Stud Club; U Of AR; Apprsr.

HACKER, AMY; Dollarway HS; Pine Bluff, AR; (4); #18 in class; HOBY; Co-Capt Pep Clb; Sec Science Clb; Acpl Chr; Sec Chorus; AR St U.

HACKNEY, CHARLES R; Hot Springs HS; Pearcy, AR; (4); 13/154; Art Clb; Church Yth Grp; VP French Clb; VP Math Clb; Natl Beta Clb; Science Clb; High Hon Roll; Kiwanis Awd; NHS; All Amer Schlr; U Of AR; Arch.

HACKNEY, DANA K; Lake Hamilton Sr HS; Hot Springs Natio, AR; (3); 92/232; Church Yth Grp; FCA; FBLA; FHA; Hosp Aide; Spanish Clb; Teachers Aide; Sftbl; Trk; Vllybl; Henderson ST; Erly Chldhd.

HADDOCK, SHANNON M; Marion HS; Marion, AR; (2); French Clb; Mu Alpha Theta; Quiz Bowl; French Hon Soc; High Hon Roll; NHS; Natl Jr Beta Club; Stdnt Cncl; Med Rsrchr.

HADDOX, CARRIE; Glen Rose HS; Benton, AR; (2); FCA; FBLA; Hosp Aide; Spanish Clb; School Musical; Ofcr Soph Cls; Ofcr Stu Cncl; Bsktbl; Chrldng; Gym; STOP; CHAMPS; Jr Ms GRJHS.

HADLEY, LAWRENCE R; Gravette HS; Gravette, AR; (3); Var Bsbl; Var Bsktbl; Var Ftbl; High Hon Roll; NHS; Pres Acad Fit Awd.

HADLEY, STEPHANIE A; Riverview HS; Kensett, AR; (2); Church Yth Grp; Cmnty Wkr; FHA; GAA; Pep Clb; Spanish Clb; SADD; Church Choir; School Play; Yrbk; ASU; Prof Bsktbl.

HAGA, KIMBERLY A; Booneville Jr Sr HS; Booneville, AR; (3); Church Yth Grp; FBLA; FTA; Treas Key Clb; Natl Beta Clb; Pres Chorus; Church Choir; Variety Show; Pres Capt Jr Cls; Pres VP Stu Cncl; Ldr Of Yth Alv, Chrstn Org; Ldrshp Awd For Soph Yr, Wn Lcl Cty Fr Tlnt Cntst Of95; Sng At Rst Hm; Msc Mnstr.

HAGAN, KIMBERLY A; Greene Co Tech HS; Paragould, AR; (4); 10/163; Am Leg Aux Girls St; Church Yth Grp; Drama Clb; FTA; Red Cross Aide; Band; Chorus; Mrchg Band; NHS; U Of Cntrl AR; Ed.

HAGAR, LESLIE F; Heber Springs HS; Heber Springs, AR; (3); 6/100; Am Leg Aux Girls St; Art Clb; Church Yth Grp; FCA; FBLA; Chrldng; Sftbl; Tennis; Vllybl; NHS.

HAGGARD, TYLER N; Southside HS; Fort Smith, AR; (3); 56/507; Church Yth Grp; FCA; Letterman Clb; Teachers Aide; Rep Sr Cls; L Bsktbl; High Hon Roll; NHS.

HAGGE, JANA; Cabot HS; Cabot, AR; (2); 1/500; Church Yth Grp; Debate Tm; German Clb; Key Clb; Band; Chorus; School Musical; High Hon Roll; Jr NHS; Stu Congress; Frgn Lang Cmptn; 120 Hrs Mission Work.

HAGHANI, JOHNATHAN M; Mt Ida Jr Sr HS; Mount Ida, AR; (3); 6/40; Church Yth Grp; Cmnty Wkr; 4-H; French Clb; FBLA; Math Clb; Math Tm; Natl Beta Clb; Natl FFA Org; Pep Clb; USAFA; Airforce Pilot; Navagatn.

HAGLER, LATISHA D; Berryville HS; Berryville, AR; (1); Church Yth Grp; Natl FFA Org; Science Clb; Church Choir; Flag Corp; Bsktbl; Trk; Gov Hon Prg Awd; High Hon Roll; Jr NHS.

HAHN, CATHY; Mountain Home HS; Mountain Home, AR; (3); 43/281; Church Yth Grp; FCA; Sec FBLA; FTA; Pres German Clb; Sec Stu Cncl; Capt Var Chrldng; Hon Roll; Intrct Clb; Rnbws; Stdnt Chrstn Assn; Hist.

HAILE, JENNIFER L; Heber Springs HS; Heber Springs, AR; (3); 6/90; Am Leg Aux Girls St; Church Yth Grp; Drama Clb; FCA; FBLA; HOBY; Natl Beta Clb; Science Clb; Spanish Clb; Band; Godpleasers Choir.

HAIRSTON, AMMIE E; Mayflower HS; Mayflower, AR; (2); Hon Roll; Radiologist; Interior Design.

HAIRSTON, KIM; Warren Sr HS; Warren, AR; (4); 1/120; Am Leg Aux Girls St; Church Yth Grp; Model UN; Church Choir; School Play; Sec Sr Cls; Treas Stu Cncl; Gov Hon Prg Awd; Pres Schlr; Val; AR St Univ; Prelaw.

HAIRSTON, SCOTT; Vilonia HS; Conway, AR; (3); Am Leg Boys St; Church Yth Grp; Drama Clb; FBLA; Math Clb; Mu Alpha Theta; Spanish Clb; Teachers Aide; School Play; Boy Scts; Forgn Missions Wrk; Harding Univ; Mnstr.

HALBERT II, RICKY L; Catholic HS; North Little Rock, AR; (3); ROTC; Rep Soph Cls; Ftbl; Pres Acad Fit Awd; U MEMPHIS; Engrng.

HALBROOK, JEREMY C; Weiner Jr-Sr HS; Weiner, AR; (3); Math Clb; Mu Alpha Theta; Natl Beta Clb; Ofcr Bsbl; Bsktbl; Ftbl; Hon Roll; Jr NHS; NHS; All Conf In Bsebll; Amer Hist Awd; Wrld Hist Awd; AR St Univ.

HALE, ALLAN C; Dollarway HS; Pine Bluff, AR; (2); Hosp Aide; Science Clb; Service Clb; VICA; Acpl Chr; Chorus; Church Choir; ST Sci Fair Awd; All Regions Choir; LA Tech; DVM.

HALE, JARROD L; North Little Rock Hs-West; North Little Rock, AR; (3); 37/550; Mu Alpha Theta; Stage Crew; High Hon Roll; Hon Roll; NHS.

HALE, LINDSAY; Springdale Sr HS; Springdale, AR; (1); 1/438; Church Yth Grp; Natl FFA Org; Chorus; Ed Yrbk; Cit Awd; High Hon Roll; Hon Roll; FBLA; School Musical; Jr NHS; Cowboys For Christ; AR HS Rodeo Assn; U Of AR; Sprts Med Dr.

HALEY, HEATHER A; Piggott HS; Rector, AR; (2); FCA; French Clb; FBLA; Letterman Clb; Natl Beta Clb; Sec Jr Cls; Ofcr Stu Cncl; Var L Bsktbl; Var L Sftbl; Var Trk.

HALEY, JASON; Fountain Lake Jr Sr HS; Hot Springs, AR; (4); 1/63; FCA; Natl Beta Clb; Natl FFA Org; Spanish Clb; Pres Jr Cls; Pres Sr Cls; Rep Stu Cncl; Var Ftbl; Var Tennis; High Hon Roll; FFA Pres; Enironmental Clb; Elks Clb Stu Of Yr; Henderson ST Univ.

HALEY, RANI; Southside HS; Fort Smith, AR; (2); Art Clb; Church Yth Grp; Hosp Aide; Key Clb; Chorus; Hon Roll; Jr NHS; Pres Acad Fit Awd; Pediatrcs.

HALFERTY, VICTORIA; North Little Rock Hs-East; North Little Rock, AR; (2); 32/550; Church Yth Grp; Cmnty Wkr; Debate Tm; FBLA; Key Clb; Natl Beta Clb; Church Choir; High Hon Roll; Lawyer.

HALL, ALISON B; Dewitt HS; De Witt, AR; (3); 1/97; FCA; French Clb; FBLA; Natl Beta Clb; Science Clb; Teachers Aide; Band; Drm Mjr(t); Stage Crew; High Hon Roll; All-Rgn Band; ACTM Math Cntst Wnnr; AR Tech Univ.

HALL, ALIVIA A; Pine Bluff HS; Pine Bluff, AR; (4); 49/410; Church Yth Grp; Cmnty Wkr; Sec DECA; FBLA; FHA; FTA; Model UN; Natl Beta Clb; Pep Clb; Pres Spanish Clb; AFS Soc Drctr; Hist Clb; Yng Ladies Clb; Home Ec Rlated Occu; U Of AR; Latn Amer Studs.

HALL, ALLEN; East Poinsett Sr HS; Lepanto, AR; (1); Church Yth Grp; FBLA; Ofcr Bsbl; Bsktbl; Ftbl; Hon Roll; Jr NHS; Pres Acad Fit Awd.

HALL, ALLISON; Rison HS; Rison, AR; (1); Church Yth Grp; FHA; Natl Beta Clb; Hon Roll; NHS; Drg Awrnss Grp; AEGIS Pgm; Sec/Treas Jr Beta Clb; UCA; Tchr.

HALL, AMANDA; Rison HS; Rison, AR; (2); Natl Beta Clb; Natl FFA Org; Bsktbl; Chrldng; Hon Roll.

HALL, ASHLEY D; Corning HS; Peach Orchard, AR; (3); FBLA; FHA; Yrbk; Rptr Rptr Jr Cls; Pres Sr Cls; Sec Stu Cncl; Co-Capt Chrldng; AR ST Univ; Elem-Early Chldhd.

HALL, BECKY; Southside HS; Fort Smith, AR; (2); French Clb; Hosp Aide; Mu Alpha Theta; Band; Color Guard; School Musical; Var Tennis; Hon Roll; Jr NHS; Pres Acad Fit Awd.

HALL, CANDICE SUE; Magnolia HS; Magnolia, AR; (3); 1/230; Am Leg Aux Girls St; French Clb; Mu Alpha Theta; Quiz Bowl; Science Clb; Church Choir; Rep Stu Cncl; L Sftbl; Hon Roll; FBLA Dist Parliamentarian; AR Gov Schl; Girls St; Arer PRIDE; Duke U.

HALL, CHARLOTTE; Melbourne HS; Melbourne, AR; (3); FHA; Natl Beta Clb; Chorus; Hon Roll; His Clb.

HALL, CHERYL L; Dumas HS; Dumas, AR; (3); Sec Jr Cls; Rep Sr Cls; Sec Stu Cncl; Hon Roll; U At Monticello; Nrsng.

HALL, COURTNEY L; Sylvan Hills HS; North Little Rock, AR; (2); 17/342; French Clb; Mu Alpha Theta; Natl Beta Clb; Sftbl; Hon Roll; Jr NHS; NHS; FBLA; Science Clb; FBLA Dist Comptn 1st Pl Tmd Wrtng 95/2nd Pl Bus Math 96; Wrld His Acad Merit Awd 96; U Of AR; Acctng.

HALL, ELIZABETH M; Poyen Schl; Poyen, AR; (3); Church Yth Grp; FCA; FBLA; FHA; Library Aide; Natl Beta Clb; Teachers Aide; Church Choir; Var Chrldng; Prfct Atten Awd; Sr Hmcmng Bsktbl Maid; Vol Wk; Henderson; Bus.

HALL, FELECIA; Lee Sr HS; Marianna, AR; (2); 19/198; 4-H; Quiz Bowl; Bsktbl; Cit Awd; 4-H Awd; Hon Roll; Prfct Atten Awd; Certf Rcgntn 50% Cmpstn; AR U; Dctr Of Arch.

HALL, GRETCHEN; Sheridan Sr HS; Sheridan, AR; (3); 24/265; Church Yth Grp; FCA; 4-H; HOBY; Letterman Clb; Office Aide; Teachers Aide; Varsity Clb; Rep Frsh Cls; Sec Soph Cls; St 4-H Tn Str; Crssrds 4-H Clb Pres; Natl Ctznshp Tour Dlgt.

HALL, JAMIE; Fordyce HS; Fordyce, AR; (3); 10/84; Am Leg Aux Girls St; Church Yth Grp; FCA; Girl Scts; Natl Beta Clb; Sec Treas Science Clb; Spanish Clb; Varsity Clb; Band; Mrchg Band; U Of Monticello; Bus.

HALL, JAMIE E; Booneville Jr Sr HS; Booneville, AR; (4); 1/86; Cmnty Wkr; Drama Clb; FBLA; Natl Beta Clb; Office Aide; Speech Tm; School Play; Hon Roll; Val; AR Gov Schl; Eng Awd; Algebra II Awd; AR Tech Univ; Psych.

HALL, JASON; Morrilton Sr HS; Plumerville, AR; (3); FBLA; Math Clb; Natl Beta Clb; Natl FFA Org; Spanish Clb; Thesps; Var L Ftbl; Var Tennis; JV Trk; Cit Awd; U Ozarks Clrksvlle; TV Prdctn.

HALL, JULIA C; El Dorado Sr HS; El Dorado, AR; (3); 14/304; Am Leg Aux Girls St; Church Yth Grp; Pres Natl Beta Clb; Hist Thesps; Acpl Chr; VP Pres Chorus; Church Choir; School Play; Hon Roll; NHS; All Rgn Choir 94-95; All ST Choir 96; Ouachita Bapt Univ; Eng.

HALL, KAREN LE ANN; Morrilton Sr HS; Plumerville, AR; (2); Art Clb; Cmnty Wkr; French Clb; FHA; Thesps; Ntl Merit Ltr; Lbry Club; Inter Dsgn.

HALL, KIMBERLY R; Emerson HS; Emerson, AR; (3); 4/21; FBLA; FHA; Rep Natl Beta Clb; Natl FFA Org; Spanish Clb; Speech Tm; Bsktbl; Hon Roll; School Play; MASH Prgm; Hstrcl Blck Coll; AR ST U; PT.

HALL, LATISHA L; Cty Line HS; Ratcliff, AR; (1); FBLA; Office Aide; Quiz Bowl; Spanish Clb; Teachers Aide; Rep Stu Cncl; Cit Awd; High Hon Roll; Spanish NHS; Med Sci/Gen DR.

HALL, MICHAEL J; Lake Hamilton Sr HS; Pearcy, AR; (3); Church Yth Grp; Cmnty Wkr; Pep Clb; Band; Chorus; Church Choir; Mrchg Band; Orch; School Musical; School Play; Svc/Ldrshp Awd Band; All Rgn Bnd; Top 10 Percent Awd Band; Henderson ST Univ; Soiology.

HALL, NICOLE R; Valley Springs Schl; Harrison, AR; (2); Church Yth Grp; Library Aide; Teachers Aide; Church Choir; Rptr Nwsp; Bsktbl; Sftbl; Trk; Vllybl; Hon Roll; Tae Kwon Do Red Belt; Coll Of The Ozarks; Psych.

HALL, RACHEL; Prairie Grove HS; Prairie Grove, AR; (3); 8/93; Church Yth Grp; Ofcr Stu Cncl; Bsktbl; Chrldng; Powder Puff Ftbl; Trk; High Hon Roll; Jr NHS; NHS; Comm Bld Svcs Aide; Bsktbl Rylty; U Of AR.

HALL, SEAN C; Hall Sr HS; Little Rock, AR; (2); Church Yth Grp; Debate Tm; FBLA; Spanish Clb; Speech Tm; Band; School Play; Socr; Cit Awd; High Hon Roll; Del Stdnt Cngrs AR.

HALL, SHERI MICHELLE; Sylvan Hills HS; North Little Rock, AR; (3); 13/290; French Clb; Mu Alpha Theta; Natl Beta Clb; Sftbl; Hon Roll; NHS; Prfct Atten Awd; Pres Acad Fit Awd; Awd Mrt Cvcs; Awd Mrt Pre-Calculus; U Central AR; His.

HALL, STACI D; Junction City HS; Bernice, LA; (4); 12/32; Church Yth Grp; FCA; Teachers Aide; Church Choir; Chrldng; Sftbl; High Hon Roll; Scrkpr Gym; Powder Puff Ftbl.

HALL, TINA L; Goza Jr HS; Arkadelphia, AR; (1); Church Yth Grp; Drama Clb; Band; Color Guard; Mrchg Band; Orch; L Gym; Flag Corp; Pep Band; School Musical; All-Region 1st Band, 1st Chair; Band Ltr; Outstdng Perfmnc Amer His; Sweekstakes Awd Wnnr Band; Harding Univ; Medicine; Paramedc.

HALL, WAYNE; Sparkman Jr Sr HS; Sparkman, AR; (1); 3/37; Natl FFA Org; Spanish Clb; Ofcr Frsh Cls; Ofcr Stu Cncl; Bsktbl; Ftbl; Trk; Vllybl; Wt Lftg; High Hon Roll; Acad Awd; Jr Olympcs USA Trck/Fld Awd 1st & 2nd Pl; MVP, Off Bck Yr Awds; U AR; Mgmt.

HALLER, JENNIFER R; Mazazine HS; Booneville, AR; (3); Church Yth Grp; FHA; Spanish Clb; School Play; Bsktbl; Chrldng; Sftbl; Trk; U Of AR; Dentist.

HALLEY, TODD; Newport HS; Newport, AR; (4); 22/155; Boy Scts; Church Yth Grp; FBLA; FHA; Library Aide; Math Tm; Office Aide; VP Q&S; Spanish Clb; SADD; Lyon Coll; Bus.

HALLIBURTON, ANNETTA; Brinkley HS; Brinkley, AR; (1); Church Yth Grp; Girl Scts; Chorus; Church Choir; Nwsp; Gov Hon Prg Awd; Jr NHS; Natl Sci Mrt Awd Wnnr; Gftd & Tlntd; U Of AR Pine Bluff; Pre-Med.

HALLIBURTON, JOANIE R; Southside HS; Fort Smith, AR; (3); 65/502; FCA; French Clb; VP FBLA; Service Clb; Teachers Aide; Drill Tm; Nwsp; Ofcr Frsh Cls; Ofcr Stu Cncl; High Hon Roll; Spec Olympics Vol; FBLA VP; U Of A; Bus/Acctng.

HALLIBURTON, REANETTA; Brinkley HS; Brinkley, AR; (1); Church Yth Grp; FHA; Girl Scts; Church Choir; Pres Frsh Cls; Bsktbl; High Hon Roll; Jr NHS; Bio.

HALLMAN, CHARITY; Dermott HS; Dermott, AR; (2); Pres Church Yth Grp; VP FBLA; Natl Beta Clb; Science Clb; Spanish Clb; Band; Bsktbl; Chrldng; Sftbl; Hon Roll; Dance; All Amer Scholar; UCA; Bio.

HALLMARK III, ROBERT; Arkansas Bapt Schl; Little Rock, AR; (2); Church Yth Grp; FCA; FBLA; Natl Beta Clb; Church Choir; JV Bsbl; JV Bsktbl; Var Ftbl; Var Trk; JETS Awd; FBLA Dist Bus Math Cmptn 1st Pl 95; Acctng.

HALMAN, RENEE; Wonderview HS; Solgohachia, AR; (3); VP Church Yth Grp; Intnl Clb; Natl Beta Clb; Natl FFA Org; Rptr Nwsp; Treas Jr Cls; Bsktbl; Hon Roll.

HALPINE, MICHAEL R; Bryant Sr HS; Alexander, AR; (4); 37/346; Church Yth Grp; FBLA; Library Aide; Church Choir; Ftbl; Trk; Hon Roll; Art Awds; U Of AR Lone Rock; Bio.

HALSTEAD, KATRINA R; Conway Sr HS; Conway, AR; (3); Church Yth Grp; FBLA; Teachers Aide; Church Choir; Boy Scts Aide; UCA; Elem Ed.

HALTERMAN, BROOKE; Pulaski Acad; Little Rock, AR; (3); Am Leg Aux Girls St; Church Yth Grp; Cmnty Wkr; FCA; Sec Natl Beta Clb; Spanish Clb; Chorus; School Musical; School Play; Ed Lit Mag; Baylor Univ.

HALTOM, MICHELLE; Sylvan Hills HS; Sherwood, AR; (2); #22 in class; Church Yth Grp; Drama Clb; FTA; JA; Library Aide; Mu Alpha Theta; Natl Beta Clb; Band; Church Choir; Orch; All Region Band 3 Yrs; Ouachita Bapt Coll; Ed.

HAM, DAVID G; Dewitt HS; De Witt, AR; (2); French Clb; Natl Beta Clb; Science Clb; Sec Soph Cls; Hon Roll; Peer Tutor; Zoology; Bio.

HAMAKER, DENISE M; Jacksonville HS; Cabot, AR; (3); 87/325; Drama Clb; FBLA; Spanish Clb; School Musical; School Play; Stage Crew; Nwsp; Hon Roll; Prfct Atten Awd; Jrnlsm Awd Featre Wrtng; Vet Tech.

HAMBLIN, APRIL L; Highland HS; Cherokee Village, AR; (3); FBLA; Chrldng; High Hon Roll; Hon Roll; Prfct Atten Awd; Awds Civics/Algebra I II/BUS Law/CTI/SPNSH I/Chem/4.0 Avg; Nom Gov Schl/Girls ST/NHS; MS ST; Acctg.

HAMBY, JENNIFER L; Mountain Home HS; Mountain Home, AR; (2); 21/283; FHA; Band; Mrchg Band; Lit Mag; Bsktbl; Sftbl; Vllybl; Hon Roll; Majorette; Woodmen Of Wrld Proficncy Amer His Awd; Ed/Tchng.

HAMILTON, AMANDA S; Cutter Morning Star HS; Hot Springs, AR; (3); Art Clb; Church Yth Grp; FCA; FHA; Spanish Clb; Treas Rep Stu Cncl; Bsktbl; Sftbl; Hon Roll; Treas Frsh Cls; Champs; Bible Study; Fire Mrshl; Photo/Sprts/Med.

HAMILTON, D HUNTER; North Little Rock Hs-East; North Little Rock, AR; (2); Church Yth Grp; Drama Clb; Mu Alpha Theta; Speech Tm; Thesps; School Musical; School Play; Rep Frsh Cls; Rep Stu Cncl; High Hon Roll; Band; Play Guitar; Waterski; Snowski; Theatrical Arts; Music.

HAMILTON, DANA; Woodlawn Schl; Pine Bluff, AR; (3); Church Yth Grp; FCA; HOBY; VP Natl Beta Clb; Ed Yrbk; Ofcr Stu Cncl; JV Capt Chrldng; Cit Awd; DAR Awd; Hon Roll; Hmcmng Maid; U Of AR-MONTICELLO.

HAMILTON, DANIEL G; Hope HS; Hope, AR; (3); Var L Bsbl; Bsbl Offensive Awd.

HAMILTON, HOLLY JO; Gravette HS; Gravette, AR; (3); Church Yth Grp; Cmnty Wkr; 4-H; GAA; Rep Frsh Cls; JV Bsktbl; L Socr; L Sftbl; 4-H Awd; High Hon Roll.

HAMILTON, JACOB T; Sheridan Sr HS; Little Rock, AR; (3); 4/260; Am Leg Boys St; Cmnty Wkr; FCA; Rep Frsh Cls; Ofcr Bsbl; Bsktbl; Hon Roll; Jr NHS; Heismann Awd; Medicine.

HAMILTON, JAMIE E; Crossett Sr HS; Crossett, AR; (2); 19/207; Church Yth Grp; HOBY; Natl Beta Clb; Chorus; Church Choir; School Musical; Ofcr Stu Cncl; Hon Roll; SFC; Ouachita Bapt Univ.

HAMILTON, JASON L; Maynard Jr Sr HS; Maynard, AR; (3); High Hon Roll; Hon Roll.

HAMILTON, SARAH; Lee Acad; Forrest City, AR; (1); 1/32; FCA; Pres Frsh Cls; Co-Capt Chrldng; Gym; High Hon Roll; Prfct Atten Awd; Pres Acad Fit Awd; Homcmng Crt; U AR; Med.

HAMLING, STEPHANIE; Wonderview HS; Hattieville, AR; (2); 2/26; Church Yth Grp; FBLA; Hosp Aide; Intnl Clb; Natl Beta Clb; Natl FFA Org; Pres Soph Cls; High Hon Roll; Class Favorite; Hmcmng Hnr Maid.

HAMM, KRISTI L; Horatio HS; Horatio, AR; (3); 5/75; Church Yth Grp; Cmnty Wkr; Pres FCA; Model UN; Church Choir; Phtg Rptr Yrbk; Rep Jr Cls; Sec Sr Cls; Rep Stu Cncl; JV Var Bsktbl; Elem Ed.

HAMMER, JUSTIN C; Fayetteville Sr HS; Fayetteville, AR; (3); Church Yth Grp; Spanish Clb; SADD; Band; Mrchg Band; Orch; Pep Band; High Hon Roll; Hon Roll; Prfct Atten Awd; U Of AR; Artist; Sculptor.

HAMMER, RAFE C; Fayetteville Sr HS; Fayetteville, AR; (2); Church Yth Grp; Band; Mrchg Band; Orch; Pep Band; School Musical; Stage Crew; Hon Roll; Univ.

HAMMOND, JASON O; Dewitt HS; De Witt, AR; (1); Church Yth Grp; FBLA; Natl FFA Org; Science Clb; Ntl Merit Schol.

HAMMONS, AUSTIN; Abundant Life Schools; North Little Rock, AR; (1); 3/35; JV Bsktbl; Cit Awd; High Hon Roll; Stu Bible Study; Jr Tstmstr Prog; Duke U.

HAMON, JENNIFER; Omaha Schl; Omaha, AR; (2); FBLA; HOBY; Natl Beta Clb; SADD; Sec Frsh Cls; VP Soph Cls; Var Bsktbl; Var Sftbl; Var Vllybl; Gov Hon Prg Awd; Bus Admin.

HAMPTON, DESZAMA D; El Dorado Sr HS; El Dorado, AR; (4); Church Yth Grp; Cmnty Wkr; Library Aide; Chorus; Hon Roll; Dbtnt 96-; 2 SAU Wrtng Awds; Span 4 Stdnt.

HAMPTON, LATERSA; Holly Grove HS; Holly Grove, AR; (4); 4/28; Church Yth Grp; FBLA; FHA; Natl Beta Clb; SADD; Band; Chorus; Rep Stu Cncl; Chrldng; Hon Roll; U AR Pine Bluff; Ag Bus.

HAMPTON, LIONEL; Cloverdale Jr HS; Mabelvale, AR; (1); FBLA; Cit Awd; Hon Roll.

HAMPTON, SHAWNA R; Biggers-Reyno HS; Biggers, AR; (2); Art Clb; VP FHA; Spanish Clb; Teachers Aide; VP Soph Cls; Var Bsktbl; Hon Roll; Stdnt Cncl Rep.

HAMPTON, TEMEKIS; Hermitage Jr Sr HS; Hermitage, AR; (4); 3/46; Am Leg Aux Girls St; French Clb; FHA; Chorus; Ed Yrbk; Rep Jr Cls; Hon Roll; Prfct Atten Awd; Beta Clb; FFA; Gftd & Tlntd; MASH; Hndrsn 100 HHS Beta Clb Sec; Acad Recog Awds; FFA Outstndng Svc Awd; U Of Cntrl AR; Nrsng.

HANAWAY, CHRISTEN R; Sloan Hendrix HS; Poughkeepsie, AR; (2); FHA; Natl Beta Clb; Band; Chorus; Rptr Nwsp; Yrbk; Hon Roll; All Region 7 Frst/2nd Awds Solo-Ensmbl 9-10th Grd; Music Awds; Music Prof/Tchr.

HANCOCK, KIM; Brinkley HS; Brinkley, AR; (2); Church Yth Grp; Drama Clb; Church Choir; School Play; Stage Crew; High Hon Roll; Jr NHS; NHS; UAM; Vet.

HANDLEY, AFRICA; Dermott HS; Dermott, AR; (3); #10 in class; Dance Clb; Natl Beta Clb; Science Clb; Band; Drill Tm; Mrchg Band; Ofcr Bsbl; Pom Pon; Gov Hon Prg Awd; Hon Roll; Pre Med.

HANDLEY, CHARLEY SHANE; Bryant Sr HS; Benton, AR; (4); 13/297; Church Yth Grp; FCA; French Clb; Science Clb; Teachers Aide; Band; JV Var Ftbl; Hon Roll; Natl Schlr Ath Awd; Hnr Grad; Future Med Prfsnls Rprtr; AR ST Univ; Med.

HANER, JESSICA; Bradford Jr Sr HS; Bradford, AR; (2); Art Clb; Church Yth Grp; French Clb; FBLA; FHA; Natl Beta Clb; Bsktbl; Crs Cntry; Sftbl; Trk; Miss BJHS; Phys Sci Awd; Cmptr Tech Awd.

HANEY, AMBER M; Pine Bluff HS; Reydell, AR; (3); Church Yth Grp; Pres 4-H; Sec Key Clb; Natl Beta Clb; Chorus; Lbrn Orch; Nwsp; Phtg Yrbk; 4-H Awd; Hon Roll; SE AR All Reg Orch 3 Yrs; Pine Bluff Symphny Yth Orch; I Dare You Awd; Spch Path/Audiology.

HANEY, HEATHER N; Junction City HS; Junction City, AR; (3); Church Yth Grp; FBLA; Science Clb; Rep Soph Cls; Rep Jr Cls; Capt Chrldng; L Sftbl; NHS; Girls ST AR Givn Hnr Hse Of Reps; OCCPTNL Pdtrc Thrpy.

HANEY, JAMIE; Searcy HS; Searcy, AR; (2); Church Yth Grp; FHA; Girl Scts; Natl Beta Clb; Office Aide; Chorus; Church Choir; Yrbk; Hon Roll; Jr NHS; 9 Yrs Cookie Brigade Grl Scts; 3rd Hghst Sls Prsn GS Cookies 96; Outstdng Ecom Stdnt 95-.

HANEY, JANET M; Southside HS; Desha, AR; (1); Dance Clb; GAA; Pep Clb; SADD; Teachers Aide; Sec Frsh Cls; Bsktbl; Sftbl; Hon Roll; Prfct Atten Awd; Specl Olympics Vol; AR Tech Univ; Child Care/Tchr.

HANEY, TAMARA S; Nashville HS; Nashville, AR; (4); 42/111; FHA; GAA; Office Aide; Teachers Aide; Band; Church Choir; Sftbl; Hon Roll; UAPB; Radlgy/Jvnl Cnslr.

HANKE, TYSON; Jessieville HS; Hot Springs, AR; (3); 2/51; Church Yth Grp; Key Clb; Natl Beta Clb; Band; Church Choir; Bsktbl; Ftbl; Golf; Tennis; Trk; Baylor U; Med.

HANKINS, AMBER A; Lee Acad; Forrest City, AR; (1); Church Yth Grp; Yrbk; Sec Frsh Cls; Chrldng; Hon Roll; U Of AR; Med Dr.

HANKINS, ERICA L; Star City HS; Star City, AR; (3); Am Leg Aux Girls St; Spanish Clb; Band; Color Guard; Mrchg Band; NHS; Ntl Merit Ltr; Flying; EAA Mem; Chrch Sftbl & Vllybl Teams; Aeronautical Sci.

HANKINS, JENNIFER; Rison HS; Rison, AR; (2); 11/48; Church Yth Grp; FCA; Natl Beta Clb; Office Aide; Teachers Aide; Church Choir; Bsktbl; Trk; Cit Awd; Hon Roll; Drug Awareness Pgm Rep.

HANKINS, JESSICA M; Glen Rose HS; Malvern, AR; (1); Church Yth Grp; FBLA; FHA; Spanish Clb; Church Choir; FBLA Sec; Talent Search; Henderson Coll; Early Chldhd.

HANKINS, MISTY D; Ola Jr Sr HS; Centerville, AR; (3); Art Clb; Chess Clb; Sec Natl Beta Clb; Rptr Natl FFA Org; Spanish Clb; Band; Mrchg Band; L Bsktbl; High Hon Roll; Hon Roll; Write Poem Pblshd 94-95 Yrbk; Crmnlgy.

HANKINS, SARAH M; North Little Rock Hs-West; North Little Rock, AR; (3); FBLA; Mu Alpha Theta; Hon Roll; NHS; Prfct Atten Awd; Acad Exclnc Awd Twice; Top 10% Of Soph Class Acad; Jr Achvmnt Prjct Bus Awd; UALR.

HANKS, AMANDA K; Springdale Sr HS; Goshen, AR; (1); JV Chrldng; JV Gym; Jr NHS; Pres Schlr; Builders Clb.

HANKTON, DESTINY A; Magnolia HS; Magnolia, AR; (2); Church Yth Grp; FBLA; Band; Church Choir; Mrchg Band; Sftbl; High Hon Roll; Amer PRIDE; Intnl Bus Mgmt.

HANLEY, BETH; Calico Rock HS; Pineville, AR; (2); Art Clb; Math Clb; Natl Beta Clb; Mgr Pep Clb; Science Clb; Spanish Clb; SADD; Hon Roll; Prfct Atten Awd; Pres Schlr; Violin; Dncng; AR Yth Cncl; Lyons.

HANLON, LANA M; Russellville Sr HS; Russellville, AR; (2); Church Yth Grp; Spanish Clb; Chorus; Church Choir; AWANA; Cmptrs.

HANNA, SHANNA M; Mountain View Jr Sr HS; Mountain View, AR; (4); Drama Clb; FBLA; FHA; FTA; Hosp Aide; Library Aide; Math Clb; Natl Beta Clb; Office Aide; Science Clb; OZ CC; Elem Ed.

HANRY, WILLIAM; Junction City HS; El Dorado, AR; (3); HOBY; Quiz Bowl; Science Clb; Spanish Clb; Sec Soph Cls; Rep Stu Cncl; Var L Ftbl; 4-H Awd; High Hon Roll; NHS; Vet Med.

HANSEN, AMANDA; Cave City HS; Cave City, AR; (3); 1/75; French Clb; VP FHA; Key Clb; Library Aide; Office Aide; Nwsp; Phtg Yrbk; Bsktbl; Tennis; Hon Roll; U Central AR Conway; Phy Thrpy.

HANSEN, AMBERLEA; Stuttgart Sr HS; Stuttgart, AR; (3); Am Leg Aux Girls St; Church Yth Grp; FBLA; HOBY; Key Clb; Mu Alpha Theta; Spanish Clb; School Play; Yrbk; Chrldng; Intl Bus.

HANSEN, ANGELA; Westside HS; Bono, AR; (4); Art Clb; Church Yth Grp; FBLA; FHA; Science Clb; Spanish Clb; Teachers Aide; Chrldng; Hon Roll; DFYIT; AR ST; Radiology.

HANSEN, BEN; Lake Hamilton Sr HS; Hot Springs Natio, AR; (2); JV Bsktbl; Var Tennis; Hon Roll; U Of NE; Bus Admin.

HANSEN, STEPHANIE A; Pulaski Acad; Little Rock, AR; (3); VP Art Clb; Church Yth Grp; Cmnty Wkr; FCA; VP Natl Beta Clb; Chorus; Rep Stu Cncl; Mgr Var Crs Cntry; Var Trk; Hon Roll; Ring Ceremony Chprsn; Comm Svc Hnrs Awd; Multi-Yr Listee.

HANSON, KRISTA; Siloam Springs Sr HS; Siloam Springs, AR; (4); 6/164; Church Yth Grp; Hosp Aide; Natl Beta Clb; Teachers Aide; Church Choir; Ed Nwsp; Yrbk; High Hon Roll; Pres NHS; Prfct Atten Awd; John Brown U; Chem.

HARBER, MICHAEL; Calico Rock HS; Wideman, AR; (4); 5/31; FBLA; Natl Beta Clb; Capt Quiz Bowl; SADD; Teachers Aide; Pep Band; Ed Nwsp; Ed Yrbk; Pres Sr Cls; Hon Roll; GATE; U Of AR.

HARDCASTLE, BRANDON; Oak Grove HS; Maumelle, AR; (2); Church Yth Grp; Band; Jazz Band; Mrchg Band; Phtg Nwsp; Phtg Yrbk; Chrch Act; Playing Sports; Card Collecting; Preacher; Sports Photo.

HARDEN, CARL V; Russellville Sr HS; Russellville, AR; (2); Church Yth Grp; Band; Church Choir; Jr NHS; NHS.

HARDERSON, SHIRLEY L; Oark HS; Oark, AR; (3); Art Clb; Dance Clb; FBLA; FHA; Natl FFA Org; Sftbl; Trk; Hon Roll; Lib Clb Vp; Schl Mascot; Funeral Svcs.

HARDERSON, STEPHANIE; Jasper HS; Jasper, AR; (4); Treas FHA; Library Aide; Math Clb; Natl Beta Clb; Natl FFA Org; Cit Awd; High Hon Roll; Hon Roll; Prfct Atten Awd; Coll Of The Ozarks; Lib Media.

HARDIN, CYNTHIA R; Northside HS; Barling, AR; (3); Spanish Clb; Chorus; Yrbk; Trk; Hon Roll; Prfct Atten Awd; Spanish NHS; OK ST Univ; Wildlife Bio.

HARDIN, ERIN A; Waldron HS; Waldron, AR; (1); Mrchg Band; Band; High Hon Roll; Hon Roll; Rcvd Algebra, Civics, Eng & Word Prcssng Awds.

HARDIN, JENNA R; Dardanelle HS; Dardanelle, AR; (3); Art Clb; FBLA; FHA; Natl Beta Clb; Acpl Chr; Chorus; Nwsp; Co-Ed Yrbk; Hon Roll; U Of Cntrl AR; Med.

HARDIN, JEREMY K; Cabot HS; Cabot, AR; (1); Church Yth Grp; Drama Clb; Jr NHS; Jpnse Clb.

HARDIN, JOHN D; Dumas Jr HS; Pickens, AR; (1); 1/120; Church Yth Grp; FBLA; Band; Tennis; Hon Roll; Rep Frsh Cls; Amer Lgn Stu Of Month; Stu Of 9 Weeks.

HARDIN, JULIE; Arkansas Bapt Schl; Little Rock, AR; (2); Church Yth Grp; FCA; FBLA; Natl Beta Clb; Chorus; Church Choir; Rep Stu Cncl; Var Bsktbl; Intrml Socr; Var Sftbl; Girls Track High Point Awd 96.

HARDIN, SHARECE Y; Marmaduke HS; Marmaduke, AR; (3); 5/55; Church Yth Grp; Natl Beta Clb; Teachers Aide; Rptr Chorus; School Musical; Nwsp; Cit Awd; Hon Roll; Prfct Atten Awd; Jrnlsm Awd; PE Awd; HAD; AR St Univ; Comp Prog.

HARDING, LACEY C; Farmington Jr Sr HS; Farmington, AR; (2); Church Yth Grp; FCA; FHA; Hosp Aide; Model UN; Sec Frsh Cls; VP Soph Cls; Rep Stu Cncl; Mgr(s); Score Keeper; Univ Of AR; Bus/Cmptrs.

HARDKE, MICAH; Carlisle Jr Sr HS; Carlisle, AR; (3); 2/65; Am Leg Aux Girls St; Art Clb; Church Yth Grp; Sec FBLA; Sec FHA; Sec Spanish Clb; Co-Ed Yrbk; Sec Soph Cls; Sec Jr Cls; Bsktbl; PRIDE 93-95; GATE 3 Yrs; Biracial Cmmtte; Medcl.

HARDY, CHRISTY; Taylor HS; Taylor, AR; (4); 1/31; Church Yth Grp; Rptr FBLA; Natl FFA Org; Quiz Bowl; Band; Ed Yrbk; Sec Treas Stu Cncl; NHS; Pres Acad Fit Awd; Val; Southern AR U; Acctng.

HARDY, SHANTE O; Forrest City HS; Forrest City, AR; (3); Cmnty Wkr; Drama Clb; French Clb; FHA; Teachers Aide; Band; Church Choir; Intrml Trk; Army Reserve; Comp Technician.

HARELSON, KRISTEN; Russellville Sr HS; Russellville, AR; (4); Am Leg Aux Girls St; French Clb; Band; Church Choir; Jazz Band; Mrchg Band; Trk; High Hon Roll; NHS; Pres Schlr; Ray A Kroc Yth Achvmt Awd; AR Yth Symphny Orch 2 Yrs; Natl Hnr Bnd Amer; AR Tech U; Msc Ed.

HARGETT, KRISTIN; Arkansas Bapt Schl; Little Rock, AR; (3); Church Yth Grp; FCA; FBLA; Spanish Clb; Chorus; Yrbk; Chrldng; Gym; Hon Roll; Beta Clb; Cheer Cntrl Braves; Vol Christmas Competition; Chrldng Camps; U Of AR; Interior Decorating.

HARGIS, CASEY; Hermitage Jr Sr HS; Wilmar, AR; (4); 2/50; Debate Tm; Drama Clb; French Clb; Math Clb; Natl Beta Clb; Natl FFA Org; Science Clb; School Play; Rep Nwsp; Sec Soph Cls.

HARGIS III, EDGAR D; Horatio HS; De Queen, AR; (2); Church Yth Grp; Var Trk; High Hon Roll; 5k Rd Runs; Rcrd Hldr Regnl Med Ctr 5k; Southern U Of AR; Elec Repair.

HARGRAVES, BRANDON M; De Soto Schl; Helena, AR; (1); Letterman Clb; L Bsktbl; JV Ftbl; L Golf; JV Trk; JV Wt Lftg; Hon Roll.

HARGREAVES, JAMES R; Russellville Sr HS; Russellville, AR; (2); Office Aide; Chorus; Church Choir; Hon Roll.

HARGROVE, BRADLEY W; Dewitt HS; De Witt, AR; (2); 11/87; FCA; French Clb; FTA; Natl Beta Clb; Natl FFA Org; Science Clb; Treas Soph Cls; Rep Stu Cncl; Var Bsbl; Var Ftbl.

HARLEY, AMANDA L; Corning HS; Corning, AR; (3); 4/70; AR ST Univ; Bus.

HARLEY, KAYTIE J; Corning Jr Sr HS; Corning, AR; (2); 1/80; Math Tm; VP Frsh Cls; VP Soph Cls; VP Jr Cls; Rep Stu Cncl; JV Var Bsktbl; JV Trk; High Hon Roll; NHS.

HARMAN, ANDREW; Southside HS; Fort Smith, AR; (3); 46/502; Church Yth Grp; FCA; German Clb; Math Tm; Mu Alpha Theta; Ed Nwsp; Var Bsktbl; Var Golf; Hon Roll; Jr NHS; Math St Hnr Roll.

HARMON, AMY D; Corning HS; Lafe, AR; (1); Drama Clb; FBLA; FHA; Hosp Aide; Spanish Clb; School Play; Tennis; PRIDE; Church Yth Grps; Univ Of AR; Pediatric Crdlgst.

HARMON, DREW A; Southside HS; Fort Smith, AR; (2); Church Yth Grp; FCA; JV Bsbl; Var Ftbl; Hon Roll.

HARMON, J C; Caddo Hills Jr Sr HS; Bonnerdale, AR; (3); 12/39; Cmnty Wkr; 4-H; Natl Beta Clb; Natl FFA Org; Spanish Clb; Rep Stu Cncl; Var Bsbl; Var Bsktbl; Capt Golf; Pres Schlr; Wldlf Mgmt.

HARMON, JENNIFER; Central Ark Christian Schl; Mabelvale, AR; (2); Church Yth Grp; Hosp Aide; Spanish Clb; Socr; Jr NHS.

HARMON, LORI M; Hope HS; Hope, AR; (3); Church Yth Grp; FBLA; Hosp Aide; Natl Beta Clb; Band; Mrchg Band; Hon Roll; French Clb; Quiz Bowl; Chr Yth Choir; Natl Dirs Band Awd; 10th Grd Outstdng Mscn; 11th Grd Outstdng Brass Plyr; U Of TX Austin.

HARMON, MACKALYNN G; Parkview Arts-Science HS; Little Rock, AR; (3); 9/285; Am Leg Aux Girls St; Church Yth Grp; Dance Clb; Key Clb; Natl Beta Clb; ROTC; Color Guard; Drill Tm; Rep Jr Cls; Hon Roll; Pearl Buck Bk Awd; Retired Offcersassoc ROTC Medl; US Naval Acad; Chem.

HARMON, RALPH C; Southside HS; Fort Smith, AR; (2); Boy Scts; Church Yth Grp; Mu Alpha Theta; Band; Crs Cntry; Swmmng; Trk; High Hon Roll; Jr NHS; NHS.

HARMS, ROSS; Gosnell Jr Sr HS; Blytheville, AR; (2); 9/105; Natl Beta Clb; Quiz Bowl; Band; Mrchg Band; Pep Band; School Play; Nwsp; Hon Roll; Pres Acad Fit Awd; Science Clb; MS Cty Comm Band; Instr Music Ed.

HARMS, SHAUN; Sylvan Hills HS; Sherwood, AR; (3); 30/290; Am Leg Boys St; Library Aide; Math Tm; Mu Alpha Theta; Natl Beta Clb; Spanish Clb; Rep Frsh Cls; Rep Stu Cncl; JV Var Socr; High Hon Roll; Univ Of AR Fayetville; Accntng.

HARP, BRANDON D; St Paul Schl; Witter, AR; (1); Rptr Nwsp; JV Bsktbl; MVP Bsktbl; Articles In Local Paper.

HARP, JARED; Pea Ridge HS; Pea Ridge, AR; (2); Church Yth Grp; Quiz Bowl; Spanish Clb; Ftbl; Trk; Wt Lftg; Hon Roll; NHS.

HARP, SARAH; Brookland Jr Sr HS; Jonesboro, AR; (2); Church Yth Grp; 4-H; FBLA; Natl Beta Clb; Chorus; Church Choir; School Musical; Variety Show; 4-H Awd; Hon Roll; Outstdng Accmpnst Awd Choir Trip To NYC; 4-H Pres Local Clb; 4-H VP Cty Teen Ldr Clb; Vet.

HARPER, BRIE ANNE; Fordyce HS; Fordyce, AR; (3); 9/84; Am Leg Aux Girls St; Church Yth Grp; Natl Beta Clb; Quiz Bowl; Teachers Aide; Band; Church Choir; Drm Mjr(t); Mrchg Band; School Play; PRIDE Group; U Of AR Fayetteville.

HARPER, KELLY; Sheridan Sr HS; Mabelvale, AR; (4); 16/220; Cmnty Wkr; FBLA; Chorus; Pres Soph Cls; Pres Jr Cls; Pres Sr Cls; Sec Stu Cncl; Capt Chrldng; Hon Roll; NHS; Natl Ldrshp & Svc Awd; All Amer Schlrs Awd; 250 Hrs Cmnty Svc; U Of AR Fayetteville; Bio.

HARPER, KEVIN A; Mills HS; Little Rock, AR; (3); Boy Scts; Church Yth Grp; Pres FBLA; Natl Beta Clb; Band; Chorus; Church Choir; School Play; Ofcr Jr Cls; AR Governors Schl; Music Vocal Ed.

HARPER, SANDRA K; Star City HS; Star City, AR; (4); 16/105; Art Clb; 4-H; French Clb; Sec FBLA; Mu Alpha Theta; Rep Natl FFA Org; Office Aide; Pres SADD; Teachers Aide; Hon Roll; Rodeo Clb; GATE; U Of AR; Acctng/Agri-Bus.

HARRELL, DUSTY; Beebe Jr HS; Searcy, AR; (1); Church Yth Grp; Natl Beta Clb; Natl FFA Org; Band; Church Choir; Jazz Band; Ftbl; Trk; Hon Roll; U Of AR.

HARRELL, LEAH S; El Dorado Sr HS; El Dorado, AR; (3); 66/316; FBLA; Natl Beta Clb; Red Cross Aide; Chorus; Church Choir; Swing Chorus; Rep Soph Cls; Cmpfire Pres; U Of AR; Neo Natal Nrs.

HARRELSON, PATRICK; Warren Jr HS; Warren, AR; (1); 3/145; Math Tm; Natl Beta Clb; Spanish Clb; Rptr Nwsp; Rptr Yrbk; JV Wt Lftg; Cit Awd; High Hon Roll; Pres Schlr.

HARRINGTON, HEATHER; Morrilton Sr HS; Morrilton, AR; (2); Natl Beta Clb; Science Clb; Thesps; Drill Tm; School Musical; Sftbl; Hon Roll; Tchr Rcgntn Awd; Natl Hnr; U AR; Med.

HARRINGTON, JARED; Drew Central Jr Sr HS; Monticello, AR; (3); 2/57; Am Leg Boys St; Boy Scts; Quiz Bowl; Rep Jr Cls; Rep Stu Cncl; Var Capt Bsktbl; L Tennis; Jr NHS; NHS.

HARRINGTON, JENNIFER L; Springdale Sr HS; Lowell, AR; (3); Drama Clb; Thesps; School Play; Stage Crew; Variety Show; Hon Roll; NHS; HOSA; Drama Clb Clrk; Drama Banquet Hostess; Springdale Bapt Schl Nrsng; Nrs.

HARRIS, ANDREA L; England HS; England, AR; (3); FHA; Chorus; Hon Roll; Loyal; U Of AR; Comp Sci.

HARRIS, ASHLEY; Delight HS; Delight, AR; (2); 1/26; FBLA; Natl Beta Clb; Natl FFA Org; VP Frsh Cls; VP Soph Cls; Rep Stu Cncl; Var Bsktbl; Var Sftbl; Hon Roll; Bty Pgnts; Phrmcy.

HARRIS, ASHLEY L; Parkview Arts-Science HS; Maumelle, AR; (2); Cmnty Wkr; French Clb; Key Clb; Hon Roll.

HARRIS, BRACE; Morrilton Sr HS; Morrilton, AR; (2); Church Yth Grp; Drama Clb; French Clb; Math Tm; Natl Beta Clb; Quiz Bowl; Thesps; School Musical; School Play; Variety Show; Natl Hstry Govt Awd; Friendlst, Mst Lkly Sccd, Mst Memrbl; TV Commrcls.

HARRIS, BRANDON L; Southside HS; Batesville, AR; (2); Church Yth Grp; Band; Ofcr Bsbl; Bsktbl; High Hon Roll; Prfct Atten Awd; Eng.

HARRIS, BRANDY R; Marion HS; Marion, AR; (2); French Clb; Band; Color Guard; Mrchg Band; Rptr Nwsp; Hon Roll; Non-Schl Sftbl; AR ST; Psych; Actress.

HARRIS, BRITTNEY; Norphlet Jr Sr HS; Norphlet, AR; (4); 1/56; Sec FBLA; Sec FHA; Band; Bsktbl; Chrldng; High Hon Roll; Sec NHS; Pres Schlr; Val; Church Yth Grp; Anchr Clb Secy; Dance; U Of AR-LTL Rock; Acctng.

HARRIS, CAMI; Marion HS; Marion, AR; (2); Art Clb; French Clb; Math Clb; Mu Alpha Theta; Var Chrldng; Var Tennis; French Hon Soc; High Hon Roll; NHS; Sftbl; All Amer Chrldr; Delta Beta Sigma; Vet.

HARRIS, CECIL W; Searcy HS; Searcy, AR; (2); 36/294; Boy Scts; Church Yth Grp; Math Tm; Natl Beta Clb; Band; Jazz Band; Mrchg Band; Orch; Pep Band; Rep Soph Cls; All-ST Band; Wind Symph; Band Cncl; Music/Prfrmr/Dir.

HARRIS, CHAD E; Lake Hamilton Sr HS; Pearcy, AR; (4); 37/275; Var Bsbl; Hon Roll; Natl Yng Ldrs Conf Wshngtn DC 95; Cmmnctns.

HARRIS, CHEREKA D; Arkansas Sr HS; Texarkana, AR; (2); Church Yth Grp; Spanish Clb; Drill Tm; JV Chrldng; Hon Roll; Grambling U; Bus Mgmt.

HARRIS, CHRISTOPHER A; Van Buren Sr HS; Van Buren, AR; (3); 25/350; FBLA; Mu Alpha Theta; Science Clb; Spanish Clb; Teachers Aide; Church Choir; High Hon Roll; Jr NHS; Prfct Atten Awd; FBLA Dist Conf Acctng I 1st Place.

HARRIS, CORIE L; Magnolia HS; Magnolia, AR; (3); 1/226; FBLA; Mu Alpha Theta; Band; Drm Mjr(t); Mrchg Band; Rep Frsh Cls; Tennis; High Hon Roll; Miss Black Columbia Cty 96; Dance Studio Mem; Ballet; Dance Awds; High Point 5th Pl Showbiz Tlnt Cmptn; Rice Univ; Med.

HARRIS, DEJUAN; Brinkley HS; Brinkley, AR; (1); Church Yth Grp; Band; Church Choir; Mrchg Band; VP Frsh Cls; Rep Stu Cncl; Hon Roll; Jr NHS; GT; All Rgn Band.

HARRIS, JASON L; Lake Hamilton Sr HS; Hot Springs Natio, AR; (2); FHA; Letterman Clb; Office Aide; SADD; Teachers Aide; School Play; Bsktbl; Golf; Cit Awd; Hon Roll; IA ST; Brdcstng/Prof Bsktbl.

HARRIS, JEROME L; Arkansas Sr HS; Texarkana, AR; (2); Church Yth Grp; Office Aide; Spanish Clb; Bsktbl; Ftbl; Trk; U AR; Dr.

HARRIS, JULIE; Farmington Jr Sr HS; Farmington, AR; (2); Model UN; Band; Drill Tm; Drm Mjr(t); Mrchg Band; Pep Band; Hon Roll; NHS; Ntl Merit Ltr; Mock Trial; U Of AR; Plant Bio.

HARRIS, JUSTIN R; North Little Rock Hs-East; North Little Rock, AR; (1); 42/646; Church Yth Grp; Drama Clb; Stage Crew; Socr; High Hon Roll; AAAA Cntrl Conf, All Conf Soccer Team; All Metro Boys Soccer; Mem AR St Soccer Team; Engrng.

HARRIS, KELLI S; Fouke Jr Sr HS; Fouke, AR; (2); Natl FFA Org; Rodeo Team; Lvstck Show Team; Lvstck & Horse Jdng Teams; Vet.

HARRIS, KELLY R; Monticello HS; Monticello, AR; (3); Sec Church Yth Grp; Natl Beta Clb; Office Aide; Spanish Clb; Chorus; Church Choir; Intrml Gym; Madrigals; U Of AR; Elem Ed.

HARRIS, KIMBERLY M; John L Mcclellan Magnet HS; Little Rock, AR; (2); Church Yth Grp; French Clb; FBLA; FHA; Church Choir; Cit Awd; Hon Roll; Computerize Acctnt.

HARRIS, KRISTY R; Pea Ridge HS; Pea Ridge, AR; (2); Spanish Clb; Chorus; Yrbk; Hon Roll; Teen Ct Juror; U Of Ak; Cmptr Prgmr.

HARRIS, KYLE; Monticello HS; Monticello, AR; (3); Church Yth Grp; French Clb; FBLA; Natl Beta Clb; Quiz Bowl; Acpl Chr; Chorus; Church Choir; NHS; Debate Tm; Multi-Yr Listee.

HARRIS, MANDY; Dumas Jr HS; Dumas, AR; (1); Church Yth Grp; FBLA; Natl Beta Clb; Science Clb; Spanish Clb; JV Chrldng; JV Gym; Hon Roll; Amer Legion, Chrldng Achvt Awds; Med.

HARRIS, MARGARET D; Lewisville HS; Lewisville, AR; (4); Art Clb; 4-H; Library Aide; Ofcr Sr Cls; Bsktbl; Trk; Nrs.

HARRIS, MARY A; Rogers HS; Rogers, AR; (3); Church Yth Grp; Cmnty Wkr; FBLA; Science Clb; Spanish Clb; Nwsp; Yrbk; Chrldng; Optimist Club; Private Singing Lessons; U Of AR; Bus Mngmt.

HARRIS, MELINDA S; Fairview HS; Chidester, AR; (2); Pres Church Yth Grp; FBLA; VP FHA; FTA; Office Aide; Teachers Aide; Sec Church Choir; Hon Roll; Bus Mchns Awd; Henderson ST.

HARRIS, MONICA E; Bearden HS; Bearden, AR; (4); 3/58; Church Yth Grp; Cmnty Wkr; FBLA; FHA; FTA; Model UN; Hist Natl Beta Clb; Quiz Bowl; Mrchg Band; Sal; U Of AR Fayetteville; Advrtsng.

HARRIS, NATOSHA T; Lake Hamilton Sr HS; Royal, AR; (3); 74/212; Church Yth Grp; FBLA; Natl FFA Org; Spanish Clb; Rptr Nwsp; Bus Law Awd.

HARRIS, REGINA R; Forrest City HS; Forrest City, AR; (3); Girl Scts; Quiz Bowl; Pride; FTAD.

HARRIS, SCIPIO; Rivercrest HS; Luxora, AR; (3); 9/100; Church Yth Grp; French Clb; FBLA; FHA; Math Clb; Church Choir; VP Soph Cls; VP Jr Cls; Var Bsbl; Var Bsktbl; Washington U; Bus Accntg.

HARRIS, SONYA M; Newport HS; Newport, AR; (3); Sec French Clb; JCL; Latin Clb; Q&S; Band; Capt Flag Corp; Mrchg Band; Rptr Nwsp; Hon Roll; NHS; ACTM Rgnl Math Cntst 3rd Pl Algebra I/Hon Mntn Geometry; Law.

HARRIS, STEPHANIE; Nashville HS; Nashville, AR; (3); 15/150; Church Yth Grp; Office Aide; School Play; Ofcr Stu Cncl; Chrldng; Tennis; Cit Awd; Hon Roll; NHS; Pres Acad Fit Awd; Homcmng Participant Twice; Participated In NCA Natl Championship; Ranked 16th In St For Tnns; U Of Conway; Obstetric Nrs.

HARRIS, SUMMER D; Lee Acad; Marianna, AR; (1).

HARRIS, TARNELL; Norphlet HS; El Dorado, AR; (1); Church Yth Grp; Band; Church Choir; Mrchg Band; Bsktbl; Jr NHS; Clss VP; Yth Choir Pres; Chrch Mass Choir Sec; Grambling ST; Med.

HARRIS, THERESICA L; North Little Rock Hs-West; North Little Rock, AR; (4); 193/439; Church Yth Grp; Drama Clb; FCA; French Clb; Natl Beta Clb; Church Choir; Ofcr Stu Cncl; Capt Chrldng; Trk; Hon Roll; U Of Cntrl AR.

HARRIS, VALERIE A; Lamar HS; Lamar, AR; (2); Church Yth Grp; FBLA; FHA; Spanish Clb; Bsktbl; Sftbl; AR Teen Univ.

HARRIS, VICKIE D; Hamburg HS; Montrose, AR; (3); Church Yth Grp; Drama Clb; 4-H; French Clb; Natl FFA Org; Office Aide; SADD; Church Choir; Yrbk; Ofcr Stu Cncl; Tulane U; Phys Thrpst.

HARRISON, ALISHA; Guy Perkins Schl; Guy, AR; (1); Church Yth Grp; FBLA; FHA; Natl FFA Org; Chorus; Church Choir; VP Frsh Cls; Ofcr Stu Cncl; Hon Roll.

HARRISON, AMANDA; Devalls Bluff Jr Sr HS; De Valls Bluff, AR; (1); Church Yth Grp; FBLA; Key Clb; Natl Beta Clb; Chorus; Bible Club; Radiologist.

HARRISON, AMBER N; Bauxite Jr Sr HS; Bauxite, AR; (2); 15/85; VP FHA; Spanish Clb; SADD; Hon Roll; VFW Jr Grls Aux Sec; Otstndng Accmplshmnt/Excl Alg I; Law.

HARRISON, BETHANY; Alma HS; Alma, AR; (3); Treas Rep Church Yth Grp; Debate Tm; Sec Pres FBLA; Mu Alpha Theta; Office Aide; Spanish Clb; Treas Jr Cls; Rep Stu Cncl; Hon Roll; NHS; St Parliamentarian For FBLA; Vol Childrens Work At Chrch On Saturday; Westark; Bus.

HARRISON, CHANDA D; Blytheville Sr HS; Blytheville, AR; (2); Chorus; Hon Roll.

HARRISON, JOCELYN; Devalls Bluff Jr Sr HS; De Valls Bluff, AR; (1); Church Yth Grp; FBLA; Natl Beta Clb; Bible Club.

HARRISON, JONDA L; Star City HS; Star City, AR; (2); Natl Beta Clb; Science Clb; Spanish Clb; Band; High Hon Roll; Hon Roll; Prfct Atten Awd; U Of Conway; Bus.

HARRISON, JUANITA; Pine Bluff HS; Pine Bluff, AR; (2); 16/580; Church Yth Grp; French Clb; Girl Scts; Natl Beta Clb; Church Choir; Pres Frsh Cls; Var Chrldng; French Hon Soc; High Hon Roll; Var Girls Choir; Pathways To Coll; His Clb Choir; Jr Beta Clb; Grambling; Comps; Elem Ed.

HARRISON, KATHY R; Bradford Jr Sr HS; Bradford, AR; (2); Church Yth Grp; FHA; GAA; Natl Beta Clb; Ofcr Stu Cncl; Bsktbl; Sftbl; Trk; Hon Roll; Art Clb; St Trk Meet; St Sftbl Meet; Sr Beta; UCA Conwy; Soc Worker.

HARRISON, LEEONA; Malvern Sr HS; Little Rock, AR; (3); Church Yth Grp; Natl Beta Clb; Pep Clb; Science Clb; Acpl Chr; High Hon Roll; Jr NHS; NHS; Pres Acad Fit Awd; Peer Cnslr; Gftd & Tlntd.

HARRISON, M STEPHEN; Lakeside HS; Hot Springs, AR; (3); Am Leg Boys St; Boy Scts; FBLA; Math Clb; Mu Alpha Theta; Natl Beta Clb; Spanish Clb; Bsktbl; Golf; High Hon Roll; Dentistry.

HARRISON, MARC; White Co Central Schl; Judsonia, AR; (2); Church Yth Grp; 4-H; VP FBLA; Treas Natl FFA Org; Capt Quiz Bowl; Var L Bsktbl; 4-H Awd; Hon Roll; Pres Acad Fit Awd; Yrbk; 4-H St Vp, Teen Star & Ambassador; U Of AR; Engr.

HARRISON, MICHAEL; Dumas HS; Dumas, AR; (2); Natl Beta Clb; Band; Jazz Band; High Hon Roll; NHS; Ventures Ed; Med Prof.

HARRISON, RACHEL N; Mansfield Jr Sr HS; Huntington, AR; (2); 3/71; Model UN; Natl Beta Clb; Ofcr Stu Cncl; Sftbl; Vllybl; Hon Roll.

HARRISON, RANEY L; Arkansas Sr HS; Texarkana, AR; (3); Drama Clb; Library Aide; Spanish Clb; Drill Tm; Chrldng; Vllybl; Texarkan Coll; Radlgy Tech.

HARRISON, STEPHANIE D; Searcy HS; Searcy, AR; (3); Art Clb; Church Yth Grp; Cmnty Wkr; FCA; French Clb; GAA; Natl Beta Clb; Office Aide; Varsity Clb; Stage Crew; U Of AR; Nrsng.

HARROD, JASON E; Fountain Lake Jr Sr HS; Hot Springs Natio, AR; (3); Art Clb; Boy Scts; Church Yth Grp; Spanish Clb; Yrbk.

HARSTAN, WENDY D; Bryant Sr HS; Bryant, AR; (2); Church Yth Grp; FHA; Teachers Aide; High Hon Roll; Hon Roll; Chrstn Cncl; Phrmcy.

HART, CHRISTIE L; Morrilton Sr HS; Morrilton, AR; (2); French Clb; Band; Drill Tm; Chrldng; Trk; Hon Roll; Majorette; Zoology.

HART, J R; Arkansas Schl Math & Science; Malvern, AR; (3); Drama Clb; FBLA; German Clb; Quiz Bowl; SADD; Thesps; Acpl Chr; Chorus; School Musical; School Play; Pugwash; U Of AR Fayette.

HART, JOHN; Watson Chapel Sr HS; Pine Bluff, AR; (3); #3 in class; Am Leg Boys St; Church Yth Grp; FCA; Natl Beta Clb; Office Aide; Spanish Clb; Teachers Aide; Church Choir; Ofcr Stu Cncl; Var Ftbl.

HART, JOHN D; Nettleton HS; Jonesboro, AR; (2); Art Clb; Boy Scts; Church Yth Grp; School Musical; School Play; Trk.

HART, JONATHAN; Jessieville HS; Hot Springs, AR; (3); FBLA; Natl Beta Clb; Quiz Bowl; Teachers Aide; Hon Roll; Yng Rpblcns Clb; Future Prblm Slvng Team.

HART, LAKESHA D; Lonoke Jr HS; Lonoke, AR; (1); GAA; Science Clb; Stat Bsktbl; Mgr(s); RN.

HART, MICHAEL A; Corning Jr Sr HS; Success, AR; (4); 17/67; Natl FFA Org; Science Clb; Spanish Clb; Bsktbl; High Hon Roll; Hon Roll; Pres Acad Fit Awd; Black River Voc-Tech; CPA.

HART, TAMARA S; Springdale Sr HS; Fayetteville, AR; (1); Art Clb; Church Yth Grp; Drama Clb; Girl Scts; Teachers Aide; Chorus; Church Choir; School Play; High Hon Roll; Jr NHS; Wrtng Novel; Hons Recital; Brigham Young Univ; Psych.

HART, TARA L; Greenwood Sr HS; Greenwood, AR; (4); 44/197; Art Clb; Church Yth Grp; FBLA; Natl Beta Clb; Office Aide; Rep Pres Spanish Clb; Rep Treas Stu Cncl; Chrldng; Hon Roll; Jr NHS; Miss Teen Sebastian Cty 96; Prom Comm; AR Tech Univ; Scndry Ed.

HARTLEY, SILAS J; Arkadelphia Sr HS; Arkadelphia, AR; (3); Am Leg Boys St; Church Yth Grp; French Clb; VP FBLA; VP FHA; Natl Beta Clb; Church Choir; Rep Frsh Cls; Pres Soph Cls; Rep Jr Cls; Upward Bound Ouachita Bapt Univ; Brown Univ; Comp Engr.

HARTMAN, BEN; Greenbrier HS; Greenbrier, AR; (3); 31/200; Drama Clb; Teachers Aide; Nwsp; Phtg Yrbk; Hon Roll; Prfct Atten Awd; Crtve Wrtng Skills; U Of Cntrl AR; Novelist.

HARTMAN, LEIGH A; Sacred Heart Schl; Morrilton, AR; (3); 3/14; Am Leg Aux Girls St; Art Clb; Church Yth Grp; Drama Clb; German Clb; GAA; Key Clb; Natl Beta Clb; SADD; Stage Crew; AR Tech; Nrsg.

HARTSELL, JEFFREY H; Dollarway HS; Pine Bluff, AR; (4); 6/91; Am Leg Boys St; Church Yth Grp; Hosp Aide; Key Clb; Letterman Clb; Library Aide; Math Clb; Science Clb; Teachers Aide; Acpl Chr; U Of AR; Kinesiology.

HARTSFIELD, HOLLY R; De Soto Schl; West Helena, AR; (2); Church Yth Grp; JV DECA; High Hon Roll; Hon Roll; NHS; Eng Acad Bttrmnt Cmptn; Psych.

HARTSFIELD, MATT W; Conway Sr HS; Conway, AR; (2); Church Yth Grp; Cmnty Wkr; Teachers Aide; Rep Stu Cncl; Var JV Bsbl; Var JV Ftbl; Powder Puff Ftbl; K-Life; Hnrbl Mention Ftbl; Amer Lgn Bsbl.

HARVEY, BRIAN A; Hot Springs HS; Hot Springs, AR; (2); FBLA; Quiz Bowl; Var JV Bsbl; Mgr(s); Score Keeper; Hon Roll; Beta Clb; 9th Grade Ftbl; Sound For Pep Rallies & Sporting Events; Acctng.

HARVEY, DAVID C; Highland HS; Cherokee Village, AR; (2); Hon Roll; Prfct Atten Awd.

HARVEY, MELISSA A; Amity Jr Sr HS; Amity, AR; (3); Pres Hist FBLA; Natl FFA Org; Phtg Rptr Nwsp; Rptr Jr Cls; Mgr(s); Hon Roll; Span I; Harding Univ; Pre-Law; Acctng.

HARVEY, TANYA L; Des Arc Jr Sr HS; Des Arc, AR; (4); 12/45; FBLA; FTA; Natl Beta Clb; Science Clb; Spanish Clb; Chorus; Yrbk; Hon Roll; Foothills Tech; Sec.

HARVILL, TONYA; Humphrey Schl; Humphrey, AR; (4); 3/22; Church Yth Grp; Library Aide; Spanish Clb; Chorus; Church Choir; Hon Roll; NHS; UCA Conway; Med.

HARWOOD, LEIGH E; Huntsville HS; Huntsville, AR; (3); 1/135; FCA; Key Clb; Band; Color Guard; VP Soph Cls; VP Jr Cls; Rep Stu Cncl; Mgr Ftbl; Intrml Sftbl; NHS; :dart; UCCM.

HASLIP, MARY K; Beebe Sr HS; Beebe, AR; (2); 56/150; Drama Clb; FBLA; HOBY; Math Clb; Pep Clb; Quiz Bowl; Spanish Clb; Thesps; School Play; U Of Cntrl AR; Psych.

HASSON, MARK J; Pulaski Acad; Little Rock, AR; (3); Natl Beta Clb; Spanish Clb; VP Temple Yth Grp; NHS; Study Jerusalem Israel 96.

HASTINGS, CODY; Nevada Schl; Rosston, AR; (4); 13/65; Art Clb; Church Yth Grp; French Clb; Natl Beta Clb; Science Clb; Teachers Aide; Band; Rep Jr Cls; Sec VP Stu Cncl; Ofcr Bsbl; Harding Univ; Sales/Mktg.

HATCH, HOLLIE; North Little Rock Hs-West; Sherwood, AR; (3); 102/554; Church Yth Grp; Drama Clb; Mu Alpha Theta; Q&S; Teachers Aide; Yrbk; Hon Roll; Demi-Soloist For Ballet Arkansas; Hartford; Ballet.

HATCH, MICHAEL; Gosnell Jr Sr HS; Gosnell, AR; (4); 26/66; Science Clb; Chorus; Var Bsbl; Var Bsktbl; Var Fld Hcky; Var Capt Golf; Hon Roll; Math Cmptnsn At ASU; Hmcmng Ct Chrldr; MS Cty CC; Acctng.

HATCHETT, LORA; Leslie Schl; Leslie, AR; (2); Church Yth Grp; FBLA; Rptr Girl Scts; Rptr Key Clb; Natl Beta Clb; Teachers Aide; Rptr Soph Cls; High Hon Roll; One Of Five Start Chrstn Clb 95; Cmps Lfe Hstrn; Coll Of Ozarks.

HATFIELD, JAKE R; Prairie Grove HS; Prairie Grove, AR; (3); Church Yth Grp; 4-H; Band; Mrchg Band; Yrbk; VP Jr Cls; Ofcr Stu Cncl; 4-H Awd; Hon Roll; NHS; U Of AR; Exec Prod.

HATFIELD, JOSEPH M; Catholic HS; Little Rock, AR; (3); Pres Art Clb; ROTC; JV Ftbl; Apprenticeship At Cabinet & Furniture Shop.

HATFIELD, KRISTY R; Huntsville HS; Huntsville, AR; (3); 8/128; Church Yth Grp; Drama Clb; Hist Rptr FBLA; Science Clb; Ofcr Soph Cls; Var L Chrldng; High Hon Roll; Hon Roll; NHS; Pres Acad Fit Awd; UAR; Bus Mgmt.

HATFIELD, WENDY; Prairie Grove HS; Prairie Grove, AR; (2); Church Yth Grp; 4-H; Natl FFA Org; Spanish Clb; Band; Mrchg Band; Pep Band; 4-H Awd; High Hon Roll; Hon Roll; Vet.

HATHCOAT, MELISSA; Mansfield Jr Sr HS; Mansfield, AR; (1); 33/76; Church Yth Grp; FCA; GAA; Speech Tm; Stage Crew; Intrml JV Chrldng; Cit Awd; Envrmntl Clb; PAWS II; Westark CC; Elem Tchr.

HATLEY, ANDY L; Russellville Sr HS; Russellville, AR; (2); Church Yth Grp; Band; Mrchg Band; JV Bsktbl; Var Ftbl; Var Capt Socr; Pres Acad Fit Awd; Univ Of VA.

HAUDRICH, DARIN P; Hartford Schl; Hackett, AR; (3); VP FBLA; Treas Jr Cls; Treas Stu Cncl; Var Bsbl; Var Bsktbl; Var Ftbl; Socr; Var Trk; High Hon Roll; Hon Roll; Aeronautical Eng.

HAUK, GRACEN E; Carlisle Jr Sr HS; Carlisle, AR; (3); Am Leg Aux Girls St; Art Clb; Bus Profs of Am; Church Yth Grp; FCA; FHA; VICA; Library Aide; Math Clb; Mu Alpha Theta; Baylor Univ; Premed.

HAULTON, KIM; East End Jr Sr HS; Houston, AR; (1); Quiz Bowl; Chrldng; Powder Puff Ftbl; Hon Roll; NHS; BADD; Beta Clb; Stanford; Polysci.

HAUSTEIN, STEFFANY; Central Ark Christian Schl; North Little Rock, AR; (1); Chorus; Rep Frsh Cls; Bsktbl; Trk; Vllybl; NHS; Treas Natl Hnr Soc.

HAWBLITZEL, JEFF; Alma HS; Alma, AR; (4); 54/159; ROTC; Science Clb; Band; Color Guard; Jazz Band; Pep Band; Var Bsbl; Var Bsktbl; Var Trk; NHS; All-Reg Band; Cert Mrtrs Achvt Nvl Jr Rsrv Offcrs Trng Crps; Citatn & Mdl VFW; U Of Cntrl AR; Military Sci.

HAWKINS, CLINT L; Atkins Schl; Atkins, AR; (1); FHA; Varsity Clb; JV Bsbl; Var L Ftbl; Var Trk; Civis Awd; Svng Marine Hab; Univ Of Notre Dame; Aqua Bio.

HAWKINS, CODY C; Searcy HS; Searcy, AR; (3); FCA; Natl Beta Clb; Spanish Clb; JV Ftbl; Var Golf; High Hon Roll; Jr NHS; NHS; Pres Acad Fit Awd; Spanish NHS; U Of AR; Engnr.

HAWKINS, JOSEPH A; Pine Bluff HS; Pine Bluff, AR; (3); Am Leg Boys St; Art Clb; Boy Scts; Nwsp; Yrbk; Hon Roll; Jr NHS; NHS; Pres Acad Fit Awd; Spcl Intrst Art; Spcl Intrst Msc.

HAWKINS, MICHELLE; W Campus Tech Ctr; Bentonville, AR; (4); 7/121; Computer Clb; FBLA; FHA; Office Aide; Teachers Aide; Hon Roll; Uptown Schol; Comp Tech Cert Of Merit For Outs Accomplshmnt; Offc Syst Suppt.

HAWKINS, SKOCHU L; Fairview HS; Camden, AR; (3); Church Yth Grp; Natl Beta Clb; Teachers Aide; Band; Color Guard; Flag Corp; Mrchg Band; Pep Band; Yrbk; Cit Awd; Navy Hnrs Pgm; Spelman Coll; Engrng.

HAWKINS, TALESIA; Camden-Fairview HS; Camden, AR; (4); 10/245; Church Yth Grp; Debate Tm; FBLA; FHA; Math Clb; Mu Alpha Theta; Natl Beta Clb; Science Clb; Spanish Clb; SADD; All Amer Chrldr; U Of Cntrl AR; Phys Thrp.

HAWKINS, TRISHANNA L; Sheridan Sr HS; Sheridan, AR; (2); Cmnty Wkr; Hon Roll; U Of AR; Psychtrst.

HAWLEY, LAUREN; Sylvan Hills HS; Sherwood, AR; (1); FCA; Library Aide; Chorus; School Musical; Chrldng; Jr NHS; Tchr.

HAWLEY, TIA M; Trumann HS; Trumann, AR; (2); Church Yth Grp; French Clb; Model UN; Band; Mrchg Band; Pep Band; Hon Roll; NHS; Prfct Atten Awd; Jr/Sr HS Region Band; All-ST Band Alternate.

HAWTHORNE, ANNA K; Glen Rose HS; Malvern, AR; (3); Church Yth Grp; FBLA; Ofcr Stu Cncl; Bsktbl; Sftbl; Ouachita Tech Coll.

HAWTHORNE, LISA A; Emmet Schl; Emmet, AR; (1); Natl Beta Clb; Hon Roll; Libry Clb; Hnrs Hlth In Home Ec; Wrtng Comptr, U Of AR; Crctve Wrtng.

HAYCRAFT, CARRIE H; North Little Rock Hs-West; North Little Rock, AR; (4); Cmnty Wkr; Drama Clb; Intnl Clb; Natl Beta Clb; Q&S; School Musical; Yrbk; Ofcr Sr Cls; Var Capt Chrldng; High Hon Roll; TX Chrstn Univ.

HAYDEN, HOLLY M; Drew Central Jr Sr HS; Wilmar, AR; (2); FBLA; FHA; Teachers Aide; Hon Roll; UAM; Med.

HAYES, ADAM; Bauxite Jr Sr HS; Benton, AR; (4); 5/43; Church Yth Grp; Cmnty Wkr; FBLA; Service Clb; Spanish Clb; SADD; Teachers Aide; Cit Awd; Hon Roll; NHS; Stu Advsry Brd Prjcts Coord; Vlntr Peer Tutor Pgm Fndr & Ldr; Hendrix Coll; Psych.

HAYES, BRANDY M; Hampton Jr Sr HS; Hampton, AR; (4); Church Yth Grp; Teachers Aide; Band; Mrchg Band; Orch; Pep Band; 4 Supr Mdls/1 Exclnt Mdl Solos; CPEP Summer Classes; SAU Magnolia; Cmptr Prgrmng.

HAYES, DANA; Gillett Jr Sr HS; Gillett, AR; (1); Art Clb; Church Yth Grp; Math Tm; Pep Clb; Quiz Bowl; Bsktbl; Chrldng; Hon Roll; Jr NHS; Prfct Atten Awd.

HAYES, DAVID; Beebe Jr HS; Beebe, AR; (1); Church Yth Grp; FBLA; Natl Beta Clb; Natl FFA Org; Church Choir; Ftbl; L Trk; Hon Roll; Beta Clb.

HAYES, KITINA; North Pulaski HS; Jacksonville, AR; (4); 22/296; Church Yth Grp; Math Clb; Mu Alpha Theta; Science Clb; Band; Jazz Band; Mrchg Band; Orch; School Musical; NHS; ASU In Jonesboro; Wldlf Mgmnt.

HAYES, ROCKY; Marion HS; Marion, AR; (3); FCA; Mu Alpha Theta; Nwsp; Rep Frsh Cls; Rep Soph Cls; Capt Chrldng; Var Sftbl; French Hon Soc; Hon Roll; NHS; U Of Central AR; Medcl.

HAYES, SARA E; Crossett Sr HS; Crossett, AR; (2); GAA; Tennis; Hon Roll; Dance; Tenns Dist Sngls Rnnr Up; Water Skiing; Ne LA U; Med.

HAYES, STACY; Monticello HS; Monticello, AR; (1); Church Yth Grp; Natl Beta Clb; Chrldng; Gym; Sftbl; Hon Roll; Jr NHS.

HAYLEY, MEREDITH D; Des Arc Jr Sr HS; Des Arc, AR; (2); Church Yth Grp; Natl Beta Clb; Science Clb; Spanish Clb; VP Soph Cls; Bsktbl; Trk; Hon Roll; Rep Frsh Cls; Type A Thon St Judes Luekemia Patients; 1st Pl Team AR Woodmen Wrld ST Cnvntn; U Of AR Med Sci; Dntl Hygnts.

HAYNES, CASSIE R; Star City HS; Pine Bluff, AR; (1); Church Yth Grp; Natl Beta Clb; Chorus; School Musical; Hon Roll; U Of Centr Ark; Intl Desgn.

HAYNES, CLIFF; Gillett Jr Sr HS; Gillett, AR; (2); 1/30; Church Yth Grp; FBLA; Rptr FHA; HOBY; Capt Quiz Bowl; VP Soph Cls; Treas Stu Cncl; Var Bsktbl; Var Ftbl; NHS.

HAYNES, KATHERINE L; Arkansas Schl For Math & Sci; Conway, AR; (4); Church Yth Grp; Cmnty Wkr; Natl Beta Clb; Orch; NHS; Fllwshp Chrstn Stdnts; Intl Sci & Engrng Fair; Beta Clb; U Of Central AR; Bio.

HAYNES, LATONYA; Newport HS; Newport, AR; (2); JCL; Latin Clb; Church Choir; Ofcr Stu Cncl; Trk; Hon Roll; Univ Of AR; Trvl Agnt/Cmptr.

HAYNES, TOSH I; Alma Sr HS; Park Hill, OK; (2); NHS; Pres Acad Fit Awd; Mntrshp Pgm Atty; U Of AR Fayetteville.

HAYS, AMANDA M; Junction City HS; Junction City, AR; (2); Church Yth Grp; FBLA; Spanish Clb; Yrbk; Ofcr Stu Cncl; High Hon Roll; BASIC; Bus.

HAYS, ANGELA M; Central Sr HS; Little Rock, AR; (3); 80/540; Church Yth Grp; Cmnty Wkr; French Clb; FBLA; Girl Scts; Mu Alpha Theta; Natl Beta Clb; Pep Clb; Science Clb; Varsity Clb; TX A&M; Med.

HAYS, BRYAN; Atkins Schl; Atkins, AR; (3); 1/63; HOBY; Natl Beta Clb; Capt Quiz Bowl; Rep Jr Cls; Ofcr Stu Cncl; L Bsktbl; High Hon Roll; Pres Jr NHS; Pres Acad Fit Awd; Art Clb; AEGIS Smmr Pgm.

HAYS, JENNIFER L; Hot Springs HS; Hot Springs, AR; (4); 43/154; Drama Clb; FBLA; Natl Beta Clb; NFL; Science Clb; Spanish Clb; Thesps; School Play; Ed Yrbk; 3rd Plc Round Table Poets Soc; U Of Cntrl AR; Mass Comm.

HAYS, MELISSA; Genoa Central HS; Texarkana, AR; (4); 1/36; Church Yth Grp; Model UN; Quiz Bowl; Chorus; Church Choir; Yrbk; High Hon Roll; Hon Roll; NHS; Val; Fellowship Chrstn Stu Treas; Chrstn Newsletter; OSU; Chem Engr.

HAYWOOD, LEIGH; Rison HS; Rison, AR; (1); 1/55; Church Yth Grp; FCA; FHA; Natl Beta Clb; Sec Frsh Cls; Bsktbl; Capt Chrldng; Sftbl; High Hon Roll; NHS; Drug Awrnss Grp; Jr Beta Clb Pres; U Of AR; Comms.

HAZLEWOOD, QUIARA M; Westside HS; Bono, AR; (3); Church Yth Grp; Rptr FBLA; FTA; Girl Scts; Science Clb; Mrchg Band; Pep Band; Hon Roll; Art Clb; Teachers Aide; Regnl Bus Math Comp 4th Pl; FBLA; 17th Annual Trivium Quadrivium Symposium; Harding Univ Hnrs Symposiu; Harding Univ; Bible; Biblcl Lang.

HEAGWOOD, TIFFANY L; De Soto Schl; Helena, AR; (2); Drama Clb; Sec Frsh Cls; Sec Soph Cls; JV L Bsktbl; Var Capt Chrldng; JV L Sftbl; JV L Trk; Bapt Chrch; AR ST Univ; Soc Worker.

HEANEY, PAULA; Ark School For Math & Science; Jerusalem, AR; (3); FBLA; HOBY; Sec Natl Beta Clb; Quiz Bowl; Spanish Clb; Lit Mag; Pres Frsh Cls; Pres Soph Cls; Sec Stu Cncl; Bsktbl; U Of AR-FAYETTEVILLE; Arch.

HEARD, CASSEY; Lake Hamilton Sr HS; Hot Springs, AR; (2); Church Yth Grp; Computer Clb; Drama Clb; FCA; Natl Beta Clb; Spanish Clb; Rep Frsh Cls; Rep Soph Cls; Chrldng; Gym; Tri-Ath Awd; SASC Host; Wolf Pride Sec; SCL; Chrch Drama; JUSTICE.

HEARD, JEFFERSON R; Mills HS; Sherwood, AR; (3); 70/268; Art Clb; Church Yth Grp; French Clb; Latin Clb; Natl Beta Clb; Science Clb; Orch; All Region & All St Orch; AR Governors Schl; Duke Univ TIP Pgm; Music; Chem.

HEARD, KARLA G; Greenwood Sr HS; Greenwood, AR; (2); Pres FCA; GAA; Teachers Aide; JV Sftbl; Var Vllybl; High Hon Roll; Jr NHS; Pres Schlr; Natl Eng Merit Awd 95-; Scuba Dvng; Med Dr.

HEARD, LATESHA N; Huttig Schl; Huttig, AR; (1); FTA; VP Frsh Cls; Rep Stu Cncl; Var Bsktbl; Var Sftbl; All Rookie Bsktbl Tm 95-96; Acad Excl Outstndng Schlrshp 95-96; 7b E All Dist Hnrb Mntn 95-96; Police Acad; Ofcr.

HEARD, MISTY D; Valley View HS; Jonesboro, AR; (3); Am Leg Aux Girls St; Drama Clb; Chorus; School Musical; School Play; Yrbk; Lit Mag; Hon Roll; NHS; Jr NHS; ST Regnl Choir; ASU; Engl Prof.

HEARD, NICOLE Y; John L Mcclellan Magnet HS; Little Rock, AR; (4); Art Clb; FBLA; FHA; Spanish Clb; Band; Drill Tm; Mrchg Band; Phtg Yrbk; Rptr Sr Cls; Vllybl; Prd; Ftr 500; UCA; Bus.

HEARN, JOSH A; Southside HS; Fort Smith, AR; (2); Church Yth Grp; FCA; Band; Ftbl; NHS.

HEARN, KERI N; Dewitt HS; De Witt, AR; (2); Church Yth Grp; Cmnty Wkr; 4-H; French Clb; FBLA; Natl Beta Clb; Var L Sftbl; Prfct Atten Awd; ASU Jonesboro.

HEARNE, AMANDA; Atkins Schl; Atkins, AR; (2); 1/84; Church Yth Grp; Cmnty Wkr; Drama Clb; FBLA; FHA; Natl Beta Clb; Science Clb; Band; Color Guard; Mrchg Band; Play Piano; 5th In Regnl FBLA Cmptn; Harding Univ; Pre-Med.

HEARNSBERGER, JAN; Arkansas Bapt Schl; Little Rock, AR; (4); 2/34; Sec FCA; Sec Natl Beta Clb; Rptr Jr Cls; Rptr Stu Cncl; Var Capt Bsktbl; Chrldng; Gov Hon Prg Awd; Sal; Church Yth Grp; Homcmng Qn; Bst All Around Character, Ability & Attitude Awd; Bstkbl, Tnns Awds; Baylor U; Mrktng.

HEATHER, HUGHES D; Lockesburg Jr Sr HS; Lockesburg, AR; (4); 1/24; FCA; Pres Spanish Clb; Pres Sr Cls; Pres Stu Cncl; VP Jr NHS; Sec NHS; Val; US Army Rsrv Natl Schlr Athl Awd; All-Dist Bsktbl 94-95 & 95-96; Texarkana Coll; Nrsng.

HEBERT, JAMES M; Cedarville Jr Sr HS; Van Buren, AR; (4); 24/70; Chess Clb; Church Yth Grp; Computer Clb; Natl FFA Org; Quiz Bowl; Science Clb; SADD; Band; Church Choir; Mrchg Band; Henderson ST Univ; Music Ed.

HECKE, GEOFFREY SCOTT; Malvern Sr HS; Malvern, AR; (3); 45/170; Am Leg Boys St; Church Yth Grp; FCA; FBLA; Natl FFA Org; Rep Stu Cncl; JV Ftbl; Hon Roll; Office Aide; Spanish Clb; Governors Yth Conf; Peer Cnslr; UA Monticello; Landscape Arch.

HECKMANN, JOHN; Central Ark Christian Schl; Little Rock, AR; (1); Church Yth Grp; French Clb; Math Clb; Rep Stu Cncl; Ofcr Bsbl; Bsktbl; Ftbl; High Hon Roll; VP Jr NHS.

HEDGE, LESLIE M; Marmaduke HS; Marmaduke, AR; (4); 4/40; Church Yth Grp; Cmnty Wkr; FCA; FBLA; FHA; Natl Beta Clb; Pep Clb; Chorus; Church Choir; Nwsp; AR ST U; Bus; Mrktg.

HEDRICK, JAMES C; Oak Grove HS; Maumelle, AR; (2); Church Yth Grp; French Clb; German Clb; Library Aide; Band; Color Guard; Flag Corp; Hon Roll; TX A&M; Bio Sci.

HEFFINGTON, ANDREA; Benton Sr HS; Benton, AR; (3); #21 in class; Church Yth Grp; Hosp Aide; Key Clb; Model UN; Spanish Clb; Church Choir; High Hon Roll; Hon Roll; Jr NHS; Kiwanis Awd.

HEFFLEY, RYAN; Cty Line HS; Branch, AR; (3); 2/40; FCA; FBLA; Natl Beta Clb; Quiz Bowl; Rptr Spanish Clb; Pres Frsh Cls; L Bsktbl; Var Golf; Cit Awd; High Hon Roll.

HEFLIN, LISA A; Russellville Sr HS; Russellville, AR; (3); Art Clb; Church Yth Grp; Natl FFA Org; Teachers Aide; Hon Roll; Farmer; AR Tech Univ; Ag.

HEFNER, JUSTINE C; Lake Hamilton Sr HS; Pearcy, AR; (2); FCA; Office Aide; JV Bsktbl; Var Sftbl; JV Vllybl; Hon Roll; Schlr Ath; U Of KY; Vet.

HEGWOOD, RUTH J; Smackover HS; Smackover, AR; (1); 10/69; FBLA; Girl Scts; Spanish Clb; Band; Church Choir; Mrchg Band; Pep Band; Ofcr Frsh Cls; 1st Chair Region IV Band 95; AEGIS Pgm 96; Black Stu Assn Mem; Comp Engr.

HEINRICH, SHELLEY J; Harrison Sr HS; Harrison, AR; (3); DECA; Drama Clb; French Clb; FBLA; Thesps; School Musical; School Play; Stage Crew; High Hon Roll; Hnr Keyboardist; ST DECA Conf 1st Place; Outstdng DECA Mem Awd.

HEINRICHS, NICOLE; Charleston HS; Charleston, AR; (2); Church Yth Grp; FCA; FBLA; Natl Beta Clb; Office Aide; Spanish Clb; Yrbk; Rep Frsh Cls; Rep Soph Cls; Var Bsktbl.

HEISLER, LAURI; Wynne HS; Wynne, AR; (3); 20/200; Church Yth Grp; Cmnty Wkr; Drama Clb; FBLA; Sec FTA; Natl Beta Clb; Q&S; Spanish Clb; SADD; Acpl Chr; 4th In All-Region Choir; 20th In All-St Choir Of AR; Rnnr-Up Rayda Dilport Acting Awd; Rhodes Coll; Psych.

HELLARD, BRIAN; Fairview HS; Camden, AR; (3); Church Yth Grp; Mu Alpha Theta; Varsity Clb; Bsktbl; L Ftbl; Trk; High Hon Roll; Pres Acad Fit Awd; Spanish NHS; VP Stdnts For Christ/Local/Dist Meth Yth; Conf Rep Conf Cncl Yth Mnstrs; Yth Mnstry.

HELLER, ALICE L; Hot Springs HS; Hot Springs, AR; (4); 6/154; Art Clb; Church Yth Grp; Cmnty Wkr; Debate Tm; JA; Mu Alpha Theta; Natl Beta Clb; NFL; Science Clb; Spanish Clb; Frgn Exch Stdnt 94-95; Ecology Clb; Hendrix Coll; Bio/Med.

HELLUMS, BRIAN R; Saratoga Schl; Fulton, AR; (3); FHA; Natl FFA Org; Science Clb; Teachers Aide; School Play; Stage Crew; Nwsp; Ofcr Soph Cls; Ofcr Jr Cls; Bsktbl; Univ Of AR; Forster.

HELM, AMANDA K; Junction City HS; Junction City, AR; (1); Church Yth Grp; FHA; Flag Corp; Hon Roll; Hm Ec Awd; Prncpls Lst; NLU.

HELMICK, ROBERT W; Blevins HS; Prescott, AR; (2); Natl FFA Org; Ofcr Frsh Cls; Var Bsbl; Intrml Ftbl; Wt Lftg.

HELMS, CHAD; Rogers HS; Rogers, AR; (4); FCA; FBLA; Teachers Aide; Ofcr Bsbl; Bsktbl; High Hon Roll; Hon Roll; NHS; Frgn Lang Clb; U Of AR; Aerospc Engrng.

HELMS, CHRIS W; Gravette HS; Hiwasse, AR; (2); FBLA; Band; Hon Roll.

HELMS, CYNTHIA N; White Co Central Schl; Judsonia, AR; (2); VP FHA; Spanish Clb; Teachers Aide; Yrbk; Pres Stu Cncl; Intrml Sftbl; Jr NHS; Sftbl; Chldrns Psych.

HELMS, JACE V; Malvern Sr HS; Malvern, AR; (3); Church Yth Grp; FCA; FBLA; Natl Beta Clb; Spanish Clb; Rep Stu Cncl; Var L Bsbl; Var L Ftbl; High Hon Roll; Hon Roll.

HELMS, JEREMY; Lavaca Jr Sr HS; Lavaca, AR; (3); 7/60; Art Clb; Church Yth Grp; Natl Beta Clb; Bsktbl; Trk; Hon Roll.

HELMS, SHAREE N; Mansfield Jr Sr HS; Mansfield, AR; (2); Debate Tm; Drama Clb; FCA; Intnl Clb; Spanish Clb; Speech Tm; Teachers Aide; VP Soph Cls; High Hon Roll; Pres Acad Fit Awd; Paws II; Earth Environmental Clb; ATU; Lawyer.

HELTON, HEATHER L; Trumann HS; Trumann, AR; (3); French Clb; Library Aide; Math Clb; Science Clb; Co-Ed Yrbk; Bsktbl; Sftbl; Trk; Vllybl; High Hon Roll; Chiroprtc.

HELTON, MELLENA G; Magazine Jr Sr HS; Magazine, AR; (2); 2/18; Church Yth Grp; FCA; FHA; Office Aide; Hon Roll; Chrch Sftbl League; Natl Sci Awd; U Of AR; Corp Sec.

HELVEY, AMANDA; Dollarway HS; Pine Bluff, AR; (4); 1/93; Church Yth Grp; Key Clb; Yrbk; Rep Sr Cls; Ofcr Stu Cncl; Capt Chrldng; Hon Roll; Jr NHS; NHS; Val; U Of AR-FAYETTEVILLE.

HEMBREY, MELISSA S; Newport HS; Newport, AR; (2); Hosp Aide; Sci Awd; MADD Art.

HEMLER, JEANNIE; Fountain Lake Jr Sr HS; Hot Springs, AR; (4); 18/51; Art Clb; Natl Beta Clb; Spanish Clb; Chorus; Hon Roll; Prfct Atten Awd; All Amer Schlr; Garland Cty CC; Graphic Dsgn.

HEMUND, CRYSTAL L; Amity Jr Sr HS; Amity, AR; (4); 3/15; Church Yth Grp; FBLA; FHA; Natl Beta Clb; Yrbk; Treas Jr Cls; Ofcr Stu Cncl; Bsktbl; Sftbl; Vllybl; Henderson ST Univ.

HENCY, TRACIE; Fayetteville Sr HS; Fayetteville, AR; (4); Church Yth Grp; FCA; Key Clb; Library Aide; Q&S; Band; Mrchg Band; Pep Band; Ed Yrbk; Vllybl; Child Psych.

HENDERSON, ALESHA; Mineral Springs Schl; Mineral Springs, AR; (2); Church Yth Grp; Natl Beta Clb; Quiz Bowl; Rep Soph Cls; Drug Prevention Team; Homemcng Ct.

HENDERSON, ALLISON; Central Ark Christian Schl; Little Rock, AR; (1); Church Yth Grp; Hosp Aide; Chorus; Church Choir; Cit Awd; High Hon Roll; Hon Roll; Vet Med.

HENDERSON, AMY D; Arkansas Sr HS; Texarkana, AR; (4); Art Clb; Math Clb; Mu Alpha Theta; Q&S; Spanish Clb; Ed Nwsp; Hon Roll; Nike; Yng Democrts; Acctng.

HENDERSON, DAVID D; Walker Schl; Magnolia, AR; (3); Art Clb; Cmnty Wkr; Drama Clb; English Clb; French Clb; FBLA; FHA; Math Clb; Natl FFA Org; SADD; PE.

HENDERSON, JESSICA D; Manila HS; Manila, AR; (1); Church Yth Grp; FHA; Chorus; Church Choir; JV Bsktbl; JV Sftbl; Hon Roll; Bsktbl Jr High Girls Most Steals/Best Dfns/3-A North All-Conf; Frosh Hmcmng Maid; AR ST Univ; Erly Chldhd Ed.

HENDERSON, JESSICA M; Hermitage Jr Sr HS; Hermitage, AR; (2); Art Clb; Church Yth Grp; Computer Clb; English Clb; FHA; Math Clb; Science Clb; Church Choir; Ofcr Soph Cls; Prfct Atten Awd; Fshng; Cmpng; Acting; Hrsrdng; Bible Schl.

HENDERSON, KIMBERLY E; North Little Rock Hs-West; North Little Rock, AR; (3); Church Yth Grp; Mu Alpha Theta; Natl Beta Clb; Band; Drm Mjr(t); Stage Crew; JV Bsktbl; High Hon Roll; NHS; Future 500; Math/Cmptr Sci.

HENDERSON, LISA; Turrell Jr-Sr HS; Turrell, AR; (3); 2/43; FBLA; Natl Beta Clb; Pres Acad Fit Awd; Sal; Naval Acad; Med.

HENDERSON, LISA; Butterfield Jr HS; Van Buren, AR; (2); Drama Clb; FBLA; Speech Tm; Thesps; Stage Crew; Bsktbl; Hon Roll; Jr NHS; Theatre.

HENDERSON, NICOLE; Sylvan Hills HS; Little Rock, AR; (3); FBLA; Mu Alpha Theta; Teachers Aide; Hon Roll; Jr NHS; TOT Clb/Acad; UCA; Ed.

HENDERSON, SARAH; Bergman Schl; Harrison, AR; (3); FBLA; Model UN; Natl Beta Clb; School Play; Rptr Nwsp; Rep Jr Cls; Rep Stu Cncl; Bsktbl; Sftbl; High Hon Roll; Univ Of AR; Cvl Eng.

HENDERSON, SARAH; Walnut Vly Chrstn Acad; Little Rock, AR; (3); 2/7; Church Yth Grp; Latin Clb; Natl Beta Clb; Stage Crew; Yrbk; Rep Soph Cls; Rep Jr Cls; VP Stu Cncl; Var Capt Chrldng; Hon Roll; Winter Formal Chm; All-Star Chrldrs; Natl Yth Ldrshp Conf Nom; Interior Dsgn.

HENDERSON, TASHA; Van Buren Sr HS; Van Buren, AR; (3); 15/300; Church Yth Grp; HOBY; Mu Alpha Theta; Treas Jr Cls; Treas Stu Cncl; Capt Pom Pon; High Hon Roll; Jr NHS; NHS; Vanderbilt; Chld Psych.

HENDERSON, ZACK; Fayetteville Sr HS; Fayetteville, AR; (3); Am Leg Boys St; Church Yth Grp; Cmnty Wkr; FBLA; SADD; Teachers Aide; Band; Lit Mag; Ofcr Stu Cncl; NHS; Pres Yth Svc Awd Wnnr; Mrktg; Advertising.

HENDREN, DAVID D; Russellville Sr HS; Russellville, AR; (3); Letterman Clb; Office Aide; Band; Var Ftbl; Var Trk; Hon Roll.

HENDREX, JOSHUA M; Fountain Lake Jr Sr HS; Lonsdale, AR; (3); Church Yth Grp; FCA; Sec Natl FFA Org; NFL; Rep Spanish Clb; School Musical; School Play; Stage Crew; Bsktbl; SCA Pres; Fire Marshalls; Southern AR U; Fisheries.

HENDRICKS, AMY D; Stuttgart Sr HS; Stuttgart, AR; (3); Church Yth Grp; FBLA; FHA; Key Clb; Natl Beta Clb; Phtg Natl FFA Org; Spanish Clb; Chorus; Hon Roll; DECA; Just Say No; GCO; Grls Chrstn Org; UCA; Psychtrst.

HENDRICKS, CHRISTIANE E; Bradford Jr Sr HS; Bradford, AR; (2); FBLA; Chorus; Bsktbl; Sftbl; Hon Roll; U Of Cntrl AR.

HENDRICKS, LELIA; Conway Sr HS; Conway, AR; (3); Church Yth Grp; FBLA; German Clb; HOBY; Natl Beta Clb; Church Choir; Swmmng; High Hon Roll; Cngrss-Bndstg Schlrshp 95; Natl FBLA Intro Bus.

HENDRICKS, SARA; Vilonia HS; Conway, AR; (3); 1/110; Church Yth Grp; FBLA; HOBY; Mu Alpha Theta; Natl Beta Clb; Quiz Bowl; Pres Jr Cls; VP Stu Cncl; Hon Roll; Church Choir; Girls St; Med.

HENDRICKS, WILLIAM L; Russellville Sr HS; Russellville, AR; (2); Letterman Clb; Spanish Clb; SADD; Teachers Aide; Varsity Clb; Crs Cntry; Ftbl; Trk; Rssllvlle All Stars; Aide To Hrshys Trck/Fld Yth Prgm; OK ST Univ; Sprts Brdcstr.

HENDRICKSON, CHERI A; Bentonville Sr HS; Bella Vista, AR; (3); 30/360; VP Computer Clb; FCA; Intnl Clb; Key Clb; SADD; Pom Pon; High Hon Roll; NHS; Pres Acad Fit Awd; Miss Tn Of AR Schlrshp Rcgntn Pgnt.

HENDRIX, AMY J; Bergman Schl; Harrison, AR; (1); Church Yth Grp; Cmnty Wkr; FBLA; FHA; Natl Beta Clb; Ofcr Stu Cncl; Bsktbl; Sftbl; Hon Roll; Prfct Atten Awd; JR Beta; Harding Univ; CPA.

HENDRIX, ANTHONY K; Fountain Lake Jr Sr HS; Hot Springs, AR; (1); Quiz Bowl; Band; Church Choir; Drm Mjr(t); Jazz Band; Mrchg Band; Mgr Bsktbl; Tennis; High Hon Roll; Hon Roll; All Rgn Band; Nom Ldrshp Hot Sprngs Assn.

HENDRIX, CARMEN; Delight HS; Antoine, AR; (4); 2/24; Am Leg Aux Girls St; 4-H; FBLA; Natl FFA Org; Office Aide; Quiz Bowl; Teachers Aide; School Play; Stage Crew; Rptr Nwsp; Hrs Rdng, Barrl Rcng & Rodeos; FFA Crps Tm, St Wnr & 2nd High Indv St 95; Ntl Wnr Tms Engr Tm; Harding U; Med.

HENDRIX, CLAY; Bergman Schl; Harrison, AR; (3); Church Yth Grp; Cmnty Wkr; FBLA; Library Aide; Model UN; Natl Beta Clb; Office Aide; Pep Clb; Quiz Bowl; Spanish Clb; Pedtrcn.

HENDRIX, COURTNEY; Brinkley HS; Hunter, AR; (4); Drama Clb; French Clb; HOBY; Library Aide; Office Aide; Science Clb; Chorus; VP Frsh Cls; Hon Roll; Jr NHS; E AR CC; Nrsng.

HENDRIX, DUSTIN G; Bauxite Jr Sr HS; Bauxite, AR; (3); Spanish Clb; SADD; Teachers Aide; VP Soph Cls; Var Bsbl; Bsktbl; Ftbl; Wt Lftg; Hon Roll; NHS; Bus Mgmt.

HENDRIX, ELIZABETH; Delight HS; Antoine, AR; (1); 4-H; Natl FFA Org; Quiz Bowl; Sec Frsh Cls; JV Bsktbl; Intrml Sftbl; Hon Roll; Harding U.

HENDRIX, ERIC K; Trumann HS; Trumann, AR; (2); Church Yth Grp; Natl FFA Org; Hon Roll.

HENDRIX, HEATHER B; Lake Hamilton Sr HS; Hot Springs Natio, AR; (3); 34/212; Art Clb; Rptr FCA; Rptr FBLA; Teachers Aide; VP Thesps; School Play; Stage Crew; Hon Roll; Jr NHS; Drama Clb; Drama; Eng Prof.

HENDRIX, JEREMY E; Fountain Lake Jr Sr HS; Hot Springs, AR; (3); Am Leg Boys St; Natl Beta Clb; Spanish Clb; Band; Chorus; Church Choir; Jazz Band; Mrchg Band; Orch; Pep Band.

HENDRIX, JOSHUA T; Russellville Sr HS; Russellville, AR; (2); 4-H; Hon Roll; Cyclone Achvrs Awd; Own Pri Mech Bus.

HENDRIX, KELICIA N; Central Sr HS; Little Rock, AR; (3); Cmnty Wkr; Drama Clb; FBLA; FHA; Girl Scts; Hosp Aide; Natl Beta Clb; Spanish Clb; Church Choir; Rep Soph Cls; AR Childrens Hosp Jr Vol; Yth Ldrshp Inst; Xavier; Bio; Chem.

HENDRIX, NICOLE; Little Rock Cntrl HS; Little Rock, AR; (3); Church Yth Grp; Cmnty Wkr; Drama Clb; FBLA; FHA; Girl Scts; Hosp Aide; Natl Beta Clb; Spanish Clb; Teachers Aide; AR Yth Ldrshp Inst; Intl Models/Talent Assn ST Rep; Stdnt Cncl Sr Senator; U Of Memphis; Bio/Neo-Natal.

HENERSON, ANNA L; Yellville Summit HS; Yellville, AR; (2); Drama Clb; Office Aide; Teachers Aide; Nwsp; Cit Awd; High Hon Roll; Hon Roll; Prfct Atten Awd; Hlth Awd; Stdnt Mnth Nom; Serv Awd; Paralegal/CPA.

HENLEY, DANA C; Bauxite Jr Sr HS; Bauxite, AR; (2); Debate Tm; FBLA; Library Aide; Office Aide; SADD; Teachers Aide; Sftbl; Hon Roll; UALR; Drama.

HENLEY, JEREMY; Leslie Schl; Leslie, AR; (3); 5/18; Art Clb; Key Clb; Math Clb; Natl FFA Org; Quiz Bowl; Science Clb; Spanish Clb; Ofcr Soph Cls; Ofcr Jr Cls; Ofcr Bsbl; Perfect Attndnce; U Of AR.

HENLEY, LEAH; Warren Jr HS; Warren, AR; (1); 11/135; Church Yth Grp; Treas Natl Beta Clb; Office Aide; Sec Frsh Cls; Rep Stu Cncl; Var L Bsktbl; Var L Trk; Hon Roll; Pres Schlr.

HENRIKSEN, MEGAN; Tuckerman HS; Tuckerman, AR; (4); 1/50; Am Leg Aux Girls St; FHA; Sec Natl Beta Clb; Sec Spanish Clb; Pres Chorus; Ed Yrbk; Rptr Sr Cls; VP Stu Cncl; L Bsktbl; Val; Mock Trial Team; AR ST Univ Jonesboro.

HENRY, BRETT; Southside HS; Fort Smith, AR; (3); Spanish Clb; Church Choir; Natl Eng Merit Awd Wnnr; Relgn Act.

HENRY, BROOKE E; North Little Rock Hs-East; North Little Rock, AR; (2); Cmnty Wkr; Drama Clb; Key Clb; Math Clb; Natl Beta Clb; Drill Tm; School Musical; School Play; Stage Crew; Intrml JV Pom Pon; 2nd Pl Sci Fair 94-95; Top 10 Pcnt Class 94-; U Of AR; Nurse Anesthetist.

HENRY, EMILY L; Springdale Sr HS; Lowell, AR; (3); FCA; FBLA; GAA; Bsktbl; Trk; Hon Roll; Jr NHS; Prfct Atten Awd; Pres Acad Fit Awd; Jrnlsm.

HENRY, JADE J; Monticello HS; Monticello, AR; (3); 32/158; Art Clb; Church Yth Grp; FBLA; FHA; Natl Beta Clb; Spanish Clb; SADD; Yrbk.

HENRY, KIRSTEN; Pulaski Acad; Little Rock, AR; (1); Natl Beta Clb; Pep Clb; Spanish Clb; Band; Church Choir; Mrchg Band; Variety Show; Bsktbl; Chrldng; Sftbl; Indpndnt Tourn Sftbl Team Drm Team 3rd ASA Natls/2nd USSSA Wrld; Prv Tnns Team; Cmptv Chrldng Team.

HENRY, MATTHEW; Arkansas Bapt Schl; Little Rock, AR; (2); Church Yth Grp; FCA; VP FBLA; Natl Beta Clb; JV Bsktbl; Var Golf; Var Tennis; High Hon Roll; Baylor; Med.

HENRY, SARAH; Brinkley HS; Brinkley, AR; (4); 7/71; Am Leg Aux Girls St; French Clb; Office Aide; Q&S; Band; Yrbk; Rep Sr Cls; Rep Stu Cncl; Hon Roll; NHS; U Cntrl AR; Elem Ed.

HENRY, WILLIE; Nashville HS; Ozan, AR; (4); 24/106; Am Leg Boys St; Cmnty Wkr; FHA; School Play; Pres Frsh Cls; Rep Soph Cls; Rep Jr Cls; Rep Sr Cls; Rep Stu Cncl; Var L Bsbl; AR Tech U; Ed.

HENSLEY, BRANDY N; Rivercrest HS; Wilson, AR; (2); FBLA; Pres Key Clb; Teachers Aide; Band; Hon Roll; Jr NHS; Doc.

HENSON, CHRISTOPHER L; Vilonia HS; Vilonia, AR; (4); 13/125; VP Art Clb; Church Yth Grp; FBLA; Letterman Clb; Mu Alpha Theta; Natl Beta Clb; Office Aide; Quiz Bowl; Spanish Clb; Varsity Clb; Mst Likely To Succeed; All Conf Ftbll; Acad Achv; AR St Univ; Mgnt.

HENSON, HEATHER D; Central HS; West Helena, AR; (1); French Clb; Cit Awd; Hon Roll; Pres Acad Fit Awd; Stdnt Of Month Awd; 4 Yr Coll.

HENSON, PHOEBE M; Southside HS; Fort Smith, AR; (3); Church Yth Grp; Key Clb; Mu Alpha Theta; Pep Clb; Teachers Aide; Chorus; Church Choir; Drill Tm; School Play; Ofcr Soph Cls.

HENSON, R JASON; De Soto Schl; Lexa, AR; (3); 9/19; Am Leg Boys St; Church Yth Grp; Drama Clb; Spanish Clb; Thesps; Church Choir; Var Bsbl; JV Bsktbl; Var JV Ftbl; Var JV Trk; #1 Geometry Stu; 1st Pl Id Dist On Geometry ABC Test & Phy Sci ABC Test; AR ST Univ; Comp Sci; Engrng.

HENSON, STEPHEN F; Emmet Schl; Curtis, AR; (2); 5/13; Hon Roll; Prfct Atten Awd; Pres Acad Fit Awd; Hndrs ST U; Arln Plt.

HENSON, SUNSHINE L; Northside HS; Fort Smith, AR; (3); French Clb; FHA; Pep Clb; Quiz Bowl; Drill Tm; Orch; Co-Ed Yrbk; Hon Roll; NHS; Pres Acad Fit Awd; Hendrix Col.

HERBERT, MIRANDA C; Forrest City HS; Forrest City, AR; (4); 24/280; Art Clb; Dance Clb; Drama Clb; Girl Scts; JA; Library Aide; Natl Beta Clb; Spanish Clb; SADD; Band; Sctng Silver Awd; Gillmore Band Awd; All St Band Awds; Drama Awds; Amer Musical Acad; Perf Arts.

HERNANDEZ, MARCELO; Dequeen HS; De Queen, AR; (3); Art Clb; Ofcr Sr Cls; Cossatot De Queen; Cmptr Techlg.

HERNANDEZ, MARIA A; North Little Rock Hs-East; North Little Rock, AR; (2); ROTC; Ofcr Soph Cls; Med.

HERRERA, REYNALDA; Springdale Sr HS; Springdale, AR; (1); FHA; Chorus; JETS Awd; NHS; Pres Ed Awds Pgm; Law Enforcement.

HERRIN, JASON; Fayetteville Sr HS; Fayetteville, AR; (4); FBLA; Intnl Clb; Band; Jazz Band; Mrchg Band; Pep Band; School Musical; Stage Crew; High Hon Roll; NHS; Frosh Acad Schlrshp; Fulbright Music Schlrsp; Dir Awd; U Of AR; Intl Bus.

HERRIN, KARLI; Beebe Sr HS; Beebe, AR; (2); 19/127; Church Yth Grp; Drama Clb; FBLA; Girl Scts; Natl Beta Clb; Science Clb; Chorus; Church Choir; Capt Flag Corp; Mrchg Band; Ouachita Bapt U; Bus.

HERRIN, TINA B; Beebe Sr HS; Beebe, AR; (4); 6/92; Natl Beta Clb; Spanish Clb; Acpl Chr; Am Leg Aux Girls St; Color Guard; Pres Acad Fit Awd; Church Yth Grp; Cmnty Wkr; Drama Clb; FTA; Choir Cncl; Champ; Stu Of The Month; AR ST U Jonesboro.

HERRING, AMANDA; J A Fair Sr HS; Little Rock, AR; (3); Drama Clb; Science Clb; Spanish Clb; Temple Yth Grp; Drill Tm; Chrldng; High Hon Roll; Hon Roll; Homemcng; UCA; Dnce.

HERRING, AMANDA R; Sloan Hendrix HS; Imboden, AR; (2); Art Clb; Natl FFA Org; Pep Clb; Var Bsktbl; Cit Awd; Hon Roll; ST FFA Lnd Jdgng Tm; Beta Clb Achvmnt Awd; AR ST Univ; Phrmcy.

HERRING, DANA; Warren Sr HS; Warren, AR; (3); 1/137; Church Yth Grp; Cmnty Wkr; French Clb; VP FBLA; Quiz Bowl; SADD; Chorus; Church Choir; School Musical; School Play; Beta Clb; Hendrix; Sports Dr.

HERRING, DIANA; Swifton Schl; Swifton, AR; (4); 3/12; FBLA; Natl Beta Clb; Pep Clb; Quiz Bowl; Spanish Clb; Yrbk; Treas Stu Cncl; Bsktbl; Sftbl; Tennis; ASU; Early Chldhd Dvlpmnt.

HERRING, JULIE D; Stephens Jr Sr HS; Stephens, AR; (3); 8/42; Art Clb; Church Yth Grp; VP FBLA; FHA; Hon Roll; NHS; Soil Conservation.

HERRING, ROBERT E; Pulaski Acad; Little Rock, AR; (2); Model UN; Natl Beta Clb; Science Clb; Band; Mrchg Band; Orch; Stage Crew; Phtg Yrbk; Hon Roll; NHS.

HERRING, SARAH ELIZABETH; Pulaski Acad; Little Rock, AR; (4); Hosp Aide; Natl Beta Clb; Science Clb; Spanish Clb; High Hon Roll; Jr NHS; NHS; Rhodes Col; Bio.

HERRINGTON, ORENDA M; Star City HS; Star City, AR; (2); Mu Alpha Theta; Spanish Clb; Speech Tm; Band; Mrchg Band; Prom Comm; U Of AR Monticello; Anesthetst.

HERRMANN, SHANNON R; Southside HS; Fort Smith, AR; (2); FCA; Spanish Clb; Ed Nwsp; Var Socr; JV Vllybl; Hon Roll; Treas NHS; Barrel Racing; AR HS Rodeo Assn Mem; AR Olympic Dev Soccer Team St Select; OK ST Univ; Vet.

HERRON, DAMION R; Crossett Sr HS; Crossett, AR; (2); Church Yth Grp; Mu Alpha Theta; Natl Beta Clb; JV Bsbl; JV Ftbl; Trk.

HERRON, DANIEL; Lee Acad; Marianna, AR; (3); 5/25; Church Yth Grp; Yrbk; Rep Frsh Cls; VP Jr Cls; Var Capt Bsktbl; Var Capt Ftbl; JV Trk; Var JV Wt Lftg; Hon Roll; NHS; Ftbl Best Defnsv Plyr; Best Bsktbl Plyr; Comp Awd; Engrng.

HERRON, LINDSEY G; Lee Acad; Marianna, AR; (1); Church Yth Grp; Yrbk; Treas Frsh Cls; Var Chrldng; JV Trk; Cit Awd; Hon Roll.

HERRON, SHANNON; Harmony Grove Jr Sr HS; Camden, AR; (3); Art Clb; Church Yth Grp; FCA; Natl Beta Clb; Spanish Clb; Al; Med.

HERRON, WILLIAM D; Lee Acad; Marianna, AR; (4); Yrbk; VP Jr Cls; Var Capt Bsktbl; Var Capt Ftbl; JV Trk; Var JV Wt Lftg; High Hon Roll; Hon Roll; NHS; Prfct Atten Awd; Bsktbl MVP; Ftbl Best Defensive; EACC; Engrng.

HERTENSTEIN, STEFANIE; Greenbrier HS; Greenbrier, AR; (2); 16/143; Cmnty Wkr; Drama Clb; Hosp Aide; Natl Beta Clb; Church Choir; Var L Sftbl; Var L Vllybl; High Hon Roll; Hon Roll; Art Clb; UCA; Nrs.

HESS, DANIEL P; Heber Springs HS; Heber Springs, AR; (3); Am Leg Boys St; Natl Beta Clb; Natl FFA Org; Spanish Clb; Hon Roll.

HESS, JANA M; Wynne HS; Wynne, AR; (2); Church Yth Grp; FTA; SADD; Band; Mrchg Band; HOSA Club; JPC; MASH Camp; U Of AR; Pdtrcn.

HESS, JOEL; Sheridan Sr HS; Sheridan, AR; (3); 88/300; Church Yth Grp; Cmnty Wkr; Rptr Sec 4-H; Intnl Clb; Math Tm; Office Aide; ROTC; Service Clb; Teachers Aide; Color Guard; Supr Cadet; Sons Of Amer Rev; Battalion 51; Comp.

HESS, LESLIE M; St Joseph HS; Conway, AR; (3); Church Yth Grp; GAA; Key Clb; School Play; Var Bsktbl; Var Sftbl; Var Trk; Var Vllybl; High Hon Roll; Hon Roll; Child Psych.

HESS, LORIE D; St Joseph HS; Conway, AR; (3); Church Yth Grp; GAA; Key Clb; School Play; Var L Bsktbl; Var L Sftbl; Var L Trk; High Hon Roll; Hon Roll; Jr NHS.

HESS, NATALIE; North Little Rock Hs-West; N Little Rock, AR; (4); 42/478; Am Leg Aux Girls St; Key Clb; Mu Alpha Theta; School Musical; School Play; Ofcr Stu Cncl; NHS; Church Yth Grp; Drama Clb; FCA; Dance Tm; Governors Schl; Octagon Clb; U Of AR Fayettevl; Chem Engr.

HESSER, CASEY S; Gillett Jr Sr HS; Gillett, AR; (3); Art Clb; Church Yth Grp; FBLA; Spanish Clb; Teachers Aide; Church Choir; Rptr Nwsp; VP Frsh Cls; Ofcr Stu Cncl; Var Bsktbl; Golf; Hntng; Snwskiing; U Of AR; Brdcstng.

HESTER, WOODY A; Hartford Schl; Hartford, AR; (3); Pres VP FBLA; VP Natl FFA Org; Teachers Aide; Pres Frsh Cls; VP Soph Cls; Pres Jr Cls; Ftbl; Hon Roll; FFA Star Green Hnd 9th Grd/Turf Lndscp Awd 11th Grd; Soc Stud Awd 10th Grd.

HEWETT, MARISHA; Henderson Magnet Jr HS; Little Rock, AR; (1); Church Yth Grp; Cmnty Wkr; FHA; Band; Church Choir; Var Chrldng; Var Gym; Hon Roll; Beta Clb; ARK Mem; UCLA; Phy Thrpst.

HEWITT, LONDON; Charleston HS; Charleston, AR; (1); Church Yth Grp; FCA; Hist FBLA; Rptr Stu Cncl; Bsktbl; Powder Puff Ftbl; Sftbl; High Hon Roll; Prfct Atten Awd; U AR.

HEYDENREICH, STACY L; Mansfield Jr Sr HS; Mansfield, AR; (3); Art Clb; Church Yth Grp; FCA; Office Aide; Spanish Clb; Band; Mrchg Band; Ofcr Jr Cls; Cit Awd; Marjorette.

HIBBS, NICKOLAS; Blevins HS; Hope, AR; (4); 7/40; Church Yth Grp; FBLA; Natl Beta Clb; Natl FFA Org; Quiz Bowl; Hon Roll; Tae Kwon Do; Weight Lftng; Aviation.

HIBDON, ASHLEY; N Little Rock High E; North Little Rock, AR; (1); Drill Tm; Stage Crew; Var Chrldng; U Of AR; Phys Therapy.

HICKAM, JORDAN; Lake Hamilton Jr HS; Hot Springs, AR; (1); 6/264; FCA; Rptr FBLA; Pres Natl Beta Clb; Teachers Aide; Drill Tm; Hon Roll; Wolf Prde Drg Free Prgm; FBS; Pediatrician.

HICKERSON, AMBER L; Piggott HS; Piggott, AR; (3); Church Yth Grp; Cmnty Wkr; FCA; 4-H; French Clb; FBLA; FHA; Natl FFA Org; Science Clb; School Musical; AR ST Univ; Tchr.

HICKERSON, CRYSTAL D; Lake Hamilton Sr HS; Hot Springs, AR; (2); Church Yth Grp; FCA; Chorus; Church Choir; School Musical; School Play; High Hon Roll; Hon Roll; Prfct Atten Awd; Pres Acad Fit Awd; Sci.

HICKERSON, SHANDA; Humphrey Schl; Humphrey, AR; (3); 2/36; Sec Natl FFA Org; Capt Quiz Bowl; Spanish Clb; School Play; Rptr Nwsp; Hon Roll; Sec Treas NHS; FFA Sweetheart; Cutest; Homcmng; U Of AR Pine Bluff; Agronomy.

HICKLIN, REBECCA G; North Little Rock Hs-West; North Little Rock, AR; (4); 3/438; Mu Alpha Theta; Natl Beta Clb; Spanish Clb; Band; Hon Roll; NHS; Tri M Music Hnr Soc; AR Governors Schl; MS ST U; Vet.

HICKS, JODI M; Waldron HS; Waldron, AR; (3); FHA; Natl Beta Clb; Natl FFA Org; Spanish Clb; Rptr Yrbk; Rep Soph Cls; Sec Jr Cls; Rep Stu Cncl; JV Bsktbl; JV Trk; Algebra I Awd; AR Tech; Parks & Recrtn Admin.

HICKS, LAURA C; Dequeen HS; De Queen, AR; (3); FHA; FTA; Office Aide; Ed Rptr Nwsp; Mgr(s); Var L Sftbl; Hon Roll; NHS; Med.

HICKS, MARISA; Greenwood Sr HS; Fort Smith, AR; (2); Art Clb; Church Yth Grp; FCA; French Clb; FBLA; NFL; Drill Tm; Chrldng; Hon Roll; Art.

HICKS, MISTY M; Saratoga Schl; Saratoga, AR; (2); 4-H; FHA; Office Aide; Quiz Bowl; Science Clb; Teachers Aide; Drill Tm; School Musical; School Play; Nwsp; Tchr.

HICKS, RYAN; Bright Star Schl; Doddridge, AR; (2); Quiz Bowl; Rep Stu Cncl; Var Bsktbl; Var Crs Cntry; Hon Roll; Prfct Atten Awd.

HICKS, STEPHANY K; Sheridan Sr HS; Little Rock, AR; (2); Church Yth Grp; Cmnty Wkr; Chorus; Stngr One Nws Tm; Henderson ST; PT.

HICKS, STEVEN E; Marked Tree Jr Sr HS; Marked Tree, AR; (2); Church Yth Grp; Natl Beta Clb; Natl FFA Org; Quiz Bowl; ROTC; Chorus; Church Choir; Bsktbl; Ftbl; Wt Lftg; Ftbl & Bsktbl Awds; Lee Coll.

HICKS, TRICIA S; Parkview Arts/Sci Magnet HS; North Little Rock, AR; (2); Church Yth Grp; Cmnty Wkr; Natl Beta Clb; Rep Frsh Cls; Ofcr Soph Cls; Cit Awd; High Hon Roll; Hon Roll; Jr NHS; Pres Acad Fit Awd; Little Rock Schl Dist Acad Achvmnt Awd Eng 10 Hnrs; Natl Macy Schlr; Acad Excl Awd Jr High; WA Univ; Med.

HIEGEL, KATHLEEN J; St Joseph HS; Conway, AR; (3); 6/25; Church Yth Grp; Cmnty Wkr; GAA; Key Clb; Varsity Clb; Rep Stu Cncl; Var Bsktbl; Var Sftbl; Var Trk; Var Vllybl; AAU; BCI Bsktbl Congress Intnl; Chrstn Brothers Univ; Med.

HIGDON, SUNNY M; Magnolia HS; Waldo, AR; (3); Church Yth Grp; Dance Clb; Rptr FHA; Natl FFA Org; Southern AR Univ; Nrsng.

HIGGINBOTHAM, JENNIFER; Greenwood Sr HS; Greenwood, AR; (4); 4/200; Capt Debate Tm; Drama Clb; Rptr 4-H; French Clb; Model UN; Mu Alpha Theta; Natl Beta Clb; Quiz Bowl; Science Clb; Speech Tm; AR Govs Schl; Westark CC; Eng.

HIGGINBOTHAM, LESLIE J; Cabot HS; Cabot, AR; (3); 100/398; Church Yth Grp; Cmnty Wkr; Chorus; Church Choir; School Musical; School Play; Stage Crew; Ofcr Frsh Cls; Ofcr Stu Cncl; Bsktbl; All Regn Choir; ASU Jonesboro; Music.

HIGGINBOTHAM, STUART; Hamburg HS; Hamburg, AR; (3); Drama Clb; HOBY; Quiz Bowl; Spanish Clb; Band; Yrbk; Rep Jr Cls; Treas Stu Cncl; NHS; Law Clb VP & Reporter; Hendrix Coll; Med.

HIGGINBOTHOM, ANDREW F; Lee Acad; Marianna, AR; (3); 1/36; Church Yth Grp; Yrbk; VP Frsh Cls; VP Soph Cls; Bsktbl; Golf; Hon Roll; NHS; Trk; Prfct Atten Awd; Natl Sci Mrt Awd; Geometry Awd; Cls Favorite 95 & 96; Outstdng Stu.

HIGGINBOTHOM, DREW; Lee Acad; Marianna, AR; (2); 1/36; Church Yth Grp; Yrbk; VP Frsh Cls; VP Soph Cls; Var Bsktbl; Golf; Trk; Wt Lftg; High Hon Roll; Prfct Atten Awd; AR.

HIGGINBOTTOM, MEGAN S; Newport HS; Newport, AR; (3); Office Aide; Band; Prfct Atten Awd; Solo & Ensemble Awds; AR ST U Beebe/Newport; Dntl H.

HIGGINBOTTOM, MOLLY; Batesville Sr HS; Cave City, AR; (3); 6/164; FCA; FBLA; HOBY; Natl Beta Clb; Band; Church Choir; Bsktbl; Sftbl; DAR Awd; High Hon Roll; Med.

HIGGINS, AMBER D; Farmington Jr Sr HS; Fayetteville, AR; (3); Church Yth Grp; French Clb; Temple Yth Grp; Band; Church Choir; Color Guard; Mrchg Band; Hon Roll; NHS; Jrlsm; U Of AR.

HIGGINS, NICK; Abundant Life Schools; North Little Rock, AR; (3); Church Yth Grp; Yrbk; Var Bsktbl; Ftbl; High Hon Roll; NHS.

HIGGINS, RYAN H; Dequeen HS; Gillham, AR; (2); Art Clb; Church Yth Grp; Cmnty Wkr; Natl FFA Org; Crs Cntry; Ftbl; Score Keeper; Trk; Wt Lftg; High Hon Roll; ATV Racer; U Of AR; Carpenter.

HIGGINS, TREMAINE; Elaine Jr Sr HS; Elaine, AR; (1); Ofcr Frsh Cls; Ofcr Stu Cncl; Bsktbl.

HIGH, KRISTY D; Springdale Sr HS; Springdale, AR; (2); FCA; FBLA; Key Clb; Acpl Chr; Sec Stu Cncl; Capt JV Chrldng; L Trk; Hon Roll; Jr NHS; NHS; U Of AR.

HIGH, TONYA M; Sloan Hendrix HS; Imboden, AR; (2); FBLA; FHA; FTA; Natl Beta Clb; Band; Stage Crew; Rptr Nwsp; Hon Roll; John Philip Sousa Band Awd; Law; Music.

HIGHFILL, AMANDA C; Russellville Sr HS; Russellville, AR; (2); 116/472; Church Yth Grp; Library Aide; Chorus; NHS; Ride Horses; Harding U.

HIGHFILL, CORY D; Westside HS; Hartman, AR; (2); 3/40; FBLA; Ftbl; AR Tech Univ.

HIGHSMITH, TERRYE A; Fairview HS; Camden, AR; (2); GAA; Natl Beta Clb; Band; Treas Soph Cls; Treas Jr Cls; Mgr(s); Var Trk; JV Vllybl; Hon Roll; Ouachita Bapt Univ Talent Srch; Flag Line; U Of AR Fayetteville; Med.

HIGHT, MICHAEL L; Emerson HS; Magnolia, AR; (3); Am Leg Boys St; Boy Scts; Church Yth Grp; FBLA; FHA; HOBY; VP Natl Beta Clb; Natl FFA Org; Church Choir; Bsktbl; Eagle Scout.

HIGHTOWER, HEATHER E; Junction City HS; Junction City, AR; (1); Church Yth Grp; FBLA; Spanish Clb; Chrldng; Powder Puff Ftbl; High Hon Roll.

HIGNITE, JOAN; Oark HS; Ozone, AR; (4); 1/9; FBLA; Pres FHA; Natl Beta Clb; Ed Yrbk; Pres Soph Cls; Pres Jr Cls; Pres Sr Cls; Pres Stu Cncl; Var Capt Bsktbl; Var Sftbl; AR Tech U; Phys Thrpy.

HILBURN, JONATHAN LEO; Junction City HS; El Dorado, AR; (2); Church Yth Grp; Science Clb; Spanish Clb; Var Bsbl; Var Bsktbl; Var Ftbl; Hon Roll; LA Tech.

HILL, AMANDA A; Morrilton Sr HS; Perry, AR; (3); Art Clb; Church Yth Grp; Drama Clb; French Clb; HOBY; Speech Tm; Chorus; Prfct Atten Awd; Eng Merit Awd; Chorus Merit Awd; UCA; Teen Cnslr.

HILL, AMBER; Sacred Heart Schl; Morrilton, AR; (2); Church Yth Grp; GAA; Key Clb; Natl Beta Clb; SADD; Church Choir; School Play; Yrbk; VP Frsh Cls; Pres Soph Cls; AR Tech U; Medcl.

HILL, AMBER J; Eureka Springs Jr Sr HS; Eureka Springs, AR; (3); Church Yth Grp; Cmnty Wkr; French Clb; Rptr FBLA; Office Aide; Nwsp; Mgr(s); Score Keeper; Hon Roll; Ntl Merit Ltr; Attnd WJC Conf Held By Natl Yth Assn In Wash DC; Poetry Pub; Coll Of Ozarks; Psych; Criminlgy.

HILL, BRANDIE L; Trumann HS; Trumann, AR; (4); 1/85; Am Leg Aux Girls St; Art Clb; Cmnty Wkr; French Clb; Pres FHA; Model UN; Co-Ed Yrbk; Ofcr Stu Cncl; NHS; Val; Sci Fr Wnnrs; Gftd & Tlntd Pgrm 11 Yrs; Hnr Grad; AR ST U; Elem Ed.

HILL, BRANDON THOMAS; Benton Sr HS; Benton, AR; (3); 39/365; Am Leg Boys St; FCA; FBLA; Key Clb; Math Clb; Rep Stu Cncl; L Mgr(s); Hon Roll; Kiwanis Awd; Pres Acad Fit Awd; Futr Probl Slving; Voice Of Demo Fnlst; Jr Glf Prog; Acctng.

HILL, CANDICE; Hot Springs HS; Hot Springs, AR; (1); Church Yth Grp; Pep Clb; Chorus; Church Choir; Chrldng; Hon Roll; PRIDE; KY U; Psych.

HILL, CASSIE J; Fayetteville Sr HS; Fayetteville, AR; (1); Church Yth Grp; FCA; GAA; Bsktbl; Vllybl; U Of TX; PT.

HILL, CHARLIE A; Fountain Lake Jr Sr HS; Hot Springs Natio, AR; (3); 9/81; Church Yth Grp; Drama Clb; Key Clb; Library Aide; Natl Beta Clb; Spanish Clb; Teachers Aide; Band; Color Guard; Flag Corp; TCHR.

HILL, CHRIS; Blevins HS; Blevins, AR; (2); Rptr Art Clb; Rptr Natl FFA Org; SAU; Vet.

HILL, CHRISTINA S; Lake Hamilton Sr HS; Royal, AR; (4); #159 in class; Church Yth Grp; FCA; Natl FFA Org; SADD; Band; Chorus; Flag Corp; Mrchg Band; Orch; Pep Band; UCA; Phy Thrpst.

HILL, CHRISTOPHER D; Central Arkansas Christian HS; Jacksonville, AR; (4); Church Yth Grp; Cmnty Wkr; Math Clb; Science Clb; Spanish Clb; Rptr Nwsp; Rptr Yrbk; Hon Roll; Pres Schlr; All Amer Schlr; Natl Sci Merit Awd; Multi-Yr Listee; Harding Univ; Bio/Chem.

HILL, DARREN L; Vilonia HS; Conway, AR; (4); Church Yth Grp; 4-H; Math Clb; Mu Alpha Theta; Natl Beta Clb; Natl FFA Org; Spanish Clb; Teachers Aide; Rep Stu Cncl; Hon Roll; FFA Pres Served On Electricity & Land Judging Team; Showed Hogs & A Steer In Cty & St Fairs; Cntrl Bapt Coll.

HILL, DAVETTIA M; Central Sr HS; Little Rock, AR; (3); Church Yth Grp; Drama Clb; FBLA; FHA; FTA; German Clb; Church Choir; School Play; Bsktbl; Hon Roll; Baylor; Bus Admin.

HILL, DUSTIN E; Dierks HS; Dierks, AR; (2); Natl FFA Org; Var Bsktbl; Var Ftbl; Var Trk; Hon Roll; FFA Frmr Of Yr 96; FFA Grnhnd Awd 95; SAU Magnolia; Ag.

HILL, DUSTIN J; Dierks HS; Newhope, AR; (2); Church Yth Grp; Cmnty Wkr; Math Clb; Natl FFA Org; Rptr Frsh Cls; JV Bsktbl; JV Ftbl; JV Trk; Pride Team Mem; U Of AR-CONWAY; Vet Sci.

HILL, GEORGE A; Salem HS; Mammoth Spring, AR; (4); 12/41; FCA; Key Clb; Natl Beta Clb; Spanish Clb; Var Bsktbl; Var Ftbl; Hon Roll; Coop Ed Sgt At Arms; AR ST U; Crmnlgy.

HILL, HELEN E; Star City HS; Star City, AR; (3); Art Clb; Church Yth Grp; FCA; FBLA; Spanish Clb; Teachers Aide; Band; Chorus; Color Guard; Mrchg Band; Speech Clb Mem; NW LA U; Acctng.

HILL, ISIS; Greenland Jr Sr HS; Prairie Grove, AR; (3); FBLA; Library Aide; Quiz Bowl; Chrldng; High Hon Roll; NHS; Span Hnrs.

HILL, JAMES M; Gillett Jr Sr HS; Gillett, AR; (3); Church Yth Grp; Computer Clb; FCA; Letterman Clb; Office Aide; Band; Ftbl; Golf; Wt Lftg; Cit Awd; AR ST Univ; Ag Bus.

HILL, JASON; Brinkley HS; Brinkley, AR; (4); 1/70; Am Leg Boys St; Church Yth Grp; Drama Clb; French Clb; FBLA; Library Aide; Office Aide; Quiz Bowl; Science Clb; Teachers Aide; Chrch CYO Grp VP; In Schl Tutr; Agribus.

HILL, JEANNE; Waldron HS; Waldron, AR; (4); 15/84; Drama Clb; Natl Beta Clb; Natl FFA Org; Band; Flag Corp; School Play; Yrbk; Sec Jr Cls; Var Chrldng; JV Trk; U Of AR; Ed.

HILL, JEREMY D; Valley Springs Schl; Valley Springs, AR; (2); Art Clb; Church Yth Grp; Cmnty Wkr; Key Clb; Rep Soph Cls; Bsktbl; Hon Roll; Prfct Atten Awd.

HILL, JOSH; Clarksville HS; Clarksville, AR; (2); Church Yth Grp; FCA; FBLA; Natl Beta Clb; Var Bsbl; JV Bsktbl; JV Var Ftbl; Hon Roll; Outdr Clb; Hunt; Fish; Bsbl; Ride 4-Whlrs; Ftnss Ctr Mbr; ATU At Russellville.

HILL, KASI; Genoa Central HS; Fouke, AR; (2); 1/66; Church Yth Grp; FHA; Spanish Clb; JV Var Chrldng; High Hon Roll; NHS; Med Applctn Of Sci For Hlth Prog; U Of Cntrl AR; Nrsng.

HILL, LYNN; Arkansas Bapt Schl; Little Rock, AR; (2); Church Yth Grp; Cmnty Wkr; FCA; FBLA; Natl Beta Clb; Chorus; Church Choir; Rep Stu Cncl; JV Var Chrldng; Hon Roll.

HILL, MANDY N; Quitman Jr Sr HS; Quitman, AR; (2); Church Yth Grp; FBLA; FHA; GAA; Natl Beta Clb; SADD; Rep Stu Cncl; L Var Bsktbl; Hon Roll; Pres Acad Fit Awd; AAU Bsktbl Natls 2nd ST Trnmnt; Chmpns TX Shootout.

HILL, MELISSA; Mulberry HS; Mulberry, AR; (4); 2/30; French Clb; Science Clb; Band; Co-Ed Yrbk; Bsktbl; Sftbl; Vllybl; Hon Roll; NHS; Sal; Bio.

HILL, PENNY L; Fairview HS; Camden, AR; (4); 34/250; Church Yth Grp; French Clb; Mu Alpha Theta; Natl Beta Clb; Natl FFA Org; Science Clb; SADD; Band; Mrchg Band; Hon Roll; 1st Region Sci Fair; Acad Challenge Schlsp; Southern AR Univ; Pre-Vet.

HILL, SONJA L; Hall Sr HS; Little Rock, AR; (2); Art Clb; Church Yth Grp; Stage Crew; JV Bsktbl; Cit Awd; Hon Roll; Howard Univ; Acctng/Crmnl Jstc.

HILL, STEPHANIE R; Morrilton Sr HS; Morrilton, AR; (2); French Clb; Ed Yrbk; Stat Vllybl; Hon Roll; Tchng.

HILL, TABITHA; Wynne HS; Wynne, AR; (4); 23/174; Drama Clb; SADD; Spanish NHS; Unity; GCECA Treas; AR ST Univ; Bus.

HILL, TRACY M; Ozark Adventist Acad; Alvarado, TX; (3); Church Yth Grp; Drama Clb; Office Aide; Teachers Aide; Chorus; School Play; Rptr Nwsp; Ed Yrbk; Sec Frsh Cls; Pres Jr Cls; Stdnt Assoc Sec Soph; Adopt-A-Kid Prgm.

HILL, VIRGINIA E; Central Ark Christian Schl; Jacksonville, AR; (2); Church Yth Grp; FHA; Trk; Hon Roll; Harding Univ.

HILL, WESLEY A; Trumann HS; Trumann, AR; (2); Church Yth Grp; Chorus; Church Choir; Hon Roll; 1st Pl Sci Fair 9th Grd; 2nd Pl Sci Fair 10th Grd; Math Awd 10th Grd; Entrepreneurship Bus.

HILL, WILLIAM K; Benton Sr HS; Benton, AR; (3); 20/300; Am Leg Boys St; Church Yth Grp; Cmnty Wkr; Key Clb; Ofcr Stu Cncl; Ftbl; Hon Roll; Jr NHS; Kiwanis Awd; U Of AR Fayetteville.

HILLHOUSE, ALISSA; Taylor HS; Taylor, AR; (4); 1/28; Church Yth Grp; Cmnty Wkr; FCA; GAA; Letterman Clb; Natl FFA Org; Office Aide; Quiz Bowl; Science Clb; Teachers Aide; S AR Univ; Medicine.

HILLIS, ALISHA D; Calvary Christian Schl; Forrest City, AR; (4); 3/7; Am Leg Aux Girls St; Church Yth Grp; Church Choir; School Play; Yrbk; Treas Stu Cncl; Bsktbl; High Hon Roll; NHS; Girls Missionary Auxillary; Ctrl Bapt Coll; Speech Therapy.

HILLIS, CHARLINA L; Trumann HS; Trumann, AR; (1); Ofcr Frsh Cls; Hon Roll; Ger; Keyboarding I, II; AR ST Univ; Comp Acctng.

HILSON, ASHLEY N; Harmony Grove Jr Sr HS; Benton, AR; (2); Church Yth Grp; French Clb; FBLA; FHA; HOBY; Natl Beta Clb; Pres Frsh Cls; Rep Stu Cncl; Var Chrldng; Hon Roll; Regnl Sci Fair Biochem 1st Pl; Regnl Sci Fair Jr Acad Of Sci Papers Biochem 1st Pl; U Of A Fayetteville; Psych.

HILSON, NAPOLEON; Dumas Jr HS; Dumas, AR; (1); Boy Scts; Church Yth Grp; Natl Beta Clb; Band; Church Choir; Pep Band; Pres Stu Cncl; Ftbl; Wt Lftg; Hon Roll; U Notre Dame; Arch Engr.

HILSON, SAMUEL R; Fairview HS; Camden, AR; (3); Art Clb; Church Yth Grp; Cmnty Wkr; Drama Clb; French Clb; Natl FFA Org; French Hon Soc; Hon Roll.

HILTON, ABIGAIL E; Southside HS; Fort Smith, AR; (2); Church Yth Grp; Cmnty Wkr; Drama Clb; German Clb; Chorus; SAIL CREW.

HILTON, BRANDI; Bradley Jr Sr HS; Bradley, AR; (1); 1/33; Church Yth Grp; FBLA; FHA; Quiz Bowl; Spanish Clb; Sec Frsh Cls; Rep Stu Cncl; Co-Capt Chrldng; High Hon Roll; Pres Acad Fit Awd; Awd Wnng Dncr; Mst Schl Sprt Chrldng; Harvard U; Med.

HILTON III, CHARLEY; John L Mcclellan Magnet HS; Little Rock, AR; (4); 50/257; French Clb; Mu Alpha Theta; Yrbk; Cit Awd; Hon Roll; Navy Hnrs Prgm; U AR Ltl Rock; Acctg/Bus Mgmt.

HILTON, JENNIFER B; Lake Hamilton Sr HS; Hot Springs, AR; (2); Hon Roll; Presdntl Acad Achvt Awd.

HILTON, STEPHANIE N; Clarksville HS; Clarksville, AR; (2); 1/150; Pres Drama Clb; Key Clb; Natl Beta Clb; Spanish Clb; School Play; Rep Stu Cncl; High Hon Roll; Prfct Atten Awd; Pres Acad Fit Awd; Mem Of Odyssey Of The Mind Team Won 1st Pl In Regnls 95; Odyssey Of The Mind Won Ranatra Fussa Awd 96; Hendrix; Lbrl Arts.

HIMES, ZACKORY L; Lavaca Jr Sr HS; Lavaca, AR; (2); FCA; 4-H; Natl FFA Org; Ofcr Jr Cls; Ofcr Bsbl; Ftbl; Trk; Wt Lftg; Hon Roll; FFA Awd; Westark; Welder.

HINDMAN, BROOKE; Sylvan Hills Jr HS; North Little Rock, AR; (1); Church Yth Grp; Cmnty Wkr; FCA; FHA; Hosp Aide; Chorus; Ofcr Stu Cncl; Chrldng; Hon Roll; Jr NHS; Repng AR Mdlng, Actng, Dncng This Smr In NY At IMTA; Harding U; News Anchr.

HINES, AMANDA M; Taylor HS; Taylor, AR; (2); 6/22; Church Yth Grp; FHA; Natl FFA Org; Yrbk; Rep Jr Cls; Stat Bsktbl; High Hon Roll; Southern AR Univ; Med.

HINES, DAVID E; Gosnell Jr Sr HS; Gosnell, AR; (2); Church Yth Grp; Letterman Clb; Spanish Clb; Ftbl; Hon Roll; Ole MS.

HINES, JENNIFER; Malvern Jr HS; Malvern, AR; (3); FCA; FBLA; Quiz Bowl; Rptr Nwsp; Rep Stu Cncl; JV Capt Chrldng; High Hon Roll; Hon Roll; Jr NHS; NHS; U Of Cntrl AR; Psych.

HINES, SARAH E; Stuttgart Sr HS; Stuttgart, AR; (3); 24/180; Church Yth Grp; DECA; FCA; FBLA; GAA; Key Clb; Natl FFA Org; Spanish Clb; Chorus; Nwsp; U Cntrl AR; OT.

HINKLE, JENNIFER K; Harrison Sr HS; Harrison, AR; (4); 21/206; Church Yth Grp; French Clb; Key Clb; Band; Mrchg Band; Pep Band; Ed Yrbk; NHS; Pres Acad Fit Awd; Frangre Col; Psych.

HINKLE, KATIE; Mountain View Jr Sr HS; Mountain View, AR; (1); Church Yth Grp; FHA; Natl Beta Clb; Teachers Aide; Variety Show; Chrldng; Hon Roll; Stdnt Mo; U Of AR; Optomtry.

HINKSON, JAMES; Clinton HS; Clinton, AR; (3); Bus Profs of Am; Church Yth Grp; FBLA; HOBY; Natl Beta Clb; Science Clb; Spanish Clb; Band; Church Choir; Drm Mjr(t); Govs Yth Conf Drgs & Alchl; All-Rgn Band; U Of AR; Msc.

HINSEY, SIMEON; Fayetteville Christian Schl; Fayetteville, AR; (3); Church Yth Grp; Computer Clb; English Clb; JA; Science Clb; Spanish Clb; Yrbk; Ofcr Jr Cls; Var Bsktbl; Var Sftbl; Cmptr Sci.

HINSLEY, JILL M; Jacksonville HS; Jacksonville, AR; (2); 16/345; Rep Church Yth Grp; Drama Clb; Treas FHA; Natl Beta Clb; Chorus; Church Choir; High Hon Roll; Art Clb; Hosp Aide; School Musical; Tap Dance 11 Yrs; Flwshp Of Christn Stdnt 9-10 Grd; Natl Schlr Cand Cngrsnl Yth Ldrshp Cncl; U Of AR; Phrmy/Dance/Intr Dsgn.

HINTERTHUER, ADAM M; Harrison Sr HS; Harrison, AR; (3); 3/200; Boy Scts; Drama Clb; Office Aide; VP Science Clb; Pres Spanish Clb; Band; Jazz Band; Mrchg Band; Pep Band; Stage Crew; AR Governors Schl 96; Project CAVES Aegis Pgm; Nom Natl Yth Ldrshp Conf; Bio; Environmental Sci.

HINTON, CASEY; Marion HS; Marion, AR; (3); Church Yth Grp; French Clb; Mu Alpha Theta; Color Guard; Yrbk; Var Chrldng; French Hon Soc; Hon Roll; Jr NHS; NHS; Camping, Hiking; AR ST U; Phys Thrpst.

HINTON, EMILY A; Sylvan Hills HS; Sherwood, AR; (3); Chrmn Church Yth Grp; Drama Clb; FCA; French Clb; Key Clb; Mu Alpha Theta; VP Natl Beta Clb; Speech Tm; Treas Stu Cncl; VP NHS.

HIPES, BARRETT; Farmington Jr Sr HS; Farmington, AR; (1); FBLA; FHA; Model UN; Band; Jazz Band; Mrchg Band; Pep Band; Rptr Stu Cncl; Hon Roll; Jr NHS; Mock Trial; All Rgn Bnd; Stanford U; Pltcl Sci.

HIPPLER, ALISHA; Bryant Sr HS; Bryant, AR; (4); 29/325; Am Leg Aux Girls St; English Clb; Hosp Aide; School Play; Co-Ed Yrbk; Sec Jr Cls; Var Bsktbl; Var Trk; Jr NHS; NHS; Stu Senate Sec; U Of A; Jrnlsm & Eng.

HIPPS, KATHERINE A; John L Mcclellan Magnet HS; Little Rock, AR; (2); French Clb; FBLA; Hosp Aide; Mu Alpha Theta; Spanish Clb; Var L Sftbl; Hon Roll; NHS; Soc Work.

HISLIP, CHRISTOPHER J; Hot Springs HS; Hot Springs, AR; (2); 16/191; Chess Clb; Cmnty Wkr; Natl Beta Clb; ROTC; Color Guard; Drill Tm; Hon Roll; FRA, VFW Citation; Rifle & Pistoltm; Knowledge Mstrs; Marine Corps.

HITCHCOCK, SHAY; Gosnell Jr Sr HS; Blytheville, AR; (2); 1/102; HOBY; Natl Beta Clb; Quiz Bowl; Red Cross Aide; Ed Nwsp; Rep Stu Cncl; Pres Acad Fit Awd; Cmnty Wkr; Drama Clb; VFW Voice Dmcrcy AR St Wnnr, Natl 8th Pl; Lit Cncl Advsry Bd; All Amer Schlr; Cmmnctns.

HITT, ANDREA J; Fayetteville Sr HS; Fayetteville, AR; (2); Church Yth Grp; Cmnty Wkr; FCA; FBLA; GAA; Spanish Clb; Band; Color Guard; Drm Mjr(t); Flag Corp.

HITT, MICHAEL W; Ozark Adventist Acad; Searcy, AR; (2); Hosp Aide; Quiz Bowl; Band; Socr; Cit Awd; High Hon Roll; Hon Roll; Jr NHS; Prfct Atten Awd; Medicine; Anesthesiology.

HIVELY, STACEY N; North Little Rock Hs-East; North Little Rock, AR; (2); French Clb; Natl Beta Clb; Spanish Clb; Hon Roll; Acad Excl Awd 2 Yrs; Lyons Coll AR.

HIX, HANNAH; Southside HS; Fort Smith, AR; (3); Cmnty Wkr; Treas French Clb; VP Key Clb; Mu Alpha Theta; School Musical; Ofcr Stu Cncl; L JV Bsktbl; L Var Chrldng; French Hon Soc; NHS; Spcl Olympcs Vol Wrkr; Delta Beta Sigma Chrty Wrk; Baylor U; PT.

HLADKY, JASON P; Wilburn Schl; Searcy, AR; (4); FBLA; FHA; Letterman Clb; Varsity Clb; Yrbk; Pres Sr Cls; Bsktbl.

HO, STEPHANIE; Butterfield Jr HS; Van Buren, AR; (1); HOBY; Teachers Aide; Band; Jazz Band; Mrchg Band; Pep Band; High Hon Roll; Jr NHS; Ntl Merit Ltr; Pres Acad Fit Awd; Phi Beta Mu Awd Music; Hlpr Annual Career Day; Vanderbilt Univ; Med/Music.

HOBBS, BOONE R; Pulaski Acad; Little Rock, AR; (2); Church Yth Grp; Cmnty Wkr; Library Aide; Natl Beta Clb; Office Aide; Spanish Clb; JV Var Bsktbl; Var Crs Cntry; JV Var Vllybl; JV Var Wt Lftg; Competitive Swimming; Carpentry; Arch; Supt.

HOBBS, CHRISTOPHER A; Crossett Sr HS; Crossett, AR; (2); Var Bsktbl; Hon Roll; Art; Applied Biol Chem I Awd; Rdng Awd; U Of AR Monticello; Art.

HOBBS JR, RAY D; Catholic HS; North Little Rock, AR; (2); Church Yth Grp; French Clb; Socr.

HOBBS, SALLY K; Alma HS; Alma, AR; (4); 1/149; French Clb; FBLA; Library Aide; Math Clb; Mu Alpha Theta; Gov Hon Prg Awd; NHS; Val; Jr Exec Trng; Partners In Christ Treas.

HOBBS, SARAH; Arkansas Bapt Schl; Little Rock, AR; (4); #1 in class; Church Yth Grp; FCA; FBLA; Natl Beta Clb; Chorus; Ed Yrbk; Pres Jr Cls; Hon Roll; Ntl Merit Schol; MS ST Univ; Vet.

HOBBS, SHELLEY; Southside HS; Fort Smith, AR; (3); Church Yth Grp; Teachers Aide; Chorus; Church Choir; Hon Roll; Pres Acad Fit Awd; Natl Eng Mrt Awd; Natl Span Exam St 3rd Pl; Hendersons Honor Coll; Med Lab.

HOBBY, MELISSA G; Benton Sr HS; Benton, AR; (3); Church Yth Grp; Key Clb; Office Aide; Science Clb; Spanish Clb; Church Choir; Hon Roll; Jr NHS; Kiwanis Awd; Pres Acad Fit Awd; U Cntrl AR; Phys Thrpy.

HOBBY, PAMELA R; Benton Sr HS; Benton, AR; (3); 50/258; Hosp Aide; Key Clb; Math Clb; Spanish Clb; Band; Church Choir; Mrchg Band; Hon Roll; Prfct Atten Awd; Pres Church Star Prgm; Tght Tddlrs Cls Chrch Past Yr; Hnr Star; His/Eng Lit Tchr.

HOBBY, PATRICIA A; Sheridan Sr HS; Mabelvale, AR; (2); Church Yth Grp; Cmnty Wkr; Office Aide; Teachers Aide; Chorus; Church Choir; Jr NHS; 150 Hrs Comm Svc; Hendrix Coll; Nrs.

HODGE, KATINA R; Hall Sr HS; Little Rock, AR; (4); 17/293; FBLA; Model UN; Natl Beta Clb; Spanish Clb; Rep Frsh Cls; Rep Soph Cls; Rep Stu Cncl; High Hon Roll; NHS; Pres Acad Fit Awd; Math Tutor; Hendrix Coll; Ec; Bus.

HODGE, LISA; Atkins Schl; Russellville, AR; (2); 1/85; Drama Clb; FBLA; HOBY; Natl Beta Clb; Quiz Bowl; Science Clb; Band; Mrchg Band; Yrbk; Var Bsktbl; Psych.

HODGE, TABITHA L; Lead Hill Schl; Lead Hill, AR; (2); FCA; Yrbk; Pres Frsh Cls; Rep Soph Cls; Bsktbl; Sftbl; Trk; Hon Roll; U Of AR; PE.

HODGES, BRANDON J; Atkins Schl; Atkins, AR; (1); Natl Beta Clb; Band; L Ftbl; High Hon Roll; Prfct Atten Awd; Pres Outstdng Acad Achvmt Awd; Jr High Ftbl Mst Imprvd 95-96; Super Achvmt & Excl Band Perfmnc.

HODGES, CLINT; Bradley Jr Sr HS; Bradley, AR; (3); 1/30; Am Leg Boys St; Church Yth Grp; FBLA; HOBY; Letterman Clb; Math Clb; Natl FFA Org; Quiz Bowl; Spanish Clb; Varsity Clb; Drug Tm; U Of AR; Psych.

HODGES, DAVID H; Arkansas Bapt Schl; Little Rock, AR; (3); Church Yth Grp; FCA; FBLA; Natl Beta Clb; Chorus; Church Choir; School Play; Ed Yrbk; VP Jr Cls; Var L Socr; Yth Mission Trip 3 Weeks To Slovakia; Song Leading At Chrch Yth Group & Chrch Group Camp; Soloist; OK Bapt Univ; Musician.

HODGES, FLOYD S; Rivercrest HS; Tyronza, AR; (2); Ofcr Soph Cls; Bsktbl; Ftbl; Swmmng; Trk; Wt Lftg.

HODGES, JON M; North Little Rock Hs-West; North Little Rock, AR; (3); Art Clb; FBLA; Spanish Clb; Rep Stu Cncl; Ftbl; Var Wt Lftg; Cit Awd; Hon Roll.

HODGES, LAKITA S; Forrest City HS; Forrest City, AR; (1); FHA; Girl Scts; Church Choir; Hon Roll; U Of Houston; Plastic Surgeon.

HODGES, SARAH J; Springdale Sr HS; Springdale, AR; (3); Church Yth Grp; Acpl Chr; French Clb; Band; Chorus; Color Guard; Flag Corp; Mrchg Band; School Musical; Variety Show; Stu Mnstry Tm.

HODGES, SUSIE; Perryville Jr Sr HS; Perryville, AR; (2); Chess Clb; Church Yth Grp; Score Keeper; Debate Tm; Ofcr FBLA; Hosp Aide; Model UN; Quiz Bowl; Spanish Clb; Teachers Aide; Engl & Spnsh Awds; Civics Awd; FBLA Keybrdng Apps Dist & St Wnnr; U Of AR Fayetteville; Bus.

HODGES, TIMOTHY R; Van Buren Sr HS; Van Buren, AR; (2); 15/450; Church Yth Grp; FCA; Math Clb; Mu Alpha Theta; Band; Mrchg Band; Jr NHS; Pres Acad Fit Awd; Art Clb; FBLA; MADD Art Cont St Wnnr; Fronstiersman Camping; Natl Jr Ldrs Conf; Civil Engr.

HOFFMAN, ANNE MARIE; Crowleys Ridge Acad; Paragould, AR; (1); Church Yth Grp; Pep Clb; Chorus; Orch; Hon Roll; Arts Encounter AEGIS Summer Project Nom 96; Oral Commnctn Awd 96; Eng Awd 96; Visual Artist; Vet.

HOFFMAN, HEATHER D; Alma HS; Rudy, AR; (3); Church Yth Grp; Pres FBLA; Office Aide; Science Clb; Band; Church Choir; Color Guard; Drill Tm; Flag Corp; Mrchg Band; FBLA Dist I Prlmntrn; Color Guard Flagline Cptn; Drill Team Cptn; AR Tech U; HS Amer His Tchr.

HOFFMAN, LISA; Southside HS; Fort Smith, AR; (3); Church Yth Grp; FHA; Mu Alpha Theta; Pep Clb; Teachers Aide; Band; Chorus; Church Choir; Mrchg Band; Hon Roll.

HOGAN, DAVID M; Trumann HS; Trumann, AR; (2); Church Yth Grp; Science Clb; Spanish Clb; Var Bsbl; Var Bsktbl; Var Ftbl; Hon Roll; NHS; U Of AR; Phys Therapy; PE.

HOGAN, ERIN; Gosnell Jr HS; Blytheville, AR; (1); Cmnty Wkr; Drama Clb; Sec French Clb; Key Clb; Quiz Bowl; Science Clb; SADD; School Play.

HOGAN, NATHAN M; Trumann HS; Trumann, AR; (2); Church Yth Grp; French Clb; Library Aide; Band; Mrchg Band; Pep Band; Rep Yrbk; Bsktbl; Ftbl; Golf; Golf 2 Dist Chmpnshps; Medalist Dist Golf Tournament; AA ST Golf Tournament 2 Appearances; Univ Of AK; Astronamy.

HOGGARD, JULIE D; England HS; England, AR; (4); 1/52; Am Leg Aux Girls St; Church Yth Grp; Drama Clb; French Clb; Library Aide; Natl Beta Clb; Drm Mjr(t); School Play; High Hon Roll; Val; LOYAL Mem; All Amer Schlr; Amer Legion Auxiliary Girls St Cnslr; U Of Cntrl AR; Nrsng.

HOGGATT, STEPHANIE; Brinkley HS; Brinkley, AR; (4); 14/71; Am Leg Aux Girls St; Church Yth Grp; VP Drama Clb; French Clb; Science Clb; Band; Drm Mjr(t); Mrchg Band; Hon Roll; NHS; Comp Sci Awd; East AR CC; Bus.

HOGNER, MELODY; Farmington Jr Sr HS; Farmington, AR; (1); Church Yth Grp; FHA; Chorus; Church Choir; Jazz Band; Hon Roll; Jr NHS; Southern Nazarene U; Ed.

HOGUE, CHERYL L; Western Yell Co HS; Belleville, AR; (2); Church Yth Grp; FBLA; Natl Beta Clb; Office Aide; Pep Clb; Teachers Aide; Stage Crew; Treas Frsh Cls; Sec Soph Cls; Hon Roll.

HOGUE, LARKEN H; Magnolia HS; Magnolia, AR; (2); Church Yth Grp; FBLA; Pep Clb; Band; Church Choir; Color Guard; Mrchg Band; Pep Band; High Hon Roll; Hon Roll; U Of AR Fayetteville; Bus.

HOGUE, MARY K; Southside HS; Fort Smith, AR; (2); 78/500; Church Yth Grp; FCA; GAA; Spanish Clb; Drill Tm; Bsktbl; Trk; Vllybl; Hon Roll; NHS; Bsktbl Cngrs Intl; All Amer Team.

HOHN, NATALIE J; Newport HS; Weiner, AR; (3); Art Clb; FBLA; FHA; Library Aide; Natl FFA Org; Office Aide; Science Clb; SADD; Yrbk; Treas Soph Cls; Natl Ldrshp Frm 10th Grd; Art Work Used For HS; Memphis Coll Of Art; Spec Effct.

HOHRINE, KATY; Malvern Sr HS; Malvern, AR; (2); Church Yth Grp; FBLA; Rptr Natl Beta Clb; SADD; Band; Church Choir; Ofcr Stu Cncl; High Hon Roll; Jr NHS; NHS; Peer Cnslng Grp Ldr 95-96; Regnl Band 94-95; 1st Div Band 94-95.

HOKE, TRACY L; Springdale Sr HS; Springdale, AR; (3); Key Clb; Pres Soph Cls; Pres Jr Cls; Rep Sr Cls; VP Stu Cncl; Chrldng; Tennis; Trk; Jr NHS; NHS; U Of AR; Medicine.

HOLBERT, SUNSHYNE G; Bergman Schl; Wickes, AR; (1); 1/80; Church Yth Grp; Dance Clb; Drama Clb; Letterman Clb; Natl Beta Clb; Pep Clb; Quiz Bowl; SADD; Band; Jazz Band; Smr Gftd/Tlntd Prgm; Hon Eng; U Of AK; Med Dr/Spclst.

HOLBROOK, SUSAN E; Lee Acad; Marianna, AR; (2); Bsktbl; Trk; Hon Roll; NHS; Ntl Merit Schol; AR ST Univ; Lawyer; Acctnt.

HOLCOMB, AUDREY A; Corning HS; Corning, AR; (3); Church Yth Grp; FCA; FHA; Spanish Clb; Trk; Hon Roll; AR ST Univ; Bus.

HOLCOMB, JANET O; Des Arc Jr Sr HS; Carlisle, AR; (4); 4/45; Am Leg Aux Girls St; Church Yth Grp; FBLA; Natl Beta Clb; Jazz Band; Mrchg Band; Pres Sr Cls; Rep Stu Cncl; High Hon Roll.

HOLCOMB, LINDA; Lee Sr HS; Marianna, AR; (1); Quiz Bowl; High Hon Roll; PHD; Kndrgrtn Tchr.

HOLCOMB, OLIVIA; Des Arc Jr Sr HS; Carlisle, AR; (4); 4/45; Am Leg Aux Girls St; FBLA; FHA; Natl Beta Clb; Jazz Band; Mrchg Band; Pres Sr Cls; Rep Stu Cncl; High Hon Roll; St Schlr; Electronics.

HOLCOMB, PETER J; Arkansas Bapt Schl; Maumelle, AR; (2); Church Yth Grp; FCA; FBLA; Natl Beta Clb; Chorus; Socr; Hon Roll; Prfct Atten Awd; Cmptr.

HOLDER, KIRK; Hatfield Schl; Hatfield, AR; (1); 2/40; Church Yth Grp; FBLA; Math Tm; Natl FFA Org; Quiz Bowl; Bsktbl; Trk; Hon Roll; Pres Acad Fit Awd; Frstry Tm; Elctrcty Tm; Harding U.

HOLDERFIELD, RAE L; Oak Grove HS; Maumelle, AR; (2); Church Yth Grp; Drama Clb; FCA; FBLA; Letterman Clb; Mu Alpha Theta; Bsktbl; Vllybl; Hon Roll; Pres Acad Fit Awd; Sthrn Nazarene U; Ed.

HOLEMAN, LISA L; Searcy HS; Searcy, AR; (4); Drama Clb; Spanish Clb; Teachers Aide; Thesps; VICA; Chorus; School Musical; School Play; Stage Crew; Variety Show; ASU Jnsboro; Hist.

HOLFELTZ, STEVEN C; Hall Sr HS; Little Rock, AR; (2); Church Yth Grp; Cmnty Wkr; Acpl Chr; School Musical; Socr; Cit Awd; Hon Roll; Jr NHS; Sci Prjcts; Outstndng Acad Achvt Awds; U AR Conway; Vet.

HOLLADAY, MEGGAN; Sheridan Sr HS; Sheridan, AR; (2); 23/286; FCA; FBLA; GAA; Teachers Aide; Varsity Clb; Var L Bsktbl; Var L Sftbl; JV L Trk; JV L Vllybl; High Hon Roll.

HOLLAND, ALLISON B; Pulaski Acad; Little Rock, AR; (4); Church Yth Grp; Cmnty Wkr; English Clb; German Clb; Natl Beta Clb; Science Clb; Spanish Clb; Band; Mrchg Band; Lit Mag; Saxophone; Crtv Wrtng; Rice U.

HOLLAND, BRANDI N; North Little Rock Hs-West; North Little Rock, AR; (4); 75/554; Art Clb; Cmnty Wkr; Girl Scts; Mu Alpha Theta; ROTC; Color Guard; Drill Tm; Powder Puff Ftbl; High Hon Roll; Hon Roll; Vol Museum Of Sci/His; Peer Ldrshp; STAR.

HOLLAND, EMILY A; Springdale Sr HS; Springdale, AR; (4); Sec French Clb; FBLA; Key Clb; Office Aide; Q&S; Chorus; Yrbk; Chrldng; French Hon Soc; Hon Roll; U Of AR; Elem Ed.

HOLLAND, J DANIEL; Cabot HS; Austin, AR; (2); Cmnty Wkr; Jazz Band; Hon Roll; Jr NHS; Elctrncs.

HOLLAND JR, JIMMIE WAYNE; Benton Sr HS; Benton, AR; (4); Am Leg Boys St; Key Clb; Var L Ftbl; High Hon Roll; Jr NHS; Kiwanis Awd; NHS; Pres Acad Fit Awd; Art Clb; Church Yth Grp; Optimist Clb Awd; All-Conf Ftbl; AR ST Univ; Ath Trng.

HOLLAND, JONI; Greenwood Sr HS; Fort Smith, AR; (1); Chrldng; Cit Awd; High Hon Roll; Jr NHS; U Of AR; Tchng.

HOLLAND, JULIE; Bryant Sr HS; Bryant, AR; (3); 20/330; Pres Church Yth Grp; VP FTA; Church Choir; Drill Tm; School Musical; Rep Stu Cncl; Co-Capt Chrldng; Hon Roll; VP NHS; Jr NHS; NCA All-Amer Chrldr; Church Co-Pianst; Multi Yr Listing.

HOLLAND, MARK R; Rogers HS; Rogers, AR; (3); Church Yth Grp; FCA; FBLA; Key Clb; Office Aide; Rep Soph Cls; Rep Jr Cls; Rep Sr Cls; Rep Stu Cncl; JV Var Ftbl; Chamber Of Commerce Acad Awd; Governors Schl; Hendrix; Pre-Med.

HOLLAND, MATTHEW G; Cty Line HS; Branch, AR; (3); 10/40; Am Leg Boys St; FCA; FBLA; Natl Beta Clb; Quiz Bowl; VP Jr Cls; VP Stu Cncl; Var L Bsbl; Var L Bsktbl; Spanish NHS; UCA; Phy Thrpst.

HOLLAND, MICHAEL; North Little Rock Hs-East; North Little Rock, AR; (3); Boy Scts; Debate Tm; Math Clb; Natl Beta Clb; Hon Roll; Prfct Atten Awd; Engr.

HOLLAND, SHANNON B; Yellville Summit HS; Yellville, AR; (3); Teachers Aide; Chorus; Chrldng; Crs Cntry; Trk; Vllybl; Hon Roll; Engrng.

HOLLAND, SHELLEY D; Newport HS; Newark, AR; (4); 1/143; Girl Scts; Natl Beta Clb; Spanish Clb; SADD; Teachers Aide; Band; Mrchg Band; Orch; High Hon Roll; NHS; Bible Clb; U Of Cntrl AR; Speech Patholgy.

HOLLAND, STEVEN L; Lamar HS; Clarksville, AR; (4); Am Leg Boys St; Church Yth Grp; FCA; L Capt Bsbl; Capt L Ftbl; JV Trk; Var Wt Lftg; Cit Awd; Hon Roll; Coll Of Ozarks; Bio.

HOLLAND, TARA; Mansfield Jr Sr HS; Huntington, AR; (1); Church Yth Grp; Debate Tm; Drama Clb; FCA; Intnl Clb; Speech Tm; Varsity Clb; School Play; Stage Crew; Variety Show; 10 Yrs Dance; Law.

HOLLANDSWORTH, LORI B; Salem HS; Salem, AR; (3); Church Yth Grp; FCA; FBLA; FHA; Treas Key Clb; Natl Beta Clb; Spanish Clb; Rep Jr Cls; Var Bsktbl; High Hon Roll; 5th Pl Word Procssng FBLA St Conv; Pre-Med.

HOLLEMAN, BRANDI NICOLE; Sheridan Sr HS; Hensley, AR; (1); FCA; Chrldng; DAR Awd; Hon Roll; Taekwondo Red Blt; Spec Olympcs Vol; RCG All Star Chrldr; U Of AR; Chld Psych.

HOLLEY, JONITA L; Lynn Schl; Black Rock, AR; (2); 2/17; Sec Art Clb; Model UN; Quiz Bowl; Sec Spanish Clb; Teachers Aide; Chorus; Rep Frsh Cls; Cit Awd; High Hon Roll; Hon Roll; Supts Roll; Lion Awd; PALS; Eng; Jrnlsm.

HOLLEY, MISSY; Pine Bluff HS; Pine Bluff, AR; (2); #7 in class; Intnl Clb; Spanish Clb; Acpl Chr; Orch; Cit Awd; High Hon Roll; Jr NHS; Pres Acad Fit Awd; Pine Bluff Sngrs; Psych.

HOLLEY, QUATRES D; Lynn Schl; Black Rock, AR; (3); 11/23; Art Clb; Cmnty Wkr; Library Aide; Office Aide; Chorus; Church Choir; School Musical; Rptr Nwsp; Ed Lit Mag; Capt Bsbl; UCLA; Biological Scis.

HOLLEY, SHARON; Dumas HS; Dumas, AR; (4); 12/124; Church Yth Grp; Cmnty Wkr; FBLA; FHA; FTA; Library Aide; Pep Clb; Spanish Clb; Church Choir; Stage Crew; Upwrd Bnd; Deb Teen Clb; AR ST Univ; Pre-Med.

HOLLIMAN, CINDY L; Marshall Jr-Sr HS; Harriet, AR; (4); 3/54; Church Yth Grp; Cmnty Wkr; VP FBLA; VP Math Clb; Natl FFA Org; Red Cross Aide; Spanish Clb; Teachers Aide; Sec Sr Cls; Hon Roll; Lcl, Reg, St Sci Fair; FBLA Lcl, Dist, St Comps; U Of Cntrl AR; Ed.

HOLLIMAN, DENENE E; Quitman Jr Sr HS; Quitman, AR; (3); Natl Beta Clb; Natl FFA Org; Teachers Aide; Bsktbl; Hon Roll; Algebra I & II Awds; Amer Govt Awd; UCA.

HOLLIMAN, JOHN S; Quitman Jr Sr HS; Quitman, AR; (2); 4-H; Natl Beta Clb; Natl FFA Org; Hon Roll.

HOLLINGSWORTH, ANDY D; Springdale Sr HS; Springdale, AR; (3); Bsktbl; Hon Roll.

HOLLINGSWORTH, JOEL; Sparkman Jr Sr HS; Sparkman, AR; (3); Church Yth Grp; Natl FFA Org; Spanish Clb; Rptr Sr Cls; Ftbl; Hon Roll; Quachita Bapt Univ.

HOLLINSHED, JANICE; Dumas Jr HS; Dumas, AR; (1); VP FBLA; Bsktbl; High Hon Roll; Hon Roll; Amer Lgn Cert; Word Prcssng.

HOLLIS, AMANDA L; Southside HS; Batesville, AR; (2); Church Yth Grp; Drama Clb; Key Clb; Natl Beta Clb; Sec Natl FFA Org; Science Clb; Acpl Chr; Chorus; Church Choir; School Musical; Madrigals; Top Math & Ag Awd; Lawyer.

HOLLIS, AMANDA S; Greenwood Sr HS; Greenwood, AR; (2); Cit Awd; High Hon Roll; Hon Roll; Ntl Merit Ltr; World His Cls Hnr; Bus; Eng.

HOLLIS, MICHAEL J; Piggott HS; Greenway, AR; (3); Church Yth Grp; FCA; 4-H; French Clb; Natl FFA Org; School Musical; Bsktbl; Ftbl; Trk; 4-H Awd; Bsktbl 3AA Dist, Cty/Conf Chmps; Trck 3AA Shot Put, North/Team Chmpns; Ldrshp Team.

HOLLIS, MICHAEL S; Crossett Sr HS; Crossett, AR; (3); 35/223; Church Yth Grp; Math Clb; Mu Alpha Theta; Band; Church Choir; Mrchg Band; Hon Roll; NHS; AR ST Hstry Day Chmpn; La Tech Univ; Pre-Med/Engr.

HOLLIVERSE, TRAMEKIA; Arkansas Sr HS; Texarkana, AR; (4); FBLA; FHA; FTA; Girl Scts; Church Choir; Drill Tm; School Musical; Var Chrldng; Var Trk; JV Vllybl; NIKE; Do Right Gang; UCA Conway.

HOLLOWAY, AMANDA M; Star City HS; Star City, AR; (3); 1/105; Church Yth Grp; FCA; French Clb; Mu Alpha Theta; Nwsp; Yrbk; Chrldng; NHS; Cmnty Wkr; Drama Clb; AP Eng; GATE; Med.

HOLLOWAY, CHRISTINA J; Bryant Sr HS; Benton, AR; (2); FBLA; Crs Cntry; Trk; Sftbl; Socr; Univ Of Conway AK; PT/PHRMCST.

HOLLOWAY, HEATHER; Norphlet HS; Norphlet, AR; (1); Church Yth Grp; FBLA; GAA; Sec Frsh Cls; Capt Bsktbl; Capt Chrldng; Jr NHS; Art Clb; Church Choir; Hon Roll; All Cnty In Bsktbl; Cls Favorite; Frosh Homcmng Maid; U Of Cntrl AR.

HOLLOWAY, JIMMY BRENT; Smackover HS; Smackover, AR; (3); Church Yth Grp; Cmnty Wkr; FBLA; Letterman Clb; Quiz Bowl; Science Clb; Spanish Clb; Church Choir; Ofcr Bsbl; Bsktbl; Henderson ST U.

HOLLOWAY, KATIE; Southside HS; Fort Smith, AR; (3); 26/502; Church Yth Grp; Dance Clb; FCA; FBLA; Key Clb; Mu Alpha Theta; VP Spanish Clb; Drill Tm; Stat Bsktbl; Mgr(s); Hmcmng Ct Jr Maid 95-; Span Mdl Awd; Jr/Sr/Soph Cncl; Hattie Caraway Ldrshp Conf; Auburn Univ; Pharm.

HOLLOWAY, KRISTI; Southside HS; Fort Smith, AR; (3); 35/502; Church Yth Grp; Dance Clb; FCA; FBLA; Key Clb; Mu Alpha Theta; Spanish Clb; Drill Tm; Stat Bsktbl; Mgr(s); Acad Achvmnt Awd; Jr/Soph/Sr Cncl; Hattie Carraway Ldrshp Conf; Auburn Univ; Bus.

HOLLOWAY, LAKESHIA L; Central Sr HS; Little Rock, AR; (3); Band; Cit Awd; High Hon Roll; Hon Roll; Pres Acad Fit Awd; U Of AR; Sports Medicine.

HOLLOWAY, SHANNON; Murfreesboro HS; Murfreesboro, AR; (3); 2/50; Church Yth Grp; FBLA; FHA; Natl Beta Clb; Science Clb; Spanish Clb; Yrbk; Rptr Stu Cncl; Chrldng; High Hon Roll; Quachita Bptst U; Law.

HOLLOWAY, TANNIKA; Morrilton Sr HS; Morrilton, AR; (2); FBLA; Girl Scts; Spanish Clb; Drill Tm; Vllybl; Hon Roll; NHS; Stu Pride.

HOLLOWAY, TYWANA R; Central Sr HS; Little Rock, AR; (2); English Clb; Science Clb; Spanish Clb; Chorus; Cit Awd; Hon Roll; Orthopedic Surgeon.

HOLLOWAY, ZEBULON; Hot Springs HS; Hot Springs, AR; (1); Church Yth Grp; Band; Church Choir; Drill Tm; Mrchg Band; Chrldng; Hon Roll; Prfct Atten Awd; U AR Pine Bluff; News Rptr.

HOLLOWELL, EMILY J; Central Ark Christian Schl; North Little Rock, AR; (3); Church Yth Grp; Cmnty Wkr; FBLA; FHA; Spanish Clb; JV Chrldng; Powder Puff Ftbl; Psych.

HOLMAN, JEFF A; Springdale Sr HS; Springdale, AR; (2); FCA; SADD; Teachers Aide; Acpl Chr; Hon Roll; NHS; Pres Acad Fit Awd; Golf; Fly Fshng; Univ Of Miami; Pharm.

HOLMES, ALISSA; Conway Sr HS; Conway, AR; (3); Art Clb; Church Yth Grp; Cmnty Wkr; Office Aide; Teachers Aide; Rep Frsh Cls; Rep Jr Cls; Rep Stu Cncl; Cit Awd; Hon Roll; Delta Beta Sigma; Regl Sci Fair 3rd Plc Envrnmntl Ctgry; U Of AR; Art/Grphc Dsgn.

HOLMES, AMANDA K; Jacksonville HS; Cabot, AR; (4); Church Yth Grp; Drama Clb; Pres 4-H; FBLA; Natl Beta Clb; Science Clb; Spanish Clb; Speech Tm; Stage Crew; 4-H Awd; AR Apaloosa Hrs Club Yth Grp Pres; Grls Mssnry Aux Sec; U Of Cntrl AR.

HOLMES, AMY S; Harrison Sr HS; Harrison, AR; (4); 46/196; Art Clb; Church Yth Grp; Cmnty Wkr; Computer Clb; Dance Clb; Girl Scts; Library Aide; Office Aide; Q&S; SADD; Girl Scout Silver/Gold/Ldrshp Awd; Cadett Chlng Silver Awd/Ldr In Trng/Sr Challenge/Career Expl Awd; ATU; Law.

HOLMES, BRINDY M; Sylvan Hills HS; Sherwood, AR; (2); Church Yth Grp; Hosp Aide; Mu Alpha Theta; Drill Tm; Stage Crew; Yrbk; Pres Stu Cncl; Var Chrldng; Hon Roll; NHS; Sherwood Yth Cncl; Miss Sylvan Hills Jr High Pageant Wnnr.

HOLMES, HEATHER A; Van Buren Sr HS; Van Buren, AR; (2); Church Yth Grp; FCA; French Clb; Mu Alpha Theta; SADD; NHS; Earth Clb; Meteorlgy.

HOLMES, HENRY; Central HS; Helena, AR; (2); Cmnty Wkr; Natl FFA Org; Church Choir; Nwsp; Yrbk; Ftbl; Trk; High Hon Roll; Hon Roll; Art Clb; Stdnt Of Mnth; U Of AR; Ag.

HOLMES, JENNIFER N; Dewitt HS; De Witt, AR; (4); Church Yth Grp; French Clb; FBLA; FTA; Model UN; Natl Beta Clb; Q&S; SADD; Sec VICA; Phtg Nwsp; PRIDE; Cooperative Ed Clb; Southern AR Univ; Eleme D.

HOLMES, KHIELA; Mills HS; Little Rock, AR; (3); 29/298; Church Yth Grp; FBLA; FHA; Mu Alpha Theta; ROTC; Spanish Clb; Sftbl; Hon Roll; NHS; Cnslr Aide; Future 500; Assn Blck Engrs AR; Proj Strtng Block; Physics Awd Acceptd Into MITE; Hendrix Coll.

HOLMES, SARAH C; Russellville Sr HS; Russellville, AR; (3); 143/340; Church Yth Grp; Cmnty Wkr; Hosp Aide; Gym; Spanish Clb; Band; Mrchg Band; Variety Show; Nwsp; Yrbk; Voice Of Democracy VFW Speech Cont; CSU; SADD; Lads To Ldrs & Leaderettes Cmptn; Bio.

HOLMES, STACEY; Paron Schl; Benton, AR; (3); FHA; Math Clb; Science Clb; Spanish Clb; Teachers Aide; School Play; Yrbk; Bsktbl; Chrldng; UCA; Nurse.

HOLOBAUGH, FAIDRA; Rural Special Schl; Fox, AR; (4); 4/25; 4-H; FBLA; Hist FHA; Natl Beta Clb; Natl FFA Org; Spanish Clb; School Play; Pres Jr Cls; Bsktbl; Hon Roll; Yth Grp; All Amer Schlr; Hendrix Coll.

HOLT, AARON; Bismarck Jr-Sr HS; Bismarck, AR; (4); 1/67; Church Yth Grp; HOBY; Pres Natl Beta Clb; Quiz Bowl; Pres Frsh Cls; Pres Soph Cls; Pres Jr Cls; Pres Sr Cls; Var Bsktbl; Hon Roll; Ouachita Baptist U; Bus.

HOLT, AMBER C; Mc Gehee HS; Mcgehee, AR; (2); Art Clb; Church Yth Grp; FTA; Library Aide; Science Clb; Spanish Clb; Teachers Aide; Rep Frsh Cls; Tennis; Soph Server; AR ST Univ.

HOLT, C A; Fayetteville Sr HS; Fayetteville, AR; (2); Church Yth Grp; Intrml Bsbl; Intrml Bsktbl; Intrml Socr; High Hon Roll; Pres Acad Fit Awd; Pre-Med.

HOLT, CARRIE J; Lonoke Jr HS; England, AR; (1); Church Yth Grp; Science Clb; Band; Mrchg Band; Rep Stu Cncl; JV Bsktbl; Var Mgr(s); Var Score Keeper; JV Trk; Var Vllybl; Phys Therapy; Pharmacist.

HOLT, JOSH; Morrilton Sr HS; Morrilton, AR; (2); French Clb; Math Tm; Var Crs Cntry; Var Trk; Hon Roll; U Of AR; Bus Mgmt.

HOLT, MELANIE L; Clarksville HS; Clarksville, AR; (2); Church Yth Grp; DECA; FCA; FHA; GAA; JV L Bsktbl; JV L Trk; Hon Roll; PRIDE; Advertising Awd.

HOLT, MELISSA; Van Buren Sr HS; Van Buren, AR; (2); Sec FHA; Mu Alpha Theta; Teachers Aide; Band; Tennis; Jr NHS; NHS; UCA; Cnslr; Interior Decorator.

HOLT, MINDY J; Magnolia HS; Magnolia, AR; (3); 10/198; Church Yth Grp; Mu Alpha Theta; Drill Tm; Ofcr Stu Cncl; Bsktbl; Chrldng; Powder Puff Ftbl; Sftbl; Trk; Vllybl; Dance.

HOLT, STEPHANIE; Danville HS; Danville, AR; (4); 6/44; FBLA; FHA; SADD; School Play; Nwsp; Rep Stu Cncl; Jr NHS; NHS; FFA Pres, Sec, Rptr; Hnr Soc Treas; AR Tech U; Ag Bus.

HOLTHOFF, FRANK; Dumas Jr HS; Dumas, AR; (2); Church Yth Grp; FCA; FBLA; Math Clb; Science Clb; Yrbk; Var L Bsbl; Var L Ftbl; Hon Roll; Pres Acad Fit Awd; U Of AR; Mech Engrng.

HOLTHOFF, JAY; Dumas HS; Dumas, AR; (2); Church Yth Grp; FBLA; Natl Beta Clb; L Golf; High Hon Roll; Hon Roll; NHS; Pres Schlr; Boy Scts; Math Clb; Merit Awd; U Of AR Fayetteville.

HOLZHAUER, ASHLEY M; Bryant Sr HS; Benton, AR; (4); 1/336; Sec VP Church Yth Grp; Drama Clb; VP English Clb; 4-H; Quiz Bowl; Pres Science Clb; Speech Tm; Drill Tm; School Play; Lit Mag; Med Camps Vol; Bio.

HOLZHAUER, BLAKE; Gillett Jr Sr HS; Gillett, AR; (3); 4/24; Am Leg Boys St; FBLA; HOBY; Quiz Bowl; Yrbk; Ofcr Stu Cncl; Ofcr Bsbl; Ftbl; NHS; Pres Acad Fit Awd; Ntl Ftbl Hall Fame Nom; Wendy's HS Heismer Awd Nom; MS ST U.

HOMAN, AMANDA; Malvern Jr HS; Malvern, AR; (3); Church Yth Grp; Drama Clb; French Clb; SADD; Pres Thesps; School Musical; School Play; Sec Jr Cls; NHS; Pres Acad Fit Awd; Peer Cnslr; Theatre.

HONDA, DION G; John L Mcclellan Magnet HS; Mabelvale, AR; (2); Church Yth Grp; Cmnty Wkr; FBLA; Mu Alpha Theta; Natl Beta Clb; Spanish Clb; Church Choir; Hon Roll; NHS; Prfct Atten Awd; Ouachita Bapt Univ; Bus Admin.

HONNOLL, BETHANY; Valley View HS; Jonesboro, AR; (3); Church Yth Grp; German Clb; Teachers Aide; Band; Chorus; Church Choir; Hon Roll; Ger Awd; Pre-Law; Lawyer.

HOOD, MISTY F; St Joe Public Schl; Pindall, AR; (3); 7/17; FBLA; FHA; GAA; Natl FFA Org; Ofcr Frsh Cls; Bsktbl; Sftbl; Hon Roll; NHS; Sports Commentator.

HOOFMAN, TABITHA A; Searcy HS; Searcy, AR; (3); Church Yth Grp; Drama Clb; FTA; Natl Beta Clb; Thesps; Chorus; School Play; Stage Crew; Yrbk; Trk; Harding Univ; Elem Ed.

HOOK, BRIANNA; Cabot HS; Cabot, AR; (1); 1/425; ROTC; High Hon Roll; U Of AZ.

HOOKER, TARA E; Trumann HS; Trumann, AR; (2); Church Yth Grp; French Clb; Math Clb; Band; Drm Mjr(t); Mrchg Band; Pep Band; Hon Roll; NHS; Four Div I Ratgs Solo/Ensmbl Band; Mst Imprvd Soph Band.

HOOKS, MATTHEW S; Palestine-Wheatley HS; Wheatley, AR; (2); Church Yth Grp; Church Choir; Ftbl; Hon Roll; Beta Clb; U AR; Music.

HOOKS, SARAH E; Gravette HS; Hiwasse, AR; (4); 11/57; Church Yth Grp; FBLA; Pres FHA; Office Aide; Phtg Yrbk; Sec Sr Cls; High Hon Roll; Hon Roll; Jr NHS; Hist NHS; All Amer Schlr; Elem Ed.

HOOPER, ANDREW J; Springdale Sr HS; Springdale, AR; (1); Church Yth Grp; Natl FFA Org; Hon Roll; Jr NHS.

HOOPER, JESSICA R; Southside HS; Batesville, AR; (1); Art Clb; Church Yth Grp; Library Aide; Hon Roll; Beta Club; Lawyer.

HOOSIER, STEPHANIE A; Cord-Charlotte Schl; Cave City, AR; (4); Cmnty Wkr; Treas FBLA; Hosp Aide; Library Aide; Treas Natl FFA Org; Office Aide; Teachers Aide; Sec Treas Soph Cls; Treas Jr Cls; Hon Roll; Hgh Acad Awd Offc Trng Lab Bus Cls; 13th Pl Comp Cncpts FBLA Cmptn; Gateway Tech Coll; CPA.

HOOTEN, JOSHUA L; Vilonia HS; Vilonia, AR; (4); 42/120; Church Yth Grp; FBLA; FHA; Natl Beta Clb; Natl FFA Org; Church Choir; School Play; Ofcr Bsbl; Bsktbl; Ftbl; ASU; Dent.

HOOTS, DANNY; Cross Co Jr Sr HS; Wynne, AR; (4); 6/41; Church Yth Grp; Natl Beta Clb; Science Clb; Sec Stu Cncl; Hon Roll.

HOOVER, AMANDA C; Berryville HS; Berryville, AR; (3); 4/120; FBLA; Science Clb; Band; Color Guard; Mrchg Band; High Hon Roll; NHS; Frgn Lang Clb VP; Pre-Vet Med.

HOOVER, KACY; Southside HS; Fort Smith, AR; (3); Pres FCA; HOBY; Key Clb; Latin Clb; Mu Alpha Theta; Spanish Clb; Ofcr Stu Cncl; Crs Cntry; Capt Socr; NHS.

HOOVER, RYAN; Cabot HS; Austin, AR; (2); Church Yth Grp; Cmnty Wkr; FCA; Model UN; Ski Clb; Teachers Aide; Church Choir; Ofcr Bsbl; Bsktbl; Hon Roll; CO Sprngs Air Force Acad.

HOOVER, TODD P; Hazen Jr Sr HS; Hazen, AR; (3); 4/45; Am Leg Boys St; Church Yth Grp; FBLA; FHA; Natl Beta Clb; Church Choir; Mrchg Band; Ofcr Bsbl; Bsktbl; Ftbl; AR ST Univ; Sports Med.

HOOVES, JILL; J A Fair Sr HS; Little Rock, AR; (2); Sec Church Yth Grp; FBLA; Natl Beta Clb; Science Clb; Rep Frsh Cls; Chrldng; Tennis; Hon Roll; NHS; Pres Acad Fit Awd; U Of AR.

HOPE, JONATHAN L; Harmony Grove Jr Sr HS; Benton, AR; (3); 6/70; Art Clb; French Clb; Science Clb; Band; Jazz Band; Mrchg Band; Pep Band; Rep Soph Cls; Score Keeper; JETS Awd; Sci Fair Engrng 1st Pl Regnl, 3rd Pl St; Jr Acad Sci Engrng 1st Pl Regnl, 1st Pl St; Art Guild 2nd Pl; U Of AR; Civil Engrng.

HOPKINS, ADAM L; Arkansas Sr HS; Texarkana, AR; (2); Debate Tm; Key Clb; Mu Alpha Theta; Quiz Bowl; Spanish Clb; Treas Frsh Cls; Ofcr Stu Cncl; Socr; Hon Roll; Jr NHS; U Of AR; Law.

HOPKINS, EBONY; Saratoga Schl; Ozan, AR; (1); Church Yth Grp; Cmnty Wkr; 4-H; FHA; Natl Beta Clb; Quiz Bowl; Church Choir; School Musical; School Play; Ofcr Frsh Cls; AR Bapt; Nrs.

HOPKINS, HOLLI; Monticello HS; Monticello, AR; (4); 7/118; Am Leg Aux Girls St; Sec VP FBLA; Natl Beta Clb; SADD; Rep Sec Band; Capt Flag Corp; Jr NHS; Sec NHS; Pres Acad Fit Awd; AR Gov Schl; Northeast LA U; Elem Ed.

HOPKINS, JAMES A; Bearden HS; Bearden, AR; (2); Ftbl; Trk; Wt Lftg; High Hon Roll; UAM.

HOPKINS, JENNIFER E; Sheridan Sr HS; Sheridan, AR; (3); 29/258; Am Leg Aux Girls St; FCA; VP French Clb; Chorus; Yrbk; Chrldng; Co-Capt Pom Pon; NHS; Pres Acad Fit Awd; ST Recog Pnl Dept Of Educ; Chem/Bus/Mktg.

HOPKINS JR, JESSE; Rogers HS; Rogers, AR; (3); Church Yth Grp; FCA; FBLA; Intnl Clb; Hon Roll; Pub Poems; Rogers Renaissance Achvmt Awds; Excl & Recognitions Awds; Bus Field.

HOPKINS, JOHN; Coleman Jr HS; Van Buren, AR; (1); HOBY; Band; Tennis; High Hon Roll; Jr NHS; Prfct Atten Awd; Pres Acad Fit Awd; U Of AR; Bus.

HOPKINS, KIM; Van Buren Sr HS; Van Buren, AR; (4); 9/270; Ofcr Church Yth Grp; Hosp Aide; VP Q&S; School Play; Mgr Yrbk; Rptr Stu Cncl; Sec NHS; Am Leg Aux Girls St; Dance Clb; Drama Clb; Amer Red Crss Lifeguard; Jr Cotillion Instr; Dance Team Capt; Drury Coll; Med Dr.

HOPKINS, MICHAEL B; Russellville Sr HS; Russellville, AR; (3); Am Leg Boys St; Cmnty Wkr; Debate Tm; Drama Clb; French Clb; Model UN; VICA; JV Ftbl; Hon Roll; NHS; AR St Teenage Republicans Vice Chm; Model League Arah Nations; U Of AR Fayetteville.

HOPPE, JUSTIN L; Crowleys Ridge Acad; Paragould, AR; (1); Church Yth Grp; FBLA; Pep Clb; Science Clb; Spanish Clb; Capt Bsktbl; Socr; Trk; Hon Roll; Phys Thrpst.

HOPPE, RICHARD; Catholic HS; Little Rock, AR; (2); 42/191; Church Yth Grp; Cmnty Wkr; ROTC; Intrml Bsktbl; Hon Roll; Pol Awrns; Yth Conn; Chrstn Brothers; PT/ARCHTCT.

HOPPER, AARON J; Mansfield Jr Sr HS; Mansfield, AR; (3); 15/60; Church Yth Grp; FCA; Letterman Clb; JV Bsktbl; Ftbl; Hon Roll; Prfct Atten Awd; AR Tech.

HOPPER, BROOKE; Central Ark Christian Schl; Little Rock, AR; (1); French Clb; Cit Awd; Hon Roll; Jr NHS; Prfct Atten Awd; Hist Club; Art Awd; U Of AR; Law.

HOPPER, LINDSAY; Southside HS; Fort Smith, AR; (3); 37/502; Church Yth Grp; JCL; Latin Clb; Mu Alpha Theta; Teachers Aide; Acpl Chr; Chorus; High Hon Roll; Jr NHS; NHS; Jr Clscl League Hon Soc; U Of AR.

HOPPIS, MATHEW; Bergman Schl; Harrison, AR; (1); Church Yth Grp; Natl Beta Clb; Natl FFA Org; Flag Corp; Var Bsbl; Var Bsktbl; High Hon Roll; Hon Roll; Prfct Atten Awd; Pres Acad Fit Awd; Univ Of AR.

HOPPLE, RENE E; Piggott HS; Saint Francis, AR; (3); 4/70; French Clb; FBLA; Treas FHA; Natl Beta Clb; Natl FFA Org; Science Clb; Church Choir; School Play; Stage Crew; Yrbk; ASU; Med.

HOPSON, AMY ANN; Star City HS; Star City, AR; (2); Church Yth Grp; FCA; Natl Beta Clb; Band; Color Guard; Mrchg Band; Rep Soph Cls; Ofcr Stu Cncl; Capt JV Chrldng; Sftbl; Soph Class Fvrt; FCA; Teen Miss Cane Creek; Jr Miss Lincoln Cty; Intl Mdl Srch Fnlst 95.

HORINE, LYNDELL CHESTON; Springdale Sr HS; Springdale, AR; (4); 1/550; Am Leg Boys St; Church Yth Grp; Debate Tm; Band; Church Choir; Mrchg Band; Ftbl; Wt Lftg; High Hon Roll; NHS; Yth For Christ Club; Fishing Club; John Brown Univ; Pre Med.

HORN, BRANDON; Brookland Jr Sr HS; Brookland, AR; (1); Church Yth Grp; Church Choir; School Musical; Ofcr Stu Cncl; Golf; Hon Roll; Pres Acad Fit Awd; FFA; AR ST U.

HORN, CHAD; Murfreesboro HS; Murfreesboro, AR; (2); 5/55; Church Yth Grp; Cmnty Wkr; FHA; Natl Beta Clb; Spanish Clb; Yrbk; Sec Frsh Cls; Rep Soph Cls; Capt Bsbl; Bsktbl; All Dist Bsbl; GATE; Univ Of Cntrl AR.

HORN, JENNIFER E; Russellville Sr HS; Russellville, AR; (2); Church Yth Grp; Band; Flag Corp; Orch; Pep Band; Rptr Nwsp; Rptr Yrbk; High Hon Roll; Prfct Atten Awd; PHRMCY.

HORN, RAMSEY M; Southside HS; Fort Smith, AR; (2); Boy Scts; Church Yth Grp; FCA; HOBY; Rep Soph Cls; VP Jr Cls; Var JV Ftbl; L Trk; Jr NHS; Key Clb; Mst Outstndng 9th Grd Cvcs Stu; Med.

HORN, STEPHANIE; Van Buren Sr HS; Van Buren, AR; (4); Church Yth Grp; Debate Tm; Drama Clb; Pres VP FHA; Library Aide; Spanish Clb; Speech Tm; Acpl Chr; Chorus; Science Clb; Rptr ASTRA Treas; W AR CC; Bus Mrktng/Adv.

HORN, TRAVIS L; Lamar HS; Hagarville, AR; (3); 4/80; Am Leg Boys St; FCA; Pres Jr Cls; Rep Stu Cncl; Var Bsktbl; Capt Ftbl; Var Trk; High Hon Roll; U Of AR; Bus.

HORNE, GENA; Prairie Grove HS; Prairie Grove, AR; (4); 10/88; Am Leg Aux Girls St; Church Yth Grp; Math Clb; Science Clb; Spanish Clb; Teachers Aide; Capt Bsktbl; High Hon Roll; NHS; Bsktbl All Dist AAO Dream Tm; Mltpl Yr Lstng; U Of AR.

HORNE, LISA; Central Ark Christian Schl; Mabelvale, AR; (4); 9/74; Art Clb; VP Mu Alpha Theta; Science Clb; Spanish Clb; Sec Bsktbl; Var L Tennis; Var L Trk; Var Capt Vllybl; NHS; Hist Clb; Med.

HORNSBY, KRISTEL R; Lonoke Sr HS; Lonoke, AR; (3); 2/115; Church Yth Grp; FCA; 4-H; FBLA; Spanish Clb; Yrbk; Ofcr Soph Cls; Co-Capt Chrldng; High Hon Roll; NHS.

HORROCKS, JENNY; Russellville Sr HS; Russellville, AR; (3); 63/340; Am Leg Aux Girls St; Church Yth Grp; GAA; Teachers Aide; Drill Tm; Chrldng; Mgr(s); Score Keeper; Trk; Vllybl; All Strs; Natl Math Awd; AR Tech Univ; Math Tchr.

HORTON, ANDREA; Monticello HS; Monticello, AR; (3); 8/158; Am Leg Aux Girls St; Art Clb; Church Yth Grp; FBLA; FHA; Natl Beta Clb; Rptr Nwsp; Rep Stu Cncl; NHS; MACY Schlr; Engr.

HORTON, BAXTER; Forrest City HS; Forrest City, AR; (2); #1 in class; Boy Scts; Mu Alpha Theta; VP Natl Beta Clb; Band; Jazz Band; Mrchg Band; Ofcr Stu Cncl; High Hon Roll; Eagle Sct; Med Sci Clb; Mock Trial; U Of AR; Pre-Med.

HORTON, HEATHER N; Jacksonville HS; Jacksonville, AR; (4); 39/283; Church Yth Grp; Cmnty Wkr; FHA; FTA; JA; Natl Beta Clb; Science Clb; Spanish Clb; Hon Roll; Pres Schlr; ASU; RN.

HORTON, JAMES L; Searcy HS; Searcy, AR; (3); 27/286; Boy Scts; FTA; Natl Beta Clb; Band; Chorus; Mrchg Band; School Musical; Hon Roll; Jr NHS; NHS; Tchng.

HORTON, JOHN P; Booneville Jr Sr HS; Booneville, AR; (2); Natl FFA Org; Science Clb; Hon Roll; Universal Tech Inst; ASE Auto.

HORTON, MELISSA D; Hot Springs HS; Hot Springs, AR; (2); Church Yth Grp; FBLA; Key Clb; Natl Beta Clb; School Play; VP Frsh Cls; Chrldng; Future Prblm Slvng; Christns On Campus; Acctng.

HORTON, NICHOLAS; Sylvan Hills HS; Sherwood, AR; (3); French Clb; Mu Alpha Theta; Socr; Hon Roll; Jr NHS; UCA; Zlgy.

HORTON, RACHAEL; Mena HS; Mena, AR; (3); 1/153; French Clb; Sec FBLA; HOBY; Science Clb; Yrbk; Tennis; French Hon Soc; NHS; Fllwshp Chrstn Stu Rep; Explr Scts; Attorney.

HORTON, SHANNA S; Magazine Jr Sr HS; Magazine, AR; (3); 2/30; Church Yth Grp; Cmnty Wkr; FHA; Natl Beta Clb; Spanish Clb; Teachers Aide; School Musical; School Play; Nwsp; Ed Yrbk; Med.

HOSE, WILLIAM M; Mena HS; Mena, AR; (3); 12/125; Art Clb; Drama Clb; French Clb; Natl FFA Org; Science Clb; Nwsp; French Hon Soc; Hon Roll; Rural Yth Tours Essay Cont; Comm.

HOSEASON, CHARLES; Watson Chapel Sr HS; Pine Bluff, AR; (4); 36/240; ROTC; School Play; Rep Stu Cncl; JV Var Ftbl; Var Trk; DAR Awd; JETS Awd; Knowledge Masters; Fire Marshall; JETS Engrng Team; SE AR Tech Coll; Elec Tech.

HOSEY, BONNIE K; Marvell Acad; Marvell, AR; (2); Church Yth Grp; Spanish Clb; Var Chrldng; NHS; U Of AR.

HOSEY, JAIMIE; Mineral Springs Schl; Mineral Springs, AR; (3); Church Yth Grp; FBLA; Natl Beta Clb; Quiz Bowl; Church Choir; Sec Jr Cls; Rep Stu Cncl; Var Chrldng; Score Keeper; Hon Roll; Odyssy Mnd; Close Up Pgm; Bus Mgmt.

HOSKINS, TARA M; Greene Cnty Tech HS; Paragould, AR; (4); 66/160; Church Yth Grp; Drama Clb; FBLA; FTA; Teachers Aide; Band; Color Guard; Mrchg Band; School Musical; School Play; FBLA Dist Comp; Crowleys Ridgecol; Bus.

HOSMAN, JOSH A; Quitman Jr Sr HS; Quitman, AR; (1); 1/60; Chess Clb; Church Yth Grp; Natl Beta Clb; Natl FFA Org; Office Aide; Quiz Bowl; Hon Roll; Pres Acad Fit Awd; LSU; Marine Biologist.

HOSTETLER, AMANDA L; Sheridan Sr HS; Sheridan, AR; (3); 12/258; Church Yth Grp; Cmnty Wkr; Pres FHA; Stage Crew; Cit Awd; High Hon Roll; NHS; Teen Invlvmnt Prog Pres; Natl Fam Prtnrshp ST Yth Bd Mem; Grant Cty CASA Yth Bd Mem; Prmry Ed/Psych.

HOTTINGER, CHRISTOPHER E; Russellville Sr HS; Russellville, AR; (4); 1/297; Am Leg Boys St; Quiz Bowl; Spanish Clb; Stage Crew; Rep Frsh Cls; JV Crs Cntry; JV Trk; Hon Roll; NHS; Ntl Merit SF; U AR; Bio.

HOTZ, ELISABETH E; Russellville Sr HS; Russellville, AR; (2); 1/400; Church Yth Grp; Band; Church Choir; Mrchg Band; Var Gym; JV Swmmng; Cit Awd; High Hon Roll; Jr NHS; NHS; Pagnt Ctznshp Awd; Schlrsp Eckerd Coll; Duke U Tlnt Idntfctn Prgm; Chrstn Stdnt Union; Lib Clb; Swm Tm; PT.

HOUCHIN, ALEX R; Rogers HS; Rogers, AR; (3); Boy Scts; 4-H; ROTC; Science Clb; Hon Roll.

HOUCHINS, TARA L; Jacksonville HS; Jacksonville, AR; (2); FBLA; Office Aide; Spanish Clb; FBLA Comptn Won Three Awds; U Of NC; Corp Lawyer/Vetrnrn.

HOUSE, AMANDA; Delight HS; Delight, AR; (1); 2/30; 4-H; Natl FFA Org; Quiz Bowl; Rep Stu Cncl; JV Bsktbl; Var Sftbl; Hon Roll; CIA; All Amer Schlr; Natl Hnr Rll; Harding U.

HOUSE, JENNY L; Mt St Mary Acad; Little Rock, AR; (2); Church Yth Grp; Sec FHA; Natl Beta Clb; Spanish Clb; Ed Yrbk; Hon Roll; Y Teens.

HOUSE, RAYMOND; John L Mcclellan Magnet HS; Little Rock, AR; (2); Church Yth Grp; Cmnty Wkr; HOBY; Mu Alpha Theta; Natl Beta Clb; School Musical; Yrbk; Capt Bsktbl; Capt Ftbl; Trk; Mech Engrng.

HOUSE, SARAH; Mulberry HS; Mulberry, AR; (4); 3/32; FHA; Science Clb; Rptr Nwsp; Bsktbl; Vllybl; High Hon Roll; Hon Roll; NHS; Pres Acad Fit Awd; Bio.

HOUSE, STEPHANIE; Perryville Jr Sr HS; Perryville, AR; (1); Church Yth Grp; FCA; 4-H; Band; Mrchg Band; Pep Band; Bsktbl; Chrldng; Hon Roll; Jr NHS.

HOUSER, DEDRA N; England HS; England, AR; (1); Church Yth Grp; Band; Color Guard; Flag Corp; Mrchg Band; Hon Roll; Acad Awd Geometry; U Of AR Fayetville; Arch.

HOUSER, RAYMOND P; Southside HS; Fort Smith, AR; (4); 109/400; Church Yth Grp; Spanish Clb; Chorus; Church Choir; Variety Show; Hon Roll; NHS; Prfct Atten Awd; Wrttn Book Of Poems; Mssn Trip Elsalvador; Westark CC; Mnstry/Phlsphy.

HOUSTON, AMANDA; Pangburn Jr Sr HS; Pangburn, AR; (2); 1/50; FBLA; VP FHA; HOBY; Natl Beta Clb; Pres Soph Cls; Ofcr Bsbl; Cit Awd; High Hon Roll; NHS.

HOUSTON, CHRISTY; Newport HS; Bradford, AR; (4); 6/142; Am Leg Aux Girls St; Church Yth Grp; FBLA; Q&S; Pres Ski Clb; School Play; Ed Yrbk; Capt Chrldng; Hon Roll; NHS; Tutor; Math Cont ACTM; Lyon Coll; Econ/Mrktng.

HOUSTON, LORRIE B; Southside HS; Fort Smith, AR; (4); 15/459; Art Clb; Church Yth Grp; Latin Clb; Mu Alpha Theta; Q&S; Quiz Bowl; Drill Tm; Ed Nwsp; Yrbk; Hon Roll; U Of Tulsa.

HOUSTON, MICHAEL; West Memphis Sr HS; West Memphis, AR; (4); 31/256; Boy Scts; Church Yth Grp; FBLA; Mu Alpha Theta; Natl Beta Clb; Var Bsbl; Var Crs Cntry; High Hon Roll; Pres Schlr; Yrbk; U Of Memphis; Arch Engrng.

HOUSTON, RUSTY D; West Memphis Sr HS; West Memphis, AR; (4); L Ftbl; ASU.

HOUSTON, TIMOTHY J; Ridgecrest HS; Paragould, AR; (4); 9/176; Am Leg Boys St; Church Yth Grp; Pres FTA; Band; Chorus; Jazz Band; Orch; School Musical; Thesps; NHS; Coll Of Ozarks; Music Ed.

HOWARD, AMI M; Northside HS; Fort Smith, AR; (4); 41/327; German Clb; Mu Alpha Theta; Orch; Rep Stu Cncl; Chrldng; Jr NHS; NHS; Ntl Merit SF; Pres Acad Fit Awd; 1st Chair Viola At AR All ST; U Of AR; Music Ed; Prof.

HOWARD, ANGELA; Blytheville Sr HS; Blytheville, AR; (3); Key Clb; Teachers Aide; Band; Hon Roll; Cmptr Intro; Typing.

HOWARD, JULIE; Glen Rose HS; Benton, AR; (2); Art Clb; Cmnty Wkr; Pres FBLA; Office Aide; Spanish Clb; SADD; Rptr Nwsp; Phtg Yrbk; Champs; Stop Steerng Comm; Hot Spring Cty Yth Bd.

HOWARD, LEIGH; Harding Acad; Searcy, AR; (2); Church Yth Grp; Key Clb; Natl Beta Clb; Service Clb; Spanish Clb; Chorus; Var L Bsktbl; L Trk; High Hon Roll; Pres Acad Fit Awd; Cir Acad Excllnc 4 Yrs; Cty & Dist Hgh Pt Trck; Wildct Awd Prfmnc Bsktbl & Trck; Phys Thrpy.

HOWARD, MARY RACHEL; Abundant Life Schools; Sherwood, AR; (1); Church Yth Grp; CAP; Drama Clb; School Musical; High Hon Roll; Hon Roll; Piano; Tstmstrs Clb; USAF Acad; Pilot.

HOWARD, MELISSA; Murfreesboro HS; Murfreesboro, AR; (4); 4/40; Church Yth Grp; FBLA; Sec FHA; Natl Beta Clb; Sec Science Clb; Sec Spanish Clb; School Play; Yrbk; Rep Pres Stu Cncl; Capt Bsktbl; U Cntrl AR; Phys Thrpy.

HOWARD, SHATIA; Humphrey Schl; Humphrey, AR; (1); 3/32; Church Yth Grp; 4-H; FBLA; FHA; GAA; Quiz Bowl; Church Choir; Bsktbl; ADAPT; Standford U; Crmnl Law.

HOWARD, YVETTE N; Crossett Sr HS; Crossett, AR; (3); 37/201; Am Leg Aux Girls St; Church Yth Grp; Library Aide; Office Aide; Band; Church Choir; Drill Tm; Flag Corp; Mrchg Band; Pep Band; Advy Bd; Band Pres; Southern A&M.

HOWE, JAMES H; Ft Smith Christian Schl; Fort Smith, AR; (2); Church Yth Grp; Cmnty Wkr; FCA; Ofcr Frsh Cls; Hist Stu Cncl; Ofcr Bsbl; Bsktbl; Ftbl; Cit Awd; Hon Roll.

HOWE, LORINDA; Yellville Summit HS; Yellville, AR; (2); Church Yth Grp; Drama Clb; Var Chrldng; JV Var Trk; Hon Roll; NHS; Boise ST U.

HOWE, MATT; Southside HS; Fort Smith, AR; (4); 150/459; Church Yth Grp; DECA; FCA; Latin Clb; Ofcr Bsbl; Ftbl; Hon Roll; Jr NHS; NHS.

HOWELL, AMANDA; Gillett Jr Sr HS; Gillett, AR; (3); 5/23; Art Clb; FBLA; FHA; Spanish Clb; Yrbk; Bsktbl; Sftbl; Trk; High Hon Roll; Hon Roll; Mst Imprvd HS Stu; U Of Conway; Nrsng.

HOWELL, BRANDI; Riverside HS; Caraway, AR; (3); Church Yth Grp; FBLA; FTA; Key Clb; Natl Beta Clb; VP Natl FFA Org; Yrbk; VP Jr Cls; Capt Chrldng; AR ST U; Med.

HOWELL, BRANDY S; Magnolia HS; Magnolia, AR; (2); Dance Clb; FHA; Co-Ed Pep Clb; Teachers Aide; Band; Drill Tm; Mrchg Band; Chrldng; High Hon Roll; Hon Roll; Phy Thrpst.

HOWELL III, JOHN CARL; Conway Sr HS; Conway, AR; (2); Art Clb; Church Yth Grp; Cmnty Wkr; Pres FCA; Church Choir; Stage Crew; Ofcr Bsbl; Bsktbl; Ftbl; Trk; Stdnt Congrss; Med Dctr/Pediatrcs.

HOWELL, MISTY D; Greene Co Tech HS; Paragould, AR; (4); Drama Clb; FBLA; Band; Color Guard; Mrchg Band; Hon Roll; Prfct Atten Awd; Flag Line Capt; ASU; Bus/Art.

HOWELL, VICKI J; Waldron HS; Danville, AR; (3); VP Drama Clb; Pres FHA; Spanish Clb; Teachers Aide; Stage Crew; High Hon Roll; AR Tech U; Ed.

HOYT, AMANDA R; Russellville Sr HS; Russellville, AR; (2); Church Yth Grp; Spanish Clb; Band; Nwsp; Swmmng; High Hon Roll; Jr NHS; NHS.

HOYT, CHRISTY; Morrilton Sr HS; Morrilton, AR; (2); Art Clb; Church Yth Grp; Drama Clb; FBLA; Math Clb; Natl Beta Clb; Science Clb; Spanish Clb; Thesps; Rptr Yrbk.

HREN, SAMANTHA J; Hot Springs HS; Hot Springs, AR; (3); #12 in class; Cmnty Wkr; Hosp Aide; Office Aide; Chorus; High Hon Roll; Hon Roll; UC Berkeley.

HRENCHIR, GEORGE B; Hartford Schl; Hartford, AR; (2); Natl FFA Org; High Hon Roll; Hon Roll; Prfct Atten Awd; AR Schl Math & Sci; 1st Lt Huntington Police Explorers; Natl Yth Ldrshp Conf Nom; Hendrix Coll; Medicine.

HRUBY, DARLA; Cutter Morning Star HS; Hot Springs, AR; (4); 1/30; Am Leg Aux Girls St; Pres FHA; Pres Natl Beta Clb; VP Spanish Clb; Pres Soph Cls; Sec Jr Cls; Rep Stu Cncl; DAR Awd; High Hon Roll; Val; Northern IL U; Pre-Law.

HUBBARD, ANDREA G; Russellville Sr HS; Casa, AR; (2); Church Yth Grp; Drama Clb; FCA; FBLA; Natl Beta Clb; Var Capt Bsktbl; Tennis.

HUBBARD, DEMETRIUS J; North Little Rock Hs-East; North Little Rock, AR; (2); Bus Profs of Am; Church Yth Grp; FCA; FBLA; Pep Clb; Quiz Bowl; Rep Soph Cls; Var Bsbl; Ftbl; Var Trk; Business Mgmt.

HUBBARD, JEREMY T; West Jr HS; West Memphis, AR; (1); CAP; Science Clb; Band; High Hon Roll; Hon Roll.

HUBBARD, JOHN M; Lockesburg Jr Sr HS; Lockesburg, AR; (3); 1/28; Church Yth Grp; FCA; Quiz Bowl; Phtg Yrbk; Ed Nwsp; Rep Frsh Cls; Rep Soph Cls; Pres Sr Cls; L Bsktbl; Var Golf.

HUBBARD, KERCHALYN M; Pine Bluff HS; Pine Bluff, AR; (3); 10/350; VP Church Yth Grp; Cmnty Wkr; FBLA; Spanish Clb; Band; Capt Drm Mjr(t); Mrchg Band; Hon Roll; NHS; Pres Acad Fit Awd; Cert Of Awd Chem; Engrng; Ec.

HUBBLE, JENNIFER N; Corning HS; Corning, AR; (3); Church Yth Grp; FCA; 4-H; FHA; GAA; Spanish Clb; Church Choir; Rep Frsh Cls; Rep Soph Cls; Rep Sr Cls; Black River Voc Tech; Psych.

HUBERTUS, RACHEL; Strong Jr Sr HS; Strong, AR; (1); Church Yth Grp; French Clb; Office Aide; Science Clb; JV Crs Cntry; JV Sftbl; Hon Roll; Algebra I Awd; Eng I Awd; Strong Whos Who Awd 96; S AR U; Soc Wrkr Nrsng Hm.

HUBSCH, JANE G; Gillett Jr Sr HS; Gillett, AR; (3); 4/23; FBLA; FHA; Pep Clb; Teachers Aide; School Play; Var Stat Mgr(s); Trk; Hon Roll; NHS; Peer Tutor; Vet.

HUCKABEE, BRENT S; Smackover HS; Smackover, AR; (4); Art Clb; Church Yth Grp; Science Clb; Pres Spanish Clb; Tennis; Pres Schlr; MASH; Yth Writing Fest Awd; 2nd Plc Poetry Cont; SAU Magnolio.

HUCKABY, BILLY J; Fountain Lake Jr Sr HS; Lonsdale, AR; (1); Chorus; School Musical; Stage Crew; Bsktbl; Hon Roll; Sci/Math.

HUCKLEBERRY, TINA MARIE; Rogers HS; Rogers, AR; (3); Church Yth Grp; FCA; Treas FHA; SADD; Var Bsktbl; Var Vllybl; High Hon Roll; Prfct Atten Awd; Model UN; Teachers Aide; Chmbr Comm Acad Awd; Rnsnc Awd; Jr Optmst Sec; KS ST U; Elem Ed.

HUDDLESTON, CLINT; Morrilton Sr HS; Morrilton, AR; (3); Drama Clb; French Clb; FBLA; Science Clb; JV Bsbl; Var Ftbl; Var Trk; Hon Roll; NHS.

HUDDLESTON, ERIN E; Jessieville HS; Jessieville, AR; (3); 7/52; Church Yth Grp; Natl Beta Clb; Quiz Bowl; Band; Church Choir; Jazz Band; Mrchg Band; Mgr(s); Score Keeper; Hon Roll; U Of AR; Hist.

HUDDLESTON, JEREMY; Gosnell Jr Sr HS; Dell, AR; (3); 1/80; Church Yth Grp; Drama Clb; FCA; Key Clb; Mu Alpha Theta; Natl Beta Clb; Quiz Bowl; Spanish Clb; Mrchg Band; School Play; U Of AR; Med.

HUDDLESTON, LAURA; Springdale Sr HS; Springdale, AR; (4); 41/585; Am Leg Aux Girls St; Debate Tm; NFL; Q&S; Red Cross Aide; Teachers Aide; Band; Mrchg Band; Nwsp; Hon Roll; Var Bnd Prfmncs; Cert CPR Instr; U Of Cntrl AR; Org Cmmnctns.

HUDDLESTON, LISA; White Hall Sr HS; Pine Bluff, AR; (3); 2/177; Hosp Aide; HOBY; Pres Key Clb; Mu Alpha Theta; Natl Beta Clb; Chorus; Rep Stu Cncl; High Hon Roll; Voted Most Likely To Succeed; All Reg Choir; Med.

HUDDLETON, LAURA; Springdale Sr HS; Springdale, AR; (4); 41/516; Am Leg Aux Girls St; NFL; Q&S; Teachers Aide; Band; Mrchg Band; Nwsp; Hon Roll; NHS; Pres Acad Fit Awd; Cert CPR Instr; Atnd Mid West Intl Bnd/Orch Clnc; Prmr Bnd WA DC Prd/Ftr Bnd Natl Symphny Orch; U Of Central AR; Org Comm.

HUDGINS, AMANDA; Glenwood Jr Sr HS; Glenwood, AR; (4); 1/30; Am Leg Aux Girls St; Church Yth Grp; FCA; FBLA; FHA; Rep Frsh Cls; Rep Soph Cls; Sec Jr Cls; Sec Sr Cls; Pres Stu Cncl; Harding Univ; Social Work.

HUDLOW, ANDREA M; Russellville Sr HS; Russellville, AR; (2); Church Yth Grp; Cmnty Wkr; Hosp Aide; Natl Beta Clb; Church Choir; Hon Roll; Coll Alge Tchr.

HUDSON, AARON D; Drew Central Jr Sr HS; Monticello, AR; (2); Church Yth Grp; Cmnty Wkr; Var Bsbl; JV Var Bsktbl; Var Mgr(s); JV Var Tennis; Hon Roll.

HUDSON, ALANNA J; Alma HS; Alma, AR; (2); SADD; Dist Attrny.

HUDSON, AMANDA; Bright Star Schl; Doddridge, AR; (1); 1/22; Church Yth Grp; VP Frsh Cls; JV Bsktbl; Var Chrldng; JV Trk; Hon Roll; U Of AR.

HUDSON, CARIE L; Vilonia HS; N Little Rock, AR; (2); Art Clb; Church Yth Grp; FHA; Hon Roll; Beta Clb; U Of AR Little Rock; Bus Mgmt.

HUDSON, HEATHER; Nettleton HS; Jonesboro, AR; (4); 8/111; Am Leg Aux Girls St; Girl Scts; HOBY; Math Clb; Natl Beta Clb; Chorus; Sftbl; Hon Roll; Mss Rdr 95; AR Natl Tngr 3rd Rnnr Up 95; AR ST U; Med.

HUDSON, MATT S; Springdale Sr HS; Springdale, AR; (2); Church Yth Grp; FCA; Letterman Clb; L Var Ftbl; L Socr; L Trk; L Wt Lftg; High Hon Roll; Hon Roll; Jr NHS; Cook At Cafe Santa Fe; CO Univ Boulder; Cmptr Prgm.

HUDSON, MEGAN J; Southside HS; Fort Smith, AR; (3); 49/502; FBLA; Spanish Clb; Teachers Aide; Band; High Hon Roll; Hon Roll; Jr NHS; NHS; Pres Acad Fit Awd; Spanish NHS; U Of AR; PT.

HUDSON, MICHAEL A; Delaplaine Schl; O Kean, AR; (1); Natl FFA Org; Quiz Bowl; Bsktbl; Trk; Cit Awd; Hon Roll.

HUDSON, NINA; Greenland Jr Sr HS; Fayetteville, AR; (2); Church Yth Grp; FBLA; FHA; Office Aide; Band; Church Choir; Color Guard; Flag Corp; Mrchg Band; Sec Frsh Cls; 1st Pl Solo & Ensmbl Band; U Of AR; Nrsng.

HUDSON, SHANE; Rivercrest HS; Osceola, AR; (2); Band; High Hon Roll; Hon Roll; Jr NHS; NHS; Pres Acad Fit Awd; Fr/Eng/Sci/His Awds; 4.0 GPA; Upwrd Bnd Sci/Math Prgm Lyon Coll At Batesville; Sci.

HUDSON, TRACI C; Jacksonville HS; Jacksonville, AR; (2); Cmnty Wkr; Drama Clb; FHA; Natl Beta Clb; Science Clb; Band; Capt Flag Corp; Mrchg Band; School Play; Stage Crew; Outsdng FHA Awd; St/Natl Spec Olympics; Miami Univ; Marine Bio.

HUETER, JILL S; Pulaski Acad; Little Rock, AR; (4); GAA; Hosp Aide; Mu Alpha Theta; Pres Natl Beta Clb; VP Science Clb; SADD; School Musical; Mgr Yrbk; High Hon Roll; VP NHS; U Of TX Austin.

HUETT, AMANDA; Genoa Central HS; Texarkana, AR; (4); 4/35; Church Yth Grp; FHA; Quiz Bowl; Sec Spanish Clb; Church Choir; School Play; Ed Lit Mag; Sec Jr Cls; Pres Sr Cls; Rep Stu Cncl; Fllwshp Chrstn Stus; Yth Choir Ensmble; Texarkana CC; Nursng.

HUETT, JAYMIE; Morrilton Sr HS; Morrilton, AR; (2); Art Clb; Office Aide; Spanish Clb; Thesps; Drill Tm; School Play; Rep Stu Cncl; High Hon Roll; Beta Clb; Hmcmng Ct; Dntstry.

HUETT, LEANNE N; Morrilton Sr HS; Morrilton, AR; (3); Drama Clb; Library Aide; Math Clb; Natl Beta Clb; Science Clb; Spanish Clb; Band; Drm Mjr(t); Jazz Band; Mrchg Band; Marjorette Capt 9th/12th Grd; Lib Club Reporter 2 Yrs; Scrapbook Comm Beta Club; AR Tech Univ; Elem Ed.

HUFF, BESSIE V; Carlisle Jr Sr HS; Carlisle, AR; (3); 1/70; Treas Church Yth Grp; 4-H; FHA; Office Aide; Red Cross Aide; Spanish Clb; High Hon Roll; NHS; Cmpr Of Yr; Multi Yr Listee; Acctnt.

HUFF JR, MATTHEW; Mammoth Spring HS; Mammoth Spring, AR; (3); Church Yth Grp; FBLA; HOBY; Natl Beta Clb; Natl FFA Org; Pep Clb; Quiz Bowl; Band; Church Choir; Jazz Band; BAD; U Of AR; Prof Bsbl Player.

HUFFMAN, ANDREA S; Yellville Summit HS; Peel, AR; (2); 18/75; Church Yth Grp; Natl Beta Clb; SADD; Teachers Aide; Band; Mrchg Band; Bsktbl; Trk; Hon Roll; NHS; YEAC; Camp Aldersgate Cnslr Vol; Homcoming Maid; Lawyer.

HUFFMAN, ASHLEY N; Southside HS; Fort Smith, AR; (2); Church Yth Grp; Dance Clb; Drama Clb; FCA; Key Clb; Drill Tm; Hon Roll; NHS; Psych.

HUFFMAN, DAVID; Omaha Schl; Omaha, AR; (1); Church Yth Grp; JV Bsktbl; Hon Roll; Choong Sil Kwan Tae Kwon Do.

HUFFMAN, JAMIE; Rogers HS; Rogers, AR; (4); Church Yth Grp; Cmnty Wkr; Drama Clb; FCA; FBLA; Key Clb; Office Aide; Pres Spanish Clb; Thesps; School Play; Teen Crt; Natl Yth Ldrshp Frm Law & Constn; Stu Bnk Brd; William Woods U; Pre-Law.

HUFFMASTER, JENNIFER; Lavaca Jr Sr HS; Lavaca, AR; (3); 6/61; VP Drama Clb; FBLA; HOBY; Natl Beta Clb; Yrbk; Lit Mag; Trk; Hon Roll; Prfct Atten Awd; Ed.

HUFFMASTER, SUSAN; Russellville Sr HS; Russellville, AR; (2); Church Yth Grp; French Clb; Band; Church Choir; Flag Corp; Mrchg Band; Pep Band; NHS.

HUFFSTUTTER, ELIZABETH M; West Memphis Christian Schl; West Memphis, AR; (2); 1/24; Church Yth Grp; Natl Beta Clb; Quiz Bowl; VP Frsh Cls; Treas Soph Cls; Bsktbl; Chrldng; Sftbl; High Hon Roll; Pres Acad Fit Awd; Bus.

HUFFSTUTTER, PAUL J; West Memphis Christian Schl; West Memphis, AR; (4); Church Yth Grp; Cmnty Wkr; VP Frsh Cls; VP Jr Cls; Bsktbl; Ftbl; Golf; Hon Roll; Med Aprntcshp Pgm; Reg/ST Sci Fair Wnr; MS ST Univ; Ag Pest Mgmnt.

HUFFSTUTTLER, MOLLIE; Calvary Christian Schl; Colt, AR; (2); 1/20; Church Yth Grp; Church Choir; Treas Soph Cls; Var Chrldng; Var Vllybl; High Hon Roll; Prfct Atten Awd.

HUGHES, BRIAN T; Pulaski Acad; Little Rock, AR; (4); Am Leg Boys St; Church Yth Grp; Cmnty Wkr; FCA; Natl Beta Clb; VP Sr Cls; Var Bsbl; Var Ftbl; Cit Awd; High Hon Roll; Wheaton Col.

HUGHES, CHRISTOPHER L; Oak Grove HS; Maumelle, AR; (3); 7/140; Am Leg Boys St; Pres Church Yth Grp; Cmnty Wkr; French Clb; Mu Alpha Theta; Natl Beta Clb; Stage Crew; Pres Jr Cls; VP Pres Stu Cncl; High Hon Roll; DARE Role Model; HERO Anti Tobacco Campaign; Care Comm; Emory Univ; Pre-Med.

HUGHES, JARROD C; Waldron HS; Waldron, AR; (2); Drama Clb; Letterman Clb; Natl Beta Clb; Natl FFA Org; Spanish Clb; School Play; L Bsbl; L Ftbl; L Golf; L Trk; Math Awd.

HUGHES, JASON; Sylvan Hills HS; North Little Rock, AR; (4); 6/233; FCA; French Clb; Mu Alpha Theta; VP Natl Beta Clb; Acpl Chr; Rptr Yrbk; Var L Bsbl; Var L Bsktbl; Var L Ftbl; High Hon Roll; All Region Choir; All ST Choir; FCA Chmpn Awd; US Army Ath Schl; Wendy Heisman Awd Schl; AR ST Univ; Brdcst Comm.

HUGHES, JASON A; Catholic HS; Little Rock, AR; (3); 3/190; Am Leg Boys St; Church Yth Grp; Cmnty Wkr; Model UN; ROTC; Service Clb; Stage Crew; Rptr Nwsp; Rptr Yrbk; Rep Jr Cls; Expert Marksman; Women Marines Assn Outstndng Cadet Awd; Med.

HUGHES, JENNIFER; Magnolia HS; Magnolia, AR; (4); 20/207; Church Yth Grp; 4-H; Mu Alpha Theta; Natl FFA Org; Band; 4-H Awd; High Hon Roll; NHS; Pres Schlr; FFA Chptr Star Farmer; Farm Bus Mgt Distwnnr; FFA Livestock Showman; OK ST U; Agricultural Engrng.

HUGHES, KATHY R; Sheridan Sr HS; Sheridan, AR; (3); Cmnty Wkr; FHA; Teachers Aide; Chorus; Hon Roll; Jr NHS; Pres Acad Fit Awd; Ouachita Baptist Univ; Psych.

HUGHES, LA SHAY S; Northside HS; Fort Smith, AR; (4); Church Yth Grp; Drama Clb; FHA; Pep Clb; Spanish Clb; Teachers Aide; Band; Church Choir; Drill Tm; School Musical; Langston Univ; Phy Thrpst.

HUGHES, MARGARET; Oak Grove HS; Maumelle, AR; (2); Church Yth Grp; Cmnty Wkr; Drama Clb; English Clb; FCA; French Clb; FBLA; Yrbk; Rep Jr Cls; Jrnlsm.

HUGHES, MARSHALL R; Searcy HS; Searcy, AR; (3); 1/310; Am Leg Boys St; Pres FBLA; Key Clb; Natl Beta Clb; VP Frsh Cls; VP Soph Cls; VP Jr Cls; Rep Sr Cls; Pres Stu Cncl; NHS; U Of AR Fayetteville; Bus Adm.

HUGHES, RACHEL; Scranton HS; Scranton, AR; (3); Art Clb; FBLA; FHA; German Clb; Letterman Clb; Natl Beta Clb; Quiz Bowl; Var Bsktbl; Hon Roll; Comp Information Sci.

HUGHES, TARA; Gurdon HS; Gurdon, AR; (2); #8 in class; Church Yth Grp; Natl Beta Clb; Spanish Clb; Chorus; Church Choir; Rptr Nwsp; Chrldng; Tennis; High Hon Roll; U Of AR; Arch.

HUGHEY, LANCE; Gosnell Jr Sr HS; Blytheville, AR; (3); Church Yth Grp; Natl Beta Clb; Var Bsktbl; Hon Roll; Prfct Atten Awd.

HUGHEY, MILUS R; Southside HS; Batesville, AR; (2); Church Yth Grp; Key Clb; Office Aide; Guitar; Williams Baptist Coll; Music.

HULBERT, BERNADETTE M; Ozark HS; Ozark, AR; (3); SADD; Chorus; Yrbk; Sftbl; PT.

HULL, CHESSICA; Bryant Sr HS; Benton, AR; (4); 12/336; Church Yth Grp; FBLA; Spanish Clb; Teachers Aide; High Hon Roll; Hon Roll; Prfct Atten Awd; Chrstn Cncl; U Of Cntrl AR Univ Schlsp; Span Club Pres 95-; Art Awd 92-93; Sci Awd; U Of Cntrl AR; PT.

HULL, NATASSIA; Dover HS; Dover, AR; (1); Treas FBLA; Spanish Clb; JV Chrldng; Hon Roll; Jr NHS; GATE; AR Tech Univ; Dntstry.

HULLOWAY, BILL R; Mc Gehee HS; Mcgehee, AR; (2); Art Clb; Drama Clb; Science Clb; Spanish Clb; School Play; Bsktbl; Ftbl; Trk; Wt Lftg; Drama Awd; U Of AR; Trial Lwyr.

HULSEY, NICOLE; Lake Hamilton Sr HS; Hot Springs, AR; (4); Church Yth Grp; FCA; Library Aide; Natl Beta Clb; Pep Clb; Science Clb; Spanish Clb; Teachers Aide; School Play; Stage Crew; Marine Bio.

HUMMEL, MAUREEN K; Southside HS; Locust Grove, AR; (2); Church Yth Grp; Rptr Stu Cncl; Var Bsktbl; Var Trk; Hon Roll; Beta Clb; Dist Trk Meet 200m 1st; Phy Thrpst.

HUMPHREY, JENNIFER A; Russellville Sr HS; Russellville, AR; (3); 25/325; Church Yth Grp; Cmnty Wkr; Hosp Aide; Library Aide; Spanish Clb; Band; Orch; Capt Var Socr; High Hon Roll; Jr NHS; Amer Quarter Horse World Champ Qualifier 95; Harding Univ; Neurology.

HUMPHREY, NATHAN J; Lockesburg Jr Sr HS; Lockesburg, AR; (4); 3/26; FBLA; Library Aide; Quiz Bowl; Spanish Clb; Flag Corp; Ed Nwsp; Ed Yrbk; VP Sr Cls; High Hon Roll; Hon Roll; U AR Fyttvlle; Finance.

HUMPHRIES, HEATHER D; Salem HS; Sturkie, AR; (4); 8/41; FCA; Key Clb; Natl Beta Clb; Ed Nwsp; Phtg Yrbk; Rptr Jr Cls; Rep Sr Cls; Mgr(s); Sftbl; High Hon Roll; Coop Ed VP; AR ST U; Bus Mgmt.

HUMPHRIES, HEATHER M; Ft Smith Christian Schl; Van Buren, AR; (2); Church Yth Grp; FCA; FHA; Spanish Clb; Teachers Aide; Band; Chrldng; Gym; Hon Roll; NHS; Berkley CA; Ocngrphy/Psych.

HUMPHRIES, WILLIAM S; Parkers Chapel Schl; El Dorado, AR; (2); Church Yth Grp; French Clb; Natl Beta Clb; Bsktbl; Hon Roll.

HUNEYCUTT, SARA; Rogers HS; Lowell, AR; (3); Church Yth Grp; Drama Clb; FCA; FBLA; HOBY; Spanish Clb; Band; Co-Capt Drill Tm; U AR; Psych.

HUNJAN, HARJOT S; Hall Sr HS; Little Rock, AR; (4); 17/290; Natl Beta Clb; Pres Science Clb; Rep Nwsp; Pres Sr Cls; Rep Stu Cncl; L Golf; Var Tennis; Gov Hon Prg Awd; NHS; Drama Clb; Interact Clb Pres; Hendrix Coll; Bio; Medicine.

HUNNICUTT, JENNIFER M; Harmony Grove Jr Sr HS; Benton, AR; (2); French Clb; Science Clb; Chorus; School Play; Henderson; Nursing.

HUNNICUTT, SCOTT; Lavaca Jr Sr HS; Lavaca, AR; (2); Church Yth Grp; FCA; 4-H; Natl FFA Org; Church Choir; Bsktbl; Wt Lftg; Hon Roll; Prchr/Tchr.

HUNT, ADAM S; Corning HS; Corning, AR; (3); Church Yth Grp; Drama Clb; Natl FFA Org; Office Aide; Spanish Clb; Thesps; Ofcr Bsbl; Bsktbl; Ftbl; Trk; Pride.

HUNT, ASHLEY D; Lonoke Jr HS; Lonoke, AR; (1); 1/125; Church Yth Grp; Science Clb; Church Choir; Nwsp; Chrldng; Trk; High Hon Roll; NHS; Pres Acad Fit Awd; Outstndng Stu Of Yr Awd; Acad Excl Awd; Attnd AR Regnl Math Cont 96; General Practioner.

HUNT, BETH; Brookland Jr Sr HS; Brookland, AR; (3); Church Yth Grp; FCA; FBLA; Natl Beta Clb; Spanish Clb; Ofcr Stu Cncl; Bsktbl; Sftbl; Vllybl; Hon Roll; AR ST U; Phys Thrpy.

HUNT, CODY; Waldron HS; Waldron, AR; (4); 9/84; Am Leg Boys St; Church Yth Grp; 4-H; Natl Beta Clb; Quiz Bowl; Pres Spanish Clb; Band; Mrchg Band; Pep Band; Phtg Yrbk; AR Tech U; Lwyr.

HUNT, CONNIE MICHELLE; Central HS; West Helena, AR; (4); 8/195; Am Leg Aux Girls St; Church Yth Grp; Spanish Clb; Teachers Aide; Acpl Chr; Chorus; Church Choir; High Hon Roll; Hon Roll; Jr NHS; Upward Bound, Upward Bound Quiz Bowl; Acad Top 15 Hnrs; Conservation Clb; PRIDE; Trivium-Quadririum Sym; TN ST Univ; Chem; Pediatrician.

HUNT, GARY R; Ozark HS; Ozark, AR; (2); Drama Clb; Intnl Clb; Model UN; Scholastic Bowl; Chorus; Ofcr Stu Cncl; Bsktbl; GATE Prgm; Scl Stud Club; Schl Bd.

HUNT, JASON; Mt Ida Jr Sr HS; Sims, AR; (4); 4/31; Pres 4-H; Sec FBLA; HOBY; Library Aide; Pres Natl Beta Clb; Capt Quiz Bowl; Sec Treas Band; Jazz Band; Mrchg Band; Orch; Lyon Coll; Med.

HUNT, MARCUS D; Ridgecrest HS; Paragould, AR; (2); Boy Scts; Church Yth Grp; Band; Jazz Band; Pep Band; Hon Roll; Head Of Own Band; AR ST; Comp Tech; Rock Star.

HUNT, SCOSHA B; Lakeside HS; Dermott, AR; (3); 12/80; Sec Pres Drama Clb; Sec Hist FBLA; FHA; Speech Tm; School Play; Rptr Nwsp; Rep Jr Cls; Pres Sr Cls; Pres Stu Cncl; Hon Roll; Clwn Clb Pres; Pride Team; SAU Tech; Cmptrs.

HUNTER, JOEY L; Star City HS; Wilmar, AR; (2); 6/120; Math Clb; Mu Alpha Theta; Quiz Bowl; Hon Roll; AP Eng; Yrbk Staff; U Of AR; Engr; Acctng.

HUNTER, JUSTIN; Southside HS; Fort Smith, AR; (3); Church Yth Grp; FCA; French Clb; FBLA; Mu Alpha Theta; Church Choir; Bsktbl; Golf; Hon Roll; NHS; Partners In Christ Pres & VP.

HUNTER, KELLIE L; Lake Hamilton Sr HS; Hot Springs Natio, AR; (2); Church Yth Grp; FCA; FBLA; GAA; Pres Natl FFA Org; Science Clb; Spanish Clb; Church Choir; Bsktbl; Hon Roll; Wlf Prd Drg Free Prgm; SCL; Henderson ST Univ; Span Tchr.

HUNTER, KIMBERLEE; Lake Hamilton Sr HS; Royal, AR; (3); FBLA; Natl Beta Clb; Spanish Clb; Co-Ed Yrbk; Sec Frsh Cls; Sec Soph Cls; Sec Jr Cls; Rep Stu Cncl; NHS; Church Yth Grp; Optmst Awd; Garland Cty CC; RN.

HUNTER, LORI; Fayetteville Christian Schl; Stilwell, OK; (4); 4-H; Chorus; Church Choir; Yrbk; Bsktbl; Vllybl; 4-H Awd; Hon Roll; NHS; OK U; Bus.

HUNTER, REBECCA K; Northside HS; Barling, AR; (3); Computer Clb; French Clb; FBLA; Intnl Clb; Office Aide; ROTC; Cit Awd; French Hon Soc; High Hon Roll; Hon Roll; Westark; Nrsng.

HUNTINGTON, ELIZABETH M; Springdale Sr HS; Springdale, AR; (1); FBLA; Pep Clb; Teachers Aide; Chrldng; Gym; Hon Roll; Jr NHS.

HUNTON, MANDY; Farmington Jr Sr HS; Farmington, AR; (4); FBLA; FHA; Model UN; Office Aide; Treas Jr Cls; Treas Sr Cls; Chrldng; Powder Puff Ftbl; Sftbl; Hon Roll; U Of AR; Elem Ed.

HURDLE, MATT D; Weiner HS; Weiner, AR; (3); Church Yth Grp; Drama Clb; FBLA; Science Clb; Band; Church Choir; School Play; Hist Stu Cncl; JV L Bsktbl; Var Tennis; AEGIS Pgms; Comp Team; Bio.

HURST, JEFFERY D; Pleasant View Schl; Ozark, AR; (3); Drama Clb; FHA; Natl Beta Clb; Quiz Bowl; Spanish Clb; Rptr Nwsp; Ofcr Frsh Cls; Ofcr Stu Cncl; Gov Hon Prg Awd; Hon Roll; Bus Mgnt.

HURST, JOSEPH P; Van Buren Sr HS; Van Buren, AR; (2); 45/350; Church Yth Grp; FCA; Mu Alpha Theta; Church Choir; Ofcr Stu Cncl; Ftbl; Wt Lftg; Hon Roll; NHS; Prfct Atten Awd.

HURT, AARON; Devalls Bluff Jr Sr HS; Biscoe, AR; (3); 1/33; Drama Clb; French Clb; FBLA; FHA; HOBY; Key Clb; Library Aide; Natl Beta Clb; Quiz Bowl; School Play; U Cntrl AR; Phys Thrpy.

HURT, APRIL M; Sheridan Sr HS; North Little Rock, AR; (3); Church Yth Grp; Office Aide; Service Clb; Teachers Aide; Band; Mrchg Band; Rptr Ed Nwsp; Yrbk; Jr NHS; Pep Band; Yth Missions Trip Panama; Cntrl Bible Coll; Yth Ministry.

HURTADO, MONICA; Dumas Jr HS; Dumas, AR; (1); JA; Teachers Aide; Ofcr Frsh Cls; Hon Roll; Prfct Atten Awd; UCA; Phys Thrpy.

HUSKEY, AUDRA M; Cave City HS; Cave City, AR; (2); French Clb; Math Clb; Science Clb; Band; Chorus; Pep Band; High Hon Roll; Hon Roll.

HUSSAIN, RAZA; Pine Bluff HS; Pine Bluff, AR; (3); 30/481; Cmnty Wkr; French Clb; FBLA; Hosp Aide; Science Clb; Rptr Nwsp; JV Bsbl; JV Tennis; Hon Roll; Jr NHS; His Clb; AFS; Medicine.

HUTCHESON, TRESSA; Lead Hill Schl; Lead Hill, AR; (4); #1 in class; Church Yth Grp; FBLA; FHA; Girl Scts; Key Clb; Math Tm; Spanish Clb; Acpl Chr; Chorus; Church Choir; Cmnty Theatre Prod; U Of AR Fayetteville; Antrplgy.

HUTCHINSON, CAMILLE M; Lincoln HS; Lincoln, AR; (3); Debate Tm; FBLA; Key Clb; VP Natl Beta Clb; Rptr Natl FFA Org; Spanish Clb; Cit Awd; High Hon Roll; Math Clb; Drill Tm; AEGIS Cmp; Stu Cngrss; Intnl Law.

HUTCHISON, DORRIE R; Northside HS; Fort Smith, AR; (3); Church Yth Grp; Girl Scts; Hosp Aide; Sec Key Clb; Band; Mrchg Band; Var Vllybl; French Hon Soc; Jr NHS; French Clb; Outstdng Jr Musician Awd; Music Bus.

HUTCHISON, JAMACA; Newark Jr Sr HS; Newark, AR; (4); 6/41; Cmnty Wkr; FHA; Hosp Aide; Library Aide; Natl Beta Clb; Sec Natl FFA Org; Office Aide; Quiz Bowl; Red Cross Aide; Band; Henderson ST U; Phy Thrpst.

HUTCHISON, LORRIE E; Northside HS; Fort Smith, AR; (3); VP Church Yth Grp; Hosp Aide; Pres Key Clb; Chorus; Swing Chorus; Rep Stu Cncl; Chrldng; Hon Roll; Spanish NHS; Rep Frsh Cls; Jr Optimst.

HUTHMACHER, KERI S; Cabot HS; Cabot, AR; (2); Church Yth Grp; Library Aide; Rep Nwsp; Yrbk; Rep Lit Mag; Cit Awd; Hon Roll; U Of AR.

HUTSON, KIM; Murfreesboro HS; Murfreesboro, AR; (4); 8/37; FBLA; FHA; Natl Beta Clb; Sec Science Clb; Spanish Clb; Rep Frsh Cls; Rep Soph Cls; Sec Jr Cls; Sec Stu Cncl; Pres Acad Fit Awd; UCA; Mdcl Tech.

HUTSON, MELISSA; Mammoth Spring HS; Mammoth Spring, AR; (3); FBLA; Natl Beta Clb; Natl FFA Org; Quiz Bowl; Flag Corp; Rep Stu Cncl; Stat Bsktbl; Sftbl; NHS; Pres Acad Fit Awd; AR ST U; Crmnl Jstc.

HUTSON, PAUL N; White Hall Sr HS; Pine Bluff, AR; (4); Art Clb; Drama Clb; Math Clb; Natl Beta Clb; Office Aide; Science Clb; Spanish Clb; Teachers Aide; Ftbl; Hon Roll; U AR Little Rock; Bus.

HUTTO, MARCUS; South Side HS; Damascus, AR; (3); 3/31; Pres Church Yth Grp; Pres 4-H; French Clb; FBLA; HOBY; Natl Beta Clb; Natl FFA Org; Quiz Bowl; Band; School Play; Hist.

HUTTON, BECKY M; Southside HS; Fort Smith, AR; (4); Church Yth Grp; Cmnty Wkr; FCA; French Clb; Teachers Aide; Band; Mrchg Band; French Hon Soc; Gov Hon Prg Awd; Hon Roll; Elks Ldge Stu Mnth; Chrch Yth Grp Piano Accmpnst; Ouachita Bapt; Piano Prfrmnce.

HUYNH, AN T; Central Sr HS; Little Rock, AR; (3); 20/540; Hosp Aide; Sec VP Natl Beta Clb; Sec Spanish Clb; Yrbk; Lit Mag; High Hon Roll; NHS; Pres Acad Fit Awd; Art Clb; Cmnty Wkr; Piano 6 Yrs; Hnrs Reg/ST Sci Fairs; Hnrd Natl Span Exam.

HUYNH, ANNA N; Marked Tree Jr Sr HS; Marked Tree, AR; (2); 1/59; Art Clb; Church Yth Grp; Cmnty Wkr; FBLA; Library Aide; Natl Beta Clb; Quiz Bowl; ROTC; Color Guard; Drill Tm; AR Schl Math/Sci 96-; Bio/Geomtry/ROTC/ENG/SPAN Hghst Acad Achvmt; Drug Ed Fr Yth Pres.

HYDE, AMIE; Ridgecrest HS; Paragould, AR; (3); Art Clb; Computer Clb; FCA; FBLA; Church Choir; Stage Crew; Chrldng; Gym; Hon Roll; U AR; Elem Tchr.

HY-GAIL, ANGELA; Bryant Sr HS; Alexander, AR; (2); Church Yth Grp; Band; Color Guard; Drill Tm; Jazz Band; Mrchg Band; Pep Band; Var Sftbl; L Trk; NHS; First All ST Band Of AR; First All Region Bnd Region 5; Natl Adjudicators Invntnl 5th Pl; U Of Cntrl AR; Music.

HYMAN, GEORGIA C; West Memphis Christian Schl; Marion, AR; (3); Art Clb; Church Yth Grp; Cmnty Wkr; Drama Clb; Girl Scts; Math Clb; Mu Alpha Theta; Natl Beta Clb; Science Clb; Band; Advertsng.

IAMES, NIKKI L; Northside HS; Fort Smith, AR; (4); 18/350; Church Yth Grp; Drama Clb; Key Clb; Mu Alpha Theta; Pres Pep Clb; Thesps; Ofcr Sr Cls; VP Stu Cncl; NHS; Spanish NHS; Prin Ldrshp Awd; Westark CC; Phys Thrpy.

ICE, CLINTON S; Mountain Home HS; Mountain Home, AR; (3); CAP; Natl FFA Org; Office Aide; Band; Rappeling; Rock Climbing.

IMEL, PAUL D; Springdale Sr HS; Springdale, AR; (2); Church Yth Grp; High Hon Roll; Jr NHS; NHS; Prfct Atten Awd; Pres Acad Fit Awd; Epsilon Sigma Alpha Outstdng Yth Awd Fnlst; Chamber Of Commerce Acad Achvmt Awd; All-Region Choir.

IMMEL, SHANA L; Mc Crory Jr Sr HS; Mc Crory, AR; (3); Church Yth Grp; FBLA; Letterman Clb; Natl FFA Org; Spanish Clb; School Play; Chrldng; Powder Puff Ftbl; Sftbl; Tennis; Acad Exc Engl Awd; East AR CC; Law.

INEBNIT, KATIE; Lake Hamilton Sr HS; Hot Springs, AR; (2); Church Yth Grp; FCA; FBLA; Library Aide; Natl Beta Clb; Spanish Clb; Yrbk; Mgr(s); Hon Roll; Ntl Merit Ltr.

INFALT, APRIL; Hackett Schl; Hackett, AR; (4); 4/40; Pres Spanish Clb; Sec Frsh Cls; Sec Soph Cls; Sec Sr Cls; Pres Stu Cncl; Var L Bsktbl; Var Chrldng; Var L Sftbl; Hon Roll; Pres NHS; Westark JC; Scndry Educ.

INGLE, AMY D; Carlisle Jr Sr HS; Carlisle, AR; (3); 13/56; VP Church Yth Grp; Cmnty Wkr; Drama Clb; FHA; Office Aide; Spanish Clb; Teachers Aide; Church Choir; School Play; Stat Bsktbl; PRIDE Tm; Chem.

INGOLD, AMY; Lee Sr HS; Marianna, AR; (4); 13/102; Natl Beta Clb; Office Aide; Science Clb; VICA; Cit Awd; Hon Roll; Phillips Cty CC; Tchr.

INGRAHAM, DARRIN; Newport HS; Newport, AR; (3); Am Leg Boys St; Church Yth Grp; FBLA; FTA; JCL; SADD; Color Guard; Drill Tm; School Play; Stage Crew; Bible Clb Pres; U Of AR Fayettevl; Comp.

INGRAM, AMANDA; Vilonia HS; Conway, AR; (2); FBLA; Mu Alpha Theta; Natl Beta Clb; Spanish Clb; Band; Flag Corp; Mrchg Band; Pep Band; High Hon Roll; Med.

INGRAM, APRIL N; Gosnell Jr Sr HS; Blytheville, AR; (2); Church Yth Grp; Band; Flag Corp; Hon Roll; AR ST U; Med Lab.

INGRAM, CASEY; Camden Fairview HS; Camden, AR; (4); 40/243; Church Yth Grp; Natl Beta Clb; Office Aide; Church Choir; Yrbk; Var Chrldng; Hon Roll; Jr NHS; NHS; Piano 10 Yrs, Gold Cup Twice; Homcmng Maid; Concert Choir; Southern AR U Magnolia.

INMAN, AMANDA I; Batesville Sr HS; Batesville, AR; (2); Bsktbl; Sftbl; Trk; Hon Roll; All Dist & All ST Sftbl; LSU; Sftbl Bsktbl Coach.

INMAN, BRIANA D; Alma HS; Alma, AR; (3); Church Yth Grp; FCA; GAA; JV Var Bsktbl; JV Trk; JV Var Vllybl; Hon Roll; NHS; Prfct Atten Awd; Pres Acad Fit Awd; Westark; Bus.

INMAN, GEOFFREY R; Searcy HS; Kohler, WI; (3); 1/215; VP French Clb; FBLA; Natl Beta Clb; Quiz Bowl; JV Bsktbl; Var Socr; Var L Tennis; Gov Hon Prg Awd; NHS; Regnl Algebra II Cont Wnnr Qualified For ST; Natl Fr Cont ST Wnnr 5th In Nation; ST Rnnr Up; Engrng.

INMAN, JESSICA N; Southside HS; Batesville, AR; (1); 4/100; Sec 4-H; Hosp Aide; Key Clb; Natl Beta Clb; Band; Sec Stu Cncl; 4-H Awd; Hon Roll; Prfct Atten Awd; Science Clb; PRIDE; Sec/Rcptnst.

INMON, QUARTUS D; Marion HS; Marion, AR; (2); Computer Clb; FCA; 4-H; Ofcr Soph Cls; Ftbl; Wt Lftg; Cit Awd; WA U; Ftbl.

INSELL, CHRISTOPHER B; Batesville Sr HS; Desha, AR; (3); Church Yth Grp; Natl Beta Clb; Science Clb; Band; Chorus; Church Choir; Mrchg Band; Pep Band; School Musical; Mgr(s); Mssn Trp.

IRELAND, CHERONDA E; John L Mcclellan Magnet HS; Little Rock, AR; (2); Computer Clb; Dance Clb; FBLA; FHA; Math Clb; Natl Beta Clb; Spanish Clb; Chorus; Drill Tm; Yrbk; Peer Facilitators; Comp Technician.

IRIBARREN, KARA D; Prairie Grove HS; Prairie Grove, AR; (3); Drama Clb; FBLA; FHA; Band; Chorus; School Play; High Hon Roll; NHS; Indl Engr.

IRVIN, JAMEY W; Izard Co Cons Jr Sr HS; Violet Hill, AR; (3); 8/44; Natl Beta Clb; Natl FFA Org; Quiz Bowl; Spanish Clb; Var Bsbl; Var Bsktbl; Hon Roll.

IRWIN, JILL S; Central Sr HS; Little Rock, AR; (3); 11/540; Drama Clb; Mu Alpha Theta; Natl Beta Clb; VP Spanish Clb; School Musical; Yrbk; Cit Awd; High Hon Roll; Jr NHS; Pres NHS; Vtd Most Lkly To Sccd Frosh Yr; ACE Awd Otstndng Frosh; Dncd Little Rock Schl 15 Yrs; Piano 13 Yrs; U Of AR; Acct.

ISACKSEN, KATIE R; St Joe Public Schl; Saint Joe, AR; (1); Natl FFA Org; Bsktbl; Sftbl; High Hon Roll; Prfct Atten Awd; WET Tm; Envirothn Tm ST Comptn Wnnrs 96; Hrsbck Riding; Anml Sci.

ISOM, HEATHER M; Jonesboro HS; Jonesboro, AR; (3); FBLA; Rep German Clb; Quiz Bowl; VICA; Ed Nwsp; Ofcr Stu Cncl; JV Var Trk; Var Vllybl; High Hon Roll; Church Yth Grp; Jrnlsm Awd; Christmas For The Elderly Chm; Jrnlsm Reporter Editor Photo Bus Adv Mgr; AR ST U; Jrnlsm Or Law.

IVEY, AMANDA J; Lamar HS; Pottsville, AR; (2); Am Leg Aux Girls St; Cmnty Wkr; FCA; 4-H; VP Sec Natl FFA Org; Ofcr Stu Cncl; Cit Awd; 4-H Awd; High Hon Roll; Hon Roll; Natl FFA Awd; Star Frnhnd; Chptr Frmer ST Frmer; Livestock Judgeing Team; U Of AR; Ag Bus/Animal Sci.

IVEY, KEZIA KISH; Forrest City HS; Madison, AR; (4); 5/276; VP FTA; FBLA; FHA; JA; Mu Alpha Theta; Rptr Natl Beta Clb; Treas Science Clb; High Hon Roll; NHS; Ntl Merit Ltr; Prncpls Club; FHA Prlmntrn Team Chrmn; U Of Cntrl AR; Comp Sci.

IVEY, MARY; Warren Jr HS; Warren, AR; (1); 1/126; Natl Beta Clb; Band; Flag Corp; Jazz Band; Mrchg Band; High Hon Roll.

IVEY, MICHELL; Gosnell Jr Sr HS; Blytheville, AR; (4); 2/70; Am Leg Aux Girls St; Mu Alpha Theta; Natl Beta Clb; School Play; Nwsp; Ed Yrbk; Var Bsktbl; NHS; Pres Acad Fit Awd; Sal; U Of Cntrl AR; Gftd Ed.

IVY, CHRIS L; West Memphis Sr HS; West Memphis, AR; (3); FHA; Var Bsktbl; Hon Roll; AR ST.

IVY, CHRISTIE K; Weiner HS; Weiner, AR; (3); Art Clb; Drama Clb; English Clb; FBLA; FHA; Library Aide; Science Clb; SADD; Band; Chorus; Hist Hon Roll; Solo/Ensemble 2nd; Law.

IWATSURU, NIKKI J; Bismarck Jr-Sr HS; Amity, AR; (3); Rptr Nwsp; Hon Roll; Various ST Wrtng Hon; Schl AP Classes; AR ST Univ; Law.

IZQUIERDO, LAURA; Warren Sr HS; Warren, AR; (4); 1/223; Church Yth Grp; Cmnty Wkr; FBLA; Model UN; Natl Beta Clb; SADD; Tennis; NHS; Pres Acad Fit Awd; Val; Hall Of Fame; U Of AR; Acctng.

JABES, KIMBERLY D; Bald Knob HS; Bald Knob, AR; (2); Natl Beta Clb; Chorus; Hon Roll; Elem Tchg.

JACK, MADALYN; Bradley Jr Sr HS; Bradley, AR; (4); 3/24; Pres FBLA; HOBY; Quiz Bowl; Spanish Clb; Pres Sr Cls; High Hon Roll; Hon Roll; NHS; Outstndng Comp Acctng I Awd; SAU Yth Apprntcshp Pgm; 1st Pl Art Show Drwng; HOBY Ldrshp Smnr; SAU; Medcl.

JACKS, ASHLEY; Jack Robey Jr HS; Pine Bluff, AR; (1); Church Yth Grp; FCA; French Clb; Chorus; Variety Show; Rep Stu Cncl; Chrldng; Hon Roll; NHS; Mss Teen Pine Bluff 95; Mss Teen E Cntrl AR 1st Rnnr Up 95.

JACKSON, ANJANIKA; Lee Sr HS; Marianna, AR; (4); 17/102; 4-H; French Clb; FHA; FTA; Natl Beta Clb; Natl FFA Org; Nwsp; Hon Roll; Ntl Merit Ltr; Prfct Atten Awd; Southern AR U Magnolia; Comp.

JACKSON, ANTONIO; Holly Grove HS; Holly Grove, AR; (4); Cmnty Wkr; 4-H; German Clb; Var Bsktbl; Var Trk; AR Star Events Silver Medal; FHA Most Outstdng Stu 95-96; Mary Holmes; Commnctn; Brodcstng.

JACKSON, ASHLEY; Mc Rae Schl; Mc Rae, AR; (4); 2/23; Church Yth Grp; Cmnty Wkr; FCA; FBLA; Natl Beta Clb; Natl FFA Org; Office Aide; SADD; Ofcr Stu Cncl; Bsktbl; UCA; Ed.

JACKSON, BENJAMIN E; Mansfield Jr Sr HS; Booneville, AR; (3); Art Clb; 4-H; Intnl Clb; Natl Beta Clb; Natl FFA Org; Band; Pep Band; Ftbl; Cit Awd; 4-H Awd; FFA Dist Pres 96-97, St Degree 96, Chptr Degree 95, Star Greenhand 94; Upward Bound Carl Albert Coll; Comp Tech.

JACKSON, BILLY; Sulphur Rock Schl; Sulphur Rock, AR; (2); 5/22; Nwsp; Sec Treas Soph Cls; Natl FFA Org; Hon Roll; Prfct Atten Awd; Natl Engl Mrt Awd; Auto Mechnc.

JACKSON, BRIAN C; Eudora HS; Eudora, AR; (2); 1/100; FBLA; FHA; HOBY; Natl Beta Clb; Quiz Bowl; SADD; Band; Church Choir; Mrchg Band; Rep Frsh Cls; Morehouse Univ; Pre-Med.

JACKSON, CHARLES J; Sheridan Sr HS; Sheridan, AR; (3); Church Yth Grp; Church Choir; School Play; JV Bsktbl; Var Ftbl; Cit Awd; Hon Roll; Jr NHS; Kiwanis Awd; NHS.

JACKSON, CHICKETTA L; Conway Sr HS; Conway, AR; (4); 52/520; Church Yth Grp; French Clb; FBLA; Natl Beta Clb; Office Aide; Science Clb; Band; Mrchg Band; French Hon Soc; Hon Roll; U Of Cntrl AR; Bus.

JACKSON, CHRISTINA B; Lakeside HS; Hot Springs, AR; (3); French Clb; FBLA; Natl Beta Clb; VP Science Clb; Ed Yrbk; High Hon Roll; NHS; Treas Church Yth Grp; Math Clb; Office Aide; WET; All Region III Band; Amer Natl Teen Ager Schlsp Pgm & Pageant.

JACKSON, CHRISY; Forrest City HS; Forrest City, AR; (4); High Hon Roll; Hon Roll; AR ST Univ.

JACKSON, CLIFTON A; Mc Gehee HS; Dermott, AR; (4); 12/96; Art Clb; FHA; FTA; Mu Alpha Theta; Natl Beta Clb; Spanish Clb; Bsktbl; Trk; U Of A Fayetteville; Engrng.

JACKSON, DANIEL C; St Joseph HS; Conway, AR; (1); Church Yth Grp; Teachers Aide; School Play; Stage Crew; Hon Roll; Jr NHS; NHS; Toadsuck Car Clb; Engr.

JACKSON, DARLENE; Hermitage Jr Sr HS; Hermitage, AR; (3); 1/32; Church Yth Grp; French Clb; Sec FBLA; FTA; HOBY; Quiz Bowl; Band; Church Choir; Ed Nwsp; Sec Stu Cncl; AR ST U; Law.

JACKSON, DAVID; Hermitage Jr Sr HS; Hermitage, AR; (2); 1/65; Church Yth Grp; Natl Beta Clb; Natl FFA Org; Quiz Bowl; Ofcr Bsbl; Ftbl; High Hon Roll; Prfct Atten Awd; Outstndng Svc Awd; Sportsmnshp Awd; Depication Awd; U Of AR Fayetteville; Sci.

JACKSON II, DENNIS D; Parkview HS; Jacksonville, AR; (2); Chess Clb; Church Yth Grp; Debate Tm; FBLA; Key Clb; Natl Beta Clb; Quiz Bowl; JV Var Bsbl; Golf; High Hon Roll; Amer Legion Bsbl.

JACKSON, DONNY R; Southside HS; Batesville, AR; (2); FHA; Key Clb; Spanish Clb; Bsktbl.

JACKSON, GINA; Pine Bluff HS; Pine Bluff, AR; (4); 32/410; Church Yth Grp; Rptr DECA; Drama Clb; Key Clb; Natl Beta Clb; Spanish Clb; Chorus; Co-Ed Chrldng; Hon Roll; NHS; U Of AR Fayetteville; Phrmcy.

JACKSON, HEATHER M; Benton Cty Christian School; Pineville, MO; (3); Church Yth Grp; Teachers Aide; Church Choir; School Musical; School Play; Pres Rep Soph Cls; JV Chrldng; Vllybl; High Hon Roll; Hon Roll; Highest GPA Wrld Hstry Fresh Yr; Phys Thrpy.

JACKSON, JAMIE; Cord-Charlotte Schl; Batesville, AR; (3); Pres VP FHA; HOBY; Natl Beta Clb; Chorus; Co-Ed Yrbk; Pres Soph Cls; Sec Jr Cls; Var JV Bsktbl; Sftbl; Hon Roll; Kndrgrtn Tchrs Aid; Erly Chldhd Ed.

JACKSON, JAMIE; Nashville HS; Nashville, AR; (3); Am Leg Aux Girls St; Church Yth Grp; 4-H; FHA; Band; Chorus; Color Guard; Drm Mjr(t); Flag Corp; Mrchg Band; Natl Famly Partnrshp Of AR St Yth Bd; Attrny Gen Suicd Prevntn Stu Advy; FHA St Exec & Pub Rel VP; Coachita ST Univ.

JACKSON, JASON; Augusta HS; Augusta, AR; (1); Church Yth Grp; FBLA; FTA; Natl Beta Clb; Teachers Aide; Ofcr Frsh Cls; Pres Stu Cncl; Capt Bsktbl; Capt Ftbl; Trk.

JACKSON, JENNIFER R; Walnut Valley Chrstn Acad; Little Rock, AR; (4); 1/6; Church Yth Grp; Drama Clb; Natl Beta Clb; School Play; Yrbk; Sec Stu Cncl; Var L Bsktbl; Var Sftbl; Var Vllybl; Hon Roll; Bio.

JACKSON, KAREN R; Taylor HS; Taylor, AR; (2); 2/23; Church Yth Grp; Natl FFA Org; Sec Frsh Cls; Rep Soph Cls; VP Jr Cls; Rep Stu Cncl; Bsktbl; Hon Roll; FCA; 4-H; SAU; Med Sci.

JACKSON, KATIE D; Searcy HS; Searcy, AR; (3); 30/220; Am Leg Aux Girls St; Church Yth Grp; Cmnty Wkr; Dance Clb; FCA; FBLA; FTA; Key Clb; Natl Beta Clb; Office Aide; All Star Chrldng Sqd; Fair Queen Contestant; U Of MS; OT.

JACKSON, KENDRICK D; Mc Crory Jr Sr HS; Mc Crory, AR; (4); Church Yth Grp; Letterman Clb; Office Aide; Spanish Clb; SADD; Varsity Clb; Chorus; Church Choir; School Musical; School Play; Southern AR Univ; Pre-Med.

JACKSON, KESHIA L; Crossett Sr HS; Crossett, AR; (3); 48/190; Treas Art Clb; Church Yth Grp; Drama Clb; Math Clb; Science Clb; Spanish Clb; Speech Tm; Band; Church Choir; Drill Tm; Hnrs Eng; Jackson ST U; Psych/Dsgn Engr.

JACKSON JR, LE ROY D; Marvell HS; Marvell, AR; (4); 7/40; Church Yth Grp; French Clb; FBLA; FTA; Natl Beta Clb; Office Aide; Capt Quiz Bowl; Spanish Clb; Teachers Aide; School Play; Natl Frnch Hon Soc Pres; Phillips Cnty CC Upward Bnd Prgrm Pres; Apostlc Live Cntr Ch Piano/Drums; AK ST Univ; Cmptr Sci.

JACKSON, LLOYD D; Arkansas Sr HS; Texarkana, TX; (2); Church Yth Grp; Chorus; Church Choir; Rep Frsh Cls; Treas Soph Cls; JV Ftbl; Cit Awd; Hon Roll; Pres Schlr; Ray A Krog Awd; Red Rvr Cncl Prvnt Rsrce Ctr Vol, Explr Pst Pres; Chrl Music.

JACKSON, MARTHA L; Searcy HS; Searcy, AR; (3); Am Leg Aux Girls St; Church Yth Grp; VP FCA; FBLA; Sec Pres Key Clb; Natl Beta Clb; Spanish Clb; Sec Soph Cls; VP Jr Cls; Sec Stu Cncl; U Of AR Fayetteville.

JACKSON, MARY ANN; Mt St Mary Acad; Little Rock, AR; (4); Cmnty Wkr; Hosp Aide; HOBY; Model UN; Office Aide; Teachers Aide; Hon Roll; NHS; Art Clb; VP Church Yth Grp; AEGIS Intl Stds; Gov Yth Conf Cnslr; Univ Cntrl AR; Physc Thrpy.

JACKSON, MARY E; Rogers HS; Lowell, AR; (2); Church Yth Grp; FCA; FBLA; High Hon Roll; Rogers Renaissance; U Of MI; Law.

JACKSON, MELANIE D; Mills HS; Little Rock, AR; (3); 68/298; FBLA; Latin Clb; Temple Yth Grp; Sftbl; Jr Cabinet; St Vincent; Radiolgy.

JACKSON, MIRANDA J; Sloan Hendrix HS; Imboden, AR; (4); Art Clb; FBLA; FHA; FTA; Natl Beta Clb; Natl FFA Org; Pep Clb; Sftbl; Hon Roll; Black River Votech.

JACKSON II, PHILLIP J; Marvell Acad; Holly Grove, AR; (2); Sec Frsh Cls; Pres Soph Cls; Boy Scts; Spanish Clb; L Bsktbl; L Ftbl; L Trk; Hon Roll; Jr NHS; NHS.

JACKSON, QUARTORIA L; Dumas HS; Dumas, AR; (2); Church Yth Grp; FCA; FBLA; Natl Beta Clb; Science Clb; L Bsktbl; JV Ftbl; Var Trk; NHS; Ntl Merit Ltr; Comp Tech.

JACKSON, RESHA; Elaine Jr Sr HS; Crumrod, AR; (3); 1/37; Cmnty Wkr; 4-H; Girl Scts; Drill Tm; Rep Sec Stu Cncl; L Bsktbl; L Chrldng; Cit Awd; Hon Roll; Prfct Atten Awd; Global Stds Clb Pres; Stu Mon; Prom Cmmtte; Omega Little Brother Hnr Awd; TOYS; U AR Pine Bluff; Bus Exec.

JACKSON, RUSTY D; Delight HS; Delight, AR; (2); FBLA; Natl Beta Clb; Natl FFA Org; Ofcr Bsbl; Bsktbl.

JACKSON, SHANTELL L; Tuckerman HS; Tuckerman, AR; (2); Church Yth Grp; FBLA; GAA; Natl Beta Clb; Spanish Clb; Chorus; Church Choir; Variety Show; Ofcr Stu Cncl; Bsktbl; AR ST Univ; RT.

JACKSON, STEFANIE; Murfreesboro HS; Murfreesboro, AR; (4); 1/37; Church Yth Grp; FBLA; FHA; Natl Beta Clb; Quiz Bowl; Church Choir; Chrldng; High Hon Roll; Pres Acad Fit Awd; Val; Peer Cnslng; Danforth Achvt Awd; CHAMPS; Hendrix Coll; Med.

JACKSON, STEPHANIE; Gentry HS; Gentry, AR; (3); Church Yth Grp; FCA; FBLA; HOBY; Spanish Clb; Treas Frsh Cls; Treas Soph Cls; Bsktbl; Sftbl; NHS; Pride Team; Prncpls Hnr Roll.

JACKSON, STEPHANIE M; Lake Hamilton Sr HS; Hot Springs, AR; (3); 32/300; FCA; German Clb; Natl Beta Clb; Var JV Bsktbl; Var Sftbl; Var Vllybl; Hon Roll; Prfct Atten Awd; Woodmn Of World; Vlybl All-St & All-Trnmt Teams; Nursng.

JACKSON, TANNER G; Central Sr HS; Little Rock, AR; (2); 44/504; Church Yth Grp; Natl Beta Clb; Spanish Clb; Church Choir; Var JV Tennis; High Hon Roll; Hon Roll; NHS; Church Mscl; Rep Sr HS Church Yth Cncl; Vet Med/Psych.

JACKSON, TASALON S; John L Mcclellan Magnet HS; Little Rock, AR; (2); 3/10; Dance Clb; FHA; Pep Clb; Spanish Clb; Acpl Chr; Drill Tm; Swing Chorus; Variety Show; Pom Pon; Cit Awd; UCA; Nrsng; Comp Technician.

JACKSON, TIFFANY D; Parkview Arts-Science HS; Little Rock, AR; (2); Church Yth Grp; FCA; 4-H; FBLA; FTA; Natl Beta Clb; Teachers Aide; Drill Tm; Pres Stu Cncl; Hon Roll; Prins Awd; Odyssey Of Mind; U Of AR; Cmptr Prgmr.

JACKSON, TIFFANY L; Yellville Summit HS; Yellville, AR; (2); Church Yth Grp; Cmnty Wkr; FCA; FBLA; HOBY; Teachers Aide; Yrbk; Var Bsktbl; Var Sftbl; Cit Awd; Dist VI FBLA Treas.

JACKSON, TIFFANY P; Hope HS; Hope, AR; (3); Church Yth Grp; Natl Beta Clb; Band; Color Guard; Mrchg Band; High Hon Roll; Hon Roll; U Of AR; Speech Path.

JACKSON, TONYA A; Mc Crory Jr Sr HS; Mc Crory, AR; (3); FBLA; FTA; Letterman Clb; Treas Spanish Clb; School Play; L Bsktbl; Powder Puff Ftbl; L Tennis; L Trk; NHS; Harding Univ; PT.

JACKSON, WILLIAM GREGORY; Dewitt HS; De Witt, AR; (1); Hon Roll; Ntl Merit Ltr.

JACKSON MC GHE, CARL C; Rison HS; Rison, AR; (3); #28 in class; Art Clb; Library Aide; Teachers Aide; Band; Church Choir; Mrchg Band; Ofcr Frsh Cls; Ofcr Stu Cncl; Ofcr Bsbl; Bsktbl; U Of AR; Law.

JACOBS, ERIN N; Russellville Sr HS; Russellville, AR; (3); Art Clb; Jr NHS; NHS; Ped.

JACOBS, STANTON; Omaha Schl; Omaha, AR; (3); Quiz Bowl; VICA; Stage Crew; Yrbk; Ofcr Stu Cncl; Bsktbl.

JACOBY, CHRISTINE; Farmington Jr Sr HS; Farmington, AR; (4); Church Yth Grp; FCA; FBLA; FHA; Model UN; SADD; Teachers Aide; Bsktbl; Sftbl; High Hon Roll; Miss Teen Of America Schlrshp/Recgntn Pgnt; U Of AR Fayettevl; Ed.

JAEGERMAN, JANEVA D; Junction City HS; Junction City, AR; (1); Church Yth Grp; English Clb; Spanish Clb; Teachers Aide; Church Choir; School Play; Ofcr Frsh Cls; Powder Puff Ftbl; Hon Roll; BASIC; Sci Clb.

JAHAN, SHORMI S; Pine Bluff HS; Pine Bluff, AR; (3); Am Leg Aux Girls St; Sec Church Yth Grp; Model UN; Natl Beta Clb; Science Clb; Ed Nwsp; Cit Awd; High Hon Roll; NHS; Key Clb; Amer Field Svc Clb; U Central AR; Bio.

JAKES, NIKISHA; Central HS; West Helena, AR; (3); Church Yth Grp; Spanish Clb; Acpl Chr; Chorus; Church Choir; Chrldng; Tennis; Hon Roll; Chrldng Capt; UA Little Rock; Crimnl Law.

JAKUS, CHRISTINA H; Sheridan Sr HS; Sheridan, AR; (4); 56/212; Church Yth Grp; Chorus; Church Choir; Lit Mag; Hon Roll; GCE; DAYA Jr Mbr; Chldrns Outreach; Performance/Ldrshp Schlrsp; U Of AR; Ed/Schl Cnslr.

JAMES, AMANDA J; Bryant HS; Benton, AR; (3); 62/354; Church Yth Grp; FBLA; Spanish Clb; JV Var Bsktbl; JV Var Vllybl; Hon Roll; Children Of Amer Revolution; Sftbl League; AR ST U; Optomitry.

JAMES, CARRIE R; Pulaski Acad; Little Rock, AR; (2); Church Yth Grp; Cmnty Wkr; Key Clb; Natl Beta Clb; Spanish Clb; Orch; School Play; Cit Awd; Hon Roll; Jr NHS; Archaeology.

JAMES, CHRISTINA M; Sylvan Hills HS; North Little Rock, AR; (3); Art Clb; Pres Church Yth Grp; FBLA; Sec Acpl Chr; Swing Chorus; Score Keeper; Var Vllybl; Hon Roll; BASIC; Ed.

JAMES, DAVID W; Huntsville HS; Huntsville, AR; (3); 4/115; Church Yth Grp; FCA; Intnl Clb; Band; Jazz Band; Pep Band; Ofcr FBLA; Ofcr Soph Cls; Ofcr Jr Cls; L Bsbl; Odyssey Mind Team.

JAMES, DON K; Gillett Jr Sr HS; Gillett, AR; (4); 3/20; Am Leg Boys St; Church Yth Grp; FBLA; GAA; Office Aide; Red Cross Aide; Temple Yth Grp; School Play; Yrbk; Ofcr Bsbl; Bob Cover Awd-Best Team Mate; Natl Ftbl Fndtn & Coll Hall Of Fame; Henderson ST Coll; Aviation.

JAMES, JASON D; Mt Ida Jr Sr HS; Story, AR; (3); 5/30; FBLA; Natl Beta Clb; Band; Jazz Band; Mrchg Band; Treas Sr Cls; Rep Stu Cncl; Bsktbl; Ftbl; High Hon Roll; U Of AR Little Rock; Law.

JAMES, JOSH J; Nettleton HS; Jonesboro, AR; (3); Am Leg Boys St; Church Yth Grp; FCA; FBLA; Math Clb; Teachers Aide; Bsktbl; Ftbl; Trk; Wt Lftg; U Of AR; Sprtsmed.

JAMES, KRISTI S; Newport HS; Newport, AR; (3); 12/133; Am Leg Aux Girls St; Church Yth Grp; JCL; Q&S; Spanish Clb; Mgr Drill Tm; School Play; Co-Ed Nwsp; Yrbk; Mgr(s); Elem Ed.

JAMES, KURT; Gillett Jr Sr HS; Gillett, AR; (4); 3/20; Am Leg Boys St; Church Yth Grp; FBLA; German Clb; Quiz Bowl; School Play; Yrbk; Ftbl; High Hon Roll; NHS; Bob Cover Best Team Mate Awd; Henderson ST U; Aviation.

JAMES, LEAH; Northside HS; Fort Smith, AR; (1); Drama Clb; Key Clb; Speech Tm; Mrchg Band; School Play; Ofcr Frsh Cls; Chrldng; Trk; Cit Awd; 4-H Awd.

JAMES, OLAN C; Northside HS; Fort Smith, AR; (3); Drama Clb; Key Clb; Spanish Clb; Thesps; Band; Jazz Band; Mrchg Band; School Play; Ofcr Soph Cls; Ofcr Jr Cls; Sebastain Cty Yng Demcrts; Jr Optmst Club; Grizzly Pride; Comm.

JAMES, RENEE D; Dequeen HS; De Queen, AR; (2); 49/115; Church Yth Grp; FBLA; FHA; FTA; Natl FFA Org; Office Aide; Rep SADD; Chorus; All Region Choir; Harding Univ; Tchr.

JAMES, RYAN M; Huntsville HS; Hindsville, AR; (4); Am Leg Boys St; 4-H; Natl FFA Org; Quiz Bowl; Band; Mrchg Band; Pep Band; Rep Jr Cls; Rep Sr Cls; Ofcr Stu Cncl; U Of AR; Poultry Sci.

JAMES, STEPHANIE L; Dollarway HS; Pine Bluff, AR; (2); Church Yth Grp; Cmnty Wkr; FHA; GAA; ROTC; Church Choir; Lit Mag; Ofcr Frsh Cls; Bsktbl; Score Keeper; TN MSU; Commnctn.

JAMES, TAMI J; Fountain Lake Jr Sr HS; Lonsdale, AR; (3); 36/84; FCA; Key Clb; Spanish Clb; Mrchg Band; Nwsp; Yrbk; Var Bsktbl; Jr Maid Bsktbl Hmcmng.

JAMESON, AMANDA; Magnolia HS; Magnolia, AR; (4); 50/205; Church Yth Grp; Mu Alpha Theta; Band; Church Choir; Mrchg Band; Yrbk; Hon Roll; NHS; FBLA; Science Clb; Outstdng Stu Awd In Band; Chrch Musical-Play; Southern AR Univ.

JAMESON, ERIN R; Huntsville HS; Huntsville, AR; (3); 12/128; Church Yth Grp; FCA; GAA; Key Clb; Office Aide; Science Clb; Var Capt Bsktbl; L Trk; Cit Awd; High Hon Roll; Phys Thrpy.

JAMIESON, CARA; Hughes Jr-Sr HS; Hughes, AR; (1); Church Yth Grp; Debate Tm; Math Clb; Natl Beta Clb; Science Clb; Band; Color Guard; Drill Tm; Mrchg Band; School Musical; ASU; Lwyr.

JANES, TERI; Gosnell Jr Sr HS; Blytheville, AR; (3); #6 in class; Spanish Clb; Teachers Aide; Chorus; Yrbk; Powder Puff Ftbl; High Hon Roll; Natl Hstry & Govt Awd; Cotton Boll Tech Ins; LPN.

JANSEN, JOHN A; Greenwood Sr HS; Fort Smith, AR; (3); Art Clb; Church Yth Grp; Computer Clb; Spanish Clb; Teachers Aide; Bsktbl; Hon Roll; NHS; U Of AR; Engrng.

JANSEN, MICHAEL R; Catholic HS; Sherwood, AR; (2); 2/200; Church Yth Grp; Latin Clb; Math Tm; Var Capt Bsktbl; High Hon Roll; Cntrl AR Chargers Yth Org; NLR Boys & Girls Clb; Keystone Clb; Yth Connection; TX A&M; Chemical Engrng.

JARNAGAN, KRISTI L; Decatur HS; Gentry, AR; (2); Church Yth Grp; Dance Clb; FHA; JV Var Bsbl; JV Var Bsktbl; JV Chrldng; Gym; JV Score Keeper; JV Var Hon Roll; Northeastern OK; Law.

JARRELL, ANTHONY SHAWN; Oak Grove HS; Maumelle, AR; (1); 5/100; Church Yth Grp; Cmnty Wkr; Natl Beta Clb; High Hon Roll; Hon Roll; 2nd In Cls Span I; CO; Lawyer.

JARRELL, CHRISTOPHER S; Oak Grove HS; Maumelle, AR; (2); Boy Scts; Church Yth Grp; Cmnty Wkr; Drama Clb; Temple Yth Grp; School Play; Stage Crew; Hon Roll; Prfct Atten Awd; Scuba Diving Cerftd; Tae Kwon Do; Running; Jogging; Annapolis Naval Acad; Navy Seal.

JARRELL, KELLY L; Southside HS; Fort Smith, AR; (3); Am Leg Aux Girls St; Church Yth Grp; Debate Tm; FCA; Quiz Bowl; Spanish Clb; Acpl Chr; Var Bsbl; L Var Gym; Pres Acad Fit Awd; Intnl Bus.

JARRETT, ADRIENNE; Lee Sr HS; Marianna, AR; (1); #4 in class; Cmnty Wkr; 4-H; French Clb; Church Choir; Sec Frsh Cls; High Hon Roll; Hon Roll; Prfct Atten Awd; Pundital Hi Dreamers:YEW; MWA.

JARRETT, SUSAN; Marion Co Rural Schl; Saint Joe, AR; (4); 4/19; FHA; Spanish Clb; Band; Pep Band; School Play; Cit Awd; Hon Roll; NHS; North AR Comm & Tech Coll.

JASMIN, AUBREY N; Mena HS; Mena, AR; (1); Church Yth Grp; Cmnty Wkr; FBLA; Band; Church Choir; Drm Mjr(t); Mrchg Band; Hon Roll; 4-H; Girls Ath; Hon Roll; U Of AK; Pre-Med.

JAYNES, JASPER L; Trumann HS; Trumann, AR; (3); Var Ftbl; JV Trk; Var Wt Lftg; Pres Acad Fit Awd; AR Spinal Cord Injury Commission Peer Cnslt; Reach For A Star Personal Achvmt Awd 95; AR ST Univ; Physical Thrpst.

JEAN, MATTHEW C; Magnolia HS; Magnolia, AR; (4); 50/210; Am Leg Boys St; Art Clb; Boy Scts; FBLA; Natl FFA Org; Capt Quiz Bowl; Science Clb; Nwsp; VP Frsh Cls; Hon Roll; St Legislative Page; AR ST U.

JEANICE, LAWLER R; Blevins HS; Blevins, AR; (2); Church Yth Grp; Natl Beta Clb; Yrbk; Ofcr Stu Cncl; Bsktbl; Chrldng; Sftbl; Hon Roll; Capt, Co-Capt; Med.

JEFFERIS, LEAH M; Booneville Jr Sr HS; Booneville, AR; (4); FBLA; FTA; Spanish Clb; Band; Pres Chorus; Mrchg Band; Pep Band; Hon Roll; AR ST Univ; Tchr.

JEFFERS, MAURICE; Morrilton Sr HS; Morrilton, AR; (3); 21/223; French Clb; Natl Beta Clb; Var Bsktbl; Hon Roll; Bsktbl All Conf, All St.

JEFFERSON, BRITTANY E; Searcy HS; Searcy, AR; (4); 30/201; Church Yth Grp; Cmnty Wkr; FCA; Girl Scts; JA; Library Aide; Pep Clb; Spanish Clb; SADD; Teachers Aide; Natl BETA Clb; Hnr Grad; Badminton Championship; ASU; Med Tech.

JEFFERSON, OCTAVIA T; Blytheville Sr HS; Blytheville, AR; (4); 30/230; Am Leg Aux Girls St; Church Yth Grp; Natl Beta Clb; Chorus; Church Choir; Cit Awd; High Hon Roll; Hon Roll; NHS; Pres Acad Fit Awd; U AR Pine Bluff; Nrs.

JEFFERSON, TAWALA R; Huttig Schl; Huttig, AR; (3); 1/26; Church Yth Grp; FBLA; FTA; Natl Beta Clb; Band; Chorus; Church Choir; Nwsp; Ofcr Stu Cncl; Hon Roll; Sngng; All Regn Chr; Acctng.

JEFFERSON, TEHRELL H; Hall Sr HS; Little Rock, AR; (2); Church Yth Grp; French Clb; Band; Church Choir; Jazz Band; Mrchg Band; School Musical; Ftbl; Bus Law; Mrktg.

JEFFERSON, TONITA L; Huttig Schl; Huttig, AR; (2); 1/26; Church Yth Grp; FBLA; FTA; Natl Beta Clb; Science Clb; Band; Chorus; Church Choir; Rptr Nwsp; Hon Roll; GATE; All Rgn Choir 94-; UCLA; Law/Psych.

JEFFERSON, YOLANDA MICHELLE; North Little Rock Hs-East; North Little Rock, AR; (2); Dance Clb; FCA; Library Aide; Office Aide; Varsity Clb; Drill Tm; Chrldng; L Pom Pon; Powder Puff Ftbl; Vllybl; Hnrbl Mntn Vlybl; Drl Tm Capt/Ltr; Lwyr.

JEFFESON, JAMES A; Huttig Schl; Huttig, AR; (2); German Clb; Varsity Clb; VP Frsh Cls; Ofcr Bsbl; Bsktbl; High Hon Roll; Hon Roll.

JEFFREY, CARMA; Newark Jr Sr HS; Newark, AR; (3); 13/52; Church Yth Grp; Pres 4-H; FHA; HOBY; Natl FFA Org; Pres Frsh Cls; Rep Soph Cls; Sec Jr Cls; VP 4-H Awd; Hon Roll; Pride; Reg, St, Cty & Dist Lvstck Jdgng Wnnr; 4-H Pres; U Of AR; Agri-Bus.

JEFFUS, BETSY; Fairview HS; Camden, AR; (4); 1/150; Am Leg Aux Girls St; Mu Alpha Theta; Natl Beta Clb; Spanish Clb; Acpl Chr; Band; NHS; Spanish NHS; Val; Majorette; U Of Centr AR; Pharm.

JENKINS, AMANDA; Calico Rock HS; Calico Rock, AR; (3); 1/35; Am Leg Aux Girls St; Church Yth Grp; FBLA; FHA; Science Clb; SADD; Band; Treas Jr Cls; Sftbl; Prfct Atten Awd; AR ST Univ; Vet Medicine.

JENKINS, DELICIA M; Conway Sr HS; Collierville, TN; (4); 90/524; Church Yth Grp; Cmnty Wkr; VP FBLA; Natl Beta Clb; Office Aide; Pres Spanish Clb; Teachers Aide; Chorus; Church Choir; Nwsp; Hnr Grad Conway HS Class Of 96; Natl Vo Tech Hnr Scty; Multi Yr Listee; OH St Univ; Bus Admin.

JENKINS, ELIZABETH D; Central Sr HS; Little Rock, AR; (2); Church Yth Grp; FBLA; Hosp Aide; Pep Clb; ROTC; Teachers Aide; Church Choir; Drill Tm; Cit Awd; Hon Roll; Stdnt Of Month; Skating; Singing Church Choir St Thomas Meml Bapt Church; UCA; PT/CMPTR Tech.

JENKINS, EVA; Calico Rock HS; Calico Rock, AR; (4); 1/32; FCA; FBLA; Natl Beta Clb; Science Clb; SADD; Yrbk; VP Stu Cncl; Var Bsktbl; Val; Pres Acad Fit Awd; Sftbl; Govrnrs Schl AR; U Of Cntrl AR.

JENKINS, JEFF B; Central Ark Christian Schl; Little Rock, AR; (2); Art Clb; French Clb; Science Clb; Teachers Aide; JV Bsktbl; JV Ftbl; Hon Roll; Ntl Merit Ltr; Hist Club; FL ST Univ; Bus Admin.

JENKINS, TIMOTHY R; Arkansas Schl For Math And Sci; Maumelle, AR; (3); Computer Clb; Math Tm; Science Clb; Band; Stage Crew; Hon Roll; Ntl Merit Ltr; Frgn Lang Awd; Cmptr Prgrmmr.

JENKINS, VERONICA D; Central Sr HS; Little Rock, AR; (3); FBLA; Hosp Aide; Natl Beta Clb; Pep Clb; Spanish Clb; Band; Church Choir; Mrchg Band; Treas Sr Cls; Cit Awd; Clarke Atlanta; Med/Psych.

JENNINGS, BRANDON A; Fairview HS; Camden, AR; (2); Church Yth Grp; Drama Clb; Key Clb; Natl Beta Clb; Natl FFA Org; Chorus; School Play; Ftbl; Wt Lftg; Hon Roll; Wrld His Ky Awd; Orl Comms Ky Awd; U Of Cntrl AR.

JENNINGS, CHRISSY L; Mills HS; North Little Rock, AR; (3); Latin Clb; Natl Beta Clb; Pep Clb; Sec Frsh Cls; Sec Soph Cls; Sec Jr Cls; Sec Stu Cncl; Var Chrldng; Powder Puff Ftbl; Jr NHS.

JENNINGS, CHRISTOPHER S; Van Buren Sr HS; Van Buren, AR; (2); Church Yth Grp; FCA; Chorus; School Play; JV Bsbl; JV Bsktbl; JV Ftbl; Van Buren HS Stdnt Wk; Voc Med.

JENNINGS, CLARK F; Catholic HS; Little Rock, AR; (3); 14/190; JV Var Socr; Hon Roll; Ntl Merit SF.

JENSEN, SUZANNE; Conway Sr HS; Conway, AR; (4); 5/520; Church Yth Grp; FBLA; Natl Beta Clb; Spanish Clb; High Hon Roll; Hon Roll; Spanish NHS; AR Gov Schl Alt 95; Smmr ER Tech; Hendrix Coll; Pre-Med.

JERKINS, ROBIN; St Paul Schl; Saint Paul, AR; (3); Art Clb; FHA; Quiz Bowl; SADD; Pres Frsh Cls; Pres Soph Cls; High Hon Roll; Hon Roll; Jr NHS; Psych.

JERNIGAN, BRYAN D; Alma HS; Alma, AR; (2); FCA; JV L Bsktbl; Hon Roll; U Of AR.

JERNIGAN, CODY M; Bald Knob HS; Searcy, AR; (3); 22/130; Natl Beta Clb; VICA; Band; Hon Roll; Pres Acad Fit Awd; NE LA Univ; Pharm.

JERNIGAN, KALI S; East Poinsett Cty HS; Lepanto, AR; (2); 1/77; Church Yth Grp; VP Natl Beta Clb; Band; Capt Color Guard; Drm Mjr(t); Mrchg Band; Yrbk; Sec Frsh Cls; High Hon Roll; NHS; Phy Therapy.

JERRY, BRANDI M; El Dorado Sr HS; El Dorado, AR; (2); Church Yth Grp; Cmnty Wkr; GAA; Natl Beta Clb; Church Choir; Var Socr; Anchor Clb; REACH/PRIDE; BASIC.

JERRY, JARROD; Strong Jr Sr HS; El Dorado, AR; (3); 1/55; French Clb; FBLA; Natl Beta Clb; Quiz Bowl; Science Clb; Pres Frsh Cls; Pres Soph Cls; Var Bsbl; Var Bsktbl; High Hon Roll; Stu Cncl; Chrch Yth Group; Citizenship Awd.

JESSEN, BETH E; Black Rock Jr Sr HS; Imboden, AR; (2); 4/46; Church Yth Grp; Band; Chorus; Church Choir; School Musical; Bsktbl; Sftbl; High Hon Roll; Hon Roll; CPR Lifguard Cert-1st Aid; Cls Favorite-Female; Most Rebounds Bsktbl Plaque; Best Hitter Sftbl Plaque; Three Rivers CC; RN.

JESTER, MISSY K; Glenwood Jr Sr HS; Glenwood, AR; (2); 1/38; FCA; Sec FBLA; HOBY; Yrbk; Pres Frsh Cls; Pres Soph Cls; Capt Co-Capt Chrldng; Sftbl; High Hon Roll; NHS; Harvard; Lwyr.

JETER, JOSHUA D; Bismarck Jr-Sr HS; Malvern, AR; (2); FCA; Natl Beta Clb; Var Bsbl; Var Ftbl; Var Trk; Hon Roll; Odyssey Of The Mind; Gftd & Tlntd; Math; Sci.

JETER, W BRANDON; Crossett Sr HS; Crossett, AR; (2); 26/207; Church Yth Grp; Natl Beta Clb; Office Aide; Var L Bsbl; Var L Ftbl; JV Tennis; Hon Roll; Harding Univ; Bus; Hlth; Ftnss.

JEWELL, JEREMY; Arkansas Schl Math & Science; Benton, AR; (4); Cmnty Wkr; Computer Clb; Model UN; Mu Alpha Theta; Natl Beta Clb; Phtg Yrbk; High Hon Roll; Hon Roll; NHS; Pres Acad Fit Awd; U Of AR; Mech Engr.

JIMMERSON, SHIRILANA; Genoa Central HS; Fouke, AR; (3); Church Yth Grp; FHA; Spanish Clb; Cit Awd; High Hon Roll; Hon Roll; NHS; Prfct Atten Awd; Church Mnstry Outrchs/Most Courteous; Star Evnt/Gld Mdl Wnr/Plmntry Prcdr Team; FCS; SW Assmbly Of God; Music/Voice.

JINES, SARA E; Hot Springs HS; Hot Springs, AR; (3); 6/150; Am Leg Aux Girls St; Rep Church Yth Grp; Pres Key Clb; Mu Alpha Theta; Natl Beta Clb; NFL; Q&S; Science Clb; Pres Spanish Clb; Thesps; Cert Acad Achvmt; Acctng.

JINES, WALT G; Pulaski Acad; Little Rock, AR; (2); Spanish Clb; Ftbl; Hunting/Fishing/Water Skiing; U Of AR; Wldlf Mgmnt.

JOBE, TEMPLE L; Lake Hamilton Sr HS; Royal, AR; (3); Drama Clb; FCA; Science Clb; Spanish Clb; Thesps; School Play; Stage Crew; Nwsp; Ofcr Stu Cncl; Trk; Drame II Awd; AR Tech; Engrng.

JOHN, SINDHIA M; Mt St Mary Acad; Little Rock, AR; (2); Girl Scts; JCL; Latin Clb; Mu Alpha Theta; Natl Beta Clb; SADD; Rptr Nwsp; MD.

JOHNS, CARRIE; Harrisburg HS; Harrisburg, AR; (4); 10/53; FCA; Library Aide; Science Clb; Spanish Clb; Phtg Rptr Yrbk; Pres Frsh Cls; Ofcr Stu Cncl; Var Chrldng; L Tennis; High Hon Roll; Quachita Bapt U; Acctng.

JOHNS, CHRISTIAN J; Springdale Sr HS; Springdale, AR; (1); Church Yth Grp; Cmnty Wkr; Dance Clb; FCA; FBLA; FHA; Pep Clb; Spanish Clb; Chorus; Church Choir; Dance; Cls Favorite; Frosh Hall Of Fame Best All Around; U Of AR; Chld Psych.

JOHNS, ERIC P; Crowleys Ridge Acad; Paragould, AR; (3); Church Yth Grp; FBLA; Science Clb; Chorus; School Play; Bsktbl; Trk; Hon Roll; NHS; Pres Acad Fit Awd; Harding Univ; Pediatrics.

JOHNS, JENNIFER R; Russellville Sr HS; Russellville, AR; (3); 51/325; GAA; Band; Drill Tm; Mrchg Band; Pep Band; JV Vllybl; High Hon Roll; Jr NHS; NHS; JV Bsktbl; Bty Pgnts; AR ST Univ; Radio/TV/BRDCST.

JOHNSON, AARON; Brookland Jr Sr HS; Jonesboro, AR; (4); 2/50; Drama Clb; Natl Beta Clb; Capt Quiz Bowl; Chorus; School Play; Variety Show; Var Bsbl; Var Bsktbl; Hon Roll; Sal; All-St Choir; All-Dist & Cty Bsbl Team; Optimist Clb Super Sr; AR ST Univ.

JOHNSON, AARON F; Beebe Sr HS; Beebe, AR; (3); 5/126; Drama Clb; Math Clb; Natl Beta Clb; Pep Clb; Science Clb; Spanish Clb; Nwsp; JV Ftbl; Intrml Vllybl; High Hon Roll.

JOHNSON, AMANDA; Cabot HS; Cabot, AR; (3); Spanish Clb; Band; Mrchg Band; Pep Band; Nwsp; Hon Roll; Jr NHS; Span Cmp; All Rgn Bnd; Eng/Span.

JOHNSON, AMANDA D; Biggers-Reyno HS; Corning, AR; (2); 2/16; Church Yth Grp; FBLA; FHA; Natl Beta Clb; Quiz Bowl; Band; School Play; Rep Nwsp; Stat Bsktbl; High Hon Roll; Psych.

JOHNSON, AMY M; Lonoke Sr HS; Jerusalem, AR; (4); Church Yth Grp; FCA; FBLA; Math Clb; Natl FFA Org; Spanish Clb; Sec SADD; Teachers Aide; Vllybl; Hon Roll.

JOHNSON, ANDREA; Little Rock Cntrl HS; Roland, AR; (4); 29/420; Sec Chess Clb; Church Yth Grp; German Clb; High Hon Roll; Hon Roll; NHS; Ntl Merit Schol; Hum Soc Pulaski Cty Vol; Hendrix Coll; Veterinary Med.

JOHNSON, ANDREA D; Clarksville HS; Clarksville, AR; (3); Art Clb; VP Drama Clb; Key Clb; Math Clb; Model UN; Natl Beta Clb; Science Clb; Spanish Clb; Ed Yrbk; High Hon Roll; Odyssey Of Mind; Engl.

JOHNSON, APRILE; Hall Sr HS; Little Rock, AR; (4); 15/280; Am Leg Aux Girls St; Church Yth Grp; FBLA; Key Clb; Natl Beta Clb; Spanish Clb; Chorus; VP Sr Cls; Ofcr Stu Cncl; Chrldng; Wellesley Bk Awd; A Philip Randolph Awd; Southwestern Bell Stu Salute Awd; Clarkk Atlanta Univ.

JOHNSON, BRANDON; Sloan Hendrix HS; Walnut Ridge, AR; (3); 8/30; Chess Clb; Church Yth Grp; HOBY; Quiz Bowl; Pres Band; Rep Stu Cncl.

JOHNSON, BRANDY T; Drew Central Jr Sr HS; Monticello, AR; (2); Dance Clb; Teachers Aide; Yrbk; Cit Awd; High Hon Roll; Pres Acad Fit Awd; Law; Interior Dsgn.

JOHNSON, BRYCE; Southside HS; Fort Smith, AR; (4); Church Yth Grp; FCA; FBLA; Mu Alpha Theta; Spanish Clb; Var L Bsbl; Var L Ftbl; Var L Trk; Hon Roll; NHS; U AR; Acctng.

JOHNSON, BUFFY D; Augusta HS; Augusta, AR; (1); 11/46; Art Clb; 4-H; FHA; FTA; Natl Beta Clb; Spanish Clb; Mrchg Band; Work With Children; Reading; Riding Bicycles; Talking On Phone; Sci/Eng/Alg/Home Ec I 1st Pl; Eng 2nd Pl; UAMS; Ped.

JOHNSON, CASEY D; Star City HS; Star City, AR; (1); #1 in class; FCA; Science Clb; Spanish Clb; Chorus; School Musical; Variety Show; Ofcr Stu Cncl; Prfct Atten Awd; AP Eng.

JOHNSON, CHRIS S; Mena HS; Mena, AR; (3); 30/150; Cmnty Wkr; French Clb; FBLA; Math Clb; Math Tm; Natl FFA Org; Speech Tm; Var Bsbl; Var Bsktbl; Var Ftbl; Pediatrician.

JOHNSON, CLAY S; Ozark HS; Ozark, AR; (3); 1/100; Church Yth Grp; Intnl Clb; Natl Beta Clb; Acpl Chr; Band; VP Jr Cls; Treas Stu Cncl; Hon Roll; AR All St Choir; Harding Univ; Mus Ed.

JOHNSON, CLIFTON; Bright Star Schl; Doddridge, AR; (3); Quiz Bowl; Band; Var Bsktbl; Var Trk; High Hon Roll; Hon Roll; Prfct Atten Awd.

JOHNSON, CLINT N; Conway Sr HS; Conway, AR; (3); 1/550; Am Leg Boys St; Debate Tm; FBLA; JA; Natl Beta Clb; High Hon Roll; Prfct Atten Awd; Named One Of AR Top 100 Jrs 96; Attnd AR Governors Schl 96; Pre-Med; Dr.

JOHNSON, DANIEL P; Russellville Sr HS; Russellville, AR; (2); Boy Scts; Church Yth Grp; Band; Church Choir; Mrchg Band; Hon Roll; NHS; Chrch Yth Cncl; Crs Lftr Drama Grp; Order Arrow Vigil Hnr Sec; Jr NHS.

JOHNSON, DAVID E; Arkansas Sr HS; Texarkana, AR; (3); 25/369; Quiz Bowl; Spanish Clb; Ftbl; Jr NHS; NHS; Natl His & Govt Awd; All-Amer Schlr; Sprts Med.

JOHNSON, ERIKA L; Rivercrest HS; Keiser, AR; (3); Band; Flag Corp; Mrchg Band; Hon Roll; Jr NHS; TAD.

JOHNSON, FRANCES K; Cty Line HS; Ozark, AR; (3); Church Yth Grp; FCA; FBLA; Rptr Nwsp; Hon Roll; Vet.

JOHNSON, FREDDY; Forrest City HS; Forrest City, AR; (1); Band; Mrchg Band; UAPB; Cmptr Tech.

JOHNSON, GREGORY C; Lakeside HS; Lake Village, AR; (2); Art Clb; Church Yth Grp; Cmnty Wkr; Drama Clb; 4-H; FBLA; FHA; Bsktbl; Ftbl; Natl Hnr Scty 96; U Of AR; Bus Admin.

JOHNSON, HALIE J; Calvary Christian Schl; Forrest City, AR; (3); 4/11; Am Leg Aux Girls St; Church Yth Grp; Letterman Clb; Office Aide; Ski Clb; Church Choir; School Play; Nwsp; Sec Treas Frsh Cls; Sec Treas Soph Cls; Homcmng Frosh & Soph; Bus Ldrs Of Tomorrow; AR Tech; Mrktg; Advertising; Bus.

JOHNSON, HOLLY; Amity Jr Sr HS; Amity, AR; (2); FBLA; FHA; Natl Beta Clb; School Play; Rptr Frsh Cls; Sec Soph Cls; Bsktbl; Trk; Hon Roll; Tlnt Srch; CATS; Prin Lst; Ram Schlr; Clss Fvrte; Multi Yrs Lstd; Henderson; Med.

JOHNSON, HOLLY; Jessieville HS; Mountain Pine, AR; (4); 13/39; Art Clb; Church Yth Grp; VP Drama Clb; VP FBLA; Natl Beta Clb; VP Speech Tm; Ed Yrbk; VP Soph Cls; VP Jr Cls; Bsktbl; Cty Rd Beautification Prjct Awd; Garden Clb Speech Wnnr; 2nd Pl VFW Essay Cont; Garland Cty CC; Nrs.

JOHNSON, HOLLY; Hermitage Jr Sr HS; Hermitage, AR; (2); 8/60; Church Yth Grp; 4-H; GAA; HOBY; Natl Beta Clb; Natl FFA Org; Sec Frsh Cls; Rep Stu Cncl; Bsktbl; Chrldng; Lions Clb Sprtsmnshp Awd 95; U Of AR Monticello.

JOHNSON, JA JUAN S; Osceola HS; Osceola, AR; (2); Cmnty Wkr; FBLA; FHA; VP Stu Cncl; Church Yth Grp; Church Yth Grp; Cmnty Wkr; Dance Clb; Debate Tm; French Clb; Mr Ebony 96; Yth Opportunties Unltd; POWER OHS Mediation Team; PRIDE; Project Alpha; Pub Speaking; Hampton Univ; Mass Media.

JOHNSON, JAMIE; West Side Christian Schl; El Dorado, AR; (4); 3/17; Church Yth Grp; Drama Clb; VP Mu Alpha Theta; Natl Beta Clb; Rep Sr Cls; Rep Stu Cncl; Capt Chrldng; OM; Acteens; Chrch Yth Grp Ldrshp Cncl; Ouachita Bapt; Speech Pthlgy.

JOHNSON, JENNIFER; Conway Sr HS; Conway, AR; (2); Church Yth Grp; Debate Tm; 4-H; Math Tm; Natl Beta Clb; Office Aide; Spanish Clb; Teachers Aide; Church Choir; 4-H Awd; Quachita Baptst Univ; Tchr.

JOHNSON, JENNIFER C; North Little Rock Hs-West; North Little Rock, AR; (3); 61/554; Church Yth Grp; FCA; Math Clb; Mu Alpha Theta; Drill Tm; Stage Crew; Hon Roll; NHS; UCA; Tchng; Elem.

JOHNSON, JENNIFER J; St Paul Schl; Witter, AR; (2); FHA; SADD; Pres Frsh Cls; Pres Jr Cls; Bsktbl; Hon Roll; SLA; U Of AR; Nurse Practitioner.

JOHNSON, JEREMY; Warren Sr HS; Warren, AR; (4); #16 in class; Am Leg Boys St; Church Yth Grp; FBLA; Treas Latin Clb; Model UN; Natl Beta Clb; VP SADD; Ofcr Bsbl; High Hon Roll; Hon Roll; U Of Cntrl AR; Occptnl Thrpy.

JOHNSON, JONI R; Dierks HS; Dierks, AR; (2); Art Clb; Treas Frsh Cls; Treas Soph Cls; Treas Jr Cls; JV Bsktbl; JV Chrldng; Natl His & Govt Awd Nom; East TX ST Univ; Phy Thrpst.

JOHNSON, KATIE A; Russellville Sr HS; Russellville, AR; (3); 64/367; Sec FCA; GAA; SADD; Stage Crew; Var Crs Cntry; Var Trk; High Hon Roll; Jr NHS; NHS; Pres Acad Fit Awd.

JOHNSON, KEESHA; Caddo Hills Jr Sr HS; Glenwood, AR; (3); 1/45; Pres FCA; Natl Beta Clb; Spanish Clb; SADD; Church Choir; Pres Soph Cls; Sec Stu Cncl; Var JV Bsktbl; Sftbl; High Hon Roll; PRIDE; AAU Bsktbl; Grlnd Cty Coll Pres Lst; Otstndng HS Stu; Natl, St Tlnt Wnnr; St Bty Wnnr; Oucchita Bapt U; Cmmnctns.

JOHNSON, KELLI F; Siloam Springs Sr HS; Siloam Springs, AR; (3); Art Clb; Church Yth Grp; Drama Clb; Hosp Aide; Key Clb; Natl Beta Clb; Office Aide; Band; Flag Corp; High Hon Roll; Nom Best Yng Actor/Actress Awrd.

JOHNSON, KIM R; West Memphis Sr HS; West Memphis, AR; (3); Church Yth Grp; Cmnty Wkr; FHA; Office Aide; Band; Church Choir; Mrchg Band; Hon Roll; Sec Stdnt Cncl Frosh Yr; Yth Rec Wrkr Cit W Memphis; Future Drvrs Amer; Spelman Coll; Pdtrcn.

JOHNSON, KRISTY; Southside HS; Fort Smith, AR; (3); 66/459; Key Clb; Office Aide; Rep Soph Cls; Chrldng; Hon Roll; Jr NHS; NHS; Natl Eng Merit Awd; Law Enf Explr Crprl; Hnr Grd; U Of AR; Crmnl Jstc.

JOHNSON, LA CRISTI L; Searcy HS; Searcy, AR; (3); Art Clb; Cmnty Wkr; FHA; Natl Beta Clb; Spanish Clb; Trk; NHS; Spanish NHS; Received Schlr & Span III Awds; Harding U; Arch; Interior Desgnr.

JOHNSON, LANCE E; Arkansas Schl Math & Science; North Little Rock, AR; (3); 1/140; Church Yth Grp; FCA; FBLA; Mu Alpha Theta; Spanish Clb; Stat Bsktbl; Mgr(s); Powder Puff Ftbl; Hon Roll; NHS; We The People Natl Cmptn At DC; AEGIS Chem Pgm; FBLA St Bus Math Cmptn; Comp Engr.

JOHNSON, LARHONDA; Marked Tree Jr Sr HS; Marked Tree, AR; (3); 6/60; Am Leg Aux Girls St; FBLA; FHA; Library Aide; Natl FFA Org; Capt ROTC; Bsktbl; Trk; NHS; ASU Upward Bound Prgm ST Univ; AR ST Univ Jonesboro.

JOHNSON, LINDA M; Clay Co Central Jr Sr HS; Rector, AR; (4); 6/59; FBLA; German Clb; Science Clb; Yrbk; Bsktbl; Sftbl; Hon Roll; NHS; Gftd/Tlntd; Renssnce Cmmttee; AR ST U; Law.

JOHNSON, LOMA GAIL; Carthage Schl; Carthage, AR; (3); Art Clb; English Clb; French Clb; FBLA; Library Aide; Math Clb; Nwsp; Ofcr Jr Cls; Ofcr Stu Cncl; Hon Roll; TX Bus Coll; CPA.

JOHNSON, MARIAH; AR Schl For Math & Scis; North Little Rock, AR; (3); 1/120; Church Yth Grp; Dance Clb; French Clb; Mu Alpha Theta; Sec Natl Beta Clb; Band; Mrchg Band; Rptr Lit Mag; VP Sr Cls; Rep Stu Cncl; Outstdng Civics Stu; Outstdng Hnrs Bio Stu; Outstdng Hum Stu; Eng; Philosophy.

JOHNSON, MARSHA; Vilonia HS; Conway, AR; (2); Church Yth Grp; FBLA; Girl Scts; Mu Alpha Theta; Natl Beta Clb; Spanish Clb; Band; Flag Corp; Mrchg Band; High Hon Roll; Yale; US Pres.

JOHNSON, MATTHEW S; Magnolia HS; Magnolia, AR; (3); Church Yth Grp; FBLA; Science Clb; Band; Church Choir; Drm Mjr(t); Jazz Band; Nwsp; Sec Stu Cncl; Hon Roll.

JOHNSON, MELISSA; Bright Star Schl; Doddridge, AR; (4); Rptr Drama Clb; Hosp Aide; Ed Nwsp; Ed Yrbk; Pres Stu Cncl; Var Chrldng; Hon Roll; NHS; Prfct Atten Awd; Texakana Coll.

JOHNSON, MELISSA; Scranton HS; Scranton, AR; (3); 1/33; Pres 4-H; Pres FBLA; Natl Beta Clb; Acpl Chr; Pres Jr Cls; L Bsktbl; L Sftbl; 4-H Awd; Vc Dmcrcy Wnnr; Stdnt Cncl VP.

JOHNSON, MELISSA A; Southside HS; Fort Smith, AR; (2); Church Yth Grp; Office Aide; Pep Clb; Teachers Aide; School Play; Hon Roll; Lawyer/Pol Sci/His Tchr.

JOHNSON, MELISSA J; Pine Bluff HS; Pine Bluff, AR; (2); Boy Scts; Cmnty Wkr; French Clb; Library Aide; Math Tm; ROTC; Teachers Aide; Color Guard; Intrml Sftbl; Hon Roll; Natl Sojourners ROTC Awd; Sftbl; Kitty Hawk Hnr Soc; Comp Scis.

JOHNSON, MICHAEL; Mountainburg Jr Sr HS; Mountainburg, AR; (4); 3/48; Treas FBLA; Model UN; Natl Beta Clb; Quiz Bowl; Science Clb; Pres SADD; Rptr Nwsp; Rep Jr Cls; Sec Sr Cls; Ofcr Bsbl; Mr Mntnbrg HS Sr Yr; Sci Fr 2nd Pl Math/3rd Pl Dist; Dstrct FBLA; U Of AR; Bio-Physics.

JOHNSON, MICHELLE R; Quitman Jr Sr HS; Greenbrier, AR; (2); FBLA; HOBY; Sec Natl Beta Clb; Teachers Aide; Nwsp; Yrbk; Sec Treas Stu Cncl; Sftbl; Cit Awd; Hon Roll; Jr Beta Pres 9th Grd; Bus/Cmptrzd Acctng.

JOHNSON, MIKEY; Dewitt HS; Saint Charles, AR; (2); 18/98; Church Yth Grp; 4-H; Natl FFA Org; Ofcr Bsbl; Bsktbl; Trk; FFA Land Judging & Parlimentary Procedure Teams; Soil Scis.

JOHNSON, MINDY; Ashdown Jr HS; Ashdown, AR; (1); 28/149; Church Yth Grp; Cmnty Wkr; Natl Beta Clb; Band; Mrchg Band; School Musical; Rep Frsh Cls; Pres Stu Cncl; Chrldng; U Of AR; Occptnl Thrpy.

JOHNSON, NATALIE N; North Little Rock Hs-East; Little Rock, AR; (1); Church Yth Grp; Debate Tm; Drama Clb; Office Aide; Spanish Clb; School Musical; Stage Crew; Cit Awd; High Hon Roll; Hon Roll; Upward Bound Project; Stu Congress; Spellman Univ; Jrnlsm.

JOHNSON, NATALIE S; Piggott HS; Piggott, AR; (2); French Clb; FBLA; Boy Scts; Science Clb; School Play; Rep Soph Cls; Ofcr Stu Cncl; Chrldng; Hon Roll; Prfct Atten Awd; Governors Yth Cncl; Three Rivers; CPA.

JOHNSON, NICHOLAS S; Magnolia HS; Magnolia, AR; (3); Church Yth Grp; French Clb; FBLA; Band; Church Choir; Drm Mjr(t); Jazz Band; Mrchg Band; Pep Band; Hon Roll.

JOHNSON, PATRICE R; Booneville Jr Sr HS; Booneville, AR; (4); 26/86; Church Yth Grp; French Clb; Rptr FBLA; Key Clb; Science Clb; VP Sec Chorus; Church Choir; School Play; Cit Awd; St Acteens Panel Alt; Named Friendliest In Sr Cls; Nrsng Home Vol; Southwest Bapt Univ; Psych.

JOHNSON, RAESHAUNA A; Central HS; West Helena, AR; (2); Trk; Hon Roll; Direct Instr Tutor; WA Univ St Louis; RN.

JOHNSON, RAY; Bright Star Schl; Doddridge, AR; (3); Band.

JOHNSON, REBECCA; Lee Acad; Marianna, AR; (3); Varsity Clb; Yrbk; VP Soph Cls; Pres Jr Cls; Var Bsktbl; Var Sftbl; Var Trk; Hon Roll; NHS.

JOHNSON, ROSEMARY A; Oak Grove HS; Maumelle, AR; (2); Church Yth Grp; Cmnty Wkr; Math Clb; Mu Alpha Theta; Natl Beta Clb; Red Cross Aide; Spanish Clb; Chorus; Sec Frsh Cls; Ofcr Stu Cncl; TN ST; Cmptr Sci/Engr/Music.

JOHNSON, RUTH M; Southside HS; Fort Smith, AR; (2); Church Yth Grp; French Clb; Teachers Aide; Band; Capt Drill Tm; Ofcr Stu Cncl; Chrldng; High Hon Roll; Jr NHS; Lawyer.

JOHNSON, RYAN L; Searcy HS; Searcy, AR; (2); 18/260; Church Yth Grp; FCA; FBLA; Key Clb; Natl Beta Clb; Spanish Clb; Var Bsktbl; Var L Tennis; High Hon Roll; Spanish NHS; PT/MED.

JOHNSON, SHAFFON; Dermott HS; Dermott, AR; (3); 7/60; Am Leg Aux Girls St; FBLA; Math Clb; Natl Beta Clb; Office Aide; Spanish Clb; Sec Frsh Cls; Sftbl; Hon Roll; Pres Acad Fit Awd; LA Tech; Acctg.

JOHNSON, SHALAWNA S; Holly Grove HS; Holly Grove, AR; (2); 14/26; Church Yth Grp; FHA; Girl Scts; Band; Church Choir; Drill Tm; School Musical; School Play; Nwsp; Yrbk; TSU; Engrng; Police Ofcr.

JOHNSON, SHARA N; Searcy HS; Searcy, AR; (2); Church Yth Grp; Cmnty Wkr; Library Aide; U Of Cntrl AR; Acctg.

JOHNSON, SHELIA M; Elaine Jr Sr HS; Elaine, AR; (3); Church Yth Grp; Drama Clb; FHA; Hon Roll; Ntl Merit Ltr; De Vry; Comp Technician.

JOHNSON, STARLA; Bradford Jr Sr HS; Bradford, AR; (3); FHA; Natl Beta Clb; High Hon Roll; Prfct Atten Awd; Bus Ed & Frgn Lang Awds; Math Tlnt Srch; Comps.

JOHNSON, STEPHEN A; Bauxite Jr Sr HS; Bauxite, AR; (2); Teachers Aide; Fire Marshall.

JOHNSON, TABITHA; Swifton Schl; Swifton, AR; (3); 3/22; FBLA; JA; Library Aide; Natl Beta Clb; Natl FFA Org; Office Aide; Spanish Clb; Teachers Aide; High Hon Roll; Pres Acad Fit Awd; AR ST U; Law.

JOHNSON, TABITHA S; Holly Grove HS; Holly Grove, AR; (3); 5/38; Rptr FBLA; FHA; German Clb; Natl Beta Clb; Quiz Bowl; Rptr Nwsp; Rep Stu Cncl; Bsktbl; Trk; Hon Roll; AR ST Univ; Soc Wrk.

JOHNSON, TAJ A; Elkins Jr Sr HS; Fayetteville, AR; (4); Am Leg Boys St; Church Yth Grp; FBLA; FHA; Math Tm; Quiz Bowl; Teachers Aide; Varsity Clb; School Play; Yrbk; All St & All Conf Sr Hi Bsbl; US Army Schlr Ath Awd; Mst Outstndg HS Stu; U Of AR; Mech Engr.

JOHNSON, TENETRIC; Dumas Jr HS; Dumas, AR; (1); Am Leg Aux Girls St; Bus Profs of Am; FBLA; FHA; Chrldng; Swmmng; Trk; Pres Schlr; Sal; Val; Sftbl; Vllybl; Jr NHS; Grambling ST; Band; Tchr.

JOHNSON, TIUNTAY M; Junction City HS; Junction City, AR; (2); Ofcr Jr Cls; Bsktbl.

JOHNSON, TONI S; Central HS; West Helena, AR; (2); Cmnty Wkr; Computer Clb; French Clb; FHA; Girl Scts; Teachers Aide; Band; Church Choir; Hon Roll; Xvaier; Pre Med.

JOHNSON, TORI; Atkins Schl; Atkins, AR; (2); 4/90; Church Yth Grp; Drama Clb; FBLA; Natl Beta Clb; Science Clb; Spanish Clb; Band; Church Choir; Mrchg Band; Pep Band; AR Tech Univ.

JOHNSON, TRENT D; Southside HS; Fort Smith, AR; (3); 22/502; Church Yth Grp; FCA; Mu Alpha Theta; Spanish Clb; Teachers Aide; Hon Roll; Jr NHS; NHS; U Of AR; Pre-Med.

JOHNSON JR, WALLACE L; Magnolia HS; Magnolia, AR; (4); 23/215; Boy Scts; Mu Alpha Theta; Office Aide; Science Clb; Church Choir; VP Sr Cls; Ftbl; Trk; Hon Roll; NHS; All Dist Crnrbck; Hon Mntn All ST Crnr; Rnr Up AAA Chmpnshp Team; UCA; Nrsng.

JOHNSON, WENDY B; Conway Sr HS; Conway, AR; (4); Drama Clb; VICA; Stage Crew; Phtg Nwsp; Phtg Yrbk; U Of Cntl AR; Photo.

JOHNSON, WILLENA C; Holly Grove Jr Sr HS; Holly Grove, AR; (3); 2/39; Am Leg Aux Girls St; Church Yth Grp; 4-H; FBLA; VP FHA; German Clb; Pep Clb; Quiz Bowl; Church Choir; Drill Tm; Norfolk ST-VA; Acctng.

JOHNSON, WILLIAM J; Robinson HS; Roland, AR; (2); Church Yth Grp; FCA; Spanish Clb; Crs Cntry; Ftbl; Trk; Wt Lftg; U Of AR Fayetteville; Ag Bus.

JOHNSONS, FELICIA L; Fountain Lake Jr Sr HS; Hot Springs Natio, AR; (2); 20/150; Church Yth Grp; Dance Clb; FCA; FHA; GAA; Key Clb; Natl Beta Clb; Pep Clb; Quiz Bowl; Red Cross Aide; DBU.

JOHNSTON, CARRIE; Monticello HS; Monticello, AR; (1); Church Yth Grp; Acpl Chr; Chorus; Rep Stu Cncl; Chrldng; Sftbl; High Hon Roll; Jr NHS; Prfct Atten Awd; Pres Acad Fit Awd.

JOHNSTON, CHRIS H; Searcy HS; Rose Bud, AR; (4); 74/195; Church Yth Grp; Natl Beta Clb; Natl FFA Org; Graphic Arts Awd Outstndg Accmplshmnt; ASU Beebe.

JOHNSTON, CHRISTIAN D; Atkins Schl; Atkins, AR; (2); Church Yth Grp; FBLA; Office Aide; Science Clb; Spanish Clb; Var L Bsbl; Var L Ftbl; Trk; Wt Lftg; Amer Legion Bsbl Assn; Reach-Out Clb; U Of AR; Ath Coach.

JOHNSTON, HEATHER; Mulberry HS; Alma, AR; (1); Natl FFA Org; Band; VP Frsh Cls; Rep Stu Cncl; Capt Chrldng; U Of AR; Phys Thrpy.

JOHNSTON, JESSICA E; Mena HS; Mena, AR; (2); 1/150; Church Yth Grp; French Clb; FBLA; Science Clb; Ofcr Frsh Cls; Bsktbl; Chrldng; Tennis; Vllybl; Hon Roll.

JOHNSTON, JOSIAH; St Paul Schl; Saint Paul, AR; (2); Art Clb; Church Yth Grp; FBLA; Quiz Bowl; SADD; Ofcr Frsh Cls; Rptr Soph Cls; Ofcr Stu Cncl; High Hon Roll; Hon Roll; MIT; Mech Engr.

JOHNSTON, LAURA L; Robinson HS; Little Rock, AR; (3); Church Yth Grp; Debate Tm; Natl Beta Clb; Spanish Clb; Thesps; Rep Jr Cls; Rep Stu Cncl; Hon Roll; NHS; Pres Acad Fit Awd.

JOHNSTON, SARAH B; Gillett Jr Sr HS; Gillett, AR; (2); Art Clb; Church Yth Grp; FBLA; FHA; Library Aide; Spanish Clb; Teachers Aide; Hon Roll; NHS; Peer Tutor.

JOHNSTON, STEPHANIE; Lakeside HS; Hot Springs, AR; (4); 6/114; Church Yth Grp; French Clb; Math Clb; Natl Beta Clb; Office Aide; Teachers Aide; Thesps; Chorus; Church Choir; Hon Roll; Frederic Chopin Piano Awd 94/96; Natl Schl Choral Awd 96; Summa Cum Laude Grad; Ouachita Bapt Univ; Music Ed.

JOHNSTON, SUMMER; Heber Springs HS; Heber Springs, AR; (4); 8/91; Am Leg Aux Girls St; Church Yth Grp; FCA; FBLA; Natl Beta Clb; Science Clb; Spanish Clb; Teachers Aide; Thesps; Band; Chng Wrld Schlrshp SAGU; Sw Assmbly God U; Bus.

JOHNSTON, TIMOTHY J; Oak Grove HS; Maumelle, AR; (2); 18/235; Am Leg Boys St; Church Yth Grp; FCA; French Clb; FBLA; Key Clb; Letterman Clb; Math Clb; Teachers Aide; Varsity Clb; Physician.

JOHSON, LANCE E; Arkansas Schl Math & Science; North Little Rock, AR; (3); 1/147; Church Yth Grp; Cmnty Wkr; FCA; FBLA; Mu Alpha Theta; Natl Beta Clb; Spanish Clb; Stat Bsktbl; High Hon Roll; NHS; Summer Chrch Cmp; Chem Eng Tst 5thplc; Chem AEGIS Cmp; Comp Eng.

JOLLY, AMY E; John L Mcclellan Magnet HS; Little Rock, AR; (3); 1/282; Drama Clb; French Clb; FBLA; Key Clb; Mu Alpha Theta; Sftbl; Gov Hon Prg Awd; High Hon Roll; Pres NHS; Pres Acad Fit Awd.

JOLLY, DEATRA L; Pine Bluff HS; Pine Bluff, AR; (4); Art Clb; Cmnty Wkr; FTA; GAA; Model UN; Mrchg Band; Sec Frsh Cls; L Bsktbl; French Clb; FHA; Crdntd Cr Ed Pres; Pn Blff PRIDE, Hist Blf Treas; U Of AR At Pine Bluff; Hist.

JONES, AMANDA; Wynne HS; Wynne, AR; (3); Am Leg Aux Girls St; Church Yth Grp; FTA; Spanish Clb; SADD; Capt Chrldng; Hon Roll; Spanish NHS; AR All St Chrldng Team; Pres Jr Progressive Clb, FTA, Spanish Honor Soc; AR ST; Comp Sci.

JONES, AMANDA L; Goza Jr HS; Arkadelphia, AR; (1); Church Yth Grp; FBLA; FHA; GAA; Church Choir; Mgr(s); Vllybl; Jr NHS.

JONES, AMANDA RENEE; Westside HS; Clarksville, AR; (2); Church Yth Grp; FHA; Natl Beta Clb; School Musical; School Play; Ofcr Stu Cncl; JV Var Bsktbl; JV Var Trk; Hon Roll; Prfct Atten Awd; 2nd Rnr Up 94-95; Johnson Co Teen Miss Pgnt; Ftbl Hmcng Cand Soph; Cls Fvrt Frosh/Soph Yr; Law Schl.

JONES, ANNE CAMERON; Central Sr HS; Little Rock, AR; (3); Church Yth Grp; Cmnty Wkr; French Clb; FBLA; Chrldng; Hon Roll; TX A&M Univ.

JONES, APRIL L; Forrest City HS; Forrest City, AR; (1); Dance Clb; FBLA; FHA; Hosp Aide; Band; Sftbl; Trk; Hon Roll; GA Tech; Phys Thrpy.

JONES, ASHLEY L; Forrest City HS; Forrest City, AR; (4); 13/275; Art Clb; Church Yth Grp; FBLA; Mu Alpha Theta; Natl Beta Clb; Office Aide; Church Choir; Ofcr Stu Cncl; Tennis; Hon Roll; AR ST U; Psych.

JONES, BECKY; Kirby HS; Glenwood, AR; (3); Church Yth Grp; FBLA; Pep Clb; Rptr Frsh Cls; Chrldng; Hon Roll; Dental Asst/Ped Nrs/Csmtlgst.

JONES, BRANDON; Lee Acad; Palestine, AR; (2); Bsktbl; Cmnty Wkr; Trk; Cit Awd; Hon Roll; U Of AR; Bus.

JONES, BRIDGETTE N; Southside HS; Batesville, AR; (4); 3/75; FBLA; FHA; Key Clb; Natl Beta Clb; Science Clb; Spanish Clb; Yrbk; Var Capt Chrldng; Cit Awd; Hon Roll; PRIDE; U Of Central AR.

JONES, CARA L; Greenwood Sr HS; Greenwood, AR; (3); 41/201; French Clb; FHA; Natl Beta Clb; Nwsp; Pom Pon; Hon Roll; Beta Clb Sec; ST & Natl Beta Clb Conventions.

JONES, CARABETH; Bentonville Sr HS; Bentonville, AR; (3); 14/332; FBLA; Red Cross Aide; Lit Mag; High Hon Roll; Teen Ct Attorney; U Of AR Upward Bound; Upward Bound Stu Of The Yr; U Of AR; Criminal Justice.

JONES, CARRIE B; Trumann HS; Trumann, AR; (3); Church Yth Grp; French Clb; FBLA; Library Aide; Natl FFA Org; Science Clb; High Hon Roll; Hon Roll; NHS; Ntl Merit Ltr; U Of AR Fayetteville; Pre-Med.

JONES, CASSANDRA L; Central Sr HS; Little Rock, AR; (3); Church Yth Grp; Cmnty Wkr; Pep Clb; ROTC; VICA; Band; Pep Band; Cit Awd; High Hon Roll; Hon Roll; Troubadors; UAPB; Law Enforcement.

JONES, CATHY J; Clarksville HS; Clarksville, AR; (4); 11/97; Art Clb; VP French Clb; Key Clb; Math Clb; Natl Beta Clb; Science Clb; Yrbk; Rep Frsh Cls; High Hon Roll; Pres Acad Fit Awd; Hlth Assoc Soclgy Awd; Bus Law Awd; Deans Schol; U Of Ozarks; Env Sci.

JONES, CHANDRIA EVETTE; Fairview HS; Camden, AR; (4); 45/245; Church Yth Grp; French Clb; FBLA; Mu Alpha Theta; Spanish Clb; Church Choir; Hon Roll; NHS; Pres Schlr; Spanish NHS; U Of Central AR; Psych.

JONES, CHRIS A; Jacksonville HS; Jacksonville, AR; (4); 36/283; Am Leg Boys St; Art Clb; FBLA; Natl Beta Clb; Spanish Clb; Teachers Aide; L Bsbl; Var Bsktbl; High Hon Roll; Hon Roll; U Of AR; Bus; Fin.

JONES, CHRISTEN E; Booneville Jr Sr HS; Booneville, AR; (2); Spanish Clb; Band; Mrchg Band; Pep Band; ASU Jonesboro; Music; Bus.

JONES, CHRYSTAL; Hall Sr HS; Little Rock, AR; (4); Church Yth Grp; French Clb; FBLA; VP Natl Beta Clb; Quiz Bowl; Church Choir; School Play; Rptr Nwsp; Var Vllybl; AR HS Press Assn Super Rating; U Of AR Little Rock; Bus Admin.

JONES, CINDY; Southside HS; Fort Smith, AR; (3); Church Yth Grp; French Clb; Pep Clb; Teachers Aide; Church Choir; Chrldng; Gym; Law.

JONES, COURTNEY D; Glenwood Jr Sr HS; Glenwood, AR; (1); 5/40; Church Yth Grp; FCA; FHA; GAA; Ofcr Stu Cncl; Bsktbl; Chrldng; High Hon Roll; Hon Roll; NHS; U Of AR Fayettville.

JONES, CRYSTAL; Central HS; West Helena, AR; (2); ROTC; Drill Tm; Trk; Cit Awd; Hon Roll; FFA; LA ST U; Pre-Law.

JONES, DAVID L; Beebe Sr HS; Beebe, AR; (3); Art Clb; FHA; Natl FFA Org; JV Ftbl; Var Mgr(s); US Nvl Acad; Pilot.

JONES, DEON; Dumas HS; Dumas, AR; (3); Am Leg Boys St; Church Yth Grp; Cmnty Wkr; FCA; Var Capt Bsbl; Var Capt Ftbl; Wt Lftg; High Hon Roll; Hon Roll.

JONES, DEZRAE S; Fairview HS; Camden, AR; (3); Church Yth Grp; FBLA; Natl Beta Clb; Natl FFA Org; Office Aide; Spanish Clb; Teachers Aide; Band; Mrchg Band; Cit Awd; Mst Outs Beta Clb; US Air Force.

JONES, DONALD F; Robinson HS; Little Rock, AR; (3); Art Clb; Band; Jazz Band; Mrchg Band; Gov Hon Prg Awd; Outstndg Achvmt Music; Tech Awd; Hendrix; Comp Prgmr.

JONES, ELENA D; Dequeen HS; De Queen, AR; (2); Church Yth Grp; FBLA; Spanish Clb; SADD; Teachers Aide; Chorus; Hon Roll; Hnr Engl Classes; Law.

JONES, GARRICK; North Little Rock Hs-West; North Little Rock, AR; (3); FCA; Hosp Aide; JA; Teachers Aide; Stage Crew; Variety Show; Ftbl; Trk; Hon Roll; Ntl Merit Ltr; Sigma Phi Beta Achvmt Awd; Blue Card Hldr; KS ST; Arch Eng.

JONES, HEATHER M; Searcy HS; Searcy, AR; (2); Church Yth Grp; Hosp Aide; Natl Beta Clb; SADD; Chorus; Co-Capt Yrbk; JV Trk; Hon Roll; Jr NHS; Spanish NHS; Harding Univ; Pre-Med; Dr.

JONES, HOLLY R; De Soto Schl; Helena, AR; (3); Am Leg Aux Girls St; Church Yth Grp; Drama Clb; Pres Thesps; Church Choir; School Musical; School Play; Yrbk; Rep Stu Cncl; L Bsktbl; Rotry Yth Ldrshp Awd; Camp Cnslr.

JONES, JAMES E; Springdale Sr HS; Springdale, AR; (1); Church Yth Grp; Math Tm; High Hon Roll; Jr NHS; Pres Acad Fit Awd; Comp Eng.

JONES, JASON; Conway Sr HS; Conway, AR; (4); 11/545; Am Leg Boys St; Art Clb; Church Yth Grp; Drama Clb; French Clb; FBLA; Natl Beta Clb; Q&S; Teachers Aide; Church Choir; Rnssnc Gld Cd; Hnr Grad; Hendrix Coll; Med.

JONES, JENNIFER G; Huntsville HS; Huntsville, AR; (4); 9/120; Art Clb; FBLA; FTA; Intnl Clb; Model UN; Science Clb; Teachers Aide; High Hon Roll; All Amer Schlr; Xerox Awd Humnties, Socl Sci; Art Awd; Engl II, World Hstry, US Hstry Awds.

JONES, JENNIFER N; Drew Central Jr Sr HS; Monticello, AR; (2); FBLA; FHA; Band; Pep Band; Phtg Yrbk; Sec Frsh Cls; High Hon Roll; Hon Roll; Jr NHS; Med.

JONES, JEREMIAH D; Shepherds Staff Chrstn Schl; Melbourne, AR; (1); 1/5; Art Clb; Chess Clb; Church Yth Grp; CAP; Computer Clb; Cit Awd; High Hon Roll; Prfct Atten Awd; Mountain Biking; Philately.

JONES, JEREMY S; Searcy HS; Searcy, AR; (3); Natl Beta Clb; L Var Socr; Hon Roll; NHS; Harding Univ; Math.

JONES, JERROD M; Hope HS; Hope, AR; (3); 1/240; FBLA; Key Clb; Natl Beta Clb; Office Aide; Ftbl; Trk; Wt Lftg; High Hon Roll; NHS; Engrng.

JONES, JESSICA A; Alma HS; Rudy, AR; (3); Church Yth Grp; VP 4-H; French Clb; Sec Natl FFA Org; Science Clb; Teachers Aide; Band; Color Guard; Mrchg Band; Hon Roll; GCE Clbs Of AR; Westark; Rsprtry Thrpy.

JONES, JESSICA L; Trumann HS; Trumann, AR; (2); Church Yth Grp; FHA; Model UN; Spanish Clb; Chorus; Hon Roll; NHS; AR ST U; Hstry Tchr.

JONES, JOANELLE L; John L Mcclellan Magnet HS; Little Rock, AR; (3); Church Yth Grp; Drama Clb; FCA; FBLA; Mu Alpha Theta; Natl Beta Clb; Spanish Clb; Drill Tm; JV Bsktbl; Hon Roll; ULAR; Radiology.

JONES, JONATHAN; Marked Tree Jr Sr HS; Marked Tree, AR; (3); FHA; Natl FFA Org; Quiz Bowl; ROTC; Ed Nwsp; Ed Yrbk; Rep Frsh Cls; Bsktbl; Trk; AR ST Univ; Phys Therapy.

JONES, JONATHAN D; Springdale Sr HS; Springdale, AR; (4); Church Yth Grp; Math Tm; Natl Beta Clb; Q&S; Quiz Bowl; Scholastic Bowl; Band; Jazz Band; Mrchg Band; Pep Band.

JONES, JOSHUA E; Jessieville HS; Mountain Pine, AR; (2); Art Clb; Church Yth Grp; Teachers Aide; Hist; Civil War Battle Fields.

JONES, JULIE C; Nemo Vista Jr Sr HS; Springfield, AR; (3); Church Yth Grp; Spanish Clb; Speech Tm; Teachers Aide; Rptr Nwsp; Bsktbl; Cit Awd; Gov Hon Prg Awd; Hon Roll; Ntl Merit Ltr; Hendrix.

JONES, JUSTIN O; Ozark HS; Ozark, AR; (3); Church Yth Grp; FCA; Intnl Clb; Chorus; Stage Crew; Ofcr Bsbl; Ftbl; Golf; Trk; Hon Roll; GCE Work Clb; U Of AR; Military.

JONES, KAREN M; Russellville Sr HS; London, AR; (2); 53/444; Church Yth Grp; SADD; Band; Church Choir; Flag Corp; Mrchg Band; Pep Band; Hon Roll; NHS; Spanish Clb; CSU Ofcr; U Of AR; Cmptr Animtn.

JONES, KASI L; Magnolia HS; Magnolia, AR; (3); Am Leg Aux Girls St; Church Yth Grp; Rep FBLA; Mu Alpha Theta; Band; Church Choir; Color Guard; Mrchg Band; Nwsp; Yrbk; AR ST Univ; Broadcast-Jrnlsm.

JONES, KATIE D; El Dorado Sr HS; El Dorado, AR; (3); Church Yth Grp; Cmnty Wkr; Natl Beta Clb; Chorus; Rep Stu Cncl; Socr; Anchor Clb; Guidance Office Aide; Campfire Girls; Kndgtn Tchr.

JONES, KENNY; Elaine Jr Sr HS; Elaine, AR; (2); Spanish Clb; Band; Church Choir; Mrchg Band; School Musical; Var Bsbl; L Bsktbl; L Ftbl; Trk; Hon Roll; Engrng.

JONES, KIZZIA; Arkadelphia Sr HS; Arkadelphia, AR; (3); Am Leg Aux Girls St; Treas Pres FBLA; Natl Beta Clb; Band; Mrchg Band; Rep VP Stu Cncl; Cit Awd; Hon Roll; Math Awd; Eng Awd; Close Up Del; U Of Cntrl AR; Dental Dygiene.

JONES, KRISTI J; Crossett Sr HS; Crossett, AR; (2); Church Yth Grp; FTA; Natl Beta Clb; Var Crs Cntry; JV Trk; Hon Roll; Stdnts For Christ Clb; Audiology.

JONES, LAKECIA N; Hermitage Jr Sr HS; Hermitage, AR; (3); 3/40; Church Yth Grp; Dance Clb; French Clb; FBLA; Natl Beta Clb; Drm Mjr(t); Ed Yrbk; VP Stu Cncl; Bsktbl; Chrldng; AR ST Univ; Med.

JONES, LAKESHA; Hope HS; Hope, AR; (3); Band; Color Guard; Mrchg Band; Hon Roll; Beta Club; Stdnt Of Month; Henderson ST Univ; Pre Med.

JONES, LANE; Catholic HS; Cabot, AR; (2); 53/205; Church Yth Grp; Cmnty Wkr; Stage Crew; Cit Awd; Hon Roll; Lcl Awd Heroism For Svng Mans Life.

JONES, LAUREN; Clarksville HS; Clarksville, AR; (2); 39/150; Drama Clb; Natl Beta Clb; Spanish Clb; Hon Roll; Prfct Atten Awd; Builders Clb 9th Grd.

JONES, LISA; Fairview HS; Camden, AR; (4); 1/250; Am Leg Aux Girls St; Drama Clb; Mu Alpha Theta; Natl Beta Clb; Chorus; Var Chrldng; French Hon Soc; Gov Hon Prg Awd; NHS; Val; Ouachita Bapt Univ; Phy Thrpy.

JONES, LORNE; Mountain View Jr Sr HS; Marcella, AR; (3); FBLA; Natl Beta Clb; Quiz Bowl; Science Clb; Spanish Clb; Church Choir; Var Ftbl; Var Trk; Var Wt Lftg; Cit Awd; Engrng.

JONES, MARY MARGARET; Russellville Sr HS; Russellville, AR; (3); Church Yth Grp; French Clb; Model UN; Band; Chrldng; Gym; Hon Roll; Law.

JONES, MELISSA D; Russellville Sr HS; Russellville, AR; (2); Church Yth Grp; Acpl Chr; Sec Chorus; Gym; Swmmng; Hon Roll; Jr NHS; French Clb; Hosp Aide; Teachers Aide; West Cntrl All Rgn Choir; AR All ST Choir; All Stars Stdnts Agnst Alcohol/Drugs; Cntrl Bapt Coll; Music.

JONES, MICHAEL D; Beebe Sr HS; Beebe, AR; (4); 7/98; Drama Clb; Math Clb; Temple Yth Grp; VP Thesps; School Play; Stage Crew; High Hon Roll; NHS; Ntl Merit SF; ASU Beebe; Engrng.

JONES, MORGAN; Bergman Schl; Harrison, AR; (1); Natl Beta Clb; Natl FFA Org; JV Bsktbl; Hon Roll; Prfct Atten Awd.

JONES, NATE C; Southside HS; Batesville, AR; (2); Key Clb; Mrchg Band; Quiz Bowl; School Play; VP Soph Cls; Intrml Vllybl; Hon Roll; Upwrd Bnd; NCEOA Ldrshp Conf Rep Of AR; Video Yrbk; KS Univ; Pol/Lwyr.

JONES, NATHAN A; Jessieville HS; Hot Springs Natio, AR; (2); Church Yth Grp; FCA; Natl Beta Clb; Band; Var Ftbl; Var Trk; Var Wt Lftg; Hon Roll; Outstdng 10th Grd Stdnt Awd 95-.

JONES, NICK; Southwest Christian Acad; Mabelvale, AR; (1); 1/11; Church Yth Grp; Chorus; Church Choir; Yrbk; Score Keeper; High Hon Roll; Prfct Atten Awd; Southern Nazarene U.

JONES, PATRICIA L; Arkansas Sr HS; Texarkana, AR; (3); Art Clb; Church Yth Grp; French Clb; Church Choir; Ofcr Stu Cncl; Jr NHS.

JONES, PAUL C; Rogers HS; Rogers, AR; (3); 7/566; Church Yth Grp; Cmnty Wkr; Science Clb; Band; Church Choir; Mrchg Band; High Hon Roll; NHS; Ntl Merit Ltr; Pres Acad Fit Awd; Chrch Bsktbl/Sftbl; Slctd Nazarene Yth Cngrss; Reg Math Fnlst; Aerospc Engrng.

JONES, PHYLESHA; Nashville HS; Nashville, AR; (2); 38/155; FBLA; FHA; GAA; Bsktbl; Capt Chrldng; Gym; Trk; Hon Roll; Math Cont Geom; Tutor; U Of AR Fayetteville; Pedtrcn.

JONES, RACHAEL L; West Fork HS; West Fork, AR; (1); Church Yth Grp; Cmnty Wkr; Chorus; Church Choir; Chrldng; Med.

JONES, REBECCA M; Newport HS; Newport, AR; (3); Office Aide; Spanish Clb; SADD; School Play; Nwsp; Lit Mag; Mgr Chrldng; Hon Roll; Pres Acad Fit Awd; AR St Univ; Optom.

JONES, RICHARD L; Benton Cty Christian School; Pineville, MO; (4); Var Bsktbl; Vllybl; U Of AR; Sports Medicine.

JONES, SARAH; Lake Hamilton Jr HS; Hot Springs, AR; (1); 6/264; Library Aide; Natl Beta Clb; Band; Mrchg Band; Pep Band; Crs Cntry; Trk; Hon Roll; Ntl Merit Schol; 1st Pl, Hnrb Mntn Schl Reflections Cont/Hnrb Mntn Music; Henderson ST U; Instrmntl Musi.

JONES, SHALIMAR L; John L Mcclellan Magnet HS; Little Rock, AR; (2); Church Yth Grp; FBLA; Girl Scts; Key Clb; Natl Beta Clb; Band; Church Choir; Mrchg Band; Cit Awd; Hon Roll; Cmptr Bus Acctng.

JONES, SHANNON; J A Fair Sr HS; Little Rock, AR; (3); 9/292; Drama Clb; French Clb; FBLA; Hosp Aide; HOBY; Capt Drill Tm; School Play; Rep Jr Cls; Rep Stu Cncl; Trk; CARE Cmte Stu Chrprsn; Arch.

JONES, SHELBY; Saratoga Schl; Saratoga, AR; (4); 3/21; Church Yth Grp; Natl Beta Clb; Natl FFA Org; Quiz Bowl; Teachers Aide; School Play; Ed Nwsp; Computer Clb; Hon Roll; Ntl Merit Ltr; Red River Tech; Graphic Dsgn.

JONES, STACIE; Poyen Schl; Malvern, AR; (3); 2/46; FCA; FHA; German Clb; Natl Beta Clb; Sec Jr Cls; Var Capt Chrldng; Sftbl; High Hon Roll; Ntl Merit Ltr; Marine Bio.

JONES, STACIE; Northside HS; Fort Smith, AR; (3); Church Yth Grp; Cmnty Wkr; FCA; Pep Clb; Band; Mrchg Band; Pep Band; Rptr Nwsp; Rptr Yrbk; Capt Chrldng; Westark CC; Psych.

JONES, STEPHANIE; Lamar HS; Lamar, AR; (3); Church Yth Grp; FCA; FHA; HOBY; Natl Beta Clb; Band; Sec Frsh Cls; Sec Soph Cls; Sec Jr Cls; Rep Stu Cncl; Henderson ST U; Pblc Rels.

JONES, STEPHANIE L; Farmington Jr Sr HS; Fayetteville, AR; (4); 32/78; Art Clb; Church Yth Grp; Drama Clb; FBLA; FHA; Office Aide; SADD; Chorus; Church Choir; School Play; NW AR CC; Comp Pgmng.

JONES, STEPHANIE R; Lake Hamilton Sr HS; Hot Springs, AR; (2); Art Clb; Church Yth Grp; Girl Scts; Natl Beta Clb; Band; Church Choir; School Play; Hon Roll; NHS; Pres Acad Fit Awd.

JONES, TAMMY; Lee Sr HS; Palestine, AR; (2); 5/178; Church Yth Grp; Drama Clb; Natl Beta Clb; SADD; Teachers Aide; Ofcr Stu Cncl; Cit Awd; Hon Roll; Prfct Atten Awd; ASU; Comp Engrng.

JONES, TANEADRA; Lee Sr HS; Marianna, AR; (1); #3 in class; FHA; Natl Beta Clb; Science Clb; Spanish Clb; Band; Church Choir; Mrchg Band; Nwsp; Yrbk; Cit Awd; Pondtcl Hgh Drmrs; Univ AR; Pedtrcn.

JONES, TASHA D; Biggers-Reyno HS; Biggers, AR; (2); 1/20; VP FHA; Natl Beta Clb; Quiz Bowl; Yrbk; Pres Frsh Cls; VP Soph Cls; Sec Stu Cncl; Var Bsktbl; Var Sftbl; Hon Roll.

JONES, TASHA N; Mt Ida Jr Sr HS; Mount Ida, AR; (1); Church Yth Grp; High Hon Roll; Hon Roll; U Of AR; Cmptr Analyst.

JONES, TEMEKA R; Magnolia HS; Magnolia, AR; (2); Church Yth Grp; FHA; GAA; Library Aide; Office Aide; Church Choir; Sec Frsh Cls; Pres Soph Cls; Bsktbl; Vllybl; U Of AR; Ed.

JONES, TEYA M; Alma HS; Alma, AR; (2); FBLA; Sec Treas SADD; VP Soph Cls; Ofcr Stu Cncl; Var Chrldng; Cit Awd; Hon Roll; NHS; Mgr(s); Soph Hmcmnb Maid; Nrse.

JONES, THELMA L; Delta HS; Tillar, AR; (4); 3/23; Am Leg Aux Girls St; FHA; Natl Beta Clb; Pres Chorus; Rptr Yrbk; Pres Sr Cls; Pres Stu Cncl; L Bsktbl; Cit Awd; Hon Roll; Shot Put; Ger Clb; Physics Clb; AR ST Univ; Jrnlsm/Advrtsng.

JONES, VINESSA K; Corning Jr Sr HS; Corning, AR; (2); Church Yth Grp; Cmnty Wkr; Drama Clb; Spanish Clb; Variety Show; High Hon Roll; Hon Roll; NHS; 2nd Plc 96 Reg OM Comp; 1st Plc 95 Reg OM Comp; Souther Nazarene Univ; Psych.

JONES, WADE; Springdale Sr HS; Springdale, AR; (3); Am Leg Boys St; Church Yth Grp; FBLA; FTA; Intnl Clb; JA; SADD; Acpl Chr; Band; Church Choir; Yth For Christ; Bus.

JONES, WESLEY D; Gosnell Jr Sr HS; Blytheville, AR; (3); 21/75; Drama Clb; Key Clb; Natl FFA Org; Science Clb; Teachers Aide; Varsity Clb; Var Bsbl; Var Ftbl; Var Wt Lftg; Hon Roll; AR ST Univ; Mech Engr.

JONESHILL, DANE F; Crowleys Ridge Acad; Paragould, AR; (2); Church Yth Grp; Pep Clb; Acpl Chr; School Play; Variety Show; Wt Lftg; Hon Roll; Harding Univ.

JONGEWAARD, MELISSA D; Huntsville HS; Wesley, AR; (2); 4/160; Science Clb; Band; Drm Mjr(t); Jazz Band; Mrchg Band; Pep Band; Ofcr Frsh Cls; High Hon Roll; Hon Roll; Prfct Atten Awd; U AR; Medcl Sci.

JOPLIN, JENNIFER E; Southside HS; Fort Smith, AR; (2); Church Yth Grp; FBLA; Spanish Clb; Hon Roll; NHS; Pres Schlr; Partners In Chrst VP.

JORDAN, AMANDA; Ozark Adventist Acad; Round Rock, TX; (4); 3/54; Church Yth Grp; Drama Clb; Scholastic Bowl; School Play; Nwsp; Ed Yrbk; Vllybl; High Hon Roll; Hon Roll; NHS; Cmnty Svc Adopt A Kid/Grandparent; Schl Stud Senate; Dental.

JORDAN, CHRISTY; St Paul Schl; Pettigrew, AR; (3); French Clb; Natl Beta Clb; Rep Frsh Cls; Rep Soph Cls; Treas Jr Cls; Rep Stu Cncl; Trk; Hon Roll; NHS; Ntl Merit Ltr; Psych.

JORDAN, CLAY C; El Dorado Sr HS; El Dorado, AR; (1); Boy Scts; Church Yth Grp; Ftbl; Socr; Steering Comm.

JORDAN, CRYSTAL L; Lincoln HS; Lincoln, AR; (3); Church Yth Grp; FBLA; Key Clb; Model UN; Natl Beta Clb; Church Choir; School Play; Ed Nwsp; Var Chrldng; High Hon Roll; Hendrix; Phys Thrpy.

JORDAN, DEVONA M; Midland HS; Pleasant Plains, AR; (3); 10/42; Bus Profs of Am; Drama Clb; FBLA; FHA; Girl Scts; Natl Beta Clb; Pep Clb; Spanish Clb; Band; School Play; Apple Prjct 4 Yrs; Harding; Med.

JORDAN, EMILY; Ozark Adventist Acad; Round Rock, TX; (1); Teachers Aide; Yrbk; High Hon Roll.

JORDAN, JON M; Crowleys Ridge Acad; Senath, MO; (3); Art Clb; Church Yth Grp; Computer Clb; Drama Clb; FBLA; Pep Clb; Science Clb; Spanish Clb; School Play; Pres Frsh Cls.

JORDAN, KIMBERLY R; Hughes Jr-Sr HS; Hughes, AR; (1); 8/70; Church Yth Grp; Natl Beta Clb; Spanish Clb; SADD; Church Choir; Color Guard; Nwsp; Rep Frsh Cls; Cit Awd; High Hon Roll; His Mdl; Comm, Spch Mdl; G/T; AR Bapt Coll; Med.

JORDAN, LEE ANN; Glen Rose HS; Malvern, AR; (2); Church Yth Grp; FHA; Library Aide; Natl Beta Clb; Spanish Clb; Teachers Aide; Rep Stu Cncl; JV Mgr(s); JV Score Keeper; JV Vllybl; Homecoming; Henderson ST U; Elem Ed.

JORDAN, MARCHELL; Dumas Jr HS; Dumas, AR; (1); Bsktbl; Trk; Hon Roll; Pres Acad Fit Awd; Cert Schlsp; U AR; Navy.

JORDAN, MICHAEL A; J A Fair Sr HS; Little Rock, AR; (4); FBLA; Spanish Clb; Yrbk; Bsktbl; Ftbl; Golf; High Hon Roll; Hon Roll; UAR-FAYETTEVILLE.

JORDAN, MICHAEL P; Augusta HS; Little Rock, AR; (2); Teachers Aide; Church Choir; School Play; Ofcr Bsbl; Bsktbl; Trk; Vllybl; Cit Awd; U Of AR; Bus Occupation; Clercl.

JORDAN, NYTALYA C; Bearden HS; Thornton, AR; (2); 2/63; Sec Church Yth Grp; Sec FBLA; Sec FHA; Natl Beta Clb; Quiz Bowl; Pep Clb; Rep Stu Cncl; Chrldng; High Hon Roll; Pres Acad Fit Awd; U AR Fyttvl; Corp Law.

JORDAN, PHILLI N; Riverside HS; Lake City, AR; (3); Church Yth Grp; French Clb; FBLA; FHA; FTA; JA; Rep Frsh Cls; Rep Soph Cls; Pres Jr Cls; Var Bsbl; MCCC; Law Enfrcmnt.

JORDAN, SHANN R; Crossett Sr HS; Crossett, AR; (2); Church Yth Grp; Hosp Aide; Mu Alpha Theta; Natl Beta Clb; Hon Roll; Pres Acad Fit Awd.

JORDAN, SHARHONDA; Hall Sr HS; Little Rock, AR; (4); 20/290; FBLA; Natl Beta Clb; Spanish Clb; Cit Awd; High Hon Roll; Hon Roll; Jr NHS; NHS; Coop Offc Ed; Future 500; U Of AR; Comp Tech Eng.

JORDAN, STACIE D; Fordyce HS; Fordyce, AR; (4); 13/88; Church Yth Grp; Sec FBLA; Natl Beta Clb; Science Clb; Spanish Clb; Band; Chorus; Mrchg Band; Stage Crew; Hon Roll; Hnr Grad; Cntrl Bapt Coll.

JORDAN, SUSAN E; North Little Rock Hs-West; North Little Rock, AR; (3); Church Yth Grp; Cmnty Wkr; Drama Clb; Intnl Clb; Key Clb; Math Clb; Mu Alpha Theta; Natl Beta Clb; Spanish Clb; Speech Tm; Outstdng Advanced Speech & Drama Stu; St Speech Trnmt 2nd Pl 96; Theatre Arts.

JORGENSEN, JOSH A; Conway Sr HS; Conway, AR; (2); Church Yth Grp; Band; Mrchg Band; Pep Band; JV Bsbl; JV Var Bsktbl; High Hon Roll; All Amer Fitness Awd; Arch/Dsgn.

JOSEPH, BRIAN A; Arkansas Schl For Math/Sci; Jonesboro, AR; (4); Am Leg Boys St; FBLA; Mu Alpha Theta; Natl Beta Clb; Quiz Bowl; Var Socr; Var Tennis; Hon Roll; NHS; WA U At St Louis; Bus.

JOSIFEK, JINDRICH; Sylvan Hills HS; Sherwood, AR; (3); Mu Alpha Theta; Spanish Clb; Socr; Tennis; NHS; U Of The Ozarks; Law.

JOYCE, DAVID T; Van Buren Sr HS; Alma, AR; (2); Church Yth Grp; Cmnty Wkr; FCA; French Clb; FBLA; Math Clb; Mu Alpha Theta; Quiz Bowl; SADD; Teachers Aide; U Of AR; Chem Eng.

JOYNER, JESSICA L; Parkview Arts-Science HS; North Little Rock, AR; (2); Church Yth Grp; Cmnty Wkr; French Clb; Math Tm; Natl Beta Clb; Quiz Bowl; Band; Church Choir; Mrchg Band; Powder Puff Ftbl; Frgn Langs.

JUMPER, AMANDA; Calvary Christian Schl; Palestine, AR; (3); 1/11; Church Yth Grp; School Play; VP Frsh Cls; VP Soph Cls; VP Stu Cncl; Bsktbl; Sftbl; Vllybl; High Hon Roll; NHS; Southwestern Assemblies Of God.

JUMPER, PAMELA S; Calvary Christian Schl; Forrest City, AR; (4); 2/7; Chorus; School Musical; School Play; Yrbk; Hist Frsh Cls; Sec Jr Cls; Sec Stu Cncl; High Hon Roll; NHS; Sal; Tap & Jazz Dancing; Classical Piano; Talent Shows Contestant Wnnr; Miss AR & Miss USA Pageants; E AR CC.

JUNEARICK, SHAWNEQUA; Blytheville Sr HS; Blytheville, AR; (4); 5/226; Am Leg Aux Girls St; Church Yth Grp; FHA; Natl Beta Clb; Pep Clb; Spanish Clb; SADD; Church Choir; Variety Show; Ed Nwsp; Outrch Clb; Yng Ladies Clb; Everyones A Hero; U Of AR Pine Bluff; Pediatrcs.

JUNEAU, ANTHONY W; Pine Bluff HS; Pine Bluff, AR; (3); 12/425; Boy Scts; Church Yth Grp; FBLA; Science Clb; Nwsp; Yrbk; VP Stu Cncl; High Hon Roll; Jr NHS; NHS; Harding Univ; OB/GYN.

JUNIOR, BRIAN L; Hampton Jr Sr HS; Hampton, AR; (3); Church Yth Grp; Teachers Aide; Rep Stu Cncl; Pride Of Amer; Martin Luther King Jr Jr Cmmsnr; U Of AR Pine Bluff; Educl Fld.

JUNYOR, SCOTT A; Nettleton HS; Jonesboro, AR; (2); Cmnty Wkr; FHA; Natl FFA Org; Spanish Clb; Ofcr Soph Cls; Ftbl; Score Keeper; Trk; Wt Lftg; Prfct Atten Awd; Environmental & Protection Svcs Outstndg Achvmt; AR ST Univ; Sci Tchr.

JUSTUS, ALLISON; Harding Acad; Searcy, AR; (2); Church Yth Grp; Key Clb; Natl Beta Clb; Pep Clb; Chorus; Bsktbl; Trk; Harding Univ.

KAATZ, TASHA M; Fountain Lake Jr Sr HS; Hot Springs, AR; (2); FHA; Key Clb; School Musical; School Play; Var Chrldng; Var Score Keeper; JV Var Sftbl; High Hon Roll; Hon Roll; Med.

KAMPS, AARON J; Highland HS; Hardy, AR; (3); Am Leg Boys St; Church Yth Grp; Natl Beta Clb; Acpl Chr; Chorus; Church Choir; Variety Show; Ofcr Stu Cncl; Var Bsbl; JV Var Bsktbl; RAD; SOUL Highland Chrstn Clb; Williams Bapt Coll; Bus.

KAMPS, DAVID; Hall Sr HS; Little Rock, AR; (4); 23/273; VP Natl Beta Clb; Ed Yrbk; Rep Sr Cls; Crs Cntry; Var Socr; High Hon Roll; NHS; Camp Anytown Attendee; Explorer Post; Interact Clb; Lyon Coll Batesville; Jrnlsm.

KAMRUDDIN, REHANA B; Dequeen HS; De Queen, AR; (2); Church Yth Grp; FBLA; SADD; Chorus; Sec Frsh Cls; Rep Soph Cls; JV Var Bsktbl; Cit Awd; Hon Roll; Soph Homcmng Maid; FCS; U Of AR Fayetteville.

KANE, NICOLE; Vilonia HS; Conway, AR; (4); 11/125; Art Clb; Church Yth Grp; Mu Alpha Theta; Natl Beta Clb; Spanish Clb; Rep Stu Cncl; Var L Bsktbl; Var L Sftbl; High Hon Roll; Teachers Aide; Schlr Athl Club Sec; Univ Cntrl AR; Intr Dsgn.

KANEY, MELISSA L; Fountain Lake Jr Sr HS; Hot Springs, AR; (1); Natl Beta Clb; Spanish Clb; Band; Jazz Band; Mrchg Band; Hon Roll; NHS; Prfct Atten Awd; All American Schlr Awd 95; Envrnmntl Clb; Univ Cntrl AR; Vetnry Med.

KANNETT, KEITH; Pleasant View Schl; Mulberry, AR; (2); Church Yth Grp; Treas Drama Clb; VP 4-H; Treas FBLA; Natl Beta Clb; Treas Natl FFA Org; Capt Quiz Bowl; Spanish Clb; Rep Stu Cncl; Capt Var Bsktbl.

KANNETT, KEVIN; Pleasant View Schl; Mulberry, AR; (1); Church Yth Grp; Drama Clb; Natl Beta Clb; Natl FFA Org; Quiz Bowl; Var Bsktbl; Var Trk; High Hon Roll.

KAPSOS, CASSANDRA M; Lead Hill Schl; Lead Hill, AR; (2); Art Clb; German Clb; Band; Chorus; Sftbl; Hon Roll; Kids Tchng Kids; Poem Pbllshd; 1 Solo Band 3 Yrs; Art.

KARAGAS, GERRILYN; Southside HS; Fort Smith, AR; (3); 58/502; Drama Clb; Hosp Aide; Mu Alpha Theta; Band; Drm Mjr(t); Mrchg Band; School Play; Jr NHS; NHS; Spanish NHS; Band Dirs Awd; Pre-Med.

KARIGAN-WINTER, ANGELINE; Huntsville HS; Huntsville, AR; (3); Am Leg Aux Girls St; Quiz Bowl; Band; Mrchg Band; Pep Band; Treas Soph Cls; Treas Jr Cls; L Trk; High Hon Roll; NHS; Wendys HS Heisman Awd; All Rgn Band; All St Jazz Band.

KARN, BRANDON R; Cutter Morning Star Jr Sr HS; Hot Springs, AR; (4); 8/28; Cmnty Wkr; FHA; Model UN; Quiz Bowl; Science Clb; Pres Spanish Clb; Treas Soph Cls; Treas Jr Cls; Treas Sr Cls; Treas Stu Cncl; VFW Spch Cont Wnnr; U Of Ozarks; Bio.

KARN, TIFFANY M; Cutter Morning Star HS; Hot Springs, AR; (2); Art Clb; FHA; Library Aide; Office Aide; Quiz Bowl; Red Cross Aide; Spanish Clb; VP Frsh Cls; JV Chrldng; Hon Roll; Advrtsmnt.

KARNES, JAMES E; Trumann HS; Trumann, AR; (3); Church Yth Grp; Cmnty Wkr; Natl FFA Org; Science Clb; Spanish Clb; Band; Jazz Band; Mrchg Band; Pep Band; Band Ltr; Helped With Yth Sports Pgms; Ducks Unltd St Francis Lake Assn Mem; Wildlife Mgmt.

KARR, JARED K; Dequeen HS; De Queen, AR; (3); 20/150; Church Yth Grp; Cmnty Wkr; FHA; Rptr Natl FFA Org; Office Aide; Teachers Aide; Sec Chorus; Church Choir; School Musical; Hon Roll; Priv Pilots License 96; US Precision Flight Tm; Downhill Skier; Roller Blader; Fly Fisher; Wtr Skier; 4 Yr; Military/Comm Pilot.

KARSCHNER, JENNIFER; Newport HS; Newport, AR; (4); 14/149; Teachers Aide; School Play; Chrldng; Gym; High Hon Roll; Hon Roll; 2nd Pl Speech Awd; AR ST U; Television Brdcstng.

KARSON, MATTHEW S; Parkview Arts-Science HS; Little Rock, AR; (2); Chess Clb; Key Clb; Natl Beta Clb; School Play; Ofcr Stu Cncl; Tennis; Trk; High Hon Roll; Jr NHS; NHS; Lbrl Arts Schl; Molecular Bio.

KARWOSKI, MELINDA B; Russellville Sr HS; Russellville, AR; (2); Church Yth Grp; Cmnty Wkr; Hosp Aide; Natl Beta Clb; Teachers Aide; Drill Tm; Capt Chrldng; Gym; Hon Roll; Capt/All Star Chrldg Squad; U Of OK; PT.

KASNICKA, RICHARD J; Springdale Sr HS; Springdale, AR; (3); Band; Jazz Band; Mrchg Band; Pep Band; U Of AR; Arch.

KASPER, NOEL L; Westside HS; Hartman, AR; (3); Church Yth Grp; Spanish Clb; Speech Tm; Chorus; Church Choir.

KASSEES, NATALIE; Sylvan Hills HS; Sherwood, AR; (3); Rptr Art Clb; Church Yth Grp; HOBY; Q&S; Spanish Clb; Teachers Aide; Ed Nwsp; Rep Jr Cls; Rep Stu Cncl; Hon Roll; Merit Awds Engl 9-10 Grd; Prin Awd Nwspr Jrnlsm 10th Grd; Semifnls Gratorical Fstvl; UALR; Corp Law.

KAUFMAN, DANIEL D; Hope HS; Washington, AR; (4); Church Yth Grp; Cmnty Wkr; Speech Tm; Band; Jazz Band; Mrchg Band; High Hon Roll; Hon Roll; Amer Musical Fnd Band Hnrs; Outstdng Brass Instrmntlst; Law.

KAUFMAN, ERIC M; Hope HS; Hope, AR; (3); 28/230; FBLA; Natl Beta Clb; Band; Color Guard; Drm Mjr(t); Jazz Band; Mrchg Band; Orch; Pep Band; Variety Show; Sec Mus Ed.

KAUFMAN, GRETCHEN M; Mc Gehee HS; Mcgehee, AR; (2); FTA; Mu Alpha Theta; Natl Beta Clb; Science Clb; Spanish Clb; Var Chrldng; Hon Roll; NHS.

KAUFMAN, KENDRA L; Russellville Sr HS; Russellville, AR; (3); Cmnty Wkr; Band; Color Guard; Mrchg Band; Pep Band; Hon Roll; Jr NHS; NHS; Pres Acad Fit Awd; All Stars; OSU; Vet.

KAULFURST, MICHAEL A; Gosnell Jr Sr HS; Blytheville, AR; (1); Church Yth Grp; Natl FFA Org; Var Bsbl; JV Bsktbl; Var Ftbl; Hon Roll; Hnrb Mntn Alg I St Math Cmptn; LSU; Coach.

KAUPP, SUZANNE; Fayetteville Sr HS; Fayetteville, AR; (4); 1/400; Am Leg Aux Girls St; Church Yth Grp; Cmnty Wkr; Mu Alpha Theta; SADD; High Hon Roll; NHS; Val; 26 Clb; U Of AR; Law.

KAWAGOE, THERESA N; Beebe Sr HS; Beebe, AR; (3); 8/115; Church Yth Grp; FHA; Math Clb; Pep Clb; Science Clb; Spanish Clb; Chorus; Yrbk; Hon Roll; UCA.

KEASTER, BRANDY; Strong Jr Sr HS; Strong, AR; (4); 16/58; Am Leg Aux Girls St; Church Yth Grp; French Clb; FBLA; Science Clb; Varsity Clb; Band; Drm Mjr(t); Nwsp; Chrldng; Grad Ushr; Mst Bsh; L; Sha-Magnolia; Prmdc.

KEATING, AMBER; Mt St Mary Acad; North Little Rock, AR; (3); 75/170; Church Yth Grp; Cmnty Wkr; Spanish Clb; Chorus; JV Co-Capt Chrldng; U Of Cntrl AR; Phys Thrpy.

KEATON, CARMEN R; Fairview HS; Camden, AR; (3); 8/259; Am Leg Aux Girls St; FBLA; Mu Alpha Theta; Natl Beta Clb; Service Clb; Band; Rep Stu Cncl; Var JV Chrldng; NHS; Spanish NHS; U Of AR; Law.

KEATON, MANDY; Hot Springs HS; Hot Springs, AR; (1); 7/300; Church Yth Grp; Cmnty Wkr; Natl Beta Clb; Thesps; Chrldng; Gym; Tennis; High Hon Roll; Pres Acad Fit Awd; PRIDE; Tap Dnce; U AR Fyttvlle; Law.

KECK, CINECA S; Springdale Sr HS; Lowell, AR; (2); Cmnty Wkr; Natl FFA Org; Red Cross Aide; Yrbk; Ofcr Jr Cls; Gym; Jr NHS; NHS; Pep Clb; Quiz Bowl; Nom Natl Yth Ldshp Forum; Fishing Clb Brd; Renaissance Clb; Law.

KEE, AMANDA R; Clarendon Jr Sr HS; Monroe, AR; (1); FBLA; Band; Mrchg Band; Hon Roll; Leo Clb; UIAR; Phy Thrpst.

KEE, RONDI M; Kingston Jr Sr HS; Berryville, AR; (3); 40/17; Church Yth Grp; 4-H; VP FBLA; FHA; Capt GAA; Office Aide; Quiz Bowl; Teachers Aide; Capt Bsktbl; JV Trk; Pride Team; Big Brother & Big Sister Pgm; North AR CC; PE.

KEELE, LAYNE S; Hope HS; Hope, AR; (3); 1/175; Church Yth Grp; Debate Tm; FCA; Treas FBLA; Natl Beta Clb; NFL; Quiz Bowl; Speech Tm; L Tennis; NHS; FBLA Extemporaneous Speaking Natls.

KEELING, AMANDA GAIL; Rogers HS; Rogers, AR; (3); Church Yth Grp; Drama Clb; FCA; Model UN; NFL; Speech Tm; Teachers Aide; Church Choir; School Play; Hon Roll; SW Bapt U; Elem Tchr.

KEELING, APRIL; Batesville Sr HS; Batesville, AR; (4); 1/155; Am Leg Aux Girls St; Cmnty Wkr; Hosp Aide; Sec Key Clb; JA; Band; Yrbk; VP Sr Cls; Ofcr Stu Cncl; Chrldng; PRIDE St Lcl Tms; U Of AR; Chem Eng.

KEELING, LARA A; St Joe Public Schl; Saint Joe, AR; (1); 3/18; Church Yth Grp; Cmnty Wkr; 4-H; Natl FFA Org; Bsktbl; 4-H Awd; High Hon Roll; Quiz Bowl; Church Choir; VP Frsh Cls; Best Freethrow; Asst Awd; Rebound Awd; Pepsi Shootum Up Age Group Champion; WET Team; Creed Speaking Awd; U Of AR.

KEELING, TERRI M; Bald Knob HS; Bald Knob, AR; (3); 38/121; Church Yth Grp; Drama Clb; Office Aide; Spanish Clb; Teachers Aide; Band; Church Choir; Color Guard; Mrchg Band; School Musical; Beta; Yth Group Natl Gen Assembly In IN; HS Band Competes In Peach Bowl At Atlanta GA; Lee Coll; Bio Sci.

KEEN, KRISTIE D; Springdale Sr HS; Springdale, AR; (3); FCA; Library Aide; Natl FFA Org; Band; Chorus; Church Choir; Mrchg Band; Pep Band; High Hon Roll; Hon Roll; Natl Jr Hnr Soc; ASBDA Natl Conv 94; U Of AR; Social Work.

KEENER, CHARITY L; Danville HS; Ola, AR; (4); 10/49; Church Yth Grp; 4-H; French Clb; FBLA; Spanish Clb; SADD; Teachers Aide; Band; Church Choir; Mrchg Band; Chrch Yth Ldr; Chrch Song Ldr.

KEENER, MANDY N; Russellville Sr HS; Russellville, AR; (3); Model UN; Spanish Clb; Band; Socr; High Hon Roll; Hon Roll; Jr NHS; NHS; U Of AR; Int Desgn.

KEENER, TIFFANEY; North Little Rock Hs-East; North Little Rock, AR; (1); Pres Church Yth Grp; Cmnty Wkr; Band; Church Choir; Ofcr Stu Cncl; Chrldng; Grambling; Medcl.

KEENER, YOLANDA; Arkansas Sr HS; Texarkana, AR; (3); Mu Alpha Theta; Quiz Bowl; Church Choir; Var L Bsktbl; Chrldng; Var L Trk; Capt L Vllybl; Hon Roll; Jr NHS; NHS; Nurs.

KEETER, ERIC T; Lavaca Jr Sr HS; Lavaca, AR; (4); FCA; FHA; Office Aide; Science Clb; SADD; Ofcr Frsh Cls; Ofcr Sr Cls; Bsktbl; Ftbl; Cit Awd; Frosh/Jr/Sr Cls Fvrt; Mr Lavaca High; Prom King; U Of Cntrl AR; Cmptr Pgmng.

KEETER, JESSICA J; Valley Springs Schl; Harrison, AR; (2); Art Clb; Church Yth Grp; Library Aide; Sec Natl FFA Org; Yrbk; Bsktbl; Trk; Vllybl; Church Newsletter; U Of AR; Acctnt.

KEEVER, JOEL L; Bryant Sr HS; Bryant, AR; (2).

KEFFER, LEE; Dewitt HS; Stuttgart, AR; (1); #33 in class; Natl FFA Org; Science Clb; JV Ftbl; JV Trk.

KEIM, AMBER; Ola Jr Sr HS; Ola, AR; (1); Church Yth Grp; Spanish Clb; Rep Stu Cncl; Bsktbl; Chrldng; 4-H Awd; High Hon Roll; Sal; All Conf Bsktbl Hnrs; Frosh Hmcmng Maid; Univ Of AR; Pre-Med.

KEIRN, WILLARD; West Fork HS; West Fork, AR; (4); 5/72; Church Yth Grp; Cmnty Wkr; NFL; Spanish Clb; Band; Mrchg Band; Pep Band; Sec Soph Cls; Sec Sr Cls; Var Bsbl; U Of AR; Engrng.

KEITH, AMANDA; Charleston HS; Charleston, AR; (4); 1/57; Am Leg Aux Girls St; Church Yth Grp; Treas FBLA; Pres FHA; Natl Beta Clb; Ed Nwsp; Ed Yrbk; Stat Bsktbl; Val; STAR Evnts Wnnr; PRIDE Team; Spirit Girls; Westark CC; Accntng.

KEITH, BECKY; Charleston HS; Charleston, AR; (1); Church Yth Grp; FCA; Treas FBLA; Treas Frsh Cls; Bsktbl; Powder Puff Ftbl; Sftbl; Trk; Hon Roll; Westark CC.

KEITH, MICHAEL K; Fouke Jr Sr HS; Texarkana, TX; (3); Boy Scts; Church Yth Grp; Natl FFA Org; Spanish Clb; JV Bsbl; Var Bsktbl; Var Ftbl; Var Trk; Pres Acad Fit Awd; YORAD; Flagler Coll; Pre-Law.

KEITHLY, SABRINA; Omaha Schl; Omaha, AR; (4); 4/21; Chess Clb; Church Yth Grp; FBLA; Library Aide; Office Aide; SADD; Teachers Aide; Band; School Play; Stage Crew; Cmptrs; Cmptr Sci.

KELCEY, KARA L; Greenwood Sr HS; Fort Smith, AR; (2); Art Clb; Cit Awd; Hon Roll; Jr NHS; Girls V-14 Trvlng Sccr Team; Natl Eng Merit Awd; Illstr.

KELLER, JUSTIN P; Russellville Sr HS; Russellville, AR; (2); 73/405; Cmnty Wkr; Computer Clb; Model UN; Band; Mrchg Band; JV Ftbl; Hon Roll; Jr NHS; NHS; Pep Band; Model League Of Arab States; All Region Bnd 2 Yrs; Pre Med.

KELLEY, BOBBI J; Alma HS; Alma, AR; (3); French Clb; Teachers Aide; Band; Mrchg Band; Rptr Nwsp; Ed Lit Mag; Hon Roll; NHS; Westark CC; Vet.

KELLEY, JOHN; West Side Christian Schl; El Dorado, AR; (2); 4-H; Natl Beta Clb; Ftbl; 4-H Awd; Vet.

KELLEY, JULIE L; Booneville Jr Sr HS; Booneville, AR; (2); 1/120; Church Yth Grp; FBLA; FTA; Key Clb; Natl Beta Clb; Science Clb; Rptr CAP; Var Chrldng; High Hon Roll; Hon Roll; U Of AR; Architecture.

KELLEY, LESHA A; Decatur HS; Decatur, AR; (3); FHA; SADD; U Of AR.

KELLEY, MESHA L; Decatur HS; Decatur, AR; (3); FHA.

KELLEY, PHILLIP R; Magnolia HS; Waldo, AR; (4); 36/192; Church Yth Grp; FBLA; Library Aide; Mu Alpha Theta; Quiz Bowl; Scholastic Bowl; Band; Chorus; Church Choir; Mrchg Band; Stdnt Cncl VP Upwrd Bnd Pgm; Oral Roberts Univ; Cmptr Sci.

KELLEY, RHETT; Coleman Jr HS; Van Buren, AR; (2); Debate Tm; Mu Alpha Theta; Science Clb; JV Bsktbl; Cit Awd; High Hon Roll; Hon Roll; U Of AR; Med.

KELLY, CARLISSA M; Dumas HS; Dumas, AR; (2); FBLA; GAA; Library Aide; Intrml Trk; Hon Roll; Med.

KELLY, HAILA; Genoa Central HS; Texarkana, AR; (4); 1/36; Church Yth Grp; Pres VP FBLA; FHA; Model UN; Church Choir; School Play; Yrbk; Var Capt Bsktbl; Var Capt Chrldng; Var Trk; Fllwshp Chrstn Stdnts; Pres Schlrshp; AR ST U; AR ST U; Comms.

KELLY, KAREN J; Russellville Sr HS; Russellville, AR; (4); 5/282; Church Yth Grp; Teachers Aide; Band; Co-Capt Drill Tm; Chrldng; NHS; Pres Acad Fit Awd; Dance Clb; Spanish Clb; Mrchg Band; Edtor Of Yth Newslttr First United Mthdst Chrch; First Natl Bank Stubrd; Univrsl Dnce Assoc Dnce Str; U Of AR; Induseng.

KELLY, KATASHA M; Central Sr HS; Little Rock, AR; (2); Chldrns Phys.

KELLY, REBEKAH; Cabot HS; Cabot, AR; (4); 15/290; Church Yth Grp; Key Clb; Spanish Clb; Band; Flag Corp; Mrchg Band; Pep Band; Lit Mag; Ofcr Jr Cls; Ofcr Sr Cls; Acad Ltr; Hnr Grad; Medallion Wnnr; Multi-Yr Listee; Lyon Coll; Ec.

KELLY, SARA; Glen Rose HS; Benton, AR; (3); 17/60; Am Leg Aux Girls St; Art Clb; Church Yth Grp; FCA; FBLA; GAA; Spanish Clb; SADD; Ofcr Stu Cncl; Var Bsktbl; Gov Yth Conf; Ftbl Hmecmg Maid; Bsktbl Hmecmg Maid; Forensic Pthlgy.

KELLY, TERRIE C; Greenwood Sr HS; Greenwood, AR; (2); Cmnty Wkr; Library Aide; Spanish Clb; Teachers Aide; Chorus; Color Guard; Mrchg Band; Stage Crew; Swing Chorus; Psych.

KELSEY, ELIZABETH; Dermott HS; Tillar, AR; (4); 4/90; Am Leg Aux Girls St; Church Yth Grp; Cmnty Wkr; FBLA; FTA; GAA; Math Clb; Natl Beta Clb; Office Aide; Band; U Of AR Pine Bluff; Dr.

KEMP, APRIL L; Strong Jr Sr HS; Strong, AR; (2); French Clb; Science Clb; Teachers Aide; Band; Mrchg Band; Hon Roll; 4 Sts Hnr Bnd; USWBA; Henderson ST U; Med Dr.

KEMP, AUDRA L; Mountain Home HS; Mountain Home, AR; (3); Am Leg Aux Girls St; Pres Art Clb; FBLA; Quiz Bowl; Spanish Clb; Teachers Aide; Nwsp; VP Sr Cls; Hon Roll; Blue/Gold Queen; Homecoming Royality; Walt Disney Animation.

KEMP, CAROLINE A; Alma HS; Alma, AR; (4); 25/150; FCA; FBLA; Mu Alpha Theta; Spanish Clb; Band; Ofcr Stu Cncl; Chrldng; Pom Pon; Hon Roll; NHS; Westark CC; Acctg.

KEMPER, MECHELE; Morrilton Sr HS; Plumerville, AR; (2); Art Clb; Church Yth Grp; 4-H; French Clb; Library Aide; Natl Beta Clb; High Hon Roll; Hon Roll; Art; Grphc Art.

KEMPF, SHELBY A; West Memphis Christian Schl; Marion, AR; (1); 2/32; Natl Beta Clb; Pres Frsh Cls; JV Bsktbl; Var Sftbl; JV Trk; JV Vllybl; High Hon Roll; Hon Roll; Pres Acad Fit Awd; Algebra II Highest GPA; Miss Hustle Bsktabl; Harding Univ; Lawyer.

KENDRICK, AMBER B; Russellville Sr HS; Russellville, AR; (3); Church Yth Grp; Cmnty Wkr; Spanish Clb; Band; Drm Mjr(t); Mrchg Band; Pep Band; High Hon Roll; Jr NHS; NHS; Majrtte Ln Capt; Bio.

KENDRICK, CARRIE; Springdale Sr HS; Springdale, AR; (3); 1/500; Computer Clb; Acpl Chr; Band; Chorus; Mrchg Band; Variety Show; Hon Roll; NHS; Ntl Merit SF; Physics/Psych.

KENDRICK, ERIN L; Pulaski Acad; Venetia, PA; (2); Cmnty Wkr; Natl Beta Clb; Spanish Clb; Orch; Rptr Yrbk; Sftbl; High Hon Roll; NHS; Interact Clb.

KENDRICK, ROBERT J; Osceola HS; Osceola, AR; (4); 49/102; Church Yth Grp; Key Clb; Library Aide; Math Clb; Science Clb; Spanish Clb; Band; Mrchg Band; Rptr Nwsp; Ed Yrbk; AR ST U; Ed.

KENNEDY, BRANDY K; Cabot HS; Cabot, AR; (2); Cmnty Wkr; French Clb; Key Clb; Rptr Yrbk; Tennis; French Hon Soc; Hon Roll; Jr NHS; NHS; Pres Acad Fit Awd; Natl Fr Exam Top 15 Prcnt; PSAT; UCA; Bus.

KENNEDY, JOSH L; Lake Hamilton Sr HS; Hot Springs, AR; (2); 1/320; Boy Scts; Church Yth Grp; FCA; FBLA; Natl Beta Clb; Spanish Clb; Stat Bsktbl; High Hon Roll; NHS; Stu Chrstn Life; Piano-Natl Piano Gld-5; Baylor; Orthpdc.

KENNEDY, JULIE; Camden-Fairview HS; Camden, AR; (3); 2/289; HOBY; Mu Alpha Theta; Pres Natl Beta Clb; VP Science Clb; SADD; Treas Frsh Cls; Ofcr Soph Cls; Treas Jr Cls; Church Yth Grp; Cmnty Wkr; Natl Yth Ldrshp Frm Def, Intllgnce, Dplmcy Rep; Louis Feinstein Hmntrn Awd; Ouachita Bapt U; Med.

KENNEDY, KRISTY; Gosnell Jr Sr HS; Blytheville, AR; (3); Church Yth Grp; FHA; Science Clb; Band; Co-Capt Flag Corp; Nwsp; Sftbl; Hon Roll; ASU; Medicine; Pediatrician.

KENNEDY, KRYSTAL S; Dumas HS; Dumas, AR; (2); #32 in class; Church Yth Grp; Church Choir; Bsktbl; Trk; Wt Lftg; Hon Roll; U Of TN; Astronomy; Nutrition.

KENNEDY, SONYA G; Forrest City HS; Forrest City, AR; (3); DECA; Vllybl; Hon Roll; EACC; RN.

KENNEDY, TORRIE R; Morrilton Sr HS; Morrilton, AR; (4); 13/150; Church Yth Grp; Natl Beta Clb; Thesps; Nwsp; Vllybl; U Of Cntrl AR; Pre-Med.

KENNETT, LORI A; Ridgecrest HS; Paragould, AR; (3); 42/207; Church Yth Grp; Drama Clb; GAA; Chorus; School Musical; Yrbk; Bsktbl; Vllybl; Hon Roll; Pres Acad Fit Awd; ASU; Primary Tchr; Scndry Tchr.

KENNEY, KAREN V; Mayflower HS; Mayflower, AR; (2); 6/70; Church Yth Grp; Drama Clb; French Clb; FBLA; Hosp Aide; Natl Beta Clb; Quiz Bowl; Band; Chorus; Church Choir; Odsy Mnd; AEGIS Prgm; Faulkner Cty Ldrshp Prgm; U Of Cntrl AR; Msc Tchr/Dir.

KENT, AMANDA; Ashdown Sr HS; Ashdown, AR; (2); Church Yth Grp; FHA; Natl FFA Org; Church Choir; Chrldng; Cit Awd; Engl/Hlth/Algebra I/Civics Awds; Cosmetology.

KENT, RHONDA; Sulphur Rock Schl; Sulphur Rock, AR; (4); 3/21; Am Leg Aux Girls St; FBLA; FHA; GAA; Key Clb; Natl Beta Clb; Yrbk; VP Frsh Cls; VP Jr Cls; VP Sr Cls; Hmcmng Qn; Bsktbl All Conf Tm; Natl Eng Mrt Awd; U Of AR; Bus.

KEOWN, AMANDA; Hall Sr HS; Little Rock, AR; (3); French Clb; Natl Beta Clb; Church Choir; Drill Tm; Sec Sr Cls; Ofcr Stu Cncl; French Hon Soc; High Hon Roll; NHS; Engr.

KERBY, JOSEPH; Greene Co Tech HS; Paragould, AR; (3); 1/180; Sec Computer Clb; French Clb; FBLA; HOBY; Office Aide; Quiz Bowl; Teachers Aide; Yrbk; Ofcr Stu Cncl; NHS; Eagle Schlr Ctzn; Cmptr Sci.

KERBY, KARLYN R; De Soto Schl; West Helena, AR; (2); 1/25; Church Yth Grp; Drama Clb; School Play; Bsktbl; Chrldng; Golf; High Hon Roll; NHS; 95 UCA All-Star Chrldr; 96 NCA All-Amer Chrldr; 95 Hmcmng Crt; Med.

KERR, BRADLEY G; Highland HS; Hardy, AR; (2); 2/101; Church Yth Grp; Natl Beta Clb; Var Bsktbl; Var Ftbl; Var Trk; Cit Awd; Hon Roll; Prfct Atten Awd; Hi-Gate; Mock Trial Team.

KERR, SHANE M; Pine Bluff HS; Pine Bluff, AR; (2); 7/540; Church Yth Grp; French Clb; Library Aide; Natl Beta Clb; Office Aide; Chorus; Lit Mag; Var L Golf; High Hon Roll; Hon Roll; Sci Fair 1st Pl Schl/3rd Pl Regnl 96.

KERSH, WILLIAM G; Valley Springs Schl; Harrison, AR; (3); Boy Scts; French Clb; Band; Pep Band; School Play; Hon Roll; Voted Best Musician In Band; Sr Scholars; U Of AR Monticello; Music Ed.

KETCHAM, WESLEY K; Parkview Arts-Science HS; Little Rock, AR; (3); 22/272; Chess Clb; Cmnty Wkr; Latin Clb; Model UN; Natl Beta Clb; Ftbl; Hon Roll; NHS; Ntl Merit Ltr; Mech Eng.

KETCHUM, APRIL B; Russellville Sr HS; Russellville, AR; (2); 100/428; French Clb; Natl Beta Clb; Band; Color Guard; Flag Corp; Mrchg Band; Pep Band; NHS; All Region Band 3 Yrs; All ST Band 1st Band/1st Chair; Duke; Med.

KETRON, NIKKI; Calico Rock HS; Calico Rock, AR; (3); 8/32; Rptr FHA; Mgr Bsktbl; Mgr(s); Hon Roll; FFA; Var Boys/Girls Mgr; Sci Clb; SADD; Berea Coll; Crnvl Ind.

KETTER, GREG; Charleston HS; Charleston, AR; (2); Church Yth Grp; FCA; FBLA; Natl Beta Clb; Quiz Bowl; Pres Soph Cls; Rep Stu Cncl; Var L Bsbl; L Var Ftbl; L Var Trk; Law Enfrcmnt.

KEYES, MORGAN G; Pulaski Acad; Little Rock, AR; (4); Am Leg Boys St; Boy Scts; Church Yth Grp; FCA; Letterman Clb; Rep Soph Cls; L Bsktbl; L Ftbl; Eagle Sct; All AR Ftbl; U Of AR; Premed.

KEYS, ANGELA; Ft Smith Christian Schl; Fort Smith, AR; (3); 3/38; Church Yth Grp; FCA; Church Choir; VP Frsh Cls; Pres Soph Cls; Rep Stu Cncl; Bsktbl; JV Var Chrldng; Trk; High Hon Roll; Westark CC; CPA.

KHAMIS, ROMMY M; John L Mcclellan Magnet HS; Little Rock, AR; (2); Church Yth Grp; Dance Clb; FBLA; Natl Beta Clb; Spanish Clb; Church Choir; Var Cit Awd; High Hon Roll; Hon Roll; Prfct Atten Awd; Yth Ldrshp Inst; PRIDE; Fnlst AGOC Oratorical Fstvl Little Rock/Memphis; Henderson ST Univ; Crmnl Justc.

KHAN, AMIR S; Russellville Sr HS; Russellville, AR; (4); 18/300; Am Leg Boys St; Cmnty Wkr; French Clb; Quiz Bowl; Crs Cntry; Trk; Hon Roll; Jr NHS; NHS; Pres Acad Fit Awd; AR Governors Schl 95; Governors Yth Cmssn; HS All-Stars; U Of AR; Arabic; Medicine.

KIFER, KENDRA; Southside HS; Fort Smith, AR; (1); Church Yth Grp; FCA; Chorus; Chrldng; Gym; High Hon Roll; Jr NHS.

KILBREATH, MARCUS G; Corning HS; Mc Dougal, AR; (3); 43/80; Natl FFA Org; Spanish Clb; L Bsbl; L Bsktbl; L Ftbl; Wt Lftg; Cit Awd; U Of AR; Phy Thrpst.

KILBURN, JUSTIN; Dumas HS; Dumas, AR; (2); FBLA; Letterman Clb; Natl Beta Clb; Spanish Clb; Varsity Clb; Yrbk; Golf; Hon Roll; NHS; Pres Acad Fit Awd.

KILGORE, HEATHER; Southside HS; Fort Smith, AR; (4); Capt Dance Clb; French Clb; Key Clb; Mu Alpha Theta; Capt Drill Tm; Ofcr Stu Cncl; Capt Chrldng; High Hon Roll; NHS; Pres Acad Fit Awd; Ft Smith Ldrshp Explr Post; Dnc Tchr; Dmnstrtr; Ms Strmkr Dnc Awd; OKC U; Dnc Prfmnc.

KILGORE, JASON; Jasper HS; Jasper, AR; (4); Art Clb; Debate Tm; JA; Math Clb; Rptr Natl FFA Org; Cit Awd; High Hon Roll; Hon Roll; Prfct Atten Awd; Prlmntry Prcdr; Dairy Fds & Elec Jdgng Teams; Drftng & Survey Of Fine Arts Awds; AR Tech U; Ag Bus.

KILLIAN, CANDINA D; Mena HS; Kirby, AR; (2); French Clb; FBLA; Science Clb; JV Bsktbl; JV Sftbl; JV Vllybl; French Hon Soc.

KILLIAN, JEREMY B; Fouke Jr Sr HS; Fouke, AR; (2); Church Yth Grp; SADD; JV Bsktbl; L Ftbl; JV Trk; YORAD; Yth Alv; U Of TX; Bus Entrprnr.

KILLIAN, MELISSA M; Mountain View Jr Sr HS; Mountain View, AR; (4); FHA; Office Aide; Spanish Clb; Teachers Aide; Chorus; Variety Show; Cit Awd; High Hon Roll; Pres Acad Fit Awd; ASU; Crim Just.

KILLOUGH, AARON; Coleman Jr HS; Van Buren, AR; (2); Hon Roll; NHS; Prfct Atten Awd; Poli Sci.

KILLOUGH, AMANDA M; Mayflower HS; Mayflower, AR; (3); FBLA; Service Clb; Teachers Aide; Hon Roll; Medicine.

KIM, SOL ME; Fayetteville Sr HS; Fayetteville, AR; (3); Art Clb; Math Clb; Math Tm; Model UN; Mu Alpha Theta; Natl Beta Clb; Quiz Bowl; Science Clb; Spanish Clb; Rep Frsh Cls; Judo Tournmt Awds; ST Sci Fair Engrng 3rd Pl Awd; Sigma Xi Recgntn Cert Awd; Engrng.

KIM, TIFFANIE; Harrison Sr HS; Harrison, AR; (2); Drama Clb; Band; Mrchg Band; School Play; Stage Crew; Drama/Music/Piano; U Of AK; Music/Actor.

KIMBALL, AARON V; Benton Cty Christian School; Rogers, AR; (3); Spanish Clb; Teachers Aide; Var Bsktbl; Var Socr; Wt Lftg; Hon Roll; Prfct Atten Awd; John Brown Univ; Phy Ftnss.

KIMBERLIN, CANDICE E; Midland HS; Pleasant Plains, AR; (3); Church Yth Grp; Drama Clb; FBLA; FHA; Girl Scts; Natl Beta Clb; Quiz Bowl; Spanish Clb; Band; School Play.

KIMBLE, LAQUELIA S; Star City HS; Star City, AR; (2); Church Yth Grp; Mu Alpha Theta; Natl Beta Clb; Office Aide; Church Choir; Ofcr Stu Cncl; Cit Awd; DAR Awd; Hon Roll; Prfct Atten Awd; U Of Cntrl AR; Pre Med.

KIMBRELL, KAREN; Morion HS; West Memphis, AR; (2); French Clb; Hosp Aide; Band; Mrchg Band; Pep Band; Hon Roll; Jr NHS; All Amer Schlr; Concert Band; Band All Region Awd; AK ST Univ; Bus.

KIMBROUGH, DEMETRIA R; Mills HS; Little Rock, AR; (3); 41/298; Office Aide; Yrbk; Ofcr Frsh Cls; Ofcr Jr Cls; Bsktbl; Vllybl; Hon Roll; Fisk Univ; Chem.

KIMERY, TODD; Murfreesboro HS; Murfreesboro, AR; (1); 4/45; Church Yth Grp; FHA; Quiz Bowl; Spanish Clb; Mrchg Band; Bsktbl; Ftbl; Trk; Hon Roll; Scuba Diving; Hunting; Harding Coll; Vet Medicine.

KIMES, AMANDA M; Huntsville HS; Huntsville, AR; (4); 4/125; Key Clb; Natl FFA Org; Sec Jr Cls; Sec Sr Cls; Rep Stu Cncl; Chrldng; Mgr(s); Rep NHS; Church Yth Grp; Library Aide; Pride VP; MASH Pres; U Cntrl AK; Phys Thrp.

KIMES, WENDY J; Northside HS; Fort Smith, AR; (2); Church Yth Grp; FHA; German Clb; Hosp Aide; Key Clb; Hon Roll; UCA; Phys Thpy.

KINARD, CHRISTY; Tuckerman HS; Newport, AR; (3); Am Leg Aux Girls St; Church Yth Grp; Cmnty Wkr; Rptr FBLA; Sec Natl Beta Clb; Sec Frsh Cls; Treas Soph Cls; Bsktbl; Sftbl; Hon Roll; Music Clb Rprtr; Hist Clb Sec; Mck Trl; Bus.

KINARD, WENDY E; Arkadelphia Sr HS; Arkadelphia, AR; (4); Art Clb; Cmnty Wkr; Quiz Bowl; Teachers Aide; Ed Nwsp; Yrbk; High Hon Roll; Hon Roll; Jr NHS; NHS; Close Up WA; Henderson ST U; Sports Med.

KINCADE, ADRIAN L; Eudora HS; Eudora, AR; (4); 15/65; Cmnty Wkr; Rptr FBLA; FHA; Library Aide; Mrchg Band; ROTC; Drill Tm; Bsktbl; Rptr Gen Coop Ed; Philander Smith Coll; Bus.

KINDLE, LEAH; Victory Christian Schl; Camden, AR; (1); 1/7; Church Yth Grp; Drama Clb; 4-H; GAA; Pep Clb; Church Choir; School Play; Var Bsktbl; Var Chrldng; Var Sftbl.

KING, AKESHA L; Star City HS; Star City, AR; (2); French Clb; FBLA; FHA; Math Clb; Mu Alpha Theta; Natl Beta Clb; Science Clb; Spanish Clb; Band; Cit Awd; AR U; Comp Tchr.

KING, ALISHA; Delta Special Schl; Tillar, AR; (1); 4/22; Church Yth Grp; Cmnty Wkr; JA; Natl Beta Clb; SADD; Church Choir; VP Frsh Cls; Cit Awd; Hon Roll; U Of Pine Bluff; Med.

KING, ARWEN; Beebe Jr HS; Beebe, AR; (1); Girl Scts; Natl Beta Clb; Band; Church Choir; Drm Mjr(t); Jazz Band; Trk; High Hon Roll; JAM Cncl.

KING, BOBBY; Pea Ridge HS; Garfield, AR; (1); 4/40; Church Yth Grp; Natl FFA Org; Hon Roll; NHS; Star Greenhand Degree In FFA; Renaissance Reward; U Of AR; Comp Sales & Repair.

KING, CHASITY L; Newport HS; Diaz, AR; (3); FHA; Spanish Clb; Cit Awd; Hon Roll; Coll Of The Ozarks; RN.

KING, CHRISTY D; Clarksville HS; Clarksville, AR; (3); Church Yth Grp; French Clb; Girl Scts; Key Clb; Math Clb; Natl Beta Clb; Science Clb; High Hon Roll; Pres Acad Fit Awd; Flag Corp; Cvl Engrng.

KING, DEMETRIA; Pine Bluff HS; Pine Bluff, AR; (2); Church Yth Grp; French Clb; FHA; FTA; GAA; Girl Scts; Natl Beta Clb; Scholastic Bowl; Science Clb; Band; Psych.

KING, DEREK C; Rogers HS; Rogers, AR; (3); Church Yth Grp; FCA; Ftbl; Wt Lftg.

KING, DONNA R; El Dorado Sr HS; Lawson, AR; (3); Church Yth Grp; Natl Beta Clb; Teachers Aide; Church Choir; NHS; Piano.

KING, DORRIE L; Russellville Sr HS; Russellville, AR; (3); Church Yth Grp; FCA; Natl Beta Clb; Band; Color Guard; Jazz Band; Mrchg Band; Pep Band; JV Var Sftbl; JV Var Vllybl; All Reg Band; CSU; Vet Med.

KING, DUSTIN; De Soto Schl; West Helena, AR; (1); Dance Clb; Stage Crew; Golf; Hon Roll; Hntg; Fshng.

KING, FELICIA S; Ola Jr Sr HS; Dardanelle, AR; (3); Art Clb; Church Yth Grp; Computer Clb; Natl Beta Clb; Spanish Clb; Church Choir; Bsktbl; High Hon Roll; Hon Roll; AR Tech U; Bus Mgmt.

KING, GLADYS E; Oak Grove HS; Little Rock, AR; (3); Church Yth Grp; Computer Clb; Dance Clb; FBLA; GAA; Office Aide; Pep Clb; Band; Church Choir; School Musical; Law.

KING V, JAMES B; Parkers Chapel Schl; El Dorado, AR; (3); Church Yth Grp; FBLA; Natl Beta Clb; Quiz Bowl; Spanish Clb; Teachers Aide; Band; Jazz Band; Mrchg Band; Stage Crew; Pianist; Span Awd.

KING, JAMES L; Central HS; Helena, AR; (3); Acpl Chr; Hon Roll; NHS; Prfct Atten Awd; Bsktbl; Video Games; AR ST; Sports Commentator.

KING, JEFF S; Harrison Sr HS; Harrison, AR; (4); Key Clb; Letterman Clb; Rep Stu Cncl; L Bsbl; L Bsktbl; L Ftbl; L Golf; L Trk; Hon Roll; NHS; U Of AR; Bus.

KING, JON D; Arkansas Schl Math & Science; Wynne, AR; (4); Am Leg Boys St; Boy Scts; Church Yth Grp; FBLA; Mu Alpha Theta; Natl Beta Clb; Spanish Clb; Ofcr Sr Cls; Bsktbl; Ftbl; Physics Olympiad Tm 96; Nom Natl Sci Mrt Awd Wnr; GA Inst Of Tech; Elec Engr/Bus.

KING, KELLEY A; Star City HS; Star City, AR; (3); 9/95; Art Clb; Church Yth Grp; English Clb; French Clb; FBLA; FHA; Mu Alpha Theta; Hon Roll; NHS; Sftbl; Phy Ther.

KING, KELLY R; Black Rock Jr Sr HS; Portia, AR; (2); 4-H; FHA; School Musical; Ofcr Frsh Cls; Ofcr Soph Cls; Bsktbl; Sftbl; Cit Awd; 4-H Awd; Hon Roll; FHA Ofcr & Parlimentarian; Law; Child Care.

KING, KEVIN G; Springdale Sr HS; Springdale, AR; (3); 1/800; Natl Beta Clb; Office Aide; Quiz Bowl; Yrbk; Intrml Bsktbl; JV Trk; High Hon Roll; Hon Roll; NHS.

KING, KYLA A; Clarksville HS; Clarksville, AR; (3); Church Yth Grp; DECA; Drama Clb; English Clb; French Clb; FBLA; Math Clb; Natl Beta Clb; Science Clb; Rptr Nwsp; Miss Teen Of AR Schlsp & Recognition Pgm Participant; Acad Excl Awd; AR Tech Univ; Jrnlsm.

KING, LAURA L; Ft Smith Christian Schl; Van Buren, AR; (2); Church Yth Grp; FCA; FBLA; Teachers Aide; Band; Church Choir; Chrldng; Hon Roll; Westark CC; Jrnlsm; Broadcstng.

KING, MARLO; Lee Sr HS; Marianna, AR; (2); Cmnty Wkr; Natl Beta Clb; Quiz Bowl; Band; Ftbl; High Hon Roll; Hon Roll; Prfct Atten Awd; Engr.

KING, MATT; Jasper HS; Jasper, AR; (4); Church Yth Grp; FBLA; FHA; Library Aide; Math Clb; Math Tm; Natl FFA Org; Science Clb; Spanish Clb; Varsity Clb; NACTC; Bus Mgmt.

KING, MICHAEL T; Southside HS; Batesville, AR; (2); Church Yth Grp; HOBY; Key Clb; Spanish Clb; Mrchg Band; Pep Band; Pres Soph Cls; Golf; Hon Roll; Kiwanis Awd; AR State Univ.

KING, NORISHA; Eudora HS; Eudora, AR; (4); 7/57; French Clb; FHA; Natl Beta Clb; Capt Bsktbl; Capt Chrldng; Trk; NHS; Ntl Merit Ltr; Miss Chicot Cty Fair Qn; St Track Team; Number 7 Cls Of 57; Alcorn ST U; Comp Sci.

KING, STEPHANIE; Mulberry HS; Mulberry, AR; (3); 1/37; FBLA; Pres Natl FFA Org; Science Clb; Teachers Aide; Sec Jr Cls; Var L Bsktbl; Var Sftbl; Var Vllybl; High Hon Roll; NHS; Greenhand Awd FFA; U Of AR; Ag Bus.

KING, TIFFANIE C; Central Sr HS; Little Rock, AR; (3); 157/540; FBLA; FHA; FTA; Natl Beta Clb; Spanish Clb; Ofcr Drill Tm; Rep Frsh Cls; Chrldng; Vllybl; Hon Roll; Top Teens Of Amer; Progssve Ldrs; Spellman Univ; Premed.

KING, YOLANDA R; Central HS; Helena, AR; (1); ROTC; Band; Color Guard; Drill Tm; Mrchg Band; Pep Band; Columbia Univ.

KINNEY, KIMBERLY A; Arkansas Sr HS; Texarkana, AR; (2); 37/471; Church Yth Grp; Hosp Aide; Sec Spanish Clb; Rep Jr Cls; JV Bsktbl; Stat L Mgr(s); Hon Roll; Pres Acad Fit Awd; Nrsng.

KINSELLA, RONNA; Benton Sr HS; Benton, AR; (2); Spanish Clb; Band; Chorus; Drm Mjr(t); Phtg Rptr Nwsp; Phtg Rptr Yrbk; Rep Stu Cncl; Jr NHS; Kiwanis Awd; Pres Acad Fit Awd; Natl Sci Merit Awd Winner; All Amer Scholar Nom; American Univ; Intl Relations.

KIRBY, ANGELA K; Cty Line HS; Barling, AR; (3); Church Yth Grp; FCA; FBLA; FHA; Hosp Aide; Natl Beta Clb; Quiz Bowl; Yrbk; Chrldng; Sftbl.

KIRBY, BRIAN C; North Little Rock Hs-West; North Little Rock, AR; (3); 96/554; Am Leg Boys St; Church Yth Grp; FCA; Mu Alpha Theta; Natl Beta Clb; Teachers Aide; Var L Bsbl; L Bsktbl; Hon Roll; All Conf Bsbl 2 Yr; All ST Bsbl 2 Yr; Team MVP Bsbl 95-.

KIRCHHOFF, CRYSTAL; Caddo Hills Jr Sr HS; Glenwood, AR; (3); 1/39; FCA; FBLA; FHA; Treas Natl Beta Clb; Quiz Bowl; Spanish Clb; Mrchg Band; VP Jr Cls; Bsktbl; Sftbl; U Of AR; Pltcl Sci/Law.

KIRK, COLIN W; Sloan Hendrix HS; Ravenden, AR; (2); Natl Beta Clb; Quiz Bowl; Band; High Hon Roll; Prfct Atten Awd; Gifted/Talented Prgm; Project WET.

KIRK, DAVID P; Springdale Sr HS; Springdale, AR; (2); VICA; Chorus; School Musical; Jr NHS; NHS; Pres Acad Fit Awd; Plays Guitar/Drums; Chrch Bnd.

KIRK, LINDSEY G; Lincoln HS; Lincoln, AR; (1); Natl FFA Org; Vet.

KIRK, LYNNETTE D; Lincoln HS; Lincoln, AR; (4); 4/59; FBLA; Natl Beta Clb; Spanish Clb; Band; Mrchg Band; Pep Band; Cit Awd; High Hon Roll; Prfct Atten Awd; John Phillip Sousa Awd; All Rgn Awd; Northeastern; Acctng.

KIRK, MARY AMANDA; Morrilton Sr HS; Morrilton, AR; (2); Art Clb; Dance Clb; Drama Clb; French Clb; Thesps; UCA Yth Theater Group; U Of Cntrl AR; Art/Drama.

KIRK, WHITNEY; Cabot HS; Cabot, AR; (2); Church Yth Grp; French Clb; Band; School Musical; School Play; Stage Crew; Rep Frsh Cls; Rep Soph Cls; Rep Sr Cls; Chrldng; Forensics Squad.

KIRKCONNELL, EVAN S; Russellville Sr HS; Russellville, AR; (2); Church Yth Grp; Band; Var L Swmmng; Var Trk; High Hon Roll; Jr NHS; NHS.

KIRKLAND, KELLY J; Cabot HS; Cabot, AR; (4); Church Yth Grp; Natl FFA Org; Office Aide; Spanish Clb; Band; Mrchg Band; Hon Roll; Kiwanis Awd; NHS; Spanish NHS; PALS; Harding Univ; Psych.

KIRTLEY, JENNIFER; Oak Grove HS; North Little Rock, AR; (2); FCA; Letterman Clb; Natl Beta Clb; Teachers Aide; Bsktbl; Chrldng; Trk; Vllybl; Hon Roll; Mrktg.

KIRTLEY, JOHN; Fairview HS; Camden, AR; (4); 2/240; Boy Scts; Church Yth Grp; Cmnty Wkr; Drama Clb; French Clb; Key Clb; Math Clb; Mu Alpha Theta; Natl Beta Clb; Quiz Bowl; Governors Schlr; AR Times Acad All Star; Eagle Sct; Ouachita Bapt Univ; Pre-Med.

KISER, HALEY; Hatfield Schl; Hatfield, AR; (1); 1/35; FBLA; Natl FFA Org; Quiz Bowl; JV Bsktbl; Sftbl; High Hon Roll.

KITCHENS, ALICIA D; Umpire Schl; Dierks, AR; (2); 5/13; Church Yth Grp; FBLA; GAA; Natl FFA Org; Phtg Yrbk; Bsktbl; Trk; High Hon Roll; Drug Prvtn Grp; USBEA; Nrs.

KITCHENS, JAMES; Lewisville HS; Lewisville, AR; (3); 1/42; Church Yth Grp; FBLA; HOBY; Office Aide; Spanish Clb; Band; Drm Mjr(t); Ofcr Stu Cncl; Hon Roll; NHS; Natl Ldrshp Mrt Awd; All-Amer Schlr.

KITTRELL, EMILY B; Springdale Sr HS; Springdale, AR; (2); Library Aide; Teachers Aide; Band; Drm Mjr(t); Mrchg Band; Hon Roll; Jr NHS; Pres Schlr.

KIVELL, WILLIAM D; Catholic HS; Little Rock, AR; (2); Boy Scts; Church Yth Grp; Cmnty Wkr; Debate Tm; 4-H; French Clb; Letterman Clb; Chorus; Rep Yrbk; Sec Stu Cncl; Nrsng Home Vol; Little League Bsbl Asst Coach; Altar Boy; Tulane; Pediatrician; Lawyer.

KIZER, AMBER; Mulberry HS; Mulberry, AR; (4); 1/28; Am Leg Aux Girls St; Church Yth Grp; French Clb; FBLA; FHA; HOBY; Natl FFA Org; Nwsp; High Hon Roll; NHS; Chem & SMASH Clubs; VIP Day.

KIZER, ANGELA A; Southside HS; Fort Smith, AR; (3); 141/502; French Clb; Teachers Aide; Band; Flag Corp; Mrchg Band; Hon Roll; NHS; Intgeract; Sail.

KIZER, HEATHER; Atkins Schl; Atkins, AR; (2); FBLA; Science Clb; Ofcr Stu Cncl; High Hon Roll; Hon Roll; AR Tech; CPA.

KIZER, TARA J; Southside HS; Fort Smith, AR; (2); FCA; Teachers Aide; Band; Mrchg Band; Hon Roll; U Of AZ; PT.

KLAIS, KRISTY; Cabot HS; Cabot, AR; (2); 14/400; French Clb; Hon Roll; Ntl Merit Ltr; Natl Fr Exam; 1st Pl Poetry Recitation; Psych.

KLAWETTER, HEATHER D; East End Jr Sr HS; Bigelow, AR; (2); Cmnty Wkr; Drama Clb; FHA; Girl Scts; Natl Beta Clb; Chorus; Yrbk; Chrldng; Hon Roll; Miss Teen AR Pgnt Contstnt; Tchr.

KLECK, ANGIE; Scranton HS; Scranton, AR; (3); FBLA; FHA; German Clb; Letterman Clb; Natl Beta Clb; Science Clb; VP Soph Cls; Stat Bsbl; Var Bsktbl; Var Chrldng; AR Tech Univ.

KLEINMENZ, SARAH; Hot Springs HS; Hot Springs, AR; (1); Church Yth Grp; FBLA; Natl Beta Clb; Office Aide; Thesps; School Musical; Chrldng; Hon Roll; Tchr; Fshn Merchandising.

KLEPPER, BARBARA K; Harrison Sr HS; Harrison, AR; (3); Church Yth Grp; Cmnty Wkr; Drama Clb; Thesps; Band; Church Choir; Flag Corp; Mrchg Band; Pep Band; School Musical; Hendrix Conway AR; Behvrl Psyc.

KLINETOB, LIESEL M; Lake Hamilton Sr HS; Hot Springs, AR; (4); 54/271; Church Yth Grp; Cmnty Wkr; GAA; Office Aide; Spanish Clb; Co-Capt Vllybl; Hon Roll; Ramon Rozzel Spnsh Schlrshp; John Brown U; Brdcstng.

KLING, JULIE; Farmington Jr Sr HS; Fayetteville, AR; (2); FBLA; Model UN; Spanish Clb; Band; Color Guard; Drill Tm; Hon Roll; NHS; Mock Trial; U Of AR; Psycht.

KLONOWSKI, BETHANY; Newark Jr Sr HS; Newark, AR; (3); 1/85; Am Leg Aux Girls St; Church Yth Grp; FBLA; Quiz Bowl; Pres Spanish Clb; VP Frsh Cls; Ofcr Soph Cls; VP Stu Cncl; Chrldng; Sftbl; PRIDE St Tm 3 Yrs; Tutor.

KNAPER, MICHAEL W; Lake Hamilton Sr HS; Hot Springs Natio, AR; (3); 59/212; FCA; VP Frsh Cls; Var Bsbl; L Bsktbl; Hon Roll; NHS; Pres Acad Fit Awd.

KNAPP, MARY A; Pangburn Jr Sr HS; Heber Springs, AR; (3); FHA; Chrldng; Gym.

KNIGHT, DANIELLE L; Dardanelle HS; Dardanelle, AR; (2); Church Yth Grp; Dance Clb; Drama Clb; Natl Beta Clb; Band; Mrchg Band; Pep Band; School Play; Ofcr Stu Cncl; Cit Awd; Med.

KNIGHT, JEANNA J; Westside HS; Hartman, AR; (2); 4-H; HOBY; Natl Beta Clb; Chorus; 4-H Awd; Hon Roll; Prfct Atten Awd; AR Tech.

KNIGHT, KATHRINE A; Pulaski Acad; Little Rock, AR; (1); Art Clb; Church Yth Grp; Cmnty Wkr; Dance Clb; FCA; Natl Beta Clb; Spanish Clb; Variety Show; Sftbl; Vllybl; Law; Medicine.

KNIGHT, MARK A; Weiner HS; Weiner, AR; (2); Church Yth Grp; Drama Clb; FBLA; HOBY; Church Choir; School Play; Ofcr Soph Cls; Bsktbl; Jr NHS; Prfct Atten Awd; Theatrical Arts.

KNIGHT, TIARRA; Drew Central Jr Sr HS; Monticello, AR; (3); #2 in class; Drama Clb; FBLA; HOBY; Science Clb; Chorus; School Play; Yrbk; VP Frsh Cls; Sec Rep Soph Cls; Hon Roll; U Of AR Monticello; Med.

KNIGHTEN, MELINDA; Foreman Jr Sr HS; Foreman, AR; (4); 2/49; Sec FBLA; Teachers Aide; Ed Yrbk; Rep Stu Cncl; High Hon Roll; NHS; Sal; Texarkana CC; Pediatric Nrs.

KNIGHTON, TERRANCE M; North Little Rock Hs-East; North Little Rock, AR; (2); FBLA; Math Clb; Spanish Clb; Ofcr Bsbl; Bsktbl; Ftbl; Tennis; High Hon Roll; Hon Roll; VA Tech; Elec Engrng.

KNIPSCHEER, CHRISTINE E; Conway Sr HS; Conway, AR; (4); 15/520; Cmnty Wkr; Sec Natl Beta Clb; Sec Sr Cls; Ofcr Stu Cncl; Capt Pom Pon; Powder Puff Ftbl; French Hon Soc; High Hon Roll; Delta Beta Sigma; Boatmens Stu Advy Bd; Rhodes Coll; Bus.

KNISELEY, MARINEL; Rogers HS; Rogers, AR; (3); Am Leg Aux Girls St; Church Yth Grp; Cmnty Wkr; Drama Clb; FCA; Orch; School Play; Crs Cntry; Socr; 4-H Awd; Chamber Of Comm Awd Acad Achvmt; Music; Eng.

KNOBLE, MATTHEW L; Harmony Grove Jr Sr HS; Haskell, AR; (2); Church Yth Grp; French Clb; FBLA; Model UN; Natl Beta Clb; Band; Mrchg Band; Pep Band; Phtg Yrbk; High Hon Roll.

KNOBLOCH, JASON; Southside HS; Fort Smith, AR; (3); Latin Clb; Mu Alpha Theta; Band; Mrchg Band; Mgr(s); High Hon Roll; Jr NHS; NHS; Latin Natl Hnr Soc; Summa Cum Laude 2 Yrs Natl Latin Exam.

KNOWLTON, BRIAN C; Central HS; West Helena, AR; (2); Boy Scts; Library Aide; Teachers Aide; Ofcr Jr Cls; Bsktbl; Ftbl; Trk; Wt Lftg; Hon Roll; Jr NHS; Bus Ed.

KNOX, KRIS; Heber Springs HS; Heber Springs, AR; (3); 15/90; Am Leg Boys St; Church Yth Grp; FCA; FBLA; FHA; Natl Beta Clb; Spanish Clb; Speech Tm; L Bsktbl; Hon Roll; Stu Salute; Commnctn Awd; U Of Ar.

KNOX, MALIA S; Rogers HS; Rogers, AR; (3); Church Yth Grp; FCA; Intnl Clb; Church Choir; Drill Tm; Intrml Pom Pon; U Of A; Ed; Elem Tchr.

KO, ROBERT; Lee Acad; Marianna, AR; (2); Rep Soph Cls; Trk; High Hon Roll; Hon Roll; Prfct Atten Awd.

KOCH, JOYLYN D; Heritage Christian Schl; Little Rock, AR; (2); Church Yth Grp; SADD; Chrldng; Var Vllybl; Nrsng.

KODAY, MISHAEL J; Oakdale Jr HS; Rogers, AR; (1); Church Yth Grp; CAP; 4-H; Hosp Aide; Model UN; 4-H Awd; Hon Roll; Prfct Atten Awd; U Of AR; Nrsng.

KOEHLER, ADAM M; Catholic HS; Sherwood, AR; (3); Boy Scts; Church Yth Grp; Hosp Aide; ROTC; Stage Crew; Yth Connecton; TV Crew; Graphics Dsgn; Elec Engr.

KOEHLER, LAURA; Paris HS; Paris, AR; (4); 2/78; Am Leg Aux Girls St; Church Yth Grp; Library Aide; Capt Quiz Bowl; School Play; Ed Yrbk; Ofcr Stu Cncl; NHS; Sal; St Schlr; DARE; Cath Yth Ministry St Convention 2 Yrs; Grad With Overall Soc Stud Awd Cumulative 4 Yrs; Hendrix Coll.

KOEHLER, TAMMY C; North Little Rock Hs-West; North Little Rock, AR; (3); 13/554; Church Yth Grp; Dance Clb; German Clb; Treas Key Clb; Mu Alpha Theta; Natl Beta Clb; Church Choir; School Musical; School Play; Phtg Yrbk; Top 10 Pct Soph Cls Achvmnt Awd; Bio Awd 9th Grd; Mercentile Svngs Bond 11th Grd; PSYCH/INTR Deco.

KOEN, CLINT D; Dewitt HS; De Witt, AR; (2); 1/100; Church Yth Grp; FCA; French Clb; Natl Beta Clb; Natl FFA Org; Quiz Bowl; Science Clb; Rep Frsh Cls; Rep Soph Cls; Rep Jr Cls; Duke; Pre-Med.

KOETTEL, WESLEY A; Evening Shade Schl; Evening Shade, AR; (3); Boy Scts; FBLA; FHA; FTA; SADD; Ofcr Bsbl; Bsktbl; Cit Awd; Hon Roll; Prfct Atten Awd; ASU.

KONDO, SHINJI; Pine Bluff HS; Pine Bluff, AR; (2); Sec French Clb; Natl Beta Clb; Sec Science Clb; Orch; Yrbk; Lit Mag; Jr NHS; Key Clb; Quiz Bowl; Chorus; Amateur Astronomy; AR Yth Symphony; Pathways To Coll.

KONEY, BECCA L; Crossett Sr HS; Crossett, AR; (2); Church Yth Grp; Natl Beta Clb; Band; Church Choir; Flag Corp; Mrchg Band; Hon Roll; Stu Of Month Awd; Stdnts For Christ; U Magnolia; Soc Worker.

KONUPCIK, DANNY P; Ozark Adventist Acad; Gentry, AR; (3); Church Yth Grp; Band; Chorus; Church Choir; Treas Frsh Cls; VP Soph Cls; Rep Stu Cncl; Intrml Bsktbl; Intrml Powder Puff Ftbl; Intrml Socr; Union Coll; Bus.

KONUPCIK, YVETTE V; Ozark Adventist Acad; Gentry, AR; (4); Band; Pres Jr Cls; Var Bsktbl; Var Ftbl; Var Socr; Var Sftbl; Capt Vllybl; Hon Roll; NHS; Pres Acad Fit Awd; Maranatha Clb; Handbell Choir; Mission Trip Mexico; Southern Coll; Bus Admin.

KORDSMEIER, STEVEN C; Catholic HS; Sherwood, AR; (2); 47/172; ROTC; U Of AR.

KORGAN, STEPHANIE; Ozark Adventist Acad; Claremore, OK; (3); Hosp Aide; Band; Yrbk; Gym; Powder Puff Ftbl; Socr; Capt Vllybl; Cit Awd; High Hon Roll; SA Pres; St Guild Piano; Phys Thrpy.

KORKAMES, KRISTEN; Southside HS; Fort Smith, AR; (3); 59/502; FCA; FBLA; Math Tm; Mu Alpha Theta; Spanish Clb; Teachers Aide; JV Bsktbl; High Hon Roll; NHS; Pres Acad Fit Awd; Acctng.

KOUDELKA, GENEVIEVE; Lake Hamilton Sr HS; Hot Springs, AR; (4); 14/279; Am Leg Aux Girls St; Sec FBLA; Sec Natl Beta Clb; Science Clb; Variety Show; Rep Stu Cncl; Chrldng; NHS; Rotary Stu; Piano Guild Awd; Optimist Yth Awd; U Of AR; Arch.

KOURAKIS, JASON R; Cave City HS; Cave City, AR; (2); 15/100; Church Yth Grp; French Clb; Natl FFA Org; Band; Pep Band; Hon Roll; Prfct Atten Awd; Upward Bound Prgm Lyon Coll 95; AR Scholars 9-10th Grd; Lyon Coll; Chem Eng.

KOVACH, KRYSTAL; Fayetteville Christian Schl; Fayetteville, AR; (4); 1/12; Church Yth Grp; Chorus; Church Choir; School Play; Ed Phtg Yrbk; Treas Jr Cls; Bsktbl; High Hon Roll; NHS; Val; Piano Mdl; Bsktbl Mst Imprvd Plyr; John Brown U; Elem Ed.

KOVACH, KYNDEL; Fayetteville Christian Schl; Fayetteville, AR; (1); Church Yth Grp; Teachers Aide; Church Choir; High Hon Roll; Hon Roll; Piano; Sunday Schl Tchr; Nrsng.

KOZETTE MORSE, SARAH KATHRYN; Arkansas Bapt Schl; Little Rock, AR; (3); FBLA; Natl Beta Clb; Spanish Clb; Phtg Yrbk; Ofcr Jr Cls; High Hon Roll; Hon Roll; Fellowship Of Chrstn Ath; John Brown Univ; Elem Ed.

KOZLOWSKI, NICHOLAS A; North Little Rock Hs-West; North Little Rock, AR; (4); 99/439; Art Clb; French Clb; Latin Clb; Math Clb; Mu Alpha Theta; VICA; Hon Roll; Skate Club; Acoustic/Elec Guitar; Univ Of AR Fayetteville; Arch.

KRAMER, ASHLEY L; Southside HS; Rosie, AR; (2); FBLA; FHA; Key Clb; Vllybl; Hon Roll; Prfct Atten Awd; U Of Cntrl AR; Elem Ed.

KRANER, KARA; Rogers HS; Rogers, AR; (4); 44/468; Church Yth Grp; FCA; FBLA; Spanish Clb; Var Bsktbl; High Hon Roll; NHS; Hon Roll; Rtry Awd; Chmbr Cmmrce Acad Awd; Rnssnce Awd Pgm; Drury Coll; Bus Ecs.

KRATOCHVIL, JOEY; Calico Rock HS; Pineville, AR; (2); 3/40; Church Yth Grp; Natl Beta Clb; Pep Clb; Spanish Clb; SADD; High Hon Roll; Lyon Coll; Bus.

KREJCI, BILL; West Fork HS; West Fork, AR; (3); Church Yth Grp; FCA; Letterman Clb; Pres Stu Cncl; Ftbl; Trk; Wt Lftg; Gov Hon Prg Awd; Am Leg Boys St; High Hnrs Alg I/Soc Studies/2nd Agri; Ouachita Bapt Univ.

KRELL, AMANDA; Marshall HS; Marshall, AR; (4); 6/52; FBLA; Sec Natl Beta Clb; Natl FFA Org; VP Spanish Clb; Pres Sr Cls; Pres Stu Cncl; Var Bsktbl; Var Chrldng; JV Trk; Var Vllybl; U Of Fayetteville; Psych.

KREMER, JUSTIN; Scranton HS; Scranton, AR; (3); Am Leg Boys St; Church Yth Grp; FBLA; German Clb; Letterman Clb; Natl Beta Clb; Natl FFA Org; Science Clb; Rep Frsh Cls; VP Rep Soph Cls; Greenhand Awd FFA; U Of AR; Bio; Engrng.

KREMERS, NICHOLAS D; Clarksville HS; Clarksville, AR; (2); FBLA; Ofcr Bsbl; Bsktbl; Crs Cntry; Ftbl; Swmmng; Trk; Wt Lftg; Hon Roll; Prfct Atten Awd; PRIDE; Bio.

KRETZ, JEREMY D; Nevada Schl; Rosston, AR; (2); FBLA; Natl Beta Clb; Yrbk; High Hon Roll; Hon Roll; Var JV Bsbl; JV Bsktbl; 1st Pl Dist FBLA; Hnrd In Natl His & Govt Awd; Prof Bsbl Player; Marine Bio.

KRISANITS, REY; Green Forest Jr Sr HS; Green Forest, AR; (3); #2 in class; Drama Clb; FBLA; HOBY; Natl Beta Clb; SADD; VP Jr Cls; Rep Stu Cncl; Var Bsktbl; Var Ftbl; Capt Trk; U Of AR.

KRONE JR, ROBERT O; Robinson HS; Roland, AR; (3); Art Clb; Church Yth Grp; VP DECA; FCA; French Clb; FBLA; Letterman Clb; Library Aide; Natl Beta Clb; Pres VICA; AR Tech; Elec Engrng.

KRONE, THOMAS E; Hope HS; Hope, AR; (3); 4-H; French Clb; Natl Beta Clb; Quiz Bowl; Nwsp; Yrbk; Ftbl; Cit Awd; DAR Awd; 4-H Awd; Writer; Buddhism; Eng Prof.

KROUSE, TARA J; Van Cove HS; Cove, AR; (3); FBLA; FHA; Natl FFA Org; Pep Clb; Acpl Chr; Chorus; School Musical; School Play; Variety Show; Yrbk; Upward Bound Pgm; Admin Of Justice; Pub Relations.

KROUT, PHILLIP T; Russellville Sr HS; Russellville, AR; (3); JV Bsktbl; Cit Awd; Hon Roll; NHS; Prfct Atten Awd; AR Tech U; Graphic Design.

KRULIN, KIMBERLY; Pulaski Acad; Little Rock, AR; (1); Cmnty Wkr; GAA; Natl Beta Clb; Spanish Clb; Ofcr Frsh Cls; Var Bsktbl; Var Chrldng; High Hon Roll; Jr NHS; U Of VA; Vet.

KRUPITSKY, EUGENE; Central Sr HS; Little Rock, AR; (2); VP German Clb; HOBY; Mu Alpha Theta; Quiz Bowl; VP Temple Yth Grp; Rep Soph Cls; Jr NHS; HOBY Wrld Ldrshp Conf; 2nd Deg Blck Blt & Asst Instr Tae Kwon Do; 6th Intl Sakharov Rdngs; Bus.

KUEFFNER, KELLY M; Russellville Sr HS; Russellville, AR; (3); Band; Chorus; Mrchg Band; Pep Band; Gov Hon Prg Awd; Hon Roll; Jr NHS; NHS; Ntl Merit Ltr.

KUEHN, LESHA M; Springdale Sr HS; Springdale, AR; (2); Drama Clb; FBLA; Teachers Aide; Chorus; School Musical; School Play; Hon Roll; NHS; Comm Thtrf; Actng.

KUHN, JENNIFER; Gurdon HS; Gurdon, AR; (1); Church Yth Grp; Chrldng; GATE Prgm; Psych.

KULBETH, NATOSHA S; Monticello HS; Monticello, AR; (3); Am Leg Aux Girls St; Church Yth Grp; FHA; Spanish Clb; Drm Mjr(t); Hon Roll; Jr NHS; NHS; Radiologist.

KULBETH, S NATOSHA; Monticello HS; Monticello, AR; (3); Am Leg Aux Girls St; Church Yth Grp; FHA; Natl Beta Clb; Spanish Clb; Drm Mjr(t); Mrchg Band; Jr NHS; NHS; All Amer Schlr; Natl Sci Awd; Radiologist.

KUMMER, BENJAMIN D; Bald Knob HS; Bradford, AR; (2); Church Yth Grp; Band; Jazz Band; Mrchg Band; Pep Band; Hunting; Fishing.

KUMPURIS, FRANK; Pulaski Acad; Little Rock, AR; (3); Am Leg Boys St; FCA; Pres Model UN; Mgr Yrbk; Ed Lit Mag; Ofcr Stu Cncl; Crs Cntry; Ftbl; Trk; High Hon Roll; Order Of Excl; Just Say No Teen Ldrs; TRUCE.

KUONEN, BENJY; Dardanelle HS; Dardanelle, AR; (4); 29/97; Church Yth Grp; Rptr FBLA; Teachers Aide; Band; Drm Mjr(t); Mrchg Band; Ed Nwsp; Lit Mag; High Hon Roll; Hon Roll; Outstdng Bus Stdnt; His Club; Stdnt Prin Advy Comm; AR Tech; Metrlgy/Brdcst Jrnlsm.

KUSSMAUL, JASON; Guy Perkins Schl; Quitman, AR; (2); 1/29; Church Yth Grp; FBLA; FHA; Natl Beta Clb; Spanish Clb; Sec Soph Cls; Intrml Bsbl; High Hon Roll; Intl Forgn Lang Awd; Cntrl Baptist Col.

KUYKENDALL, KRISTINA M; Ozark HS; Ozark, AR; (4); 10/92; FCA; FBLA; Intnl Clb; Natl Beta Clb; Chorus; Variety Show; Rep Frsh Cls; Rep Soph Cls; Rep Jr Cls; Rep Sr Cls; APR Tech Univ; Psych.

KUZNECHENKOVA, MARIA V; Prairie Grove HS; Prairie Grove, AR; (3); Church Yth Grp; Drama Clb; FBLA; FHA; School Play; Ofcr Jr Cls; High Hon Roll; NHS; Chrch Choir; Intnl Reltns.

KYLE, CARRIE J; Mc Crory Jr Sr HS; Mc Crory, AR; (3); Computer Clb; FBLA; Letterman Clb; Natl FFA Org; Spanish Clb; Teachers Aide; Varsity Clb; School Play; Rep Frsh Cls; Rep Sec Soph Cls; Math I Awd; Math II Awd; Art Awd; FBLA Rprtr; ASU; Plant Sci.

KYMER, CARLY J; Ft Smith Christian Schl; Barling, AR; (1); Church Yth Grp; Hosp Aide; High Hon Roll; Marine Bio.

KYUKENDALL, TRENA; Southside HS; Fort Smith, AR; (3); ROTC; Wt Lftg; Hon Roll; U Of AR; Entrepreneur.

LAASON, MARY A; Forrest City HS; Heth, AR; (3); FHA; Chorus; Church Choir; Hon Roll; SE Coll Of Tech; Cmptr Pgmr.

LACAZE, TERRY J; Fountain Lake Jr Sr HS; Hot Springs Natio, AR; (2); Art Clb; Hon Roll; Comic Book Art; Wrtng Short Stories; J Kubert Schl Of Art.

LACEFIELD, ANGIE; Pea Ridge HS; Pea Ridge, AR; (1); GAA; Bsktbl; Powder Puff Ftbl; Trk; Hon Roll; NHS; Habitat For Humanity; Rdng; U Of Ar; Acctng; Nrsng.

LACKEY, JUSTIN; Forrest City HS; Forrest City, AR; (2); #2 in class; Math Clb; Mu Alpha Theta; Natl Beta Clb; Office Aide; Teachers Aide; High Hon Roll; NHS.

LACKEY, LOGAN; Forrest City HS; Forrest City, AR; (3); #2 in class; Mu Alpha Theta; Natl Beta Clb; Q&S; Quiz Bowl; Science Clb; Teachers Aide; Phtg Yrbk; Golf; High Hon Roll; NHS; AZ ST.

LACKIE, KYLE E; Lonoke Sr HS; Lonoke, AR; (4); Am Leg Boys St; FBLA; Boy Scts; Natl FFA Org; Spanish Clb; Ftbl; Hon Roll; U Of AR; Pharm.

LA COMB, JESSICA L; Alma HS; Alma, AR; (2); Drama Clb; FBLA; Library Aide; Natl FFA Org; ROTC; SADD; Teachers Aide; Band; Drm Mjr(t); Mrchg Band; Nom Poet Of Yr Intnl Soc Of Poets 3 Yrs; Poems Publshd Illiad Press/Natl Lib Poetry/HS Literary Mag; Psych.

LACY, ANGELA R; Fountain Lake Jr Sr HS; Hot Springs, AR; (1); Church Yth Grp; Cmnty Wkr; FCA; Hosp Aide; Natl Beta Clb; Office Aide; Spanish Clb; Church Choir; School Play; JV Tennis; Church Bus Minstry, Nursng Hm Minstry, Soulwinning; Hyles-Anderson.

LACY, CARRIE; Morrilton Sr HS; Morrilton, AR; (3); Am Leg Aux Girls St; Church Yth Grp; Rptr Natl Beta Clb; Spanish Clb; Thesps; Capt Drill Tm; School Play; Pres Soph Cls; VP Stu Cncl; Art Clb; Govs Schl Nom; Prin Ldrshp Awd; U AR Fyttvlle.

LACY, JOSH; Farmington Jr Sr HS; Farmington, AR; (2); 4-H; French Clb; Model UN; Band; Var Bsbl; Cit Awd; High Hon Roll; NHS.

LACY, KATRINA; Gordon HS; Gurdon, AR; (1); Church Yth Grp; FHA; Church Choir; Ofcr Soph Cls; Ofcr Stu Cncl; Chrldng; Pep Stepper; Caught Being Good Awd; Hlth Hnr Awd; UABP; Psychology.

LACY, LAURA L; Fayetteville East HS; Fayetteville, AR; (4); 1/382; Am Leg Aux Girls St; Church Yth Grp; FCA; Key Clb; Mu Alpha Theta; SADD; Var L Bsktbl; High Hon Roll; NHS; Church Choir; Schlr Ath; Distngshd Hnr Grad; Univ Of AR Fayetteville; Acctg.

LADD, TARA M; Arkansas Sr HS; Texarkana, TX; (2); Church Yth Grp; Drama Clb; FCA; French Clb; Hon Roll; Pres Acad Fit Awd; AV Media; Jrnlsm; ; TV Brdcstg.

LADD, WILLIAM J; Augusta HS; Augusta, AR; (1); Art Clb; Church Yth Grp; FTA; Natl Beta Clb; Pep Clb; Spanish Clb; Band; Mrchg Band; Mgr Yrbk; AEGIS; UCA At Conway.

LAFALETTE, JAMES T; Alma HS; Alma, AR; (2); Church Yth Grp; FBLA; Office Aide; Band; Mrchg Band; Pep Band; School Musical; Stat Bsbl; High Hon Roll; Hon Roll; Golf; Fncng; U Of CO; Law Enfrcmnt.

LAFAYETTE, AMY E; Fouke Jr Sr HS; Fouke, AR; (2); Hosp Aide; Band; Mrchg Band; Cit Awd; Hon Roll; Prfct Atten Awd.

LA FOND, DANIELLE; Conway Sr HS; Conway, AR; (2); Church Yth Grp; FBLA; Girl Scts; Hosp Aide; JA; Natl Beta Clb; Office Aide; Science Clb; Spanish Clb; High Hon Roll; Marine Bio.

LA FRANCE, CHANTELL; Waston Chapel HS; Pine Bluff, AR; (4); 27/240; Cmnty Wkr; English Clb; Key Clb; Natl Beta Clb; Red Cross Aide; Hon Roll; Pres Acad Fit Awd; U Of AR; Comp Sys Engrng.

LAKEY, CHAD; Perryville Jr Sr HS; Adona, AR; (3); Chess Clb; Church Yth Grp; Computer Clb; FCA; Spanish Clb; L Bsktbl; L Ftbl; DAR Awd; High Hon Roll; Hon Roll.

LAMB, BRANDY A; Hughes Jr-Sr HS; Hughes, AR; (3); Art Clb; Church Yth Grp; Cmnty Wkr; Science Clb; Bsktbl; Cit Awd.

LAMB, DANTANESE L; Monticello HS; Monticello, AR; (3); FHA; Natl Beta Clb; Bsktbl; Gym; Sftbl; Hon Roll.

LAMB, HEATH; Nettleton HS; Jonesboro, AR; (4); 4/125; Am Leg Boys St; Math Clb; Natl Beta Clb; Spanish Clb; Teachers Aide; Varsity Clb; School Play; L Bsktbl; L Ftbl; Hon Roll; Rotry Yth Ldrshp Awd; U Cntrl AR; Phy Thrpst.

LAMB, RICHARD W; Russellville Sr HS; Russellville, AR; (2); Art Clb; VICA; Var Ftbl; Var Socr; Automtv Engrng.

LAMBER, ALESHA; Dumas HS; Dumas, AR; (4); 13/146; FTA; Natl Beta Clb; Church Choir; VP Stu Cncl; Capt Chrldng; Hon Roll; NHS; Pres Acad Fit Awd; Spanish NHS; Church Yth Grp; Vntrs Ed; Span Hnr Soc; U Of Cntrl AR; Optmtry/Pre-Law.

LAMBERSON, BETH B; Bay Jr Sr HS; Bay, AR; (3); 8/45; Cmnty Wkr; FCA; FBLA; Science Clb; VP Frsh Cls; VP Soph Cls; VP Jr Cls; JV Var Bsktbl; Var Sftbl; JV Capt Vllybl; Med Applications Sci For Hlth Prgm; Co Cty Wide Yth Drug Free Bd; Univ Of Cntrl AR; PT.

LAMBERSON, NIKKI N; Highland HS; Ash Flat, AR; (3); Church Yth Grp; FHA; Chorus; Stage Crew; Hon Roll; Prfct Atten Awd; SOUL; RAD; Highland Choralle Select Choir; ASU; Early Childhood Dev.

LAMBERT, ALESHA; Dumas HS; Dumas, AR; (4); 13/146; Church Yth Grp; FBLA; FTA; Natl Beta Clb; Band; VP Stu Cncl; Capt Var Chrldng; Hon Roll; NHS; Pres Acad Fit Awd; Span Hnr Soc; Ventures & Ed Pgm; U Cntrl AR; Optometry; Pre-Law.

LAMBERT, BILLIE T; Russellville Sr HS; Russellville, AR; (2); Drill Tm; Gym; Bus.

LAMBERT, HOLLIE M; Arkansas Sr HS; Texarkana, AR; (2); Drill Tm; Rptr Yrbk; Bsktbl; Vllybl; High Hon Roll; Hon Roll; Yng Republicans; U Of AR; Pedtrcn.

LAMBERT, LATWAYLA; Dumas HS; Dumas, AR; (2); Church Yth Grp; FBLA; FTA; Library Aide; Church Choir; Yrbk; Capt Chrldng; Trk; Hon Roll; NHS; Ventures In Ed; Amer Axlry Of Month; AK ST Univ.

LAMBERT, TRINISHA L; Fordyce HS; Fordyce, AR; (4); 5/89; Rep Am Leg Aux Girls St; Sec Treas FBLA; Natl Beta Clb; VP Spanish Clb; Rep Frsh Cls; Pres Soph Cls; Pres Jr Cls; Pres Sr Cls; Capt Bsktbl; High Hon Roll; U Of AR; Acctng.

LAMBERTH, JOSIE N; Fountain Lake Jr Sr HS; Hot Springs Natio, AR; (3); Drama Clb; Natl FFA Org; Spanish Clb; School Play; Treas Stu Cncl; JV Var Chrldng; JV Vllybl; Hon Roll; Commnctn; Bus.

LAMBETH, JENNIFER K; Dequeen HS; De Queen, AR; (3); Church Yth Grp; FBLA; FTA; Library Aide; SADD; Teachers Aide; Chorus; School Musical; School Play; Rptr Nwsp; Elem Ed Tchr.

LAMKIN, CHAD B; Stephens Jr Sr HS; Stephens, AR; (2); 1/50; Church Yth Grp; FBLA; HOBY; Quiz Bowl; Yrbk; Hon Roll; SAAR; AEGIS.

LAMKIN JR, ROGER D; Nettleton HS; Jonesboro, AR; (2); Church Yth Grp; Spanish Clb; Chorus; Golf; Mgr(s); Hon Roll; AR ST Univ.

LAMON, JAMES L; Stephens Jr Sr HS; Camden, AR; (2); Drama Clb; FBLA; Speech Tm; Chorus; Church Choir; Hon Roll; Current Evnts Cls; Prncpls Clb; Stdnt Cncl VP 96-; GA Univ; Cmtr Sci/Engr.

LAMOUREUX, LISA; Dover HS; Dover, AR; (4); 9/89; Drama Clb; FBLA; GAA; Library Aide; Natl Beta Clb; Spanish Clb; School Play; Var Bsktbl; Var Chrldng; Powder Puff Ftbl; ACT ATU Schlrshp; Span, Bus Awd 95; Bsktbl All Conf, All Reg Tnrmnt Tm, Ldng Free Throw Shooter; AR Tech U; Span.

LAMPKIN, AHMAD J; Malvern Sr HS; Malvern, AR; (3); Am Leg Boys St; Church Yth Grp; Drama Clb; FCA; Natl Beta Clb; SADD; Band; Stage Crew; Pres Stu Cncl; Var Ftbl; UCLA Los Angeles; Law.

LAMPKIN, AMBER L; Trumann HS; Trumann, AR; (2); French Clb; FHA; Hon Roll; NHS; AR ST Univ Jonesboro; PT.

LAMPP, JENNIFER L; Southside HS; Batesville, AR; (3); Art Clb; FBLA; Key Clb; Office Aide; Science Clb; Spanish Clb; Band; Chrldng.

LANCASTER, APRIL R; Mountain View Jr Sr HS; Mountain View, AR; (3); Am Leg Aux Girls St; Church Yth Grp; Natl Beta Clb; Drm Mjr(t); Yrbk; Gov Hon Prg Awd; Pres Acad Fit Awd; Drama Clb; FHA; Spanish Clb; Marching Band Drum Major Awd-Lt Govs Cup 2nd Div 94-95; Gftd & Tlntd; U Of AR Fayettville; Psych.

LANCASTER, BRENT M; Melbourne HS; Melbourne, AR; (2); Quiz Bowl; Bsktbl; His Clb; Lib Clb; LSU.

LANCASTER, CATHERINE L; Hot Springs HS; Hot Springs, AR; (2); Cmnty Wkr; VP FBLA; Key Clb; Natl Beta Clb; Q&S; Thesps; Band; Jazz Band; Mrchg Band; Pep Band; U Of KY.

LANCASTER, CYNTHIA S; Marion HS; Crawfordsville, AR; (4); 11/183; Rptr FBLA; Mu Alpha Theta; Quiz Bowl; Sec Spanish Clb; Band; Chorus; Co-Capt Color Guard; Mrchg Band; Pep Band; Cit Awd; 1st Pl FBLA Conf/5th Pl ST Conf Cmptr Applctns; 3rd Pl Frgn Lang Fstvl Rctng Span Poem; AR ST Univ; Bio.

LANCASTER, KRISTA; Mountain View Jr Sr HS; Mountain View, AR; (1); Church Yth Grp; FHA; Library Aide; Natl Beta Clb; Chrldng; Hon Roll; All-Star Staff; Dncng; Orthdntst.

LANCASTER, LESLIE M; Mt St Mary Acad; Little Rock, AR; (2); Cmnty Wkr; Hosp Aide; Natl Beta Clb; VP SADD; High Hon Roll; U Of AR Fayetteville; RN.

LANCASTER, STACEY K; Westside HS; Altus, AR; (4); 4/62; Spanish Clb; Teachers Aide; Capt Bsktbl; Acctng; Tchr.

LANCASTER, TARA N; Mills HS; Little Rock, AR; (2); 12/449; Band; Mrchg Band; Pep Band; Hon Roll; Jr NHS; NHS; Nom Atnd Ssn Natl Yth Ldrshp Forum Law/Cntstn; Med/Law.

LAND, CASSANDRA S; El Dorado Sr HS; El Dorado, AR; (1); Band; Mrchg Band; Hon Roll; U AR Pine Bluff.

LANDERS, PETER L; Valley Springs Schl; Harrison, AR; (3); Art Clb; Church Yth Grp; FBLA; Key Clb; Church Choir; School Play; Hon Roll; Sr Schlrs Pgm; BASIC; Chrch Drama Clb; Cntrl Bible Coll; Bible; Preachr.

LANDRETH, LINDSEY; Magnet Cove HS; Malvern, AR; (2); Church Yth Grp; FCA; FBLA; FTA; HOBY; Math Clb; Natl Beta Clb; Science Clb; Bsktbl; Sftbl.

LANDRUM, CHARLES; Newport HS; Newport, AR; (2); French Clb; Cit Awd; Hon Roll.

LANDRUM, JACOB A; Ridgecrest HS; Paragould, AR; (2); 5/171; Church Yth Grp; FCA; French Clb; Key Clb; Letterman Clb; Chorus; Rep Frsh Cls; Rep Soph Cls; Rep Jr Cls; Ofcr Stu Cncl; AR St Univ.

LANDRUM, RACHEL; Cabot HS; Cabot, AR; (3); Church Yth Grp; Hosp Aide; Teachers Aide; Band; Church Choir; Mrchg Band; Pep Band; Chrldng; Chrch Nrsry Wrkr; UCA; Mtrlgy.

LANDRUM, RYAN; Coleman Jr HS; Alma, AR; (1); JV Ftbl; JV Trk; Cit Awd; High Hon Roll; Jr NHS; Prfct Atten Awd; VIP Ldrshp Trng; Schlstc Achvmt Awd.

LANDRY, AMBER; Fayetteville Christian Schl; Fayetteville, AR; (2); Church Yth Grp; High Hon Roll; Hon Roll; John Brown U; Bus.

LANDRY, EUPHRAISE L; Nevada Schl; Rosston, AR; (2); Church Yth Grp; FBLA; FHA; Natl Beta Clb; Natl FFA Org; Band; Chrldng; Vetrnrn.

LANE, BIRCH D; Springdale Sr HS; Springdale, AR; (2); Church Yth Grp; FCA; Letterman Clb; Intrml Bsktbl; Var Capt Ftbl; Var L Trk; Var L Wt Lftg; Hon Roll; Southwest Jr HS Boys Ftbl Outstndg Offnse Plyr 95-96 & Boys High Point Athl Trk/Fld Evnts 95-96.

LANE, DONALD T; Rogers HS; Rogers, AR; (3); 3/600; Am Leg Boys St; Quiz Bowl; SADD; High Hon Roll; Jr NHS; Henderson 100 Pgm; Natl Macy Schlr; Med.

LANE, JOANN; Camden Fairview HS; Camden, AR; (3); Drama Clb; French Clb; Natl Beta Clb; Acpl Chr; Chorus; Church Choir; School Musical; School Play; Chrldng; Gym; Anchor Clb; Red Cross Certified Lifeguard; U Of Cntrl AR.

LANE, MIRANDA; Alpena Schl; Harrison, AR; (4); 3/28; Church Yth Grp; FHA; Math Clb; Math Tm; Sec Natl Beta Clb; ROTC; Science Clb; Spanish Clb; Teachers Aide; Chorus; Gmtry High Grd; Northwest AR Comm Tech Coll.

LANE, REBECCA D; Springdale Sr HS; Springdale, AR; (2); Church Yth Grp; Cmnty Wkr; Yrbk; High Hon Roll; Hon Roll; NHS; Pres Acad Fit Awd; Computer Clb; Jr NHS; Chrdnc Chrch Yth Grp; Vlybl Chrch Yth Grp; Grls Rep Chrch Yth Cncl; TV Prdctns All Pstns Hld; U Of AR; Bus Mgr.

LANE, SHANNON C; Rogers HS; Rogers, AR; (4); 43/450; Church Yth Grp; FCA; Model UN; Teachers Aide; Band; Mrchg Band; Orch; School Play; Cit Awd; Hon Roll; Church Orch; Forgn Lang Clb; Chrch Sftbll; U Of AR; Cvl Eng.

LANE, SHAWNA; Vilonia HS; Vilonia, AR; (3); Cmnty Wkr; Drama Clb; FBLA; Stage Crew; Yrbk; Hon Roll; Cntrl Bapt Coll; His/Tchr.

LANE, STEVE R; El Dorado Sr HS; El Dorado, AR; (2); Key Clb; Quiz Bowl; Teachers Aide; Var L Bsbl; Ftbl; Hon Roll; Amer Lgn Bsbl; OK ST Univ; Vet Med.

LANG, CANDICE M; Oak Grove HS; Maumelle, AR; (1); 1/189; FBLA; Natl Beta Clb; Spanish Clb; Var Vllybl; Dance Clb; Marine Bio.

LANG, ERIN L; Greenwood Sr HS; Greenwood, AR; (2); Church Yth Grp; FCA; French Clb; FBLA; Teachers Aide; JV Var Bsktbl; JV Var Trk; Cit Awd; High Hon Roll; Hon Roll.

LANG, KELLIE N; Oak Grove HS; Maumelle, AR; (2); Church Yth Grp; Drama Clb; HOBY; Mu Alpha Theta; Natl Beta Clb; Speech Tm; School Play; Stage Crew; High Hon Roll; Pres Acad Fit Awd; UCA; PT.

LANG, LISA C; Lake Hamilton Sr HS; Royal, AR; (2); 5/320; Art Clb; FCA; Natl Beta Clb; Spanish Clb; Lit Mag; Mgr Bsktbl; Mgr(s); Sftbl; Trk; High Hon Roll; Reflections Conts 1st Pl Vsl Arts 94-95, 2nd Pl Lit 95-96; 3rd Pl Sci Fair; Cty Essay Cont Wnnr; Art.

LANG, TARAH; Mansfield Jr Sr HS; Mansfield, AR; (1); Art Clb; Church Yth Grp; FCA; Spanish Clb; Church Choir; School Play; Stat Bsbl; L Bsktbl; JV Chrldng; JV Crs Cntry; West AR CC; Kindergarten Tchr.

LANGDON, AMBER KRISTEL; Drew Central Jr Sr HS; Monticello, AR; (3); GAA; Teachers Aide; Stage Crew; Bsktbl; Wt Lftg; Cit Awd; Hon Roll; Jr NHS; Pres Schlr; Whos Who Best Dressed; Eng Awd; U Of Monticello; Pharmacist.

LANGDON, KENYA; Deer Jr Sr HS; Ozone, AR; (4); 1/23; HOBY; Pres Latin Clb; Quiz Bowl; Rptr Lit Mag; Sec Frsh Cls; VP Sr Cls; Rptr Stu Cncl; Hon Roll; Val; Art Clb; Natl Ltn Exm Mgn Cm Ld; AEGIS Grmn Immrsn Pgm; Wl Mrt Schlrshp Rcpnt; Lyon Coll; Crtv Wrtr.

LANGDON, LANA; Genoa Central HS; Genoa, AR; (4); 8/39; FBLA; FHA; Hosp Aide; HOBY; Model UN; Capt Quiz Bowl; Spanish Clb; NHS; Band; Pres Jr Cls; HOBY Almni Assn AR Chptr VP; Govs Schl; UCA Hnrs Coll Prsdntl Schlrshp; U Cntrl AR Hnrs Coll; Law.

LANGE, COURTNEY N; Marmaduke HS; Paragould, AR; (3); Treas Church Yth Grp; English Clb; VP 4-H; FBLA; Natl Beta Clb; Chorus; Var Bsktbl; Var Sftbl; Hon Roll; Ntl Merit Ltr; AR ST U; Med Dr.

LANGFORD, JACOB M; Conway Sr HS; Conway, AR; (4); Natl FFA Org; VICA; Vol Fireman; HS FFA Pres; Natl Voc Tech Hnr Soc; De Kalb Ag Awd; Cntrl Bapt Coll; Ag Engr; Firemn.

LANGFORD, SARAH; Woodlawn Schl; Rison, AR; (3); 1/38; Church Yth Grp; FCA; 4-H; FHA; Quiz Bowl; Church Choir; School Play; Yrbk; L Bsktbl; L Trk; UAR.

LANGHORN, SHANNON; Hall Sr HS; Little Rock, AR; (3); 58/233; FCA; FTA; Spanish Clb; Ofcr Stu Cncl; Trk; Hon Roll; Gov Schl Nom; Tribe/Kachinas Peer Sprt Grp; HS Heroes Sprt Grp; Taek Wondo/Rdng/Wrtng; UCA; Bio/Doctor.

LANGLE, SARAH; Morrilton Sr HS; Morrilton, AR; (2); Church Yth Grp; FBLA; Math Clb; Natl Beta Clb; Quiz Bowl; Spanish Clb; Band; Church Choir; Jazz Band; Mrchg Band; Southern Nazarene U; Music Ed.

LANGLEY, JASEN; Valley View HS; Jonesboro, AR; (4); Art Clb; Church Yth Grp; FCA; Natl FFA Org; Quiz Bowl; Band; Mrchg Band; Var Bsbl; L Bsktbl; L Ftbl; Univ Of AR; Arch.

LANGLEY, JOE R; Arkansas Sr HS; Texarkana, AR; (2); Hon Roll; Art; Hntng; Fshng; UALR Fyttvlle; Arch.

LANGLEY, ROSCOE B; Mc Crory Jr Sr HS; Mc Crory, AR; (3); 5/69; Am Leg Boys St; Boy Scts; Church Yth Grp; FCA; Pres FBLA; FTA; Letterman Clb; Natl FFA Org; Spanish Clb; SADD; Chrch Yth Group Ldr; Summer Sftbl Team Capt; All Dist Bsbl & Hitting Champ; Quachita Bapt Univ; Bus; Tchr.

LANGSTON, ELIZABETH A; Russellville Sr HS; Russellville, AR; (3); 46/340; Am Leg Aux Girls St; Church Yth Grp; Cmnty Wkr; Office Aide; Band; Church Choir; Mrchg Band; Stage Crew; Variety Show; High Hon Roll; Celebration Of Excellence; Bio.

LANIER, PHILIP; Bright Star Schl; Doddridge, AR; (2); 1/18; Church Yth Grp; Computer Clb; Drama Clb; FBLA; Church Choir; School Play; Bsktbl; Trk; Wt Lftg; High Hon Roll; Schltc Ath; Drama, Span, Algebra, Phys Sci & Bio Awds; LSU; Bsbl; Med.

LANING, KATIE; Pulaski Acad; Little Rock, AR; (1); Church Yth Grp; Cmnty Wkr; FCA; Natl Beta Clb; Spanish Clb; Var Bsktbl; Var Chrldng; High Hon Roll; Jr NHS; Piano 8 Yrs; All-Star Chrldng 8 Yrs Squad Placed 8th Natls; Ambassador To New Stdnts.

LANINGHAM, ANNIE L; Huntsville HS; Huntsville, AR; (2); Church Yth Grp; Drama Clb; FBLA; Science Clb; Band; Church Choir; Mrchg Band; School Play.

LANINGHAM, DONALD M; Fayetteville Sr HS; Fayetteville, AR; (2); Church Yth Grp; Office Aide; Spanish Clb; Band; Mrchg Band; Pep Band; Hon Roll; Pres Acad Fit Awd; Univ Of AR; Arch/Drafting.

LANKFORD, LAKISHA; West Memphis Sr HS; West Memphis, AR; (2); Drama Clb; French Clb; Math Clb; Mu Alpha Theta; Sec Natl Beta Clb; Office Aide; Pres Science Clb; Ed Nwsp; Rep Yrbk; Capt Chrldng; Bus.

LAPINGTON, JAMIE; Mount Saint Marys Acad; Little Rock, AR; (2); Church Yth Grp; French Clb; Crs Cntry; French Hon Soc; High Hon Roll; Prfct Atten Awd; Y-Teens; Wilderness Clb; All Star Chrldng Squad; Hendrix Coll; Bus.

LARA, BERG; Southside HS; Fort Smith, AR; (3); German Clb; Pres Q&S; Ed Nwsp; Yrbk; NHS; Law.

LARK, LAKEISHA R; El Dorado Sr HS; El Dorado, AR; (1); Church Yth Grp; FBLA; Teachers Aide; Church Choir; Bsktbl; Hon Roll; Comp Tech.

LARKIN JR, RANDY P; Pea Ridge HS; Jay, OK; (3); FBLA; Natl FFA Org; Band; Mrchg Band; Ftbl.

LARMOYEUX, CHRISTOPHE; Central Arkansas Chrstn HS; Little Rock, AR; (4); 20/80; Church Yth Grp; HOBY; Mu Alpha Theta; Chorus; Pres Frsh Cls; Pres Sr Cls; Rep Stu Cncl; Var Co-Capt Bsbl; Var Capt Ftbl; Treas NHS; Mr CAC; I Dare You Ldrshp; Natl Govt/Hstry Awd.

LARRY, LA SONYA; Bright Star Schl; Doddridge, AR; (2); FBLA; FHA; GAA; Pres Frsh Cls; Rep Stu Cncl; Var Bsktbl; Hon Roll; Prfct Atten Awd; Pres Acad Fit Awd; All Rgn Bsktbl Tm; FBLA Pres; FHA VP; Grambling U; Comp Sci.

LARRY, LASONYA F; Bright Star Schl; Doddridge, AR; (2); FBLA; FHA; Church Choir; VP Frsh Cls; Rep Soph Cls; Ofcr Stu Cncl; Bsktbl; Hon Roll; All-Region; Texarkana Coll; Comp.

LARSON, LAURA T; Newport HS; Newport, AR; (4); 26/150; Am Leg Aux Girls St; Church Yth Grp; Drama Clb; English Clb; French Clb; FBLA; Library Aide; Office Aide; Q&S; SADD; Most Likely To Be Remembered; AR ST U Jonesboro; Engl.

LASH, SARAH; Viola HS; Viola, AR; (3); 2/36; FBLA; FHA; Natl FFA Org; Band; Pep Band; Yrbk; Var Bsktbl; Var Sftbl; High Hon Roll; Pres Acad Fit Awd.

LASSITER, LEIGH; Monticello HS; Monticello, AR; (3); 1/150; Church Yth Grp; FCA; VP Math Clb; Natl Beta Clb; VP Science Clb; Teachers Aide; Band; Var Chrldng; L Tennis; NHS; Ballet; Piano.

LASWON, CRAIG W; Tuckerman HS; Tuckerman, AR; (2); Natl Beta Clb.

LATE, MARCIA; Maynard Jr Sr HS; Maynard, AR; (4); 4/29; Am Leg Aux Girls St; FBLA; Natl Beta Clb; Ofcr Stu Cncl; Ofcr Bsbl; Bsktbl; Trk; Hon Roll; French Clb; FHA; Ldrs Only; Amer Hmcmng Qn Fnlst; Ar ST U; Finance.

LATHAM, BRANDI J; Trumann HS; Trumann, AR; (2); Science Clb; Spanish Clb; Band; Color Guard; Drm Mjr(t); Flag Corp; Jazz Band; Mrchg Band; Pep Band; Bsktbl; U Of MA Amherst; Vet Med.

LATHAM, SARAH; Nashville HS; Nashville, AR; (3); 36/144; Church Yth Grp; Church Choir; High Hon Roll; Hon Roll; NHS; U Of Central AR; PT.

LATHROP, JENI; Van Buren Sr HS; Van Buren, AR; (3); Mu Alpha Theta; Office Aide; Science Clb; Spanish Clb; Band; Jazz Band; Mrchg Band; Pep Band; Cit Awd; NHS; Comp Sci.

LATTA, LARISSA M; Morrow Valley Christian Acad; Canehill, AR; (3); 1/3; Church Yth Grp; Hon Roll; Prfct Atten Awd; Hghst Ovrll Avg HS Clss All Sbjcts 94-95; Scrptre Mmry Awds; Swthrt Bnqt Queen 95; Baptist Schl Of Nrsng; RN.

LAU, BETSY M; North Little Rock Hs-East; North Little Rock, AR; (1); 50/646; FCA; GAA; Girl Scts; Math Clb; Mu Alpha Theta; Science Clb; Band; Church Choir; Mrchg Band; Pep Band; Tri-M; Mu Alpha Theta; Vet Medicine.

LAUBACH, TRAVIS L; Fayetteville Sr HS; Farmington, AR; (2); Boy Scts; German Clb; Red Cross Aide; Chorus; L Crs Cntry; Swmmng; Trk; Hon Roll; Prfct Atten Awd.

LAUNG, ANITA C; Arkansas Schl Math & Science; Hot Springs, AR; (4); FBLA; Key Clb; Mu Alpha Theta; Service Clb; Spanish Clb; Hon Roll; Jr NHS; Ntl Merit SF; Pres Acad Fit Awd; AR Gov Schl; Beta Clb, 3rd Pl St Math; Bio.

LAUNIUS, ZACHARY H; Bearden HS; Bearden, AR; (4); #1 in class; Am Leg Boys St; Church Yth Grp; Cmnty Wkr; 4-H; FBLA; FHA; FTA; HOBY; Model UN; Natl Beta Clb; Yth Ctr; South AR U; Bus Admin.

LAUSTEN, RYAN; Pine Bluff HS; Pine Bluff, AR; (3); Cmnty Wkr; French Clb; HOBY; Quiz Bowl; School Play; Bsktbl; Crs Cntry; Ftbl; Trk; Vllybl; FBI.

LAVELLE, KRISTEN; Cty Line HS; Ratcliff, AR; (2); 1/50; FCA; FBLA; Natl Beta Clb; Quiz Bowl; Spanish Clb; Treas Frsh Cls; Ofcr Stu Cncl; Bsktbl; High Hon Roll; Psych.

LAVENDER, LACI; Blevins HS; Mc Caskill, AR; (4); Natl Beta Clb; Natl FFA Org; Teachers Aide; Varsity Clb; Yrbk; Bsktbl; Chrldng; Sftbl; Trk; Cit Awd; Red River Tech Coll.

LA VOICE, ALLISON; Foreman Jr Sr HS; Foreman, AR; (2); 4/42; Cmnty Wkr; Quiz Bowl; Spanish Clb; Capt Var Chrldng; Powder Puff Ftbl; JV Sftbl; High Hon Roll; Hon Roll; Jazz, Tap & Ballet Dancing For 13 Yrs; NCA All-Amer Chrldr; U Of AR; Pub Relations.

LAW, LINDSAY; Hamburg Jr HS; Hamburg, AR; (1); 6/140; Church Yth Grp; Cmnty Wkr; Quiz Bowl; Band; Jazz Band; Mrchg Band; Pep Band; School Play; Rep Stu Cncl; Tennis; Piano; Juliard; Music.

LAWLER, JEANICE; Blevins HS; Blevins, AR; (2); #2 in class; Natl Beta Clb; Bsktbl; Capt Chrldng; Sftbl; Hon Roll; Sal; MASH; UCA All Star Chrldr-Thanksgiving Day Parade; Med.

LAWRENCE, ELISABETH A; Conway Sr HS; Conway, AR; (3); Cmnty Wkr; Debate Tm; Drama Clb; Q&S; Science Clb; Pres Frsh Cls; Rep Soph Cls; Rep Jr Cls; Ofcr Stu Cncl; FBLA; Faulkner Cty Yth Ldrshp Inst; Natl Young Ldrs Conf; Delta Beta Sigma; Rhodes Memphis; Psych.

LAWRENCE, HEATHER S; Abundant Life Schools; Sherwood, AR; (3); Church Yth Grp; FBLA; Pres FHA; Natl Beta Clb; Teachers Aide; Church Choir; Ed Yrbk; Hon Roll; NHS; Pub Author In Natl Lib Of Poetry; UCA; Eng.

LAWRENCE, JOSH; Ola Jr Sr HS; Ola, AR; (3); 1/45; Chess Clb; Natl Beta Clb; Quiz Bowl; Spanish Clb; Ofcr Bsbl; Bsktbl; Ftbl; High Hon Roll; All-Conf Ftbl & Bsktbl.

LAWRENCE, LAHOMA M; Mena HS; Mena, AR; (4); Office Aide; Spanish Clb; Teachers Aide; Band; Mrchg Band; School Musical; Mgr(s); Ntl Merit Ltr; AR Tech; Elem Ed.

LAWRENCE, MATTHEW C; Southside HS; Fort Smith, AR; (2); Church Yth Grp; Latin Clb; Math Clb; Math Tm; Mu Alpha Theta; Quiz Bowl; Church Choir; Hon Roll; Jr NHS; NHS; GATE.

LAWRENCE, STACY; J A Fair Sr HS; Little Rock, AR; (4); 12/300; Model UN; Capt Drill Tm; Var Capt Bsktbl; Var Capt Sftbl; Var Vllybl; High Hon Roll; VP Jr NHS; NHS; Pres Acad Fit Awd; U Of Cntrl AR; Phy Thrpst.

LAWRENCE, VALARIE; Warren Jr HS; Warren, AR; (4); 18/140; Church Yth Grp; Dance Clb; Natl Beta Clb; Variety Show; Ofcr Frsh Cls; Ofcr Soph Cls; VP Jr Cls; Ofcr Stu Cncl; Bsktbl; Chrldng; Mst Athl; All Dist Bsktbll.

LAWRY, CYNDA; Ozark Adventist Acad; Mena, AR; (3); Church Yth Grp; Library Aide; Quiz Bowl; Bsktbl; Socr; Vllybl; Cit Awd; High Hon Roll; NHS; Prfct Atten Awd; Puppet Team; Girls Clb Adv; Adopt A Grandparent; Southwestern Adventist Coll.

LAWS, ALICE A; Hampton Jr Sr HS; Hampton, AR; (3); 8/64; FBLA; Pres FHA; Natl Beta Clb; Band; Jazz Band; Rep Stu Cncl.

LAWSON, BYRON; Lonoke Jr HS; Scott, AR; (1); 4-H; Bsktbl; Ftbl; Hon Roll; NHS; Stdnt Cncl; Ecology Clb; AR ST Univ; Sci/Math.

LAWSON, CASEY C; Van Buren Sr HS; Van Buren, AR; (2); Art Clb; Church Yth Grp; FBLA; NFL; Science Clb; SADD; Pom Pon; High Hon Roll; NHS; Ntl Merit Ltr; Earth Club; All Amer Schlr; Spr Rtngs Dance Camp; U Of AR; Pharm.

LAWSON, HEATHER D; Bentonville Sr HS; Bentonville, AR; (3); Church Yth Grp; Debate Tm; NFL; Science Clb; Speech Tm; Thesps; School Play; Bsktbl; High Hon Roll; NHS; U Of OK; Ath Trng.

LAWSON, JEREMY; Sheridan Sr HS; Leola, AR; (1); Church Yth Grp; ROTC; Band; Hon Roll.

LAWSON, LA SHUNDA D; North Little Rock Hs-West; North Little Rock, AR; (3); 125/535; CAP; Computer Clb; FBLA; FHA; VP FTA; Key Clb; Math Clb; Office Aide; Spanish Clb; Band; Acctg/Morturary Sci.

LAWSON, STEPHANIE; Malvern Jr HS; Malvern, AR; (4); 41/169; Am Leg Aux Girls St; Church Yth Grp; Natl Beta Clb; Science Clb; Spanish Clb; SADD; Band; Church Choir; Cit Awd; DAR Awd; Univ Of Cntrl AR; Psych.

LAWSON, TONJA; East End Jr Sr HS; Houston, AR; (1); FBLA; Natl Beta Clb; Nwsp; Yrbk; Capt Bsktbl; Hon Roll.

LAWSON, TRICIA; Forrest City HS; Forrest City, AR; (3); Am Leg Aux Girls St; FBLA; Mu Alpha Theta; Natl Beta Clb; Office Aide; Science Clb; Ofcr Stu Cncl; High Hon Roll; Hon Roll; U Of AR; Eng Prof.

LAY, VANESSA D; Mena HS; Mena, AR; (2); 22/150; Art Clb; Church Yth Grp; FCA; French Clb; FBLA; GAA; Science Clb; Var Bsktbl; Intrml Sftbl; Var Vllybl.

LAYROCK, TONY K; Searcy HS; Searcy, AR; (2); 41/243; Church Yth Grp; French Clb; Natl Beta Clb; Natl FFA Org; Band; Mrchg Band; French Hon Soc; Hon Roll; Arntcl Engr.

LAYTON, BILLY J; Oden Schl; Oden, AR; (4); 2/17; Am Leg Boys St; Church Yth Grp; Cmnty Wkr; Debate Tm; FBLA; Natl Beta Clb; Quiz Bowl; Scholastic Bowl; Teachers Aide; School Play; Hustle Awd At Every Camp Attended For Bsktbl; Outstdng Stu 3 Yrs; Natl All-Amer Schlr In Math; Southern Nazarene Univ.

LAYTON, JERMAINE; Arkansas Sr HS; Texarkana, AR; (2); Church Yth Grp; Cmnty Wkr; Band; Church Choir; Drm Mjr(t); Mrchg Band; Pep Band; Hon Roll; VA Kndlr Mem Schlrshp Awd; Prvntn Rsrc Cltn; MSC.

LAZENBY, JAMIE N; North Little Rock Hs-West; North Little Rock, AR; (4); 131/439; Church Yth Grp; Cmnty Wkr; Drama Clb; FCA; Natl Beta Clb; Q&S; Drill Tm; Rptr Yrbk; Cit Awd; Hon Roll; NCA Danc Cmptn Medl For Best Leaps; Dancd In Bob Hope Spcl; Votd Best Jazz Dancr For Var Danc Team; U Of AR; Bus Admin.

LE, JOSEPH T; Southside HS; Fort Smith, AR; (2); Mu Alpha Theta; Var Bsktbl; Hon Roll; Prfct Atten Awd.

LEA, KEVIN J; Russellville Sr HS; Russellville, AR; (3); 107/378; Am Leg Boys St; Church Yth Grp; Model UN; Bsktbl; Crs Cntry; Trk; Hon Roll; Jr NHS; U AR; Engr.

LEACH, JANELL M; Cabot HS; Cabot, AR; (3); 33/398; Art Clb; Cmnty Wkr; Spanish Clb; Rptr Nwsp; Tennis; High Hon Roll; Jr NHS; Kiwanis Awd; NHS; Spanish NHS; Govrnrs Schl; U Of AR; Anthrplogy.

LEACH, MELISSA J; Sylvan Hills HS; Sherwood, AR; (4); 85/233; Art Clb; Church Yth Grp; Teachers Aide; Gov Hon Prg Awd; 95 AR Govs Schl For Visual Arts; NFAA Score 7; Memphis Coll Of Art; Art Thrpy.

LEAHY, ERIN L; Lake Hamilton Sr HS; Hot Springs, AR; (2); Dance Clb; FCA; FBLA; HOBY; Natl Beta Clb; Spanish Clb; Teachers Aide; Varsity Clb; Drill Tm; VP Rptr Stu Cncl; Acoylyte 2 Yrs; Vlntr DAR.

LEAK, CHIQUITA L; Forrest City HS; Colt, AR; (3); FHA; Band; Hon Roll; Fort Valley ST Coll; Acctng.

LEAKE, JILL S; Junction City HS; Junction City, AR; (3); FBLA; Science Clb; Spanish Clb; Band; Mrchg Band; Var Stu Cncl; High Hon Roll; NHS; Basic Clb; ST Sci Fair Participant; MASH Stu-Med Application Of Sci For Hlth Pgm; LA Tech.

LEAKS, TAMIKA M; Nevada Schl; Rosston, AR; (2); FBLA; FTA; Pres Natl Beta Clb; Quiz Bowl; Teachers Aide; Church Choir; Rptr Nwsp; Hon Roll; Upward Bound Mem; Ranked 1 In Cls; Drug Team Mem; Phy Therapy.

LEAMONS, AMBER R; Sparkman Jr Sr HS; Sparkman, AR; (2); Church Yth Grp; FBLA; Natl Beta Clb; Office Aide; Quiz Bowl; Spanish Clb; Church Choir; Yrbk; NHS; Natl Yth Ldshp Forum On Law And Const; Natl Hnr Roll.

LEAMONS, RENEE; Sparkman Jr Sr HS; Sparkman, AR; (2); Church Yth Grp; FBLA; FHA; Office Aide; Quiz Bowl; Spanish Clb; Church Choir; Yrbk; JV Chrldng; High Hon Roll; Gifted & Talented Pgm.

LEAPHEART, KRISTY; Morrilton Sr HS; Morrilton, AR; (4); 1/150; Am Leg Aux Girls St; Math Clb; Natl Beta Clb; Science Clb; Thesps; Drill Tm; Pres Stu Cncl; Trk; Cit Awd; High Hon Roll; UA Fayetteville; Cmptr Engrng.

LEASURE, CLAYTON A; Southside HS; Fort Smith, AR; (3); 112/502; FCA; German Clb; Orch; Stat Bsktbl; Mgr(s); Hon Roll; NHS; Pres Acad Fit Awd; Comp Sci; Comp Prgmr.

LEASURE, ERIC D; Harrisburg HS; Harrisburg, AR; (2); 3-D Club; Interact Club; Float Comm Frosh/Soph Yrs.

LEAVY, LATECA N; North Little Rock Hs-West; North Little Rock, AR; (3); Band; Mrchg Band; Powder Puff Ftbl; Cit Awd; Hon Roll; Prfct Atten Awd; Pres Acad Fit Awd; Band Awds; Solo Ensmbl Awds; Phy.

LE BLANC, BRENT M; Mountainburg Jr Sr HS; Mountainburg, AR; (3); FCA; Science Clb; SADD; JV Bsbl; Var Bsktbl; L Var Ftbl; Var Trk; Var Wt Lftg; Hon Roll; PE.

LE BLEU, DUSTIN; Omaha Schl; Harrison, AR; (1); Church Yth Grp; JV Bsbl; JV Capt Bsktbl; AR U; Phys Ed.

LEBOW, HANNAH M; Springdale Sr HS; Springdale, AR; (2); Church Yth Grp; French Clb; FBLA; Chorus; High Hon Roll; Hon Roll; Jr NHS; NHS; Pres Acad Fit Awd; Yth For Chrst; U Of AR; Brdcstng.

LEDBETTER, JODI; Malvern Sr HS; Malvern, AR; (3); FCA; Pres 4-H; FBLA; Natl Beta Clb; Science Clb; Teachers Aide; Rep Nwsp; Rep Stu Cncl; JV Bsktbl; Powder Puff Ftbl; U Of Cntrl AR; Child Psych.

LEDFORD, KRISTI M; Bald Knob HS; Bald Knob, AR; (2); Church Yth Grp; Natl Beta Clb; VICA; Band; Color Guard; Mrchg Band; Ofcr Soph Cls; Hon Roll; Prfct Atten Awd; Pres Acad Fit Awd.

LEDFORD, KYLE J; Southside HS; Fort Smith, AR; (3); 87/502; French Clb; Mu Alpha Theta; Band; Mrchg Band; Pep Band; Ed Nwsp; Hon Roll; NHS; Pres Acad Fit Awd; Drum Line Capt; Intnl Kart Fed Rcng; All ST Drummer; OK ST Univ; Vet.

LEDING, MARANDA L; Altus Denning HS; Ozark, AR; (3); 5/23; FBLA; Natl Beta Clb; Sec Soph Cls; Capt Bsktbl; Capt Sftbl; Hon Roll; All Dist In Bsktbl; All St In Sftbl; Broke Bsktbl Record; Sports Medicine.

LEDING, TEIKA M; Ozark HS; Ozark, AR; (3); 12/101; FCA; FBLA; SADD; Pres Frsh Cls; Pres Soph Cls; Rep Jr Cls; Rep Stu Cncl; L Bsktbl; Var L Sftbl; Hon Roll; Poetry Pub; MO Western; Psych.

LEDRICK, JONATHAN A; North Little Rock Hs-East; North Little Rock, AR; (2); Church Yth Grp; Computer Clb; FBLA; Natl Beta Clb; Office Aide; Band; Church Choir; Mrchg Band; Hon Roll.

LEE, AMBER R; John L Mcclellan Magnet HS; Woodson, AR; (3); Church Yth Grp; FHA; Spanish Clb; Teachers Aide; Band; Church Choir; Hon Roll; Stu Of Week; Type-A-Thon For Leukemia; Grambling ST Univ; Psych.

LEE, ANGEL; Parkview Arts-Science HS; North Little Rock, AR; (4); 44/260; Cmnty Wkr; VP German Clb; Key Clb; Mu Alpha Theta; Natl Beta Clb; Pres Q&S; Flag Corp; Co-Ed Nwsp; Rep Stu Cncl; Capt Vllybl; Schl Nwsp Constitution & Spirt Eds Of Yr 95-96; U Of AR; Chemical Engrng.

LEE, BRANDY; Rogers HS; Rogers, AR; (4); 38/468; Church Yth Grp; Teachers Aide; Rptr Nwsp; Ed Yrbk; High Hon Roll; NHS; Chrstns Actn Pres; Chmbr Cmmrce Awd; Elem Tutor; AR ST U; Elem Ed.

LEE, CANAA; Brinkley HS; Brinkley, AR; (3); 1/89; Pres 4-H; Rptr French Clb; VP FHA; Girl Scts; HOBY; Quiz Bowl; Band; Mrchg Band; Pres Stu Cncl; Tennis; Jr High All Reg, Sr High All Reg; Best Musican Awd; AR ST U; Band Dir.

LEE, CHELLI; Dover HS; Dover, AR; (4); 2/84; Am Leg Aux Girls St; Hosp Aide; Model UN; Natl Beta Clb; Spanish Clb; Teachers Aide; Band; Flag Corp; Pres Soph Cls; Var Golf; Harding Univ; Mkting.

LEE, ELIZABETH K; Westside HS; Cash, AR; (3); Art Clb; FBLA; FTA; Science Clb; Spanish Clb; Teachers Aide; Chorus; Variety Show; High Hon Roll; Pres Acad Fit Awd; NHS; Jr Beta Clb; Span I/II Awds; AR ST Univ; PT.

LEE, JACOB; Perryville Jr Sr HS; Perryville, AR; (3); Chess Clb; FCA; FBLA; Spanish Clb; Sec Jr Cls; Ftbl; Golf; Ntl Merit Ltr; Law Enforcement.

LEE, JENNIFER D; Russellville Sr HS; Russellville, AR; (2); Church Yth Grp; FCA; GAA; Natl Beta Clb; Teachers Aide; Rep Jr Cls; Rep Stu Cncl; Sftbl; Vllybl; Hon Roll; AR Tech Univ; Nrs.

LEE, KANDY S; Rogers HS; Rogers, AR; (3); FBLA; Science Clb; Band; Rptr Nwsp; Treas Frsh Cls; JV L Chrldng; Var Tennis; Hon Roll; Pres Acad Fit Awd; Frgn Exch Stdnt Australia 96.

LEE, KRISTIE; Gosnell Jr Sr HS; Blytheville, AR; (1); Drama Clb; French Clb; Key Clb; Quiz Bowl; Band; Mrchg Band; Pep Band; Stage Crew; Trk; Hon Roll; U AR Fayetteville; Math.

LEE, MANDY M; Manila HS; Manila, AR; (1); Church Yth Grp; FHA; Natl Beta Clb; Quiz Bowl; Chorus; Sec Frsh Cls; Bsktbl; Hon Roll; Beta Club Pres; Marine Bio.

LEE, MICHELLE L; Hartford Schl; Hartford, AR; (2); Church Yth Grp; Teachers Aide; Band; Church Choir; Mrchg Band; Pep Band; Yrbk; Bsktbl; High Hon Roll; NHS; Brigham Young Univ.

LEE, RYAN; Pulaski Acad; Little Rock, AR; (3); Church Yth Grp; FCA; German Clb; Natl Beta Clb; Rep Stu Cncl; Var Bsktbl; Var L Ftbl; Var L Socr; Hon Roll; NHS; Ftbl All Metro/Tp Jr ST 96; Spr Soph Ftbl 95; Scr 4 Yr Ltrmn/ST Slct 90-; ST Chmps 89/91/93/95-; Pre Med.

LEE, SHANNON D; Ozark Adventist Acad; Gentry, AR; (2); Temple Yth Grp; Chorus; Church Choir; School Musical; Bsktbl; Socr; Vllybl; Cit Awd; Hon Roll; Prfct Atten Awd; Psychrst.

LEE, SHAWANA M; Eudora HS; Eudora, AR; (4); 8/64; Drama Clb; Sec FHA; Speech Tm; Church Choir; Nwsp; Phtg Yrbk; Rep Jr Cls; Cit Awd; Hon Roll; Ntl Merit Ltr; RN.

LEE, TEKOAH; Delight HS; Delight, AR; (3); 7/30; Church Yth Grp; 4-H; FBLA; Natl Beta Clb; Natl FFA Org; Yrbk; VP Frsh Cls; Sec Soph Cls; Sec Jr Cls; Ofcr Stu Cncl.

LEE, TONYA SUE; Devalls Bluff Jr Sr HS; De Valls Bluff, AR; (3); Church Yth Grp; Cmnty Wkr; Drama Clb; 4-H; FBLA; FHA; Library Aide; Natl Beta Clb; Office Aide; Chorus; Singing Cmptn Top 3; Piano; Tlnt & Beauty Pgnts; ASU Beebe; Educ.

LEE, VALORIE; Timbo Schl; Onia, AR; (3); 1/30; Church Yth Grp; Dance Clb; Pres FBLA; Pres FHA; HOBY; Sec Natl Beta Clb; Pres Natl FFA Org; Quiz Bowl; Bsktbl; Sftbl; Fire Marshall; Lyon Coll.

LEE, WENDY L; Ashdown Sr HS; Ashdown, AR; (3); Art Clb; Church Yth Grp; French Clb; Church Choir; Flag Corp; Mrchg Band; Ofcr Jr Cls; Powder Puff Ftbl; Prfct Atten Awd; Cert Hnr Eng III; Pride Club; SAU Magnolia; Peditrcn/RN.

LEECH, PAUL D; Star City HS; Star City, AR; (3); 14/100; Art Clb; Bus Profs of Am; Church Yth Grp; Cmnty Wkr; FCA; FBLA; Letterman Clb; Math Clb; Mu Alpha Theta; Natl Beta Clb; Hendrix; Phrmcy.

LEEDS, LUKE T; Lamar HS; Lamar, AR; (3); Am Leg Boys St; Church Yth Grp; FCA; Letterman Clb; Math Clb; Natl Beta Clb; Science Clb; Spanish Clb; Church Choir; L Bsbl.

LEEPER, CORTEZ; Delight HS; Okolona, AR; (1); 6/37; Church Yth Grp; Cmnty Wkr; FCA; 4-H; FBLA; FHA; Natl Beta Clb; Natl FFA Org; Quiz Bowl; Red Cross Aide; Upward Bound Eng & Sci Awd; Mst Outstdng Male Dramatist; U Of AR; Theater Arts; Med Dr.

LEES, ALICE; Mt Holly Schl; Magnolia, AR; (2); Natl FFA Org; Bsktbl; Cit Awd; Hon Roll; NHS; All Amer Schl Awd Pgm; Homcmng Maid 95-96; Horseback Rdng Brrl Rcng; Vet Med.

LEESON, SUMMER A; Alpena Schl; Alpena, AR; (3); FBLA; FHA; Library Aide; Natl Beta Clb; Office Aide; Spanish Clb; Speech Tm; VP Soph Cls; Pres Jr Cls; Rep Stu Cncl; Tchr.

LEGGITT, TABBITHA A; Riverview Bapt Christian Sch; Perry, AR; (2); Vllybl.

LEHMAN, COREY A; Lee Acad; Asheville, NC; (1); Ftbl; Hon Roll; Jr NHS.

LEISURE, BRANDY D; Ridgecrest HS; Paragould, AR; (2); Pres Church Yth Grp; Office Aide; Thesps; Chorus; Church Choir; School Play; Hon Roll; Elem Tchr.

LEISURE, NATALIE D; Springdale Sr HS; Springdale, AR; (3); Cmnty Wkr; Office Aide; Chorus; Hon Roll; Renaissance Prgm 2 Yrs.

LELAND, LUCINDY R; Lonoke Jr HS; Lonoke, AR; (1); Science Clb; Band; Mrchg Band; Cit Awd; Hon Roll; NHS; His; Tchr.

LELIEVRE, CRISTY S; Pottsville Schl; Pottsville, AR; (3); FBLA; Natl Beta Clb; Natl FFA Org; Hon Roll; Psych.

LEMKE, KYLE M; Gentry HS; Gentry, AR; (3); 12/65; FBLA; Math Clb; Spanish Clb; Teachers Aide; Band; Ofcr Stu Cncl; Bsktbl; Golf; Trk; NHS; AHSME AR Hnr Roll; U Of AR; Engrng.

LEMLE II, JAMES E; Catholic HS; Little Rock, AR; (3); Am Leg Boys St; Church Yth Grp; Latin Clb; Varsity Clb; Jazz Band; JV Var Bsktbl; Cit Awd; Hon Roll; Prfct Atten Awd; Sports Medicine; Phy.

LEMLEY, C ABIGAIL; Ft Smith Christian Schl; Fort Smith, AR; (4); Church Yth Grp; Cmnty Wkr; FBLA; Library Aide; Teachers Aide; Acpl Chr; Chorus; Church Choir; School Musical; School Play; Music/Bus Mngmnt.

LEMLEY, KEVIN; Conway Sr HS; Conway, AR; (4); 15/530; Cmnty Wkr; Math Tm; Model UN; Teachers Aide; Rptr Band; Jazz Band; Mrchg Band; Pep Band; School Musical; JV Bsbl; U Of Central AR; Fin; Mass Comm.

LEMON, TERESA A; Fayetteville Sr HS; Fayetteville, AR; (2); Band; Chorus; Color Guard; Pep Band; Hon Roll; All Reg Band/Choir; Prfrmng Arts.

LEMONS, CHRISTY M; England HS; England, AR; (2); #1 in class; FBLA; FHA; Spanish Clb; Band; Mrchg Band; Sec Soph Cls; Hon Roll; Henderson ST Univ; Bus.

LEMONS, HEATHER R; Cty Line HS; Charleston, AR; (3); Treas FHA; Hosp Aide; Natl Beta Clb; Quiz Bowl; Spanish Clb; Rep Chorus; School Play; Capt Var Chrldng; Hon Roll; Prfct Atten Awd; U Of AR; Med Tech.

LENT, AMANDA; Sylvan Hills HS; Colorado Springs, CO; (2); 52/342; FBLA; Hosp Aide; Mu Alpha Theta; Teachers Aide; Yrbk; High Hon Roll; Hon Roll; Jr NHS; Yrbk Merit Awd; Lcnsd Prctcl Nrse.

LENTZ, CHRISTY E; Sacred Heart Schl; Morrilton, AR; (2); Art Clb; Church Yth Grp; Natl Beta Clb; SADD; Sec Frsh Cls; Sec Soph Cls; Chrldng; Mgr(s); Hon Roll; Key Clb.

LEONARD, AMANDA L; Greenwood Sr HS; Greenwood, AR; (2); 18/150; Church Yth Grp; FCA; FBLA; Natl Beta Clb; Office Aide; Spanish Clb; Chrldng; High Hon Roll; NHS; Presdntl Acad Achvmt Awd; U Of AR; Bus.

LEONARD, BRIAN B; Harrison Sr HS; Harrison, AR; (3); FBLA; Hon Roll.

LEOPOULOS, THADDEUS; Parkview Arts-Science HS; Maumelle, AR; (3); 8/270; Am Leg Boys St; Church Yth Grp; Natl Beta Clb; Band; Jazz Band; Mrchg Band; Pep Band; Ofcr Soph Cls; VP Jr Cls; Pres Stu Cncl; Mercantile Bank Bd Rep; Soccer Ref; Harvard Book Awd.

LEREW, GLENDA; Hope HS; Hope, AR; (4); 2/210; Am Leg Aux Girls St; Church Yth Grp; Treas FBLA; Hosp Aide; Natl Beta Clb; Hon Roll; NHS; Prfct Atten Awd; Henderson ST Univ.

LESLIE, ANN M; Wynne HS; Wynne, AR; (4); Church Yth Grp; FTA; Q&S; Spanish Clb; Chorus; Church Choir; Yrbk; Cit Awd; Hon Roll; Spanish NHS; U Of Central AR; Elem Ed.

LESLIE, CARRIE A; Mt Holly Schl; Mount Holly, AR; (3); 11/22; FBLA; FHA; FTA; Office Aide; Band; Chorus; Yrbk; Ofcr Jr Cls; Ofcr Stu Cncl; Bsktbl; Magnolia SAU; RN.

LESLIE, LEAH; Robinson HS; Little Rock, AR; (2); 20/150; Natl Beta Clb; Yrbk; Chrldng; Chrldng Squan Chosen Top 5; U Of AR; Orthopedic Therapy.

LESLIE, STEPHEN A; Booneville Jr Sr HS; Booneville, AR; (3); #1 in class; Church Yth Grp; Natl Beta Clb; Spanish Clb; Band; Mrchg Band; Pep Band; High Hon Roll; Soc Sci/Span II Awds 11th Grd; Church Piano Plyr; Attnd AR Schl Gospel Music Smmr 96; Music.

LESS, SAMANTHA M; Pulaski Acad; Little Rock, AR; (2); Cmnty Wkr; Debate Tm; French Clb; Model UN; Natl Beta Clb; Teachers Aide; Temple Yth Grp; Chorus; Var Sftbl; Var Tennis; Frgn Lang Fstvl Awd Fr Poetry; Bio Acad Excl Awd; Debate Acad Excl Awd; Biolgcl Life Sci.

LESSEL, GEOFFREY P; Pulaski Acad; Little Rock, AR; (2); Church Yth Grp; FCA; Natl Beta Clb; Spanish Clb; Chorus; School Musical; JV Ftbl; JV Wt Lftg; Hon Roll; NHS; Interact Clb; Outstdng Soph Chorus Mem.

LESSENBERRY, COURTNEY A; Robinson HS; Little Rock, AR; (2); Art Clb; Church Yth Grp; FCA; French Clb; Hosp Aide; Library Aide; Natl Beta Clb; Yrbk; Pom Pon; Hon Roll; U Of CNTRL AR.

LESTER, WILLIAM H; Robinson HS; Little Rock, AR; (2); High Hon Roll; Hon Roll; Bible Study Clb; Math & Eng Awds; Army ROTC; Army; Trade Work.

LEVER, JOANNA E; Northside HS; Fort Smith, AR; (4); 42/329; Church Yth Grp; FCA; Key Clb; Mu Alpha Theta; Church Choir; Ofcr Soph Cls; Ofcr Jr Cls; Ofcr Sr Cls; Var L Chrldng; Var L Gym; Grizzly Pride; TRAX; Ftbl Trainer; U Of Cntrl AR; Kinesiology.

LEVIN, BEN; Oark HS; Ozark, AR; (1); 4-H; Natl FFA Org; Ofcr Frsh Cls; Ofcr Bsbl; Bsktbl; 4-H Awd; High Hon Roll; Hon Roll; Med.

LEWALLEN, WAYLON E; Hope HS; Hope, AR; (4); 37/195; FBLA; Natl Beta Clb; Band; Jazz Band; Mrchg Band; Orch; Pep Band; Stage Crew; Variety Show; Hon Roll; Band Schlsp; U Of AR Hope; Criminal Justice.

LEWELLYN, AMBER M; Lonoke Jr HS; Lonoke, AR; (1); Yrbk; Chrldng; Trk; Hon Roll; Ecology Club; ASU; Med.

LEWERS, EMILY S; Greenbrier HS; Greenbrier, AR; (3); 7/170; Art Clb; Drama Clb; FCA; FBLA; Natl Beta Clb; Teachers Aide; Yrbk; VP Soph Cls; Capt Co-Capt Chrldng; High Hon Roll.

LEWIS, BETHANY; Farmington Jr Sr HS; Farmington, AR; (1); FBLA; FHA; Natl FFA Org; Chrldng; Sftbl; High Hon Roll; Jr NHS; Pres Acad Fit Awd; Phys Thrpy.

LEWIS, CALANDRA F; Harmony Grove Jr Sr HS; Camden, AR; (2); 6/72; Church Yth Grp; FBLA; FHA; Natl Beta Clb; Yrbk; JV Bsktbl; JV Chrldng; Var Trk; High Hon Roll; Prfct Atten Awd; Grambling ST Univ; Comp Engr.

LEWIS, CARLA J; Jacksonville HS; Jacksonville, AR; (2); Church Yth Grp; GAA; Var Bsktbl; JV Var Sftbl; Var Trk; JV Var Vllybl; High Hon Roll; Hon Roll; Prfct Atten Awd; Snow Skiing; Bus.

LEWIS, COREY D; Bright Star Schl; Doddridge, AR; (1); Band; Astronomer.

LEWIS, CRYSTAL; Lake Hamilton Jr HS; Royal, AR; (3); Drama Clb; FBLA; FHA; German Clb; Natl FFA Org; Science Clb; Thesps; School Musical; School Play; Sftbl; FFA Pub Spkng Won Subarea; MASH; Sftbl Wrld Series 2 Yrs; Baylor; Med.

LEWIS, DREW A; Fayetteville Sr HS; Fayetteville, AR; (3); Computer Clb; FBLA; Mu Alpha Theta; Hon Roll; Pres Acad Fit Awd; Comp Sci.

LEWIS, HEATHER D; Hot Springs HS; Hot Springs Natio, AR; (4); Church Yth Grp; Cmnty Wkr; Drama Clb; French Clb; Office Aide; Q&S; Science Clb; Thesps; Band; Mrchg Band; U AR Pine Bluff; Commcnt.

LEWIS, JACOB M; Little Rock Central HS; Little Rock, AR; (2); Chess Clb; Drama Clb; German Clb; Mu Alpha Theta; Science Clb; Service Clb; Temple Yth Grp; Band; Mrchg Band; High Hon Roll; Kodak Yth Ldrshp Awd.

LEWIS, JEFFREY; Mt Holly Schl; Mount Holly, AR; (4); Church Yth Grp; HOBY; Natl Beta Clb; Spanish Clb; Pres Sr Cls; Bsktbl; 4-H Awd; High Hon Roll; Natl FFA Forestry Team 1st Pl 94; U Of AR; Arch.

LEWIS, JENIFER J; Valley View HS; Jonesboro, AR; (2); Church Yth Grp; FBLA; Natl FFA Org; Spanish Clb; Chorus; School Play; Cit Awd; High Hon Roll; Hon Roll; Fin Analysis/Math/Bus.

LEWIS, JESSICA; Alread Schl; Clinton, AR; (4); 1/5; 4-H; Pres VP FBLA; German Clb; Quiz Bowl; Teachers Aide; Ed Yrbk; Pres Frsh Cls; VP Soph Cls; Pres Jr Cls; Sec Sr Cls; HOBY Awd; U Of Cntrl AR; Med.

LEWIS, JUSTIN P; El Dorado Sr HS; El Dorado, AR; (2); Library Aide; JV Golf; U AR.

LEWIS, KARI; Hazen Jr Sr HS; De Valls Bluff, AR; (4); 7/27; Am Leg Aux Girls St; French Clb; FBLA; Pres FTA; Pres Natl Beta Clb; Phtg Yrbk; Sec Stu Cncl; Capt Bsktbl; Trk; NHS; Stu Of Yr Awd 96; Qn Mallard Beatuy & Schlrsp Wnnr; Certfd Red Crss Lifeguard; U Of Cntrl AR; Speech Patholgy.

LEWIS, KELLY M; Smackover HS; Mount Holly, AR; (3); #3 in class; Am Leg Aux Girls St; Pres Drama Clb; VP Mu Alpha Theta; Stage Crew; Ed Yrbk; Sec Jr Cls; Sec Stu Cncl; Sec NHS; Fndr/Pres START; Pres Elec Anchr Clb; Grphc Dsgn.

LEWIS, KRISTY; Bearden HS; Thornton, AR; (3); Church Yth Grp; FCA; FBLA; FHA; Model UN; Natl Beta Clb; Phtg Nwsp; Rptr Yrbk; Treas Soph Cls; High Hon Roll; Henderson ST; Psych.

LEWIS, LAURA R; Huntsville HS; Hindsville, AR; (4); 15/123; FTA; Key Clb; VP Frsh Cls; VP Soph Cls; Rep Jr Cls; Rep Sr Cls; Stat Bsbl; L Mgr(s); L Trk; High Hon Roll; Civics Awd; U Of AR; Comp Sci.

LEWIS, LOLA; Norphlet HS; El Dorado, AR; (3); 1/36; Church Yth Grp; FBLA; Service Clb; Spanish Clb; Chorus; Yrbk; Rep Stu Cncl; Cit Awd; High Hon Roll; Hon Roll; Conway; Bus.

LEWIS, LYDIA M; Fairview HS; Camden, AR; (2); 1/250; FBLA; Spanish Clb; Band; Mrchg Band; Yrbk; Sec Frsh Cls; VP Soph Cls; High Hon Roll; JETS Awd; Outstdng Bandsman Awd; All-Region Band; Acctnt.

LEWIS, MARC A; Forrest City HS; Forrest City, AR; (3); Church Yth Grp; Cmnty Wkr; FHA; Hosp Aide; Natl Beta Clb; Spanish Clb; Church Choir; Ofcr Bsbl; Bsktbl; Trk; Deans List; UCA; Pre-Med.

LEWIS, MARCUS M; Parkview Arts-Science HS; Little Rock, AR; (3); Art Clb; Church Yth Grp; Cmnty Wkr; FBLA; Bsktbl; Hon Roll; Cmmrcl Art.

LEWIS, MEGAN K; Mills HS; Jacksonville, AR; (3); 25/298; Am Leg Aux Girls St; French Clb; Natl Beta Clb; Q&S; Ed Nwsp; Jr NHS; NHS; Proj WET; AEGIS Fr Immrsn Prgm; Sci Fair 2nd Pl Schl/3rd Regnl 94-95; Cmpeted ST Envrnmntl Sci Cat; Comm/Jrnlsm.

LEWIS, MIRANDA M; Mountain Home HS; Mountain Home, AR; (3); 37/300; FBLA; FHA; Natl Beta Clb; Spanish Clb; Band; Mgr Yrbk; Powder Puff Ftbl; Hon Roll; Hendrix; Bus.

LEWIS, ROBERT; Butterfield Jr HS; Van Buren, AR; (1); Drama Clb; School Play; Bsktbl; Ftbl; Cit Awd; Hon Roll; Jr NHS; G-T Class; Student Cncl; U Of AR; Prof Sports.

LEWIS, ROOSEVELT; John L Mcclellan Magnet HS; Little Rock, AR; (2); Church Yth Grp; Cmnty Wkr; FCA; Spanish Clb; Band; Mrchg Band; Socr; Sftbl; Cit Awd; High Hon Roll; Carpentry; UCA Conway; Carpenter.

LEWIS, SUZANNE; Arkansas Bapt Schl; Little Rock, AR; (2); Church Yth Grp; FCA; FBLA; Natl Beta Clb; Church Choir; Var L Bsktbl; Sftbl; High Hon Roll; Missionary.

LI, HANBING; Central Sr HS; Little Rock, AR; (3); French Clb; Intnl Clb; Nwsp; Yrbk; Socr; SECME Clb; Sci Fair Awds.

LIEBLONG III, WARREN G; Mountain Pine Jr Sr HS; Royal, AR; (3); Am Leg Boys St; Key Clb; Natl Beta Clb; Ofcr Bsbl; Bsktbl; Ftbl; Hon Roll; Natl Ftbl Hall Of Fame Schlr Ath Awd.

LIEU, MINH T; Northside HS; Fort Smith, AR; (4); #23 in class; Mu Alpha Theta; Spanish Clb; Hon Roll; Pres Acad Fit Awd; Spanish NHS; Westark CC.

LIEUX, CHRIS; Southside HS; Fort Smith, AR; (4); 89/464; Am Leg Boys St; German Clb; Office Aide; Nwsp; Mgr(s); Hon Roll; NHS; Ft Smith Boys Clb Yth Of Yr 95; Westark CC; Psych.

LIEVSAY, LAURA F; Huntsville HS; Huntsville, AR; (2); 1/153; Sec Church Yth Grp; FCA; FTA; Quiz Bowl; Rptr Science Clb; Rep Frsh Cls; Rep Soph Cls; L Bsktbl; Mgr Ftbl; L Trk; Scrd 4 AP Govt Exm; Solo/Ensmbl Piano I Rtngs; Bsktbl Dist Trnmnt Chmps; Chld Psych.

LIGEKIS, SARAH; Norfork Jr Sr HS; Mountain Home, AR; (3); Art Clb; Church Yth Grp; English Clb; FBLA; FHA; Math Clb; Science Clb; Band; Yrbk; High Hon Roll; Frnsc Med.

LIGHT, ADAM C; Central Sr HS; Little Rock, AR; (3); 6/540; German Clb; Mu Alpha Theta; Quiz Bowl; Science Clb; Service Clb; Stage Crew; Gov Hon Prg Awd; High Hon Roll; Ntl Merit SF; Yng Democrats Treas; Neurolgst.

LIGHT, CHRISTIE; Woodlawn Schl; Rison, AR; (3); Church Yth Grp; GAA; Natl Beta Clb; Yrbk; Rep Jr Cls; Bsktbl; Chrldng; Sftbl; High Hon Roll; Span Awd; Dntl Hyg.

LIGON, LESLIE J; Marvell Acad; Marvell, AR; (3); 1/29; Am Leg Aux Girls St; Church Yth Grp; Nwsp; Co-Capt Yrbk; Var Bsktbl; Var Sftbl; Var Trk; VP Cit Awd; VP Jr NHS; Pres NHS; Law.

LILES, PAIGE; Huntsville HS; Huntsville, AR; (2); 14/155; Church Yth Grp; Pep Clb; Band; Jazz Band; Mrchg Band; Hon Roll; Pres Acad Fit Awd; UCCM; Renaissance Pgm; U Of AR; Music.

LILLARD, JUSTIN; Mineral Springs Schl; Mineral Springs, AR; (4); 1/29; HOBY; Capt Quiz Bowl; Rep Soph Cls; Rep Jr Cls; Pres Stu Cncl; Capt Ftbl; Trk; Gov Hon Prg Awd; High Hon Roll; Val; U Of Cntrl AR; Athl Trng.

LIM, FERDINAND T; Catholic HS; Little Rock, AR; (4); 67/158; Phy Ftnss Mem; U Of AR; Biomed Engrng.

LIMGO, KIM ANNE B; Russellville Sr HS; Russellville, AR; (2); Church Yth Grp; Chorus; Church Choir.

LIN, JENNIFER; Central Sr HS; Little Rock, AR; (4); Am Leg Aux Girls St; Drama Clb; FBLA; Pres Sec Natl Beta Clb; VP Rptr Spanish Clb; School Play; Rep Frsh Cls; Ofcr Stu Cncl; Hon Roll; VP NHS; Accept No Boundaries Steering Comm, Pub Chm & Sr Rep; Mercantile Bnk Stu Bd Dirs Sec; Peer Facilitator; Hendrix Coll.

LINCOLN, ELIZABETH; Jacksonville HS; Conway, AR; (4); Drama Clb; French Clb; Model UN; Rep Band; Jazz Band; Pep Band; School Musical; School Play; Stage Crew; Solo/Ensmbl 4 Yrs; Music Schlsp UCA; Hnrs Soc 3 Yrs; 1CA; Music.

LINCOLN, NICOLE C; Jacksonville HS; Jacksonville, AR; (3); Church Yth Grp; Drama Clb; French Clb; Chorus; School Musical; School Play; Hon Roll.

LINCOURT, ELAINE C; Central Sr HS; Little Rock, AR; (3); 31/540; Cmnty Wkr; Mu Alpha Theta; Natl Beta Clb; Yrbk; Gov Hon Prg Awd; NHS; Accpt No Boundaries; Film.

LINDER, SARAH; Malvern Sr HS; Malvern, AR; (3); Church Yth Grp; Natl Beta Clb; Spanish Clb; Acpl Chr; Chorus; Chrldng; High Hon Roll; Hon Roll; Jr NHS; NHS; UCA All-Star Chrldr 93; NCA All-Amer Chrldr 95; Miss Hot Spring Cty Sweetheart 94; Homcmng Qn 93; U Of AR Fayetteville; Medicine.

LINDLEY, GRAYSON; Mc Gehee HS; Mcgehee, AR; (2); Church Yth Grp; FTA; Mu Alpha Theta; Natl Beta Clb; Rep Stu Cncl; L Bsbl; Wt Lftg; High Hon Roll; Hon Roll; NHS; Acad Achvmt In Bio & Phys Sci; 3rd Pl Zoology Sci Fair; LA Tech; Engrng.

LINDSEY, JAMIE D; Lake Hamilton Sr HS; Hot Springs Natio, AR; (2); Computer Clb; Debate Tm; Letterman Clb; Math Clb; Math Tm; Natl FFA Org; Red Cross Aide; SADD; Teachers Aide; Varsity Clb; U Of AR; Cnslr; Psych.

LINDSEY, JAQUITA; Victory Christian Schl; Camden, AR; (2); Church Yth Grp; Nwsp; Yrbk; Bsktbl; Sftbl; Vllybl; Gospel Singer.

LINDSEY, JERRY R; Midland HS; Pleasant Plains, AR; (2); VP Drama Clb; Treas Natl FFA Org; Natl Beta Clb; Quiz Bowl; Spanish Clb; School Play; Stage Crew; Rep Frsh Cls; VP Soph Cls; Rep Stu Cncl; Radiologist.

LINDSEY, KRISTIN; Camden-Fairview HS; Camden, AR; (2); Church Yth Grp; Teachers Aide; School Musical; School Play; Ed Nwsp; Yrbk; Chrldng; Gym; Beta Clb; U Of AR Fayetteville.

LINDSEY, LATONYA D; Fairview HS; Camden, AR; (2); Bus Profs of Am; Church Yth Grp; FBLA; Band; Flag Corp; Mrchg Band; Hon Roll; Choices; BSU; Henderson ST Univ; Bus/Soc Sci.

LINDSEY, RYAN; Bearden HS; Bearden, AR; (4); 6/58; Church Yth Grp; 4-H; FBLA; FTA; Natl Beta Clb; Office Aide; Band; Rptr Nwsp; Rptr Yrbk; Rep Stu Cncl; Woodmen Of Wrld Amer Hstry Awd; Natl Engl Merit Awd; U Of AR Fayetteville; Law.

LINGAR, JEREMY R; Westside HS; Coal Hill, AR; (2); Natl FFA Org; Scholastic Bowl; Ofcr Bsbl; Bsktbl.

LINGENFELTER, SHONIA J; Mayflower HS; Mayflower, AR; (2); Drama Clb; FBLA; FHA; School Play; Yrbk; Co-Capt Chrldng; Hon Roll; Highest GPA Algebra Awd; AR ST U; Law.

LINGO, LINDSAY R; Lonoke Jr HS; Lonoke, AR; (1); FHA; Science Clb; Hon Roll; NHS; Lawyer.

LINGO, MONICA S; Northside HS; Barling, AR; (3); 26/418; Am Leg Aux Girls St; Spanish Clb; Teachers Aide; Orch; High Hon Roll; Hon Roll; Jr NHS; NHS; Pres Acad Fit Awd; Spanish NHS; All ST Orch; All Region Orch; Pre-Med/PT.

LINGO, SARAH; Murfreesboro HS; Murfreesboro, AR; (1); Art Clb; Girl Scts; Natl Beta Clb; Band; Drm Mjr(t); Mrchg Band; High Hon Roll; Pres Acad Fit Awd.

LINSON, KAREN; Southside HS; Barling, AR; (2); Church Yth Grp; Spanish Clb; Rptr Nwsp; Ofcr Stu Cncl; Hon Roll; NHS; Pres Acad Fit Awd; 4th Pl ST Natl Span Exam.

LINZ, AMANDA; Central Ark Christian Schl; Little Rock, AR; (2); Rep Church Yth Grp; Natl Beta Clb; Spanish Clb; Chorus; Church Choir; Var Capt Chrldng; High Hon Roll; Jr NHS; NHS; Med.

LIPE, SHAUNA M; Ft Smith Christian Schl; Cedarville, AR; (1); Church Yth Grp; FBLA; GAA; Spanish Clb; Speech Tm; JV Bsktbl; JV Chrldng; Sftbl; Hon Roll; Prfct Atten Awd; Child Psych.

LIPSEY, MATTHEW J; Catholic HS; Sherwood, AR; (3); 22/180; Church Yth Grp; Cmnty Wkr; ROTC; Band; Church Choir; Color Guard; Drill Tm; Jazz Band; Pep Band; Math Tm; Daedalian ROTC Awd; Duke.

LIPSMEYER, JUSTIN K; Fayetteville Sr HS; Fayetteville, AR; (2); Chorus; Hon Roll; U Of AR; Cmptr Pgrmng.

LIPSMEYER, KARA E; Central Sr HS; Little Rock, AR; (3); Church Yth Grp; Debate Tm; Hosp Aide; Latin Clb; Natl Beta Clb; Hon Roll; Jr NHS; Church Play.

LIPSMEYER, PAUL W; St Joe Public Schl; Morrilton, AR; (3); Church Yth Grp; Hosp Aide; Natl Beta Clb; Spanish Clb; Ofcr Bsbl; Bsktbl; Tennis; U Of Cntrl AR; Pre-Med.

LISEMBY, TENNIA A; Kingsland Schl; New Edinburg, AR; (3); 3/27; Church Yth Grp; French Clb; Natl Beta Clb; Rptr Nwsp; Stat Yrbk; VP Stu Cncl; Capt Bsktbl; Wt Lftg; High Hon Roll; Elem Tchr.

LISKO, JENNIFER; Hazen Jr Sr HS; Hazen, AR; (2); 4/50; FBLA; FHA; FTA; Natl Beta Clb; Var Bsktbl; Var Chrldng; Var Trk; Hon Roll; Stu Of The Yr.

LISLE, DIANA M; Huntsville HS; Huntsville, AR; (3); 12/126; Church Yth Grp; Key Clb; Library Aide; Science Clb; Church Choir; School Play; Stage Crew; High Hon Roll; Hon Roll; NHS; UCCM Sec; Mash; Phys Thrpy.

LISTER, DONALD J; North Little Rock Hs-East; North Little Rock, AR; (2); 90/567; FBLA; Band; School Play; Stage Crew; High Hon Roll; Hon Roll; Bus.

LISZEWSKI, APRIL L; Vilonia HS; Conway, AR; (2); Church Yth Grp; FBLA; FHA; Natl Beta Clb; Hon Roll; Home Ec Awd 94-95; Fam Dynmcs Awd 95-96; Univ Of Cntrl AR; Home Ec Tchr.

LITTLE, ASHLEY; Mansfield Jr Sr HS; Mansfield, AR; (1); Church Yth Grp; FCA; GAA; Speech Tm; Church Choir; Bsktbl; Chrldng; Crs Cntry; Powder Puff Ftbl; Score Keeper.

LITTLE, DENNIS M; Springdale Sr HS; Springdale, AR; (1); Hon Roll; Jr NHS; Pres Acad Fit Awd; Harvard.

LITTLE, JAMIE D; Springdale Sr HS; Springdale, AR; (1); Church Yth Grp; Girl Scts; Band; Color Guard; Mrchg Band; Gym; Cit Awd; Hon Roll; Jr NHS; Prfct Atten Awd; Stdnt Mnstry Team; Swpstks 2 Yrs; U Of AR; Cmptr Trnr.

LITTLE, JARED B; Huttig Schl; Huttig, AR; (1); 1/15; Church Yth Grp; German Clb; Rptr Nwsp; Var Bsbl; JV Bsktbl; Hon Roll; Cmptr Engr.

LITTLE, KIMBERLY D; Mc Crory Jr Sr HS; Mc Crory, AR; (4); FBLA; FTA; Office Aide; Spanish Clb; Temple Yth Grp; School Play; Rep Stu Cncl.

LITTLE, KIZZY; Brinkle HS; Brinkley, AR; (4); 23/71; French Clb; FBLA; FHA; Science Clb; Co-Ed Nwsp; Pres Jr Cls; Pres Sr Cls; Hon Roll; Jr & Sr Cls Favorite; BHS Sweetheart Pagaent Frosh & Jr; Homcmng Qn 95; Stu Of Week; TOP; East AR CC; Bus Admin.

LITTLE, WILLIAM CLINTON; Dequeen HS; De Queen, AR; (3); Var L Bsktbl; Var L Ftbl; Hon Roll; NHS; U Of AR.

LITTLEMYER, WILLIAM C; Nettleton HS; Jonesboro, AR; (4); Art Clb; French Clb; Office Aide; Teachers Aide; Bsktbl; Ftbl; Cmptr Tech Class; Sr Class Wittiest/Best Personality; AR ST Univ; PT.

LITTLER, NICK A; Ozark HS; Ozark, AR; (3); Church Yth Grp; FCA; Model UN; Natl Beta Clb; Quiz Bowl; Chorus; Rep Sr Cls; Ofcr Stu Cncl; Ofcr Bsbl; Bsktbl; Soccer; Soccer Referee; K-Life; PE.

LITTLES JR, JAMES RANDY; Poyen Schl; Malvern, AR; (3); FHA; Natl Beta Clb; ROTC; School Play; Yrbk; Pres Jr Cls; Intrml Bsktbl; Art; Mltry.

LITTRELL, BRIAN F; Huntsville HS; Huntsville, AR; (3); 7/128; Quiz Bowl; Science Clb; Hon Roll; Mrtl Art; Fncng; Odyssey Mind.

LIVELY, DANIEL B; Southside HS; Fort Smith, AR; (2); Motorcross Racing; Univ Of AR; Mech Engrng.

LIVELY, DARIN; Lavaca Jr Sr HS; Lavaca, AR; (2); #1 in class; FCA; Natl Beta Clb; Pres Frsh Cls; Var Bsktbl; High Hon Roll; Honored For Dsgng Schl Flag; Eng Awd; MIT; Comp Sci.

LIVERETT, HAZEL K; Genoa Central HS; Fouke, AR; (3); 4-H; Model UN; Science Clb; Spanish Clb; Yrbk; Cit Awd; High Hon Roll; NHS; Ntl Merit Ltr; Phy.

LIVERETT, KATHY; Genoa Central HS; Fouke, AR; (3); Computer Clb; Service Clb; Spanish Clb; Yrbk; Cit Awd; High Hon Roll; Hon Roll; NHS; Pre-Med.

LIVERS, NATHAN; Arkansas Bapt Schl; Little Rock, AR; (3); FCA; FBLA; Natl Beta Clb; Church Choir; Yrbk; Var L Bsbl; Capt Var Ftbl; High Hon Roll; US Navy Math Awd; Medcn.

LIVINGSTON, TONEY; Bismarck Jr-Sr HS; Bismarck, AR; (4); 2/62; Am Leg Boys St; Church Yth Grp; FCA; Natl Beta Clb; Natl FFA Org; Ftbl; Wt Lftg; DAR Awd; Hon Roll; Sal; Henderson ST U; Engrng.

LLOYD, CHAD J; Drew Central Jr Sr HS; Monticello, AR; (3); Church Yth Grp; Natl FFA Org; U At Monticello.

LLOYD, LEAH M; Arkadelphia Sr HS; Arkadelphia, AR; (3); Church Yth Grp; Cmnty Wkr; Sec 4-H; FHA; Natl Beta Clb; Teachers Aide; Rptr Nwsp; High Hon Roll; NHS; CHAMPS; Nrsng Home Vol; Henderson ST Univ; Nrsng/Crim.

LOCKARD, RACHEL; Omaha Schl; Omaha, AR; (2); Drama Clb; FBLA; Chorus; School Play; Lit Mag; Church Choir; Variety Show; Ofcr Stu Cncl; Bsktbl; Chrldng; Psych.

LOCKARD, RALYN; Omaha Schl; Omaha, AR; (2); Natl Beta Clb; Band; School Musical; Cit Awd; Hon Roll; Cmpng; Tnns; Wrtng; Arch.

LOCKHART, ANGEL; Mc Neil HS; Mc Neil, AR; (4); 3/25; Bus Profs of Am; Church Yth Grp; Church Choir; Pres Jr Cls; Pres Sr Cls; Bsktbl; Trk; Hon Roll; NHS; Anderson St Univ; Acctnt.

LOCKHART, ANNE M; Conway Sr HS; Conway, AR; (2); Church Yth Grp; French Clb; Bsktbl; Tennis; Vllybl; French Hon Soc; High Hon Roll; Hon Roll.

LOCKHART, JOSH; Conway Sr HS; Conway, AR; (2); Cmnty Wkr; Letterman Clb; Teachers Aide; Ofcr Bsbl; Ftbl; Hon Roll; Jr NHS; Prfct Atten Awd; Pre-Med.

LOCKWOOD, JENNIFER E; Southside HS; Fort Smith, AR; (3); Church Yth Grp; French Clb; Intnl Clb; Mu Alpha Theta; Pep Clb; Teachers Aide; Drill Tm; Hon Roll; NHS; Pres Acad Fit Awd; RAIN Vol.

LOEBIG, AMY V; Arkansas Sr HS; Texarkana, AR; (2); Church Yth Grp; Drama Clb; French Clb; FHA; Pres Acad Fit Awd; PRIDE.

LOFTIS, MARY A; North Little Rock HS; Jacksonville, AR; (3); Church Yth Grp; Dance Clb; FBLA; Math Clb; Mu Alpha Theta; Chorus; Drill Tm; Yrbk; Jr NHS; NHS; Jr Ldrshp Cncl Del 96; PT/NRS/ANSTHTST.

LOFTON, ARTIS T; North Little Rock Hs-East; North Little Rock, AR; (2); Natl Beta Clb; ROTC; Science Clb; Church Choir; Color Guard; Socr; Cit Awd; DAR Awd; Hon Roll; NHS; JROTC Meritorious Svc Awd; 1st Pl Achvmt Awd Sci Fair 95-; North Little Rock HS Acad Excl Awd; West Point Military Acad; Bus.

LOFTON, KADESHA C; Arkansas Sr HS; Texarkana, AR; (3); Art Clb; Church Yth Grp; FBLA; FHA; Church Choir; Chrch Mscn.

LONG, AMBER N; England HS; Scott, AR; (3); FBLA; Band; Flag Corp; Jazz Band; Mrchg Band; Cit Awd; High Hon Roll; Hon Roll; Pres Acad Fit Awd; Acad Excl 95; Acad Excl 96; Natl Sci Olympiad 4th Plc 96; All Reg Bnd 95-.

LONG, CHRISTY M; Bald Knob HS; Bald Knob, AR; (1); Band; Mrchg Band; High Hon Roll; ASU Jonesboro.

LONG, DELTA; Hatfield Schl; Hatfield, AR; (3); 3/23; Church Yth Grp; FCA; Natl Beta Clb; Natl FFA Org; Quiz Bowl; Church Choir; Bsktbl; Trk; Gifted & Talented Clb; All Amer Schlr; U Of AR Fayettvl; Phys Thrpy.

LONG, JAYME M; Searcy HS; Searcy, AR; (3); 40/350; Church Yth Grp; FCA; Key Clb; Natl Beta Clb; Office Aide; Spanish Clb; Sec Jr Cls; Bsktbl; Tennis; Jr NHS; U Of AR; Acctg.

LONG, JENNIFER A; Marion HS; Marion, AR; (2); French Clb; Nwsp; Hon Roll; Jr NHS; PRIDE; TEAMATES Gfted & Tlntd Pgm; Novelist.

LONG, JUSTIN M; Van Buren Sr HS; Rudy, AR; (2); Boy Scts; Band; Mrchg Band; Hon Roll; AR Tech; Band Tchr.

LONG, LATOSHA M; Forrest City HS; Madison, AR; (3); Natl Beta Clb; Chorus; Church Choir; Hon Roll; Spanish NHS; Deans List; Concert Choir; Der Sinkeris; East AR CC; Medcl.

LONG, MATTHEW K; Mountain View Jr Sr HS; Mountain View, AR; (4); Church Yth Grp; Natl Beta Clb; Natl FFA Org; Spanish Clb; Var Bsbl; JV Ftbl; Hon Roll; Pres Acad Fit Awd; Welding Cls Awd; Chptr Star Farmer Awd; AR ST Univ; Vet Med.

LONG, RAYE M; Lake Hamilton Sr HS; Pearcy, AR; (2); Church Yth Grp; Computer Clb; FCA; FBLA; Natl FFA Org; Chorus; Church Choir; Rptr Nwsp; Rptr Yrbk; Mgr(s); Wolf Pride; 1st Pl Microbio Awd.

LONG, RYAN S; Nettleton HS; Jonesboro, AR; (2); 4/140; Rep Church Yth Grp; Pres French Clb; Band; Jazz Band; Mrchg Band; Cit Awd; Hon Roll; Prfct Atten Awd; Pres Acad Fit Awd; Boy Scts; All St Band; Sons Of Amer Revolution; U Of NE; Music; Band Dir.

LONG, WHITNEY J; Searcy HS; Searcy, AR; (4); 1/202; Church Yth Grp; Key Clb; Natl Beta Clb; Variety Show; Yrbk; Rptr Stu Cncl; Pres NHS; Ntl Merit SF; Spanish NHS; Val; Harding U; Sprts Med.

LONGINO, TRACY M; Gosnell Jr Sr HS; Blytheville, AR; (2); Church Yth Grp; FHA; Science Clb; Spanish Clb; Sftbl; Hon Roll; RN/MED.

LOONEY, MEGAN E; Benton Cty Christian School; Lowell, AR; (1); Chorus; Church Choir; School Musical; Rep Stu Cncl; Var Bsktbl; High Hon Roll; Essay 3rd Pl Reg; High GPA; Harvard; MD.

LORETZ JR, DANNY; Carlisle Jr Sr HS; Carlisle, AR; (4); 1/48; Am Leg Boys St; VP FBLA; Pres VP FHA; HOBY; VP Pres Band; Rep Stu Cncl; Pres NHS; Val; Treas Church Yth Grp; Quiz Bowl; PRIDE; All St Band; Comp Sci.

LOTER, BRIEANNA R; Mt Vernon-Enola HS; Mount Vernon, AR; (3); Church Yth Grp; Quiz Bowl; Spanish Clb; Yrbk; Sec Soph Cls; Ofcr Stu Cncl; Bsktbl; Chrldng; Sftbl; High Hon Roll; FFA; Class Favrt; Stdnt Of Month; UCA; Nrsng/Tchng.

LOTT, JOLEEN; Hackett Schl; Hackett, AR; (3); 1/36; FBLA; Spanish Clb; Co-Capt Color Guard; Sec Jr Cls; L Bsktbl; L Sftbl; NHS; Ntl Merit Ltr; Church Yth Grp; Band; Sci.

LOTT, RACHEL; Vilonia HS; Vilonia, AR; (3); 1/140; FBLA; Model UN; Mu Alpha Theta; Natl Beta Clb; Quiz Bowl; Spanish Clb; Speech Tm; School Play; High Hon Roll; Ntl Merit Ltr; AR Governors Schl; Pre-Med.

LOUTON, EDWARD L; Lake Hamilton Sr HS; Hot Springs, AR; (2); Church Yth Grp; FBLA; German Clb; Natl Beta Clb; Band; Mrchg Band; Cit Awd; High Hon Roll; Hon Roll; NHS.

LOVE, LATONYA; Holly Grove HS; Holly Grove, AR; (4); 5/27; Am Leg Aux Girls St; Church Yth Grp; Drama Clb; 4-H; FBLA; FHA; German Clb; Natl Beta Clb; Natl FFA Org; Office Aide; Engrg Bnd; Grl ST Cnslr; U Of AR Pine Bluff; Crim Just.

LOVELACE, KURT; Bergman Schl; Harrison, AR; (3); 12/46; Am Leg Boys St; Model UN; Natl Beta Clb; Natl FFA Org; Band; Jazz Band; Pep Band; Pres VP Stu Cncl; Cmnty Wkr; 4-H; Coll Of The Ozarks; Ag.

LOVELL, KRISTIN; Sylvan Hills Jr HS; Sherwood, AR; (1); Church Yth Grp; Chorus; Church Choir; Ed Yrbk; High Hon Roll; Jr NHS; Ballet; Advanced Eng Cls; Top 10 Cls Awd; Pediatrician.

LOVENSTEIN, AUSTIN M; Catholic HS; Sherwood, AR; (2); 40/200; High Hon Roll; Immaculate Conception Religion Awd; CYM Tutoring Awd; Sr CYM.

LOVETT, AMANDA L; Waldron HS; Waldron, AR; (1); Drama Clb; Band; Mrchg Band; Hon Roll; AR Tech Univ; Psychiatrist.

LOVETT, LINDSEY L; Star City HS; Star City, AR; (4); 27/105; Church Yth Grp; French Clb; FBLA; FHA; Natl FFA Org; Teachers Aide; Band; Flag Corp; Sec Stu Cncl; Hon Roll; U Of AR; Premed.

LOVINS, CHRISTIE L; Nettleton HS; Jonesboro, AR; (4); Church Yth Grp; French Clb; FBLA; Science Clb; Band; Church Choir; Color Guard; Flag Corp; Mrchg Band; Phtg Yrbk; ASU; Psych.

LOW, SCOTT M; Siloam Springs Sr HS; Siloam Springs, AR; (4); 60/170; Am Leg Boys St; Church Yth Grp; FCA; Spanish Clb; Band; Crs Cntry; Swmmng; Trk; U Of AR; Lndscp Arch.

LOWE, BRANDON D; Greenwood Sr HS; Greenwood, AR; (4); FCA; French Clb; Natl Beta Clb; Natl FFA Org; Q&S; Variety Show; Yrbk; Cit Awd; Hon Roll; Ntl Merit Ltr; Harris Achvmt Awd Non, Beta Clb.

LOWE, JONATHAN PAUL; Fairview HS; Camden, AR; (4); Am Leg Boys St; Boy Scts; Church Yth Grp; Debate Tm; Drama Clb; FCA; Key Clb; Math Clb; Math Tm; Mu Alpha Theta; Yth Advsry Brd; Ouachita Cnty Crime Prev Prog; Gov Yth Conf; Natl Cngrssnl Yth Cmte; Quachita Baptist Univ; Poli Sci.

LOWE, MYRON E; Hughes Jr-Sr HS; Hughes, AR; (2); Cmnty Wkr; Natl FFA Org; Spanish Clb; JV Bsktbl; Intrml Ftbl; High Hon Roll; Hon Roll; Prfct Atten Awd; GATE; MS ST Univ; Bus Mgmt.

LOWE, SANDY; Bismarck Jr-Sr HS; Bismarck, AR; (2); Natl Beta Clb; Office Aide; Band; Hon Roll; Intr Decorator.

LOWERY, JAYSON; Kirby HS; Glenwood, AR; (2); 4/36; Church Yth Grp; FCA; FBLA; HOBY; Natl Beta Clb; Natl FFA Org; Quiz Bowl; Pres Soph Cls; Bsktbl; High Hon Roll.

LOWERY, JEFF; El Dorado Sr HS; El Dorado, AR; (3); Boy Scts; Church Yth Grp; FCA; FBLA; Key Clb; Natl Beta Clb; Ofcr Sr Cls; Var L Bsbl; Var Ftbl; Hon Roll; U Of AR.

LOWERY, JOHN W; Junction City HS; El Dorado, AR; (1); Church Yth Grp; Cmnty Wkr; VP FBLA; Science Clb; Band; Church Choir; Mrchg Band; Cit Awd; Hon Roll; BASIC Bro/Sis In Christ; 2nd Pl Lcl/Regnl Sci Fair; Ouachita Bapt Univ.

LOWERY, SHACARA A; North Little Rock Hs-East; North Little Rock, AR; (2); Church Yth Grp; Cmnty Wkr; Debate Tm; FBLA; JA; Key Clb; Natl Beta Clb; ROTC; Trk; Vllybl; Dance Tm; OK U; Law.

LOWMAN, LOUISE ELIZABETH; Cabot HS; Cabot, AR; (3); 66/398; Church Yth Grp; Cmnty Wkr; VP FHA; Pres German Clb; Math Clb; Office Aide; Quiz Bowl; Teachers Aide; Gov Hon Prg Awd; Hon Roll; PRIDE Club; Acadmc Ltr; Pub 5 Times Schl Litrcy Mag; Natnl Right To Life; March For Life; Freed-Hardeman Univ; Engrng.

LOWNIUS, TIMOTHY B; Victory Christian Schl; Camden, AR; (3); Church Yth Grp; Nwsp; Yrbk; Bsktbl; Hon Roll; ASL; South AR U Magnolia; Law.

LOWRY, JAIME C; Pine Bluff HS; Pine Bluff, AR; (3); 34/381; French Clb; FHA; Acpl Chr; Church Choir; Lit Mag; High Hon Roll; Hon Roll; Jr NHS; Chrstn Clb VP; Ch Sftbl; Piano; Ouachita Bapt Univ; Nrsg.

LOY, KTRINA A; Lake Hamilton Sr HS; Hot Springs, AR; (3); 28/258; GAA; Natl Beta Clb; Natl FFA Org; Science Clb; Thesps; Crs Cntry; Trk; High Hon Roll; NHS; Pres Acad Fit Awd; 5th Pl St Poultry Cont; Crss Cntry Rnnrs-Up; Harding; Tchr.

LOYD, AMY L; Wickes Schl; Grannis, AR; (3); 4/35; Church Yth Grp; Natl FFA Org; Spanish Clb; Chorus; Church Choir; School Musical; Hon Roll; An Awd In Geom Highest Grd; Awd In Principles Of Tech Highest Grd; Mountain View Sch Cosmetology.

LOYD, AMY R; Central Sr HS; Little Rock, AR; (3); Cmnty Wkr; Natl Beta Clb; Spanish Clb; Hon Roll; Jr NHS; Law.

LOYD, JUDY; Beebe Sr HS; Beebe, AR; (3); FHA; Spanish Clb; Band; School Play; Pres Frsh Cls; VP Jr Cls; Sec Stu Cncl; Var JV Chrldng; Powder Puff Ftbl; Trk; Emrgng Wmn Hattie Caraway Conf Del; Jr Clss Favorite; FHA Dist II Pres; Harding Univ; Brdcst Jrnlsm.

LOYD, TARA; Dumas Jr HS; Dumas, AR; (1); 1/160; Church Yth Grp; FBLA; Natl Beta Clb; Spanish Clb; Church Choir; Ofcr Stu Cncl; Capt Chrldng; Gym; Cit Awd; High Hon Roll; Amer Lgn Aux Stu Qtr; Dnce; Piano.

LOYD, TRACY L; Booneville Jr Sr HS; Booneville, AR; (2); GAA; Science Clb; Sftbl; Hon Roll; Best Batting Avg, All Dist Awd 95-96 Lady Cats Sftbl Team.

LUCAS, DERRICK M; Lakeside HS; Lake Village, AR; (3); 15/70; Drama Clb; FBLA; FHA; Teachers Aide; Chorus; School Play; Stage Crew; JV Bsktbl; Mgr(s); Powder Puff Ftbl; Math Tchr.

LUCAS, DUANE A; Arkansas Schl Math & Science; De Valls Bluff, AR; (2); Natl Beta Clb; Quiz Bowl; Teachers Aide; Bsktbl; FFA Rptr.

LUCAS, ZACHARY S; North Little Rock Hs-West; North Little Rock, AR; (3); Boy Scts; Church Yth Grp; JA; Var Bsbl; Var Bsktbl; Var Ftbl; Var Trk; Var Wt Lftg; Hon Roll; Legend Poetry Contest Hnbl Mention; Overall Nwscst Amiga Operator Runner Up; Cmptr Sci/Engrg.

LUCERO, ANGEL F; Morrilton Sr HS; Morrilton, AR; (3); Spanish Clb; School Musical.

LUCKY, MICHELLE B; Monticello HS; Monticello, AR; (3); FCA; Natl Beta Clb; SADD; Rep Jr Cls; Rep Stu Cncl; Chrldng; High Hon Roll; NHS; Pom Pon.

LUEBKE, BRETT L; Dewitt HS; De Witt, AR; (4); 2/72; Am Leg Boys St; FBLA; FTA; Model UN; Natl Beta Clb; Office Aide; Quiz Bowl; Science Clb; Nwsp; Yrbk; U Of MS; Chem Engrng.

LUEBKE, LESLEY S; Dewitt HS; De Witt, AR; (3); 8/90; French Clb; FBLA; FHA; FTA; Natl Beta Clb; Quiz Bowl; Science Clb; Band; Pep Band; School Play.

LUKER, MITCH A; Sheridan Sr HS; Mabelvale, AR; (2); Church Yth Grp; Cmnty Wkr; Teachers Aide; Band; Yrbk; Cit Awd; Hon Roll; Med/Doctor.

LUM, JACQUELINE N; Huttig Schl; Huttig, AR; (1); 4/14; Church Yth Grp; FTA; German Clb; Band; Church Choir; Mrchg Band; School Play; Rep Stu Cncl; Cit Awd; Hon Roll; Huttigs Kids For Christ; GYC; Encounter 95.

LUMMES, AMBERLY; Bright Star Schl; Doddridge, AR; (1); 3/22; Art Clb; Church Yth Grp; English Clb; GAA; JV Bsktbl; Var Chrldng; Var Trk; Hon Roll; Most Rebounds Bsktbl; Best Offensive Bsktbl; Best Free Throw Bsktbl; STOPP Prgm; PT.

LUMPKIN, ADRIENNE; Jonesboro HS; Jonesboro, AR; (4); 33/260; Church Yth Grp; FBLA; Key Clb; Mu Alpha Theta; Spanish Clb; Rep Stu Cncl; Var L Chrldng; Hon Roll; NHS; Ntl Merit SF; AR ST U; Engrng.

LUNCEFORD, KEVIN T; Searcy HS; Searcy, AR; (3); Art Clb; Church Yth Grp; FCA; Natl Beta Clb; Spanish Clb; Bsktbl; JV Ftbl; Won Several Art/Poster Cntsts; TIP Prgm Through Duke Univ; Gifted/Talented Prgm; AR ST Univ; Advrtsng/Mrktng.

LUNSFORD, SAYRE T; Waldron HS; Waldron, AR; (1); Art Clb; Computer Clb; Teachers Aide.

LUONG, KHAMLA; Southside HS; Fort Smith, AR; (4); Chess Clb; Church Yth Grp; French Clb; Key Clb; Mu Alpha Theta; Science Clb; Socr; Cit Awd; DAR Awd; High Hon Roll; U Of AR; Elec Engrg.

LUSBY, DANYELLE; Ft Smith Christian Schl; Fort Smith, AR; (4); 1/25; Church Yth Grp; FCA; FBLA; Sec Jr Cls; Pres Sr Cls; Bsktbl; Trk; Hon Roll; NHS; U Of Cntrl AR; Phys Thrp.

LUSSIER, MARK A; Oak Grove HS; Maumelle, AR; (1); Letterman Clb; Natl Beta Clb; Var Bsktbl; Var Ftbl; Babe Ruth Bsbl; Pres Awd Ed Excl.

LUSSIER, NICOLE M; Oak Grove HS; Maumelle, AR; (3); Drama Clb; Socr; High Hon Roll; Hon Roll; U Of Central AR; Psych.

LUSTER, AMBER N; Trumann HS; Trumann, AR; (2); FHA; Spanish Clb; Chorus; Trk; Vllybl; AR ST Univ; Nrsg.

LUSTER, EBONI C; Trumann HS; Trumann, AR; (4); 34/86; Art Clb; FHA; Library Aide; Spanish Clb; Ofcr Stu Cncl; Bsktbl; Trk; Vllybl; Hon Roll; NHS; VP Prgms FHA; AR ST Univ; Mgmnt Info Systms.

LUSTER, TAQUINA T; Pine Bluff HS; Pine Bluff, AR; (2); Church Yth Grp; Science Clb; Spanish Clb; Band; Church Choir; Mrchg Band; Pep Band; Lit Mag; Cit Awd; Hon Roll; Macys Schlr Minorities In Med; Howard; Pre-Med/Sprts Med/Peds.

LUTHER, GRETA E; Mountain Home HS; Mountain Home, AR; (3); 114/253; Drm Mjr(t); FTA; German Clb; Band; Mrchg Band; Pep Band; Ger Amer Partnrshp Prmg Germany Trvl 95; U Of AR; Psych/Bus.

LUTTON, FELICIA T; Rivercrest HS; Luxora, AR; (2); Band; Chorus; Church Choir; Flag Corp; Mrchg Band; School Play; Nwsp; Yrbk; Hon Roll; Prfct Atten Awd; Spelling/Math/Rcgntn Awds; Spelmon Coll; MD.

LUTZ, TAMMY; Beebe Sr HS; Beebe, AR; (2); 27/136; Church Yth Grp; FCA; FBLA; FHA; FTA; Natl Beta Clb; Pep Clb; Spanish Clb; Teachers Aide; Band; Fresh Cls Favorite; Nrs.

LUYET, KELLY SUZANNE KHRIS-NIKO; St Joseph HS; Conway, AR; (1); Church Yth Grp; GAA; Bsktbl; Var Chrldng; Var Sftbl; JV Var Trk; JV Var Vllybl; Hon Roll; All-Stars; Drama.

LY, HAO; Southside HS; Fort Smith, AR; (4); 97/459; 4-H; FBLA; Intnl Clb; Key Clb; Office Aide; Hon Roll; Pres Jr NHS; Pres Acad Fit Awd; Spcl Olympcs, Co Picnic Vol; Natl Engl Mrt Awd; U AR; Crmnl Psych.

LYBL, LEAH; Rogers HS; Rogers, AR; (4); 26/481; Bus Profs of Am; French Clb; Science Clb; SADD; Band; Var L Socr; Sftbl; Var L Vllybl; Med.

LYBRAND, JEFFREY N; Sheridan Sr HS; Grapevine, AR; (2); 11/286; Cmnty Wkr; VP Rptr 4-H; Cit Awd; 4-H Awd; High Hon Roll; Hon Roll; Jr NHS; Jrnlsm Poem Awd; Washington Univ; Law/Med/Poltcs.

LYKINS, LEISHA L; Piggott HS; Piggott, AR; (2); Church Yth Grp; French Clb; FHA; Natl Beta Clb; Science Clb; Band; Color Guard; Mrchg Band; School Musical; Hon Roll; Harding U; Jrnlsm Broadcasting.

LYNCH, CHARLES W; Searcy HS; Searcy, AR; (2); 46/232; Drama Clb; French Clb; FBLA; FTA; Natl Beta Clb; Chorus; School Play; Nwsp; Yrbk; Sec Soph Cls; All St Choir; All Region Choir; Yale; Jrnlsm; Oral Commnctn.

LYNCH, JAMIE; Kirby HS; Kirby, AR; (1); 1/40; FHA; GAA; Natl Beta Clb; Sec Frsh Cls; L Bsktbl; L Trk; L Wt Lftg; High Hon Roll; Hrs Shwng; Tea Kwon Do.

LYNCH, KILEY; Southside HS; Fort Smith, AR; (2); Church Yth Grp; FCA; Spanish Clb; SADD; Orch; Rep Frsh Cls; Rep Soph Cls; JV Ftbl; Wt Lftg; DAR Awd; Yth Cong; Mayors Cncl On Yth Crm Prvntn; Bio.

LYNCH, KRISTEN L; Atkins Schl; Russellville, AR; (1); Drama Clb; Natl Beta Clb; Chorus; Tennis; Hon Roll; Pres Acad Fit Awd.

LYNN, ISAAC O; Springdale Sr HS; Springdale, AR; (3); Am Leg Boys St; Boy Scts; Church Yth Grp; Science Clb; Chorus; School Musical; Sec Soph Cls; JV Var Ftbl; JV Var Trk; NHS; ST Sci Fair; GSI Camp.

LYNN, PHILIP M; Catholic HS; Little Rock, AR; (2); 32/198; Church Yth Grp; Cmnty Wkr; ROTC; Golf; Hon Roll; AZ ST Univ; Pre Med.

LYNN, SHELLEY; Mt St Mary Acad; Little Rock, AR; (3); Church Yth Grp; Cmnty Wkr; FCA; French Clb; Chorus; JV Var Chrldng; Hon Roll; Cheer Cntrl Braves All Star Chrldng Sqd/Rvr City Diamonds All Star Chrldng Sqd; UCA All Star Chrldr; U Of AR; Law.

LYON, DAVID; Van Buren Sr HS; Van Buren, AR; (2); Mu Alpha Theta; Quiz Bowl; Science Clb; Band; Mrchg Band; High Hon Roll; NHS; Schl Sci Fair Ovrll Wnnr; Moleclr Bio.

LYONS, VERONICA E; Wynne HS; Wynne, AR; (4); 8/152; FBLA; FTA; Pres Key Clb; SADD; Rep Stu Cncl; Hon Roll; NHS; Treas Spanish NHS; HOSA; Rotary Club Stu Of Week; U Of AR Fayetteville; Dentist.

LYTLE, HOWARD B; Sylvan Hills HS; Sherwood, AR; (3); Church Yth Grp; Science Clb; Spanish Clb; Chorus; Hon Roll; Jr NHS; NHS; AR Tech; Crtv Wrtng.

LYTLE, STEPHANIE; Farmington Jr Sr HS; Farmington, AR; (2); Church Yth Grp; FCA; FHA; Natl Beta Clb; Science Clb; Chorus; Chrldng; Vllybl; High Hon Roll; Law.

MABREY, ANNA F; Central Sr HS; Little Rock, AR; (3); 77/550; Church Yth Grp; Cmnty Wkr; Sec French Clb; Intnl Clb; Natl Beta Clb; Science Clb; Yrbk; Rep Sr Cls; Chrldng; Hon Roll; Y-Teens; Fellowship Of Chrstn Stdnts; Philosophy; Sci.

MABREY, LANCE; Clay Co Central Jr Sr HS; Rector, AR; (4); 1/56; Church Yth Grp; FBLA; Band; VP Stu Cncl; Ofcr Bsbl; Bsktbl; Golf; Hon Roll; Pres NHS; Val; U Cntrl AR; Phys Thrpy.

MACK, VERTIE; Dollaway HS; Pine Bluff, AR; (3); 4-H; FHA; HOBY; Band; Drm Mjr(t); Mrchg Band; Pep Band; ASU; Med.

MACK, WANDALYN R; Walker Schl; Magnolia, AR; (2); Sec Drama Clb; FBLA; Chorus; Mrchg Band; Bsktbl; Capt Chrldng; Trk; High Hon Roll; AEGIS Pgm; Commnctn.

MACKAY, JENNIFER L; Danville HS; Belleville, AR; (3); 12/36; SADD; Bsktbl; Trk; Wt Lftg; Bus Mngmt.

MACKE, JONNIE J; Fayetteville Sr HS; Fayetteville, AR; (3); Cmnty Wkr; Var L Bsktbl; Var L Trk; High Hon Roll; NHS; Peer Hlpr; Hkng Club.

MACKE, MANDY; Fayetteville Sr HS; Fayetteville, AR; (4); 28/372; Am Leg Aux Girls St; VP DECA; FBLA; Mu Alpha Theta; SADD; Hon Roll; NHS; Red Crs Peer Drug Edctr; Peer Helper Pres; Diamond Doll Bsbl Team; U AR Fayetteville.

MACKLOM, SANDI; Rogers HS; Rogers, AR; (3); Office Aide; Chorus; Stat Bsktbl; Mgr(s); JV Sftbl; Var Tennis; Hon Roll; Pres Acad Fit Awd; Scndry Ed/His.

MACLEAN, JENNIFER A; Valley Springs Schl; Harrison, AR; (2); FBLA; Band; High Hon Roll; Hon Roll; Prfct Atten Awd; Pres Schlr; Attnd 3 Weeks Regis Pgm Called Arts Encounter At AR Tech Univ; Theatre; Actor.

MAC LEAN, MARCIE; Huntsville HS; Huntsville, AR; (2); 5/154; Church Yth Grp; FCA; GAA; Science Clb; Band; Mrchg Band; VP Frsh Cls; Ofcr Soph Cls; Ofcr Stu Cncl; Bsktbl; All-Rgn HS 1st Band 3rd Chair; U Of AR.

MACON, KENNY D; Rison HS; Rison, AR; (2); Art Clb; Church Yth Grp; 4-H; Letterman Clb; Library Aide; Office Aide; Varsity Clb; Chorus; Church Choir; School Play; Bsktbl.

MADAR, BEN M; Carlisle Jr Sr HS; Carlisle, AR; (4); 2/56; Church Yth Grp; FBLA; Office Aide; Spanish Clb; Band; Yrbk; Cit Awd; High Hon Roll; Hon Roll; NHS; AR Challenge Schlsp; ASU Schlsp; ASU Jonesboro.

MADDEN, CARRIE J; Sylvan Hills HS; Sherwood, AR; (3); 89/290; Hon Roll; Jr NHS; Prfct Atten Awd; UALR; Bus Mgmt.

MADDEN, JAMESHA Z; Dumas HS; Dumas, AR; (2); Library Aide; Band; Mrchg Band; Rep Frsh Cls; Rep Soph Cls; Cit Awd; High Hon Roll; Hon Roll; Math Awds; Mst Imprvd Band Awd; Grambling Univ; Acctng/Pre-Med.

MADISON, BART E; Marion HS; Marion, AR; (4); 5/180; Am Leg Boys St; Church Yth Grp; FCA; French Clb; Math Clb; Mu Alpha Theta; L Bsktbl; L Ftbl; L Golf; French Hon Soc; Anytown USA; U Of Central AR; Vet Med.

MADISON, DIEREK; Augusta HS; Augusta, AR; (1); Science Clb; Ftbl; Golf; Wt Lftg; High Hon Roll; U Of AR; Civil Engnr.

MADISON, REGINA G; West Memphis Sr HS; West Memphis, AR; (4); 55/256; FHA; Band; Church Choir; Mrchg Band; High Hon Roll; Hon Roll; U Of Memphis; Spcl Ed.

MADISON, WENDY; Augusta HS; Augusta, AR; (4); 3/54; Am Leg Aux Girls St; English Clb; FBLA; FTA; Natl Beta Clb; VP Jr Cls; Pres Sr Cls; VP Stu Cncl; Capt Chrldng; VP NHS; U Of AR; Phrmcy.

MADSON, MATT A; Lake Hamilton Sr HS; Pearcy, AR; (2); Chess Clb; FCA; Ofcr Bsbl; Bsktbl; Ftbl; Trk; Wt Lftg; Cit Awd; High Hon Roll; Pres Acad Fit Awd.

MAESTRI, CANDICE L; Mountain Home HS; Mountain Home, AR; (4); Church Yth Grp; Drama Clb; German Clb; Key Clb; Band; Chorus; Flag Corp; Mrchg Band; Pep Band; School Play; U Of AR; Intr Dsgn.

MAGBY, ERIC W; Harmony Grove Jr Sr HS; Camden, AR; (3); Art Clb; Natl FFA Org; Stage Crew; L Ftbl; ASU Jonesboro; Arch.

MAGDALENO, JENNIFER L; Cabot HS; Cabot, AR; (2); Church Yth Grp; Band; Church Choir; Jr NHS; EMT 1st Responder; OBU; Pediatrician.

MAGIE, ERIKA R; St Joseph Jr Sr HS; Conway, AR; (3); 4/24; Church Yth Grp; Key Clb; VP Frsh Cls; Treas Jr Cls; Rep Stu Cncl; Var Bsktbl; Var Golf; Sftbl; Hon Roll; Jr NHS; U Of Cntrl AR; Med.

MAGLOTHIN, DOUGLAS L; Crowleys Ridge Acad; Jonesboro, AR; (2); 4/25; Church Yth Grp; FCA; FBLA; Natl Beta Clb; Science Clb; Spanish Clb; Acpl Chr; Jazz Band; School Musical; Variety Show.

MAHAFFEY, LEIGH C; Southside HS; Fort Smith, AR; (3); 6/458; French Clb; Key Clb; Math Clb; Mu Alpha Theta; Quiz Bowl; Nwsp; French Hon Soc; Hon Roll; Jr NHS; NHS; Premed.

MAHAN, JOE P; Montrose Acad; Dermott, AR; (3); 1/9; Natl Beta Clb; Treas Frsh Cls; Pres Soph Cls; Treas Jr Cls; Ofcr Stu Cncl; Ofcr Bsbl; Bsktbl; Ftbl; Tennis; NHS.

MAHAR, LAURA; Conway Sr HS; Conway, AR; (3); Church Yth Grp; FBLA; Natl Beta Clb; VICA; Band; Flag Corp; Mrchg Band; Phtg Yrbk; JV Var Sftbl; Hon Roll; UCA.

MAIN, BRYAN D; Cabot HS; Cabot, AR; (4); 7/285; Am Leg Boys St; Boy Scts; Pres Church Yth Grp; FCA; Band; L Crs Cntry; L Trk; Hon Roll; Kiwanis Awd; NHS; Big Bro/Big Sister; US Army Rsrv Schlr-Ath Awd; Hnr Grad; John Brown Univ; Math.

MAIN, JOSHUA; Cabot HS; Cabot, AR; (4); Key Clb; Math Clb; Spanish Clb; L Tennis; NHS; Pres Acad Fit Awd; Govr Schl 6 Wks Summer; Miami.

MAINER, KARA L; Southside HS; Fort Smith, AR; (3); Drama Clb; Pep Clb; Spanish Clb; Teachers Aide; Chorus; Church Choir; School Musical; Hon Roll; Prjct Erth; All Region Choir 3 Yrs; U Of A; Anml Sci.

MALHAM, ALEXIS; Cabot HS; Cabot, AR; (3); 20/322; Church Yth Grp; FCA; GAA; Key Clb; Spanish Clb; Band; Mrchg Band; Rep Frsh Cls; Rep Soph Cls; Rep Jr Cls; ASU Jnsboro; Engrng.

MALIK, NATHAN R; Mills HS; Little Rock, AR; (3); 12/298; Church Yth Grp; Mu Alpha Theta; Natl Beta Clb; Science Clb; Spanish Clb; Rep Soph Cls; Rep Jr Cls; High Hon Roll; Jr NHS; NHS; Prjct WET; AR Boys St Alt; Chem Engrng.

MALLAND, MAMIE; Mt Pleasant Jr Sr HS; Mount Pleasant, AR; (4); 1/20; Art Clb; Church Yth Grp; Sec FBLA; Pres FHA; Pres Natl Beta Clb; Quiz Bowl; Yrbk; Rep Frsh Cls; Rep Soph Cls; Pres Jr Cls; Govt, Alg & Spnsh Awds; Homcmng Qn; U Of AR Fayetteville; Med.

MALLARD, BEN; Coleman Jr HS; Van Buren, AR; (1); Church Yth Grp; Cmnty Wkr; FCA; Office Aide; L Bsktbl; High Hon Roll; Hon Roll; Jr NHS; Prfct Atten Awd; Pres Acad Fit Awd; Boys Clb Bsbl; Yth Cncl Heritage United Meth Church; OK ST U; Sports Med.

MALLETT, CTASHA D; Star City HS; Pine Bluff, AR; (2); Chrldng; Trk; RN.

MALLETT, MATTHEW R; St Joseph HS; Conway, AR; (2); Var Bsktbl; L Golf; Var Trk; Hon Roll; Pres Jr NHS; NHS; Frosh Cls Fvrt; Law.

MALLETTE, LANCE A; Dequeen HS; De Queen, AR; (3); 3/102; Church Yth Grp; Chorus; High Hon Roll.

MALLORY, JODY J; Magnolia HS; Magnolia, AR; (3); Boy Scts; Rep Soph Cls; Ofcr Stu Cncl; Bsktbl; Hon Roll; US Army Natl Guard; Southern AR Univ; Bus.

MALLOY, JOE; Farmington Jr Sr HS; Farmington, AR; (2); 1/100; French Clb; Model UN; Band; Cit Awd; High Hon Roll; Jr NHS.

MALLOY, NICK; Farmington Jr Sr HS; Farmington, AR; (1); FBLA; FHA; Quiz Bowl; School Musical; School Play; Nwsp; Ofcr Bsbl; Bsktbl; Wt Lftg; Cit Awd.

MALONE, ANGIE M; Rivercrest HS; Dyess, AR; (2); Church Yth Grp; Office Aide; Teachers Aide; High Hon Roll; Hon Roll; Jr NHS; NHS; Algebra I II Awds; Supt List; Nom Dist Stdnt Awd; U Of AR; Med.

MALONE, BRANDY; Hamburg Jr HS; Hamburg, AR; (1); Church Yth Grp; Acpl Chr; Band; Church Choir; Mrchg Band; Chrldng; Sftbl; U Of AR; Comp.

MALONE, STEPHANIE S; Rogers HS; Rogers, AR; (4); 75/442; Church Yth Grp; Cmnty Wkr; FCA; FBLA; GAA; Model UN; Office Aide; SADD; Varsity Clb; Var L Bsktbl; U Of AR; Poli Sci.

MALONE, TREVOR J; Weiner HS; Fisher, AR; (3); Am Leg Boys St; Chess Clb; Pres 4-H; Treas Natl FFA Org; Science Clb; Spanish Clb; Teachers Aide; VP Frsh Cls; VP Soph Cls; VP Jr Cls.

MALONEY, ALANDRA; Fayetteville Christian Schl; Fayetteville, AR; (2); VP Frsh Cls; Var Bsktbl.

MANASCO, CODY; Mt Holly Schl; Magnolia, AR; (3); 1/21; FBLA; FHA; FTA; Natl Beta Clb; Chorus; Yrbk; Pres Jr Cls; Ofcr Stu Cncl; JV Var Bsktbl; High Hon Roll; UCLA; Drama.

MANER, RYAN E; Greenwood Sr HS; Greenwood, AR; (2); FCA; VP FBLA; Rep Stu Cncl; JV Var Bsktbl; Hon Roll; Jr NHS; NHS.

MANES, BRANDON; Bergman Schl; Harrison, AR; (1); Pres Natl Beta Clb; Capt Quiz Bowl; JV Bsktbl; High Hon Roll; Prfct Atten Awd; Interested Cmptr/Med Fields.

MANES, JENNIFER L; Alma HS; Alma, AR; (4); 13/149; Sec Treas Art Clb; Church Yth Grp; Mu Alpha Theta; Spanish Clb; Teachers Aide; Band; Mrchg Band; Hon Roll; Sec NHS; Arts Live Yng Playwrights Comp Fnlst; U Of Centr AR; Art.

MANGRUM, CHRISTY D; Nettleton HS; Jonesboro, AR; (2); FHA; Spanish Clb; School Play; Yrbk; Trk; Cit Awd; Hon Roll; Nrsng; Psych.

MANGRUM, MIMI B; Crowleys Ridge Acad; Paragould, AR; (2); Church Yth Grp; FBLA; Hosp Aide; Pep Clb; Quiz Bowl; Science Clb; Spanish Clb; School Play; Yrbk; Pres Frsh Cls; FBLA VP; KIDS; Spansh Clb Vp; FBLA Lcl Chptr Pres; U Of AR; Bus Law.

MANIS, CRYSTAL L; Dewitt HS; Almyra, AR; (2); French Clb; FBLA; Library Aide; Natl Beta Clb.

MANKINS, JOHN E; Northside HS; Fort Smith, AR; (4); 80/393; Am Leg Boys St; Church Yth Grp; FBLA; Spanish Clb; SADD; Band; Church Choir; Hon Roll; Jr NHS; NHS; Westark CC; Elec Eng.

MANKINS, MICHAEL W; Northside HS; Fort Smith, AR; (3); 101/410; Am Leg Boys St; Church Yth Grp; Cmnty Wkr; FBLA; Spanish Clb; Acpl Chr; Band; Chorus; Church Choir; Mrchg Band; Music.

MANN, ELIZABETH; Benton Cty Christian School; Rogers, AR; (3); Sec Jr Cls; JV Var Chrldng; High Hon Roll; Hon Roll; John Brown Univ; Ed.

MANNING, COLLIN; Newport HS; Newport, AR; (3); Church Yth Grp; Stage Crew; Ofcr Bsbl; Bsktbl; Ftbl; Cit Awd; Hon Roll; Prfct Atten Awd.

MANNING, DONALD D; Monticello HS; Monticello, AR; (3); Church Yth Grp; Cmnty Wkr; FCA; FBLA; Chorus; Church Choir; Ofcr Bsbl; Bsktbl; Ftbl; Hon Roll; Henderson ST Univ; Bus Admin.

MANNING, FRED; Beebe Jr HS; Beebe, AR; (1); 1/126; FBLA; Sec Treas Math Clb; Natl Beta Clb; Pres Nwsp; Rep Stu Cncl; High Hon Roll; Hon Roll; Library Clb VP; Arch.

MANNING, JULIE E; Pine Bluff HS; Pine Bluff, AR; (3); 26/426; Am Leg Aux Girls St; French Clb; Key Clb; VP Acpl Chr; Ed Yrbk; VP Frsh Cls; VP Soph Cls; Hon Roll; Jr NHS; VP NHS; Ole Miss; Jrnlsm.

MANNING, MELISSA E; Huttig Schl; Huttig, AR; (3); 4/26; Am Leg Aux Girls St; Church Yth Grp; FBLA; FTA; Natl Beta Clb; Church Choir; VP Stu Cncl; Cit Awd; High Hon Roll; Hon Roll; Summer Med Pgm; MASH; Completed 1 Yr Med Pgm At S AR Comm Coll; Med-Pro Ed; U Of Little Rock; Family Practc.

MANNING, MICA; West Memphis Sr HS; West Memphis, AR; (3); Art Clb; Church Yth Grp; Cmnty Wkr; FCA; GAA; JA; Library Aide; Math Clb; Mu Alpha Theta; Natl Beta Clb; Miss Livin The Levee Pgnt Wnr; Cncrnt Stdnt Lcl CC; Wmns Sftbl League; Univ Of AR.

MANNING, RODNEY R; Hot Springs HS; Hot Springs, AR; (2); 9/174; Natl Beta Clb; ROTC; Color Guard; Drill Tm; High Hon Roll; Hon Roll; Prfct Atten Awd; Band; Jazz Band.

MANNING, SANDRA L; Harmony Grove Jr Sr HS; Camden, AR; (3); Art Clb; 4-H; FBLA; Natl FFA Org; Chorus; Hon Roll.

MANNIS, TIFFANY P; Dewitt HS; De Witt, AR; (1); Church Yth Grp; FCA; GAA; Science Clb; Band; Color Guard; L Bsktbl; L Trk; Hon Roll.

MANOS, TRACI R; Siloam Springs Sr HS; Siloam Springs, AR; (3); Church Yth Grp; Natl Beta Clb; Band; Drm Mjr(t); Flag Corp; Nwsp; Rep Sr Cls; Hon Roll; Sec NHS; Pres Acad Fit Awd; Outstndg Femle Band Stu 1995, 1996; 1996 Outstndg Crtve Wrtng Awd, Shrt Stry Awd; Ordr Of Confed Rose; Engl.

MANSFIELD, JENNIFER M; Springdale Sr HS; Springdale, AR; (2); English Clb; Band; Mrchg Band; Nwsp; Dance Clb; High Hon Roll; Hon Roll; Pres Schlr; Vet.

MANUEL, JANET; Norfork Jr Sr HS; Norfork, AR; (2); Art Clb; FBLA; FHA; Math Clb; VP Science Clb; Sec Treas Frsh Cls; VP Soph Cls; Bsktbl; Capt Chrldng; Trk; FL ST U; Marine Bio.

MANY, JULIE; Clinton HS; Clinton, AR; (4); 1/63; FBLA; Pres VP Natl Beta Clb; Science Clb; Pres Jr Cls; Sec Stu Cncl; Var Chrldng; High Hon Roll; Church Yth Grp; Drama Clb; FBLA; Mst Lkly To Sccd; Mst Crts; PRICE & I-CARE; STAND; U Of AR; Zlgy.

MAO, YEJUN; Fayetteville Sr HS; Fayetteville, AR; (2); Church Yth Grp; Intnl Clb; Math Clb; Mu Alpha Theta; Spanish Clb; Band; Mrchg Band; High Hon Roll; Hon Roll; Pres Acad Fit Awd; Fin/Bnkng.

MAPLES, DAWNA; Siloam Springs Sr HS; Siloam Springs, AR; (4); 1/161; Church Yth Grp; Natl Beta Clb; Band; Church Choir; Flag Corp; Mrchg Band; Orch; High Hon Roll; NHS; Pres Acad Fit Awd; John Brown Univ; Math Ed.

MAPLES, MISTY JO; Newport HS; Bradford, AR; (4); 1/145; Am Leg Aux Girls St; French Clb; FBLA; Q&S; Quiz Bowl; Band; Mrchg Band; School Play; Nwsp; DAR Awd; U Of AR; Landscp Arch.

MAPLES, VANESSA; St Joe Public Schl; Saint Joe, AR; (3); 2/18; Pres FBLA; Sec FHA; Natl FFA Org; Quiz Bowl; Sec Frsh Cls; Rep Soph Cls; Treas Jr Cls; Var Bsktbl; Var Sftbl; Cit Awd; Hendrix Univ; Bus.

MARASHI, KERIM B; Crossett Sr HS; El Dorado, AR; (2); JV Ftbl; Var Trk; Var Wt Lftg; Selected Participant In Eagle High Flyer Renaissance Pgm; LA Tech; Comp Sci.

MARBERRY, KRISTINA L; Flippin Jr Sr HS; Flippin, AR; (3); Cmnty Wkr; FBLA; SADD; VP Soph Cls; Hon Roll; NHS; ST FBLA Conf 3rd Plc Acctng; Blck Belt Tae Kwon Do; Multi-Yr Listee; Harding; Bus Acctng/Mgmt.

MARBLE, JENNIFER R; Altus Denning HS; Altus, AR; (2); 1/16; Church Yth Grp; FBLA; Natl Beta Clb; Pres Soph Cls; Bsktbl; Sftbl; Cit Awd; Hon Roll; Pres Acad Fit Awd; U Of AR; Bus.

MARKHAM, KATHERINE E; Central Sr HS; Little Rock, AR; (3); 125/540; Art Clb; Church Yth Grp; Cmnty Wkr; French Clb; Mu Alpha Theta; Natl Beta Clb; Service Clb; Pom Pon; Tennis; Hon Roll; Pre-Law.

MARKS, BRANDY R; John L Mcclellan Magnet HS; Little Rock, AR; (4); 26/247; FBLA; FHA; Mu Alpha Theta; Natl Beta Clb; Yrbk; Ofcr Stu Cncl; NHS; Pres Acad Fit Awd; Yth Govt; PRIDE; JAG; U Of Memphis; Soc Psych.

MARKS, DONNA; Hackett Schl; Hackett, AR; (3); Spanish Clb; Teachers Aide; Band; Chorus; Color Guard; Flag Corp; School Musical; Chrldng; Hon Roll; Westark CC; Mrtcn.

MARKS, ERICA N; Pulaski Acad; Little Rock, AR; (2); Church Yth Grp; Model UN; Spanish Clb; Var Bsktbl; JV Vllybl; High Hon Roll; NHS; Order Of Excl; Interact Clb; Natl His Day Participant.

MARKS, JASON; Arkansas Bapt Schl; Little Rock, AR; (3); French Clb; High Hon Roll; NHS; Beta Clb.

MARKS, MEAGAN; Norphlet HS; Norphlet, AR; (1); 1/45; Church Yth Grp; Var Bsktbl; Var Chrldng; High Hon Roll; Jr NHS; Stdnt Cncl Rep; PT.

MARLER, GREG W; Mountain Home HS; Mountain Home, AR; (3); Church Yth Grp; FCA; Office Aide; Chorus; Bsktbl; Mgr(s); Hon Roll; Commnctn.

MARLEY, LAURA; Ft Smith Christian Schl; Fort Smith, AR; (1); Church Yth Grp; FCA; Spanish Clb; JV Bsktbl; JV Trk; Cit Awd; High Hon Roll; Hon Roll; UCLA; Sports Med.

MARLOWE, STEPHANIE L; Mc Crory Jr Sr HS; Mc Crory, AR; (2); Church Yth Grp; GAA; Ofcr Stu Cncl; L Bsktbl; Powder Puff Ftbl; Sftbl; Tennis; Trk; Wt Lftg; Jr NHS; Music; Traveling; Coach/PT.

MARNEY, MATTHEW A; Gravette HS; Gravette, AR; (2); 3/115; Church Yth Grp; FCA; FBLA; Church Choir; Phtg Rptr Yrbk; Sec Treas Soph Cls; Ofcr Bsbl; High Hon Roll; NHS; Prfct Atten Awd; Hghst Hnrs Awds Bio, Span, Algebra, Comp Tech; U Of AR; Elec Engrng.

MAROTTI, ANNA; Hughes Jr-Sr HS; Hughes, AR; (3); 1/73; Natl Beta Clb; Band; Church Choir; Jazz Band; Mrchg Band; Yrbk; Tennis; Cit Awd; Hon Roll; Pres Acad Fit Awd; Cvcs Awd; Wrld His Awd; Gmtry Awd; Engl II Awd; Amro Msc Awd; All Rgn Band 4 Yrs; Med Field.

MARRALL, SARAH; Lake Hamilton Jr HS; Hot Springs, AR; (1); Natl Beta Clb; Natl FFA Org; Bsktbl; Sftbl; Trk; Vllybl; Cit Awd; Hon Roll; Pres Acad Fit Awd; Vet.

MARSH, CHRISTOPHER L; Mc Crory Jr Sr HS; Mc Crory, AR; (2); Church Yth Grp; FBLA; Letterman Clb; Office Aide; Spanish Clb; Golf; Jr NHS; NHS; Hendrix; PT.

MARSH, MARY; Pulaski Acad; Little Rock, AR; (2); Church Yth Grp; Cmnty Wkr; Natl Beta Clb; Var Chrldng; Gym; Sftbl; High Hon Roll; Hon Roll; Jr NHS; NHS; Prin List; Cheer Cntrl Braves Co-Ed Chrldng Sqd 4th Pl NCA Natls; Reflexology.

MARSH, STEPHEN E; Star City HS; Pine Bluff, AR; (2); 22/91; Swing Chorus; FCA; Math Clb; Mu Alpha Theta; Science Clb; Lit Mag; Bsktbl; Ftbl; Wt Lftg; Hon Roll; Wn Acad Awd 95-96; Wtr Skng, Hntng, Fshng; U Of TN; Bus.

MARSHALL, AMANDA L; Palestine-Wheatley HS; Palestine, AR; (3); 8/58; Am Leg Aux Girls St; FHA; Library Aide; Natl Beta Clb; Natl FFA Org; Ofcr Stu Cncl; Bsktbl; Atnd Cls Up In DC; Atnd Gvrnrs Yth Conf In Searcy AR; Georgetown; Bus Admin.

MARSHALL, DAVID A; Southside HS; Fort Smith, AR; (4); 84/453; VP Church Yth Grp; FBLA; Spanish Clb; Mrchg Band; Var Tennis; Hon Roll; NHS; Pres Acad Fit Awd; Spanish NHS; All ST Tennis; U Of AR; Chem Eng.

MARSHALL, ERICA D; Dewitt HS; Almyra, AR; (4); 17/86; French Clb; FBLA; HOBY; Natl Beta Clb; Teachers Aide; Chorus; School Play; Ntl Merit Ltr; Prfct Atten Awd; AR ST Univ; Bus Admin.

MARSHALL, HAROLD R; Marked Tree Jr Sr HS; Marked Tree, AR; (1); Art Clb; Boy Scts; ROTC; Ftbl; Wt Lftg; AR ST Univ.

MARSHALL, JEFF D; Pottsville Schl; Atkins, AR; (2); Natl Beta Clb; Crs Cntry; Trk.

MARSHALL, JONATHAN R; Robinson HS; Little Rock, AR; (3); FCA; FBLA; FHA; Natl Beta Clb; Treas Bsktbl; L Bsktbl; L Ftbl; Hon Roll; NHS; Chemical Engr.

MARSHALL, KENNETTA; Mc Gehee HS; Mc Gehee, AR; (3); FTA; HOBY; Mu Alpha Theta; Natl Beta Clb; Science Clb; Spanish Clb; Flag Corp; Nwsp; Sec Jr Cls; High Hon Roll; Baylor; Med.

MARSHALL, MIKE A; Fountain Lake Jr Sr HS; Hot Springs Natio, AR; (3); 22/72; Church Yth Grp; FCA; Pres Key Clb; Natl Beta Clb; Spanish Clb; School Play; Bsktbl; Hon Roll; Environmental Clb.

MARSHALL, MINDI; Gravette HS; Gravette, AR; (2); Library Aide; Chrldng; Sftbl; Hon Roll; Vet.

MARSHALL, TIFANY M; Bryant Sr HS; Benton, AR; (2); Church Yth Grp; Hosp Aide; Office Aide; Trk; Hon Roll; Pres Acad Fit Awd; Outstdng Achvmt Awd; Child Psych; Cnslng.

MARTAR, JAMIE L; Lakeside HS; Lake Village, AR; (3); 2/90; Church Yth Grp; Drama Clb; Pres FBLA; FHA; Hosp Aide; Church Choir; School Musical; School Play; Stage Crew; NHS; U Of AR Monticcello; Med Dr.

MARTER, BRANDI S; Marion HS; Marion, AR; (2); Art Clb; FBLA; Mu Alpha Theta; Band; Color Guard; Orch; Rptr Frsh Cls; French Hon Soc; High Hon Roll; NHS.

MARTILLO, JENNIE; Valley View HS; Jonesboro, AR; (3); Church Yth Grp; HOBY; ROTC; Spanish Clb; Chorus; Color Guard; Drill Tm; Vllybl; Hon Roll; Prfct Atten Awd; YOU; SAC Pres; U Of AR Fayetteville; Drama.

MARTIN, ALEXANDRIA B; Parkview Magnet HS; Maumelle, AR; (2); Cmnty Wkr; Dance Clb; Treas Drama Clb; FCA; Spanish Clb; Chorus; Ed Rptr Nwsp; Rptr Phtg Yrbk; JV Bsktbl; Var L Chrldng; Model; Lfgrd; Swm Instrctr; Cmp Cnslr; Trojan Nite; U Of AR.

MARTIN, ANDREA R; Arkansas Sr HS; Texarkana, AR; (2); Church Yth Grp; FCA; Pep Clb; ROTC; SADD; Teachers Aide; Acpl Chr; Hon Roll.

MARTIN, APRIL; Wynne HS; Wynne, AR; (3); Drama Clb; Q&S; Band; Nwsp; Ed Yrbk; Hon Roll; Spanish NHS; All-Region Band; All-St Band; ASU; Music.

MARTIN, ASHLEY E; Benton Sr HS; Benton, AR; (3); Art Clb; French Clb; FHA; Model UN; Band; Chorus; Flag Corp; Mrchg Band; Cit Awd; Taekwondo 4 Yrs.

MARTIN, BRAD A; Dequeen HS; Green Forest, AR; (1); Church Yth Grp; FCA; Quiz Bowl; SADD; Sec Frsh Cls; Var Capt Bsktbl; Cit Awd; Hon Roll; Pres Acad Fit Awd.

MARTIN, BRANDY L; Horatio HS; Shidler, OK; (2); Debate Tm; Treas FHA; Sec Natl FFA Org; Spanish Clb; Treas Frsh Cls; High Hon Roll; Hon Roll; NHS; Gifted & Talented; AR Schl For Math & Sci.

MARTIN, CAROL; Stuttgart Sr HS; Stuttgart, AR; (4); 3/150; Am Leg Aux Girls St; FBLA; Pres Mu Alpha Theta; Pres Science Clb; Spanish Clb; School Play; Rep Nwsp; Sec Stu Cncl; JV Bsktbl; Hon Roll; AR ST Univ; Acctng/Law.

MARTIN, CAROLINE R; Searcy HS; Searcy, AR; (2); Church Yth Grp; FTA; Hosp Aide; Natl Beta Clb; SADD; Band; Chorus; Mrchg Band; Hon Roll; Yth To Yth; All Region Band; All Region Choir; Harding Univ; Daycare Owner.

MARTIN, CHAD; Magnet Cove HS; Malvern, AR; (2); 3/50; Church Yth Grp; FCA; Math Clb; Natl Beta Clb; Spanish Clb; Band; Pep Band; Bsktbl; Ftbl; Trk; U Of A-Fayetteville; Engr.

MARTIN, CHARLES E; Southside HS; Fort Smith, AR; (3); 116/502; Boy Scts; French Clb; Hosp Aide; Mu Alpha Theta; Band; Mrchg Band; Pep Band; Hon Roll; NHS; Ntl Merit Ltr; Dctr.

MARTIN, DAVID; Gosnell Jr Sr HS; Blytheville, AR; (2); 40/105; Art Clb; Church Yth Grp; Teachers Aide; Chorus; Church Choir; JV Bsktbl; GATE; Male Ensmbl; U Of AR; Orthdntst.

MARTIN, DEANNA; Sulphur Rock Schl; Batesville, AR; (2); 2/28; VP 4-H; Key Clb; Natl Beta Clb; Quiz Bowl; Science Clb; Pres SADD; VP Chorus; School Play; Stage Crew; Yrbk; Mod Wdmn Amer Hist Awd; Ansthslgy.

MARTIN, JACQULYN E; Trumann HS; Trumann, AR; (2); Church Yth Grp; FHA; Model UN; Chorus; Church Choir; Rptr Nwsp; JV Var Trk; Hon Roll; NHS; Upward Bound; U Of Cntrl AR; Phy Thrpst.

MARTIN, JAMIE S; Ridgecrest HS; Paragould, AR; (3); FCA; French Clb; Key Clb; Office Aide; VP Soph Cls; Cit Awd; Hon Roll; Leo Clb Sec; TV Media Clb Mem; Natl Yth Ldrshp Conf In Washington DC Nom.

MARTIN, JEREMY W; Biggers-Reyno HS; Reyno, AR; (2); Church Yth Grp; Drama Clb; FBLA; Natl Beta Clb; Spanish Clb; Chorus; Church Choir; School Play; Var Bsbl; JV Bsktbl.

MARTIN, JOHN; Nashville HS; Nashville, AR; (3); Am Leg Boys St; Church Yth Grp; Ofcr Bsbl; Bsktbl; Ftbl; NHS.

MARTIN, KEITH; Morrilton Sr HS; Morrilton, AR; (4); 1/150; Am Leg Boys St; Church Yth Grp; French Clb; Pres Math Clb; Natl Beta Clb; Science Clb; Thesps; Pres VP Band; Jazz Band; Yrbk; U Of AR; Mech Engrng.

MARTIN, KELLY; J A Fair Sr HS; Little Rock, AR; (4); 30/300; FHA; Natl Beta Clb; Science Clb; Spanish Clb; Hon Roll; Jr NHS; NHS; Pres Acad Fit Awd; U Of AR Little Rock.

MARTIN, KENDRA K; Jonesboro HS; Jonesboro, AR; (3); Church Yth Grp; FBLA; FHA; Natl Beta Clb; Office Aide; VP Spanish Clb; Chorus; Church Choir; School Musical; Hon Roll; Girls Chorus MVP 93-94; AR ST U; Pharmcy.

MARTIN, LATANGIE S; Pine Bluff HS; Pine Bluff, AR; (4); 89/410; Church Yth Grp; French Clb; FHA; FTA; Band; Mrchg Band; Pep Band; Trk; Hon Roll; Prfct Atten Awd; U Of AR Pine Bluff; Nrsng.

MARTIN, LAURA; Pulaski Acad; Little Rock, AR; (4); 2/72; Am Leg Aux Girls St; Church Yth Grp; French Clb; Letterman Clb; Mu Alpha Theta; Natl Beta Clb; Lit Mag; Treas Jr Cls; Rep Stu Cncl; Var Capt Bsktbl; Natl Hstry Day Cmptn St Wnnr; Korean Essay Cont Natl Fnlst; Middlebury Coll; Engl.

MARTIN, LORI MICHELLE; Rivercrest HS; Keiser, AR; (2); 1/110; FBLA; HOBY; VP Math Clb; SADD; Teachers Aide; Band; Mrchg Band; Yrbk; High Hon Roll; Jr NHS; Lib Clb; Distgnd Stdnt Fnlst; Zoology/Optmtrst.

MARTIN, MANDY L; Alma HS; Alma, AR; (2); Church Yth Grp; FCA; FHA; Natl FFA Org; Red Cross Aide; ROTC; Teachers Aide; Trk; Vllybl; High Hon Roll; Alma Karate Acad; Old Ft Days Dandies; CCHA; OK ST; Vet.

MARTIN, MARY S; Shirley Jr Sr HS; Shirley, AR; (3); Natl FFA Org; Teachers Aide; Yrbk; High Hon Roll; Hon Roll; Pres Acad Fit Awd.

MARTIN, MATTHEW F; Rogers HS; Rogers, AR; (3); Am Leg Boys St; Church Yth Grp; FBLA; Band; Jazz Band; Crs Cntry; L Trk; Hon Roll; Science Clb; AR All-St Band; U Of AR Fayttvll; Pre-Dntl.

MARTIN, MEREDITH; Gentry HS; Gentry, AR; (4); 3/80; Art Clb; Model UN; Spanish Clb; Teachers Aide; Chorus; Yrbk; Sec Frsh Cls; Sec Soph Cls; Sec Jr Cls; Chrldng; Prd Tm; Jet; Mdl Pioneer; NW AR Comm Coll; Grphc Art.

MARTIN, MICHELE; Marion HS; West Memphis, AR; (2); Church Yth Grp; French Clb; GAA; Mu Alpha Theta; Ofcr Soph Cls; Ofcr Stu Cncl; Chrldng; Sftbl; Tennis; Hon Roll; Ecology Field Stds Tm; Girls Clb; Ed.

MARTIN, MICHELLE J; Sheridan Sr HS; Hensley, AR; (2); 6/294; Cmnty Wkr; Quiz Bowl; Chorus; Hon Roll; Jr NHS; 9th Grd Eng Hnrs Awd.

MARTIN, MONICA; Magnet Cove HS; Malvern, AR; (2); Church Yth Grp; Cmnty Wkr; FCA; FBLA; Natl Beta Clb; Science Clb; Spanish Clb; Phtg Rptr Yrbk; Ofcr Stu Cncl; Chrldng; Ouachita Baptist U; Psych.

MARTIN, PATRICIA BETH; Marvell Acad; Brinkley, AR; (3); FBLA; Treas Spanish Clb; Teachers Aide; Stage Crew; Nwsp; Yrbk; Treas Frsh Cls; Hon Roll.

MARTIN, REBECCA C; White Co Central Schl; Judsonia, AR; (4); Church Yth Grp; Cmnty Wkr; 4-H; FBLA; FHA; 4-H Awd; Hon Roll; AR ST Univ Beebe; Food Sci.

MARTIN, RICHARD; Calico Rock HS; Wideman, AR; (4); 17/32; Am Leg Boys St; VP Art Clb; Church Yth Grp; FCA; FBLA; Sec Treas Natl FFA Org; Spanish Clb; SADD; Rep Stu Cncl; Capt Bsktbl; Var Ldrshp Awds; ADD Image Awd; Harold Ray Jeffery Ath Schlsp; Mr Pirate Awd; Harps Comm Svc Awd; OK ST Univ; Diesel/Hvy Eqpmt.

MARTIN, RUSS W; Pulaski Acad; Little Rock, AR; (3); Am Leg Boys St; FCA; Natl Beta Clb; Spanish Clb; Chorus; Church Choir; Var Bsbl; Var Capt Ftbl; Cit Awd; Church Yth Grp; Co Ed Chrldng; Bus.

MARTIN, SARAH; Wonderview HS; Solgohachia, AR; (4); 6/28; Church Yth Grp; Sec FBLA; German Clb; Hosp Aide; HOBY; Intnl Clb; Natl Beta Clb; Rptr Natl FFA Org; Teachers Aide; Co-Ed Yrbk; U Cntrl AR; Nrs.

MARTIN, SARAH; Southside HS; Fort Smith, AR; (2); Church Yth Grp; FCA; Drill Tm; Orch; Ed Nwsp; Crs Cntry; Trk; NHS; Pres Ed Awd; Correspondence Photo.

MARTIN, SONDRA; Hatfield Schl; Hatfield, AR; (1); 3/42; GAA; Natl Beta Clb; Natl FFA Org; Varsity Clb; JV Bsbl; JV Bsktbl; Sftbl; Trk; Cit Awd; High Hon Roll; U AR; Coach.

MARTIN, SONYA; J A Fair Sr HS; Little Rock, AR; (3); 17/269; FBLA; Yrbk; Rep Stu Cncl; Var Chrldng; High Hon Roll; NHS; All-Star Chrldng RCD Ranked 8th Natls; U Of AR Fayetteville.

MARTIN, TARIA A; White Hall Sr HS; Pine Bluff, AR; (2); 95/214; Key Clb; Chrldng; Sftbl; Trk; Med Field.

MARTIN, TOMEKA S; North Little Rock Hs-West; North Little Rock, AR; (3); FCA; VP FBLA; Teachers Aide; Band; Drill Tm; Mrchg Band; Sec Sr Cls; Rep Stu Cncl; Var Sftbl; Hon Roll; Tri-M Hnr Soc; Engrng.

MARTIN, TONYA; Magnet Cove HS; Malvern, AR; (3); 1/50; Church Yth Grp; FCA; FHA; Math Clb; Office Aide; Science Clb; Spanish Clb; Band; Color Guard; Flag Corp; Baylor; Pre-Med.

MARTIN, VICKIE R; St Joe Public Schl; Western Grove, AR; (2); Church Yth Grp; FBLA; FHA; Girl Scts; Natl FFA Org; Quiz Bowl; Phtg Yrbk; Sftbl; Hon Roll; NHS; Prjct WET; Bsktbl; GT Prgm.

MARTINDALE, SAMANTHA D; Bryant Sr HS; Alexander, AR; (2); Church Yth Grp; Cmnty Wkr; FCA; FBLA; Hosp Aide; Teachers Aide; Rep Stu Cncl; NHS; Jrnlsm; UALR; Elem Schl Tchr.

MARTINDALE, STEPHANIE K; Alma HS; Alma, AR; (2); Hosp Aide; SADD; Chorus; Hon Roll; NHS; Psych.

MARTINEZ, SHANTAN B; Scotland Schl; Scotland, AR; (1); Art Clb; Church Yth Grp; Cmnty Wkr; Drama Clb; FBLA; Library Aide; Pep Clb; Teachers Aide; Band; Church Choir.

MARTINEZ, TERESA; Fayetteville Christian Schl; Rogers, AR; (4); 3/12; Church Yth Grp; Yrbk; VP Jr Cls; VP Sr Cls; Var Capt Chrldng; High Hon Roll; Hon Roll; Sec NHS; NW AR CC; Bus.

MARTZ, MICHAEL A; Bentonville Sr HS; Bentonville, AR; (3); #1 in class; Church Yth Grp; Computer Clb; FBLA; High Hon Roll; NHS; Pres Acad Fit Awd; ACE; Jr Bnk Brd Mmbr; Praise Tm Singer; Med.

MARVEL, JONI; Westside HS; Hartman, AR; (3); 1/40; Am Leg Aux Girls St; Church Yth Grp; FBLA; HOBY; Spanish Clb; Chorus; Bsktbl; Sftbl; High Hon Roll; Pres Acad Fit Awd; Pride Pres.

MARVIN, JULIE E; North Little Rock Hs-East; North Little Rock, AR; (2); Drama Clb; Math Clb; Natl Beta Clb; Spanish Clb; School Musical; School Play; High Hon Roll; Hon Roll; Cmnty Wkr; Regnl Sci Fair Awd.

MARVIN, LUKE J; Fayetteville Sr HS; Fayetteville, AR; (4); Chess Clb; Church Yth Grp; Cmnty Wkr; FCA; German Clb; Key Clb; Mu Alpha Theta; SADD; Church Choir; Sec Soph Cls; U Of AR; Psych.

MARY, MICHELLE N; Robinson HS; Roland, AR; (3); Church Yth Grp; Natl Beta Clb; Science Clb; Drill Tm; Jazz Band; Mrchg Band; Sec Soph Cls; Rep Stu Cncl; Hon Roll; NHS.

MASCOE, RYAN M; Mills HS; North Little Rock, AR; (2); 11/435; Church Yth Grp; JCL; Mu Alpha Theta; Band; Phtg Yrbk; Hon Roll; Jr NHS; FCA; Latin Clb; Math Clb; Kings Clb; ASBOA All Region Band First Band 9th Grd/Second Bnd 10th Grd.

MASK, TIFFANY B; Bryant Sr HS; Bryant, AR; (2); Church Yth Grp; FBLA; Office Aide; Ofcr Frsh Cls; Ofcr Soph Cls; Ofcr Jr Cls; UCA; Police Offcr.

MASON, AMANDA M; Junction City HS; Junction City, AR; (2); Church Yth Grp; FBLA; Science Clb; Band; Mrchg Band; Rep Stu Cncl; Var Sftbl; JV Trk; High Hon Roll; Hon Roll; Outs Soph Mus Awd; LSU; Nutrtn.

MASON, ANTHONY B; Bald Knob HS; Bradford, AR; (2); Church Yth Grp; Drama Clb; Spanish Clb; VICA; L Capt Ftbl; Trk; Wt Lftg; Chiropractor.

MASON, BENJAMIN; Vilonia HS; Vilonia, AR; (2); FBLA; Mu Alpha Theta; Natl Beta Clb; Marine Bio.

MASON, CAROL F; Eudora HS; Eudora, AR; (2); 10/120; Library Aide; Rptr Natl Beta Clb; ROTC; Band; Church Choir; Drm Mjr(t); Mrchg Band; Cit Awd; Hon Roll; U Of AR Fayetteville.

MASON, JACLYN B; Russellville Sr HS; Russellville, AR; (3); French Clb; FHA; Hosp Aide; Natl Beta Clb; Band; Mrchg Band; School Play; Stage Crew; Rptr Yrbk; Hon Roll; All-Stars Rptr; Child Psychitrist.

MASON, SHUNA; Mc Clellan HS; Little Rock, AR; (3); 13/341; FBLA; HOBY; Key Clb; Natl Beta Clb; Spanish Clb; Cit Awd; High Hon Roll; NHS; Pres Acad Fit Awd.

MASSANELLI, ROBIN; Hope HS; Hope, AR; (3); Church Yth Grp; FBLA; Natl Beta Clb; Spanish Clb; Rep Frsh Cls; Rep Soph Cls; Rep Jr Cls; Ofcr Stu Cncl; Chrldng; Hon Roll; NCA All Amer Tm 95; Fshn Mktg.

MASSANELLI, VINCE J; Fayetteville Sr HS; Fayetteville, AR; (2); Stage Crew; JV Bsktbl; Var Golf; Hon Roll; Golf Team; U Cntrl AR; Bus.

MASSARDO, JAMES R; Valley Springs Schl; Valley Springs, AR; (2); 18/70; Boy Scts; Church Yth Grp; Natl FFA Org; Teachers Aide; Band; Jazz Band; Mrchg Band; Pep Band; School Musical; Hon Roll; Ed Tlnt Srch; Pioneer Scchlrs; AEGIS Prgm/Bach/BYTES; Cmptr Engr.

MASSENGALE, BRENT W; White Co Central Schl; Searcy, AR; (4); 1/28; Am Leg Boys St; Church Yth Grp; Pres FBLA; Capt Quiz Bowl; Sec Frsh Cls; Capt L Bsbl; Capt L Bsktbl; Capt L Crs Cntry; Val; Math Tm; U Of Cntrl AR; Pharm.

MASSEY, BRENTLY A; Corning HS; Corning, AR; (3); Spanish Clb; Hon Roll; Pres Acad Fit Awd; Art.

MASSEY, GREGORY L; Conway Sr HS; Conway, AR; (2); Church Yth Grp; FBLA; Band; Mrchg Band; Cit Awd; Hon Roll.

MASSEY, JEREMY M; Bryant Sr HS; Benton, AR; (4); 11/336; Church Yth Grp; Cmnty Wkr; FBLA; Math Tm; Capt Quiz Bowl; Teachers Aide; Hon Roll; Jr NHS; Ntl Merit Ltr; Pres Acad Fit Awd; Reach Drug Free Clb; Mock Trial Tm Rgn 1st Pl/ST 4th Pl; Tutoring; U Of AR; Physics.

MASSEY, KRIS J; Highland HS; Ash Flat, AR; (3); Natl FFA Org; Office Aide; Band; Church Choir; Mrchg Band; Pep Band; Hon Roll; Prfct Atten Awd; U Of AR Fayetteville.

MASSEY, LAURA; Searcy HS; Searcy, AR; (4); 12/201; FBLA; FTA; Key Clb; Natl Beta Clb; Spanish Clb; Ofcr Stu Cncl; Chrldng; Tennis; NHS; Spanish NHS; U Of AR Fayetteville; Nrsng.

MASSEY, LESLIE DENISE; Glen Rose HS; Traskwood, AR; (1); 9/70; Church Yth Grp; FCA; Natl Beta Clb; Ofcr Stu Cncl; JV Capt Bsktbl; JV Capt Chrldng; Trk; GATE; 9th Grd Hmcmng Maid; Champs; PE Coach/Tchr.

MASSEY, OLLIE; Lee Sr HS; Marianna, AR; (3); 8/170; Treas French Clb; Pres FBLA; FHA; Sec FTA; Natl Beta Clb; Quiz Bowl; Pres Frsh Cls; Ofcr Stu Cncl; Var Chrldng; Hon Roll; TIE; PHD; Tchr.

MASSEY, TARA; Humphrey Schl; Humnoke, AR; (3); Art Clb; Drama Clb; FHA; Library Aide; Natl Beta Clb; Natl FFA Org; Spanish Clb; Teachers Aide; Cit Awd; Hon Roll; U AR Beebe; Psych.

MASTERS, CHRISTINA; Southside HS; Fort Smith, AR; (3); Church Yth Grp; Cmnty Wkr; FCA; GAA; JA; Letterman Clb; Mu Alpha Theta; Red Cross Aide; Spanish Clb; Teachers Aide; Med.

MASTERS, LESA; East Poinsett Sr HS; Lepanto, AR; (4); Am Leg Aux Girls St; Church Yth Grp; Pres Sec FHA; HOBY; Sec Library Aide; Band; Chorus; Drm Mjr(t); Mrchg Band; Pep Band; Atten AEGIS Pgm; Laureate Intl Stds; Atten Natl Ldrshp Forum Harding U; Harding U; Chil Spclst.

MASTERS, SARA A; Oak Grove HS; Maumelle, AR; (2); Church Yth Grp; Cmnty Wkr; Drama Clb; Spanish Clb; Teachers Aide; Hon Roll; U Of Cntrl AR; Pharmacology.

MATCHETT, ANDREA L; Vilonia HS; Vilonia, AR; (3); Church Yth Grp; FHA; Girl Scts; Spanish Clb; Teachers Aide; Hon Roll; Full Soil Ctr Rcrdng Arts; Engr.

MATHENY, MATTHEW R; Batesville Sr HS; Batesville, AR; (4); 15/155; Am Leg Boys St; Treas Chess Clb; Church Yth Grp; Drama Clb; FBLA; Library Aide; Natl Beta Clb; Capt Quiz Bowl; Pres Science Clb; Band; 1st Pl Acad Day Tests Bio/Chem; Library Clb Pres; Lyon Coll; Hstry Professor.

MATHENY, RUSTY D; Sloan Hendrix HS; Ravenden, AR; (2); Art Clb; Natl Beta Clb; Office Aide; Pep Clb; Bsktbl; Sftbl; Hon Roll; Pres Acad Fit Awd; Sal; Fayetville; Law/Psych.

MATHEWS, BRANDI N; Lee Acad; Marianna, AR; (2); Church Yth Grp; Library Aide; Church Choir; JV Bsktbl; JV Trk; High Hon Roll; Hon Roll; NHS; Prfct Atten Awd; Sftbl; Model.

MATHEWS, ERIC C; Pulaski Acad; Little Rock, AR; (3); Cmnty Wkr; FCA; French Clb; Intl Clb; Natl Beta Clb; Teachers Aide; Mgr Stage Crew; JV Var Bsktbl; Var Socr; High Hon Roll; JETS; Winner Belle Emerson Keith Schlrshp Keith Schl; Winner Holy Ghost Prep Hdmstrs Schlrshp.

MATHEWS, MOLLY J; Alpena Schl; Green Forest, AR; (2); Church Yth Grp; FCA; FBLA; FHA; Natl Beta Clb; Quiz Bowl; Spanish Clb; School Play; Phtg Ed Yrbk; Treas Jr Cls; GATE; Lit Clb; U Of AR Fayetteville; Lawyer.

MATHIS, AMANDA A; Blytheville Sr HS; Blytheville, AR; (3); Church Yth Grp; Pep Clb; ROTC; Spanish Clb; Church Choir; Ofcr Stu Cncl; Vllybl; Wt Lftg; Cit Awd; AR ST; Nrsng.

MATHIS, AMY; Beebe Sr HS; Beebe, AR; (3); 16/129; Church Yth Grp; Natl Beta Clb; Spanish Clb; Church Choir; Sec Soph Cls; Rep Jr Cls; Var Capt Bsktbl; Var Co-Capt Chrldng; Sftbl; Hon Roll; Jonesboro; Med.

MATIAS, EUGENIA R; Batesville Sr HS; Batesville, AR; (4); Sec Art Clb; Sec FBLA; Pres FHA; Hosp Aide; Key Clb; Office Aide; Red Cross Aide; Spanish Clb; Teachers Aide; Band; Aegus; Global Cultures; Stu Of The Month; FFA; Pride Team; Breakfast Clb; Upward Bound; Boy Scts Of Amer; U Of AR-FAYETTEVILLE; Pre-Med.

MATLOCK, AMANDA L; Springdale Sr HS; Springdale, AR; (1); FCA; FBLA; GAA; Model UN; Pep Clb; Chorus; Sftbl; High Hon Roll; Jr NHS; Baylor; Neurologist.

MATLOCK, ANGELA L; Central Sr HS; Little Rock, AR; (3); 243/540; Cmnty Wkr; FBLA; FHA; Natl Beta Clb; Trk; Hon Roll; Pre-Medicine.

MATLOCK, CANDY; Farmington Jr Sr HS; Farmington, AR; (3); Church Yth Grp; FBLA; Model UN; Natl FFA Org; Drill Tm; Treas Frsh Cls; Cit Awd; Hon Roll; NHS; U AR; PE.

MATLOCK, SARAH J; Omaha Schl; Omaha, AR; (2); Church Yth Grp; FBLA; FHA; FTA; Natl Beta Clb; School Play; Lit Mag; Rep Frsh Cls; Sec Soph Cls; Var Bsktbl; OTAD; Math Tchr.

MATTHEWS, AARON W; Southside HS; Fort Smith, AR; (3); Cmnty Wkr; FBLA; Spanish Clb; JV Bsbl; Bsktbl; Hon Roll; NHS; Pres Acad Fit Awd; Pres Schlr; Guest Sports Wrtr Gazette Nwspr; All Star Babe Ruth Leag; AR Tech; Engrng/Jrnlsm.

MATTHEWS, CARMEN M; Fouke Jr Sr HS; Fouke, AR; (3); Rptr FBLA; FHA; Natl Beta Clb; Co-Ed Yrbk; Treas Soph Cls; Hon Roll; Cnslr.

MATTHEWS, ENNIS L; John L Mcclellan Magnet HS; Little Rock, AR; (3); Church Yth Grp; ULAR; Law.

MATTHEWS, GRANT J; Cabot HS; Cabot, AR; (3); 15/400; Church Yth Grp; Office Aide; Spanish Clb; Teachers Aide; Mgr Bsktbl; Mgr(s); Score Keeper; High Hon Roll; Hon Roll; Kiwanis Awd; Showing Amer Quarter Horses; AR Jr Quarter Horse Assn Pres; U Of AR Fayetteville; Bus.

MATTHEWS, JENNIFER L; Sloan Hendrix HS; Imboden, AR; (3); 5/48; Church Yth Grp; English Clb; French Clb; FBLA; Treas Key Clb; Natl Beta Clb; Office Aide; Teachers Aide; Band; Chorus; Washington U; Medcl.

MATTHEWS, JOSH P; Cave City HS; Smithville, AR; (2); Pres Church Yth Grp; French Clb; FHA; Sec Natl Beta Clb; Natl FFA Org; Church Choir; Rep Frsh Cls; Ofcr Bsbl; Bsktbl; Tennis.

MATTHEWS, MAEGEN G; Arkansas Sr HS; Texarkana, AR; (2); Chorus; School Musical; Ofcr Soph Cls; Hon Roll; Author Bk Poetry; Texarkana CC; Voice.

MATTHEWS, NICKOLAS P; Horatio HS; Horatio, AR; (2); FCA; Rep Frsh Cls; Rep Jr Cls; Var Bsbl; JV Bsktbl; Hon Roll; NHS; Golf; Henderson ST U; Occptnl Thrpst.

MATTHEWS, SARAH E; Oak Grove HS; N Little Rock, AR; (1); 15/150; Church Yth Grp; FCA; 4-H; French Clb; Natl Beta Clb; Teachers Aide; Church Choir; Chrldng; Trk; Vllybl; Hmcmng Queen 9th Grd; U Of AR-FAYETTEVILLE.

MATTHEWS, SARAH M D; Arkansas Schl Math & Science; Sherwood, AR; (3); Am Leg Aux Girls St; Church Yth Grp; Key Clb; Mu Alpha Theta; Band; Mrchg Band; Treas Jr Cls; Sec Stu Cncl; Co-Capt Chrldng; NHS; Aerobics; Chem.

MATTHEWS, ZACHARY; Rogers HS; Lowell, AR; (1); Church Yth Grp; FCA; Model UN; Quiz Bowl; Science Clb; Band; Mrchg Band; Rep Stu Cncl; High Hon Roll; Prfct Atten Awd; Duke U; Pol Sci/Law.

MATTINGLY, JOSHUA A; Lake Hamilton Sr HS; Hot Springs, AR; (3); Church Yth Grp; Cmnty Wkr; Teachers Aide; Hon Roll; Chrprctr.

MATTINGLY, REJEANA G; Rogers HS; Rogers, AR; (3); Church Yth Grp; Drama Clb; FBLA; Spanish Clb; Church Choir; Stat Mgr(s); Stat Vllybl; High Hon Roll; Hon Roll; Prfct Atten Awd; Chamber Of Commerce & Highest Grd In 9th Grd Eng Awds; Yc Sftbl 1st Pl Dist; U Of AR; Psych.

MATYSKIELA, CHRISSY; J A Fair Sr HS; Little Rock, AR; (3); 15/290; Am Leg Aux Girls St; Church Yth Grp; Cmnty Wkr; FBLA; Science Clb; Spanish Clb; Church Choir; Drill Tm; High Hon Roll; Hon Roll; Teens For Christ; Stu Congress; SCAT; U Of Cntrl AR; Ed; Sign Lang.

MAULDIN, ROBYN D; Mt St Mary Acad; North Little Rock, AR; (4); 25/125; VP Church Yth Grp; Cmnty Wkr; Hosp Aide; JCL; Latin Clb; Library Aide; Model UN; Mu Alpha Theta; Teachers Aide; Gov Hon Prg Awd; Pres Frnds Hlpng Frnds; Ltrgy Plnng; Christian Bros U; Med.

MAUNEY, CRYSTAL R; Norphlet HS; Norphlet, AR; (4); 12/55; Hist FHA; HOBY; Mgr Nwsp; Ed Yrbk; Rep Frsh Cls; Treas Stu Cncl; Cit Awd; NHS; Pres Schlr; Church Yth Grp; Southern AR Univ; Acctng.

MAUPIN, REBECCA; Perryville Jr Sr HS; Perryville, AR; (3); FBLA; FHA; Pep Clb; Spanish Clb; Teachers Aide; Band; Mrchg Band; Pep Band; Jr NHS; NHS; Teach Deaf/Pedtrc Nrsng.

MAUPPINS, DANA; Wynne HS; Wynne, AR; (2); Church Yth Grp; Drama Clb; FBLA; FTA; Spanish Clb; JV Var Chrldng; Var Trk; Hon Roll; JPC; U Of Fayetteville; Med.

MAUPPINS, DESIREE; Wynne HS; Wynne, AR; (4); 4/175; Am Leg Aux Girls St; Key Clb; Rep Stu Cncl; Var Capt Chrldng; Var Trk; Hon Roll; Kiwanis Awd; NHS; Drama Clb; FCA; Hmcmng Queen 95-; U Of Cntrl AR.

MAXWELL, LAURA L; Marion HS; West Memphis, AR; (4); #55 in class; French Clb; FBLA; Office Aide; Hon Roll; Prfct Atten Awd; Outstdng Achvmt Awd In Eng; PRIDE & GCECA Clbs; AR ST Univ; Acctng.

MAXWELL, LAUREN E; Pine Bluff HS; Pine Bluff, AR; (2); Church Yth Grp; Cmnty Wkr; French Clb; Church Choir; Orch; Tennis; Jr NHS; U Of AR Fayetteville.

MAXWELL, NICHOLAS; Perryville Jr Sr HS; Perryville, AR; (1); 6/55; Church Yth Grp; FCA; Teachers Aide; Bsktbl; Jr NHS.

MAXWELL, SETH S; Booneville Jr Sr HS; Booneville, AR; (4); 14/85; Am Leg Boys St; Church Yth Grp; FCA; FBLA; Natl Beta Clb; Spanish Clb; Var Bsbl; Var Ftbl; Hon Roll; Hnrs Grad; Westark CC; Optometry.

MAY, ABBY; Hughes Jr-Sr HS; Hughes, AR; (3); 1/72; Pres Art Clb; Church Yth Grp; Math Tm; Mu Alpha Theta; Treas Natl Beta Clb; Quiz Bowl; Rptr Mgr Nwsp; Rep Yrbk; Sec Jr Cls; Pres Acad Fit Awd; Tae Kwon Do Grn Blt.

MAY, BROOKE; Sparkman Jr Sr HS; Sparkman, AR; (1); 2/34; Church Yth Grp; Spanish Clb; Yrbk.

MAY, JENNIFER A; Arkansas Sr HS; Texarkana, AR; (4); Art Clb; Church Yth Grp; Cmnty Wkr; FHA; Spanish Clb; Church Choir; Hon Roll; Pres Acad Fit Awd; Teenage Rpblcns; Fllwshp Chrstn Stu; Ouachita Bapt U; Vet Med.

MAY, JERUSHA L; Sparkman Jr Sr HS; Sparkman, AR; (3); Am Leg Aux Girls St; Church Yth Grp; Natl Beta Clb; Natl FFA Org; Chorus; Church Choir; Ed Yrbk; L Bsktbl; Mgr(s); Hon Roll; Fllwshp Of Chrstn Stu.

MAY, JOE D; Sparkman Jr Sr HS; Sparkman, AR; (2); Church Yth Grp; Natl Beta Clb; Natl FFA Org; Quiz Bowl; Spanish Clb; Church Choir; Rep Soph Cls; Hon Roll; L Var Bsktbl; L Var Ftbl; U Of AR; Pre-Med.

MAY, KRISTI M; Pulaski Acad; Maumelle, AR; (3); Church Yth Grp; Cmnty Wkr; FCA; Natl Beta Clb; Pres Chorus; Church Choir; Variety Show; Ed Nwsp; Var Bsktbl; Var Vllybl; City Of Maumelle Stdnt Brd Of Dir; Merchntl Bank Stdnt Brd Of Dir; AR Governors Schl; Comm/Jrnlsm.

MAY, MICAH; Magnet Cove HS; Malvern, AR; (2); Church Yth Grp; Pres FCA; FBLA; Pres Natl Beta Clb; VP Science Clb; Band; Rep Stu Cncl; Var Bsbl; Var Bsktbl; Var Ftbl; FPS; Hot Spring Cty Drug Preventn Yth Brd; U AR Fayetteville; Mech Engrg.

MAY, SARAH E; North Pulaski HS; Sherwood, AR; (3); Church Yth Grp; Drama Clb; FBLA; Hosp Aide; Science Clb; Ski Clb; Speech Tm; School Musical; School Play; Stage Crew; Pres SASS 96-97, VP 95-96; DARE Role Model.

MAY, TARA L; Russellville Sr HS; Russellville, AR; (3); Cmnty Wkr; French Clb; Natl Beta Clb; Teachers Aide; Band; Flag Corp; Mrchg Band; Orch; Variety Show; Yrbk; SPCH Pthlgy.

MAYERHOFF, DAVIN M; Parkview Arts-Science HS; Maumelle, AR; (2); Church Yth Grp; Cmnty Wkr; Natl Beta Clb; Red Cross Aide; Socr; High Hon Roll.

MAYES, SHARA K; Van Buren Sr HS; Van Buren, AR; (2); Church Yth Grp; Cmnty Wkr; FTA; GAA; Teachers Aide; Varsity Clb; Church Choir; Bsktbl; Trk; Vllybl; Grambling Univ; Pdtrcn.

MAYFIELD, LAURA L; Bald Knob HS; Bald Knob, AR; (4); 8/85; Letterman Clb; Natl Beta Clb; Band; Jazz Band; Mrchg Band; Bsktbl; Golf; Powder Puff Ftbl; High Hon Roll; FBLA; Hon Grad; Lyon Coll; Optmtry.

MAYHAN, CYNTHIA R; Oak Grove HS; N Little Rock, AR; (2); FCA; VP FHA; FTA; Natl Beta Clb; Spanish Clb; Drill Tm; Variety Show; Rep Frsh Cls; Chrldng; Pres Acad Fit Awd; Paging For State/Local Rep; Part In Advncd Subjcts Eng/His/Math; Attnd Many ABEA/TCHR Seminars; U Of Memphis; Arch.

MAYHEW, DUSTIN L; Springdale Sr HS; Springdale, AR; (1); Church Yth Grp; High Hon Roll; Pres Schlr; Yth For Christ; OK Chrstn; Arch.

MAYLAND, MATTHEW; Hoxie Schl; Hoxie, AR; (2); 1/80; Natl FFA Org; Quiz Bowl; Spanish Clb; Rep Jr Cls; Bsktbl; High Hon Roll.

MAYNARD, CAREY; Berryville HS; Berryville, AR; (3); FBLA; Key Clb; Science Clb; Yrbk; Ofcr Stu Cncl; Chrldng; Hon Roll; Jr NHS; Kiwanis Awd; NHS; Elem Ed.

MAYNARD, ROARK; Augusta HS; Augusta, AR; (1); Art Clb; Church Yth Grp; FTA; Treas Natl Beta Clb; Pep Clb; Science Clb; Spanish Clb; Band; Mrchg Band; Pep Band; GATE; Hendrix; Engr.

MAYNARD, WILLIAM DAVID; Ft Smith Christian Schl; Van Buren, AR; (3); Spanish Clb; Band; Pep Band; VP Frsh Cls; Pres Jr Cls; Ofcr Bsbl; Bsktbl; Cit Awd; Hon Roll; Prfct Atten Awd; Westark CC.

MAYO, APRIL DAWN; AR HS For Math And Sci; Texarkana, AR; (3); Art Clb; Cmnty Wkr; French Clb; Am Leg Boys St; Quiz Bowl; Chorus; High Hon Roll; Jr NHS; NHS; Pres Acad Fit Awd; Comm Svc Clb; Stu At AR Schl For Math And Sci; Marine Bio.

MAYO, ASHLEA R; Valley Springs Schl; Harrison, AR; (3); Art Clb; Church Yth Grp; Cmnty Wkr; French Clb; FBLA; FHA; GAA; Key Clb; Var Mgr Bsktbl; Mgr(s); Lee Col.

MAYO, ROBERT; Sublac Acad; Magazine, AR; (3); Boy Scts; Church Yth Grp; Natl Beta Clb; Quiz Bowl; Science Clb; Spanish Clb; Var Bsbl; Var JV Bsktbl; Var JV Trk; Cit Awd; Eagle Sct; Natl Young Ldrs Conf.

MAYS, APRIL D; Gosnell Jr Sr HS; Blytheville, AR; (1); Church Yth Grp; FHA; GAA; Pres Frsh Cls; Capt Bsktbl; Intrml Score Keeper; Capt Intrml Sftbl; Pres Schlr.

MAYS, HEATHER D; Hamburg HS; Hamburg, AR; (4); Bus Profs of Am; Church Yth Grp; FBLA; Library Aide; Spanish Clb; Acpl Chr; Chorus; Church Choir; Trk; NHS; Military.

MAYVILLE, JULIE; Elaine Jr Sr HS; Elaine, AR; (1); 1/30; Church Yth Grp; 4-H; Hon Roll; NHS.

MAZAR, ELIZABETH; Blytheville Sr HS; Blytheville, AR; (4); 1/240; Am Leg Aux Girls St; HOBY; Sec Key Clb; Hist Natl Beta Clb; Pres SADD; Thesps; Band; Capt Flag Corp; French Hon Soc; NHS; Hendrix Coll; Engl.

MC ADAMS, KRISTIE; Bright Star Schl; Doddridge, AR; (2); FBLA; Office Aide; Hon Roll; Fresh, Soph Bsktbl Maid; Fresh, Soph Cls Favorite; Texarkana Coll; Acctng.

MC AFEE, JASON D; Harrison Sr HS; Harrison, AR; (3); 16/193; Science Clb; Spanish Clb; Acpl Chr; Chorus; Var Crs Cntry; Var Socr; Hon Roll; Jr NHS; NHS; Ntl Merit Ltr; U Of Cntrl AR; Pre-Med.

MC ALISTER, JEFF; Lake Hamilton Sr HS; Hot Springs, AR; (3); Church Yth Grp; FCA; Natl Beta Clb; Science Clb; Spanish Clb; Cit Awd; High Hon Roll; Hon Roll; NHS; Pres Acad Fit Awd; SCL; Ouachita Bapt U.

MC ALLISTER, ASHLEY; Van Buren Sr HS; Van Buren, AR; (3); Art Clb; Church Yth Grp; FBLA; Mu Alpha Theta; Q&S; Red Cross Aide; Science Clb; Speech Tm; SADD; Capt Pom Pon.

MC ANALLY, MATTHEW; Amity Jr Sr HS; Amity, AR; (3); Church Yth Grp; FBLA; Natl FFA Org; Church Choir; School Play; Ofcr Stu Cncl; Ofcr Bsbl; Bsktbl; Golf; Trk; Ouachita Bapt U; Bio.

MC ANALLY, SARA E; Beebe Sr HS; Beebe, AR; (3); Am Leg Aux Girls St; Church Yth Grp; French Clb; FHA; SADD; Church Choir; Hon Roll; Jr NHS; Kiwanis Awd; NHS; Orthopedic Surg.

MC ANULTY, JODI A; Russellville Sr HS; Russellville, AR; (3); FCA; FBLA; JV Bsktbl; JV Vllybl; Hon Roll; Photo; Wildlife; Sales.

MC BRIDE, JARED; Nashville HS; Nashville, AR; (3); 40/150; Var Bsktbl; Var Ftbl; Var Tennis; Hon Roll; Jr NHS; NHS; Pres Acad Fit Awd; AR Single Season Passing Record Holder; All St Ftbl; Southwest AR Offensive Player Of Yr; Phys Therapy.

MC BRIDE, JEREMY H; Dewitt HS; De Witt, AR; (1); 37/200; Pres Frsh Cls; L Ftbl; JV Trk; JV Wt Lftg; JV Hon Roll; JV Ntl Merit Ltr; JV Pres Acad Fit Awd; Univ Of AR.

MC BRIDE, JORDAN M; Smackover HS; Smackover, AR; (1); 9/65; Var L Ftbl; Hon Roll.

MC BRIDE, LACI L; Sheridan Sr HS; Little Rock, AR; (2); 25/300; Church Yth Grp; Hosp Aide; Church Choir; School Play; Yrbk; Rep Frsh Cls; Rep Stu Cncl; Co-Capt Chrldng; Hon Roll; Vol Srts Trnr; Athl Trnr/PT.

MC BRIDE, RACHEL; Farmington Jr Sr HS; Farmington, AR; (3); Church Yth Grp; FBLA; Chorus; Church Choir; School Musical; Co-Ed Nwsp; Hon Roll; Ntl Merit Ltr; U Of AR; Acctng.

MC BRIDE, SHAWN; Conway Sr HS; Conway, AR; (3); U Of Cntrl AR; Bus/Mrktg.

MC BRYDE, GREG W; Star City HS; Star City, AR; (2); Church Yth Grp; Ofcr Bsbl; Wt Lftg; Hon Roll.

MC CABE, TERRA; Farmington Jr Sr HS; Fayetteville, AR; (3); FBLA; Model UN; School Play; Stage Crew; Pres Soph Cls; Cit Awd; Hon Roll; Jr NHS; Kiwanis Awd; NHS; U AR Upwrd Bnd VP; SW MO ST U; Dietcn.

MC CAFFERTY, PRESTON M; Marion HS; Marion, AR; (2); Band; Mrchg Band; Pep Band; Acad Achvmnt Awd Wrd Prcssng/Cmptrs; Lttr Band Awd Grd 9; Most Outstdng Band Awd Grd 10; Band/Cmptrs.

MC CAIN, KATHERINE A; West Memphis Sr HS; West Memphis, AR; (3); 37/292; Church Yth Grp; Cmnty Wkr; FCA; GAA; Library Aide; Natl Beta Clb; Bsktbl; Trk; Hon Roll; Prfct Atten Awd; Meals On Wheels Vol; Amateur Athl Union; Psych.

MC CALL, CHRIS; Woodlawn Schl; Rison, AR; (3); 1/40; Church Yth Grp; Computer Clb; FCA; 4-H; Natl Beta Clb; Office Aide; Teachers Aide; Church Choir; School Play; Rep Soph Cls; Scuba Diving; VP Friendship Yth Rally Assn; Ouachita Bapt U.

MC CANCE, RONALD C; Midland HS; Pleasant Plains, AR; (3); 7/50; FBLA; Natl Beta Clb; Pep Clb; Spanish Clb; Speech Tm; Pres Frsh Cls; Sec Soph Cls; VP Jr Cls; Ofcr Bsbl; Bsktbl.

MC CANDLESS, C MICHELLE; Springdale Sr HS; Springdale, AR; (3); High Hon Roll; Ntl Merit SF; Obtained Position In Tri-City Comp Tech Yth Apprenticeship Pgm; U Of AR Fayetteville; Comp Sci.

MC CANDLESS, LESSA; Van Cove HS; Cove, AR; (3); 1/32; FBLA; FHA; HOBY; Quiz Bowl; SADD; Yrbk; VP Stu Cncl; Bsktbl; Hon Roll; Fllwshp Chrstn Stus; Upwrd Bound; TX A&M; Marine Bio.

MC CANN, SUSAN M; Bearden HS; Bearden, AR; (3); FBLA; FHA; Rep Jr Cls; Rep Stu Cncl; Bsktbl; Chrldng; Trk; Hon Roll; Ntl Merit Schol; S AR U; Pharmacy.

MC CARLEY, JAMES R; Lakeside HS; Hot Springs, AR; (4); #1 in class; French Clb; FBLA; Math Clb; Natl Beta Clb; Cit Awd; High Hon Roll; NHS; Ntl Merit SF; Pres Acad Fit Awd; YMCA Swim Team; Vanderbilt; Bio-Med Engrng.

MC CARN, KEVIN; Mountain View Jr Sr HS; Mountain View, AR; (4); 1/87; Church Yth Grp; Pres FCA; Natl Beta Clb; Pres Soph Cls; Var L Bsbl; Var L Bsktbl; Var L Ftbl; Var L Trk; Hon Roll; Pres Acad Fit Awd; Arch Engrng.

MC CARROLL, NATHAN; Cabot HS; Cabot, AR; (2); Co-Capt Debate Tm; German Clb; Quiz Bowl; Speech Tm; Band; Mrchg Band; Stage Crew; 96 AR Chmpn Amer Legion Oratrcl Cont; Law.

MC CARTNEY, ANGELA; Kimmons Jr HS; Fort Smith, AR; (1); Church Yth Grp; FCA; Pep Clb; Chorus; Church Choir; Chrldng; Hon Roll; Fresh Chrldr; Puppet Team.

MC CARTNEY, NATHAN; Northside HS; Fort Smith, AR; (4); 5/360; Church Yth Grp; German Clb; Mu Alpha Theta; Quiz Bowl; Church Choir; Orch; Ofcr Sr Cls; Hon Roll; Jr NHS; NHS; U Of AR; Cmptr Systs Engr.

MC CARTT, MICHAEL S; Van Buren Sr HS; Van Buren, AR; (3); Church Yth Grp; Cmnty Wkr; FCA; FBLA; FHA; Teachers Aide; Band; Mrchg Band; Hon Roll; Intrml Bsbl; 9th/10th Grd Acad Awds; Cmptr Sci/PT.

MC CARTY, CARREE K; Bentonville Sr HS; Bentonville, AR; (4); 46/242; FCA; FBLA; GAA; Key Clb; Office Aide; SADD; School Play; Stage Crew; Capt Var Bsktbl; Trk; OK Univ; Metrlgy.

MC CARTY, ELIZABETH; Southside HS; Fort Smith, AR; (3); Church Yth Grp; Drama Clb; FCA; Ski Clb; Church Choir; Hon Roll; NHS; SADL Crew; Prtnrs In Chrst; Elem Ed.

MC CARTY, JON D; Bentonville Sr HS; Bentonville, AR; (3); Church Yth Grp; CAP; Acpl Chr; Band; Mrchg Band; Hon Roll; Boys & Girls Clb; Air Force; Aerospace Engrng.

MC CARTY, JOSHUA L; Huntsville HS; Huntsville, AR; (2); Church Yth Grp; Cmnty Wkr; FCA; Science Clb; SADD; JV Bsktbl; JV Ftbl; High Hon Roll; Ouachita Bapt U.

MC CARTY, MARY K; De Soto Schl; Helena, AR; (3); Drama Clb; Spanish Clb; Thesps; Stage Crew; Rep Jr Cls; Ofcr Stu Cncl; Chrldng; Hon Roll; NHS; U Of AR; Pol Sci.

MC CAULEY, JASON; Van Buren Sr HS; Van Buren, AR; (4); Church Yth Grp; Cmnty Wkr; French Clb; VP FBLA; Mu Alpha Theta; Sec Treas Q&S; Quiz Bowl; Ed Nwsp; Cit Awd; NHS; Stdnt Week 3 Tms; Acad Ltr 4 Yrs; Crawford Cty Ret Tchrs Assn Comm Svc Awd; U Of AR; Jrnlsm.

MC CLAIN, HEATHER C; Ft Smith Christian Schl; Van Buren, AR; (2); FBLA; FHA; Natl Beta Clb; Quiz Bowl; Band; High Hon Roll; Hon Roll; NHS; Outstndng Achvmt In Acad; Rdng; Swimming; Pre-Med.

MC CLAIN, HEATHER R; North Little Rock Hs-West; North Little Rock, AR; (3); Church Yth Grp; Cmnty Wkr; Key Clb; Office Aide; Rep Stu Cncl; Bsktbl; Powder Puff Ftbl; Sftbl; Trk; Hon Roll; Sports Med.

MC CLAIN, JASON P; Bald Knob HS; Bald Knob, AR; (3); Church Yth Grp; FBLA; Natl Beta Clb; Acpl Chr; Band; Chorus; Church Choir; Mrchg Band; Pep Band; School Musical; Church Missionary Invlvmnts; All Region Band/Choir; Lyon; Dentistry/Pharmacy.

MC CLAREN, RANDY E; Atkins Schl; Atkins, AR; (3); Church Yth Grp; Letterman Clb; Natl Beta Clb; Speech Tm; L Ftbl; L Trk; L Wt Lftg; Hon Roll; Cath Yth Treas; ATU; Elect Eng.

MC CLELLAND, LESLYE D; Buffalo Island Central HS; Lake City, AR; (2); 2/60; Church Yth Grp; VP FBLA; Girl Scts; Spanish Clb; VP Band; Rep Stu Cncl; Cit Awd; NHS; Pres Acad Fit Awd; Buffalo Island Yth Ldrshp Group; AR ST Univ; Occptnl Thrpst.

MC CLENAHAN, SARA M; Glen Rose HS; Malvern, AR; (2); Hist FBLA; Spanish Clb; Teachers Aide; Chorus; School Musical; School Play; Variety Show; Hon Roll.

MC CLENDON, JAMES M; Hartford Schl; Hackett, AR; (1); Church Yth Grp; Debate Tm; Natl FFA Org; Varsity Clb; Ftbl; Wt Lftg; High Hon Roll; Hon Roll; FFA 1st Pl 95-; Ftbl All Conf 95-; Dfnsv Back Of Yr 95-; U Of Notre Dame; HS Ftbl Coach.

MC CLENDON, JESSICA R; Springdale Sr HS; Springdale, AR; (2); Acpl Chr; Cit Awd; High Hon Roll.

MC CLENNY, CHRIS; Mena HS; Mena, AR; (3); Am Leg Boys St; Church Yth Grp; Science Clb; Spanish Clb; Stage Crew; Ed Phtg Yrbk; Ofcr Bsbl; Ftbl; Dist Frbll Hnrbl Mntn; Ftbll Conf Champs; Bsbll Dist Champs; Ouachita Bapt Univ; Eng.

MC CLUNG, MICHELLE L; Nettleton HS; Jonesboro, AR; (2); Debate Tm; Natl FFA Org; Science Clb; Spanish Clb; St FFA Parliamentary Cont Wnnr; Ag Bus.

MC CLURE, MATT; Butterfield Jr HS; Van Buren, AR; (1); Church Yth Grp; Band; Jazz Band; Cit Awd; Pres Jr NHS; U Of AR; Arch.

MC CLUSKEY, KATALA ROSE; Fayetteville Sr HS; Fayetteville, AR; (2); Church Yth Grp; FBLA; Spanish Clb; Band; Pom Pon.

MC COLLUM, BRITTANY; Lake Hamilton Jr HS; Hot Springs, AR; (1); 4/264; Church Yth Grp; FCA; Hist FBLA; Treas Natl Beta Clb; Office Aide; Rep Stu Cncl; Stat Ftbl; High Hon Roll; Wolf Pride; Rec Bsktbl.

MC COLLUM, KELLY L; Evening Shade Schl; Evening Shade, AR; (4); 4/16; FBLA; German Clb; Natl Beta Clb; Ed Nwsp; Yrbk; Sec Frsh Cls; Sec Stu Cncl; Capt Chrldng; Sftbl; High Hon Roll; Fire Marshall; ASU Jonesboro; Poltcl Sci.

MC COMAS, GLORIA R; Highland HS; Cherokee Village, AR; (2); Church Yth Grp; FBLA; FHA; Natl Beta Clb; Band; Chorus; Church Choir; Mrchg Band; Hon Roll; HS Intern Pgm; 1st Aide; CPR Cert; Little Rock Med Coll; Ped Srgn.

MC CONE, ALICIA; Hamburg HS; Hamburg, AR; (4); 1/5; Church Yth Grp; Drama Clb; GAA; Church Choir; School Play; Bsktbl; Trk; Cit Awd; High Hon Roll; Hon Roll; Law Clb; MVP; All Str In Bsktbll; UAM.

MC CONE, JUSTIN A; Monticello HS; Monticello, AR; (3); Church Yth Grp; Natl Beta Clb; Intrml Bsbl; JV Ftbl; JV Wt Lftg; High Hon Roll; Hon Roll; NLU; Dntstry.

MC CONNELL, ABBY L; Huntsville HS; Huntsville, AR; (2); 4/160; Church Yth Grp; Quiz Bowl; Science Clb; Band; Mrchg Band; Ofcr Stu Cncl; High Hon Roll; UAR.

MC COOL, MARY E; Russellville Sr HS; Russellville, AR; (3); Chorus; Drill Tm; Pom Pon; AR Tech Univ; Med.

MC COOL, PHILLIP R; Kingsland Schl; Rison, AR; (3); 11/21; French Clb; FHA; Natl Beta Clb; Ofcr Bsbl; Bsktbl; Wt Lftg; U Of AR; Phys Ed.

MC CORKLE, AMANDA M; Marion HS; Marion, AR; (2); Art Clb; Drama Clb; Girl Scts; Ofcr Soph Cls; Jr NHS; AR ST Univ; X-Ray Tech.

MC CORKLE, BITSY; Hope HS; Hope, AR; (3); 1/250; Am Leg Aux Girls St; Church Yth Grp; French Clb; FBLA; Natl Beta Clb; Band; Church Choir; Mrchg Band; Ofcr Soph Cls; Pres Jr Cls; Quacheta Bapt U.

MC CORKLE, CHRISTINA K; Hope HS; Hope, AR; (4); 1/199; Church Yth Grp; Sec French Clb; Pres Natl Beta Clb; Band; Rep Jr Cls; Sec Stu Cncl; VP NHS; Val; FBLA; Quiz Bowl; Govnr Schl; Life 1 Chrstn Clb Pres; Ouachita Baptist Univ; Law.

MC CORKLE, ELIZABETH A; Hope HS; Hope, AR; (3); 1/250; Am Leg Aux Girls St; VP Pres French Clb; FBLA; Hist Sec Natl Beta Clb; Quiz Bowl; Band; Pres Jr Cls; Pres Stu Cncl; NHS; Church Yth Grp; LIFE One; Ouachita Bapt Univ.

MC CORKLE, GENA R; Conway Sr HS; Conway, AR; (4); 54/520; Church Yth Grp; FBLA; Intnl Clb; JA; Spanish Clb; VICA; Band; Flag Corp; Mrchg Band; School Musical; Outstdng Band Stu Jr & Sr Yr; AR All-St Band Jr & Sr Yr; U Of AR; Law.

MC CORMICK, AMBER; Gosnell Jr Sr HS; Blytheville, AR; (2); 14/102; Church Yth Grp; FHA; Natl Beta Clb; Science Clb; Chorus; Hon Roll; AR ST U; Bus.

MC CORMICK III, CHARLEY G; Conway Sr HS; Conway, AR; (3); Boy Scts; FBLA; JA; Hon Roll; TX A&M; Bus Admin.

MC CORMICK, JAMES T; Marvell Acad; Marvell, AR; (3); Church Yth Grp; French Clb; Natl Beta Clb; Office Aide; L Bsbl; L Bsktbl; L Ftbl; L Trk; NHS.

MC CORMICK, SEAN M; Crossett Sr HS; Crossett, AR; (2); 7/216; Band; Mrchg Band; Intrml Bsktbl; JV Var Ftbl; Hon Roll; Jr Beta Clb; U Of AR; Elec Engr/Accnt.

MC COWAN, DAN A; Cushman Schl; Batesville, AR; (2); Church Yth Grp; FBLA; FHA; Quiz Bowl; Ofcr Stu Cncl; Ofcr Bsbl; Bsktbl; Crs Cntry; Trk; Hon Roll.

MC COY, AMBER; Forrest City HS; Forrest City, AR; (3); Church Yth Grp; Cmnty Wkr; Math Clb; Mu Alpha Theta; VP Natl Beta Clb; Sec Science Clb; Band; Drm Mjr(t); Ofcr Stu Cncl; High Hon Roll; Outstdng Mscn Awds; Beta Clb VP; US Math Awd; U Of AR; Bus Ec.

MC COY, ANGELA; Lakeside HS; Eudora, AR; (2); #3 in class; Church Yth Grp; Drama Clb; 4-H; FBLA; FHA; School Play; 4-H Awd; High Hon Roll; Hon Roll; Jr NHS; Med.

MC COY, CRAIG A; Sloan Hendrix HS; Imboden, AR; (2); 7/60; Cmnty Wkr; Natl Beta Clb; Natl FFA Org; Chorus; Church Choir; Rptr Nwsp; Cit Awd; Hon Roll; Black River Tech Col; Auto Dies.

MC COY, JOHN C; Clarendon Jr Sr HS; Holly Grove, AR; (1); 4-H; Ftbl; Trk; 4-H Awd; Hon Roll; Phillips Cnty CC.

MC COY, KRISTIE D; John L Mcclellan Magnet HS; Little Rock, AR; (2); Key Clb; Natl Beta Clb; Spanish Clb; VP VICA; Cit Awd; Hon Roll; NHS; Statesmans Awd; Pride; Peer Helper.

MC COY JR, LARRY; Newport HS; Newport, AR; (4); 10/140; Am Leg Boys St; Church Yth Grp; Office Aide; ROTC; Spanish Clb; SADD; Band; Color Guard; Drill Tm; Lit Mag; All Conf/ST Ftbl; ACTM Reg Math Cntst; HOT; Sthwstrn Bell Mnrty Intrnsp; ROTC Batln Staff; Mgzn Capt; U Of AR; Cmptr Sys Eng.

MC COY, TONYA; Rison HS; Rison, AR; (2); Church Yth Grp; Cmnty Wkr; FCA; French Clb; FBLA; FHA; Natl Beta Clb; Science Clb; Chrldng; Law Enfrcmnt.

MC COY, WHITNEY B; Jonesboro HS; Jonesboro, AR; (3); Church Yth Grp; French Clb; Hosp Aide; Key Clb; Natl Beta Clb; Band; Chorus; Mrchg Band; School Musical; NHS; AR Govs Schl; Med.

MC CRACKEN, RAMEY S; Mountain Home HS; Mountain Home, AR; (3); 24/267; Am Leg Aux Girls St; Church Yth Grp; French Clb; Key Clb; Natl Beta Clb; Spanish Clb; Hon Roll; SCA; Interact Clb; HS Dance Tm; U Of AR.

MC CRARY, ALEXIA; Lakeside HS; Hot Springs, AR; (2); Sec FCA; FBLA; Hosp Aide; Natl Beta Clb; Drill Tm; Ofcr Stu Cncl; Chrldng; Trk; Vllybl; Jr NHS.

MC CRARY, LEE ANN; Elaine Jr Sr HS; Mellwood, AR; (3); FBLA; Spanish Clb; Yrbk; Rep Stu Cncl; Cit Awd; Hon Roll; Schl Imprvmnt Plnng Comm Jr Class Rep.

MC CRARY, SHAWNECE; John L Mcclellan Magnet HS; Little Rock, AR; (2); Church Yth Grp; FBLA; Natl Beta Clb; Var Bsktbl; Var Chrldng; Intrml Gym; Var Vllybl; Cit Awd; High Hon Roll; Hon Roll; Howard Univ; Medicine.

MC CRAW, RYAN; Fayetteville Christian Schl; Goshen, AR; (3); Am Leg Boys St; Church Yth Grp; 4-H; Yrbk; VP Soph Cls; VP Jr Cls; Var JV Bsktbl; Hon Roll; Spec Olympcs Vol; Chrstn Chrctr Awd; U Of AR.

MC CREERY, CRYSTAL; Bright Star Schl; Doddridge, AR; (1); Church Yth Grp; Hosp Aide; Pres Frsh Cls; Var Bsktbl; Var Chrldng; JV Trk; AR ST U; Psych.

MC CUIEN, CORNEL D; North Little Rock Hs-East; Little Rock, AR; (2); Art Clb; Church Yth Grp; Science Clb; Chorus; Church Choir; Nwsp; Cit Awd; High Hon Roll; Hon Roll; U Of AR; Arch Eng.

MC CULLARS, DAVID; Conway Sr HS; Conway, AR; (2); Math Tm; Q&S; Quiz Bowl; Band; Jazz Band; School Musical; School Play; Ofcr Stu Cncl; Var Capt Socr.

MC CULLOUGH, COLLEEN E; Russellville Sr HS; Russellville, AR; (4); 12/299; Treas Church Yth Grp; Cmnty Wkr; Library Aide; Model UN; Office Aide; Spanish Clb; Teachers Aide; Sec Jr Cls; Var Socr; High Hon Roll; Srch Ldrshp Stff; Yth Advy Cncl; Rnssnc Ldrshp Pgm; U Of AR.

MC CULLOUGH, DUSTIE; Murfreesboro HS; Nashville, AR; (3); 10/38; Art Clb; Church Yth Grp; FBLA; FHA; Natl Beta Clb; Science Clb; Spanish Clb; Band; Mrchg Band; Pep Band; 4 States Band; AR Tech; Vet.

MC CULLOUGH, MONICA L; Clarendon Jr Sr HS; Clarendon, AR; (2); Church Yth Grp; FBLA; Spanish Clb; Acpl Chr; Band; Church Choir; Drm Mjr(t); Yrbk; Bsktbl; Trk.

MC CULLOUGH, PATRICK J; Russellville Sr HS; Russellville, AR; (3); #45 in class; Library Aide; Rep Frsh Cls; Hon Roll; Jr NHS; NHS; U Of AR.

MC CULLOUGH, STEPHANIE M; Mountain Home HS; Mountain Home, AR; (3); 80/253; Art Clb; Church Yth Grp; Church Choir; Flag Corp; Mrchg Band; Pep Band; Lit Mag; Socr; Tchrs Aide For Art; Photographer; Dr; Tchr.

MC CUTCHEN, BRENNAN; Mountain Home HS; Mountain Home, AR; (3); Church Yth Grp; FCA; Var L Bsktbl; Cit Awd; Hon Roll; All Conf AAAA Cntrl Bsktbl 95-; Stdnt Wk 95-.

MC CUTCHEON, DAVID; Mt Judea Schl; Mount Judea, AR; (3); Church Yth Grp; Drama Clb; 4-H; FBLA; Natl Beta Clb; Quiz Bowl; Speech Tm; School Musical; School Play; Yrbk; OM; AR Tech U; Sci Tchr.

MC CUTCHEON, FELISHA; Mt Judea Schl; Mount Judea, AR; (4); Church Yth Grp; Drama Clb; 4-H; Library Aide; Model UN; Speech Tm; Church Choir; School Musical; School Play; Yrbk; NACTC.

MC CUTCHEON, TANA L; Mt Judea Schl; Hasty, AR; (3); 1/18; Hist FBLA; Natl Beta Clb; Pres Soph Cls; Treas Jr Cls; Tennis; Hon Roll; NHS; Recd 1st Pl Acctng II FBLA Dist Cmptn; N AR Cmnty Tech Coll; Acctng.

MC DADE, JOSH; Lakeside HS; Hot Springs, AR; (3); Am Leg Boys St; FCA; FBLA; Varsity Clb; Bsktbl; Golf; Trk; Hon Roll; LA ST U; Pre-Vet Med.

MC DANIEL, ALISON N; Arkansas Sr HS; Texarkana, AR; (2); Art Clb; Church Yth Grp; Drama Clb; FCA; Library Aide; Spanish Clb; Rep Stu Cncl; L Gym; Hon Roll.

MC DANIEL, AUTUMN A; Trumann HS; Trumann, AR; (2); French Clb; Ofcr Stu Cncl; Vllybl; High Hon Roll; Hon Roll; NHS; GATE 1st-10th; ASU; Orthdntst.

MC DANIEL, CHAD; Palestine-Wheatley HS; Palestine, AR; (3); 4-H; Natl FFA Org; Ftbl; Wt Lftg; Ntl Merit Ltr; Drwng; Fshng; U Of Memphis; Tech Eng.

MC DANIEL, CRYSTAL D; Wynne HS; Wynne, AR; (3); Church Yth Grp; Cmnty Wkr; FHA; Quiz Bowl; Church Choir; 4-H Awd; Ntl Merit Ltr; Prfct Atten Awd; 4-H; Cit Awd; Unity Bibl Clb; Upward Bound Stu At Harding Univ; MASH Camp; Harding Univ; Nurs.

MC DANIEL, DALE J; Robinson HS; Roland, AR; (3); Church Yth Grp; FCA; Letterman Clb; Spanish Clb; Ofcr Bsbl; Ftbl; Golf; Wt Lftg; Water Skiing; U Of AR; Bus/Automotive.

MC DANIEL, DEWANA I; Morrilton Sr HS; Morrilton, AR; (2); Trk.

MC DANIEL, JENNIFER J; Alma HS; Alma, AR; (3); Debate Tm; FCA; French Clb; GAA; Math Clb; Science Clb; Band; Drill Tm; Mrchg Band; Bsktbl; ATU; Psych.

MC DANIEL, KALA J; Marshall HS; Marshall, AR; (3); 7/50; Natl Beta Clb; Hon Roll; North AR Comm Tech Coll; Bus.

MC DANIEL, LANE BV; Arkansas Sr HS; Texarkana, AR; (4); 45/388; Art Clb; Church Yth Grp; Computer Clb; FCA; Key Clb; Mu Alpha Theta; Red Cross Aide; Spanish Clb; JV Bsktbl; Var Golf; UCA; Phys Thrpy.

MC DANIEL, MARION E; Black Rock Jr Sr HS; Black Rock, AR; (2); Church Yth Grp; FHA; Natl Beta Clb; Natl FFA Org; School Musical; School Play; Stage Crew; Intrml Bsktbl; Capt Bsktbl; High Hon Roll.

MC DANIEL, MATTHEW GUTHRIE; Van Buren Sr HS; Van Buren, AR; (4); 50/320; Chess Clb; Church Yth Grp; Cmnty Wkr; FCA; Math Clb; Mu Alpha Theta; Quiz Bowl; Science Clb; Spanish Clb; School Play; West Ark CC; CIS.

MC DANIEL, SHANELL; Jacksonville HS; Jacksonville, AR; (3); FHA; FTA; Spanish Clb; Church Choir; Ofcr Stu Cncl; Bsktbl; Chrldng; Trk; Vllybl; Hon Roll; Memphis Univ; Comm.

MC DANIEL, TERRI L; Cutter Morning Star HS; Hot Springs, AR; (2); FHA; Natl Beta Clb; Spanish Clb; Band; Pep Band; Hon Roll.

MC DANIEL, YVONNE M; North Little Rock Hs-East; North Little Rock, AR; (1); Ofcr Frsh Cls; Hon Roll; Black His; Harvard.

MC DERMOTT, JAMES A; Lake Hamilton Sr HS; Hot Springs, AR; (4); 39/236; FCA; Var Bsktbl; Var Crs Cntry; Var Ftbl; Var Trk; Hon Roll; Natl Govt & Hist Awd; Natl Ldrshp & All-Amer Schlr Awds.

MC DERMOTT, MICHAEL B; Jacksonville HS; Jacksonville, AR; (3); Am Leg Boys St; Art Clb; Church Yth Grp; Debate Tm; Drama Clb; FCA; Spanish Clb; Yrbk; Var Chrldng; Var L Ftbl; Pres Of DCYM; CCYM; U Of AR; Arch Dsgn.

MC DONALD, DEIDERA D; Farmington Jr Sr HS; Fayetteville, AR; (3); French Clb; FBLA; FHA; Girl Scts; Natl FFA Org; Hon Roll; U Of AR; Microbio.

MC DONALD, GREG L; Beebe Sr HS; El Paso, AR; (4); 2/98; Am Leg Boys St; Pres Natl Beta Clb; Rep Stu Cncl; Var L Bsbl; Var L Ftbl; Var Trk; Var Wt Lftg; Cit Awd; Pres Acad Fit Awd; Sal; UCA; PT.

MC DONALD, JAMI; Hamburg HS; Hamburg, AR; (2); 14/150; Church Yth Grp; Cmnty Wkr; Drama Clb; GAA; Pep Clb; Chorus; Church Choir; Mgr Bsktbl; Co-Capt Chrldng; Mgr Trk.

MC DONALD, JAMIE S; Marmaduke HS; Lafe, AR; (3); Pres 4-H; Sec FBLA; Natl Beta Clb; Capt Quiz Bowl; Chorus; Yrbk; Church Yth Grp; Pep Clb; Hon Roll; 4-H Ambsdr; Soclgy Awd; PRIDE.

MC DONALD, JEREMY S; Bergman Schl; Harrison, AR; (1); Boy Scts; Natl Beta Clb; Cit Awd; Gov Hon Prg Awd; Hon Roll; Prfct Atten Awd; U Of AR; Comp Sys Engrng.

MC DONALD, KRIS; Mammoth Spring HS; Mammoth Spring, AR; (4); Treas Natl Beta Clb; Natl FFA Org; Quiz Bowl; Science Clb; L Bsbl; L Bsktbl; L Crs Cntry; Jr NHS; VP NHS; ASU Beebe; Dsgn.

MC DONALD, KRISTIN L; Beebe Sr HS; El Paso, AR; (3); 3/112; Am Leg Aux Girls St; Church Yth Grp; VP FBLA; Sec Natl Beta Clb; Pres Jr Cls; VP Stu Cncl; Trk; Cit Awd; Hon Roll; Pres Acad Fit Awd; 2nd Pl FBLA Grphc Arts Cntst 10th Grd/11th Grd; U Of Central AR; Cmrcl Art.

MC DONALD, MICHAEL E; Marion HS; West Memphis, AR; (2); Church Yth Grp; Spanish Clb; Band; Mrchg Band; Pep Band; Cit Awd; Hon Roll; Prfct Atten Awd; Pres Acad Fit Awd; Band Achvmt Awd; Solo Ensemble #1 4 Times.

MC DONALD, REBEKAH K; Bauxite Jr Sr HS; Benton, AR; (1); 1/50; Church Yth Grp; Office Aide; Quiz Bowl; Rep Soph Cls; Bsktbl; Co-Capt Chrldng; Trk; High Hon Roll; VP Jr NHS; Pediatric Nurse.

MC DONALD, SARA; Norphlet HS; Norphlet, AR; (3); 1/40; Am Leg Aux Girls St; FBLA; FHA; Spanish Clb; Teachers Aide; Yrbk; Ofcr Stu Cncl; Var Chrldng; High Hon Roll; NHS; Del Natl Yth Ldrshp Forum On Law & The Constitution; Pres-Elect Anchor Clb; Mem Natural Helpers Assoc; U Of AL-FAYETTEVILLE; Pol Sci.

MC DONALD, SHYLA; Mammoth Spring HS; Mammoth Spring, AR; (2); FHA; Natl Beta Clb; Pep Clb; Quiz Bowl; SADD; Band; Jazz Band; Mrchg Band; Pep Band; Ofcr Soph Cls; Notre Dame; Med.

MC DONALD, TERAH L; Pottsville Schl; Pottsville, AR; (3); Natl Beta Clb; Natl FFA Org; JV Bsktbl; Var Crs Cntry; Hon Roll; AR Tech U; Med.

MC DONLEY, DA SHUNDA; Dollarway HS; Pine Bluff, AR; (2); Math Clb; Math Tm; Office Aide; ROTC; Variety Show; Ofcr Stu Cncl; Var Chrldng; Cit Awd; Hon Roll; Jr NHS; Dollarway HS Med Clb; Howard.

MC DOUGALD, ANITA; Warren Sr HS; Warren, AR; (3); 1/156; Am Leg Aux Girls St; Church Yth Grp; French Clb; FBLA; Natl Beta Clb; Chorus; Church Choir; School Musical; High Hon Roll; Pres Acad Fit Awd; Dist Math Cmptns 2nd & 1st Pl; Eng Cmptn Awds; Select Girls Ensemble Chorus Mem; U Of AF Monticello; Pre-Med.

MC DOWELL, JACOB M; Fayetteville Christian Schl; Fayetteville, AR; (2); Church Yth Grp; Bsktbl; Bus Mgmt.

MC DOWELL, JEREMY J; Hartford Schl; Huntington, AR; (3); Natl FFA Org; Teachers Aide; Var Bsbl; JV Var Bsktbl; Var Ftbl; JV Var Wt Lftg; Hon Roll; Coach.

MC DOWELL, LORI; Mountain Home HS; Mountain Home, AR; (4); 75/221; FBLA; German Clb; HOBY; Key Clb; Quiz Bowl; Powder Puff Ftbl; U Of FL; Geology.

MC ELMURRY, BRANDY L; Quitman Jr Sr HS; Quitman, AR; (2); Church Yth Grp; FBLA; FHA; Natl Beta Clb; SADD; Rep Stu Cncl; Bsktbl; Sftbl; Hon Roll; Harding U; Archeology.

MC ELMURRY, SHANNON M; Parkview Arts-Science HS; Little Rock, AR; (3); 18/270; French Clb; Girl Scts; Natl Beta Clb; ROTC; Chorus; Drill Tm; High Hon Roll; NHS; Fr II & III Schlr Awd; Hattie Caraway Conf For Emerging Women; U Of AR Fayettville; His; Arch.

MC ELROY, AMANDA D; Sheridan Sr HS; Sheridan, AR; (2); Church Yth Grp; Library Aide; Band; Church Choir; Mrchg Band; Yrbk; Hon Roll; Jr NHS; Prfct Atten Awd.

MC ELROY, LAURA A; Hazen Jr Sr HS; Hazen, AR; (3); 17/44; Am Leg Aux Girls St; Pres 4-H; FBLA; FHA; Chorus; Rptr Nwsp; Cit Awd; 4-H Awd; Hon Roll; Prfct Atten Awd; U Of Cntrl AR; Accntng/CPA.

MC ELROY, MICHAEL M; John L Mcclellan Magnet HS; Little Rock, AR; (3); JA; Spanish Clb; Band; Mrchg Band; Pep Band; UAPB.

MC ELROY, RYAN M; Jacksonville HS; Jacksonville, AR; (2); Treas Church Yth Grp; Natl Beta Clb; Spanish Clb; Band; Drm Mjr(t); Mrchg Band; Pep Band; Yrbk; Var Trk; High Hon Roll; Tae Kwon Do 2nd Degree Blck Belt/Asst Instr Natl Tae Kwon Do Fed; Dentistry.

MC ELROY, SEMEKIA T; El Dorado Sr HS; El Dorado, AR; (1); Church Yth Grp; Band; Church Choir; Mrchg Band; High Hon Roll; NRSNG/DR.

MC ELROY, SHERI M; Springdale Sr HS; Springdale, AR; (3); Rptr FBLA; Treas Key Clb; Acpl Chr; Chorus; Drill Tm; Rep Sr Cls; Powder Puff Ftbl; Tennis; Trk; High Hon Roll; Yth For Christ; U Of AR.

MC ELYEA, DAVID B; Booneville Jr Sr HS; Booneville, AR; (3); Church Yth Grp; JV Var Bsbl; JV Var Bsktbl; Var Trk.

MC ENTYRE, STEWART P; Dardanelle HS; Dardanelle, AR; (4); 23/97; Church Yth Grp; Cmnty Wkr; Intnl Clb; Natl Beta Clb; ROTC; Varsity Clb; Capt L Bsbl; Var L Ftbl; JV Trk; Var Wt Lftg; AR Tech Univ; Eng.

MC FADDEN, STEPHANIE; Dermott HS; Dermott, AR; (4); 2/57; Am Leg Aux Girls St; FBLA; Math Clb; Natl Beta Clb; VP Science Clb; Spanish Clb; Yrbk; Ofcr Stu Cncl; Cit Awd; Hon Roll; U Of AR At Pine Bluff; Acctng.

MC FALL, WHITNEY D; Norfork Jr Sr HS; Norfork, AR; (3); 3/38; Art Clb; Church Yth Grp; FBLA; FHA; Math Clb; Science Clb; Teachers Aide; Var Bsktbl; Hon Roll; Pre-Medicine.

MC FARLAND, AARON M; Cabot HS; Lonoke, AR; (3); 1/398; Am Leg Boys St; Boy Scts; Var Ftbl; Tennis; Jr NHS; Kiwanis Awd; NHS; Spanish NHS; Acad All Conf Ftbl; Eng.

MC FARLAND, JOHN; Cross Co Jr Sr HS; Hickory Ridge, AR; (3); Church Yth Grp; Math Tm; Quiz Bowl; JV Var Ftbl; High Hon Roll; Hon Roll; NHS; U Of Cntrl AR; Optometrist.

MC FARLAND, JULIE A; Southside HS; Fort Smith, AR; (3); 147/502; Spanish Clb; Band; Jazz Band; Mrchg Band; Pep Band; Hon Roll; NHS; Spanish NHS; Ed.

MC FARLIN, MELINDA G; Buffalo Island Central HS; Monette, AR; (2); 5/60; Church Yth Grp; Girl Scts; HOBY; Church Choir; Rep Soph Cls; Ofcr Stu Cncl; Sftbl; Hon Roll; NHS; Pres Acad Fit Awd; AR ST Univ.

MC FEE, CRYSTAL L; Huntsville HS; Huntsville, AR; (2); 6/154; Church Yth Grp; JV Sftbl; Cit Awd; High Hon Roll; Prfct Atten Awd; Pres Acad Fit Awd; United Chrstns Campus Mnstry; U Of AR; Elem Ed.

MC FERRAN, BECKY; Charleston HS; Charleston, AR; (1); FBLA; Quiz Bowl; Band; Mrchg Band; High Hon Roll; GATE; Med.

MC GAHHEY, REAGAN N; Dewitt HS; De Witt, AR; (3); 18/94; Am Leg Aux Girls St; FCA; FBLA; FTA; School Play; Rep Jr Cls; Sec Stu Cncl; Var Chrldng; Hon Roll; Pres Acad Fit Awd; Piano; Sing; Chld Psych.

MC GARRAH, REBECCA A; Bergman Schl; Harrison, AR; (4); 11/54; Natl Beta Clb; Pep Clb; Spanish Clb; Teachers Aide; Chorus; Nwsp; Chorus Awd Outstdng Achvmts; VFW Essay Awd/$50 Savngs Bond; Grad Hnrs; Coll Of Ozarks; Elem Schl Tchr.

MC GEE, JOSH B; Farmington Jr Sr HS; Farmington, AR; (1); Church Yth Grp; L Bsktbl; L Ftbl; Trk; Hon Roll; Jr NHS; Lads To Leaders Leaderettes Natl Convention Debate Participant.

MC GEE, KRISHA; Gentry HS; Gentry, AR; (3); 1/90; Am Leg Aux Girls St; Church Yth Grp; Drama Clb; FCA; FBLA; FHA; Math Tm; Model UN; Quiz Bowl; Spanish Clb; Natl Engl Merit Awd; Psych.

MC GEHEE, AMY; Ozark Adventist Acad; Inola, OK; (3); Church Yth Grp; Band; Chorus; Mrchg Band; Variety Show; Yrbk; Pres Frsh Cls; VP Soph Cls; Ofcr Jr Cls; Var Vllybl; Sw Adventist Coll; Med.

MC GEHEE, CHRISTINA; Greenwood Sr HS; Greenwood, AR; (4); #23 in class; Debate Tm; Drama Clb; French Clb; FBLA; Sec Natl Beta Clb; Speech Tm; Teachers Aide; Ofcr Sr Cls; Hon Roll; NHS; AR Girls ST Delegate; 3rd Pl Miss Teen Sebastian Cty; Stdnt Congrs Delgt/Elected Clrk Hse; Westar K CC; BA Bus Admin.

MC GHEE, ALLAN L; El Dorado Sr HS; El Dorado, AR; (4); Church Yth Grp; FCA; Spanish Clb; Band; Church Choir; Mrchg Band; High Hon Roll; Hon Roll; Henderson ST.

MC GHEE, APRIL N; Crossett Sr HS; Crossett, AR; (2); 46/208; Natl Beta Clb; Band; Mrchg Band; Hon Roll; Univ Of AR; Math.

MC GHEE, DANIEL; Star City HS; Star City, AR; (4); 26/120; Church Yth Grp; FCA; Pres Natl FFA Org; Pres Stu Cncl; Ofcr Bsbl; Bsktbl; Ftbl; Golf; Cit Awd; NHS; Class Fvrt Grd 9-; Sr Ftbl Qrtrbck; AK HS Bsbl Coaches Ascn All-Star 96; U Of AK Fayetteville; Ag/Bus.

MC GHEE, FUNIKA; Saratoga Schl; Mineral Springs, AR; (3); 1/25; 4-H; FHA; HOBY; Quiz Bowl; Science Clb; School Play; Rptr Nwsp; Rptr Yrbk; Ofcr Stu Cncl; Var Bsktbl; U AR Medcl Sci Outreach Pgm; FL A&M; Med.

MC GHEE, SHAMOND L; Dollarway HS; Pine Bluff, AR; (2); Church Yth Grp; Math Clb; Science Clb; Chorus; Church Choir; JV Var Bsbl; Var Bsktbl; Var Ftbl; Hon Roll; Jr NHS; U Of AR; Acctg.

MC GHEE, TONYA; Norphlet HS; Calion, AR; (2); Church Yth Grp; FHA; Office Aide; Band; Church Choir; Ofcr Stu Cncl; Chrldng; Hon Roll; NHS; Prfct Atten Awd; Ntrl Hlprs.

MC GILL, MARK; Nashville HS; Nashville, AR; (3); Church Yth Grp; Cmnty Wkr; Office Aide; Spanish Clb; Church Choir; School Play; Stage Crew; Ofcr Bsbl; Bsktbl; Ftbl; Bus Mgmnt.

MC GILL, NEAL A; Greenwood Sr HS; Fort Smith, AR; (4); 61/197; Art Clb; Church Yth Grp; FCA; French Clb; Ftbl; Faculty Hnr Roll; Hghst Avg; U Of AR; Arch.

MC GINISTER, ETTA N; Phillips Co Christian Schl; West Helena, AR; (2); Church Yth Grp; Dance Clb; Office Aide; Church Choir; Orch; Ed Yrbk; High Hon Roll; Hon Roll; Blck-Blt Taekwn Do Fed; 10 Yrs Pno Lssns.

MC GINTY, JANEL L; North Little Rock Hs-West; Sherwood, AR; (3); Art Clb; Church Yth Grp; Dance Clb; Drama Clb; FCA; Key Clb; Drill Tm; School Play; Stage Crew; Hon Roll; Star Stu 96; VICA; 2nd Pl Literary/Art Magzne 96; Missn Trip Dallas TX 96; Sidewalk Sundy Schl.

MC GOOGAN, MICHAEL BRIAN; Russellville Sr HS; Russellville, AR; (3); 64/384; JV Bsbl; Var Ftbl; Hon Roll; Jr NHS; NHS; Nom Natl Ftbl Hall Fame 96; U Of AR.

MC GOUGH, MELINDA; Prescott HS; Prescott, AR; (4); 13/78; Church Yth Grp; FBLA; Key Clb; School Play; Rep Sr Cls; Capt Chrldng; Trk; Hon Roll; Kiwanis Awd; NHS; Ouachita Bapt U; Acctng.

MC GOUGH, TIFFANY R; Horatio HS; Forman, AR; (2); 3/36; Computer Clb; FHA; Acpl Chr; Word Processing; Keyboarding-Typing; Speec-Workplace Readiness; Texerkana Coll; Data Base Prgmr.

MC GOVERN, MARLIE M; Springdale Sr HS; Springdale, AR; (4); 8/513; Church Yth Grp; Dance Clb; 4-H; Band; Color Guard; Drill Tm; Mrchg Band; Orch; Cit Awd; 4-H Awd; U Of AR; Bio.

MC GOWAN, MARK; Greene Co Tech HS; Paragould, AR; (4); 1/160; Am Leg Boys St; Church Yth Grp; FCA; Model UN; Quiz Bowl; Spanish Clb; Bsktbl; Golf; Hon Roll; NHS; Egl Schlr Ctzn; TV Chnnl 49 Prdcr; Pg AR Snt; Ouachita Bapt U; Ntrl Sci.

MC GOWAN, MATT; Greene Co Tech HS; Paragould, AR; (4); Am Leg Boys St; FCA; Model UN; Quiz Bowl; Bsktbl; Golf; Hon Roll; Pres Acad Fit Awd; DARE HS Role Mod; TV Prdcr; Bsktbl All St; Williams Baptist Coll; Phys Ed.

MC GOWAN, MICHELLE; Mc Gehee HS; Winchester, AR; (3); Am Leg Aux Girls St; FTA; Mu Alpha Theta; Natl Beta Clb; Science Clb; Spanish Clb; Band; Mrchg Band; Ofcr Stu Cncl; NHS; Auxillary Line; Sci Awd 3rd Pl; U Of AR Conway; Pre-Med.

MC GOWN, ANN M; Lakeside HS; Montrose, AR; (3); 14/90; Church Yth Grp; Cmnty Wkr; FHA; GAA; Church Choir; Bsktbl; Trk; Hon Roll; NHS; Prfct Atten Awd.

MC GRATH, CHRISTOPHER RYAN; Jonesboro HS; Jonesboro, AR; (3); 45/300; Am Leg Boys St; Natl Beta Clb; Spanish Clb; Var Bsbl; Hon Roll; NHS; Pres Acad Fit Awd; Pres Of Chrch Yth Group; AR Senator Page; AR ST Univ; Phy.

MC GRATH, MICHAEL J; Booneville Jr Sr HS; Booneville, AR; (1); Boy Scts; Church Yth Grp; Cmnty Wkr; FCA; Library Aide; Band; Church Choir; Pep Band; School Play; Var L Bsktbl.

MC GREGER, AMANDA; Gosnell Jr Sr HS; Blytheville, AR; (2); Church Yth Grp; FCA; Key Clb; Quiz Bowl; Red Cross Aide; Science Clb; Spanish Clb; SADD; Chorus; Church Choir; U Of MS; Lawyer.

MC GREW, MELISSA; Butterfield Jr HS; Van Buren, AR; (1); FBLA; Drill Tm; Jr NHS; Westark CC; Tchr.

MC GREW, STACI R; Mountain Pine Jr Sr HS; Hot Springs Natio, AR; (2); 18/57; Church Yth Grp; FCA; French Clb; FHA; Science Clb; Band; Flag Corp; Mrchg Band; Pep Band; Yrbk; U Of A Conway; Ed; B-Ball Coach.

MC GRIFF, CHAD; Monticello HS; Star City, AR; (4); Am Leg Boys St; Drama Clb; French Clb; Pres FBLA; Natl Beta Clb; Speech Tm; SADD; Chorus; School Musical; School Play; U Of AR Monticello.

MC GUIRE, ERIC; Rogers HS; Rogers, AR; (4); Rptr Nwsp; Yrbk; Pblc Rltns.

MC GUIRE, SAMUEL A; Catholic HS; Little Rock, AR; (2); 28/200; Boy Scts; ROTC; Acpl Chr; Band; Jazz Band; Mrchg Band; Variety Show; Hon Roll; Sct Patrol Ldr, Sr Patrol Ldr & Troop Guide; Arch.

MC GUIRE, STACY R; Jonesboro HS; Jonesboro, AR; (3); FHA; Girl Scts; Spanish Clb; Band; Hon Roll; Pres Acad Fit Awd; Alpha Beta Clb; Animal Rights Activist; AR ST Univ; Scndry Ed; His.

MC INTOSH, BLAKE W; Arkansas Sr HS; Texarkana, AR; (3); Am Leg Boys St; Art Clb; Church Yth Grp; French Clb; Mu Alpha Theta; Bsktbl; Ftbl; Trk; All Amer Schlr; Harding U; Commnctns.

MC INTOSH, CHRIS M; Alma HS; Rudy, AR; (4); 18/149; Church Yth Grp; FCA; French Clb; Mu Alpha Theta; ROTC; Jazz Band; Orch; Pep Band; Rep Stu Cncl; Bsktbl; All Acad Team 10th/12th; Harding Univ; Comp Sci/Math.

MC INTOSH, JERRI M; Forrest City HS; Forrest City, AR; (4); Art Clb; Pres DECA; Library Aide; Office Aide; School Play; Rptr Phtg Nwsp; Bsktbl; Chrldng; High Hon Roll; Pres Acad Fit Awd; Pres Of Dstrbtng Ed; Mem Of Dlta Beta Sigma; Tp 25% Of Cls Of 96; Psych.

MC INTOSH, JOHNNY; Plainview Rover Schl; Plainview, AR; (4); 4/20; Church Yth Grp; French Clb; FBLA; Natl Beta Clb; SADD; Rptr Nwsp; Phtg Yrbk; Capt Bsktbl; High Hon Roll; Hon Roll; US Army Reserve Natl Schlt/Athl Awd; AR Tech U; Phys Ed.

MC INTYRE, LAURA M; Central Sr HS; Little Rock, AR; (1); 1/260; Church Yth Grp; Cmnty Wkr; Natl Beta Clb; Office Aide; Varsity Clb; VP Frsh Cls; VP Stu Cncl; Var Chrldng; High Hon Roll; Jr NHS; Peer Mediation; Y-Teens; Georgetown.

MC KAMIE, CINDY M; Hope HS; Hope, AR; (4); 14/195; French Clb; FBLA; FTA; Natl Beta Clb; Chorus; High Hon Roll; Hon Roll; Kiwanis Awd; NHS; Stu Of Mnth 2x; Henderson ST U; Ed.

MC KAMIE, JA QUITA; Charleston HS; Charleston, AR; (3); 4/43; FBLA; Natl Beta Clb; Quiz Bowl; Spanish Clb; Rptr Nwsp; Yrbk; Sec Frsh Cls; VP Soph Cls; Rep Stu Cncl; Stat Bsktbl; U Of AR; Med.

MC KAMIE, WESLEY A; Nevada Schl; Rosston, AR; (4); 3/60; Ed Yrbk; VP Sr Cls; Church Yth Grp; French Clb; FBLA; Natl Beta Clb; Band; Var Bsbl; Pres Acad Fit Awd; U Of Cntrl AR; Pre-Med.

MC KAV, TIFFANIE K; Dewitt HS; De Witt, AR; (2); 7/105; FCA; FBLA; GAA; Natl Beta Clb; Science Clb; Sec Frsh Cls; VP Stu Cncl; Chrldng; Sftbl; Hon Roll; Hoby Conv; UCA.

MC KAY, CHRISTOPHER A; Hampton Jr Sr HS; Camden, AR; (3); Church Yth Grp; Teachers Aide; Var Bsbl; High Hon Roll; Pres Acad Fit Awd; Beta Clb; U Of AR; Chemical Engr.

MC KAY, ERIN K; Arkadelphia Sr HS; Gurdon, AR; (3); 1/165; Church Yth Grp; French Clb; Speech Tm; Band; Ed Nwsp; Yrbk; Mgr(s); Jr NHS; Kiwanis Awd; NHS; Knowledge Masters Open Team; Peer Hlth Ed Cnslr; Marine Bio/Sports Med.

MC KEE, CHRISTOPHER K; Wynne HS; Wynne, AR; (2); Church Yth Grp; Drama Clb; VICA; Band; Mrchg Band; AR ST Univ; Arch Engrng.

MC KEE, JOSH A; Ozark HS; Ozark, AR; (2); FBLA; FHA; Office Aide; SADD; Teachers Aide; Cit Awd; Class Favorite; Class Funniest; Auto Body Repair.

MC KELLER, ROBYN; Lakeside HS; Hot Springs, AR; (4); 9/110; Rep Am Leg Aux Girls St; VP FCA; Mu Alpha Theta; Sec Thesps; Rptr Nwsp; Rep Stu Cncl; Capt Var Trk; Capt Var Vllybl; Treas NHS; Ntl Merit Schol; Rhodes Coll.

MC KELVIN, SHAUN; Harmony Grove Jr Sr HS; Camden, AR; (1); Church Yth Grp; Natl FFA Org; Quiz Bowl; JV L Ftbl; JV Wt Lftg; GATE Act; Ag Mech Achvmt; Pres Awd Educl Excl.

MC KELVY, R ADAM; Dequeen HS; De Queen, AR; (2); FBLA; Var L Crs Cntry; Var L Trk; Hon Roll.

MC KENZIE, AUBREY M; Northside HS; Fort Smith, AR; (4); French Clb; Mu Alpha Theta; Pep Clb; Teachers Aide; Band; Drill Tm; Mrchg Band; Pep Band; Hon Roll; NHS; WCC.

MC KENZIE, MELISSA J; Ozark HS; Ozark, AR; (3); Cmnty Wkr; FCA; FBLA; Intnl Clb; Math Clb; Natl Beta Clb; Spanish Clb; Chorus; Bsktbl; Trk; Ozark Summer Swim Tm; Engl Awd; Busawd; Spch Awd; Wrk Plc Rdinss Awd; Engl Awd; U Of AR; Premed.

MC KEWEN, JASON C; Dewitt HS; De Witt, AR; (4); 1/76; Am Leg Boys St; FBLA; FTA; Natl Beta Clb; Q&S; Mgr Nwsp; Yrbk; Ofcr Bsbl; DAR Awd; Val; Ouachita Bapt Univ; Pharmacist.

MC KINDRA, FATIMA J; Central Sr HS; Little Rock, AR; (3); Church Yth Grp; Debate Tm; FBLA; Natl Beta Clb; Pres Frsh Cls; Rep Soph Cls; Ofcr Jr Cls; Cit Awd; Gov Hon Prg Awd; High Hon Roll; Martin Luther King Jr Comssnr; Little Rock Ed Comssnr Only Stu; SECME Pres; Xavier; Pre-Med Or Biochem.

MC KINNEY, JOHN R; Ashdown Sr HS; Ashdown, AR; (3); Natl FFA Org; Science Clb; Welder/Auto Repairs.

MC KINNEY, LAURIE M; Russellville Sr HS; Russellville, AR; (3); Church Yth Grp; Spanish Clb; Teachers Aide; Band; Mrchg Band; Pep Band; NHS; AR Tech U; Htl/Rest Mgmt.

MC KINNEY, MELANIE D; Trumann HS; Trumann, AR; (2); French Clb; FBLA; FHA; Math Clb; Office Aide; Science Clb; Teachers Aide; Chorus; Vllybl; Cit Awd; Rdg Awd; PT/DNTST Asst.

MC KINNEY, TARA; Northside HS; Fort Smith, AR; (4); 14/329; Rptr FBLA; VP Mu Alpha Theta; Pep Clb; Sec Spanish Clb; Teachers Aide; Ofcr Soph Cls; Sec Jr Cls; Ofcr Sr Cls; Capt Chrldng; Gym; St Scholastica Monastery Vol; St Marys Presdntl Mrt Schlrshp; St Marys Coll; Chem.

MC KINNEY, TEVIA L; Nevada Schl; Rosston, AR; (1); Church Yth Grp; Library Aide; Quiz Bowl; Church Choir; Chrldng; Univ Of AR; 2nd Gde Tchr.

MC KINNIE, BENJAMIN S; Magnolia HS; Magnolia, AR; (2); Church Yth Grp; Band; Church Choir; Mrchg Band; Pep Band; Hon Roll.

MC KINNON, DAVID; Murfreesboro HS; Murfreesboro, AR; (4); Church Yth Grp; FBLA; Pres Natl Beta Clb; Capt Quiz Bowl; Science Clb; Spanish Clb; School Play; Rep Sr Cls; Ftbl; Wt Lftg; I Dare You Awd.

MC KINZIE, DEMETRIUS L; Dumas HS; Dumas, AR; (3); 42/167; Var Bsbl; Var Bsktbl; Hon Roll; ASU; Cmptr Tech.

MC KINZIE, SCOTT D; Conway Sr HS; Conway, AR; (2); Band; Jazz Band; Mrchg Band; Pep Band; Ftbl; Trk; Prfct Atten Awd; All Conf Ftbl Player; All Region Band; AR; Arch.

MC KINZIE, SETH W; Gravette HS; Gravette, AR; (2); FCA; Treas FBLA; Quiz Bowl; Phtg Yrbk; Pres Soph Cls; Var L Bsbl; Var L Bsktbl; Var L Ftbl; High Hon Roll; Hon Roll; Sprts Med.

MC KNIGHT, CHARLOTTE E; Forrest City HS; Forrest City, AR; (2); FHA; Band; Hon Roll; Nrs.

MC KNIGHT, DONNA D; Corning HS; Corning, AR; (3); Art Clb; Church Yth Grp; Drama Clb; FHA; Thesps; Band; Church Choir; Mrchg Band; School Play; Band Awd; Southern Nazarene Univ; Music.

MC KNIGHT, JASON B; Bald Knob HS; Bald Knob, AR; (3); VICA; Acpl Chr; Band; Church Choir; Jazz Band; Mrchg Band; Pep Band; Ftbl; Wt Lftg; AR ST Univ; Mus.

MC KNIGHT, PAUL; Rison HS; Rison, AR; (1); Church Yth Grp; FCA; Natl Beta Clb; Natl FFA Org; Quiz Bowl; Science Clb; Ftbl; Hon Roll; Pres Acad Fit Awd; Aegis Camp; U Of Cntrl AR; Hstry.

MC KNIGHT, RICHARD P; Rison HS; Rison, AR; (1); Church Yth Grp; FCA; Natl FFA Org; Quiz Bowl; Ftbl; Cit Awd; Hon Roll; Pres Acad Fit Awd; AEGIS Cmps; Ath Awd; Engl Awd; U Of Cntrl AR.

MC KNIGHT, STEPHANIE D; Star City HS; Star City, AR; (4); 23/105; Art Clb; Church Yth Grp; FCA; French Clb; FBLA; Quiz Bowl; Treas Science Clb; SADD; Teachers Aide; Band; AP Eng I, II, III & IV; Stdnt Cngrss; Vol Wk; Henderson ST; Sprts Med.

MC KOIN, RACHEL A; Mt St Mary Acad; Little Rock, AR; (2); French Clb; Chorus; School Play; Hon Roll; Tri-M Music Hon Soc; Acteens; Anytown; Child Psych.

MC LAIN, JASON M; Tuckerman HS; Tuckerman, AR; (2); Church Yth Grp; Natl Beta Clb; Rep Soph Cls; L Bsbl; L Bsktbl.

MC LAUGHLIN, JONATHAN; Shirley Jr Sr HS; Fairfield Bay, AR; (4); 4/31; Am Leg Boys St; Church Yth Grp; FCA; Quiz Bowl; School Play; L Var Bsktbl; L Var Ftbl; Capt Var Tennis; Hon Roll; Summer Mssn Trip All-Star Bsktbl Tm Caracas Venezuela; All-State Tnns; All Rgn Bsktbl; Ouachita Bapt Univ; Sprt Mngmt.

MC LAUGHLIN, MICHAEL E; Bryant Sr HS; Bryant, AR; (2); Art Clb; English Clb; FBLA; Science Clb; L Crs Cntry; L Trk; Hon Roll; Spec Olympics Vol; AR ST Hnr Rol Amer HS Math Cntst; Natl Lgue Jr Cotillions Vol.

MC LEAN, MATT; Lake Hamilton Sr HS; Pearcy, AR; (2); 50/320; FCA; Natl Beta Clb; Science Clb; Spanish Clb; JV L Bsktbl; Hon Roll; Pres Acad Fit Awd; AR Tech.

MC LEESE, SHIRLEY; El Dorado Sr HS; El Dorado, AR; (3); Church Yth Grp; Cmnty Wkr; FBLA; Office Aide; Acpl Chr; Chorus; Music.

MC LELLAND, LEAH B; Rogers HS; Rogers, AR; (3); Cmnty Wkr; FCA; Sec Treas FBLA; Hosp Aide; Science Clb; SADD; Drill Tm; Orch; NHS; Pres Acad Fit Awd; Univ Of Cntrl AR; PT.

MC LEMORE, EVAN M; Northside HS; Fort Smith, AR; (2); Boy Scts; FCA; Latin Clb; Quiz Bowl; Teachers Aide; Stage Crew; Ftbl; Trk; Hon Roll; NHS; Vet Med.

MC LEMORE, JULIE A; Abundant Life Schools; North Little Rock, AR; (2); Church Yth Grp; Drama Clb; Hosp Aide; Hon Roll.

MC LEMORE, STEPHANIE; Rogers HS; Rogers, AR; (4); Church Yth Grp; VP Drama Clb; Model UN; Spanish Clb; VP Thesps; School Play; Socr; Hon Roll; NHS; Pres Acad Fit Awd; Dance Co; Piano; Teen Ct; U Of AR; Law.

MC LEOD, ALICIA; Oak Grove HS; North Little Rock, AR; (1); Church Yth Grp; FCA; Letterman Clb; Natl Beta Clb; Chrldng; High Hon Roll; Pres Acad Fit Awd; Animal Care.

MC LOUD, MISTY L; Huntsville HS; Huntsville, AR; (4); 6/120; Key Clb; Science Clb; SADD; Teachers Aide; Sec Frsh Cls; VP Jr Cls; L Bsktbl; L Mgr(s); L Trk; Hon Roll; Wendys Heismn; Phys Sci, Bio Awds; U AR; Phrmcy.

MC MAHAN, ANDY J; Crossett Sr HS; Crossett, AR; (2); 30/220; Church Yth Grp; French Clb; Natl Beta Clb; Cit Awd; Hon Roll.

MC MAHAN, TARA; Ouachita Jr Sr HS; Donaldson, AR; (3); Church Yth Grp; Treas FBLA; VP FHA; Math Clb; Math Tm; Natl Beta Clb; Spanish Clb; Teachers Aide; School Musical; Co-Ed Yrbk; Girls ST Dlgt 96; Frndlst Frosh; Class Fvrt Soph/Jr Yrs; Henderson ST.

MC MANUS, MEGANN; West Side Christian Schl; El Dorado, AR; (3); Cmnty Wkr; 4-H; Mu Alpha Theta; Natl Beta Clb; Chorus; Church Choir; Var Chrldng; Var Sftbl; Var Vllybl; Hon Roll; Nom Schlr Cngrsl Yth Ldrshp Cncl.

MC MILLAN, APRIL E; Alpena Schl; Green Forest, AR; (3); Chorus; School Play; Hon Roll; Math & Three CCVE Awds; NACTC Harrison; Finance.

MC MILLAN, CHRISTOPHER; El Shaddai Chrstn Acad; Sherwood, AR; (1); Church Yth Grp; CAP; Cmnty Wkr; Drill Tm; Piano; NM ST Univ; Doctor.

MC MILLAN, MATTHEW; El Shaddai Chrstn Acad; Sherwood, AR; (2); Church Yth Grp; CAP; Church Choir; Piano/Chrch; USF Acad; Pilot.

MC MILLIN, ANN; Rogers HS; Rogers, AR; (4); 64/468; VP FCA; Key Clb; Spanish Clb; SADD; Drill Tm; Sec Treas Soph Cls; Sec Treas Jr Cls; Sec Sr Cls; Sec Stu Cncl; High Hon Roll; Tn Ct Atty; Rtry Stu Mo; Hmcmng Ct; OK ST U; Dntl.

MC MILLION, MICHELLE; Brinkley HS; Brinkley, AR; (3); 10/100; Drama Clb; French Clb; Band; Church Choir; Flag Corp; Bsktbl; High Hon Roll; Hon Roll; NHS; Early Chldhd Dev.

MC MILLON, AMY; Palestine-Wheatley HS; Wheatley, AR; (4); 5/53; Am Leg Aux Girls St; Pres FBLA; VP FHA; Natl Beta Clb; Natl FFA Org; Office Aide; Teachers Aide; Rep Stu Cncl; Hon Roll; AR ST Univ; Bus Ed.

MC MORAN, CASSIE C; Sylvan Hills HS; Sherwood, AR; (2); 57/300; Art Clb; Church Yth Grp; Chorus; Rptr Yrbk; Prin Gold Awd In Art; U Of Cntrl AR; Jrnlsm.

MC MULLAN, KATY; Hope HS; Hope, AR; (4); 1/195; Treas Am Leg Aux Girls St; Church Yth Grp; French Clb; Natl Beta Clb; Rep Sr Cls; Rep Stu Cncl; Co-Capt Chrldng; Var Tennis; Hon Roll; NHS; NCA All Amer Chrldr/Perf Macys Thnksgvng Day Parade; Beryl Henry Mst Outstndng Sr; Acad Schlrshps; U Cntrl AR; Phrmcy.

MC MULLEN, WILLIAM D; Fayetteville Sr HS; Fayetteville, AR; (2); Church Yth Grp; Band; Mrchg Band; Orch; Hon Roll; Biking Club; Univ Of AR.

MC MURTRY, D SCOTT; Fayetteville Sr HS; Fayetteville, AR; (3); Treas French Clb; Band; School Play; Ed Lit Mag; Gov Hon Prg Awd; High Hon Roll; NHS; Pres Acad Fit Awd; Yng Democrats Sec.

MC NAIR, JOSEPH DILLON; Forrest City HS; Forrest City, AR; (3); Church Yth Grp; 4-H; Letterman Clb; Natl Beta Clb; Office Aide; Teachers Aide; Ofcr Bsbl; Hon Roll; Amer Legn Bsbl; City Leag Bsbl 10 Yrs; AR ST-JONESBORO.

MC NAIR, MATT; Marion Co Rural Schl; Bruno, AR; (4); #1 in class; FBLA; Natl FFA Org; Capt Quiz Bowl; Pres Sr Cls; Pres Stu Cncl; Var Bsktbl; Hon Roll; NHS; Pres Schlr; Val; AR Tech Univ; Commnctn.

MC NALLEY, LAUREN; East End Jr Sr HS; Bigelow, AR; (1); Church Yth Grp; Natl Beta Clb; SADD; Nwsp; Co-Ed Yrbk; Bsktbl; Cit Awd; High Hon Roll; NHS; Pres Acad Fit Awd; U Of Central AR; Phy Thrpst.

MC NEAL, AMY; Perryville Jr Sr HS; Perryville, AR; (3); Church Yth Grp; FBLA; Office Aide; Red Cross Aide; Spanish Clb; Teachers Aide; Band; Pep Band; NHS; Prfct Atten Awd; U Of AR At Fayetteville; PT.

MC NEAL, LEWATIS DARNELL; Brinkley HS; Brinkley, AR; (3); Am Leg Boys St; FBLA; Teachers Aide; Ofcr Bsbl; Bsktbl; Tennis; Hon Roll; Jr NHS; Prfct Atten Awd; Pres Acad Fit Awd; STOPP; U Of AR; Ed.

MC NEELY, AMANDA; Gosnell Jr Sr HS; Blytheville, AR; (2); 9/102; Church Yth Grp; FCA; FHA; Key Clb; Natl Beta Clb; Spanish Clb; Chrldng; High Hon Roll; Pres Acad Fit Awd.

MC NEIL, AMBER; Humphrey Schl; Humphrey, AR; (1); Church Yth Grp; 4-H; FBLA; FHA; GAA; Quiz Bowl; Bsktbl; Sftbl; Vllybl; Memphis ST; Med.

MC NEILL, JEANNE; Batesville Sr HS; Batesville, AR; (2); 14/160; Church Yth Grp; Cmnty Wkr; Natl Beta Clb; Chorus; Ofcr Stu Cncl; Chrldng; Tennis; Trk; High Hon Roll; PRIDE; U Of AR Fayetteville; Med.

MC NEILL, JOYCE M; North Little Rock Hs-West; North Little Rock, AR; (3); 103/554; French Clb; Key Clb; Mu Alpha Theta; Band; Lit Mag.

MC NEW, KERI M; Robinson HS; Little Rock, AR; (3); 2/96; Am Leg Aux Girls St; FCA; GAA; Letterman Clb; Library Aide; Math Tm; Natl Beta Clb; Spanish Clb; Thesps; VP Soph Cls; Govs Schl.

MC NIECE, J J; Conway Jr HS; Conway, AR; (2); Church Yth Grp; French Clb; Hon Roll; K-Life; All-Stars; Boston U; Bio.

MC NULTY, KELLY W; Pine Bluff HS; Pine Bluff, AR; (3); 29/481; Am Leg Boys St; Boy Scts; Church Yth Grp; Letterman Clb; Office Aide; Varsity Clb; Rptr Yrbk; Var L Bsbl; Var L Ftbl; Var L Trk; Rhodes Col; FBI Agnt.

MC NULTY, MARK W; Pine Bluff HS; Pine Bluff, AR; (3); 10/430; Am Leg Boys St; Cmnty Wkr; Spanish Clb; Rptr Yrbk; Tennis; High Hon Roll; NHS; Pres Acad Fit Awd; Rptr Nwsp; Rtry Writng Contst Wnnr; Rhodes Col; Law.

MC NULTY, SHAWN T; Pine Bluff HS; Sherrill, AR; (3); Am Leg Boys St; Church Yth Grp; Science Clb; Spanish Clb; Chorus; Ofcr Bsbl; Ftbl; Tennis; High Hon Roll; Hon Roll; Envrnmntl Sci.

MC NULTY, SHAWN T; Pine Bluff HS; Pine Bluff, AR; (3); Am Leg Boys St; Church Yth Grp; Science Clb; Spanish Clb; Chorus; Ofcr Bsbl; Ftbl; Tennis; High Hon Roll; Jr NHS; Regnl Sci Fair Wnnr; Bio.

MC PHERSON, AARON M; North Pulaski HS; North Little Rock, AR; (3); 13/262; Pres Church Yth Grp; Mu Alpha Theta; Spanish Clb; Band; Mrchg Band; Yrbk; High Hon Roll; Hon Roll; NHS; Ntl Merit SF; Delta Brigade Drum & Bugle Corps Intnl Cmptn; Comp Sci.

MC PHERSON, CRAIG L; Dewitt HS; Almyra, AR; (2); Natl Beta Clb; Quiz Bowl; Science Clb; Hon Roll; Local & Regnl Sci Fair 1st Pl; ACTM Math Cmptn 1st Pl Geom; Natl Eng Merit Awd; Comp Sci.

MC PHERSON, DOUGLAS P; Magnolia HS; Magnolia, AR; (2); FCA; Church Choir; Var Ftbl; Hon Roll; Offensive Line MVP At Jay Novacek Ftbl Camp 95; Ouachita Bapt U.

MC PHERSON, GEOFF A; Conway Sr HS; Conway, AR; (4); VP Sec Spanish Clb; Band; Mrchg Band; Var L Bsbl; Hon Roll; Ntl Merit Schol; Spanish NHS; Trinity U; Bio.

MC PHERSON, SHERRY; Gravette HS; Maysville, AR; (4); 3/56; Am Leg Aux Girls St; 4-H; FBLA; FHA; HOBY; Natl FFA Org; Teachers Aide; Sftbl; High Hon Roll; NHS; U Of AR; Acctng.

MC QUAY, KEARSTON R; Hamburg HS; Hamburg, AR; (3); Church Yth Grp; Rep FBLA; GAA; Spanish Clb; Church Choir; Bsktbl; Trk; Cit Awd.

MC RAE, ANDREA; Victory Christian Schl; Camden, AR; (1); 2/6; Church Yth Grp; Debate Tm; Drama Clb; 4-H; Speech Tm; Bsktbl; Chrldng; Sftbl; Vllybl; Wt Lftg; Nrsng.

MC RAE, JAMI L; Dierks HS; Dierks, AR; (2); 1/50; Church Yth Grp; FBLA; FHA; Quiz Bowl; Rep Soph Cls; Rep Stu Cncl; Bsktbl; Hon Roll; NHS; U Of A.

MC RAE, SARA B; Dierks HS; Dierks, AR; (2); 2/50; FBLA; HOBY; Drm Mjr(t); Mrchg Band; Rep Jr Cls; Treas Stu Cncl; JV Bsktbl; Score Keeper; Hon Roll; NHS; Pride Tm; Fire Marshall; Modern Musmasters Hnr Scty; U Of Cntrl AR.

MC SHEEHY, AMBERMARIE; Russellville Sr HS; Russellville, AR; (2); Church Yth Grp; Band; Chorus; Church Choir; Mrchg Band; Jr NHS; NHS; Cmnty Wkr; Acpl Chr; Pep Band; CSU 9-10 Grd; All ST Chr 10 Grd; AU Rgn Chr 9-10 Grd; Mst Outstdng Sngr Awd 9-10 Grd; U Of North TX; Music/Voice.

MC SPADDEN, CHERI R; Newport HS; Newport, AR; (2); ROTC; Drill Tm; Pres Soph Cls; Ofcr Stu Cncl; Natl Soc Sons Of Amer Rvltn; Airforce Acad.

MC VAY, BILLY K; Morrilton Sr HS; Morrilton, AR; (3); Science Clb; Spanish Clb; Thesps; Chorus; Stage Crew.

MC VEY, ASHLEY D; Southside HS; Fort Smith, AR; (3); FCA; Key Clb; Church Choir; Yth At Chrch-Mission Trips To El Salvador; Bapt Coll.

MC WILLIAMS, JEFFREY G; Emerson HS; Emerson, AR; (4); 2/30; Am Leg Boys St; FBLA; Sec Natl Beta Clb; Pres Jr Cls; Pres Sr Cls; Pres Stu Cncl; Var L Bsktbl; Var L Tennis; Var L Trk; Sal; U Of Houston; Medicine.

MC WILLIAMS, LAUREN; El Dorado Sr HS; El Dorado, AR; (3); Church Yth Grp; FBLA; GAA; Girl Scts; Key Clb; Natl Beta Clb; Chrldng; Socr; Trk; Hon Roll; Anchor Clb; Steering Comm; U Of AR; Medicine.

MC WILLIAMS, MARGARET; Bauxite Jr Sr HS; Little Rock, AR; (1); 1/60; Church Yth Grp; Teachers Aide; Church Choir; Sec Rep Stu Cncl; Bsktbl; Capt Chrldng; Gym; L Trk; High Hon Roll; Hon Roll; 4.0 Grd Point Avg Every Yr; Dist Chmpn 110 Meter Hrdls; All Amer Chrldr.

MEALY, JARRAH L; Russellville Sr HS; Russellville, AR; (3); FBLA; Chorus; AR Tech Univ; Acctg.

MEANS, TRACI M; Russellville Sr HS; Russellville, AR; (2); 1/444; Church Yth Grp; FCA; Pres French Clb; Hosp Aide; Church Choir; L Bsktbl; L Trk; L Vllybl; Jr NHS; NHS; Chrch Band; 1st Pl Natl Fr Cntst; Vol Awd; Mssnry Dctr.

MEARS, AMY; Parkview Arts-Science HS; Little Rock, AR; (4); 10/260; Church Yth Grp; FBLA; Key Clb; Natl Beta Clb; Office Aide; Church Choir; High Hon Roll; Jr NHS; NHS; Pres Acad Fit Awd; U Of Cntrl AR; Pharm.

MEBANE, SUSAN; White Hall Sr HS; Pine Bluff, AR; (4); 6/161; Am Leg Aux Girls St; Church Yth Grp; Cmnty Wkr; Key Clb; Mu Alpha Theta; Natl Beta Clb; Pep Clb; Teachers Aide; Chorus; Hon Roll; Henderson ST Univ; Scndry Ed.

MEDFORD, BRANDON; Brinkley HS; Brinkley, AR; (4); 6/71; Pres Drama Clb; French Clb; Quiz Bowl; Science Clb; VP Jr Cls; L Bsbl; Hon Roll; Jr NHS; NHS; GATE; UCA Conway.

MEDINA, JOSE A; Lavaca Jr Sr HS; Lavaca, AR; (4); 23/56; Pres Art Clb; FBLA; Science Clb; Teachers Aide; Nwsp; Var Capt Bsbl; Var Bsktbl; Var Ftbl; Var Trk; High Hon Roll; Hon Roll 2 1/2 Yrs; All-ST/ALL-RGNLS/ALL-DIST Sr Yr Bsbl; All-Conf Hnrbl Mntn Ftbl; Westark; Cmptr Engr.

MEDLOCK, BRIANNE; Bismarck Jr-Sr HS; Bonnerdale, AR; (2); FHA; Yrbk; Hon Roll; Pres Acad Fit Awd; Beta Clb; Giftd/Tlntd; Psych.

MEDLOCK, DONNIE L; Scotland Schl; Scotland, AR; (1); Cmnty Wkr; FBLA; Bsktbl; Hon Roll; Fire Marshall.

MEDLOCK, JERED; Mulberry HS; Mulberry, AR; (2); 1/35; Church Yth Grp; Cmnty Wkr; FBLA; FHA; Quiz Bowl; Band; Jazz Band; Pep Band; Pres Soph Cls; Var L Bsktbl; Eng Awd; Bio, Geom & Advanced Keyboarding Awds; All Dist Bsktbl; Lyon Coll; Opthamology.

MEDLOCK, KENNY R; Alma HS; Alma, AR; (2); Church Yth Grp; Library Aide; SADD; Hon Roll; Insurance.

MEEK, AMANDA D; Gravette HS; Gravette, AR; (2); Church Yth Grp; Drama Clb; FCA; Library Aide; Spanish Clb; School Play; Stage Crew; Var Bsktbl; Var Powder Puff Ftbl; Cit Awd; 1st Runner Up Ms HS; Elem Ed.

MEEK, DUSTY; East Poinsett Sr HS; Tyronza, AR; (4); 2/53; FHA; Natl FFA Org; Yrbk; Pres Frsh Cls; Var L Bsbl; Bsktbl; Var L Ftbl; Hon Roll; Jr NHS; VP Pres NHS; U Of Cntrl AR; Tchr.

MEEKER, TERRAL W; Greenwood Sr HS; Greenwood, AR; (2); Boy Scts; FCA; FBLA; Natl FFA Org; Ofcr Stu Cncl; Ofcr Bsbl; Bsktbl; Ftbl; Trk; Hon Roll; U Of AR; Ftbl; Play Fiddle.

MEEKER, TOMMY H; Siloam Springs Sr HS; Siloam Springs, AR; (2); Church Yth Grp; FCA; Library Aide; Natl Beta Clb; Teachers Aide; Bsktbl; Cit Awd; Hon Roll; Prfct Atten Awd; Most Valuable Plyr Bsktbl; Univ Of AR; Bus.

MEEKS, BRYAN B; Southside HS; Fort Smith, AR; (4); Church Yth Grp; Spanish Clb; Hon Roll; Pres Acad Fit Awd; Spanish NHS; Henderson ST U.

MEEKS, KRISTIN L; Southside HS; Fort Smith, AR; (2); Drama Clb; FCA; FBLA; Key Clb; Speech Tm; Drill Tm; School Play; Trk; High Hon Roll; Jr NHS.

MEEKS, LAURA; Monticello HS; Monticello, AR; (4); 18/125; Art Clb; Church Yth Grp; Drama Clb; Treas Hist FBLA; Math Clb; Natl Beta Clb; Spanish Clb; SADD; Teachers Aide; High Hon Roll; Southern AR U; Art Ed.

MEEKS, SARAH; Hamburg HS; Hamburg, AR; (2); Drama Clb; Band; Yrbk; Rep Stu Cncl; Var Chrldng; L Crs Cntry; L Trk; Cit Awd; Hon Roll; NHS; BASIC; U Of AR; Psych.

MEFFORD, MELISSA N; Highland HS; Ash Flat, AR; (2); 6/92; Church Yth Grp; Natl FFA Org; Flag Corp; Mrchg Band; Rep Stu Cncl; Hon Roll; Prfct Atten Awd; SOUL.

MEHTA, NEHA N; Arkansas Schl Math & Science; Russellville, AR; (3); Cmnty Wkr; FBLA; Hosp Aide; Mu Alpha Theta; Natl Beta Clb; Spanish Clb; Chorus; Ofcr Frsh Cls; Ofcr Soph Cls; Ofcr Jr Cls; Odyssey Of Mind Team; Medical.

MEIER, AARON; Dover HS; Dover, AR; (3); Church Yth Grp; Natl Beta Clb; Q&S; Spanish Clb; Ed Nwsp; Co-Capt Yrbk; Trk; High Hon Roll; Jr NHS; NHS; Wildlife Admin.

MEIER, LETITIA; Vilonia HS; Vilonia, AR; (3); FBLA; Mu Alpha Theta; Natl Beta Clb; Spanish Clb; School Play; High Hon Roll; Faulkner Co Yth Ldrshp Inst; Acctng/Corp Law.

MEISNER, GINGER L; Goza Jr HS; Arkadelphia, AR; (1); 8/183; Drama Clb; Band; Color Guard; Nwsp; Yrbk; Hon Roll; Outstdng Perf Jrnlsm; Ltrmn Awd For Band; Obstetrician.

MELCHOORS, ROB; Lakeside HS; Hot Springs, AR; (4); 4/114; Church Yth Grp; FCA; Math Clb; Model UN; Mu Alpha Theta; Natl Beta Clb; Office Aide; Science Clb; Chorus; Pres Rep Stu Cncl; Schlr Ath & Ray Kroc Yth Achvmt Awds; Natl Ftbl Fndtn & Coll Hall Of Fame:outstdn Ldrshp; Purdue Univ; Chemical Engr.

MELLOW, HOLLY; Brookland Jr Sr HS; Brookland, AR; (2); Church Yth Grp; Drama Clb; Hosp Aide; Natl Beta Clb; Rptr Spanish Clb; Chorus; Chrldng; Hon Roll; Office Aide; School Musical; All-Region Choir 94-95; AR ST Univ; Pdtrc Nrs.

MELOON, ANNE M; Sylvan Hills HS; North Little Rock, AR; (2); Drama Clb; French Clb; FTA; Girl Scts; Quiz Bowl; Teachers Aide; Chorus; Yrbk; Jr NHS; NHS; Boston U; Architecture.

MELTON, JAMIE; Ouachita Jr Sr HS; Leola, AR; (4); 2/30; Church Yth Grp; Pres FBLA; Natl Beta Clb; Spanish Clb; VP Pres Stu Cncl; Swmmng; Hon Roll; Prfct Atten Awd; Pres Acad Fit Awd; Sal; Henderson ST Univ; Span.

MELTON, MELISSA L; Midland HS; Batesville, AR; (3); 1/35; VP FHA; Library Aide; Treas Natl Beta Clb; Pep Clb; Spanish Clb; Ed Yrbk; Math & Sci Clb; Navy Hnrs Pgm Cert Of Achvmnt; Stu Cncl Rep.

MENDENHALL, NATHAN L; Southside HS; Fort Smith, AR; (2); FCA; Pres Stu Cncl; Var Bsbl; Var Bsktbl; Var Ftbl; Hon Roll; Jr NHS; Prfct Atten Awd; GATE.

MENDEZ, MARCELINA L; Lavaca Jr Sr HS; Lavaca, AR; (3); Art Clb; Church Yth Grp; Cmnty Wkr; Drama Clb; 4-H; GAA; Natl FFA Org; Speech Tm; Color Guard; Mrchg Band; Chicago Art Inst; Ad.

MENDOZA, CHRISTINA; Conway Sr HS; Conway, AR; (3); Art Clb; Church Yth Grp; Cmnty Wkr; FBLA; Science Clb; Hon Roll; RN.

MENDOZA, ERIC C; Rogers HS; Rogers, AR; (3); Church Yth Grp; Cmnty Wkr; FBLA; Spanish Clb; High Hon Roll; Hon Roll; Prfct Atten Awd; Pres Schlr; Chamber Of Commerce Acad Awd; Renaissance Acad Awd; Engrng.

MENKE, AMANDA J; Hartford Schl; Hackett, AR; (3); Church Yth Grp; FBLA; Teachers Aide; School Play; Mgr Yrbk; Hon Roll; NHS; Upward Bound/Math/Sci Prgm; GATE Prgm; U Of AR; CPA.

MERCER, BRANDON D; Booneville Jr Sr HS; Booneville, AR; (3); Church Yth Grp; Drama Clb; English Clb; FCA; FHA; Speech Tm; School Play; Var L Bsbl; Var L Ftbl; Var L Trk; U Of West FL; Radio/TV Brdcst.

MEREDITH, JENNIFER L; Greene Co Tech HS; Paragould, AR; (4); 13/160; Drama Clb; French Clb; Band; Flag Corp; Mrchg Band; School Play; NHS; Pres Schlr; Telecomm; All Rgn Bana; U Of AL; Music Ed.

MEREDITH, KURT; Lakeside HS; Hot Springs, AR; (4); 10/130; Church Yth Grp; HOBY; Model UN; Thesps; Acpl Chr; Mrchg Band; Phtg Mgr Yrbk; NHS; AR Govs Schl; Natl Yth Ldrshp Forum Med; U Of AR Fayetteville; Med.

MEREDITH, MANDY; Rogers HS; Rogers, AR; (4); 11/468; Ofcr Am Leg Aux Girls St; Church Yth Grp; HOBY; Pres Model UN; Ed Nwsp; Co-Capt Pom Pon; Hon Roll; NHS; Church Choir; AR St Mck Trl Team; Natl Schlstc Jrnlsm Assn Awd Of Excllnc Edtrl Wrtng; Comm Svc Yng Amer Mdl; U Of MO-COLUMBIA; Jrnlsm.

MEREDITH, MARK; Lake Hamilton Jr HS; Hot Springs, AR; (1); 6/264; Library Aide; Natl Beta Clb; Band; Mrchg Band; Pep Band; Stage Crew; Hon Roll; All-Reg Band; 1st Pl Mdls Schl Band & Orch Assn Solo-Ensmbl; Instrmntlst Mag Mrt Awd; Instrmntl Msc.

MEREDITH, MONICA; Augusta HS; Augusta, AR; (2); Church Yth Grp; FBLA; FTA; Natl Beta Clb; Science Clb; Spanish Clb; Chorus; Chrldng; Hon Roll.

MERIDETH, ERIC; Morrilton Sr HS; Solgohachia, AR; (2); Boy Scts; Church Yth Grp; French Clb; Math Clb; Natl Beta Clb; Scholastic Bowl; Science Clb; Ftbl; Trk; Wt Lftg; Med.

MERRIFIELD, LAYLA C; Jonesboro HS; Jonesboro, AR; (4); Cmnty Wkr; Pres German Clb; Treas Library Aide; Mu Alpha Theta; VP Natl Beta Clb; Quiz Bowl; Science Clb; Yrbk; Var L Bsktbl; Hon Roll; Hendrix Coll.

MERRY, BRYAN C; Southside HS; Fort Smith, AR; (2); FCA; Key Clb; Mu Alpha Theta; Spanish Clb; Ofcr Frsh Cls; Ofcr Soph Cls; Hist Stu Cncl; Bsktbl; Ftbl; Tennis.

MERRYMAN, ANTHONY L; Pottsville Schl; Russellville, AR; (2); Natl Beta Clb; Tennis; Hon Roll.

MERSEAL, WILLIAM R T; Rogers HS; Rogers, AR; (3); Boy Scts; Church Yth Grp; Cmnty Wkr; Wt Lftg; High Hon Roll; Hon Roll; Multi-Yr Listee; Superior Acad Achvmt Chamber Commerce; Upward Bound/Educl Talent Search; U Of AR; Cmptr Eng.

MESKILL, JULIA; Southside HS; Fort Smith, AR; (4); 80/460; Church Yth Grp; Drama Clb; FBLA; Mu Alpha Theta; Spanish Clb; Thesps; School Play; Stage Crew; NHS; Spanish NHS; Drama Team Destiny Church Mnstry; Church Musical; Jr HS Ldr; Sunday Schl Tchr 5th Grd; Evangel Coll; Comm.

MESKO, BRIAN B; Walnut Vly Chrstn Acad; Hot Springs, AR; (3); 2/7; Art Clb; Church Yth Grp; Natl Beta Clb; Yrbk; Cit Awd; High Hon Roll; Hon Roll; Jr NHS; NHS; Play Guitar & Drums; Jazz Guitar Lessons; Music.

MESSENGER, WAYNE J; Riverview HS; Judsonia, AR; (2); Upward Bnd; Harding Univ; Cmptrs.

MESSMER, DANA M; Springdale Sr HS; Springdale, AR; (2); 167/638; FBLA; Hosp Aide; Teachers Aide; Band; Mrchg Band; Rptr Phtg Nwsp; Ed Yrbk; High Hon Roll; NHS; Cmnty Wkr; Mdcl Explr; U Of KY; Med.

METCALF, APRIL M; Bradford Jr Sr HS; Bradford, AR; (4); FHA; Hon Roll; Glee Clb; Choir; FHA Star Events In Illustrated Talk Bronze Medal; ASU Beebe; Soc Sci.

METCALF, BOB E; Crowleys Ridge Acad; Jonesboro, AR; (1); Church Yth Grp; Science Clb; Spanish Clb; Hon Roll.

METCALF, JIMMY L; Hartford Schl; Hartford, AR; (2); FBLA; VP Soph Cls; Var L Bsbl; Var L Bsktbl; Var L Crs Cntry; Var L Trk; Var Wt Lftg; High Hon Roll; Hon Roll; NHS; FFA; U Of AR; Acctg.

METCALF, JOHNNA I; Rogers HS; Rogers, AR; (4); 72/467; Hon Roll; Jr NHS; AR Tech U; Wldlf Bio.

METCALF, JOSHUA T; Ola Jr Sr HS; Ola, AR; (2); Spanish Clb; Var Bsbl; Var Bsktbl; Var Ftbl; High Hon Roll; Hon Roll; 4a All Dist Ftbl, Dist Hnrb Mntn Bsktbl.

METHENY, MELISSA A; Conway Sr HS; Conway, AR; (4); 18/520; FBLA; Natl Beta Clb; Office Aide; Pep Clb; High Hon Roll; Hon Roll; Natl Vo Tech Hon Soc; U Of Cnrl AR.

METHENY, RYAN; Hughes Jr-Sr HS; Hughes, AR; (1); 6/56; Church Yth Grp; Cmnty Wkr; FBLA; Quiz Bowl; Science Clb; Ofcr Frsh Cls; Capt Chrldng; Gym; Pom Pon; French Hon Soc; AR St U; Bus/Art.

METHVIN, BRYAN; Bergman Schl; Harrison, AR; (1); Church Yth Grp; 4-H; FBLA; Pep Clb; Var Bsbl; Var Bsktbl; Hon Roll; Bsktbl All Conf Team; FBLA Frosh Most Points; 2nd Pl FFA Land Judging Team; Univ Of AR; Agri Bus.

METHVIN, JUSTIN M; Lead Hill Schl; Lead Hill, AR; (1); Church Yth Grp; FHA; Quiz Bowl; School Play; Rep Stu Cncl; Ofcr Bsbl; Bsktbl; Hon Roll.

METZNER, BRANDY; Morrilton Sr HS; Morrilton, AR; (2); Church Yth Grp; Treas FBLA; Math Clb; Natl Beta Clb; Rptr Science Clb; Thesps; Band; Drill Tm; School Musical; Hon Roll; Comp Sci.

MEYER, APRIL; Abundant Life Schls; North Little Rock, AR; (1); Church Yth Grp; Chorus; Church Choir; Var Chrldng; High Hon Roll.

MEYER, JONATHAN S; Yellville Summit HS; Yellville, AR; (3); #10 in class; Cmnty Wkr; Math Clb; Natl Beta Clb; Science Clb; Service Clb; Teachers Aide; Band; Mrchg Band; VP Soph Cls; Ofcr Jr Cls; U Of AR; Cmptr Prgm Dsgnr.

MEYER, JUSTIN I; Batesville Sr HS; Batesville, AR; (3); Church Yth Grp; Natl FFA Org; JV Bsbl; L Crs Cntry; Hon Roll.

MEYER, MARC K; Pulaski Acad; Little Rock, AR; (4); Am Leg Boys St; Church Yth Grp; Cmnty Wkr; FCA; Natl Beta Clb; Spanish Clb; Varsity Clb; Chorus; Capt Bsktbl; Capt Ftbl; Miami Of OH.

MEYERS, RYAN P; Northside HS; Fort Smith, AR; (4); 69/329; Am Leg Boys St; Church Yth Grp; Cmnty Wkr; FCA; Mu Alpha Theta; Chorus; Var Bsbl; Var Capt Ftbl; High Hon Roll; Spanish NHS; AR Tech Univ; Arch; Civil Engrn.

MICKELS, KATHRYN; West Side HS; Higden, AR; (3); 1/40; Drama Clb; FCA; FBLA; FHA; HOBY; Quiz Bowl; Teachers Aide; School Play; Nwsp; Yrbk; Pblc Rltns.

MICKENS, AMY M; Lake Hamilton Sr HS; Hot Spgs Ntl Pk, AR; (4); Church Yth Grp; FCA; FHA; German Clb; Hosp Aide; Office Aide; Pep Clb; SADD; Teachers Aide; Variety Show; VP, Pres FHA; Vrty Shw; Stu Chrstn Lf; Explr Pst Hosp Sec; GCCC; Ped Lk Hmltn Pgnt; Govrs Yth Cncl Ldr; Garland County CC; Nrsng.

MICKEY, MINDI D; North Little Rock Hs-West; North Little Rock, AR; (3); 105/654; Cmnty Wkr; Drama Clb; FHA; Key Clb; Pep Clb; Spanish Clb; School Play; Stage Crew; Powder Puff Ftbl; Cit Awd; Peer Leadershp; UCA.

MIDDAUGH, APRIL; Wilburn Schl; Heber Springs, AR; (3); Pres FBLA; Sec FHA; HOBY; Sec Natl Beta Clb; Phtg Yrbk; Sec Frsh Cls; Sec Soph Cls; Pres Jr Cls; Pres Stu Cncl; Bsktbl; UAMS.

MIDDLEBROOKS, JASON; Searcy HS; Searcy, AR; (3); Boy Scts; Church Yth Grp; French Clb; FBLA; Library Aide; Natl Beta Clb; Jr NHS; NHS; Ntl Merit SF; Ouachita Bapt Univ; Vet.

MIDDLECAMP, MATTHEW A; Southside HS; Batesville, AR; (2); 24/105; Church Yth Grp; Key Clb; Science Clb; Teachers Aide; Band; Church Choir; Hon Roll; Prfct Atten Awd.

MIDDLETON, AMANDA K; Oak Grove HS; Maumelle, AR; (3); Church Yth Grp; FCA; Natl Beta Clb; Band; Mrchg Band; High Hon Roll; NHS; Pres Acad Fit Awd; Vet Vol; Vet.

MIDDLETON, AMY M; Greene Co Tech HS; Paragould, AR; (4); 22/172; FCA; GAA; Hosp Aide; Key Clb; Pres Pep Clb; Quiz Bowl; Spanish Clb; Rep Frsh Cls; Rep Soph Cls; VP Jr Cls; AR ST U; Elem Ed.

MIDDLETON, GWENDOLYN C; Eudora HS; Eudora, AR; (2); 3/102; Natl Beta Clb; Drm Mjr(t); Mrchg Band; Ofcr Stu Cncl; Cit Awd; High Hon Roll; Jr NHS; Debate Tm; FHA; Library Aide; Yth Opp Unlimited; Upward Bound; King Salaman M B Church; AR ST Univ; Mktg.

MIDDLETON, LUKE; Sulphur Rock Schl; Batesville, AR; (3); 7/19; Church Yth Grp; Cmnty Wkr; FCA; FBLA; VP Key Clb; Math Clb; Natl Beta Clb; Natl FFA Org; Quiz Bowl; Science Clb; Music.

MIDDLETON, SHAWNA L; Alma HS; Alma, AR; (4); 13/159; Drama Clb; French Clb; HOBY; Mu Alpha Theta; SADD; Lbrn Chorus; Church Choir; Hon Roll; NHS; Pres Acad Fit Awd; All Acad Team; AR Tech U; Elem Ed.

MIESNER, ANDREA; River Valley HS; Strawberry, AR; (3); Church Yth Grp; VP FBLA; VP FHA; Girl Scts; HOBY; Model UN; Natl Beta Clb; Sec Natl FFA Org; Quiz Bowl; Teachers Aide; UCA Conway; Phys Thrpy.

MIKEL, CHRIS L; Southside HS; Fort Smith, AR; (2); Church Yth Grp; Cmnty Wkr; Key Clb; Red Cross Aide; Band; Drm Mjr(t); Mrchg Band; Pep Band; Stage Crew; Hon Roll; PADI Cert; Hot Air Blln Crew/Natl Fnls; Red Crs Cert Lfgrd.

MIKLES, KATHERINE L; Lavaca Jr Sr HS; Central City, AR; (3); Grayce Dewitt Dance Studio; Ft Smith Police Explorer Post 260; HOPE Ldr; Acctng/Law.

MIKLES, LINDA K; Greenwood Sr HS; Greenwood, AR; (4); 47/198; Church Yth Grp; FCA; FBLA; FHA; French Clb; Sec Natl FFA Org; Spanish Clb; Band; Flag Corp; Hon Roll; Hrsbck Qdrll; Westark; Bus Admin.

MILAM, SARAH J; Cabot HS; Ward, AR; (3); Church Yth Grp; FCA; Pres Sr Cls; Ofcr Stu Cncl; Var Capt Bsktbl; Trk; Kiwanis Awd; Girls St; Homcmng Court.

MILAM, THOMAS W; Greenwood Sr HS; Greenwood, AR; (4); 42/198; Ofcr CAP; Natl Beta Clb; Pres Natl FFA Org; Teachers Aide; Band; Jazz Band; Mrchg Band; Hon Roll; AR Tech U; Photo.

MILES, AMBER M; Lake Hamilton Sr HS; Hot Springs, AR; (3); FCA; FBLA; German Clb; Natl Beta Clb; Drill Tm; Sftbl; Vllybl; High Hon Roll; NHS; Pres Acad Fit Awd.

MILES, NATASHA J; Jacksonville HS; Jacksonville, AR; (2); Natl Beta Clb; Band; Flag Corp; Mrchg Band; Pep Band; Sftbl; Vllybl; Hon Roll; Band Letterman; Letterman On Var Vllybl Team; U Of Cntrl AR; Psych.

MILES, SHAUNDA M; Parkview Arts-Science HS; Mabelvale, AR; (2); Church Yth Grp; French Clb; FBLA; FHA; Natl Beta Clb; Office Aide; Science Clb; Drill Tm; High Hon Roll; Jr NHS.

MILES, THERSEA; Warren Jr HS; Warren, AR; (1); Church Choir; Cit Awd; High Hon Roll; Upwrd Bound; Roger ST Coll Cmp; Hendrix ST Coll; Ed.

MILKS, CALLIE; Bryant Sr HS; Benton, AR; (4); 4/336; Church Yth Grp; English Clb; French Clb; FTA; Hosp Aide; Teachers Aide; Band; Hon Roll; Prfct Atten Awd; Harding Univ; Math/Tchng.

MILKS, TERREL D; Bryant Sr HS; Benton, AR; (2); Church Yth Grp; FBLA; Office Aide; Band; Hon Roll; UCA; Math.

MILLER, ALLISON; Arkansas Bapt Schl; Maumelle, AR; (2); Church Yth Grp; FCA; FBLA; Natl Beta Clb; Church Choir; JV Var Chrldng; High Hon Roll; Chrstn Svc Clb.

MILLER, AMANDA; Lake Hamilton Sr HS; Hot Springs, AR; (3); 15/212; FCA; FBLA; German Clb; Natl Beta Clb; Science Clb; Spanish Clb; High Hon Roll; Jr NHS; NHS; Pres Acad Fit Awd; Bus.

MILLER, AMANDA M; Corning Jr Sr HS; Corning, AR; (3); Drama Clb; Speech Tm; Thesps; Band; Drm Mjr(t); School Play; NHS; Spanish Clb; Mrchg Band; Cit Awd; Bnd Sec Sctn Ldr; AR St U Bnd Cmp & Drm Mjr Cmp; Ply Clrnt, Sax, Flt; AR ST U; Msc Ed.

MILLER, ANDREA M; Parkview Arts-Science HS; Little Rock, AR; (3); Pres Church Yth Grp; French Clb; FBLA; FHA; Band; Church Choir; Mrchg Band; Powder Puff Ftbl; Cit Awd; Hon Roll; Future 500 Comp Clb.

MILLER, ANN; Mc Crory Jr Sr HS; Mc Crory, AR; (2); Church Yth Grp; Library Aide; Spanish Clb; Yrbk; Hon Roll; Jr NHS; Prfct Atten Awd; Pediatric Nrs; Psycht.

MILLER, ASHLEY M; Harrison Sr HS; Harrison, AR; (3); Drama Clb; French Clb; GAA; Key Clb; Thesps; Stage Crew; L Var Bsktbl; Hon Roll; NHS; Pres Acad Fit Awd; U Of AR.

MILLER, CALLIE L; Lake Hamilton Sr HS; Pearcy, AR; (2); Church Yth Grp; FCA; Sec Pres FHA; Girl Scts; Natl Beta Clb; JV Var Bsktbl; JV Vllybl; DAR Awd; Hon Roll; Home Ec.

MILLER, CHRISTINA; Cabot HS; Cabot, AR; (4); 11/250; Church Yth Grp; French Clb; Treas Service Clb; JV Var Socr; Var L Sftbl; High Hon Roll; Hon Roll; Jr NHS; NHS; Pres Acad Fit Awd; U Of Cntrl AR; Bus Admin.

MILLER, CORINNE R; Russellville Sr HS; London, AR; (2); Church Yth Grp; FCA; Teachers Aide; Band; Church Choir; Mrchg Band; Pep Band; School Play; Hon Roll; Horsebck Ridng; Preachd Sermon Neighbors Grove Wesleyan Church; U Of AR; Yth Minstry.

MILLER, CRISTY L; Horatio HS; Horatio, AR; (2); Girl Scts; Teachers Aide; Chorus; Variety Show; Yrbk; Hon Roll; Pres Acad Fit Awd; Lawyer/Cmptr Tech.

MILLER, DARA D; Arkansas Sr HS; Texarkana, AR; (3); Am Leg Aux Girls St; Church Yth Grp; Debate Tm; Drama Clb; Mu Alpha Theta; School Play; Chrldng; Golf; Hon Roll; NHS; Law.

MILLER, EDDIE D; El Dorado Sr HS; El Dorado, AR; (3); FBLA; ROTC; Band; Church Choir; Capt Drill Tm; Mrchg Band; Pep Band; Rep Frsh Cls; JROTC Battalion SGM; Multi Yr Listee; AR ST Univ Jonesboro; Anatomy.

MILLER, ERIC M; Arkansas Schl Math & Science; Hot Springs, AR; (3); FBLA; Mu Alpha Theta; Natl Beta Clb; Science Clb; Spanish Clb; Rep Soph Cls; VP Sr Cls; Ofcr Jr Cls; Hon Roll; NHS; Biochem.

MILLER, HEATH; Devalls Bluff Jr Sr HS; Biscoe, AR; (1); 4-H; Natl Beta Clb; Bsktbl; 4-H Awd; High Hon Roll; Phy; Med Field.

MILLER, JAMES E O; Booneville Jr Sr HS; Booneville, AR; (3); FBLA; Spanish Clb; Acad Achvmt Awd; Paramedic.

MILLER, JANET A; Van Cove HS; Cove, AR; (4); Church Yth Grp; 4-H; FHA; Office Aide; SADD; Band; Yrbk; Hon Roll; Prfct Atten Awd; FFA; Educl Tlnt Search; Army; Phy Thrpst.

MILLER, JAUNITA L; Delaplaine Schl; Peach Orchard, AR; (1); Bus Profs of Am; FCA; FHA; GAA; Math Clb; Pep Clb; Quiz Bowl; Rptr Spanish Clb; SADD; Teachers Aide; Hmcmng Maid Of Hnr; TX A&M Univ; Pdtrc Nrse.

MILLER, JENNIFER; Gentry HS; Gentry, AR; (3); 8/64; Am Leg Aux Girls St; Church Yth Grp; Pres VP Natl FFA Org; Spanish Clb; Rptr Nwsp; Ed Yrbk; NHS; Miss Gentry Pageant/Miss Congeniality; Ag Law.

MILLER, JENNIFER A; Harding Acad; Searcy, AR; (4); 3/30; FBLA; Key Clb; Natl Beta Clb; Chorus; Swing Chorus; High Hon Roll; Kiwanis Awd; Am Leg Aux Girls St; Church Yth Grp; Cmnty Wkr; Circle Of Acad Exc For Outs Achv In Acad; Optimist Clb Yth Of Mnth; Searcy Srhks Swm Tm; Harding Univ; Premed.

MILLER, JENNIFER M; Arkansas Sr HS; Texarkana, AR; (4); 45/364; DECA; Drama Clb; School Musical; School Play; Variety Show; High Hon Roll; Pres Acad Fit Awd; French Clb; Drill Tm; Stage Crew; Yng Demo Sec And Treas; Grad With Hon; NIKE Treas; Stu Of Yr Aw For Frnch 2; Amer Acad Of Dramtc Arts; Actrs.

MILLER, JENNY; Izard County HS; Horseshoe Bend, AR; (2); FBLA; VP FHA; Natl Beta Clb; Office Aide; Pep Clb; Spanish Clb; VP Frsh Cls; Ofcr Stu Cncl; High Hon Roll; Pres Acad Fit Awd; FHA Star Events Gold Star; U Of AR; Bus.

MILLER, JONATHAN A; Huntsville HS; Huntsville, AR; (2); 16/154; Church Yth Grp; Var L Bsktbl; Var L Trk; Hon Roll; Prfct Atten Awd.

MILLER, JONATHAN B; Lamar HS; Knoxville, AR; (3); Church Yth Grp; FCA; Var L Bsbl; Var L Ftbl; Hon Roll; Ntl Merit Ltr; All Dist Bsbl Trnmnt Tm 96; All Vly Ftbl Tm 95; AR Tech Univ; Elec Engr.

MILLER, KELLEY D; Lake Hamilton Sr HS; Hot Springs Natio, AR; (3); Chess Clb; Cmnty Wkr; FHA; Band; Flag Corp; Mrchg Band; Nwsp; Yrbk; Hon Roll; 2 Poems Pub In Natl Anthologies; Won 6 Wrtng Cont Awds; Cottey; Soc Work.

MILLER, KELLY; Pea Ridge HS; Pea Ridge, AR; (1); Cmnty Wkr; Drama Clb; Quiz Bowl; Spanish Clb; Stage Crew; Variety Show; Rep Stu Cncl; Educntl Tlnt Srch; UAR.

MILLER, KRISTI; Junction City HS; El Dorado, AR; (4); 4/58; FBLA; Office Aide; Science Clb; Chorus; School Play; Sec Treas Sr Cls; Ofcr Stu Cncl; Var Co-Capt Chrldng; Mgr(s); High Hon Roll; BASIC Gnrl Cncl; Choir Awd; Page In Hse Of Reps; U Of Centr Ark; Bio.

MILLER, LARRY; Piggott HS; Pollard, AR; (4); 12/66; French Clb; Hist Natl Beta Clb; Natl FFA Org; Science Clb; JV Bsktbl; Var Capt Ftbl; JV Var Wt Lftg; High Hon Roll; Hon Roll; Pres Acad Fit Awd; Field Crops & Bio II Awds; Agronomy Teammem Which Placed 1st In Dist & 10th In St; AR ST Univ; Agribusiness.

MILLER, LESLIE A; Bergman Schl; Harrison, AR; (1); Church Yth Grp; Pep Clb; Spanish Clb; Bsktbl; Tennis; Hon Roll; Prfct Atten Awd; Beta Clb.

MILLER, MANDY M; White Co Central Schl; Judsonia, AR; (2); FBLA; Rptr Sec FHA; ROTC; School Play; Ed Co-Ed Yrbk; Crs Cntry; Cit Awd; High Hon Roll; Ntl Merit Ltr; Airplane Pilot/PA.

MILLER, MARIAN M; Mt St Mary Acad; Little Rock, AR; (2); Church Yth Grp; French Clb; Natl Beta Clb; Variety Show; Var Co-Capt Chrldng; Hon Roll; All Star Chrldr.

MILLER, MATHEWS M; Catholic HS; Little Rock, AR; (4); Church Yth Grp; Letterman Clb; Ofcr Stu Cncl; Capt Var Bsktbl; Capt Var Ftbl; L Var Tennis; Ftbl Vrsty Capt, 2 Yr Starter Qtrbck, All St, Metro; U AR Fayetteville.

MILLER, MELINDA; Smackover HS; Smackover, AR; (4); 20/49; Am Leg Aux Girls St; Church Yth Grp; Drama Clb; FBLA; Spanish Clb; Acpl Chr; Band; Chorus; Church Choir; Gov Hon Prg Awd; HOBY Awd; Henderson ST U; Music Ed.

MILLER, MELISSA; Elaine Jr Sr HS; Elaine, AR; (4); 4/21; Pres Art Clb; Church Yth Grp; Drama Clb; Office Aide; Spanish Clb; Rep Stu Cncl; Capt Chrldng; High Hon Roll; Miss EHS; Stu Mon; U AR Monticello; Acctng.

MILLER, MELISSA A; Mena HS; Mena, AR; (4); French Clb; FBLA; Library Aide; Model UN; Science Clb; Teachers Aide; Band; Flag Corp; Mrchg Band; Pep Band; Acad Explr Post 109; All Rgn Bnd Mmbr; Henderson St Univ.

MILLER, MICHAEL D; Bergman Schl; Harrison, AR; (1); Ofcr Frsh Cls; Cit Awd; NACTC Educl Talent Search Awd Of Recognition; Natl Geographic Soc Mem; NACTC; Anthropologist.

MILLER, MICHAEL F; Arkansas Sr HS; Texarkana, AR; (4); 1/370; Am Leg Boys St; Boy Scts; Key Clb; Pres Mu Alpha Theta; Spanish Clb; Treas Stu Cncl; Var Bsktbl; NHS; Pres Acad Fit Awd; U Of AR; Finance.

MILLER, MIRANDA; Farmington Jr Sr HS; Farmington, AR; (2); 1/105; FCA; FBLA; FHA; Quiz Bowl; Pres Frsh Cls; Pres Soph Cls; Var Bsktbl; Var Sftbl; High Hon Roll; NHS; U Of AR; Massage Thrpy.

MILLER, PAUL T; Catholic HS; Sherwood, AR; (3); 12/190; Church Yth Grp; ROTC; High Hon Roll; Hon Roll; Pres Acad Fit Awd; Competed Rgnl ACTM Test Finished 2nd Alg Div; Hon Mentn Geomtry Div Rgnl ACTM.

MILLER, RAE T; El Dorado Sr HS; El Dorado, AR; (3); Church Yth Grp; FBLA; Band; Church Choir; Mrchg Band; Hon Roll; Pres Acad Fit Awd; Beta Clb; U Of AR; Psych.

MILLER, REBEKAH; Sheridan Jr HS; Hensley, AR; (1); 80/294; Church Yth Grp; FCA; Chrldng; All Star Chrldr Rivercity Gym Squad Natls; 5 ST Titles Modeling/Talent Pageants; U Of AR; Epidermiologist.

MILLER, ROBIN G; Hampton Jr Sr HS; Hampton, AR; (3); 8/40; Church Yth Grp; 4-H; FBLA; Girl Scts; Natl FFA Org; Office Aide; Red Cross Aide; Teachers Aide; Band; Nwsp.

MILLER, ROBIN M; Cloverdale Jr HS; Little Rock, AR; (1); Church Yth Grp; Cmnty Wkr; Computer Clb; Hist FBLA; Library Aide; Natl Beta Clb; Pep Clb; Quiz Bowl; Band; Rptr Nwsp; SECME Head Leader; Med.

MILLER, RYAN A; Clarksville HS; Clarksville, AR; (2); Church Yth Grp; FBLA; Natl Beta Clb; Band; High Hon Roll.

MILLER, RYAN L; Van Buren Sr HS; Van Buren, AR; (2); Computer Clb; FBLA; Mu Alpha Theta; Quiz Bowl; Science Clb; Teachers Aide; High Hon Roll; Jr NHS; NHS; Ntl Merit Ltr; Holt Krock Clinic Math-A-Thon; ACTM Math Cmptn.

MILLER, SARA J; Arkansas Schl Math & Science; Kingston, AR; (3); Cmnty Wkr; FBLA; Orch; Bsktbl; High Hon Roll; NHS; Pres Acad Fit Awd; Pugwash Org Pres; Folk Music; Dance.

MILLER, SARAH J; Southside HS; Batesville, AR; (2); Church Yth Grp; Key Clb; Spanish Clb; Church Choir; Rep Stu Cncl; Var Bsktbl; Var Sftbl; Hon Roll; U Of Cntrl AR; Spts PT.

MILLER, TERIKA D; John L Mcclellan Magnet HS; Little Rock, AR; (2); Art Clb; FBLA; FHA; Pep Clb; Yrbk; Cit Awd; Hon Roll; TAG; Career Clb; PRIDE; Chgo Art Inst; Arch Eng.

MILLER, WENDY G; Mills HS; Little Rock, AR; (3); 9/298; Art Clb; Church Yth Grp; Natl Beta Clb; Teachers Aide; Church Choir; Ofcr Jr Cls; High Hon Roll; Jr NHS; NHS; Ntl Merit SF; AR Tech Univ; Wildlife Bio.

MILLIGAN, JASON K; Tuckerman HS; Tuckerman, AR; (2); 1/60; Rep Art Clb; Rep FBLA; Math Tm; Mrchg Band; Quiz Bowl; Spanish Clb; Teachers Aide; Rptr Yrbk; High Hon Roll; Natl His Day U Of MD 96; Natl Bsktbl Assn Scout.

MILLIGAN, STEVEN O; Tuckerman HS; Tuckerman, AR; (3); Church Yth Grp; FBLA; Natl Beta Clb; Spanish Clb; Ofcr Stu Cncl; Ofcr Bsbl; Bsktbl; Hon Roll; Pres Acad Fit Awd; AR Univ; Marine Bio.

MILLIGAN, TIFFANY; Bryant Sr HS; Alexander, AR; (2); English Clb; FBLA; Rep Stu Cncl; Capt Chrldng; Hon Roll; NHS; Pres Acad Fit Awd; Chrstn Cncl; Champs Peer Ldr; NADT Awd.

MILLS, AMANDA B; Ashdown Sr HS; Ashdown, AR; (3); Church Yth Grp; Cmnty Wkr; Drama Clb; French Clb; FBLA; Model UN; Natl Beta Clb; Quiz Bowl; Pres Science Clb; Thesps; Odyssy Of Mind St Fnls; Gftd & Tlntd; Piano; Med.

MILLS, CASSIE M; Arkansas Sr HS; Texarkana, AR; (3); Church Yth Grp; Drama Clb; FCA; French Clb; GAA; Math Clb; Mu Alpha Theta; Q&S; Variety Show; Yrbk; Piano; Dance; Henderson 100 Prgm; PT/SPRTS Med.

MILLS, KRISTI L; Harrisburg HS; Harrisburg, AR; (4); 6/53; Sec FCA; FBLA; Sec Library Aide; Natl FFA Org; Science Clb; Spanish Clb; Pres Soph Cls; Pres Jr Cls; Pres Sr Cls; Rep Stu Cncl; Interact Clb Bd Mem; AR ST Univ; Phy Thrpst.

MILLS, LAMONT; Hermitage Jr Sr HS; Warren, AR; (1); Church Yth Grp; 4-H; Natl Beta Clb; Natl FFA Org; Chorus; Church Choir; 4-H Awd; Hon Roll; UAM; Ag Tchr.

MILLS, LATISHA D; Hazen Jr Sr HS; Hazen, AR; (4); Church Yth Grp; French Clb; FBLA; FTA; Natl Beta Clb; Band; Chorus; Church Choir; Mrchg Band; Sprt Ed Nwsp; GATE; Henderson ST Univ; Bus.

MILLS, MELISSA; Sulphur Rock Schl; Batesville, AR; (2); 2/27; Drama Clb; FBLA; Key Clb; Natl Beta Clb; Chorus; School Play; Ed Nwsp; Ofcr Soph Cls; High Hon Roll; St Schlr; U Of NC; Cosmetology; Med.

MILLS, SHANNON; Lake Hamilton Jr HS; Pearcy, AR; (1); Church Yth Grp; FCA; 4-H; Pres Natl FFA Org; Pep Clb; Teachers Aide; Chorus; Drill Tm; Cit Awd; Hon Roll; FFA Ldrshp Awrd; FFA Grnhand Pres; FFA Jr Advsr; Vet.

MILLS, STAN; Mountain View Jr Sr HS; Mountain View, AR; (4); Am Leg Boys St; Church Yth Grp; FCA; Natl Beta Clb; Office Aide; Quiz Bowl; Science Clb; Spanish Clb; Teachers Aide; Chorus.

MILLS, TAMMY L; West Fork HS; West Fork, AR; (1); Yrbk; Chrldng; Hon Roll; Prfct Atten Awd; Eng Awd; Algebra Awd; Jrnlsm Awd; U Of AR; RN/LPN.

MILLWOOD, NICHOLAS; Dumas HS; Pickens, AR; (3); Church Yth Grp; Cmnty Wkr; Chorus; Church Choir; Cit Awd; High Hon Roll; Hon Roll; NHS; Prfct Atten Awd; Merit Awds.

MILNES, RUTH A; Monticello HS; Monticello, AR; (3); Natl Beta Clb; Natl FFA Org; Speech Tm; SADD; Hon Roll; LA Tech Univ; Graphic Arts.

MINAHAN, PATRICK M; Russellville Sr HS; Russellville, AR; (2); Church Yth Grp; Cmnty Wkr; Pres VP 4-H; Speech Tm; Band; Mrchg Band; Rptr Ed Nwsp; Hon Roll; 4-H Teen Star & Ambassador; AR Horse Show Assn Awds; U Of AR; Lawyer.

MINCER, TONY M; Valley Springs Schl; Harrison, AR; (2); 1/66; Church Yth Grp; HOBY; Band; Church Choir; Pres Soph Cls; Rep Stu Cncl; Var Bsktbl; Cit Awd; Hon Roll; Prfct Atten Awd; Outstndng Stu Sr High Awd; Sr Schlrs Prgrm; Sr Schlrs Schlrshp Clng; Pol Sci.

MINCY, JAMES K; Trumann HS; Trumann, AR; (3); Natl FFA Org; JV L Ftbl; Hon Roll; Ducks Unltd; NRA; U Of AR.

MINER, RHONDA M; Ozark HS; Alix, AR; (2); 70/99; Library Aide; Teachers Aide; Band; Chorus; Choir Hnrs; Pediatrician.

MINGE, LEAH; Mountain Home HS; Mountain Home, AR; (2); 1/288; Church Yth Grp; SADD; Spanish Clb; Var Capt Chrldng; Var Powder Puff Ftbl; JV Sftbl; High Hon Roll; All Star Chrldr Awd, All Amer Chrldr Awd.

MINKEL, JUSTIN; Fayetteville Sr HS; Fayetteville, AR; (4); 1/400; Cmnty Wkr; Key Clb; Mu Alpha Theta; Band; Lit Mag; Intrml Bsktbl; Var Tennis; Ntl Merit SF; Top 30 NCTE Wrtng Awd; 200+ Rock Clmbng Clb; Wrld Cltrs Clb Fndr & Pres; Cornell U; Engl.

MINOR, CANDACE; Devalls Bluff Jr Sr HS; De Valls Bluff, AR; (1); FBLA; Natl Beta Clb; Pres Frsh Cls; Bsktbl; Sftbl; Hon Roll.

MINOR, MARCI M; Mt St Mary Acad; Maumelle, AR; (2); FBLA; Hosp Aide; Science Clb; Sftbl; Hon Roll; Mcauley Achv Awd Schol; Hendrix Univ; EPA.

MINOR, REBEKAH M; Heritage Christian Schl; Little Rock, AR; (1); 4/15; Church Yth Grp; Ofcr Stu Cncl; Co-Capt Chrldng; Hon Roll; ASU; Bus; Interior Dsgn.

MINTON, CHRISTOPHER L; Russellville Sr HS; Russellville, AR; (2); Art Clb; Church Yth Grp; Cmnty Wkr; Spanish Clb; Teachers Aide; Var L Bsktbl; Hon Roll; NHS; Prfct Atten Awd; Chem/Prof Bsktbl Plyr.

MINTON, MELISSA M; Bryant Sr HS; Alexander, AR; (4); 14/336; Am Leg Aux Girls St; Cmnty Wkr; Drama Clb; English Clb; French Clb; Teachers Aide; Band; Mrchg Band; School Play; Gov Hon Prg Awd; Governors Yth Vol Awd; U Of Cntrl AR.

MIRABELLA, ANTHONY; Brinkley HS; Brinkley, AR; (1); Drama Clb; Thesps; Band; Mrchg Band; Orch; Pep Band; School Play; Stage Crew; NHS; Pres Acad Fit Awd; AR ST U; Music Ed.

MISENHEIMER, BRETT A; Smackover HS; El Dorado, AR; (1); #1 in class; Church Yth Grp; FBLA; JV Bsktbl; Hon Roll; Knwldg Mstr Open; Kybrdng Awd; GATE.

MITCHAM, SHELLY M; Junction City HS; El Dorado, AR; (4); 9/68; Church Yth Grp; French Clb; Pres FHA; Quiz Bowl; Science Clb; Spanish Clb; Band; Church Choir; Mrchg Band; Ofcr Stu Cncl; Majorette Capt; BAIS; NE LA Univ; Elem Ed.

MITCHELL, AARON; C V White Jr Sr HS; Helena, AR; (3); 2/18; Band; Chorus; VP Frsh Cls; VP Soph Cls; Pres Jr Cls; Rep Stu Cncl; Bsktbl; Cit Awd; Hon Roll; Chrch Musician; Upward Bnd; Univ Of AR; Ag Engr.

MITCHELL, ALISSA; Bentonville Sr HS; Seneca, MO; (3); Church Yth Grp; FCA; FBLA; Key Clb; SADD; Pres Frsh Cls; Pres Soph Cls; Pres Jr Cls; Pres Stu Cncl; Chrldng; Harding Univ; Phy Thrpst.

MITCHELL, APRIL L; Tuckerman HS; Weiner, AR; (2); FHA; Natl Beta Clb; Hon Roll.

MITCHELL, ASHLEY; Malvern Sr HS; Malvern, AR; (4); Am Leg Aux Girls St; Church Yth Grp; English Clb; Natl Beta Clb; Acpl Chr; Church Choir; Yrbk; Pres Sr Cls; High Hon Roll; NHS.

MITCHELL, ASHLEY R; Pine Bluff HS; Pine Bluff, AR; (3); Church Yth Grp; French Clb; Key Clb; Teachers Aide; Sec Acpl Chr; Church Choir; Orch; School Musical; Lit Mag; Jr NHS; Pine Bluff Yth Symphony Instrument Schlsp; Jr Soc Clb; Elem Ed.

MITCHELL, AUBREY D; Mountain Pine Jr Sr HS; Mountain Pine, AR; (2); Church Yth Grp; FCA; Natl Beta Clb; Quiz Bowl; Band; Church Choir; Mrchg Band; High Hon Roll; Ntl Merit Ltr; Var Bsktbl; Piano 8 Yrs; Bus.

MITCHELL, BRANDI; Jessieville HS; Hot Springs, AR; (4); Church Yth Grp; FTA; Key Clb; Red Cross Aide; Band; Chorus; Church Choir; Pep Band; Yrbk; Hon Roll; All Reg Hnr, 6 Yrs St, 3 Yrs All Star, 2 Yrs All Reg Jazz Band; ARK-LA-TEX Hnr Band; Beta Clb; Music Ed.

MITCHELL, CHRISTINA K; Harmony Grove Jr Sr HS; Benton, AR; (2); Sec Treas FHA; French Clb; FBLA; Model UN; Natl Beta Clb; Science Clb; Band; Mrchg Band; Hon Roll; Harmony Grove Peer Cnslr/DATE; AR Tech; CPA.

MITCHELL, DARLA J; Mountain Home HS; Mountain Home, AR; (4); Church Yth Grp; Drama Clb; French Clb; FBLA; Chorus; School Play; AR Acad Schlsp; UOFA; Pre-Law.

MITCHELL, DERNITTA; Dumas HS; Dumas, AR; (3); Church Yth Grp; Cmnty Wkr; FBLA; FHA; FTA; GAA; Chorus; Church Choir; Drill Tm; Trk; Spcl Awds Ath; UAM; Surgical Nrs.

MITCHELL, DON P; Emmet Schl; Emmet, AR; (1); Library Aide; Natl Beta Clb; Pres Frsh Cls; Capt Bsktbl; Sthrn AR U; Rnchr.

MITCHELL, JEFFREY G; Eudora HS; Eudora, AR; (3); Church Yth Grp; ROTC; Mrchg Band; Hon Roll; U Of AR Little Rock; Comp Pgmr.

MITCHELL, JENNIFER R; Osceola HS; Osceola, AR; (4); Sec Art Clb; FHA; Pep Clb; Science Clb; Spanish Clb; Band; Mrchg Band; Nwsp; Hon Roll; NHS; U Of AR Faytvl; Fshn Mrchndsng.

MITCHELL, JOSHUA L; Bryant Sr HS; Bauxite, AR; (2); Bsktbl; Hon Roll; Dr.

MITCHELL, KELLEE; Lee Sr HS; Marianna, AR; (4); 6/107; Church Yth Grp; Cmnty Wkr; Natl Beta Clb; Science Clb; VP Frsh Cls; Sec Soph Cls; Rptr Stu Cncl; High Hon Roll; Hnr Banquet Hnr; YAC Sec; U AR Fayetteville; Med.

MITCHELL, LORI A; Sheridan Sr HS; Hensley, AR; (3); 53/263; Sec Church Yth Grp; FCA; Teachers Aide; Pres Chorus; Hon Roll; Jr NHS; Teen Imprvmnt; Cantatrice; U Of Cntrl AR; Elem Ed.

MITCHELL, MANDI; White Hall Sr HS; Pine Bluff, AR; (4); 17/161; Am Leg Aux Girls St; Church Yth Grp; VP FCA; Treas FBLA; Mu Alpha Theta; Natl Beta Clb; Var Bsktbl; Var Sftbl; Var Trk; Hon Roll; US Schlr Ath Awd; Wendys HS Heisman Awd Nom; Hnr Grad; U Of AR Monticello; Bus Admin.

MITCHELL, MYRANDA L; Ozark HS; Ozark, AR; (3); Church Yth Grp; FBLA; FHA; Intnl Clb; Natl Beta Clb; Chorus; High Hon Roll; Hon Roll.

MITCHELL, REKETA D; Osceola HS; Osceola, AR; (2); FHA; GAA; Pep Clb; Spanish Clb; Church Choir; Bsktbl; Hon Roll; NHS; Typing Awd; Just Say No Clb; U Of AR; Pediatrician.

MITCHELL, SIDNEY; Amity Jr Sr HS; Amity, AR; (3); 2/15; 4-H; FBLA; FHA; Natl Beta Clb; Natl FFA Org; Rep Soph Cls; Ofcr Bsbl; Bsktbl; Swmmng; High Hon Roll; TX Tech; Ag.

MITCHELL, TESSIE R; Riverview HS; Judsonia, AR; (2); FHA; Natl Beta Clb; Band.

MITCHELL, TRACI; Dumas HS; Dumas, AR; (3); Church Yth Grp; FTA; GAA; Band; Mrchg Band; Var Bsktbl; Var Trk; Hon Roll; Prfct Atten Awd; All Conf Bsktbl; U AR At Pine Bluff; Elem Tchr.

MITCHELL, TRAYCE; J A Fair Sr HS; Little Rock, AR; (3); 26/332; FBLA; Science Clb; Drill Tm; Sec Frsh Cls; Sec Soph Cls; Rep Jr Cls; Bsktbl; Chrldng; Vllybl; NHS; UCA Conway; Pharm.

MITCHELL, TRISA; Little Rock Cntrl HS; Little Rock, AR; (4); 102/401; Drama Clb; FBLA; FHA; Intnl Clb; Spanish Clb; Band; Mrchg Band; High Hon Roll; Hon Roll; Jr NHS; Co Capt For Flagline; UAPB; Bus Mgnt.

MITCHUSSON, KELLI M; Mississippi Co Christian Acad; Luxora, AR; (3); Church Yth Grp; French Clb; Key Clb; Math Clb; Science Clb; SADD; Ed Yrbk; Var Bsktbl; High Hon Roll; Hon Roll; AR ST Univ; RN/PT.

MITCHZLL, TRENA L; Central Sr HS; Little Rock, AR; (2); Church Yth Grp; FBLA; Spanish Clb; Pres Frsh Cls; Var Bsktbl; Cit Awd; Flagline; UAPB; Bus Mgmt.

MIXON, AMBER; Dermott HS; Dermott, AR; (1); Church Yth Grp; Natl Beta Clb; Band; Jazz Band; Mrchg Band; Chrldng; Cit Awd; Hon Roll; Dance; Nrsng.

MIXON II, JAMES S; Greenwood Sr HS; Greenwood, AR; (4); 8/200; Computer Clb; FCA; FBLA; Math Clb; Mu Alpha Theta; Natl Beta Clb; Quiz Bowl; Science Clb; Sec Soph Cls; U Of AR; Cmptr Systms Engrng.

MIXON, JENNY M; Hartford Schl; Hackett, AR; (3); FBLA; FHA; Girl Scts; Hon Roll; Prfct Atten Awd; Girl Sct Slvr Awd; Hm Ec Awd; West AR.

MIXON, RANDALL; Crossett Sr HS; Crossett, AR; (3); Church Yth Grp; Chorus; Church Choir; Variety Show; Lit Mag; CHS Madrigals; Stdnts Christ; All Region/All ST Choir; Savannah Coll Arts/Dsgn; Cartns.

MIZE, MICHAEL; Ozark Adventist Acad; Noel, MO; (3); Church Yth Grp; Bsktbl; Gym; Trk; Hon Roll; Prfct Atten Awd.

MIZEUR, KELSEY; Fayettevill HS; Fayetteville, AR; (4); 1/382; Cmnty Wkr; Letterman Clb; Math Clb; Mu Alpha Theta; SADD; Varsity Clb; Band; Mrchg Band; School Musical; Stage Crew; Schl Msct; U Of MO Columbia; Brdcst Jrnls.

MOBLEY, KIMBERLY L; Lincoln HS; Lincoln, AR; (3); FBLA; FHA; Chorus; High Hon Roll; Hon Roll; CSF; Acctng.

MOBLEY, LAWANNA R; Palestine-Wheatley HS; Palestine, AR; (3); Church Yth Grp; Library Aide; Natl Beta Clb; Office Aide; SADD; Acpl Chr; Church Choir; School Play; Capt Chrldng; Hon Roll; Piano; U Of AR; Law.

MOBLEY, SARA; AR Schl For Math And Science; Kensett, AR; (3); Church Yth Grp; FCA; HOBY; Mu Alpha Theta; Natl Beta Clb; Quiz Bowl; Pres Frsh Cls; Pres Soph Cls; Rep Stu Cncl; Var Sftbl.

MOBLEY, SARA K; AR School For Math & Science; Kensett, AR; (3); Church Yth Grp; FCA; Mu Alpha Theta; Natl Beta Clb; Pres Frsh Cls; Pres Soph Cls; Rep Stu Cncl; Bsktbl; Sftbl; NHS.

MOCK, STEPHANIE N; Jessieville HS; Hot Springs Natio, AR; (2); 3/50; Church Yth Grp; FCA; Natl Beta Clb; Treas Soph Cls; Var Bsktbl; Var Trk; Cit Awd; DAR Awd; Hon Roll; FHA; All-Amer Schlr; HS Hero Lung Assn; HS Ambassador; Comp Animation.

MODE, RACHAEL; Guy Perkins Schl; Greenbrier, AR; (1); Church Yth Grp; FHA; Natl FFA Org; Hon Roll; Prfct Atten Awd; FFA Star Grnhnd Awd/Crd Spkng Awd; Chptr Srvc Prjct FHA; S ST Coll Magnolia AZ; Ag Tch.

MOE, MARIN A; Rogers HS; Rogers, AR; (4); 44/422; Cmnty Wkr; Office Aide; Spanish Clb; Teachers Aide; Var Capt Socr; JV Var Vllybl; AR Olympic Dev Pgm Soccer Team; Reach Clb Sec; Chamber Of Commerce Acad Awd; Rennaisance Pgm Acad Awd; Green Mtn Coll; Envirnmntl Stud.

MOE, ROLIN A; Rogers HS; Rogers, AR; (3); 60/600; Am Leg Boys St; Church Yth Grp; Debate Tm; NFL; Band; Ed Nwsp; Ed Lit Mag; Treas Stu Cncl; JV Socr; NHS; King Fahd Model Arab League Excl Del Awd.

MOELLERS, CHRISSIE M; Ft Smith Christian Schl; Van Buren, AR; (3); Band; Sec Sr Cls; Hon Roll; NHS; Prfct Atten Awd; Westlark CC; Ed/Cnslng.

MOFFETT, SHANE E; Smackover HS; Smackover, AR; (2); 12/58; Art Clb; Ftbl; Wt Lftg; Rodeo Team Roping; ASU At Montecello; Agri Bus.

MOFFITT, KRISTI; Sulphur Rock Schl; Batesville, AR; (3); 3/20; Am Leg Aux Girls St; FBLA; Key Clb; Natl Beta Clb; Chorus; Rptr Nwsp; Ed Yrbk; Treas Jr Cls; Sec Stu Cncl; Hon Roll; Miss City Beautiful Btsvlle Pgnt; All St Choir; ASU Jnsboro; Music Prfrmnce.

MOHN, AARON; Southside HS; Fort Smith, AR; (4); 175/459; Art Clb; Boy Scts; Church Yth Grp; Cmnty Wkr; FCA; French Clb; FHA; Intnl Clb; Key Clb; SADD; Sunday Schl Tchr; U Of AR Fayetteville; Art Thrp.

MOIX, AMANDA M; St Joseph HS; Conway, AR; (2); GAA; Hosp Aide; Key Clb; Teachers Aide; Bsktbl; Trk; Vllybl; Hon Roll; NHS; Art Achvmt Awd; U Of Cntrl AR.

MOIX, JEREMY M; St Joseph HS; Conway, AR; (2); Boy Scts; Teachers Aide; Pres Soph Cls; Var Bsktbl; Var Trk; High Hon Roll; Jr NHS; NHS.

MOLATCH JR, JOHN M; Hackett Schl; Fort Smith, AR; (2); #2 in class; KY Coll; Cmptr Eng.

MOLDER, BRADLEY S; Ozark HS; Ozark, AR; (3); 1/83; Church Yth Grp; Natl Beta Clb; Quiz Bowl; Band; Church Choir; Rep Frsh Cls; Pres Sr Cls; Rep Stu Cncl; Hon Roll; Pres Acad Fit Awd; Weight Lifting; OK Bapt U; Pre-Law.

MONDIER, MARK A; Van Buren Sr HS; Van Buren, AR; (2); Church Yth Grp; JV Bsktbl; Hon Roll; U Of OK; Meteorology.

MONEY, CRYSTAL G; Bradford Jr Sr HS; Bradford, AR; (3); Art Clb; Sec 4-H; French Clb; FBLA; FHA; Quiz Bowl; Bsktbl; Crs Cntry; Sftbl; Trk; Engl Awd 94; 2nd Plc MADD Essay Cntst 94; Vet.

MONEY, DANA M; Midland HS; Bradford, AR; (2); Church Yth Grp; Drama Clb; FBLA; FHA; Quiz Bowl; Spanish Clb; Mgr(s); Hon Roll; MASH Camp; AEGIS Perfrmng Arts Prgm; Hosp Vltr; RN.

MONROE, DAMON M; Fouke Jr Sr HS; Fouke, AR; (3); 36/82; Church Yth Grp; Natl FFA Org; Church Choir; Intrml Bsbl; YORAD; Comp Tech.

MONROE, LAUREN; Sylvan Hills HS; Sherwood, AR; (4); 28/233; Church Yth Grp; FCA; Mu Alpha Theta; Sec Natl Beta Clb; Church Choir; Var Capt Bsktbl; Var Sftbl; Var L Vllybl; Jr NHS; NHS; Army Schlr Ath; AR Actvt Assn Actv Schlrawd; Pres Awd Educl Excllnc; U Of Southern MS; Hmn Prfrmnc.

MONTAG, REECA R; Alma HS; Rudy, AR; (2); 4-H; FBLA; Library Aide; Natl FFA Org; Band; Mrchg Band; School Musical; 4-H Awd; Hon Roll; NHS; Vet.

MONTAGUE, ROBERT L; Cabot HS; Ward, AR; (3); 4-H; Natl FFA Org; 4-H Awd; ST Farmer Degree FFA; Livestock Judging; Showing Livestock.

MONTGOMERY, APRIL M; Northside HS; Fort Smith, AR; (3); Church Yth Grp; Key Clb; Spanish Clb; Band; Mrchg Band; Pep Band; Chrldng; Hon Roll; NHS; Spanish NHS; OK ST Univ; Vet Med/Math/Sci.

MONTGOMERY, BRAD; East Poinsett Sr HS; Lepanto, AR; (4); Church Yth Grp; FHA; Quiz Bowl; Band; Jazz Band; Pres Frsh Cls; VP Jr Cls; Pres Sr Cls; Rep Stu Cncl; Var Ftbl; Zrx Awd; Cmtr Sci.

MONTGOMERY, DEAN B; Des Arc Jr Sr HS; Des Arc, AR; (3); UA Fayetteville; Petro Engr.

MONTGOMERY, KARMELLA R; Harrison Sr HS; Harrison, AR; (4); Var FBLA; Key Clb; Teachers Aide; Yrbk; JV Var Bsktbl; Mgr(s); Intrml Vllybl; Hon Roll; NHS; Pres Acad Fit Awd; Harding U; Psych.

MONTGOMERY, RICHARD B; Hoxie Schl; Walnut Ridge, AR; (3); 4-H; Natl FFA Org; Teachers Aide; Hon Roll; Prfct Atten Awd.

MONTOYA, JOHN D; Hartford Schl; Midland, AR; (2); Chorus; Var Ftbl; Var Trk; Var Wt Lftg; Cit Awd; High Hon Roll; Prfct Atten Awd; Sci.

MONTS, CLAY G; Arkansas Sr HS; Texarkana, AR; (3); Church Yth Grp; Drama Clb; Sec Key Clb; Q&S; Quiz Bowl; Ed Nwsp; VP Stu Cncl; Art Clb; Cmnty Wkr; French Clb; Yth Advy Cncl; Outstdng Yth Mrt Awd; Search Ldrshp Staff; Theatre.

MOODY, BRENT D; Riverview HS; Searcy, AR; (3); 4/63; Church Yth Grp; FBLA; Natl Beta Clb; Natl FFA Org; Quiz Bowl; Spanish Clb; Church Choir; High Hon Roll; Pres Acad Fit Awd.

MOODY, JESSICA L; Riverview HS; Searcy, AR; (2); 6/68; Church Yth Grp; FBLA; FHA; Natl Beta Clb; Spanish Clb; VP Church Choir; Hon Roll; ASU; Bus.

MOODY, JOSHUA D; Blytheville Sr HS; Blytheville, AR; (3); Am Leg Boys St; Art Clb; Boy Scts; Natl Beta Clb; Spanish Clb; Jazz Band; Mrchg Band; Orch; Rptr Nwsp; Yrbk; Jr Olym Swmng; Order Of Arrow Outstdng New Mem Of Yr; Boys ST Band; AR ST Univ; Eng.

MOODY, LUCAS B; Russellville Sr HS; Russellville, AR; (3); Church Yth Grp; Debate Tm; Drama Clb; Model UN; Spanish Clb; Band; Pep Band; Gov Hon Prg Awd; High Hon Roll; Jr NHS; AR Gov Schl; Boys Girls Clb Bsktbl; Yth Rep Chrch Fin Comm; Yth Ldrshp Inst.

MOODY, NUBIA M; Gillett Jr Sr HS; Dumas, AR; (2); Cmnty Wkr; Natl Beta Clb; Quiz Bowl; Hon Roll; Homcmng Court; Law.

MOODY, RAGUN; Woodlawn Schl; Rison, AR; (2); Natl Beta Clb; Genetic Engrng.

MOODY, STACI N; Sylvan Hills HS; Sherwood, AR; (3); Spanish Clb; Drill Tm; U Of Cntrl AR.

MOON, AMANDA L; Augusta HS; Augusta, AR; (1); Jr Beta.

MOON, ANDRIA R; Trumann HS; Trumann, AR; (2); Art Clb; Church Yth Grp; French Clb; FHA; Science Clb; High Hon Roll; Hon Roll; NHS; Stu Cncl; Gftd & Tlntd.

MOON, MELISSA A; Augusta HS; Augusta, AR; (3); Art Clb; Cmnty Wkr; English Clb; Natl Beta Clb; Spanish Clb; Band; Pep Band; Hon Roll; NHS; Ladies Auxiliary To The VFW; Nrsng.

MOON, SAMUEL L; Huttig Schl; Huttig, AR; (2); Natl Beta Clb; Yrbk; Ofcr Bsbl; Hon Roll; Ger I Awd; All-Dist Bsbl Awd; All-Regnl Bsbl Awd; Engrng.

MOONEY, CRYSTAL L; Greenbrier HS; Greenbrier, AR; (2); 165/479; French Clb; Swmmng; Hon Roll.

MOONEY, JAMES B; Central HS; West Helena, AR; (3); French Clb; Teachers Aide; Art; Music; Sprts; Art.

MOONEY, JIMMY R; Parkers Chapel Schl; El Dorado, AR; (2); Boy Scts; Church Yth Grp; Cmnty Wkr; French Clb; FBLA; Hosp Aide; HOBY; Natl Beta Clb; Quiz Bowl; Science Clb; U Of A Fayetteville; Med Sci.

MOONEY, KARA; Clarksville HS; Clarksville, AR; (3); Church Yth Grp; FCA; Letterman Clb; Natl Beta Clb; Varsity Clb; Rep Stu Cncl; Crs Cntry; Sftbl; High Hon Roll; NHS.

MOONEY, KRISTY; Cross Co Jr Sr HS; Cherry Valley, AR; (3); 6/50; Art Clb; Girl Scts; Natl Beta Clb; Spanish Clb; Nwsp; Yrbk; Bsktbl; Hon Roll; Tae Kwon Do; TAD.

MOONEYHAN, AMANDA L; Marion HS; West Memphis, AR; (2); Spanish Clb; Hon Roll; NHS; Ecology Studies; Med Doctor.

MOONEYHAN, CHRISTOPHER E; Arkansas Sr HS; Texarkana, AR; (4); #45 in class; Key Clb; Mu Alpha Theta; Spanish Clb; Hon Roll.

MOONEYHAN, GINA M; Clay Co Central Jr Sr HS; Rector, AR; (2); Pres Church Yth Grp; German Clb; Science Clb; Hon Roll; Jr NHS; Gifted/Talented; Med.

MOORE, ALAN; Wynne HS; Wynne, AR; (4); 22/174; Church Yth Grp; FTA; Natl FFA Org; Red Cross Aide; SADD; Hon Roll; Acad Of Model Aeronautics; Hntng/Fshng; Gen Cooprtv Ed Clb Of Amer; Henderson ST Univ; Aviation.

MOORE, ALEXANDER D; Southside HS; Fort Smith, AR; (3); 84/502; Boy Scts; Church Yth Grp; Drama Clb; Latin Clb; Acpl Chr; Band; Chorus; Church Choir; Jazz Band; Mrchg Band; Mus Perf.

MOORE, ALEXIS R; Tuckerman HS; Tuckerman, AR; (2); Art Clb; FHA; Girl Scts; Natl Beta Clb; Spanish Clb; Teachers Aide; Acpl Chr; Chorus; Variety Show; Cit Awd; Crwnd Ms Tuckerman 95-; High Profile Univ; Child Psych.

MOORE, ALISON B; Van Buren Sr HS; Van Buren, AR; (3); FCA; FBLA; Mu Alpha Theta; Pep Clb; SADD; Pom Pon; Hon Roll; Jr NHS; GATE; U Of AR.

MOORE, AMANDA L; Jacksonville HS; Jacksonville, AR; (2); Art Clb; VP Church Yth Grp; FHA; Office Aide; Red Cross Aide; Spanish Clb; Pom Pon; Trk; Hon Roll; Flwshp Chrstn Stdnt; HI Pcfc U.

MOORE, AMANDA R; Dierks HS; Dierks, AR; (1); 1/56; Church Yth Grp; 4-H; FHA; Quiz Bowl; Yrbk; Rep Frsh Cls; Rep Soph Cls; Bsktbl; Chrldng; Trk; Horse Back Riding; Harding Univ; PT.

MOORE, AMY; Rogers HS; Rogers, AR; (4); 68/468; Church Yth Grp; FBLA; Teachers Aide; Gnrl Coop Ed; Rgrs Chmbr Comm Acad Achvmnt Awd; NWACC; Phys Thrpy.

MOORE, ANDREW D; Valley Springs Schl; Everton, AR; (2); 11/66; Art Clb; Pres Church Yth Grp; Key Clb; Quiz Bowl; Teachers Aide; Rptr Frsh Cls; Sec Soph Cls; Var Bsktbl; JV Trk; Hon Roll; US Nvl Acad.

MOORE, ANGIE; N Little Rock West Campus HS; North Little Rock, AR; (4); 128/504; Cmnty Wkr; Gov Hon Prg Awd; Drama Clb; FCA; FBLA; JA; Q&S; Speech Tm; Varsity Clb; Church Choir; Sr Cbnt; Ftr 500; AR ST U-Jonesboro; TV Prdctn.

MOORE, ANTHONY; Saratoga Schl; Washington, AR; (3); Natl Beta Clb; Natl FFA Org; Quiz Bowl; Church Choir; School Musical; L Bsktbl; Wt Lftg; Gov Hon Prg Awd; Hon Roll; Intl Frgn Lang Awd; U Of AR; Electrnc Engrng.

MOORE, APRIL; Van Buren Sr HS; Rudy, AR; (3); Church Yth Grp; FCA; HOBY; Mu Alpha Theta; Pep Clb; Spanish Clb; Speech Tm; Teachers Aide; Drill Tm; Rep Jr Cls; Miss Teenage Amer Nom; Schlsp To Westark; Attnd Dance Ofcrs Trng Camp; U Of AR.

MOORE, APRIL L; Midland HS; Concord, AR; (1); Church Yth Grp; Pep Clb; Chrldng; High Hon Roll; Chrldr Awd.

MOORE, BENJAMIN; Hackett Schl; Hackett, AR; (4); #12 in class; Church Yth Grp; Band; Church Choir; Drm Mjr(t); Mrchg Band; Boy Scts; FBLA; Spanish Clb; Teachers Aide; Pep Band; All Dist Bsbl 9-12th Grd 3 Yr Ltr Ftbl/Bsbl/Bsktbl; All Dist Ftbl 12th Grd; Gldn Glve Bsbl 9-11th Grd; Carl Albert ST Coll; Nrsng.

MOORE, BEVERLY A; Hampton Jr Sr HS; Hampton, AR; (3); 22/63; Church Yth Grp; 4-H; FTA; Teachers Aide; Chorus; Church Choir; 4-H Awd; Hon Roll; Reach Amer; PRIDE; TSU; Law.

MOORE, BRANDY; Casa Schl; Ola, AR; (4); #3 in class; Pres FHA; Treas Natl Beta Clb; Ed Yrbk; Sec Frsh Cls; Sec Treas Soph Cls; Sec Jr Cls; Sec Sr Cls; Capt Bsktbl; Sftbl; High Hon Roll; Petit Jean Tech Coll; Ag Bus.

MOORE, COLIN H; Southside HS; Fort Smith, AR; (2); 1/450; Rice Univ.

MOORE, CORVELLA M; Barton HS; Poplar Grove, AR; (3); Art Clb; Church Yth Grp; English Clb; 4-H; FHA; Spanish Clb; Speech Tm; Band; Church Choir; Mrchg Band; FHA Pres; Med Engr/Tech.

MOORE, DANNY; Southside HS; Fort Smith, AR; (3); 84/502; Boy Scts; Drama Clb; Mu Alpha Theta; Band; Chorus; School Musical; School Play; Rptr Nwsp; NHS; Pres Acad Fit Awd; Mus Perf.

MOORE, DONALD MARQ; Pine Bluff HS; Pine Bluff, AR; (4); 21/330; Am Leg Boys St; DECA; Office Aide; Chorus; L Bsktbl; L Golf; High Hon Roll; Hon Roll; NHS; Pres Acad Fit Awd; U Of AR Fayetteville.

MOORE, DUSTY J; Atkins Schl; Atkins, AR; (1); Church Yth Grp; Ski Clb; Most Imprvd Stu; Tnns; U Of AR; Comp Prgmr.

MOORE, GLENDA A; Mississippi Co Christian Acad; Blytheville, AR; (3); 5/14; Art Clb; Computer Clb; Pres French Clb; Sec Key Clb; Math Clb; Natl Beta Clb; Office Aide; Pep Clb; Science Clb; Pres SADD; Soph Fr Awd; Fayetteville.

MOORE, JAMIE E; Russellville Sr HS; Russellville, AR; (3); Church Yth Grp; GAA; Hosp Aide; Model UN; Office Aide; Varsity Clb; Band; Mrchg Band; Stage Crew; Variety Show; EF Guildes Tour; ATU; Speech Pethlgy.

MOORE, JASON; Sparkman Jr Sr HS; Sparkman, AR; (4); 1/24; Church Yth Grp; HOBY; Natl Beta Clb; Spanish Clb; Yrbk; Sec Stu Cncl; Var L Bsktbl; Hon Roll; Natl Ldrshp Forum; Beta Clb Pres; U Of AR; Comp Systms Engrng.

MOORE, JENNIFER M; Lonoke Jr HS; Lonoke, AR; (1); Church Yth Grp; Sec FHA; Church Choir; Hon Roll; NHS; Eclgy Club; Tap/Ballet/Jazz Dancng; Jonsboro; Primary Tchr.

MOORE, JEREMY E; Bryant Sr HS; Mabelvale, AR; (3); 22/347; Church Yth Grp; English Clb; French Clb; Office Aide; Teachers Aide; Crs Cntry; Trk; Hon Roll; Jr NHS; AR Chrstn Yth Flwshp Regnl Cabinet; Behavioral Sci; Ministry.

MOORE, JOHNATHAN W; Bay Jr Sr HS; Bay, AR; (3); 2/40; Natl Beta Clb; Natl FFA Org; Quiz Bowl; Scholastic Bowl; Science Clb; Pres Frsh Cls; Pres Soph Cls; Stat Bsktbl; Score Keeper; Cit Awd; Woodmen Of The World; U Of AR-LITTLE Rock; Pre-Med.

MOORE, JUNEVA; Farmington Jr Sr HS; Farmington, AR; (3); FBLA; Band; Color Guard; Mrchg Band; Pep Band; School Musical; High Hon Roll; Hon Roll; NHS; Pres Acad Fit Awd; U Of AR.

MOORE, KATIE P; Poyen Schl; Sheridan, AR; (3); 14/48; Church Yth Grp; Drama Clb; FCA; GAA; Natl Beta Clb; Church Choir; Yrbk; Sec Stu Cncl; Golf; Sftbl; Piano; AR Act Assn St Sftbl Champ Awd; Cert Outstdng Achvmnt German By Satellite; U Of Cntrl AR.

MOORE, KATINA T; Taylor HS; Taylor, AR; (3); Church Yth Grp; 4-H; FHA; Science Clb; Band; Rptr Jr Cls; Hon Roll; Dance Factory Dance Team; Miss Smiles Christmas Pageant; Homcmng Bsktbl Maid At Lage; Psych.

MOORE, KELLEY D; Lake Hamilton Sr HS; Royal, AR; (3); 25/258; 4-H; FBLA; Natl Beta Clb; Science Clb; Spanish Clb; Chrldng; High Hon Roll; NHS; Ntl Merit Ltr; Pres Acad Fit Awd; UCA; Optometry.

MOORE, KRISTEN M; West Memphis Christian Schl; Crawfordsville, AR; (2); VP Church Yth Grp; Stage Crew; Rep Soph Cls; Bsktbl; Sftbl; Trk; Vllybl; Hon Roll.

MOORE, LASHONDA; Cross Co Jr Sr HS; Wynne, AR; (3); 7/50; Church Yth Grp; FHA; Church Choir; Hon Roll; Beta Clb; Schltc Banquet; AR ST U; Bus Admin.

MOORE, LUCAS; Cabot HS; Ward, AR; (4); 18/299; Am Leg Boys St; French Clb; Pres Key Clb; NFL; Thesps; School Musical; School Play; VP Stu Cncl; NHS; Drama Clb; HS Frnscs Stu Dir; ASU Jonesboro; Theatre.

MOORE, MANDY L; Magnolia HS; Magnolia, AR; (4); 3/205; Church Yth Grp; FBLA; Hosp Aide; Mu Alpha Theta; Science Clb; Band; Color Guard; High Hon Roll; NHS; Pres Schlr; Stu Rotarian; Ouachita Bptst U; Med.

MOORE, MELISSA K; Magnolia HS; Magnolia, AR; (2); Church Yth Grp; FBLA; Band; Pres Soph Cls; Hon Roll; Pnthr Prd Drg Free Org; SAU; Phrmcst.

MOORE, MICHAEL; Vilonia HS; Vilonia, AR; (3); Am Leg Boys St; FBLA; Hosp Aide; Model UN; Natl Beta Clb; Spanish Clb; Teachers Aide; Med Explorer Post 446 Capt; Vilonia Quiz Bwl Tm Capt; Mu Alpha Theta VP; Pre Med.

MOORE, MICHELLE P; Nettleton HS; Jonesboro, AR; (3); 14/160; Sec French Clb; FBLA; Natl Beta Clb; Ed Nwsp; Hon Roll; Pres Acad Fit Awd; Best Personality Of Jr Cls; Select Choir; AR ST Univ; Pre-Med.

MOORE, NICOLE; Pangburn Jr Sr HS; Searcy, AR; (1); Church Yth Grp; Drama Clb; FBLA; FHA; Natl Beta Clb; Sec Frsh Cls; Bsktbl; Sftbl; Cit Awd; High Hon Roll; Stu Cncl & MPACT Pres; Chrch Camp Str Cmpr; Williams Bptst; Drama.

MOORE, NOELLE C; Crossett Sr HS; Crossett, AR; (2); 10/225; Church Yth Grp; HOBY; Natl Beta Clb; Yrbk; Lit Mag; VP Soph Cls; Var L Chrldng; Hon Roll; French Clb; FTA; Natl Sci Merit Awd; Renaissance Pgm; Vanderbilt Univ; Med; Dr.

MOORE, RICHARD L; Arkansas Sr HS; Texarkana, TX; (4); 32/299; Art Clb; Mu Alpha Theta; Office Aide; Pres VICA; Ed Nwsp; High Hon Roll; Jr NHS; NHS; Pres Acad Fit Awd; U Of AR; Elec Eng.

MOORE, ROSE M; Deer Jr Sr HS; Deer, AR; (3); 7/30; Church Yth Grp; Treas FBLA; Hist FHA; Treas Latin Clb; Math Clb; Teachers Aide; Chorus; Rptr Ed Nwsp; Rep Frsh Cls; Treas Soph Cls; AR All-ST Bsktbl 96; WET; First Rspndr; Envrmntl Studies/PT.

MOORE, SHELLEY A; Lake Hamilton Sr HS; Royal, AR; (3); Church Yth Grp; Cmnty Wkr; Treas FCA; 4-H; FBLA; Sec Natl Beta Clb; Office Aide; Science Clb; Spanish Clb; Var Chrldng; UCA; Optometry.

MOORE, SUMMER L; Lake Hamilton Sr HS; Hot Springs, AR; (2); Art Clb; FCA; Natl Beta Clb; Spanish Clb; Var Tennis; High Hon Roll; Hon Roll; Piano; OM 95.

MOORE, TARYNNE; Dierks HS; Newhope, AR; (4); 2/36; Church Yth Grp; Treas FHA; School Play; Yrbk; Rptr NHS; Sal; Art Clb; Quiz Bowl; Ofcr Sr Cls; Bsktbl; Amer Pride; Prjct Reach/Drug Team; GATE; Henderson ST U; Acctng.

MOORE, TINA M; Izard Co Cons Jr Sr HS; Oxford, AR; (3); FHA; Key Clb; Natl Beta Clb; Pep Clb; Spanish Clb; Teachers Aide; Yrbk; Hon Roll; Ntl Merit Ltr; Pres Acad Fit Awd; CHASE; Acad Awds Cvcs, Consmrs Ed, Spch; Mock Trial Tm; Plq All A 95-96; U Of AR Fayetteville; Pol Sci.

MOORE, TRISTA; Lamar HS; Lamar, AR; (1); Chorus; Church Choir; Chrldng; Gym; Prfct Atten Awd; U Of AR; Phy.

MORAGNE, CURTIS L; Parkview Arts-Science HS; North Little Rock, AR; (3); Cmnty Wkr; German Clb; Capt Var Bsktbl; Cit Awd; Hon Roll; Gntlmn's Club; Blck Comm Dvlprs Awd; Ath Club; Morris Brown Univ; Bus Econ.

MOREAU, JENNIFER A; Yellville Summit HS; Yellville, AR; (3); Pres Church Yth Grp; FBLA; Pres Girl Scts; Band; Chorus; Church Choir; Flag Corp; Ed Yrbk; Hon Roll; NHS; Schlstc Achvmt Vet Of Frgn Wars Post 5742 Savings Bond; U Of Cntrl AR; Elem Ed.

MOREAU, SARAH ELIZABETH; Mc Gehee HS; Lake Village, AR; (3); 29/101; Church Yth Grp; Cmnty Wkr; FBLA; FTA; Natl Beta Clb; Science Clb; Spanish Clb; Church Choir; Chorus; Hon Roll; U Of AR; Speech Therapy.

MOREFIELD, TANISHA; Wynne HS; Wynne, AR; (3); Church Yth Grp; FHA; Office Aide; Q&S; Spanish Clb; SADD; Rptr Nwsp; Ed Yrbk; Lit Mag; Stat Bsktbl; Acad Schlsp; EACC; Primary Ed.

MORELOCK, SAMANTHA J; Bauxite Jr Sr HS; Benton, AR; (2); Pres FHA; Spanish Clb; Teachers Aide; Jr NHS; Medicine.

MOREN, BOBBYE; J A Fair Sr HS; Little Rock, AR; (3); Art Clb; Church Yth Grp; Computer Clb; Drama Clb; FCA; FBLA; FHA; GAA; Natl Beta Clb; Office Aide; Teens For Christ; PT/COREOGRAPHER.

MORENO, AMBERLY; N Little Rock HS W; North Little Rock, AR; (3); 18/554; Drama Clb; Math Clb; Mu Alpha Theta; Natl Beta Clb; Stage Crew; High Hon Roll; Hon Roll; NHS; AR Govnr Schl; Hendrix Col; Bio.

MORGAN, AIMEE M; Gosnell Jr Sr HS; Cooter, MO; (3); Church Yth Grp; FHA; Key Clb; Mu Alpha Theta; Science Clb; Nwsp; Rep Frsh Cls; Rep Soph Cls; Rep Jr Cls; Chrldng; Dance; ASU; Bus Mgmt.

MORGAN, ALLISON BETH; Forrest City HS; Forrest City, AR; (4); 12/275; Am Leg Aux Girls St; Art Clb; Church Yth Grp; FBLA; Sec Mu Alpha Theta; Natl Beta Clb; Science Clb; Spanish Clb; Co-Capt Chrldng; High Hon Roll; Outstdng Chrldng Awd; Pre-Cal Awd; Prin Clb All A'S; ASU Beebe; Dntstry.

MORGAN, AMY L; Osceola HS; Osceola, AR; (2); Art Clb; French Clb; FBLA; Science Clb; Ofcr Stu Cncl; JV Capt Chrldng; Hon Roll; NHS; Crown Club; Trivium Quad Sympsm; AR ST; Tchr.

MORGAN, AMY L; Rural Special Schl; Fox, AR; (4); FHA; Teachers Aide; Chorus; Church Choir; School Play; Yrbk; Cit Awd; High Hon Roll; Hon Roll; Phys Thrpst.

MORGAN, CINDY M; Rural Special Schl; Fox, AR; (2); FHA; Spanish Clb; VP Frsh Cls; Rep Soph Cls; Bus Mngmt.

MORGAN, DAVID E; Blytheville Sr HS; Blytheville, AR; (3); Am Leg Boys St; Cmnty Wkr; Ofcr Bsbl; Ftbl; Cit Awd; Hon Roll; Cmptrs.

MORGAN, DEBRA R; Gosnell Jr Sr HS; Blytheville, AR; (1); Church Yth Grp; FCA; Teachers Aide; Capt L Bsktbl; Intrml Powder Puff Ftbl; Hon Roll; MS ST Univ; Sports Medicine.

MORGAN, GERON O; Russellville Sr HS; Pottsville, AR; (3); 140/340; Church Yth Grp; Cmnty Wkr; Band; Mrchg Band; Pep Band; JV Bsktbl; JV Vllybl; Cit Awd; Hon Roll; Pres Acad Fit Awd; ST/REGNL Majorette; AR HS Rodeo Assn; Amer Yth Qrtr Hrs Assn; ARKANSAS Vly Hrs Shw Assn; Model UN; Equine Med/Vet.

MORGAN, JASON; Farmington Jr Sr HS; Fayetteville, AR; (1); Band; Pep Band; Cit Awd; Hon Roll; Jr NHS; Pres Acad Fit Awd.

MORGAN, JIM; Southside HS; Fort Smith, AR; (4); Church Yth Grp; FCA; Mu Alpha Theta; Office Aide; Spanish Clb; Teachers Aide; Church Choir; School Play; Bsktbl; Ftbl; Westark CC; Engrng.

MORGAN, JONATHAN P; Rogers HS; Rogers, AR; (1); FBLA; Hon Roll; Prfct Atten Awd; Aquatic Biologist.

MORGAN, KRISTEN D; Mc Crory Jr Sr HS; Mc Crory, AR; (2); Spanish Clb; Teachers Aide; Chrldng; Applied Math I Awd; RN.

MORGAN, MELISSA L; Bergman Schl; Harrison, AR; (1); Church Yth Grp; Cmnty Wkr; FBLA; FHA; Natl Beta Clb; Pep Clb; Band; Chorus; Jazz Band; Pep Band; Received Awd For Highest Grd In Choir; Nrs; Vet.

MORGAN JR, PERRY A; Parkview Arts-Science HS; Mabelvale, AR; (3); All Region Orch; Sprts/Music/Sci.

MORGAN, RACHAEL; Guy Perkins Schl; Greenbrier, AR; (3); 2/25; Church Yth Grp; FBLA; FHA; GAA; Natl Beta Clb; Spanish Clb; Band; Chorus; Church Choir; Sftbl; Gilbert Chandler CC; Chld Ed.

MORGAN, RHIANNON; Ridgecrest HS; Paragould, AR; (4); 22/171; Church Yth Grp; FCA; Pres Scholastic Bowl; Lit Mag; VP Spanish Clb; Var Chrldng; NHS; US Bus Ed Awd; Trivium Quadrivium Sympsmprtcpnt; AR ST U.

MORGAN, RONIKA J; Northside HS; Fort Smith, AR; (4); Art Clb; Church Yth Grp; Drama Clb; Teachers Aide; Thesps; Band; Capt Flag Corp; Ofcr Sr Cls; Hon Roll; Partners In Christ; AR Tech Univ; Elem Ed.

MORGAN, SARAH; Star City HS; Star City, AR; (4); 17/107; Pres Church Yth Grp; Cmnty Wkr; Pres FCA; HOBY; VP Mu Alpha Theta; Church Choir; Pres Sr Cls; Rep Stu Cncl; Capt Chrldng; NHS; Whos Who Best All Arnd; U Of AR-MNTCLLO; Soc Wrkr.

MORGAN, SARAH ELIZABETH; Southside HS; Fort Smith, AR; (2); Church Yth Grp; Key Clb; Latin Clb; Service Clb; Band; Flag Corp; High Hon Roll; NHS; Pres Acad Fit Awd; Cmnty Wkr; Latin Natl Hnr Soc; Med Dr.

MORING, VICTORIA; Watson Chapel Sr HS; Pine Bluff, AR; (4); 2/240; Pres Church Yth Grp; French Clb; VP FBLA; HOBY; Model UN; Natl Beta Clb; School Play; Pres Sr Cls; Rep Stu Cncl; Sal; Lyon; Econ.

MORLEY, VICTORIA V; Elaine Jr Sr HS; Elaine, AR; (4); 8/2100; Art Clb; Church Yth Grp; VP Drama Clb; Quiz Bowl; VP Spanish Clb; Teachers Aide; Thesps; Church Choir; School Play; Rptr Yrbk; G/T; Hnr Roll; UAM; Cmptr Sci.

MORNINGSTAR, KENYA; Wynne HS; Wynne, AR; (2); Church Yth Grp; Drama Clb; Chorus; Church Choir; School Musical; Stage Crew; Chrldng; High Hon Roll; Hon Roll; Spanish NHS; Frgn Lang.

MORPHIS, AMANDA; Dermott HS; Dermott, AR; (3); Church Yth Grp; Natl Beta Clb; Science Clb; Band; Cit Awd; Hon Roll; Ntl Merit Ltr; Hendrix; Psych.

MORPHIS, CHRISTY; Lakeside HS; Lake Village, AR; (3); 5/82; Church Yth Grp; Drama Clb; FBLA; FHA; Chorus; School Play; Sec Stu Cncl; Hon Roll; NHS; Jr Cnslr Camp; Pride Tem; U Of AR Fayetteville; Msc Ed.

MORRELL, BROOKE N; Alma HS; Alma, AR; (2); Church Yth Grp; FCA; Treas French Clb; FBLA; Drill Tm; Ofcr Stu Cncl; Pom Pon; Swmmng; Vllybl; NHS.

MORRIES, KIP; Manila HS; Manila, AR; (3); Church Yth Grp; Cmnty Wkr; Pres Natl Beta Clb; Natl FFA Org; Red Cross Aide; Varsity Clb; Chorus; School Musical; School Play; Var Bsbl.

MORRIES, WHITNEY D; Manila HS; Manila, AR; (1); Church Yth Grp; FHA; Natl Beta Clb; Chorus; Church Choir; Hon Roll; Fire Marshall; Nrs.

MORRIS, AARON K; Glen Rose HS; Malvern, AR; (3); Art Clb; Church Yth Grp; FCA; French Clb; FBLA; Spanish Clb; Teachers Aide; Church Choir; Pres Frsh Cls; Ofcr Bsbl; Evangel; Hist.

MORRIS, ANDREW E; Mills HS; Little Rock, AR; (3); 17/298; Art Clb; Boy Scts; Cmnty Wkr; FCA; Var Capt Ice Hcky; High Hon Roll; Hon Roll; NHS; Roller Hockey; Camping Ecology Group.

MORRIS, ANTHONY R; Watson Chapel Sr HS; Pine Bluff, AR; (4); Universal Techinst; Auto Mech.

MORRIS, BRANDI; Green Forest Jr Sr HS; Berryville, AR; (4); 4/69; Am Leg Aux Girls St; Drama Clb; French Clb; FBLA; FHA; Intnl Clb; Natl Beta Clb; Teachers Aide; Var Chrldng; Hon Roll; VP, Pres FHA; Multi Yr Lstngs; N AR CC; Elem Ed.

MORRIS, BRENDA; Lee Sr HS; West Memphis, AR; (3); 7/166; Church Yth Grp; Natl Beta Clb; Spanish Clb; Church Choir; Bsktbl; Trk; Hon Roll; HOSA; FFA; U Of Pine Bluff; Psycht.

MORRIS, BRET P; Rogers HS; Rogers, AR; (2); Church Yth Grp; FCA; FBLA; JV Bsbl; OU; Ath Act; Coaching.

MORRIS, BRIDGETTE; Harrisburg HS; Harrisburg, AR; (4); 1/51; Am Leg Aux Girls St; Church Yth Grp; FBLA; Office Aide; Science Clb; Teachers Aide; Rptr Soph Cls; Rptr Jr Cls; Sec Treas Sr Cls; Rep Stu Cncl; AR ST U; Communictv Disorders.

MORRIS, CHRISTINA L; Mountain Home HS; Mountain Home, AR; (3); Church Yth Grp; Spanish Clb; Church Choir; Chrch Mssnry Tm; AR ST Univ; Spch Pathlgy.

MORRIS, DARIOUS L; Dequeen HS; De Queen, AR; (1); Church Yth Grp; 4-H; Natl FFA Org; SADD; Church Choir; JV Var Bsbl; JV L Bsktbl; JV L Ftbl; JV L Trk; High Hon Roll; Vet.

MORRIS, DEKARA; Crawfordsville HS; Crawfordsville, AR; (4); 2/24; Church Yth Grp; French Clb; FHA; Natl FFA Org; Pep Clb; Quiz Bowl; Chorus; Church Choir; Capt Chrldng; High Hon Roll; Published Poem 94-95; Most Athl & Popular 95-96; Hmcmng Qn 95-96; AR ST U; Ed.

MORRIS, DEVIN; Lake Hamilton Sr HS; Hot Springs, AR; (1); Dance Clb; FHA; Pep Clb; Spanish Clb; Bsktbl; Chrldng; Gym; Trk; Pres Acad Fit Awd; UCA; PT/OT.

MORRIS, ERICA; Melbourne HS; Melbourne, AR; (2); FCA; FBLA; Natl Beta Clb; Band; Sec Frsh Cls; Treas Soph Cls; Sftbl; Hon Roll; HOT; Bus.

MORRIS, ERIN B; J A Fair Sr HS; Little Rock, AR; (2); Church Yth Grp; FBLA; FTA; Natl Beta Clb; Teachers Aide; Church Choir; Nwsp; Ed Yrbk; High Hon Roll; Hon Roll; U Of Cntrl AR; Lawyer.

MORRIS, JACOB F; Black Rock Jr Sr HS; Portia, AR; (2); Boy Scts; FBLA; FHA; Natl FFA Org; Chorus; 1st Pl In Art Cont Show.

MORRIS, JOSHUA L; Dumas HS; Winchester, AR; (4); 4/127; Am Leg Boys St; Boy Scts; Cmnty Wkr; JA; Natl Beta Clb; Phtg Yrbk; Cit Awd; High Hon Roll; Kiwanis Awd; NHS; Stu Of Yr Amer Legion; Amer Legion Stu Of Month; Mrt Awd In Geog; Sci Fair Wnnr; U Of AR; Bus Acctng; CPA.

MORRIS, KELLIE; Mountain Home HS; Mountain Home, AR; (3); 54/253; Am Leg Aux Girls St; Sec FCA; FBLA; Sec FHA; Rep Spanish Clb; Key Clb; Sec Sr Cls; Var Chrldng; Hon Roll; Score Keeper; AR ST Univ; Nrsng.

MORRIS, LAURA E; Conway Sr HS; Conway, AR; (3); Church Yth Grp; FBLA; Natl Beta Clb; Q&S; Spanish Clb; Church Choir; Orch; Ed Yrbk; Hon Roll.

MORRIS, LUCAS A; Fordyce HS; Bearden, AR; (2); 18/98; Church Yth Grp; FCA; Quiz Bowl; Lit Mag; Ofcr Bsbl; Bsktbl; Ftbl; Trk; High Hon Roll; Amer Leg Bsbll.

MORRIS, MELISSA D; Cabot HS; Austin, AR; (2); Church Yth Grp; Key Clb; Spanish Clb; Hon Roll; Jr NHS; JUST Club; Pride Club; Baylor U; Mnstry/Hm Mssns.

MORRIS, MICHELLE M; Lincoln HS; Lincoln, AR; (1); FBLA; Spanish Clb; Band; Mrchg Band; High Hon Roll; Ftr Prblm Slvrs Tm.

MORRIS, MISTY; Dequeen HS; Gillham, AR; (3); Office Aide; Hon Roll; NHS.

MORRIS, NICOLE V; Lincoln HS; Lincoln, AR; (1); FBLA; Science Clb; Spanish Clb; Bsktbl; Chrldng; Gym; Sftbl; High Hon Roll; U AR; Med.

MORRIS, PAUL R; Piggott HS; Piggott, AR; (4); 10/60; Church Yth Grp; FCA; French Clb; JA; Natl Beta Clb; Natl FFA Org; Science Clb; Church Choir; School Play; Stage Crew; FFA VP; FFA Jr Adv; AR Tech Univ; Ag Bus.

MORRIS, SHANNA E; Mountain Home HS; Mountain Home, AR; (4); FBLA; Natl Beta Clb; AR Tech U; Wldlf.

MORRIS, TAMELA N; Marked Tree Jr Sr HS; Marked Tree, AR; (2); Art Clb; Computer Clb; FHA; GAA; Natl FFA Org; Office Aide; ROTC; Band; Chorus; Yrbk; Nrsng; Modeling; Law.

MORRIS, TORI; Rural Special Schl; Mountain View, AR; (3); 1/19; Church Yth Grp; FBLA; FHA; Natl Beta Clb; Natl FFA Org; Quiz Bowl; Spanish Clb; Acpl Chr; VP Frsh Cls; Pres Soph Cls.

MORRISON, ANDREA; Concord Jr Sr HS; Concord, AR; (4); 3/27; FBLA; FHA; Quiz Bowl; Science Clb; Band; Hon Roll; Navy Hnrs Pgm; Pres Ed Awds Pgm; Julian Martin Schlsp; Gateway Tech Coll.

MORRISON, COURTNEY E; Bismarck Jr-Sr HS; Bismarck, AR; (2); Church Yth Grp; Natl Beta Clb; Church Choir; Phtg Yrbk; Sec Soph Cls; Stat Bsktbl; Mgr(s); Score Keeper; Sftbl; Hon Roll; Nrsng; Tchr.

MORRISON, GABRIEL; Rural Special Schl; Fox, AR; (4); 3/25; Church Yth Grp; FBLA; Natl Beta Clb; Natl FFA Org; Spanish Clb; Chorus; Church Choir; Hon Roll; Bsktbl Team Mgr; U Of AR.

MORRISON, HEATHER S; Hot Springs HS; Hot Springs Natio, AR; (2); Art Clb; Church Yth Grp; Spanish Clb; Thesps; School Play; Hon Roll.

MORRISON, JAMES L; Parkers Chapel Schl; El Dorado, AR; (4); 3/46; Am Leg Boys St; FBLA; Natl Beta Clb; Science Clb; Spanish Clb; Teachers Aide; Acpl Chr; Band; Chorus; Jazz Band; PRIDE; AR Acad Chlng Schol; U Of Cntrl AR; Music.

MORRISON, JANA; Pea Ridge HS; Pea Ridge, AR; (2); FHA; Spanish Clb; Yrbk; Hon Roll; NHS; Educl Talent Srch; Med/Bus.

MORRISON, LINDY R; Magnolia HS; Magnolia, AR; (2); Pep Clb; Band; Bsktbl; Pom Pon; Vllybl; Hon Roll; SAU; LPN; RN; Respirtry Thrpst.

MORRISON, MICHAEL; Cabot HS; Cabot, AR; (4); CAP; French Clb; Hosp Aide; ROTC; Teachers Aide; Color Guard; Drill Tm; School Musical; Lit Mag; Hon Roll; Retrd Ofcrs Assn & Amer Legn Miltry Excl Awds; Otstdng Aerospc Sci III Cadt; Barksdale AFB SLS Grad; US Air Force; RN.

MORRISON, STACY; Cedarville Jr Sr HS; Uniontown, AR; (4); 1/65; Chess Clb; Church Yth Grp; Quiz Bowl; Science Clb; Teachers Aide; Bsktbl; Hon Roll; NHS; Pres Acad Fit Awd; Val; Westark CC.

MORRISON, TAMEKA N; Blevins HS; Hope, AR; (3); Art Clb; 4-H; FBLA; FHA; Church Choir; School Play; Yrbk; Treas Jr Cls; Rep Stu Cncl; Bsktbl; Math & Sci Upwrd Bnd; Rsprtry Thphs.

MORROW, AMANDA L; De Soto Schl; West Helena, AR; (2); Drama Clb; Hon Roll; Rhodes.

MORROW, HEATHER D; Riverview HS; Georgetown, AR; (3); Am Leg Aux Girls St; Church Yth Grp; Cmnty Wkr; Drama Clb; French Clb; FBLA; FHA; Band; Chorus; Church Choir.

MORTON, ASHLEY O; Mt St Mary Acad; Little Rock, AR; (2); Church Yth Grp; Cmnty Wkr; FCA; Drill Tm; Sec Frsh Cls; Pres Soph Cls; Ofcr Stu Cncl; Var Trk; French Hon Soc; Hon Roll.

MORTON, DOMINIK D; John L Mcclellan Magnet HS; Little Rock, AR; (2); FBLA; FHA; FTA; Girl Scts; Drill Tm; Cit Awd; Hon Roll; DARE; PRIDE; Future 500; Pediatrcn.

MORTON, JOSEPH A; Bradford Jr Sr HS; Bradford, AR; (3); Art Clb; FHA; Natl Beta Clb; Natl FFA Org; Hon Roll; ASU-BEEBE; Diesel Mechanic.

MORTON, SARAH E; Harrison Sr HS; Harrison, AR; (3); 15/200; Am Leg Aux Girls St; Church Yth Grp; Drama Clb; GAA; Key Clb; Science Clb; Spanish Clb; Thesps; School Play; Yrbk; Shared In St Girls Crss Cntry Championship; Theatric Production; Acting.

MOSELEY, JOSEPH SALEM; Warren Jr HS; New Edinburg, AR; (1); 15/135; Church Yth Grp; FCA; VICA; Church Choir; Stage Crew; Ed Nwsp; Ed Yrbk; JV L Ftbl; Wt Lftg; Outstdng Acad Achvmt In Pres Ed Awds Pgm; FL ST U; Elec Engr.

MOSELEY, MELISSA C; Fairview HS; Camden, AR; (2); Church Yth Grp; Drama Clb; Letterman Clb; Natl Beta Clb; Natl FFA Org; Office Aide; Church Choir; School Musical; Socr; Var L Tennis; UALR; Pharmacist.

MOSELEY, SUSANNE; Warren Sr HS; Warren, AR; (4); Art Clb; French Clb; FBLA; Natl Beta Clb; Band; Var Bsktbl; Tennis; Trk; Hon Roll; NHS; YMCA Sftbl; UAM; Acctng.

MOSER, LESLIE G; North Little Rock Hs-East; North Little Rock, AR; (2); Teachers Aide; Band; Mrchg Band; Hon Roll; Rainbows For Girls; Sewing; Tchr/Music/Marine Bio.

MOSER, MELANIE A; Cushman Schl; Batesville, AR; (3); Church Yth Grp; FBLA; FHA; Library Aide; Math Clb; VP Natl Beta Clb; Office Aide; Rptr Science Clb; Teachers Aide; Sec Band; Span Awd; Einstein Awd; Beta Clb VP 95-96; Coll Of Ozarks; Elem Ed.

MOSES, BRANDIE N; Booneville Jr Sr HS; Booneville, AR; (3); 15/82; FBLA; FHA; FTA; Letterman Clb; Natl Beta Clb; Science Clb; VP Frsh Cls; Sec Jr Cls; Var L Bsktbl; Var Tennis; Univ Of Central AR; PT.

MOSES, GREG; Southside HS; Fort Smith, AR; (3); 41/502; Church Yth Grp; Drama Clb; Mu Alpha Theta; Quiz Bowl; Pres Thesps; Church Choir; Orch; School Musical; School Play; NHS.

MOSHER, SAMANTHA; Lake Hamilton Sr HS; Hot Springs, AR; (1); 1/264; Natl Beta Clb; Spanish Clb; Chrldng; Gym; Computer Clb; High Hon Roll; Hon Roll; Ntl Merit Ltr; Frosh Valntn Rylty Maid.

MOSHINSKIE, LAURA; Lake Hamilton Sr HS; Hot Springs, AR; (4); 23/249; Library Aide; Natl Beta Clb; Natl FFA Org; Spanish Clb; Cit Awd; High Hon Roll; NHS; Pres Acad Fit Awd; Wolf Pride; All Amer Schlr Awd; Natl Ldrshp/Svc Awd.

MOSLEY, ANITA; Hughes Jr-Sr HS; Hughes, AR; (3); Band; Church Choir; Color Guard; Mrchg Band; School Musical; VP Frsh Cls; Pres Soph Cls; Pres Stu Cncl; Hon Roll; Math Clb; Gftd/Tlntd; 17th Annual Trivium Quodrivium Sympsm; IN U Kokomo; Electrnc Engrng.

MOSLEY, MARCUS A; Lake Hamilton Sr HS; Hot Springs, AR; (3); 12/258; Boy Scts; Church Yth Grp; CAP; Office Aide; Spanish Clb; Church Choir; Color Guard; Rep Stu Cncl; Hon Roll; Tae-Kwon-Do; Product Tester Cnsmr Rprts; Air Force Acad; Aerontcl Engrng.

MOSS, ANGELA; Woodlawn Schl; Rison, AR; (4); 4/23; Am Leg Aux Girls St; FBLA; FHA; Natl Beta Clb; Band; Drm Mjr(t); School Musical; Rptr Nwsp; Phtg Yrbk; VP Jr Cls; AR St Bwlng Yth Ldrs Pgm Sec 94-95; Pine Blff Yth Bwlng Assn Sec; Acctng.

MOSS, CLAUDETTE D; Nevada Schl; Waldo, AR; (1); Church Yth Grp; FHA; Natl Beta Clb; Quiz Bowl; Teachers Aide; Church Choir; VP Frsh Cls; Hon Roll; NHS; Homcmng Maid; Tnlt Search; Environmental Clb; UALR; Lawyer.

MOSS, DESIREE; Farmington Jr Sr HS; Farmington, AR; (3); Pres Frsh Cls; VP Jr Cls; VP Stu Cncl; Bsktbl; Chrldng; Trk; High Hon Roll; NHS; Ntl Merit Ltr; Hmcmng Bsktbl Ct 9th Grd Frosh Maid; Hmcmng Ftbl Jr Maid; Natl Cand For Ms Tn Of Amer; U Of KS; Pre-Med.

MOSS, ELONDA Y; Lewisville HS; Lewisville, AR; (3); 8/35; Church Yth Grp; English Clb; SADD; Band; Church Choir; School Play; Bsktbl; Applied Bio & Chem Awd; Hairstyling; SAU; Phy Therapy Asst.

MOSS, JAVANA J; Central Sr HS; Little Rock, AR; (4); 141/540; Church Yth Grp; FBLA; HOBY; Natl Beta Clb; VP Spanish Clb; Co-Capt Drill Tm; Pres Soph Cls; Rep Stu Cncl; Cit Awd; High Hon Roll; Black Culture Soc; Teen Talk; Clark U; Psych.

MOSS, JENNY A; Newport HS; Newport, AR; (3); 1/130; Am Leg Aux Girls St; Church Yth Grp; Latin Clb; Q&S; Spanish Clb; Drill Tm; Nwsp; Ofcr Stu Cncl; Tennis; Jr NHS; N AR Conf Cncl On Yth Ministries.

MOSS, MYISHA N; Palestine-Wheatley HS; Palestine, AR; (3); 18/52; Am Leg Aux Girls St; FHA; Office Aide; Chorus; Church Choir; Ofcr Stu Cncl; Chrldng; Hon Roll; Prfct Atten Awd; Drg Fr Club; Hannibal-Lagrange Coll; Elem Ed.

MOTE, RICHELLE; Van Buren Sr HS; Van Buren, AR; (4); 30/264; Art Clb; French Clb; FBLA; FHA; Mu Alpha Theta; Band; Color Guard; Mrchg Band; Pep Band; Ed Lit Mag; Woodwind Quintet; Silhouette Winter Guard Mem.

MOTLEY, JOHN D; Vilonia HS; Vilonia, AR; (3); 51/151; Church Yth Grp; CAP; Drama Clb; FCA; FBLA; Model UN; Speech Tm; Church Choir; School Play; Stage Crew.

MOTT, MICHAEL; Bald Knob HS; Bald Knob, AR; (3); 1/125; Am Leg Boys St; Church Yth Grp; FBLA; Natl Beta Clb; Quiz Bowl; Spanish Clb; Acpl Chr; Band; Chorus; Church Choir; Dixieland Band; Brass Quintet; TUBA; Julliard Schl Of Music; Music.

MOUNCE, ANGELA M; Rogers HS; Lowell, AR; (2); Church Yth Grp; Chorus; Hon Roll; Horseback Riding; Univ Of AR; Elem Ed.

MOUNCE, BRANDI J; Nevada Schl; Emmet, AR; (3); French Clb; FBLA; Letterman Clb; Natl Beta Clb; Teachers Aide; Band; Rptr Nwsp; VP Frsh Cls; Hon Roll; Drug Free Tm; Lib Clb; Rad.

MOUNTS, CORY N; Dierks HS; Newhope, AR; (2); 3/50; Church Yth Grp; Quiz Bowl; Pres Frsh Cls; Rep Soph Cls; VP Stu Cncl; Bsktbl; Ftbl; Golf; NHS; Prfct Atten Awd; Henderson ST.

MOURNING, MARTENE L; Lincoln HS; Prairie Grove, AR; (2); #1 in class; Church Yth Grp; Debate Tm; FBLA; Natl Beta Clb; Quiz Bowl; Spanish Clb; Band; Mrchg Band; Cit Awd; High Hon Roll; Law.

MOUROT, MATTHEW G; Sacred Heart Schl; Morrilton, AR; (3); #4 in class; Am Leg Boys St; Art Clb; Key Clb; Natl Beta Clb; SADD; Pres Soph Cls; VP Stu Cncl; Bsktbl; High Hon Roll; NHS.

MOURTON, MANDY R; Waldron HS; Waldron, AR; (3); 10/110; Church Yth Grp; Letterman Clb; Natl Beta Clb; Var Bsktbl; Var Sftbl; Var Vllybl; Hon Roll; Henderson ST Univ; Sports Med.

MOVER, ALYSSA K; Dewitt HS; De Witt, AR; (2); French Clb; FBLA; Band; Mrchg Band; Pep Band; Perfect Atdnc 2nd Sem 10th Grd.

MOXLEY, TORI; Mc Gehee HS; Mc Gehee, AR; (3); 6/100; Cmnty Wkr; FBLA; FTA; Library Aide; Mu Alpha Theta; Natl Beta Clb; Science Clb; Spanish Clb; Band; Church Choir; NHS Exec Comm; Med.

MOYE, BRANDI M; Cave City HS; Cave City, AR; (2); #1 in class; Church Yth Grp; French Clb; Key Clb; Math Clb; Science Clb; Teachers Aide; Bsktbl; Sftbl; High Hon Roll; Cavemen Agnst Drugs; Sr Beta Club.

MUCKELBERG, MEGAN; Bald Knob HS; Bald Knob, AR; (2); 1/115; Church Yth Grp; FBLA; Spanish Clb; Var Chrldng; Var Sftbl; Var Trk; High Hon Roll; Beta Clb; Psych.

MUDD, MINDY; Rogers HS; Rogers, AR; (4); FCA; Office Aide; SADD; Band; Rptr Stu Cncl; Var JV Bsktbl; Var Sftbl; Trk; Vllybl; Hon Roll; Chamber Of Cmmrce Acad Awds; Elem Ed.

MUEHLER, VANESSA L; Flippin Jr Sr HS; Mountain Home, AR; (2); Treas Art Clb; Church Yth Grp; Rep Drama Clb; FBLA; GAA; Sec Key Clb; Pres Science Clb; Sec SADD; Band; Church Choir; Interact Clb; Hnrs Awd Eng, Sci & Art.

MUELLER, JEREMY; Arkansas Schl Math & Science; Van Buren, AR; (4); 4-H; Mu Alpha Theta; Quiz Bowl; Speech Tm; Band; Jazz Band; Mrchg Band; Orch; School Play; Stage Crew; Westark CC; Comp Sci.

MULDREW, DURAND C; Saratoga Schl; Ozan, AR; (3); Church Yth Grp; Cmnty Wkr; 4-H; FHA; Natl FFA Org; Science Clb; SADD; Teachers Aide; Church Choir; School Play; Outstdng Music Awd; Cmptrs; Piano; Texarkana Coll; Acctng.

MULL, JONI; Little Rock Acad; Little Rock, AR; (4); 12/20; Am Leg Aux Girls St; Band; School Musical; Nwsp; Phtg Yrbk; Var Bsktbl; Var Chrldng; Var Sftbl; Var Vllybl; Hon Roll; UALR; Elem Ed Tchr.

MULL, MARSHALL L; Holly Grove HS; Holly Grove, AR; (4); 11/28; Boy Scts; 4-H; FBLA; FHA; German Clb; Natl FFA Org; Var Bsktbl; Trk; 4-H Awd; Hon Roll; Mary Holmes Coll; Cmptr Tech.

MULLEN, JILL; Rogers HS; Rogers, AR; (4); 18/468; Church Yth Grp; FCA; FBLA; Model UN; Band; Trk; Vllybl; High Hon Roll; Pres Acad Fit Awd; Am HS Math Exm St Rcgntn; Sthrn Nazrne U; Bus Admin.

MULLEN, MELISSA A; Rogers HS; Rogers, AR; (3); 26/596; Church Yth Grp; FBLA; Sec FHA; Teachers Aide; Bsktbl; Crs Cntry; Trk; Vllybl; High Hon Roll; NHS; AR Tech Univ; Acctng.

MULLENIX, LORI; Mt Ida Jr Sr HS; Mount Ida, AR; (3); Dance Clb; FCA; Natl Beta Clb; Natl FFA Org; Rep Stu Cncl; JV Var Bsktbl; Capt Var Chrldng; Var Sftbl; Var Trk; Hon Roll; AAU Bsktbl; All Dist, Hnrb Mntn, All Conf, All Region MVP, All St Bsktbl; All St Track; Nurse.

MULLIGAN, HOLLY L; Sheridan Sr HS; Sheridan, AR; (2); 35/286; Church Yth Grp; Cmnty Wkr; FCA; Var Mgr Bsktbl; JV Var Vllybl; Jr NHS; Teen Invlvmnt Teen Ldrs.

MULLINS, YULONDA R; Magnolia HS; Magnolia, AR; (4); #84 in class; Teachers Aide; Bsktbl; Powder Puff Ftbl; Tennis; Vllybl; Cit Awd.

MUNN, BONNIE; Perryville Jr Sr HS; Houston, AR; (1); Church Yth Grp; FCA; 4-H; School Play; VP Frsh Cls; JV Bsktbl; JV Chrldng; JV Trk; Pres Acad Fit Awd; 4-H Awd; CTT; U Of AR; Tchng.

MUNNS, HALIKAH D; Mills HS; Jacksonville, AR; (3); 43/255; Church Yth Grp; FBLA; FTA; Math Clb; Natl Beta Clb; Science Clb; Spanish Clb; SADD; Band; Church Choir; Majorette; AP Hnrs; U Of Memphis; Pre-Law.

MUNROE, JENNIFER; Highland HS; Ash Flat, AR; (3); 1/110; Church Yth Grp; Sec 4-H; HOBY; Treas Key Clb; Natl Beta Clb; Rep VP Natl FFA Org; Quiz Bowl; Teachers Aide; Treas Jr Cls; Ofcr Stu Cncl; NYLC 96; Vet.

MURPHREE, JENNIFER; Parkers Chapel Schl; El Dorado, AR; (4); 3/45; Am Leg Aux Girls St; FBLA; Natl Beta Clb; Spanish Clb; Teachers Aide; School Play; Ed Phtg Yrbk; Bsktbl; Cit Awd; Hon Roll; Camp Fire; South AR CC; Elem Ed.

MURPHREE, MOLLIE; Mt Ida Jr Sr HS; Mount Ida, AR; (2); 2/45; FHA; Natl Beta Clb; Natl FFA Org; Sec Rep Stu Cncl; Var Chrldng; Hon Roll; Pres Acad Fit Awd; PRIDE; Vanderbilt; Pharm.

MURPHY, AARON B; Sloan Hendrix HS; Imboden, AR; (3); 1/30; Church Yth Grp; Cmnty Wkr; FBLA; Natl Beta Clb; Pep Clb; Quiz Bowl; VP Frsh Cls; Treas Jr Cls; VP Stu Cncl; Ofcr Bsbl.

MURPHY, ALYSHA M; Cabot HS; Cabot, AR; (3); Art Clb; Church Yth Grp; Spanish Clb; Teachers Aide; Band; Mrchg Band; Pep Band; All Rgn Band 3 Yrs; Solo Ensmbl 3 Yrs.

MURPHY, AMY N; Mc Crory Jr Sr HS; Wynne, AR; (3); FBLA; FHA; FTA; Letterman Clb; Spanish Clb; School Play; Powder Puff Ftbl; L Tennis; Hon Roll; NHS; FFA; Medcl.

MURPHY, BOBBY; Russellville Sr HS; Russellville, AR; (3); Church Yth Grp; Spanish Clb; Band; Mrchg Band; High Hon Roll; Jr NHS; Prfct Atten Awd; Pres Acad Fit Awd; All-Stars Jr Mem; Mech Engrng.

MURPHY, BREE; Yerger Jr HS; Hope, AR; (1); Office Aide; Rep Frsh Cls; Rep Stu Cncl; Var Chrldng; Var Gym; High Hon Roll.

MURPHY, CANDACE; Morrilton Sr HS; Menifee, AR; (2); Church Yth Grp; FHA; Hosp Aide; Spanish Clb; Ofcr Soph Cls; Bsktbl; Trk; Vllybl; Hon Roll.

MURPHY, JAMAE; Westside Jr Sr HS; Bono, AR; (4); 6/79; Church Yth Grp; HOBY; Spanish Clb; Teachers Aide; Sec Band; Mrchg Band; Rep Stu Cncl; Hon Roll; NHS; Pres Acad Fit Awd; Chrstns Mkng A Dffrnc Pres; AR ST U; Msc Ed.

MURPHY, JESSICA E; Bentonville Sr HS; Bentonville, AR; (2); Church Yth Grp; Computer Clb; French Clb; Girl Scts; Band; Drill Tm; VP Frsh Cls; Chrldng; High Hon Roll; Jr NHS; Engrng.

MURPHY, JOSEPH P; Bryant Sr HS; Alexander, AR; (2); Band; Jazz Band; Mrchg Band; Pep Band; Hon Roll; UA Fayetteville; Comp Scis.

MURPHY, MARILYN R; Nevada Schl; Chidester, AR; (2); FHA; FTA; Natl Beta Clb; Rptr Nwsp; Hon Roll; Pres Acad Fit Awd; Drug Team; Tch Drw Awrns Elem; Henderson; Tchr/PT.

MURPHY, MARSHA L; Glen Rose HS; Malvern, AR; (2); FHA; Math Clb; Spanish Clb; Teachers Aide; Drill Tm; Bsktbl; Trk.

MURPHY, RICKY F; Southside HS; Fort Smith, AR; (2); Band; Mrchg Band; Swmmng; Trk; Hon Roll; NHS; Pres Acad Fit Awd; Ping Pong Clb.

MURPHY, STORMY; Magnolia HS; Hampton, AR; (3); 29/230; Church Yth Grp; French Clb; Hosp Aide; Mu Alpha Theta; Natl FFA Org; Science Clb; Teachers Aide; Yrbk; Powder Puff Ftbl; Hon Roll; Elem Ed.

MURRAY, ANGELA E; Harmony Grove Jr Sr HS; Benton, AR; (2); 1/60; Model UN; Capt Quiz Bowl; Ed Yrbk; Pres Soph Cls; Rep Stu Cncl; DAR Awd; Hon Roll; NHS; Rep French Clb; Natl Beta Clb; AR Jr Sci & Hum Symposium Del; All-St Band; Math Prof.

MURRAY, APRIEL; Norphlet HS; El Dorado, AR; (2); 1/57; Church Yth Grp; FBLA; Quiz Bowl; Spanish Clb; Band; Color Guard; Mrchg Band; Ofcr Stu Cncl; Stat Bsktbl; High Hon Roll; Schltc Awd.

MURRAY, BRANDY; Clay Co Central Jr Sr HS; Rector, AR; (4); 1/59; Sec Hist FBLA; Sec Treas Science Clb; Yrbk; Capt Chrldng; Tennis; Pres Jr NHS; NHS; Val; VP Frsh Cls; Homcmng Royalty 92-93 & 95-96; Lib Clb Pres 95-96; Dist FBLA Intro To Bus Cmptn 2nd Pl; AR ST U; Accntng.

MURRAY, JAMES A; Cabot HS; Cabot, AR; (3); Church Yth Grp; Hosp Aide; ROTC; Teachers Aide; Color Guard; Drill Tm; Hon Roll; Natl Yth Ldrshp Frm; Span Total Immrsn-AEGIS; AFJROTC Ldrshp Schl; U Of AR-FAYETTEVILLE; Pilot.

MURRAY, JONATHAN D; Trumann HS; Trumann, AR; (3); French Clb; Math Clb; Natl FFA Org; Science Clb; Bsktbl; Hon Roll; NHS; Chrstn; Excl Acad Awds; AR ST U.

MURRAY, NATHAN E; Harding Acad; Searcy, AR; (4); 8/30; FBLA; Key Clb; Sec Treas Natl Beta Clb; Acpl Chr; School Musical; Nwsp; Bsktbl; Ftbl; Trk; Church Yth Grp; Crtr Of Advncd Math Prgm; 5th Pl ST FBLA Comp Dsktp Pblshng; Harding Univ; Physc/Engrng.

MURRAY, SABIAN D; West Memphis HS; West Memphis, AR; (3); Church Yth Grp; Varsity Clb; Ed Yrbk; Var JV Bsktbl; Hon Roll; Prfct Atten Awd; AR ST Univ; Cmptr Pgm/NBA.

MURRAY, TRACY L; Clay Co Central Jr Sr HS; Lafe, AR; (2); Church Yth Grp; German Clb; JV Var Bsktbl; Var Sftbl; Hon Roll; Jr NHS; NHS; Ntl Yth Ldrshp Conf Nom; Stu Cncl Vvp Nom; Hindrix Univ; Phy Ed.

MURRELL, KEISHA R; Central HS; West Helena, AR; (2); Church Yth Grp; 4-H; Math Clb; ROTC; Teachers Aide; Chorus; Church Choir; Drill Tm; 4-H Awd; Hon Roll; MS ST; Ed.

MURRY, APRIL M; Magnolia HS; Magnolia, AR; (4); 13/207; Church Yth Grp; Mu Alpha Theta; Band; Church Choir; Mrchg Band; Yrbk; Powder Puff Ftbl; High Hon Roll; NHS; FBLA; Natl Yth Ldshp Forum On Med; S AR Univ; X-Ray Tech.

MURRY, TAMARA A; Sheridan Sr HS; Mabelvale, AR; (2); 5/250; Cmnty Wkr; FCA; Chorus; School Play; Nwsp; Lit Mag; Rptr Soph Cls; Chrldng; Jr NHS; Drama Clb; All Reg Choir.

MUSCHONG, DANIELLE; Norfork Jr Sr HS; Norfork, AR; (2); Art Clb; Church Yth Grp; FBLA; FHA; Math Clb; Spanish Clb; High Hon Roll; Hon Roll; Ntl Merit Ltr.

MUSE, AMANDA; Delight HS; Antoine, AR; (2); 4-H; FBLA; Natl Beta Clb; Natl FFA Org; Quiz Bowl; Yrbk; Ofcr Frsh Cls; Ofcr Soph Cls; Hon Roll; JETS Awd.

MUSE, SHANNON; Hazen Jr Sr HS; Hazen, AR; (3); French Clb; FBLA; FHA; Office Aide; Teachers Aide; Chorus; Rptr Nwsp; Var Chrldng; Var Gym; Hon Roll; USCAA Chrldng Awd; U Of Cntrl AR Conway; Rept Thr.

MUSKHELISHVILI, MICHAEL; Catholic HS; Little Rock, AR; (3); German Clb; Yrbk; High Hon Roll; Hon Roll; Perf In Civics Awd 94; Awd In Ger; Awd Attndng AEGIS Pgm 94.

MUSLER, SUE M; Hot Springs HS; Hot Springs Natio, AR; (4); Hon Roll; Pres Acad Fit Awd; Legal Sec; Lega Asst.

MUSTAIN, BRANDON; Arkansas Sr HS; Texarkana, AR; (2); Debate Tm; Drama Clb; Key Clb; Mu Alpha Theta; Quiz Bowl; Spanish Clb; Rptr Yrbk; VP Frsh Cls; Rep Soph Cls; Hon Roll; TX A&M; Anesthesiolgy.

MUSTAIN, SABRINA M; Norfork Jr Sr HS; Mountain Home, AR; (3); English Clb; FBLA; FHA; Math Clb; Science Clb; Spanish Clb; Teachers Aide; Sec Frsh Cls; Sec Soph Cls; Var Bsktbl.

MUSTON, TOMMY; Evening Shade Schl; Evening Shade, AR; (4); 3/20; FBLA; FHA; Pres German Clb; Sec Natl Beta Clb; Pres Natl FFA Org; Yrbk; Bsktbl; DAR Awd; Gov Hon Prg Awd; Hon Roll; FFA, Star Grnhnd & Chap Frmr Awd; Agribus.

MYATT, JAMIE; Norphlet HS; Norphlet, AR; (2); 1/57; Art Clb; Church Yth Grp; FBLA; GAA; Quiz Bowl; Spanish Clb; Band; Church Choir; Mrchg Band; Ofcr Stu Cncl; Schlstc Awd.

MYERS, AERREN; Butterfield Jr HS; Van Buren, AR; (1); 1/175; Church Yth Grp; FBLA; HOBY; Band; Mrchg Band; School Play; Rep Stu Cncl; Chrldng; Sftbl; Vllybl; Harding U; Bus.

MYERS, BRITTNEY A; Southside HS; Fort Smith, AR; (2); Dance Clb; FCA; Drill Tm; JV L Pom Pon; Hon Roll; All Amer Awd Super Star Dncr; Won Prvldge Go To Macys Thnksgvng Prde; Vlybl/Bsktbl/Swmmng/Snow Skiing; Kilgore.

MYERS, CAROLINE B; Ft Smith Christian Schl; Fort Smith, AR; (2); Church Yth Grp; Drama Clb; FCA; GAA; Spanish Clb; Church Choir; Bsktbl; Trk; Cit Awd; Hon Roll; Ctznshp/Ldrshp Awd 95; Oua Chita Bapt Univ.

MYERS, JEMECIA S; Dollarway HS; Pine Bluff, AR; (2); Church Yth Grp; Girl Scts; Pep Clb; ROTC; Teachers Aide; Church Choir; Drm Mjr(t); Var Chrldng; Trk; TX Southern.

MYERS, JOSEPH B; Ridgecrest HS; Paragould, AR; (3); FHA; Band; Jazz Band; Mrchg Band; Orch; Pep Band; School Musical; Hon Roll; Pres Acad Fit Awd; Band Cncl Treas; AR ST Univ; Bus/Mngmnt.

MYERS, KENNETH; Northside HS; Fort Smith, AR; (3); FCA; Varsity Clb; Yrbk; Var L Bsktbl; Var L Ftbl; Var L Trk; Ftbl, Bsktbl Trck Ltrs; Yng Dmcrts; Natl Hnr Soc; Fllwshp Chrstn Ath; Grambling ST U; Engrng.

MYERS, MARIAH; Ozark HS; Ozark, AR; (4); 1/95; Drama Clb; FBLA; HOBY; Intnl Clb; Model UN; Natl Beta Clb; Office Aide; Chorus; Rep Jr Cls; Sec Stu Cncl; U Of AR.

MYERS, ONETRA D; Oak Grove HS; North Little Rock, AR; (4); 8/100; Church Yth Grp; FBLA; FHA; FTA; Sec FTA; Mu Alpha Theta; Natl Beta Clb; Office Aide; Science Clb; Spanish Clb; U Of Cntrl AR.

MYERS, ROBERT B; Ft Smith Christian Schl; Fort Smith, AR; (3); Church Yth Grp; FCA; Spanish Clb; Band; Stage Crew; Ofcr Bsbl; Bsktbl; Trk; Cit Awd; Hon Roll; Heath Class; Westark Coll.

MYERS, SHAREL E; Rogers HS; Rogers, AR; (3); 137/567; Church Yth Grp; Drama Clb; Thesps; Church Choir; School Musical; School Play; Stage Crew; Yrbk; High Hon Roll; Hon Roll; Ed Theatre Assn; Natl Yth Ldrshp Forum On Law & The Constitution Nom; Bible Bowl; Civil Suit Attorney.

MYERS, STEPHANIE; Van Buren Sr HS; Van Buren, AR; (3); Art Clb; Church Yth Grp; Mu Alpha Theta; Spanish Clb; Band; Color Guard; Pep Band; High Hon Roll; Jr NHS; NHS; Asst Mgr Tm; Nrsng.

MYERS, STEVEN H; Rogers HS; Rogers, AR; (3); Am Leg Boys St; FBLA; HOBY; Natl Beta Clb; Quiz Bowl; Spanish Clb; Band; High Hon Roll; Jr NHS; NHS; U Of AR At Hendrix; Lawyer.

MYKLEBUST, MARY K; Parkview HS Magnet; Maumelle, AR; (3); Church Yth Grp; Dance Clb; FCA; 4-H; French Clb; German Clb; Key Clb; Letterman Clb; Math Clb; Natl Beta Clb; Dnc Blt/Tap/Jazz/Mdrn; Piano; 4 Yr Coll; Pre-Med.

MYLES, CRESHUN A; Lakeside HS; Lake Village, AR; (3); 14/87; Sec Drama Clb; FBLA; Natl FFA Org; Band; Drm Mjr(t); Mrchg Band; Rep Stu Cncl; High Hon Roll; Hon Roll; Drum Majorette Trophy; Close-Up; Grambling ST Univ; Pre-Med.

NABERS, ARLENE B; Clarksville HS; London, AR; (2); French Clb; Hosp Aide; Key Clb; Natl Beta Clb; Band; Mrchg Band; High Hon Roll; Hon Roll; AR Schl Of Math & Sic.

NABERS, DAVID; ASMS HS; London, AR; (3); Math Clb; Mu Alpha Theta; Natl Beta Clb; Quiz Bowl; Acpl Chr; JV Bsbl; NHS; Ntl Merit Ltr; WA Univ; Bio Prof.

NABERT, SHERRY; Heber Srpings HS; Heber Springs, AR; (4); 5/96; Am Leg Aux Girls St; Church Yth Grp; Pres VP Drama Clb; Treas FBLA; Natl Beta Clb; Yrbk; VP Frsh Cls; VP Soph Cls; Rep Stu Cncl; Var Tennis; Voice Of Democracy Cont Local & Dist Wnnr; Pub Speaking ST Top 10; FBLA Pub Speaking Cmptn Dist 1st; SW Assemblies Of God U.

NAIL, ERIC; Devalls Bluff Jr Sr HS; Biscoe, AR; (2); 2/44; Church Yth Grp; French Clb; FBLA; Natl Beta Clb; Church Choir; Ofcr Bsbl; Bsktbl; Hon Roll; Agribus.

NALE, CHRIS H; El Dorado Sr HS; El Dorado, AR; (3); Am Leg Boys St; Boy Scts; Church Yth Grp; Cmnty Wkr; Drama Clb; FCA; FBLA; Key Clb; Letterman Clb; Natl Beta Clb; Boy & Girl Clb Yth Of Yr; Sports Med.

NALL, SHAUN F; Corning HS; Corning, AR; (3); Church Yth Grp; Natl FFA Org; Ftbl; Air Force Coll; Air Force.

NALLEY, MARGARET ELISABETH; J A Fair Sr HS; Little Rock, AR; (4); 4/300; VP Drama Clb; Pres French Clb; Mu Alpha Theta; Speech Tm; School Play; Capt Chrldng; NHS; High Hon Roll; Pres Acad Fit Awd; Hall Of Fame; Super Acad Achvmt Awds AP Eng & Fr; Dance; U Of AR Fayetteville.

NANCE, SAMANTHA; Jacksonville HS; Jacksonville, AR; (2); 21/360; Sec FBLA; Pep Clb; Yrbk; Var JV Chrldng; Powder Puff Ftbl; Hon Roll.

NANEY, AMANDA K; Dequeen HS; De Queen, AR; (2); FHA; GAA; SADD; Var Crs Cntry; Var Trk; Hon Roll; Phy Ther.

NANNEMANN, SARAH; Bismarck Jr-Sr HS; Donaldson, AR; (2); Church Yth Grp; Cmnty Wkr; Natl Beta Clb; Band; Mrchg Band; Pep Band; High Hon Roll; Sftbl; Bsktbl; Civics, Hugh O'Brien, Phys Sci, Clthng, PE Awds; Henderson.

NAPIER, DAVID J; North Little Rock Hs-West; North Little Rock, AR; (3); 112/594; Am Leg Boys St; Church Yth Grp; FCA; Key Clb; Band; Bsktbl; Ftbl; Trk; Hon Roll; Pres Acad Fit Awd; Bsktbl Announcer On Schl TV Station; Comp Animation; Bus.

NAPOLITANO, DARRYL S; Flippin Jr Sr HS; Flippin, AR; (2); Drama Clb; Drama Clb; SADD; Bsktbl; JV Trk; Blue Belt Tae Kwon Do Gold Medalist; Wrtng Poetry; Bus; Psych.

NARAGON, NATASHA; Rogers HS; Rogers, AR; (4); FBLA; Key Clb; Teachers Aide; Thesps; Chorus; School Play; High Hon Roll; Pres Acad Fit Awd; AR Gov Schl; Bntn Co Tn Ct; Hendrix Coll; Pre-Law.

NARENS, COLLEEN V; Arkansas Sr HS; Texarkana, AR; (4); Art Clb; Church Yth Grp; Cmnty Wkr; Drama Clb; Girl Scts; Red Cross Aide; Spanish Clb; School Musical; Stage Crew; Yrbk; U Of A In Fayetteville; Psych.

NARENS, JENNIFER K; Rogers HS; Rogers, AR; (2); Chorus; Church Choir; Nwsp; Sftbl; Hon Roll; Multicultural Clb; Acad Achvmt Awd; Rogers Renaissance Awd.

NARENS, JESSICA A; Arkansas Sr HS; Texarkana, AR; (3); Art Clb; Church Yth Grp; Dance Clb; Office Aide; Pep Clb; Spanish Clb; Teachers Aide; Drill Tm; Rep Stu Cncl; Gftd & Tlntd Prgm; Nike Clb; Rxrbck Prd; U Of AR; Phys Thrpst.

NARROW, MONICA J; Bryant Sr HS; Benton, AR; (3); Am Leg Aux Girls St; French Clb; FBLA; Teachers Aide; Drill Tm; Ofcr Stu Cncl; Hon Roll; HS Heros; Poli Sci.

NARVESON, NICOLE R; Russellville Sr HS; Russellville, AR; (3); Church Yth Grp; GAA; Hosp Aide; Band; Flag Corp; Mrchg Band; Rep Frsh Cls; JV Var Bsktbl; Mgr(s); Var Socr; U Of AR; Bus/Intr Dcrtng.

NASH, AMANDA G; North Little Rock HS; North Little Rock, AR; (3); 54/594; Cmnty Wkr; FHA; Latin Clb; Math Clb; Mu Alpha Theta; Teachers Aide; Drill Tm; Chrldng; High Hon Roll; NHS; LSU; Bus.

NASH, MARCIE L; Dumas HS; Gould, AR; (3); Church Yth Grp; 4-H; FBLA; Quiz Bowl; Science Clb; Spanish Clb; Band; Church Choir; Drm Mjr(t); Jazz Band; U Of AR; Vet Med.

NASH, TESHA A; Abundant Life Schools; Conway, AR; (3); Church Yth Grp; Office Aide; Teachers Aide; Chorus; Church Choir; Bsktbl; Sftbl; U Of Cntrl AK; Pre-Med.

NAUMAN, JAMYE B; Rogers HS; Rogers, AR; (4); Church Yth Grp; FCA; SADD; Band; Mrchg Band; Pep Band; Hon Roll; NW AR CC; Comps.

NAVE, DARRYL J; Northside HS; Fort Smith, AR; (4); 27/408; Art Clb; Boy Scts; Church Yth Grp; VP Intnl Clb; Mu Alpha Theta; Spanish Clb; Ofcr Jr Cls; Hon Roll; NHS; Spanish NHS; U AR; Biochem.

NEAL, ADAM M; Rogers HS; Rogers, AR; (2); 1/700; Church Yth Grp; Cmnty Wkr; Library Aide; Model UN; Gov Hon Prg Awd; High Hon Roll; Pres Schlr; Teen Court Vol; Habitat For Hum Vol.

NEAL, CRYSTAL Y; Dequeen HS; De Queen, AR; (4); 6/78; Am Leg Aux Girls St; Pres Church Yth Grp; 4-H; Band; Drm Mjr(t); Mrchg Band; Hon Roll; Sec NHS; Pres Schlr; Navy Hnrs Pgm; Bus Mgmt.

NEAL, ERICA; Arkansas Sr HS; Texarkana, AR; (1); French Clb; GAA; Sec Stu Cncl; Bsktbl; Chrldng; Trk; Vllybl; French Hon Soc; Prfct Atten Awd; Md Hnr Hmcmng Ct 95; Fayetteville U AR; Bus.

NEAL, JAMIE L; Gosnell Jr Sr HS; Gosnell, AR; (2); Church Yth Grp; French Clb; Sec Key Clb; Library Aide; Natl Beta Clb; Science Clb; Teachers Aide; Band; Mrchg Band; Pep Band; AR ST U; Law.

NEAL, KYLIE A; Russellville Sr HS; Russellville, AR; (3); Church Yth Grp; Cmnty Wkr; GAA; Band; Mrchg Band; Pep Band; JV Bsktbl; Var Vllybl; Cit Awd; Egyptology.

NEAL, LESLIE Y; Mc Crory Jr Sr HS; Mc Crory, AR; (2); 4-H; FHA; Library Aide; Office Aide; Spanish Clb; Acpl Chr; Church Choir; Flag Corp; Var Bsktbl; Powder Puff Ftbl; ASU; Dr.

NEAL, PRISCILLA; Hughes Jr-Sr HS; Hughes, AR; (4); 15/47; FHA; Library Aide; Spanish Clb; Pres Soph Cls; EACC 2 Yr Tuition; Geometry Awd; EACC; Computerized Pub Acctnt.

NEAL, ZACHARY; Central Ark Christian Schl; North Little Rock, AR; (3); HOBY; Science Clb; Chorus; Pres Soph Cls; Rep Stu Cncl; Var L Bsktbl; Var L Trk; Hon Roll; Jr NHS; NHS; Harding U; Bible.

NEBLETT, LEO M; Crossett Sr HS; Crossett, AR; (2); Mu Alpha Theta; Natl Beta Clb; High Hon Roll; Babe Ruth Bsbl.

NEEL, ERICA; Trumann HS; Trumann, AR; (4); 16/85; French Clb; FHA; Sec German Clb; HOBY; Model UN; VP Band; Mrchg Band; Hon Roll; NHS; Hnr Stu; All Reg Band; Delta Bridgae Drum & Bugle Corps; U Cntrl AR; Poly Sci.

NEEL, JENNIFER L; Dierks HS; Langley, AR; (2); Church Yth Grp; Bsktbl; Trk; Hon Roll; Henderson; Vet.

NEEL, PATRICK HENRY; Trumann HS; Trumann, AR; (3); Am Leg Boys St; Church Yth Grp; Natl FFA Org; Science Clb; Spanish Clb; L Bsktbl; L Golf; Hon Roll; NHS; Trigonometry Awd; Span I/II Awd; GPA Awd; Acctng.

NEELEY, JOCELYN R; Dequeen HS; De Queen, AR; (2); FHA; FTA; SADD; Band; Chorus; Flag Corp; Mrchg Band; Yrbk; Sec Jr Cls; Hon Roll; Ed.

NEELY, EBONY S; Mills HS; Little Rock, AR; (3); 76/298; FBLA; FTA; Natl Beta Clb; Q&S; ROTC; Chorus; Church Choir; Variety Show; Rep Soph Cls; Rep Jr Cls; 1st Rnnr Up 96 Ms Mlls Pgnt; U Of Central AR; Psych.

NEELY, RACHEL M; Smackover HS; Camden, AR; (1); FBLA; FTA; GAA; Teachers Aide; JV Var Chrldng; High Hon Roll; Hon Roll; Alge Awd; Kybrdng Applctns Awd; Southern AR Univ; Tchr.

NEFF, ASHLEY D; Lincoln HS; Lincoln, AR; (1); 1/97; Model UN; Natl Beta Clb; Natl FFA Org; Quiz Bowl; Spanish Clb; Band; Mrchg Band; Pep Band; Sftbl; Hon Roll; OK ST U; Anml Sci.

NEIGHBORS, JENNIFER; Joe T Robinson HS; Little Rock, AR; (4); FBLA; FHA; Spanish Clb; Ofcr Stu Cncl; Capt Var Bsktbl; Var Chrldng; Var Trk; Var JV Vllybl; Hon Roll; Med.

NEIGHBORS, MELISSA MICHELLE; Alma HS; Alma, AR; (2); Church Yth Grp; FHA; SADD; Hon Roll; Westark CC; Ped.

NEIGHBORS, NATHAN J; Fountain Lake Jr Sr HS; Hot Springs, AR; (1); Art Clb; Church Yth Grp; Spanish Clb; Ofcr Frsh Cls; Pres Stu Cncl; Var Bsbl; JV Capt Bsktbl; Gov Hon Prg Awd; Chrch Yth Grp Pres; Miami; Art/Bsbl.

NEIGHBORS, NICOLE L; Brookland Jr Sr HS; Jonesboro, AR; (3); Art Clb; FHA; Natl Beta Clb; SADD; AR St Univ.

NEIGHBORS, SHANNA; Bradford Jr Sr HS; Bradford, AR; (1); Art Clb; FBLA; FHA; Hosp Aide; Natl Beta Clb; Pres Frsh Cls; Capt Chrldng; Hon Roll; PRIDE; Stu Cncl Rep; Zoology.

NEISSL, MATTHEW R; Charleston HS; Charleston, AR; (3); Am Leg Boys St; Church Yth Grp; FCA; FBLA; Natl Beta Clb; Chorus; Church Choir; School Play; VP Jr Cls; Var Bsbl.

NELMS, ANDREA; Brookland Jr Sr HS; Brookland, AR; (3); 2/71; Church Yth Grp; Drama Clb; Pres Natl Beta Clb; Spanish Clb; Sec Chorus; Sec Stu Cncl; Var Bsktbl; Var Sftbl; Var Vllybl; High Hon Roll; Acad Awds In Govt, Span, Bio & Amer His; Lawyer.

NELMS, STACI; Central Ark Christian Schl; Little Rock, AR; (4); 24/73; Church Yth Grp; Science Clb; Spanish Clb; Teachers Aide; Var Bsktbl; Var Tennis; Var Vllybl; High Hon Roll; Hon Roll; NHS; His Club; Ath/Yr; All Conf Vlybl; All Dist Bsktbl; Freed-Hardeman U.

NELSON, AMANDA; Bright Star Schl; Doddridge, AR; (2); Church Yth Grp; Cmnty Wkr; Drama Clb; FBLA; GAA; Church Choir; Rep Stu Cncl; Var JV Bsktbl; Var Score Keeper; Var JV Trk; Grambling; Med.

NELSON, AMANDA M; Marmaduke HS; Lafe, AR; (3); 12/55; Drama Clb; FBLA; Natl Beta Clb; Natl FFA Org; Pep Clb; Chorus; School Play; Var Chrldng; Hon Roll; AR ST U; Ag Bus.

NELSON, CHANDRA D; Pine Bluff HS; Pine Bluff, AR; (4); 6/357; Am Leg Aux Girls St; Natl Beta Clb; Quiz Bowl; Science Clb; Church Choir; Yrbk; Trk; Hon Roll; NHS; Pres Acad Fit Awd; Sci Fair 2nd Pl; Knowledge Masters Open; U Of AR Fayetteville; Nrsng.

NELSON, CHARLETT L; Hope HS; Hope, AR; (3); Church Yth Grp; Spanish Clb; Church Choir; Trk; Hon Roll; Texarkana Coll; Juvenile Cnslr.

NELSON, DAVID G; Southside HS; Fort Smith, AR; (2); Church Yth Grp; FCA; Mu Alpha Theta; Quiz Bowl; Chorus; Church Choir; School Musical; Bsktbl; High Hon Roll; NHS.

NELSON, JENNIFER L; Smackover HS; Smackover, AR; (4); 4/46; Art Clb; FBLA; FHA; FTA; Science Clb; Spanish Clb; Teachers Aide; Nwsp; JV Chrldng; Hon Roll; Hnr Grad; Close-Up; Anchor Clb Historian; FL ST U; Bus.

NELSON, KENDRA; Malvern Sr HS; Malvern, AR; (2); 1/220; FBLA; JV Var Bsktbl; JV Var Sftbl; Var Trk; JV Var Vllybl; Jr NHS; Ntl Merit Ltr; Peer Cnslr; Natl Jr Beta Clb.

NELSON, KENDRA D; Central Sr HS; Little Rock, AR; (3); 148/500; Chess Clb; Computer Clb; Dance Clb; FHA; JA; Latin Clb; Color Guard; Drill Tm; Flag Corp; Rep Frsh Cls; U Of Cntrl AR; Eng.

NELSON, KIRSTEN; Pea Ridge HS; Bentonville, AR; (1); 2/69; Church Yth Grp; Chorus; School Musical; Variety Show; Sftbl; Trk; Hon Roll; NHS; Marine Bio.

NELSON, PARREN D; Pine Bluff HS; Pine Bluff, AR; (3); Church Yth Grp; Cmnty Wkr; Office Aide; Spanish Clb; Ofcr Stu Cncl; Bsktbl; Hon Roll; Prfct Atten Awd; 95-96 Stu Of The Month; Multi-Yr Listee.

NELSON, SHAMIKA C; North Little Rock Hs-East; North Little Rock, AR; (2); Church Yth Grp; Cmnty Wkr; Debate Tm; Library Aide; Spanish Clb; Teachers Aide; Chorus; VP Stu Cncl; L Pom Pon; Hon Roll; Spellman; Med.

NELSON, SHANNON D; Forrest City HS; Forrest City, AR; (3); Church Yth Grp; VP FBLA; FTA; Mu Alpha Theta; Natl Beta Clb; Ofcr Stu Cncl; Gov Hon Prg Awd; High Hon Roll; Ntl Merit Ltr; Morehouse Coll; Pre-Med.

NELSON, SHERMIKA; Marvell HS; Marvell, AR; (4); 2/39; French Clb; FBLA; Natl Beta Clb; Quiz Bowl; Teachers Aide; Church Choir; VP Sr Cls; VP Stu Cncl; Pres Hon Soc; Sal; U Of Central AR; Bus Info Syst.

NELSON, STEPHEN D; Parkers Chapel Schl; El Dorado, AR; (3); FBLA; Natl Beta Clb; Science Clb; Spanish Clb; School Play; L Bsktbl; Hon Roll; All Cty Bsktbl; Comp Tech Awd.

NEN STIEL, LEE H; Bentonville Sr HS; Rose, OK; (4); 24/242; Church Yth Grp; Library Aide; High Hon Roll; NHS; Pres Acad Fit Awd; HI-Q; ACE; U Of OK.

NERVIG, WENDI S; Robinson HS; Little Rock, AR; (2); Church Yth Grp; FCA; Girl Scts; Natl Beta Clb; Quiz Bowl; VP Spanish Clb; Band; Chorus; Mrchg Band; Var Bsktbl; Accompanist Swing Choir Combo.

NESBITT, BRAD R; Booneville Jr Sr HS; Booneville, AR; (3); Cmnty Wkr; FHA; Key Clb; Spanish Clb; Capt Bsbl; Var Bsktbl; Var Ftbl; Var Trk; Bio.

NESBITT, ERICA; Cabot HS; Cabot, AR; (2) Drama Clb; Library Aide; NFL; Chorus; School Musical; School Play; Variety Show; Chrldng; All Rgn Choir.

NESBITT, MARY; Fayetteville Christian Schl; Springdale, AR; (1); Church Yth Grp; Church Choir; JV Capt Chrldng; Var Sftbl; High Hon Roll; Hon Roll; Piano; Sunday Schl Tchr; Childrn.

NESBITT, SAKORA; Stephens Jr Sr HS; Stephens, AR; (4); 3/37; Art Clb; Church Yth Grp; Cmnty Wkr; English Clb; 4-H; FBLA; German Clb; Library Aide; Math Clb; Office Aide; Pride; Prins Acad Awd; Acad Awd; Henderson ST U; Nrsng.

NESLIN, SHEILA L; Arkadelphia Sr HS; Arkadelphia, AR; (4); 51/156; Church Yth Grp; Cmnty Wkr; Drama Clb; English Clb; Sec FCA; FBLA; Hosp Aide; Natl Beta Clb; Science Clb; Spanish Clb; Ouchita Bapt Univ; Spch Pthlgst.

NETHERTON, KELLIE A; Springdale Sr HS; Springdale, AR; (4); 36/516; Science Clb; Band; Mrchg Band; Bsktbl; Capt Crs Cntry; Powder Puff Ftbl; Trk; High Hon Roll; Jr NHS; NHS; HOSA; U Of AR; Pre-Med.

NEUMANN, CHRISTY L; Atkins Schl; Atkins, AR; (2); Church Yth Grp; Natl Beta Clb; Office Aide; Band; Church Choir; Mrchg Band; Rodeo & Horse Clb; AR Tech U; Vet; Ag.

NEW, JENNIFER D; Junction City HS; Junction City, AR; (2); Church Yth Grp; Science Clb; Band; Church Choir; Mrchg Band; High Hon Roll; BASIC.

NEWBERRY, JERRITT D; Springdale Sr HS; Springdale, AR; (3); Natl FFA Org; Ftbl; Animal Sci Achvmt Awd; Bareback Rodeo; Motocross; Bull Riding; Animal Tech; Botany; Ranching; U Of AR; Mountain Rescue.

NEWBORN, CHANSON SHANTEZ; Forrest City HS; Colt, AR; (3); Am Leg Boys St; Art Clb; Church Yth Grp; 4-H; FBLA; FHA; FTA; Band; Chorus; Jazz Band; Xavier; Pharmacy; Art.

NEWCOMB, NATALIE N; Harmony Grove Jr Sr HS; Benton, AR; (2); Sec Church Yth Grp; Cmnty Wkr; French Clb; Quiz Bowl; Science Clb; Band; Chorus; Church Choir; Co-Capt Color Guard; Mrchg Band; Majorette, Feature Twirler; Peer Cnslng; Med Camp Vol; U Central AR; Chld Phy Thrpst.

NEWCOME, REBECCA D; Hamburg HS; Portland, AR; (2); Cmnty Wkr; Hosp Aide; Natl Beta Clb; Spanish Clb; Chorus; Bsktbl; Chrldng; Tennis; High Hon Roll; NHS.

NEWELL, KATHY Y; Sheridan Sr HS; Mabelvale, AR; (2); Church Yth Grp; Cmnty Wkr; Service Clb; Teachers Aide; Chorus; Church Choir; High Hon Roll; Hon Roll; Jr NHS; Pres Schlr; Teen Ldr Teen Invlvmnt; Awds Hghst Algbra Grd; UALR; Cardiologst.

NEWMAN, CRISSY M; Mansfield Jr Sr HS; Mansfield, AR; (1); 3/80; Drama Clb; FBLA; Intnl Clb; Model UN; Quiz Bowl; Band; High Hon Roll; Ntl Merit Ltr; Pres Schlr; Top Phys Sci Stdnt; Top Span II Stdnt; U Of AR Fayetville; Law.

NEWMAN, GRACE L; Salem HS; Salem, AR; (3); Church Yth Grp; FCA; Key Clb; Natl Beta Clb; Yrbk; Var Bsktbl; High Hon Roll; Hon Roll; Prfct Atten Awd; 1st Plc Medl In Physlgy In Reg Sci Comp; Nurs.

NEWMAN, JENNIFER M; Lavaca Jr Sr HS; Lavaca, AR; (2); 7/75; FCA; FBLA; Natl Beta Clb; Spanish Clb; Speech Tm; Band; Chorus; Sec Stu Cncl; Church Yth Grp; FHA; Outstdng 10th Grd Stdnt Plaque; Hmcmng 10th Grd Maid; Westark CC.

NEWMAN, STEFANIE D; Russellville Sr HS; Russellville, AR; (2); Church Yth Grp; Chorus; Jr NHS; NHS; Model League Of Arab Sts; AR Tech U; Acctng.

NEWSOM, JULIE; Harding Acad; Searcy, AR; (2); Church Yth Grp; Key Clb; Pep Clb; Spanish Clb; Chorus; School Musical; JV Bsktbl; Var Capt Chrldng; Var Trk; High Hon Roll; 1st Pl Rotary Clb Essay Cont; 2nd Pl ACTM Reg Algebra 2 Cont; 2 Prvt Art Shows Local Gallery; Harding U; Dietician.

NEWTON, BRIANNE; Lake Hamilton Sr HS; Hot Springs, AR; (3); FBLA; Natl Beta Clb; Quiz Bowl; Spanish Clb.

NEWTON, CRYSTAL L; Star City HS; Star City, AR; (1); 4/140; Church Yth Grp; FCA; Natl Beta Clb; Office Aide; Color Guard; Mrchg Band; Rep Stu Cncl; Chrldng; Sftbl; High Hon Roll; Frosh Class Favorite.

NEWTON, ELISHA; Whirley HS; Fairfield Bay, AR; (3); 1/42; Am Leg Aux Girls St; VP FCA; HOBY; Natl Beta Clb; Quiz Bowl; Pres Science Clb; Pres Jr Cls; L Bsktbl; L Tennis; L Trk; Ouachita U; Phrmcy.

NEWTON JR, GABRIEL J; Van Buren Sr HS; Van Buren, AR; (2); FBLA; Mu Alpha Theta; Ofcr Stu Cncl; Bsktbl; Ftbl; High Hon Roll; Jr NHS; Stu Panel; George Washington; Med.

NEWTON, JESSICA J; Conway Sr HS; Conway, AR; (2); Church Yth Grp; GAA; Letterman Clb; Library Aide; Rep Stu Cncl; Bsktbl; Hon Roll; Lbry Clb Pres; Renaissance Card Hldr; K-Life; Scndry Ed.

NEWTON, JOSEPH M; Star City HS; Yorktown, AR; (2); 1/150; Mu Alpha Theta; Capt Quiz Bowl; Band; Church Choir; Mrchg Band; Cit Awd; High Hon Roll; VP Church Yth Grp; FCA; Math Clb; Cty Yth Rally Pres; AP Eng; Accepted To AR Schl For Math & Sci; Mech Engrng.

NEWTON, KRISTI L; Viola HS; Elizabeth, AR; (3); FBLA; FHA; Band; Pres Soph Cls; Ofcr Stu Cncl; Sftbl; Cit Awd; High Hon Roll; Hon Roll; Pres Acad Fit Awd; Gifted Talented Prog; AR St Univ; Erly Chld Devlp.

NEWTON, LUCY; Southside HS; Fort Smith, AR; (3); French Clb; FBLA; Key Clb; Math Clb; Mu Alpha Theta; Teachers Aide; Drill Tm; Chrldng; High Hon Roll; Hon Roll; Sec Of Columbians; 1 Of 7 Top Drill Tm; Hmcmng Maid; Jr/Sr Cncl; U Of AR; Bus/Sprts Nutrtn.

NEWTON, SHANIQUAL R; Strong Jr Sr HS; Strong, AR; (3); Am Leg Aux Girls St; Drama Clb; French Clb; Pres FHA; Natl Beta Clb; Quiz Bowl; Science Clb; Band; Ofcr Jr Cls; Chrldng; SAU Magnolia; Phy Thrpst.

NGO, TINA; Van Buren Sr HS; Van Buren, AR; (4); FBLA; Mu Alpha Theta; Science Clb; Speech Tm; Teachers Aide; Band; Color Guard; Mrchg Band; Cit Awd; Jr NHS; U Of AR Fayetteville; Pharm.

NGONER, BRIAN A; Hot Springs HS; Hot Springs Natio, AR; (2); Drama Clb; Library Aide; Office Aide; School Play; Golf; Hon Roll; Garland Cnty Comm Coll.

NGUYEN, HOA K; Jonesboro HS; Jonesboro, AR; (4); 17/287; FBLA; Hosp Aide; JV Mu Alpha Theta; Natl Beta Clb; Office Aide; Quiz Bowl; Science Clb; Spanish Clb; Chorus; Church Choir; Future Medcl Careers Clb Treas; Attend AR Gov Schl; All Reg Choir; U Cntrl AR; Phrmcy.

NGUYEN, JENNIFER; John L Mcclellan Magnet HS; Little Rock, AR; (2); Church Yth Grp; French Clb; Cit Awd; High Hon Roll; Hon Roll; NHS; Prfct Atten Awd; Comp Pgm.

NGUYEN, JOHNNY T; Northside HS; Barling, AR; (3); Mu Alpha Theta; VP Spanish Clb; Rep Jr Cls; Hon Roll; Jr NHS; NHS; Pres Acad Fit Awd; Pres Spanish NHS; AGATE Prog; AGS; Physcn.

NGUYEN, KEVIN L; Southside HS; Batesville, AR; (2); Key Clb; Teachers Aide; Golf; Hon Roll; St Golf Championships.

NGUYEN, KHOI H; Southside HS; Fort Smith, AR; (3); Art Clb; FBLA; Key Clb; Teachers Aide; Crs Cntry; Trk; Cit Awd; High Hon Roll; Hon Roll; Prfct Atten Awd; U Of AR; Law.

NGUYEN, STEVEN; Nashville HS; Nashville, AR; (3); Church Yth Grp; FBLA; Spanish Clb; Nwsp; Yrbk; Var L Ftbl; Hon Roll; NHS; U Of A.

NGUYEN, THINH D; Northside HS; Barling, AR; (3); 8/400; Mu Alpha Theta; Spanish Clb; Teachers Aide; Hon Roll; NHS; Prfct Atten Awd; Pres Acad Fit Awd; Spanish NHS; 1st Pl Regl Sci Fr; U Of AR; Pre-Med.

NGUYEN, TONY; Fayetteville Sr HS; Fayetteville, AR; (2); Art Clb.

NGUYEN, VAN T; Rogers HS; Rogers, AR; (4); 19/468; Church Yth Grp; French Clb; FBLA; Pep Clb; Teachers Aide; Pom Pon; High Hon Roll; NHS; Renaissance & Rogers Chmbr Of Cmmrc Awds; Wal-Mart Cshr Of Mnth; U Of AR-FAYETTEVILLE; Med.

NICHOLAS, BRANDON K; Lavaca Jr Sr HS; Lavaca, AR; (4); Library Aide; ROTC; Science Clb; Teachers Aide; Hon Roll; Military Carrer.

NICHOLS, ANDREW D; Southside HS; Fort Smith, AR; (2); French Clb; Math Clb; Hon Roll.

NICHOLS, EMMA K; Pulaski Acad; Little Rock, AR; (2); Church Yth Grp; Natl Beta Clb; Spanish Clb; Acpl Chr; Church Choir; School Musical; Mgr Yrbk; Vllybl; Hon Roll; Jr NHS; Interact Clb Charter Mem & Treas; All Region Choir; Just Say No Teen Ldr; Engrng.

NICHOLS, JASON W; North Pulaski HS; North Little Ro, AR; (2); Office Aide; Band; Mrchg Band; Ofcr Soph Cls; Hon Roll; Jr NHS; Med.

NICHOLS, JILLIAN; Pocahontas HS; Pocahontas, AR; (3); #1 in class; Church Yth Grp; HOBY; Natl Beta Clb; Spanish Clb; Band; Treas Soph Cls; Treas Stu Cncl; Cit Awd; Hon Roll; Pres Acad Fit Awd; Hendrix; Med.

NICHOLS, JOHN A; St Joseph HS; Conway, AR; (2); Church Yth Grp; JV Ftbl; Var Socr; Var Wt Lftg; Hon Roll; U Of AR; Bus.

NICHOLS, PHYLLIS L; Springdale Sr HS; Fayetteville, AR; (3); 35/535; Church Yth Grp; French Clb; FBLA; Model UN; VP NFL; Q&S; Chorus; Phtg Yrbk; NHS; Pres Acad Fit Awd.

NICHOLS, RACHEL; Van Buren Sr HS; Van Buren, AR; (3); Church Yth Grp; Dance Clb; FCA; FHA; Library Aide; Mu Alpha Theta; Pep Clb; Q&S; Science Clb; Spanish Clb; Dance Tm Sr Lt; Westark CC; Nrsng.

NICHOLS, SARAH M; Sheridan Sr HS; Mabelvale, AR; (4); Church Yth Grp; Dance Clb; Pep Clb; Chorus; Drill Tm; Chrldng; Pom Pon; Hon Roll; AR Tech; Psych.

NICHOLSON, CARLA; Cross Co Jr Sr HS; Cherry Valley, AR; (3); 1/48; 4-H; Pres FBLA; HOBY; Natl Beta Clb; Spanish Clb; Co-Ed Nwsp; Phtg Yrbk; L Bsktbl; Var Sftbl; 4-H Awd; 95 Miss Crss Cty Rice; Miss AR Natl Teen Cont Ctznshp Wnnr; 4-H Teen Star & Ambssdr; Coop Ext Agnt.

NICHOLSON, RUSTY E; Vilonia HS; Conway, AR; (3); Pres Art Clb; FBLA; Natl Beta Clb; Teachers Aide; Bsktbl; Ftbl; Hon Roll; Pres Acad Fit Awd; Pres Art Clb Sr Yr; Wnnr Chss Tournmnt; Hendrix.

NICKLES, LAURA; Cross Co Jr Sr HS; Cherry Valley, AR; (4); 5/38; Am Leg Aux Girls St; FBLA; FHA; Natl Beta Clb; Spanish Clb; VP Jr Cls; VP Stu Cncl; Capt Chrldng; Tennis; Hon Roll; UCA All Star Chrldr; 3rd Pl Girls Tnns Dbls 3AA S; Phys Thrpy.

NICKOLSON, SARAH; Delta Special Schl; Tillar, AR; (4); 2/12; Sec Natl Beta Clb; Band; School Musical; Ofcr Stu Cncl; Hon Roll; Pres Acad Fit Awd; Beta Awd; J A Rigos Schlsp; AR Acad Achvmt Schlsp; Henderson ST Univ; Juvnl Psych.

NIMMO, WAYNE; Crossett Sr HS; Crossett, AR; (3); 3/200; Mu Alpha Theta; Natl Beta Clb; Quiz Bowl; Science Clb; Rptr Nwsp; High Hon Roll; NHS; Pres Acad Fit Awd; Stu For Chrst; Fulbright Schl Of Pub Affairs; MIT; Aeronautical Engrng.

NIPPER, DANIEL; West Side HS; Edgemont, AR; (4); Church Yth Grp; Drama Clb; FCA; FBLA; HOBY; Office Aide; Teachers Aide; Church Choir; School Play; Ed Nwsp; Ouachita Bapt U; Comp Sci.

NIVENS, JAMES; Blevins HS; Prescott, AR; (4); 2/35; FBLA; Natl Beta Clb; Natl FFA Org; Quiz Bowl; Yrbk; Var Bsbl; High Hon Roll; Sal; ADAPT; Voted Mst Likely To Succeed; LA Tech Coll; Elec Engrng.

NIX, GINGER K; Central Sr HS; Little Rock, AR; (3); Art Clb; Church Yth Grp; Cmnty Wkr; DECA; Office Aide; Spanish Clb; SADD; Chorus; Church Choir; Powder Puff Ftbl; AR Presbytery Comms; Ed.

NIX, KRISSY; Wynne HS; Wynne, AR; (3); Church Yth Grp; Drama Clb; FCA; SADD; Church Choir; Var L Chrldng; Cit Awd; Hon Roll; NHS; Spanish NHS; Unity Bible Clb Pres; Preliminary Talent Wnner To Mid So Fair Talent Review; Multi-Yr Listee; Piano; Pre-Vet.

NIX, LESLIE N; Hampton Jr Sr HS; Hampton, AR; (3); 7/85; Church Yth Grp; Natl Beta Clb; Pres Natl FFA Org; Teachers Aide; Phtg Yrbk; High Hon Roll; Hon Roll; FFA St Fair Reserve Champ 94, 95, Mem Of Yr, Animal Husbandry Awd, Right Hand Awd, Star Chptr Farmr; SAU Magnolia; Agri Bus.

NIX, MISTY A; Dequeen HS; De Queen, AR; (1); Church Yth Grp; Dance Clb; FBLA; SADD; Chorus; Sftbl; Cit Awd; Hon Roll; Prfct Atten Awd; Pres Acad Fit Awd; Dance 9 Yrs; Med.

NIX, REBECCA; Gentry HS; Gentry, AR; (4); 1/80; Art Clb; Math Clb; Spanish Clb; Chorus; High Hon Roll; NHS; Val; Church Yth Grp; Ofcr Stu Cncl; All St Chorus; Hi-Q Ace Tms; John Brown Univ; Mus Ed.

NIXON, ALICE A; Pine Bluff HS; Pine Bluff, AR; (3); 10/400; Am Leg Aux Girls St; Church Yth Grp; French Clb; Hosp Aide; Treas Key Clb; Office Aide; Acpl Chr; Variety Show; Yrbk; Ed Lit Mag; Jr Pollyanna Club Treas; Knowledge Masters; Speech Path/Audiology/Med.

NIXON, COURTNEY E; Springdale Sr HS; Springdale, AR; (2); Thesps; Band; Chorus; Mrchg Band; Pep Band; Stage Crew; Hon Roll; Symph Musicn.

NIXON, JAMIE; Bismarck Jr-Sr HS; Bismarck, AR; (4); 9/69; FCA; FBLA; Natl Beta Clb; Red Cross Aide; Stage Crew; Phtg Nwsp; Ed Yrbk; Rep Frsh Cls; VP Soph Cls; Rep Jr Cls; Henderson ST U; Nrsng.

NIXON, JEREMY; Bismarck Jr-Sr HS; Bismarck, AR; (2); Natl Beta Clb; Quiz Bowl; Band; Jazz Band; Mrchg Band; Pep Band; Ed Yrbk; Rep Stu Cncl; Hon Roll; Pres Acad Fit Awd; Hendrix; Pre-Law.

NIXON, MIRANDA L; Alma HS; Alma, AR; (2); Art Clb; Cmnty Wkr; ROTC; Hon Roll; Westark CC; RN.

NIXON, MORGAN; Mc Rae Schl; Mc Rae, AR; (1); FHA; Natl Beta Clb; Sec Frsh Cls; Ofcr Stu Cncl; Bsktbl; Trk; High Hon Roll; Gftd/Tlntd; Rice; Psych.

NOBLE, ASHLEY M; Pulaski Acad; Little Rock, AR; (2); VP Church Yth Grp; Cmnty Wkr; Natl Beta Clb; Spanish Clb; Band; Chorus; Church Choir; Mrchg Band; School Musical; VP Jr Cls; Interact Clb Sec.

NOBLE, KRISTY D; Riverview HS; Judsonia, AR; (2); Natl Beta Clb; Sec Band; Mrchg Band; Pep Band; High Hon Roll; Hon Roll; Bus/Cmptr Tchr.

NOBLES, C ELIZABETH; El Dorado Sr HS; El Dorado, AR; (4); 16/246; Am Leg Aux Girls St; Natl Beta Clb; Service Clb; Pres Frsh Cls; Rep Stu Cncl; Pom Pon; L Tennis; High Hon Roll; Hon Roll; Pres NHS; Barrett Hamilton Young AR Artists Awd; Wearer Of The Gold; William Woods U; Equestrn Sci.

NOBLIN, ELIZABETH R; Cabot HS; Cabot, AR; (3); 51/385; Church Yth Grp; French Clb; Key Clb; Teachers Aide; Acpl Chr; Band; Chorus; Mrchg Band; Orch; Pep Band; All Region Choir 93-95; All Region Band 93-; All ST Band 95-; Harding Univ; Music/PT.

NOE, JASON D; Farmington Jr Sr HS; Farmington, AR; (1); L Bsktbl; L Trk; Hon Roll.

NOLAN, KATIE P; Lake Hamilton Sr HS; Hot Springs, AR; (3); 3/224; FBLA; Natl Beta Clb; Science Clb; Spanish Clb; High Hon Roll; NHS; Pres Acad Fit Awd; Wolf Pride Sec, Treas; HEART; Nrs.

NOLAN, STORM; Southside HS; Ft Smith, AR; (2); Drama Clb; Mu Alpha Theta; Ski Clb; Spanish Clb; Ofcr Jr Cls; Ftbl; Trk; Wt Lftg; NHS; Harvard; Bus Ownrshp.

NOLDER, ABBY R; John L Mcclellan Magnet HS; Hensley, AR; (3); 2/280; Am Leg Aux Girls St; French Clb; FBLA; Mu Alpha Theta; Capt Chrldng; High Hon Roll; NHS; Mgn Cm Ld Natl Ltn Exm; Natl Yth Ldrshp Frm Med; Frnch I, II & III Awds; U Of AR; Med.

NOLEN, SHEREE; Delight HS; Delight, AR; (3); 2/34; 4-H; FBLA; Natl Beta Clb; Natl FFA Org; Quiz Bowl; Ofcr Stu Cncl; Hon Roll; JETS Awd; NHS; Gftd/Tlntd; Henderson ST U; Nrsng.

NOLES, GLENDA M; Oak Grove HS; North Little Rock, AR; (3); Art Clb; Cmnty Wkr; French Clb; FBLA; Mu Alpha Theta; Band; High Hon Roll; UCA.

NOONER, MICHEAL D; Mt Vernon-Enola HS; Vilonia, AR; (3); Art Clb; Quiz Bowl; Scholastic Bowl; Science Clb; Teachers Aide; Acting Awd.

NORCROSS, SARAH A; Mountain Home HS; Mountain Home, AR; (4); 27/180; Pres Art Clb; Church Yth Grp; 4-H; FBLA; FHA; HOBY; Key Clb; Natl Beta Clb; Quiz Bowl; Spanish Clb; AR Yng Artsts Assc VP 95-/Sec 94-95; Outstdng Eng Stu Awd/Summa Cum Laude Grad; AR Gov Schl Cand; U Of AR Fayetteville.

NORDIN, AMANDA D; Russellville Sr HS; Russellville, AR; (3); French Clb; Band; Drm Mjr(t); Mrchg Band; High Hon Roll; Jr NHS; NHS; All-Region Band; All-St Band; AR Tech Univ; Music Ed.

NORDIN, DEIDRE A; Russellville Sr HS; Russellville, AR; (2); Band; Mrchg Band; High Hon Roll; Jr NHS; NHS; All Reg Bnd 2 Yr; AR Tech Univ; Corp Lat.

NORFUL, ANDRIA S; Smackover HS; Smackover, AR; (3); #20 in class; FHA; FTA; Teachers Aide; Chorus; Trk; S AR Univ; Phy Thrpst.

NORMAN, BILL; Brinkley HS; Brinkley, AR; (4); 3/70; Am Leg Boys St; Church Yth Grp; Cmnty Wkr; Drama Clb; French Clb; FBLA; Science Clb; VP Sr Cls; Ofcr Bsbl; Pres NHS; All Amer Schlr; U Cntrl AR; Bus.

NORMAN, CHRISTY; Brinkley HS; Brinkley, AR; (2); Church Yth Grp; Cmnty Wkr; Drama Clb; Girl Scts; Band; Church Choir; Drm Mjr(t); Mrchg Band; Sec Frsh Cls; Rep Soph Cls; Prsdntl Acad Awd; ASU; Nrsng.

NORMAN, DANYALE C; Strong Jr Sr HS; Strong, AR; (2); Drama Clb; French Clb; Quiz Bowl; Science Clb; Pres Soph Cls; Var Bsbl; JV Bsktbl; Var Ftbl; Var Wt Lftg; Hon Roll; NLU; Mus Prod/Ftbl Plyr.

NORMAN, JEFF; Brinkley HS; Brinkley, AR; (3); Drama Clb; French Clb; Sec FBLA; Library Aide; Ofcr Jr Cls; Ftbl; Tennis; Hon Roll; Jr NHS; NHS; Chrch Yth Grp; Gftd & Tlntd; U Of Cntrl AR; Acctng.

NORMAN, TANELIA A; Russellville Sr HS; Russellville, AR; (2); FCA; Var JV GAA; Band; Mrchg Band; Var JV Bsktbl; Trk; Var JV Vllybl; Hon Roll; Jr NHS; Prfct Atten Awd; Age To Age Fnd Tutor; Math Acad Awd; TN Univ; Med Dr.

NORRELL, NELLY P; Mills HS; North Little Rock, AR; (2); 2/450; Church Yth Grp; Hosp Aide; Mu Alpha Theta; Natl Beta Clb; Spanish Clb; Teachers Aide; High Hon Roll; NHS.

NORRIS, BRANDY; Monticello Jr HS; Monticello, AR; (2); 15/160; Church Yth Grp; FCA; Natl Beta Clb; Pep Clb; Spanish Clb; Band; Drill Tm; Rep Stu Cncl; Chrldng; High Hon Roll; Nrsng.

NORRIS, HEATHER M; Huttig Schl; Huttig, AR; (3); FHA; GAA; Bsktbl; Sftbl; SAU.

NORRIS, LAURA E; Mc Gehee HS; Mcgehee, AR; (2); Church Yth Grp; Drama Clb; FBLA; FTA; Mu Alpha Theta; Natl Beta Clb; Spanish Clb; Yrbk; Treas Stu Cncl; NHS; Piano.

NORTHCUTT, LINDSAY L; Marvell Acad; Moro, AR; (4); 2/31; Pres Church Yth Grp; Rptr Nwsp; Yrbk; Sec Frsh Cls; JV Var Bsktbl; Capt Sftbl; Capt Var Trk; High Hon Roll; Jr NHS; Rep NHS; Recipient Of Elctrc Yth Tr 1995; U Of Cntrl AR; Nrsng.

NORTON, ASHLEY B; Central Sr HS; Little Rock, AR; (3); Drama Clb; FBLA; German Clb; Sftbl; Vllybl; Hon Roll; Jr NHS; Duke U Tlnt ID Pgm 92; Vlybl Outstndng Ath Achvt Awd 94; Nrsng.

NORTON, GAINES B; Catholic HS; Little Rock, AR; (3); 76/172; JV Var Tennis; Var Hon Roll; Bus.

NOUANJAVANE, KHEMPON K; Van Buren Sr HS; Van Buren, AR; (2); 43/352; FCA; FBLA; Mu Alpha Theta; VP Frsh Cls; High Hon Roll; NHS; Ntl Merit Ltr; U Of AR Little Rock; Bio.

NOVAK, JULIE M; Mountain Home HS; Midway, AR; (3); 55/267; Boy Scts; Church Yth Grp; German Clb; Girl Scts; Natl Beta Clb; Quiz Bowl; Band; Lit Mag; Mrchg Band; Pep Band; Chrch Yth Handbell Choir Dir; Ger-Amer Partnrshp Pgm 95; Governors Schl 96; Chrch Lector & Altar Server.

NOVERO, SETH L; Russellville Sr HS; Russellville, AR; (3); Art Clb; Church Yth Grp; Drama Clb; FCA; JA; Office Aide; Spanish Clb; Teachers Aide; Varsity Clb; School Play; CSU; All-Stars; Washington Univ; Biomed Engr.

NOVICK, JOHNNY T; El Dorado Sr HS; El Dorado, AR; (3); FCA; Var Ftbl; JV Var Trk; Tang Soo Do Karate 1st Cup & 1st & 3rd Medals; USAF Acad; MD.

NOWLIN, BOBBY J; Nevada Schl; Rosston, AR; (2); Art Clb; French Clb; FBLA; Natl Beta Clb; Quiz Bowl; Band; Hon Roll; Mock Trial; Drug Free Team; All-Region Band; Band Dir.

NUCKOLLS, NATALIE N; Southside HS; Batesville, AR; (2); 1/150; Church Yth Grp; FCA; Key Clb; Natl Beta Clb; Science Clb; Band; Church Choir; Ofcr Stu Cncl; Golf; Sftbl; PRIDE; Gftd & Tlntd; William Baptist Coll; Phys Thrp.

NUCKOLLS, SAM; Southside HS; Batesville, AR; (4); 1/75; Church Yth Grp; Cmnty Wkr; Drama Clb; FCA; FBLA; HOBY; Key Clb; Math Clb; Natl Beta Clb; Office Aide; PRIDE Tm; STOP; Tnns Tm; Ouachita Baptist Coll; Religion.

NUGENT, COURTNEY R; Central Sr HS; Little Rock, AR; (2); Drama Clb; Natl Beta Clb; Spanish Clb; High Hon Roll; Hon Roll.

NUMAN, PATRICK; Delta Special Schl; Rohwer, AR; (2); Natl Beta Clb; Natl FFA Org; Ofcr Stu Cncl; Ofcr Bsbl; Bsktbl; Cit Awd; Hon Roll.

NUNALLY, JENNIFER D; Black Rock Jr Sr HS; Black Rock, AR; (3); Church Yth Grp; FBLA; FHA; Natl FFA Org; Chorus; Church Choir; School Musical; Treas Frsh Cls; Treas Soph Cls; Treas Jr Cls; FBLA Treas 96-; FFA Sec 95-; Declined Natl Yng Ldrs Conf 96; Vet/Pediatric Nurse.

NUNLEY, NICK; Southside HS; Fort Smith, AR; (3); French Clb; Math Clb; Mu Alpha Theta; JV Ftbl; JV Golf; JV Wrstlng; Hon Roll; NHS; Snow Skiing; Restor Antique Mustangs; Chem Eng/Military.

NUNN, CRIS A; Rogers HS; Rogers, AR; (3); Church Yth Grp; Drill Tm; Swmmng; Hon Roll; Rogers Chamber Of Commerce Awd; Rogers Rrnaissance; Tchr.

NUNNALLY, ADRIENNE; Harding Acad; Searcy, AR; (3); Am Leg Aux Girls St; Church Yth Grp; Key Clb; Natl Beta Clb; JCL; School Musical; Pres Jr Cls; Co-Capt Chrldng; JV Var Trk; High Hon Roll; Harding U.

NUTT, CRISTY; East End Jr Sr HS; Bigelow, AR; (1); VP Church Yth Grp; Pres 4-H; VP FBLA; Treas Natl Beta Clb; SADD; Church Choir; Ed Nwsp; Ed Yrbk; Rep Stu Cncl; TV News Rptr.

NWANKWO, LA REITHA; Dollarway HS; Pine Bluff, AR; (3); Chorus; Drill Tm; Ofcr Stu Cncl; Ofcr Bsbl; Cit Awd; High Hon Roll; Prfct Atten Awd.

NWANKWO, LAKEITHA; Dollarway HS; Pine Bluff, AR; (3); Church Yth Grp; Chorus; Church Choir; Drill Tm; Bsktbl; Cit Awd; High Hon Roll; Prfct Atten Awd.

NYE, BRAD; Abundant Life Schools; Sherwood, AR; (1); Drama Clb; Speech Tm; High Hon Roll; Mar Bio.

NYLES, KLYUANA K; Robinson HS; Little Rock, AR; (3); 5/100; Church Yth Grp; Cmnty Wkr; FHA; FTA; Library Aide; Pep Clb; Chorus; Church Choir; Drill Tm; School Musical; Lawyer.

O'BANION, KRISTIE L; Newport HS; Newport, AR; (3); Church Yth Grp; Spanish Clb; SADD; Band; Flag Corp; Mrchg Band; Vet.

O BAR, KRISTIE M; Pleasant View Schl; Mulberry, AR; (4); Sec Drama Clb; FBLA; FHA; Natl Beta Clb; Phtg Yrbk; Rep Soph Cls; Rep Jr Cls; Sec Sr Cls; Ofcr Stu Cncl; Bsktbl; Sr Lady Hrnts Regnl Wnnrs; AR Tech Univ.

O'BIER, AUTUMN M; Lake Hamilton Sr HS; Hot Springs Natio, AR; (3); Church Yth Grp; Computer Clb; FBLA; Spanish Clb; Thesps; VP Chorus; Pres Jr Cls; Sec Stu Cncl; Co-Capt Chrldng; NHS; Ldrshp Hot Springs Partnership With Yth.

O'BRIEN, ASHLEY; Mount St Marys Acad; Little Rock, AR; (3); Cmnty Wkr; Q&S; Spanish Clb; Rptr Nwsp; JV Socr; HS Eng Tchr.

O'BRIEN, EVIE; Mt St Mary HS; Little Rock, AR; (3); Church Yth Grp; Cmnty Wkr; French Clb; Model UN; Co-Ed Nwsp; Var Chrldng; French Hon Soc; High Hon Roll; NHS; Vol Wrk; Eng/Wrtng.

OCAMPO, CAROLYN J; Oak Grove HS; North Little Rock, AR; (2); Mu Alpha Theta; Natl Beta Clb; Spanish Clb; Hon Roll; Outstdng Acad Achvmt; U Of AR; Med Scis.

O'DANIEL, BECKY; Southside HS; Fort Smith, AR; (2); Church Yth Grp; German Clb; Teachers Aide; Swmmng; Hon Roll; Jr NHS; NHS; Pres Acad Fit Awd; Ft Smith Tideriderders Swim Tm; All St Swimmer; Rgn 8 U S Swimmer; Jr Natl Relay Qlfr.

O'DANIEL, GINGER; Mills HS; North Little Rock, AR; (3); 5/298; Mu Alpha Theta; Natl Beta Clb; Orch; Ofcr Soph Cls; Ofcr Jr Cls; Ofcr Stu Cncl; Chrldng; Hon Roll; NHS; Pres Acad Fit Awd; CAR ST Pres/ST VP/ST Chpln; AR Governors Schl; Bus.

ODEGARD, SARAH L; Ozark HS; Ozark, AR; (3); 30/99; VP Sec Church Yth Grp; Cmnty Wkr; 4-H; FBLA; Natl Beta Clb; Speech Tm; Band; Chorus; Church Choir; Drm Mjr(t); MIDI-AEGIS Camp; All Reg 1st Band 3 Yrs; St Solo/Ensemble Medals 2 Yrs; Music Composition.

O DELL, DAVID M; Arkansas Bapt Schl; Bryant, AR; (3); Church Yth Grp; VP FCA; FBLA; Spanish Clb; Chorus; Church Choir; School Musical; School Play; Pres Jr Cls; Var L Bsktbl; All Conf/All Rgn Bsktbl 95-.

ODLE, CHRIS; Hackett Schl; Fort Smith, AR; (1); Spanish Clb; Bsktbl; Hon Roll; Jr NHS; Prfct Atten Awd; High Hon Roll.

ODLE, MEREDITH M; Lamar HS; Knoxville, AR; (4); 12/104; Sec Treas FBLA; Hosp Aide; Natl Beta Clb; Nwsp; Yrbk; Mgr(s); Hon Roll; NHS; 10th, 11th & 12th Grd Homcmng Maid; 95 Johnson Cty Fair Qn 1st Rnnr Up; Delta ST Univ; Nrsng.

ODOM, AMANDA M; Bauxite Jr Sr HS; Bauxite, AR; (2); Hosp Aide; Office Aide; Chorus; Flag Corp; Hon Roll; Bauxite Flag Line Capt; Sci Bio/Pdtrcn.

ODOM, ANDREA N; Bald Knob HS; Bald Knob, AR; (1); Natl Beta Clb; Teachers Aide; Band; Color Guard; Mrchg Band; Ofcr Stu Cncl; Hon Roll; All Region Band; Phys Therapy.

ODOM, BOBBI K; Wilburn Schl; Heber Springs, AR; (3); 4/11; Am Leg Aux Girls St; Church Yth Grp; VP 4-H; Sec FBLA; FHA; HOBY; Natl Beta Clb; Teachers Aide; Church Choir; School Play; Premed.

OGDEN III, EARL; Prairie Grove HS; Prairie Grove, AR; (4); #1 in class; Am Leg Boys St; Church Yth Grp; Cmnty Wkr; FCA; Letterman Clb; Sec Rep Natl FFA Org; Quiz Bowl; Spanish Clb; Varsity Clb; Var L Bsbl; Univ Of AR; Agri Bus.

OGDEN, MELISSA; Morrilton Sr HS; Perry, AR; (2); Church Yth Grp; French Clb; Natl Beta Clb; Office Aide; Hon Roll; UCA; Med.

OGDEN, NATHAN LOREN; Prairie Grove HS; Prairie Grove, AR; (3); #19 in class; Am Leg Boys St; Church Yth Grp; Cmnty Wkr; FCA; Math Clb; Pres Natl FFA Org; Quiz Bowl; Scholastic Bowl; Science Clb; Spanish Clb; Tae Kwon Do Recvd Black Belt; Intnl Law.

OGILVIE, AMY L; Southside HS; Batesville, AR; (3); Church Yth Grp; Cmnty Wkr; Hosp Aide; Key Clb; Natl Beta Clb; Science Clb; Teachers Aide; Band; Pep Band; Stage Crew; UCCA; Nrsng.

OGLE, SAMMY W; Magnolia HS; Magnolia, AR; (4); Church Yth Grp; Drama Clb; FBLA; Library Aide; Mu Alpha Theta; Science Clb; Chorus; Church Choir; JV Bsktbl; Var L Ftbl; Southern AR Univ.

OGLESBY, DEMESIA L; Pine Bluff HS; Pine Bluff, AR; (3); 45/485; Cmnty Wkr; FBLA; FHA; Office Aide; Pep Clb; Spanish Clb; Teachers Aide; Band; Mrchg Band; Pep Band; WA ST; Pre Phrmcy.

OGLESBY, KEISHA; Parkin Jr Sr HS; Parkin, AR; (2); 1/28; FHA; FTA; Science Clb; Chorus; Church Choir; Jazz Band; VP Soph Cls; Chrldng; High Hon Roll; Ntl Merit SF; Cmptr Tech.

OHBRIANT, HEATHER; Delta Special Schl; Dumas, AR; (4); 2/10; Church Yth Grp; Math Clb; Natl Beta Clb; Spanish Clb; VP Jr Cls; VP Sr Cls; Rep Stu Cncl; Hon Roll; NHS; Sal; Girls Ensmbl; Religion.

OKAFOR, VERONIQUE N; John L Mcclellan Magnet HS; Little Rock, AR; (4); 14/246; Mgr Drama Clb; FBLA; FTA; Natl Beta Clb; Quiz Bowl; Spanish Clb; Thesps; Acpl Chr; Band; Chorus; Deer Facilitator; SECME; Yth & Govt Clb; Hofstra Univ; Cinematography.

O'KEEFE, BRENT W; Blytheville Sr HS; Blytheville, AR; (4); 30/247; Am Leg Boys St; FCA; Key Clb; Natl Beta Clb; Rep Frsh Cls; Rep Jr Cls; Rep Stu Cncl; JV Var Ftbl; Var Golf; Pres Acad Fit Awd; Multi Yr Listee; U Of AR; Eng.

O'KEEFE, LORI B; Nevada Schl; Rosston, AR; (1); FBLA; Natl Beta Clb; Quiz Bowl; Teachers Aide; Band; High Hon Roll; Hon Roll; Drug Team; Solo Ensemble; U Of AR; Psych.

O'KELLEY, CLINTON A; Bauxite Jr Sr HS; Bauxite, AR; (2); Church Yth Grp; Office Aide; Band; Bsktbl; Jr NHS; Prfct Atten Awd.

OKUWOASH, OMETRA V; North Little Rock Hs-West; North Little Rock, AR; (3); 48/554; FHA; FTA; Math Clb; Mu Alpha Theta; Band; Mrchg Band; Pep Band; School Musical; High Hon Roll; Hon Roll; Acad Committment For Excl 96; Jr Band Awd 96; U Of Little Rock; Medicine.

OKWUOSA, PAULINE; Central Sr HS; Little Rock, AR; (3); FBLA; Pep Clb; Science Clb; Drill Tm; Nwsp; Rep Soph Cls; Ofcr Stu Cncl; Gym; Cit Awd; Hon Roll; Xavier U; Pre-Med.

OLBRICHT, THEODORE; Mammoth Spring HS; Mammoth Spring, AR; (4); 1/42; FBLA; HOBY; Natl Beta Clb; Pres VP Natl FFA Org; Treas Jr Cls; Treas Stu Cncl; L Bsktbl; High Hon Roll; Pres NHS; Pres Acad Fit Awd; Harding U; Bio.

OLGUIN, RHIANNON L; Harmony Grove Jr Sr HS; East Camden, AR; (3); Drama Clb; FCA; FBLA; FTA; Science Clb; Bsktbl; Chrldng; Trk; Pride; REACH Amer Drug/Alcohol Prvntn Awd; Southern AR Univ.

OLIENYK, ELIZABETH; Northside HS; Fort Smith, AR; (4); 81/327; Cmnty Wkr; DECA; French Clb; Key Clb; Teachers Aide; Band; Drm Mjr(t); Ed Nwsp; Hon Roll; Publc Rltn Drct For AR St Yth Ldr Prog; Natl Fnlst In CDC; DECA; OK St Univ; Grphc Dsgn.

OLIVER, ARCENIA; Garle HS; Crawfordsville, AR; (4); 4/50; French Clb; FBLA; FHA; Library Aide; Natl Beta Clb; Office Aide; Pep Clb; Teachers Aide; Chorus; Yrbk; Ft Valley ST Coll; Bio.

OLIVER, BROOKE; Cabot HS; Cabot, AR; (1); French Clb; Tennis; High Hon Roll; Jr NHS; MS ST U; Mtrlgst.

OLIVER, BRUCE; Gosnell Jr Sr HS; Blytheville, AR; (2); 37/119; Ftbl; Trk; Wt Lftg.

OLIVER, DEVAN; Nashville HS; Nashville, AR; (4); 7/120; Am Leg Aux Girls St; Church Yth Grp; Quiz Bowl; School Play; Chrldng; Gym; Jr NHS; NHS; Pres Acad Fit Awd; FHA; All Amer Chrldr; LA Tech; Eng.

OLIVER, JASON H; Hampton Jr Sr HS; Harrell, AR; (3); Church Yth Grp; FCA; Teachers Aide; Band; Mrchg Band; Ftbl; Trk; Wt Lftg; High Hon Roll; Hon Roll; Chem Awd.

OLIVER, KENDRA J; Rivercrest HS; Wilson, AR; (2); 28/128; Church Yth Grp; Girl Scts; ROTC; Church Choir; Color Guard; Capt Drill Tm; VP Soph Cls; Pres Jr Cls; Rep Stu Cncl; Cit Awd; RAA Clb; TAD Clb; UCLA; Legal Asst.

OLIVER, PATRICIA; Blevins HS; Hope, AR; (1); SADD; Ofcr Stu Cncl; Hon Roll; Ouachita Baptist U; Lawyer.

OLIVER, SHARISSA; Bauxite Jr Sr HS; Bauxite, AR; (3); Church Yth Grp; Cmnty Wkr; Dance Clb; GAA; JA; Office Aide; Spanish Clb; SADD; Teachers Aide; Drill Tm; Henderson ST U.

OLIVER, WENDY E; Gosnell Jr Sr HS; Blytheville, AR; (3); 4/74; Mu Alpha Theta; Natl Beta Clb; Teachers Aide; Mrchg Band; Pep Band; Yrbk; Cit Awd; Hon Roll; Pres Acad Fit Awd; Natl Young Ldrs Conf; AR ST Univ; Jrnlsm; News Ed.

OLLISON, RASHOD; Slyvan Hills HS; Little Rock, AR; (4); 24/233; 4-H; FBLA; FTA; Library Aide; Math Clb; Q&S; Quiz Bowl; Ed Nwsp; Lit Mag; Ofcr Stu Cncl; HOBY Ldrshp Awd; Natl Beta Clb; Crtv Wrtng Awd; U Of AR Fayetteville; Engl.

OLSON, ASIA; Deer Jr Sr HS; Jasper, AR; (3); Art Clb; Cmnty Wkr; Computer Clb; English Clb; 4-H; FBLA; FHA; HOBY; Latin Clb; Math Clb; Summerstage 95; Harrison Theater Co; Green Belt Shotokan Karate; Lead Singer Lcl Band; U Of AR; Music Theater.

OLSON, CHRISTA A; Clarksville HS; Clarksville, AR; (3); Church Yth Grp; FCA; FBLA; GAA; Spanish Clb; Church Choir; Bsktbl; Crs Cntry; Sftbl; Trk; Coached Girls Club Bsktl; Prd Club; U Of Central AR; Ansthslgst.

OLSON, CHRISTINA; Izard Co Cons Jr Sr HS; Horseshoe Bend, AR; (2); 30/40; FHA; Natl Beta Clb; Spanish Clb; Chorus; Yrbk; Sec Soph Cls; Var Chrldng; JV Gym; High Hon Roll; Hon Roll; ASU; Dr; Bus.

OLSON, MEGAN B; Lake Hamilton Sr HS; Hot Springs, AR; (2); FCA; FBLA; Natl Beta Clb; Spanish Clb; Drill Tm; Tennis; High Hon Roll; NHS; Pres Acad Fit Awd; Natl Lge Jr Ctlln; Wolf Prde; Natl Piano Plyng Adtns; FL ST.

OLSON, MELISSA P; Lake Hamilton Sr HS; Hot Springs, AR; (2); FCA; FBLA; Natl Beta Clb; Spanish Clb; Drill Tm; Var Tennis; Hon Roll; NHS; Pres Acad Fit Awd; Teachers Aide; Natl Lge Jr Ctlln; Wlf Prde; Natl Piano Plyng Adtns; FL ST.

OLTMANN, MICHAEL; Brinkley HS; Brinkley, AR; (3); Drama Clb; French Clb; FBLA; Ftbl; Trk; Wt Lftg; High Hon Roll; NHS; Aerontcs.

OLTMANS, CORAL D; Bryant Sr HS; Alexander, AR; (2); Church Yth Grp; Office Aide; Hon Roll; NHS; Phy Thrpst.

O'MELL, BUCKLEY; Lee Acad; Marianna, AR; (2); Cmnty Wkr; Red Cross Aide; Temple Yth Grp; Yrbk; Bsktbl; High Hon Roll; Hon Roll; St Page; Stu Of Month; Bus.

O'MELL, LEWIS B; Lee Acad; Marianna, AR; (2); Temple Yth Grp; Phtg Yrbk; Golf; Trk; Cit Awd; High Hon Roll; NHS; AR House Of Rep Page; Dept Awd Span World His Comp; Bus.

ONALE, ROBERT N; Junction City HS; Junction City, AR; (1); FBLA; Quiz Bowl; Science Clb; Hon Roll; 1st Plc Physics Local Sci Fair; 1st Plc Poster/Culture Bwl Reg Span Cmptn; Chrch Yth Grp; Aeronautical Eng/Military.

O'NEAL, BETHANEE A; Bentonville Sr HS; Bentonville, AR; (3); 59/323; Church Yth Grp; Acpl Chr; Chorus; Variety Show; Rep Stu Cncl; Hon Roll; Gftd & Tlntd Pgm; U Of AR; Eleme D.

O'NEAL, STEPHEN J; Rogers HS; Rogers, AR; (3); Church Yth Grp; Spanish Clb; Church Choir; Stage Crew; Yrbk; Crs Cntry; Socr; Swmmng; Trk; Hon Roll; Sci; Phy Thrpst.

O'NEAL, WHITNEY; Delight HS; Delight, AR; (4); 2/24; Natl Beta Clb; Natl FFA Org; Church Choir; School Play; Ed Yrbk; Sec Sr Cls; Var Chrldng; High Hon Roll; Ntl Merit Ltr; Sal; U Of AR-FAYETTEVILLE; Nrsng.

OPELA, MELISSA D; Fayetteville Sr HS; Fayetteville, AR; (2); Church Yth Grp; Spanish Clb; Hon Roll; Comm Arts Ctr Prod; Peer Helper Cnslng; Pals Prgm; U Of AR.

OPITZ, JONATHAN C; Benton Sr HS; Benton, AR; (3); 21/260; Am Leg Boys St; Church Yth Grp; FCA; Key Clb; Rep Stu Cncl; Var L Bsktbl; Kiwanis Awd; NHS; Stu Bd Benton St Bnk; Governors Yth Conf Del.

ORLANSKY, ALLISON L; Marvell Acad; Holly Grove, AR; (2); Computer Clb; FBLA; Latin Clb; Office Aide; Spanish Clb; Hist Rptr Soph Cls; Trk; Hon Roll; Jr NHS; NHS; Stu Of Month; Pre-Law.

ORR, AMANDA; Mann Magnet Jr HS; Little Rock, AR; (1); Church Yth Grp; Dance Clb; Spanish Clb; Church Choir; Ed Yrbk; Cit Awd; Hon Roll; Jr NHS; Pres Peer Facltrs; Tourng Hndbl Grp Chrch; Sthrn Meth U; Televsn Brdcstng.

ORR, BRANDI N; Highland HS; Ash Flat, AR; (3); Am Leg Aux Girls St; Pres 4-H; Treas Key Clb; Pres Natl Beta Clb; Quiz Bowl; Chorus; Church Choir; Var Bsktbl; 4-H Awd; Hon Roll; AR Govr Schl Nom.

ORR, MICHAEL M; Russellville Sr HS; Russellville, AR; (2); Church Yth Grp; Cmnty Wkr; FCA; Natl Beta Clb; JV Var Crs Cntry; JV Var Trk; Var Wrstlng; Chrch Plays; MX Mission Trip; Habitat For Humanity.

ORRELL, ASHLEY D; Berryville HS; Berryville, AR; (2); Church Yth Grp; FHA; Intnl Clb; Teachers Aide; Band; Church Choir; Mrchg Band; Hon Roll; Jr NHS; NHS; Yth Alive; Chrch Orch; Med.

ORRELL, JUSTIN; Lake Hamilton Jr HS; Pearcy, AR; (1); 13/264; Art Clb; Cmnty Wkr; Natl FFA Org; FFA Grnhnd Dgr, Sprt Awd 2nd Pl Tl ID, Res Cnty Fr Chmp Str 94, Grnd Chmp Str 95; Outstndg Yng Art; Comp Prgmr.

ORTIZ, NORA; Manila HS; Manila, AR; (3); Art Clb; FTA; Library Aide; Natl Beta Clb; Natl FFA Org; Teachers Aide; Chorus; School Play; Ofcr Soph Cls; Jr Cls Favorite; PRIDE; Nrs.

ORVIN, CODY H; Conway Sr HS; Conway, AR; (2); Office Aide; Hon Roll; All Amer Schlr; Pdtrcn.

OSBORN, AMANDA; Atkins Schl; Atkins, AR; (2); 7/80; Art Clb; Church Yth Grp; FBLA; Natl Beta Clb; Spanish Clb; Stat Bsktbl; Co-Capt Chrldng; Var Score Keeper; L Sftbl; High Hon Roll; Span Awd; U AR; Medicine.

OSBORN, MICHAEL R; Catholic HS; Little Rock, AR; (2); Math Tm; High Hon Roll; Soccer ASA Clb Team; Chrch Yth Group; Tutoring.

OSBORNE, ALLISON E; Russellville Sr HS; Russellville, AR; (2); Band; Drm Mjr(t); Mrchg Band; Orch; Media.

OSBORNE, BILLIE J; Booneville Jr Sr HS; Booneville, AR; (3); Church Yth Grp; FBLA; Natl Beta Clb; Band; Chorus; Mrchg Band; High Hon Roll; Hon Roll; Science Clb; Church Choir; Nrs Aide Cert; Marjorette; Westark CC; RN.

OSBUN, JOSH W; Southside HS; Fort Smith, AR; (2); Church Yth Grp; FCA; Mu Alpha Theta; Spanish Clb; High Hon Roll; Hon Roll; Jr NHS; NHS.

OSBURN, APRIL; Lake Hamilton Jr HS; Hot Springs, AR; (1); 3/264; Cmnty Wkr; FBLA; Natl Beta Clb; Natl FFA Org; Teachers Aide; Hon Roll; AR Cncl Tchrs Math Alg Cntst; PTA Dist Reflctns Cntst 1st, 2nd Pl Visual Arts; Wolf Pride Clb; Herptlgst.

O'SHIELDS, LAUREN J; Mc Crory Jr Sr HS; Mc Crory, AR; (2); Church Yth Grp; FBLA; Office Aide; Spanish Clb; School Play; Powder Puff Ftbl; Hon Roll; Jr NHS; NHS; Pres Acad Fit Awd; GATE Prgm; AR ST Univ; Acctng.

OSIER, THERESA A; Augusta HS; Augusta, AR; (2); FBLA; FTA; Girl Scts; Natl Beta Clb; Band; Drm Mjr(t); Mrchg Band; Yrbk; Sftbl; Spanish NHS; Jr/Sr GATE; AR ST Univ; Bus Acctng.

OTIS, CYNTHIA; Hughes Jr-Sr HS; Hughes, AR; (2); 10/73; Art Clb; Church Yth Grp; FBLA; Math Clb; Natl Beta Clb; Spanish Clb; Hon Roll; Prfct Atten Awd; Stanford U; Med.

OTT, SHANNON M; Ozark HS; Ozark, AR; (2); VP Church Yth Grp; Cmnty Wkr; Natl Beta Clb; SADD; Chorus; Church Choir; Ofcr Jr Cls; JV Bsktbl; Var Sftbl; High Hon Roll; United Meth Womens Elizabeth Circle VP.

OTTINGER, JENNIFER K; Hot Springs HS; Hot Springs Natio, AR; (2); 7/174; Cmnty Wkr; FBLA; Mu Alpha Theta; Natl Beta Clb; Spanish Clb; Chorus; High Hon Roll.

OTTS, ANGELA; Little Rock Acad; Mabelvale, AR; (4); Drama Clb; SADD; School Play; Yrbk; Chrldng; High Hon Roll; Jr NHS; NHS; Pres Schlr; Val; PRIDE; Voice Dmcrcy 1st Plc Wnnr.

OUZTS, MELANIE A; Russellville Sr HS; Russellville, AR; (3); Church Yth Grp; Cmnty Wkr; Band; Drill Tm; Mrchg Band; Variety Show; Chrldng; Trk; High Hon Roll; Jr NHS; All-Stars; UCA All-Star.

OVERMAN, VALERIE M; Lakeside HS; Lake Village, AR; (2); 8/80; Church Yth Grp; Cmnty Wkr; Drama Clb; FBLA; FHA; Church Choir; Hon Roll; Jr NHS; NHS; Pres Acad Fit Awd.

OVERTON, AMBER L; England HS; England, AR; (3); FCA; GAA; Natl Beta Clb; Spanish Clb; School Play; Ed Nwsp; Ofcr Stu Cncl; Bsktbl; Trk; Hon Roll; U Of AR.

OVERTON, JANA; Gosnell Jr Sr HS; Blytheville, AR; (4); 5/65; FHA; Natl Beta Clb; Office Aide; Science Clb; Spanish Clb; Teachers Aide; Chorus; L Bsktbl; High Hon Roll; NHS; TONE Conf Involvmnt; ASU; Pharmcy.

OWEN, ANTHONY; Woodlawn Schl; Star City, AR; (2); 1/45; Art Clb; Church Yth Grp; Natl Beta Clb; Quiz Bowl; Spanish Clb; Ftbl; Trk; Wt Lftg; Hon Roll.

OWEN, ANTHONY A; Star City HS; Star City, AR; (3); 10/88; Computer Clb; FHA; Math Clb; Mu Alpha Theta; Quiz Bowl; Band; Jazz Band; Mrchg Band; School Play; NHS; Star City Yth Cncl Pres; Music Perfmnc; Music Ed.

OWEN, BROOKE; Gosnell Jr Sr HS; Blytheville, AR; (2); Church Yth Grp; Key Clb; Natl Beta Clb; Science Clb; Teachers Aide; Chorus; Chrldng; High Hon Roll; Hon Roll; NHS.

OWEN, BROOKE; Van Buren Sr HS; Van Buren, AR; (3); 5/300; Mu Alpha Theta; Q&S; Science Clb; Speech Tm; Drill Tm; VP Soph Cls; VP Jr Cls; Treas Stu Cncl; NHS; Mgr Yrbk; Westminster; Pol Sci/Intl Rel.

OWEN, DENISE; Dumas Jr HS; Dumas, AR; (1); Church Yth Grp; FBLA; Natl Beta Clb; Science Clb; Spanish Clb; Band; Drm Mjr(t); Rptr Stu Cncl; Hon Roll; Church Choir; Ouachita Bapt U; Spch Pthlgst.

OWEN, JANICE M; Stamps HS; Buckner, AR; (4); 5/50; Art Clb; Church Yth Grp; Drama Clb; Math Clb; Mu Alpha Theta; Science Clb; Spanish Clb; School Play; Phtg Yrbk; Powder Puff Ftbl; Natl Merit Sci Awd; E TX St Univ.

OWEN, KELLI; Gosnell Jr Sr HS; Blytheville, AR; (4); 1/71; Church Yth Grp; FHA; HOBY; Key Clb; Natl Beta Clb; Science Clb; Teachers Aide; Chorus; VP Jr Cls; Bsktbl; AR ST U; Medcl.

OWEN, MEREDITH; White Hall Sr HS; Pine Bluff, AR; (2); Church Yth Grp; FCA; HOBY; Natl Beta Clb; Spanish Clb; Church Choir; School Musical; Rep Stu Cncl; Var Chrldng; High Hon Roll.

OWEN, NATE; Fayetteville Sr HS; Fayetteville, AR; (2); Church Yth Grp; Cmnty Wkr; Computer Clb; FCA; JA; Science Clb; Ski Clb; High Hon Roll; Hon Roll; Jr NHS; NWAJC; U Of AR; Bus Comm/Sci.

OWEN, SARAH; Monticello HS; Monticello, AR; (2); Art Clb; FCA; FBLA; Letterman Clb; Natl Beta Clb; Ofcr Soph Cls; Var Bsktbl; Var Co-Capt Chrldng; Var Sftbl; Hon Roll; Sports Med.

OWENS, ABBIE; Cabot HS; Cabot, AR; (3); 3/398; Church Yth Grp; FCA; French Clb; German Clb; Hosp Aide; Math Clb; Quiz Bowl; Teachers Aide; Orch; Rep Jr Cls; Mascot 1 Yr; Frnch Legion Of Hnr.

OWENS, ALLISON; Pulaski Acad; Little Rock, AR; (3); Church Yth Grp; Cmnty Wkr; FCA; French Clb; Natl Beta Clb; Var Chrldng; Hon Roll; NHS; All Amer Chrldr; U Of AR.

OWENS, AMBER E; Nettleton HS; Jonesboro, AR; (3); FHA; Teachers Aide; School Musical; Hon Roll; AR ST U.

OWENS, ANNA K; Arkansas Sr HS; Texarkana, AR; (3); Bus Profs of Am; Cmnty Wkr; Drama Clb; GAA; Mu Alpha Theta; Stage Crew; Yrbk; Mgr(s); Tennis; Hon Roll; 3rd Pl St Sew With Cotton; Henderson ST U; Fshn Dsgn.

OWENS, CARRIE F; Corning HS; Corning, AR; (3); Art Clb; Cmnty Wkr; SADD; Ed Yrbk; Mid-South Schlstc Vsl Art Awd; Photo.

OWENS, CHAD M; Waldron HS; Waldron, AR; (2); Pres Church Yth Grp; Natl Beta Clb; Spanish Clb; Ofcr Bsbl; Bsktbl; Ftbl; Golf; Wt Lftg; Hon Roll; AR Tech Univ; Coach; Tchr.

OWENS, CHRISTOPHER S; Benton Sr HS; Benton, AR; (3); Church Yth Grp; French Clb; FHA; Office Aide; VP Church Choir; JV Var Bsktbl; Church Sftbl; Univ Of CO; Chem/Physicist.

OWENS, CLAUDIA L; Springdale Sr HS; Springdale, AR; (1); Acpl Chr; Band; Chorus; Flag Corp; Mrchg Band; Pep Band; High Hon Roll; Jr NHS; Pres Acad Awd; All Region Bnd; Vanderbilt Univ; Music Tchr.

OWENS, DANIEL W; Rivercrest HS; Keiser, AR; (3); 2/100; Church Yth Grp; FBLA; FHA; JA; Key Clb; Math Clb; Office Aide; Quiz Bowl; Scholastic Bowl; Teachers Aide; 4 Time Mem Of All-Region Choir; 2 Time Qualifier For All-St Choir; AR ST Univ; Radiology.

OWENS, DEBRA R; Ozark HS; Ozark, AR; (2); 16/104; Yrbk; Hon Roll.

OWENS, JOHN; Arkansas Bapt Schl; Jacksonville, AR; (4); 1/34; Church Yth Grp; FCA; FBLA; Natl Beta Clb; Spanish Clb; School Play; Var Bsbl; Capt Bsktbl; NHS; Val; Ouachita Bapt Univ; Bible Mnstr.

OWENS, JOSH; Devalls Bluff Jr Sr HS; De Valls Bluff, AR; (1); Church Yth Grp; FBLA; Natl Beta Clb; Quiz Bowl; Rep Frsh Cls; Ofcr Bsbl; JV Bsktbl; Hon Roll; Bible Clb.

OWENS, KODI L; Pine Bluff HS; Pine Bluff, AR; (3); Art Clb; Band; Church Choir; Mrchg Band; Pep Band; School Musical; Hon Roll; Jr NHS.

OWENS, KRISTI L; Glenwood Jr Sr HS; Glenwood, AR; (2); 3/30; Church Yth Grp; Dance Clb; FCA; FHA; Chrldng; High Hon Roll; NHS; Span, Global Stud & His Awds; UCA; Med; Dental Field.

OWENS, LE ANN; Westside HS; Bono, AR; (4); Pres Sec FHA; Natl FFA Org; Science Clb; Teachers Aide; Band; Chorus; School Musical; Ofcr Stu Cncl; Hon Roll; AR ST Univ; Phys Therapy.

OWENS, MELINDA; Amity Jr Sr HS; Amity, AR; (4); 6/14; Church Yth Grp; Sec FBLA; Treas FHA; Natl Beta Clb; School Play; Yrbk; Treas Frsh Cls; Treas Soph Cls; Rep Sr Cls; Capt Bsktbl; Hmcmng Qn; Ram Schlr; CHAMPS; Henderson ST U.

OWENS, MELODY; Mc Clellan Magnet HS; Little Rock, AR; (2); 30/218; Drama Clb; FCA; Letterman Clb; Natl Beta Clb; Church Choir; Rep Soph Cls; Chrldng; Mgr(s); Hon Roll; Prfct Atten Awd; 2nd Deg Blck Blt ATA Tae Kwon Do; Nrsng.

OWENS, SARA C; West Memphis Sr HS; West Memphis, AR; (4); Rptr DECA; French Clb; Office Aide; VP Science Clb; Chorus; Flag Corp; Stage Crew; Ed Nwsp; Hon Roll; Explrs; Mid South CC.

OWENS, SHEILA; Mountain View Jr Sr HS; Mountain View, AR; (4); 14/87; Am Leg Aux Girls St; Natl Beta Clb; Yrbk; Pres Jr Cls; Pres Stu Cncl; Hon Roll; Natl Engl Merit Awd; Hnr Grad; Sr Video; An Income Of Her Own; New Girl Times Reprtr; Multi Yr Listing.

OWENS, TREVA L; Stuttgart Sr HS; Roe, AR; (4); 10/153; Sec Church Yth Grp; Cmnty Wkr; Debate Tm; Drama Clb; FBLA; HOBY; Math Clb; Mu Alpha Theta; Pres Natl Beta Clb; VP Pres Science Clb; GFCWA Shrt Story Cntst 3rd; Coca-Cola Schol Semifnlst; Mdl Of Hnr; U Of Cntrl AR; Pre-Med.

OWOH, JEREMY; Camden-Fairview HS; Camden, AR; (3); 41/310; Am Leg Boys St; Boy Scts; Pres Church Yth Grp; Key Clb; Math Clb; Mu Alpha Theta; Natl Beta Clb; Science Clb; Spanish Clb; SADD; U Of A Fayetteville; Cmptr Eng.

PABIN, CHRIS; Vilonia HS; Conway, AR; (3); 5/145; FBLA; Ofcr FHA; Model UN; Pres Mu Alpha Theta; Pres Natl Beta Clb; Quiz Bowl; Jazz Band; Pep Band; School Play; Crs Cntry; U Of Cntrl AR; Nclr Med Tchncn.

PACE, ADRIENNE L; Hope HS; Hope, AR; (3); FBLA; FHA; GAA; Natl Beta Clb; Natl FFA Org; Band; Mrchg Band; Trk; Wt Lftg; High Hon Roll; Natl Eng Merit Awd; Audio Engr/TV Brdcstng.

PACE, AMY; Monticello HS; Monticello, AR; (4); 1/117; Church Yth Grp; FBLA; SADD; Band; Church Choir; Flag Corp; Pres Soph Cls; Pres Jr Cls; Pres Sr Cls; NHS; Ouachita Bapt Univ.

PACE, SARAH B; Searcy HS; Searcy, AR; (3); Am Leg Aux Girls St; Church Yth Grp; FTA; Key Clb; Natl Beta Clb; Spanish Clb; Thesps; School Musical; School Play; Stage Crew; Harding U; Elem Ed.

PACK, SARA A; Springdale Sr HS; Springdale, AR; (3); Am Leg Aux Girls St; Church Yth Grp; French Clb; FBLA; Chorus; Rptr Nwsp; Rep Stu Cncl; Ofcr Co-Capt Pom Pon; Jr NHS; NHS; All Amer Schlr; All Reg Schlr; Intl Bus.

PACKARD, CLAY P; Central Sr HS; Little Rock, AR; (2); Pres Church Yth Grp; FCA; Mu Alpha Theta; Natl Beta Clb; Quiz Bowl; JV Bsbl; Var Ftbl; Socr; Tennis; Wt Lftg; Supt Stdnt Cabinet 9th; 1st Jr Acad Engrng 9th; Fayetteville; Elec Engr.

PACKER JR, KARL; Jacksonville HS; Jacksonville, AR; (4); Boy Scts; Church Yth Grp; Drama Clb; French Clb; FBLA; Teachers Aide; Chorus; Cit Awd; DAR Awd; AK Tech Univ; Elec Eng.

PADGETT, SARA J; Central Sr HS; Little Rock, AR; (2); French Clb; German Clb; Natl Beta Clb; High Hon Roll; AALA Mem; Little Rock Schl Dist Supts Cabinet Mem 94-95; Rhodes.

PAGE, DANIEL; Harrisburg HS; Harrisburg, AR; (4); 3/53; Boy Scts; Pres Church Yth Grp; HOBY; Quiz Bowl; Science Clb; Orch; High Hon Roll; NHS; Prfct Atten Awd; Spanish Clb; All St Bnd; All St Choir; All St Sci Fair; Intrlchn Arts Cmp; Nrsng Hm Mnstry; Chrch Cert Lay Spkr; GATE; Sthrn Meth U; Music Ed.

PAGE, LATOSHA; Huttig Schl; Huttig, AR; (1); 2/15; Church Yth Grp; FBLA; FHA; FTA; German Clb; Band; Church Choir; School Musical; Pres Frsh Cls; Ofcr Soph Cls; OT.

PAGE, NICOLE H; North Little Rock Hs-West; North Little Rock, AR; (4); Art Clb; GAA; Teachers Aide; Stage Crew; Vllybl; Artist Of Yr 95; Commercial Art.

PAGE, SARAH; Beebe Jr HS; Beebe, AR; (1); Church Yth Grp; FHA; GAA; Natl Beta Clb; Band; L Bsktbl; L Trk; Cit Awd; High Hon Roll; Hon Roll; Med Field.

PAGE, SHANNON N; Oak Grove HS; Maumelle, AR; (1); FCA; Letterman Clb; Natl Beta Clb; Drill Tm; High Hon Roll; Hon Roll; Pres Schlr; Arts/Interior Dcrtng.

PAGE, SUSAN G; Dumas HS; Dumas, AR; (2); FBLA; FHA; Rptr Nwsp; Sec Soph Cls; Cit Awd; High Hon Roll; Jr NHS; NHS; Prfct Atten Awd; Quachita Bapt Univ; Bus Ed.

PAINE, DERRICK L; C V White Jr Sr HS; Helena, AR; (4); 6/23; FBLA; Natl FFA Org; Band; Jazz Band; Mrchg Band; Pep Band; School Musical; Yrbk; Ofcr Jr Cls; Bsktbl; Higest Ranking Stu Phy Sci; Speech; Cert Recognition Poem Cont; UAPB.

PAINTER, CRYSTAL M; Bryant Sr HS; Alexander, AR; (3); Pep Clb; Science Clb; Spanish Clb; Teachers Aide; Band; Mrchg Band; Pep Band; School Play; Bsktbl; Sftbl; UCA; Hy; Music Ed.

PAIR, ANGELA D; Greenwood Sr HS; Fort Smith, AR; (3); GAA; Treas Natl Beta Clb; Spanish Clb; Drill Tm; Pom Pon; Sftbl; Vllybl; Gov Hon Prg Awd; High Hon Roll; Pres NHS; Certfd 1st Aid, CPR & Lifeguard; U Of AR; Dentistry.

PALADINO, ALLISON M; Mc Gehee HS; Mc Gehee, AR; (4); 11/101; Church Yth Grp; Computer Clb; Pres FBLA; Mu Alpha Theta; Natl Beta Clb; Art Clb; Cmnty Wkr; FHA; Library Aide; Math Clb; Lions Clb Schlrshp; U Of AR; Spch Path/Eng.

PALADINO, ANNA M; Nemo Vista Jr Sr HS; Center Ridge, AR; (2); 1/35; Church Yth Grp; VP FBLA; FHA; Treas Natl Beta Clb; Spanish Clb; Sec Frsh Cls; VP Soph Cls; Capt Bsktbl; Hon Roll; AAU Bsktbl; 1st Pl Dist FBLA Kybrdng Comp; Hmcmng Maid 9th/10th; Acctng/Bus.

PALADINO, JASON A; Nemo Vista Jr Sr HS; Center Ridge, AR; (3); Art Clb; Cmnty Wkr; Spanish Clb; Teachers Aide; Band; Nwsp; Bsktbl.

PALADINO, MICHAEL J; Catholic HS; Little Rock, AR; (3); 7/200; Church Yth Grp; Pres Frsh Cls; Rep Soph Cls; Intrml Bsktbl; JV Ftbl; Var Wt Lftg; High Hon Roll; Ntl Merit Ltr.

PALIK, MICHELLE; Cabot HS; Cabot, AR; (2); French Clb; Chorus; School Musical; Hon Roll; Dnce Tm; BASIC; Cncrt Grls Ensm.

PALMER, CHRISTI M; Trumann HS; Trumann, AR; (3); Spanish Clb; Band; Color Guard; Mrchg Band; Pep Band; Hon Roll; NHS; AR ST Univ.

PALMER, JAMIE N; Quitman Jr Sr HS; Quitman, AR; (3); Church Yth Grp; FBLA; Natl Beta Clb; Natl FFA Org; SADD; Church Choir; Rptr Nwsp; Cit Awd; Hon Roll; NHS; U Of Central AR; Comp Pgmg.

PALMER, JEREMIAH A; Benton Cty Christian School; Bentonville, AR; (3); Church Yth Grp; Rptr Yrbk; Treas Jr Cls; Cit Awd; Hon Roll; Woodmen Of Wrld Life Ins Soc Amer His Outstdng Profcncy Awd; ACSI Distngd Chrstn Stdnt Awd; Centre Coll; Bus.

PALMER, JUSTIN; Pulaski Acad; Little Rock, AR; (2); Cmnty Wkr; French Clb; JV Var Bsktbl; High Hon Roll; AAU Bsktbl 2 ST Chmpnshps; 10 Natl Trnmnts; Top 10 Natl Fr Exam 95-; Penn.

PALMER, MISSI; Benton Cty Christian School; Bentonville, AR; (1); Church Yth Grp; Dir Of Nursery Dept At Calvary Bapt Chrch; Art; Kitchen Aid At Schl; Northwest AR CC; Interr Dsgn.

PALMER, SHEVONDA N; North Little Rock Hs-East; Little Rock, AR; (2); Drama Clb; French Clb; FBLA; FHA; FTA; Church Choir; Color Guard; School Musical; Stage Crew; Cit Awd.

PAN, DANIEL C; Central Sr HS; Little Rock, AR; (2); French Clb; FBLA; Intnl Clb; Math Clb; Mu Alpha Theta; Natl Beta Clb; Quiz Bowl; Science Clb; Orch; Cit Awd; Accept No Boundaries; Gentlemens Club.

PANGLE, BETHANY B; Yellville Summit HS; Yellville, AR; (2); 6/70; Church Yth Grp; Teachers Aide; Ed Rptr Nwsp; High Hon Roll; Hon Roll; Pres Acad Fit Awd; Atndng AR Schl For Math/Sci; Scndry Tchng.

PANKEY, CANDACE B; Prairie Grove HS; Prairie Grove, AR; (2); Art Clb; Church Yth Grp; FHA; Science Clb; Spanish Clb; Rptr Nwsp; High Hon Roll; NHS; GATE; Acad Excl Awd; U Of AR.

PANNELL, NATALIE A; Osceola HS; Osceola, AR; (2); Church Yth Grp; Drama Clb; 4-H; Pres FBLA; Math Clb; Natl Beta Clb; Science Clb; Spanish Clb; SADD; Band; Psych.

PANNELL, VICTORIA; Dierks HS; Dierks, AR; (4); 3/35; Am Leg Aux Girls St; Church Yth Grp; French Clb; FBLA; HOBY; Quiz Bowl; Band; Drill Tm; Rptr Nwsp; NHS; U Of AR Fayetteville; Pre-Vet.

PARIS, MARY A; Southside HS; Fort Smith, AR; (2); FCA; French Clb; Office Aide; Teachers Aide; Chorus; Church Choir; Ofcr Soph Cls; Mgr(s); Hon Roll; Jr NHS; NHS; U Of CO Boulder; Interior Dsgn.

PARISH, JASON K; Gosnell Jr Sr HS; Blytheville, AR; (2); Drama Clb; Quiz Bowl; Band; Mrchg Band; Pep Band; School Play; Yrbk; Hon Roll.

PARISH, JENNIFER L; Nemo Vista Jr Sr HS; Center Ridge, AR; (3); 10/35; Church Yth Grp; FBLA; FHA; Teachers Aide; Nwsp; Yrbk; Sec Frsh Cls; Sec Jr Cls; VP Stu Cncl; JV Var Bsktbl; FFA 9-11 Grd; FFA Showteam 10/11 Grd; U Of Cntrl AR.

PARISH, KYLE; Gosnell Jr Sr HS; Blytheville, AR; (1); Drama Clb; Natl Beta Clb; Quiz Bowl; Band; Mrchg Band; Pep Band; School Play; Variety Show; Hon Roll; Prfct Atten Awd; Drums.

PARISH, LYNETTE; Malvern Sr HS; Donaldson, AR; (2); FBLA; High Hon Roll; Hon Roll; Jr NHS.

PARISH, MICHAEL J; Blytheville Sr HS; Blytheville, AR; (4); FBLA; FHA; Library Aide; Natl Beta Clb; Var L Bsbl; Var Ftbl; Wt Lftg; Hon Roll.

PARK, ROBERT; Arkansas Sr HS; Texarkana, AR; (4); Am Leg Boys St; Key Clb; ROTC; Spanish Clb; Var Ftbl; Texarkana Coll; Bar/Grill Ownr.

PARKE, LAURA E; Southside HS; Fort Smith, AR; (2); Church Yth Grp; FCA; FHA; Key Clb; Rep Soph Cls; Var Tennis; Cit Awd; Hon Roll; Jr NHS; NHS; Sportsmanship Awd In Tnns.

PARKER, ASHLEY; Dermott HS; Dermott, AR; (2); Church Yth Grp; Dance Clb; Drama Clb; FCA; Sec FBLA; Math Clb; Natl Beta Clb; Science Clb; Co-Capt Drill Tm; French Hon Soc; All Amer Schlr; Natl Merit Sci Awd; Psych.

PARKER, BARBI M; Springdale Sr HS; Springdale, AR; (2); Church Yth Grp; English Clb; Chorus; Rep Frsh Cls; High Hon Roll; Hon Roll; Jr NHS; NHS; Hendrix; Bus.

PARKER, BRANDON H; Cabot HS; Cabot, AR; (2); Church Yth Grp; Thesps; JV Bsktbl; U Of MS; Bus Admin/Cmptr Tech.

PARKER, CHRISTY M; Rison HS; Rison, AR; (1); Church Yth Grp; Cmnty Wkr; FHA; Library Aide; Band; Church Choir; Drm Mjr(t); Mrchg Band; Nwsp; Yrbk; Lttr R Awd Phys Sci; Pride Team; Drug Awrnss Clb; UAM Of Monticello; Fine Arts.

PARKER, CRYSTAL; Gillett Jr Sr HS; Tichnor, AR; (2); Art Clb; FBLA; Pep Clb; Quiz Bowl; Spanish Clb; Bsktbl; Hon Roll; Jr NHS; NHS; Pres Acad Fit Awd.

PARKER, DAVID K; Crossett Sr HS; Crossett, AR; (3); Church Yth Grp; Var Bsbl; JV Ftbl; Hon Roll; LA Tech.

PARKER, ERIC W; Omaha Schl; Omaha, AR; (2); Natl Beta Clb; School Play; Pres Soph Cls; Var Bsbl; Var Bsktbl; Cit Awd; Hon Roll; Pres Ed Awd; AR Activities Assoc Reg Bsbll All Tourn Tm, All St Bsbll.

PARKER, ERICA LYNN; Mt St Mary Acad; Little Rock, AR; (4); Art Clb; Church Yth Grp; Cmnty Wkr; Debate Tm; FBLA; Hosp Aide; Library Aide; Spanish Clb; SADD; Teachers Aide; Culture Clb; Chrstn Brother Univ; Pre-Med.

PARKER, ERIN; North Little Rock Hs-West; N Little Rock, AR; (3); Am Leg Aux Girls St; Church Yth Grp; Cmnty Wkr; Drama Clb; FCA; Key Clb; Math Clb; Mu Alpha Theta; Natl Beta Clb; Spanish Clb; Top Ten Percent Awd; Jr Ldrshp Prgm.

PARKER, HEATHER; Calvary Christian Schl; Palestine, AR; (3); 2/11; Church Yth Grp; School Play; Stage Crew; Pres Frsh Cls; Pres Soph Cls; Pres Jr Cls; Var Capt Bsktbl; Score Keeper; Var Vllybl; High Hon Roll; All Conf Tm; Sports Med.

PARKER, JASON; Mc Neil HS; Mc Neil, AR; (3); #1 in class; Computer Clb; French Clb; HOBY; Office Aide; Science Clb; Teachers Aide; Rptr Nwsp; Rep Stu Cncl; Hon Roll; Comp Pgm.

PARKER, JASON M; Norphlet HS; Calion, AR; (4); 24/58; FBLA; Spanish Clb; Rep Jr Cls; VP Sr Cls; Var L Bsbl; Var L Bsktbl; Var L Ftbl; Hon Roll; Jr NHS; S AR Univ; Psych.

PARKER, KELLI R; Springdale Sr HS; Springdale, AR; (1); FBLA; Band; Chorus; Mrchg Band; Hon Roll; Jr NHS; Pres Schlr; Awd All Reg Band 95-; 1st Pl Zoology Sr HS Div Sci Fair 95-; Peer Hlpr 96-; Animal Sci.

PARKER, KENDRA; Southside HS; Fort Smith, AR; (3); Church Yth Grp; Cmnty Wkr; FCA; Mu Alpha Theta; Spanish Clb; Band; Chorus; Drm Mjr(t); Mrchg Band; School Musical; Interact Svc Clb; SAIL.

PARKER, LATISHA; J A Fair Sr HS; Little Rock, AR; (4); Computer Clb; FBLA; FHA; Natl Beta Clb; VICA; Hon Roll; NHS; CCE; Multi-Yr Listee.

PARKER, LESLEY KAY; Rogers HS; Bentonville, AR; (3); Church Yth Grp; FCA; FBLA; GAA; Letterman Clb; Office Aide; Bsktbl; Sftbl; Trk; Hon Roll; Chamber Of Commerce Acad Achvmt Awd.

PARKER, LYNNE; Camden Fairview HS; Camden, AR; (3); Church Yth Grp; Drama Clb; Sec French Clb; FBLA; Sec Natl Beta Clb; Office Aide; Science Clb; Chorus; School Musical; School Play; UCA All-Star Chrldr; Anchor Clb Sr Brd; Natl Yth Ldrshp Forum On Med; U Of AR Fayetteville; Med.

PARKER, MELISSA D; Arkansas Sr HS; Texarkana, AR; (4); 76/374; Art Clb; Natl FFA Org; Band; Flag Corp; Mrchg Band; Pep Band; Rep Frsh Cls; Mst Outstndg Engl Stu 93-94; NIKE; Do-Right Gang; Sweepstakes Band; Radiolgy Tech.

PARKER, MICHAEL R; Mena HS; Mena, AR; (2); 11/141; French Clb; Model UN; Quiz Bowl; Band; Phtg Nwsp; Rep Stu Cncl; Var Tennis; French Hon Soc; High Hon Roll; Pres Acad Fit Awd; Explorer Scouts; Elks Ldg Stdnt Mnth; All-Rgn Symph Bnd; Auburn Univ; Marine Bio.

PARKER, MICHAEL S; Dollarway HS; Pine Bluff, AR; (2); Church Yth Grp; ROTC; Rep Soph Cls; Ofcr Stu Cncl; JV Bsbl; JV Bsktbl; JV Ftbl; Jr NHS; Certfd Lifegrd/CPR; FL ST; Molecular Bio.

PARKER, NATHAN G; Berryville HS; Berryville, AR; (3); Quiz Bowl; Science Clb; Var Bsbl; Var Bsktbl; Gov Hon Prg Awd; High Hon Roll; Hon Roll; NHS; Pres Acad Fit Awd; Cmptr Prgmng.

PARKER, OSLIN MICHAEL; Alma HS; Rudy, AR; (2); Church Yth Grp; Band; Mrchg Band; Pep Band; Hon Roll; NHS; All Rgn Bnd; 2nd Bnd In Fresh Yr; Reg Solo And Ensmble Comp.

PARKER, RACHEL; Carlisle Jr Sr HS; Carlisle, AR; (3); Am Leg Aux Girls St; Treas Church Yth Grp; FBLA; VP FHA; Spanish Clb; Teachers Aide; School Play; Rptr Frsh Cls; Treas Jr Cls; Sec Stu Cncl; NCA All-Amer Chrldr 93-95; All-Star Chrldr For Cheer Cntrl Brvs; Gftd & Tlntd.

PARKER, TOMMY; Parkview Arts-Science HS; Little Rock, AR; (3); Am Leg Boys St; Church Yth Grp; Cmnty Wkr; FCA; Key Clb; Math Clb; Varsity Clb; Ofcr Bsbl; Crs Cntry; Ftbl; De Molay; Vanderbilt; Physics/Math.

PARKER, WENDY N; Dardanelle HS; Dardanelle, AR; (4); 1/100; Art Clb; Church Yth Grp; Intnl Clb; Natl Beta Clb; Band; Chorus; Tennis; Gov Hon Prg Awd; High Hon Roll; Val; Won Voice Of Dmcrcy Audio/Essay Cntst; U Of AR.

PARKES, JOHN; Farmington Jr Sr HS; Farmington, AR; (3); 14/95; Church Yth Grp; FCA; FBLA; FHA; Natl FFA Org; Var L Bsktbl; Var L Ftbl; Cit Awd; High Hon Roll; Hon Roll.

PARKS, ALICIA P; John L Mcclellan Magnet HS; Little Rock, AR; (2); Natl Beta Clb; Computer Clb; FBLA; FHA; FTA; Math Clb; Spanish Clb; Chorus; Church Choir; Vllybl; MIT; Cmptr Sci.

PARKS, AMANDA L; Hartford Schl; Hackett, AR; (2); VP FBLA; Band; Mrchg Band; Co-Ed Yrbk; Trk; High Hon Roll; NHS; Prfct Atten Awd; FBLA Dist I Pres; Music St Of Yr Awds.

PARKS, CHARLES; Cross Co Jr Sr HS; Wynne, AR; (3); 2/50; Natl Beta Clb; Natl FFA Org; Science Clb; Spanish Clb; Bsktbl; Ftbl; Hon Roll; ASU Math Cmptn Hnrb Mntn Geom; Bio.

PARKS, CHARLIE; Rogers HS; Rogers, AR; (3); Univ Of AR; Cmptr.

PARKS, JOSHUA C; Westside Jr Sr HS; Alicia, AR; (2); Church Yth Grp; Cmnty Wkr; FCA; Quiz Bowl; Sec Spanish Clb; Hon Roll; NHS; Pres Acad Fit Awd; Natl Beta Clb; Natl FFA Org; Fire Marshall; Cty Wide Drug Yth Bd; Interact Clb Treas; AR ST Univ; Wildlife Mgmt.

PARKS, KATHY; Evening Shade Schl; Evening Shade, AR; (3); 4/35; FBLA; School Play; Rep Jr Cls; Bsktbl; Sftbl; Hon Roll.

PARKS, KIMBERLY D; Marshall HS; Marshall, AR; (2); 4-H; FBLA; Natl Beta Clb; Spanish Clb; Band; High Hon Roll; NHS.

PARKS, KRISTEN; Sylvan Hills HS; Sherwood, AR; (1); Church Yth Grp; Dance Clb; Math Tm; Office Aide; Chorus; Chrldng; Hon Roll; Jr NHS; NHS; U Of AR Fayetteville; Dentist.

PARKS, STEPHANIE L; Mountain Home HS; Mountain Home, AR; (4); 86/227; FCA; FBLA; GAA; Natl FFA Org; Band; School Play; Var Capt Vllybl; Hon Roll; Kiwanis Awd; Mst Imprvd In Vllybl; Outstdng Hitter In Vllybl; AR Tech Univ; Comp Sci.

PARNELL JR, SAMUEL G; Arkansas Sr HS; Texarkana, AR; (4); 13/375; French Clb; Math Clb; Office Aide; Quiz Bowl; Cit Awd; Hon Roll; Jr NHS; NHS; Pres Acad Fit Awd; Qz Bwl Tm Capt; Yng Demcrts VP; Pld Regnlmath Comps; Hendrix Coll.

PARRISH, LATOYA S; Bradley Jr Sr HS; Bradley, AR; (4); 4-H; Library Aide; Band; Chorus; Church Choir; School Play; Ofcr Sr Cls; Sftbl; Vllybl; 4-H Awd; Art I/II; Dsgnr.

PARRISH, LINDSEY; Magnolia HS; Magnolia, AR; (3); French Clb; FBLA; HOBY; Quiz Bowl; Science Clb; Band; Mrchg Band; Pep Band; Rep Stu Cncl; Tennis; Band Cncl; Mu Alpha Theta.

PARRISH, ROBERT L; Ozark HS; Ozark, AR; (3); 8/100; FCA; Chorus; Var Bsbl; Var Bsktbl; Hon Roll; Soc Stud Club; K-Life; U Of AR; Elctrcl Eng.

PARRISH, TOMMIE A; Marvell Acad; Holly Grove, AR; (2); FBLA; Office Aide; Spanish Clb; Teachers Aide; Hon Roll; Rep Jr NHS; NHS; Attnd Amer Studies Inst Natl Ldrsp Forum; Attnd Acad Enrchmnt For Gftd In Summr Prgm.

PARSONS, JAMES BRANDON; Jonesboro HS; Jonesboro, AR; (4); Am Leg Boys St; Band; Ftbl; Socr; High Hon Roll; Stu Ath Alumni Schlsp; U Of Cntrl AR; Pre-Med.

PARSONS, RAMIE A; Waldron HS; Waldron, AR; (4); 14/75; FBLA; Natl Beta Clb; School Play; Phtg Nwsp; Phtg Yrbk; Hon Roll; NHS; Pres Acad Fit Awd; Drama Clb; FHA; All-Reg Choir 3 Yrs; Natl Ldrshp Forum; AR Govs Schl; U Of AR Fayetteville; Jrnlsm.

PASCHALL, CHRIS L; Springdale Sr HS; Springdale, AR; (4); Art Clb; Boy Scts; Bus Profs of Am; Cmnty Wkr; 4-H; FBLA; Math Tm; 4-H Awd; Hon Roll; Prfct Atten Awd; Bsktbl; Ftbl; Wghtlftng; Bus.

PASCHALL, JEREMY L; Springdale Sr HS; Springdale, AR; (2); Boy Scts; Church Yth Grp; Cmnty Wkr; French Clb; FBLA; Hon Roll; Jr NHS; NHS; Pres Schlr; Yth Fr Christ; Just Say No; Fr/Alge Outstdng Awds; Dist Sci Fair 1st Pl; U Of AR; Bus Admin.

PASIERB, SUSAN M; St Joseph HS; North Little Rock, AR; (2); Church Yth Grp; Key Clb; School Play; VP Soph Cls; JV Var Bsktbl; JV Golf; JV Var Sftbl; JV Var Trk; JV Var Vllybl; Cit Awd.

PASLEY, CARLIE N; Searcy HS; Searcy, AR; (3); 52/255; Church Yth Grp; 4-H; French Clb; FTA; Natl Beta Clb; Thesps; Stage Crew; Rptr Nwsp; French Hon Soc; Hon Roll; U Of Cntrl AR.

PASLEY, MELANIE; Lake Hamilton Jr HS; Hot Springs, AR; (1); 12/264; Church Yth Grp; Cmnty Wkr; FBLA; Library Aide; Spanish Clb; SADD; Teachers Aide; Acpl Chr; Band; Chorus; All Rgn 1st Band; Psych.

PASSALAQUA, SHAUNDA C; Hoxie Schl; Hoxie, AR; (4); 20/60; Art Clb; Church Yth Grp; FHA; Chorus; Church Choir; Ed Yrbk; Trk; Vllybl; Hon Roll; Prfct Atten Awd; Pride Tm; Annl Qn 1st Rnnr Up; Ar ST U; Psych.

PATE, AMBER; Alpena Schl; Alpena, AR; (2); Church Yth Grp; FCA; FBLA; FHA; GAA; Spanish Clb; Church Choir; School Play; Bsktbl; Chrldng; NACTC; X-Ray Tech.

PATE, JAMIE; Pangburn Jr Sr HS; Pangburn, AR; (4); 1/45; Am Leg Aux Girls St; French Clb; FBLA; FHA; Pres Natl Beta Clb; Yrbk; VP Stu Cncl; Bsktbl; Sftbl; NHS; All St; Harding U; Math.

PATE, KRISTIE M; Junction City HS; Junction City, AR; (1); Church Yth Grp; FBLA; Science Clb; JV Chrldng; Sec Mgr(s); Var Powder Puff Ftbl; Stat Score Keeper; Var Sftbl; Tae Kwon Do; 3rd Degree Brown Belt Asst Instr.

PATE, STEPHANIE E; Poyen Schl; Leola, AR; (3); Natl Beta Clb; Spanish Clb; Teachers Aide; Church Choir; Yrbk; Lit Mag; Ofcr Soph Cls.

PATE, WENDY N; Weiner HS; Weiner, AR; (2); Church Yth Grp; FBLA; Treas FHA; Rptr Science Clb; Church Choir; School Play; Rptr Nwsp; Ed Yrbk; Hon Roll; NHS; AEGIS Prgm; G T Stdnt; U Of AR; Chld Psych/Opera Sngr.

PATEL, HEENA G; Jonesboro HS; Jonesboro, AR; (3); FBLA; Spanish Clb; Hon Roll; Prfct Atten Awd; Home Ec Cert; Math Awd; Home Ec Trophy; AR ST Univ; Acctnt.

PATEL, JATIN B; Hope HS; Hope, AR; (3); 21/220; Ofcr Bsbl; Ftbl; Trk; Hon Roll; UALR; Bus Fin.

PATEL, PUNAM A; Corning HS; Corning, AR; (1); Spanish Clb; Band; Mrchg Band; Pep Band; Hon Roll; Band Achvmnt Awd.

PATERAK, JENNIFER M; Russellville Sr HS; Russellville, AR; (3); 207/340; Drama Clb; Teachers Aide; Acpl Chr; Chorus; Stage Crew; Prfct Atten Awd; Poetry; All ST Choir 1 Yr; All Regn Choir 4 Yrs; AR Tech Univ; Eng/Ed.

PATRICK, BRANDY N; Timbo Schl; Timbo, AR; (2); Church Yth Grp; FBLA; Treas FHA; Sec Natl Beta Clb; Natl FFA Org; Pep Clb; Quiz Bowl; Drill Tm; Rep Frsh Cls; Sec Soph Cls; ST Track 95 96; Lyon Coll; Psych.

PATRICK, CANDY; St Paul Schl; Pettigrew, AR; (4); Art Clb; Drama Clb; VP FBLA; FHA; Natl Beta Clb; Science Clb; SADD; Acpl Chr; School Play; Ed Nwsp; FBLA Dist Cmptn-Plcd Acctng; U Ozarks; Bus Mgmt.

PATRICK, DARLA L; Morrilton Sr HS; Morrilton, AR; (2); Art Clb; Church Yth Grp; Natl Beta Clb; Spanish Clb; Church Choir; Trk; Hon Roll; NHS; Prfct Atten Awd; Grphc Art.

PATRICK, LINDSAY B; Bergman Schl; Bergman, AR; (2); Pep Clb; Phtg Rptr Yrbk; L Bsktbl; SMSU; Dr.

PATRICK, SPENCER A; Watson Chapel Sr HS; Pine Bluff, AR; (4); 1/240; Am Leg Boys St; Church Yth Grp; FCA; Hosp Aide; Key Clb; Model UN; Natl Beta Clb; Spanish Clb; Art Clb; Drama Clb; Knwldg Mstrs Co-Cptn; AR Mck Trl Lwyr/Wtns; U Of AR; Pre-Dntstry.

PATRIDGE, ASHLEY J; Booneville Jr Sr HS; Booneville, AR; (3); Church Yth Grp; FBLA; Natl Beta Clb; Band; Drm Mjr(t); Mrchg Band; Pep Band; Phtg Lit Mag; Rep Soph Cls; Rep Jr Cls; Attnd Prjct Caves Hlcst; GATE.

PATTERSON, AMY E; Springdale Sr HS; Springdale, AR; (3); 4/650; Church Yth Grp; FBLA; Natl FFA Org; Teachers Aide; Band; Co-Capt Flag Corp; Mrchg Band; Mgr Nwsp; Band Cncl Ofcr; Natl Hnr Jrnlst; Mrktng & Modeling.

PATTERSON, ANDREA L; Lavaca Jr Sr HS; Lavaca, AR; (3); 10/65; VP Pres Art Clb; Natl Beta Clb; Sec Science Clb; Spanish Clb; Speech Tm; Phtg Yrbk; Ofcr Soph Cls; Ofcr Jr Cls; Stat Bsktbl; L Trk; Schl Flag Holder; Art Awd; Jrnlsm Awd; U Of Cntrl AR; Wildlife Mgmt.

PATTERSON, BETHANY A; Mt St Mary Acad; Little Rock, AR; (2); Art Clb; Church Yth Grp; JCL; Latin Clb; Mu Alpha Theta; Hon Roll; Dncg; Law.

PATTERSON, BRYAN J; Bentonville Sr HS; Bentonville, AR; (3); 2/350; Church Yth Grp; Key Clb; SADD; High Hon Roll; NHS; Pres Acad Fit Awd; Jr Bnk Brd; Snd Rm Fcltr; Lions Clb Yth Vlntr; U Of AK Fayetteville; Engr.

PATTERSON, CARRI; Lakeside HS; Hot Springs, AR; (2); Church Yth Grp; Sec FCA; French Clb; FBLA; Natl Beta Clb; Office Aide; Sec Frsh Cls; VP Soph Cls; Rep Stu Cncl; Capt Var Chrldng; Yth To Yth Rep; Phys Thpy.

PATTERSON, CORY R; Mountain Pine Jr Sr HS; Mountain Pine, AR; (2); Church Yth Grp; FCA; Hon Roll; Hunt & Fish.

PATTERSON, DAVINA L; Central Sr HS; Little Rock, AR; (4); 49/401; Am Leg Aux Girls St; Girl Scts; Natl Beta Clb; Jazz Band; Mrchg Band; Yrbk; Ofcr Stu Cncl; NHS; Pres Acad Fit Awd; AR Govnr Yth Commsn; Jackson St Univ; Mass Comm.

PATTERSON, JENNIFER; Cabot HS; Cabot, AR; (2); Cmnty Wkr; French Clb; Key Clb; High Hon Roll; Hendrix.

PATTERSON, JOSH S; Osceola HS; Osceola, AR; (2); #1 in class; FBLA; Math Tm; Spanish Clb; Cit Awd; High Hon Roll; NHS.

PATTERSON, KENDRA D; Rogers HS; Rogers, AR; (3); 90/400; FCA; Hosp Aide; Teachers Aide; Chrldng; High Hon Roll; Hon Roll; Rogers Chamber Of Commerce Awd; Local Womens Shelter Vol; Psych; Sociology.

PATTERSON, NICK A; Ctl Ar Christian Jr Sr Schl; Sherwood, AR; (3); Bus Profs of Am; Church Yth Grp; Science Clb; Spanish Clb; Var JV Ftbl; Var Var Wt Lftg; FL ST Univ; Dr; Bus Admin.

PATTERSON, SAMANTHA; Manila HS; Manila, AR; (2); Art Clb; FBLA; Hon Roll; Bus Acad; Acctng.

PATTERSON, STEPHIE; Pulaski Acad; Little Rock, AR; (3); 1/92; Chrldng; Vllybl; NHS.

PATTIE, JODY A; Harrison Sr HS; Harrison, AR; (3); Am Leg Aux Girls St; Church Yth Grp; 4-H; Natl FFA Org; Office Aide; Science Clb; NHS; Key Clb; Spanish Clb; Chorus; FFA Lvstck Judge Team ST Qlfrs At Dist 96; High Pt Indvl Lvstck Judg Super Cow Clinic 96; Ag.

PATTON, ANDREW B; Searcy HS; Searcy, AR; (3); 57/218; Rep Am Leg Boys St; Church Yth Grp; Cmnty Wkr; Nwsp; Ed Yrbk; Rep Stu Cncl; Kiwanis Awd; NHS; Drama Clb; FCA; Yth To Yth; STAGE Pres; Governors Yth Cncl Drugs & Alcohol; Jr Beethovan Clb; Ouachita Bapt U; Commnctn; Bible.

PATTON, JUSTIN B; Wynne HS; Wynne, AR; (4); 7/180; Church Yth Grp; Q&S; Quiz Bowl; L Golf; Cit Awd; High Hon Roll; NHS; Ntl Merit SF; Spanish NHS; Spanish Clb; Hnr Stu; Hendrix Coll; Math.

PATTON, KRISTI A; Nevada Schl; Rosston, AR; (3); 6/51; Treas Church Yth Grp; Sec VP FBLA; Pres VP Natl Beta Clb; Quiz Bowl; Band; Co-Capt Chrldng; High Hon Roll; Pres Acad Fit Awd; FCA; French Clb; Drug-Free Team Ldr; Gftd/Tlntd; LA Tech Univ; Pre-Med.

PATTON, LEIGH ANNE; Central Ark Christian Schl; Little Rock, AR; (3); Cmnty Wkr; Office Aide; Spanish Clb; Church Choir; Stage Crew; Ed Yrbk; Rep Stu Cncl; JV Bsbl; NHS; Acctng.

PATTON, MARTIN D; Booneville Jr Sr HS; Booneville, AR; (4); 8/86; Am Leg Boys St; Church Yth Grp; FBLA; Natl Beta Clb; Spanish Clb; Var Trk; OK Baptist U; Rdlgy.

PAUL, AMANDA G; Bald Knob HS; Bald Knob, AR; (1); Drama Clb; FHA; Natl Beta Clb; Band; Chorus; Mrchg Band; Hon Roll; Symphonic Band.

PAUL, JASON; Mt Holly Schl; Mount Holly, AR; (3); 4-H; Natl FFA Org; 4-H Awd; Southern AR U; Comp Prgrmmng.

PAULLEY, MANDY; East End Jr Sr HS; Bigelow, AR; (1); Church Yth Grp; Sec 4-H; Natl Beta Clb; Church Choir; Nwsp; Yrbk; Treas Frsh Cls; Bsktbl; Cit Awd; Hon Roll; Orng Blt In Teakwondo; U Of KY; Peds.

PAXTON, ERIC J; Sylvan Hills HS; Sherwood, AR; (3); Spanish Clb; Hon Roll; Prfct Atten Awd; FBLA; Comp Sci.

PAYNE, ANTHONY J; Woodlawn Schl; Rison, AR; (3); FCA; 4-H; Natl Beta Clb; Quiz Bowl; Crs Cntry; Ftbl; Trk; 4-H Awd.

PAYNE, DEBBIE; John L Mcclellan Magnet HS; Little Rock, AR; (2); Church Yth Grp; FBLA; FHA; Natl Beta Clb; Church Choir; Yrbk; Bsktbl; Cit Awd; High Hon Roll; Pres Acad Fit Awd; Med.

PAYNE, KIMBERLY B; Amity Jr Sr HS; Amity, AR; (2); FBLA; FHA; Natl Beta Clb; Natl FFA Org; Church Choir; Bsktbl; Trk; Hon Roll; Treas Soph Cls; Med.

PAYNE, TIFFANY A; Morrilton Sr HS; Morrilton, AR; (2); Church Yth Grp; Science Clb; Spanish Clb; Thesps; Band; Chorus; Church Choir; Drm Mjr(t); Mrchg Band; School Musical; All Rgn Choir.

PAYSINGER, ZEDA; Evening Shade Schl; Evening Shade, AR; (3); Sec FBLA; Hist FHA; German Clb; Math Clb; Natl Beta Clb; Sec Natl FFA Org; Science Clb; SADD; Teachers Aide; School Play; Hstry & Govt Awd; Recycling; Lyon Coll; Engl/Telecommnctns.

PAYTON, SARAH V; Farmington Jr Sr HS; Fayetteville, AR; (3); FBLA; Model UN; SADD; Hon Roll; Psych.

PEACE, FLESHA S; Blytheville Sr HS; Blytheville, AR; (2); Church Yth Grp; Dance Clb; GAA; Acpl Chr; Drill Tm; School Musical; Variety Show; Ofcr Soph Cls; Bsktbl; Score Keeper; Grambling ST U; Vocal Music.

PEACE, TREVA; Gosnell Jr HS; Blytheville, AR; (1); Art Clb; Church Yth Grp; Drama Clb; FHA; Church Choir; School Play; Sftbl; Trk; Hon Roll; Grambling ST U; Acctng.

PEACOCK, AMANDA N; Mc Gehee HS; Mc Gehee, AR; (4); Spanish Clb; Band; Mrchg Band; Pep Band; Hon Roll; Hnr Pride Awd; John Phillip Bousa Band Awd; U Of AR Monticello; Elem Ed.

PEACOCK, CRAIG; Central Ark Christian Schl; North Little Rock, AR; (4); 6/74; Art Clb; Cmnty Wkr; FCA; FBLA; Math Clb; Chorus; Treas Stu Cncl; Var L Bsbl; Capt L Bsktbl; Capt Var Socr; Cngrssnl Schlr Natl Yng Ldrs Conf; US Naval Acad Smmr Smnr; Peope To People Stu Ambssdr Pgm; U Of AR Fayetteville.

PEAK, CHANDRA D; Marion HS; West Memphis, AR; (4); 58/180; Cmnty Wkr; French Clb; FBLA; FHA; Hosp Aide; Quiz Bowl; Band; Mrchg Band; Mgr Nwsp; Rep Soph Cls; STAR Event Awd Silver Group Cmptn; Hnrb Mntn FBLA; Acad Hnr Awd Home Ec; Chrstn Brothers Univ; Pre-Law.

PEARCE, HEATHER M; Mills HS; Sherwood, AR; (3); 40/296; Cmnty Wkr; Drama Clb; Natl Beta Clb; Q&S; Science Clb; Mrchg Band; School Play; Variety Show; Co-Ed Nwsp; Drill Tm; Project WET; Close-Up; Coastal Carolina; Marine Bio.

PEARCE, LESLIE A; Newport HS; Newport, AR; (2); 1/160; Art Clb; Church Yth Grp; 4-H; FBLA; Spanish Clb; Church Choir; Drill Tm; Nwsp; Mgr(s); Tennis; 9th Grd Awrds PE/SPAN/BIO/DUCK Stamp; 10 Grd Rgnl Math Adv Algebra/His/Hlth Occptns; AR ST U; Nrs.

PEARCE, ROGER C; Russellville Sr HS; Russellville, AR; (2); 50/405; Church Yth Grp; Letterman Clb; Math Tm; Spanish Clb; Band; Chorus; Church Choir; High Hon Roll; NHS; Pres Acad Fit Awd; Cntrl Bapt Coll; Pastr; Math Tch.

PEARSON, ALEXANDRA L; Fayetteville Sr HS; Fayetteville, AR; (3); Am Leg Aux Girls St; Art Clb; Church Yth Grp; Cmnty Wkr; FCA; SADD; Yrbk; Hon Roll; NHS; 26 Club; Med.

PEARSON, BROOKE R; Conway Sr HS; Conway, AR; (4); 70/520; Church Yth Grp; FBLA; Chorus; School Musical; Hon Roll; U Of Cntrl AR.

PEARSON, CASEY; Mineral Springs Schl; Nashville, AR; (4); 8/29; Church Yth Grp; FHA; Sec HOBY; Natl Beta Clb; Quiz Bowl; Science Clb; Spanish Clb; Band; Ed Yrbk; Var L Chrldng; AR Govs Schl Stu 95; CHAMPS; Gftd & Tlntd; U Of Central AR Conway.

PEARSON, TODD ALAN; Smackover HS; Smackover, AR; (3); 4/46; Am Leg Boys St; Art Clb; Church Yth Grp; Cmnty Wkr; FCA; FBLA; Science Clb; Spanish Clb; Bsktbl; Trk; Navy Hnrs Awd 96; Ec.

PEARSON, WENDY; Taylor HS; Taylor, AR; (3); 10/30; Church Yth Grp; 4-H; Natl FFA Org; Sec Jr Cls; Pres Stu Cncl; Bsktbl; Sftbl; 4-H Awd; High Hon Roll; NHS; Ldrshp Awd; Stu Cncl Awd; St FFA Degree; 4-H Teen Star & Ambssdr; S AR Univ; Ag Bus.

PEASE, AMY K; Southside HS; Batesville, AR; (1); VP Church Yth Grp; Dance Clb; FBLA; Key Clb; Science Clb; Drill Tm; Kiwanis Awd; Dance Team Mem; STOP; Pride; Hendrix; Law; Tchng.

PEASTER, MICHAEL J; Valley View HS; Jonesboro, AR; (3); Library Aide; Spanish Clb; Stage Crew; Yrbk; L Var Ftbl; Hon Roll; U Of Cntrl AR; Occptnl Therapy.

PECK, ALLISON; Black Rock Jr Sr HS; Black Rock, AR; (4); 7/24; FBLA; Treas FHA; Intnl Clb; Hist Natl Beta Clb; Rptr Nwsp; Phtg Yrbk; High Hon Roll; Key Clb; Chorus; School Musical; Beta Clb Lit Awd; Pres Ed Awd Otstdng Edcl Imprmnt; Interact Clb Treas; U Of A Fayetteville; Crim Just.

PECK, AMY L; North Little Rock Hs-East; North Little Rock, AR; (2); Church Yth Grp; Mu Alpha Theta; Natl Beta Clb; Church Choir; Drm Mjr(t); Mrchg Band; Sec Stu Cncl; High Hon Roll; Hon Roll; NHS; Piano; Girls Msnry Aux Dist/ST Ofcrs.

PECK, JONATHAN; Morrilton Sr HS; Morrilton, AR; (2); Church Yth Grp; Math Clb; Natl Beta Clb; Office Aide; Spanish Clb; Ftbl; Wt Lftg; DAR Awd; High Hon Roll; Hon Roll.

PEDERSON, MICHAEL A; Fayetteville Sr HS; Fayetteville, AR; (4); 1/382; Mu Alpha Theta; Band; Var Capt Ftbl; Var Socr; Wt Lftg; NHS; Ntl Merit SF; Pres Acad Fit Awd; Val; AR Govs Schl.

PEDERSON, T J; Springdale Sr HS; Springdale, AR; (2); Art Clb; Boy Scts; Drama Clb; FCA; Quiz Bowl; Teachers Aide; Thesps; Chorus; School Play; Stage Crew; Outstdng Achvmt In Oral Commnctn; Adress Presenter; Attorney For Washington Cty Teen Court; Talk Show Host.

PEDIGO, SHANE M; West Memphis Sr HS; West Memphis, AR; (3); Church Yth Grp; Cmnty Wkr; FCA; Ftbl; Trk; Wt Lftg; Hon Roll; U Of AR; Conservtn.

PEDRON, JAN; Kirby HS; Kirby, AR; (1); 1/40; Church Yth Grp; FHA; Natl Beta Clb; Pres Frsh Cls; L Bsktbl; L Trk; L Wt Lftg; High Hon Roll.

PEELER, SARAH J; Bryant Sr HS; Benton, AR; (2); Sec Stu Cncl; Var Crs Cntry; Var Trk; Hon Roll; Chrstn Cncl; Cmpr Applctns; Tchng.

PEER, DEBBIE; Van Buren Sr HS; Van Buren, AR; (4); Am Leg Aux Girls St; Church Yth Grp; FBLA; Mu Alpha Theta; Q&S; Band; Co-Capt Flag Corp; Yrbk; NHS; Library Aide; Band Cncl; Earth Club; Acad Ltr; Univ Of AR.

PELAYO, ALONDRA; Pleasant View Schl; Mulberry, AR; (2); Church Yth Grp; Drama Clb; FBLA; Natl Beta Clb; Quiz Bowl; Spanish Clb; High Hon Roll.

PEMMARAJU, NAVEEN; Arkansas Schl Math & Science; Hot Springs, AR; (3); French Clb; FBLA; HOBY; Model UN; Quiz Bowl; Orch; Yrbk; Lit Mag; VP Stu Cncl; Intrml Bsktbl; Co Prdcd/Co Hstd Teen Talk Radio Show; Bio, Frnch II, Wrld Hstry, Engl, Oral Cmmnctns Outstndng Stu; Med.

PENA, JOSHUA J; Mayflower HS; Mayflower, AR; (3); Drama Clb; French Clb; Quiz Bowl; School Play; Rptr Nwsp; Phy Thrpy.

PENDERDRAFT, MICHAEL Z; Blevins HS; Blevins, AR; (3); FBLA; Cit Awd; High Hon Roll.

PENDERGRAFT, AMANDA; Blevins HS; Blevins, AR; (3); Am Leg Aux Girls St; FBLA; Natl Beta Clb; Yrbk; Bsktbl; Chrldng; Sftbl; Trk; Cit Awd; Hon Roll.

PENDERGRAFT, MICHAEL Z; Blevins HS; Blevins, AR; (2); Church Yth Grp; Natl Beta Clb; Hon Roll.

PENDERGRASS, ERIC; Charleston HS; Charleston, AR; (1); FBLA; Letterman Clb; Ofcr Bsbl; Ftbl.

PENDLETON, ANTONIO S; Forrest City HS; Madison, AR; (3); Boy Scts; Church Yth Grp; Cmnty Wkr; FTA; Office Aide; Band; Chorus; Church Choir; Mrchg Band; High Hon Roll; FTA St Pres; Hnr Roll; John Of Supton Coll; Funrl Svc.

PENDLETON, MICHAEL A; Fayetteville Sr HS; Fayetteville, AR; (2); Band; Yrbk; Ofcr Soph Cls; Bsktbl; Swmmng; Cit Awd; Hon Roll.

PENICK, ERICA; Pulaski Acad; Little Rock, AR; (4); Church Yth Grp; FCA; French Clb; Math Clb; Mu Alpha Theta; Natl Beta Clb; Service Clb; Chorus; Rep Soph Cls; Rep Jr Cls; Just Say No Ldr; Cum Laude Grad; U AR Fayetteville.

PENIX, LINDLEY G; Newport HS; Newport, AR; (3); Church Yth Grp; JCL; Q&S; Spanish Clb; Church Choir; Drill Tm; Ed Nwsp; Yrbk; Lit Mag; Ofcr Stu Cncl; AR Governors Schl.

PENNINGTON, APRIL L; Dumas HS; Dumas, AR; (2); FBLA; Natl Beta Clb; Spanish Clb; Rptr Yrbk; Rep Frsh Cls; NHS; Pres Acad Fit Awd; U Of Cntrl AR; Pharmacy.

PENNINGTON, DARRELL W; West Fork HS; West Fork, AR; (2); Church Yth Grp; FCA; Natl FFA Org; Ofcr Soph Cls; Trk; Wt Lftg; Cit Awd; High Hon Roll; Hon Roll; Collect CD'S; Woodman Of The World His Awd.

PENNINGTON, JENNIFER; Dumas Jr HS; Dumas, AR; (1); Church Yth Grp; FBLA; Natl Beta Clb; Science Clb; Spanish Clb; Band; Var Cit Awd; High Hon Roll.

PENNINGTON, MICHELLE L; Drew Central Jr Sr HS; Monticello, AR; (4); 7/59; Church Yth Grp; Cmnty Wkr; FBLA; FHA; Science Clb; Chorus; Sec Sr Cls; Hon Roll; Jr NHS; NHS; Regnl His Fair-3rd; AR ST U; Nrsng.

PENNINGTON, SHANDA; Arkansas Schl Math & Science; Van Buren, AR; (3); Teachers Aide; Band; Jazz Band; Mrchg Band; Pep Band; Cit Awd; High Hon Roll; Jr NHS; NHS; Pres Acad Fit Awd; Accepted MASH Pgrm; Med.

PENNINGTRON, APRIL; Dumas HS; Dumas, AR; (2); FBLA; Natl Beta Clb; Spanish Clb; Phtg Yrbk; Rep Frsh Cls; Intrml Sftbl; High Hon Roll; NHS; Pres Acad Fit Awd; 90th Prcntl Stanford 8; Ventures In Ed; Twrlr In Band; Pharm.

PENNY, KORTNEY; Lake Hamilton Sr HS; Hot Springs, AR; (3); 10/245; FCA; FBLA; Natl Beta Clb; Spanish Clb; Chorus; School Musical; Ed Nwsp; Hon Roll; NHS; Pres Acad Fit Awd; Wolf Pride; Commnctns.

PEOPLES, JENNFIER M; Springdale Sr HS; Lowell, AR; (1); Church Yth Grp; FCA; FHA; Drill Tm; Drm Mjr(t); Mrchg Band; Ed Yrbk; Var Pom Pon; Hon Roll; Jr NHS; Pres Ed Awd Outstdng Acad Achvmt; Outstdng Ldrshp Awd Yrbk; Peer Helper; Psych.

PEPPER, HEATH A; North Little Rock Hs-East; North Little Rock, AR; (1); Church Yth Grp; Drama Clb; FCA; Math Clb; Stage Crew; Ftbl; Cit Awd; Hon Roll; Prfct Atten Awd; Tp 10% Awd Frosh Cls.

PERET, CARMEN A; Hot Springs HS; Hot Springs, AR; (2); Boy Scts; Debate Tm; Quiz Bowl; Teachers Aide; Band; Church Choir; Orch; Tennis; Cit Awd; High Hon Roll; St Josephs Explorer Ost 88, Hosp Vol; Chrch Band; Chrch Orch; UAR Little Rock; Medicine.

PEREZ, ANGELICA; Dequeen HS; De Queen, AR; (3); Church Yth Grp; French Clb; FBLA; Natl Beta Clb; Band; Mrchg Band; High Hon Roll; Hon Roll; NHS; Intnl Bus.

PEREZ, ANGIE M; Cabot HS; Cabot, AR; (2); Church Yth Grp; Cmnty Wkr; Key Clb; Spanish Clb; Teachers Aide; Band; Hon Roll; NHS; Prfct Atten Awd; Biling Asst Frgn Exchng Stdnts Span; Med.

PERKEY, BETH M; Evening Shade Schl; Evening Shade, AR; (3); Church Yth Grp; Cmnty Wkr; FCA; FBLA; FHA; FTA; German Clb; Office Aide; Teachers Aide; School Play; Ouachita Bapt Univ; Acctng.

PERKINS, DEBBY G; Van Buren Sr HS; Van Buren, AR; (2); Church Yth Grp; Cmnty Wkr; FCA; FBLA; Science Clb; SADD; Chorus; Hon Roll; Tchr.

PERKINS, GAIL; West Memphis Sr HS; West Memphis, AR; (4); 11/270; Church Yth Grp; FBLA; FHA; Math Clb; Natl Beta Clb; Spanish Clb; Band; Church Choir; Mrchg Band; Orch; All Region, All St, U Of M Hnr Band; Math, Engl, Sci Awds; Rep HOBY Fndtn Smnr; MS ST U; Phys Thrpy.

PERKINS, JACOB A; Jessieville HS; Jessieville, AR; (2); Church Yth Grp; VP Key Clb; Jazz Band; Mrchg Band; VP Orch; Pep Band; Rptr Nwsp; Hon Roll; Cls Ambsdr.

PERKINS, JACOB S; Morrilton Sr HS; Morrilton, AR; (4); 15/132; Math Clb; Natl Beta Clb; Quiz Bowl; Spanish Clb; Ftbl; Tennis; High Hon Roll; Pres Schlr; Knowledge Master Open Tm; Quest Tm; U Of AR; Bus.

PERKINS, JERMAINE; Nevada Schl; Buckner, AR; (4); 10/60; FHA; Quiz Bowl; Band; Rep Stu Cncl; JV Var Bsktbl; JV Var Trk; Hon Roll; NHS; Upward Bnd; Tlnt Srch; UAPB; Psych.

PERKINS, JESSE; Malvern Jr HS; Malvern, AR; (2); Church Yth Grp; FBLA; Natl Beta Clb; Quiz Bowl; Teachers Aide; Band; Mrchg Band; Pep Band; Cit Awd; High Hon Roll; Comp Prog.

PERKINS, SELENA C; John L Mcclellan Magnet HS; Little Rock, AR; (2); FBLA; Natl Beta Clb; Drill Tm; Hon Roll; Career Club.

PERKINS, WILLIAM J; Hughes Jr-Sr HS; Hughes, AR; (1); Art Clb; Math Clb; Spanish Clb; Ofcr Frsh Cls; Ofcr Stu Cncl; Bsktbl; Ftbl; Trk; Hon Roll.

PERKINSON, KRISTEN; Greenwood Sr HS; Greenwood, AR; (3); Church Yth Grp; Debate Tm; Drama Clb; HOBY; Model UN; Mrchg Band; Quiz Bowl; Office Aide; Pep Clb; Acpl Chr; U Of Cntrl AR; Med.

PERMENTER, ETHAN B; West Memphis Christian Schl; West Memphis, AR; (1); Church Yth Grp; JV Bsktbl; JV Ftbl; Golf; Trk; Sci Fair Wnnr.

PERMENTER, MATTHEW G; Conway Sr HS; Conway, AR; (2); Church Yth Grp; FCA; FBLA; Natl Beta Clb; Church Choir; JV Bsbl; Var Bsktbl; Ftbl; Hon Roll; Bus/Insrnc.

PERMENTER, SETH W; West Memphis Christian Schl; West Memphis, AR; (4); Church Yth Grp; Ftbl; High Hon Roll; Hon Roll; Prfct Atten Awd; Dist Sci Fair; Acad Betterment Com; U Of AR; Engrng.

PERNA, CHRISTINA A; Searcy HS; Searcy, AR; (3); French Clb; FHA; Natl Beta Clb; Office Aide; Band; Color Guard; Jazz Band; Mrchg Band; Hon Roll; Jr NHS; Yth To Yth Sec; OBU; Pediatrician.

PERRY, AMBER L; Alma HS; Alma, AR; (2); U Of AR Fayetteville.

PERRY, BRITNEY Y; Lake Hamilton Sr HS; Pearcy, AR; (2); FBLA; Natl Beta Clb; Natl FFA Org; Science Clb; Spanish Clb; Teachers Aide; High Hon Roll; NHS; Ntl Merit Ltr; Wolf Pride; Odyssey Mind; Geneticist.

PERRY, GINA K; Malvern Sr HS; Malvern, AR; (3); Am Leg Aux Girls St; French Clb; FBLA; Natl Beta Clb; Office Aide; SADD; Band; Drm Mjr(t); Yrbk; Jr NHS; Peer Cnslr; Tutor; AR ST Univ; Ecology; Wildlife.

PERRY, JAMAICA; Mann Magnet Jr HS; Little Rock, AR; (1); Natl Beta Clb; School Play; Capt Chrldng; Cit Awd; Hon Roll; Jr NHS; Prfct Atten Awd; Outstdng Achvmnt Dance Prfrmnc Awd; Outstdng Effort/Imprvmnt Algebra I GT Awd; Fashion Dsgnr.

PERRY, JEREMY A; J A Fair Sr HS; Little Rock, AR; (2); 50/800; Church Yth Grp; Computer Clb; FBLA; JA; Math Clb; Math Tm; Red Cross Aide; Science Clb; Band; Mrchg Band; Outstndng Hnrs In Hlth; U Of AR; Sales Pres.

PERRY, KENDRA R; Central Sr HS; Little Rock, AR; (4); German Clb; Natl Beta Clb; Band; Jazz Band; Mrchg Band; Pep Band; Rep Stu Cncl; Var L Bsktbl; Var L Trk; Hon Roll; Natl Engl Merit Awd; Macy Schol; Hampton Univ; Bio.

PERRY, STEPHANIE; West Side HS; Higden, AR; (3); 3/38; FBLA; Boy Scts; Teachers Aide; Ed Yrbk; Treas Stu Cncl; High Hon Roll; Hon Roll; Jr NHS; VP NHS; Physics/Hlth/Algebra II Awds; Cmptr Medal; Straight A's For Two Years; Harding Univ; Bus Mngmt.

PERRY, SU-LAUREN E; Central Sr HS; Little Rock, AR; (2); Drama Clb; French Clb; Mu Alpha Theta; Natl Beta Clb; High Hon Roll; Hon Roll; Acpt No Bndrs Clb Strng Comm; Vanderbuilt; Med.

PERRY, TERETHA R; North Little Rock Hs-West; North Little Rock, AR; (3); Cmnty Wkr; FHA; Chorus; School Musical; Hon Roll; Salvation Army Vol & Tchr; Creighton; Medicn; Pediatrician.

PERRY, TIA QUANDA S; J A Fair Sr HS; Little Rock, AR; (2); Dance Clb; Natl Beta Clb; Drill Tm; Vllybl; Hon Roll; Jr NHS; Spellman; Engrng.

PERRYMAN, EMILY B; Pulaski Acad; Bigelow, AR; (2); Cmnty Wkr; Drama Clb; Natl Beta Clb; Spanish Clb; School Musical; School Play; Stage Crew; JV Vllybl; Interact Clb; PA Ambassadors Clb.

PERSON, KRISTEN; West Memphis Sr HS; West Memphis, AR; (1); Church Yth Grp; Math Clb; Science Clb; Chorus; Ofcr Stu Cncl; Chrldng; Hon Roll; Pres Schlr; Beta Clb; Gymnastics; U Of AR; MD.

PESCH, SARA; Prairie Grove HS; Fayetteville, AR; (3); SADD; School Play; Powder Puff Ftbl; High Hon Roll; Hon Roll; Jr NHS; NHS; Violin; Jr Bank Bd.

PETERS, BRANDON D; Alma HS; Mountainburg, AR; (4); Art Clb; French Clb; FBLA; Nwsp; Lit Mag; Prfct Atten Awd; Gujv-Kai Karatae-Do Brown Belt; AR HS Assn Jrnlstc Exclnc Awds; AR Press Women Hnrbl Mention; Band; Jrnlsm.

PETERS, BRANDON K; Alma HS; Alma, AR; (3); Art Clb; Church Yth Grp; FCA; Teachers Aide; Rep Stu Cncl; Var Ftbl; Var Trk; Var Wt Lftg; Hon Roll; Prfct Atten Awd; Natl Art Recgntn Awd; 4on4 Champs-ATU Bsktbl Camp; Westark CC; Arch.

PETERS, CHERYL; Pleasant View Schl; Mulberry, AR; (1); #2 in class; Drama Clb; English Clb; FCA; FBLA; FHA; FTA; Natl Beta Clb; Natl FFA Org; Quiz Bowl; Speech Tm; Westark; Phrmcy.

PETERS, JASON M; Cabot HS; Cabot, AR; (4); Art Clb; Spanish Clb; Lit Mag; Hon Roll; Japanese Clb VP; Cinema Clb; Tchng.

PETERS, JESSICA L; Central Sr HS; Little Rock, AR; (2); Cmnty Wkr; Debate Tm; Natl Beta Clb; Rep Jr Cls; Var L Socr; Var L Tennis; Pres Schlr; Drama Clb; FBLA; FTA; RYLA; Interact Comm Serv Chrm; Rotary Yth Exchng Prgm Summer France; Envrmntl Sci/Marine Bio.

PETERS, RYAN G; Catholic HS; Maumelle, AR; (2); 48/200; Art Clb; Church Yth Grp; ROTC; Service Clb; Hon Roll; AAU Bsktbl/Babe Ruth All Star Team; Yth Cnnctn Cath HS/POL Awrns Club.

PETERSEN, CASEY; Crossett Sr HS; Crossett, AR; (2); Church Yth Grp; French Clb; Math Clb; Mu Alpha Theta; Natl Beta Clb; Mrchg Band; Rptr Yrbk; Hon Roll; LA Tech Univ.

PETERSON, AMY C; Harmony Grove Jr Sr HS; Traskwood, AR; (2); French Clb; Model UN; Natl Beta Clb; Science Clb; Band; Mrchg Band; Peer Cnslr; Champs; Henderson.

PETERSON, ANTHONY R; Jacksonville HS; Jacksonville, AR; (2); 56/320; French Clb; FHA; Acpl Chr; Chorus; JV Var Bsktbl; High Hon Roll; Hon Roll; Choia VP.

PETERSON, ASHLEY A; Conway Sr HS; Conway, AR; (4); French Clb; FBLA; Natl Beta Clb; Science Clb; Teachers Aide; Intrml Sftbl; Var Tennis; JV Vllybl; Hon Roll; Congress Bundestag Schol; German Intl Bus.

PETERSON, JASON R; Sylvan Hills HS; North Little Rock, AR; (3); Bus Profs of Am; FCA; FBLA; Spanish Clb; U Of AR; Crmnl Jstc.

PETERSON, MICHAEL; Rison HS; Rison, AR; (1); Quiz Bowl; Bsktbl; Ftbl; Wt Lftg; Hon Roll; Beta Clb; Drug Awarenss.

PETERSON, MICHELLE L; Rogers HS; Garfield, AR; (2); 1/750; Church Yth Grp; Drama Clb; Model UN; Var Capt Socr; High Hon Roll; Pres Acad Fit Awd; Top Span Stu; MVP & Gift Of Fury Var Soccer Awds; Elem Ed; Sociology.

PETERSON, RANA N; Bentonville Sr HS; Rogers, AR; (3); Church Yth Grp; FCA; Acpl Chr; Church Choir; Rep Stu Cncl; Var Chrldng; Var Trk; Hon Roll; Super Ranking In Fed For Piano; Modeling; Prom Comm; St Guide At NASC Conf.

PETERSON, TIA N; Smackover HS; Louann, AR; (3); Church Yth Grp; Cmnty Wkr; FHA; FTA; Girl Scts; Library Aide; Science Clb; Spanish Clb; Church Choir; Anchor Clb; Close-Up; S AR CC; Nrs.

PETERSON, ZACH; Gosnell Jr HS; Blytheville, AR; (1); USTA Tennis.

PETTIGREW, SHERRI C; Pine Bluff HS; Pine Bluff, AR; (3); Art Clb; Pres FBLA; FHA; FTA; Ed Nwsp; Hon Roll; Jr NHS; NHS; COE; Acctng; Comp Sci Engr.

PETTY, AMIE D; Greene Co Tech HS; Walcott, AR; (3); Church Yth Grp; Dance Clb; FCA; FBLA; FHA; Office Aide; Teachers Aide; Drill Tm; Ed Nwsp; Yrbk; ASU; Nrsng.

PETTY, EMILY; Jasper HS; Jasper, AR; (4); 2/45; Cmnty Wkr; Natl Beta Clb; Pres Sr Cls; Sec Stu Cncl; Var L Crs Cntry; Var L Trk; High Hon Roll; Sal; Sec Art Clb; Church Yth Grp; Indr Trck Capt; Hmcmng Qn; Wdmn Wrld Amer Hstry Awd; Pittsburg ST U; Ed.

PETTY, KIM; Hazen Jr Sr HS; Hazen, AR; (3); 4/45; Church Yth Grp; Cmnty Wkr; FBLA; FHA; FTA; Natl Beta Clb; Office Aide; Varsity Clb; Church Choir; Swing Chorus; Miss Princess Rice; Jr Miss Prairie Cty; Miss AR Ntl Teen America 1st Rnnr-Up; Spina-Bifida Sweethrt; U Of Cntrl AR; Dntl Asst.

PETTZ, SUZANNE R; Huntsville HS; Huntsville, AR; (2); Church Yth Grp; Drama Clb; 4-H; Natl Beta Clb; Band; Color Guard; Flag Corp; Mrchg Band; Pep Band; Stage Crew; Marine Bio.

PEVEY, LISA M; Star City HS; Pine Bluff, AR; (1); Church Yth Grp; English Clb; Natl Beta Clb; Office Aide; Pep Clb; Quiz Bowl; Teachers Aide; Acpl Chr; Band; Church Choir; Work In Class Spec Ed; Univ Cntrl AR; HS Eng Tchr.

PEYTON, DANNY A; Ridgecrest HS; Paragould, AR; (3); Church Yth Grp; Band; Jazz Band; Stage Crew; Ftbl; Trk; Hon Roll; Ham Radio Gen Cls License; ASU.

PEYTON, TIMMY R; Rison HS; Rison, AR; (3); FCA; Natl FFA Org; Ftbl; Wt Lftg; Wrstlng.

PFEFFER, CARRIE ANN; Des Arc Jr Sr HS; Des Arc, AR; (3); FBLA; FHA; FTA; Natl Beta Clb; Spanish Clb; Speech Tm; Ofcr Jr Cls; NHS; Art Clb; English Clb; Hmcmng Maid 95; Sigma Alpha Omega; Harding U.

PHAM, PHU; Hall Sr HS; Little Rock, AR; (3); FBLA; Natl Beta Clb; Science Clb; Cit Awd; Hon Roll; NHS; Explr Post 8.

PHARIS, BILLY; Butterfield Jr HS; Van Buren, AR; (1); Church Yth Grp; Debate Tm; FBLA; Speech Tm; VP Frsh Cls; Bsktbl; Hon Roll; Written Kids Beat Reports For Local Fox TV Station Kids Clb; Sports Medicine; Nba.

PHARR, TANJA; Drew Central Jr Sr HS; Wilmar, AR; (3); Am Leg Aux Girls St; FBLA; Science Clb; Yrbk; Ofcr Jr Cls; Hon Roll; WET Pres; UAM; Pedtrc Nrs.

PHARRIS, HEATH; Morrilton Sr HS; Morrilton, AR; (4); 16/150; Church Yth Grp; Drama Clb; Math Clb; Natl Beta Clb; Science Clb; Thesps; Church Choir; School Musical; School Play; High Hon Roll.

PHELAN, KIM; Mills HS; Little Rock, AR; (2); 6/350; Cmnty Wkr; FHA; Hosp Aide; Mu Alpha Theta; Natl Beta Clb; Q&S; Science Clb; Spanish Clb; SADD; Phtg Yrbk; 1st Pl Sci Fair Physics; 1st Pl Regnl Jr Acad Of Sci Physics; Dance; Medicine.

PHELPS, ANDREA L; Conway Sr HS; Conway, AR; (4); 43/523; Art Clb; Church Yth Grp; French Clb; Office Aide; French Hon Soc; Hon Roll; NHS; UCA.

PHELPS, CONIE; Lee Acad; Marianna, AR; (2); Church Yth Grp; HOBY; Rep Frsh Cls; Rep Soph Cls; Bsktbl; Chrldng; Trk; Hon Roll; Page To Rep Bob Mc Ginnis; U Of AR-FAYETTEVILLE; Med.

PHILLIPS, AMANDA L; Morrilton Sr HS; Plumerville, AR; (3); Art Clb; English Clb; JA; Math Clb; Science Clb; Spanish Clb; Chorus; Yrbk; U Of Cntrl AR; Arch.

PHILLIPS, AMY; Jasper HS; Jasper, AR; (4); 8/43; Church Yth Grp; Cmnty Wkr; FBLA; FHA; Math Clb; Natl Beta Clb; Natl FFA Org; Science Clb; Pres Soph Cls; VP Sr Cls; 1st Pl Dist 2nd Pl St JET; 1st Pl Entrprnrshp FBLA Dist Conf; Coll Crdt Offc Acctng & Kybrdng; N AR Comm Tech Coll; Nrsng.

PHILLIPS, BRYAN D; Bentonville Sr HS; Bentonville, AR; (4); Debate Tm; FCA; Speech Tm; School Play; Ftbl; Lcrss; Wt Lftg; Hon Roll; Multi-Yr Listee; U Of AK; Arch.

PHILLIPS, CHRIS; Humphrey Schl; Pine Bluff, AR; (3); Art Clb; FHA; Natl Beta Clb; Spanish Clb; Ofcr Bsbl; GATE; Math Awds; UALR; Med.

PHILLIPS, CHRISTINA F; Fountain Lake Jr Sr HS; Hot Springs Natio, AR; (3); 10/80; FCA; Natl Beta Clb; Spanish Clb; Phtg Nwsp; Phtg Yrbk; Var Tennis; Var Vllybl; High Hon Roll; Ntl Merit Ltr; Schlr Ath.

PHILLIPS, DAVID; Lee Sr HS; Marianna, AR; (4); 6/107; Church Yth Grp; Debate Tm; English Clb; Math Clb; Natl Beta Clb; Office Aide; Quiz Bowl; Scholastic Bowl; Science Clb; Spanish Clb; U Of AR; Med.

PHILLIPS, ELIZABETH A; Weiner HS; Weiner, AR; (2); Sec Natl FFA Org; Science Clb; Spanish Clb; Teachers Aide; Bsktbl; Hon Roll; NHS; Crops Judging Team; Parliamentary Team; Project Pals; AR ST Univ.

PHILLIPS, HOLLY A; Southside HS; Batesville, AR; (3); Church Yth Grp; FBLA; FHA; Teachers Aide; School Play; Hon Roll; Harding Univ; Bus.

PHILLIPS, JACINDA; Maynard Jr Sr HS; Pocahontas, AR; (3); Am Leg Aux Girls St; Chess Clb; French Clb; FBLA; Natl Beta Clb; School Play; Bsktbl; Sftbl; Hon Roll; Prfct Atten Awd; Stu Of Week; 4th Pl In Keyboarding Cmptn In FBLA Dist II; AR ST Univ; Phy Therapy.

PHILLIPS, JENNIFER L; Marion HS; Marion, AR; (2); Drama Clb; FCA; French Clb; Stage Crew; Ofcr Stu Cncl; Hon Roll; AR ST Univ; Nrs.

PHILLIPS, JENNIFER L; Mountain Home HS; Mountain Home, AR; (3); Church Yth Grp; 4-H; VP FHA; VP Natl FFA Org; Pep Clb; Spanish Clb; Teachers Aide; Chorus; Stage Crew; Variety Show; Outstndng Hm Ec Stu; Star FFA Grnhnd; Best Defnsve Sftbl Plyr; Vet Med.

PHILLIPS, KRISTI; Malvern Sr HS; Malvern, AR; (4); Am Leg Aux Girls St; Church Yth Grp; Cmnty Wkr; Dance Clb; Pres FCA; 4-H; FBLA; FHA; FTA; Natl Beta Clb; GMA Pres; Pensacola Chrstn Coll.

PHILLIPS, MEGAN B; Rogers HS; Rogers, AR; (3); Cmnty Wkr; FCA; FBLA; Spanish Clb; Drill Tm; Capt Chrldng; Sftbl; Hon Roll; NHS; Jr Optimist; Chmbr Of Comm Acad Awd; Interior Design.

PHILLIPS, MELODY A; North Little Rock Hs-West; North Little Rock, AR; (3); 461/554; Church Yth Grp; Cmnty Wkr; Girl Scts; Band; Mrchg Band; Hon Roll; Crm Stpprs, Ldys Gntlmns & Pr Ldrshp Clbs; ULAR; Cmptr Tech.

PHILLIPS, MICHAEL W; Mayflower HS; Conway, AR; (2); Cmnty Wkr; FHA; Ftbl; Trk; Class Fav 3 Yrs; Guitar; U Of A.

PHILLIPS, RYAN; Lynn Schl; Black Rock, AR; (4); 1/13; Boy Scts; Rep Church Yth Grp; Treas FBLA; HOBY; Math Clb; Treas Natl Beta Clb; Treas Natl FFA Org; Quiz Bowl; Science Clb; Spanish Clb; AR ST U; Ag Bus.

PHILLIPS, RYAN M; Russellville Sr HS; Russellville, AR; (3); Church Yth Grp; Band; Mrchg Band; Var Ftbl; AR Tech Univ; Psych.

PHILLIPS, STEPHANIE; Fort Lake Schl; Hot Springs, AR; (1); FCA; Hosp Aide; Model UN; Spanish Clb; Chorus; School Musical; Nwsp; Chrldng; Powder Puff Ftbl; Ntl Merit Schol; OBU; Med.

PHILLIPS, SUSAN; Sylvan Hills HS; Sherwood, AR; (4); 31/233; FBLA; Hosp Aide; Mu Alpha Theta; Natl Beta Clb; Office Aide; Spanish Clb; Band; Mrchg Band; High Hon Roll; Hon Roll; Baptist Schl Of Nrsg; Nrsg.

PHILLIPS, TIFFINY J; Siloam Springs Sr HS; Siloam Springs, AR; (2); Church Yth Grp; FCA; Natl Beta Clb; Teachers Aide; Band; Flag Corp; Tennis; High Hon Roll; Prfct Atten Awd; LIFERS & PRIDE Group; U Of AR; Psych.

PHILPOT, BECKY; Van Buren Sr HS; Van Buren, AR; (3); 42/301; Church Yth Grp; Mu Alpha Theta; Science Clb; Spanish Clb; SADD; Teachers Aide; Chorus; Church Choir; Lit Mag; Ofcr Stu Cncl; AR ST Univ; PT.

PHIPPS, JENNIFER R; Mills HS; North Little Rock, AR; (2); 9/449; Cmnty Wkr; French Clb; Hosp Aide; Math Clb; Mu Alpha Theta; High Hon Roll; Hon Roll; Jr NHS; FADDS; Y-Teens; Close-Up USA; Med.

PHOSAVANG, SILANY; Van Buren Sr HS; Van Buren, AR; (2); Art Clb; FBLA; Library Aide; Mu Alpha Theta; Science Clb; Jr NHS; NHS.

PHOUMIVONG, ONH; Spring Hill HS; Springdale, AR; (4); 57/486; Pres Drama Clb; HOBY; Model UN; Quiz Bowl; School Play; Co-Ed Yrbk; Rep Soph Cls; Rep Stu Cncl; NHS; Chess Clb; Odyssy Mnd.

PIANALTO, SHELLY S; Springdale Sr HS; Fayetteville, AR; (4); 1/485; Church Yth Grp; FBLA; Key Clb; Drill Tm; Pom Pon; Powder Puff Ftbl; Hon Roll; NHS; U Of AR-FAYETTEVILLE.

PICKERING, LEIGH-ANNE; Horatio HS; Horatio, AR; (2); Church Yth Grp; FCA; Library Aide; Natl FFA Org; Quiz Bowl; Rep Soph Cls; Bsktbl; Chrldng; Sftbl; Trk; Many Overall Subjct Awds; G/T Pgm; Hmcmng Crt; U Of Central AR; Phys Thrpy.

PICKETT, BRANDY; J A Fair Sr HS; Mabelvale, AR; (2); Church Yth Grp; Natl Beta Clb; Spanish Clb; Yrbk; Ofcr Jr Cls; Chrldng; Sftbl; Jr NHS; NHS; Pres Acad Fit Awd; U Cntrl AR; Med.

PICKETT, MELANIE; Bradley Jr Sr HS; Taylor, AR; (4); 2/23; Church Yth Grp; FBLA; FHA; Math Clb; Quiz Bowl; Spanish Clb; Band; Church Choir; Yrbk; NHS; Drug Tm; S AR U.

PICKETT, ROBERT A; Arkansas Sr HS; Texarkana, TX; (2); Church Yth Grp; HOBY; Church Choir; Yrbk; Pres Frsh Cls; Pres Soph Cls; JV Ftbl; JV Trk; Hon Roll; Jr NHS; Sprts Lwyr.

PICKINGS, BENJEAR M; Magnolia HS; Magnolia, AR; (2); Church Yth Grp; Band; Church Choir; Mrchg Band; Ftbl; Wt Lftg; Hon Roll; Drummer Southern Gspl Aires; Sci Fair 1st Pl Engrng; Northwestern.

PIECHOCKI, JON P; Catholic HS; Sherwood, AR; (2); 10/195; Latin Clb; JV Bsktbl; High Hon Roll; U Of AR; Pre Med.

PIERCE, ANDREW W; Pine Bluff HS; Pine Bluff, AR; (2); 1/700; Church Yth Grp; Math Tm; Quiz Bowl; Acpl Chr; Ed Lit Mag; Var Bsktbl; Var Golf; Jr NHS; Chrch Yth Group Ldrshp Team.

PIERCE JR, ARNOLD; Watson Chapel Sr HS; Pine Bluff, AR; (3); Spanish Clb; Band; Mrchg Band; Pep Band; Ftbl; Trk; Wt Lftg; Washington Coll-St Louis; Comps.

PIERCE, CASEY S; Central Sr HS; Little Rock, AR; (4); 70/400; Cmnty Wkr; French Clb; Hosp Aide; JA; Natl Beta Clb; Science Clb; Hon Roll; Jr NHS; NHS; Vol At Pinnacle St Park; UALR; Bio.

PIERCE, DEREK R; Pine Bluff HS; Pine Bluff, AR; (3); Church Yth Grp; Cmnty Wkr; French Clb; Letterman Clb; Quiz Bowl; Science Clb; Teachers Aide; Hon Roll; Pres Acad Fit Awd; Pres Schlr; Tulane; Physcn.

PIERCE, JARED R; Pine Bluff HS; Pine Bluff, AR; (3); 10/430; Rep Am Leg Boys St; Boy Scts; Church Yth Grp; Sec FBLA; Key Clb; Acpl Chr; Co-Ed Nwsp; Yrbk; Lit Mag; NHS; Madrigal Singers.

PIERCE, LISA M; Rose Bud Jr Sr HS; Rose Bud, AR; (1); Church Yth Grp; Drama Clb; FBLA; Spanish Clb; Band; School Play; Hon Roll; GATE; CPA.

PIERCE, MELISSA C; Ft Smith Christian Schl; Fort Smith, AR; (1); Church Yth Grp; Cmnty Wkr; FCA; Library Aide; Office Aide; Spanish Clb; JV L Bsktbl; JV L Trk; Hon Roll.

PIERCE, MONA J; Stamps HS; Buckner, AR; (3); 3/63; Am Leg Aux Girls St; FBLA; Library Aide; Mu Alpha Theta; Natl FFA Org; Spanish Clb; Band; Mrchg Band; School Play; Rep Jr Cls; Mst Outstdng In Jr Cls; UALR; Pre-Med.

PIERCE, SAM; Rison HS; Rison, AR; (2); 1/50; French Clb; FBLA; Natl Beta Clb; Quiz Bowl; Science Clb; Band; Drm Mjr(t); Treas Stu Cncl; High Hon Roll; Pres Acad Fit Awd; Drug Awarnss; Consultng.

PIERCE, SHANNA; North Little Rock Hs-East; North Little Rock, AR; (3); 7/567; FCA; GAA; Math Clb; Mu Alpha Theta; Natl Beta Clb; Science Clb; Band; Flag Corp; Mrchg Band; Vllybl; Schlr Athl 2 Yrs; Acctng.

PIERCE, WRONA R; Pulaski Acad; Little Rock, AR; (4); Church Yth Grp; Cmnty Wkr; English Clb; Model UN; Natl Beta Clb; Chorus; Orch; High Hon Roll; NHS; Ntl Merit SF.

PIERRE, CHRISTINA; Cutter Morning Star HS; Hot Springs, AR; (2); 4-H; Spanish Clb; Hon Roll; Amer Rabbit Breeders Assn; Winner Schl Spelling Bee; 4 Yr Coll; Marines/Law Schl.

PIGG, THOMAS E; Cabot HS; Austin, AR; (2); Hon Roll; NHS; Law.

PIKER, JERROD R; Bald Knob HS; Judsonia, AR; (2); Pres Church Yth Grp; Drama Clb; FBLA; Pres Natl Beta Clb; Acpl Chr; Band; Chorus; Jazz Band; Mrchg Band; Orch; U Of A; Music/Bus.

PILGRIM, KELCEY; Senior HS; Fort Smith, AR; (3); Church Yth Grp; Cmnty Wkr; French Clb; GAA; Pep Clb; Band; Church Choir; Drill Tm; Mrchg Band; Hon Roll; Counseling.

PILKINGTON, PAIGE L; Sheridan Sr HS; Sheridan, AR; (2); 6/296; Church Yth Grp; Dance Clb; FCA; Church Choir; Nwsp; Capt Var Pom Pon; Hon Roll; Jr NHS; Interact; Selctd High Expctns Comm; Cosmtlgy.

PINKERTON, DANIELLE; Lincoln HS; Lincoln, AR; (3); #6 in class; Church Yth Grp; Drama Clb; FBLA; Key Clb; Natl Beta Clb; Natl FFA Org; School Play; Rep Soph Cls; Pres Jr Cls; Cit Awd; Horseback Riding; AR Tech; Bus Admin.

PINKERTON, KIM; Nashville HS; Nashville, AR; (3); Am Leg Aux Girls St; Church Yth Grp; Cmnty Wkr; FBLA; FHA; Library Aide; Spanish Clb; Teachers Aide; School Play; Nwsp; Jr Cls Outstdng Stu; U Of Cntrl AR; Phy Thrpst.

PINNEY, TED; Central Ark Christian Schl; North Little Rock, AR; (4); 4/75; FBLA; Mu Alpha Theta; Science Clb; Spanish Clb; Pres Jr Cls; Var Capt Bsbl; Hon Roll; Pres NHS; Pres Acad Fit Awd; Natl Yng Ldrs Conf; Dntstry.

PINTER, JEFF; Morrilton Sr HS; Morrilton, AR; (3); Art Clb; FBLA; Math Clb; Natl Beta Clb; Science Clb; Spanish Clb; Thesps; Var Ftbl; Var Tennis; Hon Roll.

PINTER, MELISSA; Morrilton Sr HS; Morrilton, AR; (4); Art Clb; Church Yth Grp; FBLA; Math Clb; Natl Beta Clb; Science Clb; Spanish Clb; Thesps; Ed Yrbk; Rptr Frsh Cls; Beta Clb Treas, Scrpbk Cmte; FLBA Rep 94; U Of AR; Bus.

PIPES JR, DARRELL L; Victory Bapt Acad; Malvern, AR; (4); Church Yth Grp; FCA; Yrbk; Hon Roll; Amer Chrstn Hnr Soc.

PIPPEN, KELLEY S; Crossett Sr HS; Crossett, AR; (2); Church Yth Grp; Chorus; Church Choir; Hon Roll; Stdnts For Christ.

PIRANI, ANTHONY J; Central HS; West Helena, AR; (2); Church Yth Grp; French Clb; Quiz Bowl; ROTC; Band; Church Choir; Drill Tm; Rep Stu Cncl; Golf; Hon Roll; Accepted To AR Schl Of Math & Sci; Preached At Chrch; Stanford; Bio; Pol Sci.

PIRANI, RACHEL J; Marion HS; Marion, AR; (2); Art Clb; French Clb; Ofcr Stu Cncl; Chrldng; Hon Roll; 1st Pl Awds HS Spring Art Show 96.

PITCHER, JENNIFER; Delaplaine Schl; Delaplaine, AR; (3); 4/30; FBLA; FHA; Sec Treas Library Aide; Spanish Clb; Band; Sec Frsh Cls; Sec Soph Cls; Co-Capt Chrldng; Hon Roll; NHS; PRIDE; AIM; Med.

PITCHFORD, CLOVIS W; Mountain Home HS; Mountain Home, AR; (4); 1/230; Am Leg Boys St; Pres 4-H; French Clb; FBLA; Capt Quiz Bowl; Ofcr ROTC; Church Choir; Nwsp; Crs Cntry; Var L Ftbl; US Frst Dsgn Tm; WA U; Physcn.

PITCHFORD, LANDON H; Mountain Home HS; Mountain Home, AR; (3); 27/253; Church Yth Grp; FCA; Var L Bsktbl; High Hon Roll; Freed Hardeman Univ; Biolgst.

PITTENGER, KACI R; Alpena Schl; Green Forest, AR; (2); Church Yth Grp; FCA; Natl Beta Clb; Chorus; Phtg Yrbk; Pres Soph Cls; Chrldng; Hon Roll; Pep Clb; Spanish Clb; Reach Out; Stu Cncl.

PITTMAN, JOHN D; Hackett Schl; Hackett, AR; (1); Band; Mrchg Band; Pep Band; Var Bsbl; JV Bsktbl; JV Capt Ftbl; High Hon Roll; Jr NHS; AEGIS Pgm; Bys Clb Bsbl All Star.

PITTMAN, MINDY; Kingston Jr Sr HS; Kingston, AR; (4); 4/17; Church Yth Grp; VP FHA; Library Aide; Office Aide; Teachers Aide; Yrbk; Hist Frsh Cls; Pres Sr Cls; VP Stu Cncl; Mgr Bsktbl; FHA St Treas; NATCTC; Bus.

PITTS, ERICA; Charleston HS; Charleston, AR; (1); 1/82; Art Clb; Pres FBLA; Sec Frsh Cls; Ofcr Stu Cncl; Var L Bsktbl; Powder Puff Ftbl; L Sftbl; Var Trk; Hon Roll; Arch Engrng.

PITTS, KALISHA L; Forrest City HS; Forrest City, AR; (3); Church Yth Grp; French Clb; FHA; Mu Alpha Theta; Natl Beta Clb; Office Aide; Band; Mrchg Band; Rep Stu Cncl; High Hon Roll; Eureka Civic/Soc Club; AK ST Univ; Elem Ed.

PLAISANCE, ROBERT A; Central Sr HS; Little Rock, AR; (3); Boy Scts; Church Yth Grp; Natl Beta Clb; VICA; Var Ftbl; Cit Awd; Hon Roll; Prfct Atten Awd; Auto Tech.

PLATT, JESSICA; Central Ark Christian Schl; Little Rock, AR; (1); Church Yth Grp; Chorus; Capt Bsktbl; Crs Cntry; Trk; Jr NHS.

PLATT, MELISSA A; North Little Rock Hs-West; North Little Rock, AR; (4); 82/443; Drama Clb; French Clb; Key Clb; Library Aide; Natl Beta Clb; Science Clb; School Musical; School Play; Stage Crew; Variety Show; AR ST U; Thtr Arts.

PLEDGER, LAKEISHA D; Morrilton Sr HS; Morrilton, AR; (2); French Clb; FBLA; Natl Beta Clb; Ntl Merit Schol; Merit Awd 10th Grd Eng.

PLOSZAY, JILL K; North Little Rock Hs-West; North Little Rock, AR; (4); 4/439; Am Leg Aux Girls St; Art Clb; Church Yth Grp; Cmnty Wkr; Dance Clb; FCA; Math Clb; Mu Alpha Theta; Science Clb; Service Clb; Natl Young Ldrs Schlr; Baylor Univ; Engrng.

PLUMLE, NANCY J; Arkansas Sr HS; Texarkana, AR; (2); Art Clb; Church Yth Grp; Drama Clb; French Clb; FTA; Mu Alpha Theta; Church Choir; Drill Tm; Phtg Yrbk; Hon Roll; PRIDE; Teenage Repubs; Gymnstcs; SMU; Archtct.

PLUMLEE, RUTH L; Marvell Acad; Clarendon, AR; (4); Church Yth Grp; Computer Clb; FBLA; GAA; HOBY; Library Aide; Spanish Clb; Church Choir; School Play; Rptr Nwsp; Ouachita Bapt U; Music Prfrmnc.

PLUMLEE, RYAN T; Harrison Sr HS; Harrison, AR; (4); 2/192; FBLA; JV Bsbl; Var L Bsktbl; Var L Ftbl; JV Trk; High Hon Roll; NHS; Pres Acad Fit Awd; Builders Clb Pres; AAU Bsktbl; Fire Marshall.

PLUMMER, CHRIS O; Northside HS; Fort Smith, AR; (3); Boy Scts; Chess Clb; Church Yth Grp; French Clb; Teachers Aide; Hon Roll; Chrch Yth Drama, Choir & Ensemble; Ouachita Bapt Univ; Crimnl Just.

PLUMMER, POLLY M; Fairview HS; Camden, AR; (2); Drama Clb; FHA; Natl Beta Clb; Band; Mrchg Band; School Musical; Yrbk; Hon Roll; Dance.

PLUNKETT, LYDIA M; Monticello HS; Monticello, AR; (3); Am Leg Aux Girls St; Pres Drama Clb; VP FBLA; Pres FHA; Natl Beta Clb; SADD; Capt Band; Phtg Yrbk; Sftbl; NHS; U Of AR Fayetteville; Law.

POCKRUS, MATTHEW; Rogers HS; Rogers, AR; (4); Church Yth Grp; FCA; FBLA; Pres Model UN; Mrchg Band; Intrml Bsktbl; Hon Roll; NHS; Prfct Atten Awd; PACE Club Pres; REACH Club Prog Comm Chrmn; Mdl UN Rep Awds; Hendrix.

POE, BRANDY E; Sheridan Sr HS; Sheridan, AR; (2); 56/294; Church Yth Grp; Band; Mrchg Band; Teen Invlvmnt Drug Awrnss Prgm K-6th Grd; All Region Bnd; U Of Cntrl AR; PT.

POFF, AMANDA; Gosnell Jr Sr HS; Blytheville, AR; (2); Church Yth Grp; Cmnty Wkr; FCA; FHA; GAA; Natl Beta Clb; Quiz Bowl; Science Clb; Spanish Clb; Acpl Chr; AR St Univ; HS Tchr.

POFF, AMANDA G; Southside HS; Desha, AR; (4); 6/72; FBLA; FHA; Key Clb; Natl Beta Clb; Science Clb; Spanish Clb; Band; Capt Drill Tm; High Hon Roll; Pres Schlr; Chm Of Mentor; HTE All-Star Dancer; HTE All-Star Kick Co; AR ST Univ; Pre-Med.

POINDEXTER, JESSICA; Ridgecrest HS; Paragould, AR; (4); 13/185; FHA; Hosp Aide; Science Clb; Hon Roll; NHS; Pres Acad Fit Awd; Paragould Girls Sftbl Leag; Prsntr AGATE Conf; AR Acts Assn Active Schlr Awd; U Of AR; Pre-Med.

POINDEXTER, T C; Calvary Christian Schl; Forrest City, AR; (4); 1/7; Church Yth Grp; Yrbk; Ofcr Stu Cncl; Gov Hon Prg Awd; High Hon Roll; Kiwanis Awd; NHS; Pres Schlr; Val; Homcmng Qn; Piano; US Army Schlr Ath Awd; E AR CC; Acctng.

POINDEXTER, TOMMIE C; Calvary Christian Schl; Forrest City, AR; (4); 1/7; Church Yth Grp; Cmnty Wkr; School Play; Yrbk; Pres Stu Cncl; Bsktbl; Vllybl; High Hon Roll; NHS; Piano & Organ Lessons; East Ark CC; Acctng.

POINTS, JAMIE E; Smackover HS; Smackover, AR; (1); Church Yth Grp; Q&S; Mgr(s); Trk; Hon Roll; BASIC Pres; Law; Lawyer.

POLEY, FEATHER; Valley View HS; Jonesboro, AR; (4); 4/64; Church Yth Grp; FHA; Natl Beta Clb; Spanish Clb; Acpl Chr; Chorus; Church Choir; Ofcr Stu Cncl; High Hon Roll; Hon Roll; U Of Cntrl AR; Occup Thrpy.

POLK, RENEE E; Marvell Acad; Marvell, AR; (2); 2/36; Sec Church Yth Grp; Dance Clb; HOBY; Yrbk; Bsktbl; Chrldng; Sftbl; Trk; High Hon Roll; NHS; ABC Cntst; Stdnt Of Mnth; U Of AR; Jrnlst.

POLK, SUMMER; Nemo Vista Jr Sr HS; Center Ridge, AR; (4); 1/37; Church Yth Grp; FBLA; Spanish Clb; Natl Beta Clb; Sec Stu Cncl; Bsktbl; High Hon Roll; Natl Young Ldrs Conf Alumni; Harding Univ.

POLK, SUSAN; Nemo Vista Jr Sr HS; Center Ridge, AR; (3); 1/38; Am Leg Aux Girls St; FBLA; Rptr Natl Beta Clb; Pres Spanish Clb; Rptr Rep Stu Cncl; Bsktbl; Harding Univ.

POLKOWSKI II, GREG; Arkansas Bapt Schl; Little Rock, AR; (4); Church Yth Grp; FBLA; Pres Natl Beta Clb; Chorus; School Play; Ed Yrbk; VP Jr Cls; Pres Sr Cls; Var Capt Ftbl; FCA; All Amer Schlr In Jrnlsm & His; Natl Yth Ldrshp Forum On Med; Dir Awd; 1st Pl Desktop Pub Dist V FBLA; U AR Fayetteville; Medicine.

POLL, SARAH; Gillett Jr Sr HS; Gillett, AR; (2); 2/28; Rptr FBLA; Pres FHA; Quiz Bowl; Rptr Spanish Clb; Rptr Soph Cls; Var Bsktbl; Var Chrldng; Var Sftbl; DAR Awd; NHS; All Star Mascot 95.

POLLARD, EMILY H; Pulaski Acad; Little Rock, AR; (2); Church Yth Grp; Natl Beta Clb; Service Clb; Spanish Clb; Co-Ed Yrbk; Sftbl; JV Vllybl; High Hon Roll; Hon Roll; NHS; Natl His Day; Pediatrics; Nrsng.

POLLARD, KIMBERLY B; Bradford Jr Sr HS; Bradford, AR; (3); Church Yth Grp; 4-H; FHA; Natl Beta Clb; Teachers Aide; 4-H Awd; High Hon Roll; Prfct Atten Awd; Nurses Aide; Frnch II Hghst Grd Awd; Spch Hghst Grd Awd; ASU; Cmptr Tech.

POLLOCK, BEVERLY D; Rogers HS; Rogers, AR; (3); FBLA; Capt Band; Hon Roll; Spr Acad Achvmnt 1st/2nd Yr; COE Wrk Prgm; U Of AR; PT.

POLLOCK, MELISSA; Ridgecrest HS; Paragould, AR; (2); 6/220; FTA; Band; Mrchg Band; High Hon Roll; Video Graphics For Schl TV Station; Animation; Space Pgm.

POOL, DARLENE J; Booneville Jr Sr HS; Booneville, AR; (4); 17/87; Art Clb; Church Yth Grp; FBLA; FHA; FTA; Key Clb; Library Aide; Office Aide; Spanish Clb; Teachers Aide; DARE; Westark CC; RN.

POOL, JENNIFER; West Memphis Sr HS; West Memphis, AR; (3); French Clb; Math Clb; Mu Alpha Theta; Natl Beta Clb; Science Clb; Sec Frsh Cls; Chrldng; Tennis; Trk; High Hon Roll.

POOL, JENNIFER N; England HS; England, AR; (3); #5 in class; FCA; FBLA; FHA; Spanish Clb; Var Bsktbl; Var Chrldng; Trk; High Hon Roll; NHS; U Of AR; Dntl Hygnst.

POOL, ROSE; Norfork Jr Sr HS; Norfork, AR; (3); 1/25; Art Clb; English Clb; FBLA; FHA; Math Clb; Science Clb; SADD; Yrbk; High Hon Roll; NHS; Marine Bio.

POOL, SCOTT S; Oak Grove HS; Maumelle, AR; (1); Boy Scts; Computer Clb; Library Aide; Natl Beta Clb; Spanish Clb; Band; Mrchg Band; Rep Frsh Cls; Hon Roll; Cmptr Prgrmr/Repair.

POOLE, ANGELA N; Fayetteville Sr HS; Fayetteville, AR; (3); 4/300; Church Yth Grp; Cmnty Wkr; FBLA; Acpl Chr; Phtg Yrbk; High Hon Roll; NHS; Prfct Atten Awd; Choir; FFA Chptr Pres ST Sec; Sunday Schl Tchr; U Of A; Music Tchr.

POOLE, BRANDON D; Strong Jr Sr HS; Strong, AR; (2); French Clb; Natl Beta Clb; Nwsp; Yrbk; Ofcr Soph Cls; Ofcr Bsbl; Ftbl; Wt Lftg; French Hon Soc; SAU.

POOLE, MONCHANILLO L; Forrest City HS; Forrest City, AR; (1); SADD; Stage Crew; Nwsp; Ofcr Stu Cncl; Ofcr Bsbl; Gov Hon Prg Awd; AZ ST U; Technician.

POPE, ASHLEY; J A Fair Sr HS; Alexander, AR; (4); 21/300; Church Yth Grp; Sec Drama Clb; Mu Alpha Theta; Capt Quiz Bowl; VP Spanish Clb; School Play; Stage Crew; Co-Ed Yrbk; High Hon Roll; NHS; Piano; Sftbl; U Of Cntrl AR; Psych.

POPP, TRICIA I; Waldron HS; Waldron, AR; (2); Church Yth Grp; Natl Beta Clb; Spanish Clb; Band; Jazz Band; Mrchg Band; Pep Band; Hon Roll; Prfct Atten Awd; Music.

PORCELLI, ADRIANNE; Gurdon HS; Arkadelphia, AR; (3); Church Yth Grp; Natl Beta Clb; Spanish Clb; Chorus; Church Choir; Rep Frsh Cls; Rep Soph Cls; Rep Stu Cncl; Publshd In Shape Magzn.

PORCHAY, JAMILIA M; J A Fair Sr HS; Little Rock, AR; (4); Dance Clb; Library Aide; Pep Clb; Spanish Clb; Chorus; Hon Roll; Prfct Atten Awd; Flwshp Chrstn Stdnts; UCA; Ped.

PORCHIA, KASEY; Stephens Jr Sr HS; Stephens, AR; (3); #2 in class; 4-H; FBLA; FHA; Quiz Bowl; VP Jr Cls; Ofcr Stu Cncl; Capt Bsktbl; High Hon Roll; Hon Roll; NHS; Phys Thrpy.

PORTA, BECKY; Kimmons Jr HS; Fort Smith, AR; (1); Church Yth Grp; FCA; Church Choir; Bsktbl; Chrldng; Trk; Hon Roll; Jr NHS; U Of Central AR; Phys Thrpy.

PORTER, AMY; Huntsville HS; Elkins, AR; (4); 5/116; Drama Clb; FBLA; FTA; Treas Key Clb; Teachers Aide; Stage Crew; Rptr Nwsp; High Hon Roll; NHS; ACE/QUIZ Bowl Chief Staff.

PORTER, ASHLEY E; Mt St Mary Acad; North Little Rock, AR; (3); Hosp Aide; JCL; Latin Clb; Math Clb; Mu Alpha Theta; High Hon Roll; NHS; Pres Acad Fit Awd; Tri-M Music Natl Hnrs Soc; Pres Yth Svc Awd; Govrnrs Vol Excl Awd; Hendrix; Psych.

PORTER, CARRIE; Mineral Springs Schl; Mineral Springs, AR; (4); Church Yth Grp; FBLA; FHA; Letterman Clb; Natl Beta Clb; Office Aide; Quiz Bowl; Spanish Clb; Band; Mrchg Band; Close-Up; Chrldr Captain; Homcmng Ftbl Maid; Sr Homcmng Qn; Dist Trk Wnnr; Henderson St U; Bus Mgmt.

PORTER, GINA; Morrilton Sr HS; Conway, AR; (4); #45 in class; Art Clb; Church Yth Grp; French Clb; GAA; Pep Clb; Drill Tm; Bsktbl; Chrldng; Sftbl; Trk; U Of AR Fayetteville; Elem Ed.

PORTER, JARED; Farmington Jr Sr HS; Fayetteville, AR; (3); Am Leg Boys St; Church Yth Grp; FCA; Math Clb; SADD; Var Bsktbl; Hon Roll; Prfct Atten Awd; Stck Mrkt Clb.

PORTER, JEFF; Jacksonville HS; Jacksonville, AR; (4); 31/283; Church Yth Grp; Natl Beta Clb; VP Spanish Clb; Church Choir; JV Var Bsktbl; JV Var Ftbl; Sftbl; Hon Roll; NHS; Pres Schlr; Hnr Grad; ASU At Beebe; CPA.

PORTER, JOVANA L; John L Mcclellan Magnet HS; Little Rock, AR; (3); Art Clb; Drama Clb; FBLA; JA; Latin Clb; Jazz Band; School Musical; Bsktbl; Ftbl; Comp Animation.

PORTER, KARA; Cntrl Arkansas Chrstn Schl; Mabelvale, AR; (4); FBLA; FHA; Spanish Clb; Var Chrldng; Gym; Sftbl; Tennis; Chrldng All Star; Vlntne Ct; Harding U; Intr Dsgn.

PORTER, KIELIEMA K; Saratoga Schl; Mineral Springs, AR; (2); 4-H; Am Leg Boys St; GAA; Science Clb; School Musical; Yrbk; VP Frsh Cls; Pres Soph Cls; Bsktbl; Trk; Dietician.

PORTER, KRISTY A; Oak Grove HS; Maumelle, AR; (1); Drama Clb; FHA; Tae Kwon Do Blue Belt; U Of Cntrl AR.

PORTER, LAWANDA P; Hope HS; Hope, AR; (3); 32/150; Church Yth Grp; 4-H; Hist FHA; GAA; Girl Scts; Letterman Clb; Treas Natl Beta Clb; Band; Church Choir; Color Guard; Navy Hnrs Prgm; Hnr Card Prgm Acad Achvmnt; Pharm.

PORTER, YURIKO L; Hughes Jr-Sr HS; Hughes, AR; (2); 41/76; Art Clb; Cmnty Wkr; Math Clb; Science Clb; Spanish Clb; Bsktbl; Prfct Atten Awd; Nrs.

POSEY, SHAUNA L; Bradford Jr Sr HS; Bradford, AR; (3); Church Yth Grp; French Clb; FHA; Girl Scts; Library Aide; Natl Beta Clb; Band; Chorus; Church Choir; Variety Show; Upward Bound; Child Care; Nrsng/Lawyer.

POST, CHRIS K; Junction City HS; El Dorado, AR; (1); Church Yth Grp; FBLA; Teachers Aide; School Play; Stage Crew; High Hon Roll; Hon Roll.

POSTON, NATHAN E; Dewitt HS; Saint Charles, AR; (2); Church Yth Grp; Natl Beta Clb; Chorus; Church Choir; High Hon Roll; Hon Roll; Dr.

POTOCHNIK, ANGELA M; Rogers HS; Rogers, AR; (2); 1/850; Cmnty Wkr; Letterman Clb; Model UN; Varsity Clb; Band; Mrchg Band; Var L Crs Cntry; Var L Trk; High Hon Roll; Odyssey Of Mind.

POTTER, AMY N; Westside HS; Hartman, AR; (2); 1/48; Church Yth Grp; FBLA; Natl Beta Clb; Band.

POTTER, CRYSTAL; Calico Rock HS; Calico Rock, AR; (4); 7/31; CAP; FBLA; Natl Beta Clb; Science Clb; SADD; Band; Jazz Band; Pep Band; Pres Sr Cls; Sftbl; SADD Image Awd; Mtn Hm ASU.

POTTER, JENNIFER; Bryant Sr HS; Alexander, AR; (3); 36/394; English Clb; FCA; French Clb; Pep Clb; Pres Science Clb; Chrldng; High Hon Roll; Hon Roll; Jr NHS; NHS; Natl Ed Dev Test Awd; Pre-Med; Bio; Radiology.

POTTORFF, DARYLD; Pea Ridge HS; Pea Ridge, AR; (2); 9/72; Church Yth Grp; Letterman Clb; Varsity Clb; Band; Mrchg Band; JV Var Bsktbl; Var Trk; Hon Roll; Office Aide; U Of AR; Arch.

POTTS, PRISCELLA D; Fouke Jr Sr HS; Fouke, AR; (4); FBLA; Library Aide.

POUNDERS, JASON D; Rivercrest HS; Wilson, AR; (2); 6/110; FBLA; Pres Math Clb; Teachers Aide; Chorus; Var L Bsbl; Var Capt Bsktbl; JV L Ftbl; High Hon Roll; Hon Roll; Pres Jr NHS; TAD & Lib Clb; AAM Bsktbl Team; Jr Babe Ruth All-Star Team Made It To St Trnmt; Sports Medicine; Phy Therapy.

POUNDERS, JESSE W; Bald Knob HS; Bald Knob, AR; (3); Church Yth Grp; Debate Tm; Natl Beta Clb; Quiz Bowl; Spanish Clb; Teachers Aide; Varsity Clb; Treas Jr Cls; Ofcr Bsbl; Bsktbl; His Hnr; Prom Prince.

POUNDERS, LISA M; Izard Co Cons Jr Sr HS; Horseshoe Bend, AR; (4); 1/40; Am Leg Aux Girls St; Church Yth Grp; FBLA; Key Clb; Sec Natl Beta Clb; Spanish Clb; School Play; Co-Capt Nwsp; Ed Yrbk; Ofcr Stu Cncl; Cougars Helping Other Stu Excel Clb; AR ST Univ.

POWELL, ALISON E; Bryant Sr HS; Bryant, AR; (2); Church Yth Grp; FBLA; GAA; Bsktbl; Sftbl; Trk; Vllybl; Hon Roll; JETS Awd; Teachers Aide.

POWELL, ANDREA L; Rogers HS; Lowell, AR; (4); Sec Church Yth Grp; Drama Clb; FCA; FBLA; Pres FHA; VP Key Clb; Teachers Aide; Rep Stu Cncl; JV Socr; Pres Acad Fit Awd; AR ST Univ; Elem Ed.

POWELL, CATHY J; White Co Central Schl; Judsonia, AR; (2); Church Yth Grp; Pres 4-H; FBLA; FHA; Quiz Bowl; Lit Mag; Mgr Bsktbl; Mgr Trk; HIPPY; INTERACT Bd Mem; Gftd/Tlntd; Msc.

POWELL, CHAD A; Lee Acad; Caldwell, AR; (1); Ofcr Bsbl; Bsktbl; Ftbl; Trk; Wt Lftg; High Hon Roll; Prfct Atten Awd; U Of AR.

POWELL, CHRIS; Mc Gehee HS; Mc Gehee, AR; (4); 2/88; Am Leg Boys St; Church Yth Grp; FCA; Natl Beta Clb; Chorus; Rep Stu Cncl; Pres NHS; Sal; Prsdntl Edctn Awd; Ouachita Bapt Univ.

POWELL, CRYSTAL; Taylor HS; Taylor, AR; (1); Church Yth Grp; FCA; FHA; Quiz Bowl; Church Choir; VP Frsh Cls; High Hon Roll; Hon Roll; Crmnl Dfns Attrny.

POWELL, HEATHER; Ozark HS; Ozark, AR; (4); 16/90; Church Yth Grp; FBLA; Intnl Clb; Natl Beta Clb; SADD; Church Choir; Yrbk; Pres Frsh Cls; Pres Soph Cls; Pres Jr Cls; Ftbl Hmcmng Qn Sr Yr; Teens Chrst; GCE Employee Yr; Westlark Comm; Bus.

POWELL, JASON; Butterfield Jr HS; Van Buren, AR; (1); Band; U Of OK; Astrophysics.

POWELL, JILL; Sylvan Hills HS; Sherwood, AR; (4); 20/240; Am Leg Aux Girls St; Church Yth Grp; FCA; FBLA; FHA; Key Clb; Mu Alpha Theta; Natl Beta Clb; Spanish Clb; Drill Tm; Lyon Coll.

POWELL, JOHN; Mc Gehee HS; Mc Gehee, AR; (3); Am Leg Boys St; Church Yth Grp; FCA; FTA; Mu Alpha Theta; Natl Beta Clb; Science Clb; Nwsp; Yrbk; Hon Roll; Natl Govt Awd; All Amer Schlr; U S Achvt Acad Awd.

POWELL, JONATHAN; Southside HS; Fort Smith, AR; (4); Church Yth Grp; Intnl Clb; Mu Alpha Theta; Spanish Clb; Socr; Hon Roll; NHS; Pres Acad Fit Awd; Spanish NHS; Lyon Coll.

POWELL, KRISTI L; Nevada Schl; Rosston, AR; (1); Pres Church Yth Grp; VP 4-H; FBLA; Sec Natl FFA Org; Band; Sec Frsh Cls; Var Chrldng; Trk; 4-H Awd; Hon Roll; Singing Chrch; Rdng Hrs; Playing Piano; SNU; Vet.

POWELL, LARRY W; North Little Rock Hs-East; North Little Rock, AR; (2); 68/567; Spanish Clb; High Hon Roll; Hon Roll; Prfct Atten Awd; U Of AR; Elctrcl Eng.

POWELL, LAUREN; Warren Jr HS; Warren, AR; (1); 1/125; Church Yth Grp; Natl Beta Clb; Quiz Bowl; Chorus; Church Choir; Chrldng; High Hon Roll; Yth Ensmbl Quest Chrch; AR ST U; Nrs Prcttnr.

POWELL, MELISSA; Harding Acad; Beebe, AR; (3); Church Yth Grp; Hosp Aide; Key Clb; Pep Clb; Speech Tm; Acpl Chr; School Musical; Chrldng; Trk; DAR Awd; Harding Univ; Speech Pathology.

POWELL, NATE L; North Little Rock Hs-West; North Little Rock, AR; (4); 6/472; Art Clb; Church Yth Grp; Cmnty Wkr; Debate Tm; Mu Alpha Theta; Natl Beta Clb; VICA; Nwsp; Yrbk; Lit Mag; AR Gov Schl 95; Ownr Rcd Lbl/Pblshng Lbl Food Chn Prdctns; Singer Lcl Band Sophie Un Squad; U Of Hartford; Illustration.

POWELL, RACHEL; White Co Central Schl; Judsonia, AR; (4); 5/28; Art Clb; Church Yth Grp; Sec FBLA; Sec FHA; Quiz Bowl; Sftbl; Hon Roll; Pres Acad Fit Awd; Mexico Mission Trips; Mid TN ST Univ; Recording Ind.

POWELL, STEVEN W; Mc Gehee HS; Mcgehee, AR; (3); Church Yth Grp; Natl Beta Clb.

POWER, JENNY; Nashville HS; Nashville, AR; (4); 3/135; Church Yth Grp; Pres FBLA; HOBY; Sec Spanish Clb; School Play; Variety Show; Ed Nwsp; Sec Sr Cls; Gov Hon Prg Awd; NHS; All-Amer Chrldr; Govs Yth Crime Brd Rep; Ouachita Baptist U; Med.

POWER, JENNY M; Nashville HS; Ozan, AR; (4); 3/135; FBLA; HOBY; Spanish Clb; School Play; Variety Show; Ed Nwsp; Sec Sr Cls; Capt Chrldng; NHS; Pres Acad Fit Awd; Ouachita Bapt U; Pre-Med.

POWERS, CARA C; Lakeside HS; Hot Springs, AR; (4); 12/119; Art Clb; Church Yth Grp; Cmnty Wkr; Dance Clb; Drama Clb; German Clb; Math Clb; Mu Alpha Theta; Ski Clb; Thesps; Voice & Dance Lessons; Rock Clmbng; Oral Roberts U; Hlth/Exercise.

POWERS, LELONAH; Westside HS; Bono, AR; (4); 14/76; FBLA; VP Science Clb; Spanish Clb; Teachers Aide; Chorus; Hon Roll; Pres Acad Fit Awd; Hnr Grad; AR ST Univ; Bus Admin.

POYNER, DAVID B; Parkview HS; Little Rock, AR; (3); Church Yth Grp; Cmnty Wkr; Teachers Aide; Band; Stage Crew; Yrbk; Hon Roll; Peer Hlprs Rtrt; Chrch Camp Asst Cnslr; Comp Aided Drftng.

POYNTER, CARRIE J; Mountain Home HS; Mountain Home, AR; (2); 4/328; Church Yth Grp; German Clb; Hosp Aide; Math Tm; Band; Mrchg Band; Pep Band; Golf; Powder Puff Ftbl; Sftbl; Med.

PRATER, STEPHANIE D; Conway Sr HS; Conway, AR; (3); Church Yth Grp; FBLA; Hosp Aide; Natl Beta Clb; Pep Clb; French Hon Soc; High Hon Roll; Ntl Merit Ltr; Faulkner Cnty Yth Ldrshp Inst.

PRATER, STEPHEN K; Mills HS; Sherwood, AR; (3); 8/350; Art Clb; Boy Scts; JCL; Latin Clb; Natl Beta Clb; Quiz Bowl; Gov Hon Prg Awd; High Hon Roll; NHS; Odyssey Of The Mind; AR Young Artists Assn.

PRATT, HANNAH; Camden Fairview HS; Camden, AR; (3); 1/288; Am Leg Aux Girls St; Cmnty Wkr; Mu Alpha Theta; Natl Beta Clb; Drill Tm; School Musical; Yrbk; Sec Jr Cls; Var JV Chrldng; French Hon Soc; Anchor Club; Med.

PRATT, HOLLY R; Riverview HS; Judsonia, AR; (2); Drama Clb; FBLA; FHA; Natl Beta Clb; Service Clb; Spanish Clb; Thesps; School Play; Ofcr Stu Cncl; Hon Roll.

PRATT, NATHAN D; Clarksville HS; Clarksville, AR; (4); 20/130; Am Leg Boys St; Church Yth Grp; FCA; FBLA; Letterman Clb; Natl Beta Clb; Spanish Clb; Capt Ftbl; L Vllybl; Pride And Paws.

PRESCOTT, ROBERT S; Highland HS; Ravenden, AR; (3); Am Leg Boys St; Boy Scts; Church Yth Grp; FCA; SADD; Chorus; Church Choir; Ofcr Sr Cls; Ofcr Stu Cncl; Ofcr Bsbl; Boys St 96; Wildlife Mgmt.

PRESLEY, AMBER M; Harrisburg HS; Harrisburg, AR; (3); Church Yth Grp; FCA; GAA; Office Aide; Science Clb; Spanish Clb; Teachers Aide; Chorus; Church Choir; School Musical; Horseback Riding.

PRESLEY, JASON C; Heber Springs HS; Heber Springs, AR; (3); Am Leg Boys St; Church Yth Grp; Cmnty Wkr; FCA; FHA; Key Clb; Natl FFA Org; Office Aide; Spanish Clb; Speech Tm; U Of AR.

PRESLEY, TIFFANY N; Valley View HS; Jonesboro, AR; (2); Art Clb; Pres Church Yth Grp; FBLA; FHA; Key Clb; Spanish Clb; Co-Ed Yrbk; Rep Stu Cncl; Vllybl; High Hon Roll; Bio Awd; AR Yng Artists Assoc; Printmaking 1st Pl; ASU; Psych.

PRESSGROVE, JEREMY R; West Memphis Christian Schl; West Memphis, AR; (1); Church Yth Grp; JV L Bsktbl; JV Capt Ftbl; Hon Roll; Pres Acad Fit Awd; Dist Sci Fair Attnd/Won 2nd Schl; Cnslrs Aide; Lttrd Track.

PRESSLER, DONNA L; Brinkley HS; Brinkley, AR; (3); Church Yth Grp; French Clb; Q&S; Chorus; Church Choir; Yrbk; Ofcr Stu Cncl; Hon Roll; Var Chrldng; All Amer Schlr; U Of A; Child Psych.

PRESSNELL, AMY R; Arkansas Sr HS; Texarkana, AR; (2); Church Yth Grp; 4-H; FHA; Pep Clb; Spanish Clb; Chorus; Church Choir; Ofcr Stu Cncl; Pom Pon; Wt Lftg; Southern AR U; RN.

PRESSNELL, ANGELA L; Arkansas Sr HS; Texarkana, AR; (2); Church Yth Grp; 4-H; Pep Clb; Spanish Clb; Church Choir; Ofcr Stu Cncl; Pom Pon; 4-H Awd; Pep Sqd Capt; Occptnl Thrpy.

PRESTIDGE, ALLISON R; Black Rock Jr Sr HS; Powhatan, AR; (1); Church Yth Grp; FBLA; FHA; GAA; Natl Beta Clb; Rptr Nwsp; Bsktbl; Sftbl; Hon Roll; FBLA & Beta Rptr; Harding Univ; Phys Therapy.

PREWETT, KARI L; Lavaca Jr Sr HS; Lavaca, AR; (3); 1/60; Debate Tm; Natl Beta Clb; NFL; Spanish Clb; Speech Tm; Bsktbl; NHS; Pres Acad Fit Awd; Cmnty Wkr; Drama Clb; Woodmen Of World Awd For Outstdng Proficiency In HS; Miss Lavaca HS; Law.

PREWITT, APRIL; Dermott HS; Dermott, AR; (1); Church Yth Grp; FBLA; Natl Beta Clb; Band; Mrchg Band.

PREWITT, JENNFIER L; Central Sr HS; Little Rock, AR; (2); Cmnty Wkr; Hosp Aide; Mu Alpha Theta; Natl Beta Clb; VP Spanish Clb; Cit Awd; High Hon Roll; Jr NHS; Tchng.

PRIBBERNOW, MEGAN E; Mountain Home HS; Oakland, AR; (3); Church Yth Grp; FBLA; Pep Clb; Band; Mrchg Band; Pep Band; Spanish NHS; Majrtt; Hendrix; Psych.

PRICE, AMANDA L; Gravette HS; Gravette, AR; (2); Model UN; Quiz Bowl; Var L Bsktbl; Var Sftbl; High Hon Roll; Jr NHS; NHS; AHSME Schl Wnnr; Med.

PRICE, CINDY D; Devalls Bluff Jr Sr HS; De Valls Bluff, AR; (3); Church Yth Grp; Drama Clb; 4-H; French Clb; FBLA; FHA; Key Clb; Natl Beta Clb; School Play; Rep Jr Cls; Jonesboro; Pedtrc Dentstry.

PRICE, JHOSHUA; Arkansas Bapt Schl; Maumelle, AR; (3); 1/55; Church Yth Grp; Natl Beta Clb; Spanish Clb; High Hon Roll; Frgn Missions Clb; Navy Hnrs Pgm; Highest Acad Average Awds; Stanford U; Pre-Med; Medicine.

PRICE, JUSTIN; Lamar HS; Clarksville, AR; (3); Am Leg Boys St; Church Yth Grp; FCA; Pres FBLA; Math Clb; Natl Beta Clb; Sec Science Clb; Var Bsktbl; Var Golf; Hon Roll; Bus.

PRICE, KARA; Mc Gehee HS; Mc Gehee, AR; (4); 8/86; Am Leg Aux Girls St; Art Clb; Church Yth Grp; 4-H; FBLA; FTA; Mu Alpha Theta; Natl Beta Clb; Science Clb; Spanish Clb; U Of AR; Acctng.

PRICE, LAURA L; Hazen Jr Sr HS; Hazen, AR; (3); 6/40; FBLA; FHA; FTA; Sec Treas Band; Mrchg Band; Var Bsktbl; Trk; Church Yth Grp; Ntl Merit Ltr; Church Yth Grp; Woodsmen Of Wrld Amer His Awd; U Of A Fayetteville; Sprts Med.

PRICE, MELISSA C; Fayetteville Sr HS; Fayetteville, AR; (3); Mu Alpha Theta; Band; Capt Drm Mjr(t); Mrchg Band; Orch; Pep Band; Gov Hon Prg Awd; High Hon Roll; NHS; Frgn Lang Clb Sec; Phi Beta Mu Intl Msc Frat Awd; Band Cncl; Majorette Capt; Top 10 Pct Natl Span Exam; Engr/Law.

PRICE, NICOLE L; Cty Line HS; Branch, AR; (3); Church Yth Grp; VP FCA; FBLA; FHA; GAA; Natl Beta Clb; Rptr Yrbk; Sec Frsh Cls; Sec Soph Cls; Rep Jr Cls; Westarck CC; X-Ray Technician.

PRICE, REBECCA; Beebe Sr HS; Beebe, AR; (3); Church Yth Grp; Drama Clb; FBLA; FHA; Hosp Aide; Pep Clb; Spanish Clb; Teachers Aide; Band; Chorus; Yng Chld Dev.

PRICE, TABBITHA N; Gravette HS; Gravette, AR; (1); #3 in class; Sec Treas Frsh Cls; Var Bsktbl; Var Sftbl; Hon Roll; Pediatrics.

PRIDMORE, JENNIFER; Vilonia HS; Vilonia, AR; (3); Church Yth Grp; FBLA; Sec Mu Alpha Theta; VP Natl Beta Clb; Office Aide; Spanish Clb; School Play; Hon Roll.

PRIESTER, RUTH N; Bentonville Sr HS; Bentonville, AR; (4); Church Yth Grp; FBLA; Acpl Chr; Church Choir; Nwsp; Lit Mag; Hon Roll; NHS; Model UN; Egl Crss Awd; U Of AR; Intl Rltns.

PRIM, YAVONDA A; Fairview HS; Camden, AR; (2); Church Yth Grp; Drama Clb; Pres FBLA; GAA; Band; Chorus; Capt Flag Corp; Sftbl; Hon Roll; Pageant Overall Talent; Miss AAGC Talent 95; Pres Of Comm Girls Club; UAPB; Bus Admin.

PRIMM, JANA E; Bryant Sr HS; Benton, AR; (2); Church Yth Grp; FCA; GAA; Varsity Clb; Church Choir; Orch; Bsktbl; Crs Cntry; Trk; High Hon Roll; Priv Piano Lssns; Fstvl Piano Awds Super Plus; Priv Violin Lssns.

PRINCE, CARSON L; Central Sr HS; Little Rock, AR; (3); 7/540; Am Leg Aux Girls St; French Clb; Mu Alpha Theta; Natl Beta Clb; Rep Frsh Cls; Rep Soph Cls; Rep Jr Cls; Rep Sr Cls; Rep Stu Cncl; High Hon Roll; Natl Lib Of Poetry Cont Semi Finalst; AR Girls St Del; AR Governors Schl Stu Del; Broadcast Jrnlsm.

PRINCE, JASON D; Marion HS; West Memphis, AR; (2); FCA; Spanish Clb; Hon Roll; NHS; Psych.

PRINCE, JENNIFER M; North Little Rock Hs-West; North Little Rock, AR; (3); Q&S; Lit Mag; VP Frsh Cls; VP Stu Cncl; Stat Bsktbl; Var Mgr(s); L Trk; Stat Vllybl; Cit Awd; Hon Roll; UCA; Phys Thrpy.

PRINCE, JILL H; Magnet Cove HS; Malvern, AR; (3); 7/36; Am Leg Aux Girls St; Church Yth Grp; FCA; Math Clb; Natl Beta Clb; Science Clb; Teachers Aide; Church Choir; Yrbk; Pres Frsh Cls; Schl Choir; Optmtry.

PRINCE, KALEB; Witts Springs HS; Witts Springs, AR; (4); 2/9; 4-H; FBLA; German Clb; VP Natl Beta Clb; Capt Quiz Bowl; Science Clb; Nwsp; Yrbk; Lit Mag; Hon Roll; SMAC Club; NACTC; Bio Tech.

PRINCE, KRISTA; Brookland Jr Sr HS; Brookland, AR; (3); Art Clb; Natl Beta Clb; Natl FFA Org; Teachers Aide; Hon Roll; AR ST U.

PRINCE, ROBIN; Prairie Grove HS; Farmington, AR; (2); Math Clb; Science Clb; SADD; Pres Soph Cls; Ofcr Stu Cncl; JV Bsktbl; JV Var Chrldng; High Hon Roll; Hon Roll; Jr NHS; Taekwondo Blck Blt; Bst All Arnd; Aerospc Engnr.

PRINCE, ROY A; Monticello HS; Monticello, AR; (3); French Clb; FBLA; Natl Beta Clb; Hon Roll; Received Schlsp To UALR ABA 96; U Of AR Little Rock; Bus Admin.

PRINNER, ANGELA A; Viola HS; Viola, AR; (3); 15/36; Sec Art Clb; FBLA; FHA; Spanish Clb; Hon Roll; Prfct Atten Awd; AYAA 4th/1st Pl 95-96; Acad Imp Awd/Bst Of Shw Art; 3 Yr Art Cert; Fine Art Cls Awd; Comm Artist.

PRITCHETT, MARY E; Russellville Sr HS; Russellville, AR; (2); 1/430; Church Yth Grp; FCA; Band; Church Choir; Var Gym; High Hon Roll; Jr NHS; NHS; All Stars; Chrstn Stdnt Union.

PRIVETT, APRIL C; Black Rock Jr Sr HS; Portia, AR; (2); Church Yth Grp; 4-H; FHA; Girl Scts; Science Clb; Spanish Clb; Bsktbl; Sftbl; Hon Roll.

PRIVETT, JONATHAN S; Parkview Arts Magnet Schl; Little Rock, AR; (3); Art Clb; JA; Key Clb; Natl Beta Clb; Quiz Bowl; Scholastic Bowl; Spanish Clb; Phtg Nwsp; Phtg Yrbk; Cit Awd; Acad Achvmt Awd Amer His & Art Dsgn; Supt Cabinet Maker.

PROCTOR, JASON; Bearden HS; Sparkman, AR; (2); 4-H; FBLA; FHA; Ftbl; Trk; High Hon Roll; Hon Roll.

PROPHET, ASHLEY T; Pea Ridge HS; Pea Ridge, AR; (3); Church Yth Grp; GAA; Spanish Clb; Band; Yrbk; Ofcr Jr Cls; Ofcr Stu Cncl; Bsktbl; Crs Cntry; Mgr(s); Wendys Heisman Natl Awd Nom; AR Tech; Nrsng.

PROPPS, ANDREW P; Arkansas Sr HS; Texarkana, AR; (4); 1/370; Am Leg Boys St; Library Aide; VP Mu Alpha Theta; Quiz Bowl; Rep Stu Cncl; Sec NHS; Ntl Merit Schol; Val; French Clb; Math Clb; Yng Dem Pres; Gftd Tlntd; Natl Jr Hon Soc; U Of Cntrl AR.

PROPPS, BETH; Nashville HS; Nashville, AR; (3); FBLA; FHA; Bsktbl; Score Keeper; Hon Roll; NHS; Henderson ST Univ.

PRUETT, FLORA; Cabot HS; Ward, AR; (2); Church Yth Grp; French Clb; Nrsng.

PRUITT, AMBER D; Newport HS; Tupelo, AR; (2); FBLA; Spanish Clb; Hon Roll; All Amer Schlr; AR St Univ; PT.

PRUITT, JEANIE E; Morrilton Sr HS; Morrilton, AR; (3); Art Clb; French Clb; FBLA; Science Clb; Vllybl.

PRUITT, LAUREN; Beebe Jr HS; Beebe, AR; (1); Church Yth Grp; FBLA; FHA; Office Aide; Chorus; VP Frsh Cls; VP Stu Cncl; Chrldng; Horsebck Ridng.

PRUITT, MILLIE A; Parkview Arts-Science HS; Little Rock, AR; (3); 13/270; Am Leg Aux Girls St; Church Yth Grp; Cmnty Wkr; Natl Beta Clb; Rep Sr Cls; Trk; Hon Roll; Jr NHS; NHS; Upward Bound Proj Pres; Dentstry.

PRUSS, AMANDA R; Mt St Mary Acad; North Little Rock, AR; (3); Church Yth Grp; French Clb; Mu Alpha Theta; Office Aide; French Hon Soc; Hon Roll; Prfct Atten Awd.

PRUSS, MARGARET E; Mt St Mary Acad; North Little Rock, AR; (2); Church Yth Grp; JCL; Latin Clb; Natl Beta Clb; Bsktbl; Vllybl; High Hon Roll; Hon Roll; JOVB.

PRY, MICHAEL P; Glenwood Jr Sr HS; Glenwood, AR; (3); 13/32; Church Yth Grp; Cmnty Wkr; FBLA; Natl FFA Org; Chorus; Bsktbl; Crs Cntry; Ftbl; Trk; High Hon Roll; Ouachita Bapt Univ; Psych; Atty.

PRYOR, CRYSTAL J; Southside HS; Fort Smith, AR; (3); Church Yth Grp; Mu Alpha Theta; Pep Clb; Spanish Clb; Teachers Aide; Chorus; Hon Roll; NHS; Clogging; OK ST Univ; Vet Med.

PUCKETT, ALAN L; Lake Hamilton Sr HS; Hot Springs, AR; (2); 13/320; Church Yth Grp; FCA; Natl Beta Clb; Natl FFA Org; Spanish Clb; Sec Soph Cls; Var Bsktbl; High Hon Roll; Hon Roll; NHS; U Of AR; Sprts.

PULLEY, AUTUMN G; Southside HS; Batesville, AR; (3); Church Yth Grp; FCA; Key Clb; Office Aide; Bsktbl; Hon Roll; Prfct Atten Awd; Yth Ldrshp Conf 95-; Vanderbilt Univ.

PULLEY, BRIGETTE; Malvern Jr HS; Malvern, AR; (2); Church Yth Grp; English Clb; FCA; FBLA; GAA; Natl Beta Clb; Science Clb; Spanish Clb; SADD; Acpl Chr; Henderson ST U; Spch Pthlgy.

PULLEY, KIMBERLY; Huntsville HS; Huntsville, AR; (2); 8/154; FCA; FTA; Band; Church Choir; Mrchg Band; Pep Band; Ofcr Soph Cls; Mgr Sftbl; High Hon Roll; UAR; Elem Ed.

PULLINS, GENA D; Cushman Schl; Cushman, AR; (2); Church Yth Grp; FBLA; FHA; Office Aide; Science Clb; Cit Awd; Hon Roll; Prfct Atten Awd; Smash Prgm Hosp; Harding Univ; Mdcl/Bus Field.

PURDOM, CHERI L; Corning HS; Corning, AR; (1); Church Yth Grp; FCA; FBLA; FHA; Bsktbl; Trk; High Hon Roll; Three Rivers; Bus/Cmptrs.

PURIFOY, AMY; Greenwood Sr HS; Greenwood, AR; (1); FCA; GAA; Band; Chrldng; Trk; High Hon Roll; Jr NHS; Gymnstcs-Tumbling; Art Lessons; Chrch Yth; Art.

PURIFOY, CHRISTEL; Harmony Grove Jr Sr HS; Camden, AR; (4); 4/51; FCA; Pres 4-H; French Clb; FBLA; Natl Beta Clb; Band; Capt Color Guard; Var L Trk; NHS; Office Aide; John Philip Sousa Awd; Med.

PURIFOY, JARROD N; Bryant Sr HS; Bryant, AR; (2); Amer Legion Bsbl; U Of AR; Arch.

PURIFOY, KAREN; Genoa Central HS; Texarkana, AR; (4); Church Yth Grp; FBLA; VP Spanish Clb; School Play; Ed Yrbk; VP Frsh Cls; Bsktbl; Trk; Hon Roll; VP NHS; Southern AR U; Nrs.

PURIFOY, NATHAN J; Fayetteville Sr HS; Fayetteville, AR; (2); Church Yth Grp; FCA; Acpl Chr; Church Choir; Variety Show; Var Crs Cntry; JV Tennis.

PUTMAN, DEVIN D; Hope HS; Hope, AR; (3); Am Leg Aux Girls St; Church Yth Grp; French Clb; Pres FBLA; Natl Beta Clb; Band; Color Guard; Co-Capt Drm Mjr(t); Rep Jr Cls; Treas Stu Cncl; All Amer Majorette 94; U Of Cntrl AR; Speech Path.

PYLE, CRYSTAL L; Rogers HS; Rogers, AR; (3); Church Yth Grp; FHA; FTA; Hon Roll; Prfct Atten Awd; Renaissance Awd; Stu Of Month 96; NWACC; Kndgtn Tchr.

PYLE, JANICE; Victory Christian Schl; Bearden, AR; (3); Church Yth Grp; Spanish Clb; Speech Tm; Flag Corp; Var Bsktbl; Var Chrldng; Var Sftbl; Var Vllybl; High Hon Roll; Stu Mnstry.

QUACH, KASEY; Gosnell Jr HS; Blytheville, AR; (1); Church Yth Grp; Powder Puff Ftbl; Hon Roll; CA U.

QUALL, ASHLEY; Evening Shade Schl; Cave City, AR; (3); 3/36; Cmnty Wkr; VP Drama Clb; Rptr FBLA; Rptr FHA; German Clb; GAA; VP Natl Beta Clb; Rptr Science Clb; Teachers Aide; School Play; TAD Pres; Lyon; Jrnlsm.

QUALLS, AMANDA; Pottsville Schl; Pottsville, AR; (1); Church Yth Grp; 4-H; Natl Beta Clb; Band; Pep Band; Capt Chrldng; 4-H Awd; High Hon Roll; Pres Acad Fit Awd; 1st Pl Cty 4-H Horse Show; Amers Cover Miss Pgnt Runner-Up; Comp.

QUALLS, BOBBY H; Ozark HS; Ozark, AR; (3); Church Yth Grp; Drama Clb; Spanish Clb; Chorus; Bsktbl; Ftbl; Hon Roll.

QUALLS, LATRECE; Hazen Jr Sr HS; Hazen, AR; (4); 8/26; French Clb; FBLA; FHA; FTA; Natl Beta Clb; Church Choir; Phtg Yrbk; Cit Awd; Hon Roll; NHS; Philander Smith Coll; Bus.

QUALLS, SHELLA L; Monticello HS; Monticello, AR; (3); 37/112; Art Clb; Church Yth Grp; Debate Tm; Drama Clb; FBLA; FHA; Natl Beta Clb; Spanish Clb; Church Choir; Hon Roll; Monticello Billies Alt Mascot; Ouchita Bapt Univ.

QUALLS, TEDDY J; Mt Ida Jr Sr HS; Story, AR; (1); Church Yth Grp; Natl FFA Org; Band; Jazz Band; Mrchg Band; Pep Band; Ftbl; Hon Roll; Mst Otstdng 9th Grd; Bst Jr Hgh Counter; Amer Musical Fndtn Band Hnrs; Ouchita Bapt Univ; Seminary.

QUAST, SHYANN N; Lake Hamilton Sr HS; Hot Springs Natio, AR; (3); Church Yth Grp; FHA; GAA; Natl Beta Clb; Spanish Clb; Speech Tm; Teachers Aide; Bsktbl; Sftbl; Trk; Wolf Pride Drug Free Org.

QUERY, DESMA J; Flippin Jr Sr HS; Flippin, AR; (2); Church Yth Grp; FBLA; German Clb; SADD; Sftbl; AR ST Univ; Amer His Tchr.

QUICK, CHARLES M; Catholic HS; Little Rock, AR; (3); 17/190; Boy Scts; Church Yth Grp; ROTC; Intrml Bsktbl; Var Chrldng; Hon Roll; Yth Connctn; Svc Clb; Hendrix Col; Premed.

QUILLIN, AMANDA R; Spring Hill HS; Hope, AR; (3); French Clb; FBLA; FHA; Quiz Bowl; Speech Tm; SADD; Varsity Clb; Drill Tm; Yrbk; Ofcr Frsh Cls; U Of Cntrl AR; RN.

QUILLIN, KAREN-MARIE; Hope HS; Hope, AR; (3); 1/240; Sec Am Leg Aux Girls St; Treas French Clb; Ed Nwsp; Pres Soph Cls; Pres Sr Cls; VP Stu Cncl; Chrldng; NHS; Tennis; DAR Awd; Ftbl Trainer; NIKE; Hendrix; Med.

QUINN, AMANDA M; Conway Sr HS; Conway, AR; (3); Church Yth Grp; Cmnty Wkr; 4-H; French Clb; JA; Band; Yrbk; Ofcr Stu Cncl; French Hon Soc; High Hon Roll; All Stars Stff; Mrktng.

QUINN, JANA K; De Soto Schl; Elaine, AR; (1); Church Yth Grp; Yrbk; JV Chrldng; Hon Roll; Jr High Homcmng Qn; R Dragster Diver; 9th Grd Homcmng Maid; U MS; Marine Bio.

QUINTANA, JOSEPH F; Rose Bud Jr Sr HS; Mount Vernon, AR; (2); VP Drama Clb; Sec FBLA; HOBY; Library Aide; Model UN; Capt Quiz Bowl; Spanish Clb; Band; Art Clb; Natl FFA Org; Yth To Yth.

QUINTON, CARL; Prairie Grove HS; Prairie Grove, AR; (4); Cmnty Wkr; Letterman Clb; Math Clb; Natl FFA Org; Office Aide; Science Clb; Spanish Clb; SADD; Teachers Aide; Varsity Clb; Univ Of ARL; PT.

QUINTON, JERRA; Rivercrest HS; Luxora, AR; (4); 1/105; Church Yth Grp; Sec Pres French Clb; Ed Nwsp; VP Sr Cls; Var Chrldng; DAR Awd; Gov Hon Prg Awd; Pres Acad Fit Awd; Pres Schlr; Val; Lyon Coll; Jrnlsm.

QUINTON, REID; Rivercrest HS; Luxora, AR; (4); 19/110; Church Yth Grp; Acpl Chr; VP Soph Cls; VP Jr Cls; VP Sr Cls; Rep Stu Cncl; Var Capt Bsbl; High Hon Roll; Jr NHS; NHS; Henderson ST Univ; Sprts Med.

RABIDEAU, BROOKS; Southside HS; Fort Smith, AR; (3); 9/400; Boy Scts; Mu Alpha Theta; NHS; Tae Kwan Do Blk Belt; Pre Med.

RABY, JAMIE; Watson Chapel Sr HS; Pine Bluff, AR; (3); 1/285; Am Leg Aux Girls St; Church Yth Grp; FBLA; HOBY; Library Aide; Natl Beta Clb; Pep Clb; Science Clb; Spanish Clb; Yrbk.

RACY, MARSHAYDRICK; Dumas Jr HS; Dumas, AR; (1); Pres FBLA; Science Clb; JV Ftbl; Arch Engnr.

RADCLIFF, JULIE; Maynard Jr Sr HS; Pocahontas, AR; (3); 1/40; Am Leg Aux Girls St; Chess Clb; Church Yth Grp; VP French Clb; Sec FBLA; HOBY; Sec Natl Beta Clb; Red Cross Aide; Sec Frsh Cls; Sec Soph Cls; Gftd & Tlntd Pgm 9 Yrs; Pre-Med.

RADFORD, KENDRA D; Magazine Jr Sr HS; Magazine, AR; (3); FBLA; Treas FHA; Natl FFA Org; SADD; Drill Tm; Chrldng; Hon Roll; Prfct Atten Awd; Stephen F Austin; Indstrl Tech.

RADFORD, TOMMY W; Bryant Sr HS; Alexander, AR; (2); Church Yth Grp; Treas FBLA; Band; Mrchg Band; Pep Band; Hon Roll; Bus.

RAFFERTY, SUSAN K; Bauxite Jr Sr HS; Benton, AR; (3); 1/66; Quiz Bowl; Spanish Clb; Drill Tm; Yrbk; Rep Jr Cls; Rep Sr Cls; L Bsktbl; Var Trk; High Hon Roll; NHS; UALR.

RAGAN, CRYSTAL D; Marshall HS; Marshall, AR; (1); Spanish Clb; Hon Roll; Poem Entld Time Pblshd Mists Of Enchantment; Acad Schlsp NACTC; NACTV; Tchng/Law.

RAGAR, HEATHER N; Cabot HS; Cabot, AR; (3); FCA; Key Clb; Spanish Clb; Yrbk; Var Socr; High Hon Roll; Jr NHS; NHS; Spanish NHS; His Clb; U Of AR Fayettville; Psych.

RAGLAND, BRIAN C; Leslie Schl; Leslie, AR; (2); Chess Clb; Church Yth Grp; Natl Beta Clb; Bsktbl; High Hon Roll; Hon Roll; N AR Comm Tech Coll; Garge Att.

RAGLAND, DIONE; Leslie Schl; Leslie, AR; (4); 1/32; Sec FBLA; Key Clb; Sec Natl Beta Clb; Quiz Bowl; Band; Yrbk; Rptr Sr Cls; Var Bsktbl; High Hon Roll; Val; AR Tech U.

RAGLAND, DIXIE; Leslie Schl; Leslie, AR; (3); FBLA; FHA; Key Clb; Teachers Aide; VP Soph Cls; High Hon Roll; Hon Roll.

RAGLAND, MATTHEW; Marshall HS; Leslie, AR; (3); 3/50; Pres Art Clb; Church Yth Grp; Pres 4-H; Treas FBLA; HOBY; Treas Natl Beta Clb; Capt Quiz Bowl; Spanish Clb; Phtg Yrbk; High Hon Roll; U AR; Law.

RAGLAND, ROY D; Leslie Schl; Leslie, AR; (4); 2/32; FBLA; Key Clb; Treas VP Natl Beta Clb; Quiz Bowl; Band; Mrchg Band; Stage Crew; Yrbk; Var Bsktbl; High Hon Roll; AR Tech U.

RAGLAND, WILSON A; Hope HS; Hope, AR; (3); French Clb; FBLA; Natl Beta Clb; School Play; Hon Roll; U Of AR; Elec Engr.

RAGSDALE, CHALON A; Fayetteville Sr HS; Fayetteville, AR; (4); SADD; Thesps; Band; Jazz Band; Mrchg Band; School Musical; School Play; High Hon Roll; NHS; Ntl Merit Schol; Percussion Wnnr MTNA; Natl Hnrs Schol To U Of OK; St Fnlst In Arts Alive; U Of OK; Drama.

RAGSDALE, MISTY; Coleman Jr HS; Van Buren, AR; (1); Church Yth Grp; FBLA; FHA; Girl Scts; Library Aide; Natl Beta Clb; Science Clb; Drill Tm; High Hon Roll; Jr NHS.

RAGSDALE, SUZANNE; Ozark Adventist Acad; Benton, AR; (4); 7/54; Hosp Aide; Key Clb; Drm Mjr(t); Mrchg Band; VP Stu Cncl; Stat Socr; High Hon Roll; Jr NHS; Kiwanis Awd; Pres Acad Fit Awd; U Of AR-LITTLE Rock; Med.

RAIBLE, SHERRY; Van Buren Sr HS; Alma, AR; (4); 68/270; Mu Alpha Theta; Q&S; Band; Co-Capt Flag Corp; Mrchg Band; Nwsp; Jr NHS; NHS; Pres Acad Fit Awd; U Of AR Fayettville; Ark.

RAINBOLT, RANDAL; Leslie Schl; Marshall, AR; (4); 6/30; Drama Clb; FBLA; HOBY; Natl Beta Clb; Office Aide; Teachers Aide; Band; School Play; Stage Crew; Rep Frsh Cls; U Cntrl AR; Rdlgy.

RAINES, SARAH; White Hall Sr HS; Pine Bluff, AR; (4); 5/160; Am Leg Aux Girls St; Church Yth Grp; FBLA; Mu Alpha Theta; Natl Beta Clb; Spanish Clb; Chorus; Church Choir; Hon Roll; Pres Acad Fit Awd; Henderson St Univ; Acctng.

RAINEY, JENNIFER; Morrilton Sr HS; Morrilton, AR; (2); 1/209; Art Clb; Church Yth Grp; Dance Clb; Drama Clb; FBLA; Math Clb; Natl Beta Clb; Drill Tm; Nwsp; Trk.

RAINEY, JIA M; Mc Gehee HS; Mc Gehee, AR; (3); FBLA; Pep Clb; Chorus; School Play; Hon Roll; ITT; Comp Technician.

RAINS, BRANDON R; Atkins Schl; Atkins, AR; (1); FBLA; Band; Var JV Bsbl; Var Bsktbl; DAR Awd; Hon Roll; Pres Acad Fit Awd; Comp Engr.

RAINS, JOHN D; Forrest City HS; Forrest City, AR; (1); Library Aide; Martial Arts Trng; ASU; Arch; Vet.

RAINWATER, LANNA D; Lynn Schl; Strawberry, AR; (3); Church Yth Grp; Rptr FBLA; Rptr FHA; Rptr Natl Beta Clb; Rptr Science Clb; Ed Yrbk; Rptr Frsh Cls; Sftbl; High Hon Roll; Hon Roll; Black Rvr Techuniv; Phy Thrpy.

RAJDOVA, DANIELA; Mc Gehee HS; Mc Gehee, AR; (4); Art Clb; Drama Clb; English Clb; French Clb; German Clb; Intnl Clb; Latin Clb; Acpl Chr; Church Choir; Aise Exch Stu; Balet Dance; Snowboarding Jr World Chmpnshp Poland 95; Unulecka Acad; Arts.

RALPHO, DANNY; Springdale Sr HS; Springdale, AR; (4); Intnl Clb; School Play; Lit Mag; Ofcr Sr Cls; Bsktbl; Hon Roll; AR Razorback; Engr.

RALSTON, LESLIE A; Dardanelle HS; Dardanelle, AR; (3); 1/110; FBLA; FHA; Intnl Clb; Natl Beta Clb; School Play; Var Bsktbl; Var L Tennis; High Hon Roll; All Amrcn Schol; Natl Schol Merit Awd; Sandlizard Achvr; Premed.

RALSTON, STEPHEN S; Nettleton HS; Jonesboro, AR; (2); Church Yth Grp; Natl FFA Org; Chorus; School Musical; Ofcr Stu Cncl; Bsktbl; AR ST Univ; Animal Sci.

RAMER, DANA; Sylvan Hills HS; Sherwood, AR; (3); Church Yth Grp; Treas FBLA; Pres FHA; HOBY; Key Clb; Spanish Clb; Rep Frsh Cls; Rep Jr Cls; Pom Pon; AR ST U; Acctng.

RAMEY, ASIA; Caddo Hills Jr Sr HS; Glenwood, AR; (3); 9/30; Pres FBLA; VP Sec FHA; Natl Beta Clb; Spanish Clb; Presdntl Clssrm; Law.

RAMEY, JOSELYN K; Smackover HS; Louann, AR; (1); Church Yth Grp; FBLA; Band; Church Choir; Mrchg Band; Pres Frsh Cls; Intrml Bsktbl; Intrml Chrldng; Hon Roll; Span I Ltr Awd; LA Univ Tech.

RAMSAY, COREY; Sparkman Jr Sr HS; Sparkman, AR; (2); 1/28; Church Yth Grp; Letterman Clb; Natl Beta Clb; Natl FFA Org; Spanish Clb; Ftbl; Wt Lftg; High Hon Roll.

RAMSAY, MARVIN C; Sparkman Jr Sr HS; Sparkman, AR; (2); 1/30; Church Yth Grp; Letterman Clb; Natl Beta Clb; Natl FFA Org; Spanish Clb; Var Ftbl; High Hon Roll.

RAMSEY, AMY; Cabot HS; Cabot, AR; (4); 39/300; Church Yth Grp; Acpl Chr; Chorus; Church Choir; Cit Awd; Hon Roll; Jr NHS; Kiwanis Awd; NHS; Spanish NHS; Mdrgl Choir; AR ST U; Pre-Med/Nrsng.

RAMSEY, DALE E; Biggers-Reyno HS; Biggers, AR; (2); FHA; Natl Beta Clb; Natl FFA Org; Spanish Clb; High Hon Roll; Hon Roll; Pres Acad Fit Awd; Sal; Black River Vo-Tech; Brodsctng.

RAMSEY, DENICE; Sulphur Rock Schl; Sulphur Rock, AR; (2); 1/19; Sec FBLA; HOBY; Rptr Key Clb; Natl Beta Clb; Quiz Bowl; Sec SADD; Pres Frsh Cls; Hon Roll; Hist FHA; Sec Treas Chorus; Optmst Teen Of Mnth 95; Med Explr Post; U Of AR-FAYETTEVILLE.

RAMSEY, JOSEPH A; Star City HS; Star City, AR; (1); Quiz Bowl; High Hon Roll; Prfct Atten Awd; Acad Achvmnt.

RAMSEY, KATHRYN L; Russellville Sr HS; Russellville, AR; (2); Church Yth Grp; Hosp Aide; Sec Frsh Cls; Sec Soph Cls; Ofcr Stu Cncl; Chrldng; NHS.

RAMSEY, NICOLAS C; Sylvan Hills HS; North Little Rock, AR; (3); FBLA; Mu Alpha Theta; Natl Beta Clb; JV Var Bsktbl; High Hon Roll; Hon Roll; Jr NHS; NHS; Prfct Atten Awd; Math.

RAMSEY, WILLIAM M; Goza Jr HS; Arkadelphia, AR; (1); Church Yth Grp; FCA; Band; Church Choir; Mrchg Band; Hon Roll; Jr NHS.

RAMSEY, ZACHARY T; Bryant Sr HS; Bryant, AR; (2); Church Yth Grp; Cmnty Wkr; JV Var Ftbl; Hon Roll; UCA; Law Enfrcmnt.

RAND, GINGER L; Ozark Adventist Acad; Fort Smith, AR; (2); Church Yth Grp; Cmnty Wkr; Teachers Aide; Acpl Chr; Church Choir; Ofcr Frsh Cls; Rep Soph Cls; Hon Roll; Prfct Atten Awd; Southern Coll Of SDA; Psych.

RANDALL, MELISSA; Lake Hamilton Sr HS; Hot Springs, AR; (2); Church Yth Grp; Treas FCA; Treas FBLA; VP FHA; Natl Beta Clb; Spanish Clb; VP Soph Cls; Ofcr Stu Cncl; Chrldng; Gym; Multi Yr Listee; Sci Merit Awd; Memphis Schl Of Optom; Optom.

RANDLEMAN, KORY L; Marmaduke HS; Paragould, AR; (2); 5/60; 4-H; Natl Beta Clb; Natl FFA Org; Rep Soph Cls; Ofcr Stu Cncl; Hon Roll; Livestock Awds; AR ST Univ; Ag.

RANDOLPH, JESSICA; Van Buaren HS; Van Buren, AR; (1); Capt Chrldng; Gym; Cit Awd; Hon Roll; Jr NHS; Ntl Merit Ltr; UCLA.

RANEY, DE RON B; Lynn Schl; Smithville, AR; (3); 3/21; FBLA; Math Clb; Natl Beta Clb; Sec Natl FFA Org; Quiz Bowl; Science Clb; Ofcr Bsbl; High Hon Roll; Pres Acad Fit Awd; AR ST Univ.

RANEY, JON; Beebe Jr HS; Beebe, AR; (1); Natl Beta Clb; Natl FFA Org; Teachers Aide; Bsktbl; Ftbl; Trk; Hon Roll.

RANEY III, ROBERT WILLIAM; Pulaski Acad; Little Rock, AR; (3); Am Leg Boys St; Art Clb; Cmnty Wkr; Rep French Clb; Natl Beta Clb; Ed Lit Mag; Pres Jr Cls; Pres Stu Cncl; Ftbl; Cit Awd; Just Say No Teen Ldr; Barrett Hamilton AR Young Artists Cmptn & Exhibition 1st Place; World Traveler.

RANKIN, MELISSA; Mountainburg Jr Sr HS; Mountainburg, AR; (3); 1/60; Church Yth Grp; FCA; FHA; VP Natl Beta Clb; Science Clb; SADD; Rep Stu Cncl; Var Bsktbl; Var Sftbl; High Hon Roll.

RANSFORD, ANDY; Magnolia HS; Magnolia, AR; (2); Boy Scts; Church Yth Grp; French Clb; FBLA; Quiz Bowl; Band; Ftbl; Golf; Trk; High Hon Roll.

RANZ, JAMIE L; Mansfield Jr Sr HS; Mansfield, AR; (1); Bsktbl; FCA; GAA; Intnl Clb; Office Aide; Spanish Clb; SADD; Trk; Cit Awd; Awd High Pntr High Block Shots/Hghst In Stls/Mst Prdctve Ssn In Bsktbl; Archry; U Of The Ozarks; Bus.

RAPPE, EMILY A; Springdale Sr HS; Fayetteville, AR; (3); Church Yth Grp; FCA; FBLA; Hosp Aide; Key Clb; Pep Clb; Teachers Aide; Chorus; Variety Show; Stat Bsktbl; U AR Fayetteville; Tchr.

RAPPOLD, AMY; East End Jr Sr HS; Bigelow, AR; (3); 1/43; Church Yth Grp; Cmnty Wkr; Pres 4-H; Math Tm; Natl Beta Clb; Natl FFA Org; Rptr SADD; VICA; Ofcr Stu Cncl; Hon Roll; Grls St 96; Arch Engrng.

RASBERRY, CATHERINE N; Nettleton HS; Jonesboro, AR; (3); 1/123; Church Yth Grp; Natl Beta Clb; Band; Chorus; Color Guard; Drm Mjr(t); Mrchg Band; School Musical; VP Stu Cncl; Hon Roll; Band Cncl Rptr.

RASH, GINGER K; Vilonia HS; Vilonia, AR; (3); Church Yth Grp; FHA; Spanish Clb; Teachers Aide; Church Choir; Hon Roll; Beauty Coll; Csmtlgst.

RASMUSSEN, LAURA C; Crossett Sr HS; Crossett, AR; (2); Church Yth Grp; Natl Beta Clb; Phtg Rptr Yrbk; Lit Mag; Hon Roll; Pres Acad Fit Awd; Eagle Action Pride Team; Rensnce Prgm; Pub Reltns.

RATCLIFF, TAMEKA R; West Memphis Sr HS; West Memphis, AR; (4); FBLA; FHA; ROTC; SADD; AR ST Univ; Elem Ed.

RATELIFF, KRISTIN; Oak Grove HS; Maumelle, AR; (1); 7/189; Church Yth Grp; FCA; Letterman Clb; Acpl Chr; Chorus; Church Choir; Variety Show; Chrldng; Hon Roll; Jr NHS; U Of AR Fayetteville.

RATH JR, RUSSELL; Concord Public Schls; Concord, AR; (3); 4/34; Art Clb; HOBY; Natl Beta Clb; Quiz Bowl; Science Clb; Ed Lit Mag; Rptr Stu Cncl; Cit Awd; High Hon Roll; Hon Roll; Gftd & Tlntd; Centenary Coll; Archaeolgy.

RATLIFF, CRYSTAL S; Mc Gehee HS; Dermott, AR; (2); Mu Alpha Theta; Natl Beta Clb; Science Clb; Spanish Clb; Rptr Nwsp; Hon Roll; NHS; Law.

RATLIFF, STEPHANIE D; North Little Rock Hs-West; North Little Rock, AR; (3); 89/500; Am Leg Aux Girls St; Church Yth Grp; Drama Clb; Key Clb; Natl Beta Clb; School Musical; Stage Crew; Yrbk; Ofcr Frsh Cls; Ofcr Jr Cls; Peer Ldrshp TARS; Harding; Soc Work.

RAULS, RUSS; Rison HS; Rison, AR; (3); 1/40; Treas Art Clb; VP FCA; VP French Clb; Church Yth Grp; Natl Beta Clb; Quiz Bowl; Science Clb; Pres Frsh Cls; Pres Soph Cls; Pres Jr Cls; Clvlnd Co Hrld Awd Acad Achvt; Chnl 4 Fr Nght Flgts All-Str Ftbl; Med.

RAUSCH, LISA; Rogers HS; Rogers, AR; (1); Church Yth Grp; FCA; Quiz Bowl; Drill Tm; Chrldng; Hon Roll; Prfct Atten Awd.

RAVER, BRENT N; Valley Springs Schl; Harrison, AR; (2); Art Clb; Natl FFA Org; Stat Bsktbl; Mgr(s); Hon Roll; Prfct Atten Awd; Practice Medicine.

RAWDALL, BRENDA; Omaha Schl; Omaha, AR; (3); Church Yth Grp; FBLA; FHA; Math Clb; Science Clb; Varsity Clb; Chorus; Church Choir; Rptr Ed Nwsp; Var Chrldng; Homcmng Qn 96; Annual Qn 94-95; OTADD; Comp Pgmng.

RAWLS, AMANDA N; Crossett Sr HS; Crossett, AR; (2); 10/207; 4-H; Mu Alpha Theta; Natl Beta Clb; Natl FFA Org; Drill Tm; Pres Soph Cls; French Hon Soc; Hon Roll; Pres Acad Fit Awd; Pres Schlr; AR HS Rodeo Assn; HOBY CLEW Wrkshp; U Of Cntrl AR.

RAWSON, DOUGLAS J; Ozark Adventist Acad; Gentry, AR; (2); Church Yth Grp; Teachers Aide; Band; Stage Crew; Intrml Bsktbl; Cit Awd; High Hon Roll; Hon Roll; NHS; Prfct Atten Awd; Southern Coll; X-Ray Techncn.

RAY, AMY; Booneville Jr Sr HS; Booneville, AR; (4); 10/85; Am Leg Aux Girls St; Church Yth Grp; FCA; Pres 4-H; GAA; HOBY; Pres Key Clb; Pres Natl Beta Clb; Office Aide; Science Clb; AR Cls Up Shdw; Brrl Rcng; Lttl Lg Cch; U Of AR; Scndry Educ.

RAY, AUDREY; Booneville Jr Sr HS; Booneville, AR; (3); FBLA; HOBY; VP Key Clb; Natl Beta Clb; Office Aide; Ofcr Stu Cncl; L Bsktbl; L Sftbl; Hon Roll; Pres Acad Fit Awd; Natl Ldrshp Forum Harding U 93; Recd Sprtsmnshp Awd 93-94; Big Sister Role Mdl 95-96; UALR.

RAY, CORA L; John L Mcclellan Magnet HS; Little Rock, AR; (3); French Clb; FBLA; Chorus; Drill Tm; Pom Pon; Hon Roll; Garden Clb.

RAY, ELIZABETH L; Alma HS; Alma, AR; (3); 33/150; Church Yth Grp; Cmnty Wkr; Pres FCA; Treas FBLA; Church Choir; Rptr Stu Cncl; Var Capt Trk; Cit Awd; NHS; Pres Acad Fit Awd; Evangel; Music.

RAY, JAMIE S; Lavaca Jr Sr HS; Lavaca, AR; (3); 13/60; Church Yth Grp; FCA; FHA; Natl Beta Clb; Color Guard; Yrbk; Lit Mag; VP Soph Cls; Pres Jr Cls; Hon Roll; Westark CC.

RAY, JIMMY T; Strawberry Jr Sr HS; Strawberry, AR; (3); Church Yth Grp; Natl FFA Org; Bsktbl; Hon Roll; Prfct Atten Awd; Agri Ldrshp Awd; Elec Engrng.

RAY, JODY; Maynard Jr Sr HS; Maynard, AR; (3); Church Yth Grp; French Clb; FBLA; FHA; Natl FFA Org; School Play; Trk; Hon Roll; All-Amer Schlr.

RAY, NIKKI; Nashville HS; Nashville, AR; (4); 2/130; GAA; Bsktbl; Sftbl; High Hon Roll; Jr NHS; NHS; Pres Acad Fit Awd; U Of AR; Radiologist.

RAY, STEPHANIE A; Bryant Sr HS; Alexander, AR; (2); Chorus; School Musical; Hon Roll; Jr NHS; Chrstn Cncl; Pediatrcn.

RAY, STEPHANIE A; Lavaca Jr Sr HS; Lavaca, AR; (2); Church Yth Grp; FCA; FBLA; Office Aide; Band; Church Choir; Color Guard; Mrchg Band; Sec Frsh Cls; Sec Treas Soph Cls; Westark CC.

RAYL, MICHAEL P; Russellville Sr HS; Russellville, AR; (3); Varsity Clb; Ftbl; Socr; Hon Roll; Rolla; Cmptr Engr.

RAYMICK, JANA H; Pine Bluff HS; Pine Bluff, AR; (2); Church Yth Grp; Treas French Clb; Acpl Chr; Orch; Yrbk; Hon Roll; NHS; AFS Club; Jack Robey Singers/Angels; Stdnt Of Mo; Pine Bluff Yth Sympny Orch; AR All ST Orch; Arch.

RAYMOND, JOSEPH; Ola Jr Sr HS; Ola, AR; (2); Church Yth Grp; Band; L Ftbl; Mgr(s); Wt Lftg; High Hon Roll; Natl Sci Mrt Awd; AR Tech.

RAYMOND, MARK; Southside HS; Fort Smith, AR; (3); Chess Clb; Church Yth Grp; German Clb; Science Clb; Orch; Stage Crew; Hon Roll; 1st Pl Chem; NASA Awd; US Dept Energy Awd ST Sci Fair; All-ST Orch; U Of AR; Cmptr Engr.

RAZIAN, MARIAM; Bald Knob HS; Bald Knob, AR; (4); FHA; Natl Beta Clb; Quiz Bowl; Teachers Aide; Nwsp; Ofcr Soph Cls; Chrldng; Gym; High Hon Roll; Hnr Pgm Coll; Hnrs Clb Treas; AR ST U; Bus.

READ, ERIC D; Catholic HS; North Little Rock, AR; (2); ROTC; Color Guard; Drill Tm; Hon Roll; Yth Cnctn; Med Fld.

READING, JEREMY M; Springdale Sr HS; Springdale, AR; (2); Church Yth Grp; Cmnty Wkr; FCA; Letterman Clb; Teachers Aide; Capt L Ftbl; L Trk; Wt Lftg; High Hon Roll; Hon Roll; Bsktbl; Yth For Christ; NE; Engrng; Bus Mgmt.

REAP, MARGARET J; Crowleys Ridge Acad; Paragould, AR; (3); Church Yth Grp; Drama Clb; FBLA; Pep Clb; Science Clb; Spanish Clb; Acpl Chr; Chorus; School Musical; School Play; High Point Awd Dist Meets; KIDS; PE; Sports Medicine.

REAP, MICHELLE L; Crowleys Ridge Acad; Paragould, AR; (2); Church Yth Grp; Pep Clb; Science Clb; Spanish Clb; Chorus; Socr; Trk; Vllybl; FBLA; Harding Univ; Writer.

REAPER, AMY; Pangburn Jr Sr HS; Searcy, AR; (2); Church Yth Grp; French Clb; FBLA; FHA; Natl Beta Clb; Church Choir; Bsktbl; Sftbl; Hon Roll; NHS; MPACT Drug Free Grp; U Of A Fayetteville.

REASON, MATT J; North Little Rock Hs-West; North Little Rock, AR; (4); 23/600; Boy Scts; Math Tm; Mu Alpha Theta; Quiz Bowl; Ftbl; NHS; Ntl Merit SF.

REAVES, STEVEN R; Mc Gehee HS; Mc Gehee, AR; (4); 44/104; Art Clb; Mu Alpha Theta; Band; Jazz Band; Mrchg Band; Stage Crew; All St Band Qulfr; All Regn Bands; 18 Solo & Ensembl Awds; Brass Instrumntl Awd; John Philip Sousa Awd; U Of AR Monticello; Music; Art.

REAVIS, MATTIE E; Rogers HS; Garfield, AR; (3); Girl Scts; Hon Roll; Rogers Chamber Of Commerce Acad Awd Past2 Yrs; Tri-City Yth Apprenticeship-Rogersgroup Banking & Fin; Northwest AR CC; Assoc Bnkng.

REAVIS, STEPHANIE; Gosnell Jr Sr HS; Blytheville, AR; (1); Art Clb; Library Aide; Band; AR ST U; Jrnlsm.

RED, CARLA E; Sheridan Sr HS; Mabelvale, AR; (4); 15/220; Church Yth Grp; Cmnty Wkr; Teachers Aide; Chorus; Church Choir; Hon Roll; NHS; Prfct Atten Awd; U Of AR; Env Studs.

REDD, CARLA; West Memphis Christian Schl; Memphis, TN; (4); 1/26; Am Leg Aux Girls St; Natl Beta Clb; Ed Yrbk; VP Stu Cncl; Capt Bsktbl; Co-Capt Chrldng; Trk; NHS; Pres Acad Fit Awd; Val; Exch Stu Pgm To Hitachi Japan; Voted Most Likely To Succeed & Miss WMC; Harding Univ; Bio.

REDD, COURTNEY T; Central HS; West Helena, AR; (3); Church Yth Grp; ROTC; Color Guard; Drill Tm; Ofcr Bsbl; Ftbl; Trk; High Hon Roll; Prfct Atten Awd; PRIDE; Grambling ST; Mech Engr.

REDDICK, NAKESHA D; Malvern Sr HS; Malvern, AR; (3); 16/173; Am Leg Aux Girls St; Church Yth Grp; Natl Beta Clb; SADD; Band; Flag Corp; Rep Stu Cncl; Bsktbl; Vllybl; NHS; U Of AR Conway; Nephrologist.

REDDICK, RANDI M; Fayetteville Sr HS; Fayetteville, AR; (3); Church Yth Grp; FCA; Color Guard; Acpl Chr; Band; Chorus; Church Choir; Drm Mjr(t); Hon Roll; NHS; Peer Hlprs; Chrch Yth Ensmbl; Pre Vet Med.

REDDIN, NATHAN; Jessieville HS; Hot Springs, AR; (3); 6/51; Church Yth Grp; FBLA; FHA; Natl Beta Clb; Band; JV Bsktbl; Var Crs Cntry; Var Tennis; Var Trk; Hon Roll; Arch.

REDING, BRIAN D; Southside HS; Fort Smith, AR; (2); Church Yth Grp; Drama Clb; FCA; Band; Chorus; Church Choir; Jazz Band; Pep Band; School Musical; School Play; AR All Region & All St Choir; All Region Band; OK Bapt Univ; Music.

REECE, PRESTON S; Alpena Schl; Harrison, AR; (4); FCA; Letterman Clb; Library Aide; Natl FFA Org; Nwsp; Yrbk; Rep Frsh Cls; Rep Soph Cls; Treas Stu Cncl; Capt L Bsktbl; Chair Of Prom Comm; Litry Clb; Sec Of FFA; N AR Comm Tech Col; Policemn.

REECE, RACHELLE; Gurdon HS; Gurdon, AR; (1); Church Yth Grp; Varsity Clb; Acpl Chr; Church Choir; Chrldng; Gym; Cit Awd; Hon Roll; Prfct Atten Awd.

REECE, SHANNON L; Jonesboro HS; Jonesboro, AR; (3); Spanish Clb; Var Chrldng; Dentistry.

REED, ALISHA M; Sheridan Sr HS; Sheridan, AR; (2); Church Yth Grp; Cmnty Wkr; FCA; 4-H; GAA; Girl Scts; Band; Church Choir; Mrchg Band; Sftbl; U Of AR Fayetteville.

REED, AMY M; Smackover HS; Smackover, AR; (2); Church Yth Grp; Cmnty Wkr; FBLA; FTA; Letterman Clb; Spanish Clb; Varsity Clb; Pres Frsh Cls; Pres Soph Cls; Rep Stu Cncl; MASH Prgm; U Of AR; Neonatal Nrs.

REED, APRIL A; Ridgecrest HS; Paragould, AR; (3); Church Yth Grp; Band; Mrchg Band; Cit Awd; French Hon Soc; Hon Roll; Prfct Atten Awd; Pres Acad Fit Awd; Multi Yr Lstng; Williams Bptst Coll; Law.

REED, BARRETT B; Russellville Sr HS; Russellville, AR; (2); 4/340; Am Leg Boys St; Church Yth Grp; Teachers Aide; Treas Stu Cncl; JV Bsbl; JV Bsktbl; Var Trk; High Hon Roll; Jr NHS; NHS; MS ST; Elect/Mech Engr.

REED, BRADLEY; Cabot HS; Cabot, AR; (3); French Clb; Library Aide; French Hon Soc; Priest.

REED, CARLA; Rison HS; Rison, AR; (4); 7/53; Church Yth Grp; Treas FCA; French Clb; Pres FBLA; Natl Beta Clb; VP Natl FFA Org; Quiz Bowl; Ed Yrbk; Treas Jr Cls; Sftbl; AEGIS; Occup Thrp.

REED, CARRIE B; Fountain Lake Jr Sr HS; Lonsdale, AR; (3); 5/82; Am Leg Aux Girls St; Art Clb; Church Yth Grp; FCA; Sec Treas Key Clb; Natl Beta Clb; Treas Spanish Clb; Orch; Bsktbl; Hon Roll; Wendys Hiesman Nom; Knights Of Columbus Essay Cont Wnnr; Schlr Ath Awd; U Of Cntrl AR.

REED, CHARLA; Alma HS; Alma, AR; (3); Church Yth Grp; Debate Tm; Pres Sec FBLA; HOBY; Band; Flag Corp; Rep Stu Cncl; NHS; Drama Clb; Mu Alpha Theta; Partners In Christ Pres; Alma Swm Tm; All Rgn Band; Westark CC; Elem Ed.

REED, DAVID; Central Ark Christian Schl; Sherwood, AR; (1); 5/130; FCA; Ofcr Bsbl; Ftbl; Golf; Wt Lftg; High Hon Roll; Jr NHS; Ntl Merit Ltr; U Of Cntrl AR.

REED, ERIC L; Dierks HS; Dierks, AR; (2); Art Clb; French Clb; FBLA; Natl FFA Org; Science Clb; Stat Bsktbl; Stat Ftbl; Mgr(s); U Of AR; Med; Aviation.

REED, ERIN R; Clinton HS; Clinton, AR; (1); Church Yth Grp; FBLA; Natl Beta Clb; High Hon Roll; Hon Roll; Future Farmrs Amer Clb; Harding Univ.

REED, HEATHER A; Dequeen HS; De Queen, AR; (2); Art Clb; Church Yth Grp; FTA; SADD; Band; Chorus; Church Choir; Flag Corp; Mrchg Band; High Hon Roll; All Regn Choir For SW AR 2 Yrs; Rotary Awd In Bio Soph Yr; U Of AR Fayetteville; Vet.

REED, JAMIE L; Ft Smith Christian Schl; Fort Smith, AR; (3); FCA; Spanish Clb; Bsktbl; Co-Capt Chrldng; Trk; Hon Roll; NHS.

REED, KATHERINE L; Russellville Sr HS; Russellville, AR; (3); Office Aide; Quiz Bowl; VICA; Acpl Chr; Chorus; School Musical; Cit Awd; High Hon Roll; Hon Roll; NHS; AR VICA St Sec; Soph Choir Pres; Frosh Choir Sec; Local VICA Sec Drafting Cls; U Of AR Fayettville; Mech Engr.

REED, KELAN; Dollarway HS; Pine Bluff, AR; (2); Art Clb; VICA; Chorus; Cit Awd; Ntl Merit Ltr; Hunting/Reading; Berkeley U; Sprtscstr.

REED, LORI; Bryant Sr HS; Bryant, AR; (2); FBLA; JV Var Chrldng; Hon Roll; NHS; Spec Olympcs; Wntr Frml Ct Royalty; SIPA Conv; Radiology.

REED, MANDY A; Mena HS; Mena, AR; (3); Church Yth Grp; French Clb; FHA; GAA; Science Clb; Mrchg Band; Sec Frsh Cls; Rep Soph Cls; Bsktbl; Chrldng; Homecoming Crt; AK Tech Univ; Xray Lab Tech.

REED, MATTHEW; Southside HS; Fort Smith, AR; (2); Church Yth Grp; German Clb; Key Clb; Mu Alpha Theta; Quiz Bowl; Speech Tm; Teachers Aide; Band; Drm Mjr(t); Mrchg Band; Lyon Coll; Med.

REED, MISTY L; Valley View HS; Jonesboro, AR; (3); Church Yth Grp; Key Clb; Library Aide; Teachers Aide; Band; Chorus; Church Choir; Jazz Band; Pep Band; Hon Roll; Top Lib Awd 95-96; AR ST; Comp Pgmng.

REED, NATHAN; Lee Acad; Marianna, AR; (2); Yrbk; Ofcr Stu Cncl; L Bsktbl; L Capt Ftbl; L Trk; Wt Lftg; Hon Roll; Prfct Atten Awd; Ftbl Outstndg Defnse Plyr; Homcmng Escrt; Yrbk Stff; Centrifuge; AR Hse Reps Page; Built Churchs In MX; U Of AR; Mech Engrng.

REED, NICK; Mc Gehee HS; Mc Gehee, AR; (3); Church Yth Grp; FCA; Letterman Clb; Mu Alpha Theta; Natl Beta Clb; Science Clb; Spanish Clb; Var L Bsbl; Var L Ftbl; Cit Awd; 9 Yr Wnnr Natl Piano Guild; Hnrb Mntn All Dist Ftbl; U Of AR Fayetteville.

REED, ROBIN; Foreman Jr Sr HS; Foreman, AR; (2); Church Yth Grp; FHA; FTA; GAA; HOBY; Natl FFA Org; Quiz Bowl; SADD; Rep Frsh Cls; Bsktbl; 10 Yrs Piano; U AR; Genetic Cnslng.

REED, TAMAKA; Gould HS; Gould, AR; (3); 5/25; French Clb; FBLA; FHA; Math Clb; Science Clb; Spanish Clb; Phtg Yrbk; Treas Jr Cls; Hon Roll; Untd Math Awd; Natl Ldrshp/Svc; Grambling; Med.

REED, TAMERA N; Newport HS; Newport, AR; (2); Church Yth Grp; FBLA; FHA; FTA; Letterman Clb; Office Aide; Spanish Clb; Chorus; Church Choir; Bsktbl; Comp; Acctnt.

REED, TARA; Prairie Grove HS; Prairie Grove, AR; (3); Natl FFA Org; Var Bsktbl; Var Sftbl; High Hon Roll; Jr NHS; NHS; FBLA; Science Clb; SADD; Edctnl Tlnt Srch U AR; Spnsr Colors Day; Bsktbl Homcmng Maid; Jr Bnk Brd Farmers/Merchnt Bnk.

REED, TRACY L; Mansfield Jr Sr HS; Mansfield, AR; (3); FBLA; Natl Beta Clb; Band; Chorus; Mrchg Band; Pep Band; Cit Awd; Hon Roll; FHA; Intnl Clb; St Solo Ensemble Cont 1st Plc; St All Str Bnd; Westarck CC; Radlgy.

REEDER, BRANDY; Nashville HS; Nashville, AR; (1); Church Yth Grp; Cmnty Wkr; English Clb; 4-H; FBLA; FHA; GAA; Math Clb; Natl FFA Org; Science Clb; Explrs Hsptl Grp; ASA Sftbl Assn; U Of Conway AR; Ped Phys Thrpy.

REEDER, RACHAEL A; Mountain Home HS; Mountain Home, AR; (3); Sec Art Clb; Church Yth Grp; Spanish Clb; Band; Flag Corp; Pep Band; Socr; Sftbl; Pre-Med; Law.

REEDY, LATRONYA D; El Dorado Sr HS; El Dorado, AR; (3); Church Yth Grp; Natl Beta Clb; Band; Church Choir; Mrchg Band; Trk; NHS; Debutante; Pre-Med.

REES, AMBUR M; Southside HS; Batesville, AR; (2); Church Yth Grp; Office Aide; Science Clb; Teachers Aide; Band; Pep Band; Bsktbl; Sftbl; Hon Roll; Prfct Atten Awd; Beta Club; Five Mrshl; Top 10 Prcnt Awd; Bio.

REESE, KAYLEE; Ozark Adventist Acad; Claremore, OK; (2); 1/40; Church Yth Grp; Library Aide; Variety Show; Rptr Yrbk; VP Frsh Cls; Pres Soph Cls; Sec Stu Cncl; Vllybl; Cit Awd; High Hon Roll; Southern Coll.

REESE, WENDY; Nashville HS; Nashville, AR; (4); 23/107; Church Yth Grp; GAA; Hosp Aide; Chorus; Church Choir; School Play; Var Sftbl; Trk; Hon Roll; NHS; Comm Svc; UCA; Eng.

REEVES, AMANDA T; Mountainburg Jr Sr HS; Mountainburg, AR; (3); FHA; Natl Beta Clb; Science Clb; Spanish Clb; SADD; Band; High Hon Roll; Prfct Atten Awd; AR OM; Dist Hist Day; U Of AR; Psych.

REEVES, AMBER; Ridgecrest Jr HS; Paragould, AR; (1); Office Aide; Chrldng; Gym; Hon Roll; U Of AR; Med.

REEVES, BRANDON L; Arkansas Sr HS; Texarkana, AR; (3); Key Clb; Office Aide; Spanish Clb; Ofcr Bsbl; Ftbl; Sftbl; Trk; Wt Lftg; Hon Roll.

REEVES, CHASITY R; Nevada Schl; Rosston, AR; (1); 8/60; Church Yth Grp; FBLA; Natl Beta Clb; Quiz Bowl; Band; Var Chrldng; Hon Roll; My American Hero Essy Cntst 2nd Pl; Cert Acad Achvmnt Kybdng To Cmptrs; Bus/Sls Mgmnt.

REEVES, DANIEL; Arkansas Sr HS; Texarkana, AR; (3); Natl FFA Org; Spanish Clb; Prfct Atten Awd; Hunting, Fishing, Camping; UALR; Bio.

REEVES, JAMES N; Springdale Sr HS; Springdale, AR; (2); Am Leg Boys St; Cmnty Wkr; FCA; JV Bsbl; JV Var Ftbl; JV Var Trk; Wt Lftg; Sprts Med.

REEVES, KELLY; Hackett Schl; Hackett, AR; (2); Church Yth Grp; Drama Clb; FBLA; FHA; Spanish Clb; Speech Tm; Band; Color Guard; Mrchg Band; Pep Band; Piano; All Star Band; Marine Bio.

REEVES, MINDY; Watson Chapel Schl; Pine Bluff, AR; (1); Church Yth Grp; FCA; Natl Beta Clb; Church Choir; Sec Stu Cncl; Chrldng; Powder Puff Ftbl; Trk; Hon Roll; Ntl Merit Ltr; GATE; Gymnstcs; Chrch Drama Team; U Of AR.

REEVES, REX J; Heber Springs HS; Tumbling Shoals, AR; (3); 9/88; Am Leg Boys St; Church Yth Grp; Drama Clb; FBLA; Natl Beta Clb; Natl FFA Org; Office Aide; Science Clb; School Play; Stage Crew; Harding Univ; Psych.

REGAN, SUSAN L; Mt St Mary Acad; Sherwood, AR; (2); 1/165; Church Yth Grp; Cmnty Wkr; JCL; Latin Clb; Mu Alpha Theta; Natl Beta Clb; Q&S; SADD; Rptr Nwsp; High Hon Roll; MCAULEY Achv Awd; Im Third Awd; Natl Latn Exm Magna Cum Laude; Baylor Univ; Premed.

REICHARD, DIEDRA M; Parkview Arts/Sci Magnet HS; Little Rock, AR; (3); Art Clb; Cit Awd; Hon Roll; Natl Jr Hnr Soc.

REID, ANGIE; Jessieville HS; Jessieville, AR; (3); 1/51; FCA; Natl Beta Clb; Church Choir; Crs Cntry; Trk; DAR Awd; High Hon Roll; Hon Roll; Pres Acad Fit Awd; 2 Mile Relay Rcd St AR; Phys Thrpy.

REID, CLARENCE H; Omaha Schl; Omaha, AR; (4); 2/22; French Clb; Varsity Clb; Var Bsbl; Var Bsktbl; Gov Hon Prg Awd; Hon Roll; Pres Acad Fit Awd; Sal; US Army Reserve Natl Schlr Athl Awd; All St Bsbl; MVP Rgnl Bsbl; U Of Cntrl AR.

REID, NATALIE M; Fairview HS; Camden, AR; (3); Pres Church Yth Grp; Drama Clb; French Clb; FBLA; Mu Alpha Theta; Natl Beta Clb; Science Clb; SADD; Church Choir; School Musical; Anchr Clb; AR ST Univ.

REID, RON E; Omaha Schl; Omaha, AR; (2); 3/30; Church Yth Grp; Drama Clb; Natl Beta Clb; Quiz Bowl; Thesps; School Play; Sec Frsh Cls; Var Bsbl; Var Bsktbl; Hon Roll; PE Awd.

REID, TARA R; Weiner HS; Weiner, AR; (2); Chess Clb; FBLA; Sec FHA; Natl FFA Org; Treas Frsh Cls; Var Bsktbl; High Hon Roll; NHS.

REINHOLD, TAB; Central Ark Christian Schl; North Little Rock, AR; (1); Intrml Bsktbl; Socr; Hon Roll; Jr NHS.

REISS, REBECCA L; Lake Hamilton Sr HS; Hot Springs, AR; (3); 1/250; Church Yth Grp; FCA; FBLA; Sec Natl Beta Clb; Ofcr Stu Cncl; Bsktbl; High Hon Roll; NHS; Pres Acad Fit Awd; Rptr FHA; Stdnt Chrstn Lf Pres.

REITH, LEAH A; Southside HS; Fort Smith, AR; (4); FBLA; Key Clb; Mu Alpha Theta; Spanish Clb; Drill Tm; Bsktbl; Vllybl; Hon Roll; NHS; Spanish NHS; Westark CC; Scndry Ed.

REITZELL, MELANIE D; Prescott HS; Prescott, AR; (2); 10/93; Church Yth Grp; FBLA; Teachers Aide; Church Choir; Hon Roll; Radiologist.

RENDEL, STEPHANIE L; Jacksonville HS; Jacksonville, AR; (2); 19/300; Band; Hon Roll; Pres Acad Fit Awd; Pres Ed Awd Prgm; Yth Accdnts Prvntn; Cert Achvmt; ASU; Pediatrc Nurse.

RENFROE, CARA; Harrison Sr HS; Harrison, AR; (3); Drama Clb; School Play; Variety Show; Nwsp; JV Mgr(s); Poetry; Lit; Astrlgy/Phtgrphy.

RESOR, VALERIE; Caddo Hills Jr Sr HS; Norman, AR; (3); 4/39; FCA; Natl Beta Clb; Quiz Bowl; Scholastic Bowl; Spanish Clb; SADD; Pres Jr Cls; Pres Treas Stu Cncl; Co-Capt Bsktbl; Capt Sftbl; Best Defensive Player 92-96; Best Attitude 94; Sftbl MVP 95; Southern Nazarene U; Obsttrcn.

RESTEMAN, LUMINITA; Hot Springs HS; Hot Springs Natio, AR; (4); Church Yth Grp; FBLA; Natl Beta Clb; Office Aide; ROTC; Spanish Clb; Teachers Aide; VICA; Chorus; Hon Roll; VICA Stdnt Yr 95-.

RESTINE, MARGARET E; Mena HS; Mena, AR; (3); Pres Sec Cmnty Wkr; French Clb; French Hon Soc; CCECA ST Sec; U Of OK; Bus Mngmt/Acctg.

RETTIG, CHARLEY D; Beebe Sr HS; Beebe, AR; (3); 17/112; Art Clb; FBLA; Natl Beta Clb; Rep Soph Cls; Ftbl; Trk; Wt Lftg; Hon Roll; All Conf Ftbl; ASU At Beebe.

REUTER, JOANNA M; Arkansas Schl Math & Science; Berryville, AR; (4); 4-H; Girl Scts; Library Aide; Mu Alpha Theta; Quiz Bowl; Science Clb; 4-H Awd; Hon Roll; NHS; Ntl Merit SF; Sci Fr Papr Prsntd 5th Skhrvs Rdngs St Pptrsbrg Rssa; ASMS Stu Pgwsh; Wstnghse Sci Tlnt Srch Smi-Fnlt.

REVELL, KATHY; Lakeside HS; Hot Springs, AR; (2); Art Clb; Church Yth Grp; Cmnty Wkr; FCA; 4-H; FBLA; GAA; Math Clb; Natl Beta Clb; Red Cross Aide; Hula Bowl Chrldng Perfmnc; All-Star Chrldng Squad; St Piano Recitals Super; U Of TX; Sports Medicine.

REVELLE, ALLEN; Humphrey Schl; Humphrey, AR; (1); Ed Nwsp; JV Bsktbl; Gftd Tlntd; Cmptrs; U Of AR Fayetteville; Art Wk.

REVELS, GARY THOMAS; Lockesburgh HS; Lockesburg, AR; (3); 2/27; Am Leg Boys St; FCA; Quiz Bowl; Nwsp; Yrbk; Pres Jr Cls; Var Bsktbl; Var Golf; Hon Roll; NHS; Yrbk Sports Ed; 1st Pl In On-Site Yrbk Sports Copy At AR HS Press Assn Convention; Henderson ST; Engrng.

REYES, ELENA; Mills HS; Little Rock, AR; (3); 10/399; Church Yth Grp; Drama Clb; Mu Alpha Theta; Natl Beta Clb; Spanish Clb; School Play; Stage Crew; Ofcr Stu Cncl; L Var Sftbl; NHS; Hendrix; Lwyr/Tchr.

REYES, VIRGIL T; Catholic HS; Little Rock, AR; (2); 34/188; Boy Scts; Church Yth Grp; Cmnty Wkr; Latin Clb; ROTC; Yrbk; Hon Roll; Publicity Comm For Schl Play; Pediatrician.

REYNOLDS, JASON; Atkins Schl; Atkins, AR; (3); Church Yth Grp; Natl Beta Clb; Office Aide; Varsity Clb; Sec Frsh Cls; Ftbl; Trk; Hon Roll; Ntl Merit Ltr; Prfct Atten Awd; AR Tech.

REYNOLDS, JENNIFER; Prairie Grove HS; Fayetteville, AR; (3); FCA; 4-H; HOBY; Natl FFA Org; Spanish Clb; SADD; Var Bsktbl; Var Trk; Cit Awd; 4-H Awd; Bank Brd; Edctnl Tlnt Srch; Medcl.

REYNOLDS, JONATHAN W; El Dorado Sr HS; El Dorado, AR; (1); 11/350; Church Yth Grp; Office Aide; Rep Soph Cls; Intrml Bsktbl; Intrml Ftbl; Intrml Socr; Cit Awd; Harding Univ.

REYNOLDS, KATHRINA N; Harmony Grove Jr Sr HS; Benton, AR; (2); Art Clb; GAA; Science Clb; Speech Tm; Chorus; School Play; Bsktbl; Sftbl; Hon Roll; U Of AR; Nrs.

REYNOLDS, KIMBERLY S; Pine Bluff HS; Pine Bluff, AR; (3); Church Yth Grp; Cmnty Wkr; FHA; Spanish Clb; Teachers Aide; Chorus; Church Choir; Stu Of The Month; U AR Pine Bluff; Pre-Law.

REYNOLDS, KRISTA L; Mills HS; Jacksonville, AR; (3); 13/250; Art Clb; Church Yth Grp; Cmnty Wkr; Drama Clb; JA; Natl Beta Clb; Quiz Bowl; Science Clb; Thesps; Orch; Prjct WET; 3rd Pl Duet Acting Pulaski Cty Trny; PT.

REYNOLDS, MARILYN M; Stuttgart Sr HS; Stuttgart, AR; (4); FBLA; Sec FTA; Science Clb; Spanish Clb; Teachers Aide; Band; Mrchg Band; Hon Roll; REACH; GCO; AR ST Univ; Span Tchr.

REYNOLDS, TIMOTHY M; Pulaski Acad; North Little Rock, AR; (2); Church Yth Grp; French Clb; Natl Beta Clb; Var Crs Cntry; Var Trk; Hon Roll; NHS; Cert Scuba Diver; Black Belt Karate; Cert Lifegrd.

RHAME, MEG; Pea Ridge HS; Rogers, AR; (1); 1/90; Church Yth Grp; Hosp Aide; Spanish Clb; Trk; High Hon Roll.

RHAME, VIRGINIA; Rogers HS; Rogers, AR; (4); 1/513; Church Yth Grp; Cmnty Wkr; FCA; Intnl Clb; Model UN; Quiz Bowl; Science Clb; Spanish Clb; Acpl Chr; Chorus; GEO Clb Sec; Rnssnc Awd; John Brown U; Bio.

RHEIN, ROBIN A; Valley View HS; Jonesboro, AR; (2); Hosp Aide; Library Aide; Spanish Clb; Teachers Aide; Band; Jazz Band; Pep Band; Hon Roll; Jr NHS; NHS; Sr HS All-Region Band; Region/ST Solo Fstvl Mdls; AR ST Univ; Law.

RHEINHARDT, CINDIE; Perryville Jr Sr HS; Adona, AR; (4); 3/54; Art Clb; Church Yth Grp; FCA; FBLA; Quiz Bowl; Spanish Clb; Pres Soph Cls; Sec Jr Cls; Var Bsktbl; High Hon Roll; His Awd 2 Yrs; Bsktbl Awds & All Conf; U Of AR Fayetteville; Pre-Med.

RHEOME, AMANDA M; Lonoke Jr HS; Lonoke, AR; (1); Church Yth Grp; FHA; Nwsp; Hon Roll; Outstdng Newspaper Staff; Envrnmntl Sci/Math Cntr Rogers ST; OK ST U; Mtrlgst.

RHEW, TAMARA D; Midland HS; Pleasant Plains, AR; (3); Library Aide; Natl Beta Clb; Pep Clb; Quiz Bowl; Chorus; Church Choir; Yrbk; Mgr(s); Hon Roll; Future Problm Solving 1 Yr; Home Ec Awd 1 Yr; Gateway Tech Coll; Cmptr/Inf Sy.

RHINEHART, JIMMIE; Hampton Jr Sr HS; Hampton, AR; (4); 1/60; Church Yth Grp; HOBY; Natl Beta Clb; Capt Quiz Bowl; Church Choir; Ed Yrbk; Rep Stu Cncl; Stat Bsktbl; High Hon Roll; Ntl Merit SF; PRIDE; Chrch Nrsry Hlpr; U Of AR Fayetteville; Law.

RHOADS, JENNIFER R; North Little Rock Hs-West; North Little Rock, AR; (3); 150/554; Am Leg Aux Girls St; Church Yth Grp; Drama Clb; Key Clb; School Musical; Rep Sr Cls; Sec Stu Cncl; Gov Hon Prg Awd; Miss AR Natl Tngr 96; Oklahoma City U; Theatre/Engl.

RHODES, ADELIA J; Cabot HS; Ward, AR; (2); French Clb; Pres FHA; Key Clb; Library Aide; Bsktbl; Hon Roll; Jr NHS; NHS; JUST Clb.

RHODES, ALICIA D; Fairview HS; Camden, AR; (4); 18/245; Church Yth Grp; Drama Clb; FBLA; Letterman Clb; Mu Alpha Theta; Natl Beta Clb; Spanish Clb; Band; Color Guard; Mrchg Band; LA Tech Univ; Occup Thrpy.

RHODES, ALISHA A; Buffalo Island Central HS; Leachville, AR; (3); 2/50; Church Yth Grp; Drama Clb; FBLA; FTA; Quiz Bowl; Science Clb; Spanish Clb; Teachers Aide; Chorus; School Play.

RHODES, ANGELA; Augusta HS; Augusta, AR; (3); 11/42; FBLA; FTA; Natl Beta Clb; Office Aide; Science Clb; Spanish Clb; Band; Ed Yrbk; Hon Roll; NHS; Coll Ozarks.

RHODES, JAYSON E; Nevada Schl; Prescott, AR; (2); 14/70; FBLA; Natl Beta Clb; Pres Frsh Cls; Hon Roll; St And Dist Comp In Intro To Bus; St And Dist Comp In Comptr Concpts; Intro To Bus Awd; Eng.

RHODES, LUKE D; Lonoke Jr HS; Lonoke, AR; (2); JV Bsktbl; JV Ftbl; JV Trk; JV Wt Lftg; Hon Roll; Jr NHS; Coll; Sports Or Hlth.

RHODES, TORRY D; Rison HS; Rison, AR; (2); Cmnty Wkr; French Clb; Natl Beta Clb; Natl FFA Org; Teachers Aide; Hon Roll; U Of A Monticello.

RHONE, MARICA L; Arkansas Sr HS; Texarkana, AR; (2); Band; Mrchg Band; Pep Band; Hon Roll; Jr NHS; Pres Acad Fit Awd; 1st All Reg Band; U AR Pine Bluff; Psych.

RIBBING, JASON J; Cabot HS; Cabot, AR; (3); Church Yth Grp; Office Aide; Church Choir; JV Var Bsbl; JV Ftbl; Hon Roll; Jr NHS; Fall League Bsbl; AAU Bsbl; AMER League Bsbl; Psychlgy.

RICE, BRIAN; Southside HS; Fort Smith, AR; (3); JA; Mu Alpha Theta; Spanish Clb; High Hon Roll; Jr NHS; NHS; Ntl Merit Ltr; U AR; Engrng.

RICE, BRIAN C; England HS; England, AR; (2); Boy Scts; Church Yth Grp; Natl Beta Clb; Natl FFA Org; Quiz Bowl; Ofcr Bsbl.

RICE, BRITTNEY A; Riverview HS; Judsonia, AR; (2); Cmnty Wkr; Drama Clb; FHA; Library Aide; Pep Clb; Spanish Clb; Phtg Rptr Yrbk; Intrml L Bsktbl; Intrml L Crs Cntry; Intrml L Trk; Raider Clb Mem; Harding Coll; Modlng; Comp Work.

RICE, JARED; Charleston HS; Charleston, AR; (1); Band; Jazz Band; Mrchg Band; Orch; Pep Band; Hon Roll; OM Cmptns; U Of AR; Elec Engrng.

RICE, JEREMY W; Sylvan Hills HS; Sherwood, AR; (2); FCA; Mu Alpha Theta; Natl Beta Clb; Spanish Clb; JV Var Ftbl; Jr NHS; Vol Coch Sylvn Hlls Jr Hgh 95 Ftbll; U Of Central AR; PE.

RICE, LEASHA L; Southside HS; Batesville, AR; (4); 17/64; Am Leg Aux Girls St; Key Clb; Natl Beta Clb; Office Aide; Science Clb; Band; Pep Band; Rep Stu Cncl; JV Bsktbl; Var JV Sftbl; Piano Lssns 8 Yrs; Batesville Jr Tm Tennis; Ar ST Univ; Elem Educ.

RICE, SHANNON; Arkansas Bapt Schl; Little Rock, AR; (3); FCA; FBLA; Band; Chorus; Rep Stu Cncl; Var L Bsktbl; Var L Chrldng; Var L Trk; Ntl Merit SF; Mrchg Band; Med.

RICH, NEKITA; Cotton Plant HS; Cotton Plant, AR; (3); Church Yth Grp; 4-H; FTA; Girl Scts; HOBY; Natl FFA Org; School Play; 4-H Awd; Hon Roll; Prfct Atten Awd; Explrs Clb; YAC; U At Pine Bluff; Cmptr Tech.

RICHARD, JOE D; Valley Springs Schl; Harrison, AR; (3); 1/60; Am Leg Boys St; Art Clb; FBLA; Key Clb; Pres Soph Cls; Var Bsktbl; High Hon Roll; Hon Roll; NHS; AEGIS Prog; Eng.

RICHARDS, CORY; Mt Ida Jr Sr HS; Mount Ida, AR; (4); 7/31; FCA; FHA; Natl Beta Clb; School Play; Yrbk; Pres VP Stu Cncl; Bsktbl; Capt Chrldng; Trk; Hon Roll; Hbt Hmnty Vol; Sar Rep Ode Maddox Page; U Of AR; Law.

RICHARDSON, AMANDA B; Southside HS; Batesville, AR; (2); Church Yth Grp; Cmnty Wkr; Sec FHA; Key Clb; Natl Beta Clb; Office Aide; Teachers Aide; Band; Church Choir; Pep Band; PRIDE; Chrch Camp Cnslr; AR ST Univ; Bus Admin.

RICHARDSON, BRANDON J; Midland HS; Batesville, AR; (2); Natl Beta Clb; Natl FFA Org; Pep Clb; Quiz Bowl; JV Bsktbl; Var Trk; DAR Awd; High Hon Roll; Hon Roll; Commnctn; Sports Commentator.

RICHARDSON, BRANDON L; Greenwood Sr HS; Greenwood, AR; (2); Church Yth Grp; FBLA; Natl FFA Org; Rep Frsh Cls; Hon Roll; U Of AR; Crmnl Jstc.

RICHARDSON, CASSIE R; Trumann HS; Trumann, AR; (3); French Clb; Science Clb; Chorus; High Hon Roll; Hon Roll; NHS; Radiology.

RICHARDSON, GARY; Mc Gehee HS; Mcgehee, AR; (2); Church Yth Grp; Cmnty Wkr; 4-H; Mu Alpha Theta; Office Aide; SADD; Variety Show; Ofcr Soph Cls; Ofcr Bsbl; Ftbl; Schlr Ath Awd; PRIDE Achvmnt Awd; Merit Awd; U Of AR; Comp Eng.

RICHARDSON, JAMI A; Waldron HS; Waldron, AR; (3); Church Yth Grp; FBLA; FHA; Natl Beta Clb; Spanish Clb; Yrbk; JV Chrldng; High Hon Roll; Algebra I & II Awds; Art Forms Awd; Home Ec Awd; Harding Univ.

RICHARDSON, JEFFREY; Hatfield Schl; Hatfield, AR; (3); 2/22; Church Yth Grp; FCA; FBLA; JA; Natl Beta Clb; Natl FFA Org; Sec Jr Cls; Rep Stu Cncl; L Bsktbl; Gov Hon Prg Awd; U Of AR Monticello; Forestry.

RICHARDSON, JOHN J; Southside HS; Batesville, AR; (2); 15/110; Church Yth Grp; Key Clb; Office Aide; Teachers Aide; Band; Ofcr Bsbl; Golf; Hon Roll; Arch.

RICHARDSON, KATHLEEN C; Piggott HS; Piggott, AR; (3); Church Yth Grp; Cmnty Wkr; Dance Clb; FCA; French Clb; Natl Beta Clb; Science Clb; Band; Chorus; Church Choir; Hall Of Merit; Amer Hist Awd; All Region Band; Speech & Keyboarding Awds; Excl Solo & Ensemble; Dntl Hygiene.

RICHARDSON, KYNDRA S; Arkansas Sr HS; Texarkana, AR; (3); FTA; Spanish Clb; Band; Chorus; Church Choir; Drill Tm; Pom Pon; Southern AR U; Nrsng.

RICHARDSON, LATOYA T; Hampton Jr Sr HS; Hampton, AR; (3); 3/70; Am Leg Aux Girls St; 4-H; Natl Beta Clb; Band; Drm Mjr(t); Pres Jr Cls; Rep Stu Cncl; Var L Bsktbl; 4-H Awd; Hon Roll; Natl PRIDE; Henderson ST Univ; Law.

RICHARDSON, MATTHEW; Greene Co Tech HS; Bono, AR; (3); 23/150; Am Leg Boys St; Model UN; Quiz Bowl.

RICHARDSON, MELISSA D; Lamar HS; Lamar, AR; (2); Church Yth Grp; FBLA; Natl Beta Clb; Chorus; Church Choir; School Musical; High Hon Roll; Hon Roll; Comp Tech.

RICHARDSON, MORGAN; Warren Sr HS; Warren, AR; (4); 25/121; Am Leg Aux Girls St; VP Church Yth Grp; Drama Clb; FCA; French Clb; Model UN; Natl Beta Clb; Sec Natl FFA Org; SADD; Ed Nwsp; Natl HS Rdo Assn Mem; AR HS Rdo Assn Stu St Sec; U Of AR-FAYETTVILLE; Mrktng.

RICHARDSON, ROBIN R; Bald Knob HS; Bald Knob, AR; (1); VP Church Yth Grp; Cmnty Wkr; Dance Clb; FHA; Girl Scts; Math Tm; Natl Beta Clb; Teachers Aide; Band; Chorus; Sec Chrch Drama Tm; Asst Dir VBS.

RICHARDSON, SARA; Bryant Sr HS; Alexander, AR; (4); 5/336; Art Clb; French Clb; FBLA; Teachers Aide; Phtg Yrbk; Bsktbl; Vllybl; Jr NHS; NHS; REACH Sec; U Of Cntrl AR; Bio/Envrmtl Sci.

RICHARDSON, STACY R; Bald Knob HS; Bald Knob, AR; (3); 6/118; Am Leg Aux Girls St; Pres Church Yth Grp; Cmnty Wkr; FBLA; Pres FHA; Girl Scts; Math Tm; Natl Beta Clb; Quiz Bowl; Spanish Clb; Chptr/Dist/ST FHA Pres; Church Yth Drama Tm Pres; Tchr Chldrns Wednesday Night Church Class; Ed.

RICHART, KRISTY L; Lee Acad; Forrest City, AR; (4); 4/21; Am Leg Aux Girls St; Church Yth Grp; Nwsp; Yrbk; VP Jr Cls; VP Sr Cls; Sec NHS; EACC; Drftng.

RICHEY, CHRISTINE; Pleasant View Schl; Mulberry, AR; (4); 1/14; Church Yth Grp; Treas FBLA; VP Natl Beta Clb; Quiz Bowl; Yrbk; Pres Sr Cls; Stat Bsktbl; Trk; High Hon Roll; Prfct Atten Awd; Teen Ct Rep; U Of AR Fayetteville.

RICHEY, HEIDI; Marmaduke HS; Marmaduke, AR; (3); 1/55; HOBY; VP Natl Beta Clb; Chorus; School Play; Nwsp; VP Soph Cls; Pres Jr Cls; Rep Stu Cncl; Sftbl; High Hon Roll; AR Govs Schl; Hnds Agnst Drgs; AR Jr Natl Tngr Schlrshp Pgm.

RICHEY, KELI M; Quitman Jr Sr HS; Quitman, AR; (2); Church Yth Grp; Cmnty Wkr; Dance Clb; FBLA; FHA; HOBY; Natl Beta Clb; SADD; Teachers Aide; Cit Awd; Bio/Fr/Kybrdng/Eng/Oral Comm Awds; Nrsng.

RICHEY, KERI; West Side HS; Greers Ferry, AR; (4); 6/27; Am Leg Aux Girls St; Bus Profs of Am; Church Yth Grp; Cmnty Wkr; Dance Clb; FCA; FBLA; FHA; Library Aide; SADD; Eng & Acctng II Awds; U Of Cntrl AR; Acctng.

RICHISON, MARIE; Southside HS; Fort Smith, AR; (4); 79/432; Art Clb; Church Yth Grp; French Clb; GAA; Service Clb; Band; Color Guard; Capt Flag Corp; Mrchg Band; JV Bsktbl; U Of AR; Vet.

RICHISON, SARAH L; Southside HS; Fort Smith, AR; (2); GAA; Pep Clb; Band; Mrchg Band; JV Bsktbl; JV Chrldng; JV Vllybl; Hon Roll; Reflections Cont Wnnr.

RICHMOND, MEREDITH; Mountainburg Jr Sr HS; Mountainburg, AR; (4); 10/45; Am Leg Aux Girls St; Church Yth Grp; Drama Clb; HOBY; Model UN; Science Clb; SADD; FCA; FBLA; FHA; Gymnstcs; Cmmnty Cantana; Natl Ynd Ldrs Conf; U Ozarks; Marine Bio.

RICHTER, CRAIG; Gillett Jr Sr HS; Gillett, AR; (1); Church Yth Grp; Quiz Bowl; Pres Frsh Cls; Var Bsbl; Var Ftbl; High Hon Roll; Jr NHS.

RICHTER, WILHELM M; Arkansas Schl Math & Science; Hot Springs, AR; (4); French Clb; Key Clb; Math Clb; Math Tm; Mu Alpha Theta; Science Clb; Rep Stu Cncl; JV Socr; NHS; Ntl Merit SF; Hghst AHSME AIME Score; Chem Olympiad Stu Top 8; 1st Pl St ACTM Trig Cmptn; Elec Engr.

RICKER, SHANNON D; Plainview Rover Schl; Rover, AR; (3); Natl FFA Org; Spanish Clb; SADD; Gym; Trk; Hon Roll; Play Piano; AR Tech U; Speech Therapy.

RICKETTS, ELIZABETH E; Harmony Grove Jr Sr HS; Benton, AR; (2); 2/65; French Clb; Natl Beta Clb; Office Aide; Acpl Chr; Chorus; School Musical; Yrbk; Ofcr Stu Cncl; Chrldng; Hon Roll.

RICKETTS, JASON L; Lamar HS; Lamar, AR; (4); Am Leg Boys St; Church Yth Grp; FCA; Pres FBLA; Letterman Clb; Natl FFA Org; Science Clb; Capt L Ftbl; Wt Lftg; Cit Awd; U Of AR; Spcl Ed.

RICKETTS, KRISTEN; Southside HS; Fort Smith, AR; (3); Mu Alpha Theta; Drill Tm; Socr; High Hon Roll; NHS; Phy Thrpst.

RICKMAN, JENNI R; Lake Hamilton Sr HS; Hot Springs Natio, AR; (3); 40/213; Church Yth Grp; FCA; Bsktbl; Sftbl; Tennis; Vllybl; Hon Roll; Pres Acad Fit Awd.

RICORD, CHAD D; Conway Sr HS; Conway, AR; (2); FBLA; Band; Rlrbldng; Swrd Clctng; UCA; Acctng.

RIDDLE, COREY; Pangburn Jr Sr HS; Pangburn, AR; (4); 10/49; Am Leg Boys St; Art Clb; FBLA; FHA; Natl Beta Clb; Natl FFA Org; VP Soph Cls; VP Jr Cls; VP Sr Cls; Hon Roll; Natl Yth Ldrshp Forum; AR St Univ Schlsp; ASU; CAD.

RIDDLE, JASON C; Waldron HS; Waldron, AR; (2); Drama Clb; Spanish Clb; VICA; Hon Roll; Prfct Atten Awd; Beta Clb; Hlth, Geog, Algebra I Awds.

RIDDLE, WINDY; Hughes Jr-Sr HS; Hughes, AR; (4); 6/47; Church Yth Grp; Library Aide; Natl FFA Org; Office Aide; Teachers Aide; Chorus; Sec Soph Cls; Cit Awd; Hon Roll; Prfct Atten Awd; JTPA Tutoring; E AR CC; Bus Admin.

RIDDLING, LEIGH A; Mills HS; Little Rock, AR; (3); 29/298; Math Clb; Natl Beta Clb; Office Aide; Science Clb; Spanish Clb; Teachers Aide; Band; Mrchg Band; Yrbk; Var Sftbl; Rainbows Svc Org Chrstn Grls; Jr Cabnt; Majrtt-Twrlr; Baptist Nursing Schl; RN.

RIDER, ARTHUR T; Dierks HS; Dierks, AR; (4); Bsktbl; Hon Roll; Cossatot Tech Coll; Auto Tech.

RIDGE, DANIEL L; Rural Special Schl; Clinton, AR; (2); Natl Beta Clb; Natl FFA Org; Spanish Clb; Pres Soph Cls; JV Var Bsktbl; Hon Roll; Cls Favorite & King.

RIDGE, MELISSA; West Memphis Sr HS; Proctor, AR; (3); Cmnty Wkr; French Clb; Mu Alpha Theta; Natl Beta Clb; Science Clb; Band; High Hon Roll; Pres Acad Fit Awd; Intnl Order Of Rainbow For Girls.

RIDGELL, BRANDY; Dermott HS; Dermott, AR; (3); 9/64; FBLA; FHA; FTA; VP Math Clb; Natl Beta Clb; Spanish Clb; Band; Ofcr Stu Cncl; Trk; Hon Roll; Pre-Law.

RIDLON, ADAM P; Dequeen HS; De Queen, AR; (2); Church Yth Grp; Drama Clb; FCA; FBLA; Letterman Clb; SADD; Chorus; Rep Soph Cls; Rep Jr Cls; Var L Golf; U Of AR Fayetteville; Chem Eng.

RIDMUELLER, JENNIFER; Perryville Jr Sr HS; Perryville, AR; (4); 8/55; Am Leg Aux Girls St; FCA; FBLA; FHA; Pep Clb; Spanish Clb; Chrldng; Score Keeper; NHS; Prfct Atten Awd; 95 Yth Tour Wnnr 1st Electrc; Ms FBLA 2nd 95 & 96; Homcmng Maid 92-93 & 95-96; U Of AR Fayetteville; Nursng.

RIES, MOTA; Leslie Schl; Leslie, AR; (4); 4/33; Natl Beta Clb; Quiz Bowl; NHS; Ntl Merit SF.

RIESKE, DAVID W; Oak Grove HS; Maumelle, AR; (2); Boy Scts; Mu Alpha Theta; Natl Beta Clb; Band; Pep Band; Rptr Nwsp; HS Heros.

RIETZKE, HEATHER N; Conway Sr HS; Conway, AR; (4); 32/520; Church Yth Grp; Dance Clb; French Clb; FBLA; FTA; Natl Beta Clb; Band; French Hon Soc; High Hon Roll; Pres Schlr; UCA; Elem Ed.

RIGBY, KELLY; Batesville Sr HS; Batesville, AR; (4); 13/143; Am Leg Aux Girls St; Church Yth Grp; FBLA; Hosp Aide; Key Clb; Sec Natl Beta Clb; School Play; Yrbk; Treas Stu Cncl; Pom Pon; U Of AR Fayetteville.

RIGGIN, AMY N; Robinson HS; Little Rock, AR; (2); 9/100; Natl Beta Clb; Rptr Nwsp; Hon Roll; Jr NHS; NHS; Pres Schlr; Wrt Poetry; 3rd Pl Natl Nrth Amer Poetry Cont; Poem Publ; U Of AR Conway; Jrnlsm.

RIGGS, C BRENDON; Fayetteville Sr HS; Fayetteville, AR; (3); Am Leg Boys St; Pres Church Yth Grp; FCA; FBLA; Ftbl; Trk; Hon Roll; N AR Conf Cncl Yth Ministries 3 Yrs; Flag Ftbl Vol Coach.

RIGGS, CHARISSA; Gosnell Jr Sr HS; Blytheville, AR; (2); 1/107; Treas Art Clb; Sec Natl FFA Org; Science Clb; Teachers Aide; Chorus; Bsktbl; Mgr Ftbl; Fnlst Amer Natl Teenager Pgnt AR; AR ST U; Engl Tchr.

RIGGS, CORRY; Gosnell Jr Sr HS; Blytheville, AR; (2); Church Yth Grp; FHA; Natl Beta Clb; Science Clb; Spanish Clb; Yrbk; Powder Puff Ftbl; Hon Roll; Pres Acad Fit Awd.

RIGGS, DEREK; Coleman Jr HS; Van Buren, AR; (1); Church Yth Grp; HOBY; Band; Church Choir; Jazz Band; Mrchg Band; Pep Band; Ofcr Stu Cncl; Cit Awd; Hon Roll; Van Buren Police Explorer; Law Inforcement; Med Field.

RILEY, AMANDA; Tuckerman HS; Tuckerman, AR; (3); 2/50; Church Yth Grp; FBLA; FHA; Pres Natl Beta Clb; Hist Spanish Clb; Chorus; Church Choir; School Musical; Yrbk; Ofcr Frsh Cls; Hist & Music Clbs; AR ST U; Phys Thrp.

RILEY, CARA BRYNN; Tuckerman HS; Tuckerman, AR; (2); 1/60; VP Church Yth Grp; Rptr FBLA; GAA; Natl Beta Clb; Rptr Soph Cls; Ofcr Stu Cncl; Bsktbl; Sftbl; High Hon Roll; Jr NHS; His Club 2nd Pl Dist His Day/1st Pl ST/NATL; YES 4th Pl 94-95/2nd Pl 95-; Law/Bus Admin.

RILEY, DERRICK W; Poyen Schl; Prattsville, AR; (2); Church Yth Grp; FCA; Natl Beta Clb; Quiz Bowl; Spanish Clb; Chorus; Church Choir; VP Soph Cls; Treas Stu Cncl; Var Bsbl; ST Fine Arts Fest Male Vcl Solo Superior Rating; Natl Beta Clb Tlnt 2(d Pl; Yth Alive Mssnry; Cntrl Bible Coll; Fine Arts.

RILEY, ERIN M; Mena HS; Mena, AR; (2); Church Yth Grp; French Clb; FBLA; Science Clb; Band; Mrchg Band; Tennis; French Hon Soc; High Hon Roll; Ntl Merit Ltr.

RILEY, JOEY K; Tuckerman HS; Tuckerman, AR; (2); 2/60; Church Yth Grp; FBLA; HOBY; Natl Beta Clb; Spanish Clb; Chorus; Rep Soph Cls; JV Bsktbl; Cit Awd; High Hon Roll; AEGIS Prgm; Prins Awd; Eng/Span/Math/His/Bio Awds.

RILEY, RACHEL; Gillett Jr Sr HS; Gillett, AR; (2); Art Clb; FHA; Pep Clb; Rptr Spanish Clb; Chrldng; Sftbl; Trk; High Hon Roll; Jr NHS; NHS; All Star Chrldr 94-95.

RILEY, REBECCA; Tuckerman HS; Tuckerman, AR; (4); 1/60; Am Leg Aux Girls St; Church Yth Grp; Cmnty Wkr; FBLA; FHA; HOBY; VP Natl Beta Clb; Quiz Bowl; VP Spanish Clb; VP Chorus; Outstndng Sr; Homcmng Qn; Miss THS; Phys Thrpy.

RILEY, THOMAS M; Jonesboro HS; Jonesboro, AR; (4); 56/283; Art Clb; Natl Beta Clb; Band; Jazz Band; Mrchg Band; Hon Roll; Pres Acad Fit Awd; SEE Clb; Orch Mem For Schl Musical; U Of Memphis; Musc Recrdng Tech.

RILEY, TONYA; Blevins HS; Prescott, AR; (1); Church Yth Grp; FBLA; Quiz Bowl; Band; Church Choir; Hon Roll; Henderson ST U.

RIMKUS, JENA M; Huntsville HS; Huntsville, AR; (2); 16/257; Science Clb; Band; Mrchg Band; Ofcr Soph Cls; Hon Roll; Intl Servas; Travel; U Of AR; Arch.

RIMMER, ANGELA; Guy Perkins Schl; Greenbrier, AR; (3); 2/25; Church Yth Grp; FHA; HOBY; Natl Beta Clb; Church Choir; Pres Frsh Cls; Pres Soph Cls; Pres Jr Cls; Var Capt Chrldng; Hon Roll; Ricks Coll; Early Chldhd Ed.

RING, BRANDI; Pocahontas HS; Pocahontas, AR; (4); 10/126; Am Leg Aux Girls St; Church Yth Grp; Pres FBLA; Treas Key Clb; VP Spanish Clb; Teachers Aide; Band; Capt Flag Corp; Mrchg Band; Cit Awd; Amer Govt Awd; Ldrs Only; Beta Clb; Tp 10 Pct Cls; AR ST U; Med Tech.

RINK, CHRIS L; Booneville Jr Sr HS; Booneville, AR; (4); 18/85; Pres Church Yth Grp; Cmnty Wkr; FCA; FBLA; FTA; Natl Beta Clb; Science Clb; Spanish Clb; Pres Band; Church Choir; Directing Awds In Marching Conts; Monmouth Coll Acad Excl Schlsp; Wind Ensemble Schlsp; Concert Band; Monmouth Coll; Pre-Med.

RIORDAN, HANNAH M; Ft Smith Christian Schl; Natural Dam, AR; (2); FCA; Spanish Clb; Bsktbl; Trk; Cit Awd; NHS.

RIORDAN, JOHN MICHAEL; Ft Smith Christian Schl; Natural Dam, AR; (4); 5/25; Am Leg Boys St; Drama Clb; FCA; FBLA; Natl FFA Org; Spanish Clb; School Play; Bsktbl; Crs Cntry; Ftbl; Westark CC; Comp Sci.

RIPPER, JOHN; Lee Sr HS; Marianna, AR; (3); Church Yth Grp; Natl FFA Org; Ftbl; Hon Roll.

RIPPY, AMBER; Booneville Jr Sr HS; Booneville, AR; (2); Pres FBLA; Sec Key Clb; Pres Natl Beta Clb; VP Frsh Cls; VP Soph Cls; Var Chrldng; Cit Awd; High Hon Roll; FCA; FTA; Engl Awd; Miss FBLA 94-95; U Of AR; Orthodntcs.

RIPPY, MARK; Searcy HS; Searcy, AR; (3); 48/256; Am Leg Boys St; Church Yth Grp; FBLA; Natl Beta Clb; Science Clb; Church Choir; Yrbk; Hon Roll; NHS; AR ST Univ; Comms/Brdcstng.

RISLEY, SARAH D; Greenland Jr Sr HS; Winslow, AR; (3); Cmnty Wkr; FBLA; Hosp Aide; Quiz Bowl; Science Clb; Teachers Aide; School Play; Ed Yrbk; Hon Roll; NHS; U AR; Acctng.

RISNER, TARA; Mc Gehee HS; Mc Gehee, AR; (3); Church Yth Grp; Cmnty Wkr; Computer Clb; FBLA; FTA; Math Clb; Mu Alpha Theta; Natl Beta Clb; Spanish Clb; Teachers Aide; AR St Univ; Psych.

RITCHEY, CHRISTINA; Camden Fairview HS; Camden, AR; (2); #1 in class; Church Yth Grp; Drama Clb; Natl Beta Clb; School Musical; School Play; Nwsp; Co-Ed Yrbk; Co-Capt Chrldng; Gym; High Hon Roll; U Of AR; Psychiatry.

RITCHIE, COREY B; Dollorway Sr HS; Pine Bluff, AR; (4); 9/94; Am Leg Boys St; Church Yth Grp; Hon Roll; NHS; Bio Awd; Industrial Art Awd; AR ST Univ; Nrsng.

RITCHIE, JASON; Hazen Jr Sr HS; Hazen, AR; (4); 8/26; Boy Scts; Computer Clb; FBLA; FTA; Band; Mrchg Band; Rptr Nwsp; Rptr Yrbk; Hon Roll; Gftd & Tlntd; Navy.

RIVALDO, JAYME; Northside HS; Van Buren, AR; (2); Art Clb; Church Yth Grp; French Clb; FBLA; FHA; GAA; Science Clb; Church Choir; Capt All Star Chrldng Sqd; U AR; Phys Ther.

RIVAS, SHANNON D; Hot Springs HS; Hot Springs, AR; (4); FBLA; FHA; Natl Beta Clb; Science Clb; Thesps; Band; Jazz Band; Mrchg Band.

RIVERA, IRISH FAYE V; Ozark Adventist Acad; El Paso, TX; (4); 1/54; Church Yth Grp; Teachers Aide; Chorus; VP Jr Cls; Gym; Cit Awd; High Hon Roll; Pres Acad Fit Awd; Val; Prfct Atten Awd; Gymnstcs Instr; Stu Assn Scl VP; SW Adventist Coll; Med.

RIVERS, CHRISTIE A; Arkansas Sr HS; Texarkana, AR; (3); 9/331; Cmnty Wkr; French Clb; FTA; Mu Alpha Theta; Band; Ofcr Stu Cncl; NHS; Art Clb; Church Yth Grp; Math Clb; 4 States Hnr Band; Fllwshp Chrstn Stu; Teenage Rpblcns; Engrng.

RIX, SARAH L; New England HS; England, AR; (2); Art Clb; Church Yth Grp; FCA; French Clb; FBLA; FHA; Key Clb; Chorus; Church Choir; School Musical; OBU; Med.

ROACH, JUSTIN; Pangburn Jr Sr HS; Heber Springs, AR; (1); 2/60; French Clb; FBLA; Natl Beta Clb; Natl FFA Org; Pres Frsh Cls; Ofcr Stu Cncl; High Hon Roll; Hon Roll; MPACT; Harvard U; Cardiac Surgeon.

ROACHELL, KRISTOPHER M; Jacksonville HS; Jacksonville, AR; (3); Drama Clb; FBLA; Spanish Clb; Band; Stage Crew; Bus.

ROARK, CHAD M; Alma HS; Alma, AR; (3); Church Yth Grp; FCA; French Clb; FHA; Ftbl; Trk; Wt Lftg; Hon Roll.

ROARK, DAVID A; Poyen Schl; Poyen, AR; (3); Church Yth Grp; Cmnty Wkr; German Clb; Natl Beta Clb; Teachers Aide; VICA; Rep Stu Cncl; JV Var Bsktbl.

ROARK, ROBIN; Fordyce HS; Fordyce, AR; (4); Pres Church Yth Grp; HOBY; Pres Quiz Bowl; Band; Church Choir; School Play; Nwsp; Rep Stu Cncl; Var L Bsbl; Var L Ftbl; All Reg Band; U AR Fayetteville; Music.

ROBBERSON, DACIA L; Cty Line HS; Paris, AR; (3); 18/42; Church Yth Grp; FCA; FBLA; Sec FHA; Natl Beta Clb; Spanish Clb; Rptr Nwsp; Stat Bsktbl; JV Var Mgr(s); Hon Roll; X-Ray Tech.

ROBBINS, BROOKE; Sacred Heart Schl; Morrilton, AR; (1); #1 in class; Church Yth Grp; Cmnty Wkr; Dance Clb; Key Clb; Quiz Bowl; SADD; Ofcr Stu Cncl; High Hon Roll; Pres Acad Fit Awd; AR Nrsng Home Assn Vol Of Yr 95; Med.

ROBBINS, CHRIS; Hackett Schl; Hackett, AR; (1); Church Yth Grp; Computer Clb; FBLA; Ftbl; Cit Awd; High Hon Roll; Jr NHS; NHS; G/T; VCR Crew; Comp.

ROBBINS, JIM E; West Memphis Sr HS; West Memphis, AR; (2); CAP; JA; Color Guard; Drill Tm; Hon Roll; Prvt Pilot Lcns; Cvl Air Ptrls Billy Mitchell Awd; Memphis ST; Comm Aviation.

ROBBINS, NICHOLAS; Van Buren Sr HS; Fort Smith, AR; (3); Mu Alpha Theta; Band; Jazz Band; Mrchg Band; Pep Band; Hon Roll.

ROBBINS, PENNY; Crossett Sr HS; Crossett, AR; (4); 20/154; Var L Bsktbl; Var Tennis; High Hon Roll; Hon Roll; NHS; Girls Sftbl; All-Star Sftbl 96; U Of Cntrl AR; Comp Sci.

ROBERSON, CAMILLE; North Little Rock HS; North Little Rock, AR; (3); Q&S; Nwsp; Real Est Agent.

ROBERSON, KASEY M; Smackover HS; Smackover, AR; (1); Church Yth Grp; FTA; Girl Scts; Library Aide; Chorus; Hon Roll; Prfct Atten Awd; Pub Anthology Of Poetry Young Americans.

ROBERSON, LAGENA L; Mountain Home HS; Mountain Home, AR; (3); 7/253; FBLA; FTA; Intnl Clb; Service Clb; Church Choir; VP Capt Drill Tm; Treas Jr Cls; Rep Stu Cncl; High Hon Roll; Hon Roll; Intl Order Of Rainbow For Grls; Hendrix Univ; Ed.

ROBERTS, AMY; Gosnell Jr Sr HS; Blytheville, AR; (2); 3/100; Cmnty Wkr; Drama Clb; FHA; Girl Scts; Key Clb; Math Tm; Mu Alpha Theta; Natl Beta Clb; Spanish Clb; School Play; Med.

ROBERTS, ANDREA; Gosnell Jr HS; Blytheville, AR; (1); Drama Clb; Girl Scts; Science Clb; Band; Trk; High Hon Roll; Jrnlsm.

ROBERTS, ANGELA D; Trumann HS; Trumann, AR; (3); VP Church Yth Grp; French Clb; Science Clb; Band; Mrchg Band; Pep Band; Orthdntst.

ROBERTS, BRANDI; Rogers HS; Rogers, AR; (4); 13/468; 4-H; FBLA; Var Sftbl; 4-H Awd; High Hon Roll; NHS; FBLA; All Trnmnt Tm Cty Trnmnt; OK ST U; Biosys Engrng.

ROBERTS, CANDICE; Bergman Schl; Harrison, AR; (3); 5/52; Church Yth Grp; Sec VP FBLA; Pres FHA; Sec Natl Beta Clb; Natl FFA Org; Science Clb; Yrbk; VP Jr Cls; Powder Puff Ftbl; High Hon Roll; Nom/Attnd Girls ST; Chrstns In Actn Club; U Of AR; Anml Sci/Vet.

ROBERTS, EMILY; Murfreesboro HS; Murfreesboro, AR; (3); 10/35; Art Clb; Church Yth Grp; FBLA; FHA; Natl Beta Clb; Natl FFA Org; Speech Tm; Band; Hon Roll; Pres Acad Fit Awd; Lawyer.

ROBERTS, GALICIA W; Valley Springs Schl; Harrison, AR; (2); Art Clb; FBLA; FHA; Library Aide; Band; Yrbk; Sec Soph Cls; Hon Roll; Med.

ROBERTS, HEATHER R; Fayetteville Sr HS; Fayetteville, AR; (2); Art Clb; Church Yth Grp; Cmnty Wkr; FHA; Spanish Clb; Photo; Hendrix Coll; Soc Worker.

ROBERTS, KARLA J; Harrisburg HS; Harrisburg, AR; (3); Am Leg Aux Girls St; VP FCA; Yrbk; Pres Frsh Cls; Pres Soph Cls; Pres Sr Cls; Ofcr Stu Cncl; Var Bsktbl; Var Vllybl; NHS; Utstndng Stu Cncl Mem 2 Yrs; Ovrll Wnnr 96 Sci Fr Hrrsbrg HS; 1st Pl Cat Regl Sci Fr.

ROBERTS, KILEY; Tuckerman HS; Tuckerman, AR; (4); Am Leg Boys St; Pres Church Yth Grp; Cmnty Wkr; VP FBLA; VP FHA; Math Tm; Natl Beta Clb; Quiz Bowl; Spanish Clb; Chorus; Jr Aux Vol; AR ST U.

ROBERTS, LEANN M; Yellville Summit HS; Flippin, AR; (2); #1 in class; FBLA; Var Bsktbl; Var Sftbl; High Hon Roll.

ROBERTS, LEIGHANN; Humphrey Schl; Humphrey, AR; (3); Church Yth Grp; 4-H; FBLA; FHA; Quiz Bowl; Spanish Clb; Sec Jr Cls; Sftbl; Hon Roll; NHS; Natl Hnr Soc Svc & Ldrshp Awd.

ROBERTS, MARY E; Abundant Life Schools; North Little Rock, AR; (3); Church Yth Grp; School Play; Nwsp; Treas Jr Cls; Rep Stu Cncl; Var Bsktbl; Sftbl; Vllybl; High Hon Roll; NHS.

ROBERTS, MELISSA D; Newport HS; Newport, AR; (2); Church Yth Grp; Spanish Clb; SADD; Church Choir; Sftbl; Cit Awd.

ROBERTS, MICHAEL B; Pine Bluff HS; Pine Bluff, AR; (3); 42/540; Church Yth Grp; Office Aide; Ofcr Bsbl; Ofcr Bsbl; Hon Roll; Pres Acad Fit Awd.

ROBERTS, MIKE; Van Buren Sr HS; Van Buren, AR; (3); 19/300; FBLA; HOBY; Mu Alpha Theta; Natl Beta Clb; Q&S; Spanish Clb; Band; Jazz Band; Mrchg Band; Pep Band; Music.

ROBERTS, REBECCA; Morrilton Sr HS; Perry, AR; (4); Drama Clb; 4-H; FBLA; School Musical; Comp Tech; Data Prcssng.

ROBERTS, STACIA J; Arkansas Sr HS; Texarkana, AR; (3); 64/345; Art Clb; Church Yth Grp; GAA; Spanish Clb; Yrbk; L JV Bsktbl; Health Clb; Tnag Repblcns; Texarkana Coll.

ROBERTS, TABITHA; Bergman Schl; Harrison, AR; (3); Church Yth Grp; FBLA; Pres FHA; Natl Beta Clb; Natl FFA Org; Pres Frsh Cls; Rep Soph Cls; Pres Jr Cls; Sec Stu Cncl; Hon Roll.

ROBERTS, TAKILA; Arkansas Sr HS; Texarkana, AR; (4); 91/380; Am Leg Aux Girls St; Cmnty Wkr; VP Drama Clb; FHA; Spanish Clb; Church Choir; Co-Capt Drill Tm; School Musical; Capt Chrldng; Jr NHS.

ROBERTS, TONY; Omaha Schl; Omaha, AR; (4); Teachers Aide; VICA; Band; Cit Awd; Hon Roll; Prfct Atten Awd; Prfct Atten 10 Yrs.

ROBERTS, VICTORIA L; Ashdown Sr HS; Ashdown, AR; (2); Drama Clb; FBLA; Math Clb; Science Clb; School Play; WA Univ; Atty.

ROBERTS, VINCENT; Watson Chapel Sr HS; Pine Bluff, AR; (2); 36/280; Art Clb; Debate Tm; Drama Clb; English Clb; French Clb; FBLA; FHA; Key Clb; Model UN; Natl Beta Clb; Mock Trial; Gftd/Tlntd; First Priority Chrstn Grp; Haverford Univ; Law.

ROBERTS, WENDELL H; Hall Sr HS; Little Rock, AR; (2); Boy Scts; Church Yth Grp; Cmnty Wkr; Band; Church Choir; Mrchg Band; Acad Achvmt Awd; Hendrix; Cmptr Ad Drftng/Arch.

ROBERTS, WESLEY B; Bald Knob HS; Bald Knob, AR; (2); Church Yth Grp; FBLA; Natl Beta Clb; Band; Church Choir; Jazz Band; Mrchg Band; Pep Band; Pres Soph Cls; Ofcr Bsbl; Med.

ROBERTSON, AMANDA F; J D Leftwich HS; Magazine, AR; (3); Church Yth Grp; Cmnty Wkr; Library Aide; Natl Beta Clb; Natl FFA Org; Spanish Clb; SADD; Teachers Aide; Varsity Clb; School Play; Westark; Ed.

ROBERTSON, CHASE Q; Gillett Jr Sr HS; Gillett, AR; (4); School Play; Bsktbl; Ftbl; Art Awd; Outstdng Attndnc 2 Yrs.

ROBERTSON, CORY; Sylvan Hills HS; Sherwood, AR; (3); Mu Alpha Theta; JV Bsktbl; Jr NHS; Sports Med.

ROBERTSON, JENNIFER L; Cushman Schl; Batesville, AR; (2); 1/36; Church Yth Grp; FHA; Math Clb; Treas Natl Beta Clb; Sec Treas Science Clb; Pres Band; Chorus; Ed Nwsp; High Hon Roll; GATE Prgm.

ROBERTSON, JEREMY D; Star City HS; Star City, AR; (3); FBLA; Hosp Aide; JA; Natl Beta Clb; Spanish Clb; Bsktbl; Ftbl; Cit Awd; Prfct Atten Awd; Bdybldng; Ownng Own Bus Entrprnrshp; Vocal Music Prof Singer; U Of PA; Entrprnrshp/Fin.

ROBERTSON, JONATHAN; Lake Hamilton Sr HS; Pearcy, AR; (3); Office Aide; Teachers Aide; Var L Bsbl; Capt L Ftbl; Intrml Sftbl; Var L Trk; Intrml Wt Lftg; Hon Roll; Jr NHS; Most Points Awd; U Of AR; Architecture.

ROBERTSON, KENDRA; Green Forest Jr Sr HS; Green Forest, AR; (4); 11/69; Church Yth Grp; FBLA; Natl Beta Clb; SADD; Chorus; School Play; Yrbk; Chrldng; Cit Awd; Pres Schlr; Coll Of The Ozarks; Elem Ed.

ROBERTSON, LISA L; Springdale Sr HS; Fayetteville, AR; (4); FBLA; Model UN; Sec Acpl Chr; Chorus; Phtg Yrbk; Trk; Hon Roll; NHS; Pres Acad Fit Awd; Natl Math Awd; Church Yth Grp Secy; U Of AR; Elem Ed.

ROBERTSON, MANDI J; Taylor HS; Taylor, AR; (2); 2/22; FBLA; Sec Treas FHA; Natl FFA Org; Rep Frsh Cls; Pres Jr Cls; Rptr Stu Cncl; JV Var Bsktbl; Var L Sftbl; Hon Roll; Invited To Natl Young Ldrs Conf In Washington DC; Northeast LA U.

ROBERTSON, SAMANTHA L; Rivercrest HS; Bassett, AR; (2); 35/140; Math Clb; ROTC; Teachers Aide; VICA; Chorus; Flag Corp; Mrchg Band; School Play; Cit Awd; Hon Roll; Lib Clb; TAD Clb; AR ST Univ; Child Dev.

ROBERTSON, TISH; Greenwood Sr HS; Greenwood, AR; (2); Church Yth Grp; FBLA; Spanish Clb; Chrldng; Hon Roll; U Of Cntrl AR; PT.

ROBERTSON, WILLIAM W; Russellville Sr HS; Russellville, AR; (3); 36/340; Church Yth Grp; Var Bsktbl; High Hon Roll; Jr NHS; NHS; Stu Of Yr 94-95; Project PACE; U Of MS; Chemical Engrng.

ROBERTSON, ZACHARY R; Crossett Sr HS; Crossett, AR; (2); Church Yth Grp; Letterman Clb; Natl Beta Clb; Var Bsbl; Var Ftbl; Var Wt Lftg; Cit Awd; Hon Roll; Prfct Atten Awd; Pres Acad Fit Awd; Gabe Murray Sprtsmnshp Awd; LA Tech; Elec Engr.

ROBINETT, NIKOLA; Newark Jr Sr HS; Newark, AR; (2); Church Yth Grp; Quiz Bowl; Tennis; FFA Treas Reprtr; UCA; Philoshpy.

ROBINS, NIKKI; Cabot HS; Cabot, AR; (2); Treas French Clb; Office Aide; High Hon Roll; Hon Roll; NHS; Flan Fest Univ AR Fayetteville; Dnatl Fr Exam 18th Pl St; AAAA East St Trk Meet Vol 95; Pre-Law.

ROBINSON, A SCOTT; Pine Bluff HS; Pine Bluff, AR; (3); Am Leg Boys St; Boy Scts; Church Yth Grp; Cmnty Wkr; French Clb; Key Clb; Acpl Chr; Chorus; School Musical; Cit Awd; Eagle Sct; All Region Choir; Seabrook YMCA, T-Ball Coach Vol 2 Summrs; Bus Mgmt.

ROBINSON, ABBI B; Evening Shade Schl; Evening Shade, AR; (3); 1/35; Pres Sec FBLA; VP Sec Natl Beta Clb; School Play; Pres Frsh Cls; Pres Soph Cls; Pres Jr Cls; VP Pres Stu Cncl; Var Bsktbl; Sftbl; NHS; Bsktbl 2-B East All-Conf Awd; Accntng.

ROBINSON, BRYAN W; Russellville Sr HS; Russellville, AR; (2); 137/300; FCA; Natl Beta Clb; Spanish Clb; Varsity Clb; Var Stat Bsktbl; Var Ftbl; Score Keeper; Stat Trk; Var Wt Lftg; Hon Roll; Wldlf; Outdrs; Frnds; Washington Univ; CPA.

ROBINSON, CASSANDRA; Parkin Jr Sr HS; Parkin, AR; (2); Church Yth Grp; FHA; FTA; Natl Beta Clb; Science Clb; Church Choir; Nwsp; Pres Frsh Cls; Rep Soph Cls; High Hon Roll; Home Ec Awd For Highest Average; His Awd For Civics & Amer His; AR ST U; Nrs Practioner; RN.

ROBINSON, COREY B; Amity Jr Sr HS; Amity, AR; (2); FHA; Natl FFA Org; Rep Frsh Cls; Rep Soph Cls; Hon Roll; Clark Cty Spelling Bee 6 Yrs; GATE; Henderson ST Univ; Wldlf Blgst.

ROBINSON, DAVID A; Pulaski Acad; Little Rock, AR; (2); Art Clb; Church Yth Grp; Cmnty Wkr; Debate Tm; FCA; German Clb; Model UN; Natl Beta Clb; Chorus; School Musical; Best Rep Of A Nation In Model UN His Day Wnnr/2 Awds Sec Cncl; Senate Page 96-; Svc Trips Haiti/Hond; Pol Sci/Govt/Law.

ROBINSON, EMILY; Rison HS; Rison, AR; (1); Church Yth Grp; Cmnty Wkr; FCA; FHA; GAA; Natl Beta Clb; Teachers Aide; Bsktbl; Chrldng; Hon Roll; AEGIS.

ROBINSON, EMILY; Vlly Springs HS; Harrison, AR; (3); Debate Tm; Key Clb; Letterman Clb; Pep Clb; Red Cross Aide; SADD; Varsity Clb; Band; Church Choir; Mrchg Band; Stu Of Mnth.

ROBINSON, HEATHER; Magnet Cove HS; Malvern, AR; (4); 5/45; Pres Church Yth Grp; FCA; Natl Beta Clb; Pres Spanish Clb; Chorus; Rep Stu Cncl; Chrldng; Sftbl; High Hon Roll; Hon Roll; All-Amer Schlr Awd; Henderson ST U; Psych.

ROBINSON, JENNIFER; Arkansas City Schl; Arkansas City, AR; (3); Church Yth Grp; FHA; Girl Scts; Math Clb; Pep Clb; Science Clb; Speech Tm; Church Choir; Sec Rep Jr Cls; Sec Rep Stu Cncl; 1st Bapt Chrch; Yth Fraternity; Criminal Justice.

ROBINSON, KATHRYN E; Sylvan Hills HS; Sherwood, AR; (2); 35/261; Mu Alpha Theta; Natl Beta Clb; Spanish Clb; Band; Hon Roll; Jr NHS; NHS; Ntl Merit Ltr; Psych.

ROBINSON, KATIE L; Arkansas Bapt Schl; Keo, AR; (4); 19/34; Church Yth Grp; VP French Clb; JA; Teachers Aide; School Play; Stat Bsbl; Hon Roll; Lonoke Cnty Sr Rodeo Queen; AR St Univ; Anml Sci.

ROBINSON, KIMBERLY K; Fouke Jr Sr HS; Fouke, AR; (2); 5/69; FBLA; Natl FFA Org; Office Aide; Pep Clb; Sec Frsh Cls; Rep Soph Cls; Chrldng; Hon Roll; Univ Of AR; Phys Thpy.

ROBINSON, LA PRIA; Mayflower HS; Mayflower, AR; (1); Church Yth Grp; GAA; Drill Tm; Bsktbl; Chrldng; Sftbl; Trk; High Hon Roll; Hon Roll; Law/Mdcl.

ROBINSON, LATARA T; Stuttgart Sr HS; Stuttgart, AR; (3); Church Yth Grp; DECA; FHA; Teachers Aide; Church Choir; High Hon Roll; UALR; Nrsng.

ROBINSON, LESHIA E; Mansfield Jr Sr HS; Mansfield, AR; (4); 5/60; Pres Rep Drama Clb; Intnl Clb; VP Library Aide; Natl Beta Clb; Pres Speech Tm; School Play; Rptr Nwsp; Cit Awd; High Hon Roll; Pres Acad Fit Awd; AR Tech U.

ROBINSON, MELISSA; Genoa Central HS; Texarkana, AR; (3); Church Yth Grp; FCA; FBLA; FTA; GAA; Model UN; Quiz Bowl; Spanish Clb; Yrbk; Sec Soph Cls; Nurses & Fine Arts Clbs; Med.

ROBINSON, MICHELLE; Humphrey Schl; Humphrey, AR; (4); 2/22; Am Leg Aux Girls St; Church Yth Grp; FBLA; FHA; Spanish Clb; VP Jr Cls; VP Sr Cls; Bsktbl; AR Tech U; Elem Ed.

ROBINSON, PHILLIP M; Catholic HS; Little Rock, AR; (2); U Of AR.

ROBINSON, RENEE E; Nemo Vista Jr Sr HS; Center Ridge, AR; (2); 1/37; FBLA; FHA; Girl Scts; Natl Beta Clb; Spanish Clb; Rptr Frsh Cls; Treas Soph Cls; Ofcr Stu Cncl; Bsktbl; High Hon Roll; Psych.

ROBINSON, RYAN P; Arkansas Sr HS; Texarkana, AR; (2); Church Yth Grp; Drama Clb; Quiz Bowl; Spanish Clb; JV Bsktbl; Med.

ROBINSON, SHA NEISHA E; Star City HS; Star City, AR; (2); Church Yth Grp; 4-H; Library Aide; Natl Beta Clb; Natl FFA Org; Pep Clb; Science Clb; Band; Church Choir; Mrchg Band; UCA; Data Engr.

ROBINSON, SHANTIQUE S; Forrest City HS; Forrest City, AR; (2); FHA; Spanish Clb; Church Choir; High Hon Roll; VP FHA; Pre-Med.

ROBINSON, SHERITA; Parkin Jr Sr HS; Parkin, AR; (1); Church Yth Grp; FHA; GAA; Natl Beta Clb; Chorus; Ofcr Frsh Cls; Ofcr Stu Cncl; Bsktbl; High Hon Roll; Ntl Merit Ltr; Frgn Lang Clb; Jr Beta Pres; MIT MA; Sci Engr.

ROBINSON JR, SPENCER F; Pine Bluff HS; Pine Bluff, AR; (4); 26/440; Am Leg Boys St; Church Yth Grp; Cmnty Wkr; FHA; Spanish Clb; Pres Acpl Chr; Chorus; Church Choir; L Tennis; Cit Awd; Pres Acapella Choir; Pres HERO; AR-DAVISCUP Tnns Team; USTA Dev Tnns Team; Natl Jr Hnr Soc Mem; U Of AR-FAYETTEVILLE; Pre-Med.

ROBINSON, TERESA; Parkin Jr Sr HS; Parkin, AR; (2); FHA; Natl Beta Clb; Science Clb; Chorus; Church Choir; Ofcr Jr Cls; Ofcr Stu Cncl; Bsktbl; Chrldng; Trk; Frgn Lang Clb:var Choir; Acctg.

ROBINSON, TIFFANY L; Southside HS; Batesville, AR; (1); Church Yth Grp; Cmnty Wkr; 4-H; Key Clb; Natl Beta Clb; Science Clb; Teachers Aide; Chorus; Color Guard; Chrldng; Interpreter For Deaf.

ROBINSON, TONY W; Fouke Jr Sr HS; Fouke, AR; (3); 15/82; Natl FFA Org; Science Clb; Spanish Clb; Ofcr Bsbl; L Ftbl; Wt Lftg; Pres Acad Fit Awd; Duck Hunting; Fishing; Automotive Mechanic; Mech Engr.

ROBINSON, TRIP F; Arkansas Bapt Schl; Maumelle, AR; (3); Pres Church Yth Grp; FCA; Spanish Clb; Chorus; Church Choir; School Play; Yrbk; Var L Socr; Hon Roll; Sccr Tm Cch & Gm Ref.

ROBISON, NEELY A; Sylvan Hills HS; Sherwood, AR; (4); 69/230; FBLA; Key Clb; Spanish Clb; Teachers Aide; Var Chrldng; Hon Roll; Merit Amer His/Drama.

ROBY, DAWN; Horace Mann Magnet HS; Little Rock, AR; (1); Church Yth Grp; Dance Clb; Church Choir; School Musical; Yrbk; Bsktbl; Chrldng; Trk; Hon Roll; Pres Acad Fit Awd; Yrbk Cutest.

ROCOLE, CANDY I; Deer Jr Sr HS; Deer, AR; (3); English Clb; Rptr FBLA; FHA; Latin Clb; Math Clb; Natl FFA Org; Science Clb; Varsity Clb; Ofcr Soph Cls; Sec Jr Cls; NACTC; Bus Mgmt.

ROCOLE, TRACY A; Deer Jr Sr HS; Deer, AR; (3); 10/28; Cmnty Wkr; Capt FCA; Hist Sec FBLA; Rptr FHA; Latin Clb; Hist Sec Natl FFA Org; Chorus; Treas Jr Cls; Sec Pres Stu Cncl; JV Var Bsktbl; Show Choir; Collecting Antiques; Swimming; Camping; Future North AR Pioneer Scholar; Aegis Prgm; Coll Of The Ozarks; Wldlfe Mngm.

RODGERS, AMBER C; Crossett Sr HS; Crossett, AR; (2); Church Yth Grp; FCA; 4-H; FTA; Natl Beta Clb; Service Clb; Sec Soph Cls; Ofcr Stu Cncl; Tennis; 4-H Awd; AR HS Rodeo Assn; Stdnt Christ; Intl Pro Rodeo Assn; Dental Hygiene.

RODGERS, ANGELA; Woodlawn Schl; Rison, AR; (2); FCA; FHA; HOBY; Natl Beta Clb; Quiz Bowl; Pres Frsh Cls; Capt Bsktbl; Capt Chrldng; High Hon Roll; Pres Acad Fit Awd; Cch Pee Wee Bsktbl & Chrldrs; Bsktbl Dist Chmps; Gdnc Cnslr.

RODGERS, BOBBY L; Armorel HS; Blytheville, AR; (2); Church Yth Grp; FBLA; Natl FFA Org; Science Clb; Spanish Clb; School Play; Rep Jr Cls; Var Bsbl; Hon Roll; Prfct Atten Awd; PE.

RODGERS, G W BRANDON; Dewitt HS; Stuttgart, AR; (3); 32/104; Am Leg Boys St; VP Pres Church Yth Grp; FCA; French Clb; FBLA; FTA; HOBY; Natl Beta Clb; Treas Science Clb; Church Choir; 1st Plc Sci Fair; Natl Engl Merit Awd; Natl Ldshp And Svc Awd.

RODGERS, LISA A; Greenbrier HS; Greenbrier, AR; (3); 1/175; Church Yth Grp; Computer Clb; Drama Clb; FBLA; Natl Beta Clb; Band; Jazz Band; Mrchg Band; School Play; Yrbk; Water Ed Team; AR Yth Orch; Rgn VII Jr & Sr Band; Msc Dir.

RODGERS, MATT; Brinkley HS; Brinkley, AR; (2); Church Yth Grp; Drama Clb; Quiz Bowl; School Play; Stage Crew; Rptr Nwsp; Hon Roll; Jr NHS; NHS; Pres Acad Fit Awd.

RODGERS, MICHAEL W; West Memphis Christian Schl; Earle, AR; (2); Church Yth Grp; Rep Stu Cncl; L Bsktbl; L Ftbl; L Trk; Wt Lftg; Hon Roll; Pres Acad Fit Awd; U Of AR.

RODGERS, MISTY D; Yellville Summit HS; Yellville, AR; (2); FBLA; Natl Beta Clb; Band; Bsktbl; Hon Roll.

RODGERS, SUSANNAH; Dewitt HS; Stuttgart, AR; (2); Church Yth Grp; Cmnty Wkr; FCA; FBLA; GAA; Rptr Science Clb; Varsity Clb; Bsktbl; Chrldng; Hon Roll.

RODGERS, TINA; Fountain Lake HS; Hot Springs, AR; (2); FCA; FHA; Key Clb; Natl Beta Clb; Spanish Clb; Chorus; Stage Crew; Yrbk; Capt Chrldng; Hon Roll; Mixed Ensmble; Hmcmng Crt; Tchr.

ROE, BECKY L; Jessieville HS; Jessieville, AR; (2); Church Yth Grp; Cmnty Wkr; FHA; Speech Tm; Teachers Aide; Band; Chorus; Mrchg Band; Variety Show; Rep Stu Cncl; Hnrs Ensemble; Clinical Psycht.

ROE, JASON; Pleasant View Schl; Mulberry, AR; (2); 1/22; Church Yth Grp; Drama Clb; FBLA; Natl Beta Clb; Natl FFA Org; Quiz Bowl; Rep Stu Cncl; Bsktbl; Trk; High Hon Roll.

ROE, JUSTIN H; Fayetteville Sr HS; Fayetteville, AR; (4); Boy Scts; Latin Clb; Orch; Swing Chorus; Lit Mag; Var L Ftbl; NHS; Ntl Merit Schol; Quiz Bowl; Acpl Chr; Govs Schl; Golden Dragon Kung Fu; Marine Zoology.

ROE, REGINA; Green Forest Jr Sr HS; Green Forest, AR; (4); 14/69; Drama Clb; FCA; French Clb; FBLA; Natl Beta Clb; SADD; School Play; Yrbk; Capt Bsktbl; Cit Awd; Bsktbl Hmcmg Maid; Jr Miss 3rd Pl; Miss G F HS; Prom Svr/Comm; Sec Grd Cvl War React; Grad Atdnt; Coll Ozarks; Bus/Ed.

ROE, TRAVIS; Pleasant View Schl; Mulberry, AR; (1); Church Yth Grp; Cmnty Wkr; Drama Clb; FBLA; Math Tm; Natl Beta Clb; Natl FFA Org; Quiz Bowl; Science Clb; School Play; 2nd Pl Cty Spllng Bee; Med.

ROEWE, JEREMY A; Magnolia HS; Magnolia, AR; (4); Church Yth Grp; FCA; French Clb; FBLA; Mu Alpha Theta; Science Clb; Ftbl; Wt Lftg; High Hon Roll; NHS; Lyon Coll; Bus.

ROFKAHR, LATISHA D; Altus Denning HS; Ozark, AR; (4); 2/17; Rep FBLA; German Clb; Pres VP Natl Beta Clb; Yrbk; Pres Jr Cls; VP Stu Cncl; Var Capt Bsktbl; Var Capt Sftbl; High Hon Roll; Hon Roll; U Of Cntrl AR.

ROGERS, ALAN M; Abundant Life Schools; Jacksonville, AR; (3); Church Yth Grp; Chorus; Sec Jr Cls; JV Co-Capt Bsktbl; Hon Roll; NHS; Ntl Merit Ltr; Distngd Chrstn HS Stu; Biblical Stud.

ROGERS, AMANDA; Hazen Jr Sr HS; Hazen, AR; (1); FHA; Natl Beta Clb; Rptr Frsh Cls; Bsktbl; Capt Chrldng; Trk; Hon Roll; Prfct Atten Awd; GATE; Jr High Hmcmng Queen; Spch Pathlgy.

ROGERS, AMY M; Waldo Jr Sr HS; Waldo, AR; (3); 5/32; Church Yth Grp; FBLA; Spanish Clb; Church Choir; Nwsp; Yrbk; Rptr Stu Cncl; Hon Roll; S AR Univ; Jrnlsm.

ROGERS, ANDY; Hazen Jr Sr HS; Hazen, AR; (3); 6/43; Church Yth Grp; Cmnty Wkr; FBLA; VP FHA; FTA; Natl Beta Clb; Pres Frsh Cls; Pres Soph Cls; Rep Stu Cncl; Var Ftbl; Jr Stu Yr; Ftbl, Bsktbl MVP Jr HS; Amer Lgn Bsbl MVP; Law.

ROGERS, BRIAN JARED; Greene Co Tech HS; Paragould, AR; (3); Am Leg Boys St; Church Yth Grp; Drama Clb; Quiz Bowl; Band; Jazz Band; Mrchg Band; Orch; School Musical; School Play; Univ Of AR; Pre-Med.

ROGERS, CARRIE L; Springdale Sr HS; Springdale, AR; (3); FBLA; GAA; Varsity Clb; Chorus; Bsktbl; Powder Puff Ftbl; High Hon Roll; Hon Roll; Jr NHS; NHS; AAU Bsktbl; U KY; Phys Thrpy.

ROGERS, CHRISTINA; Blevins HS; Blevins, AR; (3); Pres Church Yth Grp; Treas CAP; Treas FBLA; Girl Scts; Natl Beta Clb; Natl FFA Org; Office Aide; Band; Chorus; Church Choir; AR Girl ST Rep.

ROGERS, CHRISTOPHER; Sprindale HS; Springdale, AR; (4); 53/481; Computer Clb; FBLA; Bsktbl; Hon Roll; Jr NHS; NHS; Pres Acad Fit Awd; Ole Miss; Elec Engrng.

ROGERS, CHRISTOPHER P; Des Arc Jr Sr HS; Des Arc, AR; (2); FCA; Am Leg Aux Girls St; Natl FFA Org; Teachers Aide; Var Bsbl; Var Bsktbl; Var Ftbl; Var Wt Lftg; Bus.

ROGERS, CRISTY D; Booneville Jr Sr HS; Booneville, AR; (2); 7/99; FCA; French Clb; FBLA; Natl Beta Clb; Science Clb; Rep Stu Cncl; Hon Roll.

ROGERS, DIXIE; Jonesboro HS; Jonesboro, AR; (4); 4/252; VP Church Yth Grp; Cmnty Wkr; Drama Clb; French Clb; FBLA; Key Clb; Mu Alpha Theta; Natl Beta Clb; Thesps; Chorus; AR Governors Schl; U Of AR; Corp Law.

ROGERS, DREW; Magnolia HS; Magnolia, AR; (2); Church Yth Grp; French Clb; Quiz Bowl; Teachers Aide; Band; Mrchg Band; Tennis; High Hon Roll; Hon Roll.

ROGERS, ELIZABETH L; Southside HS; Batesville, AR; (3); Cmnty Wkr; FBLA; Key Clb; Natl Beta Clb; Office Aide; Science Clb; Spanish Clb; Yrbk; Rep Stu Cncl; Bsktbl; U Of Cntrl AR; Pre-Law.

ROGERS, JENNIFER M; Taylor HS; Taylor, AR; (3); 8/23; Sec FBLA; FHA; Natl FFA Org; VP Stu Cncl; Bsktbl; Sftbl; Hon Roll; Church Yth Grp; FCA; Chorus; All-Dual St; All-Dist Bsktbl; All-Dist Sftbl; LA Tech Univ; Child Psych.

ROGERS, KASSIE; Foreman Jr Sr HS; Foreman, AR; (2); 1/35; Church Yth Grp; FTA; Quiz Bowl; Spanish Clb; VP SADD; Church Choir; Rep Stu Cncl; Var Bsktbl; Var Chrldng; Powder Puff Ftbl; Kids In Christ; Univ AK Fayetville; PT.

ROGERS, KATE M; Yellville Summit HS; Yellville, AR; (3); 2/75; VP Art Clb; Cmnty Wkr; Drama Clb; Girl Scts; Band; Jazz Band; Mrchg Band; Rptr Nwsp; Sftbl; High Hon Roll; Natl Young Ldrs Conf Washington DC; Comp Sci.

ROGERS, KATIE; Searcy HS; Searcy, AR; (3); Key Clb; Natl Beta Clb; Rep Frsh Cls; Rep Sr Cls; Rep Stu Cncl; Church Yth Grp; Cmnty Wkr; Drama Clb; FCA; FBLA; Natl Forum Law/Cnsttn; DCYM; CCYM; Mdrgls; U Of AR; Pre-Law/Psych.

ROGERS, MICHAEL; Lead Hill Schl; Yellville, AR; (3); 2/20; Church Yth Grp; FCA; Rep Stu Cncl; Hon Roll; Sal; Bus Mgmt.

ROGERS, MINDY; North Little Rock Hs-West; North Little Rock, AR; (4); 1/575; Church Yth Grp; Pres German Clb; Key Clb; Mu Alpha Theta; Natl Beta Clb; School Musical; Pres Sr Cls; Capt Chrldng; NHS; Ntl Merit Ltr; Duke U; Bio.

ROGERS, NICHOLAS L; North Little Rock HS; North Little Rock, AR; (2); Art Clb; Drama Clb; Natl Beta Clb; Speech Tm; School Musical; School Play; Nwsp; Lit Mag; Ofcr Frsh Cls; Ofcr Soph Cls; Duke Univ Tip; Theater Schl; Theater/Film.

ROGERS, RANDY P; Dequeen HS; De Queen, AR; (3); 60/120; Church Yth Grp; Natl FFA Org; Band; Mrchg Band; Hon Roll; Electrician; Forester.

ROGERS, SARAH; Arkansas Bapt Schl; Little Rock, AR; (3); Church Yth Grp; FBLA; Natl Beta Clb; Spanish Clb; Church Choir; School Play; Nwsp; Yrbk; Stat Socr; High Hon Roll; Frgn Missions Clb; Piano Lessons 9 Yrs; Engl.

ROGERS, SELYNNA; Mc Rae Schl; Mc Rae, AR; (2); 2/30; FHA; Sec Soph Cls; Sec Stu Cncl; Mgr(s); Sftbl; Trk; Hon Roll; Natl Assn Stu Concl.

ROGERS, VASHONDA; Oak Grove HS; Maumelle, AR; (1); Church Yth Grp; FHA; Letterman Clb; Band; Sec Frsh Cls; Var Chrldng; Hon Roll; Edtr/Pub Chrch Nwslttr; U Of AR; Lwyr.

ROGINSON, STACIE J; Rogers HS; Rogers, AR; (3); 4/605; Cmnty Wkr; Ofcr Debate Tm; NFL; Pres Science Clb; Ofcr Speech Tm; Ed Lit Mag; Crs Cntry; NHS; Drama Clb; FBLA; Chrstns In Action Pres; ACE Acad Cmptn Team; LA ST Univ; Wildlife Bio.

ROGNE, LISA; Southside HS; Fort Smith, AR; (1); Speech Tm; School Play; Ed Nwsp; Rep Stu Cncl; Var Chrldng; High Hon Roll; Hon Roll; Eng.

ROLAND, KARI; Southside HS; Fort Smith, AR; (4); Church Yth Grp; Band; Mrchg Band; High Hon Roll; Sthrn Nazarene U; Elem Ed.

ROLANDO, GUILLERMO F; Shiloh Christian Schools; Springdale, AR; (2); Church Yth Grp; FCA; Band; Mrchg Band; Vllybl; NHS; Pres Acad Fit Awd; Baylor Univ.

ROLETT, KASSIA; North Little Rock Hs-East; North Little Rock, AR; (3); 57/567; Church Yth Grp; FBLA; Hosp Aide; JA; Mu Alpha Theta; Natl Beta Clb; School Musical; School Play; Stage Crew; Cit Awd; UCA; Dlvry Room.

ROLF, MEREDITH L; Conway Sr HS; Conway, AR; (4); 7/530; FCA; French Clb; FBLA; German Clb; Intnl Clb; Letterman Clb; Natl Beta Clb; Quiz Bowl; Ed Nwsp; Var Bsktbl; Attnd Fulbright Schl Of Pub Affairs 95; U Of Dallas.

ROLLAND, KIM; East Poinsett Sr HS; Lepanto, AR; (4); 8/53; FBLA; FHA; Natl FFA Org; Office Aide; Teachers Aide; Yrbk; Ofcr Frsh Cls; L Tennis; Hon Roll; Jr NHS; Hmcmng Ct; Ducks Unltd; Pwdr Puff Ftbll; Nrs Ansthslgy.

ROMINE, JACQUELINE N; Vilonia HS; Vilonia, AR; (3); Art Clb; Church Yth Grp; Office Aide; Spanish Clb; Teachers Aide; Rep Frsh Cls; Rep Soph Cls; Rep Jr Cls; Rep Stu Cncl; Bsktbl; Art.

RONE, SHANNON L; Glen Rose HS; Traskwood, AR; (3); 9/69; FBLA; Spanish Clb; Teachers Aide; Band; Chorus; Drm Mjr(t); Mrchg Band; Pep Band; Variety Show; Hon Roll; Tlnt Srch; U Of AR Monticello; Music Ed.

RONSICK, ANNA; Mc Rae Schl; Mc Rae, AR; (1); Church Yth Grp; Natl Beta Clb; Quiz Bowl; Nwsp; High Hon Roll; Ntl Merit Ltr; GATE.

RONSICK, SARAH; Mc Rae Schl; Mc Rae, AR; (3); Am Leg Aux Girls St; Natl Beta Clb; Quiz Bowl; Hon Roll; Ntl Merit Ltr; Rssn Clb; GATE; Stdnt Mo Awd.

ROOKE, CATHERINA L; Central Sr HS; Little Rock, AR; (4); 17/428; Cmnty Wkr; Co-Capt Debate Tm; Drama Clb; Intnl Clb; Sec Mu Alpha Theta; Natl Beta Clb; VP Spanish Clb; Cit Awd; High Hon Roll; Sec NHS; Accpt No Bndrys; Dbt St Chmpn; Lttl Rck Schl Dist Dbt Awd; Loyola U Of Chicago; Bio.

ROOKS, TRAVIS J; Booneville Jr Sr HS; Booneville, AR; (2); Church Yth Grp; Spanish Clb; Band; Church Choir; Jazz Band; Mrchg Band; Pep Band; High Hon Roll; Hon Roll; Prfct Atten Awd; Natl Young Ldrs Conf DC; Cnslng; Psych.

ROONEY, THOMAS P; Catholic HS; North Little Rock, AR; (2); 29/250; ROTC; Bsktbl; Golf; Socr; High Hon Roll; Hon Roll; Outstdng Cadet ROTC 95-; VFW Loyalty Awd; ODP ST Select Soccer; U Of IN; Aerospace/Arntcl Engr.

ROOT, JAMIE L; Pea Ridge HS; Pea Ridge, AR; (3); 8/75; Church Yth Grp; FBLA; Spanish Clb; Hon Roll; NHS.

ROPER, NICK; Charleston HS; Charleston, AR; (1); 8/82; Church Yth Grp; FBLA; Ofcr Frsh Cls; Hon Roll; Westark CC.

ROREX, ENID C; Black Rock Jr Sr HS; Imboden, AR; (1); 7/50; Church Yth Grp; Sec FBLA; FHA; Treas Natl Beta Clb; Chorus; Church Choir; School Musical; Sec Stu Cncl; Capt Bsktbl; Hon Roll; Bsktbl Hnrs All Dist; Hustle & Offense Awds; FHA Cooking With Rice Cont 1st Pl; Multi-Yr Listee; U Of AR.

RORIE, JENNIFER D; Fountain Lake Jr Sr HS; Hot Springs Natio, AR; (3); 23/64; Church Yth Grp; Drama Clb; Mrchg Band; Rptr Rep Stu Cncl; Bsktbl; Vllybl; Hon Roll; Campt Of Flag Line; Chmbr Of Cmmrc Red For City Hot Springs To Japan; Stdnt Chrstn Assn Treas; U Of Central AR; Pol Sci.

ROSALEJOS, KATHERINE; Weiner HS; Fisher, AR; (2); Art Clb; FBLA; FHA; Science Clb; Spanish Clb; Tennis; Hon Roll.

ROSE, CHUCK; Fayetteville Sr HS; Fayetteville, AR; (3); Ofcr Stu Cncl; Hon Roll; Army Reservist; U Of AR; Oceanography.

ROSE, CRYSTAL; Murfreesboro HS; Murfreesboro, AR; (3); Art Clb; Church Yth Grp; Rptr FBLA; FHA; Natl Beta Clb; Science Clb; Spanish Clb; Band; Mrchg Band; School Musical; CHAMPS.

ROSE, HILLIARD J; Fayetteville Sr HS; Fayetteville, AR; (2); Boy Scts; Church Yth Grp; Band; Mrchg Band; Orch; Pep Band; Ofcr Stu Cncl; Trk; High Hon Roll; Hon Roll; Peer Hlpr.

ROSE, LATOYA M; Walker Schl; Magnolia, AR; (2); Drama Clb; FBLA; FTA; Band; Pres Soph Cls; Sec Stu Cncl; Var Capt Bsktbl; Trk; Hon Roll; Yth Of Month 96.

ROSE, MISTY; Hatfield Schl; Hatfield, AR; (1); 10/47; Church Yth Grp; Drama Clb; FCA; FBLA; FHA; GAA; Quiz Bowl; Church Choir; Gftd/Tlntd Pgm; Chrch Tlnt Expo; Spch Thrpy.

ROSE, PEYTON; Central Sr HS; Greenbrier, AR; (3); 75/540; Art Clb; Debate Tm; FBLA; Latin Clb; Natl Beta Clb; Science Clb; Capt L Bsktbl; High Hon Roll; NHS; Pres Acad Fit Awd; West Point Military Acad; Law.

ROSE, ROGER W; Ashdown Sr HS; Ashdown, AR; (3); Church Yth Grp; Cmnty Wkr; Natl Beta Clb; Spanish Clb; Varsity Clb; Var L Bsbl; Var L Ftbl; Wt Lftg; NHS.

ROSE, SHARON; Hackett Schl; Fort Smith, AR; (4); 1/40; Treas Church Yth Grp; Pres FBLA; Pres FHA; VP Soph Cls; Treas Jr Cls; Treas Stu Cncl; Co-Capt Chrldng; High Hon Roll; Pres NHS; Val; Med.

ROSE, TIMOTHY G; Valley Springs Schl; Valley Springs, AR; (2); Acpl Chr; Band; Chorus; Mrchg Band; Orch; Pep Band; Hon Roll; Prfct Atten Awd; Sr Schltc Pgm; AR Tech U; Music.

ROSEBERRY, RANDI K; Sheridan Sr HS; Sheridan, AR; (3); 38/263; Yrbk; Hon Roll; Jr NHS; Washington Jrnlsm Conf; Psych.

ROSHTO, DAVID M; Russellville Sr HS; Russellville, AR; (3); Church Yth Grp; FCA; Letterman Clb; Natl Beta Clb; Chorus; Church Choir; VP Sr Cls; Var Ftbl; Wt Lftg; Hon Roll; Natl ABA Teen Discvry 1st Pl 2 Yrs; AR Tech Univ.

ROSS, CHARNELLE; J A Fair Sr HS; Little Rock, AR; (4); 39/300; Drill Tm; Yrbk; VP Sr Cls; Hon Roll; NHS; Pres Acad Fit Awd; Peer Facilitators; Ladies Clb; Ring Staff; Clark Atlanta Univ; Bus Mgmt.

ROSS, GARY L; Russellville Sr HS; Russellville, AR; (3); Church Yth Grp; Drama Clb; Teachers Aide; Hon Roll; YABA; Forensic Team; His Tchr.

ROSS, JAMES E; Arkansas Sr HS; Texarkana, AR; (2); Spanish Clb; Bsktbl; Ftbl; Trk; Hon Roll.

ROSS, JOSHUA R; Fayetteville Sr HS; Fayetteville, AR; (2); Science Clb; Band; Mrchg Band; High Hon Roll; Cmptr Sci.

ROSS, JULIE; Sulphur Rock Schl; Sulphur Rock, AR; (1); 1/20; FHA; Key Clb; Natl Beta Clb; Natl FFA Org; Quiz Bowl; Teachers Aide; Rep Frsh Cls; Ofcr Stu Cncl; Capt Bsktbl; Trk.

ROSS, KAYSHA; Prairie Grove HS; Prairie Grove, AR; (2); 9/87; Church Yth Grp; Drama Clb; Library Aide; SADD; Church Choir; High Hon Roll; Jr NHS; Chrch Mscl Ply; Art Instrctn Schl Cont Cmptn; Intr Dsgn.

ROSS, LAURA; Sulphur Rock Schl; Sulphur Rock, AR; (4); 1/20; Am Leg Aux Girls St; HOBY; Key Clb; Yrbk; Sec Jr Cls; Pres Sr Cls; Trk; DAR Awd; High Hon Roll; Val; U Of Cntrl AR; Acctng.

ROSS, MICHELLE; Prairie Grove HS; Prairie Grove, AR; (3); Treas FHA; Spanish Clb; Jazz Band; Mrchg Band; Orch; Pep Band; Band; Color Guard; Cit Awd; High Hon Roll; Cmptr Wrtng Essay Tlnt Srch Wnnr; U Of AR; Elem Ed/Msc Thrpy.

ROSS, PHILIP; Arkadelphia Sr HS; Arkadelphia, AR; (3); 16/165; VP Church Yth Grp; HOBY; Letterman Clb; Natl Beta Clb; Ed Nwsp; Treas Jr Cls; Rep Stu Cncl; Var Swmmng; Hon Roll; Pres Acad Fit Awd; Future Prblm Slvrs St Finals; Ambssdr HOBY Wrld Conf 95; US House Rep Page 95-96; U Of NC; Pre-Law.

ROSS, RACHEL; Pine Bluff HS; Pine Bluff, AR; (3); Church Yth Grp; FBLA; Hosp Aide; Spanish Clb; Band; Lit Mag; Rep Frsh Cls; Pom Pon; Trk; Jr NHS; IMPRESS; PRIDE; Robeys Angels; U Of Pine Bluff.

ROSS, SHUWANA M; Elaine Jr Sr HS; Elaine, AR; (3); Art Clb; GAA; Bsktbl; Cit Awd.

ROSS, SUSAN; Springdale Sr HS; Springdale, AR; (4); 18/486; Church Yth Grp; FCA; Teachers Aide; Var L Bsktbl; Var L Trk; Cit Awd; High Hon Roll; Jr NHS; NHS; Pres Acad Fit Awd; HOSA; Yth For Christ; Eng Stu Of Yr; Phy Thrpst.

ROSS, TYRONDA; Stephens Jr Sr HS; Camden, AR; (3); FBLA; GAA; School Play; Bsktbl; Hon Roll; NHS; Prfct Atten Awd; Henderson ST U; Nrsng.

ROSSMAN, LESLEY; Clarksville HS; Clarksville, AR; (1); Church Yth Grp; Varsity Clb; Church Choir; Ofcr Frsh Cls; Chrldng; Gym; Trk; Vllybl; Cit Awd; Hon Roll; Prtnrs Chrst; FCA; PRIDE Pres; Vet.

ROSSON, BARBARA A; Corning HS; Success, AR; (3); #7 in class; FBLA; FHA; High Hon Roll; Hon Roll; Jr NHS; Ntl Merit Ltr; Pres Acad Fit Awd; Odyssey Of Mind Wrld Fnlsts; Pre-Law.

ROSSON, DAVID E; Corning HS; Success, AR; (3); Church Yth Grp; Bsktbl; Hon Roll.

ROSSWORN, TAMARA L; Parkview Arts-Science HS; North Little Rock, AR; (2); Drama Clb; French Clb; Church Choir; School Play; Chrldng; Hon Roll; Geomtry Hnrs Awrd; Dnc Co AR Yth Ballet; Fayette U Of Ar; Pscyh.

ROSTAN, AMANDA Y; Fountain Lake Jr Sr HS; Hot Springs Natio, AR; (2); #2 in class; Church Yth Grp; Natl Beta Clb; Natl FFA Org; Quiz Bowl; Cit Awd; DAR Awd; High Hon Roll; Hon Roll; Prfct Atten Awd; Pres Acad Fit Awd; SCA Sec 94-95.

ROTALSKY III, JOHN S; Hot Springs HS; Hot Springs Natio, AR; (2); Boy Scts; Chess Clb; Church Yth Grp; FBLA; Quiz Bowl; ROTC; Color Guard; Drill Tm; Ftbl; Cit Awd; ACE-GFTD & Tlntd Dogs; RN; Nuclear Physics.

ROTHERT, CAROLINE A; Lakeside HS; Hot Springs, AR; (4); 1/128; Church Yth Grp; Cmnty Wkr; FCA; French Clb; Hosp Aide; Math Clb; Mu Alpha Theta; Quiz Bowl; Sec Treas Science Clb; Pres Spanish Clb; AR Govs Schl; OM; Ftr Prblm Slvng.

ROTTON, HANNAH E; Rogers HS; Rogers, AR; (3); Art Clb; Church Yth Grp; Cmnty Wkr; FCA; French Clb; FBLA; Rptr Nwsp; Hon Roll.

ROUGHTON, BRYAN S; Springdale Sr HS; Springdale, AR; (2); Art Clb; Boy Scts; Chorus; Jr NHS; Eagle Sct.

ROUNDS, CHRIS; Sulphur Rock Schl; Batesville, AR; (3); 5/19; Key Clb; Natl Beta Clb; Chorus; School Play; Rep Jr Cls; Var Bsktbl; Hon Roll; Prfct Atten Awd; FFA.

ROUNDS, GARY S; Southside HS; Batesville, AR; (2); Key Clb; Natl Beta Clb; Natl FFA Org; Rep Soph Cls; Bsktbl; Hon Roll.

ROUSE, CHASTITY M; Trumann HS; Trumann, AR; (2); HOBY; Math Clb; VP Spanish Clb; VP Soph Cls; AR ST Univ.

ROUSE, ERICK S; Gosnell Jr Sr HS; Blytheville, AR; (1); Church Yth Grp; Natl FFA Org; Ofcr Bsbl; Bsktbl; Ftbl; Hon Roll; AR ST Univ.

ROWE, ELIZABETH A; Hot Springs HS; Hot Springs, AR; (2); FBLA; Band; School Musical; Pom Pon; High Hon Roll.

ROWE, LISA M; Arkansas Sr HS; Texarkana, AR; (2); Church Yth Grp; Dance Clb; Drama Clb; 4-H; French Clb; Spanish Clb; Drill Tm; Chrldng; Hon Roll; Ntl Merit Ltr; Teach Swmmng Lssns; Vlntr Boy Sct Camps; U Of AR; Pedtrcn.

ROWE, MARICIA; Camden Fairview HS; Camden, AR; (2); Sec Treas Church Yth Grp; Drama Clb; Natl Beta Clb; Flag Corp; Swing Chorus; JV Var Chrldng; L Gym; Hon Roll; Teachers Aide; Thesps; Anchor Clb; All-Amer Chrldng Squad.

ROWE, MELANIE L; Hope HS; Hope, AR; (3); 1/230; Am Leg Aux Girls St; Church Yth Grp; Pres French Clb; FBLA; Natl Beta Clb; Band; Church Choir; Mrchg Band; Yrbk; Hist Stu Cncl; LIFE 1; Nike; Pre-Med.

ROWE, MICHELE; Lake Hamilton Jr HS; Hot Springs, AR; (1); Church Yth Grp; Natl Beta Clb; Spanish Clb; Teachers Aide; Band; Church Choir; Mrchg Band; Chrch Hnd Bll Choir & Drama Clb.

ROWELL, JACLYN A; Lake Hamilton Sr HS; Hot Springs, AR; (3); 7/258; Church Yth Grp; FBLA; Natl Beta Clb; Spanish Clb; High Hon Roll; Pres Acad Fit Awd; Wolf-Pride; Garland Cty CC; Radiolgy.

ROWELL, JOSEPH A; Cave City HS; Cave City, AR; (2); #11 in class; French Clb; Key Clb; Math Clb; Science Clb; Var Co-Capt Bsktbl; Hon Roll; Lyon Col Tnmt All Tnmt Tm In Bsktbll; All St Tnmt All Tnmt Tm In Bstkbll; Lyon Col; Sprtsmed.

ROWLAND, CHRISTINE L; Rivercrest HS; Dyess, AR; (2); Key Clb; ROTC; Hon Roll; NHS; Prfct Atten Awd; ROTC Cadet Of Yr 94-95; ROTC Ctznshp Awd 96; US Army Recruiting Command Awd 96; Armed Forces.

ROWLAND, EMILIE; Farmington Jr Sr HS; Fayetteville, AR; (1); 4-H; FBLA; Quiz Bowl; Band; Mrchg Band; Pep Band; Cit Awd; 4-H Awd; High Hon Roll; Jr NHS; U AR; Arts.

ROWLAND, JEANA S; Heritage Christian Schl; Benton, AR; (3); 4/8; Church Yth Grp; Church Choir; Rep Stu Cncl; Co-Capt Chrldng; Vllybl; Hon Roll; Jr NHS; Southern AR Univ; Elem Ed.

ROWLAND, JESSICA R; Booneville Jr Sr HS; Booneville, AR; (2); French Clb; Natl Beta Clb; Science Clb; Rptr Nwsp; Ed Yrbk; Ath Trnr; Gold Circle Awd Columbia Schlstc Press Assn; AR HS Press Assn 2 Superior Awds; Marine Bio.

ROWLAND, TRICIA; J A Fair Sr HS; Little Rock, AR; (2); Church Yth Grp; Spanish Clb; Chrldng; Cit Awd; Hon Roll; NHS; Ntl Merit Ltr; All Star Chrldng Sqd 8th Pl Natl Sr Div; Natl Sci Merit Awd; Bus.

ROWLETT, AMANDA M; Mt Vernon-Enola HS; Prim, AR; (2); FBLA; FHA; Spanish Clb; Chorus; Var Sftbl.

ROWLETT, ASHLEY; Monticello HS; Monticello, AR; (4); Am Leg Aux Girls St; Drama Clb; FBLA; FHA; Math Clb; Natl Beta Clb; Science Clb; SADD; Rep Jr Cls; Rep Sr Cls; Sndy Schl Sec; Elem Tutr; U Of AR Monticello; Resp Thrp.

ROWTON, HOLLY; Clay Co Central Jr Sr HS; Rector, AR; (4); 1/59; Pres Hist FBLA; Model UN; Rep Hist Thesps; Band; Chorus; Rptr Nwsp; Sec Stu Cncl; Var Chrldng; Pres Acad Fit Awd; Val; AR Gov Schl; UCA.

ROWTON, TAMMIE R; Buffalo Island Central HS; Monette, AR; (2); Church Yth Grp; Pres VP 4-H; Treas FBLA; FTA; Girl Scts; Rptr Science Clb; Band; School Play; 4-H Awd; NHS; 2 Bwlng Lgues Trophies; Girl Scouts Gold Awd; Fire Marshall; Pharm.

ROY, CHRISTY LYNN; Rogers HS; Pea Ridge, AR; (3); Church Yth Grp; Drama Clb; FCA; GAA; Varsity Clb; Acpl Chr; Rep Stu Cncl; Capt Socr; High Hon Roll; Hon Roll; WA U; Law/Pol Sci.

ROY, CRAIG M; Lincoln HS; Lincoln, AR; (1); Letterman Clb; Natl FFA Org; Ofcr Bsbl; L Bsktbl; Capt Ftbl; Cit Awd; Hon Roll; Prfct Atten Awd; U Of AR.

ROY, MELISSA; Lincoln HS; Lincoln, AR; (3); Art Clb; Natl FFA Org; Spanish Clb; Drill Tm; Var Bsktbl; Hon Roll; U Of AR Ed Tlnt Srch; Engl Hnrs; U Of AR; Phys Thpy.

ROYSTER, MARY; West Memphis Sr HS; West Memphis, AR; (2); French Clb; Mu Alpha Theta; Natl Beta Clb; Quiz Bowl; Science Clb; Yrbk; French Hon Soc; Tuskegee; RN.

RUCKER, TRACI R; Southside HS; Fort Smith, AR; (2); Church Yth Grp; Cmnty Wkr; Drama Clb; FCA; German Clb; Speech Tm; Chorus; Church Choir; School Musical; Stage Crew; Pre-Med.

RUDDER, AUBRY M; Lonoke Jr HS; Lonoke, AR; (1); GAA; Bsktbl; Chrldng; Hon Roll; Church Yth Grp; Dance Clb; FBLA; FHA; GAA; Office Aide; U Of AR; Dental Schl.

RUDDER, HEATHER B; Marshall HS; Marshall, AR; (1); 4-H; FHA; Natl Beta Clb; Quiz Bowl; Teachers Aide; Treas Soph Cls; Vllybl; Hon Roll; Mgr(s); Sci Fair Botany 3rd Plc; Dist Sci Fair Botany 2nd Plc; U Of AL Tuscaloosa; Pub Rel.

RUDDER, MATT; Atkins Schl; Atkins, AR; (2); 5/80; Cmnty Wkr; FBLA; Natl Beta Clb; Quiz Bowl; Science Clb; Spanish Clb; Band; Mrchg Band; Var L Bsbl; Var L Bsktbl; Bsbl All Conf Awd; Univ Of AR; Cmptr Sci.

RUDDER, MELISSA PATTON; Central Sr HS; Little Rock, AR; (4); 38/401; Am Leg Aux Girls St; Natl Beta Clb; Spanish Clb; Drill Tm; Ed Yrbk; Ofcr Sr Cls; Ofcr Stu Cncl; High Hon Roll; NHS; Accept No Boudaries Steering Comm; All Amer Schlr; Natl Tchrs Eng Awd; Randolph.

RUDICK, JASON W; Mc Crory Jr Sr HS; Mc Crory, AR; (3); 9/70; Am Leg Boys St; Church Yth Grp; FTA; Letterman Clb; Spanish Clb; SADD; Varsity Clb; Ofcr Bsbl; Ftbl; Powder Puff Ftbl; Natl Yng Ldrs Amer Conf; AR ST Univ; Ag.

RUDOLPH, SHERESE D; Huntsville HS; Fayetteville, AR; (2); 10/154; Church Yth Grp; Science Clb; Band; Color Guard; Flag Corp; Mrchg Band; High Hon Roll; U Of AR; Med.

RUESTOW, MICHELE M; Northside HS; Fort Smith, AR; (4); German Clb; Hosp Aide; Mu Alpha Theta; Office Aide; Teachers Aide; Band; Mrchg Band; Hon Roll; NHS; Cmnty Wkr; Ger Hnr Soc; TAPS; Westark.

RUFF, KEVIN L; Nemo Vista Jr Sr HS; Center Ridge, AR; (3); FBLA; FHA; Natl Beta Clb; Natl FFA Org; Spanish Clb; Sec Frsh Cls; Rep Soph Cls; Rep Stu Cncl; Hon Roll.

RUFFIN, C DE-JUAN; Pocahontas HS; Pocahontas, AR; (3); 1/147; Am Leg Boys St; Boy Scts; Church Yth Grp; Cmnty Wkr; Drama Clb; FBLA; Rptr Key Clb; Math Tm; Hist Natl Beta Clb; Quiz Bowl; Bsch Lmb Hnry Sci Awds; 1ST Afcn Amer Vldctrn; AR Govs Schl; Biomed Engrng.

RUNKLES, CATHY; Farmington Jr Sr HS; Fayetteville, AR; (1); Art Clb; French Clb; FBLA; FHA; Sec Frsh Cls; Capt Chrldng; Trk; NCA All-Amer Chrldr; TIP Nom; Stu Ambassador; U Of AR; Psych.

RUNNELLS, RHONDA L; Bryant Sr HS; Alexander, AR; (3); Church Yth Grp; French Clb; FBLA; Acpl Chr; Chorus; School Musical; Hon Roll; AR ST Univ; Phy Thrpst.

RUNNELS, REBECCA; Forrest City HS; Forrest City, AR; (3); Church Yth Grp; Cmnty Wkr; Mu Alpha Theta; Natl Beta Clb; Office Aide; Science Clb; Teachers Aide; Band; Church Choir; Mrchg Band; Hendrix; Child Psych/PT.

RUPP, NICK; Hot Springs HS; Hot Springs, AR; (4); #7 in class; Am Leg Boys St; FBLA; VP Natl Beta Clb; VICA; Band; VP Sr Cls; L Trk; Cit Awd; Treas NHS; Chess Clb; Univ Scho To UCA; U Of Cntrl AR; Mus Bus.

RUSH, LEONARD V; Biggers-Reyno HS; Biggers, AR; (2); FHA; Natl FFA Org; Spanish Clb; Hon Roll.

RUSH, MERINDA; Melbourne HS; Melbourne, AR; (2); Church Yth Grp; FCA; FBLA; Natl Beta Clb; Quiz Bowl; SADD; Ofcr Stu Cncl; Bsktbl; Sftbl; Hon Roll; AR ST Univ; Bus.

RUSH, RYAN; Arkansas Schl Math & Science; Violet Hill, AR; (3); Art Clb; Chess Clb; Church Yth Grp; FCA; 4-H; FBLA; FHA; HOBY; Mu Alpha Theta; Natl Beta Clb; Georgetown U; Linguistics.

RUSHER, BRAD; Abundant Life Schools; Sherwood, AR; (2); #9 in class; Church Yth Grp; Ofcr Bsbl; Bsktbl; Ftbl; Hon Roll; NHS; Adm Frm; Mst Outstndng Chrstn Wtns; U Central AR; Comp Sci.

RUSHING, JENNIFER; Cabot HS; Cabot, AR; (4); Cmnty Wkr; 4-H; FHA; Natl FFA Org; Office Aide; Bsktbl; Vllybl; PALS P; Big Bro/Big Sis Prgm; Horse Judging Awd; AR ST U Beebe; Nrsng.

RUSIN, PETE C; Catholic HS; Fort Smith, AR; (4); Church Yth Grp; Cmnty Wkr; FCA; Varsity Clb; Pres Frsh Cls; Stat Bsktbl; Ftbl; Trk; Cit Awd; High Hon Roll; 6 Months In Australia As Exch Stu; Pol Law.

RUSSELL, AMBER; Kingsland Schl; Kingsland, AR; (3); 1/30; Church Yth Grp; FBLA; FHA; GAA; HOBY; VP Frsh Cls; Sec Soph Cls; Bsktbl; Chrldng; Var Sftbl; Chrch Drama Team; SAU; Elem Tchr.

RUSSELL, AMBER J; Huttig Schl; Huttig, AR; (3); FBLA; FTA; Hosp Aide; Natl Beta Clb; Quiz Bowl; Teachers Aide; Ofcr Jr Cls; Ofcr Stu Cncl; Hon Roll; South AR CC; Nrsng.

RUSSELL, ANNE K; Mt St Mary Acad; Little Rock, AR; (3); 30/125; Am Leg Aux Girls St; Church Yth Grp; VP French Clb; Hosp Aide; Mu Alpha Theta; Pep Clb; Phtg Yrbk; French Hon Soc; Hon Roll; NHS.

RUSSELL, BECKY D; Huntsville HS; Huntsville, AR; (4); 9/123; Church Yth Grp; FCA; Key Clb; Band; Color Guard; Flag Corp; Mrchg Band; Pep Band; Yrbk; High Hon Roll; MASH Rprtr; UCCM; DART; U Cntrl AR; Phys Thrpy.

RUSSELL, CARI; Kingsland Schl; Kingsland, AR; (3); 2/25; Church Yth Grp; FBLA; GAA; HOBY; Natl Beta Clb; Quiz Bowl; Temple Yth Grp; Treas Frsh Cls; Ofcr Soph Cls; Capt Var Bsktbl; All Dist; U Of AR; Bsktbll Coach.

RUSSELL, CLINTON L; Bearden HS; Bearden, AR; (2); 4-H; FBLA; FHA; Band; Mrchg Band; Police Explr Prog; Henderson St Univ; Pilot.

RUSSELL, JENNIFER; Oak Ridge Central Schl; Ravenden Springs, AR; (4); 2/14; VP FBLA; Pres Natl Beta Clb; School Play; Pres Jr Cls; VP Sr Cls; VP Stu Cncl; Var Bsktbl; Var Sftbl; High Hon Roll; Sal; Hon Stu; AR St Univ; Crim.

RUSSELL, JONATHAN D; Nevada Schl; Rosston, AR; (4); 7/57; Cmnty Wkr; FCA; Natl Beta Clb; Office Aide; Teachers Aide; Band; Mrchg Band; Pep Band; Stat Bsbl; Var Bsktbl; Cntrl Bapt Coll; Bblcl Stu.

RUSSELL, LANA J; Kingston Jr Sr HS; Kingston, AR; (4); 1/17; Am Leg Aux Girls St; FBLA; FHA; Quiz Bowl; Yrbk; Sec Sr Cls; Rep Stu Cncl; Mgr Bsktbl; High Hon Roll; Val; U Of Centr AR.

RUSSELL, LAURA A; Oak Grove HS; Maumelle, AR; (2); Church Yth Grp; Drama Clb; FCA; Letterman Clb; Natl Beta Clb; Band; School Play; Vllybl; Hon Roll; Soc Studies Clb VP; UCA At Conway; PT.

RUSSELL, MINDY; Warren Jr HS; Warren, AR; (1); 12/135; Natl Beta Clb; Acpl Chr; Nwsp; Yrbk; Hon Roll; Ensmbl; Pres Outstdng Acad Achvmt Awd; UAM; Pre-Med/Dr/Nrs.

RUSSELL, RUSTY A; Atkins Schl; Atkins, AR; (2); Quiz Bowl; Bsktbl; Ftbl; Hon Roll.

RUSSELL, TIANA F; Rogers HS; Rogers, AR; (4); Church Yth Grp; Cmnty Wkr; FCA; FBLA; Drill Tm; Ofcr Stu Cncl; Swmmng; Hon Roll; Jr NHS; Pres Acad Fit Awd; Color Day Crt Maid; U Of AR; Mktng.

RUSSOW, MIKE A; Gravette HS; Gravette, AR; (3); Bus Profs of Am; Church Yth Grp; Drama Clb; Library Aide; Teachers Aide; Thesps; Band; Chorus; School Play; Variety Show; WA U; Dramatic Arts.

RUST, JENNY; Booneville Jr Sr HS; Booneville, AR; (3); Church Yth Grp; Drama Clb; FBLA; Q&S; Science Clb; Speech Tm; School Play; Mgr Yrbk; Westark CC; Elem Ed.

RUTH, HILLARY; Northside HS; Fort Smith, AR; (2); Drama Clb; Hosp Aide; ROTC; Thesps; School Musical; School Play; Chrldng; Socr; Tennis; Hon Roll; Jazz & Ballet Cls; Drama Cmptns Super & Exclnt Awds; Photo.

RUTH, JAMES R; Southside HS; Fort Smith, AR; (3); Drama Clb; Mu Alpha Theta; Spanish Clb; Speech Tm; Thesps; Orch; School Musical; School Play; Stage Crew; Hon Roll; NATL Spnsh Exam; Elem Ed.

RUTHERFORD, KRISTAL; Farmington Jr Sr HS; Farmington, AR; (1); Church Yth Grp; FHA; Band; Color Guard; Hon Roll; Jr NHS; Piano; U Of AR; Bus.

RUTLEDGE, MARANDA D; Vilonia HS; Vilonia, AR; (2); Computer Clb; Drama Clb; FBLA; Natl Beta Clb; Band; Mrchg Band; Chrldng; Hon Roll; U Of Cntrl AR.

RUTLEDGE, WES; Newport HS; Newport, AR; (4); 6/147; Am Leg Boys St; Art Clb; Church Yth Grp; Q&S; Nwsp; Yrbk; Rep Stu Cncl; L Ftbl; NHS; Sal; AR Intrschlstc Star Awd; Natl Sci Merit Awd; ACTM Reg Math Cntst Hnrbl Mntn; Abilene Chrstn Univ; Arch Engr.

RUTSCHKE, MICA C; Sylvan Hills HS; Sherwood, AR; (2); Church Yth Grp; Model UN; Natl Beta Clb; Spanish Clb; Drill Tm; NHS; Swim; Vol Work Air Force Base; U Of AR; Phy Thrpst.

RYALS, PAUL C; Clarksville HS; Clarksville, AR; (2); Church Yth Grp; Drama Clb; Natl Beta Clb; Crs Cntry; High Hon Roll; Hon Roll; Jr NHS; Prfct Atten Awd; Pres Acad Fit Awd; Pres Schlr; Artistic Achvmt Awd.

RYAN, SCOTT; Gosnell Jr Sr HS; Kennett, MO; (1); Drama Clb; Library Aide; Quiz Bowl; Science Clb; Band; Mrchg Band; Pep Band; Hon Roll; SE MO.

RYAN, SCOTT A; El Dorado Sr HS; El Dorado, AR; (1); 9/436; High Hon Roll; Electronics; Art; Bio; Electrcl Engrng.

RYAN, TRACY A; Oden Schl; Oden, AR; (2); Cmnty Wkr; FBLA; Natl Beta Clb; Bsktbl; Trk; Hon Roll; Math Awd 2 Times; Eng Awd; Home Ec Awd 2 Times; Outstndng Stu Awd; Sci Awd; Span Awd; Botanis/Nursery.

RYDELL, KAREN A; Waldron HS; Mena, AR; (2); Art Clb; 4-H; Natl Beta Clb; Spanish Clb; L Var Bsktbl; L Var Trk; 4-H Awd; Hon Roll; Grand Champion Steer At AR-OK St Fair; Bsktbl MVP; Discus 5th In St.

RYDER, STUART; Russellville Sr HS; Russellville, AR; (3); 1/340; Am Leg Boys St; Church Yth Grp; Treas French Clb; Model UN; Band; Mrchg Band; Pep Band; Var Swmmng; High Hon Roll; NHS; Deacon In Church; All ST Band; Model Arab League; Vet.

RYKEN, GEOFFREY R; Conway Sr HS; Conway, AR; (2); Church Yth Grp; Drama Clb; Band; School Musical; School Play; Stage Crew; French Hon Soc; High Hon Roll; Awd Best/Highest Achvmnt Tech Theater; Theater Mgmt.

RYLEE, SANDY J; Russellville Sr HS; Russellville, AR; (2); Church Yth Grp; FCA; Hon Roll; AR ST Univ; Psychiatrist.

SACHDEVA, NEHA; Mann Magnet Jr HS; North Little Rock, AR; (1); Church Yth Grp; Hosp Aide; Natl Beta Clb; Spanish Clb; Church Choir; Phtg Yrbk; Cit Awd; High Hon Roll; Hon Roll; Jr NHS; 3rd Pl Microbio Sci Fair; Dance; Peer Facilitators Club; Emory; Phy.

SACREY, ERIN E; Springdale Sr HS; Springdale, AR; (4); Church Yth Grp; FBLA; Q&S; Science Clb; Co-Ed Yrbk; Hon Roll; Jr NHS; Pres Acad Fit Awd; U Of Cntrl AR; Bio.

SADLER, CAPRISHA MELEE; Harrisburg HS; Harrisburg, AR; (4); 7/53; FBLA; Quiz Bowl; Sec Spanish Clb; Band; Drm Mjr(t); Ed Yrbk; Sec Treas Frsh Cls; Rep Stu Cncl; Hon Roll; Lyon Coll; Med.

SAER, BETH; Mt St Mary Acad; Little Rock, AR; (3); Model UN; Mu Alpha Theta; Q&S; Ofcr Drill Tm; Co-Ed Nwsp; Ofcr Soph Cls; Ofcr Jr Cls; High Hon Roll; NHS; Spanish NHS.

SAGER, DEBORAH A; Berryville HS; Berryville, AR; (4); 11/89; Treas Natl FFA Org; Sec Spanish Clb; Band; Drm Mjr(t); Hon Roll; Jr NHS; NHS; Prfct Atten Awd; Art Clb; Church Yth Grp; Rifle Corps; AQHA Hrsbck Rdng Prgm; Chrch Bible Drill; Piano; North AR Comm Tech Comm; Eqne.

SAIN, ASHLEY N; England HS; Tucker, AR; (4); #3 in class; Art Clb; French Clb; FBLA; Library Aide; Natl Beta Clb; Yrbk; Sftbl; Cit Awd; Hon Roll; U Of Cntrl AR; Bus Admin.

SAIN, BRITTANY; Hoxie Schl; Hoxie, AR; (2); Art Clb; French Clb; FBLA; Model UN; Natl Beta Clb; Quiz Bowl; Chorus; High Hon Roll; PRIDE; French Awd; U Of AR Fayetteville; Arch.

SAIRLS, NICOLE; Brookland Jr Sr HS; Brookland, AR; (4); 5/60; Art Clb; Church Yth Grp; Sec Drama Clb; FBLA; Pres FHA; Natl Beta Clb; Spanish Clb; Pres SADD; Teachers Aide; Thesps; U Of Centrl AR; Theatrical Art.

SALDIVAR, AUDREY; Fayetteville Christian Schl; Fayetteville, AR; (3); Church Yth Grp; Church Choir; School Musical; Ed Yrbk; Pres Soph Cls; Pres Jr Cls; Var Bsktbl; High Hon Roll; NHS; Piano-Clncs, U AR Awds; Sci Prjcts Schl Awds, St Cmptn; Sun Schl Tchr; U AR; Eng.

SALERS, REGINA M; J A Fair Sr HS; Little Rock, AR; (3); Spanish Clb; Gov Hon Prg Awd; Hon Roll; NHS; UIL Impromptu Wrtng; Comms.

SALING, JAMES A; Poyen Schl; Poyen, AR; (2); Church Yth Grp; Library Aide; Natl Beta Clb; Teachers Aide; Band; Chorus; Church Choir; Jazz Band; Pep Band; High Hon Roll; Chrch Pianist; Yth Cncl Mmbr Poyen Assmbl God; Southwestern Assmbly God U; Mus.

SALISBURY, CATHERINE L; Arkansas Schl Math & Science; Malvern, AR; (4); Am Leg Aux Girls St; Cmnty Wkr; Natl Beta Clb; Spanish Clb; Band; Yrbk; Rep Jr Cls; Rep Stu Cncl; High Hon Roll; NHS; Bio.

SALMON, ANGEY C; Southside HS; Fort Smith, AR; (2); Church Yth Grp; FCA; Mu Alpha Theta; Chorus; Church Choir; Vllybl; High Hon Roll; Hon Roll; NHS; Partnrs Christ Pres 96-; SAIL Crew; OK Bapt Univ; Music.

SALOMON, LENA; Manila HS; Manila, AR; (3); 2/80; FBLA; FTA; Library Aide; Natl Beta Clb; Band; Co-Ed Yrbk; Pres Frsh Cls; Sec Jr Cls; Cit Awd; High Hon Roll; Homcmng Royalty; Natl Mrt Sci Awd; HOT; Coll Of Ozarks; Med.

SALOMON, MACARIO; Manila HS; Manila, AR; (1); 15/100; Art Clb; Natl FFA Org; Band.

SALSBURY, SUZANNE; Van Buren Sr HS; Alma, AR; (3); 10/300; Cmnty Wkr; Dance Clb; FCA; Mu Alpha Theta; Pep Clb; Science Clb; Sec Spanish Clb; SADD; Teachers Aide; Capt Pom Pon; U Cntrl AR.

SALTMARSH, JAMIE; North Little Rock Hs-East; North Little Rock, AR; (2); 41/567; Church Yth Grp; FCA; French Clb; Math Clb; Natl Beta Clb; Pep Clb; School Musical; School Play; Chrldng; Powder Puff Ftbl; 1st Pl In Dist His Day; Miss Congeniality Teen; Speech Trnmt; Theatre.

SAMBRANO, TIMOTHY F; Pulaski Acad; Little Rock, AR; (3); Am Leg Boys St; Art Clb; Church Yth Grp; FCA; Natl Beta Clb; Spanish Clb; Var Bsktbl; Ftbl; Var Socr; Tennis.

SAMPLES, ASHLEY; Farmington Jr Sr HS; Fayetteville, AR; (1); Church Yth Grp; FBLA; FHA; Treas Frsh Cls; Bsktbl; Chrldng; Cit Awd; Hon Roll; Jr NHS; Pres Acad Fit Awd; Natl Hnr Roll.

SAMPLES, DONNY R; Glen Rose HS; Benton, AR; (2); FCA; FHA; Ofcr Bsbl; Bsktbl; Ftbl; Trk; Bsktbl Offensive Player & Rebounding Awds; Top Hitting Awd Bsbl.

SAMPLES, EMMA J; Springdale Sr HS; Springdale, AR; (2); Church Yth Grp; Cmnty Wkr; French Clb; Band; Church Choir; Mrchg Band; Pep Band; Hon Roll; Bus/Cmptr Tech.

SAMUELS, MELISSA S; Dequeen HS; De Queen, AR; (3); Church Yth Grp; FHA; FTA; Office Aide; SADD; Nwsp; Yrbk; Ofcr Jr Cls; Prfct Atten Awd; Missions Trip To An Indian Reservation; An Usher At Grad; Advertising; Law.

SANCHEZ, ALEX G; Siloam Springs Sr HS; Siloam Springs, AR; (3); Bsktbl; Mgr(s); Hon Roll; NHS; Prfct Atten Awd; Outstndng Stu; U Of AR; Engrng.

SANCHEZ, BOBBIE J; Lake Hamilton Sr HS; Royal, AR; (2); Church Yth Grp; Cmnty Wkr; FBLA; Natl Beta Clb; Rptr Natl FFA Org; Science Clb; Spanish Clb; Sftbl; High Hon Roll; NHS; Intnl Comms.

SANCHEZ, ROBERT A; Mt Pleasant Jr Sr HS; Melbourne, AR; (2); FHA; Teachers Aide; Yrbk; Ofcr Bsbl; Bus.

SANDEFUR, CRYSTAL; Sulphur Rock Schl; Newark, AR; (4); Art Clb; Bus Profs of Am; Computer Clb; Debate Tm; Drama Clb; English Clb; FHA; Key Clb; Library Aide; Math Clb; Gateway Tech Coll; Nrsng/Tchng.

SANDERS, AMANDA M; Viola HS; Viola, AR; (4); 1/26; Quiz Bowl; Band; Bsktbl; Cit Awd; Gov Hon Prg Awd; High Hon Roll; Pres Acad Fit Awd; Val; Masters Col; Cnslng.

SANDERS, AMIE; Abundant Life Schools; Jacksonville, AR; (3); Church Yth Grp; Spanish Clb; Chorus; School Play; Var Bsktbl; High Hon Roll; NHS; Mssn Wk.

SANDERS, ANGELA D; Star City HS; Star City, AR; (4); 1/108; Church Yth Grp; FBLA; Mu Alpha Theta; Teachers Aide; Nwsp; Yrbk; Lit Mag; High Hon Roll; NHS; Val; Yrbk Bus Mgr; Natl Disc Mission Tour Awd; U Of AR; Pharmacy.

SANDERS, APRIL; Sylvan Hills Jr HS; Sherwood, AR; (1); 14/266; Drill Tm; Hon Roll; NHS; Schlr Athl Awd; UA At Fayetteville; Acctng.

SANDERS, BERT; Ft Smith Christian Schl; Fort Smith, AR; (3); 1/35; Church Yth Grp; Cmnty Wkr; Treas FBLA; Band; Church Choir; Var Bsbl; High Hon Roll; NHS; AR St Math Hnr Roll; 4th Pl AR Cncl Tchrs Math Cmptn; Natl Yng Ldrs Cnvntn; Duke U TIP 95.

SANDERS, BRITTNY N; North Little Rock Hs-West; North Little Rock, AR; (4); 100/427; Art Clb; Dance Clb; Key Clb; Natl Beta Clb; Drill Tm; Stage Crew; Ofcr Frsh Cls; Hon Roll; NLK E Cmps Art Cntst 2nd Pl; John Brown Univ; Psych.

SANDERS, CHAD A; Hot Springs HS; Hot Springs, AR; (3); Art Clb; Natl Beta Clb; VP Frsh Cls; Pres Soph Cls; Var Bsbl; Var Bsktbl; Var Ftbl; Var Trk; NHS; High Hon Roll; Amer Legion Bsbl.

SANDERS, COURTNEY R; Harrisburg HS; Harrisburg, AR; (2); Hosp Aide; Science Clb; Spanish Clb; Band; Mrchg Band; Hon Roll; NHS; Span Medal; Bio Medal; Eng Medal; Pre-Med; Pediatrics.

SANDERS, JEREMIAH; Danville HS; Danville, AR; (1); 4/53; Church Yth Grp; FCA; FBLA; Letterman Clb; Library Aide; L Capt Bsbl; JV L Bsktbl; JV L Ftbl; JV Trk; Jr NHS; Vet Med.

SANDERS, JILL A; Viola HS; Viola, AR; (3); 4/36; FBLA; FHA; Natl FFA Org; Spanish Clb; Chorus; Yrbk; JV Var Bsktbl; Cit Awd; High Hon Roll; Pres Acad Fit Awd; Piano Tchr 5 Yrs; U Of AR Fayetteville; Home Ec.

SANDERS, KEVIN; Calico Rock HS; Pineville, AR; (4); 9/32; Church Yth Grp; Cmnty Wkr; Rptr FCA; Pres 4-H; Treas FBLA; Hosp Aide; Natl Beta Clb; Science Clb; SADD; Hon Roll; Natl Ldrshp Forum; Teen Challenge; AR ST Univ; Pre-Med.

SANDERS, KRISTI N; Lake Hamilton Sr HS; Hot Springs Natio, AR; (4); Church Yth Grp; FHA; Office Aide; Spanish Clb; Chorus; Church Choir; Stdnt Chrstn Life Treas; Wolf Pride; Soc Wrkr/Guid Cnslr.

SANDERS, LISA; Omaha Schl; Omaha, AR; (2); Natl Beta Clb; Band; School Play; Phtg Rep Nwsp; Rptr Phtg Yrbk; Cit Awd; Hon Roll; Coll Ozarks; Bus.

SANDERS, NATLAIE R; Bryant Sr HS; Bryant, AR; (3); Church Yth Grp; English Clb; Drill Tm; Nwsp; Yrbk; Pom Pon; Jr NHS; REACH; Eng Clb; Spirit Clb; Chrstn Cncl; Fayetteville; Intr Dsgnr.

SANDERS, ROBIN R; Hughes Jr-Sr HS; Hughes, AR; (4); 10/47; Rptr Phtg Nwsp; Cit Awd; Hon Roll; FFA Rprtr; ASR; Bus.

SANDERS, RUSSELL; Hermitage Jr Sr HS; Hermitage, AR; (2); 2/60; Church Yth Grp; HOBY; Natl Beta Clb; Natl FFA Org; JV Bsbl; Var Wt Lftg; High Hon Roll; Elect Engrng.

SANDERS, SALEECE D; Stamps HS; Buckner, AR; (4); FBLA; Spanish Clb; Chorus; Bsktbl; Trk; Hon Roll; Ebony Clb; UAPB; Nurs.

SANDERS, SARAH J; Clarksville HS; Clarksville, AR; (2); 49/130; Church Yth Grp; Hon Roll; Pride & Girls Sftbl Clbs; AR Tech Univ; Bus Mgmt.

SANDERS, SHAWNDA; Southside HS; Fort Smith, AR; (3); Church Yth Grp; Debate Tm; FCA; FBLA; German Clb; High Hon Roll; Hon Roll; Jr NHS; NHS; Ntl Merit Ltr.

SANDERS, STACY; Pottsville Schl; Russellville, AR; (4); 20/66; Church Yth Grp; GAA; Natl Beta Clb; Band; Pep Band; Sec Stu Cncl; Bsktbl; Crs Cntry; Sftbl; Tennis; AR Tech U; Bio.

SANDERS, STACY A; Lake Hamilton Sr HS; Pearcy, AR; (2); Church Yth Grp; Hosp Aide; Natl Beta Clb; Chorus; Hon Roll; NHS; Pres Acad Fit Awd; Outstndg Choral Stu Awd 94-95; Hot Springs Roundtable Of Poets Cont Joseph Vanas Awd 4th Pl; Southern Nazarene U; Music.

SANDERS, TAMARIO; Morrilton Sr HS; Plumerville, AR; (3); Boy Scts; Church Yth Grp; Cmnty Wkr; FCA; Natl Beta Clb; Spanish Clb; Band; Ftbl; NHS; U Of AR; Med.

SANDERS, TAMMALA; Augusta HS; Augusta, AR; (2); Chess Clb; FHA; FTA; Teachers Aide; Church Choir; Drill Tm; Hon Roll; GATE Prgm; Devil Pride; Pres FHA; Pres Stdnt Cncl.

SANDERS, TONYA L; Timbo Schl; Alco, AR; (1); FHA; Natl Beta Clb; Sftbl; Hon Roll; 3rd Pl Stone Cty Stu Art Fair Jr Div.

SANDLIN, ADAM T; Cntrl AR Chrstn HS; Maumelle, AR; (1); Church Yth Grp; CAP; French Clb; Bsktbl; Socr; Trk; Wt Lftg; Hon Roll; Jr NHS.

SANDLIN, JOSH L; Crowleys Ridge Acad; Paragould, AR; (1); Church Yth Grp; Computer Clb; FCA; FBLA; Pep Clb; Quiz Bowl; Science Clb; Acpl Chr; Band; Chorus; Harding Univ; Dntst.

SANDLIN, KENNETH; Van Buren Sr HS; Van Buren, AR; (3); 50/301; Am Leg Boys St; Boy Scts; Church Yth Grp; Cmnty Wkr; FCA; HOBY; Key Clb; Math Clb; Mu Alpha Theta; Science Clb; 3 Time Plyr Game Ftbl; Hnrbl Mntn All Conf Ftbl.

SANENE, DANIELLE M; Arkansas Bapt Schl; Maumelle, AR; (3); Church Yth Grp; FCA; Chorus; Rptr Nwsp; Yrbk; JV Stat Bsktbl; Var Tennis; Hon Roll; Frgn Mssns Clb.

SANSING, SANDY ALLEN; Mills HS; Jacksonville, AR; (2); 10/350; Art Clb; Cmnty Wkr; Debate Tm; French Clb; JCL; Latin Clb; Mu Alpha Theta; Natl Beta Clb; Quiz Bowl; Science Clb; AR Jr Acad Of Sci Hnrb Mntn Chem; AR Stu Congrss Of Humn Reltns Excl Flor Debt; Excl Parlmntry Procd; Chem Engrng.

SANSOM, JENNIFER J; Ashdown Sr HS; Ashdown, AR; (3); 12/140; 4-H; Model UN; Natl Beta Clb; Treas Natl FFA Org; Quiz Bowl; Science Clb; Spanish Clb; School Play; Stage Crew; Cit Awd; Star Greenhand Awd 96; Beef Prod Awd 96; 2nd Pl Livestock Judging Team At AR St Cont; Acad Cls Awds; TEXARKANA; Agribusiness.

SANSOUCIE, BRIAN C; Pangburn Jr Sr HS; Pangburn, AR; (3); FBLA; Natl FFA Org; Teachers Aide; Ofcr Bsbl; Bsktbl; Sftbl; Trk; Hon Roll.

SANTANA, LUIS J; Southside HS; Fort Smith, AR; (3); 206/502; French Clb; Band; Mrchg Band; Pep Band; High Hon Roll; All Regn Bnd; All St Bnd; Shenendoah Univ; Muscn.

SANTIAGO, LUISA M; Mills HS; Cabot, AR; (3); 78/298; Church Yth Grp; FBLA; Natl Beta Clb; Q&S; Science Clb; Spanish Clb; School Play; Stage Crew; Yrbk; Ofcr Soph Cls; Project WET-ON Site Envirmnmtl Stud; Attnd Mini Camp At Gulf Coast Research Ctr Biloxi, MS; Span.

SAPASEUT, PHOUVIENG; Butterfield Jr HS; Van Buren, AR; (1); Library Aide; Natl Jr Hnr Soc; Nrsng.

SAPP, JOEL N; Tuckerman HS; Tuckerman, AR; (2); Art Clb; Cmnty Wkr; 4-H; FBLA; Natl Beta Clb; Natl FFA Org; 4-H Awd; High Hon Roll; Prfct Atten Awd.

SARGENT, KATHRYN L; Parkview Arts/Sci Magnet HS; Little Rock, AR; (2); Church Yth Grp; Cmnty Wkr; Dance Clb; 4-H; Girl Scts; Hosp Aide; Red Cross Aide; 4-H Awd; High Hon Roll; Hon Roll; Taekwondo Blk Blt; Tchng.

SAROLIA, SEJU P; Cabot HS; Cabot, AR; (3); 69/400; Hon Roll; Prfct Atten Awd; Dr.

SARTAIN, DELINA L; Wilburn Schl; Drasco, AR; (3); FHA; Library Aide; Natl Beta Clb; Yrbk; Bsktbl; Hon Roll; Prfct Atten Awd; Art 1 Acad; Cvcs & Bio Awds; Cmptrs.

SARTAIN, JENNIFER L; Wilburn Schl; Drasco, AR; (1); FHA; Teachers Aide; Stage Crew; Treas Soph Cls; Sec Jr Cls; Bsktbl; Hon Roll; St Schlr; Prevet.

SARTAIN, NICK; Sylvan Hills HS; Sherwood, AR; (3); 9/290; FCA; Mu Alpha Theta; Natl Beta Clb; Spanish Clb; Var L Bsbl; Var L Ftbl; High Hon Roll; Jr NHS; NHS; Pres Acad Fit Awd.

SARVER, MATTHEW; Jessieville HS; Hot Springs, AR; (4); 1/40; Am Leg Boys St; Church Yth Grp; Key Clb; Natl Beta Clb; JV Var Bsktbl; Var Crs Cntry; Var JV Trk; DAR Awd; Val; FCA; Hendrix Coll.

SATEE-ULLAH, KHADIJAH A; Hot Springs HS; Hot Springs Natio, AR; (3); 13/179; ROTC; Chorus; Drill Tm; Hon Roll; Prfct Atten Awd; UAPB; Med.

SATTERFIELD, MARY M; Conway Sr HS; Conway, AR; (2); Church Yth Grp; Cmnty Wkr; Drama Clb; French Clb; Orch; French Hon Soc; High Hon Roll; Hon Roll; Ozark Mssn Prjct; Delta Beta Sigma; Bus Mgmt.

SATTERWHITE, ALEXI D; Cave City HS; Cave City, AR; (4); 1/65; Church Yth Grp; Treas Natl Beta Clb; Pres Science Clb; Ed Yrbk; VP Frsh Cls; Treas Sr Cls; Ofcr Stu Cncl; Capt Var Bsktbl; Gov Hon Prg Awd; Pres Acad Fit Awd; AR ST Univ; Comp Sci.

SATTERWHITE, RACHEL A; Oak Grove HS; North Little Rock, AR; (1); Engr/Meteorolgy.

SATTLER, TAMRA; Jasper HS; Ponca, AR; (4); Church Yth Grp; Cmnty Wkr; Debate Tm; FBLA; FHA; Natl FFA Org; Church Choir; Sec Frsh Cls; JV Bsktbl; Hon Roll; NACTC; Bus.

SAUER, ANGELA Y; Sheridan Sr HS; Mabelvale, AR; (4); 10/230; FBLA; Girl Scts; Lit Mag; Sftbl; Trk; Hon Roll; Jr NHS; NHS; Interact Clb Sec; Yth For Chrst; U Of Cntrl AR; Bus.

SAUL, ABIGAIL; Devalls Bluff Jr Sr HS; De Valls Bluff, AR; (2); Church Yth Grp; French Clb; FBLA; HOBY; Key Clb; Natl Beta Clb; Varsity Clb; Pres Frsh Cls; VP Soph Cls; Rep Stu Cncl; Mens White River Sports Queen 96; Merit Roll 96; UBEA; Fayetteville U Of AR; Pharm.

SAULSBERY, CHARLA BROOKE; Southside HS; Fort Smith, AR; (4); Church Yth Grp; CAP; FCA; FBLA; Office Aide; Church Choir; Stage Crew; Hon Roll; Westark CC; Aviation.

SAUNDERS, SCOTT A; Searcy HS; Searcy, AR; (3); 91/270; Church Yth Grp; Drama Clb; 4-H; SADD; Thesps; Band; Mrchg Band; Pep Band; School Musical; Stage Crew; AR ST Univ.

SAVACOOL, ADAM; Harmony Grove Jr Sr HS; Camden, AR; (1); Church Yth Grp; Drama Clb; Natl Beta Clb; Band; Mrchg Band; Cit Awd; Chrch Organist & Pianist.

SAVAGE, ERIC J; Cty Line HS; Branch, AR; (3); 13/35; Church Yth Grp; FBLA; Natl Beta Clb; Spanish Clb; Band; Pep Band; Nwsp; Cit Awd; Hon Roll; Prfct Atten Awd; UNIV Of AR; Acctg/Bus Admin.

SAVANNAH, TAMEIKA L; El Dorado Sr HS; El Dorado, AR; (3); Church Yth Grp; Cmnty Wkr; Band; Church Choir; Mrchg Band; Rep Sr Cls; Rep Stu Cncl; Var L Bsktbl; Var L Sftbl; Futuristic Outlooks; BASIC; U Of AR; Comp Sci.

SAVELL, KENDALL L; Fouke Jr Sr HS; Fouke, AR; (3); 11/80; FHA; Ofcr Jr Cls; Ofcr Bsbl; Bsktbl; Hon Roll; Stu Cncl Treas; U Of AR; Med.

SAWYER, DESHAWN; Blevins HS; Hope, AR; (3); Rptr Art Clb; Treas FBLA; Chorus; JV Var Chrldng; Beautician; Lawyer.

SAWYER, KURT; Gosnell Jr Sr HS; Blytheville, AR; (2); 27/105; Art Clb; Church Yth Grp; Natl Beta Clb; Natl FFA Org; Science Clb; Spanish Clb; SADD; Teachers Aide; Rptr Nwsp; Rep Stu Cncl; 1st Pl Div 2 Chrstms Artwrk Arts Cncl Of MS Cty Cntst 94; U Of Cntrl AR.

SAX, STACY; Ozark HS; Altus, AR; (3); Pres VP Church Yth Grp; Pres VP 4-H; HOBY; Pres Natl Beta Clb; Sec Band; Pres Jr Cls; JV Var Bsktbl; High Hon Roll; Ntl Merit Ltr; Pres Acad Fit Awd; Med.

SAXON, JOCELYN; Southside HS; Fort Smith, AR; (3); Church Yth Grp; German Clb; Letterman Clb; Mu Alpha Theta; Band; Mrchg Band; Ofcr Soph Cls; Ofcr Jr Cls; Mgr(s); Var Socr; 96 Daimler Benz Awd Of Excl Wnnr; 94 & 96 All Region Band Mem.

SAYABANE, SENGPRUCHANH; Waldron HS; Waldron, AR; (3); Am Leg Boys St; Art Clb; Church Yth Grp; FHA; Natl Beta Clb; Spanish Clb; Teachers Aide; VP Soph Cls; Trk; Hon Roll; Eng Awd; U Of A Fayetteville.

SAYASACK, KHEK; Southside HS; Fort Smith, AR; (3); FBLA; Spanish Clb; Socr; Prfct Atten Awd; Tech Stu Assn; Cltrl Ambssdr; Law Enfrcmnt.

SAYASONE, SOUVANNY VICTORIA; Northside HS; Fort Smith, AR; (3); Drama Clb; HOBY; Key Clb; Teachers Aide; School Play; Pres Frsh Cls; Rep Soph Cls; Rep Jr Cls; Cit Awd; High Hon Roll; 3rd Pl Ms NHS Beauty Cont; WA U; Med.

SAYLOR, DANIEL; Van Buren Sr HS; Van Buren, AR; (2); Church Yth Grp; FCA; FBLA; FTA; Mu Alpha Theta; Quiz Bowl; Spanish Clb; Teachers Aide; School Play; Lit Mag; Stu Panel; AEGIS Schol Wnnr; Supr Chrch Minstry; Evangel Col; Missns.

SCAIFE, FRANCINE A; Russellville Sr HS; Russellville, AR; (2); 100/350; GAA; Band; Church Choir; Bsktbl; Sftbl; Vllybl.

SCAIFE, JEREMY M; Marvell Acad; Marvell, AR; (4); 1/31; Church Yth Grp; School Play; Ed Nwsp; Pres Jr Cls; Treas Sr Cls; Rep Stu Cncl; Var Bsktbl; Var Ftbl; Pres NHS; Val; All-Star Bsktbl; Stu Of Yr; Mr Marvel Acad; U Of AR.

SCAIFE, LA TOSHIA P; Conway Sr HS; Springfield, AR; (4); 56/520; FBLA; Natl Beta Clb; Science Clb; Spanish Clb; JV Bsktbl; High Hon Roll; Hon Roll; Spanish NHS; AR St Univ; Nurs.

SCAIFE, OLIVER B; Pine Bluff HS; Pine Bluff, AR; (2); Pres Church Yth Grp; Cmnty Wkr; French Clb; Math Tm; Teachers Aide; VICA; Church Choir; Orch; School Play; Hon Roll; Playing/Composing On Viola/Piano/Acoustic Elec Guitar; Performing Arts/Actor.

SCALES, SHANNON; Fordyce HS; New Edinburg, AR; (3); Am Leg Aux Girls St; Church Yth Grp; French Clb; Girl Scts; Science Clb; Teachers Aide; School Play; Var Chrldng; Var Powder Puff Ftbl; Sftbl; Prfrmnc Chr; Hmcmng Md 2 Yrs; Grad Ushr; U Of AR-MONTICELLO; Flght Attn.

SCARBROUGH, CHRISTINE D; Ozark Adventist Acad; Siloam Springs, AR; (3); Service Clb; Ski Clb; Teachers Aide; Band; High Hon Roll; Hon Roll.

SCARBROUGH, WILLIAM J; Southside HS; Batesville, AR; (3); Johovah Wtns 2 Yrs; New York Bethel.

SCHAAL, GEORGE; Mineral Springs Schl; Mineral Springs, AR; (1); Church Yth Grp; FBLA; Natl FFA Org; Capt Quiz Bowl; School Musical; Rep Stu Cncl; Ftbl; Hon Roll; OM St 1st Pl 95; Gftd Tlntd Educ.

SCHAAL, HENRY; Mineral Springs Schl; Mineral Springs, AR; (2); Church Yth Grp; FBLA; Natl Beta Clb; Natl FFA Org; Quiz Bowl; Ftbl; Hon Roll; OM 1st Pl St 95; FL ST U.

SCHAD, EDWARD; Subiaco Acad; Valley View, TX; (3); 2/50; HOBY; Rep Frsh Cls; Rep Soph Cls; Var L Tennis; Hon Roll; NHS; Schl Actvts & Regligous Awds; Overall Schl Applctn Stds Medal; Notre Dame U; Engr.

SCHAEFER, BAB M; Springdale Sr HS; Springdale, AR; (3); Church Yth Grp; Computer Clb; French Clb; Model UN; NFL; Quiz Bowl; Science Clb; Speech Tm; Teachers Aide; Church Choir; John Brown Univ; Comp Sci.

SCHAEFER, COURTNIE L; North Little Rock Hs-East; North Little Rock, AR; (2); Church Yth Grp; DECA; FCA; Key Clb; Math Clb; Spanish Clb; School Musical; School Play; Chrldng; Hon Roll; Sports Med Trnr; Pediatrcn.

SCHAEFER, DAVID; Benton Sr HS; Benton, AR; (4); FBLA; HOBY; Key Clb; Math Clb; Tennis; Kiwanis Awd; Pres NHS; Ntl Merit SF; Cmnty Wkr; Science Clb; Sthwstrn Bell Stu Slt Awd; Jr Rotary; AR St Math Conf Dlgt; Comp Sci.

SCHAFFER, MICHELLE K; Harrison Sr HS; Harrison, AR; (3); Church Yth Grp; Teachers Aide; Chorus; Church Choir; Gov Hon Prg Awd; Hon Roll; NHS; OK Bapt Univ; Cert Pub Acctng.

SCHAFFHAUSER, MICHAEL; Marvell HS; West Helena, AR; (4); 7/40; French Clb; Natl Beta Clb; Natl FFA Org; Capt Bsbl; Capt Ftbl; Trk; Jr NHS; Xerox Awd; ASU; Acctng.

SCHAUER, ROBERT A; Ft Smith Christian Schl; Fort Smith, AR; (1); Church Yth Grp; Teachers Aide; Band; Mrchg Band; Hon Roll; Chrch Praise Team; Yth Praise Team; Piano; Trumpet; Musician.

SCHEIN, MICHAEL M; Fayetteville Sr HS; Fayetteville, AR; (2); 1/600; French Clb; Math Clb; Math Tm; Quiz Bowl; Band; Mrchg Band; Cit Awd; High Hon Roll; Hon Roll; USA Math Tlnt Srch Grand Prz 95-; 1st Prz ST/NATL Frnch Cmptn; ST/AMER Invtnl Math Exam 1st/2nd 96.

SCHELL, LEAH M; Monticello HS; Monticello, AR; (4); Art Clb; Church Yth Grp; Drama Clb; FCA; FBLA; FHA; Letterman Clb; Natl Beta Clb, Office Aide; Speech Tm; Southern Ar Univ; Un-D.

SCHELLER, SARAH; North Little Rock HS; North Little Rock, AR; (1); Church Yth Grp; Drama Clb; FCA; Hosp Aide; Math Clb; Mu Alpha Theta; Pep Clb; Spanish Clb; School Musical; School Play; Comptv Speech I; Pre Med/Pedtrc Surgeon.

SCHENEBECK, MIRANDA; Carlisle Jr Sr HS; Carlisle, AR; (1); Church Yth Grp; 4-H; FHA; Pep Clb; Quiz Bowl; Spanish Clb; Teachers Aide; Church Choir; Chrldng; Cit Awd; UCA.

SCHENK, EDWARD; Monticello HS; Monticello, AR; (4); 24/125; Church Yth Grp; FBLA; Natl Beta Clb; Mrchg Band; Hon Roll; NHS; Pres Acad Fit Awd; Office Aide; Band; All Amer Schlr; All Region Awd In Band; UAM; Ag Bus.

SCHERER, ERIN M; Pulaski Acad; Little Rock, AR; (2); Art Clb; Drama Clb; English Clb; School Musical; School Play; Nwsp; Lit Mag; High Hon Roll; Jr NHS; NHS; Dance 12 Yrs; Hnrs Fr III/AP Art His Hnrs Cert Awded; Vol Terry Branch Lib 2 Yrs; Art/Sci Schl; Drama/Directing.

SCHERREY JR, THOMAS J; Southside HS; Fort Smith, AR; (2); FCA; Spanish Clb; JV Bsbl; L Bsktbl; L Ftbl; L Trk; Hon Roll; Scuba Diving.

SCHIBLER, JOSH S; Smackover HS; Smackover, AR; (2); 3/56; FBLA; L Var Bsbl; L Var Bsktbl; L Var Ftbl; Var L Trk; Hon Roll; Pride Team; Governors Yth Conf.

SCHIEBLE, JOHANNAH; Morrilton Sr HS; Dover, AR; (4); 11/150; Am Leg Aux Girls St; French Clb; Math Clb; Science Clb; Thesps; Band; Mrchg Band; School Musical; Ed Yrbk; Tennis; Majorette Capt; Knowledge Master Open; Quest; AR Tech U; Acctng.

SCHIEFFLER, DAVID G; De Soto Schl; Sewanee, TN; (1); 1/30; Boy Scts; Church Yth Grp; JV Bsktbl; JV Ftbl; JV Tennis; JV Trk; Cit Awd; High Hon Roll; Highest GPA Gen Sci/Algebra 2/Typing/Hlth/Eng 9; Mech Engr.

SCHIMMEL, NATHAN R; Dewitt HS; Stuttgart, AR; (4); Church Yth Grp; FCA; French Clb; Natl Beta Clb; Pres Treas Science Clb; School Play; Nwsp; Yrbk; Rep Stu Cncl; L Ftbl; Farm Bureau Ldrshp Smnr; Reydel Bapt Chrch; Comm/Radio/TV.

SCHLENKER, AARON KYLE; Trumann HS; Trumann, AR; (3); Art Clb; Natl FFA Org; Rptr Science Clb; Spanish Clb; Bsktbl; Golf; Cit Awd; High Hon Roll; Hon Roll; NHS; TAD:WON Dist AA Champs 95-96; ARSU; Coll Golf; Farming.

SCHLINKER, ANDI N; Booneville Jr Sr HS; Booneville, AR; (2); Church Yth Grp; FCA; GAA; Natl Beta Clb; Science Clb; Chorus; Church Choir; Bsktbl; Chrldng; Sftbl; AAU Bsktbl; Mr & Mrss BHS Wnnr; UAMS; Med.

SCHMIDT, BRIANA I; Greenwood Sr HS; Fort Smith, AR; (3); Church Yth Grp; Hosp Aide; Teachers Aide; Band; Mrchg Band; Hon Roll; Jr NHS; Prfct Atten Awd; Partners In Christ; Bus Mgmt; Child Care.

SCHMIDT, BROOKE E; Conway Sr HS; Conway, AR; (4); 78/520; Drama Clb; FBLA; Orch; School Musical; School Play; Stage Crew; Hon Roll; AR Governors Schl; AR Yth Symphony; Conway Civic Orch; Hendrix Coll; Psych.

SCHMIDT, COURTNEY S; Trumann HS; Trumann, AR; (3); Computer Clb; FBLA; Math Clb; Science Clb; Spanish Clb; L Var Bsbl; L Var Bsktbl; Wt Lftg; Hon Roll; NHS; AR ST Univ; Pre Law/PT.

SCHMIDT, GEOFFREY R; Central Sr HS; Little Rock, AR; (2); Pres Computer Clb; German Clb; Natl Beta Clb; Quiz Bowl; Band; Orch; Ed Yrbk; Ofcr Stu Cncl; High Hon Roll; Intl Sci/Engrg Fair 95, 96; Mock Trial; HS Math Exam; AR Cncl Tchrs Math Alg II Exam, Trig Exam; Comp Sci.

SCHMIDT, JOSH J; Riverview HS; Judsonia, AR; (2); Math Tm; Pep Clb; Quiz Bowl; Spanish Clb; Ofcr Soph Cls; Var L Bsbl; Var L Bsktbl; Var L Crs Cntry; Trk; Hon Roll; GATE; Anesthesiologist.

SCHMIEGE, MONTE E; Ozark Adventist Acad; Paris, TX; (2); Church Yth Grp; Red Cross Aide; Drill Tm; Var Swmmng; Cit Awd; Hon Roll; Prfct Atten Awd; Rdng; Lifeguard; Mt Biking; Bus Mgmt; Art.

SCHMILL, DAVID H; Springdale Sr HS; Springdale, AR; (3); Church Yth Grp; Crs Cntry; Ftbl; Var Trk; Hon Roll; Jr NHS; NHS; U Of AR; Acctg.

SCHMOKER, VIRGINIA A C; Clarksville HS; Clarksville, AR; (2); Church Yth Grp; Dance Clb; FBLA; Chorus; Ofcr Soph Cls; Trk; Hon Roll; Prfct Atten Awd; Pres Acad Fit Awd; Jazz; Ballet; Comp Prgmr.

SCHNEBELEN, ELIZABETH; Central Ark Christian Schl; North Little Rock, AR; (2); Rptr Nwsp; Rptr Yrbk; Cit Awd; High Hon Roll; Jr NHS; NHS; Ntl Merit Ltr; Barnabus Awd; Spansh Cert Of Exc; Med.

SCHNEIDER, CHAD P; Conway Sr HS; Conway, AR; (4); Office Aide; Ofcr Bsbl; Ftbl; Golf; Trk; Fish; Rdng; Bus.

SCHNEIDER, CHRISTOPHER R; Fayetteville Sr HS; Fayetteville, AR; (2); Hon Roll; Pen & Ink Drawing Fayetteville Comm Calendar; Art; Arch.

SCHNEIDER, JESSICA; Pine Bluff HS; Pine Bluff, AR; (2); Church Yth Grp; Chorus; Lit Mag; Chrldng; High Hon Roll; Hon Roll; Jr NHS; Ntl Merit Ltr.

SCHOLES, AMBER J; Rogers HS; Rogers, AR; (3); 85/550; FBLA; Spanish Clb; Drill Tm; Sec Treas Jr Cls; Treas Stu Cncl; Sftbl; Hon Roll; NHS; Prfct Atten Awd; Pres Acad Fit Awd; Chmbr Comm Cert Acad Achvmnt 2 Yrs; Renaissance Slvr 2 Yrs.

SCHOONOVER, TOMMIE; Springdale Sr HS; Springdale, AR; (4); 9/454; Am Leg Aux Girls St; Cmnty Wkr; FBLA; VP Key Clb; VP Acpl Chr; Sec Soph Cls; Sec Sr Cls; Treas Stu Cncl; Intrml Mgr Chrldng; High Hon Roll; Peer Hlpr; Yng Life; OK ST U; Elem Ed.

SCHRADER, RUSS L; Rogers HS; Rogers, AR; (3); 4-H; Natl FFA Org; SADD; VICA; Auto Racing Mini-Stock Dirt Trk; OSU; Automotive Tech.

SCHUBARTH, HEIDI; Oark HS; Oark, AR; (3); 1/14; Church Yth Grp; Pres 4-H; FHA; HOBY; Quiz Bowl; Temple Yth Grp; Sec Jr Cls; Bsktbl; 4-H Awd; Hon Roll; BYU; Med.

SCHULTE, ANNA E; Southside HS; Fort Smith, AR; (3); 42/502; Church Yth Grp; French Clb; FBLA; Drill Tm; NHS; FCA; Pep Clb; Service Clb; Rptr Nwsp; Rptr Yrbk; SAIL; U Of Cntrl AR; PT.

SCHULTE, SARAH; Mena HS; Mena, AR; (4); 11/118; Am Leg Aux Girls St; Sec Boy Scts; Church Yth Grp; Rptr FBLA; Sec Science Clb; Spanish Clb; Teachers Aide; Band; Drm Mjr(t); Mrchg Band; Piano 11 Yrs; Nom Top 8 Sr Class 96; Church/Cmnty Actvts; John Brown Univ; Grphc Dsgn.

SCHULTZ, CASEY C; Ridgecrest HS; Paragould, AR; (3); 17/210; Church Yth Grp; Drama Clb; FBLA; Chorus; Flag Corp; School Musical; Swing Chorus; Yrbk; High Hon Roll; All Reg Choir; Natl Yth Ldrshp Conf; U Of AR Fayetville/Acctg.

SCHULZ, JAMIE L; Springdale Sr HS; Springdale, AR; (1); Church Yth Grp; FBLA; Chorus; Rep Stu Cncl; Var Capt Chrldng; Sftbl; Hon Roll; Jr NHS; Pres Acad Fit Awd; All Reg Choir; Phys Thrp.

SCHUMACHER, JILL A; North Little Rock Hs-West; North Little Rock, AR; (4); Church Yth Grp; Cmnty Wkr; Debate Tm; Mu Alpha Theta; Natl Beta Clb; Band; Mrchg Band; Hon Roll; NHS; Prfct Atten Awd; Golden Knights Of Keystone; Hendrix Coll; Poltcl Sci.

SCHUMACHER, SARA L; Siloam Springs Sr HS; Siloam Springs, AR; (3); 1/161; Church Yth Grp; FCA; Pres FBLA; Rptr Stu Cncl; Var Tennis; High Hon Roll; NHS; Pres Acad Fit Awd; Jr Exec Bnkbrd; Chrch Yth Cncl Sec.

SCHWANKE, JENNIFER L; West Fork HS; West Fork, AR; (2); Hosp Aide; Band; Mrchg Band; Orch; Pep Band; High Hon Roll; NHS; Med.

SCHWANTZ, CARMEN S; Barton HS; Poplar Grove, AR; (3); FHA; Library Aide; Spanish Clb; Bsktbl; Mock Trial; Moorehead; Corporate Law.

SCHWARTZ, RYAN J; Northside HS; Fort Smith, AR; (4); 6/360; VP German Clb; Math Tm; Mu Alpha Theta; Capt Quiz Bowl; Pres Science Clb; Teachers Aide; Hon Roll; NHS; Ntl Merit SF; Pres Acad Fit Awd; AP Schlr; St Quiz Bwl Trnmnt MVP 95; Otstndng Am Hstry Stu 95; CA Inst Tech; Chem.

SCHWEIKART, BRADLEY J; Oak Grove HS; Maumelle, AR; (3); Am Leg Boys St; Art Clb; Drama Clb; Letterman Clb; Mu Alpha Theta; Quiz Bowl; Spanish Clb; Ftbl; Mgr(s); Trk; We The People Cmptn, St Champion 94-95 Wash DC; Criminal Justice.

SCHWOPE, DAVID; Arkansas Schl Math & Science; Nashville, AR; (4); Mu Alpha Theta; Natl Beta Clb; Natl FFA Org; Quiz Bowl; Teachers Aide; Band; Mrchg Band; Rep Sr Cls; NHS; Ntl Merit SF; U Of AR; Mech Engr.

SCOGGINS, JASON; Bryant Sr HS; Alexander, AR; (4); 16/336; Church Yth Grp; Cmnty Wkr; FCA; FBLA; Library Aide; Var Bsbl; Bsktbl; High Hon Roll; Hon Roll; Whos Who Sprts/His; U Of AR; Bus Admin/Advrtsng.

SCOGGINS, RYAN P; Manila HS; Manila, AR; (1); Art Clb; Church Yth Grp; Computer Clb; FBLA; Math Clb; Spanish Clb; Speech Tm; Acpl Chr; Band; Chorus.

SCOPA, REBECCA K; Fayetteville Sr HS; Fayetteville, AR; (2); Church Yth Grp; Hosp Aide; Intnl Clb; Chorus; Church Choir; Variety Show; Hon Roll; Comm Theater Plys/Mscls; Acad Enrchmnt Gftd Pgm; Art Ctr Ozarks Chldrns Chrs; Peds/ER Dr/OB.

SCOTT, ALLISON E; Rogers HS; Rogers, AR; (2); Church Yth Grp; FCA; Drill Tm; Yrbk; Chrldng; Hon Roll; Art; Interior Dsgn; Tchr.

SCOTT, AMY; Genoa Central HS; Texarkana, AR; (4); FBLA; FHA; Spanish Clb; School Play; Bsktbl; Chrldng; Trk; Hon Roll; NHS; Pres Schlr; AR ST U; Pre-Med.

SCOTT, AMY M; Marked Tree Jr Sr HS; Marked Tree, AR; (4); 11/40; Am Leg Aux Girls St; Art Clb; Church Yth Grp; FBLA; ROTC; Ed Yrbk; Co-Capt Chrldng; Hon Roll; VP NHS; Sec Soph Cls; AR ST U.

SCOTT, ANGELA M; Mountain Home HS; Mountain Home, AR; (3); FCA; FBLA; FTA; Key Clb; Var Bsktbl; Var Trk; Var Vllybl; Hon Roll; Prfct Atten Awd; Intrct Club; Rtry Intnl; 4 Yr Coll; Sprts Med/Coaching.

SCOTT, ANTWAIN; Eudora HS; Eudora, AR; (3); Cmnty Wkr; FBLA; Natl Beta Clb; ROTC; Speech Tm; Band; Church Choir; Mrchg Band; School Musical; Ofcr Frsh Cls; W Cntrl AR Regnl Sci Fair Awd; U Of Cntrl AR; Phy Thrpst.

SCOTT, BRENT W; Waldron HS; Boles, AR; (1); Band; Jazz Band; Mrchg Band; Pep Band; High Hon Roll.

SCOTT, BRUCE C; West Memphis Sr HS; West Memphis, AR; (2); Boy Scts; CAP; FCA; Letterman Clb; Library Aide; Science Clb; Color Guard; Drill Tm; Rep Frsh Cls; Ftbl; Successfully Completed AR Wing Cadet Ldrshp Sch, Civil Air Patrol; Cadet Noncommissioned Ofcr Charge; Air Force Ofcr; Marine Ofcr.

SCOTT, CHRIS; Bryant Sr HS; Bryant, AR; (4); 35/336; English Clb; Band; Jazz Band; Capt Mrchg Band; Pep Band; Pres Acad Fit Awd.

SCOTT, DUSTIN L; Lonoke Jr HS; Lonoke, AR; (1); Church Yth Grp; Cmnty Wkr; Office Aide; Science Clb; JV Ftbl; Golf; JV Trk; Hon Roll; Pres Acad Fit Awd; AAU & Aabc Bsbl; All Star Dixie League Bsbl; LA ST; Legal Field.

SCOTT, EYONA L; Crossett Sr HS; Crossett, AR; (2); Art Clb; French Clb; Science Clb; Church Choir; Drm Mjr(t); Mrchg Band; Sftbl; French Hon Soc; Hon Roll; Chrch Yth Dept; U Of Cntrl AR; Ed; Psych.

SCOTT, JUSTIN L; Jonesboro HS; Jonesboro, AR; (3); Art Clb; Church Yth Grp; Hosp Aide; Math Clb; Quiz Bowl; Spanish Clb; VICA; Stage Crew; Hon Roll; NHS; U Of AR; Arch.

SCOTT, KIMBERLY; Dermott HS; Dermott, AR; (3); 4-H; Math Clb; Natl Beta Clb; Science Clb; Spanish Clb; Band; Cit Awd; Hon Roll; Ntl Merit Ltr; Pres Acad Fit Awd; Marine Bio.

SCOTT, LEAH B; Marvell Acad; Clarendon, AR; (2); VP Church Yth Grp; FBLA; HOBY; Spanish Clb; School Play; Stat Bsktbl; Var Chrldng; Var Mgr(s); Stat Trk; Var JV Hon Roll; U Of Cntrl AR; Advertising.

SCOTT, MANDY; Van Buren Sr HS; Van Buren, AR; (3); Art Clb; Church Yth Grp; Mu Alpha Theta; Spanish Clb; Speech Tm; Chrldng; Gym; Trk; Vllybl; Hon Roll.

SCOTT, MARGARET; Lincoln HS; Morrow, AR; (2); 4/75; Church Yth Grp; FBLA; FHA; Key Clb; Math Clb; Natl Beta Clb; Science Clb; Spanish Clb; Ofcr Frsh Cls; Cit Awd; Northeastern ST U; Bus Finance.

SCOTT, MARY; John L Mcclellan Magnet HS; Little Rock, AR; (2); Church Yth Grp; French Clb; Natl Beta Clb; School Play; High Hon Roll; Ntl Merit Ltr; Pres Acad Fit Awd; Field Bio.

SCOTT, MICHAEL R; Rogers HS; Bentonville, AR; (3); Boy Scts; Church Yth Grp; FCA; FBLA; Band; Jazz Band; Mrchg Band; Pep Band; Trk; High Hon Roll; Ozark Chrstn Coll; Engr/Archtct.

SCOTT, NGOZI O; Central Sr HS; Little Rock, AR; (3); Am Leg Aux Girls St; Boy Scts; Church Yth Grp; Dance Clb; Drama Clb; Math Clb; Mu Alpha Theta; Service Clb; Spanish Clb; Band; Arch Clb; Perfmd Drmtc Arts; Hgh Stpr; U Of AR; Arch/Bus.

SCOTT, ROLANDA D; Forrest City HS; Forrest City, AR; (3); Church Yth Grp; 4-H; FBLA; FHA; FTA; Hosp Aide; Office Aide; Teachers Aide; Church Choir; Hon Roll; 5th Pl Pub Spkng 96; 2nd Pl FHA Star Events Pub Spkng 94; UAPB; Accnt.

SCOTT, SAINT M; West Memphis Sr HS; West Memphis, AR; (2); Boy Scts; CAP; FCA; Letterman Clb; Library Aide; Quiz Bowl; Scholastic Bowl; Science Clb; Color Guard; Drill Tm; Best Avg Test Score, Civil Air Patrol; Best Overall CPFT; AR Wing Cadet Ldrshp Schl Civil Air Patrol; Marines Ofcr; Biologist.

SCOTT, SHAWNA; Clarksville HS; Clarksville, AR; (4); FCA; French Clb; FBLA; Natl Beta Clb; Chorus; Variety Show; VP Sr Cls; Bsktbl; Chrldng; Trk; PRIDE Ldr; PAWS; Grad VP; Prom Cmte; Schl Stdnt Ambass; All St PRIDE Tm Vclst; Choir All Reg; Vocal Prfrmnc.

SCOTT, TRAKIETA A; Forrest City HS; Forrest City, AR; (3); Art Clb; Dance Clb; French Clb; FHA; Teachers Aide; Trk; Grambling St; Med Asst.

SCOTT, TRISHA; Harrison Sr HS; Harrison, AR; (3); 1/200; Drama Clb; Hosp Aide; Pres Science Clb; VP Spanish Clb; Pres SADD; Thesps; Band; Jazz Band; School Musical; School Play; Natl Eng Merit Schlr; All Arnd Schlr; Wmns Studies.

SCOTT, TYRONDA J; Bearden HS; Bearden, AR; (3); Church Yth Grp; Cmnty Wkr; FBLA; FHA; Natl Beta Clb; Flag Corp; Pres Frsh Cls; Pres Soph Cls; Chrldng; High Hon Roll; U AR Pine Bluff; Med.

SCOUTEN, ERIC P; Lead Hill Schl; Lead Hill, AR; (2); Boy Scts; Church Yth Grp; FCA; FHA; VP Stu Cncl; Var Bsbl; Var Bsktbl; Var Trk; Hon Roll; Prfct Atten Awd.

SCOUTEN, KIM; Lead Hill Schl; Yellville, AR; (4); 4/22; Pres Church Yth Grp; VP FBLA; Pres VP FHA; Girl Scts; Church Choir; Rep Sr Cls; Pres Stu Cncl; Var Scrkpr Chrldng; Hon Roll; NHS; U Of AR Fayetteville; Bus Mgmt.

SCRAPE, JENNIFER A; Trumann HS; Trumann, AR; (3); Science Clb; Spanish Clb; Band; Color Guard; Flag Corp; Mrchg Band; Pep Band; Yrbk; Hon Roll; NHS.

SCRAPE, REBECCA J; Trumann HS; Trumann, AR; (2); Church Yth Grp; Chorus; Church Choir; Hon Roll; AR ST; Nrsng.

SCRIBNER, TERESA; England HS; England, AR; (4); 11/63; Art Clb; Church Yth Grp; Cmnty Wkr; FCA; Sec French Clb; FBLA; HOBY; Library Aide; Natl Beta Clb; Office Aide; U Of Memphis; Comm Art.

SCRIMSHIRE, CARY L; Oden Schl; Sims, AR; (3); Art Clb; Church Yth Grp; Chorus; Sec Sr Cls; Hon Roll; Prfct Atten Awd; Chem Mrt Awd; RMCC; Vet.

SCRIVNER, JASON A; Lakeside HS; Lake Village, AR; (2); 9/90; Church Yth Grp; 4-H; FBLA; JV Ftbl; JV Wt Lftg; NHS; Prfct Atten Awd; U Of AR; Lawyer.

SEAGO, DEBORAH L; Parkview Arts-Science HS; Jacksonville, AR; (2); Natl Beta Clb; Teachers Aide; Hon Roll; Jr NHS; U Of AR Little Rock; Elem Tchr.

SEAL, KRISTEN J; Newport HS; Newport, AR; (2); Church Yth Grp; Hosp Aide; Office Aide; Spanish Clb; Church Choir; Bible Club; HOT; LA ST Univ; Elem Ed.

SEALE, DAWN A; Dierks HS; Dierks, AR; (4); Am Leg Aux Girls St; Art Clb; Church Yth Grp; FBLA; FHA; Pres Band; Church Choir; Drm Mjr(t); Mrchg Band; Pep Band; School Play; Pride Tm Secy; Hmcmng Royalty 95; U Of AR.

SEALE, SHAUN D; Dierks HS; Dierks, AR; (4); Am Leg Boys St; Church Yth Grp; VP Band; Mrchg Band; Pep Band; School Play; Ofcr Bsbl; Bsktbl; NHS; PRIDE Alchl Drg Free Tm Pres; Trim Mus Mstrs; U Of AR; Bus Admin.

SEAMAN, AL; Mc Gehee HS; Mc Gehee, AR; (3); 7/140; Boy Scts; Church Yth Grp; Library Aide; Mu Alpha Theta; Natl Beta Clb; Quiz Bowl; Science Clb; Spanish Clb; Golf; NHS; GATE; U TX Austin; Arntcl Engr.

SEAMANS, FAITH R; Sloan Hendrix HS; Imboden, AR; (2); Art Clb; Teachers Aide; Chorus; School Musical; Yrbk; Rep Frsh Cls; Var Bsktbl; Jrnlsm Mdl; Jrnlsm Schlrshp; Bus Mngmnt.

SEAMANS, HOLLY; Mc Gehee HS; Mc Gehee, AR; (4); 1/101; Am Leg Aux Girls St; Sec Natl Beta Clb; Yrbk; Treas Stu Cncl; Bsktbl; Cit Awd; Treas NHS; Pres Acad Fit Awd; Val; Trk; Ouachita Bapt Univ; Phy Thrpst.

SEAMON, CRYSTAL M; Jessieville HS; Hot Springs Natio, AR; (2); FCA; Key Clb; Band; Jazz Band; Mrchg Band; Pep Band; Pres Soph Cls; Chrldng; Amer Schlsp Awd; Poem Pub; UCA; Phy Thrpst; Sports Med.

SEAMON, MARIA E; Deer Jr Sr HS; Deer, AR; (3); 1/30; Cmnty Wkr; English Clb; FBLA; Latin Clb; Library Aide; Quiz Bowl; Chorus; High Hon Roll; Ntl Merit SF; Pres Acad Fit Awd; Summa Cum Laude Latin II Exam; Hendrix At Conway.

SEAMON, MICHAEL C; Dewitt HS; De Witt, AR; (4); 19/76; Am Leg Boys St; French Clb; FBLA; FTA; Natl Beta Clb; Q&S; Science Clb; Teachers Aide; Sprt Ed Nwsp; Ed Yrbk; U Of Cntrl AR; Phrmcy.

SEARS, EVANGELA M; Walker Schl; Magnolia, AR; (3); 1/25; Pres FBLA; Natl FFA Org; Teachers Aide; Church Choir; Yrbk; Pres Jr Cls; Pres Stu Cncl; Hon Roll; YEA-AIM; 17th Annual AR Governors Schl Eng & Lang Arts.

SEBOURN, AMANDA D; John L Mcclellan Magnet HS; Little Rock, AR; (2); #6 in class; Church Yth Grp; Cmnty Wkr; Drama Clb; French Clb; FBLA; Math Clb; Mu Alpha Theta; Natl Beta Clb; Teachers Aide; Cit Awd; U Of AR; Pharm.

SEBREN, LESLIE; Benton Sr HS; Benton, AR; (3); 27/300; FCA; FBLA; Sec FHA; Key Clb; Spanish Clb; Drill Tm; Jr NHS; Kiwanis Awd; Pres Acad Fit Awd; 1st Church Of God; PT.

SEEGER, LEIGH ANN; Batesville Sr HS; Batesville, AR; (2); 28/156; Church Yth Grp; Pres FBLA; Key Clb; VP Soph Cls; VP Stu Cncl; Var JV Chrldng; Var Score Keeper; Hon Roll; Prfct Atten Awd; Beta Club; Earth Club; Member Of Pride; Univ Of AR At Fayettevl; Med.

SEELEN, JONATHAN; Southside HS; Fort Smith, AR; (4); 119/459; Church Yth Grp; CAP; Mu Alpha Theta; ROTC; Band; Mrchg Band; Pep Band; Hon Roll; U Of OK; Cmptrs/Med/Doc USAF.

SEELEN, RAEDONNA C; Southside HS; Fort Smith, AR; (2); Church Yth Grp; ROTC; PT.

SEEMAN, SARAH E; Nettleton HS; Jonesboro, AR; (3); 11/150; FBLA; Natl Beta Clb; Pres Natl FFA Org; Chorus; Church Choir; JV Bsktbl; Var Chrldng; Var Tennis; JV Vllybl; Hon Roll; FBLA Dist Parliamentarian; Pres Of ST Winning FFA Parliamentary Team; Pres Of Portion Of Cls; TX A&M; Equine Sci.

SEGRAVES, JOSHUA D; Clarksville HS; Clarksville, AR; (2); Art Clb; FBLA; Band; Chorus; Mrchg Band; Pep Band; Ed Phtg Nwsp; Hon Roll; 3 1st Super/1 2nd Excllnt Rtngs Band Solo/Ensmbl; U AR.

SEITER, CHRISTI D; Greenwood Sr HS; Greenwood, AR; (3); Art Clb; FCA; French Clb; FBLA; FHA; Hosp Aide; Natl Beta Clb; Office Aide; Science Clb; Cit Awd; U Of AR; Chld Psych.

SELBY, DANIELLE R; Russellville Sr HS; Russellville, AR; (3); VP 4-H; Natl Beta Clb; Band; Color Guard; Flag Corp; Mrchg Band; Orch; Pep Band; Yrbk; Golf; Sci.

SELBY, KRISTEN; Butterfield Jr HS; Van Buren, AR; (1); Church Yth Grp; Cmnty Wkr; English Clb; FCA; FBLA; Office Aide; Speech Tm; Teachers Aide; Band; Church Choir; Partnrs Christ; Most Val Blzr Awd; Spch Tm Hons Eng; 2nd Rnr Up Miss BJHS Pageant; Cuachita Bapt U; Lawyr.

SELF, AMBER D; Magnet Cove HS; Malvern, AR; (1); Church Yth Grp; FCA; Band; Church Choir; Mrchg Band; Hon Roll; Explorer Post Troop 88; Pediatrician.

SELF, GREG A; Jacksonville HS; North Little Rock, AR; (3); Office Aide; Mrchg Band; Var Bsbl.

SELF, JENNIFER N; North Little Rock Hs-East; North Little Rock, AR; (2); Church Yth Grp; Church Choir; Hon Roll; Sports Medicine; Nrsng Home Visitor; Sftbl On Chrch League; U Of Cntrl AR; Phy Thrpst.

SELF, STEPHANIE D; Fayetteville Sr HS; Fayetteville, AR; (2); Drama Clb; GAA; Girl Scts; Band; Church Choir; School Play; Cit Awd; Hon Roll; Lawyer/Doctor.

SELLERS, BRANDY L; Searcy HS; Searcy, AR; (2); Natl Beta Clb; Band; Jazz Band; Mrchg Band; Hon Roll; Jr NHS; Med.

SELLERS, ERIC; Lee Acad; Marianna, AR; (2); Church Yth Grp; Yrbk; Bsktbl; Ftbl; Golf; Trk; Hon Roll; NHS; Prfct Atten Awd; U Of AR.

SELLERS, JASON; Van Buren Sr HS; Van Buren, AR; (4); Am Leg Boys St; Boy Scts; Cmnty Wkr; Mu Alpha Theta; Spanish Clb; Jazz Band; Mrchg Band; NHS; FBLA; Boy Scts Eagle Sct.

SELLERS, RHEA N; Atkins Schl; Russellville, AR; (3); Drama Clb; Science Clb; Spanish Clb; Teachers Aide; Band; Color Guard; Stage Crew; Rptr Nwsp; Var JV Bsktbl; Trk; Cngrssnl Yth Ldrshp Cncl; Grphc Art.

SELLERS, SAM R; Bryant Sr HS; Mabelvale, AR; (2); Church Yth Grp; FBLA; Hon Roll; UCA; Bio.

SELLERS, SHELLY; Vilonia HS; Vilonia, AR; (4); 1/120; Church Yth Grp; FBLA; GAA; Mu Alpha Theta; Natl Beta Clb; Pres Sr Cls; Bsktbl; High Hon Roll; NHS; Val; U Of Cntrl AR; Pre-Phrmcy.

SELVIDGE, COLLIN F; Searcy HS; Searcy, AR; (4); Church Yth Grp; Drama Clb; Math Tm; Natl Beta Clb; Spanish Clb; Thesps; School Play; Yrbk; Bsktbl; Tennis; Guitar; Harding Univ; Drama/Lit Tchr.

SEMMLER, COREY; Mineral Springs Schl; Mineral Springs, AR; (2); Boy Scts; FBLA; HOBY; Nwsp; Yrbk; Trk; Wt Lftg; Hon Roll; OM; Stdnt Nine Wks Awd; Drg Intrvntn Tm; Ouachita Baptist U.

SENYARD, ANNE; Southside HS; Fort Smith, AR; (3); Church Yth Grp; Dance Clb; Debate Tm; Drama Clb; FCA; Hosp Aide; Key Clb; Mu Alpha Theta; Pep Clb; Service Clb; Psych/Law Schl.

SERATT, DENISE; Mountainburg Jr Sr HS; Mountainburg, AR; (4); Natl Beta Clb; High Hon Roll; Hon Roll; RN.

SERATT, DONNA L; Mountainburg Jr Sr HS; Chester, AR; (3); Church Yth Grp; FCA; 4-H; FHA; Natl Beta Clb; Spanish Clb; Bsktbl; Hon Roll.

SERBOUSEK, CATHERINE M; North Little Rock Hs-West; North Little Rock, AR; (3); 69/514; Drama Clb; VP German Clb; Mu Alpha Theta; Natl Beta Clb; School Musical; School Play; Stage Crew; Powder Puff Ftbl; Socr; Ntl Merit SF; TV Prdctn; Schl Ftbl TV Sprts Announcer; NVU; Drama.

SERRANO, LESLIE M; Springdale HS; Lowell, AR; (4); Church Yth Grp; Cmnty Wkr; DECA; FCA; FBLA; FHA; Key Clb; Acpl Chr; Chorus; Drill Tm; Yth For Christ VP; All-Regn Chor 1st Rnnr Up; Donky Bsktbl For Red Cross; DECA VP & Numrs DECA Awds; U Of Cntrl AR; Mrktg; Commnctn.

SETTLAGE, KATIE E; Huntsville HS; Huntsville, AR; (3); 13/128; Drama Clb; Science Clb; Speech Tm; Teachers Aide; School Play; Stage Crew; Rptr Nwsp; Hon Roll; Hrsbck Rdng/Trnr Hntr/Jmpr Cmptn; Ag.

SETTLES, SABRINA I; Mills HS; North Little Rock, AR; (3); 47/298; FTA; Natl Beta Clb; Q&S; ROTC; Science Clb; Drill Tm; Orch; Yrbk; Ofcr Soph Cls; Ofcr Jr Cls; Upward Bnd; MITE; Engrng.

SEVAK, HEATHER; Gravette HS; Sulphur Springs, AR; (4); Am Leg Aux Girls St; Church Yth Grp; Band; Mrchg Band; Hon Roll; GEC; Elem Tchr.

SEWELL, KRISTI; Bright Star Schl; Doddridge, AR; (2); 3/23; Rptr FBLA; Office Aide; Rptr Nwsp; Pres Frsh Cls; Pres Soph Cls; Univ Of AR.

SEXTON, CASSIE; Mammoth Spring HS; Mammoth Spring, AR; (1); FHA; Natl Beta Clb; Pep Clb; Band; Mrchg Band; Ofcr Stu Cncl; Bsktbl; High Hon Roll; Jr NHS; Prfct Atten Awd; Attrny.

SEXTON, CHRISTOPHER; Magnet Cove HS; Malvern, AR; (4); Church Yth Grp; FCA; 4-H; FTA; Math Clb; Natl FFA Org; Science Clb; Teachers Aide; Rep Stu Cncl; Var L Ftbl; Southern AR U; Ag.

SEXTON, KIMBERLY A; Bryant Sr HS; Alexander, AR; (2); Church Yth Grp; Hosp Aide; Spanish Clb; Chorus; Church Choir; School Musical; Hon Roll; Acteens Ldr; Tchr Chldrns Chrch; OK Bapt Univ; Tchr.

SEXTON, MARC R; Jonesboro HS; Jonesboro, AR; (2); Church Yth Grp; Math Clb; SADD; Acpl Chr; Band; Chorus; Church Choir; Mrchg Band; All-Region Choir & Band; Outstdng Choir Mem; Perfmnc Carnegie Hall With Toronto Childrens Chorus; Vocal Trng; Music Ed.

SEXTON, SCOTT W; Clarksville HS; Clarksville, AR; (2); Chess Clb; Natl Beta Clb; Band; Mrchg Band; Hon Roll; All Region Band; 3rd Pl Fiction KUAF Wrtng Cont.

SEYDEL, MARIAH J; Jonesboro HS; Jonesboro, AR; (4); 81/275; Church Yth Grp; Drama Clb; FCA; French Clb; Mu Alpha Theta; Office Aide; Thesps; Chorus; Church Choir; School Musical; Transyvania Univ; Eng; Jrnlsm.

SHACKELFORD, SCOTT OLIVER; Shiloh Christian Schools; Springdale, AR; (3); 13/49; Am Leg Boys St; FBLA; Rep Frsh Cls; Rep Soph Cls; Rep Stu Cncl; Var Bsbl; Var Bsktbl; Var Crs Cntry; JV Ftbl; Trk; U Of AR; Pol Sci/Law.

SHADDOCK, MELISSA; Oak Grove HS; Maumelle, AR; (1); 3/189; Church Yth Grp; Cmnty Wkr; FCA; Letterman Clb; Natl Beta Clb; Church Choir; Capt Chrldng; Var Trk; Var Vllybl; Hon Roll; Odyssey Of Mind; Ballroom Dncng; U Of AR; Chem.

SHADWICK, MAX B; Dewitt HS; De Witt, AR; (2); Debate Tm; French Clb; Natl FFA Org; Quiz Bowl; Land Jdgng Tm District Wnrs.

SHAFFER, ANDREA; Southside HS; Fort Smith, AR; (3); FCA; FBLA; Key Clb; Mu Alpha Theta; Spanish Clb; Drill Tm; Rep Stu Cncl; Socr; NHS; Church Yth Grp; Natl Young Ldrs Conf.

SHAFFER, JENNIFER; Southside HS; Fort Smith, AR; (2); Church Yth Grp; FCA; FBLA; Key Clb; Mu Alpha Theta; Spanish Clb; Drill Tm; Jr NHS; NHS; Pep Clb; Pres Awd Ed Excl.

SHAFFER, LISHA; Prairie Grove HS; Prairie Grove, AR; (3); Church Yth Grp; Drama Clb; FHA; Spanish Clb; SADD; Band; Church Choir; Hon Roll; Jr NHS; NHS; Chrch Drama.

SHAHBANDAR, OUBAI M; Mann Magnet Jr HS; Little Rock, AR; (1); Chess Clb; Cmnty Wkr; French Clb; Intnl Clb; Natl Beta Clb; Quiz Bowl; Orch; Socr; Cit Awd; Hon Roll; Space Camp Schlrshp 95 & 96; Museum Of Sci & Hist Vol; Med.

SHALLENBERG, JENNIFER; Rogers HS; Rogers, AR; (4); Cmnty Wkr; Hosp Aide; Quiz Bowl; Science Clb; Teachers Aide; Band; Drm Mjr(t); Flag Corp; Mrchg Band; High Hon Roll; All Rgn Band; Hi-Q Acad Cmptn; ACE Acad Cmptn; AR ST U; Elem Ed.

SHAMLIN, REGINA C; Robinson HS; Little Rock, AR; (2); 12/156; Art Clb; French Clb; FBLA; Yrbk; Hon Roll; NHS; Beta Clb; Acad Awd Dist Cert 1st Plc Eng Mstry Lrng Tst 95; Rdng Novels; Law/Med.

SHAMSEDDIN, SOHAYLA; Farmington Jr Sr HS; Fayetteville, AR; (4); 17/80; Drama Clb; FBLA; FHA; GAA; Speech Tm; SADD; Teachers Aide; School Play; Yrbk; Bsktbl; U Of AR; Premed.

SHANNON, CHRISTIE A; Huntsville HS; Huntsville, AR; (4); 2/123; Art Clb; Church Yth Grp; Drama Clb; Treas FBLA; Pres FTA; Girl Scts; Teachers Aide; Treas Sr Cls; High Hon Roll; Treas NHS; 2nd Pl KUAF Rgnl Wrtng Cntst 95; 1st Pl Rgnl & 4th Pl St OM 95; All-Amer Schlr 96; Williams Bptst Coll; Art Ed.

SHANNON, JEFFREY; Rural Special Schl; Mountain View, AR; (4); 2/25; Am Leg Boys St; 4-H; FBLA; HOBY; Natl Beta Clb; Natl FFA Org; Quiz Bowl; Spanish Clb; Var L Bsktbl; Sal; U AR Fayetteville; Elec Engrg.

SHANNON, JOSHUA P; Rogers HS; Bentonville, AR; (3); 25/550; Chess Clb; Church Yth Grp; Library Aide; Math Tm; Quiz Bowl; High Hon Roll; Hon Roll; Roberts Chamber Commerce Awd; Rennaisaince Stdnt Band; U Of AR; Cmptr Sci.

SHANNON, LEAH; North Little Rock Hs-East; North Little Rock, AR; (2); 1/600; Church Yth Grp; FCA; Math Clb; Natl Beta Clb; Science Clb; Spanish Clb; Rptr Nwsp; Chrldng; Powder Puff Ftbl; Prfct Atten Awd; Cert Excllnc Awd Crtv Wrtng I Frosh/Eng Ii Soph/Span Ii Soph.

SHANNON, SARAH; Lincoln HS; Canehill, AR; (2); Key Clb; Chorus; High Hon Roll; Hon Roll; Med.

SHAPLEY, KRISTIE K; Hope HS; Hope, AR; (4); Church Yth Grp; French Clb; FBLA; Hist FTA; Natl Beta Clb; Nwsp; Hon Roll; Henderson St Univ.

SHARP, CLINT D; Southside HS; Fort Smith, AR; (2); Boy Scts; Church Yth Grp; Computer Clb; Quiz Bowl; Hon Roll; NHS; Cmptr Sci.

SHARP, CURTIS; Magnolia HS; Magnolia, AR; (3); #1 in class; Mu Alpha Theta; Hon Roll; Fshng; Cert Outstdng Acad Achvmt 95-; 4 Yr Alumni Schlrshp Southern AR U; Biochem/Biophysics.

SHARP, JODIE L; Valley Springs Schl; Harrison, AR; (3); 11/54; Sec Rep FBLA; Pres Key Clb; Sec Frsh Cls; Sec Soph Cls; JV Var Chrldng; JV Var Vllybl; French Hon Soc; High Hon Roll; Kiwanis Awd; NHS; Passed Lifeguard Exam; UCAR.

SHARP, JOY; North Little Rock HS; North Little Rock, AR; (1); Chrldng; Peer Ldrshp; Tchr.

SHARP, KATY; Melbourne HS; Melbourne, AR; (4); 1/32; Church Yth Grp; FCA; 4-H; Pres FBLA; FHA; Natl Beta Clb; Sec Natl FFA Org; Ed Nwsp; Yrbk; Bsktbl; Horseshows, Barrell Racing & Western Pleasure; Sportsmanship Awd N AR Horseshow Assoc; AR ST Univ; Accntng.

SHARP, TONI M; Valley Springs Schl; Harrison, AR; (2); Church Yth Grp; FHA; Key Clb; Office Aide; Sec Frsh Cls; Chrldng; Hon Roll; Sr Retirement Home Vol.

SHARPE, JESSE J; Huntsville HS; Huntsville, AR; (3); 1/135; FBLA; Quiz Bowl; Science Clb; Rep Frsh Cls; High Hon Roll; Hon Roll; NHS; Val; Odyssey Mind; ACE; Black Belt Amer Tae Kwon Do Assn; Civil Engr.

SHARPE, TONI; Alpena Schl; Alpena, AR; (3); VP Treas Church Yth Grp; FBLA; FHA; Natl Beta Clb; Pep Clb; Chorus; Church Choir; Hon Roll; Prfct Atten Awd; Horseback Riding; Work With Children.

SHASTID, RAY; Rogers HS; Rogers, AR; (4); Church Yth Grp; CAP; Cmnty Wkr; Color Guard; Var Ftbl; Var Trk; Flight Schlsp Solo; Civil Air Patrol Cadet Of The Yr; Harding U.

SHATSWELL, BRANDON K; Harrison Sr HS; Harrison, AR; (4); 1/201; Church Yth Grp; French Clb; FBLA; Key Clb; Thesps; Chorus; Jazz Band; NHS; Pres Acad Fit Awd; Chamber Of Commerce Yth Exemptary Svc Awd; U Of Central AR; Music.

SHAVER, BETH; North Little Rock Hs-West; North Little Rock, AR; (3); 60/600; FCA; Key Clb; Mu Alpha Theta; Natl Beta Clb; Yrbk; Rep Stu Cncl; Chrldng; High Hon Roll; Hon Roll; NHS.

SHAVER, KELLY; Southside HS; Fort Smith, AR; (3); 67/500; FCA; French Clb; Mu Alpha Theta; Band; Color Guard; Mrchg Band; Pep Band; Trk; High Hon Roll; NHS; Ballet/Dance; Sunday Schl Tchr; Majorette; Bio.

SHAVER, SASHA L; Marion HS; Memphis, TN; (4); 25/185; French Clb; Band; Mrchg Band; Nwsp; French Hon Soc; Hon Roll; Jr NHS; NHS; Pres Acad Fit Awd; Patriot Schlr; Team Mates; Ecol Field Stud Pgm; Grp Ldr; Chrstn Bros Univ; Vet.

SHAW, KELLYE; Newark Jr Sr HS; Oil Trough, AR; (3); 5/55; Church Yth Grp; FBLA; Math Clb; Natl Beta Clb; Sec Frsh Cls; Sec Soph Cls; Sftbl; Hon Roll; Ntl Merit Ltr; Pres Acad Fit Awd; Art II/ENGL III/CMPTR Tech/Home Ec Awds; Wht Rvr Bapt Crhch Pianist/Orgnst; Natl Engl Merit Awd; AR ST Univ; Nrsg.

SHAW, KENNETH D; Conway Sr HS; Conway, AR; (4); Orch; School Musical; Hendrix Coll.

SHAW, LAURA; Pine Bluff HS; Pine Bluff, AR; (1); French Clb; JA; Pep Clb; Chorus; Capt Chrldng; Hon Roll; Pres Schlr; Jr Soc Clb; Seabrook YMCA.

SHAW, LEANNE; Yellville Summit HS; Yellville, AR; (3); Church Yth Grp; FTA; Girl Scts; HOBY; Band; Church Choir; Flag Corp; Mrchg Band; VP Pres NHS; Rptr Nwsp; Stu Of Mnth 95; Eng II Awd 95; Mrchng Aux All-Str Perf 95; All-Amer Perf Team; Pep Band; AR ST U; Eng.

SHAW, LINDSEY; Central HS; West Helena, AR; (4); 16/195; Am Leg Aux Girls St; Church Yth Grp; Cmnty Wkr; SADD; Acpl Chr; Chorus; Church Choir; Jr NHS; French Clb; Office Aide; AR Yth Sucide Prev Comm VP; Delta Beta Sigma Sor; AR St Univ; Psych.

SHAY, SONYA L; Dover HS; Dover, AR; (4); Drama Clb; Teachers Aide; Band; Chorus; School Musical; Hon Roll; AR Tech; Forestry.

SHEA, BRIAN M; Springdale Sr HS; Springdale, AR; (2); Band; Mrchg Band; Pep Band; Cit Awd; High Hon Roll; Hon Roll; Jr NHS; Pres Acad Fit Awd; Stdnt Of Yr; All Rgn Bnd; U Of AR Rgnl Sci Fair 1st Pl; AR ST Media Cntst Hnrble Mntn; Pol Sci/Law.

SHEA, SARAH H; Dumas Jr HS; Dumas, AR; (1); Church Yth Grp; FBLA; Science Clb; Spanish Clb; Band; Church Choir; Drm Mjr(t); Yrbk; Tennis; High Hon Roll; Chrch Yth Grp; Chldrn Chrch Chr; Tulane; Pedtrcn.

SHEARER, ROBERT J; Hot Springs HS; Hot Springs Natio, AR; (2); Boy Scts; Church Yth Grp; Cmnty Wkr; FCA; FBLA; Natl Beta Clb; Quiz Bowl; Nwsp; Yrbk; Tennis; Engr.

SHEARER, RYAN; Rose Bud Jr Sr HS; Rose Bud, AR; (4); 1/40; Church Yth Grp; FCA; Pres VP FBLA; Sec Natl FFA Org; Capt Quiz Bowl; Var Bsbl; Var Bsktbl; Var Golf; Var Trk; High Hon Roll; Dentistry.

SHEETS, CHAD A; Vilonia HS; Conway, AR; (2); Art Clb; Boy Scts; Natl Beta Clb; Science Clb; Band; Mrchg Band; Pep Band; Hon Roll; UAM Schlsp 94; All Region Band 94 & 95; Music.

SHEFFIELD, JAMES B; Mc Gehee HS; Mc Gehee, AR; (2); Church Yth Grp; FTA; Letterman Clb; Mu Alpha Theta; Natl Beta Clb; VP Spanish Clb; Ftbl; Golf; Wt Lftg; NHS; UNIV OF AR; Phar.

SHEFFIELD, NATHAN K; Mountain Pine Jr Sr HS; Mountain Pine, AR; (2); 1/70; Art Clb; French Clb; FBLA; Quiz Bowl; Band; Ed Yrbk; Rep Stu Cncl; Cit Awd; High Hon Roll; Ntl Merit SF; 1st Plc Kybrdng Aplctns FBLA Dist 95-; Alva Aplng Outstdng Mscn Awd; Outstdng Jr HS Mscn 94-95.

SHELBY, ABIGAIL B; Rogers HS; Rogers, AR; (3); Church Yth Grp; Sec FCA; FBLA; Spanish Clb; Rep Frsh Cls; Rep Stu Cncl; Capt Chrldng; L Var Socr; L Trk; High Hon Roll; Benton Cnty Yth Bd; ESL Tutr Non Spkng Eng Stdnts; 5 Tm Gld Card Renaissance Wnr; Cmbr Comm Awd 2 Tms; Intl Bus/Frgn Lang.

SHELBY, LANDON P; Greenwood Sr HS; Fort Smith, AR; (3); 6/199; Church Yth Grp; English Clb; FCA; French Clb; Natl Beta Clb; Science Clb; Bsktbl; Mgr(s); Hon Roll; NHS; Bausch & Lomb Sci Awd; Natl Mrt Awd; Multi-Yr Listee; Vanderbilt; Engrng.

SHELL, MARGARET E; Pine Bluff HS; Pine Bluff, AR; (3); Church Yth Grp; 4-H; French Clb; Office Aide; Chorus; Church Choir; Hon Roll; Intnl Order Rainbow For Girls Mem; Bethel Coll; Eng Lit Tchr.

SHELLEY, BROOKE; Farmington Jr Sr HS; Farmington, AR; (1); Church Yth Grp; FCA; FBLA; FHA; GAA; Pep Clb; Church Choir; Drill Tm; JV Bsktbl; L Chrldng; Trnr/Athl PT.

SHELNUTT, CHANDRA D; Benton Sr HS; Benton, AR; (3); Art Clb; Bus Profs of Am; Church Yth Grp; Cmnty Wkr; Drama Clb; Hist French Clb; FBLA; FHA; Key Clb; Math Clb; Baptist Schl Nrsng; Nrsng.

SHELTON, BRANDON J; Yellville Summit HS; Flippin, AR; (3); Art Clb; Church Yth Grp; FCA; Natl FFA Org; Teachers Aide; Ftbl; Var Trk; Var Wt Lftg; Photo; Bsbl; Railroad-Photo & His; OK ST; Railroad Conductor.

SHELTON, CRYSTAL; Hazen Jr Sr HS; Hazen, AR; (1); Church Yth Grp; Natl Beta Clb; Treas Frsh Cls; Bsktbl; Chrldng; Hon Roll; FHA; GAA; Crs Cntry; Gym.

SHELTON, IKELA S; Fairview HS; Camden, AR; (3); Church Yth Grp; FHA; FTA; Natl Beta Clb; Spanish Clb; Band; Yrbk; Hon Roll; NHS; Spanish NHS; Elem Ed; Psych.

SHELTON, JAMIE R; North Little Rock Hs-East; North Little Rock, AR; (2); Art Clb; Church Yth Grp; Drama Clb; FBLA; Office Aide; Church Yth Grp; Stage Crew; High Hon Roll; Hon Roll; Design Stu Of Yr 94-95; 2nd Pl Art Show; Best In Show/Art Show; Memphis Coll Of Art; Artist.

SHELTON, KELLY; Mc Gehee HS; Mc Gehee, AR; (3); 1/125; Art Clb; Church Yth Grp; Drama Clb; FTA; Mu Alpha Theta; Natl Beta Clb; Office Aide; Science Clb; Spanish Clb; Band.

SHELTON, KENNY; Fountain Lake Jr Sr HS; Hot Springs, AR; (4); Am Leg Boys St; FCA; VP FBLA; Spanish Clb; Nwsp; Phtg Yrbk; Rep Stu Cncl; Var Bsbl; Var Ftbl; SAU; PE.

SHELTON, SHAYLIE C; Marmaduke HS; Paragould, AR; (2); FCA; French Clb; FBLA; Yrbk; Sec Soph Cls; Rep Stu Cncl; Var Bsktbl; Var Sftbl; JV Trk; Hon Roll; Leo Clb; AR ST Univ; Med/Psychlgy.

SHEPHERD, ANDREW; Dumas HS; Dumas, AR; (2); 1/175; Math Clb; Natl Beta Clb; Science Clb; Spanish Clb; Var Bsbl; JV Var Ftbl; Var Cit Awd; High Hon Roll; NHS; Pres Schlr; Amer Legion Stu Of Month Sept; Amer Legion Stu Of Yr; Schlr Ath Awd; U Of AR.

SHEPHERD, BROOKS A; Pine Bluff HS; Pine Bluff, AR; (2); Church Yth Grp; French Clb; FBLA; Hosp Aide; Natl Beta Clb; Science Clb; Acpl Chr; Orch; Yrbk; VP Frsh Cls.

SHEPHERD, DANA M; Alma HS; Alma, AR; (2); FCA; GAA; Letterman Clb; Spanish Clb; Varsity Clb; JV Bsktbl; Vllybl; Cit Awd; NHS; Pres Acad Fit Awd; Soph Vlybl All Conf 95; Westark; Acctng.

SHEPHERD, DREW; Dumas HS; Dumas, AR; (4); 5/163; Am Leg Aux Girls St; Math Clb; Science Clb; Ed Yrbk; Ofcr Stu Cncl; Gym; Cit Awd; High Hon Roll; NHS; Spanish NHS; U Of AR Fayetteville.

SHEPHERD, ELIZABETH; Gurdon HS; Gurdon, AR; (3); Art Clb; Church Yth Grp; Natl Beta Clb; Church Choir; School Musical; School Play; Capt Soph Cls; Capt Jr Cls; Rep Stu Cncl; Chrldng; Henderson ST U; Ed.

SHEPHERD, HOLLY C; Mountainburg Jr Sr HS; Mountainburg, AR; (3); Church Yth Grp; FCA; FHA; Natl Beta Clb; Natl FFA Org; Spanish Clb; SADD; VP Frsh Cls; VP Soph Cls; VP Jr Cls; Mtn Bkng.

SHEPHERD, TRACIE D; Huntsville HS; Huntsville, AR; (4); 3/125; Art Clb; FBLA; FTA; Key Clb; Pres Frsh Cls; Pres Soph Cls; Pres Jr Cls; Pres Sr Cls; Rptr Stu Cncl; Mgr(s); Medcl Applctn Of Sci For Hlth Treas; Drug Abuse Resistance Tm Pres; U Of Cntrl AR; Phys Thrpy.

SHEPPARD, ANDREA; Central Ark Christian Schl; Maumelle, AR; (2); French Clb; Chorus; Drill Tm; Bsktbl; Trk; High Hon Roll; Jr NHS; NHS; Natl Sci Mrt Awd; Deans Lst; Harvard; Med.

SHEPPARD, BEN T; Magnet Cove HS; Malvern, AR; (3); Church Yth Grp; FCA; FBLA; FTA; Spanish Clb; Band; Mrchg Band; School Play; Rep Frsh Cls; Sec Soph Cls; Advrtsmnt.

SHEPPARD, CRISSI D; Magnolia HS; Magnolia, AR; (2); Church Yth Grp; FBLA; Pep Clb; Band; Church Choir; Ofcr Stu Cncl; High Hon Roll; Hon Roll.

SHEPPARD, HOLLY M; Magnolia HS; Magnolia, AR; (3); French Clb; FBLA; Mu Alpha Theta; Science Clb; Band; Color Guard; Drm Mjr(t); Hon Roll; Lyon Coll; Bus.

SHEPPARD, JENNY; East Poinsett Sr HS; Lepanto, AR; (4); 6/59; Church Yth Grp; FHA; Teachers Aide; Chorus; Church Choir; High Hon Roll; Hon Roll; Jr NHS; NHS; AR ST U; Nrsng.

SHEPPARD, JULIUS; El Dorado Sr HS; El Droado, AR; (3); Am Leg Boys St; Boy Scts; Church Yth Grp; FBLA; Key Clb; Letterman Clb; Rep Frsh Cls; Rep Sr Cls; Socr; Swmmng; Law.

SHEREN, JENNY; Beebe Jr HS; Beebe, AR; (1); Church Yth Grp; FBLA; Natl Beta Clb; Pep Clb; Band; Rep Stu Cncl; Bsktbl; Chrldng; High Hon Roll; Pres Acad Fit Awd; All Amer Schlrs; Ntl Hnr Roll; Miss Jr Beebe FHA.

SHERIDAN, HEATHER L; Bauxite Jr Sr HS; Benton, AR; (1); Church Yth Grp; Office Aide; Teachers Aide; Rep Nwsp; Rep Stu Cncl; DAR Awd; Hon Roll; Jr NHS; Greater AR Mass Choir; Henderson ST; Nurse Anesthetst.

SHERMAN, YAKASHA M; Fordyce HS; Fordyce, AR; (3); #26 in class; Church Yth Grp; French Clb; FBLA; FHA; Library Aide; Natl Beta Clb; Science Clb; Powder Puff Ftbl; Hon Roll.

SHERRILL, AMBER; Central Ark Christian Schl; Sherwood, AR; (1); Capt Vllybl; High Hon Roll; Rptr Jr NHS; Valentine Ct; Intr Dsgn.

SHERRILL, SANDRA K; Farmington Jr Sr HS; Fayetteville, AR; (3); Dance Clb; FBLA; Girl Scts; Natl FFA Org; Teachers Aide; Drill Tm; Var Pom Pon; Jr NHS; NHS; Horseback Riding & Trng.

SHERROD, AMANDA G; St Joe Public Schl; Saint Joe, AR; (1); Church Yth Grp; Cmnty Wkr; FBLA; FHA; Library Aide; Rep Frsh Cls; Sang Song For FBLA Dist Meet/Vctnl Banquet.

SHERWOOD, APRIL J; Searcy HS; Searcy, AR; (2); 10/256; FCA; FTA; Natl Beta Clb; Spanish Clb; Chorus; Church Choir; Bsktbl; Jr NHS; Spanish NHS; MTNA ST Hnrs Recitalpaster Class Piano Solo; ST Yth Comm; Ch Of Jesus Christ Latter Day Sts; Dectv Homcde/Crmnl Invstgtn.

SHERWOOD, JOHN D; White Co Central Schl; Searcy, AR; (2); 8/50; Boy Scts; Church Yth Grp; FBLA; Natl FFA Org; High Hon Roll; NHS; Schl Ldrshp Group; Lion Coll; Sci; Bus.

SHEWBART, LEE ANN; Caddo Hills Jr Sr HS; Glenwood, AR; (3); #3 in class; Sec Treas Church Yth Grp; Rptr FBLA; Pres FHA; Model UN; Natl Beta Clb; Capt Quiz Bowl; Treas Jr Cls; Pres Stu Cncl; High Hon Roll; Pres Schlr.

SHICK, JASON; Hackett Schl; Hackett, AR; (4); 3/40; Spanish Clb; Band; Mrchg Band; Pep Band; High Hon Roll; NHS; Hstrn; Natl Eng Mrt Awd; Gftd/Tlntd; All-Rgn, All-Strs Bnds; AR St U Trstee Schlrshp; AR ST U; Med.

SHIELDS, DALE B; Booneville Jr Sr HS; Booneville, AR; (3); Church Yth Grp; FCA; Spanish Clb; Var Bsbl; Var Ftbl; Prfct Atten Awd.

SHIELDS, DAVID C; Gravette HS; Gravette, AR; (3); FBLA; Treas Jr Cls; Var Bsbl; Var Ftbl; Cit Awd; High Hon Roll; NHS; Engr.

SHIELDS, JASON O; Gillett Jr Sr HS; Gillett, AR; (4); German Clb; Teachers Aide; School Play; Yrbk; Ofcr Bsbl; Ftbl; Hon Roll.

SHIN, DAWNA J; Searcy HS; Searcy, AR; (2); 91/256; Church Yth Grp; French Clb; JA; Band; Chorus; Mrchg Band; Orch; Yrbk; Hon Roll; Jr NHS; All Region & All St Bands; Med Sci; Music Perfmnc.

SHINN, BENJAMIN; Jasper HS; Dogpatch, AR; (4); 3/46; Cmnty Wkr; FBLA; Pres Library Aide; Pres Math Clb; Pres Math Tm; Rptr Natl Beta Clb; Natl FFA Org; Office Aide; Capt Quiz Bowl; Sec Science Clb; AR Govs Schl; Proj GO; TEAMS; Hendrix Coll; Med.

SHINN, JOCELYN B; Huntsville HS; Huntsville, AR; (3); 14/130; Am Leg Aux Girls St; Church Yth Grp; FCA; FBLA; Band; Color Guard; Drm Mjr(t); Sftbl; Trk; NHS; U Of AR; Polysci.

SHIPLEY, JOSH A; Arkansas Schl Math & Science; Marion, AR; (3); Church Yth Grp; Drama Clb; Spanish Clb; Mrchg Band; Yrbk; Rep Soph Cls; High Hon Roll; Treas Jr NHS; NHS; Mu Alpha Theta; Navy & Marine Corps Distngd Achvmt Awd Sci Fair; Odyssey Of The Mind.

SHIPLEY, JOSLYN; Brookland Jr Sr HS; Jonesboro, AR; (4); 4/54; FBLA; Model UN; Quiz Bowl; Band; Variety Show; Ed Nwsp; Sec Frsh Cls; Rep Soph Cls; Sec Jr Cls; Sec Sr Cls; AR ST U; Eng.

SHIPMAN, ANDREA J; Yellville Summit HS; Yellville, AR; (2); #23 in class; FBLA; Natl Beta Clb; Office Aide; Teachers Aide; Band; Orch; Pep Band; Treas Stu Cncl; Hon Roll; NHS; Majorette Line 2 Yrs/Capt 1 Yr.

SHIPMAN, JAMES D; Bald Knob HS; Bald Knob, AR; (1); Quiz Bowl; Teachers Aide; Band; Cit Awd; High Hon Roll; Outstdng Perfmnc Eng; U Of AR Fayetteville; Lawyer.

SHIPMAN, JONATHAN E; Yellville Summit HS; Yellville, AR; (2); 4/76; Church Yth Grp; Cmnty Wkr; FBLA; Natl Beta Clb; Quiz Bowl; Band; Jazz Band; Mrchg Band; Ofcr Bsbl; Score Keeper; YEAC; Geomtry Awd/Phys Sci Awd 9th Grd; Algbr II Awd/Bio Awd 10th Grd; U Of MO Rolla; Mech Engr.

SHIPP, AMANDA L; Arkansas Sr HS; Texarkana, AR; (2); 7/420; Church Yth Grp; French Clb; Acpl Chr; Chorus; Rep Frsh Cls; Pres Jr NHS; Frnch Awd; Texarkana Coll; Acctng.

SHIPP, CHRIS; Arkansas Sr HS; Texarkana, AR; (2); Church Yth Grp; FCA; Church Choir; Crs Cntry; Ftbl; Trk; Mountain Of Ozarks; Minstry.

SHIREY, LINDSEY; Booneville Jr Sr HS; Booneville, AR; (2); 2/110; Church Yth Grp; FCA; GAA; Natl Beta Clb; Var Bsktbl; Var Chrldng; Var Trk; Cit Awd; High Hon Roll; Prfct Atten Awd; All Dist Bsktbl; U Of AR; Bus.

SHIRLEY, JOSHUA I; Mtn Home HS; Deer Lodge, TN; (4); 82/226; FCA; Band; Chorus; Jazz Band; Mrchg Band; Orch; Pep Band; St Schlr; TN Tech Univ; Acctng.

SHIRLEY, MELANIE D; Ridgecrest HS; Paragould, AR; (2); 79/240; FBLA; Natl FFA Org; Hon Roll; US Bus Ed Awds; All-Amer Schlr; Vet Care.

SHIRLEY, MICHAEL P; North Little Rock Hs-West; North Little Rock, AR; (3); Am Leg Boys St; Debate Tm; FBLA; German Clb; Natl Beta Clb; Hon Roll; AR Stdnt Cngrs 93-95/Spkr Of Hse 95; Yng Amer Bwlng Allnc Natl Yth Ldr Of Yr 96-; Comm/Pol Sci.

SHIRLEY, ZACH R; West Memphis Christian Schl; Crawfordsville, AR; (1); Church Yth Grp; JV Bsktbl; JV Ftbl; JV Var Trk; JV Wt Lftg; Hon Roll; Church Act; Harding Univ.

SHIRRON, MELISSA D; Sheridan Sr HS; Hensley, AR; (3); FCA; GAA; Office Aide; Pres Stu Cncl; Var Bsktbl; Var Sftbl; JV Vllybl; Cit Awd; High Hon Roll; Jr NHS; Pitcher Ntnly Rnkd Sftbl Tm; UALR; Sports Med/Athltc Trnr.

SHIU, LOUISE M; Russellville Sr HS; Russellville, AR; (2); Spanish Clb; Band; Mrchg Band; Pep Band; Ofcr Stu Cncl; High Hon Roll; Jr NHS; NHS; Pres Acad Fit Awd; Yng Repblcns; MIT; Engr.

SHOCK, CARISA E; Conway Sr HS; Conway, AR; (4); 54/550; Church Yth Grp; FCA; French Clb; GAA; Sftbl; French Hon Soc; Hon Roll; NHS; Engl Awd; Univ Scho To UCA; UCA.

SHOEMAKE, JENNIFER L; Oak Grove HS; Maumelle, AR; (1); Art Clb; FCA; Letterman Clb; Natl Beta Clb; Teachers Aide; Var L Bsktbl; Var L Vllybl; High Hon Roll; Pres Acad Fit Awd; Jr Beta Clb; Acad Awd; Medal 9 Grd Hlth; U Of Cntrl Ar; Tchr.

SHOEMAKER, MELISSA C; Fayetteville Sr HS; Fayetteville, AR; (2); GAA; Var Capt Bsktbl; Var L Sftbl; Var L Trk; High Hon Roll; Hon Roll; Frgn Lang Club; Phys Spch Thrpy.

SHOESMITH, MICHELLE; Morrilton Sr HS; Morrilton, AR; (3); Art Clb; Pres Church Yth Grp; Math Clb; Natl Beta Clb; Science Clb; Spanish Clb; Thesps; Drill Tm; School Play; Tennis; U Of Cntrl AR; Med.

SHOFFIT, JAMIE G; Elkins Jr Sr HS; Elkins, AR; (2); Cmnty Wkr; FBLA; FHA; Girl Scts; Library Aide; SADD; Teachers Aide; Band; Mrchg Band; School Play; U Of AR; Law; Politics.

SHOFFNER, WILLIAM C; Searcy HS; Searcy, AR; (2); French Clb; Natl Beta Clb; French Hon Soc; Hon Roll; Jr NHS; Beta Clb; Historian Jr Natl Hnr Soc; Engrng; Arch.

SHOFNER, MARISA M; Rogers HS; Rogers, AR; (4); Am Leg Aux Girls St; Key Clb; Drill Tm; Ofcr Frsh Cls; Treas Stu Cncl; Capt L Golf; Church Yth Grp; FCA; FBLA; Office Aide; Peer Helper; Elem Tutor; Renaissance Acad Awd; Rotry Stu Of Month; U Of Cntrl AR; Elem Schl Cnslr.

SHOFNER, TARA; Elkino HS; Fayetteville, AR; (3); Church Yth Grp; Sec FBLA; VP FHA; HOBY; Pres Natl FFA Org; Teachers Aide; Sec Soph Cls; VP Jr Cls; Ofcr Stu Cncl; Var Bsktbl; Harding U; Hstry.

SHOPPACH, JONTHAN M; Harmony Grove Jr Sr HS; Benton, AR; (2); 9/60; Church Yth Grp; Natl Beta Clb; Band; Church Choir; Mrchg Band; Pep Band; Stage Crew; Variety Show; Rep Stu Cncl; Hon Roll.

SHORES, BRENT C; Russellville Sr HS; Russellville, AR; (2); #1 in class; Church Yth Grp; Spanish Clb; Band; Church Choir; Jazz Band; Mrchg Band; JV Socr; High Hon Roll; Jr NHS; NHS; Odyssey Of The Mind; Chrstn Stu Union; Comp.

SHORES, BRIAN R; Alma HS; Alma, AR; (2); Church Yth Grp; Cmnty Wkr; FCA; Natl FFA Org; Speech Tm; Varsity Clb; Var Ftbl; Wt Lftg; NHS; Pres Acad Fit Awd; Hnr Roll; Letterman Clb; Ctznshp Awd; Westark; Forestry.

SHORES, SYREATHA J; Waldron HS; Waldron, AR; (3); Am Leg Aux Girls St; Art Clb; Cmnty Wkr; Dance Clb; Pres FHA; Girl Scts; Office Aide; Spanish Clb; Teachers Aide; Yrbk; Rich Mt Voc; Sec Sci.

SHORES, TRACY L; Russellville Sr HS; Russellville, AR; (3); 9/320; Church Yth Grp; Spanish Clb; Band; Church Choir; Rep Capt Flag Corp; Mrchg Band; Nwsp; High Hon Roll; NHS; Teachers Aide; Odyssey Of Mind; Chrstn Stu Union.

SHORT, JENNY; North Little Rock Hs-West; North Little Rock, AR; (3); 29/594; Church Yth Grp; Cmnty Wkr; Drama Clb; Key Clb; Mu Alpha Theta; Natl Beta Clb; Chrldng; High Hon Roll; NHS; Pres Acad Fit Awd; Hendrix; Med.

SHORT, LESLEE R; Magnet Cove HS; Malvern, AR; (4); Library Aide; Math Clb; Science Clb; Teachers Aide; Band; Chorus; Variety Show; Ed Yrbk; Hon Roll; U Of AR; TV Brdcst.

SHORT, MARCUS W; Crowleys Ridge Acad; Paragould, AR; (1); Church Yth Grp; FBLA; Science Clb; Socr.

SHORT, MITCH L; Nettleton HS; Jonesboro, AR; (2); French Clb; FHA; Math Clb; Quiz Bowl; Science Clb; Ofcr Soph Cls; Cit Awd; Prfct Atten Awd; Upward Bound ASU; ASU; Criminalogy.

SHORT, RACHELLE L; Dequeen HS; De Queen, AR; (1); GAA; Hosp Aide; Letterman Clb; Chorus; Yrbk; Bsktbl; Trk; Wt Lftg; Fayetteville; DR/PT/X-RAY Tch.

SHOURD, ANDREA N; Searcy HS; Searcy, AR; (3); Church Yth Grp; Spanish Clb; Chorus; Church Choir; Yrbk; Hon Roll; NHS; Spanish NHS; All Region Choir; Oauchita Bapt Univ; Eng.

SHREVE, AMBER; Farmington Jr Sr HS; Farmington, AR; (2); Band; Mrchg Band; Cit Awd; French Hon Soc; Hon Roll; NHS.

SHRYOCK, SYDNEY M; Malvern Sr HS; Malvern, AR; (3); Church Yth Grp; FCA; FBLA; Natl Beta Clb; Office Aide; Pep Clb; Acpl Chr; Chorus; Cit Awd; Hon Roll; Bach Awd; Natl Piano Guild Top Talent Awd 7 Yrs; Natl Piano Plyng Trnmnt 1st Pl Gold Mdl; Law.

SHUFFIELD, CHRISTIE L; Dover HS; Dover, AR; (2); 3/90; Spanish Clb; Var Bsktbl; High Hon Roll; Jr NHS; NHS.

SHULTS, RACHEL; Pea Ridge HS; Pea Ridge, AR; (2); Church Yth Grp; Spanish Clb; Church Choir; Var L Bsktbl; Var L Trk; Var Wt Lftg; High Hon Roll; NHS.

SHUMARD, NATALLIE; Cedarville Jr Sr HS; Natural Dam, AR; (1); Church Yth Grp; GAA; Pep Clb; Chrldng; Sftbl; Hon Roll; U Of AR; Fin Planning.

SHUMATE, TERRY R; Mountain Home HS; Mountain Home, AR; (2); French Clb; Band; Mrchg Band; Orch; Pep Band; Hon Roll.

SHUPE, HEATHER L; North Little Rock Hs-West; North Little Rock, AR; (3); 7/554; Sec Art Clb; Church Yth Grp; Cmnty Wkr; Mu Alpha Theta; Natl Beta Clb; Speech Tm; Band; Church Choir; Drill Tm; School Musical; Chrch Drama Tm Dir; Chrch Yth Ensemble; Acteens.

SHURR, ALLISON; Southside HS; Fort Smith, AR; (3); 24/502; Church Yth Grp; FCA; Key Clb; Mu Alpha Theta; Spanish Clb; SADD; Church Choir; Hon Roll; Jr NHS; NHS; PREMED/PEDIATRICN.

SHUTT, CRYSTAL; Sulphur Rock Schl; Sulphur Rock, AR; (1); 1/27; Church Yth Grp; Math Clb; Natl Beta Clb; Quiz Bowl; Science Clb; Teachers Aide; Band; Pep Band; School Play; Stage Crew; AEGIS Pgms Smmr; Tutr.

SHUTTS, RACHEL; Pea Ridge HS; Pea Ridge, AR; (2); #2 in class; Church Yth Grp; Spanish Clb; Var Bsktbl; Var Trk; High Hon Roll; NHS; Pres Acad Fit Awd; Marktng.

SIAS, PAMELA L; Crossett Sr HS; Crossett, AR; (2); Chorus; Sftbl; U Of AR Monticello; Law.

SIBLEY, RAHSHANDA K; Central Sr HS; Little Rock, AR; (4); Cmnty Wkr; Debate Tm; Hosp Aide; NFL; Service Clb; Speech Tm; Rptr Nwsp; High Hon Roll; NHS; Ntl Merit SF; Natl Achvt Fnlst; NCTE Awd; Engl.

SIDANI, ROBERT; Rogers HS; Rogers, AR; (4); FBLA; Rep Sr Cls; Var Tennis; Hon Roll; NHS; FLC Secy; PTSA & REACH; U Of AR Fayettevl; Med.

SIDES, ANDREA; Farmington Jr Sr HS; Farmington, AR; (1); 4-H; French Clb; FBLA; Band; Mrchg Band; Pep Band; 4-H Awd; Hon Roll; NHS; Ntl Merit Ltr; U Of AR.

SIEGEL, JEREMY; North Little Rock Hs-West; North Little Rock, AR; (4); Art Clb; Boy Scts; French Clb; Mu Alpha Theta; Natl Beta Clb; Science Clb; School Musical; School Play; Stage Crew; NHS; Keystone VP; TX Chrstn U; Nrsg.

SIEGEL, ROBERT BRANDON; Central Ark Christian Schl; Little Rock, AR; (2); Church Yth Grp; Cmnty Wkr; Crs Cntry; Socr; Trk; Hon Roll; Wilderness Trek Crew Ldr; Yth Group Ldrshp Comm; U Of AR; Engr.

SIEGERS, COURTNEY M; Fayetteville Sr HS; Fayetteville, AR; (3); Chorus; Var Bsktbl; Var Capt Ftbl; Trk; Wt Lftg; Hon Roll; AR Fayetteville; Dentistry.

SIHARATH, CHANSOUPHAPHON; Southside HS; Fort Smith, AR; (3); Key Clb; Mu Alpha Theta; Spanish Clb; Socr; Hon Roll; Jr NHS; NHS; Spanish NHS.

SIKES, APRIL D; Conway Sr HS; Conway, AR; (2); Church Yth Grp; FBLA; Office Aide; Crs Cntry; Swmmng; Trk; Hon Roll; Prfct Atten Awd; Aggressive Skater; Ozark Mission Proj; St Track & Crss Cntry; UCA.

SILVA, CRYSTAL S; Farmington Jr Sr HS; Farmington, AR; (2); FHA; Chorus; Hon Roll.

SILVERMAN, KATIE; Humphrey Schl; Humphrey, AR; (3); 1/35; Church Yth Grp; VP FBLA; VP FHA; Natl FFA Org; VP Science Clb; VP Spanish Clb; Ed Yrbk; Sec Frsh Cls; Pres Jr Cls; High Hon Roll; Spelman; Drmtlgy.

SILVEY, MICHAEL L; Springdale Sr HS; Springdale, AR; (1); Band; Jazz Band; Mrchg Band; High Hon Roll; NHS; Regional HS 1st Pl Sci Fair Awd Physics; 1st Chair Band Camp; Comp Engrng.

SILVEY, WILL; Murfreesboro HS; Murfreesboro, AR; (3); Art Clb; Church Yth Grp; FBLA; FHA; VP Natl Beta Clb; Science Clb; Rptr Soph Cls; Hon Roll; Awd Of Excl Henderson St Univ ACT Scores; Henderson ST Univ.

SIMCO, NICHOLAS R; Fayetteville Sr HS; Fayetteville, AR; (2); FCA; Ofcr Bsbl; Golf; Hon Roll; Pres Acad Fit Awd; Sprtsmnsp Awd Bsbl; Stock Market Game 2nd In ST; All-Star Bsbl; FSU; Law.

SIMERS, EARLE W; Highland HS; Mammoth Spring, AR; (2); Band; Chorus; Mrchg Band; Pep Band; Golf; Engrng.

SIMINGTON, SHAMEKA; Bright Star Schl; Doddridge, AR; (4); 3/22; Library Aide; Quiz Bowl; Ed Nwsp; Ed Yrbk; Sec Frsh Cls; High Hon Roll; VP NHS; Gftd/Tlntd; Afro-Amer Cnvntn; Eng Awd; U AR; Psych.

SIMMONS, AARON C; Dover HS; Dover, AR; (2); Computer Clb; Drama Clb; Model UN; Quiz Bowl; Spanish Clb; School Play; Stage Crew; Bsktbl; High Hon Roll; Hon Roll; Bus Admin.

SIMMONS, AUTUMN; Parkview Magnet HS; Little Rock, AR; (3); FBLA; HOBY; Rep Jr Cls; Hon Roll; Beta Club; Tchrs Of Tomorrow; Comp Engrng.

SIMMONS, BENJAMIN S; Marked Tree Jr Sr HS; Marked Tree, AR; (3); FBLA; Library Aide; Natl FFA Org; Quiz Bowl; Band; Jazz Band; Mrchg Band; Stage Crew; Lit Mag; Hon Roll; Mst Outstdng Cncrt Bnd; Mst Outstdng Brs; Delta Voc Schl; Auto Bdy/Mech.

SIMMONS, COREY G; Poyen Schl; Poyen, AR; (2); 2/40; Boy Scts; Church Yth Grp; Natl Beta Clb; Office Aide; Spanish Clb; Ofcr Bsbl; Var Bsktbl; Var Lcrss; Var Trk; Arch.

SIMMONS, JASON W; Hazen Jr Sr HS; Des Arc, AR; (3); 13/50; Church Yth Grp; French Clb; FBLA; FTA; Natl Beta Clb; Band; Var Bsktbl; Var Ftbl; Var Wt Lftg; Hon Roll.

SIMMONS, JENNIFER M; Lewisville HS; Lewisville, AR; (3); 3/42; Pres 4-H; FBLA; FHA; Library Aide; Spanish Clb; 4-H Awd; NHS; Pres Acad Fit Awd; Upwrd Bnd Prgm; Gftd/Tlntd; Southern AR U; Anml Sci.

SIMMONS, JOHN; Clay Co Central Jr Sr HS; Rector, AR; (3); 1/85; Church Yth Grp; Cmnty Wkr; FBLA; German Clb; HOBY; Quiz Bowl; Science Clb; Teachers Aide; Band; Church Choir; Renaissnce Stu Cmmttee.

SIMMONS, JON; Magnet Cove HS; Malvern, AR; (3); 2/40; Am Leg Boys St; FCA; Math Clb; Natl Beta Clb; Science Clb; Band; Ofcr Stu Cncl; Ofcr Bsbl; Bsktbl; High Hon Roll; Harding U Searcy AR.

SIMMONS, MELINDA R; Cutter Morning Star HS; Hot Springs, AR; (2); 1/33; Treas FBLA; Sec FHA; Hosp Aide; Natl Beta Clb; Spanish Clb; Band; Yrbk; Co-Capt Chrldng; High Hon Roll; CHAMPS; Teen Invlmnt.

SIMMONS, SABRINA M; Dollarway HS; Pine Bluff, AR; (2); Church Yth Grp; ROTC; Church Choir; Home Ec; Mechanics; Home Schl; Univ At Pine Bluff; Psych.

SIMON, GEORGENA P; Midland HS; Batesville, AR; (4); 1/40; Pres Treas FHA; Girl Scts; Library Aide; Sec Natl Beta Clb; Spanish Clb; Yrbk; High Hon Roll; Elem Ed.

SIMON, JESSICA; Booneville Jr Sr HS; Booneville, AR; (2); 2/100; Church Yth Grp; FCA; FBLA; FTA; Natl Beta Clb; Science Clb; Chrldng; Cit Awd; Hon Roll; Sci; Tchng.

SIMON, JESSICA L; St Joseph Jr Sr HS; Conway, AR; (4); 14/28; Girl Scts; Key Clb; Chorus; School Musical; School Play; Sec Soph Cls; L Bsktbl; Mgr(s); L Sftbl; L Trk; Yth Group VP; UCA; Radiology.

SIMON, MORTEN; Nettleton HS; Jonesboro, AR; (2); FBLA; Math Clb; Spanish Clb; Tennis; Bio Awd; All ST Tennis 3rd Pl/Dist Trnmnt Wnr; Ferris ST Univ; PTM.

SIMPKINS, JASON R; Blytheville Sr HS; Blytheville, AR; (3); Natl Beta Clb; Band; Jazz Band; Mrchg Band; Hon Roll; MCCC.

SIMPKINS, KRISTINA; Southside HS; Fort Smith, AR; (3); 26/502; FCA; French Clb; FHA; GAA; Math Clb; Mu Alpha Theta; Teachers Aide; Band; Mrchg Band; Trk; Ath Trnr/Mgr 9th Grd Sprts; Med.

SIMPSON, AURAYIA C; Dumas HS; Dumas, AR; (2); 8/130; Church Yth Grp; Cmnty Wkr; Computer Clb; 4-H; FBLA; Band; Church Choir; Drm Mjr(t); Jazz Band; Mrchg Band; D Mrt, Black His & Acad Improvement Awds; Music; Comp Tech.

SIMPSON, CHARLIE; Malvern Sr HS; Malvern, AR; (4); 68/171; FCA; Spanish Clb; SADD; Band; Mrchg Band; VP Sr Cls; Bsktbl; Trk; Hon Roll; CHAMPS Ldr; Peer Cnslr; All-Dist Band; U Of Cntrl AR; Mech Engrng.

SIMPSON, DAVID; Eudora HS; Little Rock, AR; (3); #2 in class; Church Choir; Var Bsktbl; Var Ftbl; High Hon Roll; Ath Awd; PE Awd; Prncpls Awd; Otsdng Achvmnt Awd Algebra; Eng Awd; High SAT Achvmnt Awd; Dermatology.

SIMPSON, JENNY; Rogers HS; Rogers, AR; (4); FBLA; Library Aide; SADD; Teachers Aide; Vllybl; Hon Roll; U S Bus Ed Awd; Renaissance Awd; U Of AR; Bus Acctng.

SIMPSON, JUSTIN; White Co Central Schl; Judsonia, AR; (3); Am Leg Boys St; Cmnty Wkr; Rptr Natl FFA Org; Yrbk; Hon Roll; Pres Acad Fit Awd; Received Sci, His & FFA Awds; NOWCO Fire Dept Vol Fireman; Game & Fish Mgmt.

SIMPSON, KERRON; Monticello HS; Monticello, AR; (4); 25/115; Am Leg Aux Girls St; French Clb; FBLA; Natl Beta Clb; Spanish Clb; Yrbk; Ofcr Sr Cls; Hnr Graduate; Outstndng Senior; Univ Of AK; Fshn Merch.

SIMPSON, LESLIE; Newport HS; Tupelo, AR; (4); #1 in class; Am Leg Aux Girls St; Spanish Clb; Band; Mrchg Band; Teachers Aide; Lit Mag; High Hon Roll; NHS; Prfct Atten Awd; Pres Schlr; U Of Cntrl AR; Occptnl Thrpy.

SIMPSON, LEVI S; Ozark HS; Ozark, AR; (2); 1/115; Cmnty Wkr; 4-H; HOBY; Natl Beta Clb; Quiz Bowl; Band; 4-H Awd; Art Clb; CAP; FBLA; DARE Role Model; AEGIS Pgm; Proj GO; Mid 1; Aerosp; 9 Yr Piano Stdnt.

SIMPSON, MARC; Ozark Adventist Acad; Siloam Springs, AR; (4); 5/50; Quiz Bowl; Band; Chorus; Variety Show; Treas Frsh Cls; Var Intrml Bsktbl; Intrml Ftbl; Cit Awd; High Hon Roll; NHS; Stu Sen; Sthwstrn Advntst Coll; Bus Mgmt.

SIMPSON, SHAWN K; Mc Gehee HS; Mcgehee, AR; (2); FTA; Spanish Clb; Golf; Trk; Hon Roll; Agri Bus.

SIMPSON, VERONICA A; Malvern Sr HS; Malvern, AR; (3); 21/170; Am Leg Aux Girls St; FCA; GAA; Natl Beta Clb; Band; Flag Corp; Vllybl; High Hon Roll; Hon Roll; NHS; Archonettes Zeta Phi Beta; 4 Yr Coll; Bus Mgmt.

SIMS, ANDRIA L; Sylvan Hills HS; Sherwood, AR; (3); Am Leg Aux Girls St; FBLA; Mu Alpha Theta; Teachers Aide; Drill Tm; Hon Roll; Jr NHS; Drama Clb; FHA; Spanish Clb; PRIDE; Sherwood Yth Cncl; Jr Exec Comm; Corp Bus.

SIMS, BILLY G; Star City HS; Moscow, AR; (3); UAM; Ag Bus.

SIMS, BILLY J; Alpena Schl; Green Forest, AR; (2); 5/51; Church Yth Grp; Natl Beta Clb; Natl FFA Org; Quiz Bowl; High Hon Roll; Hon Roll; 4-H; Spanish Clb; School Play; Lit Mag; Woodsman Of The World Awd; Pharmacist.

SIMS, BRANDON M; Dequeen HS; De Queen, AR; (2); Natl FFA Org; Church Choir; Ftbl; Hon Roll.

SIMS, HALEY; Rogers HS; Lowell, AR; (2); Church Yth Grp; FBLA; Quiz Bowl; Drill Tm; Orch; High Hon Roll; Hon Roll; Pres Acad Fit Awd; Law.

SIMS, JACQUILIN D; Sylvan Hills HS; Sherwood, AR; (3); 62/290; Am Leg Aux Girls St; French Clb; FBLA; VP FHA; Drill Tm; Ofcr Jr Cls; Hon Roll; Jr NHS; PRIDE Drg/Alcohol Free Dance Tm; HUMANS Org Keeps Schl Clean; LA ST Univ; Bus/Risk Mngmnt.

SIMS, JERRY; Southside HS; Barling, AR; (4); Latin Clb; Mu Alpha Theta; High Hon Roll; Psych.

SIMS, JOY; Cabot HS; Austin, AR; (3); 26/398; Church Yth Grp; Drama Clb; French Clb; Key Clb; Speech Tm; Teachers Aide; Thesps; School Musical; School Play; Stage Crew; St Champ Oratory ASCA Speech Trnmt; AR Tech Univ; Acctng.

SIMS, KATHERINE A; North Little Rock Hs-West; North Little Rock, AR; (3); Church Yth Grp; Band; Flag Corp; Mrchg Band; Pep Band; Stage Crew; Var Trk; Tri-M Perf Arts Clb; UCA; Occptnl Therapy.

SIMS, KOLESCHER V; Central Sr HS; Little Rock, AR; (4); 124/401; Church Yth Grp; FBLA; Hosp Aide; Band; Church Choir; Drill Tm; Mrchg Band; Pep Band; L Pom Pon; Hon Roll; Pres CSF; Sec Sunday Schl; U Of AR LR; Bio; Pre-Med.

SIMS, NACOSHA; Dollarway HS; Pine Bluff, AR; (3); Art Clb; Church Yth Grp; 4-H; French Clb; FHA; Band; Flag Corp; Mrchg Band; Pep Band; Gym.

SIMS, NATALIE L; Russellville Sr HS; Russellville, AR; (3); Cmnty Wkr; FCA; French Clb; GAA; VICA; Band; Mrchg Band; Var Swmmng; High Hon Roll; NHS; Majorette Line; Feature Twrlr; Drury; Archtct.

SIMS, SCARLET A; Atkins Schl; Atkins, AR; (4); 11/82; Drama Clb; Natl Beta Clb; Science Clb; Band; Chorus; Color Guard; Mrchg Band; School Play; Rptr Nwsp; High Hon Roll; Poem Publshd; AR Ambssdrs Of Music Travel To Europe; Summer Coll Courses ATU; Hendrix Coll; Linguistics.

SIMS, SHARRA L; John L Mcclellan Magnet HS; Little Rock, AR; (2); Church Yth Grp; Church Choir; Var Trk; JV Var Vllybl; Hon Roll; DK; RN.

SING, ADREA L; Russellville Sr HS; London, AR; (3); 159/320; French Clb; Band; Mrchg Band; Cnslr Aide; AR Tech U.

SINGH, AMANDA K; Mc Gehee HS; Mc Gehee, AR; (4); 20/101; Art Clb; Church Yth Grp; Drama Clb; FBLA; FTA; Mu Alpha Theta; Natl Beta Clb; Yrbk; AAE Art Exhibit ST Capitol 96; Univ Of AR; Cmptr Sci.

SINGH, SAMANTHA; Mc Gehee HS; Mc Gehee, AR; (3); Art Clb; Church Yth Grp; Drama Clb; FBLA; FHA; FTA; Natl Beta Clb; Science Clb; Spanish Clb; Rep Stu Cncl; UALR.

SINGLETON, ALANDRIUS M; El Dorado Sr HS; El Dorado, AR; (3); Church Yth Grp; FBLA; ROTC; Chorus; Church Choir; Drill Tm; Trk; Pride; UCA; Law/Psych.

SINGLETON, DAMON M; Fayetteville Sr HS; Fayetteville, AR; (2); Band; Jazz Band; Mrchg Band; Pep Band; JV Socr; Gov Hon Prg Awd; High Hon Roll; Hon Roll; Pres Acad Fit Awd; Rock Climbing; Musical Group Outside Of Schl-Rock Band.

SINGYOT, DALING; Waldron HS; Waldron, AR; (2); JV Bsktbl; Prfct Atten Awd; Engrng.

SINH, LINH; Central Sr HS; Little Rock, AR; (1); FHA; Spanish Clb; Yrbk; Cit Awd; Hon Roll; Jr NHS; Pres Acad Fit Awd; Save The Earth Clb; Beta Clb VP; Care Comm; Bus Ecnmcs.

SINOR, CARMEN E; Lamar HS; Clarksville, AR; (3); Hon Roll; Westark; Chld Care.

SIPES, KIMBERLY S; Crossett Sr HS; Crossett, AR; (2); Church Yth Grp; FBLA; Band; Chorus; Church Choir; Mrchg Band; Hon Roll; Majorette; Fire Baton Twirler; Dance Trng; Mid-Amer Bible Coll; Bus.

SIRMON, ADAM D; Dierks HS; Dierks, AR; (1); Church Yth Grp; Natl FFA Org; Church Choir; Hon Roll.

SIRMON, BRIDGET; Dierks HS; Dierks, AR; (4); 1/34; Art Clb; Church Yth Grp; FBLA; FHA; Church Choir; Ed Nwsp; Rep Stu Cncl; Pres NHS; Prfct Atten Awd; Val; Piano; Ouachita Bapt U; Sci.

SISCO, CHASITY; Harrison Sr HS; Harrison, AR; (4); DECA; FBLA; FHA; Spanish Clb; Band; Yrbk; 1st Pl DECA Quiz Bowl; NACTC.

SISCO, CRISSY L; Van Buren Sr HS; Van Buren, AR; (2); 11/310; Drama Clb; Mu Alpha Theta; Science Clb; Speech Tm; School Play; Cit Awd; High Hon Roll; Jr NHS; NHS.

SISEMORE, SCOTT M; Springdale Sr HS; Springdale, AR; (2); English Clb; Teachers Aide; Hon Roll; Univ Of AR; Comm.

SISNEY, ANDREA; Fountain Lake Jr Sr HS; Hot Springs, AR; (4); #2 in class; Am Leg Aux Girls St; FCA; FBLA; FHA; Key Clb; Treas Natl Beta Clb; Quiz Bowl; Sec Spanish Clb; Yrbk; Rptr Jr Cls; Rotry Stu Guest; Super Rtngs Piano Solos Natl Fed Music Clbs; Jr Fstvls; U Of Central AR; Phys Thrpy.

SISOUKRATH, THEPPHONE K; Van Buren Sr HS; Van Buren, AR; (2); Cmnty Wkr; FCA; FBLA; SADD; Ftbl; Tennis; Trk; Wt Lftg; Cit Awd; High Hon Roll; U Of AR; Bus.

SISOUPHANH, SOUNDARA J; Northside HS; Fort Smith, AR; (4); 42/360; Art Clb; FBLA; Intnl Clb; Math Clb; Mu Alpha Theta; Spanish Clb; Teachers Aide; Cit Awd; Hon Roll; Jr NHS; Westark CC.

SISSON, MIRA; Winslow Schl; Mountainburg, AR; (4); 1/13; Church Yth Grp; FBLA; FHA; VP Sr Cls; Var Bsktbl; Var Chrldng; Var Crs Cntry; Var Trk; Pres NHS; Val; AR Tech Univ; Sports Med; Nrsng.

SIZEMORE, ERIN E; Dover HS; Dover, AR; (2); 4/97; Cmnty Wkr; 4-H; Girl Scts; Hosp Aide; HOBY; Math Clb; Natl Beta Clb; Spanish Clb; VP Soph Cls; Bsktbl; 2nd Pl Regn Comp Trail Rdng Hrsbck; Ovrall Hghpnt Bio Awd; Accptd AR Schl Math Sci; Vet.

SKAGGS, MICHELLE L; Osceola HS; Osceola, AR; (3); Church Yth Grp; French Clb; FBLA; FHA; Library Aide; Office Aide; Pep Clb; Red Cross Aide; Science Clb; Chorus; Sci, Algebra & Music Awds; Crown Clb; FBLA Rptr; Multi-Yr Listee; ASU; Acctnt.

SKAIFE, KATHERINE R; Lake Hamilton Sr HS; Hot Springs, AR; (4); 10/249; Art Clb; FCA; Natl Beta Clb; Spanish Clb; SADD; Teachers Aide; Sftbl; Vllybl; Hon Roll; NHS; U Of Cntrl AR; Engrng.

SKAIFE, MARGARET; Lake Hamilton Sr HS; Hot Springs, AR; (2); 1/320; Church Yth Grp; FCA; FBLA; Natl Beta Clb; Science Clb; Spanish Clb; Lit Mag; Cit Awd; Hon Roll; NHS; Educ.

SKATES, JENNIFER M; Hot Springs HS; Hot Springs, AR; (4); 18/154; Thesps; Acpl Chr; Band; Flag Corp; Mrchg Band; School Musical; School Play; Var Swmmng; NHS; Mu Alpha Theta; NATS Reg Semi Fnlst; AR All St Choir; Ouchita Bapt U; Lndscp Arch.

SKELTON, JENNY M; Northside HS; Fort Smith, AR; (4); Mu Alpha Theta; Office Aide; ROTC; Spanish Clb; Teachers Aide; Cit Awd; Hon Roll; Pres Schlr; JROTC Donor Soc.

SKELTON, LANA; Gosnell Jr Sr HS; Blytheville, AR; (2); Church Yth Grp; French Clb; Key Clb; Math Tm; Mu Alpha Theta; Band; Chorus; Drm Mjr(t); Mrchg Band; Pep Band; Univ Of Cntrl AR; Optmtry.

SKELTON, LAURA; Hall Sr HS; Little Rock, AR; (4); 3/270; Cmnty Wkr; Hosp Aide; Intnl Clb; Treas Natl Beta Clb; Yrbk; Rep Stu Cncl; Socr; NHS; Drama Clb; Stage Crew; Explore Post 8 Sec; Tribe Peer Facilitators; Hendrix.

SKIDMORE, JUSTIN B; Cabot HS; Ward, AR; (2); Church Yth Grp; Bsktbl; Hon Roll; Jr NHS; JUST Clb.

SKIDMORE, KRISTEN A; Cabot HS; Ward, AR; (2); Church Yth Grp; VP FHA; Band; Flag Corp; Mrchg Band; Pep Band; Stat Bsktbl; Mgr(s); Jr NHS; NHS; Just Club; U Of Cntrl AR; Elem Ed.

SKILES, MANDIE E; Conway Sr HS; Conway, AR; (2); Pep Clb; Teachers Aide; Poem Publshd Natl Lib Of Poetry; Psycht Thrpy.

SKINNER, ASHLIE J; Gravette HS; Gravette, AR; (3); 4/100; FCA; FBLA; Bsktbl; Chrldng; Golf; Sftbl; High Hon Roll; NHS; Pres Acad Fit Awd; Perfmr, Sec PRIDE; Med.

SKINNER, JILLIAN C; Gravette HS; Gravette, AR; (2); 1/105; FCA; FBLA; Model UN; Quiz Bowl; VP Frsh Cls; Ofcr Stu Cncl; Bsktbl; Chrldng; Powder Puff Ftbl; Sftbl; PRIDE VP, Perfrmr; Sci.

SKINNER, JOSHUA N; Fountain Lake Jr Sr HS; Hot Springs Natio, AR; (2); Band; Jazz Band; Mrchg Band; Bsktbl; Hon Roll; Prfct Atten Awd; Med Doctor.

SKINNER, LORI D; Oak Grove HS; Maumelle, AR; (1); 14/189; FBLA; Natl Beta Clb; Spanish Clb; Cit Awd; Hon Roll; U Of AR; Psych.

SKINNER, RACHEL T; Fountain Lake Jr Sr HS; Hot Springs Natio, AR; (3); 1/83; Am Leg Aux Girls St; Pres Art Clb; Treas FBLA; Key Clb; Natl Beta Clb; Band; Sec Jr Cls; Pres Stu Cncl; High Hon Roll; Prfct Atten Awd; Univ Cntrl AR; Cardiologist.

SKIPPER, SHARLEENIA D; Marked Tree Jr Sr HS; Marked Tree, AR; (3); 7/63; Am Leg Aux Girls St; Church Yth Grp; Quiz Bowl; ROTC; Chorus; Church Choir; Capt Color Guard; Capt Flag Corp; Mrchg Band; Ed Lit Mag; Attnd Wrld Affairs Sem Whitewater WI; Attnd AR Gov Schl Choral Music; AR ST Univ; BME/MUSIC His.

SLAGLE, TODD M; Rogers HS; Rogers, AR; (3); Church Yth Grp; FBLA; Capt Socr; Gov Hon Prg Awd; Hon Roll.

SLATE, MONICA; Greenwood Sr HS; Greenwood, AR; (4); 26/197; Debate Tm; FBLA; HOBY; Model UN; Natl Beta Clb; Spanish Clb; Speech Tm; L Tennis; Hon Roll; NHS; AR Govrnrs Schl; U Of AR Fayetteville; Eng.

SLATEN, MINDY; Mt Ida Jr Sr HS; Sims, AR; (1); Church Yth Grp; FHA; Church Choir; Sec Treas Frsh Cls; Var Chrldng; High Hon Roll; Hon Roll; Homcmng Fresh Maid; 10 Yrs Betsey Schl Dance Lessons; Cmnty Perfrmng Arts.

SLATTON, LUKE; Delight HS; Delight, AR; (2); 6/21; 4-H; Natl Beta Clb; Natl FFA Org; Pres Frsh Cls; Pres Soph Cls; Ofcr Bsbl; Bsktbl; 4-H Awd.

SLATTON, SHANNON; Delight HS; Delight, AR; (3); 1/38; 4-H; FBLA; Quiz Bowl; Rep Frsh Cls; Pres Soph Cls; Pres Stu Cncl; Var Bsktbl; Var Sftbl; 4-H Awd; JETS Awd; Natl Wnng JV TEAM JETS; FFA Dairy Prod Natl 2nd Pl Tm; AR SW Dist VP.

SLAUGHTER, KEVIN M; Forrest City HS; Madison, AR; (4); 22/275; Church Yth Grp; FHA; JA; Cit Awd; Hon Roll; Jr NHS; Kiwanis Awd; Pres Acad Fit Awd; U Of AR; Eng.

SLAUGHTER, PRESTON; Pine Bluff HS; Pine Bluff, AR; (2); Church Yth Grp; French Clb; Quiz Bowl; Acpl Chr; Lit Mag; JV Bsktbl; Hon Roll.

SLAVENS, TAMMY M; Southside HS; Fort Smith, AR; (3); 22/502; Library Aide; Mu Alpha Theta; Spanish Clb; Teachers Aide; Nwsp; Hon Roll; Jr NHS; NHS; Spanish NHS; U Of AK; Ophtalmology.

SLAVENS, VERONICA; Northside HS; Fort Smith, AR; (4); 11/360; Am Leg Aux Girls St; Church Yth Grp; Cmnty Wkr; Mu Alpha Theta; Church Choir; Rep Stu Cncl; Capt Vllybl; NHS; Pres Schlr; Spanish NHS; All St In Vllybl; William Woods Univ; Mrktng; Mgmt.

SLAYTON, AMANDA K; Highland HS; Williford, AR; (2); Church Yth Grp; FBLA; Natl Beta Clb; Band; Chorus; Color Guard; Mrchg Band; Pep Band; School Musical; Prfct Atten Awd; All Rgn Band; Bus Tchr.

SLAYTON, JOSH L; Nettleton HS; Jonesboro, AR; (2); Church Yth Grp; Chorus; L Bsbl; L Bsktbl; Bsktbl Leading Assists Frosh Yr; Bsktbl Best Defensive Player Frosh Yr; Bsbl All Star Team; FL ST Univ; Mrktg.

SLEDGE, JENNIFER N; Blytheville Sr HS; Blytheville, AR; (3); Vllybl; Wt Lftg.

SLIKKER, ANNA; Hall Sr HS; Little Rock, AR; (2); Drama Clb; FBLA; Spanish Clb; Drill Tm; School Musical; School Play; Rptr Nwsp; Ofcr Stu Cncl; Vllybl; Hon Roll; Yng Life.

SLINKARD, DAWN M; Vilonia HS; Conway, AR; (3); Art Clb; Sec FBLA; Girl Scts; Model UN; Mu Alpha Theta; Natl Beta Clb; Spanish Clb; Band; Jazz Band; Mrchg Band; Rcvd Gold/Silver Ldrshp Awds; Silver Awd Girl Scouts; All Region In Band; Pediatrcn.

SLOAN, MARY V; Southside HS; Fort Smith, AR; (3); Church Yth Grp; Drama Clb; FCA; French Clb; Girl Scts; Chorus; Church Choir; School Musical; School Play; Stage Crew; Farm Bureau Action Comm Washington DC; Organ; Fr Cls Trip Europe 96; Westark CC.

SLUYTER, LORA; Lake Hamilton Sr HS; Hot Springs, AR; (4); 4/242; Am Leg Aux Girls St; Church Yth Grp; FCA; FBLA; Natl Beta Clb; Sec Spanish Clb; Sec Sr Cls; Rep Stu Cncl; L Co-Capt Chrldng; Var Gym.

SMALEC, HEATHER; Mountain Home HS; Mountain Home, AR; (2); 45/215; Church Yth Grp; French Clb; Pep Clb; Yrbk; Chrldng; Tennis; Hon Roll; Prfct Atten Awd; U Of MN; Bus.

SMALL, ALICIA; Danville HS; Danville, AR; (2); 6/38; Pres Church Yth Grp; Cmnty Wkr; FCA; VP 4-H; Quiz Bowl; SADD; Phtg Ed Yrbk; Var Capt Chrldng; Office Aide; Mrchg Band; Natl Princss Amers Tots & Teens Pagnt 95; Miss Teen Rivr Vly; 1st Rnnr Up Invars Pagnts; Spk Up Wnnr; Pharmaceutical Rep.

SMALL, BECKY; Lake Hamilton Sr HS; Hot Springs, AR; (4); 17/250; FBLA; FHA; Letterman Clb; Natl Beta Clb; Office Aide; Pep Clb; Spanish Clb; Teachers Aide; Chorus; Cit Awd.

SMALL, JENNIFER; Cedarville Jr Sr HS; Van Buren, AR; (4); 7/62; Church Yth Grp; Drama Clb; FHA; Quiz Bowl; Pres Science Clb; Pres SADD; Band; Color Guard; Drm Mjr(t); Mrchg Band; All-St AR Bnd; All-Reg AR Bnd; Westark CC; Elem Ed.

SMART, ASHLEY; Sulphur Rock Schl; Batesville, AR; (1); 7/28; Church Yth Grp; Pres FHA; Key Clb; Natl Beta Clb; Natl FFA Org; Quiz Bowl; SADD; Pres Frsh Cls; Rep Stu Cncl; Capt Bsktbl; Gftd/Tlntd.

SMEDLEY, TARA; Hatfield Schl; Hatfield, AR; (1); 2/47; FBLA; FHA; Pres Frsh Cls; Var Bsktbl; Var Chrldng; Sftbl; Trk; High Hon Roll; Pres Acad Fit Awd; U AR Fayettville; Law.

SMELKO, JOHN PAUL; Hall Sr HS; Little Rock, AR; (3); #16 in class; Am Leg Boys St; FBLA; Natl Beta Clb; Spanish Clb; Tennis; Cit Awd; High Hon Roll; Hon Roll; Jr NHS; NHS; Governors Schl Recommendation; Harvard Bk Awd; Explorers Post; Chemical Engr.

SMILEY, AMY; Glenwood Jr Sr HS; Glenwood, AR; (3); 3/35; Church Yth Grp; HOBY; Quiz Bowl; Capt Flag Corp; Ed Nwsp; Pres Jr Cls; Sec Stu Cncl; Golf; Sftbl; Rep NHS; Liberty U.

SMITH, ADRAIN; Rison HS; Rison, AR; (3); #6 in class; Am Leg Boys St; Church Yth Grp; French Clb; FHA; Natl Beta Clb; Science Clb; VP Jr Cls; Ofcr Bsbl; Ftbl; Hon Roll.

SMITH, ALICIA L; Lamar HS; Lamar, AR; (4); 4/64; FBLA; FHA; Hosp Aide; Natl Beta Clb; Band; Rptr Nwsp; Phtg Yrbk; Cit Awd; Hon Roll; Pres Acad Fit Awd; Yth Opp Unlimted Schol To UAM; Bus Stu Awd; Vol Awd; U Of Ozarks; Nurs.

SMITH, ALISON L; Benton Sr HS; Benton, AR; (3); Art Clb; Computer Clb; French Clb; FBLA; FHA; Hosp Aide; Pep Clb; Drill Tm; Cit Awd; Hon Roll; Stdnt Of Mo; Bapt Little Rock; Nrsng Schl.

SMITH, AMANDA K; Viola HS; Viola, AR; (3); 1/38; Sec FBLA; FHA; Natl FFA Org; Sec Band; Chorus; Pep Band; Rptr Nwsp; Yrbk; Treas Jr Cls; Var Mgr Bsktbl; AR St Uinv; Phys Thpy.

SMITH, AMANDA R; Nevada Schl; Rosston, AR; (2); 2/65; Church Yth Grp; French Clb; FBLA; Natl Beta Clb; Quiz Bowl; Teachers Aide; Band; Church Choir; VP Sec Frsh Cls; Rep Stu Cncl; Drug Free Team; Saxaphone; Piano; Reading; Central Bapt Coll; Nrsng.

SMITH, AMBER D; Plainview Rover Schl; Plainview, AR; (3); Art Clb; English Clb; French Clb; GAA; Natl FFA Org; Office Aide; Teachers Aide; Sec Soph Cls; Sec Jr Cls; Capt Bsktbl; AR Tech; Elem Ed; Child Care.

SMITH, ANDREA G; Arkansas Sr HS; Texarkana, TX; (2); Church Yth Grp; Band; Mrchg Band; All Reg Band; All ST Band Tryouts; Kindler Awd.

SMITH, ANGELA; Mammoth Spring HS; Mammoth Spring, AR; (3); 2/45; VP Church Yth Grp; FBLA; FHA; Sec Natl Beta Clb; Pep Clb; Science Clb; Band; Mrchg Band; VP Jr Cls; Bsktbl; Stu Cncl Sec, Rprtr, VP; U Cntrl AR; Phys Thrpy.

SMITH, ANNA; Nettleton Jr HS; Jonesboro, AR; (2); FBLA; Math Clb; Natl Beta Clb; Quiz Bowl; Science Clb; Chorus; School Musical; School Play; Hon Roll; Pres Acad Fit Awd; FBLA 1st Pl ST/1ST Pl Dist/Mocklaw; 2nd Pl ST Mock Lawyer; Stdnt Star Srch Wnnr Kiss FM Jr Axlry; WA Univ; Law.

SMITH, ASHLEY; Parkers Chapel Schl; El Dorado, AR; (4); 2/46; Pres Art Clb; FBLA; HOBY; Natl Beta Clb; VP Jr Cls; Ofcr Stu Cncl; Capt Chrldng; Tennis; High Hon Roll; Sal; Dance; UCA All Str Chrldr; UCA; Bio.

SMITH, ASHLEY; Gosnell Jr HS; Blytheville, AR; (1); Church Yth Grp; French Clb; Key Clb; Natl Beta Clb; Quiz Bowl; Science Clb; Rptr Nwsp; Sec Treas Frsh Cls; Co-Capt Chrldng; Cit Awd; Vanderbilt U; Med.

SMITH, ASHLEY A; Southside HS; Fort Smith, AR; (2); Church Yth Grp; French Clb; Mu Alpha Theta; Office Aide; Band; Capt Chrldng; Hon Roll; NHS; Delta Beta Sigma.

SMITH, ASHLEY J; Arkansas Sr HS; Texarkana, AR; (2); Church Yth Grp; Dance Clb; Drama Clb; French Clb; Math Clb; Mu Alpha Theta; Pep Clb; Drill Tm; Chrldng; Gym; Yrbk Photo; U Of AR.

SMITH, BOYD S; Van Cove HS; Cove, AR; (2); Chess Clb; FBLA; Model UN; Natl Beta Clb; Quiz Bowl; Band; Pep Band; Ofcr Jr Cls; Hon Roll; MIT; Math Prof; Comp Progrmmng.

SMITH, BRAD; Blevins HS; Mc Caskill, AR; (3); Church Yth Grp; Cmnty Wkr; Natl Beta Clb; Var Bsbl; Var Bsktbl; Var Trk; Hon Roll; TX A&M; Bus.

SMITH, BRANDI K; Sylvan Hills HS; Sherwood, AR; (3); 39/290; Am Leg Aux Girls St; Church Yth Grp; FBLA; Spanish Clb; Band; Mrchg Band; Hon Roll; Jr NHS; NHS; U Of AR Pine Bluff; Nrsng.

SMITH, BRENT A; Huttig Schl; Huttig, AR; (2); Church Yth Grp; Natl Beta Clb; Band; Mrchg Band; Hon Roll; Two Man Bch Vlybl; Tae Kwan Do; Prof Vlybl.

SMITH, BRIAN A; Northside HS; Fort Smith, AR; (3); FHA; Spanish Clb; Hon Roll; U Of AZ; Law Enfrcmnt.

SMITH, BRIDGET J; Bauxite Jr Sr HS; Benton, AR; (4); Sec FBLA; Spanish Clb; SADD; Capt Bsktbl; Capt Sftbl; Trk; DAR Awd; Hon Roll; Phtgrphy Clb Treas; US Army Rsrv Natl Schlr Ath Awd; Henderson ST Univ; Pre Vet.

SMITH, BROOKE; Sparkman Jr Sr HS; Sparkman, AR; (1); #2 in class; Church Yth Grp; Dance Clb; 4-H; FBLA; Spanish Clb; Church Choir; Yrbk; Chrldng; Hon Roll; Raider Spirit Awd For Chrldng; All Star Chrldr; U Of Cntrl AR Phys Therapy.

SMITH, BYRON S; Fouke Jr Sr HS; Fouke, AR; (3); Church Yth Grp; FHA; Natl Beta Clb; Ofcr Bsbl; Ftbl; Golf; Hon Roll.

SMITH, CACE; Pea Ridge HS; Pea Ridge, AR; (1); Church Yth Grp; FBLA; Pres Frsh Cls; Ofcr Bsbl; Bsktbl; Ftbl; Trk; Hon Roll.

SMITH, CANDICE S; Cloverdale Jr HS; Little Rock, AR; (1); FBLA; Natl Beta Clb; Quiz Bowl; Rep Frsh Cls; Rep Stu Cncl; Co-Capt Chrldng; Var Tennis; High Hon Roll; Hon Roll; Jr NHS; PSECME VP; Upward Bound; Hendrix; Corp Atty/Pol Sci.

SMITH, CHRIS B; Parkin Jr Sr HS; Parkin, AR; (3); French Clb; Natl Beta Clb; Science Clb; Ofcr Bsbl; Hon Roll.

SMITH, CHRISTAL BRANDI; Marshall HS; Marshall, AR; (3); 12/50; Rptr Art Clb; Church Yth Grp; 4-H; Rptr FBLA; Girl Scts; Natl Beta Clb; Spanish Clb; JV Sftbl; JV Trk; JV Vllybl; Photo; AR ST Univ.

SMITH, CHRISTI; Carlisle Jr Sr HS; Hazen, AR; (2); 4-H; Chorus; School Play; Ofcr Soph Cls; Chrldng; Ozarks; Wildlf.

SMITH, CHRISTOPHER L; Newport HS; Newport, AR; (1); 5/161; Church Yth Grp; FBLA; JCL; Latin Clb; Band; Jazz Band; Mrchg Band; Pep Band; School Musical; 3 First Pl Ribbons Solo Ensmbl; Atnd Intl Potpourri AR Schl Math/Sci; Won Geogrphy Awrd; U Of AR; Crmnl Lawyer.

SMITH, CINDY; Riverview Bapt Christian Sch; Morrilton, AR; (2); Church Yth Grp; Pep Clb; Church Choir; Ed Rptr Nwsp; Ed Phtg Yrbk; Var Vllybl; Hon Roll; Acpl Chr; School Play; Cit Awd; Yth Ambsdr; Jr Chrch Tchr; Rep Ldrshp Cnfrnc; Central Baptist Coll; Chrstn Ed.

SMITH, CLARISSA; Senior HS; Fayetteville, AR; (4); 2/2; Am Leg Aux Girls St; Computer Clb; Speech Tm; Nwsp; Ed Lit Mag; Gov Hon Prg Awd; High Hon Roll; Ntl Merit Schol; Web Page; Mrtl Arts; Intrctv Stry-Tllng; U Of AR; Art.

SMITH, COUNTS; Wynne HS; Wynne, AR; (3); FBLA; Sec FTA; Q&S; SADD; Ed Nwsp; Yrbk; Tennis; NHS; Spanish NHS; Church Yth Grp; Schlsp Clb; Jr Progressive Clb; Prom Decoating P Invitation Comm; U Of AR Fayetteville; Pharmacy.

SMITH, CRYSTAL DIANE; Crowleys Ridge Acad; Jonesboro, AR; (1); FBLA; Pep Clb; Chorus; JV Bsktbl; JV Trk; JV Vllybl; Hon Roll; Freed Hardemanuniv; Mktin.

SMITH, DANIELLE; Forrest City HS; Forrest City, AR; (4); Pres FBLA; FHA; FTA; Mu Alpha Theta; Hist Natl Beta Clb; Office Aide; Drill Tm; VP Stu Cncl; Chrldng; Trk; U Of AR Fayetteville; Mrktg.

SMITH, DANIELLE S; Mena HS; Mena, AR; (2); 1/145; Boy Scts; 4-H; French Clb; FBLA; Science Clb; Band; Flag Corp; Mrchg Band; French Hon Soc; High Hon Roll; Explorer Scouts Post 109 VP.

SMITH, DAVID C; Beebe Sr HS; Searcy, AR; (3); Am Leg Boys St; Science Clb; Treas Stu Cncl; Ftbl; Law.

SMITH, DENNY; Fairview HS; Camden, AR; (3); 68/300; French Clb; Mu Alpha Theta; VP Natl FFA Org; Quiz Bowl; Speech Tm; Var Ftbl; Capt Var Socr; Var Trk; Hon Roll; AR ST FFA Elec 1st Pl Team, 3rd High Indvdl; Penn ST U; Ag Engrng.

SMITH, DOROTHY A; Pea Ridge HS; Pea Ridge, AR; (2); Drama Clb; 4-H; Color Guard; Drill Tm; Flag Corp; Mrchg Band; School Play; Stage Crew; Ed Yrbk; Bsktbl; U Of AR; Sci.

SMITH, DUSTIN D; Dequeen HS; De Queen, AR; (3); Church Yth Grp; Acpl Chr; Church Choir; Stage Crew; Rep Frsh Cls; Rep Soph Cls; Rep Stu Cncl; L Bsbl; L Ftbl; Hon Roll; Poem Pblshd Natl Lbry Ptry; All Rgn Choir 4 Yrs/Strght; Ply Guitar/Harmonica; Yth Mnstry.

SMITH, ELLEN N; Pea Ridge HS; Pea Ridge, AR; (3); 15/40; Drama Clb; 4-H; Natl FFA Org; Spanish Clb; Band; Color Guard; Mrchg Band; School Play; Yrbk; Local Rabbit Club; NEO; Vet Med.

SMITH, ERIC R; Cabot HS; Cabot, AR; (3); 2/398; Am Leg Boys St; FCA; Pres Frsh Cls; Pres Soph Cls; Var Bsbl; Var Bsktbl; Jr NHS; NHS; Ntl Merit Ltr; Spanish NHS.

SMITH, ERIN; Mt Ida Jr Sr HS; Mount Ida, AR; (1); Church Yth Grp; GAA; Rep Stu Cncl; Bsktbl; Chrldng; Hon Roll.

SMITH, FLOYD T; Hope HS; Fulton, AR; (3); 23/238; Pres 4-H; FBLA; Pres Natl Beta Clb; Quiz Bowl; Band; Pres Church Choir; Drm Mjr(t); Mrchg Band; Hon Roll; AZ ST Univ; Comp Engr.

SMITH, GRAYSON; Charleston HS; Charleston, AR; (2); Church Yth Grp; FCA; FBLA; Natl Beta Clb; Spanish Clb; Ofcr Stu Cncl; Ofcr Bsbl; Ftbl; Trk; Wt Lftg; All-Dist Ftbl 94-95.

SMITH, HEATHER L; Fouke Jr Sr HS; Fouke, AR; (3); Treas Boy Scts; Church Yth Grp; Sec FBLA; Natl FFA Org; SADD; MASH; Camp Couchdale Co-Op Camp; BSA Lifenet Explorer Post 200; Henderson; Acctng.

SMITH, HOLLI; Gillett Jr Sr HS; Watson, AR; (3); 3/24; Am Leg Aux Girls St; Art Clb; Church Yth Grp; FBLA; FHA; Pep Clb; Quiz Bowl; Spanish Clb; School Play; Yrbk; Jr Beta Clb; AR ST U; Med.

SMITH, HOLLY A; Springdale Sr HS; Springdale, AR; (4); 56/532; Church Yth Grp; Drama Clb; FBLA; Key Clb; Thesps; Acpl Chr; Chorus; Drill Tm; School Musical; School Play; Natl Hnr Choir; 1st Chr All Region, All St; Ouachita Bapt U; Music Ed.

SMITH, JACOB D; North Little Rock HS West; North Little Rock, AR; (3); Church Yth Grp; Drama Clb; FCA; German Clb; Key Clb; Teachers Aide; School Play; Stage Crew; Ftbl; Hon Roll; 2nd Yr Peer Ldr.

SMITH, JAMES H; North Little Rock Hs-West; North Little Rock, AR; (3); FCA; 4-H; SADD; JV Bsktbl; Cit Awd; Hon Roll; Rotry Clb Mem; U Of A Fayetteville; Comp Sci.

SMITH, JANA D; Springdale Sr HS; Springdale, AR; (2); FCA; French Clb; FBLA; Key Clb; Office Aide; Acpl Chr; Chorus; Var Chrldng; Powder Puff Ftbl; Intrml Sftbl; All ST Supr Mact Wrt Play 1 Of 4 Plays; All Region Choir; Treas Just Say O Club; Baylor; Anesthetist/Doctor.

SMITH, JARED; Central Ark Christian Schl; Little Rock, AR; (2); Golf; Cit Awd; Hon Roll; NHS.

SMITH, JASON A; Van Buren Sr HS; Van Buren, AR; (2); Church Yth Grp; Quiz Bowl; Science Clb; Hon Roll; Cmptr Grphcs/Art.

SMITH, JASON C; Jessieville HS; Jessieville, AR; (3); L Ftbl; L Trk; All Dist & All Garland Cty-Ftbl; All Dist & Outstdng Field Events-Trk; U Of AR; Biologist.

SMITH, JASON R; North Little Rock Hs-East; North Little Rock, AR; (2); Yrbk; Ofcr Frsh Cls; Bsktbl; Philnader; Bsktbl.

SMITH, JEFFREY A; Dierks HS; Dierks, AR; (3); Church Yth Grp; Ofcr Natl FFA Org; Science Clb; Treas Stu Cncl; Var L Ftbl; Var Trk; Hon Roll; NHS; Prfct Atten Awd; ALG I Awd; SAU; Ag.

SMITH, JENNIFER; Gillett Jr Sr HS; Tichnor, AR; (1); 2/24; Art Clb; Church Yth Grp; VP Frsh Cls; JV Bsktbl; Var Chrldng; Hon Roll; Jr NHS.

SMITH, JENNIFER J; Cty Line HS; Ratcliff, AR; (3); 1/35; FBLA; Natl Beta Clb; Treas Spanish Clb; Bsktbl; Cit Awd; High Hon Roll; Hon Roll; NHS; Spanish NHS; Treas Sec Soph Cls; Westark CC.

SMITH, JERI L; Arkansas Sr HS; Texarkana, AR; (3); Art Clb; Church Yth Grp; FHA; Mu Alpha Theta; Spanish Clb; Hon Roll; Jr NHS; NHS; Yth Clb Pres; U Of Central AR Conway.

SMITH, JESSICA A; Central Ark Christian Schl; Little Rock, AR; (1); French Clb; Score Keeper; Cit Awd; Hon Roll; Jr NHS.

SMITH, JESSICA N; Junction City HS; Junction City, AR; (1); Church Yth Grp; Science Clb; Spanish Clb; Church Choir; Ofcr Frsh Cls; Ofcr Stu Cncl; Chrldng; Sftbl; High Hon Roll; Ntl Merit Ltr; St Sci Fair Winner; Schlrshp S AR Univ; Amer Govt/Home Ed Awds.

SMITH, JOEL N; Huntsville HS; Huntsville, AR; (2); 2/165; Church Yth Grp; FCA; Var Bsbl; Var JV Bsktbl; Ftbl; Hon Roll; U Of AR.

SMITH, JOHNELLE; Mills HS; Little Rock, AR; (3); 2/296; Church Yth Grp; JCL; Latin Clb; Pres Natl Beta Clb; Rep Jr Cls; Pres Stu Cncl; Capt Chrldng; Gov Hon Prg Awd; Pres NHS; Pres Acad Fit Awd; I Dare You Awd; Mercantile Bnk Bd Stdnt Rep 96; Hendrix Coll; Pre-Med/His.

SMITH, JONATHAN; Arkansas Bapt Schl; Little Rock, AR; (2); 1/65; Church Yth Grp; FBLA; Natl Beta Clb; Var Bsbl.

SMITH, JONATHAN B; Mills HS; North Little Rock, AR; (3); DECA; FBLA; Spanish Clb; High Hon Roll; Hon Roll; Pres Acad Fit Awd.

SMITH, JOSHUA M; J A Fair Sr HS; Little Rock, AR; (4); 67/300; Art Clb; Church Yth Grp; Cmnty Wkr; FCA; French Clb; Natl Beta Clb; Office Aide; Science Clb; Spanish Clb; Teachers Aide; Hmcmng Crt; U Of AR; Bus.

SMITH, JOY; Ft Smith Christian Schl; Alma, AR; (2); Band; Rep Soph Cls; JV Var Chrldng; Cit Awd; Hon Roll; NHS; Univ Of CA Fullerton; Jrnlsm.

SMITH, JUSTIN; Mineral Springs Schl; Saratoga, AR; (2); Natl Beta Clb; Natl FFA Org; Quiz Bowl; Band; Mrchg Band; VP Frsh Cls; Ftbl; Trk; Wt Lftg; Hon Roll; OM; OBU; Trnsprtn.

SMITH, KASHANA J; Strong Jr Sr HS; Strong, AR; (2); Church Yth Grp; Drama Clb; French Clb; Natl Beta Clb; Church Choir; Yrbk; Var Bsktbl; Hon Roll; Ntl Merit Ltr; Whos Who Sports; U Of AL Birmingham; PT.

SMITH, KATHLEEN; Cabot HS; Cabot, AR; (3); Church Yth Grp; VP Key Clb; Church Choir; Co-Ed Yrbk; Treas Stu Cncl; Co-Capt Chrldng; French Hon Soc; Jr NHS; Kiwanis Awd; NHS; UCA All Str Chrldr; NCA All Amerchldr; Sci.

SMITH, KATRINA MICHELLE; Robinson HS; Little Rock, AR; (3); FCA; FBLA; FTA; Hosp Aide; Natl Beta Clb; Sec Spanish Clb; Rep Frsh Cls; Rep Soph Cls; Sec Jr Cls; Co-Capt Chrldng; Friends For Life; Caring Comm.

SMITH, KAYLA S; Conway Sr HS; Conway, AR; (4); 50/520; Rptr FBLA; Natl Beta Clb; Teachers Aide; Var Sftbl; High Hon Roll; Hnr Grad; Natl Voc Tech Hnr Soc ; Received Act Schlrshp UCA; U Of Cntrl AR; Cmptr Sci/Math.

SMITH, KRISTEN R; El Dorado Sr HS; El Dorado, AR; (2); Church Yth Grp; Natl Beta Clb; Band; Drm Mjr(t); Mrchg Band; Phrmcst.

SMITH, KRISTY L; Alpena Schl; Alpena, AR; (3); FBLA; Spanish Clb; Beta Clb; Eng Awds; Span Awd; NACTC; Bus; Jrnlsm.

SMITH, LACY L; Mississippi Co Christian Acad; Wilson, AR; (3); 7/13; Church Yth Grp; French Clb; FHA; Key Clb; Math Clb; Science Clb; SADD; Chorus; Var Capt Bsktbl; Hon Roll; MVP & All Conf 94, All Trnmnt 95; WMC Wndys Clssc All Trnmnt 94, 95; MCCAS Tm Plyr Awd 94; AR ST U.

SMITH, LAKEISHA; Dermott HS; Dermott, AR; (1); Ofcr Stu Cncl; Bsktbl; Chrldng; Trk; Cit Awd; Hon Roll; Beta Clb; Acad Awd; Hmcmng Ct; Lwyr/Tchr.

SMITH, LAURA; Maynard Jr Sr HS; Maynard, AR; (4); 3/29; French Clb; FBLA; FHA; Library Aide; VP Natl Beta Clb; Teachers Aide; Yrbk; Treas Frsh Cls; Treas Soph Cls; Treas Jr Cls; AR ST U; Phy Ther.

SMITH, LAURA B; Crowleys Ridge Acad; Paragould, AR; (1); 1/30; Church Yth Grp; FBLA; Pep Clb; Science Clb; Spanish Clb; Bsktbl; Bible Bowl; Harding Univ; Pharmcst.

SMITH, LISA; De Soto Schl; West Helena, AR; (3); Pres Church Yth Grp; Drama Clb; Hosp Aide; HOBY; Spanish Clb; Thesps; Yrbk; Treas Frsh Cls; Treas Soph Cls; Treas Jr Cls; U AR; Psych.

SMITH, LISA; Sylvan Hills HS; North Little Rock, AR; (2); Church Yth Grp; Math Clb; Mu Alpha Theta; Science Clb; Spanish Clb; Chrldng; Socr; Hon Roll; NHS; All Star Chrldng Squad.

SMITH, MANDY; Gosnell Jr Sr HS; Blytheville, AR; (3); FHA; Natl Beta Clb; Chrldng; Hon Roll; Pres Schlr; Beta Clb; Cottonboll Tech Inst; Nursng.

SMITH, MANDY E; Clarendon Jr Sr HS; Monroe, AR; (1); FBLA; Yrbk; Hon Roll; Leo Clb; Northwest CC; Phych.

SMITH, MARGARET CECILIA B; Central Sr HS; Little Rock, AR; (3); Church Yth Grp; French Clb; Pres Girl Scts; Hosp Aide; Natl Beta Clb; Quiz Bowl; School Play; Gov Hon Prg Awd; Hon Roll; Jr NHS; Natl Cncl Of Tchrs Of Eng Wrtng Cmptn; Governors Schl For Gftd Stdnts In AR; Politics & Philosophy.

SMITH, MARK A; Huntsville HS; Huntsville, AR; (4); 8/123; Am Leg Boys St; Art Clb; Boy Scts; Church Yth Grp; Model UN; Band; Jazz Band; Var Bsbl; High Hon Roll; Pres Acad Fit Awd; Enrlld Drake Avation Flight Schl; U Of AR; Pilot.

SMITH, MATT; Leslie Schl; Leslie, AR; (2); 1/26; Church Yth Grp; FCA; Natl Beta Clb; Quiz Bowl; Pres Frsh Cls; Var Bsktbl; Trk; Wt Lftg; High Hon Roll; Pres Acad Fit Awd; CO Sprngs; Elec Engr.

SMITH, MEGAN R; Rogers HS; Rogers, AR; (3); Church Yth Grp; Cmnty Wkr; FCA; VP FBLA; Teachers Aide; Church Choir; Orch; JV Bsktbl; Hon Roll; NHS; Rogers Morning Rotary Clb; KUAF Wrtng Cont 3rd Pl; U Of A; Law.

SMITH, MELANIE SUE A; Huntsville HS; Hindsville, AR; (3); 18/128; Church Yth Grp; Key Clb; Library Aide; Quiz Bowl; Science Clb; SADD; Ofcr Stu Cncl; Mgr(s); Score Keeper; High Hon Roll; Mdsn Cty Rcrd Artcl Wrtr; Piano; U Of AR; Dntstry.

SMITH, MELISSA; Gillett Jr Sr HS; Tichnor, AR; (4); 1/20; Am Leg Aux Girls St; Church Yth Grp; FBLA; Ed Nwsp; Ed Yrbk; Bsktbl; Sprt Ed Chrldng; Sftbl; Hon Roll; NHS; AR ST U.

SMITH, MEREDITH; Magnet Cove HS; Malvern, AR; (3); Am Leg Aux Girls St; Church Yth Grp; Pres FBLA; HOBY; VP Natl Beta Clb; Acpl Chr; Yrbk; Pres Soph Cls; Rep Stu Cncl; Co-Capt Chrldng; Ouachita Baptist U; Bus Admin.

SMITH, MICHELLE E; Jonesboro HS; Jonesboro, AR; (3); 15/300; Church Yth Grp; Natl Beta Clb; Quiz Bowl; Ofcr Stu Cncl; L Crs Cntry; L Capt Swmmng; Hon Roll; FCA; French Clb; Mu Alpha Theta; Swmmng Lttrmn 2 Yr All St Awd; HS Swm Tm Awd Outstndng Prfmnc; Hmn Anatomy Dept Awd.

SMITH, MIKEL; East Poinsett Sr HS; Lepanto, AR; (4); Church Yth Grp; Letterman Clb; Natl FFA Org; Band; Jazz Band; Mrchg Band; Variety Show; Hon Roll; NHS; Music.

SMITH, MOLLY C; Black Rock Jr Sr HS; Black Rock, AR; (1); VP FHA; Treas Natl Beta Clb; Quiz Bowl; Pres Frsh Cls; Var Bsktbl; Sftbl; Hon Roll; GATE.

SMITH, MONIQUE A; North Little Rock Hs-West; North Little Rock, AR; (3); FHA; Key Clb; Chorus; School Musical; Cit Awd; Hon Roll; Ladies & Gentlemens Clb.

SMITH, NATASHA V; Hope HS; Fulton, AR; (3); 23/207; Church Yth Grp; Sec French Clb; Natl Beta Clb; Band; Church Choir; Color Guard; Capt Flag Corp; Mrchg Band; High Hon Roll; Hon Roll; Piano For Church; Purdue; Pre-Med.

SMITH, NELLI; Charleston HS; Lavaca, AR; (3); 4/50; Am Leg Aux Girls St; Church Yth Grp; FBLA; Pres FHA; Natl Beta Clb; Spanish Clb; Co-Ed Yrbk; Treas Jr Cls; Capt Chrldng; High Hon Roll; U Of AR; Zoo.

SMITH, NIKKI; Arkadelphia Sr HS; Arkadelphia, AR; (3); Church Yth Grp; Cmnty Wkr; Drama Clb; FCA; FBLA; FHA; Red Cross Aide; Spanish Clb; Band; Color Guard; Band-Rifle Capt; Americanos Drum & Bugle Corps; U Of AR Conway; Orthodontists.

SMITH, PATRICK R; Mills HS; Jacksonville, AR; (2); 47/449; Boy Scts; Church Yth Grp; French Clb; Library Aide; Natl Beta Clb; Science Clb; Orch; Ofcr Stu Cncl; French Hon Soc; Hon Roll; Poets Rndtbl Of AR; BSA Life Scout; Tulane; Eclgst/Rural Dr.

SMITH, R DUSTIN; Lonoke Jr HS; Lonoke, AR; (1); Church Yth Grp.

SMITH, RACHEL M; John L Mcclellan Magnet HS; Little Rock, AR; (2); FBLA; Natl Beta Clb; Office Aide; Hon Roll; Childrens Hosp Vol; UALR; Child Care; Wrtng.

SMITH, REGE L; Parkview Arts-Science HS; Little Rock, AR; (3); Church Yth Grp; Cmnty Wkr; Dance Clb; FHA; Natl Beta Clb; Church Choir; School Musical; Hon Roll; Ladies Clb; Sec Beta Cl 96-; Med.

SMITH, RHIANNON MARIE; Weiner HS; Weiner, AR; (3); Art Clb; Debate Tm; Drama Clb; Natl FFA Org; Science Clb; Spanish Clb; Treas Jr Cls; Rep Stu Cncl; Hon Roll; NHS; Cngrsnl Yth Ldrshp Conf; Natl Schlr; All Rgn Chr; 2nd Plc Ne Dist; Hrs Rdng Cntst Jrnlsm; Poetry; Vet Sci.

SMITH III, ROBERT; Poyen Schl; Malvern, AR; (3); Church Yth Grp; FCA; German Clb; Natl Beta Clb; Quiz Bowl; Rptr Yrbk; Rptr Stu Cncl; Var Bsktbl; Hon Roll; Med.

SMITH, ROGER L; Mt Ida Jr Sr HS; Story, AR; (2); 5/55; Natl Beta Clb; Natl FFA Org; Band; Jazz Band; Mrchg Band; Pep Band; Bsktbl; Hon Roll; Prfct Atten Awd; Archt.

SMITH, SABRINA L; Mc Gehee HS; Mc Gehee, AR; (2); Church Yth Grp; FBLA; FTA; Girl Scts; Spanish Clb; Yrbk; VP Soph Cls; Bsktbl; Mgr(s); Trk; Pride Awd 95-; FL ST; Actrs/Bus.

SMITH, SAMUEL; Sulphur Rock Schl; Sulphur Rock, AR; (2); 6/19; Church Yth Grp; Natl FFA Org; SADD; Ofcr Soph Cls; Ofcr Stu Cncl; Bsktbl; Trk; Hon Roll; Beta Clb; 1st Sci Fair; Apple; Lyon; Landscp Arch.

SMITH, SARAH; Southside HS; Fort Smith, AR; (3); 119/502; Church Yth Grp; French Clb; Mu Alpha Theta; Drm Mjr(t); Jazz Band; Mrchg Band; Orch; Variety Show; Hon Roll; NHS; Eqstrn Rdng Zone VII Fnlst 94-95; Amer Royal Hrs Shw; Plays Elec Bass/Violin Lcl Bnd.

SMITH, SCOTTIE; Oak Ridge Central Schl; Pocahontas, AR; (3); 3/29; Art Clb; Church Yth Grp; 4-H; FHA; German Clb; HOBY; Library Aide; Math Tm; Natl Beta Clb; Science Clb; UAM; Psych.

SMITH, SHAKITA R; Emerson HS; Emerson, AR; (3); 1/23; Am Leg Aux Girls St; Church Yth Grp; FBLA; FHA; GAA; Natl Beta Clb; Natl FFA Org; Spanish Clb; Sec Jr Cls; Sec Stu Cncl; Navy Hon Prgm; Pre-Med.

SMITH, SHANNAN; Mineral Springs Schl; Mineral Springs, AR; (2); 4-H; FBLA; HOBY; Natl Beta Clb; Varsity Clb; Bsktbl; Chrldng; Trk; Vllybl; Beauty Pgnts; U Of AR Fayetteville.

SMITH, SHARON E; Bentonville Sr HS; Bentonville, AR; (3); 34/317; Church Yth Grp; Pres VP FCA; Key Clb; Acpl Chr; Church Choir; Capt Chrldng; Cit Awd; High Hon Roll; NHS; Pres Acad Fit Awd; Ouchita Bapt U; Scndry Ed.

SMITH, SHERRI L; Prescott HS; Prescott, AR; (1); 12/76; FBLA; FHA; FTA; Hon Roll; Explorers Rprtr; Law.

SMITH, SIOBHAN E; Pine Bluff HS; Pine Bluff, AR; (2); French Clb; Model UN; Band; Drill Tm; Mrchg Band; Orch; VP Jr Cls; Ofcr Stu Cncl; High Hon Roll; NHS; Natl Beta Clb; His Clb; Prjct IMPRES; Spelman; Drama/Actress.

SMITH, STACY L; El Dorado Sr HS; El Dorado, AR; (1); Church Yth Grp; FHA; Church Choir; Rep Frsh Cls; Hon Roll; Camp Fire.

SMITH, STAR B; Mt Pleasant Jr Sr HS; Melbourne, AR; (3); Art Clb; Schlsp; ASU.

SMITH, STARLA C; Dequeen HS; Winthrop, AR; (4); 12/71; Church Yth Grp; FTA; Girl Scts; SADD; Chorus; VP Jr Cls; VP Stu Cncl; L Bsktbl; High Hon Roll; NHS; Sr Homecomng Maid; U Of Cntrl AR; Bio.

SMITH, STEVIE M; Lake Hamilton Sr HS; Hot Springs, AR; (2); 29/320; Letterman Clb; Ftbl; Wt Lftg; Cit Awd; Hon Roll; Pres Acad Fit Awd; Duke U; Ansthslgst.

SMITH, TABITHA L; White Co Central Schl; Searcy, AR; (2); Art Clb; Church Yth Grp; FBLA; FHA; GAA; Quiz Bowl; Red Cross Aide; Var Chorus; Var Bsktbl; Var Sftbl; Intrct Clb Searcy Rtry Clb; Harding Univ; Vet.

SMITH, TAMARA D; Bearden HS; Fordyce, AR; (4); 18/58; Cmnty Wkr; 4-H; FBLA; FHA; FTA; Girl Scts; Band; Chorus; Church Choir; Mrchg Band; Hnr Dplma; FHA Stu Of Yr; U Of AR; Elem Ed.

SMITH, TERRANCE A; Watson Chapel Sr HS; Pine Bluff, AR; (3); Church Yth Grp; Church Choir; Rep Stu Cncl; JV Var Bsktbl; Var Crs Cntry; JV Ftbl; Var Trk; JV Var Wt Lftg; Cit Awd; Hon Roll; U Of AR Pine Bluff; Pre-Law.

SMITH, THOMAS J; Southside HS; Fort Smith, AR; (3); Church Yth Grp; Drama Clb; Speech Tm; Band; Mrchg Band; Pep Band; School Play; Stage Crew; Hon Roll; Wrtng/Eng Tchr.

SMITH, TIFFANY; Lake Hamilton Jr HS; Royal, AR; (1); 6/264; Church Yth Grp; FCA; Hosp Aide; Natl Beta Clb; Natl FFA Org; Teachers Aide; Mgr Vllybl; Wolf Pride Pres; Fellowship Bible Study.

SMITH, TIFFANY; Norphlet HS; Norphlet, AR; (2); Church Yth Grp; VP Library Aide; Treas Soph Cls; Bsktbl; Art Clb; Church Choir; Ftbl; Yth Oppurtunities Unlmtd; Upward Bnd; Rch; Coroner.

SMITH, TIFFANY J; Greene Co Tech HS; Paragould, AR; (4); 14/150; Church Yth Grp; FBLA; Ofcr Stu Cncl; Chrldng; High Hon Roll; NHS; Ntl Merit Ltr; Flwshp Of Chrstn Spirit Ldrs Songleader; Stu Chrstn Assn VP; U Of Cntrl AR; Phy Therapy.

SMITH, TRAVIS D; Forrest City HS; Madison, AR; (2); Boy Scts; FHA; Math Tm; Natl Beta Clb; SADD; Chorus; Church Choir; Bsktbl; Ftbl; Trk.

SMITH, TREQUITA; Parkin Jr Sr HS; Parkin, AR; (3); 1/41; FHA; Natl Beta Clb; Science Clb; VP Frsh Cls; Rep Soph Cls; Pres Jr Cls; Ofcr Stu Cncl; Capt Bsktbl; Score Keeper; Trk; Frgn Lang Club/Italian; George Washington U; Frnsc Sci.

SMITH, WENDY C; Armorel HS; Blytheville, AR; (4); 2/18; Church Yth Grp; FBLA; FHA; Natl Beta Clb; Spanish Clb; Yrbk; Chrldng; Hon Roll; Sal; MS Cnty CC; Nurs.

SMITH, WHITTENY; Newport HS; Newport, AR; (3); Am Leg Aux Girls St; Church Yth Grp; Drill Tm; School Play; Lit Mag; Treas Stu Cncl; Chrldng; L Sftbl; Cit Awd; Hon Roll; U Of AR; Crim.

SMITH, WILLIAM; Palestine-Wheatley HS; Wheatley, AR; (3); #1 in class; FBLA; HOBY; Natl Beta Clb; Office Aide; Pres Soph Cls; Pres Jr Cls; Ofcr Stu Cncl; Mgr(s); Score Keeper; Hon Roll; Micro Bio.

SMITH, ZACKARY J; Weiner HS; Weiner, AR; (2); Pres Church Yth Grp; 4-H; Natl FFA Org; Science Clb; Band; Ofcr Stu Cncl; Var L Bsbl; Var L Bsktbl; Hon Roll; LIFE; AR ST Univ.

SMITHWICK, ELIZABETH M; Pine Bluff HS; Pine Bluff, AR; (4); 40/410; Bus Profs of Am; Church Yth Grp; Cmnty Wkr; French Clb; FHA; Intnl Clb; Key Clb; Scholastic Bowl; Acpl Chr; Church Choir; AR ST Univ; Bus.

SNARR, MICHAEL; Fayetteville Christian Schl; Lincoln, AR; (3); Church Yth Grp; Spanish Clb; Yrbk; Rep Jr Cls; Var Bsktbl; Hon Roll; NHS.

SNEAD, JANITA K; Gosnell Jr Sr HS; Blytheville, AR; (3); Art Clb; Drama Clb; French Clb; FHA; Library Aide; Speech Tm; Chorus; School Play; Nwsp; GCECA; DARE Clb Ed; MS Cnty CC; TV Brdcstng.

SNEED, BILLY W; Union Schl; El Dorado, AR; (3); French Clb; Natl Beta Clb; Ofcr Stu Cncl; Hon Roll; Bus Applications Cert Achvmnt; Cert To Attend Boys ST; U Of Comway.

SNELLINGS, JASON O; Valley View HS; Jonesboro, AR; (3); Quiz Bowl; ROTC; Socr; Pres Acad Fit Awd; Mock Trial Tm; Hstry Awd.

SNELSON, KELLY; Rose Bud Jr Sr HS; Romance, AR; (3); 2/36; Treas Drama Clb; Treas FBLA; GAA; Sec Natl FFA Org; Yrbk; Pres Jr Cls; Ofcr Bsbl; Bsktbl; Sftbl; Trk; Univ Of Cntrl AR; Bsktbl Coach.

SNIDER, BRANDY N; Bryant Sr HS; Bryant, AR; (2); Church Yth Grp; FCA; FBLA; GAA; JV Bsktbl; Var Sftbl; Var Trk; Var Vllybl; Var Hon Roll; Spcl Olympics Vol; U Of Cntrl AR; Pre-Med.

SNIDER, JAY; Carlisle Jr Sr HS; Carlisle, AR; (3); 10/62; Am Leg Boys St; Art Clb; Boy Scts; Church Yth Grp; Cmnty Wkr; FCA; FBLA; Office Aide; Spanish Clb; Rep Stu Cncl; Whos Who In Sports; Bsbl All-Star 94; Chrch Yth Growth Sec.

SNIDER, LEANNE R; Pulaski Acad; Little Rock, AR; (2); Church Yth Grp; Model UN; Natl Beta Clb; Spanish Clb; Bsktbl; Cit Awd; High Hon Roll; NHS; Band; Sftbl; Interact Clb VP; Just Say No Teen Ldr; Head Democratic Floor Page US Senate; Machon Schlsp Bk Awd.

SNIPES, AMBER; Ft Smith Christian Schl; Fort Smith, AR; (1); Church Yth Grp; Band; Bsktbl; Trk; Med.

SNIPES, DONELLE; Cedarville Jr Sr HS; Van Buren, AR; (4); 6/65; Debate Tm; FHA; Quiz Bowl; VP Science Clb; SADD; Color Guard; Rep Sr Cls; High Hon Roll; NHS; Pres Acad Fit Awd; Sr Yr GPA 4 Pt; Cdrvll Msnc Ldg & Crwfrd Cty Bd Rltrs Schlrshps; U Of OK; Mtrlgy.

SNIPES, GIA D; Cedarville Jr Sr HS; Van Buren, AR; (4); 6/65; Debate Tm; FHA; Quiz Bowl; VP Science Clb; SADD; Flag Corp; Rep Sr Cls; High Hon Roll; NHS; Pres Acad Fit Awd; Schol Recpt Of Cdrvill Masonic Lodge; Schol Recpt Of Crawford Co Brdof Realtrs; Hnr Grad; U Of OK; Meteorlgy.

SNIPES, SUSANNE M; Jonesboro HS; Jonesboro, AR; (3); 55/327; Church Yth Grp; FCA; French Clb; FBLA; Key Clb; Natl Beta Clb; Yrbk; Bsktbl; Vllybl; Hon Roll; MVP ST Vllybl Trnmt; Gatorade Circle Of Champions ST Awd Vllybl; ST Vllybl Champions; Purdue U; Sports Medicine.

SNODGRASS, JENNIFER E; Central Sr HS; Bauxite, AR; (3); 47/540; Am Leg Aux Girls St; Drama Clb; Natl Beta Clb; Science Clb; Spanish Clb; High Hon Roll; Hon Roll; NHS; Prfct Atten Awd; Judo Clb Pres; Physics Schl, Regnl & St Lvl Awds; TARS Pres & Treas; AR ST.

SNODGRASS, JUSTIN E; Central Sr HS; Bauxite, AR; (2); Science Clb; Spanish Clb; Var Crs Cntry; Var Trk; Hon Roll; Judo; UALR; Bio.

SNOW, MATTHEW L; Junction City HS; Junction City, AR; (2); FBLA; Quiz Bowl; Science Clb; Spanish Clb; Church Choir; Var Bsbl; Var Bsktbl; JV Ftbl; Score Keeper; High Hon Roll; BASIC.

SNOW, PHELLEP A; Marked Tree Jr Sr HS; Marked Tree, AR; (3); 28/64; Church Yth Grp; Library Aide; Quiz Bowl; ROTC; Stage Crew; Variety Show; Nwsp; Lit Mag; Rep Stu Cncl; Var Bsktbl; Upward Bound Mem & Ctznshp Awd; GATE; Jrnlsm.

SNOW, SHANE; Paris HS; New Blaine, AR; (3); Am Leg Boys St; Drama Clb; FCA; HOBY; Letterman Clb; NFL; Speech Tm; School Musical; Ftbl; Trk; Odyssey Of Mind; AR Tech U; Bio.

SNOWDEN, MARIA D; Bergman Schl; Harrison, AR; (2); Church Yth Grp; FBLA; Natl FFA Org; Hon Roll; Sci An Math.

SNYDER, ALLISON K; Marvell Acad; Marvell, AR; (4); 7/32; Church Yth Grp; Spanish Clb; Ed Nwsp; Bsktbl; High Hon Roll; NHS; Prfct Atten Awd; Pres Acad Fit Awd; Phillips County CC; Bus Mgmt.

SNYDER, AMBER D; Morrilton Sr HS; Morrilton, AR; (4); 50/150; Rep Art Clb; Cmnty Wkr; Sec French Clb; Sec FBLA; Math Clb; Office Aide; Thesps; Stage Crew; Yrbk; Trk; UAR; Psych.

SNYDER, BRADLEY W; Greene Co Tech HS; Paragould, AR; (4); 36/155; Art Clb; FBLA; Library Aide; Office Aide; Quiz Bowl; Spanish Clb; Ofcr Bsbl; Hon Roll; AR ST Univ; Criminology.

SNYDER, BRIDGET; Berryville HS; Berryville, AR; (4); 19/83; Church Yth Grp; Pres Debate Tm; Pres 4-H; Pres French Clb; German Clb; Girl Scts; VP Natl FFA Org; Pep Clb; Teachers Aide; Sec Chorus; Carroll Cty Ctlmns Bf Prncs; Ms Carroll Cty Ms Cngnlty; Natl Ldrshp Frm; WA Ldrshp Conf; U Of AR; Ag Ed.

SNYDER, NICOLE E; Southside HS; Fort Smith, AR; (2); Drama Clb; Mu Alpha Theta; Band; Drm Mjr(t); Mrchg Band; Pep Band; Stage Crew; Hon Roll; NHS; All-Region Band; Pharmacy; Med.

SNYDER, SEBRINA K; Bradford Jr Sr HS; Bradford, AR; (2); 4-H; French Clb; FHA; Rptr Nwsp; Hon Roll; Vrlgst/Microbio.

SOENTGEN, JUDITH T; Brookland Jr Sr HS; Jonesboro, AR; (3); FBLA; Spanish Clb; Variety Show; Rptr Nwsp; Bsktbl; Vllybl; Hon Roll; Mst Imprvd Ath Awd Bsktbl.

SOLANO, ELIZABETH T; Sheridan Sr HS; Sheridan, AR; (3); Cmnty Wkr; Service Clb; Chorus; Lit Mag; 4-H; Teachers Aide; Flag Corp; 4-H Awd; High Hon Roll; Jr NHS; Comm Svc Seal; Cert Literacy Tutor; Law.

SOLLEY, NANCY; Bright Star Schl; Doddridge, AR; (4); 1/22; Quiz Bowl; Rptr Nwsp; Ed Yrbk; Sec Soph Cls; VP Jr Cls; Sec Sr Cls; Rep Stu Cncl; Bsktbl; Pres NHS; Val; Henderson ST U.

SONNIER, ANNA M; Southside HS; Fort Smith, AR; (2); Debate Tm; Mu Alpha Theta; Bsktbl; Vllybl; High Hon Roll; Hon Roll; Jr NHS; NHS; Prfct Atten Awd; Pres Acad Fit Awd; Law; Politics.

SOPHABMIXAY, SETTHA; Russellville Sr HS; Russellville, AR; (3); 25/365; Church Yth Grp; French Clb; Spanish Clb; Varsity Clb; Lit Mag; JV Capt Socr; High Hon Roll; Hon Roll; NHS; Var Tennis; Med Club.

SORENSON, JENNIFER D; Williford HS; Williford, AR; (2); Teachers Aide; Chorus; Sec Soph Cls; Amer Legion Recognition; Black River Tech; Beautician.

SORENSON, JOSH M; Dequeen HS; De Queen, AR; (2); 1/130; Var Bsktbl; High Hon Roll; U Of ND; PT.

SORRELLS, ALICIA C; Lake Hamilton Sr HS; Hot Springs, AR; (4); Church Yth Grp; FHA; Office Aide; Teachers Aide; Chorus; Church Choir; Nwsp; Hon Roll; Child Care Awd; GCCC; Bus Admin.

SORRELLS, PAIGE; Kirby HS; Amity, AR; (3); 4/26; Am Leg Aux Girls St; FBLA; FHA; Yrbk; Ofcr Frsh Cls; Ofcr Soph Cls; Ofcr Jr Cls; Bsktbl; Crs Cntry; Trk; Navy Hon Pgm; Henderson ST U; Pharm.

SORY, VICKI; Bryant Sr HS; Bryant, AR; (2); Church Yth Grp; English Clb; French Clb; FBLA; Natl Beta Clb; Church Choir; Var Capt Chrldng; High Hon Roll; Jr NHS; Pres Acad Fit Awd; Chrstn Cncl; U AR Fayetteville; Phys Thry.

SOTALLARO, LEAH C; Conway Sr HS; Conway, AR; (4); 25/520; Church Yth Grp; Cmnty Wkr; Debate Tm; Drama Clb; FBLA; Natl Beta Clb; Office Aide; Spanish Clb; Band; Chorus; U Of AR; Elem Educ.

SOTO, JOSHUA D; Springdale Sr HS; Springdale, AR; (3); Church Yth Grp; Cmnty Wkr; Library Aide; Ed Phtg Yrbk; JV Ftbl; Wt Lftg; Hon Roll; NW Tech Inst.

SOUKUP, TINA W; Russellville Sr HS; Russellville, AR; (2); 153/403; Cmnty Wkr; Natl Beta Clb; Office Aide; Chorus; Drill Tm; Chrldng; Gym; Pom Pon; Swmmng; Tchr; Music.

SOUTHARD, SHERYL; Arkansas Schl Math & Science; Hot Springs, AR; (3); Cmnty Wkr; FBLA; Library Aide; Natl Beta Clb; Spanish Clb; Teachers Aide; High Hon Roll; Hon Roll; NHS; Pres Acad Fit Awd; Reg St Sci Fair; Knwldge Master Comp; ARK Cncl Of Tchrs Of Math; Bio.

SOUTHERLAND, KERRY; Dumas Jr HS; Dumas, AR; (1); 1/175; Church Yth Grp; FBLA; Natl Beta Clb; Quiz Bowl; Science Clb; Spanish Clb; Band; Church Choir; Drm Mjr(t); Mrchg Band; Sci Clb Pres; Mst Likely To Succeed & Mst Intllgnt; OM Cmptn.

SPACK, STEVEN M; Russellville Sr HS; London, AR; (3); 89/389; Art Clb; Church Yth Grp; Spanish Clb; Var L Bsbl; Mgr Ftbl; Var Trk; High Hon Roll; Hon Roll; Jr NHS; NHS; St Finals-Amer Legion Russelville AR Team 95-96.

SPAHN, KIMBERLY; Coleman Jr HS; Van Buren, AR; (1); Church Yth Grp; Pres FHA; Girl Scts; Band; Capt Drill Tm; Jazz Band; Mrchg Band; Pep Band; High Hon Roll; NHS; Prtnrs In Chrst.

SPALDING, LORI E; Southside HS; Fort Smith, AR; (2); Church Yth Grp; FCA; Band; Drill Tm; Mrchg Band; Pep Band; Score Keeper; Trk; Vllybl; Hon Roll; U Of AR; Coach/Tchr.

SPANGLER, KRIS; Farmington Jr Sr HS; Farmington, AR; (2); French Clb; Model UN; Band; Jazz Band; Mrchg Band; Hon Roll; U Of AR; Arntcl Engnr.

SPANN, HEIDI R; Fayetteville East HS; Fayetteville, AR; (4); 36/399; Intnl Clb; Red Cross Aide; VP Thesps; Acpl Chr; School Musical; School Play; Variety Show; Lit Mag; Capt Swmmng; Hon Roll; U Of KS.

SPANN, JASON C; Pine Bluff HS; Pine Bluff, AR; (3); 15/470; Am Leg Boys St; French Clb; Library Aide; Math Tm; Quiz Bowl; JV Ftbl; Hon Roll; Jr NHS; NHS; Pres Acad Fit Awd; Odyssey Of The MindAHSME Hnr Roll; Comp Sci.

SPARKS, KELLI; Southside HS; Fort Smith, AR; (4); French Clb; Intnl Clb; Key Clb; Pep Clb; Nwsp; Yrbk; Chrldng; French Hon Soc; High Hon Roll; Hon Roll; Fort Hays ST U; Frnch.

SPARKS, REYNA; Jasper HS; Jasper, AR; (4); Rep Art Clb; FBLA; VP FHA; Math Clb; Natl Beta Clb; Rep Spanish Clb; Yrbk; Hon Roll; PRIDE; A-TAD.

SPAUNHORST, STACY E; Greene Co Tech HS; Paragould, AR; (4); 9/160; Church Yth Grp; FCA; Sec 4-H; FHA; Key Clb; VP Pep Clb; Science Clb; Spanish Clb; Rep Stu Cncl; Capt Chrldng; ASU; Mgmt Information Sys.

SPEAR, JOHN P; Smackover HS; Eldorado, AR; (3); Natl FFA Org; VICA; Greenhand FFA Degree; Chptr FFA Degree; Little Rock Plumbing Cmptn; Carpenter; Plumber.

SPEARS, JAMIE L; Lonoke Sr HS; Lonoke, AR; (3); Art Clb; FBLA; Math Clb; Spanish Clb; Var Bsktbl; Var Trk; Hon Roll; NHS; PRIDE Sec; Ecology Clb; Nrs.

SPEARS, SHANE S; Blytheville Sr HS; Blytheville, AR; (4); 10/200; Church Yth Grp; Drama Clb; Key Clb; Band; School Play; Yrbk; French Hon Soc; High Hon Roll; NHS; Pres Acad Fit Awd; Hendrix.

SPEDDING, JULIE C; Bentonville Sr HS; Hiwasse, AR; (2); Church Yth Grp; FCA; FBLA; Spanish Clb; Chrldng; Tennis; High Hon Roll; Jr NHS.

SPEED, PRESTON; Dumas HS; Dumas, AR; (2); FCA; FBLA; Math Clb; Spanish Clb; L Ftbl; L Golf; Hon Roll; NHS; Pres Acad Fit Awd; Church Yth Grp.

SPEER, KEVIN M; Searcy HS; Searcy, AR; (3); 15/250; Art Clb; FCA; French Clb; FBLA; Quiz Bowl; Nwsp; JV Bsktbl; Var Tennis; French Hon Soc; High Hon Roll; Car Audio & Electronics; Poet.

SPEERS, STEVEN C; Cutter Morning Star HS; Hot Springs, AR; (2); Art Clb; Church Yth Grp; FCA; FHA; HOBY; Library Aide; Office Aide; Spanish Clb; Sec Soph Cls; L Bsktbl.

SPEIGHT, JENNIFER; Southside HS; Fort Smith, AR; (4); 206/464; French Clb; Letterman Clb; Pep Clb; Teachers Aide; Drill Tm; Chrldng; Crs Cntry; Gym; Trk; Vllybl; Westark; Hstry.

SPENCE, TAMARA F; Waldron HS; Waldron, AR; (2); Church Yth Grp; 4-H; Hosp Aide; Band; Mrchg Band; Sftbl; Hon Roll; Pres Acad Fit Awd; Vol Hosp; Holocaust Nvr Again AEGIS Cmp 95; All Rgn Bnd 94-95; Symphnc Bnd 2nd Chair; Univ Of TX; Physics.

SPENCER, COURTNEY D; Russellville Sr HS; Russellville, AR; (2); Art Clb; Dance Clb; Band; Drill Tm; Mrchg Band; Gym; High Hon Roll; Hon Roll; Jr NHS; NHS; Arch.

SPENCER, DAVID; Russellville Sr HS; London, AR; (3); 132/360; Art Clb; Quiz Bowl; VP VICA; Hon Roll; Cyclone Achvr; Wildlf Mgmt.

SPENCER, JASON P; Sheridan Sr HS; Little Rock, AR; (2); Cmnty Wkr; Intnl Clb; ROTC; Service Clb; Band; Color Guard; Drill Tm; Ed Nwsp; Yrbk; Lit Mag; Sons Of The Amer Revolution; TX A&M; Biochem.

SPENCER, SARAH A; Lee Acad; Colt, AR; (1); Church Yth Grp; Church Choir; VP Frsh Cls; High Hon Roll; U Of AR; Med Dr.

SPICER, AMANDA; Blevins HS; Mc Caskill, AR; (3); FBLA; Sec Natl Beta Clb; Natl FFA Org; Quiz Bowl; Yrbk; Bsktbl; Chrldng; Trk; Hon Roll; ADAPT; Med.

SPICKELMIER, JENNIFER; Dardanelle HS; Dardanelle, AR; (4); 18/100; Am Leg Aux Girls St; FBLA; FHA; Intnl Clb; Natl Beta Clb; Sec Sr Cls; Var Chrldng; Var Crs Cntry; L Sftbl; Trk; Miss DHS; Acad Ath; AR Tech Univ; Bus.

SPILLERS, CHIVONNE L; Fouke Jr Sr HS; Fouke, AR; (3); Art Clb; Chess Clb; Church Yth Grp; Natl FFA Org; Spanish Clb; Band; Drm Mjr(t); Jazz Band; Mrchg Band; Pep Band; Forensics.

SPILLYARDS, JEFFREY L; Pine Bluff HS; Pine Bluff, AR; (3); Am Leg Boys St; Boy Scts; Church Yth Grp; French Clb; Pres Acpl Chr; Rep Yrbk; Tennis; Hon Roll; NHS; Pres Acad Fit Awd.

SPILMAN, ANNA K; Southside HS; Fort Smith, AR; (3); 271/502; Church Yth Grp; Chorus; YAM Trip Minski Belayusin 94.

SPINKS, DARRYL; Dumas Jr HS; Dumas, AR; (2); 8/179; Pres Church Yth Grp; FCA; FTA; Natl Beta Clb; Quiz Bowl; Spanish Clb; Band; Church Choir; Mrchg Band; Pres Stu Cncl; U Of AR Fayetteville; Comp Sci.

SPINKS, SCOTT F; Mills HS; Sherwood, AR; (3); 1/300; Church Yth Grp; Mu Alpha Theta; Natl Beta Clb; Q&S; Quiz Bowl; Church Choir; Orch; Nwsp; NHS.

SPIVEY, JAMIE M; Stamps HS; Buckner, AR; (3); Art Clb; Teachers Aide; Band; Mrchg Band; Gym; Swmmng; Cit Awd.

SPIVEY, LINDSAY; Mt Ida Jr Sr HS; Mount Ida, AR; (1); Church Yth Grp; FHA; Var Chrldng; Var Sftbl; Prfct Atten Awd.

SPONER, MELISSA; Morrilton Sr HS; Morrilton, AR; (2); Art Clb; Church Yth Grp; Drama Clb; FBLA; Math Clb; Science Clb; Spanish Clb; Thesps; Drill Tm; School Play; U Central AR; Phys Ther.

SPOONER, APRIL N; Junction City HS; Junction City, AR; (1); Church Yth Grp; Band; Mrchg Band; Powder Puff Ftbl; Hon Roll.

SPRADLEY, CORY J; Cabot HS; Lonoke, AR; (1); Church Yth Grp; Cmnty Wkr; FBLA; Girl Scts; Library Aide; Office Aide; Intrml Sftbl; Hon Roll.

SPRADLING, JOSHUA R; Gravette HS; Gravette, AR; (3); Boy Scts; Church Yth Grp; Drama Clb; Thesps; School Play; Cit Awd; High Hon Roll; NHS; Natl Yng Ldrs Conf; St Hs Rep Pg.

SPRAGGINS, PAMELA M; Rogers HS; Rogers, AR; (3); Church Yth Grp; FBLA; Office Aide; Spanish Clb; SADD; Church Choir; Ed Yrbk; Bsktbl; High Hon Roll; U Of AR; Jrnlsm.

SPRATT, JACQUELINE; Forrest City HS; Forrest City, AR; (3); DECA; French Clb; FHA; FTA; Library Aide; Math Clb; Jazz Band; Office Aide; Teachers Aide; High Hon Roll; Deans List; Concord Carter Inst; Med Rcrd.

SPRINGMAN, JASON; West Fork HS; West Fork, AR; (4); 1/72; Drama Clb; FBLA; HOBY; Model UN; Band; Mrchg Band; Orch; Pep Band; High Hon Roll; Pres NHS; Upward Bnd Pgm; Hendrix Coll; Genetics Med.

SPROTT, SARAH E; Harrison Sr HS; Harrison, AR; (4); 35/207; Church Yth Grp; Cmnty Wkr; Drama Clb; FBLA; GAA; Office Aide; Red Cross Aide; Science Clb; Spanish Clb; Thesps; Most Outstdng Chrldr; Unvrsl Chrldrs Assn All Star; Cherd In London New Years Day Pard 96; U Of AR; Pre-Med; Family Phy.

SPURLIN, CANDYCE L; Pangburn Jr Sr HS; Judsonia, AR; (4); 11/43; French Clb; FBLA; FHA; Natl Beta Clb; Yrbk; Treas Frsh Cls; Rep Stu Cncl; Capt Chrldng; Swmmng; High Hon Roll; Homcmng & Sweetheart Banquet Queen; Miss PHS; ASU; Jrnlsm.

SPURLIN, KRISTI M; Southside HS; Batesville, AR; (2); FBLA; Key Clb; Band; Drill Tm; Pep Band; Mgr(s); Hon Roll.

SPURLOCK, LAURA L; Sylvan Hills HS; Sherwood, AR; (2); 19/343; Church Yth Grp; Math Clb; Mu Alpha Theta; Natl Beta Clb; Spanish Clb; Chorus; Hon Roll; Jr NHS; NHS.

SPURLOCK, LELA; Brinkley HS; Brinkley, AR; (1); Office Aide; Hon Roll; Jr NHS; Gftd & Tlnted; ASU; Med.

SPURLOCK, LESLIE A; Sylvan Hills HS; Sherwood, AR; (2); 11/343; Church Yth Grp; FCA; French Clb; FHA; Mu Alpha Theta; Natl Beta Clb; Chorus; Hon Roll; Jr NHS; NHS; Nrsng.

SQUIRE, SARAH; Mt St Mary Acad; Little Rock, AR; (4); 3/125; VP Pres Church Yth Grp; Mu Alpha Theta; Spanish Clb; Acpl Chr; Chorus; Church Choir; High Hon Roll; JETS Awd; NHS; Pres Schlr; Tri-M Music Hnr Soc; All Region & All St Choir; Rhodes Coll.

SQUIRES, DAVID A; Mills HS; Little Rock, AR; (3); Church Yth Grp; Q&S; ROTC; Color Guard; Nwsp; High Hon Roll; Hon Roll; NHS; Kings Clb; Engrng.

SQUIRES, TRAVIS W; Cty Line HS; Ozark, AR; (2); Boy Scts; Church Yth Grp; Spanish Clb; Band; Pep Band; Prfct Atten Awd.

STAATS, CHRISTIN L; England HS; England, AR; (2); Church Yth Grp; FBLA; Girl Scts; Natl Beta Clb; Band; Drm Mjr(t); Jazz Band; Mrchg Band; Hon Roll; Pres Acad Fit Awd; Horseback Riding; Coll; Music.

STAATS, TED; Gravette HS; Bentonville, AR; (2); FBLA; Yrbk; Var Bsbl; Var Bsktbl; Hon Roll; NHS; Alg I Pin Awd; Bio Awd; US Natl Awd Math; Natl Yngs Ldrs Conf Wshngtn DC Natl Schlr AR Rep.

STACEY, HEATH; Bergman Schl; Harrison, AR; (4); 2/60; Church Yth Grp; Rptr Frsh Cls; Pres Natl Beta Clb; Quiz Bowl; VP Spanish Clb; Ed Nwsp; Pres Frsh Cls; VP Soph Cls; Pres Jr Cls; VP Stu Cncl; Harrison Chmaber Of Commerce Hnr Stu Awd; NATCO Hnrs Schlsp Awd; Stu Of Yr; U Of AR; Biochem; Pre-Med.

STAFFORD, GREGORY L; North Little Rock Hs-West; North Little Rock, AR; (3); 50/554; Church Yth Grp; Mu Alpha Theta; Band; Church Choir; Jazz Band; Mrchg Band; Hon Roll; NHS; Natl Beta Clb; High Hon Roll; All Reg Cncrt/Jz Bnd; All ST Jz Bnd; All ST Cncrt Bnd Altrnt; U Of Cntrl AR; Pre Med.

STAGGER, MELANIE; Parkview Arts/Sci Magnet HS; Little Rock, AR; (4); 2/265; Am Leg Aux Girls St; Girl Scts; Sec Key Clb; Mu Alpha Theta; Pres Natl Beta Clb; Band; VP Jr Cls; Pres Sr Cls; Rep Stu Cncl; Sal; Bio.

STAGGS, ALISHA; Siloam Springs Sr HS; Siloam Springs, AR; (2); FCA; FBLA; Key Clb; Natl Beta Clb; Office Aide; Science Clb; Spanish Clb; Teachers Aide; Chrldng; Hon Roll; U Of AR; Pol Sci.

STAGGS, BRADY A; Arkansas Sr HS; Texarkana, AR; (4); 10/375; Church Yth Grp; Mu Alpha Theta; Office Aide; Quiz Bowl; Spanish Clb; Band; Mrchg Band; Pep Band; NHS; Ntl Merit Ltr; U Cntrl AR; Med.

STAIN, BILLY L; Yellville Summit HS; Yellville, AR; (2); 1/86; Church Yth Grp; Math Clb; Teachers Aide; Var Bsktbl; Hon Roll; NHS.

STALEY, ANGELA; J A Fair Sr HS; Little Rock, AR; (4); 1/300; FBLA; HOBY; Mu Alpha Theta; Yrbk; Pres Stu Cncl; Chrldng; Sftbl; Tennis; High Hon Roll; NHS; Hmcmng Qn; NHS Pres; U Of AR Fayettevl; Med.

STALEY, JASON L; Mountain Home HS; Mountain Home, AR; (3); Pep Clb; ROTC; Spanish Clb; Pres Soph Cls; Ftbl; Trk; Hon Roll.

STALEY, KYLA; J A Fair Sr HS; Little Rock, AR; (3); 22/269; Drama Clb; FBLA; Rptr Yrbk; School Play; Rep Stu Cncl; Capt Chrldng; Hon Roll; NHS; Pres Acad Fit Awd; Hosp Aide; Hmcmng Court; Teens For Christ; Univ Of AR; Comm.

STALLINGS, CRYSTAL M; Sloan Hendrix HS; Imboden, AR; (3); 5/32; Church Yth Grp; Rptr FBLA; Pres FHA; FTA; Natl Beta Clb; Pep Clb; Nwsp; Yrbk; Pres Stu Cncl; Stat Bsktbl; AR ST U.

STAMPS, HALEY; Springdale Sr HS; Springdale, AR; (3); French Clb; Q&S; Ed Rptr Nwsp; Yrbk; French Hon Soc; Hon Roll; Jr NHS; NHS; Ntl Merit SF; Pres Acad Fit Awd; AEGIS Summer Prgm; Natl Jrnlsm Awds; AR Govrs Schl Alternate; His/Jrnlsm/Sociology.

STANCLIFF, JOI; Russellville Sr HS; Russellville, AR; (3); Cmnty Wkr; Drama Clb; French Clb; Girl Scts; Hosp Aide; Teachers Aide; Chorus; High Hon Roll; Jr NHS; NHS; Crim Psych.

STANDRIDGE, ALISHA; Mt Ida Jr Sr HS; Mount Ida, AR; (3); 7/47; HOBY; Natl Beta Clb; Natl FFA Org; School Play; Ofcr Stu Cncl; Capt Bsktbl; Mgr(s); Sftbl; Hon Roll; All Amer Schlr 94-95; Homcmng Crt 93 & 95; Natl Ldrshp, Svc, Bus Ed Awds; Sprts Med.

STANDRIDGE, SUMMER F; Parkview Arts-Science HS; Scott, AR; (3); Cmnty Wkr; Debate Tm; Sec Pres 4-H; French Clb; Cit Awd; 4-H Awd; Hon Roll; Explorers; Young Amer Boy Scout Explorer; 4-H Ambassador; Teen Star; ST Record Bk Wnnr In Vet Sci; Zoology & Vet Medicine.

STANICK, JENNIFER; Greenwood Sr HS; Greenwood, AR; (2); Church Yth Grp; VP FCA; French Clb; FBLA; Stage Crew; L Var Chrldng; Mgr(s); JV Vllybl; Hon Roll; U AR; Law.

STANLEY, CHAD M; Nashville HS; Ozan, AR; (3); Church Yth Grp; 4-H; Natl FFA Org; School Play; Var Ftbl; Hon Roll; Breeder/Shwmn Cattle; Hunt; Fish; Rdng Horses; Snow Skiing; Wtr Sprgs; Southern ST Univ; Agri.

STANLEY, GREG; Sylvan Hills HS; Sherwood, AR; (2); 24/300; Church Yth Grp; FCA; French Clb; FBLA; Key Clb; Math Clb; Mu Alpha Theta; Natl Beta Clb; Acpl Chr; Church Choir; CA At Berkeley; Cmptr Sci.

STANLEY, GWEN N; John L Mcclellan Magnet HS; Little Rock, AR; (3); 22/288; Sec Art Clb; Computer Clb; Mu Alpha Theta; Cit Awd; High Hon Roll; Hon Roll; NHS; Ntl Merit Ltr; Yth/Govt; Psychlgst.

STANLEY, HEATH D; Mountain Home HS; Mountain Home, AR; (3); 89/267; FCA; Var Bsbl; JV Bsktbl; High Hon Roll.

STANLEY, LEE A; Searcy HS; Searcy, AR; (3); Sec Church Yth Grp; FCA; FBLA; Sec Key Clb; Natl Beta Clb; Office Aide; Spanish Clb; Socr; NHS; Spanish NHS; Flying Lssns; Tap/Bllt/Jazz.

STANLEY, NEAL H; Monticello HS; Wilmar, AR; (3); Church Yth Grp; Cmnty Wkr; FCA; FBLA; SADD; Church Choir; Var Bsbl; Var Bsktbl; Var Ftbl; Var Wt Lftg.

STANLEY, SARAH; Jasper HS; Dogpatch, AR; (3); Church Yth Grp; Drama Clb; FBLA; FHA; HOBY; Math Clb; Math Tm; Natl Beta Clb; VP Natl FFA Org; Rep Science Clb; Grls St Dlgt; FFA, FHA & FBLA Prlmntry Teams; 1st Ms Mrry Chrstms 95; Str Grnhnd & Chptr Frmr; Mrn Bio.

STANLEY, TABITHA A; Stuttgart Sr HS; Stuttgart, AR; (3); Church Yth Grp; Cmnty Wkr; DECA; FBLA; Key Clb; Spanish Clb; Chorus; VP Jr Cls; Rep Stu Cncl; NHS; U Of AR Fayetteville; Bus Mgmt.

STANTON, DONNA J; Conway Sr HS; Conway, AR; (4); 14/520; Church Yth Grp; FBLA; Hosp Aide; Natl Beta Clb; Teachers Aide; Chorus; Church Choir; Cit Awd; High Hon Roll; Spanish NHS; Natl Voc-Tech Hnr Soc; U Of Cntrl AR; Rad.

STANTON, MARLENE; Arkansas Schl Math & Science; Eudora, AR; (3); Church Yth Grp; FBLA; Hosp Aide; HOBY; Natl Beta Clb; Quiz Bowl; Band; Church Choir; Drill Tm; Mrchg Band; Tulane U; Med.

STANTON, STACY; Magnolia HS; Magnolia, AR; (2); #1 in class; Teachers Aide; Hon Roll; Bio.

STAPLES, KELLI M; North Little Rock Hs-West; North Little Rock, AR; (3); 77/554; Church Yth Grp; Cmnty Wkr; Debate Tm; FCA; Hosp Aide; Key Clb; Mu Alpha Theta; Spanish Clb; Church Choir; Drill Tm; Peer Ldrshp; U Of AR At Fayetteville.

STARBUCK, MATRINA R; Mena HS; Mena, AR; (4); 44/100; Church Yth Grp; Cmnty Wkr; SADD; Teachers Aide; Band; Church Choir; Mrchg Band; School Play; Ed Yrbk; Ozark Chrstiancol; Elem Ed.

STARK, CHELSEA L; Heber Springs HS; Heber Springs, AR; (3); 13/110; FBLA; FHA; Natl Beta Clb; Spanish Clb; Chorus; Church Choir; School Musical; Stage Crew; Cit Awd; High Hon Roll; Kenpo Karate Stu; Wrld His Awd; Eng Awd; U Of Cntrl AR.

STARK, INICE E; Valley View HS; Jonesboro, AR; (2); Church Yth Grp; 4-H; FHA; Library Aide; Office Aide; Spanish Clb; Teachers Aide; Hon Roll; Alg I Awd; Nom Natl Yng Ldrs Conf; Nrse.

STARKS, STEPHANIE A; John L Mcclellan Magnet HS; Little Rock, AR; (2); FBLA; Natl Beta Clb; Quiz Bowl; Church Choir; Hon Roll; U Of NC; Civil Law.

STARLING, MINDI; Delight HS; Delight, AR; (2); 2/28; FBLA; Natl Beta Clb; Natl FFA Org; Quiz Bowl; Sec Soph Cls; Bsktbl; Sftbl; Hon Roll; U AR Fyttvlle.

STARNES, JONDALYN; Harmony Grove Jr Sr HS; Camden, AR; (4); 4/48; Am Leg Aux Girls St; Church Yth Grp; Natl Beta Clb; Quiz Bowl; Mrchg Band; School Play; Rep Stu Cncl; High Hon Roll; NHS; Pres Acad Fit Awd; Mss Hrmny Grv; Henderson.

STARR, CARYNE M; John L Mcclellan Magnet HS; Little Rock, AR; (2); Church Yth Grp; Natl Beta Clb; Var Chrldng; Tennis; Hon Roll; NHS; CIA; Marine Bio.

STAUDT, CRYSTAL D; Rogers HS; Garfield, AR; (3); Hosp Aide; Model UN; Flag Corp; Mrchg Band; Mgr Socr; Mgr Vllybl; Gov Hon Prg Awd; NHS; Church Yth Grp; Teachers Aide; A M Seminary; Lettered 2 Yrs Academics; Architecture.

STAUFFER, KELLI; Southside HS; Fort Smith, AR; (4); 99/465; Pres Church Yth Grp; Cmnty Wkr; German Clb; Pres Key Clb; Service Clb; Orch; School Musical; Rep Sr Cls; Rep Stu Cncl; DAR Awd; U Of Cntrl AR; Music Ed.

STEEGER, LIESL R; Arkadelphia Sr HS; Arkadelphia, AR; (4); Church Yth Grp; FCA; French Clb; FBLA; Natl Beta Clb; Co-Capt Drill Tm; Rptr Soph Cls; High Hon Roll; NHS; Pres Acad Fit Awd; Ouachita Bapt Univ; Mrchndsng.

STEELE, NICHOLAS; Newark Jr Sr HS; Newark, AR; (2); Church Yth Grp; 4-H; Natl Beta Clb; Natl FFA Org; Quiz Bowl; Ofcr Bsbl; Bsktbl; Hon Roll; Pres Schlr.

STEELMAN, AMY; Camden Christian Acad; Sparkman, AR; (4); Church Yth Grp; 4-H; FHA; Spanish Clb; Church Choir; School Play; Yrbk; Ofcr Stu Cncl; Bsktbl; Vllybl; Ouachita Baptist U; Ed.

STEER, STEVEN T; Izard Co Cons Jr Sr HS; Oxford, AR; (4); Key Clb; Natl Beta Clb; Band; Mrchg Band; Variety Show; High Hon Roll.

STELLMON, MELISSA E; Fayetteville Sr HS; Fayetteville, AR; (2); Church Yth Grp; Band; Flag Corp; Mrchg Band; Pep Band; High Hon Roll; Hon Roll; Outstdng Bandsman Awd; U Of AR; Music.

STELLY, TIA L; Bald Knob HS; Bald Knob, AR; (2); Natl Beta Clb; Band; Chorus; Color Guard; Mrchg Band; Cit Awd; High Hon Roll; Hon Roll; Color Guard Flag Capt.

STENNIS, BRANDI M; Fairview HS; Camden, AR; (3); 7/280; Am Leg Aux Girls St; Church Yth Grp; Mu Alpha Theta; Natl Beta Clb; Spanish Clb; Church Choir; Sec Pres Frsh Cls; Rep Soph Cls; Rep Jr Cls; VP Stu Cncl; CO ST Univ; Wldlf Biol.

STEPHANIDIS, JAIME M; Hall Sr HS; Little Rock, AR; (2); Art Clb; Church Yth Grp; FBLA; JCL; Latin Clb; Spanish Clb; Speech Tm; Cit Awd; High Hon Roll; Hon Roll; Spirit Grps.

STEPHANOVA, NATALYA A; Searcy HS; Searcy, AR; (3); 1/230; Natl Beta Clb; Thesps; Chorus; Stage Crew; NHS; Schl Dinner Theatre; Jr Revue; Time-Keeper Drama Trnmnts; U Of AR Fayetteville; Intrprtr.

STEPHENS, KARLA; Bradley Jr Sr HS; Taylor, AR; (2); Church Yth Grp; VP FHA; HOBY; Math Clb; Spanish Clb; Pres Frsh Cls; Sec Stu Cncl; Var Bsktbl; Capt Chrldng; Sftbl; Southern AR U; Med.

STEPHENS, LINDA; Emmet Schl; Emmet, AR; (2); 2/15; Library Aide; Natl Beta Clb; Capt Bsktbl; Cit Awd; Hon Roll; Prfct Atten Awd; Swimming; Horseback Riding; Lib Clb; CPR 1st Aid Trng; U Of AR; Med.

STEPHENS, LIZ; Southside HS; Fort Smith, AR; (3); Church Yth Grp; FCA; Latin Clb; Band; Church Choir; Drm Mjr(t); School Musical; Rep Jr Cls; Var Tennis; Hon Roll; Natl Eng Mrt Awd; Intrct Svc Clb Sec; U Of AR.

STEPHENS, SHANE M; Rogers HS; Rogers, AR; (4); Church Yth Grp; Band; Hon Roll; Renaissance Awd; Nw AR CC; Bus.

STEPHENSON, CASEY; Dermott HS; Dermott, AR; (2); #1 in class; Church Yth Grp; FCA; FBLA; Natl Beta Clb; Ftbl; Cit Awd; DAR Awd; High Hon Roll; Hon Roll; NHS; Med.

STEPHENSON, JEANNETTE D; Parkview Arts Sci Magnet HS; Little Rock, AR; (2); Church Yth Grp; Cmnty Wkr; French Clb; Girl Scts; Hosp Aide; Key Clb; Library Aide; Natl Beta Clb; Chorus; Church Choir; Peer Facilitators; Robert Sarver Mem Vol Awd; Acctng; Bus Admin.

STEPP, HAELYN; Ozark HS; Ozark, AR; (4); 10/110; FBLA; FHA; HOBY; Intnl Clb; Natl Beta Clb; Quiz Bowl; Pres Frsh Cls; Var Bsktbl; High Hon Roll; NHS; Westark CC.

STEPP, SHEENA R; Springdale Sr HS; Springdale, AR; (3); Church Yth Grp; Dance Clb; FCA; French Clb; Chorus; Church Choir; Drill Tm; JV Var Chrldng; Gym; High Hon Roll; PEOPLE Pgm; U Of AR; Phy Thrpst Asst.

STERLING, LATRESA D; Stamps HS; Stamps, AR; (4); 5/48; Mu Alpha Theta; Spanish Clb; Sec Soph Cls; Sec Jr Cls; Sec Sr Cls; Hon Roll; NHS; 4-H; Office Aide; SADD; Ebony Club; Mst Outstdng Acctng Awd; Escort Grad Class Of 95; Red River Tech Coll; Nrsng.

STEVENS, AMY R; Searcy HS; Searcy, AR; (3); 63/286; FCA; French Clb; FTA; Key Clb; Natl Beta Clb; Band; Chorus; Drm Mjr(t); Rep Jr Cls; Hist Rep Stu Cncl; Music/PE.

STEVENS, ANDREA; Central Ark Christian Schl; Little Rock, AR; (2); Church Yth Grp; French Clb; Chorus; Drill Tm; JV Var Bsktbl; JV Var Trk; High Hon Roll; Sec Jr NHS; Powder Puff Ftbl; Var Score Keeper; Piano; All-Rgn Chrs; Harding U.

STEVENS, APRIL M; Williford HS; Williford, AR; (2); 7/20; Art Clb; FBLA; FHA; Natl Beta Clb; Yrbk; Sec Stu Cncl; Bsktbl; Sftbl; Trk.

STEVENS, CHRISTOPHER R; Southside HS; Batesville, AR; (2); Quiz Bowl; High Hon Roll; NHS; Prfct Atten Awd; Chem Eng.

STEVENS, JENNY; Junction City HS; El Dorado, AR; (2); FBLA; Spanish Clb; Sftbl; High Hon Roll.

STEVENS, MELISSA; Leslie Schl; Leslie, AR; (1); Church Yth Grp; Cmnty Wkr; FCA; 4-H; FBLA; Key Clb; Chorus; JV Bsktbl; JV Trk; Hon Roll; Chld Care Spec.

STEVENS, MICHELLE L; Timbo Schl; Fifty Six, AR; (3); 3/27; VP FBLA; FHA; Treas Natl Beta Clb; Capt Quiz Bowl; Rep Nwsp; L Bsktbl; L Sftbl; L Trk; NHS; Natl FFA Org; Lifeguard; CPR & 1st Aid Cert; AR ST U.

STEVENS, SCOTTY W; Rural Special Schl; Prim, AR; (2); FCA; Ofcr Soph Cls; Var Bsktbl; Hon Roll; GATE Hnr.

STEVENS, SHANNON; West Side Christian Schl; El Dorado, AR; (3); Drama Clb; Natl Beta Clb; Acpl Chr; Chorus; Yrbk; Sec Jr Cls; Var Vllybl; Hon Roll; Ntl Merit Ltr; Teenage Reps; Arts & Crfts; Elem Ed.

STEVENSON, ALICIA; Annie Camp Jr HS; Jonesboro, AR; (1); FBLA; Natl Beta Clb; Chorus; Var Chrldng; High Hon Roll; Hon Roll; Var Chrldr Ltr; Gymnstcs 9 Yrs; Yth Bowlng League; AR ST U.

STEVENSON, AMBER; Cross Co Jr Sr HS; Hickory Ridge, AR; (4); 4/45; Am Leg Aux Girls St; FHA; Natl Beta Clb; Science Clb; SADD; Acpl Chr; Co-Ed Nwsp; VP Jr Cls; Pres Sr Cls; Rep Stu Cncl; U Of Central AR; Pre Optmtry.

STEVENSON, MISTY M; Cave City HS; Batesville, AR; (2); #1 in class; French Clb; FHA; Key Clb; Math Clb; Science Clb; Bsktbl; Sftbl; Hon Roll.

STEVES, SARA L; Stuttgart Sr HS; Stuttgart, AR; (4); 16/160; Art Clb; Church Yth Grp; FBLA; Key Clb; Library Aide; Quiz Bowl; Science Clb; Spanish Clb; Teachers Aide; Band; AR St Univ; Bus.

STEWARD, ASHLEY; Augusta HS; Augusta, AR; (3); Am Leg Aux Girls St; Church Yth Grp; Natl Beta Clb; Sec Stu Cncl; Var Bsktbl; Var Chrldng; High Hon Roll; NHS; Tae-Kwon-Do; Dancing; FL ST U; Marine Bio.

STEWARD, DANIEL; Newark Jr Sr HS; Newport, AR; (4); 2/41; FBLA; Math Clb; Natl Beta Clb; Natl FFA Org; Spanish Clb; Hon Roll; Sal; St Schlr; All Amer Schlr; Natl Engl Merit Awd; ASU Beebe; Wldlfe Mgmt.

STEWARD, JEREMY R; West Memphis Christian Schl; West Memphis, AR; (1); Church Yth Grp; Capt Ftbl; Wt Lftg; Prof Ftbl.

STEWARD, JOSH R; West Memphis Christian Schl; West Memphis, AR; (2); Church Yth Grp; Cmnty Wkr; FCA; HOBY; School Play; Ofcr Bsbl; Wt Lftg; Law Team; FBI; DEA.

STEWART, AMBER; Dollarway HS; Pine Bluff, AR; (4); 6/92; French Clb; Hosp Aide; Key Clb; Teachers Aide; Ed Nwsp; Hon Roll; NHS; Pres Acad Fit Awd; U Of Cntrl AR; Nrsng.

STEWART, ANDRICK D; J A Fair Sr HS; Little Rock, AR; (4); Art Clb; French Clb; Spanish Clb; Bsktbl; Score Keeper; Wiley Coll; Bus Admin.

STEWART, ANGIE; Clarksville HS; Clarksville, AR; (1); 1/130; FBLA; Natl Beta Clb; Chrldng; Crs Cntry; Trk; Vllybl; Hon Roll; Mss Tn AR; Gymnstcs, Cch Non Schl Spon.

STEWART, DAVID; Mineral Springs Schl; Mineral Springs, AR; (2); Church Yth Grp; FBLA; Natl Beta Clb; Quiz Bowl; Band; Church Choir; Jazz Band; Mrchg Band; Pep Band; Pres Soph Cls.

STEWART, DELTA S; Fairview HS; Camden, AR; (2); Art Clb; Drama Clb; Letterman Clb; Natl Beta Clb; Natl FFA Org; JV Bsktbl; Mgr(s); Var L Tennis; JV L Vllybl; Hon Roll; Psych.

STEWART, DONNA L; England HS; England, AR; (2); Church Yth Grp; Office Aide; Chorus; Church Choir; Var Bsktbl; Trk; Cit Awd; UAPB; Child Care.

STEWART, EMILY; Oak Grove HS; Maumelle, AR; (2); #1 in class; VP Art Clb; Church Yth Grp; French Clb; Letterman Clb; Mu Alpha Theta; Natl Beta Clb; Church Choir; VP Stu Cncl; L Trk; Pres Acad Fit Awd; Maumelle Stdnt Bd Of Dir 95-.

STEWART, GREG M; Catholic HS; Sherwood, AR; (3); Church Yth Grp; Acpl Chr; Chorus; Swing Chorus; Socr.

STEWART, JASON A J; Arkansas Sr HS; Texarkana, AR; (4); 22/380; Art Clb; Church Yth Grp; Key Clb; Math Clb; Bsktbl; Ftbl; Trk; Gov Hon Prg Awd; High Hon Roll; Pres Acad Fit Awd; Outstndng Enriched Engl 94-95, Bio 94 & OYM 95; Minority Yth Of Yr Rnnr-Up 95; Govs Schl 95; Boys St; Bus Admin.

STEWART, JEFFERY B; Dequeen HS; De Queen, AR; (2); Church Yth Grp; Office Aide; Rep Frsh Cls; Var L Bsbl; L Ftbl; Hon Roll; Coach.

STEWART, JENNIFER L; Sloan Hendrix HS; Pocahontas, AR; (3); 1/30; Church Yth Grp; Pres Sec FBLA; FHA; FTA; VP Sec Natl Beta Clb; Sec Church Choir; Nwsp; Yrbk; Sec Stu Cncl; Chorus; Lions Clb Lamp Of Lrng Awd; Ralph Joseph Yth Ldrshp Tm Schlrshp.

STEWART, JEREMY W; Harmony Grove Jr Sr HS; Benton, AR; (2); French Clb; Band; Mrchg Band; Rep Stu Cncl; JV L Bsktbl; Trk; Hon Roll.

STEWART, JILL S; Arkansas Bapt Schl; Little Rock, AR; (4); Church Yth Grp; FBLA; Natl Beta Clb; Spanish Clb; Acpl Chr; Chorus; School Musical; Nwsp; Ed Yrbk; Pres Soph Cls; Hmcmng Maid; Schlstc Schlrshp; U Of AR-LITTLE Rock; Jrnlsm.

STEWART, JOSHUA W; White Co Central Schl; Judsonia, AR; (3); 4/35; Church Yth Grp; Cmnty Wkr; FBLA; FHA; Math Tm; Sec Natl FFA Org; Quiz Bowl; Pres Jr Cls; JV Bsbl; JV Bsktbl; Lyon Coll.

STEWART, ROBERT A; Hampton Jr Sr HS; Hampton, AR; (4); 9/63; Am Leg Boys St; Church Yth Grp; Library Aide; VP Natl Beta Clb; Band; Yrbk; Var Capt Ftbl; Wt Lftg; Hon Roll; FCA; Natl Yth Ldrshp Forum On Med; Henderson ST Univ; Chem.

STEWART, TARYN L; Central Sr HS; Little Rock, AR; (4); 124/400; Cmnty Wkr; Dance Clb; French Clb; JA; Natl Beta Clb; Quiz Bowl; ROTC; Science Clb; Service Clb; School Musical; Govrnrs Schl; Natl Libr Of Poetry 3rd Prz Wnnr; Millsaps Coll; Engl.

STICE, GARRETT L; Yellville Summit HS; Summit, AR; (1); CAP; Cmnty Wkr; Natl FFA Org; Office Aide; Teachers Aide; Ofcr Bsbl; Ftbl; Med Applctns Of Sci For Hlth HS Med Prgm; Drury Coll; Gen Practice MD.

STIEDLE, JILL M; De Soto Schl; Helena, AR; (2); Drama Clb; School Play; Pres Frsh Cls; VP Soph Cls; Ofcr Stu Cncl; Sftbl; NHS; Med.

STIERS, ASHLEY L; Cabot HS; Cabot, AR; (3); Church Yth Grp; French Clb; Hosp Aide; Chorus; School Musical; Nwsp; Yrbk; Hon Roll; Jr NHS; NHS; Williams Bapt Coll; Bus Admin.

STILL, KELLI E; Valley Springs Schl; Harrison, AR; (3); Art Clb; Hist French Clb; Treas Band; Mrchg Band; Pep Band; Yrbk; Sftbl; High Hon Roll; Hon Roll; NHS; Sr Schlrs Pgm; Sr Schlrs Schlsp Dr Co-Dir; Cty Rep Natl Ldrshp Forum.

STILL JR, MICHAEL J; Ozark Adventist Acad; Gentry, AR; (4); Intrml Bsktbl; Intrml Ftbl; Intrml Gym; Intrml Vllybl; Hon Roll; NHS; Prfct Atten Awd; Nw AR CC.

STILL, SARAH; Yerger Jr HS; Hope, AR; (1); Church Yth Grp; Chrldng; Gym; Hon Roll; U Of AR; Medcl.

STIMIS, ROBERT G; Catholic HS; Little Rock, AR; (2); 1/200; Church Yth Grp; Cmnty Wkr; Letterman Clb; ROTC; Service Clb; Varsity Clb; JV Bsktbl; JV Var Ftbl; High Hon Roll; Legion Bsbl; Chosen Best Soph Cadet In JROTC Pgm; US Naval Acad; Engrng; Medicine.

STINCHCOMB, NATALIE; Prairie Grove HS; Prairie Grove, AR; (3); Rptr Science Clb; Treas SADD; VP Frsh Cls; Rep Soph Cls; Ofcr Stu Cncl; JV Var Bsktbl; Co-Capt Chrldng; Sftbl; Cit Awd; High Hon Roll; U Of AR; Elem Ed.

STINE, CASSIE N; Mt Pleasant Jr Sr HS; Mount Pleasant, AR; (1); Art Clb; Church Yth Grp; FBLA; FHA; Natl Beta Clb; Yrbk; Treas Frsh Cls; Sftbl; Hon Roll; Edctnl Talent Srch POWER Camp; RN.

STITH, MYRTLE M; Buffalo Island Central HS; Monette, AR; (2); 10/61; Church Yth Grp; FBLA; FTA; Library Aide; Natl FFA Org; Spanish Clb; Band; Church Choir; High Hon Roll; Hon Roll; Doctor/Lawyer.

STITT, JESSICA; Cabot HS; Cabot, AR; (1); Church Yth Grp; French Clb; Band; Tennis; Hon Roll; Chrch Eldr Hope.

STOBAUGH, JEREMY; Morrilton Sr HS; Morrilton, AR; (4); 1/150; Pres Church Yth Grp; Math Clb; VP Natl Beta Clb; Science Clb; Pres Spanish Clb; Thesps; School Play; VP Sr Cls; Tennis; Hon Roll; Tndy Tech Schlr; Top Math Sci Stu 95-96; UAR; Cmptr Sci.

STOBAUGH, WM BART; Sacred Heart Schl; Atkins, AR; (3); Art Clb; Church Yth Grp; Drama Clb; German Clb; Natl Beta Clb; Ofcr Stu Cncl; Bsktbl; Hon Roll; AR Tech.

STOCKTON, T J; Nemo Vista Jr Sr HS; Springfield, AR; (4); 8/30; Art Clb; FCA; FBLA; FHA; Key Clb; Spanish Clb; Pres SADD; Bsktbl; Var Mgr(s); Var Trk; Key Clb; SADD-PRESJTPA; UCA; US Army.

STOKES, JASON; Lake Hamilton Sr HS; Hot Springs, AR; (3); Church Yth Grp; FCA; FBLA; Natl Beta Clb; Quiz Bowl; Spanish Clb; Rep Stu Cncl; Var L Bsbl; High Hon Roll; Amer Legion Bsbl.

STOKES, LAURA; Cross Co Jr Sr HS; Hickory Ridge, AR; (3); 8/45; Art Clb; Church Yth Grp; GAA; Girl Scts; Spanish Clb; SADD; Yrbk; Sec Frsh Cls; Rep Soph Cls; VP Jr Cls; All Dist Bsktbl; Ftbl Hmcmng Royalty; Bsktbl Royalty; Dist Runner Up Tennis; G/T.

STOKES, MICHELLE R; Blytheville Sr HS; Blytheville, AR; (4); 83/195; Spanish Clb; Band; Mrchg Band; Vllybl; Hon Roll; MS Cnty CC.

STOLARIK, RICK; Mountain Home HS; Mountain Home, AR; (4); 47/260; FCA; German Clb; Band; Mrchg Band; Ftbl; Trk; Wt Lftg; Hon Roll; GAPP; Lyon Coll; Bio; Pre-Med.

STONE, ANGELA; Manila HS; Manila, AR; (2); FBLA; Natl Beta Clb; Chorus; JV Var Chrldng; Hon Roll; Elem Ed.

STONE, JEFFREY P; Fayetteville Sr HS; Fayetteville, AR; (2); Church Yth Grp; Chorus; Hon Roll; Plays Bsktbl Comm Yth Cntr Team; Mtrlgcl Tech/Astrnt.

STONE, JENNIFER R; Bryant Sr HS; Benton, AR; (4); 7/336; Church Yth Grp; Cmnty Wkr; Drama Clb; English Clb; Office Aide; Science Clb; Speech Tm; Teachers Aide; School Play; Lit Mag; U Of Cntrl AR; Pre-Med/Pdtrcn.

STONE, JOSH S; Ozark HS; Ozark, AR; (2); #8 in class; Church Yth Grp; FCA; Intnl Clb; Natl Beta Clb; Quiz Bowl; Band; Var Bsktbl; Var Golf; Hon Roll.

STONE, LESLIE; Pea Ridge HS; Pea Ridge, AR; (4); 4/39; Debate Tm; FBLA; Quiz Bowl; Spanish Clb; Speech Tm; Band; Mrchg Band; Rptr Nwsp; VP Stu Cncl; High Hon Roll; U Of Cntrl AR; Phys Thrpy.

STOREY, ALLISON; Searcy HS; Searcy, AR; (4); Am Leg Aux Girls St; Church Yth Grp; FTA; Hosp Aide; Natl Beta Clb; Thesps; Chorus; School Musical; School Play; NHS; Mssn Wrk; Harding Univ; Nrsng.

STORY, EMILY; Forrest City HS; Forrest City, AR; (4); 7/275; Am Leg Aux Girls St; Church Yth Grp; Cmnty Wkr; FBLA; Mu Alpha Theta; Natl Beta Clb; Q&S; Science Clb; Yrbk; Golf; Honored In Pres Ed Awds Pgm; Delta Beta Sigma HS Sorority; Play In Ladies Sftbl League; U Of AR; Commnctn.

STORY, JOSHUA L; Riverview HS; Judsonia, AR; (2); Natl Beta Clb; Spanish Clb; Guitar; Music Prodctn; Poetry; Music Prdctn.

STORY, MARCI E; Dierks HS; Newhope, AR; (1); 2/56; Church Yth Grp; 4-H; FHA; GAA; Treas Soph Cls; Bsktbl; Trk; 4-H Awd; High Hon Roll; Hon Roll.

STORY, SARAH; Brinkley HS; Brinkley, AR; (1); Office Aide; High Hon Roll; Hon Roll; Jr NHS; Natl Sci Mrt Awd; Frshmn Maid; ASU; Nrsng.

STOTELMYER, DAVID; Central Ark Christian Schl; Sherwood, AR; (1); Church Yth Grp; Ofcr Stu Cncl; Ofcr Bsbl; Capt Bsktbl; Capt Ftbl; High Hon Roll; Jr NHS.

STOTTMAN, HEATHER L; Russellville Sr HS; Russellville, AR; (3); FBLA; Library Aide; Band; Mrchg Band; Pep Band; High Hon Roll; Jr NHS; NHS; Model Arab Leag Delg; Poem Pub Natl HS Bk Natl Poetry Soc; Bio.

STOUT, JEFFREY A; Tuckerman HS; Grubbs, AR; (2); Church Yth Grp; FCA; FBLA; Natl Beta Clb; Spanish Clb; Ofcr Bsbl; Bsktbl; Hon Roll; AR ST U.

STOUT, RANDY; Hermitage Jr Sr HS; Warren, AR; (1); Natl Beta Clb; Natl FFA Org; Band; Mrchg Band; Bsktbl; High Hon Roll; Hon Roll; Gftd & Tlntd Prog.

STOUT, TINA M; Armorel HS; Blytheville, AR; (3); 4/30; Am Leg Aux Girls St; Church Yth Grp; 4-H; FBLA; FHA; Natl Beta Clb; Natl FFA Org; Pep Clb; Spanish Clb; School Musical; MCCC; RN.

STOVALL, CHRIS J; Scranton HS; Scranton, AR; (3); Church Yth Grp; FBLA; German Clb; Natl Beta Clb; Natl FFA Org; Science Clb; Pres Soph Cls; Var Bsbl; Var Bsktbl; JV Trk; U Of Cntrl AR.

STOVER, MELISSA D; Casa Schl; Casa, AR; (2); Debate Tm; FBLA; FHA; Natl Beta Clb; Natl FFA Org; Spanish Clb; Band; Ed Yrbk; Ofcr Frsh Cls; Sec Soph Cls; Perry-Casa Acad Achvmnt Awd; UCA; Psych.

STOWERS, JENNIFER E; Norfork Jr Sr HS; Norfork, AR; (3); Art Clb; Church Yth Grp; VP FBLA; Math Clb; Rptr Jr Cls; High Hon Roll; Hon Roll; NHS; U Of AR; Bus.

STRACENER, AMANDA; North Little Rock HS East; North Little Rock, AR; (1); Church Yth Grp; Church Choir; Chrldng; High Hon Roll; Hon Roll; Chrch; Swim; Phys Thrpy.

STRACENER, CARRIE A; Midland HS; Pleasant Plains, AR; (2); Phtg Drama Clb; Hist FBLA; FHA; Natl Beta Clb; Spanish Clb; Sec Pres Band; School Play; Sec Soph Cls; Hon Roll.

STRACK, BRIDGET A; St Joseph HS; Conway, AR; (2); Church Yth Grp; Key Clb; Chrldng; Hon Roll; Jr NHS; All Stars; Jr Optmst; Photographer.

STRACK, SAM K; St Joseph HS; Conway, AR; (2); Boy Scts; Church Yth Grp; Teachers Aide; Treas Soph Cls; Bsktbl; Mgr(s); Trk; Hon Roll; Jr NHS; Univ Of Cntrl AR.

STRACK, STEPHEN J; St Joseph HS; Conway, AR; (2); 2/26; Boy Scts; Church Yth Grp; Key Clb; Teachers Aide; School Play; Var L Bsktbl; Var L Golf; L Trk; High Hon Roll; Hon Roll; UCA.

STRAIGHT, JOI; Bismarck Jr-Sr HS; Bismarck, AR; (3); 1/57; Church Yth Grp; FBLA; Natl Beta Clb; Quiz Bowl; Band; Rptr Nwsp; Rep Stu Cncl; High Hon Roll; Ntl Merit Ltr; Odyssy Mind; Ranatra Fusca Crtvty Awd; Ftr Prbml Slvng; Tae Kwon Do; Wrtng Awds; Press Clb; Dan Ford Awd; Westminster; Engl.

STRASNER, SAM S; Russellville Sr HS; Dover, AR; (3); Office Aide; Q&S; Sprt Ed Nwsp; L Golf; Hon Roll; AR HS Press Assn Sprts Layout In Nwspr Superior Awd/2nd Pl In Sprts Wrtng On Site Cmptn; AR ST Univ; Jrnlsm/Sprts Wrtr.

STRATTON, STEPHANIE D; Harrison Sr HS; Harrison, AR; (3); 1/193; Church Yth Grp; 4-H; Sec Natl FFA Org; Science Clb; Spanish Clb; Band; Drm Mjr(t); High Hon Roll; Hon Roll; NHS; Best Twirler; OK ST U; Pre-Vet.

STRAUSBERG, RACHEL; Farmington Jr Sr HS; Fayetteville, AR; (2); Model UN; Band; Color Guard; Flag Corp; Mrchg Band; Pep Band; Cit Awd; Hon Roll; Jr NHS; NHS; U Of A; Entomaly.

STRAWN, TODD; Atkins Schl; Atkins, AR; (2); 1/84; FBLA; Library Aide; Natl Beta Clb; Rep Frsh Cls; Rep Soph Cls; High Hon Roll; Prfct Atten Awd; Pres Acad Fit Awd; 9th Grd Outstdng Stdnt 94-95; 1st Pl Bus Math Dist V FBLA; 1st Pl Bus Math AR FBLA 96; U Of Cntrl AR; Cmptr Engr.

STREET, AARON J; Southside HS; Batesville, AR; (3); 11/75; Art Clb; Natl Beta Clb; Science Clb; Intrml Ftbl; Tennis; Hon Roll; Prfct Atten Awd; Amer Math Cmtn 1st Pl Schl; Bus.

STREETER, KENDRA; Crossett Sr HS; Hamburg, AR; (3); 4-H; Treas FBLA; FHA; Mu Alpha Theta; Natl Beta Clb; Church Choir; 4-H Awd; Hon Roll; NHS; Servitium; Elem Ed.

STREETER, LESLIE D; Pine Bluff HS; Pine Bluff, AR; (3); 37/420; Church Yth Grp; French Clb; Natl Beta Clb; VP Frsh Cls; Rep Soph Cls; Pres Sr Cls; Var L Bsktbl; Var L Ftbl; Hon Roll; Jr NHS; Intnl Sci & Engrng Fair Fnlst; Bio.

STREETT, NATHAN M; Yellville Summit HS; Yellville, AR; (3); Pres Art Clb; Teachers Aide; Rep Frsh Cls; JV Var Bsktbl; Cit Awd; High Hon Roll; Hon Roll; NHS; Pres Acad Fit Awd; Outstdng Underclassman; Math Awds.

STREITHORST, AMANDA G; Ozark HS; Ozark, AR; (3); Church Yth Grp; Girl Scts; SADD; Band; Chorus; Flag Corp; Mrchg Band; Trk; Westark; Chldhd Ed.

STRICKER, JENNY; Ozark Adventist Acad; Gentry, AR; (3); 1/72; Church Yth Grp; Scholastic Bowl; School Musical; Rptr Nwsp; Intrml Vllybl; High Hon Roll; Prfct Atten Awd; Puppet Team; Handbell Choir; Girls Clb Vlg Rep.

STRICKLAND, BRANDY; Pangburn Jr Sr HS; Pangburn, AR; (4); 4/50; Sec French Clb; FHA; Natl Beta Clb; School Play; Hon Roll; NHS; Sal; U Of Conway; Bus.

STRICKLAND, JOHN; Ozark Adventist Acad; Gentry, AR; (3); 1/65; Church Yth Grp; Scholastic Bowl; Ed Nwsp; Cit Awd; High Hon Roll; Prfct Atten Awd; Schl Puppet Team; Walla Walla Coll; Engr.

STRICKLAND, JOHN; Ozark Adventist Acad; Stringtown, OK; (3); 1/69; Scholastic Bowl; Co-Ed Nwsp; Cit Awd; High Hon Roll; NHS; Prfct Atten Awd; Walla Walla Univ; Eng.

STRICKLAND, MICHELLE L; Jacksonville HS; Jacksonville, AR; (4); 46/413; Drama Clb; Teachers Aide; Chorus; School Musical; School Play; Variety Show; Hon Roll; U Of AR; Nrsng.

STRICKLAND, STACEY; Arkansas Sr HS; Texarkana, AR; (4); Church Yth Grp; Cmnty Wkr; Math Clb; Mu Alpha Theta; Quiz Bowl; Spanish Clb; Band; Drm Mjr(t); Mrchg Band; Pep Band; GATE; Do Right Gang.

STRICKLAND, WARREN; John L Mcclellan Magnet HS; Mabelvale, AR; (3); 10/400; Am Leg Boys St; Church Yth Grp; FCA; FBLA; Natl Beta Clb; Spanish Clb; Ftbl; Trk; High Hon Roll; Hon Roll; Natl Hist Govt Awd; Natl Yth Ldr Conf; Beta, PRIDE & Career Clbs; Engnr.

STRICKLIN, KIMBERLY; Watson Chapel Schl; Pine Bluff, AR; (4); 7/240; Cmnty Wkr; 4-H; Key Clb; Model UN; Natl Beta Clb; Yrbk; Pres VP Stu Cncl; 4-H Awd; High Hon Roll; Hon Roll; JETS Engrng Team 12th Grd 1st In ST; AR Gov Schl 12th Grd; TRMEP Engrng Prgm Fayettvl; U Of AR Fytvl; Chem Engrng.

STRICKLIN, TERAH A; Mena HS; Mena, AR; (3); Am Leg Aux Girls St; French Clb; FBLA; Science Clb; French Hon Soc; Hon Roll; NHS; Rich Mountain CC; Bus.

STRINGFELLOW, JOHN B; Arkansas Sr HS; Texarkana, AR; (3); Am Leg Boys St; Capt Debate Tm; Key Clb; Math Clb; Mu Alpha Theta; Q&S; Quiz Bowl; Church Choir; Yrbk; Sec Soph Cls; LAW.

STRONCEK, DAVID B; Oak Grove HS; Maumelle, AR; (2); 26/139; Spanish Clb; Hon Roll; Model Car Cmptn; Restrng Late 60s Autos & Early 70s Pick-Up Trucks With Father, 1st & 2nd Pl St Cmptn.

STROTHER, CRYSTAL; Southside HS; Floral, AR; (2); FBLA; Key Clb; Natl FFA Org; Office Aide; Band; Hon Roll; Prfct Atten Awd; Psych.

STROTHER, SHANA M; Malvern Sr HS; Donaldson, AR; (3); FBLA; Spanish Clb; SADD; Chorus; Ed Yrbk; Rep Stu Cncl; L Sftbl; NHS; Church Yth Grp; FHA; Peer Cnsling; All Dist Sftbll; Henderson St Univ; Medio Comm.

STROUD, CRISSY L; Bryant Sr HS; Benton, AR; (3); Church Yth Grp; Cmnty Wkr; FCA; 4-H; FBLA; Office Aide; Teachers Aide; Church Choir; Bsktbl; Sftbl; Plyd ST Champ Sftbl Team Ctchr/Rnnr-Up Bsktbl 96; Henderson; Coach/Tch.

STROUD, DE NITA R; North Little Rock Hs-West; North Little Rock, AR; (4); Art Clb; Dance Clb; Drama Clb; FHA; FTA; Key Clb; Natl Beta Clb; Pep Clb; Chorus; Drill Tm; U Of Cntrl AR; Psych.

STROUD, JOSHUA L; Delaplaine Schl; O Kean, AR; (1); 1/21; Library Aide; Quiz Bowl; Spanish Clb; VP Frsh Cls; Rep Stu Cncl; JV Co-Ed Bsktbl; L Trk; Cit Awd; High Hon Roll; Prfct Atten Awd; Eng, Sci & Math Awds; AR ST Univ; Tchr.

STROUD, MARY; Farmington Jr Sr HS; Farmington, AR; (1); French Clb; Drill Tm; Pres Frsh Cls; Ofcr Stu Cncl; Pom Pon; Hon Roll; Jr NHS; Chrch Yth.

STROUD, THOMAS J; Maynard Jr Sr HS; Maynard, AR; (2); Natl FFA Org; Rptr Frsh Cls; Prfct Atten Awd; Welding; Pipeline Welder.

STROUT, APRIL D; Rogers HS; Rogers, AR; (2); 42/764; FHA; Band; Mrchg Band; Pep Band; Rptr Phtg Nwsp; High Hon Roll; Hon Roll; Pres Schlr; Natl Eng Mrt Awd; North AR Symphony Yth Orch; All-Region Band; U Of AR; Music; Sci.

STRUCK, ERICA A; Cabot HS; Cabot, AR; (3); 4/368; Treas Key Clb; Church Choir; School Play; Rep Soph Cls; Treas Pres Stu Cncl; Gov Hon Prg Awd; High Hon Roll; NHS; Spanish NHS; Church Yth Grp; Chem.

STUART, GINGER M; Carlisle Jr Sr HS; Carlisle, AR; (4); 1/50; Am Leg Aux Girls St; Church Yth Grp; VP Treas FBLA; Quiz Bowl; VP Spanish Clb; Hist VP Band; Mrchg Band; Pep Band; Ed Yrbk; Lit Mag; Piano 10 Yrs; CHS Math, Trig, Soc Stud, Wrld His, Eng, Esy, Sci & Physcs Awds; Tandy Tech Schlr; Hendrix Coll; Eng.

STUART, JON; Mc Gehee HS; Mc Gehee, AR; (4); 4/101; Am Leg Boys St; Art Clb; Church Yth Grp; FCA; FBLA; HOBY; Mu Alpha Theta; Natl Beta Clb; Science Clb; Spanish Clb; Rep 95-96.

STUCKEY, ANNA; Van Buren Sr HS; Van Buren, AR; (3); Church Yth Grp; Cmnty Wkr; FCA; Mu Alpha Theta; Var L Chrldng; Var L Trk; Var L Vllybl; Hon Roll; NHS; Pep Clb; Partners In Christ; Homcmng Ct Maid; Arch.

STUCKEY, JANET; Cross Co Jr Sr HS; Hickory Ridge, AR; (4); 5/41; Am Leg Aux Girls St; Church Yth Grp; Cmnty Wkr; Natl Beta Clb; Office Aide; Chorus; Church Choir; Hon Roll; Kiwanis Awd; ASU Beebe; LPN.

STUCKEY, WILL C; Ft Smith Christian Schl; Van Buren, AR; (1); Boy Scts; Band; Hon Roll; U Of AR; ER Dr.

STUCKY, SUSAN C; Arkansas Sr HS; Texarkana, AR; (4); 52/374; Sec Art Clb; Church Yth Grp; Spanish Clb; Hon Roll; Pres Acad Fit Awd; Do Rght Gng VP; Yng Dmcrts; Smmr Stg; AR Gvrnrs Schl; Hrdng U; Grphc Dsgn.

SUDMEYER, AIMEE D; Morrilton Sr HS; Morrilton, AR; (3); Church Yth Grp; French Clb; Math Clb; Thesps; Band; Mrchg Band; School Musical; School Play; High Hon Roll; Drama Clb; Majorette Capt; Band Cncl; Stu Pride Wnnr; AR Tech Univ; Ed.

SUDMEYER, CHAD; Lake Hamilton Sr HS; Pearcy, AR; (4); 5/279; Treas FBLA; Natl Beta Clb; Natl FFA Org; Spanish Clb; Teachers Aide; High Hon Roll; Hon Roll; NHS; Pres Acad Fit Awd; Lk Hmltn Tech Tm, Ldr; St Chmp Ag Mech Tm; Natl Hist Govt Awd; U Of AR Fayetteville; Cmptrs.

SUITER, JULEE L; Bradford Jr Sr HS; Russell, AR; (3); Cmnty Wkr; French Clb; FBLA; Hosp Aide; Natl Beta Clb; Quiz Bowl; Band; Yrbk; Bsktbl; Crs Cntry; U WA; Law/Cmptr Sci.

SULLIVAN, ARLENE E; Union Schl; El Dorado, AR; (3); Church Yth Grp; French Clb; FBLA; Natl Beta Clb; Yrbk; Treas Stu Cncl; Bsktbl; Sftbl; Prfct Atten Awd; MASH; Crossfire Stdnt Lead; Prof Pilot/Strm Chsr.

SULLIVAN, CAREY; Rose Bud Jr Sr HS; Romance, AR; (4); 1/37; Art Clb; Church Yth Grp; FCA; FBLA; FHA; Pres Natl Beta Clb; Natl FFA Org; Spanish Clb; Nwsp; Yrbk; Sr Engl Awd; Geom/Cgen Awd; ASY At Beebe; Cnotr Drftbg.

SULLIVAN, CHRISTY A; Bald Knob HS; Bald Knob, AR; (4); 1/80; Am Leg Aux Girls St; Church Yth Grp; FBLA; Natl Beta Clb; Band; Church Choir; Jazz Band; Mrchg Band; Pep Band; Phtg Nwsp; Lyon Coll; Chem.

SULLIVAN, DAVID N; Pine Bluff HS; Pine Bluff, AR; (3); 17/500; Am Leg Boys St; Boy Scts; Treas Acpl Chr; Church Choir; Tennis; Gov Hon Prg Awd; Hon Roll; Jr NHS; NHS; Hsstry Clb; Eagle Sct; Amer Frgn Exchng; Washington & Lee Univ; Law.

SULLIVAN, ERIN N; Mills HS; Jacksonville, AR; (3); 50/298; French Clb; FTA; Natl Beta Clb; Q&S; Science Clb; School Play; Stage Crew; Yrbk; Ofcr Jr Cls; Project WET; Sci Fair Participant; Soc Stud Clb.

SULLIVAN, JOHN D; Jacksonville HS; Jacksonville, AR; (4); 16/327; Boy Scts; Debate Tm; Drama Clb; Latin Clb; Library Aide; Natl Beta Clb; Quiz Bowl; Science Clb; Teachers Aide; Band; Govs Schl; Interact Clb; U Of OK Norman; Engrng.

SULLIVAN, JOHN R; Bald Knob HS; Bald Knob, AR; (1); Church Yth Grp; FBLA; Natl Beta Clb; Office Aide; Quiz Bowl; Band; Church Choir; Mrchg Band; Hon Roll; Harding Univ; Math.

SULLIVAN, KATHY; England HS; England, AR; (4); Church Yth Grp; Drama Clb; FBLA; Natl Beta Clb; Spanish Clb; Var L Bsktbl; L Sftbl; Hon Roll; JETS Awd; Schlr, Ath Awd-US Army Reserve; U Of Central AR; Bus.

SULLIVAN, MICHAEL F; Trumann HS; Trumann, AR; (3); Art Clb; Boy Scts; Bsktbl; Crs Cntry; Trk; Wt Lftg; Hon Roll; St Trk & Field Events; Office Aide; Inline Flr Hockey; AR ST Univ; Art; PE.

SULLIVENT, BRIAN M; Bearden HS; Bearden, AR; (4); 4-H; FBLA; FHA; FTA; Varsity Clb; Nwsp; Yrbk; L Ftbl; High Hon Roll; Hon Roll; Southern AR U; Mrktng.

SUMMERHILL, ANDREA B; Beebe HS; Beebe, AR; (3); 11/131; Church Yth Grp; FBLA; FHA; Hosp Aide; Natl Beta Clb; Quiz Bowl; Science Clb; Spanish Clb; Drill Tm; High Hon Roll; Psych.

SUMMERHILL, KELLY S; Searcy HS; Searcy, AR; (3); 30/260; FCA; Natl Beta Clb; Hist Spanish Clb; Chorus; JV Var Bsktbl; JV Var Sftbl; High Hon Roll; Hon Roll; NHS; Spanish NHS; 2nd Pl Optmst Essay Cntst; UCA; PT.

SUMMERS, MATTHEW S; Bryant Sr HS; Bryant, AR; (2); Church Yth Grp; Computer Clb; FCA; Teachers Aide; Rep Stu Cncl; Var Capt Ftbl; Var Wt Lftg; Hon Roll; UA Fayetteville; Comp; Bus; Ftbl.

SUPRISE, JASON; Southside HS; Fort Smith, AR; (2); Church Yth Grp; Computer Clb; Mu Alpha Theta; Spanish Clb; Hon Roll; NHS; Pres Acad Fit Awd; Comp Engrng.

SURFACE, STACY L; Decatur HS; Decatur, AR; (2); Church Yth Grp; Sec FHA; Pep Clb; Chrldng; Aplld Bio Chem Sci Awd; FHA Easter Seals Awd; U AR; Schl Cnslr.

SURLES, JULIE E; Southside HS; Batesville, AR; (3); Am Leg Aux Girls St; FBLA; Hosp Aide; Key Clb; Natl Beta Clb; Science Clb; Band; Bsktbl; Tennis; High Hon Roll.

SURPRISE, JASON M; Southside HS; Fort Smith, AR; (2); Church Yth Grp; Computer Clb; Mu Alpha Theta; Hon Roll; NHS; Pres Acad Fit Awd; Spanish NHS; Cmptr Eng.

SUTHERLAND, LISA G; Mayflower HS; Jacksonville, AR; (2); Church Yth Grp; Natl Beta Clb; Bsktbl; Trk; Hon Roll; Phy Thrpst.

SUTLIFF, DIANNA R; White Hall Sr HS; Pine Bluff, AR; (4); 22/161; Key Clb; Natl Beta Clb; Pep Clb; Spanish Clb; Teachers Aide; Yrbk; Pom Pon; Hon Roll; Church Yth Grp; Dance Clb; Math Awds; Homcmng Ct; U Of Cntrl AR; Pediatric Medcn.

SUTTERFIELD, JENNIFER L; Timbo Schl; Leslie, AR; (2); FHA; Natl Beta Clb; Rptr Nwsp; Pres Frsh Cls; Rep Soph Cls; Rep Stu Cncl; L Bsktbl; L Trk; Hon Roll; Altrnte For Aegis Camp; U Of A; Art/Dance.

SUTTERFIELD, MICHAEL; Sulphur Rock Schl; Batesville, AR; (2); 1/21; Church Yth Grp; Natl Beta Clb; Office Aide; Quiz Bowl; Teachers Aide; School Play; Nwsp; Pres Soph Cls; Rep Stu Cncl; Ftbl; Remedial Clsses Tchr Asst; Church Yth Choir; Military.

SUTTERFIELD, RAGAN K; Morrilton Sr HS; Solgohachia, AR; (2); Boy Scts; Church Yth Grp; Library Aide; Quiz Bowl; Science Clb; School Play; Hon Roll; Bird Audubon Soc; Stdnt Pride Wnnr; TX A&M; Ornithology.

SUTTERFILED, JEFF S; Timbo Schl; Leslie, AR; (2); Treas Frsh Cls; Treas Soph Cls; JV Capt Bsktbl; Var L Trk; Hon Roll; 8 Bsktbll Awds; 1 High Pt Awd Trck; 16 Track Ribbons; NACTC; Coaching.

SUTTLES, BRANDON W; Greenwood Sr HS; Greenwood, AR; (3); 15/200; Church Yth Grp; FBLA; FHA; Math Clb; Mu Alpha Theta; Natl Beta Clb; Science Clb; Spanish Clb; Band; Church Choir; Natl Tn Bible Qz 1st Pl 93, Tm Cap 2nd Pl 94; Numerous Tlnt Shows Vcls; UCA; Biochem.

SUTTLES, JANETTA L; Arkansas Sr HS; Texarkana, AR; (4); Church Yth Grp; Dance Clb; GAA; Girl Scts; HOBY; Office Aide; Spanish Clb; Band; Drill Tm; Hon Roll; U Of Cntrl AR; Phy Thrpst.

SUTTON, DONITIA; Rison HS; Rison, AR; (3); 1/39; French Clb; FBLA; Natl Beta Clb; Science Clb; Band; Flag Corp; Mrchg Band; VP Stu Cncl; Sftbl; DAR Awd; Poem Reflctn Lght; Attnded Proj CAVES, AEGIS Pgm; Attnd MIDI Bch Byts.

SUTTON, KARMEN D; Des Arc Jr Sr HS; Des Arc, AR; (4); Church Yth Grp; FBLA; FTA; GAA; Science Clb; Spanish Clb; Yrbk; Rep Sr Cls; Rep Stu Cncl; Bsktbl; U Of Cntrl AR.

SUTTON, MITZI; Southside HS; Fort Smith, AR; (4); 89/432; FBLA; Key Clb; Teachers Aide; Ofcr Jr Cls; Ofcr Sr Cls; Hon Roll; NHS; U Cntrl AR; Acctng.

SUTTON, NORMA J; Lynn Schl; Smithville, AR; (3); Art Clb; Teachers Aide; Ofcr Frsh Cls; Bsktbl; Sftbl.

SWAIM, MICHAEL K; Pulaski Acad; Little Rock, AR; (3); Church Yth Grp; FCA; Natl Beta Clb; Spanish Clb; Treas Jr Cls; Var Ftbl; Var Socr.

SWAIN, ERIN; Morrilton Sr HS; Perry, AR; (4); 1/150; Church Yth Grp; Hosp Aide; Math Clb; Natl Beta Clb; Ed Yrbk; Rep Stu Cncl; Chrldng; Crs Cntry; Trk; Val; Tndy Tech Schlr; Grls St Alt; U Of AR Fayetteville; Phys Thp.

SWAIN, JOHN R; Northside HS; Fort Smith, AR; (3); German Clb; ROTC; ROTC Saber Tm; ROTC Rifle Team.

SWAN, MICHELLE; Rogers HS; Rogers, AR; (4); 43/498; FCA; FBLA; Key Clb; Teachers Aide; Drill Tm; Var Chrldng; High Hon Roll; Hon Roll; Jr NHS; Chmbr Cmmrce Acad Awd Wnnr 2xs; Rnssnce Slvr Awd, Gld Awd; U AR Fyttvlle; Rdtn Thrpy.

SWEARINGEN, RACHEL A; Rogers HS; Rogers, AR; (3); Am Leg Aux Girls St; Church Yth Grp; Cmnty Wkr; FCA; FBLA; Letterman Clb; Office Aide; Spanish Clb; Teachers Aide; Sec Treas Sr Cls; Chmbr Of Comm Awd; Stdnt Of Mnth; Frmrshl; Mrktng.

SWEARINGEN, RICHARD V; Van Buren Sr HS; Van Buren, AR; (2); Hon Roll.

SWEAT, EMILY; Blevins HS; Mc Caskill, AR; (4); 1/36; 4-H; FBLA; Natl Beta Clb; Natl FFA Org; Pres Jr Cls; Pres VP Stu Cncl; Var L Bsktbl; Var L Sftbl; 4-H Awd; Hon Roll; 4-H St Recrd Bk Wnnr, St Teen Star & Ambssdr; AR Beef Princess; U Of Central AR; Phys Thrpy.

SWEAT, KYLA; Blevins HS; Mc Caskill, AR; (3); 1/50; Church Yth Grp; Natl Beta Clb; Natl FFA Org; VP Jr Cls; Treas Stu Cncl; Var Bsktbl; Var Sftbl; Var Trk; High Hon Roll; ADAPT; SAU.

SWEEDEN, BRANDY; Murfreesboro HS; Murfreesboro, AR; (2); 2/54; FBLA; Treas FHA; Natl Beta Clb; Science Clb; Spanish Clb; Band; Trk; High Hon Roll; Pres Acad Fit Awd; Church Yth Grp; Majorette Corp Capt; Dist V Prlmntrn FHA; 2nd Plc 800m Dist; Ouachita Bapt U; Mtrlgst.

SWEET, BRANDY R; Siloam Springs Sr HS; Siloam Springs, AR; (3); Church Yth Grp; Drama Clb; FCA; FHA; Key Clb; Natl Beta Clb; Spanish Clb; Chorus; School Play; JV Bsktbl; Poem Pub; RN Pediatrics.

SWEETEN, JONA L; Rogers HS; Rogers, AR; (2); 76/765; Church Yth Grp; Band; Church Choir; Mrchg Band; Variety Show; Hon Roll; Prfct Atten Awd; Chamber Of Commerce Awd; All-Region Band; Penaissance; Northwest AR CC.

SWEETEN, SAMANTHA S; Springdale Sr HS; Springdale, AR; (3); Am Leg Aux Girls St; Key Clb; Model UN; NFL; Q&S; Chorus; Ed Co-Ed Yrbk; Gov Hon Prg Awd; High Hon Roll; Jr NHS; USNSA; Hendrix Coll; Chem.

SWIFT, BRIAN C; Booneville Jr Sr HS; Booneville, AR; (2); 1/99; Church Yth Grp; Cmnty Wkr; FCA; FBLA; Key Clb; Natl Beta Clb; Quiz Bowl; Science Clb; Pres Frsh Cls; Pres Soph Cls; Soph Bio Awd/Soc Sci Awd/4.0 GPA Awd; AR Farm Bur/Teen Chllng Del/Vol Ltl Leag Ftbl/Bsbl Coach.

SWINDELL, KAREN; Lamar HS; Clarksville, AR; (4); 15/64; Am Leg Aux Girls St; Church Yth Grp; FCA; Hosp Aide; Teachers Aide; Color Guard; Rep Stu Cncl; Var Bsktbl; Stat Mgr(s); Hon Roll; Ftbll Hmcmng Queen; All Dist All Regn Bsktbll; U Of AR; Elem Ed.

SWINDLE, ERIK J; Cntrl AR Chrstn HS; Sherwood, AR; (4); Church Yth Grp; Cmnty Wkr; Spanish Clb; Teachers Aide; Ed Nwsp; Ed Yrbk; Bsktbl; Hon Roll; Spanish NHS; Science Clb; Assoc Wmn Harding Schol; Carter Adm Schol; SE Chrstn Ed Schlr; Harding Univ.

SWINEY, HEATH; Bradford Jr Sr HS; Bradford, AR; (1); Church Yth Grp; FHA; Natl Beta Clb; Natl FFA Org; Varsity Clb.

SWINNEY, LEIGH; Woodlawn Schl; Rison, AR; (3); 1/45; Church Yth Grp; GAA; Natl Beta Clb; L Bsktbl; Sftbl; High Hon Roll; UCA; Med.

SWISHER, AMY R; Waldron HS; Waldron, AR; (2); Art Clb; Church Yth Grp; FHA; Natl Beta Clb; Spanish Clb; Church Choir; Prfct Atten Awd; Barrett Hamilton Yng AR Artist Awd; Hnr Card Holder; Prntng Awd; U AR; Hstry Tchr.

SWORD, RUSS M; Springdale Sr HS; Springdale, AR; (2); Church Yth Grp; FCA; FBLA; JV Ftbl; Var Trk; JV Wt Lftg; High Hon Roll; NHS; Guitar Lssns.

SYHARATH, PAMELA; Northside HS; Fort Smith, AR; (4); 25/329; FBLA; Treas Intnl Clb; Mu Alpha Theta; Spanish Clb; Teachers Aide; Hon Roll; Jr NHS; NHS; Prfct Atten Awd; Pres Acad Fit Awd; Top 10 Stu; Garvin Grizzly Awd; U Of AR; Bus Mgmt.

SYMMES, RAYNA E; Fouke Jr Sr HS; Fouke, AR; (2); Library Aide; Office Aide; School Play; Trk; Mck Trl; Psych/Absd Chldrn.

SZWEDO, ANNA K; Mt St Mary Acad; Little Rock, AR; (2); Church Yth Grp; Hosp Aide; Latin Clb; Bsktbl; Mgr(s); Tennis; Hon Roll.

SZYMANSKI, DESIREE M; Fairview HS; Chidester, AR; (3); Art Clb; Church Yth Grp; French Clb; Natl FFA Org; Science Clb; SADD; VICA; Church Choir; Cit Awd; Hon Roll; Awded Stu Of Yr In Radio Broadcasting 95-96; Marine Biologist.

TABER, JASON L; Arkansas Sr HS; Texarkana, AR; (3); High Hon Roll.

TABOR, ASHLEY; Lonoke Jr HS; Lonoke, AR; (1); Art Clb; Church Yth Grp; FHA; GAA; Science Clb; Spanish Clb; Trk; Vllybl; Hon Roll; NHS; Med.

TABOR, MALINA A; Mc Gehee HS; Mcgehee, AR; (2); Church Yth Grp; FBLA; FTA; Mu Alpha Theta; Natl Beta Clb; Science Clb; Spanish Clb; Teachers Aide; School Play; Sec Soph Cls; Soph Srvr; Pride Awds.

TACKER, JASON; East Poinsett Sr HS; Lepanto, AR; (4); Church Yth Grp; French Clb; FBLA; Natl FFA Org; Spanish Clb; Ofcr Bsbl; Bsktbl; Ftbl; Golf; Wt Lftg.

TACKETT, MICHAEL B; Harmony Grove Jr Sr HS; Benton, AR; (2); Art Clb; Church Yth Grp; French Clb; Natl Beta Clb; Band; Mrchg Band; Bsktbl; Asst In Natl League Of Jr Cotillions; Engrng.

TAKSAKULVITH, MIT; Jacksonville HS; Jacksonville, AR; (3); Am Leg Boys St; Cmnty Wkr; Drama Clb; French Clb; Band; Mrchg Band; Pep Band; School Play; VP Stu Cncl; Hon Roll; U Of AR Fayetteville; Pre-Med.

TALAFUSE, ALBERT L; Arkansas Sr HS; Texarkana, AR; (2); Church Yth Grp; FCA; Nwsp; Yrbk; Ofcr Bsbl; Var Crs Cntry; Intrml Ftbl; Var Trk; Hon Roll; Track Team ST Chmps; Southern AR Univ; Lndscape Arc.

TALLEY, NIKEIA D; John L Mcclellan Magnet HS; Little Rock, AR; (2); FBLA; Spanish Clb; Varsity Clb; JV Var Bsktbl; Hon Roll; UCA.

TALLEY, TAMAYA K; El Dorado Sr HS; El Dorado, AR; (3); #69 in class; Natl Beta Clb; Band; Church Choir; Mrchg Band; Futuristic Outlks Clb; U Of AR Pinebluff; Cmptr Sci.

TAM, TAMMIE A; El Dorado Sr HS; El Dorado, AR; (1); Orch.

TANG, CHANG H; Crossett Sr HS; Crossett, AR; (2).

TANKERSLEY, JACOB W; Oden Schl; Oden, AR; (2); 2/24; Church Yth Grp; FBLA; Natl Beta Clb; Natl FFA Org; VP Frsh Cls; Var Bsbl; Var Bsktbl; Var Trk; Var Wt Lftg; Pres Woods & Waters; VP FBLA; VPFFA.

TANNER, JAMIE C; Conway Sr HS; Conway, AR; (3); 61/516; Drama Clb; French Clb; Natl Beta Clb; French Hon Soc; High Hon Roll; Hon Roll; U Central AR; Psych.

TANNER, LAWRENCE ROBERT; Booneville Jr Sr HS; Booneville, AR; (3); Church Yth Grp; Cmnty Wkr; FBLA; Pep Clb; Band; Mrchg Band; High Hon Roll; Hon Roll; Bus Admin.

TANNER, RICHARD H; Cabot HS; Cabot, AR; (2); Band.

TANNER, SARAH R; Booneville Jr Sr HS; Booneville, AR; (2); Natl Beta Clb; Science Clb; Spanish Clb; Band; Mrchg Band; Pep Band; Rep Stu Cncl; Hon Roll; Prfct Atten Awd; Psych.

TAPPAN, CHARLES; De Soto Schl; Helena, AR; (1); Boy Scts; Church Yth Grp; Cmnty Wkr; Bsktbl; Ftbl; Tennis; High Hon Roll; Hon Roll; MS Privt Schl Ed Assn Dist 1 W Acad Bttrmnt Comp Civics 1st Pl; US Spc & Rckt Ctr Smmr Prgm 3 Yrs; Engrng.

TAPSON, EMILY R; Cabot HS; Cabot, AR; (3); 7/398; Am Leg Aux Girls St; Church Yth Grp; Key Clb; Math Clb; Rep Frsh Cls; Rep Soph Cls; Sec Jr Cls; Rep Sr Cls; Ofcr Stu Cncl; NHS; His Clb; Hlth, Advanced Math & Trig Acad Awds.

TARLTON, JONATHAN; Marion HS; Marion, AR; (1); Rep Church Yth Grp; CAP; French Clb; Color Guard; Drill Tm; Trk; French Hon Soc; Hon Roll; CO Spr Air Frc Acad; Chem Engr.

TARPLEY, KANDI D; Corning Jr Sr HS; Lafe, AR; (2); Church Yth Grp; FBLA; FHA; Library Aide; High Hon Roll; Hon Roll; Jr NHS; NHS; Prfct Atten Awd; Natl Yth Ldrshp Law/Constitutn Forum Invitn; PRIDE; Lyons Coll; Psych/Law.

TARPLEY, KELLI R; Corning Jr Sr HS; Lafe, AR; (2); Church Yth Grp; FBLA; Library Aide; Chorus; Hon Roll; Jr NHS; PRIDE; AR ST U; Acctnt; Stock Broker.

TARPLEY, TRACY L; Highland HS; Hardy, AR; (3); Church Yth Grp; FHA; Key Clb; Chorus; Church Choir; School Musical; High Hon Roll; Hon Roll; Prfct Atten Awd; RAD; Guidance Asst; Pop Ensemble; Elem Ed; Spcl Ed.

TARRANT, ANDY H; Southside HS; Fort Smith, AR; (2); Church Yth Grp; Ofcr Bsbl; Wt Lftg; Hon Roll; Jr NHS; Pres Acad Fit Awd; 4 Yr Coll.

TARVER, KRISTIE A; Stuttgart Sr HS; Stuttgart, AR; (4); 7/160; Church Yth Grp; FBLA; Key Clb; Rptr Science Clb; Phtg Spanish Clb; Band; Mrchg Band; High Hon Roll; Rptr NHS; Pres Acad Fit Awd; AR ST Univ; Bio; Pre-Med.

TARVIN, AMELIA LYNN; Bauxite Jr Sr HS; Benton, AR; (4); 3/40; Am Leg Aux Girls St; FBLA; Pres SADD; Capt Drill Tm; School Play; Rep Stu Cncl; Capt Bsktbl; Hon Roll; NHS; Pres Acad Fit Awd; Gftd & Tlntd Prog; U Of Cntrl AR.

TARVIN, LORIE A; Bauxite Jr Sr HS; Benton, AR; (2); #3 in class; Spanish Clb; SADD; Drill Tm; Ofcr Yrbk; Pres Frsh Cls; Var Bsktbl; Sftbl; Trk; Hon Roll; Pres Acad Fit Awd.

TATE, CHRISTY R; Clarksville HS; Clarksville, AR; (2); Church Yth Grp; FCA; FBLA; Natl Beta Clb; Spanish Clb; VP Soph Cls; Chrldng; Gov Hon Prg Awd; Hon Roll; HS Gymnastics All-Star Chrldr.

TATE, HEATHER R; Springdale Sr HS; Springdale, AR; (3); Chorus; Yrbk; Marine Bio.

TATE, MELISSA D; Pea Ridge HS; Pea Ridge, AR; (2); Art Clb; Pep Clb; Spanish Clb; Var Bsktbl; Var Chrldng; Var Sftbl; Hon Roll; Most Imprvd Math Awd; Artistic Enthusiasm; Hnr Rl; Acctnt.

TATUM, FELIX; Saratoga Schl; Ozan, AR; (2); Church Yth Grp; 4-H; Natl Beta Clb; Natl FFA Org; Quiz Bowl; Band; Chorus; Church Choir; Ofcr Soph Cls; Bsktbl.

TATUM, LAKISHA D; Dollarway HS; Pine Bluff, AR; (3); Church Yth Grp; French Clb; FHA; Key Clb; Band; Church Choir; Mrchg Band; Cit Awd; Hon Roll; Prfct Atten Awd; U Of AR Pine Bluff; Comp Sci.

TATUM, TARVIS T; Hermitage Jr Sr HS; Banks, AR; (2); 15/60; Natl FFA Org; Band; Ftbl; Trk; Wt Lftg; Hon Roll; UAM Pychiatrist.

TATUM, VICTORIA; Crossett Sr HS; Crossett, AR; (4); 11/175; Am Leg Aux Girls St; Drama Clb; French Clb; FBLA; FHA; FTA; Math Clb; Mu Alpha Theta; Natl Beta Clb; Science Clb; Sec Of Servitium; Eagle Action Pride; Homcmng Maid; Sr Of Distinction; Pres FBLA; Pres Little Sisters; U Of AR; Acctng.

TAYLOR, ADAM K; Delaplaine Schl; Beech Grove, AR; (1); Church Yth Grp; Natl FFA Org; Rptr Frsh Cls; Trk; Wt Lftg; AR ST Univ.

TAYLOR, ALISSA; Southside HS; Fort Smith, AR; (4); Church Yth Grp; Dance Clb; French Clb; FBLA; Key Clb; Mu Alpha Theta; Office Aide; Pep Clb; Teachers Aide; Chorus; Cprtv Offc Ed; Westark CC; Acctng.

TAYLOR, AMANDA; St Joe Public Schl; Saint Joe, AR; (2); Church Yth Grp; French Clb; FBLA; Girl Scts; Yrbk; Hon Roll; NHS; Ntl Merit Schol; Pres Acad Fit Awd; Coll Of The Ozarks.

TAYLOR, AMY; Trumann HS; Trumann, AR; (2); 1/126; Art Clb; French Clb; Intnl Clb; Office Aide; Science Clb; Ofcr Stu Cncl; Mgr(s); Vllybl; High Hon Roll; NHS; U Of AR; Bus Mgmt; Advertising.

TAYLOR, AMY C; Dumas HS; Dumas, AR; (2); Church Yth Grp; FBLA; FTA; Teachers Aide; Band; Church Choir; Color Guard; Flag Corp; Mrchg Band; VP Frsh Cls; Outstdng Stu Of The Yr; Outstdng Stu Nine Weeks; Outstdng Flagline Mem; Memphis ST; Comp Tech; Engrng.

TAYLOR, ANDY M; Warren Sr HS; New Edinburg, AR; (2); Church Yth Grp; Drama Clb; 4-H; 4-H Awd; Hon Roll; AR Cncl Of Tchrs Of Math; 2nd Pl Regnl Geom Examination; Hnrs Geom & Hnrs Eng II Awds.

TAYLOR, ARMANDIS D; Central HS; West Helena, AR; (2); ROTC; Rptr Nwsp; Phtg Yrbk; Ed Lit Mag; Rep Soph Cls; L Ftbl; L Trk; Hon Roll; Pres Acad Fit Awd; Sprts/Mfg.

TAYLOR, ARRIKA S; Mc Crory Jr Sr HS; Mc Crory, AR; (3); Church Yth Grp; FBLA; Library Aide; Spanish Clb; SADD; Church Choir; Ofcr Stu Cncl; Hon Roll; Jr NHS; NHS; U Of Conway AR; OB-GYN.

TAYLOR, CANDICE L; Paron Schl; Paron, AR; (4); 1/14; VP FHA; Nwsp; Ed Yrbk; VP Sr Cls; Gov Hon Prg Awd; Hon Roll; NHS; Val; GAA; Math Clb; Chncllrs Ldrshp Schlshp; U Of AR Little Rock; RN.

TAYLOR, CHANDRA; Siloam Springs Sr HS; Siloam Springs, AR; (3); 2/170; Am Leg Aux Girls St; FCA; FBLA; Sec Key Clb; Treas Natl Beta Clb; School Play; Sec Soph Cls; Var Chrldng; High Hon Roll; NHS; Bus.

TAYLOR, CHARLES Z; Jonesboro HS; Jonesboro, AR; (3); 81/360; Boy Scts; Cmnty Wkr; FCA; FBLA; VP Key Clb; Natl Beta Clb; Science Clb; Spanish Clb; Thesps; Chorus; AR Govnr Schl; Eagle Sct; Rhodes Col; Econ.

TAYLOR, CHRISTA; Magnolia HS; Magnolia, AR; (2); Church Yth Grp; Band; Church Choir; Color Guard; Mrchg Band; Pep Band; Hon Roll; 1st Band 1st Chr All Region Band.

TAYLOR, CHRISTY; Walnut Ridge HS; Walnut Ridge, AR; (1); Art Clb; Church Yth Grp; Cmnty Wkr; FHA; Spanish Clb; Varsity Clb; Co-Capt Chrldng; Gym; Cit Awd; High Hon Roll; AR ST U; Phys Thrpy.

TAYLOR, CODY A; England HS; Sherrill, AR; (4); Letterman Clb; Office Aide; Church Choir; Var Bsbl; JV Ftbl; Hon Roll; Red Belt Tae Kwon Do; Henderson ST Univ; Aviation.

TAYLOR, COURTNEY R; Dumas HS; Dumas, AR; (3); 18/145; FBLA; Math Clb; Science Clb; Spanish Clb; Co-Capt Stu Cncl; Gym; Tennis; Hon Roll; U Of AR; Nrsng.

TAYLOR, DAVID M; Gosnell Jr Sr HS; Blytheville, AR; (2); Art Clb; Church Yth Grp; Natl Beta Clb; Teachers Aide; Var Bsbl; Hon Roll.

TAYLOR, DREW E; Dumas HS; Dumas, AR; (2); Church Yth Grp; FBLA; Math Clb; Natl Beta Clb; Spanish Clb; Band; Pep Band; Hon Roll; NHS; Pres Acad Fit Awd; Amro Msc Hnr Band Awd; LA ST Univ; PT.

TAYLOR, ELIZABETH; Jonesboro HS; Jonesboro, AR; (1); Letterman Clb; Natl Beta Clb; Office Aide; Chorus; Var Chrldng; Vllybl; Hon Roll; Pres Acad Fit Awd; Pres Schlr; Home Ec Outstndng Stu; 3 Yrs Schlr Athl; NCA All Amer Chrldr; U AR; Law.

TAYLOR, ELIZABETH A; Ridgecrest HS; Paragould, AR; (2); FCA; French Clb; Office Aide; Nwsp; Hon Roll; Prfct Atten Awd; Dance Team-Lt 96-97 Schl Yr; Leo Clb; Awd 3 Super Ribbons At UDA Dance Camp; Psych.

TAYLOR, ERICA; John L Mcclellan Magnet HS; Little Rock, AR; (2); Church Yth Grp; FHA; Girl Scts; Natl Beta Clb; Spanish Clb; Mgr(s); Trk; High Hon Roll; Hon Roll; NHS; U Of Fayetteville; Educ.

TAYLOR, ERICK T; Pine Bluff HS; Pine Bluff, AR; (2); 46/580; Church Yth Grp; French Clb; Teachers Aide; JV Bsktbl; Var Mgr(s); Var Score Keeper; Hon Roll; Alcorn ST; Comm/PE.

TAYLOR, ERICKA L; Sheridan Sr HS; Grapevine, AR; (4); 13/220; Treas Church Yth Grp; Cmnty Wkr; FCA; FBLA; Teachers Aide; Chorus; Church Choir; Capt Pom Pon; Hon Roll; NHS; All Star Dance Team 95-96; Spirit Stepper Of The Yr 93-94; The Prudential Spirit Of The Comm Awd; U Of Cntrl AR; Bus.

TAYLOR, FELICIA; AR Math & Science Schl; Bauxite, AR; (4); Cmnty Wkr; Mu Alpha Theta; Treas Natl Beta Clb; SADD; Ed Yrbk; Lit Mag; High Hon Roll; Hon Roll; Jr NHS; NHS; Intnl Frgn Lang Awd Ger I/II; 4 Acad Excl Awd Jrnlsm; Res Life Comm Sec; U Of Central AR; Bus Admnstrn.

TAYLOR, HAILEY; West Memphis Sr HS; West Memphis, AR; (2); Church Yth Grp; French Clb; Sec VP Math Clb; Math Tm; Mu Alpha Theta; Natl Beta Clb; Quiz Bowl; Chorus; Pres Church Choir; School Musical; Governors Yth Conf Alcohol/Drugs; Delta Beta Sigma; Law.

TAYLOR, HEATHER A; Salem HS; Salem, AR; (3); Key Clb; Natl Beta Clb; Band; Jazz Band; Yrbk; VP Soph Cls; Sftbl; Hon Roll.

TAYLOR, HEATHER E; Lake Hamilton Sr HS; Hot Springs, AR; (3); FBLA; Quiz Bowl; Science Clb; Spanish Clb; Pres Thesps; School Musical; School Play; Stage Crew; Variety Show; Bsktbl; SCL; Young Life Chrstn Group; Wolf Pride; Intl Relations.

TAYLOR, JACOB S; Dequeen HS; Gillham, AR; (2); 4-H; SADD; Chorus; Ofcr Frsh Cls; Ofcr Soph Cls; Ofcr Jr Cls; Ofcr Bsbl; Ftbl; 4-H Awd; Hon Roll.

TAYLOR, JAMES F; Robinson HS; Little Rock, AR; (2); Boy Scts; Church Yth Grp; L Bsktbl; Alg I Acad Awd; U Of AR; Bus.

TAYLOR, JASON D; Trumann HS; Trumann, AR; (3); German Clb; Natl FFA Org; Science Clb; Ofcr Bsbl; Ftbl.

TAYLOR, JEFFREY P; Pine Bluff HS; Pine Bluff, AR; (3); Church Yth Grp; Natl FFA Org; Quiz Bowl; Science Clb; Spanish Clb; Yrbk; Ofcr Bsbl; Tennis; Hon Roll; NHS; Sailing; Sea Kayaking; Mountain Biking; U Of Miami; Marine Sci.

TAYLOR, JENNIFER; Wynne HS; Wynne, AR; (4); 21/160; Church Yth Grp; Crs Cntry; L Trk; Hon Roll; Spanish NHS; Jr Progressive Clb; U Of Central AR; Dentistry.

TAYLOR, JENNIFER H; Beebe Sr HS; Beebe, AR; (3); 14/126; Pres FHA; Pres Treas Natl Beta Clb; Treas Frsh Cls; Sec Jr Cls; Var Capt Chrldng; Var Capt Sftbl; Hon Roll; Art Clb; Church Yth Grp; Drama Clb; All ST Sftbl; All Conf Bsktbl; 2 Yr Voice Demcrcy Winner; UCA.

TAYLOR, JENNIFER R; Bryant Sr HS; Alexander, AR; (3); 28/920; Church Yth Grp; FTA; Office Aide; Spanish Clb; Hon Roll; Henderson ST; Bus Mgmt.

TAYLOR, JESSICA P; Monticello HS; Monticello, AR; (4); Am Leg Aux Girls St; Church Yth Grp; FCA; FBLA; Math Clb; Office Aide; Science Clb; Spanish Clb; SADD; Ofcr Soph Cls; Homecoming Crt 2 Yrs & Queen; Natlbeta Clb Pres, VP; Outstndng Sr; U Of AR.

TAYLOR, JOSEPH A; Ridgecrest HS; Paragould, AR; (4); 81/185; Library Aide; Sec Natl FFA Org; Teachers Aide; Yrbk; Ftbl; Pres Acad Fit Awd; Pres Schlr; FFA Crops Judgng Tm 94-; Livestock Show Tm 94-; Proj PALS 95-; AR ST U; Agrnmy.

TAYLOR, JOSHUA H; White Co Central Schl; Judsonia, AR; (4); Church Yth Grp; Teachers Aide; Yrbk; Bsktbl; Hon Roll; Tool & Dye.

TAYLOR, JULIA; Bradley Jr Sr HS; Bradley, AR; (3); 7/26; Church Yth Grp; FBLA; Spanish Clb; Church Choir; Hon Roll; Prfct Atten Awd; Talent Srch; SAU; Phy.

TAYLOR, KAMI S; Dardanelle HS; Dardanelle, AR; (4); 14/98; Intnl Clb; Sec Natl Beta Clb; Band; Capt Drm Mjr(t); Mrchg Band; Co-Ed Rptr Nwsp; Rep Stu Cncl; Ofcr Bsbl; Var Tennis; Hosp Aide; AR Tech Univ Majorette 96-; AR Tech Univ; Brdcst Jrnlsm.

TAYLOR, KARLI R; Dequeen HS; De Queen, AR; (3); Boy Scts; FHA; FTA; Red Cross Aide; SADD; Chrldng; Hon Roll; Med; Phy Thrpst.

TAYLOR, KATRINA J; Landmark Baptist Acad; Salado, AR; (4); 1/5; Boy Scts; Church Yth Grp; Key Clb; Chorus; Church Choir; High Hon Roll; Hon Roll; Prfct Atten Awd; Chrch Puppet Tm; U Of Cntrl AR.

TAYLOR, KENYA R; Malvern Sr HS; Malvern, AR; (3); Church Yth Grp; Cmnty Wkr; 4-H; French Clb; Library Aide; Natl Beta Clb; Office Aide; ROTC; SADD; Teachers Aide; Attnd Henderson ST Univ Smmr Inst; Governors Yth Conf; Peer Cnslr; Jr Choir Dir; Gracenotes; Jr Cnslr; UCA; Psych.

TAYLOR, KRESTON A; Hazen Jr Sr HS; Hazen, AR; (3); 16/45; Boy Scts; Church Yth Grp; Band; Mrchg Band; Co-Ed Yrbk; JV Var Bsbl; JV Var Ftbl; Var Golf; JV Var Trk; Var Wt Lftg; UALR; Crmnl Law.

TAYLOR, LAKISHA A; Rivercrest HS; Joiner, AR; (3); #22 in class; Church Yth Grp; ROTC; Teachers Aide; Drill Tm; Hon Roll; ASU; RN.

TAYLOR, LESLIE ANN; Green Forest Jr Sr HS; Green Forest, AR; (4); FBLA; FHA; Intnl Clb; Natl Beta Clb; SADD; School Play; Chrldng; High Hon Roll; Hon Roll; N AR Tech CC; Radiology.

TAYLOR, LORI L; Greenwood Sr HS; Fort Smith, AR; (4); Church Yth Grp; French Clb; Teachers Aide; Rptr Nwsp; Rptr Yrbk; Hon Roll; Westark Comm Col6; Pre-Dntl.

TAYLOR, MARK; Gosnell Jr Sr HS; Blytheville, AR; (2); Art Clb; Church Yth Grp; Natl Beta Clb; Teachers Aide; Var Bsbl; Hon Roll; Hntng; Fshng; Engrng.

TAYLOR, MELISSA; Huntsville HS; Hindsville, AR; (3); 9/128; FCA; Model UN; Natl FFA Org; VP Science Clb; Ofcr Soph Cls; Ofcr Jr Cls; Var L Golf; L Mgr(s); Hon Roll; AR Stu Congrss; Pol Sci.

TAYLOR, MINDY R; Cave City HS; Cave City, AR; (2); Natl Beta Clb; Natl FFA Org; Teachers Aide; Sftbl.

TAYLOR, MORGAN; Gosnell Jr Sr HS; Blytheville, AR; (3); Church Yth Grp; FHA; Key Clb; Natl Beta Clb; Office Aide; Drill Tm.

TAYLOR, NANCY C; Harrison Sr HS; Harrison, AR; (4); 1/203; Church Yth Grp; FBLA; Sec Treas Key Clb; Science Clb; Spanish Clb; SADD; Teachers Aide; Rep Frsh Cls; Var L Bsktbl; Var L Tennis; All ST All Conf Vlybl Slctn; Outstdng Snr Grl 96; Schlr Ath Rcpnt; Harding U; Bio-Chem.

TAYLOR, NATHAN T; Black Rock Jr Sr HS; Portia, AR; (2); Marine Bio.

TAYLOR, PATRICK B; Alma HS; Alma, AR; (3); Church Yth Grp; FCA; Teachers Aide; VP Frsh Cls; VP Soph Cls; Rep Stu Cncl; L Bsbl; Var L Ftbl; Var L Golf; Hon Roll; All Acad Tm.

TAYLOR, ROSHADA; John L Mcclellan Magnet HS; Little Rock, AR; (4); 35/257; DECA; French Clb; FBLA; FHA; Pres Library Aide; Mu Alpha Theta; Office Aide; SADD; VICA; Ofcr Sr Cls; Military Sword; U Of AR; FBI.

TAYLOR, SARAH; North Little Rock Hs-East; North Little Rock, AR; (1); Church Yth Grp; Drama Clb; FCA; Pep Clb; School Musical; Variety Show; Ofcr Frsh Cls; Chrldng; Trk; High Hon Roll; Kindgtn Tchr.

TAYLOR, SCOTT B; Genoa Central HS; Texarkana, AR; (4); 4-H; FBLA; HOBY; Model UN; Quiz Bowl; Science Clb; Spanish Clb; Varsity Clb; Church Choir; Variety Show; S AR Horse Assn; Pep Rally Announcer Bsktbl Games; UALR; Bus.

TAYLOR, SHANNON; Flippin Jr Sr HS; Flippin, AR; (3); Drama Clb; German Clb; Hosp Aide; Key Clb; Natl FFA Org; NFL; Science Clb; SADD; Teachers Aide; Band; Music Clb; Interact; RN.

TAYLOR, SUSAN G; John L Mcclellan Magnet HS; Mabelvale, AR; (4); Computer Clb; VP French Clb; Chrmn FBLA; Office Aide; Service Clb; Teachers Aide; Chorus; High Hon Roll; Hon Roll; Yth Accident Prvntn Stu Advsry Brd; Pres Ed Awd; 1st Plc At St FBLA Comp; U Of AR; Prelaw.

TAYLOR, TAMMY; Bradford Jr Sr HS; Bradford, AR; (4); 5/36; Art Clb; 4-H; French Clb; Natl Beta Clb; Natl FFA Org; Quiz Bowl; School Play; VP Frsh Cls; Bsktbl; Sftbl; Hillbilly Horse Show Assn; UCA; Phys Thrp.

TAYLOR, THOMAS J; Southside HS; Batesville, AR; (2); Chiropractic.

TAYLOR, TONYA; Central HS; West Helena, AR; (2); FBLA; Spanish Clb; Band; Mrchg Band; Powder Puff Ftbl; Hon Roll; NHS; Pediatrician; Pediatric Nurse.

TAYLOR, VALERIE; Dollarway HS; Pine Bluff, AR; (4); 1/92; Church Yth Grp; Office Aide; Acpl Chr; Chorus; Church Choir; Hon Roll; NHS; Pres Acad Fit Awd; Val; All Amer Schlr; U Of AR Monticello; Acctng.

TAYLOR, VALERIE M; St Joseph HS; Conway, AR; (3); Church Yth Grp; Key Clb; Office Aide; Teachers Aide; School Musical; School Play; Nwsp; Capt Chrldng; Hon Roll; All-Star Club Pres.

TAYLOR, VANESSA S; Bald Knob HS; Bald Knob, AR; (4); 5/88; Sec Church Yth Grp; FBLA; FHA; Natl Beta Clb; Spanish Clb; Acpl Chr; Pres Chorus; Church Choir; School Play; Swing Chorus; Harding Univ; Pre-Med.

TAYLOR, WENDY L; Woodlawn Schl; Warren, AR; (1); Church Yth Grp; Chorus; Speech Thrpst.

TEAGUE, CLORINDA L; Marion HS; Marion, AR; (2); Church Yth Grp; Drama Clb; Spanish Clb; Speech Tm; Color Guard; School Play; JV Bsktbl; Cit Awd; Hon Roll; Mid South Ms Yth Conf Pagent For Mid Town Church Of Christ; Lib Page; Murray ST; Pre Med.

TEAGUE, JAMES D; Gillett Jr Sr HS; Gillett, AR; (2); Art Clb; Spanish Clb; Band; Ed Nwsp; NHS; Jrnlsm Awd; MASH Pgm; AR ST Univ; Med Field.

TEAGUE, JENNIFER; Sulphur Rock Schl; Batesville, AR; (1); Key Clb; Natl Beta Clb; Band; Chorus; Pep Band; Won 1st Pl Earth Sci Rgnl Sci Fair.

TEAGUE, JENNIFER L; Harrison Sr HS; Harrison, AR; (4); 99/204; 4-H; VP FBLA; NFL; Spanish Clb; School Play; Rptr Nwsp; Phtg Yrbk; JV Golf; Var Pom Pon; Var Wt Lftg; U Of AR Fayetteville; Bus.

TEAGUE, JOHN T; Lake Hamilton Sr HS; Hot Springs, AR; (2); Church Yth Grp; Natl Beta Clb; Spanish Clb; Band; Chorus; Church Choir; Mrchg Band; School Musical; High Hon Roll; Hon Roll; Henderson ST U; CPA.

TEAGUE, LEAH D; Central HS; West Helena, AR; (2); Church Yth Grp; Office Aide; Band; Mrchg Band; Tennis; Hon Roll; Dsgnr.

TEAGUE, MONICA LEE; Bryant Sr HS; Alexander, AR; (2); Church Yth Grp; Drama Clb; Hosp Aide; Teachers Aide; Band; Color Guard; Mrchg Band; Ntl Merit Ltr; Sftbl Bryant Optimist Club; U Of Conway; Sci.

TEAGUE, RACHEL E; Pulaski Acad; Little Rock, AR; (4); Church Yth Grp; Cmnty Wkr; English Clb; Spanish Clb; High Hon Roll; Hon Roll; Jr NHS; NHS; Cum Laude Soc; Horseback Ride; Governors Schl; LA ST Univ.

TEAGUE, TONYA; Calico Rock HS; Calico Rock, AR; (3); Am Leg Aux Girls St; Treas Art Clb; Church Yth Grp; FCA; FBLA; GAA; Girl Scts; Hosp Aide; Natl Beta Clb; Science Clb; Stu Ambssdr For Ozrk Tech Coll; Attnd Hattie Caraway Conf; Eng & Comp Tech Awd; Bsktbl, Bsbl Awds; Coll Of Ozarks MO; Chld Psych.

TEAS, TUER; Heber Springs HS; Heber Springs, AR; (4); 22/103; Am Leg Aux Girls St; Church Yth Grp; French Clb; FBLA; HOBY; Sec Natl Beta Clb; Quiz Bowl; Spanish Clb; Teachers Aide; Band; U Of Cntrl AR; Educ.

TEATER, MANDIE; Victory Christian Schl; Hampton, AR; (2); 2/7; Church Yth Grp; Debate Tm; Speech Tm; Ed Yrbk; Var Bsktbl; Var Vllybl; Cit Awd; High Hon Roll; Pres Acad Fit Awd; GAA; Bulldog Schlr Awd; Oral Roberts U; Med.

TEDDER, LACY S; Dierks HS; Newhope, AR; (1); Church Yth Grp; FHA; Yrbk; Sec Frsh Cls; Mgr(s); Hon Roll; Sci/Home Ec/Civics Acad Awds.

TEEGARDEN, ROXANNE G; Melbourne HS; Pineville, AR; (4); 17/35; Sec Art Clb; Church Yth Grp; FBLA; FHA; Girl Scts; Hosp Aide; Library Aide; Natl FFA Org; Office Aide; Pep Clb; ASU; Pre-Law.

TEER, AMANDA L; Arkansas Sr HS; Texarkana, AR; (2); Church Yth Grp; Dance Clb; French Clb; Office Aide; Pep Clb; Church Choir; Drill Tm; School Play; Chrldng; Pom Pon; Teenage Repblcns; Psych.

TEETS, JOSEPH A; Fountain Lake Jr Sr HS; Hot Springs Natio, AR; (3); Natl FFA Org; Spanish Clb; Var JV Ftbl; Hon Roll.

TEFTELLER, DANIEL O; Fouke Jr Sr HS; Fouke, AR; (2); Natl FFA Org; Band; Mrchg Band; Ofcr Soph Cls.

TEGGUE, JAMES K; Blevins HS; Hope, AR; (2); Natl Beta Clb; Quiz Bowl; Trk; High Hon Roll; Hon Roll; NHS; Pres Acad Fit Awd; Newscaster On Schl Television Show; ADAPT Mem; Meteorologist; Sci.

TELLEZ, ROBERT; Catholic HS; Jacksonville, AR; (3); 1/190; Church Yth Grp; Cmnty Wkr; Debate Tm; HOBY; Model UN; ROTC; High Hon Roll; Hon Roll; Amer Lgn Bsbl; Yng Rpblcn Rep & Yth Cnnctn; Natl Yng Ldrs Conf; Stanford; Poli Sci.

TEMPELMEYER, DARLA M; Lakeside HS; Hot Springs, AR; (1); Cmnty Wkr; FBLA; Band; Chorus; Church Choir; Flag Corp; Mrchg Band; Hon Roll; Jr NHS; Pres Acad Fit Awd; Solo/Ensmbl Band Two 1st Div Mdls; All Region Bnd; Symphonic Bnd 1st Chair; Harvard; Lawyer.

TEMPLE, JOHN R; Jacksonville HS; Jacksonville, AR; (2); 4/206; FBLA; Office Aide; Spanish Clb; Teachers Aide; Ofcr Bsbl; Ftbl; Trk; Hon Roll.

TEMPLE, TABITHA L; Hermitage Jr Sr HS; Warren, AR; (2); 3/60; Church Yth Grp; HOBY; Natl Beta Clb; Natl FFA Org; Band; Flag Corp; Mrchg Band; School Musical; Hon Roll; TX A&M; Marine Biologist.

TEMPLE, TIA M; Fairview HS; Camden, AR; (3); VP Church Yth Grp; Treas Drama Clb; Sec French Clb; Treas Mu Alpha Theta; Natl Beta Clb; Science Clb; Chorus; School Musical; French Hon Soc; NHS; Bus.

TEMPLETON, ASHLEY A; El Dorado Sr HS; El Dorado, AR; (3); 60/316; Am Leg Aux Girls St; Church Yth Grp; Natl Beta Clb; Office Aide; Service Clb; Hon Roll; Jr Cls Steering Comm; Jr Civitans; Camp Fire; Quachita Bapt Univ; Phy Thrpst.

TEMPLETON, BRIAN P; Swifton Schl; Swifton, AR; (3); Church Yth Grp; FBLA; FHA; Natl FFA Org; Office Aide; Pep Clb; Spanish Clb; Rptr Frsh Cls; Rptr Soph Cls; Rptr Jr Cls; AR ST Univ; Mngmt.

TENBENSEL, AMANDA K; Bentonville Sr HS; Bentonville, AR; (3); Church Yth Grp; Band; Jazz Band; Mrchg Band; Pep Band; U Of AR; Bus Mgmt.

TENCLEVE, TRISHA; Scranton HS; Scranton, AR; (4); 1/24; Am Leg Aux Girls St; FBLA; German Clb; Natl Beta Clb; Science Clb; Yrbk; Pres Soph Cls; Pres Jr Cls; Bsktbl; Val; Univ Of Cntrl AR; Spch Path.

TENNER, LAPORSHA A; North Little Rock Hs-East; North Little Rock, AR; (2); Church Yth Grp; FCA; Pres FBLA; Chorus; Church Choir; Bsktbl; Trk; Vllybl; Hon Roll; Monicello U; Cnslr.

TENNISON, SHELLY F; Yellville Summit HS; Yellville, AR; (3); 12/85; Drama Clb; Rptr FBLA; Band; Capt Co-Capt Color Guard; Capt Co-Capt Flag Corp; Mrchg Band; Pep Band; Ed Nwsp; Yrbk; Gov Hon Prg Awd; U Of AR; His; Lawyer.

TENNYSON, CHRISTOPHER KIT; Gosnell Jr Sr HS; Gosnell, AR; (4); 25/66; Quiz Bowl; Var Bsbl; Var Ftbl; Var Golf; Var Wt Lftg; Var Wrstlng; Hon Roll; NHS; Pres Acad Fit Awd.

TERRELL, JOHN D; Murfreesboro HS; Murfreesboro, AR; (2); #3 in class; FHA; Natl Beta Clb; Pres Spanish Clb; Yrbk; Sec Soph Cls; Ofcr Bsbl; Bsktbl; Ftbl; Hon Roll; Pres Acad Fit Awd; Pre Med.

TERRELL, JOY; Hermitage Jr Sr HS; Hermitage, AR; (3); Church Yth Grp; French Clb; Natl Beta Clb; Natl FFA Org; Band; Chorus; Church Choir; School Play; Variety Show; Nwsp; Marchd Macys Thanksgiving Day Parade NYC W/Universal Chrldrs 95; Crowned Miss Hermitage 96; U Of AR At Fayetteville; Dr.

TERRELL, MISTY D; Jacksonville HS; Jacksonville, AR; (3); 19/325; Am Leg Aux Girls St; Debate Tm; VP Drama Clb; FBLA; Natl Beta Clb; NFL; Spanish Clb; School Play; VP Stu Cncl; NHS; Acctng.

TERRELL, NICHOLE; Brinkley HS; Brinkley, AR; (3); Sec French Clb; Sec FBLA; Pres FHA; Quiz Bowl; Phtg Yrbk; Pres Jr Cls; Rep Stu Cncl; Var Bsktbl; NHS; U Of AR Fayetteville; Med.

TERRY, AMANDA; Watson Chapel Sr HS; Pine Bluff, AR; (1); Church Yth Grp; Cmnty Wkr; Dance Clb; Drama Clb; Natl Beta Clb; Church Choir; Chrldng; Powder Puff Ftbl; High Hon Roll; Sec Beta Club; Top Acad; 3rd Plsci Fair; UCA; OT.

TERRY, COURTNEY E; Central Sr HS; Little Rock, AR; (3); 55/560; Church Yth Grp; FCA; Service Clb; Spanish Clb; Var Socr; Hon Roll; NHS.

TERRY, FARRIS W; Van Cove HS; Cove, AR; (3); 4-H; Natl FFA Org; Yrbk; Var Bsbl; Judging Teams; GATE; Upward Bound; 4 Yr U.

TERRY, LA SHAY D; Lake Hamilton Sr HS; Pearcy, AR; (3); Church Yth Grp; Dance Clb; FCA; FBLA; Hosp Aide; Natl Beta Clb; Spanish Clb; Chorus; School Musical; Art Clb; MASH; Pre-Med.

TERRY, MICHAEL; Cabot HS; Cabot, AR; (3); 57/398; Am Leg Boys St; Boy Scts; Pres Church Yth Grp; VP German Clb; Library Aide; High Hon Roll; Kiwanis Awd; PRIDE Clb; Natl Schlr; Envrnmntl Sci.

TERRY, MONICA L; Ashdown Sr HS; Wilton, AR; (4); 53/134; Church Yth Grp; Church Choir; Amer Lgn Schl Awd; Engl II Awd; Personal Rsrce Mgnt Awd; Gen Coop Ed 1 Awd; Elem Engl Tchr.

TERRY, RACHEL; Cabot HS; Cabot, AR; (1); Church Yth Grp; German Clb; High Hon Roll; Pride Clb.

TERRY, SAM M; Southside HS; Fort Smith, AR; (2); FCA; Key Clb; Latin Clb; Mu Alpha Theta; Quiz Bowl; Swmmng; Hon Roll; NHS; Pres Acad Fit Awd; Intnl Sci Fair.

TERRY, SARAH; Lake Hamilton Sr HS; Hot Springs, AR; (3); 27/253; Church Yth Grp; Pres FBLA; HOBY; Natl Beta Clb; Q&S; Spanish Clb; Drill Tm; Co-Ed Nwsp; NHS; Pres Acad Fit Awd; Adam Dodd Memrl Awd Otstndng Frshmn; Optmst Wrtng Awd; Harding U; Cmmnctns.

TERWILLIGAR, JANA L; Lake Hamilton Sr HS; Bonnerdale, AR; (3); 20/220; Church Yth Grp; FBLA; Natl Beta Clb; Spanish Clb; Teachers Aide; Band; Mrchg Band; Pep Band; School Musical; Acad Ltrs; Solo Ensmbl Band Cont High Rtngs; Marine Bio.

TERWILLIGER, EMILY G; Russellville Sr HS; Dover, AR; (3); Church Yth Grp; SADD; Band; Chorus; Church Choir; Mrchg Band; Variety Show; Cit Awd; Jr NHS; NHS.

TETERS, MELISSA A; Springdale Sr HS; Springdale, AR; (3); Church Yth Grp; FCA; FBLA; Pres Key Clb; Teachers Aide; Var Chrldng; Powder Puff Ftbl; Tennis; Hon Roll; Judge.

THACH, DAVID; Arkansas Schl Math & Science; Barling, AR; (4); Art Clb; Sec 4-H; Rptr FBLA; HOBY; Key Clb; Model UN; Pres Mu Alpha Theta; Natl Beta Clb; Pres Soph Cls; Hon Roll; Purdue U Bk Awd; Sakharovs Rdngs Intl Sci Conf:1st Pl AR St Rflctns; Cornell U; Intl Rltns.

THACH, HAEEN; Northside HS; Fort Smith, AR; (3); Spanish Clb; Band; Capt Flag Corp; Treas Jr Cls; Hon Roll; Jr NHS; NHS; Spanish NHS.

THAI, BAO H; Southside HS; Barling, AR; (3); Boy Scts; Church Yth Grp; FCA; Chorus; Church Choir; Ofcr Jr Cls; Var Ftbl; JV Socr; JV Wt Lftg; JV Hon Roll; U Of A; Mech Engr.

THAREL, AMANDA; Booneville Jr Sr HS; Booneville, AR; (4); 4/86; Am Leg Aux Girls St; Church Yth Grp; Pres FBLA; Natl Beta Clb; Chorus; Church Choir; School Play; Rep Stu Cncl; Chrldng; FCA; St Beta Ortry Cmptn Wnnr; U AR.

THARP, MISTY; Rison HS; Rison, AR; (4); 6/53; Am Leg Aux Girls St; Rep French Clb; Pres FHA; Natl Beta Clb; Pres Science Clb; Pres Band; Mrchg Band; Ofcr Stu Cncl; Hon Roll; Ntl Merit Ltr; AR Tech U; Accntng.

THARP, MYA; Blevins HS; Hope, AR; (2); 2/38; Church Yth Grp; 4-H; FBLA; Natl Beta Clb; Rep Frsh Cls; Rep Soph Cls; Mgr(s); Cit Awd; High Hon Roll; Hon Roll; ADAPT.

THAXTON, DYLAN; Malvern Sr HS; Malvern, AR; (3); 1/220; Natl Beta Clb; Quiz Bowl; Science Clb; Lbrn Band; Mrchg Band; Ofcr Bsbl; High Hon Roll; Jr NHS; Treas NHS; Pres Schlr; 1st Plc Sci Fair; All Reg Bnd Mmbr; LA Tech Univ; Biomed Eng.

THEIS, ADAM S; Dewitt HS; De Witt, AR; (2).

THESSING, WHITNEY A; Conway Sr HS; Conway, AR; (4); 140/540; FCA; FBLA; VICA; Rep Jr Cls; Rep Sr Cls; Ofcr Stu Cncl; Pom Pon; Hon Roll; All Str Staff; Fire Marshall; U Of Cntrl AR.

THEUNISSEN, AMANDA H; Lakeside HS; Eudora, AR; (3); Drama Clb; Sec FBLA; FHA; School Play; Stage Crew; Ofcr Stu Cncl; Powder Puff Ftbl; Hon Roll; NHS; Lawyer.

THILMONT, ASHLEY A; Mountain Home HS; Mountain Home, AR; (3); 120/300; Art Clb; Rep VP FHA; Office Aide; Teachers Aide; 1st Pl Dist Art Cont; 2nd Pl St Art Cmptn; ASU; Graphic Art.

THOMAS, AMANDA; Evening Shade Schl; Evening Shade, AR; (1); FCA; FBLA; FHA; Quiz Bowl; VP Frsh Cls; Rep Stu Cncl; Bsktbl; Hon Roll; NHS; Pres Acad Fit Awd.

THOMAS, ANGELA; Central HS; West Helena, AR; (3); 2/200; Church Yth Grp; Math Tm; Church Choir; Stage Crew; Rep Frsh Cls; Rep Stu Cncl; Var L Bsktbl; High Hon Roll; Hon Roll; Jr NHS; Pride Treas; Engrng Bound; Span Clb; Tuskegee Univ; Phrmcy.

THOMAS, APRIL T; Blytheville Sr HS; Blytheville, AR; (3); Church Yth Grp; FHA; ROTC; Drill Tm; Cit Awd; Hon Roll; AR ST Univ; Nrsng.

THOMAS, BRIDGETT D; Lakeside HS; Lake Village, AR; (2); 2/100; Church Yth Grp; Drama Clb; FBLA; Band; School Play; Rep Stu Cncl; Chrldng; High Hon Roll; NHS; U Of AR; Pharm.

THOMAS, CALEB; Prairie Grove HS; Prairie Grove, AR; (4); 1/89; Church Yth Grp; Pres FCA; VP Natl FFA Org; VP Sr Cls; Var Bsbl; Var Ftbl; Var Golf; Var Tennis; NHS; Val; FCH; Abilene Chrstn U; Vet.

THOMAS, COLE; Morrilton Sr HS; Morrilton, AR; (2); Church Yth Grp; Office Aide; Quiz Bowl; Spanish Clb; Var Ftbl; Hon Roll; Law.

THOMAS, CYNTHIA; Elaine Jr Sr HS; Elaine, AR; (3); 4/39; Church Yth Grp; FBLA; FHA; Natl FFA Org; Chorus; School Musical; Phtg Nwsp; Rep Frsh Cls; Treas Stu Cncl; Hon Roll; Beauty Pagnts 2nd Rnnr Up 2 Times, Photognc 2 Times; Cosmtlgy.

THOMAS, DERRICK L; Booneville Jr Sr HS; Booneville, AR; (2); Church Yth Grp; FCA; Key Clb; Letterman Clb; Natl Beta Clb; Science Clb; JV Bsktbl; Var L Ftbl; Var L Trk; Hon Roll; U Of AR; Engrng.

THOMAS, ELIZABETH M; Arkansas Bapt Schl; Little Rock, AR; (3); Church Yth Grp; FCA; FBLA; Natl Beta Clb; Spanish Clb; Band; Church Choir; Flag Corp; Mrchg Band; Pep Band; Eqn Vet.

THOMAS, JASON; Harmony Grove Jr Sr HS; Camden, AR; (1); Church Yth Grp; FCA; Natl Beta Clb; Natl FFA Org; Band; Mrchg Band; Ftbl; Wt Lftg; Hon Roll; Pltry Tm; Henderson.

THOMAS, JENNIFER S; Springdale Sr HS; Springdale, AR; (2); Church Yth Grp; Pres FHA; Teachers Aide; Band; Capt Drm Mjr(t); Mrchg Band; Orch; Pep Band; Hon Roll; Nrsng.

THOMAS, JESTIN Z; Pine Bluff HS; Pine Bluff, AR; (3); Hosp Aide; Key Clb; Natl Beta Clb; Spanish Clb; Band; Mrchg Band; Pep Band; Hon Roll; Jr NHS; FBLA; Pathways To Coll; AR Comm Planning Group For HIV Prevention; DE ST; Sports Medicine.

THOMAS, JOSH R; Southside HS; Batesville, AR; (1); Boy Scts; Church Yth Grp; Natl Beta Clb; Science Clb; Teachers Aide; Band; Pep Band; Var Bsbl; Tennis; Trk; Top 10% Of Frosh Clss; Cmptrs.

THOMAS, KARLA; Brinkley HS; Brinkley, AR; (1); Church Yth Grp; Quiz Bowl; Teachers Aide; Band; Church Choir; Mrchg Band; Rep Stu Cncl; High Hon Roll; VP NHS; Oil Painting, Twirling & Piano.

THOMAS, KATRINA H; Lavaca Jr Sr HS; Lavaca, AR; (3); Church Yth Grp; Teachers Aide; Chorus; Church Choir; Vllybl; Cit Awd; Hon Roll; Coll Of The Ozarks; RN.

THOMAS, MAKETRIA S; Russellville Sr HS; Russellville, AR; (4); Church Yth Grp; FCA; GAA; Office Aide; VP Spanish Clb; Lit Mag; Var Trk; Hon Roll; Teachers Aide; Band; Cyclone Achvr Awd; Equity Cmmtee-Dist; UAR-FAYETTEVILLE; Chem Engrng.

THOMAS, MATTHEW A; Farmington Jr Sr HS; Farmington, AR; (2); Boy Scts; FBLA; Hon Roll; Jr NHS; Prfct Atten Awd; Pres Acad Fit Awd; U Of AR; Acctng.

THOMAS, NICOLE; Southside HS; Fort Smith, AR; (2); FCA; Spanish Clb; Intrml Vllybl; Hon Roll; Jr NHS; Grls, Coed Sftbl Non Schl Spon; Radiolgy.

THOMAS, PAYTON C; Newport HS; Newport, AR; (2); Church Yth Grp; French Clb; Band; Church Choir; Mrchg Band; Ofcr Stu Cncl; Mgr(s); Trk; Cit Awd; Hon Roll; Outstndg Brass Awrd; All Reg Bnd; U Of AR; OB/GYN.

THOMAS, REBEKAH; Ridgecrest HS; Paragould, AR; (2); Church Yth Grp; 4-H; FBLA; Hosp Aide; Band; Mrchg Band; Pep Band; Teachers Aide; Hon Roll; Prfct Atten Awd; Bus.

THOMAS, REGINA; Mtn View HS; Mountain View, AR; (3); 3/60; Church Yth Grp; Dance Clb; Drama Clb; FCA; FBLA; GAA; Natl Beta Clb; Science Clb; Spanish Clb; SADD; Beta Clb VP; Span Clb Pres; Jonesboro Univ; Dntl Hyg.

THOMAS, SARA C; Rogers HS; Rogers, AR; (3); 99/600; Church Yth Grp; Dance Clb; FCA; Band; Drm Mjr(t); Mrchg Band; Orch; Pom Pon; Hon Roll; NHS.

THOMAS, SARAH J; Valley Springs Schl; Harrison, AR; (3); FHA; Natl FFA Org; NACTC; Vet.

THOMAS, SHAWN N; Southside HS; Batesville, AR; (3); Church Yth Grp; Quiz Bowl; Band; Church Choir; Mrchg Band; Pep Band; Hon Roll; Chrch Plays & Musical Dramas; Sky Diving; ER Specialist; Pediatrics.

THOMAS, SHAWNNA M; Fouke Jr Sr HS; Fouke, AR; (3); Church Yth Grp; FBLA; Natl FFA Org; Spanish Clb; Band; Sftbl; Cit Awd; Hon Roll; NHS; Jazz Band; Pres/1st Priority; Cmptr Sci.

THOMAS, TARA O; Central Sr HS; Little Rock, AR; (4); Church Yth Grp; Dance Clb; FBLA; FHA; Spanish Clb; Church Choir; Drill Tm; Rep Sr Cls; Pom Pon; Jackson ST Univ; Pre-Med.

THOMAS, TERRI L; Marvell Acad; Poplar Grove, AR; (4); 5/30; FBLA; Spanish Clb; Teachers Aide; School Play; Stage Crew; Nwsp; Mgr Yrbk; Hon Roll; Jr NHS; NHS; MASH; Span & Algebra II ABC Awd; AR ST Univ; Eng; Span.

THOMAS, TIA S; Arkadelphia Sr HS; Arkadelphia, AR; (4); 27/160; Cmnty Wkr; FCA; FHA; Natl Beta Clb; Drill Tm; Var Capt Bsktbl; Var Capt Vllybl; High Hon Roll; Hon Roll; NHS; Henderson ST U; Psych.

THOMAS, TIFFANY E; Arkansas Sr HS; Texarkana, AR; (3); 14/341; Am Leg Aux Girls St; Church Yth Grp; Drama Clb; Mu Alpha Theta; Speech Tm; Church Choir; Drill Tm; School Play; Rep Frsh Cls; Prfct Atten Awd; 5 Yrs Piano; Ouachita Bapt U; Psych.

THOMAS, TONYA; Nashville HS; Nashville, AR; (4); 4/106; Church Yth Grp; FBLA; Letterman Clb; Quiz Bowl; Spanish Clb; Chorus; School Play; Phtg Rptr Nwsp; Phtg Rptr Yrbk; Ofcr Stu Cncl; Talented/Gifted Prgm; AR Tech Univ; Bus Admin.

THOMASON, ALICE J; Valley Springs Schl; Everton, AR; (3); 10/60; Art Clb; Church Yth Grp; Rptr French Clb; FBLA; Key Clb; Var L Bsktbl; Var L Vllybl; Hon Roll; NHS; Prfct Atten Awd; Placed 15th & 25th In Natl Fr Exam; North AR Comm Tech Coll.

THOMASON, ALICIA; Warren Sr HS; Warren, AR; (3); Church Yth Grp; French Clb; Natl Beta Clb; SADD; Chorus; Church Choir; High Hon Roll; UAM.

THOMASON, BRYAN; Bradford Jr Sr HS; Bradford, AR; (4); 5/35; Church Yth Grp; French Clb; Pres FBLA; FHA; HOBY; Natl Beta Clb; Band; Chorus; School Musical; Ed Yrbk; Gftd & Tlntd Prgrm; 3rd Pl Odyssy Of Mindcmptn Regl; U Of AR At Fayetteville.

THOMASON, CHRIS C; Amity Jr Sr HS; Amity, AR; (2); Church Yth Grp; FCA; FBLA; FHA; Natl Beta Clb; Natl FFA Org; School Play; Nwsp; Pres Frsh Cls; Rep Soph Cls; Baylor; Doctor.

THOMASON, JOHN W; Rivercrest HS; Lynnville, TN; (2); 2/145; Church Yth Grp; FBLA; Letterman Clb; Math Clb; Teachers Aide; Yrbk; VP Soph Cls; Ofcr Bsbl; Ftbl; Cit Awd; Lib Clb VP; Teens Against Drugs; David Lipscomb U; Bus.

THOMASON, KALENA; Bradford Jr Sr HS; Bradford, AR; (3); FHA; Yrbk; Rptr Frsh Cls; Treas Soph Cls; Treas Jr Cls; Bsktbl; Crs Cntry; Sftbl; Trk; Hon Roll; Home Ec.

THOMASON, KRIS L; Fouke Jr Sr HS; Fouke, AR; (3); Cit Awd; Hon Roll; Pres Acad Fit Awd; Pres Schlr; Grd Achvmnts Various Classes; Actvts Chrch Plays; Henderson Univ; Dntstry.

THOMPSON, BRYAN W; Ridgecrest HS; Paragould, AR; (3); 9/220; FCA; French Clb; Science Clb; Ofcr Bsbl; Bsktbl; Ftbl; French Hon Soc; High Hon Roll; Pres Acad Fit Awd; Three Rivers CC; PE.

THOMPSON, CANDIS L; Smackover HS; Smackover, AR; (1); VP Church Yth Grp; Computer Clb; FBLA; FTA; Spanish Clb; Church Choir; Hon Chsn Peer Mdtr By Clsmts; Being Outdoors; Hendrix Conway; PT.

THOMPSON, CASSIE; Hazen Jr Sr HS; Hazen, AR; (4); 9/27; French Clb; FBLA; FTA; Natl Beta Clb; Band; Chorus; Rptr Nwsp; Hon Roll; NHS; AR St Univ.

THOMPSON, CHRIS P; Rogers HS; Rogers, AR; (1); Church Yth Grp; CAP; Model UN; Band; Mrchg Band.

THOMPSON, CRYSTAL; Murfreesboro HS; Murfreesboro, AR; (4); 13/37; FBLA; FHA; Natl Beta Clb; Science Clb; Band; Drm Mjr(t); Rep Sr Cls; Bsktbl; Trk; St Schlr; Hmcmng Maid; Red River Techcol; RN.

THOMPSON, DACUS W; Searcy HS; Searcy, AR; (3); Church Yth Grp; Cmnty Wkr; FCA; Key Clb; Natl Beta Clb; Variety Show; Bsktbl; JV Var Ftbl; Socr; NHS.

THOMPSON, GLORIA; Ola Jr Sr HS; Dardanelle, AR; (2); Chess Clb; Cmnty Wkr; GAA; Math Tm; Office Aide; ROTC; Teachers Aide; Church Choir; School Play; Lit Mag; VALR; Cmptr Sci.

THOMPSON, HEATHER D; Marked Tree Jr Sr HS; Marked Tree, AR; (3); 1/68; Am Leg Aux Girls St; FBLA; HOBY; Spanish Clb; Capt Var Chrldng; Var Sftbl; NHS; UCA All-Star Chrldr; World Affairs Smnr Ambassador; Fnlst AR Schl For Math & Sci; U Of AR Fayetteville; Corp Law.

THOMPSON, JAMES D; Gosnell Jr Sr HS; Blytheville, AR; (1); Art Clb; Library Aide.

THOMPSON, JENNY; Wynne HS; Wynne, AR; (3); Church Yth Grp; Drama Clb; FTA; Q&S; SADD; Church Choir; Flag Corp; Mrchg Band; School Musical; School Play; ASU; Oncology Nrs Practitioner.

THOMPSON, JESSE W; Arkansas Sr HS; Texarkana, AR; (4); 16/379; Art Clb; FBLA; Pres Mu Alpha Theta; Natl FFA Org; Spanish Clb; JV Ftbl; Hon Roll; NHS; Lewis Thompson Ldrshp Awd; Spnsh Stu Of Yr; U Of The Ozarks; Engrng.

THOMPSON, KASSIE; Ridgecrest HS; Paragould, AR; (1); Chrldng; Hon Roll; Pres Acad Fit Awd; U AR; Physlgy.

THOMPSON, KATHRYN B; Southside HS; Batesville, AR; (4); 12/76; FBLA; FHA; Key Clb; Office Aide; Science Clb; Spanish Clb; Hon Roll.

THOMPSON, KAYSIE; Ashdown Sr HS; Ashdown, AR; (3); 1/132; Cmnty Wkr; French Clb; FBLA; Model UN; Natl Beta Clb; Science Clb; School Play; French Hon Soc; High Hon Roll; Hon Roll; Wdsmn Of Wrld Awd; Attnd Henderson 100 Pgm Henderson ST Univ; Odyssey Of Mind; Advrtsng.

THOMPSON, LAURA K; Arkansas Sr HS; Texarkana, AR; (2); 115/432; Pres Spanish Clb; Band; Mrchg Band; Pep Band; Treas Frsh Cls; Teen Crt.

THOMPSON, MEGAN; Harmony Grove Jr Sr HS; Camden, AR; (3); 4/52; Chess Clb; FBLA; VP FTA; Library Aide; Natl Beta Clb; Science Clb; Spanish Clb; Band; NHS; Pres Acad Fit Awd; Elem Ed.

THOMPSON, MICHELLE; Jacksonville HS; Jacksonville, AR; (3); Church Yth Grp; Drama Clb; Natl Beta Clb; Spanish Clb; Chorus; Variety Show; Yrbk; Hon Roll; Flwshp Chrstn Stdnts; Church Nursery Vol; ASU Beebe; RN.

THOMPSON, PAMELA A; Bryant Sr HS; Alexander, AR; (2); Art Clb; Church Yth Grp; Cmnty Wkr; Teachers Aide; Hon Roll; Jr NHS; Sftbl 6 Yrs; FL ST Univ; Psych.

THOMPSON, ROBERT E; Fountain Lake Jr Sr HS; Hot Springs Natio, AR; (3); Boy Scts; Church Yth Grp; FCA; Spanish Clb; Chorus; Color Guard; School Play; Stage Crew; Hon Roll; SCA Pres; Envrnmntl Clb; Eagle Sct; Elctrcl Engr.

THOMPSON, RYAN; Arkansas Bapt Schl; Little Rock, AR; (3); Natl Beta Clb; Spanish Clb; Cit Awd; Hon Roll; Pol Awareness Clb; Union U; Bus; Comp Sci.

THOMPSON, SERENA; Sheridan Sr HS; Sheridan, AR; (4); 7/220; Am Leg Aux Girls St; Church Yth Grp; Pres FHA; Pres Chorus; Sec NHS; FCA; Quiz Bowl; Mrchg Band; Orch; Hon Roll; Governors Schlshp Recipient; Young Independents Pres; NASSP Prin Ldrshp Awd; Madrigals; Schlr Awd; U AL-FAYETTEVILLE; Psych.

THOMPSON, SHELLY; Maynard Jr Sr HS; Maynard, AR; (3); Am Leg Aux Girls St; Chess Clb; Church Yth Grp; French Clb; FBLA; Natl Beta Clb; School Play; VP Frsh Cls; VP Stu Cncl; Bsktbl; Schlr Athl Awd; Med.

THOMPSON, TENETHREA; Bearden HS; Bearden, AR; (2); Church Yth Grp; 4-H; FBLA; FHA; FTA; Natl Beta Clb; Church Choir; Var Chrldng; Var Trk; Hon Roll; Carlton Smith Yth Ctr Vlntr Of Yr; U Of AR Fayetteville.

THOMPSON, TIFFANY D; Newport HS; Newport, AR; (2); Art Clb; Library Aide; Spanish Clb; Cit Awd; Hon Roll; Lib Asst Awd; Bible Club; AR ST Univ; His Prof.

THOMPSON, TRAVIS S; Searcy HS; Searcy, AR; (3); Church Yth Grp; Cmnty Wkr; FCA; Natl Beta Clb; Ofcr Bsbl; Hon Roll; Jr NHS; NHS; Ntl Merit Ltr; Optometry.

THOMPSON, TRISHA M; Huntsville HS; Huntsville, AR; (2); FCA; FBLA; FTA; Natl Beta Clb; SADD; Ofcr Frsh Cls; Ofcr Soph Cls; Ofcr Stu Cncl; Chrldng; Golf; Bus.

THOMPSON, VALERI A; North Pulaski HS; Jacksonville, AR; (3); 18/239; Drama Clb; Mu Alpha Theta; Band; Mrchg Band; Pep Band; Hon Roll; NHS; North Pulaski Band Sec/1st Chair/Sctn Ldr; All Region Band; Hon Band; Southeast MO ST U; USAF/LAW.

THOMPSON, VENTRELL; Dermott HS; Dermott, AR; (2); FCA; FBLA; Math Clb; Natl Beta Clb; Church Choir; Rep Soph Cls; Rep Stu Cncl; Bsktbl; Cit Awd; Hon Roll; U Of AR; Medicine.

THOMPSON, WESLEY G; Conway Sr HS; Conway, AR; (2); Band; Jazz Band; Mrchg Band; Orch; Pep Band; Bowling; Pro Bowler.

THORN, SHIRHONDA D; Forrest City HS; Colt, AR; (3); Drama Clb; French Clb; FBLA; Mu Alpha Theta; Natl Beta Clb; Quiz Bowl; Band; Rep Stu Cncl; Church Yth Grp; Dance Clb; Arnharts Ballet Folklorico; Govnrs Yth Conf Ldr; Drug Free Club Ofcr; Med.

THORNBURG, KLINT K; Southside HS; Fort Smith, AR; (2); Church Yth Grp; FCA; FBLA; Key Clb; Teachers Aide; Ftbl; Hon Roll; Soph Cncl; U Of AR; Engrng.

THORNTON, BRANDON; Calvary Christian Schl; Forrest City, AR; (3); 3/11; Church Yth Grp; Var Bsktbl; Var Socr; Cit Awd; High Hon Roll; Hon Roll; MASH Camp; Ntl Hstry & Govt Awd 95-96; Multiple Yr Listing; Williams Baptist Coll; Med.

THORNTON, KAREN R; North Little Rock Hs-West; North Little Rock, AR; (4); 25/439; Church Yth Grp; Cmnty Wkr; Hosp Aide; Mu Alpha Theta; Natl Beta Clb; Mgr Q&S; Mgr Yrbk; High Hon Roll; Hon Roll; NHS; Mission Trips; Top 10%; Sunday Schl Tchr; Henderson ST U; Erly Chldhd Ed.

THORNTON, LAURA E; Hermitage Jr Sr HS; Hermitage, AR; (4); 6/43; Am Leg Aux Girls St; Church Yth Grp; Debate Tm; 4-H; French Clb; GAA; Natl Beta Clb; Natl FFA Org; Varsity Clb; Band; U AR Monticello; Dntl.

THORNTON, MARY A; Hermitage Jr Sr HS; Hermitage, AR; (3); 8/68; Sec Church Yth Grp; Cmnty Wkr; 4-H; FHA; GAA; Math Clb; Natl Beta Clb; Natl FFA Org; Varsity Clb; Band; U Of AR Monticello; Pre Med.

THORPE, JENNIFER N; Bentonville Sr HS; Bella Vista, AR; (4); 22/242; Church Yth Grp; FCA; French Clb; Chorus; Tennis; Hon Roll; NHS; Hnr Grad; U Ozarks; Math.

THREADGILL, ANGELA; Foreman Jr Sr HS; Foreman, AR; (4); 8/50; Am Leg Aux Girls St; Cmnty Wkr; FTA; Teachers Aide; Church Choir; Sec Sr Cls; Chrldng; High Hon Roll; Hon Roll; NHS; U AR Pine Bluff; Elem Ed.

THRESHER, GINGER; Malvern Sr HS; Donaldson, AR; (3); FBLA; Natl Beta Clb; SADD; Teachers Aide; High Hon Roll; Jr NHS; NHS; Pres Acad Fit Awd; Peer Cnslrs; Jr Beta Clb; Rdlgy.

THRIST, ANDREA; Central Sr HS; Little Rock, AR; (2); Church Yth Grp; 4-H; Library Aide; Pep Clb; Teachers Aide; Band; Church Choir; Memphis St Univ; Spec Ed Psych.

THROCKMORTON, JOSHUA; Mountain View Jr Sr HS; Mountain View, AR; (4); 21/87; Natl Beta Clb; Spanish Clb; Bsktbl; Oral Roberts U; Optometrist.

THROGMARTIN, AMANDA C; Ridgecrest HS; Paragould, AR; (3); 2/200; Church Yth Grp; FBLA; Key Clb; Quiz Bowl; Science Clb; JV Bsktbl; Hon Roll; NHS; Pres Acad Fit Awd; Cit Awd; Crusaders For Christ; French Achvmnt Awd.

THRONEBERRY, JASON K; Pine Bluff HS; Pine Bluff, AR; (2); Church Yth Grp; French Clb; Orch; Hon Roll; Jr NHS; Pine Bluff Yth Symphony; Schl Chrstn Clb VP; Ag Govt Worker.

THROWER, ANGELA S; Arkansas Sr HS; Texarkana, AR; (3); Church Yth Grp; Band; Church Choir; Flag Corp; Mrchg Band; Hon Roll; Prfct Atten Awd; Med.

THURLKILL, CARMON E; Junction City HS; El Dorado, AR; (4); FHA; Spanish Clb; Band; Mrchg Band; NHS.

THURMAN, TAYLOR; Danville HS; Danville, AR; (2); 4-H; GAA; Ofcr Stu Cncl; Bsktbl; Capt Chrldng; Trk; 4-H Awd; Hon Roll; NHS.

TIBBETT, ZACHARY C; Dewitt HS; De Witt, AR; (1); Church Yth Grp; French Clb; Science Clb; Bus Fld.

TIBBS, VALORIE; Brookland Jr Sr HS; Brookland, AR; (3); Art Clb; FHA; Hosp Aide; Natl FFA Org; Spanish Clb; SADD; Band; Pep Band; Rptr Nwsp; Hon Roll; AR ST U; Educ.

TILGHMAN, SONYA; Lee Sr HS; Marianna, AR; (3); 28/138; Art Clb; Church Yth Grp; Science Clb; Spanish Clb; Variety Show; Cit Awd; Hon Roll; U Of AR; Nrsng.

TILL, SHARON R; Mills HS; Little Rock, AR; (2); 20/449; Girl Scts; Sec Frsh Cls; L Trk; Hon Roll; TX A&M; Vet.

TILLERY, MATTHEW E; Fountain Lake Jr Sr HS; Benton, AR; (2); FCA; Natl FFA Org; Band; Chorus; Jazz Band; Mrchg Band; Pep Band; School Musical; Ftbl; Bus.

TILLEY, JAMES; Hatfield Schl; Hatfield, AR; (3); 1/22; Sec FBLA; VP Natl Beta Clb; Sec Natl FFA Org; Capt Quiz Bowl; Ed Yrbk; VP Soph Cls; VP Jr Cls; VP Stu Cncl; Band; Score Keeper; FBLA Cmptr Applctns Dist 1st Pl 95-96, St 3rd Pl 95; FFA Frstry Tm Dist 1st Pl 95, St 2nd Pl 94; Cmptr Prgmmng.

TILLEY, JEANNIE D; Marshall HS; Marshall, AR; (4); 2/54; Pres FBLA; Rptr Natl FFA Org; Quiz Bowl; VP Sr Cls; Var Capt Sftbl; Gov Hon Prg Awd; Sal; Art Clb; Church Yth Grp; Cmnty Wkr; 1st Pl Chem Div Regnl Sci Fair; AR Biotechnology Awd; US Army Sci Awd; U Of Cntrl AR; Pre-Med.

TILLEY, RONALD E; Mountain Home HS; Mountain Home, AR; (4); German Clb; Natl FFA Org; Band; Jazz Band; Mrchg Band; Orch; Pep Band; Pres Schlr; All Regn Band; Qlfd All ST; Chem/Bio.

TILLMAN, JESSICA K; Dumas HS; Gould, AR; (3); 38/175; Church Yth Grp; Chorus; Cit Awd; Hon Roll; Lib Clb; Black Achvrs Awd; D Awd In Choir; Home Ec Awd; Book Buddy; Merit Roll; ITT Tech Inst; Comp Engr.

TILLMAN, QUELINDA; East End Jr Sr HS; Bigelow, AR; (1); Co-Capt Bsktbl; Powder Puff Ftbl; Trk; Hon Roll; BETA; UCLA; Vet.

TIMMERMAN, ANGELA S; Altus Denning HS; Altus, AR; (3); Church Yth Grp; Cmnty Wkr; Dance Clb; FBLA; Library Aide; Natl FFA Org; SADD; Chorus; Church Choir; Drill Tm.

TIMMONS, PAUL; Forrest City HS; Forrest City, AR; (3); Church Yth Grp; Mu Alpha Theta; Natl Beta Clb; Natl FFA Org; High Hon Roll; 1st Pl Spnsh Poetry Recitation FIAN Fest; Pre-Med.

TINDLE, JASON W; Russellville Sr HS; Russellville, AR; (2); Church Yth Grp; FCA; Natl Beta Clb; Pep Clb; Quiz Bowl; VICA; Band; Mrchg Band; Auto Mechanics Stu Mon April 96.

TINKLE, DWAYNE B; Jessieville HS; Hot Springs, AR; (3); 3/60; Natl Beta Clb; Church Yth Grp; FCA; FBLA; Key Clb; Quiz Bowl; Band; Bsktbl; Trk; High Hon Roll; U Of AR; Chem Engnr.

TINNELL, JACOB C; Lamar HS; London, AR; (3); FBLA; Math Clb; Natl Beta Clb; Science Clb; Hon Roll; Hnr Stdnt Awd 5 Yrs; Cmptr Sci.

TIPTON, BLAYNE H; Hazen Jr Sr HS; Hazen, AR; (4); 1/26; Am Leg Boys St; Church Yth Grp; FBLA; FTA; Natl Beta Clb; Nwsp; Yrbk; Ofcr Stu Cncl; Ofcr Bsbl; Capt Bsktbl; Stdnt Bnkng Bd; Ruth Barrett Fox Awd Schlrshp; Prncpls Awd; U Of Cntrl AR.

TIPTON, COREY A; Dierks HS; Dierks, AR; (3); Church Yth Grp; Natl FFA Org; Cossatot Vo Tech; Mechanic.

TIPTON, DYLAN D; Devalls Bluff Jr Sr HS; Biscoe, AR; (4); 2/30; Drama Clb; French Clb; FBLA; Key Clb; Natl Beta Clb; Chorus; Stage Crew; Sec Jr Cls; Rep Stu Cncl; L Bsbl; U Of AR; Phys Thrp.

TIPTON, LESLEY; Farmington Jr Sr HS; Farmington, AR; (3); Art Clb; French Clb; FBLA; Model UN; Band; Color Guard; Drill Tm; Pres Jr Cls; Hon Roll; NHS; Intl Bus Frnch.

TIPTON, TOMMY; Hartford Schl; Huntington, AR; (2); Church Yth Grp; FBLA; Natl FFA Org; Sec Frsh Cls; Treas Soph Cls; Rep Stu Cncl; Var Bsbl; JV Var Bsktbl; Var Crs Cntry; JV Var Ftbl; U Of AR.

TITUS, JENNIFER B; Smackover HS; Smackover, AR; (2); 9/56; Pres Church Yth Grp; Cmnty Wkr; FBLA; FHA; Spanish Clb; Band; Church Choir; Color Guard; Mrchg Band; Trk; Anchor Clb; Governors Yth Conf; Nurse.

TOBEY, SHERRI D; Charleston HS; Charleston, AR; (4); 7/60; FHA; Natl Beta Clb; Spanish Clb; Acpl Chr; Band; Chorus; Color Guard; Mrchg Band; Pep Band; School Musical; Cmptd/Won Many Talent Shows; Ouachita Bapt Univ; Music.

TOBIAS, ERIC M; Mountain Home HS; Mountain Home, AR; (3); Pres Drama Clb; Quiz Bowl; School Play; Ed Lit Mag; JV Bsktbl; WET Pres; SAVE Pres; FATAL Pres; ESPN 2 Outdoors Host; His Prof.

TODD, JASON L; Huntsville HS; Hindsville, AR; (2); 11/154; FCA; Natl FFA Org; Ftbl; Wt Lftg; High Hon Roll; Hon Roll; Phys Thrp.

TODD, TIFFANY D; Searcy HS; Searcy, AR; (4); Am Leg Aux Girls St; FCA; FBLA; Natl Beta Clb; Spanish Clb; Chrldng; Hon Roll; Jr NHS; NHS; Spanish NHS; Radiology.

TOKI, TAMMY; Mc Clellan HS; Mabelvale, AR; (3); Church Yth Grp; Cmnty Wkr; FBLA; Drill Tm; Lifeguard; Guid Dept Aide; Hnr Roll; Cnslr; U Of Fayetteville; Dr; Marn Bio.

TOLBERT, MELINDA R; Ozark HS; Ozark, AR; (2); Intnl Clb; Office Aide; Soc Stu Club.

TOLL, JULIE A; Devalls Bluff Jr Sr HS; De Valls Bluff, AR; (2); Church Yth Grp; 4-H; FBLA; GAA; Key Clb; Acpl Chr; Church Choir; Bsktbl; Crs Cntry; ULAR.

TOLLER, MICHAEL S; Monticello HS; Monticello, AR; (4); 49/115; Church Yth Grp; Drama Clb; FCA; FBLA; Spanish Clb; Speech Tm; Acpl Chr; Band; Chorus; Church Choir; Ouachita Bapt Univ; Music.

TOLLESON, LISA; Kirby HS; Kirby, AR; (1); 1/40; FCA; GAA; Natl Beta Clb; VP Frsh Cls; L Bsktbl; L Trk; L Wt Lftg; High Hon Roll.

TOLLESON, NIKKI; Kirby HS; Amity, AR; (2); 2/36; Debate Tm; FBLA; FHA; GAA; Natl Beta Clb; Ofcr Stu Cncl; Var Bsktbl; Var Trk; High Hon Roll; Hon Roll; Undirty Dozen; HS Heroes; Henderson ST U; Tchr.

TOLLETT, DAVID E; Nashville HS; Nashville, AR; (4); Am Leg Boys St; Church Yth Grp; Church Choir; School Play; Nwsp; Yrbk; Ftbl; Tennis; Hon Roll; NHS; Univ Of Cntrl AR; Bus.

TOLLETT, JULIE G; Dequeen HS; De Queen, AR; (1); Var Capt Bsktbl; Var Sftbl; Var Trk; Hon Roll; Amateur Ath Union; Bsktbl Congress Intnl; Coach; Tchr.

TOLLISON, STEVEN L; Westside HS; Hartman, AR; (4); 7/20; Church Yth Grp; Natl Beta Clb; Band; JV Bsbl; JV Ftbl; High Hon Roll; Prfct Atten Awd.

TOMBLIN, JOHN M; Umpire Schl; Dierks, AR; (4); 5/11; Cmnty Wkr; 4-H; Letterman Clb; Natl FFA Org; Varsity Clb; Yrbk; Treas Stu Cncl; Var Capt Bsktbl; Trk; 4-H Awd; Cossatot Univ; PE.

TOMLIN, KIMBERLY M; Greenwood Sr HS; Fort Smith, AR; (2); French Clb; FBLA; FHA; Teachers Aide; Hon Roll; Jr NHS; Washington U St Louis; Med.

TOMLIN, SAMANTHA P; El Dorado Sr HS; El Dorado, AR; (1); Church Yth Grp; Dance Clb; Var Pom Pon; Hon Roll; NHS; Anchor Club; PT.

TOMLINSON, JASON P; Mc Crory Jr Sr HS; Mc Crory, AR; (4); 15/47; Church Yth Grp; School Musical; School Play; Rptr Nwsp; Sec Frsh Cls; Sec Soph Cls; Hon Roll; Japanese Clb; Fllwshp Chrstn Stdnts; David Lipscomb Univ; Bible.

TOMLINSON, JOSH A; Clinton HS; Clinton, AR; (1); 12/107; Church Yth Grp; FBLA; Quiz Bowl; JV Stat Bsbl; Bsktbl; Ftbl; Trk; High Hon Roll; Prfct Atten Awd.

TOMLINSON, JULIE A; Springdale Sr HS; Springdale, AR; (1); Church Yth Grp; FCA; FBLA; Drill Tm; Pom Pon; Hon Roll; Jr NHS; Pres Acad Fit Awd; Sftbl; Piano; Lawyer.

TOMLINSON, LAURA N; Springdale Sr HS; Springdale, AR; (1); Church Yth Grp; Drama Clb; FCA; FBLA; Drill Tm; Pom Pon; Hon Roll; Jr NHS; Pres Acad Fit Awd; Sftbl; Piano; Law Enforcement; FBI Agent.

TOMLINSON, SARAH; Clinton HS; Clinton, AR; (2); Library Aide; Science Clb; Chrldng; High Hon Roll; Hon Roll; U Of AR; Fin.

TOMLINSON, TIMOTHY W; Jessieville HS; Hot Springs Natio, AR; (2); 24/65; Chess Clb; Church Yth Grp; FCA; Key Clb; Natl Beta Clb; Band; Jazz Band; Mrchg Band; Pep Band; Hon Roll; Harding Univ; Acctg.

TONDRO, JESSICA L; Booneville Jr Sr HS; Booneville, AR; (3); Band; Mrchg Band; Hon Roll; Swimming; ACTEENS; Beta Clb; X-Ray Technician.

TONEY, EVE N; Morrilton Sr HS; Morrilton, AR; (3); French Clb; Ofcr Sr Cls; Hon Roll; UCA; Bus.

TONEY, KATRINA; Morrilton Sr HS; Menifee, AR; (2); 1/30; Natl Beta Clb; Science Clb; Trk; Hon Roll; UAPB; RN.

TONEY, SHANIEKA; Stuttgart Sr HS; Stuttgart, AR; (4); 4-H; FHA; Girl Scts; Spanish Clb; Teachers Aide; Varsity Clb; Chorus; 4-H Awd; Sci Fair Hnrb Mntn Environmental Sci 94; UAPB; Med; Surgeon.

TONG, ALAN; Arkansas Schl Math & Science; Pine Bluff, AR; (4); FBLA; Model UN; Mu Alpha Theta; Natl Beta Clb; Capt Quiz Bowl; Cit Awd; High Hon Roll; NHS; Pres Acad Fit Awd; WA Univ At St Louis; Med.

TONG, SUSAN T; Central Sr HS; Little Rock, AR; (3); Cmnty Wkr; Mu Alpha Theta; Natl Beta Clb; Spanish Clb; Hon Roll; NHS; TX A&M; Elec Engrng.

TOOMBS, SABRINA R; Jacksonville HS; Jacksonville, AR; (4); FBLA; Natl Beta Clb; Spanish Clb; Band; Church Choir; Capt Flag Corp; Mrchg Band; Pep Band; High Hon Roll; Hon Roll; Upward Bound; Hon Miladies Brnch Spnsr Zeta Phi Beta; Dillard Univ; Cmptr Sci.

TOOMER, ROSALYND J; Dollarway HS; Pine Bluff, AR; (3); #3 in class; French Clb; Band; Church Choir; Jazz Band; Mrchg Band; Cit Awd; Jr NHS; NHS; Ntl Merit Ltr; Med.

TORKELSON, ISAAC A; Lavaca Jr Sr HS; Lavaca, AR; (2); Natl FFA Org; Office Aide; JV L Bsktbl; Var L Trk; Cit Awd; High Hon Roll; Decathlon Participent 95-96; Trk Participant 94-96; Achvmt In Bio; GATE Pgm Mem; Arch.

TORRENCE, DENISE N; Stephens Jr Sr HS; Stephens, AR; (2); 5/40; FBLA; Church Choir; VP Soph Cls; Ofcr Stu Cncl; Bsktbl; Hon Roll; Prin Awd; Stu Of Month; U Of AR Conway; Bus Mgmt.

TORRENCE, LA'SHAWNDA T; Stephens Jr Sr HS; Stephens, AR; (2); Church Yth Grp; 4-H; FBLA; Band; Chorus; Church Choir; Score Keeper; Cit Awd; Hon Roll; Prin Awd; Nurse.

TORRENCE, WILLIAM; Dermott HS; Dermott, AR; (4); 3/63; Computer Clb; DECA; FCA; FBLA; Science Clb; VP Sr Cls; Hon Roll; NHS; Ntl Merit SF; Pres Acad Fit Awd; U Of AR At Pine Bluff; Bus.

TORRES, JASON D; Bauxite Jr Sr HS; Bauxite, AR; (3); 9/75; Am Leg Boys St; Church Yth Grp; Debate Tm; FBLA; Intnl Clb; JA; Quiz Bowl; Spanish Clb; Teachers Aide; Church Choir.

TORRES, STEPHANIE E; Arkansas Sr HS; Texarkana, AR; (4); Art Clb; Drama Clb; FBLA; Spanish Clb; School Musical; School Play; TEXARKANA Coll.

TOSTON, STEVEN; Dermott HS; Dermott, AR; (4); 12/56; FBLA; FTA; VP Math Clb; Natl Beta Clb; Science Clb; Pres Soph Cls; Pres Sr Cls; Ofcr Stu Cncl; Hon Roll; Pres Acad Fit Awd; U Of AR; Elec Engr.

TOTTY, MICHAEL; East Poinsett Sr HS; Marked Tree, AR; (4); FHA; Natl FFA Org; Quiz Bowl; VP Stu Cncl; Var L Bsktbl; Var L Ftbl; Hon Roll; NHS; 3 A S All-Conf Bsktbl 94-95 & 95-96; 3 A S All-Conf Ftbl 95-96; U Of Cntrl AR; Elctrncs.

TOULSON, CHRISTOPHER M; Pulaski Acad; Little Rock, AR; (2); German Clb; Letterman Clb; Natl Beta Clb; School Play; Stage Crew; Lit Mag; Bsktbl; Ftbl; Trk; Cit Awd; Kineseology.

TOWNSEND, BRIAN; Spring Hill HS; Hope, AR; (3); Am Leg Boys St; 4-H; French Clb; FBLA; VP Natl Beta Clb; Quiz Bowl; SADD; Treas Jr Cls; L Bsktbl; Hon Roll; U Of AR-FAYETTEVILLE; Bus Mgmt.

TOWNSEND, CHRIS E; Springdale Sr HS; Springdale, AR; (3); Boy Scts; Cmnty Wkr; Teachers Aide; Hon Roll; Univ Of AR Fayetteville.

TOWNSEND, DUSTY D; Arkansas Sr HS; Texarkana, AR; (2); Church Yth Grp; Natl FFA Org; ROTC; Chorus; Church Choir; Crs Cntry; Trk; Hon Roll; Sthrn AR U.

TOWNSEND, LILAH S; Searcy HS; Searcy, AR; (3); Church Yth Grp; FTA; Natl Beta Clb; Spanish Clb; Hon Roll; Jr NHS; NHS; Spanish NHS.

TOWNSEND, MICHAEL B; Spring Hill HS; Hope, AR; (3); Am Leg Boys St; French Clb; FBLA; Natl Beta Clb; Quiz Bowl; SADD; Treas Jr Cls; L Bsktbl; Hon Roll; Natl Eng Mrt Awd; U Of AR Fayetteville; Bus Mgmt.

TOWNSEND, RAVEN N; Arkansas Sr HS; Texarkana, AR; (2); Sec Spanish Clb; Drill Tm; Shoat Rvltn; Vet.

TOWNSEND, TERRI T; Robinson HS; Little Rock, AR; (2); Art Clb; Church Yth Grp; Cmnty Wkr; FBLA; FHA; FTA; Women & Children Recovery Ctr U Of AR Med Sci Vol.

TOWNSON, MONTY W; Rivercrest HS; Dyess, AR; (2); ROTC; VICA; Hon Roll; Jr NHS; NHS; Pres Acad Fit Awd; Mltry Ord Wrld Wars/Awd Merit; RIFLE Tm; AR ST Univ; Cmptr Engr.

TRACY, BEN W; Dewitt HS; De Witt, AR; (1); Church Yth Grp; FCA; French Clb; Science Clb; JV Bsktbl; JV Ftbl; JV Trk; Pride Clb; Ltrd Bsktbl/Ftbl/Track; Med.

TRACY, NICOLE A; Nashville HS; Nashville, AR; (3); Boy Scts; Church Yth Grp; Library Aide; Quiz Bowl; Spanish Clb; Band; Ed Nwsp; Yrbk; Hon Roll; Pres Acad Fit Awd.

TRAIL, STACIE R; Southside HS; Batesville, AR; (1); Church Yth Grp; Science Clb; Hon Roll; Optometrist.

TRAMBLE, NICOLE S; Rivercrest HS; Wilson, AR; (2); French Clb; ROTC; Band; Church Choir; Color Guard; Drill Tm; Mrchg Band; Hon Roll; TAD.

TRAMEL, LESLEY A; Brookland Jr Sr HS; Jonesboro, AR; (3); FHA; Natl FFA Org; Cit Awd; AR ST; Crmnlgy.

TRAMMEL, CHANDRA E; Springdale Sr HS; Springdale, AR; (3); Church Yth Grp; Sec FBLA; Q&S; Yrbk; Hon Roll; Jr NHS; NHS; All Amer Schlrs; Chamber Of Commerce Awd; US Achvmt Acad; UA; Bus Field.

TRAMMEL, MISTI M; Elkins Jr Sr HS; Fayetteville, AR; (2); 6/70; FBLA; FHA; SADD; Band; Chorus; Church Choir; Mrchg Band; Hon Roll; AR Schl Of Math & Sci Acceptance; Media Clb, VP; Mock Trial; Pre-Med.

TRAMMELL, DENA F; Timbo Schl; Mountain View, AR; (1); 1/27; Church Yth Grp; Cmnty Wkr; FHA; Sec Natl Beta Clb; Rep Frsh Cls; French Hon Soc; Hon Roll; Prof Dance Group Mem; 2nd In Zone For Optimist Oratorical Cmptn 1st Pl Local; Attorney.

TRAMMELL, LAYNE L; Timbo Schl; Timbo, AR; (1); 3/29; FBLA; Natl Beta Clb; Ofcr Frsh Cls; Bsktbl; Sftbl; Trk; Hon Roll; ASU; Elem Tchr.

TRAN, HIEN D; Southside HS; Fort Smith, AR; (3); Church Yth Grp; FCA; Spanish Clb; Teachers Aide; Church Choir; Ftbl; Trk; Hon Roll; Jr NHS; NHS; Sail Crw; Cultural Ambssdr; U Of AR; Med Fld.

TRAN, HUNG Q; El Dorado Sr HS; El Dorado, AR; (3); 58/314; FBLA; Key Clb; Natl Beta Clb; Thesps; JV Bsbl; Var Swmmng; Hon Roll; U Of AR; Psych.

TRAN, LINDA; John L Mcclellan Magnet HS; Little Rock, AR; (4); 1/246; Am Leg Aux Girls St; Cmnty Wkr; Debate Tm; Drama Clb; FBLA; VP Key Clb; Mu Alpha Theta; Capt Quiz Bowl; Treas Spanish Clb; School Musical; Yth & Govt Clb Pres; Peer Helpers Advy Cncl Historian; WA U.

TRAN, MARY; Southside HS; Fort Smith, AR; (2); School Play; High Hon Roll; Hon Roll; Prfct Atten Awd; Natl Engl Mrt Awd; Pharmacy.

TRAN, ROBERT V; Russellville Sr HS; Russellville, AR; (4); Spanish Clb; Treas Sr Cls; Var Bsktbl; JV Var Golf; Prfct Atten Awd; Mst Tlntd; All Stars; AR Tech U; Acctng.

TRAPP, BETH; Marked Tree Jr Sr HS; Trumann, AR; (2); Natl Beta Clb; Band; Chorus; Mrchg Band; Sftbl; High Hon Roll; Hon Roll; Amer Mscl Fnd Band Hnrs Outstdng Mscl Tlnt; Sr Band Most Imprvd Prcssn; Sftbl; AR ST U.

TRAVIS, HEATHER; Brookland Jr Sr HS; Paragould, AR; (2); Church Yth Grp; Drama Clb; FBLA; Natl Beta Clb; Spanish Clb; Chorus; School Play; Rep Soph Cls; High Hon Roll; Sr All Reg Chr; All St Chr; FBLA Dist 4th; AR St Univ; Chr Music.

TRAVIS, PATRICK M; Yellville Summit HS; Yellville, AR; (3); Library Aide; Quiz Bowl; High Hon Roll; Hon Roll; Prfct Atten Awd; Hnrs Engl Awd; Stdnt Of Mnth; Jesus.

TRAVIS, SUSANNA; Ft Smith Christian Schl; Fort Smith, AR; (2); Church Yth Grp; FCA; Band; Mrchg Band; Sec Frsh Cls; Sec Soph Cls; JV Bsktbl; Var Trk; High Hon Roll; NHS; Scndry Ed.

TRAW, PERRY J; Cave City HS; Batesville, AR; (2); Band; Stat Bsbl; Mgr(s); Hon Roll; Radio & TV Broadcasting; Law; Lawyer.

TRAYLOR, CAROL E; Mansfield Jr Sr HS; Hartford, AR; (3); Art Clb; FCA; FBLA; Intnl Clb; Nwsp; Bsktbl; Cit Awd; Hon Roll; Prfct Atten Awd; Westark Univ; RN.

TRAYWEEK, JIMMY L; Gosnell Jr Sr HS; Gosnell, AR; (2); Church Yth Grp; FCA; Teachers Aide; Chorus; Ftbl.

TREADWAY, RYAN G; Hartford Schl; Hartford, AR; (2); Treas FBLA; Natl FFA Org; Teachers Aide; Pres Frsh Cls; Ofcr Soph Cls; Var L Bsktbl; Var L Crs Cntry; Capt L Ftbl; Var L Trk; Hon Roll; All Dist Ftbl & Trk; Gftd & Tlntd Cls; UCLA.

TREASTER, AIMEE D; Hot Springs HS; Hot Springs, AR; (3); 4/159; Church Yth Grp; Hosp Aide; Mu Alpha Theta; Spanish Clb; Chorus; School Play; Rptr Nwsp; High Hon Roll; Hon Roll; NHS; Future Problem Slvng; Bowling; Cert Acad Achvmnt 3 Yrs; Univ Of Cntrl AR; PT.

TREAT, SARA; Central Ark Christian Schl; North Little Rock, AR; (2); Church Yth Grp; French Clb; Chorus; Rep Frsh Cls; Sec Bsbl; Crs Cntry; Trk; Vllybl; High Hon Roll; Jr NHS; All-Rgn Chorus; Hist Clb; Harding U; Med.

TREECE, CHRISTA; Marion HS; Marion, AR; (1); Art Clb; Church Yth Grp; English Clb; Math Clb; Science Clb; Chorus; Church Choir; Ofcr Frsh Cls; Ofcr Stu Cncl; Chrldng; Voice; Piano.

TREECE, HANNAH; Midland HS; Batesville, AR; (3); Pres VP 4-H; Pres FHA; HOBY; Natl Beta Clb; Ofcr Stu Cncl; Bsktbl; Trk; DAR Awd; St 4-H Rcrd Bk Wnnr.

TREECE, JASON; Sylvan Hills HS; Sherwood, AR; (2); 24/350; FCA; Mu Alpha Theta; Natl Beta Clb; Spanish Clb; Acpl Chr; Ofcr Bsbl; Ftbl; Hon Roll; Jr NHS; NHS; All Region Choir 10th Grd; Natl Yth Ldrshp Forum On Law-Constitution.

TREMAINE, MICHAEL A; Conway Sr HS; Conway, AR; (1); Church Yth Grp.

TREMBLY, KYLE L; Gravette HS; Sulphur Springs, AR; (4); 6/57; Am Leg Boys St; FBLA; Quiz Bowl; Teachers Aide; Stage Crew; Rep Stu Cncl; Co-Capt Var Bsktbl; Cit Awd; Hon Roll; NHS; N E OK A&M; Sprts Med.

TRICE, CICELY; Pine Bluff HS; Pine Bluff, AR; (4); 80/410; Pres Art Clb; Pres DECA; Hist French Clb; Model UN; Chorus; Cit Awd; Hon Roll; Ntl Merit Ltr; Navy Hnrs Pgm; Distngd Achvmt Awd Delta Sigma Theta; Pine Bluff Yth Cncl Outstdng Yth Awd Acads & Art; UALR; Advertsng; Graphic Design.

TRIMBLE, NICOSIA; Nashville HS; Nashville, AR; (4); Am Leg Aux Girls St; FHA; Var Bsktbl; Var Trk; Hon Roll; NHS; Girls St Surveyor; ESL Vol; Family Life Ctr Tutor; U Of Cntrl AR; Phy Thrpst.

TRIMBLE, RYAN; North Little Rock Hs-West; North Little Rock, AR; (4); FCA; Key Clb; VICA; School Play; Stage Crew; JV Bsktbl; Var Chrldng; Var Ftbl; Powder Puff Ftbl; Hon Roll; NCA Staff Instr; All-Star HS Chrldr AR; U Of Cntrl AR; Engrng.

TRIMMER, FELINA S; Rogers HS; Lowell, AR; (2); JV Bsktbl; High Hon Roll; FFA; U Of AR; Dentist.

TRITCH, BRETT A; Ridgecrest HS; Paragould, AR; (3); Church Yth Grp; Natl Beta Clb; Pres Soph Cls; Var L Bsbl; Var L Bsktbl; Var L Ftbl; Cit Awd; High Hon Roll; Hon Roll.

TROTTER, LEANNE M; Southside HS; Fort Smith, AR; (3); 79/502; Church Yth Grp; FCA; Mu Alpha Theta; Service Clb; Chorus; Hon Roll; NHS; SAIL Crew; All-Region Choir; Pre-Med.

TROTTER II, STEVEN; Arkansas Schl Math & Science; Hot Springs Natio, AR; (3); Art Clb; Boy Scts; Church Yth Grp; Cmnty Wkr; Computer Clb; FBLA; JA; Library Aide; Natl Beta Clb; Spanish Clb; Virologist.

TROUTMAN, KATRENNA; Nettleton HS; Jonesboro, AR; (4); 28/124; Church Yth Grp; FBLA; Rep Math Clb; Natl Beta Clb; Office Aide; Pep Clb; Sec Spanish Clb; Teachers Aide; Chorus; Church Choir; PRIDE Membr Sec; Stu Who Care; AR St Univ.

TRUESDALE, MARTY L; Lake Hamilton Sr HS; Bonnerdale, AR; (2); 4/26; Stat Bsktbl; UALR; Bus.

TRUONG, DUYEN; John L Mcclellan Magnet HS; Little Rock, AR; (4); 3/255; VP French Clb; Sec FBLA; Treas Mu Alpha Theta; Office Aide; Co-Capt Quiz Bowl; Chrmn Service Clb; Thesps; School Musical; School Play; Stage Crew; U Of TX Austin; Engrng.

TRUSTY, JEFFREY D; Russellville Sr HS; Russellville, AR; (2); 1/350; Church Yth Grp; Band; Mrchg Band; Pep Band; VP Frsh Cls; Bsktbl; Crs Cntry; Trk; Hon Roll; High Hon Roll; Engrng-Civil.

TU, HANNAH; Southside HS; Fort Smith, AR; (2); French Clb; FBLA; Key Clb; Mu Alpha Theta; Quiz Bowl; Mgr Nwsp; Jr NHS; NHS; Pres Acad Fit Awd; Hosp Aide; SAIL Club; Soph Cncl.

TUCKEN, LISA M; Fairview HS; Camden, AR; (3); 1/296; Pres Church Yth Grp; Drama Clb; Pres 4-H; Pres Natl FFA Org; SADD; NHS; Spanish NHS; Natl Beta Clb; Pep Clb; Science Clb; 2nd In AR For FFA Prepared Pub Speaking; AR Yth Suicide Preventin Cmssn; CPYF Of AR Vice Moderatr; Ouachita Bapt Univ; Psych.

TUCKER, AMY E; Bay Jr Sr HS; Bay, AR; (4); 8/22; FBLA; FHA; Natl FFA Org; Science Clb; Teachers Aide; Nwsp; Sec Treas Frsh Cls; Sec Treas Soph Cls; Hon Roll; Campus Qn Contestant; ASU; Criminology.

TUCKER, ANGELA; Gentry HS; Gentry, AR; (4); 1/80; Am Leg Aux Girls St; FCA; FBLA; Key Clb; Bsktbl; Chrldng; Trk; NHS; Pres Acad Fit Awd; Val; SW Baptist Univ; Phys Thpy.

TUCKER, ANNA M; Gravette HS; Gravette, AR; (4); 7/56; FBLA; Treas FHA; Nwsp; Yrbk; Treas Soph Cls; Capt Chrldng; Hon Roll; NHS; All Amer Schlr; U AR; Bus.

TUCKER, ASHLEY; Pulaski Acad; Little Rock, AR; (4); Church Yth Grp; Drama Clb; FCA; GAA; HOBY; Library Aide; Pep Clb; Spanish Clb; Teachers Aide; Chorus; Little Rock All Star Dance Tm; Pres Just Say No; Pres Y Teens; U Of AR Fayetteville; Bus Admi.

TUCKER, BRYAN; Clay Co Central Jr Sr HS; Rector, AR; (3); 1/80; High Hon Roll; Hon Roll; Jr NHS; NHS; Pres Acad Fit Awd.

TUCKER, DOTTIE; Beebe Sr HS; El Paso, AR; (3); Drama Clb; FBLA; FHA; Natl Beta Clb; Spanish Clb; Treas Chorus; School Musical; Ed Nwsp; Var Chrldng; Var Vllybl; Var Msct; UCA; Comm Art.

TUCKER, EVERETT C; Central Sr HS; Little Rock, AR; (1); French Clb; Natl Beta Clb; Quiz Bowl; Bsktbl; Ftbl; Golf; High Hon Roll; Jr NHS; Pres Acad Fit Awd; Pres Schlr; Most Likly To Succeed/Schlstc/Otstndng Stdnt.

TUCKER, GWEN; Jasper HS; Jasper, AR; (4); Cmnty Wkr; Sec FBLA; VP FHA; Natl Beta Clb; Yrbk; Sftbl; High Hon Roll; Art Clb; Math Clb; Natl FFA Org; North AR CC; Elem Ed.

TUCKER, KIM D; Junction City HS; Junction City, AR; (3); Cmnty Wkr; Science Clb; Band; Mrchg Band; Yrbk; Rep Stu Cncl; U Of AR; Occptnl Therapy.

TUCKER, MICHELE; Searcy HS; Searcy, AR; (3); 27/286; French Clb; Rep VP FBLA; FHA; Hosp Aide; Natl Beta Clb; SADD; French Hon Soc; Hon Roll; Jr NHS; NHS; Yth To Yth.

TUCKER, SUSAN; Dumas HS; Dumas, AR; (2); 13/179; Girl Scts; Quiz Bowl; Band; Church Choir; Jazz Band; Mrchg Band; School Play; Variety Show; Hon Roll; NHS; Lyon Col; Arts.

TUCKFIELD, K MELISSA; Russellville Sr HS; Russellville, AR; (2); Church Yth Grp; Band; Chorus; Church Choir; Mrchg Band; Cit Awd; High Hon Roll; Jr NHS; NHS; CSU; Nrsng.

TUELL, RACHEL; Leslie Schl; Leslie, AR; (1); 1/35; Church Yth Grp; FHA; Hosp Aide; Band; Church Choir; School Play; Cit Awd; High Hon Roll; Prfct Atten Awd; Pres Schlr; Vol Nursing Ctr 95; Hendrix Coll Conway; Med.

TULL, APRIL D; Bauxite Jr Sr HS; Benton, AR; (4); 2/43; Am Leg Aux Girls St; FBLA; Red Cross Aide; Spanish Clb; Treas SADD; Co-Capt Drill Tm; VP Sr Cls; Pres Stu Cncl; L Bsktbl; NHS; U Of Cntrl AR; Acctng.

TULLIS, AMY; Hope HS; Hope, AR; (3); 1/230; Church Yth Grp; FBLA; Natl Beta Clb; Rep Stu Cncl; Var Chrldng; Var Tennis; High Hon Roll; NHS; NIKE; Grls St; UCA; Ortho.

TULLOS, MERLE A; Star City HS; Star City, AR; (3); Church Yth Grp; Mu Alpha Theta; Natl FFA Org; Quiz Bowl; Spanish Clb; Yrbk; Var L Bsbl; Cit Awd; Hon Roll; NHS; U Of AR; Ag Bus.

TULLOS, STEPHANIE N; Central Ark Christian Schl; North Little Rock, AR; (2); Church Yth Grp; Cmnty Wkr; Debate Tm; Drama Clb; English Clb; FCA; FBLA; Hosp Aide; Natl Beta Clb; Office Aide; Hrsbck Rdng; SMU; Comm/Tlvsn Anchr.

TUNNER, ALESIA L; Cave City HS; Sulphur Rock, AR; (2); Church Yth Grp; French Clb; Phtg FBLA; FHA; Key Clb; Math Clb; Science Clb; Bsktbl; Sftbl; Hon Roll; FHA AR STAR Evnts Natl Slvr Mdl Wnnr; AR Star Evnts ST Gold Mdl Wnnr.

TURBERVILLE, CEDRIE C; Parkin Jr Sr HS; Parkin, AR; (3); 8/30; Art Clb; Cmnty Wkr; FHA; Band; Church Choir; Ofcr Bsbl; Bsktbl; Chrldng; Ftbl; Mgr(s); Bsktbl; Track; Citizen Awd; Hnrs Soc; FHA; AR ST; Comm/Bus/Cmptr Tech.

TURLEY, LESLIE; Murfreesboro HS; Murfreesboro, AR; (4); FBLA; FHA; Natl Beta Clb; School Play; Rep Stu Cncl; L Bsktbl; JV Chrldng; High Hon Roll; Hon Roll; NHS; FHA Prlmntry Procdrs Won St & Natnls; U Central AR; Med.

TURNAGE, CHRIS; Central Ark Christian Schl; Little Rock, AR; (4); 16/80; Mu Alpha Theta; Acpl Chr; School Musical; School Play; Treas Stu Cncl; L Var Bsbl; JV L Bsktbl; Var L Ftbl; Var L Trk; NHS; Chsn Sing Carnegie Hall; Ouachita Bapt U; Pre Med/Bus.

TURNEG, AMANDA; Russellville Sr HS; Russellville, AR; (3); Church Yth Grp; FHA; Natl Beta Clb; SADD; Band; Church Choir; Mrchg Band; HOSA; Dentist; Pharmacist.

TURNER, ADRIENNE L; Russellville Sr HS; Russellville, AR; (3); Church Yth Grp; Hosp Aide; Office Aide; Teachers Aide; Band; Chorus; Church Choir; Drm Mjr(t); Mrchg Band; Pep Band; Music Ministry.

TURNER, ANTHONY G; Bradford Jr Sr HS; Bradford, AR; (2); Art Clb; Boy Scts; French Clb; Math Clb; Natl Beta Clb; Natl FFA Org; Quiz Bowl; Band; JV Var Bsbl; JV Bsktbl.

TURNER, ANTHONY R; Midland HS; Pleasant Plains, AR; (2); 1/60; Church Yth Grp; FBLA; HOBY; Natl Beta Clb; Quiz Bowl; Mgr Yrbk; Ofcr Stu Cncl; Mgr(s); High Hon Roll; Cmnty Wkr; Ftr Prblm Slvng; Church Camp Cnslr; Nrthrn AR 1st Alt HOBY Ldrshp Conf; U Of AR; Emerg Med Dctr.

TURNER, ASHLEY J; Piggott HS; Greenway, AR; (4); 37/100; Art Clb; Drama Clb; 4-H; French Clb; FBLA; Girl Scts; Natl FFA Org; Band; School Play; Stage Crew; AR ST U; Phys Thrp.

TURNER, BRANDY L; Lincoln HS; Lincoln, AR; (1); Natl FFA Org; Drill Tm; Hon Roll.

TURNER, BREANNE L; Pea Ridge HS; Pea Ridge, AR; (3); 14/50; Church Yth Grp; FHA; Rptr Natl FFA Org; Spanish Clb; Yrbk; VP Frsh Cls; VP Soph Cls; VP Jr Cls; Capt Chrldng; Hon Roll; Bus.

TURNER, CHERESE L; Lavaca Jr Sr HS; Lavaca, AR; (2); 3/75; Church Yth Grp; Natl Beta Clb; Quiz Bowl; Band; Church Choir; Mrchg Band; Pres Soph Cls; High Hon Roll; NHS; Odyssey Of Mind; Gftd & Tlntd; AR Coll; Tchng.

TURNER, CHRIS W; Russellville Sr HS; Russellville, AR; (2); Art Clb; Computer Clb; Natl Beta Clb; Acpl Chr; Chorus; Prfct Atten Awd; Library-Media Clb; All Region Choir; PLA; Chem.

TURNER, CHRISTOPHER L; Lockesburg Jr Sr HS; Lockesburg, AR; (3); Am Leg Boys St; Church Yth Grp; Spanish Clb; Church Choir; Rptr Nwsp; Sprt Ed Yrbk; L Bsktbl; Golf; Jr NHS; AR Press Wmns Assn HS Comm Cntst Wnr; 3 Yr Wnnr All AR Awd Outstdnt Yrbk; U Of Cntrl AZ; PT.

TURNER, DAWN M; Northside HS; Fort Smith, AR; (4); 33/360; Pres French Clb; Sec Soph Cls; Ofcr Jr Cls; Ofcr Sr Cls; JV Bsktbl; JV Capt Chrldng; Pom Pon; 4-H; Ft Smith Ldrshp Explorer Cncl; AR Actvts Assn Schlr Athl 95-96; U TN Chattanooga; Med.

TURNER, HOPE N; Lake Hamilton Sr HS; Royal, AR; (3); Church Yth Grp; FCA; Latin Clb; Spanish Clb; Band; Mrchg Band; Var Bsktbl; Var Trk; Var Vllybl; NHS.

TURNER, JEFF G; Hope HS; Hope, AR; (3); French Clb; Key Clb; Natl Beta Clb; Rptr Nwsp; Rptr Yrbk; Rep Frsh Cls; L Golf; Hon Roll; Univ Cntrl AR Conway; Law.

TURNER, JOY E; Russellville Sr HS; Russellville, AR; (2); Church Yth Grp; Dance Clb; FCA; French Clb; GAA; Red Cross Aide; Drill Tm; Pres Stu Cncl; Var Bsktbl; Var Chrldng; Ldr Of Chrstn Stu Union; Cmptn Chrldr; Top Gun Dancer At NCA Camp; Southern Meth U; Sci.

TURŃER, KATRINA; Pea Ridge HS; Garfield, AR; (3); 1/60; Church Yth Grp; FBLA; Math Clb; Spanish Clb; Yrbk; Treas Jr Cls; High Hon Roll; NHS; Pres Acad Fit Awd; Elec Engr.

TURNER, KERRI; Wynne HS; Wynne, AR; (2); Church Yth Grp; Sec Drama Clb; FBLA; FTA; Church Choir; School Musical; Ofcr Stu Cncl; Chrldng; NHS; Spanish NHS; 2nd VP Of Jr Progressive Clb.

TURNER, LANITA L; Cabot HS; Cabot, AR; (4); 39/298; French Clb; NFL; Church Choir; School Musical; School Play; Stage Crew; Variety Show; Kiwanis Awd; Pres Acad Fit Awd; Spanish NHS; Cmmnty Thtr Mscls; 2nd Pl ST Natl Span Exam; U Of MS; Thtr Arts/Actrs.

TURNER, LEAH N; Dierks HS; Newhope, AR; (2); Art Clb; FHA; Co-Ed Yrbk; 4-H Awd; U Of AR; Pre-Med.

TURNER, OLIVIA; Lake Hamilton Sr HS; Royal, AR; (1); Church Yth Grp; FCA; FBLA; Chrldng; Gym; Trk; Hon Roll.

TURNER, RAHELE D; J A Fair Sr HS; Little Rock, AR; (4); 7/300; Church Yth Grp; FBLA; Quiz Bowl; VICA; High Hon Roll; Hon Roll; NHS; Sec Frsh Cls; JV Bsktbl; JV Chrldng; 1st Plce Physcs Adv Mech Drfting; Natl Air Frce Recrtng Svc Awd Math Sci; Stu Of Yr Comp Aided Drfting; Pulaski Tech Arch Drftng; Arch.

TURNER, ROBERT D; Black Rock Jr Sr HS; Portia, AR; (2); Acpl Chr; Yrbk; GFTD & Tlntd Cls; Studio Engrng.

TURNER, TABITHA; East Poinsett Sr HS; Lepanto, AR; (4); 5/60; FBLA; FHA; Library Aide; Natl FFA Org; Tennis; Hon Roll; Jr NHS; NHS; U Of Cntrl AR; Pre-Vet.

TURNER, TAMI; Sheridan Sr HS; Sheridan, AR; (4); 42/212; Church Yth Grp; Cmnty Wkr; ROTC; VP Service Clb; Color Guard; Drill Tm; Flag Corp; Co-Ed Ed Yrbk; Hon Roll; Jr NHS; Yng Rpblcns; Natl Lib Ptry Pms Pub; U Of Cntrl AR; Psych.

TURNER, TAUDRA J; Rivercrest HS; Bassett, AR; (3); French Clb; FBLA; FHA; FTA; Key Clb; Math Clb; Science Clb; SADD; Band; Chorus; Career Awd; Art Awd; UCLA; Comp.

TURNER, THOMAS S; Hamburg HS; Crossett, AR; (4); 6/111; Church Yth Grp; Natl FFA Org; Spanish Clb; Chorus; High Hon Roll; Jr NHS; NHS; ABC Bowling League; YABA Bowling League; Two Time Tm USA Bowling Finalist; U Of AR Monticello; Pre Med.

TURNER, TROY E; Barton HS; Lexa, AR; (3); Art Clb; Natl Beta Clb; Spanish Clb; VP Frsh Cls; Pres Soph Cls; L Bsbl; L Bsktbl; L Ftbl; L Trk; ASU.

TURNER, VALERIE; Mountain View Jr Sr HS; Pleasant Grove, AR; (4); 10/86; Church Yth Grp; Library Aide; Natl Beta Clb; Spanish Clb; Teachers Aide; Church Choir; High Hon Roll; Lyon Coll; Eng Ed.

TURNEY, CHRISTY M; Lonoke Jr HS; Jacksonville, AR; (1); FHA; Office Aide; Science Clb; 2nd Pl Schl Art Cont; Schl Fund Raisers.

TURPEN, COURTNEY D; Marked Tree Jr Sr HS; Marked Tree, AR; (3); 3/65; FBLA; FHA; Sec Natl Beta Clb; Spanish Clb; Yrbk; Sec Frsh Cls; Rep Stu Cncl; Co-Capt Chrldng; Sec NHS; I Dare You Awd; AR St Univ.

TURRENTINE, JOHN D; Searcy HS; Searcy, AR; (2); Natl Beta Clb; Spanish Clb; Ftbl; Socr; Hon Roll.

TWILLEY, DIONNE; Murfreesboro HS; Murfreesboro, AR; (2); Art Clb; Bus Profs of Am; Church Yth Grp; FBLA; FHA; Natl Beta Clb; Pep Clb; Quiz Bowl; Science Clb; Spanish Clb; Pres Ed Awds Educl Excl Gmtry/Span I/Engl/Cmptr Tech; Envrnmntlist.

TWILLIE, MELINDA C; Mills HS; Little Rock, AR; (2); FCA; FHA; Latin Clb; Natl Beta Clb; Q&S; Quiz Bowl; Spanish Clb; Chorus; Nwsp; Jr NHS; Ethics Awd Sherwood Rotary Clb; 2nd Soprano, 1st Chair All Rgn; 1st Prz Zoology Mills Sci Fair; Rhodes Coll; Law.

TYLER, JASON; Sacred Heart Schl; Morrilton, AR; (3); 1/14; HOBY; Pres Key Clb; Library Aide; Natl Beta Clb; Capt Quiz Bowl; Yrbk; Pres Frsh Cls; Mgr Mgr(s); High Hon Roll; Altar Srvr; CYM VP.

TYLER, KIM; Sacred Heart Schl; Morrilton, AR; (1); 1/19; Church Yth Grp; Cmnty Wkr; Key Clb; Natl Beta Clb; SADD; Teachers Aide; Variety Show; Sec Frsh Cls; Var Bsktbl; High Hon Roll; Med.

TYLER, SARAH L; Quitman Jr Sr HS; Quitman, AR; (3); FBLA; FHA; Speech Tm; Nwsp; Ofcr Stu Cncl; Cit Awd; High Hon Roll; Hon Roll; UCA; Comp Prgmr.

TYNER, MIKE F; Cty Line HS; Charleston, AR; (3); 6/39; FBLA; FHA; Natl Beta Clb; Spanish Clb; Chorus; Rptr Nwsp; Hon Roll; Eng Ed.

TYREE, KRISTI L; Augusta HS; Augusta, AR; (1); Art Clb; Church Yth Grp; Sec Natl Beta Clb; Science Clb; Spanish Clb; Church Choir; High Hon Roll; Rives Dance Studio Dancer; Conf Cncl On Yth Ministries 1 Yr Rep; Dist Cncl On Yth Ministries 1 Yr Rep; Hygenist.

TYREE, MARY M; Bauxite Jr Sr HS; Bauxite, AR; (2); FBLA; Spanish Clb; Drill Tm; Var JV Bsktbl; Score Keeper; Sftbl; Trk; Hon Roll; Jr NHS; Law.

TYRONE, KILBY N; Russellville Sr HS; Russellville, AR; (2); GAA; Office Aide; Spanish Clb; Mrchg Band; Orch; Pep Band; L Swmmng; High Hon Roll; NHS; Elem Ed.

ULREY, BRIAN; Arkansas Schl Math & Science; Flippin, AR; (3); Church Yth Grp; Cmnty Wkr; FBLA; German Clb; Library Aide; Mu Alpha Theta; Quiz Bowl; Science Clb; SADD; Teachers Aide; NHS; Wash Univ St Louis.

UMERAH, CATHERINE U; Parkview Arts-Science HS; North Little Rock, AR; (2); Art Clb; Church Yth Grp; Intnl Clb; Natl Beta Clb; Spanish Clb; Band; Church Choir; Mrchg Band; School Musical; Hon Roll; Div I All ST Reg Bnd; Parkview Dstngshd Ladies Clb; Parkview Gospel Choir Ensmbl; Loyola; Info Mktg Spclst.

UMPHRESS, MEGAN A; Conway Sr HS; Conway, AR; (3); FBLA; Natl Beta Clb; Var L Tennis; Cit Awd; Hon Roll; Spanish NHS; K-Life Ministies; US Tennis Assn Ranked In Girls 18s Sngls/Dbls.

UNDERWOOD, AMANDA; East End Jr Sr HS; Houston, AR; (1); Church Yth Grp; FBLA; Natl Beta Clb; SADD; Yrbk; Sec Frsh Cls; Chrldng; Gym; Sftbl; Hon Roll; Hmcmng Qn; U Of AR Fayetteville; Bus.

UNDERWOOD, KERRI L; Arkansas Sr HS; Texarkana, AR; (4); Church Yth Grp; Hosp Aide; Office Aide; Spanish Clb; Drill Tm; Rep Stu Cncl; NIKE; Hlth; Yng Democratics; Teenage Rpblcns; U Of Cntrl AR; Bus Mrktng.

UNDERWOOD, ZACHARY; Charleston HS; Charleston, AR; (1); Church Yth Grp; Band; Mrchg Band; Pep Band; Ofcr Bsbl; Bsktbl; Hon Roll; Acctng.

UPCHRUCH, ASHLEY B; Arkansas Sr HS; Texarkana, AR; (3); 1/300; Art Clb; Cmnty Wkr; Math Clb; Mu Alpha Theta; Quiz Bowl; Drill Tm; Pres Stu Cncl; Chrldng; Pres NHS; Med.

UPTERGROVE, REBECCA J; Lake Hamilton Sr HS; Hot Springs Natio, AR; (3); Church Yth Grp; Office Aide; Spanish Clb; Chorus; School Play; PRIDE; Choir Lib; Yth Theatre Group; Lawyer.

UPTON, JASON; Rogers HS; Rogers, AR; (4); Am Leg Boys St; Letterman Clb; Rptr Nwsp; Sprt Ed Yrbk; Var L Ftbl; Wt Lftg; Hon Roll; Frgn Lang Club; U Of AR; PE.

URBANEK, JOEY; Mountain Home HS; Mountain Home, AR; (4); 22/227; FCA; Key Clb; Natl Beta Clb; Var Bsbl; Var Ftbl; Wt Lftg; Hon Roll; Bsbl Al ST/ALL Conf/All Star; Ftbl All ST/ALL Dist; AR Schlr Ath; AR Tech; Eng.

UREN, ADRIANNE; Nemo Vista Jr Sr HS; Springfield, AR; (4); 2/30; Am Leg Aux Girls St; Pres VP FBLA; VP Natl Beta Clb; Natl FFA Org; Treas Spanish Clb; Band; Yrbk; Var Score Keeper; Hon Roll; Sal; Attnded 1st Wrld Yth Summit; U Of AR At Fayetteville; Psych.

UREN, DREW W; Nemo Vista Jr Sr HS; Springfield, AR; (2); Spanish Clb; JV Bsbl; Hon Roll; Pres Acad Fit Awd.

USDROWSKI, SARAH; Lake Hamilton Sr HS; Royal, AR; (4); 9/279; Am Leg Aux Girls St; FCA; Pres FHA; Natl Beta Clb; VP Sr Cls; VP Stu Cncl; Crs Cntry; Trk; NHS; Pres Acad Fit Awd; Soil Consv Awd; US Frstry Cmmssn Awd; U Of AR; Chem Engrng.

UTTER, BENJAMIN D; Jessieville HS; Hot Springs Natio, AR; (2); 6/50; Church Yth Grp; FCA; HOBY; Key Clb; Natl Beta Clb; Quiz Bowl; Band; Chorus; Mrchg Band; Pep Band; Yng Rpblcns Clb VP; Annapolis; Naval/CIA.

VADEN, DANIKA B; Beebe Sr HS; Mc Rae, AR; (3); Pres Church Yth Grp; Drama Clb; FBLA; Treas Natl Beta Clb; Spanish Clb; Thesps; Ed Nwsp; Yrbk; Treas Stu Cncl; Hon Roll.

VALBRACHT, GARY W; Jacksonville HS; Cabot, AR; (4); Art Clb; Boy Scts; Chess Clb; Cmnty Wkr; Library Aide; Babe Ruth Bsbl; Philmont High Adventure Base; Amer Legion Bsbl; Packard High Adventure Base; Eagle Scout; CMSU; Engrng.

VALENCIA, DESIREE; County Line HS; Ratcliff, AR; (4); Church Yth Grp; FCA; FBLA; FHA; Yrbk; Chrldng; Mgr(s); Sftbl; Trk; Hon Roll; Westark; Comp Pgm.

VALENTINE, VICKY; Crawfordsville HS; Crawfordsville, AR; (4); 1/24; Church Yth Grp; Quiz Bowl; Chorus; School Play; Score Keeper; Cit Awd; High Hon Roll; Hon Roll; Prfct Atten Awd; Val; Harding U; Comp Tech.

VALENZVELA, CHANTAL A; Springdale Sr HS; Springdale, AR; (2); Cmnty Wkr; FBLA; Band; Chorus; Mrchg Band; Pep Band; Rptr Yrbk; High Hon Roll; Hon Roll; Jr NHS.

VAN AMBURG, CHRIS B; Cord-Charlotte Schl; Charlotte, AR; (4); Church Yth Grp; Cmnty Wkr; 4-H; Band; Chorus; Church Choir; School Musical; Variety Show; Ofcr Bsbl; Bsktbl; Schl Fire Marshal; Charter Mem Vol Fire Dept Jr Dept; Gateway Voc Coll; Bus Admin.

VAN BOSKIRK, ELIZABETH J; Yellville Summit HS; Yellville, AR; (3); 20/99; Art Clb; Church Yth Grp; Drama Clb; Band; Mrchg Band; Pep Band; Hon Roll; Prfct Atten Awd; Cmnty Wkr; Church Choir; Ballet 9-11; Art/Art Awd 9-10; Pvt Art; Hnrs Math; U Of WA; Oceanogrphy/Art/Dance.

VANCE, STUART O; Black Rock Jr Sr HS; Portia, AR; (4); 1/24; FBLA; Teachers Aide; Chorus; School Musical; Ed Yrbk; Rep Frsh Cls; Treas Jr Cls; High Hon Roll; Val; Desktop Publishing Awd FBLA Dist 2; Portia Church Of Christ Vol Work; AR ST Univ.

VANCIL, JARROD M; Piggott HS; Piggott, AR; (2); 4-H; French Clb; Natl Beta Clb; Natl FFA Org; Ofcr Soph Cls; Cit Awd; 4-H Awd; High Hon Roll; Hon Roll; Prfct Atten Awd; FFA Star Greenhand; FFA Hnr; FFA Showmanship Awd; Ag Bus.

VAN CLEVE, MIKEL W; Conway Sr HS; Conway, AR; (4); JV Bsktbl; Var Socr; Hon Roll; Jr NHS; U Of Ctrl AR; Ed.

VAN DALSEM, PYKE; Perryville Jr Sr HS; Houston, AR; (2); Boy Scts; Chess Clb; FCA; Spanish Clb; Teachers Aide; L Bsktbl; Var Golf; Var Powder Puff Ftbl; Hon Roll; Jr NHS.

VANDERFORD, GLANITA R; Lee Acad; Marianna, AR; (1); 1/35; Church Yth Grp; Bsktbl; Chrldng; Trk; Whos Who; Annual Beauty Queen.

VANDERLEEST, CHRISTOPHER R; Russellville Sr HS; Russellville, AR; (2); #44 in class; Art Clb; Church Yth Grp; Church Choir; NHS; Cmptr Prgrmg.

VAN DUSEN, LARAE J; Alpena Schl; Harrison, AR; (3); Church Yth Grp; Library Aide; Natl Beta Clb; Chorus; Church Choir; School Play; Rptr Yrbk; Hon Roll; Prfct Atten Awd; Schl Achvmt Awds Rcgnzd; Nurse.

VAN DYKE, JASON M; Russellville Sr HS; Russellville, AR; (2); 135/405; Church Yth Grp; Natl Beta Clb; SADD; Bsktbl; Golf; Hon Roll; One Of Top Jr Golfers In AR; AR ST Golf Assn; Mrktng/Bus.

VAN DYNE, RICHARD; Witts Springs HS; Marshall, AR; (2); 1/6; Computer Clb; 4-H; FBLA; Math Clb; Sec Natl Beta Clb; Quiz Bowl; VP Soph Cls; Bsktbl; High Hon Roll; NHS; Sci Awd.

VAN EVERA, PAUL M; Mountain View Jr Sr HS; Mountain View, AR; (3); Church Yth Grp; Natl Beta Clb; Quiz Bowl; Science Clb; Spanish Clb; Church Choir; JV Var Ftbl; JV Var Mgr(s); JV Var Trk; Cit Awd; Pres Of Chrch Yth Grp; Law.

VANGNESS, DAWN U; Trumann HS; Trumann, AR; (3); Art Clb; Math Clb; Science Clb; Spanish Clb; Band; Color Guard; Mrchg Band; Pep Band; Yrbk; Hon Roll; Vo Tech; Nrs.

VANHOOK, RICHARD L; Newport HS; Newport, AR; (2); Art Clb; Latin Clb; Golf; Hon Roll.

VANHOOK, TARA L; Huntsville HS; Huntsville, AR; (3); FCA; Key Clb; Science Clb; Ed Nwsp; Yrbk; Mgr Ftbl; Mgr(s); Hon Roll; UAR; Spch Path.

VAN HORN, ANNA; Ridgecrest Scndry Complex; Paragould, AR; (1); Church Yth Grp; Drama Clb; FBLA; Chorus; Church Choir; School Musical; Rep Stu Cncl; Chrldng; Gym; Hon Roll; NCA Natls Chrldng Squad 14th Pl; All Region Choir 2nd Chair; Teen Ct Lawyer; U Of AR; Criminal Lawyer.

VAN HORN, JENNIFER E; Gentry HS; Gentry, AR; (4); 36/76; Cmnty Wkr; Drama Clb; FCA; FHA; FTA; Spanish Clb; Rep Stu Cncl; Bsktbl; Sftbl; Trk; Ed Tlnt Srch; Devry Inst Of Tch; Comp Inf Sys.

VAN-HOUTEN, SARA E; Devalls Bluff Jr Sr HS; De Valls Bluff, AR; (3); Church Yth Grp; French Clb; FBLA; FHA; Sec Treas Key Clb; Library Aide; Natl Beta Clb; Chorus; Phtg Yrbk; Cit Awd; Farmers & Merchants Bnk Stu Dev Brd; AR ST U Jonesboro; Sec.

VAN KIRK, MELONY; Van Buren Sr HS; Van Buren, AR; (2); Var Bsktbl; Var Chrldng; Var Gym; Var Trk; Var Vllybl.

VAN PELT, BRIANNE M; North Little Rock Hs-West; North Little Rock, AR; (3); 169/554; Drama Clb; FCA; Pres FBLA; Spanish Clb; Chorus; School Musical; Bsktbl; Vllybl; 2 Degree Black Belt Taekwondo; Co-Captain Jr Girls Taekwondo 2 Gold Medals In Italy; Peer Ldrshp Pgm; UCA; Elem Ed.

VAN RHEENEN, SARA; Harding Acad; Searcy, AR; (4); Am Leg Aux Girls St; HOBY; Key Clb; Rptr Natl Beta Clb; Quiz Bowl; Chorus; Ed Yrbk; Co-Capt Chrldng; Tennis; Hon Roll; Miss Harding Acad; Harding U.

VAN ZANT, KAMI C; Oak Grove HS; N Little Rock, AR; (2); Church Yth Grp; Natl Beta Clb; Pep Clb; Spanish Clb; Chorus; High Hon Roll; Hon Roll; Soc Studies Clb.

VARNADO, TAMARA P; Forrest City HS; Madison, AR; (2); 4-H; FHA; Girl Scts; Science Clb; Rep Stu Cncl; Trk; Vllybl; 4-H Awd; Hon Roll; FHA Star Events; Southwestern Bell Minority Internship AR ST U; U Of Cntrl AR; Medcl Engr.

VARNELL, MISTY; Sheridan Sr HS; Sheridan, AR; (2); Church Yth Grp; Dance Clb; Chorus; Church Choir; Hon Roll; Pres Acad Fit Awd; Singing; Swimming; Dancing; Perf Arts.

VARNER, FILMORE J; Central HS; West Helena, AR; (2); #13 in class; Church Yth Grp; HOBY; Acpl Chr; Chorus; Church Choir; Rep Soph Cls; Rep Stu Cncl; Bsktbl; Ftbl; Trk; Natl Yth Forum; Chrch Org Pres; Outstdng Yth Of Yr; Morehouse; Pol Sci; Theology.

VASQUEZ, CLAUDIA; Arkansas Sr HS; Texarkana, AR; (3); Church Yth Grp; Cmnty Wkr; FHA; Spanish Clb; Temple Yth Grp; Band; Church Choir; Wt Lftg; Cnslr.

VASSAR, EMILY; Manila HS; Manila, AR; (1); Church Yth Grp; Chorus; Church Choir; Var Chrldng; Var Sftbl; Ouachita Bapt Coll.

VASSOL, LA SHONDA M; Dumas HS; Dumas, AR; (2); Church Yth Grp; FBLA; FTA; Church Choir; Cmptr Tech.

VAUGHAN, KRISTEN R; Hampton Jr Sr HS; Hampton, AR; (4); Church Yth Grp; FBLA; FHA; Teachers Aide; Church Choir; Rptr Nwsp; Ofcr Stu Cncl; Powder Puff Ftbl; Hon Roll; His Awd; FHA Svc Awd.

VAUGHN, JENNIFER S; Western Yell Co HS; Danville, AR; (2); Drama Clb; Natl Beta Clb; Band; Treas Soph Cls; Hon Roll; Schl Rep At HOBY; Law.

VAUGHN, KERRY L; Waldron HS; Waldron, AR; (2); Drama Clb; FBLA; FHA; Band; Church Choir; Flag Corp; Mrchg Band; Hon Roll; U Of AR; Bus.

VAUGHN, LORI; Mountain Home HS; Mountain Home, AR; (3); 1/265; French Clb; FBLA; HOBY; Natl Beta Clb; Rep Stu Cncl; JV Socr; JV Var Tennis; High Hon Roll; Pres Acad Fit Awd; Spanish NHS; Med Explrs; Med.

VAUGHN, MATT L; Springdale Sr HS; Springdale, AR; (2); Church Yth Grp; Pres 4-H; Band; Mrchg Band; Pep Band; Hon Roll; Bsbl.

VAUGHN, SHARIKA; Saratoga Schl; Columbus, AR; (1); FHA; Natl Beta Clb; Natl FFA Org; Rep Frsh Cls; Capt Bsktbl; Hon Roll; Ntl Merit Ltr; Gftd/Tlntd; Phys Thrpy.

VAUGHNS, PAUL; Hamburg HS; Wilmot, AR; (3); Am Leg Boys St; Church Yth Grp; Cmnty Wkr; FBLA; Spanish Clb; Church Choir; Rep Stu Cncl; Var Bsktbl; Hon Roll; NHS.

VAUGHT, JAKE; Amity Jr Sr HS; Amity, AR; (1); Church Yth Grp; Natl Beta Clb; Natl FFA Org; VP Frsh Cls; Ofcr Bsbl; Hon Roll; GT; Erly AM Smnry; Tlnt Srch; Stu Cncl; U Of AR Monticello; Consrvtn.

VAUGHT, TYLER J; Siloam Springs Sr HS; Siloam Springs, AR; (2); Church Yth Grp; Debate Tm; FCA; Natl Beta Clb; Speech Tm; Teachers Aide; School Play; Stage Crew; Rptr Ed Nwsp; Ed Yrbk; LIFERS; 2nd Pl In Regnl Sci Fair In Chem Div.

VAULNER, JEFFERY A; Nettleton HS; Jonesboro, AR; (2); Art Clb; FBLA; Natl FFA Org; Bsktbl; Golf; Tennis; Hon Roll; Eng Awd.

VAZKEZ, EZEKIEL; Dumas HS; Dumas, AR; (3); 1/170; FCA; Math Clb; Natl Beta Clb; Science Clb; Spanish Clb; Rep Frsh Cls; Pres Soph Cls; Rep Jr Cls; Rep Sr Cls; Ftbl; HS Stu Of Yr.

VEEDER, COURTNEY B; Southside HS; Batesville, AR; (1); Key Clb; Science Clb; Chrldng; Hon Roll; Prfct Atten Awd; Pride; Stop; Ldrshp Awd; ASU.

VENABLE, BRIAN T; Pine Bluff HS; Pine Bluff, AR; (2); Church Yth Grp; Teachers Aide; Acpl Chr; Church Choir; Cit Awd; Hon Roll; Pres Acad Fit Awd; U Of AR; Psych.

VENTIMIGLIA, PAM; Southside HS; Fort Smith, AR; (3); FCA; Vllybl; NHS; Hstry.

VERMA, MONICA; Abundant Life Schools; North Little Rock, AR; (2); 1/20; Drama Clb; Spanish Clb; Bsktbl; Sftbl; Hon Roll; NHS; IFLA.

VERMILLION, HILARY S; Mayflower HS; Mayflower, AR; (3); #1 in class; Am Leg Aux Girls St; Art Clb; French Clb; FHA; Natl Beta Clb; High Hon Roll; Hon Roll; Drg Free Yth St Poster Cont; Odyssey Of The Mind; Histry Prof.

VERNON, HEATHER L; Junction City HS; Junction City, AR; (2); Church Yth Grp; FCA; Science Clb; Spanish Clb; Var Powder Puff Ftbl; Var L Sftbl; High Hon Roll; BASIC; Typing Awd; Evangel.

VERRETT, SANDY R; Parkers Chapel Schl; El Dorado, AR; (2); Church Yth Grp; FBLA; Natl Beta Clb; Spanish Clb; JV Var Chrldng; Hon Roll; Gymnastics; 3 Yrs Of Piano.

VERRETTE, FRANCES L; Siloam Springs Sr HS; Siloam Springs, AR; (3); Church Yth Grp; FCA; FBLA; Key Clb; Spanish Clb; Church Choir; Ofcr Stu Cncl; Bsktbl; Sftbl; Tennis; Poetry Wrtng; Missionary; Oceanography; Marine Bio.

VESECKY, ANGELA; Leslie Schl; Leslie, AR; (4); 4/34; Drama Clb; FBLA; VP FHA; Key Clb; Pres Natl Beta Clb; Thesps; Band; Ed Yrbk; Bsktbl; Trk; NACTC; Bus Mgnt.

VESS, MARCUS L; Searcy HS; Searcy, AR; (2); Church Yth Grp; FCA; JA; Natl Beta Clb; Spanish Clb; Chorus; Church Choir; Var Bsbl; JV Bsktbl; JV Ftbl; Wildlife Conservation; Amer Legion Bsbl; Medicine.

VEST, GINA M; Mountain Home HS; Mountain Home, AR; (3); Church Yth Grp; Cmnty Wkr; Mgr FBLA; Chorus; Phtg Yrbk; JV Socr; PRIDE Skit Tm; Renaissance; Sci Achvmnt Awd; Outstdng Achvmnt Awd; U Of AR.

VESTAL, JAYME A; Bradford Jr Sr HS; Newport, AR; (4); French Clb; FBLA; FHA; GAA; Math Tm; Natl Beta Clb; Natl FFA Org; Pres Frsh Cls; Pres Soph Cls; Rep Stu Cncl; Accntng Awd; Chem Awd; His Awd; Civic Awd; Govt Awd; Nurse.

VESTAL, NICOLE; Perryville Jr Sr HS; Perryville, AR; (2); Art Clb; FCA; Office Aide; Spanish Clb; Teachers Aide; Chrldng; Golf; Hon Roll; Jr NHS.

VETETO, KELLY E; Valley View HS; Jonesboro, AR; (4); 5/65; Pres Art Clb; FHA; Spanish Clb; Teachers Aide; Treas Frsh Cls; Rep Soph Cls; L Vllybl; Hon Roll; VP Jr NHS; Pres Acad Fit Awd; Govs Schl; AR ST U; Bus.

VIALA, COURTNEY R; Cabot HS; Cabot, AR; (3); 76/312; Hosp Aide; Key Clb; Church Choir; Rptr Frsh Cls; Rptr Soph Cls; Rptr Jr Cls; Rptr Sr Cls; Capt Chrldng; Jr NHS; NHS; U Of AR; Mrktng.

VICK, JUSTIN; Danville HS; Danville, AR; (1); 4/70; Church Yth Grp; FCA; Natl FFA Org; Quiz Bowl; SADD; Ftbl; Trk; Hon Roll; Jr NHS; S AR; Phys Ed.

VICKERY, ALYSON; Pulaski Acad; Little Rock, AR; (3); FCA; Natl Beta Clb; Spanish Clb; Yrbk; Bsktbl; Chrldng; Powder Puff Ftbl; Trk; All-Star Chrldng; Gymnastics.

VIGNERY, JEANELLE M; Gravette HS; Gravette, AR; (1); #4 in class; Church Yth Grp; FBLA; VP Frsh Cls; Rep Stu Cncl; JV Var Bsktbl; JV Chrldng; Hon Roll; Jr NHS; NHS; Educl Talent Search; Cnslng.

VILLINES, HEATHER L; Harrison Sr HS; Compton, AR; (3); 54/200; Church Yth Grp; DECA; French Clb; FBLA; Office Aide; Chorus; Church Choir; High Hon Roll; Hon Roll; NHS; N AR Comm Tech Coll.

VINCENT, JULIE; North Cntrl Ar Adult Ed Ctr; Mc Rae, AR; (4); Drama Clb; FHA; HOBY; Library Aide; Math Tm; Natl Beta Clb; Office Aide; Quiz Bowl; Science Clb; SADD; Trojan Schlr; Voice Of Democrcy Schl 1st Pl Wnnr; G/T Stu; U Of Central AR; Engl Jrnlsm.

VINES, AMY L; Jonesboro HS; Jonesboro, AR; (4); 15/252; Art Clb; Church Yth Grp; FBLA; Hosp Aide; Key Clb; Mu Alpha Theta; Natl Beta Clb; Hon Roll; NHS; Pres Acad Fit Awd; David Lipscomb Univ; Arch.

VINES, TIFFANY J; Ridgecrest HS; Paragould, AR; (3); FHA; Library Aide; ROTC; Bsktbl; Bus Mgmt.

VINSON, JENNA M; Fountain Lake Jr Sr HS; Hot Springs, AR; (3); 17/75; Pep Clb; Teachers Aide; CHAMPS Club; Awd Chld Dev; Awd Wrkpl Readiness; Tchr.

VINSON, SHANNON; Batesville Sr HS; Batesville, AR; (2); FCA; FBLA; HOBY; Natl Beta Clb; Yrbk; Sec Stu Cncl; Chrldng; Golf; Sftbl; High Hon Roll; U Of AR; Poli Sci.

VIZENA, VAL; Jasper HS; Dogpatch, AR; (4); 4/50; Am Leg Aux Girls St; Treas Art Clb; Church Yth Grp; Cmnty Wkr; FBLA; Math Clb; Pres Natl Beta Clb; Office Aide; VP Science Clb; Spanish Clb; Mntrhsp; U Of AR Fayetteville; Inatl La.

VO, CALEY B; Rogers HS; Rogers, AR; (3); Church Yth Grp; Cmnty Wkr; Model UN; Speech Tm; Var Chrldng; Trk; Wt Lftg; High Hon Roll; Teachers Aide; Rogers Chamber Of Commerce Stu Acad Achvmt Awd 2 Yrs; REACH & PACE Clbs; Hendrix; Soc Scis.

VOIGT, AMBER L; Bergman Schl; Harrison, AR; (1); Church Yth Grp; GAA; Natl Beta Clb; Spanish Clb; JV L Bsktbl; Sftbl; Ntl Merit Schol; U Of AR; Vet.

VONDRAN, AMANDA M; Lee Acad; Moro, AR; (1); Trk; Phillips Co Comm Col; Jrnlsm.

VONDRAN, STEPHANIE D; Searcy HS; Searcy, AR; (2); 23/256; Church Yth Grp; Dance Clb; French Clb; Natl Beta Clb; Band; Chorus; Mrchg Band; Pep Band; Mgr(s); French Hon Soc; Tulane; FBI Agent/Law.

VONGVILATH, SOMYONG; Russellville Sr HS; Russellville, AR; (2); Church Yth Grp; Cmnty Wkr; Natl Beta Clb; Spanish Clb; Sftbl; Vllybl; Hon Roll.

VOWELL, CHANAN; North Little Rock Hs-West; North Little Rock, AR; (3); Drama Clb; French Clb; Mu Alpha Theta; Q&S; Drill Tm; Lit Mag; Songahm Tae Kwon Do.

VOYLES, ELIZABETH E; Marion HS; West Memphis, AR; (2); Church Yth Grp; FBLA; GAA; Spanish Clb; Co-Ed Yrbk; Cit Awd; Hon Roll; NHS; Rhodes Coll; Phys Therapy.

VOYTKO, DONNA R; Cabot HS; Cabot, AR; (3); Cmnty Wkr; Key Clb; Office Aide; Teachers Aide; Socr; Vol Of The Yr; Environmental Law.

VUONG, STEVEN; Southside HS; Fort Smith, AR; (3); Church Yth Grp; Cmnty Wkr; Math Clb; Mu Alpha Theta; Spanish Clb; Chorus; Church Choir; School Musical; School Play; Hon Roll; Karare; All ST Choir.

WAACK, BARBARA M; Southside HS; Fort Smith, AR; (3); Church Yth Grp; Cmnty Wkr; Key Clb; Mu Alpha Theta; Spanish Clb; Chorus; Chrldng; Vllybl; VP NHS; Piano Tchr; Candy Striper; U Of AR; Coach.

WAACK, GERRILYN; Southside HS; Fort Smith, AR; (3); 58/502; Sec Drama Clb; Hosp Aide; Mu Alpha Theta; Band; Drm Mjr(t); School Play; Hon Roll; Jr NHS; NHS; Spanish NHS; Pre-Med.

WADDILL, KAREY E; Norphlet HS; El Dorado, AR; (4); Church Yth Grp; FBLA; FHA; Spanish Clb; Mrchg Band; Rep Stu Cncl; Var L Bsktbl; Var L Chrldng; Hon Roll; NHS; Harding Univ; Pre-Pharm.

WADDILL, KELLY; Norphlet HS; El Dorado, AR; (2); Art Clb; Church Yth Grp; FBLA; Spanish Clb; Band; Rep Stu Cncl; Bsktbl; High Hon Roll; NHS; Anchor Club; Scholastic Awd; Harding Univ; Bus Admin.

WADE, AMBER L; Searcy HS; Searcy, AR; (2); Natl Beta Clb; Spanish Clb; Band; Mrchg Band; Pep Band; High Hon Roll; Hon Roll; Jr NHS; Spanish NHS; Vet.

WADE, DAWN E; Van-Cove HS; Vandervoort, AR; (4); 7/32; Art Clb; French Clb; FBLA; Library Aide; Natl Beta Clb; Yrbk; Hon Roll; NHS; Church Yth Grp; Natl Art Hnr Soc; U Of Ozarks; Art Ed.

WADE, MAISHA L; Forrest City HS; Colt, AR; (3); Church Yth Grp; Drama Clb; 4-H; FBLA; FHA; FTA; Spanish Clb; Teachers Aide; Church Choir; School Play; Essay Winner; Deans List; Beta Club; SU Louisianna; Agribus.

WADE, PAMELA E; Oak Grove HS; North Little Rock, AR; (2); Drama Clb; Natl Beta Clb; Spanish Clb; Hon Roll; Educl Imprvmnt Pres Awd; UCA.

WADE, SHANETTA; Marvel HS; Turner, AR; (2); Church Yth Grp; 4-H; FHA; FTA; Natl Beta Clb; Band; Church Choir; Mrchg Band; Pep Band; School Play; UALR; Pedtrcn.

WADE, TANYA N; Dumas HS; Dumas, AR; (3); 44/189; Church Yth Grp; Drama Clb; FBLA; FTA; Girl Scts; Spanish Clb; Church Choir; Mgr(s); Hon Roll; MASH Pgm; Chief Usher; Sec; UAM; Nrsng; Comp Sci.

WADLEY, RANDY A; Tuckerman HS; Tuckerman, AR; (2); 18/58; 4-H; Natl Beta Clb; Natl FFA Org; Spanish Clb; Teachers Aide; Cit Awd; Hon Roll; FFA Jdgng Team/Creed Spker; His Club; ASU; Law.

WAFFORD, LISA D; Sheridan Sr HS; Pine Bluff, AR; (3); FHA; Chorus; Church Choir; Merit List; GCE.

WAGES, CORY W; Arkansas Sr HS; Texarkana, AR; (2); Boy Scts; Church Yth Grp; Drama Clb; Quiz Bowl; Spanish Clb; Speech Tm; Rep Stu Cncl; Ftbl; Hon Roll.

WAGGLE, LISA K; Rose Bud Jr Sr HS; Rose Bud, AR; (3); Church Yth Grp; FHA; Upward Bound; Yth To Yth; Cosmetology; Coll Of Ozarks; Surgery Dr.

WAGNER, ERIN C; Cabot HS; Cabot, AR; (3); 149/400; Art Clb; Church Yth Grp; Key Clb; Office Aide; Teachers Aide; Drill Tm; Lit Mag; Bsktbl; Hon Roll; Best Of Art Show 11th Grd; Celebration Of Excl Awd/Art.

WAGNER, JANUARY; Pea Ridge HS; Pea Ridge, AR; (4); 1/40; FBLA; Quiz Bowl; Spanish Clb; Band; Drm Mjr(t); Cit Awd; High Hon Roll; NHS; Pres Acad Fit Awd; Val; Scott Hi-Q; U AR; Accntnt.

WAGNER, NIKKI R; Manila HS; Manila, AR; (1); Church Yth Grp; FHA; Band; Rep Frsh Cls; Gftd & Tlntd; Paleontologist.

WAGNER, SARAH; Northside HS; Fort Smith, AR; (4); 33/340; Am Leg Aux Girls St; Pres FCA; Mu Alpha Theta; Spanish Clb; Ofcr Stu Cncl; Var Bsktbl; Hon Roll; NHS; Pres Acad Fit Awd; Spanish NHS; All St Bsktbl; All AR 3rd Team Bsktbl; Northside Best Female Ath; Southwest TX ST U.

WAGNER, STACIE D; Pulaski Acad; Little Rock, AR; (2); Sec Church Yth Grp; Natl Beta Clb; Service Clb; Spanish Clb; Band; Mrchg Band; Yrbk; Hon Roll; Sec Jr NHS; NHS; Headmasters List.

WAGNON, CARISSA J; Parkers Chapel Schl; El Dorado, AR; (3); 3/63; Art Clb; Church Yth Grp; 4-H; French Clb; FBLA; Library Aide; Natl Beta Clb; School Play; Sec Frsh Cls; Treas Soph Cls; Natl History Awd; Sci Awds; UCA; Paralegal.

WAGNON, NATHAN C; Cabot HS; Lonoke, AR; (3); Am Leg Boys St; Church Yth Grp; Cmnty Wkr; Pres FCA; Key Clb; Band; School Musical; School Play; Stage Crew; Pres Jr Cls; Cabot Intrschlstc Star; Chrch Band; Evnglst.

WAGONER, ANGELA; Harmony Grove Jr Sr HS; Camden, AR; (2); FBLA; Natl Beta Clb; Spanish Clb; Hon Roll; NHS.

WAITE, AMBER LYNN; Vilonia HS; Conway, AR; (2); FBLA; Math Clb; Mu Alpha Theta; Natl Beta Clb; Band; Mrchg Band; Pep Band; High Hon Roll; Prfct Atten Awd; RT.

WAITS, BRANDI S; Northside HS; Fort Smith, AR; (2); Church Yth Grp; FCA; Chorus; Church Choir; Drill Tm; School Musical; Variety Show; Rep Soph Cls; High Hon Roll; Hon Roll; Hrsbck Rdng; Sftbl; Wtr Skiing; Snow Skiing; Vet.

WAITS, MACON M; Highland HS; Cherokee Village, AR; (3); Am Leg Aux Girls St; Cmnty Wkr; FBLA; Sec Natl Beta Clb; Teachers Aide; High Hon Roll; Hon Roll; Hosp Aide; Powder Puff Ftbl; Schlstc Achv Awd; RAD; Rnsnc Awd; Acctng/Mrktg/Bus.

WAKEFIELD, COREY; Lamar HS; Clarksville, AR; (4); FCA; FBLA; Natl Beta Clb; Natl FFA Org; Science Clb; Var Capt Bsbl; Var Capt Bsktbl; Var Capt Ftbl; Var Wt Lftg; AR Tech Univ; Ag Bus.

WAKEFIELD, MANDY; Southside HS; Fort Smith, AR; (4); 37/462; French Clb; FBLA; Key Clb; Mu Alpha Theta; Sftbl; Vllybl; Hon Roll; Jr NHS; NHS; Pres Acad Fit Awd; Natl Engl Mrt Awd; SAIL Crew; KUDOS Awd; U Cntrl AR; Occptnl Thrpy.

WAKWE, EMILY C; North Little Rock Hs-East; Little Rock, AR; (2); 61/563; Art Clb; Church Yth Grp; FCA; Hosp Aide; Trk; Vllybl; Wt Lftg; Hon Roll; Prfct Atten Awd; Natl Acad Ftnss Awd; Dr.

WALBERT, CAMERON D; Southside HS; Fort Smith, AR; (2); Church Yth Grp; Cmnty Wkr; FBLA; Key Clb; Ofcr Stu Cncl; Tennis; Hon Roll; NHS; Nom Natl Yth Ldrshp Forum Law/Constitution; Lawyer.

WALDEN, ANGELA; Central Ark Christian Schl; North Little Rock, AR; (4); 1/75; Church Yth Grp; Drama Clb; Girl Scts; Mu Alpha Theta; Natl Beta Clb; Speech Tm; School Musical; School Play; Jr NHS; NHS; Pre-Calculus Awd; AP Amer Hstry Awd; Natl Yng Ldrshp Conf; Ouachita Bapt U; Pedtrcn.

WALDEN, ERIN; Jonesboro HS; Jonesboro, AR; (1); Natl Beta Clb; Chorus; Rep Frsh Cls; Var Bsktbl; Var Chrldng; Hon Roll; All Conf Bsktbl; Mst Otsdng Bsktbl Plyr Var; Otsdng Choir Stdnt; U Of AR; Fed Law Enfrcmnt Agnt.

WALDEN, JORDAN; North Little Rock HS E Campus; North Little Rock, AR; (1); Church Yth Grp; School Musical; School Play; Rep Stu Cncl; Capt Chrldng; High Hon Roll; Med.

WALDEN, REBECCA L; North Little Rock Hs-West; North Little Rock, AR; (3); 10/554; Cmnty Wkr; Math Clb; Mu Alpha Theta; Natl Beta Clb; Q&S; Rptr Nwsp; High Hon Roll; NHS; Prfct Atten Awd; Jrnlsm Stu Of Yr 93-94; Ger Stu Of Yr 94-95.

WALDON, HOLLY G; Dequeen HS; De Queen, AR; (2); Church Yth Grp; Cmnty Wkr; 4-H; SADD; Yrbk; JV Bsbl; 4-H Awd; 95 Sprtsmnsp 4-H Awd; Choir; Harding; Tchr.

WALDRUP, DERRICK; Dermott HS; Dermott, AR; (1); 3/64; Church Yth Grp; FCA; Natl Beta Clb; Varsity Clb; Band; Mrchg Band; Rep Stu Cncl; Var Bsbl; JV Ftbl; Cit Awd; Baylor; Cardiologist.

WALES, CHRISTI D; Siloam Springs Sr HS; Siloam Springs, AR; (4); 23/296; Church Yth Grp; Cmnty Wkr; FCA; FHA; Key Clb; Library Aide; Natl Beta Clb; Natl FFA Org; Office Aide; Spanish Clb; FFA Secy; Dairy Jdgng 3rd St, 1st Rgnl; John Brown U; Psych.

WALKER, ALISA J; Decatur HS; Decatur, AR; (2); FCA; Natl Beta Clb; Yrbk; Sec Frsh Cls; JV Var Bsktbl; Pom Pon; High Hon Roll; Hon Roll; NHS; Pres Acad Fit Awd; U Of AR; Psych.

WALKER, AMBER N; Viola HS; Gepp, AR; (3); 15/36; FHA; Spanish Clb; Band; Pep Band; Mgr(s); Cit Awd; Pres Acad Fit Awd.

WALKER, AMY B; Mills HS; Jacksonville, AR; (2); FHA; FTA; ROTC; Spanish Clb; Color Guard; Hon Roll.

WALKER, ANGELA; St Joe Public Schl; Pindall, AR; (4); 1/9; Rep 4-H; Pres Rep Natl FFA Org; Rep Jr Cls; VP Sr Cls; Cit Awd; Ntl Merit Schol; Val; Project WET; St Envirothon Champ; St Dairy Judging Champ; U Of MO Columbia; Animal Sci.

WALKER, ASHLEY; Foreman Jr Sr HS; Foreman, AR; (1); Cmnty Wkr; Spanish Clb; JV Capt Chrldng; Hon Roll; U Of AR; Tchr.

WALKER, CANDIE M; Alma HS; Alma, AR; (3); Church Yth Grp; FCA; FHA; Teachers Aide; Chorus; Church Choir; Drill Tm; Chrldng; Cit Awd; Hon Roll; Westark CC; Spch Thrpst/Cnslr.

WALKER JR, D J; Abundant Life Schools; North Little Rock, AR; (2); 2/18; Drama Clb; Spanish Clb; Ofcr Bsbl; Bsktbl; Ftbl; Wt Lftg; High Hon Roll; Hon Roll; NHS; Church Yth Grp; AWANA; U Of AR; Comp Programming.

WALKER, DELORES J; Holly Grove HS; Pine Bluff, AR; (1); 1/26; FHA; Quiz Bowl; Band; Pep Band; School Musical; School Play; Rep Frsh Cls; Capt Bsktbl; High Hon Roll; Hon Roll; GATE; Great Rivers Edctnl Coop Awd Exclnc; Jr Jojo Reading Club; U Of AR Pine Bluff; Art/Music.

WALKER, DENESHA R; Mc Gehee HS; Mc Gehee, AR; (2); GAA; Science Clb; Spanish Clb; Var Chrldng; Prfct Atten Awd; Pride Awd; Northeast LA U; Civil/Chem Eng.

WALKER, DUSTIN A; Cty Line HS; Cecil, AR; (3); Church Yth Grp; FCA; 4-H; Natl Beta Clb; Natl FFA Org; Spanish Clb; Pres Soph Cls; Bsktbl; Hon Roll.

WALKER, DUSTIN H; Cotter Jr Sr HS; Gassville, AR; (3); 7/42; Quiz Bowl; Var Bsbl; 1st Pl Bio Regnl Math/Sci Cntst.

WALKER, EMILY; Central Ark Christian Schl; Little Rock, AR; (3); 2/80; Church Yth Grp; French Clb; FBLA; Science Clb; Chorus; Stage Crew; Sec Stu Cncl; Co-Capt Chrldng; High Hon Roll; NHS.

WALKER, FREDDIE; Pea Ridge HS; Pea Ridge, AR; (3); 1/57; Church Yth Grp; Cmnty Wkr; Letterman Clb; Model UN; Quiz Bowl; Spanish Clb; Nwsp; Rep Frsh Cls; VP Soph Cls; Sec Jr Cls; U AR; Phrmcy.

WALKER, JACOB T; Berryville HS; Berryville, AR; (3); 5/100; Capt Quiz Bowl; Science Clb; Rptr Nwsp; Ed Lit Mag; Rptr Frsh Cls; High Hon Roll; Jr NHS; Treas NHS; GATE Prgm; Odessy Of Mind; Teen Ct Attorney; Hendrix Coll; Pharmacy/Radlgy.

WALKER, JANEA; Central Ark Christian Schl; Sherwood, AR; (3); 7/75; VP Church Yth Grp; Science Clb; Spanish Clb; Yrbk; VP Soph Cls; Chrldng; Hon Roll; Jr NHS; NHS; Hstry Clb; Intr Desgn.

WALKER, JENNIFER J; Southside HS; Fort Smith, AR; (2); Drama Clb; Hosp Aide; Latin Clb; Red Cross Aide; Band; Mrchg Band; Hon Roll; Vet.

WALKER, LATONYA; Hughes Jr-Sr HS; Hughes, AR; (1); Church Yth Grp; Math Clb; VP Frsh Cls; Capt Bsktbl; Capt Chrldng; Capt Trk; High Hon Roll; NHS; U Of AR; Math/Bus/Law.

WALKER, LAURA; Tuckerman HS; Newport, AR; (3); Church Yth Grp; Cmnty Wkr; FBLA; FHA; Natl Beta Clb; Quiz Bowl; Yrbk; Sec Frsh Cls; Pres Soph Cls; Rep Jr Cls; Attorney.

WALKER, LIESL F; Fayetteville Christian Schl; Fayetteville, AR; (2); Church Yth Grp; 4-H; Variety Show; Yrbk; Var Bsktbl; 4-H Awd; Hon Roll; NHS; Jr Chmpn; ST Rcrd Book Wnr; Natl Congress Del; Art Ctr Ozarks Piano Hons Rctl; Yng Edison Soc Awd.

WALKER, MARTIESE S; Parkview Arts-Science HS; Little Rock, AR; (3); Church Yth Grp; FBLA; Natl Beta Clb; Teachers Aide; Rptr Yrbk; Ftbl; High Hon Roll; NHS; Prfct Atten Awd; Reading; Hampton; Law.

WALKER, SABRA; Harrison Sr HS; Harrison, AR; (2); 1/211; Key Clb; Spanish Clb; Thesps; Acpl Chr; Chrldng; High Hon Roll; Spanish NHS; Natl Engl Mrt Awd; AR Intl Lang Pgm Spnsh Immersion Camp; Harrison Theater Co Kismet & The King & I; Bus Admin.

WALKER, SARAH E; Booneville Jr Sr HS; Booneville, AR; (2); Church Yth Grp; French Clb; Natl Beta Clb; Office Aide; Science Clb; Sec Chorus; Church Choir; Mrchg Band; Sec Stu Cncl; Hon Roll; Acteens 95-96 St Panelist; Yth Alive; Ouachita Bapt Univ; Music Ed.

WALKER, SARAH E; Springdale Sr HS; Springdale, AR; (4); Church Yth Grp; Key Clb; Acpl Chr; Chorus; Ofcr Soph Cls; Ofcr Jr Cls; Ofcr Sr Cls; Chrldng; Powder Puff Ftbl; NHS.

WALKER, SHERITA; Saratoga Schl; Ozan, AR; (2); Church Yth Grp; Quiz Bowl; Science Clb; School Musical; School Play; Yrbk; Sec Soph Cls; Bsktbl; Trk; Hon Roll; Surgical Nurse.

WALKER, STACEY; Carlisle Jr Sr HS; Carlisle, AR; (3); Art Clb; Church Yth Grp; Cmnty Wkr; Drama Clb; English Clb; FBLA; GAA; Spanish Clb; Church Choir; School Play; Mdlng; Resp Thrp.

WALKER, TABITHA; Bradford Jr Sr HS; Bradford, AR; (1); Art Clb; Church Yth Grp; FBLA; FHA; Hosp Aide; Teachers Aide; Church Choir; VP Frsh Cls; Ofcr Stu Cncl; Chrldng; All Amer Schlrs; Phys Thrpy.

WALKER, WAYNITA L; Arkansas Sr HS; Texarkana, AR; (2); Teachers Aide; Chorus; High Hon Roll; Hon Roll; 3 Yrs Schl Choir Plaque; Arch.

WALL, ERIC; Forrest City HS; Forrest City, AR; (3); Computer Clb; Office Aide; Band; Jazz Band; Mrchg Band; Pep Band; Nwsp; Cit Awd; Hon Roll; NHS; Louis Armstrong Jazz Band Awd; Cmptr Prgmmr.

WALL, KELLI; Morrilton Sr HS; Morrilton, AR; (3); French Clb; Natl Beta Clb; Office Aide; Thesps; Drill Tm; Rptr Nwsp; Ed Yrbk; Hon Roll; Kndrgrtn Tchr.

WALL, MARY ELIZABETH; Dollarway HS; Pine Bluff, AR; (3); Church Yth Grp; 4-H; French Clb; Pep Clb; Chorus; Church Choir; Pom Pon; 4-H Awd; High Hon Roll; Hon Roll; Natl His/Govt Awd; U Of AR Fayetteville.

WALLACE, ELIZABETH A; North Pulaski HS; Jacksonville, AR; (3); Drama Clb; Speech Tm; Thesps; School Musical; School Play; Stage Crew.

WALLACE, JAMES; Nashville HS; Nashville, AR; (3); Church Yth Grp; Natl Beta Clb; Spanish Clb; JV Var Bsbl; JV Ftbl; Hon Roll; NHS; Talented/Gifted Prgm; U Of Miami; Marine Sci.

WALLACE, JASON M; Danville HS; Danville, AR; (4); Pres Church Yth Grp; FCA; Pres SADD; VP Stu Cncl; Bsktbl; Ftbl; Trk; NHS; Prfct Atten Awd; AR Tech Univ.

WALLACE, KENDRA D; Pine Bluff HS; Pine Bluff, AR; (2); Church Yth Grp; Cmnty Wkr; Dance Clb; Girl Scts; Church Choir; Mrchg Band; Hon Roll; Jr NHS; FHA; Pep Clb; Impress Drug Prvntn/Awarenss; Pathways To Coll; Howard Univ; Attrny.

WALLACE, LESLEY E; Lonoke Jr HS; Lonoke, AR; (1); Church Yth Grp; Dance Clb; Science Clb; Band; Drm Mjr(t); Rep Stu Cncl; Bsktbl; Trk; Hon Roll; NHS.

WALLACE, NIKKI; Rison HS; Rison, AR; (4); 8/54; Am Leg Aux Girls St; Church Yth Grp; Sec FCA; FHA; Natl Beta Clb; VP Sr Cls; Var Chrldng; Hon Roll; French Clb; FBLA; Drg Awrnss Grp; Sr Clss Frndlst; Ouachita Bapt U; Nrsng.

WALLACE, REBECCA M; Stuttgart Sr HS; Humphrey, AR; (4); 35/153; Chorus; Hon Roll; Pres Acad Fit Awd; Pres Schlr; HOSA; Phillips CC; Sec.

WALLACE, RHONDA; Monticello HS; Monticello, AR; (1); Church Yth Grp; FHA; Natl Beta Clb; Acpl Chr; Chorus; Church Choir; Treas Stu Cncl; JV Chrldng; Wt Lftg; High Hon Roll.

WALLER, KIM; Cabot HS; Cabot, AR; (2); 58/405; Dance Clb; Drama Clb; Pres FHA; GAA; Key Clb; Natl Beta Clb; Office Aide; Yrbk; Ofcr Stu Cncl; Bsktbl; UCA; Med.

WALLER, KYLE R; West Memphis Christian Schl; Marion, AR; (2); VP Frsh Cls; VP Soph Cls; Var Bsbl; Var Ftbl; Var Golf; JV Trk; Fighting Heart For Baseball; AR ST.

WALLIS, AIMEE; Magnet Cove HS; Malvern, AR; (4); Church Yth Grp; FCA; 4-H; FBLA; Math Clb; Natl FFA Org; Office Aide; Science Clb; Teachers Aide; Chorus; Ouachita Bapt Univ; Bus.

WALLIS, KEITH W; Drew Central Jr Sr HS; Monticello, AR; (4); 9/60; FBLA; Natl FFA Org; Science Clb; Ofcr Frsh Cls; Ofcr Soph Cls; Ofcr Jr Cls; Ofcr Sr Cls; Ofcr Bsbl; Hon Roll; Bio Awd; Art Awd; Acad & Art Schlsps; U Of AR-MONTICELLO; Art.

WALLRATH, JENNIFER D; Mountain Home HS; Mountain Home, AR; (4); 15/232; Church Yth Grp; FTA; GAA; Natl FFA Org; Spanish Clb; Swmmng; Trk; Vllybl; High Hon Roll; 4-H; Grad Magna Cum Laude; ASU; Sci Ed.

WALLS, BRITTANY S; Booneville Jr Sr HS; Clinton, AR; (2); Church Yth Grp; FBLA; FTA; Natl Beta Clb; Office Aide; Science Clb; Teachers Aide; Chrldng; Hon Roll; Prfct Atten Awd; Youth Alive; AR Tech Univ; Acctng.

WALLS, BRYAN; Butterfield Jr HS; Van Buren, AR; (1); Band; Jazz Band; Ed Lit Mag; Jr NHS; Ntl Merit Ltr.

WALLS, CRYSTAL M; North Little Rock Hs-West; North Little Rock, AR; (3); Church Yth Grp; Cmnty Wkr; Sec Debate Tm; Drama Clb; ROTC; Band; Color Guard; Mrchg Band; School Play; Hon Roll; Optmist Intl Zone; Nvy Lwyr.

WALLS, JAMIE A; Walker Schl; Magnolia, AR; (2); Drama Clb; FBLA; Church Choir; Sec Frsh Cls; Sec Soph Cls; Treas Stu Cncl; Var Bsktbl; Var Chrldng; Hon Roll; Upward Bound At Southern AR U; Bus Mgmt; Prsnl Recruiter.

WALNOFER, LISA; Charleston HS; Charleston, AR; (2); FCA; FBLA; FHA; Natl Beta Clb; Rptr Stu Cncl; JV Bsktbl; Chrldng; Powder Puff Ftbl; Sftbl; Trk.

WALPOLE, BRANDY C; England HS; England, AR; (3); 25/75; Church Yth Grp; Drama Clb; FCA; FBLA; Pep Clb; Spanish Clb; Mrchg Band; School Play; Chrldng; Hon Roll; UCA; CPA.

WALSH, AMY C; Bearden HS; Sparkman, AR; (3); Cmnty Wkr; 4-H; Library Aide; Natl Beta Clb; Band; Mrchg Band; Pres Jr Cls; Var Bsktbl; High Hon Roll; Pres Acad Fit Awd.

WALSH, BRAD J; Crossett Sr HS; Crossett, AR; (2); Church Yth Grp; Math Clb; Mu Alpha Theta; Natl Beta Clb; Band; Mrchg Band; Var Crs Cntry; JV Ftbl; JV Var Trk; Hon Roll; U Of AR.

WALSH, KELLY A; West Fork HS; West Fork, AR; (1); 9th Grd Engl Class Achvd Highest Grd.

WALSH, ROBBIN B; North Little Rock Hs-East; North Little Rock, AR; (3); Pres Church Yth Grp; Girl Scts; Q&S; Band; Church Choir; Mrchg Band; Lit Mag; Hon Roll; Tri M Music Hnr Scty; CCYM; DCYM; Comp Sci.

WALTER, BRIAN; Lee Sr HS; Moro, AR; (1); Elec Engrng.

WALTERS JR, CLARENCE; Jacksonville HS; Jacksonville, AR; (4); 86/300; Dance Clb; Pep Clb; Spanish Clb; Variety Show; Bsktbl; Ftbl; Trk; UALR; Bus.

WALTERS, COURTNEY L; Lake Hamilton Sr HS; Royal, AR; (2); Church Yth Grp; FCA; FBLA; Hosp Aide; Natl Beta Clb; Spanish Clb; Band; Church Choir; High Hon Roll; NHS; Stu Chrstn Life; Pedtrc Nrs.

WALTERS, TODD D; Southside HS; Fort Smith, AR; (4); 241/453; Drama Clb; French Clb; Office Aide; Teachers Aide; Acpl Chr; Chorus; Church Choir; 1st Chair Tenor II W Cntrl AR; All Region Choir; 9th Chair; 1st Chair AR All St Choir; UCA; Music.

WALTHALL, LESLEY J; Nevada Schl; Waldo, AR; (1); 1/50; FBLA; Band; Hon Roll; Southern AR Univ.

WALTHALL, LINDSAY K; Nevada Schl; Waldo, AR; (3); 1/51; FBLA; High Hon Roll; Pres Acad Fit Awd; Navy Seals Awd; Drug Tm; SAU; RN.

WALTON, DIONNE; Brinkley HS; Brinkley, AR; (1); Church Yth Grp; 4-H; FHA; Girl Scts; Band; Mrchg Band; Bsktbl; Trk; Hon Roll; Jr NHS.

WALTON, MICHAEL A; Springdale Sr HS; Springdale, AR; (1); Church Yth Grp; FCA; FBLA; Chorus; Pres Stu Cncl; JV Bsktbl; Capt JV Ftbl; Hon Roll; Jr NHS; Pres Acad Fit Awd; 9th Grd Class Favorite/Most Athltc; Sports Med.

WALTRIP, ELIZABETH F; Salem HS; Glencoe, AR; (3); Church Yth Grp; FHA; Quiz Bowl; Teachers Aide; Var Chrldng; Powder Puff Ftbl; Var Trk; Cit Awd; Hon Roll; Prfct Atten Awd; AR ST Univ.

WANG, JAMES; Evening Shade Schl; Evening Shade, AR; (1); FBLA; SADD; Ofcr Frsh Cls; Hon Roll; 2nd Deg Blk Blt Karate, Own Schl, Top 10 Wrld Natl Blk Blt Leag; Tch Karate.

WANN, SUZANNE; Siloam Springs Sr HS; Siloam Springs, AR; (4); 1/160; FCA; Natl Beta Clb; Band; L Bsktbl; L Trk; High Hon Roll; NHS; Ntl Merit Schol; Rhodes Coll; Bio; Med Rsrch.

WARD, AIMEE K; Southside HS; Fort Smith, AR; (4); 21/508; Church Yth Grp; FCA; French Clb; Mu Alpha Theta; Church Choir; Drill Tm; Stat Bsbl; Var Vllybl; French Hon Soc; Jr NHS; NHS; Scndry Ed/Math.

WARD, ANTHONY R; Robinson HS; Little Rock, AR; (2); 58/374; FBLA; Natl Beta Clb; Spanish Clb; Var Bsktbl; TOT; Tulane U; Airline Pilot.

WARD, BRIAN P; Central HS; Helena, AR; (3); FBLA; Natl FFA Org; FFA VP; Howard Univ; Med.

WARD, CHRISTINA M; Clarksville HS; Clarksville, AR; (2); Church Yth Grp; FBLA; Girl Scts; Library Aide; Natl Beta Clb; Bsktbl; Gym; Swmmng; Vllybl; Cit Awd; Pride Tm.

WARD, COREY L; Mc Gehee HS; Mc Gehee, AR; (4); Computer Clb; Spanish Clb; Ofcr Bsbl; Ftbl; U Of AR; Comp Sci.

WARD, CRYSTAL; Omaha Schl; Omaha, AR; (2); Church Yth Grp; FHA; Natl Beta Clb; Church Choir; Cit Awd; Hon Roll; Honorary Musician Awd; Arch.

WARD, JASON; Guy Perkins Schl; Guy, AR; (2); Church Yth Grp; 4-H; Pres FHA; Treas Natl FFA Org; Band; Pres Frsh Cls; Pres Soph Cls; Beta Clb; FHA Comm Svc; FHA AR Comm Svc Awd Wnnr; Chrch Lfefrce Yth Grp; Univ Of AR; Military/Law.

WARD, JASON W; Osceola HS; Osceola, AR; (3); Church Yth Grp; French Clb; FBLA; Science Clb; Band; Church Choir; Drm Mjr(t); Jazz Band; Mrchg Band; Rep Yrbk; All Amer Schlr; Natl Ldrshp & Svc Awd; Natl Sci Mrt Awd; AR ST Univ; Music Ed.

WARD, JOSHUA; Murfreesboro HS; Murfreesboro, AR; (1); Natl Beta Clb; Quiz Bowl; JV Bsbl; JV Bsktbl; JV Ftbl; JV Trk; JV Wt Lftg; Cit Awd; Hon Roll; Bapt Chrch; Sunday Schl Sec Usher; SAU.

WARD, JULIE N; Southside Schl; Damascus, AR; (4); 5/26; Church Yth Grp; French Clb; Hist FBLA; Treas FHA; VP Natl Beta Clb; Pres Natl FFA Org; Office Aide; School Play; Sec Sr Cls; Mgr(s); Class Fav; Hmcmng Maid; Fall Fstvl Queen; U Of Cntrl AR; Elem Ed.

WARD, KELLY A; Lake Hamilton Sr HS; Hot Springs, AR; (3); FBLA; German Clb; Treas Natl Beta Clb; Office Aide; Science Clb; Ofcr Stu Cncl; Trk; Vllybl; Hon Roll; NHS; OK ST U; Fash Mrchndsng.

WARD, LAURA; Oak Ridge Central Schl; Ravenden Springs, AR; (4); 3/14; Pres FBLA; Treas Natl FFA Org; Pres Jr Cls; Sec Treas Sr Cls; Capt Bsktbl; Sftbl; Hon Roll; Prfct Atten Awd; Schl Imprvmnt; All Dist, Reg & St Bsktbl; Williams Bapt; Phys Ed.

WARD, MARLA; Horatio HS; Winthrop, AR; (4); 5/30; Am Leg Aux Girls St; Church Yth Grp; Sec FCA; Pres FBLA; Sec Sr Cls; Var Bsktbl; Var Chrldng; Golf; Hon Roll; Odyssy Of Mind; U Of Cntrl AR; Rdlgy.

WARD, MARY J; Morrilton Sr HS; Morrilton, AR; (3); Spanish Clb; Phy Thrpst.

WARD, MELANIE A; Junction City HS; Junction City, AR; (3); Church Yth Grp; Model UN; Vllybl; Hon Roll; Jr NHS; NHS; Vet.

WARD, STEPHANIE; Delight HS; Murfreesboro, AR; (1); Church Yth Grp; FHA; Natl FFA Org; Chrldng; High Hon Roll; Hon Roll; All Amer Schlr Awd; Natl Ldrshp Svc Awd; Natl Hnr Rl; U Of AR Fayetteville; Bus.

WARD, TERRA K; Arkansas Sr HS; Texarkana, AR; (3); Church Yth Grp; French Clb; FBLA; Q&S; ROTC; Band; Capt Flag Corp; Mrchg Band; Ed Treas Nwsp; Nike Clb.

WARD, TIMOTHY J; Ridgecrest HS; Paragould, AR; (2); Church Yth Grp; ROTC; Band; Color Guard; Drill Tm; JV Ftbl; Cit Awd; Prfct Atten Awd; ROTC Rifle Team; Church Drama Team; Chrch Puppet Team Chldrns Chrch Tchr; Oral Roberts Univ; Cmptr Pgmr.

WARDLAW, JEFFREY; Hermitage Jr Sr HS; Hermitage, AR; (2); Church Yth Grp; FCA; 4-H; FBLA; Natl Beta Clb; Natl FFA Org; Band; Nwsp; Yrbk; 4-H Awd; Grnhnd Awd 94; Ouchita Bapt U; Vet.

WARDRUP, STEVEN D; Southside HS; Fort Smith, AR; (2); Cit Awd; Hon Roll; Prfct Atten Awd; Go-Kart Racing & KART Jr II Champ; Guitar; Westark CC; Engrng.

WARE, LATORIA D; Blytheville Sr HS; Blytheville, AR; (4); Church Yth Grp; Hosp Aide; Chorus; Church Choir; Variety Show; Ofcr Stu Cncl; Vllybl; Cit Awd; Hon Roll; Ntl Merit Ltr; Pdtrcs.

WARE, LATOSHA; Crawfordsville HS; Crawfordsville, AR; (4); 6/24; FBLA; FHA; GAA; Natl Beta Clb; Natl FFA Org; Chorus; Church Choir; Bsktbl; Cit Awd; Hon Roll; GATE; U AR Pine Bluff; Word Prcssng.

WARFORD, JANET; Greenland Jr Sr HS; Greenland, AR; (2); Church Yth Grp; FBLA; Chrldng; Sftbl; Hon Roll; Pres Acad Fit Awd; Edctnl Tlnt Srch; U AR; Math.

WARGO, SHAYNE; Delta Special Schl; Watson, AR; (1); Church Yth Grp; Natl FFA Org; Varsity Clb; Church Choir; Ofcr Frsh Cls; Ofcr Stu Cncl; Ofcr Bsbl; Bsktbl; Cit Awd; Gov Hon Prg Awd; U Of AR Fayetteville; Radiolgy.

WARNER, KAREN M; Southside Schl; Damascus, AR; (3); Cmnty Wkr; 4-H; Library Aide; Natl Beta Clb; Natl FFA Org; Quiz Bowl; School Musical; School Play; Variety Show; Sec Treas Jr Cls; Awd For Outstndg Achvmt; AR Russelvilltech; Ag.

WARNICK, JASON E; Jonesboro HS; Jonesboro, AR; (3); Pres Church Yth Grp; Band; Jazz Band; Mrchg Band; Ofcr Stu Cncl; Hon Roll; Vol Cmp Aldrgt; Ttr Aftr Schl Elem Chldrn; Oral Srgn.

WARNICK, RENEE S; Hoxie Schl; Walnut Ridge, AR; (4); 30/60; Art Clb; French Clb; Quiz Bowl; Science Clb; Teachers Aide; Nwsp; Yrbk; Trk; Vllybl; Hon Roll; Peer Cnslr; PRIDE; Lyon Coll; Psych.

WARNTJES, MELISSA S; Springdale Sr HS; Springdale, AR; (2); FCA; FHA; Intrml JV Bsktbl; Var Co-Capt Crs Cntry; Capt Trk; Hon Roll; Nrsng.

WARR, STEPHANIE K; Cabot HS; Cabot, AR; (2); Church Yth Grp; Quiz Bowl; Band; Jazz Band; Mrchg Band; Pep Band; Jr NHS; AR Jr Symphony Orch; All-Region Band.

WARREN, BRANDI D; Morrilton Sr HS; Morrilton, AR; (3); Cmnty Wkr; Dance Clb; Drama Clb; FBLA; Natl Beta Clb; Natl FFA Org; Science Clb; Spanish Clb; Thesps; Drill Tm; Drill Tm; FFA Prlmntrn; Volunteerism Awd; U Of Cntrl AR; PT.

WARREN, BRANDON B; El Dorado Sr HS; El Dorado, AR; (3); Boy Scts; Church Yth Grp; FCA; Teachers Aide; Nwsp; Yrbk; Rep Jr Cls; Ofcr Bsbl; Ftbl; Socr; Hnr Athl; Key Clb; Steerng Comm; Pre-Med.

WARREN, DEMETRICK T; Central HS; West Helena, AR; (2); ROTC; Bsktbl; Hon Roll; Memphis ST; Elec Engr.

WARREN, EDWARD; Riverview Bapt Christian Sch; Morrilton, AR; (2); Church Yth Grp; School Play; Yrbk; Bsktbl; Score Keeper; Cit Awd; High Hon Roll; Hon Roll; Woodmen Of Amer Awd; Phys Fitness Conv; Chess Cmptn Conv; Game Warden.

WARREN, JASON K; Bryant Sr HS; Alexander, AR; (4); FBLA; Teachers Aide; VICA; Acpl Chr; Church Choir; School Musical; School Play; Stage Crew; Variety Show; Mgr L Ftbl; Outstdng Choir Stdnt Awd; Chrstn Cncl 10-12th Grds; Metro 12th Elecs; Remington Cncl; Elec Engr.

WARREN, JENNIFER R; Newport HS; Newport, AR; (2); Church Yth Grp; FBLA; JCL; Latin Clb; Q&S; Ed Nwsp; Var L Sftbl; Hon Roll; Voice Of Demo Wnr 1st/3rd Pl; Iyon Coll; Pre-Med.

WARREN, JIM E; Crossett Sr HS; Crossett, AR; (2); Church Yth Grp; Mu Alpha Theta; Natl Beta Clb; Spanish Clb; Church Choir; Crs Cntry; Trk; Hon Roll; Pres Acad Fit Awd; LA Tech Univ; Elec/Mech Engr.

WARREN, LISA M; Booneville Jr Sr HS; Booneville, AR; (3); 2/85; Am Leg Aux Girls St; Church Yth Grp; FBLA; Natl Beta Clb; Treas Jr Cls; Treas Sr Cls; Var Bsktbl; Var Sftbl; Hon Roll; Ntl Merit Ltr; Natl Eng Mrt Awd; AR Tech U; Acctng.

WARREN, ROBERT K; Arkansas Sr HS; Texarkana, AR; (2); Key Clb; Var Bsbl; Var Ftbl; Cit Awd; Hon Roll; NHS.

WARREN, ROBERTA; St Paul Schl; Witter, AR; (2); FBLA; FHA; Natl Beta Clb; Sec SADD; Treas Soph Cls; Treas Stu Cncl; High Hon Roll; NHS; U Of AR; Med.

WARREN, SHANE N; West Fork HS; Elkins, AR; (1); FCA; Rep Stu Cncl; Var Bsbl; Var Bsktbl; Var Ftbl; Var Trk; Hon Roll; Sprts Med/Sprts Admin.

WARREN, TAMMIE; Concord Jr Sr HS; Drasco, AR; (4); 2/25; Sec FBLA; HOBY; Treas Natl Beta Clb; Rptr Frsh Cls; Pres Soph Cls; Sec Jr Cls; Sec Sr Cls; Capt Chrldng; Hon Roll; Cit Awd; Amer Schlr; Miss CHS 93-94; Hmcmng Crt; U Of Cntrl AR; Advrtsng.

WARREN, TRINA L; Marion HS; Marion, AR; (4); 32/180; Church Yth Grp; Cmnty Wkr; French Clb; Mu Alpha Theta; Band; Mrchg Band; Orch; French Hon Soc; Hon Roll; NHS; Chrstn Brothers Univ; Pre-Med.

WARREN, VALANTI P; Junction City HS; Junction City, AR; (2); Church Yth Grp; Cmnty Wkr; Teachers Aide; Band; Chorus; Church Choir; Mrchg Band; School Musical; Variety Show; Cit Awd; 1st Pl Loc Sci Fair/Rgnl 2nd Pl/ST; 1st Pl City Pgnt/Bst Evening Gwn; A Avg Awd Eng/Amer Govt Awd; Pine Bluff Univ; Dsgn Engr.

WARRICK, MATTHEW D; Booneville Jr Sr HS; Booneville, AR; (3); 9/84; Am Leg Boys St; Church Yth Grp; FCA; Letterman Clb; Natl Beta Clb; Spanish Clb; Var L Bsbl; Var L Bsktbl; Var L Ftbl; Var L Trk; Vol Work Spec Olympics.

WASHAM, BRITTANI; Mammoth Spring HS; Mammoth Spring, AR; (2); Natl Beta Clb; Pep Clb; Quiz Bowl; SADD; Band; Mrchg Band; Pep Band; Rep Stu Cncl; Bsktbl; Sftbl.

WASHINGTON, ALISHA LASHUN; Ashdown Sr HS; Ashdown, AR; (2); Church Yth Grp; GAA; JV Vllybl; Awd Mntng 3.3 While Ath; Sftbl; Eng/Sci/Med; Spelman; Dctr.

WASHINGTON, ELBONIE A; El Dorado Sr HS; El Dorado, AR; (3); Church Yth Grp; FBLA; SADD; Band; Color Guard; Drm Mjr(t); Mrchg Band; Cit Awd; Oralitoral Cont Dist & St Wnnr; Miss Ebony Pageant; Hnr Roll In Color Guard & Drum Major.

WASHINGTON, ERICKA; Ashdown Sr HS; Ashdown, AR; (1); Church Yth Grp; Rep French Clb; Pres Natl Beta Clb; Church Choir; Rep Frsh Cls; Chrldng; Gym; Sftbl; Hon Roll; NCA All Amer Tm; U Of AR; Pdtrcn.

WASHINGTON, RACHEL J; Parkview Arts-Science HS; Maumelle, AR; (2); Art Clb; Church Yth Grp; Pres Natl Beta Clb; Spanish Clb; Rep Frsh Cls; Crs Cntry; Capt Pom Pon; Trk; Vllybl; FCA; Dance; Fllwshp Chrstn Stud Pres.

WASHINGTON, SHANTRELL R; Arkansas Sr HS; Texarkana, AR; (2); Pres Church Yth Grp; Pres 4-H; FTA; Hosp Aide; Spanish Clb; Band; Church Choir; Color Guard; Flag Corp; Mrchg Band; DARE Awd; UAPB; Elem Ed.

WASHINGTON, TAMIKA; North Little Rock HS; North Little Rock, AR; (1); FCA; GAA; Chrldng; Trk; Hon Roll; UALR; Bus; Nrsng.

WASHINGTON, TENIKA L; Central Sr HS; Little Rock, AR; (3); FBLA; Spanish Clb; Band; Capt Vllybl; Hon Roll; Pres Acad Fit Awd.

WASHINGTON, TIMOTHY D; Jacksonville HS; Jacksonville, AR; (2); 47/360; Art Clb; Band; Church Choir; Mrchg Band; Pep Band; Cit Awd; Hon Roll; Prfct Atten Awd; Med; Surgical Dr.

WATERBURY, ALISSA; Northside HS; Fort Smith, AR; (3); Church Yth Grp; Office Aide; Teachers Aide; Chrldng; Gym; Trk; Vllybl; Hon Roll.

WATERS, DAVID; Huntsville HS; Huntsville, AR; (2); 2/154; Science Clb; Band; Mrchg Band; Pep Band; Rep Stu Cncl; Var JV Bsktbl; Hon Roll; U AR; Elec Engrng.

WATERS, JAMES R; Mc Rae Schl; Beebe, AR; (3); Math Tm; VICA; Church Choir; Variety Show; Ofcr Bsbl; Bsktbl; Crs Cntry; Trk; Hon Roll; Prfct Atten Awd; Math & Sci Awds; Fayetteville; Tchr; Coach.

WATERS, LEAH R; Hoxie Schl; Sedgwick, AR; (3); FHA; GAA; Pep Clb; Quiz Bowl; Treas Science Clb; Treas Spanish Clb; Treas Thesps; Chorus; Bsktbl; Chrldng; Rnr-Up Miss Mustang 96; 2nd Rnr-Up Miss Mustang 95; AK ST Univ; Rdlgy.

WATERS, PAT R; Valley Springs Schl; Harrison, AR; (2); Band; NACTC; Singer; Songwriter.

WATFORD, RYAN D; Southside HS; Fort Smith, AR; (2); Debate Tm; Key Clb; Band; Jazz Band; Ofcr Frsh Cls; Ofcr Stu Cncl; Var Bsktbl; Var Tennis; Hon Roll; Pres Acad Fit Awd; Doc.

WATKINS, AMANDA; Central Ark Christian Schl; Little Rock, AR; (3); FBLA; Natl Beta Clb; Science Clb; Spanish Clb; Yrbk; Chrldng; Socr; Trk; High Hon Roll; NHS; Chrldng NCA All Amer, Chr Cntrl Brvs Allstar; FBLA Dist VIII Treas.

WATKINS, ANGELA N; Mena HS; Greenwood, AR; (1); Church Yth Grp; Teachers Aide; JV Chrldng; JV Vllybl; Hon Roll; Bus Mgmt.

WATKINS, BRANDI; Brinkley HS; Brinkley, AR; (3); French Clb; Library Aide; Chorus; Ed Yrbk; Sec Jr Cls; Ofcr Stu Cncl; Capt Chrldng; Tennis; VP Jr NHS; Sec NHS; U Of AR; Med.

WATKINS, CHRIS S; Catholic HS; Little Rock, AR; (3); 51/176; Church Yth Grp; Ftbl; Baylor Univ; Acctg/Fin.

WATKINS, CHRISTOPHE; Greenland Jr Sr HS; Fayetteville, AR; (3); Church Yth Grp; FBLA; HOBY; Church Choir; School Play; Ofcr Frsh Cls; Ofcr Soph Cls; Ofcr Jr Cls; Ofcr Stu Cncl; Bsktbl; Math, Alg I, Gmtry, Lfe, Erth, Phys Sci, Eng, Amer Hstry, Fbio, Kybrdng; Insprtn Awd.

WATKINS, CHRISTY; Hope HS; Hope, AR; (3); Church Yth Grp; French Clb; FBLA; Natl Beta Clb; Variety Show; Rep Treas Stu Cncl; Chrldng; Cit Awd; High Hon Roll; NHS.

WATKINS, DEANNA; Van Buren Sr HS; Van Buren, AR; (4); 12/270; Pres Computer Clb; French Clb; JA; Math Clb; Mu Alpha Theta; Drill Tm; Jazz Band; Mrchg Band; School Play; High Hon Roll; Erth Club; Comm Thtr; Natl Ldrshp Svc Awd; Weslark CC; Cmptr Systm Eng.

WATKINS, EDWARD P; Nettleton HS; Jonesboro, AR; (3); Church Yth Grp; Spanish Clb; School Play; Hon Roll; Bsbl; AR ST; Pre-Med.

WATKINS, JOHN W; Alma HS; Alma, AR; (4); 22/186; Church Yth Grp; Computer Clb; Teachers Aide; Bsktbl; Ftbl; Wt Lftg; Hon Roll; NHS; Westark CC; Elec Engr.

WATKINS, LANDON P; Valley Springs Schl; Harrison, AR; (3); 1/58; 4-H; French Clb; FBLA; Key Clb; Natl FFA Org; Quiz Bowl; Var Bsbl; Hon Roll; NHS; Art Clb; Tm Roping; Natl FFA Org Washington Ldrshp Conf.

WATKINS, REGINA; Van Cove HS; Vandervoort, AR; (4); 2/32; Church Yth Grp; Pres FBLA; Model UN; Treas Natl Beta Clb; Natl FFA Org; Quiz Bowl; Yrbk; Hon Roll; NHS; Sal; Fire Marshall; Elks Clb Stu Of Mnth; Offc Wrkr; S AR Univ; Busag.

WATKINS, SABRINA; Horatio HS; Horatio, AR; (2); Pres Rep FHA; Chorus; Rep Yrbk; Rep Jr Cls; Henderson; Bus.

WATKINS, SHARINA; St Paul Schl; Witter, AR; (2); 1/30; FBLA; FHA; Natl Beta Clb; SADD; School Play; Sec Frsh Cls; Var Bsktbl; Trk; High Hon Roll; Ntl Merit Ltr; Pee-Wee Bsktbl Coach; U Of AR.

WATKINS, SUMMER; Augusta HS; Augusta, AR; (2); Treas FBLA; Natl Beta Clb; Science Clb; Spanish Clb; Chorus; High Hon Roll; NHS; Bus Mgmt.

WATKINS, TIFFANY A; Pulaski Acad; Little Rock, AR; (3); Church Yth Grp; Cmnty Wkr; Dance Clb; Drama Clb; Spanish Clb; Drill Tm; School Play; Rep Frsh Cls.

WATKINS, TRACI J; Van Buren Sr HS; Van Buren, AR; (2); Debate Tm; FBLA; FHA; Hosp Aide; Science Clb; Hon Roll; Aikido Assn Of Amer; 1st Pl Tm Wrk Sci Fair Awd; King Opera Hse Plyrs; Westark CC; Police Invstgtr.

WATLINGTON, BRANDY M; Midland HS; Pangburn, AR; (4); 4/45; Church Yth Grp; FBLA; FHA; Natl Beta Clb; Pep Clb; Mgr Yrbk; Pres Jr Cls; Stat Bsktbl; High Hon Roll; U Of Centr AR; CPA.

WATSON, CHRIS L; Crowleys Ridge Acad; Paragould, AR; (3); 4/24; Art Clb; Church Yth Grp; Cmnty Wkr; FBLA; Pep Clb; Science Clb; Service Clb; Spanish Clb; School Play; Treas Frsh Cls; Chmbr Of Cmmrce Yth Comm; KIDS; Harding U.

WATSON, CHRISTINA; Bald Knob HS; Bald Knob, AR; (4); 9/76; Cmnty Wkr; HOBY; Math Tm; Office Aide; Chorus; Church Choir; JV Bsktbl; Capt Powder Puff Ftbl; High Hon Roll; Hon Roll; Coe Cmmttee; Shw Choir; Madrgl Choir; Cntrl Bapt Coll; Sprts Med.

WATSON, DORSEY; Harmony Grove Jr Sr HS; Camden, AR; (1); 4/55; Church Yth Grp; Natl FFA Org; Science Clb; Church Choir; Rep Stu Cncl; JV Bsktbl; JV Ftbl; Cit Awd; Hon Roll.

WATSON, ERIC M; Searcy HS; Searcy, AR; (3); 9/300; Church Yth Grp; Natl Beta Clb; Band; Jazz Band; Mrchg Band; Pep Band; French Hon Soc; High Hon Roll; Hon Roll; Jr NHS.

WATSON, JEFF R; Lake Hamilton Sr HS; Hot Springs Natio, AR; (2); FCA; Stat Bsktbl; JV Tennis; Hon Roll; Praise Band; Chrch Easter Play.

WATSON, JONATHAN; Abundant Life Schools; Jacksonville, AR; (4); #1 in class; Church Yth Grp; Chorus; School Play; Rptr Yrbk; Var Bsbl; Capt Bsktbl; High Hon Roll; NHS; Ntl Merit Ltr; Val; Ouachita Baptist U.

WATSON, LASHUNDRA N; Arkansas Sr HS; Texarkana, AR; (3); 21/398; Am Leg Aux Girls St; Art Clb; Church Yth Grp; Dance Clb; Drama Clb; FHA; Mu Alpha Theta; Varsity Clb; Church Choir; Drill Tm; Austin Coll; Med.

WATSON, LINDSEY F; Bald Knob HS; Bald Knob, AR; (3); Art Clb; Church Yth Grp; Natl Beta Clb; Office Aide; Acpl Chr; Chorus; Church Choir; Swing Chorus; Ofcr Stu Cncl; High Hon Roll; PRIDE; Cntrl Baptist Col; Bus.

WATSON, SETH D; Arkansas Sr HS; Texarkana, AR; (3); Church Yth Grp; Key Clb; Spanish Clb; Rep Soph Cls; Rep Jr Cls; Var L Bsbl; Var Bsktbl; Var Ftbl.

WATSON, SHANDOLYN; Dumas Jr HS; Dumas, AR; (1); Church Yth Grp; FBLA; Pres Spanish Clb; Band; Church Choir; Ofcr Stu Cncl; Cit Awd; Hon Roll; Grambling ST U; Law.

WATSON, TIFFINEY S; Harmony Grove Jr Sr HS; East Camden, AR; (3); 9/65; Am Leg Aux Girls St; Treas FBLA; VP FHA; Treas Spanish Clb; VP Jr Cls; VP Stu Cncl; Var Bsktbl; Capt Chrldng; Trk; Cit Awd; U Of AR Fayetteville; Bus.

WATSON, WENDY N; Alma HS; Alma, AR; (3); Church Yth Grp; FBLA; Spanish Clb; Band; Color Guard; Flag Corp; Mrchg Band; Pep Band; Hon Roll; NHS; Waterskiing; Westark CC; Ed; Child Psych.

WATSON, WILLIAM J; Arkansas Schl Math & Science; Conway, AR; (4); Boy Scts; Church Yth Grp; Cmnty Wkr; FBLA; Intnl Clb; JA; Mu Alpha Theta; Science Clb; Spanish Clb; Ofcr Jr Cls; Chem Engrng.

WATT, NATHAN A; Magnolia HS; Magnolia, AR; (4); French Clb; Quiz Bowl; Teachers Aide; Band; Mrchg Band; Pep Band; Hon Roll; Ntl Merit SF.

WATTERS, ANGELA L; Morrilton Sr HS; Morrilton, AR; (2); Library Aide; Rptr Natl FFA Org; Wnnr Of Sub-Area FFA Creed Cont 96; Mrt Awds For Math & Sci; Ag Tchr.

WATTS, CRYSTAL; Blevins HS; Mc Caskill, AR; (3); FHA; HOBY; Natl Beta Clb; Church Choir; Bsktbl; Chrldng; Trk; Cit Awd; Hon Roll; ADAPT; Upward Bnd.

WATTS, LORI K; Timbo Schl; Harriet, AR; (2); 1/30; Church Yth Grp; FBLA; FHA; GAA; Natl Beta Clb; Yrbk; Treas Frsh Cls; Treas Soph Cls; Rep Stu Cncl; Cit Awd; Arts/Commctns.

WAYCASTER, LAURA; Shirley Jr Sr HS; Fairfield Bay, AR; (4); 2/30; Church Yth Grp; FCA; FBLA; Natl Beta Clb; Science Clb; SADD; JV Var Bsktbl; JV Var Vllybl; High Hon Roll; Sal; Skiing; Boating; Ouachita Bapt U; Pre-Optometry.

WAYMACK, EMILY; Cabot HS; Austin, AR; (3); Church Yth Grp; HOBY; Natl FFA Org; Teachers Aide; L Trk; Hon Roll; NHS; Pres Cabot FFA Chptr; Rdng Horses, Rodeo; Lonole Cty Rodeo Qn 93-94; Animal Sci.

WAYMACK, JENNIFER; Pea Ridge HS; Bentonville, AR; (3); 5/63; Church Yth Grp; Drama Clb; Pres FBLA; Spanish Clb; Band; Mrchg Band; Rptr Stu Cncl; Cit Awd; Hon Roll; Kiwanis Awd; Pres Acad Awd; U S Achvmnt Acad; U Of Cntrl AR; Med.

WEAKS, PRISCILLA E; Bay Jr Sr HS; Trumann, AR; (3); 8/42; Pres FHA; Science Clb; Chorus; Rep Soph Cls; Rep Jr Cls; Var Sftbl; High Hon Roll; Hon Roll; Prfct Atten Awd; Science Clb; Delta Voc Tech Inst; Bus/Own.

WEAR, JAIME L; Southside HS; Fort Smith, AR; (2); Church Yth Grp; Drama Clb; Band; Mrchg Band; Pep Band; School Musical; School Play; Stage Crew; Hon Roll; Pres Acad Fit Awd; Miss Teen Sebastian Cty Contestant; Novelist.

WEATHERFORD, TAMMY L; Des Arc Jr Sr HS; Des Arc, AR; (2); Cmnty Wkr; Library Aide; Teachers Aide; Yrbk; Ofcr Soph Cls; JV Var Chrldng; JV Var Pom Pon; Wt Lftg; Hon Roll; U Of AR; Law Enfrcmnt.

WEATHERLY, JOEY D; Crossett Sr HS; Crossett, AR; (2); 69/250; Natl Beta Clb; Hon Roll; Babe Ruth Bsbl; Boys & Girls Clb Of Amer; U Of AR; Sports Medicine.

WEATHERLY, ROBERT R; Southside HS; Fort Smith, AR; (2); Mu Alpha Theta; Teachers Aide; Band; Mrchg Band; Ed Nwsp; Rep Frsh Cls; Tennis; Hon Roll; Jr NHS; NHS; Black Belt Tae Kwon Do; Air Force Acad; Arntcl Engr.

WEATHERS, JENNIFER; Fayetteville Christian Schl; Fayetteville, AR; (1); Church Yth Grp; Chrldng; Socr; High Hon Roll.

WEATHERSPOON, CASIE M; West Memphis Sr HS; Marion, AR; (4); 75/357; Church Yth Grp; English Clb; French Clb; FHA; Math Clb; Band; Church Choir; Color Guard; Mrchg Band; Orch; UIDS; Mid South CC; Psych.

WEAVER, AMANDA; Cave City HS; Cave City, AR; (2); Pres French Clb; FHA; Key Clb; Natl Beta Clb; Sftbl; High Hon Roll; Prfct Atten Awd; CAD; RN.

WEAVER, AMANDA D; St Joe Public Schl; Witts Springs, AR; (2); Church Yth Grp; 4-H; FBLA; Natl FFA Org; Quiz Bowl; VP Frsh Cls; VP Soph Cls; Bsktbl; 4-H Awd; High Hon Roll; Project WET; Envirothon Team Won St; Many Photo Awds.

WEAVER, AMY S; Cave City HS; Cave City, AR; (2); 18/82; Church Yth Grp; FHA; Key Clb; Natl Beta Clb; Teachers Aide; Co-Capt Chrldng; Hon Roll; Jr Math/Sci Club; HS Eng Tchr.

WEAVER, BRANDI N; Parkin Jr Sr HS; Parkin, AR; (3); GAA; Girl Scts; Hosp Aide; Natl Beta Clb; Science Clb; SADD; Church Choir; Ofcr Jr Cls; Hon Roll; NHS; Positive Image Clb; Italian Clb; Frgn Lang Clb; Hstry Clb; Thrpy.

WEAVER, DESHARHEA M; Clarendon Jr Sr HS; Clarendon, AR; (1); Church Yth Grp; FBLA; Natl Beta Clb; Office Aide; Yrbk; Hist Frsh Cls; Chrldng; High Hon Roll; Cmnty Wkr; 4-H; LEO Clb; Lion Pride Stars; Stu Cncl; UCA; Acctng.

WEAVER, HOLLY; Sulphur Rock Schl; Sulphur Rock, AR; (3); 1/20; 4-H; HOBY; Pres Key Clb; Treas Natl Beta Clb; Chorus; Nwsp; Ed Yrbk; Treas Stu Cncl; Var Bsktbl; High Hon Roll; Med.

WEAVER, JENNIFER; West Memphis Sr HS; Proctor, AR; (4); 42/256; Church Yth Grp; FBLA; Math Clb; Mu Alpha Theta; Natl Beta Clb; Band; Mrchg Band; Hon Roll; Southwest Tech; CAD Pgm.

WEAVER, JUSTIN; Van Buren Sr HS; Van Buren, AR; (2); 17/310; Church Yth Grp; HOBY; Mu Alpha Theta; Science Clb; Rep Soph Cls; Bsktbl; JV L Ftbl; High Hon Roll; NHS; Prfct Atten Awd; Natl His/Govt Awd; All-Amer Schlr Awd; Natl Ldrshp/Svc Awds; U Of AR; Atty.

WEAVER, KIMBERLY; Jessieville HS; Jessieville, AR; (4); Pres FBLA; Sec FHA; Pres Speech Tm; Band; Chorus; Nwsp; Pres Sr Cls; Rep Stu Cncl; DAR Awd; Hon Roll.

WEAVER, LATONYA; Brinkley HS; Brinkley, AR; (3); Church Yth Grp; Cmnty Wkr; FCA; FBLA; FHA; GAA; Girl Scts; Letterman Clb; Office Aide; Q&S; All Dist Bsktbl, Chrldng; UCA Conway; Math.

WEAVER, MICHAEL E; Booneville Jr Sr HS; Booneville, AR; (2); Church Yth Grp; French Clb; Natl Beta Clb; Band; Mrchg Band; Pep Band; JV Bsbl; JV Bsktbl; NHS.

WEAVER, MICHAEL J; West Fork HS; West Fork, AR; (3); Church Yth Grp; Natl FFA Org; JV Bsktbl; Hon Roll; NHS; Star Greenhand Awd; Industrial Arts Awd; Eng, Math & Bus Law Awds; U Of AR; Ag.

WEAVER, MOLLIE E; Lavaca Jr Sr HS; Lavaca, AR; (3); 13/60; Art Clb; Church Yth Grp; Library Aide; Natl Beta Clb; Church Choir; Cit Awd; Hon Roll; HOPE; Westark CC.

WEAVER, NATHAN L; Vilonia HS; Vilonia, AR; (3); 14/148; Church Yth Grp; Model UN; Mu Alpha Theta; Natl Beta Clb; Office Aide; Var L Bsktbl; High Hon Roll; Hon Roll.

WEBB, AMBER N; Westside HS; Cash, AR; (4); 4/79; Church Yth Grp; VP FBLA; FHA; Science Clb; Teachers Aide; Chorus; High Hon Roll; NHS; Pres Acad Fit Awd; Chrstns Making A Difference; Acteens; AR ST Univ.

WEBB, ANDREA L; John L Mcclellan Magnet HS; Little Rock, AR; (2); FBLA; FHA; JA; Letterman Clb; Mu Alpha Theta; Natl Beta Clb; Yrbk; Stat Bsktbl; Mgr(s); Score Keeper; Bowling; Spelman; Criminology; Psych.

WEBB, ANDREA N; Buffalo Island Central HS; Leachville, AR; (2); Drama Clb; FBLA; FTA; Library Aide; Spanish Clb; Band; School Play; Hon Roll; NHS; AR ST Univ.

WEBB, ANTHONY; Riverside HS; Lake City, AR; (4); Church Yth Grp; French Clb; Key Clb; Natl FFA Org; Quiz Bowl; Chorus; Rep Sr Cls; Cit Awd; Hon Roll; Chrstn Clb; Cmptr Sci.

WEBB, ATHENA M; Parkview Arts-Science HS; Little Rock, AR; (2); Art Clb; Cmnty Wkr; French Clb; Natl Beta Clb; Teachers Aide; Stage Crew; Cit Awd; Hon Roll; Jr NHS; Photo; Childrens Hosp Vol; Flwshp Of Chrstn Schls; Tchr; Photo; Actress.

WEBB, COURTNEY; Lee Acad; Marianna, AR; (3); HOBY; SADD; Yrbk; Rep Frsh Cls; Rep Stu Cncl; Bsktbl; Sftbl; Trk; High Hon Roll; NHS; U Of AR.

WEBB, CRYSTAL D; Fayetteville Sr HS; Elkins, AR; (3); Debate Tm; French Clb; Teachers Aide; Band; Jazz Band; Mrchg Band; Pep Band; Nwsp; Hon Roll; Young Democrates; TX Chrstn U; Pol Sci/Intl Rel.

WEBB, DAVID E; Mt Ida Jr Sr HS; Story, AR; (3); #2 in class; Natl Beta Clb; Natl FFA Org; Ofcr Bsbl; Bsktbl; High Hon Roll; U Of AR; Eng.

WEBB, ERICA; Parkview Arts-Science HS; North Little Rock, AR; (3); 9/275; Church Yth Grp; Natl Beta Clb; Church Choir; Orch; School Play; Hon Roll; NHS; Yth Orch Univ AR Little Rock; All Dist Orch SE MO; Yth Orch SE MO ST Univ; Cntrl Bapt Coll; Law.

WEBB, JASON HARRIS; Prescott HS; Prescott, AR; (3); Am Leg Boys St; Church Yth Grp; FBLA; Treas Sr Cls; Rep Stu Cncl; L Bsbl; L Bsktbl; L Ftbl; Hon Roll; NHS; Page Intern Pgm For Senator Mike Ross; NV Cty Comm Theatre; Southern AR U.

WEBB, JESSICA H; Morrilton Sr HS; Morrilton, AR; (3); Drama Clb; Quiz Bowl; Thesps; School Musical; School Play; Ed Nwsp; Yrbk; Gov Hon Prg Awd; U Of Chicago; Jrnlsm.

WEBB, JOSEPH R; Conway Sr HS; Conway, AR; (2); Church Yth Grp; Service Clb; Teachers Aide; Church Choir; Hon Roll.

WEBB, KRISTEN M; Bald Knob HS; Bald Knob, AR; (4); 19/91; Church Yth Grp; Natl Beta Clb; Teachers Aide; Acpl Chr; Chorus; Hon Roll; Pres Acad Fit Awd; AR ST Univ; Bio.

WEBB, LAURA; J A Fair Sr HS; Little Rock, AR; (4); Art Clb; Church Yth Grp; Drama Clb; Science Clb; Band; School Play; Chrldng; Trk; Hon Roll; Univ Of Cntrl AR; Orthdnta.

WEBB, LORA; Southside HS; Batesville, AR; (3); 1/90; Church Yth Grp; FBLA; Hosp Aide; HOBY; Key Clb; Rptr Natl Beta Clb; Science Clb; Teachers Aide; Band; Bsktbl; Trck All-St; Pride Team Perfrmr; Candy Striper Pgm Miss Congenialty; U Of Central AR; Phys Thrpy.

WEBB, LOURIE N; Lonoke Jr HS; Lonoke, AR; (1); Church Yth Grp; Science Clb; Hon Roll; NHS; Odyssey Of The Mind SE AR Div; Union Coll; Pediatrics; Gen Prac.

WEBB, MEGAN C; El Dorado Sr HS; El Dorado, AR; (3); Am Leg Aux Girls St; Cmnty Wkr; Natl Beta Clb; Service Clb; Teachers Aide; Nwsp; Yrbk; NHS; Pres Acad Fit Awd; REACH & PRIDE Pgms; Civitan; Campfire, Anchor Clb; SAU; Law.

WEBB, MISTY; Danville HS; Danville, AR; (3); 5/38; Cmnty Wkr; Drama Clb; FHA; Girl Scts; Pep Clb; Speech Tm; SADD; Band; Color Guard; Flag Corp; Miss Discipline; Soph Maid For Winter Dance 96; Band Cncl Rep; AR Tech Univ; Bio; Comp Sci.

WEBB, MISTY V; Gravette HS; Gravette, AR; (2); 5/96; Church Yth Grp; FCA; FBLA; Yrbk; Var Co-Capt Chrldng; Gym; Powder Puff Ftbl; Hon Roll; NHS; Woodman Of Wrld Awd; All Amer Chrldr; Multiple Yr Listing; U Of AR; Bus.

WEBB, WILLIAM B; Southside HS; Fort Smith, AR; (2); Church Yth Grp; Key Clb; Spanish Clb; Teachers Aide; Mgr Mgr(s); Socr; Hon Roll; Tnns.

WEBSTER, JAMEELAH; North Little Rock Hs-West; North Little Rock, AR; (4); Am Leg Aux Girls St; Church Yth Grp; Dance Clb; Debate Tm; FCA; FTA; GAA; Intnl Clb; Key Clb; Pep Clb; Hmcmng Court; Modeling; Clark Univ; Pre-Med; Model.

WEBSTER, JON W; Marvell Acad; Holly Grove, AR; (4); Office Aide; Spanish Clb; Teachers Aide; School Play; Sec Sr Cls; Cit Awd; Hon Roll; Prfct Atten Awd; AR ST Univ; Ag Bus.

WEDDINGTON, KERI; Lee Acad; Forrest City, AR; (2); Sec Frsh Cls; Var Capt Chrldng; Trk; Natl Math Awd.

WEDGWORTH, VICKIE; Augusta HS; Augusta, AR; (1); Church Yth Grp; Natl Beta Clb; Science Clb; Spanish Clb; Church Choir; Pres Frsh Cls; Rep Stu Cncl; Hon Roll.

WEEKS, APRIL L; Star City HS; Star City, AR; (2); Church Yth Grp; Computer Clb; FBLA; FHA; Natl Beta Clb; Science Clb; Spanish Clb; DAR Awd; Berkley; Genetic Engrng.

WEEKS, MCKALE S; Northside HS; Fort Smith, AR; (3); Church Yth Grp; FCA; FBLA; VP Latin Clb; Letterman Clb; Teachers Aide; Band; Mrchg Band; Pep Band; Var Ftbl; All St All Region Band; Multi-Yr Listee; U Of AR; Med.

WEEKS, ROBYN L; Bentonville Sr HS; Bentonville, AR; (3); 5/340; Church Yth Grp; Key Clb; Band; Mrchg Band; Orch; Pep Band; School Musical; Ed Nwsp; Rptr Yrbk; Rptr Jr Cls; Evangell; Jrnlsm/Mnstry.

WEEMS, KRISTY L; Stamps HS; Buckner, AR; (3); 4/40; Am Leg Aux Girls St; FBLA; FHA; Mu Alpha Theta; Spanish Clb; Mrchg Band; School Play; Hon Roll; Jr NHS; NHS.

WEEMS, LATANA; Holly Grove HS; Holly Grove, AR; (2); Church Yth Grp; Cmnty Wkr; FHA; Natl FFA Org; Office Aide; Church Choir; U Of AR Pine Bluff; Elem Tchr.

WEENS, KRISTY L; Stamps HS; Buckner, AR; (3); 4/40; Am Leg Aux Girls St; Phtg FBLA; Sec FHA; Mu Alpha Theta; Natl FFA Org; Spanish Clb; Flag Corp; School Play; Hon Roll; NHS.

WEINSINGER, EMILY; Northside HS; Van Buren, AR; (4); Treas FBLA; Pep Clb; Teachers Aide; Ofcr Stu Cncl; Chrldng; Gym; Hon Roll; People To People Stu Ambsdr New Zealand/Figi; FBLA/STU Cncl Treas; Westark CC Schlrshp; Miss Nrthsd; Westark CC; Chef.

WEIR, BRIAN L; Southside HS; Fort Smith, AR; (2); Church Yth Grp; FCA; Key Clb; Letterman Clb; Mu Alpha Theta; Crs Cntry; Trk; High Hon Roll; NHS; Pres Acad Fit Awd; U Of AR; Mech; Elec Engrng.

WEIR, JILL; Hoxie Schl; Walnut Ridge, AR; (4); 1/60; Am Leg Aux Girls St; Model UN; Natl Beta Clb; Science Clb; Spanish Clb; Nwsp; Pres Jr Cls; VP Sr Cls; Rep Stu Cncl; Capt Bsktbl; Gftd/Tlntd Awd; Engl, Chem, Alg I & II & Civics Awds; AR ST U; Med.

WEIS, RACHEL C; Bergman Schl; Harrison, AR; (2); Church Yth Grp; Natl Beta Clb; Teachers Aide; Band; Chorus; NACTC; Cmptr Bus.

WEISENFELS, LIZ A; Southside HS; Fort Smith, AR; (2).

WEISENFELS, MICHELLE L; Northside HS; Fort Smith, AR; (4); 8/350; Am Leg Aux Girls St; Church Yth Grp; Sec FCA; GAA; Sec Mu Alpha Theta; Ofcr Stu Cncl; Capt L Bsktbl; NHS; Pres Schlr; Cmnty Wkr; US Army Rsrv Schlr, Athl Awd; Bsktbl All Conf, All Area Tm; Westark CC; Bio.

WELCH, AMY J; Hampton Jr Sr HS; Hampton, AR; (4); 4/63; Natl Beta Clb; Teachers Aide; Ed Yrbk; Pres Stu Cncl; L Tennis; High Hon Roll; Hon Roll; Sal; GCECA Pres; MASH; S AR Univ; RN.

WELCH, ANGELA R; Smackover HS; Louann, AR; (2); 7/50; Church Yth Grp; Cmnty Wkr; Q&S; Spanish Clb; Band; Yrbk; NHS; Drama Clb; FTA; Stage Crew; Pres Of BASIC; START Tech Clb; Gfted Tlntd Prog.

WELCH, JENNIFER L; Yellville Summit HS; Yellville, AR; (2); 7/80; FBLA; Office Aide; Teachers Aide; Band; Drm Mjr(t); Mrchg Band; High Hon Roll; NHS; Pres Acad Fit Awd; Univ Of Cntrl AR.

WELCH, KIMBERLY D; Trumann HS; Trumann, AR; (3); Art Clb; German Clb; NFL; Bsktbl; Hon Roll; NHS; Sci Awd; Swimming.

WELCH, LILY B; Smackover HS; Louann, AR; (1); Church Yth Grp; FBLA; Hon Roll.

WELCH, TIFFANY M; Vilonia HS; Conway, AR; (3); FBLA; Pres FHA; Mu Alpha Theta; Natl Beta Clb; Office Aide; Spanish Clb; Teachers Aide; School Play; Hon Roll; U Of AR Fayetteville.

WELLINGHOFF, ANN; East End Jr Sr HS; Houston, AR; (4); 1/39; Math Tm; Natl Beta Clb; Teachers Aide; Treas Soph Cls; Treas Jr Cls; Treas Sr Cls; High Hon Roll; Val; Gftd & Tlntd; Mst Likely To Succeed; U Of AR Fayettevl; Engrng.

WELLS, ANNE; Ft Smith Christian Schl; Fort Smith, AR; (3); Church Yth Grp; Cmnty Wkr; FCA; FBLA; Mrchg Band; VP Soph Cls; Stat Bsktbl; High Hon Roll; Hon Roll; NHS; Brdcstng.

WELLS, BECKY L; Waldron HS; Waldron, AR; (3); Am Leg Aux Girls St; Church Yth Grp; Pres 4-H; Girl Scts; Spanish Clb; Teachers Aide; Chorus; Church Choir; Yrbk; Score Keeper; US His Awd; Sec Ed.

WELLS, JEREMY L; Sacred Heart Schl; Solgohachia, AR; (3); Church Yth Grp; Key Clb; SADD; Phtg Yrbk; Bsktbl; Hon Roll; Prfct Atten Awd; Comp.

WELLS, JILL S; Stamps HS; Buckner, AR; (3); 7/60; Church Yth Grp; FCA; 4-H; Math Clb; Mu Alpha Theta; Natl FFA Org; Science Clb; Varsity Clb; Church Choir; Bsktbl; SAU.

WELLS, JOHN; Alma HS; Alma, AR; (3); Church Yth Grp; French Clb; Mu Alpha Theta; Office Aide; Band; Rptr Soph Cls; Sec Jr Cls; Cit Awd; Hon Roll; NHS; Tae Kwon Do; Westark; Ind Engrng.

WELLS, JOHN D; Rogers HS; Rogers, AR; (3); Bsktbl; U Of Ar; Bus Mgmt.

WELLS, KACY S; Junction City HS; El Dorado, AR; (3); 1/56; Am Leg Aux Girls St; FBLA; Science Clb; Drm Mjr(t); Jazz Band; Pres Hist Stu Cncl; Var Sftbl; High Hon Roll; NHS; Church Yth Grp; SASIC Sec; Phy Thrpy.

WELLS, KENDRA A; Sloan-Hendrix Jr Sr HS; Ravenden, AR; (4); Art Clb; FBLA; Natl FFA Org; Office Aide; Teachers Aide; Yrbk; Pres Frsh Cls; VP Sr Cls; Rep Stu Cncl; Ntl Merit Ltr; Rodeo Barrel Racing; Cottonbou Tech Inst; Nrsng.

WELLS, KILEY J; Clay Co Central Jr Sr HS; Greenway, AR; (3); Church Yth Grp; Cmnty Wkr; 4-H; German Clb; Teachers Aide; Band; Mrchg Band; Pep Band; Rptr Nwsp; Pres Stu Cncl; All Amer Schlr; US Math Acad; AR ST U.

WELLS, MELISSA; Dermott HS; Dermott, AR; (2); Church Yth Grp; Dance Clb; Drama Clb; FBLA; Natl Beta Clb; Drill Tm; School Play; Sftbl; High Hon Roll; NHS; Law.

WELLS, MELISSA A; Fayetteville Sr HS; Fayetteville, AR; (2); Church Yth Grp; GAA; Var Bsktbl; Hon Roll; U Of AR; Ath Trnr.

WELLS, SARAH; Ft Smith Christian Schl; Fort Smith, AR; (1); Band; Ofcr Frsh Cls; Cit Awd; Hon Roll; Prfct Atten Awd.

WELSCH, KIPLAN K; Lake Hamilton Sr HS; Hot Springs Natio, AR; (3); Art Clb; Natl FFA Org; Hon Roll; NHS; 2nd Pl St Ag Mechanics Team Championship; 1st Pl Dist Team Ag Mechanics Cont; GM Fin Schl; GMAC Fin Admin.

WENCK, MEGAN; Southside HS; Fort Smith, AR; (2); Pres Church Yth Grp; School Play; Rep Stu Cncl; Hon Roll; Pres Acad Fit Awd; Val; Savannah Coll; Intr Dsgn.

WERNER, RANDY; West Fork HS; West Fork, AR; (4); Church Yth Grp; FCA; VP Jr Cls; Sec Sr Cls; Var Bsbl; Var Bsktbl; Var Ftbl; Var Trk; Hon Roll; NHS; IM Bsktbl; Upward Bound; Educl Talent Search; U Of AR.

WERSCHKY, AIMEE S; Greenwood Sr HS; Fort Smith, AR; (2); Church Yth Grp; GAA; Church Choir; JV Bsktbl; Var Sftbl; Cit Awd; Hon Roll.

WESLEY, KAMEELAH; Parkview Arts-Science HS; Little Rock, AR; (4); 16/261; VP Church Yth Grp; Cmnty Wkr; VP FBLA; Mu Alpha Theta; Natl Beta Clb; Teachers Aide; Band; Church Choir; Capt Mrchg Band; School Musical; All Region 1st Band; Ladies Clb; AR Natl Guard Awd; 2nd Pl Zeta Phi Beta Awd; U Of OK; Chem Engrng.

WESLEY, RODERICK D; J A Fair Sr HS; Little Rock, AR; (3); 4-H; FTA; Band; Var Bsktbl; Var Ftbl; Cmptr Engr/Acctg.

WESLEY, TENA; Stephens Jr Sr HS; Camden, AR; (3); French Clb; Rptr FBLA; Hist FHA; Hon Roll; NHS; Prfct Atten Awd; Pres Acad Fit Awd; S AR Univ; Acctng.

WEST, ADAM; Sulphur Rock Schl; Batesville, AR; (4); Natl FFA Org; Pres Frsh Cls; VP Soph Cls; Rep Stu Cncl; Var Bsbl; Var Bsktbl; Hon Roll.

WEST, ALICIA D; Mountainburg Jr Sr HS; Mountainburg, AR; (3); FCA; Natl Beta Clb; VP Natl FFA Org; SADD; Var Bsktbl; Hon Roll; U Of AR; Chld Psychlgy.

WEST, ALLISON; Rison HS; Rison, AR; (3); 4/40; Art Clb; Church Yth Grp; Rptr FBLA; Natl Beta Clb; Science Clb; Church Choir; Yrbk; Chrldng; Hon Roll; NHS; U AR; Med.

WEST, AMANDA M; Russellville Sr HS; Russellville, AR; (3); Church Yth Grp; Q&S; Spanish Clb; Band; Mrchg Band; Yrbk; Hon Roll; Jr NHS; NHS; Natl Yth Ldrsp Forum On Med; ER Dr.

WEST, ASHLEY; El Dorado Sr HS; El Dorado, AR; (2); Church Yth Grp; FBLA; Natl Beta Clb; Ed Yrbk; High Hon Roll; NHS; Pres Schlr; Cmnty Wkr; Service Clb; Chorus; Anchor Club; Oratorio Sel Choir; BASIC; 13 Yrs Of Dance; Ouachita Bapt Univ.

WEST, JESSICA H; North Little Rock HS West; North Little Rock, AR; (3); 60/554; Church Yth Grp; FCA; Key Clb; Mu Alpha Theta; Natl Beta Clb; Drill Tm; Pom Pon; Powder Puff Ftbl; High Hon Roll; Hon Roll; Great Outdoors; STAND For Christ; Criminal Justice.

WEST, JOEDI D; Concord Jr Sr HS; Drasco, AR; (3); Sec Art Clb; Church Yth Grp; FBLA; Natl Beta Clb; Science Clb; Band; Yrbk; Mgr Bsbl; Sftbl; Hon Roll; Psychiatrist.

WEST, JOSH S; Lavaca Jr Sr HS; Lavaca, AR; (3); 3/60; Church Yth Grp; FCA; FHA; Natl Beta Clb; Quiz Bowl; Science Clb; Church Choir; Pres Frsh Cls; Treas Soph Cls; VP Jr Cls; AR Tech Univ; Orthopedic Surgn.

WEST, JOSLIN K; Southside HS; Fort Smith, AR; (2); Church Yth Grp; Drill Tm; Orch; Trk; Hon Roll; Jr NHS; NHS; U OF AR; Atty.

WEST, KRISTEN M; Marion HS; West Memphis, AR; (3); Church Yth Grp; Cmnty Wkr; Spanish Clb; Band; Church Choir; Mrchg Band; Pep Band; U Memphis Hnr Band; All Region Band 2 Yrs; Outstdng Band Stu.

WEST, PATTI; Rivercrest HS; Wilson, AR; (4); 17/110; Church Yth Grp; French Clb; FBLA; FHA; HOBY; Key Clb; Library Aide; Math Clb; Office Aide; Speech Tm; Atten Gov Yth Conf AR; Family Ldr Teens Agnst Drugs; Rhodes Coll; Intl Rltns.

WEST, TALISHA S; Taylor HS; Taylor, AR; (3); Church Yth Grp; 4-H; FBLA; FHA; Library Aide; Quiz Bowl; Teachers Aide; Band; Chorus; Church Choir; Jrnlsm Awd; CHAMPS Peer Ldrshp Grou; Govt Acad Quiz Bowl Awd; Schlr Rep AR NYLC In DC; Phy, Occptnl Thrpst; Ed.

WEST, TENA K; Dewitt HS; De Witt, AR; (4); 17/70; Church Yth Grp; DECA; French Clb; FBLA; FTA; Natl Beta Clb; SADD; Hon Roll; HOSA Treas; U Of AR; Radiology Tech.

WESTERMAN, AMBER L; Harmony Grove Jr Sr HS; Benton, AR; (3); 6/42; Church Yth Grp; French Clb; FBLA; FHA; Science Clb; SADD; Acpl Chr; Ofcr Stu Cncl; Hon Roll; Governors Yth Conf; Peer Cnslrs.

WESTFALL, AARON; Nashville HS; Nashville, AR; (3); 8/130; Church Yth Grp; Varsity Clb; Ofcr Bsbl; Ftbl; Wt Lftg; Hon Roll; NHS; Pres Chrch Yth.

WESTON, WILLIAM D; Atkins Schl; Atkins, AR; (1); Ofcr Frsh Cls; Hon Roll; Pres Awd Outstndng Acad Achv.

WETHERINGTON, SHEA; Gurdon HS; Gurdon, AR; (4); 7/49; Art Clb; HOBY; Natl Beta Clb; Spanish Clb; Chorus; School Play; Ed Nwsp; Capt Chrldng; High Hon Roll; Pres Schlr; 29th NCA Chr Cmptn; UCA; Vet.

WETSELL, JAMES J; Cabot HS; Cabot, AR; (3); 80/400; Church Yth Grp; Band; Jazz Band; Mrchg Band; Stage Crew; JV Bsktbl; NHS; Chrch Yth Cncl.

WETZEL, DIXIE; Prairie Grove HS; Prairie Grove, AR; (2); Library Aide; Spanish Clb; Pres Frsh Cls; Rep Soph Cls; L Bsktbl; Capt Chrldng; Sftbl; High Hon Roll; Jr NHS; Ldrshp Awd; X-Ray Tech.

WHALEY, MELISA R; Mc Rae Schl; Griffithville, AR; (2); Sec FBLA; Sec FHA; GAA; Math Tm; Pres Soph Cls; Capt Bsktbl; Capt Crs Cntry; Sftbl; Capt Trk; U Of AR; Family Therapy.

WHALIN, CORY M; Cabot HS; Cabot, AR; (3); 130/300; Church Yth Grp; French Clb; ROTC; Band; Jazz Band; Pep Band; School Musical; School Play; Lit Mag; JV Bsktbl; Kappa Kappa Psi Awd Mscl Achvmt; Mltry Ordr Prpl Hrt Awd Outstdng Ldrshp.

WHATLEY JR, STEPHEN LEE; Lakeside HS; Hot Springs, AR; (3); Am Leg Boys St; FBLA; Pres Math Clb; Mu Alpha Theta; Rptr Natl Beta Clb; Quiz Bowl; Science Clb; Spanish Clb; Golf; NHS; Engrng.

WHATLEY, TARA D; Bauxite Jr Sr HS; Benton, AR; (2); Church Yth Grp; Cmnty Wkr; Girl Scts; Office Aide; Church Choir; Drill Tm; Bsktbl; Trk; Horses.

WHEELER, ADAM E; Corning HS; Corning, AR; (1); Ftbl; Trk; Hon Roll; Pres Acad Fit Awd.

WHEELER, AMANDA A; Rivercrest HS; Dyess, AR; (2); 2/123; Church Yth Grp; Math Clb; Yrbk; Ofcr Stu Cncl; Bsktbl; Hon Roll; Jr NHS; NHS; Rep Frsh Cls; Trk; TAD; Lib Club; Pedtrcs/Sprts Med.

WHEELER, AMANDA K; John L Mcclellan Magnet HS; Little Rock, AR; (2); FBLA; Key Clb; Spanish Clb; VICA; Hon Roll; 1st Pl CAD Arch Cont Voc Ind Clbs Of Amer; U Of AR Fayetteville; Arch.

WHEELER, BRITTON ROSS; Fayetteville Sr HS; Fayetteville, AR; (3); 89/418; Am Leg Boys St; Boy Scts; Church Yth Grp; Cmnty Wkr; FCA; FBLA; Letterman Clb; SADD; Ofcr Bsbl; L Ftbl; Ozark Mission Project; Cotillon; Pub Svc Vol; U Of AR.

WHEELER, COURTNEY B; Southside HS; Batesville, AR; (2); Art Clb; Key Clb; Spanish Clb; Ofcr Stu Cncl; Bsktbl; Sftbl; Hon Roll; UCA; Lit Tchr; Coach.

WHEELER, JAMMIE L; Midland HS; Pleasant Plains, AR; (2); FHA; Natl Beta Clb; Pep Clb; Spanish Clb; Rep Frsh Cls; Rep Soph Cls; Rep Stu Cncl; Var Bsktbl; Var Crs Cntry; Stat Mgr(s); Jr Girls Bsktbl Awds; Jr/Sr Girls Track Awds; AR ST Track Fnlst.

WHEELER, NATALIE D; Ridgecrest HS; Paragould, AR; (2); Church Yth Grp; Band; Chorus; Church Choir; Color Guard; Mrchg Band; Hon Roll; Crusaders For Christ Clb; Band Cncl; Ouachita Bapt U; Music Ed.

WHEELER, PAUL D; Marshall HS; Marshall, AR; (3); Art Clb; 4-H; Yrbk; Var Ftbl; Var L Trk; Cit Awd; Track All Conf/ST Qualifier; Mech.

WHEELER, REBECCA M; Lamar HS; Lamar, AR; (3); Am Leg Aux Girls St; Pres VP Church Yth Grp; FCA; FBLA; Natl Beta Clb; Teachers Aide; Band; Capt Sftbl; Trk; Hon Roll; Bus; Pre-Law.

WHEELER, RONALD S; Crossett Sr HS; Crossett, AR; (2); 1/225; Mu Alpha Theta; Church Choir; Ftbl; Cit Awd; Ntl Merit Ltr; Babe Ruth Bsbll.

WHEELER, WILLIAM WAYNE; Lake Hamilton Sr HS; Hot Springs, AR; (4); 27/276; Boy Scts; Church Yth Grp; Pres Computer Clb; Drama Clb; FBLA; Letterman Clb; Natl Beta Clb; Office Aide; Teachers Aide; Thesps; VP Amateur Radio Clb; All St Bapt Band, Choir; All Region Band, Choir, Orch; Henderson ST U; Comp Sys Anlst.

WHEELEY, STEPHANIE M; Central HS; West Helena, AR; (2); Church Yth Grp; Teachers Aide; Acpl Chr; Chorus; Church Choir; Hon Roll; TCK; Tchr.

WHELPLEY, VERONICA M; St Paul Schl; Huntsville, AR; (2); FBLA; FHA; Natl Beta Clb; Quiz Bowl; SADD; Band; Hon Roll; Pres Acad Fit Awd; Presdntl Educl Excl Awd; Acad Excl N All Soph Cls; Young Ldr At DC Conf Nom; Truck Brokerage.

WHERRY, VALERY K; Fairview HS; Camden, AR; (2); Church Yth Grp; Drama Clb; French Clb; Chorus; Church Choir; School Musical; School Play; Soccer; Anytown USA; Jacksonville Bapt Coll; Ped.

WHETSEL, ANGELA M; Buffalo Island Central HS; Monette, AR; (3); Drama Clb; FBLA; FHA; FTA; Science Clb; Spanish Clb; School Play; Sftbl; Hon Roll; NHS; Med.

WHILEY, JUSTIN H; Fountain Lake Jr Sr HS; Hot Springs Natio, AR; (2); Church Yth Grp; FCA; Varsity Clb; Church Choir; Var Bsbl; Var Ftbl; Var Wt Lftg; Hon Roll; Envrnmntl Club; AR Tech; Arch.

WHIPPLE, MARY; Arkadelphia Sr HS; Arkadelphia, AR; (4); 1/172; Am Leg Aux Girls St; FBLA; HOBY; Natl Beta Clb; Chorus; Capt Drill Tm; VP Stu Cncl; L Tennis; NHS; US Snt Page; Washington & Lee U; Bus.

WHISENANT, LIESEL A; Pine Bluff HS; Pine Bluff, AR; (4); 72/410; Art Clb; Sec Church Yth Grp; Cmnty Wkr; FBLA; Intnl Clb; VP Key Clb; Red Cross Aide; Service Clb; Spanish Clb; Rep Frsh Cls; Sec Radcl Yth Invsn-CYO; Coach Grls Sftbl; Missntte Tchr; Chrch Actvts, Orgs; Henderson ST U; Nrsng.

WHISENHUNT, CARA L; Nettleton HS; Jonesboro, AR; (3); FBLA; Math Clb; Natl Beta Clb; Science Clb; Band; Chorus; Mrchg Band; Pres Acad Fit Awd; Band Cncl; Phi Beta Mu Awd; FL Coll; Chiropractic.

WHISENHUNT, CAROL; Delight HS; Delight, AR; (3); 4/34; Church Yth Grp; 4-H; FBLA; HOBY; Natl Beta Clb; Natl FFA Org; Quiz Bowl; Pres Jr Cls; Hon Roll; JETS Awd; Henderson ST U; Nrsng.

WHISENHUNT, LORI B; Dierks HS; Newhope, AR; (2); 12/53; FBLA; Pres Frsh Cls; Pres Soph Cls; Pres Jr Cls; Bsktbl; Crs Cntry; Trk; Vllybl; Hon Roll; Pres Acad Fit Awd; Hist Tchr; Coach.

WHITAKER, AMY; Brookland Jr Sr HS; Jonesboro, AR; (3); 1/69; Church Yth Grp; VP FBLA; Hosp Aide; Natl Beta Clb; Quiz Bowl; Chorus; Pres Frsh Cls; Pres Soph Cls; High Hon Roll; Hon Roll; Tchr.

WHITAKER, BILEE; Cabot HS; Cabot, AR; (3); 11/398; Church Yth Grp; Key Clb; Teachers Aide; Band; Mrchg Band; Pep Band; Ed Lit Mag; Var Tennis; JV Vllybl; High Hon Roll; Harding Univ.

WHITAKER, CALVIN C; Carthage Schl; Carthage, AR; (3); Boy Scts; French Clb; FBLA; FHA; Var Bsktbl; Cit Awd; Hon Roll; Prfct Atten Awd; Upward Bound Pgm; Bus.

WHITAKER, MANDY L; Sheridan Sr HS; Sheridan, AR; (2); Church Yth Grp; Chrldng; Hon Roll; Jr NHS.

WHITAKER, MARCY P; West Memphis Christian Schl; West Memphis, AR; (1); Church Yth Grp; Vllybl; High Hon Roll; NHS.

WHITBY, ANDROS D; Forrest City HS; Forrest City, AR; (1); Church Yth Grp; Cmnty Wkr; FBLA; FHA; Natl FFA Org; Office Aide; Nwsp; Yrbk; Ofcr Soph Cls; Hon Roll; Bus Law; Lawyer.

WHITE, AARON LANGSTON; Central Sr HS; Maumelle, AR; (3); Church Yth Grp; Pres VP FCA; Treas Latin Clb; Mu Alpha Theta; Natl Beta Clb; Quiz Bowl; Science Clb; Band; Church Choir; Jazz Band; UALR NASA Grnt; Mck Trl Team; AR Team Natl We The People Cnstitnl Cmptn; U Of AR; Poli Sci.

WHITE, ALICIO N; Nashville HS; Nashville, AR; (4); 18/135; Church Yth Grp; FHA; Spanish Clb; Hon Roll; Jr NHS; NHS; All Amer Schlr; Cossatot Tech Coll; Cmptrs.

WHITE, ALISSA D; Lamar HS; Lamar, AR; (2); FBLA; Chorus; Nwsp; Yrbk; Golf; High Hon Roll; US Naval Acad; Law/Navy.

WHITE, AMY B; Cabot HS; Cabot, AR; (1); Church Yth Grp; Capt Var Bsktbl; Var Golf; Var Trk; Hon Roll; Chrch Hndbl Choir.

WHITE, ANNA B; West Memphis Christian Schl; Earle, AR; (3); Church Yth Grp; Natl Beta Clb; Chorus; Church Choir; Yrbk; Hon Roll; Radiology.

WHITE, BETSY; Valley Springs Schl; Pindall, AR; (4); 19/51; Am Leg Aux Girls St; Church Yth Grp; French Clb; FBLA; GAA; Sec Key Clb; Speech Tm; School Play; Rptr Nwsp; Var Capt Chrldng; OSU; Comnctns.

WHITE, BRANDON L; Augusta HS; Augusta, AR; (2); 9/55; Church Yth Grp; Cmnty Wkr; FHA; FTA; Natl Beta Clb; Science Clb; Spanish Clb; Church Choir; Mrchg Band; Pep Band; Ofcr Svrl Clubs; Play Sprts; Hlp Fmly; U Of Central AR; Pre Med.

WHITE, BRIAN; Arkansas Schl Math & Science; Paragould, AR; (4); Boy Scts; Mu Alpha Theta; Natl Beta Clb; Band; Pres Sr Cls; Trk; DAR Awd; Gov Hon Prg Awd; NHS; Ntl Merit Ltr; Northwestern U; Astronaut.

WHITE, BRIAN; Cotter Jr Sr HS; Gassville, AR; (4); 1/32; FBLA; Band; Jazz Band; Mrchg Band; Pep Band; Ofcr Jr Cls; Cit Awd; High Hon Roll; Hon Roll; Val; Amer Leg Schl Awd; AR ST U; Bus Admin.

WHITE, CHRISTY; Forrest City HS; Forrest City, AR; (3); Church Yth Grp; Library Aide; Mu Alpha Theta; Natl Beta Clb; Office Aide; Science Clb; Acpl Chr; Chorus; Hon Roll.

WHITE II, CLAUD DANIEL; Abundant Life Schools; Sherwood, AR; (4); 4/18; Church Yth Grp; Cmnty Wkr; School Play; Rep Frsh Cls; VP Soph Cls; Pres Jr Cls; Ofcr Sr Cls; Ofcr Stu Cncl; L Bsbl; L Bsktbl; Twin City Bnk Stdnt Bd; Natl Gd Trng; U Of AR; Bus Adm/Cmptr Sci.

WHITE, CRYSTAL A; Hughes Jr-Sr HS; Heth, AR; (1); Spanish Clb; Band; Jazz Band; Rep Frsh Cls; Rep Stu Cncl; Hon Roll; Pres Acad Fit Awd; Alpha Beta Pres; Poem Publishd Anthology Of Poetry By Young Amers.

WHITE, DONDI R; Hope HS; Hope, AR; (3); Art Clb; FHA; Natl Beta Clb; Natl FFA Org; High Hon Roll; Hon Roll; JROTC; U Of MI; Arch Engrng.

WHITE, HOLLY D; Ridgecrest HS; Paragould, AR; (3); 57/210; Church Yth Grp; Hosp Aide; Pep Clb; Spanish Clb; Chorus; School Musical; Swing Chorus; Hon Roll; Select Wmns Ensmble Membr; Encore Membr; Homecoming Maide; AR St Univ; Elem Ed.

WHITE, JAMES C; Nashville HS; Nashville, AR; (4); 44/106; Rptr Yrbk; Boy Scts; FHA; Quiz Bowl; Band; St Schlr; UAMS Little Rock; Dr.

WHITE, JAMI R; Dierks HS; Dierks, AR; (3); 5/38; GAA; Math Clb; Natl FFA Org; School Play; VP Jr Cls; Bsktbl; Chrldng; Trk; High Hon Roll; NHS; Tm Acad Ldr; St Qualfr Track; OBU; RN.

WHITE, JENNIFER; Warren Sr HS; Warren, AR; (4); #1 in class; Am Leg Aux Girls St; Church Yth Grp; Drama Clb; FCA; FBLA; Model UN; Natl Beta Clb; Office Aide; Quiz Bowl; SADD; U Of AR.

WHITE, JIMMY L; John L Mcclellan Magnet HS; Little Rock, AR; (3); French Clb; Library Aide; Cit Awd; French Hon Soc; High Hon Roll; Hon Roll; NHS; Prfct Atten Awd; Psych.

WHITE, JODY; Monticello HS; Monticello, AR; (3); Church Yth Grp; FCA; 4-H; Letterman Clb; Natl Beta Clb; SADD; Church Choir; Sec Jr Cls; Var Chrldng; Capt Gym.

WHITE, JOHN R; Lake Hamilton Jr HS; Royal, AR; (1); Church Yth Grp; FCA; Natl Beta Clb; Ofcr Frsh Cls; Bsktbl; Wt Lftg; Hon Roll; Bwlng Lge; IABA Offcr; Wichita ST; Prof Bwlr.

WHITE, KIMBERLY M; Conway Sr HS; Conway, AR; (3); German Clb; Natl Beta Clb; Orch; Hon Roll; U Of Cntrl AR; Occptnl Therapy.

WHITE, KRISTINA M; Greene Co Tech HS; Paragould, AR; (3); Drama Clb; French Clb; FHA; FTA; Chorus; School Musical; High Hon Roll; NHS; Prfct Atten Awd.

WHITE, LAKIDA T; Dumas HS; Dumas, AR; (3); FTA; Library Aide; Spanish Clb; Chorus; Church Choir; School Play; Cit Awd; Hon Roll; All Stars Club; UCA; Med Tech.

WHITE, LAURA E; Cabot HS; Cabot, AR; (4); 12/298; Sec Treas Art Clb; Church Yth Grp; Math Clb; Spanish Clb; High Hon Roll; Kiwanis Awd; NHS; Pres Acad Fit Awd; Spanish NHS; Hnr Grad; Acad Schlsp To Harding U; Natl Span Exam; VFW Speech Cont Local Wnnr; Hnr Mntn Adv Math Regnl; Harding UCOMP Sci.

WHITE, MELISSA R; Magnolia HS; Magnolia, AR; (2); 30/221; Church Yth Grp; Office Aide; Pep Clb; Varsity Clb; Band; Church Choir; Mrchg Band; Sec Soph Cls; Chrldng; High Hon Roll; U Of AR-LITTLE Rock; Med.

WHITE, MEREDITH L; Pine Bluff HS; Pine Bluff, AR; (4); 7/410; Am Leg Aux Girls St; Church Yth Grp; Cmnty Wkr; Pres French Clb; FBLA; FHA; Natl Beta Clb; Chorus; Church Choir; Yrbk; AR Governors Schl; U Of Cntrl AR.

WHITE, MICHA; County Line HS; Ratcliff, AR; (3); FCA; FBLA; HOBY; Natl Beta Clb; Spanish Clb; Ed Yrbk; Pres Soph Cls; Var Bsktbl; Hon Roll; Church Yth Grp; Natl Yng Ldrs Conf; Cty Teen Ct; Law.

WHITE, MIRANDA G; Forrest City HS; Forrest City, AR; (3); Spanish Clb; Yrbk; High Hon Roll; Pres Schlr.

WHITE, MISTY L; Valley Springs Schl; Pindall, AR; (2); Church Yth Grp; Cmnty Wkr; FBLA; Key Clb; Office Aide; Teachers Aide; JV Var Bsktbl; JV Trk; Cit Awd; Hon Roll; Cls Favorite; 1a East All Conf Bsktbl Team; Stu Cnslr For AEGS Summer Pgm; Comp Programming.

WHITE, NICOLE; Nashville HS; Nashville, AR; (4); 18/106; Church Yth Grp; FHA; Spanish Clb; Hon Roll; Jr NHS; NHS; All Amer Schlr Awd; Prins Awd; Cossatot Tech Coll.

WHITE, RANDY A; Cabot HS; Cabot, AR; (3); Natl FFA Org; Office Aide; Band; Mrchg Band; Hon Roll; Automotive Tech I; Subject Area Awd; Auto Body; Mech.

WHITE, ROBERT B; Arkansas Schl Math & Science; Paragould, AR; (4); Boy Scts; Mu Alpha Theta; Natl Beta Clb; Band; Pres Sr Cls; Trk; DAR Awd; Ntl Merit SF.

WHITE, ROBYN L; Hope HS; Hope, AR; (4); 1/200; Am Leg Aux Girls St; Church Yth Grp; French Clb; Rptr Natl Beta Clb; Band; Pres NHS; Val; Govrnrs Schlr; Bousch & Lomb Awd; U Of AR Fayetteville.

WHITE, SARAH; Paris HS; Paris, AR; (4); 4/80; Church Yth Grp; Cmnty Wkr; Q&S; Science Clb; Speech Tm; Ed Yrbk; High Hon Roll; Kiwanis Awd; NHS; Brett Minden Fndtn Schlsp; Rotry Clb Awd; Comm Outreach Svcs Bd Of Dirs 95-96; AR Tech Univ; Bio; Pre-Med.

WHITE, SHANNON; Hartford Schl; Hartford, AR; (4); 6/29; Church Yth Grp; Sec Natl FFA Org; Treas Frsh Cls; Ofcr Stu Cncl; Stat Bsktbl; Capt Var Chrldng; Cit Awd; High Hon Roll; Sec NHS; Ntl Merit Ltr; Bst All Arnd Grl 12th; Anml Sci/Vet Asst.

WHITE, STEPHANIE M; Benton Cty Christian School; Bentonville, AR; (3); Church Yth Grp; Hosp Aide; Library Aide; Teachers Aide; Chorus; Church Choir; Chrldng; Hon Roll; Natl Sci Mrt Awd; Natl Ldrshp Svc Awd; Corp Lawyer.

WHITE, STEPHEN; Kirby HS; Umpire, AR; (3); Church Yth Grp; 4-H; FBLA; HOBY; Natl FFA Org; Pep Band; Rptr Soph Cls; Var L Bsktbl; 4-H Awd; Rcgntn Outstndng Cmnty Svc Pres Awd.

WHITE, TRACY; Camden Christian Acad; Stephens, AR; (3); #1 in class; Church Yth Grp; Drama Clb; Library Aide; Office Aide; Quiz Bowl; Spanish Clb; Teachers Aide; Church Choir; School Musical; School Play; Woodmen Wrld Amer Hstry Awd; Southwestern Assmbly God; Psych.

WHITE, TRINA G; Cedarville Jr Sr HS; Cedarville, AR; (3); 1/65; Church Yth Grp; Band; Church Choir; Ed Nwsp; Yrbk; High Hon Roll; NHS; Prtnrs Christ; Westark.

WHITE, WHITNEY; Conway Sr HS; Conway, AR; (3); Church Yth Grp; Drama Clb; VP German Clb; Natl Beta Clb; Church Choir; VP Jr Cls; Ofcr Stu Cncl; Capt Chrldng; Powder Puff Ftbl; Ger Honorary; U Of AR-FAYETTEVILLE.

WHITE, WHITNEY R; Gosnell Jr Sr HS; Blytheville, AR; (1); Key Clb; Chorus; Phys Thpy.

WHITEHEAD, A W; Lee Acad; Marianna, AR; (2); Rep Frsh Cls; Rep Soph Cls; Intrml JV Bsktbl; JV Var Chrldng; JV Var Sftbl; JV Trk; Jr Mss Lee Acad; Clss Fav; Jr Grls Bsktbl Bst Dfnsv Plyr 94-95; AR ST U; Med.

WHITEHEAD, AMY M; Magnolia HS; Magnolia, AR; (4); Co-Ed Nwsp; Church Yth Grp; French Clb; Mu Alpha Theta; Band; Flag Corp; Hon Roll; NHS; Southern AR Univ; Bus Admin.

WHITEHEAD, DYLANA; Morrilton Sr HS; Morrilton, AR; (3); 24/174; Art Clb; Church Yth Grp; Natl Beta Clb; Sec Spanish Clb; Thesps; School Play; Yrbk; Capt Chrldng; Var Sftbl; Hon Roll; U AR Fayetteville.

WHITEHEAD, MATTHEW T; Oak Grove HS; Maumelle, AR; (1); Hon Roll.

WHITEHURST, STEPHEN C; Monticello HS; Monticello, AR; (4); Church Yth Grp; FBLA; Natl Beta Clb; Band; Ftbl; Trk; High Hon Roll; Hon Roll; Jr NHS; NHS; Natl Hnr Roll; Schlr Ath Awd; Multi Yr Listee; UALR; Pre-Med.

WHITENER, JOE E; Bradford Jr Sr HS; Bradford, AR; (2); Church Yth Grp; Cmnty Wkr; Math Tm; Natl Beta Clb; Natl FFA Org; Quiz Bowl; Ofcr Stu Cncl; Ofcr Bsbl; Bsktbl; Sftbl.

WHITESIDE, WHITNY J; Gravette HS; Maysville, AR; (3); FCA; 4-H; FBLA; FHA; Natl FFA Org; Office Aide; Yrbk; Sec Soph Cls; Bsktbl; Socr; FFA Treas, St Farmer Degree; Northeastern OK; Ag Ed.

WHITFIELD, LAQUITA; Turrell HS; Turrell, AR; (3); 1/40; Church Yth Grp; Pres FBLA; FHA; HOBY; Pres Natl Beta Clb; Quiz Bowl; Scholastic Bowl; Chorus; Church Choir; School Musical; AR ST U; Srgcl Asst.

WHITIS, ANDREA L; Mississippi Co Christian Acad; Osceola, AR; (2); 2/13; Church Yth Grp; French Clb; Math Clb; Science Clb; SADD; Band; Flag Corp; Bsktbl; Chrldng; Hon Roll.

WHITLEY, MARCUS; Magnet Cove HS; Malvern, AR; (3); FCA; Natl Beta Clb; VP Frsh Cls; Rep Soph Cls; Rep Jr Cls; Hist Stu Cncl; Var Ftbl; Var Trk; High Hon Roll; Math Clb; Malvern Natl Bnk Stu Advy Bd Of Dir; Sports Medicine.

WHITLEY, STACI; Coleman Jr HS; Van Buren, AR; (1); Church Yth Grp; Library Aide; Church Choir; Rep Stu Cncl; Cit Awd; High Hon Roll; Hon Roll; Jr NHS; NHS; Stu Of The Month; Acad Honoree; Elem Ed.

WHITLOCK, JESSE C; Ozark HS; Ozark, AR; (3); FCA; SADD; Teachers Aide; Ofcr Bsbl; Crs Cntry; Ftbl; Trk; Wt Lftg; 4-H; Westark CC; Elctrcn.

WHITLOCK, REBECCA J; Lake Hamilton Sr HS; Hot Springs Natio, AR; (3); 2/250; Church Yth Grp; FCA; FBLA; Natl Beta Clb; Pres Chorus; Church Choir; Hon Roll; Pres Acad Fit Awd; Stdnt Chrstn Life Pres; Wolf Pride; Bio/Chem.

WHITLOW, JESSICA L; Yellville Summit HS; Summit, AR; (2); Church Yth Grp; Acpl Chr; Chorus; Church Choir; Drill Tm; School Musical; Sftbl; Hon Roll; Hustle Awd In Sftbl; All Conf Team In Sftbl.

WHITMIRE, ERIC M; Cabot HS; Cabot, AR; (2); Church Yth Grp; FCA; French Clb; Band; Church Choir; Ftbl; Trk; Hon Roll; Ftbll Acad All Conf; Comp Eng.

WHITMIRE, MISTY L; Nettleton HS; Jonesboro, AR; (3); FHA; Spanish Clb; Teachers Aide; Chorus; Nwsp; Yrbk; Powder Puff Ftbl; Hon Roll; AR ST Univ; Tchr.

WHITMORE, ASHLEY S; Dewitt HS; Saint Charles, AR; (2); 1/100; FCA; French Clb; Natl Beta Clb; Pres Frsh Cls; VP Soph Cls; Ofcr Stu Cncl; Bsktbl; Sftbl; Trk; High Hon Roll.

WHITNEY, APRIL D; Fairview HS; Camden, AR; (3); 16/326; Pres Church Yth Grp; Cmnty Wkr; Math Clb; Mu Alpha Theta; Natl Beta Clb; Science Clb; Spanish Clb; Band; Flag Corp; Cit Awd; Henderson Univ.

WHITNEY, CAMERON W; Bergman Schl; Harrison, AR; (2); Church Yth Grp; Natl FFA Org; Var Bsbl; JV Bsktbl; Var Chrldng; Hon Roll.

WHITNEY, DENA L; Southside HS; Fort Smith, AR; (4); 247/459; Church Yth Grp; SADD; VICA; Chorus; Variety Show; Bsktbl; Cit Awd; Hon Roll; Prfct Atten Awd; Cmnty Wkr; Emplyee Of Month; Westark CC; Legal Asst/Cmptr S.

WHITNEY, TARA; Brookland Jr Sr HS; Lake City, AR; (2); FHA; Treas Spanish Clb; SADD; Prfct Atten Awd; Home Ec Awd.

WHITSETT, TODD D; Van Buren Sr HS; Van Buren, AR; (2); Church Yth Grp; Mu Alpha Theta; Band; Cit Awd; High Hon Roll; Jr NHS.

WHITSON, CHRISTINA M; Central Sr HS; Mabelvale, AR; (3); Art Clb; Cmnty Wkr; Drama Clb; FBLA; German Clb; Natl Beta Clb; Science Clb; Mrchg Band; Nwsp; High Hon Roll; Accept No Boundaries Club; Steering Comm Histrn; Tae Kwon Do Black Belt; Young Democrats; Hendrix Coll; Marine Bio.

WHITT, AMY; Mc Crory Jr Sr HS; Mc Crory, AR; (2); 1/60; Church Yth Grp; FBLA; Spanish Clb; Teachers Aide; VP Pres Soph Cls; Ofcr Stu Cncl; Chrldng; Tennis; High Hon Roll; Jr NHS; Lyon Col.

WHITTAKER, AMBER; Northside HS; Barling, AR; (3); Dance Clb; FCA; GAA; Key Clb; Spanish Clb; Teachers Aide; Drill Tm; Rep Soph Cls; Rep Jr Cls; Rep Stu Cncl; U Of Cntrl AR Conway; Sec Ed.

WHITTED, AMY; Pea Ridge HS; Pea Ridge, AR; (2); 7/71; Drama Clb; FBLA; FHA; GAA; Spanish Clb; Yrbk; JV Bsktbl; Capt Sftbl; Cit Awd; DAR Awd; Sportmanship Awd Sftbl; Coll Of Ozarks; Coach.

WHITTEMORE, JOHN D; Central Ark Christian Schl; Little Rock, AR; (3); Boy Scts; Church Yth Grp; FCA; Chorus; School Play; Yrbk; Rep Stu Cncl; Crs Cntry; Socr; NHS; Rsrch.

WHITTINGTON, JESSICA D; Fouke Jr Sr HS; Fouke, AR; (3); Church Yth Grp; FBLA; Treas FHA; Natl Beta Clb; Office Aide; Church Choir; Hon Roll; Cmptr Sci Awd 11th Grd; Ed Choice Awd Natl Lbry/Poetry 96; Poem Pub; UCLA; Bus.

WHITTINGTON, WADE; Charleston HS; Charleston, AR; (2); 2/61; Cmnty Wkr; FCA; Rptr FBLA; Library Aide; Natl Beta Clb; Quiz Bowl; Varsity Clb; High Hon Roll; U Of AR; Hlth.

WHITTINGTON, WILLIAM; Northside HS; Fort Smith, AR; (4); Art Clb; Boy Scts; Drama Clb; ROTC; German Clb; Office Aide; Teachers Aide; Capt Ftbl; Trk; Wt Lftg; Blchr Creatures Pres; Garvin Grzzly Awds 2xs; Illstrtr.

WHITWORTH, TERRA; Morrilton Sr HS; Morrilton, AR; (2); Church Yth Grp; French Clb; Natl Beta Clb; Science Clb; Drill Tm; JV Vllybl; Hon Roll; Prfct Atten Awd; Art Clb; Nwsp; Drl Tm Capt; AR Tech; Law.

WICKARD, CARRIE R; Central Sr HS; Little Rock, AR; (3); 124/507; French Clb; Sec Treas Natl Beta Clb; Rptr Nwsp; Yrbk; Powder Puff Ftbl; Cit Awd; Hon Roll; Y Teens Sec, Treas, Hstrn; U Of A Fayetteville; Elem Ed.

WICKARD, JENNIFER; J A Fair Sr HS; Little Rock, AR; (2); Church Yth Grp; Cmnty Wkr; FBLA; Office Aide; SADD; Chorus; Church Choir; Cit Awd; Hon Roll; NHS; Ladies Club; Recruiting Comm.

WICKER, REBECCA; Sylvan Hills HS; North Little Rock, AR; (4); 1/233; Am Leg Aux Girls St; Church Yth Grp; Mu Alpha Theta; Natl Beta Clb; Pres Spanish Clb; Church Choir; Rep Jr Cls; Rep Sr Cls; Pres Treas NHS; Val; Ouachita Baptst Univ.

WICKLIFFE, SARAH E; Mayflower HS; Mayflower, AR; (2); 2/64; Church Yth Grp; Natl Beta Clb; Teachers Aide; Sec Frsh Cls; Pres Soph Cls; VP Stu Cncl; JV Var Bsktbl; Capt Chrldng; High Hon Roll; Hon Roll; Univ Of AR; Vet Sci.

WIDDICOMBE, CHRIS J; Blytheville Sr HS; Blytheville, AR; (3); 11/200; Church Yth Grp; Cmnty Wkr; Math Clb; Science Clb; Church Choir; VP Frsh Cls; Var Bsktbl; Var Socr; High Hon Roll; Hon Roll.

WIEDEMAN, COURTNEY D; Corning HS; Corning, AR; (1); FHA; Spanish Clb; High Hon Roll; Hon Roll; Pres Acad Fit Awd; Anthlgst.

WIEDEMANN, HEATHER A; Rogers HS; Rogers, AR; (3); 117/600; Hosp Aide; Office Aide; Chorus; Hon Roll; Rgrs Chmbr Cmmrc Acad Aws 2 Yrs; Pharmacist.

WIEDOWER, CAREY; Sacred Heart Schl; Morrilton, AR; (3); 1/14; Am Leg Aux Girls St; Church Yth Grp; Key Clb; Natl Beta Clb; School Play; Yrbk; Pres Jr Cls; Ofcr Stu Cncl; Bsktbl; Hon Roll; All Conf Bsktbl; Rebel Awd Bsktbl; U Of AR; Bus.

WIEDOWER, ELIZABETH; Sacred Heart Schl; Morrilton, AR; (2); Church Yth Grp; Natl Beta Clb; Yrbk; Pres Frsh Cls; Rep Soph Cls; Rep Stu Cncl; Var Bsktbl; Var Sftbl; High Hon Roll; Pres Schlr; Homcmng Qn 94-95; U Of AR Fayetteville; Medcl.

WIEMANN, TIFFANY L; Lake Hamilton Sr HS; Pearcy, AR; (3); Church Yth Grp; FCA; FBLA; Hosp Aide; Office Aide; Spanish Clb; Teachers Aide; Rep Cmnty Wkr; Ofcr Stu Cncl; Intrml Crs Cntry; HEART.

WIENANDS, MARCIE L; Bentonville Sr HS; Bentonville, AR; (4); 7/325; Church Yth Grp; Debate Tm; Hosp Aide; Key Clb; Model UN; NFL; Band; Color Guard; Mrchg Band; School Play; Harding U; Med.

WIERICK, JENNY; Rogers HS; Rogers, AR; (4); Church Yth Grp; FCA; FBLA; FTA; Key Clb; NFL; Spanish Clb; Speech Tm; Swmmng; Debate Tm; U AR; Acctng.

WIETECHA, DANIEL L; Fairview HS; Camden, AR; (2); Church Yth Grp; Drama Clb; Natl Beta Clb; Natl FFA Org; Teachers Aide; Church Choir; School Play; Stage Crew; Socr; Hon Roll.

WIGGINS, BILLIE K; Mc Crory Jr Sr HS; Mc Crory, AR; (3); Church Choir; Flag Corp; Jazz Band; Mrchg Band; Powder Puff Ftbl; Hon Roll; Nrsng.

WIGGINS, ERIN; Chaffin Jr HS; Fort Smith, AR; (1); Church Yth Grp; Cmnty Wkr; FCA; Chorus; Variety Show; L Bsktbl; L Chrldng; Var Wrstlng; L Vllybl; Hon Roll; Vanderbilt; Med.

WIGGINS, FELICIA A; Danville HS; Danville, AR; (3); 9/36; GAA; Pep Clb; Bsktbl; Chrldng; Trk; High Hon Roll; NHS; Bus Mgnt.

WIGGINS, JENNIFER R; Southside HS; Fort Smith, AR; (3); Church Yth Grp; Cmnty Wkr; FCA; FHA; Pep Clb; Spanish Clb; Teachers Aide; Band; Mrchg Band; Variety Show; Spnsh Natl Mrt Test Top 10% St; Girls St; FHA Unit/Dist Pres; Little Girls Drill Tm Tchr Orr Girls Clb; Psych.

WIGGINS, JESSICA A; Atkins Schl; Russellville, AR; (1); Art Clb; Church Choir; High Hon Roll; Jr Beta; Pres Ed Awd.

WIGGINS, KEITH C; Rogers HS; Rogers, AR; (3); 23/596; JV Bsbl; JV Bsktbl; JV Ftbl; JV Socr; Hon Roll; U Of AR; Architecture; Engrng.

WIGGINS, SHANEE L; North Little Rock Hs-East; North Little Rock, AR; (1); Church Yth Grp; Drama Clb; FCA; GAA; Band; Church Choir; Drill Tm; School Play; Trk; Hon Roll; Drill Tm Co Capt; Spelman; News Rptr.

WIGINTON, ASHLEY K; Southside HS; Fort Smith, AR; (2); Hosp Aide; Mu Alpha Theta; Office Aide; Teachers Aide; Hon Roll; Jr NHS; NHS; Pres Acad Fit Awd; Spanish NHS; Psych.

WILBANKS, JULIE M; John L Mcclellan Magnet HS; Little Rock, AR; (3); Drama Clb; French Clb; Model UN; Q&S; Quiz Bowl; Spanish Clb; School Musical; School Play; Stage Crew; Nwsp; Span Clb Exec Cncl Mem; U Of Cntrl AR; Commnctns.

WILBERT, CHRIS L; Victory Christian Schl; Camden, AR; (3); Church Yth Grp; Drama Clb; Varsity Clb; Nwsp; Yrbk; Var Bsbl; Var Bsktbl; Var Ftbl; Var Wt Lftg; Var Prfct Atten Awd.

WILBORN, CANDICE M; Blytheville Sr HS; Blytheville, AR; (2); Church Yth Grp; Girl Scts; Spanish Clb; Band; Church Choir; Cit Awd; Hon Roll; Prfct Atten Awd; Sec/Cmptrs.

WILBUR, MAURA; Rogers HS; Rogers, AR; (4); 36/468; Church Yth Grp; Hosp Aide; Key Clb; Model UN; Ed Nwsp; Ed Lit Mag; Var JV Tennis; Gov Hon Prg Awd; NHS; Search Tm; Frgn Svc.

WILBURN, SHARINA M; Valley Springs Schl; Everton, AR; (3); FBLA; FHA; Library Aide; Spanish Clb; Phtg Yrbk; Hon Roll; Lib Clb Rptr; Bus Fin.

WILCOX, ANGELA D; Alpena Schl; Alpena, AR; (4); Church Yth Grp; FBLA; FHA; Natl Beta Clb; Nwsp; Yrbk; Var Bsktbl; Cit Awd; Hon Roll; Prom Qn; Homcmng Maid; Free Throw Awd; Eng & Geog Awds.

WILCOX, CHRISTIE A; Alpena Schl; Alpena, AR; (3); Church Yth Grp; VP Natl Beta Clb; Nwsp; Yrbk; Var Bsktbl; Var Trk; Cit Awd; Hon Roll; Grad Herald; Art Awd; Bsktbl Most Dedicated.

WILCOX, NATHAN W; Mulberry HS; Mulberry, AR; (3); Art Clb; Church Yth Grp; Cmnty Wkr; 4-H; Frnch Clb; Natl FFA Org; Science Clb; SADD; Var Bsbl; Var Bsktbl; AR 4-H Teen Star; Athltc Awd Free Thrw Prctg Hgh Point; Westark CC; Lib Arts.

WILDHAGEN, RACHEL; Clinton HS; Shirley, AR; (4); Am Leg Aux Girls St; Natl Beta Clb; Pep Clb; Science Clb; Spanish Clb; VP Pres Stu Cncl; Chrldng; Trk; Hon Roll; AR Govs Yth Conf Ldr 3 Yrs; Hendrix Coll; Chem.

WILES, JENNIFER; Highland HS; Ash Flat, AR; (3); 11/108; Am Leg Aux Girls St; Church Yth Grp; FBLA; FHA; VP Pres Key Clb; Natl Beta Clb; Quiz Bowl; Ofcr Stu Cncl; Hon Roll; NHS; Rebels Against Drugs; SOUL VP; Harding Univ.

WILES, JENNIFER L; Highland HS; Cherokee Village, AR; (2); 12/92; Library Aide; Hon Roll; Acad Awds; Batesville Lyons Coll; Ed.

WILES, JOHN E; Highland HS; Hardy, AR; (3); Am Leg Boys St; Church Yth Grp; Key Clb; Natl Beta Clb; Quiz Bowl; Ftbl; Trk; Hon Roll; Prfct Atten Awd; Pres Acad Fit Awd; Supreme Court Justice Boys St; Fulbright Schl Of Pub Affairs USA; U AR; Pol Sci.

WILEY, AMANDA R; Malvern Sr HS; Malvern, AR; (3); #1 in class; FBLA; Natl Beta Clb; Acpl Chr; High Hon Roll; Jr NHS; NHS; Prfct Atten Awd; Pres Acad Fit Awd; Natl Young Ldrs Conf DC; Henderson ST Univ.

WILEY, MANDY; Cedarville Jr Sr HS; Cedarville, AR; (3); 4/60; FBLA; FHA; Science Clb; Spanish Clb; Nwsp; Yrbk; Hon Roll; NHS; Carl Albert Schol Chem 1st; Ed Talent Srch; SADA; Westark Univ; X-Ray Tech.

WILEY, SPENCER H; Southside HS; Fort Smith, AR; (3); Letterman Clb; Quiz Bowl; Teachers Aide; Stage Crew; Bsktbl; Trk; Hon Roll; Pres Acad Fit Awd; U Of AR Fayetteville.

WILFORD, RACHEL N; Central Sr HS; Little Rock, AR; (3); Am Leg Aux Girls St; Cmnty Wkr; French Clb; Natl Beta Clb; Q&S; Nwsp; Rep Stu Cncl; Hon Roll; NHS; Socr; Ltl Rock Schl Dist Supts Stu Cabnt; Rhodes Coll; Bio.

WILHITE, MANDY; Lincoln HS; Prairie Grove, AR; (3); Art Clb; Dance Clb; Natl Beta Clb; Natl FFA Org; Spanish Clb; Drill Tm; School Play; Bsktbl; Sftbl; Trk; NW AR CC; Hygienist.

WILHITE, MELISSA; Lincoln HS; Lincoln, AR; (2); #8 in class; Church Yth Grp; Debate Tm; FBLA; Key Clb; Natl FFA Org; Science Clb; Spanish Clb; Drill Tm; Hon Roll; Baptist Schl Of Nursing; Med.

WILKERSON, DANIEL W; Crowleys Ridge Acad; Paragould, AR; (2); Church Yth Grp; FBLA; Acpl Chr; Church Choir; School Play; Ofcr Bsbl; Bsktbl; Socr; Trk; Hon Roll; Crowleys Ridge Coll.

WILKERSON, GINGER L; Mayflower HS; Mayflower, AR; (2); FBLA; VP Library Aide; Natl Beta Clb; Chorus; Rep Frsh Cls; Hon Roll; Tm 3 Chrstn Org.

WILKERSON, JASON D; Smackover HS; Smackover, AR; (1); 1/70; Church Yth Grp; FBLA; Quiz Bowl; Spanish Clb; Rep Stu Cncl; JV Bsktbl; JV L Trk; Hon Roll; Rcvd 1st Pl Span Spkng Frgn Lang Fstvl; U Of AR; Archtctr.

WILKERSON, KOQUESE S; Ozark HS; Ozark, AR; (2); Church Yth Grp; Natl Beta Clb; Chorus; Church Choir; VP Frsh Cls; Pres Soph Cls; Pres Jr Cls; Pres Stu Cncl; Bsktbl; Sftbl; Natl Yth Ldrshp Forum; AAU & BCI Bsktbl; U Of AR; Sociology; Crimnl Law.

WILKERSON, RACHEL A; Marvell Acad; Elaine, AR; (3); Library Aide; Quiz Bowl; Spanish Clb; Teachers Aide; Nwsp; Rep Frsh Cls; JV Chrldng; Hon Roll; Teach Bible Schl; Coach T-Ball Local Team.

WILKERSON, REBECCA P; Parkview Arts-Science HS; Little Rock, AR; (3); Church Yth Grp; Cmnty Wkr; Drama Clb; Girl Scts; HOBY; Key Clb; Latin Clb; Natl Beta Clb; Office Aide; Teachers Aide; U Pine Bluff; Chem.

WILKERSON, SUSAN K; Bryant Sr HS; Benton, AR; (4); 10/336; English Clb; French Clb; FBLA; FTA; Science Clb; Teachers Aide; Cit Awd; DAR Awd; Hon Roll; NHS; Hnr Medal; Dist Comp Acctng II 2nd Pl; U Of AR Little Rock; Acctng.

WILKES, AMANDA; Mineral Springs Schl; Mineral Springs, AR; (1); FBLA; JA; Quiz Bowl; Sec Frsh Cls; Chrldng; Sftbl; High Hon Roll; OM; Pgnt Tm; OU; Psycht.

WILKES, BYRON N; Cave City HS; Cave City, AR; (3); 1/80; Church Yth Grp; FHA; HOBY; Key Clb; Natl Beta Clb; Pres Frsh Cls; Pres Soph Cls; Var Bsbl; Var Bsktbl; High Hon Roll; Med Spec.

WILKIE, ASHLEY; Calvary Christian Schl; Forrest City, AR; (2); Church Yth Grp; Drama Clb; Girl Scts; Office Aide; Science Clb; Church Choir; School Play; Stage Crew; Capt Chrldng; Hon Roll; NCA All Amer Chrldr Team; United Meth Chrch Dist Cncl Yth Mnstrs/Conf Cncl; Hedrix; Phrmcy.

WILKINS, MEGAN; Lamar HS; Lamar, AR; (1); FCA; Var Chrldng; High Hon Roll; NHS; All Stars Group; Med.

WILKINS, REBECCA; Mulberry HS; Mulberry, AR; (3); 1/40; French Clb; FBLA; Teachers Aide; Hon Roll; NHS; Med.

WILKINS, SUSAN K; Southside HS; Fort Smith, AR; (3); Art Clb; French Clb; FHA; Mu Alpha Theta; Spanish Clb; Teachers Aide; Hon Roll; Jr NHS; NHS; Spanish NHS; Westark; Comp Prog.

WILKINSON, ADAM D; Lee Acad; Brickeys, AR; (1); Church Yth Grp; Ftbl; Trk; Cit Awd; Hon Roll; Prfct Atten Awd.

WILKINSON, AMANDA J; Dollarway HS; Pine Bluff, AR; (2); Church Yth Grp; Computer Clb; FHA; Key Clb; Library Aide; Acpl Chr; Cit Awd; Comp Awd; Keyboarding Awd; Med Field.

WILLAMS, MARY A; Southside HS; Rosie, AR; (3); #1 in class; Am Leg Aux Girls St; Sec FBLA; Key Clb; Treas Natl Beta Clb; Science Clb; Treas Jr Cls; Rep Stu Cncl; Var Bsktbl; Var Tennis; High Hon Roll.

WILLARD, WENDY; Maynard Jr Sr HS; Pocahontas, AR; (4); 2/29; Office Aide; Hon Roll; Sal; Bausch & Lomb Sci Awd; UALR.

WILLCUTT, BRANDY E; Morrilton Sr HS; Morrilton, AR; (2); Natl Beta Clb; Natl FFA Org; Hon Roll; Natl Hon Roll; Intl Frgn Lang Awd; All Amer Schlr Awd; U Of Central AR; Bus.

WILLCUTT, DANIEL H; Atkins Schl; Atkins, AR; (1); Church Yth Grp; Natl Beta Clb; Ofcr Stu Cncl; Var Bsbl; Var L Ftbl; Hon Roll; 9th Grd Eng Awd; Gftd/Tlntd Prgm; AR Tech Univ.

WILLETT, MELISSA A; Smackover HS; El Dorado, AR; (3); 4/49; Cmnty Wkr; Drama Clb; GAA; Hosp Aide; Pres Mu Alpha Theta; Capt Quiz Bowl; Science Clb; Spanish Clb; Band; Phtg Yrbk; Anchor Clb Sec; Natl Yth Forum Med Pgm; MASH; Hendricks; Med.

WILLHITE, BRITTNEY; Brinkley HS; Brinkley, AR; (3); FBLA; Q&S; ROTC; Chorus; Rptr Nwsp; JV Var Chrldng; Gov Hon Prg Awd; High Hon Roll; Jr NHS; NHS; Hlth Occptns; Lbry Clb; Bapt Schl Nrsng; Nrsng.

WILLHOITE, SARAH J; Emerson HS; Magnolia, AR; (2); Church Yth Grp; FBLA; Natl Beta Clb; Natl FFA Org; Band; Church Choir; Orch; Chrldng; Cit Awd; Hon Roll.

WILLIAMS, ALISHA S; Blytheville Sr HS; Blytheville, AR; (3); 3/265; Am Leg Aux Girls St; FBLA; Natl Beta Clb; Spanish Clb; Band; Yrbk; Pres Stu Cncl; Bsktbl; Hon Roll; Pres Acad Fit Awd; Chem; Pharmacy.

WILLIAMS, AMANDA D; Cabot HS; Cabot, AR; (3); Church Yth Grp; Key Clb; Nwsp; Yrbk; Rep Sr Cls; Ofcr Stu Cncl; Hon Roll; Yng Authors Awd; Math Achvmnt Awd; Hstry Clb; SW Univ; Elem Ed.

WILLIAMS, AMANDA K; Lavaca Jr Sr HS; Lavaca, AR; (2); Natl Beta Clb; Band; Mrchg Band; Hon Roll; Carol Albert St Coll Math & Sci; Band Ltr; Law Enforcement.

WILLIAMS, AMANDA L; Bearden HS; Bearden, AR; (4); 1/58; 4-H; FBLA; FHA; FTA; Natl Beta Clb; Quiz Bowl; Rptr Nwsp; Rptr Yrbk; Val; Upward Bnd; Grtr Bradley Yth Choir VP; UALR; Bio.

WILLIAMS, AMBER; Mc Rae Schl; Mc Rae, AR; (3); Drama Clb; FBLA; Natl Beta Clb; Office Aide; Quiz Bowl; Rptr Nwsp; Rptr Jr Cls; L Bsktbl; Hon Roll; Prfct Atten Awd; Russn Clb.

WILLIAMS, AMBER; St Paul Schl; Elkins, AR; (4); FHA; Natl Beta Clb; Science Clb; SADD; Teachers Aide; School Play; Ed Yrbk; Bsktbl; Trk; NHS; NTI Schlrshp; Womens Sftbl; NW Sar Tech Inst; Bus.

WILLIAMS, AMIE D; Nevada Schl; Buckner, AR; (3); FBLA; Natl Beta Clb; Quiz Bowl; Rptr Nwsp; Yrbk; Pres Soph Cls; Pres Jr Cls; Sec VP Stu Cncl; Hon Roll; Pres Acad Fit Awd; U Of AR; Mktng.

WILLIAMS, ANDREW V; Scotland Schl; Center Ridge, AR; (3); #3 in class; Am Leg Boys St; Cmnty Wkr; Debate Tm; FBLA; FHA; Natl Beta Clb; Quiz Bowl; Bsktbl; Hon Roll; Chess Trnmt; COE Paige; Chirprtr.

WILLIAMS, ANGELA; Brookland Jr Sr HS; Paragould, AR; (4); Art Clb; Drama Clb; Hist FBLA; VP FHA; HOBY; SADD; Ed Yrbk; Sec Pres Stu Cncl; Hon Roll; Treas NHS; Project LAND AEGIS Pgm Summer 94; NEA Humane Soc Mascot; AR ST U; Psych.

WILLIAMS, ANGELA; Springdale Sr HS; Springdale, AR; (3); French Clb; FBLA; Q&S; Chorus; Ed Yrbk; Var Socr; Hon Roll.

WILLIAMS, ASHLEE A; Central Sr HS; Little Rock, AR; (4); 51/370; Church Yth Grp; Dance Clb; French Clb; Latin Clb; Mu Alpha Theta; Natl Beta Clb; Spanish Clb; High Hon Roll; NHS; Pres Acad Fit Awd; Harding Univ; Pre-Med.

WILLIAMS, AUTUMN; Bald Knob HS; Judsonia, AR; (4); 23/78; Church Yth Grp; FBLA; FHA; HOBY; Office Aide; Band; Chorus; Church Choir; Nwsp; Phtg Yrbk; Attnd Tone 6 3xs; Gftd/Tlntd; ASU Beebe; Cmptr.

WILLIAMS, BENNIE R; Forrest City HS; Madison, AR; (3); FBLA; Natl Beta Clb; Band; Jazz Band; Mrchg Band; Rep Frsh Cls; Hon Roll; Prfct Atten Awd; Natl Mck Trl Comp; Deans Lst; FL ST U; Comptr Engrng.

WILLIAMS, BRAD; Southwest Christian Acad; Little Rock, AR; (2); Church Yth Grp; FCA; Chorus; Stage Crew; Yrbk; Bsktbl; Trk; Cit Awd; Hon Roll; Prfct Atten Awd; Sci Fair 1st Pl; Golf; OK ST U.

WILLIAMS, BRANDI E; Lincoln HS; Lincoln, AR; (4); 2/59; Key Clb; Math Clb; Natl Beta Clb; Natl FFA Org; Science Clb; Spanish Clb; School Play; High Hon Roll; Sal; U Of AR; Spnsh.

WILLIAMS, BRANDI L; Trumann HS; Trumann, AR; (4); 20/85; Am Leg Aux Girls St; FHA; GAA; Intnl Clb; Math Clb; Natl Beta Clb; Natl FFA Org; Science Clb; Spanish Clb; Capt Bsktbl; Homecoming Queen; Friendliest Girlsr; Best Ath Of Sr Clss 95; AR St Univ; BSN.

WILLIAMS, BRENT A; Mountain Home HS; Mountain Home, AR; (3); Art Clb; School Musical; Var Bsktbl; Gov Hon Prg Awd; High Hon Roll; Hon Roll; Accepted Natl Yth Ldrshp Forum Med; Pathologist.

WILLIAMS, BRIAN G; Rogers HS; Rogers, AR; (3); Boy Scts; Church Yth Grp; Cmnty Wkr; FCA; FBLA; Intnl Clb; Letterman Clb; Spanish Clb; SADD; Ofcr Soph Cls; U Of AR; Bus; Coach.

WILLIAMS, BUDDY; Monticello HS; Monticello, AR; (3); Church Yth Grp; FCA; Math Clb; Natl Beta Clb; Science Clb; Var Bsbl; Hon Roll; Jr NHS; NHS; All Amer Scholar; Natl Sci Merit Awd.

WILLIAMS, CARNITA S; Oak Grove HS; North Little Rock, AR; (2); Church Yth Grp; FCA; FHA; FTA; Letterman Clb; Spanish Clb; Band; Church Choir; Drill Tm; Sftbl; Assn Of Black Engrs Starting Block Stu; Memphis ST; RN.

WILLIAMS, CHERI; Malvern Sr HS; Malvern, AR; (2); FCA; FBLA; Natl Beta Clb; Pep Clb; SADD; Pres Frsh Cls; Rep Stu Cncl; Hon Roll; Jr NHS; Martin Luther King Jr Comm; Math And Sci Upward Bnd; Gfted Tlnted.

WILLIAMS, CHRISTA; Carlisle Jr Sr HS; Carlisle, AR; (4); Am Leg Aux Girls St; Church Yth Grp; Cmnty Wkr; Library Aide; Spanish Clb; Teachers Aide; Band; Mrchg Band; Orch; Pep Band; Hernderson St Univ; Premed.

WILLIAMS, CHRISTINA; Warren Sr HS; Warren, AR; (4); 26/112; Church Yth Grp; Cmnty Wkr; FBLA; Natl Beta Clb; Pres SADD; Teachers Aide; High Hon Roll; Hon Roll; NHS; Pres Acad Fit Awd; Schl Hl Fame; U Of AR; Elem Ed.

WILLIAMS, CHRYSTAL M; Malvern Sr HS; Malvern, AR; (3); Church Yth Grp; Sec FBLA; Natl Beta Clb; Pep Clb; Spanish Clb; SADD; Chorus; Ofcr Stu Cncl; High Hon Roll; Jr NHS; Peer Cnslrs Group Ldr; Henderson ST Univ; Ed.

WILLIAMS, DEIDRA; Bearden HS; Bearden, AR; (2); FBLA; FTA; Church Choir; Sec Soph Cls; Bsktbl; Trk; Cit Awd; Hon Roll; Pres Acad Fit Awd; 4-H; Beta Clb; U AR.

WILLIAMS JR, EDDIE L; Forrest City HS; Forrest City, AR; (3); Boy Scts; Cmnty Wkr; FHA; Office Aide; Spanish Clb; Church Choir; Ftbl; High Hon Roll; Hon Roll; Conway; Bus; Comp.

WILLIAMS, ELIZABETH L; Henderson Magnet Jr HS; Little Rock, AR; (1); FBLA; FHA; FTA; Band; Orch; Swing Chorus; Co-Capt Chrldng; Trk; Cit Awd; Hon Roll; Y-Teens; Memphis ST; Bus Admin.

WILLIAMS, ELIZABETH L; Southside HS; Fort Smith, AR; (4); 145/459; FBLA; FHA; Key Clb; Latin Clb; Mu Alpha Theta; Band; Hon Roll; Westark CC; Bus Admin.

WILLIAMS, ERIN; Rivercrest HS; Wilson, AR; (3); 7/95; French Clb; FBLA; Math Clb; Rep Jr Cls; VP Sr Cls; JV Capt Chrldng; High Hon Roll; Jr NHS; Ntl Merit Ltr; Prfct Atten Awd; Fnlst Of Amer Natl Teenager In AR 95; Phys Therapy.

WILLIAMS, GLENDA M; Riverview HS; Kensett, AR; (2); Church Yth Grp; FHA; Band; Chorus; Church Choir; Cls A All Star Band Awd; Medicind; Music.

WILLIAMS JR, GREGORY D; El Dorado Sr HS; Monroe, LA; (1); Chess Clb; Church Yth Grp; FCA; ROTC; Church Choir; JV Bsbl; JV Ftbl; JV Trk; Hon Roll; NHS; MIT; Arch.

WILLIAMS, HAZEL R; Eudora HS; Eudora, AR; (2); Church Yth Grp; FBLA; ROTC; Church Choir; Chrldng; Cit Awd.

WILLIAMS, HEATHER; Southside HS; Fort Smith, AR; (3); Library Aide; Mu Alpha Theta; Service Clb; Spanish Clb; High Hon Roll; Hon Roll; NHS; Ntl Merit Ltr; Spanish NHS; Psych.

WILLIAMS, IRVETTE S; John L Mcclellan Magnet HS; Little Rock, AR; (2); Boy Scts; Rep FHA; Hosp Aide; Office Aide; Spanish Clb; Chorus; School Play; Sec Stu Cncl; Chrldng; Hon Roll; Randolph-Macon Womens Coll; Med.

WILLIAMS, JACKIE E; Nettleton HS; Jonesboro, AR; (2); VP FBLA; Chrldng; Gym; Powder Puff Ftbl; Hon Roll; Hmcmng Queen 9th Grd; Hmcmng Maid 10th Grd; Beta Club 9th Grd; Vanderbilt; Ansthslgst.

WILLIAMS, JAMES E; Osceola HS; Osceola, AR; (2); Art Clb; Boy Scts; Band; Jazz Band; Mrchg Band; Hon Roll; AR ST Univ.

WILLIAMS JR, JAMES R; Rogers HS; Lowell, AR; (2); Hon Roll; Odyssey Of The Mind 2nd Place At State.

WILLIAMS, JASON A; Fayetteville Sr HS; Fayetteville, AR; (2); Boy Scts; Church Yth Grp; Spanish Clb; Band; Mrchg Band; Orch; Pep Band; Univ Of AR.

WILLIAMS, JEFFREY; Southside HS; Fort Smith, AR; (2); Boy Scts; German Clb; Band; Mrchg Band; Hon Roll; WA U St Louis; Med.

WILLIAMS, JEREMI L; Holly Grove HS; Holly Grove, AR; (2); #7 in class; Church Yth Grp; 4-H; FHA; Natl FFA Org; Quiz Bowl; SADD; Band; School Musical; School Play; Stage Crew; Geltman Clb; Hrs Rcng; UAPB; NBA.

WILLIAMS, JEREMY M; North Little Rock Hs-East; North Little Rock, AR; (2); 103/567; Church Yth Grp; Cmnty Wkr; Drama Clb; Red Cross Aide; Band; Church Choir; Jazz Band; Mrchg Band; Orch; School Musical; All Reg Band; Stu Perf/Tech Asst AR Chldrn Thtr; Prin Percsnst AR Yth Orch; Perf Arts/Thtr.

WILLIAMS, JOSH L; Mansfield Jr Sr HS; Booneville, AR; (1); 5/76; Drama Clb; FCA; FBLA; Quiz Bowl; Rep Stu Cncl; JV Bsktbl; JV Golf; JV Mgr(s); High Hon Roll; Pres Acad Fit Awd; Mdl Untd Ntns; Harvard; Lawyer.

WILLIAMS, JUSTIN S; Junction City HS; El Dorado, AR; (3); Church Yth Grp; Science Clb; Spanish Clb; Ofcr Bsbl; Hon Roll; X Ray Tech.

WILLIAMS, KARA; Buffalo Island Central HS; Monette, AR; (3); 1/60; VP Pres FBLA; VP FTA; HOBY; Quiz Bowl; Spanish Clb; School Play; Rep VP Stu Cncl; Intrml Var Chrldng; Var Golf; NHS; Natl Math Awd; Natl Achvt Acad.

WILLIAMS, KATHERINE; Cabot HS; Cabot, AR; (3); French Clb; Library Aide; Quiz Bowl; Teachers Aide; Chorus; Church Choir; School Musical; French Hon Soc; High Hon Roll; Jr NHS; Fr II Hnrs Test FLAN Festival 3rd Pl; Natl Fr Exam Hnr; Fr.

WILLIAMS, KATHERINE A; Russellville Sr HS; Russellville, AR; (4); Church Yth Grp; French Clb; Library Aide; Model UN; Office Aide; Variety Show; Rep Frsh Cls; Treas Soph Cls; Treas Jr Cls; Treas Stu Cncl; Mock Trial; Odyssey Of Mind; Sccr Clb; U Of C AR.

WILLIAMS, KENNETH L; Rivercrest HS; Joiner, AR; (3); 5/99; French Clb; FHA; Bsktbl; Ftbl; NHS; AR; Engrng.

WILLIAMS, KIM D; Lonoke Jr HS; Lonoke, AR; (1); Cmnty Wkr; FHA; Band; Orch; School Musical; School Play; Stage Crew; Rptr Nwsp; Hon Roll; NHS; Mst Imprvd Bnd; Plcd 3 Sci Fair; Mdls Solos/Ensmbl; Georgetown; Psych.

WILLIAMS, KISSA; Southside HS; Fort Smith, AR; (2); Church Yth Grp; FCA; FBLA; GAA; Girl Scts; Key Clb; Spanish Clb; Var Bsktbl; Var Trk; Hon Roll; Landscaping/Crafts; Howard; Sci/Techlgy.

WILLIAMS, KORENDA; Mansfield Jr Sr HS; Mansfield, AR; (4); 16/53; Art Clb; FCA; FBLA; FHA; Natl Beta Clb; Natl FFA Org; JV Bsktbl; Var Co-Capt Chrldng; JV Vllybl; Hon Roll; All St UCA Chrldr; Prm Comm; AR Tech U.

WILLIAMS, KRISTY; Dermott HS; Montrose, AR; (2); FBLA; Natl Beta Clb; Band; Mrchg Band; VP Soph Cls; Pres Stu Cncl; Cit Awd; Hon Roll; Ntl Merit Ltr; Pres Acad Fit Awd; Med.

WILLIAMS, LAKEISHA L; John L Mcclellan Magnet HS; Little Rock, AR; (4); Church Yth Grp; Cmnty Wkr; 4-H; FBLA; Letterman Clb; Mu Alpha Theta; Office Aide; 4-H Awd; Hon Roll; Prfct Atten Awd; UCA; PT.

WILLIAMS, LANSTON S; Morrilton Sr HS; Morrilton, AR; (2); Church Yth Grp; French Clb; Natl Beta Clb; Bsktbl; Hon Roll; Ntl Merit Ltr; UCA; Cmptr Tech.

WILLIAMS, LARON F; Bearden HS; Thornton, AR; (3); Boy Scts; Church Yth Grp; 4-H; Band; Church Choir; Mrchg Band; Prfct Atten Awd; Shorter Col.

WILLIAMS, LAURA; Gosnell Jr Sr HS; Blytheville, AR; (2); Church Yth Grp; FHA; Math Clb; Mu Alpha Theta; Natl Beta Clb; Science Clb; Spanish Clb; Ofcr Bsbl; Bsktbl; Chrldng; AR ST U; Ed.

WILLIAMS, LE ANN M; Sheridan Sr HS; Sheridan, AR; (4); 53/206; FCA; GAA; Bsktbl; Sftbl; Trk; Vllybl; Miss Grant Cnty; Lettered In Vlybll; Activ Ptcpnt In Hope Pentecostalyth Grp; U Of Cntrl Ark; Phys Thpy.

WILLIAMS, LEKEYA; Tuckerman HS; Tuckerman, AR; (4); 3/46; FBLA; FHA; Library Aide; Natl Beta Clb; Quiz Bowl; Spanish Clb; SADD; Rptr Nwsp; Yrbk; Gov Hon Prg Awd; Mock Trial; His Day 1st 95 & 2nd 96; AR ST U; RN.

WILLIAMS, LEODIS; Forrest City HS; Forrest City, AR; (3); VP Church Yth Grp; Band; Church Choir; Jazz Band; Mrchg Band; High Hon Roll; Hon Roll.

WILLIAMS, LESLIE A; Van Buren Sr HS; Van Buren, AR; (2); Church Yth Grp; French Clb; Treas FBLA; Pres FHA; Mu Alpha Theta; Co-Capt Pep Clb; SADD; Rptr Soph Cls; Rep Stu Cncl; Pom Pon; Pol Sci.

WILLIAMS, LINDSAY; Van Buren Sr HS; Van Buren, AR; (4); 17/256; Cmnty Wkr; Q&S; Band; Chorus; Phtg Rptr Nwsp; Phtg Rptr Yrbk; Ofcr Stu Cncl; Crs Cntry; Cit Awd; High Hon Roll; AR Tech Westark.

WILLIAMS, MAURICE L; El Dorado Sr HS; El Dorado, AR; (1); Art Clb; Church Choir; Ofcr Frsh Cls; Ftbl; Trk; Ath Schlr; UCLA; Cmptrs.

WILLIAMS, MELINDA L; Central HS; West Helena, AR; (3); 6/214; French Clb; Teachers Aide; High Hon Roll; Hon Roll; Jr NHS; NHS; Yng Democ Stu Clb; Tching.

WILLIAMS, MELINDA S; Junction City HS; Junction City, AR; (1); 1/53; Church Yth Grp; Quiz Bowl; Science Clb; Spanish Clb; Church Choir; Yrbk; Ofcr Stu Cncl; JV Chrldng; Powder Puff Ftbl; High Hon Roll; Ouachita Bapt U; Sprts Med.

WILLIAMS, MENDY; Bearden HS; Bearden, AR; (4); 7/58; Church Yth Grp; French Clb; Science Clb; School Musical; L Crs Cntry; L Trk; Var Cit Awd; High Hon Roll; Hon Roll; Prfct Atten Awd; Hnr Grad; Prin Hnr Roll; Track & Crss Cntry; SAU; Elem Ed.

WILLIAMS, MICHAEL D; Nevada Schl; Rosston, AR; (1); Church Yth Grp; FBLA; Natl Beta Clb.

WILLIAMS, MICHELLE L; Jonesboro HS; Jonesboro, AR; (3); VP Church Yth Grp; French Clb; Math Clb; Natl Beta Clb; Office Aide; SADD; Band; Capt Flag Corp; Mrchg Band; Pep Band; Outstdng Band Mem; Outstdng Flagline Mem; Flwshp Of Chrstn Stu; ASU.

WILLIAMS, MINNIE S; Marvell Acad; Moro, AR; (4); 12/32; Church Yth Grp; Computer Clb; FBLA; Library Aide; Office Aide; Spanish Clb; Teachers Aide; Church Choir; Ed Rptr Nwsp; High Hon Roll; Poetry; Modeling; Eastern AR CC; Nrsng.

WILLIAMS, NICOLE D; Dumas HS; Dumas, AR; (2); Church Yth Grp; Cmnty Wkr; FBLA; FTA; Girl Scts; Chorus; Drill Tm; Ofcr Frsh Cls; Rep Stu Cncl; Sftbl; Enjoy Wrtng Poetry; Participated In Talent Show; Spelman; Jrnlsm.

WILLIAMS, NIKKI; Mt Vernon Jr Sr HS; Mount Vernon, AR; (3); Am Leg Aux Girls St; Pres FBLA; Pres Natl Beta Clb; Natl FFA Org; Yrbk; VP Sec Stu Cncl; Var Bsktbl; Sftbl; Hon Roll; ASU; Comp Inf Sys.

WILLIAMS, PAMELA; Parkin Jr Sr HS; Earle, AR; (2); High Hon Roll; FHA; U Of AR; Cmptr Pgmr.

WILLIAMS, RASHALD L; Fairview HS; Camden, AR; (3); Am Leg Boys St; Mu Alpha Theta; Science Clb; SADD; Chorus; Var L Bsktbl; JV Ftbl; Var L Trk; Intrml Vllybl; Cit Awd; Comp Engrng.

WILLIAMS, REBECCA A; Ozark Adventist Acad; Hot Springs, AR; (2); Church Yth Grp; Teachers Aide; Church Choir; Var Bsktbl; Intrml Sftbl; Intrml Vllybl; Prfct Atten Awd; Nrsng.

WILLIAMS, REGINA; Mc Gehee HS; Tillar, AR; (2); FHA; Spanish Clb; Church Choir; Ofcr Stu Cncl; Sftbl; Vllybl; Cit Awd; Upward Bound Pgm; Frst Rnr Up Junettnth Pagnt; Martin Luther King Jr Comm; UCA Conway.

WILLIAMS, S R; Fayetteville Sr HS; Goshen, AR; (2); Drama Clb; FBLA; Varsity Clb; Ofcr Bsbl; Bsktbl; Ftbl; Trk; Wt Lftg; Hon Roll; Prfct Atten Awd.

WILLIAMS, SARA E; Pottsville Schl; Atkins, AR; (3); 1/50; Church Yth Grp; GAA; Natl Beta Clb; Rep Jr Cls; Var Bsktbl; Var Sftbl; Hon Roll; Sociology.

WILLIAMS, SARA M; Clarksville HS; Clarksville, AR; (3); FCA; FBLA; Spanish Clb; Var Bsktbl; Var Sftbl; Var Trk; Var Vllybl; Hon Roll; Prfct Atten Awd; Pres Acad Fit Awd; Law.

WILLIAMS, SARAH; Lake Hamilton Sr HS; Hot Springs, AR; (2); Church Yth Grp; Natl Beta Clb; Band; Mrchg Band; High Hon Roll; Hon Roll; All-Regn Band 1st Band.

WILLIAMS, SHALONDA; Lee Sr HS; Marianna, AR; (1); #1 in class; Church Yth Grp; Drama Clb; Natl Beta Clb; Science Clb; Spanish Clb; School Musical; School Play; Rep Stu Cncl; High Hon Roll; Pres Acad Fit Awd; PHD; Xavier U; Phy.

WILLIAMS, SHARON; J A Fair Sr HS; Little Rock, AR; (3); Church Yth Grp; Hist Drama Clb; FCA; 4-H; Pres FBLA; GAA; Sec Natl Beta Clb; Chorus; Church Choir; School Play; Choir Acad Achvmt Awd; UALR; Cmptr Prgmng/Actng.

WILLIAMS, SHERRILL F; Carlisle Jr Sr HS; Carlisle, AR; (3); FHA; GAA; Library Aide; Spanish Clb; Teachers Aide; Chorus; Church Choir; Hon Roll; U Of Conway; Elem Ed; Nrsng.

WILLIAMS, SR; Fayetteville Sr HS; Goshen, AR; (3); FCA; FBLA; School Play; Ofcr Bsbl; Bsktbl; Ftbl; Wt Lftg; High Hon Roll; Pres Acad Fit Awd.

WILLIAMS, STEPHANIE; Dermott HS; Dermott, AR; (1); Church Yth Grp; Girl Scts; Natl Beta Clb; Band; Church Choir; Jazz Band; Cit Awd; Hon Roll; Prfct Atten Awd; Coll.

WILLIAMS, STEPHANIE D; Arkansas Sr HS; Texarkana, AR; (2); Bus Profs of Am; Church Yth Grp; Cmnty Wkr; FBLA; Office Aide; Quiz Bowl; Spanish Clb; Church Choir; Ofcr Stu Cncl; Hon Roll; UT Arlington; Criminal Justice.

WILLIAMS, TACO; El Dorado Sr HS; El Dorado, AR; (3); Library Aide; ROTC; Teachers Aide; Band; Mrchg Band; Pep Band; Treas Pres Stu Cncl; Var L Bsktbl; Steering Cmmtte; El Dorado Schlr Ath; Natl Yth Svc Day; Phys Thrpy.

WILLIAMS, TASHA D; Parkin Jr Sr HS; Earle, AR; (4); 6/33; FHA; Teachers Aide; Varsity Clb; Ofcr Jr Cls; Ofcr Sr Cls; Hon Roll; Beta Clb Sec; East AR CC; Ministry.

WILLIAMS, TIFFANY L; Lake Hamilton Sr HS; Royal, AR; (2); FCA; Var Fld Hcky; Crs Cntry; Trk; SCL Mem; All St In Crss Cntry; Greenhand FFA Degree Awd; AR Tech Univ; Wildlife Biolgst.

WILLIAMS JR, TIMMY; Morrilton Sr HS; Atkins, AR; (3); Church Yth Grp; Drama Clb; HOBY; Office Aide; Thesps; Church Choir; School Musical; School Play; Var Ftbl; Cit Awd; Boys St; U Of AR-FAYETTEVILLE; Bus.

WILLIAMS, TRACIE; Dumas HS; Dumas, AR; (3); 32/163; Bus Profs of Am; Church Yth Grp; Cmnty Wkr; FBLA; FHA; FTA; Girl Scts; Teachers Aide; Band; Chorus; Stndt Cncl Treas; Univ Cntrl AR; Bus Admn.

WILLIAMS, TRACY; Lee Sr HS; Moro, AR; (4); 13/102; School Play; High Hon Roll; Pres Acad Fit Awd; Math Acad Awd; Phillips Cty CC; Elem Ed.

WILLIAMS, WENDI; Monticello HS; Monticello, AR; (1); Church Yth Grp; FHA; GAA; Natl Beta Clb; Band; Mrchg Band; Pep Band; Pres Stu Cncl; Co-Capt L Bsktbl; Co-Capt L Chrldng.

WILLIAMS, YOLANDA D; Mc Gehee HS; Mc Gehee, AR; (4); Art Clb; FHA; Chorus; Nwsp; Merit Roll; U Of AR Monticello; Nrsng.

WILLIAMSON, AMY G; De Soto Schl; Elaine, AR; (3); 1/19; Thesps; Yrbk; VP Jr Cls; Ofcr Stu Cncl; High Hon Roll; NHS; Am Leg Aux Girls St; Spanish Clb; School Play; 2nd Pl Chem Acad Bttrmnt Cmptn 96; Navy Hnrs Prog Awd; Hghst Avg Span I & II, Wrd Prcssng, Comp Sci; Harding U; Phrmcy.

WILLIAMSON, COY R; Horatio HS; Horatio, AR; (2); FCA; Natl FFA Org; Quiz Bowl; Var Bsbl; Var Bsktbl; Var Ftbl; Hon Roll; NHS.

WILLIAMSON, DAMON; North Little Rock Hs-West; North Little Rock, AR; (3); Drama Clb; FBLA; Spanish Clb; Stage Crew; Ftbl; Trk; Wt Lftg; Hon Roll; Pol.

WILLIAMSON, HOLLI N; Conway Sr HS; Conway, AR; (2); Church Yth Grp; FBLA; Chorus; Church Choir; FBLA Creed Awd 94-95; All Region Choir 95-96; All St Yth Choir Yth Ministeries 95-96; Mexico Mission; Bus; Law; Music.

WILLIAMSON, HOLLYE A; Dequeen HS; De Queen, AR; (2); 11/100; Church Yth Grp; VP FBLA; VP FHA; SADD; Chorus; Rptr Nwsp; High Hon Roll; Cert Acad Achvmt Bio 95-; Cert Acad Achvmt Home Ec I 94-95; FHA ST STAR Evnts Gld Mdlst Sr Ill Tlk; OK ST Univ; Dr Veterinary Med.

WILLIAMSON, JESSICA D; Russellville Sr HS; Russellville, AR; (2); Sec Church Yth Grp; FCA; Band; Bsktbl; Sftbl; Trk; Vllybl; Hon Roll; NHS; Pres Acad Fit Awd.

WILLIAMSON, MARLA; Mineral Springs Schl; Mineral Springs, AR; (4); 2/29; Church Yth Grp; 4-H; FHA; Letterman Clb; Natl Beta Clb; Quiz Bowl; SADD; Varsity Clb; Co-Ed Yrbk; Rep Stu Cncl; Henderson ST U; Bus Mgmt.

WILLIFORD, COURTNEY B; Sheridan Sr HS; Sheridan, AR; (2); Treas Church Yth Grp; Cmnty Wkr; Hosp Aide; Teachers Aide; Church Choir; Variety Show; Ed Nwsp; Mgr(s); Hon Roll; Chsn Duke Univ 7th Grd Sit For Act HS Seniors; Hmcng Maid; WA Univ; Elem Ed/Pre-Med.

WILLIS, CHANDRA D; Russellville Sr HS; Russellville, AR; (2); Church Yth Grp; Spanish Clb; Band; Flag Corp; Mrchg Band; High Hon Roll; Jr NHS; NHS.

WILLIS, CHARITY L; West Fork HS; West Fork, AR; (1); FHA; Library Aide; Natl FFA Org; Teachers Aide; Trk; Hon Roll; Judge In Equine Div.

WILLIS, ERICKA R; Hot Springs HS; Hot Springs, AR; (3); Church Yth Grp; Office Aide; Pep Clb; Band; Church Choir; Flag Corp; Mrchg Band; Pep Band; Flag Corp Capt; Criminal Law.

WILLIS, JEREMY S; North Little Rock Hs-West; North Little Rock, AR; (3); Church Yth Grp; Letterman Clb; Band; Jazz Band; Mrchg Band; Pep Band; Gov Hon Prg Awd; Hon Roll; Peer Ldrshp.

WILLIS, LATASHA L; Dardanelle HS; Dardanelle, AR; (3); Church Yth Grp; Cmnty Wkr; Drama Clb; FCA; FBLA; GAA; Girl Scts; Intnl Clb; Letterman Clb; SADD; Most Improved; Lizard Achiever Awd; Dr Martin L King 3rd Pl Essay Winner; West AR CC; Kndgtn Tchr.

WILLIS, SHANNA D; Northside HS; Fort Smith, AR; (3); Church Yth Grp; Spanish Clb; Band; Church Choir; Drill Tm; Mrchg Band; Treas Soph Cls; Ofcr Jr Cls; Hon Roll; Prfct Atten Awd; STAT; TRAX & Grizzly Pride; TX Southern U; Chld Soc Wrkr.

WILLIS, STEPHANIE; Watson Chapel Sr HS; Pine Bluff, AR; (3); Church Yth Grp; FCA; FBLA; FHA; Key Clb; Spanish Clb; Chorus; Bsktbl; Mgr(s); Score Keeper; Eng Awd For Acad Awd; Nrs; Elem Schl Tchr.

WILLIS, VINCENT D; Jacksonville HS; Jacksonville, AR; (2); Church Yth Grp; Drama Clb; FHA; Church Choir; Ofcr Stu Cncl; JV Bsktbl; Hon Roll; Presdntl Acad Awd; Lawyer; Bus Mgmt.

WILLOUGHBY, FAITH M; England HS; England, AR; (1); #6 in class; FBLA; FHA; Quiz Bowl; Hon Roll; Pres Acad Fit Awd; Acad Excl; Hnr Awd Eng; LOYAL/GIFTED Talented Class; U Of AR; Cmptr Tech.

WILLS, ERIC G; Yellville Summit HS; Yellville, AR; (3); 5/95; Am Leg Boys St; Art Clb; Natl FFA Org; Quiz Bowl; Varsity Clb; Ofcr Bsbl; Bsktbl; Cit Awd; High Hon Roll; Hon Roll; Bsbl/Bsktbl Awds; Bio/Amer His Awds; MO At Rolla; Ag.

WILLS, RACHEL; Yellville Summit HS; Yellville, AR; (2); FCA; FBLA; Library Aide; Math Clb; Capt Chrldng; Crs Cntry; Trk; Cit Awd; High Hon Roll; Hon Roll; Fshn Dsgn.

WILSON, ADRIENNE; Benton Sr HS; Benton, AR; (4); 4/221; Am Leg Aux Girls St; Church Yth Grp; Cmnty Wkr; FBLA; Key Clb; Math Clb; VP Science Clb; Spanish Clb; Teachers Aide; Band; Harding Univ.

WILSON, ALICIA A; Sloan Hendrix HS; Imboden, AR; (2); 1/50; Treas FHA; GAA; HOBY; Model UN; Natl Beta Clb; Rptr Natl FFA Org; Office Aide; Pep Clb; Chorus; School Musical; Lamp Of Learning Awd; AR ST Univ; Radiologist.

WILSON, BRANDON S; Southside HS; Fort Smith, AR; (2); FCA; Teachers Aide; JV Bsktbl; Cit Awd; High Hon Roll; Hon Roll; Prfct Atten Awd; Sports Player Of Month; Boys Clb Bsktbl.

WILSON, BRIDGET R; Harrison Sr HS; Harrison, AR; (3); Church Yth Grp; FBLA; Band; Flag Corp; Mrchg Band; Ed Nwsp; Hon Roll; Debenair Clb; Acctng.

WILSON, CARMILYA A; Mc Gehee HS; Mc Gehee, AR; (2); 8/109; Church Yth Grp; FTA; GAA; Math Clb; Mu Alpha Theta; Natl Beta Clb; Science Clb; Spanish Clb; Chorus; School Play; Microbiologist.

WILSON, CELESTE P; Bryant Sr HS; Bryant, AR; (2); Church Yth Grp; Cmnty Wkr; French Clb; Hosp Aide; Band; Mrchg Band; High Hon Roll; Jr NHS; Missions 95 96; U Of Cntrl AR; Phys Thrpy.

WILSON, CHARLES S; Danville HS; Danville, AR; (2); 3/36; Church Yth Grp; FCA; VP FBLA; Capt Scholastic Bowl; School Play; Pres Soph Cls; Ofcr Stu Cncl; L Bsktbl; L Ftbl; Cit Awd; Drama.

WILSON, CHESLEA; Lamar HS; Knoxville, AR; (3); FCA; Teachers Aide; Var Chrldng; Hon Roll; AR Tech Univ; Elem Ed.

WILSON, CHRIS; Wonderview HS; Jerusalem, AR; (4); #2 in class; Am Leg Boys St; FBLA; Intnl Clb; Natl Beta Clb; Natl FFA Org; Band; Rptr Nwsp; Mgr Bsktbl; Hon Roll; Pres Acad Fit Awd; U Of Central AR; Pharmacy.

WILSON, CHRIS; Strong Jr Sr HS; Strong, AR; (1); French Clb; Science Clb; Band; Ofcr Frsh Cls; JV Bsktbl; Cit Awd; Hon Roll; Prfct Atten Awd; BASIC; Cmptr Tech.

WILSON, CRYSTAL D; Timbo Schl; Harriet, AR; (2); Church Yth Grp; FBLA; FHA; Natl Beta Clb; Natl FFA Org; Church Choir; Nwsp; Yrbk; Trk; Cit Awd; Bio; Psych.

WILSON, DAVID G; Cabot HS; Austin, AR; (3); 41/396; Church Yth Grp; Quiz Bowl; High Hon Roll; Hon Roll; Kiwanis Awd.

WILSON, DEANNA L; Rose Bud Jr Sr HS; Romance, AR; (2); FHA; Teachers Aide; Yth-To-Yth; Comm Svc Project; Legal Asst.

WILSON, DONNA; Marion HS; Marion, AR; (3); Art Clb; Church Yth Grp; French Clb; Church Choir; Nwsp; Chrldng; Alpha Beta Sigma.

WILSON, ERIN J; Cabot HS; Austin, AR; (1); 58/516; Math Clb; Vllybl; High Hon Roll; Hon Roll; JUST Club.

WILSON, JAIME; Watson Chapel Sr HS; Pine Bluff, AR; (2); Church Yth Grp; Drama Clb; French Clb; Hosp Aide; Key Clb; Natl Beta Clb; Office Aide; School Play; Yrbk; Hon Roll; U Of AR Fayetteville; Pre-Law.

WILSON, JAMES N; Fairview HS; Camden, AR; (3); Science Clb; Spanish Clb; Var JV Ftbl; Var Socr; Var Tennis; Var Wt Lftg; Hon Roll; Olympc Devlpmnt Pgm Soccer.

WILSON, JAMIE L; Abundant Life Schools; Jacksonville, AR; (2); Church Yth Grp; Drama Clb; Spanish Clb; Chorus; Church Choir; School Musical; Prfct Atten Awd; Admin Forum; Stu Devotions; See You At The Pole; Spiritual Emphasis Week; Corporate Lawyer.

WILSON, JASON C; Dewitt HS; De Witt, AR; (3); 20/92; Am Leg Boys St; Church Yth Grp; FCA; FBLA; HOBY; Natl Beta Clb; Science Clb; Var L Bsktbl; High Hon Roll; Natl Eng Mrt Awd; Ouachita Bapt Bsktbl Camp; Lifeguard.

WILSON, JEROME M; Forrest City HS; Forrest City, AR; (4); Church Yth Grp; FCA; FHA; Teachers Aide; Bsktbl; Trk; Wt Lftg; High Hon Roll; Hon Roll; Civil Engrg.

WILSON, JOSHUA C; Flippin Jr Sr HS; Flippin, AR; (3); CAP; SADD; Intrml Trk; Hon Roll; Pres Acad Fit Awd; Automobile Bdy Repair.

WILSON, JOSHUA L; Harrison Sr HS; Harrison, AR; (4); Cmnty Wkr; French Clb; Office Aide; Spanish Clb; Teachers Aide; Crs Cntry; Socr; Trk; Spanish NHS; St Span Cmptn 1st For Extemperaneous Reading Poetry & Skit; St Natl Fr Exam 10th; Span Natl Exam; Comp Prgmr; Frgn Lang.

WILSON, KARA L; West Memphis Christian Schl; Marion, AR; (3); Am Leg Aux Girls St; Church Yth Grp; Cmnty Wkr; FCA; French Clb; GAA; VP Frsh Cls; VP Soph Cls; Treas Jr Cls; Sec Stu Cncl.

WILSON, KATIE L; Bryant Sr HS; Bauxite, AR; (2); #1 in class; Church Yth Grp; English Clb; FBLA; HOBY; Science Clb; Spanish Clb; Chorus; Church Choir; School Musical; Hon Roll; Music 4 Choir Trphs, 6 Outstndg Achvt Patchs; 2 Outstndg Achvts Engl Trphs.

WILSON, KIMBERLY; Mount View HS; Mountain View, AR; (3); FHA; HOBY; Natl Beta Clb; Rptr Spanish Clb; Teachers Aide; Var Chrldng; Pres Acad Fit Awd; U Of Central AR.

WILSON, KRISTEN M; Lonoke Jr HS; Lonoke, AR; (1); Church Yth Grp; GAA; Science Clb; Bsktbl; Chrldng; Hon Roll; NHS; U Of AR; Phy Thrpst.

WILSON, LATONYA S; John L Mcclellan Magnet HS; Little Rock, AR; (3); FBLA; Rep FHA; Key Clb; Quiz Bowl; Science Clb; Spanish Clb; Pres Band; Mrchg Band; Cit Awd; High Hon Roll; TX Tech; Med.

WILSON, LAURA; Charleston HS; Charleston, AR; (3); 6/43; Church Yth Grp; FHA; Natl Beta Clb; Quiz Bowl; Chorus; School Musical; Hon Roll; Ntl Merit SF.

WILSON, LESLIE R; Harrison Sr HS; Harrison, AR; (4); 1/198; Cmnty Wkr; French Clb; Rptr Nwsp; Ed Yrbk; L Bsktbl; High Hon Roll; NHS; Val; U Of Cntrl AR; Forestry.

WILSON, LILLIE J; Bald Knob HS; Bald Knob, AR; (2); Sec Art Clb; Church Yth Grp; Drama Clb; GAA; Chorus; Church Choir; Trk; Cit Awd; High Hon Roll; Hon Roll.

WILSON, LORI; Malvern Sr HS; Malvern, AR; (4); Church Yth Grp; FCA; FBLA; FHA; Natl Beta Clb; Quiz Bowl; SADD; Drill Tm; Stage Crew; Nwsp; GATE Prizm Drama; Gov Yth Conf Ldr; CHAMPS Peer Cnslr; Joseph Baldwin Acad Nom; Ouachita Bapt Univ; Brdcst Jrnl.

WILSON, MANDY C; Junction City HS; Junction City, AR; (1); Quiz Bowl; Spanish Clb; School Play; Yrbk; Ofcr Stu Cncl; JV Mgr(s); Var Powder Puff Ftbl; High Hon Roll; BASIC; U Of AR; Phy Therapy.

WILSON, MARILYN G; Booneville Jr Sr HS; Booneville, AR; (3); Church Yth Grp; FBLA; FHA; Spanish Clb; High Hon Roll; Prfct Atten Awd; Yth Alive; Coll Of Ozarks; Pre-Law.

WILSON, MELANIE; Gurdon HS; Gurdon, AR; (3); 1/60; Am Leg Aux Girls St; Church Yth Grp; FHA; Natl Beta Clb; Spanish Clb; Band; Jazz Band; School Musical; NHS; Prfct Atten Awd; Henderson U; Spnsh Tchr.

WILSON, MELISSA A; Lake Hamilton Sr HS; Hot Springs Natio, AR; (2); 47/262; Church Yth Grp; FHA; Hosp Aide; Mgr(s); Sftbl; High Hon Roll; Sftbl All Stars 4 Yrs; Natl Hist/Govt Awd; Nrsng.

WILSON, MICHELLE; Rison HS; Rison, AR; (2); 1/50; Church Yth Grp; FCA; French Clb; FBLA; FHA; HOBY; Natl Beta Clb; Science Clb; Sec Treas Frsh Cls; Var Chrldng; Ms Tn Of AR Pgnt.

WILSON, MICHELLE L; Gosnell Jr Sr HS; Manila, AR; (2); AR ST Univ; Pediatrics.

WILSON, RANDY J; Clinton HS; Clinton, AR; (4); Boy Scts; FBLA; FHA; JV Bsktbl; JV Var Ftbl.

WILSON, RICHARD P; Bright Star Schl; Dallas, TX; (2); Art Clb; Computer Clb; Debate Tm; Drama Clb; English Clb; 4-H; FHA; Library Aide; Math Clb; Math Tm; Mrkmnshp; Archer; Cmptr Oper/Tech.

WILSON, SHANE; Nashville HS; Nashville, AR; (3); Spanish Clb; Teachers Aide; Mgr(s); Hon Roll; Jr NHS; NHS; Pres Acad Fit Awd.

WILSON, SHERIKA L; Parkview Arts-Science HS; North Little Rock, AR; (2); Church Yth Grp; FHA; Girl Scts; Church Choir; School Play; Rep Soph Cls; Hon Roll; Jr Beta Clb; Clark Atlanta; Soc Sci.

WILSON, STACEY; Gould HS; Gould, AR; (2); 2/16; Art Clb; HOBY; Science Clb; Church Choir; VP Soph Cls; Co-Ed Chrldng; High Hon Roll; Ntl Merit Ltr; Sal; Church Yth Grp; Amer Natl Teenagr; Philander Smith; Brdcstng.

WILSON, STEPHEN M; Southside HS; Fort Smith, AR; (2); Mu Alpha Theta; Spanish Clb; Bsktbl; Hon Roll; NHS; Prfct Atten Awd; GATE; Pre-Med/Pediatric Ophthlmlgy.

WILSON, TERRICA R; Osceola HS; Osceola, AR; (3); #6 in class; French Clb; FBLA; Model UN; Science Clb; High Hon Roll; Jr NHS; Kiwanis Awd; NHS; Prfct Atten Awd; Pres Acad Fit Awd; U Of Cntrl AR.

WILSON, TOBY; Poyen Schl; Prattsville, AR; (4); 3/36; Am Leg Boys St; Church Yth Grp; FCA; 4-H; HOBY; Quiz Bowl; Yrbk; Rep Frsh Cls; VP Soph Cls; Rep Sr Cls; AEGIS Pgms; Ouachita Bapt U; Ministry.

WILSON, TOMMY W; Trumann HS; Trumann, AR; (2); French Clb; FBLA; Model UN; Quiz Bowl; ROTC; Pres Science Clb; Rptr Nwsp; Speaker-AR Historical Asoc; Natl Sojourners Awd; Trumann Area Centennial Comm; Rhodes Coll; Pol Sci.

WILSON, WOODROW D; Central HS; Helena, AR; (2); Church Yth Grp; Chorus; Church Choir; Var L Ftbl; Var L Trk; Hon Roll; Prfct Atten Awd; CHS PRIDE Group; Child Psych.

WINBERRY, BENJAMIN C; Piggott HS; Piggott, AR; (3); 1/70; Am Leg Boys St; Church Yth Grp; Pres Drama Clb; FCA; French Clb; FBLA; HOBY; Key Clb; VP Natl Beta Clb; Quiz Bowl; FCA; Fren Clb; U Of AR; Pol Sci.

WINDERS, JODI D; West Memphis Christian Schl; Earle, AR; (1); Church Yth Grp; Natl Beta Clb; Ofcr Stu Cncl; Bsktbl; Chrldng; Trk; Vllybl; Hon Roll; Prin Hnr Roll; U Of AR; Phy Thrpst.

WINDERS, RICKEY J; West Memphis Christian Schl; Earle, AR; (2); L Var Bsbl; L Var Bsktbl; L Var Ftbl; Hon Roll; Prfct Atten Awd.

WINDHAM, KYLIE; Morrilton Sr HS; Morrilton, AR; (3); Church Yth Grp; French Clb; Math Clb; Natl Beta Clb; Thesps; Band; Flag Corp; Mrchg Band; French Hon Soc; Hon Roll; AR Tech U; Math.

WINE, KISTY T; John L Mcclellan Magnet HS; Little Rock, AR; (4); Church Yth Grp; Dance Clb; Drama Clb; FBLA; FHA; GAA; Library Aide; Office Aide; Spanish Clb; Varsity Clb; Stu Wk; Trck Chmpnshp; Spnsh Awd; Philander Smith Coll; Elem Ed.

WINFREY, JO D; Searcy HS; Searcy, AR; (2); 67/265; Church Yth Grp; FCA; GAA; Key Clb; Letterman Clb; Natl Beta Clb; JV Var Bsktbl; Hon Roll; French Clb; FBLA; Finalist AR Natl Tngr Schlsp Prgm; AAU ST Bsktbl Team Plyd Natnls; Coll Bsktbl; 4 Yr U; Pre-Law/Bus/Lawyer.

WINKLER, DAVID A; Wynne HS; Wynne, AR; (3); Boy Scts; Church Yth Grp; Drama Clb; FBLA; FTA; SADD; Church Choir; School Musical; School Play; Hon Roll; U Of Central AR; Educ.

WINKLER, DAWN; Parkview Arts-Science HS; Little Rock, AR; (2); Church Yth Grp; Debate Tm; French Clb; FBLA; HOBY; Natl Beta Clb; Office Aide; Rep Frsh Cls; Rep Soph Cls; Rep Jr Cls; Assn Black Engrs AR; Yng Democrats Of AR; Stanford Univ; Mech Engr.

WINKLER, JEFFREY K; Pine Bluff HS; Pine Bluff, AR; (3); Church Yth Grp; Office Aide; Spanish Clb; L Bsbl; HERO 11/12th Grds.

WINN-HOOD, MIRANDA M; Mt Vernon-Enola HS; Mount Vernon, AR; (2); FBLA; FHA; Natl Beta Clb; Quiz Bowl; Science Clb; Spanish Clb; Speech Tm; Chorus; School Musical; School Play; Jr High Choir Awd; Harding Univ; Elem Tchr.

WINSTON, LEANN; Rison HS; Rison, AR; (3); 5/40; Church Yth Grp; Sec Treas French Clb; VP FBLA; Natl Beta Clb; Science Clb; Band; Mrchg Band; Rep Frsh Cls; Hon Roll; Majorette; LA Tech U; Bus.

WINSTON, RACHEL A; Sheridan Sr HS; Sheridan, AR; (3); 7/270; Treas Sec Church Yth Grp; Cmnty Wkr; FCA; FBLA; GAA; Rep Band; Chorus; Church Choir; Mrchg Band; School Play; Participated In Miss Teen AR Pageant; Chrstn Psycht.

WINTERS, MATTHEW R; Russellville Sr HS; Russellville, AR; (2); 53/450; Rep Church Yth Grp; Band; Mrchg Band; High Hon Roll; Jr NHS; NHS; Prfct Atten Awd; All Rgn Bnd 94-95 4th Chair Trombone; AR Tech Univ; Bus.

WINTERS, MEREDITH; Southside HS; Fort Smith, AR; (2); Church Yth Grp; Rep Drama Clb; Latin Clb; Math Clb; School Musical; School Play; Stage Crew; Jr NHS; NHS; Hon Roll; 1st Pl Regnl OM; Gftd & Tlntd Pgm 9 Yrs; Chem.

WINTERS, NIKKI; Southside HS; Fort Smith, AR; (4); 63/459; Church Yth Grp; FCA; French Clb; FBLA; Mu Alpha Theta; Service Clb; Chrldng; Gym; French Hon Soc; NHS; Westark CC; Scndry Ed.

WIRGES, KEVIN C; Catholic HS; North Little Rock, AR; (3); Boy Scts; Church Yth Grp; ROTC; Drill Tm; Math.

WISE, AMANDA M; Fouke Jr Sr HS; Fouke, AR; (2); FBLA; Natl FFA Org; Yrbk; Geomtry Awd; Baylor Univ; Lawyer.

WISE, HEATHER; West Side Christian Schl; El Dorado, AR; (3); 1/30; Church Yth Grp; Drama Clb; Mu Alpha Theta; Natl Beta Clb; Acpl Chr; Chorus; School Play; Teachers Aide; Rep Soph Cls; Treas Jr Cls; Eng Awd; ORUEF Ptry Rdng Natls 6th Pl; Math & Sci Awds; Evangel Coll; Eng.

WISE, LISA M; England HS; England, AR; (2); Chorus; Hon Roll; PT.

WISLER, ANGIE; Greenbrier HS; Greenbrier, AR; (4); 5/132; FBLA; HOBY; Natl Beta Clb; Quiz Bowl; Band; Chorus; Jazz Band; Mrchg Band; Sec Frsh Cls; Cit Awd.

WISON, CARMILYA A; Mc Gehee HS; Mc Gehee, AR; (2); 8/106; Church Yth Grp; FTA; Mu Alpha Theta; Natl Beta Clb; Science Clb; Spanish Clb; Chorus; Bsktbl; Chrldng; Trk; Microbio.

WISTRAND, ROBERT; Rogers HS; Rogers, AR; (4); 55/515; Am Leg Boys St; Pres Church Yth Grp; FCA; Library Aide; Model UN; Church Choir; Ofcr Stu Cncl; Var Capt Crs Cntry; Var Trk; Cit Awd; ELCA Wshngtn DC Yth Mnstry Ldrshp Conf; AR All St Crss Cntry St Chmpn 94; Anthrplgy.

WITCHER, SHU'MIA L; Magnolia HS; Waldo, AR; (2); FHA; Teachers Aide; Band; Mrchg Band; Stage Crew; JV Trk; Hon Roll; Clark Univ; PT.

WITHERS, JEREMY D; John L Mcclellan Magnet HS; Little Rock, AR; (2); Natl Beta Clb; Spanish Clb; Band; Drm Mjr(t); Mrchg Band; Pep Band; JV Bsktbl; Cit Awd; High Hon Roll; NHS; U Of AR; Comp Tech.

WITHERSPOON, KRYSTAL; Yerger Jr HS; Hope, AR; (1); Church Yth Grp; 4-H; VP FHA; GAA; Girl Scts; Church Choir; Ofcr Stu Cncl; Ofcr Bsbl; Chrldng; Gym; Gftd & Tlnt; UCLA; Bus & Cmptng.

WITHERSPOON, NICK K; Bryant Sr HS; Bryant, AR; (3); Art Clb; Church Yth Grp; Cmnty Wkr; Drama Clb; Letterman Clb; Library Aide; Teachers Aide; Bsktbl; Hon Roll; Bsktbl/Bus.

WITT, NATHAN L; Pine Bluff HS; Pine Bluff, AR; (2); FHA; Chorus; JV Bsbl; Hon Roll; UCA; Nrsng; Bus.

WIXSON, HALEY; Weiner HS; Fisher, AR; (1); Church Yth Grp; FHA; Natl FFA Org; Science Clb; Chorus; Var Chrldng; Hon Roll; NHS; WAKE UP; Harding U; Wrkng W/Hndcpd Chldn.

WOFFORD, REBEKAH; Perryville Jr Sr HS; Perryville, AR; (2); FBLA; Spanish Clb; Teachers Aide; Hon Roll; St Wrtng Comp On Georgrphy Wnnr; Cong Of Jehovahs Wtnss Mem; Alg I, Geomtry Awds; UCA; Acctnt.

WOLF, KARA; Valley View HS; Jonesboro, AR; (3); 1/82; Church Yth Grp; Spanish Clb; Teachers Aide; Chorus; Treas Soph Cls; VP Jr Cls; Ofcr Stu Cncl; Bsktbl; Golf; Tennis; Tnns St Trnmnt 3rd Pl Dbls, Dist Title Wnnr; Fire Mrshll; Vet.

WOLF, NORMAN R; Arkansas Sr HS; Texarkana, AR; (4); 11/379; Treas Art Clb; Church Yth Grp; FBLA; Math Clb; Mu Alpha Theta; Spanish Clb; Church Choir; JV Ftbl; High Hon Roll; Hon Roll; Fellowship Of Chrstn Stus Treas; U Of AR; Arch.

WOLFE, APRIL; Mt Pleasant Jr Sr HS; Sage, AR; (1); 1/23; Art Clb; French Clb; Pres FHA; Library Aide; Natl Beta Clb; Quiz Bowl; Pres Frsh Cls; Bsktbl; Sftbl; High Hon Roll.

WOLFE, BRANDON; Mills HS; Sherwood, AR; (3); Art Clb; Mu Alpha Theta; Nwsp; Gov Hon Prg Awd; High Hon Roll; Pres Schlr; Lit Mag Ed; Coffehouse Poetry Rdngs Creator/Orgnzr.

WOLFE, JARROD S; Fairview HS; Camden, AR; (4); French Clb; Natl FFA Org; Teachers Aide; Hon Roll.

WOLFE, JEREMY; Fairview HS; Camden, AR; (4); Am Leg Boys St; Art Clb; Boy Scts; Debate Tm; French Clb; FBLA; Key Clb; Mu Alpha Theta; Natl Beta Clb; Natl FFA Org; Ouachita Bapt U; Pre-Phrmcy.

WOLFE, JONATHAN L; Fairview HS; Camden, AR; (3); Church Yth Grp; Key Clb; Mu Alpha Theta; Natl FFA Org; Chorus; Church Choir; Ftbl; Golf; Hon Roll; NHS.

WOLFE, LORI; Evening Shade Schl; Evening Shade, AR; (1); FCA; FBLA; FHA; Quiz Bowl; Teachers Aide; Hon Roll; TAD.

WOLFE, MATTHEW; Fayetteville Christian Schl; Fayetteville, AR; (4); #2 in class; Am Leg Boys St; Church Yth Grp; Yrbk; Ofcr Jr Cls; Ofcr Sr Cls; Var Capt Bsktbl; High Hon Roll; Hon Roll; NHS; Sal; John Brown Univ; Bio.

WOLFE, SARALIN; Fayetteville Christian Schl; Fayetteville, AR; (1); Church Yth Grp; Pres Frsh Cls; Var Bsktbl; High Hon Roll; NHS; Yth Bible Study; Sunday Schl Tchr.

WOLFE, TONIA; Warren Sr HS; Banks, AR; (3); 21/144; Art Clb; Church Yth Grp; Drama Clb; French Clb; FBLA; Natl Beta Clb; Ed Nwsp; Ed Yrbk; L Chrldng; L Tennis; Natl Voc Tech Hnr Soc; HOSA.

WOLFORD, BRISTY L; White Co Central Schl; Judsonia, AR; (4); 1/28; Am Leg Aux Girls St; Church Yth Grp; FBLA; FHA; FTA; Office Aide; VP Soph Cls; Pres Sr Cls; Capt Bsktbl; Sftbl; AR St Univ; Pre Law.

WOLKEN, DANIEL J; Lakeside HS; Hot Springs, AR; (3); Am Leg Boys St; VP Natl Beta Clb; Capt Quiz Bowl; Treas Temple Yth Grp; Sprt Ed Nwsp; Treas Soph Cls; NHS; Rptr French Clb; FBLA; Sec Math Clb; Odyssey Of Mind 10 Yrs; Futr Problm Solvng Intnl Fnlst; 1st Pl In AR Press Womns Assn Sports Wrtng; Broadcast Jrnlsm.

WOMACK, STEVEN M; Central Sr HS; Little Rock, AR; (2); Band; JV Bsktbl; Cit Awd; MO Univ; Sports Medicine.

WOMACK, TRISHA J; Huttig Schl; Huttig, AR; (3); FBLA; FHA; FTA; JA; Bsktbl; Sftbl; Cit Awd; Hon Roll; FHA 2 Yrs, Sec 1 Yr; FTA; Nurseanethicist.

WOMBLE, GRETCHEN R; North Pulaski HS; Jacksonville, AR; (3); Church Yth Grp; Cmnty Wkr; DECA; Drama Clb; French Clb; FBLA; FHA; Teachers Aide; DECA Sr VP; ALSU; Mrktg Mgmnt.

WOOD, ALLISON R; Hope HS; Hope, AR; (3); 1/238; Church Yth Grp; FBLA; Natl Beta Clb; Yrbk; Hist Stu Cncl; Tennis; DAR Awd; High Hon Roll; French Clb; Band; Natl Yth Ldrshp Forum; Nike; U Of AR Fayetteville; Law.

WOOD, ANGEL D; Junction City HS; El Dorado, AR; (2); Church Yth Grp; FBLA; Quiz Bowl; Spanish Clb; Chrldng; Sftbl; High Hon Roll.

WOOD, CLINTON N; Fourche Valley Schl; Bluffton, AR; (4); 1/12; Am Leg Boys St; Church Yth Grp; Pres 4-H; Natl Beta Clb; Pres Sr Cls; Pres Stu Cncl; Var Bsktbl; NHS; Val; Drama Clb; AR Tech Univ; Med.

WOOD, DIELLA D; Drew Central Jr Sr HS; Monticello, AR; (3); FBLA; FHA; Chorus; Rep Frsh Cls; VP Jr Cls; Sec Stu Cncl; Hon Roll; Jr NHS.

WOOD, JASON E; Central Sr HS; Little Rock, AR; (2); Cit Awd; Prfct Atten Awd; Fr Mrshl; Pulaski Tech; Cmptr Repair.

WOOD, JULIE K; Greene Co Tech HS; Paragould, AR; (4); 5/140; Am Leg Aux Girls St; Pres Art Clb; Lit Mag; Cit Awd; Gov Hon Prg Awd; High Hon Roll; NHS; Prfct Atten Awd; Pres Acad Fit Awd; Pres Schlr; Hendrix Coll.

WOOD, KEITH J; Fairview HS; Camden, AR; (3); Church Yth Grp; Mu Alpha Theta; Natl FFA Org; Spanish Clb; Hon Roll; Spanish NHS.

WOOD, MARCUS L; Hampton Jr Sr HS; Hampton, AR; (3); 10/76; Ofcr Am Leg Boys St; Pres FCA; Pres FBLA; Pres Frsh Cls; Pres Sr Cls; VP Stu Cncl; Capt Bsktbl; Tennis; Trk; Hon Roll; Multicultural Achvmnt Schlr; Reach; Air Force Recruit Awd; FL St Univ; Eng.

WOOD, MATTHEW N; North Little Rock Hs-East; North Little Rock, AR; (2); 44/567; Art Clb; Church Yth Grp; Debate Tm; French Clb; Treas Natl Beta Clb; Quiz Bowl; School Musical; School Play; Golf; High Hon Roll; Top 10 Pct Class Awd.

WOOD, MICHAEL B; Cushman Schl; Cushman, AR; (4); 2/15; FHA; Natl FFA Org; School Play; Rep Stu Cncl; Var L Bsbl; High Hon Roll; Sal; St Schlr.

WOOD, MICHAEL D; North Little Rock Hs-West; North Little Rock, AR; (4); Debate Tm; Drama Clb; Mu Alpha Theta; Mrchg Band; School Musical; School Play; Gov Hon Prg Awd; Ntl Merit SF; Prfct Atten Awd.

WOOD, MICHELLE D; Clarksville HS; Clarksville, AR; (2); Church Yth Grp; FCA; Spanish Clb; Church Choir; JV Var Bsktbl; JV Var Sftbl; JV Trk; JV Vllybl; Hon Roll; Pres Acad Fit Awd; Paws Club; Pride Club; AR Tech Univ; Cmptr Sci.

WOOD, TYLER H; Van Buren Sr HS; Van Buren, AR; (2); Church Yth Grp; Debate Tm; FCA; Mu Alpha Theta; Science Clb; SADD; Var Bsktbl; High Hon Roll; NHS; Pres Acad Fit Awd.

WOOD, WENDY; Prairie Grove HS; Prairie Grove, AR; (3); FHA; Hosp Aide; Chorus; Nwsp; Rep Frsh Cls; Rep Stu Cncl; High Hon Roll; Jr NHS; Kiwanis Awd; John Brown.

WOODALL, MATTHEW; Pangburn Jr Sr HS; Heber Springs, AR; (4); 1/48; French Clb; FBLA; HOBY; Natl Beta Clb; Capt Quiz Bowl; Pres Soph Cls; Ofcr Stu Cncl; Hon Roll; Pres NHS; Law.

WOODARD, ELIZABETH K; Conway Sr HS; Conway, AR; (4); 151/502; Church Yth Grp; Cmnty Wkr; Drama Clb; German Clb; JA; Office Aide; Chorus; Var Pom Pon; JV Sftbl; U Of AR; Law.

WOODARD, JEREMY S; Corning HS; Success, AR; (3); Natl FFA Org; AR ST Univ; Wildlife Mngmt.

WOODELL, ALISSA E; Valley Springs Schl; Harrison, AR; (2); Art Clb; Church Yth Grp; FHA; Band; Chorus; Church Choir; Rep Frsh Cls; Ofcr Stu Cncl; Score Keeper; Campus Chrstn Group; Commnctn.

WOODIE, LINDSEY S; Arkansas Sr HS; Texarkana, AR; (1); Art Clb; Dance Clb; GAA; Hosp Aide; Math Clb; Spanish Clb; Drill Tm; Variety Show; Phtg Yrbk; Chrldng; Texarkana Boys & Girls Clb Bd Mem; Outstdng Span Awd 96.

WOODLEY, TAMEKA A; John L Mcclellan Magnet HS; Little Rock, AR; (2); FBLA; Natl Beta Clb; Vllybl; Hon Roll; Chldcare Dev.

WOODMANSEE, SUMMER; Watson Chapel Sr HS; Pine Bluff, AR; (1); Natl Beta Clb; Band; Chrldng; Powder Puff Ftbl; 13 Dance Awds, Dance Comp Team; 1st Degree Black Belt Taekwondo; Watson Chapel Band Qn; Dance Chrgrphy.

WOODRUFF, AMY; Nashville HS; Nashville, AR; (4); 6/106; Am Leg Aux Girls St; Church Yth Grp; Q&S; Quiz Bowl; Spanish Clb; Band; Flag Corp; Mrchg Band; School Play; Co-Ed Nwsp; Prtflo Jrnl Entry Pub Tchrs Wrk Bk; Edtr Yr Awd AR Schl Press Assn; U Of Cntrl AR; Med.

WOODRUFF, AMY G; Lavaca Jr Sr HS; Lavaca, AR; (2); Church Yth Grp; FCA; FHA; GAA; Hosp Aide; Office Aide; Spanish Clb; VP Soph Cls; Stat Bsktbl; Mgr(s); Bsktbl Stats; Soph Homcmng Maid Bsktbl; Rptr; Med.

WOODRUFF, HEATHER O; Siloam Springs Sr HS; Siloam Springs, AR; (2); Band; Chorus; Church Choir; Mrchg Band; Orch; Pep Band; Hon Roll; Sftbl; Music.

WOODRUFF, KATIE L; Conway Sr HS; Conway, AR; (4); 15/502; Am Leg Aux Girls St; Church Yth Grp; Cmnty Wkr; Drama Clb; French Clb; FBLA; Hosp Aide; Library Aide; Natl Beta Clb; Office Aide; U Of AR; Pharmacy.

WOODRUFT, HOLT; Nashville HS; Nashville, AR; (4); 2/106; Am Leg Boys St; Church Yth Grp; Spanish Clb; Band; Chorus; Church Choir; Mrchg Band; School Play; High Hon Roll; Hon Roll; Henderson ST U.

WOODS, COURTNEY J; Arkansas Schl Math & Science; Hot Springs Natio, AR; (3); FBLA; Natl Beta Clb; Quiz Bowl; ROTC; Church Choir; Mrchg Band; Var L Bsbl; Intrml JV Bsktbl; Intrml JV Ftbl; NHS; Schl Comm Ldr; Odyssey Of The Mind; Morehouse Coll; Pediatrics.

WOODS, LEVI J; Norfork Jr Sr HS; Norfork, AR; (3); Am Leg Boys St; Art Clb; FBLA; FHA; Library Aide; Office Aide; Science Clb; Spanish Clb; Speech Tm; Teachers Aide; Coll Of The Ozarks; Phys Ed.

WOODS, MYIA M; Parkview Arts-Science HS; Little Rock, AR; (2); Church Yth Grp; Cmnty Wkr; FHA; Hosp Aide; Teachers Aide; Chorus; Church Choir; School Musical; Vllybl; Cit Awd; Philander Smith; Chld Dev.

WOODS, ROYALLE D; Hughes Jr-Sr HS; Hughes, AR; (1); Church Yth Grp; Pres Math Clb; Band; Church Choir; Mrchg Band; Pep Band; Bsktbl; Trk; Soloist; Gramlin U; Bus Admin.

WOODS, SHARIEKA D; England HS; Tucker, AR; (2); Church Yth Grp; FHA; High Hon Roll; UALA; Educl Psych.

WOODS, TIFFANY A; Lavaca Jr Sr HS; Lavaca, AR; (2); 13/28; Art Clb; Church Yth Grp; Drama Clb; FCA; FHA; Science Clb; Spanish Clb; Speech Tm; Church Choir; Bsktbl; USA Vllybl League; NE; Coll Coach; Lawyer.

WOODS, WHITNEY; Prairie Grove HS; Prairie Grove, AR; (3); FBLA; Spanish Clb; Teachers Aide; Capt Chrldng; High Hon Roll; NHS; Jr Bnk Brd; Ldrshp Awd; UCA All Star Chrldr.

WOODWARD, KARRIE; Southside HS; Fort Smith, AR; (4); 41/535; Church Yth Grp; Drama Clb; FCA; Key Clb; Mu Alpha Theta; Spanish Clb; Chorus; School Musical; School Play; Stage Crew; U AR.

WOOLBRIDHT, JORDAN C; Benton Sr HS; Benton, AR; (3); 10/265; Am Leg Boys St; Church Yth Grp; French Clb; HOBY; Key Clb; Variety Show; Pres Soph Cls; Pres Jr Cls; Var Bsktbl; High Hon Roll; Benton ST Bnk Stdnt Bd; Main St Benton Stdnt Advy Bd; Cntrl AR Comm Plyrs.

WOOLBRIGHT, JORDAN CURTIS; Benton Sr HS; Benton, AR; (3); FCA; French Clb; HOBY; Key Clb; VP Church Choir; Pres Soph Cls; Pres Jr Cls; Var Bsktbl; High Hon Roll; Kiwanis Awd; U Of AR Fayetteville.

WOOLDRIDGE, BROCK; Ridgecrest HS; Paragould, AR; (3); Church Yth Grp; FCA; HOBY; Key Clb; Natl Beta Clb; VP Stu Cncl; Var L Bsbl; Var L Bsktbl; Var L Ftbl; Var L Socr; Ntl Bus Ed Awd; Ftbl Camp Best Camper; Multiple Yr Listing; U Of AR; Med.

WOOLEY, KATHERINE D; Hall Sr HS; Little Rock, AR; (4); 6/273; Drama Clb; FBLA; Intnl Clb; Natl Beta Clb; Quiz Bowl; Science Clb; Service Clb; Spanish Clb; Speech Tm; Teachers Aide; Bsch/Lmb Awd; HS Hall Fame; Mst Dpndble 96; Explrrs Pres; Spnsh V & VI Super; 1st Pl Sci Dbte, FBLA; Hendrix Coll; Biochem.

WOOLLEY, TROY; Woodlawn Schl; Rison, AR; (3); 1/45; Rptr Nwsp; Hon Roll; Gftd Tlntd; Beta Clb Rprtr.

WOOLSEY, B JILL; Lincoln HS; Lincoln, AR; (4); 8/59; Church Yth Grp; 4-H; Model UN; Natl Beta Clb; Band; 4-H Awd; Hon Roll; FHA; Office Aide; Spanish Clb; All Amer Schlr Awd; Semper Fedelis Awd Band; U Of AR Fayettevl; Amer Hstry.

WOOLSEY, LISA M; Russellville Sr HS; Russellville, AR; (2); 1/400; Church Yth Grp; Spanish Clb; Band; Church Choir; Flag Corp; Mrchg Band; Pep Band; High Hon Roll; NHS; AR Fed Teenage Republicans Sec; Chrstn Stu Union; Pol Sci.

WOOTEN, DALE; Genoa Central HS; Texarkana, AR; (3); Church Yth Grp; FBLA; Quiz Bowl; Spanish Clb; Yrbk; Var Bsktbl; Cit Awd; Prfct Atten Awd.

WOOTEN, LISA L; West Memphis Sr HS; West Memphis, AR; (4); 101/305; Cmnty Wkr; DECA; FHA; JA; Natl Beta Clb; Chrldng; Hon Roll; Jr NHS; Prfct Atten Awd; Maid Of Hnr; Fire Marshall; Schl Announcer; Le Moyne-Owen Coll.

WOOTEN, PAM; West Side Christian Schl; El Dorado, AR; (4); 2/17; VP Church Yth Grp; Pres Mu Alpha Theta; Natl Beta Clb; Office Aide; Chorus; Church Choir; Sec Jr Cls; Sec Sr Cls; High Hon Roll; Pres Acad Fit Awd; Wdmn Wrld Amer Hstry Awd; S AR CC.

WORD, KEITH; Brinkley HS; Brinkley, AR; (4); Am Leg Boys St; French Clb; FBLA; Ftbl; Trk; DAR Awd; Hon Roll; NHS; Intrsclstc Star Awd-Stu Athlt; AR ST U.

WORDLAW, JOSHUA; Parkview Arts-Science HS; Little Rock, AR; (4); Art Clb; Bus Profs of Am; Church Yth Grp; Drama Clb; FTA; German Clb; Teachers Aide; School Play; Nwsp; Ofcr Stu Cncl; Nom Jr Hmcmng King 96; Radio/Brdcstng/Engr.

WORKMAN, CRISTY L; Cty Line HS; Paris, AR; (3); Church Yth Grp; FCA; Rptr FBLA; FHA; Natl Beta Clb; Spanish Clb; Stage Crew; Nwsp; Hon Roll.

WORKS, CHARLES R; Clinton HS; Clinton, AR; (2); Natl FFA Org; Var Ftbl; Var Wt Lftg; Hon Roll; George Bush Presdntl Awd; NE LA ST Univ; Firefighter.

WORLEY, BRENT B; Searcy HS; Searcy, AR; (2); 12/256; Natl Beta Clb; Band; Jazz Band; Mrchg Band; JV Ftbl; Var Tennis; Jr NHS; Orthpdc Surg.

WORTHAM, TANYA D; Arkadelphia Sr HS; Arkadelphia, AR; (3); Pres Drama Clb; French Clb; Sec Natl Beta Clb; Quiz Bowl; Scholastic Bowl; Band; Mrchg Band; School Play; Var Socr; Martial Arts; Law; Medicine.

WORTHAM, TERMAYNE O; Trumann HS; Trumann, AR; (4); FBLA; German Clb; Science Clb; Spanish Clb; Var Capt Bsktbl; Var Ftbl; Score Keeper; Var Tennis; Wt Lftg; Univ Of AR; Cmptr Sci.

WORTHINGTON, JULIE A; Swifton Schl; Swifton, AR; (2); 1/13; Rptr FBLA; HOBY; Natl Beta Clb; Quiz Bowl; Ed Nwsp; Pres Frsh Cls; Pres Soph Cls; Rptr Stu Cncl; Hist.

WORTHINGTON, LESLIE; Swifton Schl; Swifton, AR; (4); 2/9; Am Leg Aux Girls St; Church Yth Grp; FBLA; Natl Beta Clb; Natl FFA Org; Office Aide; Yrbk; Sec Sr Cls; Cit Awd; Sal; High Hnr Roll; Farmers Electrc WA DC Yth Tour Essay Cont Wnnr; Spnsh Clb; ASU; Rdlgc Tech.

WRAY, HUNTER M; Russellville Sr HS; Russellville, AR; (3); Church Yth Grp; Cmnty Wkr; FCA; Letterman Clb; Varsity Clb; Acpl Chr; Chorus; Var Stu Cncl; JV Var Bsbl; Var L Ftbl; Natl HS Rodeo Finals 10th Pl Boys Cutting 95, St Champ 96 & Top 15 Natl 96; OSU; Vet.

WRIGHT, ALICIA; Mountainburg Jr Sr HS; Mountainburg, AR; (3); #3 in class; Drama Clb; FHA; Natl Beta Clb; Science Clb; Teachers Aide; Pres Band; Mrchg Band; Pep Band; School Play; High Hon Roll; UAR.

WRIGHT, ALISHA D; Bentonville Sr HS; Cave Springs, AR; (4); Am Leg Aux Girls St; Intnl Clb; SADD; Drill Tm; Stage Crew; Hon Roll; Pres Acad Fit Awd; Miss Cave Sprgs; DECA; NW AR CC.

WRIGHT, ALLISON; Gosnell Jr Sr HS; Blytheville, AR; (2); Pres FCA; Mu Alpha Theta; Pres Natl Beta Clb; Quiz Bowl; VP SADD; Pres Soph Cls; Capt Bsktbl; Capt Trk; Hon Roll; Pres Acad Fit Awd; Bus Admin.

WRIGHT, AMY B; Bearden HS; Bearden, AR; (4); 5/58; Am Leg Aux Girls St; Cmnty Wkr; 4-H; Sec Natl Beta Clb; Band; Rptr Nwsp; Rptr Yrbk; Trk; Hon Roll; Ntl Merit Ltr; Hnr Grad; SAU Magnolia; Occptnl Thrpy.

WRIGHT, ANDREW M; North Little Rock Hs-West; North Little Rock, AR; (3); Church Yth Grp; Band; Jazz Band; Mrchg Band; Stage Crew; Gov Hon Prg Awd; Hon Roll; Henderson ST Univ; Music.

WRIGHT, ATO O; Pine Bluff HS; Pine Bluff, AR; (2); French Clb; Science Clb; Band; Mrchg Band; Pep Band; Pres Soph Cls; Ofcr Stu Cncl; JV Ftbl; Socr; Var Trk; Stdnt Mnth April 95; Stdnt Mnth Oct 96; Duke; Bio/Pre-Med.

WRIGHT, BRANDY; Cty Line HS; Ratcliff, AR; (4); 2/40; Church Yth Grp; Pres FCA; Treas FBLA; Pres FHA; VP Natl Beta Clb; Capt Bsktbl; Capt Sftbl; Cit Awd; High Hon Roll; Sal; All St, Rgnl MVP Bsktbl; Educ.

WRIGHT, CHRIS S; Arkansas Sr HS; Texarkana, AR; (2); Church Yth Grp; Drama Clb; 4-H; Key Clb; Mu Alpha Theta; Spanish Clb; School Play; Trk; Hon Roll; Jr NHS; Stu Cncl Rep; Ouachita Bapt U; Commnctns.

WRIGHT, COURTNEY R; Lakeside HS; Hot Springs Natio, AR; (3); Church Yth Grp; Natl Beta Clb; Band; Mgr Yrbk; Rep Stu Cncl; Hon Roll; Jr NHS; NHS; FBLA; Math Clb; Odyssey Of Mind; Future Problem Solving; Ed.

WRIGHT, CRENISHA M; Forrest City HS; Forrest City, AR; (2); FHA; Natl Beta Clb; Science Clb; Spanish Clb; Band; Mrchg Band; High Hon Roll; Band Mrt Awd; All-Region Band Awd; Gramblin ST Univ; Comp Sci.

WRIGHT, DANETTA; Bearden HS; Bearden, AR; (2); 4-H; FBLA; Band; Church Choir; Mrchg Band; School Musical; Ofcr Frsh Cls; High Hon Roll; Prfct Atten Awd; U Of AL; Law.

WRIGHT, DREW; Central Ark Christian Schl; Little Rock, AR; (1); Sec Church Yth Grp; Cmnty Wkr; Hosp Aide; Treas Math Clb; L Ftbl; High Hon Roll; Jr NHS; Ntl Merit Ltr; Rankd 14th St AR For Tennis Novce 14s; Notre Dame; Comp Sci.

WRIGHT, ERICA; Weiner HS; Weiner, AR; (3); Sec Art Clb; Chess Clb; Church Yth Grp; Drama Clb; Rep FBLA; Pres FHA; Natl FFA Org; Pep Clb; Rep Science Clb; Speech Tm; Recvd Awds In Engl, Jrnlsm, Sci, Bnd; Ag Sci Drvr Ed Medls; Arch.

WRIGHT, GERRIAND L; Bearden HS; Bearden, AR; (2); FBLA; Natl Beta Clb; Bsktbl; Trk; Hon Roll; Engr.

WRIGHT, JANNA M; Dewitt HS; De Witt, AR; (1); 1/110; Church Yth Grp; French Clb; Science Clb; Church Choir; High Hon Roll; Ntl Merit Ltr; Algebra/Eng/Phys Sci Awds; ACTM Regnl Math Contest 1st Pl; UAM; Cert Lifeguard; Pharm.

WRIGHT, JEANETTA L; Bearden HS; Bearden, AR; (2); 5/22; 4-H; FBLA; FHA; FTA; Band; Chorus; Mrchg Band; Pep Band; School Musical; School Play; Bnd Capt Jr; WA U In St Louis; Eng.

WRIGHT, JENNIFER; Central Ark Christian Schl; North Little Rock, AR; (2); Church Yth Grp; French Clb; Acpl Chr; Variety Show; Trk; High Hon Roll; Pres Jr NHS; AR All-St Choir; Jr & Sr All-Regn Choirs; Harding U; Bio.

WRIGHT, JENNIFER G; Sloan Hendrix HS; Imboden, AR; (3); 3/30; Rptr FBLA; FTA; Pres Natl Beta Clb; Sec Pres Natl FFA Org; Pep Clb; Nwsp; Yrbk; Treas Soph Cls; Pres Jr Cls; Ofcr Stu Cncl; Gftd & Tlntd Soc; Annual Qn; Stu Cncl Chm Of Pub Relations; Lions Clb Acad Awd; ASU; CPA.

WRIGHT, JOSH; Calico Rock HS; Calico Rock, AR; (1); 2/33; Church Yth Grp; FCA; Natl Beta Clb; Natl FFA Org; Capt Quiz Bowl; SADD; Var Bsbl; JV Bsktbl; Hon Roll; Prfct Atten Awd; U Of AR.

WRIGHT, KATHRYN E; Lonoke Jr HS; Lonoke, AR; (1); 1/150; Church Yth Grp; Band; Nwsp; Mgr Bsktbl; High Hon Roll; NHS; Eclgy Clb; Otstdng Stdnt; Bsktbl; 4 Yr Coll; Vet.

WRIGHT, KATHY L; Berryville HS; Berryville, AR; (2); Church Yth Grp; FHA; Intnl Clb; Science Clb; Rptr Band; Capt Color Guard; Mrchg Band; Hon Roll; Jr NHS; NHS; Bus.

WRIGHT, KIM; Hope HS; Hope, AR; (2); 1/260; Church Yth Grp; Natl Beta Clb; Natl FFA Org; Variety Show; Rep Frsh Cls; Rep Stu Cncl; Capt Var Chrldng; High Hon Roll; Hon Roll; U Of AR; Econ.

WRIGHT, KIMBERLY K; Norphlet HS; Norphlet, AR; (4); 14/56; FBLA; FHA; Spanish Clb; Capt Band; Jazz Band; Capt Mrchg Band; Pep Band; Hon Roll; NHS; S AR CC; Crimjust.

WRIGHT, LEAH M; Berryville HS; Berryville, AR; (2); Church Yth Grp; Dance Clb; Drama Clb; Girl Scts; Science Clb; Spanish Clb; Band; Hon Roll; Jr NHS; NHS; Yth Alive; Bible Schl Tchr; Psych; Drama.

WRIGHT, LETICIA; Dollarway HS; Pine Bluff, AR; (3); 6/200; Dance Clb; Drama Clb; Hosp Aide; Key Clb; Band; Chorus; Mrchg Band; School Musical; Rep Stu Cncl; Trk; Biomed Engrg.

WRIGHT, MALORIE; Morrilton Sr HS; Morrilton, AR; (3); Church Yth Grp; FHA; Natl Beta Clb; Thesps; Drill Tm; School Play; Ofcr Jr Cls; Bsktbl; Hon Roll; Ntl Merit Ltr; U Of AR.

WRIGHT, MICHELLE N; Lake Hamilton Sr HS; Hot Springs Natio, AR; (3); Church Yth Grp; Dance Clb; FCA; Pres FBLA; FHA; Natl Beta Clb; Spanish Clb; Co-Capt Drill Tm; School Musical; Yrbk; UDA Univ Dnc Assn All Star Tchng Dnc; U Of AR; Diet.

WRIGHT, RITA C; Smackover HS; Smackover, AR; (2); 8/70; Church Yth Grp; Cmnty Wkr; FBLA; FHA; FTA; GAA; Office Aide; Quiz Bowl; Spanish Clb; Teachers Aide; PRIDE Team Pres; Governors Yth Conf Yth Ldr; Psych.

WRIGHT, SHAMEKIA L; Nevada Schl; Buckner, AR; (2); Art Clb; French Clb; FBLA; FHA; FTA; Natl Beta Clb; Office Aide; Speech Tm; Teachers Aide; Band; Poem Publshd; FHA Sec; Drug Tm 3 Yrs; U Of AR Pine Bluff; PT.

WRIGHT, SHANNON E; Jacksonville HS; Cabot, AR; (4); 3/283; Drama Clb; FBLA; FHA; Natl Beta Clb; Spanish Clb; Band; Yrbk; High Hon Roll; NHS; Library Aide; Intract; U Of Central AR.

WRIGHT, STACEY; Gentry HS; Gentry, AR; (4); 16/85; Sec Art Clb; Church Yth Grp; Cmnty Wkr; FBLA; Model UN; Spanish Clb; Teachers Aide; Church Choir; Nwsp; Var Bsktbl; John Brown Univ; Elem Ed.

ARKANSAS

WRISER, AMBER R; Bauxite Jr Sr HS; Bauxite, AR; (2); Church Yth Grp; Dance Clb; Sec FBLA; GAA; HOBY; Spanish Clb; Teachers Aide; Drill Tm; School Play; Nwsp; LA Tech; Tchr.

WROTEN, AMY; East Poinsett Sr HS; Dyess, AR; (2); Church Yth Grp; FHA; Church Choir; High Hon Roll; Jr NHS; NHS; AR ST U; Legal Sec.

WULFF, CHRISTINA A; Highland HS; Cherokee Village, AR; (4); 11/80; FBLA; Office Aide; Chorus; Yrbk; High Hon Roll; Hon Roll; RAD; Williams Bapt Coll.

WUNDER, LAURIE; Robinson HS; Roland, AR; (3); 18/130; Drama Clb; Natl Beta Clb; Q&S; Treas Spanish Clb; Chorus; School Musical; Nwsp; Capt Chrldng; Trk; Hon Roll; NCA All Amer Chrldr 95-96; Auburn U; Phys Thrpy.

WYATT, MICHAEL A; Southside HS; Batesville, AR; (1); Church Yth Grp; FCA; FBLA; Quiz Bowl; Band; Sec Treas Frsh Cls; Hist Stu Cncl; JV Bsktbl; JV Golf; JV Trk; Williams Bapt; Tchng.

WYATT, MICHELLE C; Cabot HS; Cabot, AR; (3); 22/400; Office Aide; ROTC; Science Clb; High Hon Roll; Hon Roll; Chatham Coll; Envrmnl Sci.

WYLES, ERIC; Lamar HS; Lamar, AR; (4); 1/65; Am Leg Boys St; Church Yth Grp; FCA; HOBY; Capt Quiz Bowl; VP Science Clb; Var Bsbl; Var Capt Bsktbl; High Hon Roll; Val; Comp Sci.

WYLES, LEA A; Lamar HS; Lamar, AR; (2); FCA; FBLA; VP Pres Frsh Cls; VP Pres Soph Cls; Pres Jr Cls; Capt Var Bsktbl; Hon Roll; AR Tech Univ.

WYLIE, GLENDA N; Gravette HS; Gravette, AR; (1); 1/100; Church Yth Grp; FHA; Band; Church Choir; Mrchg Band; Pep Band; Pres Frsh Cls; High Hon Roll; Jr NHS; Law/Bus.

WYMER, WENDY L; Bald Knob HS; Bald Knob, AR; (1); Drama Clb; Band; Color Guard; Mrchg Band; Bsktbl; Trk; Hon Roll; ASU Beebe; Phys Thrpy.

WYNN, OMEGA; Farmington Jr Sr HS; Fayetteville, AR; (3); Church Yth Grp; FBLA; Natl FFA Org; School Play; Sftbl; Cit Awd; Hon Roll; Jr NHS; NHS; Pres Acad Fit Awd.

WYNNE, KRISTI M; Forrest City HS; Forrest City, AR; (3); 4-H; Library Aide; Spanish Clb; Church Choir; Drill Tm; Hon Roll; Jackson ST; Pedtrcn/Cosmtlgy.

WYNNE, WESLEY G; Ozark Adventist Acad; Waskom, TX; (2); Church Yth Grp; Hosp Aide; Band; School Play; Ed Phtg Yrbk; Pres Frsh Cls; VP Soph Cls; High Hon Roll; Hon Roll; LSU; Rad.

WYSS, VIRGINIA E; Clay Co Central Jr Sr HS; Greenway, AR; (4); FHA; Natl FFA Org; Band; Flag Corp; Mrchg Band; Mrchg Band; Pep Band; High Hon Roll; Hon Roll; Prfct Atten Awd; AR ST Univ; Comp Tech; Acctnt.

XAYAVONG, PHANAVANH IENG; Northside HS; Fort Smith, AR; (2); Drama Clb; FBLA; Intnl Clb; Socr; Hon Roll; NHS; Spanish NHS; Jr Optimist Pres; Cultural Ambssdrs; Westark CC; Bio.

XAYAVONGSA, SANGKHOM; Kimmons Jr HS; Fort Smith, AR; (2); French Clb; Spanish Clb; Cit Awd; Hon Roll; Prfct Atten Awd.

XAYSANASY, KELLY J; Southside HS; Fort Smith, AR; (3); 82/502; Key Clb; Latin Clb; Mu Alpha Theta; Hon Roll; Jr NHS; NHS; Cltrl Ambssdr; Sail Crew; U Of AK; Psych.

YACAVONE, AARON M; Mississippi Co Christian Acad; Osceola, AR; (3); 6/13; French Clb; JA; Math Clb; Science Clb; Tennis; U Of TN; Fin.

YAGER, SCOTT T; Oak Grove HS; Maumelle, AR; (2); FCA; Pres Letterman Clb; VICA; Var Bsbl; Var Bsktbl; Var Ftbl; Var Trk; Hon Roll; Gary Henderson Awd; U Of Cntrl AR; Elec Engr.

YANCEY, JESSICA; Izard Co Cons Jr Sr HS; Horseshoe Bend, AR; (1); Church Yth Grp; 4-H; Key Clb; Natl Beta Clb; Pep Clb; Spanish Clb; Teachers Aide; Band; Church Choir; Variety Show; CHASE; AR ST U; Speech Ther.

YANCY, CARISSA J; Russellville Sr HS; Russellville, AR; (3); 55/320; Church Yth Grp; Spanish Clb; Chorus; Lit Mag; Hon Roll; Jr NHS; Pres Acad Fit Awd; Mission Trip To Mexico; AR Tech Univ.

YANG, CINDY; Fayetteville East HS; Fayetteville, AR; (4); FBLA; FHA; SADD; High Hon Roll; Hon Roll; Prfct Atten Awd; Natl Hnr Soc; U Of AR; Fin.

YARBRO, AMANDA G; Hartford Schl; Hartford, AR; (1); Cit Awd; Hon Roll; Gftd/Tlntd Prgrm; Phrmcy/Floristry; Hartford Pride Team; Phrmcy.

YARBRO JR, BOBBY W; Manila HS; Manila, AR; (1); Prfct Atten Awd; Renaissance; AR ST U; Auto Mchnc.

YARBRO, SCOTT P; Forrest City HS; Forrest City, AR; (3); Drama Clb; Mu Alpha Theta; Natl Beta Clb; Natl FFA Org; Spanish Clb; Teachers Aide; Stage Crew; High Hon Roll; Hon Roll; U Of AR; Lawyer.

YARBROUGH, ELAINA D; Lake Hamilton Sr HS; Hot Springs Natio, AR; (3); 117/212; Drama Clb; Teachers Aide; Thesps; VP Chorus; School Musical; L Mgr(s); L Trk; Pres Acad Fit Awd; All Rgn Grls Choir 95-; Comm Theatre 93-94; Henderson ST U; Prfrmng Arts.

YARBROUGH, KEELY; Fayetteville Sr HS; Fayetteville, AR; (3); Am Leg Aux Girls St; Church Yth Grp; Cmnty Wkr; FCA; Key Clb; Letterman Clb; Math Clb; Mu Alpha Theta; SADD; Var L Bsktbl; Phys Therapy; Sports Medicine.

YARBROUGH, TERESHIA L; El Dorado Sr HS; El Dorado, AR; (2); Church Yth Grp; Chorus; Church Choir; Girls All-Region Choir; SAU Yth Apprenticeship Pgm Certfd Nrsng Asst; South AR Univ; Obstetrician.

YARBROUGH, VAN; Van Buren Sr HS; Van Buren, AR; (3); Mu Alpha Theta; High Hon Roll; Hon Roll.

YATES, BILLY J; Highland HS; Hardy, AR; (2); Ftbl; Wrstlng.

YATES, CASEY A; Fouke Jr Sr HS; Fouke, AR; (3); 3/100; Chess Clb; English Clb; FBLA; Spanish Clb; Speech Tm; Sec Sr Cls; Var Golf; High Hon Roll; Hon Roll; NHS; Univ Of AR; Turfologist/Golf.

YATES, EDDIE; Cabot HS; Austin, AR; (3); FCA; FBLA; Math Tm; Natl Beta Clb; NFL; JV Bsktbl; Var Ftbl; Var Wt Lftg; Hon Roll; Kiwanis Awd; Acctng.

YATES, JAMES E; Marmaduke HS; Marmaduke, AR; (3); Church Yth Grp; Natl Beta Clb; Natl FFA Org; Ofcr Bsbl; Hon Roll; AR ST U; Engrng.

YATES, KELLIE A; Fayetteville Christian Schl; Springdale, AR; (2); 5/16; FCA; Yrbk; Treas Frsh Cls; Var L Bsktbl; High Hon Roll; Hon Roll; NHS; Alpha Chi Epsilon; U Of AR; Acctng.

YATES, THOMAS; Bright Star Schl; Doddridge, AR; (4); 5/21; Drama Clb; HOBY; Office Aide; Ed Nwsp; Ed Yrbk; Pres Soph Cls; Treas Jr Cls; Treas Sr Cls; Hon Roll; NHS; Jr Cls Favorite; Sr Most Tlntd; Drama Clb Treas; Texarkana Coll; Bus.

YAZETTI, DAYANEE M; Mena HS; Mena, AR; (3); #9 in class; Am Leg Aux Girls St; Mgr Art Clb; Drama Clb; 4-H; French Clb; FBLA; Natl FFA Org; Science Clb; Mrchg Band; Rptr Nwsp; Univ AR; Plant/Soil Sci.

YEAGER, MINDY D; Robinson HS; Roland, AR; (1); 7/156; Church Yth Grp; Drama Clb; FBLA; FHA; Natl Beta Clb; Spanish Clb; Chorus; Hon Roll; NHS; Auburn Univ; Marine Bio.

YEAGER, TIFFANY M; Arkansas Sr HS; Texarkana, AR; (3); Church Yth Grp; Drama Clb; FHA; Pep Clb; Church Choir; School Play; Variety Show; E TX Bapt U; Drama Tchr.

YEARBER, ESTHER V; Yellville Summit HS; Yellville, AR; (2); 14/80; Church Yth Grp; Teachers Aide; Band; Mrchg Band; Orch; Pep Band; Variety Show; High Hon Roll; Hon Roll; Acad Ldrshp Awds; All Reg Band; Bst Stndt Intro Med Prof; U Of AR; Psych.

YEKTA, SAM; Rogers HS; Rogers, AR; (3); Bsktbl; Ftbl; Wt Lftg; Hon Roll; U Of AR; Med.

YELVINGTON, LORI K; Stuttgart Sr HS; Stuttgart, AR; (3); Church Yth Grp; Cmnty Wkr; Drama Clb; FBLA; Key Clb; Natl FFA Org; Office Aide; Spanish Clb; Teachers Aide; Chorus; Delta Beta Sigma Chpln; U Of AR Conway; Bus/Cmptr.

YEUNG, THOMAS G; Pulaski Acad; Little Rock, AR; (2); Boy Scts; HOBY; Latin Clb; High Hon Roll; Ordr Excl; NHS; Natl Beta Club.

YIELDING, NICHOLAS B; Cabot HS; Cabot, AR; (3); 71/324; Key Clb; Spanish Clb; Band; Mrchg Band; Pep Band; Jr NHS; Sr All Regn Band 95-; Jr All Regn Band 94; Acad Ltr 93-95; Nom Natl Young Ldrs Conf; AR Tech Univ; Park/Rec.

YOCUM, KEVIN; Southside HS; Fort Smith, AR; (4); 50/440; Church Yth Grp; FCA; FBLA; Key Clb; Mu Alpha Theta; Office Aide; Ofcr Bsbl; Bsktbl; Hon Roll; NHS; Westark; Engrng.

YORK, BRANDY; Blytheville Sr HS; Blytheville, AR; (4); 40/244; Drama Clb; French Clb; FHA; Key Clb; Chrldng; Gym; Hon Roll; Gymnstcs St 5th Pl Ranking; U Of AL Tuscaloosa; Sprts Med.

YORK, JONATHAN L; Pine Bluff HS; Pine Bluff, AR; (3); Church Yth Grp; Office Aide; Spanish Clb; Ftbl; Hon Roll; Amer Fld Svcs; A Tm.

YORK, JOSH; Hermitage Jr Sr HS; Hermitage, AR; (1); #1 in class; Church Yth Grp; Var Bsbl; JV Bsktbl; JV Ftbl; High Hon Roll; FFA; Med.

YORK, KERI; Heber Springs HS; Heber Springs, AR; (4); 1/100; Am Leg Aux Girls St; Rptr Drama Clb; VP FBLA; HOBY; Treas Natl Beta Clb; Treas Soph Cls; VP Sr Cls; Rptr Stu Cncl; Capt Chrldng; FCA; Am Lgn Ortrcl St Wnnr; FBLA Job Intrvw St Wnnr; U AR Fyttvlle; Kiniesiolgy.

YORK, MELLISSA K; Hartford Schl; Hackett, AR; (4); Ed FBLA; FHA; Color Guard; Ed Nwsp; Yrbk; Hon Roll; PRIDE Pres 2 Yrs; West AR CC; Scndry Eng Tchr.

YORK, REGGIE D; Star City HS; Star City, AR; (4); 35/105; Church Yth Grp; 4-H; Natl FFA Org; Rptr Nwsp; Rep Jr Cls; Var Bsktbl; Cit Awd; 4-H Awd; Hon Roll; The Young Gentlemens Clb; S Awd; SAU Tech; Cmptr Tech.

YORK, RICKIE M; Mc Gehee HS; Mcgehee, AR; (2); World His Awd; Vet.

YORK, SHERMIKA; Gould HS; Gould, AR; (3); 1/25; Art Clb; French Clb; Sec FBLA; VP FHA; Math Clb; Natl Beta Clb; Office Aide; Sec Science Clb; Pres Jr Cls; Bsktbl; Natl Yng Ldrs Conf; U Of AR; Med.

YORK, TAMIKIA L; Hermitage Jr Sr HS; Hermitage, AR; (2); #9 in class; FBLA; Natl Beta Clb; Chorus; Church Choir; Yrbk; Hon Roll; U Of Cntrl AR.

YOUNG, AMANDA; Marion Co Rural Schl; Everton, AR; (2); 4-H; FHA; Math Clb; Science Clb; School Play; Bsktbl; Hon Roll; FHA Sec; Evirothon Team; Coll Of The Ozarks; Ed.

YOUNG, BRIANNA; Kirby HS; Kirby, AR; (2); 3/35; Chess Clb; Debate Tm; FBLA; FHA; GAA; Natl Beta Clb; Pep Clb; Quiz Bowl; Speech Tm; Varsity Clb; Gfted And Tlnted Prog; Henderson St Univ; Com Prog.

YOUNG, CHRIS C; Springdale Sr HS; Springdale, AR; (3); 136/520; Intrml Bsktbl; Hon Roll; Jr NHS; Glbl Chal Schl Wnnr Top 2 Pct In Natn; Tchr.

YOUNG, DANIEL B; Springdale Sr HS; Springdale, AR; (2); Church Yth Grp; FCA; Band; Mrchg Band; Pep Band; Var Crs Cntry; Var Tennis; Var Trk; Hon Roll; Jr NHS; U Of AR; Computer Tech.

YOUNG, DANIEL R; Rogers HS; Rogers, AR; (3); Church Yth Grp; Science Clb; Band; Jazz Band; Mrchg Band; Orch; Ed Nwsp; High Hon Roll; Jr NHS; Pres Acad Fit Awd.

YOUNG, DAVID R; Osceola HS; Osceola, AR; (2); 5/150; Church Yth Grp; HOBY; Band; Ofcr Bsbl; Ftbl; Wt Lftg; High Hon Roll; NHS.

YOUNG, JEREMY; Lincoln HS; Summers, AR; (2); 12/68; Church Yth Grp; Model UN; Natl Beta Clb; Natl FFA Org; Science Clb; Band; Church Choir; Mrchg Band; NFL; Ofcr Frsh Cls; Bptst Prchr; Central Bptst; Mnstr.

YOUNG, JESSICA L; Hot Springs HS; Hot Springs Natio, AR; (3); 25/200; Am Leg Aux Girls St; Church Yth Grp; FCA; GAA; Natl Beta Clb; Spanish Clb; School Play; Treas Stu Cncl; Bsktbl; Var Socr.

YOUNG, JONATHAN J; Lake Hamilton Sr HS; Hot Springs, AR; (3); Church Yth Grp; Cmnty Wkr; FCA; Church Choir; Yrbk; Pres Stu Cncl; Var Bsbl; Var Bsktbl; Var Ftbl; Var Golf.

YOUNG, KATHLEEN; Mammoth Spring HS; Hardy, AR; (3); 1/45; FBLA; HOBY; Natl Beta Clb; Pep Clb; SADD; Band; Jazz Band; Pres Frsh Cls; Var L Bsktbl; High Hon Roll; Jrnlsm.

YOUNG, KATIE; Lincoln HS; Morrow, AR; (2); Church Yth Grp; Debate Tm; FBLA; HOBY; Key Clb; Natl Beta Clb; Spanish Clb; Chorus; Rep Stu Cncl; Cit Awd.

YOUNG, KEN; Woodlawn Schl; Warren, AR; (2); Church Yth Grp; Natl Beta Clb; Ofcr Bsbl; Bsktbl; Hon Roll.

YOUNG, KRISTEN E; Bryant Sr HS; Benton, AR; (2); Church Yth Grp; Rptr Hist Stu Cncl; Co-Capt Chrldng; DAR Awd; High Hon Roll; Jr NHS; NHS; Caring Comm Hlp Teen With Fmly/Prsnl Prblms; REACH; Chrstn Cncl Treas/VP.

YOUNG, LANCE; Morrilton Sr HS; Morrilton, AR; (3); 15/175; Church Yth Grp; Math Clb; Natl Beta Clb; Office Aide; Spanish Clb; Thesps; School Play; Stage Crew; Ofcr Bsbl; Hon Roll.

YOUNG, LAURA; Jessieville HS; Hot Springs Natio, AR; (4); 10/39; Am Leg Aux Girls St; HOBY; Sec Key Clb; Natl Beta Clb; Drm Mjr(t); Pres Stu Cncl; Var L Bsktbl; DAR Awd; Art Clb; Outstndng Key Clb, & Band; All Star, Reg, Mid South Hnr Bands; AR Tech U; Nrsng.

YOUNG, LEE; Booneville Jr Sr HS; Booneville, AR; (2); Art Clb; Church Yth Grp; Science Clb; Hon Roll; Martial Arts; Music; Art; Art.

YOUNG III, LEON D; Searcy HS; Searcy, AR; (3).

YOUNG, MARK; Nashville HS; Nashville, AR; (3); 1/120; Am Leg Boys St; School Play; Var Tennis; Gov Hon Prg Awd; High Hon Roll; NHS; Boy Scts; FBLA; FHA; Quiz Bowl; All Rgn Bnd 93-95; All Rgn Choir 93-95; All St Choir 95-; Outstdng 11th Grd Bndsmn; Chem Awd; U Of AR.

YOUNG, MARY M; Valley Springs Schl; Everton, AR; (3); French Clb; FHA; Key Clb; Mgr Bsktbl; Mgr Sftbl; Hon Roll.

YOUNG, MICHELLE E; Bryant Sr HS; Bryant, AR; (3); English Clb; FCA; Office Aide; Science Clb; Speech Tm; Teachers Aide; JV Var Bsktbl; U Of AR Fayetteville; Engr/PT.

YOUNG, NEELY C; Pulaski Acad; Little Rock, AR; (3); Church Yth Grp; Dance Clb; FCA; FBLA; Teachers Aide; Drill Tm; Nwsp; Rep Stu Cncl; High Hon Roll; Hon Roll; Achvmt/Math Awds; Just Say No Clb; Comm Svc; Acctng/Bus.

YOUNG, ROY N; Crossett Sr HS; Crossett, AR; (2); Art Clb; Church Yth Grp; Cmnty Wkr; Drama Clb; French Clb; Natl Beta Clb; Science Clb; Band; School Musical; School Play; Jrnlsm.

YOUNG, SARAH A; Lake Hamilton Sr HS; Hot Springs Natio, AR; (3); Church Yth Grp; Computer Clb; German Clb; Teachers Aide; Co-Ed Yrbk; U Of Cntrl AR; Comm/Pub Rltns.

YOUNG, SHELLY; Rison HS; Rison, AR; (3); Art Clb; HOBY; Natl Beta Clb; Flag Corp; U Of AR Monticello; Nursng.

YOUNG, STEPHANIE; Ft Smith Christian Schl; Lavaca, AR; (2); Drama Clb; FCA; Spanish Clb; Bsktbl; Hon Roll; NHS; U Of AR; Bus Admin.

YOUNG, SUSAN; Morrilton Sr HS; Morrilton, AR; (2); Church Yth Grp; Library Aide; Natl Beta Clb; Science Clb; Spanish Clb; Thesps; Band; Mrchg Band; School Musical; 4-H Awd; Stu PRIDE Awd; Sci Olympid Hi Score.

YOUNG, YAEL; Benton Sr HS; Benton, AR; (3); 3/250; Key Clb; Math Clb; Model UN; Quiz Bowl; Hist Spanish Clb; Mrchg Band; Orch; High Hon Roll; Jr NHS; Kiwanis Awd; Future Problem Solving Team 1st In St & 4th In Intnl; 3rd Pl In St Cmptn Sci Fair; Early Grad; LA Tech Univ; Architecture.

YOUNGBLOOD, JERRY; Wickes Schl; Wickes, AR; (3); 1/32; Church Yth Grp; 4-H; Science Clb; JV Var Bsbl; JV Var Bsktbl; JV Trk; Hon Roll; FFA Offcr, Star Greenhand Awd & Dairy Jdgng Tm; Show Cattle; OK ST U; Ag.

YOUNGBLOOD, TIFFANY S; Alpena Schl; Alpena, AR; (2); VP Church Yth Grp; FBLA; Treas FHA; Spanish Clb; Chld Dev Hgh Stu Awd; Coll Of The Ozarks; Tchng.

YOUNGBLOOD, TOBY W; Mena HS; Mena, AR; (4); 9/127; Am Leg Boys St; Church Yth Grp; Cmnty Wkr; FCA; French Clb; Pres VP FBLA; Model UN; Quiz Bowl; Science Clb; Teachers Aide; AR Govs Schl; Govs Yth Cmmssn; U Of AR; Law.

YOUNGER, AMY M; Nashville HS; Ozan, AR; (3); 37/144; Church Yth Grp; FBLA; FHA; Teachers Aide; Henderson ST; Cmptr Prgmmr.

YOUNGMAN, ROBERT M; Hoxie Schl; Hoxie, AR; (3); 3/60; Treas Am Leg Boys St; Church Yth Grp; FBLA; Treas FHA; Model UN; Natl Beta Clb; Natl FFA Org; Thesps; Ed Yrbk; Hon Roll; Fulbright Schl Pub Affairs Grad; Harvard; Investment Bnkng.

YOW, REBECCA A; Salem HS; Glencoe, AR; (4); 7/41; Key Clb; Natl Beta Clb; Spanish Clb; Teachers Aide; Yrbk; Hon Roll; Nursng.

ZACHARY, CA'LYN; Morrilton Sr HS; Plumerville, AR; (2); French Clb; Natl Beta Clb; Ofcr Bsbl; Ftbl; Hon Roll.

ZARATE, JUANITA; Dequeen HS; De Queen, AR; (2); 39/100; Church Yth Grp; Band; Mrchg Band; Var L Sftbl; Cit Awd; Hon Roll.

ZEEK, MELISSA A; Smackover HS; Louann, AR; (3); Church Yth Grp; Drama Clb; FHA; Pres VP Girl Scts; Spanish Clb; Pres VP Chorus; Church Choir; Stage Crew; Hon Roll; NHS; Anchor Clb; U Of AR Magnolia; Tchr.

ZEILER, CHRISTIE L; Westside HS; Coal Hill, AR; (4); Am Leg Aux Girls St; FBLA; Natl Beta Clb; Pep Clb; Spanish Clb; Teachers Aide; Band; Chorus; Rep Nwsp; Pres Stu Cncl; Westerk CC; Phys Thrp.

ZEILER, MARLO R; Cty Line HS; Ratcliff, AR; (3); FCA; FBLA; Treas Pres FHA; Office Aide; Spanish Clb; Ofcr Stu Cncl; Bsktbl; Cit Awd; Hon Roll; Prfct Atten Awd; Spnsh Clb; Homecmng Maid; Miss CLHS; Bus Mrchngdising.

ZEMAN, ALAN J; Jessieville HS; Mountain Pine, AR; (3); CAP; Wt Lftg; Drafting; Drafter.

ZERR, JULIE A; Harrison Sr HS; Harrison, AR; (3); 66/186; FBLA; GAA; Crs Cntry; Trk; Hon Roll; All-St Crss Cntry; Whos Who In HS Aths.

ZHOU, LILY; Central Sr HS; Little Rock, AR; (3); Intnl Clb; Mu Alpha Theta; Natl Beta Clb; Gov Hon Prg Awd; High Hon Roll; Hon Roll; Jr NHS; NHS; Pres Acad Fit Awd; Regnl Sci & St Sci Fairs; Natl Jr Sci & Hum Symposia; Chem.

ZIELSTRE, SCOTT A; Conway Sr HS; Conway, AR; (2); Band; Mrchg Band; Pep Band; High Hon Roll; Hon Roll.

ZIEMSKI, RYAN V; Jacksonville HS; Jacksonville, AR; (1); Boy Scts; 4-H; Math Clb; Teachers Aide; Chorus; School Play; Socr; Trk; Wrstlng; Hon Roll; Jr Math Leag; FSU; Hotel Mgr.

ZINAMON, BRANDI L; Oak Grove HS; North Little Rock, AR; (3); 43/125; Am Leg Aux Girls St; Art Clb; FCA; 4-H; French Clb; Letterman Clb; Rep Frsh Cls; Rep Jr Cls; Var Capt Bsktbl; Var Capt Powder Puff Ftbl; Memphis ST; Sports Med/OT.

ZITZELBERGER, CHRISTIE; Pocahontas HS; Maynard, AR; (4); 1/129; Pres FHA; HOBY; Sec Natl Beta Clb; Red Cross Aide; Pres Jr Cls; Pres Schlr; Val; Art Clb; Sec Church Yth Grp; Cmnty Wkr; Leo Clb Pres; AEGIS Med, Laureate Intnl Stud; U Cntrl ARFMED.

ZUBOW, MARGARET A; Flippin Jr Sr HS; Flippin, AR; (2); Drama Clb; 4-H; Pres FBLA; German Clb; Key Clb; SADD; School Play; Phtg Yrbk; Sec Frsh Cls; Sec Soph Cls.

ZWICKER, MEGAN M; Mountain Home HS; Mountain Home, AR; (3); Art Clb; Church Yth Grp; Natl Beta Clb; Quiz Bowl; Spanish Clb; Yrbk; Hon Roll; Prfct Atten Awd; Spanish NHS; Interact Club; Stdnt Chrstn Assn; Yrbk Supr Awd; Hendrix Coll; Bio/Pre-Med.

KANSAS

AAGAARD, CHRISTOPHER J; Wichita Heights HS; Wichita, KS; (3); 21/242; Boy Scts; French Clb; Science Clb; Hon Roll; NHS; Acad Ltr 3 Yrs; Sci Olympd Ltr; Engrg.

AARSTAD, KRYSTAL D; Newton Sr HS; Newton, KS; (3); Dance Clb; Key Clb; Office Aide; SADD; Chorus; Bsktbl; Diving; Gym; Mgr(s); High Hon Roll; KS St Univ; Sec Ed.

ABANISHE, SHADE A; Washington HS; Kansas City, KS; (4); 60/220; Drama Clb; Key Clb; Office Aide; Spanish Clb; Band; Treas Sr Cls; Rep Stu Cncl; Trk; Wt Lftg; Hon Roll; Peer Sprt; Rl Mdl; Gspl Chr; Kansas City CC; Pre Med.

ABASTA, BERENICE; Chaparral HS; Harper, KS; (3); 6/65; Mgr Nwsp; Phtg Yrbk; High Hon Roll; Hon Roll; NHS; Participated In St Photo Cont; Acctng; Real Estate.

ABBOTT, CHANTEL M; Pleasant Ridge HS; Platte City, MO; (4); Church Yth Grp; Debate Tm; Drama Clb; FCA; French Clb; FBLA; Q&S; Spanish Clb; Speech Tm; SADD; Mltry.

ABBOTT, JESSICA L; Holton HS; Mayetta, KS; (2); HOBY; Letterman Clb; Model UN; NFL; Quiz Bowl; Drill Tm; School Musical; High Hon Roll; NHS; Chorus; Wmns Chorus.

ABBOTT, RANDI N; Oskaloosa HS; Oskaloosa, KS; (2); Cmnty Wkr; FBLA; Pres FHA; Girl Scts; Letterman Clb; Pep Clb; SADD; Chorus; Var Bsktbl; Var Sftbl; KS Univ; Pediatrics.

ABBOTT, SEAN G; Holton HS; Mayetta, KS; (1); Model UN; NFL; Scholastic Bowl; Band; Mrchg Band; Pep Band; School Musical; JV Ftbl; Hon Roll.

ABBOTT, TIM; Blue Valley HS; Stanley, KS; (4); 76/230; Church Yth Grp; Pres VP 4-H; Office Aide; Band; Mrchg Band; Pep Band; Var Capt Trk; 4-H Awd; Hon Roll; KS ST; Hrtcltr.

ABEL, BEN C; Emporia HS; Emporia, KS; (2); Church Yth Grp; Band; Mrchg Band; JV Swmmng.

ABELDT, JOSH L; Chapman HS; Hope, KS; (3); Church Yth Grp; VP 4-H; VP Natl FFA Org; SADD; Teachers Aide; Acpl Chr; Chorus; Variety Show; VP Sr Cls; Treas Stu Cncl; KS ST U; Ag Eng.

ABERNATHY, AVERY; Manhattan HS; Manhattan, KS; (3); Am Leg Boys St; French Clb; FBLA; Teachers Aide; School Play; Ofcr Stu Cncl; JV Bsbl; Var Crs Cntry; Var Capt Socr; JV Trk; Baker U; Architecture.

ABERNETHY, LINDSAY; Bishop Miege HS; Leawood, KS; (2); 3/163; Church Yth Grp; Cmnty Wkr; Debate Tm; GAA; Hosp Aide; HOBY; SADD; Pres Soph Cls; Pres Jr Cls; Bsktbl; Forensics; Unitown; Peer Hlpr; Boston Coll; Med.

ABERNETHY, STACY A; St Thomas Aquinas HS; Leawood, KS; (4); 65/231; French Clb; School Play; Nwsp; Rep Soph Cls; Bsktbl; Crs Cntry; Powder Puff Ftbl; Socr; Sftbl; Trk; Nom Pwdr Puff Queen; 15 Hrs Coll Credit; Front Page Ed; Bakers Natl Ed Fndtn Schlrshp KS ST; U Of KS; Bus.

ABITZ, LYNETTE; Onaga HS; Emmett, KS; (4); 3/22; Sec FHA; HOBY; Pres SADD; Ed Yrbk; Sec Frsh Cls; Bsktbl; Capt Chrldng; Vllybl; 4-H Awd; NHS; KS ST U; Jrnlsm.

ABNER, NATHAN S; Riley Cty HS; Manhattan, KS; (3); Art Clb; School Play; Swing Chorus; Yrbk; Ofcr Bsbl; Bsktbl; Ftbl; Mgr(s); Trk; Wt Lftg; All Schl Publication Art Layouts & Comp Work; Schl Plays; KS ST; Graphic Artist.

ABPLANALP, ALLISON L; Washburn Rural HS; Topeka, KS; (2); 2/380; Debate Tm; FCA; NFL; Church Choir; Ed Nwsp; Rep Jr Cls; L Bsktbl; JV Socr; High Hon Roll; SADD; Earthbnd; Untd Meth Yth Cnc; Acad Ltrmn; U Of KS; Patholgy.

ABRAHAMS, NATHAN J; Newton Sr HS; Newton, KS; (1); Art Clb; Church Yth Grp; Model UN; Hon Roll; Knwldge Mstr; Phtgrphy Clb; Gld Crd.

ABRAHAMSON, TY J; Olathe South Sr HS; Olathe, KS; (4); Debate Tm; Sec Drama Clb; NFL; Sec Thesps; Chorus; School Musical; School Play; Church Yth Grp; Capt Letterman Clb; Teachers Aide; KS All-St HS Hnr Choir 3 Yr Medallion; Soloist; Natl Choral Awd; Natl & Regnl ACDA Hnr Choirs 93-96; KS Univ; Stage Perfmnc.

ABRAM, BRIAN J; Bishop Miege HS; Prairie Village, KS; (1); 19/250; Pres Frsh Cls; Bsktbl; Var L Socr; Var L Trk; High Hon Roll; Spirit Awd.

ABRAMS, KARIN; Holton HS; Mayetta, KS; (4); 11/63; FHA; L Letterman Clb; Teachers Aide; Rep Nwsp; Rep Yrbk; Mgr(s); Sftbl; Hon Roll; Treas NHS; Ftr Hmmkrs Of Amer Mem Of Yr; Cloud County CC; Socl Wrk.

ABU-YOUSIF, ADNAN; Blue Valley Northwest HS; Overland Park, KS; (4); Debate Tm; JV Ftbl; Var Wrstlng; Hon Roll; NHS; Biomedical Engrng.

ACE, LINDSAY T; Emporia HS; Emporia, KS; (3); Am Leg Aux Girls St; Church Yth Grp; FCA; Rep Jr Cls; Rep Sr Cls; Treas Stu Cncl; Intrml JV Bsktbl; Var Capt Crs Cntry; Var Trk; High Hon Roll; HS Heisman Trophy Nom; Sprts Med.

ACHESON, DARRELL; Morland Jr Sr HS; Morland, KS; (3); 1/9; Church Yth Grp; Cmnty Wkr; Quiz Bowl; SADD; Teachers Aide; Varsity Clb; Band; Chorus; Church Choir; Pep Band; Dentistry.

ACHESON, SAPRINA M; Russell HS; Russell, KS; (2); Church Yth Grp; Cmnty Wkr; Band; Mrchg Band; Pep Band; Stage Crew; Bsktbl; Crs Cntry; Sftbl; Hon Roll; BCCC; Rec Therapist.

ACHTERBERG, ELLIOTT; F L Schlagle HS; Kansas City, KS; (4); 36/173; CAP; Office Aide; Q&S; SADD; Teachers Aide; Band; Drm Mjr(t); Mrchg Band; Pep Band; Yrbk; Teen Advy Cncl Of Mayor; US Marine Corps Corps Delayed Entry Pgm To Active Duty; NYLF-SDID; KCKCC; US Marine Corps.

ACKERMAN, AMY L; Spearville Jr Sr HS; Spearville, KS; (2); 1/32; HOBY; Sec Treas Pep Clb; Quiz Bowl; Band; Chorus; Pep Band; Pres Frsh Cls; Hon Roll; NHS; Pres Acad Fit Awd.

ACKERMAN, DEREK B; Blue Valley HS; Stilwell, KS; (2); Wt Lftg; Hon Roll; Comp Pgmng & Math Conts; K-ST.

ACKERMAN, ERIC M; Dodge City HS; Dodge City, KS; (2); Church Yth Grp; Cmnty Wkr; Office Aide; Var Bsbl; Var Bsktbl; Var Ftbl; Var Wt Lftg.

ACKERMAN, JENNIFER L; Garden City Sr HS; Garden City, KS; (2); Church Yth Grp; Cmnty Wkr; Math Tm; Teachers Aide; Varsity Clb; Var Bsktbl; Var Sftbl; Var Vllybl; Cit Awd; High Hon Roll; 1st Team All League-Fast Pitch Sftbl; Med/Vet.

ACKERMAN, KIMBERLY D; Blue Valley HS; Stilwell, KS; (4); Pres FHA; SADD; Mgr(s); High Hon Roll; Hon Roll; NHS; KS ST U; Acctng.

ACKERMAN, SHAWN L; Sabetha HS; Sabetha, KS; (3); 13/78; FCA; FHA; Sec Natl FFA Org; Pep Clb; Chorus; Var Chrldng; High Hon Roll; Hon Roll; NHS; Pres Acad Fit Awd; Showing Horses; ABRA Reserve Wrld Chmpns; Livestock Judging Camps; Speech Contests; KS ST Univ; Acctng/Bus Admin.

ACKERMAN, STEPHANIE A; Spearville Jr Sr HS; Spearville, KS; (3); Office Aide; Pep Clb; Quiz Bowl; Speech Tm; VP Frsh Cls; Rep Stu Cncl; Stat Mgr(s); Var L Trk; JV Vllybl; Hon Roll; Phy Thrpst.

ACKLIN, RANDY N; Yates Ctr HS; Yates Center, KS; (2); Dance Clb; NFL; Hon Roll.

ACKORS, FRANCENE T; J C Harmon HS; Kansas City, KS; (4); 42/362; Art Clb; Church Yth Grp; Cmnty Wkr; FTA; GAA; Spanish Clb; JV Var Vllybl; High Hon Roll; Hon Roll; NHS; Dual Enrollment Coll; Schlr All Amer Awds; Grd Schl Tchr Intern; UMKC; Elem Ed.

ACOSTA, CARMEN J; Council Grove HS; White City, KS; (3); Cmnty Wkr; FCA; FBLA; VP Rep Key Clb; Office Aide; Pep Clb; SADD; Teachers Aide; Band; Chorus; Rest Home Vol; Attend & Assist The Local Kiwanis Clb In Act; Attnd The Key Clb Dist & Intl Convention; KS Univ; Ed.

ACOSTA, SARA M; Turner HS; Kansas City, KS; (4); #17 in class; Bus Profs of Am; Science Clb; SADD; Band; Jazz Band; Mrchg Band; Pep Band; High Hon Roll; Hon Roll; Jr NHS; SADD Clb Pres; Kansas City CC; Vet.

ADAM, NATHAN; Pittsburg HS; Pittsburg, KS; (4); 10/168; Church Yth Grp; Debate Tm; Mrchg Band; High Hon Roll; Pres Schlr; St Schlr; Am Leg Boys St; Drama Clb; FCA; Band; Rotry Clb Schlsp; Pittsburg St Univ Schlsp & Hnrs Schlsp; Pittsburg ST Univ.

ADAM, TAMMY; Tipton HS; Tipton, KS; (4); 2/12; Church Yth Grp; Pep Clb; Teachers Aide; School Play; Mgr Yrbk; Pres Soph Cls; Pres Jr Cls; Rep Stu Cncl; L Bsktbl; L Trk; Emporia St T*ests Hnrb Mntn Chem; Outstndng Achvt Latin II, Acctng, Bio; Outstndng Achvt Amer Lit; Acctng.

ADAMS, ANI L; Russell HS; Russell, KS; (2); Church Yth Grp; 4-H; SADD; Band; Chorus; Church Choir; Stat Bsktbl; JV Sftbl; Var JV Vllybl; 4-H Awd; Ft Hays ST; Phys Therapy.

ADAMS, BRIAN J; Baldwin HS; Baldwin City, KS; (4); 19/80; Boy Scts; Church Yth Grp; Letterman Clb; School Musical; JV Var Crs Cntry; JV Var Tennis; Hon Roll; Pittsburg ST Univ; Engr.

ADAMS, CHAD; Liberal HS; Liberal, KS; (3); Church Yth Grp; FCA; Letterman Clb; Teachers Aide; Var Ftbl; Var Trk; Var Wt Lftg; Prfct Atten Awd; 2nd Team Offnsv Tackl All-Area SW KS; Natl Yth Ldrshp Form Defns Intel & Diplomacy; Multi-Yr Listee; Ed; PE.

ADAMS, CHERIELLE; Yates Ctr HS; Yates Center, KS; (4); 1/34; Am Leg Aux Girls St; 4-H; HOBY; Natl FFA Org; Bsktbl; Sftbl; Vllybl; 4-H Awd; NHS; Val; Natl Yng Ldrs Conf; KSU; Finance.

ADAMS, CLAYTON; El Dorado HS; El Dorado, KS; (2); Yrbk; High Hon Roll; Debate; Southwestern; Law.

ADAMS, DANELLE; St Thomas Aquinas HS; Shawnee, KS; (3); 2/268; Cmnty Wkr; Key Clb; Math Tm; Pep Clb; Ski Clb; Drill Tm; Ed Yrbk; Socr; High Hon Roll; NHS; Exmplry Dscpln Awd; KU Regnl Jrnlsm Cmptn; Mrktng/Advrtsng.

ADAMS, JANELLE; Centralia Schl; Corning, KS; (1); Drama Clb; FHA; Letterman Clb; Pep Clb; Chorus; School Musical; JV Bsktbl; JV Chrldng; Var Sftbl; Var Trk; KS ST U.

ADAMS, JESS; Blue Valley Northwest HS; Overland Park, KS; (2); Ftbl; Trk; Wt Lftg; Hon Roll.

ADAMS, JOHN; Kapaun-Mt Carmel HS; Wichita, KS; (4); 32/185; HOBY; Q&S; Thesps; Acpl Chr; School Musical; Nwsp; Pres Jr Cls; Ftbl; JETS Awd; Pres Acad Fit Awd; U IA; Mgzne Jrnlst.

ADAMS, JOHN C; Douglass HS; Douglass, KS; (3); FCA; 4-H; Quiz Bowl; Science Clb; Teachers Aide; Chorus; Jazz Band; Mrchg Band; Orch; Pep Band.

ADAMS, JOHN M; Kapaun-Mt Carmel HS; Wichita, KS; (4); 30/180; Chess Clb; Q&S; Thesps; School Musical; Ed Nwsp; Pres Jr Cls; Var Ftbl; High Hon Roll; NHS; Pres Schlr; Avila Coll; Thtr.

ADAMS, JOSHUA D; Lawrence HS; Lawrence, KS; (3); Church Yth Grp; Library Aide; Spanish Clb; Orch; Intrml Bsktbl; Intrml Ftbl; Intrml Trk; Hon Roll; Pres Schlr; Aeronautical Engrng; Pilot; Arch.

ADAMS, KATE; Spring Hill HS; Spring Hill, KS; (4); 23/110; Church Yth Grp; Capt Dance Clb; FCA; 4-H; Hosp Aide; Pep Clb; SADD; Drill Tm; High Hon Roll; Hon Roll; Johnson Cty CC; PT.

ADAMS, KAYLENE; Crest HS; Kincaid, KS; (1); Pep Clb; Chorus; Flag Corp; Chrldng; Golf; Pom Pon; Vllybl; High Hon Roll; Piano.

ADAMS, LAURIE; Riley Cty HS; Manhattan, KS; (3); FCA; FBLA; FHA; Pep Clb; SADD; Var Chrldng; JV Sftbl; Var Vllybl; Hon Roll; U Of KS; Bio/Pre Med.

ADAMS, NICK B; Ft Scott HS; Fort Scott, KS; (2); Computer Clb; Debate Tm; NFL; Quiz Bowl; Science Clb; Speech Tm; Hon Roll; Gifted Ed; U Of KS; Pharmacy.

ADAMS, PETE; St Marys HS; Maple Hill, KS; (4); 5/55; Letterman Clb; Natl FFA Org; Office Aide; Teachers Aide; Bsktbl; Var Ftbl; Hon Roll; NHS; Pres Acad Fit Awd; St Schlr; KS ST Univ; Animal Sci; Bus.

ADAMS, RAUSHANAH; Wichita West HS; Wichita, KS; (3); 37/300; Cmnty Wkr; DECA; French Clb; Hosp Aide; Pep Clb; Teachers Aide; Sec Jr Cls; Ofcr Stu Cncl; Co-Capt Chrldng; NHS; All Amer Chrldr; Hnr Roll Hnrb Mntn; VP Of DECA; U Of KS; Comp Sys Analyst.

ADAMS IV, RAYMOND; St Marys HS; Maple Hill, KS; (4); 5/35; 4-H; Letterman Clb; Natl FFA Org; Teachers Aide; Var L Bsktbl; Var L Ftbl; Hon Roll; NHS; Pres Acad Fit Awd; Schlr Athl Awd; KS ST U; Animal Sci.

ADAMS, SARAH J; Anderson Cty Jr Sr HS; Garnett, KS; (2); Intnl Clb; Pep Clb; SADD; Vllybl; Hon Roll.

ADAMS, SHERLYN; Shawnee Mission East HS; Leawood, KS; (3); 17/350; Church Yth Grp; Cmnty Wkr; Natl Beta Clb; Pep Clb; Q&S; Spanish Clb; Speech Tm; Varsity Clb; Rptr Yrbk; JV Var Bsktbl; Horseback Riding; U Of CO; Psych; Pre-Med; Pre Vet.

ADAMS, THOMAS TYLER; Blue Valley Northwest HS; Overland Park, KS; (2); Debate Tm; JCL; Latin Clb; NFL; Band; Mrchg Band; Nwsp; Lit Mag; Trk; Hon Roll; KS JCL Conv 1st Plc Latin; Debate ST Qlfr.

ADAMS, TROY D; Andover HS; Andover, KS; (4); 18/138; Church Yth Grp; FCA; SADD; Teachers Aide; Var Socr; Hon Roll; NHS; Andovers Acad Fitness Awd; Soccer Awds 1st Team All League-All Reg/2nd Team All ST/MV Pat; OK Chrstn Univ Of Sci/Art.

ADAMS, YOLANDA; Leavenworth HS; Leavenworth, KS; (1); Church Yth Grp; English Clb; ROTC; Speech Tm; Chorus; Bsktbl; Vllybl; Hon Roll; Good Fellows; IN Univ; Natl Guards Crim Psyc.

ADANY, ANIKO; Shawnee Mission N HS; Roeland Park, KS; (4); 60/360; Cmnty Wkr; Hosp Aide; Pep Clb; Church Choir; Orch; School Musical; Stage Crew; High Hon Roll; Hon Roll; Pres Schlr; Amnesty Intl Vp; Natl Merit Cmmnded Schol; KU; Bio.

ADDINGTON, AMY; Olathe South Sr HS; Olathe, KS; (4); Church Yth Grp; Dance Clb; French Clb; Pep Clb; Band; Drill Tm; Pom Pon; High Hon Roll; NHS; Pres Acad Fit Awd; U Of KS; Elem Ed.

ADDIS, JOEL S; Derby HS; Derby, KS; (3); Church Yth Grp; FCA; Band; Church Choir; Jazz Band; Mrchg Band; Pep Band; Ofcr Stu Cncl; Future Problem Solvers; Odyssey Of The Mind; KU Stock Market Group; Law.

ADDIS, TREVOR A; Oswego HS; Oswego, KS; (1); Letterman Clb; Band; Pep Band; Var Bsbl; Var Ftbl; Wt Lftg; High Hon Roll.

ADDISON, ALICIA; St John Jr Sr HS; Saint John, KS; (3); 1/44; Ofcr 4-H; SADD; Band; Sec Frsh Cls; Treas Soph Cls; Treas Jr Cls; Rep Stu Cncl; Tennis; 4-H Awd; High Hon Roll; KAY Org Pres & VP; KS ST Univ; Bus.

ADELHARDT, STEPHANIE; Chaparral HS; Harper, KS; (4); 1/60; Church Yth Grp; FCA; Key Clb; Pep Clb; Scholastic Bowl; Teachers Aide; Chorus; Church Choir; School Musical; Stage Crew; NHS Pres; Jr HS Math Tm Asst Coach; Tandy Awd Wnnr; Ldrshp Awd; Washburn U; Math.

ADELL, ADRIENNE; Olathe South Sr HS; Olathe, KS; (3); Church Yth Grp; Cmnty Wkr; School Musical; Powder Puff Ftbl; JV Socr; JV Vllybl; High Hon Roll; NHS; Pres Acad Fit Awd; Spanish NHS; Phy Ther.

ADKINS, NICOLE L; Clifton-Clyde HS; Clifton, KS; (4); Drama Clb; FBLA; Natl FFA Org; Sec Sr Cls; Rep Stu Cncl; Mgr(s); Cit Awd; High Hon Roll; NHS; KAY Clb Pres, VP, Wrld Svc Drctr; Inst Of Ntrl Hlng Sci; Massge.

ADMIRE, CHRISTINA; Arkansas City HS; Arkansas City, KS; (3); Am Leg Aux Girls St; Debate Tm; FCA; NFL; Office Aide; SADD; Teachers Aide; Band; Church Choir; Flag Corp; KAY Activity Dir; KU; Jrnlsm.

ADOLPH, JESSICA L; Labette Co HS; Edna, KS; (4); 72/128; FCA; FBLA; Library Aide; Natl FFA Org; Rep Frsh Cls; Sec Soph Cls; Rep Stu Cncl; Bsktbl; Tennis; Vllybl; Nashburn Univ; Elem Ed.

ADORANTE, ASHLEY B; Shawnee Mission S Sr HS; Overland Park, KS; (3); Church Yth Grp; Cmnty Wkr; Intnl Clb; Pep Clb; Sec Service Clb; Teachers Aide; JV L Gym; JV Trk; Hon Roll; DECA.

ADUDDELL, JERALD R; Haven HS; Haven, KS; (4); Church Yth Grp; Cmnty Wkr; FCA; SADD; Chorus; School Musical; School Play; Variety Show; Var L Ftbl; Var L Trk; KS Music Edctrs Festival Choir Mem; KS ST Univ Honor Choir; KS Assn For Yth; Harding Univ; Music Ed.

AFZAL, NAEEM; Maur Hill Prep Schl; Atchison, KS; (3); 7/73; Office Aide; Socr; Trk; Vllybl; Wt Lftg; Wrstlng; High Hon Roll; Hon Roll; Dntstry.

AGA, CHRISTINA T; Blue Valley Northwest HS; Overland Park, KS; (3); Debate Tm; NFL; Scholastic Bowl; Science Clb; Band; Drm Mjr(t); JV Crs Cntry; Var Capt Socr; High Hon Roll; NHS; KS Assn Yth Svcs; Acad Decathlon Team; U Of KS; Bus; Engrng.

AGNEW, BRYCE C; Goddard HS; Wichita, KS; (1); Hon Roll; AYSO Sccr; Ind Smmr League Trnmnt Sccr; Ks ST Univ; Vetrnrn.

AGUILERA, RYAN J; Garden City Sr HS; Garden City, KS; (2); Acpl Chr; School Musical; Ftbl; Wt Lftg; Wrstlng; Mntr Cls; KU; Bus.

AGUSTIN, ANGELA; Kapaun-Mt Carmel HS; Wichita, KS; (3); Church Yth Grp; Treas French Clb; Hosp Aide; SADD; Chorus; School Musical; School Play; Stage Crew; NHS; Wchta Yth Symphny; Dist/ST Orchs; Coca Cola Choir For Olympc Trch Crmny; Music/Microbio.

AHL, CHRISTY M; Washburn Rural HS; Topeka, KS; (4); Church Yth Grp; Cmnty Wkr; Hosp Aide; Spanish Clb; Teachers Aide; Chorus; Church Choir; School Musical; Variety Show; Nwsp; KS Univ.

AHLQUIST, AMY; Bern Schl; Bern, KS; (3); Church Yth Grp; Letterman Clb; Pep Clb; SADD; Band; Chorus; Drill Tm; Mrchg Band; Pep Band; Treas Stu Cncl; Washburn Univ; Xray Tech.

AHLVERS, JENNIFER; Waconda East HS; Glen Elder, KS; (2); 5/23; Church Yth Grp; Letterman Clb; Quiz Bowl; Speech Tm; Band; Chorus; School Play; JV Bsktbl; High Hon Roll; Hon Roll; Cnslr/Eng Tchr.

AHUJA, NEEL K; Washburn Rural HS; Topeka, KS; (2); Computer Clb; Debate Tm; FBLA; Hosp Aide; Model UN; NFL; Rptr Nwsp; High Hon Roll.

AITA, COURTNEY B; Blue Valley HS; Stilwell, KS; (2); Debate Tm; Latin Clb; Socr; Hon Roll.

AKAGI, CAM; Ulysses HS; Ulysses, KS; (3); Art Clb; Letterman Clb; Spanish Clb; SADD; Var L Bsbl; Var L Bsktbl; High Hon Roll; Prfct Atten Awd.

AKERBERG, CASLE L; Lawrence HS; Lawrence, KS; (2); Orch; Rep Soph Cls; Var Bsktbl; Var Chrldng; Var Socr; Var Trk; High Hon Roll; Hon Roll; Yale; Chem Engrng.

AKERS, LORI K; Concordia Jr Sr HS; Concordia, KS; (3); 1/102; NFL; Hist Science Clb; Sec Spanish Clb; Band; Chorus; Church Choir; Var Crs Cntry; Var Trk; High Hon Roll; Hist NHS; Spcl Ed; Span.

AKIN, JEFF A; Shawnee Mission E Sr HS; Shawnee Mission, KS; (2); Church Yth Grp; Rptr Nwsp; JV Tennis; Cit Awd; Hon Roll; Hab For Hum; Psych.

AKRED, REBECCA S; Haven HS; Mount Hope, KS; (3); Church Yth Grp; FCA; SADD; Church Choir; Var Sftbl; Hon Roll; Chorus; School Musical; Sec Frsh Cls; Intrml Chrldng; KAY, Bd Mem, Sec & VP; Bus; Acctng.

ALBERS, AMY E; Midway Schl; Denton, KS; (2); Church Yth Grp; Pep Clb; Quiz Bowl; Band; Mrchg Band; Pep Band; School Play; Yrbk; Var L Bsktbl; Var L Trk; KS ST U; Vet/Dr.

ALBERS, DAVID; Colby Sr HS; Colby, KS; (3); Wrstlng; KS Hwy Patrol Cadet Law Enforcement Acad; Rotry Ldrshp Conf Manhattan; Washburn Univ; Hwy Patrol.

ALBERS, MARK C; Midway Schl; Bendena, KS; (3); 1/23; Church Yth Grp; School Play; VP Jr Cls; Ofcr Stu Cncl; Var L Bsktbl; Var L Ftbl; Cit Awd; High Hon Roll; NHS; Prfct Atten Awd; KS ST Univ; Ag Ec.

ALBERT, JACOB M; Yates Ctr HS; Yates Center, KS; (3); Natl FFA Org; Var Bsktbl; Hon Roll; Eng/Mech.

ALBERT, MARK V; Tonganoxie HS; Tonganoxie, KS; (4); 1/118; Debate Tm; Math Tm; Quiz Bowl; VP Science Clb; VP Teachers Aide; VP Variety Show; JV Var Socr; VP Gov Hon Prg Awd; VP High Hon Roll; VP Kiwanis Awd; Acclrtd Math; Voice Of Dmcry Awd; KU Math Dept May Landis Schol; Pittsburgh St; Chem.

ALBERT, MEGAN M; Olpe Schl; Olpe, KS; (3); Office Aide; Teachers Aide; Nwsp; Yrbk; Var Bsktbl; Var Vllybl; Hon Roll; ESU.

ALBERTSON, AARON L; Shawnee Mission N HS; Shawnee, KS; (1); Pep Clb; Bsktbl; Trk; Hon Roll; Art Painting/Drawing; Math.

ALBIN, LANCE D; Quinter Jr Sr HS; Quinter, KS; (2); Debate Tm; FCA; HOBY; Quiz Bowl; Speech Tm; VP Frsh Cls; Pres Soph Cls; Trk; High Hon Roll; NHS; Sterling Coll; Law.

ALBINO, MARIA L; Leavenworth HS; Gatesville, TX; (4); Drama Clb; NFL; Thesps; Acpl Chr; School Musical; School Play; Stage Crew; Ed Nwsp; High Hon Roll; Church Yth Grp; St Mary Coll; Bus.

ALBINO, ROSIN L; Leavenworth HS; Fort Leavenworth, KS; (3); 72/346; Church Yth Grp; Drama Clb; Thesps; Church Choir; School Play; Stage Crew; High Hon Roll; Hon Roll; Ltrd Drama; Tech Sprt Prof Theater Group; Elem Ed/Theater.

ALBRECHT, ANDREA; Herington HS; Herington, KS; (1); Church Yth Grp; Drama Clb; FCA; Pep Clb; Quiz Bowl; Band; Chorus; Church Choir; Mrchg Band; Pep Band; Peer Cnslr.

ALBRECHT, ANDY L; Marion HS; Marion, KS; (2); Band; Jazz Band; Mrchg Band; Pep Band; Swing Chorus.

ALBRECHT, SARAH; Dodge City HS; Dodge City, KS; (2); Church Yth Grp; 4-H; Chorus; Orch; School Musical; Variety Show; Rep Stu Cncl; Crs Cntry; Trk; 4-H Awd; Piano.

ALBRECHT, SARAH J; Liberal HS; Liberal, KS; (3); FHA; FTA; Teachers Aide; Chorus; Bsktbl; Mgr(s); High Hon Roll; Jr NHS; NHS; Ntl Merit Schol.

ALBRIGHT, ERIN C; Goddard HS; Wichita, KS; (2); Church Yth Grp; Var Golf; High Hon Roll; Comp Engrng.

ALBRIGHT, ROB W; Olathe East Sr HS; Olathe, KS; (2); Church Yth Grp; Spanish Clb; Varsity Clb; Band; Mrchg Band; Capt Swmmng; Hon Roll; Yr Round Swimming; KS Univ.

ALBRITTON, ELIZABETH A; Olathe East Sr HS; Overland Park, KS; (3); Church Yth Grp; French Clb; Latin Clb; Letterman Clb; School Play; Stage Crew; Rptr Nwsp; Var Crs Cntry; Powder Puff Ftbl; Var Socr; Jv Soccer Capt; Commnctn; Bio.

ALBRO, CHRISTINA J; Andale HS; Goddard, KS; (3); Church Yth Grp; Scholastic Bowl; SADD; Band; Chorus; School Play; Hon Roll; NHS; Lang Clb; Teens As Tchrs; KS Newman Col; Pharm.

ALCALA, DONNA; Ulysses HS; Ulysses, KS; (2); Hon Roll; Msc; Wrtng; Film Dir.

ALCANTAR, MELISSA A; Topeka West HS; Topeka, KS; (3); Spanish Clb; JV Tennis; Hon Roll; Spirit Clb Pres; White Rose; Teens Hope; SADD; Wghtlftrs; KA Univ; Radiology.

ALENA, JENNIFER A; Bishop Miege HS; Shawnee, KS; (3); 21/170; Church Yth Grp; French Clb; Pep Clb; SADD; Var Trk; Var Vllybl; High Hon Roll; NHS; Pres Acad Fit Awd; Vlybl All-Trnmt Team; Psych.

ALEXANDER, AUDREY; Clay Ctr Cmty HS; Clay Center, KS; (4); 1/98; Drama Clb; HOBY; VP Natl FFA Org; Spanish Clb; Speech Tm; Crs Cntry; Vllybl; Hon Roll; NHS; Jr Miss Pgnt; Bausch & Lomb Hnry Sci Awd; KS ST U; Ag Engrng.

ALEXANDER, BRANDY J; Sumner Acad Of Arts & Science; Kansas City, KS; (1); Church Yth Grp; Dance Clb; Pep Clb; Spanish Clb; Band; Church Choir; Drill Tm; Bsktbl; Gym; Trk; Model For Project Save A Child; AAU Cougars KS Trk Team; Ed.

ALEXANDER, ERIKA; Satanta Jr Sr HS; Satanta, KS; (4); 1/18; Pres VP Church Yth Grp; Pres FCA; Pres Sec 4-H; HOBY; Chorus; Rep Stu Cncl; Stat Bsktbl; Var Trk; Hon Roll; NHS; Natl Piano Gld Auds, Natl Pgm; St Musc Fstvls Piano, Vc Smll Vcl Ensmbl; Treas St Chrch God Yth Fllwsh; Mid-Amer Bibl Coll; Sec Ed.

ALEXANDER, JENA; Lawrence HS; Lawrence, KS; (2); Hosp Aide; Key Clb; Model UN; Spanish Clb; Hon Roll; Amnesty Intl; Alliance For Soc Awareness.

ALEXANDER, KEVIN B; Topeka West HS; Topeka, KS; (3); 25/239; French Clb; Pep Clb; Q&S; SADD; Teachers Aide; Phtg Nwsp; Capt Socr; High Hon Roll; Hon Roll; NHS; Columbia Schol Press Photo Awd 4th; Bus.

ALEXANDER, LESLEY; Maize HS; Wichita, KS; (4); 4/235; Am Leg Aux Girls St; Church Yth Grp; Cmnty Wkr; HOBY; Math Tm; Pres Q&S; Service Clb; Spanish Clb; SADD; High Hon Roll; KS Rgnts Hnrs Acad; Nvl ROTC Schlrshp; Georgetown U.

ALEXANDER, SHELLY P; Campus HS; Haysville, KS; (3); 19/201; Am Leg Aux Girls St; Drama Clb; Thesps; Acpl Chr; Chorus; School Musical; School Play; High Hon Roll; NHS; Pres Acad Fit Awd; Psych.

ALEXANDER, TRACY; Shawnee Heights Sr HS; Berryton, KS; (3); 15/245; FBLA; Intnl Clb; Key Clb; Stage Crew; Ed Yrbk; Var Bsktbl; Var Trk; Var JV Vllybl; High Hon Roll; NHS; AFS Frgn Exch Stu Paraguay.

ALEXANDER, VALERIE J; Wichita South HS; Wichita, KS; (1); #1 in class; Church Yth Grp; Cmnty Wkr; GAA; Girl Scts; Letterman Clb; Teachers Aide; JV Sftbl; High Hon Roll; Hon Roll; Pres Acad Fit Awd; Chrldng Coach; Amer Indian Clb; U KS; Tchr.

ALFORD, HAVEN D; Jewell HS; Hutchinson, KS; (1); 2/24; FHA; Pep Clb; Quiz Bowl; Speech Tm; Trk; Vllybl; High Hon Roll; Hon Roll; KS ST Univ; Arch.

ALFORD, STEPHANIE; Kapaum Mt Carmel HS; Wichita, KS; (4); 79/170; Church Yth Grp; Cmnty Wkr; GAA; Chorus; Intrml Bsktbl; Var Trk; Hon Roll; Pres Acad Fit Awd; St Schlr; Outstdng Achvmnt Algebra II; Brd Of Regents Schlr; U Of KS; Bio.

ALGER, ROBYN L; Lawrence HS; Lawrence, KS; (4); 52/615; Cmnty Wkr; Dance Clb; Key Clb; Spanish Clb; Teachers Aide; Chorus; Rep Stu Cncl; Chrldng; Gym; Powder Puff Ftbl; Magna Cum Laude Natl Latin Exam; KS Univ; Occptnl Therapy.

ALIANI, STEPHANIE; Caney Valley Jr Sr HS; Caney, KS; (3); Church Yth Grp; FCA; Chrldng; Vllybl; Hon Roll; NHS; Multi-Yr Listee; Ozark Chrstn Coll.

ALISHIE, TYSON; Garden City Sr HS; Garden City, KS; (3); 79/296; Church Yth Grp; Debate Tm; Band; Chorus; Church Choir; Jazz Band; Mrchg Band; Orch; Pep Band; Hon Roll; Washburn Univ; Optom.

ALLAM, COURT R; Hutchinson HS; Hutchinson, KS; (3); 22/346; Pep Clb; SADD; Rptr Nwsp; Rptr Yrbk; Bsktbl; JV Ftbl; JV Golf; High Hon Roll; Prfct Atten Awd; KS ST Univ; Comm/Radio/TV.

ALLEN, ALICIA M; Leavenworth HS; Fort Leavenworth, KS; (3); Church Yth Grp; Cmnty Wkr; Teachers Aide; Bsktbl; Gov Hon Prg Awd; High Hon Roll; Hon Roll; Prfct Atten Awd; Good Fellows; Earth Clb; Pre-Med.

ALLEN, ALISSA R; Centralia Schl; Centralia, KS; (3); Church Yth Grp; Cmnty Wkr; Dance Clb; Letterman Clb; Science Clb; Teachers Aide; Chorus; Capt Drill Tm; School Play; Ed Yrbk; KAYS; Johnson Cty CC; Occpnl Thr Ast.

ALLEN, AMY M; Turner HS; Kansas City, KS; (4); 19/191; Bus Profs of Am; DECA; Drill Tm; Ofcr Sr Cls; Ofcr Stu Cncl; Vllybl; Hon Roll; NHS; Pres Schlr; SADD; YES Tlnt Srch Schlrshp Prog; Mark Of Excllnc; Mntr; KSKCC; Law Enf.

ALLEN, ANGIE M; Basehor Linwood HS; Bonner Springs, KS; (4); French Clb; VP FBLA; Girl Scts; Math Clb; Office Aide; Teachers Aide; Hon Roll; U Of KS; Children Dr.

ALLEN, ANGIE R; Norwich HS; Norwich, KS; (3); 6/16; Church Yth Grp; FCA; Quiz Bowl; SADD; Band; Chorus; Flag Corp; Mrchg Band; School Musical; Variety Show; Kayettes; Worship Ldr.

ALLEN, BRAD T; Burlington HS; Burlington, KS; (2); Church Yth Grp; FBLA; Var L Ftbl; Hon Roll; Prfct Atten Awd.

ALLEN, CARRIE; Manhattan HS; Manhattan, KS; (4); FCA; French Clb; Pep Clb; Band; Mrchg Band; Pep Band; Ofcr Stu Cncl; JV Var Chrldng; Trk; Hon Roll; KS ST U; Scndry Ed.

ALLEN, ELESHA; Columbus HS; Scammon, KS; (4); 2/87; Bus Profs of Am; Church Yth Grp; Cmnty Wkr; FCA; FHA; Letterman Clb; Math Tm; Pep Clb; Quiz Bowl; Scholastic Bowl; Pittsburg State Unif; Nrsng/Med.

ALLEN, GLENDA; Newton Sr HS; Newton, KS; (4); 59/211; Cmnty Wkr; French Clb; FTA; Teachers Aide; Acpl Chr; Chorus; Church Choir; School Musical; JV Sftbl; JV Swmmng; Church Yth Choir Dir; Emporia ST U; Music Ed.

ALLEN, HEATHER; Wichita West HS; Wichita, KS; (4); 83/365; Church Yth Grp; Cmnty Wkr; DECA; Office Aide; Pep Clb; Red Cross Aide; ROTC; SADD; Teachers Aide; Chorus; U Of KS; Mass Commnctns.

ALLEN, HEATHER R; Nemaha Valley HS; Seneca, KS; (3); 18/48; Art Clb; Church Yth Grp; Teachers Aide; School Play; Stage Crew; Hon Roll; NHS; Prfct Atten Awd; KS Assn Youth Asst Pgm Dir; Forensics.

ALLEN, JENIFER A; Wichita East HS; Wichita, KS; (4); 5/300; Bus Profs of Am; DECA; Quiz Bowl; Teachers Aide; Sftbl; Vllybl; Hon Roll; Butler Cty CC; Elem Ed.

ALLEN, JENNIFER M; Sacred Heart HS; Salina, KS; (3); Church Yth Grp; Cmnty Wkr; FBLA; Teachers Aide; Sec Jr Cls; Var L Bsktbl; Powder Puff Ftbl; Var L Sftbl; Var L Vllybl; Wt Lftg; Swthrt Queen.

ALLEN, JOE M; Chanute Sr HS; Chanute, KS; (2); 1/300; Art Clb; Rep Church Yth Grp; Cmnty Wkr; English Clb; FCA; 4-H; French Clb; Math Clb; Math Tm; Pep Clb; Slng; Altr Srvr Cath Yth Org; Otstndng Tech Awd Frosh.

ALLEN, KUIANA; Sumner Acad Of Arts & Science; Kansas City, KS; (3); Latin Clb; Pep Clb; Spanish Clb; Band; Chorus; JV Var Chrldng; JV Trk; U Of MO Kansas City; Med.

ALLEN, QUENTIN T; Valley Falls HS; Valley Falls, KS; (3); Red Cross Aide; Band; Pep Band; Intrml Bsbl; Var L Bsktbl; Var L Ftbl; Intrml Gym; Intrml Swmmng; Var L Trk; Intrml Wt Lftg; Washburn Univ.

ALLEN, RACHEL E; Sumner Acad Of Arts & Science; Kansas City, KS; (2); Church Yth Grp; French Clb; French Hon Soc; High Hon Roll; Hon Roll; NHS; Psych.

ALLEN, RHONDA G; Labette Co HS; Oswego, KS; (2); 9/158; Church Yth Grp; FCA; FBLA; Church Choir; Bsktbl; Var Crs Cntry; Var Trk; High Hon Roll; Piano; UMYF Missions.

ALLEN, SARAH; Hays HS; Hays, KS; (4); 1/200; Cmnty Wkr; Hosp Aide; Ed Yrbk; Gov Hon Prg Awd; High Hon Roll; Jr NHS; NHS; St Schlr; Val; Intrnshp Local Vet; Tandy Tech Schlrs Acad Top 2 Percnt; Natl Schltc Press Assn InKC; Hnrb Mntn; KS ST U; Engrng.

ALLEN, TEIAH; Stafford Jr Sr HS; Stafford, KS; (4); 5/24; Church Yth Grp; FHA; HOBY; Yrbk; VP Jr Cls; Pres Sr Cls; Rep Stu Cncl; NFL; Pep Clb; Teachers Aide; FHA St VP 94-95, St Pres 95-96; Conf Cncl On Yth Ministries; KS U; Poltcl Sci.

ALLEN, TERESA; Syracuse Jr Sr HS; Syracuse, KS; (4); 2/29; Girl Scts; Speech Tm; Band; Chorus; School Play; Pres Soph Cls; Pres Jr Cls; Pres Sr Cls; Pres Rep Stu Cncl; NHS; Msct; U Of KS; Med.

ALLEN, TERESA A; Jefferson West HS; Ozawkie, KS; (1); 1/73; JV Bsktbl; Vllybl; High Hon Roll; Engl Hnr; Keybrding Hnr; Ortho Surg.

ALLEN, TONYA; Greensburg HS; Greensburg, KS; (4); 2/34; Library Aide; Ofcr Frsh Cls; Ofcr Soph Cls; Pres Jr Cls; Ofcr Sr Cls; Var Bsktbl; Var Vllybl; NHS; Pres Schlr; Sal; Northwestern OK ST U.

ALLEN, YVONNE L; Topeka West HS; Topeka, KS; (2); Cmnty Wkr; English Clb; French Clb; Model UN; Nwsp; Lit Mag; High Hon Roll; TEA Party Sec.

ALLER, TARYN; Hiawatha HS; Hiawatha, KS; (4); 3/87; Treas Church Yth Grp; Cmnty Wkr; FCA; Sec VP Natl FFA Org; Science Clb; Band; Mrchg Band; Cit Awd; Hon Roll; NHS; 94 FFA Russn Ldrshp Exch; 95 Bio Clb Fld Stdy; 95 KS St Lions Band; Highland CC; Agribus.

ALLERS, BRIDGET; Blue Valley North HS; Leawood, KS; (4); 19/173; FCA; Key Clb; Drill Tm; Crs Cntry; Socr; Trk; Vllybl; High Hon Roll; NHS; Pres Acad Fit Awd; Kay Clb; Wichita ST U; Phys Thrpy.

ALLEY, JOSHUA D; Blue Valley Northwest HS; Overland Park, KS; (2); Church Yth Grp; Computer Clb; Drama Clb; Science Clb; Spanish Clb; SADD; Acpl Chr; Chorus; School Musical; School Play.

ALLEYNE, KHALIL C; Topeka HS; Auburn, KS; (2); Hon Roll; Ntl Merit Ltr; Emory Univ; Pulmonologst.

ALLISON, AMANDA M; Riley Cty HS; Riley, KS; (3); FHA; Pep Clb; SADD; Teachers Aide; FHA Offcr; Manhattan Area Tech Ctr; RN.

ALLISON, ANDREA R; Lawrence HS; Lawrence, KS; (2); Chorus; Ger; Animals; Vllybl; Tnns; U Of KS; Plastic Surgeon.

ALLISON, DUSTIN L; Washburn Rural HS; Topeka, KS; (3); 46/370; FCA; Ftbl; Trk; Wt Lftg; Wrstlng; High Hon Roll; Hon Roll; Prfct Atten Awd; SMSU; Engrng.

ALLISON, TARA R; Wichita West HS; Wichita, KS; (3); 1/857; Cmnty Wkr; JA; Pep Clb; Band; Mrchg Band; Orch; Pep Band; School Musical; High Hon Roll; Bus Ed.

ALLISON-GALLIMORE, BOBBY; Home Schooled; Spring Hill, KS; (2); Am Leg Boys St; Pres 4-H; Pres JA; Chorus; Church Choir; School Musical; 4-H Awd; Cmnty Wkr; Orch; Hon Roll; Johnson Cty Mr 4-H; Natl 4-H Congress Delegate; Natl Assn Of Parliamentarians Mem.

ALLMON, CORTNEY C; Hutchinson HS; Hutchinson, KS; (2); Key Clb; Chorus; Drill Tm; Rep Frsh Cls; Rep Soph Cls; Rep Jr Cls; Bsktbl; Tennis; High Hon Roll; Prfct Atten Awd; Peer Hlpr; KS Univ.

ALLMON, DEANA; Ellsworth HS; Ellsworth, KS; (4); Cmnty Wkr; SADD; Varsity Clb; Chorus; Stage Crew; Swing Chorus; Rep Stu Cncl; Hon Roll; Church Yth Grp; Drama Clb; Kyts; Kyt Bd; Dstngd Schlstc Achvmt Awds; Ft Hays ST U; Cmptr/Info Systm.

ALLMOND, KENDA A; Pittsburg HS; Pittsburg, KS; (4); 17/165; Drama Clb; FHA; NFL; Thesps; Chorus; School Musical; School Play; Stage Crew; Rep Stu Cncl; NHS; Intl Ordr Rnbw Grls; Pittsburg ST U; Music Ed.

ALLOWAY, ASHLEY; Conway Springs HS; Conway Springs, KS; (3); 2/30; Ed Yrbk; VP Frsh Cls; Pres Soph Cls; Pres Jr Cls; Pres Stu Cncl; JV Var Chrldng; Pom Pon; JV Var Tennis; Hon Roll; NHS; Pres Clb; Steering Cmmtte; St Tennis 321-A Cmptn 6th Pl Singles.

ALLOWAY, ROBYN J; Labette Co HS; Parsons, KS; (2); Sec Church Yth Grp; FCA; FBLA; Natl FFA Org; SADD; Bsktbl; Sftbl; Tennis; High Hon Roll; PT.

ALLSUP, KELLY; Sterling HS; Sterling, KS; (4); 6/32; FHA; Red Cross Aide; Science Clb; Varsity Clb; Var Bsktbl; Var Vllybl; High Hon Roll; NHS; Art Clb; Church Yth Grp; Act Dir Big Bros/Big Srs; Drury Coll Springfield.

ALMELING, DAVID S; Washburn Rural HS; Topeka, KS; (2); Debate Tm; Socr; Tennis; High Hon Roll; Forensics.

ALMOS, HEIDI J; Garden City Sr HS; Garden City, KS; (1); Church Yth Grp; Cmnty Wkr; FHA; Spanish Clb; Band; Mrchg Band; Pep Band; Intrml Mgr Bsktbl; Hon Roll; KS U; Med.

ALONZO, STACY M; Topeka HS; Topeka, KS; (3); Church Yth Grp; Cmnty Wkr; Teachers Aide; Acpl Chr; Band; Chorus; Church Choir; Drill Tm; Jazz Band; Mrchg Band; Intnl Soccer USA 4 Summers; KS ST Olympic Dev Team Soccer; Schlrshp KA Univ Mdwstrn Music Camp; Liberal Arts.

ALSOP, BETSY; Garden City Sr HS; Garden City, KS; (4); 37/330; Am Leg Aux Girls St; Debate Tm; Hosp Aide; Model UN; NFL; Speech Tm; Crs Cntry; Swmmng; Hon Roll; Kiwanis Awd; KSU; Speech Coach.

ALSTON, DOUG R; Wichita East HS; Wichita, KS; (2); German Clb; Band; Mrchg Band; Orch; Hon Roll; Ger NHS; KS All St Orch; Veterans Admin Vol.

ALSTROM, ANGIE J; Hoxie HS; Hoxie, KS; (4); 6/34; Church Yth Grp; Cmnty Wkr; FCA; FHA; GAA; Natl FFA Org; Speech Tm; Teachers Aide; Band; Chorus; STAND; KSU; Marine Biology.

ALT, KATIE; Abilene HS; Abilene, KS; (2); 1/118; FCA; Spanish Clb; Chorus; Stage Crew; VP Soph Cls; Var Chrldng; JV Tennis; High Hon Roll; Hon Roll; Piano; Dolphins; Marine Bio.

ALTEVOGT, GRETCHEN; Wabaunsee HS; Alma, KS; (1); Church Yth Grp; FBLA; FHA; Pep Clb; Speech Tm; Var L Bsktbl; Powder Puff Ftbl; Var L Sftbl; JV Vllybl; High Hon Roll.

ALTHOUSE, ANDREA L; El Dorado HS; El Dorado, KS; (3); FCA; Letterman Clb; Math Clb; NFL; SADD; Varsity Clb; Orch; Ed Yrbk; Mgr(s); Powder Puff Ftbl.

ALTMAN, CHRISTY L; Blue Valley Northwest HS; Overland Park, KS; (2); 209/430; Church Yth Grp; Drama Clb; Pep Clb; School Play; Stage Crew; Hon Roll; KS Univ.

ALTOBELLO, STEVE; Manhattan HS; Manhattan, KS; (4); 98/385; Chess Clb; Science Clb; Spanish Clb; Band; Mrchg Band; Pep Band; Intrml Bsktbl; Var L Ftbl; L Trk; Intrml Vllybl; KS ST U; Vet.

ALVA, MICHAEL R; Washburn Rural HS; Topeka, KS; (3); 57/350; Ofcr Sr Cls; Var L Tennis; High Hon Roll; Hon Roll; KS Univ.

ALWIN, MARC S; Colby Sr HS; Colby, KS; (2); Boy Scts; Church Yth Grp; Spanish Clb; Bsktbl; Eagle Prjct.

AMANI-TALESHI, AZADEH; Shawnee Mission N HS; Shawnee Mission, KS; (4); 82/347; Cmnty Wkr; German Clb; Letterman Clb; Pep Clb; Varsity Clb; Ofcr Stu Cncl; Var Chrldng; Var Socr; Var Tennis; Wt Lftg; Jewish Womn Intnl Cert Of Recgntn; All-Amer Chrldr Awd; Top 10 Homcmng & Spring Ct Candidate; LUC; Pre-Med.

AMARO, JOHN A; Olathe East Sr HS; Olathe, KS; (2); Letterman Clb; Spanish Clb; Variety Show; Intrml Bsbl; JV Ftbl; Wt Lftg; Var Wrstlng; Hon Roll; Dfnsv Lnmn Of Yr Frosh Yr; Bus/Dntstry.

AMAYA, ISABEL; Pierson Jr HS; Kansas City, KS; (1); Drill Tm; Bsktbl; JV Var Trk; Vllybl; High Hon Roll; Hon Roll; Jr NHS; Pres Schlr; Prtcptd March/Dimes Walk Amer; Peer Mediator; Chem Eng.

AMBORN, ANDY; Olathe North Sr HS; Olathe, KS; (3); FCA; French Clb; Drill Tm; Variety Show; Rep Sr Cls; Bsktbl; Powder Puff Ftbl; Var Cmnty Wkr; Trk; French Hon Soc.

AMBRISTER, TAMRA; Heights HS; Wichita, KS; (4); 84/252; Church Yth Grp; VP CAP; Pep Clb; Teachers Aide; Varsity Clb; Swmmng; Hon Roll; Water Safety Instrctr; Life Guard Cert; KS ST U; Scndry Ed.

AMERIN, CORY I; Stanton Co HS; Johnson, KS; (1); Church Yth Grp; Bsktbl; Crs Cntry; Trk; High Hon Roll; Smmr Bsktbl Trvlng Team SW Sundevils.

AMERSHEK, AUSTIN L; Southeast HS; Mc Cune, KS; (3); 3/65; Church Yth Grp; Math Tm; Scholastic Bowl; Var Bsbl; Bsktbl; Var Ftbl; Wt Lftg; Hon Roll; NHS; KY ST; Eng.

AMES, JEREMY R; Derby HS; Derby, KS; (2); Drama Clb; Pep Clb; Varsity Clb; Acpl Chr; Chorus; School Musical; Wt Lftg; High Hon Roll; Prfct Atten Awd; Wichita ST Univ; Fire Fighter.

AMES, NATALIE A; Downs HS; Downs, KS; (1); Pep Clb; Band; Chorus; Mrchg Band; Pep Band; High Hon Roll; Hon Roll; Story Publshd HS Wrtr; K ST; Psychtrst.

AMES, SHARI; Clearwater HS; Clearwater, KS; (3); Letterman Clb; SADD; Band; Chorus; Rep Stu Cncl; Capt Chrldng; Score Keeper; Hon Roll; Relay For Life; Hutchinson CC.

AMEY, BENJAMIN L; Wichita Heights HS; Wichita, KS; (4); 6/240; Capt Quiz Bowl; Chorus; JV Var Bsktbl; Hon Roll; Pres NHS; Ntl Merit SF; Boy Scts; Church Yth Grp; German Clb; SADD; KS Regents Hnrs Acad; Sci Olympia; IA ST U; Elec Engrng.

AMMAR, ALEX S; Wichita East HS; Wichita, KS; (4); Art Clb; Cmnty Wkr; French Clb; Acpl Chr; Chorus; Orch; School Musical; Variety Show; Rep Frsh Cls; Rep Soph Cls; Intl Baccalaureate; Douglas Express Singers Fndr/Dir; Centerstage Co Perfmr; Northwestern Univ; Msc.

AMMERMAN, JESSICA Q; Circle HS; El Dorado, KS; (2); FCA; Chorus; School Musical; Variety Show; Var Bsktbl; JV Sftbl; JV Vllybl; Hon Roll.

AMON, PATRICK L; Holton HS; Holton, KS; (2); Letterman Clb; Rep Soph Cls; Var L Bsktbl; Var L Ftbl; Var L Golf; Cit Awd; Hon Roll; Prfct Atten Awd; Amer Lgn Bsbl Ptchr/Shrtstp/Clean Up Bttr.

AMOS, MATT; Andale HS; Goddard, KS; (1); Church Yth Grp; SADD; Bsktbl; Var Crs Cntry; Trk; Hon Roll; AYSO Sccr; Sp Olympcs Vol; U Of KS.

AMPHONE, BOUAVONE; Wichita East HS; Wichita, KS; (2); Church Yth Grp; Debate Tm; Teachers Aide; Bsktbl; Vllybl; Hon Roll; Washburn Univ; Law.

AMRSTRONG, BRANDI; Garden City Sr HS; Garden City, KS; (4); Church Yth Grp; NFL; Thesps; Band; School Play; Lit Mag; High Hon Roll; NHS; Pres Acad Fit Awd; Drama Clb; Var Dance Tm; Bible Stdy; Sterling Coll.

AMSAUGH, ALICIA; Acad Of Mt St Scholastica; Atchison, KS; (3); 2/50; Cmnty Wkr; GAA; NFL; Pep Clb; Chorus; VP Frsh Cls; Bsktbl; Vllybl; High Hon Roll; Pres Schlr; Spnsh Awds; Benedictine Coll; Clncl Psych.

AMSBAUGH, ALICIA M; Acad Of Mt St Scholastica; Atchison, KS; (3); Cmnty Wkr; NFL; Pep Clb; Chorus; School Musical; VP Frsh Cls; Bsktbl; Vllybl; High Hon Roll; NHS; Span Awds; All Lge Hnrble Mntn Vllbll; U Of KS; Elem Ed.

ANCIAUX, SARA A; Blue Valley Northwest HS; Overland Park, KS; (4); 50/343; FCA; Teachers Aide; Varsity Clb; Ofcr Jr Cls; Ofcr Sr Cls; Bsktbl; Var Co-Capt Tennis; NHS; SW MO ST; Bus.

ANDERS, PAUL W; Wichita East HS; Wichita, KS; (2); Church Yth Grp; Crs Cntry; Trk; NHS; Japanese Clb.

ANDERSEN, SUSAN R; Moundridge HS; Moundridge, KS; (2); Church Yth Grp; FCA; Pep Clb; Band; Chorus; Mrchg Band; Pep Band; School Musical; Mgr(s); Sftbl.

ANDERSON, ADRIAN C; Sumner Acad Of Arts & Science; Kansas City, KS; (1); Boy Scts; Church Yth Grp; Cmnty Wkr; Office Aide; Teachers Aide; Band; Mrchg Band; Pep Band; Rep Frsh Cls; Rep Soph Cls; Yth Tchr Sunday Schl; Ftbl Awds; Comp & Electronics; FL ST Univ; Comp; Elctrncs Spc.

ANDERSON, ADRIANNE M; Shawnee Mission Nw Sr HS; Lenexa, KS; (3); 30/428; Treas Pres Art Clb; Church Yth Grp; Model UN; NFL; Teachers Aide; Socr; High Hon Roll; NHS; Yth In Govt; Govt; Psych.

ANDERSON, ASHLEY; Hillcrest Schl; Agenda, KS; (1); VP 4-H; Sec Pep Clb; Speech Tm; Band; Drill Tm; Jazz Band; Mrchg Band; Pep Band; Pres Frsh Cls; JV Bsktbl; KPHA Resrv Chmpn Yth; APHA; Med.

ANDERSON, BECKY; Derby HS; Derby, KS; (4); 42/345; Ofcr DECA; Teachers Aide; VICA; Rep Stu Cncl; Mgr Bsbl; Mgr Bsktbl; High Hon Roll; NHS; Pres Acad Fit Awd; Pres Schlr; Wichita ST U; Elem Ed.

ANDERSON, BOBBY J; Smoky Valley HS; Mc Pherson, KS; (2); Chorus; Hon Roll; PT.

ANDERSON, BRIAN; Shawnee Mission N HS; Merriam, KS; (3); 3/370; Debate Tm; Treas NFL; Pep Clb; Spanish Clb; Cit Awd; High Hon Roll; NHS; Ntl Merit Ltr; FBI Agt.

ANDERSON, BRYCE A; Wichita Northwest HS; Wichita, KS; (3); Bus Profs of Am; Church Yth Grp; Acpl Chr; Rckt Clb; Wichita ST Univ; Bus Admin.

ANDERSON, CHABLISE R; Wichita South HS; Wichita, KS; (4); 22/294; Church Yth Grp; Church Choir; High Hon Roll; NHS; Prfct Atten Awd; KS Hnr Schlr; Butler Cnty CC:ED.

ANDERSON, CHRIS A; Pittsburg HS; Pittsburg, KS; (1).

ANDERSON, CHRISTOPHER R; Galena HS; Galena, KS; (2); Church Yth Grp; Letterman Clb; Math Tm; Quiz Bowl; L Var Bsbl; Var L Bsktbl; JV Ftbl; Acctng.

ANDERSON, CRISTY R; Berean Acad; Valley Center, KS; (3); Letterman Clb; Scholastic Bowl; Spanish Clb; Drill Tm; School Play; Ed Yrbk; VP Soph Cls; Bsktbl; Vllybl; High Hon Roll; KS ST Univ.

ANDERSON, DARIN; Iola Sr HS; Iola, KS; (3); Office Aide; Var Crs Cntry; Mgr(s); Score Keeper; Trk; Cit Awd; Hon Roll; Prfct Atten Awd; Pres Acad Fit Awd; KS ST; Food Sci.

ANDERSON, DAVID R; St John's Military Schl; Westminster, CO; (2); Chess Clb; ROTC; DAR Awd; High Hon Roll; Blue Beret Clb; Spartans Clb.

ANDERSON, ERICK J; Hutchinson HS; Hutchinson, KS; (1); Boy Scts; Church Yth Grp; Key Clb; Scholastic Bowl; Spanish Clb; High Hon Roll; Prfct Atten Awd; Pres Acad Fit Awd.

ANDERSON, ERIKA; Leroy HS; Westphalia, KS; (3); 1/21; Am Leg Aux Girls St; Church Yth Grp; Quiz Bowl; Band; Chorus; Bsktbl; Trk; Vllybl; High Hon Roll; Ozark Chrstn Coll; Ed.

ANDERSON, GILLIAN N; Maize HS; Wichita, KS; (1); NFL; Thesps; Chorus; Variety Show; Hon Roll; Karate Martial Arts; U Of KS.

ANDERSON, ISAAC; Shawnee Mission Northwest Schl; Lenexa, KS; (4); Church Yth Grp; Cmnty Wkr; Teachers Aide; Band; Mrchg Band; Pep Band; Bsktbl; JV Socr; High Hon Roll; Hon Roll; Young Life; KS ST Univ.

ANDERSON, JASON; Clay Ctr Cmty HS; Green, KS; (3); Am Leg Boys St; Church Yth Grp; Natl FFA Org; Ofcr Bsbl; Bsktbl; Hon Roll.

ANDERSON, JASON K; Galena HS; Galena, KS; (1); Church Yth Grp; FHA; Quiz Bowl; JV Bsktbl; JV Golf; Mgr(s); Hon Roll; Prfct Atten Awd.

ANDERSON, JASON P; Wichita East HS; Wichita, KS; (2); Library Aide; Hon Roll; Bsbel SW Boys Clb Right Fielder.

ANDERSON, JOY R; Salina HS Central; Salina, KS; (4); 62/228; Church Yth Grp; Cmnty Wkr; Debate Tm; Drama Clb; NFL; SADD; Teachers Aide; Church Choir; Orch; School Musical; Spec Olympcs Cch; Prsbytry N KS Yth Cncl Rep & Hist; Hbt Hmnty Vol; Sterling Coll Sterling; Med.

ANDERSON, KANDIS; Goodland HS; Goodland, KS; (2); 15/100; Church Yth Grp; FHA; Varsity Clb; School Musical; Pres Soph Cls; Var Crs Cntry; Wt Lftg; Prom Server; U Of KS.

ANDERSON, KATIE M; Basehor Linwood HS; Basehor, KS; (2); Church Yth Grp; Cmnty Wkr; VP NFL; Spanish Clb; SADD; Variety Show; JV Vllybl; Hon Roll; Smmr Sftbl Team 10 Yrs; Dance/Gymnstc Outside Schl; Reach; KS U; Med.

ANDERSON, LINDSAY J; Jefferson West HS; Topeka, KS; (2); FTA; Letterman Clb; Teachers Aide; Drill Tm; Ofcr Jr Cls; Bsktbl; Pom Pon; Hon Roll.

ANDERSON, MEGAN; Andover HS; Andover, KS; (1); 1/216; Pep Clb; Band; Jazz Band; Mrchg Band; Pep Band; Yrbk; Chrldng; High Hon Roll; Hon Roll; Pres Schlr.

ANDERSON, MELVA; Wyandotte HS; Kansas City, KS; (3); Church Yth Grp; Cmnty Wkr; Hosp Aide; Orch; High Hon Roll; NHS; Med Careers Clb.

ANDERSON, MINDY L; Newton Sr HS; Newton, KS; (3); 6/250; Church Yth Grp; Cmnty Wkr; VP French Clb; Hosp Aide; Key Clb; Orch; L Var Golf; High Hon Roll; NHS; KS Univ; Bus Admin.

ANDERSON, MIRANDA J; Humboldt HS; Humboldt, KS; (3); Teachers Aide; Chorus; PSU; Elem Ed.

ANDERSON, NATE; Blue Valley Northwest HS; Overland Park, KS; (2); 1/418; Church Yth Grp; Var Socr; Var Trk; High Hon Roll; Jr Irish U-17 Sccr Champs 96; Arch.

ANDERSON, NIKITA L; Wichita East HS; Wichita, KS; (2); Chorus; Hon Roll.

ANDERSON, PETER J; Newton Sr HS; Newton, KS; (4); Am Leg Boys St; Church Yth Grp; SADD; Teachers Aide; Band; Pep Band; Nwsp; Var L Ftbl; Var L Trk; KS ST Univ; Commnctns.

ANDERSON, RACHAEL E; Shawnee Mission E Sr HS; Prairie Village, KS; (2); French Clb; Chorus; Var Gym; Intrml Socr; Hon Roll; Art; Clb Gymnastics; KS City Art Inst; Architecture.

ANDERSON, RYAN S; Hays HS; Hays, KS; (1); Church Yth Grp; JV Ftbl; JV Wt Lftg; L High Hon Roll; U Of CO; Wldlf Blgst.

ANDERSON, SCOTT; Manhattan HS; Manhattan, KS; (3); 123/433; Am Leg Boys St; FCA; NFL; Chorus; School Musical; Swing Chorus; Variety Show; Var L Golf; Hon Roll; NHS; Westminster Coll; Law.

ANDERSON, SCOTT C; Bishop Miege HS; Kansas City, MO; (4); 14/165; Church Yth Grp; Cmnty Wkr; Acpl Chr; School Musical; School Play; Phtg Yrbk; VP Stu Cncl; Bsktbl; Var Crs Cntry; Var Golf; Aquinas Awd; KS Hnrs Schlr; Donkey Talk; Miami U Of OH; Bus.

ANDERSON, SHANNON R; Pierson Jr HS; Kansas City, KS; (1); Art Clb; Thesps; School Play; Rep Stu Cncl; Wrtng Poems/Short Stories; Read Books; Art; Artist/Wrtr/Archlgst.

ANDERSON, STARR; Hillsboro HS; Hillsboro, KS; (3); 13/65; Band; Nwsp; Nwsp; Var Chrldng; Var Crs Cntry; High Hon Roll; NHS; Cmnty Wkr; German Clb; Chorus; Natl Hnr Roll; All Amer Schlstc Schlr; Fort Hays ST; Bus.

ANDERSON, TERESA M; Thayer HS; Thayer, KS; (3); Drama Clb; FCA; Scholastic Bowl; Speech Tm; Thesps; School Play; Phtg Yrbk; Sec Frsh Cls; Sec Soph Cls; Sec Jr Cls; NCCC; Acctng.

ANDERSON, VERNE Y; Sumner Acad Of Arts & Science; Kansas City, KS; (1); Girl Scts; Chorus; Ofcr Stu Cncl; Bsktbl; Girl Scouts Silver Awd; MAT 7 Score Abv Avg; Ansthslgy Dr.

ANDRA, KELLY M; Shawnee Mission Nw Sr HS; Lenexa, KS; (4); 1/400; Pep Clb; SADD; Var L Bsktbl; Var L Crs Cntry; Var L Trk; High Hon Roll; NHS; Ntl Merit Schol; Pres Acad Fit Awd; St Chmpn 3200 M Run & St Rnnr-Up 1600 M Run 95; Crss Cntry St Rnnr-Up & Leag Chmpn 95; Tandy Stu; Med.

ANDRE, ASHLEY C; Shawnee Mission N HS; Shawnee, KS; (1); Church Yth Grp; Hosp Aide; Pep Clb; Band; Hon Roll; Chrch Drama; Yth Drama Chrch; Veterinarian.

ANDREWS, DEIADRE D; Wyandotte HS; Kansas City, KS; (2); Resp Thrpy.

ANDREWS, JOSHUA S; El Dorado HS; El Dorado, KS; (2); 7/177; Drama Clb; FCA; NFL; SADD; Church Choir; School Musical; Var Mgr(s); Swmmng; NHS; NEMA Natl Engl Merit Awd Wnnr; ENCORE Show Choir; KS St Univ; Lwyr.

ANDREWS, KERI; Columbus HS; Columbus, KS; (3); Bus Profs of Am; FCA; 4-H; VP FHA; Sec Stu Cncl; Var Bsktbl; Golf; Var Trk; Hon Roll; NHS; Brice/Verna Durbin Ldrshp Awd; KS ST U.

ANDREWS, KIMBERLY M; Salina HS South; Salina, KS; (3); 123/256; Church Yth Grp; Cmnty Wkr; Office Aide; SADD; Teachers Aide; Band; Spec Olympcs; Habitat For Humnty; Admin.

ANDREWS, SARAH; Spring Hill HS; Olathe, KS; (2); Church Yth Grp; Cmnty Wkr; Debate Tm; NFL; Spanish Clb; Band; Mrchg Band; Pep Band; Stage Crew; Bsktbl; 6 Yrs Chldrns Dept Chrch; Bronze Cngrsnl Awd; HOBY Awd; Law.

ANDREWS, STEPHANIE; Columbus HS; Columbus, KS; (3); 14/115; FHA; GAA; Treas Frsh Cls; Sec Soph Cls; Sec Jr Cls; Treas Sr Cls; Stat Bsktbl; Powder Puff Ftbl; Sftbl; Trk; Pittsburg ST U; Scndry Ed.

ANDREWSON, RACHEL A; Mc Pherson HS; Mc Pherson, KS; (2); Church Yth Grp; Spanish Clb; Mgr(s); Stat Socr; Var Vllybl; Cit Awd; Hon Roll; Bd Mbr Teen Ctr; Chldcr Head Start Prgm/Spec Needs Chldrn; Elem Ed.

ANDUSS, MINDY; Peabody-Burns Jr Sr HS; Peabody, KS; (3); Church Yth Grp; Cmnty Wkr; Letterman Clb; SADD; Varsity Clb; Band; Chorus; Church Choir; Mrchg Band; Pep Band; Anatomy; Music; K U; Pre-Med; Phy Thrpst.

ANEJA, TIA; Wichita East HS; Wichita, KS; (3); Cmnty Wkr; Hosp Aide; Intnl Clb; JA; Letterman Clb; Office Aide; Q&S; Red Cross Aide; SADD; Teachers Aide; Law; Psych; Medicine.

ANGELL, SARAH S; Gardner-Edgerton HS; Edgerton, KS; (4); 21/109; FBLA; Spanish Clb; Band; School Musical; Rep Sr Cls; Rep Stu Cncl; High Hon Roll; Hon Roll; Pres Acad Fit Awd; Spanish NHS; Natural Hlprs; Hnr Bnd; Pensacola Christian Coll; El Ed.

ANGELO, MATT D; Blue Valley Northwest HS; Overland Park, KS; (3); Key Clb; Ski Clb; Bsktbl; Socr; Tennis; High Hon Roll; Hon Roll; NHS; Bus.

ANGELO, TOM J; Kapaun-Mt Carmel HS; Wichita, KS; (2); Boy Scts; School Musical; Stage Crew; JV Ftbl; JV Trk; JV Wrstlng; Hon Roll; Jr NHS; Eagle Sct Awd Boy Scts; Math Tutor Jr HS Stdntsf; U Of KS; Bio/Gntcs.

ANGLE, MELISSA; Wichita NW HS; Wichita, KS; (2); 63/300; L Debate Tm; Q&S; L Speech Tm; Ed Nwsp; Rep L Frsh Cls; Rep Soph Cls; Ofcr Stu Cncl; Vllybl; High Hon Roll; Pres Acad Fit Awd; Mus Instrmnt; Natl Frnsic Lge Mmbr; Poli Sci.

ANNELER, TY L; Central Christian Schl; Hutchinson, KS; (4); 8/18; Church Yth Grp; Drama Clb; Teachers Aide; Varsity Clb; Sec Stu Cncl; Var Bsktbl; Hon Roll; Amer Lgn Schl Awrds; Hutchinson CC; Acctng.

ANNELER, TYRELL L; Central Christian Schl; Hutchinson, KS; (4); 8/18; Church Yth Grp; Drama Clb; Teachers Aide; Varsity Clb; Sec Stu Cncl; L Bsktbl; Cit Awd; Hon Roll; Amrcn Legn Cert; Hutchinson JC; Bus Mgnt.

ANSCHULTZ, MELISSA; Hays HS; Hays, KS; (4); 18/231; Am Leg Aux Girls St; Debate Tm; NFL; Speech Tm; Nwsp; Sec Stu Cncl; Hon Roll; NHS; Church Yth Grp; Teachers Aide; Natl Forensics League Pres & Sec; U Of KS; Medicine.

ANSCHUTZ, CARL E; Great Bend Sr HS; Great Bend, KS; (3); 3/255; Cmnty Wkr; Drama Clb; German Clb; Intnl Clb; Band; Jazz Band; Mrchg Band; Pep Band; Stage Crew; Variety Show; Ger Stdnt Exch Prgm; Natl Yth Ldrshp Med Forum; Dstngshd Schlstc Achvmt Awd; U Of KS; Pre-Med.

ANSCHUTZ, CYNTHIA D; Great Bend Sr HS; Great Bend, KS; (1); Cmnty Wkr; Drama Clb; German Clb; Intnl Clb; Service Clb; Band; Color Guard; Flag Corp; Mrchg Band; Pep Band; Distngshd Schlstc Achvmt; Pep/Cncrt Bands Awds; KS Univ; Pedtrcn/Psychtrst.

ANSCHUTZ, JOSHUA B; Great Bend Sr HS; Great Bend, KS; (1); Boy Scts; Church Yth Grp; Pep Clb; Band; Chorus; Mrchg Band; Pep Band; Hon Roll; KS ST Univ; Vet.

ANSCHUTZ, JUDITH Y; Russell HS; Gorham, KS; (1); Church Yth Grp; 4-H; Acpl Chr; Band; Chorus; Mrchg Band; Pep Band; School Musical; Variety Show; Lit Mag.

ANSCHUTZ, MELISSA; Hays HS; Hays, KS; (4); 19/231; Am Leg Aux Girls St; Debate Tm; Pres NFL; Speech Tm; Nwsp; Sec Stu Cncl; Hon Roll; NHS; Church Yth Grp; Teachers Aide; KU Hnr Schlr; Pr Lit Tutr; U Of KS; Med.

ANSLEY, JERROD R; Garden City Sr HS; Garden City, KS; (1); Church Yth Grp; Drama Clb; FCA; Math Tm; Band; School Play; Stage Crew; Ftbl; Golf; Wt Lftg; Little Lg Bsbl Coach; Univ Of KS; Sprts Brdcstng.

ANSLEY, MICHELLE; Olathe South Sr HS; Olathe, KS; (4); 22/384; GAA; Var Capt Sftbl; JV Var Vllybl; High Hon Roll; Hon Roll; NHS; St Schlr; NW MO ST.

ANSPAUGH, JODIE; Washburn Rural HS; Topeka, KS; (3); 37/351; Cmnty Wkr; French Clb; Hosp Aide; Pres Intnl Clb; SADD; Band; Mrchg Band; Orch; Pep Band; JV Socr; Treas Marien Explr Post 712 Scubadiving Club.

ANSPAUGH, KIRSTEN G; Salina HS Central; Salina, KS; (3); Drama Clb; Teachers Aide; Band; Mrchg Band; Pep Band; School Play; Stage Crew; Hon Roll; KS ST Univ; Psych/Meteorlogy.

ANSTAETT, TAYLOR; Deerfield HS; Garden City, KS; (4); 12/25; Church Yth Grp; FHA; Office Aide; Pep Clb; Teachers Aide; Thesps; Band; Mrchg Band; Pep Band; School Play; Forensics; Dodge City CC; Athltc Trng.

ANTES, EMILY; Atchison Sr HS; Atchison, KS; (1); Church Yth Grp; French Clb; Band; Mrchg Band; Pep Band; Golf; Vllybl; High Hon Roll; Highland CC; Dntst/Dntl Hygnst.

ANTHONY, DANA M; Shawnee Mission W Sr HS; Shawnee Mission, KS; (3); 39/415; Church Yth Grp; Intnl Clb; Lit Mag; Crs Cntry; Socr; NHS; Comm Svc; Intnl Bus/Japanese.

ANTHONY, TIFFANY; Summer Acad; Kansas City, KS; (2); French Clb; JCL; Latin Clb; Chorus; Hon Roll; NYU; French Interpreter.

ANTHONY, TYAUNA C; Highland Park HS; Topeka, KS; (2); Cmnty Wkr; JA; Office Aide; SADD; Teachers Aide; Yrbk; Pom Pon; Powder Puff Ftbl; Score Keeper; Wt Lftg; Univ; Photogrphr.

ANTISDEL, KATIE; Louisburg HS; Louisburg, KS; (2); Bus Profs of Am; Letterman Clb; Pep Clb; Spanish Clb; SADD; Chorus; Variety Show; JV Bsktbl; Var Chrldng; Var Sftbl; Equestrian; KS U; Med.

ANTONE, LORI R; Wichita East HS; Wichita, KS; (2); German Clb; Teachers Aide; Chrldng; Trk; Hon Roll; Ger NHS; PT/SPRTS Med.

ANTONIO, MICHELLE; Peabody-Burns Jr Sr HS; Peabody, KS; (4); 10/31; Letterman Clb; Varsity Clb; Mrchg Band; School Musical; Ed Nwsp; Var Bsktbl; Var Chrldng; Var Sftbl; Var Vllybl; NHS; Whichita ST Univ; Dntl Hygiene.

ANTRIM, AMY B; Salina HS Central; Salina, KS; (3); Church Yth Grp; Drama Clb; Teachers Aide; Thesps; Chorus; School Musical; Stage Crew; JV Vllybl; Jr Ldrshp.

ANTROBUS, CHRIS M; Olathe East Sr HS; Overland Park, KS; (2); Am Leg Boys St; Natl Beta Clb; Spanish Clb; SADD; Ofcr Bsbl; Trk; Wt Lftg; High Hon Roll; Hon Roll; NHS.

APPEL, MEAGAN J; Liberal HS; Liberal, KS; (3); Am Leg Aux Girls St; Art Clb; Church Yth Grp; Cmnty Wkr; Thesps; School Musical; School Play; Ed Yrbk; Hon Roll; Kiwanis Awd; Jr Ldrshp Liberal; Webster U; Jrnlsm.

APPIER, ERIC; Frontenac Jr Sr HS; Frontenac, KS; (4); 5/36; Art Clb; Spanish Clb; Teachers Aide; Varsity Clb; Var L Bsktbl; Var Ftbl; High Hon Roll; NHS; Prfct Atten Awd; Pres Acad Fit Awd; Eagle Sct 94; Comp Sci.

APPLE, ALLISON D; Louisburg HS; Louisburg, KS; (2); Sec Art Clb; Letterman Clb; Spanish Clb; SADD; Phtg Yrbk; Treas Frsh Cls; Treas Soph Cls; Treas Jr Cls; Var L Sftbl; Hon Roll.

APPLEBAUM, JEREMY; Blue Valley Northwest HS; Overland Park, KS; (3); Q&S; Temple Yth Grp; Phtg Yrbk; Var Crs Cntry; JV Trk; Hon Roll; Sec NHS; Bnai Brith Yth Org; Comm Svc; Law; Bus.

APPLEBEE, CRYSTAL; Concorida HS; Concordia, KS; (4); 1/100; Debate Tm; Drama Clb; Science Clb; Spanish Clb; Speech Tm; Varsity Clb; Acpl Chr; School Musical; Swing Chorus; Pres Frsh Cls; Cloud County CC; Optmtry.

APPLEGARTH, HEATHER M; Washington HS; Washington, KS; (2); French Clb; FBLA; Band; Chorus; JV Vllybl; High Hon Roll; St KS Schlrshp Tsts; Ft Hays St Math Rlys; Natl Frnch Cncrd; Phys Thrp.

APPLEGATE, PAMELA; Piper HS; Kansas City, KS; (2); FHA; GAA; Mgr(s); Sftbl; Vllybl; Cit Awd; High Hon Roll; Hon Roll; Jr NHS; Smmr Leag Sftbl; Baker ST; PE Tchr.

APPLEQUIST, EMILY; Mc Pherson HS; Mc Pherson, KS; (1); Church Yth Grp; Band; JV Var Chrldng; JV Trk; High Hon Roll; Pres Phys Ftnss Awd; Gymnstcs; Sccr; Swm Tm; Flute; KS U; Phys Ed.

APPS, MELISSA; Sedgwick HS; Sedgwick, KS; (4); 2/24; Am Leg Aux Girls St; Capt Quiz Bowl; Band; Ed Nwsp; Ed Yrbk; Pres VP Stu Cncl; Bsktbl; High Hon Roll; Treas NHS; Prncpls Ldrshp, Jrnlsm & Eng Awds; KS ST U; Jrnlsm.

AQUILAR, CRYSTAL; Emporia HS; Emporia, KS; (2); Church Yth Grp; Bsktbl; Chrldng; Vllybl; High Hon Roll; Hon Roll; Kayettes; Rec Sftbl; Cheer Camp NCA; KS U; Bus.

AQUILAR, YOLANDA; J C Harmon HS; Kansas City, KS; (4); 25/201; Am Leg Aux Girls St; Cmnty Wkr; FCA; Girl Scts; Service Clb; Pres Spanish Clb; Band; Vllybl; Hon Roll; NHS; Psych.

ARANDA, JEANNETTE; Elkhart HS; Elkhart, KS; (3); 10/35; Church Yth Grp; Cmnty Wkr; Hosp Aide; HOBY; Pres Frsh Cls; Var Bsktbl; Var Trk; High Hon Roll; Hon Roll; NHS; OK Pnhndl ST U; Law.

ARANJO III, TIMO; Olathe North Sr HS; Olathe, KS; (4); 10/351; Am Leg Boys St; VP Debate Tm; Math Tm; NFL; Pres Science Clb; Band; Mrchg Band; Pep Band; Capt Crs Cntry; Trk; Eric Dowell Forensics Awd Outstdng Sr Forensics; HS Outstdng Sr Math/Sci Dean Of Engrng Awd; KS ST; Chem Engr.

ARBEC, MICHELLE; Columbus HS; Hallowell, KS; (3); 16/91; FHA; Teachers Aide; High Hon Roll; Hon Roll; Drftng Club; Wrtn Titans Sec; U Of KS; Aerospace Engr.

ARBUCKLE, REBECCA A; Wichita East HS; Wichita, KS; (3); 17/274; Chorus; School Musical; Variety Show; VP Frsh Cls; Pres Soph Cls; Var Capt Pom Pon; High Hon Roll; NHS; Untd Way Wallace Yth Vntr Grnt Comm; NCA Dnc All-Amer; Vol Work; U Of KS.

ARCHER, ERIN J; Anderson Cty Jr Sr HS; Garnett, KS; (1); Intnl Clb; SADD; Bsktbl; Vllybl; DAR Awd; High Hon Roll; Octgn Clb; Kay Clb; Gftd Ed; Dgpnd Clb; Ansthslgst.

ARCHER, KEVIN W; Lyons HS; Lyons, KS; (2); Art Clb; Pep Clb; Phtg Yrbk; Ofcr Bsbl; Bsktbl; Golf; Hon Roll; NHS; Soph Server At Jr-Sr Prom; Rod & Gun Clb; KS ST Univ.

ARCHER, VADA A; Clearwater HS; Wichita, KS; (4); Letterman Clb; SADD; Teachers Aide; Chorus; School Play; Stage Crew; Trk; Vllybl; Hon Roll; Kayettes Vp; Cowley Cty Comm Coll; Phy Ftnss.

ARCHIE, CHARLENE A; Junction City HS; Junction City, KS; (3); Church Yth Grp; Cmnty Wkr; Cit Awd; Hon Roll; Sndy Schl Tchr; Pres Of Chrch Yth Grp; Albany St Col; Nurs.

ARD, DAN J; Wellsville Jr Sr HS; Wellsville, KS; (2); Boy Scts; Treas Drama Clb; FCA; Math Tm; Band; Mrchg Band; Stage Crew; Ftbl; High Hon Roll; Rec Soccer; Cmptr Sci/Tech.

ARD, KEVIN L; Maize HS; Maize, KS; (2); 1/250; Church Yth Grp; FCA; German Clb; Math Tm; NFL; Scholastic Bowl; Science Clb; Church Choir; Var Crs Cntry; NHS; Future Prblm Slvng; Sci Olympiad; Bio/Eng.

ARDERY, RUSTIN; South Gray HS; Copeland, KS; (2); Church Yth Grp; Cmnty Wkr; 4-H; HOBY; Letterman Clb; Spanish Clb; JV Bsktbl; Var Ftbl; Var Trk; Cit Awd.

AREA, KRYSTAL; Shawnee Heights Sr HS; Topeka, KS; (2); Church Yth Grp; Debate Tm; Girl Scts; Pep Clb; SADD; Orch; Var Chrldng; High Hon Roll; NHS; Cmnty Church Drama Team; Concordia Coll; Chrstn Ed Admn.

AREBALO, LISA M; Wellington Sr HS; Wellington, KS; (2); Church Yth Grp; Chorus; JV Bsktbl; JV Sftbl; JV Var Vllybl; Hon Roll; Friends Univ.

AREHEART, BRADLEY; Emporia HS; Emporia, KS; (3); Am Leg Boys St; FCA; VP FBLA; VP NFL; Pres Stu Cncl; Var Ftbl; NHS; US Senate Page In Wash DC For US Senator Thurmond; Attnd Amer Acad Of Achvmt.

ARELLANO, CHRIS; Hugoton HS; Hugoton, KS; (3); 10/69; Church Yth Grp; Rep Stu Cncl; Var Bsbl; Var Bsktbl; Var Ftbl; Cit Awd; High Hon Roll; Hon Roll; NHS; Pres Acad Fit Awd; Ftbl All-League 1st Tm Hnrb Mntn, All-Area 1st Tm Hnrb Mntn & Outstndg Bck; Bsbl Offnse Plyr Of Yr; KS U; Law.

ARENDT, KATHLEEN J; Colby Sr HS; Colby, KS; (2); Church Yth Grp; FCA; Spanish Clb; SADD; Chorus; School Play; Variety Show; Rep Soph Cls; Var Chrldng; Miss High Plains Teen Pageant; Sweet Adelines; Bible Clb; Washburn; Law.

ARENSDORF, CHERYL M; Bishop Carroll Catholic HS; Wichita, KS; (3); 3/176; Debate Tm; Quiz Bowl; Acpl Chr; Church Choir; Rep Frsh Cls; High Hon Roll; Hon Roll; NHS; Ntl Merit Ltr; Church Yth Grp; US House Of Reps Page.

ARGOSINO, SHEILA F; Wichita Collegiate Schl; Wichita, KS; (4); Drama Clb; Hosp Aide; Chorus; School Play; Yrbk; Golf; Tennis; Hon Roll; Homecoming Queen; U Of San Diego.

ARIAS, JOSE; Great Bend Sr HS; Great Bend, KS; (3); Am Leg Boys St; German Clb; Pep Clb; Teachers Aide; Chorus; Hon Roll; Kiwanis Awd; Folk Dance Pres; Cinco De Mayo Comm Clb; Outdoor Soccer; KS ST.

ARKENBERG, LOGAN J; Shawnee Heights HS; Tecumseh, KS; (2); Church Yth Grp; JV Bsbl; Crs Cntry; Trk; Wrstlng; High Hon Roll; Hon Roll; KS U.

ARMIJO, PHILLIP A; El Dorado HS; El Dorado, KS; (2); Church Yth Grp; Debate Tm; FCA; NFL; Spanish Clb; Stage Crew; Phtg Yrbk; Diving; Ftbl; Swmmng; KS Assn Yth VP; Med.

ARMOUR, LINDSEY F; Olpe Schl; Olpe, KS; (2); Pep Clb; JV Vllybl; Hon Roll; NHS.

ARMSTRONG, ALLISON B; Wichita Heights HS; Wichita, KS; (3); 23/250; Am Leg Aux Girls St; Church Yth Grp; Q&S; Chorus; Variety Show; Ed Yrbk; Rep Stu Cncl; L Var Pom Pon; JV Sftbl; High Hon Roll; U Of KS; PT.

ARMSTRONG, BEVERLY; Frankft HS; Frankfort, KS; (4); 12/29; Am Leg Aux Girls St; FHA; Girl Scts; Library Aide; SADD; Yrbk; Rptr Stu Cncl; Var L Bsktbl; Var L Vllybl; Hon Roll; Emporia ST U; Phys Thrp.

ARMSTRONG, BRADLEY P; Topeka HS; Topeka, KS; (3); Cmnty Wkr; Debate Tm; Latin Clb; Model UN; NFL; Ed Nwsp; Cit Awd; High Hon Roll; NHS; Child Psych.

ARMSTRONG, BRANDI; Garden City Sr HS; Garden City, KS; (4); 37/314; Church Yth Grp; Drama Clb; NFL; Thesps; Band; School Play; Lit Mag; High Hon Roll; NHS; FHA; Dance Team; Sterling Coll; Theater Arts.

ARMSTRONG, CHRISTINE M; Dodge City HS; Dodge City, KS; (3); 65/350; Cmnty Wkr; Drama Clb; SADD; Acpl Chr; Chorus; School Musical; School Play; Sftbl; Wt Lftg; Hon Roll; Jr Ldrshp Dodge; Madrigals Singing Group; Music Perfmnc.

ARMSTRONG, JAY R; Wichita Southeast HS; Wichita, KS; (2); Boy Scts; Church Yth Grp; Debate Tm; Var Bsbl; JV Bsktbl; Prfct Atten Awd; Brigham Young Univ; Law.

ARMSTRONG, JEFFREY A; Ft Scott HS; Fort Scott, KS; (3); 1/140; Am Leg Boys St; FCA; Key Clb; Science Clb; Var Bsktbl; Var Capt Crs Cntry; Var Tennis; Var Trk; Hon Roll; NHS; MO Rolla; Civil Engrng.

ARMSTRONG, MATT; Campus HS; Haysville, KS; (3); Am Leg Boys St; Church Yth Grp; Intnl Clb; Q&S; Quiz Bowl; Scholastic Bowl; Speech Tm; Nwsp; Ofcr Stu Cncl; Hon Roll; 2nd Pl At St Jrnlsm Cont In Advertising Dsgn; U Of KS; Advertising Dsgn.

ARMSTRONG, MATT D; Topeka HS; Topeka, KS; (3); Cmnty Wkr; Var Mgr Bsktbl; Var Mgr(s); High Hon Roll; NHS; Jc Penney Gldn Rule Awd Nominee; Athltc Trng.

ARMSTRONG, SALENA R; Topeka HS; Topeka, KS; (3); Teachers Aide; High Hon Roll; Schlsp From Concordia Lang Village In MN; Office Admin.

ARMSTRONG, SHANE M; Garden City Sr HS; Garden City, KS; (2); Chess Clb; Church Yth Grp; Var Ftbl; Var Mgr(s); Wt Lftg; Hon Roll.

ARNDT, RYAN R; Emporia HS; Emporia, KS; (2); 22/327; FCA; 4-H; JV L Ftbl; Var L Wrstlng; Cit Awd; High Hon Roll; Whos Who Amer HS Ath; KS ST Univ; Ag.

ARNETT, ANGELA M; Bonner Springs HS; Bonner Springs, KS; (3); 9/120; Church Yth Grp; Quiz Bowl; SADD; Varsity Clb; Acpl Chr; Chorus; Church Choir; School Musical; Stage Crew; Bsktbl; PEER; 4 Yr Coll; Prfrmr.

ARNETT, MATT; Dodge City HS; Dodge City, KS; (1); JV Bsbl; Bsktbl; KS ST U; Banking.

ARNETT, TRESSA D; Pratt HS; Pratt, KS; (3); HOBY; Ed Yrbk; Treas Frsh Cls; Pres Soph Cls; VP Jr Cls; Sec Stu Cncl; Var Sftbl; High Hon Roll; Pres NHS; JV Tennis; 1st Pl Div Wnnr In KS Fedrl Jr Duck Stamp Dsgn Cont; League Smmr Yrs 92 & 94; Red Crss Safty Instr.

ARNETTE, DEANA; Olathe East Sr HS; Overland Park, KS; (3); Art Clb; Cmnty Wkr; Dance Clb; Drama Clb; Girl Scts; Hosp Aide; Letterman Clb; Pep Clb; Teachers Aide; VICA; Cert Nurs Asst; KS St Univ; Racing Boats.

ARNHOLD, COLLEEN M; Trinity Catholic HS; Hutchinson, KS; (1); 7/38; Debate Tm; 4-H; Band; Chorus; Mrchg Band; Pep Band; Sec Frsh Cls; Bsktbl; Golf; Tennis; 1st In Horticulture Judging At St, 14th Individually & 6th Team In Nation; Art Awd; Horticulture.

ARNHOLD, LEAH; Miltonvale HS; Marion, KS; (2); 1/10; 4-H; HOBY; Letterman Clb; NFL; Pep Clb; Quiz Bowl; Band; Chorus; Mrchg Band; Pep Band; 2nd ST Bio-Emoria Schlrshp Tests; Cty Champion 4-H Photo/Woodwrkng; Pharmcst/Bus.

ARNOLD, AUDRA A; Maize HS; Wichita, KS; (2); 75/300; Church Yth Grp; Hon Roll; Play Piano 12 Yrs; Num Music Auditions Wichita ST Univ; Wichita ST Univ; Bus Admin.

ARNOLD, BECKY; Ashland HS; Ashland, KS; (4); Office Aide; Pep Clb; Speech Tm; Chorus; School Musical; Yrbk; Bsktbl; Chrldng; Crs Cntry; Golf; 1st Annual Clark Cty Fair Queen 94; Sidneys Schl Of Hair/Design.

ARNOLD, DARLITA; Leroy HS; Le Roy, KS; (1); 1/16; Quiz Bowl; Scholastic Bowl; Pres Frsh Cls; High Hon Roll; KS U; Dr.

ARNOLD, DAYLA; Leroy HS; Le Roy, KS; (4); 1/16; Am Leg Aux Girls St; Hosp Aide; Math Tm; Quiz Bowl; Speech Tm; Chorus; School Musical; Gov Hon Prg Awd; High Hon Roll; Hon Roll; Nursng.

ARNOLD, EMANUEL J; Junction City HS; Junction City, KS; (2); Boy Scts; German Clb; Pep Clb; ROTC; Varsity Clb; Orch; JV Bsktbl; Var Socr; Hon Roll; Presdntl Phys Ftnss Awd; K-ST; Law Enfrcmt.

ARNOLD, EMILY S; Baldwin HS; Baldwin City, KS; (4); Letterman Clb; Pep Clb; Bsktbl; Vllybl; High Hon Roll; NHS; St Schlr; Regeants Scholar; KS Univ.

ARNOLD, JOSH T; Wellsville Jr Sr HS; Wellsville, KS; (1); FBLA; Hon Roll; NHS; Oceangrpr.

ARNOLD, KELLIE M; Washburn Rural HS; Wakarusa, KS; (4); 10/268; Cmnty Wkr; French Clb; Band; Variety Show; Phtg Yrbk; Intrml Bsktbl; Powder Puff Ftbl; JV Var Socr; High Hon Roll; NHS; Piano Conts; Lifeguard; Lettered 4 Yrs In Acads; KS ST Univ; Engrng.

ARNOLD, LAURIE A; Baxter Springs HS; Baxter Springs, KS; (3); 4/50; Church Yth Grp; FCA; FHA; Girl Scts; Scholastic Bowl; Band; Treas Jr Cls; Treas Sr Cls; Var L Trk; NHS; Bus.

ARNOLD, LISA R; Shawnee Mission Nw Sr HS; Lenexa, KS; (3); 96/460; Cmnty Wkr; Hosp Aide; Intnl Clb; Teachers Aide; Band; Mrchg Band; Crs Cntry; Hon Roll; Karate Instr; 6th Rank Blue Belt; Flute; Speech Pathology; Audiology.

ARNOLD, NATHAN B; Midway Schl; Bendena, KS; (3); 3/25; Church Yth Grp; FCA; Letterman Clb; Quiz Bowl; Chorus; School Play; Nwsp; Pres Frsh Cls; Pres Soph Cls; Var L Bsktbl; Med/Missnry.

ARNOLD, STEPHANIE; Baldwin HS; Baldwin City, KS; (1); Church Yth Grp; FHA; Chorus; Church Choir; JV Chrldng; JV Vllybl; Marine Bio.

ARNOLD, TIMOTHY; Washington HS; Kansas City, KS; (4); German Clb; Office Aide; KS Univ; CPA.

ARNOTT, SARAH J; Olathe East Sr HS; Lenexa, KS; (2); Sec Church Yth Grp; Pep Clb; Spanish Clb; Band; Chorus; Capt Drill Tm; School Musical; L Pom Pon; High Hon Roll; Hon Roll; Dance At Studio & Perform At Several Charity; KS Univ; Ed.

ARRAMBIDE, KATE; St Thomas Aquinas HS; Overland Park, KS; (2); 57/280; FCA; French Clb; Hosp Aide; Key Clb; Pep Clb; Church Choir; Chrldng; Diving; Powder Puff Ftbl; Hon Roll; Jr Vol St Jo Hlth Ctr; CPR Cert Amer Red Cross.

ARRINGTON, ASHLEY; Rose Hill HS; Rose Hill, KS; (3); SADD; Lawyer/Dsgnr.

ARTMAN, BETH A; El Dorado HS; El Dorado, KS; (2); Church Yth Grp; FCA; French Clb; Math Clb; Math Tm; SADD; Orch; JV Bsktbl; Mgr(s); Powder Puff Ftbl; ST Music Festival Superior Rating; Auditioned/Awd Acceptance Wichita Yth Symphony 2 Yrs; Cmptr Engrg/Mngmt.

ARZATE, MERCEDES; Emporia HS; Emporia, KS; (2); Band; Chorus; Church Choir; Mrchg Band; Pep Band; Red Belt In Tae Kwon Do; White Belt In Hap Ki Do; Play Piano; Dancing Lessons; Psych.

ASCHENBRENNER, JOHN W; Colby Sr HS; Colby, KS; (4); Drama Clb; French Clb; Science Clb; SADD; Band; Chorus; Jazz Band; Mrchg Band; Pep Band; Hon Roll.

ASHBURN, JAYLON M; Troy HS; Troy, KS; (2); Boy Scts; Church Yth Grp; Cmnty Wkr; Drama Clb; Letterman Clb; Natl FFA Org; School Play; Stage Crew; JV Bsktbl; Var Ftbl; Mic-O-Say; Life Rank In Boy Scts.

ASHBY, JENNIFER L; Southeast HS; Wichita, KS; (4); 68/232; Church Yth Grp; Teachers Aide; Acpl Chr; Chorus; Church Choir; Variety Show; Hon Roll; Ntl Merit Ltr; U Of KS.

ASHCRAFT, DESIREE J; Hutchinson HS; Hutchinson, KS; (3); 63/290; DECA; Teachers Aide; Hon Roll; Prfct Atten Awd; Psych.

ASHCRAFT, DIANE P; Andale HS; Colwich, KS; (2); Church Yth Grp; Letterman Clb; Spanish Clb; Band; Mrchg Band; Pep Band; Trk; Hon Roll; Zoology/Marine Bio.

ASHCRAFT, LEANNA; Field Kindley Mem Sr HS; Coffeyville, KS; (2); French Clb; German Clb; Var L Chrldng; Swmmng; Hon Roll; All Trnmt Chrldr; Best All Around Frosh Chrldr; Washington Univ; Comp Prgmr.

ASHER, AMANDA K; Great Bend Sr HS; Great Bend, KS; (3); Rep Spanish Clb; Acpl Chr; Band; Jazz Band; Mrchg Band; Swing Chorus; Variety Show; High Hon Roll; Church Yth Grp; Chorus; 1st Alt 2nd Plc In St RMTA Pianoaudtn; 1st Plc In Parnassus Clb Piano Audtns; I Rating At St Piano; Bethany Col; Mus Ed.

ASHER, JANA; Turner HS; Kansas City, KS; (3); Rep FHA; SADD; Chorus; Rep Stu Cncl; Mgr(s); Hon Roll; Univ KS; RN.

ASHER, RACHEL; Ottawa HS; Ottawa, KS; (4); Am Leg Aux Girls St; HOBY; Service Clb; Spanish Clb; School Play; Variety Show; Yrbk; Ofcr Stu Cncl; Chrldng; High Hon Roll; KS U; Bus.

ASHFORD, AMY A; Bonner Springs HS; Bonner Springs, KS; (3); 1/189; Office Aide; Band; Mrchg Band; Pep Band; Var Chrldng; Var Trk; JV Vllybl; Hon Roll; Rtry Intl Schol Awd; SADD Clb; KS St Univ; Anml Sci.

ASHLEY, TARA; Jefferson West HS; Ozawkie, KS; (3); 10/83; Church Yth Grp; Drama Clb; FBLA; FHA; FTA; Spanish Clb; SADD; Chorus; School Play; Stage Crew; Emporia ST; Elem Ed.

ASHMORE, CHRISTIE; Syracuse Jr Sr HS; Syracuse, KS; (3); Am Leg Aux Girls St; Chorus; Church Choir; Bsktbl; Chrldng; Crs Cntry; Powder Puff Ftbl; 4-H Awd; Hon Roll; Letterman Clb; Miss Hmltn Cnty 1995-96; Ag.

ASHTON, EMILY L; Salina HS South; Salina, KS; (2); Debate Tm; NFL; Yrbk; Sec Soph Cls; Pres Jr Cls; Pom Pon; Swmmng; Cit Awd; Hon Roll; Pres Acad Fit Awd; Young Woman Cls 98 Rep; Optimist Oratorical Awd 2nd Pl; Show Troupe Dance Team; KS ST Univ; Soc Work.

ASHTON, KATHRYN A; Shawnee Heights Sr HS; Topeka, KS; (2); Church Yth Grp; Cmnty Wkr; Debate Tm; NFL; Orch; Chrldng; High Hon Roll; Hon Roll; Lang Arts/Sci/Frgn Lang/Math Acad Awds; KS ST Histrcl Soc Summer Yth Vol; Ed/ESL.

ASHWORTH, AMANDA L; Topeka West HS; Topeka, KS; (4); Art Clb; Rptr Yrbk; Hon Roll; SADD; U Of KS; Mktg.

ASKREN, NICHOLAS; Garden City Sr HS; Garden City, KS; (4); 21/313; Church Yth Grp; Math Tm; Band; Jazz Band; Mrchg Band; Pep Band; High Hon Roll; Pres Acad Fit Awd; Garden City CC.

ASKREN, NIKKI; Jackson Heights HS; Netawaka, KS; (3); 4-H; FBLA; FHA; Pep Clb; SADD; Chorus; School Musical; Bsktbl; Vllybl; Hon Roll.

ASLIN, LINDSEY; Shawnee Mission E Sr HS; Shawnee Mission, KS; (3); Church Yth Grp; Varsity Clb; Jazz Band; Orch; School Musical; Var L Swmmng; Hon Roll; Swmmng St Champ & Rcrd Hldr.

ASQUITH, AARON R; Olathe South Sr HS; Olathe, KS; (3); Cmnty Wkr; Letterman Clb; Teachers Aide; Varsity Clb; Band; Jazz Band; Mrchg Band; Phtg Nwsp; Phtg Yrbk; Ftbl; Phtgrphy; Top 16 Awds ST Swmmng Mt; Bus/Advrtsng.

AST, BOB; Kapaun-Mt Carmel HS; Wichita, KS; (2); 15/200; Debate Tm; Hosp Aide; Q&S; Quiz Bowl; Sprt Ed Nwsp; High Hon Roll; Print Media.

AST, JASON M; Conway Springs HS; Conway Springs, KS; (3); 6/32; Church Yth Grp; Quiz Bowl; Var Bsktbl; JV Ftbl; Var Tennis; High Hon Roll; Hon Roll; NHS; KS Univ; Sports Med.

AST, JULIETTE; Wichita East HS; Wichita, KS; (3); Phtg Nwsp; Cmnty Wkr; Dance Clb; JA; Chorus; School Musical; Pom Pon; High Hon Roll; NHS; Natl Ger Hnrs Soc VP; Hangar Bd; Acad Lttr 96; Intl Bcclrt; Pre-Med/Bus Admin.

ASTEN, STACY L; Bonner Springs HS; Kansas City, KS; (4); 35/135; Quiz Bowl; Scholastic Bowl; SADD; Teachers Aide; Flag Corp; Pep Band; Var L Mgr(s); Hon Roll; Acad Decath; ROTC Schol; KCKCC Pres Schol; Xavier Univ; Mltry Nurs.

ATHA, SCOTT W; Washburn Rural HS; Topeka, KS; (3); 14/351; Church Yth Grp; Math Tm; Model UN; Ed Nwsp; VP Frsh Cls; Pres Soph Cls; Var Ftbl; Var Golf; High Hon Roll; NHS; Stu Brd Pres Of KS Schol Press Assoc; U Of KS.

ATKINSON, ANDREA; White City HS; White City, KS; (4); 3/11; Office Aide; Quiz Bowl; SADD; Teachers Aide; VP Frsh Cls; Pres Stu Cncl; High Hon Roll; Hon Roll; NHS; Peer Helpers; Gov Ctr Teen Ldrshp Grp; Cloud Cty CC; Medcl Sec.

ATKINSON, BRADLEY J; White City HS; White City, KS; (3); Quiz Bowl; Scholastic Bowl; SADD; School Musical; School Play; Stage Crew; Nwsp; Yrbk; Rep Stu Cncl; Var Ftbl; Pre-Med.

ATKINSON, JAYME; Iola Sr HS; Iola, KS; (4); 2/95; Cmnty Wkr; FBLA; Service Clb; Spanish Clb; SADD; Rep Stu Cncl; Var Capt Crs Cntry; Var Trk; High Hon Roll; NHS; Phy Ther.

ATKINSON, NICOLE D; Wichita North HS; Wichita, KS; (4); Office Aide; Acpl Chr; Band; Church Choir; Jazz Band; Mrchg Band; Pep Band; Variety Show; Cit Awd; Hon Roll; Base Clb; Gspl Choir Sec; Wichita ST U; Crmnl Law.

ATLAS, JONATHAN B; Shawnee Mission E Sr HS; Shawnee Mission, KS; (3); 35/420; Natl Beta Clb; Q&S; Ed Nwsp; Pres Sr Cls; Intrml Bsktbl; French Hon Soc; High Hon Roll; NHS; Intnl Clb; Latin Clb; Co-Chm Of House That East Built Hab For Hum House; Intnl Baccalaureate Pgm; Bus; Medicine.

ATTAR, ROULA T; NW HS Wichita; Wichita, KS; (4); 1/365; Debate Tm; Pres Intnl Clb; Math Clb; Office Aide; Red Cross Aide; Scholastic Bowl; School Play; Socr; NHS; Val; PTSA Sec; Audit Tm; Untd Way Vol; Wichita St Univ; Law.

ATTARZADEH, CHUCK H; Wichita Southeast HS; Wichita, KS; (2); 1/437; Cmnty Wkr; French Clb; Service Clb; Orch; Ofcr Bsbl; Hon Roll; NHS; His; Hiking; Bsbl; Architecture.

ATWOOD, JENNIFER E; Smoky Valley HS; Lindsborg, KS; (1); Drama Clb; Thesps; School Musical; School Play; Stage Crew; Chrldng; Tennis; Hon Roll.

ATWOOD, JOHN C; Osawatomie HS; Osawatomie, KS; (1); Church Yth Grp; Science Clb; Chorus; School Musical; School Play; Variety Show; Ofcr Stu Cncl; Intrml Bsbl; High Hon Roll; Pres Acad Fit Awd; Emporia ST; Elem Tchr/Engr.

AUBERT, JARED J; Marmaton Valley Jr Sr HS; La Harpe, KS; (2); 2/30; 4-H; Math Tm; Band; Pep Band; JV Golf; High Hon Roll; Tech Stdnts Assn; KS ST; Engrng.

AUDIESS, HAILEY M; Chanute Sr HS; Chanute, KS; (2); Church Yth Grp; Spanish Clb; Varsity Clb; Var Sftbl; Hon Roll.

AUFDEMBERGE, KATY L; Basehor Linwood HS; Basehor, KS; (2); High Hon Roll; Prfct Atten Awd; Sci Olympiad; REACH; Acad Excl Awd.

AUGUSTINE, BARRON D; Thomas More Prep-Marion HS; Hays, KS; (4); Church Yth Grp; Crs Cntry; Trk.

AUGUSTINE, CHRISTOPHER S; Salina HS South; Salina, KS; (3); Ftbl; Wt Lftg; Wrstlng; High Hon Roll; Hon Roll; NHS; Prfct Atten Awd; Pres Acad Fit Awd; KA ST Univ; Acctng.

AUGUSTINE, GRETCHEN M; Thomas More Prep-Marion HS; Hays, KS; (1); 25/75; Church Yth Grp; Varsity Clb; Chorus; Chrldng; Crs Cntry; Trk; Hon Roll.

AUGUSTINE, RACHELLE; Buhler HS; Hutchinson, KS; (3); 4-H; FHA; HOBY; Church Choir; School Musical; 4-H Awd; High Hon Roll; Church Yth Grp; Chorus; Variety Show; Cmnty Thtr; Spec Olympcs Cch/Vol; Soph Sngrs Shw Choir; Med.

AUGUSTINE, SARAH; Thomas More Prep-Marion HS; Ellis, KS; (4); 5/93; Church Yth Grp; 4-H; Model UN; Band; Church Choir; School Musical; Ed Nwsp; Sftbl; Var Vllybl; Ntl Merit SF; TX A&M U; Mrn Bio.

AUGUSTINE, SHANNON C; Thomas More Prep-Marion HS; Ellis, KS; (2); Church Yth Grp; 4-H; HOBY; Band; Church Choir; School Musical; Co-Ed Nwsp; JV Vllybl; Cit Awd; Local Chldcr Ctr Vol; Washington DC Prtst Agnst Abrtn Trip; Annl Pro-Life March; Hmls Shltr Vol; Elem/Spec Ed.

AUGUSTINE, TARA A; Ellis HS; Ellis, KS; (4); 20/40; Church Yth Grp; FHA; Band; Chorus; Mrchg Band; Pep Band; School Play; Phtg Yrbk; Vllybl; Kayettes Treas; U Of KS; Photojrnlsm.

AUMAN, LISA E; Riverton Schl; Riverton, KS; (4); 2/56; Church Yth Grp; Cmnty Wkr; FHA; Math Clb; Science Clb; School Play; JV Vllybl; High Hon Roll; NHS; Sal; PSU; Occptnl Thrpy.

AUNE, JENNA; Wabaunsee HS; Alma, KS; (1); Church Yth Grp; FHA; Rptr Nwsp; Lit Mag; Powder Puff Ftbl; JV Tennis; Hon Roll; Ntl Merit Schol; 3rd Pl St Short Story Wrtng Cont.

AUSBORN, CODY; Sublette HS; Sublette, KS; (1); Church Yth Grp; Ofcr Bsbl; Bsktbl; High Hon Roll.

AUSBORN, RYAN; Sublette HS; Sublette, KS; (2); Church Yth Grp; Debate Tm; NFL; High Hon Roll; KS Assn Yth; AFS.

AUSTIN, JENNIFER A; Bishop Miege HS; Prairie Village, KS; (2); 37/163; Sec Stu Cncl; High Hon Roll; Campus Ministry Team Peer Helper; KU.

AUSTIN, JEREMY C; Parsons HS; Parsons, KS; (2); 10/143; Pres FTA; Pres Spanish Clb; Pres SADD; Jazz Band; VP Stu Cncl; Mgr(s); Tennis; High Hon Roll; NHS; Prfct Atten Awd; Sports Clb; Pre-Med.

AUSTIN, KALA; Lansing HS; Lansing, KS; (1); Church Yth Grp; Cmnty Wkr; 4-H; Office Aide; Pep Clb; Teachers Aide; Band; VP Frsh Cls; Var Chrldng; Hon Roll; Kayetts Clb; KS ST; Nursng.

AUTRY, NICHOLAS A; Baxter Springs HS; Baxter Springs, KS; (2); Church Yth Grp; 4-H; French Clb; Var Golf; High Hon Roll; Gifted Ed Pgm; Med.

AUXTER, ARIANNA M; Independence HS; Independence, KS; (1); Church Yth Grp; Orch; Pres Frsh Cls; Pres Soph Cls; Bsktbl; Powder Puff Ftbl; Swmmng; Vllybl; Pittsburgh ST; Sports Medicine.

AVALOS, TONI; Wellington Sr HS; Wellington, KS; (2); Church Yth Grp; Key Clb; Pep Clb; Red Cross Aide; Band; Mrchg Band; Pep Band; Var Crs Cntry; JV Trk; Hon Roll; Emporia ST U.

AVERILL, CECILIA; Atchison Sr HS; Atchison, KS; (2); 1/121; Cmnty Wkr; Debate Tm; Quiz Bowl; School Musical; School Play; Ed Nwsp; Rep Frsh Cls; Rep Soph Cls; Hon Roll; Odyssey Of Mind Rgnl Wnnr; Natl Hstry Day Rgnl Wnnr; Voice Of Dmcrcy Essay Dist Wnnr; KS U; Cardiothrc Srgn.

AVERY, CANDICE B; Wichita Southeast HS; Wichita, KS; (3); 71/378; Bsktbl; Hon Roll; Multicultural Group; Leo Clb; Black Awareness Group; TX Southern Univ; Law; Psych.

AVERY, MARY E; Manhattan HS; Manhattan, KS; (4); Cmnty Wkr; 4-H; FBLA; Spanish Clb; SADD; JV Bsktbl; JV Sftbl; Var Tennis; High Hon Roll; Jr NHS; Medcl Explr; HS Rodeo; FL ST; Pre-Med.

AVERY, TAWNY C; Salina HS Central; Salina, KS; (3); Teachers Aide; Wt Lftg; Hon Roll; Tae Kwon Do; K-ST.

AVEY, RACHEL E; Bishop Carroll Catholic HS; Wichita, KS; (3); Debate Tm; Hon Roll.

AVILA, BLANCA E; Liberal HS; Liberal, KS; (3); Church Yth Grp; Bsktbl; Tennis; Vllybl; Hon Roll; MVP Tennis; SCCC.

AVILA, JOSE E; Wichita East HS; Wichita, KS; (2); French Clb; German Clb; Swmmng; Hon Roll; NHS; Intl Bcclrt Prgm; Exchng Stdnt Ger; Eng.

AVILA, VICENTE; Derby HS; Derby, KS; (2); Church Yth Grp; FCA; Church Choir; Ftbl; Swmmng; Hon Roll.

AXMAN, JENNIFER M; Larned HS; Larned, KS; (2); Church Yth Grp; Band; Mrchg Band; Vllybl.

AYERS, ERIN ELIZABETH; Berean Christian Schl; Olathe, KS; (4); 1/8; Church Yth Grp; Chorus; School Musical; Rep Stu Cncl; Capt Bsktbl; Capt Vllybl; High Hon Roll; Ntl Merit Ltr; Pres Acad Fit Awd; Val; Amer Chrstn Hnrs Scty; Sterling Coll.

AYERS, SUMMER; Derby HS; Derby, KS; (4); 37/341; Church Yth Grp; Drama Clb; SADD; Thesps; Sec Frsh Cls; Sec Soph Cls; Co-Capt Var Chrldng; High Hon Roll; NHS; Pres Schlr; Cowler Cty CC Pres Schlsp; Natl Yth Ldrshp Forum On Medicine; Kay Clb; U Of KS; Medicine.

AYERS, ZACHERY J; Ingalls Jr Sr HS; Cimarron, KS; (2); Bus Profs of Am; 4-H; Natl FFA Org; Pep Clb; Band; Pep Band; JV Bsktbl; Sftbl; Wt Lftg; Hon Roll; FFA Speech Awd; Sci.

AYRES, CHARLES; Shawnee Mssn E HS; Prairie Village, KS; (4); 21/500; Dance Clb; Drama Clb; Intnl Clb; Natl Beta Clb; Thesps; School Musical; School Play; Stage Crew; High Hon Roll; Hon Roll; AFS; Sister Cty Exchang Stu; Geo Washingtonuniv; Asian Stds.

AYRES, JOHN; Washburn Rural HS; Topeka, KS; (3); 5/351; Debate Tm; HOBY; JA; Model UN; JV Bsktbl; Var L Crs Cntry; Var L Tennis; High Hon Roll; NHS; KS Bd Rgnts Hnrs Acad; Ken Berry & Babe Ruth Bsbl; US Naval Acad; Law.

AZEMBER, JILL S; Girard HS; Girard, KS; (4); 1/69; Spanish Clb; SADD; Teachers Aide; School Play; Var Chrldng; Var Golf; High Hon Roll; NHS; Pres Acad Fit Awd; Ku Hnr Schlr; Ft Scott CC.

BABCOCK, GRACE; Circle HS; Towanda, KS; (3); Acpl Chr; Band; Chorus; Church Choir; Mrchg Band; Pep Band; School Musical; School Play; Variety Show; High Hon Roll; Reg St Music Fest Sup Rtngs; Vcl Hnr Choir; U Fest HS Band.

BABER, PHILLIP; Central Christian Schl; Hutchinson, KS; (3); 2/14; Church Yth Grp; Debate Tm; Quiz Bowl; School Play; Rptr Nwsp; Rep Frsh Cls; Rep Soph Cls; Rep Jr Cls; Pres Sr Cls; Pres Stu Cncl; Natl Young Ldrs Conf DC 96; Radio Talk Show Host/MC Frosh Yr; Sterling Coll; Theology.

BACA, SUZANNE; St John Jr Sr HS; Saint John, KS; (1); Key Clb; Pep Clb; SADD; Band; Jazz Band; Pep Band; School Musical; Var L Crs Cntry; Var L Trk; Var Wt Lftg; ST Cross Cntry 14th Pl; ST Track 10th Pl; Regnl CC Track 3rd Pl.

BACCUS, MINDY K; Minneapolis HS; Ada, KS; (2); 1/63; Church Yth Grp; Debate Tm; French Clb; VP FHA; Math Clb; Quiz Bowl; Speech Tm; Band; School Play; KS Rgnts Hnr Acad; Law.

BACH, BRAD; Jetmore HS; Jetmore, KS; (3); 2/21; Boy Scts; Church Yth Grp; FCA; Natl FFA Org; Quiz Bowl; Scholastic Bowl; Thesps; Hon Roll; Var Bsktbl; Var Ftbl; Nom Wendys HS Heisman Schlrshp; KY ST; Cmptr Engrg.

BACH, HUYEN N; Newton Sr HS; Newton, KS; (4); Art Clb; Spanish Clb; Ofcr Jr Cls; Crs Cntry; Sftbl; High Hon Roll; HS Art Shows Ribbons; Big Brothers & Big Sisters; Whitewing Schlsp; Washburn U; Bio.

BACHERT, JENNIFER J; Oak Grove Baptist Schl; Kansas City, KS; (3); 5/12; Church Yth Grp; Letterman Clb; School Play; Rep Frsh Cls; JV Bsktbl; Capt L Chrldng; Var L Vllybl; Cit Awd; Hon Roll; Pres Acad Fit Awd; Chrstn Chrctr Awd Cls, Chrldng; Sci Fair; Teen Apprntc Pgm; Elem Ed.

BACHMAN, AMY D; Hesston HS; Newton, KS; (1); Church Yth Grp; FCA; Quiz Bowl; Band; Chorus; Jazz Band; Pep Band; Vllybl; High Hon Roll; Acad Dcthln; Mssnry Pilot.

BACHMAN, CHRIS J; Field Kindley Mem Sr HS; Coffeyville, KS; (1); French Clb; German Clb; Var Bsbl; Bsktbl; Crs Cntry; Hon Roll; Prfct Atten Awd; U KS.

BACHMAN, RICHARD A; Bishop Carroll Catholic HS; Wichita, KS; (2); Art Clb; FCA; Spanish Clb; Var Crs Cntry; Var Trk; Indian Hills Swm Tm; Commrcl Art.

BACHUS, MEECHIE; Sumner Acad; Kansas City, KS; (1); Debate Tm; French Clb; Pep Clb; Church Choir; Orch; Chrldng; Howard Univ; Airnautical Eng.

BACKES, THOMAS D; Kapaun-Mt Carmel HS; Wichita, KS; (1); Church Yth Grp; Debate Tm; Math Clb; Math Tm; Spanish Clb; JV Crs Cntry; Wichita ST U Chem 111 5 Hrs Credit; Currently Enrolled In Chem 112 5 Hrs Credit.

BACKUES, STEVEN K; Garden City Sr HS; Garden City, KS; (1); Chess Clb; Church Yth Grp; Quiz Bowl; Band; Chorus; Church Choir; School Play; High Hon Roll; Prin Hnr Rl; Outstndng Sci Stdnt; Math Relays; Sci Olympiad; Genetics.

BACON, ANNE; Topeka HS; Topeka, KS; (1); Church Yth Grp; Letterman Clb; Pep Clb; Band; Chorus; Mrchg Band; School Musical; Tennis; Hon Roll; Fearless Clb.

BACON, LANA R; South Haven Schl; Wellington, KS; (2); Church Yth Grp; Pep Clb; Treas Frsh Cls; Sec Soph Cls; L Trk; JV Vllybl; Hon Roll; NHS.

BACON, TYLER D; Circle HS; El Dorado, KS; (2); FCA; SADD; Acpl Chr; Band; Variety Show; Var L Bsktbl; Var L Crs Cntry; Var L Golf; High Hon Roll; Madrigals; Tchr.

BADER, CARRIE; Shawnee Mission E Sr HS; Shawnee Mission, KS; (3); Thesps; School Musical; School Play; Stage Crew; Yrbk; High Hon Roll; Hon Roll; Pres Schlr.

BADSKY, SARAH E; Shawnee Heights Sr HS; Berryton, KS; (4); 4-H; SADD; Teachers Aide; Band; Mrchg Band; Pep Band; Treas Frsh Cls; Treas Soph Cls; Var Capt Bsktbl; JV Var Sftbl; Ctznshp Awd; Bsktbl Schlsp; Johnson Cty CC; Engrng.

BADURA, CHAD; Rossville HS; Rossville, KS; (4); Letterman Clb; Teachers Aide; L Var Bsktbl; L Var Ftbl; L Var Trk; Wt Lftg; NHS; KS Area Tech; Htg/Cooling.

BAE, KEITH J; Blue Valley North HS; Overland Park, KS; (2); Church Yth Grp; Model UN; Chorus; JV Bsktbl; JV Ftbl; JV Trk; High Hon Roll; Hon Roll.

BAE, YEOUL; Lawrence HS; Lawrence, KS; (3); Computer Clb; Hosp Aide; Intnl Clb; Teachers Aide; Lit Mag; Hon Roll; Prfct Atten Awd; Korean Yth Assn Ldr; Dir Btfctn; Dir Engl; IM Eng Ortrcl Cntst; Korean Yth Assn Awd; IM Poem Comp; Med/Chem.

BAEHLER, MICHELLE; Wallace Cty HS; Sharon Springs, KS; (1); Church Yth Grp; Drama Clb; FCA; Pep Clb; Quiz Bowl; Scholastic Bowl; Spanish Clb; SADD; Teachers Aide; Chorus; Panhandle ST U; Tchr.

BAENIG, MARIE E; Shawnee Heights Sr HS; Topeka, KS; (3); Church Yth Grp; Debate Tm; NFL; Speech Tm; Band; Mrchg Band; Pep Band; Socr; High Hon Roll; NHS.

BAER, JULIE; Manhattan HS; Manhattan, KS; (4); 128/364; SADD; JV Bsktbl; Var Crs Cntry; Mgr(s); Powder Puff Ftbl; Var Trk; High Hon Roll; Kiwanis Awd; NHS; FCA; Stu Co Gnrl Asmbly; Emporia ST Univ; PE Tchr.

BAERG, DUSTIN L; Inman Jr Sr HS; Inman, KS; (2); Church Yth Grp; Natl FFA Org; Spanish Clb; Chorus; Church Choir; School Musical; School Play; Variety Show; Hon Roll; Pres Acad Fit Awd.

BAESEL, CHRIS; Wichita Northwest HS; Wichita, KS; (4); Am Leg Boys St; FCA; L Bsktbl; Var Ftbl; Hon Roll; NHS; U Of KS; Orthodontist.

BAGBY, DARREN; Frederic Remington HS; Wichita, KS; (3); Am Leg Boys St; Boy Scts; Letterman Clb; Band; Mrchg Band; Pep Band; Ofcr Stu Cncl; Var Ftbl; Var Wrstlng; Hon Roll; Grad From Yth Ldrshp Butler; Engrng.

BAGGETT, SARAH; Shawnee Mission E Sr HS; Prairie Village, KS; (3); 9/409; Band; Mrchg Band; Orch; Pep Band; Lit Mag; French Hon Soc; High Hon Roll; Jr NHS; NHS; Ntl Merit Ltr; Prvt Lsns Flute; KS Regents Hon Acad; Chem Engr.

BAGLEY, KYLE H; Holton HS; Holton, KS; (1); Chorus; Nwsp; Bsktbl; Ftbl; Wt Lftg.

BAGSHAW, JOSHUA A; Olathe East Sr HS; Olathe, KS; (2); Drama Clb; French Clb; Thesps; Acpl Chr; Chorus; School Musical; School Play; Stage Crew; Variety Show; Intrml Mgr Ftbl; Law.

BAHARI, SARAH L; Washburn Rural HS; Topeka, KS; (2); Cmnty Wkr; SADD; Ed Yrbk; JV Vllybl; Wt Lftg; High Hon Roll; Jr Olympc Vllybll.

BAHL, BRANDON K; Ulysses HS; Ulysses, KS; (1); Church Yth Grp; FBLA; Spanish Clb; SADD; Bsktbl; High Hon Roll.

BAHNER, KARI M; Wamego HS; Belvue, KS; (2); Natl FFA Org; Science Clb; SADD; JV Golf; Var Sftbl; JV Vllybl; Cit Awd; Hon Roll; Kayettes; Ftbl & Bsktbl Chrldr; Genetics.

BAHNS, CHRISTI A; Dodge City HS; Dodge City, KS; (3); Church Yth Grp; FHA; Intnl Clb; Spanish Clb; SADD; Teachers Aide; JV Vllybl; High Hon Roll; Hon Roll; Bus.

BAHR, BRAD J; Liberal HS; Liberal, KS; (3); Boy Scts; Church Yth Grp; French Clb; Teachers Aide; High Hon Roll; NHS; BYU; Chrprctr.

BAHR, CAMBRIA; Otis Bison HS; Olmitz, KS; (4); 5/25; Sec 4-H; SADD; Chorus; Chorus; School Play; Nwsp; Yrbk; Sec Frsh Cls; Pres Stu Cncl; 4-H Awd; KS ST U; Commnctns.

BAHR, LISA M; Otis Bison HS; Otis, KS; (2); Church Yth Grp; Pep Clb; SADD; Band; Chorus; JV Bsktbl; Score Keeper; JV Vllybl; Cit Awd; Hon Roll; KAYS; Coach Little Kids Bsktbl; Dance Cmmtte.

BAHRE, SHANNON N; Washburn Rural HS; Topeka, KS; (2); 4/400; French Clb; Intnl Clb; Natl FFA Org; NFL; SADD; Hlpng Hnds Humane Soc Vol.

BAILEY, AMBER M; Galena HS; Galena, KS; (3); FHA; GAA; Scholastic Bowl; Science Clb; SADD; Varsity Clb; Chrldng; Vllybl; Hon Roll; School Play; Miss Galena 96; PSU; Pre-Med.

BAILEY, APRIL; Valley Ctr HS; Valley Center, KS; (1); 16/219; Hon Roll; US Swimming; KU; Tchr; Swim Coach.

BAILEY, CHAD N; Salina HS Central; Salina, KS; (2); Church Yth Grp; Hon Roll; Prfct Atten Awd; Engr/Arch.

BAILEY, CHRISTA C; Riverton Schl; Galena, KS; (2); Church Yth Grp; FCA; FHA; Spanish Clb; Chorus; Flag Corp; School Musical; Rep Frsh Cls; Vllybl; Hon Roll; KS U; Rdlgy.

BAILEY, DEVON L; Galena HS; Galena, KS; (1); Church Yth Grp; FCA; FHA; Band; Jazz Band; Mrchg Band; Pep Band; Var L Bsktbl; JV Vllybl; High Hon Roll; Pittsburg ST Univ.

BAILEY, DUSTIN R; Garden City Sr HS; Garden City, KS; (3); Intrml Bsktbl; Var L Ftbl; Var L Trk; High Hon Roll.

BAILEY, ERIN M; Atchison Sr HS; Atchison, KS; (1); Art Clb; Computer Clb; Chorus; Cit Awd; Hon Roll; Cosmetologist.

BAILEY, EVAN G; Lawrence HS; Lawrence, KS; (3); NFL; Spanish Clb; Chorus; Rep Frsh Cls; Rep Soph Cls; Rep Jr Cls; Ofcr Stu Cncl; JV Bsbl; JV Bsktbl; Cit Awd; Commnctn.

BAILEY, GABRIEL K; Ellsworth HS; Ellsworth, KS; (2); Church Yth Grp; Letterman Clb; Quiz Bowl; Band; Chorus; Church Choir; Mrchg Band; Pep Band; School Play; Stage Crew; KS Rep Natl Episcpl Yth Evnt; KS Kids Wrstlng Trnmnt 2 Yrs.

BAILEY, HENRY; Clearwater HS; Clearwater, KS; (2); JV Bsktbl; JV Ftbl; Var Trk.

BAILEY, LINDA; Lawrence HS; Lawrence, KS; (4); Acpl Chr; JV Bsktbl; JV Chrldng; JV Gym; JV Trk; JV Vllybl; SW Col; Marinebio.

BAILEY, MATT; Silver Lake Jr Sr HS; Silver Lake, KS; (2); 17/60; Crs Cntry; Trk; Wt Lftg; Hon Roll.

BAILEY, MITCHELL; Ellsworth HS; Ellsworth, KS; (4); 10/68; Q&S; Band; Ed Nwsp; Yrbk; Ofcr Bsbl; Capt Var Bsktbl; Capt Var Ftbl; Var Trk; High Hon Roll; Pres Schlr; Ottawa U; Eng.

BAILEY, OWEN R; Osawatomie HS; Osawatomie, KS; (2); 18/96; Chess Clb; Science Clb; Band; Mrchg Band; Pep Band; Hon Roll; Fshng; Camping; Clay Shooting.

BAILEY, ROBIN; Dodge City HS; Dodge City, KS; (1); Church Yth Grp; 4-H; Band; Flag Corp; Jazz Band; Mrchg Band; 4-H Awd; Rodeo; Ft Hays.

BAILEY, WENDY L; Otis Bison HS; Otis, KS; (2); Letterman Clb; SADD; Band; Chorus; Sec Frsh Cls; Var L Bsktbl; Var L Trk; Var L Vllybl; High Hon Roll; NHS; Phy Therapy; Speech Pathology.

BAILEY, WILLIAM; St Thomas Aquinas HS; Lenexa, KS; (3); 63/260; Am Leg Boys St; Boy Scts; Debate Tm; NFL; Treas Science Clb; Var Crs Cntry; Var Trk; High Hon Roll; Hon Roll; NHS; Engrng; Arch.

BAIN, JEDIDIAH J; Bazine Jr Sr HS; Brownell, KS; (4); 2/6; Church Yth Grp; Quiz Bowl; Spanish Clb; Band; Yrbk; VP Frsh Cls; VP Soph Cls; Pres Sr Cls; VP Stu Cncl; Var L Bsktbl; Ft Hays ST Univ; Acctg.

BAIN, JOSEPH; Ness City HS; Ness City, KS; (2); Church Yth Grp; Natl FFA Org; Quiz Bowl; Rep Frsh Cls; JV Var Bsktbl; Mgr(s); High Hon Roll; Hon Roll; NHS; JV Tennis; Acad Team; Fort Hays ST U; Law.

BAIN, MATT; Ness City HS; Ness City, KS; (4); 2/29; Am Leg Boys St; Church Yth Grp; Cmnty Wkr; FCA; Letterman Clb; Rptr Natl FFA Org; Pep Clb; Scholastic Bowl; Pres Sr Cls; VP Stu Cncl; Recrd Bk Bck; Ft Hays ST U; Big-Game Biolgst.

BAIN, TORRI A; Ness City HS; Ness City, KS; (4); Church Yth Grp; Cmnty Wkr; FHA; Letterman Clb; Pep Clb; Thesps; Chorus; Ofcr Jr Cls; L Trk; Var L Vllybl; Jr Legion Auxiliary Clb; Ft Hays ST.

BAINTER, RAQUELLE F; Hoxie HS; Hoxie, KS; (3); Church Yth Grp; Cmnty Wkr; FCA; FHA; Natl FFA Org; Red Cross Aide; Teachers Aide; Varsity Clb; School Musical; School Play; Chrstn Yth Grp; KS St Univ; Psych.

BAIRD, JESSICA A; Canton-Galva HS; Galva, KS; (3); Church Yth Grp; FBLA; Letterman Clb; SADD; Band; Pep Band; Mgr(s); Sftbl; Vllybl; Hon Roll; Ft Hays Univ.

BAIRD, JILL A; Wichita East HS; Wichita, KS; (2); German Clb; Girl Scts; Band; Jazz Band; Mrchg Band; Pep Band; High Hon Roll; NHS; Church Yth Grp; Variety Show; Germn Natl Hnr Scty; Chrch Bell Choir.

BAIRD, MANDY; Hoisington HS; Hoisington, KS; (3); Church Yth Grp; Intnl Clb; Letterman Clb; Office Aide; Pep Clb; SADD; Band; Mrchg Band; Pep Band; Variety Show; Pre-Dntl.

BAIRD, SAMANTHA R; Canton-Galva HS; Galva, KS; (2); FBLA; Band; Chorus; SADD; Bsktbl; Vllybl; Hon Roll.

BAKER, AMANDA; Sedgwick HS; Sedgwick, KS; (2); Cmnty Wkr; Spanish Clb; Teachers Aide; Mgr(s); Hon Roll; KAYS; U Of KS; Med.

BAKER, AMANDA L; Riverton Schl; Riverton, KS; (1); Church Yth Grp; FHA; Science Clb; Band; Mrchg Band; Orch; Pep Band; Sftbl; Wt Lftg; Hon Roll; KAYS.

BAKER, AMY C; Maize HS; Wichita, KS; (2); 1/300; Treas Thesps; School Musical; School Play; Variety Show; VP Soph Cls; Pom Pon; High Hon Roll; NHS; Ofcr Stu Cncl; Drama Clb; 95 Sweetheart Queen; Awd All Amer NCA Dance Cmp; I Rtng Rgnl Solo Cntst; KHYS VP; Friends Univ.

BAKER, ANDY J; Oskaloosa HS; Oskaloosa, KS; (2); Church Yth Grp; Cmnty Wkr; FBLA; FHA; Quiz Bowl; SADD; Var Bsbl; JV Bsktbl.

BAKER, ANGELA; Wichita Co HS; Marienthal, KS; (3); Church Yth Grp; Cmnty Wkr; 4-H; HOBY; Natl FFA Org; Pep Clb; Band; Chorus; Mrchg Band; Pep Band; Frnscs; Educ.

BAKER, BARBARA L; Junction City HS; Junction City, KS; (2); Church Yth Grp; Dance Clb; Drama Clb; Chorus; School Musical; School Play; Pom Pon; High Hon Roll; NHS; KMEA Dist 3 Hnr Choir; 1 Rating KS ST Music Fstvl Voice; KSU; Early Chldhd; Elem Ed.

BAKER, BROCK; Garden City Sr HS; Garden City, KS; (4); Church Yth Grp; VP Pres 4-H; Treas Natl FFA Org; Teachers Aide; 4-H Awd; Natl Little Britches Rodeo Assn; Garden City HS Rodeo Team; Garden City CC; Ag.

BAKER, CANDICE M; Seaman Sr HS; Topeka, KS; (3); Drama Clb; English Clb; FBLA; German Clb; NFL; Band; Mrchg Band; Orch; Pep Band; School Musical; Psych.

BAKER, DANIEL; Arkansas City HS; Arkansas City, KS; (3); Am Leg Boys St; Church Yth Grp; FCA; Natl FFA Org; Office Aide; SADD; Teachers Aide; VP Sr Cls; JV Bsbl; Wrstlng; KS ST Univ; Engr.

BAKER, DAVID C; Hillsboro HS; Hillsboro, KS; (3); 16/60; Church Yth Grp; Acpl Chr; Band; Chorus; Church Choir; Jazz Band; Mrchg Band; Pep Band; School Musical; School Play; Sprtsmnshp/Ldrshp Awd Smmr Tnns Cmp 2 Yrs; Im Third Rnnr-Up Kanakuk-Kanakomo Kamp; Bus Adm.

BAKER, ERIN L; Goddard HS; Goddard, KS; (2); Science Clb; Nwsp; Yrbk; Sftbl; Tennis; Vllybl; High Hon Roll; Piano; KAYS Clb; U KS; Jrnlsm.

BAKER, JACQUELYN T; El Dorado HS; El Dorado, KS; (2); Math Clb; Spanish Clb; Sec Treas SADD; Teachers Aide; Varsity Clb; Chorus; Var Bsktbl; Powder Puff Ftbl; Var Sftbl; JV Vllybl; Earth Care Clb; Law Enforcement.

BAKER, JENNIFER; Goddard HS; Wichita, KS; (3); #1 in class; Band; Drill Tm; Pres Jr Cls; Pres Sr Cls; NHS; Pep Clb; Science Clb; SADD; Mrchg Band; Pep Band; All Amer Schlr; KAYS; Bible Clb; Med.

BAKER, KIMBERLY A; Leavenworth HS; Leavenworth, KS; (1); Church Yth Grp; Piano; St Marys Coll; Tchg/Law.

BAKER, LAURA M; Cheney Jr Sr HS; Cheney, KS; (4); Church Yth Grp; Chorus; Stage Crew; Co-Ed Rptr Yrbk; Mgr(s); Hon Roll; Forensics; KS St Univ; Brdcst Jrnlsm.

BAKER, MAUREEN; Immaculata HS; Leavenworth, KS; (3); 1/43; Am Leg Aux Girls St; Girl Scts; Hosp Aide; Math Tm; School Musical; School Play; Ed Yrbk; Capt Chrldng; NHS; Sci Olympd; Creighton Univ.

BAKER, MELISSA; North Cntrl HS; Haddam, KS; (4); 5/10; FBLA; Sec Treas Letterman Clb; Natl FFA Org; Pep Clb; Yrbk; Sec Treas Soph Cls; Var Capt Bsktbl; Chrldng; Var Crs Cntry; Trk; KS St Univ; Vet Med.

BAKER, MICHAEL L; Iola Sr HS; Iola, KS; (4); 24/121; Am Leg Boys St; Church Yth Grp; Drama Clb; Letterman Clb; SADD; Thesps; Varsity Clb; Chorus; School Play; Swing Chorus; U Of KS; Scndry Ed; Coaching.

BAKER, NATASHA A; Washington HS; Kansas City, KS; (2); ROTC; Spanish Clb; Acpl Chr; Drill Tm; Variety Show; Promise Project Adult-Yth Partnership Awd; Ed Talent Search Mem; Concert Choir; Spelman Coll; Psych.

BAKER, NIKKI; Sedgwick HS; Sedgwick, KS; (1); 4/25; Band; Mrchg Band; Pep Band; Trk; Vllybl; High Hon Roll; St Band; U Of KS; Med.

BAKER, PATRIECE M; Washington HS; Morrowville, KS; (3); 10/40; French Clb; FHA; Letterman Clb; Treas Jr Cls; Var Bsktbl; Var Trk; Var Vllybl; French Hon Soc; High Hon Roll; NHS.

BAKER, REBECCA; Atchison Sr HS; Atchison, KS; (2); Pres 4-H; Spanish Clb; Mgr(s); Stat Vllybl; 4-H Awd; High Hon Roll; Hon Roll; Lnchn Of Champs; KS ST U; Bio.

BAKER, RUSTY A; Liberal HS; Liberal, KS; (4); 4/210; Debate Tm; French Clb; Teachers Aide; Lit Mag; High Hon Roll; NHS; GPA 4.0; Wichita ST Univ; CPA.

BAKER, RYAN J; Goddard HS; Wichita, KS; (1); Church Yth Grp; Debate Tm; Band; Mrchg Band; Variety Show; JV Bsbl; JV Socr; KS ST.

BAKER, SCOTT A; Caney Valley Jr Sr HS; Caney, KS; (3); 12/93; Church Yth Grp; Cmnty Wkr; Letterman Clb; Pep Clb; Varsity Clb; Ofcr Bsbl; Bsktbl; Crs Cntry; Wt Lftg; High Hon Roll; U Of KS; Pharmacy; Law; Psych.

BAKER, SHAY; Leavenworth HS; Leavenworth, KS; (4); Band; Drm Mjr(t); Mrchg Band; Pres Frsh Cls; Pres Soph Cls; Pres Jr Cls; Pres Sr Cls; Chrldng; Church Yth Grp; Hosp Aide; Hmcmng Rylty; Wntr Rylty; 2nd Rnr Up Leavenworth Co Jr Ms Prgm; KS ST Univ.

BAKER, SHERI; Wellington Sr HS; Wellington, KS; (2); Church Yth Grp; Cmnty Wkr; French Clb; Library Aide; Yrbk; Hon Roll; Jr NHS; Lions Awd Nom.

BAKER, TERESA J; Ottawa HS; Ottawa, KS; (2); GAA; Spanish Clb; Pres Frsh Cls; Bsktbl; Powder Puff Ftbl; Sftbl; Vllybl; High Hon Roll; Hon Roll; USAF.

BAKER, TRIECE M; Washington HS; Morrowville, KS; (3); 10/40; French Clb; FHA; Letterman Clb; Treas Jr Cls; Var Bsktbl; Var Trk; Var Vllybl; French Hon Soc; High Hon Roll; NHS.

BAKER, TYLER; Maize HS; Wichita, KS; (3); Boy Scts; Debate Tm; Letterman Clb; NFL; Spanish Clb; SADD; JV Var Crs Cntry; JV Var Tennis; Hon Roll; Law/Bus.

BAKER, WESLEY P; Prairie View Jr Sr HS; La Cygne, KS; (4); 13/70; Letterman Clb; Natl FFA Org; Intrml Nwsp; Intrml Yrbk; Sec Soph Cls; VP Jr Cls; Var Bsbl; Var Bsktbl; Var Ftbl; Var Trk; Pittsburg ST Univ; Nrsng.

BALCH, ANDREA D; El Dorado HS; El Dorado, KS; (3); Letterman Clb; Math Clb; SADD; Teachers Aide; Band; Mrchg Band; Pep Band; School Musical; JV Bsktbl; Mgr Ftbl; Hist/Pre-Law.

BALDASSARO, RYAN M; Independence HS; Independence, KS; (1); Church Yth Grp; JV Ftbl; JV Wrstlng; Renaissance Hnr Soc; Sprts Med.

BALDEN, ANDREW D; Jefferson Co North HS; Winchester, KS; (3); 13/45; Band; Mrchg Band; Orch; Pep Band; School Musical; KS Univ; Cmptr Sci.

BALDRIDGE, JASON; Olathe North Sr HS; Olathe, KS; (2); Church Yth Grp; JV Socr; Var Swmmng; High Hon Roll; Pres Acad Fit Awd; Magna Cum Laude Awd Natl Ltn Exm.

BALDWIN, ADAM S; Inman Jr Sr HS; Mc Pherson, KS; (2); Phtg 4-H; Rptr Natl FFA Org; Spanish Clb; Band; Chorus; Mrchg Band; School Musical; School Play; Variety Show; Bsktbl; KS ST Univ; Crop Dstr.

BALDWIN, AMY K; Wichita North HS; Wichita, KS; (1); Var Swmmng; Jobs Dghtrs Bethel 74.

BALDWIN, GREG S; Olathe East Sr HS; Olathe, KS; (3); Church Yth Grp; Spanish Clb; Teachers Aide; Band; Intrml Bsbl; Intrml Bsktbl; High Hon Roll; Hon Roll; Prfct Atten Awd; Pres Acad Fit Awd; Spcl Olympics Vol; Fall Conditioning; KS Univ; Engrng; Bus.

BALDWIN, JENNIFER E; Blue Valley Northwest HS; Overland Park, KS; (4); 9/340; Cmnty Wkr; Chrmn Pep Clb; Powder Puff Ftbl; High Hon Roll; Chrmn NHS; Ntl Merit Ltr; St Schlr; Natl Art Hnrs Soc; Spndt Awd; U Of IL; Cvl Eng.

BALDWIN, LISA; Larned HS; Larned, KS; (3); 13/80; Am Leg Aux Girls St; Pres Church Yth Grp; VP SADD; Acpl Chr; Band; Church Choir; Jazz Band; Mrchg Band; Pep Band; Capt Chrldng; Pittsburg ST Univ; Music Ed.

BALDWIN, MARK A; Santa Fe Trail Jr HS; Olathe, KS; (1); Church Yth Grp; Office Aide; Spanish Clb; Teachers Aide; Band; Intrml Socr; Hon Roll.

BALDWIN, MELISSA D; Field Kindley Mem Sr HS; Coffeyville, KS; (3); Debate Tm; French Clb; NFL; Mgr Yrbk; Var Chrldng; Var Swmmng; Var Tennis; Hon Roll; NHS; Ad.

BALDWIN, MOLLIE E; Shawnee Heights Sr HS; Topeka, KS; (2); Church Yth Grp; Cmnty Wkr; Drama Clb; NFL; Pep Clb; Ski Clb; Thesps; Band; Chorus; Church Choir; Advrtsng.

BALDWIN, SARAH E; Hays HS; Hays, KS; (2); Pep Clb; Drill Tm; Pom Pon; Hon Roll; Ft Hays ST.

BALES, BRIAN J; Shawnee Mission W Sr HS; Overland Park, KS; (2); 82/500; Drama Clb; NFL; Thesps; School Musical; School Play; Stage Crew; JV Swmmng; Hon Roll; Ntl Merit Ltr; Master Of Comedy Awd 95-96; Sr Awd; Best Novice Awd; Amer Acad; Film Actor.

BALES, CHRISTOPHER A; Olathe East Sr HS; Overland Park, KS; (2); Band; Mrchg Band; Pep Band; School Play; Hon Roll; Jrnlsm/Meteorlgy.

BALES, ERIN A; Cheney Jr Sr HS; Cheney, KS; (3); 30/40; Church Choir; Hnr Rl Hnrbl Mntn; Hutchinson CC; Arch.

BALES, NICOLE M; Washburn Rural HS; Topeka, KS; (3); Chorus; Variety Show; Co-Ed Nwsp; Var L Golf; High Hon Roll; Red Crss Certfd Lifeguard.

BALL, JASON C; Emporia HS; Emporia, KS; (3); Bsktbl; Wt Lftg; High Hon Roll; Pres Schlr; Pittsburg ST; Electronics Tech.

BALL, JESSICA A; Blue Valley Northwest HS; Overland Park, KS; (2); Church Yth Grp; Girl Scts; Pep Clb; Teachers Aide; Band; Chorus; Church Choir; Golf; Socr; Hon Roll; KC Art Inst; Art; Pantng-Drawng.

BALL, JESSICA O; Ft Scott HS; Fulton, KS; (3); Am Leg Aux Girls St; Debate Tm; Pres FTA; Sec NFL; Office Aide; Band; Stage Crew; Hon Roll; NHS; Intl Order Of Rainbow For Grls Stof KS.

BALL, MARK A; Central Heights Sr HS; Rantoul, KS; (2); Church Yth Grp; Natl FFA Org; Science Clb; Stage Crew; Ftbl; Trk; High Hon Roll; Hon Roll; Ottawa; Math/Engr.

BALLENTINE JR, JOE; Onaga HS; Onaga, KS; (2); Natl FFA Org; Treas Jr Cls; High Hon Roll; Hon Roll; K ST.

BALLINGER, MARK; Belle Plaine HS; Belle Plaine, KS; (2); Letterman Clb; Ofcr Bsbl; JV Bsktbl; JV Var Ftbl; Cit Awd; Hon Roll; Wichita ST U; Architecture.

BALLINGER, THOMAS J; Atchison Co Cmty HS; Atchison, KS; (3); Letterman Clb; Band; Jazz Band; Pep Band; VP Frsh Cls; Var Ftbl; Var Wt Lftg; Hon Roll.

BALLUCH, JASON A; Trego Comm HS; Wa Keeney, KS; (2); Church Yth Grp; Varsity Clb; Ftbl; Trk; Wt Lftg; High Hon Roll; Pres Acad Fit Awd; Archtctr.

BALSINGER, KARLA A; Shawnee Mission N HS; Shawnee Mission, KS; (2); #43 in class; Church Yth Grp; Drama Clb; Pep Clb; Thesps; Band; Jazz Band; Mrchg Band; Pep Band; School Musical; Stage Crew; Johnson County CC.

BALSLY, EDEN M; Blue Valley Northwest HS; Overland Park, KS; (2); Cmnty Wkr; Pep Clb; Rep Stu Cncl; Hon Roll; Excl Eng Awd 94-95; Teenstar Frlncr 94-95; Teenstar 95-; Crrspndnt & Bd Mem; Duke U; Jrnlsm.

BALSMEIER, WILLIAM K; Manhattan HS; Manhattan, KS; (3); Am Leg Boys St; Boy Scts; Scholastic Bowl; Thesps; VICA; Band; Chorus; Church Choir; Mrchg Band; School Play; Auto Engr/Bus.

BALTER, CHAD; Olathe North Sr HS; Olathe, KS; (2); Latin Clb; Var Chrldng; Intrml Ftbl; Intrml Wt Lftg; Var Wrstlng; Hon Roll; Science.

BALZANO, LAURA K; St Thomas Aquinas HS; Overland Park, KS; (3); 1/260; Am Leg Aux Girls St; Cmnty Wkr; FCA; Sec French Clb; Math Clb; NFL; Capt Socr; High Hon Roll; NHS; Church Yth Grp; Film Clb; Duke TIP Natl Hnr Awd.

BANDA, ISABEL C; Deerfield HS; Deerfield, KS; (4); Church Yth Grp; Pep Clb; Teachers Aide; Yrbk; JV Bsktbl; Var Crs Cntry; Var Trk; Garden City CC; Plce Offcr.

BANDY, CRYSTAL L; Halstead HS; Bentley, KS; (3); Church Yth Grp; Cmnty Wkr; Letterman Clb; Spanish Clb; Teachers Aide; Chorus; Church Choir; School Musical; Bsktbl; Mgr(s); Span Clb VP; Kayette Bd Mem; John Brown U; Sports Medicine.

BANDY, SARA G; El Dorado HS; El Dorado, KS; (2); Kay Club; KS U; Nrsng.

BANERJEE, BIDISHA; Lawrence HS; Lawrence, KS; (2); Pres Chess Clb; Debate Tm; Drama Clb; German Clb; NFL; Quiz Bowl; Scholastic Bowl; Thesps; Chorus; School Play; Outsdng Nove Frnscs Stdnt; Pub Poem Anthlgy.

BANISTER, GAVIN M; Douglass HS; Douglass, KS; (3); 9/70; FCA; Letterman Clb; Rep Frsh Cls; Rep Soph Cls; Rep Jr Cls; Var L Bsbl; Var L Bsktbl; Var L Ftbl; High Hon Roll; Hon Roll; Phys Thpy.

BANKS, KATIE; El Dorado HS; El Dorado, KS; (3); Am Leg Aux Girls St; Pres Drama Clb; NFL; Thesps; School Musical; Pres Frsh Cls; Chrldng; High Hon Roll; NHS; Peer Cnslng; Jr Ambsdrs; Elem Ed.

BANKS, KRISTY L; Eureka Jr Sr HS; Toronto, KS; (3); Pres Church Yth Grp; Cmnty Wkr; French Clb; FHA; Intnl Clb; SADD; Chorus; Church Choir; Stage Crew; Pres Acad Fit Awd; Intl Club/Rainbow Girls; Lwyr.

BANKS, KYLE J; Pratt HS; Pratt, KS; (3); Church Yth Grp; SADD; Chorus; School Musical; Bsktbl; Crs Cntry; Golf; Hon Roll.

BANKS, PAUL; Washburn Rural HS; Topeka, KS; (1); Boy Scts; Church Yth Grp; Cmnty Wkr; Library Aide; Model UN; SADD; Cit Awd; Hon Roll; Prfct Atten Awd; Pres Acad Fit Awd; Eagle Scout W/ 3 Palms/Ord Of Arrow; Sons Of Amer Rev Awd; Arch/Drftng/Engrng.

BANVELOS, ANTONIO; Garden City Sr HS; Garden City, KS; (2); Socr; Garden City CC.

BARABAN, MELISSA A; Blue Valley Northwest HS; Overland Park, KS; (1); Orch; Hon Roll.

BARBA, COREEN L; Immaculata HS; Leavenworth, KS; (2); Church Yth Grp; Girl Scts; Hosp Aide; HOBY; Sec Intnl Clb; Stage Crew; French Hon Soc; High Hon Roll; NHS.

BARBER, JUDITH; Burrton Schl; Burrton, KS; (4); 3/21; Sec Latin Clb; Natl Beta Clb; Nwsp; Sec Treas Jr Cls; VP Sr Cls; Var Chrldng; NHS; Teachers Aide; Chorus; School Musical; Interact Clb; Tlntd Arts Pgm Art I/II & Drama; KS ST U; Commnctns.

BARBER, KELLY S; Wichita West HS; Wichita, KS; (2); 19/431; Cmnty Wkr; Hosp Aide; HOBY; Intnl Clb; Var Trk; Var Wt Lftg; Hon Roll; Afrcn Amrcn Clb; Med.

BARBER, KEVIN DAVID; Olathe South Sr HS; Olathe, KS; (4); 46/381; Spanish Clb; Band; Jazz Band; Capt Mrchg Band; Pep Band; High Hon Roll; NHS; Pres Acad Fit Awd; Spanish NHS; Div 1 Rtng Dist, St Solo Cmptns Trumpet; Dist Band 1 Yr; Johnson Cty CC; Comp Engrng.

BARBER, MARCUS A; Wichita South HS; Wichita, KS; (2); Church Yth Grp; Scholastic Bowl; Band; Church Choir; Mrchg Band; Pep Band; VP Soph Cls; Intrml Bsktbl; L Var Wrstlng; High Hon Roll; City Lge Wrstlng Champ; Multi Yr Listee; Stanford Univ; Cognative Sci.

BARBER, SABRINA D; Ellsworth HS; Ellsworth, KS; (1); 20/70; Church Yth Grp; English Clb; FCA; French Clb; GAA; NFL; Chorus; Church Choir; Mrchg Band; School Play; Kayetts; Music/Drama.

BARCLAY, HEIDI; Arkansas City HS; Arkansas City, KS; (3); 8/189; Am Leg Aux Girls St; Scholastic Bowl; Teachers Aide; Chorus; Orch; Hon Roll; NHS; Jr Ldrshp; Wichita Symph Yth Orch; U Of Ks; Pre-Med.

BARCLAY, JOHN J; Smoky Valley HS; Lindsborg, KS; (1); Church Yth Grp; Band; Chorus; Jazz Band; Pep Band; Treas Frsh Cls; Bsktbl; Var Tennis; High Hon Roll; Pep Clb; Lindsborg Swedish Folk Dancers; Crime Stoppers; Pre-Med.

BARCUS, BETH A; Olathe East Sr HS; Overland Park, KS; (2); Church Yth Grp; GAA; Intnl Clb; Letterman Clb; Spanish Clb; Teachers Aide; Varsity Clb; Chorus; Church Choir; JV Crs Cntry; Outstdng Span Awd; Pres Exec Awd; ST Trck Meet.

BARDEEN, JAMES; Pittsburg HS; Pittsburg, KS; (3); 5/200; Am Leg Boys St; Church Yth Grp; FCA; Spanish Clb; Band; Jazz Band; Mrchg Band; School Musical; Golf; NHS; St Golf 11th; Comp Eng.

BARDSLEY, LELAND R; Santa Fe Trail HS; Scranton, KS; (4); 1/92; FBLA; Capt Scholastic Bowl; Band; Drm Mjr(t); Mrchg Band; L Crs Cntry; High Hon Roll; Pres NHS; Val; Math Tm; Dist Hnr Band 3 Yrs; Cornell U; Pediatrcs.

BARE, JESSICA B; Shawnee Mission W Sr HS; Lenexa, KS; (3); Art Clb; Church Yth Grp; Dance Clb; Drama Clb; Drill Tm; School Play; Stage Crew; Rep Soph Cls; Ofcr Jr Cls; Var Pom Pon; Modern Dance 10 Yrs; U Of KS; Bio.

BARFOOT, BROOKE A; Leavenworth HS; Leavenworth, KS; (2); ROTC; Chorus; Drill Tm; High Hon Roll; Hon Roll; Karate; Piano; KS ST Univ; Lrg Anml Vet.

BARGER, GREYSON; Sedgwick HS; Sedgwick, KS; (3); FCA; Scholastic Bowl; School Musical; School Play; Var L Bsktbl; Var L Ftbl; Wt Lftg; High Hon Roll; Prfct Atten Awd; Pres Acad Fit Awd; KS ST; Comp Sci.

BARGMANN, RYAN J; Hayden HS; Topeka, KS; (2); Intnl Clb; Spanish Clb; Chorus; Church Choir; Bsktbl; Socr; Hon Roll.

BARKER, ARIANE; Independence HS; Independence, KS; (4); Am Leg Aux Girls St; Church Yth Grp; Cmnty Wkr; Drama Clb; FCA; JA; Pep Clb; Red Cross Aide; Spanish Clb; SADD; U Of KS; Psych.

BARKER, BRANDI L; Maize HS; Wichita, KS; (1); Drama Clb; SADD; Thesps; High Hon Roll; ST Acad Olympcs; WSU.

BARKER, BRANDIE; Marmaton Valley Jr Sr HS; Moran, KS; (4); 1/20; Pres 4-H; HOBY; Pres Natl FFA Org; Band; Drm Mjr(t); School Play; Co-Ed Yrbk; Pres Sr Cls; 4-H Awd; Am Leg Aux Girls St; Schlr Bowl.

BARKER, HALEY; Independence HS; Independence, KS; (1); Pep Clb; Sec Frsh Cls; JV Chrldng; Ballet 9 Yrs; Univ Of KS; Photographer.

BARKER, JIMMY; Wichita Collegiate Schl; Wichita, KS; (4); Am Leg Boys St; Church Yth Grp; Pep Clb; Acpl Chr; School Musical; Variety Show; Var Tennis; High Hon Roll; Chess Clb; SADD; IM Ultimate Frisbee; Indstrl Engrng.

BARKER, KRISTIN L; Field Kindley Mem Sr HS; Coffeyville, KS; (2); 1/175; Church Yth Grp; French Clb; Chorus; School Musical; High Hon Roll; Piano Tchr & Accompaniest; Piano Perf.

BARKYOUMB, CAMMIE J; Blue Valley HS; Overland Park, KS; (2); Sftbl; Vllybl; Hon Roll.

BARLOW, HILLARY B; Yates Ctr HS; Toronto, KS; (3); VP Sec Church Yth Grp; FCA; Pres Sec 4-H; FHA; Letterman Clb; Office Aide; Science Clb; SADD; Band; Church Choir; Miss Trnto.

BARLOW, MINISA R; Wichita HS SE; Wichita, KS; (3); 37/355; Cmnty Wkr; German Clb; SADD; Flag Corp; Bsktbl; Chrldng; JV Socr; Var Vllybl; High Hon Roll; NHS; FFA Dist Chmp; Embry-Riddle Univ; Prof Pilot.

BARNABY, STEPHANIE; Seaman Sr HS; Topeka, KS; (3); Am Leg Aux Girls St; FBLA; FHA; Key Clb; SADD; Rep Stu Cncl; Chrldng; Socr; High Hon Roll; NHS; KSU; Chem.

BARNES, CARINDA; Sumner Acad Of Arts & Science; Kansas City, KS; (4); 63/198; Church Yth Grp; Cmnty Wkr; FTA; GAA; JA; JCL; Q&S; Co-Ed Yrbk; French Hon Soc; High Hon Roll; YMCA Swim Instr, Lifeguard & Swim Team; Rel Ed Instr; St Mary Coll; Elem Ed.

BARNES, ERIN M; Kapaun-Mt Carmel HS; Wichita, KS; (3); French Clb; Hosp Aide; Service Clb; SADD; Chorus; School Musical; Stage Crew; Nwsp; Rep Frsh Cls; Rep Soph Cls; Ecology Clb Pres; Drama Dept; KS ST U; Veterinary Medicine.

BARNES, JASON; Louisburg HS; Louisburg, KS; (3); Letterman Clb; SADD; Band; Drm Mjr(t); Mrchg Band; Pep Band; Stage Crew; Variety Show; Hon Roll; Prfct Atten Awd; KS Univ; Law.

BARNES, SHAUNNA R; Washington HS; Washington, KS; (3); 13/40; Art Clb; Dance Clb; French Clb; Letterman Clb; Office Aide; Pep Clb; Teachers Aide; Chorus; Color Guard; Drill Tm; Grphc Arts.

BARNES, SONIA J; Elkhart HS; Elkhart, KS; (3); 19/40; Church Yth Grp; Thesps; Band; Chorus; School Musical; School Play; Stage Crew; Hon Roll; Ozark Chrstn Col.

BARNES, TRAVIS; Newton Sr HS; Newton, KS; (3); Church Yth Grp; Band; Jazz Band; Mrchg Band; Orch; Pep Band; Hon Roll; Acctng.

BARNETT, AMANDA S; Atchison Co Cmty HS; Holton, KS; (2); Church Yth Grp; HOBY; Letterman Clb; Quiz Bowl; Band; Mrchg Band; Pep Band; Sec Frsh Cls; JV Var Bsktbl; Var Trk; U Of NE; Pediatric Onclgst.

BARNETT, BARNEY J; Jefferson West HS; Topeka, KS; (2); 17/70; Church Yth Grp; Drama Clb; 4-H; Speech Tm; Bsktbl; Wt Lftg; 4-H Awd; High Hon Roll; Prfct Atten Awd; Local 4-H Clb Pres; Cty 4-H Cncl Treas; 4-H Cty King 95; 4-H Ambassador; Washburn U; Law.

BARNETT, BRANDI D; Smoky Valley HS; Lindsborg, KS; (1); Church Yth Grp; Drama Clb; FCA; Speech Tm; Band; Chorus; Rep Stu Cncl; Var Trk; JV Vllybl; High Hon Roll.

BARNETT, CASSIE; Riverton Schl; Baxter Springs, KS; (3); Church Yth Grp; French Clb; Girl Scts; HOBY; Teachers Aide; Chorus; Yrbk; Hon Roll; Ntl Merit Schol; PSU; Occptnl Thrpy.

BARNETT, DANELLE K; Winfield HS; Winfield, KS; (2); Church Yth Grp; FCA; School Musical; Stage Crew; JV Sftbl; JV Vllybl; High Hon Roll; Hon Roll; Med Rsrch.

BARNETT, DEE L; Beloit Jr Sr HS; Beloit, KS; (2); Church Yth Grp; Letterman Clb; Chorus; School Musical; School Play; Variety Show; Var L Bsbl; Var L Bsktbl; Hon Roll; Amer Legion Bsbl; AAU Bsktbl; Outstndg Vocal Musician Awrd; Elem Schl Tchr/Coach.

BARNETT, GARY M; Hope HS; Hope, KS; (2); Church Yth Grp; Scholastic Bowl; Pres SADD; Band; Pep Band; Treas Soph Cls; Var L Bsbl; Var L Bsktbl; High Hon Roll; Pres Acad Fit Awd; Tchr.

BARNETT, JEFF R; Maur Hill Prep Schl; Lawrence, KS; (3); Debate Tm; French Clb; Teachers Aide; Thesps; Chorus; Orch; School Play; Stage Crew; Variety Show; Pres Stu Cncl; Asst Prefect.

BARNETT, JENI; El Dorado HS; El Dorado, KS; (3); Spanish Clb; SADD; Band; Orch; VP Jr Cls; Var Chrldng; High Hon Roll; NHS; Church Yth Grp; Mrchg Band; LIFE; KAY; Jr Ambassador; KS ST U; Eng Ed.

BARNETT, SASHA N; Garden City Sr HS; Garden City, KS; (2); Church Yth Grp; FHA; Key Clb; Science Clb; Spanish Clb; Band; Church Choir; Hon Roll; Piano; Mssn Trps; PT.

BARNHART, ANDY S; Ottawa HS; Ottawa, KS; (4); Letterman Clb; Rep Frsh Cls; JV Var Bsktbl; JV Var Ftbl; High Hon Roll; Hon Roll; Amer Lgn Bsbl To ST 3 Yrs; Univ Of KS; Bus Admn.

BARNHART, SHANNAN D; Andover HS; Andover, KS; (4); 38/148; Band; Drm Mjr(t); Mrchg Band; Pep Band; Socr; Sftbl; Hon Roll; Butler Cnty CC; Acctng.

BARNOW, TARA; Eureka Jr Sr HS; Eureka, KS; (2); Debate Tm; FHA; Letterman Clb; Yrbk; Bsktbl; Vllybl; High Hon Roll; Trk; Teachers Aide; For Lang Clb; Emporia ST U; For Lang Tchr.

BARNTHOUSE, MICHAEL; Arkansas City HS; Arkansas City, KS; (3); 6/189; Am Leg Boys St; Boy Scts; Church Yth Grp; FCA; Hosp Aide; HOBY; Phtg Nwsp; Phtg Yrbk; Bsktbl; Var L Tennis; BSA Eagle Sct 94; Order Arrow Arrowman Yr 95; AR City Jr Ldrshp First Grad Class 96; KS ST U; Chem/Envrnmntl Engr.

BARR, BRANDON; Lebo Schl; Lebo, KS; (4); 6/26; Am Leg Boys St; Cmnty Wkr; Dance Clb; 4-H; FBLA; Natl FFA Org; Teachers Aide; Band; Pep Band; Pres Frsh Cls; FFA St Farmer, Dairy Proficiency 96; KS St Dairy Judging Team; KS Key Awd Wnnr; KS ST Univ; Vet; Dairy Sci.

BARR, BROOK R; Lawrence HS; Lawrence, KS; (2); Church Yth Grp; Office Aide; Teachers Aide; Acpl Chr; Chorus; Church Choir; School Musical; School Play; Variety Show; Ed Rptr Nwsp; Jrnlsm; Music; Astronaut.

BARR, EMILY; St Thomas Aquinas HS; Overland Park, KS; (3); 66/291; Spanish Clb; SADD; Capt Bsktbl; JV Var Sftbl; JV Var Vllybl; High Hon Roll; NHS; Vlybl 5a ST Chmps 95/Dfnsve Awd ST Vlybl; 3rd Pl ST Mst Imprvd Awd Sftbl 96; PT.

BARR, WENDY D; Parsons HS; Parsons, KS; (3); #17 in class; Key Clb; Pep Clb; Spanish Clb; JV Tennis; Hon Roll; Labette CC; Sprts Mdcn/PT.

BARRETO, ERIC D; Olathe East Sr HS; Olathe, KS; (2); #1 in class; Church Yth Grp; Debate Tm; French Clb; HOBY; NFL; School Play; Ed Yrbk; Rep Stu Cncl; High Hon Roll; Pres Acad Fit Awd.

BARRETT, BRITTNEY; Shawnee Mission S Sr HS; Overland Park, KS; (4); 126/420; Church Yth Grp; Cmnty Wkr; Dance Clb; Drama Clb; FCA; Intnl Clb; Letterman Clb; SADD; Teachers Aide; Varsity Clb; Hmcmng Queen; Hentage Royalty Yrbk Queen; U Of AZ; Comm.

BARRETT, CARA L; Council Grove HS; Alta Vista, KS; (2); 19/98; Drama Clb; FHA; SADD; Var Crs Cntry; Var Trk; High Hon Roll; Mammalogist.

BARRETT, DEBBIE; Deerfield HS; Deerfield, KS; (1); Church Yth Grp; FHA; Phtg Yrbk; Rep Frsh Cls; Var Chrldng; Var JV Vllybl; Hon Roll; Pres Acad Fit Awd.

BARRETT, ERIKA; Jewell HS; Randall, KS; (4); 1/15; School Play; Ed Yrbk; Treas Stu Cncl; Bsktbl; Chrldng; Vllybl; Gov Hon Prg Awd; High Hon Roll; NHS; Val; Sterling Coll.

BARRETT, KIRSTEN; Jewell HS; Randall, KS; (2); FCA; FHA; Office Aide; Pep Clb; Band; Mrchg Band; Pep Band; Sec Treas Soph Cls; Var Bsktbl; Var Chrldng; St High Jmp 5th Pl; Vlybl 1st Tm AU Clss; Bsktbl 2nd Tm AU Area; Cnslng.

BARRETT, MICHELLE; Washburn Rural HS; Auburn, KS; (3); Teachers Aide; Chrldng; Powder Puff Ftbl; Sftbl; Trk; Vllybl; High Hon Roll; KSU.

BARRETT, TIM A; Osawatomie HS; Osawatomie, KS; (1); Letterman Clb; Science Clb; Ofcr Bsbl; Ftbl; Wt Lftg; Wrstlng; High Hon Roll; NHS.

BARRON, BRENT K; Topeka West HS; Topeka, KS; (3); 96/247; Art Clb; Math Clb; Office Aide; Spanish Clb; Crs Cntry; Trk; Hon Roll; UCLA; Cmmrcl Dsgn.

BARRY, DENNIS EDWARD; Leavenworth HS; Leavenworth, KS; (3); Crs Cntry; High Hon Roll; Pittsburg St Univ; Mech Eng Tec.

BARSICK, LAURA; Washington HS; Kansas City, KS; (4); Debate Tm; Drama Clb; NFL; Q&S; Teachers Aide; Thesps; School Play; Stage Crew; Nwsp; High Hon Roll; Kansas City KS CC; Comp Grphc.

BARTA, AMBER D; Ellsworth HS; Wilson, KS; (2); 26/70; 4-H; Letterman Clb; Band; Chorus; Jazz Band; Mrchg Band; Pep Band; Rptr Nwsp; JV Bsktbl; Var Chrldng; Forensics; Pops Elite Singing Grp; Kayettes; KS Univ; Crmnlgy.

BARTEL, ANDY; Hillsboro HS; Hillsboro, KS; (2); 3/46; Church Yth Grp; 4-H; Natl FFA Org; Quiz Bowl; Band; Pep Band; JV Bsktbl; JV Ftbl; Intrml Sftbl; High Hon Roll.

BARTEL, JENNIFER; Hillsboro HS; Hillsboro, KS; (1); 15/71; Band; Chorus; Mrchg Band; Pep Band; Trk; Vllybl; High Hon Roll; Hon Roll; KS ST U; Vet.

BARTEL, LACIE; Senior HS; Atlanta, KS; (2); 2/30; Church Yth Grp; Teachers Aide; Band; Drill Tm; Pep Band; Sec Soph Cls; Ofcr Stu Cncl; Var Bsktbl; Var Sftbl; Var Vllybl.

BARTEL, ZACHARY; Hillsboro HS; Hillsboro, KS; (3); 5/64; Church Yth Grp; Natl FFA Org; Band; Mrchg Band; Pep Band; Var Tennis; High Hon Roll; NHS.

BARTELLI, BRAD; Parsons HS; Parsons, KS; (2); 8/138; Church Yth Grp; FTA; Key Clb; JV Bsbl; JV Bsktbl; JV Ftbl; Intrml Wt Lftg; Hon Roll; NHS.

BARTH, ERIC W; Wichita South HS; Wichita, KS; (4); 2/272; Church Yth Grp; Library Aide; Pres Scholastic Bowl; Gov Hon Prg Awd; Hon Roll; NHS; Sal; St Schlr; U Of KS; Poli Sci.

BARTHEL, SARAH; Atchison Sr HS; Atchison, KS; (1); Spanish Clb; High Hon Roll; Pres Acad Fit Awd.

BARTHELMAN, ELI D; Maize HS; Wichita, KS; (3); Art Clb; Science Clb; Hon Roll; ST/REGNL Medal Sci Olympiad 2 Yrs; Chem.

BARTHELME, SHANNON; Valley Ctr HS; Valley Center, KS; (2); Chorus; Variety Show; Chrldng; Hon Roll; Yth Alive; Wmns Ansmble; Pittsburg U.

BARTHOL, LAUREN; St Thomas Aquinas HS; Leawood, KS; (4); 19/242; Am Leg Aux Girls St; Debate Tm; German Clb; Model UN; NFL; Band; Phtg Nwsp; Lit Mag; High Hon Roll; NHS; German Clb; Nrsng.

BARTHOLOMEW, KARA L; Inman Jr Sr HS; Inman, KS; (2); Pep Clb; Chorus; Hon Roll; Prfct Atten Awd; U Of KS; Lawyer; Politician.

BARTHULY, JODIE; St Marys HS; Saint Marys, KS; (4); 1/53; FBLA; Quiz Bowl; Band; Ed Yrbk; Ofcr Stu Cncl; L Vllybl; High Hon Roll; NHS; Val; FCA; KS Hnr Soc; KS ST U; Cmptr Sci.

BARTKO, ANNIE J; Bishop Miege HS; Mission, KS; (1); 120/260; Chorus; Drill Tm; Pom Pon; Tennis; Trk; Hon Roll.

BARTKOSKI, BRANDON; Burlingame HS; Burlingame, KS; (3); 3/33; High Hon Roll; Sons Of VFW; KS ST U; Scndry Ed.

BARTLETT, ABBEY L; Holton HS; Holton, KS; (1); Church Yth Grp; Cmnty Wkr; Dance Clb; Acpl Chr; Band; Chorus; Church Choir; Mrchg Band; Orch; Pep Band; Piano; Baker U; Soc Work.

BARTLETT, TAUSHA; Haviland HS; Haviland, KS; (3); Church Yth Grp; Pep Clb; Teachers Aide; Chorus; Sec Frsh Cls; Sec Soph Cls; Sec Jr Cls; Sec Sr Cls; Ofcr Stu Cncl; Chrldng.

BARTLEY, SHANE; Hutchinson HS; Hutchinson, KS; (4); 7/216; Am Leg Boys St; Pres Art Clb; Church Yth Grp; JV Bsbl; Var L Bsktbl; L Mgr(s); High Hon Roll; NHS; Pres Acad Fit Awd; Marimba Natl Chmpshp; Hutchinson CC; Music.

BARTON JR, CURTIS E; Wichita East HS; Wichita, KS; (2); Church Yth Grp; Drama Clb; Hosp Aide; Spanish Clb; Teachers Aide; School Musical; School Play; Trk; Hon Roll; Demolay; Med.

BARTZ, NICOLE; El Dorado HS; El Dorado, KS; (4); 17/155; Am Leg Aux Girls St; Church Yth Grp; Debate Tm; Letterman Clb; NFL; School Play; Var Chrldng; Co-Capt Powder Puff Ftbl; Var Tennis; High Hon Roll; KU.

BASEL II, WENDELL R; Lawrence HS; Lawrence, KS; (4); Church Yth Grp; FCA; Teachers Aide; Intrml Bsktbl; Var Mgr(s); JV Var Trk; Hon Roll; Pres Acad Fit Awd; KS Univ; Ath Trng Sci.

BASGALL, JESSICA R; Otis Bison HS; Otis, KS; (2); Church Yth Grp; Quiz Bowl; SADD; Band; Mrchg Band; Pep Band; Stage Crew; Vllybl; High Hon Roll; KAYS; Ed.

BASINSKI, BRIAN A; Louisburg HS; Louisburg, KS; (3); Teachers Aide; Yrbk; Trk; Wt Lftg; High Hon Roll; Hon Roll; Prfct Atten Awd; Navy/Coll.

BASKA, KATHLEEN M; Bishop Miege HS; Shawnee Mission, KS; (4); 25/160; Teachers Aide; Drill Tm; School Play; Rep Frsh Cls; Rep Soph Cls; Capt Socr; Vllybl; Hon Roll; Spirit Clb; Campus Ministry Team; U Of MO Columbia; Animal Sci.

BASLER, PAUL; Olathe East Sr HS; Olathe, KS; (3); Boy Scts; Letterman Clb; Spanish Clb; Varsity Clb; Ofcr Bsbl; Var Ftbl; Var Trk; Var Wrstlng; Hon Roll.

BASOW, ANNIE; Lawrence HS; Lawrence, KS; (3); 187/632; Cmnty Wkr; GAA; Hosp Aide; Latin Clb; Teachers Aide; Hon Roll; Stu Imprvmnt Awd; Poli Sci.

BASS, CAMILLE; Sumner Acad Of Arts & Science; Kansas City, KS; (3); 46/148; Latin Clb; Pep Clb; Spanish Clb; Acpl Chr; Chorus; L Chrldng; High Hon Roll; Hon Roll; NHS; Ntl Merit Ltr; 2 Yrs Tutor Pgm; KU; Med.

BASS, KIMBERLY; Topeka West HS; Topeka, KS; (4); 5/236; Art Clb; Church Yth Grp; Library Aide; Pep Clb; Teachers Aide; High Hon Roll; St Schlr; Washburn Univ.

BASS, SAMUEL C; Goddard HS; Wichita, KS; (2); JA; Library Aide; Math Tm; Office Aide; Science Clb; Spanish Clb; Teachers Aide; Golf; Socr; Wrstlng; Kays Clb; OK Univ; Lawyer.

BASSELL, CANDICE M; Wichita Collegiate Schl; Wichita, KS; (3); Debate Tm; Sec Treas English Clb; German Clb; NFL; Quiz Bowl; Scholastic Bowl; Var Tennis; High Hon Roll; Piano Spec Rcgntn KMTA Fall Auditions 94; Rnkd 13 KS Tennis Grls Singles 95; Wichita Chldrns Hm Vol; Chem/Physcn.

BASSETT, TAMMY; Central Jr Sr HS; Salina, KS; (4); 7/196; Debate Tm; Math Tm; Pres NFL; Speech Tm; SADD; Var Chrldng; High Hon Roll; NHS; Pres Acad Fit Awd; St Schlr; Washburn Univ; Law.

BASTIN, HOLLY L; Olathe East Sr HS; Lenexa, KS; (2); Art Clb; Church Yth Grp; Latin Clb; Letterman Clb; Orch; Variety Show; Rep Frsh Cls; Trk; Hon Roll; Pres Acad Fit Awd; Area Youth Symphony Grds; Lettered Orch/Track; Music Ed Natl Conf; Music Ed.

BASYE, MICHELLE R; Salina HS Central; Salina, KS; (2); Church Yth Grp; Acpl Chr; Chorus; Church Choir; Hon Roll; KS Music Edctrs Assn St Choir, Dist Choir; Mid-America Nazarene Coll; Ed.

BATCHMAN, STACI L; Otis Bison HS; Olmitz, KS; (3); 3/25; Church Yth Grp; Cmnty Wkr; Dance Clb; GAA; Pres Letterman Clb; Pep Clb; Pres Treas SADD; Teachers Aide; Varsity Clb; Band; KAY Clb Rep, VP, Prog Dir; KY St Univ; Phy Thrpy.

BATES, DERRICK D; Seaman Sr HS; Topeka, KS; (3); Church Yth Grp; Cmnty Wkr; Pres 4-H; FBLA; JA; SADD; Band; Mrchg Band; Pep Band; Bsktbl; Arch Eng.

BATES, JOLYNN; Wichita East HS; Wichita, KS; (2); Library Aide; Teachers Aide; Chorus; Tchr.

BATES, MATTHEW M; Lansing HS; Leavenworth, KS; (4); 3/143; Scholastic Bowl; School Play; Ed Nwsp; Ofcr Stu Cncl; Var Capt Bsktbl; Socr; Tennis; NHS; Ntl Merit SF; Debate Tm; Mst Likely To Succeed; KAYS Lansing Chptr VP; Chem Engrng.

BATES, MICHAEL J; Sumner Acad Of Arts & Science; Kansas City, KS; (2); Church Yth Grp; Latin Clb; Spanish Clb; JV Ftbl; Var Trk; Hon Roll; Wrk/Mssn Trp Restr Orlndo FL 96; Mid-Amer Nazarene Coll; Archtct.

BATES, RYAN S; Hoisington HS; Hoisington, KS; (3); Am Leg Boys St; Church Yth Grp; L Var Bsktbl; L Var Tennis; Hon Roll; LEAD Yth Forum; DARE Role Model.

BATES, TYRONE; Wyandotte HS; Kansas City, KS; (4); 7/196; Pres Church Yth Grp; Drama Clb; FCA; JA; Letterman Clb; Band; Chorus; Rep Stu Cncl; Capt Crs Cntry; Capt Trk; SCLS Schlrshp/Awd Wnnr; Stu Of Month 95; Crss Cntry League Chmpn 3 Yrs; Medcl Careers; Teen Hope; Peer; Fisk U; Med.

BATH, KIRK T; Washburn Rural HS; Topeka, KS; (3); 89/320; Intrml Bsktbl; Var L Golf; High Hon Roll; Hon Roll; KS U; Dntstry.

BATHELME, LUKE A; Bishop Carroll Catholic HS; Wichita, KS; (3); Church Yth Grp; Ftbl; Wt Lftg; Pres Acad Fit Awd; Meteorology.

BATHOLOMEW, DENISE R; Olathe North Sr HS; Olathe, KS; (4); Church Yth Grp; Thesps; School Musical; School Play; Stage Crew; Rep Stu Cncl; Cit Awd; NHS; Pres Acad Fit Awd; Drama Clb; Brigham Young U; Elem Ed.

BATHURST, DOLLY; Chapman HS; Abilene, KS; (4); 4/107; Natl FFA Org; Chorus; Church Choir; Pres Frsh Cls; Rep Soph Cls; Sec Treas Stu Cncl; Var Trk; JV Var Vllybl; 4-H Awd; High Hon Roll; Emmnls Mssn Team To Mexico; Sterling Coll; Ed.

BATHURST, NEELEY R; Chapman HS; Abilene, KS; (3); Church Yth Grp; 4-H; School Play; Rep Frsh Cls; Rep Soph Cls; Rep Jr Cls; Ofcr Stu Cncl; Var Capt Crs Cntry; Var Trk; Hon Roll; Jr-Sr Ensemble; AFG Club; I Rating Soloist ST Vocal Cmptn; Elem Ed.

BATIN, CHRIS; Ulysses HS; Ulysses, KS; (2); SADD; Var Bsktbl; Var Ftbl; Var Trk; Var Wt Lftg; High Hon Roll; NHS.

BATTENFIELD, COURTNEY; Washburn Rural HS; Topeka, KS; (4); 13/268; Church Yth Grp; French Clb; Band; Mrchg Band; Bsktbl; Var L Chrldng; Intrml Gym; Intrml Powder Puff Ftbl; NHS; KS St Univ; Eng.

BATTESE, KELLY; Olathe North Sr HS; Olathe, KS; (3); Church Yth Grp; FCA; Spanish Clb; Var Bsbl; Var Bsktbl; High Hon Roll; NHS; Prfct Atten Awd; Spanish NHS; Phy Therapy.

BATY, KENDRA; Olathe South Sr HS; Olathe, KS; (4); Pres French Clb; Acpl Chr; Chorus; Church Choir; School Musical; Mgr(s); High Hon Roll; NHS; St Schlr; Mid Amer Nazarence Coll; Soc.

BAUCK, AARON; Anderson Cty Jr Sr HS; Garnett, KS; (3); 2/74; Am Leg Boys St; Church Yth Grp; Library Aide; Pep Clb; Scholastic Bowl; SADD; Ofcr Stu Cncl; Var Golf; High Hon Roll; NHS; Red Cross Bd; Octgn VP; Emporia ST U; Bus.

BAUCK, LYLE E; Anderson Cty Jr Sr HS; Garnett, KS; (1); Church Yth Grp; Cmnty Wkr; Pep Clb; Scholastic Bowl; SADD; JV Ftbl; Golf; High Hon Roll; Octagon; Modl Leg; Bsbl.

BAUER, BRANDON; Mulvane Sr HS; Mulvane, KS; (4); 1/144; Cmnty Wkr; FCA; French Clb; Letterman Clb; Math Tm; SADD; Teachers Aide; Varsity Clb; Phtg Yrbk; Treas Jr Cls; Yth Prvntn Tm; SW Hnrs Smnr; U Of KS Hnr Schlr; U Of KS; Phys Ther.

BAUER, CORY J; Northern Valley HS; Almena, KS; (1); Natl FFA Org; Speech Tm; Chorus; School Musical; JV Bsktbl; JV Ftbl; Hon Roll; Prfct Atten Awd.

BAUER, DANIEL; Louisburg HS; Louisburg, KS; (3); Boy Scts; JV Bsktbl; JV Var Ftbl; JV Var Trk; Var L Wrstlng; Crpntr/Supt/Prjct Mgr.

BAUER, LUKE D; Buhler HS; Hutchinson, KS; (2); Letterman Clb; Spanish Clb; SADD; Acpl Chr; School Musical; Swing Chorus; Rep Stu Cncl; Var Bsbl; Wt Lftg; Hon Roll.

BAUER, STARSKY L; Ness City HS; Ness City, KS; (1); Church Yth Grp; Ofcr Frsh Cls; Wt Lftg; Hon Roll; Med.

BAUGHMAN, JENNIFER; Washington HS; Kansas City, KS; (3); Debate Tm; Drama Clb; Spanish Clb; SADD; Rptr Nwsp; Powder Puff Ftbl; Sftbl; Vllybl; KS ST Univ; DVM; Veterinarian.

BAUGHNS JR, ANDREW H; Wichita East HS; Wichita, KS; (2); Hon Roll; Sci Olympiad Received 2nd Pl In St Level; IB Stu; Stud Rigorous Math & Physics; Washington U; Thertcl Physics.

BAUM, MELISSA M; Northwest HS Wichita; Wichita, KS; (4); Church Yth Grp; VP Intnl Clb; Red Cross Aide; Band; Capt Color Guard; Hon Roll; NHS; Pres Acad Fit Awd; Spanish NHS; Cmnty Wkr; SW MO State Univ; Entreprenru.

BAUMAN, ASBBIE A; Quinter Jr Sr HS; Quinter, KS; (3); Church Yth Grp; FCA; FHA; Band; Mrchg Band; Pep Band; School Musical; School Play; Ofcr Frsh Cls; Ofcr Jr Cls; All ST Choir; Music Cntsts; KU; Music Thrpy.

BAUMAN, KARLENE; Sabetha HS; Sabetha, KS; (4); 21/60; Pres 4-H; Rep German Clb; Rep Natl FFA Org; Pep Clb; Co-Capt Flag Corp; Mrchg Band; Pep Band; Bsktbl; 4-H Awd; Hon Roll; KS Brwn Swiss Prncss 94-95; KS Dairy Brwn Swss Awd; Natl Diary Conf; Chrch Yth Grp Pres, VP, Sec; KS ST U.

BAUMANN, SKY; West Smith Cty HS; Franklin, NE; (4); 10/26; Letterman Clb; Natl FFA Org; Pep Clb; SADD; Yrbk; L Bsktbl; L Chrldng; L Trk; L Vllybl; Hon Roll; Fort Hays ST U; Agribusiness.

BAUMGARTNER, MEGAN E; Phillipsburg HS; Phillipsburg, KS; (2); 5/63; Sec FBLA; Scholastic Bowl; Band; Chorus; School Musical; School Play; Ed Nwsp; Rep Frsh Cls; Mgr Jr Cls; Rep Stu Cncl; Natl Young Ldr Conf Nom; Natl Schlr.

BAUS, LEIGH A; Pratt HS; Pratt, KS; (3); Church Yth Grp; Mrchg Band; Orch; Pep Band; JV Bsktbl; JV Var Golf; High Hon Roll; Hon Roll; Cmnty Wkr; Library Aide; Stdnt Of Wk 3 Times; 6th/7th Grd Coach Rec Bsktbl Undefeated; Pratt CC; Aviation.

BAXA, JULIE; Ulysses HS; Ulysses, KS; (2); FBLA; Band; Flag Corp; Jazz Band; Mrchg Band; Var L Chrldng; Hon Roll; Pres Acad Fit Awd; Ecology Clb; Natl Lions Clb Band; Ft Hays ST U; Jrnlsm.

BAXA, KARLA; Hillcrest Schl; Cuba, KS; (1); 1/20; Church Yth Grp; FCA; FHA; Natl FFA Org; Quiz Bowl; Jazz Band; Treas Frsh Cls; Mgr(s); Vllybl; High Hon Roll; Elem Educ.

BAXTER, KYE J; Sedan HS; Sedan, KS; (2); 2/33; Church Yth Grp; Treas FHA; Letterman Clb; Speech Tm; Chorus; School Play; Variety Show; Var L Bsbl; Var Bsktbl; Var L Ftbl; Dist Choir; Knowledge Bowl; Sci; Eng.

BAXTER, LUKE; Onaga HS; Onaga, KS; (2); 2/49; Church Yth Grp; Cmnty Wkr; Letterman Clb; Spanish Clb; Ofcr Soph Cls; Rep Stu Cncl; Var L Bsktbl; Var L Ftbl; Var L Trk; High Hon Roll; Yth Bsktbl Ofcl Vol; Christmas Events; KS ST Univ; Medicine.

BAYER, INGRID; Trinity Catholic HS; Mc Pherson, KS; (4); 1/28; Church Yth Grp; Debate Tm; Hosp Aide; NFL; Band; Church Choir; Jazz Band; School Play; High Hon Roll; NHS; Author Schl Play; Forensics Team; Psycht.

BAYER, KRISTEN R; Great Bend Sr HS; Great Bend, KS; (3); Church Yth Grp; German Clb; Office Aide; SADD; Teachers Aide; Chorus; Hon Roll; Barten Cty 2 Yrs.

BAYES, REBEKAH D; Great Bend Sr HS; Great Bend, KS; (2); Church Yth Grp; Drama Clb; FCA; Pep Clb; Spanish Clb; Teachers Aide; Chorus; Variety Show; Stat Bsktbl; Golf; Kayettes; KS ST U; Elem Ed.

BAYLOR, KRISTEN; Ottawa HS; Ottawa, KS; (4); Am Leg Aux Girls St; Church Yth Grp; FCA; French Clb; Office Aide; Varsity Clb; Chorus; Drill Tm; School Musical; School Play; Hmcmng Qn; KS ST U; Scl Work.

BAYNE, MARGARET E; Shawnee Mission N HS; Overland Park, KS; (3); Pep Clb; ROTC; Chorus; Church Choir; Color Guard; Drill Tm; School Musical; School Play; Stage Crew; Swing Chorus; TX Natl Choir; Super Rating St Solo & Choir Cmptns; 7th Pl Drill Down ROTC Drill Meet; Music Ed; Music Performace.

BAYOUTH, DAN P; Lawrence HS; Lawrence, KS; (2); Band; Mrchg Band; Socr; Hon Roll; Pres Acad Fit Awd; Comp Sci.

BAYS, AIMEE N; Topeka West HS; Topeka, KS; (4); 2/235; Cmnty Wkr; French Clb; Girl Scts; Math Clb; Office Aide; Q&S; Scholastic Bowl; Teachers Aide; Co-Ed Ed Yrbk; Gov Hon Prg Awd; Natl Frnch Exm IV Lvl 1st ST/5TH Nation; Upwrd Bnd; U Of KS.

BAZIL, AUDREY R; Rose Hill HS; Rose Hill, KS; (3); Girl Scts; Capt Scholastic Bowl; Band; Mrchg Band; Pep Band; School Musical; Ed Yrbk; High Hon Roll; Girl Scout Gold Awd; His.

BEACHY, JANE W; Shawnee Mission E Sr HS; Prairie Village, KS; (3); 43/430; Church Yth Grp; Cmnty Wkr; Drama Clb; Natl Beta Clb; SADD; Thesps; Chorus; Church Choir; School Musical; School Play; Thtr.

BEALBY, ALICIA; Russell HS; Russell, KS; (3); 1/87; Church Yth Grp; Cmnty Wkr; Dance Clb; Debate Tm; Drama Clb; FCA; Key Clb; Letterman Clb; Natl FFA Org; NFL; KS St Univ; Phy Thrpy.

BEALE, CHRIS K; Beloit Jr Sr HS; Beloit, KS; (2); Science Clb; Hon Roll; KS Univ; Cardiologist.

BEALE, CORY J; Norton Comm HS; Norton, KS; (3); Church Yth Grp; Cmnty Wkr; Pep Clb; Quiz Bowl; Scholastic Bowl; Band; Pep Band; School Musical; JV Bsktbl; Hon Roll; Kays; Knwldg Mstr Open; Schlstc Ltr; Manhattan Chrstn Coll.

BEALL, OLIVER P; Pleasant Ridge HS; Easton, KS; (3); 4-H; Natl FFA Org; Teachers Aide; Cit Awd; 4-H Awd; Hon Roll; NHS; Ag.

BEAM, KRISTEN L; Washburn Rural HS; Topeka, KS; (3); Church Yth Grp; JA; Sftbl; Trk; High Hon Roll; Prfct Atten Awd; Pol Sci/Lawyer.

BEAMER, SARAH; Grinnell HS; Oakley, KS; (3); 2/15; Pres Church Yth Grp; HOBY; Math Clb; Pep Clb; Quiz Bowl; Science Clb; Chorus; Mrchg Band; Pep Band; School Play.

BEAMON, ANDRIA C; Bishop Miege HS; Shawnee Mission, KS; (1); Debate Tm; High Hon Roll; Hon Roll.

BEAN, AMANDA M; Kingman HS; Pretty Prairie, KS; (2); Church Yth Grp; FBLA; Library Aide; SADD; Teachers Aide; School Play; Stage Crew; Yrbk; Bsktbl; Var Golf; Yth Govt; Teens Today Ldrs Tomorrow; Emporia AST Univ; Ed.

BEAN, BRODERICK G; Onaga HS; Onaga, KS; (2); Office Aide; VP SADD; Chorus; School Musical; Hon Roll; Singing Comm Weddings; Career Day Organizer 2 Yrs; Bus Mngmt/Acctng.

BEAN, JULIE; Kingman HS; Pretty Prairie, KS; (4); 1/70; Church Yth Grp; FCA; Sec Treas French Clb; FBLA; Library Aide; SADD; Teachers Aide; High Hon Roll; Pres VP NHS; Pres Acad Fit Awd; Teens Today Ldrs Tomorrow Cabinet; Gov Schlr; KS Newman Coll; Biochem.

BEAN, MELANIE S; Beloit Jr Sr HS; Beloit, KS; (3); Sec 4-H; Natl FFA Org; Spanish Clb; Phtg Rptr Nwsp; Ofcr Jr Cls; 4-H Awd; High Hon Roll; Lvl I KS St Spnsh Tst 23rd Pl; Kytt Mem; AFS Clb VP; Fort Hays ST.

BEAN, RODERICK D; Onaga HS; Onaga, KS; (2); Chorus; Rptr Nwsp; Phtg Yrbk; Hon Roll; Beloit Vo-Tech; Hvy Equip Oper.

BEARD, SHANNON R; Kapaun-Mt Carmel HS; Wichita, KS; (2); Pres Church Yth Grp; Debate Tm; Spanish Clb; Sec SADD; Chorus; Rep Frsh Cls; Treas Stu Cncl; Score Keeper; Hon Roll; NHS; Yth Prvntn Tm; Prish Cncl Yth Rep; Peer Lstng Grp.

BEASHORE, RYAN P; Shawnee Mission N HS; Shawnee Mission, KS; (3); 180/497; Cmnty Wkr; Office Aide; Pep Clb; Teachers Aide; Ofcr Bsbl; Bsktbl; Ftbl; Golf; High Hon Roll; Hon Roll; KS U; Phys Thrp.

BEATON, AARON J; Scott Comm HS; Scott City, KS; (3); 1/65; Am Leg Boys St; 4-H; Natl FFA Org; Var L Crs Cntry; Var Trk; 4-H Awd; Hon Roll.

BEATON, LINDSAY S; Scott Comm HS; Scott City, KS; (3); 7/79; Church Yth Grp; 4-H; Pep Clb; Band; Flag Corp; Jazz Band; Pep Band; Rep Stu Cncl; Stat Bsktbl; JV Trk; Hstd Japanese Frgn Exchng Stu; Frgn Exchng Stu In Japan 1 Mnth; KS ST Univ; Law/Bus.

BEATSON, BRANDI M; Olathe East Sr HS; Olathe, KS; (3); 58/360; Cmnty Wkr; Pres Pep Clb; Spanish Clb; Teachers Aide; Drill Tm; Rep Frsh Cls; Rep Sr Cls; Powder Puff Ftbl; Hon Roll; NHS; KS Univ; OT.

BEAVERS, MATTHEW R; Cheney Jr Sr HS; Cheney, KS; (2); 2/55; Letterman Clb; Varsity Clb; Chorus; Variety Show; VP Soph Cls; JV Bsktbl; L Var Ftbl; L Var Trk; High Hon Roll; Pres Acad Fit Awd; Bethany Univ; Premed.

BEBERMEYER, MELISSA D; Maize HS; Wichita, KS; (3); Dance Clb; Office Aide; Science Clb; Spanish Clb; SADD; Teachers Aide; Wt Lftg; Hon Roll; Prfct Atten Awd; Pres Acad Fit Awd; Soccer; KAYS Mem; KS Newman; Phy Thrpst.

BEBOUT, JESSAMEE D; Downtown Law Magnet HS; Wichita, KS; (3); Latin Clb; Library Aide; Stage Crew; Hon Roll; NHS; Pottery.

BECHARD, APRIL; Clifton-Clyde HS; Clifton, KS; (4); 10/34; Am Leg Aux Girls St; Church Yth Grp; 4-H; FBLA; Pep Clb; Phtg Yrbk; VP Jr Cls; Pres Sr Cls; Treas Stu Cncl; L Bsktbl; Kayettes; Highland CC; Sprts Phys Thrpy.

BECHARD, DAYNA A; Tescott HS; Culver, KS; (3); Cmnty Wkr; Quiz Bowl; School Play; Pres Stu Cncl; L Trk; Hon Roll; NHS; Ottawa Cty Yth Task Force; Vac Bible Schl Asst Tchr; Frnscs 1st Pl ST Fstvl; Fort Hays ST; Cmrcl Art/Jrnlsm.

BECHDOLDT, KRISSY; Maize HS; Wichita, KS; (2); Church Yth Grp; 4-H; Spanish Clb; SADD; Bsktbl; Sftbl; Vllybl; High Hon Roll; Hon Roll; NHS; Pittsburg ST U; Elem Ed.

BECHDOLDT, LAUREN; Maize HS; Wichita, KS; (3); 8/200; Art Clb; Church Yth Grp; Cmnty Wkr; Math Tm; Science Clb; Spanish Clb; SADD; High Hon Roll; NHS; Pres Acad Fit Awd; Avila Coll; Phys Asst.

BECHELMAYR, KELLY E; Turner HS; Kansas City, KS; (4); 31/200; Art Clb; Bus Profs of Am; Dance Clb; Band; Drill Tm; Mrchg Band; School Musical; Variety Show; Rep Sr Cls; High Hon Roll; Johnson Cnty CC.

BECHTEL, MEGAN; Winfield HS; Winfield, KS; (3); Debate Tm; French Clb; HOBY; NFL; Pep Clb; Quiz Bowl; Scholastic Bowl; Teachers Aide; Var Bsktbl; High Hon Roll; Amer Fld Svc Chptr Co-Pres; KS; Sec Math Ed.

BECHTELHEIMER, JESSICA; Bishop Carroll Catholic HS; Wichita, KS; (2); 20/201; Church Yth Grp; French Clb; SADD; French Hon Soc; High Hon Roll; Hon Roll; Alge Tutor 1 Yr; CYO Mbr Of Yr; Heritage Pnl; Wichita ST Univ; Grphc Dsgn.

BECK, ARIANE L; Blue Valley Northwest HS; Shawnee Mission, KS; (3); 1/350; Math Clb; Model UN; Band; Jazz Band; Mrchg Band; Pep Band; High Hon Roll; NHS; Cmnty Wkr; Drama Clb; KAYS Clb; Sfty City Vol; Elect Engnr.

BECK, CHRISTINA D; Liberal HS; Liberal, KS; (2); TX A&M; Marine Bio.

BECK, JENNIFER M; Clearwater HS; Clearwater, KS; (4); FCA; SADD; Chorus; Church Choir; School Musical; School Play; Stage Crew; Kayette Brd; Show Choir; Rainbow Girl St Ofcr; Ft Hays ST U; Brdcstng.

BECK, MEGAN; Maranatha Acad; Shawnee Mission, KS; (4); 7/34; Am Leg Aux Girls St; HOBY; School Musical; School Play; Rep Frsh Cls; Rep Soph Cls; VP Jr Cls; Var Capt Bsktbl; High Hon Roll; NHS; Law.

BECK, MICAH; Maranatha Acad; Shawnee, KS; (1); Church Yth Grp; Drama Clb; English Clb; School Play; Stage Crew; Ofcr Frsh Cls; Ofcr Stu Cncl.

BECK, NAOMI; Clay Ctr Cmty HS; Clay Center, KS; (4); 23/95; Sec Art Clb; Church Yth Grp; Drama Clb; NFL; Chorus; Ed Nwsp; Ed Yrbk; DAR Awd; Hon Roll; NHS; Clay Cty Jr Miss Prgm 1st Rnr Up; 2 Mssn Trps; Forensics SQ Qlfyr 2 Yrs; Ozark Chrstn Coll; Mssns.

BECK, SHAWNNA M; Northern Hghts HS; Americus, KS; (3); Church Yth Grp; Girl Scts; Office Aide; Chorus; JV Bsktbl; Hon Roll; Girl Scouts; Yth Group Pres; Nrsng Home Vol; Phys Therapy.

BECK, TIFFANY; Sumner Acad Of Arts & Science; Kansas City, KS; (2); Church Yth Grp; Debate Tm; Latin Clb; Pep Clb; Spanish Clb; Chorus; JV L Chrldng; Gym; High Hon Roll; Hon Roll; U KS; Nrsng.

BECKER, ANGIE; Centralia Schl; Centralia, KS; (1); 10/34; Drama Clb; Band; Chorus; Mrchg Band; Pep Band; School Play; Chrldng; Trk; Vllybl; Cit Awd; Air Force Acad; Military Offcr.

BECKER, GABBIE; Downs HS; Downs, KS; (3); Church Yth Grp; FCA; FHA; Pep Clb; Spanish Clb; Band; Chorus; Mrchg Band; Pep Band; School Musical; Ed.

BECKER, JOANNA M; Shawnee Heights HS; Topeka, KS; (1); Drama Clb; Orch; School Musical; KU.

BECKER, KENT R; Hayden HS; Topeka, KS; (2); Var Bsbl; Var Bsktbl; Var Ftbl; Hon Roll; Hnrb Mntn All City K/P, Rushing & Punting; Ftbl 1st Team Hnrb Mntn; Bsktbl Ltr; 2nd Team All City Bsbl.

BECKER, NEIL C; Wichita North HS; Wichita, KS; (2); VP Boy Scts; Drama Clb; Latin Clb; Chorus; School Musical; Var JV Wrstlng; High Hon Roll; Church Yth Grp; Teachers Aide; Church Choir; Comp Mgmt; United Way Yth Day Of Caring 95 Vol; Outdoor Camping.

BECKER, ROBIN; Hiawatha HS; Hiawatha, KS; (2); 10/110; Drama Clb; Pep Clb; Drill Tm; Chrldng; Trk; Bio Club; KAYS.

BECKER, SHANE A; Great Bend Sr HS; Great Bend, KS; (4); German Clb; Pep Clb; Band; Jazz Band; Mrchg Band; Pep Band; Variety Show; Rep Frsh Cls; Var Mgr Bsbl; Barton Cty CC; Justice Admin.

BECKER, SHAWN J; Centralia Schl; Centralia, KS; (3); 1/22; Computer Clb; VP Letterman Clb; Sec Natl FFA Org; Quiz Bowl; Science Clb; Nwsp; Pres Frsh Cls; Pres Soph Cls; Ofcr Stu Cncl; Var L Bsktbl; Ag Eng.

BECKER, STEPHANIE; Goodland HS; Goodland, KS; (4); Am Leg Aux Girls St; Church Yth Grp; FHA; GAA; Chorus; School Musical; Yrbk; VP Jr Cls; VP Sr Cls; JV Bsktbl.

BECKHAM, R JASON; Piper HS; Kansas City, KS; (4); Var L Ftbl; Cit Awd; Hon Roll; Prfct Atten Awd; Pres Schlr; Ptry Publ Anthlgy Winds Acrss Plains Lbry Of Cngrs 96; Accptd Hnrs Prgm/Pres Schlsp KCKCC; KCKCC.

BECKMAN, MATTHEW S; Grinnell HS; Grinnell, KS; (3); 5/14; Church Yth Grp; Math Clb; Math Tm; Science Clb; Spanish Clb; Chorus; Rep Stu Cncl; JV Bsktbl; Var Ftbl; Mgr(s).

BECKMANN, NICHOLAS M; Smith Ctr Jr Sr HS; Smith Center, KS; (3); 3/48; Church Yth Grp; Drama Clb; Letterman Clb; Math Tm; Quiz Bowl; Scholastic Bowl; Science Clb; Chorus; School Play; Var L Crs Cntry; Rgnts Hnrs Acad; St Chem Awd; 3 Sprt St Qulfr; U Of KS.

BECKMON, NATHAN; Crest HS; Kincaid, KS; (4); 7/25; FBLA; VICA; Chorus; Treas Soph Cls; Var Capt Bsktbl; Var Capt Ftbl; Trk; Wt Lftg; High Hon Roll; Hon Roll; All Leag 1st Team B-Ball/F-Ball; 1st Team All Leag Offnsv End/2nd Team Dfnsv Back All ST B-Ball; Allen County.

BECKWITH, JOE; Sedgwick HS; Sedgwick, KS; (3); Letterman Clb; Band; Chorus; School Musical; Variety Show; VP Frsh Cls; VP Soph Cls; VP Jr Cls; Rep Stu Cncl; Var L Bsktbl.

BECKWITH, JULIE K; Pleasant Ridge HS; Leavenworth, KS; (4); 1/65; Church Yth Grp; FCA; Hosp Aide; SADD; School Musical; School Play; Ed Nwsp; Cit Awd; NHS; Val; Natl Yth Ldrshp Frm On Med 95; Psych.

BEDELL, DANIELLE; Wellsville Jr Sr HS; Wellsville, KS; (4); 1/49; Am Leg Aux Girls St; FCA; Ed Yrbk; VP Jr Cls; VP Sr Cls; Cit Awd; High Hon Roll; NHS; St Schlr; Val; KAY VP; Elem Libry Asst; U Of KS.

BEEBE, KELLY DENISE; Wichita North HS; Wichita, KS; (3); 66/260; Cmnty Wkr; Drama Clb; Ski Clb; Thesps; School Musical; School Play; Stage Crew; Swing Chorus; Variety Show; Ofcr Stu Cncl; KS St Jr Skier; Thspn Offcr; Marine Bio.

BEEGHLY-HILLS, JENNIFER L; Burlington HS; Burlington, KS; (3); 7/87; Drama Clb; Hist FBLA; Quiz Bowl; Thesps; School Musical; School Play; Rep Jr Cls; Ofcr Stu Cncl; Var Bsktbl; Var Sftbl; FBLA ST Exec Brd Dist 1 VP; Natl Yng Ldrs Conf; KS Rgnts Hnrs Acad; U Of KS; Arspc Engrng.

BEEMER, CHRISTA A; Arkansas City HS; Arkansas City, KS; (3); 1/200; Drama Clb; Office Aide; SADD; Chorus; Orch; School Musical; School Play; Hon Roll; NHS; Teenage Comms Theatre Troupe.

BEEMS, TIFFANY; Clay Ctr Cmty HS; Clay Center, KS; (3); Art Clb; Debate Tm; Drama Clb; Chorus; Rptr Nwsp; Rep Stu Cncl; Var L Golf; NHS; Church Yth Grp; Speech Tm; KS Rgnts Hnrs Acad; FOG/ENVRMNTL Clb; Lifeguard; KU.

BEER, JANESSA E; Bishop Miege HS; Kansas City, MO; (2); 30/163; French Clb; Drill Tm; Pom Pon; High Hon Roll; U KS.

BEER, JENNIFER; Olathe East Sr HS; Olathe, KS; (3); French Clb; Letterman Clb; Pep Clb; Drill Tm; Ofcr Frsh Cls; Ofcr Stu Cncl; High Hon Roll; Hon Roll; Pres Acad Fit Awd; Pdtrc Nrsng.

BEERY, HEATH C; Cimarron HS; Kalvesta, KS; (2); Church Yth Grp; FCA; Letterman Clb; Pep Clb; Spanish Clb; Band; Treas Frsh Cls; Var Bsbl; Var Bsktbl; JV Ftbl; 4 Yr Coll.

BEERY, RONDA R; Labette Co HS; Mound Valley, KS; (2); Art Clb; Church Yth Grp; Dance Clb; FCA; FHA; Pep Clb; SADD; Vllybl; Cit Awd; Hon Roll; Chrch Bsbl; Nrs; Dr; Tchr.

BEESON, IRENE L; Lawrence HS; Lawrence, KS; (2); Church Yth Grp; Spanish Clb; Orch; JV Trk; Hon Roll; Pres Acad Fit Awd; Fellwshp Chrstn Studs; Manhattan Chrstn Coll; Tchr.

BEETS, ASHLEY; Ottawa HS; Ottawa, KS; (2); 1/195; Letterman Clb; SADD; Teachers Aide; Varsity Clb; Rep Soph Cls; VP Jr Cls; Bsktbl; Trk; Vllybl; High Hon Roll; Teenport.

BEFORT, CHERYL; Wichita Heights HS; Wichita, KS; (4); 27/249; Am Leg Aux Girls St; Cmnty Wkr; Debate Tm; HOBY; Pres NFL; Phtg Yrbk; Rep Stu Cncl; L Swmmng; Hon Roll; NHS; Peer Ldr; Site Cncl Rep; Wichita ST U; Sports Med.

BEGNOCHE, SHERI R; Downs HS; Downs, KS; (3); Ofcr FHA; Band; Drill Tm; School Play; Nwsp; Yrbk; Pres Soph Cls; Pres Jr Cls; Bsktbl; High Hon Roll.

BEHNK, PAM; Haven HS; Haven, KS; (4); Dance Clb; Pep Clb; Chorus; Drill Tm; Chrldng; Tennis; Hon Roll; Independence CC; Nutri.

BEHRENS, MELISSA S; Great Bend Sr HS; Great Bend, KS; (4); Nwsp; Hon Roll; Prfct Atten Awd; BCCC.

BEHRENS, MICHAEL C; Great Bend Sr HS; Great Bend, KS; (1); Intrml Ftbl.

BEHRENS, RICHARD R; Leavenworth HS; Leavenworth, KS; (1); Church Yth Grp; Hon Roll; MIT; Electrncs.

BEHRENS, STACIE; Turner HS; Kansas City, KS; (3); Bus Profs of Am; Church Yth Grp; SADD; Church Choir; Hon Roll; NHS; Schlrshps To 3 Or 4 Diffrnt Chrstn Schls; Bible Bowl; U Of KS; Pediatrc Nursng.

BEISNER, KYLE D; Lawrence HS; Lawrence, KS; (2); Church Yth Grp; Debate Tm; DECA; Teachers Aide; Var Golf; Hon Roll; KU.

BELCHER, BRANDI; Maranatha Acad; Olathe, KS; (3); Church Yth Grp; Drama Clb; Pep Clb; Teachers Aide; School Musical; School Play; Rptr Nwsp; Rep Sec Stu Cncl; JV Var Chrldng; Hon Roll; Mdlng I/II; Toni & Guys Hair Acad; Csmtlgst.

BELCHER, CHRISTIE D; Ft Scott HS; Fort Scott, KS; (3); SADD; Chorus; Rep Stu Cncl; High Hon Roll; Hon Roll; Natural Helpers; Elem Ed.

BELDEN, KATIE L; Hays HS; Hays, KS; (4); Teachers Aide; Band; Chorus; Flag Corp; Mrchg Band; School Play; Nwsp; Yrbk; JV Bsktbl; Sftbl; Ft Hays ST Univ; Ed.

BELDEROL, ERICA L; Wichita East HS; Wichita, KS; (3); Church Yth Grp; Chorus; Church Choir; School Musical; Variety Show; NHS; Pres Acad Fit Awd; Tae Kwon Do; Chrch Drama Grp; Friend Univ; Educ.

BELDING, TAMI A; Halstead HS; Halstead, KS; (2); Girl Scts; Hosp Aide; Flag Corp; Jazz Band; Mrchg Band; Pep Band; JV Var Bsktbl; Cit Awd; Hon Roll; Church Yth Grp; OK ST U; Music Tchr.

BELL, BRANDEE D; Shawnee Mission W Sr HS; Overland Park, KS; (4); Church Yth Grp; Cmnty Wkr; Teachers Aide; Band; Church Choir; Mrchg Band; Pep Band; High Hon Roll; Stu Tchng; Washburn U.

BELL, CASSANDRA M; Wichita South HS; Wichita, KS; (2); 20/300; Church Yth Grp; Debate Tm; NFL; Scholastic Bowl; Church Choir; Drill Tm; Pres Frsh Cls; Rep Stu Cncl; High Hon Roll; NHS; KRHA; Harvard; Pol Sci/Law.

BELL, CHRIS J; Wellsville Jr Sr HS; Wellsville, KS; (3); 19/55; Band; Pep Band; JV Bsktbl; Var Ftbl; Mgr(s); Var Trk; Cit Awd; Hon Roll; Amer Legion Cadet Law Camp; Shot Put St 3a 6th 95 & 5th 96; Scndry Ed; Sports Medicine.

BELL, JA MEYA L; Wichita North HS; Wichita, KS; (2); Cmnty Wkr; DECA; Key Clb; Pep Clb; Spanish Clb; Church Choir; Drill Tm; Mrchg Band; Variety Show; Ofcr Stu Cncl; Wichita ST; Pol Sci/Crmnl Law.

BELL, JEFF C; Washburn Rural HS; Topeka, KS; (3).

BELL, JENNIFER; Dodge City HS; Dodge City, KS; (4); 36/254; Teachers Aide; Band; Chorus; Drill Tm; Mrchg Band; School Musical; JV Chrldng; Hon Roll; Presidents Awd; Acad Distincton Grad; Fine Arts Stu Of Month Choir; Washburn U; Acturial Sci.

BELL, JENNIFER; Junction City HS; Lawrenceville, GA; (3); Church Yth Grp; Cmnty Wkr; Debate Tm; Red Cross Aide; Scholastic Bowl; JV Bsktbl; High Hon Roll; Jr NHS; NHS; Pres Acad Fit Awd; Blue Jay Pride; Soph Comm; Duke.

BELL, JENNIFER C; Silver Lake Jr Sr HS; Silver Lake, KS; (3); 14/52; Dance Clb; Debate Tm; FHA; NFL; Pep Clb; Spanish Clb; Speech Tm; Teachers Aide; Band; Drill Tm; Natl Frnscs Lgue Natl Qlifr 1st Pl Mdlst; Cath Frnscs Lgue Natl Qlifr 1st Pl Mdlst Oratory; ST Champ; Pub Rltns/Advtsng Exec.

BELL, MICHELLE; Maize HS; Wichita, KS; (4); 6/212; Cmnty Wkr; Sec German Clb; Var NFL; Red Cross Aide; Scholastic Bowl; Band; High Hon Roll; NHS; Pres Acad Fit Awd; Mrchg Band; KS Regents Hnrs Acad; Pittsburg ST Univ; Pre-Med.

BELL, STUART K; Bishop Miege HS; Kansas City, KS; (3); 72/178; Cmnty Wkr; Pep Clb; Spanish Clb; SADD; Rptr Nwsp; Rep Frsh Cls; Treas Jr Cls; JV Crs Cntry; JV Trk; Hon Roll; Stdnts/Tchrs Pgm; Eng Explrs Pgm; U Of KS; Eng.

BELL, SUSAN E; Maranatha Acad; Shawnee Mission, KS; (3); Band; Mrchg Band; Orch; Pep Band; Socr; Tennis; Hon Roll; NHS; Involvmnt In Chrch Yth Grp; Goldeneagle Awd; Chrstn Chrctr Awd In Sccr.

BELL, TARA K; Shawnee Heights Sr HS; Topeka, KS; (4); 1/237; Hosp Aide; Model UN; Pep Clb; Scholastic Bowl; SADD; Teachers Aide; Acpl Chr; Gov Hon Prg Awd; High Hon Roll; NHS; Jr Civitan Pres; KSU; Psych.

BELL, WILLIAM E; Russell HS; Russell, KS; (1); Church Yth Grp; FCA; Natl FFA Org; Chorus; Church Choir; JV Ftbl; Wt Lftg; Hon Roll; UA.

BELLAFIORE, TONI; St Thomas Aquinas HS; Overland Park, KS; (4); 27/232; Am Leg Aux Girls St; Church Yth Grp; Hosp Aide; SADD; Pres Stu Cncl; Capt CAP; Cit Awd; High Hon Roll; NHS.

BELLES, DUWAYNE N; Beloit Jr Sr HS; Beloit, KS; (4); Sec Drama Clb; Quiz Bowl; Spanish Clb; Band; Mrchg Band; School Musical; School Play; NHS; Pres Acad Fit Awd; St Schlr; KU.

BELLINDER, ELIZABETH; Rock Creek Jr Sr HS; Saint George, KS; (4); 15/50; Am Leg Aux Girls St; Bus Profs of Am; Church Yth Grp; FHA; Math Tm; Teachers Aide; Bsktbl; Sftbl; Hon Roll; Peer Tutor; KS ST; Law Enf.

BELLINGER, LEAH K; Bishop Miege HS; Kansas City, MO; (3); 13/174; Hosp Aide; Office Aide; Pep Clb; Pep Band; JV Sftbl; High Hon Roll; NHS; Sec Church Yth Grp; Band; Hmrm Coll Rep; Stdnt Ath Trnr; Acad Excl Awd 2 Yrs; PT.

BELOT, ELLEN; Lawrence HS; Lawrence, KS; (2); Ofcr FCA; Rep Frsh Cls; Sec Soph Cls; Bsktbl; Var Swmmng; Vllybl; High Hon Roll; Pres Acad Fit Awd; Church Yth Grp; Chorus; Schl N Ews Anchor; Chorale & Hnr Choir; Knowledge Master Open; Jrnlsm.

BELT, AIMEE C; Paola HS; Paola, KS; (3); 28/133; Am Leg Aux Girls St; Drama Clb; SADD; Teachers Aide; Chorus; Var L Sftbl; JV Vllybl; Hon Roll; NHS; Bus Mngmt.

BELT, JENNY; Hutchinson HS; Hutchinson, KS; (4); 4/266; Am Leg Aux Girls St; Key Clb; Pep Clb; Thesps; Acpl Chr; School Musical; School Play; High Hon Roll; NHS; Med.

BELTZ, TIMOTHY J; Enterprise Sda Acad; Kansas City, MO; (4); Boy Scts; Drama Clb; Ski Clb; Band; Chorus; School Play; Stage Crew; Sec Frsh Cls; Pres Soph Cls; Capt Gym; Gymnst Of Yr Awd; Chrstn Recog; Bst Actr Awd; Union Coll; Phys Asst.

BEMIS, KRISTIN; Hays HS; Hays, KS; (4); 19/202; Pres 4-H; Pres Natl FFA Org; Teachers Aide; Phtg Nwsp; Phtg Yrbk; Ofcr Stu Cncl; NHS; 96 Miss Rodeo KS Prncss; All Amer Schlr; 95 Miss Rodeo Beef Empire Days; Ft Hays ST Univ; Equine Sci.

BENAE, MELISSA; Conway Springs HS; Conway Springs, KS; (2); Pep Clb; Varsity Clb; Ofcr Soph Cls; Var Bsktbl; Var Chrldng; Powder Puff Ftbl; Var Vllybl; Hon Roll; Cardinalaires; Elem Ed.

BENAGE, MARIETTE M; Ft Scott HS; Fort Scott, KS; (2); Church Yth Grp; FCA; Pep Clb; Chorus; Church Choir; Ofcr Stu Cncl; JV Bsktbl; Var Powder Puff Ftbl; JV Sftbl; Hon Roll; Notre Dame; Zoologist.

BENAVIDEZ, MICHAEL; Shawnee Heights HS; Topeka, KS; (4); 33/250; Cmnty Wkr; FBLA; JA; Red Cross Aide; SADD; Teachers Aide; High Hon Roll; Hon Roll; Pres Schlr; KS St Univ; Elec Eng.

BENCOMO, ELIZABETH A; Dodge City HS; Dodge City, KS; (1); Church Yth Grp; Cmnty Wkr; SADD; Band; Church Choir; Flag Corp; Mrchg Band; High Hon Roll; Hon Roll; Elem Schl Tchr.

BENCOMO, SONIA; Ulysses HS; Ulysses, KS; (3); Art Clb; Church Yth Grp; Cmnty Wkr; FBLA; FHA; SADD; Chrldng; Swmmng; Hon Roll; Eclgy Clb; Frgn Lang Class; Bus Ed.

BENDER, ELIZABETH M; Wichita East HS; Wichita, KS; (2); Girl Scts; Band; Mrchg Band; Orch; Pep Band; Intnl Baccalaureatte Pgm; Dist 6 Band; Wichita Wind Ensemble; Wichita ST Univ; Music Ed.

BENDER, JON; Ellsworth HS; Ellsworth, KS; (4); 4/67; Church Yth Grp; Debate Tm; SADD; Teachers Aide; Mrchg Band; Pep Band; School Play; Var Golf; High Hon Roll; NHS; Concordia Coll; Rlgn.

BENDER, JOSHUA M; Wichita East HS; Wichita, KS; (4); 53/280; Sec Boy Scts; Science Clb; Spanish Clb; School Play; Phtg Nwsp; Lit Mag; Rep Frsh Cls; Var Crs Cntry; Var Trk; Wt Lftg; Heart Of Amer; Gutenburg Printing Cmptn; ST Wrestling & Crss Cntry Cmptn; Prom King Nom; KS ST Univ; Arch.

BENEFIELD, JOSHUA; St Mary's Colgan HS; Pittsburg, KS; (1); 5/48; Cmnty Wkr; L Trk; High Hon Roll; Hon Roll; Ntl Merit Ltr; Sci Fair; 5th In 800 M At Jr Olympic Gualification Meet; Medalist In Western Sectional Mens Fig Skate; U Of Notre Dame; Sports Med.

BENFER, KATIE; Clay Ctr Cmty HS; Longford, KS; (2); Sec Church Yth Grp; Cmnty Wkr; Pres 4-H; FHA; Natl FFA Org; JV Bsktbl; 4-H Awd; High Hon Roll; Frgn Lang Clb; KS ST U; Ag.

BENFER, SARAH L; Salina HS Central; Salina, KS; (4); Art Clb; High Hon Roll; NHS; Pres Acad Fit Awd; St Schlr; Ft Hays ST U; Art.

BENHAM, MIKE B; Blue Valley North HS; Leawood, KS; (2); Church Yth Grp; Model UN; Ski Clb; Varsity Clb; Acpl Chr; Chorus; Church Choir; Variety Show; JV Ftbl; Var Swmmng; US Swim Team KC Blazers; Scuba Diving; Vet Med.

BENITZ, ALLISHA; Troy HS; Troy, KS; (1); Church Yth Grp; Letterman Clb; Speech Tm; Treas Frsh Cls; JV Bsktbl; Var Chrldng; Var Crs Cntry; Var Trk; JV Vllybl; Hon Roll; Med.

BENJAMIN, FELICIA M; Anderson Cty Jr Sr HS; Garnett, KS; (1); Church Yth Grp; Acpl Chr; Chorus; Hon Roll; SADD; Law.

BENJAMIN, KELLI J; Salina HS South; Salina, KS; (4); 17/215; Pep Clb; Drill Tm; Mrchg Band; Orch; Pep Band; Trk; Gov Hon Prg Awd; High Hon Roll; Hon Roll; NHS; Vvtts Dnc Std; KS ST U; Acctng.

BENNEFELD, JOY; Olathe East Sr HS; Olathe, KS; (4); Intnl Clb; Model UN; Science Clb; Teachers Aide; Mgr Swmmng; NHS; Fshn Mrchndsng Clb; Fmly/Csmr Sci; Johnson Cty CC.

BENNETT, AMBER R; Buhler HS; Moundridge, KS; (2); Church Yth Grp; Cmnty Wkr; FCA; French Clb; Chorus; Church Choir; Variety Show; JV Bsktbl; Intrml Wt Lftg; High Hon Roll; Hutchinson CC; Law Enforcement.

BENNETT, ANGELA D; Girard HS; Girard, KS; (4); 9/69; Treas FHA; Girl Scts; Library Aide; Math Tm; Science Clb; Spanish Clb; SADD; Band; Mrchg Band; Pep Band; Kayetts Dir Of Prgm; Ft Scott; Acctg/Bus.

BENNETT, ARVILLA; Winfield HS; Winfield, KS; (2); Church Yth Grp; Cmnty Wkr; Hosp Aide; SADD; Thesps; Band; Chorus; Mrchg Band; Pep Band; School Play; AP Amer His; U Of NE Lincoln; Eng.

BENNETT, BRANDY M; Syracuse Jr Sr HS; Syracuse, KS; (1); Child Dev.

BENNETT, BROOKE; Campus HS; Haysville, KS; (4); 2/213; Am Leg Aux Girls St; Church Yth Grp; Debate Tm; Nwsp; Capt L Chrldng; High Hon Roll; NHS; Scholastic Bowl; Service Clb; Speech Tm; Stu Ath Wk; KS Hnr Schlr; Wcht Bus Jrnl Pblshd; Wichita ST U; Comms.

BENNETT, CHARLIE; Halstead HS; Halstead, KS; (2); Church Yth Grp; Debate Tm; HOBY; Spanish Clb; Pres Frsh Cls; Pres Soph Cls; Pres Stu Cncl; Var Ftbl; Var Trk; High Hon Roll; 96 3-A 4x100m Relay St Chmpn; 3rd Pl 1-4 A Novce Debate St Trnmt; Debate Point Speakr Avg 95-96; Harvard; Law.

BENNETT, CRAIG M; Topeka HS; Topeka, KS; (2); Boy Scts; Computer Clb; Model UN; Science Clb; Teachers Aide; High Hon Roll; Hon Roll; Ntl Merit Ltr; KS St Mountain Bike Champion 95; Freelance Internet Web Page Developer; Russian Clb; Engrng.

BENNETT, JASON; Goddard Jr HS; Wichita, KS; (1); Church Yth Grp; Cmnty Wkr; Debate Tm; Ed Nwsp; Ed Yrbk; Crs Cntry; JV Trk; Cit Awd; High Hon Roll; Pres Acad Fit Awd.

BENNETT, JENNIFER E; Independence HS; Independence, KS; (3); Nwsp; Var Sftbl; Hon Roll.

BENNETT, JOHN W; Halstead HS; Halstead, KS; (3); Church Yth Grp; FCA; Letterman Clb; Spanish Clb; L Ftbl; L Trk; High Hon Roll; Hon Roll; NHS; Bus Mgmt.

BENNETT, LESLIE M; Blue Valley Northwest HS; Overland Park, KS; (2); Church Yth Grp; Drama Clb; Latin Clb; Thesps; School Play; JV Sftbl; Tchng.

BENNETT, MATTHEW E; Santa Fe Trail Jr HS; Olathe, KS; (1); French Clb; Teachers Aide; Ofcr Bsbl; High Hon Roll; Pres Schlr; Bus.

BENNETT, MINDY J; Sterling HS; Sterling, KS; (4); 1/31; Capt Quiz Bowl; Teachers Aide; Ed Nwsp; Ed Yrbk; Ed Lit Mag; Gov Hon Prg Awd; Hon Roll; Prfct Atten Awd; Pres Acad Fit Awd; Val; KS St Univ; Sec Ed.

BENNETT, MOLLY W; Shawnee Mission N HS; Shawnee Mission, KS; (3); Pres Thesps; Sec Stu Cncl; NHS; Church Yth Grp; Drama Clb; Math Tm; Pep Clb; Band; Church Choir; Jazz Band; Piano Lessons; Regnl/ST Contest Solo; Hrsbck Rdng.

BENNETT, TODD W; Southeast HS; Mc Cune, KS; (3); Letterman Clb; Natl FFA Org; Science Clb; Varsity Clb; Capt Bsktbl; Capt Trk; Hon Roll; OK Chrstn.

BENNETT-GIDEON, REBECCA L; Wyandotte HS; Kansas City, KS; (1); Drama Clb; High Hon Roll; Hon Roll; Hnrs Classes; Pediatrician.

BENNINGA, TRACI; Manhattan HS; Manhattan, KS; (3); Church Yth Grp; Intnl Clb; Spanish Clb; Teachers Aide; Band; Church Choir; Mrchg Band; Pep Band; School Musical; High Hon Roll; KS ST U; Elem Ed.

BENNINGTON, SCOTT G; El Dorado HS; El Dorado, KS; (2); Debate Tm; Letterman Clb; NFL; SADD; Rep Soph Cls; Ofcr Stu Cncl; JV Bsktbl; Var Crs Cntry; Var Trk; Hon Roll; HS Math Tchr/Bsktbl/Track.

BENOIT, NICHOLE R; Palco HS; Damar, KS; (3); 3/18; Church Yth Grp; Model UN; Pep Clb; Band; Pep Band; School Play; Ed Nwsp; Ed Yrbk; Treas Soph Cls; Rep Jr Cls; Ft Hays ST Univ; Nurse.

BENSEL, TARA; Hugoton HS; Hugoton, KS; (2); 10/87; FCA; Spanish Clb; Band; Jazz Band; Mrchg Band; Bsktbl; Sftbl; Vllybl; Hon Roll; Triple A Awd.

BENSON, ERIC F; Sumner Acad Of Arts & Science; Kansas City, KS; (3); Church Yth Grp; German Clb; Latin Clb; JV Var Ftbl; Var Tennis; High Hon Roll; Hon Roll; Asia Clb Sec & Pres; Bio.

BENSON, STEPHANIE; Maranatha Acad; Overland Park, KS; (4); 2/32; Hosp Aide; School Play; Treas Jr Cls; Mgr(s); Vllybl; High Hon Roll; VP NHS; Pres Schlr; Sal; Ed Yrbk; Mexico Mssns Trps; Rockhurst Coll; Pre-Med/Ped.

BENTCH, SARA D; Bishop Ward HS; Kansas City, KS; (1); 14/115; Office Aide; Pep Clb; Var Crs Cntry; Mgr(s); Score Keeper; JV Trk; Hon Roll; Schlarshps; Var Ltr Crs Cntry; Univ Of KS.

BENTEMAN, ANNETTE L; Yates Ctr HS; Yates Center, KS; (3); Art Clb; Church Yth Grp; Cmnty Wkr; FCA; FHA; Letterman Clb; Library Aide; Scholastic Bowl; Stat Sftbl; Cit Awd; Natl Yth Ldrshp Forum On Medicine; Qn Candidate For Winter Ball; KS Univ; Medicine.

BENTLEY, SARAH; Topeka HS; Topeka, KS; (3); Teachers Aide; Chorus; Hon Roll; Rowing.

BENTON, ABBY; Topeka West HS; Topeka, KS; (4); 18/240; Church Yth Grp; Rep French Clb; FBLA; Letterman Clb; Pep Clb; Q&S; Teachers Aide; Varsity Clb; Yrbk; Var L Bsktbl; KS Hnrs Schlr; KS ST U; Acctng.

BENTON, JESSICA; Ingalls Jr Sr HS; Ingalls, KS; (1); Letterman Clb; Pep Clb; Rep SADD; Drill Tm; Co-Ed Yrbk; Var L Bsktbl; Var L Chrldng; Var L Vllybl; VP Frsh Cls; Pres Soph Cls; K ST.

BENTON, THERESA; Ingalls Jr Sr HS; Ingalls, KS; (1); 1/22; Church Yth Grp; Letterman Clb; Pep Clb; Quiz Bowl; SADD; School Play; Phtg Rptr Yrbk; Pres Frsh Cls; Rep Stu Cncl; High Hon Roll; Crmnl Law.

BERANEK, JENNIE; Liberal HS; Liberal, KS; (4); Am Leg Aux Girls St; Key Clb; Band; Mrchg Band; Pep Band; Wt Lftg; Ky Clb Intl Cnvntn Dlgt; Seward Cty CC; Med.

BERARD, CARLY D; Blue Valley HS; Overland Park, KS; (3); 12/251; Art Clb; Debate Tm; NFL; High Hon Roll; Hon Roll; NHS; Pre-Law.

BERENBOM, ANNE; Shawnee Mission E Sr HS; Shawnee Mission, KS; (3); Cmnty Wkr; Math Tm; Natl Beta Clb; Q&S; Service Clb; Spanish Clb; Yrbk; Sftbl; High Hon Roll; NHS; Penzner Piano Cmptn Fnlst-Jewish Comm Ctr Of KS City; Hebrew Tchr; Nesiya Inst Israel; Phy.

BERENS, JAMIE; Thomas More Prep-Marion HS; Hays, KS; (1); Library Aide; Crs Cntry; Hon Roll.

BERG, BRANDON; Maur Hill Prep Schl; Valley Falls, KS; (3); Library Aide; Math Tm; NFL; Intrml Bsktbl; JV Ftbl; Hon Roll; NHS; Pres Acad Fit Awd; Morningside; Med.

BERG, BRIAN D; Robert E Clark Jr HS; Bonner Springs, KS; (1); 1/178; Boy Scts; Church Yth Grp; Cmnty Wkr; Band; Jazz Band; Mrchg Band; Pep Band; Co-Ed Yrbk; Bsktbl; Ftbl; KS Ist Music Cntst; Top Ten Eng Awd; Hoop It Up 3 On 3 Bsktbl Trnmnt; U Of KS; Architectural Engrng.

BERG, DAVID; Olathe North Sr HS; Olathe, KS; (2); Boy Scts; Church Yth Grp; Debate Tm; Spanish Clb; Teachers Aide; JV Var Trk; Var Wrstlng; High Hon Roll; Hon Roll; Pres Acad Fit Awd; Math.

BERG, KIM; Lyndon HS; Vassar, KS; (1); Church Yth Grp; FBLA; Chorus; Church Choir; VP Soph Cls; Var Chrldng; Trk; High Hon Roll; Lyon Cty League 3rd Pl Algebra; Tabor Coll; Ophthamology.

BERGEN, ERICA; Garden City Sr HS; Garden City, KS; (4); Hosp Aide; High Hon Roll; Prfct Atten Awd; Outstndng Anatony/Phosiology Sr Stu; Presidential Schlrshp; Garden City CC; Nrsng.

BERGER, ABBIE; Remington HS; Whitewater, KS; (2); Church Yth Grp; Debate Tm; FHA; Spanish Clb; Thesps; School Musical; School Play; Variety Show; Chrldng; Hon Roll; Pre-Med.

BERGER, CLAIRE; Blue Vlly N HS; Leawood, KS; (3); French Clb; NFL; Varsity Clb; Lit Mag; Powder Puff Ftbl; Tennis; Wt Lftg; High Hon Roll; Hon Roll; NHS; Princeton Univ; Eng.

BERGER, ERIN R; Horton HS; Everest, KS; (3); 3/38; Cmnty Wkr; FCA; Band; Sec Jr Cls; Pres Sr Cls; Rep Stu Cncl; JV Var Bsktbl; JV Vllybl; Hon Roll; NHS; Church Organist; KS Univ; Pre-Med.

BERGER, NICHOLE L; Horton HS; Hiawatha, KS; (4); 16/63; Church Yth Grp; 4-H; Office Aide; Pep Clb; Teachers Aide; Band; Mrchg Band; Pep Band; School Play; Nwsp; Fort Hays ST; Spch Pthlgst.

BERGER, SUZETTE; Valley Heights Jr Sr HS; Barnes, KS; (4); 16/27; Am Leg Aux Girls St; Church Yth Grp; FCA; 4-H; FHA; Letterman Clb; Model UN; Natl FFA Org; NFL; Quiz Bowl; Emporia ST U; Hstry Ed.

BERGERON, TANYA M; Attica Public Schl; Attica, KS; (2); Cmnty Wkr; Drama Clb; Hosp Aide; Quiz Bowl; Chorus; School Play; Hon Roll; Washington U St Louis; Eng Prof.

BERGKAMP, LORI; Sedgwick HS; Valley Center, KS; (2); 3/36; FHA; Scholastic Bowl; Phtg Nwsp; Phtg Yrbk; VP Frsh Cls; Treas Soph Cls; Ofcr Stu Cncl; JV Bsktbl; Trk; JV Vllybl; Photo-Jrnlsm.

BERGKAMP, SARAH; Valley Heights Jr Sr HS; Blue Rapids, KS; (4); 5/30; Am Leg Aux Girls St; Church Yth Grp; Letterman Clb; Model UN; Teachers Aide; Band; Chorus; Drill Tm; School Play; Nwsp; KS ST U; Ftnss & Ntrtn.

BERGKAMP, THERESE M; Andale HS; Mount Hope, KS; (2); Church Yth Grp; Quiz Bowl; Scholastic Bowl; Spanish Clb; SADD; Chorus; School Play; High Hon Roll; Hon Roll; NHS.

BERGMAN, JAMI; Smith Ctr Jr Sr HS; Lebanon, KS; (2); 6/60; Math Tm; Quiz Bowl; SADD; Acpl Chr; Band; VP Frsh Cls; VP Soph Cls; Chrldng; Trk; High Hon Roll; KAYS; KS Ambssdrs Of Music; Shrine Bowl Band KS; Lifegrd; KS ST U; Vet Med.

BERGMAN, MARIAH L; Campus HS; Haysville, KS; (3); 1/200; Capt Am Leg Aux Girls St; VP Pres Church Yth Grp; Hosp Aide; Intnl Clb; SADD; Chorus; Co-Capt Pom Pon; Capt L Powder Puff Ftbl; High Hon Roll; Hon Roll; Chem Awd; Won Miss Cntrl KS Tenn USA; 1st Runner Up In Miss KS Teen USA Pageant; Dent.

BERGMAN, MEGHAN R; Onaga HS; Onaga, KS; (2); 4/45; Dance Clb; Letterman Clb; Pep Clb; Quiz Bowl; SADD; Teachers Aide; Varsity Clb; Drill Tm; Nwsp; Mgr Yrbk; KAYS; Green-Alert; Adopt-A-Hwy; KS Univ; Physcns Asst.

BERGMAN, RUSSELL; Nemaha Valley HS; Seneca, KS; (2); 4-H; Letterman Clb; Treas Soph Cls; Bsktbl; Ftbl; Trk; 4-H Awd; High Hon Roll.

BERGMAN, SARAH A; Bailey-Benedict Jr Sr High; Seneca, KS; (2); Treas Church Yth Grp; FBLA; FHA; Quiz Bowl; Church Choir; Pep Band; Pres Soph Cls; Var Chrldng; JV Vllybl; High Hon Roll.

BERGMAN, SHAWN J; Bailey-Benedict Jr Sr High; Seneca, KS; (4); 1/7; Rep Pres Church Yth Grp; Capt Quiz Bowl; Band; Rep Sr Cls; VP Rep Stu Cncl; L Capt Bsktbl; NHS; Ntl Merit SF; Pres Acad Fit Awd; Val; KS Stu Univ; Chem Eng.

BERGMANN, RAYMOND M; Marysville HS; Beattie, KS; (2); Natl FFA Org; Bsktbl; Ftbl.

BERGMEIER, RAYMOND O; Kingman HS; Kingman, KS; (1); JV Ftbl; Var Wrstlng; High Hon Roll; Hon Roll; Yth & Govt; Ath Trng; Hunting; Ft Hays ST Univ; Bacteriology.

BERGQUIST, VALERIE A; Osage City HS; Osage City, KS; (3); 8/28; Church Yth Grp; Cmnty Wkr; 4-H; Pep Clb; Q&S; Science Clb; Spanish Clb; Teachers Aide; Yrbk; Treas Jr Cls; Ray Clb; Emporia ST Univ; Cmptr Engr.

BERGSTEN, MELISSA A; Wamego HS; Wamego, KS; (2); Cmnty Wkr; FCA; VP FBLA; Treas Rptr FHA; Intnl Clb; Scholastic Bowl; Science Clb; SADD; Drill Tm; Nwsp; Kayette Clb-Fresh Rep, Pres, VP; U Of KS; Med Sci.

BERGSTROM, LYNELLE R; Clifton-Clyde HS; Clyde, KS; (3); Pep Clb; Band; Church Choir; Pep Band; Variety Show; Pres Sr Cls; Var Bsktbl; L Trk; L Vllybl; Wt Lftg; Bsktbl 2nd Rnrup ST 96; Vlybl ST Chmpns 96; Fort Hays.

BERHARDT, JODI; Marion HS; Marion, KS; (4); 5/56; Art Clb; Church Yth Grp; Natl FFA Org; Office Aide; Teachers Aide; Yrbk; Var Bsktbl; Var Crs Cntry; Var Trk; High Hon Roll; Artist Awd; FFA Degree; Recrdng Keeping Awd; Pratt Comm Coll; Animal Sci.

BERLAND, VALERIE A; Palco HS; Damar, KS; (3); 1/19; Sec Treas Church Yth Grp; Debate Tm; Letterman Clb; Pep Band; School Play; Pres Jr Cls; VP Pres Stu Cncl; Var Capt Chrldng; Var Vllybl; NHS; Peer Power Theatre; Washburn U; Bus Mngmt.

BERLIN, JESSICA; Leavenworth HS; Leavenworth, KS; (2); 62/423; Model UN; SADD; Rep Stu Cncl; Var L Crs Cntry; Var L Trk; High Hon Roll; Pres C Cntry Clb; Peer Medtr; Good Fellows.

BERMAN, ALYSSA M; Blue Valley Northwest HS; Overland Park, KS; (3); Office Aide; Teachers Aide; Varsity Clb; Bsktbl; Var Capt Vllybl; Hon Roll; Aide To Blind; Sports Thrpst; Phy Thrpst.

BERMEO, GABRIEL A; Bishop Miege HS; Roeland Park, KS; (4); Service Clb; Spanish Clb; School Musical; School Play; Variety Show; Lit Mag; Var Crs Cntry; Var Trk; High Hon Roll; NHS; Minority HS Stu Med Apprenticeship; Pgm Under Womens Rsrch Inst & Ku Med Schl; Northwestern U.

BERNA, MARY J; Blue Valley Northwest HS; Overland Park, KS; (2); 25/400; Church Yth Grp; Debate Tm; German Clb; Girl Scts; Intnl Clb; Band; High Hon Roll; Hon Roll; Rappel Mstr; Nrsng Hm Vstr; Congress Bundestag Schlrshp Rcpnt.

BERNAL, ANTHONY J; Shawnee Mission N HS; Shawnee Mission, KS; (3); Drama Clb; Latin Clb; Letterman Clb; Thesps; Acpl Chr; Chorus; Orch; School Musical; School Play; Stage Crew; Music Tchr.

BERNARD, JEREMY D; Russell HS; Russell, KS; (3); Boy Scts; Church Yth Grp; Cmnty Wkr; German Clb; Natl FFA Org; Band; Mrchg Band; Ftbl; Tennis; Wt Lftg; FFA; Ft Hays ST U; Frgn Lang Tchr.

BERNBECK, MICHELLE D; Quinter Jr Sr HS; Gove, KS; (4); 10/26; FHA; Letterman Clb; Library Aide; Math Tm; Quiz Bowl; SADD; Teachers Aide; Thesps; Band; Chorus; Wichita State Univ; Music Educ.

BERND, KATHY M; Labette Co HS; Dennis, KS; (2); FCA; SADD; Chrldng; Hon Roll; Piano Ltr; Power Tumbling.

BERNEY, DEANNA J; Circle HS; Benton, KS; (4); 2/91; Library Aide; SADD; Nwsp; Bsktbl; Sftbl; Tennis; High Hon Roll; Hon Roll; Pres Acad Fit Awd; Sal; Butler Cnty CC; Acctng.

BERNHARD, ELIZABAETH M; St Marys HS; Maple Hill, KS; (3); Sec FBLA; Pep Clb; Drill Tm; Sec Sr Cls; Chrldng; Golf; JV Vllybl; JV Wrstlng; High Hon Roll; Hon Roll; Med.

BERNHARD, LONI M; Blue Valley Northwest HS; Overland Park, KS; (2); Church Yth Grp; Socr; 4 Yr Schl; Ed/Child Psych.

BERNHARDT, JODI K; Marion HS; Marion, KS; (4); 5/60; Art Clb; Church Yth Grp; Cmnty Wkr; Natl FFA Org; Office Aide; Teachers Aide; Yrbk; Var Bsktbl; Var Crs Cntry; Var Trk; Art Awd; FFA Prfncy Awd; Pratt CC; Animal Sci.

BERNHARDT, LISA M; Lyons HS; Lyons, KS; (3); Office Aide; Pep Clb; Phtg Yrbk; JV Tennis; Hon Roll.

BERQUIST, ERIN; Shawnee Mission Northwest HS; Shawnee Mission, KS; (4); Cmnty Wkr; Key Clb; Band; Mrchg Band; Pep Band; High Hon Roll; Hon Roll; NHS; Sftbl; Drum Line; KU; Intl Bus; Mrktng With Japan.

BERRY, CHRIS M; Kingman HS; Murdock, KS; (3); Hon Roll; Ski Diving; Zoology; Zoologist.

BERRY, DAVID D; Galena HS; Galena, KS; (3); Church Yth Grp; Cmnty Wkr; FCA; FBLA; FHA; Letterman Clb; Office Aide; SADD; Nwsp; Yrbk; MO Southern ST Coll; Crimnlgy.

BERRY, JENNIFER R; Independence HS; Independence, KS; (1); NFL; Band; Mrchg Band; Orch; Pep Band; Sftbl; Vllybl; Wichita ST Univ; Model/Actress.

BERRY, KRISTA; Holcomb HS; Holcomb, KS; (4); 5/41; VP FHA; Pres Key Clb; Chorus; Yrbk; Sec Sr Cls; Var Capt Chrldng; Var Trk; Hon Roll; NHS; Pres Schlr; Ft Hays ST Univ; Elem Ed.

BERRY, MATTHEW A; Emporia HS; Emporia, KS; (3); Pep Clb; Band; Var Socr; Var Trk; Hon Roll; SMILE Comm & Schl Ling Pgm; Washburn Univ; Pre-Law.

BERRY, RYAN M; Garden City Sr HS; Garden City, KS; (2); Church Yth Grp; Cmnty Wkr; Key Clb; JV Bsktbl; Var Golf; High Hon Roll; Prfct Atten Awd; Dentistry.

BERRY, SHAWNDA R; Maize HS; Wichita, KS; (3); French Clb; JA; Science Clb; Teachers Aide; Hon Roll.

BERRY, TIM; Wichita West HS; Wichita, KS; (3); 10/230; French Clb; Teachers Aide; Band; Chorus; Jazz Band; Mrchg Band; Orch; Pep Band; School Musical; San Diego; Bus Admn/FBI.

BERRYMAN, JACOB W; Ashland HS; Ashland, KS; (3); 2/28; FCA; Letterman Clb; Math Tm; Quiz Bowl; Varsity Clb; Pres Frsh Cls; JV Bsktbl; Var Capt Ftbl; L Golf; High Hon Roll; GATE; Ath Clb; Acad Olympics; KS Univ; Engrng; Arch; Medicine.

BERTHOLF, MATTHEW; Hutchinson HS; Hutchinson, KS; (3); 32/400; Am Leg Boys St; Key Clb; Letterman Clb; Pep Clb; Var L Bsbl; JV Bsktbl; Var L Ftbl; Wt Lftg; Cit Awd; Hon Roll; Bus Admin.

BERTRAM, APRIL; Chase HS; Raymond, KS; (4); 3/15; Church Yth Grp; Pres FHA; Ed Nwsp; Ed Yrbk; Pres Soph Cls; Pres Sr Cls; Ofcr Stu Cncl; Chrldng; Hon Roll; Pres NHS; Washburn U; Psych.

BERTRAND, ANNETTE; Olathe East Sr HS; Olathe, KS; (3); French Clb; Sec Pep Band; Rep Soph Cls; Ofcr Jr Cls; High Hon Roll; Hon Roll; Pres Acad Fit Awd; Church Yth Grp; Teachers Aide; JV Powder Puff Ftbl; Stdnt Amer Dance Ctr 8 Yrs; Amer Yth Ballet Prfrmng Yth Co 7 Yrs; Prof Dncr.

BERTRAND, EMILY K; Blue Valley North HS; Overland Park, KS; (2); Hosp Aide; Model UN; Science Clb; Chorus; School Musical; High Hon Roll; St Schlr; Church Yth Grp; Office Aide; Thesps; Apprentice Prof Ballet Co; Natl Young Leaders Conf; 15 Plus Ballet Schlsps; Prof Ballet.

BERTRAND, LIZ ANN M; Bishop Carroll Catholic HS; Wichita, KS; (2); Church Yth Grp; Drama Clb; Hosp Aide; Chrldng; Hon Roll; KSU; Nrs.

BERTRAND, TRACY M; Wellington Sr HS; Wellington, KS; (3); 5/165; Church Yth Grp; SADD; Var Capt Bsktbl; Var L Sftbl; Var Capt Vllybl; High Hon Roll; Hon Roll; Jr NHS; NHS.

BESENYI, JENNIFER M; Topeka West HS; Topeka, KS; (1); Cmnty Wkr; SADD; Chorus; Rep Frsh Cls; Rep Stu Cncl; Var Mgr(s); JV Sftbl; Intrml Vllybl; Hon Roll; Trk & Field, Bsktbl, Tumbeling & Bowling; KS Univ.

BESPERAT, AARON D; Otis Bison HS; Timken, KS; (2); Quiz Bowl; Speech Tm; Band; Pep Band; School Play; Variety Show; Pres Frsh Cls; JV Bsktbl; Trk; High Hon Roll; Acctng.

BETTEGA, NICK P; Yates Ctr HS; Yates Center, KS; (2); 1/60; Art Clb; Church Yth Grp; FCA; FHA; Quiz Bowl; Spanish Clb; VP Stu Cncl; Ofcr Bsbl; Bsktbl; Ftbl; Pharmacy.

BETTIS, MARK T; Washburn Rural HS; Topeka, KS; (3); 90/400; Church Yth Grp; Cmnty Wkr; Rptr Yrbk; Rptr Lit Mag; Var Bsktbl; JV Golf; Powder Puff Ftbl; Wt Lftg; High Hon Roll; Hon Roll; Engrng; Bus.

BETZ, PATRICK T; Liberal HS; Liberal, KS; (3); Debate Tm; FTA; Math Tm; NFL; Quiz Bowl; Science Clb; Rep Jr Cls; Crs Cntry; Swmmng; High Hon Roll; USAF Acad; Engrng.

BETZEN, DOUG M; South Haven Schl; Geuda Springs, KS; (3); 1/17; Natl FFA Org; School Play; VP Soph Cls; Treas Sr Cls; Cit Awd; High Hon Roll; Hon Roll; NHS; Prfct Atten Awd; All Amer Schlr.

BETZEN, SHARON M; South Haven Schl; Geuda Springs, KS; (1); Sec Frsh Cls; Sec Treas Soph Cls; Cit Awd; High Hon Roll; Prfct Atten Awd; All-Amer Schlrs Awd.

BEUGESDIJK, BEN H; Trinity Catholic HS; Halstead, KS; (1); Church Yth Grp; Cmnty Wkr; Debate Tm; NFL; Ofcr Stu Cncl; Tennis; Hon Roll; Sccr Plyr Ref.

BEUKE, NOELLE M; Andover HS; Andover, KS; (4); 9/138; Teachers Aide; Acpl Chr; School Musical; Variety Show; Var Capt Chrldng; High Hon Roll; NHS; Pres Acad Fit Awd; Pres Schlr; St Schlr; Fall Homcmng Qn Ct; Cum Laude Grad; KS ST Univ; Psych.

BEVER, JAMES F; Campus HS; Wichita, KS; (3); Office Aide; VICA; Hon Roll; Architecture.

BEVINS, RYAN; Frontenac Jr Sr HS; Pittsburg, KS; (3); 1/40; Pep Clb; VP Frsh Cls; Var L Bsbl; Var L Bsktbl; Var Ftbl; Var Wt Lftg; Hon Roll; KU Lawrence; Math.

BEVIS, ANDREA L; Olathe North Sr HS; Olathe, KS; (3); Church Yth Grp; Cmnty Wkr; Drama Clb; Science Clb; Spanish Clb; Teachers Aide; Thesps; Acpl Chr; Chorus; Church Choir; Mid Amer Nazarene Col; Engl.

BEYAH, KHAJRIYYAH N; Northeast Magnet HS; Wichita, KS; (1); 9/150; Church Yth Grp; FCA; Girl Scts; Pep Clb; Spanish Clb; Church Choir; L Chrldng; Trk; Hon Roll; Langston U; Medicine.

BEYDLER, BECKI; Trego Comm HS; Wa Keeney, KS; (1); Dance Clb; Letterman Clb; Drill Tm; Ofcr Frsh Cls; Ofcr Stu Cncl; Var Chrldng; Var Trk; JV Vllybl; Hon Roll; Kays/Kayettes; KS ST U; Phy Thrpst.

BEYER, JAMES E; Riverton Schl; Baxter Springs, KS; (1); Church Yth Grp; Math Tm; Scholastic Bowl; Band; Chorus; Orch; High Hon Roll; Ntl Merit Ltr; Pres Acad Fit Awd; Flwshp Of Chrstn Stdnts.

BEYER, JASON E; Santa Fe Trail Jr HS; Olathe, KS; (1); Church Yth Grp; Drama Clb; Church Choir; Hon Roll; Church Quiz Team; Guitar.

BEYNON, MATT S; St John's Military Schl; Wichita, KS; (2); Letterman Clb; ROTC; Varsity Clb; Color Guard; Drill Tm; Var Ftbl; Capt Wrstlng; High Hon Roll; VFW Distngd Medal Of Hnr For Outstdng Achvmt & Exceptional Ldrshp Ability; Schwan Schlsp.

BEZDEK, ANGIE; Shawnee Heights Sr HS; Topeka, KS; (4); 14/237; Hosp Aide; Orch; School Musical; Mgr Yrbk; Var Co-Capt Crs Cntry; Var Trk; High Hon Roll; Hon Roll; Treas NHS; Pres Schlr; U Of KS; Acctng.

BHATNAGAR, RADHA L; Smoky Valley HS; Lindsborg, KS; (2); Drama Clb; 4-H; FHA; Band; Chorus; Jazz Band; Mrchg Band; Orch; Pep Band; School Play.

BIANCARELLI, GINA; Girard HS; Girard, KS; (4); 19/69; Cmnty Wkr; Science Clb; Pres Spanish Clb; SADD; Teachers Aide; Yrbk; Var Crs Cntry; Golf; Vllybl; NHS; Pittsburg ST Univ.

BICKEL, TIMOTHY E; Wichita West HS; Wichita, KS; (4); 58/260; Bsktbl; Socr; Hon Roll; Natl Libry Of Poetry Publsee; Emporia St Univ; Engl.

BIDWELL, MICHAEL P; Manhattan HS; Manhattan, KS; (3); 35/450; JV Var Tennis; Hon Roll; U KS; Meterology.

BIECHELE, BARB M; Shawnee Mission S Sr HS; Shawnee Mission, KS; (4); DECA; Acpl Chr; Hon Roll; NHS; DECA Natls/ST Comps; OJT; Northland Coll; Envrnmntl Sci.

BIELEFELD, ROSS; Hope HS; Hope, KS; (3); Pres FBLA; Natl FFA Org; Scholastic Bowl; Treas SADD; Yrbk; Ofcr Stu Cncl; Bsktbl; Trk; 4-H Awd; NHS; Govs Ctr Teen Ldrshp; Site Base Cncl; KS ST U; Arch.

BIELFELDT, LEAH E; Garden City Sr HS; Garden City, KS; (2); Church Yth Grp; Debate Tm; French Clb; Latin Clb; Orch; High Hon Roll; Natl Guild Of Piano Tchrs Wnnr; Comm Orch; Future Problm Solvrs Intnl Cmptn; Odyssey Of Mind; Cello; His.

BIENHOFF, JACKIE D; Eastern Heights Jr Sr HS; Agra, KS; (3); 6/9; Drama Clb; Letterman Clb; Pep Clb; Speech Tm; School Play; Bsktbl; Score Keeper; Trk; Vllybl; Hon Roll; Horse Trnr.

BIGGERSTAFF, CLAYTON P; Arkansas City HS; Arkansas City, KS; (1); High Hon Roll; Hon Roll; OK ST Univ; Engrng; Drafting.

BIGGERSTAFF, SHALON; Frontenac Jr Sr HS; Frontenac, KS; (2); 5/63; Pep Clb; Spanish Clb; Yrbk; Pres Soph Cls; Ofcr Stu Cncl; Vllybl; Hon Roll; STUCCO; Crim.

BIGGS, NICHOLAS J; Buhler HS; Hutchinson, KS; (3); Church Yth Grp; FCA; Spanish Clb; Mrchg Band; Orch; Pep Band; Stage Crew; Ftbl; Trk; Wt Lftg; Sports Medicine; Phys Therapy.

BIGONGIARI, JEFFREY; Wichita Collegiate Schl; Wichita, KS; (4); Pres Chess Clb; Debate Tm; Capt Scholastic Bowl; Science Clb; Rptr Nwsp; VP Frsh Cls; Pres Soph Cls; VP Jr Cls; VP Sr Cls; VP Stu Cncl; Tulane.

BILDERBACK, CHAD; Atchison Sr HS; Atchison, KS; (2); Bsktbl; Ftbl; Hon Roll; KS ST; Vet.

BILDERBACK, REBECCA A; Labette Co HS; Altamont, KS; (4); 14/128; Church Yth Grp; FCA; French Clb; FBLA; Library Aide; Var Crs Cntry; JV Var Trk; Hon Roll; NHS; Pres Schlr; Coffeyville CC.

BILLING, MEGAN; Seaman Sr HS; Topeka, KS; (3); Art Clb; Church Yth Grp; Drama Clb; Sec French Clb; Band; Chorus; Mrchg Band; School Musical; Hon Roll; NHS; KS ST U; Cmmnctns.

BILLINGER, DAWN M; Thomas More Prep-Marion HS; Hays, KS; (3); 46/77; NFL; Pep Clb; Var L Sftbl; Wt Lftg; Hon Roll; Forencis Ltr 2 Yrs; NLSA Awds 96; USSSA Sftbl Wmn League; KS Univ.

BILLINGS, ALICIA A; Blue Valley Northwest HS; Overland Park, KS; (2); 83/409; Hon Roll; Empuria ST Univ; Wrtr/Jrnlsm.

BILLINGS, RICHARD P; Bishop Ward HS; Kansas City, KS; (2); 3/93; Drama Clb; School Musical; Stage Crew; Var Ftbl; JV Golf; High Hon Roll; NHS; NHS Treas; Cert Of Awds Frgn Lang/Soc Sci 96.

BILLINGSLEY, KARI M; Independence HS; Independence, KS; (3); Church Yth Grp; FCA; SADD; Chorus; Church Choir; High Hon Roll; NHS; French Clb; Pep Clb; Teachers Aide; Pittsburg ST Univ Deans Schlsp; Phi Kappa Phi Hnr Soc Awd; Amateur Radio Operator; Yth Minister.

BILLINGSLEY, SAMANTHA A; Sumner Acad; Kansas City, KS; (3); 1/142; Drama Clb; Hosp Aide; Intnl Clb; JCL; Key Clb; Latin Clb; Pep Clb; Spanish Clb; Thesps; School Musical.

BILLMAN, BRET R; Wichita East HS; Wichita, KS; (2); Church Yth Grp; JV Bsbl; Hon Roll; Intnl Bcclrte Prgm.

BILLS, JENNIFER; Seaman Sr HS; Topeka, KS; (3); Church Yth Grp; Cmnty Wkr; FBLA; Math Clb; Mu Alpha Theta; SADD; Church Choir; Jazz Band; High Hon Roll; NHS; Sunday Schl Treas; Avid Star Trek Collectr; Physics.

BILYEU, JOSHUA W; Turner HS; Kansas City, KS; (2); Trk; Hon Roll; Pres Acad Fit Awd; Comp.

BILYK, TYLER; Sedan HS; Pawhuska, OK; (2); 7/40; 4-H; Letterman Clb; Natl FFA Org; Quiz Bowl; Jazz Band; VP Soph Cls; Var L Bsbl; Var L Bsktbl; Var L Ftbl; Hon Roll; All League Qrtrbck Ftbl; All Leg Infld Bsbl; AZ ST U; Sprts Med.

BINA, NICHOLE; Centre Jr Sr HS; Lincolnville, KS; (3); Church Yth Grp; FBLA; HOBY; SADD; Pres Frsh Cls; Pres Soph Cls; Sec Jr Cls; Capt L Bsktbl; Capt L Vllybl; NHS; Bus.

BINA, NIKKI; Centre Jr Sr HS; Lincolnville, KS; (3); Church Yth Grp; FBLA; HOBY; SADD; Sec Jr Cls; Bsktbl; Trk; Vllybl; Hon Roll; NHS.

BINDEL, NICOLE R; Sabetha HS; Sabetha, KS; (3); FBLA; Pep Clb; Teachers Aide; Chorus; Rep Stu Cncl; Var L Bsktbl; Var L Trk; Var L Vllybl; Hon Roll; Prfct Atten Awd; Bus Admin.

BINGAMAN, RACHELLE J; Wichita Collegiate Schl; Wichita, KS; (3); Church Yth Grp; Debate Tm; NFL; SADD; School Musical; Sec Sr Cls; Pom Pon; High Hon Roll; SHARP; Yng Life; Baylor Univ; Eng/Comm.

BIRCHER, MOLLY; Ellsworth HS; Ellsworth, KS; (4); 7/66; Am Leg Aux Girls St; Church Yth Grp; Capt Debate Tm; Pres 4-H; Pres Varsity Clb; Band; L Bsktbl; Capt Crs Cntry; Capt Trk; 4-H Awd; Ft Hays ST U; Pol Sci.

BIRD, DEBORAH J; Clearwater HS; Clearwater, KS; (2); SADD; Chorus; High Hon Roll.

BIRD, JEANE M; Clearwater HS; Clearwater, KS; (4); 1/87; Letterman Clb; SADD; Chorus; Nwsp; Capt Chrldng; Gov Hon Prg Awd; High Hon Roll; NHS; St Schlr; KS ST Univ; Bio-Med Engrng.

BIRD, JEFF A; Deerfield HS; Deerfield, KS; (2); Church Yth Grp; Pep Clb; Science Clb; Var Bsktbl; Hon Roll.

BIRD, TARI A; Topeka West HS; Topeka, KS; (3); 45/249; Church Yth Grp; Debate Tm; VP French Clb; NFL; Rep Pep Clb; SADD; Teachers Aide; Crs Cntry; Powder Puff Ftbl; Vllybl; DARE; Tea Party; Teens Hope; U Of KS; Law; Math.

BIRK, MANDY L; Burlington HS; Burlington, KS; (3); Sec FBLA; Pres VP FHA; Model UN; Band; Capt Flag Corp; Mrchg Band; Pep Band; Sec Soph Cls; High Hon Roll; Hon Roll; PT.

BIRKBECK, TAMARA; Burlington HS; Burlington, KS; (4); 1/80; Church Yth Grp; FBLA; FHA; GAA; Natl FFA Org; Pep Clb; Teachers Aide; Ofcr Soph Cls; Ofcr Jr Cls; Ofcr Sr Cls; Debbie Roth Schl Sprt Awd; Dale Dennis Excl Ed Awd; All-ST Hnrbl Mntn Team; All-ST Bsktbl Acad Team; KS ST Univ; Anml Sci.

BIRMINGHAM, MARK; Parsons HS; Parsons, KS; (3); 1/120; VP FCA; Ed Key Clb; Ed Yrbk; VP Soph Cls; Var Bsktbl; Var Ftbl; JV Trk; Cit Awd; High Hon Roll; NHS; Wrld Hstry Awd; Sports Clb; Tutor; Med.

BIRRELL, ABIGAEL W; Topeka West HS; Topeka, KS; (3); Debate Tm; English Clb; German Clb; Model UN; Q&S; Quiz Bowl; Scholastic Bowl; Speech Tm; Teachers Aide; Thesps; Topeka Capitol Jrnl Yth Staff Writer.

BIRZER, STACIE; Ellinwood Jr Sr HS; Ellinwood, KS; (3); 10/46; FCA; Teachers Aide; Band; Flag Corp; Mrchg Band; Pep Band; Stage Crew; JV Bsktbl; Var Chrldng; Stat Mgr(s); STAR Pgm; KS Assn Yth.

BISBY, KATHERINE; Shawnee Mission N HS; Merriam, KS; (3); 53/429; Pres Church Yth Grp; Q&S; Spanish Clb; Band; Mrchg Band; Pep Band; Ed Phtg Yrbk; JV Var Swmmng; Hon Roll; NHS; KS ST.

BISHOP, BECKY M; Lincoln Jr Sr HS; Lincoln, KS; (2); Letterman Clb; Pep Clb; Trk; Hon Roll; KU; Psychiatry.

BISHOP, CARMALETTA C; Washington HS; Kansas City, KS; (2); Dance Clb; ROTC; Spanish Clb; Acpl Chr; Drill Tm; High Hon Roll; RN.

BISHOP, CORY J; Ulysses HS; Ulysses, KS; (4); 18/93; Am Leg Boys St; FBLA; Letterman Clb; Spanish Clb; SADD; Ofcr Stu Cncl; Var Bsbl; NHS; Ntl Merit Ltr; West TX A&M; Psych.

BISHOP, JESSICA M; Lawrence HS; Lawrence, KS; (4); 91/520; Church Yth Grp; Teachers Aide; Band; Jazz Band; Mrchg Band; Pep Band; School Play; Variety Show; Hon Roll; Ntl Merit Ltr; Spiritual Integrity From Flwshp Of Chrstn Stdnts Awd; U Of KS.

BISSEY, JENNIFER L; Tonganoxie HS; Tonganoxie, KS; (4); 15/118; Art Clb; Church Yth Grp; FCA; Sec FBLA; Office Aide; Science Clb; Spanish Clb; SADD; Teachers Aide; Drill Tm; U Of KS; Bio.

BITNOFF, NATASHA M; Macksville HS; Belpre, KS; (3); 4/20; JV Bsktbl; JV Powder Puff Ftbl; JV Vllybl; Hon Roll; NHS; Kayette Clb; NW KS Voc Tech; Arch Drafting.

BITTEL, TONYA L; Thomas More Prep-Marion HS; Hays, KS; (2); Hosp Aide; Scholastic Bowl; Band; Church Choir; Mrchg Band; Pep Band; School Musical; Nwsp; Yrbk; High Hon Roll; Med Field.

BITTER, GREGG A; Garden City Sr HS; Garden City, KS; (3); 116/300; Church Yth Grp; Office Aide; Teachers Aide; Band; Mrchg Band; Pep Band; Tennis; Hon Roll; KS ST Univ; Comp Tech.

BJURSTROM, BRANDA L; Wichita Co HS; Leoti, KS; (4); Art Clb; Hosp Aide; Natl FFA Org; VP Pep Clb; Band; Chorus; Mrchg Band; Pep Band; School Musical; School Play; Chrldng, Dnc; Hon Rll; Flg Corps; Colby CC; Nrsng.

BLACK, ADAM J; Prairie View Jr Sr HS; Paola, KS; (3); 20/88; 4-H; Natl FFA Org; Band; Ftbl; Trk; Wt Lftg; Wrstlng; Hon Roll; Aviation.

BLACK, CHARLENE M; El Dorado HS; El Dorado, KS; (3); 44/144; Pres Sec 4-H; French Clb; Math Clb; SADD; Teachers Aide; Orch; JV Crs Cntry; 4-H Awd; Pres Hon Roll; Eastern OK ST Coll; Vet Med.

BLACK, ELIZABETH; Emporia HS; Emporia, KS; (4); Sec Church Yth Grp; Key Clb; Church Choir; Orch; School Musical; Cit Awd; Hon Roll; Natl Tchrs Hl Fm Choir; Wldlf/Bckpckng Clb; Marine Biol.

BLACK, HEATHER L; Halstead HS; Sedgwick, KS; (3); Church Yth Grp; German Clb; Girl Scts; Chorus; Nwsp; JV Trk; JV Vllybl; Hon Roll; German Clb Sec, Treas; Marine Bio.

BLACK, KEELY R; Ottawa HS; Ottawa, KS; (2); Church Yth Grp; Debate Tm; Drill Tm; School Musical; School Play; Variety Show; NFL; Pom Pon; High Hon Roll; NHS; Univ KS; Pre-Med; Cardiovascul.

BLACK, KRISTEN K; Halstead HS; Sedgwick, KS; (1); Church Yth Grp; Drama Clb; German Clb; Girl Scts; School Play; Trk.

BLACK, NATALIE; Wichita North HS; Wichita, KS; (3); Church Yth Grp; German Clb; Teachers Aide; Orch; School Musical; Rep Soph Cls; Treas Jr Cls; VP Stu Cncl; JV Var Chrldng; Var Swmmng; I Dare You Awd; Wichita Yth Symphony; WSU; Neo-Natal Nrsng.

BLACK, STAR L; Salina HS South; Salina, KS; (3); 117/277; Drama Clb; Thesps; School Musical; School Play; Ofcr Stu Cncl; KS Univ; Art His.

BLACK, TYLER J; Mc Pherson HS; Mc Pherson, KS; (3); French Clb; Science Clb; Var Bsbl; JV Bsktbl; Hon Roll; Math Rly; Chem Engr.

BLACKBURN, AMANDA M; Labette Co HS; Parsons, KS; (2); SADD; Hon Roll; KAYS.

BLACKBURN, RYAN M; Labette Co HS; Dennis, KS; (2); FCA; Natl FFA Org; VICA; Wrstlng; High Hon Roll; Hon Roll; Individual Achvmt Awd; KS ST Univ; Agronomy.

BLACKERBY, SHAILA A; Maize HS; Wichita, KS; (3); Phtg Nwsp; Hon Roll; Free Lance Photgrphy; Cmptr; Free Lance Wrtr; Wichita ST Univ; Phtgrphr.

BLACKETER, ANGELICA L; Leavenworth HS; Leavenworth, KS; (1); Church Yth Grp; Cmnty Wkr; ROTC; Band; Chorus; Church Choir; Mrchg Band; Pep Band; School Musical; High Hon Roll; Band Cncl Frosh Rep; ROTC Drum/Bugle Corps; Cadet Chorus ROTC; Outstdng Acad Awd; Massage THRPST/AIR Force.

BLACKFORD, BEAU; Buhler HS; Hutchinson, KS; (3); Am Leg Boys St; Computer Clb; Science Clb; Band; Chorus; Jazz Band; Mrchg Band; Orch; Pep Band; Stage Crew; Sr Squad Ldr For Marching Band; Amer Red Cross Blood Mobile Vol; KS ST Univ; Comp Sci.

BLACKMAN, TODD D; Shawnee Mission S Sr HS; Overland Park, KS; (4); Pres Temple Yth Grp; Acpl Chr; High Hon Roll; Hon Roll; NHS; Ntl Merit Schol; Piano Prfmnce; U KS; Cmptr Engrng.

BLACKWELDER, AMY D; Cimarron HS; Cimarron, KS; (4); 4/50; Church Yth Grp; Cmnty Wkr; Math Tm; Pres Pep Clb; Capt Quiz Bowl; Spanish Clb; Teachers Aide; Band; Flag Corp; Mrchg Band; KS ST U; Grphc Design.

BLACKWELL, KARI L; Olathe North Sr HS; Olathe, KS; (4); 137/357; Dance Clb; Office Aide; Spanish Clb; Drill Tm; Hon Roll; U Of KS.

BLACKWILL, STACY M; Quinter Jr Sr HS; Quinter, KS; (3); Debate Tm; Drama Clb; FHA; School Play; Pres Frsh Cls; Rep Jr Cls; Pres Sr Cls; Sec Stu Cncl; Hon Roll; Commnctn; Pub Speaking.

BLAIR, MICKI; Central Jr Sr HS; Atlanta, KS; (4); 1/26; Church Yth Grp; FCA; School Play; Ed Yrbk; Pres Jr Cls; Pres Sr Cls; VP Stu Cncl; Var Bsktbl; Var Chrldng; Var Vllybl; Emporia ST U; Ed.

BLAKE, CARL A; Derby HS; Derby, KS; (1); Boy Scts; Intrml Bsktbl; JV Crs Cntry; Var Trk; High Hon Roll; Eagle Scout.

BLAKE, CASSIE L; Pawnee Heights East HS; Rozel, KS; (1); Band; Chorus; Mrchg Band; Pep Band; Ofcr Frsh Cls; Bsktbl; Chrldng; Vllybl; High Hon Roll; Hon Roll.

BLAKE, CHARLENE M; Topeka HS; Topeka, KS; (2); 3/558; Dance Clb; Science Clb; Spanish Clb; Band; Drill Tm; Mrchg Band; Pom Pon; Sftbl; High Hon Roll; Natl Sci Mrt Awd; Schltc Hnrs; Pre-Medicine.

BLAKE, MARGARET A; Shawnee Mission Nw Sr HS; Lake Quivira, KS; (4); 71/451; Mgr Drama Clb; NFL; Thesps; School Musical; School Play; Stage Crew; High Hon Roll; Hon Roll; Theatre.

BLAKE, MELISSA; Udall HS; Udall, KS; (3); Church Yth Grp; Spanish Clb; Speech Tm; Acpl Chr; Band; Chorus; Church Choir; Drill Tm; Mrchg Band; Pep Band; Won Miss KS Natl Tngr 95.

BLAKE, SHANNON; Manhattan HS; Manhattan, KS; (4); 1/364; Church Yth Grp; Pep Clb; Spanish Clb; SADD; Teachers Aide; Mrchg Band; Capt Chrldng; Mgr(s); High Hon Roll; Hon Roll; 2nd Pl Natl Span Exam Span I; Volntr Elem Schl; St Of KS Schlr; KSSU; Ed.

BLAKELY, ALISON H; Shawnee Heights HS; Berryton, KS; (3); 47/217; Church Yth Grp; Hosp Aide; SADD; Band; Mrchg Band; Pep Band; Hon Roll; Chrch Chrstn Ed Bd; Care Co; PT/OT.

BLAKESLEY, NATHANAEL L; Ottawa HS; Ottawa, KS; (3); 45/146; Am Leg Boys St; Debate Tm; Thesps; Chorus; School Musical; Swing Chorus; Variety Show; Hon Roll.

BLAKESLEY, STACY; Garden City Sr HS; Garden City, KS; (4); KS Univ; Med.

BLANCAS, ANTHONY E; Highland Park HS; Topeka, KS; (3); Am Leg Boys St; Church Yth Grp; Cmnty Wkr; Spanish Clb; Sec Stu Cncl; Var Bsbl; Var Socr; High Hon Roll; Hon Roll; NHS; Med.

BLANCO, ANTHONY L; Topeka West HS; Topeka, KS; (4); Church Yth Grp; Cmnty Wkr; Spanish Clb; SADD; Hon Roll; Var L Bsktbl; Var L Ftbl; Var L Trk; Homcmng King; I-70 Lge Hnrbl Mntn Ftbll; Washburn Univ; Psych.

BLAND, JULIE; Marmaton Valley Jr Sr HS; Moran, KS; (3); #1 in class; Church Yth Grp; FCA; GAA; HOBY; Math Tm; Natl FFA Org; Pep Clb; Quiz Bowl; Band; Mrchg Band.

BLANKENSHIP, BENJAMIN A; Olathe East Sr HS; Olathe, KS; (3); Church Yth Grp; Cmnty Wkr; Letterman Clb; Spanish Clb; Teachers Aide; Varsity Clb; Band; Co-Capt Bsbl; Sec L Bsktbl; Var L Ftbl; Optmtry.

BLANTON, APRIL; Cheney Jr Sr HS; Murdock, KS; (2); Art Clb; Spanish Clb; Chorus; Variety Show; Trk; Hon Roll; Ntl Merit Ltr; Acad Excl Awd; Girls Glee; Art Jury; Hutchison CC; Law Enforcement.

BLASI, BLAKE C; Bishop Carroll Catholic HS; Wichita, KS; (3); 20/176; Var Bsbl; Var Ftbl; Hon Roll; NHS.

BLASI, NATHAN; Goddar HS; Wichita, KS; (2); Church Yth Grp; Var Bsbl; Var Ftbl; Var Wt Lftg; High Hon Roll; NHS; Bible & Chess Clbs; U Of CO; Architecture.

BLASI, VINCENT L; Wichita West HS; Wichita, KS; (3); 40/283; Am Leg Boys St; Church Yth Grp; Teachers Aide; Chorus; Ofcr Jr Cls; Prfct Atten Awd; Army.

BLASING, JEREMY; Washburn Rural HS; Topeka, KS; (3); Ofcr Bsbl; Bsktbl; Crs Cntry; Ftbl; Trk; Wt Lftg; Wrstlng; Hon Roll; Lifeguard; Cert Of Mrt For Outstdng Perfmnc & Dedicated Svc; Hunting; Fishing; Swimming; Play Guitar; KS ST; Pol Sci; Pub Admin.

BLASINGAME, JEANNA; Valley Falls HS; Denison, KS; (3); 4-H; Math Tm; Scholastic Bowl; Teachers Aide; Var Chrldng; Var Vllybl; 4-H Awd; Hon Roll; NHS; Letterman Clb; KS Pinto Assn High Point Awd.

BLASOR, JASON R; Parsons HS; Parsons, KS; (2); Church Yth Grp; Var JV Ftbl; JV Golf; Pittsburg ST Univ; Artist.

BLASS, KENDA D; Hayden HS; Fort Worth, TX; (2); Cmnty Wkr; Latin Clb; Office Aide; Pep Clb; SADD; Chorus; Var Mgr Bsktbl; Var Mgr(s); Var Score Keeper; Var JV Tennis; Help Church Vacation Bible Schl; KS Univ; Pol Sci/Zoology.

BLATTNER, BARTON; Atchison Sr HS; Atchison, KS; (2); 10/123; Church Yth Grp; Cmnty Wkr; Pres Frsh Cls; Rep Soph Cls; JV Var Bsbl; JV Var Bsktbl; JV Var Ftbl; Wt Lftg; High Hon Roll; Pres Acad Fit Awd; Natl Yng Ldrs Conf Wshngtn DC; USAA US Natl Math Awd; KS ST U.

BLATTNER, ERIC; Atchison Sr HS; Atchison, KS; (1); Church Yth Grp; Cmnty Wkr; JV Bsbl; Bsktbl; JV Ftbl; Wt Lftg; Gov Hon Prg Awd.

BLAUFUSS, MELINDA JO; Anderson Cty Jr Sr HS; Welda, KS; (2); FHA; SADD; Chorus; JV Bsktbl; Var Bsktbl; Hon Roll; Received Acad Awd In Lang Arts; Received Bronze Awd In Renaissance Pgm.

BLAUTUSS, LISA; Olpe Schl; Olpe, KS; (4); 1/26; 4-H; VP FBLA; Capt Quiz Bowl; Treas Frsh Cls; Treas Jr Cls; Treas Sr Cls; Ofcr Stu Cncl; Var L Bsktbl; Var L Trk; Var L Vllybl; Emporia ST U; Acctng.

BLAYLOCK, BRANDI N; Wichita Southeast HS; Wichita, KS; (2); Church Yth Grp; Acpl Chr; Church Choir; Orch; High Hon Roll; Hon Roll; NHS; Habt Hmnty Vol; UCLA.

BLAYLOCK, REBECCA L; Olathe North Sr HS; Olathe, KS; (4); 35/320; Pep Clb; Yrbk; Rep Jr Cls; Rep Stu Cncl; Mgr(s); French Hon Soc; High Hon Roll; NHS; Pres Acad Fit Awd; Pres Schlr; Johnson County CC; Phys Thrpy.

BLAZEK, A J; Maize HS; Wichita, KS; (3); 20/250; Boy Scts; Letterman Clb; Spanish Clb; SADD; VP Thesps; VP Varsity Clb; Orch; School Play; Rep Frsh Cls; Rep Jr Cls; Eagle Sct; Coll; Scndry Ed.

BLAZIC, ADAM; Girard HS; Girard, KS; (3); 1/85; Natl FFA Org; Office Aide; Science Clb; Spanish Clb; SADD; Teachers Aide; JV Var Bsbl; JV Var Ftbl; JV Var Trk; Wt Lftg; Engrng.

BLENDER, CALLIE J; Chase Co HS; Emporia, KS; (2); Church Yth Grp; Pres 4-H; Pep Clb; Quiz Bowl; Spanish Clb; Band; Chorus; Church Choir; Mrchg Band; Pep Band; KAYS ST Yth Org.

BLENDER, CORINNE L; Chase Co HS; Emporia, KS; (2); Church Yth Grp; Sec Treas 4-H; Pep Clb; Quiz Bowl; Sec Spanish Clb; Band; Chorus; Church Choir; Mrchg Band; Pep Band; KAYS ST Yth Org.

BLESS, RAYNE; Lakin HS; Lakin, KS; (3); Dance Clb; Pep Clb; Quiz Bowl; Chorus; Var L Chrldng; Var L Pom Pon; High Hon Roll; Hon Roll; KS ST Univ; Bus; Acctng.

BLEVINS, BRANDY M; Independence HS; Independence, KS; (1); Church Yth Grp; FCA; French Clb; Pep Clb; Chorus; Church Choir.

BLEVINS, CHRIS; Highland HS; Highland, KS; (3); 4-H; Letterman Clb; Natl FFA Org; Chorus; School Musical; School Play; Swing Chorus; Rptr Nwsp; Phtg Yrbk; Pres Frsh Cls; AJQHA Wrld Show Top 10; KS ST U; Vet Med.

BLEVINS, DENISE; Highland HS; Highland, KS; (2); Church Yth Grp; Pres 4-H; Natl FFA Org; Pep Clb; Chorus; School Musical; Ofcr Frsh Cls; Ofcr Soph Cls; Ofcr Stu Cncl; JV Var Bsktbl; KS ST; Bus.

BLEVINS, DEREK A; Maize HS; Maize, KS; (4); Church Yth Grp; SADD; Teachers Aide; Varsity Clb; Var L Socr; Wt Lftg; Hon Roll; Pres Acad Fit Awd; WSU; Bus Mngmnt.

BLEVINS, JULIE M; Field Kindley Mem Sr HS; Coffeyville, KS; (4); Church Yth Grp; Band; Church Choir; Color Guard; Jazz Band; Mrchg Band; School Musical; Hon Roll; NHS; Prfct Atten Awd; Lions Intnl Band Mem; Stu Tchr; Played Natl Anthem At Grad; Multi-Yr Listee; Coffeyville Comm Coll; HS Band.

BLISS, KYLEE; Little River Jr Sr HS; Windom, KS; (1); Ski Clb; Band; Mrchg Band; Pep Band; Stat Bsktbl; Var Chrldng; JV Var Mgr(s); Var Pom Pon; Stat Vllybl; 4-H Awd; Marine Bio.

BLISS, MAUREEN E; Colby Sr HS; Colby, KS; (2); 9/140; Church Yth Grp; FCA; Science Clb; Spanish Clb; Chorus; Sftbl; Tennis; Trk; Wt Lftg; Hon Roll; Taekwondo; AZ ST U.

BLOBAUM, HEIDI A; Blue Valley Northwest HS; Overland Park, KS; (3); 14/364; Debate Tm; Sec Drama Clb; Model UN; Pres NFL; Speech Tm; Thesps; School Play; Stage Crew; High Hon Roll; Hon Roll.

BLOESING, G JARED; Wichita South HS; Wichita, KS; (2); 10/273; Boy Scts; Band; Jazz Band; Var L Swmmng; Var L Tennis; Hon Roll; Eagle Scout; Var Schlrs Bowl; Acad Ltrman; U Of KS; Meteorlgy.

BLOMGREN, SHARON L; Wichita Heights HS; Wichita, KS; (4); 42/246; FHA; Hon Roll; NHS; Pres Acad Fit Awd; Stu Rep At Chrch; Drama Tm; Sterling Col; Spec Ed Tchr.

BLOMQUIST, JENNIFER; Salina HS Central; Salina, KS; (2); Hosp Aide; HOBY; SADD; School Play; VP Soph Cls; Bsktbl; Chrldng; Crs Cntry; Trk; Pres Acad Fit Awd; KS U; Med.

BLOODWORTH, BRIAN E; Junction City HS; Fort Riley, KS; (4); Sec VP Computer Clb; Drama Clb; Model UN; Speech Tm; Phtg Nwsp; Phtg Yrbk; Var Capt Socr; Var Swmmng; High Hon Roll; NHS; TX A&M; Marine Biologist.

BLOOM, ERIC J; Eudora HS; Eudora, KS; (3); 1/70; Church Yth Grp; FBLA; JA; Quiz Bowl; Scholastic Bowl; Spanish Clb; Band; Treas Frsh Cls; Treas Soph Cls; Treas Jr Cls; Cmptr Sci.

BLOOM, GINNY; Andover HS; Wichita, KS; (4); 1/144; Cmnty Wkr; Hosp Aide; Scholastic Bowl; SADD; Teachers Aide; Ed Nwsp; Var L Socr; Gov Hon Prg Awd; High Hon Roll; Treas NHS; Univ Of PA.

BLOOM, KRISTEN M; Wichita Collegiate Schl; Wichita, KS; (4); Dance Clb; French Clb; Teachers Aide; Varsity Clb; School Musical; Chrldng; Socr; Sftbl; Trk; Vllybl; Trk 7th St Discus 96; Toys For Tots Recognition 95-96; ISAS Fine Arts Festival Perfmnc; U Of KS.

BLOOMER, AMY E; Clearwater HS; Clearwater, KS; (2); 1/98; Letterman Clb; Math Tm; Science Clb; Spanish Clb; SADD; Varsity Clb; Treas Church Yth Grp; Var L Bsktbl; Var L Trk; Var L Vllybl; Pediatrics.

BLOOMFIELD, JOHN; Wabaunsee HS; Alma, KS; (3); Letterman Clb; Pres Sec Natl FFA Org; Quiz Bowl; Crs Cntry; Trk; High Hon Roll; NHS; Ntl Merit SF; St Exec Comm Rep FFA; St Trk Medalist; KS ST; Vet Med.

BLOSSER, TARA; Shawnee Mission South HS; Overland Park, KS; (4); 224/413; Ofcr DECA; NFL; Pep Clb; Teachers Aide; Ofcr Acpl Chr; Ed Nwsp; Stat Bsktbl; JV Golf; Var L Trk; U Of KS; Medicine; Mrktg.

BLOSSER, VIOLET; Central Jr HS; Lawrence, KS; (1); JA; Math Tm; Chorus; Orch; Variety Show; L JV Crs Cntry; JV Socr; Cit Awd; High Hon Roll.

BLOUIN, MICHAEL T; Derby HS; Derby, KS; (3); Church Yth Grp; Band; Jazz Band; Mrchg Band; Pep Band; Hon Roll; Elec Engr.

BLOUNT, CATHERINE; Marion HS; Marion, KS; (4); Am Leg Aux Girls St; Girl Scts; Quiz Bowl; School Musical; School Play; Rep Stu Cncl; Var L Crs Cntry; Hon Roll; NHS; Trk; Oz-Heartland Racing Team; Cycling.

BLOUNT, ELLA S; Marion HS; Marion, KS; (4); FHA; Girl Scts; Natl FFA Org; Scholastic Bowl; Stage Crew; Phtg Yrbk; Rep Stu Cncl; Var L Crs Cntry; Mgr Ftbl; St Schlr; U Of KS; Span.

BLOUSTINE, JEFF; Louisburg HS; Louisburg, KS; (3); Am Leg Boys St; Letterman Clb; SADD; Band; Var Bsbl; Bsktbl; JV Ftbl; Hon Roll; KS U; Crmnlgy.

BLUBAUGH, STEPHANIE K; Labette Co HS; Parsons, KS; (3); FCA; FBLA; Spanish Clb; Nwsp; Yrbk; Ofcr Stu Cncl; JV Var Bsktbl; JV Var Trk; JV Var Vllybl; Hon Roll; Optometry; Phy Therapy.

BLUM, DIANA J; Shawnee Mission W Sr HS; Lenexa, KS; (3); Church Yth Grp; Office Aide; Church Choir; Stage Crew; Yrbk; Chrldng; High Hon Roll; Hon Roll; Chrldg Ltr; Span Cls Ltr Frosh; UNL; Med Dr.

BLUME, MATTHEW J; Thomas More Prep-Marion HS; Hays, KS; (2); Church Yth Grp; Cmnty Wkr; ROTC; Speech Tm; School Play; Pres Frsh Cls; Ofcr Soph Cls; Bsktbl; Ftbl; Trk; Natrl Hlprs; Washington St Louis; Arch.

BLUNK, HEIDI R; Wellington Sr HS; Wellington, KS; (2); Intnl Clb; Key Clb; SADD; Band; Church Choir; L Bsktbl; L Vllybl; High Hon Roll; Jr NHS; Pres Acad Fit Awd; Lions Clb Awd; KS U Med Schl; Med.

BLUNT, BONNIE R; Great Bend Sr HS; Great Bend, KS; (2); Church Yth Grp; Drama Clb; German Clb; Hosp Aide; SADD; Band; Church Choir; Mrchg Band; Pep Band; School Play; Kayetts; OSU; Meterology.

BLUNT, KELLY; Palco HS; Palco, KS; (1); Debate Tm; FHA; Pep Clb; Speech Tm; Treas Frsh Cls; Var JV Bsktbl; Chrldng; Trk; JV Vllybl; Hon Roll; Medcl.

BOAZ, REBECCA L; Troy HS; Troy, KS; (4); Church Yth Grp; Cmnty Wkr; Quiz Bowl; Speech Tm; Teachers Aide; School Play; Pres 4-H Awd; Sec NHS; St Schlr; Acad, Band, Quiz Bowl, Speech & Chorus Ltrs; Camp Cnslr; Vocal Solo St 1st Pl; Summer Mission Mexico; Grace Univ; Psych.

BOBBITT, JODI R; Hoisington HS; Hoisington, KS; (3); 1/68; Intnl Clb; Pep Clb; Sec Treas SADD; Varsity Clb; Band; JV Var Bsktbl; Var Sftbl; JV Var Vllybl; High Hon Roll; NHS; Pediatric Nrsng.

BOCK, NATALIE E; Bishop Miege HS; Merriam, KS; (2); 26/170; Church Yth Grp; Cmnty Wkr; GAA; SADD; Drill Tm; Rep Frsh Cls; Crs Cntry; Swmmng; High Hon Roll; Hon Roll; Outdoors Club; Spirit Club; CMT; KU; Prmry Ed.

BOCKEN, JOE; Marmaton Valley Jr Sr HS; La Harpe, KS; (3); 14/29; FCA; Math Tm; Natl FFA Org; Band; Var L Bsktbl; Var L Ftbl; Var L Trk; Hon Roll; Ntl Merit Ltr; Multiple Yr Listing; KS ST; Vet Sci.

BODANSKE, SARAH E; Blue Valley Northwest HS; Overland Park, KS; (2); Orch; Bsktbl; Tennis; Hon Roll; Yth Camp Horsemanship Cnslr.

BODDIE, CHELSEA; Wyandotte HS; Kansas City, KS; (4); 22/130; Church Yth Grp; Band; Church Choir; Jazz Band; Mrchg Band; Pep Band; Bsktbl; Trk; Vllybl; High Hon Roll; U Of AR Pine Bluff; Med.

BODEN, JASON W; Jewell HS; Esbon, KS; (1); Church Yth Grp; FCA; 4-H; Natl FFA Org; SADD; Chorus; JV Bsktbl; Var Ftbl; 4-H Awd; Hon Roll.

BODINE, TONI L; Rock Creek Jr Sr HS; Manhattan, KS; (3); Hosp Aide; SADD; Phtg Rptr Yrbk; VP Frsh Cls; JV Var Bsktbl; Var Chrldng; JV Var Trk; JV Vllybl; Hon Roll; Pep Clb; ST Track Frosh Yr; Bowling; Nrs.

BODWELL, BROOK A; Independence HS; Independence, KS; (3); Church Yth Grp; French Clb; Science Clb; Chorus; Nwsp; Wt Lftg; Hon Roll; NHS; TLT Mem.

BOECKEL, REBECCA L; Olathe East Sr HS; Olathe, KS; (2); Church Yth Grp; Math Tm; Spanish Clb; VP Band; Pres Mrchg Band; Orch; Pep Band; Var Capt Gym; High Hon Roll; Pres Acad Fit Awd; Solo/Ensmbl Fstvl I Rating ST.

BOECKMAN, KELLY L; Wetmore Schl; Goff, KS; (2); Church Yth Grp; Letterman Clb; Pep Clb; Band; Chorus; Mrchg Band; Pep Band; School Musical; School Play; Pres Frsh Cls; KAY Clb Schl Svc Dir; Emporia ST Univ; Bus; Acctng.

BOECKMANN, COURTNEY M; Holton HS; Holton, KS; (2); Church Yth Grp; FHA; Letterman Clb; Q&S; Spanish Clb; Varsity Clb; Phtg Nwsp; Phtg Yrbk; Var Mgr(s); Var Sftbl; KS U; Tchng.

BOECKMANN, LAURA A; Holton HS; Holton, KS; (1); Church Yth Grp; Rptr Natl FFA Org; Quiz Bowl; Sftbl; Prfct Atten Awd; KS Univ; Tchr.

BOEDING, CARRIE R; Shawnee Heights HS; Topeka, KS; (2); Church Yth Grp; Intnl Clb; Spanish Clb; SADD; Cit Awd; High Hon Roll; Hon Roll; Pres Acad Fit Awd; Guth Awd For Otstndng Acad/Ctznshp; Inside-Out Club; KS ST Emporia; Tch.

BOEH, SARAH J; Troy HS; Troy, KS; (2); 7/44; Pres Church Yth Grp; Pres 4-H; Letterman Clb; Natl FFA Org; VP Soph Cls; Var Bsktbl; Var Crs Cntry; Sftbl; Var Trk; JV Var Vllybl; Church Orgnst; Accpnst For Choirs/Solos; KS ST Univ; Archt.

BOEHM, DUSTIN; Paola HS; Paola, KS; (3); Pres Drama Clb; Teachers Aide; Thesps; School Play; Stage Crew; Ed Nwsp; Hon Roll; U Of KS; Scndry Egn Ed; Theater.

BOEHMER, ERIC M; Bern Schl; Bern, KS; (3); 1/12; Letterman Clb; Quiz Bowl; SADD; Band; VP Sr Cls; Var Bsktbl; Var Ftbl; Var Trk; Hon Roll; NHS; Highland CC; Agri.

BOEHNER, RYAN S; Oswego HS; Oswego, KS; (2); 2/35; Church Yth Grp; Math Tm; Scholastic Bowl; Band; Var Bsktbl; JV Ftbl; Capt Golf; High Hon Roll; Pres Acad Fit Awd.

BOEHNKE, JOHN P; Great Bend Sr HS; Great Bend, KS; (1); Boy Scts; Band; Mrchg Band; Pep Band; High Hon Roll; Prfct Atten Awd.

BOEKEN, JOSEPH L; Marmaton Valley Jr Sr HS; La Harpe, KS; (3); 8/33; Am Leg Boys St; FCA; Math Tm; Natl FFA Org; Pep Clb; Band; Mrchg Band; Pep Band; Var L Bsktbl; Var L Ftbl; All Leg Lnbckr Hnrbl Mnt 94-95 & 95-96; 1st Tm All Leg Grd 95-96; All Leg Lnbckr Hnrbl Mtn; Emporia; Vet Sci.

BOELLING, ELIZABETH; Herington HS; Herington, KS; (4); 4/40; Church Yth Grp; Drama Clb; FHA; Pep Clb; Teachers Aide; Band; Drill Tm; Drm Mjr(t); Jazz Band; Mrchg Band; KS Hnrs Pgm; CVL Hnr Band; DARE Offcr; KS Wesleyan U; Psych.

BOESE, CHRISTINE A; Maize HS; Wichita, KS; (2); Hosp Aide; Spanish Clb; SADD; Chorus; Wt Lftg; Hon Roll; Scuba Diving; Creative Wrtr; Med.

BOESE, JEFFREY; Garden City Sr HS; Garden City, KS; (3); Var Bsktbl; Intrml Sftbl; Var Trk; Intrml Wt Lftg; Hon Roll; Ldrshp Conf Lamp.

BOGENHAGEN, NICOLE; Wallace Cty HS; Wallace, KS; (4); 3/22; FCA; 4-H; Pep Clb; Scholastic Bowl; SADD; Chorus; School Musical; Sec Treas Sr Cls; High Hon Roll; NHS; Doane Coll; Medicine.

BOGER, KRISTINA L; Hoisington HS; Hoisington, KS; (3); 1/72; Cmnty Wkr; Dance Clb; Debate Tm; NFL; Science Clb; Color Guard; Drill Tm; Flag Corp; Mrchg Band; Variety Show; Yth Forum; Bio; Botany; Medicine.

BOGGS, KRISTIN; Jefferson West HS; Ozawkie, KS; (3); 6/83; Letterman Clb; Spanish Clb; SADD; Band; Jazz Band; Mrchg Band; Pep Band; Var Bsktbl; Powder Puff Ftbl; Var Sftbl.

BOGGS, TIFFANY L; Campus HS; Haysville, KS; (3); Church Yth Grp; Cmnty Wkr; Teachers Aide; Chorus; Swing Chorus; High Hon Roll; Jr NHS; NHS; Comm Daycare; Butler CC; Ped Nurse.

BOGLE, TRACETTE M; Winfield HS; Winfield, KS; (2); 3/219; Art Clb; Church Yth Grp; Debate Tm; DECA; Drama Clb; FCA; Hosp Aide; HOBY; NFL; Speech Tm; Red Ribbon Comm; Southwesterner Rotry Ldrshp Team Player Awd; Lubbuck Chrstn Coll; Intnl Bus.

BOGNER, CHERYL; Spearville Jr Sr HS; Wright, KS; (2); 5/29; Art Clb; 4-H; Letterman Clb; Stat Ftbl; Trk; Wt Lftg; 4-H Awd; Hon Roll; Film Producer Girls/Boys Bsktbl Teams.

BOGNER, JULIE A; South Barber HS; Kiowa, KS; (4); 3/28; Church Yth Grp; Girl Scts; Quiz Bowl; Speech Tm; SADD; Band; Chorus; Flag Corp; Pep Band; School Play; Wichita ST U; Vocal Music Ed.

BOGNER, REBEKAH GRACE; Winfield HS; Winfield, KS; (4); 8/160; Church Yth Grp; Drama Clb; NFL; Scholastic Bowl; Teachers Aide; Acpl Chr; Band; Jazz Band; School Play; Swing Chorus; Emporia ST Univ; Scndry Ed.

BOGNER, SEAN P; Labette Co HS; Parsons, KS; (2); VICA; Band; Jazz Band; Mrchg Band; Pep Band; High Hon Roll; Hon Roll; Indvdl Achvmnt Awd; Pittsburg ST U; Wood Tech/Musc.

BOHANNON, CHRISTOPHE; Blue Valley Northwest HS; Overland Park, KS; (4); 102/354; Church Yth Grp; German Clb; HOBY; Library Aide; Pep Clb; Teachers Aide; Pres Varsity Clb; Capt L Crs Cntry; Powder Puff Ftbl; Trk; Crss Cntry; Schls Drg/Alchl Plcy Innvtr; Hlth Sci.

BOHANNON, JAIMEE; El Dorado HS; El Dorado, KS; (3); 8/173; Am Leg Aux Girls St; Debate Tm; French Clb; Pres Letterman Clb; Math Clb; NFL; SADD; Mrchg Band; Var L Bsktbl; Var L Trk; Chmbr Of Cmmrce Jr Ambssdr; Chem Engr.

BOHANNON, STEPHANY; El Dorado HS; El Dorado, KS; (2); French Clb; Letterman Clb; Yrbk; Var Bsktbl; Var Trk; JV Vllybl; High Hon Roll; Hon Roll; Jr Ambsdrs; Earthcare Coordntr; NFL; Oceanogrphy.

BOHI, JENNIFER A; Olathe East Sr HS; Olathe, KS; (2); Art Clb; Church Yth Grp; Cmnty Wkr; Spanish Clb; Teachers Aide; Orch; Yrbk; Gov Hon Prg Awd; High Hon Roll; Pres Schlr; Mission Trips; Wrk With Hmls; Mid Amer Nazarene Coll; Vet Med.

BOHME, BROOKE; Goodland HS; Goodland, KS; (2); 5/87; Art Clb; Dance Clb; German Clb; GAA; Letterman Clb; Math Tm; SADD; Drill Tm; Bsktbl; Pom Pon; Smmr Trvlng Team 3rd ST; Arctctl Eng.

BOHN, JERROD; Seaman Sr HS; Topeka, KS; (3); 12/260; Church Yth Grp; Debate Tm; FBLA; Model UN; NFL; JV Tennis; High Hon Roll; NHS.

BOHON, SEAN P; Bishop Miege HS; Prairie Village, KS; (3); 90/188; Church Yth Grp; Pep Clb; Varsity Clb; Acpl Chr; Chorus; Var L Bsbl; JV Wrstlng; Hon Roll.

BOHR, JAMI J; Field Kindley Mem Sr HS; Coffeyville, KS; (3); Spanish Clb; Teachers Aide; Ed Yrbk; Hon Roll; Prfct Atten Awd; Elem Ed.

BOIES, MATT; Olathe East Sr HS; Olathe, KS; (2); Letterman Clb; Rep Frsh Cls; Ofcr Bsbl; Ftbl; Hon Roll; Pres Acad Fit Awd; Lawyer.

BOKNECHT, MARK; Atchison Sr HS; Atchison, KS; (4); 19/125; Am Leg Boys St; DECA; Spanish Clb; Var L Bsktbl; Var L Ftbl; Var L Tennis; Var L Trk; Hon Roll; U KS; Bus Adm.

BOLDEN, CRISTAL A; F L Schlagle HS; Kansas City, KS; (1); Dance Clb; SADD; Teachers Aide; Pep Band; Chrldng; Trk; Hon Roll; Lincoln Univ; Lawyer.

BOLDENOW, MICHAEL A; Salina HS South; Salina, KS; (3); Church Yth Grp; Band; Jazz Band; Mrchg Band; Pep Band; School Play.

BOLDRIDGE, IEESNA L; Atchison Sr HS; Atchison, KS; (4); 23/143; SADD; Band; Mrchg Band; Pep Band; School Musical; Yrbk; Rep Frsh Cls; Rep Soph Cls; Rep Jr Cls; Rep Sr Cls; Kytts Pres; KS ST Univ; Bus Mgmt.

BOLEN, CHRISTOPHER B; Junction City HS; Junction City, KS; (3); Hon Roll; Comp Prog.

BOLEN, JOLENE C; Wellsville Jr Sr HS; Wellsville, KS; (2); FBLA; Intnl Clb; Math Tm; Spanish Clb; Var Chrldng; Hon Roll; NHS; Warhburn Univ; Law.

BOLEN, KRISTIE; Otis Bison HS; Timken, KS; (4); 3/25; Am Leg Aux Girls St; Band; Chorus; School Play; VP Frsh Cls; Treas Jr Cls; VP Sr Cls; Stat Ftbl; High Hon Roll; Pres NHS; Appalachian ST U; Psych.

BOLEN, KRISTIE; Otis Bison HS; La Grange, NC; (4); 3/25; Am Leg Aux Girls St; Speech Tm; Band; Chorus; Variety Show; Treas Jr Cls; VP Sr Cls; Mgr(s); High Hon Roll; Pres NHS; Appalachian ST Univ; Psych.

BOLES, JOHN; Emporia HS; Emporia, KS; (3); 35/267; Am Leg Boys St; Boy Scts; FBLA; Key Clb; NFL; Phtg Rptr Yrbk; JV Var Bsbl; NHS; Church Yth Grp; Intrml Wt Lftg; Comm Area Recycling Excl Awd 95; BSA World Conservation Awd; Wildlife Resources Mgmt; Photo.

BOLES, PAUL M; Wichita South HS; Wichita, KS; (3); Boy Scts; Chess Clb; Church Yth Grp; CAP; Debate Tm; Drama Clb; Letterman Clb; NFL; ROTC; Teachers Aide.

BOLIN, COLLEEN; St Thomas Aquinas HS; Overland Park, KS; (4); 13/231; Am Leg Aux Girls St; Sec Sr Cls; Ofcr Stu Cncl; Trk; Vllybl; High Hon Roll; NHS; St Schlr; KSU; Bus.

BOLLENBACH, JON F; Bishop Carroll Catholic HS; Wichita, KS; (3); 32/176; Drama Clb; Spanish Clb; Acpl Chr; Chorus; School Musical; Cit Awd; Hon Roll; KS Newman; Ed.

BOLLER, SARAH M; Junction City HS; Junction City, KS; (3); Church Yth Grp; FCA; Pres 4-H; Mrchg Band; Pres Stu Cncl; Co-Capt Vllybl; 4-H Awd; High Hon Roll; NHS; Quiz Bowl.

BOLLIG, CHRISTA; Trego Comm HS; Wa Keeney, KS; (4); 1/50; Debate Tm; NFL; Band; Rep Stu Cncl; Chrldng; Vllybl; NHS; St Schlr; All A Hnr Rll; Miss Teen Amer Schlrshp/Rcgntn Pgnt; Govt Actn Yth Tour Washngtn DC; Chem.

BOLLIG, JUSTIN M; Trego Comm HS; Wa Keeney, KS; (3); 14/48; Science Clb; Band; Mrchg Band; Pep Band; Trk; High Hon Roll; Hon Roll; Elec Repair.

BOLLIG, KATIE; Thomas More Prep-Marion HS; Hays, KS; (4); 7/93; Model UN; Chorus; School Musical; Nwsp; Yrbk; Rep Stu Cncl; Bsktbl; Trk; Vllybl; High Hon Roll; Fort Hays ST U.

BOLLIG, NICOLE R; Trego Comm HS; Wa Keeney, KS; (2); 20/49; Church Yth Grp; FHA; Letterman Clb; Math Tm; Pep Clb; Science Clb; SADD; Band; Mrchg Band; Pep Band; KS Assn Yth Points Chrm/Treas; Emporia ST Univ; Accntnt.

BOLLIG, PATRICK; Silver Lake Jr Sr HS; Topeka, KS; (1); 1/52; Chess Clb; NFL; Quiz Bowl; Capt Scholastic Bowl; Speech Tm; Variety Show; JV Ftbl; Intrml Wt Lftg; Var L Wrstlng; Gov Hon Prg Awd; Juggling.

BOLLIN, KATIE L; Pleasant Ridge HS; Easton, KS; (4); 6/64; Drama Clb; FCA; Pres VP 4-H; FBLA; Letterman Clb; Pres Treas Natl FFA Org; Scholastic Bowl; Ofcr SADD; Band; Mrchg Band; Coffeyville CC; Pre-Vet Med.

BOLLING, MELANIE; Ft Scott HS; Fort Scott, KS; (4); 1/130; Am Leg Aux Girls St; Key Clb; Orch; Treas Sr Cls; Var Crs Cntry; High Hon Roll; NHS; Intnl Yth Frm; Frnscs; Physcs Clb Pres.

BOLLMAN, HEATHER; Chaparral HS; Anthony, KS; (4); 16/60; Church Yth Grp; Sec FCA; Key Clb; Sec Pep Clb; Teachers Aide; Band; Chorus; Church Choir; Mrchg Band; Pep Band; Ottawa Univ; Jrnlsm.

BOLMER, STEFFANI; Dodge City HS; Dodge City, KS; (2); Band; Color Guard; Mrchg Band; School Musical; Variety Show; Chrldng; Hon Roll; Comp Dance Tm; U Of KS; Perf Arts.

BOLT-BENJAMIN, SARAH; Baldwin HS; Baldwin City, KS; (4); FHA; HOBY; SADD; Chorus; School Musical; Rptr Nwsp; Phtg Yrbk; Intrml Vllybl; Hon Roll; FHA & FAA VP; KS U; Zoology.

BOLTON, KARI; Marysville HS; Marysville, KS; (4); 7/83; Treas Church Yth Grp; Band; Sec Jr Cls; Pres Sr Cls; Rep Stu Cncl; Var Bsktbl; Var Tennis; High Hon Roll; Kiwanis Awd; NHS; U Of KS.

BOLYARD, BRAD; Olathe South Sr HS; Olathe, KS; (3); Letterman Clb; Q&S; Mgr Nwsp; Lit Mag; JV Bsbl; JV Bsktbl; Hon Roll; NHS; Pres Acad Fit Awd; Johnson Cty Yth Ct Prog; 4 Yr Coll; Bus/Adv Mrktng.

BOLYARD, ELIZABETH M; Pratt HS; Pratt, KS; (4); FCA; Teachers Aide; Band; Pep Band; Nwsp; Rep Frsh Cls; Bsktbl; Sftbl; Vllybl; High Hon Roll; KS St Univ; Eng.

BOLYARD, TABITHA J; Trinity Catholic HS; South Hutchinson, KS; (1); Teachers Aide; Chorus; Drill Tm; Trk; Cit Awd; High Hon Roll; Hon Roll; Kiwanis Awd; Schlrshp 1st Yr Span; Ed/Tchr.

BOLZ, ANNA; Washburn Rural HS; Topeka, KS; (2); 7/380; Church Yth Grp; Model UN; NFL; Chorus; Church Choir; School Musical; School Play; Variety Show; Lit Mag; Trk; Music; Drama.

BOMBARDIER, BRYAN; Concordia Jr Sr HS; Concordia, KS; (3); 7/110; Am Leg Boys St; Church Yth Grp; Computer Clb; Letterman Clb; Math Tm; Office Aide; Pep Clb; Quiz Bowl; Spanish Clb; Pres Frsh Cls; KS Univ; Pharmacy.

BOMHOFF, GREGORY; Bishop Carroll Catholic HS; Wichita, KS; (4); HOBY; Spanish Clb; School Play; Crs Cntry; Trk; NHS.

BONCZKOWSKI, NOAH J; Chanute Sr HS; Chanute, KS; (3); Letterman Clb; Spanish Clb; Pres Band; Jazz Band; Mrchg Band; Pep Band; Ftbl; Wt Lftg; Hon Roll; Prfct Atten Awd; Prof Jazz Musician; Dist/ST Solo/Ensemble 95-; Symphony Of Winds 95-; Wichita ST Univ; Crim Just.

BOND, AMBER L; Williamsburg Schl; Waverly, KS; (2); 3/25; Natl FFA Org; Capt Drill Tm; Co-Capt Flag Corp; School Play; Sec Jr Cls; Var Bsktbl; Var Sftbl; Var Vllybl; Hon Roll; Sec NHS; KAYS Treas; Pediatric Phy Thrpst.

BOND, BEN K; Washington HS; Washington, KS; (3); Am Leg Boys St; Boy Scts; FCA; French Clb; Letterman Clb; Pep Clb; Band; Mrchg Band; Pep Band; Var Bsktbl; Fort Hays ST U; Athl Trng.

BOND, DAPHNE; Coldwater Jr Sr HS; Coldwater, KS; (4); 1/20; Letterman Clb; Quiz Bowl; Ofcr Sr Cls; Ofcr Stu Cncl; Bsktbl; Crs Cntry; Trk; High Hon Roll; Jr NHS; NHS; KS ST U; Nrsng.

BOND, ERIC; Bonner Springs HS; Kansas City, KS; (3); JV Bsbl; Hon Roll; KS Univ; Firefighting.

BOND, KELLY; Emporia HS; Emporia, KS; (3); Pep Clb; SADD; Ofcr Jr Cls; JV Capt Chrldng; JV Trk; JV Vllybl; Hon Roll; Kayettes Attend KAY Camp; Stu Members Ldrshp Emporia; Ad.

BOND, LACY R; Lakin HS; Lakin, KS; (2); Art Clb; Chorus; School Musical; Hon Roll; Csmtlgst.

BOND, LOGAN W; Gardner-Edgerton HS; Gardner, KS; (4); 12/116; French Clb; School Musical; Rptr Nwsp; Var L Bsktbl; Var L Crs Cntry; Var L Trk; Drury Coll; Sports Mgmt.

BONEBRAKE, KEEGAN; Atchison Sr HS; Atchison, KS; (1); 1/131; Socr; U Of KS.

BONEBRAKE, KELLY L; Eudora HS; Eudora, KS; (4); 1/43; Sec Drama Clb; FBLA; German Clb; SADD; Band; Mrchg Band; Pep Band; School Musical; School Play; Stage Crew; Outstdng Sci Stdnt; Outstdng Eng Stdnt; U Of KS.

BONEBRAKE, MICHAEL L; Topeka HS; Topeka, KS; (3); Boy Scts; Letterman Clb; Model UN; NFL; Crs Cntry; Tennis; Trk; High Hon Roll; NHS.

BONEBRAKE, MICHAEL S; Manhattan HS; Manhattan, KS; (4); Art Clb; Boy Scts; Dance Clb; FCA; German Clb; Letterman Clb; Varsity Clb; Band; Bsktbl; Crs Cntry; Altar Server; KSU.

BONEBRAKE, TYLER; Atchison Sr HS; Atchison, KS; (3); 12/100; Spanish Clb; Pres Rep Frsh Cls; Rep Soph Cls; Var Capt Bsktbl; Var L Trk; L Vllybl; High Hon Roll; Hon Roll; NHS; Luncheon Of Chmpns 3 Yrs; Multicultrl Ldrshp Acad; U Of NC; Ed.

BONER, PATRICK F; Burlingame HS; Burlingame, KS; (3); Church Yth Grp; Rep Spanish Clb; Stage Crew; JV Bsktbl; High Hon Roll; Hon Roll; NW MO St Univ; Comp Prog.

BONEWITZ, RYAN; Newton Sr HS; Newton, KS; (3); Am Leg Boys St; Church Yth Grp; SADD; Teachers Aide; Ofcr Bsbl; Bsktbl; Ftbl; Hon Roll; KS ST Univ.

BONHAM, HAYLEY E; Lawrence HS; Lawrence, KS; (2); Computer Clb; Ger; Softbl; Meteorology; IN U Bloomington; Music.

BONJOUR, JESSICA D; Centralia Schl; Centralia, KS; (3); Letterman Clb; Pep Clb; Science Clb; Chorus; Drill Tm; Ed Yrbk; VP Frsh Cls; Capt Pom Pon; Hon Roll; Drl Tm Sqd Co Capt Sr Yr; Emporia ST Schlrsp Awds Frosh/Soph/Jr Yr; ST Msc Chrs 3 Yrs; Colby CC; Vet Asst.

BONNELL, STEPHANIE; Goddard HS; Wichita, KS; (3); 76/169; HOBY; Pep Clb; Science Clb; SADD; Chorus; Drill Tm; VP Stu Cncl; Socr; High Hon Roll; Church Yth Grp; Dist/St Choir; Madrigals; Ed/Music.

BONNER, ALI; Haysville Campus HS; Haysville, KS; (4); 67/198; Church Yth Grp; Girl Scts; Intnl Clb; SADD; Teachers Aide; Orch; Ofcr Stu Cncl; Chrldng; Powder Puff Ftbl; Swmmng; Swm Hysvll Swm Clb; U Of NE At Kearney; Elem Ed.

BONTRAGER, ANDREA J; Haven HS; Haven, KS; (3); Am Leg Aux Girls St; Pres Church Yth Grp; FCA; Thesps; Chorus; Church Choir; School Musical; Variety Show; Ed Nwsp; Rep Frsh Cls; CO Chrstn Univ; Behavioral Sci.

BOOK, RENEE M; Circle HS; Towanda, KS; (2); Cmnty Wkr; Drama Clb; School Musical; School Play; Stage Crew; High Hon Roll; Hon Roll; Pres Acad Fit Awd.

BOOKLESS, JULIA E; Buhler HS; Hutchinson, KS; (4); 1/140; Church Yth Grp; FCA; Letterman Clb; Service Clb; Spanish Clb; SADD; Band; Chorus; Mrchg Band; Pep Band; NW MO St Univ; Bus.

BOOMER, JODI; Glasco HS; Glasco, KS; (3); 1/7; Am Leg Aux Girls St; Church Yth Grp; Band; Pres Frsh Cls; Pres Soph Cls; Pres Jr Cls; VP Stu Cncl; Var Bsktbl; Var Vllybl; NHS.

BOONE, SUSAN L; Blue Valley Northwest HS; Overland Park, KS; (4); 76/343; Church Yth Grp; Cmnty Wkr; SADD; Teachers Aide; Chorus; Bsktbl; Powder Puff Ftbl; High Hon Roll; Hon Roll; Capt NHS; U Of Dayton; Elem Ed.

BOOR, RICHARD TODD; Hoisington HS; Hoisington, KS; (4); 8/60; Am Leg Boys St; FCA; Letterman Clb; Quiz Bowl; Var L Bsbl; Var L Bsktbl; Hon Roll; NHS; Ft Hays ST Univ; Pre-Med.

BOOS, LEE A; Ellis HS; Ellis, KS; (4); 2/40; Cmnty Wkr; Math Tm; Pep Clb; Chorus; School Play; Variety Show; Rep Jr Cls; VP Rep Sr Cls; Score Keeper; High Hon Roll; KU Hnrs Pgm; U Of KS; Cytotechnology.

BOOS, MARTIN D; Hayden HS; Topeka, KS; (2); NFL; Quiz Bowl; Var Crs Cntry; Var Trk; Hon Roll; NHS.

BOOTH, JESSICA; Eureka Jr Sr HS; Eureka, KS; (2); 5/70; 4-H; Quiz Bowl; Science Clb; Spanish Clb; SADD; Chorus; Stat Var Bsktbl; Mgr(s); High Hon Roll; Kiwanis Awd.

BOOTS, KARI R; Caney Valley Jr Sr HS; Independence, KS; (3); Art Clb; Drama Clb; Rep GAA; Teachers Aide; School Play; Nwsp; Sprt Ed Yrbk; Sec Frsh Cls; VP Jr Cls; VP Sr Cls; U Of KS.

BOOTSMA, AUNDREA; Louisburg HS; Louisburg, KS; (1); Church Yth Grp; VP 4-H; Natl FFA Org; Band; Color Guard; Mrchg Band; Pep Band; Ofcr Frsh Cls; Chrldng; Hon Roll; Soccer; VP 4-H; Rn.

BOREL, BROOKE E; Topeka HS; Topeka, KS; (2); Cmnty Wkr; Chorus; School Musical; High Hon Roll; Horseback Rdng; Piano; Russian Clb; Engr.

BOREN, MELANIE K; Field Kindley HS; Coffeyville, KS; (3); Sec Drama Clb; Red Cross Aide; Thesps; Band; Chorus; Mrchg Band; Pep Band; School Musical; School Play; Stage Crew; Intl Thespian; Intl Lions Band; Pittsburg ST Univ; Bus.

BOREN, SARAH K; Bishop Miege HS; Leawood, KS; (4); 9/160; SADD; Phtg Nwsp; Phtg Yrbk; Rep Soph Cls; Treas Jr Cls; Pres Stu Cncl; Var Capt Socr; High Hon Roll; NHS; St Schlr; Aquinas Awd Wnnr; El Centro Tutor; Amigos De Las Americas; U Of MO Columbia; Med.

BORG, STARLA L; Council Grove HS; Alta Vista, KS; (3); FCA; 4-H; Pres Natl FFA Org; SADD; JV Bsktbl; JV Vllybl; Hon Roll; Pres NHS; Pres Acad Fit Awd; Kayettes VP; 1st Pl CVL Acctg; FFA Star Chptr Farmer; KS ST Univ; Animal Sci.

BORGEN, DEBBIE; Lyons HS; Lyons, KS; (4); 28/76; Am Leg Aux Girls St; FCA; Letterman Clb; Office Aide; Pres Pep Clb; Teachers Aide; School Play; Bsktbl; Chrldng; Vllybl; KS ST U; Ed.

BORGER, MELISSA; Jetmore HS; Jetmore, KS; (1); Church Yth Grp; Pep Clb; Band; Chorus; Pep Band; Var JV Bsktbl; Var Chrldng; JV Golf; Var Trk; JV Var Vllybl; Ft Hays ST Univ; Psych.

BORGER, MICHELLE; Jetmore HS; Jetmore, KS; (3); 1/18; FCA; Girl Scts; Quiz Bowl; Scholastic Bowl; Drm Mjr(t); VP Stu Cncl; Trk; Vllybl; St Schlr; Val; KS ST U; Chem Engrng.

BORHANI, BEHROOZ; Shawnee Mission N HS; Mission, KS; (3); High Hon Roll; Jr NHS; Med.

BORN, JOHN B; Kapaun-Mt Carmel HS; Wichita, KS; (1); Bsktbl; Hon Roll; Phys.

BORNE, CHERYL M; Circle HS; El Dorado, KS; (2); VP Church Yth Grp; VP 4-H; Band; Jazz Band; Mrchg Band; Pep Band; JV Sftbl; JV Vllybl; 4-H Awd; Hon Roll; Bio; Nrsng.

BORNIGER, CHRISTOPHER T; Kapaun-Mt Carmel HS; Wichita, KS; (3); 5/200; Drama Clb; VP Q&S; Capt Scholastic Bowl; Spanish Clb; Thesps; Chorus; School Musical; Ed Nwsp; High Hon Roll; NHS; Review Wrtng, Jrnlsm Ed Assn Write Off Excllnt Awd; Law.

BORTHWICK, LORI B; Ulysses HS; Ulysses, KS; (1); Cmnty Wkr; Debate Tm; VP 4-H; FBLA; Natl FFA Org; NFL; Spanish Clb; SADD; Treas Frsh Cls; Rep Stu Cncl; U Of KS; Spts Med.

BORUM, ANGELLA D; Prairie View Jr Sr HS; Parker, KS; (2); 6/90; FBLA; Math Clb; Math Tm; Quiz Bowl; Scholastic Bowl; Spanish Clb; Mgr Bsbl; Mgr Bsktbl; Mgr(s); Mgr Vllybl; Treas Future Bus Ldrs Amer; Ped.

BORYS, DAVID N; Blue Valley Northwest HS; Overland Park, KS; (1); CAP; JV Wrstlng; Hon Roll; Soc Sci Excl Merit Awd; AF Acad.

BOSLEY, CARL J; Washburn Rural HS; Topeka, KS; (3); Treas Chess Clb; Pres Computer Clb; Debate Tm; Model UN; Quiz Bowl; NHS; Math Olympiad Pgm Participant 95-96; USA Math Olympiad Wnnr; Mem US Team To Intl Math Olympiad 96; Math.

BOSSE, BRIAN K; Independence HS; Independence, KS; (3); 13/146; Am Leg Boys St; FCA; Pep Clb; SADD; Chorus; School Musical; Swing Chorus; Var L Tennis; Hon Roll; NHS; Med.

BOSSE, WEYLAN J; Onaga HS; Onaga, KS; (2); Boy Scts; 4-H; HOBY; Natl FFA Org; Quiz Bowl; Band; JV Bsktbl; JV Ftbl; High Hon Roll; Hon Roll; FFA Rprtr 2 Yrs/Pub Speakng/Ag Comm Prfcncy Awds; KS ST Univ; Ag Ed.

BOSSERT, ALAN T; Colby Sr HS; Colby, KS; (2); Art Clb; Boy Scts; Church Yth Grp; Cmnty Wkr; Bsktbl; Crs Cntry; Trk; Hon Roll.

BOTT, KYLE; Linn Schl; Palmer, KS; (4); 9/26; Hist Church Yth Grp; Treas FBLA; Natl FFA Org; High Hon Roll; Hon Roll; Prfct Atten Awd; Spcl Olympics; Autistic; Von Verbal.

BOTTGER, JENNIFER; Phillipsburg HS; Phillipsburg, KS; (3); Church Yth Grp; 4-H; Natl FFA Org; Spanish Clb; SADD; Mgr Soph Cls; Mgr Jr Cls; Mgr Sr Cls; 4-H Awd; High Hon Roll; Chmbr Comm Stdnt Grds 9-11; Kayette Bd 10-11 Grds/VP Grd 12; U Of KS; Archtct/Acctnt.

BOTTIGER, JONATHAN; Wathena Schl; Denton, KS; (4); 2/37; FCA; Math Clb; Band; Pep Band; Pres Stu Cncl; Crs Cntry; High Hon Roll; Sal; St Schlr; U Of Miami; Bus.

BOTTIGER, STEPHANIE E; Midway Schl; Denton, KS; (2); Church Yth Grp; School Play; JV Bsktbl; L Mgr(s); L Trk; JV Vllybl; Hon Roll.

BOTTOM, TRACEE; Jackson Heights HS; Soldier, KS; (3); FHA; Natl FFA Org; Pep Clb; Spanish Clb; Drill Tm; Var Bsktbl; Var Chrldng; High Hon Roll; KS HS Rodeo Assoc; Vet.

BOTTORFF, TIMOTHY J; Olathe East Sr HS; Olathe, KS; (4); 1/310; Chess Clb; French Clb; Quiz Bowl; Rptr Nwsp; JV Bsbl; French Hon Soc; High Hon Roll; NHS; Ntl Merit SF; Val; Wartburg Col.

BOUDINOT, ALYSON M; Shawnee Mission West HS; Overland Park, KS; (3); Church Yth Grp; Cmnty Wkr; FBLA; Acpl Chr; Church Choir; School Play; Ofcr Stu Cncl; Chrldng; Swmmng; Hon Roll; Chrch Preschl Choir Tchr; After Schl Recreational Dir; KS ST Univ; Spcl Ed Tchr.

BOUDREAUX, KRISTEN; Wichita Southeast HS; Wichita, KS; (3); Art Clb; Teachers Aide; Band; Var Sftbl; Tennis; Hon Roll; Optometrist/PT.

BOURELL, GRETCHEN; Liberal HS; Liberal, KS; (2); Key Clb; Band; Chorus; Flag Corp; Mrchg Band; Pep Band; Chrldng; Swmmng; Hon Roll; Jr NHS; Roller Blading; Cosmetology; Interior Dsgn.

BOUTROS, NICHOLAS D; Shawnee Mission W Sr HS; Overland Park, KS; (2); 16/400; Chess Clb; Church Yth Grp; Latin Clb; Model UN; Q&S; Spanish Clb; Lit Mag; High Hon Roll; Hon Roll; NHS; Frosh/Soph/Jr Acad Ltr; Wrtr.

BOUTZ, BRYAN; Seaman Sr HS; Topeka, KS; (3); Church Yth Grp; Drama Clb; 4-H; Key Clb; Chorus; Church Choir; School Musical; Stage Crew; High Hon Roll; NHS; Cmptr Tech Fcltr.

BOVAIRD, KELLY A; Washburn Rural HS; Topeka, KS; (4); 7/268; Church Yth Grp; Chorus; School Musical; Variety Show; Var L Crs Cntry; Intrml Powder Puff Ftbl; JV Socr; High Hon Roll; NHS; St Schlr; Baker Univ; Bio Rsrch.

BOVAIRD, ROBERT A; Washburn Rural HS; Topeka, KS; (2); 16/356; Drama Clb; Orch; School Musical; School Play; Socr; Trk; Wrstlng; High Hon Roll; Tchng; Engrng.

BOWDEN, AMANDA R; Morland Jr Sr HS; Hill City, KS; (1); Church Yth Grp; Scholastic Bowl; Band; Church Choir; Mrchg Band; Pep Band; Treas Frsh Cls; JV Vllybl; Hon Roll; KAY Member; Educ.

BOWDEN, ASHLEY; Louisburg HS; Bucyrus, KS; (3); Bus Profs of Am; Letterman Clb; Pep Clb; Spanish Clb; SADD; Var Bsktbl; Var Chrldng; Var Vllybl; High Hon Roll; NHS; Pittsburg ST Univ; Elem Ed.

BOWDEN, ERICA; Shawnee Heights HS; Topeka, KS; (4); 1/229; Pres Drama Clb; FBLA; Pres Thesps; Drill Tm; School Play; Ed Lit Mag; High Hon Roll; NHS; Pres Acad Fit Awd; St Schlr; KS St Univ; Arch Eng.

BOWDEN, TIM; St John Jr Sr HS; Saint John, KS; (1); 1/50; Letterman Clb; Math Tm; Pep Clb; Quiz Bowl; Varsity Clb; Band; Bsktbl; Ftbl; Trk; High Hon Roll.

BOWE, LASHAWNA L; Field Kindley Mem Sr HS; Coffeyville, KS; (4); NFL; Co-Capt Quiz Bowl; Chorus; Mrchg Band; High Hon Roll; NHS; Ntl Merit SF; Cmmnty Theatre; Dist Choir; IA ST U; Theatre.

BOWELL, LINDSAY; Abilene HS; Abilene, KS; (4); 50/118; Am Leg Aux Girls St; 4-H; HOBY; NFL; Teachers Aide; Var Powder Puff Ftbl; Var Sftbl; Var Trk; 4-H Awd; Hon Roll; HOBY Ldrshp Conf Jr Cnslr 95; KS ST U; Med.

BOWEN, DESIREE D; Kapaun-Mt Carmel HS; Wichita, KS; (3); Church Yth Grp; SADD; Art; United Crusaders; Crusaders Life; Sunday Schl Aid.

BOWEN, JENNIFER L; Shawnee Mission W Sr HS; Lenexa, KS; (1); Latin Clb; SADD; Capt Chrldng; JV Socr; Wt Lftg; Hon Roll; Rice; Pharmaceutical Chemist.

BOWEN, MITCHELL W; Horton HS; Horton, KS; (2); 8/80; Cmnty Wkr; JV Bsktbl; JV Var Ftbl; Wt Lftg; High Hon Roll; Hon Roll; Pres Acad Fit Awd; KS ST; Optometry; Anesthlgy.

BOWEN, NICOLE C; Shawnee Mission W Sr HS; Overland Park, KS; (2); 84/425; Rep Soph Cls; Ofcr Stu Cncl; Bsktbl; Crs Cntry; Var Pom Pon; Hon Roll; KS Unv.

BOWEN, RICHARD W; Blue Valley HS; Lawton, OK; (4); 4/16; Bus Profs of Am; FHA; Office Aide; SADD; Chorus; Rep Frsh Cls; VP Soph Cls; VP Jr Cls; Sec Sr Cls; Pres Stu Cncl; Highland Comm Coll; Ath Trnng.

BOWEN, RONALD S; Lucas Luray HS; Lucas, KS; (3); Boy Scts; Speech Tm; SADD; School Play; JV Bsktbl; JV Ftbl; Var Trk.

BOWEN, SCOTT R; Wichita South HS; Wichita, KS; (4); Boy Scts; ROTC; Teachers Aide; Band; Mgr(s); JV Tennis; Hon Roll; Eagle Sct; Band Ltr; Acad Ltr; Friends Univ; His; Ed; Tchr.

BOWENS, JERMAINE; Wyandotte HS; Kansas City, KS; (3); 7/18; Ofcr Jr Cls; Ofcr Bsbl; Bsktbl; Chrldng; Crs Cntry; Ftbl; Mgr(s); Socr; Sftbl; Swmmng; KS Univ; Bus.

BOWERS, CHRISTINA B; Emporia HS; Emporia, KS; (2); Debate Tm; Chorus; Church Choir; Drill Tm; School Musical; Sec Soph Cls; JV Sftbl; JV Tennis; High Hon Roll; Hon Roll; Ballet; Piano; Emporia ST U; Arts.

BOWLER, JAMES N; Northeast Magnet HS; Wichita, KS; (2); 65/148; Chess Clb; Drama Clb; Mgr Stage Crew; Rep Stu Cncl; Prfct Atten Awd; Joe Kuburt Schl Cmrcl Dsgn; Art.

BOWLER, TAMARA N; Wichita North HS; Wichita, KS; (3); 73/395; Church Yth Grp; FCA; GAA; Teachers Aide; Bsktbl; Sftbl; Swmmng; Vllybl; Wt Lftg; Hon Roll; Neonatal Nrse.

BOWLING, KIM M; Leavenworth HS; Leavenworth, KS; (2); Chorus; Stat Ftbl; Stat Mgr(s); Stat Wrstlng; Hon Roll; Pioneer All Acad Awd; KS City KS CC; Nurse.

BOWLING, STACEY D; Derby HS; Derby, KS; (3); 28/384; Cmnty Wkr; Teachers Aide; Band; Mrchg Band; Ofcr Stu Cncl; Var Swmmng; Hon Roll; NHS; U Of KS; Biomedical Engrng.

BOWMAN, CRYSTAL D; Leroy HS; Le Roy, KS; (2); Intnl Clb; Pep Clb; Drill Tm; Yrbk; Chrldng; Vllybl; High Hon Roll.

BOWMAN, ERIN E; Buhler HS; Hutchinson, KS; (2); VP Church Yth Grp; FCA; Spanish Clb; Band; Mrchg Band; Pep Band; Hon Roll.

BOWMAN, HEATHER; Prairie View Jr Sr HS; La Cygne, KS; (3); 25/67; Church Yth Grp; FHA; Natl FFA Org; Quiz Bowl; Spanish Clb; Co-Ed Nwsp; Phtg Yrbk; JV Sftbl; JV Vllybl; Hon Roll; FHA Treas 96-; Most Imprvd Jrnlsm Awd.

BOWMAN, JAMES S; Topeka HS; Topeka, KS; (3); Hon Roll; Rowing Clb Pres; KS ST Univ.

BOWMAN, JENNIFER A; Pleasant Ridge HS; Easton, KS; (3); Rep FBLA; Letterman Clb; Pep Clb; SADD; Phtg Nwsp; VP Stu Cncl; Var Bsktbl; Var Trk; Var Vllybl; Hon Roll; KS ST; Bus.

BOWMAN, KERRY; Atchison County Cmnty HS; Holton, KS; (4); 8/60; Sec Art Clb; VP 4-H; Letterman Clb; Treas SADD; Capt Drill Tm; Nwsp; Sec Stu Cncl; Chrldng; Pom Pon; High Hon Roll; Hnrbl Mntn Jr Duck Stmp Cntst; Ft Hays ST U; Anml Sci.

BOWMAN, MELISSA; Shawnee Mission Northwest HS; Shawnee Mission, KS; (2); 78/450; JV Chrldng; High Hon Roll; Young Life; Bus.

BOWMAN, MIRIAM; Goodland HS; Goodland, KS; (2); 1/91; Sec Church Yth Grp; HOBY; Chrmn Intnl Clb; Math Tm; Scholastic Bowl; Chrmn Band; Jazz Band; Sec Soph Cls; JV Tennis; High Hon Roll; Med/PT.

BOWSER, JESSICA; Jackson Heights HS; Netawaka, KS; (1); Pep Clb; Band; Chorus; Mrchg Band; Pep Band; School Musical; Ofcr Bsbl; Crs Cntry; Trk; High Hon Roll; Dist Schlstc Achvmnt Crs Cntry/Bnd; Acad Awd 3.5 GPA; 2nd Tm All Leag Hon Crs Cntry; ST Solo I Rtng; Washburn; Mallet Percussion.

BOWSER, LINDSAY E; Topeka HS; Topeka, KS; (3); Band; Mrchg Band; Pep Band; Powder Puff Ftbl; Trk; Vllybl; High Hon Roll; Hon Roll; Washburn U.

BOXBERGER, STEPHANIE; Mc Pherson HS; Mc Pherson, KS; (2); Church Yth Grp; German Clb; Q&S; Ed Yrbk; Var JV Bsktbl; JV Trk; Hon Roll; KAYS; Barton CC; Acctnt.

BOXUM, RAQUEL; Smith Ctr Jr Sr HS; Lebanon, KS; (4); Am Leg Aux Girls St; FHA; Quiz Bowl; SADD; Yrbk; Pres Sr Cls; L Bsktbl; Co-Capt Chrldng; High Hon Roll; NHS; Homcmng Qn Attendnt.

BOY, HEATH; Syracuse Jr Sr HS; Syracuse, KS; (4); 4/29; Cmnty Wkr; Sec Treas Drama Clb; 4-H; Letterman Clb; Pep Clb; Quiz Bowl; Speech Tm; Band; Chorus; Jazz Band.

BOYCE, BRANDILYN; Spring Hill HS; Olathe, KS; (2); Church Yth Grp; Cmnty Wkr; Intnl Clb; Science Clb; Chorus; Swing Chorus; Hon Roll; Jr NHS; KU.

BOYD, CHERYL; Turner HS; Kansas City, KS; (4); 50/230; Chess Clb; Church Yth Grp; Cmnty Wkr; FTA; SADD; Rep Jr Cls; Rep Sr Cls; Rep Stu Cncl; JV Chrldng; JV Sftbl; Phy Thrpst.

BOYD, CHRISTINA; Valley Falls HS; Valley Falls, KS; (4); 13/35; Dance Clb; Drama Clb; 4-H; FHA; Pep Clb; Speech Tm; Drill Tm; School Play; Stage Crew; Phtg Nwsp; Emporia ST Univ; Art Thrpy.

BOYD, DANA; Summer Acad; Kansas City, KS; (4); 27/195; Church Yth Grp; HOBY; Pep Clb; Spanish Clb; SADD; Acpl Chr; Church Choir; Rep Soph Cls; Rep Jr Cls; Rep Sr Cls; Acad Dcthln; Gspl Chr Sec; Purdue U; Chem Engrng.

BOYD, DEENA; Shawnee Mission W Sr HS; Lenexa, KS; (3); 43/440; Church Yth Grp; Cmnty Wkr; Pep Clb; Spanish Clb; Chorus; Drill Tm; School Musical; JV Var Gym; High Hon Roll; NHS; Camp Cnslr Yth Chrstn Camp; Anti-Substance Abuse Clb.

BOYD, DUSTY; Valley Falls HS; Valley Falls, KS; (3); FHA; Ofcr Stu Cncl; Ofcr Bsbl; Wt Lftg; Hon Roll; NHS; Comm Svc; KS ST Univ; Engrng.

BOYD, FREDERICK J; Wyandotte HS; Kansas City, KS; (2); Art; Drwng; Drwng/Arts.

BOYD, JAMES A; Great Bend Sr HS; Great Bend, KS; (2); Boy Scts; Church Yth Grp; German Clb; Math Tm; Scholastic Bowl; Band; Mrchg Band; High Hon Roll; Acctng.

BOYD, JENNY; Jefferson Co North HS; Nortonville, KS; (2); 5/53; Church Yth Grp; Drama Clb; FHA; Letterman Clb; SADD; School Play; Ofcr Soph Cls; Trk; Vllybl; High Hon Roll; FBLA; Skiing; Poetry; KU; Med.

BOYD, JON J; Baldwin HS; Baldwin City, KS; (4); Boy Scts; Church Yth Grp; Letterman Clb; Acpl Chr; Chorus; Nwsp; Yrbk; Var Crs Cntry; Var Trk; Hon Roll; BSA Eagle Sct Awd; Yng Ntrlst Awd; KS Ornthlgy Soc; Karl & Leone Butell Schlrshp Awd; Baker U; Bio.

BOYD, LEAH M; Meade HS; Meade, KS; (3); 1/40; Church Yth Grp; Treas FCA; Treas Key Clb; Pep Clb; Quiz Bowl; Spanish Clb; Speech Tm; Band; Chorus; Church Choir; Keyette Brd Mmbr; KS St Univ; Arion Awd Wnnr; Lwyr.

BOYD, MELISSA; Humboldt HS; Humboldt, KS; (3); 2/63; Drama Clb; Quiz Bowl; Band; Swing Chorus; Var Capt Golf; NHS; Sal; 4-H; GAA; JA; KS Regents Hnr Acad; Dist Treas; Air Force Acad Summer Scientific Seminar; Cmptrs/Psych.

BOYD, MELISSA J; Shawnee Mission E Sr HS; Shawnee Mission, KS; (2); Natl Beta Clb; Thesps; School Play; Stage Crew; Tennis; Hon Roll; AZ Univ; Intr Dsgn/Arch.

BOYD, MOLLY; Wichita East HS; Wichita, KS; (3); 32/337; Am Leg Aux Girls St; Church Yth Grp; Spanish Clb; Jazz Band; Variety Show; Sec Jr Cls; Capt Chrldng; Hon Roll; NHS.

BOYD, RYAN; Kinsley HS; Offerle, KS; (4); 1/36; Am Leg Boys St; Boy Scts; Quiz Bowl; VP Sr Cls; JV Var Bsktbl; L Golf; Hon Roll; NHS; Ntl Merit Ltr; KSU; Engr.

BOYD, TIARA R; Newton Sr HS; Newton, KS; (1); SADD; Bsktbl; Vllybl; WEBOK Awd; CPA.

BOYD, VERONICA D; Washington HS; Kansas City, KS; (4); Drama Clb; NFL; Pep Clb; Spanish Clb; SADD; Teachers Aide; Thesps; Chorus; Church Choir; School Play; NAACP; Piano; Sax; Jackson ST U; Comp Sci.

BOYDEN, MARY; Hayden HS; Topeka, KS; (3); 7/135; Church Yth Grp; Hosp Aide; Pep Clb; Chorus; Yrbk; JV Socr; High Hon Roll; NHS; YABA Bowling League; Creighton Univ; Medicine.

BOYDSTON, AMANDA R; Olathe East Sr HS; Overland Park, KS; (2); Church Yth Grp; Cmnty Wkr; French Clb; Pep Clb; Spanish Clb; Drill Tm; Ofcr Frsh Cls; Ofcr Stu Cncl; High Hon Roll; Hon Roll; Dir Of Vol Work.

BOYER, JENIFER; El Dorado HS; El Dorado, KS; (4); 2/155; Am Leg Aux Girls St; Church Yth Grp; Cmnty Wkr; French Clb; Letterman Clb; Office Aide; SADD; Teachers Aide; Drill Tm; Yrbk; Jr Ambass; Marquette U; Dntl.

BOYES, JARRETT R; Galena HS; Galena, KS; (1); Church Yth Grp; FHA; Letterman Clb; Ofcr Stu Cncl; Ofcr Bsbl; Bsktbl; Ftbl; Wt Lftg; Hon Roll; All CNC Hnrbl Mntn Bsbl.

BOYES, STEFFANIE; Columbus HS; Columbus, KS; (2); Bus Profs of Am; Math Tm; Drill Tm; JV Bsktbl; JV Golf; Var Sftbl; High Hon Roll; Hon Roll; 2nd Pl St BPA Document Formatting.

BOYKIN, DA MEEKA M; Wyandotte HS; Kansas City, KS; (2); Church Yth Grp; Acpl Chr; Church Choir; School Musical; OK Bapt U; Fshn.

BOYKO, MEGAN A; Olathe East Sr HS; Olathe, KS; (2); Church Yth Grp; French Clb; Office Aide; Teachers Aide; Mgr(s); Hon Roll; Prfct Atten Awd; Aviator.

BOYLE, JEFF D; Norton Comm HS; Norton, KS; (3); 14/63; Church Yth Grp; Cmnty Wkr; FHA; Pep Clb; Teachers Aide; Band; Treas Frsh Cls; Treas Soph Cls; Var Capt Ftbl; L Tennis; All St Wrstlng; All St Hnrbl Mntn Ftbl; Exercise Sci.

BOYLES, DEIDRA M; White Rock HS; Superior, NE; (2); 3/15; Letterman Clb; Pep Clb; SADD; Band; Chorus; Golf; Hon Roll; NHS; NE Chrstn Coll New Ways Singers; Play Band KS Shrine Bowl; Fort Hays; Psych.

BOYLES, NICK; Conway Springs HS; Mayfield, KS; (3); 4/34; JV Ftbl; High Hon Roll; Hon Roll; Cowley Cty; Welding.

BOYLES, SCOTT B; White Rock HS; Burr Oak, KS; (3); 4/7; Am Leg Boys St; Church Yth Grp; Drama Clb; Letterman Clb; Natl FFA Org; Pep Clb; Quiz Bowl; Speech Tm; SADD; School Play; KS ST.

BOZEMAN, ANGELA; Seaman Sr HS; Topeka, KS; (4); 2/248; Church Yth Grp; Sec Treas Math Clb; Mu Alpha Theta; Sec Soph Cls; Sec Jr Cls; Pres Stu Cncl; Ofcr Stu Cncl; Var L Socr; Var L Vllybl; High Hon Roll; KS ST U; Bio.

BRACE, SHANNON E; Derby HS; Derby, KS; (3); Church Yth Grp; Girl Scts; SADD; Chorus; Church Choir; Orch; JV Crs Cntry; Var Trk; Hon Roll; NHS; Music.

BRACHER, BRIAN D; Field Kindley Mem Sr HS; Coffeyville, KS; (2); Boy Scts; Church Yth Grp; Debate Tm; NFL; Chorus; Church Choir; High Hon Roll; Hon Roll; Prfct Atten Awd; Church Choir Chimes; Lwyr/Fed Agnt.

BRACK, HOLLY A; Lacrosse HS; La Crosse, KS; (3); 2/30; Cmnty Wkr; Pep Clb; Band; Mrchg Band; Pep Band; Var Bsktbl; Var Vllybl; High Hon Roll; NHS; Prfct Atten Awd; Acad Cont; KS U; Pharmacy.

BRACK, SHANNON L; Otis Bison HS; Otis, KS; (2); Church Yth Grp; Band; JV Bsktbl; Var Sftbl; L Trk; JV Vllybl; Cit Awd; High Hon Roll; Ft Hays; Bus.

BRACKEEN, NICOLE; Great Bend Sr HS; Great Bend, KS; (2); Church Yth Grp; FCA; Pep Clb; Chorus; Variety Show; Var Chrldng; JV Sftbl; Prfct Atten Awd; Kayettes Clb.

BRACKETT, PETER; Colby Sr HS; Oakley, KS; (2); Church Yth Grp; HOBY; Math Tm; Science Clb; Spanish Clb; Church Choir; Orch; Pep Band; Hon Roll; Prfct Atten Awd; Colby Comm Coll; Gntc Eng.

BRACY, DANICA J; Salina HS South; Salina, KS; (3); Mrchg Band; Pep Band; Yrbk; Mgr(s); Hon Roll; Prfct Atten Awd; Natl Ltn Exam Awd; KS ST U; Crmnl Jstc.

BRACY, KARA; Andover HS; Andover, KS; (3); 16/157; Cmnty Wkr; Red Cross Aide; SADD; Rep Jr Cls; Ofcr Stu Cncl; Var L Chrldng; L Trk; High Hon Roll; NHS; Pep Clb; Yth Ldrshp Butler; Bus.

BRADBURN, RYAN; Emporia HS; Emporia, KS; (4); Church Yth Grp; Band; Pres Chorus; Mrchg Band; Pep Band; School Play; Swing Chorus; Cit Awd; Gov Hon Prg Awd; Hon Roll; All St Choir; Manhattan Chrstn Coll; Music.

BRADBURY, DIANA M; Wichita Hgts HS; Wichita, KS; (4); 32/236; Drama Clb; French Clb; Hosp Aide; Thesps; Chorus; French Hon Soc; High Hon Roll; NHS; Pres Schlr; Teachers Aide; Pres Of Wmns Ensmbl; VP Of Thespins; Sec Of Frnch Clb; U Of KS; Nrsing.

BRADBURY, MATTHEW E; Mc Pherson HS; Mc Pherson, KS; (3); Boy Scts; Church Yth Grp; Letterman Clb; SADD; Chorus; Drm Mjr(t); Pep Band; School Musical; Var Swmmng; NHS; St Choir; Music.

BRADFIELD, JANA; Shawnee Mission Nw Sr HS; Lenexa, KS; (3); Am Leg Aux Girls St; Church Yth Grp; Cmnty Wkr; Intnl Clb; JA; Stage Crew; Bsktbl; Socr; High Hon Roll; NHS.

BRADFORD, JUSTIN; Olathe South Sr HS; Olathe, KS; (4); 11/380; Scholastic Bowl; Science Clb; Band; Ed Nwsp; High Hon Roll; NHS; Ntl Merit Ltr; Pres Acad Fit Awd; Spanish NHS; St Schlr; Cmptr Prgrmmng; Yth In Govt; Sci Olympiad; U Of KS; Bio Chem/Mlclr Bio.

BRADFORD, KATHY A; Topeka HS; Topeka, KS; (2); Church Yth Grp; 4-H; Girl Scts; Office Aide; Pep Clb; Spanish Clb; Teachers Aide; Var JV Sftbl; JV Vllybl; Wt Lftg; Marine Bio.

BRADFORD, KRISTIN M; Seaman Sr HS; Topeka, KS; (3); Church Yth Grp; Cmnty Wkr; Debate Tm; VP FBLA; Key Clb; Math Clb; Mu Alpha Theta; NFL; Spanish Clb; Band; Pre-Med.

BRADLEY, AMANDA K; Independence HS; Independence, KS; (4); 19/141; French Clb; JCL; Scholastic Bowl; Orch; School Musical; High Hon Roll; NHS; Pres Acad Fit Awd; Pres Schlr; St Schlr; KS Assn Of Yth; Acad Decathlon; Carleton Coll; Pathologist.

BRADLEY, RYAN P; Atchison Sr HS; Atchison, KS; (1); Boy Scts; Band; JV Crs Cntry; Eagle Scout.

BRADSHAW, APRIL C; Garden City Sr HS; Garden City, KS; (1); Church Yth Grp; Chorus; Church Choir; Hon Roll; Bio; OB-GYN Medicine.

BRADSTREET, DERRICK A; Goddard HS; Goddard, KS; (1); Church Yth Grp; 4-H; Band; Pep Band; Ftbl.

BRADSTREET, DUSTIN; Goddard HS; Goddard, KS; (3); Treas 4-H; SADD; Band; Mrchg Band; Pep Band; Ftbl; Mgr(s); Wrstlng; 4-H Awd; High Hon Roll; KS Univ; Sports Trainer.

BRADSTREET, ERIC C; Hutchinson HS; Hutchinson, KS; (1); 1/400; Science Clb; Spanish Clb; Varsity Clb; Crs Cntry; Trk; Wt Lftg; Cit Awd; High Hon Roll; Prfct Atten Awd; Pres Acad Fit Awd.

BRADSTREET, SARA; Garden City Sr HS; Garden City, KS; (3); Drama Clb; Thesps; Chorus; Church Choir; School Musical; School Play; Lit Mag; Swmmng; Hon Roll; Modern Choir; St Choir 96; Music Ed.

BRADY, JEREMY P; Clearwater HS; Clearwater, KS; (2); Church Yth Grp; Cmnty Wkr; Band; Jazz Band; Mrchg Band; Pep Band; Bsktbl; Var Golf; Wt Lftg; High Hon Roll; Sci; Engrng.

BRADY, KEITH D; Garden City Sr HS; Garden City, KS; (2); Church Yth Grp; Band; Jazz Band; Mrchg Band; Pep Band; JV Trk; Hon Roll; KS ST; Chem.

BRADY, KIMBERLY; Otis Bison HS; Albert, KS; (3); 11/28; Church Yth Grp; 4-H; Quiz Bowl; School Play; Nwsp; Bsktbl; Chrldng; Vllybl; 4-H Awd; Hon Roll; VFW Schlrshp; 2nd Pl Sci Fair Awd; KSU; Law.

BRADY, KRISTY L; Garden City Sr HS; Garden City, KS; (2); Church Yth Grp; Band; Orch; High Hon Roll; Southwestern.

BRADY, LESLIE; Derby HS; Derby, KS; (1); JV Chrldng; Hon Roll; Pres Acad Fit Awd.

BRAKE, SARAH; Kinsley HS; Kinsley, KS; (2); Church Yth Grp; Debate Tm; Quiz Bowl; Band; Bsktbl; Trk; Vllybl; Hon Roll; NHS; Med.

BRAKEL, SHEILA; Iola Sr HS; Iola, KS; (4); 13/100; FBLA; SADD; Band; Chorus; Mrchg Band; Pep Band; High Hon Roll; Hon Roll; Coffeyville CC; Educ.

BRAMBALL, KYLIE L; Frankft HS; Frankfort, KS; (3); Am Leg Aux Girls St; Church Yth Grp; FHA; Hosp Aide; Pep Clb; SADD; Chorus; Yrbk; Sec Sr Cls; Hon Roll; Johnson County CC; Csmtlgst.

BRAMLAGE, ANDREW C; Troy HS; Troy, KS; (2); Church Yth Grp; Drama Clb; Letterman Clb; Library Aide; Natl FFA Org; Pep Clb; Quiz Bowl; Scholastic Bowl; Speech Tm; Pep Band; KS St Univ; Bus Mgnt.

BRANCH, CARLISA; East HS; Wichita, KS; (4); Am Leg Aux Girls St; DECA; Band; Church Choir; Mrchg Band; Pep Band; Hon Roll; Butler Cty CC; Jrnlsm.

BRANCH, CHANTA M; F L Schlagle HS; Kansas City, KS; (1); SADD; Drill Tm; Orch; School Musical; Bsktbl; Crs Cntry; Trk; Vllybl; Cit Awd; Hon Roll.

BRAND, KENT A; Andale HS; Colwich, KS; (2); Church Yth Grp; Spanish Clb; High Hon Roll; Hon Roll; JV Bsktbl; Glf; Black And Gold Hnr Roll; KS St Univ.

BRANDAU, JACK R; Washburn Rural HS; Topeka, KS; (3); CAP; Cmnty Wkr; Red Cross Aide; Spanish Clb; Bsktbl; Golf; Jr NHS; KS ST Univ; Pre-Med.

BRANDENBURG, CHELSEA; Garden City Sr HS; Garden City, KS; (4); 30/315; Church Yth Grp; Debate Tm; Drama Clb; French Clb; Model UN; NFL; High Hon Roll; Pres Acad Fit Awd; Pres Schlr; St Schlr; Ldr Schl Bible Study; Manhattan Chrstn Coll; Missions.

BRANDSTED, TIM W; Washburn Rural HS; Topeka, KS; (3); Boy Scts; Church Yth Grp; Jazz Band; Variety Show; High Hon Roll; Hon Roll.

BRANDT, KRISTEN N; Andover HS; Andover, KS; (4); 16/137; Cmnty Wkr; Debate Tm; NFL; Speech Tm; SADD; Nwsp; Socr; High Hon Roll; Hon Roll; NHS; Studio Art; Regnl Jrnlsm Cont 2nd Pl; Congressional Art Cmptn 3rd Pl; U Of KS; Museum Curator.

BRANDT, LAURI M; Smoky Valley HS; Roxbury, KS; (2); Chorus; Bsktbl; High Hon Roll; PA ST; PT.

BRANICK, MISTY D; Russell HS; Russell, KS; (3); Church Yth Grp; Key Clb; SADD; Chorus; School Musical; Var L Chrldng; Var L Trk; High Hon Roll; NHS; Dance Clb; KAY Club; U Of KS; Med/Pharm.

BRANT, CHARLES E; Arkansas City HS; Arkansas City, KS; (3); 23/225; Am Leg Boys St; Church Yth Grp; Pres Scholastic Bowl; School Musical; School Play; Stage Crew; Ofcr Stu Cncl; Var Socr; NHS; Yng Amer Soccer Ambssdrs Rep; Schl Imprvmnt Cmmtte; Arch Engr.

BRANUM, KAREN; Russell HS; Russell, KS; (2); FCA; Pep Clb; SADD; Chorus; Rep Stu Cncl; High Hon Roll; Pediatrician.

BRASSFIELD, JO ANNA; Basehor Linwood HS; Basehor, KS; (2); Science Clb; Rep Stu Cncl; JV Sftbl; High Hon Roll; Rch Envrmntl Club; 4 Yr Schl; Hlth Admin.

BRASWELL, RACHAEL L; Blue Valley Northwest HS; Overland Park, KS; (1); Church Yth Grp; Stage Crew; Hon Roll; Top Ten Frosh In Amer HS Math Exam; Judge For Odyssey Of Mint Dist Level Vol; Northwestern Univ; Medicine.

BRAUNGARDT, JOSHUA L; Douglass HS; Douglass, KS; (4); 20/43; Letterman Clb; Teachers Aide; Ftbl; Wt Lftg; Wrstlng; Hon Roll; Pres Schlr; Cowley Cnty CC; Phy Thrpy.

BRAXTON, DERRICK E; Sumner Acad Of Arts & Science; Kansas City, KS; (3); Church Yth Grp; Spanish Clb; Acpl Chr; Church Choir; School Musical; Ed Yrbk; Ftbl; Hon Roll; Africn Amer Stu Achv Awd; KSU; Acctng.

BRAZEAL, GREGORY; Blue Valley North HS; Leawood, KS; (3); 1/300; French Clb; School Musical; Pres Soph Cls; Rep Jr Cls; Treas Stu Cncl; High Hon Roll; NHS; Piano; Juggling; Natl Art Hnrs Soc; Philosophy.

BRAZIER, CARRIE A; Southeast HS; Wichita, KS; (3); 46/385; Church Yth Grp; Cmnty Wkr; Debate Tm; Drama Clb; Girl Scts; NFL; SADD; Thesps; Chorus; Church Choir; Sienra Teens; Bus Law.

BREAULT, BEN B; Sacred Heart HS; Salina, KS; (3); Church Yth Grp; FBLA; Pep Clb; Quiz Bowl; Scholastic Bowl; Rptr Nwsp; Pres Stu Cncl; Var Bsktbl; Var L Golf; Wt Lftg.

BREAULT, KAREN D; Wichita West HS; Wichita, KS; (1); 15/416; Chorus; Variety Show; Hon Roll; Acad Ltr.

BRECKENRIDGE, ROBERT L; Valley Heights Jr Sr HS; Waterville, KS; (3); Am Leg Boys St; Church Yth Grp; Letterman Clb; Band; Pep Band; School Play; Ofcr Stu Cncl; Trk; NHS; Cmnty Wkr; Teen Ctr Bd 6 Yrs; Butler CC; Hotel/Rstrnt Mngmt.

BREDAHL, JESSICA M; Sabetha HS; Sabetha, KS; (4); 13/60; Church Yth Grp; German Clb; Pep Clb; Yrbk; Bsktbl; Vllybl; High Hon Roll; Hon Roll; NHS; MO Western ST Coll; Comm Art.

BREDEHOFT, TIMOTHY S; Lawrence HS; Lawrence, KS; (3); Am Leg Boys St; Church Yth Grp; Acpl Chr; Band; Chorus; Church Choir; Mrchg Band; Pep Band; Variety Show; Rep Frsh Cls.

BREDEMEIER, JASON; Nemaha Valley HS; Seneca, KS; (3); Sec Church Yth Grp; Rep Letterman Clb; Capt Quiz Bowl; Speech Tm; Ed Yrbk; Var Bsktbl; Var L Ftbl; NHS; Cmnty Wkr; Drama Clb; Babe Ruth Bsbl St; Pony Leg Bsbl; Reprtd Bsktbl Gams On KMZA Rad; Compt On & Coch Swim Tem; Lifeguard; U Of KS; Tchng; Jrnlsm.

BREDFELDT, NICHOLE; Dodge City HS; Dodge City, KS; (1); Church Yth Grp; 4-H; Orch; 4-H Awd; Yth Rep S Cntrl Stock Horse Assn; KS Amer Qtr Horse Yth Assn; U Of KS; Med.

BREEDEN, SARAH; Hays HS; Hays, KS; (1); Church Yth Grp; Band; Church Choir; Mrchg Band; Pep Band; Bsktbl; Swmmng; Vllybl; Hon Roll; Teens For Christ; Interior Dsgn; Landscape.

BREEDING, EMMA M; Shawnee Mission E Sr HS; Prairie Village, KS; (2); Office Aide; Hon Roll; KS ST; Vet.

BREES, JESSICA; Goddard HS; Wichita, KS; (2); Church Yth Grp; Drama Clb; Pep Clb; Teachers Aide; Chorus; School Play; Var Ofcr Chrldng; High Hon Roll; Hon Roll; Pres Acad Fit Awd; Var Cheer Sqd Rcvd Top Tm/Spirit Awds NCA Cmp 95; Wichita ST; Eng Tchr/Med.

BREINER, RYAN; Wabaunsee HS; Alma, KS; (1); 1/50; 4-H; FHA; Letterman Clb; Natl FFA Org; VP Frsh Cls; Pres Soph Cls; Var Bsbl; JV Bsktbl; Var L Ftbl; High Hon Roll; KS ST Univ; Anml Sci/Indstry.

BREMER, SCOTT T; Olathe South Sr HS; Olathe, KS; (3); Pres Church Yth Grp; Office Aide; Teachers Aide; Wrstlng; Hon Roll; Grls Fst Ptch Sftbl Ofcl; Sccr Ofcl; Sccr; Bsbl; Bsktbl; Bus.

BRENN, BROOKS; Colby Sr HS; Colby, KS; (4); 18/96; Am Leg Boys St; Boy Scts; Church Yth Grp; Drama Clb; Natl FFA Org; Speech Tm; Teachers Aide; Chorus; Mrchg Band; School Musical; Churc Choir; FFA Pres 95-; Lt Sheriffs Explorers 94-; CCC; Music Therapy.

BRENNAN, CANDACE L; Greensburg HS; Greensburg, KS; (3); FHA; Pep Clb; Teachers Aide; Yrbk; Northwestern OK ST; Elem Ed.

BRENNAN, SEAN; Leavenworth HS; Fort Leavenworth, KS; (3); 34/371; Church Yth Grp; Debate Tm; Q&S; Quiz Bowl; Scholastic Bowl; Thesps; Band; Mrchg Band; Pep Band; School Musical; Chrch Lector & Greeter; Hubbard Summer Acad Future Tchrs Participant; Bethany Univ; Amer His Prof.

BRENNAN, SHANNON; Washington HS; Kansas City, KS; (4); 1/220; Key Clb; Spanish Clb; Pres Jr Cls; VP Pres Stu Cncl; JV Var Bsktbl; JV Var Crs Cntry; Var L Sftbl; L Capt Vllybl; Gov Hon Prg Awd; High Hon Roll; NW MO St Univ; Med.

BRENNER, ADAM; Thomas More Prep-Marion HS; Hays, KS; (2); Church Yth Grp; French Clb; Latin Clb; Pep Clb; Bsktbl; Ftbl; Wt Lftg; Hon Roll; Pres Acad Fit Awd.

BRENNER, JEFF S; Shawnee Mission W Sr HS; Overland Park, KS; (2); Boy Scts; Church Yth Grp.

BRENNER, KEVIN D; Chapman HS; Woodbine, KS; (3); Church Yth Grp; Natl FFA Org; Varsity Clb; Var Capt Crs Cntry; Var Trk; Hon Roll; Beloit Tech Schl; Diesel Mech.

BRENZIKOFER, NATASHA; Peabody-Burns Jr Sr HS; Burns, KS; (3); 8/30; Church Yth Grp; FCA; Math Tm; Natl FFA Org; Ed Phtg Nwsp; Rep Sec Stu Cncl; Var Vllybl; High Hon Roll; Hon Roll; St Schlr; Barrell Race, Many Gold & Silver Belt Buckles Awds; Vet Asst; Lifeguard; Teach Horse Back Riding; KS ST Univ; Vet; Phy Thrpst.

BRETHAVER, JOSEPH; J C Harmon HS; Kansas City, KS; (4); Am Leg Boys St; Band; Jazz Band; Mrchg Band; Pep Band; Var Bsbl; Var Wrstlng; Hon Roll; U Of KS.

BRETTHAUER, MEGAN N; Tonganoxie HS; Tonganoxie, KS; (4); 2/138; Bus Profs of Am; Debate Tm; FBLA; FHA; Spanish Clb; SADD; Drill Tm; Ofcr Frsh Cls; Ofcr Jr Cls; Bsktbl.

BRETZ, JENNIFER; Morland Jr Sr HS; Studley, KS; (4); 4/12; 4-H; Math Tm; Office Aide; Scholastic Bowl; Teachers Aide; Drill Tm; Rep Sr Cls; Sec Treas Stu Cncl; Var Bsktbl; Var Vllybl; 1st In Algebra II At League Acad Cntst; Ft Hays ST Univ; Bus.

BRETZ, KYLE G; Lucus-Luray HS; Lucas, KS; (3); Cmnty Wkr; SADD; Chorus; L Bsktbl; L Ftbl; L Trk; Wt Lftg; Elem Ed.

BREUER, SHANNON L; Atchison Sr HS; Atchison, KS; (1); Church Yth Grp; Cmnty Wkr; Hon Roll; Upward Bound Prjct Focus; U Of KS; Schl Cnslr.

BREWER, ANGELA; Olathe North Sr HS; Olathe, KS; (2); French Clb; Teachers Aide; Orch; Hon Roll; Prfct Atten Awd.

BREWER, DANE A; Kapaun-Mt Carmel HS; Andover, KS; (3); Church Yth Grp; Cmnty Wkr; JA; Teachers Aide; Var L Socr; Intrml Wt Lftg; Var L Wrstlng; High Hon Roll; Creighton Univ; Premed.

BREWER, ELIZABETH C; Coldwater Jr Sr HS; Coldwater, KS; (1); FHA; Pep Clb; Band; Chorus; Mrchg Band; Pep Band; School Musical; School Play; Variety Show; Hon Roll; KS ST.

BREWER, HEATHER M; Olathe East Sr HS; Olathe, KS; (2); Church Yth Grp; Spanish Clb; Chorus; Church Choir; Socr; High Hon Roll; Doctor.

BREWER, WILLIAM A; Washington HS; Kansas City, KS; (2); FCA; ROTC; Science Clb; Teachers Aide; Varsity Clb; Acpl Chr; Chorus; Stage Crew; JV Bsktbl; Var Ftbl; Gspl Choir; Bio.

BREWINGTON, JOSHUA D; Blue Valley HS; Olathe, KS; (2); Church Yth Grp; Debate Tm; Red Cross Aide; Acpl Chr; Chorus; School Musical; Variety Show; Bsktbl; Hon Roll; Pvt Voice Lssns; Lfgrdng; Ynglf; 4 Year Schl; Cmptr Fld/Mltry.

BREWINGTON, RICHARD RYAN; Blue Vlly HS; Olathe, KS; (4); 15/205; Church Yth Grp; Cmnty Wkr; Debate Tm; Math Tm; Teachers Aide; Acpl Chr; Chorus; School Musical; Swing Chorus; Variety Show; Natl Merit Cmnded Schol; Blue Vllymntr Prog; Pittsburg St Univ; Premed.

BREWSTER, JENNIFER D; Blue Valley HS; Stilwell, KS; (3); 16/300; Cmnty Wkr; Letterman Clb; Teachers Aide; Pres Sr Cls; JV Var Bsktbl; Var Socr; Vllybl; High Hon Roll; Hon Roll; Jr NHS; Elem Schl Tutor; Elem Ed.

BRICKELL, KRISTA L; Burlington HS; Burlington, KS; (4); 9/80; Office Aide; Nwsp; Yrbk; L Bsktbl; L Trk; High Hon Roll; Hon Roll; NHS; Emporia ST U; Psych.

BRIDGES, JESSICA; Shawnee Mission South HS; Overland Park, KS; (3); Church Yth Grp; DECA; Intnl Clb; Math Clb; Quiz Bowl; Band; Capt Socr; Hon Roll; NHS; Ntl Merit Ltr; Intnl Bus; Mrktg.

BRIDGES, KELLY; Olathe East Sr HS; Olathe, KS; (4); 26/278; Spanish Clb; Rep Soph Cls; VP Jr Cls; VP Sr Cls; Rep Stu Cncl; Var Capt Chrldng; High Hon Roll; NHS; Pres Acad Fit Awd; Pres Schlr; U Of KS.

BRIGG, MICHAEL J; Immaculata HS; Leavenworth, KS; (4); 1/48; Am Leg Boys St; Capt Var Quiz Bowl; Pres Sr Cls; Treas Stu Cncl; Var L Ftbl; Gov Hon Prg Awd; High Hon Roll; Var NHS; Ntl Merit SF.

BRIGGEMAN, BRIAN C; Pratt HS; Iuka, KS; (4); 2/96; Church Yth Grp; Cmnty Wkr; FCA; Teachers Aide; Rep Stu Cncl; Var Bsbl; Var Ftbl; NHS; Sal; St Schlr; NHS Pres; All Lg Bsbl/Ftbl; KS ST Univ; Ag Ec.

BRIGGEMAN, STEVEN M; Pratt HS; Iuka, KS; (3); 4/95; Church Yth Grp; FCA; 4-H; Teachers Aide; Mrchg Band; Pep Band; Ofcr Stu Cncl; Crs Cntry; Trk; Hon Roll; FCA VP; KS ST Univ; Ag/Music.

BRIGGS, CHRISTY; Garden City Sr HS; Garden City, KS; (4); 45/313; Art Clb; Drama Clb; Thesps; School Musical; School Play; Stage Crew; Ed Nwsp; High Hon Roll; Kiwanis Awd; NHS; Ft Hayes ST; Art.

BRIGGS, JOSS E; Dighton HS; Gove, KS; (3); 4/28; Am Leg Boys St; Chess Clb; Church Yth Grp; FCA; Math Tm; Pep Clb; Speech Tm; Sec Jr Cls; Var L Bsktbl; Capt Ftbl; All Area/League/ST/COACHES Pale Honbl Ment Bskbl; KS ST Univ; Civil Engr.

BRIGGS, MARY; Leavenworth HS; Leavenworth, KS; (4); Church Yth Grp; SADD; Acpl Chr; Church Choir; School Musical; Chrmn Stu Cncl; JV Chrldng; High Hon Roll; NHS; Pres Acad Fit Awd; Southern UT Univ; Music; Psych.

BRIGHAM, CARRIE T; Ottawa HS; Ottawa, KS; (3); Church Yth Grp; French Clb; Treas Key Clb; VP Pres SADD; High Hon Roll; Hon Roll; Treas Of Rcyclng Envr Club; Myrs Yth Smmt; Ottw Swim Club; Pittsburg ST; Acct.

BRIGHAM, JON R; Iola Sr HS; Iola, KS; (3); Hon Roll.

BRIGHT, JAMES N; Chanute Sr HS; Chanute, KS; (2); Church Yth Grp; Band; Mrchg Band; Pep Band; Trk; Hon Roll; MIT; Aero Eng.

BRIGHTON, MICHAEL R; Manhattan HS; Manhattan, KS; (4); FCA; Var Crs Cntry; Var Trk; High Hon Roll; Kiwanis Awd; NHS; KS ST U; Bio.

BRIGMAN, CHERIE E; Buhler HS; Buhler, KS; (3); Church Yth Grp; Cmnty Wkr; FHA; Hosp Aide; Chorus; Church Choir; Stage Crew; Var Mgr(s); Score Keeper; Stat Sftbl; Hutchinson JC; Human Relations.

BRILL, BRANDON; Girard HS; Girard, KS; (4); Am Leg Boys St; Letterman Clb; Teachers Aide; Pres Frsh Cls; Pres Soph Cls; Pres Jr Cls; Ofcr Bsbl; Ftbl; Wt Lftg; Hon Roll; U Of KS Lawrence; Elem Ed.

BRIM, HEATHER L; Basehor Linwood HS; Basehor, KS; (3); GAA; SADD; Mrchg Band; Pep Band; Var L Chrldng; Var L Crs Cntry; Var L Sftbl; High Hon Roll; Hon Roll; Art Clb; Supt Stu Advy Cncl Mem; Stu Of The Month; KCKCC; Spcl Ed Tchr.

BRIMMERMAN, DAVID L; Wichita West HS; Wichita, KS; (4); Church Yth Grp; Cmnty Wkr; DECA; Letterman Clb; Q&S; Quiz Bowl; Scholastic Bowl; Teachers Aide; Thesps; Stage Crew; DECA Cls Ofcr; Eagle Achvmt Awd; Mentor & Career Clb; Butler CC; Tchr.

BRINEY, STEPHANIE; Goodland HS; Goodland, KS; (3); 27/87; Church Yth Grp; 4-H; German Clb; Band; Mrchg Band; Orch; Pep Band; Var Trk; JV Vllybl; Wt Lftg; Vet.

BRINGHAM, DARIN A; Meade HS; Meade, KS; (1); Church Yth Grp; 4-H; Math Tm; Pep Clb; Quiz Bowl; Scholastic Bowl; Speech Tm; Acpl Chr; Band; Chorus; 1st Tm All League Schlrs Bwl 1st Frosh To Receive Hnr In Leagues His; Future Astronaut Trng Prgm II.

BRINK, LISA D; Ft Scott HS; Fort Scott, KS; (4); 17/124; Church Yth Grp; Cmnty Wkr; Dance Clb; FCA; GAA; Key Clb; Pep Clb; Science Clb; SADD; Teachers Aide; His Clb Pres; Honduras Mssn Trp; Slct Ensmbl; Wmns Ensmbl; Japan/Toyota 6 Wks Exchg Stu; SCUM; Ottawa U KS; Bio.

BRINKER, MATTHEW; Manhattan HS; Manhattan, KS; (3); Debate Tm; NFL; Quiz Bowl; Band; Mrchg Band; School Musical; Bsktbl; Crs Cntry; Trk; Hon Roll; KS ST; Engrng.

BRINKERHOFF, DAVID; Derby HS; Derby, KS; (4); Am Leg Boys St; VP Bus Profs of Am; SADD; Band; Church Choir; Ofcr Stu Cncl; Hon Roll; NHS; Cowley Co CC; Acctng.

BRINKLEY, SARAH E; Buhler HS; Hutchinson, KS; (3); Computer Clb; FHA; German Clb; Science Clb; SADD; Band; Chorus; Church Choir; Mrchg Band; Pep Band; Cosmetology; Nrs.

BRISTOW, MIKE K; Immaculata HS; Leavenworth, KS; (2); Art Clb; Church Yth Grp; Cmnty Wkr; Library Aide; Office Aide; Spanish Clb; SADD; School Play; Stage Crew; Yrbk; Ken Kersten Bsktbl Awd; Leavenwroth Times All Area Soccer 2nd Team; Art Awd; MVP Bsbl Amer Legion; Med.

BRITTAN, CODY R; Scott Comm HS; Scott City, KS; (3); 10/90; Letterman Clb; Library Aide; Teachers Aide; Chorus; Ofcr Bsbl; Bsktbl; Ftbl; Wt Lftg; Cit Awd; Hon Roll; Hutchinson JC; Sprts Med.

BRITTIAN, REBECCA A; Downtown Law Magnet HS; Wichita, KS; (3); Church Yth Grp; Cmnty Wkr; JA; Spanish Clb; Band; Mrchg Band; Var Capt Golf; Var L Swmmng; Cit Awd; Wichita Rvr Fstvl Schnr Mate 96; Lfgrd; Cmptv Glfr; Law/Crmnl Jstc.

BRITTON, MATTHEW W; Lawrence HS; Lawrence, KS; (2); JA; Hon Roll; Roller Hky; KS Univ; Bus.

BRIZENDINE, KRISTEN A; Blue Valley HS; Overland Park, KS; (2); Church Yth Grp; Acpl Chr; Church Choir; Flag Corp; School Musical; Variety Show; High Hon Roll; Hon Roll; Piano; Dance; Coll.

BROADHEAD, ERIC W; Wichita South HS; Wichita, KS; (4); Art Clb; Computer Clb; Science Clb; Pres Yrbk; K-ST Salina; Mech Engrng.

BROBERG, BROOKE; Shawnee Mission W Sr HS; Lenexa, KS; (3); Pres DECA; Ofcr Stu Cncl; Chrldng; Hon Roll; NHS; Shawnee Mission Cotillion; DECA KS ST Pres 96; U Of KS; Meteorology.

BROBST, JEREMY N; Scott Comm HS; Scott City, KS; (3); VP Pres 4-H; Treas Natl FFA Org; Teachers Aide; Bsktbl; Var L Crs Cntry; Var L Trk; Wt Lftg; 4-H Awd; Hon Roll; Pres Acad Fit Awd; FFA Dist Lndjdgng High Indvdl 1st Tm/Natl Land Jdgng 95; Natl FFA Knwldg Test 95; Ag Ed.

BROCE, KRISTA; Arkansas City HS; Arkansas City, KS; (4); Am Leg Aux Girls St; Church Yth Grp; FCA; SADD; Acpl Chr; Chorus; School Musical; Rep Frsh Cls; Bsktbl; Chrldng; Cowley Cty CC; Dental Hygn.

BROCK, DUSTIN R; Derby HS; Derby, KS; (1); Bsktbl; Ftbl; Wt Lftg; High Hon Roll; Hon Roll; St Rnkngs KSU Stock Mrkt Game; Math/Sci/Cmptr.

BROCK, MANDY; Highland HS; Hiawatha, KS; (3); #2 in class; Temple Yth Grp; Chorus; School Musical; Swing Chorus; VP Soph Cls; Pres Jr Cls; Rep Stu Cncl; Mgr(s); NHS; Stu Offrng Spprt; Phys Thrpy.

BROCK, MELANIE; Emporia HS; Emporia, KS; (3); Treas Pep Clb; SADD; Ofcr Jr Cls; Chrldng; Pom Pon; Cit Awd; Hon Roll; Kayettes; KS ST Univ.

BROCK, SARAH; Topeka HS; Topeka, KS; (3); 48/315; Church Yth Grp; French Clb; GAA; SADD; Teachers Aide; Rep Sr Cls; Var Capt Stu Cncl; L Vllybl; High Hon Roll.

BROCKLING, VALERIE M; Olathe North Sr HS; Olathe, KS; (2); Church Yth Grp; Pep Clb; Spanish Clb; Teachers Aide; Chrldng; Gym; Trk; Wt Lftg; Cit Awd; High Hon Roll; KS U; Elem Tchr.

BROCKWAY, MATT; Olathe East Sr HS; Olathe, KS; (3); Pep Clb; Spanish Clb; Band; Jazz Band; Mrchg Band; Orch; Pep Band; Var Crs Cntry; Var Trk; High Hon Roll.

BROCKWAY, RYAN M; Olathe East Sr HS; Olathe, KS; (3); Pep Clb; Spanish Clb; Mrchg Band; Orch; Pep Band; Var Crs Cntry; Var Trk; Hon Roll; NHS; Spanish NHS; Bus.

BRODERSEN, CATHERINE; Junction City HS; Fort Leavenworth, KS; (1); 1/409; Church Yth Grp; Cmnty Wkr; Red Cross Aide; Bsktbl; Var L Sftbl; Tennis; High Hon Roll; Acad Ltr Awd; Acad Ath Awd; Cls Awd.

BRODIE, ELIZABETH; Shawnee Mission E Sr HS; Prairie Village, KS; (4); 79/408; Church Yth Grp; Dance Clb; Girl Scts; Hosp Aide; Math Tm; Model UN; Natl Beta Clb; Science Clb; SADD; Stage Crew; Yth In Govt; Optmst Mdl Leg/Attrny Gen; SHARE Chprsn; Pres Ed Awd.

BRODINE, LUKE W; Shawnee Mission S Sr HS; Shawnee Mission, KS; (3); 16/448; Church Yth Grp; Band; Church Choir; Drm Mjr(t); Jazz Band; Mrchg Band; Pep Band; JV Tennis; High Hon Roll; NHS; Mus.

BROECKELMAN, BARRY M; Maize HS; Wichita, KS; (2); 1/294; Cmnty Wkr; SADD; School Play; Pres Soph Cls; Pres Jr Cls; Rep Stu Cncl; JV Bsktbl; JV Golf; High Hon Roll; NHS; Bst Actr Awd Sprng Play; Rep Attnd Stdnt Cncl Wrkshp; Slctd Prtnrs Comm Ldrshp Prgm; Med.

BROKER, JONATHAN; Iola Sr HS; Iola, KS; (4); 7/100; Am Leg Boys St; Church Yth Grp; Letterman Clb; Library Aide; Teachers Aide; Varsity Clb; Church Choir; Var L Bsktbl; L Ftbl; Var L Golf; I Dr You Awd; RYLA Cmp; Engr.

BRONAUGH, MELISSA D; St Marys HS; Saint Marys, KS; (4); 19/54; Church Yth Grp; FBLA; FHA; Natl FFA Org; Pep Clb; Band; Capt Drill Tm; Ed Yrbk; Rep Frsh Cls; Rep Soph Cls; Ft Hays St Univ; Elem Ed.

BRONNENBERG, MELISSA A; Caney Valley Jr Sr HS; Caney, KS; (3); Am Leg Aux Girls St; Debate Tm; Pres Drama Clb; NFL; School Musical; School Play; Nwsp; Yrbk; Sec Stu Cncl; NHS; Southwestern Coll; Comm.

BRONSON, LENA; Winfield HS; Winfield, KS; (2); Cmnty Wkr; Dance Clb; VP Soph Cls; Chrldng; Swmmng; Hon Roll; Church Yth Grp; Debate Tm; Drama Clb; Hosp Aide; Natl Interschlstc Ath Admin Assn; Music Festival Piano ST/REGNL; Music.

BRONSON, TRACY R; Hays HS; Hays, KS; (1); Dance Clb; Pep Clb; Drill Tm; Pom Pon; Powder Puff Ftbl; Sftbl; Wt Lftg; Hon Roll; Dance; Bsbl Team Mgr; KU.

BROOCKERD, SHAY E; Blue Valley HS; Stilwell, KS; (2); Thesps; Acpl Chr; Chorus; Drill Tm; Flag Corp; School Musical; School Play; Treas Frsh Cls; Rep Stu Cncl; Hon Roll; Film/Sound Editing/Music/Arts.

BROOKE, ELIZABETH A; Atchison Co Cmty HS; Atchison, KS; (3); 1/64; Cmnty Wkr; Hist 4-H; Treas Math Clb; Mu Alpha Theta; Quiz Bowl; Pres Science Clb; Bsktbl; 4-H Awd; High Hon Roll; NHS; CO ST; Vet.

BROOKE, JOSHUA E; Seaman Sr HS; Topeka, KS; (3); 4-H; FBLA; German Clb; Yrbk; Var L Ftbl; Var Trk; Var Wt Lftg; 4-H Awd; Hon Roll; KS Univ; Sports Medicine.

BROOKE, TARYN; Seaman Sr HS; Topeka, KS; (4); 17/248; Debate Tm; VP FBLA; Pres Model UN; VP Stu Cncl; Var L Bsktbl; Var L Vllybl; St Schlr; 4-H; HOBY; Key Clb; Ms Teen KS 95; Natl Frnscs Lg Dist Ortn Champ & Natl Cmptr; FBLA St Champ Entrprnrshp & Natl Cmptr; Bus Admin.

BROOKS, ADAM; Blue Valley Northwest HS; Overland Park, KS; (1); Boy Scts; Debate Tm; Band; Mrchg Band; Orch.

BROOKS, ALICIA L; Ottawa HS; Ottawa, KS; (2); Church Yth Grp; Quiz Bowl; Spanish Clb; Band; Jazz Band; Mrchg Band; Orch; Pep Band; JV L Crs Cntry; Var Trk; U Of KS.

BROOKS, AMANDA; Turner HS; Kansas City, KS; (3); Bus Profs of Am; Science Clb; SADD; High Hon Roll; Hon Roll; Jr NHS; NHS; Prfct Atten Awd; Pres Acad Fit Awd; Kansas City CC; Animal Care.

BROOKS, ASHLEY; Protection Schl; Protection, KS; (3); 1/16; Letterman Clb; Pep Clb; Band; Chorus; Drill Tm; Flag Corp; School Musical; Ofcr Stu Cncl; Chrldng; Vllybl.

BROOKS, CARLA A; Jefferson West HS; Meriden, KS; (2); 20/69; Pep Clb; Band; Pep Band; Ed Rptr Nwsp; Var Chrldng; Stat Trk; High Hon Roll; Hon Roll; W KY Univ; Spec Ed.

BROOKS, CARRIE J; Axtell Schl; Axtell, KS; (2); VP FHA; Letterman Clb; Chorus; Rep Frsh Cls; Rep Soph Cls; Var Bsktbl; Trk; Vllybl; Hon Roll; Kay Clb.

BROOKS, CATHERINE; St Thomas Aquinas HS; Lenexa, KS; (3); Cmnty Wkr; Pep Clb; Acpl Chr; Church Choir; School Musical; Ofcr Stu Cncl; Stat Bsktbl; JV Var Chrldng; Var Swmmng; Hon Roll; U Of KS; Pedtrc Psycht.

BROOKS, CHRISTOPER L; Lawrence HS; Lawrence, KS; (3); Library Aide; Ofcr Jr Cls; JV Bsktbl; Var L Socr; Var L Tennis; Intrml Vllybl; Hon Roll; Prfct Atten Awd; Jr Cls Plnng Comm.

BROOKS, CHRISTOPHER P; Chapman HS; Chapman, KS; (3); Church Yth Grp; SADD; Rep Sr Cls; JV Bsktbl; Var Tennis; High Hon Roll; Hon Roll; Pres Schlr; St Schlr; Hi-Y Govt Group; KS ST Univ; Arch Engr/Arch.

BROOKS, DARREN S; Manhattan HS; Manhattan, KS; (4); 25/368; Boy Scts; Band; Jazz Band; Mrchg Band; Orch; Pep Band; School Musical; Variety Show; High Hon Roll; NHS; Gymnatstic; John Phillip Sousa Bndawd; Eagle Sct; KS St Univ; Mus Ed.

BROOKS, DAVID S; Manhattan HS; Manhattan, KS; (4); 1/375; Teachers Aide; High Hon Roll; NHS; USGF Gymnastics Participant; Gymnastics Coach; KS Hnr Schlr; KS ST U; Chemical Engrng.

BROOKS, JODY L; Healy Schl; Healy, KS; (4); 1/10; Hosp Aide; Pep Clb; Quiz Bowl; Scholastic Bowl; Teachers Aide; Band; Chorus; Church Choir; Mrchg Band; Pep Band; KU Hnrs Scholar; KS Newman Col; Pre-Med.

BROOKS, JOSH G; Northwest HS; Wichita, KS; (4); School Play; Var Ftbl; JV Wrstlng; Hon Roll; Wichita ST Univ.

BROOKS, LAURA; Atchison Sr HS; Atchison, KS; (1); 1/131; Church Yth Grp; Dance Clb; Band; Mrchg Band; Pep Band; VP Frsh Cls; Rep Stu Cncl; Chrldng; Mgr(s); High Hon Roll; Multcltrl Clb; Lunch Champs; Ortho Surgry.

BROOKS, NATE J; Leroy HS; Le Roy, KS; (2); Church Yth Grp; Cmnty Wkr; Rep Stu Cncl; Ftbl; Wt Lftg; Hon Roll; Yth Grp Bnd; Yth Grp Drama Tm; Engrg.

BROOKSHIRE, DANIEL; Wellington Sr HS; Wellington, KS; (4); 15/116; Boy Scts; German Clb; Math Clb; Math Tm; Capt Quiz Bowl; Capt Scholastic Bowl; JV Bsbl; Var Ftbl; Var Trk; NHS; Wichita ST U; Aerospc Engrng.

BROOMFIELD, ANGELA N; Circle HS; Towanda, KS; (2); Scholastic Bowl; SADD; Chorus; School Musical; School Play; Variety Show; Nwsp; Hon Roll; Pres Acad Ftnss Awd; JC Juco; Jrnlsm.

BROSIUS, ANDRA; Concordia Jr Sr HS; Concordia, KS; (3); 6/102; Church Yth Grp; Science Clb; Spanish Clb; Band; Var Bsktbl; Var Tennis; Var Trk; Var Vllybl; High Hon Roll; NHS; KS ST Univ; Envrnmntl Chmst.

BROTHERSON, ERIC W; Santa Fe Trail Jr HS; Olathe, KS; (1); Dance Clb; Letterman Clb; Drill Tm; Stage Crew; Bsktbl; JV Socr; High Hon Roll; Pres Acad Fit Awd; Olathe Soccer Clb; St Ranked Skier.

BROTHERTON, BETHANY; Chaparral HS; Anthony, KS; (3); 49/80; Church Yth Grp; Debate Tm; Drama Clb; Girl Scts; NFL; Speech Tm; School Play; Hon Roll; Bowling 10 Yrs; Stock Mrkt Game Capt; Forensics Team; Univ Of CA; Psych.

BROTSKY, DESIREE; Campus HS; Haysville, KS; (3); Church Yth Grp; FCA; Q&S; SADD; Teachers Aide; Band; Mrchg Band; Yrbk; Sec Frsh Cls; Sec Soph Cls; Natural Helpers; Phys Therapy.

BROWER, JULIE; Olathe South Sr HS; Olathe, KS; (2); Church Yth Grp; Spanish Clb; Yrbk; Bsktbl; JV Var Vllybl; High Hon Roll; Pres Acad Fit Awd; Chrch Yth Gpr Svc Prjcts; Mid Amer Nazarene Grp; Phys Thr.

BROWN, ALEXIS; Bishop Carroll Catholic HS; Wichita, KS; (3); Church Yth Grp; FCA; Spanish Clb; SADD; Band; Mrchg Band; Pep Band; Var Co-Capt Chrldng; Var L Tennis; JV Trk; GCTL; KS Teens As Tchrs Tobacco Prevention Team; Chrldng Top Team Awd; Med/Frgn Lang/Astrnmy/Archlgy.

BROWN, AMANDA A; Ft Scott HS; Fort Scott, KS; (3); Drama Clb; Pep Clb; Thesps; Chorus; Church Choir; School Musical; School Play; Variety Show; Nwsp; Hon Roll.

BROWN, ANGIE; Ashland HS; Ashland, KS; (1); Church Yth Grp; Pep Clb; Band; Chorus; Mrchg Band; Pep Band; Rep Stu Cncl; Trk; 4-H Awd; Hon Roll.

BROWN, APRIL D; Neodesha Jr Sr HS; Neodesha, KS; (2); Art Clb; Church Yth Grp; Cmnty Wkr; Library Aide; Pep Clb; SADD; Teachers Aide; Church Choir; Hon Roll; Johnson/Wheals Schlsp; Modling Schlsp; Cmptr Engrng.

BROWN, ARIANNE M; Colby Sr HS; Colby, KS; (2); Rep Church Yth Grp; Cmnty Wkr; FCA; Girl Scts; Science Clb; Spanish Clb; SADD; Phtg Yrbk; Crs Cntry; Mgr(s); Colby CC; CDC/PEDIATRIC PT.

BROWN, ARIKA J; Wichita Heights HS; Wichita, KS; (4); Church Yth Grp; Letterman Clb; Office Aide; Teachers Aide; Varsity Clb; Trk; Vllybl; Hon Roll; Pratt Comm Coll; Med.

BROWN, BRIAN M; Bluestom HS; Augusta, KS; (3); Math Tm; Pep Clb; Band; Jazz Band; Mrchg Band; Pep Band; Yrbk; Rep Sr Cls; High Hon Roll; KEMA Hnr Band 2 Yrs; Natl Hnr Soc 2 Times; Aerospace Engrg.

BROWN, BRIANNE; Lawrence HS; Lawrence, KS; (4); 25/521; Key Clb; Office Aide; Spanish Clb; Teachers Aide; Var Capt Chrldng; JV Gym; Hon Roll; Treas NHS; KS Hnr Schlr; Pres Awd For Educl Excl; Dnce; U Of KS; Pdtrcn.

BROWN, CHANDA R; Colby Sr HS; Colby, KS; (2); Pres 4-H; Intnl Clb; Spanish Clb; Ed Nwsp; Yrbk; Rep Frsh Cls; JV Vllybl; 4-H Awd; Church Yth Grp; Cmnty Wkr; Nwsppr Awd; ST Fair Phto Chsn To Be Pub.

BROWN, CHANTELLE; Great Bend Sr HS; Great Bend, KS; (4); Am Leg Aux Girls St; Pep Clb; School Play; VP Frsh Cls; Rep Soph Cls; Stat Bsktbl; JV Var Chrldng; JV Sftbl; JV Var Tennis; JV Vllybl; Barton County CC; Optmety.

BROWN, CHARLOTTE; Turner HS; Kansas City, KS; (3); Math Tm; Rep Jr Cls; Rep Stu Cncl; Var Chrldng; High Hon Roll; Sec Jr NHS; Pres Acad Fit Awd.

BROWN, CRYSTAL; Maize HS; Wichita, KS; (4); 12/230; Church Yth Grp; Cmnty Wkr; Debate Tm; FCA; NFL; SADD; Teachers Aide; Varsity Clb; Acpl Chr; Chorus; KS Assn For Yth Bd Mbr; CHAOS Pres; OK Bptst U; Elem Ed.

BROWN, DANIEL J; Concordia Jr Sr HS; Concordia, KS; (3); Art Clb; Letterman Clb; Ftbl; Trk; Wt Lftg; Hon Roll; Prfct Atten Awd; Art.

BROWN, DANIEL L; Wellington Sr HS; Wellington, KS; (4); Am Leg Boys St; Church Yth Grp; Cmnty Wkr; JV Bsktbl; High Hon Roll; Hon Roll; Jr NHS; NHS; Prfct Atten Awd; U KS.

BROWN, DAVID J; Great Bend Sr HS; Great Bend, KS; (3); Ofcr Bsbl; Sprts Med.

BROWN, DAVID M; Topeka HS; Topeka, KS; (3); Church Yth Grp; Cmnty Wkr; Debate Tm; Hosp Aide; Intnl Clb; Letterman Clb; NFL; High Hon Roll; Ntl Merit Ltr; Cvl Engrng.

BROWN, DENISE; Turner HS; Kansas City, KS; (2); Cmnty Wkr; FBLA; Hosp Aide; JA; Science Clb; SADD; Yrbk; Ofcr Frsh Cls; Ofcr Soph Cls; Ofcr Stu Cncl; Soph Cls Rep For Winter Act; Jr Cls Pres For Jr Exec Cncl; VP Of Stu Cncl; Nrsng; Marine Biologist.

BROWN, DESIREE M; Wichita South HS; Wichita, KS; (2); Church Yth Grp; JA; Church Choir; Co-Capt Rep Stu Cncl; Vllybl; Hon Roll; Sftbl; Modeling; Awd For Raising GPA; Interior Dsgn.

BROWN, DIANE M; Bishop Carroll Catholic HS; Wichita, KS; (3); 5/176; Girl Scts; Scholastic Bowl; Hon Roll; NHS; Phy Thrpy.

BROWN, DUSTIN P; Washburn Rural HS; Auburn, KS; (2); Chorus; Variety Show; JV Bsbl; JV Bsktbl; Var Socr; Hon Roll; Attndnc Cnsl.

BROWN III, GEORGE L; Sedan HS; Sedan, KS; (4); 3/28; FCA; 4-H; Natl FFA Org; Teachers Aide; School Play; Sec Jr Cls; Var Bsbl; Var Bsktbl; High Hon Roll; NHS; Ft Hays ST U; Acctng.

BROWN, GINGER; Sacred Heart HS; Salina, KS; (3); 1/40; Church Yth Grp; Rptr FBLA; HOBY; Pep Clb; Quiz Bowl; School Musical; VP Soph Cls; Pres Jr Cls; Var Bsktbl; Var L Sftbl; Scl Wrk.

BROWN, GINGER; Topeka West HS; Topeka, KS; (4); 12/238; Am Leg Aux Girls St; Cmnty Wkr; Spanish Clb; Jazz Band; Mrchg Band; Pep Band; Chrmn Stu Cncl; High Hon Roll; NHS; St Schlr; Peer Hlpr; Bnd Cncl Rep; U KS; Phrmcy.

BROWN, JAMIE; Goddard HS; Wichita, KS; (4); 25/156; Church Yth Grp; Cmnty Wkr; Debate Tm; Drama Clb; FCA; NFL; Pep Clb; Red Cross Aide; Scholastic Bowl; Spanish Clb; Trk & Field; Bsktbl; Sr Cls Best Personality; Sci; Music; Acad Schlsp; Friends Univ; Bio; Ed.

BROWN, JASON D; Wichita Southeast HS; Wichita, KS; (1); Debate Tm; NFL; Hon Roll; Harvard Univ; Law.

BROWN, JENNIFER; St Mary's Colgan HS; Pittsburg, KS; (4); Am Leg Aux Girls St; HOBY; Q&S; Scholastic Bowl; Ed Yrbk; Hon Roll; NHS; Church Yth Grp; Cmnty Wkr; All Amer Schlr; SEK Orch; Lions Clb Outstndng Sr; Drury Coll; Commnctns.

BROWN, JENNIFER; Atwood HS; Atwood, KS; (4); 26/40; Art Clb; Church Yth Grp; Cmnty Wkr; Letterman Clb; Library Aide; Natl FFA Org; Scholastic Bowl; Varsity Clb; Chorus; School Play; Natl & St FFA Convntns; Farm Bureau 95 Capital Experience Tour; 95 Rawlins Cty Jr Miss; Colby CC; Office Tech.

BROWN, JESSI; Plainville HS; Plainville, KS; (3); 7/48; Church Yth Grp; Drill Tm; Rptr Nwsp; Rep Jr Cls; Rep Sr Cls; Rep Stu Cncl; Var Bsktbl; High Hon Roll; Hon Roll; NHS; Ft Hays ST U; Radiology.

BROWN, JILL R; Maize HS; Wichita, KS; (3); Q&S; SADD; Teachers Aide; Mgr Yrbk; Var Socr; Hon Roll; KS Newman Coll; Elem Ed.

BROWN, JONATHAN D; Trego Comm HS; Wa Keeney, KS; (2); 1/49; Church Yth Grp; Debate Tm; Drama Clb; German Clb; Math Tm; Pep Clb; SADD; Band; Chorus; Mrchg Band.

BROWN, JOSH W; Junction City HS; Fort Riley, KS; (1); Boy Scts; Church Yth Grp; Debate Tm; German Clb; L Socr; High Hon Roll; Jr NHS; Eagle Sct Awd.

BROWN, JULIA A; Independence Bible Schl; Independence, KS; (3); 1/8; Church Yth Grp; Chorus; Church Choir; School Musical; Swing Chorus; Rptr Nwsp; Ed Yrbk; High Hon Roll; Hon Roll; Val; Jr Mrshll Grdtn; Tght Bsc Span; Lttrd Acad; Gods Bible Coll; Sngr.

BROWN, JULIE A; Blue Valley Northwest HS; Overland Park, KS; (3); Church Yth Grp; Cmnty Wkr; Drama Clb; Teachers Aide; School Play; Stage Crew; Powder Puff Ftbl; Hon Roll; Drama Awd; KS Univ; Jrnlsm.

BROWN, KATHERINE; Blue Vlly HS; Stilwell, KS; (4); 53/229; NFL; Band; School Play; Var L Chrldng; Hon Roll; NHS; Yng KS Writers; BVHS Outs Sr Writr Awd; KS St Univ; Engl.

BROWN, KERRI E; Atchison Sr HS; Atchison, KS; (1); Spanish Clb; Band; Mrchg Band; Hon Roll.

BROWN, KRISTY; Ellis HS; Ellis, KS; (2); 6/40; Church Yth Grp; FHA; Pep Clb; Spanish Clb; SADD; Church Choir; Drill Tm; Ofcr Bsbl; Bsktbl; Chrldng; Kayettes; Lcl Wrtng Cont 2nd Pl; KS U; Medcl.

BROWN, KRISTY J; Ft Scott HS; Fulton, KS; (3); Church Yth Grp; FCA; Natl FFA Org; Pep Clb; Chorus; Church Choir; JV Bsktbl; JV Trk; Wt Lftg; 2 Yrs ST Lvstck Jdng; 3 Yrs Dist Choir; Ft Scott CC.

BROWN, LAUREN; Garden City Sr HS; Garden City, KS; (3); Church Yth Grp; French Clb; Red Cross Aide; SADD; Teachers Aide; Acpl Chr; Chorus; Church Choir; Ofcr Soph Cls; JETS Clb; Ksu; PT Med.

BROWN, LISA; Seaman Sr HS; Topeka, KS; (4); 20/252; Art Clb; Church Yth Grp; VP French Clb; Key Clb; Spanish Clb; SADD; Band; Flag Corp; Swmmng; NHS; OK Christian U Of Sci & Arts.

BROWN, LORI L; Ft Scott HS; Fort Scott, KS; (3); Church Yth Grp; Computer Clb; Science Clb; Orch; Hon Roll; Rdlgst.

BROWN, MANDY; Olatehe East HS; Olathe, KS; (4); Drama Clb; FHA; Letterman Clb; Office Aide; Science Clb; Teachers Aide; Acpl Chr; Chorus; Drill Tm; School Play; U Of KS.

BROWN, MARCUS J; Maize HS; Wichita, KS; (1); Boy Scts; Math Tm; Scholastic Bowl; Chorus; School Musical; Variety Show; Rep Frsh Cls; Hon Roll; Sci Olympiad; Odyssey Of The Mind; Future Problem Solving; KS Univ.

BROWN, MATTHEW; St John's HS; Beloit, KS; (3); 3/12; Church Yth Grp; HOBY; Quiz Bowl; Capt Var Ftbl; Var Trk; Cit Awd; High Hon Roll; NHS; Pres Acad Fit Awd; Spirit Awd; Mrktng.

BROWN, MEGAN E; Blue Valley Northwest HS; Overland Park, KS; (1); Church Yth Grp; Chorus; Church Choir; High Hon Roll; Piano Mlt Piano Plq/Awd/Mscnshp Cert; Saltelight Club For Schl Bible Study; Non-Schl Vlybl; OK; Vet Med.

BROWN, MELISSA; Hesston HS; Hesston, KS; (4); 5/53; Drama Clb; FCA; Ed FBLA; Scholastic Bowl; Teachers Aide; School Musical; School Play; High Hon Roll; Washburn Univ; Theatre/Spec Ed.

BROWN, MONIQUE C; Wichita Heights HS; Wichita, KS; (2); Church Yth Grp; Cmnty Wkr; Office Aide; Speech Tm; Teachers Aide; Chorus; Church Choir; Drill Tm; High Hon Roll; Clark Univ; Phys Thpy.

BROWN, NICHOLAS G; Nickerson HS; South Hutchinson, KS; (2); Church Yth Grp; FCA; VP FBLA; JV Golf; Hon Roll; FL Chrstn Coll; Yth Mnstr.

BROWN, PAM L; Pratt HS; Preston, KS; (2); 4-H; FHA; SADD; Band; Mrchg Band; Pep Band; Var L Crs Cntry; JV Trk; 4-H Awd; Hon Roll.

BROWN, PATRICIA E; Field Kindley Mem Sr HS; Coffeyville, KS; (4); 4/146; Church Yth Grp; Cmnty Wkr; Drama Clb; French Clb; Hosp Aide; JA; Chorus; Church Choir; School Musical; School Play; SW MO St Univ.

BROWN, PATRICK K; Shawnee Mission N HS; Shawnee Mission, KS; (4); 102/374; Boy Scts; Pep Clb; Sec Frsh Cls; Treas Soph Cls; VP Jr Cls; Intrml Bsbl; Intrml Bsktbl; Var Socr; Hon Roll; NHS; Orgnl One Act Play Wrtn/Prdcd; Radio/Tlvsn Comm.

BROWN, RONALD H; Labette Co HS; Mound Valley, KS; (3); 27/136; Band; Chorus; Church Choir; Mrchg Band; School Musical; Rep Stu Cncl; Stat Bsktbl; Mgr(s); NHS; Stu Co Rep SADD 2 Yrs; Ozark Christian Coll; Music Min.

BROWN, RONNIE; Syracuse Jr Sr HS; Coolidge, KS; (3); Cmnty Wkr; Library Aide; Band; Chorus; Mrchg Band; Pep Band; Var L Bsktbl; Var L Ftbl; Var L Trk; Hon Roll; High Plains League Acad Awd; KSHSAA Cert Outstndng Achvt Track.

BROWN, SARAH L; Topeka West HS; Topeka, KS; (3); 21/240; Church Yth Grp; Chrmn German Clb; Rep Frsh Cls; Rep Soph Cls; Rep Jr Cls; VP Stu Cncl; Var L Bsktbl; Var L Trk; Var L Vllybl; High Hon Roll; Nom For Natl Wendys Heisman Awd; Asthma Spclst.

BROWN, SCOTT; Kapaun-Mt Carmel HS; Wichita, KS; (3); Church Yth Grp; Var Trk; Hon Roll; Pres Acad Fit Awd; Peopl To Peopl Stu Ambssdr; Fin.

BROWN, SHAMEKA D; Washington HS; Kansas City, KS; (2); Church Yth Grp; Cmnty Wkr; Debate Tm; FCA; GAA; Intnl Clb; Letterman Clb; Pep Clb; Varsity Clb; Church Choir; Wrk With Chldrn/Advc; Chrch Act; Ply Bsktbl/Vlybl; TX Southern; Bus/Law.

BROWN, SHANNON; Labette Co HS; Mound Valley, KS; (3); 38/140; FCA; HOBY; Chorus; Drm Mjr(t); School Musical; Pres Frsh Cls; Rep Soph Cls; Chrldng; Hon Roll; Hnrs Soc; Dist & St Choir; Coffeyville CC; Music.

BROWN, SHELLY; Bucklin Schl; Ford, KS; (3); 12/50; Church Yth Grp; FCA; Quiz Bowl; SADD; Band; Mrchg Band; Pep Band; VP Rep Stu Cncl; Bsktbl; Trk; Serendipity Cmnty Svc Grp.

BROWN, SONYA; Quivira Heights HS; Bushton, KS; (3); 3/26; FCA; Math Tm; Office Aide; Quiz Bowl; Band; Chorus; Pres Stu Cncl; Tennis; Hon Roll; NHS; Santa Clara Univ; Law/Crim Jstc.

BROWN, STACEY; Spring Hill HS; Spring Hill, KS; (4); 5/98; Boy Scts; Hosp Aide; Pres Science Clb; Sec Treas SADD; Teachers Aide; Intrml Bsktbl; Intrml Vllybl; High Hon Roll; NHS; Teens Tchr; KS Hnrs Schlr; Fire Explr Pst Sec, Tres; Johnson Cty CC; Nrsng.

BROWN, STACEY M; Blue Valley Northwest HS; Overland Park, KS; (2); Church Yth Grp; Cmnty Wkr; JA; Teachers Aide; Band; Church Choir; Jazz Band; Mrchg Band; Pep Band; Hon Roll; Heartlands Schl Of Ridng-Therptc Horsbck Ridng For Mentlly & Physiclly Challngd Kids Vol; Spcl Needs Presch Tchr.

BROWN, STACY L; Oskaloosa HS; Oskaloosa, KS; (2); HOBY; Letterman Clb; SADD; School Musical; Var Bsktbl; Var Crs Cntry; Var Trk; Cit Awd; Drama Clb; Office Aide; Teen As Tchrs; Jefferson Cty Yth Sbstnc Abuse Task Force.

BROWN, SUMMER; Clay Ctr Cmty HS; Clay Center, KS; (4); 1/95; Church Yth Grp; Cmnty Wkr; Drama Clb; Sec FBLA; Spanish Clb; Band; Chorus; Church Choir; Drm Mjr(t); Jazz Band; KS ST Univ; Scndry Music Ed.

BROWN, TAMARA L; Wallace Cty HS; Wallace, KS; (3); Rptr Church Yth Grp; NFL; Scholastic Bowl; VP Chorus; Nwsp; Rep Frsh Cls; Rep Sr Cls; Ofcr Stu Cncl; Hon Roll; FCA; Piano Perf.

BROWN, TANDA; Kinsley HS; Offerle, KS; (3); Church Yth Grp; Chorus; School Play; Bsktbl; Vllybl; High Hon Roll; Hon Roll; Target Clb; Phys Thrpy.

BROWN, TERYN E; Liberal HS; Liberal, KS; (4); 18/245; Office Aide; Pres Band; Chorus; Jazz Band; Pres Mrchg Band; Pres Pep Band; School Musical; School Play; Variety Show; High Hon Roll; DARE Role Model; Bethany Coll.

BROWN, TONYA; Goddard HS; Goddard, KS; (3); 16/169; Science Clb; SADD; Teachers Aide; Band; Var Capt Bsktbl; Var Sftbl; Var Vllybl; High Hon Roll; NHS; Pres Acad Fit Awd; Med.

BROWN, TREY; Kansas City Area Voc Tech Sch; Leavenworth, KS; (4); Bus Profs of Am; JV Ftbl; JV Trk; Hon Roll; Pres Acctng Clss; Devry; Acctng.

BROWN, WADE D; Central Heights Sr HS; Richmond, KS; (1); Church Yth Grp; Letterman Clb; JV Bsktbl; Var L Crs Cntry; High Hon Roll; Babe Ruth Bsbl.

BROWNBACK, KYLE R; Lyndon HS; Lyndon, KS; (2); 1/45; Church Yth Grp; Cmnty Wkr; 4-H; FBLA; Scholastic Bowl; Band; JV Ftbl; JV Golf; Hon Roll; NHS; Del Ctznshp WA Focus; Ldrshp Amer Jr Ldr 96; Sam Brownback For Senate Vol; Engr.

BROWNE, CASEY K; Great Bend Sr HS; Great Bend, KS; (1); Drama Clb; German Clb; Band; Mrchg Band; Pep Band; Sftbl; Tennis; KS Assoc For Yth; KS Univ.

BROWNELL, AARON; St Marys HS; Emmett, KS; (2); FBLA; Band; Jazz Band; Mrchg Band; Pep Band; Var Bsbl; Var Bsktbl; Var Crs Cntry; High Hon Roll; NHS; Acad Ath Awd; Graphic Design.

BROWNELL, KATIE A; St Marys HS; Emmett, KS; (4); FBLA; Letterman Clb; Pep Clb; Band; Jazz Band; Mrchg Band; Var Capt Chrldng; Crs Cntry; Trk; Vllybl; Multi Yr Listee; KS ST Univ; Acctng.

BROWNEWELL, TIFFANY J; Parsons HS; Parsons, KS; (4); Treas FHA; Hosp Aide; Spanish Clb; SADD; Teachers Aide; Treas Band; Mrchg Band; Yrbk; Pom Pon; Vllybl; Full Orch; Mrt Schlsp; Labette CC; Elem Ed.

BROWNING, JESSICA; Chanute Sr HS; Chanute, KS; (2); 14/130; FCA; FTA; Math Tm; Spanish Clb; Sec Soph Cls; JV Vllybl; Ed.

BROWNING, MICHAEL; Winfield HS; Winfield, KS; (3); 13/170; Am Leg Boys St; Church Yth Grp; Cmnty Wkr; Debate Tm; FCA; NFL; Pep Clb; Scholastic Bowl; Speech Tm; Rep Jr Cls.

BROWNING, NIKI; Independence HS; Independence, KS; (3); Pres FCA; Pep Clb; Orch; Ed Nwsp; Rep Soph Cls; Rep Jr Cls; Var Chrldng; Powder Puff Ftbl; Hon Roll; NHS; OK City Univ; Pub Rel.

BROWNING, TARRAH; Shawnee Mission S Sr HS; Overland Park, KS; (4); Am Leg Aux Girls St; Debate Tm; Model UN; VP NFL; Quiz Bowl; Service Clb; Speech Tm; Rep Stu Cncl; JV Var Chrldng; High Hon Roll; Peer Cnslng; Mock Trial; Spec Olympcs Vol; Harvesters Vol; Pltcs.

BROXTERMAN, BARRY K; Axtell Schl; Axtell, KS; (3); 5/20; FCA; Letterman Clb; Teachers Aide; Varsity Clb; Sec Frsh Cls; Pres Soph Cls; Pres Jr Cls; Bsktbl; Ftbl; Wt Lftg; St Bsktbl Team Startr; St Chmpnshp Ftbl Team; Emporia ST; Bus Admin.

BROXTERMAN, STACIE R; Bailey-Benedict Jr Sr High; Baileyville, KS; (2); Church Yth Grp; FHA; Pep Clb; Quiz Bowl; Band; VP Soph Cls; Var Trk; JV Vllybl; Cit Awd; Hon Roll.

BROYLES, MANDY; Olpe Schl; Madison, KS; (3); 6/30; Church Yth Grp; Cmnty Wkr; FBLA; Pep Clb; Band; Chorus; Mrchg Band; Pep Band; School Play; Treas Frsh Cls.

BRUBACHER, KATE E; Newton Sr HS; North Newton, KS; (2); 22/280; Art Clb; Church Yth Grp; Drama Clb; German Clb; Key Clb; Model UN; Thesps; Church Choir; Orch; School Play; Slct Cmnty Choir; Chrch Yth Grp & Key Clb Offcr.

BRUBAKER, DARIN A; Shawnee Heights Sr HS; Topeka, KS; (2); FBLA; Scholastic Bowl; Bsktbl; JV Ftbl; JV Var Trk; High Hon Roll; NHS; Prfct Atten Awd; KS Bd Of Regents Hnrs Acad Smmr 96; Sci Olympiad Gold Medalist 95-96.

BRUBAKER, KELLIE J; Shawnee Heights HS; Topeka, KS; (1); Intnl Clb; NFL; Pep Clb; Chorus; Drill Tm; Hon Roll; Ballet, Tap & Jazz Classes; Piano & Vocal Lessons; KS ST U; Elem Tchr.

BRUCE, BRAD T; Shawnee Mission N HS; Roeland Park, KS; (2); Boy Scts; Debate Tm; Pep Clb; ROTC; Color Guard; Drill Tm; Socr; Hon Roll; Mtn Biking; Johnson Cnty Prmr Sccr League; KS Univ.

BRUCE, CYNTHIA L; Independence HS; Independence, KS; (2); French Clb; FTA; Teachers Aide; Band; Chorus; Flag Corp; School Musical; Hon Roll; KAYS; Pittsburg St Univ; Elem Ed.

BRUCE, HOPE; St Thomas Aquinas HS; Shawnee Mission, KS; (2); Cmnty Wkr; Model UN; Ski Clb; Pres Stu Cncl; JV Chrldng; Var Mgr(s); Var Powder Puff Ftbl; Hon Roll; Pres Acad Fit Awd; Show Choir; U Of KS; Medicine.

BRUCKER, JENNY; Syracuse Jr Sr HS; Syracuse, KS; (2); 6/30; Art Clb; Church Yth Grp; Cmnty Wkr; Drama Clb; 4-H; Letterman Clb; Pep Clb; Quiz Bowl; Speech Tm; Band; KS U; Med Tech.

BRUCKERHOFF, TRACI L; Manhattan HS; Manhattan, KS; (4); 150/368; Church Yth Grp; FCA; French Clb; Natl FFA Org; SADD; JV Crs Cntry; Powder Puff Ftbl; Var Socr; JV Trk; Stat Wrstlng; Rodeo Clb Sec/Treas; KS ST U; Rec/Park Admin.

BRUEY, JAROD D; Caldwell Jr Sr HS; Caldwell, KS; (3); 4-H; Math Tm; JV Bsktbl; L Ftbl; Trk; Hon Roll.

BRUGGEMAN, NICOLE; Golden Plains HS; Rexford, KS; (3); 5/16; Church Yth Grp; Letterman Clb; Pep Clb; Chorus; Co-Ed Yrbk; Sec Frsh Cls; Rep Jr Cls; Rep Sr Cls; Sec Stu Cncl; JV Var Bsktbl; Cnstsnt Shrdn Cty Jr MS Aug; Ft Hays ST; Acctg.

BRULEZ, KRISTY; St Thomas Aquinas HS; Olathe, KS; (3); Cmnty Wkr; Ski Clb; Rep Soph Cls; Chrldng; Diving; Powder Puff Ftbl; NCA Chrldr; KU.

BRUMBACK, JEANA M; Arkansas City HS; Arkansas City, KS; (3); Church Yth Grp; FCA; Red Cross Aide; SADD; Chorus; Church Choir; Rep Stu Cncl; Stat Trk; Hon Roll; Paramedic.

BRUMBACK, JESSICA; Columbus HS; Columbus, KS; (2); Bus Profs of Am; Band; Drill Tm; Mrchg Band; Rptr Phtg Nwsp; Golf; Hon Roll; 1st Pl 4a Yrbk Photo Reg Schlstc Press Assn; KS Assn Ldrshp Conf 1st Pl Document Formatting BPA; Med.

BRUMLEY, AARON K; Logan Jr HS; Topeka, KS; (1); 1/150; Band; Jazz Band; L Ftbl; JV Tennis; Cit Awd; High Hon Roll; Pres Acad Fit Awd; Band; Sci; Math; Sci Field.

BRUMLEY, WILLIAM J; Lawrence HS; Lawrence, KS; (2); Rep Drama Clb; Thesps; Acpl Chr; Band; School Play; Stage Crew; Variety Show; Cit Awd; High Hon Roll; Hon Roll; Smmr Yth Theatr; Mus Theatr.

BRUMMER, JENNIFER; Tipton HS; Tipton, KS; (3); Math Tm; Quiz Bowl; Drm Mjr(t); Pep Band; Sec Jr Cls; Var L Bsktbl; Var Chrldng; Var Trk; Var L Vllybl; NHS; KS ST U; Dieticn.

BRUMMER, LAURA; St John's HS; Beloit, KS; (3); Sec Treas Church Yth Grp; Pres VP Pep Clb; Quiz Bowl; Speech Tm; SADD; Band; Chorus; Pep Band; Yrbk; Sec Soph Cls; Math Relays; Careers 2000; Scl Work.

BRUMMER, TARA; Tipton HS; Hunter, KS; (4); 5/12; Am Leg Aux Girls St; Yrbk; Treas Frsh Cls; Treas Soph Cls; Sec Sr Cls; Treas Stu Cncl; Capt Bsktbl; Capt Chrldng; Capt Vllybl; Pres Acad Fit Awd; Hnr Roll; Ft Hays St U; Bus.

BRUMSEY, JEHAN; Lawrence HS; Lawrence, KS; (3); Red Cross Aide; Phtg Nwsp; Phtg Yrbk; Rep Soph Cls; Ofcr Stu Cncl; L Bsktbl; L Chrldng; L Var Trk; L Vllybl; RIT; Photojournalism.

BRUMWELL, SEAN C; Shawnee Mission E Sr HS; Shawnee Mission, KS; (4); Natl Beta Clb; Band; Mrchg Band; Swing Chorus; JV Trk; Intrml Vllybl; High Hon Roll; NHS; Ntl Merit SF; KS City Flute Choir; Natl Mrt Fnlst & KS Hnrs Schlr; 4r Natl Fncng Olympcs; U Of KS; Engrng Physics.

BRUNA, KRIS A; Hanover Schl; Hanover, KS; (4); 11/22; Pres FBLA; VP FHA; Letterman Clb; Hist Natl FFA Org; Office Aide; Stage Crew; Nwsp; Yrbk; Treas Stu Cncl; High Hon Roll; Vlybl; Southeast CC; Agribus.

BRUNA, TRACY; Hanover Schl; Hanover, KS; (4); 4/23; Am Leg Aux Girls St; Church Yth Grp; FHA; Letterman Clb; Teachers Aide; Treas Jr Cls; Vllybl; High Hon Roll; Hon Roll; NHS; Christmas Ball Qn; Elem Educ.

BRUNE, DANIEL K; Olathe South Sr HS; Olathe, KS; (4); 43/359; Boy Scts; Church Yth Grp; Q&S; Science Clb; Spanish Clb; Orch; Rptr Nwsp; Rep Frsh Cls; Hon Roll; NHS; Eagle Scout; Schl Lit Magazine; Sci Olympiad; U Of KS; Ed; Soc Stud.

BRUNER, JASON E; Central Heights Sr HS; Richmond, KS; (1); FCA; 4-H; Spanish Clb; Band; Mrchg Band; Pep Band; JV Bsktbl; Var Crs Cntry; Var Trk; High Hon Roll; Lawyer.

BRUNER, JEREMY E; Augusta Sr HS; Augusta, KS; (3); Band; Mrchg Band; Pep Band; Rep Frsh Cls; Rep Soph Cls; Rep Jr Cls; Pres Sr Cls; Rep Stu Cncl; NHS; Office Aide; Renaissance Comm; Schl Dist Imprvmnt Comm; Emporia ST Univ; Msc Ed.

BRUNER, JOSEPH L; Clearwater HS; Clearwater, KS; (2); Zoologist.

BRUNGARDT, AMANDA L; Victoria HS; Gorham, KS; (4); 8/25; 4-H; FHA; Letterman Clb; Model UN; NFL; Pep Clb; SADD; Chorus; Bsktbl; Powder Puff Ftbl; Voice Dmcrcy 2nd Plc; Ft Hays ST Univ.

BRUNGARDT, BRANDON J; Garden City Sr HS; Garden City, KS; (2); Church Yth Grp; Spanish Clb; Rep Soph Cls; Var Bsbl; Bsktbl; JV Var Ftbl; Wt Lftg; Hon Roll; Chf Squir For Knights Of Columbus; Pres For Comm Vision Now Yth Advsry Comm; Topeka Univ; Optom.

BRUNGARDT, COLETTE L; Wichita East HS; Wichita, KS; (4); Treas Church Yth Grp; Chorus; School Musical; Stage Crew; French Hon Soc; NHS; Intl Bcclrt Pgm; Grl Sct Gld Slvr Awds; Msc Thtr Wcht Intrn; Thtr Arts.

BRUNGARDT, JESSICA L; Hays HS; Hays, KS; (4); Art Clb; Church Yth Grp; Band; Chorus; Mrchg Band; Pep Band; Hon Roll; Video Prod; Ft Hays ST U; Telecomm.

BRUNGARDT, NICK J; Hays HS; Hays, KS; (1); Church Yth Grp; Ftbl; Wt Lftg; Hon Roll.

BRUNHOEBER, AMY C; Wichita Southeast HS; Wichita, KS; (2); Church Yth Grp; Cmnty Wkr; Drama Clb; Girl Scts; Hosp Aide; Varsity Clb; Church Choir; Orch; School Musical; Stage Crew; KU; Musical Thrpst.

BRUNING, BRETT P; Ellsworth HS; Ellsworth, KS; (2); 7/90; Treas Church Yth Grp; Band; Chorus; Mrchg Band; Swing Chorus; Pres Frsh Cls; Pres Soph Cls; JV Crs Cntry; Var Tennis; High Hon Roll; KMEA Fest Choir; Ellswth HS Outschoir; KS Masonc All St HS Bnd; KSU.

BRUNK, JAMIE A; Berean Acad; Wichita, KS; (4); Church Yth Grp; Office Aide; Speech Tm; School Play; Ed Nwsp; Ed Yrbk; Cit Awd; Hon Roll; Hosp Vistation Group; Babysitter; John Brown U; Print Jrnlsm.

BRUNKHARDT, AUSTIN; Sublette HS; Garden City, KS; (2); Church Yth Grp; Band; Mrchg Band; Pep Band; Garden City Comm Coll; Comp Sci.

BRUNN, DANIELLE; Rossville HS; Rossville, KS; (2); 11/40; Debate Tm; FBLA; HOBY; Letterman Clb; NFL; Speech Tm; Chorus; Var Chrldng; Var Golf; Pres Acad Fit Awd; John Halula Memrl Awd; CO ST; Microbio.

BRUNS, ADAM; Olathe East Sr HS; Olathe, KS; (3); Church Yth Grp; Letterman Clb; Spanish Clb; SADD; Varsity Clb; Band; Church Choir; JV Computer Clb; Hon Roll.

BRUNS, AMANDA L; Blue Valley North HS; Overland Park, KS; (3); Church Yth Grp; Cmnty Wkr; Debate Tm; Math Clb; Math Tm; Model UN; Q&S; Teachers Aide; Stage Crew; Ed Yrbk; Truman ST U; Math.

BRUNTON, KYLIE; Wichita North HS; Wichita, KS; (4); 17/274; Church Yth Grp; Drama Clb; Q&S; Chorus; Drill Tm; School Musical; Variety Show; Yrbk; Rep Frsh Cls; Rep Soph Cls; Environmental Clb; Prom Comm; Psych.

BRUSCHI, DENISE E; Blue Valley HS; Leawood, KS; (4); 2/230; 4-H; Intnl Clb; Letterman Clb; Red Cross Aide; Chrmn Band; Drm Mjr(t); Mrchg Band; Pep Band; School Musical; Capt Socr; Intl Exch Stu; Stu Trnr; U Of NC; Physcl Thpy.

BRYAM, BRANDI; Shawnee Mission E Sr HS; Mission Woods, KS; (4); School Play; Chrldng; Gym; Powder Puff Ftbl; Tennis; Wt Lftg; High Hon Roll; Hon Roll; NHS; 1st Yr Schlrshp Pen; U Of KS; Liberal Arts.

BRYAN, ERICH; Heights HS; Wichita, KS; (4); 90/247; Church Yth Grp; German Clb; SADD; Teachers Aide; Var Capt Bsbl; JV Var Crs Cntry; Hon Roll; St Schlr; Galaxy Awd 96; Bsbl 2nd Tm All City/All ST 94/1st Tm All City/All ST 95-; MVP 95-; Wichita ST Univ; Pre-Med.

BRYAN, JAMIE E; Lansing HS; Lansing, KS; (4); Church Yth Grp; French Clb; Hon Roll; Bio.

BRYAN, JANNA L; Blue Valley HS; Overland Park, KS; (2); 4-H; Pres Frsh Cls; Pres Soph Cls; Pres Jr Cls; Rep Stu Cncl; Var Tennis; Var Trk; Phtg 4-H Awd; Hon Roll; Optimist Club Awd; KS ST Univ; Law Enfrcement.

BRYAN, JASON P; Ottawa HS; Ottawa, KS; (3); Boy Scts; Church Yth Grp; FCA; 4-H; SADD; Teachers Aide; Ftbl; High Hon Roll; Hon Roll; Natl Grd Boy Sct Explorer Grp Adv; KS ST Univ; Engr/ROTC.

BRYAN, JOAN R; Valley Ctr HS; Valley Center, KS; (3); Church Yth Grp; Chorus; Church Choir; School Musical; Stage Crew; Variety Show; Yth Alive.

BRYAN, LAURA; Wichita North HS; Wichita, KS; (4); 14/247; Church Yth Grp; Q&S; Ed Yrbk; VP Sr Cls; Ofcr Stu Cncl; Var L Chrldng; Var L Socr; L Capt Vllybl; NHS; St Schlr; Baker U; Med.

BRYANT, CHRISSY; Atwood HS; Atwood, KS; (3); Am Leg Aux Girls St; Church Yth Grp; GAA; Letterman Clb; School Play; Var Bsktbl; Var Chrldng; Var Vllybl; Wt Lftg; Hon Roll; Xenon; Csmtlgy.

BRYANT, EMILY; Olathe East Sr HS; Lenexa, KS; (3); 1/380; Dance Clb; Debate Tm; Drama Clb; French Clb; NFL; Powder Puff Ftbl; Var Trk; High Hon Roll; VP NHS; Pres Schlr; Publshd Natl Lib Of Poetrys Memories Of Tomorrow 96; Dance/PT.

BRYANT, JENNIFER A; Topeka West HS; Topeka, KS; (4); 138/239; Math Tm; U Of KS; Nurs.

BRYANT, JOSHUA R; Central Heights Sr HS; Princeton, KS; (2); Church Yth Grp; Letterman Clb; Scholastic Bowl; Science Clb; Spanish Clb; Band; Chorus; High Hon Roll; Prfct Atten Awd; Pres Acad Fit Awd; Meteorology.

BRYANT, KENDRA M; Liberal HS; Liberal, KS; (3); Church Yth Grp; Pres Drama Clb; NFL; Chorus; Drill Tm; School Musical; VP Soph Cls; VP Jr Cls; Var Chrldng; NHS; Show Choir; HOBY Fnlst.

BRYANT, MC CLAIN E; Sumner Acad Of Arts & Science; Kansas City, KS; (1); French Clb; Latin Clb; Chorus; Trk; Vllybl; Pres Acad Fit Awd; Explorer Scouts At KU Med Ctr; MO Democratic Party Vol; Freedom Inc Vol; Howard; Med.

BRYANT, MICHAEL; South Gray HS; Copeland, KS; (3); Letterman Clb; Spanish Clb; Chorus; Var Bsktbl; Var Ftbl; Trk; Hon Roll; NHS.

BRYANT, REBECCA J; Washington HS; Washington, KS; (3); 1/40; Art Clb; Church Yth Grp; FHA; HOBY; Band; Var L Trk; Var L Vllybl; NHS; FCA; Girl Scts; Girl Sct Slvr Awd, Pres.

BRYSON, JESSICA; Riley Cty HS; Riley, KS; (4); 3/36; Am Leg Aux Girls St; Debate Tm; Treas FHA; Pep Clb; SADD; Teachers Aide; School Play; Stage Crew; Yrbk; Treas Jr Cls; KS Spclty Dog Svc Puppy Rsr; Med.

BUBLITZ, ERICH; Lawrence HS; Lawrence, KS; (3); Am Leg Boys St; Boy Scts; Computer Clb; Debate Tm; Drama Clb; NFL; Thesps; Stage Crew; Hon Roll; Lawrence Assn Of Particle Physics Stud; Lawrence Pub Schls Comp Dev Group; Info Sys.

BUCCIGROSSI, MICHELLE A; Salina HS South; Salina, KS; (2); 60/300; VP Church Yth Grp; FCA; Band; Mrchg Band; Pep Band; Sec Jr Cls; Rep Stu Cncl; Var Golf; Hon Roll; Prfct Atten Awd; Habitat For Hmnty; KS St Univ; Ed.

BUCHANAN, AMBER; Shawnee Heights Sr HS; Topeka, KS; (4); Church Yth Grp; Speech Tm; Teachers Aide; Thesps; Band; School Musical; School Play; Stage Crew; Nwsp; Hon Roll; Emporia U; Animation.

BUCHANAN, BRENT; Goddard HS; Goddard, KS; (4); Science Clb; Spanish Clb; Teachers Aide; Var Bsbl; Var Bsktbl; Wt Lftg; Hon Roll; NHS; Friends Univ; Bus Admin.

BUCHANAN, BRYCE W; Minneola Schl; Minneola, KS; (3); 4-H; Math Tm; Speech Tm; Band; Chorus; Church Choir; Jazz Band; Mrchg Band; Pep Band; School Musical; Chrstn Yth Work Camp Did Repairs From Hurricane Andrew.

BUCHANAN, JESSICA Y; Wichita North HS; Wichita, KS; (2); 61/160; Office Aide; Chorus; Variety Show; VP Frsh Cls; High Hon Roll; Hon Roll; Clb 98; KS Newman; Neo-Natal Nrsng.

BUCHANAN, JULIE E; Southeast HS; Wichita, KS; (4); 23/300; Cmnty Wkr; Teachers Aide; Band; Church Choir; Mrchg Band; Orch; Hon Roll; NHS; AP Dstngshd Schlr; Rehab Hosp Vol; U Of KS; Occupthrpy.

BUCHE, AARON; Frontenac Jr Sr HS; Frontenac, KS; (4); #1 in class; Am Leg Boys St; Art Clb; Spanish Clb; Varsity Clb; Pres Frsh Cls; Pres Soph Cls; Pres Jr Cls; Pres Sr Cls; L Bsbl; L Bsktbl.

BUCHER, JAKE W; Oskaloosa HS; Oskaloosa, KS; (2); Church Yth Grp; FCA; FBLA; Letterman Clb; Scholastic Bowl; SADD; JV Var Bsbl; JV Var Bsktbl; Var Crs Cntry; JV Ftbl; U Of AZ; Crim Just.

BUCHHEISTER, MENDY D; Manhattan HS; Manhattan, KS; (3); Church Yth Grp; Cmnty Wkr; FCA; GAA; Spanish Clb; SADD; Chorus; Church Choir; Variety Show; Bsktbl; Piano; Show Choir; Chld Psych.

BUCHMUELLER, DANIEL J; Pratt HS; Pratt, KS; (3); FCA; Scholastic Bowl; Speech Tm; SADD; Band; Chorus; School Musical; Hon Roll; Church Yth Grp; Key Clb; Southwestern Coll; OT.

BUCHWALD, BRENT A; Salina HS South; Salina, KS; (2); 118/292; Church Yth Grp; Letterman Clb; Band; Mrchg Band; Ftbl; Hon Roll; KS ST U; Engrng.

BUCK, BRIAN D; Bishop Miege HS; Roeland Park, KS; (2); 79/155; Church Yth Grp; Socr; Trk; Cit Awd; Hon Roll.

BUCK, JORDAN R; Washburn Rural HS; Topeka, KS; (2); 68/380; Cmnty Wkr; JV Bsbl; JV Ftbl; JV Wt Lftg; High Hon Roll; U Of KS; Bus.

BUCKLAND, CARRIE E; Topeka HS; Topeka, KS; (3); 4/348; Cmnty Wkr; Intnl Clb; Service Clb; Spanish Clb; Cit Awd; High Hon Roll; NHS; Soujourners, Fearless & Anti Violence Clbs.

BUCKLEY, MELISSA A; Wyandotte HS; Kansas City, KS; (1); Church Yth Grp; 4-H; Hosp Aide; SADD; Nrsng Home Vol; KS Univ; Vet Asst.

BUCKMAN, LUKE J; Anderson Cty Jr Sr HS; Greeley, KS; (2); Church Choir; JV Bsktbl; JV Ftbl; High Hon Roll; KS U.

BUCL, LUCAS; Sublette HS; Sublette, KS; (2); 1/40; Boy Scts; Church Yth Grp; Letterman Clb; Pres Soph Cls; Rep Stu Cncl; JV Bsktbl; Var Ftbl; JV Golf; High Hon Roll; NHS.

BUCZINSKI, ERICA M; Goddard HS; Wichita, KS; (1); Church Yth Grp; Chorus; High Hon Roll; Pres Acad Fit Awd; Honor Choir; Acad Letter; Jrnlsm/Psych.

BUDDEN, SARA; Abilene HS; Abilene, KS; (4); 1/125; Am Leg Aux Girls St; Cmnty Wkr; Pres Sr Cls; Ofcr Stu Cncl; Bsktbl; Trk; High Hon Roll; NHS; Pres Acad Fit Awd; Val; Jr HS Girls Bsktbl Coach; KS ST U.

BUDHRAM, GAVIN R; Olathe South Sr HS; Olathe, KS; (4); 1/350; Drama Clb; Math Clb; Spanish Clb; Band; Mrchg Band; Pep Band; School Musical; School Play; Stage Crew; Rptr Nwsp; Slvr Mdl Natl Ltn Exam; Natl Hspnc Schlr; KS ST U; Med.

BUDHRAM, IAN; Indian Trail Jr HS; Olathe, KS; (2); Debate Tm; Quiz Bowl; Science Clb; Teachers Aide; Chorus; Crs Cntry; High Hon Roll; Knowledge Bowl.

BUDIG, HEATHER J; Great Bend Sr HS; Great Bend, KS; (2); Church Yth Grp; Pep Clb; Spanish Clb; Variety Show; Rep Frsh Cls; Ofcr Stu Cncl; Var Chrldng; Gym; Sftbl; Hon Roll; Frosh & Soph Peer Cnslr; Kayettes; U Of KS; Med.

BUDKE, STACEY; Tipton HS; Tipton, KS; (4); 1/12; Drama Clb; Math Tm; Pep Clb; Speech Tm; Teachers Aide; Band; Chorus; Church Choir; Mrchg Band; Pep Band; Brwn Mck Coll; Crmnl Jstc.

BUECHMAN, JOSEPH R; Larned HS; Larned, KS; (3); 20/100; Am Leg Boys St; Church Yth Grp; Teachers Aide; Rptr Yrbk; JV Var Ftbl; Var L Golf; Var L Wrstlng; Hon Roll; Golf Course Supt.

BUEHLER, JANA; North Central HS; Haddam, KS; (3); 3/10; Pres FBLA; VP FHA; Natl FFA Org; Speech Tm; Pres SADD; School Play; Swing Chorus; Pres Jr Cls; Ofcr Stu Cncl; Var Bsktbl; Commnctn.

BUENO, RENEE G; Garden City Sr HS; Garden City, KS; (1); FHA; Spanish Clb; Orch; Bsktbl; JV Sftbl; High Hon Roll; Orch Awds/Letter.

BUESSING, DALE; Axtell Schl; Axtell, KS; (4); 3/16; VP Letterman Clb; Quiz Bowl; Teachers Aide; Band; Chorus; Pep Band; Bsktbl; Ftbl; Trk; High Hon Roll; Manhatten Ave Vo Tech; Elec Pwr.

BUESSING, JAMES; Marysville HS; Marysville, KS; (4); 13/83; Debate Tm; Drama Clb; FCA; NFL; Band; Mrchg Band; Pep Band; Pres Stu Cncl; Wrstlng; High Hon Roll; KS ST U; Bus Admin.

BUESSING, SHAWN; B & B HS; Baileyville, KS; (3); 2/13; Church Yth Grp; CAP; 4-H; FBLA; HOBY; Quiz Bowl; Scholastic Bowl; Band; Orch; Pep Band; CYO Pres; 4-H Clb Pres; Geolgy, Frstry Clb Ldr; KS ST U; Engrng.

BUETZER, CASEY; Nemaha Valley HS; Seneca, KS; (2); 4-H; Speech Tm; Drill Tm; School Play; Rep Stu Cncl; Var Chrldng; Var Trk; JV Vllybl; High Hon Roll; Prfct Atten Awd; KS ST U; Advrtsng.

BUETZER, SARA; Nemaha Valley HS; Seneca, KS; (4); 6/54; Drama Clb; 4-H; Letterman Clb; SADD; Drill Tm; Pep Band; Swing Chorus; Yrbk; Pres Jr Cls; Pres Stu Cncl; Prin Ldrshp Awd; KSU Ldrshp Awd; KS U Manhattn; Elem Ed.

BUFFINGTON, AMY M; Labette Co HS; Altamont, KS; (2); Hosp Aide; SADD; Hon Roll; KS Assn Of Yth Club.

BUFFINGTON, JENNIFER A; Labette Co HS; Altamont, KS; (2); FHA; Hosp Aide; SADD; Hon Roll; Paramedics Club; KS Assn Of Yth Club; Psych.

BUFFINGTON, SAMI J; Southeast HS; Cherokee, KS; (4); 4/52; French Clb; German Clb; Scholastic Bowl; Science Clb; School Play; Nwsp; Sec Jr Cls; Sec Sr Cls; High Hon Roll; NHS; Col Of Ozarks; Dietcs.

BUGGELN, MICHELLE; Augusta Sr HS; Augusta, KS; (4); Am Leg Aux Girls St; Church Yth Grp; Band; Chorus; Capt Flag Corp; School Musical; Rep Stu Cncl; Mgr(s); High Hon Roll; NHS; OK Chrstn U Sci/Arts; Scpl Ed.

BUI, THANH M; Wichita East HS; Wichita, KS; (4); JV Ftbl; Var Trk; Hon Roll; Wichita ST; Psych.

BUITRON, GABRIELA D; Sumner Acad Of Arts & Science; Topeka, KS; (4); 27/193; Church Yth Grp; French Clb; Pep Clb; Stage Crew; French Hon Soc; High Hon Roll; Hon Roll; NHS; 1st Pl Wmns Rghts Essay Cntst; Cnsrvtry; Chrch Drama Dir; Mid-Amer Nazarene Coll; Comms.

BULK, JANA; Humboldt HS; Humboldt, KS; (4); Church Yth Grp; Dance Clb; Girl Scts; Chorus; Church Choir; Orch; School Musical; School Play; Stage Crew; Variety Show; Psych; Piano; KS ST Univ; Vet.

BULL, CHAD M; Shawnee Heights HS; Topeka, KS; (1); Boy Scts; Math Tm; Model UN; Office Aide; Hon Roll; Pres Acad Fit Awd.

BULLARD, COURTNEY F; Bishop Miege HS; Shawnee, KS; (1); 27/265; French Clb; Ofcr Frsh Cls; Ofcr Bsbl; Bsktbl; JV Socr; High Hon Roll.

BULLARD, KATHY; Shanee Heights HS; Topeka, KS; (3); Debate Tm; Pep Clb; Thesps; Band; Chrldng; Trk; Hon Roll; Prfct Atten Awd; Bio-Engrng.

BULLER, CARMEN; Hillsboro HS; Hillsboro, KS; (3); 11/67; Rep Church Yth Grp; Quiz Bowl; Band; Chorus; Mrchg Band; Pep Band; School Play; JV Trk; High Hon Roll; Sec Ed.

BULLER, ERICA A; Hesston HS; Hesston, KS; (2); Church Yth Grp; FCA; Pres FBLA; Chorus; School Musical; Var L Bsktbl; Mgr(s); Var L Tennis; Var L Trk; Hon Roll; Worship Team-Chrch; Tchr.

BULLER, PATRICK; Hillsboro HS; Hillsboro, KS; (1); 6/71; Church Yth Grp; Band; Chorus; Mrchg Band; Pep Band; JV Crs Cntry; JV Golf; High Hon Roll.

BULLER, WADE T; Clearwater HS; Clearwater, KS; (4); 15/87; SADD; Chorus; School Musical; School Play; Rep Frsh Cls; Rep Soph Cls; Rep Jr Cls; Rep Sr Cls; Rep Stu Cncl; Var Bsktbl; Cowley Cty CC; Bus; Acctnt.

BULLOCK, BRITTIAN M; Olathe East Sr HS; Olathe, KS; (2); Boy Scts; Q&S; Spanish Clb; Teachers Aide; Thesps; Acpl Chr; School Musical; School Play; Lit Mag; Hon Roll; SASH; Columbia Univ; Frgn Pol Anlyst.

BULLOCK, DAVID; Syracuse Jr Sr HS; Syracuse, KS; (4); 5/29; Church Yth Grp; Drama Clb; Letterman Clb; Varsity Clb; Band; Chorus; Yrbk; Var L Ftbl; Var Wt Lftg; Hon Roll; Music.

BULLOCK, KELLI A; Olathe East Sr HS; Olathe, KS; (3); Cmnty Wkr; French Clb; Teachers Aide; Mgr(s); Swmmng; Hon Roll; Vol YMCA; U Of KS; Spec Ed/Elem Ed.

BUMGARNER, JENNIFER; Field Kindley Mem Sr HS; Coffeyville, KS; (4); 8/141; Am Leg Aux Girls St; Debate Tm; Drama Clb; NFL; Band; School Musical; School Play; Trk; High Hon Roll; NHS; Coffeyville CC; Psycht.

BUNCE, JOSH A; Riverton Schl; Baxter Springs, KS; (2); Math Clb; Math Tm; Art Clb; Church Yth Grp; Pep Clb; Quiz Bowl; Spanish Clb; Ofcr Soph Cls; Score Keeper; Hon Roll; KS U; Ministry.

BUNCE, TOM J; Riverton Schl; Baxter Springs, KS; (3); Art Clb; Church Yth Grp; Natl FFA Org; Central Univ; Ranger.

BUNCH, MALENA J; Sumner Acad Of Arts & Science; Kansas City, KS; (1); Church Yth Grp; Latin Clb; Pep Clb; Spanish Clb; Chorus; Church Choir; Bsktbl; KU.

BUNCK, BOBBIE A; Horton HS; Everest, KS; (4); 9/59; Church Yth Grp; Library Aide; Pep Clb; Teachers Aide; Treas Jr Cls; Treas Sr Cls; Var Bsktbl; Var Chrldng; Var Trk; Var Vllybl; KS ST Univ; Agribus.

BUNCK, MARIE A; Horton HS; Everest, KS; (2); 1/80; Church Yth Grp; Pres 4-H; Scholastic Bowl; Band; Jazz Band; Bsktbl; Chrldng; Crs Cntry; Trk; High Hon Roll; KS ST Univ.

BUNKER, LESLIE J; Olathe East Sr HS; Olathe, KS; (2); Church Yth Grp; Office Aide; Pep Clb; Teachers Aide; Chorus; Orch; Hon Roll; Jr NHS; Peds Nrs.

BUNTAIN, JESSICA R; Topeka HS; Topeka, KS; (2); Pres French Clb; Girl Scts; Model UN; Band; Mrchg Band; Pep Band; Bsktbl; JV Socr; High Hon Roll; Hrsbk Rdg; Astrnmy/Astro Physics.

BURBACH, DARSHA H; Trego Comm HS; Collyer, KS; (2); 39/60; Church Yth Grp; Letterman Clb; Pep Clb; Bsktbl; Mgr(s); Powder Puff Ftbl; Tennis; Wt Lftg; Hon Roll; Ofcr FHA; KS ST Univ; Dr.

BURCH, TODD; Syracuse Jr Sr HS; Syracuse, KS; (2); FCA; Letterman Clb; Teachers Aide; Var Bsktbl; Var Ftbl; OK ST Univ.

BURCH, WENDEE; Holcomb HS; Holcomb, KS; (3); 1/63; Church Yth Grp; HOBY; Pres Key Clb; Pres Natl FFA Org; Quiz Bowl; Chorus; Ofcr Stu Cncl; Vllybl; High Hon Roll; VP NHS; S W OK ST U; Phrmcy.

BURCHAM, GREGG A; Caldwell Jr Sr HS; Caldwell, KS; (2); 2/32; Church Yth Grp; FCA; Math Tm; Pep Clb; Quiz Bowl; Scholastic Bowl; Speech Tm; SADD; Band; Chorus; TEAMS.

BURCHETT, CASSIE L; Independence HS; Independence, KS; (1); Church Yth Grp; FCA; NFL; Pep Clb; SADD; Band; Chorus; Church Choir; Mrchg Band; Orch; KS U.

BURCHETT, JAMI D; Paola HS; Paola, KS; (4); 17/123; Cmnty Wkr; FCA; Science Clb; SADD; Teachers Aide; Chorus; Ofcr Stu Cncl; Trk; Vllybl; High Hon Roll; Ftbl Statctn; USVBA Clb Natl Qlfr; Envrnmntl Clb; Barton Cty CC; PT.

BURCHETT, JENNIFER; Wakefield Schl; Longford, KS; (2); Church Yth Grp; FHA; Pep Clb; SADD; Band; Mrchg Band; Pep Band; Var Bsbl; JV Bsktbl; Var Chrldng; Chrch Yth Grp Pres; Pediatrician.

BURCHETT, JONI; Paola HS; Paola, KS; (3); Cmnty Wkr; FCA; FHA; Pep Clb; SADD; Teachers Aide; Var Chrldng; Var Vllybl; Hon Roll; Jr Olympic Vllybl; Tutoring; KAYS; Elem Ed; Kndgtn Tchr.

BURCHETT IV, LAWRENCE R; St Thomas Aquinas HS; Overland Park, KS; (3); 16/261; Am Leg Boys St; Cmnty Wkr; FBLA; Rptr Nwsp; Rep Soph Cls; VP Stu Cncl; Var L Ftbl; NHS; Ntl Merit Ltr; JV Bsbl; Presdtnl Hnr Roll; Clean Team ATOD Free; Forensics; Pre Med/Cardvsclr Surg.

BURDETTE, DONALD E; Washington HS; Kansas City, KS; (2); Church Yth Grp; Spanish Clb; Band; Church Choir; Bsktbl; Hon Roll; NHS; KS U; Engrng.

BURDGE, AMY; Meade HS; Meade, KS; (3); Library Aide; Hon Roll; Super Reader Awd.

BURDGE, SARAH J; Meade HS; Meade, KS; (1); Cit Awd; Hon Roll; Prfct Atten Awd.

BURDICK, AMY; Andover HS; Andover, KS; (1); 1/210; Church Yth Grp; Pep Clb; Band; Flag Corp; Yrbk; Chrldng; High Hon Roll; Running; Theater; KS ST U; Dietician.

BURDICK, JUSTIN M; Jackson Heights HS; Whiting, KS; (2); Natl FFA Org; JV Ftbl; Hon Roll; Prfct Atten Awd.

BURGARDT, SHANNON; Hays HS; Hays, KS; (4); Cmnty Wkr; Hosp Aide; Red Cross Aide; Spanish Clb; High Hon Roll; Hon Roll; Pres Acad Fit Awd; Ft Hays ST Univ.

BURGE, ENOCKISHAD M; Shawnee Mission E Sr HS; Shawnee Mission, KS; (4); 105/400; Natl Beta Clb; High Hon Roll; Hon Roll; NHS; Prfct Atten Awd; Pres Schlr; Minority Yth Rcgntn Awd; Devry; Bus Hmn Rsrcs.

BURGER, PATRICK S; Bishop Miege HS; Lenexa, KS; (1); 74/247; Boy Scts; NFL; Quiz Bowl; SADD; Wrstlng; Hon Roll; Pres Acad Fit Awd; Univ Of KSED.

BURGESS, ANDREA L; White Rock HS; Esbon, KS; (4); 8/17; Church Yth Grp; Letterman Clb; Pep Clb; SADD; Yrbk; Sec Sr Cls; Var L Bsktbl; Var L Chrldng; Var L Crs Cntry; Var L Trk; Crs Cntry/Trck Schlsp; USAR Natl Schlr Ath Awd; All Lg Vlybl; Hnr Mntn Bsbl; ST Trck; Colby CC; PT Asst.

BURGESS, CARMEN; Colby Sr HS; Colby, KS; (4); 2/99; VP Church Yth Grp; FCA; Pres French Clb; Band; Swing Chorus; Rep Nwsp; Capt Bsktbl; Var Crs Cntry; Var Trk; Var Vllybl; KU Hnr Schlr; US Army Rsrv Natl Schlr, Athl Awd; Tandy Tech Schlrs Chmpns; Evangel; Phys Asst.

BURGESS, JUSTIN; Ulysses HS; Ulysses, KS; (3); Church Yth Grp; Debate Tm; NFL; SADD; Chorus; School Musical; Swing Chorus; Var Golf; High Hon Roll; NHS.

BURGESS, KEVIN M; Sumner Acad Of Arts & Science; Shawnee Mission, KS; (4); 40/200; Cmnty Wkr; Debate Tm; 4-H; French Clb; SADD; Trk; Hon Roll; NHS; KCK CC.

BURGEY, DAWN R; Fairfield HS; Sylvia, KS; (3); Church Yth Grp; FCA; Hosp Aide; Speech Tm; SADD; Acpl Chr; Chorus; School Musical; School Play; Hon Roll; Friends Univ.

BURHENN, JASON P; Great Bend Sr HS; Great Bend, KS; (3); Church Yth Grp; DECA; FHA; Pep Clb; Teachers Aide; Bsktbl; Ftbl; Trk; Wt Lftg; Hon Roll; KS ST; Tchr.

BURKART, RYAN D; Maur Hill Prep Schl; Rushville, MO; (1); Boy Scts; Church Yth Grp; Ofcr Bsbl; Bsktbl; High Hon Roll; Dr.

BURKDOLL, JEFFREY S; Marais Des Cygnes Valley HS; Melvern, KS; (3); Am Leg Boys St; 4-H; Letterman Clb; Natl FFA Org; Stage Crew; Nwsp; Yrbk; Treas Frsh Cls; Treas Soph Cls; Rep Jr Cls.

BURKDOLL, SHANNON F; Central Heights Sr HS; Rantoul, KS; (3); Sec Art Clb; Sec Rep 4-H; FBLA; Letterman Clb; Hist Natl FFA Org; Spanish Clb; Rptr Nwsp; JV Var Crs Cntry; High Hon Roll; NHS; Allen Cty CC; Jrnlsm/Agribus.

BURKE, ALLISON; Prairie View Jr Sr HS; La Cygne, KS; (4); 2/65; Church Yth Grp; Dance Clb; 4-H; Pres FBLA; FHA; VP Letterman Clb; Quiz Bowl; Spanish Clb; Teachers Aide; Chorus; Pittsburg ST U; Nrsng.

BURKE, DANIEL; Maur Hill Prep Schl; Atchison, KS; (3); Pres Frsh Cls; Pres Soph Cls; Pres Jr Cls; Var L Bsbl; Capt L Bsktbl; Var L Ftbl; Var Golf; High Hon Roll; Hon Roll; NHS; Piano; Creighton; Sprts Med.

BURKE, HEATHER E; Wichita West HS; Wichita, KS; (2); Church Yth Grp; Debate Tm; JA; Latin Clb; NFL; Office Aide; Teachers Aide; Ofcr Frsh Cls; Ofcr Soph Cls; Hon Roll; Wasburn Univ; Law.

BURKE, JIMI; Hamilton HS; Hamilton, KS; (1); 1/8; 4-H; FBLA; Quiz Bowl; Pres Frsh Cls; Var Bsktbl; Var Trk; Var Vllybl; 4-H Awd; High Hon Roll; Stu Cncl.

BURKE, KIMBERLY A; Sumner Acad Of Arts & Science; Kansas City, KS; (4); 65/192; VP French Clb; Key Clb; Latin Clb; Pep Clb; Q&S; SADD; Capt Drill Tm; Orch; Yrbk; Swmmng; KS Univ.

BURKE, ROBIN; Topeka West HS; Topeka, KS; (2); Church Yth Grp; Drama Clb; Hosp Aide; JA; Spanish Clb; Chorus; Swmmng; Med Rsrch.

BURKE, SAMANTHA R; Chanute Sr HS; Walnut, KS; (2); FCA; French Clb; Chorus; Phtg Yrbk; Bsktbl; Mgr(s); Hon Roll; Photographer Of Yr 96; KS ST; Zoology.

BURKE, SARA; Frontenac Jr Sr HS; Frontenac, KS; (2); 1/55; Hosp Aide; HOBY; Pep Clb; Spanish Clb; Teachers Aide; Rep Stu Cncl; Bsktbl; Vllybl; Hon Roll; U Of CT; Med.

BURKHART, ERICA; Kinsley HS; Kinsley, KS; (4); 5/36; Chorus; School Musical; Yrbk; Mgr Bsktbl; Var Vllybl; Hon Roll; Pres Schlr; KS Wesleyan U Presdntl Schlrshp; Hnrs Stu; KAYS Sec/Treas, VP; KS Wesleyan U; Elem Ed.

BURKHART, HOLLIE J; Hayden HS; Topeka, KS; (2); Intnl Clb; Pep Clb; Variety Show; Yrbk; Var Chrldng; Hon Roll; Competitive Dance.

BURKHART, KRISTI N; Spearville Jr Sr HS; Spearville, KS; (3); 6/28; Church Yth Grp; Pres Pep Clb; Quiz Bowl; Speech Tm; Teachers Aide; Band; Chorus; Mrchg Band; Pep Band; School Play; Ft Hays ST Univ; Pharm.

BURKHART, LORI; Pratt HS; Pratt, KS; (1); Church Yth Grp; FHA; Pep Clb; Chrldng; Tennis; Trk; Hon Roll.

BURKIN, DAVID T; Tonganoxie HS; Tonganoxie, KS; (4); Letterman Clb; Pep Clb; SADD; Varsity Clb; Bsktbl; High Hon Roll; Pres Acad Fit Awd; Johnson Cty CC.

BURKINDINE, EMILY; St Thomas Aquinas HS; Leawood, KS; (2); #4 in class; Hist FCA; French Clb; Math Tm; Rptr Nwsp; Lit Mag; Var Chrldng; Powder Puff Ftbl; Var Trk; High Hon Roll; Piano; Pub Relations; Commnctn.

BURNETT, ARLO J; Shawnee Mission W Sr HS; Shawnee Mission, KS; (4); High Hon Roll; Pres Acad Fit Awd; KS Hnr Schlr; CO ST U.

BURNETT, JULIA M; Goodland HS; Goodland, KS; (2); 12/87; FHA; VP Frsh Cls; Var Vllybl; Wt Lftg; Hon Roll.

BURNETT, KRIS C; Halstead HS; Halstead, KS; (4); Letterman Clb; Spanish Clb; Var L Bsktbl; JV Golf; Trk; Hon Roll; Ft Hays ST U; Bus Mgmt.

BURNETT, KRISTINA; Prairie View Jr Sr HS; La Cygne, KS; (4); 7/66; Sec Treas Church Yth Grp; Pres 4-H; HOBY; Band; Sec Chorus; Drill Tm; Ed Yrbk; Sec Sr Cls; Vllybl; High Hon Roll; KSU; Nutrition.

BURNETT, LATOYA B; Highland Park HS; Topeka, KS; (1); Orch; Hon Roll; Crtv Wrtng.

BURNETT, LINDSAY; Anderson Cty Jr Sr HS; Garnett, KS; (4); 4/79; Dance Clb; Intnl Clb; NFL; SADD; L Var Chrldng; Var L Mgr(s); Hon Roll; Church Yth Grp; Pep Clb; Quiz Bowl; Octagon Clb; Model Legislature Sgt At Arms; Gifted Hnr Cls; Pittsburg ST Coll; Phy Thrpst.

BURNETT, SEASON; Maize HS; Wichita, KS; (3); Church Yth Grp; Cmnty Wkr; Drama Clb; NFL; Science Clb; Spanish Clb; SADD; Thesps; Chorus; Variety Show; All I Ratings St Reg Solo Comp Vcl; City Lge Swim Tm; Perf Arts.

BURNOR, AMIE S; Independence HS; Cherryvale, KS; (4); 60/141; Pres Church Yth Grp; Pres Sec 4-H; FHA; Hist JCL; NFL; Co-Capt Scholastic Bowl; Science Clb; SADD; Band; Mrchg Band; U Of KS; Jrnlsm.

BURNS, BETHANY D; Newton Sr HS; Newton, KS; (4); Cmnty Wkr; Office Aide; Teachers Aide; Chorus; Swing Chorus; High Hon Roll; Hon Roll; Pres Schlr; St Schlr; KS Hnrs & KS Brd Regent Schlr; Hutchinson CC; Phrmcy.

BURNS, BRANDI; Lakin HS; Lakin, KS; (1); FCA; Pep Clb; Spanish Clb; L Bsktbl; L Chrldng; L Trk; Hon Roll.

BURNS, DARCIE J; Blue Valley Northwest HS; Overland Park, KS; (3); Debate Tm; NFL; Hon Roll; Natl Eng Mrt Awd; Intnl Relations.

BURNS, JENNIFER L; Norton Comm HS; Norton, KS; (4); Pres Church Yth Grp; Model UN; Pep Clb; SADD; Swing Chorus; Nwsp; Yrbk; Rep Stu Cncl; High Hon Roll; Drama Clb; KS Assn For Yth VP; Fort Hays ST Univ; Elem Ed.

BURNS, KELLY M; Bishop Ward HS; Kansas City, KS; (3); 16/76; Debate Tm; JCL; Latin Clb; NFL; Office Aide; Pep Clb; Spanish Clb; SADD; Swing Chorus; Mgr Wrstlng; KU; Sports/Vet Med.

BURNS, TAMMY; Prairie View Jr Sr HS; Osawatomie, KS; (3); 13/70; Band; Co-Capt Drill Tm; Yrbk; Sec Jr Cls; JV Bsktbl; Var Trk; Var Vllybl; High Hon Roll; NHS; Prfct Atten Awd; KS ST Univ; Vet Med.

BUROW, EVAN; Bonner Springs HS; Bonner Springs, KS; (3); Am Leg Boys St; Church Yth Grp; FCA; Quiz Bowl; SADD; Teachers Aide; Chorus; Var Trk; Hon Roll; NHS; Bus.

BURR, KELLI; Goodland HS; Goodland, KS; (4); 5/75; Church Yth Grp; Debate Tm; FHA; VP GAA; Pres SADD; Teachers Aide; Chorus; VP Frsh Cls; VP Soph Cls; Ofcr Stu Cncl; Western ST Coll Of CO.

BURRESS, JESSICA; Erie HS; Erie, KS; (4); 4/42; Art Clb; Church Yth Grp; FCA; HOBY; Office Aide; Pep Clb; Science Clb; Church Choir; Variety Show; Rptr Nwsp; Trgt; Frgn Lang Clb; Schlstc Mdl; Emporia ST U; Phy Ther.

BURRIES, RYAN W; Arkansas City HS; Arkansas City, KS; (1); JV Ftbl.

BURRIS, ANDREW B; Derby HS; Derby, KS; (1); Quiz Bowl; ROTC; Scholastic Bowl; Mrchg Band; JV Socr; JV Trk; Hon Roll.

BURRIS, JACQUELINE; Caney Vly USD 436; Havana, KS; (4); 10/50; FCA; 4-H; FBLA; FHA; GAA; Spanish Clb; Teachers Aide; Color Guard; Var Sftbl; Var Vllybl; Trnr Var Bsktbl; Coffeyville CC; Med.

BURRIS, JOHN R; Field Kindley Mem Sr HS; Coffeyville, KS; (2); 21/163; Debate Tm; NFL; Scholastic Bowl; Speech Tm; Extended Learing Pgm; KS Univ; Jrnlsm; Sports Brodcst.

BURRIS, PAM S; Parsons HS; Parsons, KS; (2); FHA; Acpl Chr; Var Bus Profs of Am; JV Sftbl; JV Var Tennis; Wt Lftg; Hon Roll; Sprts Clb.

BURRIS, SANDY; Parsons HS; Parsons, KS; (4); 20/120; FCA; Key Clb; Office Aide; Var Capt Bsktbl; Var Sftbl; JV Var Tennis; Wt Lftg; Cit Awd; Hon Roll; Kiwanis Awd; Sprts Clb; Labelle CC; Bus.

BURROUGHS, CHAD D; Great Bend Sr HS; Great Bend, KS; (1); Church Yth Grp; Band; Chorus; Mrchg Band; Stage Crew; Variety Show; Crs Cntry; Trk; Cit Awd; High Hon Roll; Frosh Ensmbl Grp Choir; Frosh/Soph Mens Ensmbl Choir; Symph Band; KS Univ.

BURROUGHS, JEFFREY R; Bishop Miege HS; Kansas City, MO; (3); 10/172; Boy Scts; French Clb; JV Bsbl; Var L Ftbl; Hon Roll; Treas NHS; Eagle Scout; Pres Chldrn Mercy Hosp Explorers Post; Wendys HS Heisman Awd Nom.

BURROWS, BRANDI R; Rolla HS; Rolla, KS; (4); Church Yth Grp; Drama Clb; FCA; Pep Clb; Speech Tm; Band; Chorus; Flag Corp; Mrchg Band; Pep Band.

BURRUSS, SHANNA R; Cair Paravel - Latin Schl; Topeka, KS; (3); Church Yth Grp; Pres VP Dance Clb; Debate Tm; Quiz Bowl; Spanish Clb; School Play; JV Vllybl; Vol At Topeka Zoo, Hosp; Aviatn Pstboy Scts Of Amer Pres VP; KS St Univ.

BURT, DARON L; Ft Scott HS; Fort Scott, KS; (2); Art Clb; Church Yth Grp; Pep Clb; Acpl Chr; Chorus; School Musical; School Play; Stage Crew; Swing Chorus; Variety Show; 1st Pl Solo, Choir & Ensmbl; 1st Pl Solo & Choir & 2nd Pl Ensmbl At St; Gtr Plyr.

BURTCH, ERIN J; Topeka HS; Topeka, KS; (3); 6/330; Church Yth Grp; Intnl Clb; Model UN; Nwsp; Yrbk; Lit Mag; High Hon Roll; Tower Awd; PPI; Langs; Anthropology.

BURTON, AMBER; Frankft HS; Frankfort, KS; (3); 1/37; FHA; Girl Scts; SADD; Teachers Aide; Chorus; Bsktbl; Vllybl; High Hon Roll; City Swim Team Coach/Lfgrd; Wildcat Singers.

BURTON, BENJAMIN; Enterprise Sda Acad; Manhattan, KS; (2); Band; Chorus; Drill Tm; School Play; Stage Crew; Gym; High Hon Roll; Val; Natl HS Math Exm Top Score.

BURTON, BRIAN; Enterprise Sda Acad; Wichita, KS; (3); Church Yth Grp; Model UN; Band; Pres Frsh Cls; Pres Soph Cls; Var Capt Bsktbl; Var Gym; Var Socr; Var Trk; High Hon Roll; Med.

BURTON, CHRIS; Enterprise Sda Acad; Wichita, KS; (4); Church Yth Grp; Model UN; Band; School Play; Ofcr Sr Cls; Ofcr Stu Cncl; Var Bsktbl; Gym; High Hon Roll; Camp Cnslr; Deans List; Missions Mexico; Friends U; Sports Med.

BURTON, EMILY S; Axtell Schl; Summerfield, KS; (4); 2/15; FCA; Pres Natl FFA Org; Pep Clb; Spanish Clb; Teachers Aide; Band; Chorus; Vllybl; High Hon Roll; VP NHS; Spnsh Awd; All Leag Schlrs; Manhattan Tech Ctr; Drftng.

BURTON, KIMBERLY S; Blue Valley HS; Overland Park, KS; (2); Church Yth Grp; Chorus; Church Choir; Var L Trk; Vllybl; High Hon Roll; Hon Roll; Chrstn Clb; Wrtng Awd 2nd Optimist Poetry Cntst; SA ST Trck/Fld Qualification; 4 Yr Coll; Math/Engrng.

BURTON, LU JUANA M; Topeka HS; Topeka, KS; (3); 76/323; Cmnty Wkr; Math Clb; Drill Tm; Orch; Var L Bsktbl; Var Trk; JV Vllybl; Hon Roll; NHS; Pres Acad Fit Awd; Japanese Clb; STRAPP; Bus; Acctng.

BURTON, MICHELLE A; Olathe East Sr HS; Olathe, KS; (2); Drama Clb; French Clb; Hon Roll; Jr NHS; Part Forensics Soph Yr; U Of Miami; Marine Bio.

BURTON, STACI M; Ft Scott HS; Fort Scott, KS; (3); FHA; Natl FFA Org; Office Aide; Teachers Aide; Color Guard; Mgr(s); Tiger Paw Awd; Labette Comm Coll; Radiologist.

BUSCH, ANGELINE; Dodge City HS; Dodge City, KS; (4); 22/253; Am Leg Aux Girls St; SADD; Var Bsktbl; Var Vllybl; Cit Awd; High Hon Roll; NHS; Prfct Atten Awd; Church Yth Grp; FCA; Peer Helper; DARE.

BUSCH, NOAH; Marysville HS; Home, KS; (3); Am Leg Boys St; Debate Tm; Letterman Clb; NFL; Band; Chorus; School Play; Rep Soph Cls; Rep Jr Cls; Pres Stu Cncl; Adj Gen Of KS Medal For Excl; Governors Ctr For Teen Ldrshp; Marysville Yth Coalition Pres; Northland; Environmental Stud.

BUSCHER, JENNIFER; Hayden HS; Topeka, KS; (4); 3/119; Dance Clb; French Clb; Intnl Clb; Pep Clb; Speech Tm; SADD; Drill Tm; Pom Pon; Gov Hon Prg Awd; High Hon Roll; Ballet Midwest; Pro-Life Clb; Star Dancer; U Of KS; Jrnlsm.

BUSENITZ, AMBER M; Berean Acad; Benton, KS; (3); Church Yth Grp; Drama Clb; Teachers Aide; Pep Band; Phtg Yrbk; Rep Soph Cls; Treas Sr Cls; High Hon Roll; NHS; Math Tm; Hnrb Mntn KS Voices Cont Prose; Jrnlsm.

BUSH, DENEEN; Shawnee Heights Sr HS; Topeka, KS; (4); Sec Church Yth Grp; Ofcr Drama Clb; NFL; Speech Tm; Sec Treas Thesps; Mrchg Band; School Musical; School Play; Ed Nwsp; Hon Roll; Tpk Cap Jrnl Mst Vlbl Stffr Awd; SHHS Natl Jrnlsm Conv Rep; KS ST; Jrnlsm.

BUSICK, MISTY; Parsons HS; Parsons, KS; (4); Cmnty Wkr; FBLA; NFL; Q&S; Speech Tm; School Play; Ed Nwsp; Ntl Merit Ltr; FHA; Red Cross Aide; Delta Psi Omega; Comm Theatre; Pub Wrtng; KS ST Univ; Theatre.

BUSSE, ANDREA; Cheylin West Jr Sr HS; Bird City, KS; (4); 1/14; Am Leg Aux Girls St; Church Yth Grp; Capt Quiz Bowl; Drm Mjr(t); Yrbk; Pres Sr Cls; VP Stu Cncl; Bsktbl; Vllybl; NHS; St Olaf; Bio.

BUSSEN, JENNY; Wallace Cty HS; Wallace, KS; (4); 3/23; Pres Church Yth Grp; Office Aide; Sec Pep Clb; Treas SADD; Sec Treas Band; Mrchg Band; Pep Band; Ofcr Stu Cncl; High Hon Roll; Sec NHS; Barton Cnty CC; Ofc Tech.

BUSTAMANTE, PHILLIP J; Garden City Sr HS; Garden City, KS; (1); 8/25; Ofcr Bsbl; Bsktbl; Ftbl; Wt Lftg; Cty All Stars Bsbl.

BUSTAMANTE, SAMUEL A; Bishop Miege HS; Kansas City, MO; (2); Bsktbl; Crs Cntry; Hon Roll; Biking; Over 200 Hrs Comm Svc.

BUTCHER, LORA M; Wichita West HS; Wichita, KS; (3); 11/183; Am Leg Aux Girls St; Church Yth Grp; Treas SADD; Church Choir; Ofcr Jr Cls; Var Tennis; High Hon Roll; NHS; Cmpltd KS Rgnts Hnrs Acad; Wichita ST U; Mech Engrng.

BUTLER, ANGIE K; Great Bend Sr HS; Great Bend, KS; (2); Church Yth Grp; Hosp Aide; SADD; Band; Mrchg Band; Pep Band; Ed Nwsp; Swmmng; Hon Roll; Jrnlsm I Splmnt Proj; J-I Cls Did Lst Issue Pnthr Tls Nwsp; Rprtr.

BUTLER, BRIAN; Hays HS; Hays, KS; (4); Teachers Aide; Var Ftbl; Var Trk; Var Wt Lftg; Hon Roll; Ft Hays ST U; Elem Ed.

BUTLER, CAREN M; Wamego SeniorHS; Wamego, KS; (4); 1/93; Church Yth Grp; Science Clb; Acpl Chr; Band; Chorus; Jazz Band; Mrchg Band; School Musical; Swing Chorus; Gov Hon Prg Awd; KS ST U; Music Ed.

BUTLER, DEREK S; Wichita Southeast HS; Wichita, KS; (3); CAP; Debate Tm; Drama Clb; NFL; Speech Tm; Varsity Clb; School Musical; School Play; Stage Crew; Variety Show; Prof Theater Tech; Pilots License; Aeronautics/Theatre.

BUTLER, LISA A; St Paul HS; Walnut, KS; (2); 3/25; Math Tm; Natl FFA Org; Quiz Bowl; Speech Tm; Hon Roll; NHS; Rcvd A Stdnts Better Than Ever Recognition; Morie Spcl With Comps.

BUTLER, NIKKI; Silver Lake Jr Sr HS; Silver Lake, KS; (3); 13/52; Church Yth Grp; Debate Tm; Pres FHA; NFL; Pep Clb; Teachers Aide; Band; Drill Tm; Mrchg Band; Pep Band; USVBA Vllybl; Positive Attitude Awd; Yth Project; Layout Ed; Soc Worker.

BUTLER, SHRRI E; Leavenworth HS; Leavenworth, KS; (3); 103/398; ROTC; Teachers Aide; Nwsp; Bsktbl; Mgr(s); Trk; High Hon Roll; Hon Roll; Spcl Olympc Vlntr; Med.

BUTLER, STACIE; Wamego HS; Wamego, KS; (4); 6/92; FCA; FHA; Letterman Clb; SADD; Sec Soph Cls; Var Tennis; High Hon Roll; Hon Roll; NHS; Emporia ST U; Law.

BUTRICK, JEFF; Highland HS; Highland, KS; (3); 1/15; Cmnty Wkr; Natl FFA Org; Chorus; School Musical; School Play; Stage Crew; Rptr Nwsp; Rptr Yrbk; Var Trk; Hon Roll; SOS; Memphis U; Crmnl Jstc.

BUTTENHOFF, DENISE; Lincoln Jr Sr HS; Lincoln, KS; (4); 3/35; Am Leg Aux Girls St; Church Yth Grp; FHA; Letterman Clb; Pep Clb; Teachers Aide; Band; Chorus; Church Choir; Mrchg Band; Sterling Coll; Music Ed.

BUTTONHOFF, DEIDRA; Lincoln Jr Sr HS; Lincoln, KS; (2); 2/32; Treas Church Yth Grp; Letterman Clb; Pep Clb; Scholastic Bowl; Band; Chorus; Church Choir; Mrchg Band; Pep Band; School Musical; Nursing/Sci Mjr.

BUTTREY, THOMAS P; Council Grove HS; Council Grove, KS; (2); Church Yth Grp; FCA; Key Clb; Letterman Clb; Pep Clb; SADD; Var L Bsbl; Var L Ftbl; Intrml Wt Lftg; JV Wrstlng; Peer Helper.

BUTTS, DACIA R; Derby HS; Wichita, KS; (1); Church Yth Grp; French Clb; Church Choir; Cit Awd; French Hon Soc; Hon Roll; Service Clb; Environmental Clb; Ldrshp Awd.

BUTTS, GAYLYNN; Chase HS; Chase, KS; (2); Church Yth Grp; FHA; GAA; Math Tm; Pep Clb; Spanish Clb; Band; VP Soph Cls; Var Bsktbl; Var Chrldng.

BUTTS, JENNIFER E; Washburn Rural HS; Topeka, KS; (2); 1/380; Pres Soph Cls; VP Jr Cls; Ofcr Stu Cncl; Bsktbl; Var Trk; High Hon Roll; Pr Mdtn; Tns Tchrs; KS ST Univ; Elem/Sec Ed.

BUTTS, JENNIFER L; Lyons HS; Lyons, KS; (3); 15/60; Art Clb; German Clb; Treas Girl Scts; Pep Clb; Teachers Aide; Silver Awd Girl Scouts; MO Western ST Coll; Navy.

BUTTS, RYAN; Protection Schl; Protection, KS; (2); Speech Tm; Band; Chorus; Pep Band; School Musical; JV Bsktbl; JV Var Ftbl; L Trk; High Hon Roll; School Play; Show Choir.

BYERLEY, LACY; Anderson Cty Jr Sr HS; Garnett, KS; (1); Pep Clb; Chorus; School Musical; VP Frsh Cls; Var Chrldng; JV Vllybl; High Hon Roll.

BYERLEY, SARA; Anderson Cty Jr Sr HS; Garnett, KS; (3); HOBY; Sec Treas Intnl Clb; Sec Pep Clb; Science Clb; Teachers Aide; Chorus; Swing Chorus; VP Jr Cls; JV Vllybl; Hon Roll.

BYERLY, ALLEN E; Pratt HS; Pratt, KS; (3); French Clb; Math Tm; NFL; Scholastic Bowl; Yrbk; Tennis; High Hon Roll; Boy Scts; Cmnty Wkr; Debate Tm; 3 Time Debate/Spch Qlfr; Won Town/Zone Optmst Ortrcl Cntst; 6 Time Wnr Top Stu Wk Awd; Bus.

BYERS, DAVID P; Blue Valley HS; Overland Park, KS; (4); Am Leg Boys St; Church Yth Grp; Letterman Clb; Varsity Clb; Band; JV Bsktbl; Ftbl; Trk; Cit Awd; Hon Roll; All EKL Team; All Sun Cntry; All City Track.

BYERS, JACOB L; Blue Valley HS; Stilwell, KS; (3); Church Yth Grp; JV Bsbl; Intrml Bsktbl; Score Keeper; Hon Roll.

BYFIELD, MICHELLE; Herington HS; Herington, KS; (3); FCA; FHA; Math Tm; Pep Clb; Chorus; Capt Chrldng; JV Var Trk; High Hon Roll; Hon Roll; NHS; Psych.

BYLER, JASON R; Wellington Sr HS; Wellington, KS; (3); JV Ftbl; Var Golf; High Hon Roll; Jr NHS; Chem Engrng.

BYRD, DAWN M; Labette Co HS; Mound Valley, KS; (3); Church Yth Grp; Hosp Aide; SADD; Chorus; Church Choir; Flag Corp; School Musical; Swing Chorus; Ofcr Stu Cncl; Hon Roll; Washburn Univ; Lawyer.

BYRD, KENDRA J; Blue Valley HS; Shawnee Mission, KS; (3); 49/251; Church Yth Grp; Cmnty Wkr; Varsity Clb; Drill Tm; Sec Stu Cncl; Var Bsktbl; Var Sftbl; Var Vllybl; Hon Roll; NHS; Stu Based Ldrshp Comm; HS Heisman Trophy Nom; Bus Mgmt.

BYRNE, JANELLE; Shawnee Mission W Sr HS; Lenexa, KS; (3); 9/415; Church Yth Grp; Chorus; Chrldng; Sftbl; High Hon Roll; NHS; Peer Tutr; JAWS; U KS.

CADEK, JASON L; Wellington Sr HS; Howard, OH; (2); 6/181; Church Yth Grp; SADD; Rep Stu Cncl; JV Bsbl; JV Var Ftbl; Var Trk; JV Var Wrstlng; High Hon Roll; Jr NHS; Lions Clb Plq; Rtry Top 10%.

CADY, KRISTOPHER A; Jewell HS; Jewell, KS; (1); Hon Roll; Prfct Atten Awd.

CADY, STEPHEN M; Olathe South Sr HS; Olathe, KS; (3); 1/400; Boy Scts; Church Yth Grp; Dance Clb; Drama Clb; NFL; Pep Clb; Speech Tm; Thesps; Varsity Clb; Acpl Chr; Pres Dist Cncl Yth Mnstrs; Coord Team Conf Cncl Yth Mnstrs; Repertory Theatre; Theatre.

CAELLNER, KELLY L; Salina HS South; Salina, KS; (3); French Clb; SADD; Pres Frsh Cls; VP Soph Cls; Sec Jr Cls; Treas Sr Cls; Capt Swmmng; Cit Awd; NHS; Pres Acad Fit Awd; Natl Fnlst US Swimming/4 Times ST Chmpn; Pre Med.

CAFFREY, APRIL; Frankfort Jr/Sr HS; Vermillion, KS; (2); Cmnty Wkr; FHA; Chorus; Church Choir; School Play; Bsktbl; Chrldng; KSU; Nursing.

CAGE, TARAH L; Maranatha Acad; Shawnee Mission, KS; (3); Cmnty Wkr; Chorus; Hon Roll; Goldn Eagle Awd 96; Elem Ed.

CAGWIN, ANNE R; Desoto HS; Shawnee, KS; (3); Cmnty Wkr; Drama Clb; French Clb; Intnl Clb; Letterman Clb; Science Clb; SADD; Cit Awd; High Hon Roll; Hon Roll; 10 Day Stu Exch With Germny; Pittsburgh St Univ; Eng Tech.

CAHOJ, LINDSEY; Eureka Jr Sr HS; Eureka, KS; (3); 5/50; Science Clb; SADD; Sec Jr Cls; Var Bsktbl; Var Chrldng; JV Vllybl; High Hon Roll; Kiwanis Awd; Kytts; NEDC; KS ST U; Int Dsgn.

CAHOW, JOSHUA W; Blue Valley HS; Stilwell, KS; (3); Hon Roll; Motors; Hot Rods; Drag Racing; Sound Sys; Pittsburg ST; Auto Engrng.

CAHOW, LESLIE E; Blue Valley Northwest HS; Overland Park, KS; (3); Church Yth Grp; Powder Puff Ftbl; Trk; Hon Roll; U Of KS; Med Field.

CAIN, PATRICK; Hayden HS; Topeka, KS; (3); Church Yth Grp; Cmnty Wkr; Computer Clb; Drama Clb; FBLA; Intnl Clb; JA; Library Aide; Model UN; Office Aide; 1st Grnd Awd; KS City Sci Fair; Gertrude Awd; Bst Snd Dsgn Schl Mus; Optmst Ortrcl Cntst 94 3rd/95 2nd; KS ST Univ; Elec Engr.

CAIRNS, MICHELLE L; Wichita East HS; Wichita, KS; (3); 14/350; Cmnty Wkr; Stage Crew; High Hon Roll; NHS; Wichita ST Univ; Acctg.

CAIRNS, NICHOLE; Washington HS; Greenleaf, KS; (4); Am Leg Aux Girls St; French Clb; FHA; Varsity Clb; Drill Tm; Bsktbl; Chrldng; Golf; Trk; Vllybl; Cloud Co CC.

CALAWAY, APRIL; Wichita Northwest HS; Wichita, KS; (4); 32/334; Cmnty Wkr; FCA; Q&S; Ed Nwsp; Var L Crs Cntry; Mgr(s); Var L Trk; High Hon Roll; Pres Schlr; Ath Schlr Trk; Butler Cty Comm Coll; Jrnlsm.

CALCARA, MEGAN C; Bishop Miege HS; Kansas City, MO; (3); Phtg Nwsp; Phtg Yrbk; Rep Soph Cls; Sec Stu Cncl; Intrml Bsktbl; Var Crs Cntry; Capt Swmmng; Architecture.

CALDERWOOD, JESSICA; Nemaha Valley HS; Seneca, KS; (3); Drama Clb; Letterman Clb; Speech Tm; Varsity Clb; Drill Tm; Pep Band; School Play; Ofcr Frsh Cls; Ofcr Soph Cls; Ofcr Jr Cls; Elem Math Tchr.

CALDWELL, JESSICA G; Olathe North Sr HS; Olathe, KS; (4); Church Yth Grp; Cmnty Wkr; Science Clb; Acpl Chr; L Swmmng; Hon Roll; Stu Ntrlst Prog; Mid-Amer Nzrn Coll.

CALDWELL, MATT A; Anderson Cty Jr Sr HS; Garnett, KS; (3); Am Leg Boys St; VP Intnl Clb; Natl FFA Org; SADD; Rep Jr Cls; Sec Stu Cncl; Bsktbl; Golf; High Hon Roll; NHS; Pre-Law.

CALES, JAIME K; Winfield HS; Winfield, KS; (4); 47/148; Bus Profs of Am; Church Yth Grp; Sec 4-H; SADD; Orch; Var Swmmng; Var JV Vllybl; Hon Roll; Emporia ST Univ; Bus.

CALHOUN, APRIL; Cimarron HS; Cimarron, KS; (3); Pep Clb; Sec Spanish Clb; Band; Nwsp; Yrbk; Rep Soph Cls; Sec Jr Cls; Var Chrldng; Hon Roll; NHS; Erly Chldhd Ed.

CALHOUN, MISTY; Kansas City Chrstn Acad; Grandview, MO; (4); Church Yth Grp; Cmnty Wkr; Debate Tm; 4-H; German Clb; Speech Tm; Teachers Aide; Acpl Chr; Chorus; Church Choir.

CALLAHAN, CHRISTOPHER; J C Harmon HS; Kansas City, KS; (4); 5/200; Chess Clb; Cmnty Wkr; French Clb; Hosp Aide; Teachers Aide; High Hon Roll; NHS; Pres Schlr; St Schlr.

CALLANAN, MARK A; Circle HS; Benton, KS; (3); 10/120; Boy Scts; Church Yth Grp; FCA; Capt Math Tm; Quiz Bowl; SADD; Rptr Nwsp; JV Bsktbl; Var Capt Tennis; High Hon Roll; KS U; Med.

CALLAWAY, JESSICA E; Campus HS; Haysville, KS; (2); Computer Clb; Orch; Stage Crew; High Hon Roll; Hon Roll; Prfct Atten Awd; Voc/Csmtlgy.

CALLEN, SHANNA T; Wichita East HS; Wichita, KS; (2); Art Clb; Church Yth Grp; Office Aide; Spanish Clb; Hon Roll; Natl Art Hnr Soc; Psych.

CALLIER, SARAH B; Bishop Miege HS; Overland Park, KS; (1); 23/245; GAA; Var Bsktbl; Var Trk; Vllybl; High Hon Roll; Mary Ann Lucas Schlsp; AAU Bsktbl.

CALLOWAY, CHAZ R; Wichita North HS; Wichita, KS; (3); Computer Clb; Science Clb; Spanish Clb; Bsktbl; Hon Roll; Prfct Atten Awd; CPR Certfd.

CALORE, ANNE M; Olathe North Sr HS; Olathe, KS; (4); Drama Clb; Letterman Clb; Thesps; Treas Acpl Chr; Chorus; Church Choir; School Musical; School Play; Swing Chorus; Variety Show; Mem Of Northwinds A Select Vocal Jazz Ensemble; Rcvd Schlsp To Vocal Music Inst At KS ST Univ.

CALOVICH, JENNY D; Piper HS; Kansas City, KS; (3); Church Yth Grp; 4-H; Spanish Clb; Teachers Aide; Chorus; Ed Yrbk; Var L Chrldng; Sftbl; Vllybl; High Hon Roll; Swmmng; Ldrshp 2020; KU.

CALVERT, ELIZABETH; Wichita East HS; Wichita, KS; (3); Cmnty Wkr; French Clb; Science Clb; SADD; Ofcr Stu Cncl; French Hon Soc; NHS; KS St Univ; Med.

CALVERT, JAMES R; Topeka West HS; Topeka, KS; (3); 22/239; Art Clb; French Clb; Letterman Clb; Pep Clb; Q&S; Phtg Yrbk; Var L Ftbl; Var Wt Lftg; High Hon Roll; Var L Golf; U Of KS; Bus.

CALVERT, KATHERINE E; Topeka West HS; Topeka, KS; (1); French Clb; Girl Scts; Pep Clb; SADD; Bsktbl; Sftbl; Vllybl; High Hon Roll; Hon Roll; Pres Acad Fit Awd; City Day Camp Vol; HS Peer Helper Cnslr.

CALVERT, SAMATHA; Lansing HS; Lansing, KS; (2); Dance Clb; Office Aide; Drill Tm; Pom Pon; Hon Roll; Starmakers Dnc Chorgrphy 4 Star Awd; NCA Danz All Amer Nom; City Sponsrd Sftbl; Kayette Clb; Dnc.

CAMERON, ANDREW W; Blue Valley Northwest HS; Overland Park, KS; (2); Debate Tm; Trk; Hon Roll; Novice Debater Of Yr 95-; U Of KS; Law.

CAMERON, GEREMY A; Holton HS; Holton, KS; (3); Art Clb; Letterman Clb; Spanish Clb; Teachers Aide; Golf; Mgr(s); Score Keeper; Hon Roll; Highland CC; Bus.

CAMERON, LAKISHA Y; Highland Park HS; Topeka, KS; (2); Church Yth Grp; Debate Tm; Drill Tm; Stat Bsktbl; Chrldng; Mgr(s); Sftbl; Trk; Vllybl; Hon Roll; Clark Atlanta; Atty; Family Law.

CAMERON, SARA; Ulysses HS; Ulysses, KS; (4); 27/93; FCA; VP NFL; SADD; Varsity Clb; Chorus; School Musical; Pres VP Stu Cncl; Var Chrldng; NHS; U KS; Brdcst Nws.

CAMFIELD, JUSTIN M; Maize HS; Colwich, KS; (1); Church Yth Grp; High Hon Roll; Hon Roll; Bsbl; Yth Pstr; Venard.

CAMPBELL, AMY L; Riverton Schl; Riverton, KS; (3); Church Yth Grp; FCA; Letterman Clb; Chorus; Church Choir; Pep Band; Sftbl; Vllybl; Hon Roll; Ntl Merit Ltr; Central Bible Coll; Missnry.

CAMPBELL, ASHLEY; Shawnee Heights Sr HS; Topeka, KS; (4); Church Yth Grp; SADD; Thesps; Drill Tm; School Musical; School Play; Yrbk; Pom Pon; High Hon Roll; NHS; Jr Cvtns VP; KS Hnr Schlr; All Amer Schlr; KS ST U.

CAMPBELL, CARA; Garden City Sr HS; Garden City, KS; (4); 28/334; Drama Clb; Thesps; Acpl Chr; Band; Color Guard; Mrchg Band; Stage Crew; Ed Yrbk; Ed Lit Mag; NHS; Garden City CC.

CAMPBELL, CHRISTINA K; Liberal HS; Liberal, KS; (2); Church Yth Grp; Chorus; Church Choir; Mgr(s); Vllybl; Hon Roll; NHS.

CAMPBELL, HOLLY S; Hoxie HS; Hoxie, KS; (3); 4/44; Pres Church Yth Grp; FCA; 4-H; FHA; School Musical; Swing Chorus; VP Frsh Cls; Rep Soph Cls; VP Jr Cls; VP Pres Stu Cncl; Schl Record Co-Holder In 800 M Run.

CAMPBELL, JAMI K; Cedar Vale HS; Cedar Vale, KS; (3); 2/23; FHA; Letterman Clb; Pep Clb; SADD; Varsity Clb; Band; Jazz Band; Mrchg Band; Pep Band; School Play; Georgetown; Cmptr Sci/Jrnlsm.

CAMPBELL, JEREMY B; Hayden HS; Topeka, KS; (2); Band; Mrchg Band; Pep Band; Varsity Clb; Ftbl; Wt Lftg; Wrstlng; Hon Roll; Server Of Mass At Church; Recgntn For No Detentions; Washburn Univ.

CAMPBELL, JUSTIN B; Wichita South HS; Wichita, KS; (2); 21/430; Computer Clb; Math Clb; Science Clb; Spanish Clb; Teachers Aide; Swmmng; Trk; Cit Awd; High Hon Roll; NHS; WSU; Horticulture.

CAMPBELL, KATIE; Goodland HS; Goodland, KS; (2); Church Yth Grp; FHA; SADD; School Play; Vllybl; Hon Roll; Kayettes Devotions; Colby; Med.

CAMPBELL, KELLI; Ulysses HS; Ulysses, KS; (4); Sec Art Clb; Rep NFL; SADD; Band; Mrchg Band; Rep Sr Cls; Rep Stu Cncl; Mgr Bsktbl; Var L Golf; High Hon Roll.

CAMPBELL, KELLY N; Hoxie HS; Hoxie, KS; (3); 6/43; Church Yth Grp; FCA; School Musical; Yrbk; Var Bsktbl; Var Trk; Var Vllybl; Hon Roll; NHS; Pres Acad Fit Awd; Kent St Univ.

CAMPBELL, KIMBERLY A; Hays HS; Hays, KS; (2); 1/231; Church Yth Grp; Chorus; School Musical; High Hon Roll; Prfct Atten Awd; Hays Arts Cncl Crtv Wrtng Cntst 1st Pl Poetry/HS Artst Pstcrd Cntst 3rd Pl; Dead Poets Soc; Ft Hays ST Univ.

CAMPBELL, KRISTIN; Leavenworth HS; Leavenworth, KS; (4); 13/339; Cmnty Wkr; HOBY; ROTC; Acpl Chr; Chorus; Church Choir; Ofcr Stu Cncl; Cit Awd; High Hon Roll; NHS; U Of KS; Phy Ther.

CAMPBELL, MARTHA R; Derby Christian Schl; Derby, KS; (1); Drama Clb; School Play; Bsktbl; Hon Roll; Prncpls Awd; Friends Univ; Ed.

CAMPBELL, MELISSA A; Troy HS; Troy, KS; (2); Church Yth Grp; Drama Clb; FCA; School Play; Bsktbl; Chrldng; Crs Cntry; Mgr(s); Sftbl; High Hon Roll; Nom All Amer Frosh Yr; 4 Yr Univ; HS Math Tch/Coach.

CAMPBELL, MELISSA S; Blue Valley HS; Overland Park, KS; (2); GAA; Bsktbl; Sftbl; Vllybl; Hon Roll; 2 Tiger Pride Awds For Acad; KU.

CAMPBELL, MELONIE G; Leavenworth HS; Leavenworth, KS; (3); Church Yth Grp; ROTC; Mgr(s); JV Vllybl; K ST; Nrsng.

CAMPBELL, MICHAEL; F L Schlagle HS; Kansas City, KS; (4); Art Clb; Church Yth Grp; Cmnty Wkr; Letterman Clb; Varsity Clb; Rep Jr Cls; Var Bsktbl; Var Golf; Hon Roll; Jr NHS; Eng Bus/Spts Agt.

CAMPBELL, TAMARA M; Washington HS; Kansas City, KS; (2); French Clb; JV Vllybl.

CAMPTON, NICOLE L; Pleasant Ridge HS; Leavenworth, KS; (3); Pres 4-H; VP FBLA; Natl FFA Org; SADD; School Musical; School Play; Pres Frsh Cls; Pres Soph Cls; Pres Jr Cls; Pres Sr Cls; KS ST Univ.

CANADY, KRISTINA R; Washburn Rural HS; Topeka, KS; (2); 140/360; Church Yth Grp; Debate Tm; NFL; Spanish Clb; Church Choir; Orch; School Musical; Hon Roll; Mdcn OB-GYN.

CANDELARIO, PHILIP M; Sumner Acad Of Arts & Science; Kansas City, KS; (4); 1/196; NFL; Rep Sr Cls; Socr; High Hon Roll; NHS; Ntl Merit SF; Spanish NHS; St Schlr; Debate Tm; Spanish Clb; U Of KS.

CANFIELD, BRAD; Mulvane Sr HS; Mulvane, KS; (3); Church Yth Grp; FCA; Key Clb; Letterman Clb; Spanish Clb; SADD; Band; Mrchg Band; Treas Stu Cncl; Bsktbl.

CANIPE, LIZ D; Blue Valley Northwest HS; Overland Park, KS; (2); 68/409; Church Yth Grp; Cmnty Wkr; Pep Clb; Teachers Aide; Band; Mrchg Band; Pep Band; Hon Roll; Salt & Light Club.

CANN, NICHOLE; Topeka HS; Topeka, KS; (4); 30/354; Church Yth Grp; High Hon Roll; Hon Roll; Outs Bus Stu Awd For Topeka HS; 1st Plc Washburn Univ Acad Contst For Accntng 1; KS St Univ; Acctng.

CANNON, ALI; Shawnee Mission E Sr HS; Fairway, KS; (4); Chrmn Natl Beta Clb; Q&S; Ed Nwsp; VP Sr Cls; Sftbl; French Hon Soc; High Hon Roll; Hon Roll; NHS; Pres Schlr; U Of MO; Brdcst Jrnlsm.

CANNON, CORY; Emporia HS; Emporia, KS; (4); FCA; 4-H; HOBY; Pres Model UN; NFL; Sec Quiz Bowl; VP Soph Cls; Stat Bsktbl; JV Trk; Hon Roll; Tns/Tchrs; Sci Olympd; 4-H Ambass; Emporia ST U; Polysci.

CANSLER, JESSICA; Turner HS; Kansas City, KS; (4); 3/196; SADD; Band; Drm Mjr(t); Mrchg Band; Sftbl; High Hon Roll; Hon Roll; Jr NHS; NHS; Pres Acad Fit Awd; U Of KS.

CANTRALL, SETH; Greensburg HS; Greensburg, KS; (1); 14/40; Band; Chorus; Mrchg Band; Pep Band; School Musical; School Play; Stage Crew; Var Bsbl; Intrml JV Bsktbl; JV Var Tennis; Slct Vcl MYF Chrch Grp.

CANTRELL, JACEE L; South Barber HS; Waldron, KS; (2); 8/21; HOBY; Rep Frsh Cls; Rep Soph Cls; VP Stu Cncl; Bsktbl; Chrldng; Trk; Vllybl; High Hon Roll; Hon Roll; Kayette Clb Treas; CH Dance Prod Perf Troupe; Bronze Acad Pin; Nrs.

CANTRELL, MARCIA K; Field Kindley Mem Sr HS; Coffeyville, KS; (4); #71 in class; Church Yth Grp; French Clb; Hosp Aide; Teachers Aide; High Hon Roll; Hon Roll; Coffeyville CC; Nrsng.

CANTRELL, NICHOLAS D; Washburn Rural HS; Topeka, KS; (2); Var Bsbl; Bsktbl; Ftbl; High Hon Roll.

CANTU, CHRISTINA; Olathe South Sr HS; Olathe, KS; (4); Church Yth Grp; Cmnty Wkr; Letterman Clb; Pep Clb; Spanish Clb; Teachers Aide; Chorus; Stage Crew; Variety Show; Chrldng; Chldrn Mercy Gentics Mmbrshp; DARE Role Model; Mothers Hands; Drake Univ; Bio.

CANTU, JENNIFER L; Olathe East Sr HS; Olathe, KS; (2); Pep Clb; Spanish Clb; Varsity Clb; Var Chrldng; Var Gym; Var Trk; Hon Roll; Dr.

CAO, LONG HONG N; Garden City Sr HS; Garden City, KS; (3); Church Yth Grp; French Clb; Band; Jazz Band; Mrchg Band; Prfct Atten Awd; U Of KS; Engr.

CAO, MINH Q; Derby HS; Wichita, KS; (3); High Hon Roll; Hon Roll; NHS; Wichita St Univ; Elec Eng.

CAPPS, JENNIFER M; Wichita East HS; Wichita, KS; (4); Band; Mrchg Band; Pep Band; School Musical; Hon Roll; Emporia State Univ; Elem Educ.

CAPREZ, MECHELLE; Dighton HS; Dighton, KS; (2); Church Yth Grp; Cmnty Wkr; FCA; Pep Clb; Band; Chorus; Mrchg Band; Pep Band; KS U; Soc Worker.

CARDAMONE, HEATHER; Saint Xavier HS; Junction City, KS; (4); Am Leg Aux Girls St; Church Yth Grp; FHA; SADD; Teachers Aide; Chorus; Church Choir; School Musical; Var Vllybl; Hon Roll; Forensics; Servant Squad; Elem Ed.

CARDEN, MELINDA K; Olathe North Sr HS; Lenexa, KS; (4); Debate Tm; Drama Clb; NFL; Spanish Clb; School Musical; School Play; Ed Yrbk; Lit Mag; Sec Sr Cls; JV Trk; U Of KS.

CARDER, JENNIFER; Hoxie HS; Hoxie, KS; (4); Church Yth Grp; FCA; Pres FHA; Teachers Aide; Band; Mrchg Band; Ofcr Stu Cncl; Chrldng; Hon Roll; Ballet 14 Yrs; USMC.

CARDER, NICOLE G; Holton HS; Holton, KS; (1); Band; Mrchg Band; Orch; Pep Band; Forensics Team.

CAREY, LISA K; Washburn Rural HS; Topeka, KS; (3); GAA; Teachers Aide; Bsktbl; Sftbl; Vllybl; High Hon Roll; Hon Roll; Pres Acad Fit Awd; All-City & Playr Of Yr, All-St 1st Tem, USA Today Hnrb Mntn Bsktbl; All-City, Nsca All-Amer Sftbl; OK Univ; Nutritionist.

CAREY, STEPHANIE M; Leavenworth HS; Leavenworth, KS; (1); Dance Clb; Acpl Chr; Band; Chorus; Church Choir; Mrchg Band; School Musical; Swing Chorus; High Hon Roll; Hon Roll; U Of KS.

CARHART, LAUREN E; Blue Valley North HS; Leawood, KS; (2); Church Yth Grp; Hosp Aide; Spanish Clb; Yrbk; Hon Roll.

CARLEY, CARA L; Hartford HS; Reading, KS; (2); 1/50; Church Yth Grp; Cmnty Wkr; FHA; Letterman Clb; Bsktbl; Trk; Vllybl; Wt Lftg; Cit Awd; Hon Roll; Emporia ST Univ.

CARLIN, MIKE; Manhattan HS; Manhattan, KS; (3); Church Yth Grp; Chorus; School Play; Swing Chorus; VP Jr Cls; Var JV Bsbl; Intrml Bsktbl; High Hon Roll; NHS; St Schlr; U Notre Dame; Bus Admin.

CARLINI, MEGAN L; Kapaun-Mt Carmel HS; Wichita, KS; (4); Church Yth Grp; Debate Tm; French Clb; Mgr Q&S; VP SADD; Stage Crew; Rptr Yrbk; Rep Frsh Cls; Hon Roll; NHS; Yth Prevention Team; Governors Ctr For Teen Ldrshp; Ecology Clb; Ft Hays ST Univ; Elem Ed.

CARLSON, BRANDON C; Lyons HS; Lyons, KS; (2); Art Clb; Church Yth Grp; FCA; 4-H; HOBY; Math Tm; Pep Clb; Scholastic Bowl; Intrml Bsbl; JV Bsktbl; Air Force Acad; Engrng.

CARLSON, BRENT; Pike Valley HS; Courtland, KS; (4); 19/26; FBLA; Natl FFA Org; Speech Tm; Bsktbl; Trk; KS FFA ST Deg; Pike Vly FFA Star Chptr Frmr; Cloud Cty CC; Agbus.

CARLSON, CARMEN L; Smoky Valley HS; Lindsborg, KS; (2); Church Yth Grp; FCA; Letterman Clb; Math Tm; Pep Clb; Varsity Clb; Band; Chorus; Mrchg Band; Pep Band; Art; Washington Univ; Bio-Med Engrng.

CARLSON, JOSHUA A; Clifton-Clyde HS; Clifton, KS; (4); FBLA; Natl FFA Org; Scholastic Bowl; Pres Jr Cls; Pres Stu Cncl; Var L Bsktbl; Var L Ftbl; Hon Roll; NHS; School Play; Forensics Team; KS Univ; Jrnlsm.

CARLSON, LAURA; Topeka HS; Topeka, KS; (2); 38/446; Cmnty Wkr; German Clb; Hosp Aide; Science Clb; Spanish Clb; Hon Roll; RN.

CARLSON, LUCAS; Centre Jr Sr HS; Lincolnville, KS; (2); 1/19; Treas Church Yth Grp; Pres 4-H; Rptr Natl FFA Org; Pres Frsh Cls; Pres Soph Cls; Var Bsktbl; Var Ftbl; Var Trk; Var Wt Lftg; High Hon Roll; KS ST U; Animal Sci.

CARLSON, MINDI; Ottawa HS; Ottawa, KS; (2); Church Yth Grp; FCA; 4-H; French Clb; GAA; Spanish Clb; SADD; Chorus; Church Choir; School Musical; Stu Of Month; KS ST Univ; Marine Bio.

CARLSON, RACHEL L; Maranatha Acad; Smithville, MO; (4); Church Yth Grp; Teachers Aide; Mgr School Play; Stage Crew; Mgr Bsktbl; High Hon Roll; Gldn Eagle Awd; All Amer Schlr; Evangel Coll; Soc Wrk.

CARLSON, SARAH; Lawrence HS; Lawrence, KS; (4); 138/521; Key Clb; Office Aide; Teachers Aide; Chorus; JV Var Chrldng; JV Var Gym; Hon Roll; Pres Schlr; Dance Lyrcl/Jazz/Tap/Chrdnce; U Of KS; PT.

CARLSON, TONYA; Mulvane Sr HS; Mulvane, KS; (4); 22/144; Letterman Clb; SADD; Thesps; Chorus; Stage Crew; High Hon Roll; Hon Roll; NHS; Ntl Merit Ltr; Prfct Atten Awd; KS ST U; Acctng.

CARLTON, CHRIS R; Larned HS; Larned, KS; (2); 25/110; Letterman Clb; Teachers Aide; Rep Frsh Cls; Rep Soph Cls; Rep Stu Cncl; L Var Ftbl; JV Trk; L Var Wrstlng; Hon Roll; Prfct Atten Awd.

CARLTON, ROBERT S; Hiawatha HS; Hiawatha, KS; (3); 20/115; Am Leg Boys St; Quiz Bowl; Teachers Aide; JV Bsktbl; Var Ftbl; Wt Lftg; Hon Roll; Treas NHS; Ntl Merit Ltr; Pres Acad Fit Awd; Hiawatha Episcopal Chrch Bishops Comm; Comp Animation Artist.

CARLTON, WENDY; Leroy HS; Le Roy, KS; (4); 6/16; Am Leg Aux Girls St; Church Yth Grp; Dance Clb; FCA; Sec VP 4-H; HOBY; Math Tm; Pres Band; Chorus; Capt Drill Tm; Natl Grd Schlstc Ath Awds; All Amer Dncr; Pittsburg ST U; Pre Med.

CARMAN, BRIAN M; Blue Valley Northwest HS; Overland Park, KS; (1); Boy Scts; Church Yth Grp; Debate Tm; Ftbl; Wt Lftg; Hon Roll; Bushidokaty Karate; Reg Karate Light Kickboxing Trnmt Wnnr; Eagle Sct; Outdoor Clb; KS ST; Comp Engr.

CARMICHAEL, TRENT; Garden City Sr HS; Garden City, KS; (3); German Clb; Math Tm; Golf; Wt Lftg; Hon Roll; Odyssey Mind.

CARMODY, KEVIN; Sabetha HS; Sabetha, KS; (3); 40/90; Am Leg Boys St; Bus Profs of Am; Church Yth Grp; FCA; Office Aide; Pep Clb; Spanish Clb; Band; Jazz Band; Pep Band; Brdcstng.

CARMONA, MARGIE R; Bishop Ward HS; Kansas City, KS; (4); Church Yth Grp; Dance Clb; Pep Clb; Drill Tm; Var Pom Pon; Trk; High Hon Roll; Hon Roll; Rockhurst Coll; Phys Thrpy.

CARNAL, MATT J; Parsons HS; Parsons, KS; (3); 18/108; Pep Clb; SADD; Var Bsbl; Var Crs Cntry; Wt Lftg; Hon Roll.

CARNAL, NATHAN; Parsons HS; Parsons, KS; (4); 5/118; FBLA; Teachers Aide; JV Var Bsbl; JV Var Crs Cntry; High Hon Roll; NHS; Pres Acad Fit Awd; St Schlr; U Of Tulsa; CIS; Acctng.

CARNAO, CAROL L; Bishop Miege HS; Kansas City, MO; (3); 16/170; Dance Clb; Drama Clb; French Clb; Rptr Nwsp; Ed Lit Mag; High Hon Roll; NHS; People To People Stdnt Ambssdr 96 Stdnt Ldrshp Prgm; E Durten Meml Schlsp Awd; Acad Excl Awd 10/11 Yr; Scndry Eng/Fre Ed.

CARNEY, TIM; Northeast Magnet HS; Wichita, KS; (2); 1/120; Church Yth Grp; Rep Soph Cls; JV Bsbl; High Hon Roll; Hon Roll; Prfct Atten Awd; Natl Eng Design Callenge Team Capt; Eng.

CARNEY, VINCENT N; Bishop Carroll Catholic HS; Wichita, KS; (2); Cmnty Wkr; English Clb; JA; Letterman Clb; Math Tm; Spanish Clb; Ofcr Bsbl; Golf; Score Keeper; Socr; KS Newman; Pyrotechnician.

CARPENTER, AARON; Hayden HS; Topeka, KS; (4); #5 in class; Cmnty Wkr; Debate Tm; Latin Clb; Letterman Clb; NFL; Office Aide; Yrbk; Score Keeper; Cit Awd; Gov Hon Prg Awd; Dlgte To Cngrtnl Ldrshp Cncl 96; KS ST Univ; Nclr Engr.

CARPENTER, BRIAN P; Blue Valley Northwest HS; Overland Park, KS; (4); Drama Clb; Pep Clb; Teachers Aide; Acpl Chr; Chorus; Mrchg Band; School Musical; Swing Chorus; JV Ftbl; Hon Roll; Natl Deans List; DARE Role Model; U Of KS; Microbio.

CARPENTER, TRAVIS A; Blue Valley HS; Stilwell, KS; (2); 7/220; High Hon Roll; Karate, Bsktbl; Vllybl; Socceer; Skiing; Duke; Bus Mgmt.

CARPENTIER, JAMIE; Elwood Schl; Elwood, KS; (2); HOBY; Pep Clb; Band; Chorus; Pres Frsh Cls; Pres Soph Cls; Sec Jr Cls; Rep Stu Cncl; Bsktbl; Chrldng; KS ST U; Bus.

CARPINELLI, ANNE; Acad Of Mt St Scholastica; Atchison, KS; (3); 1/30; Church Yth Grp; Cmnty Wkr; NFL; Pep Clb; Quiz Bowl; Service Clb; Teachers Aide; Acpl Chr; Chorus; School Musical; Med.

CARR, ALICIA D; Augusta Sr HS; Augusta, KS; (3); 23/147; Church Yth Grp; English Clb; French Clb; JA; SADD; Varsity Clb; Band; Chorus; Capt Var Sftbl; U Of WA; Bus.

CARR, MARY D; Manhattan HS; Manhattan, KS; (4); 32/388; Church Yth Grp; Cmnty Wkr; German Clb; Girl Scts; Chorus; Jazz Band; School Musical; Swing Chorus; Rep Stu Cncl; NHS; St Chr; KS Hnr Schlr; Solo Smr Chrl Inst; VOCAL Perf.

CARR, MATTHEW; Southeast Saline Schl; Gypsum, KS; (3); Rep Am Leg Boys St; Cmnty Wkr; Varsity Clb; VP Soph Cls; VP Jr Cls; VP Sr Cls; Var L Bsbl; Var L Bsktbl; Var L Ftbl; Cit Awd; US Naval Acad; Aerospace Engrn.

CARR, MELISSA A; Maize HS; Wichita, KS; (2); Church Yth Grp; Letterman Clb; Q&S; Service Clb; SADD; Chorus; Variety Show; Phtg Ed Yrbk; VP Frsh Cls; Ofcr Stu Cncl; USAV Vlybl Tm 4 Yrs; Several Phtgrphy Awds; Advtsng/Photo Jrnlsm.

CARR, PAUL; Cair Paravel - Latin Schl; Topeka, KS; (2); 2/24; Church Yth Grp; Debate Tm; Drama Clb; Math Tm; Chorus; School Musical; JV Var Bsktbl; High Hon Roll; City Swim Tm; Mitch Holthaus Sprtscstng Acad Grad; Bible Quiz Team; Radio/TV Brdcstng.

CARRERA JR, ANTOLIN; Shawnee Mission N HS; Shawnee Mission, KS; (4); 24/346; Church Yth Grp; Cmnty Wkr; Spanish Clb; Teachers Aide; Socr; Trk; Wrstlng; Hon Roll; NHS; Ntl Merit SF; LULAC; Natl Hspnc Mrt Schlr; Clgt Wrld Series 95; KS Schlr; K ST; Sci.

CARRICO, SHERRI A; Basehor Linwood HS; Bonner Springs, KS; (3); 6/101; Sec 4-H; Hosp Aide; Math Clb; SADD; School Play; Ed Yrbk; 4-H Awd; High Hon Roll; NHS; Prfct Atten Awd; Sci Olympiad; Leavenworth Cty Jr Ldrs Historian; Pre Mdcn.

CARRITHERS, SARA E; Wichita North HS; Wichita, KS; (2); Church Yth Grp; Cmnty Wkr; Chorus; Church Choir; Orch; School Musical; Ed Lit Mag; Rep Stu Cncl; High Hon Roll; Hon Roll; Univ Eng Prfsr/Wrtr.

CARROLL, ANDREA; Olathe North Sr HS; Olathe, KS; (2); 1/400; Hosp Aide; Math Tm; Science Clb; Band; Mrchg Band; Rep Stu Cncl; Sftbl; Vllybl; High Hon Roll; Pres Schlr; Sci Olympd Tm; Med.

CARROLL, JAMES T; Burlingame HS; Burlingame, KS; (1); Band; Rep Stu Cncl; Var JV Bsktbl; Var L Ftbl; Var L Trk; Hon Roll; Candidate For Qn Of Courts.

CARROLL, JOHN W; Great Bend Sr HS; Great Bend, KS; (3); 102/230; Library Aide; Teachers Aide; Hon Roll; Boys St Nom; KS Law Enforcement Schl; Barton Cty CC.

CARROLL, RENE; Garden City Sr HS; Garden City, KS; (4); Cmnty Wkr; FHA; Hosp Aide; Science Clb; SADD; Band; Drill Tm; Mrchg Band; Pep Band; Var Pom Pon; Garden City CC; Crmnl Jstc.

CARSON, DENA C; Parsons HS; Mound Valley, KS; (1); L Vllybl; Sprts Clb; Cmptrs.

CARSON, JENNIFER L; Labette Co HS; Parsons, KS; (2); FCA; Natl FFA Org; SADD; JV Bsktbl; JV Tennis; JV Var Trk; Hon Roll; Stu Pilot License; KS ST U; Vet Medicine.

CARSTEDT, KAREN; Marmaton Valley Jr Sr HS; Moran, KS; (3); Am Leg Aux Girls St; Church Yth Grp; Drama Clb; FCA; 4-H; Hosp Aide; Math Tm; Natl FFA Org; Pep Clb; Band; Chrch Cmp.

CARTER, ANDREA B; Berean Acad; Newton, KS; (4); 4/32; Letterman Clb; Teachers Aide; Orch; School Play; Rep Jr Cls; Rep Sr Cls; Trk; Cit Awd; High Hon Roll; NHS; Calvary Bible Coll.

CARTER, ANGELA D; Russell HS; Russell, KS; (1); SADD; Chorus; School Musical; Hon Roll; Kay Clb; Tutor; Comm Art/Elem Ed.

CARTER, BECKY; Washburn Rural HS; Topeka, KS; (3); Dance Clb; Pep Clb; Varsity Clb; Variety Show; Var L Chrldng; KU; Tchr; Psychology.

CARTER, CARYN E; Blue Valley HS; Leawood, KS; (2); Debate Tm; NFL; Temple Yth Grp; Tennis; Hon Roll; Lawyer/Bus.

CARTER, DANIELLE D; Topeka West HS; Topeka, KS; (4); Church Yth Grp; Spanish Clb; SADD; Teachers Aide; Rep Sr Cls; Ofcr Stu Cncl; Tennis; Hon Roll; 10th ST Tennis; VP Spnsh Clb; Washburn Univ; Elem Ed.

CARTER, ERIC; Santa Fe Trail HS; Overbrook, KS; (3); 25/94; Am Leg Boys St; Church Yth Grp; Cmnty Wkr; FBLA; Letterman Clb; Rep Stu Cncl; Var L Bsbl; Var L Bsktbl; Var Crs Cntry; Hon Roll; All St 4A 1st Team Bsktbl, Ord Team All St Bsktbl.

CARTER, IVY M; Highland Park HS; Topeka, KS; (2); Math Clb; SADD; Drill Tm; Mgr(s); Vllybl; Hon Roll; Nrsng Home Vol; Cert Kybrdng I/II; VOTEC; Med Sec.

CARTER, JOSHUA; Garden City Sr HS; Garden City, KS; (3); Church Yth Grp; Debate Tm; Math Tm; NFL; Speech Tm; Band; Mrchg Band; High Hon Roll; NHS; Prfct Atten Awd; Acad Ltr.

CARTER, JULIE V; Blue Valley HS; Stilwell, KS; (2); Q&S; Teachers Aide; Chorus; Variety Show; Rptr Nwsp; Crs Cntry; Trk; Hon Roll; KU; Brdcst Jrnlsm.

CARTER, KAREN L; Wichita South HS; Wichita, KS; (4); Church Yth Grp; SADD; Band; Mrchg Band; Pep Band; High Hon Roll; Hon Roll; Butler Cty CC; Acctng; Mrktg.

CARTER, MICHAEL P; Blue Valley Northwest HS; Overland Park, KS; (2); 1/404; Church Yth Grp; Acpl Chr; Church Choir; School Musical; Bsktbl; High Hon Roll.

CARTER, RACHEL S; Blue Valley North HS; Leawood, KS; (2); Model UN; Drill Tm; Flag Corp; Hon Roll; Danceing 11 Yrs; ISU; Mtrnty Nrs.

CARTHEN, KALISHA J; Wichita Southeast HS; Wichita, KS; (2); 40/436; Church Yth Grp; Cmnty Wkr; French Clb; Office Aide; Teachers Aide; Var Chrldng; Var Trk; JV Vllybl; Hon Roll; Acad Ltr; Gspl Choir; Blck Awrnss VP; All-Star Chrldr; UCA Cmp; Howard U; Pedtrcn.

CARTHEN, WARNELL D; Wichita East HS; Wichita, KS; (3); Library Aide; Teachers Aide; Band; Chorus; Engrng.

CARTLIDGE, JENNIFER M; Great Bend Sr HS; Great Bend, KS; (3); 10/230; Church Yth Grp; Cmnty Wkr; FCA; Pep Clb; SADD; Teachers Aide; Acpl Chr; Swing Chorus; Variety Show; Rep Frsh Cls; KS ST Univ; Law.

CARTWRIGHT, CHRIS; Arkansas City HS; Arkansas City, KS; (4); 26/180; Scholastic Bowl; Socr; Hon Roll; NHS; Pres Schlr; U Of MO Rolla; Aerosp Engrng.

CARTY, ANNE; Lansing HS; Lansing, KS; (2); #2 in class; Art Clb; Drama Clb; French Clb; Sftbl; French Hon Soc; High Hon Roll; Co-Pres Of Art Clb; Ntl Art Hnr Soc; Snowboarding; Art His; Anthropology.

CARTY, ELIZABETH B; Blue Valley Northwest HS; Shawnee Mission, KS; (4); Pep Clb; Teachers Aide; Mgr(s); Powder Puff Ftbl; Score Keeper; Johnson Cty CC; Hotel/Res Mgmt.

CARVER, DALE TRAVIS; Blue Valley HS; Overland Park, KS; (2); 32/237; Cmnty Wkr; FCA; Mgr Nwsp; Var Socr; Capt Swmmng; Hon Roll; Jr Natl Caliber Swimmer; Atll Amer Consideration Time Standard In Swimming.

CASEY, CATHLEEN E; Pierson Jr HS; Kansas City, KS; (1); Rep Soph Cls; Rep Stu Cncl; Var L Chrldng; L Vllybl; Cit Awd; High Hon Roll; Jr NHS; Pres Schlr; Peer Mediation Team; Suicide Prevention Trng; Bus.

CASEY, CHRIS M; Halstead HS; Halstead, KS; (2); 15/65; Rptr Nwsp; Hon Roll; Wichita St Univ; Premed.

CASEY, THERESA M; Olathe North Sr HS; Olathe, KS; (2); Cmnty Wkr; HOBY; Teachers Aide; Band; Chorus; Mrchg Band; High Hon Roll; Hon Roll; Pres Acad Fit Awd; Vol Help Elem Schl Chldrn; Aided Comm Envrnmntl Svcs; Advncd Algebra/Trig; Hnrs Eng/Chem Cls; Genetics/Biochem.

CASEY, TRACIE; Olathe North Sr HS; Olathe, KS; (2); Church Yth Grp; Cmnty Wkr; Spanish Clb; Band; Mrchg Band; Pep Band; High Hon Roll; Hon Roll; Pres Acad Fit Awd; Family & Consumer Sci Clb; Comm Beautification Svc; Genetics; Chem.

CASEY, TRINA; South Gray HS; Copeland, KS; (1); 1/31; 4-H; Quiz Bowl; Band; Chorus; Pep Band; JV Var Bsktbl; JV Vllybl; 4-H Awd; High Hon Roll; Val.

CASH, JARED D; Troy HS; Troy, KS; (2); Boy Scts; Drama Clb; 4-H; Quiz Bowl; School Play; Var JV Crs Cntry; JV Ftbl; Var Trk; Var Wrstlng; NHS; Pittsburg ST Coll; Comp Pgmng.

CASH, LISA; Udall HS; Udall, KS; (1); Hosp Aide; School Play; Hon Roll; Poem Pblshd Natl Lit Of Poetry Pblctn Shadows & Light 96.

CASHER, NICHOL R; Derby HS; Wichita, KS; (3); Library Aide; Pep Clb; ROTC; SADD; Teachers Aide; Color Guard; Ed Yrbk; JV Var Chrldng; JV Trk; Hon Roll; Tns As Tchrs, Anti Smkng Grp; SADD; Med Fld.

CASHMAN, MEGAN S; Downs HS; Downs, KS; (2); FCA; 4-H; FHA; Natl FFA Org; Band; VP Soph Cls; Bsktbl; Sftbl; Hon Roll; St Schlr; Pub Lit Magazine; Profcncy Awd Sheep Prdctn Twice FFA; Ride Horses; KSU; Vet.

CASIDA, KELLI D; Jayhawk-Linn HS; Prescott, KS; (3); Church Yth Grp; 4-H; Band; Chorus; Church Choir; Mrchg Band; Pep Band; Crs Cntry; Trk; 4-H Awd; ST Trk; ST Music Festival; Fort Scott Comm Coll; Music Ed.

CASNER, JARROD L; Bishop Ward HS; Kansas City, KS; (2); 34/99; Church Yth Grp; Drama Clb; JCL; Latin Clb; NFL; Band; JV Bsbl; JV Ftbl; JV Wrstlng; Hon Roll; Wrestler Of Yr; Qualifier St Forensics.

CASPER, ROBERT T; Fredonia HS; Fredonia, KS; (3); 1/75; Church Yth Grp; Cmnty Wkr; FCA; VP 4-H; Pres Natl FFA Org; Quiz Bowl; Science Clb; 4-H Awd; High Hon Roll; Prfct Atten Awd; 1st Pl Team Natl FFA Champs Ag Mech; Engrng.

CASSAW, COREY D; Colby Sr HS; Colby, KS; (2); Art Clb; Church Yth Grp; FCA; Bsktbl; Ftbl; Trk; Wt Lftg; KS ST Univ.

CASSELL, EMILY; Wichita East HS; Wichita, KS; (3); Debate Tm; Hosp Aide; NFL; Spanish Clb; Chorus; School Musical; JV Var Chrldng; Hon Roll; NHS; Spanish NHS; Intl BA.

CASSIDY, CHRISTINE M; Colby Sr HS; Colby, KS; (2); 73/103; Debate Tm; Office Aide; Spanish Clb; Chorus; Ed Yrbk; Mgr Vllybl; Cit Awd; Hon Roll.

CASTANEDA, ANA M; Sumner Acad Of Arts & Science; Kansas City, KS; (4); Art Clb; French Clb; Spanish Clb; SADD; French Hon Soc; High Hon Roll; NHS; Spanish NHS; Mutlcltrl Yth Tgthr Spkr; Intl BADIPLMA Cndt Magna Cum Laude; Psych; Crim Psych.

CASTANEDA, SALINA M; Wyandotte HS; Kansas City, KS; (2); Church Yth Grp; Intnl Clb; Variety Show; Phtg Yrbk; Hon Roll; LULAC; Upward Bound; Acad Of Art Coll; Photogrphr.

CASTEEL, COREY; Abilene HS; Abilene, KS; (3); Am Leg Boys St; Debate Tm; Drama Clb; FCA; Natl FFA Org; NFL; School Play; Rep Soph Cls; Rep Jr Cls; Rep Sr Cls; Jr Lions; PE; Coach.

CASTELLANOS, ELIZABETH G; Chaparral HS; Dixon, CA; (2); Key Clb; Pep Clb; Band; Chorus; Mrchg Band; Pep Band; Var Chrldng; Var Trk; Vllybl; High Hon Roll; Med.

CASTENS, BENJAMIN; Wichita Heights HS; Wichita, KS; (4); 12/226; Am Leg Boys St; Church Yth Grp; German Clb; SADD; Chorus; Variety Show; Var Socr; Hon Roll; NHS; Pres Acad Fit Awd; Concordia Coll; Civil Engrng.

CASTLEBERRY, AMY M; Central Heights Sr HS; Rantoul, KS; (2); FCA; FHA; Letterman Clb; Pep Clb; Swing Chorus; High Hon Roll; Hon Roll; NHS; Natl Brrl Horse Assn; FHA Dist Sec; Amer Hstry Medal; Ft Scott; Psych.

CASTROP, KELLIE A; St Thomas Aquinas HS; Lenexa, KS; (3); Art Clb; Cmnty Wkr; French Clb; GAA; Science Clb; Spanish Clb; SADD; Intrml Bsktbl; JV Socr; High Hon Roll; Vol Work; Art Cls; U Of FL; Veterinary Medicine.

CATES, KELSEY B; Bishop Carroll Catholic HS; Wichita, KS; (2); Var Chrldng; JV Socr; JV Vllybl.

CATHCART-RAKE, KATE M; Salina HS Central; Salina, KS; (4); Church Yth Grp; Cmnty Wkr; Debate Tm; Drama Clb; NFL; Quiz Bowl; SADD; Church Choir; Orch; School Musical; William Jewellcol; Bus Admin.

CATLIN, AARON D; Clay Ctr Cmty HS; Clay Center, KS; (3); Am Leg Boys St; Church Yth Grp; Yrbk; VP Soph Cls; Pres Sr Cls; Var L Bsbl; JV Bsktbl; Var L Ftbl; Var L Trk; Hon Roll; Tiger Cncl; Stu Rep Schl Site Cncl; Med.

CATLIN, MICAH D; Salina HS South; Salina, KS; (3); Am Leg Boys St; Church Yth Grp; Cmnty Wkr; Debate Tm; Quiz Bowl; Spanish Clb; Band; Mrchg Band; Orch; Pep Band.

CATLIN, MINDY C; Salina HS South; Olathe, KS; (4); 1/225; Dance Clb; Drama Clb; Hosp Aide; JA; Math Tm; NFL; Pep Clb; Quiz Bowl; SADD; Teachers Aide; Pres Ldshp Awd; Xerox Humntes Awd; KS Regents Hnr Acad; KS St Univ.

CATON, MOLLY M; Bishop Miege HS; Shawnee Mission, KS; (1); 1/245; Church Yth Grp; GAA; NFL; Pep Clb; Service Clb; School Play; Rep Frsh Cls; Rep Stu Cncl; Sftbl; Vllybl; Frosh Class High GPA Awd; Spirit Awd; Med Fld.

CATRON, CHERYL L; Washburn Rural HS; Topeka, KS; (2); 42/380; Church Yth Grp; Cmnty Wkr; Letterman Clb; Chorus; Church Choir; Variety Show; Yrbk; Tennis; High Hon Roll; Med/Sci Fld.

CATTERSON, CARRIE J; Chanute Sr HS; Chanute, KS; (2); 4-H; French Clb; Red Cross Aide; Spanish Clb; 4-H Awd; High Hon Roll; Prncpls Ldrshp Tm; Chiro.

CAUBLE, JUSTIN R; Riverton Schl; Baxter Springs, KS; (2); Art Clb; Church Yth Grp; Computer Clb; Math Clb; Math Tm; Ski Clb; Ofcr Soph Cls; Hon Roll; Ntl Merit Ltr.

CAUDILLO, SARA M; Wellington Sr HS; Wellington, KS; (2); Girl Scts; Library Aide; Band; Mrchg Band; Pep Band; Mgr(s); Score Keeper; Hon Roll; CCD Aide; Altar Srvr; U Of KS; Med.

CAULFIELD, SUSAN; St Thomas Aquinas HS; Leawood, KS; (4); 2/231; Am Leg Aux Girls St; Church Yth Grp; Pres VP FCA; German Clb; GAA; Pep Clb; Scholastic Bowl; SADD; Treas Frsh Cls; VP Jr Cls; FCA Pres, VP; Peer Mnstr; Prncpl Ldrshp Awd 95; U Notre Dame; Comp Engr.

CAULKINS, ANGELA L; Field Kindley Mem Sr HS; Coffeyville, KS; (3); 20/180; Church Yth Grp; Drama Clb; Band; Jazz Band; Mrchg Band; Pep Band; School Play; Mgr(s); Hon Roll; NHS; Natl HS 1st Chr Trombone Awd Jr Yr; ST Qual Brss Quintet Soph Yr; Intl Frgn Lang Awds Wnnr Fre 11; Elem Ed.

CAUTHON, A SUSANNE; Shawnee Hghts HS; Topeka, KS; (4); 45/230; Church Yth Grp; Cmnty Wkr; FCA; Pep Clb; Rptr Nwsp; Var Tennis; High Hon Roll; Hon Roll; Swm Tm; Pres Awd Educ Excl; KS Univ; Grphc Dsgn.

CAVANAUGH, CHRISTY; Goddard HS; Goddard, KS; (4); Spanish Clb; Teachers Aide; Bsktbl; Tennis; High Hon Roll; Hon Roll; NHS; Pittsburg ST Univ.

CAVANAUGH, TRISHA A; Goddard HS; Goddard, KS; (1); Church Yth Grp; Bsktbl; Sftbl; High Hon Roll; Ed Awd Prog Pres; Gov Cntr Teen Ldrshp; Pittsburg St Univ.

CAVE, TALISHA K; Wichita West HS; Wichita, KS; (3); 16/286; Office Aide; Spanish Clb; Teachers Aide; Church Choir; High Hon Roll; Hon Roll; Prfct Atten Awd; WSU; Pdtrcn.

CAVNAR, ANNA L; St Thomas Aquinas HS; Overland Park, KS; (3); 33/265; French Clb; NFL; Speech Tm; High Hon Roll; NHS; Jazz Band; Prfct Atten Awd; Hrsbckrdng Comp; Piano Comp; Teens For Life Club; Vol Heartlands Schl Of Rdng Hndcp; AIDS Hospice; Intnl Bus.

CAYLOR, ANGELA D; Central Heights Sr HS; Ottawa, KS; (4); 11/42; FCA; Letterman Clb; Pep Clb; Science Clb; Spanish Clb; Band; Ofcr Stu Cncl; Bsktbl; Chrldng; Trk; St Bsktbll; St Track; Ft Scott CC.

CAYWOOD, BRAD W; Sterling HS; Sterling, KS; (3); 1/60; Church Yth Grp; Letterman Clb; Quiz Bowl; Scholastic Bowl; Science Clb; Varsity Clb; Tennis; High Hon Roll; Army Natl Guard; Church Missions Comm Mem; Qualified For St Tnns Cmptn; KS ST; Engrng.

CEBALLOS, MELISSA A; Olathe East Sr HS; Olathe, KS; (2); Church Yth Grp; Orch; High Hon Roll; Spanish NHS; KU.

CEBULA, ADAM P; Goodland HS; Goodland, KS; (3); Church Yth Grp; Band; Mrchg Band; Pep Band; JV Bsktbl; Stat JV Crs Cntry; Var L Golf; Intrml Wt Lftg; Hon Roll; NHS.

CECH, JESSICA A; Goodland HS; Goodland, KS; (2); ROTC; JV Chrldng; JV Tennis; KSU; Bio.

CENTLIVRE, BROCK J; Olathe South Sr HS; Olathe, KS; (2); 118/466; Boy Scts; Bsktbl; Ftbl; Trk; Wt Lftg; High Hon Roll; Hon Roll; Notre Dame; Engrng; Drafting.

CERADSKY, RYAN L; J C Harmon HS; Kansas City, KS; (3); 4-H; Acpl Chr; Chorus; Drill Tm; Flag Corp; Mrchg Band; Ofcr Frsh Cls; Ofcr Soph Cls; Ofcr Jr Cls; Hon Roll; KU; Psychlgst.

CERNECH, CHRISTY A; Basehor Linwood HS; Bonner Springs, KS; (3); Church Yth Grp; Debate Tm; Drama Clb; FCA; French Clb; Girl Scts; NFL; Spanish Clb; SADD; School Play; K ST; Chld Psych.

CERSOVSKY, JACOB; Colby Sr HS; Colby, KS; (3); 16/97; JV Var Ftbl; JV Golf; JV Trk; JV Var Wrstlng; Hon Roll; NHS; Natl Lang Arts Olympiad; Rel Ed Classes; Eng/Arch.

CHACEY, MICHAEL D; Derby HS; Derby, KS; (3); 17/350; Boy Scts; Church Yth Grp; Debate Tm; NFL; Church Choir; Mrchg Band; High Hon Roll; NHS; Future Prblm Slvng ST Chmpnshp; Intl Cmptn Prtcpnt; Odyssey Of Mind; Sci/Bio.

CHADD, JAE; Ulysses HS; Ulysses, KS; (3); Art Clb; Pres FHA; HOBY; Red Cross Aide; Acpl Chr; Chorus; School Musical; Var L Chrldng; High Hon Roll; NHS; Lifegrd; Cert Wtr Sfty Instr; KS St U; Archtr.

CHAFFEE, ALLEN; Clay Ctr Cmty HS; Clay Center, KS; (4); 11/109; Am Leg Boys St; FBLA; Band; Jazz Band; Mrchg Band; Pep Band; School Musical; Var Bsktbl; Var L Ftbl; Var L Golf; Bus; Own Bus.

CHAFFIN, MEAGAN L; Wichita North HS; Wichita, KS; (3); Church Yth Grp; Cmnty Wkr; Drama Clb; 4-H; Spanish Clb; Teachers Aide; Thesps; Church Choir; School Musical; School Play; Manhatten Chrstn Col; Psych.

CHAI, SHAWN P; Russell HS; Russell, KS; (2); Boy Scts; Natl FFA Org; SADD; JV Bsktbl; Var JV Ftbl; JV Trk; High Hon Roll; Hon Roll; Prfct Atten Awd; FFA Ofcr; Lawyer.

CHAIRS, BRITTNI F; Wichita North HS; Wichita, KS; (3); Church Yth Grp; Cmnty Wkr; Girl Scts; JA; ROTC; Church Choir; Variety Show; Prfct Atten Awd; Honor Med Soc; Langton U.

CHALFANT, LINDSEY N; Cair Paravel - Latin Schl; Topeka, KS; (4); 7/15; Acpl Chr; Chorus; School Musical; Sec Jr Cls; Stat Mgr(s); Var Swmmng; JV Vllybl; Hon Roll; Piano; U Of KS; Intl Bus.

CHALFANT, MELINDA R; Mc Louth Schl; Mc Louth, KS; (3); 2/38; Am Leg Aux Girls St; Church Yth Grp; FBLA; FHA; Pep Clb; Quiz Bowl; SADD; Teachers Aide; Band; Chorus; Shrine Bowl Bnd Camp; Ottowa Univ; Spch Thpy.

CHALLACOMBE, DARIN J; Cair Paravel - Latin Schl; Topeka, KS; (4); Boy Scts; Church Yth Grp; Drama Clb; School Musical; School Play; Stage Crew; Ed Nwsp; Yrbk; Rep Stu Cncl; Stat Bsktbl; Jrnlst Of The Yr Awd; Comm Actor & Crew Mem; Medicine & Cross-Cultural Mssn.

CHALOUPKA, STACEY L; Belle Plaine HS; Belle Plaine, KS; (2); Letterman Clb; Pep Clb; SADD; Yrbk; Bsktbl; Crs Cntry; Trk; High Hon Roll; NHS; Prfct Atten Awd; Outstndng Prfrmncs St Cmptn Trck, Crs Cntry; Pittsburg ST U; Bus Mgmt.

CHALOUPKA, TRACEY D; Belle Plaine HS; Belle Plaine, KS; (2); French Clb; Letterman Clb; SADD; Var Crs Cntry; Trk; Wt Lftg; Hon Roll; Pittsburg Univ; Acctng.

CHAMBERLAND, REGAN; Sedan HS; Sedan, KS; (4); 5/27; Letterman Clb; Teachers Aide; Chorus; School Musical; Rptr Yrbk; Sec Stu Cncl; Co-Capt Chrldng; Sftbl; Vllybl; Hon Roll; Pittsburg ST U.

CHAMBERS, CARRIE L; Yates Ctr HS; Yates Center, KS; (3); 4/54; FCA; Sec SADD; Chorus; VP Frsh Cls; VP Jr Cls; VP Sr Cls; Var Bsktbl; Var Sftbl; Var Vllybl; High Hon Roll.

CHAMBERS, HEATHER; Turner HS; Kansas City, KS; (3); 10/260; FTA; GAA; Letterman Clb; Varsity Clb; Band; Jazz Band; Mrchg Band; Pep Band; Var L Bsktbl; Var L Crs Cntry; Tn Advsry Cncl KCK Ldrshp 2020; All Conf Sftbl; All KS Sftbl; All Huron Bsktbl; All Soph Tm Bsktl; Ed.

CHAMPLIN, DAVID G; Blue Valley Northwest HS; Overland Park, KS; (4); 1/343; Hosp Aide; Band; School Musical; Var Crs Cntry; Var Trk; High Hon Roll; VP NHS; Ntl Merit SF; All St Band.

CHAN, BRADY C; Manhattan HS; Manhattan, KS; (3); 30/430; Church Yth Grp; FCA; Spanish Clb; Teachers Aide; Rep Stu Cncl; Var L Socr; Var L Trk; High Hon Roll; NHS; Pres Acad Fit Awd; Study Abrd Mexico; U Of KS.

CHANANELL, NICOLE; Jetmore HS; Jetmore, KS; (4); 1/15; Church Yth Grp; FCA; Pep Clb; Quiz Bowl; Scholastic Bowl; Teachers Aide; Band; Chorus; Mrchg Band; Pep Band; Outstdng Math/Sci Stdt Awd; Outstdng Band Stdt; Hutchinson Comm Coll.

CHANCE, JILL M; Maize HS; Wichita, KS; (2); 62/280; Church Yth Grp; SADD; Var JV Chrldng; Hon Roll; Kays; KS Univ; Lwyr.

CHANCE, RAYMOND D; Cheney Jr Sr HS; Cheney, KS; (3); Church Yth Grp; Pres 4-H; Band; Chorus; Drm Mjr(t); Jazz Band; Mrchg Band; Pep Band; Golf; 4-H Awd; Mechncl Engrng.

CHANDLER, CARLY; Shawnee Mission Northwest HS; Shawnee Mission, KS; (2); 170/458; Church Yth Grp; Cmnty Wkr; Dance Clb; Debate Tm; Pep Clb; Church Choir; Drill Tm; Hon Roll; Young Life & Campaigners Clbs.

CHANDLER, LAURA L; Northwest Schl; Wichita, KS; (3); Debate Tm; Intnl Clb; Math Clb; Math Tm; NFL; Science Clb; Tennis; Trk; High Hon Roll; NHS; K ST; Orthodontist; Dentist.

CHANDLER, WENDY; Louisburg HS; Louisburg, KS; (3); 5/78; Church Yth Grp; Pres Math Clb; Teachers Aide; Temple Yth Grp; Nwsp; Ed Lit Mag; High Hon Roll; NHS; Yth Planning Comm; TSA.

CHANDRA, SAPANA; St Mary's Colgan HS; Pittsburg, KS; (2); Pep Clb; Science Clb; Hon Roll; Prfct Atten Awd; Schlrs Bowl; Piano; Drawing/Art; KS Univ; Bus.

CHANEY, ADAM; Smoky Valley HS; Lindsborg, KS; (4); Boy Scts; Church Yth Grp; FCA; Letterman Clb; Teachers Aide; Varsity Clb; Band; Mrchg Band; Pep Band; Variety Show; Top 25 ST Receivers; ST Clss 4a Trple Jump 5th Pl 95-; Bethany Coll; Admin Of Jstce.

CHANG, ALBERT M; Blue Valley HS; Overland Park, KS; (3); 2/251; Am Leg Boys St; Debate Tm; JCL; Latin Clb; Crs Cntry; Tennis; High Hon Roll; NHS; KS Assn Of Yth; Comp Engrng.

CHANG, JACK; Topeka West HS; Topeka, KS; (1); Tae Kwon Do; MIT; Cmptr.

CHANG, JESSE; Olathe East Sr HS; Overland Park, KS; (2); Boy Scts; Computer Clb; Letterman Clb; Orch; Yrbk; Crs Cntry; Trk; Wrstlng; Hon Roll; TSA Frst Pl ST Cmptr Constr/Appl; Pittsburgh ST Univ; Cmptr Sci.

CHANG, JESSICA; Topeka West HS; Topeka, KS; (2); French Clb; Pep Clb; Hon Roll; Prtcptd Natl Fre Cntst Frosh/Soph Yr; KA ST Univ; Phrmcst.

CHANG, NATHAN; Olathe East Sr HS; Olathe, KS; (2); Church Yth Grp; Band; Mrchg Band; Bsktbl; JV Ftbl; Mgr(s); JV Trk; Hon Roll; Astrnmy.

CHANG, TINA; Southeast HS; Wichita, KS; (3); 9/376; Math Clb; Math Tm; Teachers Aide; High Hon Roll; NHS; Asian Club Sec Jr Yr; Pittsburg North Rly Algbr Smplfctn 2nd Pl Soph Yr; Algbr Eqtns/Inql Alg Smplfct; U Of Southern CA; Fin.

CHAPIN, NIKI; Desoto HS; Shawnee Mission, KS; (3); #3 in class; Church Yth Grp; Sec Treas 4-H; French Clb; Math Tm; SADD; Sec Pres Thesps; Band; Pres Chorus; Church Choir; Jazz Band; Frnscs.

CHAPMAN, BEN J; Ottawa HS; Ottawa, KS; (2); Church Yth Grp; French Clb; Letterman Clb; Band; Jazz Band; Mrchg Band; Pep Band; Variety Show; JV Var Golf; Mgr(s); Baker Univ.

CHAPMAN, EMILY; Olathe East Sr HS; Lenexa, KS; (3); 16/375; Church Yth Grp; French Clb; Letterman Clb; Math Tm; Pep Clb; Teachers Aide; Chorus; Rptr Phtg Yrbk; Sftbl; Vllybl; Piano; Wheaton IL Coll; Bio; Chem.

CHAPMAN, FRANKLIN A; Labette Co HS; Mound Valley, KS; (4); 70/130; Church Yth Grp; 4-H; FBLA; Natl FFA Org; VICA; L Bsbl; Ftbl; Golf; 4-H Awd; Pres Acad Fit Awd; Labette CC; Wood Tech.

CHAPMAN, KRISTINE; Shawnee Mission Nw HS; Lenexa, KS; (3); 32/460; Church Yth Grp; Sec Intnl Clb; Sec Key Clb; Q&S; SADD; Thesps; Acpl Chr; Nwsp; Ed Lit Mag; High Hon Roll; Jrnlsm, Choir & Acad Ltrs; U Of KS.

CHAPMAN, KRISTY A; Leavenworth HS; Leavenworth, KS; (1); JV Var Bsktbl; JV Crs Cntry; Var Sftbl; High Hon Roll; Hon Roll; All Amer Schlr Awd.

CHAPMAN, MANDY J; Garden City Sr HS; Garden City, KS; (2); Debate Tm; Science Clb; Speech Tm; JV Var Bsktbl; Var L Trk; JV Vllybl; Var Wt Lftg; High Hon Roll; Hon Roll; Pres Acad Fit Awd; World Yth Environmental Ldr; U Of Rochester; Virology.

CHAPMAN, SETH T; Beloit Jr Sr HS; Beloit, KS; (1); Band; Mrchg Band; Pep Band; JV Ftbl; JV Golf; High Hon Roll; Pres Acad Fit Awd; Future Med Clb; KS ST; Phrmcst.

CHAPMAN, STACIE J; Shawnee Mission Nw Sr HS; Shawnee Mission, KS; (3); Cmnty Wkr; Teachers Aide; Drill Tm; Mrchg Band; High Hon Roll; Hon Roll; NHS; Fashion Careers; Mrktg; KU; Acctng; Mrktg.

CHAPPELOW, SARAH E; Santa Fe Trail Jr HS; Olathe, KS; (1); Church Yth Grp; Drama Clb; Key Clb; Chorus; Church Choir; School Play; Variety Show; Rptr Nwsp; Mgr(s); Vllybl; Pres Awd For Educl Excl; NY; Theatre Actress.

CHAPPIE, MARTKETTA D; J C Harmon HS; Kansas City, KS; (1); FCA; Office Aide; Pep Clb; SADD; Teachers Aide; Drill Tm; Ofcr Frsh Cls; Chrldng; Crs Cntry; Trk.

CHAPUT, EDDIE J; Clifton-Clyde HS; Clifton, KS; (4); Church Yth Grp; Band; Jazz Band; Mrchg Band; Pep Band; Ofcr Bsbl; Bsktbl; Ftbl; Sftbl; Trk; Cloud Cty Coll; Phy Thrpst.

CHARAY, JASON; Washburn Rural HS; Topeka, KS; (2); 58/450; Boy Scts; Church Yth Grp; Phtg Nwsp; Phtg Yrbk; VP Frsh Cls; Rep Soph Cls; Treas Jr Cls; JV Bsktbl; Intrml Ftbl; Var Trk; Eagle Scout; King Wntr Dnc Cls; Ynamed Yth Cnsl Prsbytry; Med/Bus.

CHARAY, JULIE; Washburn Rural HS; Topeka, KS; (2); Church Yth Grp; FCA; JV Bsktbl; Var L Socr; High Hon Roll.

CHARBONEAU, ANGELA T; Derby Christian Schl; Haysville, KS; (2); Church Yth Grp; Drama Clb; Band; Stage Crew; Yrbk; Rep Soph Cls; Ofcr Stu Cncl; Var Bsktbl; Hon Roll; Chrstn Charature Awd Soph Cls; Soul Wng Clb; Hmcmng Rep Soph Cls; Elem Ed.

CHARBONNEAU, SHANNON R; Silver Lake Jr Sr HS; Silver Lake, KS; (3); 10/53; Am Leg Aux Girls St; Chorus; School Musical; Rptr Nwsp; Sec Stu Cncl; Var L Bsktbl; Var L Chrldng; Var L Vllybl; Hon Roll; Treas NHS; Acad All League 3 Yrs; KS Univ; Occupthrpy.

CHARBONNEAU, TIFFANY M; Phillipsburg HS; Phillipsburg, KS; (2); Am Leg Aux Girls St; Church Yth Grp; Dance Clb; GAA; Pep Clb; Spanish Clb; Speech Tm; Drill Tm; Flag Corp; Rep Jr Cls; SADD; Kays.

CHARLES, CRYSTAL; Wyandotte HS; Kansas City, KS; (2); Dance Clb; FBLA; Pep Clb; Spanish Clb; SADD; Church Choir; School Musical; School Play; Ofcr Soph Cls; Ofcr Stu Cncl; Teen Hope; Peer; Lawyer/Paralegal.

CHARLES, NICHOLAS; Derby Christian Schl; Wichita, KS; (1); Church Yth Grp; Cmnty Wkr; Hosp Aide; Library Aide; Teachers Aide; Church Choir; School Play; Yrbk; Score Keeper; Hon Roll; Best Chrstn Character Prin Awd; KS ST Coll; Sociology.

CHARLES, SARA A; Hoisington HS; Hoisington, KS; (2); Intnl Clb; Letterman Clb; Pep Clb; SADD; Band; Pep Band; Rep Soph Cls; L Crs Cntry; L Trk; Hon Roll; LEAD Youth Forum; Ft Hays ST Univ.

CHARPENTIER, NICOLE; Shawnee Mission Nw Sr HS; Lenexa, KS; (3); 23/450; Church Yth Grp; Capt Drill Tm; Mrchg Band; JV Sftbl; High Hon Roll; Hon Roll; NHS; Acad Ltr; Drill Tm Var Capt; Straight A's 6 Smstrs; Med.

CHASE, HEATHER S; St Thomas Aquinas HS; Shawnee Mission, KS; (3); 58/263; Church Yth Grp; Cmnty Wkr; Spanish Clb; SADD; Teachers Aide; Acpl Chr; Church Choir; School Musical; Variety Show; Var L Tennis; MO Vly Tennis Rankg Sngls/Dbls; Ms Lexexa Pagnt Fnlst; Elem Ed.

CHASE, SPRING K; Parsons HS; Parsons, KS; (4); 26/130; Hosp Aide; Office Aide; Red Cross Aide; SADD; Yrbk; Capt Chrldng; Hon Roll; NHS; Pres Acad Fit Awd; Library Aide; Pre-Med Clb; Sports Clb; SAVE Clb; KS ST Univ; Pre-Phy Thrpst.

CHASE, TINA; Ulysses HS; Ulysses, KS; (4); Cmnty Wkr; FBLA; Letterman Clb; SADD; Var Capt Chrldng; Var Trk; High Hon Roll; Hon Roll; NHS; NCA All Amer Chrldr; KS ST; Med.

CHASTAIN, JACKIE L; El Dorado HS; El Dorado, KS; (2); Chorus; JV Sftbl; KS Univ; Police Ofcr/Lawyer.

CHAU, THOMAS P; Derby HS; Derby, KS; (1); Orch; Brdcstng.

CHAU, TIM P; Derby HS; Derby, KS; (1); Orch; Hon Roll.

CHAUNCEY, DANIELLE M; Wichita East HS; Wichita, KS; (4); Church Yth Grp; Red Cross Aide; Chorus; School Musical; School Play; Stage Crew; Variety Show; Phtg Nwsp; Phtg Yrbk; Var L Bsktbl; Harp; Law.

CHAUVIN, KELLYE L; Baldwin HS; Baldwin City, KS; (3); Church Yth Grp; FBLA; Intnl Clb; Math Tm; NFL; Office Aide; School Musical; Pom Pon; Tennis; Hon Roll; Comp Dnce Tm; Fashn Inst Of NY; Fash Merch.

CHAVEZ, CONSUELO; Sedgwick HS; Sedgwick, KS; (3); #4 in class; VP Computer Clb; HOBY; Ofcr Intrml Band; Color Guard; Mrchg Band; Pep Band; School Musical; Variety Show; Trk; WSU; Music Ed.

CHEATHAM, ERIN; Wichita Northwest HS; Wichita, KS; (3); Am Leg Aux Girls St; Church Yth Grp; Cmnty Wkr; NFL; Chorus; Rep Jr Cls; Chrldng; Hon Roll; NHS; Elem Educ.

CHEATHAM, TIM; Sumner Acad Of Arts & Science; Kansas City, KS; (3); Treas German Clb; Latin Clb; Golf; Mgr(s); High Hon Roll; NHS; Ger Natl Hnr Soc; Mech-Civil Engrng.

CHEATUM, TRAVIS; Syracuse Jr Sr HS; Syracuse, KS; (3); 6/37; Church Yth Grp; Drama Clb; 4-H; Letterman Clb; Pep Clb; Speech Tm; Chorus; Church Choir; School Play; Stage Crew; Outdr Clssrm; Manhatten Bible Coll; Vet Sci.

CHEE, BERNARD A; Derby HS; Wichita, KS; (2); Church Yth Grp; JV Trk; Hon Roll; PHYS.

CHEESMAN, KELSEY; Mc Pherson HS; Mc Pherson, KS; (4); Art Clb; Church Yth Grp; Letterman Clb; Q&S; SADD; Phtg Nwsp; Ofcr Jr Cls; Intrml Powder Puff Ftbl; Var L Sftbl; JV Var Tennis; Pres Local Teen Ctr-Back Alley; Natl Jrnlsm Conf Super; Hnrs At Art Shows; Regional Jrnlsm Cmptn 2nd Pl; Emporia ST Univ; Scndry Art Ed.

CHEN, CHINGWEI W; Topeka West HS; Topeka, KS; (1); 1/350; French Clb; Math Clb; Math Tm; Model UN; Quiz Bowl; L Tennis; High Hon Roll; Stu At Washburn U; Stu At U Of KS; Pre-Med; Microbiology.

CHENEY, JASON A; Sylvan Unified HS; Hunter, KS; (3); 3/19; Church Yth Grp; Math Tm; Quiz Bowl; Scholastic Bowl; Speech Tm; SADD; Band; Chorus; Pep Band; School Musical; Medicine.

CHENEY, JENNY; Syracuse Jr Sr HS; Syracuse, KS; (4); 5/30; Cmnty Wkr; Drama Clb; GAA; Letterman Clb; NFL; Pep Clb; Quiz Bowl; Speech Tm; Teachers Aide; Varsity Clb; Writng Conts 1st Pl College Level, 2nd Pl Dist; Photo; GCCC; Commnctns.

CHENG, WAISHENG; Lawrence HS; Lawrence, KS; (3); Chess Clb; Hosp Aide; Intnl Clb; Key Clb; Library Aide; Office Aide; Spanish Clb; Hon Roll; Hnrs Rctl; Hnrlbl Mntn KMTA; KA Univ; Bio.

CHENGAPPA, TINA; Manhattan HS; Manhattan, KS; (1); Cmnty Wkr; Pep Clb; Chrldng; Hon Roll; Gymnstcs; Piano; Dance; KU; Med.

CHENOWETH, SHAWN; Burlingame HS; Burlingame, KS; (3); #1 in class; Letterman Clb; Spanish Clb; Band; Treas Jr Cls; Ftbl; Wrstlng; Hon Roll; NHS; KS ST Univ; Mech Engr.

CHERNEY, CARRIE C; Hillcrest Schl; Agenda, KS; (2); 1/9; Dance Clb; HOBY; Quiz Bowl; Yrbk; VP Soph Cls; Bsktbl; Trk; Vllybl; High Hon Roll; NHS; KS ST U; Elem Ed.

CHERNEY, ERICA; Hillcrest Schl; Agenda, KS; (3); #2 in class; Treas 4-H; Sec FHA; Natl FFA Org; Quiz Bowl; Capt Drill Tm; Ed Yrbk; Pres Jr Cls; Var L Bsktbl; Var L Vllybl; NHS; KS ST U; Arch Dsgn.

CHESMORE, PHILLIP C; Shawnee Heights HS; Topeka, KS; (2); Band; Ftbl; Wt Lftg; Wrstlng.

CHESTER, JANA L; Phillipsburg HS; Glade, KS; (2); Church Yth Grp; Rptr 4-H; Rptr FBLA; Quiz Bowl; Ed Nwsp; Rep Stu Cncl; Tennis; High Hon Roll; Mrchg Band; Pep Band; KS Schol Press Assoc Stu Brd; KAY.

CHIARELLI, CHARLES M; Hillsboro HS; Durham, KS; (2); Computer Clb; Quiz Bowl; Rep Frsh Cls; Rep Soph Cls; Ftbl; Cit Awd; High Hon Roll; Hon Roll; KS ST; Tech.

CHIARELLI, DEREK; Hillsboro HS; Durham, KS; (1); 20/71; Ftbl; Golf; Hon Roll; NHS; Nrsng.

CHIGURUPATI, RADHA; Washburn Rural HS; Topeka, KS; (3); 17/360; Cmnty Wkr; Intnl Clb; JA; SADD; Band; Mrchg Band; Pep Band; School Play; High Hon Roll; NHS; Top Sales Person Of Yr 94 Jr Achvmt; Play Flute; KU; Music.

CHILDERS, DONNA M; Lawrence HS; Lawrence, KS; (3); 253/637; Church Yth Grp; Cmnty Wkr; FTA; Key Clb; Office Aide; Spanish Clb; Church Choir; Yth Ldr Core; Cntrl TX Coll; Elem Ed.

CHILDERS, ROBIN L; Chanute Sr HS; Chanute, KS; (3); 1/120; Church Yth Grp; FCA; Spanish Clb; Nwsp; Rep Stu Cncl; Var Bsktbl; Var Trk; Var Vllybl; Hon Roll; Prins Ldrshp Team.

CHILES, TRACY; Shawnee Mission N HS; Shawnee Mission, KS; (2); 15/463; Pep Clb; School Musical; School Play; Stage Crew; Rep Frsh Cls; Rep Soph Cls; Ofcr Stu Cncl; Var Chrldng; Hon Roll; Acad Ltr.

CHILSON, JOSH; Wellington Sr HS; Wellington, KS; (1); 4/175; Debate Tm; Library Aide; NFL; Scholastic Bowl; SADD; Ed Nwsp; Bsktbl; High Hon Roll; Jr NHS; Rotary Intnl Mrt Awd; Politician; Attorney.

CHITWOOD, ROBYN I; Wellington Sr HS; Mayfield, KS; (3); 28/165; Bus Profs of Am; Cmnty Wkr; Key Clb; SADD; High Hon Roll; Hon Roll; Jr NHS; NHS; Prfct Atten Awd; Bus Pro Amer Reg St Cmptn; KAY; Tn Ldrshp Cmte; Emporia; Acctng.

CHITWOOD, RYAN E; Wellington Sr HS; Mayfield, KS; (4); 29/122; Pres Natl FFA Org; Hon Roll; Treas Jr NHS; Prfct Atten Awd; Lions Awd; FFA Natl Ldrshp Conf In Washington DC; Hutchinson CC; Farm/Ranch Mgmt.

CHMELKA, ADAM J; Washburn Rural HS; Topeka, KS; (2); Boy Scts; Chess Clb; Debate Tm; German Clb; NFL; Orch; Star Trek Clb Chief Engr.

CHMIDLING, KAREN; Jefferson Co North HS; Nortonville, KS; (2); Sec FBLA; Letterman Clb; SADD; Band; Chorus; Drm Mjr(t); Mrchg Band; Pep Band; School Musical; Church Yth Grp; All-Lg Hnr Roll; 1 Rnkng St Solo Voice; KS U; Rdlgy.

CHO, GRACE W; Blue Valley Northwest HS; Overland Park, KS; (2); 65/413; Band; Mrchg Band; Rep Jr Cls; Rep Stu Cncl; JV Chrldng; JV Trk; High Hon Roll; Hon Roll; Pep Band; Multi-Cultural Clb; Korean Schl Greater KS City Grad.

CHOONCHAROEN, STEVE D; Washburn Rural HS; Auburn, KS; (3); 84/470; Am Leg Boys St; Teachers Aide; Var L Bsbl; Intrml Bsktbl; Var Capt Ftbl; Intrml Wt Lftg; High Hon Roll; NHS.

CHOROMANSKI, ROBERT L; St Thomas Aquinas HS; Lenexa, KS; (4); 23/231; Am Leg Boys St; Boy Scts; Debate Tm; Key Clb; Model UN; Var L Swmmng; NHS; Amer Lgn Boys Nation 95; Eagle Scout; U Of KS; Pol Sci.

CHOW, KRISTIN N; Sumner Acad Of Arts & Science; Kansas City, KS; (4); 69/199; Debate Tm; JA; Latin Clb; Orch; Ed Nwsp; Crs Cntry; Tennis; Hon Roll; NHS; Pres Schlr; Bates Coll; Bio-Psych.

CHOWNING, JOEY D; Turner HS; Kansas City, KS; (2); Church Yth Grp; Var L Bsbl; Bsktbl; Var L Socr; High Hon Roll; Hon Roll; Jr NHS; NHS; Prfct Atten Awd; Pres Acad Fit Awd; Strght A Frosh Sci; Span Mark/Excl; Pittsburgh State Univ; Bus Ownr.

CHRINSTENSEN, RENEE; South Barber HS; Kiowa, KS; (4); 1/28; Am Leg Aux Girls St; Church Yth Grp; Drama Clb; Quiz Bowl; Service Clb; Speech Tm; SADD; Acpl Chr; Band; Chorus; Kayettes Treas; Oration/Info Speech St Chmpnshps; KSU; Acctng.

CHRISLIP, ABRAM M; Eudora HS; Eudora, KS; (3); Church Yth Grp; FBLA; Letterman Clb; Scholastic Bowl; Rep Frsh Cls; Rep Soph Cls; Rep Jr Cls; Rep Stu Cncl; Var L Bsbl; Var L Bsktbl; Arch; Engrng.

CHRISMAN, SARAH E; Southeast Saline Schl; Assaria, KS; (3); 24/54; Church Yth Grp; FHA; Pep Clb; Science Clb; Varsity Clb; Band; Chorus; Flag Corp; Mrchg Band; Pep Band; FHA Star Events Parlaw Natls Gold Medal.

CHRISTENSEN, KYLE J; Wichita East HS; Wichita, KS; (2); Boy Scts; Church Yth Grp; Cmnty Wkr; Ftbl; Wt Lftg; Hon Roll; Ynl Life Chrstn Yth Fllwshp Org.

CHRISTENSEN, REBECCA A; Topeka HS; Topeka, KS; (2); Cmnty Wkr; German Clb; Model UN; SADD; Mrchg Band; Orch; Variety Show; Rep Frsh Cls; Treas Soph Cls; High Hon Roll.

CHRISTIANSEN, JON; Hillsboro HS; Durham, KS; (4); 2/45; 4-H; Natl FFA Org; Quiz Bowl; Yrbk; Pres Stu Cncl; L Var Bsktbl; L Var Crs Cntry; L Var Ftbl; NHS; Sal; KS ST U; Engrng.

CHRISTIANSEN, TERESA; Smoky Valley HS; Gypsum, KS; (4); 1/76; Pres Bus Profs of Am; Church Yth Grp; FCA; Pres Stu Cncl; Co-Capt Bsktbl; Var L Trk; Co-Capt Vllybl; DAR Awd; VP NHS; Ntl Merit Ltr.

CHRISTIASON, MICHELLE M; Lyndon HS; Lyndon, KS; (3); FBLA; Library Aide; Spanish Clb; Drill Tm; School Play; Stage Crew; Rptr Nwsp; Mgr(s); Score Keeper; Vllybl; Commnctns.

CHRISTIE, HOLLIE K; Olathe South Sr HS; Olathe, KS; (2); Church Yth Grp; Letterman Clb; Office Aide; Teachers Aide; Varsity Clb; Var Chrldng; Var Gym; Hon Roll; Pres Acad Fit Awd; Chrch Organized Work & Witness Trips Participant; Mid-Amer Nazarene Coll; Psych.

CHRISTMAN, LINDSAY; Wichita Collegiate Schl; Wichita, KS; (3); Church Yth Grp; SADD; Acpl Chr; Chorus; School Play; Variety Show; Tennis; High Hon Roll; Black Belt Tae Kwon Do; Pre-Med.

CHRISTNER, ROB; Hesston HS; Hesston, KS; (4); Church Yth Grp; Acpl Chr; Band; Chorus; Jazz Band; Pep Band; Variety Show; Crs Cntry; Trk; High Hon Roll; Odyssey Of The Mind; Goshen Coll; Engrng.

CHRISTOPHER, ADAM R; Smoky Valley HS; Falun, KS; (1); Drama Clb; FCA; NFL; Thesps; Band; Jazz Band; Orch; High Hon Roll; Church Yth Grp; Chorus; Fort Hays Univ 4 Art Projcts Outstdng Work Awds; Arch.

CHRISTOPHER, MATT; Wathena Schl; Wathena, KS; (3); 5/45; Church Yth Grp; Letterman Clb; Nwsp; Rep Soph Cls; Pres Jr Cls; Pres Sr Cls; Var Ftbl; Trk; Hon Roll; NHS; MO Western ST Coll; Crim Jstc.

CHRISTOPHER, SHANNON M; Olathe South Sr HS; Olathe, KS; (4); Church Yth Grp; Cmnty Wkr; Letterman Clb; Teachers Aide; Acpl Chr; Chorus; Church Choir; Acad Hnrs; Play Piano 12 Yrs; Tch Theory To Piano Stdnts; Tchng.

CHRISTY, ERICA L; Maize HS; Wichita, KS; (2); Church Yth Grp; Letterman Clb; Q&S; SADD; Chorus; Variety Show; Ed Yrbk; Tennis; Hon Roll; NHS; Forenscs; Kndgtn Tchr/Mar Bio.

CHRONISTER, LEVI; Pittsburg HS; Pittsburg, KS; (3); 1/200; Am Leg Boys St; Pres Q&S; Spanish Clb; Co-Ed Nwsp; Pres Soph Cls; L Capt Tennis; Hon Roll; NHS; Ntl Merit SF.

CHUDY, LAURA; St Thomas Aquinas HS; Shawnee Mission, KS; (4); 52/231; Pep Clb; Co-Capt Chrldng; Swmmng; High Hon Roll; Hon Roll; NHS; TX Chrstn U; Mrktng.

CHUMBLEY, DANIEL W; Newton Sr HS; Newton, KS; (2); Boy Scts; Church Yth Grp; NFL; Ftbl; Hwy Ptrl.

CHURCH, BECKY; Emporia HS; Emporia, KS; (3); Capt Drill Tm; Co-Capt Chrldng; Cit Awd; Hon Roll; Prfct Atten Awd; Dir MS Dance Tm; 2 Tms NCA All Amer Tm; Starfire Dance Co 6 Yrs; Ofc Tech.

CHURCH, BRYAN M; South Haven Schl; South Haven, KS; (2); Church Yth Grp; Math Tm; Natl FFA Org; Pep Clb; Quiz Bowl; JV Bsktbl; Var L Ftbl; Var L Trk; Hon Roll; NHS; Ag Bus.

CHURCH, CALEB; Langing HS; Lansing, KS; (3); Am Leg Boys St; Church Yth Grp; Debate Tm; NFL; Rep Sr Cls; Tennis; Wt Lftg; High Hon Roll; Hon Roll; Prfct Atten Awd; Kay Clb; KS Univ.

CHURCHWELL, BILLY M; Bishop Ward HS; Kansas City, KS; (1); 12/120; Rep Stu Cncl; Intrml Bsbl; JV Ftbl; Var Wrstlng; High Hon Roll; Outstdng Frosh Ldrshp & Svc Awd; All-KS Newcomer Of Yr Awd & Raymond Segura Outstndg Wrestling; Med.

CIARLA, JOEY; Buhler HS; Hutchinson, KS; (3); Church Yth Grp; FCA; Q&S; Spanish Clb; Phtg Yrbk; Phtg Nwsp; JV Crs Cntry; JV Golf; Var Trk; Renaissance Choice Awd; Commted 2 Chrst; Yth Mnstry.

CICERO, ANGELA B; Sumner Acad Of Arts & Science; Kansas City, KS; (2); Art Clb; French Clb; Girl Scts; JCL; Latin Clb; Band; Jazz Band; Mrchg Band; Pep Band; Sftbl; Arch/Cvl Engr.

CINDRIC, ANDREA; Shawnee Mission E Sr HS; Leawood, KS; (3); 105/409; Debate Tm; Sec NFL; Speech Tm; Ed Yrbk; Intrml Sftbl; Hon Roll; NHS; Stu Response Team; Ger Exch Stu Pgm; U Of KS; Law.

CINK, AMY L; Baldwin HS; Baldwin City, KS; (4); 2/80; Art Clb; Church Yth Grp; Intnl Clb; Math Tm; Teachers Aide; JV Tennis; JV Vllybl; High Hon Roll; NHS; Pres Acad Fit Awd; Baker Univ; Vet.

CISNEROS, CHRISTIAN M; Atwood HS; Herndon, KS; (4); 10/39; Pres Church Yth Grp; Spanish Clb; Chorus; Church Choir; School Play; Swing Chorus; JV Var Bsktbl; Score Keeper; JV Var Trk; Male Vclst Of Yr; Natl Chrl Soc; N Park Coll; Hstry.

CLAAS, DAVID M; Nemaha Valley HS; Seneca, KS; (3); Capt Quiz Bowl; Ofcr Bsbl; Bsktbl; Swmmng; High Hon Roll; Bowling League; KS St.

CLAAS, JENNIFER D; Bailey-Benedict Jr Sr High; Seneca, KS; (1); Church Yth Grp; FBLA; FHA; Pep Clb; Mrchg Band; Orch; Pep Band; Band; Sec Frsh Cls; Var Bsktbl; Zoologist.

CLAAS, LAUREN E; Bishop Miege HS; Leawood, KS; (1); 33/250; Church Yth Grp; GAA; Church Choir; Bsktbl; Sftbl; Vllybl; High Hon Roll; Mid-Amer Games Vol.

CLAASSEN, BRANDON W; Maize HS; Goddard, KS; (3); Art Clb; Church Yth Grp; Spanish Clb; Teachers Aide; Bsktbl; Ftbl; Trk; Wt Lftg; Hon Roll; Flying.

CLABURN, HILLARY L; Wichita North HS; Wichita, KS; (3); ROTC; Band; Jazz Band; Mrchg Band; Orch; Pep Band; Var Score Keeper; JV Socr; Hon Roll.

CLACHER, RAYLYN A; Maize HS; Wichita, KS; (4); FCA; French Clb; Key Clb; SADD; Church Choir; Variety Show; High Hon Roll; NHS; Friends U; Scndry Eng Tchr.

CLAIBORN, DAVE C; Olathe East Sr HS; Olathe, KS; (2); Var Debate Tm; NFL; Chorus; School Play; Rep Stu Cncl; Intrml Bsbl; Intrml Bsktbl; Ftbl; JV Tennis; Hon Roll; SASH Advy Bd.

CLANTON, CYNTHIA M; Trego Comm HS; Wa Keeney, KS; (4); FHA; Library Aide; Sec SADD; Chorus; School Musical; Stage Crew; Variety Show; Nwsp; Yrbk; Hon Roll; Kayettes; Pep Clb; Forensics; Colby CC; Bus Mgmt.

CLAPSADDLE, STACY R; Leavenworth HS; Leavenworth, KS; (1); High Hon Roll.

CLARE, JESSICA L; Jefferson West HS; Meriden, KS; (3); Sec 4-H; FHA; Letterman Clb; Natl FFA Org; Band; Mrchg Band; Pep Band; Bsktbl; JV Crs Cntry; Var Trk.

CLARK, AMANDA L; Quivira Heights HS; Bushton, KS; (3); Church Yth Grp; Drama Clb; FCA; Pep Clb; Speech Tm; Band; Chorus; Church Choir; Mrchg Band; Pep Band; Hnrbl Men St Spllng Tst; KS ST U; Frnsc Anthrplgy.

CLARK, ANNESSA D; Newton Sr HS; Newton, KS; (2); Church Yth Grp; Girl Scts; SADD; Acpl Chr; Chorus; Vllybl; Hon Roll; Grl Sct Slvr Awd.

CLARK, ASHLEY D; Hayden HS; Topeka, KS; (3); Cmnty Wkr; Dance Clb; French Clb; Intnl Clb; Pep Clb; Chorus; Drill Tm; Var L Diving; Var L Pom Pon; JV Swmmng; Natl Yng Ldrs Conf; NCA Danz All Amer; Bio.

CLARK, BRANDON; Valley Ctr HS; Valley Center, KS; (3); 61/169; Church Yth Grp; French Clb; Teachers Aide; Varsity Clb; Treas Jr Cls; Treas Sr Cls; Rep Stu Cncl; Bsktbl; Ftbl; Trk.

CLARK, BRITTANY A; Chanute Sr HS; Chanute, KS; (1); French Clb; Band; Mrchg Band; JV Chrldng; JV Sftbl; Hon Roll.

CLARK, CALEB; Valley Falls HS; Valley Falls, KS; (3); Am Leg Boys St; FHA; Teachers Aide; Band; Chorus; Pep Band; Ofcr Bsbl; Ftbl; Wt Lftg; Hon Roll.

CLARK, CASEY MICHAEL; Manhattan HS; Manhattan, KS; (3); Sec Church Yth Grp; FCA; FBLA; Pep Clb; SADD; Var L Bsbl; Intrml Capt Bsktbl; Hon Roll; NHS; Dr.

CLARK, CASSIE L; Derby HS; Derby, KS; (1); Church Yth Grp; Girl Scts; Mgr Yrbk; Hon Roll.

CLARK, DAKOTA D; Valley Falls HS; Valley Falls, KS; (3); Cmnty Wkr; Drama Clb; 4-H; FHA; Band; Mrchg Band; School Play; Ofcr Stu Cncl; Rep Frsh Cls; KSU.

CLARK, DAYNA; Valley Falls HS; Valley Falls, KS; (4); 20/35; Am Leg Aux Girls St; FHA; Teachers Aide; Band; Chorus; Drill Tm; Mrchg Band; Pep Band; Rep Frsh Cls; Rep Jr Cls; Intl Bsktbl Trnmnt In Belgium; Kaw Area Tech Schl; Nrsng.

CLARK, DOUG; Lansing HS; Lansing, KS; (3); 22/142; Church Yth Grp; French Clb; Math Tm; Quiz Bowl; Scholastic Bowl; Teachers Aide; Mgr Bsktbl; JV Mgr Ftbl; Mgr(s); Score Keeper; NFHS Treas; KS St Amer Leg Bys St Alt; U Of KS; Chem Engrng.

CLARK, ERICA; Washington HS; Kansas City, KS; (3); Dance Clb; Acpl Chr; Drill Tm; Ofcr Jr Cls; Bsktbl; Clark Coll; Bus.

CLARK, HEATHER; Atchison Co Cmty HS; Lancaster, KS; (2); Dance Clb; GAA; Letterman Clb; Natl FFA Org; Pep Clb; Varsity Clb; Band; Drill Tm; Jazz Band; Sec Soph Cls; All Amer Chrldr; Histrn Chptr FFA; Dance; U Of AZ; PT.

CLARK, JAMIE; Oak Grove Baptist Schl; Kansas City, KS; (4); 2/8; Church Yth Grp; Letterman Clb; Teachers Aide; Sec Soph Cls; VP Sr Cls; Capt L Bsktbl; Var Capt Vllybl; Hon Roll; Pres Acad Fit Awd; Sal; Natl Chrstn Hnr Soc; KS City KS CC; Nrsng.

CLARK, JENNIFER J; Junction City HS; Junction City, KS; (4); 18/250; Church Yth Grp; Dance Clb; Pres Pep Clb; Chorus; Mrchg Band; School Musical; School Play; Ed Lit Mag; Powder Puff Ftbl; Sftbl; Elem Bsktbl Coach Vol; Cromwell Book Awd; Baccalaureate Comm; Mid Amer Nazarene Coll; Sec Ed.

CLARK, JENNIFER M; Topeka West HS; Topeka, KS; (3); 56/240; Church Yth Grp; Cmnty Wkr; Dance Clb; Pep Clb; SADD; Drill Tm; Swmmng; Tennis; High Hon Roll; NHS.

CLARK, JESSICA R; Topeka HS; Topeka, KS; (1); 53/538; Church Yth Grp; Service Clb; Chorus; Variety Show; JV Tennis; Hon Roll.

CLARK, JIM; Seaman Sr HS; Topeka, KS; (3); Boy Scts; Church Yth Grp; Debate Tm; FBLA; VP Pres Key Clb; Model UN; Teachers Aide; Stage Crew; Mgr Bsktbl; Hon Roll; Bus Admin.

CLARK, JO ELLEN; Hiawatha HS; Falls City, NE; (4); 11/86; Am Leg Aux Girls St; French Clb; Treas Intnl Clb; Quiz Bowl; Teachers Aide; High Hon Roll; NHS; KAYS; Intl Bus.

CLARK, JUSTIN W; Garden City Sr HS; Garden City, KS; (1); Church Yth Grp; Letterman Clb; Varsity Clb; Chorus; Var Trk; Georgetown Univ; Eng/Math.

CLARK, KARRIE; Burlington HS; Burlington, KS; (1); Church Yth Grp; Dance Clb; FBLA; School Musical; School Play; Stage Crew; Var Chrldng; Var Pom Pon; JV Vllybl; Hon Roll; Attendant Ftbl Hmcmng; Ld Dancer Nutcracker Ballet.

CLARK, KELLI; Manhattan HS; Manhattan, KS; (1); Church Yth Grp; Drama Clb; FCA; Pep Clb; Stage Crew; Chrldng; High Hon Roll; Hon Roll; Tchng.

CLARK, KRISSY; Lawrence HS; Lawrence, KS; (3); Art Clb; Hosp Aide; Trk; High Hon Roll; Hon Roll; Yth Group; Jr Planning; Span.

CLARK, KYE A; Wichita Heights HS; Wichita, KS; (4); Hon Roll; NHS; Pres Acad Fit Awd; St Schlr; Wichita ST Univ; Bio; Dr.

CLARK, LAURA M; Halstead HS; Halstead, KS; (3); GAA; Letterman Clb; Teachers Aide; Band; Jazz Band; Mrchg Band; Pep Band; Var Bsktbl; Var Swmmng; Var Trk; KU Med Center; Pre-Med.

CLARK, LESLIE; Holton HS; Holton, KS; (2); Dance Clb; Girl Scts; Letterman Clb; Band; JV Bsktbl; Var Crs Cntry; Vllybl; Hon Roll; NHS.

CLARK, LORA M; Hill City HS; Hill City, KS; (3); 5/31; Treas Church Yth Grp; Sec FHA; NFL; Pep Clb; SADD; Chorus; Co-Ed Nwsp; Ed Yrbk; High Hon Roll; Prfct Atten Awd; Schl Bible Study; Teens As Tchrs/Teen Bsln Trng; KS Assn Of Yth; Scndry Math Ed.

CLARK, MARY E; Holton HS; Holton, KS; (3); FHA; Teachers Aide; Chorus; Mgr(s); Vllybl; Hon Roll; NHS; Kays 9-11 Offcr Spec Prgms; SADD 9-10; PSU; OT.

CLARK, MELINDA K; Dodge City HS; Dodge City, KS; (3); Church Yth Grp; Cmnty Wkr; Pres Intnl Clb; SADD; Chorus; High Hon Roll; NHS; U Of KS; Occup Thrp.

CLARK, NATHAN; Cair Paravel - Latin Schl; Topeka, KS; (1); Boy Scts; Church Yth Grp; Acpl Chr; Chorus; School Musical; Bsktbl; Hon Roll.

CLARK, NICOLE R; Shawnee Mission E Sr HS; Roeland Park, KS; (3); Church Yth Grp; Letterman Clb; Pep Clb; Teachers Aide; Band; Church Choir; Mrchg Band; Orch; Pep Band; School Musical; Dist Hnr Band 2nd Chair; St Solo Festival I Rating.

CLARK, PATRICIA C; Midway Schl; Bendena, KS; (2); Pres Church Yth Grp; Capt Quiz Bowl; Band; Mrchg Band; School Play; Yrbk; Sec Soph Cls; Mgr(s); JV Vllybl; High Hon Roll; Ltrd Acad 2 Yrs; Pl 3rd Algebra II Cls; Media/Gymnstcs Coach.

CLARK, RYAN L; Conway Springs HS; Conway Springs, KS; (3); 18/32; Church Yth Grp; Rep Frsh Cls; Co-Capt Bsktbl; Swmmng; Tennis; Wt Lftg; Hon Roll; Prfct Atten Awd; U Of KS; Phys Thpy.

CLARK, SCOTT T; Wichita East HS; Wichita, KS; (3); 1/500; Dance Clb; Debate Tm; Quiz Bowl; Scholastic Bowl; Science Clb; Spanish Clb; Orch; Hon Roll; NHS; Spanish NHS; Physics.

CLARK, SEAN; Maur Hill Prep Schl; Atchison, KS; (4); 5/46; Cmnty Wkr; Capt Math Tm; Model UN; Capt NFL; VP Stu Cncl; Ofcr Bsbl; Capt Ftbl; Trk; Wrstlng; High Hon Roll; Span Awd; U Of KS; Bus Admin.

CLARK, SHANA E; Conway Springs HS; Conway Springs, KS; (2); 3/56; Church Yth Grp; FHA; Pep Clb; Chrldng; Tennis; High Hon Roll; Hon Roll; Ntl Merit SF; U Of KS; Chem Pharmcy.

CLARK, SHANTE; Wyandotte HS; Kansas City, KS; (4); 9/180; Acpl Chr; Church Choir; Variety Show; Rep Jr Cls; Rep Sr Cls; L Var Bsktbl; L Var Vllybl; High Hon Roll; Hon Roll; NHS; KS Scholar; KS ST; Nrsng.

CLARK, STEVEN A; Hutchinson HS; Hutchinson, KS; (2); 65/250; Church Yth Grp; Cmnty Wkr; Key Clb; Letterman Clb; Band; Var Bsbl; JV Var Bsktbl; Var Ftbl; Cit Awd; 4-H Awd; Super Salthawk; Southern CA; Sprts Med.

CLARKE, CAROL; Medicine Lodge HS; Medicine Lodge, KS; (4); 2/54; Church Yth Grp; HOBY; Sec Letterman Clb; School Play; Var Golf; High Hon Roll; NHS; Var Frsh Cls; Var Bsbl; K101 Hnr Band; Sadie Hawkins Royalty; Page St KS Senator; KSU; Math Ed.

CLARKE, CATHERINE L; Desoto HS; Shawnee, KS; (4); Drill Tm; Devonshire Dancers KS Renfest & Shakespeares Festival Perfmnc; Johnson Cty CC; Acctng.

CLARKE, KACEY S; Yates Ctr HS; Yates Center, KS; (3); 13/60; FCA; Pres 4-H; Sec FHA; Office Aide; Teachers Aide; Chorus; School Musical; Mgr(s); Trk; Vllybl; Frgn Lang Club; Natl Helpers; Pittsburg ST Univ; Home Ec.

CLARKE, MATTHEW B; Sumner Acad Of Arts & Science; Kansas City, KS; (1); Chess Clb; Church Yth Grp; French Clb; SADD; Band; Mrchg Band; Orch; Pep Band; Mgr(s); Hon Roll; KS ST Univ; Vet Medicine.

CLARKSON, ERIC; Cimarron HS; Cimarron, KS; (3); 13/45; Church Yth Grp; Cmnty Wkr; FCA; HOBY; Letterman Clb; Pep Clb; Quiz Bowl; Spanish Clb; Band; Jazz Band; Chrch Mssn Wrk-Mexico, Phoenix, Kansas City, Colorado Sprngs, Pueblo; Mid Am Nzrne Coll; Engrng.

CLARY, ADAM; Troy HS; Troy, KS; (2); Letterman Clb; Var Bsbl; Var Bsktbl; Var Crs Cntry; Var Ftbl; Var Trk; Hon Roll; Prfct Atten Awd; Arch.

CLARY, CHRISTOPHER O; Wichita Northwest HS; Wichita, KS; (2); 63/400; Boy Scts; Cmnty Wkr; Debate Tm; Math Tm; NFL; Speech Tm; Hon Roll; Spanish NHS.

CLARY, HEATHER M; Midway Schl; Denton, KS; (2); Church Yth Grp; Pep Clb; School Play; Yrbk; Chrldng; Mgr(s); Var Vllybl; Hon Roll; Pres Acad Fit Awd; Travel; Tourism.

CLASEN, ALICIA; Udall HS; Udall, KS; (4); Sec Church Yth Grp; FHA; Math Tm; Office Aide; Band; Ofcr Stu Cncl; JV Bsktbl; Trk; Vllybl; High Hon Roll; Hnrb Mntn Vllybl Lg; Bsktbl Mst Imprvd, Coachs Awds; Cowley Cnty CC; Acctntng.

CLASEN, CARRIE L; Belle Plaine HS; Belle Plaine, KS; (3); 8/59; Church Yth Grp; Cmnty Wkr; Math Tm; Pep Clb; Spanish Clb; SADD; Sec Jr Cls; JV Vllybl; Hon Roll; NHS; KAYS; KS St Univ.

CLASEN, DARREN J; Udall HS; Udall, KS; (3); Church Yth Grp; Band; Mrchg Band; Pep Band; Var Bsbl; Var Bsktbl; Crs Cntry; All League Hnrbl Mntn Bsktbl.

CLASEN, MARSHA; Udall HS; Udall, KS; (1); Church Yth Grp; Band; Ofcr Frsh Cls; Bsktbl; Vllybl; High Hon Roll; Hon Roll; Prfct Atten Awd; Dntl Hgnst.

CLATTERBUCK, CHRIS; Shawnee Mission E Sr HS; Shawnee Mission, KS; (4); 7/400; Boy Scts; Capt Debate Tm; French Clb; Model UN; Pres NFL; Quiz Bowl; French Hon Soc; JETS Awd; Ntl Merit Schol; Stanford U; Intl Rltns.

CLAWSON, STEPHANIE; Springa Hill HS; Olathe, KS; (4); Am Leg Aux Girls St; Church Yth Grp; Cmnty Wkr; Letterman Clb; Pep Clb; SADD; Acpl Chr; Yrbk; VP Sr Cls; Capt Bsktbl; Vlybl, Bsktbl, Sftbl, Bsbl Offcte; KS ST U; Elem Ed.

CLAY, SANDRA A; Gardner-Edgerton HS; Gardner, KS; (3); Church Yth Grp; Drama Clb; Chorus; Church Choir; School Musical; School Play; Stage Crew; Rep Frsh Cls; Hon Roll; Intnl Thsbn Scty; Stge Mgr; Stdnt Dir; Lwyr.

CLAYCAMP, JEFF; Hillcrest Schl; Cuba, KS; (3); 4-H; Letterman Clb; Rptr Natl FFA Org; Quiz Bowl; Teachers Aide; Var L Bsktbl; Var L Crs Cntry; Var L Trk; High Hon Roll; NHS.

CLAYTON, JEFF A; Washburn Rural HS; Topeka, KS; (3); Natl Beta Clb; Quiz Bowl; Ed Nwsp; High Hon Roll; Hon Roll; Washburn U; Jrnlsm.

CLAYTON, JENNIFER; Topeka West HS; Topeka, KS; (2); Church Yth Grp; FCA; FHA; Intnl Clb; Science Clb; SADD; Chrldng; Powder Puff Ftbl; High Hon Roll; Hon Roll; Washburn; Psych.

CLEARWATER, JACOB T; Maur Hill Prep Schl; Atchison, KS; (1); Boy Scts; Debate Tm; Speech Tm; Chorus; Church Choir; School Play; Rep Soph Cls; JV Ftbl.

CLEEVES, BEN R; Hutchinson HS; Hutchinson, KS; (2); 1/346; Church Yth Grp; Debate Tm; Key Clb; NFL; Science Clb; Speech Tm; Band; High Hon Roll; PAS; Yng Republicans Clb.

CLEMANS, JESSICA L; St John Jr Sr HS; Saint John, KS; (4); SADD; Teachers Aide; Varsity Clb; Yrbk; Var Vllybl; Hon Roll; Chrch Mem; ASU; Law; His; Criminal Law.

CLEMENCE, CHRIS; Valley Ctr HS; Valley Center, KS; (3); Church Yth Grp; Capt Quiz Bowl; Band; Mrchg Band; Pep Band; Var Crs Cntry; Wt Lftg; Chess Clb; French Clb; Capt Scholastic Bowl; Promise Keepers; Jr Eng Tech Soc; Poli Sci.

CLEMENS, OLIVIA J; Basehor Linwood HS; Basehor, KS; (3); 19/99; FBLA; Treas VP FHA; Hosp Aide; SADD; Treas Soph Cls; Treas Jr Cls; VP Sr Cls; Hon Roll; VP NHS; Prfct Atten Awd; U Of KS; Bus/Mngmt.

CLEMENT, MITCH; Garden City Sr HS; Garden City, KS; (4); 1/315; Church Yth Grp; Pres Key Clb; Math Tm; Acpl Chr; Var L Bsbl; Var Capt Ftbl; Kiwanis Awd; Pres NHS; Ntl Merit Ltr; Wheaton Coll; Biblcl Stds.

CLEMENTS, ANDY L; Northwest HS Wichita; Wichita, KS; (3); 1/375; Am Leg Aux Girls St; Cmnty Wkr; Girl Scts; Hosp Aide; Intnl Clb; Math Clb; Math Tm; Spanish Clb; Teachers Aide; Church Choir; JC Penny Golden Rule Awd; CO Schl Of Mines Medal Of Achvmt In Math & Sci; Bausch & Lomb Sci Awd; Chem Engrng; Drug Rsrch.

CLEMENTS, RAYMOND J; Wichita East HS; Wichita, KS; (3); Church Yth Grp; Band; Chorus; Church Choir; Drm Mjr(t); Jazz Band; Mrchg Band; Orch; Pep Band; School Musical; All ST Concert Band; Dist VI Jazz Band; IAJE Awd Recipient For Outstdng Musicianshp; Music Edctr/Performer.

CLERK, NIKKI; Minneola Schl; Dodge City, KS; (1); Church Yth Grp; FCA; Math Clb; Math Tm; Spanish Clb; Band; Chorus; Jazz Band; Pep Band; School Musical.

CLEVELAND, SARAH E; Circle HS; Towanda, KS; (3); Church Yth Grp; Quiz Bowl; SADD; Acpl Chr; Band; Church Choir; School Musical; School Play; High Hon Roll; Drama Clb; Local City Offcs Vol; Washburn Univ; CPA.

CLEVENGER, ADAM J; Bucklin Schl; Ford, KS; (3); Church Yth Grp; Band; Mrchg Band; Pep Band; Hon Roll.

CLICK, AMY L; Great Bend Sr HS; Great Bend, KS; (2); Church Yth Grp; Drama Clb; Scholastic Bowl; Band; Mrchg Band; Stage Crew; Hon Roll; OK ST Univ; Bio.

CLICK, TIM; Great Bend Sr HS; Great Bend, KS; (4); 9/216; Am Leg Boys St; Church Yth Grp; Quiz Bowl; Band; Mrchg Band; School Play; High Hon Roll; NHS; Hon Roll; Prfct Atten Awd; Amateur Radio; Comp Pgmng; Northwestern OK; Med; Comp Sci.

CLIFT, PATRICK; Wellington Sr HS; Wellington, KS; (3); SADD; Rep Frsh Cls; Rep Stu Cncl; Bsktbl; Ftbl; Golf; Wt Lftg; Hon Roll; Jr NHS; Prfct Atten Awd.

CLIFT, RICHARD; Wellington Sr HS; Wellington, KS; (4); Church Yth Grp; Letterman Clb; Library Aide; SADD; Varsity Clb; Rep Stu Cncl; Var L Ftbl; Var L Golf; Wt Lftg; High Hon Roll; Ftbl All Time Schl Record Holder & All St Running Back.

CLIFTON, TRINA T; Parsons HS; Parsons, KS; (3); Church Yth Grp; Girl Scts; Pep Clb; Teachers Aide; Band; Mrchg Band; Pep Band; Ofcr Frsh Cls; Ofcr Soph Cls; Hon Roll.

CLINE, ANGIE; Enterprise Sda Acad; Wellsville, KS; (4); Drama Clb; Model UN; Band; School Play; Nwsp; Yrbk; Ofcr Stu Cncl; Bsktbl; High Hon Roll; Cmnty Wkr; Southwestern Adventist; Nursng.

CLINE, JASON; Atchison Sr HS; Atchison, KS; (2); #17 in class; Church Yth Grp; Cmnty Wkr; Ofcr Frsh Cls; Ofcr Soph Cls; Rep Stu Cncl; L Var Bsbl; L JV Bsktbl; L Var Ftbl; Wt Lftg; Cit Awd; Cngrssnl Yth Ldrshp Cncl; Ks St; Acctng.

CLINE, MATTHEW B; Wichita East HS; Wichita, KS; (2); German Clb; Band; Mrchg Band; Pep Band; All City Band; Wichita ST U; His.

CLINE, MELISSA; Northwest HS; Wichita, KS; (3); 1/350; Church Yth Grp; Cmnty Wkr; Hosp Aide; HOBY; Intnl Clb; Math Tm; Treas Soph Cls; Rep Jr Cls; Bsktbl; Var L Socr; Outstndng Sci Stu 2xs; Teens Hope-Aids Ed.

CLINE, SHEA R; Berean Acad; Valley Center, KS; (4); Church Yth Grp; Teachers Aide; Varsity Clb; Chorus; School Play; Chrldng; High Hon Roll; Hon Roll; Distngd Chrstn HS Stdnt Awd 95-; Chrldng Cmp Chmpnshps Fnlst; Pittsburg ST; Intr Dsgn/Vet.

CLIVER, IRONA MARCELLA; Wichita South HS; Wichita, KS; (2); 53/394; Cmnty Wkr; Pep Clb; School Musical; School Play; Rep Frsh Cls; Rep Soph Cls; Var Diving; Var Swmmng; JV Tennis; Hon Roll; SHAB Pres; March Of Dimes For South Capt; KS U Of Lawrence; Heart Surgn.

CLOSE, MELISSA A; Maize HS; Maize, KS; (3); Pres Spanish Clb; SADD; Thesps; Band; Chorus; Nwsp; Chrldng; Pom Pon; Socr; Hon Roll; KAKE Chnl 10 Intern; Produce Kids TV Pgm; Pom Camp All-Amer Dancer Nom; ST Cmptn Newscast 1st Team; U Of KS; Broadcast Jrnlsm.

CLOUD, LESLIE A; Olathe North Sr HS; Olathe, KS; (1); Band; Drill Tm; Variety Show; Hon Roll; Dance Clb; Drama Clb; Girl Scts; Pep Clb; Var Swmmng; Marine Bio.

CLOWER, LEXY; Winfield HS; Winfield, KS; (1); Girl Scts; Intnl Clb; Pep Clb; Chorus; Chrldng; Hon Roll; Cowley Cty CC Chrldng Clinic Spirit Stick 96.

CLUBINE, JAMIE S; Independence HS; Independence, KS; (4); 48/160; Cmnty Wkr; FHA; Teachers Aide; Orch; JV Tennis; Hon Roll; KARM; Orch Ltr 4 Yrs; Strolling Strings 4 Yrs; Renaissance 3 Yrs; Coffeyville CC; Ag.

CLUBINE, JASON E; Independence HS; Independence, KS; (1); Church Yth Grp; Band; Mrchg Band; Pep Band; Hon Roll; Renaissance Mem.

CLYMER, JEREMY J; Hugoton HS; Hugoton, KS; (1); Boy Scts; Church Yth Grp; Wt Lftg; Hon Roll; Wrestling; Band; Jazz Band; KS ST Univ; Mech Engr.

COATS, CHANTAL; Olathe East Sr HS; Olathe, KS; (3); Spanish Clb; Teachers Aide; Fashn Clb; Clark Atlnta Univ; Phys Thpy.

COATS, JASON E; Shawnee Mission N HS; Shawnee Mission, KS; (3); 18/420; Q&S; Thesps; Band; School Play; Stage Crew; Lit Mag; High Hon Roll; NHS; Reperatory Theatre Stagewriter; Stonelion Puppet Theatre Apprentice; Natl Merit Commended Schlr; Elem Ed.

COBB, MICHELLE L; Russell HS; Russell, KS; (1); Church Yth Grp; Dance Clb; Key Clb; Rptr Natl FFA Org; SADD; Band; Mrchg Band; Ofcr Stu Cncl; Bsktbl; Trk.

COBB, RENA; Faith Bapt Christian Schl; Central City, KY; (3); 1/1; Church Yth Grp; Church Choir; Hon Roll; Prfct Atten Awd.

COBLE, ABBY C; Salina HS Central; Salina, KS; (4); Church Yth Grp; Girl Scts; Teachers Aide; Chorus; Church Choir; Var L Swmmng; High Hon Roll; Hon Roll; NHS; Prfct Atten Awd; Ft Hays ST U; Phrmcy.

COBLE, SUZANNE R; Circle HS; Towanda, KS; (2); Church Yth Grp; FHA; Spanish Clb; SADD; Chorus; Stage Crew; Variety Show.

COBURN, KATHARINE; Arkansas City HS; Arkansas City, KS; (4); 50/172; Am Leg Aux Girls St; Drama Clb; Pres FHA; Teachers Aide; School Musical; School Play; Ofcr Stage Crew; Phtg Nwsp; Phtg Yrbk; Hon Roll; Washington Close Up 96; Cowley Cty CC; Hotel Mgmt.

COCHENER, JOHN T; Wichita Collegiate Schl; Wichita, KS; (3); Debate Tm; Quiz Bowl; Scholastic Bowl; Acpl Chr; Band; Jazz Band; Pep Band; Trk; High Hon Roll; People To People Stu Ambassador; Engrng.

COCHRAN, CORY; Spring Hill HS; Spring Hill, KS; (4); Am Leg Boys St; Debate Tm; French Clb; Letterman Clb; Scholastic Bowl; Mrchg Band; L Crs Cntry; Capt L Wrstlng; High Hon Roll; Hon Roll; KS St Univ; Eng.

COCHRAN, RYAN L; Wellington Sr HS; Wellington, KS; (2); Office Aide; SADD; Golf; Hon Roll; Jr NHS; NHS; Prfct Atten Awd; Duke U ACT Assesmnt Tst; KS U.

COCHRAN, TRACI; Wellington Sr HS; Wellington, KS; (3); Key Clb; Office Aide; Drill Tm; Rep Stu Cncl; Var Trk; JV Vllybl; Hon Roll; St Capital Page; KS St Univ; Psych.

COCHRANE, ANDREW R; Topeka West HS; Topeka, KS; (3); Church Yth Grp; Teachers Aide; JV Bsbl; High Hon Roll.

COCHRANE, NATHAN E; Topeka West HS; Topeka, KS; (2); Church Yth Grp; High Hon Roll; Bsbl; Rdng/Sci-Fi-Mrdr Mystry; Grphc Arts.

COCHREN, LUCAS; Jackson Heights HS; Whiting, KS; (1); 10/35; Church Yth Grp; Cmnty Wkr; Pep Clb; Acpl Chr; Band; Chorus; Church Choir; Drm Mjr(t); Mrchg Band; Pep Band; Kent ST; Arch.

CODAY, IAN S; Marmaton Valley Jr Sr HS; Elsmore, KS; (2); 3/33; Math Tm; Band; Mrchg Band; Orch; Pep Band; JV Golf; Hon Roll; Tech Stu Assn; Ftr Farmers Of Amer.

CODER, JENNIFER K; Independence HS; Independence, KS; (1); Pep Clb; Orch; VP Frsh Cls; Ofcr Stu Cncl; Bsktbl; Var L Sftbl; Vllybl; KS Univ.

COE, TRACY M; Hamilton HS; Hamilton, KS; (3); 3/12; FBLA; FHA; Treas Jr Cls; Var L Vllybl; Cit Awd; High Hon Roll.

COEN, MICHELLE; Garden City Sr HS; Garden City, KS; (3); FTA; Office Aide; Pres Service Clb; Teachers Aide; Bsktbl; Var Chrldng; High Hon Roll; Hon Roll; Wt Lftg; Job Corp Vol; DARE Role Mdl; Emporia ST; Elem Ed.

COERBER, BERNIE; Lakin HS; Lakin, KS; (3); Am Leg Boys St; Church Yth Grp; Debate Tm; School Play; Ed Nwsp; Yrbk; Rep Soph Cls; Rep Jr Cls; Pres Stu Cncl; High Hon Roll; U Of AR; Corp Law.

COFER, ANGIE; Baschor-Linwood HS; Basehor, KS; (1); Church Yth Grp; 4-H; Pep Clb; Var Chrldng; 4-H Awd; High Hon Roll; Dncng; Gymnstcs; KS U; Nrsng.

COFFEY, AMY L; Arkansas City HS; Arkansas City, KS; (1); FCA; 4-H; Band; Mrchg Band; Pep Band; Var Tennis; Hon Roll; Accmplshd Pianist.

COFFEY, BEN J; Louisburg HS; Paola, KS; (2); Church Yth Grp; Letterman Clb; Spanish Clb; Var Bsktbl; Var Ftbl; Var Trk; Var Wt Lftg; Hon Roll; KS ST Univ; Nursery Mgmt.

COFFIE, TRUDY C; Topeka HS; Topeka, KS; (2); Hon Roll; Acad Schlr Ltr; Psych; Soc Work.

COFFIN, BRANDY B; Washburn Rural HS; Topeka, KS; (2); 91/397; Cmnty Wkr; JA; Pep Clb; Red Cross Aide; SADD; Teachers Aide; Hon Roll; Elem Ed/Tchr.

COFFMAN, NATHAN N; Lawrence HS; Lawrence, KS; (3); Acpl Chr; Variety Show; Var L Bsbl; Var L Ftbl; Co-Capt L Wrstlng; Cit Awd; Hon Roll; NHS; Prfct Atten Awd; Ftbl 2nd Team All Sunflower League Def Back; 4th In St Wrestling; Explorers Post Engrng; Engrng; Law Enforcement.

COFIELD, CARLA S; Muncie Christian Schl; Kansas City, KS; (3); Church Yth Grp; School Play; Yrbk; Ofcr Jr Cls; Bsktbl; Chrldng; Vllybl; Nrsng.

COFIELD, JULIE M; St Xavier's HS; Junction City, KS; (2); Church Yth Grp; Cmnty Wkr; SADD; Pres Frsh Cls; JV Trk; JV Vllybl; Hon Roll; Ntl Merit Ltr; KS ST U.

COLBERG, KRISTA D; Lyons HS; Lyons, KS; (2); Dance Clb; Pep Clb; Spanish Clb; Chorus; Drill Tm; Chrldng; Tennis; Hon Roll; U Of KS; Pharmcy.

COLBERT, LORI; Columbus HS; Columbus, KS; (3); 2/100; Bus Profs of Am; Pres Sec 4-H; Math Tm; Gov Hon Prg Awd; High Hon Roll; Hon Roll; NHS.

COLBERT, TAYLOR; Manhattan HS; Manhattan, KS; (3); 1/430; Pep Clb; School Play; Ed Nwsp; Yrbk; Rep Stu Cncl; Powder Puff Ftbl; Var Sftbl; Cit Awd; High Hon Roll; NHS; GFWC Ctznshp Crtv Wrtng Schlrshp Conf St & Dist Wnnr; Heritage Panel; SHARE Brd & Vlntr; KS ST U; Med.

COLBY, TIA D; Beloit Jr Sr HS; Beloit, KS; (1); 11/98; Church Yth Grp; Hist 4-H; FHA; SADD; Band; Chorus; Mrchg Band; Orch; Pep Band; School Play; KAY Clb Pres; Musician.

COLCLAUSURE, STEPHANIE C; Olathe North Sr HS; Olathe, KS; (3); French Clb; Letterman Clb; Teachers Aide; Band; Phtg Yrbk; JV Bsktbl; Powder Puff Ftbl; Vllybl; High Hon Roll.

COLE, AARON O; Olpe Schl; Emporia, KS; (1); 8/24; Boy Scts; Band; Mrchg Band; Ofcr Bsbl; JV Var Ftbl; Var Trk; Var Wt Lftg; Cit Awd; High Hon Roll; Hon Roll; Natl Frgn Lang Awd; Natl Hnr Roll; KS ST; Eng.

COLE, ANGIE; Hays HS; Hays, KS; (2); Dance Clb; Spanish Clb; Swmmng; Wt Lftg; Hon Roll; Spanish NHS; Chrldng; Vet Med/Psych.

COLE, BRIAN; Minneapolis HS; Minneapolis, KS; (3); Church Yth Grp; Cmnty Wkr; Debate Tm; Hosp Aide; Teachers Aide; Capt Var Ftbl; Capt Var Golf; Capt Wt Lftg; NHS; Pres Acad Fit Awd; Bio; Pre-Med; Family Phy.

COLE, EMILY; Lincoln Jr Sr HS; Beverly, KS; (1); Church Yth Grp; Var Bsktbl; Var Trk; JV Vllybl; Hon Roll; Phy Thrpst.

COLE, JAIME L; Seaman Sr HS; Topeka, KS; (4); Drama Clb; FBLA; Ofcr Pres FHA; Pep Clb; Spanish Clb; SADD; Teachers Aide; Rep Frsh Cls; Rep Stu Cncl; Powder Puff Ftbl; Washburn U; Dctr Ob/Gyn Fld.

COLE, JAMIE; St John Jr Sr HS; Seward, KS; (3); 8/90; Church Yth Grp; Treas Pres SADD; Flag Corp; School Musical; School Play; Ed Yrbk; Treas Jr Cls; Var Crs Cntry; Var Trk; NHS; Poetry ST Spch/Drama; KS ST U; Adv/His.

COLE, JASON E; Olpe Schl; Emporia, KS; (2); Boy Scts; Drama Clb; Rep Stu Cncl; JV Ftbl; Sftbl; Trk; Wt Lftg; Hon Roll.

COLE, KYLE D; Olpe Schl; Olpe, KS; (2); Church Yth Grp; VP Frsh Cls; VP Jr Cls; Bsktbl; Ftbl; Trk; Hon Roll; Emporia ST U.

COLE, MICHAEL A; Washington HS; Kansas City, KS; (2); French Clb; Letterman Clb; Varsity Clb; Var L Bsbl; JV Bsktbl; High Hon Roll; DECA; Peer Ldr.

COLE, MISTY D; Washington HS; Washington, KS; (3); Church Yth Grp; Dance Clb; French Clb; FHA; GAA; Girl Scts; Letterman Clb; Pep Clb; Band; Drill Tm; Tching.

COLE, NICHOLAS; Olathe East Sr HS; Olathe, KS; (3); Boy Scts; Church Yth Grp; Intnl Clb; Model UN; Spanish Clb; Band; Jazz Band; Mrchg Band; Pep Band; Socr; KS Univ; Elec Engrng.

COLE, RACHEL; Mulvane Sr HS; Mulvane, KS; (3); 14/135; Church Yth Grp; Cmnty Wkr; FCA; Office Aide; SADD; Stage Crew; Hon Roll; NHS; Prfct Atten Awd; Pres Acad Fit Awd; Mulvane CC; Phy Ther.

COLE, REBECCA L; Blue Valley Northwest HS; Overland Park, KS; (2); Chorus; Yrbk; Sftbl; Wt Lftg; High Hon Roll; Hon Roll; Nrs; Phy Thrpst; Jrnlsm.

COLEMAN, ANIKA D; Wyandotte HS; Kansas City, KS; (4); Hon Roll; Tchrs Of Tomorrow; KS Univ; Elem Ed.

COLEMAN, BRIAN A; Garden City Sr HS; Garden City, KS; (1); Computer Clb; High Hon Roll; Geolgy Spec Achvmt; Cmptr Tech.

COLEMAN, CHRISTOPHER; Valley Falls HS; Valley Falls, KS; (3); Cmnty Wkr; FHA; Letterman Clb; Band; Pep Band; Ofcr Bsbl; Bsktbl; Ftbl; Wt Lftg; High Hon Roll; KS ST U.

COLEMAN, JENNIFER; Miltonvale HS; Miltonvale, KS; (4); 1/7; Am Leg Aux Girls St; Church Yth Grp; Quiz Bowl; Co-Ed Yrbk; Pres Frsh Cls; Pres Soph Cls; Pres Jr Cls; Pres Sr Cls; High Hon Roll; NHS; Cloud Cty CC; Scl Wrk.

COLEMAN, SCOTT D; Manhattan HS; Manhattan, KS; (3); Boy Scts; Church Yth Grp; Band; Mrchg Band; Pep Band; Tennis; Hon Roll; Eagle Sct.

COLEMAN, TARA L; Newton Sr HS; Newton, KS; (2); 92/279; Girl Scts; Teachers Aide; Orch; U Of Cntrl OK; Forensic Sci.

COLES, KRISTY; Olathe South HS; Cabot, AR; (4); Church Yth Grp; Letterman Clb; Pep Clb; Spanish Clb; Varsity Clb; Variety Show; Var Capt Chrldng; Powder Puff Ftbl; High Hon Roll; Hon Roll; All-Star Cheer Sq; ASC Top Star Jmpr; UCA All Star; Lyon Coll.

COLGAN, AMANDA; Washburn Rural HS; Topeka, KS; (4); 3/267; Debate Tm; Hosp Aide; NFL; JV Bsktbl; Var L Golf; JV Vllybl; High Hon Roll; Ntl Merit Ltr; Pres Schlr; St Schlr; NHS; Washburn Univ; Bio; Pre-Med.

COLLARD, JUSTIN B; Lansing HS; Leavenworth, KS; (4); 9/143; Boy Scts; Debate Tm; Drama Clb; NFL; Band; Jazz Band; Pep Band; Var L Ftbl; High Hon Roll; NHS; U KS; Comp Sci.

COLLE, TREY M; Nickerson HS; Sterling, KS; (4); 30/101; Church Yth Grp; 4-H; Band; Chorus; Jazz Band; Mrchg Band; Pep Band; Bsktbl; Ftbl; Tennis; Stu Ldrshp Smnr; Natl Hnr Soc; Yth Ldrshp Prog; Natl Hnr Soc VP; York Col; Optom.

COLLENE, BESS; Maranatha Acad; Bonner Springs, KS; (2); Church Yth Grp; Cmnty Wkr; HOBY; Chorus; School Musical; Ed Nwsp; Rep Stu Cncl; Socr; Vllybl; NHS; US Natl Math Awd; Dstngshd A Hnr Rll; Prss Twrd Mrk Awd; Hstry.

COLLETTE, ANDY B; Maize HS; Wichita, KS; (2); Letterman Clb; JV Bsbl; Mgr(s); Var Socr; Notre Dame; Med.

COLLETTE, JENNIE; Salina HS Central; Salina, KS; (2); Cmnty Wkr; Drama Clb; Science Clb; SADD; School Play; Stage Crew; Rep Soph Cls; Rep Stu Cncl; Var Chrldng; Meteorologist.

COLLETTE, JOSHUA M; Concordia Jr Sr HS; Aurora, KS; (2); Church Yth Grp; Letterman Clb; Quiz Bowl; Spanish Clb; Trk; Wt Lftg; Hon Roll; NHS; Astron.

COLLIER, TRACEY D; Washburn Rural HS; Topeka, KS; (3); Cmnty Wkr; Hosp Aide; Spanish Clb; SADD; Teachers Aide; Crs Cntry; Trk; Wt Lftg; High Hon Roll; Hon Roll; Lifeguarding Mgr; Head Lifeguard; Winter Royalty Nom 94-95; U Of KS; Pediatrician.

COLLING, BECKY L; Caldwell Jr Sr HS; Caldwell, KS; (3); Church Yth Grp; Drama Clb; German Clb; Pep Clb; Speech Tm; Chorus; Flag Corp; School Play; Swing Chorus; Ed Nwsp; Kayettes; Cowley Cty CC; Ed Dsgn.

COLLINS, ALANA J; Lansing HS; Lansing, KS; (4); 34/150; Church Yth Grp; Band; Chorus; Drm Mjr(t); L Var Bsktbl; Var L Trk; Var L Vllybl; Hon Roll; Debate Tm; DARE Rl Mdl; Highland CC; PT.

COLLINS, AMANDA; Spring Hill HS; Olathe, KS; (2); GAA; Letterman Clb; Chorus; Church Choir; Stat Bsktbl; Mgr(s); Stat Sftbl; High Hon Roll; Hon Roll; Choir; KS ST U; Psych.

COLLINS, AMBER M; Parsons HS; Parsons, KS; (2); 23/138; Sec Church Yth Grp; Cmnty Wkr; FBLA; Sec FHA; FTA; Pep Clb; Band; Church Choir; Mrchg Band; Pep Band; Sports Clb; Pittsburg ST Univ; Tchr; Bus.

COLLINS, AMY; Atchison Sr HS; Atchison, KS; (3); Chorus; NHS; KS U; Sports Med.

COLLINS, ANDREA; Highland HS; Highland, KS; (1); 1/25; Church Yth Grp; Cmnty Wkr; Natl FFA Org; Quiz Bowl; Band; Swing Chorus; Pres Frsh Cls; L Var Bsktbl; Chrldng; Trk; Med.

COLLINS, ANDREA S; Yates Ctr HS; Piqua, KS; (2); FCA; FHA; Letterman Clb; Spanish Clb; Treas Stu Cncl; Var L Bsktbl; JV Vllybl; Hon Roll; Art Clb; SADD; Acad Lttr; KS ST Univ; Sprts Trnr.

COLLINS, BECKY J; Hayden HS; Topeka, KS; (2); JV Tennis; Hon Roll; Hosp Vlntr; KS U; Photo.

COLLINS, BROOKE; Wichita North HS; Wichita, KS; (2); 1/394; Church Yth Grp; Debate Tm; Drama Clb; NFL; Thesps; Chorus; Church Choir; School Musical; School Play; Stage Crew; Medicine.

COLLINS, DOROTHY E; Northeast HS; Arma, KS; (4); 1/43; Drama Clb; Chorus; School Play; VP Sr Cls; Capt L Bsktbl; Var Capt Vllybl; Gov Hon Prg Awd; Val; High Hon Roll; NHS; All-St All-Cls 3a Hnrb Mntn Bsktbl; St Vocal Soloist; All-Cuc 1st Team Vllybl & Bsktbl; U Of KS; Law.

COLLINS, ERICA B; Circle HS; Benton, KS; (3); Ed Nwsp; Ed Yrbk; Var L Bsktbl; Var L Trk; Wt Lftg; Multi Yr Listee; Sprts Med.

COLLINS, FLOYD E; Leavenworth HS; Leavenworth, KS; (3); Church Yth Grp; Letterman Clb; Spanish Clb; Varsity Clb; JV Crs Cntry; Var L Ftbl; Var L Trk; Hon Roll; Atmsphr Sci.

COLLINS, GREGORY L; F L Schlagle HS; Kansas City, KS; (1); JV Bsktbl; Var L Ftbl; Wt Lftg; Hon Roll; Peer Ldr; Orthodontist.

COLLINS, JOHN S; Parsons HS; Parsons, KS; (1); 34/139; JV Bsbl; Hon Roll.

COLLINS, KRISTEN A; Parsons HS; Parsons, KS; (1); 23/148; Church Yth Grp; Drama Clb; Pep Clb; SADD; Chorus; School Musical; School Play; Acad Lttr; Spec Ed.

COLLINS, MATTHEW; Northwest HS Wichita; Wichita, KS; (3); Band; Mrchg Band; Pep Band; Score Keeper; Hon Roll; Fndr NW Hrtg Panel; Aviation.

COLLINS, PATRICIA D; Wichita North HS; Wichita, KS; (4); Church Yth Grp; Chorus; Church Choir; School Musical; Variety Show; Socr; Tennis; Hon Roll; WSU.

COLLINS, REBECCA; Manhattan HS; Manhattan, KS; (4); Church Yth Grp; FCA; Hosp Aide; Letterman Clb; Office Aide; Pep Clb; Varsity Clb; Orch; Powder Puff Ftbl; Trk; Stu Ath Trainer; CNA; St Fnlst Miss Amer KS Coed Pageant; KS ST U; Exercise Sci.

COLLINS, SARAH K; Garden City Sr HS; Garden City, KS; (2); Church Yth Grp; FHA; Hosp Aide; Key Clb; Spanish Clb; Acpl Chr; Var Bsktbl; Var Trk; Var Vllybl; High Hon Roll; KS U.

COLLINS, TABITHA A; Washington HS; Kansas City, KS; (3); Church Yth Grp; Dance Clb; German Clb; Pep Clb; Teachers Aide; Acpl Chr; Capt Drill Tm; Rep Frsh Cls; Rep Stu Cncl; Hon Roll; Tn Hp; Hmn Bhvr Sci/Chld Psychlgst.

COLLINS, TENILLE K; Triplains Schl; Winona, KS; (2); Pep Clb; Rep Frsh Cls; Sec Soph Cls; Cit Awd; High Hon Roll; Hon Roll; Jr NHS; Pres Acad Fit Awd; Kayettes 2 Yrs; Bus Admin.

COLLINS, THOMAS W; Frontenac Jr Sr HS; Frontenac, KS; (3); Am Leg Boys St; Library Aide; Am Leg Boys St; Scholastic Bowl; Spanish Clb; Yrbk; Var Golf; Hon Roll; NHS; Prfct Atten Awd; Amer Lgn Boys St Bst City Awd; KS ST U; Arch.

COLLINS, TIFFANY J; Liberal HS; Liberal, KS; (2); Band; Chorus; Mrchg Band; Pep Band; Swing Chorus; Variety Show; Hon Roll; NHS; Singing Solos; Horseback Riding; Competitive Forensics; Vet.

COLLMAN, CANDICE L; Washburn Rural HS; Topeka, KS; (2); Church Yth Grp; Letterman Clb; SADD; Band; Church Choir; Mrchg Band; Pep Band; Var L Swmmng; Hon Roll; Trvl Holland Sprts For Undrstndng Swim Team; KS ST Univ; PT.

COLLMANN, JULIE L; Belleville HS; Cuba, KS; (2); Art Clb; Drama Clb; FBLA; Letterman Clb; NFL; Pep Clb; Speech Tm; Thesps; School Play; Stage Crew; UNC; Kndgtn Tchr.

COLSON, JASON L; Goodland HS; Goodland, KS; (3); Letterman Clb; Office Aide; Ftbl; Wt Lftg; Wrstlng; Yth Group; Hunting.

COLSTON, DEBORAH; Lansing HS; Lansing, KS; (3); 1/142; French Clb; German Clb; Math Tm; Quiz Bowl; Band; Ed Nwsp; French Hon Soc; High Hon Roll; Jr NHS; NHS; KS Regents Hnrs Acad.

COLSTROM, LAURA D; Osage City HS; Osage City, KS; (3); 8/28; Art Clb; Church Yth Grp; Library Aide; Pep Clb; Science Clb; Spanish Clb; Band; Pep Band; JV Var Sftbl; JV Var Vllybl; Art Clb Treas; Emporia St Univ; Elem Ed.

COLTRANE, ARON; Iola Sr HS; La Harpe, KS; (4); 1/95; Am Leg Boys St; Church Yth Grp; Natl FFA Org; VP Jr Cls; VP Sr Cls; Var Capt Bsktbl; JV Crs Cntry; High Hon Roll; NHS; Val; GCTL; KS ST U; Ag.

COLTRANE, SISSY; Southeast HS; Cherokee, KS; (3); Pres FHA; Library Aide; Pep Clb; Science Clb; Yrbk; Pres Stu Cncl; Bsktbl; Vllybl; Hon Roll; NHS; KS Assn Of Yth; Labette CC; Nrsng.

COLVARD, CANDACE; Cunningham HS; Cunningham, KS; (4); 8/18; Am Leg Aux Girls St; Drama Clb; Quiz Bowl; Speech Tm; SADD; Teachers Aide; Band; Chorus; Pep Band; Ed Yrbk; Natl Eng Mrt Awd; Panhandle ST U; Music Ed.

COLYER, NICOLE; Maranatha Acad; Olathe, KS; (4); 1/32; Church Yth Grp; Chorus; School Musical; Rep Stu Cncl; L Var Trk; High Hon Roll; Pres NHS; Val; NFL; Pep Clb; Church Worship Tm; Schl Select Vocal Ensmbl; SW Baptist U; Music.

COMBES, LORETTA D; Humboldt HS; Humboldt, KS; (4); 5/40; Teachers Aide; Band; Mrchg Band; Pep Band; High Hon Roll; Supts Gold Awd; Allen Cty CC; Bus.

COMBEST, BRAD; Lansing HS; Leavenworth, KS; (1); Debate Tm; Drama Clb; NFL; School Play; Rep Frsh Cls; JV Bsktbl; JV Socr; Hon Roll; Forensics Ltr; Edinburgh U; Brdcstng/Virology.

COMBEST, VICTORIA; Dodge City HS; Dodge City, KS; (2); Church Yth Grp; Girl Scts; Intnl Clb; Chorus; Emporia St Univ; Elem Ed.

COMBS, HANNAH E; Chatauqua Cty HS; Sedan, KS; (4); 16/26; FHA; Speech Tm; Teachers Aide; Band; Chorus; Pep Band; School Play; Stage Crew; Sftbl; Trk; Hutchison CC; Bio Ed.

COMBS, JEREMY; Wichita West HS; Wichita, KS; (3); 25/283; Am Leg Boys St; Debate Tm; Letterman Clb; NFL; Office Aide; Teachers Aide; Varsity Clb; VP Sr Cls; Var L Crs Cntry; Var L Trk; AAU Trck Jr Olympcs; KS ST; Eng/Bus.

COMBS, SARA; Lawrence HS; Lawrence, KS; (4); 72/5210; Cmnty Wkr; Key Clb; Acpl Chr; Band; Chorus; Drm Mjr(t); Jazz Band; Mrchg Band; Orch; Pep Band; Music Schlrshp Univ KS Clarinet; Kiwanis Club Schlrshp Music; KMEA ST Orch 2 Yrs; U Of KS.

COMER, LYNDA; Onaga HS; Onaga, KS; (3); Church Yth Grp; Girl Scts; Pep Clb; Service Clb; Spanish Clb; Band; Mrchg Band; Pep Band; Stage Crew; Rptr Stu Cncl; Drafting Awd; KAYS Pres; Highland CC; Arch Dsgn.

COMFORT, RIKKI; Minneapolis HS; Minneapolis, KS; (4); 9/37; Teachers Aide; Band; Drill Tm; Mrchg Band; Pep Band; School Play; Treas Soph Cls; Treas Jr Cls; Treas Sr Cls; Var Chrldng; KS ST U; Kinesiology.

COMMER, KRISTIN D; Shawnee Mission N HS; Shawnee Mission, KS; (3); 2/377; Church Yth Grp; Pep Clb; Spanish Clb; Teachers Aide; Orch; School Musical; High Hon Roll; NHS; Columbia Univ Bk Awd.

COMPTON, DESIRAE L; Uniontown HS; Bronson, KS; (3); 8/24; FCA; Spanish Clb; Hon Roll; KS Univ; Hist Tchr.

COMPTON, ELIZABETH; Ness City HS; Ness City, KS; (1); Church Yth Grp; NFL; Pep Clb; Scholastic Bowl; Thesps; Chorus; Stage Crew; Hon Roll; Marine Bio.

COMPTON, JEFF R; Horton HS; Hiawatha, KS; (3); 12/45; Natl FFA Org; Band; Church Choir; Jazz Band; Mrchg Band; Pep Band; Var Bsktbl; Var Ftbl; Hon Roll; Prfct Atten Awd; KS St Univ; KS St Univ.

COMSTOCK, EMILY; Shawnee Heights HS; Topeka, KS; (3); Church Yth Grp; FCA; FBLA; HOBY; Key Clb; SADD; Band; Chorus; Mrchg Band; Ofcr Stu Cncl; U Of KS; Psych.

COMSTOCK, JENNIFER L; Wichita Heights HS; Wichita, KS; (2); 61/336; German Clb; Girl Scts; NFL; Chorus; School Musical; Ofcr Stu Cncl; Hon Roll; FL ST; Marine Biologist.

CONARD, DANIELLE L; Central Christian Schl; Hutchinson, KS; (4); Church Yth Grp; Debate Tm; Pep Clb; Acpl Chr; Band; Chorus; Pep Band; School Play; Stage Crew; Rptr Nwsp; Highest Praise; Distngd Chrstn HS Stu Awd For Music; Hutchinson CC; Travl & Tourism.

CONARD, HAYLEY; Hoxie HS; Hoxie, KS; (3); Church Yth Grp; FHA; School Musical; School Play; Var Capt Chrldng; Hon Roll; NHS; FHA Meals On Wheels Delivery; Bus Mgmt.

CONAWAY, JULIE K; Bishop Ward HS; Bonner Springs, KS; (1); 43/114; Hon Roll; KS ST Univ.

CONDLEY, ELIZABETH A; Topeka West HS; Topeka, KS; (2); Art Clb; Church Yth Grp; French Clb; Pep Clb; Swmmng; Hon Roll.

CONDON, TRAVIS A; Labette Co HS; Altamont, KS; (2); Boy Scts; Church Yth Grp; FCA; Band; Chorus; Mrchg Band; Pep Band; School Musical; Rep Frsh Cls; JV Trk; Dist/ST Hnrs Choir 95-; ST Vcl Solo 1st Rtng 94-; Li'L Abner HS Musical 95-; Northwest MO ST; Music P Arts.

CONES, MELANIE; Inman Jr Sr HS; Hutchinson, KS; (4); 11/29; Sec Art Clb; Church Yth Grp; Cmnty Wkr; Pres FHA; Math Tm; Pep Clb; Teachers Aide; Varsity Clb; Rep Band; Chorus; KS ST; Aviation.

CONGDON, ADRIEL; Cair Paravel - Latin Schl; Topeka, KS; (2); 2/24; Church Yth Grp; Acpl Chr; Chorus; Church Choir; Orch; School Musical; Var Bsktbl; High Hon Roll; Won Voice/Strings Musical Awds In Reg & Natl Cmptns; Perfrmd Violin Solo In Hnrs Concrt; Wheaton Coll; Missnry.

CONKLIN, BLAKE; Topeka HS; Topeka, KS; (3); 12/365; French Clb; Yrbk; Rep Soph Cls; JV Var Bsktbl; Var Golf; Var Socr; High Hon Roll; Acad & Ctznshp Tower Awd; Sports Med; Phy Thrpst.

CONKLIN, LISA M; Wichita Heights HS; Wichita, KS; (3); 61/389; Church Yth Grp; Teachers Aide; Church Choir; Jazz Band; Orch; Variety Show; Yrbk; Pom Pon; Hon Roll; Prfct Atten Awd; Bus.

CONKLING, JENNY; Shawnee Mission N HS; Roeland Park, KS; (4); 31/346; GAA; Hosp Aide; Latin Clb; Pep Clb; Q&S; Sprt Ed Yrbk; Var Bsktbl; Var Sftbl; Var Vllybl; Hon Roll; Comm Bld Donor; Habitat For Humnty; KS St Univ; Mgnt Inf.

CONLEY, NICOLE R; Emporia HS; Emporia, KS; (2); Bckstg Mgr Passion Play; Flint Hills Voc Tech Coll; Rcpt.

CONN, JASON M; Downs HS; Harlan, KS; (1); FHA; Natl FFA Org; Band; Chorus; Mrchg Band; Pep Band; JV Bsktbl; L Trk; Hon Roll; Pres Acad Fit Awd; Star Greenhand Awd Local FFA Chptr; Ft Hays ST Univ; Ag Ed.

CONNEALY, CASEY; St Thomas Aguinas HS; Leawood, KS; (3); 54/277; Am Leg Boys St; Cmnty Wkr; NFL; Band; Jazz Band; School Musical; Variety Show; JV Golf; Socr; Var Swmmng; St Piano Music Fstvl; KS Boys St Del; KU.

CONNELL, JEFF; Olathe North Sr HS; Olathe, KS; (4); Cmnty Wkr; FCA; Ofcr Stu Cncl; Var Capt Bsbl; Var Capt Ftbl; High Hon Roll; NHS; Pres Acad Fit Awd; Pres Schlr; St Schlr; Natl Ftbl Fndtn Coll Hall Of Fame Schlr Ath Awd; Emporia ST Univ; Bus; Mktg.

CONNELLY, KELLY; Bishop Miege HS; Belton, MO; (4); 6/167; Debate Tm; French Clb; HOBY; NFL; Pep Clb; Speech Tm; SADD; School Play; Vllybl; High Hon Roll; Dncd W/Wstprt Bllt Thtre; Cmps Mnstry Tm; Envrnmntl Awrnss Clb; Rcrtmnt Spkr; Rtry 4 Wy Spch Cont Fnlst; Dnce.

CONNELLY, KERRY; Topeka West HS; Topeka, KS; (4); 4/236; Cmnty Wkr; Math Clb; Pep Clb; Spanish Clb; Band; Jazz Band; School Musical; Variety Show; High Hon Roll; Treas NHS; KS Univ.

CONNER, BRIANA M; Metro Boulevard Alt HS; Wichita, KS; (4); Lit Mag; Butler Cty CC.

CONNER, SUSAN; Shawnee Mssn NW HS; Lenexa, KS; (4); 16/400; Q&S; SADD; Ofcr Drill Tm; Ed Nwsp; Ed Yrbk; High Hon Roll; NHS; Ntl Merit Ltr; Pres Schlr; KS State Univ; Medicine.

CONNOR, DAVID; Wichita West HS; Wichita, KS; (3); 4/389; Am Leg Boys St; Church Yth Grp; FCA; Band; Jazz Band; Mrchg Band; Pep Band; School Musical; Variety Show; Ofcr Frsh Cls; Wichita River Festival Prairie Schooner Mate 96; Investigative Summer Sci Participant; KS Univ; Bio.

CONOVER, AMANDRA; Ulysses HS; Ulysses, KS; (2); Church Yth Grp; FHA; Chorus; Church Choir; Stat Bsktbl; Mgr(s); JV Vllybl; Hon Roll; KS ST U; Ed.

CONOVER, THERESA M; Goddard HS; Wichita, KS; (3); Church Yth Grp; Office Aide; Science Clb; SADD; Teachers Aide; Stage Crew; Ofcr Sr Cls; Sftbl; High Hon Roll; Hon Roll; Wichita ST U; Child Psycht.

CONRAD, BRANDON L; Labette Co HS; Oswego, KS; (3); 4-H; Natl FFA Org; Quiz Bowl; Scholastic Bowl; Ofcr Bsbl; Ftbl; Cit Awd; 4-H Awd; Hon Roll.

CONRAD, JESSICA; Fairfield HS; Sylvia, KS; (3); Cmnty Wkr; School Musical; School Play; Treas Soph Cls; Sec Jr Cls; Rep Stu Cncl; Bsktbl; Vllybl; Wt Lftg; Cit Awd; U Of KS; Premed.

CONRAD, KIMBERLY L; Field Kindley Mem Sr HS; Coffeyville, KS; (2); 19/157; Church Yth Grp; Cmnty Wkr; L Debate Tm; German Clb; Rep Stu Cncl; Var L Ftbl; Var L Mgr(s); Var L Swmmng; Tennis; High Hon Roll; Tomorrows Ldrs Of Comm; Tree Bd Assoc Mem; Vol Tutor.

CONRAD, MICHAEL W; Field Kindley Mem Sr HS; Coffeyville, KS; (4); 33/132; Church Yth Grp; Cmnty Wkr; Debate Tm; French Clb; Teachers Aide; L Orch; School Play; Variety Show; Var Golf; Var L Swmmng; Elem Schl Tutor Vol; Amer Red Cross Blood Donor; Meals On Wheels Driver & Deliverer; CA Poly Tech; Aeron Engr.

CONRAD, RYAN LEE; Hutchinson HS; Hutchinson, KS; (4); 60/250; Church Yth Grp; Cmnty Wkr; Hist DECA; Key Clb; Quiz Bowl; Service Clb; SADD; Chorus; Church Choir; JV Trk; KS Boys Choir Alumni; Mktg Stdnt Of Yr Schlrshp; 3rd Pl ST DECA Comp; U Of KS; Bus/Cmptrs.

CONRAD, TED T; Blue Valley HS; Stilwell, KS; (3); Boy Scts; Church Yth Grp; Acpl Chr; Chorus; Church Choir; School Musical; JV Golf; Hon Roll; NHS; Boy/Eagle Sct Awds; All-St Choir 96.

CONRADY, KELLY S; Caldwell Jr Sr HS; Caldwell, KS; (3); Nwsp; Yrbk; Var L Ftbl; Trk; Hon Roll; Prfct Atten Awd; Nom Amer Lgns Boys ST; Plcd 5th ST Track Intrmdt Hrdls 95; Qlfd ST Hrdls High Intrmdt 96; PT.

CONSIGLIO, DAVID N; Shawnee Mission Northwest HS; Shawnee Mission, KS; (4); 175/390; Cmnty Wkr; Var Ftbl; Hon Roll; Mid Amer Hazarene Coll; Bus Adm.

CONWAY IV, LAWRENCE; Leavenworth HS; Fort Leavenworth, KS; (3); Boy Scts; Chess Clb; Church Yth Grp; Debate Tm; Drama Clb; Latin Clb; NFL; Thesps; School Musical; School Play; Acting.

CONWELL, ANDREW M; Wellington Sr HS; Wellington, KS; (4); Scholastic Bowl; Ofcr Bsbl; Ftbl; Trk; Hon Roll; Jr NHS.

COOK, ANNE; Spring Hill HS; Spring Hill, KS; (4); 17/97; Am Leg Aux Girls St; Church Yth Grp; Cmnty Wkr; Q&S; Science Clb; SADD; Ed Yrbk; Ofcr Stu Cncl; Capt Vllybl; Hon Roll; Sth Johnson Cty Fire Explrs; JCCC; PT Asst.

COOK, BETHANY L; Lawrence HS; Lawrence, KS; (4); Church Yth Grp; Debate Tm; Latin Clb; Band; Chorus; Mrchg Band; Ed Yrbk; VP Stu Cncl; Intrml Stat Vllybl; High Hon Roll; Histrcl Paper ST Cmptn 2nd In Regnls; Natl Latin Finalist; 4 Yr Coll; Pre-Med/Bus Ad/His.

COOK, CASSONDRA D; Solomon Jr Sr HS; Solomon, KS; (2); 2/37; FHA; Band; Chorus; Trk; Vllybl; Wt Lftg; High Hon Roll; Hon Roll; Bethany Coll; Acctng.

COOK, CHRIS G; Ft Scott HS; Fort Scott, KS; (2); 50/150; Church Yth Grp; Treas VP 4-H; Latin Clb; Natl FFA Org; JV Ftbl; Wt Lftg; 4-H Awd; Hon Roll; KS ST; Wldlf Bio.

COOK, CHRISTINA M; Wellington Sr HS; Wellington, KS; (2); Church Yth Grp; Cmnty Wkr; French Clb; Key Clb; Chorus; Church Choir; JV Bsktbl; Var Tennis; Cit Awd; Hon Roll; Chrch Mssn Trp; Trnsltn; Cowley CC; Trnsltr.

COOK, COURTNEY D; Liberal HS; Liberal, KS; (3); Church Yth Grp; Cmnty Wkr; Key Clb; Chorus; Church Choir; School Musical; Stage Crew; JV Vllybl; High Hon Roll; Hon Roll; Med Explrs; Physcl Rhbltn.

COOK, CRYSTAL M; Riverton Schl; Riverton, KS; (3); FCA; French Clb; FHA; Letterman Clb; Natl FFA Org; Acpl Chr; Chorus; JV Var Bsktbl; Var JV Sftbl; High Hon Roll; Church Vlybl; Natural Helpers; PSU; Nrsng.

COOK, JULIE A; Eudora HS; Eudora, KS; (4); FBLA; NFL; Spanish Clb; Varsity Clb; School Play; JV Var Bsktbl; JV Sftbl; JV Var Vllybl; Drama Clb; Office Aide; Peer Tutor; Extended Learning Excelled Prgm; U Of KS; Sci/Premed.

COOK, LESTIE J; Circle HS; Benton, KS; (4); SADD; Teachers Aide; Acpl Chr; Band; Church Choir; School Musical; Rep Stu Cncl; Var L Chrldng; Hon Roll; NHS; Natl Hnr Roll; Presdntl Awd Educl Excl; Butler; Acctng.

COOK, MICHELLE; Ashland Jr-Sr HS; Ashland, KS; (4); Pres Sec Church Yth Grp; Quiz Bowl; Speech Tm; Var Chrldng; Var Crs Cntry; Var Trk; High Hon Roll; Hon Roll; NHS; Pres Acad Fit Awd; Pittsburg ST U; Med.

COOK, MICHELLE R; Washington HS; Greenleaf, KS; (4); 4/30; Pres French Clb; FHA; Library Aide; Pep Clb; Drill Tm; School Musical; School Play; Chrldng; JV Golf; High Hon Roll; Elks Hnr Stu; Intl Frgn Lang Awd Frnch; Schltc Awd; KS ST U; Phys Thrpy.

COOK, MONICA; Russell HS; Bunker Hill, KS; (4); 10/68; FCA; Treas Rptr 4-H; SADD; Rep Jr Cls; Rep Sr Cls; Var Capt Chrldng; High Hon Roll; VP NHS; Key Clb; Letterman Clb; KS Assn Of Yth Vp, Points Dir, Bd Mem; Adopt-A-Mile Pgm; Ft Hays ST Univ; Pre-Pharmacy.

COOK, NEAL W; Burlington HS; Burlington, KS; (3); Church Yth Grp; Office Aide; Var L Wrstlng; Hon Roll.

COOK, REBEKAH; Shawnee Hghts HS; Topeka, KS; (4); 1/237; Church Yth Grp; Cmnty Wkr; FCA; Model UN; Red Cross Aide; Acpl Chr; Band; Chorus; Church Choir; Mrchg Band; Natl Stu Of Yr Yth For Christ USA 95-96; John Brown Univ.

COOK, SARA; Peabody-Burns Jr Sr HS; Peabody, KS; (3); 3/30; L Band; L Chorus; School Musical; Ed Yrbk; Treas Soph Cls; Var L Chrldng; High Hon Roll; Pres Acad Fit Awd; Natl Sci Mrt Awd; Hrt Amer Lge Hnr Bnd.

COOK, SARA LUANNE; Elwood Schl; Faucett, MO; (4); 1/17; Band; Drill Tm; Yrbk; Ofcr Stu Cncl; Chrldng; Gym; Gov Hon Prg Awd; NHS; Pres Acad Fit Awd; Val; MO Western ST Coll.

COOKSON, SAMANTHA; Madison Jr Sr HS; Madison, KS; (4); 3/20; Am Leg Aux Girls St; German Clb; Band; Chorus; Ofcr Frsh Cls; Ofcr Soph Cls; Sec Sr Cls; Bsktbl; Var Chrldng; Var Vllybl; KU; Nrsng.

COOLEY, ANNE; Hayden HS; Topeka, KS; (4); 7/110; Hosp Aide; Intnl Clb; Office Aide; JV Var Tennis; Intrml Vllybl; High Hon Roll; Hon Roll; U Of KS; Premed.

COOLEY, SARAH; Circle HS; Augusta, KS; (4); Am Leg Aux Girls St; Q&S; Spanish Clb; SADD; School Musical; Nwsp; Ed Yrbk; Tennis; High Hon Roll.

COOLEY, SARAH D; Campus HS; Haysville, KS; (2); JV Bsktbl; Var Sftbl; JV Vllybl; Butler Cty CC.

COOLEY, VANESSA A; Lakin HS; Lakin, KS; (3); Art Clb; Church Yth Grp; Var L Golf; Hon Roll; Forensics Ltr; All League Acad Hon Mntn; KU; Pre Med.

COOLIDGE, SARAH E; Shawnee Heights Sr HS; Topeka, KS; (3); Church Yth Grp; Intnl Clb; Key Clb; Band; Mrchg Band; Pep Band; Cit Awd; High Hon Roll; Hon Roll; Prfct Atten Awd; Bible Clb; Yth For Chrst; Lttr In Acadmcs; Phys Thpy.

COOMES, HEATHER L; St Paul HS; Saint Paul, KS; (3); 3/16; Church Yth Grp; NFL; Quiz Bowl; Scholastic Bowl; Band; Chorus; Mgr(s); Trk; Vllybl; Hon Roll; St Trk 1600m Relay Champs 96.

COOMES, NICHOLAS E; Girard HS; Girard, KS; (4); 1/69; Church Yth Grp; Var Bsbl; Var Capt Bsktbl; Var Capt Ftbl; Trk; Gov Hon Prg Awd; High Hon Roll; NHS; Pres Schlr; St Schlr; KS Regents Hnrs Acad; Pittsburg ST Univ; Engrng Tech.

COON, BRANDI N; Highland Park HS; Topeka, KS; (2); 1/150; Church Yth Grp; Cmnty Wkr; Hosp Aide; Science Clb; Church Choir; School Musical; Swing Chorus; Sec Soph Cls; Chrldng; High Hon Roll; STRAPP; Teens HOPE; BSU; KS U; Med.

COON, JODI; Wabaunsee HS; Alma, KS; (1); Church Yth Grp; Band; Chorus; Pep Band; School Musical; Sftbl; Tennis; Hon Roll; Emporia ST U; Elem Ed.

COONFIELD, BRANDON J; Coldwater Jr Sr HS; Coldwater, KS; (1); Boy Scts; Chess Clb; Cmnty Wkr; Letterman Clb; Pep Clb; Science Clb; VICA; Band; Chorus; Mrchg Band; KS ST Chmpnshp Ftbl Div I Tm; Bw/Rfl Hntng; Fshng; K ST; NBA/WLDLF Cnsrvtnst.

COONLEY, DANIEL S; Blue Valley Northwest HS; Overland Park, KS; (4); 78/341; Rptr Nwsp; Ed Lit Mag; Art Clb; Quiz Bowl; Service Clb; Gov Hon Prg Awd; Hon Roll; NHS; Pres Schlr; NY Univ; Film Production.

COONS, JOSHUA; Turner HS; Kansas City, KS; (3); Boy Scts; Bus Profs of Am; JV Wrstlng; Hon Roll; Cmptr Scis.

COONS, KEVIN V; Ottawa HS; Ottawa, KS; (3); Intrml Ftbl; Hon Roll.

COOPER, ALLEN B; Udall HS; Udall, KS; (3); Church Yth Grp; Band; Mrchg Band; Pep Band; Ftbl; Prfct Atten Awd; Air Craft.

COOPER, ELIZABETH ANNE; Wichita East HS; Wichita, KS; (2); Church Yth Grp; French Clb; Band; Chorus; Mrchg Band; Orch; Pep Band; School Musical; French Hon Soc; Hon Roll; Intl Baccal Stdnt Advsry Cncl; Music Ed/Vocal/Instrm.

COOPER, JACOB A; Circle HS; El Dorado, KS; (2); 4-H; Acpl Chr; Bsktbl; Wt Lftg; 4-H Awd; Hon Roll; Bsktbl Awds; U Of KS; Park Rngr/Game Wrdn.

COOPER, JOHN G; Colby Sr HS; Colby, KS; (4); 24/110; Art Clb; Boy Scts; Library Aide; Office Aide; Spanish Clb; Speech Tm; SADD; Teachers Aide; Nwsp; Yrbk; Crmnl Justice.

COOPER, KIM; Wellington Sr HS; Wellington, KS; (2); Church Yth Grp; French Clb; Key Clb; Scholastic Bowl; SADD; Band; Church Choir; Mrchg Band; Pep Band; Tennis.

COOPER, MELISA; Seaman Sr HS; Topeka, KS; (4); 20/189; Church Yth Grp; Debate Tm; FBLA; Key Clb; Model UN; VP Spanish Clb; Nwsp; Chrldng; KS ST U; Acctng.

COOPER, MONICA D; Madison Jr Sr HS; Madison, KS; (3); Church Yth Grp; FBLA; VICA; Band; Mrchg Band; Trk; Vllybl; Wt Lftg; Hon Roll; GAA; Tsk Frc Rep.

COOPER, REBECCA; Desoto HS; Shawnee Mission, KS; (4); 2/106; Church Yth Grp; Band; Church Choir; Drm Mjr(t); Chrldng; Vllybl; Gov Hon Prg Awd; High Hon Roll; NHS; Sal; Johnson Cty CC; Music.

COOPER, RON A; Independence HS; Independence, KS; (2); Hon Roll; KS ST Univ; Engr.

COOPER, SONYA; Hoxie HS; Hoxie, KS; (4); 1/33; Church Yth Grp; FHA; Girl Scts; Gov Hon Prg Awd; Hon Roll; NHS; St Schlr; Val; Cmnty Wkr; Chorus; Natl His Day; KS ST His Day Stdnt Of Yr; Bethel Coll; His/Bus.

COOTS, AARON A; Maur Hill Prep Schl; Atchison, KS; (1); Boy Scts; Chorus; School Play; Stage Crew; Hon Roll.

COOTS, ALAN J; Maur Hill Prep Schl; Atchison, KS; (1); Boy Scts; Chorus; High Hon Roll.

COP, CARRIE; Shawnee Mission N HS; Merriam, KS; (3); Church Yth Grp; Drama Clb; Pep Clb; Thesps; Chorus; School Musical; School Play; Stage Crew; Intrml Gym; Hon Roll; PHQ.

COP, TRACY; Turner HS; Kansas City, KS; (3); 19/275; Drama Clb; German Clb; Teachers Aide; Variety Show; Sec Treas Frsh Cls; Treas Jr Cls; Sec Treas Stu Cncl; Mgr(s); Cit Awd; High Hon Roll; DECA Mrktng; Math Awds; KCC; Elem Ed.

COPE, GERRY W; Great Bend Sr HS; Great Bend, KS; (2); Church Yth Grp; Key Clb; Pep Clb; Acpl Chr; Band; Church Choir; Mrchg Band; Variety Show; Ofcr Bsbl; Ftbl; Peer Cnslr; KAY Clb; Homcmng Candidate.

COPELAND, ELIZABETH A; Wichita East HS; Wichita, KS; (3); 20/337; Church Yth Grp; Cmnty Wkr; Chorus; Church Choir; School Musical; Variety Show; VP Jr Cls; Vllybl; High Hon Roll; NHS; Schooner Mate; KS ST Univ; Elem Ed.

COPELAND, ERIN R; Santa Fe Trail Jr HS; Olathe, KS; (1); Drama Clb; French Clb; Pep Clb; Teachers Aide; Drill Tm; School Play; Swmmng; French Hon Soc; Hon Roll; Pres Schlr.

COPELAND, JENNIFER; Shawnee Mission NW HS; Lenexa, KS; (4); 92/390; Q&S; Teachers Aide; Ed Nwsp; Hon Roll; Pres Of Fash Careers; U Of KS; Magzne Jrnlsm.

COPELAND, PAMELA J; Dodge City HS; Dodge City, KS; (1); Chorus; Orch; Vocal Music.

COPELAND, RACHEL A; Wellington Sr HS; Wellington, KS; (2); Church Yth Grp; Red Cross Aide; SADD; Acpl Chr; Chorus; Church Choir; Swmmng; Trk; Vllybl; Jr NHS.

COPP, ERIKA; Oskaloosa HS; Ozawkie, KS; (4); Debate Tm; FBLA; NFL; Thesps; School Musical; School Play; Ed Yrbk; Chrldng; High Hon Roll; Prfct Atten Awd; GATE; U Of KS; Hist.

CORBETT, KENDRA RENEE; Salina HS South; Salina, KS; (4); Teachers Aide; Band; Rep Soph Cls.

CORBY, VICTORIA M; Salina HS Central; Salina, KS; (2); High Hon Roll; Pres Schlr; Salvation Army Tutor; 4 Yr Univ; Sci/.ath.

CORCIMIGLIA, REGINA; Wichita West HS; Wichita, KS; (4); 19/260; Am Leg Aux Girls St; Cmnty Wkr; French Clb; Office Aide; Teachers Aide; Rep Soph Cls; Rep Jr Cls; Rep Sr Cls; JV Sftbl; Hon Roll; KS Hnrs Pgm; Photo.

CORCORAN, CARA; Washburn Rural HS; Topeka, KS; (3); Church Yth Grp; Cmnty Wkr; FBLA; SADD; Variety Show; Phtg Nwsp; Phtg Yrbk; JV Var Chrldng; Powder Puff Ftbl; High Hon Roll; Dnc Cmptns; KU; Nrsng.

CORCORAN, JAMIE; Belle Plaine HS; Belle Plaine, KS; (3); Letterman Clb; Pep Clb; SADD; Bsktbl; Trk; Vllybl; Wt Lftg; Kays Clb.

CORCORAN, KELLIE K; Hutchinson HS; Hutchinson, KS; (3); Am Leg Aux Girls St; Cmnty Wkr; Key Clb; Orch; School Musical; Variety Show; Bsktbl; High Hon Roll; Hon Roll; Jr NHS; Chrch Choir; Kayettes Clb; KS ST Univ; Vet Med.

CORCORAN, MARY K; Lawrence HS; Lawrence, KS; (2); Debate Tm; HOBY; Pep Clb; Teachers Aide; Thesps; Band; Chorus; Mrchg Band; Pep Band; Phtg Ed Nwsp; Jr Asst Coord For KATM; Bike Across KS; U Of KS; Graphic Arts; Oral Com.

CORCORAN, MATTHEW; St Thomas Aquinas HS; Lenexa, KS; (3); 22/261; Am Leg Boys St; Sec Key Clb; Rptr Yrbk; Var Swmmng; High Hon Roll; NHS; Stdnts As Tchrs Tutoring Pgm; Engrng.

CORCORAN, SANDY C; Stockton HS; Stockton, KS; (4); 7/33; FHA; Key Clb; Q&S; Red Cross Aide; Teachers Aide; Ed Yrbk; Mgr(s); Hon Roll; Photo; Wrtng; Med Start; KS ST U; Med.

CORDER, STUARTT; Spring Hill HS; Olathe, KS; (4); 1/97; Am Leg Boys St; Chess Clb; Church Yth Grp; Debate Tm; HOBY; Letterman Clb; NFL; Capt Quiz Bowl; Capt Scholastic Bowl; Speech Tm; Prjct KARM Stu Dir; KU; Arspc Engr.

CORDIA, JESSICA M; Liberal HS; Liberal, KS; (3); Hon Roll; Acctnt.

CORFMAN, MYRINDA; Berean Acad; Whitewater, KS; (3); Church Yth Grp; HOBY; NFL; Thesps; Acpl Chr; Band; School Musical; School Play; VP Frsh Cls; Rep Soph Cls; PTP Ambssdr; Heirborne England 95; Teens As Tchrs; Prfrmng Arts.

CORKE, ERIC; Goodland HS; Goodland, KS; (3); 26/89; Wt Lftg; Northwest KS Area Vo-Tech Sch.

CORLE JR, ALDON E; Independence HS; Independence, KS; (4); 14/139; Boy Scts; Pep Clb; Spanish Clb; Teachers Aide; JV Ftbl; High Hon Roll; Hon Roll; NHS; Pres Acad Fit Awd; PUPPS; KS Schlr Awd; ICC; Vet.

CORMODE, JILL; Atchison Co Cmty HS; Lancaster, KS; (1); Church Yth Grp; Natl FFA Org; Band; Mrchg Band; Pep Band; JV Chrldng; Hon Roll; Kays; Med Fld.

CORN, JANUARY; Quivira Heights HS; Holyrood, KS; (2); 1/17; Church Yth Grp; VP Frsh Cls; VP Soph Cls; Var L Tennis; Var L Trk; High Hon Roll; KAYS; Peer Cnslr; Bus Admin.

CORNE, DANIELLE A; Northeast Magnet HS; Wichita, KS; (3); 23/99; Boy Scts; Drama Clb; Orch; School Play; Variety Show; Nwsp; Rep Frsh Cls; Rep Soph Cls; Hon Roll; Prfct Atten Awd; Jr Aviation Explorers Pres; Achieving Woman In Sci Awd; HS Outdoor Wildlife Ctr Founder; Military; Bus; Aviation.

CORNEJO, TIFFANY M; Wichita South HS; Wichita, KS; (2); Debate Tm; Drama Clb; GAA; Latin Clb; Letterman Clb; NFL; Office Aide; Speech Tm; Bsktbl; Sftbl; 4 Yr Coll; Law.

CORNELIUS, SARA; Coldwater Jr Sr HS; Coldwater, KS; (1); FHA; Letterman Clb; Band; Chorus; Variety Show; Rep Frsh Cls; Rep Stu Cncl; Bsktbl; Chrldng; Vllybl.

CORNETT, J RYAN; Garden City Sr HS; Garden City, KS; (1); Church Yth Grp; Ofcr Bsbl; Bsktbl; Wt Lftg; Hon Roll; Prfct Atten Awd; Hnrs Bio/Eng/Algbr II Soph; YMCA Bsktbl Tm Coach; Law/Math.

CORNETT, STEVEN R; Fredonia HS; Fall River, KS; (3); Chorus; School Play; Stage Crew; Hon Roll; Wichita ST Univ; Comp Engrng.

CORNWELL, LESLEY B; Wichita East HS; Wichita, KS; (3); 97/293; Church Yth Grp; Cmnty Wkr; Spanish Clb; Church Choir; Drill Tm; Hon Roll; Sunday Schl Tchr; Pediatrics.

CORONA, MARK T; Sumner Acad Of Arts & Science; Kansas City, KS; (1).

CORPORON, JAY A; Topeka West HS; Topeka, KS; (3); Math Clb; Spanish Clb; High Hon Roll; Physics.

CORRELL, KELLY; Columbus HS; Columbus, KS; (2); Bus Profs of Am; 4-H; Math Tm; Spanish Clb; Bsktbl; Mgr(s); Powder Puff Ftbl; Sftbl; Wt Lftg; 4-H Awd; Kay Clb.

CORRELL, NICOLE M; Spearville Jr Sr HS; Spearville, KS; (2); Pep Clb; Quiz Bowl; Varsity Clb; Band; Chorus; Mrchg Band; Pep Band; Sec Soph Cls; Bsktbl; Trk; Acctng.

COSLETT, BETHANY R; Chaparral HS; Harper, KS; (2); Church Yth Grp; 4-H; Key Clb; Natl FFA Org; Quiz Bowl; Chorus; JV Bsktbl; JV Crs Cntry; JV Trk; 4-H Awd; Natl 4-H Erth Tm; Japanese 4-H Exch; Natl TSA Cmptn; KS ST Univ; Animal Sci.

COSNER, AMANDA J; Lakin HS; Lakin, KS; (2); Church Yth Grp; Drama Clb; French Clb; FHA; Hosp Aide; Speech Tm; School Play; JV Chrldng; Hon Roll; NHS; Chrldng Hnr; KS Univ; Bus.

COSSMAN, LISA M; Dodge City HS; Dodge City, KS; (3); Math Tm; Office Aide; SADD; Drill Tm; JV Bsktbl; Var Trk; Var Vllybl; NHS; KS Assn Yth Brd; Drg Awrnss Restnc Ed; Srgcl Nrs.

COSTELLO, CYMBRE; Atchison Sr HS; Atchison, KS; (4); 13/123; Church Yth Grp; Spanish Clb; Teachers Aide; Band; Chrldng; Capt L Socr; Vllybl; Hon Roll; NHS; NYLC Delg; All Huron Leag 2nd Tm Soccer; Benedictine Coll; Elem Ed.

COSTELLO, STACY G; Dodge City HS; Dodge City, KS; (3); Church Yth Grp; Drama Clb; Band; Mrchg Band; School Play; Wt Lftg; Hon Roll; Ntl Merit Ltr; Peer Hlpr Cnslr; Southwestern Coll; Marine Bio.

COSTIN, HEATHER; Altoona Midway HS; Altoona, KS; (4); 2/27; Teachers Aide; Drm Mjr(t); Pres Frsh Cls; Pres Soph Cls; Pres Jr Cls; Pres Sr Cls; High Hon Roll; VP NHS; Sal; St Spch, Drama Cmptr; St Band Cmptr; Micro Dsgn Pres; Emporia ST U; Elem Ed.

COSTLEY, COLIN; Glasco HS; Glasco, KS; (3); 1/7; Quiz Bowl; Treas Frsh Cls; VP Soph Cls; Ofcr Stu Cncl; JV Bsktbl; Var Ftbl; Trk; High Hon Roll; NHS; Emporia St U Math & Geom Tests Hnrb Mntn; Schl Site Cmmttte; KS Sst U Engrng & Sci Inst; Engr.

COSTLEY, MISTY D; Salina HS South; Salina, KS; (2); Hon Roll; Chrch Yth Grp; KS ST U; Bus.

COTE, JIMMY M; Blue Valley HS; Shawnee Mission, KS; (4); Am Leg Boys St; Boy Scts; Band; Mrchg Band; Pep Band; Hon Roll; NHS; Accepted & Attnd US Naval Acad Summer Smnr.

COTE, KRISTAL M; Osage City HS; Osage City, KS; (4); Bus Profs of Am; Drama Clb; French Clb; Office Aide; Chorus; School Play; Hon Roll; Natl Engl Merit Awd; Better Than Ever Awd; Flint Hills Tech Col; Grphc Art.

COTHRAN, MICHELLE; Sumner Acad Of Arts & Science; Kansas City, KS; (1); Latin Clb; Pep Clb; Spanish Clb; Intrml Chrldng; JV Sftbl; Hon Roll.

COULSON, JENNIFER L; Baxter Springs HS; Baxter Springs, KS; (4); 10/63; Church Yth Grp; FCA; FHA; Pep Clb; Science Clb; Spanish Clb; Band; Church Choir; Drm Mjr(t); Mrchg Band; Outs Stu In Inst Mus; Acad Achv Awd; Mid Amer Nazarene Col; Rdlgy.

COULTER, ADAM H; Garden City Sr HS; Garden City, KS; (2); Letterman Clb; Varsity Clb; Rep Jr Cls; Ofcr Stu Cncl; JV Bsktbl; L Ftbl; Var L Trk; Hon Roll; Stuco Clss Rep.

COULTER, CHRIS; Mulvane Sr HS; Mulvane, KS; (4); 11/144; Boy Scts; FCA; Scholastic Bowl; SADD; Teachers Aide; Thesps; School Play; Ed Nwsp; Yrbk; NHS; Arch Engrng.

COULTER, ERICA; Wichita Northwest HS; Wichita, KS; (4); 10/333; Church Yth Grp; Cmnty Wkr; Debate Tm; GAA; Hosp Aide; Intnl Clb; NFL; Office Aide; Crs Cntry; Trk; Bethel Coll.

COULTER, LEA B; Colby Sr HS; Colby, KS; (2); Church Yth Grp; Spanish Clb; Chorus; Ofcr Soph Cls; Hon Roll.

COULTER, SARAH M; Topeka HS; Topeka, KS; (1); Church Yth Grp; Dance Clb; 4-H; Band; Mrchg Band; Pep Band; 4-H Awd; High Hon Roll; Hon Roll; Prtcptd 4 Local Prdctns The Nutcracker; Prtcptd Swan Lake/Mudsummer Nights Dream/Firebird.

COULTER, SETH L; Topeka HS; Topeka, KS; (4); Boy Scts; Debate Tm; Jazz Band; Nwsp; Lit Mag; Pres Jr Cls; Rep Sr Cls; High Hon Roll; Hon Roll; NHS; Eagle Sct Awd; U Of KS; Radio Broadcasting.

COUNSIL, DOUG; Neodesha Jr Sr HS; Neodesha, KS; (4); 5/41; Am Leg Boys St; Math Clb; Math Tm; Pep Clb; Teachers Aide; Mgr Nwsp; VP Stu Cncl; High Hon Roll; Hon Roll; Pres Acad Fit Awd; Renaissance; Publctns Bus Mngr.

COUNTER, KATHARINE; Salina HS Central; Salina, KS; (4); Am Leg Aux Girls St; Church Yth Grp; Debate Tm; SADD; Thesps; School Musical; Stage Crew; Swing Chorus; Swmmng; Hon Roll; NW MO ST U; Rec Admin.

COUNTRYMAN, KAREN R; Caldwell Jr Sr HS; Caldwell, KS; (2); Church Yth Grp; Pep Clb; SADD; Stage Crew; Mgr Bsktbl; Mgr(s); Hon Roll; Prfct Atten Awd; Univ Of KS.

COURSEN, BRIAN M; Burlingame HS; Burlingame, KS; (2); 15/35; Church Yth Grp; Pep Clb; Band; Mrchg Band; JV Bsktbl; Var L Ftbl; Var L Trk; Var Wt Lftg; Var L Wrstlng; Hon Roll.

COURSON, NICOLE L; Great Bend Sr HS; Great Bend, KS; (3); Hosp Aide; JV Vllybl; Hon Roll; Prfct Atten Awd; U Of KS; Med.

COURTER, PAUL; Jefferson Co North HS; Nortonville, KS; (3); VP Drama Clb; Ofcr FBLA; Letterman Clb; Speech Tm; SADD; School Play; Stage Crew; Pres Soph Cls; Var L Ftbl; Var L Trk.

COURTRIGHT, ERICA D; Newton Sr HS; Newton, KS; (2); Art Clb; Pres Church Yth Grp; Sec 4-H; French Clb; Model UN; Nwsp; Rep Frsh Cls; Sec Treas Soph Cls; Ofcr Stu Cncl; JV Bsktbl; Future Problem Solving; Sci Olympia.

COURTWAY, EDGAR N; Ft Scott HS; Fort Scott, KS; (4); Boy Scts; Church Yth Grp; Debate Tm; NFL; Science Clb; Teachers Aide; Band; Mrchg Band; Pep Band; Ftbl.

COVER, SARA C; Ottawa HS; Ottawa, KS; (2); Art Clb; Church Yth Grp; VP Key Clb; Spanish Clb; SADD; JV Socr; High Hon Roll; NHS; Med.

COVEY, MARK; Mulvane Sr HS; Mulvane, KS; (4); 1/144; Debate Tm; HOBY; Scholastic Bowl; Thesps; School Musical; School Play; Ed Nwsp; Pres Stu Cncl; NHS; Val; KS Assn For Yth; Show Choir.

COWAN, MIKE; Sedgwick HS; Sedgwick, KS; (1); 7/28; Letterman Clb; Pres Frsh Cls; Var JV Bsktbl; Var JV Ftbl; Hon Roll.

COWDEN, CHRISTOPHER M; Olathe East Sr HS; Olathe, KS; (3); Church Yth Grp; Spanish Clb; Ftbl; Hon Roll; Johnson Cty CC; Crmnl Jstc.

COWELL, SARAH M; Derby HS; Derby, KS; (3); Church Yth Grp; Cmnty Wkr; FCA; Thesps; Orch; VP Frsh Cls; Pres Soph Cls; VP Pres Stu Cncl; High Hon Roll; NHS; OK Bapt Univ; Scndry Ed.

COWGILL, MICHAEL; Rock Creek Jr Sr HS; Saint George, KS; (2); 2/72; Boy Scts; Church Yth Grp; Debate Tm; Math Tm; Quiz Bowl; Scholastic Bowl; Var Bsbl; Var Bsktbl; Var Ftbl; High Hon Roll; Athltc Acad; Marine Bio.

COX, AIMEE; Rose Hill HS; Rose Hill, KS; (3); 1/135; Quiz Bowl; Scholastic Bowl; Thesps; Band; School Musical; Stage Crew; Yrbk; Sftbl; High Hon Roll; Ntl Merit Ltr; Yrbk Ed; Dist Hnr Band; Wichita Wind Ensemble; Law.

COX, ANGELA C; Wichita North HS; Wichita, KS; (2); French Clb; Rptr Nwsp; Rep Soph Cls; Rep Jr Cls; Pom Pon; Hon Roll; Clb 98; Segwick Cty Zoo Vol; Photojrnlsm.

COX, BENJAMIN R; Salina HS South; Salina, KS; (2); Church Yth Grp; Cmnty Wkr; Hon Roll; Renaissance Stdnt; KA ST Univ; Arch/Gen Contrctg.

COX, BRENT D; Beloit Jr Sr HS; Beloit, KS; (2); L Bsbl; JV Ftbl; High Hon Roll; Hon Roll.

COX, HEATHER J; Meade HS; Meade, KS; (3); Church Yth Grp; Letterman Clb; NFL; Pep Clb; Spanish Clb; Band; Chorus; Mrchg Band; Pep Band; School Play; Kayettes; Hutchinson CC; Pre Law.

COX, JAMES A; J C Harmon HS; Kansas City, KS; (4); 12/230; Key Clb; Office Aide; Teachers Aide; Mrchg Band; Capt L Bsbl; Capt L Ftbl; Intrml Trk; Capt L Wrstlng; High Hon Roll; NHS; US Army Schol Ath; Metro Classic All Str Ftbll Gme.

COX, JEFFREY A; Chaparral HS; Anthony, KS; (3); Church Yth Grp; Natl FFA Org; Office Aide; Var Bsktbl; Var Ftbl; Var Trk; Wt Lftg; High Hon Roll.

COX, MELISSA; Liberal HS; Liberal, KS; (3); Am Leg Aux Girls St; Teachers Aide; Chrldng; Sftbl; Vllybl; Hon Roll; NHS; KS U; Optometry.

COX, MELODY; Madison Jr Sr HS; Madison, KS; (4); 1/26; Am Leg Aux Girls St; 4-H; German Clb; Letterman Clb; Quiz Bowl; Bsktbl; Chrldng; Trk; Vllybl; High Hon Roll; Girls St; Emporia ST U; Accntng.

COX, MONICA M; Holton HS; Holton, KS; (2); Q&S; Rptr Nwsp; Chorus; Rep Stu Cncl; Vllybl; Hon Roll; Ntl Merit Ltr; Kayettes; KS Univ; Tchng.

COX, SHELLEY K; Andover HS; Wichita, KS; (4); 19/138; Church Yth Grp; FCA; 4-H; Chorus; Church Choir; School Musical; 4-H Awd; High Hon Roll; Hon Roll; NHS; Received I Rating At Regnl Solo Cont; Received I Rating At St Solo Cont; Butler Cty CC; RN.

COY, ALLISON M; Topeka West HS; Topeka, KS; (4); Dance Clb; Teachers Aide; Acpl Chr; Chorus; Drill Tm; Hon Roll; KS U; Psych.

COY, CATI; Wathena Schl; Wathena, KS; (4); 5/37; Church Yth Grp; Drama Clb; HOBY; Letterman Clb; Math Clb; Science Clb; Band; Chorus; Var L Chrldng; High Hon Roll; Grls St; U Of KS; Acctng.

COYLE, MARIA L; Wyandotte HS; Kansas City, KS; (2); Church Yth Grp; Band; Church Choir; Mrchg Band; JV Var Trk; Hon Roll; NHS; Prfct Atten Awd; Ch Play; Vet/Schl Tchr.

COZADD, SHANNON J; Jefferson West HS; Meriden, KS; (1); 1/76; Quiz Bowl; Spanish Clb; JV Crs Cntry; High Hon Roll; Prfct Atten Awd.

COZZI, HEATHER R; Jefferson West HS; Meriden, KS; (3); 15/76; Church Yth Grp; FHA; Hosp Aide; NFL; SADD; Band; School Play; Chrldng; NHS; USCAA Chrldng Spirit Awd; FHA Ofcr Of The Yr; Med Missions.

CRABBE, KHAD; Junction City HS; Fort Riley, KS; (3); 25/300; Am Leg Boys St; Chorus; Church Choir; Jazz Band; School Musical; School Play; Stage Crew; Swing Chorus; Rep Soph Cls; JV Ftbl; Outstdng Music Stu; Math Technician.

CRABLE, CORY H; Olathe North Sr HS; Olathe, KS; (3); Cmnty Wkr; Drama Clb; English Clb; Library Aide; Q&S; Thesps; Acpl Chr; School Play; Swing Chorus; Hon Roll; Emporia ST Univ; Eng Lit.

CRAFT, JASON; Seaman Sr HS; Topeka, KS; (3); 4/250; Church Yth Grp; FBLA; Library Aide; Nwsp; Yrbk; Trk; High Hon Roll; Prfct Atten Awd; Local Hstry Day Cmptn 2nd Pl, St Cmptn Qualfr; Seaman Step Squad; Local Senator & Rep Page; Cardiolgy.

CRAFT, MARIO S; Washington HS; Kansas City, KS; (2); FCA; Chorus; Church Choir; JV Crs Cntry; Hon Roll; Comp Pgm.

CRAFT, SHAUN R; Marion HS; Marion, KS; (2); Church Yth Grp; Letterman Clb; Math Tm; Treas Soph Cls; Treas Jr Cls; Var L Bsbl; JV Bsktbl; Var L Ftbl; JV Trk; High Hon Roll; Stu Cncl Rep For NHS.

CRAFTON, DAWN; Turner HS; Kansas City, KS; (4); 13/200; Bus Profs of Am; Math Tm; Science Clb; Spanish Clb; Drill Tm; School Play; Sftbl; Hon Roll; Jr NHS; NHS; U Of KS; Bio-Med Engrng.

CRAIG, DEIDRA; Baldwin HS; Baldwin City, KS; (2); Intnl Clb; Spanish Clb; JV Var Bsktbl; Var Chrldng; High Hon Roll; Hon Roll; Pres Acad Fit Awd; Kays; NE Univ; Med.

CRAIG, JASON; Blue Valley North HS; Shawnee Mission, KS; (3); Boy Scts; Church Yth Grp; Bsktbl; Ftbl; Hon Roll; Architectural Engrng.

CRAIG, KIMBERLY A; Great Bend Sr HS; Great Bend, KS; (3); Church Yth Grp; Cmnty Wkr; Dance Clb; German Clb; Pep Clb; Acpl Chr; Band; Chorus; Color Guard; Mrchg Band; Kytts; Acad/Band/Choir/Tnns Lttrs; KS ST Univ; Engrng/Cmptr Sci.

CRAIG, NATHAN G; Goodland HS; Goodland, KS; (2); 17/90; Cmnty Wkr; Band; Pep Band; JV Var Cmnty Wkr; JV Var Trk; Wt Lftg; JV L Wrstlng; Hon Roll; Church Yth Grp; 4-H; Amer Legions Bsbl/Sftbl Coach; Kempo Karate.

CRAIG, SARAH R; Wichita Northwest HS; Maize, KS; (2); Q&S; Sprt Ed Nwsp; Rep Jr Cls; JV Bsktbl; JV Crs Cntry; Var Socr; Hon Roll; All Amercn Rnking; KS Schol Pressassoc Hdline Wrtng Contest; Env Eng.

CRAIG, SASHA; Humboldt HS; Humboldt, KS; (3); 11/63; Dance Clb; Church Choir; Swing Chorus; Yrbk; Chrldng; Hon Roll; Pres Acad Fit Awd; Med.

CRAIG, STACIE M; Shawnee Heights Sr HS; Topeka, KS; (2); Church Yth Grp; Cmnty Wkr; Debate Tm; FCA; 4-H; Pep Clb; SADD; Church Choir; Var Trk; JV Vllybl; Church Bell Choir.

CRAINE, ANNIE; Olathe East Sr HS; Overland Park, KS; (3); Church Yth Grp; Letterman Clb; Pep Clb; Teachers Aide; Chorus; Sec Soph Cls; Sec Jr Cls; Sec Sr Cls; Bsktbl; Powder Puff Ftbl; TX Christian U.

CRAMER, ALEETA L; Leavenworth HS; Leavenworth, KS; (4); 70/330; Treas Drama Clb; Treas NFL; Treas Thesps; School Play; Stage Crew; High Hon Roll; NHS; Science Clb; SADD; Teachers Aide; Dirctd Full Length Play The Crucible; Boston Univ; Stage Light Dsgnr.

CRAMER, BEN; Healy Schl; Healy, KS; (3); 1/10; FCA; Quiz Bowl; School Play; Mgr Yrbk; VP Frsh Cls; VP Soph Cls; Sec Jr Cls; Ofcr Bsbl; Bsktbl; Ftbl.

CRAMER, JERROD L; Labette Co HS; Mound Valley, KS; (2); FCA; Natl FFA Org; SADD; VICA; JV Bsbl; JV Bsktbl; Intrml Ftbl; Hon Roll; NHS; Pres Schlr; Elec Engr.

CRAMER, RANDALL S; Wellington Sr HS; Wellington, KS; (3); 3/165; Church Yth Grp; FCA; Quiz Bowl; Var Crs Cntry; Var Tennis; High Hon Roll; NHS; Lions Awd; Arch.

CRANDALL, JESSICA; Little River Jr Sr HS; Little River, KS; (2); Church Yth Grp; FHA; German Clb; Math Tm; Quiz Bowl; Band; Chorus; Mrchg Band; Pep Band; Pres Frsh Cls.

CRANDALL, KAYLA L; Topeka HS; Topeka, KS; (3); Church Yth Grp; Model UN; Band; Mrchg Band; Pep Band; Powder Puff Ftbl; L Swmmng; Trk; Hon Roll; NHS; Chrch Drama Team; Natl Span Test; Washburn U; Intl Mnstry.

CRANE, BRAD J; Maize HS; Wichita, KS; (3); Church Yth Grp; Debate Tm; NFL; Q&S; Nwsp; Bsktbl; Golf; Hon Roll; KS U.

CRANE, BREANN; Ottawa HS; Ottawa, KS; (3); 12/170; Church Yth Grp; FCA; Key Clb; Spanish Clb; SADD; Flag Corp; Yrbk; Ofcr Stu Cncl; JV Tennis; High Hon Roll; Chamber Of Commerce Awd; Peer Tutor; Karate; U Of Southern CA; Pol Sci.

CRANE, CHRISTYN L; Lawrence HS; Lawrence, KS; (2); Rep Frsh Cls; JV Var Sftbl; JV Vllybl; High Hon Roll; Hon Roll; Bsktbl As Soph; Elem Ed.

CRANE, ERIC M; Spearville Jr Sr HS; Wright, KS; (3); 7/30; Church Yth Grp; Drama Clb; Letterman Clb; Pep Clb; Speech Tm; Thesps; Varsity Clb; Chorus; School Musical; School Play; All-League Hnrs Var Sprts; Tchrs Aide; Amer Legion Bsbl; Fort Hays ST U; Bus.

CRANE, KENT J; Washburn Rural HS; Auburn, KS; (3); Boy Scts; Debate Tm; NFL; Band; Mrchg Band; Orch; Pep Band; Variety Show; JV Ftbl; High Hon Roll.

CRANE, RACHEL; Macksville HS; Larned, KS; (2); 1/30; Church Yth Grp; Key Clb; Letterman Clb; Quiz Bowl; Band; School Play; Rep Soph Cls; Var L Bsktbl; Var L Chrldng; Var L Trk; Natl Sci Mrt Awd.

CRANE, RICKI; Shawnee Mission N HS; Overland Park, KS; (3); Pep Clb; Q&S; Band; Mrchg Band; Pep Band; Ed Yrbk; Mgr(s); Hon Roll; Emporia ST U; HS Eng Tchr.

CRANE, ROBERT E; Riverton Schl; Baxter Springs, KS; (1); Church Yth Grp; FCA; FHA; Spanish Clb; School Play; VP Frsh Cls; Ofcr Stu Cncl; Bsktbl; Ftbl; Trk.

CRANE, ZACHARY; Macksville HS; Larned, KS; (3); Cmnty Wkr; Letterman Clb; Var Bsktbl; Var Ftbl; JV Trk; Var Wt Lftg; Hon Roll; Prfct Atten Awd; Comp Drafting; Grphc Dsgn.

CRANGLE, SUSAN; Lincoln Jr Sr HS; Lincoln, KS; (3); 3/30; Debate Tm; Drama Clb; Key Clb; Letterman Clb; Math Tm; Pep Clb; Quiz Bowl; Scholastic Bowl; Speech Tm; SADD; KS Assn For Yth Club; Russian; Math.

CRANMER, CHANDRA R; Maize HS; Wichita, KS; (3); Science Clb; Spanish Clb; SADD; Var Socr; High Hon Roll; Hon Roll; Sec NHS; US Jr Olympic Tae Kwon Do Red Belt 4th Pl 95; Intnatnl Bus/Corp Law.

CRANSTON, JAKE J; Colby Sr HS; Colby, KS; (2); 1/121; 4-H; Natl FFA Org; Quiz Bowl; JV Ftbl; 4-H Awd; Hon Roll.

CRARY, LAURA; Lansing HS; Leavenworth, KS; (1); Church Yth Grp; Debate Tm; Pep Clb; Church Choir; Chrldng; Hon Roll; Acad Debate Awd; Debate & Chrldng Ltr; Baker U; Tchr.

CRAWFORD, AMANDA R; Hartford HS; Neosho Rapids, KS; (2); Hosp Aide; Letterman Clb; Stat Bsktbl; Var L Trk; Var L Vllybl; Var Wt Lftg; Tae Kwon Deo; Emporia ST; Persnl Trnr/Trck.

CRAWFORD, BETSY; Atchison Sr HS; Ozawkie, KS; (4); 34/124; Pres Church Yth Grp; Sec 4-H; HOBY; Sec Spanish Clb; Band; Flag Corp; Mrchg Band; Pep Band; Hon Roll; Pres NHS; Multi-Cltrl Ldrshp Prog; Mrtrs Achvt; Lnch Of Champs; Highland CC; Psych.

CRAWFORD, CHRISTINA D; Belle Plaine HS; Belle Plaine, KS; (4); 17/72; Letterman Clb; Pep Clb; Library Aide; Phtg Yrbk; Rep Stu Cncl; Var Capt Bsktbl; Var Capt Chrldng; Var Sftbl; Var Vllybl; Hon Roll; KAYS; Emporia ST Univ; Scndry Ed Bus.

CRAWFORD, CLINT J; Hartford HS; Emporia, KS; (2); SADD; JV Ftbl; OK ST; Law Enforcement.

CRAWFORD, HEATHER R; Anderson Cty Jr Sr HS; Garnett, KS; (2); Church Yth Grp; Drama Clb; FHA; Pep Clb; Chorus; School Play; Stage Crew; Rep Stu Cncl; Bsktbl; Chrldng; KS Assn Yth; Jr Olympc Vlybl; Nrsng.

CRAWFORD, JILL A; Halstead HS; Halstead, KS; (1); Church Yth Grp; Pep Clb; Spanish Clb; Pep Band; School Musical; Powder Puff Ftbl; Trk; Vllybl; Hon Roll; KS ST.

CRAWFORD, KATIE; Valley Heights Jr Sr HS; Blue Rapids, KS; (3); 2/30; Debate Tm; FHA; Girl Scts; HOBY; Letterman Clb; Model UN; Pep Clb; Scholastic Bowl; Band; Flag Corp; KS ST U; Cvl Engrng.

CRAWFORD, KATIE; Mc Louth Schl; Mc Louth, KS; (1); Church Yth Grp; Pep Clb; Quiz Bowl; Scholastic Bowl; Spanish Clb; Acpl Chr; Chorus; Swing Chorus; High Hon Roll; Hon Roll; Belmont Univ; Msc Prod.

CRAWFORD, MICHAEL A; Blue Valley Northwest HS; Overland Park, KS; (1); 3/26; Church Yth Grp; Bsktbl; Ftbl; KS Univ; Arch.

CRAWFORD, SUMMER; Chetopa Schl; Welch, OK; (2); 2/20; Church Yth Grp; 4-H; Pep Clb; Quiz Bowl; Scholastic Bowl; Band; Chorus; Church Choir; Mrchg Band; Pep Band; NEO; Nrsng.

CRAWLEY, WILLIAM; Eudora HS; Eudora, KS; (4); 4/43; Varsity Clb; Var Trk; JV Wrstlng; High Hon Roll; Hon Roll; NHS; Pres Schlr; St Schlr; Devry Inst; Cmptr Info Sys.

CRAYTON, ANGELA L; Morland Jr Sr HS; Morland, KS; (1); 2/10; Church Yth Grp; Cmnty Wkr; Pep Clb; Band; Chorus; Pep Band; School Play; Pres Frsh Cls; JV Bsktbl; Var Chrldng; Colby CC; Actress.

CRAYTON, CHRISTIE S; Morland Jr Sr HS; Morland, KS; (2); Church Yth Grp; GAA; Math Tm; Pep Clb; Band; Chorus; Mrchg Band; Pep Band; School Musical; School Play.

CRAYTON, SHAUN A; Morland Jr Sr HS; Morland, KS; (3); Math Tm; Pep Clb; Ski Clb; Band; Pep Band; School Play; Nwsp; Rep Jr Cls; Ftbl; Golf; Ft Hays Univ.

CREED, ANNIE; North HS; Wichita, KS; (3); Church Yth Grp; Letterman Clb; Q&S; Teachers Aide; Varsity Clb; Ed Yrbk; Rptr Lit Mag; Rep Jr Cls; Golf; Sftbl; All City Hnrb Mntn Outfield Sftbl; Ltr In Vllybl, Sftbl & Golf; Friends Univ; PE; Sports Admin.

CREEKMORE, DANIEL L; Campus HS; Wichita, KS; (1); Church Yth Grp; Scholastic Bowl; SADD; High Hon Roll; Trmpt Prvt Lssns; Rec Coord Local Vctn Bible Schl Prgm; Mgr Of Mtrls/Prod Mass Prod Unit Gnl Tech Crs; Engrng/Archt.

CRIBBS, BRYAN J; Eudora HS; Eudora, KS; (4); 2/42; Church Yth Grp; Letterman Clb; Var Capt Bsbl; Var Crs Cntry; Var Capt Ftbl; JV Trk; Var Wt Lftg; Gov Hon Prg Awd; High Hon Roll; NHS; Johnson Cty CC.

CRINER, BRYAN M; Turner HS; Kansas City, KS; (4); 19/200; Wt Lftg; Hon Roll; Jr NHS; KS Univ; Nrs.

CRIPPS, KINDRA; Mission Valley HS; Harveyville, KS; (3); 10/58; Church Yth Grp; Letterman Clb; Q&S; SADD; Nwsp; Sec Stu Cncl; Var Capt Bsktbl; Var Capt Sftbl; Var Capt Vllybl; Hon Roll; Kays; 5 Club; Bio Awd Stght As.

CRISER, ANGIE E; Wichita East HS; Wichita, KS; (3); Teachers Aide; Variety Show; Rptr Yrbk; JV Vllybl; High Hon Roll; Hon Roll; NHS.

CRISLER, HILARY A; Wellington Sr HS; Wellington, KS; (3); Var Co-Capt Tennis; Hon Roll; Jr NHS; NHS; KS ST U.

CRISLER, LAURA M; Wamego HS; Wamego, KS; (2); Church Yth Grp; Cmnty Wkr; 4-H; FHA; Service Clb; Teachers Aide; Band; Mrchg Band; Pep Band; School Musical; Dickens Ave Chrch Of Chrst Yth Crp; Comm Theatr Prog; Comm Bnd; KS St Univ; Sec Ed.

CRISLER, MEGAN L; Wellington Sr HS; Wellington, KS; (3); 12/150; Key Clb; Red Cross Aide; SADD; Band; Var Bsktbl; Var Sftbl; Var Vllybl; Hon Roll; VP Jr NHS; NHS; Rotary Awd.

CRISPIN, JESSA; Lincoln Jr Sr HS; Lincoln, KS; (4); 3/31; Am Leg Aux Girls St; Debate Tm; Drama Clb; Pres FHA; Girl Scts; Letterman Clb; Library Aide; Quiz Bowl; Nwsp; Treas NHS; Baylor U; Engl Tchr.

CRISPIN, PENNY; Lincoln Jr Sr HS; Lincoln, KS; (1); 1/52; Girl Scts; Capt Quiz Bowl; L Trk; Hon Roll; Outstdng Perfmnc For Vol Svc Awd; Peer Helper; Writer; Tchr.

CRIST, ELISSA; Scott Comm HS; Scott City, KS; (3); 13/73; Church Yth Grp; GAA; HOBY; Teachers Aide; Var Bsktbl; Var Crs Cntry; Wt Lftg; Hon Roll; KS St Salina ACE Acad Schlrshp; Sociology.

CRISTOBAL, EUNICE E; Emporia HS; Emporia, KS; (3); Church Yth Grp; Chorus; Church Choir; Hon Roll; Macy Minorities Med Prgm Natl Macy Schlr; Pre-Med.

CRITTENDEN, CHAD; Wellington Sr HS; Wellington, KS; (2); Church Yth Grp; Cmnty Wkr; L JV Bsktbl; L Crs Cntry; L Tennis; High Hon Roll; Jr NHS; Rotary Awd Nom; Pgm Chm Jr Ntl Hnr Soc; Top 20 Cls Frosh; Pharm.

CROCKER, NIKKI; Derby HS; Wichita, KS; (4); 106/396; Church Yth Grp; Cmnty Wkr; Teachers Aide; Ofcr Stu Cncl; Hon Roll; Miss NAACP; Miss Schol; Miss Mcconnel Teen Miss Tlnt; KS St Univ; Chem Eng.

CROCKETT, TRACY; Udall HS; Udall, KS; (2); Church Yth Grp; Girl Scts; Band; Chorus; Drill Tm; Drm Mjr(t); Mrchg Band; Rep Frsh Cls; Pres Soph Cls; Ofcr Stu Cncl; Girl Sct Silver Awd; Chrldng Co-Capt 96-97; Television Brdcstng.

CROCKFORD, JENNIFER; Buhler HS; Hutchinson, KS; (4); 1/143; Am Leg Aux Girls St; Pres Sec 4-H; HOBY; Letterman Clb; Rep Stu Cncl; Chrldng; 4-H Awd; Hon Roll; NHS; Ntl Merit Ltr; Bus.

CROFT, DANIEL J; Manhattan HS; Manhattan, KS; (2); Chess Clb; FCA; Red Cross Aide; Band; Mrchg Band; Crs Cntry; Golf; Wrstlng; Hon Roll; Duke U; Pre-Law.

CROME, CARRIE I; Washington HS; Washington, KS; (4); Art Clb; Church Yth Grp; FHA; Letterman Clb; SADD; Phtg Yrbk; Vllybl; Hon Roll; 4-H; Varsity Clb; Emporia ST U; Elem Ed.

CROME, GRETCHEN; Washington HS; Washington, KS; (1); Church Yth Grp; FHA; Letterman Clb; Band; Ofcr Frsh Cls; Bsktbl; Chrldng; Vllybl; High Hon Roll; Hon Roll; Elem Ed.

CROMWELL, MEGAN L; Burlingame HS; Burlingame, KS; (1); 7/28; FBLA; Science Clb; Service Clb; Band; Mrchg Band; Pep Band; School Musical; Stage Crew; Bsktbl; Vllybl.

CRONK, MICHELLE N; Emporia HS; Emporia, KS; (4); FBLA; Bsktbl; Sftbl; Cit Awd; Hon Roll; Pres Ed Awds Prgm Awd Ed Exclnc; Latinas Unidos; Kayettes; SADD; Emporia ST U; Bus.

CRONN JR, DARREL E; Smith Ctr Jr Sr HS; Smith Center, KS; (4); 16/45; Am Leg Boys St; Church Yth Grp; Letterman Clb; Natl FFA Org; SADD; Ed Yrbk; Pres Jr Cls; Ftbl; Trk; Wt Lftg; U Of KS; Geology Engrng.

CROOKS, BILL; Silver Lake Jr Sr HS; Silver Lake, KS; (3); 6/70; Am Leg Boys St; Church Clb; Chorus; Rptr Nwsp; VP Frsh Cls; Treas Soph Cls; Treas Jr Cls; VP Stu Cncl; Var Bsbl; Var Bsktbl.

CROSLAND, JOSHUA D; Santa Fe Trail HS; Carbondale, KS; (3); Church Yth Grp; Treas FBLA; Math Tm; Math Clb; Var Ftbl; Var Golf; High Hon Roll; Hon Roll; Treas NHS; Grad Ldrshp Osage Co 96; Whos Who KS FBLA 96; Intl Bus Conf 96; KS ST Univ; Eng.

CROSS, ANGI M; Southeast HS; Wichita, KS; (3); 5/378; Cmnty Wkr; FCA; VP Spanish Clb; VP SADD; Thesps; Var Gym; Var Ofcr Pom Pon; High Hon Roll; NHS; Dance Clb; Bible Clb Co-Ldr; U Of KS; Psychiatry; Dance.

CROSS, BRIAN S; Skyline Schl; Pratt, KS; (4); 1/31; Church Yth Grp; Q&S; Capt Quiz Bowl; Band; Stage Crew; Ed Nwsp; L Crs Cntry; Trk; Pres NHS; Ntl Merit SF; KS ST U; Comp Sci.

CROSS, DAVID D; Circle HS; Towanda, KS; (2); Church Yth Grp; Cmnty Wkr; Acpl Chr; Band; Chorus; Mrchg Band; Variety Show; Ofcr Jr Cls; Socr; Tennis; Spec Intrst Small Engns.

CROSS, GINA S; Wichita East HS; Wichita, KS; (3); Cmnty Wkr; Teachers Aide; High Hon Roll; NHS; Spanish NHS; Sunnyside Superstar; Intl Baccalaureate Prgm; Med.

CROSS, LANETTA J; Derby HS; Wichita, KS; (1); Church Yth Grp; FCA; Hosp Aide; Band; Chorus; Crs Cntry; Sftbl; JV Var Trk; Wt Lftg; Hon Roll; DRC Sftbl; PT.

CROSS, SHAWNA N; Russell HS; Russell, KS; (2); Church Yth Grp; FCA; Key Clb; Letterman Clb; Pep Clb; SADD; Chorus; School Musical; School Play; VP Frsh Cls; Mission Ed Tour 96; KS Wesleyan Univ; Elem Ed.

CROSSLAND, MICHELLE; Columbus HS; Columbus, KS; (4); Bus Profs of Am; Church Yth Grp; Cmnty Wkr; Dance Clb; FHA; Letterman Clb; Math Tm; SADD; Drill Tm; Var L Chrldng; KAY Clb Brd 2 Yrs; Comm Svc Awd; SW MO ST U.

CROTINGER, ANGELA; Liberal HS; Liberal, KS; (4); Treas Am Leg Aux Girls St; Cmnty Wkr; Drama Clb; FHA; Hosp Aide; Key Clb; Office Aide; Teachers Aide; Thesps; Band; 5 States Hnr Band Hall Of Fame 4 Yrs; KMEA Dist Hnr Band 5th Chr; Solo/Ensmbl Rtng Reg I, St II; Acctng.

CROUCH, DARLA M; Wichita West HS; Wichita, KS; (2); 16/250; Church Yth Grp; Teachers Aide; Hon Roll; Prfct Atten Awd; Wichita St Univ; Elem Ed.

CROUCH, KRISTI; Holton HS; Holton, KS; (4); Sec VP 4-H; VP Letterman Clb; Red Cross Aide; Acpl Chr; Church Choir; Mrchg Band; Pep Band; School Musical; Var Crs Cntry; Var Pom Pon; Summer Choral Inst Mem; Kay Clb; Butler Cty Comm Coll; Hospitali.

CROUCHER, DEBBIE; Osage City HS; Osage City, KS; (4); Am Leg Aux Girls St; Pep Clb; Science Clb; Teachers Aide; Band; Chorus; Mrchg Band; Pep Band; Hon Roll.

CROUDER, JOHN C; Basehor Linwood HS; Basehor, KS; (3); Debate Tm; French Clb; Ftbl; Sci Olympiad.

CROUGH, SHEILAH; Garden City Sr HS; Garden City, KS; (4); 132/313; Teachers Aide; Chorus; Var Capt Chrldng; JV Sftbl; Hon Roll; Yng Life Clb; Washburn U; Spch Path.

CROUSE, MARIE; Rose Hill HS; Rose Hill, KS; (3); Church Yth Grp; Letterman Clb; Teachers Aide; Chorus; Church Choir; School Musical; Variety Show; Sec Jr Cls; Hon Roll; Princeton Coll; Paralegal.

CROUSE, TAMI S; Canton-Galva HS; Galva, KS; (3); 16/40; FBLA; SADD; Ofcr Stu Cncl; JV Var Bsktbl; Powder Puff Ftbl; Score Keeper; Sftbl; Hon Roll; Annual Deaf-Walk-A-Thon; K-ST; Kineslgy.

CROW, CHRISTOPHER S; Independence HS; Independence, KS; (2); 1/189; French Clb; VP Science Clb; Chorus; Pres Frsh Cls; Pres Soph Cls; Var Golf; High Hon Roll; Hon Roll.

CROW, CHRISTY E; Shawnee Heights Sr HS; Tecumseh, KS; (2); Church Yth Grp; Letterman Clb; Varsity Clb; Orch; School Play; VP Soph Cls; VP Jr Cls; Var JV Socr; JV Tennis; Hon Roll; Topeka Yth Symphony; Dir Play For Schl; Adv From Regionals To St Cont In Violin; OK Bapt Univ; Emporia ST.

CROW, JUSTIN M; Quivira Heights HS; Holyrood, KS; (2); 3/18; Pep Clb; Quiz Bowl; Band; Mrchg Band; Pep Band; JV Bsktbl; Hon Roll; Prfct Atten Awd; Pres Acad Fit Awd; Schlrs Bowl Team Co-Capt; Chem.

CROW, KASEY; Dexter Jr Sr HS; Dexter, KS; (3); Am Leg Boys St; 4-H; Letterman Clb; Math Tm; Science Clb; Band; Mrchg Band; Pep Band; School Musical; Pres Frsh Cls; Eng.

CROWDER, JASON; Spring Hill HS; Spring Hill, KS; (2); 8/90; FCA; Science Clb; SADD; JV Bsbl; Var Bsktbl; Var Crs Cntry; High Hon Roll; Hon Roll; Jr NHS; Odyssey Mind; Med.

CROWDER, JEANETTE M; Spring Hill HS; Spring Hill, KS; (4); Letterman Clb; Q&S; Acpl Chr; Chorus; School Musical; Variety Show; Yrbk; Pres Frsh Cls; Sec Soph Cls; Sec Jr Cls; Madrigals; KMEA St Hnrs Choir; St Choir Cmptns; Singer.

CROWDER, JEREMY M; Washington HS; Kansas City, KS; (2); Band; Mrchg Band; Pep Band; Ftbl; High Hon Roll; Hon Roll; Pres Acad Fit Awd; QUEST Prgm; U Of KS; Gntcs/Anatomy Phslgy.

CROWE, KERSTAN L; Maize HS; Wichita, KS; (3); Cmnty Wkr; Debate Tm; Math Tm; NFL; Spanish Clb; SADD; JV Trk; High Hon Roll; NHS; Pres Schlr; 2nd Pl KS Grp Prjct Ctgry/Advncd Natls Natl His Day; I Dare You Ldrshp Awd; La Aguila Awd; Bus/Med.

CROWE, MELINDA M; Maize HS; Wichita, KS; (3); Ski Clb; Spanish Clb; SADD; Teachers Aide; Hon Roll; Competed In St Ski Trnmt Won 1st & 2nd In 3 Events; Wichita ST Univ; Bus.

CROWNOVER, NICHOLAS A; Chanute Sr HS; Chanute, KS; (3); 98/150; Boy Scts; Cmnty Wkr; Band; Jazz Band; Variety Show; Trk; Cit Awd; Psychology.

CROY, ANDREW D; Junction City HS; Fort Riley, KS; (3); Am Leg Boys St; FCA; German Clb; Quiz Bowl; ROTC; Scholastic Bowl; JV Bsbl; Intrml Bsktbl; Wt Lftg; High Hon Roll; Duke TIP Pgm; Westpoint; Psych.

CROY, KEVIN P; Junction City HS; Fort Riley, KS; (2); German Clb; HOBY; ROTC; Color Guard; Drill Tm; Sec Stu Cncl; High Hon Roll; Prfct Atten Awd; Sabre Guard; Air Force Acad; Aeronautics.

CROY, NATHAN; Olathe East Sr HS; Olathe, KS; (2); Church Yth Grp; Drama Clb; Band; Chorus; Mrchg Band; School Play.

CRUBEL, ROBERT; St Marys HS; Saint Marys, KS; (4); 7/51; Letterman Clb; Band; Jazz Band; School Musical; Bsktbl; Ftbl; Var L Golf; High Hon Roll; VP NHS; Trumpet Choir; KS ST U; Arch Engr.

CRUM, BRANDI LEE; Perry Lecompton HS; Perry, KS; (3); Church Yth Grp; Sec Drama Clb; FBLA; FHA; Girl Scts; Treas Intnl Clb; Letterman Clb; Office Aide; Pep Clb; SADD; Engrng.

CRUM, KYLE E; Shawnee Mission E Sr HS; Prairie Village, KS; (2); Band; Jazz Band; Mrchg Band; Pep Band; High Hon Roll; Hon Roll; Mus.

CRUMB, LAURIE; Mission Valley HS; Burlingame, KS; (4); 12/61; Pres 4-H; Pres FHA; Letterman Clb; Natl FFA Org; Q&S; Speech Tm; Teachers Aide; Chorus; Yrbk; Hon Roll; KAYS-FRGN Lang Clb; MVHS Site Cncl; VFW VOD Speech Cont; MV Pride Inside Force; 5 Clb; FHA STAR; Emporia ST Univ; Elem Ed.

CRUME, TIFFANY D; Seaman Sr HS; Topeka, KS; (4); FHA; Key Clb; Yrbk; FHA VP; SADD; Tarrant Cty Comm.

CRUMRINE, SARAH E; Olathe South Sr HS; Olathe, KS; (3); Church Yth Grp; Letterman Clb; Spanish Clb; Orch; Co-Ed Nwsp; Lit Mag; High Hon Roll; NHS; Ntl Merit SF; Spanish NHS; Ks City Yth Symp; Viola Perf.

CRUNDER, CHAD; St John Jr Sr HS; Saint John, KS; (3); Quiz Bowl; SADD; School Musical; School Play; VP Stu Cncl; Var L Bsktbl; Var L Trk; High Hon Roll; Ntl Merit SF; Boy Scts; Kay Clb Pres.

CRUZ, DALELA N; Ingalls Jr Sr HS; Pierceville, KS; (2); Letterman Clb; Pep Clb; Quiz Bowl; Band; Chorus; School Musical; Bsktbl; Vllybl; Hon Roll; Washington Univ; Tchg/Music.

CRUZ, RAINIER T; St Xavier's HS; Ft Riley, KS; (2); Red Cross Aide; Rptr Yrbk; Bsktbl; Ftbl; Trk; Wrstlng; Cit Awd; Hon Roll; Kiwanis Awd; Pres Acad Fit Awd; Schltc Awd; Physician.

CUBBAGE, GILLIAN; Wellington Sr HS; Wellington, KS; (4); 28/180; Am Leg Aux Girls St; French Clb; SADD; Phtg Nwsp; Hon Roll; Wchta ST U; Psych.

CUDNEY, KRIS; St Mary's Colgan HS; Pittsburg, KS; (3); Pep Clb; JV Var Bsktbl; Var Sftbl; JV Var Vllybl; High Hon Roll; NHS; Ntl Merit Ltr; Pittsburg ST Univ.

CUELLAR, AUTUMN A; Derby HS; Derby, KS; (3); 9/380; Church Yth Grp; FCA; Key Clb; Band; Capt Flag Corp; Ofcr Stu Cncl; JV Socr; High Hon Roll; VP NHS; Quiz Bowl; Envrnmntl Clb VP; USAF Acad; Cmptr Engr.

CUEVAS, AMBER; Ottawa HS; Ottawa, KS; (2); #1 in class; Spanish Clb; Drill Tm; Variety Show; Rep Frsh Cls; Vllybl; High Hon Roll; U Of KS; Pre-Med.

CUEVAS, BLAKE R; Shawnee Heights Sr HS; Topeka, KS; (2); Pep Clb; Ftbl; Wt Lftg; Hon Roll; Nom People To People/Whos Who Amng Amer HS Stdnts 94-95; HALO Club; Air Force Acad.

CUEVAS, JESSE T; Shawnee Mission E HS; Leawood, KS; (3); 9/421; Boy Scts; Cmnty Wkr; Math Tm; Model UN; Scholastic Bowl; Spanish Clb; Ofcr Stu Cncl; Bsktbl; Wt Lftg; High Hon Roll; Macys Schol; Stanford Univ.

CULBERTSON, ASHLEY K; El Dorado HS; El Dorado, KS; (2); Church Yth Grp; Debate Tm; FCA; Math Clb; NFL; SADD; Orch; Bsktbl; Vllybl; Spanish Clb; Novice Debator Of Yr; KS ST Univ; Envrnmntl Lawyer.

CULLEN, LISA; Bonner Springs HS; Edwardsville, KS; (3); 1/100; Key Clb; Band; Mrchg Band; Pep Band; Chrldng; Sftbl; Vllybl; High Hon Roll; NHS; Ldrs Clb Bd; KS U; Med.

CULLENS, JARRETT T; Wallace Cty HS; Sharon Springs, KS; (2); Church Yth Grp; 4-H; Pep Clb; School Play; Bsktbl; Ftbl; Trk; Wt Lftg; Hon Roll; Colby CC; Sprts Med/PE.

CULLOP, NICHOLAS O; Chaparral HS; Anthony, KS; (1); Natl FFA Org; Bsktbl; Ftbl; Golf; Hon Roll.

CULLUM, AMY L; Halstead HS; Bentley, KS; (3); 26/57; High Hon Roll; Nrsng.

CULP, CHRISTINE; St Thomas Aquinas HS; Lenexa, KS; (4); 57/230; Am Leg Aux Girls St; Cmnty Wkr; Debate Tm; Hosp Aide; Model UN; Ed Nwsp; L Tennis; Trk; High Hon Roll; Pres NHS; Bus.

CULP, TERRI A; Chanute Sr HS; Walnut, KS; (2); Church Yth Grp; Math Tm; Pep Clb; Chorus; School Play; Stat JV Bsktbl; Mgr(s); JV Trk; High Hon Roll; Hon Roll; U Of NE; Arch.

CULVER, CRYSTAL J; Ashland HS; Hereford, TX; (2); Art Clb; 4-H; Speech Tm; JV Bsktbl; KS HS Rodeo Assn; Art Tchr.

CUMMING, SARIAH; Garden City Sr HS; Garden City, KS; (4); 49/313; Church Yth Grp; German Clb; Letterman Clb; NFL; Acpl Chr; Color Guard; School Play; NHS; Cmnty Wkr; Debate Tm; 95 KS Ambssdrs Music Euro Tour; Recording Wrkshp; Studo Engrng.

CUMMINGS, CASEY L; Wichita Southeast HS; Wichita, KS; (3); Teachers Aide; Hon Roll; KU; Phy.

CUMMINGS, COREY L; Wichita Southeast HS; Wichita, KS; (2); Teachers Aide; Hon Roll; KU; Dentist.

CUMMINS, COURTNEY A; Buhler HS; Hutchinson, KS; (2); Band; Chorus; Church Choir; Jazz Band; Mrchg Band; Pep Band; School Musical; Stage Crew; Mgr(s); Wt Lftg; Natl Bnd Assn Outstndg Music Cmprs Awd; KS Univ; Interior Dsgn.

CUMMINS, ERIN; Wichita North HS; Wichita, KS; (4); Church Yth Grp; Teachers Aide; Chorus; Variety Show; Cit Awd; Hon Roll; Cmnty Wkr; TV Internship; Environmental Awareness Clb; N Environmental Water Testing Group; Manhattan Chrstn Coll.

CUMMINS, TARA; Wichita North HS; Wichita, KS; (2); Church Yth Grp; Cmnty Wkr; Thesps; Acpl Chr; Chorus; School Musical; School Play; Variety Show; Var Chrldng; NHS; Wichita ST Univ; Theater Arts.

CUMMINS, WILLIAM; Gridley HS; Gridley, KS; (3); Boy Scts; Church Yth Grp; HOBY; Quiz Bowl; School Play; Rep Frsh Cls; Pres Soph Cls; JV Bsktbl; Var Ftbl; Hon Roll; Vlntr Fire Fightr; Fire Sci.

CUNHA, VANESSA L; Council Grove HS; Alta Vista, KS; (4); 32/75; Cmnty Wkr; Drama Clb; FCA; NFL; School Play; Mgr Yrbk; Mgr(s); Trk; High Hon Roll; Hon Roll; Kayette Team Ldr; KS Bd Of Regents Completer; Emporia ST U; Bus Ed.

CUNNINGHAM, AMY; Modesto HS; Neodesha, KS; (3); Pep Clb; Teachers Aide; Chorus; Drill Tm; Capt Pom Pon; Tennis; Hon Roll; Neodesha FFA Org; Tchr; Lawyer.

CUNNINGHAM, ANDREA M; Sumner Acad Of Arts & Science; Kansas City, KS; (4); Church Yth Grp; French Clb; Spanish Clb; Chorus; Church Choir; Var Bsktbl; Stat Ftbl; Var Trk; French Hon Soc; NHS; KS City CC; Fr & Span.

CUNNINGHAM, KIM L; Southeast HS; Wichita, KS; (4); JA; Socr; Butler Cty Jr Col.

CUNNINGHAM, LA TISHA D; Hays HS; Hays, KS; (2); Church Yth Grp; Debate Tm; Hosp Aide; HOBY; NFL; SADD; Hon Roll; U Of CO; Atty.

CUNNINGHAM, MARIN D; Pierson Jr HS; Kansas City, KS; (1); Dance Clb; Debate Tm; Drama Clb; Lit Mag; Ldrshp Team; Kemp Marshal Alt; Lawyer; Bus Mgmt.

CUNNINGHAM, STACY M; Trinity Catholic HS; Hutchinson, KS; (1); Church Yth Grp; Office Aide; JV Bsktbl; Hon Roll; Pres Awd Educl Excl; Natl Phys Ftns Awd; U Of KY.

CURNUTT, CARRI L; El Dorado HS; El Dorado, KS; (2); Church Yth Grp; SADD; Chorus; Hon Roll; Erth Care Club; Spec Olympcs Vol Coach; SPREE; Butler Cty CC; Law Enf.

CURREY, CHRISTINA; Manhattan HS; Manhattan, KS; (4); 70/365; Church Yth Grp; Dance Clb; FCA; German Clb; Intnl Clb; Teachers Aide; Thesps; School Play; Stage Crew; JV Swmmng; Sci Olympiad; Intntl Thespian Soc; Piano; Johnson Cty CC; Dental Hygiene.

CURRIER, GINNY B; Liberal HS; Liberal, KS; (2); Church Yth Grp; GAA; Key Clb; Chorus; Church Choir; Stage Crew; JV Bsktbl; JV Sftbl; High Hon Roll; Hon Roll; Math; Sci; Aeronautics.

CURRIER, RYAN; Sedgwick HS; Sedgwick, KS; (3); 2/40; Letterman Clb; Boy Scts; Stage Crew; Rep Soph Cls; VP Stu Cncl; Var L Bsktbl; Var L Ftbl; Socr; Wt Lftg; High Hon Roll; All-Lg Fllbck, Lnbckr & Plc Kckr; Hnrb Mntn All-Lg Pntr; Hnr Mntn All-St Running Bck; Med.

CURRY, AMANDA; Garden City Sr HS; Garden City, KS; (3); FHA; German Clb; Quiz Bowl; Science Clb; VICA; JV Chrldng; Var Wt Lftg; High Hon Roll; NW KS Area Vo-Tech Drafting Exhbit Grnd Chmpn 95; PA ST U; Arch Engrng.

CURRY, JENNIFER; Shawnee Mission W Sr HS; Lenexa, KS; (4); 45/377; Debate Tm; NFL; Q&S; Band; Pep Band; School Play; Ed Nwsp; High Hon Roll; Treas NHS; Ntl Merit Ltr; U Of KS; Jrnlsm.

CURRY, JENNIFER L; Blue Valley Northwest HS; Overland Park, KS; (2); 1/400; Cmnty Wkr; Debate Tm; Q&S; Stage Crew; Yrbk; Lit Mag; High Hon Roll.

CURRY, MISTY; Waverly HS; Waverly, KS; (4); 5/21; Church Yth Grp; Cmnty Wkr; Quiz Bowl; Teachers Aide; Band; Chorus; Pep Band; School Musical; School Play; Rptr Nwsp; KS U; Nrsng.

CURRY, PATRICK NATHANIEL; Southeast KS Spec Ed Coop; Galena, KS; (4); 2/35; Debate Tm; VP FHA; Scholastic Bowl; Pres Stu Cncl; Capt Ftbl; Wt Lftg; High Hon Roll; NHS; Pres Acad Fit Awd; Sal; Pittsburg ST U.

CURTIS, DENNIS A; Buhler HS; Hutchinson, KS; (2); Boy Scts; Church Yth Grp; FCA; Letterman Clb; Chorus; School Musical; School Play; Ftbl; Wt Lftg; Wrstlng; Sports Medicine.

CURTIS, ELLEN M; Chanute Sr HS; Chanute, KS; (4); #28 in class; Debate Tm; FCA; Letterman Clb; NFL; Spanish Clb; Varsity Clb; Var Sftbl; Var Trk; Var Vllybl; Hon Roll; Principles Ldrshp Tm; Stdnt Cncl.

CURTIS, EMILY; Hays HS; Hays, KS; (3); 35/200; Church Yth Grp; Rep Frsh Cls; Rep Soph Cls; Rep Jr Cls; Ofcr Sr Cls; Treas Stu Cncl; JV Sftbl; Var L Tennis; Hon Roll; Jr NHS.

CURTIS, KERRY E; Burlingame HS; Burlingame, KS; (2); Letterman Clb; Drill Tm; School Musical; School Play; Nwsp; Sec Jr Cls; VP Stu Cncl; Mgr(s); Pom Pon; Vllybl; KS U.

CURTIS, MARCIE R; Conway Springs HS; Conway Springs, KS; (3); Church Yth Grp; Rptr Nwsp; Sec Jr Cls; Vllybl.

CUSACK, ERYN C; Blue Valley HS; Stilwell, KS; (3); Band; Jazz Band; Mrchg Band; Pep Band; Yrbk; Hon Roll; Envrnmntl Clb; VA Medcl Ctr Mentorship Pgm; Bst Of Cls Awds Spnsh I, Engl II; Psych.

CUSICK, NICHOLE M; Louisburg HS; Louisburg, KS; (2); Bus Profs of Am; Church Yth Grp; FCA; Letterman Clb; SADD; Chorus; Rep Stu Cncl; Bsktbl; Chrldng; Sftbl.

CUSTARD, NAIISHA L; Wichita North HS; Wichita, KS; (2); ROTC; Band; Church Choir; Jazz Band; Mrchg Band; School Play; Trk; Hon Roll; Black His Finale; Jrnlsm; Bus; Clark Univ.

CUSTER, TYLER; Goodland HS; Goodland, KS; (2); 11/91; Church Yth Grp; Debate Tm; German Clb; Quiz Bowl; Varsity Clb; Band; Jazz Band; Pep Band; Var L Crs Cntry; Var L Trk; MENSA; Chem/Elec Eng.

CUTLER, VANESSA L; Washburn Rural HS; Wakarusa, KS; (3); Art Clb; Church Yth Grp; French Clb; Band; Mrchg Band; Orch; Pep Band; School Musical; High Hon Roll; NHS; Dist Band; St Orch; Topeka Yth Wind Ensemble; BYU.

CYPHERS, BRYSON J; Holton HS; Holton, KS; (1); Letterman Clb; Chorus; Pres Frsh Cls; Intrml Bsbl; Intrml Bsktbl; Intrml Ftbl; Intrml Golf; Intrml Cit Awd; High Hon Roll; KS ST.

CYPHERS, MATT; Holton HS; Holton, KS; (4); 10/69; Boy Scts; FHA; Letterman Clb; Model UN; SADD; Teachers Aide; Chorus; School Musical; Pres Frsh Cls; Pres Soph Cls; Kays Brd Mem; Nuclear Med.

CZIR, JULIE E; Blue Valley Northwest HS; Overland Park, KS; (2); 94/409; Church Yth Grp; Cmnty Wkr; Capt JV Bsktbl; JV Sftbl; Wt Lftg; Hon Roll; Medicine.

DA CUNHA, KARY C; Santa Fe Trail Jr HS; Olathe, KS; (1); Cmnty Wkr; Intrml Bsbl; Intrml Wt Lftg; L JV Wrstlng; Hon Roll; Psych/Coach/Cnslr.

DAESCHNER, SUSAN R; Wichita Southeast HS; Wichita, KS; (2); Church Yth Grp; Drama Clb; JA; Thesps; Chorus; School Play; Stage Crew; Rptr Nwsp; Pres Soph Cls; High Hon Roll.

DAILEY, ERIN; Ottawa HS; Ottawa, KS; (4); Letterman Clb; Red Cross Aide; Scholastic Bowl; SADD; Drill Tm; Stage Crew; Variety Show; JV Bsktbl; Powder Puff Ftbl; Trk; Outs Sr Math Sci Awd; Duke Costa Rica Trp; Ottawa Arts Cncl Vol Of Yr; KS St Univ; Premed.

DAILEY, NICHOLAS A; Independence HS; Independence, KS; (2); JV Bsbl; JV Bsktbl; Hon Roll.

DAILEY, SARAH; Atchison Sr HS; Atchison, KS; (2); Church Yth Grp; Debate Tm; Band; Church Choir; Mrchg Band; Mgr(s); JV Vllybl; High Hon Roll; Small Ensmbl ST Music Fstvl II Rtng; YMCA Gymnastcs Team 2 Yrs; Kayettes.

DALBERG, FAWN M; Horton HS; Horton, KS; (3); Church Yth Grp; Band; Chorus; Jazz Band; Mrchg Band; Trk; Vllybl; Wt Lftg; Asbury Coll; Law.

DALBOM, CHRISTOPHR; Shawnee Mission Northwest HS; Shawnee Mission, KS; (3); 6/450; HOBY; Key Clb; Pres Jr Cls; Rep Stu Cncl; Var L Crs Cntry; JV Trk; High Hon Roll.

DALBOM, ERIC P; Clearwater HS; Clearwater, KS; (3); 18/65; Am Leg Boys St; Church Yth Grp; Cmnty Wkr; NFL; Band; Chorus; Ofcr Bsbl; Bsktbl; Socr; Church Choir; Show Choir.

DALE, JESSE J; Arkansas City HS; Arkansas City, KS; (3); FCA; Letterman Clb; Teachers Aide; Varsity Clb; JV Bsbl; Var Ftbl; Wrstlng; Hon Roll; Prfct Atten Awd.

DALE, MARY ANN B; Hutchinson HS; Hutchinson, KS; (4); 77/252; Church Yth Grp; Drama Clb; French Clb; Pep Clb; Chorus; School Play; Var L Chrldng; Powder Puff Ftbl; Wt Lftg; High Hon Roll; Hutchinson CC; Sports Med.

DALE, RACHEL N; Shawnee Mission Nw Sr HS; Shawnee Mission, KS; (3); Church Yth Grp; Model UN; Bsktbl; High Hon Roll; NHS; Explorng Childhd; Elem Ed.

DALE, RYAN T; Great Bend Sr HS; Great Bend, KS; (2); Band; Mrchg Band; High Hon Roll; Tae Kwon Do; Art; Tnns.

DALEY, JOSEPH M; Campus HS; Haysville, KS; (3); Science Clb; SADD; Teachers Aide; JV Ftbl; NHS; Dfnsmn Rllr Hcky Team; Bllrdr; KS ST Univ; Vet.

DALEY, MIKE M; Parsons HS; Parsons, KS; (2); Church Yth Grp; VICA; Nwsp; Yrbk; Stat Bsktbl; JV Golf; U Of KS; Comma Art.

DALKE, DAWN; Wichita North HS; Wichita, KS; (4); 1/250; Science Clb; Band; Rep Sr Cls; Rep Stu Cncl; Var Chrldng; Var Socr; Gov Hon Prg Awd; Hon Roll; Sec NHS; Val; KS ST Univ; Chem.

DALKE, DENAI; Wichita North HS; Wichita, KS; (1); 1/300; Scholastic Bowl; Teachers Aide; Band; Mrchg Band; Pep Band; Rep Frsh Cls; Rep Stu Cncl; Intrml Chrldng; JV Socr; High Hon Roll.

DALKE, JUSTIN D; Moundridge HS; Moundridge, KS; (3); Church Yth Grp; Natl FFA Org; Quiz Bowl; Band; Treas Sr Cls; Var Ftbl; Mgr(s); Var Trk; Wt Lftg; Hon Roll; Mech Engr.

DALKE, NATHAN; Ulysses HS; Ulysses, KS; (4); 1/93; Am Leg Boys St; Church Yth Grp; FBLA; SADD; VP Sr Cls; Var L Bsbl; Var Capt Bsktbl; Var L Band; Pres NHS; Homcmng King.

DALKE, REMINGTON S; Hutchinson HS; Hutchinson, KS; (2); Church Yth Grp; Cmnty Wkr; French Clb; High Hon Roll; Teen Missions Intl In Costa Rica 8 Weeks; Vet.

DALLAM, LYNLEY M; Shawnee Mission E Sr HS; Shawnee Mission, KS; (2); Rep Pep Clb; Varsity Clb; Rep Frsh Cls; Rep Soph Cls; Bsktbl; Var Diving; Hon Roll; League Diving 2nd Pl; KS Univ; Dental Practice.

DALTON, CAROLINE S; Shawnee Heights Sr HS; Topeka, KS; (2); 2/400; Ofcr Girl Scts; Hosp Aide; SADD; Rptr Yrbk; High Hon Roll; Acad Lttr; Acad Awds In Math Lang Arts Forgn Lang.

DALTON, MAEGAN; Topeka West HS; Topeka, KS; (4); 21/238; Church Yth Grp; Cmnty Wkr; Pep Clb; Q&S; Spanish Clb; Co-Ed Yrbk; Var Chrldng; High Hon Roll; Hon Roll; NHS; YWCA Future Ldr Nom; Jane C Stormont Womens Ctr Intern; Frank Blackburn Memrl Schlsp Recipient; KS ST Univ; Wildlife Bio.

DALTON, STEPHANIE L; Northeast HS; Pittsburg, KS; (3); 8/49; Library Aide; Chorus; Pres Jr Cls; Ofcr Stu Cncl; Bsktbl; Golf; Hon Roll; Pittsburg ST Univ; Elem Ed.

DALY, MEGAN; Olathe East Sr HS; Olathe, KS; (3); Church Yth Grp; Debate Tm; French Clb; Letterman Clb; Pep Clb; Acpl Chr; Church Choir; Var Swmmng; Hon Roll; Prfct Atten Awd; Elem Ed.

DAMM, KRISTY; Larned HS; Larned, KS; (3); Girl Scts; Letterman Clb; L Stat Bsbl; Hon Roll; Genetic Engrng.

DANE, ERIN; Olathe East Sr HS; Olathe, KS; (2); Teachers Aide; School Play; Hon Roll; Fshn Mrchndsng Clb; Engl Achvt Awd; Fashion Show; Fashion Dsgn.

DANG, JOHN T; Southeast HS; Wichita, KS; (4); 25/320; Chess Clb; Library Aide; Office Aide; Red Cross Aide; VP Scholastic Bowl; High Hon Roll; Jr NHS; NHS; KU; Pre Med.

DANG, THANH; Maize HS; Wichita, KS; (2); Chess Clb; Quiz Bowl; Science Clb; High Hon Roll; Hon Roll; NHS; Pres Acad Fit Awd; Sci Olympiad.

DANG, THO; Maize HS; Wichita, KS; (2); Chess Clb; Quiz Bowl; Scholastic Bowl; Science Clb; Tennis; Cit Awd; Hon Roll; Prfct Atten Awd; Pres Acad Fit Awd; Mdl Sci Olympiad Comp.

D'ANGELO, BRIAN; St Thomas Aquinas HS; Olathe, KS; (4); Boy Scts; Spanish Clb; Ftbl; Hon Roll; Intl Bus.

DANIEL, MATTHEW; Great Bend Sr HS; Great Bend, KS; (1); 31/242; Spanish Clb; Band; Mrchg Band; Pep Band; High Hon Roll; Hon Roll; Prfct Atten Awd; KS ST HS Act; Dstng Schlstc Achvmt Awd; Acad Lttr; U Of KS.

DANIELS, ANGIE D; El Dorado HS; El Dorado, KS; (3); Art Clb; Church Yth Grp; Debate Tm; SADD; Teachers Aide; Wt Lftg; Hon Roll; Butler Cty CC; Psych.

DANIELS, CHAD; Pleasant Ridge HS; Leavenworth, KS; (2); 15/75; FBLA; Spanish Clb; SADD; Varsity Clb; JV Var Bsktbl; Var Crs Cntry; Var Trk; Prfct Atten Awd.

DANIELS, DACIA; Stanton Co HS; Johnson, KS; (3); 3/35; Church Yth Grp; FBLA; Quiz Bowl; Scholastic Bowl; Chorus; VP Jr Cls; Chrldng; Hon Roll; NHS; Prfct Atten Awd; Explrs; KS ST Univ; CPA.

DANIELS II, JOSEPH W; Southeast Saline Schl; Gypsum, KS; (2); Art Clb; Church Yth Grp; FHA; Pep Clb; Band; Mrchg Band; Bsktbl; Crs Cntry; Wt Lftg; Hon Roll; Sprts Med.

DANIELS, STACIE; Topeka West HS; Topeka, KS; (4); Am Leg Aux Girls St; Church Yth Grp; Math Clb; Model UN; Spanish Clb; Chorus; Church Choir; Co-Ed Lit Mag; High Hon Roll; NHS; KS ST U; Elem Ed.

DANIELSON, EMILY J; Topeka HS; Topeka, KS; (2); French Clb; Pep Clb; Chorus; Drill Tm; Ed Yrbk; Treas Frsh Cls; Chrldng; Pom Pon; Tennis; Hon Roll; KS ST Univ; Psych.

DANIELSON, MATT A; Lenora HS; Lenora, KS; (2); Quiz Bowl; SADD; Rep Nwsp; Yrbk; Lit Mag; VP Soph Cls; Var L Ftbl; Var L Trk; Var Wt Lftg; Sprts Med.

DANIHER, MARK A; Garden City Sr HS; Garden City, KS; (3); Church Yth Grp; Teachers Aide; Ftbl; Wt Lftg; Wrstlng; Vol & Speaker Wrestling Demo HS; Vol Yth Wrestling & Ftbl; Yth Wrestling To St; Racquet Ball; CO; Ath Trainer.

DANNEFER, ERIC; Rossville HS; Rossville, KS; (4); 2/44; Church Yth Grp; FBLA; Quiz Bowl; Scholastic Bowl; Band; Jazz Band; Mrchg Band; Pep Band; School Musical; VP Frsh Cls; KS Hnrs Schlr; Topeka Chmbr Cmmrce Hnrs Bnqt Top 5% Cty Grads; All Star Bsktbl-Cty; Manhttn Chrstn Coll; Yth Mnstry.

DAO, ROBERT H; Wichita South HS; Wichita, KS; (3); Teachers Aide; Hon Roll; NHS; DECA Clb; Qualify For Natl DECA; Childrens Art Museum Festival Vol; Wichita ST U; Mrktg.

DARBY, HEIDI M; Gardner-Edgerton HS; Gardner, KS; (2); Drama Clb; FBLA; NFL; Drill Tm; School Musical; School Play; Co-Ed Nwsp; Ed Yrbk; VP Jr Cls; Trk; U Of KS; Jrnlsm; Drama.

DARBY, LEAH M; Wellington Sr HS; Wellington, KS; (4); 3/130; Am Leg Aux Girls St; Church Yth Grp; Key Clb; Quiz Bowl; Acpl Chr; Band; Chorus; Mrchg Band; Yrbk; Ofcr Stu Cncl; UKS; Musc Thtr.

DARDEN, AARON; Eureka Jr Sr HS; Eureka, KS; (3); Am Leg Boys St; Church Yth Grp; Debate Tm; FHA; HOBY; Letterman Clb; Quiz Bowl; Red Cross Aide; Science Clb; Spanish Clb; KS U; Poli Sci.

DARDENNE, ELISSA; Galena HS; Galena, KS; (1); Church Yth Grp; FCA; JV Sftbl; Hon Roll; Lawyer.

DARE, CARIE; Faith Chrstn Acad; Uniontown, KS; (1); 3/5; Church Yth Grp; Cmnty Wkr; Drama Clb; Band; Chorus; School Play; Bsktbl; Crs Cntry; Socr; Sftbl; ACE ST 1st Voc Solo/Duet; ACE Intnl 4th Voc Solo; Piano 7 Yrs; Evangel Bible Coll; Msc.

DARK, PHIL; Bishop Ward HS; Kansas City, KS; (2); 8/93; Capt L Bsktbl; L Crs Cntry; High Hon Roll; AAU Bsktbl Natl Comptn 3rd 95; Math Cntst Wnnr Schlsp 94; PT.

DARNALL, DANIEL C; Glasco HS; Beloit, KS; (2); 3/13; Church Yth Grp; Pep Clb; VP Soph Cls; JV Bsktbl; L Ftbl; Wt Lftg; Hon Roll.

DARNAUER, JENNIFER C; Goodland HS; Goodland, KS; (4); 1/80; Church Yth Grp; GAA; Band; Treas Stu Cncl; Var L Bsktbl; Var L Vllybl; High Hon Roll; Pres NHS; St Schlr; Val; Manhattan Chrstn Coll; Cnslng.

DARNELL, LATISHIA S; Wichita Southeast HS; Wichita, KS; (2); Church Yth Grp; Debate Tm; Speech Tm; Chorus; Church Choir; High Hon Roll; Hon Roll; Bible & Eblers Modeling Clbs; Pastors Hnr Roll; MI ST U; Criminal Law; Psych.

DARNELL, MELISSA M; Palco HS; Damar, KS; (4); 4/14; Cmnty Wkr; Pres VP FHA; Pres VP Letterman Clb; Model UN; Office Aide; Pep Clb; Varsity Clb; Band; Mrchg Band; Pep Band; Dist Ath Awd; Teens As Tchrs; Vol Spec Olympcs; Washburn Univ; Radiation Thrpy.

DARNELL, TYLER A; Palco HS; Damar, KS; (1); 1/11; Boy Scts; Debate Tm; Drama Clb; Letterman Clb; Pres Frsh Cls; Var Bsktbl; Var Ftbl; Var L Trk; High Hon Roll; Pres Awd Ed Excl; Chiro.

DARR, AMANDA S; Arkansas City HS; Arkansas City, KS; (2); Trk; Hon Roll; Prfct Atten Awd; KS ST U; Prchsng Agent.

DARRAH, BROOKE; Wichita Collegiate Schl; Wichita, KS; (3); School Musical; Ed Yrbk; Var L Sftbl; JV Vllybl; Hon Roll; Lit Clb.

DARSNEK, VIMINDA M; Blue Valley HS; Overland Park, KS; (3); Church Yth Grp; Cmnty Wkr; Intnl Clb; SADD; Church Choir; Rep Stu Cncl; Cit Awd; High Hon Roll; Hon Roll; Jr NHS; NAL; KAY Clb Svc Dir; Emrgncy Med.

DA SILVA, HEATHER; Immaculata HS; Leavenworth, KS; (2); Church Yth Grp; Intnl Clb; Spanish Clb; Chorus; School Musical; School Play; Stage Crew; Var Chrldng; Pom Pon; Vllybl; Homer Davis Meml Schlsp; Multi-Yr Listee; Comm Svc; KCKCC; Pub Hlth/Nrsng.

DAUBER, TIA L; Central Burden Jr/Sr HS; Burden, KS; (4); 1/30; Cmnty Wkr; FCA; Letterman Clb; Pep Clb; Teachers Aide; Varsity Clb; School Play; Sec Frsh Cls; Sec Soph Cls; Var Bsktbl; Emporia ST U; Ped Nrs.

DAUER, MENDI L; Smoky Valley HS; Lindsborg, KS; (2); Bus Profs of Am; Church Yth Grp; German Clb; Pep Clb; Chorus; Rep Jr Cls; JV Capt Bsktbl; Crs Cntry; Vllybl; High Hon Roll; BPA Natls 13th Pl.

DAUGHERTY, BRANDI; Shawnee Mission N HS; Merriam, KS; (2); 60/452; French Clb; NFL; Pep Clb; Q&S; Band; Mgr Nwsp; Phtg Yrbk; Lit Mag; Diving; Swmmng; Chicago Art Inst; Commrcl Art.

DAUPHIN, QUINN; Washburn Rural HS; Topeka, KS; (3); 47/403; Cmnty Wkr; Dance Clb; Teachers Aide; Band; Jazz Band; Pep Band; Variety Show; Intrml Bsktbl; JV Var Chrldng; Powder Puff Ftbl; Topeka Yth Prjct Vol; Dnc Cmp Vol Cnslr; North TX ST Univ; Crim Psych.

DAUTEL, JENNY; Goodland HS; Goodland, KS; (4); FHA; SADD; Teachers Aide; Vllybl; High Hon Roll; NHS; Pres Acad Fit Awd; St Schlr; Amer Fld Svc VP; FL Southern Coll.

DAUTEL, NICOLE R; Chapman HS; Hope, KS; (4); 24/107; Pep Clb; SADD; Chorus; Rep Frsh Cls; Sec Soph Cls; Rep Sr Cls; JV Bsktbl; Var Chrldng; JV Vllybl; High Hon Roll; KS Teens As Tchr; Piano; KS ST Univ; Nutrition Sci.

DAVENPORT, MELISSA A; Anderson Cty Jr Sr HS; Garnett, KS; (3); Cmnty Wkr; Intnl Clb; Pep Clb; SADD; Chorus; Church Choir; School Musical; Variety Show; Ofcr Soph Cls; Bsktbl; KAY Clb; Bus.

DAVENPORT, VANESSA; Udall HS; Udall, KS; (2); School Play; Var Pom Pon; JV Vllybl; Cit Awd; Gov Hon Prg Awd; High Hon Roll; Pres Acad Fit Awd; Pres Schlr; Govs Ctr For Teen Ldrshp Stu Cncl Rep; Stanford; Bus.

DAVID, CRYSTAL; Marmaton Valley Jr Sr HS; Moran, KS; (4); #4 in class; Natl FFA Org; Teachers Aide; Band; Flag Corp; Mrchg Band; Pep Band; Ofcr Frsh Cls; Ofcr Soph Cls; Ofcr Sr Cls; Ofcr Stu Cncl; St FFA Degree, Chptr Star Agribusnsmn, Star Greenhnd, Hnrb Mntn; Vllybl Tm Ldr Awd; Vllybl/Bsktbl Capt; Allen Cty CC.

DAVIDSON, ANNIE; Russell HS; Russell, KS; (1); Key Clb; SADD; Band; Chorus; Church Choir; Mrchg Band; Pep Band; School Musical; School Play; High Hon Roll; St MTNA Perfmnc Cmptn Hnrb Mntn; Womens Federated Auditions Cmptn; KMEA Dist IV & League Hnr Band; U Of KS.

DAVIDSON, BRIANN K; Greeley Co Schl; Tribune, KS; (3); 2/19; VP Natl FFA Org; SADD; Yrbk; VP Frsh Cls; Ofcr Stu Cncl; Var L Bsktbl; Var L Chrldng; Var L Tennis; High Hon Roll; Med.

DAVIDSON, CHAD C; Desoto HS; Shawnee Mission, KS; (4); 64/101; Church Yth Grp; Cmnty Wkr; Office Aide; Teachers Aide; Church Choir; JV Var Socr; Var Trk; Hon Roll; Chsrtn Clb Pres; YFC Bible Quiz Tm; SW Baptist Univ.

DAVIDSON, HEATHER; Spring Hill HS; Spring Hill, KS; (4); 6/100; Office Aide; Pep Clb; Science Clb; Service Clb; SADD; Teachers Aide; Hon Roll; St Schlr; Acctng.

DAVIDSON, PATRICIA; Burlingame HS; Burlingame, KS; (2); 11/34; Science Clb; VP Soph Cls; Bsktbl; Chrldng; Vllybl; Hon Roll; Kays Clb; Homcmng Atten; KU.

DAVIDSON, PATTIE M; Glasco HS; Glasco, KS; (3); Chorus; Sec Frsh Cls; Sec Soph Cls; Sec Jr Cls; Hon Roll; NHS; Brown Mackie; Acctng/Bus Mngmt.

DAVIDSON, SETH J; Blue Valley HS; Overland Park, KS; (4); 32/230; Church Yth Grp; Debate Tm; Drama Clb; FCA; Acpl Chr; Chorus; School Musical; School Play; Swing Chorus; Variety Show; Young Life; KS ST; Yth Ministry.

DAVIED, SUSAN L; Lyndon HS; Lyndon, KS; (3); 1/40; 4-H; FBLA; FHA; Quiz Bowl; Band; Chorus; Mrchg Band; Pep Band; JV Trk; JV Vllybl; KS ST Univ; Vet Med.

DAVIES, ANDY N; Field Kindley Mem Sr HS; Bushton, KS; (2); Boy Scts; Church Yth Grp; Debate Tm; French Clb; NFL; Band; Church Choir; Ftbl; Hon Roll.

DAVIES, APRIL M; Lawrence HS; Lawrence, KS; (4); Spanish Clb; Band; Chorus; Mrchg Band; Pep Band; School Play; Hon Roll; Pres Acad Fit Awd; U Of KS.

DAVIES, ASHLEIGH L; Horton HS; Hiawatha, KS; (4); Art Clb; Church Yth Grp; Cmnty Wkr; Computer Clb; Drama Clb; FHA; GAA; JA; Library Aide; Office Aide; Achvt Awd Jrnlsm; Edtng Awd Jrnlsm; Highlnd CC; Jrnlsm.

DAVIES, JEFF W; Hiawatha HS; Hiawatha, KS; (4); 4/86; Pres Church Yth Grp; Cmnty Wkr; FCA; 4-H; Key Clb; Letterman Clb; Pep Clb; Teachers Aide; JV Bsktbl; Capt L Ftbl; Horatio Alger Natl Schol; KS St Univ Col Of Eng Hnrs Prog; KSU Found Schol; KS St Univ; Aero Eng.

DAVIES, LUKE W; Horton HS; Hiawatha, KS; (3); Church Yth Grp; Cmnty Wkr; Computer Clb; JA; Natl FFA Org; Spanish Clb; Teachers Aide; Varsity Clb; L Var Bsktbl; L Var Ftbl; Prin Hnr Roll; Acad Sportsmanship Awd; Dist Cham Ag Mechanics; FFA Dist Achvmt Awd; KS ST Univ; Ag Ec.

DAVIGNON, JANELE L; Palco HS; Damar, KS; (1); FHA; Natl FFA Org; Pep Clb; JV Vllybl; Cit Awd; Pres Ed Awd; Brown Macki; Acctng.

DAVIS, AARON K; Washburn Rural HS; Auburn, KS; (3); 65/361; JV Bsktbl; Capt Ftbl; Var Trk; Var Wt Lftg; High Hon Roll; NHS; Soph Ath Of Yr; Ftbl All League Hnrb Mntn; All City Hnrb Mntn.

DAVIS, ABIE L; Goodland HS; Goodland, KS; (3); 21/82; Church Yth Grp; Band; Flag Corp; Pep Band; Mgr Stage Crew; Chrldng; Golf; Vllybl; Pres NHS; Kayettes Schl Svc Offcr; Ottawa; Msc Ther.

DAVIS, ALICIA; Wichita South HS; Wichita, KS; (2); School Musical; Pres Soph Cls; JV Var Chrldng; High Hon Roll; Dancer; Vol Work.

DAVIS, ALISON; Oak Grove Baptist Schl; Mission, KS; (4); 1/8; Ed Yrbk; VP Jr Cls; Pres Sr Cls; VP Stu Cncl; Var Capt Bsktbl; Var Chrldng; Var Capt Vllybl; Cit Awd; Val; Church Yth Grp; Chrstn Hnr Soc; Johnson Cty CC.

DAVIS, BLAKE; Halstead HS; Halstead, KS; (3); Church Yth Grp; Band; Chorus; Mrchg Band; Pep Band; School Musical; School Play; Stage Crew; Sec Sr Cls; Chrldng; KS St Univ; Intr Dsgn.

DAVIS, BOBBY J; Downs HS; Lebanon, KS; (1); Scholastic Bowl; Ofcr Frsh Cls; Cit Awd; High Hon Roll; Pres Acad Fit Awd; Sal.

DAVIS, BRAD W; Washburn Rural HS; Topeka, KS; (3); 126/343; Cmnty Wkr; Hosp Aide; Spanish Clb; School Musical; School Play; Stage Crew; Variety Show; Wt Lftg; High Hon Roll; Hon Roll; Peer Mediation; Teens As Tchrs; Comptn Small Bore Riflery; KS ST U; Mech Engr.

DAVIS, BRIAN J; Andale HS; Colwich, KS; (1); Hon Roll; Tutoring Grd Schl Stdnts Eng/Math; Ed/Eng Tchr.

DAVIS, BRIAN S; Northwest HS; Wichita, KS; (4); DECA; Var L Wrstlng; Hon Roll; Acad All Amer In Wrestling; 6th Overall St DECA; St Wrestling Qualifier; Ft Hays ST Univ; Bus; Mrktg.

DAVIS, BRYNN K; Shawnee Heights Sr HS; Topeka, KS; (2); Church Yth Grp; Band; Mrchg Band; Pep Band; L Var Trk; High Hon Roll; Hon Roll; Marching Band Squad Ldr; 1st Acad Ltr; 2nd Band Ltr; U Of KS; Architecture.

DAVIS, CLIFF; Northern Heights HS; Reading, KS; (3); Treas Art Clb; HOBY; Pep Clb; Capt Quiz Bowl; Capt Scholastic Bowl; Treas Science Clb; SADD; Stage Crew; Pres Soph Cls; Pres Jr Cls; Schl Mascot; Videogrphr; Lightng Coordntr; Forensic Pathlgy.

DAVIS, DARCY; Olathe North Sr HS; Olathe, KS; (4); 1/350; Am Leg Aux Girls St; Cmnty Wkr; German Clb; Math Tm; Acpl Chr; Band; Church Choir; Lit Mag; NHS; Val; Vandercook Coll Of Music.

DAVIS, DENENE R; Southeast HS; Mc Cune, KS; (3); Church Yth Grp; VP FHA; Science Clb; Band; Var L Bsktbl; Crs Cntry; Vllybl; Hon Roll; NHS; Labette CC.

DAVIS, ELIZABETH; Garden City Sr HS; Garden City, KS; (3); 69/310; Church Yth Grp; Cmnty Wkr; Teachers Aide; Band; Church Choir; Mgr Sftbl; High Hon Roll; Hon Roll; Chldrns Chrch Mnstrs; Garden City CC; Ed.

DAVIS, ERIC F; Immaculata HS; Bonner Springs, KS; (2); 1/55; Math Tm; Quiz Bowl; Scholastic Bowl; Science Clb; Rep Soph Cls; Rep Stu Cncl; Var L Socr; Var L Tennis; High Hon Roll; Hon Roll; Top GPA In Cls; 3rd Pl Sci Olympd-Watr Qulty Regnl & St; 1st Pl Algbr II Math Rely; Comp Sci.

DAVIS, ERIKA; Belleville HS; Belleville, KS; (3); 5/38; Am Leg Aux Girls St; Drama Clb; FBLA; Science Clb; Spanish Clb; Band; Chorus; Flag Corp; Mrchg Band; Pep Band; KS Univ; Law.

DAVIS, ERIN; Wichita East HS; Wichita, KS; (3); Church Yth Grp; Spanish Clb; Treas Frsh Cls; Var L Swmmng; High Hon Roll; NHS; Spanish NHS; MO Vly Athl Rep US Swimming.

DAVIS, JACOB D; Wetmore Schl; Wetmore, KS; (4); 1/15; Letterman Clb; Quiz Bowl; Scholastic Bowl; VP Stu Cncl; Var Trk; Gov Hon Prg Awd; High Hon Roll; NHS; Pres Schlr; Val; KS ST U; Engrng.

DAVIS, JAIME L; Chapman HS; Enterprise, KS; (3); Church Yth Grp; Girl Scts; SADD; Chorus; Bsktbl; Hon Roll; Prfct Atten Awd; K ST.

DAVIS, JAMIE; Shawnee Heights Sr HS; Topeka, KS; (2); Church Yth Grp; Pep Clb; Rptr Nwsp; Var Tennis; Var Trk; High Hon Roll; All-Amer Schlr; Care Co; KS ST U; Jrnlsm.

DAVIS, JASON; Hill City HS; Hill City, KS; (3); Am Leg Boys St; Church Yth Grp; 4-H; Natl FFA Org; Pep Clb; Rep Stu Cncl; 4-H Awd; Hon Roll; Pres Acad Fit Awd.

DAVIS, JASON L; Labette Co HS; Bartlett, KS; (3); Ed Nwsp; Amer Hstry St 2nd; Comp Sci.

DAVIS, JASON R; Manhattan HS; Manhattan, KS; (4); 1/368; Church Yth Grp; Key Clb; Quiz Bowl; Scholastic Bowl; Intrml Tennis; High Hon Roll; Kiwanis Awd; NHS; St Schlr; Val; Acad Ltr Wnnr; SW MO ST U; Comp Sci.

DAVIS, JEFF; Hayden HS; Topeka, KS; (3); 2/150; FBLA; Quiz Bowl; Scholastic Bowl; Acpl Chr; Church Choir; Jazz Band; School Musical; High Hon Roll; Hon Roll; NHS; James H Parke Mem Schol Natl Wnnr; Dar Outs Yth Vol Natl Wnnr; Attrny.

DAVIS, JENNY M; Blue Valley Northwest HS; Overland Park, KS; (2); Debate Tm; Drama Clb; NFL; VP Treas Temple Yth Grp; School Musical; School Play; Hon Roll; ST Qual Forensics; Natl Yth Ldrshp Law/Constn; KU Stanford; Psych/Lawyer.

DAVIS, JOE R; Great Bend Sr HS; Great Bend, KS; (2); Boy Scts; Church Yth Grp; German Clb; Band; Mrchg Band; Pep Band; Intrml Socr; Hon Roll; CO Schl Of Mines; Chem Engr.

DAVIS, JONATHAN W; Newton Sr HS; Newton, KS; (2); 1/279; Var L Ftbl; Var L Golf; High Hon Roll; U Of KS; Med Dr.

DAVIS, JULIE A; Jefferson West HS; Meriden, KS; (3); FHA; Spanish Clb; SADD; High Hon Roll; Prfct Atten Awd; U Of KS; Nrsng.

DAVIS, KESIA M; Olathe East Sr HS; Olathe, KS; (2); Cmnty Wkr; Letterman Clb; Pep Clb; Chorus; Drill Tm; Pres Frsh Cls; Pres Stu Cncl; JV Swmmng; High Hon Roll; Hon Roll; K ST; Marine Bio/Law/Bus.

DAVIS, KYLIE; Manhattan HS; Manhattan, KS; (3); Am Leg Aux Girls St; French Clb; FBLA; Pres Pep Clb; SADD; Treas Jr Cls; Stat Bsktbl; Intrml Sftbl; FCA; Hon Roll; KS ST Univ; Bus Mgmt.

DAVIS, LACEY; Newton Sr HS; Newton, KS; (1); 5/294; 4-H; Natl FFA Org; 4-H Awd; High Hon Roll; Star Grnhnd Awd FFA 96; Dist Dairy Judgng Frosh 1st Pl; Equine Sci Ag Prfcncy Awd Entrprnshp 1st 96; KS ST Univ; Equine Sci.

DAVIS, LINDSEY L; Arkansas City HS; Arkansas City, KS; (1); FCA; Letterman Clb; SADD; Rep Frsh Cls; Rep Soph Cls; JV Sftbl; Var L Vllybl; Hon Roll; Cowley Cntry CC; Elem Tchr.

DAVIS, MARANDA J; Highland Park HS; Topeka, KS; (3); Church Yth Grp; Pep Clb; Church Choir; School Musical; Swing Chorus; High Hon Roll; NHS; Gifted Cls; Chrch Camp Cnslr; Ministry.

DAVIS, MATT; Salina HS Central; Salina, KS; (3); 17/267; Am Leg Boys St; Church Yth Grp; Band; Var L Bsktbl; Var L Ftbl; L Golf; High Hon Roll; NHS; Ntl Merit SF; Pres Acad Fit Awd; Engrng.

DAVIS, MATTHEW N; Topeka West HS; Topeka, KS; (3); 19/227; Q&S; Spanish Clb; Ofcr Stu Cncl; Var Bsktbl; Var Capt Crs Cntry; Var Capt Trk; Cit Awd; High Hon Roll; NHS; TV Video Magazine; Wendys Jr Heisman Natl Nom.

DAVIS, MELANIE L; Hutchinson HS; Buhler, KS; (2); Church Yth Grp; Girl Scts; Hosp Aide; Key Clb; Cit Awd; High Hon Roll; Hon Roll; KS Univ; Pediatrician.

DAVIS, MICHELLE; St Xavier's HS; Junction City, KS; (1); German Clb; SADD; Var JV Bsktbl; JV Vllybl; High Hon Roll; CYO; Servant Squad; Elem Educ.

DAVIS, MINDY; South HS; Wichita, KS; (4); Church Yth Grp; Letterman Clb; Teachers Aide; Varsity Clb; Band; Chorus; Mrchg Band; Orch; Pep Band; School Musical; NCA All Amer Chrldr; Acad Ltr; SHABB & Young Life Clbs; Friends U; Music Ed.

DAVIS, MISTY D; Labette Co HS; Oswego, KS; (4); 11/129; Church Yth Grp; French Clb; FHA; Science Clb; Spanish Clb; SADD; High Hon Roll; Jr NHS; NHS; Pres Schlr; Paramedics Clb; Univ KS Alumni Hnr Awd; KS ST Regents Awd; Pittsburg ST Univ; Phy Thrpy.

DAVIS, PRAIRIE L; Circle HS; Benton, KS; (2); Q&S; Chorus; School Play; Variety Show; Yrbk; Pres Soph Cls; Pres Jr Cls; JV Chrldng; High Hon Roll; Hon Roll; U Southern CA.

DAVIS, RACHAEL M; Hillsboro HS; Hillsboro, KS; (2); 18/48; Church Yth Grp; Stage Crew; Bsktbl; Intrml Sftbl; Trk; Vllybl; Grls Ensmble; Mxd Chorus; Soc Wrk/Cnsnlr.

DAVIS, ROBERT B; Goddard HS; Goddard, KS; (2); 49/150; Science Clb; Ftbl; Trk; Wt Lftg; Wrstlng; Hon Roll; VA Military Inst; Phys Ftnss.

DAVIS, SCOTT B; Lewis Schl; Lewis, KS; (2); 5/18; Boy Scts; Church Yth Grp; Speech Tm; Acpl Chr; Band; Color Guard; Pep Band; School Musical; Rep Frsh Cls; L Ftbl; Cntrl Bible Coll.

DAVIS, SUSAN K; Garden City Sr HS; Garden City, KS; (3); FHA; Band; Ed Yrbk; Crmstprs Soph VP/JR Treas; Garden City CC; Nrsg/Bus.

DAVIS, TANNER J; Blue Valley HS; Olathe, KS; (3); Q&S; Quiz Bowl; Ed Nwsp; Hon Roll; NHS; Allied Signal Wrkshp.

DAVIS, TRACY A; Washburn Rural HS; Topeka, KS; (2); Cmnty Wkr; Debate Tm; Model UN; NFL; High Hon Roll; Optimist Oratorical Cont 2nd & 3rd Pl; Human Rights Clb; Earthbound; Columbia U; Biochemistry.

DAVIS, WHITNEY; Sublette HS; Sublette, KS; (2); Church Yth Grp; Letterman Clb; Sec Soph Cls; Ofcr Stu Cncl; Bsktbl; Trk; Vllybl; NHS; KAYS; GCTL Sec.

DAVISON, SCOTT W; Washington HS; Kansas City, KS; (3); Letterman Clb; Varsity Clb; Acpl Chr; Crs Cntry; Ftbl; Trk; Wrstlng; Hon Roll; Pres NHS; Prfct Atten Awd.

DAVOLT, JULIA A; Independence Bible Schl; Independence, KS; (3); Church Yth Grp; Band; Chorus; School Musical; School Play; Yrbk; Pres Frsh Cls; Rep Stu Cncl; 5th In Span Cmptn At Indep CC; Gods Bible Schl; Music; Nrsng.

DAWLEY, SCOTT M; Garden City Sr HS; Garden City, KS; (2); Church Yth Grp; Computer Clb; Band; Jazz Band; Mrchg Band; Pep Band; Hon Roll; Prfct Atten Awd.

DAWSON, ERIC L; Chanute Sr HS; Chanute, KS; (1); 44/143; Boy Scts; French Clb; JV Bsktbl; JV Ftbl; Var Golf.

DAWSON, JUSTIN; Leavenworth HS; Leavenworth, KS; (4); 8/326; Am Leg Boys St; SADD; Rep Jr Cls; VP Sr Cls; Rep Stu Cncl; L Crs Cntry; JV Tennis; High Hon Roll; NHS; KS ST Univ; Cmptr Engrg.

DAWSON, NICK S; Buhler HS; Hutchinson, KS; (2); FCA; Office Aide; Varsity Clb; Band; Jazz Band; Mrchg Band; Pep Band; Stage Crew; JV Bsktbl; Var Ftbl; Coll; Bus/Coaching.

DAWSON, SERENA; Northwest HS; Wichita, KS; (4); 30/333; Cmnty Wkr; School Musical; Variety Show; Rep Frsh Cls; Rep Soph Cls; Rep Jr Cls; VP Stu Cncl; Cit Awd; NHS; St Schlr; Peer Ambsdr; Natl Assn Stdnt Cncls; Bible Schl Tchr; Friends Univ; Elem Ed.

DAY, JENNIFER A; Shawnee Mission S Sr HS; Overland Park, KS; (2); 96/482; Intnl Clb; Pep Clb; Teachers Aide; Hon Roll; Show-Me-South; Peer Cnslng; U Of CO; Chld Psychtrst.

DAY, LEAH L; Yates Ctr HS; Yates Center, KS; (2); 19/61; Art Clb; Cmnty Wkr; FHA; Letterman Clb; Spanish Clb; Powder Puff Ftbl; Sftbl; Vllybl; High Hon Roll.

DAY, LISA; Council Grove HS; Council Grove, KS; (1); Church Yth Grp; FCA; 4-H; Key Clb; SADD; Band; Chorus; Church Choir; Mrchg Band; Pep Band; Kayettes; Bsktbl All-Trnmnt Team.

DAY, LORI M; Wichita Collegiate Schl; Wichita, KS; (3); Church Yth Grp; Cmnty Wkr; Yrbk; Ed Lit Mag; Var Golf; Var Capt Sftbl; High Hon Roll; Ntl Merit Ltr; Playing Piano; Harpsichord Bldg/Playing; Promo Wise/More Unvrsl Use Duct Tape; Wheaton Coll; Hist.

DAY, MELISSA; Shawnee Heights Sr HS; Topeka, KS; (4); 1/237; Hist FBLA; Intnl Clb; Drill Tm; Ed Nwsp; Ed Yrbk; Co-Capt Trk; High Hon Roll; NHS; St Schlr; MO Univ; Photojrnlsm.

DAY, RYAN C; Cimarron HS; Cimarron, KS; (2); Church Yth Grp; FCA; Natl FFA Org; Pep Clb; Spanish Clb; Band; Jazz Band; Pep Band; Sec Frsh Cls; JV Bsktbl; Var Ftbl; KS ST Univ; Vet Med.

DAY, TINA J; Elwood Schl; Elwood, KS; (2); 5/16; Pep Clb; Red Cross Aide; Teachers Aide; Treas Soph Cls; L Var Bsktbl; Mgr(s); Hon Roll; Upward Bound; Emporia ST Univ.

DAYTON, MELISSA A; Blue Valley Northwest HS; Overland Park, KS; (3); 117/364; Cmnty Wkr; FCA; Varsity Clb; Powder Puff Ftbl; Swmmng; Vllybl; Hon Roll; Infant Dev Ctr Aide; 2 Yrs HS Swmng St Chmpn.

DEALY, NOLAN J; Halstead HS; Halstead, KS; (3); Church Yth Grp; Debate Tm; Drama Clb; Letterman Clb; Quiz Bowl; Scholastic Bowl; Service Clb; Band; Mrchg Band; Pep Band; Cmptr Sci.

DEAN, ANDREW N; Washburn Rural HS; Topeka, KS; (3); Spanish Clb; Band; Mrchg Band; Socr; Wt Lftg; Hon Roll; Amer Leg Cadet Law Enforcement Acad; KS ST Univ; Criminal Justice.

DEAN, CHRIS S; Maize HS; Wichita, KS; (3); Math Tm; Spanish Clb; Teachers Aide; Bsktbl; High Hon Roll; Hon Roll; Wichita ST Univ; Bus/Acctng.

DEAN, ERIN M; Maize HS; Wichita, KS; (1); Hosp Aide; SADD; Bsktbl; Socr; Wt Lftg; KS Univ; Pharm.

DEAN, JERED; St Mary's Colgan HS; Pittsburg, KS; (1); Boy Scts; Church Yth Grp; Hon Roll; Ntl Merit Ltr; Play Bass Guitar/Harmonica; Race Radio Cntrl Trucks; Dsgn/Fly/Bld Radio Cntrl Airplanes; Purdue U; Elect/Mech Engrng.

DEAN, LEANNA M; Scott Comm HS; Scott City, KS; (3); Library Aide; SADD; Chorus; School Musical; Mgr Crs Cntry; Emporia St Univ; Comp.

DEAN, MOLLY R; Louisburg HS; Bucyrus, KS; (2); Bus Profs of Am; Letterman Clb; Math Clb; Spanish Clb; Bsktbl; Sftbl; High Hon Roll; Exceptnl Atndc; Lang Arts Outstdng Acad Achvmt; Sci Outstdng Acad Achvmt; KS Univ; Med Doctor.

DEAN, RONNIE L; Hoisington HS; Susank, KS; (3); Church Yth Grp; Pep Clb; Band; Mrchg Band; Pep Band; Mgr(s); Hon Roll; KS ST; Chld Psych.

DEAN JR, THOMAS L; Cherryvale HS; Cherryvale, KS; (3); Church Yth Grp; Cmnty Wkr; Drama Clb; FCA; FBLA; FHA; NFL; Quiz Bowl; Scholastic Bowl; Speech Tm; Yth Pastors; Dist Hnr Choir; Ozark Chrstn Coll; Elem Ed.

DEARDORFF, AARON B; Ottawa HS; Ottawa, KS; (3); Letterman Clb; Chorus; Variety Show; Pres Frsh Cls; JV Bsktbl; Var Ftbl; Socr; Var Trk; Hon Roll.

DEARINGER, STEVEN; South Gray HS; Montezuma, KS; (3); 6/21; HOBY; Letterman Clb; Sprt Ed Nwsp; Ed Yrbk; Pres Soph Cls; VP Jr Cls; Var L Ftbl; Hon Roll; NHS.

DE BERRY, ELIZABETH C; Fredonia HS; Fredonia, KS; (3); 9/80; Art Clb; Cmnty Wkr; FCA; Rep NFL; Office Aide; Pep Clb; Scholastic Bowl; Science Clb; Spanish Clb; Speech Tm; Art Awds; St Forensics; Pittsburgh St Univ Engl Comp Schol; U Of KS; Phys Thpy.

DEBES, CYNTHIA E; Clifton-Clyde HS; Clyde, KS; (3); 1/32; Church Yth Grp; Scholastic Bowl; Band; Mrchg Band; Pep Band; VP Jr Cls; JV Bsktbl; JV Var Vllybl; High Hon Roll; Pres NHS; Frnscs Tm 2 Yr ST Qualfr; Hnrs Engl Prtcpnt; Nwspr Articles Pub.

DE BEY, EPHANIE K; Salina HS Central; Salina, KS; (4); 40/238; Pres Church Yth Grp; Cmnty Wkr; Girl Scts; Teachers Aide; Band; Orch; School Musical; Hon Roll; NHS; Pres Acad Fit Awd; SW Coll; Bio.

DEBNAM, NIKKI; South Gray HS; Montezuma, KS; (1); 3/29; Pep Clb; Band; Chorus; Pep Band; JV Bsktbl; Hon Roll.

DEBOER, JEFF T; Olathe South Sr HS; Olathe, KS; (3); Drama Clb; Office Aide; School Musical; School Play; Intrml Ftbl; Hon Roll; Summer Dinner Theatre; Acting.

DE BROT, DAVID E; Topeka HS; Topeka, KS; (2); Church Yth Grp; Drama Clb; German Clb; NFL; Speech Tm; Thesps; Acpl Chr; Chorus; School Musical; School Play; Natl Forensics League Natl Trnmnt; Wrkng With/Tchng Chldrn; Northwestern; Psych/Theatre.

DE BUSK, ANGELA; Holton HS; Holton, KS; (2); Church Yth Grp; Letterman Clb; Quiz Bowl; Teachers Aide; Var Chrldng; Mgr(s); Hon Roll; Frnscs Tm; KS ST.

DE CAIGNY, RYAN; Bishop Ward HS; Kansas City, KS; (2); Boy Scts; Latin Clb; Spanish Clb; JV Bsbl; High Hon Roll; Hon Roll; Pilot; CPA.

DECHAND, DAWN M; Washburn Rural HS; Topeka, KS; (2); Debate Tm; Girl Scts; Cit Awd; High Hon Roll; JC Pennys Golden Rule Awd; 1st Pl In Natl Keep Amer Beautiful Awds; St & Comm Vol.

DECHANT, ANDREA; Ness City HS; Ness City, KS; (4); 6/29; Am Leg Aux Girls St; Church Yth Grp; Cmnty Wkr; Office Aide; Band; School Play; Sec Stu Cncl; Chrldng; High Hon Roll; NHS; Law.

DECHANT, JASON M; Thomas More Prep-Marion HS; Hays, KS; (1); Boy Scts; JV Bsbl; Bsktbl; JV Var Ftbl; Hon Roll; Architecture; Drawing; Art.

DECHANT, LINZIE E; Larned HS; Larned, KS; (2); Church Yth Grp; FHA; Chorus; Yrbk; Var Bsktbl; JV Computer Clb; Wt Lftg; Psych.

DECHANT, RYAN; Sacred Heart HS; Salina, KS; (4); 10/23; Am Leg Boys St; Church Yth Grp; Cmnty Wkr; Pep Clb; Bsktbl; Crs Cntry; Golf; Trk; Cit Awd; Sedes Sapientiae Awd; KS ST Univ; Arch.

DECHANT, TAMMY R; Dodge City HS; Dodge City, KS; (4); 93/254; Church Yth Grp; Girl Scts; SADD; Teachers Aide; Chorus; Orch; Elem Aide; Fort Hays ST; Ed.

DE CICCO, ANNE M; Bishop Carroll Catholic HS; Wichita, KS; (2); Church Yth Grp; Score Keeper; Var Trk; Hon Roll; USUBA 2 Yrs; Summer Sftbl League; Medicine; Pediatrics.

DECKER, ANGIE; Mc Pherson HS; Mc Pherson, KS; (4); 52/194; Church Yth Grp; German Clb; Band; Chorus; Color Guard; Flag Corp; School Musical; Chrldng; Pom Pon; Hon Roll; KS Reg & St Vocal Cont; Mxd Ensmbl; Butler Cty CC; Music Ed.

DECKER, ANTHONY M; Topeka West HS; Topeka, KS; (2); Art Clb; Spanish Clb; Ftbl; Wt Lftg; Wrstlng; KS ST Univ; Engrng.

DECKER, BRANDY; Garden City Sr HS; Garden City, KS; (3); Debate Tm; NFL; Red Cross Aide; Science Clb; Band; Color Guard; Mrchg Band; Pep Band; JV Vllybl; NHS; Ku; Microbio.

DECKER, RUSTI D; Wellington Sr HS; Wellington, KS; (3); Key Clb; Band; Jazz Band; Mrchg Band; VP Jr Cls; Rep Stu Cncl; Var Sftbl; Var Vllybl; Hon Roll; NHS; Lions Awd; Mass Commnctns.

DE DONDER, CURTIS; St Marys HS; Saint Marys, KS; (4); 6/54; FBLA; Letterman Clb; Teachers Aide; Var JV Bsktbl; Var JV Ftbl; Wt Lftg; High Hon Roll; Hon Roll; Sec NHS; KS ST U; Accntng.

DE DONDER, KIMBERLY L; Lebo Schl; Reading, KS; (3); 10/30; 4-H; FBLA; Quiz Bowl; Scholastic Bowl; Teachers Aide; Chorus; Rptr Nwsp; Rptr Yrbk; High Hon Roll; Hon Roll; Comm Svc Prjct; Rennisance Prgm.

DE DONDER, LISA C; St Marys HS; Saint Marys, KS; (2); FHA; Pep Clb; Band; Jazz Band; Mrchg Band; Pep Band; Bsktbl; Crs Cntry; Trk; Wt Lftg; Caterer.

DEE, JESSICA K; Acad Of Mt St Scholastica; Lawrence, KS; (3); Church Yth Grp; Cmnty Wkr; French Clb; Girl Scts; Intnl Clb; Library Aide; Office Aide; Pep Clb; Chorus; Orch; Sirch Clb; Dorm Cncl; Spcl Olympics Vol; Dartmouth; Wildlife Bio.

DEEDS, ZACHARY; Shawnee Mission Nw Sr HS; Shawnee, KS; (3); 9/448; Treas Science Clb; L Crs Cntry; L Trk; High Hon Roll; NHS; Spirit Clb-Bd Mem; Prom Comm.

DEERY, LOU; St Thomas Aquinas HS; Shawnee Mission, KS; (3); 44/261; Am Leg Boys St; FCA; German Clb; Ofcr Bsbl; Var Capt Bsktbl; Wt Lftg; High Hon Roll; NHS; Spcl Olympics Vol; Bsktbl Camps Asst Coach; Bus; Psych.

DEES, MICHELLE; Paola HS; Paola, KS; (4); 34/124; Art Clb; Treas Bus Profs of Am; Church Yth Grp; Sec Drama Clb; SADD; Band; Chorus; Flag Corp; Mrchg Band; School Musical; KS U At Lawrence; PT.

DEETS, LUKE A; Manhattan HS; Manhattan, KS; (3); 22/426; Am Leg Boys St; Chess Clb; Church Yth Grp; 4-H; SADD; School Play; Intrml Bsktbl; High Hon Roll; NHS; KS ST Univ; Arch.

DE FAZIO, MIA C; Wichita East HS; Wichita, KS; (2); Pres Church Yth Grp; French Clb; Girl Scts; Var Bsktbl; Var L Socr; JV Tennis; Sec VP French Hon Soc; High Hon Roll; NHS; Sprt Cbnt.

DE FILIPPO, KRISTEN L; Derby HS; Derby, KS; (3); 11/300; Church Yth Grp; SADD; Band; Jazz Band; Ed Lit Mag; Trk; High Hon Roll; Jr NHS; NHS; Vol Tutor; Church Musician; Futr Prblm Slvrs; Chem Engr.

DEGAND, LISSA; Royal Valley HS; Mayetta, KS; (4); 12/54; Pres VP 4-H; Pres Rep Natl FFA Org; SADD; Phtg Yrbk; VP Stu Cncl; Var Capt Bsktbl; Capt Var Vllybl; Hon Roll; NHS; Highland CC.

DEGENHARDT, JESSICA D; Russell HS; Russell, KS; (2); Drama Clb; FCA; Key Clb; Pep Clb; SADD; Flag Corp; Bsktbl; Chrldng; Trk; Wt Lftg; Barton Cnty Univ.

DEGENHARDT, STEVEN M; Bishop Carroll Catholic HS; Wichita, KS; (2); 28/209; Church Yth Grp; JV Bsbl; JV Ftbl; Var Wt Lftg; Hon Roll; U Of Notre Dame; Eng.

DE GRAFTENREED, LEANDA M; Washington HS; Kansas City, KS; (3); 9/220; Drama Clb; NFL; ROTC; SADD; Var Bsktbl; Var Crs Cntry; Trk; High Hon Roll; NHS; Ntl Merit Ltr; Rockhurst Coll; Elem Ed.

DEGRUSON, DEBRA; Wichita Heights HS; Kechi, KS; (4); Bus Profs of Am; Church Yth Grp; French Clb; Teachers Aide; Band; Mrchg Band; Socr; Hon Roll; Emporia ST U; Acctng.

DEGUERRE, DANIELLE K; St Thomas Aquinas HS; Overland Park, KS; (2); 24/460; Church Yth Grp; French Clb; SADD; Lit Mag; Rep Frsh Cls; Var Socr; JV Vllybl; High Hon Roll; Pres Acad Fit Awd; CSF; U Of Santa Clara; Bus.

DEHNER, MICHELLE; Atchison Sr HS; Atchison, KS; (2); Church Yth Grp; HOBY; Band; Church Choir; Jazz Band; Mrchg Band; Pep Band; Var JV Bsktbl; JV Sftbl; JV Vllybl.

DEIBERT, JOSHUA J; Garden City Sr HS; Garden City, KS; (2); Church Yth Grp; Cmnty Wkr; Band; Jazz Band; Mrchg Band; Pep Band; JV Golf; Var Socr; Cit Awd; Hon Roll; Smmr Swm Tm; Mountain Biking; Plyng In Alternative Bnd; 4 Yr Coll.

DEIBERT, MICHELLE L; Mankato Jr Sr HS; Mankato, KS; (2); Drama Clb; VP FHA; Quiz Bowl; Chorus; JV Vllybl; Hon Roll.

DEIBERT, NIKKI A; Colby Sr HS; Colby, KS; (3); Church Yth Grp; French Clb; Office Aide; Science Clb; Teachers Aide; Nwsp; Yrbk; CCD; Ft Hays ST Univ; Acctng.

DEIBERT, RENELLE D; Great Bend Sr HS; Great Bend, KS; (1); German Clb; Girl Scts; Hosp Aide; Math Tm; Pep Clb; Service Clb; Band; Jazz Band; Mrchg Band; Pep Band; Medical Prof.

DEICHERT, ALISON; Mulvane Sr HS; Mulvane, KS; (3); SADD; Yrbk; Pres Jr Cls; Ofcr Stu Cncl; Var Chrldng; High Hon Roll; NHS; Prfct Atten Awd; KSU; Psychlgy.

DEIDRA, BOYLES; White Rock HS; Superior, NE; (2); 5/15; Church Yth Grp; Girl Scts; Math Tm; Pep Clb; Quiz Bowl; Speech Tm; Band; Chorus; Church Choir; Orch; KS Hs Rep Pg; NCC; Psych.

DEIGHTON, KRISTIN; Macksville HS; Macksville, KS; (2); Church Yth Grp; Band; Rptr Nwsp; Sec Soph Cls; JV Var Bsktbl; JV Var Chrldng; Var Trk; JV Var Vllybl; High Hon Roll; Intrml Powder Puff Ftbl; Piano.

DEINES, ERIN E; Chapman HS; Chapman, KS; (2); 6/105; Church Yth Grp; Math Tm; Natl FFA Org; Band; Pep Band; JV Tennis; High Hon Roll; Quiz Bowl; Church Choir; Mrchg Band; AFS; FFA Natl Land Judging & St Meats Judging; KS ST; Engrng; Vet.

DEINES, NATHAN A; Chapman HS; Chapman, KS; (4); 6/107; Church Yth Grp; Quiz Bowl; Scholastic Bowl; School Play; Stage Crew; Var JV Bsktbl; Var JV Ftbl; High Hon Roll; NHS; Ntl Merit Schol; KS Hnr Schlr; Careers 2000; NHS Tutorial Comm Chprsn; KS ST U; Comp Pgmng.

DEINES, SALLY R; Trego Comm HS; Wa Keeney, KS; (3); 16/48; Debate Tm; Drama Clb; FHA; German Clb; NFL; Office Aide; Science Clb; Speech Tm; SADD; Drill Tm; FHSU.

DEINES, TIMOTHY; Trego Comm HS; Wa Keeney, KS; (4); 12/47; Church Yth Grp; Cmnty Wkr; Debate Tm; Drama Clb; German Clb; Letterman Clb; Math Tm; Natl FFA Org; NFL; Scholastic Bowl; Wa Keeney FFA Sec & Pres; Frgn Lang Clb Pres; St FFA Degree; NW Dist FFA Treas; KS ST Univ; Pre-Vet; Pre-Law.

DEKAT, SHANIA; Rock Creek Jr Sr HS; Saint George, KS; (1); High Hon Roll; Hon Roll; NHS; KS ST U.

DE KNEGT, JEFF; Maranatha Acad; Lenexa, KS; (2); Church Yth Grp; Letterman Clb; Acpl Chr; Chorus; Church Choir; School Musical; School Play; Hon Roll; NHS; Church Worship Ldr, Praise Team; Quartet; Music Ministry.

DELACOUR, JERAD; Cherryvale HS; Independence, KS; (3); 1/42; Scholastic Bowl; Band; Chorus; Church Choir; Var Trk; High Hon Roll; NHS; Church Yth Grp; FHA; Mrchg Band; Tri-M Mus Hon Soc VP/PRES; KS ST Univ Hon Choir; ST Mus Fstvl-Solo; Cmptr Engr.

DELAMAIDE, AMY C; Northwest HS; Wichita, KS; (2); 1/375; Art Clb; Girl Scts; Quiz Bowl; Red Cross Aide; Scholastic Bowl; Band; Mrchg Band; Orch; Pep Band; High Hon Roll; Odyssey Of Mind World Finals 23rd Pl 96; Girl Sct Silver Awd; Soc Sci; Intnl Relations.

DELANEY, MEGAN ANNE; Bishop Miege HS; Prairie Village, KS; (3); 23/170; Church Yth Grp; Cmnty Wkr; Ed Yrbk; High Hon Roll; NHS; Amgs De Las Amers; 1st Pl Jrnlsm 95-; Chldrns Pl Teen Bd.

DELATORRE, KELLY A; Chanute Sr HS; Chanute, KS; (2); 49/149; Drama Clb; 4-H; JA; Spanish Clb; Teachers Aide; Chorus; School Play; Phtg Yrbk; VP Frsh Cls; Ofcr Stu Cncl; KS ST U; Ag.

DELATORRE, NICHOLAS M; Chanute Sr HS; Chanute, KS; (2); Church Yth Grp; Cmnty Wkr; Dance Clb; FBLA; Spanish Clb; Chorus; Treas Frsh Cls; Ofcr Stu Cncl; Hon Roll; K ST Ldrshp Cmp; Uppr Resptry Thrpy/X-Ray Tech.

DELEON, DANIELLE; Sumner Acad Of Arts Of Sci; Kansas City, KS; (4); 29/193; Spanish Clb; Acpl Chr; Mrchg Band; Pep Band; Var Sftbl; High Hon Roll; Hon Roll; NHS; Pres Schlr; Spanish NHS; Grad Cum Laude; Pittsburgh ST Univ; Psych.

DELGADO, CAROL J; Bishop Ward HS; Kansas City, KS; (3); 6/76; Ofcr Am Leg Aux Girls St; Church Yth Grp; Cmnty Wkr; 4-H; Pep Clb; SADD; High Hon Roll; NHS; Hispanic Ldrshp Opportunity Pgm; Stdnts As Tchrs; Teen Ct; Ldrshp 2020; Antropology.

DELGADO, DIANA M; Wichita Heights HS; Wichita, KS; (2); Church Yth Grp; Spanish Clb; Band; Mrchg Band; Pep Band; Law.

DELIMONT, DIANA J; Beloit Jr Sr HS; Beloit, KS; (1); 11/98; Church Yth Grp; German Clb; Letterman Clb; Band; Jazz Band; Mrchg Band; Pep Band; Sftbl; High Hon Roll; Hon Roll; Kayettes Club; Sterling Coll.

DELLADIO, HEATHER N; Bonner Springs HS; Bonner Springs, KS; (3); 1/128; Office Aide; Phtg Nwsp; VP Jr Cls; Cit Awd; High Hon Roll; Hon Roll; NHS; Prfct Atten Awd; Kayettes; Ldrs Clb; KS Univ; Acctng; Bus.

DELLINGER, HILARY A; Protection Schl; Protection, KS; (2); 6/20; Letterman Clb; Pep Clb; Band; Mrchg Band; Pep Band; L Var Bsktbl; L Var Crs Cntry; Mgr Ftbl; Hon Roll.

DELLINGER, LAURA L; Wichita Heights HS; Wichita, KS; (2); 1/336; Church Yth Grp; Orch; High Hon Roll; Sci Olympiad, Natls 96, Team 16th; Dance; Wichita Symphony Yth Orch.

DELMEZ, SHANNON M; Olathe East Sr HS; Olathe, KS; (3); Debate Tm; French Clb; Hosp Aide; Q&S; Band; Chorus; Stage Crew; Ed Yrbk; Lit Mag; Stat Wrstlng.

DE LOS SANTOS, LEYLA D; Derby HS; Derby, KS; (4); Church Yth Grp; Cmnty Wkr; FCA; Acpl Chr; Pres Chorus; School Musical; Variety Show; Hon Roll; Vocal Music & FCA Outstndg Ldrshp Awds; Dist Choir 94; Miss KS Pgnt Miss Derby 96; Friends U; Elem Ed.

DELOW, CLINTON; Labette Co HS; Edna, KS; (3); 41/146; VICA; Hon Roll; Military; Electronics.

DEL PERCIO, MARLO; Sumner Acad Of Arts & Science; Kansas City, KS; (1); GAA; JCL; Latin Clb; Spanish Clb; Thesps; Chorus; School Play; JV L Sftbl; Var L Vllybl; High Hon Roll.

DELZEIT, RANEE; Dodge City HS; Dodge City, KS; (1); Church Yth Grp; Debate Tm; 4-H; Bsktbl; Vllybl; 4-H Awd; Hon Roll; Vlybl Coach.

DE MARCO, JOHN A; Bishop Miege HS; Leawood, KS; (3); 15/185; Ed Nwsp; Hon Roll; Acad Achvmnt Awd.

DEMAREE, JESSICA; Arkansas City HS; Arkansas City, KS; (1); Church Yth Grp; SADD; Band; Mrchg Band; Pep Band; Ofcr Frsh Cls; Ofcr Stu Cncl; Vllybl; Cowley Cty CC.

DE MARIA, CARA; Lansing HS; Lansing, KS; (2); Drama Clb; French Clb; Math Tm; Science Clb; Thesps; Band; Mrchg Band; School Play; Lit Mag; High Hon Roll; League, Regnl & St Music Festivals With Solo & Trio All 1 Ratings; Jr Recorder Soc.

DEMBY-PENNINGTON, DANIELLE D; Lawrence HS; Lawrence, KS; (3); Cmnty Wkr; JA; Library Aide; Quiz Bowl; Chorus; Church Choir; Ofcr Stu Cncl; Cit Awd; Afrcn Amer Clb Grls Pres; Gspl Sng Wrtr; Ldrs Tmrrw; U Of Southern CA; Med.

DEMEL, DUSTIN M; Hoisington HS; Hoisington, KS; (2); Church Yth Grp; Letterman Clb; Varsity Clb; Band; Jazz Band; Pep Band; Stage Crew; Variety Show; Var Bsbl; JV Bsktbl; LEAD.

DEMEL, MELISSA R; Great Bend Sr HS; Great Bend, KS; (1); Church Yth Grp; Drama Clb; Band; Mrchg Band; Pep Band; Stage Crew; Variety Show; Cit Awd; Hon Roll; Pgm VP Explores Grp; 101 Comms; Visits Sr Citzns; Barton Cty; Graphcs Desgn.

DE MEO, ANNIE E; Hayden HS; Topeka, KS; (2); 12/170; Debate Tm; Intnl Clb; NFL; Quiz Bowl; Speech Tm; Sec Treas SADD; Band; Drm Mjr(t); High Hon Roll; NHS; CFL Natl Speech Qualifier.

DEMORET, TIM; Trego Comm HS; Wa Keeney, KS; (4); 1/50; Church Yth Grp; Letterman Clb; Quiz Bowl; Science Clb; SADD; Band; Var L Ftbl; High Hon Roll; NHS; West Coast Baptist Coll.

DEMOSS, BRAD; Prairie View USD 362; Parker, KS; (4); 21/67; Natl FFA Org; Hon Roll; FFA Dgrees East Cntrl Dist 95-/ST Frmr 95-/Grnhnd 93-94/Swne Prdctn Awd 94-95; Bible Schl Asst; Agribus.

DE MOSS, KELLI A; Newton Sr HS; Newton, KS; (3); Church Yth Grp; FCA; Key Clb; SADD; Orch; Ftbl; Sftbl; Hon Roll.

DEMOTT, SUSIE I; Baldwin HS; Baldwin City, KS; (4); 28/78; Drama Clb; NFL; Varsity Clb; Chorus; Mgr(s); Sftbl; Var JV Tennis; JV Vllybl; High Hon Roll; Hon Roll; BPW Schlrsp; Vc Dmcrcy Schlrsp; Johnson Cty CC; Intrprtr Trng.

DE MOTTE, SARAH; Basenor-Linwood HS; Bonner Springs, KS; (1); Church Yth Grp; Cmnty Wkr; 4-H; Var L Chrldng; JV Sftbl; 4-H Awd; High Hon Roll; Hon Roll; KU; Tch; Nrs.

DEMPSEY, SHAWNA D; Mankato Jr Sr HS; Mankato, KS; (2); 1/30; Church Yth Grp; 4-H; Math Tm; Natl FFA Org; NFL; Quiz Bowl; Speech Tm; Varsity Clb; Rep Frsh Cls; Rep Soph Cls; Lawyer.

DEMUTH, SHANNON; Hays HS; Hays, KS; (3); JA; Acpl Chr; Chorus; Orch; School Musical; Capt Pom Pon; High Hon Roll; NHS; Ntl Merit Ltr.

DENEAULT, ERIC M; Concordia Jr Sr HS; Concordia, KS; (4); Am Leg Boys St; Church Yth Grp; Band; Mrchg Band; Pep Band; Ofcr Bsbl; Tennis; Hon Roll; Prfct Atten Awd; Cloud Cnty CC; Wldlfe Cons.

DENEKE, JODI L; Beloit Jr Sr HS; Beloit, KS; (3); Cmnty Wkr; FBLA; Letterman Clb; Science Clb; Spanish Clb; L Trk; Hon Roll.

DENK, TERESA M; Shawnee Mission W Sr HS; Overland Park, KS; (2); 66/426; Pep Clb; Teachers Aide; Rep Frsh Cls; Vllybl; Hon Roll; Schlr Ath Awd; Nrsng Home Vol; KS ST; Psych; Span.

DENMAN, STACI L; Washburn Rural HS; Topeka, KS; (3); 65/343; Cmnty Wkr; Teachers Aide; JV Sftbl; High Hon Roll; Hon Roll; Peer Mediation; Teens As Tchrs; U Of KS; Med.

DENNETT, SHAWNA D; Oskaloosa HS; Mc Louth, KS; (3); 6/65; Treas FBLA; SADD; Band; Co-Ed Yrbk; Sec Soph Cls; Treas Jr Cls; Var L Sftbl; JV Var Vllybl; High Hon Roll; Forensic Psych.

DENNIS, ERIN L; Independence HS; Independence, KS; (3); Church Yth Grp; Pep Clb; Chorus; School Play; Rep Ski Clb; Rep Jr Cls; Rep Stu Cncl; Bsktbl; Powder Puff Ftbl; Vllybl; KS Univ.

DENNIS, TAMRA L; Shawnee Heights Sr HS; Berryton, KS; (2); Church Yth Grp; Band; Church Choir; Mrchg Band; Pep Band; Hon Roll; Vet.

DENNIS, W R; Blue Valley HS; Shawnee Mission, KS; (3); Church Yth Grp; Cmnty Wkr; Cit Awd; Hon Roll; Prfct Atten Awd; HS Chem Tchr.

DE NOON, NICOLE E; Manhattan HS; Manhattan, KS; (3); Pep Clb; Spanish Clb; Chorus; Church Choir; School Musical; Swing Chorus; Variety Show; Cit Awd; High Hon Roll; Hon Roll; Teens Leading Teens Drug Prevention Ldrshp; Dancing; KS ST Univ; Arch; Engrng.

DENTON, ASHLEY R; Dodge City HS; Dodge City, KS; (2); Red Cross Aide; JV Vllybl; KS Univ.

DENTON, CARRIE; Pittsburg HS; Pittsburg, KS; (3); 1/240; Church Yth Grp; 4-H; HOBY; Pep Clb; Spanish Clb; Swing Chorus; Sec Jr Cls; Var L Trk; NHS; Cmnty Wkr; KS Rgnts Hnrs Acad; Tchr.

DENTON, JAIME; Shawnee Mission N HS; Merriam, KS; (4); 93/360; Pep Clb; Spanish Clb; Chrldng; Sftbl; Wt Lftg; Hon Roll; Pittsburgh ST U; Elem Ed.

DENTON, KEVIN; Maur Hill Prep Schl; Atchison, KS; (3); Boy Scts; Computer Clb; Drama Clb; HOBY; School Play; Nwsp; Bsktbl; Tennis; High Hon Roll; NHS; Engrng.

DEPENBUSCH, CARRIE; Columbus HS; Columbus, KS; (3); 5/105; Pres Bus Profs of Am; 4-H; HOBY; Math Tm; Treas Stu Cncl; 4-H Awd; Hon Roll; NHS; HOBY St Rcrtmnt Comm; 4th Pl Team BPA Prlmntry Prcdr At Natl Conf; U Of KS; Acctng.

DE PRIEST, JESSICA J; Louisburg HS; Bucyrus, KS; (3); 7/90; Letterman Clb; Math Clb; Math Tm; Spanish Clb; Band; Drill Tm; High Hon Roll; NHS; Prfct Atten Awd; Debate Tm; TSA; KS ST Univ; Civil Engrng.

DERINGTON, GABRIELLE L; Pierson Jr HS; Kansas City, KS; (2); Drama Clb; German Clb; Band; Jazz Band; Mrchg Band; Pep Band; School Musical; Cit Awd; Hon Roll; Jr NHS; Prfrmng Arts/Actng.

DERSTEIN, CHRISTOPHER B; El Dorado HS; El Dorado, KS; (2); FCA; Letterman Clb; SADD; Band; Chorus; Mrchg Band; Ofcr Bsbl; Bsktbl; Tennis; Hon Roll; State Piano; Encore Hnr Choir; Wichita Wind Ensmbl Hnr Band; Music/Tchng/Concert Piano.

DERSTEIN, RACHEL; Bucklin Schl; Ford, KS; (1); Church Yth Grp; 4-H; NFL; Pep Clb; Speech Tm; SADD; Band; Mrchg Band; Pep Band; School Play.

DERSTEIN, RYAN; Bucklin Schl; Ford, KS; (3); Church Yth Grp; FCA; 4-H; Quiz Bowl; Var Bsktbl; Var Ftbl; Var Wt Lftg; 4-H Awd; Hon Roll; CO Mountain Coll; Vet Asst.

DE RUYSCHER, SIMON O; Immaculata HS; Leavenworth, KS; (2); Art Clb; Church Yth Grp; Cmnty Wkr; Pep Clb; SADD; Socr; Congressional Yth Ldrhp Cnsl Rep; MADD Art Cont Wnnr; Artist; Soccer Player.

DE SALVO, ALLEGRA M; Lawrence HS; Lawrence, KS; (4); 1/521; Key Clb; Spanish Clb; Teachers Aide; School Play; Sec Sr Cls; Capt Pom Pon; Co-Capt Socr; Cit Awd; DAR Awd; Gov Hon Prg Awd; Universal Dance Assn All-Star; U Of KS; Acctng.

DESBIEN, ANGELA; Thomas More Prep-Marian HS; Hays, KS; (4); 3/93; VP Frsh Cls; Rep Soph Cls; Rep Jr Cls; Rep Sr Cls; Var Trk; Var Co-Capt Vllybl; St Schlr; Church Yth Grp; Hosp Aide; Model UN; All Amer Schlr; Schlstc Awd Highest GPA Cls; Ambsdr Grp; Med.

DETERS, JEFF G; Centralia Schl; Centralia, KS; (3); Natl FFA Org; Science Clb; Nwsp; Ftbl; Wt Lftg; Hon Roll.

DETERS, MELISSA R; Hayden HS; Topeka, KS; (2); Crs Cntry; Trk; Wt Lftg; High Hon Roll; Music & Painting; Guitar; Math.

DE THAMPLE, STEPHANIE C; Wichita South HS; Wichita, KS; (1); Debate Tm; NFL; Stage Crew; Hot Rod Cars/Bsktbl/Gardening/Bike Riding; UCLA; DJ.

DETRIXHE, ALAN J; Clifton-Clyde HS; Concordia, KS; (4); FBLA; Natl FFA Org; Phtg Yrbk; VP Frsh Cls; VP Soph Cls; Ofcr Stu Cncl; Co-Capt Ftbl; High Hon Roll; NHS; Hnrs Bus; Cloud Cty Comm Coll; Broadcstng.

DETRIXHE, MONICA; Concordia Jr Sr HS; Concordia, KS; (3); #1 in class; Church Yth Grp; Debate Tm; Pres 4-H; HOBY; NFL; Band; VP Jr Cls; Var Tennis; NHS; Cncrda Yth Tsk Frce; Pltcl Sci.

DETWEILER, ERIC W; Axtell Schl; Summerfield, KS; (2); 4/15; Church Yth Grp; Letterman Clb; Varsity Clb; Chorus; Ofcr Bsbl; Bsktbl; Ftbl; Sftbl; Wt Lftg; Hon Roll.

DETWILER, JON; Eureka Jr Sr HS; Eureka, KS; (2); Church Yth Grp; Drama Clb; Letterman Clb; Spanish Clb; Chorus; School Play; Sec Soph Cls; Var L Ftbl; Var L Trk; Var L Wrstlng; De Molay.

DEUTSCH, JEREMY; Trinity Acad; Wichita, KS; (2); 1/25; Church Yth Grp; Ed Nwsp; Yrbk; Pres Soph Cls; Var Bsbl; Var Bsktbl; Var Socr; High Hon Roll.

DEUVALL, KRISTINE L; Olathe North Sr HS; Olathe, KS; (3); Cmnty Wkr; Latin Clb; Office Aide; Ski Clb; Teachers Aide; Hon Roll; Eng Awd; Peer Mediation; KS Univ; Phy Thrpst.

DE VADER, EMILY; St Marys HS; Saint Marys, KS; (4); 9/56; Pep Clb; Drill Tm; Treas Frsh Cls; Treas Soph Cls; Pres Jr Cls; Sec Sr Cls; Pres Stu Cncl; Capt Var Chrldng; Sftbl; NHS; Ft Hays ST U; Sociology.

DE VADER, TRAVIS; Holton HS; Holton, KS; (4); 3/66; Am Leg Boys St; Model UN; Pres Speech Tm; VP Jr Cls; Rep Stu Cncl; High Hon Roll; Sec NHS; Gov Bill Graves Cmpgn Dist Chrmn; Bob Dole For Pres Cmpgn; KS Gov Optmst Mdl Yth In Govt; Loyola U; Poli Sci.

DE VICTOR, DARCY E; Lawrence HS; Lawrence, KS; (2); Church Yth Grp; French Clb; Science Clb; School Play; Rep Soph Cls; JV Vllybl; Hon Roll; Cmnty Wkr; Chorus; Variety Show; Church Msn Wk Cumberland Pines TN; Jr Olympic Tm Vlybl; Sml Vocal Ensemble ST Music Festival.

DEVLIN, IAN J; Washburn Rural HS; Topeka, KS; (3); JV Bsktbl; Var Crs Cntry; JV Socr; Var Trk; Wt Lftg; High Hon Roll.

DEVLIN, TRAVIS; Smith Ctr Jr Sr HS; Lebanon, KS; (4); 9/42; Natl FFA Org; SADD; JV Bsktbl; JV Var Golf; Hon Roll; KS ST U; Milling Sci.

DEVORA, HEIDI; Lansing HS; Lansing, KS; (3); 1/140; Science Clb; Spanish Clb; Teachers Aide; Rep Stu Cncl; Var Capt Chrldng; Var Trk; High Hon Roll; NHS; Prfct Atten Awd; Letterman Clb; Kayettes Brd; Roylty Crt; Natl Chrldrs Assn All-Amer; U Of KS; Med.

DEVORE, CHARLES A; Field Kindley Mem Sr HS; Coffeyville, KS; (2); 10/217; Debate Tm; German Clb; Red Cross Aide; Rep Soph Cls; JV Crs Cntry; Var L Swmmng; High Hon Roll; Pres Acad Fit Awd.

DEWALD, CHRIS R; Russell HS; Russell, KS; (4); 4-H; Key Clb; Pep Clb; JV Ftbl; Var Wt Lftg; KS ST Univ.

DE WALD, JESSICA MARIE; Trego Comm HS; Wa Keeney, KS; (4); 1/50; Boy Scts; Debate Tm; Girl Scts; Jr NHS; NHS; Am Leg Aux Girls St; Math Tm; Model UN; Quiz Bowl; Science Clb; Philmont Boy Sct Ranch 50 M Iler Cnsrvtn Awd, All Girls Trek Crew Ldr, PTC Trng Staff; Cottey Coll; Envrnmntl Sci.

DE WALD, SHANE R; Otis Bison HS; Otis, KS; (3); 5/27; Pep Clb; VP SADD; Band; Chorus; Mrchg Band; Pep Band; Variety Show; Ed Nwsp; Pres Frsh Cls; VP Soph Cls.

DEWEY, NAOMI; Hillsboro HS; Hillsboro, KS; (3); Church Yth Grp; 4-H; Natl FFA Org; NHS; Vet.

DEWEY, NOAMI J; Hillsboro HS; Hillsboro, KS; (3); 11/62; Church Yth Grp; 4-H; Natl FFA Org; Science Clb; School Play; Stage Crew; Intrml Sftbl; High Hon Roll; NHS; Kayettes; Pre Vet Med.

DEWEY, STEVEN M; Great Bend Sr HS; Great Bend, KS; (1); Church Yth Grp; Band; Mrchg Band; JV Tennis; Hon Roll; Prfct Atten Awd.

DEWITT, NICOLE; Wichita West HS; Wichita, KS; (3); 20/283; Sec Treas Church Yth Grp; Pep Clb; Acpl Chr; JV Var Chrldng; Hon Roll; Jr NHS; NHS; Chorus; Church Choir; School Musical; Asst Dir Of Inner-City After Schl Pgm; Participant In Coca-Cola Olympic Torch Hnr Choir; Southwestern Coll; Pre-Med.

DE WITT, PATRICK; Northwest HS; Wichita, KS; (2); Art Clb; Boy Scts; Church Yth Grp; Spanish Clb; Church Choir; Rep Jr Cls; JV Bsbl; Hon Roll; Missionary; Ft Hays.

DEWOODY, REBECCA S; Independence HS; Independence, KS; (1); Church Yth Grp; 4-H; Girl Scts; Math Tm; NFL; Pep Clb; Quiz Bowl; Scholastic Bowl; Acpl Chr; Orch; Episcol Dicesan Yth Strng Comtee; Sewanee Univ; Med.

DEXTER, ANGIE R; Wichita South HS; Wichita, KS; (3); Church Yth Grp; Cmnty Wkr; Debate Tm; Drama Clb; FTA; NFL; Red Cross Aide; Service Clb; Speech Tm; Thesps; Thspn Treas; NHS Pres.

DEXTER, BRANDON L; Ness City HS; Ness City, KS; (3); Art Clb; Boy Scts; Church Yth Grp; Yrbk; Var L Bsktbl; Var L Ftbl; Var L Golf; Var Wt Lftg; High Hon Roll; Hon Roll; Play Bsbl; Bowling Yth League; Drafter.

DEZOTELL, GARY E; Campus HS; Haysville, KS; (1); Chorus; Intrml Bsbl; Intrml Wt Lftg; Cit Awd; High Hon Roll; Good U; Archlgst/His Tchr.

DIAMOND, ZACHARIAH B; Smoky Valley HS; Lindsborg, KS; (2); FCA; Letterman Clb; Band; Pep Band; Pres Soph Cls; Var L Bsktbl; Var L Crs Cntry; Var L Trk; Hon Roll; Church Yth Grp.

DIAS, BENJAMIN S; Blue Valley North HS; Overland Park, KS; (3); Boy Scts; Drama Clb; German Clb; Thesps; School Musical; School Play; Stage Crew; Acad Decathalon Team.

DIAZ, DAVID; Derby HS; Derby, KS; (1); Chess Clb; Church Yth Grp; ROTC; Band; Drill Tm; Mrchg Band; Pep Band; Hon Roll; Prfct Atten Awd; Air Force.

DIAZ, JOSHUA; Wichita West HS; Wichita, KS; (2); 128/431; Church Yth Grp; Prfct Atten Awd; WUS; Cmptr Rpr/Arntc Pilot.

DIBBERN, ASHLEY; Shawnee Heights Sr HS; Topeka, KS; (2); 1/300; Church Yth Grp; FBLA; Pep Clb; Church Choir; Ed Yrbk; Pres Frsh Cls; Pres Soph Cls; Var Tennis; High Hon Roll; Sprt Club Offcr; KS ST.

DIBBLE, ANDREW; Hays HS; Hays, KS; (3); 25/237; Boy Scts; Var JV Bsbl; Var JV Bsktbl; Var JV Crs Cntry; Intrml Wt Lftg; High Hon Roll; NHS.

DIBBLE, SARA A; Santa Fe Trail HS; Scranton, KS; (3); Art Clb; Church Yth Grp; FBLA; Math Tm; Quiz Bowl; Spanish Clb; Teachers Aide; Var Crs Cntry; JV Trk; Hon Roll; KAYS; Psych.

DIBLE, JERI; Iola Sr HS; Neosho Falls, KS; (4); 14/96; Am Leg Aux Girls St; Cmnty Wkr; French Clb; VP FBLA; FHA; Key Clb; SADD; Yrbk; Treas Sr Cls; High Hon Roll; KS ST U; Acctng.

DICE, JENNIFER S; Blue Valley HS; Stilwell, KS; (4); 85/229; Dance Clb; Library Aide; Teachers Aide; Sftbl; Hon Roll; Heart To Heart Vol; KS Univ; Acctng.

DICK, DUSTIN L; Rossville HS; Rossville, KS; (3); FBLA; Letterman Clb; VP Frsh Cls; VP Soph Cls; VP Jr Cls; VP Sr Cls; Var Bsktbl; Var Ftbl; Var Golf; Wt Lftg; PT.

DICK, MELISSA; Rossville HS; Rossville, KS; (2); 7/35; FBLA; Yrbk; Rep Frsh Cls; Rep Stu Cncl; JV Bsktbl; Var Chrldng; Var Golf; Var Sftbl; High Hon Roll; Hon Roll; Ms Tn Of Amer Schlrshp & Recognition Pgm; Emporia ST U; Ed.

DICK, PAMELA D; Russell HS; Russell, KS; (1); SADD; Hon Roll.

DICK, TANYA M; Blue Valley HS; Stanley, KS; (2); Church Yth Grp; Bsktbl; Vllybl; Concordia Coll.

DICKASON, DEVON D; Turner HS; Kansas City, KS; (2); Drama Clb; French Clb; NFL; Drill Tm; School Play; Sec Stu Cncl; Pom Pon; Vllybl; Jr NHS; Pres Acad Fit Awd; Pittsburg ST U.

DICKASON, MICHELLE L; Emporia HS; Emporia, KS; (3); Church Yth Grp; FCA; JV L Socr; High Hon Roll; Hon Roll.

DICKE, BENJAMIN T; Sunrise Chrstn Acad; Wichita, KS; (3); Church Yth Grp; Cmnty Wkr; Chorus; Church Choir; School Musical; School Play; Stage Crew; Var L Bsbl; Var L Socr; Hon Roll; Cmnty Plays; Dance; Schl Mascot; Theatre.

DICKENS, BLOSSOM M; Labette Co HS; Cherryvale, KS; (2); Church Yth Grp; Cmnty Wkr; FBLA; Band; Jazz Band; Mrchg Band; Orch; Pep Band; School Musical; Mgr(s); Regnl Solo/Ensmbl II Solo/I Duet/II Trio/I/SOLO Flute Four; ST Solo Ensmbl I Solo; Pittsburg ST Univ; Elem Ed.

DICKERSON, JOSHUA M; Chaparral HS; Manchester, OK; (1); Cmnty Wkr; Marine Bio.

DICKEY, ELIZABETH; Shawnee Mission Nw Sr HS; Leawood, KS; (2); JV Var Chrldng; Intrml Sftbl; KS ST Univ.

DICKHOFF, DANIEL B; Hayden HS; Topeka, KS; (3); 65/131; Boy Scts; Intnl Clb; Spanish Clb; SADD; JV Bsktbl; Ftbl; Trk; Hon Roll; Video Tech; Hnbl Mntn All Cty.

DICKINSON, MICHAEL S; Caney Valley Jr Sr HS; Tyro, KS; (4); Church Yth Grp; FCA; Letterman Clb; Office Aide; Varsity Clb; Treas Jr Cls; Treas Sr Cls; Var Capt Bsbl; Var L Bsktbl; Var L Ftbl; Ftbl/Bsbl 2 Yrs; Independence CC; PT.

DICKINSON, SHARON E; Leavenworth HS; Leavenworth, KS; (3); Drama Clb; French Clb; Hosp Aide; ROTC; Teachers Aide; Thesps; Acpl Chr; Chorus; Stage Crew; Hon Roll; Natl Piano Plyng Adtns Of Amer Coll Mus 4 Yrs; Exclnt Rtng Rgnl Mus Fstvl.

DICKMAN, ADAM; Colby Sr HS; Colby, KS; (2); Church Yth Grp; Spanish Clb; Intrml Ftbl; Sftbl; JV Tennis; Hon Roll; KS ST; Archtct.

DICKMAN, GREGORY C; Grinnell HS; Grinnell, KS; (2); 1/14; Church Yth Grp; HOBY; Math Clb; Quiz Bowl; Science Clb; Speech Tm; Band; Pep Band; Ofcr Frsh Cls; Var L Bsktbl.

DICKMAN, MATTHEW C; Grinnell HS; Rexford, KS; (3); 1/14; Quiz Bowl; Scholastic Bowl; VP Frsh Cls; Rep Soph Cls; VP Jr Cls; Rep Stu Cncl; Var L Bsktbl; JV Var Crs Cntry; High Hon Roll; NHS.

DICKSON, KARI; Newton Sr HS; Newton, KS; (2); French Clb; Hosp Aide; Key Clb; Stat Bsktbl; Stat Trk; Hon Roll; Hutchinson CC.

DIECKMANN, ERIN; Olathe North Sr HS; Olathe, KS; (2); Spanish Clb; Stage Crew; Gym; Hon Roll; Pres Schlr; KS Univ.

DIEDERICH, JEANETTE; Hanover Schl; Greenleaf, KS; (4); 6/23; Church Yth Grp; Drama Clb; 4-H; FHA; Speech Tm; Chorus; School Play; Stage Crew; Yrbk; Forensics; Psych.

DIEHL, AMANDA; White Rock HS; Burr Oak, KS; (3); 1/7; Am Leg Aux Girls St; Drama Clb; HOBY; Letterman Clb; Pep Clb; Quiz Bowl; Scholastic Bowl; SADD; Band; Chorus; Msc.

DIEHL, AMY; Wabaunsee HS; Alma, KS; (4); 3/35; Am Leg Aux Girls St; Sec FBLA; FHA; Rptr Nwsp; Treas Stu Cncl; JV Var Bsktbl; Var Vllybl; Hon Roll; NHS; Prfct Atten Awd; KS ST U.

DIEHL, JENNI L; Mc Pherson HS; Mc Pherson, KS; (2); 12/245; Math Tm; Scholastic Bowl; Pres Spanish Clb; JV Bsktbl; JV Sftbl; JV Vllybl; High Hon Roll; Clb Soccer; Aerobics; Medicine.

DIEHL, STEPHANIE A; Liberal HS; Liberal, KS; (3); Am Leg Aux Girls St; Church Yth Grp; Key Clb; Band; Flag Corp; School Musical; Ed Nwsp; Stat Bsktbl; Hon Roll; NHS; Commnctn; Pre-Law.

DIEHN, MIKE; Osawatomie HS; Osawatomie, KS; (1); Computer Clb; Science Clb; Hon Roll; Keyboarding; KU.

DIEKER, RYAN C; Maize HS; Maize, KS; (3); 12/240; Church Yth Grp; Debate Tm; NFL; Spanish Clb; SADD; Teachers Aide; Band; Pep Band; High Hon Roll; NHS; Chem.

DIEL, SARAH J A; Gardner-Edgerton HS; Gardner, KS; (2); Band; Chorus; Church Choir; Mrchg Band; Orch; Pep Band; School Play; Vllybl; High Hon Roll; Hon Roll; KU K ST; Chld Ed.

DIEL-WINTERS, SARAH J A; Gardner-Edgerton HS; Gardner, KS; (2); Drama Clb; Band; Church Choir; Mrchg Band; Orch; Pep Band; Mgr(s); High Hon Roll; Hon Roll; Prfct Atten Awd; Child Eed.

DIENER, RACHEL M; Lyons HS; Lyons, KS; (2); VP Church Yth Grp; Debate Tm; Letterman Clb; NFL; Pep Clb; Band; Pep Band; School Play; Intrml Bsktbl; Score Keeper; Dance Tm; Actrs/DNA Rsrch.

DIENST, KILEY R; Meade HS; Meade, KS; (2); 4-H; Pep Clb; Quiz Bowl; Band; Chorus; Pep Band; School Musical; Tennis; Trk; Cit Awd; Phy Ther.

DIEPENBROCK, J RYAN; Shawnee Mission Nw Sr HS; Lenexa, KS; (4); 100/450; Bus Profs of Am; FBLA; Spanish Clb; Varsity Clb; Var Chrldng; JV Crs Cntry; JV Socr; Hon Roll; AZ ST Univ; Acctng.

DIEPENBROCK, STEPHANIE L; Wichita East HS; Wichita, KS; (2); Church Yth Grp; Hosp Aide; Office Aide; Teachers Aide; Rptr Yrbk; Hon Roll; KS ST U; Eng.

DIES, ANDREW; Hillsboro HS; Lehigh, KS; (2); 4/73; Church Yth Grp; Band; Mrchg Band; Pep Band; Rep Frsh Cls; Bsktbl; Ftbl; Golf; Wt Lftg; High Hon Roll.

DIESEL, CHRISTY L; St Marys HS; Rossville, KS; (3); FBLA; Pep Clb; JV Sftbl; JV Vllybl; Hon Roll; UMASS; Engrng.

DIETZ, CINDY; Mulvane Sr HS; Peck, KS; (4); 21/144; FHA; Q&S; SADD; Thesps; Chorus; Yrbk; Chrldng; Hon Roll; NHS; Yrbk Edtr; KS Assn Of Yth Pres; FHA Chptr & Dist Offcr; York Coll.

DIETZE, LAWRENCE F; Lawrence HS; Lawrence, KS; (4); 141/632; Cmnty Wkr; German Clb; Office Aide; Teachers Aide; Var Swmmng; High Hon Roll; Ntl Merit SF; Pres Schlr.

DIGGS, LYNETREA C; Bonner Springs HS; Kansas City, KS; (4); 35/175; Drama Clb; FHA; Key Clb; Pep Clb; SADD; Acpl Chr; Band; Chorus; Drill Tm; Flag Corp; Johnson Cty CC; Nursing.

DILL, BRAD; Wichita Heights HS; Wichita, KS; (2); Boy Scts; Church Yth Grp; Spanish Clb; Rep Stu Cncl; Var L Socr; Hon Roll; Peer Ldr Heights HS; All Cty Hnrbl Mntn Sccr; Stck Market Clb; Bus Ldshp.

DILL, MEGAN M; Hartford HS; Hartford, KS; (2); 3/39; Church Yth Grp; 4-H; FBLA; HOBY; Letterman Clb; NFL; Scholastic Bowl; Band; Mrchg Band; Pep Band; Stdnt Cncl Sec 10/VP 11; KA ST Univ; Bio/Pathologst.

DILLINGER, CAMILLA L; Altoona Midway HS; Buffalo, KS; (3); Quiz Bowl; Scholastic Bowl; Speech Tm; SADD; Chorus; High Hon Roll; VP NHS; ST Frnscs Qlfr; Eng/Creative Wrtng.

DILLINGER, DANIEL L; Emporia HS; Emporia, KS; (4); Key Clb; Latin Clb; Chrmn Sr Cls; Intrml Bsktbl; Ftbl; Cit Awd; High Hon Roll; Prfct Atten Awd; Pres Schlr; Schl Recycling; Good Samaritan Awd; Renaissance Schlsp; Emporia ST Univ; Pre-Med.

DILLMAN, EVAN; Highland HS; Highland, KS; (1); Church Yth Grp; Cmnty Wkr; Pep Clb; Chorus; Bsktbl; Crs Cntry; Ftbl; Mgr(s); Trk; Hon Roll; Emporia ST; Sprts Med.

DILLON, DAVID N; Northeast Magnet HS; Wichita, KS; (2); 20/119; Church Yth Grp; Math Tm; Church Choir; Ofcr Stu Cncl; Hon Roll; 1st Pl In Magnet Fair For Sci Project 95; Natl Engrng Design Challenge Team Mem 96-97; Comps; Sci.

DILLON, JOSHUA L; Parsons HS; Parsons, KS; (3); Debate Tm; Key Clb; NFL; Q&S; Spanish Clb; Speech Tm; Teachers Aide; Ed Nwsp; Hon Roll; Treas NHS; Lib Arts.

DILLON, TREY; Manhattan HS; Manhattan, KS; (4); Cmnty Wkr; FBLA; Ed Nwsp; VP Sr Cls; Var Bsktbl; JV Crs Cntry; JV Sftbl; Cit Awd; Fl Hmcmng Qn 95; KS ST Univ; Pub Rltns.

DILTS, BRAD; Wichita Collegiate Schl; Sedgwick, KS; (2); Church Yth Grp; 4-H; 4-H Awd; High Hon Roll; Optmst Clb Unsng Hero Awd; Lattner Schlrshp; KS ST U; Ag Engrng.

DI MATTIA, CHRISTINA A; Junction City HS; Fort Riley, KS; (3); 5/268; Am Leg Aux Girls St; Church Yth Grp; Girl Scts; Scholastic Bowl; Band; Church Choir; Mrchg Band; School Musical; High Hon Roll; NHS; Boston Univ; Biomedical Engr.

DINGES, ANDREA; Victoria HS; Victoria, KS; (4); Church Yth Grp; Sec FBLA; Letterman Clb; Pep Clb; SADD; Varsity Clb; Tennis; Hon Roll; Girl Scts; Powder Puff Ftbl; Natl Hnr Soc; Fort Hays ST Univ; Sec Admin.

DINKEL, ADAM J; Quinter Jr Sr HS; Quinter, KS; (3); Boy Scts; VP Church Yth Grp; Debate Tm; FCA; Letterman Clb; Speech Tm; Color Guard; Stage Crew; Var Bsktbl; Var L Ftbl; U Of KS; Cvl Drftng.

DINKEL, MATTHEW; Plainville HS; Plainville, KS; (3); 5/45; Church Yth Grp; Cmnty Wkr; HOBY; Letterman Clb; Pep Clb; Var Bsbl; Var Ftbl; Var Wrstlng; High Hon Roll; Prfct Atten Awd.

DIRKS, MELODEE D; Garden City Sr HS; Garden City, KS; (2); Church Yth Grp; Sec 4-H; Orch; KS ST; Elem Ed.

DIRKS, NANCY S; Wyandotte HS; Kansas City, KS; (3); Cit Awd; Hon Roll; TX Southern U; Pharmcy.

DISHMAN, SARA; Goddard HS; Wichita, KS; (3); Pep Clb; Science Clb; Spanish Clb; SADD; Teachers Aide; Co-Ed Yrbk; Capt Var Socr; French Hon Soc; High Hon Roll; NHS; KS Olympic Dev Soccer Pool Team.

DISHON, KELLY J; Troy HS; Troy, KS; (3); Drama Clb; Letterman Clb; Library Aide; Pep Clb; Speech Tm; School Play; Nwsp; Yrbk; Vllybl; Hon Roll; U Of KS.

DISKIN, MARY K; St Paul HS; Saint Paul, KS; (4); Church Yth Grp; Pep Clb; Speech Tm; Chorus; Church Choir; Rep Soph Cls; Treas Jr Cls; Sec Treas Stu Cncl; Var L Bsktbl; Var L Vllybl.

DISKIN, MONICA A; St Paul HS; Walnut, KS; (3); Church Yth Grp; Quiz Bowl; Scholastic Bowl; Yrbk; VP Frsh Cls; Var JV Vllybl; Hon Roll; NHS; Prfct Atten Awd.

DISRUD, GINGER A; Blue Valley HS; Olathe, KS; (2); Church Yth Grp; Cmnty Wkr; Computer Clb; FCA; Hosp Aide; Church Choir; Drill Tm; Flag Corp; Mrchg Band; Variety Show; Accmplshd Pianist 9 Yrs; Asst Dnc Instrctr; Crmnl Psych/Med.

DITCH, BRANDI; Seaman Sr HS; Topeka, KS; (3); Church Yth Grp; FBLA; FHA; Sec Key Clb; Pep Clb; SADD; Drill Tm; Yrbk; Hon Roll; NHS; KU; Scl Wrk.

DITMER, PAUL A; Seaman Sr HS; Topeka, KS; (3); Church Yth Grp; Cmnty Wkr; Drama Clb; French Clb; Speech Tm; Band; Nwsp; Yrbk; Swmmng; Tennis; Jrnlsm.

DITTMAN, CRYSTAL; White City HS; Woodbine, KS; (2); 2/12; FHA; HOBY; SADD; Chorus; VP Soph Cls; Chrldng; Trk; Vllybl; Hon Roll; NHS; KS ST U; Trvl Agnt.

DITTMAN, MEGAN K; Hope HS; Hope, KS; (4); 4/11; Sec Pres Church Yth Grp; Sec 4-H; FBLA; Pep Clb; SADD; Teachers Aide; Band; Chorus; Yrbk; Ofcr Frsh Cls; Fort Hays ST U; Elem Ed.

DIX, DANICA; Emporia HS; Emporia, KS; (4); Am Leg Aux Girls St; Debate Tm; Letterman Clb; NFL; Sec Pep Clb; Q&S; Nwsp; Treas Jr Cls; Capt Chrldng; Var Trk; Emporia ST U; Bus.

DIX, JANUARI J; Stockton HS; Stockton, KS; (3); VP FHA; Pep Clb; Band; Drill Tm; Pep Band; Stage Crew; Treas Jr Cls; Var Chrldng; Var Pom Pon; NHS; Ft Hays St Univ; Lgl Asst.

DIXON, AMBER; Wichita East HS; Wichita, KS; (4); 111/296; Drama Clb; Girl Scts; Var Capt Chrldng; Var Capt Diving; Var Capt Gym; Var L Pom Pon; Var L Swmmng; Hon Roll; NCA All Amer Chrldng Team, All Star Chrldng Squad; Barton Cty CC; Scl Work.

DIXON, ANITA F; Ottawa HS; Ottawa, KS; (4); 27/145; Art Clb; Cmnty Wkr; 4-H; Teachers Aide; Bsktbl; Powder Puff Ftbl; Score Keeper; Sftbl; Trk; Vllybl; All Acad Tm Bsktbll; Acad Renaissance Awds; Ottawa Univ; Pk& Rec.

DIXON, ARONDA; Wyandotte HS; Kansas City, KS; (4); 18/185; Church Yth Grp; Computer Clb; Library Aide; Office Aide; Teachers Aide; VICA; High Hon Roll; NHS; KU Endwmnt Mrt Prtcpnt; KS Almni Assn Prtcpnt; KS U; Bus.

DIXON, CORY R; Olathe East Sr HS; Olathe, KS; (4); 54/305; German Clb; Intnl Clb; Math Tm; Office Aide; Red Cross Aide; Capt Wrstlng; High Hon Roll; NHS; Hnrble Mntn For Photo; HS Wrstlnghawk Schol; Johnson Cnty CC; Elec Eng.

DIXON, ERIKA J; Halstead HS; Sedgwick, KS; (3); Pep Clb; Spanish Clb; Band; Chorus; Mrchg Band; Pep Band; Var Chrldng; Sftbl; Vllybl; NHS; Stdnt Of Mnth; Girls H-Clb; Kayettes; Advrtsng/Comm/Fash Dsgn.

DIXON, ILSE C; Louisburg HS; Louisburg, KS; (2); Treas Art Clb; Letterman Clb; Math Clb; NFL; Spanish Clb; SADD; Chorus; School Play; Variety Show; JV Var Mgr(s); Ldrshp Awd; U Of KS; Interior Dsgn.

DIXON, JENNY; Ulysses HS; Ulysses, KS; (4); 8/93; Am Leg Aux Girls St; Debate Tm; Teachers Aide; Chorus; School Musical; Tennis; Trk; NHS; TV Pblc Brdcstng; Show Choir; KU; Med.

DIXON, KATIE; Salina HS South; Salina, KS; (1); Church Yth Grp; Pep Clb; Chrldng; Pom Pon; Sftbl; Wt Lftg; Cit Awd; Hon Roll; Pres Acad Fit Awd; Pres Schlr; Tchr.

DIXON, MATT R; Scott City Sr HS; Scott City, KS; (4); Acpl Chr; Band; Chorus; Jazz Band; Mrchg Band; Pep Band; School Musical; Stage Crew; Ofcr Stu Cncl; Golf; KS Salina; Mech Engrng.

DIXON, MELISSA R; Berean Acad; Wichita, KS; (3); Church Yth Grp; Chorus; Church Choir; High Hon Roll; Yth Drama; Teen Ldrshp Cncl.

DIXON JR, PHIL S; Turner HS; Kansas City, KS; (4); 23/189; Am Leg Boys St; Q&S; Ed Nwsp; Pres Stu Cncl; Bsktbl; JV Wrstlng; High Hon Roll; Hon Roll; Jr NHS; NHS; KS Hnr Pgm; Natural Hlprs; Hmcmng King; Bus Admin.

DJAJICH, MIKE T; Olathe East Sr HS; Olathe, KS; (4); 30/300; Church Yth Grp; Band; Jazz Band; Mrchg Band; Pep Band; Variety Show; Bsktbl; Socr; NHS; Pres Acad Fit Awd; Tulane Univ; Arch.

DO, DUY P; Sumner Acad Of Arts & Science; Kansas City, KS; (1); Church Yth Grp; Var Tennis; High Hon Roll.

DOBBINS, JESSICA L; Wichita North HS; Wichita, KS; (3); 22/274; Am Leg Aux Girls St; Cmnty Wkr; GAA; Pep Clb; Varsity Clb; Orch; School Musical; Rep Soph Cls; Rep Jr Cls; Ofcr Stu Cncl; KS St Univ; Arch Eng.

DOBBS, DEBORAH; Kansas City Christian Schl; Gladstone, MO; (4); 15/37; Church Yth Grp; Debate Tm; Office Aide; Pep Clb; Church Choir; Score Keeper; Socr; Vllybl; High Hon Roll; Hon Roll; Piano 1st Pl Awds; Moody Bible Inst; Missionary.

DOBNICK, THY K; Wichita East HS; Wichita, KS; (4); Church Yth Grp; French Clb; Thesps; Chorus; Church Choir; School Musical; School Play; Stage Crew; Variety Show; Rep Frsh Cls; Intnl Baccalaureat Diploma Candidate; U Of KS; Pre-Med; Human Bio.

DOBRATZ, JENNIFER D; Great Bend Sr HS; Dodge City, KS; (2); Math Tm; Band; Flag Corp; Mrchg Band; Vllybl; Hon Roll; Prfct Atten Awd; Env Clb.

DOBRATZ, RYAN A; Shawnee Mission E Sr HS; Shawnee Mission, KS; (2); Latin Clb; Pep Clb; JV Bsktbl; JV Golf; Wt Lftg; Hon Roll.

DOBRAUC, MARY; St Mary's Colgan HS; Pittsburg, KS; (2); 1/42; Scholastic Bowl; Var Bsktbl; Var Sftbl; Var Trk; JV Vllybl; High Hon Roll; Prfct Atten Awd; Math Rlys; Jr Ldrshp/Crwfrd Cty; All Amer Schlr.

DOBRAUC, RACHEL; St Mary's Colgan HS; Pittsburg, KS; (2); 1/40; Quiz Bowl; Bsktbl; Sftbl; Vllybl; Hon Roll; Cmmnctns.

DOBSKI, KEVIN M; Lawrence HS; Lawrence, KS; (2); Church Yth Grp; Cmnty Wkr; Office Aide; Science Clb; Rptr Nwsp; Rptr Yrbk; Rep Frsh Cls; Rep Soph Cls; Intrml Bsktbl; Intrml Ftbl; Nate Awd; Stu Of Mnth 3 Times; Ltrd Ftbl/Bsktbl; Exec Bd Stu Cncl; Boston Coll; Bus/Sprts Adu.

DOBSON, JEAN M; Arkansas City HS; Arkansas City, KS; (2); Church Yth Grp; Drama Clb; FCA; SADD; Church Choir; Orch; School Musical; School Play; Stage Crew; Rep Soph Cls; Fr Comptn 1st Pl; Orch/Drama Lettered; Amer Field Svc; Sprts Physcn.

DOBYNS, SHASTA; Ingalls Jr Sr HS; Ingalls, KS; (3); Cmnty Wkr; GAA; Letterman Clb; Pep Clb; SADD; Teachers Aide; Varsity Clb; Band; Mrchg Band; Pep Band; Most Inspirational Vllybl; Most Imprvd Vllybl; Most Inspirational Trk; GCCC; Math Tchr.

DODD, BONNIE; Clay Ctr Cmty HS; Clay Center, KS; (2); Art Clb; 4-H; FHA; Natl FFA Org; JV Bsktbl; JV Sftbl; 4-H Awd; Hon Roll; Prfct Atten Awd; U Of KS.

DODDER, JAY M; Silver Lake Jr Sr HS; Silver Lake, KS; (3); 18/51; NFL; Quiz Bowl; Scholastic Bowl; Speech Tm; Swing Chorus; Var Bsbl; Var L Bsktbl; Var L Ftbl; Hon Roll; NHS; Bus Admin.

DODDS, LAURA A; Kapaun-Mt Carmel HS; Wichita, KS; (3); Church Yth Grp; Cmnty Wkr; Hosp Aide; Spanish Clb; High Hon Roll; NHS; United Crusaders VP; Crusaders For Life; Ecology Clb.

DODSON, AARON P; Atchison Sr HS; Atchison, KS; (1); Bsktbl; Hon Roll; Dr.

DOEBELE, DUSTIN; Silver Lake Jr Sr HS; Silver Lake, KS; (3); 3/53; Debate Tm; NFL; Scholastic Bowl; Cit Awd; High Hon Roll; NHS; Forensics; Elec Eng.

DOEBLIN, MELISSA R; Wichita Collegiate Schl; Wichita, KS; (3); German Clb; Science Clb; Service Clb; SADD; Nwsp; Tennis; Hon Roll; Envir Club VP; Lit Club; Bio Adventure Club; Bio.

DOHE, KRIS; Sylvan Unified HS; Lincoln, KS; (4); 4/15; Church Yth Grp; Cmnty Wkr; Library Aide; Math Tm; Pep Clb; SADD; Teachers Aide; Band; Mrchg Band; Pep Band; 4-H Camp Cnslr; Frm Bru Ldrshp Camp; Colby CC.

DOHERTY, ANDREW D; Ft Scott HS; Fort Scott, KS; (3); FBLA; JV Bsbl; Intrml Bsktbl; Intrml Wt Lftg; Tiger Paw Awd; Pittsburg ST Univ; MBA.

DOHERTY, KRISTI L; Paola HS; Paola, KS; (4); 13/119; Art Clb; Bus Profs of Am; FCA; FHA; Office Aide; SADD; Vllybl; High Hon Roll; NHS; Prfct Atten Awd; Penn Vly CC; Radiologic Tech.

DOHL, LYLE; Sylvan Unified HS; Sylvan Grove, KS; (3); 3/18; 4-H; Pep Band; School Musical; L Bsktbl; L Ftbl; L Trk; NHS; Church Yth Grp; Quiz Bowl; Speech Tm; St Speech Fest Gold Medal; Ftbl St Chmpns 95; Bsktbl St Chmpns 95-96.

DOHL, MEGAN R; Sylvan Unified HS; Sylvan Grove, KS; (2); Church Yth Grp; Dance Clb; 4-H; Math Tm; Pep Clb; Quiz Bowl; SADD; Band; Chorus; Mrchg Band; AAU Bsktbl Recruit/Miss Bsktbl Showcase 96; Farm Bureau Ldrshp Camp Schlsp 96; 4-H KS City Conf Wnr.

DOHRMAN, APRIL; Rossville HS; Delia, KS; (3); 10/45; Church Yth Grp; FBLA; Letterman Clb; Pep Clb; Teachers Aide; Varsity Clb; Band; Rep Frsh Cls; Rep Soph Cls; Rep Jr Cls; Emporia ST U; Scndry Ed.

DOILE, TRACY; El Dorado HS; El Dorado, KS; (3); 1/137; Am Leg Aux Girls St; VP Sec FCA; Letterman Clb; Flag Corp; Rep Stu Cncl; L Pom Pon; L Sftbl; L Vllybl; High Hon Roll; NHS; Jr Ambassadors Co-Chm; Psych.

DOLAN, AMY J; Shawnee Heights HS; Topeka, KS; (4); Pep Clb; SADD; Teachers Aide; Hon Roll; Schl Play Chldrns Thtr; Care Co; Rtrmnt Hms/Red Cross Wrppng/Day Cr Vol; U Of KS; Psych.

DOLAN, JESSICA C; Salina HS South; Salina, KS; (2); Chorus; Chrldng; KS Univ; Psych.

DOLAN, SHARON; Salina HS South; Salina, KS; (2); Pep Clb; Chorus; Variety Show; JV Chrldng; Hon Roll; Invlvd In Sftbl On A Recrtn Tm; Psych.

DOLEZAL, AIMEE M; Ellsworth HS; Kanopolis, KS; (1); Hon Roll; KS ST Univ; Bus.

DOLINA, JACQUALINE; Eudora HS; Eudora, KS; (4); 10/44; Drama Clb; FBLA; Pep Clb; SADD; Varsity Clb; Drill Tm; Pep Band; School Musical; School Play; Ed Yrbk; Baker U; Phys Thrpy.

DOLL, AMANDA A; Wichita East HS; Wichita, KS; (3); 15/300; Church Yth Grp; Teachers Aide; Yrbk; High Hon Roll; Natl Yth Ldrshp Forum On Med; Wichita ST Univ; Dermatology.

DOLL, JAKE; Rock Creek Jr Sr HS; Westmoreland, KS; (2); 1/65; Math Tm; Quiz Bowl; Band; Jazz Band; Pep Band; Ofcr Stu Cncl; Ofcr Bsbl; Bsktbl; Ftbl; Golf.

DOLSKY, RON A; Wichita Southeast HS; Wichita, KS; (2); 23/408; High Hon Roll; Hon Roll.

DOMANN, MICHELLE R; Jefferson Co North HS; Nortonville, KS; (4); 13/39; SADD; Teachers Aide; Chorus; School Musical; Rep Stu Cncl; Trk; JV Vllybl; Wt Lftg; Hon Roll; KAW Area Techschl; Offc Tech.

DOMEN, CHRISTOPHER H; Wichita East HS; Wichita, KS; (2); Tennis.

DOMINGUEZ, HEATHER R; Oak Grove Baptist Schl; Kansas City, KS; (3); Church Yth Grp; Letterman Clb; Office Aide; Pep Clb; Teachers Aide; Varsity Clb; Chorus; Church Choir; School Musical; Yrbk; Chrstn Character Awd In Bsktbl; JCCC; Dntl Hygiene.

DOMNANISH, SUZANNE E; Central Heights Sr HS; Richmond, KS; (1); Dance Clb; Pep Clb; Science Clb; Spanish Clb; Band; Drill Tm; Mrchg Band; Pep Band; JV Bsktbl; Var Pom Pon; Violin 13 Yrs; KS Univ.

DOMSKY, STEPHANIE M; Atchison Sr HS; Atchison, KS; (1); Hosp Aide; Spanish Clb; Band; Mrchg Band; JV Bsktbl; JV Sftbl; JV Vllybl; High Hon Roll; Hon Roll; Lnchn Chmpns Hnr Rl Stdnts; Crdlgst; KS U; Crdlgst.

DONAHEY, BRENDA R; Blue Valley HS; Stilwell, KS; (4); 1/230; Debate Tm; GAA; Chorus; Ofcr Stu Cncl; Crs Cntry; Sftbl; Gov Hon Prg Awd; High Hon Roll; NHS; Val; NHS; Supt Awd; KS ST U; Archtrl Engrng.

DONAHEY, JASON L; Blue Valley HS; Stilwell, KS; (3); 28/250; Teachers Aide; Varsity Clb; Var Bsktbl.

DONALD, JULIE; Shawnee Mission E Sr HS; Shawnee Mission, KS; (2); Church Yth Grp; Cmnty Wkr; Natl Beta Clb; Q&S; Church Choir; Drill Tm; Rptr Nwsp; High Hon Roll; Spanish NHS; Ambassadors.

DONALDSON, REBECCA; Atchison Sr HS; Atchison, KS; (2); Church Yth Grp; Girl Scts; Band; Yrbk; Sec Soph Cls; Var Bsktbl; Var L Sftbl; Var Vllybl; Stat Wrstlng; Hon Roll; Law.

DONLEY, CLINT; Ellsworth HS; Lincoln, KS; (4); 7/69; 4-H; Treas Natl FFA Org; VP Varsity Clb; Treas Sr Cls; Capt Ftbl; Capt Wrstlng; High Hon Roll; Pres Acad Fit Awd; Band; Mrchg Band; KS Rgnts Hon Schlr; KS St U; Anml Sci/Indstry.

DONLEY, JENNY L; Ellsworth HS; Lincoln, KS; (2); Church Yth Grp; Drama Clb; 4-H; GAA; Natl FFA Org; Pep Clb; Band; Chorus; Church Choir; Mrchg Band; Horses; Natl Mrt Sci Awd; KS ST Univ; Ag Bus; Mgmt.

DONLEY, LAURA E; Ellsworth HS; Ellsworth, KS; (2); 28/100; 4-H; GAA; Letterman Clb; Sec Natl FFA Org; Band; Mrchg Band; Pep Band; Ofcr Stu Cncl; Var L Bsktbl; Hon Roll; Kayettes Schl Svc Chprsn; Pediatric Nrsng.

DONLEY, MARTHA; Crest HS; Colony, KS; (3); 1/24; Church Yth Grp; Treas Rptr Drama Clb; FHA; German Clb; HOBY; Letterman Clb; Natl FFA Org; School Play; Bsktbl; High Hon Roll; KS Health Care Assn Yng Adult Vol Yr 95; Trvlng Bsktbl Tm; Top 10% German Stu; Ecology.

DONLEY, MARY ANNE; Ellsworth HS; Ellsworth, KS; (4); 5/69; Church Yth Grp; Cmnty Wkr; 4-H; Service Clb; Teachers Aide; Band; Chorus; Church Choir; High Hon Roll; St Schlr; Sterling Coll; Elem Ed.

DONN, TRAVIS; Turner HS; Bonner Springs, KS; (4); 10/196; Chess Clb; Letterman Clb; Science Clb; Ftbl; Wrstlng; High Hon Roll; Hon Roll; Jr NHS; NHS.

DONNELL, MARIA; Sumner Acad Of Arts And Sci; Kansas City, KS; (2); Church Yth Grp; Latin Clb; Pep Clb; Spanish Clb; SADD; Church Choir; Orch; Capt Var Chrldng; Spellman Coll; Dntstry.

DONNELLY, AMY M; Bishop Miege HS; Leawood, KS; (1); 8/250; Church Yth Grp; Debate Tm; Hosp Aide; Treas Soph Cls; Capt Sftbl; High Hon Roll; Forensics; Dr.

DONNELLY, BETH; Rossville HS; Silver Lake, KS; (4); 6/40; Dance Clb; FBLA; Letterman Clb; Teachers Aide; Band; Drill Tm; Pep Band; School Musical; Golf; Mgr(s); Washburn U; Math Ed.

DONNELLY, CHRIS L; Olathe East Sr HS; Olathe, KS; (2); Drama Clb; Quiz Bowl; Spanish Clb; Thesps; Stage Crew; Ed Yrbk; Hon Roll; KS ST Univ; Elec Eng.

DONNELLY, KRISTEN; Washington HS; Kansas City, KS; (2); Church Yth Grp; Drama Clb; Hosp Aide; Pep Clb; Chorus; School Musical; Rptr Nwsp; Hon Roll; Navy Ofcr/Pediatric Nurse.

DONNELLY, KYLE; Manhattan HS; Manhattan, KS; (4); 70/388; Boy Scts; Church Yth Grp; Science Clb; Spanish Clb; Teachers Aide; Var Ftbl; Var Trk; Var Wt Lftg; High Hon Roll; NHS; Bowlng League; Smmr League Bsbl; IM Bsktbl; KS ST U; Engrng.

DONNER, DOUG K; Thomas More Prep-Marion HS; Hays, KS; (2); 39/85; Boy Scts; Church Yth Grp; Debate Tm; Band; Mrchg Band; Pep Band; Var L Golf; Math Tm; Wt Lftg; Hon Roll; Math.

DONOHUE, TIM A; Bishop Miege HS; Overland Park, KS; (2); 7/172; French Clb; Quiz Bowl; High Hon Roll; Natl Yng Ldrs Conf; Acad Excl.

DONOVAN, CATIMA M; Horton HS; Horton, KS; (3); 3/39; Church Yth Grp; FCA; Quiz Bowl; SADD; Band; Rep Stu Cncl; Stat Trk; High Hon Roll; Hon Roll; NHS; Acad Lttr; MO Western ST Coll; Pre-Med.

DONOVAN, JENNY C; Bishop Carroll Catholic HS; Wichita, KS; (3); Church Yth Grp; Red Cross Aide; SADD; Band; Mrchg Band; Orch; Pep Band; Sec Frsh Cls; Bsktbl; Vllybl; Art.

DOOLEY, RYAN MICHAEL; Maur Hill Prep Schl; Atchison, KS; (2); School Play; Rptr Nwsp; Bsktbl; Ftbl; Wt Lftg; High Hon Roll; Riding 4 Wheeler; KS ST U.

DOOLITTLE, PHILLIP; Sumner Acad Of Arts & Science; Kansas City, KS; (3); Cmnty Wkr; JA; Quiz Bowl; Spanish Clb; Ofcr Stu Cncl; High Hon Roll; NHS; Spanish NHS; Chem/Envmntl Eng.

DOORNBOS, CALE J; El Dorado HS; El Dorado, KS; (4); 32/150; Am Leg Boys St; Church Yth Grp; 4-H; Letterman Clb; Var L Ftbl; Var L Wrstlng; Hon Roll; NHS; Prfct Atten Awd; Spanish Clb; 2x Hnrb Mntn Wrstlng, Hnrb Mntn All St Acad Wrstlng; KS ST U; Landscp Arch.

DOORNBOS, JACK; El Dorado HS; El Dorado, KS; (2); 4-H; Letterman Clb; SADD; Capt Frsh Cls; Capt Soph Cls; JV Var Ftbl; Wt Lftg; Var Wrstlng; Wrstlng St Qlfr 96; Scndry Ed.

DOORNBOS, JAY A; El Dorado HS; El Dorado, KS; (3); 29/144; Am Leg Boys St; Church Yth Grp; 4-H; Letterman Clb; SADD; Treas Frsh Cls; Treas Soph Cls; Treas Jr Cls; JV Var Ftbl; Wt Lftg; Ldrs Inflncng Ftr Exclnc; Sec Ed.

DOOSE, JASON R; Blue Valley Northwest HS; Loveland, OH; (1); Church Yth Grp; Gym; Hon Roll; Floyd Krteck Awd; MO And KS St Champ Lvl 4 In Gymnstcs; KU; Eng.

DORELL, CHEYENNE; Highland HS; Highland, KS; (2); Church Yth Grp; Cmnty Wkr; 4-H; Pep Clb; Acpl Chr; Band; Chorus; Drill Tm; Mrchg Band; Orch; Cast Mem In Comm Play; Singer In Chrch Praise Band; Babysit For Several Families; Interpreter For Hearing Imprd.

DORHMAN, APRIL Y; Rossville HS; Delia, KS; (3); 9/46; Cmnty Wkr; French Clb; FBLA; Letterman Clb; Teachers Aide; Varsity Clb; Drill Tm; Var L Vllybl; High Hon Roll; NHS; St Trk & Bsktbl; Elem Or Scndry Ed.

DORN, JESSICA S; Goodland HS; Goodland, KS; (2); 18/87; Chorus; Cit Awd; Hon Roll; AFS; Citizenship Awd For Helping Handicapped Stu; Bus.

DORNES, JOEY D; Wellsville Jr Sr HS; Rantoul, KS; (2); Sec Frsh Cls; Hon Roll; BUS.

DORR, CHRISTINE; Bishop Ward HS; Kansas City, KS; (2); 16/100; Drama Clb; Pep Clb; School Musical; Sec Frsh Cls; Pres Soph Cls; JV Chrldng; Hon Roll; Peer; KS ST U; Interior Dsgn.

DORSEY, BROOKE A; Topeka West HS; Topeka, KS; (2); Church Yth Grp; French Clb; Drill Tm; Rep Stu Cncl; Capt Chrldng; Trk; Hon Roll; Pres Acad Fit Awd; ROTC; Mgr(s); Selected For Schl Conflict Mgr Team; Black Stu Union; Spellman; Surgeon.

DORSSOM, ERIN; Perry Lecompton HS; Lecompton, KS; (4); 1/70; VP FHA; Pep Clb; SADD; VP Stu Cncl; Tennis; Gov Hon Prg Awd; NHS; Pres Acad Fit Awd; St Schlr; Val; U Of KS; Ed; Tchr.

DORSSOM, STEPHANIE S; Atchison Sr HS; Atchison, KS; (4); Debate Tm; Teachers Aide; DECA; Highland Univ; Paralgl.

DORT, RACHEL L; Washington HS; Kansas City, KS; (3); Key Clb; Teachers Aide; Band; Mrchg Band; Pep Band; Sftbl; Wt Lftg; KS Univ.

DORVILLERS, SUMMER; Baldwin HS; Baldwin City, KS; (2); FHA; Varsity Clb; Chrldng; Golf; Mgr(s); Vllybl; Wrstlng; Co Medial Test; KS U; Child Psych.

DORZWEILER, ERIC; Ellis HS; Ellis, KS; (4); 19/41; Church Yth Grp; Natl FFA Org; School Play; 4-H Awd; Hon Roll; Prfct Atten Awd; St Schlr; Cmnty Wkr; Sec Treas 4-H; Quiz Bowl; De Kalb Ag Accmplshmnt Awd; Hugh O'Brien Ldrsp Awd; Farm Bureau Ldrsp Amer Conf Rep KS; Northwest KS Tech Schl; Comm.

DORZWEILER, RICHARD; Hays HS; Catharine, KS; (4); 29/209; Teachers Aide; Bsktbl; Crs Cntry; Mgr(s); Trk; Wt Lftg; Cit Awd; DAR Awd; Hon Roll; NHS; All Acad-Ath Team; Var Ltr Wnnr; Hardest Worker Awd; Ft Hays ST Univ; German.

DOSS, ADAM; Wichita Heights HS; Wichita, KS; (3); Bus Profs of Am; Debate Tm; German Clb; Hosp Aide; VP JA; NFL; Quiz Bowl; Scholastic Bowl; Science Clb; Speech Tm; Sci Olympd; Intl Stdnt Forum; Stock Mrkt Club.

DOSS, JOSHUA L; Turner HS; Kansas City, KS; (2); Var Ftbl; JV Trk; Wt Lftg; Optimist Intnl Essay Cont 3rd Pl; Eng Tchr.

DOSS, LINDSAY M; Turner HS; Kansas City, KS; (3); German Clb; Science Clb; SADD; Thesps; Varsity Clb; Chorus; Chrldng; Trk; Vllybl; Vol St Marys Food Kitchen; Habitat Humanity; NE; Criminologist.

DOTSON, ABBY L; Shawnee Heights HS; Topeka, KS; (1); Church Yth Grp; Pep Clb; Church Choir; High Hon Roll; Hon A Clb.

DOTSON, BRANDI A; Wichita Heights HS; Wichita, KS; (4); 1/259; Bus Profs of Am; Church Yth Grp; Cmnty Wkr; SADD; Teachers Aide; JV Vllybl; Hon Roll; NHS; Pres Acad Fit Awd; Val; Stock Market Clb 2nd In ST; Galaxy Awd Nom For Bus Entrepreneurship; Wichita ST Univ; Child Psych.

DOTY, NATHAN; Home Schl; Wichita, KS; (3); Church Yth Grp; Church Choir; Yrbk; Var Capt Socr; Philadelphia Coll Of The Bible.

DOTY, SHANNON L; Arkansas City HS; Arkansas City, KS; (3); 25/200; Cmnty Wkr; Hosp Aide; SADD; Teachers Aide; High Hon Roll; Pres Acad Fit Awd; OK ST U; Acctng.

DOTZOUR, MELANIE L; Wichita Southeast HS; Wichita, KS; (2); 25/418; Church Yth Grp; FCA; Acpl Chr; Chorus; Church Choir; Variety Show; JV Socr; Hon Roll; NHS.

DOUBRAVA, TRINA D; Ellsworth HS; Ellsworth, KS; (2); 1/90; Church Yth Grp; Sec Treas Key Clb; Letterman Clb; Band; Chorus; Mrchg Band; Pep Band; Rptr Nwsp; Bsktbl; Tennis; Pops Choir; Natl Ldrshp/Svc Awd; All Amer Schlr; Certfd Nrs Aide; CNA; U Of KS; PT.

DOUD, AMANDA A; Mankato Jr Sr HS; Mankato, KS; (3); Church Yth Grp; Drama Clb; 4-H; Natl FFA Org; NFL; Pep Clb; Quiz Bowl; Thesps; Band; Chorus; Natl FFA Chorus; St Hnr Choir; Cath Yth Org VP; Cloud Cty CC; Nrsng.

DOUGHTY, BRYAN; Maize HS; Maize, KS; (4); Debate Tm; German Clb; Letterman Clb; Science Clb; SADD; Hon Roll; Lawyer.

DOUGHTY, VAN O; Marmaton Valley Jr Sr HS; Kincaid, KS; (2); Natl FFA Org.

DOUGLAS, AARON J; Lansing HS; Lansing, KS; (4); 43/138; Hon Roll; Taekwondo; Explorers Police Cadet Pgm; Military Svc.

DOUGLAS, JONATHAN E; Olathe East Sr HS; Olathe, KS; (2); Church Yth Grp; French Clb; Spanish Clb; Church Choir; JV Bsktbl; JV Ftbl; Hon Roll; Prfct Atten Awd; U Of KS; Bus Mngmt.

DOUGLAS, KACY B; Marmaton Valley Jr Sr HS; Iola, KS; (3); 2/38; Church Yth Grp; Drama Clb; 4-H; VP FBLA; Letterman Clb; Math Tm; NFL; Pep Clb; Chorus; Pep Band; Yth Ctr Vol; Chm 4 H Comm; Natl Yth Ldrshp Conf; Cmptrs/Grphc Dsgn/Cmmrcl Art.

DOUTHART, HEATHER C; Washburn Rural HS; Auburn, KS; (2); Yrbk; FHA; Acpl Chr; JV Vllybl; Cit Awd; High Hon Roll; Hon Roll; Emporia ST Univ; Scndry Ed.

DOVE, KATE; Kapaun-Mt Carmel HS; Wichita, KS; (4); 39/164; Church Yth Grp; French Clb; Hosp Aide; Quiz Bowl; Service Clb; SADD; Teachers Aide; Varsity Clb; Chorus; High Hon Roll; Rockhurst; Pre-Med.

DOVER, JAMEY A; Newton Sr HS; Newton, KS; (2); Boy Scts; Church Yth Grp; Library Aide; Stage Crew; Variety Show; Var L Ftbl; Var Trk; Wt Lftg; BYU; Forestry.

DOVER, LAURA A; Bishop Miege HS; Shawnee Mission, KS; (3); #8 in class; Church Yth Grp; Hosp Aide; SADD; Chorus; Rep Stu Cncl; Var Trk; Var Vllybl; High Hon Roll; NHS; Campus Ministry Team.

DOWD, KELLY E; Bishop Miege HS; Overland Park, KS; (3); 54/170; French Clb; Hosp Aide; JV Socr; Intrml Vllybl; Hon Roll; KS St Univ; Ed.

DOWDALL, JAYME; Blue Valley HS; Olathe, KS; (2); Church Yth Grp; Chorus; Co-Capt Drill Tm; School Musical; Sec Frsh Cls; Sec Soph Cls; High Hon Roll; Hon Roll; Church Choir; All St Choir; 1 Rating At St Vocal Solo Cont; Blue Valley Optimist Clb Excl In Ldrshp Awd; Music Ed.

DOWELL, JOHN R; Ottawa HS; Ottawa, KS; (3); Cmnty Wkr; FCA; Band; Jazz Band; Pep Band; Variety Show; Crs Cntry; Trk; DAR Awd; Hon Roll; KS ST; Engrng.

DOWLING, TAMMIE; Protection Schl; Protection, KS; (1); Letterman Clb; Pep Clb; Band; Chorus; Mrchg Band; Pep Band; School Play; JV Var Bsktbl; JV Var Vllybl; High Hon Roll; Bus Mgmt.

DOWLING, TANNER; Minneola Schl; Dodge City, KS; (2); Church Yth Grp; FCA; 4-H; Letterman Clb; Speech Tm; Chorus; Bsktbl; Ftbl; Golf; 4-H Awd; Livestck Judgng Team; KS Livestck Assn; Livestck Assn; KS ST U.

DOWLING, THOMAS; Thomas More Prep-Marion HS; Hays, KS; (1); Church Yth Grp; Debate Tm; 4-H; Service Clb; Spanish Clb; Speech Tm; Band; JV Bsktbl; JV Ftbl; JV Golf; KSU; Law.

DOWLING, TREESA J; Wellsville Jr Sr HS; Wellsville, KS; (3); 1/60; Church Yth Grp; FCA; FBLA; Intnl Clb; Math Tm; Band; Church Choir; Mrchg Band; Vllybl; High Hon Roll; KS City Yth Symphony; Interlochen Arts Camp; World Yth Symphony Orch; Ottawa Suzuki Stings; Music Violin & Conducting.

DOWNEY, ERIN E; Newton Sr HS; Newton, KS; (4); 10/211; Church Yth Grp; French Clb; VP Key Clb; Office Aide; Chorus; Swing Chorus; Var L Bsktbl; Var L Trk; Var L Vllybl; High Hon Roll; DARE Role Model; U Of KS; Nrsing.

DOWNING, JAMES; Wichita South HS; Wichita, KS; (4); Am Leg Boys St; German Clb; ROTC; Band; Jazz Band; Variety Show; VP Stu Cncl; Var Tennis; Hon Roll; St Schlr; KS Univ; Law.

DOWNING, JULIE A; Salina HS South; Salina, KS; (2); Church Yth Grp; FCA; Teachers Aide; Chorus; Church Choir; Sftbl; Trk; Vllybl; Hon Roll; Mid Amer Nazarene.

DOWNING, MATT D; Topeka HS; Topeka, KS; (3); Chorus; Church Choir; Haskell JC.

DOWNING, SHAYE; Atchison Sr HS; Atchison, KS; (2); 1/114; Church Yth Grp; Debate Tm; Spanish Clb; SADD; Varsity Clb; Band; Drill Tm; Mrchg Band; Pep Band; Sec Frsh Cls; Kayetes; Law.

DOWNING, TARA B; Field Kindley Mem Sr HS; Coffeyville, KS; (3); Cmnty Wkr; French Clb; German Clb; Yrbk; Chrldng; Mgr(s); Tennis; Hon Roll; NHS; Debate Tm; Cath Yth Org VP; Pittsburg ST Univ; Phys Ther.

DOWNS, JESSE A; Buhler HS; Hutchinson, KS; (2); Church Yth Grp; Cmnty Wkr; Science Clb; Chorus; Church Choir; Mrchg Band; Pep Band; Stat Bsktbl; Mgr(s); High Hon Roll; KS Univ; Comp Pgmng.

DOWNS, NATHAN V; Baxter Springs HS; Joplin, MO; (3); FBLA; Psych.

DOXON, ELIZABETH D; Trego Comm HS; Ogallah, KS; (2); Debate Tm; Math Tm; NFL; Quiz Bowl; Scholastic Bowl; Science Clb; Spanish Clb; SADD; Pep Band; High Hon Roll; Zoolgy/Vet Sci.

DOYLE, CHRIS M; St Thomas Aquinas HS; Overland Park, KS; (4); FCA; Ofcr Bsbl; Ftbl; Wt Lftg; Hon Roll; All Metro Ftbl Team; MVP 95-96; Outstdng Schltc Achvmt Awd; KU.

DOYLE, KEELY S; Tipton HS; Cawker City, KS; (4); 3/12; Church Yth Grp; Cmnty Wkr; Drama Clb; Math Tm; Pep Clb; Band; Chorus; Church Choir; Mrchg Band; Pep Band; Voice Of Dem Schl Wnnr; Twin Lakeslge Schol Ath Awd; Barton CC.

DOYLE, LAURA M; Labette Co HS; Parsons, KS; (2); FBLA; Band; Hon Roll; Sigma Mu; Lang Masters.

DOYLE, RYAN P; Sumner Acad Of Arts & Science; Kansas City, KS; (3); Hosp Aide; Latin Clb; Spanish Clb; Ftbl; Hon Roll; Taking IB Class; KS U; Sci/Bio/Chem.

DRAGOO, VANESSA R; Northeast Magnet HS; Wichita, KS; (3); 24/99; Art Clb; Church Yth Grp; Cmnty Wkr; Drama Clb; Girl Scts; ROTC; Teachers Aide; Drill Tm; School Play; Phtg Nwsp; Achvng Wmn Sci; Natl Hnr Art Soc; KS Univ; Ed/Bus.

DRAKE, ADAM D; Bishop Miege HS; Leawood, KS; (2); 32/163; Boy Scts; JV Bsktbl; JV Crs Cntry; JV Ftbl; Var L Trk; High Hon Roll; Hon Roll; Eagle Scout.

DRAKE, ALICIA D; Great Bend Sr HS; Great Bend, KS; (4); 73/263; Pep Clb; Spanish Clb; SADD; Yrbk; Sftbl; Vllybl; High Hon Roll; Hon Roll; Pres Acad Fit Awd; Pres Schlr; Intrntnl Ordr Of Jbs Dghtrs; Barton CCC; Lbrl Arts.

DRAKE, ANGELA; Kansas City Christian Schl; Leawood, KS; (3); Chorus; Rptr Soph Cls; Var L Chrldng; Var L Trk; High Hon Roll; NHS; Var Chrldng Discipline Awd 96; Chrldng Enthusiasm Awd 93; Var Trck Displn Awd 96.

DRAKE, DAMON; Eureka Jr Sr HS; Eureka, KS; (3); 6/50; Office Aide; Thesps; Band; Mrchg Band; Pep Band; School Play; Stage Crew; Golf; High Hon Roll; Hon Roll; Emporia St; Music.

DRAKE, DAPHNE L; South Barber HS; Kiowa, KS; (4); 14/28; Red Cross Aide; SADD; Teachers Aide; Band; Chorus; Sec Soph Cls; Treas Jr Cls; VP Sr Cls; Sec Stu Cncl; Var Capt Bsktbl; Bronze, Silver & Gold Hnr Pins; Ftbl Homccmng Qn 95-96; Pop Choir; Pratt CC; Pre-Elem Ed.

DRAKE, HEIDI; Peabody-Burns Jr Sr HS; Burns, KS; (3); 1/30; Church Yth Grp; 4-H; Girl Scts; Band; Chorus; Mrchg Band; Pep Band; School Musical; Swing Chorus; Frnscs; Auto Mech.

DRAKE, LINNAH A; Peabody-Burns Jr Sr HS; Burns, KS; (3); School Musical; Yrbk; VP Frsh Cls; JV Var Bsktbl; High Hon Roll; NHS.

DRAKE, MICAH; Louisburg HS; Louisburg, KS; (2); FCA; Letterman Clb; Chorus; JV Var Bsktbl; JV Var Ftbl; Var Trk; Hon Roll.

DRAKE, NICHOLAS J; Pleasanton HS; Pleasanton, KS; (2); Church Yth Grp; JV Bsktbl; High Hon Roll; Hon Roll; NHS; Harvard; Law.

DRAPER, CRYSTAL H; Turner HS; Kansas City, KS; (2); Band; Mrchg Band; JV Bsktbl; Var Chrldng; JV Sftbl; Hon Roll; Jr NHS; Coll Plnng Club; U Of KS; Nrsng.

DRAPER, TANYA; Colby Sr HS; Colby, KS; (4); 11/99; Church Yth Grp; Sec French Clb; Sec Spanish Clb; Teachers Aide; VP Frsh Cls; VP Soph Cls; VP Jr Cls; Pres Stu Cncl; JV Bsktbl; 4-H Awd; KS ST U; Scl Work.

DRAY, MELISSA L; Lawrence HS; Lawrence, KS; (2); Dance Clb; 4-H; Thesps; Acpl Chr; Band; School Play; JV Var Chrldng; Var Gym; JV Var Trk; Hon Roll; 1st Pl Natl Dance Cmptn Soloist; Song Ldr For Chrch; Perf Arts.

DREES, CHRIS T; Thomas More Prep-Marion HS; Hays, KS; (2); 38/74; Ofcr Stu Cncl; JV Bsktbl; JV Var Ftbl; JV Var Trk; Wt Lftg; Hon Roll; Natural Hlprs; Columbian Squires.

DREHER, CARY; Quinter Jr Sr HS; Quinter, KS; (1); Church Yth Grp; Debate Tm; FCA; Chorus; Church Choir; School Play; Rptr Nwsp; Var Chrldng; Cit Awd; High Hon Roll; Frosh Ensemble; St Forensics & Music.

DREHER, JENNIFER A; El Dorado HS; El Dorado, KS; (2); Church Yth Grp; Drama Clb; FCA; SADD; Thesps; Chorus; School Musical; School Play; High Hon Roll; Hon Roll; KAY Bd Soph Yr; Med.

DREHER, JESSICA R; Halstead HS; Halstead, KS; (1); Church Yth Grp; German Clb; Pep Clb; Service Clb; Rep Frsh Cls; JV Bsktbl; JV Vllybl; Hon Roll.

DREHER, KIMBERLY; Thomas More Prep-Marion HS; Hays, KS; (4); 26/98; Church Yth Grp; Trk; Vllybl; High Hon Roll; Hon Roll; Hnrbl Mntn Tm Vlybl; Three Tm ST Trck Qlfr; Fort Hays ST Univ; Bus/Fin.

DREHER, LEANN; Trego Comm HS; Wa Keeney, KS; (2); Pres Church Yth Grp; Dance Clb; German Clb; Letterman Clb; Math Tm; Pep Clb; Science Clb; SADD; Band; Chorus; Lions Clb Awd; KAYS Sec & VP; FT Hays ST U; Eng Tchr.

DREIER, PATRICK M; Salina HS Central; Salina, KS; (2); Church Yth Grp; Natl FFA Org; Band; Mrchg Band; Pep Band; Golf; Pres Acad Fit Awd; OK ST Univ; Sci.

DREILING, BRETT F; Victoria HS; Victoria, KS; (2); Letterman Clb; SADD; VICA; Bsktbl; Ftbl; Trk; Wt Lftg; Hon Roll; NHS; Pres Acad Fit Awd.

DREILING, ERIN M; Buhler HS; Hutchinson, KS; (2); Boy Scts; Office Aide; Band; Jazz Band; Mrchg Band; Pep Band; School Musical; JV Bsbl; Intrml Wt Lftg; JV Wrstlng; Ordthdntcs.

DREILING, KENDRA; Hays HS; Hays, KS; (4); DECA; Teachers Aide; Nwsp; Yrbk; Intrml Powder Puff Ftbl; Hon Roll; St DECA Cmptn 1st Pl; DECA Silver Mrt Awd; Outstdng Comm Svc Awd; Natl DECA Conf; Mrktg.

DRELING, NATASHA M; Victoria HS; Victoria, KS; (2); Letterman Clb; SADD; Varsity Clb; Rep Frsh Cls; Rep Soph Cls; Rep Jr Cls; Rep Stu Cncl; Var L Trk; Cit Awd; NHS; Ft Hays ST.

DRENNAN, LINDSAY A; Riverton Schl; Galena, KS; (3); 3/60; Church Yth Grp; Cmnty Wkr; FCA; Letterman Clb; Science Clb; Rep Stu Cncl; Bsktbl; Cit Awd; 4-H Awd; High Hon Roll; FHA St Ofcr; Bio.

DRESCHER, ARWEN E; Goddard HS; Goddard, KS; (3); Cmnty Wkr; Drama Clb; German Clb; Girl Scts; Pep Clb; Q&S; Thesps; Chorus; Stage Crew; Variety Show; Creative Wrtng.

DRESSLER, DEANNA; Shawnee Mission N HS; Shawnee Mission, KS; (4); 47/346; Church Yth Grp; Q&S; Sec Spanish Clb; Pres Acpl Chr; Var Capt Bsktbl; Var Vllybl; High Hon Roll; NHS; Pres Schlr; St Schlr; Cornell Coll; Pre-Law/Hum.

DRESSLER, MICHAEL J; Manhattan HS; Manhattan, KS; (2); 1/430; Chess Clb; Quiz Bowl; Scholastic Bowl; Spanish Clb; Band; Orch; NHS; Natl Fnlst MJNA Selmer Wdwnd Cmptn 95; Emerson Elec Co Gvrnrs Schlrshp Interlocken Arts Camp 96; Med/Msc.

DREVITS, ELIZABETH; Atchison Sr HS; Atchison, KS; (1); Band; Mrchg Band; Pep Band; Tennis; High Hon Roll; Hon Roll; Comm Theater; Piano Lessons; Voice Lessons/Recitals.

DRICKEY, KIRSTEN; Norton Comm HS; Norton, KS; (4); 6/43; Am Leg Aux Girls St; Church Yth Grp; Model UN; Pep Clb; Q&S; Scholastic Bowl; SADD; Band; Drill Tm; Flag Corp; 2nd Pl Infogrphcs KSPA Cont; Jrnlsm.

DRIETZ, RAGAN P; Liberal HS; Liberal, KS; (4); 67/210; FTA; Office Aide; Teachers Aide; Var Bsbl; Bsktbl; Var Ftbl; Wt Lftg; Hon Roll; All-Western Ath Conf Ftbl; Power Trng Stu Of The Yr; Offensive Lineman Of The Yr; Wichita St Univ; Phy Thrpst.

DRIVER, LAURA J; Williamsburg Schl; Pomona, KS; (2); 1/23; Pres 4-H; Pres Natl FFA Org; Band; VP Frsh Cls; Var L Bsktbl; Ofcr Stu Cncl; Var L Vllybl; High Hon Roll; VP NHS; 4-H Awd.

DRIVER, LEE A; Williamsburg Schl; Pomona, KS; (1); 1/20; FCA; 4-H; Natl FFA Org; Acpl Chr; Band; Chorus; Pres Frsh Cls; Var L Bsktbl; Var L Ftbl; L Var Trk.

DROGE, JUSTIN LEON; Shawnee Heights Sr HS; Tecumseh, KS; (2); FBLA; JV Bsbl; High Hon Roll.

DROST, SERITA M; Hayden HS; Topeka, KS; (2); Cmnty Wkr; Spanish Clb; Teachers Aide; Orch; Crs Cntry; Trk; Hon Roll; 1st Pl MADD Poster Cont; Rel Cls Asst Tchr; Optimist Clb Concession Stand Vol; Emporia ST Univ; HS Eng Tchr.

DROSTE, NICHOLAS C; Manhattan HS; Manhattan, KS; (2); Thesps; Nwsp; JV Ftbl; JV Trk; Wt Lftg; JV Wrstlng; Hon Roll; Armed Forces.

DROWN, ELI J; Basehor Linwood HS; Tonganoxie, KS; (3); Art Clb; Chess Clb; Church Yth Grp; JA; Quiz Bowl; Scholastic Bowl; Teachers Aide; JV Bsbl; JV Var Ftbl; JV Wt Lftg; 4 Yr Univ; Grphc Engr/Md.

DRUM, BRANDI; Silver Lake Jr Sr HS; Silver Lake, KS; (1); 8/52; Church Yth Grp; Chorus; Yrbk; Stat Bsktbl; Score Keeper; JV Var Sftbl; Trk; Vllybl; Hon Roll.

DRUMM, TIA M; Labette Co HS; Altamont, KS; (2); Church Yth Grp; FCA; Letterman Clb; SADD; Chorus; School Musical; Var Chrldng; Hon Roll; Libry Clb; Ozark Chrstn Col.

DRUMRIGHT, LEANNE; Ottawa HS; Ottawa, KS; (2); JV Var Bsktbl; JV Var Trk; JV Vllybl; Cit Awd; High Hon Roll; Pres Acad Fit Awd; Teenport; O Clb; U KS; Medicine.

DRUMRIGHT, WHITNEY; Ottawa HS; Ottawa, KS; (3); Am Leg Aux Girls St; GAA; Rep Soph Cls; Rep Jr Cls; Pres Stu Cncl; Var Bsktbl; Var Trk; Var Vllybl; High Hon Roll; NHS; Attnd City Cmmssn Bnqt For Top 5% Of Class; K ST; Pre-Med/Rdlgy.

DRYDEN, JAIME; St John Jr Sr HS; Saint John, KS; (3); 9/45; Church Yth Grp; Cmnty Wkr; FHA; Pep Clb; Red Cross Aide; SADD; Band; Chorus; Church Choir; Mrchg Band; Kayettes; Natl Amer Hist Awd; Lettrd Sprts; ST Tennis; Barton Cty CC; Med Fld.

DRYDEN, SARAH; Larned HS; Larned, KS; (2); Church Yth Grp; Pep Clb; Band; Chorus; Sec Jazz Band; Mrchg Band; Pep Band; Sftbl; High Hon Roll; Hon Roll; Les Chantees Pres; Elem Educ.

DUARTE, LOURDES M; Arkansas City HS; Arkansas City, KS; (4); 47/170; Drama Clb; Sec FTA; Quiz Bowl; Scholastic Bowl; Teachers Aide; Band; Drm Mjr(t); Mrchg Band; Orch; Pep Band; ST Union Bnk Schlsp; Outstdng Stdnt; Cowley Cty CC; Intnl Bus.

DUBBERT, RACHEL; Downs HS; Downs, KS; (4); 1/21; Treas FHA; Girl Scts; HOBY; Treas Sr Cls; Bsktbl; Chrldng; Trk; High Hon Roll; Val; Pres Acad Fit Awd; Dwns Hnr Soc; KS ST U; Gen Engrng.

DUBIN, JOSEPH; Blue Valley North HS; Leawood, KS; (3); 8/222; Cmnty Wkr; Quiz Bowl; Scholastic Bowl; Temple Yth Grp; Mrchg Band; Orch; Var Tennis; Var Wrstlng; NHS; St Schlr; Tympanist; Acad Decathlon; Racquetball.

DUBIN, SARA; Olathe North Sr HS; Olathe, KS; (3); 33/391; Church Yth Grp; Sec Drama Clb; Spanish Clb; Thesps; Church Choir; Stage Crew; JV Swmmng; High Hon Roll; NHS; Pres Acad Fit Awd; Chrstn Ldrshp Inst; Cnslr.

DUBIN, WILLIAM J; Santa Fe Trail Jr HS; Olathe, KS; (1); Church Yth Grp; Nwsp; L Ftbl; JV Swmmng; L Trk; High Hon Roll; Prfct Atten Awd; Pres Acad Fit Awd; Babe Ruth Bsbl; Sci Olympiad; US Naval Acad; Soc Sci.

DUCHAN, ANDY L; Field Kindley Mem Sr HS; Coffeyville, KS; (4); 1/130; Church Yth Grp; French Clb; Teachers Aide; High Hon Roll; NHS; Val; Wichita ST U; Arspc Engrng.

DUCKETT, SHIRIKA L; Wichita North HS; Wichita, KS; (3); Teachers Aide; Band; Ofcr Frsh Cls; Ofcr Soph Cls; Ofcr Jr Cls; Ofcr Stu Cncl; Crs Cntry; Trk; Hon Roll; Early Chldhd Ed.

DUDLEY, TIFFANY J; Topeka West HS; Topeka, KS; (3); Spanish Clb; SADD; Chorus; Orch; Mgr(s); Swmmng; Hon Roll.

DUFFETT, SHANNON R; Paola HS; Paola, KS; (3); Drama Clb; Teachers Aide; School Play; Stage Crew; High Hon Roll; NHS; Enviro Clb; Mar Bio.

DUFFEY, DAVID W; Salina HS South; Salina, KS; (3); 10/300; Am Leg Boys St; Church Yth Grp; Computer Clb; Debate Tm; Math Tm; NFL; Quiz Bowl; Science Clb; Teachers Aide; Band; Sr Pres ; Gctl; ESSI/KSU; KS ST U.

DUFFY, COLLEEN; Eureka Jr Sr HS; Eureka, KS; (3); 1/53; Am Leg Aux Girls St; Science Clb; Spanish Clb; VP Frsh Cls; Pres Soph Cls; Pres Jr Cls; High Hon Roll; Kiwanis Awd; Kayette Pres; K-ST; Med.

DUFFY, JENNIFER KATHLEEN; Manhattan HS; Manhattan, KS; (3); Cmnty Wkr; FBLA; Teachers Aide; Stat Bsktbl; Mgr(s); High Hon Roll; Hon Roll; NHS; KS St Univ; Med.

DUGGER, AMANDA B; Yates Ctr HS; Yates Center, KS; (2); Church Yth Grp; FCA; Letterman Clb; Red Cross Aide; SADD; Chorus; Bsktbl; Sftbl; Vllybl; Hon Roll; Butler Cty; Occptnl Thrpst.

DULING, ANGELA K; Bishop Carroll Catholic HS; Wichita, KS; (2); 46/201; Church Yth Grp; Chorus; Variety Show; Ofcr Stu Cncl; Hon Roll; Golden Eagle Acad Achvmnt Awd; KS ST Univ; Vet Med.

DULING, SHANNON R; Kapaun-Mt Carmel HS; Wichita, KS; (3); 69/170; Spanish Clb; Var Bsktbl; JV Socr; JV Vllybl; Eco Club; Sprts Admin.

DUNAVAN, MARCUS; Seaman Sr HS; Topeka, KS; (3); 1/250; Chess Clb; VP Church Yth Grp; Debate Tm; English Clb; Pres FBLA; HOBY; Key Clb; VP Math Clb; Math Tm; Model UN; Physics.

DUNAWAY, CANDI F; Buhler HS; Hutchinson, KS; (2); Church Yth Grp; FCA; Spanish Clb; SADD; Rptr Yrbk; Hon Roll; Tchrs Choice Awd; Reno Cty Yth Alliance Cncl; Wesley Towers Vol.

DUNAWAY, CRYSTAL; Basehor Linwood HS; Basehor, KS; (4); FHA; Hosp Aide; Pep Clb; Q&S; SADD; Teachers Aide; Yrbk; Bsktbl; Vllybl; Hon Roll; Johnson Cty CC.

DUNBACK, CHRISTOPHER DEANE; Belleville HS; Belleville, KS; (4); 1/47; Band; Jazz Band; Mrchg Band; Swing Chorus; Yrbk; Pres Frsh Cls; Pres Soph Cls; Rep Jr Cls; VP Stu Cncl; Capt Bsktbl; Ku Honor Schlr; Ftbl Cls 3-A St Champs; Discus Schl Record; KU; Pharmacy.

DUNBAR, AARON R; Central Heights Sr HS; Richmond, KS; (2); 4-H; Natl FFA Org; Band; Sec Frsh Cls; Treas Soph Cls; JV Bsktbl; JV Ftbl; 4-H Awd; High Hon Roll; Baseball.

DUNBAR, JANNA; Central Heights Sr HS; Richmond, KS; (4); 5/42; Am Leg Aux Girls St; HOBY; Letterman Clb; Natl FFA Org; Pres Jr Cls; Pres Sr Cls; Pres Stu Cncl; Var Capt Bsktbl; Vllybl; 4-H Awd; KSU; Ag.

DUNCAN, CHRIS; Leavenworth HS; Leavenworth, KS; (3); 1/349; Am Leg Boys St; Boy Scts; Quiz Bowl; Treas Science Clb; SADD; JV Var Tennis; High Hon Roll; NHS; Ntl Merit Ltr; Pres Acad Fit Awd; Eagle Sct; Pre-Med; Bio.

DUNCAN, CHRISTY L; Desoto HS; De Soto, KS; (3); Cmnty Wkr; Pres VP FHA; Teachers Aide; Vllybl; Wt Lftg; Cit Awd; Hon Roll; Pres Acad Fit Awd; JCCC; Elem Ed.

DUNCAN, JENNIFER M; Buhler HS; Buhler, KS; (2); Church Yth Grp; FCA; Science Clb; Band; Chorus; Mrchg Band; Pep Band; JV Chrldng; Vllybl; Hon Roll; AWANA Var Clb Ldr In Trng; Poetry Pub; Seminary; Missionary.

DUNCAN, JEREMIAH J; Hutchinson HS; Hutchinson, KS; (2); Teachers Aide; Thesps; School Play; Spcl Olympics Sponsor; Santas Wrkshp; TECH Awds Helper; Psych; Arts.

DUNCAN, JOSHUA; Dodge City HS; Dodge City, KS; (1); 4-H; 4-H Awd.

DUNCAN, KAREN; Manhattan HS; Manhattan, KS; (3); Girl Scts; Natl Beta Clb; Spanish Clb; Band; Mrchg Band; Orch; Pep Band; School Musical; Variety Show; Swmmng; KS ST U.

DUNCAN, KIMBERLY S; Columbus HS; Crestline, KS; (3); Church Yth Grp; FHA; Chorus; Church Choir; High Hon Roll; Hon Roll; Tchr.

DUNCAN, MARANATHA J; Manhattan HS; Dupont, WA; (4); Church Yth Grp; FCA; FTA; Girl Scts; Pep Clb; SADD; Teachers Aide; Ofcr Stu Cncl; Mgr Ftbl; Mgr(s); Highland CC; Elem Ed/Sprts Med.

DUNCAN, PATRICIA; Olathe South Sr HS; Olathe, KS; (4); 1/398; Cmnty Wkr; French Clb; Letterman Clb; Drill Tm; Ofcr Stu Cncl; Sftbl; Gov Hon Prg Awd; VP NHS; Pres Acad Fit Awd; Val; KS Hnr Schlr; KS ST U; Hotel/Rstrnt Mngmt.

DUNEHOO, ALISON L; Shawnee Mission N HS; Shawnee Mission, KS; (2); 6/489; Church Yth Grp; Latin Clb; Pep Clb; Q&S; Thesps; School Musical; School Play; Stage Crew; Yrbk; Rep Frsh Cls; Med; Pediatrics.

DUNGEY, AMBER N; Maize HS; Wichita, KS; (2); Church Yth Grp; Science Clb; Service Clb; SADD; School Play; Variety Show; Yrbk; JV Socr; High Hon Roll; NHS.

DUNHAM, KEELY A; Topeka HS; Topeka, KS; (4); French Clb; Office Aide; Teachers Aide; Hon Roll; Tae Kwon Do; Rdng; Weight Lifting; Exercise; KS ST Univ; Forensic Sci.

DUNHAM, MARCY E; Great Bend Sr HS; Great Bend, KS; (1); Pep Clb; Variety Show; Hon Roll.

DUNLAVY, TONY G; Belle Plaine HS; Belle Plaine, KS; (2); Church Yth Grp; Letterman Clb; Spanish Clb; SADD; Band; Mrchg Band; School Play; Bsktbl; Mgr(s); Hon Roll; Roller Hockey; US Air Force Acad; Pilot.

DUNMIRE, ELLY; Bern Schl; Bern, KS; (2); 1/15; Church Yth Grp; Cmnty Wkr; 4-H; Pep Clb; Scholastic Bowl; SADD; Varsity Clb; Band; Chorus; Drm Mjr(t); KSU; Jrnlsm.

DUNN, ADAM P; Clearwater HS; Clearwater, KS; (4); 1/78; Library Aide; Math Tm; Scholastic Bowl; Bus Profs of Am; Nwsp; NHS; Pres Schlr; St Schlr; Val; Pittsburg ST Univ; Pre-Med.

DUNN, ALEXANDRIA S; Holton HS; Holton, KS; (1); Church Yth Grp; Dance Clb; Drama Clb; NFL; Speech Tm; Band; Mrchg Band; Orch; Pep Band; JV Crs Cntry; Baker Univ; Attorney.

DUNN, COREY A; Baldwin HS; Baldwin City, KS; (3); Church Yth Grp; 4-H; FHA; Intnl Clb; Letterman Clb; Pep Clb; Band; Pep Band; Pres Sr Cls; Var Bsktbl; Ivan Boyd Mapleleaf Schlsp; KS ST Univ.

DUNN, CORTLAND R; St John's Military Schl; Englewood, CO; (3); Cmnty Wkr; FCA; Letterman Clb; ROTC; Varsity Clb; Acpl Chr; Chorus; Church Choir; Color Guard; Drill Tm; Work With Adolescences Suffer Attentikon Deficit Hyperactive Disorder/Depression; Military Acad; Med Dr.

DUNN, EMILY R; Clearwater HS; Clearwater, KS; (2); #1 in class; Art Clb; Letterman Clb; Math Tm; Spanish Clb; SADD; Var JV Bsktbl; Mgr(s); Var Trk; JV Vllybl; Hon Roll.

DUNN, JOEL D; Shawnee Heights HS; Topeka, KS; (1); Church Yth Grp; FCA; Band; Jazz Band; Mrchg Band; Orch; Pep Band; JV Bsbl; Bsktbl; High Hon Roll.

DUNN, JOHN D; Shawnee Heights HS; Topeka, KS; (3); #1 in class; Church Yth Grp; FCA; Chorus; Church Choir; Orch; School Musical; Swing Chorus; Var L Bsbl; Hon Roll; NHS; Gospel Singing Duo; Oral Roberts Univ; Bus; Music.

DUNN, KATIE; Paola HS; Paola, KS; (2); Cmnty Wkr; Debate Tm; Drama Clb; NFL; SADD; Thesps; Chorus; School Play; High Hon Roll; Acpl Chr; Hrs Back Rdng; Set Constr Drama Prdctns.

DUNNELL, JENNIFER A; East HS; Wichita, KS; (4); Church Yth Grp; Debate Tm; NFL; Teachers Aide; Chorus; School Musical; Mgr L Bsbl; Var L Chrldng; Var Gym; Mgr Wrstlng; OK Chrstn Univ Of Sci; Chem.

DUNSTAN, NANETTE S; Mankato Jr Sr HS; Mankato, KS; (2); Church Yth Grp; 4-H; FHA; HOBY; Math Tm; Speech Tm; Band; Chorus; Flag Corp; Mrchg Band.

DUONG, MYANH T; Wichita East HS; Wichita, KS; (3); Math Clb; Church Choir.

DURAN, LUIS; Garden City Sr HS; Garden City, KS; (3); Sftbl; Wt Lftg; High Hon Roll; Prfct Atten Awd; DECA Clb; Chrch; KU; Comp Layout.

DURAN, RAUL; Garden City Sr HS; Garden City, KS; (3); #1 in class; Computer Clb; DECA; Teachers Aide; High Hon Roll; NHS; Ntl Merit Ltr; Prfct Atten Awd; Soph Yr Aca Ltr; Earth Sci Stu Yr; Schl Chldrn Aide; WSU; Comp Sci.

DURAN, REYES A; Garden City Sr HS; Garden City, KS; (2); Church Yth Grp; Latin Clb; Mgr Nwsp; High Hon Roll; Natl Latin Exam Slvr Medal 95; Natl Latin Exam Magna Cum Laude 96.

DURBIN, DUSTIN; Winfield HS; Winfield, KS; (3); 13/175; Am Leg Boys St; Church Yth Grp; Debate Tm; Drama Clb; FCA; Thesps; School Musical; School Play; Ed Nwsp; Yrbk; KS St Press Assn Stu Bd 96-97; Tulsa Univ; Sports Admin.

DURBIN, JON M; Emporia HS; Emporia, KS; (2); Church Yth Grp; JV Socr; Hon Roll; Prfct Atten Awd; Pres Acad Fit Awd; Rgnl Art Cntst Gold Key; KS Univ; Architect.

DUREE, TYLER J; Lakin HS; Lakin, KS; (1); Boy Scts; Scholastic Bowl; Band; Jazz Band; Microbioligist.

DURHAM, BENJAMIN J; Oak Grove Baptist Schl; Kansas City, KS; (3); Church Yth Grp; DECA; Intnl Clb; Key Clb; Chorus; Rep Stu Cncl; Var L Bsktbl; Var L Socr; High Hon Roll; Pres Acad Fit Awd; U Of KS; Bus.

DURHAM, JESSICA S; Blue Valley HS; Overland Park, KS; (2); Church Yth Grp; FCA; Band; Am Leg Aux Girls St; Church Choir; Pep Band; School Musical; VP Frsh Cls; High Hon Roll; Hon Roll; Pre-Med.

DURKEE, DAVID; Kansas City Bible Clg High; Overland Park, KS; (4); Chess Clb; Church Yth Grp; Drama Clb; Chorus; Church Choir; School Musical; School Play; Variety Show; VP Sr Cls; JV Bsktbl; KCCBS; Vet Med.

DURLER, ANNE; Dodge City HS; Dodge City, KS; (1); Church Yth Grp; Cmnty Wkr; Pres 4-H; Bsktbl; Vllybl; 4-H Awd.

DURR, DUSTIN D; Trego Comm HS; Wa Keeney, KS; (3); 9/48; Boy Scts; Letterman Clb; Science Clb; SADD; L Var Ftbl; L Var Golf; L Var Trk; L Var Wrstlng; High Hon Roll; NHS; KAYS.

D'URSO, SIMON; Paola HS; Paola, KS; (3); Pres Chess Clb; VP Science Clb; Band; Jazz Band; Mrchg Band; Pep Band; NHS; KS ST; Engrng.

DUSIL II, ANTONE L; Sumner Acad Of Arts & Science; Kansas City, KS; (3); 82/148; Sec Boy Scts; Latin Clb; Spanish Clb; Yrbk; JV Var Crs Cntry; JV Var Trk; High Hon Roll; Hon Roll; Hnrbl Mntn All KS Crs Cntry; Sr Ptrl Ldr Asst Sr Ptrl Ldr Trp Guide; Brthrhd Ordr Arrow; KU; Physics/His.

DUSIN, BRIANNE; Hays HS; Hays, KS; (3); 1/210; Nwsp; Yrbk; Pres Soph Cls; Pres Stu Cncl; Sftbl; Vllybl; High Hon Roll; Hon Roll; Jr NHS; NHS; Nom Wendy's 's Heisman Schlrshp; Aths; Ctznshp Awd; Most Sprtd Awd Vlybl/Sftbl; Vol Red Crs; Trck/Treat; KS ST Univ; Hmn Ecology/Bus.

DUTCHER, SARAH L; El Dorado HS; Augusta, KS; (2); Church Yth Grp; SADD; Orch; Sci/Marine Bio; U Of NC; Marine Biolgst.

DUTROW, NATALIE B; Mc Pherson HS; Mc Pherson, KS; (3); 6/200; Church Yth Grp; French Clb; Letterman Clb; Science Clb; Church Choir; School Musical; Var L Trk; Hon Roll; NHS; Pres Acad Fit Awd; 4 Yr Coll; Chem/Envir Sci.

DUTTON, JEREMY; Hoisington HS; Hoisington, KS; (3); #29 in class; Church Yth Grp; Debate Tm; HOBY; Letterman Clb; Office Aide; SADD; Variety Show; L Bsktbl; L Crs Cntry; L Trk; All-Lg X-Cntry; All-Area Bsktbl; SADD VP; Bio.

DUTTON, SALEENA; Macksville HS; Macksville, KS; (3); #3 in class; Church Yth Grp; 4-H; VP Jr Cls; Ofcr Stu Cncl; Var L Bsktbl; Var L Chrldng; L Trk; Var L Vllybl; High Hon Roll; NHS.

DUVALL, JESSICA; Williamsburg Schl; Pomona, KS; (3); 5/20; Sec 4-H; Natl FFA Org; Pep Clb; Spanish Clb; Band; Chorus; Mrchg Band; School Play; Phtg Nwsp; High Hon Roll; Kay Clb; Emporia St U Schlrshp Tests; Vol; Emporia ST U; Elem Ed.

DVORAK, NICHOLAS A; Dodge City HS; Dodge City, KS; (3); Church Yth Grp; Office Aide; Tennis.

DWOOGHE, JAMIE M; Labette Co HS; Bartlett, KS; (3); Church Yth Grp; FCA; 4-H; GAA; Pep Clb; SADD; VICA; Church Choir; Drill Tm; Variety Show; MSSC.

DWYER, ALPHA L; Topeka West HS; Topeka, KS; (3); 71/238; Art Clb; Church Yth Grp; Cmnty Wkr; Hosp Aide; Math Clb; Office Aide; SADD; Teachers Aide; Chorus; Church Choir; KS Olympic Dev Prog Soccr Tm; KSU Yth Ldrshp Conf; KS Yth Ldrshp Series; Tchr.

DWYER, JENNIFER; Wellington Sr HS; Wellington, KS; (1); 1/200; Office Aide; SADD; Band; Chrldng; High Hon Roll; Jr NHS; Lions/Rotary Club Awrds; U Of KS; Sports Med.

DYCHES, SEAN D; Blue Valley Northwest HS; Overland Park, KS; (3); Boy Scts; Church Yth Grp; German Clb; Church Choir; Orch; Hon Roll; Eagle Sct; Sec Sls.

DYCK, ALAN W; Blue Valley Northwest HS; Overland Park, KS; (2); German Clb; Orch; Hon Roll; KS ST Univ; Archtctrl Engrng.

DYCK, HEIDI J; Berean Acad; Newton, KS; (3); Church Yth Grp; Letterman Clb; Varsity Clb; Rptr Nwsp; Tennis; Trk; Hon Roll.

DYE, LA JASMIA N; Wyandotte HS; Minneapolis, MN; (1); Drill Tm; Trk; Black His Pgm; Spelman Coll; OB.

DYE, MINDY; Independence HS; Independence, KS; (2); 52/194; Church Yth Grp; FCA; Letterman Clb; Pep Clb; SADD; Varsity Clb; Chrldng; Score Keeper; Sftbl; Hon Roll; Girl Scts; Piano; Gymnastcs; KS U; Preschl Ed.

DYKE, MARIE; Gridley HS; Gridley, KS; (2); 1/9; Band; Pep Band; JV Var Bsktbl; Var Trk; Var L Vllybl; Hon Roll; Allen Cty CC; Tchr.

DYKE, RAELLA; Sunrise Acad; Haysville, KS; (3); Art Clb; Cmnty Wkr; FHA; Natl Beta Clb; Spanish Clb; Church Choir; Orch; 4-H Awd; High Hon Roll; Prfct Atten Awd; Bio.

DYKSTRA, JEAN E; Blue Valley Northwest HS; Shawnee Mission, KS; (4); 33/340; Drill Tm; Mrchg Band; JV Var Chrldng; Var Trk; High Hon Roll; Hon Roll; NHS; Pres Acad Fit Awd; St Schlr; KS Brd Of Rgnst Acad Awd; U Of KS; Chem Eng.

DYMACEK, KRISTEN M; Eudora HS; Eudora, KS; (4); 3/43; Pres 4-H; Pres SADD; Rptr Nwsp; Rptr Yrbk; Rep Stu Cncl; Capt L Bsktbl; Capt L Sftbl; NHS; St Schlr; KS ST U; Pre-Veterinary Medcn.

EARLE, ERIN K; Andover HS; Andover, KS; (2); Church Yth Grp; FCA; FTA; Band; Chorus; Mrchg Band; Orch; School Musical; School Play; Pres Acad Fit Awd.

EARLES, ERIN; Immaculata HS; Somerset, KY; (2); Church Yth Grp; Cmnty Wkr; Teachers Aide; Rep Frsh Cls; Sec Stu Cncl; JV Bsktbl; JV Sftbl; JV Vllybl; Hon Roll; Pres Acad Fit Awd; Jr Lfgrd; Jrnlsm.

EARLY, ALLISON; Shawnee Mission E Sr HS; Shawnee Mission, KS; (4); 104/398; GAA; Letterman Clb; Pep Clb; SADD; Varsity Clb; Var L Chrldng; Var Pom Pon; Tennis; High Hon Roll; NHS; SHARE; U Of KS; Mass Commnctn.

EARNHART, MELANIE D; Blue Valley HS; Olathe, KS; (4); Art Clb; Cmnty Wkr; Teachers Aide; Nwsp; Swmmng; Hon Roll; NHS; Schltcs Eng, Wrtng & Arts, Ceramics; Helped With Swimming Portion Of Spcl Olympics.

EASH, JAMES; Northwest HS; Wichita, KS; (3); 12/327; Am Leg Boys St; Office Aide; Lit Mag; Pres Frsh Cls; Var Bsbl; Var Bsktbl; Var Socr; High Hon Roll; NHS.

EASTBURN, SARAH E; Blue Valley Northwest HS; Overland Park, KS; (3); 54/430; Art Clb; Church Yth Grp; Pep Clb; Phtg Yrbk; Sec Jr Cls; Socr; Tennis; Natl Yng Ldr.

EASTERDAY, DARA J; Meade HS; Meade, KS; (3); Church Yth Grp; FCA; 4-H; Pep Clb; Spanish Clb; Band; Chorus; Mrchg Band; Pep Band; School Musical; I Dare You Awd; Madrigals; Belmont Univ; Music Bus.

EASTERDAY, EMILY; St John Jr Sr HS; Overland Park, KS; (4); 21/250; Am Leg Aux Girls St; Church Yth Grp; FCA; Key Clb; Office Aide; Bsktbl; Var JV Crs Cntry; Var L Socr; JV Tennis; High Hon Roll; Stu Ambssdr; Benedctine; Tchr.

EASTES, BEAU; Pratt HS; Pratt, KS; (3); Key Clb; Teachers Aide; Phtg Yrbk; Rep Stu Cncl; L Bsbl; L Bsktbl; Capt Ftbl; Wt Lftg; Hon Roll; 4th Pl Acad Olympic Awd In Sports Photo; Starter On 95 4a St Ftbl Champion.

EASTWOOD, ALISON K; Blue Valley HS; Overland Park, KS; (2); Cmnty Wkr; Dance Clb; Hosp Aide; Drill Tm; Flag Corp; Vllybl; Hon Roll; Prfct Atten Awd; Dance Studio Instr; Explorers; KS ST Univ.

EASTWOOD, JAMES J; Ft Scott HS; Fort Scott, KS; (2); Debate Tm; NFL; Chorus; Crs Cntry; All-St Choir 96; Law.

EATINGER, JENNIE L; Wellsville Jr Sr HS; Wellsville, KS; (2); Church Yth Grp; 4-H; FBLA; Mrchg Band; Pep Band; Vllybl; 4-H Awd; High Hon Roll; NHS; KS Univ.

EATON, AARON; Ellis HS; Ellis, KS; (2); Sec Church Yth Grp; SADD; Band; Color Guard; Rep Stu Cncl; Var Bsktbl; Capt Chrldng; Var Sftbl; Var Trk; JV Var Vllybl; Wrtng Cont Awds; St Forensics Qualfr 94-95.

EATON, HEATHER L; Riley Cty HS; Riley, KS; (3); 1/44; Am Leg Aux Girls St; Church Yth Grp; SADD; Chorus; Drm Mjr(t); School Play; Cit Awd; Hon Roll; Treas NHS; Cmnty Wkr; KS Lions St Band; KS Dist III Hnr Choir; BVL Hnr Choir & Band; Broadcast Jrnlsm; Drama.

EATON, JEREMY D; Wichita East HS; Wichita, KS; (2); Church Yth Grp; Band; Mrchg Band; Pep Band; Ftbl; Trk; Wt Lftg; Hon Roll; Wichita Wind Ensmbl; MIT; Engrng.

EBABEN, ANDRE; Centre Jr Sr HS; Lincolnville, KS; (3); Boy Scts; CAP; 4-H; Letterman Clb; Natl FFA Org; Pep Clb; Band; Chorus; Mrchg Band; Pep Band; Cmptr Aided Dsgn.

EBEL, KAREN; Hiawatha HS; Hiawatha, KS; (4); 12/87; Am Leg Aux Girls St; Church Yth Grp; French Clb; Intnl Clb; Key Clb; Letterman Clb; Pep Clb; SADD; Band; Mrchg Band; Sun Schl Tchr; U KS; Phys Thrpy.

EBELING, PAMELA; Dodge City HS; Dodge City, KS; (3); Church Yth Grp; FCA; Treas 4-H; Intnl Clb; SADD; Band; Church Choir; Color Guard; Mrchg Band; Hon Roll; Octagon Clb; KU; Bus Law.

EBERHART, KATIE; Labette Co HS; Parsons, KS; (2); Church Yth Grp; FCA; FBLA; Letterman Clb; Library Aide; SADD; Ofcr Soph Cls; Ofcr Stu Cncl; Var Crs Cntry; Var Trk; Pittsburg ST U; Nrsng.

EBERT, AMANDA; Rock Creek Jr Sr HS; Wamego, KS; (4); 6/64; FHA; Natl FFA Org; Treas SADD; Teachers Aide; Band; Jazz Band; Mrchg Band; Pep Band; Gym; L Trk; Childcare Ctr In Home.

EBERT, BRICE S; Rock Creek Jr Sr HS; Westmoreland, KS; (4); 8/43; Bus Profs of Am; Teachers Aide; Treas Frsh Cls; VP Jr Cls; Var L Bsbl; L Bsktbl; Var L Ftbl; Var L Golf; Hon Roll; Tutor & Mentor For Elem Stdnts; Stu Entrepreneur Awd Wichita ST Univ; KS Hwy Patrol Trng Acad.

EBERT, MEGAN; Rossville HS; Rossville, KS; (3); 2/50; Treas 4-H; VP FBLA; Scholastic Bowl; Band; School Musical; Var L Bsktbl; Var L Sftbl; Var L Vllybl; High Hon Roll; NHS; All-Lg Vlybl & Sftbl Tm; St Proj Wnnr FBLA; KS ST U; Intr Archtctr.

EBERT, NEIL; Rock Creek Jr Sr HS; Saint George, KS; (4); 12/52; Am Leg Boys St; Boy Scts; Cmnty Wkr; Debate Tm; Math Tm; Natl FFA Org; Pep Clb; Scholastic Bowl; Teachers Aide; Sec Jr Cls; FFA Star Greenhand/Sentinel/Sec; SADD VP; KS ST U; Agri Sci.

EBRIGHT, EMILY A; Lyons HS; Lyons, KS; (2); Art Clb; Church Yth Grp; Computer Clb; Dance Clb; Drama Clb; FCA; NFL; Pep Clb; Quiz Bowl; Scholastic Bowl; Dance.

ECK, DEANA; Osborne HS; Osborne, KS; (4); 5/26; Am Leg Aux Girls St; FHA; Band; Chorus; School Musical; Sec Sr Cls; Hon Roll; Prfct Atten Awd; Pep Clb; Mrchg Band; FHA Offcr Pts, Chrmn, Treas.

ECK, JANET; Andale HS; Goddard, KS; (4); 3/70; Church Yth Grp; German Clb; Letterman Clb; SADD; Treas Sr Cls; L Bsktbl; L Trk; L Vllybl; High Hon Roll; Hon Roll; US Army Rsrv Natl Schlr/Ath Awd; Acad All St Bsktbl; Hnr Grad; Ft Hays U; Med.

ECK, KRISTINE; Lawrence HS; Lawrence, KS; (4); Am Leg Aux Girls St; Cmnty Wkr; Key Clb; Model UN; Service Clb; Teachers Aide; Hon Roll; Ntl Merit SF; Pres Acad Fit Awd.

ECK, LUKE H; Andale HS; Goddard, KS; (2); Church Yth Grp; Letterman Clb; Scholastic Bowl; Spanish Clb; Bsktbl; Ftbl; Trk; High Hon Roll.

ECK, MARLA J; Attica Public Schl; Attica, KS; (2); Church Yth Grp; 4-H; Quiz Bowl; Chorus; School Play; Rep Stu Cncl; Trk; High Hon Roll; Ntl Merit Ltr; PT.

ECKELS, MELODY R; Ness City HS; Ness City, KS; (3); Church Yth Grp; Pep Clb; Quiz Bowl; Scholastic Bowl; Speech Tm; Thesps; Chorus; Church Choir; School Play; Rep Stu Cncl; Speech, Poetry & Int St Chmpn 95; St Hnrs Acad 95; KS ST; Music Thrpy.

ECKERT, MICHELLE D; South Barber HS; Kiowa, KS; (2); Church Yth Grp; Drama Clb; SADD; Band; Chorus; Mrchg Band; Pep Band; Tennis; Hon Roll; Frnscs; Piano.

ECKERT, SABRINA; Atchison Co Cmty HS; Effingham, KS; (4); 6/57; Pres Church Yth Grp; Pres Sec 4-H; VP FBLA; Sec VP Natl FFA Org; Sec Science Clb; Var L Bsktbl; Var L Vllybl; NHS; Letterman Clb; Math Clb; US Army Rsrv Natl Schlr/Ath Awd; KAYS Pres; KS ST U; Elem Ed.

ECKHARDT, AMANDA; Columbus HS; Columbus, KS; (2); Church Yth Grp; FCA; 4-H; Jazz Band; Mrchg Band; Chrldng; Trk; Vllybl; DAR Awd; 4-H Awd; Chrch Pianist; Yth Cnslr.

ECKHARDT, ERIKA A; Junction City HS; Junction City, KS; (1); Pep Clb; High Hon Roll; Frosh Comm; NY U; Jrnlsm.

ECKHART, KYLE M; Belle Plaine HS; Belle Plaine, KS; (2); 5/60; Church Yth Grp; Quiz Bowl; Band; VP Soph Cls; Bsktbl; Ftbl; Socr; High Hon Roll; NHS; Ntl Merit Schol; U Of WA.

ECKHOFF, MELISSA S; Buhler HS; Hutchinson, KS; (4); 49/146; FCA; Sec German Clb; Science Clb; SADD; Teachers Aide; Hon Roll; NHS; Prfct Atten Awd; SMAD Recycling Clb; Phy Thrpst Vol; Hutchinson CC; Phys Therp Asst.

ECKLES, JAMES P; Dodge City HS; Dodge City, KS; (3); Var Wrstlng; 2-Time ST Placer Wrstlg.

EDDY, SARAH; Syracuse Jr Sr HS; Syracuse, KS; (2); Drama Clb; Quiz Bowl; Band; Chorus; Mrchg Band; Pep Band; School Play; Trk; Hon Roll; KSU; Food Svc.

EDEN, JESSICA; Peabody-Burns Jr Sr HS; Peabody, KS; (2); Church Yth Grp; Treas FHA; Chorus; JV Bsktbl; Mgr(s); JV Vllybl; Hon Roll; Bus Mktg.

EDGAR, JENNIFER; Basehor Linwood HS; Basehor, KS; (3); 13/100; VP FHA; GAA; Sec Frsh Cls; Sec Soph Cls; JV Vllybl; High Hon Roll; Hon Roll; SADD; U Of KS; Psych.

EDGER, CARISSA J; Meade HS; Meade, KS; (1); Church Yth Grp; Drama Clb; FCA; Chorus; Pep Band; Rep Frsh Cls; Bsktbl; Trk; Vllybl; Cit Awd; Kayetts.

EDGINGTON, MARCI D; Lakin HS; Ulysses, KS; (2); Cmnty Wkr; 4-H; Quiz Bowl; Band; Pep Band; Golf; 4-H Awd; Hon Roll; NHS.

EDIGER, CALEB E; Chaparral HS; Harper, KS; (1); Church Yth Grp; 4-H; Natl FFA Org; Quiz Bowl; Band; Mrchg Band; Pep Band; Crs Cntry; Tennis; 4-H Awd; Tech Stdnt Assn; KU; Medcl.

EDIGER, KYLIE J; Halstead HS; Halstead, KS; (1); Dance Clb; Pep Clb; Band; Drill Tm; Mrchg Band; Pep Band; School Musical; Bsktbl; Vllybl; Hon Roll; Bus.

EDINGTON, AMANDA D; Chase Co HS; Emporia, KS; (2); Church Yth Grp; Dance Clb; Spanish Clb; Teachers Aide; Acpl Chr; Band; Chorus; Church Choir; Drill Tm; Mrchg Band; Bethany Coll; Music Ed.

EDMONDS, KATHERINE A; Great Bend Sr HS; Great Bend, KS; (3); Treas Church Yth Grp; Rep French Clb; Treas Service Clb; SADD; Acpl Chr; Band; Church Choir; Orch; NHS; Scholastic Bowl; Madrigal Pops Singers; Bio.

EDMONDS, LISA; Buhler HS; Hutchinson, KS; (3); Church Yth Grp; Cmnty Wkr; Computer Clb; Intnl Clb; Q&S; Quiz Bowl; Scholastic Bowl; Spanish Clb; SADD; Teachers Aide; Retirement Ctr Vol; Gifted Pgm; TX A&M Univ; Span; Bus.

EDMONDSON, SHAUN; Lawrence HS; Lawrence, KS; (4); Am Leg Boys St; Teachers Aide; Rptr Nwsp; Rptr Yrbk; Pres Frsh Cls; Rep Jr Cls; Ofcr Stu Cncl; Var Bsbl; Var Bsktbl; Ftbl; Pro Bsbl.

EDMONSTON, CONNIE; Protection Schl; Protection, KS; (4); 1/12; Band; Chorus; Pres Stu Cncl; Var Capt Bsktbl; Capt Chrldng; Capt Vllybl; Cit Awd; Gov Hon Prg Awd; High Hon Roll; NHS; Arion Awd-Highst Instrumntl Awd; All Area Acad Tem; All-Arond Girl Awd; Panther Pride Awd; Show Choir; Hutchinson CC; Phys Therapy.

EDVALDS, BRETT A; Shawnee Mission N HS; Shawnee Mission, KS; (2); 84/580; Church Yth Grp; Pep Clb; Teachers Aide; Varsity Clb; Ofcr Bsbl; Bsktbl; Ftbl; Wt Lftg; Hon Roll; Sprts Med/PT.

EDWARDS, ADRIANE; Northern Heights HS; Emporia, KS; (2); 4-H; HOBY; Band; Chorus; JV Bsktbl; Var Chrldng; Var Trk; Hon Roll; Pres Acad Fit Awd; Church Yth Grp; Forensics; Law.

EDWARDS, BRENT A; Scott Comm HS; Scott City, KS; (3); Church Yth Grp; Natl FFA Org; Teachers Aide; Var L Bsktbl; Var Capt Ftbl; Var L Trk; Var L Wt Lftg; Hon Roll; NWKL 1st Team; SWK 2nd Team; St Champion In Weight Lifting; Bus & Ag.

EDWARDS, CHRIS; Wichita East HS; Wichita, KS; (3); Boy Scts; JV Crs Cntry; High Hon Roll; Jr NHS; NYLC; Ed.

EDWARDS, DANIEL J; Bishop Miege HS; Kansas City, MO; (3); 50/170; Church Yth Grp; Hosp Aide; Pep Clb; Teachers Aide; Phtg Nwsp; Phtg Yrbk; Intrml Bsktbl; Var Capt Socr; Var Trk; Hon Roll; Cmps Mnstry Tm; Sprts Med/Athltc Trng.

EDWARDS, EMILY M; Greeley Co Schl; Tribune, KS; (2); Church Yth Grp; Drama Clb; SADD; Chorus; Rep Stu Cncl; JV Tennis; High Hon Roll; Hon Roll; Art Clb; Pep Clb; Peer Hlprs; Dodge City Dist Yth Chprsn; Jurisdictional Yth Team Rep; Southwestern; Theology/Religion.

EDWARDS, JASON; Meade HS; Fowler, KS; (4); Art Clb; Church Yth Grp; FCA; Key Clb; Letterman Clb; NFL; Pep Clb; Spanish Clb; Varsity Clb; Chorus; All-League Puntr 96; Schl Track Records Holdr & Co-Holdr; St Track 2nd & 4th Pl 4x100 & 4x400 95; Friends U; Vet Med.

EDWARDS, NICOLE E; Colby Sr HS; Colby, KS; (2); French Clb; Chorus; School Musical; Chrldng; French Hon Soc; Hon Roll; Writing; Dancing; Reading; NYU; Lit/Tchr/Writer.

EDWARDS, PAULA M; Wellington Sr HS; Wellington, KS; (2); Red Cross Aide; Mgr Bsktbl; Score Keeper; L Tennis; L Trk; Hon Roll; Jr NHS; NHS; Soc Svcs.

EDWARDS, PETER M; Independence HS; Independence, KS; (3); Boy Scts; Church Yth Grp; Cmnty Wkr; Color Guard; Rptr Nwsp; L Ftbl; Var L Wt Lftg; Var L Wrstlng; Hon Roll; Prfct Atten Awd; Renassance Acad Awd; MO Southern ST Coll; Cmptr Pg.

EDWARDS, REBECCA L; Independence HS; Independence, KS; (1); Church Yth Grp; L Orch; Powder Puff Ftbl; Prfct Atten Awd; KSHSAA Regnl Musc Festvl 1st Div String Ensembl; KSHSAA St Muscl Festvl 2nd Div String Ensembl.

EDWARDS, VINCENT; Wichita West HS; Wichita, KS; (3); 20/283; Church Yth Grp; Cmnty Wkr; ROTC; Band; Drill Tm; Jazz Band; Mrchg Band; Pep Band; Ofcr Jr Cls; Bsktbl; Vol Untd Way; K ST; Law.

EFFLANDT, KAREN M; Wichita Collegiate Schl; Wichita, KS; (3); Service Clb; SADD; Chorus; JV Tennis; High Hon Roll; Hon Roll; Ballet.

EFTINK, LANCE; Sedgwick HS; Sedgwick, KS; (1); 2/30; Church Yth Grp; Quiz Bowl; Band; Mrchg Band; Pep Band; Rep Stu Cncl; JV Bsktbl; JV Ftbl; Wt Lftg; High Hon Roll; Stu Tech Assn; KSU; Arch Engr.

EGAN, DAVID L; Caney Valley Jr Sr HS; Caney, KS; (2); FCA; JV Bsbl; Stat Bsktbl; Hon Roll; NHS; Soph Srvr.

EGBERT, KRISTY D; Circle HS; Benton, KS; (3); #13 in class; Letterman Clb; Spanish Clb; Varsity Clb; Band; Pep Band; Variety Show; Mgr Nwsp; Pom Pon; High Hon Roll; Jet Skiing; Karate; KS ST.

EGGERS, JESSICA; Ellinwood Jr Sr HS; Ellinwood, KS; (1); Dance Clb; Debate Tm; FCA; Key Clb; Band; Chorus; Flag Corp; Var Chrldng; Var Pom Pon; JV Vllybl; Ft Hays Univ; Pre-Law.

EGGERS, SHANNA; Yates Ctr HS; Yates Center, KS; (3); 3/56; Am Leg Aux Girls St; FCA; 4-H; Treas FHA; Quiz Bowl; Spanish Clb; Yrbk; Var L Chrldng; 4-H Awd; High Hon Roll; Ed.

EHMKE, LAYTON R; Dighton HS; Healy, KS; (1); Chess Clb; Drama Clb; 4-H; Intnl Clb; Pep Clb; Quiz Bowl; Speech Tm; SADD; Bus Profs of Am; Band.

EICHELBERGER, JEANNE MARIE; Wichita East HS; Wichita, KS; (3); Church Yth Grp; Cmnty Wkr; Debate Tm; Hosp Aide; NFL; Spanish Clb; Pres SADD; High Hon Roll; NHS; Spanish NHS; The Intnl Baccallaureate Pgm; Acad Ltr; Rdng; Swimming; Vllybl; Bus Admin.

EICHER, JOSH L; Hesston HS; Newton, KS; (1); German Clb; Var Trk; Hon Roll; Ger Hnr Awd; KS ST Univ.

EICHMAN, CARA L; Wamego HS; Wamego, KS; (3); Church Yth Grp; Cmnty Wkr; HOBY; Intnl Clb; Letterman Clb; Science Clb; SADD; Band; Drill Tm; Mrchg Band; Summer Sftbl Pgm; Sight Cncl Mem; KS ST U.

EICHMAN, HEIDI; St Marys HS; Saint Marys, KS; (4); Debate Tm; 4-H; FBLA; FHA; HOBY; Pres NFL; School Musical; Ed Yrbk; NHS; St Schlr; I Dare You Awd; Teen Advsry Cncl; Teen Pages Edtr; KS ST U; Mass Commnctns.

EICHMAN, MICHELLE K; St Thomas Aquinas HS; Lenexa, KS; (3); 70/263; JV Bsktbl; Var Socr; Var Tennis; High Hon Roll; NHS; 4th Pl SA Doubles In Tnns 95; Soccer 1st Pl 4 Times; Child Psych.

EICKHOLT, ERIC D; Junction City HS; Junction City, KS; (2); CAP; ROTC; Color Guard; Drill Tm; Hon Roll; KS ST Univ; Ag.

EIGSTI, MELISSA DAWN; Hesston HS; Hesston, KS; (3); Sec Church Yth Grp; 4-H; Band; Chorus; Jazz Band; School Musical; School Play; JV Var Tennis; 4-H Awd; High Hon Roll; Goshen Coll; Nrsng.

EIGSTI, SHANNA E; Haven HS; Hutchinson, KS; (4); 15/69; Pres Sec Church Yth Grp; VP SADD; Rep Band; Chorus; Flag Corp; Pep Band; Variety Show; VP Stu Cncl; JV Vllybl; Hon Roll; FCA Pres; Kay Svc Org Sec; Hesston Col; Acctnt.

EILAND, DAWN E; Rolla HS; Rolla, KS; (3); 2/14; Church Yth Grp; FCA; Pep Clb; VP Band; Rep Chorus; Pep Band; Ed Nwsp; Sec Frsh Cls; VP Soph Cls; VP Jr Cls; KMEA Hnr Band; All Area Vllybl & Bsktbl Teams; Santa Fe Trail League Vllybl & Bsktbl.

EILERT, HEATHER J; Wichita East HS; Wichita, KS; (4); Drama Clb; FHA; Latin Clb; Teachers Aide; Band; Mrchg Band; High Hon Roll; Hon Roll; HERO; WSU; Nrsng.

EILERT, MANDY; St John's HS; Beloit, KS; (1); Church Yth Grp; Pep Clb; Chorus; School Musical; JV Var Bsktbl; Var Chrldng; L Var Trk; JV Vllybl; High Hon Roll; Hon Roll; Emporia ST Schlrshp Contest 3rd Pl; Psych.

EILRICH, STEVEN; Mc Pherson HS; Mc Pherson, KS; (4); Cmnty Wkr; Natl FFA Org; Speech Tm; Band; Mrchg Band; Pep Band; Cit Awd; Hon Roll; KS ST U; Vet/Sci.

EISENHUT, CHRISTA D; Topeka HS; Topeka, KS; (4); Office Aide; Pep Clb; SADD; Teachers Aide; High Hon Roll; NHS; Allen County CC; Bus Admn.

EISENMAN, LYNN M; Shawnee Mission S Sr HS; Overland Park, KS; (4); 40/450; Intnl Clb; Pep Clb; Q&S; Teachers Aide; Stage Crew; Phtg Yrbk; High Hon Roll; NHS; Ntl Merit SF; BBYO Chapter Pres.

EK, MELISSA D; Canton-Galva HS; Galva, KS; (3); FBLA; Letterman Clb; SADD; Sec Treas Soph Cls; Pres Stu Cncl; Powder Puff Ftbl; Sftbl; Vllybl; Wt Lftg; Hon Roll; Ed.

ELAM, KANDI M; Jewell HS; Lincoln, NE; (3); Debate Tm; Library Aide; NFL; Speech Tm; Band; Flag Corp; Bus Mgnt.

ELAM, KELLY; Wichita Heights HS; Wichita, KS; (4); 19/242; Treas Bus Profs of Am; Pep Clb; VP SADD; Var Crs Cntry; Var Sftbl; Hon Roll; NHS; KS Hon Schlr; Wichita St U; Bus Admn.

ELDER, JANEL R; Washington HS; Washington, KS; (3); 1/40; Natl FFA Org; Pep Clb; Scholastic Bowl; Band; Jazz Band; Swing Chorus; Pres Frsh Cls; Var Bsktbl; JV Vllybl; High Hon Roll; Ed.

ELDER, JOHN M; Maize HS; Wichita, KS; (3); 24/242; Church Yth Grp; Debate Tm; Letterman Clb; Office Aide; Science Clb; Service Clb; Pres Spanish Clb; Pres SADD; Teachers Aide; Thesps; All Chisholm Trail League Bsbl; All ST Class 5-A Bsbl; Pre-Med/Coaching.

ELDER, SAMANTHA L; Humboldt HS; Humboldt, KS; (2); #18 in class; Cmnty Wkr; FHA; Pep Clb; Chorus; Swing Chorus; Var Mgr(s); Var Score Keeper; Socr; Trk; Vllybl; ACCC; Rdtn Tech.

ELDER, SHAY S; Washburn Rural HS; Topeka, KS; (2); Church Yth Grp; Cmnty Wkr; Debate Tm; Letterman Clb; NFL; Speech Tm; Church Choir; High Hon Roll; Hon Roll; Mrchg Band; Bio; Environmental Law.

EL HADDAD, HEBA; Field Kindley Mem Sr HS; Coffeyville, KS; (2); Dance Clb; Drama Clb; French Clb; Hosp Aide; Church Choir; Stage Crew; JV Tennis; Hon Roll; Piano; Pharmacy.

ELKINS, JENNIFER; Olathe South Sr HS; Olathe, KS; (3); French Clb; Capt Band; Church Choir; Drm Mjr(t); Mrchg Band; School Musical; Var Tennis; High Hon Roll; Hon Roll; NHS; Div I Rtngs Solo/Ensmbl Perf Clrnt; 8th Pl Natl/6th Pl ST Fr Test; Hnrs His/Engl/Math; Advncd Sci.

ELLENZ, KELLY L; Andale HS; Colwich, KS; (2); Church Yth Grp; Spanish Clb; SADD; Stat Mgr(s); High Hon Roll; Hon Roll; KS Univ; Med.

ELLENZ, KENDRA L; Andale HS; Colwich, KS; (1); Church Yth Grp; Spanish Clb; Hon Roll; KS Univ.

ELLENZ, KIMBERLY L; Andale HS; Colwich, KS; (1); Church Yth Grp; Spanish Clb; Hon Roll; KS U.

ELLERMAN, RACHEL L; Williamsburg Schl; Williamsburg, KS; (2); 2/30; Natl FFA Org; Band; Chorus; Mrchg Band; Pep Band; Stage Crew; Hon Roll; Treas NHS; ST/INTL Lions Bnd; U Of TX San Antonio.

ELLERMAN, REBEKAH A; Williamsburg Schl; Williamsburg, KS; (3); 1/18; Treas French Clb; Sec Natl FFA Org; Band; Pres Frsh Cls; VP Soph Cls; Sec Treas Jr Cls; Ofcr Stu Cncl; High Hon Roll; Rep NHS; Chorus; KS Regents Hnrs Acad; St Winning FFA Dairy Foods Team; Comp Drftng.

ELLINGTON, CHRIS M; Maize HS; Wichita, KS; (3); Boy Scts; Wichita Area Voc Tech Col; Wichita St Univ; Auto Indust.

ELLIOT, CHRISTINA; Shawnee Mission W Sr HS; Overland Park, KS; (4); 6/3; FCA; Q&S; Pres SADD; Ed Yrbk; Var L Crs Cntry; Var L Trk; High Hon Roll; NHS; Peer Tutor; KS Hnr Schlr; Outstdng Sr In Sci & Math; KS ST Univ; Chem Engrng.

ELLIOT, STEVEN; Hays HS; Hays, KS; (1); Band; Mrchg Band; Ftbl; Hon Roll; Law.

ELLIOTT, ADAM S; Russell HS; Russell, KS; (4); Boy Scts; Church Yth Grp; Key Clb; Letterman Clb; Natl FFA Org; Pep Clb; SADD; JV Bsktbl; Var JV Ftbl; JV Tennis; Eagle Scout; KS St Univ; Wldlf Bio.

ELLIOTT, BRENDA G; Chaparral HS; Danville, KS; (1); Chorus; Chrldng; Hon Roll; FFA Medal; KS Newman Coll.

ELLIOTT, CODY L; Great Bend Sr HS; Great Bend, KS; (1); Ftbl; Mgr(s); Wt Lftg; Hon Roll; Prfct Atten Awd; Sports Card Collecting, Over 7000 Cards Total; Ftbl; Typed 75 Page Report On 75th Anniv NFL; Comp Tech; Acctnt; Ftbl.

ELLIOTT, EMILY M; Derby HS; Derby, KS; (1); Church Yth Grp; Cmnty Wkr; ROTC; Chorus; Church Choir; Drill Tm; Hon Roll; Military Order Of The World Wars Awd ROTC; 2nd Place Individual Drill Cmptn ROTC; Geology.

ELLIOTT, JACOB J; Maize HS; Maize, KS; (2); Drama Clb; Thesps; School Play; Stage Crew; JV Ftbl; Var Wrstlng; Hon Roll.

ELLIOTT, JASON; Mc Pherson HS; Mc Pherson, KS; (4); Art Clb; Church Yth Grp; Cmnty Wkr; Office Aide; Teachers Aide; Chorus; Var L Socr; Var L Trk; Hon Roll; Prfct Atten Awd; DARE Rep; Several Chrch Mission Trips; Freed-Hardeman Univ.

ELLIOTT, JENNIFER L; Oxford HS; Oxford, KS; (2); 1/50; Letterman Clb; Spanish Clb; Varsity Clb; Rptr Nwsp; Phtg Yrbk; JV Bsktbl; Var Chrldng; Var Crs Cntry; High Hon Roll; Hon Roll; Creative Wrtng.

ELLIOTT, JENNIFER S; Andover HS; Andover, KS; (4); 11/138; Art Clb; Teachers Aide; Chorus; Bsktbl; Mgr(s); Sftbl; Vllybl; High Hon Roll; Pres Acad Fit Awd; KS Bd Of Regents Schlr; KU Hnrs Schlr; Butler Cty CC; Tchr; Cnslr.

ELLIOTT, JOHANNA V; Russell HS; Russell, KS; (1); Church Yth Grp; Cmnty Wkr; Drama Clb; Key Clb; SADD; Chorus; School Play; Stage Crew; JV L Chrldng; High Hon Roll; KS ST Univ.

ELLIOTT, KATIE; Kapaun-Mt Carmel HS; Wichita, KS; (3); Church Yth Grp; Cmnty Wkr; Hosp Aide; Spanish Clb; SADD; High Hon Roll; Jr Assembly Whichita Mem; United Crusaders Clb.

ELLIOTT, KRISTI; Garden City Sr HS; Garden City, KS; (3); Math Tm; Red Cross Aide; Band; Mrchg Band; Pep Band; Ed Nwsp; Ed Lit Mag; Stat Bsktbl; JV Tennis; NHS; Jrnlsm.

ELLIOTT, KRYSTYNA F; Lawrence HS; Lawrence, KS; (2); 4-H; Natl FFA Org; Science Clb; Acpl Chr; Chorus; Color Guard; Flag Corp; Mrchg Band; Orch; School Musical; Quarter Horse Shows; K ST; Vet.

ELLIOTT, LAURA; St Thomas Aquinas HS; Paola, KS; (1); VP Math Clb; Math Tm; Mu Alpha Theta; Science Clb; High Hon Roll; Hon Roll; JETS Awd; Mission To Planet Eart Natl Winner; Mars Scientific Expermnt Propolsal Regnl Winner; Sci.

ELLIOTT, LESLIE; Goddard HS; Goddard, KS; (4); Drama Clb; French Clb; Science Clb; Spanish Clb; Score Keeper; Tennis; NHS.

ELLIOTT, LIBBY; Hill City HS; Hill City, KS; (4); Am Leg Aux Girls St; FCA; Sec FHA; Natl FFA Org; Rep Pep Clb; VP Ski Clb; SADD; Teachers Aide; Chorus; Church Choir; KAY VP; Fort Hays ST U; Spec Ed.

ELLIOTT, MEGAN; Spearville Jr Sr HS; Wright, KS; (3); 10/27; Sec 4-H; Pep Clb; Speech Tm; Stage Crew; Ofcr Frsh Cls; Ofcr Soph Cls; Ofcr Jr Cls; JV Vllybl; 4-H Awd; Rodeo; Art; Juco; Art.

ELLIOTT, RODNEY R; Haven HS; Mount Hope, KS; (2); Ofcr Bsbl; JV Bsktbl; Ftbl; High Hon Roll; Mid-Amer Yth Bsktbl; Farming; Play Guitar; KAYS; Ag; Ed; Coaching.

ELLIOTT, SHANA; Spearville Jr Sr HS; Wright, KS; (1); 4-H; Quiz Bowl; Sec Frsh Cls; 4-H Awd; High Hon Roll; Hon Roll; Lwyr.

ELLIS, ADAM R; Thayer HS; Thayer, KS; (3); 1/13; Church Yth Grp; FCA; Pep Clb; Quiz Bowl; Scholastic Bowl; Science Clb; Speech Tm; Thesps; Band; Jazz Band; Med Schl/Ansthlgy.

ELLIS, ASHLEY R; Morland Jr Sr HS; Penokee, KS; (1); 1/10; 4-H; Scholastic Bowl; Speech Tm; Band; Chorus; School Play; Mgr(s); Wt Lftg; High Hon Roll; KS Univ; Med Dr.

ELLIS, CHAD; Independence HS; Independence, KS; (4); Am Leg Boys St; Church Yth Grp; Science Clb; Teachers Aide; Chorus; Church Choir; Ofcr Bsbl; Bsktbl; Hon Roll; Certfd PADI; Southern Nazarene Univ; Pilot.

ELLIS, JOSH R; Morland Jr Sr HS; Penokee, KS; (2); 2/11; Treas 4-H; Scholastic Bowl; Band; L Bsktbl; L Ftbl; Wt Lftg; 4-H Awd; High Hon Roll; NHS; KS Univ.

ELLIS, KATHERINE; Emporia HS; Emporia, KS; (4); Sec Pres Art Clb; Church Yth Grp; Q&S; SADD; Chorus; Church Choir; Ed Nwsp; Var Capt Swmmng; Cit Awd; Hon Roll; Emporia ST U.

ELLIS, KODY J; St John Jr Sr HS; Saint John, KS; (4); 5/27; Church Yth Grp; Band; Chorus; Jazz Band; Pep Band; School Musical; Swing Chorus; L Chrldng; Var L Ftbl; Hon Roll; Hnrbl Mntn All Leag Lineman/All Area Lineman Ftbl 95; Barton Cty CC; Music.

ELLIS, TAMMY R; Galena HS; Galena, KS; (3); Cmnty Wkr; FBLA; Girl Scts; Library Aide; Math Tm; Office Aide; Pep Clb; Red Cross Aide; Scholastic Bowl; SADD; Phi Kappa Phi Deans Schlsp; Pittsburg ST Univ; Comp Prgmr.

ELLISON, APRIL M; Wyandotte HS; Kansas City, KS; (2); Teachers Aide; Reading; Singing; Listening To Radio; KS ST Univ; RN.

ELLISS, DENITA K; Anderson Cty Jr Sr HS; Westphalia, KS; (4); 5/76; Treas Art Clb; Sec Treas Church Yth Grp; Sec Sr Cls; Capt L Chrldng; Capt L Crs Cntry; High Hon Roll; Pres NHS; Pres Schlr; Sal; St Schlr; Acad Awds Math/Eng/Sci/Social Sci; Gifted Stdnt; Pittsburg ST Univ; Coml Grphcs.

ELLSAESSER, LALANE; Hugoton HS; Moscow, KS; (3); 6/69; Church Yth Grp; FCA; 4-H; Band; Pres Frsh Cls; Bsktbl; Crs Cntry; Trk; High Hon Roll; NHS; KS ST U; Vet.

ELLSWORTH, TYLER; Central Jr HS; Lawrence, KS; (1); Band; Chorus; L Crs Cntry; JV Trk; Lawrence Yth Symphony.

ELMER, CHAD M; Eudora HS; Linwood, KS; (4); Art Clb; Computer Clb; FBLA; Spanish Clb; Varsity Clb; Pres VICA; Var L Bsbl; Var L Bsktbl; Var L Ftbl; Hon Roll; Johnson Cty CC; Grphc Art.

ELMORE, ANDI; Sedgwick HS; Valley Center, KS; (3); 4/30; Speech Tm; Chorus; School Musical; Rptr Nwsp; Yrbk; Pres Frsh Cls; Pres Soph Cls; Pres Jr Cls; Rep Stu Cncl; High Hon Roll; Commnctns.

ELMORE, JASON; Sedan HS; Sedan, KS; (3); 7/30; Church Yth Grp; FCA; FHA; HOBY; Letterman Clb; Spanish Clb; Varsity Clb; Band; Chorus; Pep Band; Bus Admin.

ELMORE, JERRY; Argonia Jr Sr HS; Argonia, KS; (3); Church Yth Grp; Letterman Clb; Quiz Bowl; Scholastic Bowl; Band; Pep Band; Stage Crew; Pres Frsh Cls; Sec Stu Cncl; High Hon Roll; League Chmpn Quiz Bowl Squad; ST Schlr Bowl; Cmptr Sys Anlyst.

ELROD, BREE; Topeka HS; Topeka, KS; (4); Intnl Clb; NFL; Pres Thesps; Acpl Chr; Chorus; Drill Tm; School Musical; School Play; Variety Show; Phtg Ed Nwsp; Homcmng Qn; NHS Outstdng Sr; Stu Govt Outstdng Sr; Drill Team Outstdng Sr; Knox Coll; His.

ELSASSER, LESLIE; Olathe South Sr HS; Olathe, KS; (4); 19/350; Q&S; Yrbk; Lit Mag; Var Capt Gym; High Hon Roll; Hon Roll; NHS; KS Hnr Schlr; KS Dist Schlr; Show-Me-South; KS ST Univ.

ELSER, ABBY; Wakefield Schl; Wakefield, KS; (3); 1/25; Church Yth Grp; Cmnty Wkr; HOBY; Quiz Bowl; SADD; Teachers Aide; School Play; Rptr Nwsp; Phtg Yrbk; Pres Stu Cncl; U Of KS; Elem Educ.

ELSEY, SHANDI; Sublette HS; Sublette, KS; (2); Church Yth Grp; HOBY; Letterman Clb; Band; Pres Frsh Cls; Rep Stu Cncl; Var Chrldng; Var Vllybl; Hon Roll; Pep Clb; GCTL; Kays Clb; KS Univ; Psych.

ELSTEN, ERIC; Baxter Springs HS; Baxter Springs, KS; (3); 4/65; Am Leg Boys St; Cmnty Wkr; FBLA; FHA; Library Aide; Scholastic Bowl; Science Clb; Spanish Clb; Teachers Aide; School Play; Natl Yth Ldrshp Conf; Comp Sys Analyst.

ELWELL, AARON; Washburn Rural HS; Topeka, KS; (3); Varsity Clb; Var Bsktbl; JV Crs Cntry; High Hon Roll; Mtn Bk Rcng; Norba; KS ST; Arch/Bldg Sci.

EMEL, CRYSTAL B; Hutchinson HS; Hutchinson, KS; (2); 16/386; Church Yth Grp; Treas 4-H; French Clb; NFL; Band; High Hon Roll; NHS; Debate Tm; Speech Tm; Drm Mjr(t); Hutchfest Brd; Peer Cnslng; Poli Sci.

EMERSON, TRENDI G; Hayden HS; Topeka, KS; (2); SADD; Stat Var Bsktbl; Var Mgr(s); Var Score Keeper; JV Sftbl; JV Vllybl; Wt Lftg; Hon Roll; KS ST Univ.

EMERT, BONNIE J; Sumner Acad Of Arts & Science; Kansas City, KS; (3); 69/150; Church Yth Grp; Drama Clb; French Clb; Sec Pres German Clb; Latin Clb; NFL; Pep Clb; Stage Crew; Var Stat Ftbl; Hon Roll; Ft Hays; Rn.

EMERY, BROOKE; Shawnee Mission Northwest HS; Shawnee Mission, KS; (4); 105/390; Church Yth Grp; Office Aide; Pep Clb; Q&S; Teachers Aide; Ed Yrbk; Socr; Hon Roll; Fashion Careers I & II Ofcr; Awd Of Excl In Yrbk Wrtng From Ball ST 95; U Of KS; Bio.

EMIG, JAYSON R; Hope HS; Hope, KS; (2); Church Yth Grp; FBLA; Natl FFA Org; SADD; Chorus; Jazz Band; Var L Bsktbl; Var L Ftbl; High Hon Roll; NHS; Jr High Dances DJ Vol.

EMMERT, TERRYE L; Riverton Schl; Riverton, KS; (4); 5/57; Am Leg Aux Girls St; Letterman Clb; VP Soph Cls; Sec Jr Cls; Rep Stu Cncl; Cit Awd; NHS; Ntl Merit Ltr; Art Clb; KU Hnr Stu; MSSC; Criminal Justice.

EMO, ABBY D; Olathe East Sr HS; Overland Park, KS; (2); Cmnty Wkr; French Clb; Ofcr Jr Cls; Chrldng.

ENDICOTT, LORI A; Ft Scott HS; Fort Scott, KS; (2); Pep Clb; Chorus; School Musical; School Play; Rptr Soph Cls; Hon Roll; Nurse.

ENDRESS, CHRIS; Eureka Jr Sr HS; Eureka, KS; (4); 3/64; Letterman Clb; Quiz Bowl; Spanish Clb; Teachers Aide; Varsity Clb; Church Choir; Swing Chorus; Ftbl; Kiwanis Awd; NHS; Empora ST U; Scndry Ed Sci.

ENFIELD, AMANDA S; Wellsville Jr Sr HS; Wellsville, KS; (1); Church Yth Grp; FCA; FBLA; Intnl Clb; Math Tm; Church Choir; Yrbk; High Hon Roll; Baker.

ENGEBRETSON, MEGAN; Lansing HS; Lansing, KS; (1); Debate Tm; Math Tm; JV L Chrldng; High Hon Roll; Hon Roll; Elem Ed.

ENGEL, KELLY A; Clearwater HS; Clearwater, KS; (4); Girl Scts; Letterman Clb; Library Aide; SADD; Chorus; Bsktbl; Vllybl; Hon Roll; Kayettes Dir Of Recreation; WORD Rel Group; Friends Univ; Graphic Dsgn.

ENGELBERT, JOANNE; St John's HS; Beloit, KS; (2); Church Yth Grp; Speech Tm; SADD; Rep Stu Cncl; Bsktbl; Trk; Vllybl; High Hon Roll; NHS; Pres Acad Fit Awd; Piano Lssns; St Piano Cont; KS ST; Bus.

ENGELBERT, JOSH L; Beloit Jr Sr HS; Beloit, KS; (1); SADD; Var Bsbl; L Ftbl; High Hon Roll.

ENGELKEMIER, MONTE; Blue Valley HS; Overland Park, KS; (4); Church Yth Grp; Debate Tm; 4-H; HOBY; Math Tm; NFL; Speech Tm; Rep Jr Cls; Rep Sr Cls; Rep Stu Cncl; HOBY Jr Cnslr; Blue Vly USD Mentorshp Pgm; Natl 4-H Congrss; KS ST; Mech Engrng.

ENGELKEN, NATE J; Nemaha Valley HS; Seneca, KS; (3); Art Clb; Church Yth Grp; Letterman Clb; School Play; Stage Crew; Rep Stu Cncl; Crs Cntry; Trk; Prfct Atten Awd; Auto Body Repair.

ENGELMANN, ALISON; Andover HS; Wichita, KS; (3); Pep Clb; Chorus; School Play; Variety Show; Mgr Nwsp; Sec Soph Cls; VP Jr Cls; Capt Chrldng; Hon Roll; Pres Acad Fit Awd; U KS; Ad.

ENGELS, JEREMY D; Wichita Northwest HS; Wichita, KS; (2); 1/380; FCA; Intnl Clb; Science Clb; Spanish Clb; Teachers Aide; Orch; Var Bsbl; Intrml Wt Lftg; Cit Awd; High Hon Roll; Wichita Yth Symphony Repetory Orch Prin Bassist; Top Sci Stu Awd; Pre-Med; Phy.

ENGLE, RYAN; Madison Jr Sr HS; Madison, KS; (3); HOBY; Quiz Bowl; Jazz Band; Pres Frsh Cls; Pres Jr Cls; VP Jr Cls; Var L Bsktbl; Var L Ftbl; Var L Trk; NHS; KS ST; Accntng.

ENGLEMAN, AMY J; Goodland HS; Goodland, KS; (3); 19/82; Church Yth Grp; FHA; JV Tennis; Hon Roll; NHS; AFS Pres; Bus/Psych.

ENGLEMAN, MEGAN L; Great Bend Sr HS; Great Bend, KS; (3); Pep Clb; Teachers Aide; Band; Flag Corp; Mrchg Band; Pep Band; Stage Crew; Hon Roll; Prfct Atten Awd; Kyts Bd 96-; Jz Dnc 8 Yrs; Florist.

ENGROFF, JENNIFER; Hayden HS; Topeka, KS; (4); 9/117; Debate Tm; Letterman Clb; Var Capt Bsktbl; Var L Vllybl; Gov Hon Prg Awd; High Hon Roll; NHS; Pres Acad Fit Awd; Pres Schlr; St Schlr; AZ ST; Acctng.

ENGSTROM, APRIL D; Fredonia HS; Fredonia, KS; (4); 7/73; Art Clb; Cmnty Wkr; Drama Clb; French Clb; Pep Clb; Science Clb; Service Clb; Spanish Clb; School Play; Ed Nwsp; Pittsburg St U; Eng Ed.

ENGSTROM, KRISTIN A; Canton-Galva HS; Galva, KS; (3); German Clb; SADD; Yrbk; Ofcr Stu Cncl; Sftbl; Hon Roll; FBLA; KS U; Pediatric Nrs.

ENGSTROM, NICHOLAS J; Wamego HS; Wamego, KS; (3); Am Leg Boys St; Church Yth Grp; Letterman Clb; Pres Science Clb; Band; Mrchg Band; Pep Band; JV Bsktbl; JV Crs Cntry; Var Trk.

ENLEE, BROOKE; Atchison Sr HS; Atchison, KS; (2); Church Yth Grp; Debate Tm; NFL; Spanish Clb; Church Choir; Sftbl; JV Vllybl; High Hon Roll; Pres Acad Fit Awd; Chrch Spon Musicl; Piano; Med.

ENLOW, KRISTIE; Dodge City HS; Dodge City, KS; (3); Cmnty Wkr; 4-H; Natl FFA Org; Speech Tm; Band; Mrchg Band; Bsktbl; 4-H Awd; Hon Roll; 4-H Clb Sec, VP, Pres; FFA VP, Sent; Livestock Jdgng, Speech, Land Jdng Conts; Vet.

ENNEKING, CHAD D; Bern Schl; Bern, KS; (3); Letterman Clb; Var Bsktbl; Var Ftbl; Cit Awd; Prfct Atten Awd.

ENNS, DAVID; Hillsboro HS; Hillsboro, KS; (1); 1/73; Church Yth Grp; Natl FFA Org; Scholastic Bowl; Band; Mrchg Band; Pep Band; Bsktbl; Ftbl; High Hon Roll.

ENOCH, MATTHEW M; Riley Cty HS; Manhattan, KS; (3); Church Yth Grp; FBLA; Pep Clb; Teachers Aide; VP Frsh Cls; VP Soph Cls; Rep Stu Cncl; JV Bsktbl; L Ftbl; L Trk; St Weightlng Champ; KS St Univ; Park Mgnt.

ENOS, KIMBERLY B; Northwest HS Wichita; Wichita, KS; (3); 28/327; Cmnty Wkr; Intnl Clb; Orch; Hon Roll; NHS; Pres Acad Fit Awd; NAHS Pres; Regnl Wnnr In Stock Market Game Hosted By KS ST U; Fnlst In David Losew Photo Cmptn; Columbia Coll; ASL Interpreter.

ENSIGN, DERIK K; Olathe East Sr HS; Olathe, KS; (2); Tennis; High Hon Roll; All City Tnns Team; KY; Cardiovascular Surgeon.

ENSLEY, JILL RAE ANNE; Seaman Sr HS; Topeka, KS; (4); 98/280; Pres Art Clb; Cmnty Wkr; French Clb; Model UN; SADD; Sec Thesps; Band; Drill Tm; School Musical; Ed Lit Mag; 1st Pl Regnl His Day Cmptn Individual Media; Young Democrats Pres; Topeka Arts Cncl Mem; KS Univ; Fine Arts; Wrtng.

ENSLINGER, JEFFREY A; Dodge City HS; Dodge City, KS; (3); Cit Awd; Acctng.

ENSZ, ANDREW P; Newton Sr HS; Newton, KS; (4); 1/212; Am Leg Boys St; Church Yth Grp; Science Clb; Var L Bsktbl; Var L Golf; NHS; Pres Schlr; Val; Amer Legion Outstdng Stu; Governors Schlr; U Of KS; Biomedical Engrng.

ENSZ, JEREMY; Inman Jr Sr HS; Inman, KS; (2); Church Yth Grp; Math Tm; Quiz Bowl; Scholastic Bowl; Spanish Clb; VP Frsh Cls; Ftbl; Golf; Mgr(s); Wt Lftg; 5th Pl Natl Glbl Chllng Crrnt Evnts Tst; St Quiz Bwl Team; Nclr Engrng.

ENTWISTLE, ANIKA; Shawnee Mission E Sr HS; Leawood, KS; (3); Q&S; Nwsp; Crs Cntry; Trk; French Hon Soc; Hon Roll; NHS; Jrnlsm; Ed.

ENTZ, KYLE B; Berean Acad; Whitewater, KS; (3); 4/45; Church Yth Grp; Letterman Clb; Science Clb; Band; Pep Band; Rep Frsh Cls; Pres Jr Cls; Var Bsktbl; High Hon Roll; NHS; Moody Bible Inst; Intnl Relatns.

ENZ, NICHOLAS J; Newton Sr HS; Newton, KS; (2); Treas Church Yth Grp; Band; Jazz Band; Mrchg Band; Pep Band; JV Socr; JV Tennis; High Hon Roll; Hon Roll; Dntst.

EOFF, JENNIFER; Mc Pherson HS; Defiance, OH; (4); Church Yth Grp; Letterman Clb; Spanish Clb; Chorus; School Musical; Ofcr Stu Cncl; Chrldng; Swmmng; Hon Roll; NHS; LDS Yng Women Medlln; Mixed Ensmble 2 Yrs; Utah Valley ST Coll; Elem Ed.

EPLER, CORY; Columbus HS; Hallowell, KS; (4); 5/95; Am Leg Boys St; Math Tm; Pres VP Natl FFA Org; Chorus; Pres Jr Cls; VP Sr Cls; Pres Stu Cncl; L Var Bsktbl; L Var Trk; Pres NHS; KS Assn Yth Trea; KS Hnr Schlr; KS St FFA Degree; KSU.

EPLEY, CURTIS; Kingman HS; Kingman, KS; (3); Am Leg Boys St; Cmnty Wkr; FBLA; Office Aide; JV Bsktbl; Var Trk; Friends; Acctng; Stock Broker.

EPP, STEPHANIE M; Newton Sr HS; Newton, KS; (1); Church Yth Grp; SADD; Hon Roll; Med.

EPPERSON, JOSHUA; Peabody-Burns Jr Sr HS; Peabody, KS; (1); 2/35; Church Yth Grp; FCA; Quiz Bowl; Band; School Musical; JV Ftbl; Var Trk; High Hon Roll; Drama Clb; Math Tm; Lge Schlrshp Cont Brnz Mdl; Natl Bible Bwl 2nd Pl.

EPPLER, BETH A; Blue Valley North HS; Leawood, KS; (2); Church Yth Grp; Dance Clb; Drill Tm; Mrchg Band; School Musical; Variety Show; Pom Pon; Hon Roll; Miller & Marlee Entertainers Troupe Mem; Theater In The Park Mem; Dance Instr; KS ST Univ; Psych.

EPPS, COLBY; Topeka West HS; Topeka, KS; (4); SADD; Band; Jazz Band; Mrchg Band; Orch; Pep Band; JV Var Bsbl; JV Var Bsktbl; JV Socr; Cit Awd; Snowball King 96; Citation For Outstndng Musicianshp Band Pres; KS ST HS Acts Assn Citizenshp Awd; KS ST; Bus.

ERB, TRAVIS L; Ness City HS; Ness City, KS; (1); Church Yth Grp; Natl FFA Org; Var Bsbl; Stat Bsktbl; Stat Ftbl; Var Golf; Greenhand FFA Awd; Hnrs Every Semester; Fort Hays ST; Pub Relations.

ERBACHER, MEGAN; Thomas More Prep-Marion HS; Hays, KS; (1); Debate Tm; Latin Clb; JV Bsktbl; Vllybl; High Hon Roll; Gftd Stu Prog.

ERICKSON, ALICIA K; Washburn Rural HS; Wakarusa, KS; (3); Art Clb; French Clb; Band; Mrchg Band; Orch; Pep Band; School Musical; High Hon Roll; NHS; Topeka Yth Symph; Dist Hnr Orch; All St Hnr Orch.

ERICKSON, CARRIAN B; Blue Valley HS; Shawnee Mission, KS; (3); Spanish Clb; Teachers Aide; Varsity Clb; Drill Tm; Flag Corp; Variety Show; Bsktbl; Var Chrldng; Var Pom Pon; Var Sftbl; U Of KS; Ed.

ERICKSON, GENEVA J; Smoky Valley HS; Lindsborg, KS; (3); Pep Clb; Varsity Clb; Band; Mrchg Band; Pep Band; Var Chrldng; JV Vllybl; High Hon Roll; High Hon Roll; Acctng.

ERICKSON, KRISTEN M; Desoto HS; Olathe, KS; (3); French Clb; Band; Mrchg Band; Pep Band; Nwsp; Yrbk; Hon Roll; U Of KS.

ERICSON, MYNON M; Mission Valley HS; Maple Hill, KS; (4); 15/61; Church Yth Grp; Sec VP FHA; Letterman Clb; Pep Clb; Spanish Clb; SADD; Teachers Aide; Acpl Chr; Band; Chorus; FHA Natl Lvl 9th Grd/ST Lvl 10th Grd; KS ST Univ; Social Worker.

ERIKSON, MICHELLE; El Dorado HS; El Dorado, KS; (4); 1/156; Church Yth Grp; Cmnty Wkr; Debate Tm; HOBY; Letterman Clb; NFL; Pep Clb; Speech Tm; SADD; Varsity Clb; HOBY Alumni Assn, Jr Cnslr; Completed HS 3 Yrs W/4 GPA; KS ST U; Medcl.

ERIKSON, SHELLEY L; El Dorado HS; El Dorado, KS; (3); 1/140; Church Yth Grp; Debate Tm; French Clb; GAA; HOBY; NFL; Office Aide; SADD; Varsity Clb; Bsktbl; KS ST Univ; Physcns Asst.

ERIVES, ABEL; Sublette HS; Sublette, KS; (3); 18/36; Macy Minorities In Medicine Pgm Awd; Med Dr.

ERKMANN, JOHN J; Blue Valley Northwest HS; Overland Park, KS; (2); Computer Clb; Debate Tm; High Hon Roll; Hon Roll; Phy.

ERNST, BRITTA; Seaman Sr HS; Topeka, KS; (4); 16/245; Am Leg Aux Girls St; Church Yth Grp; Hosp Aide; Key Clb; Pres Spanish Clb; SADD; Chorus; Stat Bsktbl; Var Trk; High Hon Roll; AFS; KS ST U; Arch.

ERNST, TIFFANY A; Hays HS; Hays, KS; (3); Church Yth Grp; Hosp Aide; NFL; SADD; Acpl Chr; Chorus; Church Choir; School Musical; School Play; Stage Crew; Music.

ERNZEN, CHAD N; Leavenworth HS; Leavenworth, KS; (3); Var Bsktbl; Hon Roll.

ERVIN, MELANIE N; Liberal HS; Liberal, KS; (3); Art Clb; Drama Clb; Hosp Aide; Teachers Aide; Thesps; School Play; Rptr Phtg Yrbk; JV Tennis; Hon Roll; NHS; U Of NM; Radiology.

ERWAY, DEE; Larned HS; Larned, KS; (2); Art Clb; Intnl Clb; Letterman Clb; Pep Clb; Spanish Clb; Acpl Chr; Chrldng; Hon Roll.

ERWIN, ASHLEY D; Maize HS; Wichita, KS; (2); VP Church Yth Grp; Drama Clb; GAA; SADD; Chorus; Variety Show; Sftbl; Trk; Wt Lftg; Hon Roll; KS Univ; Pediatrician.

ERWINE, ARIELE; Olathe East Sr HS; Olathe, KS; (2); Art Clb; Drama Clb; French Clb; Teachers Aide; School Play; Trk; Vllybl; Hon Roll; Drm Awds; Phtgrphy; Coll; Art Tchr.

ESCHKE, STACY; Riley Cty HS; Riley, KS; (1); 25/49; Church Yth Grp; Cmnty Wkr; FCA; 4-H; FHA; Pep Clb; SADD; Band; Chorus; Church Choir; St Msc; HS Reg Msc Solos & Ensmbls; NCA Camp 95-96; KS ST U; Fshn Dsgn.

ESHELMAN, MELISSA; Manhattan HS; Manhattan, KS; (2); Church Yth Grp; SADD; Chrldng; Sftbl; Hon Roll; Jazz Dance; KS ST U; Psych.

ESLICK, AMANDA L; Salina HS South; Salina, KS; (3); Teachers Aide; Hon Roll; Renaissance Card Holder & Awd Wnnr; .5 Clb; Psych.

ESPE, ANGELA R; Bishop Miege HS; Olathe, KS; (1); 2/245; Church Yth Grp; JV Bsktbl; Var Sftbl; Intrml Vllybl; High Hon Roll; Ed Tchr/Coach.

ESPINOSA, RACHEL I; Dodge City HS; Dodge City, KS; (3); Cmnty Wkr; French Clb; Model UN; Quiz Bowl; Scholastic Bowl; SADD; Teachers Aide; Chorus; French Hon Soc; NHS; Pre-Med.

ESPINOSA, SILVIA A; Wichita West HS; Wichita, KS; (2); 101/431; Spanish Clb; Nwsp; Yrbk; Ofcr Soph Cls; Hon Roll; Prfct Atten Awd; Wichita ST Univ; Psych.

ESPINOZA, IRIS E; Rolla HS; Rolla, KS; (2); Band; Chorus; Mrchg Band; Pep Band; Sec Soph Cls; Var Bsktbl; Var Trk; Vllybl; Prfct Atten Awd; Phys Ed Tchr.

ESPINOZA, MARCIANO A; Rolla HS; Rolla, KS; (3); FCA; Chorus; Ed Nwsp; Var Cmnty Wkr; Var Trk; High Hon Roll; Hon Roll; Eng Tchr.

ESPINOZA, PATRICIA; Wichita North HS; Wichita, KS; (4); Girl Scts; Hon Roll; Acad Achvmnt Awd; Unsung Hero Awd; Hispanic Womens Ntwrk Schlsp; Wichita ST Univ; Physicn Asst.

ESSEX, MATTHEW A; Syracuse Jr Sr HS; Syracuse, KS; (2); Church Yth Grp; Cmnty Wkr; Letterman Clb; Pep Clb; VP Frsh Cls; JV Var Ftbl; Var Trk; Var Wt Lftg; Hon Roll; Guitar; IM Bsktbl; All-League Acad Trk & Ftbl; Mid Amer Nazarene.

ESSLINGER, ANTHONY J; Bern Schl; Bern, KS; (2); Var Scholastic Bowl; SADD; Band; Chorus; Mrchg Band; Pep Band; School Play; Mgr Bsktbl; Var Ftbl; Trk.

ESSLINGER, VANESSA D; Campus HS; Clearwater, KS; (3); Treas Drama Clb; Q&S; Thesps; Chorus; School Musical; School Play; Stage Crew; Ed Nwsp; High Hon Roll; NHS; Campus Singers; Best Supporting Actress Awd; Hnr Bar Thespian; Julliard; Musical Theatre.

ESSMAN, RUSSELL F; Oskaloosa HS; Oskaloosa, KS; (3); FBLA; SADD; Teachers Aide; Varsity Clb; Ofcr Bsbl; Bsktbl; Ftbl; Golf; Wt Lftg; Wrstlng; KS ST; Aeronautics.

ESSMILLER, ADLEE Y; Manhattan HS; Manhattan, KS; (4); 66/354; Art Clb; Computer Clb; FBLA; Spanish Clb; SADD; Teachers Aide; Varsity Clb; JV Golf; Var Tennis; High Hon Roll; Acad Excl Awd; KSHSAA Outstdng Achvmt Awd; Pres Acad Achvmnt Awd; KS ST Univ; Bus.

ESTES, CHRIS J; Remington HS; Potwin, KS; (4); 5/25; Letterman Clb; Office Aide; Band; Capt Bsktbl; Capt Ftbl; Capt Trk; Wt Lftg; High Hon Roll; NHS; Ft Scott CC; Crmnl Jstc.

ESTES, IEISHA R; Pittsburg HS; Pittsburg, KS; (1); Chorus; Intrml Bsktbl; Hon Roll; RN.

ESTES, JEREMIAH H; Topeka West HS; Topeka, KS; (1); Boy Scts; Teachers Aide; Chorus; Church Choir; School Musical; School Play; High Hon Roll.

ESTES, MICHAEL G; Halstead HS; Halstead, KS; (2); Letterman Clb; Varsity Clb; Var Bsktbl; Var Ftbl; Var Wt Lftg; Hon Roll; Bsktbl Var MVP, MCAA Hnrb Mntn, All-League, All-Area Team Hnrb Mntn; U Of KS; Phys Thrpy.

ETCHESON, JENNIFER N; Pittsburg HS; Pittsburg, KS; (2); Cmnty Wkr; GAA; Bsktbl; Crs Cntry; Sftbl; High Hon Roll; Hon Roll; Engrng.

ETCHISON, EMILY; Quivira Heights HS; Holyrood, KS; (3); 6/24; Church Yth Grp; FCA; HOBY; Letterman Clb; Speech Tm; Chorus; Sec Jr Cls; Var L Vllybl; Hon Roll; CNA; Music Thrpy.

ETLING, TINA M; Cimarron HS; Ensign, KS; (4); 7/49; Church Yth Grp; FCA; Band; Chorus; Church Choir; Capt Drill Tm; School Musical; Ed Nwsp; Ed Yrbk; Tennis; Pratt CC; Elem Ed.

ETTER, KAMI D; Wellington Sr HS; Mayfield, KS; (2); Dance Clb; Drama Clb; SADD; Teachers Aide; Drill Tm; NHS; Natl FFA Org; KSU.

EUBANK, ROBIN; Protection Schl; Protection, KS; (2); 1/21; Church Yth Grp; Treas 4-H; VP Pep Clb; Var Scholastic Bowl; Speech Tm; Pres Soph Cls; Rep Stu Cncl; 4-H Awd; High Hon Roll; Kayettes Bd Mem; Advtsng Mgmt.

EUBANKS, BRIAN W; Field Kindley Mem Sr HS; Coffeyville, KS; (3); Church Yth Grp; Math Tm; Spanish Clb; High Hon Roll; Hon Roll; NHS; KS U; Civil Engnr.

EUBANKS, SARA D; Valley Ctr HS; Valley Center, KS; (3); 30/162; Church Yth Grp; Hosp Aide; Chorus; Church Choir; School Musical; Hon Roll; Bible Bwl; Chrch Drama Tm.

EUCKER, STEPHANIE A; Wichita Heights HS; Wichita, KS; (3); 1/250; German Clb; Math Tm; Science Clb; Band; Mrchg Band; Var L Tennis; L Trk; High Hon Roll; Hon Roll; Pres NHS.

EUCTICE, HEATHER; Concordia Jr Sr HS; Concordia, KS; (4); Am Leg Aux Girls St; Dance Clb; Drama Clb; NFL; Thesps; Band; Drm Mjr(t); Pep Band; Chrldng; Hon Roll; ST Qlfr Frnscs; 96 Cld Cnty Jr Miss; Cld Cnty CC; Scndry Drmtc Arts.

EVANHOE, LAURELIN; Derby HS; Derby, KS; (4); 7/341; Sec Art Clb; Drama Clb; Speech Tm; Teachers Aide; High Hon Roll; NHS; St Schlr; Stage Crew; Envir Clb Pres; KS Hnr Schlr; Pres Awd Ecudl Excl; U Of KS; Envir Sci.

EVANOFF, KRISTINA M; Blue Valley HS; Overland Park, KS; (3); Bsktbl; Var Socr; Vllybl; High Hon Roll; Hon Roll; SADD; Tax Law.

EVANS, AARON D; Labette Co HS; Parsons, KS; (4); Chess Clb; Church Yth Grp; FCA; Library Aide; Science Clb; JV Ftbl; JV Trk; High Hon Roll; Hon Roll; NHS; Labette CC; Phy Ther.

EVANS, AMANDA L; El Dorado HS; El Dorado, KS; (2); Cmnty Wkr; HOBY; Letterman Clb; Rep Stu Cncl; Var L Bsktbl; Var L Sftbl; Var L Vllybl; High Hon Roll; NHS; Peer Cnslng; Pathlgst.

EVANS, CLINT R; Smoky Valley HS; Lindsborg, KS; (3); Boy Scts; Church Yth Grp; Sec Soph Cls; Ofcr Bsbl; JV Bsktbl; JV Ftbl; High Hon Roll; Hon Roll; KAYS; Cnstrctn.

EVANS, DANIAL P; South Barber HS; Kiowa, KS; (3); VICA; Band; Chorus; Mrchg Band; Pep Band; School Play; Var Trk; Wt Lftg; High Hon Roll; NHS.

EVANS, DESIREE R; Washington HS; Kansas City, KS; (2); Church Yth Grp; Cmnty Wkr; Rptr Nwsp; Swmmng; Vllybl; Wrtng; Roller Skating; Sing; Dance; KS City Comm Coll; Author.

EVANS, ELISHA D; Olathe South Sr HS; Olathe, KS; (4); Orch; Hon Roll; NHS; Pltcl Sci.

EVANS, ERIC; Topeka HS; Topeka, KS; (1); Church Yth Grp; Band; Mrchg Band; Pep Band; Bsktbl; Ftbl; JV Trk; Hon Roll; BSU; STRAPP.

EVANS, JACQUELINE N; Oskaloosa HS; Oskaloosa, KS; (2); FBLA; FHA; Letterman Clb; Pep Clb; Ski Clb; SADD; Ofcr Frsh Cls; Chrldng; Pom Pon; High Hon Roll.

EVANS, JEREMY L; Bucklin Schl; Bucklin, KS; (3); Church Yth Grp; Band; Chorus; Var L Bsktbl; Var L Ftbl; Hon Roll; Ag.

EVANS, JOSH; Eureka Jr Sr HS; Neal, KS; (3); 1/60; Drama Clb; NFL; Quiz Bowl; Scholastic Bowl; Ski Clb; Band; School Play; Pres Stu Cncl; High Hon Roll; NHS; Acting.

EVANS, REBECCA C; Olathe North Sr HS; Olathe, KS; (4); Office Aide; Spanish Clb; Teachers Aide; Hon Roll; Rockhurst Coll; Nrsng.

EVANS, RYAN W; Great Bend Sr HS; Great Bend, KS; (2); 10/263; Math Tm; Band; Jazz Band; Mrchg Band; Pep Band; Variety Show; Bsktbl; Socr; High Hon Roll; KS Univ; Cmptr Syst Anlyst.

EVANS, TREVER M; Hoisington HS; Hoisington, KS; (3); 12/72; Am Leg Boys St; Boy Scts; Church Yth Grp; Cmnty Wkr; Debate Tm; Letterman Clb; Ofcr Bsbl; Bsktbl; Hon Roll; NHS; KS Univ; Pre-Med.

EVANSON, DENAE; Bishop Ward HS; Kansas City, KS; (1); Debate Tm; 4-H; NFL; Pep Clb; Speech Tm; Bsktbl; JV Chrldng; Pom Pon; Hon Roll; UCLA; Crmnl Law.

EVEL, KEVIN; Sacred Heart HS; Salina, KS; (3); Cmnty Wkr; FBLA; Letterman Clb; Math Tm; Pep Clb; Golf; High Hon Roll; NHS; Prfct Atten Awd.

EVERETT, JULIE L; Campus HS; Haysville, KS; (3); 15/250; Church Yth Grp; Cmnty Wkr; Intnl Clb; Q&S; Science Clb; SADD; Ed Nwsp; Rep Jr Cls; Ofcr Stu Cncl; High Hon Roll; Opt Clb Stu Of Mnth; Jrnlsm Merit Awd; Cathlc Yth Org Comm Offcr; Acctng.

EVERETT, NIKKI; Lansing HS; Lansing, KS; (3); 5/142; Church Yth Grp; Pres French Clb; Teachers Aide; Chorus; Sec Drill Tm; Mgr(s); Pom Pon; Treas French Hon Soc; High Hon Roll; NHS; Ballet/Jazz Classes; Piano/Vocal Lessons; League Music Festival Vocal Solo I Rating; OK Univ; Architect.

EVERETT, REINA C; Washington HS; Kansas City, KS; (3); Cmnty Wkr; Band; Mrchg Band; Pep Band; Stage Crew; Treas Soph Cls; Anthropology.

EVERETTE, RICARDO D; Junction City HS; Apo, AE; (3); 34/292; Am Leg Boys St; Church Yth Grp; Letterman Clb; Spanish Clb; Rptr Yrbk; Ofcr Stu Cncl; JV Trk; Cit Awd; High Hon Roll; East Carolina Univ; Jrnlsm.

EVERHART, CLINTON; Haysville Campus HS; Wichita, KS; (4); 10/198; Am Leg Boys St; Drama Clb; Intnl Clb; Science Clb; Thesps; Chorus; Orch; School Musical; School Play; Stage Crew; 1st Runner Up WSU Distngd Schlsp Invitational; Wichita ST Univ.

EVERINGHAM, KRISTINA; Wichita East HS; Wichita, KS; (2); Church Yth Grp; Cmnty Wkr; Spanish Clb; Teachers Aide; Chorus; Church Choir; High Hon Roll; Lived/Studies Puerto Rico Frosh Yr; St Anthonys Fmly Shltr Vol; ESL Tutor Vol; Sunday Schl Tchr; Span/Ed/Mssnry/HS Tchr.

EVERITT, BRANDI N; Leavenworth HS; Leavenworth, KS; (3); Pres Church Yth Grp; Hosp Aide; Pres Intnl Clb; ROTC; Chrmn SADD; School Play; Yrbk; Socr; Hon Roll; Drama Clb; ROTC Hnr Grd Wthout Wpns Commndr; Air Frc; Lwyr.

EVEROSKI, ROBERT D; Halstead HS; Halstead, KS; (4); 28/51; Hon Roll; Prfct Atten Awd; Vol Weatherman For Halstead Schl Dist Wth Cntr; Hutchinson CC; Comp Sci.

EVERS, JANA L; St Thomas Aquinas HS; Leawood, KS; (3); 4/263; Church Yth Grp; Cmnty Wkr; German Clb; Ed Nwsp; Intrml Bsktbl; High Hon Roll; NHS; Ntl Merit Ltr; Teens For Life Pres; Phys Thpy.

EVERT, NICKOLAS C; Goodland HS; Goodland, KS; (3); 6/97; Boy Scts; 4-H; FHA; Band; Jazz Band; Mrchg Band; Pep Band.

EVERY, ADAM D; Parsons HS; Parsons, KS; (4); Church Yth Grp; FTA; Spanish Clb; SADD; Teachers Aide; School Musical; Crs Cntry; Wt Lftg; Hon Roll; Prfct Atten Awd; U Of KS; Optometry.

EVERY, JASON C; Wichita South HS; Wichita, KS; (3); School Play; Hon Roll; Archery; Bowhunter Ed Cert; British/European Motorcycle Show; Wichita ST Univ; PT.

EVINGER, BROOKE A; Cimarron HS; Cimarron, KS; (4); 1/50; Sec Pep Clb; Treas Spanish Clb; Teachers Aide; Rep Jr Cls; High Hon Roll; NHS; Ntl Merit SF; U Of Notre Dame; Intl Bus Admin.

EWBANK, CRISTI; Parsons HS; Mc Cune, KS; (4); 41/144; Spanish Clb; SADD; Teachers Aide; Yrbk; Hon Roll; Sprts Clb; Pre-Med Clb; Wrstlng Cheerldr; Wichita St Univ; Elem Ed.

EWELL, JORDAN ALICIA; Washburn Rural HS; Topeka, KS; (2); Orch; School Musical; Hon Roll; Chrch Act Vol; KS Univ; Jrnlsm; Commnctn.

EWERT, JILL; Canton-Galva HS; Canton, KS; (2); FBLA; SADD; Band; School Play; Ofcr Stu Cncl; Var Bsktbl; Var Chrldng; Var Trk; Var Vllybl; High Hon Roll; Pwdr Puff Ftbl Qrtrbck; Hrt Amer Leg Schlsp Tstng Gld Mdlst; Drama.

EWERT, LIBBY E; Anderson Cty Jr Sr HS; Parker, KS; (2); Cmnty Wkr; FHA; Intnl Clb; Library Aide; Pep Clb; SADD; Hon Roll; Acad Awds; KAY Clb; FHA Sec & Treas; Emporia ST; Elem Ed.

EWING, ADAM T; Wellington Sr HS; Wellington, KS; (2); 1/175; Boy Scts; Church Yth Grp; Scholastic Bowl; Church Choir; Wrstlng; Cit Awd; High Hon Roll; Hon Roll; Jr NHS; Prfct Atten Awd.

EWING, ANGELA S; Independence HS; Independence, KS; (1); Church Yth Grp; Cmnty Wkr; VP 4-H; Orch; JV Sftbl; 4-H Awd; High Hon Roll.

EWING, KELLY M; Turner HS; Kansas City, KS; (3); Bus Profs of Am; Pep Clb; SADD; Prfct Atten Awd; Car Shows; KS Assn Of Yths; Drag Racing; Pittsburgh ST Univ.

EWING, SHANNON; Eric HS; Erie, KS; (4); 1/41; FCA; SADD; Yrbk; VP Frsh Cls; VP Soph Cls; VP Jr Cls; VP Sr Cls; Bsktbl; Vllybl; Gov Hon Prg Awd; KS Assn Of Yth; All ST Acad Awd; U Of KS; Sports Sci/PT.

EWING, TAYLOR J; Shawnee Heights Sr HS; Tecumseh, KS; (2); Church Yth Grp; FCA; FBLA; Pep Clb; Quiz Bowl; Ftbl; High Hon Roll; Hon Roll; Bsbl; PAL Bsktbl.

EWY, AARON; Dodge City HS; Dodge City, KS; (4); 28/254; Teachers Aide; High Hon Roll; Bio.

EWY, DAVID; Maize HS; Wichita, KS; (4); Debate Tm; Math Tm; Science Clb; Spanish Clb; High Hon Roll; Hon Roll; NHS; St Schlr; Wichita St Univ; Comp Sci.

EYBERG, KATHERINE T; Blue Valley Northwest HS; Overland Park, KS; (1); Vllybl; High Hon Roll.

EYE, WYMETTA L; Campus HS; Wichita, KS; (3); Intnl Clb; Quiz Bowl; Scholastic Bowl; SADD; Band; Mrchg Band; Pep Band; High Hon Roll; Hon Roll; NHS; MIT; Eng.

EYLAR, NEAL L; Troy HS; Atchison, KS; (2); Var Bsbl; Hon Roll; NHS; Prfct Atten Awd; KS Univ.

EZELL, JEREMY H; Galena HS; Galena, KS; (1); FCA; FBLA; FHA; Rep Stu Cncl; L Bsktbl; L Cmnty Wkr; Wt Lftg; High Hon Roll; KS Univ; Law.

EZELL, NATHAN A; Galena HS; Galena, KS; (3); Am Leg Boys St; Church Yth Grp; FHA; Ofcr Stu Cncl; JV Var Bsktbl; JV Var Ftbl; High Hon Roll; NHS; Prfct Atten Awd; Natl Young Ldrshp Conf; KS Newman Coll Investigative Summer Sci; Bus; Comps.

EZELL, SAMMIE; Galena HS; Galena, KS; (4); 1/33; Am Leg Aux Girls St; Pres FHA; HOBY; Scholastic Bowl; VP Stu Cncl; Pres NHS; St Schlr; Val; FCA; FBLA; KS Regents Hnrs Acad; 3rd Rnnr Up Miss Teen KS Pgnt; KS ST U; Bus Admin.

FABER, NICOLE L; Udall HS; Wichita, KS; (2); Band; Lit Mag; Hon Roll; Band Ltr; Wichita ST U; PT.

FABER, RACHEL; Goddard HS; Wichita, KS; (3); Drama Clb; Pep Clb; Chorus; School Musical; Variety Show; Chrldng; Socr; High Hon Roll; Hon Roll; NHS; Phy.

FABRIZIUS, AMANDA; Trego Comm HS; Wa Keeney, KS; (3); 1/48; Drama Clb; Pres Science Clb; SADD; Band; Mrchg Band; Pep Band; Rep Jr Cls; Ofcr Stu Cncl; High Hon Roll; NHS; 4 Yr Coll.

FABRIZIUS, JENNY; Solomon Jr Sr HS; Solomon, KS; (4); 4/15; FHA; Letterman Clb; Band; School Play; Pres VP Stu Cncl; L Var Bsktbl; L Var Vllybl; High Hon Roll; NHS; Dance Clb; DARE Role Model; KS ST Univ; Elem Ed.

FAGAN, BRANDY D; Arkansas City HS; Arkansas City, KS; (1); English Clb; Library Aide; Red Cross Aide; SADD; Teachers Aide; Flag Corp; Crs Cntry; Trk; FFA Clb; Work With Disabled.

FAGAN, TODD; Mulvane Sr HS; Mulvane, KS; (3); FCA; Band; Jazz Band; Rep Soph Cls; Treas Jr Cls; Var Bsbl; Var Ftbl; Hon Roll; NHS; Prfct Atten Awd; Emporia ST; Sports Med.

FAGEN, AUBREY L; Jetmore HS; Spearville, KS; (4); 3/15; Teachers Aide; Nwsp; Yrbk; Pres Frsh Cls; Ofcr Stu Cncl; Bsktbl; Var Vllybl; Hon Roll; Stdnt Cncl Pres Sr; Crums Beauty Coll.

FAGER, JAKE T; Salina HS South; Salina, KS; (4); Am Leg Boys St; Church Yth Grp; NFL; Teachers Aide; Thesps; Chorus; School Musical; Stage Crew; Variety Show; Bsktbl; KS ST U; Engrng.

FAIMON, CARYN; Burlingame HS; Auburn, KS; (4); 2/36; 4-H; FBLA; HOBY; Letterman Clb; Band; Jazz Band; Pres Sr Cls; VP Stu Cncl; Var Bsktbl; Capt Vllybl.

FAIR, J.D.; Manhattan HS; Manhattan, KS; (4); Am Leg Boys St; Pres Chess Clb; Letterman Clb; SADD; Varsity Clb; Ftbl; Swmmng; Trk; High Hon Roll; NHS; KS ST Univ.

FAIR, JAMES D; Manhattan HS; Manhattan, KS; (4); Am Leg Boys St; Pres Chess Clb; Letterman Clb; Varsity Clb; Ofcr Stu Cncl; Ftbl; Swmmng; Trk; High Hon Roll; NHS; KS ST U; Med.

FAIRCHILD, JENNIFER; St John Jr Sr HS; Saint John, KS; (3); Church Yth Grp; 4-H; FHA; Band; Chorus; Church Choir; Var Bsktbl; Var Trk; Var Vllybl; Hon Roll; Psychlgy/Ed.

FAISON, TYRONE; Junction City HS; Junction City, KS; (2); Trk; Wrstlng; Hon Roll.

FAJARDO, ANN; Topeka West HS; Topeka, KS; (4); 17/239; Church Yth Grp; Cmnty Wkr; French Clb; German Clb; Intnl Clb; Library Aide; Math Clb; Model UN; Science Clb; Spanish Clb; TEA Party Env Clb; Stu Advsry Cncl Mmbr; Heritage Panel Mmbr; USC; Bio.

FALCONE, JASON C; Blue Valley Northwest HS; Overland Park, KS; (3); Cmnty Wkr; JCL; Latin Clb; Stage Crew; Rptr Nwsp; JV Mgr(s); JV Var Socr; Hon Roll; KJCL Convntn Latn Cmptn 5th Pl; Odyssey Of The Mind Tem Cmptn St Levl; DARE Rol Modl For Polc Dept; Criminal Justice; Law.

FALK, AARON; Jefferson Co North HS; Nortonville, KS; (4); 5/37; Art Clb; JV Bsktbl; Hon Roll; Prfct Atten Awd; Outstndng Indstrl Arts Stu; NHS; KS ST U; Arch.

FALK, BRANDON D; Onaga HS; Wheaton, KS; (3); Church Yth Grp; Cmnty Wkr; 4-H; Letterman Clb; Natl FFA Org; Quiz Bowl; Teachers Aide; Varsity Clb; Band; Pep Band; Olympic Wghtlftng.

FALK, JEANNE S; Atchison Co Cmty HS; Atchison, KS; (2); 1/65; 4-H; Math Clb; Band; Mrchg Band; Pep Band; 4-H Awd; Hon Roll; Twrlng Squad Baton; KS ST Univ; Animal Sci.

FALKE, AMY M; Anderson Cty Jr Sr HS; Westphalia, KS; (3); 6/70; Drama Clb; Intnl Clb; Pep Clb; Thesps; Acpl Chr; Band; Chorus; Mrchg Band; Pep Band; School Musical; Kndgtrn Bible Schl Tchr; After Schl Tutor.

FALKE, JAKE; Anderson Cty Jr Sr HS; Westphalia, KS; (1); Chorus; JV Golf; High Hon Roll.

FALLIS, BART; Buhler HS; Hutchinson, KS; (2); Boy Scts; Church Yth Grp; Letterman Clb; Science Clb; Band; Mrchg Band; Pep Band; School Musical; Ftbl; Trk; Goju Karate-Gold In Natls; 3rd Pl In AAU Jr Olympics For St; Ranked 1st In Natl Magazines 92-95; Law Enforcement.

FAN, ERICA; Washburn Rural HS; Topeka, KS; (2); 8/400; Rep French Clb; Hosp Aide; Intnl Clb; Model UN; NFL; SADD; Orch; School Musical; JV L Tennis; High Hon Roll; Forensics.

FANGMAN, RANDY H; Bailey-Benedict Jr Sr High; Seneca, KS; (4); Ofcr Bsbl; Sftbl; Wt Lftg; Hon Roll; Prfct Atten Awd; KAW Area Tech Schl; Auto Body.

FANGROW, JESSICA R; Canton-Galva HS; Canton, KS; (2); 9/30; FBLA; SADD; Chorus; Vllybl; Hon Roll; Prfct Atten Awd; KS ST; Cmptrs/Bus.

FANKHAUSER, DUSTAN D; Garden City Sr HS; Garden City, KS; (2); Church Yth Grp; Cmnty Wkr; French Clb; Key Clb; Letterman Clb; Varsity Clb; Bsktbl; Ftbl; Tennis; Wt Lftg; Acad Ltr; Sprts Med.

FANKHAUSER, GRANT; Wichita Collegiate Schl; Wichita, KS; (2); Tennis; High Hon Roll; Polo; Bus.

FANN, KEVIN C; Buhler HS; Hutchinson, KS; (2); Church Yth Grp; FCA; SADD; Band; Chorus; Jazz Band; School Musical; Variety Show; JV Bsktbl; High Hon Roll; Acctnt.

FANNING, ROCHELLE A; Kapaun-Mt Carmel HS; Derby, KS; (2); Church Yth Grp; Cmnty Wkr; GAA; JV Bsktbl; Var Socr; Hon Roll; 49ers Soccr Clb.

FANSKA, JOE; Spring Hill HS; Spring Hill, KS; (2); 3/90; JV Bsbl; JV Bsktbl; High Hon Roll; Sci Clb; Ntrl Hlprs; Knwldg Mstr Open; Engrng.

FARBER, MANDIE; Hoxie HS; Hoxie, KS; (1); FCA; FHA; Natl FFA Org; Pep Clb; Chorus; Chrldng; Wt Lftg; Hon Roll; Law.

FARBER, RACHEL R; Hoxie HS; Hoxie, KS; (3); Church Yth Grp; 4-H; Natl FFA Org; Chorus; Yrbk; Rep Stu Cncl; 4-H Awd; 4-H Ctznshp WA Fcs Trp; Northwest KS Voc Tech Schl.

FARKES, HELEN M; Shawnee Mission S Sr HS; Overland Park, KS; (4); 89/413; Church Yth Grp; Intnl Clb; Sec SADD; Teachers Aide; Band; Mrchg Band; Mgr Trk; High Hon Roll; Hon Roll; NHS; Chrch Yth Ldrshp Band; Natl/Prvncl/Diocese Yth Events/Confs; Truman ST U; Acctng.

FARLOW, ROXANNE E; Independence HS; Independence, KS; (4); 29/141; Church Yth Grp; Orch; Ed Yrbk; Hon Roll; NHS; Strllng Strngs; Independence CC; Acctng.

FARMER, CRYSTAL D; Anderson Cty Jr Sr HS; Welda, KS; (2); FHA; SADD; Hon Roll; Renaissance Awd From ACHS; Var Choir Mem; Criminal Lawyer; Bus.

FARMER, RACHEL S; Blue Valley HS; Overland Park, KS; (2); Var Bsktbl; JV Var Vllybl; Hon Roll; KS Belles AAU Bsktbl 94-; Hnrbl Mntl All EKL Bsktbl 96.

FARMER, SABRINA R; Clearwater HS; Viola, KS; (2); SADD; School Musical; School Play; Hon Roll; Kayettes; KS ST U; HS Bio Tchr.

FARNEN, ANDREA N; St Thomas Aquinas HS; Leawood, KS; (3); Key Clb; Office Aide; Powder Puff Ftbl; Hon Roll; Forstry.

FARNEY, CHRISTOPHER J; Shawnee Mission N HS; Merriam, KS; (1); 16/521; JCL; Latin Clb; Pep Clb; JV Bsktbl; JV Ftbl; Trk; Wt Lftg; Bst Ofnsv/Dfnsv Plyr Multi ST Trny; Frosh Rgnl Trck Mt 1T Pl Dscs/2nd Pl Shtpt; TIP Natl Awd.

FARR, JANESE; Valley Falls HS; Valley Falls, KS; (2); FBLA; FHA; Ed Nwsp; Yrbk; VP Frsh Cls; VP Soph Cls; Var Bsktbl; JV Vllybl; High Hon Roll; Prfct Atten Awd; KS Assn Yth Treas; Jrnlsm Staff; Y Teens; KS ST U.

FARR, JESSICA; Valley Falls HS; Valley Falls, KS; (4); 1/31; Co-Capt Dance Clb; VP FBLA; Band; Pres Stu Cncl; Var L Bsktbl; Var L Trk; Var L Vllybl; High Hon Roll; Pres NHS; Val; Acctng.

FARRAN, PAUL K; Bishop Carroll Catholic HS; Wichita, KS; (2); 32/190; Boy Scts; Church Yth Grp; HOBY; Scholastic Bowl; Spanish Clb; Band; Ofcr Soph Cls; Crs Cntry; Trk; Hon Roll; Camp Vlntr; Boy Sct Awd; U Of KS; Med.

FARRANT, JANELLE; Jefferson West HS; Meriden, KS; (3); 11/85; Art Clb; Chess Clb; Dance Clb; French Clb; FBLA; Letterman Clb; Natl FFA Org; Pep Clb; SADD; Drill Tm; KS U; Medcl.

FARRAR, BRANDON; Hugoton HS; Hugoton, KS; (4); 1/66; 4-H; Teachers Aide; Band; Jazz Band; Rep Stu Cncl; Var Ftbl; Gov Hon Prg Awd; NHS; Val; W TX; Engrng.

FARRAR, JODY; Hugoton HS; Hugoton, KS; (2); 1/89; FCA; Band; Chorus; Pres Soph Cls; Chrldng; High Hon Roll; Triple A Awd.

FARRELL, BRETT; Olathe North Sr HS; Olathe, KS; (2); Cmnty Wkr; Math Tm; Science Clb; Band; Jazz Band; Mrchg Band; Orch; Ofcr Stu Cncl; High Hon Roll; Hon Roll; Dir Awd Orch; Outstdng Musician; 1st Pl St Solo & Ensemble Festival; KS Univ.

FARRELL, CARLY E; Blue Valley Northwest HS; Shawnee Mission, KS; (3); 26/371; FCA; Sec Frsh Cls; Sec Soph Cls; Var Crs Cntry; Var Swmmng; High Hon Roll; Hon Roll; NHS; All Sun Cntry Swmmr Of Yr; All KC Area 1st Team For Swimming; Pub Mc Gregor-Hill Poetry Anthology; Ed.

FARRELL, KELLIE C; Blue Valley Northwest HS; Shawnee Mission, KS; (4); Church Yth Grp; German Clb; Chrldng; Diving; Hon Roll; NHS; Pres Schlr; St Schlr; Natl Art Hnr Soc; KS ST U; Arch.

FARREN, TENA M; Chanute Sr HS; Chanute, KS; (4); Church Yth Grp; French Clb; FBLA; Teachers Aide; Var L Bsktbl; Var L Vllybl; Hon Roll; NHS; Ntl Merit Ltr; Pres Acad Fit Awd; Neosho Cty CC; Intnl Bus.

FARRINGER, PAUL D; Santa Fe Trail Jr HS; Olathe, KS; (1); JV Socr; Var L Swmmng; Hon Roll; Rappelling; KS ST; Bus.

FARRIS, JANET L; Prairie View Jr Sr HS; La Cygne, KS; (3); 12/69; Church Yth Grp; FHA; Spanish Clb; Co-Ed Yrbk; JV Var Bsktbl; JV Var Vllybl; Hon Roll; Prfct Atten Awd; Frt Hayes ST Univ; Intr Dsgn.

FARRIS, MARANDA J; Neodesha Jr Sr HS; Neodesha, KS; (1); FHA; Pep Clb; Band; Mrchg Band; Pep Band; Swmmng; JV Vllybl; Wt Lftg; Hon Roll.

FARRIS, MATT; Goddard HS; Goddard, KS; (3); 1/170; Boy Scts; Debate Tm; NFL; Science Clb; Band; Mrchg Band; High Hon Roll; NHS; Prfct Atten Awd; Pres Acad Fit Awd; Eagle Sct; Order Of The Arrow; Arch.

FARRIS, PAT H; St John's Military Schl; Oklahoma City, OK; (2); Drama Clb; French Clb; ROTC; Spanish Clb; Speech Tm; SADD; Thesps; Chorus; Church Choir; Flag Corp; Schl Pres Schltc Awd; U Of CA Berkeley.

FARRIS, REBECCA A; Wichita East HS; Wichita, KS; (2); Church Yth Grp; Cmnty Wkr; Dance Clb; Drama Clb; Girl Scts; Intnl Clb; Letterman Clb; Spanish Clb; Varsity Clb; Acpl Chr.

FARSON, EMERY L; Washburn Rural HS; Topeka, KS; (3); 38/351; Debate Tm; FCA; NFL; Chorus; Variety Show; Sec Frsh Cls; JV Bsktbl; Var Powder Puff Ftbl; Intrml Trk; Intrml Vllybl; Pre-Med.

FARWELL, DANA; Bern Schl; Seneca, KS; (2); 4/14; Sec Treas Church Yth Grp; Pres Sec 4-H; Letterman Clb; Band; Var Bsktbl; Sftbl; Trk; Var Vllybl; 4-H Awd; Hon Roll; KS ST U; Hlth.

FARWELL, ROBERT D; Bern Schl; Seneca, KS; (3); 2/14; Church Yth Grp; Cmnty Wkr; Letterman Clb; Pep Clb; Quiz Bowl; SADD; Band; Chorus; Pep Band; School Play; K-ST.

FARWELL, TANGELA; Lyndon HS; Lyndon, KS; (3); Sec FBLA; FHA; SADD; Band; Pep Band; School Play; Stage Crew; Sec Soph Cls; Sec Jr Cls; Bsktbl; Wendy's HS Hsmn Schlrsp Ath Ctznsp; Haskel Indian Coll; Tchng.

FASSE, JAMES D; Atchison Co Cmty HS; Effingham, KS; (2); Church Yth Grp; 4-H; Natl FFA Org; Pep Clb; Quiz Bowl; Scholastic Bowl; Acpl Chr; Band; Chorus; Church Choir; FFA Awds.

FAST, ADRIANNE N; Newton Sr HS; Newton, KS; (2); Church Yth Grp; German Clb; Band; Chorus; Mrchg Band; Pep Band; Mgr(s); JV Vllybl; Hon Roll.

FAST, AMY; Inman Jr Sr HS; Inman, KS; (4); 1/29; FHA; Pep Clb; Band; Chorus; School Musical; Variety Show; Rep Stu Cncl; L Chrldng; Pres NHS; Val; Music Thrpy.

FAST, EMMYLOU J; Salina HS Central; Salina, KS; (4); 1/228; Church Yth Grp; Cmnty Wkr; Quiz Bowl; Jazz Band; Orch; School Musical; Gov Hon Prg Awd; Hon Roll; NHS; Ntl Merit SF; All ST Roch Mdln; Untd Peers Christ Pres; Wheaton Coll; Mus/Math.

FAUCHER, LYSETTE A; Lawrence HS; Lawrence, KS; (2); Drama Clb; Girl Scts; JA; Chorus; Orch; School Play; Cit Awd; Hon Roll; Pres Acad Fit Awd; Church Yth Grp; Hnr Choir; KS Univ; Music Ed/Engrng.

FAUDEL, LORRY A; Halstead HS; Halstead, KS; (1); Church Yth Grp; German Clb; SADD; Band; Mgr Bsktbl; JV Golf; Hon Roll; Jazz Band; Mrchg Band; Pep Band; Wichita Wind Ensemble-Play Trombone; Went To St With Trombone Solo & Received II Rating; Kayettes Mem; U Of KS; Instrumental Music Ed.

FAULHABER, JENNIFER L; Washburn Rural HS; Topeka, KS; (3); Ed Yrbk; High Hon Roll; Prfct Atten Awd; Designed Pgm For Drama Dept Productions; U Of KS; Criminal Psych.

FAVAND, ALISON; Topeka HS; Topeka, KS; (2); Pep Clb; High Hon Roll; Hon Roll; Jr NHS; Prfct Atten Awd; MD2B Club; Hosp Vol; Med.

FAVITTA, LISA L; Field Kindley Mem Sr HS; Coffeyville, KS; (4); 28/141; Spanish Clb; NHS; Chrprctr.

FAWCETT, ROCHELLE; Dodge City HS; Dodge City, KS; (1); GAA; Band; Mrchg Band; Pep Band; JV Bsbl; Bsktbl; Chrldng.

FEAGINS, GREG D; Uniontown HS; Redfield, KS; (4); 4/32; FHA; Math Clb; Math Tm; Pep Clb; Spanish Clb; Band; Pep Band; Bsktbl; Ftbl; High Hon Roll; Ft Scott CC.

FEARS, REGINALD L; Sumner Acad Of Arts & Science; Kansas City, KS; (4); 5/195; Boy Scts; Cmnty Wkr; Spanish Clb; Rep Stu Cncl; Var Ftbl; Var Trk; Gov Hon Prg Awd; High Hon Roll; NHS; Pres Schlr; Natl Achvmnt Smfnlst; Dist Stdnt Of Mnth; Peer; Stanford Univ; Hmn Bio.

FEASTER, RACHEL L; Hays HS; Kansas City, MO; (1); Drama Clb; NFL; Pep Clb; Speech Tm; Hon Roll; KS Univ; Clncl Psychlgst.

FECHTER, AMBER J; El Dorado HS; El Dorado, KS; (2); Church Yth Grp; Math Clb; Orch; Treas Jr Cls; JV Capt Chrldng; Sftbl; High Hon Roll; FCA; Spanish Clb; SADD; Rt Ldr Bkng Acrss KS; Jr Ambssdr; Acclyt Chrch 4 Yrs.

FEDORCHUK, MICHELLE; Junction City HS; Junction City, KS; (4); 25/250; Am Leg Aux Girls St; Debate Tm; Key Clb; Quiz Bowl; Band; Jazz Band; Mrchg Band; Pep Band; School Musical; School Play; Pr Mdtn; Nclr Engnr.

FEE, LAWRENCE; Turner HS; Kansas City, KS; (3); 37/225; Key Clb; Math Clb; Math Tm; Teachers Aide; Wt Lftg; Hon Roll; Smmr Marchng Band 8 Yrs; Japanse Stdy 1 Yr; Pittsburg ST; Auto Engrng.

FEELEY, RYAN; Manhattan HS; Manhattan, KS; (3); Church Yth Grp; Band; Mrchg Band; Pep Band; Var L Ftbl; Var L Wrstlng; High Hon Roll; NHS; Awds St Of KS Schlrshp Tests; Piano Lssns 11 Yrs; Mech Engr.

FEGAN, CLINT D; Hartford HS; Hartford, KS; (2); Church Yth Grp; Letterman Clb; JV L Bsktbl; Var L Crs Cntry; Hon Roll.

FEHLING, MARK I; Blue Valley North HS; Leawood, KS; (2); Hon Roll; Acctng.

FEHR, BEN L; Marysville HS; Marysville, KS; (3); Church Yth Grp; Cmnty Wkr; Debate Tm; Treas Drama Clb; Letterman Clb; Sec NFL; School Play; Stage Crew; VP Jr Cls; Var Crs Cntry; Wrtng; U Of AZ; Theatre; Jrnlsm.

FEHR, TAMMY; Emporia HS; Emporia, KS; (4); 28/286; Church Yth Grp; SADD; Chorus; Drill Tm; Flag Corp; Chrldng; Cit Awd; High Hon Roll; KS Hnr Schlr; Butler Cty CC; Elem Ed.

FEINBERG, SAMUEL E; Blue Valley Northwest HS; Overland Park, KS; (2); Chess Clb; Debate Tm; Latin Clb; Chorus; Rep Frsh Cls; JV Tennis; Hon Roll; Engrng.

FEIST, ANDREW R; Claflin Jr Sr HS; Claflin, KS; (4); 1/27; Library Aide; Math Tm; Capt Quiz Bowl; Speech Tm; Band; Chorus; School Play; L Tennis; NHS; Ntl Merit SF; Acad Ltr; Multiple Yr Listing; Tchr.

FELDKAMP, BRADLEY J; Manhattan HS; Manhattan, KS; (3); Band; Mrchg Band; Pep Band; Intrml Bsktbl; Var Crs Cntry; High Hon Roll; Hon Roll; NHS; KS ST Univ.

FELDKAMP, MELISSA; Centralia Schl; Centralia, KS; (4); 7/23; 4-H; Letterman Clb; Science Clb; Teachers Aide; Band; Chorus; Mrchg Band; Pep Band; Nwsp; Yrbk; Smmr Sftbl; Creighton U; Psych.

FELDKAMP, RENEE; Centralia Schl; Centralia, KS; (1); 4-H; Chorus; Stage Crew; Bsktbl; Chrldng; Vllybl; 4-H Awd; Hon Roll.

FELDKAMP, TERRI; Seaman Sr HS; Topeka, KS; (4); 11/248; FBLA; Math Clb; Mu Alpha Theta; Treas Spanish Clb; SADD; JV Bsktbl; Trk; Cit Awd; High Hon Roll; NHS; Plc Athltc Lg Scrkpr; Rlgn Tchr Aide; Washburn U; Elem Ed.

FELDKAMP, TY J; Sylvan Unified HS; Sylvan Grove, KS; (3); 1/19; Church Yth Grp; VP 4-H; Math Tm; Quiz Bowl; Scholastic Bowl; Band; Chorus; Mrchg Band; Pep Band; VP Jr Cls; Agribusiness.

FELDMAN, LEILANI N; Shawnee Mission W Sr HS; Lenexa, KS; (3); Art Clb; Church Yth Grp; Speech Tm; Teachers Aide; Acpl Chr; Church Choir; Chrldng; Socr; Vllybl; Hon Roll; Medtn; Minrty Succss Frm; Exec Wmns Intl; OK Baptist U; Yth Ldr.

FELDT, AMANDA K; Lenora HS; Lenora, KS; (2); Quiz Bowl; Rptr Nwsp; Yrbk; VP Frsh Cls; Pres Soph Cls; JV Var Bsktbl; Var Chrldng; Vllybl; High Hon Roll; Hon Roll.

FELDT, REBECCA J; Lenora HS; Lenora, KS; (1); Church Yth Grp; Pep Clb; Quiz Bowl; SADD; Drill Tm; Pres Frsh Cls; JV Bsktbl; JV Vllybl; High Hon Roll.

FELLERS, JENNIFER J; Great Bend Sr HS; Great Bend, KS; (4); Church Yth Grp; Debate Tm; Drama Clb; NFL; Speech Tm; SADD; School Play; Stage Crew; Mgr(s); Hon Roll; 2nd Plce Voice Of Dem Wnnr; VP Ofdrama Clb; DECA; Barton CC; Bus.

FELVER, RICHARD R; Goodland HS; Goodland, KS; (2); 11/87; Boy Scts; Church Yth Grp; Letterman Clb; Varsity Clb; Band; Jazz Band; Pep Band; Pres Jr Cls; Var L Bsktbl; Var L Ftbl; KS ST.

FENG, SEAN H; Olathe East Sr HS; Overland Park, KS; (3); Computer Clb; Hosp Aide; Spanish Clb; Teachers Aide; High Hon Roll; Hon Roll; U Of CA; Intnl Bus.

FENNER, MICHAEL J; Goodland HS; Goodland, KS; (4); Church Yth Grp; FHA; Letterman Clb; Stage Crew; Bsktbl; Ftbl; Trk; Wt Lftg; Wrstlng; Hon Roll; FHA Mem Of Month 96; Colby CC; PT.

FENTON, JAMES R; Manhattan HS; Manhattan, KS; (3); Boy Scts; Church Yth Grp; German Clb; Red Cross Aide; Band; Orch; School Musical; Variety Show; Swmmng; High Hon Roll; Eagle Scout; Order Of The Arrow Chptr Chief.

FERGUSON, JENNIFER E; Washington HS; Kansas City, KS; (3); 22/300; Church Yth Grp; Hosp Aide; Red Cross Aide; Acpl Chr; Drill Tm; Rptr Yrbk; Vllybl; Hon Roll; NHS; Bio; Phy Thrpst.

FERGUSON, MARY E; Marais Des Cygnes Valley HS; Melvern, KS; (3); Church Yth Grp; Hosp Aide; Quiz Bowl; Scholastic Bowl; Spanish Clb; Church Choir; JV Bsktbl; JV Vllybl; Cit Awd; Page At St Capital For Rep Hummerickhouse.

FERGUSON, OLIVIA P; Kensington Jr Sr HS; Kensington, KS; (3); 3/21; 4-H; Letterman Clb; Library Aide; Natl FFA Org; Quiz Bowl; Scholastic Bowl; Speech Tm; Rep Stu Cncl; JV Vllybl; Hon Roll; KS ST Univ; Lib Sci.

FERIL, ORRIN; St John Jr Sr HS; Saint John, KS; (2); Church Yth Grp; FHA; Pep Clb; Quiz Bowl; Scholastic Bowl; SADD; Band; Mrchg Band; School Musical; Treas Soph Cls; Lubbock Chrstn U/Lubbock TX.

FERMAN, CHRIS; Mulvane Sr HS; Mulvane, KS; (2); 19/150; FCA; SADD; Chorus; Rptr Yrbk; Pres Frsh Cls; Sec Soph Cls; Chrldng; Trk; Hon Roll; Pres Acad Fit Awd; Emporia ST U; Elem Ed.

FERMIN, LORI R; Wichita South HS; Wichita, KS; (1); 206/489; Church Yth Grp; Latin Clb; Spanish Clb; JV Bsktbl; JV Sftbl; JV Vllybl; KS ST Univ; Intr Dsgn.

FERNANDEZ, AMOS O; Emporia HS; Emporia, KS; (2); Church Yth Grp; JV Bsbl; Stat Bsktbl; Cit Awd; Hon Roll; Amer Lgn Bsbl; Emporia ST U; Sci.

FERNANDO, HARENDRA N; Larned HS; Larned, KS; (2); Debate Tm; Drama Clb; HOBY; Acpl Chr; Chorus; VP Soph Cls; Rep Stu Cncl; Var Tennis; Hon Roll; Med/Drama.

FERNKOPF, LURA D; Holton HS; Holton, KS; (1); Drama Clb; Speech Tm; Acpl Chr; Band; Chorus; Church Choir; Mrchg Band; Pep Band; Stage Crew; Variety Show; *%tnl Music Fstvl Voice/Flute; ST Music Fstvl Voice; Chamber Choir; Nrsng.

FERREE, JESSICA; Arkansas City HS; Arkansas City, KS; (3); 58/189; Rptr VP 4-H; Natl FFA Org; Treas NFL; Teachers Aide; VP Soph Cls; Rep Jr Cls; Tennis; 4-H Awd; Hon Roll; Close-Up WA; Sr Cls Pres 96-97; Natl Forensics League VP 96-97; Emporia ST; Elem Ed.

FERREL, MISTY; Sedgwick HS; Sedgwick, KS; (4); 2/24; Am Leg Aux Girls St; Cmnty Wkr; FCA; Letterman Clb; Pres Sr Cls; Rep Sec Stu Cncl; Var Capt Bsktbl; Var Vllybl; High Hon Roll; NHS; KS Hnr Schlr; HOA All Leag Vllybl Hnrb Mntn 94 95; Sedgwick Invitational Trnmt Team Bsktbl; KS Newman Coll; Acctng.

FERRELL, JEFFREY W; Shawnee Mission S Sr HS; Shawnee Mission, KS; (4); 67/451; Boy Scts; HOBY; Jazz Band; Mrchg Band; School Play; Pres Soph Cls; Pres Stu Cncl; Hon Roll; NHS; Church Yth Grp; Hmcmng Kng; Yng Life/Bnd, Guitar; Jhnsn Cty Yth Bsbl-Ctchr; U KS; Tchr.

FERRELL, JUSTIN L; Topeka West HS; Topeka, KS; (2); Church Yth Grp; Spanish Clb; Rep Jr Cls; Var L Ftbl; Hon Roll; Slct Actrs Gld; Med.

FERRELL, MATT; Caney Valley Jr Sr HS; Caney, KS; (3); Church Yth Grp; Cmnty Wkr; Computer Clb; English Clb; Science Clb; Teachers Aide; Band; Church Choir; Jazz Band; Mrchg Band; U Of KS; Pharmacist.

FERRER, JODY M; Yates Ctr HS; Yates Center, KS; (3); Art Clb; Church Yth Grp; SADD; Chorus; School Musical; School Play; High Hon Roll; Hon Roll; Mc Pherson Coll; Art His/Hums.

FERRIS, JENNIFER L; Maize HS; Christiansburg, VA; (1); 119/308; Hon Roll; Jobs Daughters; Sftbl; Wrtng Poetry; WSU; PT.

FERRIS, MICHELLE L; Madison Jr Sr HS; Yates Center, KS; (3); Church Yth Grp; Cmnty Wkr; Drama Clb; FBLA; German Clb; Pep Clb; Quiz Bowl; Scholastic Bowl; Speech Tm; Thesps; Odessy Of Mind; Cnslr Mentally Challenged; ST Forensics; Baker Univ; Psych Mntly Chlngd.

FERRUGIA, LISA; Shawnee Mission East HS; Prairie Village, KS; (4); Church Yth Grp; Dance Clb; Q&S; Church Choir; School Musical; Ed Yrbk; Hon Roll; NHS; Ntl Merit SF; Dance; Perf With Prof Co; Carnegie Mellon Univ; Eng.

FESENMEYER, KATHERINE M; Robert E Clark Jr HS; Bonner Springs, KS; (1); Chorus; School Musical; Var Tennis; High Hon Roll; Tchr.

FETTIS, BRANDY; TMP-MARIAN HS; Hays, KS; (3); Debate Tm; JCL; Latin Clb; NFL; Band; Pep Band; Ed Yrbk; Chrldng; High Hon Roll; Hon Roll; Regnls I Ratng Flute Solo; St I Ratng Flute Trio; Piano Clinis I Ratng, I W/Hnrs; KS U; Optmtry.

FEUERBORN, NATALIE; Anderson Cty Jr Sr HS; Greeley, KS; (4); Am Leg Aux Girls St; Church Yth Grp; Drama Clb; SADD; Pres Chorus; School Musical; School Play; Sec Stu Cncl; Chrldng; NHS; U Of KS.

FEWINS, PHILLIP D; Chanute Sr HS; Humboldt, KS; (1); 1/170; FCA; Math Tm; Chorus; Swing Chorus; Rep Stu Cncl; JV Bsktbl; JV Ftbl; High Hon Roll; Physcl Sci Awd; Ntrl Hlprs.

FICK, ALISSA A; Manhattan HS; Manhattan, KS; (2); Church Yth Grp; 4-H; Pep Clb; Church Choir; 4-H Awd; Hon Roll; Wrestling Mgr; KSU; Vet; Nrsng.

FIDLER, GARY L; Galena HS; Galena, KS; (1); KS Univ; Chiropractor.

FIEF, APRIL; South Gray HS; Copeland, KS; (4); 7/21; Church Yth Grp; English Clb; Letterman Clb; Teachers Aide; Nwsp; Yrbk; VP Soph Cls; Var Bsktbl; L Vllybl; High Hon Roll; Garden City CC; Jrnlsm.

FIELDS, NIKKI; Wichita Heights HS; Wichita, KS; (3); 28/250; Church Yth Grp; Teachers Aide; Band; Church Choir; Mrchg Band; Treas Jr Cls; High Hon Roll; Hon Roll; Multicultural Clb; Exec HS Internshp; Rotary Clb Career Day; Clark-Atlanta Univ; Bus Admin.

FIELDS, NIKKI S; Olathe East Sr HS; Overland Park, KS; (4); Drama Clb; English Clb; Letterman Clb; Science Clb; Spanish Clb; SADD; Teachers Aide; Capt Drill Tm; School Musical; Variety Show; Hmcmng/Prom Rylty Crt; Dctd Stdnt Dnc 15 Yrs/Dnc Tchr 2 Yrs; I Of KS; OT.

FIELDS, RYAN D; Hartford HS; Hartford, KS; (2); Church Yth Grp; Cmnty Wkr; Letterman Clb; Scholastic Bowl; Var L Bsktbl; Var L Crs Cntry; Var Wt Lftg; High Hon Roll; NHS; KS ST; Elec Engr.

FIELDS, SUNNY; Frontenac Jr Sr HS; Frontenac, KS; (3); 3/30; Am Leg Aux Girls St; Cmnty Wkr; FHA; Sec Pep Clb; Pres Spanish Clb; Nwsp; VP Jr Cls; Stat Ftbl; L Sftbl; NHS; Pittsbrgh St Univ; Med.

FIELITZ, FRANK; Newton Sr HS; Germany, XX; (4); Computer Clb; German Clb; Latin Clb; Socr; Tennis; Ger & Eng Fluent; Russian & Latin Skills; Went To Germany & USA Schl; Fin Mgr.

FIEST, KARA; White City HS; White City, KS; (4); Am Leg Aux Girls St; Church Yth Grp; SADD; Drill Tm; Yrbk; VP Stu Cncl; Var Capt Bsktbl; Var Capt Vllybl; Hon Roll; NHS; Dentistry.

FIFE, KATE; Spring Hill HS; Spring Hill, KS; (4); Debate Tm; Office Aide; Spanish Clb; Speech Tm; Teachers Aide; Rep Stu Cncl; JV Bsktbl; Var Sftbl; Gov Hon Prg Awd; Hon Roll; Frnscs-Qlfd To St In Serious Solo Actng & Poetry; Johnson Cty CC.

FIFER, DON G; Campus HS; Haysville, KS; (3); Church Yth Grp; Intnl Clb; SADD; Teachers Aide; VICA; Ofcr Soph Cls; Ofcr Jr Cls; Rep Sr Cls; Bsktbl; Ftbl; Dist Chrch Group Ldrshp Team; Best Example For Yr 94-95; CO Chrstn; Yth Ministry/Bus.

FIGGINS, JENNIFER R; Mankato Jr Sr HS; Mankato, KS; (3); Rptr Natl FFA Org; Quiz Bowl; Teachers Aide; Band; Chorus; Mrchg Band; Pep Band; Ofcr Stu Cncl; High Hon Roll; Hon Roll; KS ST Univ; Ag Bus.

FIKE, VERINDA J E; Maranatha Acad; Shawnee Mission, KS; (3); Band; Mrchg Band; Pep Band; School Musical; School Play; VP Jr Cls; Pres Sr Cls; JV Var Bsktbl; Var Capt Socr; High Hon Roll; Cia Agent.

FILBERT, KELLI S; Ness City HS; Ness City, KS; (2); Church Yth Grp; Cmnty Wkr; Drama Clb; FHA; Pep Clb; Quiz Bowl; Scholastic Bowl; Thesps; Band; Chorus; Dist V Hnr Band; Western Plains Festival Of Winds Hnr Band; U Of NE.

FILE, BRIAN; Seaman Sr HS; Topeka, KS; (4); FBLA; SADD; Rep Stu Cncl; L Bsktbl; L Crs Cntry; L Trk; NHS; Prfct Atten Awd; Pres Acad Fit Awd; U Of KS.

FILE, COURTNEY J; Beloit Jr Sr HS; Beloit, KS; (3); 1/66; Church Yth Grp; Letterman Clb; Science Clb; Spanish Clb; Chorus; Variety Show; JV Bsktbl; Mgr(s); L Var Trk; Wt Lftg; Ftr Med Clb VP; U Of KS; Ob.

FILSINGER, STACIE; Spring Hill HS; Spring Hill, KS; (4); Am Leg Aux Girls St; Church Yth Grp; Cmnty Wkr; FCA; French Clb; Intnl Clb; Letterman Clb; Library Aide; Office Aide; Pep Clb; Intl Stu Host; Page Area Rep St Capital; KU; Med.

FILSON, HIEDI; Protection Schl; Protection, KS; (2); Letterman Clb; Pep Clb; Varsity Clb; Band; Chorus; Mrchg Band; Pep Band; School Musical; School Play; Swing Chorus.

FINAN, SHEILA; Rock Creek Jr Sr HS; Blaine, KS; (2); 9/61; FHA; SADD; Treas Soph Cls; Mgr(s); JV Vllybl; Hon Roll; NHS.

FINCH, GERA; Garden City Sr HS; Garden City, KS; (3); Cmnty Wkr; Teachers Aide; Var Golf; Hon Roll; Ft Hays ST Univ; Acctng.

FINCHAM, BRIAN S; Louisburg HS; Louisburg, KS; (3); Am Leg Boys St; Church Yth Grp; FCA; Sec 4-H; SADD; School Play; Stage Crew; JV Bsktbl; Var Socr; Pres Acad Fit Awd; Faith Bapt Bible Coll; Comp Pgm.

FINCHAM, RACHEL E; Leavenworth HS; Leavenworth, KS; (4); 24/289; Church Yth Grp; German Clb; Spanish Clb; Teachers Aide; High Hon Roll; Acad Ltr; KS Hnrs Schlr; Multi-Yr Listee; KS City CC; Pre-Med; Pre-Pharm.

FINCHER, MAILE S; Parsons HS; Parsons, KS; (1); 28/145; Church Yth Grp; Orch; School Musical; Hon Roll; Univ KS; His.

FINDLEY, JESSICA M; Turner HS; Kansas City, KS; (2); Chorus; Yrbk; Ofcr Stu Cncl; JV Var Bsktbl; Var Chrldng; Var Crs Cntry; Var Sftbl; Cit Awd; Hon Roll; Jr NHS.

FINDLEY, LEAH; Ulysses HS; Ulysses, KS; (3); Church Yth Grp; Debate Tm; Drama Clb; NFL; Chorus; School Musical; High Hon Roll; Hon Roll; NHS; Mid-Amer Nazarene Coll; Elem Ed.

FINDLEY, NATHAN A; Shawnee Mission E Sr HS; Prairie Village, KS; (4); Church Yth Grp; Cmnty Wkr; Drama Clb; Natl Beta Clb; NFL; Thesps; Chorus; School Musical; School Play; Stage Crew; AIDS Awareness-Aids Week; Greater KS City Aids Cncl; U Of KS.

FINGER, AMANDA; Andover HS; Andover, KS; (3); 14/160; Church Yth Grp; Band; Mrchg Band; Var Chrldng; Var Sftbl; High Hon Roll; NHS; Bus Admin.

FINGER, KELSEY J; Quinter Jr Sr HS; Quinter, KS; (2); Church Yth Grp; Debate Tm; FCA; FHA; Letterman Clb; Chorus; JV Bsktbl; Var Trk; JV Vllybl; Hon Roll; KS ST Univ.

FINK, AMANDA J; Chase Co HS; Cottonwood Falls, KS; (2); 2/39; Math Tm; Quiz Bowl; Spanish Clb; Chorus; School Musical; Ofcr Frsh Cls; Ofcr Soph Cls; Chrldng; Hon Roll; NHS; KAYS Clb; REL; KS ST; Vet; Pediatrics.

FINK, KEVIN W; Meade HS; Meade, KS; (3); French Clb; NFL; Quiz Bowl; Varsity Clb; Acpl Chr; School Musical; VP Frsh Cls; Rep Sec Stu Cncl; Var L Crs Cntry; Hon Roll.

FINK, MICKAYLA; Ulysses HS; Ulysses, KS; (2); 11/110; Debate Tm; FBLA; SADD; Mgr(s); Hon Roll; Frgn Lang Clb; Effrt Awd; Acad Awd; Washburn; Law.

FINKEMEIER, HOLLYN A; Olathe North Sr HS; Kansas City, KS; (2); Church Yth Grp; Dance Clb; Drama Clb; 4-H; Red Cross Aide; Speech Tm; Teachers Aide; Acpl Chr; Chorus; Church Choir; Mck Trl; Jb Shdwng; Washburn U; Law.

FINLAY, TERI; Syracuse Jr Sr HS; Kendall, KS; (2); 4-H; Band; Chorus; Mrchg Band; Bsktbl; Powder Puff Ftbl; Vllybl; 4-H Awd; Hon Roll.

FINLAYSON, ELIZABETH N; Marysville HS; Marysville, KS; (4); 3/87; 4-H; NFL; Acpl Chr; Jazz Band; Swing Chorus; Art Clb; Drama Clb; Teachers Aide; Band; Chorus; Kayettes Brd Of Music 4 Yrs; Apprntc Shw Dog Hndlr; Piano; Tch Piano Lssns 3 Yrs; KS ST U; Music.

FINLEY, JASON A; Goodland HS; Goodland, KS; (2); 23/87; Church Yth Grp; FHA; Letterman Clb; Pep Clb; SADD; Band; Mrchg Band; Pep Band; JV Bsktbl; JV Ftbl.

FINLEY, JENNIFER L; Basehor Linwood HS; Kansas City, KS; (3); Church Yth Grp; French Clb; Girl Scts; NFL; Office Aide; Science Clb; Teachers Aide; School Play; Ed Nwsp; Treas Frsh Cls; Poem Pblshd Young Authors Of Amer 92; Scndry Ed.

FINLEY, TERESA M; Derby HS; Derby, KS; (2); 1/450; Cmnty Wkr; DECA; SADD; Ofcr Soph Cls; Ofcr Stu Cncl; High Hon Roll; NHS; Kay Club; GTC Prgm; Pittsburg ST Math Relays 3rd Algebraic Eqtns/Inqlts; KS ST Univ; Vet Med.

FINLEY, ZACHARY A; Shawnee Mission West HS; Lenexa, KS; (3); DECA; Q&S; Yrbk; Sec Jr Cls; VP Sr Cls; Ofcr Stu Cncl; Trk; Wt Lftg; High Hon Roll; Church Yth Grp; Forensics; Radio TV Clb; Prom Comm; Bus Admin.

FINNEY, BRIAN D; Bishop Ward HS; Kansas City, KS; (2); 37/93; Boy Scts; Drama Clb; Chorus; Church Choir; School Musical; Stage Crew; Swing Chorus; Score Keeper; Wrstlng; Hon Roll; Christ The King Pastrs & Fr Heliadore Mejak Schlsps; Chrch Lectr; Chrch Art & Envrnmnt Comm Mem; Telecommnctn.

FINNEY, JEROD R; Olathe East Sr HS; Olathe, KS; (2); Ftbl; Trk; Wt Lftg; Wrstlng; Cit Awd; High Hon Roll; Prfct Atten Awd; Pres Schlr; Martial Arts; Talent Srch; Capt Frosh Ftbl Team.

FINNEY, MEGAN; Winfield HS; Winfield, KS; (3); Church Yth Grp; Cmnty Wkr; Girl Scts; Hosp Aide; Varsity Clb; Chorus; JV Var Chrldng; JV Var Pom Pon; High Hon Roll; Hon Roll; Amer Bptst Grls Cmmsn.

FINNEY, SARAH K; Manhattan HS; Manhattan, KS; (2); Church Yth Grp; Cmnty Wkr; French Clb; Hosp Aide; Library Aide; Hon Roll; KS ST Univ; Vet Med.

FINNIGIN, KEVIN; Lansing HS; Leavenworth, KS; (3); 11/156; Cmnty Wkr; Math Tm; Service Clb; Band; Mrchg Band; Pep Band; JV Bsbl; Mgr L Bsktbl; Var L Ftbl; Trk; Royalty Attendant; Excllnc In Comp Application Awd; Design Engr.

FISCHER, AVERY; Hays HS; Hays, KS; (3); 1/237; Am Leg Aux Girls St; Church Yth Grp; 4-H; Band; Orch; School Musical; Rptr Nwsp; High Hon Roll; Model UN; Scholastic Bowl; Winning Essay 96; Hnrbl Mention HS Woodwinds 96; Woodwinds Schlrshp; Eng/Jrnlsm.

FISCHER, BROOKE R; Hutchinson HS; Hutchinson, KS; (2); 4/300; Church Yth Grp; Pep Clb; Orch; School Musical; Cit Awd; High Hon Roll; Prfct Atten Awd; Wichita Yth Symphony; Hutchinson Symphony; Peer Cnslr; Phy Thrpst.

FISCHER, CARISA L; Hutchinson HS; Hutchinson, KS; (4); 40/252; Church Yth Grp; Pep Clb; Band; Mrchg Band; Pep Band; Cit Awd; High Hon Roll; NHS; Prfct Atten Awd; Hutchison Regnl Yth Symphony; George & Belle Pearce Schlsp; NEA Schlsp; Hutchinson CC; Elem Ed.

FISCHER, DATHAN; Leroy HS; Le Roy, KS; (2); Church Yth Grp; 4-H; Ofcr Stu Cncl; Bsktbl; Ftbl; Trk; High Hon Roll; Hnrbl Mntn All Leag Qtrbck.

FISCHER, HEIDI E; Hutchinson HS; Hutchinson, KS; (2); 36/436; Church Yth Grp; Band; Chorus; Mrchg Band; Pep Band; School Musical; School Play; Stage Crew; High Hon Roll; Htchnsn Yth Symphony.

FISCHER, HEIDI M; Washburn Rural HS; Topeka, KS; (3); Church Yth Grp; 4-H; Band; Mrchg Band; Pep Band; High Hon Roll; Hon Roll; Emporia ST Univ; Elem Tchr.

FISCHER, HELEN; Arkansas City HS; Arkansas City, KS; (2); Church Yth Grp; FCA; JV Bsktbl; JV Sftbl; Hon Roll; Acad Excel Awd Union ST Bank; Certfd Stndrd 1st Aid/CPR; Whale Trnr.

FISCHER, LAURA D; Shawnee Mission W Sr HS; Shawnee Mission, KS; (4); ROTC; SADD; Hon Roll; Peer Hlprs; Sndy Schl; DAR Clnsts; Johnson Cty CC; Intr Dsgn.

FISCHER, NICOLE; St John Jr Sr HS; Great Bend, KS; (1); Church Yth Grp; VP 4-H; FHA; Pep Clb; Quiz Bowl; SADD; Band; Chorus; Jazz Band; Mrchg Band.

FISCHER, NIKOLAS; Maur Hill Prep Schl; Atchison, KS; (2); 12/56; Debate Tm; Chorus; School Musical; School Play; Intrml Bsktbl; JV Var Socr; Hon Roll; Johnson Cty CC; Ag Bus.

FISCHER, RENEE L; Salina HS South; Salina, KS; (3); FCA; Letterman Clb; Band; Mrchg Band; Rptr Stu Cncl; Stat Crs Cntry; Stat Trk; High Hon Roll; Hon Roll; NHS; K-ST; Bus/Compu App.

FISCHER, STACI M; Ellis HS; Ellis, KS; (3); Church Yth Grp; FHA; Model UN; Pep Clb; SADD; Chorus; School Play; Phtg Yrbk; Rep Frsh Cls; Rep Soph Cls; Photography; Tnns; Walking; KS Newman; OB Nrsng.

FISHER, AMANDA J; Hays HS; Hays, KS; (4); Church Yth Grp; Pep Clb; Teachers Aide; Band; Church Choir; Powder Puff Ftbl; Sftbl; Wt Lftg; High Hon Roll; NHS; Fort Hays ST U; Bus.

FISHER, ANGIE; Thomas More Prep-Marion HS; Hays, KS; (1); Stage Crew; High Hon Roll; Hon Roll; Cmnty Svc; Tae Kwon Do; Fort Hays ST U; Elem Ed.

FISHER, BRANDON; Burrton Schl; Burrton, KS; (2); 1/30; Boy Scts; Church Yth Grp; FCA; Math Tm; Pep Clb; Quiz Bowl; VP Soph Cls; Bsktbl; Golf; High Hon Roll; KS ST U; Cvl Engrng.

FISHER, CODY C; Herndon Schl; Herndon, KS; (2); Pres Frsh Cls; Pres Soph Cls; Var Bsktbl; High Hon Roll; Odyssey Of Minds; CO Univ; Drftg/Cmptr.

FISHER, ERIN; Manhattan HS; Manhattan, KS; (4); 1/483; Am Leg Aux Girls St; Church Yth Grp; FCA; 4-H; Pep Clb; Chorus; Swing Chorus; Stat Bsktbl; Stat Ftbl; 4-H Awd; Pres FCA; Pep Clb; Sub-Deb Sorority; Riley Cty 4-H Ambssdr; KS ST U; Pre-Phys Thrpy.

FISHER, GARRETT; Burrton Schl; Burrton, KS; (3); 1/28; Church Yth Grp; FCA; Scholastic Bowl; Band; Chorus; Mrchg Band; Pep Band; Treas Jr Cls; Var Bsktbl; Var Wt Lftg; Hutchinson CC.

FISHER, HELEN C; Blue Valley HS; Shawnee Mission, KS; (2); Cit Awd; Hon Roll; Math & Fr Cmptns.

FISHER, KATHY S; Shawnee Mission Nw Sr HS; Shawnee, KS; (3); 41/461; Church Yth Grp; Variety Show; JV Bsktbl; JV Vllybl; High Hon Roll; Hon Roll; NHS; Natl Schlr; Acad Ltr; FBI Agent.

FISHER, MELISSA A; Ingalls Jr Sr HS; Ingalls, KS; (4); 4/15; Church Yth Grp; Pep Clb; Band; Sec Jr Cls; Ofcr Sr Cls; Sec Stu Cncl; Trk; Cmnty Wkr; Computer Clb; Letterman Clb; John Phillip Sousa Band Awd; Tabor Coll; Spec Ed.

FISHER, MICHAEL A; Ingalls Jr Sr HS; Ingalls, KS; (3); Church Yth Grp; Pep Clb; SADD; Band; Mrchg Band; Pep Band; Bsktbl; Mgr Ftbl; Mgr Trk; Hon Roll; Mssns Trps.

FISHER, NEVA M; Junction City HS; Junction City, KS; (1); Church Yth Grp; 4-H; Pep Clb; Teachers Aide; Ofcr Frsh Cls; Chrldng; High Hon Roll; KS ST Univ; Ed.

FISHER, NICOLE R; Onaga HS; Havensville, KS; (2); Treas FHA; Pep Clb; Spanish Clb; Yrbk; Var Chrldng; High Hon Roll; Dr.

FISHER, NIKKI; Onaga HS; Onaga, KS; (2); 3/48; Capt Dance Clb; GAA; Natl FFA Org; Capt Pep Clb; SADD; Chorus; Drill Tm; School Musical; School Play; Rptr Nwsp; KS ST.

FISHER, NOLAN; Little River Jr Sr HS; Windom, KS; (4); 5/22; Church Yth Grp; Cmnty Wkr; FCA; 4-H; FHA; Math Tm; Model UN; Spanish Clb; Varsity Clb; Rptr Nwsp; Work Tech Pgm; KS ST Univ; Park Rsrc Mgmt.

FISHER, REBECCA A; Highland Park HS; Topeka, KS; (3); Church Yth Grp; CAP; Math Clb; SADD; Church Choir; Drill Tm; Rep Frsh Cls; JV Var Bsktbl; Cit Awd; Hon Roll; UPWARD Bound Prog; Pres Of Chrch Yth Dept; Sec Treas Of Yth Dept; Pres Yth Choir; OK Univ; Trvl Agnt.

FISHER, REBECCA L; Hays HS; Hays, KS; (1); Church Yth Grp; Pep Clb; Powder Puff Ftbl; Sftbl; Hon Roll.

FISHER, TAMMY R; Garden Plain Jr Sr HS; Garden Plain, KS; (3); Church Yth Grp; Red Cross Aide; Spanish Clb; SADD; Ed Nwsp; Ed Yrbk; Rep Frsh Cls; Treas Stu Cncl; JV Var Bsktbl; Var Chrldng; Bus.

FISHER, TIM; Conway Springs HS; Conway Springs, KS; (3); 5/32; Church Yth Grp; Scholastic Bowl; School Play; Treas Soph Cls; Treas Jr Cls; Treas Stu Cncl; Hon Roll; NHS; U Of KS; Physics.

FISHMAN, LEVI G; Hyman Brand Hebrew Acad; Shawnee Mission, KS; (3); School Play; Intrml Crs Cntry; Score Keeper; Prfct Atten Awd; Engl Awd; Dir.

FITCH, ANGELA M; Blue Valley North HS; Overland Park, KS; (4); 10/169; Var Capt Bsktbl; Var Powder Puff Ftbl; Var Capt Sftbl; Var Capt Vllybl; High Hon Roll; NHS; Dartmouth Coll Book Awd; Emporia ST Schlrsp/Cntst Acctng 1st Pl/Hnr Mntl ST; Pres Awd Edcl Excl; U Of KS.

FITCH, LESLIE D; Blue Valley North HS; Overland Park, KS; (2); GAA; Var L Bsktbl; Var L Sftbl; Var L Vllybl; High Hon Roll; Hon Roll; Yth Ldrshp Inst; U Of KS.

FITCH, LISA; Baxter Springs HS; Baxter Springs, KS; (4); 2/67; Am Leg Aux Girls St; Church Yth Grp; Cmnty Wkr; FCA; Pres FHA; Pep Clb; Scholastic Bowl; Science Clb; Teachers Aide; Thesps; Natl Awd Wnng Prlmntry Law Tm Pres; KS Rgnt Hnr Stu; DARE Rle Mdl; Ottawa U; Scndry Eng.

FITTS, CARISSA C; Sumner Acad Of Arts & Science; Kansas City, KS; (3); Art Clb; Church Yth Grp; Key Clb; Spanish Clb; SADD; Rep Jr Cls; JV Sftbl; JV Trk; Hon Roll; Pep Clb; Violin; NAACP; STOP; Industrial Dsgn.

FITZGERALD, BRANDON M; Wichita Co HS; Leoti, KS; (3); Cmnty Wkr; SADD; Teachers Aide; Yrbk; Prfct Atten Awd; Acctng.

FITZGERALD, BRENDAN T; Immaculata HS; Leavenworth, KS; (4); 8/48; JA; Office Aide; Ofcr Jr Cls; Treas Sr Cls; Ofcr Stu Cncl; Var Capt Bsktbl; Var Capt Ftbl; Cit Awd; High Hon Roll; NHS; IBAC; Summer Bsbl; Stdnts That Care; Avila Coll; Bus Fin.

FITZGERALD, CARRIE E; Bishop Miege HS; Shawnee Mission, KS; (3); 5/180; Pep Clb; SADD; Phtg Nwsp; Phtg Yrbk; Rep Stu Cncl; Var L Bsktbl; JV Crs Cntry; Var L Socr; Cit Awd; High Hon Roll; Notre Dame; Ed; Bus; Sales.

FITZGERALD, ERIN P; Bishop Miege HS; Shawnee, KS; (1); Church Yth Grp; French Clb; Pep Clb; SADD; JV Sftbl; JV Vllybl; Hon Roll; Nurse.

FITZGERREL, KELVIE ANN; Ransom Jr Sr HS; Ransom, KS; (4); 1/17; Church Yth Grp; Pres FCA; Ed Yrbk; Sec Treas Jr Cls; Rep Stu Cncl; Var Chrldng; Var Crs Cntry; Var Trk; Gov Hon Prg Awd; High Hon Roll; All Amer Schlr Natl Awd; KS Hnrs Pgm Awd; U Of KS; Acctng.

FITZGIBBON, TRAVIS W; Topeka HS; Topeka, KS; (2); Yrbk; Hon Roll; Outstdng Bus Stu 95-96; Acctng.

FITZMAURICE, STEPHANIE J; Olathe East Sr HS; Olathe, KS; (2); 159/409; Church Yth Grp; Cmnty Wkr; French Clb; Girl Scts; Teachers Aide; Acpl Chr; Chorus; Vllybl; Cit Awd; Hon Roll; Girl Scouts Silver Awd; Emporia ST Univ; Ed.

FITZPATRICK, HEIDI M; Wellington Sr HS; Wellington, KS; (3); 13/165; 4-H; Natl FFA Org; Spanish Clb; Chorus; Ofcr Stu Cncl; Crs Cntry; Mgr(s); Swmmng; Trk; 4-H Awd; St FFA Degree; KS ST U; Ag.

FJELL, SARAH; Manhattan HS; Manhattan, KS; (1); Church Yth Grp; 4-H; Pep Clb; Band; Mrchg Band; Chrldng; JV Socr; 4-H Awd; Hon Roll; Dist Schlstc Achvmnt Awrd Chrldg/Band; Piano Guild KMTA; Dnc Tap Jazz.

FLACK, KARI; Marmaton Valley Jr Sr HS; Moran, KS; (2); Church Yth Grp; FCA; FHA; Natl FFA Org; NFL; Pep Clb; School Play; Bsktbl; Chrldng; Vllybl.

FLAGLER, MICHAEL G; Trego Comm HS; Wa Keeney, KS; (3); 1/48; Pres Church Yth Grp; Math Tm; Science Clb; Rep Frsh Cls; Pres Soph Cls; Sec Jr Cls; Rep Stu Cncl; High Hon Roll; NHS; Intnl Clb; I Dare You Ldrshp Awd; K ST Coll Of Tech; Cmptr Sci.

FLAHART, LESLIE M; Washburn Rural HS; Topeka, KS; (2); Band; Mrchg Band; Lit Mag; High Hon Roll; Tech Theatre; Dance; Dance.

FLAMING, KRISTAL D; Newton Sr HS; Newton, KS; (1); Sftbl; Trk; Vllybl; High Hon Roll; Hon Roll; Photo.

FLAMING, STEVE G; Manhattan HS; Manhattan, KS; (2); 69/500; Church Yth Grp; Cmnty Wkr; Debate Tm; Orch; Ofcr Bsbl; Score Keeper; Gov Hon Prg Awd; High Hon Roll; Hon Roll; Pres Acad Fit Awd; Amer Legion Bsbl; OK Jr Golf Trnmnts.

FLANAGAN, JILL; Sumner Acad; Kansas City, KS; (1); French Clb; Latin Clb; Pep Clb; Chrldng; Gym; Hon Roll; U KS; Med.

FLANAGIN, QUINTIN; Colby Sr HS; Colby, KS; (2); Church Yth Grp; FBLA; Letterman Clb; Band; Mrchg Band; Pep Band; Stat Bsktbl; Var Crs Cntry; Var Tennis; Hon Roll; Fort Hays ST Univ; Optmtrst.

FLATT, EMILY; Seaman Sr HS; Topeka, KS; (2); Church Yth Grp; Cmnty Wkr; FBLA; FHA; Band; Drill Tm; Mrchg Band; Rptr Yrbk; Var Swmmng; High Hon Roll; Pre-Med; Psych.

FLAVIN, MATTHEW D; Mankato Jr Sr HS; Mankato, KS; (2); 2/32; Church Yth Grp; Math Tm; Natl FFA Org; Quiz Bowl; Yrbk; JV Bsktbl; Var L Golf; High Hon Roll; Voice Democracy Awd.

FLAX, PAMELA; Dodge City HS; Wright, KS; (1); Church Yth Grp; Cmnty Wkr; Drama Clb; Chorus.

FLAX, TOM D; Thomas More Prep-Marion HS; Hays, KS; (1); 30/71; Band; Bsktbl; Ftbl; Trk; Wt Lftg; High Hon Roll; Colombian Squires.

FLEEK, KELLY; Lansing HS; Lansing, KS; (3); Drill Tm; Ofcr Soph Cls; Ofcr Jr Cls; Ofcr Sr Cls; Ofcr Stu Cncl; Chrldng; Trk; High Hon Roll; Hon Roll; NHS; AZ Univ; Physclthrpy.

FLEER, BRIAN; Olathe South Sr HS; Olathe, KS; (4); 36/386; German Clb; Letterman Clb; Teachers Aide; Varsity Clb; Var Capt Bsbl; Ftbl; High Hon Roll; Hon Roll; NHS; Scndry Ed.

FLEETWOOD, COURTNEY; Goddard HS; Goddard, KS; (3); Church Yth Grp; Science Clb; Spanish Clb; Yrbk; Sftbl; High Hon Roll; Hon Roll; NHS; KAYS; Chrch Vol; Pre-Med; Arch.

FLEIG, JOSH; Arkansas City HS; Arkansas City, KS; (3); Church Yth Grp; Debate Tm; Drama Clb; Band; Chorus; Jazz Band; Pep Band; Variety Show; Rep Stu Cncl; Chrstn Rock Band; Cowley Cty CC; Music; Band Dir.

FLEIG, WALTER; Schlagle HS; Kansas City, KS; (4); Wt Lftg; Hnr Rl; Ftbl; Wght Lftg; KCKCC; Bus/Cmptr Repair.

FLEISCHER, AIREANA S; Washington HS; Kansas City, KS; (2); Drama Clb; Spanish Clb; SADD; JV Vllybl; Hon Roll.

FLEMING, JENNY; Lawrence HS; Lawrence, KS; (3); Debate Tm; Teachers Aide; Rep Stu Cncl; JV Var Chrldng; JV Gym; Hon Roll; NHS; NCA All Amer Cheerldr; Bus.

FLEMING, SARAH; Wichita Collegiate Schl; Wichita, KS; (4); 2/75; Chorus; School Play; Yrbk; Ed Lit Mag; Sftbl; Var Tennis; High Hon Roll; Ntl Merit SF; St Schlr; Tennis St Champ; Cum Laude Soc; Rnsslr Awd For Math & Sci.

FLENNER, SCOTT A; Lyons HS; Lyons, KS; (2); Band; Intrml Bsktbl; Var Golf; Frosh Var Golf ST Qlfr; KGA ST Qlfr Golf 2 Yrs; K ST; Golf Clb Pro.

FLERLAGE, RYAN A; St Marys HS; Saint Marys, KS; (4); 16/55; Boy Scts; FCA; FBLA; Pep Clb; Teachers Aide; Band; Jazz Band; Mrchg Band; Pep Band; School Musical; Emporia St Univ; Elem Ed.

FLESKE, CAREY L; Great Bend Sr HS; Great Bend, KS; (3); Rep Am Leg Boys St; Boy Scts; Church Yth Grp; Rptr Debate Tm; German Clb; Pep Clb; Rptr Speech Tm; Nwsp; JV Bsktbl; JV Golf.

FLETCHER, BRIAN G; Columbus Unified HS; Columbus, KS; (4); 27/95; Art Clb; Math Tm; Hon Roll; Pittsburg ST Univ; Acctng.

FLETCHER, GINA; Burlington HS; Burlington, KS; (3); 21/85; Dance Clb; Office Aide; Pep Clb; Chorus; Drill Tm; Nwsp; Var Chrldng; Var Pom Pon; High Hon Roll; Hon Roll; Psych.

FLETCHER, JASON W; Ellsworth HS; Ellsworth, KS; (2); Letterman Clb; Chorus; Phtg Nwsp; Bsktbl; Crs Cntry; Trk; Hon Roll.

FLETCHER, JENNIFER L; Shawnee Mission W Sr HS; Overland Park, KS; (3); 171/415; Church Yth Grp; Intnl Clb; Latin Clb; NFL; Speech Tm; Teachers Aide; Chorus; Church Choir; Hon Roll; Chrch Eng Handbell Choir; Western ST Coll Of CO; Mrktg.

FLICK, MELISSA; Macksville HS; Haviland, KS; (3); 2/24; Letterman Clb; Quiz Bowl; Band; Pres Jr Cls; Sec Stu Cncl; Bsktbl; Vllybl; DAR Awd; NHS; Kayette VP; Med.

FLICK, RYAN T; Great Bend Sr HS; Great Bend, KS; (2); Boy Scts; Church Yth Grp; Varsity Clb; Acpl Chr; Band; Chorus; Mrchg Band; Variety Show; L Bsktbl; Ftbl; Phys Therapy.

FLICK, VALERIE; Macksville HS; Haviland, KS; (2); 3/30; HOBY; Letterman Clb; Band; VP Soph Cls; Ofcr Stu Cncl; Var Bsktbl; Var Chrldng; Var Trk; Var Vllybl; DAR Awd.

FLINT, STEPHANIE J; Kensington Jr Sr HS; Kensington, KS; (3); Letterman Clb; Spanish Clb; SADD; Band; Mrchg Band; Pep Band; School Musical; Ofcr Stu Cncl; Hon Roll; NHS; KMEA Hon Bnd; Prairie Haven Nurs Cntr; Voice Of Dem Wnnr In Schl; Phys Thpy.

FLOCK, JOANNA; Eureka Jr Sr HS; Madison, KS; (4); 7/63; 4-H; FHA; Spanish Clb; School Play; VP Frsh Cls; Rep Stu Cncl; Capt Chrldng; Capt Vllybl; Kiwanis Awd; NHS; Olympic Torch Escort Runner; FHA Outstndng Dist Sr; Regents Schlr; KS ST U; Speech Pthlgy.

FLOHRSCHUTZ, WILLIE R; Holton HS; Denison, KS; (2); Quiz Bowl; Ed Nwsp; Rptr Yrbk; Lit Mag; JV Bsktbl; High Hon Roll; Hon Roll; Gtr Rck Band; Smmr Bsbl; KS U; Wrtr.

FLORENCE JR, SARAH; West HS; Wichita, KS; (4); Am Leg Aux Girls St; Bus Profs of Am; Church Yth Grp; Cmnty Wkr; Dance Clb; Debate Tm; GAA; Girl Scts; JA; Office Aide; Blck Ldrshp; Ldr Of Tmmrw; Wichita ST; Medcl.

FLORES, ADRIAN; Spearville Jr Sr HS; Spearville, KS; (2); Pep Clb; Quiz Bowl; Speech Tm; Chorus; Stage Crew; Bsktbl; Ftbl; Mgr(s); Wt Lftg; High Hon Roll; Chiropractor.

FLORES, SUSAN M; Buhler HS; Hutchinson, KS; (2); Church Yth Grp; Sec 4-H; Hosp Aide; Red Cross Aide; Science Clb; Spanish Clb; Chorus; Stage Crew; Bsktbl; Vllybl; Med.

FLORIO, ANGELA M; Kapaun-Mt Carmel HS; Mulvane, KS; (2); Church Yth Grp; Stage Crew; Hon Roll; CYO; KS ST; Fshn Dsgnr/Actress.

FLORQUIST, LANE; Syracuse Jr Sr HS; Syracuse, KS; (3); 2/37; Church Yth Grp; Varsity Clb; Band; Chorus; Sec Treas Jr Cls; Var Bsktbl; Var Ftbl; Var Tennis; High Hon Roll; NHS; Phys Thrpy.

FLORY, ERIN; Mc Pherson HS; Mc Pherson, KS; (4); Church Yth Grp; German Clb; Science Clb; Spanish Clb; Band; Chorus; Orch; School Musical; Hon Roll; NHS; St Piano Fstvl; St Solo & Ensemble Fstvl.

FLORY, MICHELLE; Jefferson Co North HS; Nortonville, KS; (2); 4/52; Pres Rep 4-H; FBLA; HOBY; Speech Tm; Chorus; School Musical; 4-H Awd; High Hon Roll; Hon Roll; Pres Acad Fit Awd.

FLOURNOY, RHONDA A; Manhattan HS; Manhattan, KS; (2); Hon Roll; KS ST.

FLOWER, ERICA; Chapman HS; Junction City, KS; (4); Dance Clb; Drama Clb; NFL; SADD; School Play; Stage Crew; Var Pom Pon; High Hon Roll; Hon Roll; Stu Dir In All Schl Production; KS ST U.

FLOYD, BRIAN A; Kapaun-Mt Carmel HS; Wichita, KS; (4); Church Yth Grp; Drama Clb; French Clb; Thesps; Acpl Chr; Chorus; School Musical; School Play; Stage Crew; JV Ftbl.

FLYNN, BREANNA; Gardner-Edgerton HS; Gardner, KS; (2); Drama Clb; FCA; French Clb; Pep Clb; SADD; Teachers Aide; School Play; Yrbk; Var Capt Chrldng; Trk; HOBY Candidate; Nom Natl Young Ldrs Conf.

FLYNN, KATIE A; Great Bend Sr HS; Great Bend, KS; (1); Church Yth Grp; Drama Clb; Band; Chorus; Mrchg Band; School Musical; Variety Show; Manhatten Chrstn Col; Mnstry.

FLYNN, RACHEL; Olathe East Sr HS; Overland Park, KS; (4); 98/300; Church Yth Grp; Cmnty Wkr; Natl Beta Clb; Teachers Aide; Band; Color Guard; Hon Roll; Fshn Mrchndsng Club; Family & Consumer Sci Clb; U Of NE Kearney; Phys Thrpy.

FOGELBERG, STACIE; Hoisington HS; Great Bend, KS; (4); Model UN; SADD; Pres Band; Sec Jr Cls; Sec Sr Cls; Rep Stu Cncl; L Crs Cntry; L Trk; High Hon Roll; Hon Roll; GPA Hnr Awd; Homecoming Queen; Stdnt Naturalist Club Pres; Sterling Coll; Nrsng.

FOLCK, LINDSAY A; Lyons HS; Lyons, KS; (2); Sec 4-H; NFL; Band; Jazz Band; VP Frsh Cls; Var L Tennis; High Hon Roll; NHS; Pres Acad Fit Awd; Art Clb; Church Accmpnst; Bio.

FOLEY, ALICIA; Goddard HS; Goddard, KS; (3); Church Yth Grp; Pres VP 4-H; Science Clb; Band; Mrchg Band; Pep Band; Tennis; 4-H Awd; High Hon Roll; NHS; Rsrv Champion Horse Judging Team CO 4-H Classic; Hrsmanshp.

FOLEY, ROSS G; Cheney Jr Sr HS; Cheney, KS; (2); 21/47; Church Yth Grp; 4-H; Scholastic Bowl; Band; Chorus; Mrchg Band; Pep Band; JV Bsktbl; Var L Ftbl; Var L Trk; Chrch Cncl On Ministeries HS Rep.

FOLLMER, HOLLY; Washburn Rural HS; Topeka, KS; (4); 30/268; Church Yth Grp; Cmnty Wkr; French Clb; Treas SADD; Band; Mrchg Band; Pep Band; Var Capt Chrldng; Swmmng; High Hon Roll; Baylor Univ.

FOLSCROFT, RYAN J; Sumner Acad Of Arts & Science; Kansas City, KS; (4); 6/196; Art Clb; Spanish Clb; SADD; Band; Jazz Band; Nwsp; Yrbk; NHS; Spanish NHS; St Jazz Band; U Of MO-KANSAS City; Acctng.

FOLSOM, REBECCA P; Osawatomie HS; Osawatomie, KS; (1); Science Clb; High Hon Roll; NHS; KU; Ed.

FONG, RICHARD S; Blue Valley Northwest HS; Overland Park, KS; (1); Chess Clb; Debate Tm; NFL; Treas Soph Cls; Crs Cntry; Hon Roll; Bus.

FONSECA, DEBORAH E; Lawrence HS; Lawrence, KS; (4); Church Yth Grp; Debate Tm; Sec Treas French Clb; NFL; Ed Yrbk; Rep Soph Cls; Rep Jr Cls; Rep Sr Cls; Rep Stu Cncl; Capt Socr; Sr Planning Comm; Ruby Level Of Excl In Natl Forensic League Points; Flagler Coll; Ed; Broadcasting.

FOOS, JENDEE; Lacrosse HS; La Crosse, KS; (3); SADD; Band; Chorus; Jazz Band; Pep Band; Yrbk; Var Capt Bsktbl; Trk; Vllybl; Hon Roll; All-Trnmnt Bsktbl Team; Crmnl Jstc.

FOOS, MATTHEW D; Bazine Jr Sr HS; Bazine, KS; (4); 1/6; Band; Yrbk; Pres Frsh Cls; Pres Soph Cls; Pres Stu Cncl; Var L Bsktbl; Var L Ftbl; Var L Trk; High Hon Roll; Val; All League Ftbl 95/Hon Mention 94; Ft Hays ST Univ; Agribus.

FOOS, SHANNA; Bazine Jr Sr HS; Ness City, KS; (4); 3/6; Church Yth Grp; Drama Clb; Office Aide; Band; Chorus; Drm Mjr(t); Mrchg Band; Pep Band; School Play; Yrbk; Fornscs; Barton Cty CC; Ofc Ed.

FOOTE, DANIELLE L; Northeast Magnet HS; Wichita, KS; (3); Church Yth Grp; Cmnty Wkr; Dance Clb; Girl Scts; JA; Pep Clb; Spanish Clb; School Play; Stage Crew; Variety Show; Natl Yng Ldrs Conf; Wichita Bar Assoc Summr Intrn; Wichita St U Mentor For 95 96 Schl Yr Outs Ptpct; Spelman Univ.

FOOTE-MC KENNA, HEIDI D; Manhattan HS; Manhattan, KS; (2); VP German Clb; Thesps; Stage Crew; Trk; Hon Roll; KS ST Jr Rowing Crew 10th; 3rd Pl TOSHIBA Awds 9th; Nom Natl Hnrs Soc 10th; Univ Of NC; Arcn/Anthlgy.

FORACH, JASON T; Blue Valley North HS; Overland Park, KS; (4); 54/172; Boy Scts; Cmnty Wkr; Drama Clb; Speech Tm; Chorus; Mrchg Band; School Play; Nwsp; Yrbk; Lit Mag; U Of MO Columbia; Music.

FORAN, PAMELA; Ellsworth HS; Ellsworth, KS; (3); 4/64; Church Yth Grp; Pres 4-H; Girl Scts; HOBY; Letterman Clb; Rptr Natl FFA Org; Band; L Var Trk; 4-H Awd; High Hon Roll; Kayettes Bd Mem.

FORBES, MARY A; Parsons HS; Parsons, KS; (1); Chrldng; Hon Roll; KS Univ; Phy Thrpst.

FORBES, NANCY J; J C Harmon HS; Kansas City, KS; (2); Church Yth Grp; FCA; GAA; Key Clb; Quiz Bowl; Chorus; School Play; Bsktbl; Hon Roll; Acad Decathln; KS ST U; Accntg.

FORD, GRANT; Wichita East HS; Wichita, KS; (2); 98/350; Ofcr Bsbl; Socr; Hon Roll.

FORD, JENNIFER; Circle HS; Wichita, KS; (4); 5/90; Spanish Clb; Chorus; School Play; Ed Nwsp; Capt Pom Pon; Sftbl; Tennis; High Hon Roll; NHS; US Natl Ldrshp Mrt Awd; All Amer Schlr; Commnctns.

FORD, JENNY L; Troy HS; Troy, KS; (2); Art Clb; Pep Clb; Band; Mrchg Band; Pep Band; Hon Roll; Kndrgrtn Tchr.

FORD, KIM S; Wichita North HS; Wichita, KS; (3); 40/260; Drama Clb; French Clb; Thesps; Acpl Chr; School Musical; Variety Show; Rptr Yrbk; Rep Jr Cls; Var Chrldng; Var Tennis.

FORD, LYALL L; Garden City Sr HS; Garden City, KS; (2); Boy Scts; Church Yth Grp; Debate Tm; NFL; Band; Crs Cntry; JV Tennis; E F Schlsp Trip, England, Belgium & France; Natl Wnnr His Day, Wash DC; 2 Time St Wnnr His Day.

FORD, MELISSA R; Wichita North HS; Wichita, KS; (2); 80/395; Church Yth Grp; Cmnty Wkr; Pep Clb; Teachers Aide; Chorus; Rep Soph Cls; Rep Stu Cncl; Bsktbl; Var Pom Pon; Hon Roll; KS Univ; Bus.

FORD, MIRANDA S; Campus HS; Haysville, KS; (2); Church Yth Grp; Girl Scts; SADD; Teachers Aide; High Hon Roll; Bus Owner.

FORD, STEPHANIE; Lawrence HS; Lawrence, KS; (4); Pres Am Leg Aux Girls St; Girl Scts; Key Clb; Latin Clb; Model UN; Teachers Aide; Acpl Chr; Band; Chorus; Church Choir; Allnc Soc Awrnss Pres; Yth Lcl Govt; KS U.

FOREMAN, ANNA; Hugoton HS; Liberal, KS; (2); 3/85; Church Yth Grp; HOBY; Band; Chorus; Chrldng; Trk; Vllybl; High Hon Roll; Hon Roll; Prfct Atten Awd; Art; Piano; NASA Spc Cmp; Friends U.

FOREMAN, NATHAN; Hugoton HS; Liberal, KS; (3); 2/69; Boy Scts; Church Yth Grp; Debate Tm; Quiz Bowl; Band; Chorus; Ftbl; High Hon Roll; NHS; Prfct Atten Awd; Eagle Sct; Friends U; Pre-Med.

FORMAN, ALISHA J; Lawrence HS; Lawrence, KS; (2); Church Yth Grp; Cmnty Wkr; Hosp Aide; Science Clb; Teachers Aide; Chorus; Pres Frsh Cls; High Hon Roll; Gospel Choir; Awd For ST Mus Ensmbl; Vet.

FORMAN, KIMBERLY E; Jefferson West HS; Meriden, KS; (3); Girl Scts; Pep Clb; High Hon Roll; Hon Roll; Photo; Highland CC; Photo.

FORNSHELL, JAMIE N; Maize HS; Wichita, KS; (4); Debate Tm; Science Clb; Spanish Clb; SADD; Teachers Aide; Varsity Clb; JV Var Bsktbl; Var Socr; Var Vllybl; Var Wt Lftg; KS St Univ.

FORREST, CALAH N; Argonia Jr Sr HS; Argonia, KS; (3); 7/22; Church Yth Grp; Letterman Clb; Pep Clb; Band; School Play; Bsktbl; Sftbl; Trk; Vllybl; Hon Roll; OT.

FORSSBERG, STEVEN P; Logan HS; Logan, KS; (4); 1/15; Boy Scts; Church Yth Grp; Capt Scholastic Bowl; School Play; Capt Bsktbl; Ftbl; Golf; Cit Awd; St Schlr; Val; Phillips Cty Grand Champ; Sec Treas Soph & Jr Cls; 50 Mile Afoot & Afloat Awd; KS ST Univ; Mech Engr.

FORSYTHE JR, STEVEN A; Highland Park HS; Topeka, KS; (2); 4/200; High Hon Roll; Pres Acad Fit Awd; Bsktbl; Stanford; Fin Adv.

FOSE, JAYME; Trego Comm HS; Wa Keeney, KS; (1); 1/46; FHA; Pep Clb; Science Clb; Speech Tm; Drill Tm; Mrchg Band; Bsktbl; Chrldng; Trk; High Hon Roll.

FOSKUHL, JASON; Dodge City HS; Dodge City, KS; (1); Debate Tm; Educl Talent Search Through Dodge City CC Mem; Quiz Bowl Open; 1st Pl Jr Engrng Tech Soc; KS Univ; Attorney.

FOSKUHL, MANDY R; Bucklin Schl; Bucklin, KS; (4); Library Aide; Math Tm; Speech Tm; SADD; Teachers Aide; Varsity Clb; Band; Chorus; Mrchg Band; Pep Band; DCCC; Phy Thrpst Asst.

FOSNIGHT, RENETTA S; Goddard HS; Wichita, KS; (2); Church Yth Grp; Debate Tm; Office Aide; Science Clb; Spanish Clb; Speech Tm; Mgr Band; Church Choir; Mrchg Band; Pep Band; Comm Svc Chrch Yth Grp; Mssns Trp Costa Rica Chrch Yth Grp; Med/Phrmctcl/Optmtrst.

FOSTER, BILL; Field Kindley Mem Sr HS; Coffeyville, KS; (4); Church Yth Grp; FCA; JA; Letterman Clb; Math Tm; Var Capt Bsktbl; Var Capt Ftbl; High Hon Roll; Prfct Atten Awd.

FOSTER, BRANDON A; Great Bend Sr HS; Great Bend, KS; (2); Pep Clb; JV Bsktbl; JV Golf; Intrml Socr; High Hon Roll; Hon Roll; Pres Acad Fit Awd; Pres Schlr; Presdntl Achvmnt Awd; Babe Ruth Bsbl Leag; Hap Dumont Bsbl Leag.

FOSTER, CANDI; Wichita West HS; Wichita, KS; (3); 2/283; Church Yth Grp; Cmnty Wkr; Band; Church Choir; Var L Socr; Var L Trk; Var L Vllybl; Hon Roll; NHS; Prfct Atten Awd; Yth Grp Missions Trip; Elem Ed.

FOSTER, CHRISTOPHER M; Washburn Rural HS; Topeka, KS; (3); 30/350; Am Leg Boys St; Boy Scts; Debate Tm; Red Cross Aide; Band; Mrchg Band; Pep Band; JV Bsktbl; Var Trk; High Hon Roll; Eagle Scout; Amer Lgn; Penn ST; Crmnl Jstce/Acctng.

FOSTER, GREGORY A; Labette Co HS; Oswego, KS; (2); 44/158; Natl FFA Org; Pep Clb; Science Clb; SADD; VICA; Var L Bsbl; Hon Roll.

FOSTER, JANICE; Junction City HS; Saint Louis, MO; (2); 14/277; FBLA; Key Clb; Office Aide; Variety Show; Rep Frsh Cls; Rep Soph Cls; JV Capt Chrldng; Hon Roll; Jr NHS; UCLA; Pediatrician.

FOSTER, KRISTI M; Marmaton Valley Jr Sr HS; Savonburg, KS; (2); 1/32; Math Tm; Scholastic Bowl; Speech Tm; Stage Crew; Var Trk; High Hon Roll; ST Trck Meet Frosh/Soph; ST Frnscs Soph; Drwng/Rdng/Wrtng; Chldrns Author/Eng Tchr.

FOSTER, LAURISSA M; Berean Acad; Wichita, KS; (3); Church Yth Grp; Math Tm; Band; Church Choir; Orch; Pep Band; High Hon Roll.

FOSTER, NANCY K; Jefferson West HS; Meriden, KS; (2); 12/75; Church Yth Grp; FBLA; FHA; Spanish Clb; Var Powder Puff Ftbl; JV Sftbl; Var L Vllybl; High Hon Roll.

FOSTER, NATALIE; Hutchinson HS; Hutchinson, KS; (3); 25/400; Church Yth Grp; Debate Tm; French Clb; HOBY; Key Clb; NFL; Pep Clb; Speech Tm; School Play; Rptr Frsh Cls; Future Prblm Slvng; Amnesty Intl; Stu Congress Team.

FOSTER, NATHAN C; Downs HS; Downs, KS; (1); Church Yth Grp; 4-H; Band; Mrchg Band; Pep Band; School Musical; JV Bsktbl; JV Ftbl; Var L Golf; 4-H Awd; Bus.

FOSTER, SHEYENE M; Clay Ctr Cmty HS; Clay Center, KS; (4); Am Leg Aux Girls St; Art Clb; Church Yth Grp; Cmnty Wkr; Debate Tm; Drama Clb; Natl FFA Org; Quiz Bowl; Scholastic Bowl; Spanish Clb; Atnd Natl Envrthn Cmptn 3 Cnsctv Yrs Tm Rep KS; KS ST Univ; Pblc Rltns.

FOSTER, THERESA M; Walnut Creek HS; Eskridge, KS; (3); 1/1; Church Yth Grp; Pres 4-H; Orch; 4-H Awd; V A Vol; KS ST Univ; Nrsng Home Admin.

FOSTER, TIM D; Northeast Magnet HS; Wichita, KS; (4); 1/63; Church Yth Grp; Math Tm; Science Clb; VP Jr Cls; Capt L Socr; Hon Roll; NHS; Ntl Merit Schol; Pres Schlr; St Schlr; U Of AR; Elec Eng.

FOTOVICH, BRIAN; Piper HS; Kansas City, KS; (3); Am Leg Boys St; Letterman Clb; Yrbk; Rep Stu Cncl; Var Bsbl; JV Bsktbl; Var Ftbl; High Hon Roll; NHS; Cmnty Wkr; Gftd Pgm Mem; Ice Hockey; Engrng.

FOUNTAINE, ELIZABETH A; Arkansas City HS; Arkansas City, KS; (2); Pres Church Yth Grp; FCA; SADD; Orch; School Play; Rep Soph Cls; Rep Jr Cls; Var L Crs Cntry; Var Trk; NHS; Usherettes; KS ST Univ; Psychlgst.

FOURAKER, SARAH L; Maranatha Acad; Shawnee, KS; (4); Pres Band; Color Guard; Jazz Band; Mrchg Band; Pep Band; School Musical; JV Chrldng; JV Vllybl; High Hon Roll; NHS; Piano; Flying Lessons; Orcher Local Summer Theater; Music Bus.

FOUTS, KARLI L; Highland Park HS; Topeka, KS; (2); Cit Awd; Hon Roll; Graphic Arts.

FOUTS, KEITH; Ottawa HS; Ottawa, KS; (3); Am Leg Boys St; Letterman Clb; Scholastic Bowl; Treas Spanish Clb; Var Crs Cntry; Var Trk; DAR Awd; High Hon Roll; NHS; Pres Acad Fit Awd; Aeronautics; Comp Sci.

FOWLER, JOHN; Parsons HS; Parsons, KS; (3); Church Yth Grp; Debate Tm; NFL; Band; Tennis; Hon Roll; NHS; Philsphy.

FOWLER, ROBINA; Turner HS; Kansas City, KS; (3); Church Yth Grp; Chorus; Yrbk; Ofcr Stu Cncl; Bsktbl; Vllybl; Hon Roll; Jr NHS; NHS; Acptd To Sumr Tm Admtnc Misn Prgm With Chrch 3 Yrs; Chrstn Ministrys.

FOWLER, SHARA; Atchison Sr HS; Atchison, KS; (1); Church Yth Grp; Cmnty Wkr; Debate Tm; Spanish Clb; Band; Mrchg Band; Pep Band; Chrldng; Hon Roll.

FOWLER, TOM D; Hutchinson HS; Hutchinson, KS; (3); 22/350; Am Leg Aux Girls St; Debate Tm; French Clb; NFL; Speech Tm; Band; Jazz Band; Mrchg Band; Rep Sr Cls; Ofcr Stu Cncl; Stdng Cngrs; Pol Sci/Ec.

FOWLER, TRICIA M; Parsons HS; Parsons, KS; (3); 5/108; Teachers Aide; Chorus; Spirit Clb; Psych.

FOX, CAROLEE; Waverly HS; Waverly, KS; (4); 7/17; NFL; Quiz Bowl; Teachers Aide; Band; Chorus; Pep Band; School Musical; L Trk; JV L Vllybl; High Hon Roll; OK Chrstn; Elem Ed.

FOX, HEATHER; St Marys HS; Saint Marys, KS; (2); FHA; Pep Clb; Band; Jazz Band; Pep Band; Var Bsktbl; Var Crs Cntry; Var Sftbl; Var Trk; High Hon Roll; KS U; Med.

FOX, JAMES P; Wellington Sr HS; Wellington, KS; (4); 11/119; High Hon Roll; Hon Roll; KS ST U; Comp Sci.

FOX, TRENT; St John Jr Sr HS; Saint John, KS; (2); Pep Clb; School Play; Sec Frsh Cls; Pres Soph Cls; VP Jr Cls; JV Bsktbl; JV Ftbl; High Hon Roll; NHS; Ntl Merit Ltr; Horses/Cattle; TX Tech; Anml Sci.

FOXX, MARIANNE; Wakefield HS; Milford, KS; (4); FHA; Pep Clb; Red Cross Aide; Spanish Clb; Speech Tm; Teachers Aide; Varsity Clb; Chorus; Ed Yrbk; Var Capt Vllybl; Southern Bapt Church; KS ST U; Crmnlgy.

FRAIRE, BRENDA; Liberal HS; Liberal, KS; (4); Am Leg Aux Girls St; Church Yth Grp; Cmnty Wkr; FHA; Key Clb; Office Aide; Quiz Bowl; Spanish Clb; Varsity Clb; Var Bsktbl; Chem.

FRAKER, NICOLE; Jefferson Co North HS; Winchester, KS; (2); Cmnty Wkr; FBLA; FHA; SADD; Band; Flag Corp; Mrchg Band; Pep Band; School Musical; Rep Soph Cls.

FRAKES, STEVEN T; Douglass HS; Atlanta, KS; (2); 26/78; Letterman Clb; Teachers Aide; Var L Ftbl; Var L Wrstlng; Hon Roll; 3rd Regnl Wrestling 95 2nd 96 ST 6th; 1st Team CPL League Wrestling; Outstdng Wrestler Awd.

FRALIN, GOLDA; Wichita East HS; Wichita, KS; (2); Church Yth Grp; Cmnty Wkr; Dance Clb; Debate Tm; Girl Scts; Math Clb; Model UN; Church Choir; Drill Tm; Yrbk; Langston; Law Schl.

FRANCIS, ANNETTE M; Chaparral HS; Anthony, KS; (4); 19/60; Key Clb; Pep Clb; Band; Chorus; School Musical; Rep Stu Cncl; Var Bsktbl; Var Trk; Var Vllybl; High Hon Roll; Teens As Tchrs; KS Jr Acad Bio; U Of KS; Occu Thpy.

FRANCIS, JEFF H; Blue Valley Northwest HS; Overland Park, KS; (2); Letterman Clb; Varsity Clb; JV Bsbl; Var L Crs Cntry; Ftbl; Var L Swmmng; High Hon Roll; Hon Roll.

FRANCIS, JENNIFER L; Blue Valley North West HS; Shawnee Mission, KS; (4); 1/340; Cmnty Wkr; FCA; GAA; Letterman Clb; Varsity Clb; Band; Mrchg Band; Orch; School Musical; Capt L Crs Cntry; All St Crss Cntry Team; Supt Awd; Whos Who In Ath; KS ST Univ; Pre-Vet.

FRANCIS, JULIA H; Blue Valley Northwest HS; Shawnee Mission, KS; (3); Hosp Aide; Intnl Clb; Key Clb; Math Clb; Band; Church Choir; Mrchg Band; Orch; High Hon Roll; NHS; BSA Explorer; Eng/Soc Stud/Physics Merit Awds; Natl Span Exam High Score; UN Essay Contest Winner; Pre-Med/Physician.

FRANCIS, LINDY; Garden City Sr HS; Garden City, KS; (4); 39/333; Bus Profs of Am; Church Yth Grp; 4-H; FHA; Chorus; Church Choir; Var L Chrldng; Wt Lftg; 4-H Awd; High Hon Roll; Baker U.

FRANCIS, TY D; Scott Comm HS; Scott City, KS; (3); Boy Scts; Band; Jazz Band; Pep Band; School Musical; Yrbk; JV Var Bsktbl; Var Tennis; High Hon Roll; NHS; Top Ratings At St Music Festival; Dist Hnr Concert Band & Hnr Jazz Band; Music Production; Bus.

FRANK, ALEC J; Blue Valley HS; Stilwell, KS; (2); Hon Roll; Med.

FRANK, CHRIS; Manhattan HS; Manhattan, KS; (3); Am Leg Boys St; Boy Scts; Hon Roll; Boy Sct Order Of The Arrow & Eagle Sct; KS ST Univ; Comp Sci.

FRANK, DEONNA D; Dodge City HS; Dodge City, KS; (4); 49/254; Office Aide; Teachers Aide; Orch; Bsktbl; Var Sftbl; Hon Roll; DARE; Dodge City CC; PTA.

FRANK, SHANNON; Shawnee Mission S Sr HS; Shawnee Mission, KS; (2); 135/400; Church Yth Grp; GAA; Pep Clb; Teachers Aide; Chrldng; Hon Roll; U Of KS; Fshn Merch.

FRANKE, HEATH; Herndon Schl; Oberlin, KS; (4); 3/6; 4-H; Math Tm; Model UN; Scholastic Bowl; Phtg Nwsp; Chrmn Yrbk; Pres Frsh Cls; Pres Soph Cls; Pres Sr Cls; Rep Stu Cncl; X-Cntry/Trck Schol; 4-H Found Awd; Canon Photo Mstrs; Colby CCACCTNG.

FRANKE, TRAVIS W; Topeka West HS; Topeka, KS; (2); Church Yth Grp; French Clb; Band; Jazz Band; Mrchg Band; Pep Band; School Musical; JV Socr; JV L Tennis; High Hon Roll.

FRANKEL, LESLIE M; Blue Valley Northwest HS; Overland Park, KS; (1); Acpl Chr; Chorus; Pep Clb; Flag Corp; School Musical; Hon Roll; Acad Awd Fr; Div I Rtng ST Vcl Msc Solo; Chldrn Perf Dnce Trpe; Comm Thtr; Mscl Thtr.

FRANKEN, ANDREW W; Troy HS; Troy, KS; (2); 4/40; Church Yth Grp; Cmnty Wkr; Letterman Clb; Var L Bsktbl; Var L Ftbl; Wt Lftg; High Hon Roll; NHS.

FRANKLIN, AMBER M; Blue Valley Northwest HS; Leawood, KS; (4); 1/343; Debate Tm; Pres FCA; Math Clb; Rep Sr Cls; Capt Swmmng; Gov Hon Prg Awd; Pres Schlr; St Schlr; Val; US Swmmng KS Cty Blzrs; U Of KS; Pol Sci.

FRANKLIN, CHRISTIE L; Louisburg HS; Louisburg, KS; (2); Hon Roll; 4 Yr Coll; PT.

FRANKLIN, PATRICIA A; Girard HS; Hepler, KS; (4); 32/69; Sec FHA; Natl FFA Org; Spanish Clb; SADD; Teachers Aide; Band; Mrchg Band; Pep Band; School Play; Mgr(s); Ft Scott CC; Vet Tech.

FRANKLIN, TARA; Arkansas City HS; Arkansas City, KS; (1); Church Yth Grp; Cmnty Wkr; Band; Church Choir; Mrchg Band; Pep Band; Mgr(s); Hon Roll; Actv Chrch/Yth Grp; Play Piano/Violin; SW Bapt Univ; Art.

FRANKS IV, JAMES H; Washburn Rural HS; Topeka, KS; (3); FBLA; SADD; Yrbk; Lit Mag; High Hon Roll; Hon Roll; Builders Clb; Washburn Univ Topeka; Psycht.

FRANKS, SETH A; Hyman Brand Hebrew Acad; Leawood, KS; (3); Hosp Aide; Math Tm; Office Aide; Temple Yth Grp; School Play; Stage Crew; Rptr Nwsp; Ed Yrbk; Mgr Bsktbl; Mgr(s).

FRANTZ, KELLY J; Shawnee Heights HS; Topeka, KS; (3); Debate Tm; Hosp Aide; SADD; Teachers Aide; Chorus; Orch; High Hon Roll; Hon Roll; Jr NHS; Prfct Atten Awd; Law.

FRANZ, JENNIFER E; Maize HS; Wichita, KS; (2); Church Yth Grp; FCA; Letterman Clb; NFL; Science Clb; Chorus; Church Choir; Variety Show; Hon Roll; NHS; KAYS; Music Therapy.

FRANZ, KARL N; Olathe East Sr HS; Overland Park, KS; (3); Church Yth Grp; Spanish Clb; Chorus; Bsktbl; High Hon Roll; Hon Roll.

FRANZ, LEAH J; Blue Valley Northwest HS; Overland Park, KS; (3); Chorus; School Play; Lit Mag; VP Frsh Cls; Pres Soph Cls; Hon Roll; Yth For Christ Drama Tm Vlntr; Ecology Clb; Northwestern; Engl.

FRANZ, NATASHA; Wichita Southeast HS; Tulsa, OK; (4); Library Aide; Q&S; SADD; Teachers Aide; Ed Yrbk; JV Var Swmmng; JV Trk; Mgr Vllybl; High Hon Roll; Hon Roll; KS Hnr Schlr; Acad Ltr; Ath Ltr; U Of KS; Jrnlsm; Advertising.

FRANZEN, JUSTIN L; Topeka HS; Topeka, KS; (2); Church Yth Grp; Acpl Chr; Band; Chorus; Church Choir; Mrchg Band; School Musical; Variety Show; High Hon Roll; Pres Acad Fit Awd.

FRASCO, MANDY N; Maize HS; Wichita, KS; (2); Letterman Clb; Q&S; Spanish Clb; SADD; Yrbk; Var Bsktbl; Var Sftbl; JV Vllybl; Hon Roll; Sftbl Var Hnrb Mntn Pitcher; Kay Clb Mem; 2nd Team Utility; Psych.

FRASER, PHILIP M; Campus HS; Wichita, KS; (2); 5/375; Church Yth Grp; High Hon Roll; NHS; Natural Hlprs; Med.

FRATZEL, CHRISTOPHER A; Immaculata HS; Basehor, KS; (2); Boy Scts; Scholastic Bowl; Thesps; Ftbl; Golf; Hon Roll; Schl Awd Excl Cmptr Pgmng.

FRAZEE, JACOB M; Maize HS; Wichita, KS; (1); Band; Jazz Band; Mrchg Band; Pep Band; Prfct Atten Awd; Pres Acad Fit Awd; KS ST.

FRAZEE, JASPER; Sabetha HS; Sabetha, KS; (3); 27/80; Church Yth Grp; Pres FCA; Pres 4-H; Pres Chorus; School Play; Rep Stu Cncl; Var Bsktbl; Var Ftbl; Var Trk; Hon Roll; Airclt Maint.

FRAZELL, ROBERT L; J C Harmon HS; Kansas City, KS; (2); Hon Roll.

FRAZELL, TARA D; Chanute Sr HS; Chanute, KS; (3); 16/160; FCA; GAA; Letterman Clb; Pep Clb; Red Cross Aide; SADD; Teachers Aide; Varsity Clb; Nwsp; Rep Frsh Cls; Jr Lions Clb; Orthodontics.

FRAZER, JENNIFER T; Shawnee Mission Nw Sr HS; Shawnee, KS; (4); 5/395; Church Yth Grp; Debate Tm; Math Tm; Scholastic Bowl; Science Clb; Band; NHS; Ntl Merit SF; Acad Dcthln; Rsrch Sci.

FRAZIER, RACHEL ELIZABETH; Newton Sr HS; Newton, KS; (4); 10/235; Dance Clb; French Clb; Key Clb; Letterman Clb; Varsity Clb; VICA; Chorus; Swing Chorus; JV Var Bsktbl; JV Crs Cntry; Comm Internship; Eclipse Clb; Emporia ST Univ; Elem Ed.

FRAZIER, WHITNEY J; Wichita Southeast HS; Wichita, KS; (2); Socr; Hon Roll; Prfct Atten Awd; Marine Bio.

FREDEN, ANNE V; Topeka West HS; Topeka, KS; (4); 4/240; Cmnty Wkr; Q&S; Sec Spanish Clb; Ed Yrbk; L Co-Capt Tennis; High Hon Roll; Sec NHS; Wellesley Col.

FREDERICK, JOE L; Wabaunsee HS; Alma, KS; (3); Church Yth Grp; 4-H; FBLA; FHA; Letterman Clb; Natl FFA Org; VP Frsh Cls; Pres Jr Cls; Rep Stu Cncl; JV Var Bsktbl; KS St Univ.

FREDERICK, JUSTIN D; Shawnee Heights Sr HS; Topeka, KS; (2); Church Yth Grp; Cmnty Wkr; Intnl Clb; Model UN; Pep Clb; Treas SADD; Thesps; Orch; High Hon Roll; Hon Roll; Co Chair Fundraising Orch; Emporia St Univ; Elem Tchr.

FREDERKING, MATTHEW D; Beloit Jr Sr HS; Beloit, KS; (2); Church Yth Grp; Letterman Clb; Natl FFA Org; Chorus; School Musical; Stage Crew; Ofcr Frsh Cls; Ofcr Soph Cls; JV Bsktbl; Var Ftbl; Jdgng Cttl; K ST; Ag.

FREDIN, JAYNANN E; Maize HS; Wichita, KS; (3); Church Yth Grp; Letterman Clb; Spanish Clb; SADD; Teachers Aide; Chorus; Church Choir; Variety Show; Hon Roll; RAYS, KS Assoc Of Yth.

FREELON, SHANNA N; Leavenworth HS; Leavenworth, KS; (3); Art Clb; Church Yth Grp; School Play; Ofcr Jr Cls; Var Crs Cntry; Var Trk; Wt Lftg; U Of KS; Pre Law.

FREEMAN, AUBREY; Pratt HS; Pratt, KS; (1); Church Yth Grp; Cmnty Wkr; FHA; Hosp Aide; Pep Clb; Varsity Clb; Church Choir; Drill Tm; Chrldng; Gym; U Of KS; Anesthetist.

FREEMAN, DANI; Lansing HS; Lansing, KS; (4); Church Yth Grp; Cmnty Wkr; L Drama Clb; 4-H; Ofcr French Clb; Intnl Clb; Key Clb; Office Aide; Science Clb; Teachers Aide; Riding/Skating Clubs; KS ST U; Vet Med.

FREEMAN, ELIZABETH; Paola HS; Paola, KS; (2); 6/150; Art Clb; Church Yth Grp; Debate Tm; Drama Clb; FCA; NFL; SADD; Thesps; Stage Crew; Pres Soph Cls.

FREEMAN III, GRANVILLE T; Southeast HS; Wichita, KS; (3); 64/360; Cmnty Wkr; Drama Clb; Hosp Aide; Red Cross Aide; Teachers Aide; Thesps; School Musical; School Play; Stage Crew; Ed Yrbk; Future Ldrs Of Amer; Commnctns.

FREEMAN, JEANNA L; Topeka HS; Topeka, KS; (3); Chorus; Chansonette Select Womens Choir; ETC Selection Of Actors; BSU; Savannah Coll; Intr Dsgn.

FREEMAN, JENNY D; Ellsworth HS; Kanopolis, KS; (2); 19/85; Church Yth Grp; Band; Chorus; Flag Corp; Mrchg Band; Pep Band; Sec Frsh Cls; Bsktbl; Trk; Vllybl; Natl Sci Merit Awd; All Amer Schlr; Sterling Coll; Tchng/Coaching.

FREEMAN, MELISSA; Washburn Rural HS; Topeka, KS; (2); Drama Clb; SADD; Ed Yrbk; Var Chrldng; JV Trk; High Hon Roll; Dance; Gymnastics; Coaching Gymnastics; U Of GA.

FREHE, MARK E; Silver Lake Jr Sr HS; Silver Lake, KS; (4); 20/46; Cmnty Wkr; Letterman Clb; Varsity Clb; Acpl Chr; Band; Chorus; Jazz Band; Mrchg Band; Pep Band; School Musical; Emporia ST Univ.

FREHE, MATT; Silver Lake Jr Sr HS; Silver Lake, KS; (2); Band; Chorus; Mrchg Band; School Musical; JV Bsktbl; Var L Crs Cntry; Var L Ftbl; Var L Trk; Cit Awd; Hon Roll; KS Univ; Firefighter.

FREIDLIN, ERIC W; Maize HS; Wichita, KS; (3); Teachers Aide; Band; Mrchg Band; Pep Band; Mgr Bsktbl; Capt Mgr(s); Trk; Play Marching Baritone In Band; Software Engrng.

FRENCH, EMILY; Hugoton HS; Hugoton, KS; (3); 4/69; Am Leg Aux Girls St; Church Yth Grp; Treas FCA; Band; Treas Soph Cls; Sec Jr Cls; Var L Chrldng; Hon Roll; NHS; Hmcmng Ct.

FRENCH, JOHN M; Buhler HS; Hutchinson, KS; (2); Church Yth Grp; Letterman Clb; Var L Bsbl; Bsktbl; JV L Ftbl; Hon Roll; Prfct Atten Awd; Amer Legion Bsbl 95 St Champions; U Of OK.

FRENCH, LANCE M; Trego Comm HS; Wa Keeney, KS; (3); 30/48; Boy Scts; Band; Mrchg Band; Pep Band; Phtg Yrbk; Mgr Bsktbl; Phtg Ftbl; Tennis; Mgr Vllybl; Private In US Army; KS ST Univ; Fshn Photo.

FRENCH, MATT; Buhler HS; Buhler, KS; (3); 1/175; Am Leg Boys St; FCA; Band; Chorus; Drm Mjr(t); Jazz Band; Mrchg Band; Pep Band; School Play; Rep Stu Cncl; U Of KS; Premed.

FRENCH, SHONDA; Udall HS; Udall, KS; (2); Church Yth Grp; Drama Clb; Quiz Bowl; Red Cross Aide; Scholastic Bowl; Band; Jazz Band; Mrchg Band; Pep Band; School Play; KS ST U.

FRESE, AMY L; Council Grove HS; Alta Vista, KS; (4); 19/77; Church Yth Grp; FCA; FBLA; FHA; Key Clb; SADD; Teachers Aide; Band; Mrchg Band; Pep Band; Hrtlnd Acad Dnc; Key Club Adpt-A-Grndprnt Prog; KAY Club; KS ST U; Elem Ed.

FRESE, JOE R; Basehor Linwood HS; Bonner Springs, KS; (2); Boy Scts; Church Yth Grp; Cmnty Wkr; Math Tm; Pep Clb; Hon Roll; Engr.

FREUND, PETER; Maranatha Acad; Olathe, KS; (3); 6/49; Band; School Musical; School Play; Stage Crew; Ed Nwsp; Ed Yrbk; Treas Jr Cls; Rep Stu Cncl; NHS; Chess Clb; All Amer Schlr; Jrnlsm; Pol.

FREY, DIANE L; Olathe South Sr HS; Olathe, KS; (3); Church Yth Grp; Drama Clb; NFL; Pep Clb; Teachers Aide; Thesps; Chorus; Drill Tm; School Musical; School Play; Thtrcl Arts/Hair Stylst.

FREY, JACE R; Wichita East HS; Wichita, KS; (4); 1/350; Debate Tm; English Clb; NFL; Speech Tm; Acpl Chr; Chorus; School Musical; Variety Show; Ofcr Stu Cncl; Capt Swmmng; Rice U.

FREY, KARI E; Olathe East Sr HS; Olathe, KS; (2); Church Yth Grp; French Clb; Letterman Clb; Band; Jazz Band; Mrchg Band; Pep Band; Ed Yrbk; High Hon Roll; Pres Acad Fit Awd; Ed.

FREY, KATRINA L; Newton Sr HS; North Newton, KS; (3); Art Clb; Church Yth Grp; German Clb; Model UN; Orch; JV Bsktbl; Var JV Crs Cntry; Var Mgr(s); JV Trk; NHS; Northland Coll; Biol.

FREY, KENNY; Inman Jr Sr HS; Mc Pherson, KS; (2); 10/50; Church Yth Grp; Natl FFA Org; NFL; Band; Mrchg Band; Pep Band; Var L Ftbl; Trk; Hon Roll; Prfct Atten Awd; US Air Force Acad; Aviatn.

FRICK, CHRISSIE J; Trego Comm HS; Wa Keeney, KS; (3); 13/50; Debate Tm; Drama Clb; German Clb; NFL; Quiz Bowl; Scholastic Bowl; Science Clb; Speech Tm; SADD; Rptr Nwsp; Harvard Law Schl; Crim Law.

FRICK, MEGAN E; Shawnee Mission W Sr HS; Lenexa, KS; (1); 75/434; Dance Clb; Debate Tm; GAA; Latin Clb; Letterman Clb; Pep Clb; Varsity Clb; JV Var Bsktbl; Var Golf; Var Sftbl; Sports Medicine.

FRICK, MELISSA; Larned HS; Larned, KS; (4); 19/90; 4-H; Spanish Clb; Acpl Chr; Band; Pep Band; Bsktbl; Chrldng; Tennis; Trk; NHS; KSU; Bakery Sci.

FRIDY, MELINDA K; Liberal HS; Liberal, KS; (2); 3/320; Church Yth Grp; FCA; Sec Treas Key Clb; NFL; Sec Treas Science Clb; Band; Flag Corp; JV Vllybl; High Hon Roll; NHS; Downhill Snow Skiing; KS Univ; Psych.

FRIEDL, RACHEL M; Hayden HS; Topeka, KS; (2); Intnl Clb; SADD; Mgr(s); Hon Roll; Spirit Clb.

FRIEDLY, DAWN R; Phillipsburg HS; Phillipsburg, KS; (2); Debate Tm; HOBY; High Hon Roll; Art Clb; Church Yth Grp; Drama Clb; German Clb; NFL; Pep Clb; Speech Tm; Kay; Chmbr Cmrc; KU; Intr Dsgn.

FRIEDSTROM, EMILY J; Topeka West HS; Topeka, KS; (3); Am Leg Aux Girls St; Church Yth Grp; Cmnty Wkr; French Clb; SADD; Band; Mrchg Band; Pep Band; Stage Crew; JV Stat Bsktbl; Spirit Clb VP; Te Prty; Mscl Stagemgr; Washburn Univ.

FRIEND, ANDREA E; Clearwater HS; Clearwater, KS; (4); 10/80; Rep Key Clb; Letterman Clb; SADD; Rep Sr Cls; JV Bsktbl; Var Trk; JV Vllybl; High Hon Roll; VP NHS; Mgr(s); GCTL; U Of KS; Scl Work.

FRIEND, GARY; Northeast Magnet HS; Wichita, KS; (1); JETS Awd; Natl Engrg Dsgn Chlng 6th Plc Natl Cmptn; GATE Pgm; Stdnt Mo 96; MIT; Engrg.

FRIEND, JANA S; Southeast HS; Wichita, KS; (4); 83/378; Church Yth Grp; Hosp Aide; Teachers Aide; Pre Med.

FRIERSON, SEDRIC T; Wyandotte HS; Kansas City, KS; (2); Nwsp; Yrbk; Ofcr Jr Cls; Bsktbl; Ftbl; Trk; Bus Mgmt.

FRIESEN, CHRISTOPHER D; Hesston HS; Hesston, KS; (3); Church Yth Grp; FCA; FBLA; Model UN; Quiz Bowl; Band; Chorus; Pep Band; Bsktbl; High Hon Roll.

FRIESEN, KELLY; Hutchinson HS; Hutchinson, KS; (4); Church Yth Grp; Letterman Clb; Band; Jazz Band; Mrchg Band; Pep Band; Capt Var Ftbl; Var L Swmmng; Var L Trk; Ftbl Schlrshp To HCC; Chrch Sftbl; Hutchinson CC.

FRIESEN, KERRY; Hillsboro HS; Hillsboro, KS; (3); 2/62; Church Yth Grp; Dance Clb; Chorus; School Musical; Chrldng; Var L Tennis; High Hon Roll; NHS; Kayettes VP; Sprt N Clbrtn; Music Prfrmnc.

FRIESEN, KIM A; Hutchinson HS; Hutchinson, KS; (4); Church Yth Grp; Letterman Clb; Band; Mrchg Band; Pep Band; Capt L Ftbl; Capt L Swmmng; Var L Trk; Wt Lftg; Hnrb Mntn Hnr Roll; Hutchinson CC.

FRIESEN, KRISTY M; Elyria Christian Schl; Mc Pherson, KS; (3); 2/4; Church Yth Grp; Drama Clb; NFL; Speech Tm; Teachers Aide; School Play; Ed Yrbk; Stat Bsktbl; Hon Roll; Church Choir; Sunday Schl Tchr; Pre-Law.

FRIESEN, LARESSA M; Meade HS; Meade, KS; (1); Church Yth Grp; Key Clb; Pep Clb; Band; Chorus; Pep Band; Sec Frsh Cls; Bsktbl; Swmmng; High Hon Roll.

FRIESEN, LISA M; Meade HS; Meade, KS; (4); 5/24; Church Yth Grp; FCA; Letterman Clb; Band; Chorus; Church Choir; School Musical; Var Capt Tennis; High Hon Roll; NHS; John Brown Univ; Biochem.

FRIESEN, TRACY D; Berean Acad; Galva, KS; (4); 1/32; Church Yth Grp; Cmnty Wkr; Math Tm; Band; Gov Hon Prg Awd; High Hon Roll; Pres Sec NHS; Prfct Atten Awd; Val; Chorus; Hnrs Choir; Cedarville Coll; Bible/Msns.

FRIESS, KATY; Conway Springs HS; Argonia, KS; (2); Church Yth Grp; Drama Clb; FHA; Spanish Clb; School Play; Rptr Nwsp; VP Stu Cncl; Diving; Powder Puff Ftbl; Trk; Flt Attndt.

FRIEZE, STEPHANIE; Andover HS; Wichita, KS; (4); 28/140; Pres French Clb; Scholastic Bowl; Acpl Chr; School Musical; Rptr Yrbk; Var Golf; JV Sftbl; High Hon Roll; Prfct Atten Awd; Madrigals; Trinity U.

FRIHART, MONICA A; Field Kindley Mem Sr HS; Coffeyville, KS; (2); Dance Clb; French Clb; German Clb; Drill Tm; Rep Frsh Cls; Rep Stu Cncl; Mgr(s); Var Pom Pon; Var Trk; Hon Roll; Bus Mgmt.

FRISBIE, MEGHAN; Herington HS; Herington, KS; (1); Church Yth Grp; Dance Clb; Drama Clb; FHA; Pep Clb; Band; Mrchg Band; Var Chrldng; High Hon Roll; Hon Roll; Jz; Bllt Pnt; Miami; Fshn Dsgn.

FRITZMEIER, SHARI; Stafford Jr Sr HS; Stafford, KS; (3); 1/24; Church Yth Grp; FCA; Math Tm; Quiz Bowl; Science Clb; Bsktbl; Trk; Vllybl; Wt Lftg; High Hon Roll; 2 A St Discus Chmpn; Scndry Math Ed.

FROETSCHNER, CHRISTOPHER D; Larned HS; Larned, KS; (2); VP Jr Cls; Var Bsbl; Var Bsktbl; Hon Roll; Prfct Atten Awd.

FROST, HEATHER L; Meade HS; Meade, KS; (1); Church Yth Grp; NFL; Band; Chorus; Mrchg Band; Pep Band; School Musical; School Play; Cit Awd; High Hon Roll; Kayettes.

FROST, WAYNE; White Rock HS; Esbon, KS; (4); #2 in class; Am Leg Boys St; Letterman Clb; Math Tm; Natl FFA Org; Pep Clb; Quiz Bowl; SADD; Pres Sr Cls; Ftbl; High Hon Roll; Ft Hays St U; Ag Bus.

FRUIN, KELLY L; Blue Valley Northwest HS; Overland Park, KS; (4); Teachers Aide; Var Capt Bsktbl; Var Sftbl; Var Vllybl; Cit Awd; High Hon Roll; NHS; Pres Acad Fit Awd; St Schlr; Varsity Clb; U Of KS.

FRUIT, TRACI L; Pratt HS; Haviland, KS; (4); 6/99; Cmnty Wkr; Debate Tm; Hosp Aide; SADD; Teachers Aide; Chorus; Stage Crew; Ed Nwsp; L Vllybl; High Hon Roll; Washburn Univ; Chem.

FRY, CHERRY; West Elk Jr Sr HS; Elk Falls, KS; (3); #1 in class; Church Yth Grp; 4-H; JA; School Play; Yrbk; Cit Awd; 4-H Awd; High Hon Roll; Hon Roll; NHS; Coll Of Ozarks; Elem Ed.

FRY, DOUGLAS M; Coldwater Jr Sr HS; Coldwater, KS; (2); 4/24; Church Yth Grp; FCA; Letterman Clb; VICA; Band; Chorus; Pep Band; School Musical; JV Bsktbl; JV Ftbl.

FRY, JAMIE A; El Dorado HS; El Dorado, KS; (2); Letterman Clb; NFL; Spanish Clb; Band; Bsktbl; JV Sftbl; JV Var Tennis; Hon Roll; SADD; Mrchg Band; Jr Ambassador; Earth Care Clb.

FRY, LAURA; Sedgwick HS; Sedgwick, KS; (2); Letterman Clb; Scholastic Bowl; Chorus; School Musical; Sec Soph Cls; Chrldng; Trk; Vllybl; Hon Roll.

FRY, LORI; Coldwater Jr Sr HS; Wilmore, KS; (2); Band; Chorus; School Musical; Variety Show; Treas Soph Cls; JV Var Bsktbl; Trk; JV Var Vllybl; High Hon Roll; Hon Roll; KSU.

FRY, TOBY J; Bishop Ward HS; Kansas City, KS; (2); Church Yth Grp; Drama Clb; Intnl Clb; NFL; Pep Clb; Speech Tm; SADD; School Musical; School Play; Stage Crew; Good Samaritan Proj; GIFT Bishop Wards Envrmntl Clb; Campus Mnstry Tm; Notre Dame; Law/Crmnlgy.

FRYE, JENNY; Wallace Cty HS; Sharon Springs, KS; (2); Pep Clb; Chorus; Drill Tm; Chrldng; Pom Pon; Nurses Aide Trng Through Colby CC; Drafter.

FRYE, LAURA K; Topeka HS; Topeka, KS; (1); 1/530; Cmnty Wkr; Hosp Aide; Model UN; Pep Clb; Spanish Clb; Drill Tm; High Hon Roll.

FRYE, NATHAN; Hays HS; Hays, KS; (3); Boy Scts; Scholastic Bowl; Science Clb; Band; Jazz Band; Orch; Pep Band; School Musical; NHS; Ntl Merit SF.

FRYMAN, LYNNLEA; Garden City Sr HS; Garden City, KS; (4); 31/313; Drama Clb; Pres 4-H; FHA; Key Clb; Pres SADD; Acpl Chr; Chorus; School Musical; School Play; Rep Sr Cls; I Dare You Awd; Fort Hays ST U; Vocal Music.

FUCHS, KIM; Shawnee Mission N HS; Shawnee Mission, KS; (3); 32/380; Drama Clb; Thesps; Varsity Clb; School Play; Stage Crew; Sec Soph Cls; Sec Pres Stu Cncl; Var Capt Chrldng; High Hon Roll; NHS; Tae Kwon Do Stu; Cotillion Mem; Psych.

FUCHS, MEGAN M; Bishop Miege HS; Shawnee Mission, KS; (3); 28/180; Church Yth Grp; Office Aide; SADD; Drill Tm; Yrbk; Hon Roll; NHS; Acad Excl Awd; Spirit Clb; Hnrs Schlsp From Miege.

FUGATE, JOSHUA C; Turner HS; Kansas City, KS; (4); 9/200; Bus Profs of Am; Church Yth Grp; Q&S; Varsity Clb; Ed Nwsp; Var Bsbl; Var Bsktbl; High Hon Roll; Hon Roll; Jr NHS; Sun Schl Tchr; Bus Admin.

FUHLHAGE, MARLA; Leroy HS; Le Roy, KS; (4); 7/16; Am Leg Aux Girls St; Office Aide; Band; Sec Frsh Cls; Sec Soph Cls; Sec Jr Cls; Sec Sr Cls; Bsktbl; High Hon Roll; St Schlr; Emporia St U; Elem Ed.

FUHRMANN, ADELE C; Lawrence HS; Lawrence, KS; (2); Church Yth Grp; Spanish Clb; Chorus; Church Choir; Variety Show; JV Trk; Hon Roll; Flwshp Chrstn Stdnts; Respite Care Vol; KA Music Ed Assoc Part.

FUKUNAGA, EDWIN T; Blue Valley Northwest HS; Overland Park, KS; (1); Chess Clb; Orch; School Musical; Hon Roll; Scor 64/80 Natl Span Exam Lvl 2; Tech Aide; AllST Prgm Interlochen Fine Arts Camp; Hghst Scr AHSME; Cmptr Sci/Elec Engr.

FULK, ALI; Gardner-Edgerton HS; Gardner, KS; (1); Church Yth Grp; FCA; Pep Clb; Chorus; School Musical; School Play; Chrldng; Hon Roll; Ftbl, Wrestling & Bsktbl Chrldng Ltr; Schltc Achvmt Ltr.

FULLEN, JASON T; Leavenworth HS; Leavenworth, KS; (3); 46/409; FBLA; Var Bsktbl; Cit Awd; High Hon Roll; Hon Roll; NHS; Pres Acad Fit Awd; Stanford Univ.

FULLER, MATT P; Beloit Jr Sr HS; Beloit, KS; (2); Church Yth Grp; Letterman Clb; L Ftbl; JV Trk.

FULLHART, THOMAS R; Central Jr Sr HS; Grenola, KS; (4); 5/25; Computer Clb; Math Tm; Capt Scholastic Bowl; Spanish Clb; Sec Speech Tm; L Stat Trk; Hon Roll; NHS; Ntl Merit SF; Pres Acad Fit Awd; Regents Hnr Acad Pittsburg St U; KS ST U; Comp Sci.

FULMER, JUSTIN; Washburn Rural HS; Topeka, KS; (3); FBLA; Teachers Aide; School Musical; School Play; Yrbk; Hon Roll; 1st Washburn Univ Acad Cont In Comp Literacy; Vol Of The Yr; Bus Stu Of The Yr; Washburn Univ; Graphic Dsgn.

FULTON, ALICIA; Triplains Schl; Winona, KS; (3); HOBY; Letterman Clb; Quiz Bowl; Church Choir; School Play; Var L Bsktbl; L Trk; Hon Roll; Jr NHS; NHS; CCC; Nrsng.

FULTZ, JOSHUA; Atchison Sr HS; Atchison, KS; (4); Pres Art Clb; Math Clb; Mrchg Band; Orch; Ftbl; Hon Roll; Moikan Artist; Highland CC; Art Ed.

FUNCHESS, APRIL D; Southeast HS; Wichita, KS; (2); Church Yth Grp; Teachers Aide; Intrml Socr; High Hon Roll; KS St Univ; Med.

FUND, MELISSA; Wamego HS; Wamego, KS; (2); 25/125; Church Yth Grp; Debate Tm; 4-H; FHA; Science Clb; Band; Mrchg Band; Nwsp; Cit Awd; 4-H Awd; Extended Learning Pgm; Highest Rating For Fr Horn Solo, Fr Horn IV & Brass Choir At St Cmptn; Jrnlsm; Vet Med.

FUNK, COREY D; Maize HS; Wichita, KS; (3); 64/281; Church Yth Grp; Letterman Clb; L Ftbl; High Hon Roll; Hon Roll.

FUNK, CORY; Russell HS; Russell, KS; (3); 12/78; Am Leg Boys St; Pres Church Yth Grp; Key Clb; Pep Clb; SADD; Band; Chorus; Jazz Band; L Mrchg Band; L Pep Band; ST St Singers Show Choir; Ft Hays ST U; Vocal Music Tchr.

FUNK, DERRICK S; Hillsboro HS; Hillsboro, KS; (3); 23/48; Church Yth Grp; Cmnty Wkr; JV Bsktbl; Var L Ftbl; Wt Lftg; Hon Roll; KS ST; Engr.

FUNK, EVAN J; El Dorado HS; El Dorado, KS; (3); 1/200; Letterman Clb; Spanish Clb; Teachers Aide; Varsity Clb; Var Bsktbl; Var Ftbl; Var Trk; Intrml Wt Lftg; Hon Roll; NHS.

FUNK, JACOB S; Newton Sr HS; Newton, KS; (2); JV Bsbl; JV Bsktbl; Wt Lftg; High Hon Roll; U Of KS; Surgeon.

FUNK, JESSICA D; Mc Louth Schl; Mc Louth, KS; (2); Church Yth Grp; Cmnty Wkr; Drama Clb; FHA; GAA; Pep Clb; Spanish Clb; SADD; Teachers Aide; Varsity Clb; KS Univ; Pharmacy.

FUNK, NATHAN L; Hillsboro HS; Hillsboro, KS; (2); 23/48; Boy Scts; Church Yth Grp; Cmnty Wkr; Letterman Clb; Natl FFA Org; Yrbk; Bsktbl; Ftbl; Intrml Sftbl; Hon Roll.

FUNK, THOMAS D; Leavenworth HS; Leavenworth, KS; (3); Boy Scts; Ski Clb; Nwsp; School Musical; Wrstlng; Jrnlsm Ed Assn Natl Wrt Off Hnrbl Mntn; KS Prs Wm/Prs Assn K Schlstc 3rd Plc; MENSA; K ST.

FUQUA, AMY; Inman Jr Sr HS; Inman, KS; (2); Art Clb; Church Yth Grp; Acpl Chr; Band; Chorus; Church Choir; Mrchg Band; Pep Band; Variety Show; Var Bsktbl.

FUQUA, KELSEY I; Douglass HS; Douglass, KS; (3); 7/60; Teachers Aide; High Hon Roll; Hon Roll; Awd For Outstdng Perfmnc In Comp Applications; Span II Awd; Wildlife Bio.

FURSMAN, ERIKA L; Anderson Cty Jr Sr HS; Garnett, KS; (1); Cmnty Wkr; French Clb; Intnl Clb; Letterman Clb; Pep Clb; SADD; Band; Mrchg Band; Pep Band; Score Keeper; KAY Clb; Dog Pound; KS Univ; Fine Arts; Jrnlsm.

FURST, KARA; St Thomas Aquinas HS; Overland Park, KS; (3); Cmnty Wkr; FBLA; GAA; Sftbl; Hon Roll; Music/Fishing/Camping; Soc Wrk; Envrnmntlst.

FUSCO, AUDREY C; Wichita Southeast HS; Wichita, KS; (2); 11/436; Cmnty Wkr; Debate Tm; NFL; Office Aide; Orch; High Hon Roll; Hon Roll; Sierra Clb.

FYE, SUNSHINE C; Summer Acad Of Arts & Sci; Kansas City, KS; (4); 3/196; Hist Drama Clb; Co-Capt FCA; Pres 4-H; Pres German Clb; Pres Scholastic Bowl; School Musical; Var Capt Crs Cntry; Cit Awd; NHS; Ntl Merit Schol; Ger Hnr Soc; Intnl Baccalaureate; Wheaton Coll; Pol Sci; Art.

FYFFE, BENJAMIN J; Circle HS; Towanda, KS; (2); Church Yth Grp; FCA; Rep Frsh Cls; Rep Soph Cls; JV Bsbl; JV Bsktbl; Mgr Ftbl; Hon Roll; Spartan Schl Of Aeronautics.

FYLER, ERIN; Sublette HS; Sublette, KS; (1); Church Yth Grp; Pep Clb; Acpl Chr; Band; Chorus; Pep Band; School Musical; Chrldng; Vllybl.

FYLER, JEREMY; Otis Bison HS; Olmitz, KS; (1); Church Yth Grp; 4-H; Acpl Chr; Band; Chorus; Church Choir; Mrchg Band; Pep Band; Bsktbl; Hon Roll; Fort Hays ST Univ; Bus; CPA.

FYOCK, SUMMER L; Jayhawk-Linn HS; Prescott, KS; (3); Art Clb; Church Yth Grp; Cmnty Wkr; Math Clb; Math Tm; Band; Mrchg Band; Pep Band; School Play; Var Bsktbl; Top 20; Natl Yth Ldrshp Forum Law/Constitution; U Of KS; Law.

GAAS, KELLY R; Thomas More Prep-Marion HS; Hays, KS; (2); Bsktbl; Mgr(s); TX A&M; Acctng.

GABB, JAMI S; Piper HS; Kansas City, KS; (4); French Clb; VP FHA; Library Aide; Sec Spanish Clb; SADD; Chorus; Cit Awd; High Hon Roll; Jr NHS; Pres Acad Fit Awd; Eng Lit Achvmt Awd; Bd Of Regents Cert; Stu Of The Month; KC KS CC; Pre-Pharmacy.

GABEHART, REBECCA J; Washburn Rural HS; Auburn, KS; (2); 31/372; SADD; Intrml Bsktbl; JV Socr; Acad Lttr; Archtctr; Art Drwng; Archtctr.

GABLE, WILLIAM; Wichita West HS; Wichita, KS; (4); 69/271; Debate Tm; NFL; Var L Crs Cntry; Var L Trk; Hon Roll; EOA; U Of AZ; Comp Sci.

GADELKARIM, SAFIA S; Wichita East HS; Wichita, KS; (2); 9/420; Math Clb; Spanish Clb; School Play; Bsktbl; Hon Roll; Pdtrcn.

GADER, ANDREA R; Washburn Rural HS; Topeka, KS; (2); Church Yth Grp; Teachers Aide; Chorus; School Musical; Rptr Lit Mag; Hon Roll; Karate.

GAFFORD, KRIS; Nemaha Valley HS; Seneca, KS; (4); 8/54; 4-H; Letterman Clb; SADD; Band; Pep Band; School Play; Stage Crew; Ed Yrbk; VP Soph Cls; Ofcr Jr Cls; Forensics; KAYS; Images; KS ST U.

GAGE, JESSICA L; Russell HS; Russell, KS; (3); 9/100; Sec Church Yth Grp; Cmnty Wkr; Dance Clb; Debate Tm; FCA; Girl Scts; Key Clb; Letterman Clb; Pep Clb; SADD.

GAGE, SHILO; Circle HS; El Dorado, KS; (2); Church Yth Grp; 4-H; Girl Scts; Quiz Bowl; Band; Chorus; Church Choir; Mrchg Band; Pep Band; Variety Show; APHA & SCSHA; KS ST U; Vet.

GAGE, SHON M; Circle HS; El Dorado, KS; (2); 15/144; 4-H; Pep Clb; Quiz Bowl; SADD; Band; Chorus; Church Choir; Mrchg Band; Pep Band; Variety Show; 4-H Clb Sec; Presdntl Ctznshp Awd; Jay R Ginther Awd; KS ST Univ; Equine Vet.

GAGER, AMBER; Dodge City HS; Dodge City, KS; (2); Intnl Clb; Spanish Clb; SADD; Yrbk; Karate; Local Coll Night Cls; K-ST; Med.

GAGER, RACHAEL R; Eastern Heights Jr Sr HS; Kirwin, KS; (3); 2/11; Church Yth Grp; Drama Clb; 4-H; Math Tm; School Play; Trk; Vllybl; 4-H Awd; High Hon Roll; NHS; Colby Comm; Vet.

GAHAGAN, MERICA L; Goodland HS; Goodland, KS; (4); 14/78; Chorus; Yrbk; Chrldng; Mgr(s); Vllybl; High Hon Roll; NHS; Pres Acad Fit Awd; School Musical; School Play; Sherman Cty Jr Ms; KS House Of Rep Page; NW KS Tech Schl; Acctng.

GAINES, KEVIN M; Bern Schl; Sabetha, KS; (4); Letterman Clb; SADD; Teachers Aide; Band; Jazz Band; Mrchg Band; Pep Band; Var Capt Bsktbl; L Capt Ftbl; Var L Trk; Hmcmng King; Highland CC; Bus.

GAINES, RONALD JAMES RJ; El Dorado HS; Cassoday, KS; (3); 26/150; Am Leg Boys St; Church Yth Grp; NFL; SADD; Band; Mrchg Band; School Musical; Swing Chorus; Ofcr Stu Cncl; NHS; LIFE; KAY; Chmbr Of Cmrc Jr Ambsdr; KS ST U; Msc.

GALE, DEREK M; Blue Valley Northwest HS; Overland Park, KS; (2); Chess Clb; Cmnty Wkr; Temple Yth Grp; L Socr; Hon Roll; Span II Awd; Enrichmnt Prog.

GALLAGHER JR, LARRY D; Liberal HS; Liberal, KS; (4); 44/210; Church Yth Grp; Cmnty Wkr; French Clb; FTA; Key Clb; Office Aide; Teachers Aide; Church Choir; Tennis; Hon Roll; Seward County CC; Engrng.

GALLAGHER, VICTORIA; Gardner-Edgerton HS; Gardner, KS; (4); 47/114; French Clb; Hosp Aide; Library Aide; Pep Clb; SADD; Teachers Aide; Orch; Pittsburg ST Univ; Nrsng.

GALLARDO, ALEXIS; Deerfield HS; Deerfield, KS; (4); 1/22; HOBY; Quiz Bowl; VP Sr Cls; Pres Stu Cncl; Capt Var Bsktbl; Var Chrldng; Capt Var Vllybl; High Hon Roll; NHS; 1st Rnnr Up Miss Garden City; Benedictine Coll; Med.

GALLARDO, JUSTIN C; Wichita North HS; Wichita, KS; (2); Church Yth Grp; Teachers Aide; Var Crs Cntry; JV Golf; Hon Roll; Prfct Atten Awd.

GAMALO, SANTIPONG; Northeast Magnet HS; Wichita, KS; (2); Teachers Aide; Band; Ofcr Stu Cncl; JV Golf; Var Swmmng; JETS Awd; MIT; Nclr Physcs.

GAMBLE, KODY; Fairfield HS; Abbyville, KS; (2); #1 in class; 4-H; Quiz Bowl; Chorus; School Play; Yrbk; Rep Stu Cncl; Var Bsktbl; Var Vllybl; High Hon Roll; Pres Schlr; FAD; FTSA; Lawyer.

GAMBLE, LIZ; Meae HS; Meade, KS; (4); 10/25; Church Yth Grp; French Clb; Letterman Clb; Pep Clb; Band; Chorus; School Musical; Sec Jr Cls; Var Capt Chrldng; High Hon Roll; Emporia ST U; Educ.

GAMBLE, MARGI; Olathe North Sr HS; Olathe, KS; (3); Sec Bus Profs of Am; Church Yth Grp; Cmnty Wkr; French Clb; Pep Clb; Chorus; High Hon Roll; Hon Roll; Jr NHS; Pres Acad Fit Awd; U Of KS; Intnl Bus; Acctng.

GAMBLE, SEAN J; Blue Valley Northwest HS; Leawood, KS; (4); 25/340; VP Drama Clb; NFL; Service Clb; Thesps; Varsity Clb; School Musical; School Play; High Hon Roll; NHS; Creighton Univ; Med.

GAMBREL, MATT R; Oswego HS; Oswego, KS; (1); Band; Chorus; Mrchg Band; School Musical; JV Var Bsktbl; JV Var Ftbl; Intrml Wrstlng; Hon Roll; Law.

GAMIL, MARIA-THERESA; Junction City HS; Fort Riley, KS; (2); #1 in class; Church Yth Grp; Scholastic Bowl; Bsktbl; NHS; Duke Univ; Pediatrician.

GAMMILL, SANDRA F; Attica Public Schl; Attica, KS; (2); 1/25; Church Yth Grp; VP Sec 4-H; Quiz Bowl; Speech Tm; Chorus; JV Bsktbl; Var Trk; JV Vllybl; Hon Roll; Vet; Horse Trainer.

GANDHI, ANN; Washburn Rural HS; Topeka, KS; (2); Orch; Tennis.

GANN, MEGAN E; Bishop Ward HS; Kansas City, KS; (2); 25/99; Church Yth Grp; Drama Clb; Sec Pep Clb; SADD; School Musical; School Play; Stage Crew; Bsktbl; Powder Puff Ftbl; Score Keeper; Creight Univ; Pharm.

GANO, TRAVIS J; Hays HS; Hays, KS; (3); Church Yth Grp; Natl FFA Org; Pep Clb; SADD; JV Bsktbl; Var JV Ftbl; Var JV Trk; Wt Lftg; Hon Roll; Ft Hays ST Univ.

GANSKE, GRETA; Russell HS; Russell, KS; (3); 1/86; Dance Clb; HOBY; Math Tm; Model UN; Quiz Bowl; Sec Jr Cls; L Tennis; 4-H Awd; High Hon Roll; NHS; Danforth I Dare You Awd; NHS Stu Of Yr.

GANTZ, BRYAN L; Sterling HS; Sterling, KS; (3); Church Yth Grp; Debate Tm; FHA; Letterman Clb; Science Clb; Teachers Aide; Band; Mrchg Band; Pep Band; Variety Show; Honrbl Mntn All-League Bsktbl.

GAONA, JAIME J; Shawnee Mission N HS; Mission, KS; (2); Church Yth Grp; Pep Clb; School Play; Stage Crew; Rep Soph Cls; Ofcr Jr Cls; JV Var Ftbl; Score Keeper; Var Wt Lftg; KS ST; Contractor; Criminology.

GARACH, SHALLY; Shawnee Mission S Sr HS; Overland Park, KS; (4); Debate Tm; Ofcr Intnl Clb; JV Trk; High Hon Roll; NHS; Pres Schlr; St Schlr; Sci Knowledge Bowl 3rd 95/5th 96; Sci Olympiad; Women Of Conscience Pres Awareness Clb; U Of KS; Chem Engr/Pre Med.

GARARD, DANA; Erie HS; Erie, KS; (4); Am Leg Aux Girls St; Art Clb; Church Yth Grp; Debate Tm; Drama Clb; FCA; NFL; Drill Tm; Nwsp; Chrldng; Allen Cty CC.

GARBER, BENJAMIN M; Anderson Cty Jr Sr HS; Garnett, KS; (4); 24/75; Boy Scts; Church Yth Grp; Pep Clb; SADD; Band; Jazz Band; Mrchg Band; Pep Band; Yrbk; Hon Roll; Ozard Chrstn Col; Theology.

GARBER, KRISTI C; Labette Co HS; Coffeyville, KS; (2); Church Yth Grp; FCA; FBLA; Hosp Aide; Letterman Clb; VICA; Rep Stu Cncl; JV Var Bsktbl; Var L Sftbl; JV Vllybl; Summr Trvlng Sftbl Team; KS Exprss Sftb L Team; Eurpn Tour 96-Summr In Hollnd; Qulfyr Natl VICA Cont; MO Southern U; Med Field; Nrsng.

GARCIA, ADRIENNE; Northeast Magnet HS; Wichita, KS; (2); Cmnty Wkr; Drama Clb; Red Cross Aide; Chorus; Pres Soph Cls; Ofcr Stu Cncl; Hon Roll; NHS; Variety Show; KS Rgnts Hnrs Acad; Natl Engr Dsgn Chlng; Stdnt Ambsdr; KS Univ.

GARCIA, CARLA M; Yates Ctr HS; Yates Center, KS; (2); 1/60; Art Clb; FHA; Letterman Clb; NFL; Spanish Clb; SADD; Var L Bsktbl; Var L Sftbl; JV Vllybl; High Hon Roll.

GARCIA, CARLOS; Wyandotte HS; Kansas City, KS; (3); Intnl Clb; Ofcr Frsh Cls; Ofcr Soph Cls; High Hon Roll; Hon Roll; KS U; Med.

GARCIA, CHRISTINA M; Turner HS; Kansas City, KS; (2); Drama Clb; GAA; Girl Scts; Math Clb; Office Aide; Pep Clb; Quiz Bowl; Science Clb; SADD; Chorus; U Of KS; Lawyer.

GARCIA, JUAN; Trinity Catholic HS; Hutchinson, KS; (1); Math Tm; VP Frsh Cls; JV Ftbl; JV Trk; High Hon Roll.

GARCIA, LORELEI; Mc Louth Schl; Mc Louth, KS; (2); Church Yth Grp; Pep Clb; Spanish Clb; SADD; School Play; Sec Soph Cls; Var Var Chrldng; JV Vllybl; High Hon Roll; Hon Roll; Bsktbl; KU; Chrprctc.

GARCIA, OSCAR A; Wichita North HS; Wichita, KS; (1); 1/449; Church Yth Grp; Church Choir; JV Socr; High Hon Roll.

GARCIA, YOLANDA; Wabaunsee HS; Paxico, KS; (3); FBLA; FHA; Letterman Clb; Band; Pres Soph Cls; Var L Bsktbl; Var L Trk; Var L Vllybl; High Hon Roll; NHS; U Of KS; Psych.

GARDNER, CHRISTINE A; Bishop Ward HS; Kansas City, KS; (2); 22/93; Pep Clb; SADD; Pres Frsh Cls; Var Bsktbl; Powder Puff Ftbl; JV Vllybl; Hon Roll; NHS; KS ST U; Vet Med.

GARDNER, DANA M; Hartford HS; Hartford, KS; (2); Church Yth Grp; Drama Clb; Letterman Clb; School Play; Var L Chrldng; Var L Trk; Var L Vllybl; High Hon Roll; FBLA; FHA; Acad Awd; Fort Hays ST Univ; PT.

GARDNER, JAMES L; Topeka HS; Topeka, KS; (4); 15/344; Church Yth Grp; Acpl Chr; Chorus; Church Choir; School Musical; Variety Show; Hon Roll; NHS; Bible Study Clb Ldr; KSHSAA Numerous I Rtngs Piiano, Vocal & Instrumntl Perfs; Martial Arts Clb VP; Piano Perf.

GARDNER, LUCAS; Shawnee Mission E HS; Shawnee Mission, KS; (2); 120/485; Boy Scts; Cmnty Wkr; Intrml Bsbl; Intrml Socr; High Hon Roll; Hon Roll; SM East Drftng Prgm; Arch/Engr.

GARDNER, NATHAN; Mc Louth Schl; Mc Louth, KS; (4); 8/37; Letterman Clb; Pep Clb; Teachers Aide; Var Bsktbl; Var Ftbl; Var Trk; Wt Lftg; Cit Awd; High Hon Roll; NHS; Coffeyville CC.

GARDNER, RYAN A; Bishop Ward HS; Kansas City, KS; (3); Am Leg Boys St; Drama Clb; SADD; Rptr Nwsp; Pres Frsh Cls; Intrml Bsktbl; Var Ftbl; JV Trk; Hon Roll; NHS; KS St Univ; Med.

GARDOS, MARY E; Sumner Acad Of Arts & Science; Kansas City, KS; (4); Art Clb; Key Clb; Pep Clb; SADD; Band; Orch; JCL; Latin Clb; Spanish Clb; Mrchg Band; Visual Arts.

GARMAN, GAVIN K; White Rock HS; Burr Oak, KS; (2); 3/15; Letterman Clb; Math Tm; Natl FFA Org; Pep Clb; Quiz Bowl; SADD; Chorus; Pres Frsh Cls; Pres Soph Cls; Var Bsktbl.

GARMAN, GERIT; White Rock HS; Burr Oak, KS; (4); 1/17; Capt Quiz Bowl; Rep Frsh Cls; Sec Soph Cls; Sec Jr Cls; VP Sr Cls; Pres Stu Cncl; Var Capt Bsktbl; Var Capt Ftbl; High Hon Roll; NHS; Jr Lgn Bsbl; KS St U; Engrng.

GARNER, AMANDA M; Wichita West HS; Wichita, KS; (3); Drama Clb; Nwsp; Lit Mag; Crtv Wrtng; Hnr Roll; Butler CC; Jrnlsm Tchr.

GARNER, CHRISTOPHER M; Dodge City HS; Victoria, VA; (2); Art Clb; German Clb; Math Clb; Office Aide; Quiz Bowl; Capt JV Bsktbl; Hon Roll; Jr NHS; OK Univ; Dr.

GARNER, ERIN K; Caney Valley Jr Sr HS; Caney, KS; (1); Drama Clb; School Play; Hon Roll; Pittsburgh St Univ; Nrse.

GARNER, JENNIFER; Turner HS; Kansas City, KS; (3); 3/270; Band; Drill Tm; Rep Jr Cls; Var Trk; High Hon Roll; Hon Roll; Jr NHS; NHS; Pres Acad Fit Awd; UDA Dance Star 93-94.

GARNER, SABRINA; Lansing High Schl Gardner; Lansing, KS; (4); French Clb; Teachers Aide; Acpl Chr; Chorus; JV Capt Chrldng; Mgr Socr; Hon Roll; Highland CC; Sml Bus Mgmt.

GARNICA, CHRIS; Wichita Heights HS; Wichita, KS; (3); 52/250; Am Leg Boys St; Debate Tm; NFL; Spanish Clb; Rep Stu Cncl; Var Ftbl; Var Trk; Var Wrstlng; Hon Roll; NHS; U KS; Psych.

GARRELS, BRIAN A; Maize HS; Wichita, KS; (3); Science Clb; Spanish Clb; Ftbl; High Hon Roll; Hon Roll; Plcemn/Frefghtr.

GARRETT, BRANDON M; Great Bend Sr HS; Great Bend, KS; (2); 29/263; VP German Clb; Hosp Aide; JV Bsktbl; JV Ftbl; Intrml Socr; Var Trk; Intrml Wt Lftg; High Hon Roll; Hon Roll; Prfct Atten Awd; Natl Hnr Soc Jr Yr; 4th At ST Level Ger Contest; Schulerkongrep/History/Geog; Urban Dev/PT.

GARRETT, JENNIFER; Junction City HS; Fort Riley, KS; (1); Band; Mrchg Band; Sftbl; High Hon Roll.

GARRETT, MICHAEL; Olathe East Sr HS; Olathe, KS; (3); Computer Clb; French Clb; Teachers Aide; Lbrn Band; Jazz Band; Mrchg Band; Pep Band; School Musical; Hon Roll; Cmptr Intern Word Tech; KS U; Cmptr Sci.

GARRETT, TERRY M; Prairie View Jr Sr HS; La Cygne, KS; (2); 26/88; 4-H; Math Clb; Math Tm; Quiz Bowl; Scholastic Bowl; Spanish Clb; Thesps; VP Jr Cls; JV Bsktbl; Hon Roll; Eng Awd; U Of KS; Cvl Engrng.

GARRIOTT, JEFFREY A; Wichita Southeast HS; Wichita, KS; (2); 1/436; Church Yth Grp; Cmnty Wkr; Math Tm; Scholastic Bowl; Church Choir; Mrchg Band; Pep Band; High Hon Roll; Prfct Atten Awd; French Clb; I Rating At St Piano Festival Frosh & Soph Yr.

GARRISON, ELVIS; Wyandotte HS; Kansas City, KS; (4); 22/180; Computer Clb; Hon Roll; KCK CC.

GARRISON, HEATHER L; Derby HS; Derby, KS; (4); 30/315; Cmnty Wkr; Thesps; Chorus; School Musical; Rep Jr Cls; Rep Sr Cls; Hon Roll; NHS; Pres Schlr; St Schlr; KS ST Univ; Music Ed.

GARRISON, JARED D; Wichita South HS; Wichita, KS; (4); 25/300; Church Yth Grp; Debate Tm; NFL; Teachers Aide; Ofcr Stu Cncl; JV Bsktbl; Var Socr; JV Wrstlng; High Hon Roll; Homcmng King; South High Studs Mem; Acad & Sports Ltrs; Wichita ST U; Pol Sci; Law.

GARRISON, KATHY A; Kingman HS; Kingman, KS; (3); Church Yth Grp; FCA; FBLA; Jazz Band; Mrchg Band; Orch; School Play; NHS; Pres Acad Fit Awd; Quiz Bowl; Awded Trip To Washington DC By KS Rural Electric Corp; U Of KS; Psych; Theater.

GARST, JULIE; Glasco HS; Glasco, KS; (2); Church Yth Grp; HOBY; Letterman Clb; Pep Clb; Quiz Bowl; Varsity Clb; Chorus; JV Bsktbl; Var Capt Chrldng; Var L Golf; VFW Voice Of Democracy; Learn & Serve Vol; KS ST; Medicine.

GARTEN, CODY W; Cunningham HS; Spivey, KS; (3); 5/30; Letterman Clb; Pep Clb; Quiz Bowl; Science Clb; SADD; Varsity Clb; Bsktbl; Ftbl; Trk; Prfct Atten Awd; Colby Univ; Vet.

GARTEN, CORY; Cunningham HS; Spivey, KS; (3); 2/27; Letterman Clb; Quiz Bowl; Pres Jr Cls; Var Bsktbl; Var Tennis; High Hon Roll; Hon Roll; Hugh Obrian Yth Ldrshp Ambsdr; Pre-Med.

GARTNER, CODY; Seaman Sr HS; Topeka, KS; (3); SADD; Crs Cntry; Ftbl; Trk; High Hon Roll; NHS; Prfct Atten Awd; Yth Actn Coaltn; Bddy Sys; Vet Med.

GARTRELL, NICOLE L; Stockton HS; Stockton, KS; (2); 4-H; Math Tm; Pep Clb; Band; Chorus; Jazz Band; Mrchg Band; Pep Band; Var L Trk; 4-H Awd; Stdnt Mo Awd; Frnscs.

GARWICK, ELISABETH M; Manhattan HS; Manhattan, KS; (4); 44/350; Cmnty Wkr; Hosp Aide; Library Aide; Bsktbl; Golf; Mgr(s); Mgr Stat Swmmng; Mgr Stat Vllybl; Kiwanis Awd; NHS; La Sertoma Svc Awd; Natl Yth Ldrshp Forum On Medicine; U Of KS; Bio; Genetics.

GARY, JOHN D; Junction City HS; Junction City, KS; (3); Church Yth Grp; Natl FFA Org; Band; Chorus; JV Var Socr; Wrstlng; Duke; Doctor.

GASCHLER, CARRI; Wichita South HS; Wichita, KS; (1); Church Yth Grp; Cmnty Wkr; Hosp Aide; Pep Clb; Chrldng; High Hon Roll; Hon Roll; NHS; Pres Acad Fit Awd; Indoor Soccer; Psycht.

GASKELL, KAREN L; Horton HS; Horton, KS; (2); 26/80; Church Yth Grp; Drama Clb; Pep Clb; Band; Chorus; Church Choir; Jazz Band; Mrchg Band; Pep Band; School Musical; Poem Publshd HS Writter; Spcl Ed Vlntr; Emporia; Spcl Ed.

GASKILL, TREVOR R; Wichita Heights HS; Wichita, KS; (3); Varsity Clb; JV Bsbl; JV Ftbl; Var L Swmmng; Hon Roll; NHS; Eagle Scout; Ordr Of Arrw; Chrch Aclyt; St Swim Mt Qulfr; KS ST.

GASPER, JULIE; Lawrence HS; Lawrence, KS; (2); 19/681; Band; Chorus; Bsktbl; Var L Sftbl; JV Var Vllybl; Cit Awd; High Hon Roll; Prfct Atten Awd; Pres Acad Fit Awd.

GASPER, LAURA A; Stockton HS; Stockton, KS; (2); FHA; Natl FFA Org; Pep Clb; Drill Tm; Co-Ed Nwsp; Rep Frsh Cls; Sec VP Stu Cncl; Bsktbl; Pom Pon; Hon Roll; CYO Treas; KS ST; Jrnlsm; Photo.

GASSEN, MATTHEW W; Washburn Rural HS; Topeka, KS; (2); Cmnty Wkr; FBLA; SADD; Phtg Nwsp; Phtg Yrbk; Soph Rep To Schl SITE Cncl; Mem Of Alternative Ed Drafting & Dev Bd For Schl Dist; Oncologist.

GASSMAN, TARA R; Jennings Schl; Dresden, KS; (1); FHA; Pep Clb; Band; Pep Band; Pres Frsh Cls; Var L Bsktbl; Var L Vllybl; Hon Roll; KU; Phy Thrpst.

GASSMANN, BRENDA; Jennings Schl; Dresden, KS; (2); Church Grp; VP FHA; Quiz Bowl; Band; Sec Treas Frsh Cls; Sec Soph Cls; V Bsktbl; L Trk; JV Var Vllybl; Hon Roll.

GAST, AMELIA L; Leavenworth HS; Leavenworth, KS; (1); Church Y Grp; Cmnty Wkr; ROTC; Color Guard; Drill Tm; Var Mgr(s); Var Socr; C Awd; High Hon Roll; ROTC Hrn Guard Without Weapons; KS ST; AF Aca

GAST, BRYAN FRANCIS; Louisburg HS; Bucyrus, KS; (2); Natl FFA Org High Hon Roll; Prfct Atten Awd; Math Awd 94-95; Soc Sci Awd 94-95; Lang Arts Awd 95-96; Sci Awd 95-96; Ag Proficiency Awd 96; Johnson Cty CC; Bus.

GAST, KAREN; Jefferson Co North HS; Valley Falls, KS; (4); #8 in class; FBLA; SADD; Var Chrldng; Vllybl; High Hon Roll; Hon Roll; NHS; Emporia ST U; Elem Ed.

GASTION, REYNA; West HS; Wichita, KS; (2); Church Yth Grp; HOBY; Teachers Aide; Chorus; Church Choir; Drill Tm; School Musical; Variety Show; Bsktbl; Chrldng; All-Amer Chrldng Team; Hoop It Up; KS U; Medcl Tech.

GASTON, AMANDA L; Baxter Springs HS; Baxter Springs, KS; (3); Church Yth Grp; Cmnty Wkr; Pep Clb; Band; Church Choir; Jazz Band; Mrchg Band; Orch; Pep Band; School Musical; MO Southern ST Coll.

GASTON, RENAE; Columbus HS; Pittsburg, KS; (4); 4/91; Bus Profs of Am; VP FCA; Math Tm; Treas Jr Cls; Treas Sr Cls; Treas Stu Cncl; Var L Bsktbl; Var L Sftbl; High Hon Roll; NHS; Pittsburg ST U; Bus Admin.

GATES, AMBER N; Wichita Heights HS; Wichita, KS; (2); 12/336; Orch; Hon Roll; Dist, St Orchstrs; Prncpl Chr Wichita Yth Symphny; KS U.

GATES, CARA M; Chanute Sr HS; Chanute, KS; (3); Church Yth Grp; Cmnty Wkr; Treas FCA; French Clb; FBLA; Pres FTA; GAA; Sec Frsh Cls; Ofcr Stu Cncl; Bsktbl; Prins Ldrshp Team VP; DARE Vol; KS Univ; Law.

GATES, SUSAN J; Leavenworth HS; Easton, KS; (3); 4-H; FBLA; Letterman Clb; SADD; Acpl Chr; Church Choir; Var L Bsktbl; Var L Sftbl; Var L Trk; Var L Vllybl; Def Plr, Off Plr, Bttng Champ Sftbll.

GATEWOOD, AMBER D; Columbus HS; Columbus, KS; (3); 13/95; Am Leg Aux Girls St; Church Yth Grp; Dance Clb; 4-H; Key Clb; Letterman Clb; Math Tm; Varsity Clb; Drill Tm; Rptr Nwsp; Drftng Clb; KS ST Univ; Arch/Arch Engrng.

GATEWOOD, CHARLIE L; Council Grove HS; Council Grove, KS; (4); Band; Mrchg Band; Pep Band; JV Bsktbl; Var Ftbl; JV Wt Lftg.

GATEWOOD, JORDAN T; Shawnee Mission S Sr HS; Overland Park, KS; (2); 66/463; Pep Clb; Socr; Hon Roll; KS Univ.

GATTIS, JOSHUA M; Colby Sr HS; Colby, KS; (2); Church Yth Grp; JV Ftbl; JV Trk; Hon Roll; Algebra I Awd; Span II Awd; TX Tech Univ; Arch.

GATTSHALL, TRAVIS; Goodland HS; Goodland, KS; (2); 8/87; Church Yth Grp; 4-H; Math Tm; Bsktbl; 4-H Awd; Hon Roll; KS St Fair Livestock Judging Team.

GATZ, MICAH D; Baldwin HS; Baldwin City, KS; (2); 9/115; Boy Scts; Church Yth Grp; Letterman Clb; Ftbl; JV Golf; Tennis; High Hon Roll; NHS; Local Soccer Team; His; Prof.

GAUGHAN, AMY; Spring Hill HS; Spring Hill, KS; (2); 13/97; Debate Tm; Girl Scts; NFL; Pep Clb; Band; Mrchg Band; Pep Band; Var Chrldng; High Hon Roll; Hon Roll; Natural Helpers; Schl Bsktbl Trnmt Hostess; Psych.

GAUGHAN, CHRISTOPHER M; St Thomas Aquinas HS; Kansas City, MO; (2); Math Tm; Spanish Clb; Var Swmmng; Hon Roll; Law.

GAUL, CHRISTOPHER; Atchison Sr HS; Atchison, KS; (3); Church Yth Grp; Band; Church Choir; Jazz Band; Mrchg Band; Pep Band; JV Bsbl; JV Bsktbl; Var Socr; High Hon Roll.

GAUL, MIKE; Atchison Sr HS; Atchison, KS; (4); 3/125; Am Leg Boys St; Church Yth Grp; Band; Church Choir; Jazz Band; Var Golf; Var Socr; High Hon Roll; NHS; Pep Band; Natl Yng Ldrs Conf.

GAUNT, MARTHA E; Wichita East HS; Wichita, KS; (2); Church Yth Grp; Drama Clb; French Clb; German Clb; Stage Crew; Socr; Tennis; High Hon Roll; Wichita ST Univ.

GAUNT, STACI L; Great Bend Sr HS; Great Bend, KS; (3); Boy Scts; Church Yth Grp; Pep Clb; Spanish Clb; Vllybl; Hon Roll; KS ST Univ; Bus.

GAUS, SHARON J; Campus HS; Haysville, KS; (2); Church Yth Grp; Intnl Clb; Science Clb; High Hon Roll; Hon Roll; OK ST U; Law.

GAVIN, SEAN M; Leavenworth HS; Leavenworth, KS; (1); Cmnty Wkr; JA; ROTC; Var Trk; High Hon Roll; Cadet Of Month/Hnr Co/Commendation Cert JROTC; Amer Cancer Soc Relay For Life Vol; ST Senate Page.

GAVIN, STEPHANIE R; Wichita Heights HS; Wichita, KS; (3); 33/250; Church Yth Grp; Cmnty Wkr; Hosp Aide; Band; Church Choir; Mrchg Band; Pep Band; High Hon Roll; Hon Roll; NHS; PT.

GAYLEY, SCOTT A; Bishop Miege HS; Prairie Village, KS; (4); 12/168; Am Leg Boys St; Boy Scts; Treas VP Debate Tm; Hosp Aide; NFL; Capt Quiz Bowl; Pres Science Clb; Treas Speech Tm; School Play; High Hon Roll; Aquinas Fnlst; Emp Explr Post Capt; Aviation Explr Post; KU; Med.

GEAN, ERICA J; Protection Schl; Coldwater, KS; (3); Speech Tm; Band; Chorus; School Musical; School Play; Yrbk; Pres Sr Cls; Ofcr Stu Cncl; High Hon Roll; Hon Roll; KAYS VP; Rep KS With KS Ambassdrs Of Music To Europe 95; 3rd In Prose At ST Speech Cont 95-96; KS Univ; Pol Sci; Comm Studs.

GEANES, MICHAEL T; Blue Valley HS; Olathe, KS; (4); 47/230; Boy Scts; Debate Tm; FHA; NFL; Hon Roll; NHS; Ntl Merit Ltr; Pres Schlr; U Of KS.

GEAR, MATTHEW D; Bishop Carroll Catholic HS; Wichita, KS; (2); French Clb; Spanish Clb; JV Var Ftbl; Var L Wrstlng.

GEBHARD, MARVIN J; Northern Valley HS; Long Island, KS; (2); Natl FFA Org; Band; Jazz Band; Pep Band; Sec Soph Cls; Var Bsktbl; Var Ftbl; Var Trk; Var Wt Lftg; Hon Roll; KS Univ; Sports Medicine.

GEBHART, WHITNEY E; Salina HS Central; Salina, KS; (2); 32/278; Cmnty Wkr; Rep Soph Cls; JV Bsktbl; JV Vllybl; Hon Roll; Pres Acad Fit Awd; Brkfst Bddy Undrprvlgd Chldrn.

GEE, JODI; Ulysses HS; Ulysses, KS; (4); 1/93; Am Leg Aux Girls St; FBLA; SADD; Varsity Clb; Tennis; High Hon Roll; NHS; Frgn Lang Clb; Outstndng Math & Sci Stu.

GEESLING, ALAN; Fairfield HS; Turon, KS; (2); 4-H; SADD; Acpl Chr; Chorus; School Play; Stage Crew; VP Soph Cls; VP Jr Cls; Var Ftbl; Var Trk; Fairfield Tech Club; Pratt CC; Ag.

GEFFERT, KERI A; Haven HS; Haven, KS; (2); Treas Church Yth Grp; Pres 4-H; Natl FFA Org; Chorus; Church Choir; Variety Show; Sec Frsh Cls; Treas Soph Cls; JV Sftbl; JV Vllybl; KS Hereford Assn Qn; KS Jr Hereford Assn Rptr; KS ST Univ; Ag.

GEGEN, SARAH; Andale HS; Colwich, KS; (2); Art Clb; Spanish Clb; SADD; Bsktbl; Chrldng; Vllybl; Hon Roll.

GEHRT, JESSE; Wabaunsee HS; Alma, KS; (1); Church Yth Grp; Treas 4-H; Natl FFA Org; JV Bsbl; Score Keeper; High Hon Roll; KS ST Univ.

GEIER, AMANDA; Garden City Sr HS; Garden City, KS; (3); Church Yth Grp; Teachers Aide; Ed Nwsp; JV Var Vllybl; High Hon Roll; Hon Roll;

[illegible]R, ELIJAH; Royal Valley HS; Hoyt, KS; (4); Letterman Clb; Band; [illegible]and; School Musical; Pres Jr Cls; VP Stu Cncl; L Ftbl; L Wrstlng; [illegible]Hon Roll; NHS; K ST; Mech Engr.

[illegible]ER, JULIE; Leavenworth HS; Leavenworth, KS; (3); Var Bsktbl; [illegible]ennis; Var Trk; Var Vllybl; Hon Roll; NHS; Ntl Merit Ltr; Phys Thpy.

[illegible], SARAH G; Troy HS; Troy, KS; (2); VP 4-H; HOBY; Treas [illegible]n Clb; Sec Natl FFA Org; Pep Clb; Ofcr Stu Cncl; Bsktbl; Vllybl; [illegible]on Roll; NHS; Frst FFA NE Dist Pub Spkng Cont 2 Yrs; [illegible]r/Supts 4h Projs; Cont Cncl Rep; Own/Raise Livestck; KS ST Univ;

[illegible], JENNIFER; Mc Pherson HS; Mc Pherson, KS; (4); Church Yth Grp; [illegible]an Clb; Letterman Clb; Red Cross Aide; SADD; Ofcr Stu Cncl; Bsktbl; [illegible]ntry; Swmmng; High Hon Roll; Care Prvdr/Disbld Chldrn; Church Yth Treas; Amer Pres Ed Awd; KS ST Univ; Nrsg.

[illegible]IS, METTA A; Dodge City HS; Dodge City, KS; (3); Am Leg Aux Girls [illegible], Church Yth Grp; Cmnty Wkr; French Clb; Intnl Clb; Office Aide; SADD; [illegible]on Roll; NHS; KSDS; Outward Bnd Class Exprnc; Sr Ldrshp Dodge; Frnsc [illegible]thlgst.

GEISENDORF, GINA S; Atchison Sr HS; Atchison, KS; (1); Church Yth Grp; Cmnty Wkr; French Clb; Hosp Aide; JV Chrldng; JV Trk; Prfct Atten Awd; Dance Club.

GEISENDORF, WILLIAM; Atchison Sr HS; Atchison, KS; (4); Am Leg Boys St; Church Yth Grp; Teachers Aide; Ftbl; Trk; Wt Lftg; High Hon Roll; Natl Yth Ldrshp Conf Wshngtn DC; Ldrshp Conf; Sci Olympd.

GEISER, JEREMY; Garden City Sr HS; Garden City, KS; (3); Boy Scts; Church Yth Grp; Cmnty Wkr; Debate Tm; French Clb; Math Tm; Natl FFA Org; Ofcr Bsbl; Bsktbl; Ftbl.

GEISER, RYAN R; Garden City Sr HS; Garden City, KS; (2); Church Yth Grp; German Clb; Math Tm; Science Clb; Ofcr Bsbl; VICA.

GEISLER, LINDSEY R; Washburn Rural HS; Topeka, KS; (2); 16/380; Girl Scts; Band; Mrchg Band; L Pep Band; High Hon Roll; Dist Wide Newsletter; Acad Lttr; Bnd Lttr; Hon Engl And Math Prog; Eng.

GEITZ, JEFF M; Emporia HS; Emporia, KS; (2); Cmnty Wkr; Debate Tm; FCA; Pep Clb; Teachers Aide; Rep Frsh Cls; Rep Jr Cls; Pre-Med.

GEMBALA, JESSICA K; Concordia Jr Sr HS; Concordia, KS; (3); Church Yth Grp; Cmnty Wkr; Drama Clb; Science Clb; Spanish Clb; Band; Mrchg Band; Pep Band; School Musical; High Hon Roll; Washburn; Phy Thrpst; Psych.

GENCUR, KIMBERLY; Shawnee Mission Nw Sr HS; Shawnee Mission, KS; (4); 72/403; Church Yth Grp; Dance Clb; HOBY; Pep Clb; SADD; Teachers Aide; Varsity Clb; Drill Tm; Flag Corp; Ed Nwsp; Yng Lif; Pres Prom Cmmtte; Stu Response Tm; Sci Proj; Lg Regnl Tennis; William Jewell Coll; Intl Bus.

GENEREUX, AARON; Hillcrest Schl; Cuba, KS; (4); 1/16; Church Yth Grp; Letterman Clb; Quiz Bowl; Ed Yrbk; Pres Stu Cncl; Var L Bsktbl; Var L Ftbl; Var L Trk; High Hon Roll; NHS; Scndry Ed.

GENEREUX, SARA; Hillcrest Schl; Cuba, KS; (3); 1/13; VP FHA; Quiz Bowl; Band; Ed Yrbk; Treas Jr Cls; Sec Stu Cncl; Var Bsktbl; Var Chrldng; Var Vllybl; NHS.

GENTRY, ALLISON J; Wichita Heights HS; Wichita, KS; (2); 1/400; Church Yth Grp; Drama Clb; Thesps; Chorus; Church Choir; School Play; Stage Crew; Variety Show; Hon Roll; KS Math Assessment; Abilene Chrstn Univ.

GENTRY, SHANA; Rossville HS; Rossville, KS; (1); 7/45; Church Yth Grp; Cmnty Wkr; Debate Tm; Drama Clb; FBLA; GAA; Letterman Clb; NFL; Pep Clb; SADD; Pt.

GEORG, AMBER L; Lacrosse HS; Rush Center, KS; (3); 1/29; 4-H; Speech Tm; Band; Sec Jr Cls; VP Stu Cncl; L Bsktbl; L Golf; L Vllybl; High Hon Roll; NHS; KS; Psych.

GEORGE, BRUCE E; Great Bend Sr HS; Great Bend, KS; (4); Office Aide; Pep Clb; Spanish Clb; Band; Mrchg Band; JV Bsbl; JV Intrml Bsktbl; Intrml Socr; Hon Roll; Barton Cty CC; Engrng.

GEORGE, DENISE K; Uniontown HS; Uniontown, KS; (1); FCA; 4-H; FHA; Math Clb; Math Tm; Natl FFA Org; JV Bsktbl; JV Vllybl; 4-H Awd; Hon Roll.

GEORGE, GINA L; Oswego HS; Oswego, KS; (3); Ofcr FHA; Speech Tm; Thesps; Rep Stu Cncl; JV Var Bsktbl; Var Sftbl; JV Var Vllybl; Var Wt Lftg; Hon Roll; NHS; WA Univ; Bio/Phtgrphy.

GEORGE, JAMIE D; Wichita East HS; Wichita, KS; (2); 23/339; JA; Var L Sftbl; JV Vllybl; High Hon Roll.

GEORGE, LES; Berean Acad; Wichita, KS; (3); Church Yth Grp; Teachers Aide; High Hon Roll; Hon Roll; Knife/Swrdsmth.

GEORGE, LYNDSAY N; Goodland HS; Goodland, KS; (3); FHA; GAA; JV Bsktbl; Var Crs Cntry; Var Sftbl; Var Trk; Cit Awd; Hon Roll.

GEORGE, MELISSA; ACC HS; Nortonville, KS; (2); Art Clb; 4-H; Quiz Bowl; Band; JV Var Chrldng; Trk; Vllybl; High Hon Roll; Kiwanis Awd; NHS.

GEORGE, NATHAN; Seaman Sr HS; Topeka, KS; (3); Boy Scts; Church Yth Grp; FBLA; Math Clb; Math Tm; Mu Alpha Theta; Ski Clb; Bsktbl; Golf; Swmmng; KSU; Engrng.

GEORGE, STACEY; Gardner-Edgerton HS; Gardner, KS; (4); 8/110; Am Leg Aux Girls St; Thesps; Drill Tm; Mrchg Band; Treas Frsh Cls; Treas Soph Cls; Tennis; NHS; Drama Clb; French Clb; Roles Of Annie & Adelaide Schl Plays; KU Hnr Schlr.

GEPNER, JOSEPH E; Tonganoxie Schl; Leavenworth, KS; (2); Debate Tm; JV Bsktbl; Var Crs Cntry; Var Socr; Var Trk; Hon Roll; Scuba Diving.

GERALD, ASHLEY; Shawnee Mission N HS; Shawnee Mission, KS; (3); 120/430; Church Yth Grp; Cmnty Wkr; GAA; Letterman Clb; Pep Clb; Acpl Chr; Pres Chorus; Church Choir; Mgr(s); Vllybl; US Vlyblb Assn 3 Yrs; Vol Mission 4 Yrs; Vac Bible Schl 4 Yrs; U Of KS; Peds.

GERANT, KIMBERLY Z; Ft Scott HS; Fort Scott, KS; (3); 1/110; 4-H; VP FHA; VP Pres Natl FFA Org; Teachers Aide; Orch; Trk; 4-H Awd; Hon Roll; NHS; Ft Scott CC; Agronomy.

GERARD, AARON L; Stanton Co HS; Ulysses, KS; (1); Quiz Bowl; VP Frsh Cls; JV Bsktbl; JV Var Ftbl; Trk; Hon Roll; KU; Engrng.

GERBER, MINDY L; Garden City Sr HS; Garden City, KS; (2); Church Yth Grp; Cmnty Wkr; FHA; Letterman Clb; Varsity Clb; Chorus; Church Choir; Rptr Yrbk; Var Chrldng; Hon Roll; K ST; Optmtry.

GERBER, TIFANNE L; Stanton Co HS; Manter, KS; (3); Church Yth Grp; FBLA; Band; Chorus; School Play; Variety Show; Hon Roll; KAYS Bd Mem-Schl Svc; Pre-Med.

GERBERDING, MICHELLE D; Wellington Sr HS; Mayfield, KS; (4); Church Yth Grp; French Clb; Math Tm; Band; Church Choir; Bsktbl; Mgr(s); Score Keeper; Trk; High Hon Roll; Yth Rep; Rainbow Girls; Church Camp Cnslr; K-ST; Vet Med.

GERDES, CRAIG A; Wichita South HS; Wichita, KS; (1); Boy Scts; ROTC; Band; Color Guard; Drill Tm; Mrchg Band; Pep Band; School Musical; Var Crs Cntry; Var Trk.

GERDES, SARA; South HS; Salina, KS; (2); Art Clb; Church Yth Grp; Dance Clb; Chrldng; Gym; Hon Roll; Cnlsng.

GERETY, KAREN; Lansing HS; Lansing, KS; (2); Art Clb; French Clb; JV Sftbl; French Hon Soc; High Hon Roll; Art Hnr Scty.

GERETY, KELLY; Lansing HS; Lansing, KS; (4); JV Var Bsbl; JV Var Ftbl; JV Trk; JV Var Wrstlng; Hon Roll; KS City CC.

GERFEN, KEITH M; St Thomas Aquinas HS; Shawnee, KS; (4); 90/231; Treas 4-H; Band; Pep Band; School Musical; School Play; Stage Crew; 4-H Awd; Hon Roll; MS150 3 Yrs; Johnson Cty CC; Engrng.

GERHARDT, REBECCA L; Holton HS; Holton, KS; (2); Pres Church Yth Grp; NFL; Q&S; Quiz Bowl; Speech Tm; Stage Crew; Ed Nwsp; Yrbk; Hon Roll; NHS.

GERHART, KELLY; Blue Valley Northwest HS; Overland Park, KS; (2); 1/325; Church Yth Grp; FCA; Yrbk; Ofcr Frsh Cls; Ofcr Soph Cls; Vllybl; High Hon Roll.

GERING, SHANNON; Hesston HS; Hesston, KS; (2); Church Yth Grp; 4-H; FBLA; JV Tennis; Hon Roll.

GERKEN, SCOTT; Paola HS; Paola, KS; (4); 26/94; Am Leg Boys St; Church Yth Grp; Natl FFA Org; Teachers Aide; Ftbl; Welding Clb Ofcr; North Cntrl KS Area Vo-Tech.

GERMAN, SARA D; Yates Ctr HS; Neosho Falls, KS; (3); FHA; Scholastic Bowl; Yrbk; High Hon Roll; KAYS World Sci Ofcr 2 Yrs; Pittsburg ST Univ; Bio.

GERRITZ, GAYLE; Shawnee Mission E HS; Shawnee Mission, KS; (4); 24/373; Stage Crew; Nwsp; Pep Clb; Rep Soph Cls; Ofcr Stu Cncl; Var Chrldng; Capt Socr; L Tennis; High Hon Roll; Hon Roll; SHARE Big Bro/Big Sis Chm; AFS Hst Sblng; Prin Ldrshp Awd; U Of KS; Bus.

GERROND, AUBREY; Hugoton HS; Hugoton, KS; (3); 10/70; Letterman Clb; Quiz Bowl; Teachers Aide; Varsity Clb; Acpl Chr; Band; Chorus; Drm Mjr(t); Mrchg Band; Pep Band; Med Field.

GERSON, STACY L; Blue Valley Northwest HS; Overland Park, KS; (2); Spanish Clb; Temple Yth Grp; High Hon Roll; Hon Roll; Camp Cnslr Camp Rainbow; VP Prgm Temple Yth; Sec Temple Yth.

GERSTENKORN, CHRIS B; Great Bend Sr HS; Great Bend, KS; (3); Spanish Clb; JV Crs Cntry; Hon Roll; Barton County CC.

GERSTENKORN, LESLIE J; Shawnee Heights HS; Topeka, KS; (1); Church Yth Grp; Intnl Clb; Pep Clb; Chorus; Bsktbl; Sftbl; Wt Lftg; High Hon Roll.

GERSTNER, EMILY S; Great Bend Sr HS; Great Bend, KS; (3); Pep Clb; Teachers Aide; Band; Color Guard; Mrchg Band; Swmmng; Vllybl; Hon Roll; Prfct Atten Awd; Kayettes; Wichita ST Univ; Bus Mgmt; Mktg.

GERSTNER, NICOLE L; Trego Comm HS; Collyer, KS; (2); 1/49; Letterman Clb; Math Tm; SADD; School Musical; Rep Frsh Cls; Rep Stu Cncl; JV Var Bsktbl; Var L Trk; Var L Vllybl; High Hon Roll; Kays/Kayettes Clb VP; ST Qlfr Trck 200m Dash; KS Univ; Sprts Medcn.

GERSTNER, RYAN; Frankft HS; Vermillion, KS; (3); 1/35; Letterman Clb; Quiz Bowl; Sec Treas Soph Cls; Pres Jr Cls; Var L Bsktbl; Var L Ftbl; High Hon Roll; NHS; Prfct Atten Awd; U Of KS Lawrence; Accntng.

GETCHELL, SARA E; Buhler HS; Hutchinson, KS; (2); Church Yth Grp; Computer Clb; Debate Tm; German Clb; NFL; Science Clb; Spanish Clb; Speech Tm; Hon Roll; 4th St Debate; Lawyer; Debate Tchr.

GETTLER, TOBY; Independence HS; Independence, KS; (4); Am Leg Boys St; Cmnty Wkr; JA; Spanish Clb; SADD; Mgr Bsktbl; Trk; Hon Roll; Church Yth Grp; Teachers Aide; PUPPS 2 Yrs; Chrch Deacon; Boys St Delegate; Independence CC; Bus Mgmt.

GEURIAN, BRIENNA B; Hutchinson HS; Hutchinson, KS; (3); Bus Profs of Am; French Clb; Office Aide; Swmmng; Hon Roll; Prfct Atten Awd; KS ST U; Bus Admin.

GEYER, DEBBIE; Olathe South Sr HS; Olathe, KS; (3); Dance Clb; Pep Clb; Teachers Aide; Drill Tm; Bsktbl; Trk; High Hon Roll; Hon Roll; Track Most Valuable Plyr Awd; Phys Therapist.

GEYER, STACY L; Beloit Jr Sr HS; Beloit, KS; (1); Church Yth Grp; Letterman Clb; SADD; JV Bsktbl; Var L Crs Cntry; Var L Trk; High Hon Roll; U Of KS; Med.

GFELLER, HEATHER L; Chapman HS; Chapman, KS; (3); Church Yth Grp; 4-H; SADD; Chorus; Pres Jr Cls; Pres Stu Cncl; Var Bsktbl; Var Sftbl; Var Vllybl; Hon Roll; OK U; Meteorology.

GFELLER, KIMBERLY A; Chapman HS; Chapman, KS; (4); 5/115; Church Yth Grp; FCA; 4-H; SADD; Teachers Aide; Nwsp; Ed Yrbk; Treas Frsh Cls; Treas Soph Cls; Pres Jr Cls; KS HS Rodeo Assn; Comm Food Dr & Blood Dr Vol; KS ST Univ; Vet Medicine.

GHARTEY-TAGOE, AMMA Y; Manhattan HS; Manhattan, KS; (3); 1/453; Debate Tm; Scholastic Bowl; Mrchg Band; School Play; Pres VP Stu Cncl; JV Bsktbl; JV Trk; NHS; Dance Clb; NFL; Natl His Day Grnd Prz Natl Champ 96; Dual St Spch Champ Info Spkng, Poetry 96; SHARE Brd Yth Svc Org; Microbio.

GHATE, SUJATA M; Southeast HS; Wichita, KS; (2); Debate Tm; Drama Clb; GAA; Thesps; School Musical; School Play; Stage Crew; Socr.

GIANG, JONNEY P; Liberal HS; Liberal, KS; (2); Key Clb; Science Clb; Tennis; Hon Roll; NHS; KS Univ; Med.

GIBBS, CURT; Olathe North Sr HS; Olathe, KS; (2); Boy Scts; Drama Clb; German Clb; Library Aide; Thesps; School Musical; School Play; Rptr Nwsp; High Hon Roll; Hon Roll; Eagle Scout; KU; Geneticist.

GIBBS, KATRINA; Wyandotte HS; Kansas City, KS; (4); #7 in class; Church Yth Grp; Cmnty Wkr; SADD; Teachers Aide; Ofcr Soph Cls; Ofcr Jr Cls; Ofcr Sr Cls; High Hon Roll; Hon Roll; Rptr NHS; NW MO ST; Scndry Educ.

GIBLER, BEN M; Lawrence HS; Lawrence, KS; (2); German Clb; Band; JV Ftbl; High Hon Roll; Hon Roll; Pres Acad Fit Awd; KS Univ; Bus Mngmt.

GIBSON, AMBER R; Wichita South HS; Wichita, KS; (3); 1/300; Church Yth Grp; Drama Clb; FTA; Scholastic Bowl; Thesps; Church Choir; School Musical; Ed Nwsp; NHS; Library Aide; Mentoring At Kelly Elem Schl; Preschl-Elem Tchr.

GIBSON, JEFF; Marysville HS; Marysville, KS; (4); Teachers Aide; Varsity Clb; Capt Ftbl; Wt Lftg; L Var Wrstlng; Hon Roll; Coffeyville CC; Acctng.

GIBSON, JULIE F; Nickerson HS; South Hutchinson, KS; (4); Spanish Clb; Phtg Ed Yrbk; JV Bsktbl; JV Var Chrldng; Hon Roll; Cls Of 96 Schlrshp; Rno Cty Schlrshp; Tonyflores Hspnc Schlrshp; KS ST U; Mrktng.

GIBSON, RODNEY; Turner HS; Kansas City, KS; (4); Am Leg Boys St; Bus Profs of Am; Chess Clb; Letterman Clb; Varsity Clb; JV Bsbl; Var Ftbl; Var Trk; Var Wrstlng; Ftbl All Huron League Hnrbl Mntn; 2nd Tm All Kansan Wrstlng; HS Gldn Glry Wrstlng; Cntrl Meth Coll; Arch Eng.

GIDEON, KAYLEEN S; Kapaun-Mt Carmel HS; Wichita, KS; (3); Church Yth Grp; Cmnty Wkr; Spanish Clb; SADD; Teachers Aide; Chorus; Church Choir; Orch; KS ST U; Hotel Restaurant Mgt.

GIEFER, JEFFREY A; Kingman HS; Spivey, KS; (3); Church Yth Grp; Natl FFA Org; Wt Lftg; Hon Roll; Comp Prgmr; Tech.

GIEFER, RENAE J; Pretty Prairie HS; Cheney, KS; (4); 6/21; Church Yth Grp; Chorus; Sec Frsh Cls; Pres Jr Cls; Sec Sr Cls; Var L Bsktbl; Sftbl; Var L Trk; Var L Vllybl; High Hon Roll; Sterling Col; Phy Thrpy.

GIER, KATRINA; Buhler HS; Hutchinson, KS; (4); 14/148; Am Leg Aux Girls St; Church Yth Grp; CAP; NFL; Chorus; School Musical; Pres Stu Cncl; Capt Crs Cntry; High Hon Roll; NHS; Aid Assn Luth Brnch 2886 VP; Pub Lib Yng Adult Advsry Brd Co Chprsn; Renaissance Stu Advsry Brd; West Pt Military Acad.

GIER, KRISTI N; Shawnee Mission E Sr HS; Leawood, KS; (4); Church Yth Grp; Church Choir; Co-Ed Lit Mag; Ofcr Stu Cncl; Ntl Merit SF; US Acad Dcthln; KS ST U; Med.

GIER, TINA M; Girard HS; Hepler, KS; (4); 14/69; Spanish Clb; SADD; Teachers Aide; Var Bsktbl; JV Vllybl; Hon Roll; NHS; Kayettes; CNC Hon Ment Bsktbl Jr Yr; Ft Scott CC; Bus.

GIERSCH, CRYSTAL A; Southeast Saline Schl; Salina, KS; (2); 1/63; FHA; NFL; Pep Clb; Varsity Clb; Band; Rep Stu Cncl; Var L Sftbl; Var L Vllybl; Cit Awd; High Hon Roll.

GIESEL, JOSHUA J; Riverton Schl; Riverton, KS; (3); FCA; FHA; Letterman Clb; VP Frsh Cls; Rep Stu Cncl; Var Bsbl; Var Bsktbl; Var Ftbl; Var Golf; Var Trk; Kays; Frgn Lang Club; Pittsburgh ST U; Bus.

GIESICK, MELISSA; Buhler HS; Buhler, KS; (3); FCA; Q&S; Band; Mrchg Band; Pep Band; Ed Yrbk; Powder Puff Ftbl; Var Vllybl; Hon Roll; B-Club; Emporia ST Univ; Med Tech.

GIESS, TYLER L; Hays HS; Hays, KS; (3); Intrml Bsktbl; High Hon Roll; NHS; Accntng.

GIESSEL, ANDREW J; Larned HS; Larned, KS; (1); 1/111; Church Yth Grp; FCA; Scholastic Bowl; Ofcr Stu Cncl; JV Crs Cntry; JV Var Tennis; Intrml Wt Lftg; High Hon Roll; Prfct Atten Awd.

GIESSEL, MANDY; Hayden HS; Topeka, KS; (4); 12/109; Hosp Aide; Intnl Clb; SADD; Rep Soph Cls; JV Crs Cntry; Var Swmmng; JV Trk; Cit Awd; High Hon Roll; NHS; KS Hnr Schol; Winter Sprts Queen Candte; Meals On Wheels Vol; KS St Univ; Exercis Sci.

GIESSEL, SARAH A; Hayden HS; Topeka, KS; (2); 14/150; Hosp Aide; VP Intnl Clb; Pep Clb; JV Crs Cntry; L Var Socr; L Var Swmmng; L Var Trk; Chrch Candle Bearer; Piano; Intnl Travel; KS Univ; Nrsng.

GIFFORD, JASON C; Shawnee Heights Sr HS; Topeka, KS; (2); Boy Scts; Church Yth Grp; Band; Jazz Band; Mrchg Band; Pep Band; High Hon Roll; Hon Roll; Brigham Young Univ; Engr.

GIFFORD, MANDY L; Ottawa HS; Ottawa, KS; (3); Library Aide; Office Aide; Teachers Aide; Bsktbl; Hon Roll; Cosmetology.

GIGER, BENJAMIN W; Chase Co HS; Elmdale, KS; (3); 1/45; Church Yth Grp; Acpl Chr; Chorus; Var Ftbl; High Hon Roll; NHS; Val; Farming; Ranching; KS ST U; Ag.

GIGER, JACOB L; South Haven Schl; Geuda Springs, KS; (1); Church Yth Grp; FCA; VP 4-H; Math Tm; Natl FFA Org; Quiz Bowl; Band; Mrchg Band; Pep Band; School Play.

GIGLIOTTI, ALISSA K; Blue Valley HS; Leawood, KS; (2); 27/282; Art Clb; Debate Tm; Phtg Nwsp; Rep Stu Cncl; Var Crs Cntry; Var Trk; High Hon Roll; Hon Roll; Schltc Art Awd; All Metro Crss Cntry.

GILBERT, CASEY; Shawnee Mission S Sr HS; Lenexa, KS; (3); 80/400; Intnl Clb; Pep Clb; Chrldng; Gym; Trk; Vllybl; Hon Roll; NHS; Pres Acad Fit Awd; Piano; Youth Ldrshp Inst; Schrshp Pin; Soc Psych.

GILBERT, GRAHAM N; Dodge City HS; Dodge City, KS; (3); Church Yth Grp; FCA; Quiz Bowl; Teachers Aide; Chorus; Var Bsktbl; Var Ftbl; Var Trk; Wt Lftg; Pres Acad Fit Awd.

GILBERT, JANELLE; Clay Ctr Cmty HS; Morganville, KS; (4); #34 in class; Pres 4-H; Treas Natl FFA Org; Treas Jr Cls; Stat Bsktbl; Swmmng; Ecology Clb Pres; Main Street HS Advy Bd; Show Choir Pianist; KS ST Univ; Vet Med.

GILBERT, MONICA; Leroy HS; Burlington, KS; (2); Church Yth Grp; Chorus; Chrldng; Vllybl; High Hon Roll.

GILBERT, NICOLE A; Andale HS; Colwich, KS; (2); Church Yth Grp; Debate Tm; Spanish Clb; Band; Flag Corp; Mrchg Band; Pep Band; Intrml Bsktbl; Var Chrldng; Var Vllybl.

GILBERT, REBECCA A; Shawnee Mission Northwest HS; Kansas City, KS; (4); 64/400; Hosp Aide; Q&S; Spanish Clb; SADD; Teachers Aide; Ed Nwsp; Bsktbl; Sftbl; Vllybl; Hon Roll; Johnson Cty CC; Occptnl Therpy.

GILCHRIST, CARRIE C; Salina HS South; Salina, KS; (4); 42/214; Drama Clb; NFL; Thesps; Jazz Band; School Musical; School Play; Ofcr Stu Cncl; NHS; Speech Tm; Band; Lovewell Inst For Creatve Arts Smmrs 92-95; Family Matters Cmnty Show Trpe; Musicl Theatr.

GILCHRIST, NICHOLAS; Valley Ctr HS; Valley Center, KS; (4); Art Clb; Church Yth Grp; Spanish Clb; SADD; Ed Lit Mag; Pres Jr Cls; Pres Sr Cls; Rep Stu Cncl; Var Ftbl; Powder Puff Ftbl; JETS Prblm Slvng Tm 1st Div ST; KS Wslyn Univ Crtv Wrtng Cntst; Poets Forum; Wichita ST Univ; Bio/Pre-Med.

GILE, CURTIS; Washburn Rural HS; Topeka, KS; (3); Boy Scts; Church Yth Grp; Band; Mrchg Band; Pep Band; High Hon Roll; KS ST U; Engrng; Survey.

GILES, JENNY; Bucklin Schl; Bucklin, KS; (3); Church Yth Grp; FCA; 4-H; Quiz Bowl; Scholastic Bowl; Speech Tm; SADD; Band; Mrchg Band; Pep Band; FCA VP; KS ST; Ag Ec.

GILES, KATIE; Bucklin Schl; Bucklin, KS; (1); 4/40; FCA; 4-H; NFL; Pep Clb; Speech Tm; SADD; Band; Mrchg Band; Pep Band; School Play.

GILFILLAN, SARAH; Hiawatha HS; Hiawatha, KS; (1); 8/107; Church Yth Grp; Pep Clb; JV Capt Chrldng; High Hon Roll; Elem Ed.

GILL, ADAM M; Blue Valley North HS; Overland Park, KS; (2); JV Var Ftbl; JV Var Wrstlng; Hon Roll.

GILL, AUSTIN; Riley Cty HS; Leonardville, KS; (3); 1/45; Debate Tm; FBLA; Quiz Bowl; Scholastic Bowl; School Play; Var Crs Cntry; Var Trk; Hon Roll; NHS; Pres Acad Fit Awd; KS Regents Hnrs Acad 96; Engrng.

GILL, JULIE; Fairfield HS; Sylvia, KS; (3); 2/35; VP Church Yth Grp; Quiz Bowl; Teachers Aide; VP Chorus; Rep Jr Cls; Sec Rep Stu Cncl; Var Bsktbl; Var Crs Cntry; High Hon Roll; NHS; U Of KS; Pharmacy.

GILL, LARA; Wellington Sr HS; Wellington, KS; (1); #4 in class; Church Yth Grp; Drama Clb; Math Tm; Office Aide; SADD; Yrbk; Chrldng; High Hon Roll; Jr NHS; Piano.

GILLEN, HEATHER; Silver Lake Jr Sr HS; Silver Lake, KS; (2); 11/60; FHA; NFL; Pep Clb; Band; Church Choir; Mrchg Band; Pep Band; Stage Crew; Ofcr Stu Cncl; JV Bsktbl; Vet.

GILLERAN, LINDSAY B; Blue Valley Northwest HS; Overland Park, KS; (3); Band; Orch; School Musical; Crs Cntry; Trk; Hon Roll; NHS; Kansas City Yth Symphny; Landscpe Arch.

GILLESPIE, EDDIE; Wichita East HS; Wichita, KS; (2); Stat Bsktbl; Ftbl; High Hon Roll; Hon Roll; Grambling Univ; Law.

GILLESPIE, KEVIN G; Campus HS; Wichita, KS; (3); SADD; Teachers Aide; Intrml Bsktbl; High Hon Roll; Hon Roll; NHS.

GILLESPIE, SEAN M; Derby HS; Derby, KS; (2); Computer Clb; Drama Clb; Thesps; Stage Crew; 1st Plc Htch Drftng Expo; CAD Dvsn; Cmptr Pgrmmr.

GILLESPIE, TAMI; Mulvane Sr HS; Mulvane, KS; (3); 15/140; Am Leg Aux Girls St; FCA; Q&S; SADD; Rep Frsh Cls; JV Var Chrldng; High Hon Roll; NHS; Prfct Atten Awd; Pres Acad Fit Awd; KS ST U.

GILLETT, JANELL H; Mankato Jr Sr HS; Esbon, KS; (3); 4/26; VP Natl FFA Org; Quiz Bowl; Band; Chorus; Church Choir; Mrchg Band; Pep Band; Swing Chorus; Rep Frsh Cls; VP Jr Cls; Pike Trl League All League Bsktbl 95-96, Hnrb Mntn Vllybl 95-96; KS ST U; Sprts Med.

GILLETTE, ALLISON; Goodland HS; Goodland, KS; (2); 14/89; Church Yth Grp; Letterman Clb; Band; Color Guard; Pep Band; Stage Crew; JV Bsktbl; Var Crs Cntry; Hon Roll; Best Girl Weigh Lifter.

GILLGANNON, MINDY; Seaman Sr HS; Topeka, KS; (4); 68/248; Am Leg Aux Girls St; Church Yth Grp; 4-H; FBLA; FHA; GAA; Library Aide; Pep Clb; SADD; Teachers Aide; Sun Schl Tchr; Cdt Tchr For Hndcppd Class; U Of KS; Chld Psych.

GILLIG, MELISSA I; South Barber HS; Kiowa, KS; (3); 1/24; Sec VP Church Yth Grp; Rptr Natl FFA Org; VP Pres NFL; SADD; Teachers Aide; Acpl Chr; Chorus; VP Frsh Cls; Treas Soph Cls; VP Jr Cls; Baker Univ; Dentistry.

GILLIGAN, ANDREA; Emporia HS; Emporia, KS; (3); Church Yth Grp; Cmnty Wkr; Key Clb; Band; Church Choir; Drm Mjr(t); Mrchg Band; Orch; Pep Band; School Musical; Emporia ST U; Music Ed.

GILLIGAN, ROBERT F; Emporia HS; Emporia, KS; (4); 124/288; Am Leg Boys St; Church Yth Grp; Cmnty Wkr; Debate Tm; 4-H; Key Clb; Model UN; NFL; Quiz Bowl; Scholastic Bowl; Emporia ST Univ; Spch Comm.

GILLIHAN, MEGAN K; Louisburg HS; Bucyrus, KS; (3); Art Clb; Bus Profs of Am; Pep Clb; Spanish Clb; SADD; Teachers Aide; School Play; JV Bsktbl; Hon Roll; Interior Dsgn.

GILLIKIN, ANGELA; Olathe East Sr HS; Overland Park, KS; (4); 1/300; Church Yth Grp; HOBY; Science Clb; Service Clb; Band; Chorus; Mrchg Band; Pep Band; Stat Trk; NHS; Chem.

GILLILAND, JESSICA L; Bonner Springs HS; Shawnee Mission, KS; (2); Dance Clb; Chorus; Chrldng; Sftbl; Ldrs Clb; Certfd Amer Red Crss Lifegrd; Johnson CTY CC; Elem Educ.

GILLILAND, ROBYN R; El Dorado HS; El Dorado, KS; (2); Church Yth Grp; Cmnty Wkr; Office Aide; SADD; Teachers Aide; Chorus; Powder Puff Ftbl; Sftbl; Hon Roll; KAY; Business.

GILLISPIE, JENNIFER; Maize HS; Wichita, KS; (3); 43/250; Church Yth Grp; Debate Tm; FCA; Letterman Clb; NFL; Service Clb; SADD; Var Socr; Var Tennis; NHS; Sunflower Girls St; 5th Pl In Calculating Machines At Pratt; Acctng.

GILLMAN, AMANDA D; Field Kindley Mem Sr HS; Independence, KS; (4); 13/134; Cmnty Wkr; Debate Tm; NFL; Spanish Clb; Band; Vllybl; Cit Awd; High Hon Roll; NHS; Pres Schlr; KS ST Debate Chmpnshp 96; KS U; Marine Bio.

GILLMORE, JAMES W; Moundridge HS; Moundridge, KS; (2); 4-H; Natl FFA Org; Quiz Bowl; Scholastic Bowl; Ftbl; 4-H Awd; AQHA Riding/Star Prgm; Horse Journal Pub/Ed; KS ST Univ.

GILLUM, KATHLEEN F; Wichita Southeast HS; Wichita, KS; (2); Debate Tm; NFL; Band; Mrchg Band; Nwsp; Hon Roll; Pol Sci.

GILMORE, BRYAN A; Olathe South Sr HS; Olathe, KS; (3); Drama Clb; Letterman Clb; Chorus; Ftbl; Hon Roll; KS Schlsp Test 2nd Pl Schl & Hnrbl Mntn; Engr.

GILMORE, NATASHA J; Galena HS; Galena, KS; (3); FHA; GAA; SADD; Ed Nwsp; Yrbk; Ofcr Frsh Cls; Ofcr Soph Cls; Pres Jr Cls; Bsktbl; NHS.

GILMORE, REBEKAH A; Lawrence HS; Lawrence, KS; (3); 73/643; VP Church Yth Grp; English Clb; German Clb; Key Clb; Pep Clb; Varsity Clb; Acpl Chr; Band; Chorus; Church Choir; Chrch Bell Choir, Guitar & Cont Music Ensemble; Natl His Day St Cmptn; Natl Choral Awd Central Jr High; Chrch Music.

GILPIN, AMANDA N; Wichita Southeast HS; Wichita, KS; (1); 1/430; Church Yth Grp; Band; Mrchg Band; Pep Band; Var Socr; Var Vllybl; High Hon Roll; Hon Roll; Play Alto Sax/HS Stg Band 97; Chrch Yth Grp Actvty Dcsn Mkrs; 2nd Chair Cncrt Band.

GILREATH, CHRISTOPHER D; Oswego HS; Oswego, KS; (1); Church Yth Grp; FHA; Scholastic Bowl; Pres Frsh Cls; JV Bsbl; JV Ftbl; Leg Art Mt 1st Pl Prntmkng; Cmptr Grphcs.

GILREATH, KRISTI A; Salina HS South; Salina, KS; (3); Church Yth Grp; Cmnty Wkr; FCA; Red Cross Aide; Band; Church Choir; Drm Mjr(t); Jazz Band; Mrchg Band; Orch; 1st Chair Clrntst Wnd Ensmbl; Chrch Pianist; Span Acad Hnrs; KS ST Univ; Sports Med/Jrnlsm.

GILSON, GENEVIEVE; Hays HS; Hays, KS; (3); Church Yth Grp; Sec 4-H; NFL; Band; Mrchg Band; JV Golf; AP Amer His; Part ST Frnscs; ST Music Fstvl; Psych/His.

GIMPLE, KIMBERLY A; Emporia HS; Emporia, KS; (1); Church Yth Grp; FCA; Chorus; Stage Crew; Swing Chorus; Variety Show; High Hon Roll; KS Music Edctrs Assn All-ST Choir; Natl Tchrs Hall Fame Chorus; Music.

GINDER, MOLLY J; Bishop Miege HS; Kansas City, MO; (1); 41/250; Hosp Aide; SADD; Intrml Bsktbl; Var L Socr; High Hon Roll; Campus Minstry Team; Clb Soccr; Elem Boys Sccr Team Coach.

GINDLESBERGER, ABBEY; Ulysses HS; Ulysses, KS; (3); 1/140; Am Leg Aux Girls St; Church Yth Grp; Letterman Clb; SADD; VP Frsh Cls; VP Soph Cls; Ofcr Stu Cncl; Bsktbl; Golf; NHS; Frgn Lang Clb; TX Chrstn U; Phys Thrpy.

GING, VANESSA; Sedgwick HS; Sedgwick, KS; (4); 12/24; Am Leg Aux Girls St; FHA; SADD; Teachers Aide; School Musical; School Play; Ftbl; Stat Vllybl; Hon Roll; Letterman Clb; KS Assn For Yth; Intl Ordr Rainbow For Girls; Dodge City CC; Medcl.

GINIE, RYAN; Olathe South Sr HS; Olathe, KS; (3); Cmnty Wkr; Letterman Clb; Teachers Aide; Varsity Clb; Ofcr Stu Cncl; JV Bsbl; JV Bsktbl; High Hon Roll; NHS; Pres Acad Fit Awd.

GINN, KELLI; North Central HS; Reynolds, NE; (4); 3/10; Am Leg Aux Girls St; Pres Drama Clb; FHA; Quiz Bowl; Speech Tm; School Play; Nwsp; Yrbk; Rep Stu Cncl; High Hon Roll; FHA Dist D Pres, Dist D VP.

GINN, SHALINN; Oxford HS; Oxford, KS; (1); 1/50; Church Yth Grp; Drama Clb; Varsity Clb; Chorus; School Play; Chrldng; Trk; Vllybl; High Hon Roll; Red Cross Aide; Piano Perfrmnce; KS U; Med.

GINTER, ANGIE; Shawnee Heights Sr HS; Topeka, KS; (3); FBLA; Hosp Aide; Pep Clb; Sec Frsh Cls; Sec Soph Cls; Sec Jr Cls; Co-Capt Capt Chrldng; Var L Trk; High Hon Roll; NHS; KS Univ; Pharmacist.

GIPSON, CHRIS L; Wichita North HS; Wichita, KS; (2); #1 in class; Rep Soph Cls; JV Bsktbl; Var L Trk; Hon Roll; Team Physician.

GIRARD, KRISTINA M; Hayden HS; Topeka, KS; (2); Cmnty Wkr; Pep Clb; Yrbk; JV Chrldng; Hon Roll; Smmr Leg Sftbl; Emporia ST U; Ed.

GIRST, BETH; Central Christian Schl; Hutchinson, KS; (4); 1/18; Lit Mag; Teachers Aide; Pres Soph Cls; Rep Stu Cncl; Capt L Chrldng; L Powder Puff Ftbl; Var L Vllybl; Gov Hon Prg Awd; High Hon Roll; Val; Trinity Intrntnl U; Elem Ed.

GIRTH, NICOLE; Frontenac Jr Sr HS; Frontenac, KS; (1); Church Yth Grp; FHA; Pep Clb; Ofcr Stu Cncl; Var Chrldng; Var Sftbl; Var Vllybl; Hon Roll; Pittsburg ST U; Nursing.

GIRTY, JANELLE D; South Barber HS; Kiowa, KS; (2); 5/20; SADD; Band; Chorus; Swing Chorus; Sec Soph Cls; Bsktbl; Chrldng; Tennis; High Hon Roll; Hon Roll; Bronze/Gold Hnr Point Pins; Acad Exclnc Awd GPA; NWOSU; RN.

GISH, SAM L; Washburn Rural HS; Topeka, KS; (3); 112/351; Letterman Clb; Q&S; Teachers Aide; Rptr Yrbk; Ofcr Bsbl; Ftbl; Hon Roll; Legion All Star Bsbl Team; All Amer Schlr; Winter Dance King Candidate.

GISLER, JENNIFER; Shawnee Mission East HS; Shawnee Mission, KS; (3); 117/409; Q&S; Yrbk; JV Crs Cntry; JV Trk; High Hon Roll; Hon Roll; NHS; North Star Mentoring Pgm-Teen Advy Bd Mem; Psych.

GISSELBECK, TIFFANY; Clay Ctr Cmty HS; Miltonvale, KS; (3); Band; Yrbk; Treas Frsh Cls; Treas Soph Cls; Treas Jr Cls; VP Sr Cls; Var L Bsktbl; Var L Vllybl; High Hon Roll; NHS; NCKL Hnrbl Mntion; KS St Univ; Neonatolgst.

GIVENS, TAMMY E; Holton HS; Holton, KS; (1); Girl Scts; SADD; Stat Bsktbl; Mgr(s); Stat Trk; Stat Vllybl.

GLAESER, ANNA; Shawnee Mission W Sr HS; Overland Park, KS; (4); Cmnty Wkr; Teachers Aide; Band; Variety Show; Rep Stu Cncl; Var Chrldng; Hon Roll; KS ST U; Bus.

GLANCY, PATRICK J; Atchison Co Cmty HS; Cummings, KS; (3); Math Clb; Mu Alpha Theta; Natl FFA Org; Nwsp; Yrbk; Treas Jr Cls; JV Bsktbl; Hon Roll.

GLASGOW, AMBER C; Winfield HS; Winfield, KS; (3); Church Yth Grp; Red Cross Aide; Orch; Pres Rep Nwsp; Pres Yrbk; Hon Roll; NHS; AFS; Frgn Cultre Clb.

GLASGOW, GRANT S; Wellington Sr HS; Wellington, KS; (2); 12/182; Church Yth Grp; Library Aide; Golf; High Hon Roll; Hon Roll; Jr NHS; Rtry Schlr.

GLASGOW, JENNI L; Wellington Sr HS; Wellington, KS; (2); 19/182; Church Yth Grp; Office Aide; Ofcr Stu Cncl; Chrldng; High Hon Roll; Hon Roll; Jr NHS; Jr Lions Awd.

GLASGOW, STEPHANIE; Shawnee Heights HS; Topeka, KS; (1); Dance Clb; Var Chrldng; High Hon Roll; Hnr A Prgm; Spirit Clb Rep; Care Co; KS Univ; Prfrmng Arts.

GLASS, SHANA M; Blue Valley Northwest HS; Overland Park, KS; (2); Temple Yth Grp; Hon Roll; Bnai Brith Yth Org Pres/VP Of Chptr/Mmbr In Trng Of Yr KC Cncl.

GLASSMAN, KELLI A; Salina HS South; Salina, KS; (3); Church Yth Grp; Hosp Aide; Chorus; Ofcr Stu Cncl; Hon Roll; NHS; Ft Hays ST Univ; Pre-Med.

GLASSMAN, URSULA A; Russell HS; Russell, KS; (3); 22/90; FCA; Letterman Clb; Pep Clb; SADD; Church Choir; School Musical; Var Crs Cntry; JV Var Trk; High Hon Roll; NHS; Ft Hays ST Univ; Pre-Med.

GLAVAS, ADRIANNE N; Shawnee Mission E Sr HS; Prairie Village, KS; (3); Cmnty Wkr; Hosp Aide; Hon Roll; Multi-Yr Listee; Ed; His.

GLAVINICH, JILL M; Bishop Miege HS; Shawnee Mission, KS; (4); 19/180; Cmnty Wkr; Debate Tm; German Clb; NFL; Pep Clb; Teachers Aide; Yrbk; Chrldng; High Hon Roll; NHS.

GLEASON, KATIE; Halstead HS; Halstead, KS; (1); 4-H; Spanish Clb; Treas Frsh Cls; Chrldng; Vllybl; 4-H Awd; HS Rodeo; Booster Clb; Kayettes; Fort Hays ST Univ; Ed.

GLEASON, RYAN; Garden City Sr HS; Garden City, KS; (3); Math Tm; Band; Mrchg Band; Pep Band; High Hon Roll; St Reg Math Relay Three Man Tm 1st Pl; JETS; Tbl Tnns; KS ST U; Engrng.

GLEASON, SADIE; Dodge City HS; Wright, KS; (1); Orch; Horses; Rodeo Rope; KS ST; Vet/Pro Rodeo.

GLEASON, SHEENA; Halstead HS; Halstead, KS; (3); 1/60; Am Leg Aux Girls St; Swing Chorus; 4-H; Band; School Play; Ofcr Stu Cncl; Bsktbl; High Hon Roll; NHS; Debate Tm; KS Assn Yth Treas, Brd.

GLENDENING, ADAM C; Stockton HS; Stockton, KS; (2); Church Yth Grp; Band; Mrchg Band; Pep Band; Pres Soph Cls; Bsktbl; Ftbl; Hon Roll.

GLENN, AMY; Bishop Ward HS; Kansas City, KS; (4); 15/96; SADD; Nwsp; Yrbk; Var L Bsktbl; Var Capt Sftbl; Hon Roll; NHS; Pres Schlr; St Schlr; Pep Clb; Schlr-Athl 95-96; Rockhurst; Phys Thrpy.

GLENN, CHERITH; Wellington Sr HS; Wellington, KS; (2); Drama Clb; French Clb; SADD; School Play; Trk; Hon Roll; KS Univ; Med Dr.

GLENN, JENNIFER L; Leavenworth HS; Leavenworth, KS; (4); Teachers Aide; Chorus; Ed Yrbk; Powder Puff Ftbl; US Natl Jrnslm Awd.

GLENN II, JOHN R; Circle HS; Benton, KS; (2); Boy Scts; Math Tm; School Musical; School Play; Stage Crew; Hon Roll; Prfct Atten Awd; Boy Scts Of Amrca Order Of The Arrow.

GLENN, RYAN P; Dodge City HS; Dodge City, KS; (1); Boy Scts; Rptr Natl FFA Org; FFA.

GLENNIE, AMBER S; Wichita East HS; Wichita, KS; (2); Yrbk; Mgr Bsktbl; Mgr(s); Photography; Modeling.

GLOTZBACH, KEITH; Wabaunsee HS; Paxico, KS; (2); FBLA; Key Clb; Quiz Bowl; Var Bsbl; JV Bsktbl; JV Crs Cntry; High Hon Roll; Natl Eng Mrt Awd.

GLOVER, RHONDA J; Fredonia HS; Fall River, KS; (3); 4-H; FHA; NFL; Pep Clb; Science Clb; Spanish Clb; Rptr Nwsp; Var Chrldng; 4-H Awd; Hon Roll; Psych.

GNAD, BRANDY L; Thomas More Prep-Marion HS; Hays, KS; (2); 22/85; Library Aide; Pep Clb; Rep Frsh Cls; Rep Soph Cls; Rep Stu Cncl; L Chrldng; Sftbl; Wt Lftg; Hon Roll; Ambsdrs; Cntr Rsrch Serv Awrd; Lctr/Cmntr Serv; Ft Hays ST Univ; Soc Wrkr.

GOATEE, KATHLEEN E; Udall HS; Udall, KS; (2); 10/36; Speech Tm; Chorus; School Play; Hon Roll; UCLA; Intrprtor/FBI.

GODDARD, DARREN J; Manhattan HS; Manhattan, KS; (2); 1/499; Church Yth Grp; Drama Clb; FCA; Treas 4-H; Scholastic Bowl; Thesps; Band; Mrchg Band; Pep Band; Stage Crew; Sunset Zoo Explorer.

GODDARD, JASON D; Beloit Jr Sr HS; Glasco, KS; (4); Letterman Clb; Pres Science Clb; Sec Treas SADD; Teachers Aide; Band; Variety Show; Bsktbl; Var Capt Ftbl; Wt Lftg; Hon Roll; KS ST U; Pre-Vet.

GODFREY, CHRISTOPHER; Junction City HS; Junction City, KS; (3); Am Leg Boys St; German Clb; Cit Awd; High Hon Roll; Martial Arts.

GODFREY, DIANE; Rock Creek Jr Sr HS; Saint George, KS; (1); 1/45; Scholastic Bowl; Rptr Nwsp; High Hon Roll; Senate Page; Med.

GODFREY III, JAMES R; Salina HS South; Salina, KS; (4); Am Leg Boys St; Pres Church Yth Grp; Drama Clb; NFL; Thesps; Drm Mjr(t); Mrchg Band; School Musical; School Play; Swing Chorus; Diocesan Yth Cncl 2 Yrs; Mark Malone Awd For Dramatic Excl; Ft Hays ST Univ; Commnctn.

GODFREY, JANA M; Labette Co HS; Parsons, KS; (4); 18/128; Church Yth Grp; Pres Sec 4-H; Hosp Aide; Band; Flag Corp; Mrchg Band; Pep Band; 4-H Awd; High Hon Roll; NHS; KS Jr Polled Hereford Assn; KAY Pgm & Svc Dir; KS ST U; Ag Jrnlsm.

GODFREY, VANESSA; St John Jr Sr HS; Saint John, KS; (4); 11/28; 4-H; Pep Clb; SADD; Teachers Aide; School Musical; Ed Yrbk; Pres Soph Cls; Pres Stu Cncl; Capt L Vllybl; Hon Roll; Natl His & Govt Awd; Named All Amer Team In Vllybl; OK Chrstn Univ; Mrktng.

GODINEZ, MATTHEW; Chanute Sr HS; Chanute, KS; (2); 54/152; Church Yth Grp; Spanish Clb; Chorus; Mrchg Band; JV Bsbl; JV Var Ftbl; Var Trk; Wt Lftg; Hon Roll; Cmnty Wkr; Principal Ldshp Tm; U Of KS; Bus Alw.

GODOWN, CASEY; Maize HS; Maize, KS; (3); 36/342; Church Yth Grp; FCA; French Clb; Letterman Clb; Scholastic Bowl; Teachers Aide; Church Choir; Stage Crew; JV Bsktbl; Hon Roll; Acad Ltr 95 & 96; KS ST U; Arch.

GODSIL, JOSH T; Dodge City HS; Dodge City, KS; (3); Church Yth Grp; ROTC; Stat Bsktbl; Hon Roll; Manhattan Chrstn Coll.

GOEBEL, KELLY R; Bishop Carroll Catholic HS; Wichita, KS; (2); Church Yth Grp; Cmnty Wkr; Drama Clb; Spanish Clb; SADD; Chorus; School Play; Stage Crew; Ofcr Jr Cls; Ofcr Stu Cncl; Jr HS Tutor; Jr Golfer Tm Plyr; KS Univ; Pre Med/Thrpst.

GOECKEL, JESSICA; Hanover Schl; Hanover, KS; (4); VP Church Yth Grp; Treas FHA; Natl FFA Org; SADD; Flag Corp; School Play; Stage Crew; Yrbk; Capt Var Vllybl; High Hon Roll; Girls ST Alternate; Christmas Ball Candidate; Forensics ST Festival Rating 1; Cloud Cty CC; Med Tchnlgy.

GOERING, ANGIE D; Halstead HS; Hutchinson, KS; (3); Drama Clb; Hosp Aide; Library Aide; Pep Clb; Spanish Clb; SADD; Chorus; School Musical; Rptr Nwsp; Kayettes; Hutchinson CC; Acctng.

GOERING, BRETT; Washburn Rural HS; Topeka, KS; (2); Church Yth Grp; Sprt Ed Nwsp; JV Bsbl; Bsktbl; High Hon Roll; Washburn Rural HS Jrnlsm Rookie Of Yr 96; Jrnlsm.

GOERING, CASSANDRA B; Meade HS; Meade, KS; (1); 12/34; Pep Clb; JV Vllybl; Hon Roll; Kayettes; Ldrshp Amer; Ft Hays Univ; Elem Ed.

GOERING, CLAUDIA A; Moundridge HS; Moundridge, KS; (3); Church Yth Grp; Debate Tm; 4-H; Natl FFA Org; Chorus; Church Choir; Ofcr Stu Cncl; High Hon Roll; Hon Roll; NHS.

GOERING, JAMIE; Inman Jr Sr HS; Inman, KS; (4); 5/28; Church Yth Grp; Cmnty Wkr; Chorus; Variety Show; Pres Stu Cncl; High Hon Roll; NHS; FHA; German Clb; Math Clb; Chrch Yth Grp VP & Pres; Vctn Bible Schl Asst Sng Ldr; Hutchinson CC; Phrmcy.

GOERING, KATHRYN F; Lawrence HS; Lawrence, KS; (4); German Clb; Science Clb; Chorus; Orch; School Musical; Trk; NHS; Vlntr Wildcare; St Orch; Highst Rtngs St Solo Cmptn Violin; KU; Vet.

GOERING, MEGAN K; Moundridge HS; Moundridge, KS; (2); Church Yth Grp; FCA; Pep Clb; Band; Chorus; Mrchg Band; Pep Band; School Musical; Co-Ed Yrbk; Ofcr Frsh Cls.

GOERING, SUZIE; Hesston HS; Newton, KS; (3); 1/67; Church Yth Grp; Pres 4-H; FBLA; Treas Natl FFA Org; Band; Chorus; School Musical; School Play; Tennis; High Hon Roll; KS ST Univ.

GOERTZ, MARVIN; Dodge City HS; Dodge City, KS; (4); 5/250; Quiz Bowl; Teachers Aide; Var Crs Cntry; Var Socr; JV Tennis; JV Wrstlng; Jr NHS; NHS; KS ST; Vet Med.

GOERTZEN, APRIL R; Stanton Co HS; Johnson, KS; (2); Church Yth Grp; Quiz Bowl; Band; Chorus; School Play; Rep Yrbk; Mgr Crs Cntry; High Hon Roll; NHS; Prfct Atten Awd; Optom.

GOERTZEN, WILLIAM; Hillsboro HS; Hillsboro, KS; (2); 1/45; Church Yth Grp; Chorus; Church Choir; School Musical; Tennis; High Hon Roll; Tabor Coll.

GOETSCH, LISA; Pierson Jr HS; Kansas City, KS; (1); Art Clb; Church Yth Grp; Computer Clb; Office Aide; Yrbk; Trk; Cit Awd; Hon Roll; Jr NHS; Prfct Atten Awd.

GOETSCH, PATRICE; Turner HS; Kansas City, KS; (3); Cmnty Wkr; Debate Tm; Math Clb; Math Tm; School Musical; Rptr Yrbk; Pres Jr Cls; NHS; Prfct Atten Awd; Art Clb; Frnscs Clb; Ntrl Hlprs; Site Cncl; YES Pgm; Fash Dsgn.

GOETZ, ADAM H; Leavenworth HS; Leavenworth, KS; (4); Church Yth Grp; Rep DECA; VP Intnl Clb; Pres Science Clb; VP SADD; Ed Nwsp; High Hon Roll; NHS; Cultural Diversity Clb VP; Acad Awd; Goodfellows; U Of MO Rolla; Metallurgcl Eng.

GOETZ, ASTRID R; Russell HS; Russell, KS; (2); Church Yth Grp; Natl FFA Org; Pep Clb; Chorus; School Musical; Hon Roll; Pres Acad Fit Awd; Psych/Social Work.

GOETZ, DOUG A; Wheatland Middle Sr HS; Park, KS; (4); 7/16; Nwsp; Yrbk; VP Soph Cls; Rep Jr Cls; Pres Sr Cls; Var L Bsktbl; Hon Roll; Homecoming Crt; Ft Hays St Univ; Tech Stds.

GOETZ, JENNIFER B; Leavenworth HS; Leavenworth, KS; (3); Intnl Clb; SADD; High Hon Roll; NHS; Goodfellows Rep; Discover Tribute Awd Gold Schlsp KS; Leavenworth Area Disability Advocacy Assn; Tchng.

GOETZ, JENNIFER J; Thomas More Prep-Marion HS; Hays, KS; (2); 26/76; Spanish Clb; Speech Tm; Yrbk; Hon Roll; Designing.

GOETZ, MAEGAN M; Victoria HS; Victoria, KS; (2); Church Yth Grp; FHA; Pep Clb; Chorus; Powder Puff Ftbl; Tennis; Hon Roll; NHS; Cosmo.

GOETZ, TAMMY; Cunningham HS; Zenda, KS; (4); 1/18; SADD; Chorus; Pres Jr Cls; Pres Stu Cncl; Trk; Var Capt Vllybl; Gov Hon Prg Awd; Hon Roll; Pres Acad Fit Awd; Val; Show Choir; CYO; Hutchinson CC; Acctng.

GOETZ, TIFFANY; Cunningham HS; Zenda, KS; (3); 1/28; SADD; School Play; VP Jr Cls; Rep Stu Cncl; Bsktbl; Chrldng; Trk; Vllybl; High Hon Roll; Pres Acad Fit Awd; Med.

GOFFIN, SABRA J; Shawnee Mission E Sr HS; Leawood, KS; (4); 55/407; Natl Beta Clb; Temple Yth Grp; Mrchg Band; Pep Band; Intrml Vllybl; High Hon Roll; Hon Roll; NHS; Intnl Clb; Library Aide; Frgn Travel; Japnse; Smith Coll; Japnse/Intl Rltns.

GOINS, ADRIAN D; Independence Bible Schl; Thayer, KS; (2); Church Yth Grp; 4-H; Band; Chorus; Rptr Nwsp; Sec Frsh Cls; Hon Roll.

GOLBUFF, JOHN C; Olathe East Sr HS; Olathe, KS; (2); French Clb; Letterman Clb; Trk; Hon Roll; Bio.

GOLDEN, CASEY L; Derby HS; Wichita, KS; (2); ROTC; Teachers Aide; Rptr Nwsp; Karate Red Belt; Elem Schl Tutor; Butler County CC; Dentstry.

GOLDEN, STACEY E; Wichita Southeast HS; Wichita, KS; (1); Art Clb; French Clb; JV Sftbl; Vllybl; Hon Roll.

GOLDEN, SUSAN N; Riley Cty HS; Riley, KS; (3); 17/54; Church Yth Grp; Natl FFA Org; Pep Clb; Scholastic Bowl; SADD; Teachers Aide; JV Bsktbl; Var Chrldng; High Hon Roll; Hon Roll; Trng Horses; Agribus.

GOLDSBERRY, JONI A; Washington HS; Washington, KS; (3); Church Yth Grp; French Clb; Band; Church Choir; Jazz Band; Mrchg Band; Pep Band; School Musical; School Play; High Hon Roll; Rgnl & St Piano Fests; Ozark Chrstn Coll; Msc.

GOLDSBERRY, KATIE L; Meade HS; Meade, KS; (2); Church Yth Grp; 4-H; Letterman Clb; Pep Clb; Band; Chorus; Mrchg Band; Pep Band; School Musical.

GOLDSTEIN, DAVID K; Blue Valley North HS; Leawood, KS; (3); 42/222; Ofcr Drama Clb; Ofcr French Clb; Model UN; NFL; Ofcr Thesps; Ofcr Chorus; School Musical; School Play; Stage Crew; Rep Jr Cls; Pres Stdnt Ambsdrs; Ofcr SBL Cncl; Awd Bst Spkr Serbian Subcomm/Hse Rep; Natl Yth Ldrshp Forum.

GOLTL, RYANN J; Morland Jr Sr HS; Morland, KS; (3); Capt Quiz Bowl; Band; School Play; VP Frsh Cls; Pres Soph Cls; VP Pres Stu Cncl; Var Bsktbl; Var Vllybl; Hon Roll; NHS; U Of KS.

GOLTRA, JAMIE; Ft Scott HS; Fort Scott, KS; (3); Key Clb; NFL; Chorus; Ed Lit Mag; Pres Soph Cls; Pres Sr Cls; Rep Stu Cncl; Var Capt Pom Pon; Hon Roll; NHS; Southwest MO ST U; Commnctns.

GOLTRA, SARAH L; Ft Scott HS; Fort Scott, KS; (2); Pep Clb; Chorus; Orch; High Hon Roll; Hon Roll; Pride Clb.

GOLUBSKI, ADAM L; Sumner Acad Of Arts & Science; Kansas City, KS; (3); Church Yth Grp; Latin Clb; Spanish Clb; Chrmn Stu Cncl; JV Bsbl; Var Golf; High Hon Roll; NHS; Wnnr 2 Math Awds; Part Camp Entrprs/Rotary Clb; Civil/Arch Engr.

GOLUBSKI, KATE B; Washington HS; Kansas City, KS; (4); 2/220; FCA; French Clb; Key Clb; Teachers Aide; Band; Mrchg Band; Orch; Pep Band; Rep Frsh Cls; Rep Soph Cls; Johnson County CC; Comp Sci.

GOMEZ, ANGELA N; Bishop Ward HS; Kansas City, KS; (2); 10/99; Drama Clb; Pep Clb; SADD; Chorus; School Musical; School Play; Stage Crew; Swing Chorus; High Hon Roll; Hon Roll; St Marys; Teaching.

GOMEZ, ERICA D; Topeka HS; Topeka, KS; (4); 125/354; French Clb; Intnl Clb; Yrbk; Lit Mag; Intrml Socr; Hon Roll; Poem Publshd Natl Libry Of Poetry 94; U Of KS; Psych/Jrnlsm.

GOMEZ, IVAN C; Wichita Heights HS; Wichita, KS; (3); 46/250; Letterman Clb; Varsity Clb; Rep Stu Cncl; Var L Socr; Hon Roll; NHS; Play Bsktbl; Wichita ST.

GOMEZ, JENIFER L; Topeka HS; Topeka, KS; (4); Church Yth Grp; Spanish Clb; Band; Chorus; Drill Tm; Orch; Socr; Gov Hon Prg Awd; High Hon Roll; NHS; Washburn Univ; Poli Sci.

GONZALES, AMY L; Turner HS; Kansas City, KS; (2); Hosp Aide; Hon Roll; Jr NHS; U Of KS; Soc Wrk/Cnslr.

GONZALES, CARESS M; J C Harmon HS; Kansas City, KS; (1); Cmnty Wkr; Flag Corp; Mrchg Band; Cit Awd; High Hon Roll; Hon Roll; Tech Prep Magnet Prgm.

GONZALEZ, JENNIFER L; Shawnee Heights HS; Topeka, KS; (3); Cmnty Wkr; Debate Tm; Letterman Clb; NFL; Pep Clb; SADD; Teachers Aide; Chorus; Socr; Trk; Nrsng Home Vol; Sec/Treas HALO; Emporia ST Univ; PT.

GONZALEZ, MARCIE R; Perry Lecompton HS; Perry, KS; (2); Drama Clb; FBLA; SADD; School Musical; School Play; VP Jr Cls; Var Golf; Hon Roll; Intnl Clb; Chorus; Sngrs; Dncg; Prfrmng Arts.

GOOCH, SARA; Liberal HS; Liberal, KS; (4); Am Leg Aux Girls St; Cmnty Wkr; FCA; Hosp Aide; Math Tm; Quiz Bowl; Yrbk; Sec Treas Stu Cncl; Var Chrldng; High Hon Roll; Natl Hnr Soc; KS ST U; Acctng.

GOOD, FREDERICK D; Berean Acad; Towanda, KS; (4); Church Yth Grp; 4-H; Letterman Clb; Teachers Aide; Chorus; Church Choir; Crs Cntry; Trk; 4-H Awd; Pensacola Chrstn Coll; Pre-Med.

GOOD, LAURA; Blue Valley HS; Olsburg, KS; (1); Bus Profs of Am; VP 4-H; FHA; Band; Chorus; School Play; VP Frsh Cls; JV Bsktbl; JV Vllybl; 4-H Awd; Piano.

GOOD, LISA M; Ottawa HS; Ottawa, KS; (3); French Clb; FBLA; SADD; High Hon Roll; Hon Roll; U Of KS; Psych.

GOOD, SHELLEY A; Derby HS; Derby, KS; (2); Church Yth Grp; FCA; Band; Mrchg Band; Rep Soph Cls; Rep Stu Cncl; JV L Gym; High Hon Roll; NHS; Stdnt Of Mnth; U Of San Diego; Marine Bio.

GOODALE, JEREMY; Hays HS; Hays, KS; (2); Church Yth Grp; Letterman Clb; Acpl Chr; Ofcr Frsh Cls; JV Bsktbl; JV Var Crs Cntry; Var Trk; Var Wt Lftg; Hon Roll; Pres Acad Fit Awd; Bus Admin.

GOODE, JAMIE M; Shawnee Mission W Sr HS; Lenexa, KS; (4); 50/360; Cmnty Wkr; Hosp Aide; Pep Clb; Spanish Clb; Speech Tm; Teachers Aide; Bsktbl; JV Crs Cntry; Mgr(s); Var Swmmng; U Of KS; Elem Ed.

GOODISON, ERIN; Jayhawk-Linn HS; Mound City, KS; (4); 1/36; Am Leg Aux Girls St; Natl FFA Org; School Play; VP Soph Cls; Sec Jr Cls; Ofcr Stu Cncl; Var Capt Bsktbl; Var L Vllybl; NHS; Val; Grls Ntn KS Rep; FFA Wshngtn Ldrshp Conf; U KS; Chld Wlfre.

GOODLOE, AMY; Ottawa HS; Ottawa, KS; (1); Debate Tm; 4-H; NFL; Drill Tm; School Play; Stage Crew; Variety Show; Ofcr Stu Cncl; High Hon Roll; Ballet Dncr; Stu Of Mnth-Feb 96; Debater Of Yr Awd 95.

GOODMAN, HOLLY M; Silver Lake Jr Sr HS; Silver Lake, KS; (4); 7/44; Church Yth Grp; Pep Clb; SADD; Teachers Aide; Chorus; Mrchg Band; Pep Band; School Musical; Stage Crew; Nwsp; Highlight Video Videogrphr; Hubbard Summer Acad; Allen Cty CC; Elem Ed.

GOODNO, JAMIE; St John Jr Sr HS; Seward, KS; (1); Church Yth Grp; Pep Clb; SADD; Band; Chorus; JV Bsktbl; Var Chrldng; JV Trk; JV Vllybl; Hon Roll.

GOODPASTURE, AMANDA R; Atchison Sr HS; Atchison, KS; (1); Church Yth Grp; Hon Roll; Kayettes; KS Univ; RN.

GOODPASTURE, TOM; Maur Hill Prep Schl; Atchison, KS; (4); #5 in class; JV Crs Cntry; Intrml Gym; Capt L Trk; Capt L Wrstlng; Hon Roll; NHS; Coll Of The Ozarks; Bus.

GOODROW, CRYSTAL B; Ness City HS; Ness City, KS; (3); 20/39; Church Yth Grp; Treas Sec 4-H; Pep Clb; Thesps; Chorus; Church Choir; School Musical; School Play; Stage Crew; JV Vllybl; Sang/Plyd Flute For Long Term Care; Ft Hays ST Univ; Engl.

GOODWIN, JENNIE L; Claflin Jr Sr HS; Claflin, KS; (4); 20/27; Church Yth Grp; Debate Tm; FHA; Pep Clb; Yrbk; Wt Lftg; Hon Roll; Vol Work At Battered Womens Shelter; Barton Cty CC; Socialogist.

GOODWIN, KEVIN; Derby HS; Derby, KS; (4); 14/347; Church Yth Grp; FCA; Letterman Clb; ROTC; Varsity Clb; Var L Bsbl; Var L Ftbl; Hon Roll; NHS; Pres Schlr; Air Force Rotc Schol; TX A&M Univ; Mech Eng.

GOODWIN, MEGAN; Sublette HS; Sublette, KS; (1); Church Yth Grp; Pep Clb; JV Bsktbl; Var Trk; JV Vllybl; High Hon Roll; Pres Acad Fit Awd; Pres Schlr.

GOODWIN, NATALIE E; Shawnee Mission E Sr HS; Fairway, KS; (3); 99/600; Church Yth Grp; Math Clb; Natl Beta Clb; Pep Clb; Service Clb; Band; Church Choir; Mrchg Band; Orch; Pep Band; Music Ed.

GOOSEY, AMANDA F; Arkansas City HS; Arkansas City, KS; (1); Church Yth Grp; 4-H; Natl FFA Org; Band; Mrchg Band; Pep Band; 4-H Awd; Vet.

GORDAN, JANEY; Valley Falls HS; Valley Falls, KS; (2); 4-H; VP FHA; Band; Chorus; Rep Frsh Cls; Chrldng; Sftbl; Vllybl; 4-H Awd; High Hon Roll; Coalition Essential Schls; KS ST; Vet.

GORDEE, HOLLIE D; Great Bend Sr HS; Great Bend, KS; (3); Church Yth Grp; Cmnty Wkr; Debate Tm; German Clb; NFL; Speech Tm; Nwsp; Mgr Sftbl; Hon Roll; NHS; Ger Exch; OK Bapt U; Info Sys/Intl Bus.

GORDON, CHERYL K; Rossville HS; Rossville, KS; (3); Letterman Clb; Band; Drill Tm; Jazz Band; Nwsp; JV Var Bsktbl; Var Trk; JV Var Vllybl; Hon Roll; Emporia ST; Art.

GORDON, VAREE; Rock Creek Jr Sr HS; Westmoreland, KS; (2); 10/65; 4-H; Scholastic Bowl; Band; Chorus; Church Choir; Jazz Band; School Play; 4-H Awd; NHS; Church Yth Grp; Photo Clb.

GORDY, JENNY; Cair Paravel - Latin Schl; Topeka, KS; (1); Church Yth Grp; Drama Clb; Chorus; School Play; JV Chrldng; Vllybl; High Hon Roll; Piano; Educ.

GORE, BETHANY S; Norwich HS; Norwich, KS; (3); 2/19; Church Yth Grp; FCA; Quiz Bowl; SADD; Band; Chorus; Flag Corp; Mrchg Band; School Musical; Variety Show; Kayettes; KS Stateline.

GORE, JEFF D; Nickerson HS; Hutchinson, KS; (2); FCA; JV Bsbl; Wt Lftg; Entrprnrshp.

GORGES, CRYSTAL D; Andale HS; Andale, KS; (3); Letterman Clb; Scholastic Bowl; Teachers Aide; Band; Mrchg Band; Pep Band; L Ftbl; Mgr(s); L Mgr Wrstlng; Hon Roll; Ath Trnr Ftbl & Wrestling; Phy Thrpst.

GORGES, DANIEL J; Maize HS; Colwich, KS; (2); Church Yth Grp; Debate Tm; Science Clb; SADD; Chorus; Variety Show; High Hon Roll; Hon Roll; Jr NHS; NHS; Natl Forensics League; Med.

GORGES, JANA; Bishop Carroll Catholic HS; Goddard, KS; (3); Art Clb; Church Yth Grp; Mgr Nwsp; Yrbk; Hon Roll; St Francis Hosp Vol; Eye Surgeon.

GORGES, PAUL D; Andale HS; Andale, KS; (1); High Hon Roll.

GORMAN, TRENTON K; Parsons HS; Parsons, KS; (3); Debate Tm; NFL; Rptr Nwsp; Treas Jr Cls; HS Natl Debate Trnmnt; Natl Mngmt Assn Speech Contest Winner; Pre Law.

GORMLEY, JENNI M; Wichita East HS; Wichita, KS; (2); Bus Profs of Am; Pep Clb; Spanish Clb; Teachers Aide; Orch; Hon Roll; Play Piano/Prvt Cello Lssns; Fin Mgr.

GORRELL, KARI M; Wichita Northwest HS; Wichita, KS; (2); Debate Tm; NFL; Q&S; Ed Yrbk; Rep Soph Cls; Bsktbl; JV Sftbl; JV Vllybl; Hon Roll; Pres Acad Fit Awd.

GORUP, GEOFF; Maize HS; Wichita, KS; (2); 34/300; Debate Tm; Drama Clb; NFL; Thesps; School Play; Stage Crew; JV Socr; Hon Roll; Law/Sci.

GOSS, DANIELLE R; Leavenworth HS; Leavenworth, KS; (3); Drama Clb; NFL; SADD; Thesps; Acpl Chr; Chorus; School Musical; School Play; Stage Crew; High Hon Roll; Hon Roll; Stella Prod Drm Club/Tspns Offcr; St Mary Coll; Elem Ed/Drm.

GOSSETT, JENNIFER L; Derby HS; Derby, KS; (4); 60/400; Church Yth Grp; Yrbk; High Hon Roll; Hon Roll; NHS; Elem Tutor; Friends Univ; Eng.

GOSSMAN, CHEYENNE V; Wellington Sr HS; Wellington, KS; (3); Bus Profs of Am; Library Aide; SADD; Hon Roll; Emporia St Univ; Lib.

GOSSMAN, MELISSA A; St Thomas Aguinas HS; Leawood, KS; (2); Girl Scts; Key Clb; Spanish Clb; SADD; Teachers Aide; Church Choir; JV Crs Cntry; Var Socr; High Hon Roll; Hon Roll.

GOTH, AMANDA; Waconda East HS; Beloit, KS; (2); Church Yth Grp; Dance Clb; FHA; Band; Drill Tm; Pep Band; Variety Show; Chrldng; Trk; Hon Roll.

GOTT, CHRISTOPHER M; Northeast Magnet HS; Wichita, KS; (3); Church Yth Grp; Spanish Clb; Multi Yr Listing; WSU; Law Enfrcmnt.

GOTTAL, JENNIFER M; Topeka HS; Topeka, KS; (1); 85/400; Hosp Aide; Gov Hon Prg Awd; Hon Roll; Speech Pathologist.

GOTTESBUREN, PAUL; Sumner Acad Of Arts & Science; Kansas City, KS; (3); 27/148; HOBY; JCL; Key Clb; Chorus; Spanish Clb; Thesps; Stage Crew; High Hon Roll; NHS; Chem; Comps.

GOTTLOB, RUSSELL O; Arkansas City HS; Arkansas City, KS; (2); 4-H; Natl FFA Org; 4-H Awd; High Hon Roll; Hon Roll; NHS; Pres Acad Fit Awd; KS State Univ; Architectur Eng.

GOTTSCHALK, JENNIFER; Leavenworth HS; Leavenworth, KS; (2); 21/389; Debate Tm; Hosp Aide; Drill Tm; Mrchg Band; VP Soph Cls; Var Pom Pon; Var Stat Trk; High Hon Roll; Symphonic Band; Acad Ltr; Ft Hays ST Univ; Bio Sci.

GOTTSCHALK, RYAN C; Thomas More Prep-Marian HS; Hays, KS; (4); VP Soph Cls; Ofcr Stu Cncl; Var L Bsbl; Var L Bsktbl; Hon Roll; Fort Hays ST Univ; :PT.

GOUGE, ANDREA; Wichita North HS; Wichita, KS; (4); 48/250; Bus Profs of Am; Church Yth Grp; Office Aide; Teachers Aide; Orch; Hon Roll; Acad Lttr; Pres Bus Prof Of Amer, Local Chptr; Attnd Natl Conf, Bus Prof Of Amer 96; Friends Univ; Elem Ed.

GOUGH, ERIN L; Newton Sr HS; Newton, KS; (2); 1/300; Key Clb; Model UN; Thesps; Chorus; School Musical; Nwsp; Lit Mag; Hon Roll; Histry Day; Jrnlsm.

GOUGH, JILL; Wellington Sr HS; Wellington, KS; (1); Church Yth Grp; Band; Chorus; Jazz Band; Mrchg Band; Pep Band; Cit Awd; High Hon Roll; Hon Roll; VP Jr NHS; I Ratng At Regnl & St Pin Festvls; 1st Pl Pin & Singng & 2nd Pl Fiddl At KS St Old Tim Musc Festvl; Oral Roberts U.

GOULD, JEFF; Jackson Heights HS; Netawaka, KS; (2); 7/36; Sec Chess Clb; Treas FBLA; Pep Clb; Var Scholastic Bowl; Band; Pep Band; School Musical; Rep Stu Cncl; Var L Trk; High Hon Roll; Air Force Acad; Aerontcl Engr.

GOULD, MELISSA D; Derby HS; Derby, KS; (1); Church Yth Grp; Drama Clb; FCA; Hosp Aide; SADD; Chorus; Hon Roll.

GOURLEY, ERIC S; Beloit Jr Sr HS; Beloit, KS; (2); Var L Bsbl; JV Var Ftbl; High Hon Roll; Natl Span Tst Span I Plcd 13th.

GOWEN, ANDREA; Madison Jr Sr HS; Hartford, KS; (3); 4-H; German Clb; Band; Chorus; Flag Corp; Mrchg Band; Pep Band; School Play; Bsktbl; Chrldng; KS ST; Vet.

GOWLER, RACHEL E; Shawnee Mission N HS; Shawnee Mission, KS; (3); VP Church Yth Grp; Pep Clb; Spanish Clb; Church Choir; Co-Capt Drill Tm; Rep Soph Cls; Ofcr Stu Cncl; Co-Capt Pom Pon; Swmmng; High Hon Roll; Smmr Sci/Math Inst; Dance Schl; Acad Lttr; PT.

GRABER, JENNIFER L; Kingman HS; Kingman, KS; (4); 7/72; Sec French Clb; Q&S; Yrbk; Sec Sr Cls; JV Tennis; High Hon Roll; NHS; St Schlr; Church Yth Grp; FCA; KS Hnr Stu; Teens Today Ldrs Tomorrow; Southwestern Coll; Bio.

GRABER, JOSHUA M; Berean Acad; Newton, KS; (3); 1/44; Church Yth Grp; Letterman Clb; Math Tm; Scholastic Bowl; Varsity Clb; Chorus; Rep Stu Cncl; L Bsktbl; L Socr; L Trk; Sci Team; Math Tutor; Church Yth Grp Stu Ldr.

GRABER, KAREN H; Kingman HS; Kingman, KS; (3); FBLA; Natl FFA Org; NFL; Office Aide; Spanish Clb; SADD; Bsktbl; Vllybl; High Hon Roll; Chrch Choir.

GRABER, MICHAEL A; Kingman HS; Kingman, KS; (1); 1/8; Boy Scts; FCA; FBLA; Scholastic Bowl; Band; Chorus; Jazz Band; Mrchg Band; High Hon Roll; Quiz Bowl; Eagle Scout Awd.

GRABER, ROCHELLE; Hayden HS; Topeka, KS; (3); Art Clb; Intnl Clb; High Hon Roll; NHS; St Schlr; Hayden Pro-Life Chptr; Hayden Chamber Singers; Creighton U; Medicine.

GRACE, AIMEE L; Topeka HS; Topeka, KS; (3); Cmnty Wkr; Sec Thesps; School Musical; School Play; Variety Show; High Hon Roll; NHS; Sec Drama Clb; NFL; Office Aide; Fearless Clb; Sojurners; Utopia Clb-Sec; 4th NFL, 5th St Forensics; Congregssional Yth Ldrshp Cncl.

GRACE, JILL C; Hayden HS; Topeka, KS; (2); FBLA; Intnl Clb; Pep Clb; SADD; Bsktbl; Crs Cntry; Wt Lftg; High Hon Roll; Hon Roll; Bus Mgmt.

GRACE, JOHN; Hayden HS; Topeka, KS; (4); 19/110; Art Clb; Var Bsbl; JV Bsktbl; JV Crs Cntry; High Hon Roll; NHS; Prfct Atten Awd; Washburn Univ; Acctng.

GRACE, LEE ANNE R; Beloit Jr Sr HS; Beloit, KS; (1); Church Yth Grp; Chorus; Church Choir; Orch; L Var Crs Cntry; L Var Trk; High Hon Roll; SADD; JV Bsktbl; ST Violin Solo; ST Track; KS Assn Yth Sec; PT.

GRADIN, SAMUEL M; Riverton Schl; Galena, KS; (4); Math Tm; Service Clb; Ofcr Sr Cls; Trk; NHS; YES Pgm; Eng.

GRAF, KELLY; Bishop Carroll Catholic HS; Wichita, KS; (3); VP Frsh Cls; VP Soph Cls; VP Jr Cls; VP Stu Cncl; JV Bsktbl; Var Crs Cntry; Var Trk; High Hon Roll; GCTL; Acad Achvmnt Awd; Friends Univ; Bus.

GRAF, LINDSEY; Leavenworth HS; Leavenworth, KS; (3); 6/367; Church Yth Grp; Cmnty Wkr; SADD; Teachers Aide; Var Bsktbl; JV Trk; Var Vllybl; High Hon Roll; NHS; Camp Bsktbl Cnslr; PT.

GRAFEL, KATHRYN A; Herndon Schl; Herndon, KS; (2); Math Tm; Model UN; Quiz Bowl; Scholastic Bowl; Speech Tm; Band; Chorus; Pep Band; Swing Chorus; Ed Yrbk; Stu Of The Mnth.

GRAFOS, GINA L; Wichita East HS; Wichita, KS; (2); 26/425; Church Yth Grp; Spanish Clb; Phtg Yrbk; Hon Roll; NHS; Spanish NHS; Phtgrphy Club.

GRAGERT, SARAH; Wichita East HS; Wichita, KS; (2); #1 in class; Church Yth Grp; Debate Tm; Sec NFL; Thesps; Chorus; School Musical; School Play; Var Gym; NHS; Spanish NHS; Horseback Riding 9th Pl Quarter Horse World Champs Jumping; Law.

GRAHAM, CODY L; Hays HS; Hays, KS; (1); Natl FFA Org; Chorus; Var Bsbl; Var Bsktbl; Var Ftbl; Wt Lftg; High Hon Roll; Hon Roll; Pres Acad Fit Awd; Natl FFA Greenhand Awd; KS ST; Ag Engrng.

GRAHAM, JOHN V; Norton Comm HS; Norton, KS; (2); 1/75; Boy Scts; Church Yth Grp; Drama Clb; HOBY; Band; School Play; Swing Chorus; Rep Stu Cncl; JV Ftbl; L Tennis; Vacation Bible Schl Vol; Astronaut Trng Pgm KS.

GRAHAM, LAURISA A; Minneola Schl; Minneola, KS; (3); Church Yth Grp; Library Aide; Math Tm; Spanish Clb; Speech Tm; Chorus; School Musical; School Play; Ed Yrbk; Pres Soph Cls; Ldrshp Amer 96.

GRAHAM, LINDSAY M; Salina HS South; Salina, KS; (2); Church Yth Grp; Cmnty Wkr; Drama Clb; Chorus; Sec Frsh Cls; Intrml Bsktbl; JV Sftbl; Intrml Vllybl; Var Wt Lftg; Hon Roll; Spcl Hnr Awd 5 Club Rnsnc Club; KS U; Art.

GRAHAM, NICHOLAS A; Shawnee Mission E Sr HS; Prairie Village, KS; (3); 4/415; Quiz Bowl; Var L Swmmng; Pres French Hon Soc; High Hon Roll; JETS Awd; NHS; Ntl Merit Ltr; Intl Baccalaureate Prog.

GRAHAM, TIFFANY L; F L Schlagle HS; Kansas City, KS; (1).

GRAMKOW, JEREMIAH C; Meade HS; Meade, KS; (2); Boy Scts; Sec Key Clb; Letterman Clb; Pep Clb; Chorus; School Musical; JV Bsktbl; Var L Crs Cntry; Var L Trk; Prfct Atten Awd; Law.

GRANADOS, LETICIA I; Wichita North HS; Wichita, KS; (2); Church Yth Grp; Teachers Aide; Wt Lftg; Hon Roll; Prfct Atten Awd.

GRANDON, LEIGH; Paola HS; Paola, KS; (3); 13/133; Am Leg Aux Girls St; Pres Church Yth Grp; Drama Clb; FCA; FHA; Service Clb; SADD; School Play; JV Bsktbl; Var L Sftbl; Sunflower Girls St; Hubbard Summer Acad; KS ST Univ; Elem Ed.

GRANT, ADAM J; Liberal HS; Liberal, KS; (3); Am Leg Boys St; Yrbk; VP CAP; High Hon Roll; NHS; Psych.

GRANT, AMY; Rock Creek Jr Sr HS; Saint George, KS; (2); Debate Tm; Natl FFA Org; Pep Clb; Spanish Clb; SADD; Band; Pep Band; Var Chrldng; High Hon Roll; Hon Roll; Vol Wrk; KS ST U; Psych.

GRANT, ERIC C; Larned HS; Larned, KS; (2); Church Yth Grp; Quiz Bowl; Scholastic Bowl; Band; Chorus; Pep Band; Ftbl; Trk; High Hon Roll; Hon Roll; Comp Sci.

GRANT, RYAN C; Derby HS; Derby, KS; (3); 28/394; Church Yth Grp; Key Clb; Ofcr Stu Cncl; Bsktbl; Var Capt Crs Cntry; Var Capt Tennis; High Hon Roll; NHS; I Dare You Ldrshp Awd; Yth Eldr Presbytn Chrch; U Of KS; Lawyer.

GRANT, SARAH B; Arkansas City HS; Arkansas City, KS; (2); Debate Tm; FCA; 4-H; Treas Natl FFA Org; NFL; Rep Soph Cls; Ofcr Stu Cncl; Var Chrldng; 4-H Awd; High Hon Roll; Ushrtts; Lvstck Jdg Team; KS ST U.

GRATTAN, KELLI; Sedgwick HS; Sedgwick, KS; (4); Am Leg Aux Girls St; Pres Letterman Clb; Chorus; Yrbk; Sec Jr Cls; Treas Sr Cls; Var Capt Chrldng; Var Trk; Var Capt Vllybl; High Hon Roll; KS ST U; Elem Educ.

GRAUE, CHRISTINE E; Blue Valley HS; Overland Park, KS; (3); Library Aide; Spanish Clb; Teachers Aide; School Musical; Nwsp; Chrldng; Cit Awd; High Hon Roll; Hon Roll; Kay Clb; Vol Work; U Of KS; Pre-Schl Tchr.

GRAUERHOLZ, JESSELYN; Spring Hill HS; Olathe, KS; (3); Debate Tm; NFL; SADD; School Musical; School Play; Rptr Nwsp; VP Frsh Cls; High Hon Roll; Hon Roll; NHS; Ntrl Hlprs.

GRAUNKE, LAURA E; Shawnee Mission E Sr HS; Overland Park, KS; (3); 75/400; Church Yth Grp; Natl Beta Clb; SADD; JV Vllybl; Hon Roll; NHS; Ozark Chrstn Coll; Deaf Mnstry.

GRAVERHOLZ, JESSELYN L; Spring Hill HS; Olathe, KS; (3); Sec NFL; Pep Clb; Q&S; SADD; School Musical; School Play; Ed Nwsp; High Hon Roll; Hon Roll; NHS; U Of KS.

GRAVES, AMY L; Nickerson HS; Nickerson, KS; (3); 10/101; Am Leg Aux Girls St; Key Clb; Math Tm; Band; Mrchg Band; Pep Band; Swing Chorus; Powder Puff Ftbl; Tennis; Hon Roll; Tchng.

GRAVES, CHARISSE M; Buhler HS; Hutchinson, KS; (4); 1/144; Church Yth Grp; FCA; Band; Chorus; Church Choir; Orch; High Hon Roll; NHS; Intnl Clb; Mrchg Band; KMEA All-St Orch 3 Yrs, Princpl Clarinet 2 Yrs; Interlochen Arts Camp Smmr 95; Music.

GRAVES, JOE D; Labette Co HS; Bartlett, KS; (2); Church Yth Grp; FCA; Science Clb; JV Bsktbl; JV Crs Cntry; JV Ftbl; Var Tennis; Hon Roll.

GRAVES, KIMBERLY A; Wellington Sr HS; Wellington, KS; (2); Church Yth Grp; Var Bsktbl; Intrml Mgr(s); Var Trk; Hon Roll; Jr NHS; KS.

GRAVES, SARAH; Wichita South HS; Wichita, KS; (1); 45/489; Band; Mrchg Band; Pep Band; Variety Show; Chrldng; Var Swmmng; Hon Roll; Wrtng; Singing; KS U; Chld Psych.

GRAVES, SERAH J; Shawnee Heights Sr HS; Tecumseh, KS; (3); SADD; Chorus; High Hon Roll; Hon Roll; KU.

GRAVES, TRACI L; Dodge City HS; Dodge City, KS; (3); Church Yth Grp; Band; Chorus; Church Choir; Mrchg Band; Pep Band; Variety Show; NHS; Peer Cnlr; Stu Of Mnth.

GRAY, ADAM E; Wichita Southeast HS; Wichita, KS; (2); Boy Scts; Church Choir; Orch; Stage Crew; Ftbl; High Hon Roll; Hon Roll; WA Univ St Louis; Cmptr Tech.

GRAY, ALYSSA E; Flinthills HS; Rosalia, KS; (2); FCA; 4-H; Letterman Clb; Quiz Bowl; SADD; Band; School Play; JV Var Vllybl; High Hon Roll; NHS; Forenscs.

GRAY, AMY L; Udall HS; Arkansas City, KS; (4); 2/36; Church Yth Grp; Quiz Bowl; Scholastic Bowl; Teachers Aide; Band; Chorus; Jazz Band; Mrchg Band; Pep Band; School Play; Friends Univ; Med.

GRAY, DUSTIN; Turner HS; Kansas City, KS; (3); 12/225; SADD; Varsity Clb; Var CAP; Var Ftbl; Var Socr; High Hon Roll; Hon Roll; NHS; Peer Cnslng; Kays.

GRAY, JEREMY J; Liberal HS; Liberal, KS; (2); Boy Scts; Capt Debate Tm; Math Tm; NFL; Office Aide; Quiz Bowl; Science Clb; Speech Tm; High Hon Roll; NHS; Chem/Alg II/SPAN/ENG II/DEBATE/FORENSICS Top Stdnt Awds; Yng Republcns; Law.

GRAY, KRISTIANE; Shawnee Mission Northeast HS; Lenexa, KS; (4); 49/411; Debate Tm; NFL; Pep Clb; Speech Tm; VP Rep Stu Cncl; JV Crs Cntry; JV Trk; Hon Roll; NHS; Graduation Speaker; U Of KS; Law.

GRAY, MELISSA; Lyndon HS; Quenemo, KS; (3); 13/40; Pres FBLA; Band; Rep Stu Cncl; Bsktbl; Chrldng; Sftbl; Trk; Vllybl; Hon Roll; Prfct Atten Awd; Law.

GRAY, SHELLY L; Field Kindley Mem Sr HS; Coffeyville, KS; (2); 1/163; German Clb; Bsktbl; Score Keeper; Sftbl; Wt Lftg; High Hon Roll; Hon Roll; Prfct Atten Awd; Natural Helpers Org; Native Amer Clb.

GRAY, STEVEN; Olathe North Sr HS; Dallas, TX; (4); School Play; Bsktbl; Ftbl; Trk; Hon Roll; NHS; Pre-Med.

GRECIAN, KELLY A; Palco HS; Palco, KS; (3); 2/20; Church Yth Grp; Debate Tm; Drama Clb; 4-H; Letterman Clb; Natl FFA Org; Band; Chorus; Pep Band; School Play; KS ST Univ; Dietician.

GREEMORE, KELLY R; Holton HS; Holton, KS; (3); 34/78; Church Yth Grp; FHA; Letterman Clb; Teachers Aide; Acpl Chr; Chorus; Church Choir; School Musical; Lit Mag; Mgr Crs Cntry; Mgr(s); St Music Rating I Ensemble; Regnl Solo Music II; Haskell Emporia; Tchng.

GREEN, ANGELA; Hugoton HS; Hugoton, KS; (4); 5/66; Church Yth Grp; FCA; FHA; Chorus; School Musical; Ofcr Stu Cncl; Vllybl; High Hon Roll; NHS; Wrk/Study Pgm; Hesston Coll; Mrktng.

GREEN, CHRIS; Hutchinson HS; Hutchinson, KS; (3); Am Leg Boys St; Church Yth Grp; French Clb; Key Clb; Quiz Bowl; Scholastic Bowl; Science Clb; Service Clb; Sprt Ed Nwsp; Rep Sr Cls; Acad Excl Awd; 2nd Pl KS Schlsp Cont Word Processing 95; 3rd Pl ST Of KS Schlsp Cont Geog 96.

GREEN, DENYSE; Udall HS; Douglass, KS; (3); Church Yth Grp; Drama Clb; Math Tm; Ed Nwsp; Sec Nwsp; VP Soph Cls; VP Jr Cls; JV Vllybl; Dance Clb; Multi Yr Listing; Scndry Ed.

GREEN, GLENDA; Southeast Saline Schl; Assaria, KS; (2); Art Clb; Church Yth Grp; Cmnty Wkr; English Clb; NFL; Varsity Clb; Chorus; Stage Crew; Var Chrldng; Wt Lftg; Genetic Engrng.

GREEN, JANA M; Emporia HS; Emporia, KS; (3); Church Yth Grp; FCA; Stage Crew; Rep Jr Cls; Var Gym; Cit Awd; High Hon Roll; Hon Roll; Mexico Missions Drama Tm.

GREEN, JOHNNA L; Olathe East Sr HS; Wichita, KS; (4); Spanish Clb; Teachers Aide; Yrbk; JV Var Bsktbl; Powder Puff Ftbl; JV Sftbl; Vllybl; Hon Roll; NHS; Pres Acad Fit Awd; U Of KS.

GREEN, JOY; South Gray HS; Copeland, KS; (1); 7/30; Church Yth Grp; GAA; Chorus; School Musical; School Play; Swing Chorus; JV Var Bsktbl; Var Chrldng; Var Trk; JV Var Vllybl; ST Chorus; KS ST U; Cmptr Pgrmg/Music.

GREEN, JULIA R; Southeast KS Spec Ed Coop; Baxter Springs, KS; (3); Pep Clb; Scholastic Bowl; Science Clb; Spanish Clb; Band; Mrchg Band; School Musical; Chrldng; High Hon Roll; NHS; Chem Engrng.

GREEN, KYLE P; Nickerson HS; South Hutchinson, KS; (2); 6/102; L Bsktbl; L Crs Cntry; L Socr; Hon Roll; U Of OK; Bus.

GREEN, LISA; Wyandotte HS; Kansas City, KS; (3); High Hon Roll; Hon Roll; Phy Thrpst.

GREEN, MEAGAN; Quivira Heights HS; Lorraine, KS; (2); 2/18; Drama Clb; HOBY; Scholastic Bowl; Varsity Clb; Band; Chorus; Var L Tennis; Var L Trk; High Hon Roll; Pres Acad Fit Awd; 1st Pl Amer HS Math Exam; TTA; EAA Eagle Flight; USAF Acad; Astrontcl Engr.

GREEN, MEGAN M; Manhattan HS; Manhattan, KS; (3); Church Yth Grp; Cmnty Wkr; Spanish Clb; SADD; JV Trk; Hon Roll; NHS.

GREEN, TOBY; Dodge City HS; Dodge City, KS; (4); 86/254; Am Leg Boys St; JV Bsbl; JV Bsktbl; JV Crs Cntry; Presdntl Acad Imprvmt Awd; Pittsburg ST Univ; Civil Engr.

GREENBAUM, STACY L; Blue Valley HS; Overland Park, KS; (2); Debate Tm; Drama Clb; Intnl Clb; NFL; Spanish Clb; Temple Yth Grp; Chorus; Orch; School Musical; High Hon Roll; Natl Yth Group; BBY Group; BBYO Paper Ed; BBYO KS Chptr Programming VP; Pol Sci Clb.

GREENE, ALICIA; Jackson Heights HS; Circleville, KS; (2); Church Yth Grp; Pep Clb; Vllybl; High Hon Roll; Prfct Atten Awd; Emporia ST U; Tchr.

GREENE, JOY E; Wichita Heights HS; Wichita, KS; (4); Debate Tm; JA; NFL; Teachers Aide; Church Choir; Rptr Yrbk; Trk; Optimist Clb; Gospel Clb; Judge.

GREENE, NATHAN S; Jewell HS; Jewell, KS; (1); 2/23; FCA; Math Tm; Natl FFA Org; Pep Clb; Quiz Bowl; Scholastic Bowl; Band; Mrchg Band; Orch; Pep Band.

GREENFIELD, TAMMY C; Emporia HS; Emporia, KS; (4); 41/271; Cmnty Wkr; FBLA; Cit Awd; High Hon Roll; Hon Roll; SMILE; Emporia ST U; Bus.

GREENLEAF, JARED S; Greensburg HS; Greensburg, KS; (1); Boy Scts; Church Yth Grp; Cmnty Wkr; Band; Mrchg Band; Pep Band; Pres Frsh Cls; Bsktbl; Tennis; Hon Roll; PCL.

GREENLEAF, JUSTIN P; Greensburg HS; Greensburg, KS; (1); Boy Scts; Church Yth Grp; Cmnty Wkr; Band; Mrchg Band; Pep Band; Treas Frsh Cls; Bsktbl; Tennis; High Hon Roll; PCL.

GREENWALD, JESSE R; El Dorado HS; El Dorado, KS; (3); Cmnty Wkr; Sec Debate Tm; Sec NFL; Nwsp; Ed Yrbk; High Hon Roll; KS Regents Hnrs Acad; Duke TIP; MIT; Comp Sci; Elec Engrng.

GREENWALL, JAMIE; Iola Sr HS; Iola, KS; (4); 3/95; Church Yth Grp; Pres Drama Clb; Spanish Clb; Speech Tm; Thesps; Chorus; Church Choir; School Musical; School Play; Sec Soph Cls; KS Hnrs Schlr; KS Regnts Hnrs Acad; Kayette Clb Pres; BYU; Advertsng.

GREENWALL, NATHAN S; Iola Sr HS; Iola, KS; (4); 2/158; Am Leg Boys St; Art Clb; Church Yth Grp; Drama Clb; Nwsp; Intrml Golf; Cit Awd; High Hon Roll; Hon Roll; NHS; Hnr Piano Clb; Jr Cls Prom; Art; Act Worker; BYU; Art.

GREENWOOD, STACY M; Shawnee Heights HS; Topeka, KS; (2); High Hon Roll; Achvmt Hgh Hnrs Eng/Span/Cmptrs/Sci/Bus/Home Ec; Chrch Grnds Cr; U Of KS; Cmptr Sci.

GREEP, NATASHA R; Derby Christian Schl; Derby, KS; (1); Church Yth Grp; Drama Clb; Rep Frsh Cls; Ofcr Stu Cncl; Bsktbl; Cit Awd; Hon Roll; Prfct Atten Awd; Pensacola Chrstn Col; Phy Thpry.

GREER, CEZANNE; Mc Pherson HS; Mc Pherson, KS; (3); HOBY; Letterman Clb; Red Cross Aide; Science Clb; Spanish Clb; Chorus; School Musical; Swmmng; Tennis; NHS.

GREGG, ADAM T; Newton Sr HS; Newton, KS; (2); 1/270; Key Clb; Model UN; SADD; Temple Yth Grp; Band; Jazz Band; Tennis; High Hon Roll.

GREGORY, ANGELA; Bishop Ward HS; Kansas City, KS; (4); 6/91; Cmnty Wkr; HOBY; Pep Clb; SADD; Treas VP Stu Cncl; Capt Chrldng; Hon Roll; NHS; Pres Schlr; St Schlr; St Mary Coll; Bus.

GREGORY, CHRISTINA K; Valley Ctr HS; Valley Center, KS; (3); 13/162; Church Yth Grp; Cmnty Wkr; French Clb; Girl Scts; Hosp Aide; Science Clb; SADD; Chorus; Lit Mag; NHS; Girl Scouts Silver Awd; Sedgwick Cty Zoo Pin Awd; Zoology.

GREGORY, JASON L; Cheney Jr Sr HS; Cheney, KS; (4); 5/50; Church Yth Grp; Chorus; School Play; Co-Ed Yrbk; Pres Sr Cls; Sec Stu Cncl; Var L Ftbl; Var L Trk; High Hon Roll; NHS; ST Rcrd 4x400 Meter Rly Cls 3a; KS ST Univ; Ag Eng.

GREGORY, KAREN H; Washington HS; Kansas City, KS; (2); Spanish Clb; Mgr(s); Prfct Atten Awd; Art Schltc Hnr Roll & Bd Rm Exhibit; Vet.

GREGORY, VERRA T; Shawnee Mission N HS; Overland Park, KS; (3); French Clb; Key Clb; Pep Clb; Orch; Tennis; High Hon Roll; Hon Roll; NHS; Premed.

GRENNAN, JENNIFER; Silver Lake Jr Sr HS; Silver Lake, KS; (3); 1/52; NFL; Band; Chorus; School Musical; School Play; Pres Frsh Cls; JV Vllybl; Hon Roll; Pres NHS; Pep Clb; Chrch Vol; KS St U.

GRESNICK, TRISHA; Baldwin HS; Baldwin City, KS; (3); 20/97; Am Leg Aux Girls St; Cmnty Wkr; HOBY; Letterman Clb; Spanish Clb; Rep Sr Cls; Chrldng; Pom Pon; Tennis; High Hon Roll; Fort Hays ST U; Intl Bus.

GRETENCORD, AMY R; Anderson Cty Jr Sr HS; Garnett, KS; (1); Church Yth Grp; GAA; Intnl Clb; Pep Clb; SADD; Acpl Chr; Chorus; Swing Chorus; Variety Show; Intrml Bsktbl; Spelling Bee Champ; Drama.

GRETENCORD, MICHELLE L; Anderson Cty Jr Sr HS; Garnett, KS; (2); Church Yth Grp; GAA; Intnl Clb; SADD; Nwsp; Yrbk; Ofcr Frsh Cls; Ofcr Soph Cls; Ofcr Stu Cncl; Var Bsktbl; KAY Clb; Octogon; KS Univ; Nrs Practioner.

GREVE, JENNIFER; Iola Sr HS; Iola, KS; (4); 13/95; Church Yth Grp; FBLA; Library Aide; SADD; Band; Color Guard; Mrchg Band; Orch; Pep Band; JV Bsktbl; Phi Theta Kappa; Emporia St U Schlrshp; ACCC Acad; Emporia ST U; Med.

GRIEB, LAUREN M; Blue Valley HS; Stilwell, KS; (3); Q&S; Varsity Clb; Mgr Nwsp; Rptr Yrbk; VP Frsh Cls; Bsktbl; Socr; Tennis; Trk; Hon Roll; Germn 3 Poetry Rding 1st Plc; All Star Tm NECIS Bsktbll Tnmt; Luxembourg Wmns Natl Sccr Tm; KS St Univ; Intr Dsgnr.

GRIER, TIFFANY D; Sedan HS; Peru, KS; (2); Spanish Clb; Bsktbl; Vllybl; Ed.

GRIFFETH, ERIN C N; Lawrence HS; Lawrence, KS; (3); 122/627; Am Leg Aux Girls St; Girl Scts; Hosp Aide; Spanish Clb; Band; Mrchg Band; Ofcr Frsh Cls; High Hon Roll; NHS; Pres Acad Fit Awd; Flute Section Ldr; Douglas Cty Sci Fair Awd; Engrng; Music.

GRIFFIN, ANGIE; Ulysses HS; Ulysses, KS; (3); Art Clb; Debate Tm; FBLA; NFL; Yrbk; Crs Cntry; Trk; High Hon Roll; Pre-Law.

GRIFFIN, ASHLEY A; Maize HS; Maize, KS; (1); Cmnty Wkr; High Hon Roll; Ftr Prblm Slvng; Excl Span.

GRIFFIN, JACQUELINE N; Washburn Rural HS; Topeka, KS; (2); SADD; Chorus; School Musical; Stage Crew; Variety Show; Ed Nwsp; Tns Tchrs; KS Ambass Music; Hrsbck Rdng Jmpr & Hntr; Vet.

GRIFFIN, LILA G; J C Harmon HS; Kansas City, KS; (2); Cmnty Wkr; Computer Clb; GAA; Key Clb; Pep Clb; Quiz Bowl; Scholastic Bowl; Church Choir; Ofcr Soph Cls; Chrldng; UMKC.

GRIFFIN, TARA M; Colby Sr HS; Colby, KS; (3); Church Yth Grp; Cmnty Wkr; VP Girl Scts; Library Aide; Natl FFA Org; Office Aide; Spanish Clb; Teachers Aide; Rptr Phtg Nwsp; JV Bsktbl; Silver Awd In Girl Scouting; Colby CC.

GRIFFIN, TRISTAN S; Cimarron HS; Cimarron, KS; (3); Church Yth Grp; Cmnty Wkr; Computer Clb; Letterman Clb; Spanish Clb; Band; Jazz Band; Mrchg Band; Pep Band; Ofcr Bsktl; BSA; Bus.

GRIFFITH, HEATHER; Shawnee Heights HS; Topeka, KS; (4); 13/237; Church Yth Grp; Intnl Clb; Pep Clb; Science Clb; SADD; Teachers Aide; Chorus; School Musical; Variety Show; Var Capt Chrldng; Dance 14 Yrs; Piano 11 Yrs; UKS; Bio.

GRIFFITH, KIM; Paola HS; Paola, KS; (3); Cmnty Wkr; 4-H; FHA; Hosp Aide; Pep Clb; SADD; Stat Bsktbl; Stat L Vllybl; Hon Roll; Pittsburg ST Univ; RN; Neonatl.

GRIFFITHS, TONYA R; Abilene HS; Abilene, KS; (3); 20/123; Am Leg Aux Girls St; FCA; VP FBLA; Pres Spanish Clb; Drill Tm; Ed Nwsp; Sec Soph Cls; Sec Jr Cls; Sec Sr Cls; Var Bsktbl; Reason Chrstin Singing Group; Intnl Order Of Jobs Daughters, Local & St Offices; KS ST Univ; HS Art Tchr.

GRIGSBY, MEGAN; Attica Public Schl; Attica, KS; (1); Pres Church Yth Grp; Chorus; School Play; Var Bsktbl; Var Trk; Var Vllybl; Hon Roll; Med.

GRILLIOT, ADAM; Syracuse Jr Sr HS; Syracuse, KS; (3); 6/37; Treas 4-H; Pep Clb; Band; Chorus; Pep Band; Pres Soph Cls; Var Bsktbl; Var Crs Cntry; Var Trk; Hon Roll; Vet.

GRILLIOT, PAUL; Syracuse Jr Sr HS; Syracuse, KS; (2); 8/30; 4-H; Letterman Clb; Pep Clb; Band; Chorus; Pep Band; JV Bsktbl; Var L Golf; 4-H Awd; Hon Roll; Tchr.

GRILLOT, KRYSTAL; Labetle Cty HS; Parsons, KS; (3); FCA; FBLA; Letterman Clb; Natl FFA Org; Pep Clb; Chrldng; Sftbl; Cit Awd; Hon Roll; NHS.

GRIMES, ALICIA C; Buhler HS; Hutchinson, KS; (2); Church Yth Grp; FCA; Sec French Clb; Hosp Aide; NFL; Speech Tm; Chorus; Church Choir; Intrml Sftbl; Intrml Tennis; Stdnts Mkng Difference; Bus Mgmt.

GRIMES, STEVE S; Wichita Northwest HS; Wichita, KS; (4); Hon Roll; Educl Excel Prestl Awd; Friends Univ; Bus.

GRIMM, AMANDA; Conway Springs HS; Conway Springs, KS; (2); FHA; Band; Chorus; Mrchg Band; Variety Show; Bsktbl; Chrldng; Tennis; Trk; Cardinalaires.

GRIMM, KARA S; Sabetha HS; Morrill, KS; (3); 49/91; Church Yth Grp; Pres 4-H; FHA; NFL; Chorus; Church Choir; School Musical; JV Vllybl; 4-H Awd; Prfct Atten Awd; Bus Clb; Respiratory Clb; X-Ray Tech.

GRIMM, SARA J; Sabetha HS; Morrill, KS; (2); 3/64; Church Yth Grp; FCA; Pres Spanish Clb; Ofcr Stu Cncl; JV Bsktbl; L Crs Cntry; Trk; High Hon Roll; NHS; Natl Bible Quiz; Regnl Piano Festival; Odyssey Singers; Calvary Bible Coll; Elem Ed.

GRIMM, SHAUN M; Blue Valley North HS; Leawood, KS; (4); 61/166; FCA; Letterman Clb; Model UN; SADD; Capt Socr; Var Trk; Hon Roll; Prfct Atten Awd; KS ST; Engrng.

GRIMSLEY, TRICIA D; Maize HS; Wichita, KS; (3); Sec Letterman Clb; Science Clb; Spanish Clb; Ofcr Stu Cncl; Var Chrldng; Sftbl; Hon Roll; Treas Frsh Cls; Treas Soph Cls; Sftb 1st Team & MVP.

GRINDEL, KATHRYN G; Turner HS; Kansas City, KS; (4); 27/190; Rep Bus Profs of Am; Pres Debate Tm; Hosp Aide; Treas NFL; Teachers Aide; Rep Jr Cls; Rep Sr Cls; Hon Roll; Rep Jr NHS; Rep NHS; Ldrshp 2020; Commnctns.

GRINSELL, CHARLENE; Cheney Jr Sr HS; Cheney, KS; (2); Church Yth Grp; Drama Clb; Chorus; School Play; Swing Chorus; High Hon Roll; Perform In Many Plays & Musicals In The Wichita Area; Ratings In Drama & Music Vocal Solo Cmptn; UCLA; Actress.

GRINSTAFF, KRISTY; Udall HS; Udall, KS; (2); Church Yth Grp; Band; Mrchg Band; Pep Band; Rep Soph Cls; L Bsktbl; Var L Chrldng; L Trk; L Vllybl; Hon Roll; Nursng.

GRISELL, VINCENT A; Topeka West HS; Topeka, KS; (2); Church Yth Grp; Drama Clb; French Clb; Pep Clb; Thesps; Variety Show; Nwsp; Rep Soph Cls; VP Jr Cls; High Hon Roll.

GRISHOM, SHAREE S; Junction City HS; Junction City, KS; (3); Church Yth Grp; Church Choir; Ofcr Jr Cls; Vllybl; Hon Roll; Grambling Univ; Lawyer.

GRIZZELL, APRIL; Larned HS; Macksville, KS; (4); Am Leg Aux Girls St; 4-H; Girl Scts; Letterman Clb; Teachers Aide; Acpl Chr; Band; Mrchg Band; Pep Band; Yrbk; Kayettes; Pblshd HS Wrtr; KU.

GROAT, MIKE E; Rose Hill HS; Derby, KS; (3); Yrbk; Intrml Bsktbl; Var L Crs Cntry; Intrml Ftbl; Var L Trk; High Hon Roll; Gold Key Schlstc Art Comp; KS ST; Engrng.

GROENING, JAMI D; Marion HS; Marion, KS; (4); 24/62; Treas Church Yth Grp; Sec 4-H; FHA; Natl FFA Org; Office Aide; Teachers Aide; Sec Band; Flag Corp; Mrchg Band; Pep Band; Tabor Coll; Elem Educ.

GROENING, JENNY; Marion HS; Marion, KS; (4); 2/51; Am Leg Aux Girls St; Church Yth Grp; Dance Clb; Drm Mjr(t); Capt Flag Corp; School Musical; Swing Chorus; Ed Yrbk; Capt Chrldng; NHS; DARE Role Model; Multiple Yr Listing; Emporia ST U; Sec Engl Ed.

GROESBECK, ELI J; Washburn Rural HS; Topeka, KS; (3); Chess Clb; Cmnty Wkr; Computer Clb; Debate Tm; Model UN; NFL; Speech Tm; Band; Mrchg Band; Pep Band; Sam Brownback Senate Campaign Vol Staff 96.

GROFF, MICHAEL R; Manhattan HS; Manhattan, KS; (2); Chess Clb; FCA; FBLA; Spanish Clb; Var L Swmmng; Hon Roll; NHS; Manhattan Marlins USS Swm Clb; St Thomas More CYO; Engr/Arch.

GROGAN, TRISHIA R; Basehor Linwood HS; Basehor, KS; (3); 5/99; Math Clb; Chorus; Mgr Rptr Nwsp; High Hon Roll; U Of KS; Tchng/Bus.

GRONNIGER, MATT; Olathe North Sr HS; Olathe, KS; (2); French Clb; Quiz Bowl; Science Clb; Band; Mrchg Band; Pep Band; School Musical; Variety Show; JV Tennis; JV Wrstlng; Chrch Orch; Architecture.

GROOM, REBECCA A; Quinter Jr Sr HS; Quinter, KS; (3); Church Yth Grp; Chorus; Church Choir; School Musical; School Play; Stage Crew; Rptr Yrbk; Mgr(s); Hon Roll; Ntl Merit Schol; Colby CC; Eng.

GROSE, EMILY; Bern Schl; Bern, KS; (3); Letterman Clb; Band; Chorus; Mrchg Band; Sec Stu Cncl; Var Bsktbl; Vllybl; DAR Awd; Hon Roll; NHS; STUCO Sec 3 Yrs; KAYS VP/PRES; Elem Ed.

GROSS, APRIL N; Blue Valley HS; Stilwell, KS; (2); JV Sftbl; Hon Roll; Sftbl; Medicine.

GROSS, GEOFFREY; Larned HS; Larned, KS; (3); 8/85; Am Leg Boys St; Church Yth Grp; FCA; 4-H; Chorus; JV Var Bsktbl; L Var Ftbl; L Var Golf; Hon Roll; NHS; Natl Yng Ldrs Conf; KS 4 A St Golf Trnmnt; Bsktbll Ref; KS ST; Pre Med.

GROSS, JEFF; Canton-Galva HS; Galva, KS; (3); 3/48; Am Leg Boys St; FBLA; HOBY; Quiz Bowl; SADD; Pres Soph Cls; Treas Jr Cls; Ofcr Stu Cncl; Var Bsktbl; High Hon Roll; Meteorology.

GROSS, JESSICA; Ness City HS; Bazine, KS; (3); 3/38; Pep Clb; Quiz Bowl; Scholastic Bowl; Service Clb; VP Jr Cls; JV Bsktbl; High Hon Roll; NHS; KS ST; Anml Sci.

GROSS, LACY D; Hays HS; Hays, KS; (1); Pep Clb; Ft Hays ST Univ; Comps.

GROSS, MARSHALL A; Shawnee Mission South Ctr; Overland Park, KS; (3); Church Yth Grp; JA; Teachers Aide; Pres Acad Fit Awd; Lang, Cultural, Geo Pol Of Russia; Intnl Bus.

GROSS, MEGAN; Winfield HS; Winfield, KS; (3); 33/148; Bus Profs of Am; Church Yth Grp; Orch; Var L Tennis; Hon Roll; NHS; Spts Med.

GROSS, MICHAEL L; Canton-Galva HS; Galva, KS; (2); 1/35; VP FBLA; HOBY; Quiz Bowl; Pres SADD; Pres Frsh Cls; Pres Jr Cls; Ofcr Stu Cncl; High Hon Roll; NHS; Prfct Atten Awd; US Air Force Acad; Arntcs/Plt.

GROSS, TIFFANY D; Silver Lake Jr Sr HS; Silver Lake, KS; (4); 14/43; Library Aide; Teachers Aide; Band; Chorus; Capt Flag Corp; Mrchg Band; Pep Band; School Musical; Vllybl; Hon Roll; Washburn Univ; Comp Tech.

GROSSARDT, AMBER L; Claflin Jr Sr HS; Claflin, KS; (4); 2/27; VP Treas FHA; Pep Clb; Scholastic Bowl; Band; Pep Band; Variety Show; Sec Frsh Cls; Sec Soph Cls; Pres Jr Cls; Pres Sr Cls; Barton Cnty CC; Nrsng.

GROSSER, MICHAEL R; Junction City HS; Junction City, KS; (3); #2 in class; Am Leg Boys St; Scholastic Bowl; Ofcr Jr Cls; Ftbl; Trk; Wt Lftg; High Hon Roll; NHS; Pres Acad Fit Awd; Dare Role Model; Tutor.

GROSSMAN, ANDREW M; Blue Valley North HS; Leawood, KS; (2); Cmnty Wkr; Model UN; Orch; School Musical; Rep Frsh Cls; Rep Soph Cls; Sec Jr Cls; Intrml Bsbl; JV Socr; Hon Roll; Spirit Clb.

GROTHER, LAURA; Northern Heights HS; Americus, KS; (2); 1/60; Church Yth Grp; FBLA; Sec Science Clb; SADD; School Musical; Chrldng; Hon Roll; NHS; Pep Clb; Quiz Bowl; VIP Show Choir; Genetic Engrng.

GROTHUSEN, DALLAS; Scott Comm HS; Scott City, KS; (4); 16/75; Church Yth Grp; Sec Treas 4-H; Treas Intnl Clb; Sec Natl FFA Org; Sec Soph Cls; VP Sr Cls; Var L Tennis; 4-H Awd; Hon Roll; Kiwanis Awd; 4-H Cncl Rptr; K-ST Solina; Elctrncs Eng.

GROVE, ANDREW R; Shawnee Mission N HS; Overland Park, KS; (1); 121/500; Pep Clb; Golf; Fire Dept Explr; U Of KS; Firefighter.

GROVER, JON; Weskan Schl; Weskan, KS; (2); 2/12; Pep Clb; Quiz Bowl; Speech Tm; Band; Chorus; School Play; Yrbk; VP Soph Cls; Bsktbl; High Hon Roll; KS ST; Engr.

GROVER, LORI; Field Kindley Mem Sr HS; Coffeyville, KS; (4); 1/133; Ofcr Frsh Cls; Var Bsktbl; Pom Pon; Var Sftbl; High Hon Roll; NHS; Pres Schlr; St Schlr; Val; Coffeyville CC; Elem Ed.

GROVER, SCOTT; North Central HS; Morrowville, KS; (4); 6/10; Pres 4-H; FBLA; Pres Natl FFA Org; SADD; Chorus; School Musical; Swing Chorus; Capt Bsktbl; Cit Awd; 4-H Awd; Southeast CC; Agricultural Ed.

GROW, AMANDA; Central Jr Sr HS; Atlanta, KS; (3); 1/35; Teachers Aide; School Play; Ed Nwsp; Pres Jr Cls; Var L Bsktbl; Capt Chrldng; Var L Sftbl; Var L Vllybl; High Hon Roll; NHS; Chld Spch Thrpst.

GRUBB, ANNA M; Iola Sr HS; Iola, KS; (3); Church Yth Grp; SADD; Church Choir; Jazz Band; JV Crs Cntry; Mgr(s); Hon Roll; Hon Piano Clb Pres; Poem Pub; Emporia ST Univ; Tchg/Psych.

GRUBB, LESAH J; Quivira Heights HS; Holyrood, KS; (3); 7/26; Am Leg Aux Girls St; Letterman Clb; Band; Chorus; Var L Bsktbl; Var L Trk; Var L Vllybl; High Hon Roll; Hon Roll; FCA; Kays Clb; Bio.

GRUBER, KELLI; Hope HS; Hope, KS; (2); FBLA; FHA; Natl FFA Org; Scholastic Bowl; SADD; Chorus; Rep Stu Cncl; Bsktbl; Chrldng; 4-H Awd; KS ST U; Vet.

GRUENBAUM, MICHAEL; Immaculata HS; Leavenworth, KS; (3); Am Leg Boys St; Cmnty Wkr; Dance Clb; Intnl Clb; Teachers Aide; Socr; Tennis; French Hon Soc; High Hon Roll; FIFA Soccer Referee; KS ST Awd; Hnrb Mntn In Span; Creighton; Lang; Intnl Relations.

GRUNBACHER, LORI R; Andale HS; Mount Hope, KS; (1); Church Yth Grp; Cmnty Wkr; 4-H; Spanish Clb; SADD; Varsity Clb; Band; Chorus; Drm Mjr(t); Mrchg Band; Emporia ST Hnrble Mntn Gen Math Clss/ST Awd 96.

GRUNDER, JENNIFER; St John Jr Sr HS; Saint John, KS; (1); Church Yth Grp; Pep Clb; SADD; Band; Pep Band; School Play; JV Var Bsktbl; JV Var Crs Cntry; JV Var Trk; High Hon Roll; Kayetts Brd Mem 2 Yrs; KU; PT.

GRUNDY, JENNIFER R; Field Kindley Mem Sr HS; Coffeyville, KS; (4); Church Yth Grp; FCA; Spanish Clb; Teachers Aide; Mrchg Band; JV Var Bsktbl; JV Var Sftbl; JV Var Vllybl; Coffeyville CC; Prim Ed Tchr.

GRUNER, BETHANY C; Eureka Jr Sr HS; Eureka, KS; (4); Church Yth Grp; FHA; Letterman Clb; Quiz Bowl; Scholastic Bowl; Science Clb; Spanish Clb; SADD; Yrbk; Lit Mag; Dana Col; Grphcdesgn.

GRUNEWALD, MICHAEL G; Wamego HS; Wamego, KS; (1); Cmnty Wkr; FCA; FBLA; Scholastic Bowl; SADD; Treas Frsh Cls; Bsktbl; Golf; Cit Awd; Hon Roll; CPA.

GRUNOY, CHAD A; Field Kindley Mem Sr HS; Coffeyville, KS; (2); 1/175; Church Yth Grp; Office Aide; Teachers Aide; Var L Bsktbl; Var L Crs Cntry; Var L Trk; High Hon Roll; Pres Acad Fit Awd.

GRUSHANSKAYA, ANNA; Blue Valley HS; Overland Park, KS; (2); Office Aide; Teachers Aide; JV Tennis; High Hon Roll; Hon Roll; KU; Psych.

GRUWELL, SARAH; Waconda East HS; Glen Elder, KS; (4); Cmnty Wkr; FHA; Varsity Clb; Band; School Play; Yrbk; Chrldng; Golf; Vllybl; Hon Roll; Barton Cty; Chld Dev.

GRZENDA, ADRIENNE; Holton HS; Holton, KS; (3); 1/73; VP Sec Model UN; Var Capt Quiz Bowl; Speech Tm; Band; Ed Nwsp; Mgr Bsktbl; JV Sftbl; High Hon Roll; NHS; CNFL Natl Alt Ortn; St Rtng Of I Brss Qntet & Extmprns Spkng; U Of KS; Med.

GUATNEY, ADAM D; Yates Ctr HS; Yates Center, KS; (4); Art Clb; FCA; FHA; Spanish Clb; SADD; Rep Stu Cncl; Var L Bsbl; Var L Bsktbl; Var L Ftbl; Hon Roll; US Navy; Cmptr Oper.

GUATNEY, NICHOLAS J; Yates Ctr HS; Yates Center, KS; (2); Art Clb; FCA; SADD; JV Bsbl; JV Bsktbl; JV Var Ftbl; Hon Roll; Navy.

GUCCIONE, GRETCHEN; Abilene HS; Abilene, KS; (2); Church Yth Grp; Sec German Clb; NFL; School Play; Chrldng; Tennis; High Hon Roll; Stu Of Wk In Ftns Cls; CPR Cert & Lfgrd Cert; Brigham Young U; Ed.

GUENTHER, MARTIN R; Blue Valley Nw HS; Overland Park, KS; (3); Boy Scts; Church Yth Grp; German Clb; Band; Mrchg Band; Pep Band; Hon Roll; KS ST; Engr.

GUERRA, TINA M; Oskaloosa HS; Oskaloosa, KS; (2); 5/90; Church Yth Grp; Rptr FBLA; Letterman Clb; SADD; Pres Soph Cls; Var Bsktbl; Co-Capt Pom Pon; High Hon Roll; NHS; Debate Tm; Johnson Cty CC; Dntl Hygiene.

GUESS, DENEIKA; Washington HS; Kansas City, KS; (1); Pep Clb; Spanish Clb; Var Chrldng; Spellman.

GUETTERMAN, LEIGH; Louisburg HS; Bucyrus, KS; (1); Church Yth Grp; Cmnty Wkr; Ofcr Frsh Cls; Ofcr Stu Cncl; Var Chrldng; Var Vllybl; Hon Roll; KSU; Tchr.

GUEVARA, DINA; Garden City Sr HS; Garden City, KS; (4); 53/313; French Clb; SADD; Teachers Aide; Sec Sr Cls; High Hon Roll; Hon Roll; Prfct Atten Awd; La Familia VP; Bus Admin.

GUINN, BILLY E; Wichita South HS; Wichita, KS; (3); 25/250; Ftbl; DECA Clb Pres; DECA St Cconf 6th Pl; Wichita ST Univ; Mrktg; Bus.

GUINN, KEVAN K; Maize HS; Wichita, KS; (3); Letterman Clb; Office Aide; SADD; Acpl Chr; Band; Chorus; Jazz Band; Mrchg Band; Pep Band; School Musical; Drum Line Section Ldr; Teach Percussion To Yng People; KS ST Univ; Music/Bus.

GUINN, LISA L; Wellington Sr HS; Wellington, KS; (3); Boy Scts; Bus Profs of Am; 4-H; Natl FFA Org; Vllybl; 4-H Awd; NHS; Prfct Atten Awd; Lions Jr Awd; FFA WA Ldrshp Conf; Whos Who Govt Stu; Horticulture.

GULICK, CARRIE E; Ft Scott HS; Fort Scott, KS; (4); #1 in class; Office Aide; Pep Clb; Spanish Clb; SADD; Chorus; Rptr Nwsp; Trk; Vllybl; Hon Roll; NHS; Physics Clb Treas; Ft Scott CC; Nrsng.

GULINSON, ELIZABETH E; Blue Valley Northwest HS; Overland Park, KS; (3); Drama Clb; NFL; Thesps; Chorus; School Musical; School Play; Socr; Tennis; Hon Roll; Debate Tm; Poem Pub/Taped Natl Lib Congress; Coterie Theatres Plywrghts Rngtbl VP; Rotary 4/Wy Spch Schlsp Cont; Ed/Bus Mngmt.

GULLETT, MELISSA G; Leavenworth HS; Leavenworth, KS; (4); 56/289; Natl Beta Clb; SADD; Teachers Aide; Thesps; Acpl Chr; Mrchg Band; Swing Chorus; Chrldng; High Hon Roll; NHS; U Of KS; Nrsng.

GULLICKSON, ERIN; Blue Valley Northwest HS; Overland Park, KS; (4); 30/425; Church Yth Grp; Cmnty Wkr; FCA; Hosp Aide; Q&S; Church Choir; Rptr Nwsp; Bsktbl; Powder Puff Ftbl; Swmmng.

GULLINO, ALYCEE M; J C Harmon HS; Kansas City, KS; (3); Cmnty Wkr; FCA; JA; Key Clb; School Play; Yrbk; Cit Awd; High Hon Roll; Drama Clb; French Clb; Upward Bound; FCA & Theater Dept Publicist; KU; Art; Mass Commnctns.

GUNLOCK, KRISTAL I; Leroy HS; Le Roy, KS; (3); Am Leg Aux Girls St; Church Yth Grp; Math Tm; Drill Tm; Capt Chrldng; Var Trk; Capt Vllybl; High Hon Roll; Band; Treas Frsh Cls; Medicine.

GUNNOE, DELYLA M; Acad Of Mt St Scholastica; Atchison, KS; (3); Church Yth Grp; GAA; Pep Clb; Chorus; JV Bsktbl; JV Trk; JV Var Vllybl; Hon Roll; Jr NHS; Spanish NHS; Bsktbl; Vlybl; Trck; Occptnl Thrpst.

GUNTHER, CORINNE S; Lawrence HS; Lawrence, KS; (2); Library Aide; Office Aide; Band; Chorus; School Musical; School Play; Chrldng; Vllybl; Project Freedom; KS Univ; Bus/Ed.

GUNTHER, CRAIG; Valley Falls HS; Valley Falls, KS; (3); Cmnty Wkr; Teachers Aide; Acpl Chr; Chorus; Jazz Band; Bsktbl; Hon Roll.

GUPTA, NIHAR P; Blue Valley North HS; Leawood, KS; (2); Church Yth Grp; Cmnty Wkr; Debate Tm; French Clb; Math Tm; Model UN; NFL; Temple Yth Grp; High Hon Roll; Cngrssnl Yth Ldrshp Cncl WA DC; 1st, 2nd, 3rd Pl Mdls KCATM Math Cmptn.

GURIES, ERICA L; Salina HS Central; Salina, KS; (3); 7/350; Cmnty Wkr; Debate Tm; Sec NFL; VP Pres Thesps; School Play; Phtg Rptr Nwsp; Rep Stu Cncl; Pom Pon; NHS; Ntl Merit Schol; Intnl Bus; Mrktg.

GUSTAFSON, ERIC C; Olathe East Sr HS; Overland Park, KS; (2); Art Clb; Church Yth Grp; Latin Clb; Teachers Aide; Schol Art Awd; WI Luth Univ; Med.

GUSTAFSON, ERIC S; Shawnee Heights HS; Berryton, KS; (1); High Hon Roll; Prfct Atten Awd; HS Rodeo; Farm; Ranch; Rodeo.

GUSTUS, CLIFFORD D; Ellsworth HS; Geneseo, KS; (2); VP Frsh Cls; JV Bsktbl; Var Ftbl; Var Golf; Var Trk; Hon Roll.

GUTHRIE, JAMIE L; Dodge City HS; Dodge City, KS; (3); Church Yth Grp; Cmnty Wkr; Intnl Clb; Yrbk; Vllybl; Emporia; Psych.

GUTIERREZ, ERICA E; Andover HS; Andover, KS; (3); Quiz Bowl; Band; Jazz Band; Mrchg Band; Pep Band; Var Tennis; Hon Roll; Regional & St Music Contests; Macy Schlr; Pre-Med.

GUTIERREZ, JENNY A; Leavenworth HS; Leavenworth, KS; (1); Church Yth Grp; Cmnty Wkr; Drama Clb; Hosp Aide; Band; Chorus; Mrchg Band; School Musical; School Play; High Hon Roll; Blt; Cndy Strpng; Kds FACE; Meteorology.

GUTOWSKI, NICOLE M; Washburn Rural HS; Topeka, KS; (2); 76/380; Church Yth Grp; Debate Tm; SADD; Rptr Yrbk; High Hon Roll; Hon Roll; Lifeguard; Wrtng Stories; KS Univ.

GUY, KATIE; Trinity Catholic HS; Newton, KS; (1); Band; Chorus; Pep Band; Var Bsktbl; JV Var Trk; JV Vllybl; High Hon Roll; Pres Schlr; Pol Sci.

GUY, SHERRA; Jefferson West HS; Meriden, KS; (2); Letterman Clb; Pep Clb; Band; Mrchg Band; Pep Band; Powder Puff Ftbl; Vllybl; Hon Roll; Teens As Tchrs; Jefferson Cty Teen Drug/Alchl Cltn; Soc Svcs.

GUYER, DONNA B; Highland Park HS; Topeka, KS; (3); Cit Awd; High Hon Roll; Hon Roll; Bus Stu Of Month; U Of KS; Bio.

GWARTNEY, CARA L; St Thomas Aquinas HS; Overland Park, KS; (4); 143/231; Church Yth Grp; Key Clb; SADD; Teachers Aide; Acpl Chr; Cit Awd; Hon Roll; Fewfer Awd; Chrstn Ldrshp Awd; Dinner Theaters; Plays; KS ST Univ.

GWIN, STAPHNI K; Silver Lake Jr Sr HS; Silver Lake, KS; (3); 5/51; Church Yth Grp; NFL; School Musical; School Play; Swing Chorus; Pres Soph Cls; Pres Jr Cls; Bsktbl; Chrldng; NHS; IN Wesleyan Univ; Music.

GWIN, STEPHANI; Silver Lake Jr Sr HS; Silver Lake, KS; (3); 5/60; Church Yth Grp; NFL; Speech Tm; Acpl Chr; Ofcr Soph Cls; Ofcr Jr Cls; JV Var Bsktbl; Var Chrldng; High Hon Roll; NHS; Music.

HA, STACY; Salina HS Central; Salina, KS; (3); 28/290; Drama Clb; French Clb; Quiz Bowl; Teachers Aide; VP Thesps; School Musical; School Play; Stage Crew; Ed Yrbk; High Hon Roll; 1st Reg KS Schlstc Press Assn Cntst; 1st ST KS Schlstc Prs Assn Cntst; Perf ST Thespian Conf Show; Fordham Univ.

HAACK, LINDSEY; Cheylin HS; Bird City, KS; (4); 2/14; Am Leg Aux Girls St; Treas Church Yth Grp; Dance Clb; FHA; SADD; Band; Church Choir; Drill Tm; Mrchg Band; Pep Band; 96 Cheyenne Cty Jr Miss 1st Rnnr-Up; U Of KS; Sprts Jrnlsm.

HAAG, ERIC; Leavenworth HS; Leavenworth, KS; (4); Am Leg Boys St; Cmnty Wkr; Drama Clb; Letterman Clb; Math Tm; NFL; Pres Q&S; Teachers Aide; Thesps; Varsity Clb; Schlr Dstnctn; 2nd Pl John Etheridge Mmrl Prfrmng Arts Schlrshp; I At ST Solos/Ensembles; Pittsburg ST Univ; Vclst/Actr.

HAAG, MICHAEL R; Leavenworth HS; Leavenworth, KS; (2); Cmnty Wkr; Science Clb; Chorus; School Musical; Swing Chorus; Socr; High Hon Roll.

HAAS, ANNE; Thomas More Prep-Marion HS; Hays, KS; (3); Latin Clb; Nwsp; Yrbk; Rep Frsh Cls; Pres Soph Cls; Rep Jr Cls; Bsktbl; Vllybl; High Hon Roll; Hon Roll; Psych.

HAAS, KATY B; Blue Valley Northwest HS; Overland Park, KS; (3); Powder Puff Ftbl; Var Tennis; NHS; KAYS Clb Mem; Husky Awd Mem.

HAAS, TY; Olathe South Sr HS; Olathe, KS; (3); Cmnty Wkr; Ofcr Frsh Cls; Pittsburgh Univ; His.

HAASE, MICAH; Galena HS; Galena, KS; (3); JV Bsbl; Hon Roll.

HABIGER, TYLER J; Quivira Heights HS; Bushton, KS; (1); Church Yth Grp; Letterman Clb; Band; Rep Frsh Cls; Ofcr Stu Cncl; JV Bsktbl; JV Ftbl; Var Golf; High Hon Roll; Hon Roll.

HABLUETZEL, SUZANNE M; Washington HS; Washington, KS; (4); 1/30; Am Leg Aux Girls St; Church Yth Grp; FCA; Girl Scts; SADD; Band; School Play; Treas Sr Cls; JV Golf; NHS; Elks Schlr; St Schlrshp Tests; Ft Hays St Math Relays; Emporia ST U; Scndry Ed.

HACKING, CHARITY; Fairfield HS; Turon, KS; (3); Church Yth Grp; Letterman Clb; NFL; SADD; Teachers Aide; Chorus; School Play; Rptr Yrbk; Pres Soph Cls; Sec Jr Cls.

HACKLER, JEREMIAH G; Washburn Rural HS; Topeka, KS; (2); 13/380; Debate Tm; Model UN; Quiz Bowl; Band; Mrchg Band; Orch; Pep Band; Swmmng; High Hon Roll; Topeka Yth Symphony & Wind Ensemble; Sci Field.

HACKLEY, MARLENA L; Wichita East HS; Wichita, KS; (4); 29/278; Chorus; Lit Mag; Hon Roll; Acad Ltr; Dance; Story, Art Pub Schl Lit Mgzn; Wichita ST U; Creative Wrtng.

HACKNEY, COLEY G; Herndon Schl; Oberlin, KS; (3); Band; Chorus; Mrchg Band; Pep Band; Var Bsktbl; Var Ftbl; Var Trk; Hon Roll; Chem.

HACKNEY, SHANELE D; Protection Schl; Protection, KS; (3); 6/17; Church Yth Grp; Letterman Clb; Sec Treas Pep Clb; Band; Chorus; Drm Mjr(t); Flag Corp; Yrbk; Var Bsktbl; Var Sftbl.

HACKNEY, TYLER J; Herndon Schl; Oberlin, KS; (2); Ftbl; Hon Roll; Warrens Occptnl Tech Inst; Auto.

HADLEY, LAURA; Hillsboro HS; Hillsboro, KS; (3); Church Yth Grp; Girl Scts; Band; Chorus; Mrchg Band; Pep Band; Sec Soph Cls; Vllybl; High Hon Roll; NHS.

HADORN, BETHANY D; Wellington Sr HS; Wellington, KS; (2); Church Yth Grp; Band; Church Choir; Ofcr Stu Cncl; Mgr(s); Swmmng; Hon Roll; Jr NHS; Mrchg Band; Bsktbl; Lions Awd; Piano Guild; KS ST U; RN.

HADSALL, LACEY V; St Marys HS; Emmett, KS; (1); Church Yth Grp; Debate Tm; FBLA; Sec FHA; Hosp Aide; Pep Clb; Band; Chorus; JV Bsktbl; Hon Roll; Biochem/Microbio.

HAFFNER, KAREN A; Junction City HS; Junction City, KS; (3); 12/300; Am Leg Aux Girls St; Church Yth Grp; Service Clb; SADD; Band; Church Choir; Mrchg Band; Pep Band; Ofcr Soph Cls; High Hon Roll; Emporia St Univ; Ed.

HAGAR, KELLIE L; Wellington Sr HS; Wellington, KS; (2); Church Yth Grp; Cmnty Wkr; Natl FFA Org; Spanish Clb; Pres SADD; L Bsktbl; L Sftbl; L Tennis; High Hon Roll; Jr NHS; Med.

HAGEDORN, AMY E; Robert E Clark Jr HS; Bonner Springs, KS; (1); Church Yth Grp; Band; Chorus; Mrchg Band; Rep Frsh Cls; Rep Stu Cncl; Bsktbl; Vllybl; High Hon Roll; Hon Roll; Dist Band; St Choir.

HAGEDORN, SCOTT; Bonner Spgs HS; Bonner Springs, KS; (3); Am Leg Boys St; Church Yth Grp; Spanish Clb; Band; Pep Band; Var Crs Cntry; Cit Awd; NHS; Ntl Merit Ltr; Dist Band; Sci Olympiad-Mgr-Natl Cmptn.

HAGEMAN, BILL; Kingman HS; Kingman, KS; (3); Church Yth Grp; 4-H; FBLA; Spanish Clb; Var Bsbl; JV Bsktbl; JV Ftbl; JV Wt Lftg; High Hon Roll.

HAGEMAN, DAVID R; Hoxie HS; Hoxie, KS; (3); 13/43; Boy Scts; Debate Tm; Office Aide; JV Bsktbl; JV Ftbl; Hon Roll; Eagle Scout; Comp Sci; Comp Prgmr.

HAGEMAN, MICHAEL; Abilene HS; Abilene, KS; (4); 9/125; Am Leg Boys St; Pres Church Yth Grp; Sec FCA; Chorus; School Musical; Rep Stu Cncl; Var Crs Cntry; Var Trk; Var L Wrstlng; High Hon Roll; KS ST Univ; Civil Engrng.

HAGEMAN, ROBBIE R; Fowler HS; Fowler, KS; (4); 5/12; Church Yth Grp; Cmnty Wkr; Math Tm; Spanish Clb; Speech Tm; Teachers Aide; Varsity Clb; Stage Crew; Bsktbl; Cit Awd; Dodge City Comm Coll; Pre-Engrn.

HAGEMAN, SHERRI; Kingman HS; Spivey, KS; (2); #1 in class; FBLA; SADD; JV Bsktbl; Var L Chrldng; Powder Puff Ftbl; Sftbl; JV Vllybl; High Hon Roll; NHS; Treas Church Yth Grp; Acad All Lge Awd; CYO Vlybl.

HAGEMAN, STEVE; Kingman HS; Spivey, KS; (4); 2/70; FBLA; VP Rep Sr Cls; Ofcr Stu Cncl; Var L Ftbl; Var L Trk; Cit Awd; High Hon Roll; NHS; Sal; Ntl Merit Schol; CYO Vllybl; Coed Sftbl; I Dare You Awd; KS ST U; Engrng.

HAGEMANN, MICHELLE; Girard HS; Hepler, KS; (4); 7/69; Am Leg Aux Girls St; Church Yth Grp; 4-H; SADD; Band; Yrbk; Var L Bsktbl; 4-H Awd; High Hon Roll; NHS; Pittsburg ST U; Bus Admin.

HAGEN, JENNY; Hillsboro HS; Hillsboro, KS; (1); 1/73; Church Yth Grp; Chorus; Vllybl; High Hon Roll.

HAGER, ANNA N; Quivira Heights HS; Bushton, KS; (3); Church Yth Grp; FCA; German Clb; Hosp Aide; Letterman Clb; Office Aide; Pep Clb; Teachers Aide; Chorus; Church Choir; Gary Nordstrom Photo Awd; Hays Artshw.

HAGER, JENNIFER M; Gardner-Edgerton HS; Edgerton, KS; (4); 21/109; Church Yth Grp; Pres FCA; Pres French Clb; Band; School Musical; Yrbk; Rep Stu Cncl; Capt Var Bsktbl; Var L Sftbl; JV Vllybl; Natural Hlprs; Mid Amer Nazarene Coll; Soc Sci.

HAGER, MEGAN; Gardner-Edgerton HS; Edgerton, KS; (2); Church Yth Grp; FCA; Pep Clb; Spanish Clb; Band; Mrchg Band; Pep Band; School Play; Var Capt Chrldng; Hon Roll; NCA All Amer Chrldng Tm; Natural Helper; Mid Amer Nazarene Coll; Chld Ps.

HAGERMAN, ABIGAIL E; South Haven Schl; South Haven, KS; (1); Scholastic Bowl; Band; Jazz Band; Mrchg Band; Pep Band; JV Bsktbl; Var Chrldng; JV L Vllybl; High Hon Roll; Pres Acad Fit Awd; Quiz Bowl; FHA; FCA; U Of Sks; Neurosurgeon.

HAGERMAN, SARA; South Haven Schl; South Haven, KS; (4); 2/15; Church Yth Grp; FCA; FHA; HOBY; Letterman Clb; Natl FFA Org; Pep Clb; Quiz Bowl; Band; Chorus; Semper Fidelis Awd; Yth For Music; KSU Hnr Band; Emporia ST U; Music Ed.

HAGERMAN, STEPHEN; Blue Valley HS; Overland Park, KS; (2); Church Yth Grp; Speech Tm; Band; Mrchg Band; Pep Band; Var Bsktbl; Var Tennis; Var Trk; Intrml Wt Lftg; High Hon Roll; Bus.

HAGLER, AMANDA; Dodge City HS; Dodge City, KS; (2); Debate Tm; Intnl Clb; Spanish Clb; SADD; Rptr Yrbk; JV Chrldng; Kansas Univ.

HAGMAN, KATHERINE K; Norton Comm HS; Lenora, KS; (3); 8/56; Drama Clb; Sec VP 4-H; VP FHA; Library Aide; Model UN; Pep Clb; Q&S; SADD; Acpl Chr; Band; KAYS; Attnd Ctznshp Washington Focus Trip 96; Attnd Natl 4-H Congress 96; KS ST Univ; Interior Dsgn.

HAGUE, MICHAEL; Peabody-Burns Jr Sr HS; Peabody, KS; (1); Church Yth Grp; Cmnty Wkr; FCA; Quiz Bowl; Band; Bsktbl; Ftbl; Trk; Mrchg Band; Pep Band; Peer Helper; Sound Tech For Schl Prgms.

HAHN, SARAH L; Hanston Jr Sr HS; Hanston, KS; (4); 6/13; Church Yth Grp; Teachers Aide; Ed Nwsp; Phtg Yrbk; Pres Frsh Cls; Pres Soph Cls; Pres Jr Cls; Capt Bsktbl; Trk; Capt Vllybl; Ft Hays St Univ; Elem Ed.

HAIL, STEPHANIE; Garden City Sr HS; Garden City, KS; (3); FHA; Key Clb; Math Tm; Acpl Chr; Rep Stu Cncl; Bsktbl; Trk; Vllybl; NHS; Share Tm Stu Spprt Grp; KS Ambssdrs Choir Toured Europe.

HAILE, JENNIFER W; Blue Vlly HS; Shawnee Mission, KS; (3); Debate Tm; High Hon Roll; Hon Roll; NHS; Elem Schl Tutr; Math Tm; Criminolgy.

HAIN, RACHELLE L; Wellington Sr HS; Wellington, KS; (3); Pres SADD; Band; Mrchg Band; Pep Band; Var Trk; Var Vllybl; High Hon Roll; Jr NHS; Office Aide; Hon Roll; Chrch Yth Grp; Rtry Awd; Tri St Music Fstvl I Rtng; Rgnl Music Fstvl I Rtng; WSU.

HAINES, BRIAN T; Olathe South Sr HS; Olathe, KS; (3); German Clb; Band; JV Crs Cntry; JV Socr; Var Trk; JV Wrstlng; Hon Roll; NHS; Pres Acad Fit Awd.

HAINES, CARINA L; Wichita North HS; Wichita, KS; (3); Church Yth Grp; Library Aide; Hon Roll; NHS; Hrsbck Rdng; Anml Scis.

HAINES, DARLA A; Salina HS South; Salina, KS; (3); Spanish Clb; Band; Chorus; Mrchg Band; Variety Show; High Hon Roll; Hon Roll; KS ST U; Educ.

HAINES, DEREK G; Wellington Sr HS; Wellington, KS; (3); 28/161; Cmnty Wkr; Natl FFA Org; Var Bsktbl; Var Ftbl; Hon Roll; NHS; KS U; Sprts Med.

HAINES, MELANIE J; Stockton HS; Stockton, KS; (2); #1 in class; FHA; HOBY; Natl FFA Org; Band; L Bsktbl; Trk; Vllybl; 4-H Awd; High Hon Roll.

HAINES, TRACI R; Garden Plain Jr Sr HS; Garden Plain, KS; (2); 2/30; Church Yth Grp; Letterman Clb; Quiz Bowl; Spanish Clb; Speech Tm; SADD; VP Frsh Cls; Var Crs Cntry; Var Trk; High Hon Roll.

HAJEK, MICHELLE; Centre Jr Sr HS; Lost Springs, KS; (3); 4/16; Band; Chorus; Sec Frsh Cls; Rep Soph Cls; VP Jr Cls; Capt Chrldng; High Hon Roll; Hon Roll; NHS; Pres Acad Fit Awd; Butler; Asst PT.

HAKE, KATIE B; Buhler HS; Hutchinson, KS; (2); 12/190; Sec Pres Church Yth Grp; Ofcr FCA; Band; Chorus; School Musical; Rep Stu Cncl; Tennis; Crimestoppers Club; In-ST Univ.

HALBLEIB, ERIN E; Ness City HS; Ness City, KS; (2); Sec Church Yth Grp; Quiz Bowl; Band; School Play; Var Chrldng; Tennis; High Hon Roll; NHS; Cmnty Wkr; NFL; KAYS Bd Mem; Acad Team 1st In League; KS ST Univ; Comp Engrng.

HALDERSON, BJORN; Cunningham HS; Cunningham, KS; (2); Cmnty Wkr; 4-H; Letterman Clb; Pep Clb; Science Clb; SADD; Varsity Clb; Pres Frsh Cls; VP Soph Cls; Var L Bsktbl; KAY Clb Sec; STUCO Rep; KS ST U; Bus Mgmt.

HALE, ANGELA; Waconda East HS; Cawker City, KS; (3); 4/21; Treas FHA; HOBY; Scholastic Bowl; Varsity Clb; Band; Drill Tm; Treas Stu Cncl; Chrldng; High Hon Roll; NHS; U Of KS; Phy Ther.

HALE, ANGELA M; Belle Plaine HS; Belle Plaine, KS; (2); Library Aide; Pep Clb; Spanish Clb; SADD; Band; Jazz Band; Mrchg Band; Pep Band; KAYS; Wichita ST U; Comp Sci.

HALE, CHAD WESLEY; Topeka West HS; Topeka, KS; (3); Boy Scts; Cmnty Wkr; JA; School Musical; School Play; Variety Show; Crs Cntry; Golf; High Hon Roll; Pres Acad Fit Awd; KS Univ; Medical.

HALE, SARAH; Maize HS; Wichita, KS; (4); 32/217; Chrmn Church Yth Grp; Letterman Clb; NFL; Pres Q&S; Chorus; SADD; Teachers Aide; Varsity Clb; Ed Nwsp; JV Bsktbl; Stu Voting Task Force Rep; Yth Action Cncl Bd; High Hnr Roll; U Of KS; Jrnlsm; Span.

HALEY, AMANDA M; Goodland HS; Kanorado, KS; (2); 4-H; Chorus; DECAI Pres 95-; Sci/Bus/Ed.

HALEY, CLINT; Paola HS; Paola, KS; (3); 1/133; Am Leg Boys St; Pres Church Yth Grp; FCA; VP Pres 4-H; Pres Natl FFA Org; Scholastic Bowl; Ftbl; Golf; 4-H Awd; High Hon Roll; All-Amer Schlr; I Dare You Awd; KS ST Univ; Bus.

HALEY, CRYSTAL K; El Dorado HS; El Dorado, KS; (2); Bus Profs of Am; FHA; Spanish Clb; SADD; Tennis; Enjy Rdng/Wrtng Poetry; Stephen F Austin; Nrsg.

HALL, ABBY; Fairfield HS; Sylvia, KS; (1); 4-H; School Play; Bsktbl; Vllybl; Hon Roll; Hi Q; FAD; Forensics.

HALL, ADRIAN L; Liberal HS; Liberal, KS; (4); Church Yth Grp; Teachers Aide; Chorus; Church Choir; Ftbl; Mgr(s); Trk; Wrstlng; KS ST U; Commnctns.

HALL, ANDI; Campus HS; Wichita, KS; (3); 10/206; Church Yth Grp; Science Clb; SADD; VICA; Chorus; Ofcr Stu Cncl; High Hon Roll; Hon Roll; NHS; Acad Letter 3 Yrs; Brd Arth KS VICA Comp 2nd Pl; KS ST Univ; Arch.

HALL, ANDREW N; Maize HS; Wichita, KS; (3); 19/242; Boy Scts; Church Yth Grp; French Clb; Band; Mrchg Band; Pep Band; JV Golf; High Hon Roll; Hon Roll; NHS; Adv Wichita Wind Ensemble; Odyssey Of The Mind; M-Club; OK St Univ; Engrng.

HALL, BETHANY; Caney Valley Jr Sr HS; Caney, KS; (3); 4/85; Debate Tm; Drama Clb; Treas FHA; HOBY; NFL; School Play; Co-Ed Nwsp; Yrbk; Bsktbl; Trk; KS ST U; Law.

HALL, CHARLES R; Junction City HS; Junction City, KS; (3); Cmnty Wkr; German Clb; VICA; Yrbk; Treas Frsh Cls; Var L Ftbl; JV Golf; Trk; Wt Lftg; JV Wrstlng; Own Car Customizing Shop.

HALL, CHRIS D; Newton Sr HS; Newton, KS; (4); 72/217; Boy Scts; Chorus; Golf; Socr; Swmmng; Hon Roll; Recreational Ice Hockey; KS ST Univ; Architecture.

HALL, ERIC W; Topeka HS; Topeka, KS; (3); German Clb; High Hon Roll; Philosophy Clb; KS ST Univ; Cinematography.

HALL, JEREMIAH W; Lakin HS; Lakin, KS; (2); FCA; Band; Chorus; Jazz Band; Mrchg Band; Pep Band; Ofcr Bsbl; Bsktbl; Ftbl; Tennis.

HALL, KRYSTLE K; Riverton Schl; Baxter Springs, KS; (1); 1/70; Church Yth Grp; Cmnty Wkr; FCA; 4-H; FHA; Key Clb; Lbrn Pep Clb; Treas Band; Chorus; Church Choir.

HALL, LINDSAY M; Field Kindley Mem Sr HS; Coffeyville, KS; (2); Church Yth Grp; Drama Clb; FCA; German Clb; Chorus; Mrchg Band; School Musical; School Play; JV Vllybl; High Hon Roll.

HALL, LORI A; Northwest HS Wichita; Wichita, KS; (3); 19/327; Church Yth Grp; Intnl Clb; Teachers Aide; Hon Roll; Jr NHS; Math Tutor; Worked With ESL Stdnts On Basic Skills; Sunday Schl Aide; Elem Ed.

HALL, MELISSA M; Haven HS; Hutchinson, KS; (3); Band; Mrchg Band; Orch; Pep Band.

HALL, STEPHANIE H; Olathe East Sr HS; Overland Park, KS; (2); Church Yth Grp; Cmnty Wkr; Pep Clb; Spanish Clb; Chorus; Drill Tm; High Hon Roll; Prin Hnr Roll; KS Univ; Tch; Ed.

HALL, STEPHANIE L; Atchison Co Cmty HS; Effingham, KS; (2); Church Yth Grp; Pep Clb; Band; Church Choir; Mrchg Band; Pep Band; Variety Show; JV Chrldng; Vllybl; High Hon Roll; Baton Twirler; KS ST.

HALL, TAMARA L; Oskaloosa HS; Oskaloosa, KS; (2); Debate Tm; FBLA; Letterman Clb; Pep Clb; SADD; Varsity Clb; School Musical; School Play; Var Bsktbl; Var Chrldng; Phrmcy.

HALL, TIFFANY L; Atchison Co Cmty HS; Effingham, KS; (2); Church Yth Grp; Pep Clb; Band; Chorus; Church Choir; Mrchg Band; Pep Band; Variety Show; Vllybl; High Hon Roll; Baton Twirler; KS ST U.

HALL, TRACY R; Jefferson West HS; Meriden, KS; (2); 16/72; Church Yth Grp; FBLA; FHA; Pep Clb; SADD; Stage Crew; Powder Puff Ftbl; Trk; Vllybl; Hon Roll; Recreational Thrpst.

HALL, ZACHARY A; Kansas City Christian Schl; Lenexa, KS; (4); Church Yth Grp; Drama Clb; Thesps; Chorus; School Play; Treas Frsh Cls; Pres Jr Cls; Pres Sr Cls; Mgr(s); NHS; Liefguard; Camp Cnslr; Johnson Cty CC; Scdnry Ed.

HALLACY, AMY; St Mary's Colgan HS; Pittsburg, KS; (4); 4/25; Am Leg Aux Girls St; Church Yth Grp; Cmnty Wkr; French Clb; Girl Scts; Math Tm; Pep Clb; Science Clb; Treas Sr Cls; Sec Stu Cncl; KSU; Vet.

HALLER, JENNIFER R; Wabaunsee HS; Mc Farland, KS; (4); 12/35; Rep VP FBLA; FHA; Office Aide; School Play; Ed Nwsp; Yrbk; Pres Sr Cls; Rep Stu Cncl; Var Bsktbl; Powder Puff Ftbl; KS ST U; Publc Rltns.

HALLER, REBECCA J; Marysville HS; Home, KS; (2); Church Yth Grp; Band; Jazz Band; Mrchg Band; Pep Band; School Play; Tennis; Hon Roll; Kiwanis Awd; Prfct Atten Awd; 1st & 2nd Yr Ltr Var & Jazz Band; OK Bapt Univ; HS Band Tchr.

HALLIBURTON, BRANDI L; Field Kindley Mem Sr HS; Coffeyville, KS; (1); Church Yth Grp; German Clb; Chrldng; Gym; Sftbl; Hon Roll; Club Brit.

HALLIBURTON, KRISTIN L; Field Kindley Mem Sr HS; Coffeyville, KS; (4); #13 in class; JA; Spanish Clb; Chrldng; Trk; NHS; Pres Schlr; KS Hnr Schlr; All-Star Chrldr; KS U; Bus.

HALLING, MELISSA A; Atchison Co Cmty HS; Atchison, KS; (3); 5/51; Hosp Aide; Pres Math Clb; Mu Alpha Theta; Teachers Aide; Treas Frsh Cls; JV Capt Bsktbl; Powder Puff Ftbl; Var Vllybl; Wt Lftg; High Hon Roll; MO Western; Acctng.

HALLORAN, BRAD S; Garden City Sr HS; Garden City, KS; (1); Church Yth Grp; Debate Tm; L Golf; JV Wrstlng; Hon Roll; Motorcycle ATV Rcng; CO Univ; Medicine.

HALLUM, TROY J; Derby HS; Derby, KS; (1); JV Bsbl; JV Ftbl; L Wrstlng; High Hon Roll; Hon Roll.

HALPAIN, KRISTY; Wichita Northwest HS; Wichita, KS; (3); Bus Profs of Am; Church Yth Grp; Office Aide; Hon Roll; OK St U; Bus/Acctg.

HALSTEAD, RACHEL M; Leavenworth HS; Leavenworth, KS; (2); Chorus; KCKCC; Acctng; Arts.

HALTERMAN, KELLY; Shawnee Mission Northwest HS; Shawnee Mission, KS; (3); Church Yth Grp; GAA; Teachers Aide; Capt Var Chrldng; Sftbl; Hon Roll; NHS; Acad Ltr.

HAMBLET, BRIE E; Wabaunsee HS; Alma, KS; (4); 13/35; Drama Clb; French Clb; SADD; Yrbk; Powder Puff Ftbl; Hon Roll; Photo; Schl Play; KS St Univ; Theatr Arts.

HAMEL, ERIN J; South Haven Schl; South Haven, KS; (3); Church Yth Grp; FHA; Natl FFA Org; Pep Clb; Hon Roll; Stu Of Month; Psych.

HAMEL, NICHOLE R; Salina HS South; Salina, KS; (3); 3/250; Math Tm; Pep Clb; Capt Drill Tm; Mrchg Band; Orch; VP Stu Cncl; Capt Pom Pon; JV Var Sftbl; JV Vllybl; Hon Roll; Tn Ambcs Sec; PSAT Cmndd Stu.

HAMER, REBECCA Y; Holton HS; Denison, KS; (1); Church Yth Grp; Band; Chorus; Mrchg Band; Pep Band; High Hon Roll; Nrsng.

HAMILTON, AMANDA; Holton HS; Holton, KS; (1); Phtg Nwsp; Phtg Yrbk; Pres Soph Cls; Bsktbl; Var Chrldng; JV Var Sftbl; Vllybl; Hon Roll.

HAMILTON, AMBER N; Blue Vlly HS; Shawnee Mission, KS; (3); 10/250; Cmnty Wkr; Hon Roll; NHS; Sop Wrtng Awd; Grls St Rep; Publc Reltns.

HAMILTON, ASHLEY K; Belle Plaine HS; Belle Plaine, KS; (2); 1/60; Church Yth Grp; SADD; Drm Mjr(t); VP Frsh Cls; Pres Soph Cls; Pres Jr Cls; Pom Pon; Trk; High Hon Roll; Math Tm; KAYS; Med.

HAMILTON, ERINN B; Oxford HS; Oxford, KS; (2); Church Yth Grp; Letterman Clb; Pep Clb; JV Bsktbl; Var Chrldng; Var Crs Cntry; Var Trk; Hon Roll.

HAMILTON, JANELL C; Marais Des Cygnes Valley HS; Melvern, KS; (3); Letterman Clb; Chorus; School Musical; VP Soph Cls; VP Jr Cls; Rep Stu Cncl; Var L Bsktbl; Computer Clb; High Hon Roll; NHS; Emporia ST Univ; Home Ec.

HAMILTON, JULIE; Wichita East HS; Wichita, KS; (4); 58/296; Debate Tm; Treas Girl Scts; NFL; Office Aide; Teachers Aide; Socr; Tennis; Hon Roll; NHS; Prom Cmmtee; Grl Sct Schol; Wmn Hstry Awd; Salem St Col; Nrsing.

HAMILTON, LYNEDA; Spring Hill HS; Olathe, KS; (4); 34/97; Am Leg Aux Girls St; Church Yth Grp; FCA; 4-H; Letterman Clb; Pep Clb; Spanish Clb; SADD; Teachers Aide; Chorus; KS ST U.

HAMILTON, MICHELLE; Wichita South HS; Wichita, KS; (4); 5/292; Church Yth Grp; NFL; Scholastic Bowl; Thesps; Chorus; Sec Frsh Cls; Hist NHS; St Schlr; Campus Life Vp; Friends Univ; Pre Med.

HAMILTON, REBECCA; Smith Ctr Jr Sr HS; Smith Center, KS; (3); 4-H; FHA; Natl FFA Org; SADD; Band; Chorus; Var Capt Chrldng; Trk; 4-H Awd; Hon Roll; KAYS; Fort Hays ST Univ; Hotel Mngmt.

HAMLIN, JASON; Newton Sr HS; Newton, KS; (1); Model UN; Scholastic Bowl; Ftbl; Trk; Wt Lftg; WEBOK Awd 95.

HAMLIN, LESLI J; Douglass HS; Douglass, KS; (2); 12/85; Church Yth Grp; Cmnty Wkr; FCA; GAA; Science Clb; Bsktbl; Vllybl; Cit Awd; Hon Roll; St Schlr; Chrysalis; Wichita ST; Archeology.

HAMM, FAYE L; Goddard HS; Goddard, KS; (2); Church Yth Grp; Drama Clb; German Clb; NFL; Ofcr Band; Jazz Band; School Play; Var L Crs Cntry; JV L Socr; Science Clb; Best Bit Awd; Church Drama Grp; Piano 12 Yrs.

HAMM, JASON D; El Dorado HS; El Dorado, KS; (2); Cmnty Wkr; Letterman Clb; SADD; Chorus; JV Bsktbl; L Ftbl; Capt Trk; Cit Awd; Hon Roll; Gridiron Grt; CO St Univ.

HAMMACK, SCOTT; Leavenworth HS; Fort Leavenworth, KS; (3); Am Leg Boys St; Boy Scts; ROTC; SADD; Band; Jazz Band; JV Var Socr; High Hon Roll; NHS; Pres Acad Fit Awd; Mech Engrng.

HAMMAN, KELLY A; Shawnee Mission E Sr HS; Prairie Village, KS; (4); 159/407; Church Yth Grp; Cmnty Wkr; Office Aide; Pep Clb; SADD; Teachers Aide; Mgr(s); Hon Roll; Emporia ST Univ.

HAMMAN, RUEBEN K; Yates Ctr HS; Toronto, KS; (2); 5/60; Church Yth Grp; FCA; 4-H; FHA; Letterman Clb; Quiz Bowl; Scholastic Bowl; Service Clb; Ski Clb; Spanish Clb.

HAMMEL, SALLY; Clay Ctr Cmty HS; Clay Center, KS; (4); 1/97; Church Yth Grp; Band; Chorus; Drill Tm; Mrchg Band; Pep Band; School Play; Ed Yrbk; Sec Frsh Cls; L Var Golf; Chrysler Jr Golf Schlsp 95; KS Regnl Golf Championship Trnmt Wnnr 94, 95; KS St Golf Cmptn 2nd Pl 95; Mercer Univ; Bus; Golf Pro.

HAMMER, CATHY; Maranatha Acad; Leavenworth, KS; (3); Math Tm; Band; Chorus; Color Guard; Mrchg Band; Pep Band; School Musical; Ofcr Sr Cls; Var Chrldng; High Hon Roll; Leavenworth Cty Jr Miss 96-97; Ballet.

HAMMER, ERIN J; Ellinwood Jr Sr HS; Ellinwood, KS; (2); Church Yth Grp; Debate Tm; Quiz Bowl; Spanish Clb; Teachers Aide; Band; Mrchg Band; Pep Band; JV Bsktbl; Var Mgr(s); KAY Ofcr.

HAMMERSCHMIDT, BECKY; Hayden HS; Topeka, KS; (3); FBLA; Intnl Clb; Sec SADD; Drill Tm; High Hon Roll; NHS.

HAMMERSCHMIDT, SCOTT; Hays HS; Hays, KS; (4); 6/200; Science Clb; Band; Jazz Band; Mrchg Band; Orch; Pep Band; School Musical; Phtg Nwsp; Phtg Yrbk; Gov Hon Prg Awd; KS ST U; Elec Engrng.

HAMMES, SHAUN D; Nemaha Valley HS; Seneca, KS; (3); L Bsktbl; L Var Ftbl; JV Golf; L Var Mgr(s); Var Trk; Intrml Wt Lftg; Hon Roll; Prfct Atten Awd; St Schlr; Acctng.

HAMMIG, STACY D; Lawrence HS; Lawrence, KS; (2); FTA; German Clb; JA; High Hon Roll; Pres Acad Fit Awd; Law.

HAMMON, COURTNEY L; Bishop Carroll Catholic HS; Wichita, KS; (3); Spanish Clb; SADD; Yrbk; High Hon Roll; Hon Roll; KS St Univ; Law.

HAMMOND, ASHLEY B; Northern Valley HS; Long Island, KS; (1); Church Yth Grp; Band; Jazz Band; JV Bsktbl; JV Ftbl; Var Golf; Hon Roll; Prfct Atten Awd; KS U; Bus.

HAMMOND, FLETCHER; Eureka Jr Sr HS; Eureka, KS; (2); 1/50; Boy Scts; Church Yth Grp; French Clb; Quiz Bowl; SADD; Thesps; School Play; Yrbk; JV Golf; Kiwanis Awd; York Coll; Aerospc Engr.

HAMMOND, KRISTAN; Leroy HS; Le Roy, KS; (2); Church Yth Grp; HOBY; Pres Frsh Cls; VP Soph Cls; Ofcr Stu Cncl; Var JV Bsktbl; Var Chrldng; Var Trk; Var Vllybl; Hon Roll; Chrch Yth Band; Evangel; Art.

HAMMOND, KRISTEN; Shawnee Mission East HS; Shawnee Mission, KS; (3); 45/410; Church Yth Grp; French Clb; Natl Beta Clb; Q&S; SADD; Varsity Clb; Orch; Sprt Ed Nwsp; JV Capt Bsktbl; Var L Crs Cntry; Schlsp Pin; Jrnlsm.

HAMON, SUE; Topeka HS; Topeka, KS; (2); 3/446; Treas French Clb; Model UN; Band; Mrchg Band; Orch; Pep Band; School Musical; JV Vllybl; High Hon Roll; Natl Sci Mrt Awd; Chem.

HAMOR, EMILY; Coldwater Jr Sr HS; Coldwater, KS; (4); 3/20; FHA; Letterman Clb; Band; Pep Band; Ofcr Jr Cls; Sec Stu Cncl; Var Bsktbl; Var Vllybl; High Hon Roll; NHS; KS ST U; Elem Ed.

HAMPEL, AIMEE R; Garden Plain Jr Sr HS; Garden Plain, KS; (3); 10/35; Scholastic Bowl; SADD; Sec Frsh Cls; Pres Soph Cls; Pres Jr Cls; High Hon Roll; Hon Roll; NHS; Church Yth Grp; Red Cross Aide; Bus Acctg.

HAMPEL, ERIN M; Garden Plain Jr Sr HS; Garden Plain, KS; (2); Art Clb; Church Yth Grp; GAA; Spanish Clb; SADD; Vllybl; Hon Roll; Essay Publshd Nwspr; Photography/Radlgy Tear.

HAMPTON, AMBER; Ulysses HS; Ulysses, KS; (3); Art Clb; Spanish Clb; Var Trk; Hon Roll; Grphc Dsgn.

HAMPTON, CAROL; Lansing HS; Colorado Springs, CO; (1); Church Yth Grp; French Clb; Var L Chrldng; JV Sftbl; Hon Roll; Adv Acrobatics Dance Class 95-96; 4 Natl Acrobat Cmptns 2 Gold, 2 Silver, 2 Bro Ze Medals & 4th Pl; CO St Univ; Bio.

HAMPTON, SHAUN M; Independence HS; Independence, KS; (3); Am Leg Boys St; Cmnty Wkr; Teachers Aide; Band; Jazz Band; Mrchg Band; Pep Band; Hon Roll; Time Warner Internship; Sr Band Rep; Sunflower St Games Soccer Player; Pitt ST; Mass Commnctn.

HAMPTON, SHILEESE; Washington HS; Kansas City, KS; (3); Church Yth Grp; FCA; ROTC; SADD; Acpl Chr; Church Choir; Capt Var Chrldng; Powder Puff Ftbl; Hon Roll; NHS; Teen Hope; Langston.

HANCOCK, BROOK; Hugoton HS; Hugoton, KS; (4); 14/66; Am Leg Aux Girls St; Church Yth Grp; FCA; Quiz Bowl; Teachers Aide; Sec Treas Frsh Cls; VP Treas Stu Cncl; Bsktbl; Mgr(s); Trk; Girls Trackster Awd 94; Teens As Tchrs St Pgm; Emporia ST U; Bus.

HANCOCK, GENNIFER A; Hartford HS; Hartford, KS; (3); 4/17; FBLA; Letterman Clb; Quiz Bowl; Chrldng; Vllybl; High Hon Roll; NHS; WI St Univ; Spch Path.

HANDKE, BRIAN; Atchison Co Cmty HS; Atchison, KS; (3); Letterman Clb; Natl FFA Org; Office Aide; Band; Jazz Band; Mrchg Band; Pep Band; School Musical; Var Ftbl; Hon Roll; KS ST U.

HANDKE, MEGAN; Atchison Sr HS; Atchison, KS; (2); NFL; Quiz Bowl; JV Var Bsktbl; JV Var Socr; NHS.

HANDKE, MIRANDA E; Atchison Sr HS; Atchison, KS; (1); JV Bsktbl; JV Var Socr; Hon Roll; Univ Of Berekly.

HANDLEY, LARISSA; Troy HS; Troy, KS; (1); Church Yth Grp; Letterman Clb; Pep Clb; Var Chrldng; Hon Roll; Horsbck Rdng.

HANDLOS, DAVID; Junction City HS; Milford, KS; (3); 16/310; Am Leg Boys St; Church Yth Grp; School Musical; JV Ftbl; JV Trk; Cit Awd; High Hon Roll; NHS; Amateur Radio; KS ST Univ; Physics.

HANDS, JEREMY; Garden City Sr HS; Garden City, KS; (4); 7/313; Church Yth Grp; Key Clb; Band; JV Var Ftbl; JV Var Trk; Kiwanis Awd; NHS; St Schlr; JV Var Wt Lftg; Wild Life Sponsor; Acad Ltr; Friends U; Religion.

HANDSHUMAKER, STACY M; Field Kindley Mem Sr HS; Coffeyville, KS; (2); Drama Clb; German Clb; GAA; Thesps; Band; Mrchg Band; School Play; Stage Crew; Chrldng; Sftbl; Pittsburg Univ; Eng Tchr.

HANDSON, LA TISHA G; Wyandotte HS; Kansas City, KS; (3); Band; Drm Mjr(t); Jazz Band; Mrchg Band; Pep Band; Rep Frsh Cls; Rep Soph Cls; Rep Jr Cls; Ofcr Stu Cncl; Chess Clb; Stu Cncl Swthrt Dnc Chm; Frosh Hon Bnd; TX S Univ.

HANDY, SHAWN E; Shawnee Mission N HS; Shawnee Mission, KS; (4); 86/425; Church Yth Grp; Cmnty Wkr; Pep Clb; Spanish Clb; Teachers Aide; Ftbl; Tennis; Wt Lftg; Wrstlng; Hon Roll; Attnd Natl Yng Ldrs Conf 94; Pittsburg ST Univ; Arch Eng.

HANDZEL, CHRIS J; Bishop Miege HS; Kansas City, KS; (4); 7/160; Am Leg Boys St; Pep Clb; Var Bsbl; High Hon Roll; NHS; Pres Schlr; St Schlr; Bsebl SA ST Champs; KS ST Univ; Arch.

HANES, JARED S; Eastern Heights Jr Sr HS; Republican City, NE; (3); Drama Clb; 4-H; Letterman Clb; School Play; Phtg Ed Nwsp; Phtg Ed Yrbk; L Capt Bsktbl; L Var Ftbl; Wt Lftg; Hon Roll; 1 Rating ST Forensics; Beloit Voc Tech; Farming.

HANES, MARIE L; Otis Bison HS; Pawnee Rock, KS; (3); 4-H; Pep Clb; Chorus; NHS; Rodeo.

HANES, SARAH; Valley Ctr HS; Valley Center, KS; (4); 42/135; GAA; Letterman Clb; SADD; Varsity Clb; Chorus; Bsktbl; Powder Puff Ftbl; Sftbl; Trk; Vllybl; KS ST U; Bio.

HANEY, DAVID W; Central Heights Sr HS; Richmond, KS; (4); Church Yth Grp; Natl FFA Org; Quiz Bowl; Science Clb; Spanish Clb; Teachers Aide; Bsktbl; Ku 95 Comp Engrng Cont 1st Place; Ku 96 Speaker Dsgn Cmptn 1st Place; Ottawa Univ.

HANEY, ELIZABETH; Spring Hill HS; Spring Hill, KS; (4); Church Yth Grp; Pep Clb; Teachers Aide; Chorus; Flag Corp; School Musical; Swing Chorus; Variety Show; Hon Roll; Best Fml Actor Awd Jr Yr; Solo I Rating At Regnl Solo/Sml Ensmbl Festvl II At ST; RN.

HANEY, JEANINE; Greensburg HS; Greensburg, KS; (3); 4-H; FHA; Band; Mrchg Band; Pep Band; Tennis; 4-H Awd; Hon Roll; Acctng.

HANKE, MIRANDA; Atchison Sr HS; Atchison, KS; (1); NFL; JV Bsktbl; JV Var Socr; Var Hon Roll.

HANKEN, SARAH C; Larned HS; Larned, KS; (3); Church Yth Grp; FCA; Letterman Clb; Band; Chorus; Flag Corp; Mrchg Band; Pep Band; Var Bsktbl; Hon Roll; KS ST U; Mrktng.

HANKS, CURTIS; Girard HS; Girard, KS; (3); 10/75; Am Leg Boys St; Church Yth Grp; Cmnty Wkr; Pres 4-H; Natl FFA Org; SADD; Teachers Aide; 4-H Awd; High Hon Roll; NHS; Page For KS Senator; Govt In Action Yth Tour To Washington DC; Treas FFA Org.

HANLEY, CHRISTY M; Topeka HS; Topeka, KS; (2); 6/446; Church Yth Grp; Hosp Aide; Model UN; NFL; Acpl Chr; Drill Tm; School Musical; Variety Show; VP Frsh Cls; High Hon Roll; Participated In Dance Classes.

HANLEY, JESSICA J; Blue Valley NW HS; Leawood, KS; (2); JCL; Latin Clb; Band; Jazz Band; Mrchg Band; High Hon Roll; All ST Band 1st Chair; 2 Gold Mdls Natl Latin Exam.

HANNA, GREG; Central Christian Schl; Hutchinson, KS; (2); 1/20; Church Yth Grp; Quiz Bowl; Band; Chorus; Mrchg Band; Pep Band; School Play; JV Bsktbl; High Hon Roll; Rec I Rating ST Clarinet Solo; Music Ed/Cmptr Sci.

HANNE, BEN C; Wichita East HS; Wichita, KS; (2); Church Yth Grp; Drama Clb; German Clb; Thesps; Acpl Chr; Chorus; School Musical; School Play; Stage Crew; Variety Show; Smmr Trp To Germany Btwn 10/11 Grd Exch Stdnt; Voc Ensmbl Douglas Exprss Raised Money For Charity.

HANNEBAUM, KARMEN L; Salina HS South; Salina, KS; (3); 1/200; Church Yth Grp; Cmnty Wkr; FCA; Teachers Aide; Var L Bsktbl; Var L Sftbl; Wt Lftg; Hon Roll; NHS; Pres Acad Fit Awd; Teen Too Ambucs; All I-70 League Slctn Sftbl 96; Renaissance Gold Card Hldr; Yth Mnstr Slctn Comm; KA ST Univ; Elem Ed.

HANNEY, ASHLEY K; Shawnee Heights HS; Tecumseh, KS; (1); Church Yth Grp; 4-H; Service Clb; Chorus; Church Choir; School Musical; Lit Mag; Crs Cntry; 4-H Awd; High Hon Roll; VFW Essay Wnnr.

HANNI, SAM M; Bern Schl; Bern, KS; (4); 5/12; Letterman Clb; Varsity Clb; Band; Jazz Band; Pep Band; VP Sr Cls; Pres Stu Cncl; Var L Bsktbl; Var L Ftbl; KS ST Univ; Vet.

HANNON, BRIAN J; Basehor Linwood HS; Bonner Springs, KS; (3); 4/99; Church Yth Grp; Debate Tm; Treas Math Clb; NFL; Scholastic Bowl; SADD; Rep Stu Cncl; JV Bsktbl; Var Crs Cntry; Var Golf; USAA Natl Math Awd; Baush/Lomb Sci Awd; Natl Cngrsnl Youth Ldrshp Nmntn; Mech Eng.

HANRAHAN, BRENDA K; Topeka HS; Topeka, KS; (4); English Clb; French Clb; Intnl Clb; Letterman Clb; Pep Clb; SADD; Orch; Nwsp; Yrbk; Lit Mag; Rwng Clb; Vygrs Intl Ambass KS; Washburn U; Jrnlsm.

HANSEN, HEATHER N; Wichita Northwest HS; Wichita, KS; (4); Debate Tm; Intnl Clb; NFL; Q&S; Scholastic Bowl; Ed Nwsp; Hon Roll; NHS; Ntl Merit SF; St Schlr; KS ST U; Engl Ed.

HANSEN, JESSICA D; Victoria HS; Victoria, KS; (2); FBLA; Pep Clb; SADD; Varsity Clb; JV Var Bsktbl; JV Powder Puff Ftbl; JV Trk; JV Var Vllybl; Cit Awd; Hon Roll; KS ST Univ; Sports Ed.

HANSEN, PHILIP C; Independence HS; Independence, KS; (1); Church Yth Grp; French Clb; Science Clb; Spanish Clb; Chorus; Stat Bsktbl; JV Trk; Hon Roll; Acad Ltr Awd; Harvard; Dr.

HANSEN, SHANNON K; Wichita Southeast HS; Wichita, KS; (3); #9 in class; Church Yth Grp; Girl Scts; Teachers Aide; Acpl Chr; Chorus; Church Choir; Stage Crew; Swing Chorus; Variety Show; Sftbl; Creighton Univ; Math Tchr.

HANSON, KALE W; Blue Valley HS; Stilwell, KS; (2); Rep Church Yth Grp; Debate Tm; Math Tm; SADD; Socr; Sftbl; Hon Roll; Chrstn Clb; Chrstn Camp Jr Srvnt Vol; Yth Drama Mnstries; Concordia Coll; Chrstn Ed Dir.

HANSON, MANDY L; Marion HS; Marion, KS; (3); 1/40; Math Tm; NFL; Teachers Aide; Drill Tm; School Musical; Swing Chorus; Yrbk; Ofcr Stu Cncl; Chrldng; Mgr(s); Sarfire Dnce Compny; Stu Ldshp; KS Univ; Jrnlsm.

HAPPEL, LYNN C; Blue Valley HS; Stilwell, KS; (4); Hosp Aide; Intnl Clb; SADD; Band; Mrchg Band; Pep Band; School Musical; School Play; Intrml Vllybl; Hon Roll; U Of MO; Med.

HARBAUGH, ERIC M; Belle Plaine HS; Belle Plaine, KS; (4); Church Yth Grp; Drama Clb; Letterman Clb; Math Clb; Math Tm; Pep Clb; Quiz Bowl; Scholastic Bowl; SADD; Teachers Aide; F; US Mil Acad; Mech Engr.

HARBAUGH, ERIN; Field Kindley HS; Coffeyville, KS; (4); Am Leg Aux Girls St; FCA; NFL; Spanish Clb; Chorus; Church Choir; School Musical; School Play; Pres Stu Cncl; NHS; Stu Of Yr; John C Stennis Natl Stu Congress; Amer Red Crss Exec Brd; Coffeyville CC; Broadcast News.

HARBER, JESSICA D; Shawnee Mission W Sr HS; Lenexa, KS; (1); Church Yth Grp; Pep Clb; SADD; Drill Tm; Rptr Nwsp; Jr NHS; Pharm.

HARCLERODE, JONATHAN K; Emporia HS; Emporia, KS; (4); 1/275; Boy Scts; VP Debate Tm; Pres Key Clb; VP Orch; Crs Cntry; Trk; Ntl Merit Schol; St Schlr; VP Model UN; Lbrn Science Clb; U Of KS; Pre-Med; Chem Engrng.

HARDAWAY, RYAN; Ulysses HS; Ulysses, KS; (3); FCA; SADD; JV Bsbl; Var JV Bsktbl; Var L Ftbl; Hon Roll; NHS.

HARDCASTLE, MICHELLE; Shawnee Mission S Sr HS; Lenexa, KS; (2); Cmnty Wkr; GAA; Pep Clb; Drill Tm; JV Var Chrldng; Gym; Hon Roll; Shawnee Mission Cotillion; MO U.

HARDEN, BYRON J; Valley Falls HS; Valley Falls, KS; (3); Cmnty Wkr; VP Frsh Cls; Pres Soph Cls.

HARDEN, CINDY K; Ashland HS; Ashland, KS; (2); 1/22; Church Yth Grp; HOBY; NFL; Quiz Bowl; Speech Tm; Band; Ofcr Stu Cncl; Tennis; Var Trk; High Hon Roll; Fnlst Valory-Hetzel Potry Cntst; 5th Drmtc Solo ST Speech; U Of KS; Med.

HARDER, CHELSI; Elkhart HS; Elkhart, KS; (3); 2/33; VP Church Yth Grp; Treas Girl Scts; VP Letterman Clb; Office Aide; Varsity Clb; Chorus; School Musical; School Play; Stage Crew; Ed Nwsp; Nrsng.

HARDER, JENNIFER S; Topeka HS; Topeka, KS; (3); Church Yth Grp; German Clb; Teachers Aide; Co-Capt Flag Corp; Dance Clb; Teens HOPE; Animal Trng.

HARDER, ROBIN S; Berean Acad; Newton, KS; (4); 6/32; Church Yth Grp; Quiz Bowl; Band; Chorus; Church Choir; Pep Band; School Play; Stage Crew; Var L Tennis; High Hon Roll; John Brown U.

HARDER, TRACY D; Onaga HS; Wheaton, KS; (3); 4/30; Pres 4-H; VP FHA; Office Aide; Co-Capt Drill Tm; Sec Stu Cncl; Bsktbl; Sftbl; Vllybl; High Hon Roll; Pres NHS; KS Assn For Yth; KS Univ; Phy Thrpst.

HARDERS, KRISTOPHER R; Olathe East Sr HS; Overland Park, KS; (4); 1/305; VP French Clb; Spanish Clb; Intrml Bsbl; DAR Awd; Gov Hon Prg Awd; High Hon Roll; Pres NHS; Ntl Merit Ltr; Pres Acad Fit Awd; St Schlr; U Of Miami; Intl Bus.

HARDIMAN, SHANNON L; F L Schlagle HS; Kansas City, KS; (1); Church Yth Grp; Math Clb; Office Aide; Pep Clb; Science Clb; SADD; Acpl Chr; Band; Church Choir; Mrchg Band; Essay & Creative Wrtng; OB-GYN.

HARDIN, MISSY; Junction City HS; Junction City, KS; (1); Church Yth Grp; ROTC; Drill Tm; Yrbk; Art, Draw, Sketch & Paint; Wrtng; KS Univ; Pediatric Nrs.

HARDING, AMY; Louisburg HS; Louisburg, KS; (3); 1/87; Bus Profs of Am; Hosp Aide; Letterman Clb; Spanish Clb; SADD; Var L Bsktbl; Var L Vllybl; Wt Lftg; High Hon Roll; NHS; Top 10 Pct Math/Sci/Bus/Soc Sci/Lang Arts Acad Awds; MAST; All Frntr Leag Hon Mntn Vlybl 2 Yrs; U Of KS; Pre-Med.

HARDING, JENNY L; Maize HS; Wichita, KS; (3); Debate Tm; Hon Roll; Foensics; KS ST; Tchr.

HARDING, JESSICA A; Holton HS; Mayetta, KS; (1); JV Bsktbl; Mgr(s); Score Keeper; JV Vllybl; Emporia ST; Tchr.

HARDING, MAREN; Royal Valley HS; Mayetta, KS; (3); 9/65; Art Clb; Dance Clb; Drama Clb; Girl Scts; Letterman Clb; Band; Drill Tm; Flag Corp; Mrchg Band; Pep Band; USAV Vllybll; 2 Schol Gld Keys Art Clb; AAV Bsktbll; Grl Sct Slvr Awd; Marine Bio.

HARDMAN, DEE ANNA L; Parsons HS; Parsons, KS; (4); 50/119; Cmnty Wkr; VP FBLA; Office Aide; Pep Clb; SADD; Band; Mrchg Band; Pep Band; Yrbk; Vllybl; KS ST Univ; Acctng/Fin.

HARDMAN, GABE R; Great Bend Sr HS; Great Bend, KS; (3); 26/230; Church Yth Grp; Spanish Clb; Band; Mrchg Band; Pep Band; Ofcr Bsbl; Mgr(s); High Hon Roll; Hon Roll; Prfct Atten Awd; Amer Lgn Bsbl; KS Univ; Sprts Psych.

HARDY, ERIKA V; Salina HS South; Salina, KS; (3); Dance Clb; Library Aide; Pep Clb; Teachers Aide; Drill Tm; Pom Pon; Hon Roll; Habitat For Humnty; Taught Dance DARE Camp; Banton Cty Sci Co; Tchr.

HARDY, KELLY; Ellis HS; Hays, KS; (4); 13/40; Am Leg Aux Girls St; Treas Sec FHA; Office Aide; SADD; School Musical; Ed Nwsp; Rep Stu Cncl; Capt Var Chrldng; Var L Vllybl; Hon Roll; Hmcmng Queen; Kayettes; Forensics; Fort Hays ST U; Bus.

HARE, ERICA M; Hayden HS; Topeka, KS; (2); Church Yth Grp; Hosp Aide; Intnl Clb; SADD; Band; Pep Band; Tennis; Hon Roll; KS U; Music.

HARE, RACHEL S; Shawnee Mission N HS; Mission, KS; (3); 51/380; German Clb; GAA; Pep Clb; Acpl Chr; Chorus; Sftbl; Hon Roll; Best Cntr Fielder; Acad Awd; Var Sftbl Awd; Speech Pathology.

HAREMZA, JESSICA L; Colby Sr HS; Colby, KS; (3); Am Leg Aux Girls St; Church Yth Grp; Debate Tm; 4-H; Math Tm; Science Clb; Spanish Clb; Chorus; High Hon Roll; NHS; Med.

HARGIS, TERI A; Field Kindley Mem Sr HS; Coffeyville, KS; (3); GAA; FTA; Teachers Aide; Sprt Ed Yrbk; Var Capt Bsktbl; Co-Capt Pom Pon; Var Sftbl; Var Trk; Var Vllybl; Hon Roll; Stardancr Awd; 2 All Star Bsktbl Awds; Coffeyville CC; Phys Asst.

HARGROVE, JEFF D; Maur Hill Prep Schl; Saint Joseph, MO; (1); Boy Scts; Drama Clb; Bsktbl; Tennis; High Hon Roll; Hon Roll; All Amer Schlr; Rocky Mountain Schlr; Natl Eng Merit Awd; KS ST; Engrng.

HARKINS, DAWN M; Central Heights Sr HS; Richmond, KS; (2); 8/41; Science Clb; Spanish Clb; Chorus; High Hon Roll; Prfct Atten Awd; Modern Woodman Of Amer Sec; Rec Sftbl.

HARKINS, MATTHEW; Bluestem HS; El Dorado, KS; (4); 4/61; HOBY; Drm Mjr(t); School Play; Ed Nwsp; Var L Wrstlng; Cit Awd; High Hon Roll; Pres NHS; Debate Tm; 4-H; KS Regnts Hnrs Acad Pittsburg St; CYO Parish Pres, Dicosean-Regnl Rep; KS ST U; Comp.

HARKLEROAD, ALEX D; Blue Valley HS; Bucyrus, KS; (4); Boy Scts; Church Yth Grp; ROTC; Band; Mrchg Band; Pep Band; Var Socr; Capt Var Swmmng; Var Trk; Natl Yth Ldrshp Forum; Im Sports; Water Safety Instr; U Of KS; Cmp Sci; Engrng.

HARKLEROAD, ALLEN D; Blue Valley HS; Bucyrus, KS; (4); 42/230; Boy Scts; Church Yth Grp; Band; Mrchg Band; Pep Band; School Musical; School Play; Stage Crew; Intrml Bsktbl; Var Ftbl; Swimming Instr; U Of KS; Archaeology.

HARLAN, BILL; Hanover Schl; Hanover, KS; (4); 3/23; Pres Sec 4-H; Letterman Clb; Pres Natl FFA Org; Pres Soph Cls; Pres Jr Cls; Var Capt Bsktbl; Var Trk; 4-H Awd; High Hon Roll; NHS; Connie Belin Natl Recognth Pgm For HS Schlrs; St FFA Farmer Degree; KS ST U; Ag Ed.

HARLIN JR, WILLIAM R; Wyandotte HS; Kansas City, KS; (1); JV Ftbl; Var Ftbl; Wt Lftg; Hon Roll; Rel; Peer Ldr Asst Recognition; KS Univ; Prof Ftbl; Engr.

HARLOW, BRETT D; Wellsville Jr Sr HS; Wellsville, KS; (2); Church Yth Grp; CAP; Debate Tm; FCA; FBLA; Sec Intnl Clb; ROTC; Speech Tm; VP SADD; Varsity Clb; NE Univ; Engrng.

HARLOW, JOSHUA D; Holton HS; Holton, KS; (1); Band; Bsktbl; Ftbl; Hon Roll; Air Frce Acad.

HARLOW, KOLISSA; White City HS; Herington, KS; (1); Drama Clb; FHA; SADD; Band; Chorus; Drill Tm; Bsktbl; Trk; Vllybl; High Hon Roll.

HARMA, TRISHA; Derby HS; Derby, KS; (3); Church Yth Grp; Drama Clb; Ofcr Stu Cncl; Chrldng; Powder Puff Ftbl; Socr; High Hon Roll; Jr NHS; NHS; Pres Acad Fit Awd; Kay Clb; ASAP2.

HARMON, JENNIFER E; Leavenworth HS; Leavenworth, KS; (1); Hon Roll; Animal Care; Tech; Vet.

HARMON, TAI; Protection Schl; Protection, KS; (1); Letterman Clb; Pep Clb; Band; Chorus; Mrchg Band; Pep Band; School Musical; Variety Show; JV Bsktbl; L Trk.

HARMS, DAN R; Garden City Sr HS; Garden City, KS; (2); Church Yth Grp; CAP; Natl FFA Org; VICA; Orch; Hon Roll; Garden City CC; Farming.

HARMS, GREG; Ulysses HS; Ulysses, KS; (4); 11/90; Am Leg Boys St; Church Yth Grp; FCA; FBLA; School Musical; Rep Stu Cncl; Var L Crs Cntry; High Hon Roll; NHS; Hillsdale Coll; Engrng.

HARMS, KELSIE L; Maize HS; Wichita, KS; (3); Church Yth Grp; Cmnty Wkr; FCA; Science Clb; Spanish Clb; SADD; Band; Chorus; Church Choir; Mrchg Band; Tabor Coll; Cnslng.

HARMS, TRACI; Pratt HS; Pratt, KS; (1); FHA; Pep Clb; Band; Chorus; Color Guard; Flag Corp; Mrchg Band; Pep Band; JV Chrldng; 4-H Awd; Girls Ensemble.

HARNDEN, ANGELA M; Attica Public Schl; Attica, KS; (3); Pres Soph Cls; Var L Bsktbl; Var L Chrldng; Var L Vllybl; Hon Roll; Emporia Univ; Phy Thrpst.

HARNESS, COURTNEY; Highland HS; Highland, KS; (4); Cmnty Wkr; FCA; Q&S; Quiz Bowl; Rep Phtg Nwsp; Ed Yrbk; Treas Stu Cncl; Var Capt Chrldng; Var Mgr Trk; High Hon Roll.

HARNESS, HILARY; Highland HS; Highland, KS; (2); Church Yth Grp; FCA; Natl FFA Org; Quiz Bowl; Pres Stu Cncl; Var L Chrldng; Var L Vllybl; Hon Roll; NHS; Girl Scts; KS Rivers & Streams Team.

HAROLD, TATUM; Weskan Schl; Weskan, KS; (4); 3/6; Art Clb; Church Yth Grp; 4-H; HOBY; Pep Clb; Quiz Bowl; Scholastic Bowl; Speech Tm; Teachers Aide; Band; Engl Merit Awd; KS Wesleyan; Hlth.

HARP, MIKE R; Field Kindley Mem Sr HS; Coffeyville, KS; (4); Church Yth Grp; Cmnty Wkr; JA; Pres Spanish Clb; Chorus; Church Choir; Wt Lftg; Hon Roll; NHS; Show Choir; Bus.

HARPER, JOSH; Jackson Heights HS; Soldier, KS; (2); Church Yth Grp; Quiz Bowl; Chorus; Church Choir; School Musical; School Play; Yrbk; Rep Stu Cncl; Crs Cntry; Socr; Bst All-Arnd Stndt; Cmbrdge; Law.

HARPER, MEAY C; Ft Scott HS; Fort Scott, KS; (3); Letterman Clb; Teachers Aide; Var Bsktbl; Var Sftbl; Var Vllybl; Hon Roll; Prfct Atten Awd; Pres Acad Fit Awd.

HARPER, ROBIN L; Liberal HS; Liberal, KS; (3); Am Leg Aux Girls St; Church Yth Grp; Teachers Aide; Chorus; Rep Frsh Cls; Var Soph Cls; Ofcr Stu Cncl; Var Capt Chrldng; JV Sftbl; Wt Lftg; FL ST; Optmtry.

HARPER, SAMANTHA; Hays HS; Hays, KS; (2); Church Yth Grp; Dance Clb; 4-H; Ski Clb; Chorus; School Musical; 4-H Awd; Hon Roll; Teach 2-3 Danc Classes; Dance In Various Exclusive Productions, Dance Cmptns, Talent Shows & Recitals; KS U; Dancing; Bio-Chem.

HARPER, SHAWN J; J C Harmon HS; Kansas City, KS; (2); Church Yth Grp; Cmnty Wkr; Chorus; Church Choir; School Musical; Ofcr Soph Cls; Gym; High Hon Roll; Hon Roll; Gi Con Do-Orange Belt Karate; Acting In Plays; Kempo Yellow Belt; BSU Mem; Yth Net Mem In KCMO; Drama.

HARRIES, BRIAN J; Lyndon HS; Vassar, KS; (2); Church Yth Grp; FBLA; Math Tm; Quiz Bowl; Scholastic Bowl; Band; Church Choir; Mrchg Band; Pep Band; School Play; Lit Clb; I Rating At St Music Cmptn.

HARRINGTON, DIANE R; Blue Valley Northwest HS; Overland Park, KS; (3); Church Yth Grp; Cmnty Wkr; Pep Clb; Teachers Aide; Chorus; Rptr Yrbk; Wt Lftg; Hon Roll; Mrt Awd Wrtng Smpl Prfct Scr; Pres Salt/Light Club; Pblshd Sparrowgrass Poetrys; KS ST U.

HARRINGTON, EMILY P; Blue Valley Northwest HS; Overland Park, KS; (2); 1/427; Debate Tm; FCA; Latin Clb; JV Bsktbl; L Crs Cntry; L Socr; High Hon Roll; Slvr Ky Pntng Natl Schlstc Art & Wrtng Awds; KS Sccr Tm.

HARRINGTON, JODI; Garden City Sr HS; Garden City, KS; (4); 17/313; Church Yth Grp; Key Clb; Science Clb; SADD; Church Choir; Var Bsktbl; Var Sftbl; Var Vllybl; High Hon Roll; Hon Roll; Grdn City Comm Coll; Ath Trng.

HARRINGTON, KATHERINE; Olathe South Sr HS; Olathe, KS; (4); Spanish Clb; Orch; Ed Nwsp; JV Var Tennis; Trk; Vllybl; High Hon Roll; Hon Roll; Prfct Atten Awd; Pres Acad Fit Awd; Baker U; Psych.

HARRIS, ADAM L; Independence HS; Independence, KS; (1); Church Yth Grp; Bsktbl; Crs Cntry; Socr; Swmmng; Trk; 4-H Awd; Karate; KS U.

HARRIS, AMANDA S; South Haven Schl; Geuda Springs, KS; (1); Church Yth Grp; Pep Clb; Pres Soph Cls; Stat Vllybl; High Hon Roll.

HARRIS, CHIQUITA N; Sumner Acad Of Arts & Science; Kansas City, KS; (4); French Clb; Pep Clb; Chorus; High Hon Roll; Hon Roll; NHS; Intl Baccalaureate Cand; Langston Univ; Elem Ed.

HARRIS, CHRISTOPERH M; Washburn Rural HS; Topeka, KS; (2); Cmnty Wkr; Natl FFA Org; Office Aide; Orch; School Musical; Ftbl; Trk; Wt Lftg; Hon Roll; Church Yth Grp; US Naval Sea Cadets; Mltry.

HARRIS, EMILY J; Wichita East HS; Wichita, KS; (3); Church Yth Grp; Cmnty Wkr; Girl Scts; Spanish Clb; Band; Mrchg Band; Pep Band; Socr; NHS.

HARRIS, JACOB B; Olathe East Sr HS; Overland Park, KS; (2); Boy Scts; Church Yth Grp; Computer Clb; French Clb; Stage Crew; Eagle Sct Awd; BYU; Comp Sci.

HARRIS, JODI L; Emporia HS; Augusta, KS; (2); Church Yth Grp; Debate Tm; Chorus; Rptr Nwsp; Intrml Chrldng; Var L Gym; Var L Trk; High Hon Roll; Church Yth Grp Mission Trips To Panama/Inner City Dallas; EHS Scholar Ath; Pre Med.

HARRIS, KATHLEEN A; Washburn Rural HS; Topeka, KS; (3); 19/351; Church Yth Grp; SADD; Teachers Aide; Band; Mrchg Band; Pep Band; High Hon Roll; Pittsburg ST Univ; Micro Bio.

HARRIS, MARGARET L; Blue Valley HS; Olathe, KS; (1); Chorus; Church Choir; Rptr Nwsp; High Hon Roll; Hon Roll; Duke Tlnt Idntfctn Prgm 95-; Natl Span Exam Gold Mdl Level II; ST Music Cntst Vcl Ensmble I Rtng.

HARRIS, MATT; Valley Ctr HS; Valley Center, KS; (3); 19/160; Church Yth Grp; Letterman Clb; Quiz Bowl; Scholastic Bowl; Spanish Clb; Varsity Clb; Golf; Wt Lftg; High Hon Roll; Hon Roll; Huntng/Fishng; Ophthalmologist.

HARRIS, MICHAEL E; St John's Military Schl; Mayer, AZ; (3); Boy Scts; Chess Clb; Church Yth Grp; Drama Clb; Letterman Clb; NFL; ROTC; Band; Church Choir; Drill Tm; ASU-AZ; Crmnl Jstc.

HARRIS, MICHELLE L; Junction City HS; Junction City, KS; (3); Cmnty Wkr; 4-H; Girl Scts; Band; School Musical; Ofcr Jr Cls; Bsktbl; High Hon Roll; NHS; Prfct Atten Awd.

HARRIS, MIRANDA; Goddard Jr HS; Wichita, KS; (2); Church Yth Grp; Chorus; Church Choir; Variety Show; Var JV Bsktbl; Var Sftbl; Var Vllybl; High Hon Roll; Pres Acad Fit Awd; Sprts Med.

HARRIS, NICOLE; Hugoton HS; Liberal, KS; (3); 8/69; Church Yth Grp; 4-H; Natl FFA Org; 4-H Awd; High Hon Roll; Hon Roll; NHS; 4-H Awd Wnnr; KS ST U; Comp Engrng.

HARRIS, PAULA N; Wichita Southeast HS; Wichita, KS; (4); 6/378; Cmnty Wkr; Drama Clb; Spanish Clb; SADD; Thesps; Orch; School Musical; School Play; Capt Chrldng; NHS; Psych.

HARRIS, ROBERT W; Minneapolis HS; Minneapolis, KS; (4); Pres Church Yth Grp; Library Aide; Pres Math Clb; SADD; Band; Cit Awd; High Hon Roll; Treas NHS; Prfct Atten Awd; St Schlr; Plyd Kybrd Show Choir; 1 Rating ST Ensmbld; 2 Rating ST Piano Solo; KS ST Univ Salina; Cmptr Sci.

HARRIS, SARAH; Acad Of Mt St Scholastica; Atchison, KS; (3); 2/30; Church Yth Grp; Cmnty Wkr; HOBY; Pep Clb; Pres Service Clb; Chorus; Rep Stu Cncl; Var Bsktbl; Var Vllybl; High Hon Roll; Gov Ctr For Teen Ldrshp; Benedictine Coll.

HARRIS, STEPHEN WELSH; Shawnee Mission E Sr HS; Fairway, KS; (4); Church Yth Grp; JV Socr; JV Tennis; High Hon Roll; Hon Roll; JETS Awd; Jr NHS; NHS; Ntl Merit Ltr; Net Global LLC Co Co-Owner; U Of KS.

HARRIS, TANYON R; Lawrence HS; Lawrence, KS; (3); Church Yth Grp; Chorus; Rep Soph Cls; JV Bsktbl; JV Ftbl; Var Trk; JV Wt Lftg; Intrml Hon Roll; Own Bus.

HARRIS, VERNETTA L; Sumner Acad Of Arts & Science; Kansas City, KS; (4); 1/193; Church Yth Grp; French Clb; Key Clb; Quiz Bowl; Var Bsktbl; Cit Awd; French Hon Soc; Gov Hon Prg Awd; High Hon Roll; NHS; Trinity Univ; Med.

HARRIS, VICTOR C; Holton HS; Holton, KS; (1); Computer Clb; FHA; Acpl Chr; Chorus; Church Choir; School Musical; Bsktbl; Ftbl; Trk; Hon Roll; Vocal Solo At Washburn Univ Singing Festival; Dance; Nicole Amon Awd For Most Dedicated Dancer 96; KS U; Family Dr.

HARRIS, WILLIAM; Great Bend Sr HS; Great Bend, KS; (2); Cmnty Wkr; Drama Clb; Acpl Chr; Band; Chorus; Mrchg Band; Pep Band; Stage Crew; Variety Show; Hon Roll; Bus.

HARRISON, ALICIA K; Wichita East HS; Wichita, KS; (4); Am Leg Aux Girls St; Cmnty Wkr; Hosp Aide; Chorus; Bsktbl; Trk; High Hon Roll; NHS; St Schlr; Spanish Clb; Natl Mrt Cmmnded; Saint Olaf Coll; Bio.

HARRISON, AMBER D; Wichita Southeast HS; Wichita, KS; (3); 32/400; SADD; Mgr(s); Pom Pon; Hon Roll; Wichita ST Univ; Vet.

HARRISON, JOHN; Silver Lake Jr Sr HS; Silver Lake, KS; (3); 7/56; Am Leg Boys St; Church Yth Grp; Computer Clb; Debate Tm; Letterman Clb; Scholastic Bowl; Teachers Aide; Varsity Clb; Ofcr Stu Cncl; Var Bsbl; 3A ST Bsbl Champs 96.

HARRISON, LA TISHUA D; Northeast HS; Arcadia, KS; (2); Library Aide; Office Aide; Pep Clb; Teachers Aide; Band; Chorus; Color Guard; JV Golf; Hon Roll.

HARRISON, LISA; St John Jr Sr HS; Saint John, KS; (4); FHA; VP Spanish Clb; Sec Treas Band; Pres Jr Cls; Sec Sr Cls; Var L Crs Cntry; Var L Trk; Hon Roll; NHS; Colby CC.

HARRISON, MARK; Goodland HS; Goodland, KS; (2); 3/100; Pres Church Yth Grp; Rep 4-H; Band; Jazz Band; Pep Band; Var Bsktbl; JV Ftbl; JV Golf; High Hon Roll; Pres Acad Fit Awd.

HARRISON, TABITHA; Olathe North Sr HS; Olathe, KS; (4); Am Leg Aux Girls St; Debate Tm; NFL; Pep Clb; Speech Tm; Varsity Clb; Nwsp; Ofcr Jr Cls; Ofcr Sr Cls; Var L Chrldng; Baker; Psych.

HARRITY, BRYAN J; Sumner Acad Of Arts & Science; Kansas City, KS; (1); Art Clb; Latin Clb; Spanish Clb; Ftbl; Hon Roll.

HARRITY, SHANNON M; Sumner Acad Of Arts & Science; Kansas City, KS; (3); Key Clb; Latin Clb; NFL; SADD; Drill Tm; School Play; Stage Crew; Phtg Yrbk; High Hon Roll; Drama Clb; JILL; KS Univ; Nrsng.

HARROLD, JASEY; Ulysses HS; Ulysses, KS; (2); Church Yth Grp; VP FHA; SADD; Band; Jazz Band; Rptr Nwsp; Yrbk; Rep Soph Cls; Ofcr Stu Cncl; Var Chrldng.

HARROLD, JOSHUA C; Buhler HS; Hutchinson, KS; (3); 10/200; Am Leg Boys St; Church Yth Grp; Pres Computer Clb; FCA; Service Clb; Sec SADD; Chorus; Var L Tennis; Hon Roll; Letterman Clb; Interactives Clb; Pepperdine Univ; Psych.

HARSHA, ELIZABETH; Shawnee Mission W Sr HS; Lenexa, KS; (3); Church Yth Grp; FCA; Acpl Chr; Treas Chorus; Sec Stu Cncl; Capt JV Chrldng; JV Var Trk; NHS; Rep Frsh Cls; Rep Soph Cls; Peer Mediation Conflict Resltn; Young Life; N Park Coll; Scndry Ed/Bio.

HARSHBARGER, ALICIA E; Maize HS; Wichita, KS; (4); SADD; Sec Frsh Cls; Sec Soph Cls; Sec Jr Cls; Treas Sr Cls; Var Sftbl; Var Vllybl; NHS; Church Yth Grp; Debate Tm; KAYS; M-Clb Treas.

HARSHMAN, BURTON L; Chase Co HS; Cedar Point, KS; (3); #6 in class; Spanish Clb; Mrchg Band; VP Jr Cls; Ofcr Stu Cncl; Var Bsbl; Var Bsktbl; Var Ftbl; Trk; Hon Roll; NHS; Crmnl Jstc.

HART, BETSEY C; Olathe East Sr HS; Shawnee Mission, KS; (4); Church Yth Grp; Girl Scts; Band; Ofcr Soph Cls; Mgr Bsktbl; Mgr Vllybl; High Hon Roll; NHS; Pres Acad Fit Awd; Trk; Chrch Productions; KU.

HART, JOHN I; Olathe East Sr HS; Overland Park, KS; (3); Boy Scts; Church Yth Grp; Letterman Clb; Math Clb; Church Choir; Jazz Band; Phtg Rptr Nwsp; Var L Wrstlng; High Hon Roll; Hon Roll.

HART, JOMARIE; Blue Valley HS; Stilwell, KS; (2); Art Clb; Tennis; Hon Roll; KS City Art Inst; Comm Art.

HART, MELISSA S; Hayden HS; Topeka, KS; (4); SADD; Band; Drm Mjr(t); Mrchg Band; Pep Band; School Musical; Hon Roll.

HART, MEREDITH C; Galena HS; Galena, KS; (2); Church Yth Grp; FHA; Math Tm; SADD; Treas Frsh Cls; Rep Soph Cls; Rep Stu Cncl; Golf; Vllybl; Wt Lftg; KU; Pol Sci.

HART, MICHELE; Hayden HS; Topeka, KS; (3); SADD; Band; Mrchg Band; Pep Band; High Hon Roll.

HART, NIKI; Nickerson HS; Nickerson, KS; (1); 1/132; Church Yth Grp; Drama Clb; NFL; Thesps; Mrchg Band; School Play; Var Chrldng; JV Tennis; High Hon Roll; Band; Dance Clss; Steel Drum Band; UCLA; Marine Bio.

HART, RACHAEL C; Wichita North HS; Wichita, KS; (2); Church Yth Grp; Vllybl; Hon Roll; Stdnt Mo; Chrch Cmp Cnslr; WSU; Nrsng.

HART, SKY-LEANNE; Leavenworth HS; Leavenworth, KS; (3); German Clb; Stage Crew; Rptr Nwsp; Ed Yrbk; JV Bsktbl; Hon Roll; Leavenworth Times Carrier Of The Yr 95; Mortuary Sci.

HART, STEPHANIE; Goodland HS; Goodland, KS; (3); 3/82; Church Yth Grp; Cmnty Wkr; GAA; SADD; Band; Mrchg Band; Pep Band; School Play; Stage Crew; Pres Frsh Cls; AFS; Hnrbl Mntn Ann Arlys Bowler Poetry Prize; Coll; Pre-Med/Mssns.

HART, TRACY A; Basehor Linwood HS; Bonner Springs, KS; (2); Church Yth Grp; GAA; Girl Scts; Hosp Aide; SADD; JV Bsktbl; JV Sftbl; High Hon Roll; Hon Roll; Lifeguard; Swim Team; Phy Thrpst.

HARTE MITCHELL, TIM J; Blue Valley HS; Overland Park, KS; (2); Cmnty Wkr; Debate Tm; Var Letterman Clb; NFL; Orch; Cit Awd; Hon Roll; Big Bro, Sr Of Amer; Natl Hd Injury Fnd; Soph Of Yr; Emporia ST U; Phlsphy.

HARTER, ERREN; Emporia HS; Emporia, KS; (3); Am Leg Boys St; Church Yth Grp; Debate Tm; FCA; 4-H; Socr; Tennis; 4-H Awd; High Hon Roll; CO ST; Acctng; Backpacking CO.

HARTER, LANCE M; Colby Sr HS; Colby, KS; (2); 17/106; Church Yth Grp; Cmnty Wkr; 4-H; Bsktbl; Ftbl; Wt Lftg; Hon Roll.

HARTIG, TIMOTHY B; Sumner Acad Of Arts & Science; Kansas City, KS; (3); Church Yth Grp; Math Clb; Spanish Clb; Ofcr Bsbl; High Hon Roll; NHS; Bowling; Chrch Sound System; Vol With Comm Projects; Engrng.

HARTING, MATTHEW H; Derby HS; Derby, KS; (4); Am Leg Boys St; Boy Scts; Mrchg Band; Ofcr Stu Cncl; Var L Bsbl; Var L Socr; Var L Wrstlng; High Hon Roll; NHS; Ntl Merit Ltr; USAF Acad; Aeronautical Engr.

HARTLEY, ANTONIA C; Baxter HS; Baxter Springs, KS; (2); 1/100; Pres FHA; Capt Scholastic Bowl; L Band; School Musical; VP Frsh Cls; Stu Cncl; Var L Trk; Var L Vllybl; Hon Roll; Pres Acad Fit Awd; NSF; STARS Pgm.

HARTLEY, KATIE M; Goddard HS; Wichita, KS; (3); VP Church Yth Grp; Science Clb; SADD; Acpl Chr; Chorus; School Musical; School Play; Variety Show; Yrbk; Hon Roll; Choir Trip To London; KS Ambsdrs Of Msc European Tour; ST Solo Contest; Dist Choir; Cmnctns.

HARTMAN, ANDREA; Emporia HS; Emporia, KS; (4); Am Leg Aux Girls St; FCA; NFL; Pep Clb; Ofcr Jr Cls; Ofcr Sr Cls; JV Capt Chrldng; Var Swmmng; Cit Awd; Hon Roll; Kayettes Bd; SMILE; Peer Mdtr; U Of KS; Bus Admin.

HARTMAN, AUTUMN M; Arkansas City HS; Arkansas City, KS; (1); Church Yth Grp; FCA; SADD; Band; Flag Corp; Mrchg Band; Pep Band; Rep Frsh Cls; Var Chrldng; JV Tennis; Rd Crs Lfgrd Cert; KS Univ.

HARTMAN, BROOKE TAMARRON; Wichita Northwest HS; Wichita, KS; (3); Church Yth Grp; Drama Clb; Drill Tm; School Play; Bsktbl; Pom Pon; Sftbl; Vllybl; High Hon Roll; NHS; Law; Secret Svc Agent.

HARTMAN, JAMES B; Dighton HS; Dighton, KS; (2); Chess Clb; Stat Bsktbl; Stat Ftbl; Prfct Atten Awd; Spch Cls One Act Play 2nd Pl; Goodland KS Vo Tec; Mech/Elctr.

HARTMAN, SHANNON; Turner HS; Kansas City, KS; (3); Debate Tm; Math Tm; NFL; Spanish Clb; Ofcr Jr Cls; Capt Var Chrldng; Hon Roll; Jr NHS; NHS.

HARTNETT, DAVID; Manhattan HS; Manhattan, KS; (3); Art Clb; Church Yth Grp; FCA; 4-H; Quiz Bowl; Scholastic Bowl; Intrml Vllybl; 4-H Awd; Hon Roll; NHS.

HARTSELL, MEGGIN E; Great Bend Sr HS; Great Bend, KS; (3); Church Yth Grp; Drama Clb; Pep Clb; Service Clb; Teachers Aide; Acpl Chr; Chorus; Church Choir; Stage Crew; Swing Chorus; Fine Arts Festival Natl Wnnr 95; I Rating St Music Festival Solo; Chrch Musical; Cntrl Bible Coll; Elem Ed; Music.

HARTTER, BENJAMIN E; Sabetha HS; Morrill, KS; (2); 7/65; Church Yth Grp; FCA; Pep Clb; Spanish Clb; Ofcr Bsbl; Ftbl; Golf; Mgr(s); Wt Lftg; Hon Roll; U Of KS; Sports Med.

HARTTER, CARA S; Bern Schl; Bern, KS; (2); Church Yth Grp; GAA; Letterman Clb; Pep Clb; Quiz Bowl; Spanish Clb; SADD; Varsity Clb; Band; Chorus; KSU; Bus.

HARTTER, JAIMIE M; Troy HS; Effingham, KS; (4); 4/35; Cmnty Wkr; Drama Clb; FHA; VP Key Clb; Sec Treas Letterman Clb; Math Tm; Pep Clb; Q&S; Quiz Bowl; Scholastic Bowl; Stu Of Month Awd; William Hart, Chamber Of Commerce Schlsp; KS ST Achvmt Schlsp; KS ST Alumni Awd; KS ST Univ; Jrnlsm.

HARTTER, JODY E; Bern Schl; Bern, KS; (4); 2/12; Drama Clb; Quiz Bowl; Scholastic Bowl; Chorus; School Play; VP Stu Cncl; Vllybl; Hon Roll; NHS; Church Yth Grp; KAYS Pres 95-96; KS ST U; Sales/Mrktng.

HARTTER, KRISTIN K; Sabetha HS; Sabetha, KS; (3); 2/91; Bus Profs of Am; Church Yth Grp; Pres FHA; German Clb; Ofcr Stu Cncl; Tennis; Vllybl; High Hon Roll; NHS; Pres Acad Fit Awd; KS St Univ; Hortcltr.

HARTWICK, KACIE D; Dodge City HS; Dodge City, KS; (4); 1/253; Church Yth Grp; French Clb; SADD; Band; Sftbl; Cit Awd; Gov Hon Prg Awd; Hon Roll; NHS; Val; U Of KS; Nrsng.

HARTZFELD, JESSICA J; Northeast HS; Arma, KS; (2); 1/50; Band; Mrchg Band; Pep Band; Phtg Nwsp; JV Bsktbl; Var Chrldng; JV Var Sftbl; JV Vllybl; Hon Roll; Prfct Atten Awd; Bible Schl Tchr; Med.

HARVEY, CHAD; Pratt HS; Pratt, KS; (3); 20/114; Am Leg Boys St; Church Yth Grp; Cmnty Wkr; FCA; VP 4-H; JA; Red Cross Aide; Science Clb; Rep SADD; Teachers Aide; 4-H KS St Del Natl Yth Ldrshp Conf; 7th Pl St Tnns; Leag Champ Crss Cntry; Numerous 4-H Awds; Comm Vol; Emporia ST; Hlth Field.

HARVEY, KIM; Columbus HS; Hallowell, KS; (4); 29/91; Bus Profs of Am; FHA; Office Aide; Chorus; Flag Corp; High Hon Roll; Hon Roll; NHS; Prfct Atten Awd; Mgr Boys Bsktbl Team; Pittsburg ST U.

HARVEY, RACHEL M; Topeka HS; Topeka, KS; (2); Church Yth Grp; Girl Scts; Chorus; Hon Roll; AFS Mem.

HARWOOD, ELLEN; Chanute Sr HS; Chanute, KS; (3); 1/140; Church Yth Grp; FCA; VP 4-H; Spanish Clb; Acpl Chr; School Musical; Ofcr Stu Cncl; Chrldng; High Hon Roll; NHS; Prins Ldrshp Tm; KS ST Univ.

HASAN, HEATHER L; Halstead HS; Newton, KS; (1); Hosp Aide; Letterman Clb; Spanish Clb; Drill Tm; School Musical; School Play; Stage Crew; Bsktbl; Pom Pon; Powder Puff Ftbl; Buster Clb.

HASELHORST, JASON M; Great Bend Sr HS; Great Bend, KS; (3); Church Yth Grp; Drama Clb; Natl FFA Org; Pep Clb; Acpl Chr; Variety Show; Hon Roll; FFA Org; 1st Soph Pres His Of GBHS; Wildlf Bio.

HASH, NICOLE; Louisburg HS; Louisburg, KS; (3); 1/87; Debate Tm; Drama Clb; Q&S; SADD; School Play; Ed Nwsp; Lit Mag; Vllybl; High Hon Roll; NHS; Truman ST Univ; Cmptr Sci/Comm.

HASHMI, MICHELLE C; Emporia HS; Emporia, KS; (2); Debate Tm; FCA; Key Clb; NFL; Cit Awd; Hon Roll; Piano 10 Yrs; Univ Of KS; Pre Med.

HASKELL, NATHAN; Kinsley HS; Kinsley, KS; (2); Band; VP Soph Cls; Var L Bsktbl; JV Ftbl; Var Golf; High Hon Roll; Hon Roll; Trgt Clb; Art.

HASLETT, CASSI; Syracuse Jr Sr HS; Syracuse, KS; (1); Church Yth Grp; 4-H; Pep Clb; Spanish Clb; VP Frsh Cls; JV Var Bsktbl; Var Powder Puff Ftbl; Var Sftbl; Var Trk; Var Vllybl.

HASSELLE, SUZANNE M; Lawrence HS; Lawrence, KS; (4); Cmnty Wkr; Debate Tm; Key Clb; Model UN; Science Clb; Orch; Hon Roll; NHS; Ntl Merit Ltr; Prfct Atten Awd; Photo; Amherst.

HASTINGS, CLIFF R; Wabaunsee HS; Maple Hill, KS; (4); Art Clb; Church Yth Grp; 4-H; Letterman Clb; SADD; Bsktbl; Ftbl; Tennis; Hon Roll; Tarant Co JC; Phys Asst.

HASTINGS, JUSTIN P; Olathe South Sr HS; Olathe, KS; (4); Boy Scts; French Clb; Teachers Aide; Stage Crew; Trk; French Hon Soc; Hon Roll; JETS Awd; Eagle Sct With Palms; KS ST Champion-TSA-COMP Aided Drftng & Dsgn 96; Johnson Cty CC; Arch Engrng.

HASTINGS, LOGAN W; Parsons HS; Parsons, KS; (2); FTA; Key Clb; Pep Clb; Spanish Clb; SADD; Golf; Hon Roll; KS U; Architectural Drafting.

HASTY, HERNDON S; Blue Valley Northwest HS; Overland Park, KS; (2); Boy Scts; Drama Clb; Thesps; Band; Mrchg Band; School Musical; School Play; Intrml Ftbl; Hon Roll; Sci Bwl Team; Psych.

HASTY, SCOTT P; Blue Valley Northwest HS; Overland Park, KS; (3); 18/400; Boy Scts; Cmnty Wkr; Intnl Clb; Math Clb; Science Clb; Spanish Clb; High Hon Roll; U Of IL; Chemcl Engr; Comp Engr.

HATCHER, MANDY; Goodland HS; Goodland, KS; (3); 17/85; Church Yth Grp; Sec 4-H; VP FHA; Band; Flag Corp; Jazz Band; Pep Band; Golf; 4-H Awd; Hon Roll; Kayettes Pts Chm; 4-H Yth Issues 95 Memphis; KS ST U; Intr Arch.

HATCHER, WES; Goodland HS; Goodland, KS; (1); Church Yth Grp; 4-H; Natl FFA Org; Band; Jazz Band; Pep Band; Ofcr Bsbl; Bsktbl; Ftbl; Trk; Grand Champion Geology; 4-H Jr Ldrs; Dist 4-H Record Winner.

HATFIELD, CHRISTINA; Larned HS; Larned, KS; (2); Church Yth Grp; Quiz Bowl; Band; Mrchg Band; Pep Band; Bsktbl; Sftbl; Trk; Vllybl; Wt Lftg; Wichita ST U; Photo.

HATHAWAY, KEISHA N; Derby HS; Derby, KS; (3); Church Yth Grp; Cmnty Wkr; ROTC; Band; Church Choir; Drill Tm; Mrchg Band; Rep Soph Cls; Rep Jr Cls; Rep Stu Cncl; ROTC Ldrshp Awd; Stdnt Cncl Ldrshp Awd; ROTC Queen 95; NC A&T Univ; Behavior Sci.

HATLEY, MARY A; Chaparral HS; Harper, KS; (3); FCA; NFL; Band; Flag Corp; Chrldng; Trk; Vllybl; Debate Tm; Mrchg Band; Pep Band; NFL Chptr Treas & Pres; Stephens Coll; Pre-Law.

HATMAKER, CORY J; Douglass HS; Douglass, KS; (3); 23/60; Teachers Aide; Hon Roll; Wldng; Auto Mechs.

HATRIDGE, JILL; Olathe South Sr HS; Olathe, KS; (4); Pres Drama Clb; French Clb; NFL; Chorus; School Musical; School Play; Chrmn Stu Cncl; Powder Puff Ftbl; High Hon Roll; NHS; Pres Awd Educl Excl; AFS Exch Pgm; Truman ST; Speech Pathology.

HATTAN, JUSTIN; Concordia Jr Sr HS; Concordia, KS; (4); 1/102; Am Leg Boys St; Boy Scts; Pres Bus Profs of Am; Pres Church Yth Grp; Cmnty Wkr; Debate Tm; Drama Clb; Pres 4-H; Pres FBLA; HOBY; Coca-Cola Ldrshp Awd Natl Fnlst; Am Lgn Natl Ortrcl Cmptn St Chmpn; Close Up Wshngtn Del; Ecs.

HATTRUP, CHRISTINE L; St Thomas Aquinas HS; Overland Park, KS; (4); 1/231; Church Yth Grp; Debate Tm; Key Clb; Math Clb; Ed Nwsp; Var Sftbl; High Hon Roll; Ntl Merit SF; Pres Schlr; Shw Me Aqns Clb Pres; Chem.

HATTRUP, KIMBERLY L; Spearville Jr Sr HS; Offerle, KS; (3); Quiz Bowl; Band; Chorus; School Play; Var Bsbl; Var Bsktbl; Var Chrldng; Tennis; Var Vllybl; High Hon Roll.

HAUCK, CHAD; Minneapolis HS; Ada, KS; (3); 12/62; Am Leg Boys St; Debate Tm; 4-H; Pres Natl FFA Org; NFL; Quiz Bowl; SADD; 4-H Awd; Hon Roll; Hist NHS; KS St Univ; Vet.

HAUG, AARON M; Maur Hill Prep Schl; Atchison, KS; (1); Church Yth Grp; Debate Tm; Chorus; High Hon Roll; Acoustic Guitar.

HAUG, SUSAN J; Frankft HS; Frankfort, KS; (2); FHA; SADD; Band; Drill Tm; School Play; JV Vllybl; Cit Awd; Hon Roll; NHS; Mrchg Band; Forensics.

HAUGAARD, RYAN T; Colby Sr HS; Colby, KS; (2); Art Clb; Hosp Aide; SADD; Variety Show; Nwsp; Yrbk; JV Bsbl; Var Bsktbl; Var Crs Cntry; JV Ftbl; Grand Champ Arch; Washington Univ; Nuclear Engrng.

HAUGH, JUSTIN C; Washburn Rural HS; Topeka, KS; (3); 3/357; Boy Scts; VP Chess Clb; Church Yth Grp; Computer Clb; VP Debate Tm; Model UN; VP NFL; Speech Tm; Sec Sr Cls; JV Tennis; Knwldg Mstr Opn Prtcpnt; Amer Indvdl Math Exm Partcpnt; Natl Merit Cmnd Schlr.

HAUKAP, JAYSA A; Garden Plain Jr Sr HS; Garden Plain, KS; (3); 1/37; Red Cross Aide; Sec Spanish Clb; Treas Soph Cls; JV Var Bsktbl; Co-Capt Pom Pon; Sftbl; Var Vllybl; High Hon Roll; NHS.

HAUSCHILD, HEIDI; Sterling HS; Sterling, KS; (3); Church Yth Grp; Letterman Clb; Band; Chorus; Flag Corp; Rptr Yrbk; VP Sr Cls; Chrldng; High Hon Roll; Prfct Atten Awd; Big Brother Big Sister; CO Inst Of Art; Decorating.

HAVERAMP, ERIKA L; Nemaha Valley HS; Seneca, KS; (3); Church Yth Grp; Quiz Bowl; Scholastic Bowl; SADD; Teachers Aide; Vllybl; Hon Roll; NHS; KAY Club; U Of KS; Pdtrcn.

HAVERKAMP, ERIKA L; Nemaha Valley HS; Seneca, KS; (3); Church Yth Grp; Cmnty Wkr; Quiz Bowl; Scholastic Bowl; SADD; Teachers Aide; Vllybl; Hon Roll; NHS; Prfct Atten Awd; KS Assn Yth Clb; U Of KS; PT.

HAVERKAMP, QUINN M; Bern Schl; Bern, KS; (2); Church Yth Grp; Letterman Clb; Band; Chorus; Mrchg Band; Treas Soph Cls; JV Bsktbl; JV Vllybl; Cit Awd; Hon Roll; KS Univ; Bus.

HAVLICEK, REBECCA L; Manhattan HS; Manhattan, KS; (2); Church Yth Grp; Cmnty Wkr; 4-H; GAA; Letterman Clb; Teachers Aide; Varsity Clb; Bsktbl; Sftbl; Trk.

HAWBAKER, MEGAN M; Quinter Jr Sr HS; Quinter, KS; (3); Church Yth Grp; FCA; FHA; Letterman Clb; Math Tm; Pep Clb; Quiz Bowl; Band; Chorus; Mrchg Band.

HAWK, MEGAN D; Washburn Rural HS; Topeka, KS; (2); 10/380; Cmnty Wkr; Debate Tm; Model UN; NFL; Red Cross Aide; SADD; Teachers Aide; High Hon Roll; Hon Roll; KS Optmst Modl Leg Asst Sec ST; Sec ST; Psych/Soc/Soc Wk.

HAWKINS, ANDY; West Elk Jr Sr HS; Grenola, KS; (2); 2/37; Pres 4-H; Letterman Clb; Math Tm; Sec Natl FFA Org; Band; Pep Band; School Play; Rep Frsh Cls; Sec Stu Cncl; JV Var Bsktbl; KS ST; Pre-Vet Sci.

HAWKINS, CHRISTINA L; Leavenworth HS; Leavenworth, KS; (3); Art Clb; Chess Clb; SADD; Hon Roll; Prfct Atten Awd; Schlsp; Stu Of Month; Stock Markt, Spcl Art, Excl In Math & GREAT Awds; Prof Artst; Acctng & Puzzle Clb; Norfolk ST Univ; Acctng; Bus.

HAWKINS III, FLOYD; Sumner Acad Of Arts & Science; Kansas City, KS; (3); Latin Clb; Spanish Clb; Band; Mrchg Band; Pep Band; Var L Bsktbl; Var L Crs Cntry; Var Tennis; Hon Roll; Langston Univ; Bus.

HAWKINS, JESSICA; Garden City Sr HS; Garden City, KS; (3); Science Clb; VICA; Band; Jazz Band; Hon Roll.

HAWKINS, MELISA R; Shawnee Mission N HS; Shawnee Mission, KS; (2); Dance Clb; Drama Clb; Latin Clb; Teachers Aide; Chorus; School Play; High Hon Roll; Hon Roll; Hoffman Intl Mdlng Schl; Johnson Cty CC; Mtrlgst.

HAWKINS, NISHON J; Junction City HS; Junction City, KS; (2); High Hon Roll.

HAWKINS, REBECCA; Junction City HS; Manhattan, KS; (3); Church Yth Grp; Teachers Aide; Chorus; School Musical; High Hon Roll; Liberty Univ; Law Enforcement.

HAWKINS, SCOTT M; Washburn Rural HS; Topeka, KS; (3); 120/400; Church Yth Grp; Computer Clb; Teachers Aide; Band; Church Choir; Mrchg Band; Pep Band; JV Golf; High Hon Roll; Mus Cmp; 1st Chr Prcsn; Drum Line Cmp; Chrch Hndbl Chr; Drms Cntmpry Wrshp Svc; Chrch Msn Wrk; Hsptl Vol; KS ST; Acctng/Cmptr Tech.

HAWKINSON, JOHN T; Inman Jr Sr HS; Mc Pherson, KS; (2); Hon Roll.

HAWKS, KAMI; Northern Valley HS; Almena, KS; (4); 1/10; Am Leg Aux Girls St; HOBY; Chorus; Pres Jr Cls; Pres Stu Cncl; Var Capt Bsktbl; Var Capt Chrldng; Var Capt Vllybl; High Hon Roll; Val; KS ST U; Psych.

HAWKS, MEGAN E; Wellington Sr HS; Wellington, KS; (3); #13 in class; Cmnty Wkr; Drama Clb; Band; Jazz Band; School Play; Ofcr Stu Cncl; Var Chrldng; Stat Wrstlng; High Hon Roll; NHS; Piano Top Hnrs Tri-St; Rollerblading & Gymnstcs; KS U; Ed.

HAWLEY, STEPHANIE V; Riverton Schl; Riverton, KS; (3); Church Yth Grp; VP Band; Orch; Pres Frsh Cls; Pres Soph Cls; Capt Bsktbl; Capt Chrldng; Var Socr; Var Trk; High Hon Roll; Vp Adv Brd; Pittsburg St Univ; Human Bio.

HAWPE, DENISE; Hays HS; Hays, KS; (3); 16/247; Pres Church Yth Grp; VP 4-H; Quiz Bowl; Church Choir; Stage Crew; Stat Bsktbl; Stat JV Vllybl; 4-H Awd; High Hon Roll; NHS; Acad Lttr; Prjct Ldr; Ft Hays ST Univ; Scndry Tchr.

HAWTHORNE, APRIL M; Great Bend Sr HS; Great Bend, KS; (2); Church Yth Grp; 4-H; Pep Clb; Band; Jazz Band; Pep Band; JV Vllybl; High Hon Roll; Prfct Atten Awd; Chrch Piano & Spcl Music; 1st Chair Clarinet, Sect Ldr & Marching Band; KU; Acctng; Bus.

HAWTHORNE, NICOLE; Goddard HS; Goddard, KS; (2); Church Yth Grp; Office Aide; Chorus; Var Socr; Var Vllybl; High Hon Roll; Hon Roll; Pres Acad Fit Awd.

HAWTHORNE, SKYE LENEE; Hays HS; Hackensack, NJ; (3); Church Yth Grp; Girl Scts; Pep Clb; Orch; School Musical; Mgr Variety Show; Hon Roll; NHS; Sternberg Museum Vol; Dead Poet Soc; Ft Hays ST Univ; Archeaology.

HAY, BRANDON N; Bishop Carroll Catholic HS; Wichita, KS; (3); Church Yth Grp; Letterman Clb; Var L Bsbl; JV Var Bsktbl; Intrml Ftbl.

HAY, JASON A; Northeast HS; Arma, KS; (2); 21/45; Rptr Yrbk; Var Bsbl; JV Bsktbl; JV Ftbl.

HAYES, BEN; Hutchinson HS; Hutchinson, KS; (4); 6/255; Am Leg Boys St; Boy Scts; Church Yth Grp; HOBY; Key Clb; Science Clb; Church Choir; Ed Yrbk; Rep Frsh Cls; JV Crs Cntry; Hastings Coll.

HAYES, BRIGETTE; Topeka West HS; Topeka, KS; (4); Church Yth Grp; German Clb; Q&S; Nwsp; Lit Mag; Socr; Hon Roll; Debate Tm; Math Clb; Atheneum Wrtng Clb Hospitality Chair; Forensics; KS Bd Of Regents Schlr.

HAYES, JAMIE; Baldwin HS; Baldwin City, KS; (4); 17/78; Church Yth Grp; FHA; Intnl Clb; Teachers Aide; Math Tm; Band; Mrchg Band; Pep Band; Var Capt Crs Cntry; Var L Trk; U Of Evansville.

HAYES, ROBERT H; Anderson Cty Jr Sr HS; Garnett, KS; (2); JV Var Bsktbl; Var Crs Cntry; Intrml Wt Lftg; High Hon Roll; Pres Acad Fit Awd.

HAYES, ROBIN; Seaman Sr HS; Topeka, KS; (3); FBLA; FHA; Hosp Aide; Key Clb; SADD; Ofcr Stu Cncl; High Hon Roll; Jr NHS; NHS; Peer Mediation; Psycht.

HAYES, SAM; Kingman HS; Kingman, KS; (3); 32/80; 4-H; FBLA; Natl FFA Org; SADD; Teachers Aide; Bsktbl; Ftbl; Golf; Sftbl; 4-H Awd; KS ST U; Arch Engrng.

HAYES, TERRA M; Douglass HS; Augusta, KS; (3); Church Yth Grp; Cmnty Wkr; FCA; Hosp Aide; Office Aide; Swing Chorus; Ofcr Sr Cls; Mgr(s); Vllybl; High Hon Roll; PT/ATH Trnr.

HAYMOND, BETH C; Ellsworth HS; Ellsworth, KS; (2); 5/90; Church Yth Grp; Pres VP 4-H; Girl Scts; Band; Chorus; Church Choir; Mrchg Band; Pep Band; School Play; Swing Chorus; Ft Hays ST Univ; Early Chldhd.

HAYNES, CHRISTINA L; Topeka West HS; Topeka, KS; (3); Cmnty Wkr; Debate Tm; FTA; NFL; Rep Pep Clb; Spanish Clb; Speech Tm; SADD; Teachers Aide; JV Bsktbl; Teens HOPE; TEA Party; K ST; Elem Ed.

HAYNES, KEVIN H; Russell HS; Russell, KS; (1); 4-H; Pep Clb; Quiz Bowl; Scholastic Bowl; Science Clb; Band; Chorus; Church Choir; Mrchg Band; Pep Band.

HAYNIE, NICOLE; Goddard HS; Goddard, KS; (3); 77/171; Church Yth Grp; Hosp Aide; Science Clb; Spanish Clb; SADD; Teachers Aide; Band; Church Choir; Mrchg Band; Pep Band; Child Care Provider; Far Weest Optimist Club; Exercising; Elem Ed.

HAYS, ANNE; Shawnee Mission E Sr HS; Fairway, KS; (3); 53/450; Church Yth Grp; Cmnty Wkr; French Clb; GAA; Natl Beta Clb; Q&S; Chorus; Church Choir; Phtg Nwsp; Bsktbl; Childrens Hosp Vol; KS U; Psych.

HAYS, ERIN H; Shawnee Mission W Sr HS; Lenexa, KS; (2); Church Yth Grp; Dance Clb; Pep Clb; Band; Drill Tm; Mrchg Band; Hon Roll; Pres Acad Fit Awd; Tchr At Dance Studio.

HAYS, JAMIE A; Pratt HS; Pratt, KS; (2); Church Yth Grp; FHA; Pep Clb; SADD; Chorus; School Musical; Var Sftbl; JV Vllybl; Hon Roll; KS Univ; Med.

HAYS, REBEKAH; Northern Valley HS; Logan, KS; (3); 1/16; Am Leg Aux Girls St; Chorus; Pres Jr Cls; Pres Sr Cls; VP Stu Cncl; Bsktbl; Chrldng; Trk; Vllybl; High Hon Roll; U Of KS; Pedtrcn.

HAZELRIGG, JESSICA; Junction City HS; San Antonio, TX; (1); 1/409; Church Yth Grp; Quiz Bowl; Red Cross Aide; Bsktbl.

HEAD, SARA; Yates Ctr HS; Yates Center, KS; (3); FHA; Girl Scts; Spanish Clb; Teachers Aide; Band; Mrchg Band; Pep Band; Chrldng; Vllybl; Cit Awd; Cadet Law Enfrcmt Acad; Pittsburg ST U; Comp.

HEAD, TRACEY L; Oskaloosa HS; Ozawkie, KS; (3); Church Yth Grp; French Clb; FBLA; Sftbl; High Hon Roll; Hon Roll; OK Bptst U; Eng.

HEADINGS, ANDREA; Central Christian Schl; Hutchinson, KS; (2); Church Yth Grp; Band; Chorus; Church Choir; Mrchg Band; Pep Band; Chrldng; Hon Roll; Home Ec.

HEADLEY, MATT; Hutchinson HS; Hutchinson, KS; (4); Art Clb; Church Yth Grp; Rep Soph Cls; Rep Jr Cls; Rep Sr Cls; Rep Stu Cncl; Var Ftbl; Hon Roll; Amnesty Intl Clb; Rising Star Art Pgm; Boys St; KS Univ Lawrence; Art.

HEADLEY, MIKE; Wellington Sr HS; Wellington, KS; (2); Church Yth Grp; Natl FFA Org; SADD; Var JV Bsktbl; Var Crs Cntry; Var Trk; Hon Roll; Jr NHS.

HEALEY, REANNA; Atchison Sr HS; Atchison, KS; (1); Spanish Clb; Chorus; Upward Bnd; Art Dsgnr.

HEALY, ANTHONY J; Bishop Carroll Catholic HS; Wichita, KS; (3); FCA; Ski Clb; Rep Sr Cls; Ftbl; Socr; Ntl Merit Ltr; Pre-Med.

HEALY, JENNIFER; Lansing HS; Lansing, KS; (4); 9/150; Am Leg Aux Girls St; Key Clb; NFL; Office Aide; Spanish Clb; School Play; Pom Pon; High Hon Roll; NHS; U KS Hnr Schlr; KSU; Wildlife Bio.

HEALY, WENDY; Spring Hill HS; Spring Hill, KS; (2); Church Yth Grp; Cmnty Wkr; 4-H; Acpl Chr; Chorus; Church Choir; School Musical; JV Var Bsktbl; Var Sftbl; 4-H Awd; Reg & St HS Piano Fest.

HEARD, JOHN C; Wichita East HS; Wichita, KS; (3); Treas Drama Clb; Sec French Clb; Pres SADD; Treas Thesps; School Play; Stage Crew; VP Stu Cncl; NHS; Debate Tm; School Musical; Spirit Cabinet; Music Thtr; Intl Rltns/Thtr.

HEARD, SCOTT; Iola Sr HS; Iola, KS; (3); Am Leg Boys St; French Clb; FBLA; Ftbl; Golf; High Hon Roll; Hon Roll; NHS; KS ST Univ.

HEARNE, BENJAMIN L; Manhattan HS; Norman, OK; (2); Intrml Bsbl; JV Socr; Hon Roll; Bsktbl; Cmptr Prgrm.

HEARNE, TRICIA D; Independence HS; Independence, KS; (1); 1/200; Church Yth Grp; Cmnty Wkr; FCA; Pep Clb; SADD; Chorus; High Hon Roll; Hon Roll; Church Choir; Powder Puff Ftbl; ST/DIST Choir.

HEARTING, AMY I; Trego Comm HS; Wa Keeney, KS; (2); 24/55; Church Yth Grp; Debate Tm; Drama Clb; NFL; Pep Clb; Science Clb; Speech Tm; SADD; Band; Mrchg Band; Sci; Lawyer.

HEARTING, HOLLY; Trego Comm HS; Wa Keeney, KS; (4); 1/45; Church Yth Grp; Debate Tm; FHA; German Clb; Girl Scts; Quiz Bowl; Science Clb; SADD; Band; Mrchg Band; Explrr Scts; Peer Mdtr; U Of KS; Eng.

HEATH, ANGEL V; Leavenworth HS; Leavenworth, KS; (2); Church Yth Grp; Cmnty Wkr; GAA; ROTC; SADD; Teachers Aide; Band; Chorus; Church Choir; Variety Show; ST Bsktbl 4th Pl; ST Trck Lng Jmp 2nd Pl/200m 5th Pl; Hustle Awd Vlybl; Mst Imprvd JV/V Bsktbl; U Of NC; Fine Arts/Comm.

HEATH, MICHELLE L; Chase Co HS; Cedar Point, KS; (3); Church Yth Grp; Math Tm; Spanish Clb; Mrchg Band; Pep Band; Sftbl; Vllybl; Hon Roll; NHS; KAYS; ESU; Bus/Acctng.

HEATHERMAN, REBECCA A; Kingman HS; Kingman, KS; (1); 4/90; Church Yth Grp; 4-H; FBLA; SADD; Intrml Bsktbl; Mgr(s); Var Trk; JV Intrml Vllybl; High Hon Roll; Summer Swim Tm; Running Long Dist; TTLT; Emporia ST Univ; Psych.

HEATON, DANNIELL A; Russell HS; Russell, KS; (3); Drama Clb; SADD; Band; Chorus; Church Choir; Mrchg Band; Pep Band; School Musical; School Play; Hon Roll; Fr Camp; KS ST Univ; Music Ed.

HEAVEY, BRANDON A; Blue Valley Northwest HS; Overland Park, KS; (2); Boy Scts; Science Clb; Band; Mrchg Band; Pep Band; Hon Roll; Prfct Atten Awd; Roller Hcky Team Capt; Eagle Sct; Comp Sci.

HEAVRIN, SARAH E; Parsons HS; Parsons, KS; (1); Pep Clb; Chorus; JV Var Chrldng; Hon Roll; Pre-Med Clb; Sports Clb; All-Star Chrldr Awd; KS Univ.

HECHT, TRAVIS W; Bern Schl; Seneca, KS; (3); 3/17; Church Yth Grp; Cmnty Wkr; Drama Clb; FCA; Letterman Clb; Pep Clb; Quiz Bowl; Scholastic Bowl; Spanish Clb; SADD; KS St Univ; Bus.

HECK, KATIE E; Lawrence HS; Lawrence, KS; (2); FCA; Band; Sec Jr Cls; Rep Stu Cncl; Mgr(s); JV Socr; Stat Vllybl; Hon Roll; Spec Ed.

HECK, MAGGIE M; Baldwin HS; Lawrence, KS; (4); 20/77; GAA; Sec Intnl Clb; Sec Letterman Clb; Pep Clb; Sec Varsity Clb; Yrbk; Ofcr Stu Cncl; Var Tennis; Var Vllybl; High Hon Roll; Comm Svc Projects; U Of KS; Intnl Bus.

HECKERSON, NICHOLAS R; Holton HS; Holton, KS; (2); JV L Golf; Hon Roll; KS St Water Ski Championships Top 3; KS ST Univ; Bus.

HECKLER, ARIEL; Newton Sr HS; Newton, KS; (4); 6/211; Am Leg Aux Girls St; Art Clb; German Clb; Orch; Swing Chorus; High Hon Roll; NHS; Elem Schl Vol; Bethel Coll; Genetcs.

HECKMAN, BROOKE; Yates Ctr HS; Yates Center, KS; (3); FCA; FHA; Spanish Clb; SADD; Pres Frsh Cls; Rptr Jr Cls; Ofcr Stu Cncl; Chrldng; High Hon Roll; NHS; Pittsburg ST U; Nrsng.

HEDGE, BRIAN D; Thomas More Prep-Marion HS; Hays, KS; (2); Var Bsbl; Var Ftbl; Hon Roll.

HEDGER, JAY; Hutchinson HS; Hutchinson, KS; (3); Office Aide; Prfct Atten Awd; Ftbl/Trck Var Trnr; Sprts Med.

HEDGES, ROBIN R; Shawnee Heights Sr HS; Topeka, KS; (2); Pep Clb; SADD; Chorus; Ofcr Drill Tm; Pom Pon; Hon Roll; KS Univ; Pediatric Nrs.

HEDMAN, BREE; Manhattan HS; Manhattan, KS; (3); 1/433; Treas Church Yth Grp; Cmnty Wkr; FCA; Pep Clb; Church Choir; Intrml Bsktbl; Var L Crs Cntry; Var L Trk; Intrml Vllybl; High Hon Roll.

HEDRICK, BRYAN M; Holton HS; Denison, KS; (1); Chorus; Rep Frsh Cls; Rep Stu Cncl; Intrml Bsktbl; Intrml Ftbl; Intrml Wt Lftg; Washburn; Meteorlgy.

HEDRICK, JAIMEE A; Wichita East HS; Wichita, KS; (3); Church Yth Grp; Cmnty Wkr; Chorus; Church Choir; Orch; Variety Show; Soc Wrk/Psych.

HEETER, ABIGEAL; Shawnee Mission Nw Sr HS; Shawnee Mission, KS; (4); 101/408; Pep Clb; Var L Diving; High Hon Roll; NHS; Pres Acad Fit Awd; Pres Schlr; St Schlr; KS Hnr Schlr; Prom Comm; Ballet Dancer; Northeast MO ST; Bio; Med.

HEFFNER, AMANDA S; Wichita East HS; Kechi, KS; (2); #1 in class; Drama Clb; German Clb; Thesps; Chorus; School Musical; School Play; High Hon Roll; Variety Show; Hon Roll; Ballet; Jazz; Tap; Choreographer; Intern Co Mem Music Theatre; Musical Theatre; Film; TV.

HEFFRON, TYLER E; Wellington Sr HS; Wellington, KS; (2); Church Yth Grp; Debate Tm; NFL; Office Aide; Red Cross Aide; Scholastic Bowl; Speech Tm; SADD; Rep Frsh Cls; Rep Soph Cls; KAY Rep; Lawyer.

HEGEDUS, JESSICA; Blue Vlly NW HS; Overland Park, KS; (2); 70/409; Cmnty Wkr; Q&S; Rptr Nwsp; JV Trk; High Hon Roll; Hon Roll; Vol For Spec Oympcs; 2nd Plc Feature Writing Cont; Jrnlsm.

HEIDRICK, JEFFERY B; Maize HS; Wichita, KS; (2); 1/300; Debate Tm; NFL; Spanish Clb; SADD; Band; Mrchg Band; Pep Band; JV Bsbl; JV Bsktbl; High Hon Roll.

HEIER, CARRIE L; Wheatland Middle Sr HS; Park, KS; (3); 2/15; Art Clb; Church Yth Grp; Quiz Bowl; Chorus; School Play; Bsktbl; Chrldng; Vllybl; Hon Roll; Ft Hays ST U; Bus.

HEIKKILA, CHRISTINA R; Great Bend Sr HS; Great Bend, KS; (1); Debate Tm; Drama Clb; German Clb; NFL; Speech Tm; Band; Prfct Atten Awd.

HEIL, TARA; Ulysses HS; Ulysses, KS; (4); 13/93; Art Clb; Church Yth Grp; Nwsp; Yrbk; NHS; Early Chldhd Educ.

HEILI, JASMINE; Garden City Sr HS; Garden City, KS; (4); 1/311; Am Leg Aux Girls St; Church Yth Grp; Science Clb; Spanish Clb; SADD; Treas Stu Cncl; Var Chrldng; NHS; Tandy Tech Schlr; Emporia ST U; Optmtry.

HEIM, JUSTIN; St Marys HS; Saint Marys, KS; (2); 8/50; Var L Bsktbl; Var L Ftbl; High Hon Roll; NHS; Acctng.

HEIM, RYAN M; Shawnee Mission N HS; Roeland Park, KS; (1); Cmnty Wkr; JV Bsbl; Hon Roll; OK ST Univ; Fire Engrng.

HEIMAN, AMY; Olathe North Sr HS; Olathe, KS; (3); 1/390; Church Yth Grp; GAA; Math Tm; Orch; Rep Soph Cls; Treas Jr Cls; Var Sftbl; High Hon Roll; NHS; Pres Acad Fit Awd.

HEIMAN, JAMIE L; Bailey-Benedict Jr Sr High; Baileyville, KS; (1); 1/20; Church Yth Grp; FBLA; FHA; Letterman Clb; Treas Pep Clb; Quiz Bowl; Scholastic Bowl; Band; Mrchg Band; Pep Band; KS Univ; Pharm/Spts Med.

HEIMAN, MICHAELA M; Bailey-Benedict Jr Sr High; Baileyville, KS; (1); Church Yth Grp; FBLA; FHA; Pep Clb; Band; Pep Band; Pres Frsh Cls; JV Bsktbl; Var Chrldng; Var Powder Puff Ftbl.

HEIMILLER, NICHOLAS; Washburn Rural HS; Topeka, KS; (3); Debate Tm; Science Clb; Hon Roll; Rptr Nwsp; Lit Mag; Earthbnd Clb Treas 96-; Star Trek Clb; Human Rghts; U Of CO; Eng/Bio.

HEIN, CARMEN; Hillsboro HS; Hillsboro, KS; (1); 15/71; Church Yth Grp; Spanish Clb; Chorus; Ofcr Bsbl; JV JV Bsktbl; Sftbl; Trk; Vllybl; Hon Roll; NHS.

HEIN, TERESA M; Great Bend Sr HS; Great Bend, KS; (3); Pep Clb; SADD; Hon Roll; Ntl Merit Ltr; Prfct Atten Awd; Pre-Law.

HEINE, RACHEL L; Chase HS; Chase, KS; (2); 1/18; Church Yth Grp; FHA; Letterman Clb; Math Clb; Math Tm; Quiz Bowl; Spanish Clb; Band; Pep Band; Pres Frsh Cls.

HEINE, SARA J; Chase HS; Ellinwood, KS; (2); 1/20; Hist Church Yth Grp; FHA; Letterman Clb; Quiz Bowl; Spanish Clb; Band; Pep Band; Sec Treas Frsh Cls; Sec Treas Soph Cls; High Hon Roll; KS ST; Cmptr Sci.

HEINEMANN, LINDSAY R; Wichita North HS; Wichita, KS; (4); Red Cross Aide; Thesps; Acpl Chr; School Musical; Rep Frsh Cls; Rep Soph Cls; 5th Plc Nats Natl Sngng Comp; Olympic Torch Coca Cola Choir; Wichita ST Univ; Music Perf.

HEINEN, DANA; Nemaha Valley HS; Seneca, KS; (3); HOBY; Letterman Clb; SADD; Sec Frsh Cls; Var Capt Bsktbl; L Trk; Var Capt Vllybl; Hon Roll; Prfct Atten Awd; Church Yth Grp; KAYS Brd, Wrld Svc, Cmmnty Svc, Sec; Nrsng Hm Cert Nrses Aide; PE.

HEINEN, DAVID E; Valley Falls HS; Valley Falls, KS; (4); 10/32; Am Leg Boys St; Cmnty Wkr; FCA; Band; Mrchg Band; Pep Band; JV Var Ftbl; Wt Lftg; Cit Awd; Hon Roll; Devry Inst Tech; Elec Eng.

HEINEN, GLENN; Nemaha Valley HS; Seneca, KS; (3); Pres Frsh Cls; Pres Soph Cls; Pres Jr Cls; Var Bsktbl; Var Crs Cntry; Ftbl; 4-H Awd; High Hon Roll; NHS; Pres Acad Fit Awd.

HEINEN, JENNIFER J; Axtell Schl; Axtell, KS; (3); FCA; Letterman Clb; Band; Chorus; Mrchg Band; Pep Band; School Musical; Yrbk; Sec Frsh Cls; Sec Jr Cls; KAYS Mem, Bd & VP; Non School Spon Sftbl; Nrsng.

HEINEN, LUCAS W; Horton HS; Denton, KS; (4); 5/65; Church Yth Grp; Natl FFA Org; Teachers Aide; Bsktbl; High Hon Roll; NHS; Ag Bus.

HEINEN, MISTY; Valley Falls HS; Valley Falls, KS; (2); Church Yth Grp; Drama Clb; FBLA; NFL; Key Clb; School Play; High Hon Roll; Y-Teens; KAY.

HEINEN, TODD J; Desoto HS; De Soto, KS; (3); 1/150; Treas 4-H; Band; Bsktbl; Var Ftbl; Cit Awd; High Hon Roll; NHS; Pres Acad Fit Awd.

HEINIGER, LESLIE J; Bern Schl; Bern, KS; (2); Pep Clb; Quiz Bowl; Spanish Clb; SADD; Chorus; Var Bsbl; Var L Ftbl; Mgr(s); Cit Awd; Hon Roll; Pitcher On HS Girls Sftbl Team; Golf; Sports Medicine.

HEINIGER, PETE C; Williamsburg Schl; Williamsburg, KS; (3); 4-H; French Clb; Natl FFA Org; Varsity Clb; Acpl Chr; Band; Chorus; Jazz Band; Pep Band; School Play; Sing; Square Dance; KS ST Univ; Vocal Perfrmnc.

HEINITZ, KATINA; Ulysses HS; Ulysses, KS; (2); Boy Scts; Church Yth Grp; Letterman Clb; SADD; Band; School Musical; Sec Stu Cncl; Bsktbl; Crs Cntry; Hon Roll; Spnsh Peaks Sct Ranch Staff; Rock Clmbng; Marian Medal.

HEINS, CRYSTAL G; Olpe Schl; Olpe, KS; (2); Church Yth Grp; 4-H; Band; Church Choir; Mrchg Band; Pep Band; School Play; Pres Soph Cls; Var Bsktbl; Var Vllybl.

HEINTZ, HILARY M; Blue Valley Northwest HS; Overland Park, KS; (1); Church Yth Grp; Cmnty Wkr; Service Clb; Church Choir; Bsktbl; Crs Cntry; Trk; Hon Roll; Art & Eng Awds; Med.

HEINTZELMAN, DAWN M; Leavenworth HS; Leavenworth, KS; (4); 80/360; Church Yth Grp; Cmnty Wkr; ROTC; Teachers Aide; Varsity Clb; Chorus; Color Guard; Drill Tm; Flag Corp; School Musical; Drill Tm Capt; Drill/Weapons 6th Pl Nation; Pharm.

HEINTZELMAN, DREW B; Tonganoxie HS; Tonganoxie, KS; (3); Art Clb; Church Yth Grp; Cmnty Wkr; Math Tm; Science Clb; Spanish Clb; SADD; Teachers Aide; High Hon Roll; Kiwanis Awd; U Of KS; Pre-Med.

HEINTZELMAN, MOLLY K; Blue Valley HS; Overland Park, KS; (2); Spanish Clb; SADD; Ed Yrbk; Hon Roll; Yng Life.

HEINZ, TIMOTHY J; Garden City Sr HS; Garden City, KS; (1); Church Yth Grp; Science Clb; Bsktbl; Ftbl; Wt Lftg; Hon Roll; KS Univ; Math; Sci.

HEIRONIMUS, MICHAEL K; Central Heights Sr HS; Greeley, KS; (3); Quiz Bowl; Science Clb; Spanish Clb; Speech Tm; Teachers Aide; Rep Nwsp; Treas Soph Cls; High Hon Roll; Pres Acad Fit Awd; Comp Engrng.

HEISERMAN, JENNY A; Shawnee Heights HS; Topeka, KS; (3); Church Yth Grp; Cmnty Wkr; Pep Clb; Chorus; High Hon Roll; Prfct Atten Awd; Care Co Fcltr; Page For Senate.

HEISKELL, SARAH M; Derby HS; Derby, KS; (3); Art Clb; Chorus; Rptr Lit Mag; Hon Roll; Pres Acad Fit Awd; Modeling; Prin Hnr Roll; KU; Pharmacy.

HEITMAN, ETHAN; Manhattan HS; Manhattan, KS; (4); Band; Phtg Nwsp; Phtg Yrbk; Ftbl; Wt Lftg; Boys ST 96 Mayor Of City; K ST; Portrait Photo.

HEITMANN, LORRAINE K; Coldwater Jr Sr HS; Coldwater, KS; (2); Church Yth Grp; Debate Tm; Drama Clb; FHA; Band; Chorus; Church Choir; School Play; Variety Show; High Hon Roll.

HEITZ, CHRISTIN H; Maize HS; Wichita, KS; (3); Church Yth Grp; French Clb; NFL; Office Aide; Thesps; School Play; Stage Crew; Tennis; Hon Roll; KAYS; Wichita ST Univ; Med; Hlth.

HELLER, JESSICA R; Sylvan Unified HS; Hunter, KS; (3); Am Leg Aux Girls St; Math Tm; Quiz Bowl; Speech Tm; Band; Chorus; Bsktbl; Vllybl; 4-H Awd; NHS; Lions St Band; Shriner St Band; KS ST; Human Ecology.

HELLERUD, LESLEY M; Junction City HS; Junction City, KS; (4); 9/224; Church Yth Grp; Acpl Chr; School Musical; Treas Soph Cls; Treas Jr Cls; Rep Sr Cls; Rep Stu Cncl; Chrldng; Tennis; Cit Awd; KS ST U; Fshn Merchandising.

HELLERUD, LORI L; Junction City HS; Junction City, KS; (1); Church Yth Grp; Pep Clb; Acpl Chr; Ofcr Frsh Cls; Chrldng; High Hon Roll; KU; Obstetrical Nrs.

HELLWIG, DIANE J; Labette Co HS; Altamont, KS; (2); 1/163; Church Yth Grp; VP 4-H; FBLA; Hosp Aide; Natl FFA Org; Chorus; Yrbk; JV Chrldng; JV Crs Cntry; High Hon Roll; FBLA St Parlimentarian; Local Sec.

HELM, AMBER; Kingman HS; Kingman, KS; (4); 5/72; VP FCA; Pres 4-H; HOBY; Rep Natl FFA Org; Quiz Bowl; Church Choir; Variety Show; Rep Stu Cncl; Var L Golf; High Hon Roll; Dansforth I Dare You Awd; OK Soc Rng Mgmt Rng Yth Acad Top Cmpr 94; KS 4-3-2-1a Rgnl Glf Indvl Chmpn; Scndry Educ.

HELM, CARRIE L; Maize HS; Wichita, KS; (3); Drama Clb; Letterman Clb; Science Clb; SADD; Thesps; Stage Crew; Capt Pom Pon; Wt Lftg; Hon Roll; Cleveland Schl Chiroprtc.

HELM, DENISE R; Cheney Jr Sr HS; Cheney, KS; (2); 10/50; Art Clb; Chorus; Church Choir; High Hon Roll; Hon Roll; Pres Schlr; Bus; Engr.

HELM, KRISTINA A; Turner HS; Kansas City, KS; (2); Drill Tm; School Musical; Variety Show; Ofcr Jr Cls; Ofcr Stu Cncl; Cit Awd; Hon Roll; Jr NHS; NHS; Pres Acad Fit Awd; U Of KS; Phtgrphr.

HELM, REBECCA D; Pierson Jr HS; Kansas City, KS; (1); Drill Tm; School Musical; Nwsp; Ofcr Stu Cncl; Pom Pon; Trk; Hon Roll; Drill Team; Intr Dsgnr.

HELMERS, SHAWNA M; Campus HS; Haysville, KS; (2); Church Yth Grp; SADD; Chorus; Visit Chldrn Hosp; KS Univ; DR RN/BUS Mgmt.

HELMS, ANNELIES M; Oskaloosa HS; Oskaloosa, KS; (4); 5/47; Debate Tm; FBLA; VP FHA; NFL; SADD; Band; Jazz Band; Pep Band; School Musical; Ed Nwsp; Frnch Horn Lessons; KMEA Dist Band; U Of KS; Jrnlsm.

HELMS, LAURA; Frontenac Jr Sr HS; Pittsburg, KS; (4); 4/38; Pres Drama Clb; Pep Clb; Scholastic Bowl; Sec Spanish Clb; Band; Drm Mjr(t); School Play; Pres Stu Cncl; Var Capt Chrldng; NHS; Hnr Band; St Music Festival 1st Pl; Pittsburg ST U; Ed.

HELSEL, AMY; Dexter Jr Sr HS; Dexter, KS; (3); Math Tm; Band; Drm Mjr(t); VP Jr Cls; VP Stu Cncl; Bsktbl; Chrldng; Vllybl; Hon Roll; NHS; Photojrnlsm.

HELSTROM, CLARK A; Maize HS; Wichita, KS; (3); Church Yth Grp; Teachers Aide; Hon Roll; Pre-Med.

HELTEN, AMANDA A; Garden Plain Jr Sr HS; Cheney, KS; (2); 3/30; Church Yth Grp; Scholastic Bowl; Spanish Clb; Acpl Chr; Chorus; High Hon Roll; Hon Roll; St Joe CYO Sec 9th Grd/Treas 10th Grd; Bus/Eng/Art.

HELTON, ANGELA C; Ft Scott HS; Fort Scott, KS; (4); 4-H; FTA; Key Clb; Pres VP Natl FFA Org; Pep Clb; Spanish Clb; Teachers Aide; Yrbk; 4-H Awd; Ft Scott CC.

HELTON, CALEB A; Riverton Schl; Galena, KS; (3); Art Clb; Yrbk.

HELTON, JOSH J; Syracuse Jr Sr HS; Syracuse, KS; (2); Quiz Bowl; Scholastic Bowl; Hon Roll; Cmptr Prgmr.

HEMBERGER, EMILY R; Argonia Jr Sr HS; Argonia, KS; (3); 4/21; Letterman Clb; Band; Chorus; Pep Band; Sec Frsh Cls; Sec Soph Cls; Sec Jr Cls; Var Bsktbl; Var Chrldng; Var Trk; 4 Yr Coll; Bus/Fin.

HEMBERGER, JESSICA; Argonia Jr Sr HS; Argonia, KS; (2); 2/17; Quiz Bowl; Band; School Play; Trk; JV Vllybl; High Hon Roll; Comp Tech.

HEMBREE, DEREK F; Ness City HS; Ness City, KS; (3); Boy Scts; Church Yth Grp; Office Aide; Thesps; Band; Chorus; Church Choir; Mrchg Band; Pep Band; School Musical; Chrch Choir, Trumpet, Lector & Server; I Dare You Awd; U Of KS; Acctng.

HEMBREE, JENNIFER S; Ness City HS; Ness City, KS; (1); Church Yth Grp; Girl Scts; Pep Clb; Band; Chorus; Church Choir; Mrchg Band; Pep Band; School Musical; Stage Crew; Chrch Choir, Clarinet & Server; Nrsng.

HEMBREE, KELLI M; Labette Co HS; Parsons, KS; (3); #1 in class; Chess Clb; FCA; Letterman Clb; Yrbk; Pres Soph Cls; Var Bsktbl; JV Sftbl; Var Trk; Var Vllybl; High Hon Roll; Optometry.

HEMMEN, ADAM G; Topeka West HS; Topeka, KS; (1); 17/341; Church Yth Grp; French Clb; German Clb; Math Clb; Pep Clb; Spanish Clb; SADD; Church Choir; Rep Frsh Cls; Rep Soph Cls.

HEMPHILL, JONATHAN; Central Jr HS; Lawrence, KS; (1); Church Yth Grp; Band; Chorus; Church Choir; Rep Stu Cncl; Crs Cntry; Swmmng; Trk; Hon Roll.

HEMPHILL, KIRK A; Dodge City HS; Dodge City, KS; (3); Boy Scts; French Clb; Band; Chorus; Mrchg Band; School Musical; High Hon Roll; Eagle Scout.

HEMPHILL, NICK W; Nickerson HS; Nickerson, KS; (2); Chess Clb; Math Tm; Science Clb; Intrml Bsktbl; Var Trk; Hon Roll; Vol Work; Astrnmy; Math; U Of AZ; Astrnmy.

HEMPHILL, TIFFANY J; Beloit Jr Sr HS; Beloit, KS; (1); Art Clb; Spanish Clb; Band; Orch; Pep Band; Rep Frsh Cls; Bsktbl; Vllybl; KS Span I Stu Hnr; Stu Cncl.

HENDERSON, AMY C; Shawnee Mission West HS; Lenexa, KS; (3); Church Yth Grp; Cmnty Wkr; DECA; FCA; Pep Clb; SADD; Teachers Aide; Chrldng; Hon Roll; Pres Schlr; Ballet & Jazz Dance; KS ST Univ; Bus; Mrktg.

HENDERSON, AMY J; Lyndon HS; Vassar, KS; (3); Church Yth Grp; FTA; GAA; Pep Clb; Spanish Clb; Teachers Aide; Band; Chorus; Church Choir; Mrchg Band; Hmcmng Attndt; Athl Recogntns Hgh Jmp, Lng Jmp Hnrs; KS U-Lawrence; Lwyr.

HENDERSON, AMY J; Topeka West HS; Topeka, KS; (3); Cmnty Wkr; Drama Clb; NFL; Pep Clb; Spanish Clb; Speech Tm; Thesps; School Musical; School Play; Stage Crew; Topeka West Players-Acting Group; KS Univ.

HENDERSON, ELIZABETH N; Atchison Sr HS; Atchison, KS; (2); Hon Roll; Hnrb Mntn; Meritorious Achvmt; KU; X-Ray Tech; Zoologist.

HENDERSON, HEATH W; Yates Ctr HS; Yates Center, KS; (2); Art Clb; Boy Scts; VP Church Yth Grp; Cmnty Wkr; Debate Tm; Drama Clb; VP FCA; 4-H; FHA; Letterman Clb; Baker; PE; PE Tchr.

HENDERSON, JILL R; Frontenac Jr Sr HS; Frontenac, KS; (4); Cmnty Wkr; Dance Clb; Girl Scts; Library Aide; Pep Clb; SADD; Teachers Aide; Rptr Nwsp; Phtg Yrbk; Sec Soph Cls; Comm Vol; PSU.

HENDERSON, KEITH C; Topeka West HS; Topeka, KS; (4); 23/250; Pres Debate Tm; Model UN; Pres NFL; Band; Mrchg Band; Orch; Pep Band; Gov Hon Prg Awd; Hon Roll; KS Univ; Comm Stds.

HENDERSON, KRISTI L; Topeka West HS; Topeka, KS; (1); German Clb; Band; Mrchg Band; Pep Band; School Musical; Tennis; High Hon Roll; Pres Acad Fit Awd; Rtng Regnl Solo Cntst Flute; Bus Awd Kybrdng/Intgrtd Cmptr Applctns.

HENDERSON, MARIA A; Baldwin HS; Baldwin City, KS; (2); Church Yth Grp; Intnl Clb; Pep Clb; Tennis; Pres Ed Awd; Hnr Stu Excl Awd; Distngd Schltc Achvmt Awd; Marine Biologist.

HENDERSON, MEGAN; Independence HS; Independence, KS; (1); Church Yth Grp; Debate Tm; Sec NFL; Chorus; School Musical; High Hon Roll; Bible Stud Cell Group Ldr.

HENDERSON, STEPHANIE D; Derby HS; Wichita, KS; (1); Church Yth Grp; SADD; Chorus; Rptr Nwsp; Comm Rec Leagues Bsktbl/Sftbl.

HENDERSON, TINA L; Wichita Southeast HS; Wichita, KS; (2); Church Yth Grp; Band; Chorus; Church Choir; Mrchg Band; Variety Show; Hon Roll; Elem Ed.

HENDERSON, TODD; Washington HS; Kansas City, KS; (2); Church Yth Grp; SADD; Band; Church Choir; Drm Mjr(t); Jazz Band; Mrchg Band; Orch; Pep Band; Bsktbl; Mentor & Tutor For At Risk Stus Elem & Ms; Music Ed.

HENDRICH, BRIDGETTE M; Colby Sr HS; Portis, KS; (4); 15/99; Church Yth Grp; Drama Clb; FHA; NFL; Pep Clb; Quiz Bowl; Chorus; School Play; Yrbk; Sec Soph Cls; Bob Jones U.

HENDRICKS, BRIAN; Blue Valley Northwest HS; Overland Park, KS; (1); Church Yth Grp; Orch; School Musical; Ofcr Bsbl; Crs Cntry; Hon Roll; Yth Symphony; KS ST Solo Cmptn Excl Rating Cello; Outward Bd Yth Ldrshp Pgm.

HENDRICKS, JEREMY C; Nickerson HS; Hutchinson, KS; (3); Church Yth Grp; Cmnty Wkr; Office Aide; Teachers Aide; Intrml Crs Cntry; Hon Roll; Police Cadet; Eagle Scout; Hutchinson Comm Coll; Criminal.

HENDRICKSON, CASSY; Paola HS; Paola, KS; (3); Bus Profs of Am; Pep Clb; Band; Chorus; Mrchg Band; Pep Band; Var Chrldng; High Hon Roll; NHS; Prfct Atten Awd; KS ST Univ; Optometry.

HENDRICKSON, ERIC; Olpe Schl; Olpe, KS; (4); 3/26; Church Yth Grp; Quiz Bowl; Scholastic Bowl; VP Sr Cls; Rep Stu Cncl; Var Bsktbl; Var Ftbl; Var Trk; Cit Awd; High Hon Roll; KS U HS Hnrs 96; Amer Legion Bsbl Pgm 93-96; Emporia ST U; Engrng.

HENDRIX, ANN R; Blue Valley North HS; Overland Park, KS; (2); 47/272; Drill Tm; Vllybl; Hon Roll; Dance; Engrng.

HENDRIX, TESSA L; Flinthills HS; Cassoday, KS; (3); Art Clb; FCA; Sec 4-H; SADD; Treas Soph Cls; Treas Jr Cls; Mgr(s); JV Vllybl; Hon Roll.

HENKE, KLINT; Hillcrest Schl; Cuba, KS; (1); 3/22; Church Yth Grp; 4-H; FHA; Letterman Clb; Natl FFA Org; Pep Clb; Speech Tm; Band; Jazz Band; Pep Band; KS ST U.

HENLEY, ANNIE L; Bishop Miege HS; Prairie Village, KS; (1); 44/245; Church Yth Grp; Cmnty Wkr; Pep Clb; SADD; Rep Stu Cncl; Var Bsktbl; Var Crs Cntry; Var Socr; Vllybl; High Hon Roll; Mary Ann Lucas Schlrshp Otstdng Cath Stdnt; Chldrns Mercy Hosp Vol.

HENLEY, JASON D; J C Harmon HS; Kansas City, KS; (2); Ftbl; JV Wrstlng; Hon Roll.

HENNE, MARLA; Quirira Heights HS; Holyrood, KS; (4); 4/21; Am Leg Aux Girls St; Church Yth Grp; Drama Clb; FCA; Speech Tm; Band; Chorus; Church Choir; Color Guard; Drill Tm; Bethany; Phrmcy.

HENNESSY, BRIAN M; Clearwater HS; Clearwater, KS; (3); Wrstlng; Acctng.

HENNESSY, JENNIFER L; Clearwater HS; Clearwater, KS; (4); 1/74; Letterman Clb; Math Tm; SADD; Ofcr Stu Cncl; High Hon Roll; Treas NHS; St Schlr; Val; Kayettes Sec; KS ST Univ; Environmental Eng.

HENNIG, JASON S; Chanute Sr HS; Chanute, KS; (3); Band; High Hon Roll.

HENNIGH, DAVID SHANE; Ulysses HS; Ulysses, KS; (4); Am Leg Boys St; Cmnty Wkr; HOBY; Letterman Clb; Natl FFA Org; SADD; Capt Bsktbl; NHS; Whos Who In Sports; All St Hnrb Mntn Bsktbl; Industrial Arts Clb; Dodge City CC.

HENNING, CLARKE; Kingman HS; Kingman, KS; (1); JV Bsbl; Bsktbl; Ftbl; Var Wt Lftg; High Hon Roll; Hon Roll; U Of KS; Arch.

HENNING, CRAIG; Goddard HS; Wichita, KS; (3); 48/172; Q&S; Red Cross Aide; Chorus; Jazz Band; Lit Mag; Ftbl; Tennis; Wrstlng; High Hon Roll.

HENNING, JULIE; Hays HS; Hays, KS; (3); 69/205; Church Yth Grp; Science Clb; Crs Cntry; Swmmng; Hon Roll; NHS; Pres Acad Fit Awd; KA ST Univ; Kinesiology.

HENOCH, BRANDY; Salina HS South; Salina, KS; (2); Church Yth Grp; Pep Clb; Band; Drm Mjr(t); Mrchg Band; Pep Band; Chrldng; High Hon Roll; U Of KS; Elem Ed.

HENRIKSON, SARAH L; Emporia HS; Emporia, KS; (4); Cmnty Wkr; 4-H; GAA; Letterman Clb; Pep Clb; Varsity Clb; Ed Yrbk; Rep Sr Cls; Capt L Bsktbl; L Crs Cntry; KS St Univ; Vet.

HENRY, DEANNE M; Nemaha Valley HS; Seneca, KS; (4); 16/51; Church Yth Grp; Pres SADD; Teachers Aide; Letterman Clb; Treas Chorus; Swing Chorus; Ofcr Frsh Cls; Treas Soph Cls; Treas Jr Cls; Treas Sr Cls; KAY Pres, Treas & Historian; KSHSAA Wanda Mae Vinson Schlsp; Citizens St Bnk Schlsp; Emporia ST Univ; Bus Admin.

HENRY, SARAH I; Washburn Rural HS; Topeka, KS; (4); Church Yth Grp; FCA; Church Choir; High Hon Roll; Chr Drama; Chr Wrshp Band; 3rd Pl Washburn Univ Area HS Art Cntst; Looking Up; Org Chrstn Cncrt; Allen Cty CC; Elem Ed.

HENSLER, ROBERT M; Blue Valley HS; Leawood, KS; (2); Ftbl; High Hon Roll; Ftbl Vars Ltr Awd; KS ST; Engr.

HENSLEY, BENJAMIN A; Salina HS South; Salina, KS; (4); Am Leg Boys St; Drama Clb; NFL; Thesps; Chorus; School Musical; School Play; Cit Awd; Tae Kwon Do; Piano; Bst Spprtng Actr; Mscl Theatre.

HENSLEY, CALEB T; Pittsburg HS; Pittsburg, KS; (4); 33/163; Am Leg Boys St; Boy Scts; Church Yth Grp; FCA; French Clb; FTA; Letterman Clb; Red Cross Aide; Science Clb; Band; Explorers Adventure Clb; Exlplorers Med Clb; FTA Ltr; Ftbl Ltr; Pittsburg ST Univ; Bus Admin.

HENSLEY, JERI D; Spearville Jr Sr HS; Spearville, KS; (3); FHA; Natl FFA Org; Pep Clb; Quiz Bowl; Speech Tm; Stage Crew; Sec Soph Cls; Hon Roll; Sec NHS; Prfct Atten Awd.

HENSLEY, ZACH; Bucklin Schl; Ford, KS; (2); #7 in class; Band; Chorus; Mrchg Band; Pep Band; Var L Bsktbl; Var L Ftbl; Var L Trk; Wt Lftg; Hon Roll; Pres Acad Fit Awd; Smmr Bsbl; All-Star Team 3 Yrs; Peer Hlpr.

HENTZEN, BRANDON J; Parsons HS; Parsons, KS; (3); 4/116; Boy Scts; Debate Tm; Band; Jazz Band; Mrchg Band; Pep Band; Var Ftbl; JV Golf; Var Wt Lftg; High Hon Roll; Boy Scout Eagle Awd; Master Scuba Diver; Pittsburg ST Univ; Engr.

HENTZEN, JAMIE C; Bishop Carroll Catholic HS; Wichita, KS; (2); 78/208; Church Yth Grp; Cmnty Wkr; French Clb; German Clb; SADD; Nwsp; JV Sftbl; JV Tennis; French Hon Soc; KS ST Univ; Schl Admin.

HEPHNER, KEITH A; Campus HS; Haysville, KS; (3); Library Aide; Office Aide; Science Clb; Chorus; Bsktbl; Ftbl; Mgr(s); High Hon Roll; Hon Roll; Car Clb; Wichita ST U; Pilot.

HEPLER, VALERIE A; Wichita West HS; Wichita, KS; (2); Red Cross Aide; Band; Mrchg Band; Pep Band; Nwsp; Cit Awd; Hon Roll; All City Band; Flute Solo; Hnrb Mntn.

HEPNER, PAULA; Ottawa HS; Ottawa, KS; (3); 11/149; Am Leg Aux Girls St; Church Yth Grp; FCA; Letterman Clb; Chorus; School Musical; School Play; Stage Crew; Variety Show; Pres Soph Cls; Stdnt Cncl Camp 95; Emporia ST Univ Hubbard Summer Acad Future Tchrs 96; Elem Ed.

HERBERS, CHAD; Winfield HS; Winfield, KS; (3); 36/150; FCA; Letterman Clb; Pep Clb; Varsity Clb; Rep Stu Cncl; Var Bsbl; Var Ftbl; Hon Roll; All Ark Vly Hnrb Mntn Catcher; Am Legion Cenark League All Star Catcher & Outfielder; Engrng.

HERBERT, ERIN E; Lawrence HS; Lawrence, KS; (3); Model UN; Orch; Nwsp; Lit Mag; Crs Cntry; Hon Roll.

HERBERT, TONI L; Maize HS; Wichita, KS; (2); Science Clb; Spanish Clb; SADD; Chorus; Hon Roll; Pres Acad Fit Awd; People/People Stdnt Ambsdr; Acad Lttr; Bio.

HERBISON, ALYSIA M; Basehor Linwood HS; Basehor, KS; (2); Debate Tm; FHA; NFL; SADD; Chorus; Rptr Nwsp; Hon Roll; REACH.

HERBST, KATIE M; Hayden HS; Topeka, KS; (2); NFL; JV Tennis; JV Trk; High Hon Roll; Hon Roll; Art Fest; Art Fair.

HERBSTER, JUDD L; Sabetha HS; Morrill, KS; (3); 12/85; Am Leg Boys St; Church Yth Grp; FCA; Pres 4-H; VP FHA; German Clb; Letterman Clb; Pep Clb; Spanish Clb; Rptr Swing Chorus; KS ST Univ; Law.

HERD, AMY; Goddard HS; Goddard, KS; (3); Letterman Clb; Spanish Clb; SADD; Teachers Aide; Band; Mrchg Band; Pep Band; Var Vllybl; High Hon Roll; Prfct Atten Awd; KS Univ; Elem Ed.

HERKEN, BRYAN T; Leavenworth HS; Leavenworth, KS; (4); Boy Scts; Church Yth Grp; ROTC; Color Guard; Drill Tm; Var L Socr; Capt Swmmng; High Hon Roll; NHS; Chess Clb; OK Chrstn; Bus.

HERKEN, EMILY D; Pleasant Ridge HS; Easton, KS; (3); FBLA; Pep Clb; Treas Frsh Cls; Treas Soph Cls; Treas Jr Cls; Var Chrldng; Vllybl; Hon Roll; NHS; Prfct Atten Awd; SADD; KU; Bus; Acctng.

HERKEN, MICHELLE; Jefferson West HS; Ozawkie, KS; (3); 4/85; Chess Clb; French Clb; FBLA; SADD; School Musical; School Play; Stage Crew; High Hon Roll; Hon Roll; NHS; Chem Engr.

HERL, CLINTON; Victoria HS; Victoria, KS; (2); Church Yth Grp; 4-H; Letterman Clb; SADD; Varsity Clb; VP Frsh Cls; Pres Soph Cls; Pres Jr Cls; JV Bsktbl; Var L Ftbl.

HERLEIN, JAMIE M; Ottawa HS; Ottawa, KS; (3); Letterman Clb; Varsity Clb; L Ftbl; Var Wrstlng; Hon Roll; Pres Acad Fit Awd; Univ Of KS; Law.

HERMAN, ALISSA; Concordia Jr Sr HS; Concordia, KS; (3); 20/110; Church Yth Grp; SADD; Varsity Clb; Band; Church Choir; Bsktbl; Crs Cntry; High Hon Roll; NHS; Pres Acad Fit Awd; Yth Cncl Chrch; Ft Hays; RN.

HERMAN, ASHLEY L; Dighton HS; Dighton, KS; (2); FCA; SADD; Band; Pep Band; Yrbk; Sec Soph Cls; Var L Bsktbl; Vllybl; Hon Roll; Chess Clb; KS Univ; Mrktg/Adv.

HERMAN, CHRIS C; Kingman HS; Kingman, KS; (1); Church Yth Grp; FCA; Pres 4-H; Acpl Chr; Band; Chorus; Intrml Bsktbl; Var L Tennis; 4-H Awd; High Hon Roll.

HERMAN, ROBIN; Hayden HS; Topeka, KS; (3); JA; Powder Puff Ftbl; Var L Trk; Var L Vllybl; Intrml Wt Lftg; Hon Roll; DARE Role Model; KS ST Univ; Indstrl Engr.

HERMANN, JAMI L; Oskaloosa HS; Ozawkie, KS; (2); 10/70; FBLA; FHA; SADD; Rptr Nwsp; Cit Awd; High Hon Roll; Hon Roll; Ntl Merit Ltr; Awd In Stock Mkt Game; Washburn; Law.

HERMESCH, NATHAN E; Centralia Schl; Goff, KS; (4); 1/22; VP Letterman Clb; VP Science Clb; School Play; Rptr Nwsp; Pres Frsh Cls; Capt Var Bsktbl; Capt Var Ftbl; L Var Trk; Gov Hon Prg Awd; Hon Roll; KSU Deans Awd & Schlr; Homcmng King; Tandy Tech Schlr; KS ST Univ; Mech Engr.

HERMON, DUSTIN E; South Barber HS; Kiowa, KS; (4); 2/28; Church Yth Grp; Office Aide; Speech Tm; School Play; Stage Crew; Ed Nwsp; Sec Frsh Cls; VP Soph Cls; High Hon Roll; Sal; Outstdng Sr Sci & Math; Wichita ST Univ; Phy Asst.

HERMRECK, ELIZABETH R; Anderson Cty Jr Sr HS; Garnett, KS; (2); Drama Clb; Pep Clb; Band; Jazz Band; Mrchg Band; Pep Band; Stage Crew; Ed Nwsp; High Hon Roll; Schl Plays/Musicals/Comm Perfmng Arts Light Techcns; Frnscs Tm Extemp Speaker; At Risk Studts Tutor; Lab Techn/PT.

HERNANDEZ, CATHERINE R; Cherryvale HS; Cherryvale, KS; (4); 36/40; Church Yth Grp; FHA; Scholastic Bowl; Spanish Clb; SADD; Chorus; Rep Soph Cls; Rep Jr Cls; Pom Pon; Wt Lftg; KS Hnr Schlr; Prom Qn; PSU 1st Pl; Main St, Nrsng Home Vol; KS St House Of Reps Page; U Of KS; Psychiatrist.

HERNANDEZ, DAWN V; Sumner Acad Of Arts & Science; Kansas City, KS; (3); French Clb; Latin Clb; Spanish Clb; High Hon Roll; Hon Roll; NHS; Med.

HERNANDEZ, JESUS V; Garden City Sr HS; Garden City, KS; (2); Chess Clb; Latin Clb; Science Clb; Jazz Band; Mrchg Band; Orch; Pep Band; JV Crs Cntry; JV Tennis; High Hon Roll; All-St Chess Team; St Odyssey Of The Mind Fnlst; All-Amer Schlr Sci; Cal Tech; Physics.

HERNANDEZ, MARISSA M; Bishop Miege HS; Kansas City, KS; (2); Sec Treas Church Yth Grp; SADD; Pep Band; JV Var Chrldng; Pres Acad Fit Awd; Val; Holy Name Chrch Srvr; Hlpng St Marys Food Ktchn; Nom 94 Scty Of Intnl Acad Excl; U Of MO; Med Prof.

HERNANDEZ, OSWALDO; Garden City Sr HS; Garden City, KS; (1); Socr; Engr.

HERNANDEZ, TWYLA E; Seaman Sr HS; Topeka, KS; (4); 65/242; Cmnty Wkr; Pres Rptr 4-H; Key Clb; Office Aide; Spanish Clb; SADD; Teachers Aide; Stage Crew; 4-H Awd; Hon Roll; Nrsng.

HERNDON, JENNIFER A; Blue Valley Northwest HS; Overland Park, KS; (2); Mgr(s); Hon Roll; KS Univ; CPA.

HERNDON, KATY L; Goddard HS; Goddard, KS; (1); Church Yth Grp; Office Aide; Var L Socr; Cit Awd; High Hon Roll; Pres Schlr; Natl Merit Sci Awd; KS Univ; Med Field.

HEROLD, ANGIE; Great Bend Sr HS; Great Bend, KS; (2); Pep Clb; Chorus; Variety Show; Pres Soph Cls; Var Chrldng; Var Swmmng; Medcl.

HEROLD, SHIREEN; Hays HS; Hays, KS; (4); Church Yth Grp; Cmnty Wkr; Dance Clb; Office Aide; SADD; Teachers Aide; Chorus; Intrml Powder Puff Ftbl; Intrml Socr; Mgr Trk; Spcl Olympics Vl; Ft Hays ST Univ; Elem Ed.

HERPOLSHEIMER, JUSTIN W; Belle Plaine HS; Belle Plaine, KS; (2); Spanish Clb; Hon Roll; Ntl Merit Ltr; Comp Prmng; Microbiology; Chem; Anatomy; Physiology; Physics.

HERR, JANIS M; Wichita East HS; Wichita, KS; (4); Drama Clb; Teachers Aide; Treas Thesps; Color Guard; Orch; School Play; Stage Crew; Hon Roll; KS St Thespian Brd; HERO; Butler Cnty CC; Bus Admin.

HERR, POUNG; J C Harmon HS; Kansas City, KS; (3); 1/200; Sec Church Yth Grp; FBLA; HOBY; Library Aide; Q&S; Chorus; Ed Nwsp; Treas Jr Cls; Ofcr Stu Cncl; High Hon Roll.

HERREN, REBECCA J; Wichita Southeast HS; Wichita, KS; (2); Church Yth Grp; Hosp Aide; Socr; Trk; High Hon Roll; Hon Roll; NHS; U Of KS; Chld Psych/Tchng.

HERRIAGE, CHRIS; Blue Valley Northwest HS; Overland Park, KS; (4); 67/343; Band; Jazz Band; Capt Mrchg Band; Orch; Pep Band; School Musical; JV Socr; High Hon Roll; Hon Roll; Pres Schlr; Wichita ST Univ; Music Perfmnc.

HERRING, KENT L; Valley Falls HS; Valley Falls, KS; (3); Pep Clb; Band; Pep Band; Ofcr Jr Cls; Ofcr Stu Cncl; Ftbl; Trade Schl; Electronics.

HERRING, SCOTT E; Jefferson West HS; Ozawkie, KS; (2); FBLA; Bsktbl; High Hon Roll; "cmptr/Bus.

HERRINGTON, MATTHEW T; Hill City HS; Hill City, KS; (2); Church Yth Grp; FCA; Pep Clb; SADD; JV Bsktbl; Var Trk; Var Wt Lftg; Hon Roll; KAYS Recr Ldr.

HERRMAN, ALAN; Dodge City HS; Dodge City, KS; (1); Debate Tm; Ofcr Bsbl; Bsktbl; Ftbl.

HERRMAN, ANDREA L; Salina HS South; Salina, KS; (3); Pep Clb; Teachers Aide; Band; Chorus; Church Choir; Mrchg Band; Orch; Pep Band; School Musical; High Hon Roll; U Of KS; Music.

HERRMAN, DARCY D; Great Bend Sr HS; Great Bend, KS; (2); Church Yth Grp; Debate Tm; Drama Clb; NFL; Pep Clb; Rep Spanish Clb; Speech Tm; Chorus; Co-Ed Nwsp; High Hon Roll; Psych.

HERRMAN, DUSTIN JAMES; Russell HS; Gorham, KS; (1); Boy Scts; Quiz Bowl; Band; Mrchg Band; JV Bsbl; JV Ftbl; JV Wrstlng; High Hon Roll; Sci Olympiad St Placer.

HERRMAN, ERIN; Great Bend Sr HS; Great Bend, KS; (3); Church Yth Grp; Pep Clb; SADD; Acpl Chr; Variety Show; Chrldng; Hon Roll; Prfct Atten Awd; Pres Acad Fit Awd; KS ST.

HERRMAN, JENNIFER A; Leavenworth HS; Leavenworth, KS; (3); Church Yth Grp; SADD; Teachers Aide; Church Choir; Socr; Hon Roll; Nrsng.

HERRMAN, JOHN A; Lacrosse HS; Liebenthal, KS; (3); Drama Clb; Quiz Bowl; Scholastic Bowl; School Play; Pres Jr Cls; Var Golf; High Hon Roll; NHS; MIT; Arspc Engrng.

HERRMANN, BERNIE; Seaman Sr HS; Topeka, KS; (3); SADD; Mrchg Band; Pep Band; Stage Crew; Var Ftbl; Var Trk; High Hon Roll; Jr NHS; Debate Tm; Pres Schlr; KS U; Arch Engrng.

HERRMANN, MARTY; Sabetha HS; Sabetha, KS; (4); 23/60; VP 4-H; Pres Natl FFA Org; NFL; Spanish Clb; Band; Pep Band; Rep Stu Cncl; Bsktbl; 4-H Awd; Amer Qtr Hors Yth Assn 6th High Indv Hors Judgng World Show 95; KS Qtr Horse Yth Assn Res High Pt 93; Garden City CC; Food Sci.

HERRMANN, RENEE M; Independence HS; Independence, KS; (4); Church Yth Grp; NFL; Pep Clb; Orch; JV Sftbl; Intrml Vllybl; High Hon Roll; Hon Roll; NHS; KS Univ; Commercl Art.

HERRMANN, TONYA; Kinsley HS; Kinsley, KS; (4); 3/37; Church Yth Grp; Cmnty Wkr; 4-H; Office Aide; Teachers Aide; Varsity Clb; School Musical; School Play; Ed Yrbk; Sec Frsh Cls; Stu City Cncl Rep; KS ST U; Spch Pthlgy.

HERRON, NATHAN; Hesston HS; Hesston, KS; (3); Am Leg Boys St; Boy Scts; FBLA; Model UN; Band; Chorus; Jazz Band; Pep Band; Var Golf; Church Yth Grp; Order Of The Arrow; KS St Univ; Prelaw.

HERSH, JEREMY S; Halstead HS; Sedgwick, KS; (4).

HERSH, JUSTIN D; Ft Scott HS; Fort Scott, KS; (4); Am Leg Boys St; Church Yth Grp; FCA; 4-H; Letterman Clb; Pep Clb; Science Clb; SADD; Teachers Aide; Chorus; Bio.

HERSHEY, SHANNON; Enterprise Sda Acad; Wichita, KS; (3); Church Yth Grp; Model UN; Teachers Aide; Chorus; Church Choir; VP Stu Cncl; Stat Bsktbl; Stat Ftbl; Stat Gym; Stat Score Keeper; Adventist Disaster Svc Cert; Comm Svc; Deans List; Butlet Cty Comm Coll; Bus Mgmt.

HERTEL, LISA; Thomas More Prep-Marion HS; Hays, KS; (1); 12/60; Band; Mrchg Band; Pep Band; High Hon Roll; Hon Roll.

HERTEL, LYN; Cheylin HS; Bird City, KS; (4); 5/14; Am Leg Aux Girls St; FHA; Girl Scts; HOBY; Scholastic Bowl; Treas Jr Cls; Sec Stu Cncl; Chrldng; Pom Pon; Hon Roll; Colby CC; Acctng.

HERTEL, MICHELLE; Thomas More Prep-Marion HS; Hays, KS; (3); Cmnty Wkr; HOBY; JCL; Pres Service Clb; Rptr Nwsp; Pres Jr Cls; Rep Stu Cncl; Var Chrldng; Hon Roll; NYLC 96; Schl Ambssdr; Natural Hlpr.

HERTZLER, JULIE L; Southeast HS; Wichita, KS; (3); 107/378; Pres French Clb; SADD; Teachers Aide; Acpl Chr; Chorus; Var L Golf; JV Sftbl; Hon Roll; Yth Mentor; KS ST Univ; Pre-Med.

HERWIG, CHRIS M; Salina HS Central; Salina, KS; (3); Church Yth Grp; Debate Tm; NFL; Tennis; Hon Roll; Ntl Merit Ltr; Stu Congress; KSU; Law.

HERZBERG, STEVEN W; Shawnee Mission W Sr HS; Overland Park, KS; (2); 42/426; Art Clb; Boy Scts; Church Yth Grp; Pep Clb; High Hon Roll; Hon Roll; Natl Art Hnr Soc.

HERZOG, KATRINA I; Quinter Jr Sr HS; Quinter, KS; (2); Church Yth Grp; FCA; Letterman Clb; Scholastic Bowl; School Play; JV Golf; Var L Trk; Var L Vllybl; NHS; High Hon Roll; Phy Thrpst.

HESKETT, KATIE D; Wamego HS; Wamego, KS; (3); 1/97; Treas FBLA; Rep SADD; Treas Frsh Cls; Treas Soph Cls; Treas Jr Cls; Treas Sr Cls; Bsktbl; Vllybl; Cit Awd; Hon Roll; Photo; KS St Univ; Acctng.

HESS, BRETT A; Humboldt HS; Humboldt, KS; (2); 4/65; 4-H; Natl FFA Org; Band; JV Var Bsktbl; 4-H Awd; High Hon Roll; Prfct Atten Awd; Kays; KS Univ; Dctr.

HESS, CHRIS A; Kapaun-Mt Carmel HS; Wichita, KS; (4); 2/175; Cmnty Wkr; Debate Tm; VP Q&S; Ed Nwsp; Ofcr Bsbl; Cit Awd; High Hon Roll; Ntl Merit SF; Church Yth Grp; NFL; KS Schlstc Press Assn St Brd; Piano; Law.

HESS, JENNIFER M; Madison Jr Sr HS; Madison, KS; (4); Drama Clb; German Clb; Band; Chorus; Jazz Band; Mrchg Band; School Play; High Hon Roll; Hon Roll; Dist II Choir; Emporia ST Univ; Eng.

HESS, JEREMY J; Wabaunsee HS; Alma, KS; (3); Church Yth Grp; Library Aide; Natl FFA Org; Office Aide; School Play; Var L Bsktbl; Var L Ftbl; Powder Puff Ftbl; Hon Roll; FFA Greenhand Chapt Pres.

HESS, JESSICA L; Madison Jr Sr HS; Madison, KS; (3); 6/26; FBLA; German Clb; Band; Mrchg Band; Pep Band; Treas Sr Cls; JV Vllybl; High Hon Roll; Hon Roll; Emporium ST Univ; Acctng.

HESS, LEA A; Smith Ctr Jr Sr HS; Smith Center, KS; (4); 9/42; Church Yth Grp; Cmnty Wkr; Letterman Clb; Pres SADD; Chorus; VP Sr Cls; Var Stat Crs Cntry; High Hon Roll; Hon Roll; NHS; ST SAD Stu Of Yr; Ft Hays ST U; Elem Ed.

HESS, MICHAEL B; Baldwin HS; Baldwin City, KS; (3); Art Clb; Church Yth Grp; CAP; Cmnty Wkr; French Clb; FHA; FTA; Pres Letterman Clb; Office Aide; Pep Clb; Placed In St Trk; Spcl Ed; Psych.

HESS, STEPHANIE; Burlington HS; Burlington, KS; (2); 12/68; Dance Clb; Drill Tm; JV Bsktbl; Var Chrldng; Var Pom Pon; Var Sftbl; Var Vllybl; High Hon Roll; Hon Roll; NHS.

HESSELTINE, TRAVIS S; Lyndon HS; Vassar, KS; (4); 11/37; FBLA; FHA; Band; Stage Crew; JV Bsktbl; Golf; Hon Roll; Forensics; Lyon Ctyn League CAD 1st In Div 95; Butler Cty CC; Engrng.

HESTEHAVE, JOSH R; St John's Military Schl; Upland, CA; (4); 10/25; Boy Scts; ROTC; Band; Color Guard; Mrchg Band; School Musical; Ofcr Sr Cls; Golf; Wt Lftg; Hon Roll; San Diego ST.

HESTON, CHAD E; Liberal HS; Liberal, KS; (3); Am Leg Boys St; Boy Scts; Rep Jr Cls; Pres Sr Cls; JV Bsktbl; Var Ftbl; JV Trk; Hon Roll; NHS; Prfct Atten Awd; Eagle Sct.

HESTON, MICHELLE; Louisburg HS; Louisburg, KS; (4); Church Yth Grp; Letterman Clb; SADD; Teachers Aide; Chorus; Church Choir; Chrldng; Trk; High Hon Roll; Hon Roll; Johnson Cty CC; Spec Ed.

HETRICK, CASEY; Logan Jr HS; Topeka, KS; (1); Church Yth Grp; Debate Tm; Bsktbl; Ftbl; High Hon Roll; Engrng.

HETT, MARTHA E; Iola Sr HS; Deerfield, KS; (3); Church Yth Grp; Cmnty Wkr; FHA; Spanish Clb; SADD; Band; Mrchg Band; JV Var Bsktbl; JV L Trk; JV Var Vllybl; SE KS Hnrble Mntn Bsktbl 95-.

HETTENBACH, DUSTY J; Arkansas City HS; Arkansas City, KS; (1); JV Bsbl; High Hon Roll; Hon Roll; Wichita ST.

HETTINGER, KATE; Shawnee Mission Northwest HS; Lenexa, KS; (4); 5/375; Church Yth Grp; Cmnty Wkr; Debate Tm; Intnl Clb; JA; NFL; Q&S; Service Clb; Jazz Band; Rptr Nwsp; Natl Merit Commendtn; Tandy Tech Schlr; KS Hons Schlr; Drake Univ; Jrnlsm.

HETZKE, STEFANIE; Otis Bison HS; Pawnee Rock, KS; (2); 2/36; Letterman Clb; Speech Tm; SADD; Band; Chorus; JV Bsktbl; Var Chrldng; Var Trk; JV Vllybl; High Hon Roll; KAYS; Bethel Coll; Vet.

HETZLER, CHRISTINA; Manhattan HS; Manhattan, KS; (4); Church Yth Grp; Cmnty Wkr; 4-H; Pep Clb; Band; Mrchg Band; Pep Band; High Hon Roll; Hon Roll; NHS; EMT Classes; KSU; Med.

HEUERTZ, THOMAS E; Valley Falls HS; Valley Falls, KS; (2); Band; Chorus; JV Bsktbl; Var Crs Cntry; JV Ftbl; Var Trk; Pres Acad Fit Awd; Ath Schlsp In Crss Cntry & Trk; Construction.

HEWITT, DUSTIN L; Council Grove HS; Alta Vista, KS; (2); Church Yth Grp; FCA; SADD; Church Choir; JV Bsktbl; Wt Lftg; Hon Roll.

HEWITT, LISA; Baldwin HS; Baldwin City, KS; (3); Cmnty Wkr; Debate Tm; Intnl Clb; Letterman Clb; NFL; Pep Clb; Rep Stu Cncl; Bsktbl; Chrldng; Crs Cntry; Med.

HEWSON, TRACI D; Garden City Sr HS; Garden City, KS; (2); Art Clb; Church Yth Grp; NFL; Band; Chorus; Color Guard; Mrchg Band; Var Crs Cntry; Var Swmmng; High Hon Roll.

HIATT, DANIEL V; Bishop Miege HS; Prairie Village, KS; (3); 35/184; Letterman Clb; Office Aide; Teachers Aide; Varsity Clb; JV Bsktbl; Var L Tennis; High Hon Roll; Hon Roll; Pres Acad Fit Awd; Bagroom Wrkr.

HIATT, JULIE; St Thomas Aquinas HS; Kansas City, MO; (4); 70/260; Am Leg Aux Girls St; Var Debate Tm; Hist French Clb; JA; Model UN; VP NFL; Tennis; Trk; NHS; Pres Acad Fit Awd; Cert Red Cross Lifeguard; Bible Schl Tchr; HS Tutor.

HIATT, LISA A; Bishop Miege HS; Prairie Village, KS; (1); 71/245; Church Yth Grp; Acpl Chr; Chorus; Church Choir; School Musical; School Play; JV Tennis; High Hon Roll; Hon Roll; Pres Acad Fit Awd.

HIBBARD, KARIE; Olathe North Sr HS; Olathe, KS; (3); Church Yth Grp; German Clb; Pep Clb; Teachers Aide; Orch; Nwsp; Rep Treas Stu Cncl; Chrldng; NHS; Pres Acad Fit Awd; Doane Coll; Elem Ed.

HIBBS, JASON C; Golden Plains Jr Sr HS; Rexford, KS; (4); Am Leg Boys St; 4-H; Pres Letterman Clb; School Play; Pres Sr Cls; Capt Var Bsktbl; Crs Cntry; Hon Roll; NHS; Prfct Atten Awd; Construction Sci.

HIBEN, CONSTANCE N; Labette Co HS; Oswego, KS; (2); 4-H; FBLA; Letterman Clb; Natl FFA Org; Pep Clb; Red Cross Aide; Speech Tm; SADD; Varsity Clb; VICA; KS ST Univ.

HIBLER, JARROD; Halstead HS; Halstead, KS; (3); Debate Tm; Pres Sec 4-H; Scholastic Bowl; Varsity Clb; Rep Frsh Cls; Ofcr Stu Cncl; Ofcr Bsbl; Var Ftbl; Var Wrstlng; 4-H Awd; KS Regents Hnr Acad Schlr; 3a St Champion Wrestler; KS Bd Regents Recommended Curr; Phy Thrpst; Sports Trainer.

HICKERT, AUDREY O; Hill City HS; Morland, KS; (2); Treas FHA; HOBY; NFL; Pres Pep Clb; Scholastic Bowl; SADD; Var Chrldng; Vllybl; Wt Lftg; KAYS.

HICKEY, ANGEL; Liberal HS; Liberal, KS; (1); Drama Clb; Band; Mrchg Band; School Musical; School Play; Chrldng; Gym; San Antonio Wrld Games 95 Wrld Chmpn Sparring; Rincs Amer Freestyle Karate Yngst Blck Blt; CO ST; Medcl.

HICKMAN, COURTNEY D; Holton HS; Holton, KS; (1); FHA; Nwsp; Yrbk; Bsktbl; Chrldng; Crs Cntry; Sftbl; Vllybl; Hon Roll; Kayehes; Sports Medicine.

HICKMON, JAZMIN; Sumner Acad Of Arts & Science; Kansas City, KS; (3); Church Yth Grp; Cmnty Wkr; Key Clb; Latin Clb; Chorus; Church Choir; Capt Var Chrldng; Trk; Hon Roll; NCA All Amer Chrldng Team; 15 Yr Triple Jump Rcrd Brkr; Chrch God Mission Wrk Prjcts.

HICKS, AMANDA; Salina HS South; Salina, KS; (4); 55/235; Am Leg Aux Girls St; Band; Mrchg Band; Co-Ed Yrbk; VP Stu Cncl; L Golf; Prom Team Mem; Crimstprs Orgzr; Govs Cntr For Teen Ldrshp; K ST; Educ.

HICKS, JESSICA L; Riley Cty HS; Leonardville, KS; (3); FHA; Pep Clb; Teachers Aide; Band; Pep Band; Amer Legion Post 40 Mem; Jrnlsm.

HICKS, MARRKA; Wyandotte HS; Kansas City, KS; (1); Hosp Aide; Library Aide; Math Clb; Office Aide; Mrchg Band; Chrldng; Vllybl; Teachers Aide; Bsktbl; Hon Roll; UCLA; Med.

HICKS, MINDY; Horton HS; Everest, KS; (2); 26/88; Church Yth Grp; Dance Clb; Drama Clb; FHA; Pep Clb; SADD; Teachers Aide; Chorus; Drill Tm; School Musical; Rdng; KS ST U; Optometrist.

HIEBERT, KAREN; Goddard HS; Goddard, KS; (3); 15/171; Q&S; Science Clb; Spanish Clb; SADD; Stage Crew; Lit Mag; High Hon Roll; HS His Tchr.

HIEBERT, KINSEY; Maize HS; Wichita, KS; (3); 16/242; Q&S; Science Clb; Spanish Clb; SADD; Nwsp; L Tennis; High Hon Roll; NHS; Wichita ST Univ Sr Schlr; KS Assn For Yth; Dntl.

HIEBERT, LISA; Sedgwick HS; Sedgwick, KS; (4); 7/24; Am Leg Aux Girls St; FHA; HOBY; Quiz Bowl; SADD; Teachers Aide; School Musical; Rptr Nwsp; Rep Stu Cncl; Capt Bsktbl; Mc Pherson All Star Bsktbl Team; Bsktbl & Vllybl HOA All League Hnrb Mntn; Juco Schl; Sprts Med.

HIEBERT, RACHAEL L; Maize HS; Wichita, KS; (1); JV Socr; Hon Roll; Pres Acad Fit Awd.

HIEBERT, STEPHANIE I; Wichita East HS; Wichita, KS; (4); French Clb; Girl Scts; Varsity Clb; Var L Gym; Var L Swmmng; JV Wt Lftg; High Hon Roll; Hon Roll; St Schlr; KS Univ; Liberal Arts.

HIGGINBOTHAM, MICHELLE L; Williamsburg Schl; Williamsburg, KS; (4); 6/19; FCA; Drill Tm; Bsktbl; Chrldng; Trk; Vllybl; Wt Lftg; Hon Roll; Spanish Clb; Teachers Aide; Emporia ST Univ; PEDS Nrsng.

HIGGINS, COURTNEY B; Shawnee Mission N HS; Shawnee Mission, KS; (4); 4/346; French Clb; Pep Clb; VP Spanish Clb; Nwsp; Rep Frsh Cls; JV Bsktbl; Var Sftbl; JV Vllybl; Gov Hon Prg Awd; High Hon Roll; KS ST U.

HIGGINS, HANAE K; Kapaun-Mt Carmel HS; Wichita, KS; (3); Rep French Clb; Q&S; Co-Ed Yrbk; Rep Jr Cls; Mgr(s); Hon Roll; NHS; Eco Clb; United Crusaders; Crusaders For Life; U Of KS; Comm.

HIGGINS, JOHANNA; Wellington Sr HS; Wellington, KS; (2); Church Yth Grp; SADD; Band; Mgr(s); Score Keeper; Hon Roll; Jr NHS; KS Univ.

HIGGINS, TERI L; Leavenworth HS; Leavenworth, KS; (3); Score Keeper; Sftbl; Vllybl; Wt Lftg; Cit Awd; Hon Roll; KS ST; Psych.

HIGGS, TRAVIS; Newton Sr HS; Newton, KS; (4); 1/217; Teachers Aide; Lit Mag; L Swmmng; Gov Hon Prg Awd; Ntl Merit Ltr; Pres Schlr; St Schlr; Val; Am Leg Boys St; Boy Scts; US Air Force Acad; Multi-Yr Listee; USAF Acad; Aero Eng.

HIGHT, AARON D; Riverton Schl; Riverton, KS; (2); 1/60; Church Yth Grp; FCA; Letterman Clb; Band; Chorus; Jazz Band; Mrchg Band; Pep Band; Swing Chorus; High Hon Roll.

HIGHTOWER, JANETTE L; Prairie View Jr Sr HS; La Cygne, KS; (2); 25/90; VP 4-H; HOBY; Treas Natl FFA Org; Quiz Bowl; Spanish Clb; Var Crs Cntry; Var Trk; 4-H Awd; Hon Roll; NHS; KS ST; Vet.

HIGLEY, CANDICE G; Troy HS; Cummings, KS; (4); 3/35; Church Yth Grp; Drama Clb; Letterman Clb; Pep Clb; Q&S; Quiz Bowl; Spanish Clb; Teachers Aide; Band; Chorus; Voice Of Democracy Cont 1s Pl; Kayettes & Bayette Bd Mem; Benedictine Coll; Brdcst Jrnslm.

HILBISH, BETH; Shawnee Heights HS; Tecumseh, KS; (3); 1/375; Church Yth Grp; Girl Scts; Model UN; Office Aide; Mgr Quiz Bowl; Mgr Scholastic Bowl; High Hon Roll; Prfct Atten Awd; Sci Olympiad 4 Yrs; Close Up WA DC; Group Ldr Church Camp 2 Yrs; KS Univ; Scndry Ed Math.

HILDEBRAND, CASSIE L; Great Bend Sr HS; Great Bend, KS; (3); Pep Clb; Acpl Chr; Variety Show; Var Chrldng; Var Swmmng; Hon Roll; NHS; KS ST Univ.

HILDEBRAND, JESSICA; Maize HS; Wichita, KS; (3); 1/243; Rep Church Yth Grp; Debate Tm; French Clb; Girl Scts; NFL; Thesps; High Hon Roll; NHS; Drama Clb; Teachers Aide; Intnl Future Problem Solving Team; Girl Sct Ldr & Cnslr In Trng; Clincal Child Psych.

HILDEBRAND, SARA; Stafford Jr Sr HS; Stafford, KS; (2); Church Yth Grp; Cmnty Wkr; Drama Clb; FHA; Quiz Bowl; SADD; Band; Chorus; Church Choir; Mrchg Band; St Forenscis Chmpnshps Pl; St Piano Fest 1 Ratngs 2 Yrs; Cmnty Drama Guild; Sterling Coll; Phys Thrpy.

HILDEBRANDT, HENRY C; Central Heights Sr HS; Princeton, KS; (1); Art Clb; Church Yth Grp; FCA; Pep Clb; Science Clb; Bsktbl; Ftbl; Trk; High Hon Roll; Hon Roll; KS Univ; Arch Engr.

HILDRETH, BRANDY E; Perry Lecompton HS; Grantville, KS; (2); FBLA; Hosp Aide; Intnl Clb; Letterman Clb; School Musical; School Play; Sprt Ed Yrbk; Rep Soph Cls; Golf; NHS; PT.

HILGER, STEPHANIE J; Wichita South HS; Wichita, KS; (3); Dance Clb; FHA; Pep Clb; Red Cross Aide; Band; Mrchg Band; Pep Band; Rep Stu Cncl; Intrml Bsktbl; Pom Pon; Teens Hope; All City Bnd; HIV Aidsed; Phys Thpy.

HILL, AMY M; Bishop Ward HS; Kansas City, KS; (3); Am Leg Aux Girls St; Cmnty Wkr; Drama Clb; Library Aide; Office Aide; Pep Clb; Speech Tm; SADD; Teachers Aide; Chorus; Forensics; Tchr REACH; Ldrshp 2020; St Marys Leavenworth; Spec Ed.

HILL, BRIAN; Maize HS; Wichita, KS; (3); 22/242; Church Yth Grp; FCA; Teachers Aide; Golf; High Hon Roll; Hon Roll; NHS; Civil Engr.

HILL, BROOKE L; Osage City HS; Osage City, KS; (3); Church Yth Grp; Pep Clb; Q&S; Science Clb; Yrbk; Var L Bsktbl; Var Sftbl; Var L Trk; Var L Vllybl; High Hon Roll.

HILL, CASSIE; Circle HS; Towanda, KS; (2); Church Yth Grp; SADD; Acpl Chr; Orch; School Musical; School Play; Variety Show; Rptr Nwsp; Rep Soph Cls; Rep Stu Cncl; Regnl Solo Festival Received A 1 Rating; St Solo Festival Received A 2 Rating; WSU Quantico; Bachlr In Psych.

HILL, CHRISTIE M; Pierson Jr HS; Kansas City, KS; (1); Band; Stat Bsktbl; Mgr(s); Score Keeper; Stat Sftbl; Stat Vllybl; Prfct Atten Awd; Modeled For Catalogs/Many Fashion Agencies; FIT; Fshn Dsgnr/Model.

HILL, DONNA L; Labette Co HS; Altamont, KS; (3); 40/143; Cmnty Wkr; French Clb; Spanish Clb; VP SADD; JV Var Mgr(s); Stat Wrstlng; Hon Roll; NHS; Bio; Bionics; Cryobiology.

HILL, GARRETT; Liberal HS; Liberal, KS; (3); 18/256; Am Leg Boys St; Boy Scts; Band; Chorus; Mrchg Band; VP Stu Cncl; Var Bsktbl; Var Ftbl; Var Trk; NHS; Medicine.

HILL, HEATHER F; Wallace Cty HS; Sharon Springs, KS; (1); FCA; Pep Clb; SADD; Band; Chorus; Jazz Band; Mrchg Band; Pep Band; JV Trk; JV Vllybl; Nurse.

HILL, HYDA-JAMES; Manhattan HS; Manhattan, KS; (4); Band; Church Choir; Jazz Band; Mrchg Band; Orch; Pep Band; School Musical; Variety Show; Prom King; Wnnr Mr MHS Pageant; Larry Norvell Schlsp; KS ST Univ.

HILL, JASON N; Shawnee Mission S Sr HS; Overland Park, KS; (4); Pep Clb; Teachers Aide; Capt Bsktbl; JV Golf; Intrml Socr; Hon Roll; Neosho Cnty JC; Crmnl Sci.

HILL, KENDRA; Rock Creek Jr Sr HS; Westmoreland, KS; (2); 13/71; 4-H; Natl FFA Org; Var Bsktbl; Var Chrldng; Var Vllybl; 4-H Awd; Hon Roll; 2nd Rnnr Up Miss Pottawatomie Cty Fair; Natl Hnr Roll Ldrshp & Svc Awds; Cty Fair Miss Congeniality; Med.

HILL, MANDI J; Campus HS; Wichita, KS; (2); Church Yth Grp; Science Clb; SADD; Church Choir; Mgr Stat Sftbl; High Hon Roll; Hon Roll; NHS.

HILL, NATHAN L; Topeka HS; Topeka, KS; (2); Spanish Clb; Rptr Nwsp; JV Socr; JV L Tennis; High Hon Roll; Hon Roll.

HILL, NICCOLE; Olathe North Sr HS; Olathe, KS; (3); Church Yth Grp; Cmnty Wkr; Band; Drm Mjr(t); Mrchg Band; Rep Sec Stu Cncl; High Hon Roll; Hon Roll; Am Leg Aux Girls St; Young KS Writers-Poem Pub; Missionary Work-MX; Elem Ed.

HILL, SARAH; Hutchinson HS; Hutchinson, KS; (3); 1/350; Debate Tm; Key Clb; Letterman Clb; Scholastic Bowl; Chorus; Golf; Swmmng; High Hon Roll.

HILL, SHAWN R; Iola Sr HS; Iola, KS; (4); FBLA; SADD; Hon Roll; NCK Vo Tech; Bus Mgmt.

HILL, TANEKA A; Highland Park HS; Topeka, KS; (2); Church Yth Grp; JA; ROTC; Chorus; Church Choir; Cit Awd; High Hon Roll; Hon Roll; Spellman; Arch Engrg/Med.

HILL, VICKI M; Augusta Sr HS; Augusta, KS; (4); French Clb; Office Aide; Pep Clb; Teachers Aide; Thesps; Chorus; Drill Tm; Pom Pon; High Hon Roll; Solo Cmptrn Natls 2nd Pl; All Amer Dncr Awds; Dncd St Ptrcts Day Prd Dublin Ireland; Butler Cty.

HILLEARY, ALISHA; Derby HS; Wichita, KS; (1); Girl Scts; SADD; Acpl Chr; School Play; Nwsp; Hon Roll; Article Pub HS News/Grphcs; Wrtng; Jrnlst/Athr.

HILLEY, AMANDA; Stafford Jr Sr HS; Stafford, KS; (1); 1/36; Church Yth Grp; Cmnty Wkr; FCA; 4-H; Natl FFA Org; Pep Clb; Scholastic Bowl; Band; Mrchg Band; High Hon Roll; Vet.

HILLIN, ANDREW M; Lawrence HS; Lawrence, KS; (2); Band; Mrchg Band; Pep Band.

HILLMAN, CASSIE; Norton Comm HS; Norton, KS; (3); 1/55; Treas Church Yth Grp; Pres Pep Clb; Band; Chorus; School Play; Swing Chorus; Pres Stu Cncl; Bsktbl; Tennis; High Hon Roll.

HILLMAN, CHRISTINA; Frankft HS; Frankfort, KS; (2); Band; Chorus; Flag Corp; Jazz Band; Mrchg Band; Pep Band; Ofcr Soph Cls; Stat Bsktbl; Trk; JV Vllybl; Span; Psych/Tchng.

HILLS, AMANDA LYNN; Ulysses HS; Ulysses, KS; (2); 7/110; Debate Tm; Sec FHA; HOBY; Treas NFL; SADD; Stage Crew; Intrml Bsktbl; Mgr(s); JV Tennis; Hon Roll; Eclgy Clb; Frgn Lang Clb; OK U; Bus.

HILLS, ANDREW J; Parsons HS; Parsons, KS; (3); 20/108; Debate Tm; NFL; Office Aide; JV Bsbl; Wt Lftg; Var JV Wrstlng; Hon Roll; 1 Dan Shinwa Taido; KS ST U; Chem Eng.

HILLS, JASON W; Oxford HS; Geuda Springs, KS; (2); Church Yth Grp; FCA; Varsity Clb; Var Bsktbl; Var L Ftbl; Hon Roll.

HILT, BARBARA; St Mary's Colgan HS; Pittsburg, KS; (2); Pep Clb; Scholastic Bowl; Science Clb; Thesps; Chorus; Church Choir; School Musical; School Play; Stage Crew; High Hon Roll; 3rd Plc Hmrs Solo Actng ST Chmpnshps Natl Frnscs Leag.

HILTGEN, CINDY; Frankft HS; Frankfort, KS; (4); 7/29; Am Leg Aux Girls St; Letterman Clb; Chorus; Yrbk; Pres Stu Cncl; Bsktbl; Chrldng; Trk; Vllybl; NHS; Elem Educ.

HILYARD, ROBIN L; Shawnee Mission W Sr HS; Overland Park, KS; (2); 20/426; Dance Clb; Math Tm; Teachers Aide; Drill Tm; Yrbk; Var Gym; High Hon Roll; Scholar Ath; Crmnl Jstc.

HINDS, WILLIAM W; Derby HS; Wichita, KS; (3); Chess Clb; ROTC; Band; Color Guard; Drill Tm; Mrchg Band; Hon Roll; NHS; Martial Arts; OM; Billiards; Bwlng; FPS; Chem Engr.

HINEMAN, SARAH; Dighton HS; Dighton, KS; (3); 3/27; FCA; HOBY; Pep Clb; Band; Chorus; School Musical; VP Soph Cls; Sec Stu Cncl; Vllybl; High Hon Roll; Vet Med.

HINES, CHAD A; Blue Valley HS; Stilwell, KS; (4); Drama Clb; NFL; Thesps; School Play; Lit Mag; Var Socr; Hon Roll; Ntl Merit Ltr; Grinnell Coll; Eng.

HINES, MINDY JOY; Cair Paravel - Latin Schl; Topeka, KS; (3); 1/16; Church Yth Grp; Drama Clb; Acpl Chr; School Musical; School Play; JV Bsktbl; JV Vllybl; High Hon Roll; Chorus; Orch; HS Chrstn Testimony Awd; Poetry Publshd; Violin Quartet.

HINES, RACHEL L; Hutchinson HS; Hutchinson, KS; (3); 46/290; Debate Tm; NFL; Band; Chorus; Mrchg Band; Pep Band; JV Var Mgr(s); High Hon Roll; Hon Roll; Huchinson CC.

HINES, TRAVIS R; Spearville Jr Sr HS; Spearville, KS; (3); Letterman Clb; Quiz Bowl; Chorus; School Play; Var Bsbl; Var Bsktbl; Var Ftbl; Var Trk; Hon Roll; NHS.

HINGULA, ROBERT J; Leavenworth HS; Fort Leavenworth, KS; (3); 16/374; Am Leg Boys St; Church Yth Grp; Cmnty Wkr; Pres Drama Clb; NFL; Pres Thesps; Acpl Chr; Chorus; Church Choir; School Musical; Guitar; Cmmnty Thtr; AAFES; Truman U; Thtr Arts.

HINKIN, SARAH; Manhattan HS; Manhattan, KS; (4); French Clb; Spanish Clb; SADD; Teachers Aide; Chorus; Church Choir; Swing Chorus; High Hon Roll; NHS; St Schlr; U Of KS; Phrmcy.

HINKLE, KENDRA; Derby HS; Derby, KS; (4); Church Yth Grp; Varsity Clb; Mgr(s); Trk; Gov Hon Prg Awd; High Hon Roll; NHS; St Yth Cabinet; South Cntrl Dist Yth Cabinet Pres; KS ST U; Preaching Farmer.

HINKLEY, JENNIFER; Garden City Sr HS; Garden City, KS; (4); 59/313; Office Aide; Yrbk; Hon Roll; Yng Life Grp; Garden City CC; Chld Psych.

HINKLEY, JENNIFER R; Spring Hill HS; Spring Hill, KS; (2); Church Yth Grp; Cmnty Wkr; Science Clb; SADD; Chorus; Church Choir; School Musical; Hon Roll; Spirit Clb; Comm Vol Work; Madrigals; Law.

HINMAN, CARRIE A; Baxter Springs HS; Baxter Springs, KS; (4); 1/70; Sec Treas FCA; Sec FHA; Hosp Aide; Pep Clb; Science Clb; Pres NHS; Val; Parliamentary Law Team Sec; Bus Clb; Medical Explorers; Pittsburg ST Univ; Pre-Med.

HINSON, JASIE E; Bishop Carroll Catholic HS; Wichita, KS; (2); French Clb; Teachers Aide; Band; Jazz Band; L Crs Cntry; JV Socr; Hon Roll; Pro Life Clb Sec; Piano HS Regnl ST Comp.

HINSON, SAMANTHA A; Great Bend Sr HS; Great Bend, KS; (3); Church Yth Grp; Cmnty Wkr; Drama Clb; Girl Scts; Teachers Aide; Acpl Chr; Church Choir; School Play; Variety Show; Hon Roll; Girl Sct Camp Unit Ldr & Gold/Slvr Awds; Big Brothers/Big Sisters; Child Psych.

HIPP, MICHELLE R; Kapaun-Mt Carmel HS; Wichita, KS; (4); VP Boy Scts; Sec VP Church Yth Grp; Cmnty Wkr; Dance Clb; Girl Scts; Red Cross Aide; Pres Service Clb; Spanish Clb; SADD; Variety Show; Cmnty Vol; Rockhurst Col; Bus Mgmt.

HIPP, SUZIE E; Kapaun-Mt Carmel HS; Wichita, KS; (3); Pres Church Yth Grp; VP French Clb; Hosp Aide; Golf; Capt JV Socr; Hon Roll; VP NHS; United Ways Dwayne Wallace Venture Grant Yth Comm; United Crusaders VP; Reg IV Cath Yth Org VP; Soc Worker/Tchr.

HIRSCH, CHARLES; Newton Sr HS; Newton, KS; (3); 36/340; Mgr Am Leg Boys St; French Clb; VP Key Clb; Socr; Capt Trk; Wrstlng; High Hon Roll; Hon Roll; NHS; Ntl Merit Ltr; Ldrshp; High Hnrs Naval Acad Summer Seminar; US Naval Acad; Fighter Pilot.

HIRSCHFELD, SARAH M; Dodge City HS; Dodge City, KS; (3); Church Yth Grp; French Clb; Model UN; Quiz Bowl; Scholastic Bowl; SADD; Orch; Hon Roll; NHS; KAYS.

HIRSHFELD, SARAH; Dodge City HS; Dodge City, KS; (3); Church Yth Grp; French Clb; Model UN; Quiz Bowl; Scholastic Bowl; SADD; Orch; Hon Roll; NHS; Octgn Clb; Psych.

HIRT, ANDREW J; St Thomas Aquinas HS; Lenexa, KS; (3); Cmnty Wkr; Scholastic Bowl; Service Clb; Hon Roll; ST Acad Dcthln; Acctng.

HISAW, LORI R; Tonganoxie HS; Leavenworth, KS; (4); Art Clb; Church Yth Grp; 4-H; FBLA; FHA; Hosp Aide; Science Clb; Spanish Clb; SADD; NHS; Outstanding Acad Achvmnt; Library Clb; KCNCC; Scndry Ed.

HITCHCOCK, KRISTIN D; Baldwin HS; Baldwin City, KS; (3); Pres 4-H; Intnl Clb; Math Tm; Service Clb; Rptr Nwsp; Yrbk; JV Tennis; 4-H Awd; High Hon Roll; Sec Treas NHS; Intl Rltns.

HITTLE, KANE; Winfield HS; Winfield, KS; (4); 43/159; Natl FFA Org; Hon Roll; KS ST U; Agri Engr.

HITZ, LAUREN; Wichita Collegiate Schl; Wichita, KS; (2); 1/70; Cmnty Wkr; Scholastic Bowl; Sec Frsh Cls; JV Bsktbl; JV Vllybl; High Hon Roll; Lit Clb.

HIXON, HILERY A; Southeast HS; Wichita, KS; (4); Stage Crew; JV Socr; Hon Roll; NHS; US Natl Math Awd; Schltc Arts Pgm; Wichita ST Univ; Psych.

HIXON, JENNIFER; Girard HS; Pittsburg, KS; (4); Church Yth Grp; 4-H; Letterman Clb; Natl FFA Org; Quiz Bowl; Scholastic Bowl; Science Clb; Spanish Clb; SADD; Teachers Aide; Bible Quiz; Soc Sci Dept Awd; Symph Winds; Independce Comp Days; Southwest Bapt Univ; PT.

HIXON, JESSICA; Wichita Northwest HS; Wichita, KS; (3); Bus Profs of Am; Church Yth Grp; Teachers Aide; Church Choir; Hon Roll; Mid America Nazarene Coll.

HIXSON, KEVIN L; Blue Valley Northwest HS; Overland Park, KS; (3); 1/364; Chess Clb; VP Church Yth Grp; Intnl Clb; Red Cross Aide; Var L Wrstlng; High Hon Roll; NHS; Freestyle Wrestling Club; Engr.

HLADEK, AMY; Trego Comm HS; Wa Keeney, KS; (1); 1/50; Sec Church Yth Grp; Rep FHA; Speech Tm; JV Bsktbl; Var Chrldng; Var Trk; JV Vllybl; High Hon Roll; Hon Roll; Pres Acad Fit Awd.

HLADEK, KAREN; Trego Comm HS; Wa Keeney, KS; (4); 9/52; Pres Church Yth Grp; Treas Drama Clb; Sec FHA; Letterman Clb; NFL; Pep Clb; Science Clb; Service Clb; Speech Tm; VP SADD; Outstndg Jr Athl; KS ST U; Chem.

HLADIK, CHAD R; Wichita East HS; Wichita, KS; (2); Church Yth Grp; CAP; JV Bsktbl; L Socr; Hon Roll; NHS; Intl Forgn Lang Awd; Intl BA Stu.

HO, MICHAEL C; Blue Valley Northwest HS; Overland Park, KS; (2); 1/409; Church Yth Grp; Math Tm; Chorus; High Hon Roll; Amer HS Top 5 Soph Math Exam; Top 10 2 KCATM Math Cntst Evnts; Archt/Cmptr Rltd.

HO, TRANG T; Bishop Carroll Catholic HS; Wichita, KS; (2); Church Yth Grp; Cmnty Wkr; JA; NFL; Quiz Bowl; Ofcr Frsh Cls; High Hon Roll; Prfct Atten Awd; Hndmd Of Mary; CYA; Golden Eagle Awd 2 Yrs; Med.

HOANG, BE T; Maize HS; Wichita, KS; (3); 40/300; Tennis; Hon Roll; Vol Recgn Awd 95; Poetic Achvmt Awd 96; Cert Awd 96; U Of KS; Intl Bus/Csmtlgy.

HOANG, LYNN T; Maize HS; Wichita, KS; (1); SADD; Hon Roll; U Of KS, Optom.

HOANG, MICHELLE BE T; Maize HS; Wichita, KS; (3); 30/300; JV Tennis; High Hon Roll; Hon Roll; Acad Lttr Awd; Peotic Achvmnt Awd; Hnr Rl; U Of KS; Intl Bus.

HOAR, SHAWN; Dodge City HS; Dodge City, KS; (3); Church Yth Grp; Cmnty Wkr; Office Aide; Score Keeper; Hon Roll; Bus/Fire Sci.

HOBBS, ALLISON; Halstead HS; Halstead, KS; (3); Church Yth Grp; Cmnty Wkr; Letterman Clb; Pep Clb; Spanish Clb; Band; Mrchg Band; Pep Band; Pres Soph Cls; VP Jr Cls; Nrsng; Eng.

HOBER, JULIE; St John's HS; Beloit, KS; (4); 4/13; Church Yth Grp; Office Aide; SADD; Teachers Aide; Chorus; Pres Sr Cls; Rep Stu Cncl; High Hon Roll; Hon Roll; Pres Schlr; Emporia ST Schlrshp Hnrb Mntn, St Awds Engl; Ft Hays Awd Of Excl, Bronze Awd; Emporia ST U; Early Chldhd Ed.

HOCHARD, CANDACE D; Mc Louth Schl; Mc Louth, KS; (2); Church Yth Grp; Cmnty Wkr; Drama Clb; Pep Clb; SADD; Teachers Aide; Thesps; Varsity Clb; School Musical; School Play; All League Bsktbl; All St Trk 2 Yrs & St Nr Up In 2 Mile; KS Univ; Broadcasting.

HOCHSTETLER, MATTHEW; Lawrence HS; Lawrence, KS; (3); CAP; Debate Tm; German Clb; Hosp Aide; HOBY; Key Clb; Model UN; NFL; Spanish Clb; Teachers Aide; Poltcl Campgn Steering Cmmtte; KS U Courses; Poltcl Sci.

HOCKER, SARA E; Circle HS; Towanda, KS; (2); 1/125; Q&S; Quiz Bowl; Scholastic Bowl; SADD; Teachers Aide; Varsity Clb; Rptr Nwsp; Mgr(s); Tennis; Wt Lftg; Yth Ldrshp Butler Cls 96 Nom; Family Physician.

HOCKMAN, ELIZABETH D; Muncie Christian Schl; Bonner Springs, KS; (1); Church Yth Grp; School Play; Var Bsktbl; Var Vllybl.

HODGES, AMY S; Hays HS; Hays, KS; (3); Drill Tm; Capt Pom Pon; Hon Roll.

HODGES, CHRISTINA; Seaman Sr HS; Topeka, KS; (4); 37/248; Church Yth Grp; English Clb; Intnl Clb; Key Clb; Mu Alpha Theta; Sec Spanish Clb; SADD; Church Choir; Flag Corp; NHS; Exchng Stu Hst Sis; U Of KS; Intl Rltns.

HODGSON, DAN L; Olathe East Sr HS; Overland Park, KS; (2); Boy Scts; Church Yth Grp; Drama Clb; Thesps; School Play; Stage Crew; Intrml JV Socr; Hon Roll; Eagle Sct; Exchng Stdnt Ger; Del Prsbytrn Yth Triennium.

HODGSON, JON; Little River Jr Sr HS; Little River, KS; (3); Am Leg Boys St; Church Yth Grp; German Clb; Math Tm; Quiz Bowl; Scholastic Bowl; Rep Stu Cncl; JV Bsktbl; JV Var Ftbl; JV Var Trk.

HODISON, PATRICIA; Royal Valley HS; Mayetta, KS; (4); 2/53; Drama Clb; Girl Scts; Scholastic Bowl; Band; Church Choir; Yrbk; Var Co-Capt Chrldng; Cit Awd; NHS; KS Assoc For Yth Prog Dir, Sec, Pres; Emporia St Univ; Music.

HODSON, STEPHANIE M; Chaparral HS; Anthony, KS; (3); 2/63; Am Leg Aux Girls St; Church Yth Grp; VP FCA; NFL; Band; Pres Chorus; Flag Corp; Tennis; Treas NHS; U Of KS; Pharmacy.

HOELZLE, JAMES B; Blue Valley Northwest HS; Overland Park, KS; (1); Cmnty Wkr; Bsktbl; JV L Golf; High Hon Roll; Help Spec Olympcs.

HOETING, CRYSTAL E; Hill City HS; Hill City, KS; (4); 7/36; Hist Treas FHA; Girl Scts; NFL; Pres SADD; School Play; Ed Nwsp; Yrbk; Hon Roll; NHS; Lions Club Stdnt; Actrss Of Yr; Ft Hays ST Univ; Spec Ed.

HOFER, ELIZABETH A; Kensington Jr Sr HS; Cedar, KS; (3); Natl FFA Org; SADD; Teachers Aide; VP Jr Cls; Var L Bsktbl; Pom Pon; Var L Trk; Var L Vllybl; High Hon Roll; NHS.

HOFF, GEORGE E; Santa Fe Trail Jr HS; Olathe, KS; (1); Art Clb; 4-H; Teachers Aide; 4-H Awd; Hon Roll; Prfct Atten Awd; Pres Schlr; Ntl Coaliton Throwing Best Parties; Best Party Awd; Frmng.

HOFFMAN, AMANDA; North Central HS; Haddam, KS; (3); 6/10; Cmnty Wkr; Hist FBLA; HOBY; Scholastic Bowl; VP Frsh Cls; Pres Soph Cls; Sec Treas CAP; JV Var Bsktbl; Var Crs Cntry; Hon Roll; KSU Salina; Fly Airplanes.

HOFFMAN, BRADLEY A; Shawnee Mission W Sr HS; Lenexa, KS; (3); Church Yth Grp; DECA; Teachers Aide; Ofcr Stu Cncl; Socr; Trk; Hon Roll; Pres Acad Fit Awd; 1st Pl KS ST DECA, Vehicles & Petroleum Mrkting; Natl DECA Conf Orlando; Var Ltr Soccer.

HOFFMAN, CHRISTY; Greeley Co Schl; Tribune, KS; (4); 1/23; Art Clb; Church Yth Grp; Quiz Bowl; Scholastic Bowl; Speech Tm; Crs Cntry; Trk; Vllybl; Gov Hon Prg Awd; High Hon Roll; Ft Hays ST U; Art.

HOFFMAN, CORY D; Pratt HS; Pratt, KS; (2); JV Bsbl; Var Bsktbl; Var L Ftbl.

HOFFMAN, DARREN; Topeka HS; Topeka, KS; (4); Math Tm; Model UN; Jazz Band; Pep Band; Crs Cntry; Ftbl; Trk; Wrstlng; High Hon Roll; Ntl Merit Ltr; Co Fndr Topeka HS Phlsphy Club; VP Japanese Club; A P Schlr Awd; U Of KS; Coll Lbrl Arts/Sci.

HOFFMAN, DAWN E; Topeka HS; Topeka, KS; (1); Church Yth Grp; German Clb; Band; Mrchg Band; Pep Band; Stage Crew; High Hon Roll; Pres Acad Fit Awd; KS U; Soc Wrkr.

HOFFMAN, FELICIA J; Attica Public Schl; Kiowa, KS; (3); Speech Tm; Chorus; School Play; Nwsp; Yrbk; Var L Bsktbl; Var L Trk; Var L Vllybl; Hon Roll; Yrbk Ed; Newspapr Ed; Rgnl Trck Qualifier; ST Forensics Qualifier; Northwestern OK ST Univ; Bus.

HOFFMAN, JASON A; Bishop Carroll Catholic HS; Wichita, KS; (2); Boy Scts; Debate Tm; JV Bsbl; JV Ftbl; Hon Roll; Cath Yth Orch.

HOFFMAN, JENNIFER K; Newton Sr HS; Newton, KS; (1); French Clb; Tennis; Hon Roll.

HOFFMAN, KHARA K; Kapaun-Mt Carmel HS; Wichita, KS; (4); Pres Church Yth Grp; Q&S; Golf; Stage Crew; Scrkpr Yrbk; Hon Roll; NHS; Reg IV Outstndg Cathlc Yth; KS Schlstc Press Assn St Jrnlsm 2nd Pl Yrbk Layout/Dsgn; Rockhurst Coll; Comp Sci.

HOFFMAN, RYAN; Thomas More Prep-Marion HS; Hays, KS; (1); 6/66; Pres Frsh Cls; JV Bsbl; JV Ftbl; Notre Dame.

HOFFMAN, SELINA; Pittsburg HS; Pittsburg, KS; (4); 26/165; Am Leg Aux Girls St; French Clb; FTA; Library Aide; Teachers Aide; Orch; VP Sr Cls; Ofcr Stu Cncl; Vllybl; Hon Roll; Lions Clb Hnr Stu; Pittsburgh; Spch Pthlgy.

HOFFMAN, TRISHA S; Northeast HS; Mulberry, KS; (1); 8/48; GAA; Varsity Clb; Band; Mrchg Band; Pep Band; JV Bsktbl; JV Chrldng; Var Trk; JV Vllybl; Hon Roll; 5th Pl 400m 3a Regnl Track.

HOFFMAN, ZANE S; Shawnee Heights Sr HS; Topeka, KS; (2); Boy Scts; Church Yth Grp; Cmnty Wkr; Band; Mrchg Band; JV Ftbl; JV L Wrstlng; Hon Roll; Eagle Scout; Bsbl; KS U.

HOFFMANN, JOSEPH A; Bishop Miege HS; Overland Park, KS; (2); 11/163; Church Yth Grp; Quiz Bowl; Intrml Ftbl; JV Wrstlng; High Hon Roll; Acad Excel Awd.

HOGAN, BRIAN; Skyline Schl; Pratt, KS; (4); Church Yth Grp; Pep Clb; SADD; Band; Chorus; Mrchg Band; Orch; Pep Band; School Musical; School Play; Stu Of Month; Tabor Coll; PE.

HOGAN, KATHRYN R; Shawnee Mission N HS; Merriam, KS; (4); Pep Clb; Spanish Clb; Band; Mrchg Band; Pep Band; School Play; High Hon Roll; Hon Roll; Jr NHS; NHS; Shawnee Mssn Thtr Ambssdr; U Of KS; Phys Thrpy.

HOGAN, REBECCA; Seaman Sr HS; Topeka, KS; (3); Am Leg Aux Girls St; Church Yth Grp; Cmnty Wkr; Dance Clb; FBLA; Key Clb; Pep Clb; SADD; Band; Drill Tm; Advrtsng.

HOGAN, SHELLY L; Central Heights Sr HS; Lane, KS; (3); FBLA; Band; Yrbk; VP Jr Cls; Rep Stu Cncl; Var Capt Chrldng; Var Vllybl; High Hon Roll; NHS; Pres Acad Fit Awd; Bus.

HOGAN, TIMOTHY J; Blue Valley Northwest HS; Overland Park, KS; (2); Church Yth Grp; Drama Clb; NFL; Thesps; Stage Crew; Wrstlng; Tae Kwon Do Blue Belt W/Stripe.

HOGG, JOSH R; Lyons HS; Lyons, KS; (2); Art Clb; Boy Scts; JV Bsktbl; JV Ftbl; Rod & Gun Clb; KS Univ; Criminal Investigator.

HOGUE, CANDACE M; Blue Valley Northwest HS; Overland Park, KS; (3); Cmnty Wkr; Varsity Clb; Var Bsktbl; Var Sftbl; Var Vllybl; Wt Lftg; High Hon Roll; Hon Roll; Ntl Merit Ltr; Pres Acad Fit Awd; Spcl Olympics; Jr Olympc Vllybl Cptn Team; Bus/Mrktng.

HOITING, SUZANNE M; Shawnee Mission S Sr HS; Overland Park, KS; (3); 14/447; Church Yth Grp; Pep Clb; Acpl Chr; Ed Yrbk; Rep Stu Cncl; Var L Crs Cntry; High Hon Roll; NHS; Pres Schlr; Cadet Tchr.

HOLBROOKS, DAVID E; Arkansas City HS; Arkansas City, KS; (3); Rep Jr Cls; Rep Stu Cncl; Hon Roll; Army Basic Trng Grad 96; U Of ND; Airline Pilot.

HOLCOMB, APRIL; Flinthills HS; Rosalia, KS; (1); Chorus; School Play; Ofcr Frsh Cls; Ofcr Stu Cncl; Chrldng; Mgr(s); Trk; Vllybl; Hon Roll.

HOLCOMB, CASSANDRA J; Circle HS; El Dorado, KS; (4); NFL; Band; Jazz Band; Mrchg Band; Pep Band; Stage Crew; Variety Show; JV Bsktbl; JV Sftbl; Hon Roll; Crim.

HOLDEMAN, TROY A; Newton Sr HS; Halstead, KS; (2); 1/271; Letterman Clb; SADD; Varsity Clb; Var Ftbl; Wt Lftg; High Hon Roll; Pres Acad Fit Awd.

HOLDER, ERIKA K; Wichita North HS; Hoover, AL; (2); Church Yth Grp; Drama Clb; Band; Flag Corp; School Play; Stage Crew; Rep Soph Cls; Intrml Socr; Hon Roll; Play Flute In Concert Band 2 Yrs; Yth Day Of Caring Vol; NY Univ; Acting; Med Tech.

HOLE, P AARON; Erie HS; Erie, KS; (3); 4/42; Church Yth Grp; Debate Tm; NFL; Science Clb; VP Sr Cls; Var Bsbl; Var Wt Lftg; 4-H Awd; NHS; FCA; Red Crss Water Safety Instr; Amer Legion Bsbl; Farm Bureau Ldrshp Amer 94 & Cnslr 95; Environmental Bio.

HOLECEK, CURTIS J; Lucus-Luray HS; Lucas, KS; (2); SADD; Var Bsktbl; Var Ftbl.

HOLGUIN, JUSTIN M; Lewis Schl; Lewis, KS; (3); Bsktbl; Ftbl; Trk; Wt Lftg; Hon Roll; Hays CC.

HOLGUIN, MANUEL F; Lewis Schl; Lewis, KS; (4); 2/17; Am Leg Boys St; Boy Scts; Church Yth Grp; FBLA; NFL; Quiz Bowl; Teachers Aide; Band; Chorus; Jazz Band; All Lg, All St, All Star Ftbl; KS ST U; Physcs.

HOLIHAUS, KRISTIN R; Axtell Schl; Axtell, KS; (3); FCA; GAA; Pep Clb; Spanish Clb; Band; Chorus; Pep Band; Stage Crew; Yrbk; Sec Stu Cncl; Kys VP, Pres, Bd.

HOLLADAY, IAN C; Shawnee Mission W Sr HS; Overland Park, KS; (4); 1/365; Boy Scts; German Clb; Quiz Bowl; ROTC; Intrml Ftbl; High Hon Roll; NHS; Ntl Merit Schol; Pres Schlr; Val; Hnry Tribe Mic-O-Sav; U KS; Bus Admin.

HOLLAND, AMANDA J; Immaculata HS; Leavenworth, KS; (2); 11/61; Church Yth Grp; Math Tm; Scholastic Bowl; Science Clb; Stage Crew; Rep Soph Cls; JV Vllybl; Hon Roll; NHS; Chrch Vac Bible Schl Cnslr; Sunday Schl Kndgtn Tchr; Stdnts Who Care Clb; Comm.

HOLLAND, ERIN J; Immaculata HS; Leavenworth, KS; (4); 2/47; Ofcr Jr Cls; Pres Sr Cls; DAR Awd; Gov Hon Prg Awd; High Hon Roll; NHS; Pres Schlr; Sal; St Schlr; Duke U; Law.

HOLLAND, TARA A; Arkansas City HS; Arkansas City, KS; (2); Church Yth Grp; Debate Tm; NFL; JV Bsktbl; Var Golf; Hon Roll; NHS; KAY Clb Bd Mem; Meteorology.

HOLLAND, TYLER; Sublette HS; Sublette, KS; (4); 5/32; Boy Scts; Pres Church Yth Grp; VP Letterman Clb; VP Band; Chorus; Jazz Band; Pep Band; School Musical; VP Frsh Cls; VP Soph Cls; KS 2 A St Bsktbl Chmpnshp Tm 94-95; All Trnmnt Tm Hugoton Invtntl Dec 95; KSU; Vet.

HOLLE, KENT; Atwood HS; Oberlin, KS; (3); Am Leg Boys St; Rep Art Clb; Pres 4-H; Model UN; Natl FFA Org; Scholastic Bowl; School Play; Trk; Library Aide; Chorus; Music & Drama Clb Outstdng Drama Stu; Odessey Of Mind; PALS; Jr Ldr Farm Bureau Ldrshp Amer Conf; Pol Ofcr; His Tchr; Animator.

HOLLE, LORI; Hays HS; Hays, KS; (4); 28/204; Church Yth Grp; Cmnty Wkr; Library Aide; Teachers Aide; JV Tennis; Hon Roll; NHS; U Of KS; Arch.

HOLLENSBE, STEPHANIE E; Derby HS; Wichita, KS; (1); Church Yth Grp; ROTC; Hon Roll; Kndgtn Tchr.

HOLLER, JASON; Shawnee Mission N HS; Shawnee Mission, KS; (3); 36/430; Pep Clb; Chorus; High Hon Roll; Prfct Atten Awd.

HOLLER, JONATHAN K; Halstead HS; Bentley, KS; (1); Bsktbl; Hon Roll; Jr NHS; NHS; Prfct Atten Awd; PT.

HOLLIDAY, ADAM B; Stanton Co HS; Johnson, KS; (3); Boy Scts; Church Yth Grp; Band; Rep Frsh Cls; VP Stu Cncl; JV Bsktbl; Var L Ftbl; Var Trk; Cit Awd; Prfct Atten Awd; Tchr; Coach; Physical Therapy.

HOLLIDAY, CINDY A; Horton HS; Willis, KS; (2); 36/72; Library Aide; JV Vllybl; Wt Lftg; Hon Roll.

HOLLIDAY, MIKE; Olathe North Sr HS; Olathe, KS; (3); Church Yth Grp; Cmnty Wkr; Dance Clb; German Clb; Math Tm; Teachers Aide; Band; Co-Ed Lit Mag; Hon Roll; Karate; Comps; Wrtng; KS U; Physics; Chem.

HOLLIGER, JOYCE F; Mc Louth Schl; Mc Louth, KS; (3); Sec FBLA; Pep Clb; Chorus; Yrbk; Rep Stu Cncl; Hon Roll; Johnson Cty Comm Coll; Hygienis.

HOLLINGSWORTH, BARBIE; Shawnee Mission N HS; Overland Park, KS; (4); 24/370; Q&S; Acpl Chr; Band; Church Choir; Mrchg Band; Orch; School Musical; Ed Yrbk; Var Swmmng; NHS; St Orch; Dist 1 Hnr Orch; 2nd Place Layout Double Page Spread KS Schltc Press Assn Cont; KS ST U; Print Jrnlsm; Ed.

HOLLOWAY, AKILAH M; Topeka West HS; Topeka, KS; (1); Art Clb; Bsktbl; Wt Lftg; Hon Roll; Hlth/Hum Svc/Ansthslgst.

HOLLOWAY, AMANDA K; Mc Louth Schl; Mc Louth, KS; (2); Art Clb; FHA; Office Aide; Pep Clb; Quiz Bowl; SADD; Ed Phtg Yrbk; Hon Roll; Yrbk II; De Vry Tech Inst; Cmptr Prgrmr.

HOLLOWAY, ANDREA R; Russell HS; Russell, KS; (2); Chorus; Ofcr Sr Cls; Bsktbl; Trk; Wt Lftg; Hon Roll; Nrsng.

HOLLOWAY, CARA; Greensburg HS; Greensburg, KS; (4); Church Yth Grp; Pres Girl Scts; Teachers Aide; Band; Chorus; Flag Corp; Mrchg Band; Pep Band; School Musical; School Play; Amer Red Crs Lfgrd Instr/CPR/FIRST Aid Certd; Girl Scouts Silver Awd; Trng Certd; Hutcinson CC; Elem/Spec Ed.

HOLLOWELL, LINDSEY; Wichita North HS; Wichita, KS; (2); Cmnty Wkr; Pep Clb; Pom Pon; Socr; Multi-Yr Listee; Phy Thrpst.

HOLM, ADAM D; Washburn Rural HS; Topeka, KS; (3); 64/370; Chess Clb; Church Yth Grp; Debate Tm; FBLA; JA; NFL; Speech Tm; Band; Mrchg Band; Pep Band; Debate Ltr & 4th St; Forensics Ltr & 10th St; Fin; Financial Mgr.

HOLMES, AMBER M; Wichita North HS; Grand Forks AFB, ND; (4); Cmnty Wkr; Drama Clb; HOBY; Library Aide; Thesps; Chorus; School Play; Variety Show; Hon Roll; Coca Cola Olymp Torch Relay Choir; Hispn Wmn Ntwrk Schlrshp Nom; Fnlst NCCJ Schlrshp; U Of ND; Crmnl Jstc/Law.

HOLMES, ERIKA C; Anderson Cty Jr Sr HS; Garnett, KS; (4); 1/75; Debate Tm; Pep Clb; Science Clb; Band; Gov Hon Prg Awd; NHS; Pres Schlr; St Schlr; Val; Church Yth Grp; AATG/PAD Study; KS St Univ; Bio.

HOLMES, JEFFREY; Campus HS; Haysville, KS; (2); French Clb; Science Clb; SADD; Var L Bsbl; JV Bsktbl; Var L Ftbl; Wt Lftg; Hon Roll; Criminal Justice.

HOLMES, JENNIFER; Highland Park HS; Topeka, KS; (3); Church Choir; JV Tennis; Hon Roll; Prfct Atten Awd; Stu Of Mnth; Vol Church; Acad Ltr; KS ST; Zoologist.

HOLMES, NICHOLAS R; Washburn Rural HS; Topeka, KS; (3); Boy Scts; Debate Tm; Band; Jazz Band; Mrchg Band; Orch; Pep Band; Intrml Bsktbl; High Hon Roll; Tpka Yth Symphnr; Tpka Wind Ensmbl Prin Prcsn; Msnc All ST Bnd; Dist All ST Bnd; KS U; Music.

HOLMES, NIKI; Louisburg HS; Bucyrus, KS; (1); Math Clb; Math Tm; Acpl Chr; Band; Chorus; Mrchg Band; Pep Band; Chrldng; High Hon Roll; Hon Roll; Wrstlng/Bsktbl Chrldr; KS U; Med.

HOLMGREN, DAN A; Shawnee Mission S Sr HS; Shawnee Mission, KS; (4); 14/450; Boy Scts; Band; Mrchg Band; Trk; High Hon Roll; Hon Roll; Jr NHS; NHS; KS St Univ; Eng.

HOLOPIREK, MATT D; Otis Bison HS; Otis, KS; (1); 5/36; Quiz Bowl; Spanish Clb; SADD; Treas Frsh Cls; JV Bsktbl; JV Ftbl; JV Wt Lftg; High Hon Roll; Hon Roll; KAY; KS ST Univ; Zoologist.

HOLOVACH, DARIN; Manhattan HS; Manhattan, KS; (3); 35/500; 4-H; Capt Ftbl; Wt Lftg; 4-H Awd; High Hon Roll; Acctng.

HOLROYD, JANA; Southeast HS; Mc Cune, KS; (4); 1/52; FHA; Library Aide; Science Clb; High Hon Roll; NHS; Val; Kytts; Pittsburgh ST Univ.

HOLROYD, MEGAN L; Southeast HS; Mc Cune, KS; (3); 1/64; FHA; Scholastic Bowl; Science Clb; Ofcr Jr Cls; High Hon Roll; NHS; Keyettes.

HOLST, JOSH R; Shawnee Mission Nw Sr HS; Lenexa, KS; (4); 4/409; Math Tm; Science Clb; Orch; Ed Lit Mag; Intrml Socr; JV Trk; Ntl Merit SF; St Schlr; Church Yth Grp; School Musical; STEP Co-Pres; EMT; KS Rgnts Hnrs Acad 94; Psychbio.

HOLSTE, JARED; Atwood HS; Ludell, KS; (3); Church Yth Grp; Pres Sec 4-H; Treas Natl FFA Org; Hon Roll; Pres Jr Cls; Var Bsktbl; KS ST U; Vet Med.

HOLT, BECKY; Blue Valley HS; Olsburg, KS; (4); 2/16; Pres Bus Profs of Am; Pres Computer Clb; VP FHA; Pres SADD; Teachers Aide; Band; Chorus; Drm Mjr(t); Mrchg Band; Pep Band; KS Hnr Schlr; KS St U; Bus/Acctg.

HOLT, GRETCHEN M; Shawnee Mission West HS; Lenexa, KS; (4); 24/369; DECA; Girl Scts; Spanish Clb; High Hon Roll; Jr NHS; NHS; Pres Schlr; St Schlr; Peer Tutor; De Vry; Telecommunications Mgmt.

HOLT, KEILA L; Derby Christian Schl; Wichita, KS; (2); Church Yth Grp; Dance Clb; GAA; Girl Scts; Spanish Clb; SADD; Teachers Aide; Drill Tm; Var Bsktbl; Var Chrldng; Tchr/Soc Wrkr/Psych.

HOLTHAUS, CARINA M; Axtell Schl; Axtell, KS; (4); 1/14; FCA; Letterman Clb; Ofcr Stu Cncl; Bsktbl; Mgr(s); Trk; Cit Awd; High Hon Roll; Pres NHS; Val; KS Assn For Yth; Site-Bast Cncl Stu Rep; Teens As Tchrs; Benedictine KS; Med.

HOLTHAUS, KATRINA S R; Great Bend Sr HS; Great Bend, KS; (4); 53/213; Church Yth Grp; Drama Clb; Spanish Clb; Teachers Aide; Chorus; High Hon Roll; Hon Roll; Kayettes; Washburn U; Elem Ed.

HOLTHAUS, KRISTIN R; Axtell Schl; Axtell, KS; (3); FCA; GAA; Pep Clb; Spanish Clb; Band; Chorus; Church Choir; Pep Band; Stage Crew; Yrbk; Kays.

HOLTHAUS, MATTHEW R; Axtell Schl; Axtell, KS; (3); 3/20; Band; Chorus; Yrbk; Rep Soph Cls; Bsktbl; Var L Ftbl; Hon Roll; Bsbl; KS ST; Wldlf Biologist.

HOLTHAUS, RHONDA; Nemaha Valley HS; Seneca, KS; (2); Chrldng; Vllybl; Hon Roll; Prfct Atten Awd; Chrldng Ltr; Kay Clb; KS U; Commrcl Advrtsng.

HOLTORF, THERESA; Linn Schl; Palmer, KS; (3); 1/25; FBLA; Letterman Clb; Band; Mrchg Band; Pres Soph Cls; Hist Stu Cncl; L Bsktbl; High Hon Roll; NHS; KSUFMATH.

HOLTWICK, JENNIFER; Colby Sr HS; Colby, KS; (4); 4/97; Am Leg Aux Girls St; Church Yth Grp; Cmnty Wkr; Debate Tm; French Clb; Letterman Clb; Scholastic Bowl; SADD; Teachers Aide; Varsity Clb; Schl Musicals Lead Roles; Meals-On-Wheels; Med.

HOLTZ, DARRELL D; Midland Sda Schl; Overland Park, KS; (1).

HOLUB, DUSTIN T; Olathe East Sr HS; Olathe, KS; (2); Rep Frsh Cls; High Hon Roll; Hon Roll; Pres Acad Fit Awd.

HOLWAY, SUSAN A; Beloit Jr Sr HS; Beloit, KS; (2); Church Yth Grp; Spanish Clb; SADD; Chorus; Orch; School Musical; School Play; Stage Crew; Variety Show; Trk; KSHSAA St Music Cont Vocal Solo II Rating.

HOLZMAN, ANDREA M; Kapaun-Mt Carmel HS; Wichita, KS; (4); Debate Tm; Teachers Aide; Acpl Chr; Stage Crew; Prfct Atten Awd; Optimist Unsung Hero Awd; Eagle Achvmt Awd; Rockhurst Coll; Bus Mgmt.

HOLZWART, CHRISTOPHER; Olathe South Sr HS; Olathe, KS; (4); Boy Scts; Church Yth Grp; Cmnty Wkr; Debate Tm; Spanish Clb; Teachers Aide; Lit Mag; Crs Cntry; High Hon Roll; Hon Roll; KS U; Arch.

HOMAN, BRANDY N; Topeka HS; Topeka, KS; (1); High Hon Roll; Acad Ltr; Colby CC; Vet Asst.

HOMEIER, DEANNA N; Russell HS; Russell, KS; (2); Church Yth Grp; 4-H; Natl FFA Org; Band; Mrchg Band; Rep Stu Cncl; JV Capt Chrldng; JV Sftbl; 4-H Awd; High Hon Roll; Med Field.

HOMEWOOD, ANDREA N; Washburn Rural HS; Topeka, KS; (2); Chorus; Hon Roll; Smnr; BYU; Elem Schl Tchr.

HOMMERTZHEIM, KARLA J; Andale HS; Colwich, KS; (3); Church Yth Grp; GAA; Letterman Clb; Teachers Aide; JV Bsktbl; Mgr(s); Powder Puff Ftbl; Var L Trk; Var JV Vllybl; High Hon Roll; KS ST; Medicine.

HOMOLKA, LORA; Ellsworth HS; Ellsworth, KS; (4); 20/70; Am Leg Aux Girls St; Church Yth Grp; Girl Scts; Hosp Aide; Band; Chorus; Flag Corp; Mrchg Band; Pep Band; Vllybl; Girl Scouts Silver & Gold Awds; Hutchinson CC; Rdlgy.

HOOD, ERICA L; Shawnee Heights HS; Topeka, KS; (2); Church Yth Grp; Pep Clb; SADD; Chorus; Sftbl; Vllybl; Wt Lftg; High Hon Roll; Care Co; Crime Stoppers.

HOOD, SELINA ANNE; Paola HS; Paola, KS; (3); 16/136; Drama Clb; FCA; NFL; SADD; Thesps; Var Chorus; School Musical; School Play; Rptr Yrbk; Rep Frsh Cls; KAYS Sec/VP; Pre-Med/Bio.

HOOK, PATRICK; Sedgwick HS; Sedgwick, KS; (4); 2/23; Am Leg Boys St; Church Yth Grp; Capt Scholastic Bowl; Spanish Clb; SADD; Band; Nwsp; High Hon Roll; NHS; St Schlr; I Dare You Awd; Cngrssnl Yth Ldrshp Cncl; KS ST; Cmptr Sci.

HOOK, TIFFANY; Olathe South Sr HS; Olathe, KS; (4); 31/370; Am Leg Aux Girls St; Pres Church Yth Grp; Ed Q&S; Band; Ed Yrbk; High Hon Roll; NHS; German Clb; Variety Show; Lit Mag; Cngrssnl Awd; KS Hnr Soc; Untd Natl Jrnslm Awd; Acctng.

HOOKER, KEVIN J; Shawnee Mission N HS; Shawnee Mission, KS; (4); 41/375; Church Yth Grp; German Clb; Pep Clb; Var Bsbl; Var Bsktbl; JV Socr; High Hon Roll; NHS; Pres Schlr; Baker U.

HOOPER, ANDREW C; Bishop Miege HS; Kansas City, MO; (4); Boy Scts; Wrstlng; Hon Roll; Egl Sct; Truman ST Univ.

HOOPER, CLINT W; Clearwater HS; Clearwater, KS; (3); Ntl Merit SF; Guitar; Musical Engrng; Songwriter; KS ST; Bounty Hunter.

HOOPER, SARAH L; Atchison Sr HS; Atchison, KS; (1); Church Yth Grp; Spanish Clb; Band; Mrchg Band; Pep Band; JV Bsktbl; JV Sftbl; JV Vllybl; High Hon Roll; Hon Roll; UKS; Jrnlsm.

HOOPINGARNER, ERIC C; Lawrence HS; Lawrence, KS; (2); Crs Cntry; Trk; Cit Awd; High Hon Roll; Hon Roll; Pres Schlr; U Of FL; Lawyer.

HOOSER, HOLLY A; Blue Valley Northwest HS; Overland Park, KS; (3); Cmnty Wkr; Church Yth Grp; FCA; Church Choir; Var Golf; Hon Roll.

HOOSER, LINDSAY A; Blue Valley Northwest HS; Overland Park, KS; (1); Church Yth Grp; Debate Tm; Church Choir; Var Golf; Hon Roll.

HOOSIER, MATT W; Trego Comm HS; Wa Keeney, KS; (2); 1/55; Church Yth Grp; Debate Tm; Quiz Bowl; Science Clb; Speech Tm; Band; Mrchg Band; Pep Band; Golf; High Hon Roll; Medalist At Natl Cath Forensics League Debate Trnmt.

HOOTEN, JAIRA B; Blue Valley HS; Stilwell, KS; (2); SADD; Rep Stu Cncl; JV Crs Cntry; Var Swmmng; Cit Awd; Hon Roll; Natl Art HNR Soc Treas; Natl Span Contest Exclnt Rating Extmprns Reading; KS ST Univ; Ed/Psych.

HOOTEN, KIMBERLY K; Maize HS; Wichita, KS; (2); 1/250; Church Yth Grp; 4-H; Spanish Clb; SADD; Chorus; Variety Show; High Hon Roll; NHS; Pres Acad Fit Awd; KAYS.

HOOVER, ALISSA; Hanover Schl; Hanover, KS; (3); 1/16; VP Drama Clb; Sec FBLA; FHA; Letterman Clb; Band; Rep Frsh Cls; Sec Stu Cncl; Co-Capt Chrldng; Vllybl; High Hon Roll; Bus.

HOOVER, CATHERINE J; Shawnee Mission S Sr HS; Shawnee Mission, KS; (3); 22/443; Am Leg Aux Girls St; Church Yth Grp; Dance Clb; Intnl Clb; Pep Clb; SADD; Chorus; Drill Tm; School Musical; High Hon Roll; Yth Group Drama Team; Stu Cncl; Mem Of Somerset Ballet Dance Co; KS ST; Bio.

HOOVER, ERICA; Independence HS; Independence, KS; (1); French Clb; Pep Clb; Var L Bsktbl; Var Tennis; Var L Trk; High Hon Roll; French Clb; Pep Clb; Rep Stu Cncl.

HOOVER, MICHELLE; Washington HS; Greenleaf, KS; (4); 5/31; Am Leg Aux Girls St; French Clb; Pep Clb; Yrbk; Rep Stu Cncl; Var Chrldng; Golf; Var Vllybl; High Hon Roll; Homcmng Rally; CYO Hstrn; KSU.

HOOVER, TISHA; Wichita South HS; Wichita, KS; (2); Drama Clb; Pep Clb; Thesps; Chorus; School Musical; School Play; Variety Show; JV Capt Chrldng; Swmmng; Letterman Clb; Thespian Treas 96-; Miss Titan; Lifeguard; Drama.

HOPKINS, JACKIE L; Holton HS; Holton, KS; (1); FHA; Acpl Chr; Band; Chorus; Pep Band; Vllybl; Paraproffesional Aide; KS ST Univ; Paralegal; Lawyer.

HOPKINS, JULIA C; Hoisington HS; Hoisington, KS; (2); Church Yth Grp; SADD; Band; Mrchg Band; Trk; Vllybl; High Hon Roll; Oral Roberts U; Dr; Med Field.

HOPKINS, MICHELLE R; Topeka West HS; Topeka, KS; (4); French Clb; Pep Clb; Spanish Clb; Teachers Aide; Acpl Chr; Chorus; Swing Chorus; Variety Show; JV Crs Cntry; Var Sftbl; 1-70 League For Sftbl; All City Sftbl; Neosho; Nrsng.

HOPKINS, SHEILA M; Galena HS; Galena, KS; (3); FHA; JV Sftbl; Hon Roll; MO Southern ST Coll.

HOPP, SHAUNA M; Smoky Valley HS; Marquette, KS; (1); Pep Clb; Red Cross Aide; Band; Mrchg Band; Pep Band; Bsktbl; Vllybl; High Hon Roll; KAY's Svc Grp; Soph Cls Pres 96-; KS ST; Accntnt.

HOPPER, BENJAMIN L; Riley Cty HS; Leonardville, KS; (3); 3/50; Debate Tm; Drama Clb; FCA; FBLA; Natl FFA Org; Pep Clb; SADD; Band; School Play; Rep Soph Cls; KS St Univ; Pltcn.

HOPPER, HEATHER M; Cheney Jr Sr HS; Cheney, KS; (2); Church Yth Grp; Cmnty Wkr; Pep Clb; Band; Chorus; Flag Corp; School Play; Swing Chorus; Mgr(s); Hon Roll; Girls Glee; Pop Choir; KS U; Nws Brdcstng/Sprts Med.

HOPPER, STACY; Wichita East HS; Wichita, KS; (2); Girl Scts; Orch; Hon Roll.

HORALEK, JONI L; Valley Heights Jr Sr HS; Frankfort, KS; (4); Church Yth Grp; Cmnty Wkr; FHA; Pep Clb; Chorus; Variety Show; Treas Frsh Cls; Vllybl; Wt Lftg; Hon Roll; KS ST Univ; Spch Pthlgy.

HORAN, ROBIN; Abilene HS; Abilene, KS; (4); 17/111; Spanish Clb; Chorus; Drill Tm; School Musical; Capt Var Chrldng; Var Tennis; High Hon Roll; NHS; Spanish NHS; FCA; Ensemble; Ft Hays ST U; Elem Ed.

HORCHEM, TRAVIS; Ness City HS; Ness City, KS; (1); 2/32; Church Yth Grp; 4-H; Quiz Bowl; Scholastic Bowl; Band; Bsktbl; Ftbl; Wt Lftg; High Hon Roll; Hon Roll; Math.

HORIGAN, MEGAN L; Frankft HS; Frankfort, KS; (3); Letterman Clb; SADD; Chorus; Flag Corp; School Play; VP Frsh Cls; VP Soph Cls; Pres Jr Cls; Bsktbl; Mgr(s); Med Field.

HORN, AMANDA B; Royal Valley HS; Hoyt, KS; (4); 10/53; Pep Clb; SADD; Teachers Aide; Band; Chorus; Mrchg Band; Pep Band; School Musical; Mgr Chrldng; Hon Roll; Kays Publicity & Points; Emporia ST Univ; Scndry Bus Ed.

HORN, EILEEN R; St Thomas Aquinas HS; Lenexa, KS; (2); 17/280; FCA; Hosp Aide; Ed Nwsp; Bsktbl; Sftbl; Vllybl; High Hon Roll; Notre Dame; Pre-Med.

HORN, JEFFREY M; Basehor Linwood HS; Basehor, KS; (3); 13/100; Ofcr Bsbl; High Hon Roll; Hon Roll; FBLA.

HORN, JUSTIN; Humboldt HS; Humboldt, KS; (4); 3/43; Scholastic Bowl; Band; Mrchg Band; Pep Band; Variety Show; JV Var Golf; High Hon Roll; NHS; KS Hnr Schlr; Stu Of Month Feb 96; Pittsburg ST U; Comp Sci.

HORN, KELLI; Jetmore HS; Jetmore, KS; (4); 5/15; Pep Clb; Quiz Bowl; Scholastic Bowl; Speech Tm; School Play; Phtg Yrbk; VP Sr Cls; Var Chrldng; JV Vllybl; Hon Roll; J-Clb; KS Assn For Yth; Dodge City CC; Phys Thrpy.

HORN, STEVE G; Salina HS South; Salina, KS; (3); Cmnty Wkr; Teachers Aide; Rep Soph Cls; JV Var Bsktbl; JV Var Tennis; NHS; Ch Altar Boy; Vol Umpire 2 Yrs Fndrsng.

HORN, WILLIAM; Holcomb HS; Holcomb, KS; (3); CAP; French Clb; Spanish Clb; Band; Color Guard; Drill Tm; Mrchg Band; School Musical; Wrstlng; Explr Scts; Air Force Acad; Gntcst.

HORNBAKER, JENNIFER; Olathe East Sr HS; Olathe, KS; (4); 12/300; Am Leg Aux Girls St; French Clb; Chorus; School Musical; Variety Show; Ed Yrbk; Ed Lit Mag; Rep Sr Cls; Rep Stu Cncl; JV Crs Cntry; SASH; Respect Cmmtte; U Of KS; Intr Dsgn.

HORNE, NIKKI; Blue Valley Northwest HS; Overland Park, KS; (3); Var L Chrldng; Var L Diving; High Hon Roll; Pres Acad Fit Awd; Pro Cheer All Strs.

HORNE, TIFFANY D; Haven HS; Hutchinson, KS; (3); Church Yth Grp; FCA; French Clb; SADD; Band; Church Choir; Pep Band; School Musical; School Play; Variety Show; KAYS.

HORNECKER, BRANDY; Topeka HS; Topeka, KS; (4); 46/354; Cmnty Wkr; VP French Clb; Library Aide; NFL; Variety Show; High Hon Roll; Hon Roll; Pres Acad Fit Awd; Dance; Topeka HS Tower Awd; KS St Univ; Civil Engrng.

HORNER, ALLYSON R; Blue Vlly HS; Leawood, KS; (2); Debate Tm; NFL; High Hon Roll; U Of KS; Med.

HORNER, KRISTAN E; Smoky Valley HS; Lindsborg, KS; (2); Band; Mrchg Band; Pep Band; School Play; Hon Roll; Article Written For KS Writing Assessment Sent To St For Scoring; Manchester Coll; Pre-Med.

HORNER, TARYN; Mulvane Sr HS; Mulvane, KS; (4); 16/144; SADD; Teachers Aide; Ed Yrbk; Hon Roll; NHS; Prfct Atten Awd; Friends U; Acctng.

HORNING, AMY S; Syracuse Jr Sr HS; Syracuse, KS; (2); Art Clb; Church Yth Grp; Pep Clb; Chorus; Flag Corp; Rptr Nwsp; Chrldng; Powder Puff Ftbl; Vllybl; Wt Lftg; Ft Hemp ST Univ; Pre Med.

HORNING, KRISTI; Syracuse Jr Sr HS; Syracuse, KS; (2); 2/32; Church Yth Grp; Letterman Clb; Pep Clb; SADD; Teachers Aide; Chorus; Sec Soph Cls; Ofcr Sr Cls; Chrldng; High Hon Roll; Emporia U; Elem Ed.

HORNUNG, PETE T; Ottawa HS; Ottawa, KS; (3); Am Leg Boys St; Church Yth Grp; Letterman Clb; Teachers Aide; Acpl Chr; Church Choir; Ofcr Bsbl; Bsktbl; Ftbl; Golf; KS ST Univ.

HORSCH, SHANE J; Maize HS; Wichita, KS; (2); Hon Roll; NE; Wildlife Bio.

HORST, NATHAN D; Hesston HS; Newton, KS; (3); Church Yth Grp; Debate Tm; Model UN; NFL; Chorus; School Play; Variety Show; Ofcr Jr Cls; Ofcr Stu Cncl; Tennis.

HORTON, ALLISON; Inman Jr Sr HS; Inman, KS; (3); 1/40; Art Clb; Church Yth Grp; German Clb; Natl FFA Org; NFL; Quiz Bowl; School Musical; School Play; Treas Jr Cls; High Hon Roll; Mission Trps Frgn Cntries; Tambourine Mnstry.

HORTON, CHRIS; Pittsburg HS; Pittsburg, KS; (3); Am Leg Boys St; Debate Tm; FCA; FHA; NFL; Q&S; Spanish Clb; Yrbk; Crs Cntry; Pres NHS; Med Explorers Clb VP; Pittsburg ST Univ; Psych; Bus.

HORTON, MARY T; Bishop Ward HS; Kansas City, KS; (2); 4/100; Cmnty Wkr; Dance Clb; Drama Clb; Pep Clb; Science Clb; Drill Tm; School Musical; School Play; High Hon Roll; Jr NHS; KS City Theatre Co; Ballet Productions; Ballet Schlsp Wichita ST; Jazz Schlsp Chicago; Surgeon.

HORTON, MATTHEW T; Labette Co HS; Parsons, KS; (2); Chess Clb; Church Yth Grp; FCA; Letterman Clb; SADD; Rptr Nwsp; VP Frsh Cls; Var L Bsbl; JV Var Bsktbl; JV Var Ftbl; All Acad Team Bsktbl Trnmnt.

HORTON, NICOLE L; Blue Valley Northwest HS; Leawood, KS; (3); 57/400; Church Yth Grp; Cmnty Wkr; High Hon Roll; NHS.

HORTON, STACI; Inman Jr Sr HS; Inman, KS; (2); Art Clb; Church Yth Grp; German Clb; NFL; Pep Clb; Quiz Bowl; Band; Mrchg Band; Pep Band; High Hon Roll; Mission Trips; Tambourine Mnstry.

HORTON, STACIE; Elkhart HS; Elkhart, KS; (4); 2/32; HOBY; Speech Tm; Thesps; School Musical; School Play; Ed Nwsp; Yrbk; VP Sr Cls; NHS; Sal; Chrch Accmpnst; U Of OK.

HOSKINS, JOY; Goddard HS; Wichita, KS; (4); Drama Clb; German Clb; Science Clb; Chorus; School Musical; School Play; Pres Sr Cls; High Hon Roll; NHS; Pres Schlr; Creighton Univ.

HOSKINSON, JASON; Shawnee Heights Sr HS; Berryton, KS; (2); Church Yth Grp; Band; Jazz Band; Mrchg Band; Pep Band; High Hon Roll.

HOSKINSON, KEVIN; Garden City Sr HS; Garden City, KS; (4); 33/333; Boy Scts; Church Yth Grp; Cmnty Wkr; Drama Clb; Key Clb; Latin Clb; Quiz Bowl; Science Clb; Acpl Chr; Band; Silver Medalist Natl Latin Exam; Pope Pius XII Awd; Eagle Scout; Garden City CC; Drama.

HOSLER, CHRISTINA; Valley Falls HS; Valley Falls, KS; (3); Am Leg Aux Girls St; Church Yth Grp; Drama Clb; 4-H; FBLA; FHA; Band; Chorus; Drill Tm; School Play.

HOSLER, NICHOLAS J; Valley Falls HS; Valley Falls, KS; (3); Pres Frsh Cls; L Bsktbl; L Trk; Hon Roll.

HOSS, BRADLEY J; Ness City HS; Ness City, KS; (2); Church Yth Grp; Natl FFA Org; Pep Clb; Band; Mrchg Band; Pep Band; Ofcr Stu Cncl; Ftbl; Wt Lftg; Prfct Atten Awd; Ag.

HOSS, JULIE; Ness City HS; Ness City, KS; (4); 1/29; Church Yth Grp; Office Aide; VP Pep Clb; Quiz Bowl; Chorus; Pres Jr Cls; Var Capt Bsktbl; Var L Trk; Var Capt Vllybl; NHS; Female Athl Yr; Natl Army Rsrve Schlr/Athl; Wendys Heisman HS Nom; U KS; Sprts Med.

HOSS, KELLY J; Russell HS; Russell, KS; (2); Boy Scts; Church Yth Grp; Key Clb; Letterman Clb; SADD; Sec Frsh Cls; Sec Soph Cls; Ofcr Stu Cncl; JV Bsbl; JV Var Bsktbl; NHS Stu Of Yr; Teens As Tchrs.

HOSTETIER, SARA B; Maize HS; Wichita, KS; (2); 1/280; Church Yth Grp; Spanish Clb; SADD; Teachers Aide; Varsity Clb; Bsktbl; Sftbl; Trk; Vllybl; Wt Lftg.

HOTTENSTEIN, LONI A; Humboldt HS; Humboldt, KS; (2); FHA; Band; Pep Band; Phtg Rptr Nwsp; L Bsktbl; Vllybl; Hon Roll; L Trk; Allen Cty; Bus; Med Records.

HOTTMAN, SCOTT A; Abilene HS; Abilene, KS; (3); Am Leg Boys St; Ftbl; Wrstlng; Hon Roll.

HOUCHIN, ADAM B; Great Bend Sr HS; Great Bend, KS; (4); 65/250; Am Leg Boys St; Church Yth Grp; Debate Tm; NFL; Pep Clb; Quiz Bowl; Scholastic Bowl; Spanish Clb; Speech Tm; Chorus; Manger Bsktbll; Barton Cnty CC; Sprts Med.

HOUGH, MAGGIE; Clearwater HS; Clearwater, KS; (4); 26/85; Am Leg Aux Girls St; CAP; SADD; Teachers Aide; Chorus; School Musical; Nwsp; Mgr(s); Score Keeper; Hon Roll; Hutchinson CC; Elem Ed.

HOUGH, SCARLETT E; Field Kindley HS; Coffeyville, KS; (4); 1/130; Church Yth Grp; Debate Tm; English Clb; NFL; Spanish Clb; Speech Tm; Teachers Aide; Acpl Chr; Chorus; High Hon Roll; KS ST Univ; Bio/Med Rsrch.

HOUGHLAND, CANDICE L; Field Kindley Mem Sr HS; Coffeyville, KS; (2); Church Yth Grp; FCA; French Clb; Rep Stu Cncl; JV Sftbl; JV Tennis; Hon Roll; U Of KS; Tchr.

HOUK, LACI R; Oxford HS; Geuda Springs, KS; (2); 1/45; Key Clb; Pep Clb; Spanish Clb; Varsity Clb; Band; Mrchg Band; Pep Band; JV Var Bsktbl; Var Sftbl; JV Var Vllybl; Ft Nays Univ; Pharm.

HOUPT, JASON T; Topeka HS; Topeka, KS; (1); ROTC; JV Crs Cntry; JV Trk; Hon Roll; NHS; Pres Schlr; Annapolis; Military Lawyer.

HOUSE, BECKY; Mc Pherson HS; Mc Pherson, KS; (4); 1/190; VP Pres Church Yth Grp; Sec VP FTA; Sec Science Clb; Speech Tm; School Musical; JV Var Tennis; Gov Hon Prg Awd; Val; Capt Dance Clb; Drama Clb; Elem Schl Math Tutor; Dist Choir; Odyssey Of Mind; Creighton Univ; Envmntl Sci.

HOUSE, CORRIE E; Wichita Northwest HS; Wichita, KS; (2); KS ST; PT.

HOUSE, GINA L; Ottawa HS; Ottawa, KS; (3); Hosp Aide; Teachers Aide; Hon Roll; Stu Naturalist Pgm; CNA Ottawa Retirement Vlg; Voc Trng.

HOUSE, KELLY L; Great Bend Sr HS; Great Bend, KS; (3); Church Yth Grp; Pep Clb; Spanish Clb; Var Crs Cntry; Var Trk; Hon Roll; Prfct Atten Awd; Barron Cty CC; Animal Sci.

HOUSEMAN, SARAH; Eureka Jr Sr HS; Eureka, KS; (2); French Clb; Letterman Clb; Office Aide; Quiz Bowl; Science Clb; SADD; Swing Chorus; Yrbk; Lit Mag; High Hon Roll; KU; Pedtrcn.

HOUSER, NICOLE; Plainville HS; Plainville, KS; (4); 1/52; Pres Church Yth Grp; Cmnty Wkr; FHA; Pep Clb; JV Var Tennis; Gov Hon Prg Awd; High Hon Roll; Hon Roll; NHS; Prfct Atten Awd; SITE Cncl Mem & Sec; Steering Comm Mem & Sec; KS Regents Hnrs Acad; Ft Hays ST Univ; Elem Ed.

HOUSHOLDER, ANNE; Wichita Collegiate Schl; Wichita, KS; (2); Cmnty Wkr; Debate Tm; Girl Scts; Hosp Aide; Quiz Bowl; Scholastic Bowl; High Hon Roll; Hon Roll.

HOUSHOLDER, HEIDI; Syracuse Jr Sr HS; Coolidge, KS; (1); Sec 4-H; Pep Clb; Band; Chorus; Mrchg Band; Pep Band; Rep Stu Cncl; Var Bsktbl; Powder Puff Ftbl; JV Vllybl; Natl Little Britches Rodeo.

HOUSHOLDER, HOLLY; Halstead HS; Halstead, KS; (3); Pres Church Yth Grp; Cmnty Wkr; Letterman Clb; Pep Clb; Rep Spanish Clb; Temple Yth Grp; Chorus; Church Choir; Capt Drill Tm; School Musical; Kayettes Bd Mem; Viola; KS Unv; Phy Therapy.

HOUSMAN, LARAE; Jetmore HS; Jetmore, KS; (1); Church Yth Grp; Treas 4-H; Natl FFA Org; Chorus; Variety Show; Var JV Bsktbl; Var Chrldng; JV Golf; JV Var Vllybl; 4-H Awd; Farm Bureau Ldrshp Camp; Kayetts; Bsktbl.

HOUSTON, LEILANI M; Shawnee Mission Northwest HS; Shawnee, KS; (2); Art Clb; CAP; Drama Clb; Hosp Aide; Band; Mrchg Band; Pep Band; Socr; Billy Mitchell Awd CAP Flight Ofcr; Echo Flight Commander MO Wing Encampment; NCO Of Yr MO Wing; JCCC; RN.

HOVEL, SARAH; Shawnee Mission E Sr HS; Prairie Village, KS; (3); 30/409; Church Yth Grp; Natl Beta Clb; Q&S; Service Clb; JV Crs Cntry; Var L French Hon Soc; High Hon Roll; NHS; Spanish NHS; Office Aide; Piano; Columbia Bk Awd; Schltc Pin Awd; Avila Awd Recital; Phy Thrpst.

HOVER, KIMBERLY A; Maranatha Acad; Bonner Springs, KS; (3); 11/52; Church Yth Grp; Band; Mrchg Band; Bsktbl; Vllybl; High Hon Roll; Bus Mgmt.

HOWARD, ASHLEY; Garden City Sr HS; Garden City, KS; (4); French Clb; Bsktbl; Vllybl; Wt Lftg; High Hon Roll; Pres Acad Fit Awd; SW TX At San Marcos; Pre Med.

HOWARD, CARRIE; Seaman Sr HS; Topeka, KS; (4); Hist FHA; Key Clb; Library Aide; Natl FFA Org; Flag Corp; Phtg Nwsp; Phtg Yrbk; Swmmng; Vllybl; High Hon Roll; KS ST U; Bio.

HOWARD, CHELSIE; Atchison Co Cmty HS; Lancaster, KS; (2); Letterman Clb; Math Clb; Band; Church Choir; Drill Tm; Mrchg Band; Pep Band; Stage Crew; Variety Show; Treas Frsh Cls; Waterskiing; Baton Twirler.

HOWARD, HEATHER F; Ottawa HS; Ottawa, KS; (3); Church Yth Grp; Cmnty Wkr; French Clb; Teachers Aide; Chorus; Flag Corp; Yrbk; High Hon Roll; KS ST Univ; Soc Work.

HOWARD, JASON L; Halstead HS; Halstead, KS; (3); Church Yth Grp; Letterman Clb; Pep Clb; Spanish Clb; JV Var Ftbl; Var Capt Wrstlng; Hon Roll; ST Wrstlng Qlfr 9th-11th Grd; 3rd Pl ST Wrstlng 10th 4th/11th Yr; KS Natl Jr Wrstlng Tm 10th/11th; Acctg.

HOWARD, KAMSHIA R; Wichita North HS; Wichita, KS; (3); Chorus; Rep Frsh Cls; Rep Jr Cls; Rep Stu Cncl; JV Trk; Hon Roll; Prfct Atten Awd; Nth HS Concrt Choir; Nth HS Madrigal Singer; BASE Clb; U Of KS.

HOWARD, KELLY; Wichita North HS; Wichita, KS; (4); 14/247; Pep Clb; Scholastic Bowl; Science Clb; Chorus; Variety Show; Var L Socr; Hon Roll; NHS; Pres Schlr; St Schlr; Wichita ST Univ; Bio; Span.

HOWARD, MICHELE L; Northeast HS; Mulberry, KS; (3); 12/34; Band; Chorus; Rep Stu Cncl; Var L Bsktbl; Var L Sftbl; Var L Vllybl; Hon Roll; WA U; Phys Thrpy.

HOWARD, SHELLY R; Horton HS; Horton, KS; (4); 12/57; Church Yth Grp; Drill Tm; School Play; Yrbk; VP Pres Stu Cncl; Bsktbl; Capt Chrldng; Vllybl; Hon Roll; NHS; Homecoming Queen; Baker Univ; Busadmin.

HOWARD, STEPHANIE; Hiawatha HS; Hiawatha, KS; (3); 36/101; Church Yth Grp; FHA; Letterman Clb; Pep Clb; Teachers Aide; Rptr Nwsp; Chrldng; Powder Puff Ftbl; Hon Roll; Upwrd Bnd Proj Focus, Stu Sntr & Stu Snt VP; Emporia ST U; Elem Ed.

HOWE, SHAWN; Weskan Schl; Weskan, KS; (4); 2/6; Church Yth Grp; Pres 4-H; Quiz Bowl; Chorus; School Play; Stage Crew; Swing Chorus; VP Sr Cls; Hon Roll; Pres Acad Fit Awd; Coffeyville CC; Vet Med.

HOWELL, ANGELA D; Washburn Rural HS; Topeka, KS; (3); 83/351; JA; Model UN; Office Aide; Phtg Nwsp; Phtg Yrbk; Scl Wrk.

HOWELL, DARLA L; Southeast HS; Mc Cune, KS; (4); 8/54; Library Aide; Band; Jazz Band; Mrchg Band; Pep Band; School Musical; Vllybl; Hon Roll; Treas NHS; Prfct Atten Awd; John Philip Sousa Awd; Kayette Clb Bd Mem; Pittsburg ST Univ.

HOWELL, MARCUS; Basehor Linwood HS; Basehor, KS; (4); 28/121; Church Yth Grp; FCA; Office Aide; Q&S; Science Clb; Teachers Aide; Phtg Yrbk; Hon Roll; Mgr Sftbl; Homcmng Float Comm; Ran Sound Sys For Chrch Svc & Choir Practice; DARE Yth Speaker; KS ST U; Prof Pilots Pgm.

HOWELL, SCOTT; Shawnee Mission S Sr HS; Shawnee Mission, KS; (4); Am Leg Boys St; Ofcr Stu Cncl; Var Capt Crs Cntry; Var Score Keeper; Var Capt Trk; Cit Awd; Hon Roll; VP NHS; Pres Schlr; St Schlr; Claremont Mc Kenna Clg; Env Sci.

HOWELL, STEPHEN; Norton Comm HS; Norton, KS; (4); 1/41; Church Yth Grp; Quiz Bowl; Band; School Play; Pres Jr Cls; Ftbl; Tennis; NHS; Ntl Merit SF; Val; Manhattan Chrstn Coll.

HOWELL, TRAVIS J; Garden Plain Jr Sr HS; Garden Plain, KS; (2); 1/34; Chess Clb; Church Yth Grp; HOBY; Quiz Bowl; Red Cross Aide; Spanish Clb; SADD; Rep Frsh Cls; Rep Stu Cncl; JV Var Bsktbl; US Naval Acad; Engr.

HOWER, SEAN P; Manhattan HS; Manhattan, KS; (3); Science Clb; Var Socr; Hon Roll.

HOWLAND, BRAD E; Jewell HS; Jewell, KS; (1); Church Yth Grp; FCA; Quiz Bowl; SADD; Band; Chorus; Pep Band; School Play; Trk; Hon Roll; FFA.

HOWLAND, IVY; Jewell HS; Jewell, KS; (4); 2/15; Church Yth Grp; FCA; FHA; Quiz Bowl; Drm Mjr(t); School Musical; Treas Sr Cls; Cit Awd; Sal; St Schlr; Hesston Coll; Nrsng.

HOYLE, BRIDGET; Maranatha Acad; Lenexa, KS; (1); Drama Clb; Rep Stu Cncl; JV Var Bsktbl; JV Vllybl; High Hon Roll.

HOYLE, MELYNDA; Maranatha Acad; Lenexa, KS; (3); 5/50; Math Tm; Pep Clb; Pres Jr Cls; Stat Bsktbl; High Hon Roll; NHS; Bus Mngmt.

HOYLE, SHEYENE; Clay Ctr Cmty HS; Clay Center, KS; (4); 21/98; Am Leg Aux Girls St; Sec Treas Drama Clb; Pres Natl FFA Org; Spanish Clb; School Play; Ed Nwsp; Sec Sr Cls; Rep Stu Cncl; Var Crs Cntry; NHS; Gftd Prog; Teens For Chrst; Natl Envrthn Team; KS ST U; Eng.

HUA, JULIE; Manhattan HS; Manhattan, KS; (4); 1/388; Church Yth Grp; Cmnty Wkr; Treas French Clb; Hosp Aide; Intnl Clb; Pep Clb; SADD; Teachers Aide; Nwsp; Sec Soph Cls; Manhattan AIDS Pjct Vol; U Chicago; Bio.

HUBBARD, LATISHA R; Wichita East HS; Wichita, KS; (3); 8/294; Bus Profs of Am; Church Yth Grp; Chrldng; High Hon Roll; Black Ldrshp; Mnrty Wmns Ldshp; Crim Just.

HUBBARD, MICHELLE; Smith Ctr Jr Sr HS; Smith Center, KS; (4); 10/45; Am Leg Aux Girls St; Church Yth Grp; Pres FHA; SADD; Phtg Yrbk; Sec Frsh Cls; Treas Soph Cls; Hon Roll; NHS; FHA St Ofcr; KS Assn For Yth Sec; U Of KS.

HUBBLE, LISA MARIE; Meade HS; Meade, KS; (1); Church Yth Grp; Key Clb; Letterman Clb; Pep Clb; Band; Chorus; School Musical; Treas Frsh Cls; Var Tennis; Drama Clb; Kayettes.

HUBER, HEIDI R; Blue Valley HS; Stanley, KS; (2); 4/250; Church Yth Grp; Church Choir; Swmmng; Tennis; Water Skier; Clsscl Piano Lssns Since 3rd Grd; Fre Hnr Schlr.

HUBER, SARAH B; Wichita South HS; Wichita, KS; (3); 68/300; Teachers Aide; Orch; Var Socr; Var Tennis; Med.

HUBERT, AMY; Concordia Jr Sr HS; Concordia, KS; (3); 1/102; Church Yth Grp; Pres VP 4-H; NFL; Quiz Bowl; Sec Treas Science Clb; Band; NHS; Debate Tm; Drama Clb; Hosp Aide; Bausch & Lomb Honry Sci Awd; Close-Up Washington Del; Yth Tsk Frc; Sci.

HUBKA, KELLY J; Kapaun-Mt Carmel HS; Andover, KS; (3); Cmnty Wkr; French Clb; Hosp Aide; High Hon Roll; Hon Roll; Med.

HUBLER, AMY J; Anderson Cty Jr Sr HS; Garnett, KS; (1); Pep Clb; Chorus; Vllybl; Hon Roll; Law Enforcement.

HUCKE, ALAN E; Labette Co HS; Mound Valley, KS; (2); Natl FFA Org; JV Ftbl; Hon Roll.

HUCKINS, DEBRA; Hayden HS; Topeka, KS; (2); Cmnty Wkr; L Debate Tm; Intnl Clb; Rptr Ed Nwsp; Var L Socr; JV Tennis; JV Trk; High Hon Roll; Hon Roll.

HUDDLESTON, TRAVIS M; Great Bend Sr HS; Great Bend, KS; (3); 143/230; German Clb; JV Bsbl; Hon Roll; Amer Lgn Bsbl; Barton Cty CC.

HUDSON, AMANDA; St Mary's Colgan HS; Pittsburg, KS; (1); Dance Clb; Pep Clb; Ofcr Stu Cncl; Bsktbl; Pom Pon; Trk; Vllybl; High Hon Roll; U Of Miami; Interior Design.

HUDSON, KAREY; Pike Valley HS; Courtland, KS; (4); 5/28; Treas Church Yth Grp; Pres VP FBLA; Sec FHA; HOBY; Speech Tm; SADD; Sec Treas Stu Cncl; Var L Chrldng; High Hon Roll; NHS; Tutor; Span & Stu Cncl Awds; KS ST U; Dietetics.

HUDSON, RYAN; Ft Scott Christian Heights; Fort Scott, KS; (3); 1/150; HOBY; NFL; Nwsp; Ofcr Stu Cncl; Var Crs Cntry; Var Tennis; Hon Roll; NHS; Pltcl Actn Clb Pres.

HUEBER, SARAH R; Robert E Clark Jr HS; Bonner Springs, KS; (1); Church Yth Grp; Cmnty Wkr; FHA; Office Aide; SADD; Varsity Clb; Acpl Chr; Ofcr Frsh Cls; Ofcr Soph Cls; Ofcr Stu Cncl; STAR Prgm; Bus.

HUEBERT, DALLAS; Wichita Hts HS; Wichita, KS; (4); 67/344; French Clb; Teachers Aide; JV Bsktbl; JV Ftbl; JV Tennis; JV Trk; Hon Roll; Prfct Atten Awd; Natl Yth Ldshp Forum; Wichita St Univ; Phys Thpy.

HUEBERT, ERIC J; Halstead HS; Halstead, KS; (1); Cit Awd; High Hon Roll; Hon Roll; AYSO Soccer; Babe Ruth Bsbl; Highes Batt Ave Team 2nd League; All-Star Team.

HUEBERT, GREGORY D; Wichita Heights HS; Wichita, KS; (4); 67/344; French Clb; Teachers Aide; JV Bsktbl; JV Ftbl; JV Tennis; JV Trk; Hon Roll; Prfct Atten Awd; Natl Yth Ldrshp Forum; Wichita ST Univ; Phy Therapy.

HUEBNER, KELLIE; Pittsburg HS; Pittsburg, KS; (3); 16/200; Church Yth Grp; Debate Tm; FCA; FHA; NFL; Q&S; Spanish Clb; Rptr Phtg Nwsp; Bsktbl; Vllybl; Missionary.

HUEFTLE, ERIN; Hoxie HS; Menlo, KS; (3); 1/43; FCA; Quiz Bowl; School Musical; Sec Frsh Cls; Sec Soph Cls; Sec Jr Cls; Sec Sr Cls; Capt Chrldng; High Hon Roll; NHS; KA ST Univ; Bus Admin/Finc.

HUELAT, BRETT; Pittsburg HS; Pittsburg, KS; (4); 3/165; Am Leg Boys St; Pres Church Yth Grp; Treas FCA; VP Q&S; Rep Spanish Clb; Band; Jazz Band; Mrchg Band; Ed Yrbk; JV Bsktbl; 4th Pl St Interprtatn Of Poetry; St Qualifr Poetry & Duet Acting; 1st Pl Rgnls Them & Dsgn Jrnlsm; U Notre Dame; Bus Mgmt.

HUELSMAN, CHRISTOPHER J; Kapaun-Mt Carmel HS; Wichita, KS; (1); Bsktbl; Ftbl; Umpr Lttl Leg Bsbll Smmr 96.

HUERTER, STACEY; Silver Lake Jr Sr HS; Silver Lake, KS; (2); Church Yth Grp; NFL; School Musical; School Play; Sec Treas Frsh Cls; Sec Treas Soph Cls; JV Bsktbl; Var L Crs Cntry; Var L Trk; NHS.

HUEY, KRISTIN; Blue Valley HS; Olathe, KS; (4); Nwsp; Ofcr Stu Cncl; Socr; Tennis; Hon Roll; Poetry Pub Natl Lib Of Poetry; 2nd Rnnr Up Miss KS Amer Coed Pageant; SMU; Intnl Bus & Mgmt.

HUFF, LARRY; Troy HS; Troy, KS; (3); 1/27; Boy Scts; Drama Clb; Letterman Clb; Q&S; Speech Tm; Band; Mrchg Band; Pep Band; School Play; Ed Nwsp; Sports Med.

HUFF, REGINA L; Troy HS; Troy, KS; (3); 4/27; Q&S; Quiz Bowl; Speech Tm; Band; School Play; Rptr Phtg Nwsp; Stat Ftbl; Var L Vllybl; Hon Roll; NHS; Kayettes; Washburn Unib; Prelaw.

HUFF, TYLER; Quivira Heights HS; Bushton, KS; (4); 3/21; Church Yth Grp; Cmnty Wkr; Drama Clb; FCA; HOBY; Letterman Clb; Library Aide; Office Aide; Quiz Bowl; Band; KS ST U; Bus.

HUFFERD, MICHELLE R; Field Kindley HS; Coffeyville, KS; (2); Church Yth Grp; Church Choir; Poetry Pub; Author.

HUFFERD, NICOLE; Field Kinley HS; Coffeyville, KS; (1); Church Yth Grp; Church Choir; High Hon Roll; Jr NHS; Span Tchr.

HUFFMAN, CHERYL; Faith Christian Schl; Osawatomie, KS; (3); Teachers Aide; School Musical; Rptr Nwsp; Ed Yrbk; Pres Jr Cls; Var Bsktbl; Capt Chrldng; Var Vllybl; Hon Roll; Homcmng Qn; Bus.

HUFFMAN, LYNDA K; Minneapolis HS; Delphos, KS; (3); 10/70; French Clb; Teachers Aide; Ed Nwsp; Ed Yrbk; Prfct Atten Awd; Nrsng; Acctng; Jrnlsm.

HUFFMAN, TERESA; Rose Hill HS; Rose Hill, KS; (3); High Hon Roll; Story & Poem Pub; Flute; Vet Med.

HUFFORD, JOHN M; Wyandotte HS; Kansas City, KS; (2); Boy Scts; NHS; People To People Stdnt Ambsdr Prgm; Stock Brkr.

HUGGARD, LISA; Stafford Jr Sr HS; Stafford, KS; (2); Sftbl; Vllybl; Wt Lftg.

HUGGINS, AMY P; Desoto HS; Olathe, KS; (3); 11/146; Cmnty Wkr; Spanish Clb; SADD; Teachers Aide; Band; Mrchg Band; Bsktbl; Sftbl; Wt Lftg; Cit Awd; People To People Abssdr To Austrla.

HUGHES, AIMEE; Blue Valley HS; Shawnee Mission, KS; (4); 6/230; Drama Clb; Thesps; Chorus; Drill Tm; Flag Corp; School Musical; School Play; Swing Chorus; Treas Sr Cls; High Hon Roll; Tulane Univ; Intnl Relations.

HUGHES, AMY; Spring Hill HS; Spring Hill, KS; (3); Am Leg Aux Girls St; Pep Clb; SADD; Teachers Aide; Hon Roll.

HUGHES, BRIAN T; Great Bend Sr HS; Great Bend, KS; (2); Boy Scts; Church Yth Grp; Pep Clb; Chorus; Variety Show; JV Bsktbl; JV Ftbl; Var L Trk; Wt Lftg; High Hon Roll; Peer Cnslng; Explorers; PT.

HUGHES, CARRIE M; Wichita Southeast HS; Wichita, KS; (2); French Clb; JA; NFL; Acpl Chr; Chorus; Intrml Bsktbl; L Socr; Intrml JV Vllybl; Hon Roll; U Of KS; Pediatrician; Phy Thrp.

HUGHES, CURTRINA; Sumner Acad; Kansas City, KS; (1); Church Yth Grp; French Clb; Latin Clb; Pep Clb; Church Choir; Orch; Chrldng; Trk; French Hon Soc; High Hon Roll; KS City Yth Symphony; People To People Stu Ambssdr Pgm; U Of KS; Med.

HUGHES, DUGAN; Goddard HS; Goddard, KS; (4); 21/140; Spanish Clb; Wt Lftg; High Hon Roll; Prfct Atten Awd; Wichita ST U.

HUGHES, JAMIE D; Scott Comm HS; Scott City, KS; (3); Church Yth Grp; Tennis; Wt Lftg; High Hon Roll; Prfct Atten Awd; Pres Schlr; Cmptr Sci.

HUGHES, MEGAN L; South Haven Schl; South Haven, KS; (1); Drama Clb; FCA; Math Tm; Natl FFA Org; Pep Clb; School Play; Bsktbl; Trk; Vllybl; High Hon Roll; KS ST Univ; Jrnlsm.

HUGHES, MELISSA M; Olathe East Sr HS; Overland Park, KS; (2); 1/409; Church Yth Grp; French Clb; Pep Clb; Spanish Clb; Church Choir; Drill Tm; Mrchg Band; Variety Show; Yrbk; Rep Jr Cls; Drill Team Capt; Comm Svc; Acad French Awd; Frgn Lang/Missionary.

HUGHES, SARA K; Wichita East HS; Wichita, KS; (4); Hon Roll; Butler Cty CC; Pre-Med.

HUGHES, SHARLA R; Salina HS South; Salina, KS; (2); 15/305; Letterman Clb; Pep Clb; Band; Chorus; Pep Band; Chrldng.

HUGHEY, EMILY S; Blue Valley North HS; Overland Park, KS; (3); 25/200; Church Yth Grp; Intnl Clb; Model UN; Q&S; Spanish Clb; Varsity Clb; Nwsp; Swmmng; Hon Roll; Jrnlsm.

HUHLE, FERINAND J; Junction City HS; Junction City, KS; (4); French Clb; German Clb; Var Diving; Var Socr; Var Swmmng; Var Tennis; Hon Roll; NHS; Outstndng Achvmnt Tennis Cert; Tennis Most Inspirational Plyr; 3 Letter Man Club Soccer/Swmng/Tennis; KS ST.

HULA, JONATHAN; St John Jr Sr HS; Saint John, KS; (2); Church Yth Grp; Pep Clb; SADD; Band; Mrchg Band; JV Var Bsktbl; Var Trk; Hon Roll; Aeronautical Engr.

HULING, DEBORAH E; Derby HS; Derby, KS; (4); 9/350; High Hon Roll; Pres Acad Fit Awd; KS Hon Schol; Acad Letter Rcpt.

HULL, CODY B; El Dorado HS; Colorado Springs, CO; (2); Church Yth Grp; Debate Tm; Drama Clb; FCA; Math Clb; NFL; SADD; School Musical; Ofcr Frsh Cls; Ofcr Soph Cls; LIFE; Peer Cnslr 94-96; CO Univ.

HULL, CRAIG; Derby HS; Derby, KS; (2); Science Clb; Treas Frsh Cls; Ofcr Stu Cncl; High Hon Roll; NHS; Engrng/Sci Summer Inst At KS ST; Engrng.

HULL, DRU B; Lawrence HS; Lawrence, KS; (2); Church Yth Grp; Band; Chorus; Variety Show; Ofcr Bsbl; JV Bsktbl; Trk; High Hon Roll; Hon Roll; Pres Acad Fit Awd; Chrch Song Ldr; Yth Mission Team; St Music Cont I Rating; Phy Thrpst.

HULL, JACOB T; Frankft HS; Frankfort, KS; (3); Am Leg Boys St; Letterman Clb; Quiz Bowl; Band; Chorus; Church Choir; JV Bsktbl; Var L Ftbl; L Trk; Hon Roll; Ed; Music.

HULL, KATRINA; Inman Jr Sr HS; Inman, KS; (3); 1/35; Church Yth Grp; Cmnty Wkr; FHA; Math Tm; NFL; Pep Clb; Quiz Bowl; Red Cross Aide; Spanish Clb; Teachers Aide; KS U.

HULL, KRISTA J; Remington HS; Potwin, KS; (3); Cmnty Wkr; Debate Tm; FHA; Girl Scts; NFL; Band; Mrchg Band; Pep Band; Hon Roll; 4th Pl Extmprns Spkg ST Forensics; 9th Pl 2 Spkr ST Debate; Pres Natl Forensics League 2 Yrs; Govt.

HULL, MICHAEL; Iola Sr HS; Iola, KS; (4); 10/98; Am Leg Boys St; Church Yth Grp; Treas SADD; Pres Frsh Cls; Pres Soph Cls; Pres Jr Cls; Rep Stu Cncl; Var Capt Bsktbl; Var Capt Ftbl; High Hon Roll; U Of Chicago; Med.

HULL, NANCY; Sedgwick HS; Sedgwick, KS; (2); 10/40; FHA; Letterman Clb; Chorus; Stage Crew; Pres Frsh Cls; Rep Stu Cncl; Bsktbl; Var Trk; Vllybl; Wt Lftg; HOA All League Vllybl 1st Team 94 & 95.

HULL, SHANNON B; Burlington HS; Burlington, KS; (3); 21/85; FBLA; FHA; Teachers Aide; Yrbk; Ofcr Stu Cncl; JV Var Bsktbl; JV Chrldng; Var Sftbl; Hon Roll; Prfct Atten Awd; Natl Young Ldrs Conf Wash DC; U Of KS; Bus.

HULL, TARA E; El Dorado HS; El Dorado, KS; (3); Church Yth Grp; Cmnty Wkr; Debate Tm; FCA; NFL; SADD; Band; Mrchg Band; Ed Nwsp; Rep Jr Cls; LIFE; DARE; KS ST.

HULLUM, DIONNA; Sumner Acad Of Arts & Science; Kansas City, KS; (3); 82/148; Pep Clb; Spanish Clb; Orch; Bsktbl; JV Chrldng; Hon Roll; Prfct Atten Awd; Med.

HULSE, KRISTY; Wichita Heights HS; Wichita, KS; (3); JA; Teachers Aide; Var Chrldng; Pom Pon; L Socr; Wt Lftg; High Hon Roll; Peer Ldr.

HULSING, ANGIE D; Bailey-Benedict Jr Sr High; Baileyville, KS; (3); 3/13; Church Yth Grp; VP FBLA; Sec VP FHA; Sec Pep Clb; Quiz Bowl; Band; Mrchg Band; Pep Band; Yrbk; Pres Frsh Cls; KS ST; Spch Ther.

HULSING, JOHN H; Bailey-Benedict Jr Sr High; Baileyville, KS; (2); Church Yth Grp; Quiz Bowl; Scholastic Bowl; Bsktbl; Ftbl; Trk; Prfct Atten Awd; KS ST Univ.

HULSING, MELISSA M; Bailey-Benedict Jr Sr High; Baileyville, KS; (2); 6/20; Church Yth Grp; FBLA; FHA; Pep Clb; Quiz Bowl; Band; Mrchg Band; Pep Band; Yrbk; Pres Frsh Cls; KS ST; Tchr.

HULTGREN, BRICE; White City HS; White City, KS; (1); 2/22; Boy Scts; Church Yth Grp; Scholastic Bowl; Band; Chorus; Church Choir; Jazz Band; Mrchg Band; Pep Band; Ofcr Bsbl.

HUMBARD, AMANDA; Pittsburg HS; Pittsburg, KS; (4); Church Yth Grp; Q&S; Teachers Aide; School Musical; Ed Nwsp; Mgr Yrbk; Med Explorers; High Adventure Explorers; Pittsburg; Pre-Med.

HUMBARGER, TRICIA L; Shawnee Mission N HS; Merriam, KS; (4); Cmnty Wkr; Office Aide; Pep Clb; Teachers Aide; Orch; Trk; NHS; Pres Schlr.

HUMBLE, TIFFANY; Goddard HS; Wichita, KS; (3); Church Yth Grp; GAA; Pep Clb; Band; Mrchg Band; Pep Band; Sftbl; High Hon Roll; Hon Roll; Jr NHS; Friends Univ; Optmtry.

HUMMEL, CASEY; Circle HS; Towanda, KS; (4); Am Leg Boys St; Letterman Clb; Library Aide; SADD; Teachers Aide; Var L Bsktbl; Var L Ftbl; Intrml Wt Lftg; Hon Roll; Bus.

HUMPHERIES, JULIA; Hayden HS; Topeka, KS; (3); 25/140; Dance Clb; Intnl Clb; Pep Clb; SADD; Drill Tm; Pom Pon; High Hon Roll; Hon Roll; NHS; NHS Pres & Treas; NCA All Amer; Starmaker Stardancer; Pharmacy.

HUMPHREY, EMILY; South Barber HS; Kiowa, KS; (4); 7/30; Am Leg Aux Girls St; Church Yth Grp; Cmnty Wkr; Girl Scts; Office Aide; Scholastic Bowl; SADD; Ed Nwsp; Sec Stu Cncl; Var JV Tennis; Kytts VP; Brnz Slvr Gld Hnr Pns; Ftbl Hmcmng Attndnt; KS ST U; Med.

HUMPHREYS, ALICIA; Emporia HS; Emporia, KS; (4); Am Leg Aux Girls St; FBLA; Pep Clb; Teachers Aide; Ofcr Sr Cls; JV Chrldng; Hon Roll; Emporia ST U; Phys Thrpy.

HUND, AMELIA M; Wichita Southeast HS; Wichita, KS; (2); Art Clb; Church Yth Grp; Cmnty Wkr; Drama Clb; Girl Scts; Teachers Aide; Thesps; Chorus; Stage Crew; Rep Stu Cncl; Prncpls Hnr Rl; Gold Key Awrd; Wichita ST Univ; Photogrphy.

HUND, JENNIFER; Wabaunsee HS; Mc Farland, KS; (3); Treas Church Yth Grp; FBLA; Varsity Clb; Drill Tm; L Bsktbl; L Sftbl; L Vllybl; High Hon Roll; Careers 2000 Team 1st Pl; U Of KS; Surgical Nurse.

HUND, JENNIFER K; Hayden HS; Topeka, KS; (3); 42/130; Pep Clb; Spanish Clb; Bsktbl; Swmmng; Tennis; Trk; Wt Lftg; Hon Roll; U Of KS; Dntl Hygienst.

HUND, ROSA; Wabaunsee HS; Paxico, KS; (2); Church Yth Grp; Pres 4-H; FHA; HOBY; School Play; Pres Frsh Cls; JV Bsktbl; Powder Puff Ftbl; JV Tennis; High Hon Roll.

HUNDLEY, ERIKA L; Holton HS; Holton, KS; (1); Church Yth Grp; Cmnty Wkr; FHA; GAA; Girl Scts; Band; Chorus; Church Choir; School Musical; School Play; Kayettes; Washburn Univ; Soc Wkrs.

HUNDLEY, MATTHEW J; Bern Schl; Bern, KS; (2); Letterman Clb; SADD; Varsity Clb; Band; Chorus; Mrchg Band; Pep Band; Phtg Yrbk; Var Bsbl; Var Bsktbl; Coach.

HUNDLEY, RACHEL A; Bern Schl; Bern, KS; (4); Cmnty Wkr; Dance Clb; Drama Clb; Letterman Clb; Pep Clb; SADD; Varsity Clb; Band; Chorus; Church Choir; Teens As Tchrs Rep; Southwestern Coll; Crmnl Jstc.

HUNDLEY, SHELLY L; Holton HS; Holton, KS; (1); Chorus; Bsktbl; JV Var Sftbl; Vllybl; Rayettes; KS Univ; Dr/Phys Asst.

HUNLEY, FRANCES; St John Jr Sr HS; Saint John, KS; (3); 1/48; Church Yth Grp; Pres 4-H; Pres Pep Clb; SADD; Band; School Play; Ofcr Stu Cncl; Var Crs Cntry; Var Trk; NHS.

HUNSAKER, HEATHER; Highland HS; Highland, KS; (2); Natl FFA Org; Chorus; Bsktbl; Chrldng; Trk; Vllybl; Hon Roll; NHS; Highland CC; Coaching.

HUNSINGER, JAMES E; Bonner Springs HS; Bonner Springs, KS; (3); Am Leg Boys St; Boy Scts; Stage Crew; Nwsp; Pres Jr Cls; Stat Mgr Crs Cntry; Jr NHS; Peer Cnslr; Wyandotte Cty Ldrshp Cncl; KS Univ.

HUNSUCKER, JESSICA; Douglass HS; Douglass, KS; (3); 11/69; Church Yth Grp; Letterman Clb; Office Aide; Pep Clb; Teachers Aide; Bsktbl; Chrldng; Crs Cntry; Trk; Wt Lftg; Nrsng.

HUNSUCKER, MARY; Central Jr Sr HS; Burden, KS; (3); FCA; Phtg Yrbk; Ofcr Frsh Cls; Sec Jr Cls; Ofcr Stu Cncl; Var Chrldng; Var Sftbl; JV Vllybl; High Hon Roll; NHS.

HUNT, BETH; Baxter Springs HS; Baxter Springs, KS; (4); 5/66; Am Leg Aux Girls St; Pres FHA; Capt Scholastic Bowl; Ed Yrbk; Pres Sr Cls; VP Stu Cncl; NHS; St Schlr; Art Clb; Church Yth Grp; Prlmntry Law Tm Pres, St Champ, Gld Natls; GSA Gld Awd; Med.

HUNT, ELIZABETH; Mc Pherson HS; Mc Pherson, KS; (4); 58/194; 4-H; French Clb; German Clb; Library Aide; Q&S; Scholastic Bowl; Science Clb; SADD; Yrbk; Mc Pherson Coll; Elem Ed.

HUNT, JAY; Tonganoxie HS; Lansing, KS; (4); 48/120; Church Yth Grp; 4-H; Natl FFA Org; Science Clb; Wrstlng; Cit Awd; 4-H Awd; Hon Roll; Prdntl Sprt Comm Yth Awd; KACRAO Quality Ldrshp Awd; Natl FFA Trngl Awd; KS ST Univ; Vet Med.

HUNT, JERUSHA; Olathe North Sr HS; Olathe, KS; (4); 12/351; Treas Spanish Clb; Orch; School Musical; High Hon Roll; NHS; VP Spanish NHS; St Schlr; Church Yth Grp; Teachers Aide; Acpl Chr; Natl HS Hnrs Orch; Coll Chrch Nazarne Orch; Baker U; Span/Scndry Ed.

HUNT, LOIRE A; Wichita East HS; Wichita, KS; (2); FHA; High Hon Roll; Hon Roll; Tchr Hlpr.

HUNT, MICHELLE; Olathe East Sr HS; Lenexa, KS; (3); 1/385; Church Yth Grp; Drama Clb; Thesps; School Play; Stage Crew; Ed Lit Mag; High Hon Roll; NHS; Chorus; Church Choir; Fshn Mrchndng Clb; Fshn Show Coord; Costuming.

HUNTER, ALYSSA R; Scott Comm HS; Scott City, KS; (3); 9/74; Am Leg Aux Girls St; Church Yth Grp; VP Frsh Cls; VP Stu Cncl; Var L Mgr(s); Var L Sftbl; L Capt Vllybl; High Hon Roll; NHS; KS ST Univ; Vet.

HUNTER, ASHLEE S; Dexter Jr Sr HS; Dexter, KS; (3); Church Yth Grp; Cmnty Wkr; 4-H; Math Clb; Math Tm; Science Clb; SADD; Band; Chorus; Jazz Band; KS ST U; Phy Ther.

HUNTER, KELLY J; Gardner-Edgerton HS; Gardner, KS; (2); Dance Clb; Drama Clb; Pep Clb; Thesps; Chorus; Drill Tm; School Musical; School Play; Stage Crew; Yrbk; Intl Thspns Soc.

HUNTER, KORINA L; Eastern Heights Jr Sr HS; Agra, KS; (3); 4/11; Church Yth Grp; FTA; Pep Clb; Band; Chorus; Drm Mjr(t); Mrchg Band; Pep Band; School Play; Ed Nwsp; Elem Ed.

HUNTER, MARSHALL; Eureka Jr Sr HS; Eureka, KS; (3); Am Leg Boys St; Boy Scts; Church Yth Grp; Band; Mrchg Band; Pep Band; JV Bsktbl; JV Var Golf; Hon Roll; USAF.

HUNTER, TAMMY; Turner HS; Kansas City, KS; (4); Bus Profs of Am; Church Yth Grp; SADD; Band; Mrchg Band; Pep Band; Hon Roll; KS Hnr Schlr; U Of KS; Law.

HUNTINGTON, DAN T; Maize HS; Wichita, KS; (2); Church Yth Grp; Spanish Clb; Golf; Socr; High Hon Roll; NHS; Engr.

HUNTINGTON, LINDY; Maize HS; Wichita, KS; (3); 20/250; Art Clb; Pres Church Yth Grp; Hosp Aide; Spanish Clb; Rep Sr Cls; Tennis; NHS; Pres Acad Fit Awd; Socr; High Hon Roll; Prtcpnt Natl His Day Natl Lvl; Natl Yth Ldrshp Forum Prtcpnt Med; Pre-Med.

HUNTLEY, BROOKE; Shawnee Mission S Sr HS; Shawnee Mission, KS; (3); 85/439; Church Yth Grp; Cmnty Wkr; Dance Clb; GAA; Intnl Clb; Model UN; Natl Beta Clb; Pep Clb; Speech Tm; SADD; Schlrshp Pin; Rsrch/Dev Forum Grnd Awd Fr; KS Olympc Dev Prgm Grls Sccr; Pre-Med.

HUNZIGER, LUCAS; Atchison Sr HS; Atchison, KS; (3); Am Leg Boys St; Church Yth Grp; 4-H; Stat Bsktbl; Var Golf; 4-H Awd; Hon Roll; NHS.

HUOSSLER, WILLIAM W; Great Bend Sr HS; Great Bend, KS; (2); Debate Tm; Speech Tm; Band; Jazz Band; Pep Band; Variety Show; JV Bsbl; Var Swmmng; Hon Roll; Prfct Atten Awd; Wichita ST Univ; Pro Bsbl.

HUPE, JENNIFER L; Derby HS; Derby, KS; (3); Church Yth Grp; Cmnty Wkr; FCA; Office Aide; Teachers Aide; Church Choir; Hon Roll; KS Univ; Pediatrician.

HUPP, CARMEN M; Immaculata HS; Leavenworth, KS; (4); 23/48; Cmnty Wkr; Girl Scts; Hosp Aide; JA; Stage Crew; Rptr Yrbk; Chrldng; Gym; Hon Roll; Kiwanis Awd; Gold Awd Girl Scouts; Stdnts That Care Comm Svc Grp; Pittsburgh ST Univ; Vet Med.

HURD, CHARISSA J; Oswego HS; Oswego, KS; (1); 5/45; Church Yth Grp; Scholastic Bowl; Spanish Clb; Band; Mrchg Band; Vllybl; Wt Lftg; Gov Hon Prg Awd; High Hon Roll; NHS; Poem Pub; Renaissance Gold Card Holder; Ltr Of Achvmt MA Inst Of Tech; Lifter Of The Week; Pittsburg ST; Bio; Physiology.

HURLEY, ABBEY D; Buhler HS; Hutchinson, KS; (2); Letterman Clb; Band; Chorus; Mrchg Band; Pep Band; Stage Crew; JV Var Bsktbl; Var Sftbl; JV Var Vllybl; Hon Roll.

HURLEY, DAWN M; Field Kindley Mem Sr HS; Coffeyville, KS; (3); 27/150; Church Yth Grp; Cmnty Wkr; French Clb; Natl FFA Org; Teachers Aide; Yrbk; Trk; Hon Roll; NHS; Pres Acad Fit Awd; Pre Prof Career Exploration; CYO Sec & Treas; TEC; Labette CC; Nrsng.

HURLEY, JACOB M; Santa Fe Trail Jr HS; Olathe, KS; (1); Computer Clb; Dance Clb; Quiz Bowl; Spanish Clb; Teachers Aide; School Play; Ofcr Stu Cncl; Bsktbl; Ftbl; Trk; FL ST; Commnctn.

HURLEY, JUSTIN M; Labette Co HS; Mound Valley, KS; (4); 18/128; Chess Clb; FCA; Letterman Clb; VICA; JV Var Bsktbl; L Lbrn Ftbl; L Lbrn Trk; Stat Wt Lftg; Hon Roll; NHS; Ftbll MVP; All League Off Guard; Track Most Insprtnl; Southwestern Univ; PE.

HURST, KENDALL M; Wichita North HS; Wichita, KS; (3); Cmnty Wkr; Teachers Aide; Band; Jazz Band; Mrchg Band; Orch; Pep Band; Rep Stu Cncl; Hon Roll; NHS; Phrmcy.

HURST, STACEY L; Blue Valley North HS; Leawood, KS; (3); Church Yth Grp; Cmnty Wkr; Intnl Clb; Model UN; Service Clb; Rptr Nwsp; Powder Puff Ftbl; Vllybl; Hon Roll; KAYS Clb Pres; Optimist Clb Ldrshp Awd.

HURT, CARISSA D; Prairie View Jr Sr HS; La Cygne, KS; (3); 7/67; Sec Treas 4-H; FHA; Band; Chorus; School Musical; School Play; L Var Sftbl; JV L Vllybl; 4-H Awd; NHS; All Star Team Hnrb Mntn; Soc Work; Vet Sci.

HURT, DANIEL; Wichita East HS; Wichita, KS; (4); Church Yth Grp; German Clb; Letterman Clb; Quiz Bowl; Scholastic Bowl; Acpl Chr; Chorus; School Musical; School Play; Variety Show; Wrestling St Qlfr; NE MO ST U.

HURT, DEMETRIUS EDWARD; Sumner Acad Of Arts & Science; Kansas City, KS; (4); 127/201; Church Yth Grp; Cmnty Wkr; French Clb; Spanish Clb; Church Choir; Orch; French Hon Soc; Hon Roll; NHS; Spanish NHS; Yth Outreach Dir; Natl Yth Ldrshp Cong; Westack CC; Intl Law.

HURT, HEATHER; Frontenac Jr Sr HS; Pittsburg, KS; (1); 1/50; Cmnty Wkr; Pep Clb; Scholastic Bowl; Spanish Clb; Teachers Aide; Var Chrldng; Var Sftbl; Var Vllybl; High Hon Roll; Gftd Ed Pgm.

HURT, KARAH; Jayhawk-Linn HS; Mound City, KS; (3); 1/50; Pres 4-H; JA; Math Tm; Band; Ofcr Stu Cncl; Bsktbl; Trk; Vllybl; High Hon Roll; Chrldng.

HURT, KEVIN W; Olathe South Sr HS; Olathe, KS; (4); Teachers Aide; Pres Band; Jazz Band; Mrchg Band; Pep Band; School Musical; Hon Roll; Jr NHS; ST Band; Outstdng Musician; Washburn Univ Topeka; Music Ed.

HURT, MELISSA A; Lyndon HS; Lyndon, KS; (4); Church Yth Grp; Library Aide; Teachers Aide; Band; Drill Tm; Phtg Yrbk; Sec Soph Cls; Var Wt Lftg; Hon Roll; Highland CC; Studio Photogrphr.

HURTIG, TAMERA; Tescott HS; Tescott, KS; (4); 5/12; Am Leg Aux Girls St; Church Yth Grp; Girl Scts; Pep Clb; Quiz Bowl; Scholastic Bowl; Teachers Aide; Band; Chorus; Jazz Band; Lions Bnd; Yth For Music Cncrt Bnd; Claud Cty CC; Music.

HUSBAND, MIKE D; Colby Sr HS; Colby, KS; (2); 36/106; Church Yth Grp; JV Stat Bsktbl; Var Trk; Hon Roll.

HUSER, TRACY R; Fredonia HS; Fredonia, KS; (3); 6/90; Sec Pres Art Clb; Church Yth Grp; Debate Tm; Drama Clb; Sec NFL; Science Clb; Spanish Clb; Teachers Aide; School Play; Hon Roll; Bst Of Show Art Awd; Schol Bnqut; St Frnsics; U Of KS; Art.

HUSLIG, CARYN; Ellsworth HS; Ellsworth, KS; (2); 1/90; Church Yth Grp; Key Clb; NFL; Band; Chorus; Church Choir; Mrchg Band; Pep Band; High Hon Roll; Optmtry.

HUSMANN, KEVIN E; Blue Valley Northwest HS; Overland Park, KS; (1); Band; Mrchg Band; Socr; Wrstlng; Hon Roll; Play Premier Soccer For KC Legends; Soccer.

HUSSEY, JASON T; Blue Valley North HS; Leawood, KS; (2); Boy Scts; Eagle Scout; U Of KS.

HUSTEAD, LORI M; Topeka West HS; Topeka, KS; (3); 44/239; Church Yth Grp; Math Clb; Pep Clb; Spanish Clb; SADD; L Var Swmmng; Hon Roll; Elem Ed/Tchr.

HUSTON, ANNA E; Lawrence HS; Lawrence, KS; (2); Church Yth Grp; Cmnty Wkr; FCA; French Clb; Hosp Aide; Yrbk; Rep Frsh Cls; Rep Stu Cncl; Bsktbl; JV Capt Socr; Stu Of Yr Acad & All-Around.

HUSTON, NATALIE; Garden City Sr HS; Garden City, KS; (4); Pres 4-H; Rptr Nwsp; Pom Pon; Vllybl; 4-H Awd; Hon Roll; NHS; KS ST U; Health.

HUTCHINGS, SARAH K; Jennings Schl; Jennings, KS; (1); Cmnty Wkr; FHA; GAA; Pep Clb; Quiz Bowl; Band; Chorus; Pep Band; School Musical; Ofcr Stu Cncl.

HUTCHINS, EMILY; Holton HS; Holton, KS; (3); 4-H; Letterman Clb; Teachers Aide; Drill Tm; School Musical; Chrldng; Crs Cntry; Sftbl; Vllybl; NHS.

HUTCHINSON, BOURKE; Central Jr Sr HS; Salina, KS; (4); 23/225; Am Leg Boys St; Band; Ofcr Stu Cncl; Ofcr Bsbl; Swmmng; NHS; Pres Acad Fit Awd; Boy Scts; Jazz Band; At-Risk Stdnts Cnslr; U Of KS; Chem Engrng.

HUTCHINSON, KRISTINA D; Junction City HS; Junction City, KS; (2); Chorus; School Musical; Variety Show; High Hon Roll; KS ST U; Vet.

HUTCHISON, AMANDA; Russell HS; Russell, KS; (1); Church Yth Grp; Dance Clb; Key Clb; SADD; Chorus; Church Choir; Drill Tm; Variety Show; Rep Stu Cncl; JV Bsktbl; Vol Local Chld Care Cntr; Sec Plc St Elks Hoop Shoot Cntst/KS; KS Univ; Ped.

HUTCHISON, JESSICA S; Northeast HS; Mulberry, KS; (2); 12/45; Library Aide; Hon Roll; Herpetology; Environ Prot; Vet.

HUTCHISON, LAURA M; Leavenworth HS; Fort Leavenworth, KS; (3); Church Yth Grp; German Clb; Office Aide; Chorus; Mgr(s); Vllybl; Prfct Atten Awd; Army Fam Action Plan Dlgt; US Vlybl Assoc; VP Vlybl Club; CO ST Univ.

HUTFLES, ANGELA; Jefferson West HS; Meriden, KS; (3); 1/79; FHA; Chorus; Sec Jr Cls; Var Bsktbl; Var Vllybl; Cit Awd; High Hon Roll; NHS; Prfct Atten Awd; Frgn Lang Clb.

HUTLEY, PATTY; St Marys HS; Saint Marys, KS; (3); FBLA; FHA; Library Aide; Pep Clb; Band; Pep Band; Treas Jr Cls; High Hon Roll; NHS; Emporia ST U; Bus Admin.

HUTSELL, CASEY L; Bishop Miege HS; Prairie Village, KS; (3); 83/168; Church Yth Grp; Cmnty Wkr; Letterman Clb; Office Aide; Teachers Aide; Varsity Clb; Var L Bsbl; JV Bsktbl; Hon Roll; Pres Acad Fit Awd; Spirit Clb Ofcr; All Lge; All Shawnee Missn; Hnrbl Mntn All City; Ed.

HUTTING, MELANIE; Louisburg HS; Paola, KS; (4); 21/78; Debate Tm; 4-H; Letterman Clb; Natl FFA Org; Pep Clb; SADD; Chorus; Chrldng; 4-H Awd; Hon Roll; FFA Pres; KS St U; Ag Ed.

HUTTMANN, BRENDON; Olathe South Sr HS; Olathe, KS; (4); Letterman Clb; Teachers Aide; Varsity Clb; Ofcr Bsbl; Wt Lftg; Hon Roll; Outdoor Actvts/Ath; 4 Yr Coll; Vet Sci/Forestry.

HUYETT, AMANDA J; Turner HS; Kansas City, KS; (3); Church Yth Grp; Cmnty Wkr; SADD; VP Stu Cncl; Var Chrldng; Var Trk; JV Vllybl; Hon Roll; Jr NHS; Prfct Atten Awd; Army.

HUYNH, SANG K; Wichita South HS; Wichita, KS; (2); 10/394; Chess Clb; Cmnty Wkr; Scholastic Bowl; Science Clb; Teachers Aide; Sec Stu Cncl; High Hon Roll; Hon Roll; A-SAIL; Wichita ST Univ; Elect Engr/Dr.

HUYNH, THAIHOA THI; Wichita Southeast HS; Wichita, KS; (2); French Clb; Asian Clb Ofcr; DECA; Ambassadors Clb; YEK; Wichita ST Univ; Intnl Bus.

HUYNH, TONGA N; Wichita East HS; Wichita, KS; (3); French Clb; Science Clb; French Hon Soc; High Hon Roll; Hon Roll; Prfct Atten Awd; Sci Olympia; U Of KS; Hlth.

HUYNH, TRUCLY T; Wichita North HS; Wichita, KS; (3); 25/274; Scholastic Bowl; Teachers Aide; Rep Jr Cls; Hon Roll; NHS; Wichita ST Univ; Pre-Med.

HUYSER, BECKY; Blue Valley Northwest HS; Lenexa, KS; (4); 15/340; Church Yth Grp; JV Var Chrldng; Powder Puff Ftbl; L Trk; DAR Awd; High Hon Roll; Sec NHS; St Schlr; Husky Awd; U Of KS; Elem/MS Ed.

HYDE, ANDREA C; Beloit Jr Sr HS; Beloit, KS; (3); Letterman Clb; Band; Church Choir; Ofcr Soph Cls; JV Bsktbl; Var Sftbl; Var Vllybl; 4-H Awd; Hon Roll; FCA; Psych.

HYDE, HANNAH; Prairie View Jr Sr HS; Fontana, KS; (1); Church Yth Grp; 4-H; FHA; Letterman Clb; Chorus; Var Chrldng; Trk; Vllybl; High Hon Roll; Hon Roll.

HYNDMAN, AARON J; Wellsville Jr Sr HS; Edgerton, KS; (2); Computer Clb; Debate Tm; FBLA; Intnl Clb; Math Tm; Quiz Bowl; Scholastic Bowl; Ofcr Bsbl; Trk; Wrstlng.

IBACH, JULIE A; Emporia HS; Emporia, KS; (3); FBLA; Fashn Desgn.

ICE, HEATHER; St Marys HS; Saint Marys, KS; (3); 5/45; FBLA; Letterman Clb; L Pep Clb; L Band; L Jazz Band; L Mrchg Band; L Pep Band; Var Bsktbl; L Var Sftbl; L Trk; Natl Yng Ldrs Conf Alumni Rep; MEL Athltc Acads Awd; KS U; Mtrlgy.

IHNOW, GEOFFREY K; Blue Valley North HS; Overland Park, KS; (2); 11/230; Church Yth Grp; FCA; Math Tm; Quiz Bowl; Scholastic Bowl; Spanish Clb; Stat Bsbl; Chrldng; JV Socr; JV Trk; Univ Of PA; Actuarial Sci.

IHRIE, REBECCA A; Topeka HS; Topeka, KS; (4); 1/336; Pres Church Yth Grp; Pres NFL; Mrchg Band; Orch; School Musical; Var L Sr Cls; Pres NHS; Val; St Schlr; Pres Acad Fit Awd; Natl AP Schlr; All St Acad Team; Shipman & Dstngshd Legislator Schlr; U Of MI; Chem.

IMAKAWA, AKIKO; Blue Valley Northwest HS; Overland Park, KS; (1); Cmnty Wkr; Science Clb; Chorus; Orch; School Musical; Intrml Vllybl; High Hon Roll; Hon Roll; Supr I/Excl Rtng ST Piano Comp; Supr I Rtng KMEA Regnl/ST Comp; Pediatrics.

IMBER, MOLLY; Lawrence HS; Lawrence, KS; (4); 1/620; French Clb; Key Clb; Crs Cntry; Trk; NHS; Ntl Merit SF; Pres Schlr; Yth In Govt Secy; Bio.

IMEL, JOSH N; Central Heights Sr HS; Princeton, KS; (3); FCA; FBLA; FHA; Letterman Clb; Natl FFA Org; Var Bsktbl; Var Capt Ftbl; Var Trk; High Hon Roll; Hon Roll.

IMEL, WES; Bucklin Schl; Bucklin, KS; (3); Church Yth Grp; Cmnty Wkr; FCA; Pep Clb; Speech Tm; Band; Chorus; Church Choir; Mrchg Band; Pep Band; Rodeo; OSU; Chiropractor.

IMMELL, AMY; Shawnee Mission N HS; Mission, KS; (1); Drama Clb; Thesps; Acpl Chr; Orch; School Musical; School Play; Stage Crew; Hon Roll; Perf.

IMMER, JEFFREY B; Eudora HS; Eudora, KS; (4); 9/43; Cmnty Wkr; Pres Drama Clb; Spanish Clb; Speech Tm; SADD; School Play; Nwsp; Ed Yrbk; Lit Mag; Cit Awd; Envrnmntl Clb Pres; Outstdng Eng Stdnt; Outstdng Art Stdnt; Johnson Cty CC; Ed.

INGEBRETSON, CHRISTI S; Wichita East HS; Wichita, KS; (4); Church Yth Grp; Band; Chorus; Church Choir; Mrchg Band; School Musical; Variety Show; Sign Lang; KS ST Univ; Acctng.

INGELS, JOSHUA; Atchison Sr HS; Atchison, KS; (3); 4/100; Church Yth Grp; Spanish Clb; Ftbl; High Hon Roll; Hon Roll; Bio Chem Olympd Qulfr; Natl Yth Ldrshp Conf; Math.

INGELS, KRISTEN D; Maize HS; Wichita, KS; (2); Church Yth Grp; Pep Clb; Science Clb; Spanish Clb; Band; Mrchg Band; Pep Band; Tennis; Hon Roll; Pharmcst.

INGELS, LORA D; Atchison Sr HS; Atchison, KS; (1); Washburn; Law.

INGLE, JOHN; Spring Hill HS; Spring Hill, KS; (4); Cmnty Wkr; Computer Clb; 4-H; Office Aide; Pep Clb; Teachers Aide; Wrstlng; Cit Awd; 4-H Awd; Hon Roll; Johnson Cty CC; Cmptr Engrg.

INGLEHART, JOHN P; Wellsville Jr Sr HS; Wellsville, KS; (2); Church Yth Grp; FCA; Bsktbl; Ftbl; NHS.

INGRAM, JESSICA M; Washburn Rural HS; Topeka, KS; (3); 61/351; FBLA; Letterman Clb; Teachers Aide; Varsity Clb; Powder Puff Ftbl; Swmmng; Wt Lftg; High Hon Roll; Hon Roll; Stu Site Cncl; Daisy Chain; AZ ST Univ; Bus/Arch.

INGRAM, LIZ; Shawnee Mission S Sr HS; Overland Park, KS; (4); SADD; Teachers Aide; Drill Tm; Treas Sr Cls; Rep Stu Cncl; Var JV Chrldng; Var JV Trk; Cit Awd; High Hon Roll; Hon Roll; Hmcng Cndte; Speclzd Stu Wrks W/Lrng Dsblts Chldrn; KS ST; Ed.

INGUYEN, COUNG X; Wichita East HS; Wichita, KS; (4); Art Clb; Computer Clb; English Clb; Math Clb; Ofcr Sr Cls; Bsktbl; Socr; Swmmng; Vllybl.

INMAN, SARA; Topeka HS; Topeka, KS; (4); 4/336; Cmnty Wkr; VP German Clb; Hosp Aide; Rptr Nwsp; Ed Yrbk; Var Crs Cntry; High Hon Roll; Sec NHS; Pres Acad Fit Awd; Dance Clb; IL Inst Of Tech; Mech Engr.

INSLEE, BRANDI N; Cheney Jr Sr HS; Cheney, KS; (3); 7/52; Church Yth Grp; Hosp Aide; Math Tm; Chorus; JV Bsktbl; JV Vllybl; High Hon Roll; NHS; Pres Acad Fit Awd; KU; Med.

INSLEE, JOSHUA W; Attica Public Schl; Sharon, KS; (2); 3/27; Chorus; Rep Frsh Cls; Sec Soph Cls; Var Bsbl; Var Bsktbl; Var Ftbl; Var Trk; High Hon Roll; Hon Roll; US Natl Awd Eng.

INTERIANO, SARAI; Wichita East HS; Wichita, KS; (3); Spanish Clb; Teachers Aide; Hon Roll; Spanish NHS; Hangar Brd 4 Yrs; Natl Span Exam 1st; U Of KS; Med.

INTFEN, MICHAEL; Atchison Sr HS; Atchison, KS; (2); Art Clb; Church Yth Grp; Cmnty Wkr; Scholastic Bowl; School Musical; School Play; Ftbl; Mgr(s); JV Socr; High Hon Roll; Acad Tlntd Pgm; MIT; Astrophysics.

IRBY, CHRIS M; Wichita Collegiate Schl; Wichita, KS; (3); SADD; Varsity Clb; Chorus; JV Bsktbl; Var L Ftbl; Var L Trk; High Hon Roll; Hon Roll; I Dare You Ldrshp Awd; 3a ST Ftbl Chmpn Strtr; Law/Psych.

IRELAND, JENAEA; Peabody-Burns Jr Sr HS; Peabody, KS; (4); 4/34; Church Yth Grp; Dance Clb; FCA; Girl Scts; Letterman Clb; Varsity Clb; Band; Chorus; Drm Mjr(t); Jazz Band; Marion Cty Scholar; Summer Gymnstcs; KS ST U; Fshn Mrktng.

IRELAND, KATE; Jackson Heights HS; Muscotah, KS; (1); 1/41; 4-H; Scholastic Bowl; Band; Chorus; High Hon Roll; Hrs Shws & Cntsts.

IRON WING, TASHA L; Wichita North HS; Wichita, KS; (2); Teachers Aide; School Play; Hon Roll; Prfct Atten Awd; UNITY; All Ntns Yth Clb; Frnscs Tm; Bus.

IRSIK, MAX; Dodge City HS; Dodge City, KS; (3); Church Yth Grp; Debate Tm; NFL; JV Var Ftbl; JV Golf; Hon Roll; NHS; Pres Acad Fit Awd; Natl Yng Ldrs Cncl; Jr Ldrshp Dodge; DARE Role Model; Law.

IRSIK, SARA L; Uniontown HS; Mapleton, KS; (4); 10/38; Church Yth Grp; FCA; Math Clb; Teachers Aide; Chorus; Church Choir; Hon Roll; NHS; KS Schltc Bus Ed Awd; Ft Scott CC.

IRVIN, AMANDA L; Bishop Ward HS; Kansas City, KS; (2); 1/93; Sec Drama Clb; Hosp Aide; Pep Clb; SADD; Drill Tm; School Musical; Stage Crew; Powder Puff Ftbl; Intrml Vllybl; High Hon Roll; GIFT; Conflict Resolution Team.

IRVIN, DANA; Inman Jr Sr HS; Inman, KS; (4); 2/32; German Clb; Quiz Bowl; Scholastic Bowl; Band; Mrchg Band; Pep Band; Pres Soph Cls; Ofcr Stu Cncl; High Hon Roll; Hon Roll; Comp Sci, Prgrmmng; U Of AZ; Comp Sci.

IRWIN, JACCIE; Circle HS; El Dorado, KS; (3); Church Yth Grp; Drama Clb; FCA; 4-H; FHA; Hosp Aide; Letterman Clb; Library Aide; Q&S; Speech Tm; Butler Cty 4 H Ambssdr; Supr Rtng JEA NSPA Natl Cont; St Qulfr Jrnlsm, Frnscs; Pittsburg ST U; Cmmrcl Dsgn.

IRWIN, JESSICA; Russell HS; Bunker Hill, KS; (4); 1/73; Am Leg Aux Girls St; Debate Tm; German Clb; SADD; Ed Yrbk; Sec Treas Stu Cncl; Var Tennis; High Hon Roll; Pres NHS; Pres Acad Fit Awd; KS Assn Yth Exec Bd; U Of KS; Hist.

IRWIN, KENDALL D; Russell HS; Bunker Hill, KS; (1); 1/103; Cmnty Wkr; Drama Clb; School Musical; School Play; Stage Crew; Sec Treas Frsh Cls; Rep Stu Cncl; JV L Chrldng; Var L Trk; High Hon Roll; Var Choir; Acad Lttr Hnr Roll; Chrldng Lttr; KAY Club; Sprts Med.

IRWIN, KIMBERLY; Blue Valley HS; Overland Park, KS; (4); FBLA; FHA; HOBY; Math Clb; Quiz Bowl; Band; Mrchg Band; Church Yth Grp; Cit Awd; High Hon Roll; Chmthn Hnbl Mntn; KS U; Microbio.

ISAAC, MICHAEL; Hillsboro HS; Hillsboro, KS; (2); 1/45; Church Yth Grp; Quiz Bowl; Band; Church Choir; Mrchg Band; Pep Band; JV Crs Cntry; JV Tennis; High Hon Roll; Arch.

ISAAC, NANCY J; Meade HS; Meade, KS; (1); Church Yth Grp; Math Tm; Speech Tm; Band; Chorus; Church Choir; Mrchg Band; Pep Band; School Musical; Var Crs Cntry; Coll.

ISAAC, NATHAN E; Meade HS; Meade, KS; (3); Church Yth Grp; Letterman Clb; Band; Chorus; Mrchg Band; Pep Band; School Musical; Var Crs Cntry; Var Tennis; Cit Awd; Agricltrl Engrng.

ISAACS, MELISSA K; Topeka HS; Topeka, KS; (1); Church Yth Grp; Cmnty Wkr; Hosp Aide; Swmmng; Vllybl; High Hon Roll; Hon Roll; Topeka Swim Assn; Math Tchr.

ISABELL, PAUL J; Bishop Ward HS; Kansas City, KS; (2); 39/93; Band; Ofcr Bsbl; Hon Roll; U Of KS; Auto Eng.

ISBELL, BRANDI M; Riverton Schl; Galena, KS; (2); French Clb; Pep Clb; Chorus; Drill Tm; School Musical; Treas Soph Cls; Rep Stu Cncl; JV Vllybl; Hon Roll; Jr NHS; Phys Thrpy.

ISBELL, RYAN S; Beloit Jr Sr HS; Beloit, KS; (3); 3/59; Art Clb; Cmnty Wkr; Letterman Clb; Science Clb; Spanish Clb; SADD; Pres Frsh Cls; Pres Soph Cls; Pres Jr Cls; Ofcr Stu Cncl.

ISCH, JUSTIN L; Madison Jr Sr HS; Gridley, KS; (3); 8/26; Church Yth Grp; FBLA; German Clb; Letterman Clb; Church Choir; School Play; Sec Stu Cncl; L Bsktbl; L Ftbl; Cit Awd; KS ST U; Animal Sci.

ISE, GREGORY S; Blue Valley Northwest HS; Overland Park, KS; (3); JV Bsktbl; High Hon Roll; Hon Roll; NHS; Northwestern Univ; Acctng.

ISERNHAGEN, MARY L; Blue Valley HS; Overland Park, KS; (4); Lit Mag; Tennis; Hon Roll; Piano 10 Yrs, Several Schlrshps; Smmr Sftbl Team; U Of KS; Piano.

ISOM, JEFF M; Blue Valley North HS; Leawood, KS; (2); Church Yth Grp; JV Var Socr; Hon Roll; Pres Acad Fit Awd; U Of CA; Arch; Industrial Dsgn.

ISRAEL, MELISSA; Spearville Jr Sr HS; Spearville, KS; (2); 3/31; Dance Clb; GAA; HOBY; Letterman Clb; Math Tm; Pep Clb; Quiz Bowl; Scholastic Bowl; Band; Chorus; Bstr Clb Acad Achvr Awd; Acad Olympics 5th; SW KS Bus Comp 4th; Barton Cnty CC; Math.

IVERSON, KIMBERLY M; Wichita East HS; Wichita, KS; (2); 1/425; Sftbl; Vllybl; High Hon Roll; Peer Ldrshp Comm Svc; Nom Hngr Bd; Ldrshp 2000; WSU; PT.

IVEY, COURTNEY; Syracuse Jr Sr HS; Syracuse, KS; (1); 1/34; Drama Clb; Pep Clb; Chorus; JV Bsktbl; Var Powder Puff Ftbl; Trk; JV Vllybl; High Hon Roll.

IVORY, DALELA; Junction City HS; Junction City, KS; (3); Pep Clb; Ofcr Jr Cls; Bsktbl; Trk; Vllybl; High Hon Roll; Hon Roll; NHS; St Runner-Up Triple Jump Cls 6a; All-Amer Schlr; KS Univ; Med.

IWERT, NIKKI; North Central HS; Mahaska, KS; (4); 8/10; Am Leg Aux Girls St; Church Yth Grp; 4-H; FBLA; FHA; Pep Clb; Nwsp; Yrbk; High Hon Roll; Prfct Atten Awd; KS ST U.

JABLONSKI, CHRISTOPHER M; Wichita Collegiate Schl; Wichita, KS; (3); Am Leg Boys St; Church Yth Grp; Cmnty Wkr; FCA; JA; Letterman Clb; Varsity Clb; Chorus; School Musical; Variety Show; Natl Recog US Marine Corps Resvetoys For Tots Cmmdrs Awd; St Bsktbll Champ; Air Frce Acad; Plt.

JABLONSKI, JILL M; Bishop Miege HS; Overland Park, KS; (3); 4/170; Cmnty Wkr; Acpl Chr; School Musical; School Play; Rep Soph Cls; Rep Jr Cls; JV Var Socr; Hon Roll; Jr NHS; NHS; Wendys Heisman Awd; Hghst Fmle GPA In Clss; 4 Yr Schl; Ed/Math.

JACCARD, LINDSEY; Louisburg HS; Louisburg, KS; (2); FBLA; Letterman Clb; Natl FFA Org; Spanish Clb; Band; Mrchg Band; Pep Band; Intrml Mgr Trk; JV Vllybl; Hon Roll; Chldrns Tutor; Phys Thrpy.

JACKSON, AMIEE D; Wichita South HS; Wichita, KS; (4); Church Yth Grp; ROTC; Acpl Chr; Chorus; VP Soph Cls; Sec Sr Cls; Var Tennis; Rainbow Grls; Var Capt Grls Sccr; SHAB; Pittsburg ST Univ; Hosp Mngmt.

JACKSON, AMY; Salina HS Central; Salina, KS; (1); Debate Tm; Library Aide; NFL; Pep Clb; SADD; Chorus; Var L Chrldng; Hon Roll; NHS; Spelman Coll; Psycht.

JACKSON, BRIYONA; Manhattan HS; Manhattan, KS; (4); Church Yth Grp; Drama Clb; SADD; Capt Var Chrldng; Var Sftbl; JV Vllybl; Hon Roll; Upward Bnd; HIV/AIDS Peer Instr; Red Crss Certified; Heritage Panel; GA ST U; Financial Mgr.

JACKSON, CORRIE L; Eudora HS; Eudora, KS; (4); 9/43; Teachers Aide; Varsity Clb; Ed Nwsp; Yrbk; Pres Soph Cls; Pres Jr Cls; Pres Sr Cls; Var L Bsbl; Var Bsktbl; Hon Roll; 3a All-St Bsbl Pitcher 95 & 1st Base 96; Scndry Ed; Eng.

JACKSON, DEONA; J C Harmon HS; Kansas City, KS; (2); Church Yth Grp; Cmnty Wkr; Key Clb; Spanish Clb; Chorus; Church Choir; Hon Roll.

JACKSON, ERIKA C; Topeka West HS; Topeka, KS; (4); 28/240; Church Yth Grp; Intnl Clb; Pep Clb; SADD; Chorus; Drill Tm; Variety Show; Mgr Swmmng; High Hon Roll; NHS; KS ST U; Dance.

JACKSON, ERIN E; Olathe East Sr HS; Overland Park, KS; (2); Cmnty Wkr; Spanish Clb; Band; Mrchg Band; High Hon Roll; Hon Roll; Pres Schlr; Vet Med.

JACKSON, HEATHER A; Stockton HS; Stockton, KS; (2); Church Yth Grp; Pep Clb; Band; Chorus; Jazz Band; Mrchg Band; Pep Band; JV Bsktbl; Var Trk; Hon Roll; Sftbl; Chrch Orch; Law/Lawyer.

JACKSON, JAMES; Maranatha Acad; Shawnee, KS; (2); Band; Jazz Band; Mrchg Band; Pep Band; School Play; Pres Soph Cls; Var Bsktbl; Var Socr; High Hon Roll; NHS; Air Force Acad; Arntcl Engnr.

JACKSON, KALAH; Olathe North Sr HS; Olathe, KS; (2); Church Yth Grp; Cmnty Wkr; Church Choir; Orch; Nwsp; JV L Swmmng; Hon Roll; Pres Acad Fit Awd; Drama Prgm Church; Missnry Wrk Mexico; Clinical Psych.

JACKSON, KARA M; Maize HS; Wichita, KS; (3); 39/243; Church Yth Grp; Letterman Clb; Spanish Clb; SADD; Chorus; Church Choir; Variety Show; Var Bsktbl; Hon Roll; NHS; Tutoring; PT; PA.

JACKSON, KIRSTIN D; Clifton-Clyde HS; Clifton, KS; (3); 7/34; Am Leg Aux Girls St; Church Yth Grp; FBLA; Pep Clb; Teachers Aide; Band; Chorus; Church Choir; Jazz Band; Mrchg Band; Kay Club Pres; St Mary CYO Rep Parish Cncl; Cloud Cnty CC.

JACKSON, LA CRESHA R; Wyandotte HS; Kansas City, KS; (2); Church Yth Grp; Cmnty Wkr; Pep Clb; Church Choir; Drill Tm; Morehouse.

JACKSON, LA RENDA D; F L Schlagle HS; Kansas City, KS; (1); Church Yth Grp; Church Choir; Hon Roll; Piano Lessons; Chrch Jr Usher Bd; Bus.

JACKSON, LATOYA D; Wichita East HS; Wichita, KS; (2); Rptr Nwsp; Var Capt Bsktbl; Hon Roll; All Trnmt Team; All-ST Hnrb Mntn; Top 4 Frosh By Local Nwsp; Bus.

JACKSON, MOLLIE; Wichita Heights HS; Wichita, KS; (3); 1/350; Bus Profs of Am; VP Church Yth Grp; HOBY; Science Clb; Pres Spanish Clb; Treas Frsh Cls; Treas Soph Cls; Sec Jr Cls; Ofcr Sr Cls; Ofcr Stu Cncl; Peer Ldr; Hmcmng Qn Attndnt; Mediator; Med.

JACKSON, RACHEL R; Salina HS Central; Salina, KS; (2); Drama Clb; School Musical; School Play; Stage Crew; Phtg Yrbk; Hon Roll; Arch.

JACKSON, SARAH; Sedgwick HS; Sedgwick, KS; (2); 9/35; Art Clb; Letterman Clb; Band; Chorus; School Musical; Pres Soph Cls; Rep Stu Cncl; Var Chrldng; Trk; High Hon Roll; Csmtlgy.

JACKSON, SARAH E; Ellinwood Jr Sr HS; Ellinwood, KS; (2); 17/44; Church Yth Grp; Cmnty Wkr; FCA; Latin Clb; Teachers Aide; Chorus; Church Choir; JV Bsktbl; Var Trk; JV Var Vllybl; Two Time St Qualifier Trk , Plcd 5th In 4x200 Relay 96; Barton Cty CC; Bus Mgmt.

JACKSON, SHAWN I; Pratt HS; Pratt, KS; (2); SADD; Band; Ftbl; JV Var Trk; High Hon Roll.

JACKSON, STACI L; Phillipsburg HS; Phillipsburg, KS; (3); 6/42; Treas VP Church Yth Grp; Cmnty Wkr; Pres Sec 4-H; Spanish Clb; SADD; Teachers Aide; Band; Mrchg Band; Pep Band; Ofcr Stu Cncl; Wndy Heisman Awd Wnnr; Frt Hays St Univ.

JACKSON, TERA; Ft Scott HS; Fort Scott, KS; (3); Letterman Clb; Pep Clb; Varsity Clb; Chorus; Var Chrldng; Mgr(s); Sftbl; Mgr Vllybl; Hon Roll; Chrldr For 96 Shrine Bowl; Nrs.

JACOB, NICHOLAS E; Emporia HS; Emporia, KS; (2); JV Bsktbl; JV Socr; JV Trk; Intrml Wt Lftg; Cit Awd; Hon Roll; Coach Comp Yth Soccer; Marine Bio/Med.

JACOBI, AMANDA; Wichita East HS; Wichita, KS; (3); 26/292; Debate Tm; Hosp Aide; NFL; Spanish Clb; Chorus; Variety Show; JV Var Chrldng; Hon Roll; NHS; Spanish NHS; Acad Ltr; U Of KS; Bus.

JACOBS, BETHANY R; Blue Valley North HS; Overland Park, KS; (3); Church Yth Grp; Drama Clb; Thesps; Sec Chorus; Church Choir; School Musical; School Play; Stage Crew; Hon Roll; Model UN; Vol Teen AIDS Info Hotline; Elem Ed.

JACOBS, FLETCHER; Holton HS; Holton, KS; (2); Model UN; Quiz Bowl; Scholastic Bowl; Band; Mrchg Band; Pep Band; School Musical; Nwsp; Yrbk; Bsktbl; Drawing, Wrtng.

JACOBS, GENEVA L; Hayden HS; Berryton, KS; (2); Intnl Clb; JV Var Crs Cntry; JV Socr; Var L Trk; Stat Vllybl; High Hon Roll; NHS; Coll.

JACOBS, JACKY; Wichita North HS; Wichita, KS; (3); 11/234; Cmnty Wkr; Q&S; Teachers Aide; Color Guard; Co-Ed Yrbk; JV Sftbl; Var Trk; Hon Roll; NHS; Jrnlsm.

JACOBS, JENNIFER; Peabody-Burns Jr Sr HS; Peabody, KS; (2); #1 in class; FCA; Band; Flag Corp; VP Soph Cls; Rep Stu Cncl; Var L Bsktbl; Var L Chrldng; Var L Vllybl; High Hon Roll; Hon Roll; Natl Sci Mrt Awd.

JACOBS, JOE B; Blue Valley Northwest HS; Overland Park, KS; (2); Debate Tm; Letterman Clb; Pep Clb; SADD; Teachers Aide; Temple Yth Grp; Varsity Clb; Pres Jr Cls; Rep Stu Cncl; Intrml Bsbl; Snowboarding; Peer Support; Block Schedule Group; CO Univ; Bus/Mngmt.

JACOBS, JOSH C; Medicine Lodge HS; Lake City, KS; (1); Church Yth Grp; Natl FFA Org; Chorus; Ftbl; Wt Lftg; Hon Roll; Summer Rec Bsbl.

JACOBS, KORY; Maize HS; Wichita, KS; (4); French Clb; Science Clb; SADD; Var Bsktbl; Var Socr; Var Tennis; High Hon Roll; NHS; Ntl Merit Ltr; St Schlr; Phys Thpry.

JACOBS, TAMARA S; Maize HS; Wichita, KS; (3); Debate Tm; DECA; Teachers Aide; Band; Mrchg Band; Pep Band; School Play; Hon Roll; KS ST; Bus; Comps.

JACOBS, TRISHA; Argonia Jr Sr HS; Milan, KS; (3); Church Yth Grp; Cmnty Wkr; HOBY; Letterman Clb; Office Aide; Pep Clb; Teachers Aide; Band; Chorus; Yrbk; Brdcst Jrnlsm.

JACOBSEN, STEPHEN; Hiawatha HS; Hiawatha, KS; (4); 6/87; Church Yth Grp; Intnl Clb; Key Clb; Pep Clb; Spanish Clb; VP Sr Cls; Var Tennis; High Hon Roll; Hon Roll; NHS; U Of KS; Mech Engrng.

JACOS, TYSON A; Great Bend Sr HS; Great Bend, KS; (2); Spanish Clb; JV Bsbl; JV Wrstlng; CO ST U; Med.

JAGELS, RICHARD; Garden City Sr HS; Garden City, KS; (3); Church Yth Grp; Cmnty Wkr; Band; Jazz Band; Mrchg Band; Pep Band; JV Bsktbl; Wt Lftg; Hon Roll; Ldrshp Amer 95; Winter Hmcmng Attndnt 96; Phys Thrpy.

JAGGARD, MANDY; Olathe South Sr HS; Olathe, KS; (3); 18/420; Church Yth Grp; Cmnty Wkr; Math Clb; Math Tm; Pep Clb; Science Clb; Spanish Clb; Church Choir; Orch; School Musical; Sec Ed/Psych.

JAGGERS, OLIVA M; Smoky Valley HS; Mc Pherson, KS; (2); Band; Mrchg Band; Pep Band; JV Trk; Hon Roll; Kays Club.

JAHN, LAURA; Shawnee Mission N HS; Shawnee Mission, KS; (2); 80/446; Pep Clb; Q&S; Co-Ed Yrbk; Mgr(s); Acad Ltr; Asst Handicapped Stdnts Horseback Riding; Jrnlsm.

JAHNKE, JOSH P; Salina HS South; Salina, KS; (3); Cmnty Wkr; Teachers Aide; Var L Bsbl; Var L Bsktbl; Mgr Vllybl; High Hon Roll.

JAHR, CARA; Mc Louth Schl; Mc Louth, KS; (4); Pres Art Clb; Church Yth Grp; FBLA; Spanish Clb; SADD; Teachers Aide; Yrbk; Chrldng; High Hon Roll; Hon Roll; Washburn U; Elem Ed.

JAKSA III, FRANK J; Bishop Ward HS; Kansas City, KS; (1); 8/114; Varsity Clb; Var Bsbl; Stat Bsktbl; Mgr(s); Score Keeper; High Hon Roll; Rcvd Acad Schlsp 95-; Amer Lgn Bsbl Smmr 96.

JAKSON, DEBBIE L; Hays HS; Hays, KS; (1); Church Yth Grp; Cmnty Wkr; Drama Clb; Hosp Aide; Pep Clb; Quiz Bowl; Spanish Clb; Chorus; Church Choir; School Musical; Fort Hays ST; Ped.

JAMES, COREY MICHAEL; Leavenworth HS; Leavenworth, KS; (4); 50/326; Letterman Clb; Varsity Clb; Var Capt Ftbl; Hon Roll; Coffeyville CC; Phy Thpry.

JAMES, KERRY A; Dighton HS; Shields, KS; (1); Church Yth Grp; FCA; Band; Chorus; Church Choir; Mrchg Band; Pep Band; VP Frsh Cls; JV Bsktbl; Var Ftbl.

JAMES, KEVIN M; Emporia HS; Emporia, KS; (3); 34/267; Boy Scts; Church Yth Grp; Var L Ftbl; Wt Lftg; Cit Awd; High Hon Roll; Hon Roll; Eagle Scout; Engrng.

JAMES III, LEE A; Sumner Acad; Kansas City, KS; (4); 45/197; Boy Scts; Chess Clb; Cmnty Wkr; Computer Clb; Latin Clb; Office Aide; Pep Clb; Spanish Clb; Varsity Clb; Sprt Ed Yrbk; Bsktbl All League 1st Tm/League MVP/ALL Met KS 1st Tm/1st Tm All ST Class 5a; Barton Cty CC; Arch.

JAMES, LINDSAY D; Dighton HS; Shields, KS; (3); 1/27; Church Yth Grp; Cmnty Wkr; VP Pres FCA; VP Sec 4-H; Speech Tm; Sec Pres SADD; Pres Jr Cls; JV Capt Bsktbl; 4-H Awd; High Hon Roll; Psych.

JAMES, LUKE; Dighton HS; Dighton, KS; (4); 4/45; Am Leg Boys St; Art Clb; Church Yth Grp; Cmnty Wkr; FCA; 4-H; Math Tm; Quiz Bowl; Scholastic Bowl; SADD; Schl Peer Helper; Environment; KS ST Univ; Environmtl Chem.

JAMES, MELYNIE; Winfield HS; Winfield, KS; (4); 4/182; Church Yth Grp; Acpl Chr; Swing Chorus; Variety Show; Rep Soph Cls; Rep Jr Cls; Rep Sr Cls; Rep Stu Cncl; High Hon Roll; VP NHS; KS Hnrs Rgnts Acad; Ms Tn Of KS Fnlst; Plng Comms; Brigham Young U; Pub Rel.

JAMES, RON J; Newton Sr HS; Newton, KS; (2); 1/270; Boy Scts; Church Yth Grp; Band; Mrchg Band; Pep Band; Ofcr Bsbl; JV Crs Cntry; Ftbl; Var Trk; Var Wrstlng; Med.

JAMES, TODD R; Topeka HS; Topeka, KS; (3); Ofcr Bsbl; Bsktbl; Crs Cntry; Ftbl; Trk; Hon Roll; KS U; Hist.

JAMESON, LAURIE; Garden City Sr HS; Garden City, KS; (3); 24/310; Church Yth Grp; Cmnty Wkr; Varsity Clb; Band; Tennis; High Hon Roll; Hon Roll; Prfct Atten Awd; Pres Acad Fit Awd; KS ST U; Phys Thrpy.

JAMISON, CHERIE; Quinter Jr Sr HS; Quinter, KS; (2); Church Yth Grp; FCA; Letterman Clb; Natl FFA Org; Band; Chorus; Var JV Bsktbl; Var Chrldng; Trk; JV Vllybl; Law Enfrcmnt.

JAMISON, ERIC T; Baldwin HS; Lawrence, KS; (4); 11/78; Cmnty Wkr; Chorus; School Musical; School Play; Variety Show; Rptr Yrbk; JV Bsktbl; JV Tennis; Hon Roll; NHS.

JAMISON, MATTHEW C; Goodland HS; Goodland, KS; (2); FHA; Letterman Clb; Chorus; Var Bsktbl; Ftbl; Var Tennis; Wt Lftg; Hon Roll.

JAMVOLD, KIRK; Troy HS; Troy, KS; (2); Church Yth Grp; FCA; Natl FFA Org; JV Bsktbl; JV Ftbl; Prfct Atten Awd.

JANES, ARINYA; Erie HS; Erie, KS; (4); 12/42; Am Leg Aux Girls St; Art Clb; Chess Clb; Church Yth Grp; Drama Clb; Intnl Clb; Quiz Bowl; Red Cross Aide; Scholastic Bowl; Science Clb; Natl Yng Ldrs Conf; Natl Yth Ldrshp Frm On Med; Top Schlstc Fml Chss Plyr In KS 93-94; U Of N TX; Med.

JANIS, MICHAEL E; Shawnee Mission S Sr HS; Lenexa, KS; (4); 63/413; Pres Band; Drm Mjr(t); Jazz Band; Pep Band; School Musical; Rep Stu Cncl; JV Bsbl; JV Socr; Cmnty Wkr; Drama Clb; Marine Corps Smpr Fdls Awd Mus Exclnc; Heritage 1st Attndnt; KS ST Univ; Sprt Psych/Knslgy.

JANIS, MICHELLE; Horton HS; Horton, KS; (4); 3/57; Church Yth Grp; FHA; Band; Jazz Band; Ed Nwsp; Hon Roll; NHS; Pres Acad Fit Awd; MO Wstrn St Col; Acctnt.

JANKO, CORY R; Derby HS; Derby, KS; (1); Church Yth Grp; Hon Roll; Paintball; OK Univ; Md.

JANSEN, REBECCA; Hayden HS; Topeka, KS; (3); 9/140; Hosp Aide; Pep Clb; SADD; Chorus; Var Sftbl; Intrml Vllybl; High Hon Roll; NHS; Bowling Top 10 In City 95-96; Creighton Univ; Acctng.

JANSONIUS, JENNIFER A; Logan HS; Prairie View, KS; (3); 2/26; Church Yth Grp; 4-H; Pep Clb; Scholastic Bowl; Chorus; Flag Corp; School Play; Mgr Yrbk; Var L Bsktbl; Band; KSPA Regnl Cont 1st Pls; Mrktg; Advertising.

JANSSEN, HAYDEN T; Emporia HS; Emporia, KS; (3); 50/350; Church Yth Grp; FCA; Key Clb; Latin Clb; Quiz Bowl; Scholastic Bowl; Science Clb; Band; Jazz Band; Mrchg Band; St Sci Olympd Cmptn; Engl.

JANSSEN, TRAVIS J; Ellsworth HS; Geneseo, KS; (2); 5/90; 4-H; Band; Mrchg Band; Pep Band; School Musical; Mgr Ftbl; JV Golf; Wt Lftg; 4-H Awd; High Hon Roll; FFA Chptr Rptr; Acad Ltr; KS ST Univ; Animal Sci.

JANTZ, JENNIFER; South Gray HS; Montezuma, KS; (4); 9/19; Drama Clb; Speech Tm; Chorus; School Play; Sec Treas Soph Cls; Sec Treas Sr Cls; Var L Chrldng; Mgr(s); High Hon Roll; Hon Roll; United Meth Yth Grp; KAYS Pres; Bsktbl Homcmng Qn; Denver Acad Crt Rprtng; Crt Rpr.

JANTZ, KELLY L; Moundridge HS; Moundridge, KS; (3); FCA; VP Pres FHA; Pep Clb; Chorus; Drill Tm; Sec Frsh Cls; Sec Soph Cls; Ofcr Stu Cncl; Chrldng; Hon Roll; Bethany Col; Psych.

JANUARY, AMANDA M; Gardner-Edgerton HS; Edgerton, KS; (2); 41/165; Pep Clb; Chorus; Drill Tm; School Musical; School Play; Stat Bsbl; Mgr(s); Co-Capt Pom Pon; Hon Roll; Stuco Sec; Chrs Blue Blzrs; U Of KS; Dance Chrgrphy.

JANUARY, RYAN J; Lyons HS; Lyons, KS; (2); Church Yth Grp; Crs Cntry; L Var Wrstlng; Hon Roll; Cmptr Prgmng.

JANUARY, TRAVIS; Hutchinson HS; Hutchinson, KS; (3); Am Leg Boys St; Church Yth Grp; French Clb; Science Clb; Band; Pep Band; Socr; Swmmng; Cit Awd; High Hon Roll; Optometry.

JANZEN, ANGELA J; Newton Sr HS; Newton, KS; (2); 1/250; Church Yth Grp; German Clb; Key Clb; Orch; Var L Crs Cntry; L Swmmng; High Hon Roll; Explr Pst; Lbrl Arts.

JANZEN, ANNIE M; Wichita North HS; Wichita, KS; (2); 17/380; Church Yth Grp; Library Aide; Band; Church Choir; Drm Mjr(t); Mrchg Band; Pep Band; Hon Roll.

JANZEN, DUSTIN T; Scott Comm HS; Scott City, KS; (3); Cmnty Wkr; 4-H; Natl FFA Org; Yrbk; Ofcr Frsh Cls; Ofcr Soph Cls; Ofcr Jr Cls; Ofcr Sr Cls; Ofcr Stu Cncl; JV Var Bsbl; Pittsburg ST U; Bankr; Electrnc.

JANZEN, JOSHUA D; Hesston HS; Hesston, KS; (1); Band; Chorus; Ftbl; Tennis.

JANZEN, NATHAN; Colby Sr HS; Whitewater, KS; (4); 1/97; Am Leg Boys St; Natl FFA Org; NFL; Scholastic Bowl; Ftbl; DAR Awd; Gov Hon Prg Awd; NHS; St Schlr; Val; Grace Univ.

JARBOE, JANELLE R; Lakin HS; Lakin, KS; (3); Pres 4-H; Sec FHA; Quiz Bowl; School Play; Rptr Nwsp; Rptr Yrbk; Sec Soph Cls; Sec Rep Jr Cls; Rep Stu Cncl; 4-H Awd; Forensics; U Of KS; Pre-Law; Child Psych.

JARBOE, MELODY J; Lakin HS; Lakin, KS; (1); FCA; Sec 4-H; Pep Clb; Band; Jazz Band; Pep Band; Sec Frsh Cls; Pres Soph Cls; Intrml Sftbl; Hon Roll; Forensics; U Of KS; Elem Ed.

JARBOE, SONIA; Topeka West HS; Topeka, KS; (4); 31/243; Art Clb; Church Yth Grp; French Clb; Intnl Clb; Q&S; Teachers Aide; Nwsp; Crs Cntry; Socr; Trk; KS ST Univ; Archtctr.

JARDINE, JANAE L; Blue Valley Northwest HS; Overland Park, KS; (4); Church Yth Grp; Cmnty Wkr; Hosp Aide; Capt Drill Tm; Orch; School Musical; Powder Puff Ftbl; Hon Roll; NHS; Pres Schlr; Natl Eng Merit Awrd; KS ST; Nursg.

JARRATT, CLAY M; Turner HS; Kansas City, KS; (4); Art Clb; Boy Scts; NFL; Thesps; Rep Frsh Cls; Eagle Sct; Ldrshp 2020; NYLC; Johnson Cty CC; Scenic Dsgn.

JARRED, JENNIFER L; Maranatha Acad; Kansas City, KS; (3); Teachers Aide; Varsity Clb; Chorus; School Musical; Vllybl; High Hon Roll; Awd Mst Outs Choir Membr; Mus Ed.

JARRETT, ANDREW S; Columbus HS; Baxter Springs, KS; (4); 8/85; Am Leg Boys St; Math Tm; Natl FFA Org; Rep Yrbk; Ofcr Sr Cls; Rep Stu Cncl; Var Golf; VP NHS; Pres Acad Fit Awd; St Schlr; Wings Gftd Ed; Pittsburg ST U; Plastcs Enrng.

JARRETT, JUSTIN; Columbus HS; Baxter Springs, KS; (4); 7/87; Bus Profs of Am; Church Yth Grp; FCA; FHA; Letterman Clb; Math Tm; Spanish Clb; Pres Soph Cls; Ofcr Stu Cncl; Golf; Bus Prof Of Amer Prlmntry Prcdr Team Mmbr 2nd Natls; Pittsburg ST U; Atty.

JARVIS, MELISSA R; Campus HS; Haysville, KS; (3); 10/201; Sec Church Yth Grp; Pres Band; Color Guard; Flag Corp; Mrchg Band; Pep Band; High Hon Roll; Hon Roll; NHS; Cowely Cty CC; Bus Mngmnt.

JASMINE, HEILI D; Garden City Sr HS; Garden City, KS; (4); 4/313; Am Leg Aux Girls St; Math Tm; Science Clb; Spanish Clb; VP SADD; Treas Stu Cncl; Co-Capt Chrldng; Gov Hon Prg Awd; NHS; Pres Schlr; Big Brothers & Big Sisters Pgm; Emporia ST Univ; Optometry.

JASO, JEREMY M; Newton Sr HS; Newton, KS; (1); Chess Clb; Church Yth Grp; Drama Clb; Quiz Bowl; JV Socr; JV Var Wrstlng; High Hon Roll; Frnscs; Sprts Med/Ath Trnr.

JASO, SARAH M; Newton Sr HS; Newton, KS; (3); Church Yth Grp; Key Clb; Model UN; Scholastic Bowl; Band; Mrchg Band; Pep Band; JV Sftbl; High Hon Roll; KS Univ.

JAY, DAVID; Beloit Jr Sr HS; Beloit, KS; (1); Quiz Bowl; Scholastic Bowl; High Hon Roll; Astronomy; Physics; Columbia U Schl Of Engrng.

JEAN, SCOTT; Olathe South Sr HS; Olathe, KS; (2); 4-H; Letterman Clb; Teachers Aide; Ftbl; Wt Lftg; Wrstlng; 4-H Awd; High Hon Roll; Hon Roll; KS ST U; Sprts Med.

JEFFERSON, CORY; Wyandotte HS; Kansas City, KS; (2); FBLA; Pep Clb; Teachers Aide; School Play; Yrbk; Ofcr Stu Cncl; Chrldng; Hon Roll; Prfct Atten Awd; Magnet Prgm; Lulac Ed Svc Cntr; Entrepreneur.

JEFFERSON, MARK A; Labette Co HS; Parsons, KS; (4); Chess Clb; FCA; Natl FFA Org; VICA; Var Bsbl; Var Ftbl; Hon Roll; St Proficiency Awd FFA; MVP Ftbl; Mst Inspirational Player Bsbl; All-St Bsbl; All-Conf Bsbl; Pittsburg ST Univ; Wood Tech.

JEFFERY, MELISSA; Mulvane Sr HS; Mulvane, KS; (4); 17/120; Am Leg Aux Girls St; Library Aide; SADD; Teachers Aide; Band; Mrchg Band; Ed Nwsp; NHS; Pres Acad Fit Awd.

JEFFREY, HALEY L; Topeka HS; Topeka, KS; (3); Cmnty Wkr; Intnl Clb; Model UN; Teachers Aide; Stage Crew; Phtg Nwsp; Hon Roll; Jazz/Tap Dance 13 Yrs; Nwspr Photogrhr.

JEFFREY, ROBYN; Atchison Co Cmty HS; Effingham, KS; (4); 17/60; Church Yth Grp; Sec 4-H; Letterman Clb; Library Aide; Math Clb; Pep Clb; Science Clb; SADD; Band; Mrchg Band; Cty 4-H Ambsdr; Co Capt Chrldng Squad; Highland CC; Prim Ed.

JEFFRIES, JACKIE R; Riverton Schl; Baxter Springs, KS; (3); Church Yth Grp; FHA; Key Clb; Spanish Clb; Church Choir; Sftbl; Hon Roll; Horseback Riding; Dancing; Chrstn Coll; Tchr.

JEGEN, DANIELLE; Blue Valley HS; Stilwell, KS; (3); Thesps; Varsity Clb; Acpl Chr; Chorus; Drill Tm; School Musical; Swing Chorus; Variety Show; Rep Soph Cls; JV Chrldng; Leads In Var Mscls; Optmst Awd; I Rtng St Lvl Solo-Vcl; Comm Theatre; Houston U; Msc Ed.

JEKIC, NICK J; Shawnee Mission N HS; Shawnee Mission, KS; (4); #11 in class; VP French Clb; Pep Clb; Band; Mrchg Band; Orch; Pep Band; JV Tennis; Hon Roll; NHS; Pres Schlr; Letter In Acad And Bnd; U Of KS; Bus.

JELLISON, DAVID W; Protection Schl; Protection, KS; (2); Church Yth Grp; Letterman Clb; Pep Band; JV Bsktbl; Var L Ftbl; Var L Trk; Hon Roll.

JELLISON, TOMMY R; Burlingame HS; Burlingame, KS; (1); 19/36; Boy Scts; Chess Clb; FBLA; Mu Alpha Theta; Pep Clb; Thesps; Yrbk; Pres Frsh Cls; JV Ftbl; High Hon Roll; Harvard Univ; Lwyr.

JENKINS, BRIAN; Bishop Carroll Catholic HS; Wichita, KS; (4); 7/142; Cmnty Wkr; Drama Clb; FCA; Hosp Aide; Red Cross Aide; Pres SADD; Ed Nwsp; Pres Sr Cls; Capt Crs Cntry; Capt Trk; U Of KS; Chem Engrng.

JENKINS, CARRIE A; Blue Valley Northwest HS; Overland Park, KS; (2); Service Clb; High Hon Roll; Forensic Acctng.

JENKINS, ERICA L; Dodge City HS; Dodge City, KS; (3); Cmnty Wkr; Debate Tm; Intnl Clb; Spanish Clb; SADD; Band; Mrchg Band; JV Chrldng; Hon Roll; Prfct Atten Awd; Envrnmntl Studies.

JENKINS, JARED J; Bonner Springs HS; Bonner Springs, KS; (4); 9/143; Quiz Bowl; Band; Chorus; Mrchg Band; School Musical; Var Crs Cntry; Var Trk; High Hon Roll; Hon Roll; NHS; KS City KS CC; Civil Engrng.

JENKINS, JENNIFER; South Gray HS; Copeland, KS; (1); Quiz Bowl; Scholastic Bowl; Band; Chorus; Pep Band; Bsktbl; Chrldng; Pom Pon; Sftbl; High Hon Roll; KAYS; Auburn U.

JENKINS, RENEE C; Axtell Schl; Axtell, KS; (3); 7/17; Church Yth Grp; Cmnty Wkr; FCA; Letterman Clb; Spanish Clb; Varsity Clb; Chorus; School Play; Yrbk; Ofcr Jr Cls; Emporia ST; Acctng/Bus.

JENKINS, ROBERT F; Wellington Sr HS; Wellington, KS; (2); Debate Tm; Key Clb; SADD; Ftbl; Tennis; Wt Lftg; Hon Roll; NC; Lawyer Or Dr.

JENKINS, TESSIE D; Stockton HS; Stockton, KS; (3); 5/32; Church Yth Grp; FHA; Pep Clb; Band; Church Choir; Pep Band; Chrldng; Vllybl; Hon Roll; NHS; Model; Ft Hays U; Phys Thrpy.

JENKINS, TRAVIS D; Troy HS; Troy, KS; (4); 13/35; Church Yth Grp; Drama Clb; Letterman Clb; Natl FFA Org; School Play; Var Capt Bsktbl; Var L Crs Cntry; Var Capt Ftbl; Var L Trk; NHS; Male Ath Of Yr; Highland CC; Cnstrctn Engr Tec.

JENKINSON, KELLI L; Great Bend Sr HS; Great Bend, KS; (3); 28/245; Am Leg Aux Girls St; Church Yth Grp; Hosp Aide; Office Aide; Pep Clb; High Hon Roll; Hon Roll; Prfct Atten Awd; Kayettes; U Of KS; Pre-Med.

JENNINGS, AMY M; Clearwater HS; Clearwater, KS; (2); Socr; Wt Lftg.

JENNINGS, BRANDY M; Bishop Miege HS; Kansas City, KS; (2); 53/163; Cmnty Wkr; SADD; Intrml JV Bsktbl; JV Crs Cntry; Intrml Sftbl; High Hon Roll; Hon Roll; CMT Svc Comm Ldr; U Of KS; Aero Eng.

JENNINGS, JENNIFER L; Washburn Rural HS; Topeka, KS; (3); Cmnty Wkr; Debate Tm; French Clb; Girl Scts; Intnl Clb; Pep Clb; Band; Chorus; School Play; Variety Show; Poetry Pub; Selected To Audition For 96 Premier Productions For Miss Teen KS; Washburn Univ; Psycht; Author.

JENNINGS, JOSH D; Colby Sr HS; Colby, KS; (2); Church Yth Grp; Spanish Clb; SADD; Band; Pep Band; Ftbl; Golf.

JENNINGS, SCOTT K; Olathe South Sr HS; Olathe, KS; (2); Ofcr Bsbl; Bsktbl; Trk; Hon Roll; Pres Acad Fit Awd.

JENNISON, AURORA; Bluestem HS; El Dorado, KS; (3); 6/65; Church Yth Grp; Cmnty Wkr; FCA; HOBY; Scholastic Bowl; Teachers Aide; Thesps; School Play; Stage Crew; Ed Rptr Nwsp; Tn Age Repubs V-Chrprsn; Cmmnty Thtr; Knsns Lf; Friends U; Psychtrst.

JENNISON, CHERYL M; Blue Valley HS; Stilwell, KS; (3); Church Yth Grp; SADD; Teachers Aide; Band; Chorus; Church Choir; Jazz Band; Mrchg Band; Pep Band; School Musical; St Vocal Solo, Choir; Theatre.

JENSEN, ADRIENNE; Olathe North Sr HS; Olathe, KS; (2); FHA; Spanish Clb; High Hon Roll; Hon Roll; Pres Acad Fit Awd; Pres Schlr; Acad Excl Awd; Acad Pin & Gold Bar; Outstdng Achvmt Awds; Cert Of Recognition; KS U; Interior Designing.

JENSEN, ERIC W; Smoky Valley HS; Roxbury, KS; (1); Band; Mrchg Band; Pep Band.

JENSEN, G DAILEY; Olpe Schl; Olpe, KS; (4); Office Aide; Teachers Aide; Sec Sr Cls; Var L Bsktbl; Hon Roll; Bsktbl 3 Yrs-Lettered-All League 2nd Team; All St 2a-All Area 1st Team; Seward CC; Chiropractor.

JENSEN, JANAE N; Mankato Jr Sr HS; Mankato, KS; (3); 2/25; Church Yth Grp; Dance Clb; FHA; Math Tm; Natl FFA Org; Pep Clb; Quiz Bowl; Band; Chorus; Church Choir; KS ST Univ.

JENSEN, KATY; Blue Valley HS; Leawood, KS; (2); Hon Roll; KS ST; Vet.

JENSEN, LORI; Wichita North HS; Wichita, KS; (4); 1/250; Church Yth Grp; Cmnty Wkr; HOBY; Chorus; Variety Show; Rep Frsh Cls; Rep Soph Cls; Rep Jr Cls; Rep Sr Cls; Rep Stu Cncl; US Stu Cncl Awds; Intrn Wrk; Chrch Ldrshp Rls; Brigham Young U; Psych.

JENSEN, MICHELLE R; Clay Ctr Cmty HS; Clay Center, KS; (4); Church Yth Grp; Office Aide; SADD; Chorus; Color Guard; Capt Drill Tm; VP Soph Cls; Stat Bsktbl; Mgr(s); Score Keeper; Yth Ldr Core; Yth Grp Yth Cncl; Ottawa; Psych.

JENSEN, SARAH; Enterprise Sda Acad; Ottawa, KS; (1); VP Frsh Cls; Hon Roll.

JENSEN, SARAH; Neodesha Jr Sr HS; Neodesha, KS; (4); 5/41; Am Leg Aux Girls St; Cmnty Wkr; School Play; Rep Frsh Cls; Rep Soph Cls; Rep Jr Cls; VP Sr Cls; L Wt Lftg; DAR Awd; Sec NHS; Peer Hlprs; Apprentcshp Pgm; KS ST U.

JENSEN, TYLER K; Garden City Sr HS; Garden City, KS; (1); Boy Scts; Chess Clb; Debate Tm; Acpl Chr; JV Tennis; High Hon Roll; Hon Roll; Pres Acad Fit Awd; Road Biking; Karate; Garden City HS; Law Schl/FBI.

JENSEN, WENDY; Enterprise Sda Acad; Ottawa, KS; (4); Teachers Aide; School Play; Nwsp; Yrbk; High Hon Roll.

JEPSON, ANGIE; Shawnee Mission Nw Sr HS; Lenexa, KS; (2); 26/423; Dance Clb; Debate Tm; Drama Clb; Key Clb; NFL; Pep Clb; Thesps; Acpl Chr; Stage Crew; Chrldng; Pro Cheer All Star Coed Chrldng Sqd; All Amer Chrldr.

JESCHKE, EMILY; Highland HS; Troy, KS; (2); 4/32; Church Yth Grp; Cmnty Wkr; Natl FFA Org; Pep Clb; Spanish Clb; Chorus; School Musical; Swing Chorus; Sec Soph Cls; Var Bsktbl.

JESSUP, MATTHEW S; Manhattan HS; Manhattan, KS; (2); Band; Jazz Band; Mrchg Band; Variety Show; Hon Roll; Sprts; Drftng; KS ST; Engrng.

JEZMIR, ALLA; Blue Valley North HS; Overland Park, KS; (2); Drama Clb; Intnl Clb; Service Clb; Temple Yth Grp; Thesps; Chorus; School Musical; Rptr Nwsp; JV Tennis; High Hon Roll; Holocaust Expression Theater; Chorus Mem Comm Theater; Piano.

JINDRA, BRIAN N; Manhattan HS; Manhattan, KS; (3); Am Leg Boys St; VP Chess Clb; Science Clb; Teachers Aide; School Play; Rep Stu Cncl; Var L Socr; High Hon Roll; Jr NHS; NHS; Habitat For Humanity, Vol As Med Asst; Sunday Schl Tchr-Preschl; John Hopkins Univ; Pre-Med.

JIRAK, ISRAEL L; Stockton HS; Glade, KS; (4); 1/33; Math Tm; Quiz Bowl; Pres Frsh Cls; Pres Soph Cls; Pres Jr Cls; Ftbl; Hon Roll; NHS; St Schlr; Val; U Of KS; Atmsphrc Scis.

JOBE, JULIE A; Olathe North Sr HS; Olathe, KS; (4); Church Yth Grp; Drama Clb; French Clb; Thesps; Acpl Chr; Band; Church Choir; Mrchg Band; Pep Band; School Musical; Sgn Lang Intrprtr Boy Scout Camp/Ch; William Jewell Coll; Vcl Mus Ed.

JOE III, DARNELL; F L Schlagle HS; Kansas City, KS; (4); 4/190; Band; Mrchg Band; Pep Band; Variety Show; Ofcr Frsh Cls; Ofcr Soph Cls; Ofcr Jr Cls; Ofcr Sr Cls; Ofcr Stu Cncl; Ofcr Bsbl; Teen HOPE; Peer Cnslr; KS Alumni Hnr Schlr; Kansas City CC; Bus/Cmptr Sci.

JOERG, JULIE A; Jewell HS; Randall, KS; (4); 3/15; VP FHA; SADD; Yrbk; Rep Sr Cls; Treas Stu Cncl; Vllybl; Hon Roll; NHS; Pres Schlr; St Schlr; Natl Yth Ldshp Forum On Med; Fort Hays St Univ; Premed.

JOHANNSEN, CHASE C; Blue Valley North HS; Leawood, KS; (4); Art Clb; French Clb; German Clb; Orch; DAR Awd; French Hon Soc; Nationally Ranked Equestrian Hunter-Jumper; U Of KS; Dr; Lawyer.

JOHANSEN, GRETCHEN N; Hiawatha HS; Hiawatha, KS; (4); 13/87; Cmnty Wkr; FCA; Letterman Clb; Library Aide; Band; Mrchg Band; School Musical; Ed Yrbk; Treas Soph Cls; Treas Jr Cls; Mid Amer Nazarene Coll.

JOHL, BRAD E; Blue Valley North HS; Leawood, KS; (3); 26/250; Rep Frsh Cls; JV Bsbl; JV Bsktbl; Hon Roll; Best Spkr Model United Nat 10th Grade; Lawyer/Sports Brdcaster.

JOHN, STACY A; St Thomas Aquinas HS; Shawnee Mission, KS; (4); 15/231; Cmnty Wkr; Hosp Aide; Office Aide; Pep Clb; Science Clb; SADD; Teachers Aide; Socr; Vllybl; High Hon Roll; Summa Cum Laude; KU; Nrsing.

JOHNS, JEREMY; Crest HS; Kincaid, KS; (3); Am Leg Boys St; Church Yth Grp; Drama Clb; 4-H; Natl FFA Org; Bsktbl; Ftbl; Trk; 4-H Awd; Hon Roll.

JOHNSEN, RAE ANN R; Emporia HS; Emporia, KS; (3); Church Yth Grp; Cmnty Wkr; Drama Clb; FCA; Teachers Aide; Band; Mrchg Band; Orch; Pep Band; School Musical; St Comp For Bnd Qurtet; Ded Awd For Chrldng; Aero.

JOHNSMEYER, BRAD K; Blue Valley Northwest HS; Overland Park, KS; (2); SADD; Ofcr Frsh Cls; Ofcr Soph Cls; Ofcr Jr Cls; Ofcr Stu Cncl; Tennis; High Hon Roll.

JOHNSON, AARON; Winfield HS; Winfield, KS; (3); 17/158; Am Leg Boys St; Boy Scts; Church Yth Grp; Debate Tm; Drama Clb; FCA; Acpl Chr; School Play; Variety Show; Yrbk.

JOHNSON, ADAM; Blue Valley HS; Olsburg, KS; (3); 4/31; Am Leg Boys St; Boy Scts; Church Yth Grp; 4-H; FHA; Natl FFA Org; Spanish Clb; Band; Mrchg Band; Pep Band; Eagle Sct; Solo-Pilots License; KS ST U; Aeronautical Engrng.

JOHNSON, AMBER R; Topeka HS; Topeka, KS; (2); Cmnty Wkr; Science Clb; Drill Tm; Vllybl; Cit Awd; Hon Roll; Ctznshp Awd; Natl Engl Awd; Hon Roll; Creighton Univ; Med.

JOHNSON, AMY; Valley Falls HS; Valley Falls, KS; (2); 1/45; FHA; Band; Chorus; Rptr Nwsp; Rptr Yrbk; Pres Frsh Cls; Pres Soph Cls; Var JV Bsktbl; Var Chrldng; L Trk; KS ST U.

JOHNSON, ANDREW C; Washburn Rural HS; Topeka, KS; (3); 47/356; Boy Scts; Church Yth Grp; Cmnty Wkr; Debate Tm; Hosp Aide; Model UN; JV Crs Cntry; Capt Swmmng; High Hon Roll; Ntl Merit Ltr; Topeka Yth Cncl VP 2 Yrs; Attnd Natl Yth Ldrshp Forum Med; Lwyr/Doc.

JOHNSON, ANGIE K; Beloit Jr Sr HS; Beloit, KS; (1); 10/90; Church Yth Grp; 4-H; Band; Chorus; Mrchg Band; Orch; Variety Show; Var L Chrldng; 4-H Awd; High Hon Roll; SADD Clb.

JOHNSON, APRIL; Campus HS; Haysville, KS; (4); 9/213; Church Yth Grp; FCA; Pres FTA; HOBY; VP Q&S; SADD; Ed Nwsp; Pres Frsh Cls; Pres Soph Cls; Treas Stu Cncl; Campus Pride VP; 2nd Tm Ark Vly Leag Vllybl; Ark Vly Leag Champ Javelin; Elem Educ.

JOHNSON, ASHLEE B; Olathe East Sr HS; Lenexa, KS; (2); Church Yth Grp; Cmnty Wkr; Spanish Clb; Bsktbl; High Hon Roll; Hon Roll; Pres Acad Fit Awd; Spanish NHS; Span Excellence Awd Frosh Awd; U Of AK; Mass Communications.

JOHNSON, BART L; Lawrence HS; Lawrence, KS; (2); JV Ftbl; JV Trk; Hon Roll; KSU.

JOHNSON, BIANCA L; Washington HS; Kansas City, KS; (2); FCA; ROTC; Band; Chorus; Color Guard; Drill Tm; Mrchg Band; Pep Band; Mgr JV Bsktbl; Trk; FL A&M; Bus.

JOHNSON, BRAD; Troy HS; Troy, KS; (2); Church Yth Grp; JV Bsktbl; JV Ftbl; JV Wt Lftg; Hon Roll; Art Awd; Highland Jr Col.

JOHNSON, BRAD; Olathe East Sr HS; Lenexa, KS; (2); 25/409; Cmnty Wkr; Letterman Clb; Math Clb; Spanish Clb; Variety Show; JV Bsktbl; JV Golf; Wt Lftg; Gov Hon Prg Awd; High Hon Roll.

JOHNSON, BRANDEN D; Jennings Schl; Jennings, KS; (1); 4/14; Church Yth Grp; Pep Clb; Band; Pep Band; School Musical; JV Bsktbl; Hon Roll; Miltry.

JOHNSON, BRANDY L; Sumner Acad Of Arts & Science; Kansas City, KS; (3); Cmnty Wkr; Debate Tm; NFL; Spanish Clb; Church Choir; Nwsp; Ed Yrbk; Ofcr Frsh Cls; Ofcr Soph Cls; Ofcr Jr Cls; NAACP Yth Chap Pres; Frnsc Ortry/Dist/ST Top 12; HOPE; Spelman Coll; Eng/Civ Lib Law.

JOHNSON, BRETT; Olathe South Sr HS; Olathe, KS; (4); Boy Scts; Church Yth Grp; HOBY; Letterman Clb; Drill Tm; Q&S; Band; Mrchg Band; Yrbk; High Hon Roll; Rtry Exch Stu 96-97; Bio-Chem.

JOHNSON, CHAD; Iola Sr HS; Iola, KS; (3); 1/125; Am Leg Boys St; Boy Scts; Church Yth Grp; French Clb; FBLA; JV Crs Cntry; JV Trk; Cit Awd; High Hon Roll; NHS; Order Of The Arrow; Zoology.

JOHNSON, COURTNEY B; Salina HS Central; Salina, KS; (3); Cmnty Wkr; Bsktbl; Sftbl; Wt Lftg; Hon Roll; Pres Acad Fit Awd; DECA; Marine Bio.

JOHNSON, DALE L; Central Heights Sr HS; Princeton, KS; (2); FCA; FBLA; Letterman Clb; Science Clb; Spanish Clb; SADD; Sec Soph Cls; Ftbl; Wt Lftg; High Hon Roll; Law Enfrcmnt.

JOHNSON, DARLA D; Wellington Sr HS; Wellington, KS; (2); Church Yth Grp; Dance Clb; French Clb; SADD; Chorus; Church Choir; Drill Tm; Rptr Stu Cncl; Hon Roll; NHS; Cowley Cty CC; Dance.

JOHNSON, DAVI A; Wichita SE Sr HS; Wichita, KS; (4); 25/250; Church Yth Grp; Debate Tm; JCL; NFL; Q&S; Speech Tm; Ed Nwsp; Trk; Hon Roll; NHS; Samford Univ; Pre Law.

JOHNSON, ELIZABETH M; Immaculata HS; Leavenworth, KS; (2); Church Yth Grp; Cmnty Wkr; Hosp Aide; Band; Mrchg Band; Pep Band; Var Chrldng; Cit Awd; Hon Roll; Prfct Atten Awd; Bio/Pediatrician.

JOHNSON, EMILY J; Shawnee Mission N HS; Shawnee Mission, KS; (4); Pep Clb; Spanish Clb; Chorus; School Play; Rep Stu Cncl; Var Capt Chrldng; Socr; Computer Clb; Hon Roll; NHS; KS St Univ.

JOHNSON, EMILY M; Baldwin HS; Baldwin City, KS; (2); Sec Church Yth Grp; Intnl Clb; Chorus; Church Choir; Orch; School Musical; Variety Show; NHS; FHA; Treas Jr Cls; Suzuki Violin.

JOHNSON, ERIC; Maize HS; Wichita, KS; (1); Cmnty Wkr; Debate Tm; NFL; Var L Crs Cntry; Var L Trk; Hon Roll; Pres Phys Ftnss Awd; Smmr Swm Tm; Frosh Cross Cntry ST Qualifier.

JOHNSON, GENA; Buhler HS; Hutchinson, KS; (4); 7/147; Am Leg Aux Girls St; Sec Church Yth Grp; Debate Tm; VP 4-H; Letterman Clb; Pres NFL; Science Clb; Service Clb; Spanish Clb; Speech Tm; KS ST U; Ortho Srgn.

JOHNSON, GEOFFREY C; Wichita Southeast HS; Wichita, KS; (4); NHS; Wichita ST Univ; Acctng.

JOHNSON, HEATHER; Columbus HS; Columbus, KS; (4); 10/92; Am Leg Aux Girls St; Church Yth Grp; Cmnty Wkr; Dance Clb; 4-H; FHA; Letterman Clb; Math Tm; Chorus; Drill Tm; Ownr Instctr Dnc Studio; Mss Colbs 96; Pttsbrg ST U; Sprts Med.

JOHNSON, HEATHER; Mc Pherson HS; Mc Pherson, KS; (3); Art Clb; DECA; French Clb; FHA; Q&S; Science Clb; Spanish Clb; SADD; Ed Yrbk; Hon Roll; Advertising; Jrnlsm.

JOHNSON, HOLLY S; Smoky Valley HS; Smolan, KS; (1); Cmnty Wkr; Dance Clb; Band; Mrchg Band; Pep Band; High Hon Roll; Hon Roll; Swedish Dancers Of Lindsborg.

JOHNSON, JACOB G; Southeast KS Spec Ed Coop; Baxter Springs, KS; (2); 1/73; Church Yth Grp; Drama Clb; FCA; FHA; Pep Clb; Scholastic Bowl; Band; Chorus; Mrchg Band; Pep Band.

JOHNSON, JACQUELINE L; Lansing HS; Lansing, KS; (4); 7/143; Drama Clb; Chorus; Stage Crew; Ed Yrbk; Treas Sr Cls; Treas Stu Cncl; JV Vllybl; High Hon Roll; Treas NHS; Ntl Merit SF; U Of KS; Med.

JOHNSON, JAMES C; Minneola Schl; Minneola, KS; (3); Church Yth Grp; FCA; Quiz Bowl; Speech Tm; Chorus; School Musical; School Play; Swing Chorus; Ofcr Stu Cncl; JV Bsktbl; His.

JOHNSON, JAMIE L; Liberal HS; Liberal, KS; (2); Drama Clb; NFL; Chorus; Hon Roll; Redskin Chorale; Actress.

JOHNSON, JASMINE B; Leavenworth HS; Newport News, VA; (2); Intnl Clb; Red Cross Aide; ROTC; Band; Srch/Rescue Trng; Vol Nrthrn VA Trng Ctr; Hnr Awd Excptnl Vol Svc; Nurse.

JOHNSON, JASMINE N; Washington HS; Kansas City, KS; (3); French Clb; Hosp Aide; Office Aide; Chorus; Prfct Atten Awd; Wichita St Univ; Elem Ed.

JOHNSON, JENNIFER; Campus HS; Wichita, KS; (4); 59/209; Art Clb; Church Yth Grp; Debate Tm; Drama Clb; Intnl Clb; NFL; Q&S; Quiz Bowl; Scholastic Bowl; Science Clb; All Star Chr Squad Chapperal Trnmnt; Friends U; Mrktng.

JOHNSON, JENNY; Valley Falls HS; Valley Falls, KS; (4); 1/31; Am Leg Aux Girls St; Band; Co-Ed Yrbk; Pres Jr Cls; Capt Chrldng; Trk; High Hon Roll; Sec NHS; St Schlr; Dance Team; KS St U; Mass Comms.

JOHNSON, JEREMIAH C; Gardner-Edgerton HS; Gardner, KS; (2); Church Yth Grp; Cmnty Wkr; 4-H; Hosp Aide; Spanish Clb; Band; Mrchg Band; Pep Band; Wrstlng; 4-H Awd; CPR Cert; Lfgrd Cert; U Of MO Columbia; Sprts Med.

JOHNSON, JEREMY; Wichita Heights HS; Wichita, KS; (4); Boy Scts; Bus Profs of Am; Church Yth Grp; Band; Mrchg Band; BSA Eagle Sct; KS ST U; Bus.

JOHNSON, JONATHAN; Olathe North Sr HS; Olathe, KS; (4); Spanish Clb; Stage Crew; High Hon Roll; Hon Roll; Pres Schlr; St Schlr; Comp-Video Game Pgm; Digipen; Video Game Prgmr.

JOHNSON, JOSEPH E; Sumner Acad Of Arts & Science; Kansas City, KS; (2); Latin Clb; Spanish Clb; SADD; Var Ftbl; Var Trk; Hon Roll; Blck/Veatch Explr Pgm; K ST; Arch/Cvl Eng.

JOHNSON, JOSLIN O; Shawnee Mission West HS; Overland Park, KS; (3); GAA; Library Aide; Quiz Bowl; Teachers Aide; Trk; Bus/Phtgrphy.

JOHNSON, JULIE; Blue Valley Northwest HS; Overland Park, KS; (2); 2/27; Church Yth Grp; Intnl Clb; Church Choir; Hon Roll; ESL Clb; Comp Engr.

JOHNSON, JUSTIN K; Troy HS; Troy, KS; (4); 2/35; Church Yth Grp; Letterman Clb; Rep Stu Cncl; Var Bsktbl; Ftbl; Wt Lftg; High Hon Roll; Sal; Govs Ctr For Teen Ldrshp; KU Hnrs Schlr; NE KS All-Star Bsktbl Game; Highland CC; Bus.

JOHNSON, KAMARA; Sumner Acad Of Arts & Science; Kansas City, KS; (3); JA; Latin Clb; Pep Clb; Spanish Clb; Acpl Chr; Chorus; Chrldng; High Hon Roll; Hon Roll; Prfct Atten Awd; Teen HOPE Ldr; Washburn U; Medcl.

JOHNSON, KARA C; Smoky Valley HS; Lindsborg, KS; (1); Church Yth Grp; FHA; Pep Clb; Chorus; School Play; Bsktbl; JV Trk; Vllybl; Psych.

JOHNSON, KATHERINE S; Holton HS; Holton, KS; (1); Art Clb; Church Yth Grp; Cmnty Wkr; 4-H; Pres FHA; Letterman Clb; Natl FFA Org; SADD; Band; Church Choir; Daycare; KSU; Vet.

JOHNSON, KELLEY; Solomon Jr Sr HS; New Cambria, KS; (3); 3/27; FHA; Letterman Clb; SADD; Band; Nwsp; Var Bsktbl; Var Sftbl; Var Vllybl; Hon Roll; NHS; Pep Band; Pep Clb; Ofc Aide; Fort Hays; Spcl Ed.

JOHNSON, KEVIN; Shawnee Mission S Sr HS; Shawnee Mission, KS; (3); Church Yth Grp; Teachers Aide; Acpl Chr; School Musical; 4-H Awd; Hon Roll; NHS; Pres Schlr; Eng.

JOHNSON, KIRK C; Blue Valley HS; Stilwell, KS; (3); 27/251; Letterman Clb; Band; Mrchg Band; Pep Band; Phtg Nwsp; Var L Bsbl; Var L Ftbl; Hon Roll; NHS; Photo; Pre-Med.

JOHNSON, KYLE; Wabaunsee HS; Maple Hill, KS; (3); 1/50; FBLA; Quiz Bowl; Pres Frsh Cls; Var L Bsbl; Var L Ftbl; Var L Tennis; Hon Roll; NHS; Air Explr Scts; Aero Engrng.

JOHNSON, LACEY; Columbus HS; Columbus, KS; (1); Church Yth Grp; 4-H; Band; Mrchg Band; Hon Roll; Pittsburg ST U; Acctng.

JOHNSON, LEANNA M; Shawnee Heights HS; Topeka, KS; (1); Church Yth Grp; Pep Clb; Band; Jazz Band; Mrchg Band; Pep Band; School Musical; JV Trk; Hon Roll; Ntl Merit Ltr; Outstdng Symphonic Band Awd Achvmt; Pen Pal South Africa; Jazz Music; KS Univ; Med; Nurse.

JOHNSON, LORRIE M; Wichita Southeast HS; Wichita, KS; (2); Church Yth Grp; FCA; Letterman Clb; NFL; Varsity Clb; Chorus; School Musical; Stage Crew; Socr; Hon Roll; UCLA; Photo.

JOHNSON, MANDY; Ellsworth HS; Ellsworth, KS; (4); 16/67; Pres Church Yth Grp; Intnl Clb; Letterman Clb; Teachers Aide; School Play; Nwsp; Yrbk; Var Bsktbl; JV Golf; JV Vllybl; Kayette Pres, Kayettel Of Yr, Head Finance; Attn KS ST Engrng, Sci Smmr Schl; Forensic Ltrd; Highland CC; Phys Thrpst.

JOHNSON, MEGAN K; Turner HS; Kansas City, KS; (2); Chess Clb; Letterman Clb; SADD; Band; Mrchg Band; Pep Band; JV L Bsktbl; Var L Crs Cntry; Var L Trk; Hon Roll.

JOHNSON, MELINDA; Little River Jr Sr HS; Little River, KS; (1); Church Yth Grp; Band; Chorus; Mrchg Band; Pep Band; Sec Bsktbl; Mgr(s); JV Vllybl; Hon Roll.

JOHNSON, MELISSA; Frankft HS; Vermillion, KS; (4); 6/29; Am Leg Aux Girls St; FHA; Office Aide; Pep Clb; SADD; Flag Corp; VP Jr Cls; Vllybl; High Hon Roll; NHS; Washburn U; Radiologic Tech.

JOHNSON, MELISSA F; Southeast HS; Wichita, KS; (3); 79/378; Teachers Aide; Band; Mrchg Band; Pep Band; Hon Roll.

JOHNSON, MICHAEL; Mulvane Sr HS; Mulvane, KS; (3); 4/135; SADD; Jazz Band; Rptr Yrbk; Rep Jr Cls; Var Bsbl; JV Bsktbl; Var Ftbl; High Hon Roll; NHS; Prfct Atten Awd; Pharmacy.

JOHNSON, MINDY L; Great Bend Sr HS; Great Bend, KS; (2); Church Yth Grp; FCA; Pep Clb; Rep Spanish Clb; Chorus; Church Choir; Variety Show; Var Chrldng; Mgr(s); Powder Puff Ftbl; KS Univ; Pre-Law.

JOHNSON, NATHAN A; Frankft HS; Vermillion, KS; (1); 4/28; Art Clb; Cmnty Wkr; Letterman Clb; Quiz Bowl; School Play; Sec Soph Cls; Stat Ftbl; Var L Golf; High Hon Roll; Hon Roll; KS ST UnivARCH Engrng.

JOHNSON, NATHAN W; Mc Pherson HS; Mc Pherson, KS; (1); Boy Scts; Band; Jazz Band; High Hon Roll; Pres Acad Fit Awd; KS ST; Cmptr Prgrmmr.

JOHNSON, NICOLE C; Derby HS; Derby, KS; (1); Church Yth Grp; SADD; Band; Nwsp; Southwestern U; Advrtsng.

JOHNSON, PAIGE; Bucklin Schl; Kingsdown, KS; (1); Church Yth Grp; FCA; Pep Clb; Pep Band; Chrldng; Vllybl; Hon Roll.

JOHNSON, PHILIP; Labette Co HS; Parsons, KS; (4); Rep Church Yth Grp; FCA; Natl FFA Org; Ed Yrbk; Rep Stu Cncl; Capt Ftbl; Wt Lftg; Capt Wrstlng; High Hon Roll; Pres Acad Fit Awd; Natl Eng Mrt Awd; St Champion Ag Sales; 800 Lb Weightlifting Clb-Bench, Squat & Poowerclean; U Of KS; Pre-Phy Therapy.

JOHNSON, RACHEL A; Baldwin HS; Lawrence, KS; (4); Art Clb; Church Yth Grp; Debate Tm; Drama Clb; Hosp Aide; Intnl Clb; Math Clb; Math Tm; NFL; Spanish Clb; Piano; U KS; Sci; Wrtng.

JOHNSON, ROBERT C; Wichita South HS; Wichita, KS; (1); Ofcr Frsh Cls; Bsktbl; Hon Roll; Producer; Dir.

JOHNSON, RYAN; Colby Sr HS; Colby, KS; (2); Church Yth Grp; Debate Tm; Math Tm; NFL; Quiz Bowl; Scholastic Bowl; Spanish Clb; Speech Tm; Intrml Var Golf; High Hon Roll.

JOHNSON, RYAN D; Uniontown HS; Bronson, KS; (2); Math Clb; Math Tm; Band; Mrchg Band; Pep Band; High Hon Roll; Ft Scott CC.

JOHNSON, SARAH D; Topeka West HS; Topeka, KS; (4); 67/234; French Clb; Band; Mrchg Band; Pep Band; Hon Roll; Baker U.

JOHNSON, SISSY K; Nickerson HS; Nickerson, KS; (3); Church Yth Grp; Cmnty Wkr; FCA; Girl Scts; JA; Key Clb; Library Aide; Pep Clb; Science Clb; Spanish Clb; KS ST; Bus.

JOHNSON, SONYA R; Moundridge HS; Moundridge, KS; (3); Pres Church Yth Grp; Debate Tm; Drama Clb; FCA; FHA; NFL; Pres Pep Clb; Teachers Aide; Chorus; Church Choir.

JOHNSON, STACY L; Olathe North Sr HS; Olathe, KS; (3); Drama Clb; Thesps; School Musical; School Play; Stage Crew; Hon Roll; Early Chldhd Ed; Photo.

JOHNSON, TAMARA; Baldwin HS; Baldwin City, KS; (4); 1/80; Band; Chorus; Mrchg Band; Orch; Pep Band; School Musical; Gov Hon Prg Awd; High Hon Roll; Hon Roll; NHS; Chrch Pianist; Sunday Schl Tchr; Baker Univ; Elem Ed.

JOHNSON, TANNER D; Smoky Valley HS; Lindsborg, KS; (1); Band; Mrchg Band; Pep Band; JV Bsktbl; JV L Tennis; High Hon Roll; Hon Roll; Math/Algbra Tchr.

JOHNSON, TIMOTHY; Olathe North Sr HS; Olathe, KS; (2); Boy Scts; Church Yth Grp; Drama Clb; Thesps; School Musical; School Play; Variety Show; Ofcr Soph Cls; Hon Roll; Wrtng Conf Nrrtn 2nd Pl; Prose Pub Lit Mag; Russian Lang/Cltr; Tchr.

JOHNSON, TRACY E; Tescott HS; Culver, KS; (3); Pep Clb; Quiz Bowl; Teachers Aide; Varsity Clb; Band; Drill Tm; Mrchg Band; Pep Band; Bsktbl; Trk; Beech Air Club.

JOHNSON, VERONICA B; Immaculata HS; Leavenworth, KS; (2); #14 in class; Am Leg Aux Girls St; Church Yth Grp; Cmnty Wkr; Girl Scts; Intnl Clb; Spanish Clb; Band; Church Choir; Mrchg Band; Pep Band; Girl Sct Silver Awd; Guild Audition Music Awd; Howard Univ; Fertility Dctr.

JOHNSON, VIVIENNE P; Bishop Ward HS; Kansas City, KS; (3); Church Yth Grp; Drama Clb; Hosp Aide; Office Aide; SADD; Drill Tm; Pom Pon; Vllybl; Hon Roll; KS ST Univ; Vet.

JOHNSTON, ALANA; Riley Cty HS; Riley, KS; (2); 7/62; Drama Clb; FCA; VP FHA; Pep Clb; SADD; Mrchg Band; Pep Band; School Play; Var Chrldng; Hon Roll.

JOHNSTON, BETH; Enterprise Sda Acad; Abilene, KS; (4); 1/20; Church Yth Grp; Band; School Play; Ed Nwsp; Ed Yrbk; Rep Sr Cls; Rep Stu Cncl; High Hon Roll; Prfct Atten Awd; Union Coll; Phys Thrpy.

JOHNSTON, JEREMY D; Garden City Sr HS; Garden City, KS; (4); 72/313; Church Yth Grp; FCA; JV Bsbl; Capt L Bsktbl; High Hon Roll; Hon Roll; Jr NHS; 1st Tms All Leag & All Area Bsktbl 95-96; Top 10 All Time 3 Pt Percentage Fld Goals & No 1 St 95-96; Bus.

JOHNSTON, KELLI; Washburn Rural HS; Topeka, KS; (4); Church Yth Grp; Cmnty Wkr; FCA; Girl Scts; SADD; Yrbk; L Bsktbl; L Golf; Powder Puff Ftbl; Score Keeper; Golf City/League/Regnl Champion Num Awd-Achvmts; Girls Golf All ST 93-94; Runner-Up 95-; KS ST.

JOHNSTON, KIMBERLY; Independence HS; Independence, KS; (4); 40/139; Church Yth Grp; JA; SADD; Band; Color Guard; Mrchg Band; Sftbl; Vllybl; Hon Roll; NHS; Pittsburg ST U; Elem Ed.

JOHNSTON, MATTHEW A; El Dorado HS; El Dorado, KS; (3); 1/145; Am Leg Boys St; Debate Tm; Letterman Clb; Math Clb; Yrbk; Var Bsktbl; Var Ftbl; Var Trk; High Hon Roll; NHS; Engrng.

JOHNSTON, NATHAN T; Washburn Rural HS; Topeka, KS; (4); Debate Tm; JA; NFL; Orch; Lit Mag; High Hon Roll; Ntl Merit Ltr; Flimmaking; Screenwrtng; Music Compostion; U Southern CA; Filmmaking.

JOHNSTON, SHAWN; Elwood USD 486; Saint Joseph, MO; (3); #3 in class; HOBY; Library Aide; Quiz Bowl; Teachers Aide; Band; Chorus; Ed Nwsp; Ed Yrbk; Rep Frsh Cls; Rep Soph Cls; Peer Power Prog; HI Pacific U.

JOHNSTONE, JEREMY S; Wichita Southeast HS; Wichita, KS; (3); 183/480; Debate Tm; Math Tm; Quiz Bowl; Scholastic Bowl; Science Clb; Ftbl; 2nd Pl Pittsburg ST Math Relays; Japanese Club; ST Pres NSCAR; WSU; Cmptr Engr.

JOLLEY, CHARLES A; Sumner Acad Of Arts & Science; Kansas City, KS; (3); Church Yth Grp; French Clb; JA; Science Clb; Stage Crew; Variety Show; Ed Nwsp; Ed Yrbk; High Hon Roll; Hon Roll; UMKC Math Sci Prgm; Gspl Magcn; Cmptr Hrdwr, Oper Desgn/Neurl Ntwrks Resrch; Mid-Amer Nazarene Coll; Cmptr E.

JOLLIFF, SASHA; Wichita South HS; Wichita, KS; (4); Church Yth Grp; Cmnty Wkr; Teachers Aide; Nwsp; Yrbk; Chrldng; Mgr(s); Vllybl; High Hon Roll; Hon Roll; Friends U; Bio.

JONES, ADAM R; Smoky Valley HS; Marquette, KS; (1); Var L Bsktbl; Var JV Ftbl; High Hon Roll; Hon Roll; Sports Medicine.

JONES, ADRIAN; Wyandotte HS; Kansas City, KS; (4); 6/198; Pres Computer Clb; Ed Yrbk; Ofcr Jr Cls; Ofcr Sr Cls; Ofcr Stu Cncl; High Hon Roll; Hon Roll; NHS; Presdntl Schlrshp; Comp Sci Dept Tchr Asst; Multiple Yr Listing; NW MO ST U; Comp Pgm.

JONES, AIMEE L; Shawnee Heights Sr HS; Berryton, KS; (4); Library Aide; Pep Clb; SADD; Chorus; Drill Tm; Pom Pon; Hon Roll; Washburn Univ; Bus.

JONES, AMBER; Minneola Schl; Minneola, KS; (1); Dance Clb; FCA; GAA; Girl Scts; Math Tm; Pep Clb; Scholastic Bowl; Band; Chorus; Jazz Band; Washburn; Soc Wrk.

JONES, AMIE D; Derby HS; Derby, KS; (3); Art Clb; Cmnty Wkr; Drama Clb; Key Clb; Orch; Vllybl; Hon Roll; Stdnt Of Month; Panther All Star; Butler CC; Drug Enfcrmt Agcy.

JONES, ANDRENA; Maize HS; Wichita, KS; (3); Drama Clb; Office Aide; Spanish Clb; Teachers Aide; Thesps; School Play; Stage Crew; Hon Roll; Med.

JONES, ANGELA D; Augusta Sr HS; Augusta, KS; (2); French Clb; Band; Mrchg Band; Orch; Pep Band; Hon Roll; U Of KS; Archt.

JONES, ASHLEE L; Blue Valley Northwest HS; Overland Park, KS; (2); Church Yth Grp; Cmnty Wkr; Band; Chorus; Mrchg Band; Pep Band; School Musical; School Play; Mgr(s); Hon Roll; Sample Writing English Finals; Tai Kwon Do; Person To Person Awd 95; Univ Of KS.

JONES, BRANDEN L; Smoky Valley HS; Lindsborg, KS; (2); Church Yth Grp; Cmnty Wkr; Band; Ftbl; Trk; Hon Roll; Chrch Yth Srmns.

JONES, BRENT; El Dorado HS; El Dorado, KS; (3); 4-H; Teachers Aide; Bsktbl; Var JV Ftbl; Wt Lftg; 4-H Awd; Hon Roll; 4-H Cty Fair Grand Chmpn Steer Showing 95; 4-H Clb VP; Butler Cty CC; Animal Sci.

JONES, CATHERINE; Mulvane Sr HS; Mulvane, KS; (3); 1/100; Church Yth Grp; St Schlr; Sec SADD; Acpl Chr; Chorus; Treas Frsh Cls; Sec Stu Cncl; High Hon Roll; NHS; Prfct Atten Awd; Scndry Ed.

JONES, CHRISTI L; Haven HS; Mount Hope, KS; (3); Chorus; Hon Roll; Psychlgst.

JONES, CHRISTOPHER R; Emporia HS; Emporia, KS; (2); Intrml Bsktbl; Intrml Golf; Gym; Wt Lftg; High Hon Roll; Prfct Atten Awd; KS ST; Engrng.

JONES, DEREK A; Atchison Sr HS; Atchison, KS; (1); Band; Mrchg Band; Pep Band; JV Bsbl; JV Ftbl; Var Wrstlng; High Hon Roll; KS ST Univ.

JONES, DIANA L; Pleasant Ridge HS; Easton, KS; (4); 8/64; FCA; 4-H; FBLA; Letterman Clb; SADD; School Play; Chrldng; High Hon Roll; NHS; Pres Acad Fit Awd; Union Coll; Scndry Ed; Acctng.

JONES, DORY A; Wichita North HS; Wichita, KS; (4); 1/230; Cmnty Wkr; SADD; Acpl Chr; Chorus; Jazz Band; Orch; School Musical; Variety Show; Ofcr Stu Cncl; Cit Awd; Wichita Yth Symph Orch; Usher Drctr For Wichita Symph Orch; WI St Univ; Mus.

JONES, EMMA R; Junction City HS; Milford, KS; (2); Church Yth Grp; Hosp Aide; Pep Clb; Temple Yth Grp; Band; Chorus; Church Choir; Mrchg Band; Stage Crew; BYU.

JONES, GREG L; Chapman HS; Chapman, KS; (3); 5/97; Am Leg Boys St; Bsktbl; Ftbl; Trk; Wt Lftg; High Hon Roll; NHS; Prfct Atten Awd; Acad Ltr; I Dare You Awd; Schlr Ath Awd; Outstndng Schlstc Achvt Awd; Ftbl All Lg Hnrbl Mntn; KS ST U; Bus.

JONES, HEATHER E; Neodesha Jr Sr HS; Independence, KS; (1); Tennis; Trk.

JONES, JACQUEE L; Salina HS Central; Salina, KS; (2); Church Yth Grp; Debate Tm; FCA; Teachers Aide; JV Bsktbl; Var L Trk; JV Vllybl; Hon Roll; UPC; CO U; Tchr; Coach.

JONES, JALEAH D; Blue Valley HS; Overland Park, KS; (3); Church Yth Grp; Chorus; Church Choir; Orch; School Musical; High Hon Roll; Hon Roll; NHS; Johnson Cnty CC; Bus.

JONES, JANEY D; Conway Springs HS; Conway Springs, KS; (2); Drama Clb; Drill Tm; Ofcr Soph Cls; Bsktbl; Pom Pon; Powder Puff Ftbl; Vllybl; Wt Lftg.

JONES, JEFFREY R; Bishop Miege HS; Merriam, KS; (1); 51/245; Boy Scts; Cmnty Wkr; Debate Tm; Spanish Clb; Trk; Wrstlng; High Hon Roll; Hon Roll; Eagle Scout; Cngrsnl Mdl; Spirit Club; Air Force Acad.

JONES, JENNA; Olathe South Sr HS; Olathe, KS; (2); Dance Clb; Letterman Clb; Pep Clb; Teachers Aide; Ofcr Frsh Cls; Ofcr Soph Cls; Chrldng; Powder Puff Ftbl; Trk; Hon Roll; Dance.

JONES, JEREMIAH B; Olathe East Sr HS; Olathe, KS; (3); Church Yth Grp; Computer Clb; French Clb; Spanish Clb; Teachers Aide; Wt Lftg; High Hon Roll; Local Co Art Dir; Baptist Bible Coll; Chem Engrng.

JONES, JEREMY; Campus HS; Wichita, KS; (1); Intnl Clb; JV Ftbl; Wt Lftg; JV Wrstlng; High Hon Roll; Prins Hnr Roll.

JONES, JILL; Lebo Schl; Reading, KS; (4); 2/23; Church Choir; Rptr Nwsp; Sec Soph Cls; VP Sr Cls; Pres Stu Cncl; Var L Bsktbl; High Hon Roll; VP NHS; Sal; St Schlr; Triple Trio; Emporia ST Univ; Sec Ed.

JONES, JOSH; Northwest HS; Wichita, KS; (3); 40/327; Am Leg Boys St; Cmnty Wkr; Intnl Clb; Math Clb; Teachers Aide; Intrml Ftbl; Var L Tennis; High Hon Roll; NHS; KS ST Univ; Comp Sci.

JONES, KARRA A; Santa Fe Trail Jr HS; Wichita, KS; (1); Dance Clb; Drama Clb; Pep Clb; Scholastic Bowl; Spanish Clb; Temple Yth Grp; Capt Drill Tm; School Play; Stage Crew; Swing Chorus; Brown Coll; Lawyer; Psychiatrist.

JONES, KATIE A; Bishop Miege HS; Roeland Park, KS; (3); 81/170; Church Yth Grp; Cmnty Wkr; Spanish Clb; Yrbk; Lit Mag; JV Var Socr; High Hon Roll; Hon Roll.

JONES, KATIE K; Wichita Southeast HS; Wichita, KS; (2); Church Yth Grp; Drama Clb; Band; Church Choir; Mrchg Band; Stage Crew; Rep Jr Cls; Hon Roll; Mssns Tm; Friends Univ.

JONES, KAY; Colby Sr HS; Colby, KS; (3); Church Yth Grp; Library Aide; Science Clb; Service Clb; Spanish Clb; Hon Roll; Spanish NHS.

JONES, KEISHA; Wichita Collegiate Schl; Wichita, KS; (3); Chorus; School Play; Ed Lit Mag; High Hon Roll; Fay Family Awd; Natl Frnch Exam Plcr; Med.

JONES, KRISTI L; Oswego HS; Parsons, KS; (3); 4/30; Am Leg Aux Girls St; FCA; FHA; Math Tm; Pres Stu Cncl; Var Bsktbl; Var Capt Chrldng; Sftbl; Vllybl; High Hon Roll; Pittsburg Univ; Nrsng-Trama.

JONES, KYLE M; Norton Comm HS; Norton, KS; (4); 14/43; Boy Scts; Church Yth Grp; Cmnty Wkr; Pep Clb; Teachers Aide; Var L Golf; Var Wt Lftg; Var L Wrstlng; High Hon Roll; Prfct Atten Awd; Auto Racing; Fishing; Barton Cty CC; Fire Sci Tech.

JONES, LATOYA D; Shawnee Mission N HS; Overland Park, KS; (3); 121/329; Church Yth Grp; Cmnty Wkr; Key Clb; Pep Clb; Spanish Clb; Rep Jr Cls; Pres Sr Cls; Hon Roll; Inroads; KS St Univ; Textile Mktng.

JONES, LESLIE C; Washington HS; Kansas City, KS; (2); Debate Tm; Pep Clb; Church Choir; Drill Tm; Orch; Bsktbl; Hon Roll; Forensics Tm; Sec For Debate Forensic Tm; Debate Novice Of Yr; Lawyer.

JONES, LYNN; J C Harmon HS; Kansas City, KS; (2); Drama Clb; Pep Clb; SADD; School Musical; School Play; Stage Crew; Swing Chorus; Ofcr Frsh Cls; Chrldng; Crs Cntry; Peer Natural Helpers; U KS; Nrs.

JONES, MANDY R; Piper HS; Kansas City, KS; (4); Church Yth Grp; FHA; Library Aide; Spanish Clb; JV Bsktbl; JV Chrldng; JV Vllybl; Cit Awd; High Hon Roll; Hon Roll; Hnrbl Mntn ST Comp For Fed Jr Duck Stamp; Pres Schlsp KCKCC; KCKCC.

JONES, MICHELLE M; Goddard HS; Wichita, KS; (1); Church Yth Grp; Pep Clb; SADD; Band; Drill Tm; Mrchg Band; Orch; Pep Band; School Play; Variety Show; Wind Ensembles Goddard; Wichita Wind Ensemble.

JONES, NATALIE R; Shawnee Mission S Sr HS; Shawnee Mission, KS; (3); 23/440; Pres Church Yth Grp; Debate Tm; Pep Clb; Band; Church Choir; Mrchg Band; Orch; Ed Yrbk; High Hon Roll; Ntl Merit Ltr; Flute St Comp Rtng I, 1st Chr Dist I Bnd; 1st Pl Dist I KS Jrnlsm Comp Cutln Wrtng; Jrnlsm.

JONES, NIKIA M; Junction City HS; Fort Riley, KS; (2); 5/277; Dance Clb; Debate Tm; Chorus; Mrchg Band; Rep Frsh Cls; Rep Soph Cls; Capt Chrldng; High Hon Roll; NHS; Peer Mediator; All Dist Awd; All Amer Schlr; Pre Law.

JONES, PATRICK; Wyandotte HS; Kansas City, KS; (3); Church Yth Grp; Cmnty Wkr; FHA; Math Tm; Office Aide; Teachers Aide; Church Choir; Bsktbl; Hon Roll.

JONES, RANDEE L; Chase Co HS; Cottonwood Falls, KS; (3); Church Yth Grp; Cmnty Wkr; 4-H; Scholastic Bowl; Spanish Clb; Chorus; School Play; Var Bsktbl; Var Sftbl; Var Vllybl; Rec Cmssn Yth Coach For Bsktbl & Vllybl; Lifeguard; Swim Instr; Massage Thrpst.

JONES, RHIANNON C; Derby HS; Derby, KS; (1); Church Yth Grp; FCA; Band; Mrchg Band; Pep Band; Ofcr Frsh Cls; Hon Roll; Cal Poly.

JONES, ROBERT D; Junction City HS; Milford, KS; (3); Spanish Clb; SADD; JV Wrstlng; Cit Awd; Hon Roll; KS ST Univ.

JONES, SANDY L; Chanute Sr HS; Chanute, KS; (2); Drama Clb; Lit Mag; Bsktbl; Sftbl; Vllybl; Wt Lftg; Drama Hnrs & Awds For Best Set & Acting.

JONES, SARAH J; Wichita Northwest HS; Wichita, KS; (2); 40/360; Art Clb; Cmnty Wkr; Girl Scts; Intnl Clb; High Hon Roll; Hon Roll; Nalt Art Hnrs Soc Sec; KS ST Univ; Aeronautical Engr.

JONES, SHEINELLE; Wichita Heights HS; Wichita, KS; (4); 9/242; Rptr Nwsp; Pres Frsh Cls; Pres Soph Cls; Rep Stu Cncl; Capt Chrldng; Cit Awd; High Hon Roll; NHS; St Schlr; NAACP Yth Cncl; Peer Ldrshp; Jack & Jill America Inc; Northwestern U; Jrnlsm.

JONES, STACY; Mulvane Sr HS; Mulvane, KS; (3); SADD; Teachers Aide; Chorus; NHS; Prfct Atten Awd; Pres Acad Fit Awd; Sun Schl Tchr; KSU; Vet.

JONES, TEMPRESS N; Northeast Magnet HS; Wichita, KS; (2); Bus Profs of Am; Church Yth Grp; Cmnty Wkr; FCA; Girl Scts; JA; Pep Clb; Red Cross Aide; Church Choir; Drill Tm; Washburn Law Schl; Law.

JONES, TRENT; Lebo Schl; Lebo, KS; (3); 16/27; Am Leg Boys St; Boy Scts; Natl FFA Org; Var L Bsktbl; Var L Ftbl; Var L Trk; Hon Roll; KS Shrine Bowl Team Mgr 95.

JONES, WALTON; Olathe South Sr HS; Olathe, KS; (3); Church Yth Grp; HOBY; Quiz Bowl; Scholastic Bowl; Lit Mag; Spanish Clb; High Hon Roll; NHS; Ntl Merit SF; Spanish NHS; Photo; Harmnca; Guitar; Wheaton Coll; Med.

JONES, WAYLON L; Glasco HS; Glasco, KS; (2); Church Yth Grp; Quiz Bowl; Sec Soph Cls; JV Bsktbl; Var Golf; Wt Lftg; Hon Roll.

JORDAN, JEREMY M; Chanute Sr HS; Chanute, KS; (2); Church Yth Grp; FCA; Chorus; JV Bsktbl; L Ftbl; JV Trk; Hon Roll; Auburn; Cmptr Prgmr.

JORDAN, JUSTIN B; Goddard HS; Goddard, KS; (1); Band; Mrchg Band; Cit Awd; High Hon Roll; Pres Acad Fit Awd; Natl Sci Mrt/Sci Olympd Awds; Cmptv Soccer.

JORDAN, KARI; Independence HS; Independence, KS; (1); Speech Tm; Orch; School Musical; Chrldng; Hon Roll; Forensics Sqd; Sftbl & Vllybl; ICC; Vet.

JORDAN, LARIESHA C; Wyandotte HS; Kansas City, KS; (2); Church Yth Grp; Cmnty Wkr; Pep Clb; Acpl Chr; Church Choir; Trk; Hon Roll; NHS; Opera Perf; Explr Clb; Howard Univ; Med.

JORDAN, MAJA A; Olathe East Sr HS; Olathe, KS; (3); 23/374; Pres Band; Jazz Band; Pres Mrchg Band; Ed Yrbk; Rep Stu Cncl; Var Trk; High Hon Roll; NHS; Pres Acad Fit Awd; Pres Schlr; Al Amer Schlr; USNAA; KSHSAA; Baker Univ; Bio; Chem.

JORDAN, SHAUNDA T; Junction City HS; Fort Riley, KS; (3); 27/300; Church Yth Grp; Debate Tm; Red Cross Aide; Intrml Bsktbl; High Hon Roll; Ofcr Jr Cls; JV Trk; JV Vllybl; Hon Roll; Prfct Atten Awd; KAPPA; U Of Central FL; Pre-Law.

JORDON, J JOSHUA; Emporia HS; Emporia, KS; (3); 1/300; Science Clb; SADD; Rep Soph Cls; Rep Jr Cls; Rep Sr Cls; Rep Stu Cncl; Var JV Bsktbl; High Hon Roll; NHS; Boy Scts; KS Regents Hnr Acad; Gifted Prgm; Stdnt Mvmnt In Ldrshp; U Of KS.

JORGENSEN, SARAH E; Brewster Schl; Brewster, KS; (4); Church Yth Grp; Band; Pres Frsh Cls; VP Soph Cls; Pres Jr Cls; VP Sr Cls; VP Stu Cncl; Var Capt Bsktbl; Var Trk; Var Capt Vllybl; KS Assn/Yth; Colby CC; Pre-Med.

JOURNAGAN, REBECCA; Goddard HS; Wichita, KS; (4); 4/140; Church Yth Grp; Hosp Aide; SADD; Chorus; Church Choir; Sec Stu Cncl; High Hon Roll; NHS; Pres Schlr; Madrigals; Dist/ST Hon Choir; Recvd I Rating At Regnl/ST Solo Contest; Coca Cola Olympic Trch Choir; Wichita ST U; Physcn Asst.

JOY, JAY; Hillcrest Schl; Cuba, KS; (2); 1/9; FHA; Quiz Bowl; Scholastic Bowl; Band; Chorus; Jazz Band; Mrchg Band; Pep Band; Rep Soph Cls; High Hon Roll; FFA; CYO; KS ST U; Vet Med.

JOYCE, JASON T; Washburn Rural HS; Topeka, KS; (3); Cmnty Wkr; Speech Tm; Pres Frsh Cls; Rep Stu Cncl; Var Bsktbl; Var Trk; High Hon Roll; Macys Schlr; Natl Yth Ldrshp Med Forum; Med.

JOYNER, MACKALE R; Sumner Acad; Kansas City, KS; (3); 13/150; Church Yth Grp; Cmnty Wkr; French Clb; Church Choir; Rep Sr Cls; Var L Bsktbl; Crs Cntry; French Hon Soc; High Hon Roll; Jr NHS; Black Data Processing Assn Pgm; Natl Comp Cmptn; AAU Bsktbl; United Way Vol; Tutor; Sunday Schl Treas; MIT; Comp Sci.

JUAREZ, KRISTINA R; Shawnee Mission Northwest HS; Shawnee Mission, KS; (3); 85/435; Church Yth Grp; Pres 4-H; Intnl Clb; NFL; Service Clb; Rptr Nwsp; JV Vllybl; 4-H Awd; NHS; Pub Rltns Prsn Cougars United; Stu Response Team; Intl Bus.

JUENEMAN, DANIEL L; Hanover Schl; Hollenberg, KS; (3); 7/17; Church Yth Grp; Letterman Clb; Natl FFA Org; SADD; Teachers Aide; VP Frsh Cls; Rep Jr Cls; Rep Sr Cls; Rep Stu Cncl; Var L Bsktbl.

JUENEMAN, KAYLIN A; Hanover Schl; Hollenberg, KS; (3); 1/17; Am Leg Aux Girls St; Drama Clb; FHA; Natl FFA Org; Speech Tm; Band; Pres Soph Cls; Pres Jr Cls; High Hon Roll; NHS; St IA Extmprns Spkng 2nd Pl; Kent ST; Comms.

JUENEMAN, KOYLIN; Hanover Schl; Hollenberg, KS; (3); 1/17; Am Leg Aux Girls St; Drama Clb; FHA; Letterman Clb; Natl FFA Org; Band; Pres Jr Cls; Pres Sr Cls; High Hon Roll; NHS; 2nd 1a ST Extmprns Spkng; 2nd Soil Cnsrvtn Pub Spkng Area Cntst; 1st Dist BVL Hnr Band; KS ST; Comms.

JUENEMAN, MARK; Hanover Schl; Hanover, KS; (4); 5/23; Church Yth Grp; Natl FFA Org; SADD; Rptr Nwsp; Ed Yrbk; VP Frsh Cls; Ofcr Jr Cls; Rep Stu Cncl; JV Ftbl; JV Trk; Knghts Clmbs; Son Amer Leg; Cloud Cty CC; Bus Admin.

JUFFA, LAURA B; Blue Valley Northwest HS; Overland Park, KS; (2); 1/430; Church Yth Grp; FCA; Varsity Clb; VP Jr Cls; Bsktbl; Trk; Vllybl; High Hon Roll.

JUHL, BRIANA; Wathena Schl; Wathena, KS; (3); Chorus; School Play; Yrbk; Sec Rep Stu Cncl; JV Bsktbl; JV Vllybl; Cit Awd; High Hon Roll; NHS; Bus Clb Sec; Medcl Trnscrptnst.

JUHNKE, BEN N; Wichita Southeast HS; Wichita, KS; (2); Church Yth Grp; Drama Clb; Orch; Stage Crew; Hon Roll; KS ST Univ; Movie Dir.

JUHNKE, STACY D; Buhler HS; Buhler, KS; (4); Church Yth Grp; Drama Clb; FCA; Library Aide; NFL; Office Aide; Pep Clb; Spanish Clb; SADD; Teachers Aide; Tchrs Choice Awd; Tabor Coll; Mission; Drama.

JUILLERAT, LAURA A; Cair Paravel - Latin Schl; Topeka, KS; (3); Teachers Aide; Acpl Chr; Var Capt Bsktbl; Var Capt Vllybl; High Hon Roll; Hon Roll; Ballet; Acctng.

JULIAN, NICOLE D; Yates Ctr HS; Yates Center, KS; (2); Art Clb; FCA; FHA; Letterman Clb; Spanish Clb; SADD; Chorus; JV Bsktbl; Intrml Powder Puff Ftbl; Var Sftbl; Emporia ST; Bio.

JUNE-FRIESEN, KATY M; Newton Sr HS; Newton, KS; (2); Art Clb; Church Yth Grp; German Clb; Model UN; Band; Church Choir; Mrchg Band; Orch; Ed Lit Mag; Vllybl; Dance Ballet & Jazz; Future Problem Solving; Music Cont Solo & Ensembls; KMEA; Arts.

JUNGEL, SCOTT L; Solomon Jr Sr HS; New Cambria, KS; (2); 1/50; Natl FFA Org; SADD; Var Bsktbl; High Hon Roll; Prfct Atten Awd; FFA Cnvtn; K ST; Cmptr Sci.

JUST, CHRISTY; Wichita South HS; Wichita, KS; (2); Church Yth Grp; Dance Clb; Pep Clb; Teachers Aide; Rep Stu Cncl; Var L Chrldng; Hon Roll; Elem HS/TCHR Prin.

JUST, KRISTYN R; Garden City Sr HS; Garden City, KS; (1); Orch; Chrldng; Sftbl; High Hon Roll.

KABA, MELANIE J; Topeka HS; Topeka, KS; (4); 37/370; Drama Clb; French Clb; Model UN; NFL; Thesps; Chorus; Drill Tm; School Play; Variety Show; Nwsp; Fash Inst Of Tech; Int Dsgn.

KABERLINE, LACEY; Shawnee Heights HS; Topeka, KS; (3); FBLA; Key Clb; SADD; Teachers Aide; L Var Chrldng; Hon Roll; Miss KS Teen USA Pageant Participant; Emporia ST Univ; Tchr; Commnctn.

KABRIEL, CHRIS; Valley Falls HS; Ozawkie, KS; (4); 4/35; Am Leg Boys St; Cmnty Wkr; FHA; Teachers Aide; Band; Pep Band; Phtg Nwsp; Phtg Yrbk; Pres Soph Cls; VP Jr Cls; Hmcmng King; Cmnty Svc Yth Advsry Cncl; DEFALT & DARE; KS ST U; Comp Engr.

KACZOCHA, ELIZABETH S; Rose Hill HS; Derby, KS; (3); Debate Tm; Chorus; School Musical; Stage Crew; Variety Show; Hon Roll; 7 Poems Pblshd.

KADAKIA, BIMAL R; Blue Valley HS; Overland Park, KS; (4); 25/230; French Clb; Scholastic Bowl; Ed Yrbk; High Hon Roll; Hon Roll; NHS; Prfct Atten Awd; Pres Schlr; St Schlr; Mntrshp Acad Prgm; Univ Of KS; Chem/Med.

KAFER, RILIE; Highland HS; White Cloud, KS; (2); Pep Clb; Band; Chorus; Mrchg Band; Pep Band; School Musical; Pres Soph Cls; Rep Stu Cncl; High Hon Roll; NHS; SOS.

KAFKA, ZANETA; Goodland HS; Goodland, KS; (3); 1/85; Church Yth Grp; Band; Chorus; Flag Corp; Jazz Band; School Musical; Rep Stu Cncl; High Hon Roll; NHS; Ntl Merit SF; Music Ministry.

KAGAN, JENNIFER A; Blue Valley Northwest HS; Shawnee Mission, KS; (4); Cmnty Wkr; Drama Clb; Q&S; Stage Crew; Rptr Nwsp; High Hon Roll; Hon Roll; NHS; KS City Cncl Bnai Brith Yth Org Pres; NY Univ.

KAHLE, LINDA; Buhler HS; Hutchinson, KS; (3); 57/168; Computer Clb; FCA; Letterman Clb; Q&S; Science Clb; Spanish Clb; SADD; Yrbk; Intrml Powder Puff Ftbl; JV L Sftbl; Graphic Arts; Ad Dsgn.

KAHRS, STACY; Clay Ctr Cmty HS; Clay Center, KS; (3); 9/99; Church Yth Grp; Debate Tm; Drama Clb; Science Clb; Chorus; Orch; Var Crs Cntry; Var Trk; High Hon Roll; Pres NHS; Nrsng.

KAISER, AARON P; Great Bend Sr HS; Great Bend, KS; (1); Band; Mrchg Band; Pep Band; Crs Cntry; Swmmng; Trk; High Hon Roll.

KAISER, AMANDA; Buhler HS; Hutchinson, KS; (3); Church Yth Grp; Debate Tm; FCA; Science Clb; SADD; Varsity Clb; Band; Chorus; Color Guard; Flag Corp; KS Univ; Phy Thrpst.

KAISER, JEREMY D; Chase HS; Raymond, KS; (2); Pep Clb; Var Bsktbl; Var Ftbl; Wt Lftg; Hon Roll.

KAISER, KELLY; Paola HS; Paola, KS; (3); 13/127; Am Leg Boys St; Church Yth Grp; Cmnty Wkr; VP Rptr Natl FFA Org; Quiz Bowl; Teachers Aide; JV Var Ftbl; 4-H Awd; High Hon Roll; NHS; KS ST Univ; Agronomy.

KAISER, KELLY J; Great Bend Sr HS; Great Bend, KS; (3); 3/250; Pep Clb; Var Bsbl; Cls 5-A St Bsbl Champs 95 & Shortstop Hnrb Mntn.

KAISER, RYAN J; Great Bend Sr HS; Great Bend, KS; (4); 4/217; Spanish Clb; Ofcr Bsbl; Wt Lftg; High Hon Roll; NHS; Prfct Atten Awd; Pres Acad Fit Awd; Span Clb Pres; Kays Clb; Co-Ed Sftbl; IM Bsktbl; KS ST Univ; Chem.

KAISER, SCOTT D; Shawnee Mission S Sr HS; Shawnee Mission, KS; (4); 20/413; Am Leg Boys St; Pres Church Yth Grp; Debate Tm; Math Tm; Model UN; NFL; Jazz Band; High Hon Roll; Hon Roll; NHS; NFL Stu Congress Natl Qualifier; John C Stennis Stu Congress 10th Pl Superhouse; U Of KS; Engrng; Law.

KALAL, AMANDA JO; Derby HS; Wichita, KS; (2); Hon Roll; NHS; Future Problem Solving Team Qualified For St; KS ST U; Elem Tchr.

KALENDER, JESSICA; Blue Valley North HS; Leawood, KS; (2); Hosp Aide; Temple Yth Grp; Band; Mrchg Band; Pep Band; Rptr Yrbk; Sftbl; Hon Roll.

KALLENBERGER, LORA; Wichita Heights HS; Kechi, KS; (3); 25/250; Cmnty Wkr; Teachers Aide; Var Trk; Hon Roll; NHS; Ed.

KALOUS, DARIN; Junction City HS; Junction City, KS; (4); Am Leg Boys St; Ftbl; Golf; Natl Math/Acad Awds; I-70 Acad Awd; KS ST Univ; Cmptr Engr/Sci.

KALTENBACH, ERIN L; Ashland HS; Ashland, KS; (2); Church Yth Grp; Cmnty Wkr; 4-H; Pep Clb; Quiz Bowl; Scholastic Bowl; Stage Crew; Ofcr Stu Cncl; JV Var Bsktbl; Powder Puff Ftbl; Lwyr/HS His Tchr.

KALUSHA, JANA L; Olathe East Sr HS; Overland Park, KS; (2); Cmnty Wkr; Pep Clb; Spanish Clb; Drill Tm; Pom Pon; Trk; Most Impvd Hstry; Hnrbl Mtn All Amer Drill Tm; Tech/Outstdng Achvmnt Dance Awds; Bio.

KAMBAMPATI, VIKRAM; Wichita East HS; Wichita, KS; (3); Boy Scts; Spanish Clb; SADD; JV Bsbl; Hon Roll; NHS; Ntl Merit Ltr; Natl Art Hon Soc; Pre Med/Art.

KAMLOWSKY, KATIE A; Blue Valley North HS; Leawood, KS; (2); 13/231; Church Yth Grp; Cmnty Wkr; Model UN; JV Tennis; High Hon Roll; Hon Roll; Inner Delta Clb; Yng Life; St Of KS Schol Cntst.

KAMM, CHRISTINA; Desoto HS; Shawnee Mission, KS; (4); 7/111; SADD; Thesps; Ed Yrbk; Treas Soph Cls; Treas Jr Cls; Treas Sr Cls; High Hon Roll; NHS; Pres Acad Fit Awd; Snflwr Grls St.

KANAREK, STEVEN T; Blue Valley Northwest HS; Overland Park, KS; (1); High Hon Roll; Prfct Atten Awd; Acad Exclnc Cmptr Tech; Vol LIT For Jewish Comm Ctr; KU; Allergist.

KANAVY, ANNA C; Newton Sr HS; Newton, KS; (2); Church Yth Grp; Orch; High Hon Roll; Puppets.

KANE, BRIAN D; Dodge City HS; Dodge City, KS; (3); Church Yth Grp; FCA; Office Aide; Var Bsbl; Var Bsktbl; Var Ftbl; Var Golf; Wt Lftg; High Hon Roll; NHS; Acctg.

KANE, CANDACE; Atchison Sr HS; Atchison, KS; (4); 16/250; Art Clb; Bus Profs of Am; Church Yth Grp; Drama Clb; Band; Church Choir; School Musical; School Play; JV Chrldng; High Hon Roll; NEKA; Data Prcsng.

KANNGIESSER, CASSIE M; Maize HS; Wichita, KS; (2); German Clb; JV Sftbl; Hon Roll; Sec.

KANOST, LAURA M; Manhattan HS; Manhattan, KS; (3); FTA; Spanish Clb; Band; Church Choir; Mrchg Band; Orch; School Musical; Gym; High Hon Roll; NHS; KS St Univ; Ed.

KARBER, KAYLA; Southeast Saline Schl; Gypsum, KS; (4); Art Clb; Dance Clb; 4-H; FHA; Pep Clb; Chorus; School Play; Pom Pon; 4-H Awd; Hon Roll; All Amer Danz Team Mem Nom; Miss Topeka Teen USA; Talent Wnnr & 3rd Rnnr Up Qn Amer Coed Pageant; Wichita ST Univ; Fshn Dsgn.

KARLESKINT, JOSEPH D; Ft Scott HS; Fort Scott, KS; (2); Chorus; School Musical; Pres Frsh Cls; Ofcr Stu Cncl; Var Bsbl; Var Bsktbl; Var Ftbl; Hon Roll.

KARLESKINT, MATTHEW J; Ft Scott HS; Fort Scott, KS; (3); 24/178; Church Yth Grp; FCA; Letterman Clb; Pep Clb; Varsity Clb; Var Bsbl; Var Bsktbl; Var Ftbl; Var Trk; Var Wt Lftg.

KARLINGER, JEREMY J; Pittsburg HS; Pittsburg, KS; (1); Pres Frsh Cls; JV Wt Lftg; Hon Roll; Ntrl Hlprs.

KARNEY, JOSEPH S; Lawrence HS; Lawrence, KS; (4); 530/550; Sec Model UN; Quiz Bowl; Spanish Clb; Band; Mrchg Band; High Hon Roll; NHS; Pres Acad Fit Awd; St Schlr; U Of IL; Mech Engrng.

KARNS, BROOKS; Jackson Heights HS; Onaga, KS; (1); Band; Chorus; Mrchg Band; School Musical; Ofcr Stu Cncl; Bsktbl; Ftbl; Hon Roll; Prfct Atten Awd; Emporia; Tchr.

KARNS, JENNY; Holton HS; Holton, KS; (4); Art Clb; Church Yth Grp; SADD; Band; Chorus; Church Choir; Phtg Rptr Nwsp; Ed Yrbk; Pres Frsh Cls; JV Vllybl; GCTL Bd Mem; Kayette Bd; AA Awds; KS U; Psycht.

KARRER, JULIE E; St Thomas Aguinas HS; Overland Park, KS; (3); Key Clb; Drill Tm; Nwsp; Yrbk; Hon Roll; TCU; Chem Engrng.

KARST, JESSICA; Shawnee Heights HS; Topeka, KS; (1); Church Yth Grp; Hosp Aide; Pep Clb; SADD; Drill Tm; School Play; L Pom Pon; High Hon Roll; Prfct Atten Awd; Ks ST Univ; Nrsng.

KASHKA, LEE A; Goodland HS; Goodland, KS; (2); 16/87; Church Yth Grp; 4-H; Chorus; Jazz Band; School Musical; Swing Chorus; Crs Cntry; Pep Band; Treas Soph Cls; JV Bsktbl.

KASMARICK, KELLY E; Blue Valley HS; Overland Park, KS; (2); 4-H; Sftbl; Tennis; Hon Roll.

KASSELMAN, KODY W; Spearville Jr Sr HS; Spearville, KS; (2); 9/32; Letterman Clb; Pep Clb; Quiz Bowl; Varsity Clb; Chorus; Church Choir; Ofcr Stu Cncl; Bsktbl; Ftbl; Trk; Acad Achvr; Homecoming Attndnt; K-ST Engrg Prtcpnt; Sports Med.

KASSEN, BRET R; Shawnee Mission W Sr HS; Lenexa, KS; (3); 14/398; Sec Frsh Cls; Rep Soph Cls; Treas Jr Cls; Pres Sr Cls; Ofcr Stu Cncl; Var L Bsbl; Bsktbl; Var L Ftbl; Wt Lftg; High Hon Roll; Stdnt Peer Mediation/Cnflct Rsltn; Soph Hon Mntn All League Dfns Ftbl.

KASSLER, ELIZABETH A; Haven HS; Haven, KS; (3); Letterman Clb; Sec Treas SADD; Chorus; Variety Show; Trk; Vllybl; High Hon Roll; Hon Roll; NHS; KAY Pres; Peer Cnslr/Pres; 95-ST Trck Qlfr In High Jump/Hrdls; 4 Yr Coll; Anml Sci.

KASTENS, SUSAN; Atwood HS; Atwood, KS; (4); HOBY; Sec Treas Lit Mag; Sec Treas Soph Cls; Sec Treas Jr Cls; Sec Treas Sr Cls; Hon Roll; Art Clb; Letterman Clb; Spanish Clb; Chorus; KS Regents Hnr Acad; NSTA/NASA Sci Awd; Crtv Arts Clb Pres; Ft Hays St U; Bio.

KASTL, JUSTIN T; Ft Scott HS; Fort Scott, KS; (2); Debate Tm; FCA; Key Clb; NFL; Quiz Bowl; Orch; JV Crs Cntry; JV Trk; High Hon Roll; Pres Acad Fit Awd; Regents Hnrs Acad; Natural Hlprs; Comm Orch; Comm Swim Team; Med.

KATCHER, JENNIFER S; Shawnee Mission S Sr HS; Shawnee Mission, KS; (2); 23/491; Intnl Clb; School Musical; JV Var Chrldng; Var Diving; Var Gym; High Hon Roll; Jr NHS; Pres Acad Fit Awd; Pres Schlr.

KATICH, LISA M; Lawrence HS; Lawrence, KS; (3); Chorus; Orch; School Musical; Variety Show; Hon Roll; High Hon Roll; Dist Hnrs Orch 2 Yrs; All ST Hnrs Orch 2 Yrs; Orch Otstndng Musician Awd; Music Prfrmnce.

KATZ, BARBIE; Centre Jr Sr HS; Lost Springs, KS; (4); 1/17; Pres FBLA; Sec FHA; Pep Clb; Stage Crew; Ed Nwsp; VP Soph Cls; VP Jr Cls; High Hon Roll; Pres NHS; Envrnmntl Sci.

KATZ, TAMARA C; Blue Valley Northwest HS; Overland Park, KS; (1); Art Clb; Temple Yth Grp; Phtg Nwsp; Lit Mag; Powder Puff Ftbl; Hon Roll; Natl Art Hnr Soc; Temple Yth Grp Pres; IN Univ; Photography.

KATZER, VANESSA P; Anderson Cty Jr Sr HS; Garnett, KS; (1); SADD; Hon Roll.

KAUFMAN, DENILLE; Hillsboro HS; Hillsboro, KS; (2); 7/49; Church Yth Grp; Chorus; Var Chrldng; Gym; High Hon Roll; Hon Roll; Kayettes; KS ST U.

KAUFMAN, JAKE D; Elyria Christian Schl; Mc Pherson, KS; (2); Art Clb; Church Yth Grp; Drama Clb; Service Clb; Chorus; School Play; Bsktbl; Socr; Tennis; Cnstrctn.

KAUFMAN, JENNIFER R; Shawnee Mission W Sr HS; Overland Park, KS; (3); 29/415; Church Yth Grp; Pep Clb; Orch; School Musical; Mgr Bsktbl; NHS; Strolling Strings.

KAUFMAN, JOSEPH E; Buhler HS; Buhler, KS; (1); Church Yth Grp; FCA; Science Clb; JV Bsbl; JV L Wrstlng; Pres Acad Fit Awd.

KAUFMAN, RHETT; Lucus-Luray HS; Lucas, KS; (2); 2/22; Church Yth Grp; 4-H; Quiz Bowl; SADD; Ofcr Frsh Cls; Ofcr Stu Cncl; Bsktbl; Ftbl; 4-H Awd; High Hon Roll; KS ST Univ.

KAUFMANN, KARISSA; Cheney Jr Sr HS; Cheney, KS; (3); 1/50; Pres Church Yth Grp; Band; Jazz Band; Mrchg Band; Orch; Pep Band; JV Var Bsktbl; Var L Crs Cntry; Var L Trk; High Hon Roll.

KAUFMANN, KRISTOPHER J; Cheney Jr Sr HS; Cheney, KS; (4); 7/50; Band; Sec Treas Soph Cls; Sec Jr Cls; VP Sr Cls; Rep Stu Cncl; Var L Ftbl; Var L Trk; High Hon Roll; NHS; Church Yth Grp; KS Newman Col; Med.

KAUP, HALEY J; Norton Comm HS; Norton, KS; (3); Rep Church Yth Grp; Dance Clb; Drama Clb; FCA; Math Clb; Pep Clb; Science Clb; Spanish Clb; SADD; Yrbk; KAYS Rptrt.

KAUP, ILLENE; Attica Public Schl; Anthony, KS; (4); 6/21; 4-H; Girl Scts; HOBY; Pep Clb; SADD; Band; Drm Mjr(t); Mrchg Band; Pep Band; School Play; Girl Sct Gold Awd; Dodge City CC; Athltc Trng.

KAUTEN, JENNIFER R; Liberal HS; Liberal, KS; (3); French Clb; German Clb; NFL; Chorus; School Play; Stage Crew; Variety Show; Hon Roll; NHS; Prfct Atten Awd; Phychiatry/Law.

KAUTIO, DEREK A; Olathe South Sr HS; Olathe, KS; (2); Spanish Clb; Ftbl; Swmmng; Wt Lftg; Hon Roll; Pres Acad Fit Awd; Pres Schlr; Tech Clb.

KAY, PETE; Ottaws HS; Ottawa, KS; (3); 15/156; FCA; 4-H; Letterman Clb; Ofcr Stu Cncl; Ftbl; Golf; Wrstlng; 4-H Awd; High Hon Roll; NHS; Danforth Awd Winner; KS ST; Pre-Med.

KAY, SARA E; Lacrosse HS; La Crosse, KS; (4); 12/25; Debate Tm; 4-H; French Clb; Letterman Clb; Pep Clb; Speech Tm; Varsity Clb; Band; Chrldng; NHS; KS Wesleyan; Cnslng.

KEARN, BRENDAN D; Salina HS South; Salina, KS; (3); Boy Scts; Church Yth Grp; Quiz Bowl; Band; Mrchg Band; Pep Band; Golf; Hon Roll; KS Wesleyan Univ Frgn Lang Camp Cnslr.

KEARNS, KELLY A; Shawnee Mission W Sr HS; Lenexa, KS; (4); 61/352; Cmnty Wkr; Letterman Clb; Teachers Aide; Mgr(s); Score Keeper; JV Capt Socr; Mgr Vllybl; High Hon Roll; Hon Roll; Pres Acad Fit Awd; Hlth Careers Comm Svc Hosp Aide; Acad Awd Winner 3 Times; Stdnt Of Month; U Of KS; PT.

KEARNS, KELLY J; Shawnee Heights HS; Wakarusa, KS; (3); Church Yth Grp; Debate Tm; Pep Clb; SADD; Teachers Aide; Chorus; JV Trk; Hon Roll; KS U; Bus.

KEAST, JACQUE; Larned HS; Larned, KS; (4); 19/90; Am Leg Aux Girls St; Intnl Clb; Letterman Clb; Scholastic Bowl; Teachers Aide; Var Sftbl; Capt Vllybl; Hon Roll; Ed Yrbk; Jr Olympc Vlybl; KS U; Jrnlsm.

KEATING, JACKI; St Xavier's HS; Junction City, KS; (4); 7/15; Am Leg Aux Girls St; Church Yth Grp; Cmnty Wkr; FHA; SADD; Teachers Aide; Chorus; School Musical; Variety Show; Sec Stu Cncl; Natl Hnr Soc VP; Cath Yth Org VP; SADD VP; Cloud Cty CC.

KEATING, JILL D; Uniontown HS; Fulton, KS; (2); FCA; FHA; Letterman Clb; Math Clb; Natl FFA Org; Pep Clb; Spanish Clb; Band; Pep Band; Treas Frsh Cls; VP Pres For Future Hommkrs Of Amrca; Treas For FFA Jr Offcs; Pittsburg St Univ; Bus Mgnt.

KEATON, MEGAN; Jefferson West HS; Meriden, KS; (4); 12/60; Pres French Clb; Capt Pres Quiz Bowl; Acpl Chr; Pres Soph Cls; Var Capt Chrldng; Hon Roll; NHS; Cmnty Wkr; VP Drama Clb; ST FHA VP Pgms; St Bnd; Doane Coll; Frnch.

KEBERLEIN, JENNIFER; Thomas More Prep-Marion HS; Hays, KS; (1); Church Yth Grp; Cmnty Wkr; Debate Tm; VP Frsh Cls; Ofcr Stu Cncl; Bsktbl; Trk; Vllybl; Ed.

KECK, ELIZABETH A; Shawnee Mission E Sr HS; Prairie Village, KS; (4); 26/398; Cmnty Wkr; Natl Beta Clb; Teachers Aide; Orch; High Hon Roll; NHS; Ntl Merit SF; Chruch Lctr; KS Anthrplgcl Assn Fld Schl Spvr; Math.

KEEARNS, DEBORAH L; Halstead HS; Halstead, KS; (3); Church Yth Grp; Cmnty Wkr; Treas Spanish Clb; Teachers Aide; Chorus; School Play; Ed Nwsp; Mgr Bsktbl; JV Vllybl; High Hon Roll; 3 Poems Sub/Advncd To Final Round; Wrtng; Hutchinson CC; Acctng.

KEEHN, PATRICIA; Jackson Heights HS; Holton, KS; (1); Dance Clb; FHA; Pep Clb; Band; Chorus; Mrchg Band; Pep Band; School Musical; School Play; JV Crs Cntry; Notre Dame; Tchr/Dnc Instr.

KEEL, LIESEL; Central Jr HS; Lawrence, KS; (2); Acpl Chr; Band; Church Choir; School Play; VP Stu Cncl; Cit Awd; High Hon Roll; KS U; Tchng.

KEELER, JESSE M; Northeast Magnet HS; Wichita, KS; (4); 5/63; Church Yth Grp; JA; Math Tm; Quiz Bowl; Intrml Bsktbl; High Hon Roll; NHS; Scholastic Bowl; Science Clb; Intrml Ftbl; Sci Olympiad; KS Jr Acad Of Sci; Sci Fair Comp; KS St Univ; Comp Eng.

KEELER, KRISTY L; Salina HS South; Salina, KS; (4); 32/239; Boy Scts; Pep Clb; Phtg Ed Yrbk; Rep Stu Cncl; Mgr Bsktbl; Var Chrldng; Var Powder Puff Ftbl; Var Score Keeper; Vllybl; Hon Roll; Frnscs; Prom Qn; Mstrs Art Pgm; KS ST U; Psych.

KEELER, MEGHAN; Wichita East HS; Wichita, KS; (2); Art Clb; Cmnty Wkr; Red Cross Aide; Crs Cntry; Tennis; Hon Roll; Bus.

KEELEY, TOM J; Immaculata HS; Leavenworth, KS; (2); Boy Scts; Math Tm; Quiz Bowl; Speech Tm; School Play; JV Bsbl; JV Bsktbl; Var Socr; High Hon Roll; NHS.

KEENAN, CARL; Larned HS; Larned, KS; (3); Office Aide; Quiz Bowl; Rep Stu Cncl; Tennis; Hon Roll; Prfct Atten Awd; Broadcasting; Bus.

KEENAN, CARLIN; Oakley HS; Oakley, KS; (4); Church Yth Grp; 4-H; FHA; Office Aide; Speech Tm; Chorus; School Play; Rep Frsh Cls; Ofcr Stu Cncl; JV Bsktbl; Emporia ST Univ; Elem Tchr.

KEENAN, VERONICA; Larned HS; Larned, KS; (2); 11/102; Intnl Clb; Hon Roll; Frnsc Sci.

KEENE, JENNIFER J; Arkansas City HS; Arkansas City, KS; (3); Church Yth Grp; FCA; Hosp Aide; Band; Mrchg Band; Yrbk; JV Tennis; High Hon Roll; NHS; Cmnty Wkr; Usherettes; U Of KS.

KEESLING, NITA C; Cheney Jr Sr HS; Cheney, KS; (3); High Hon Roll; Acad Excl Awd Prins Hnr Roll; Vol Ministry Work; Acad Olympics; Graphic Arts; Studio Art.

KEETER, BESSIE; Salina HS Central; Salina, KS; (4); #228 in class; Office Aide; Var Co-Capt Trk; High Hon Roll; NHS; St Schlr; Acad Lttr/Gftd Prgm 9-12th Grd; AAU; U Of KS; Engrng.

KEETON, RACHEL M; Nickerson HS; South Hutchinson, KS; (3); 4/119; Church Yth Grp; FCA; SADD; Band; Chorus; Church Choir; Mrchg Band; Pep Band; School Musical; Variety Show; Symph Bnd Most Imprvd Trophy; Mrchng Bnd Squad Ldr; Band/Choir Ltr; Manhattan Chrstn Coll; Fam Cnsl.

KEHLER, JENNIFER; El Dorado HS; Leon, KS; (3); 11/190; Sec Church Yth Grp; NFL; Thesps; Chorus; School Musical; Sec Jr Cls; Var Chrldng; Var Trk; 4-H Awd; NHS; KS St Trk Meet 100 Hh 5a 94 2nd Pl, 300 Lh 5a 95 7th Pl; Chamb Comm Btlr Cty 4-H Cmnty Svc Awd; Bio.

KEIL, DAVID M; Russell HS; Russell, KS; (2); Church Yth Grp; Debate Tm; 4-H; Natl FFA Org; JV Bsbl; Bsktbl; Var Crs Cntry; 4-H Awd; High Hon Roll; FFA VP; Elem Ed.

KEIMIG, STEVEN L; Maur Hill Prep Schl; Atchison, KS; (1); SADD; Band; Mrchg Band; Pep Band; JV Ftbl; Mgr(s).

KEIRNS, LACEY L; Stockton HS; Woodston, KS; (3); Drama Clb; FHA; Pep Clb; Band; Chorus; Jazz Band; Mrchg Band; Pep Band; Mgr(s); Hon Roll; Kay Clb; KS ST; Elem Tchng.

KEISER, KEVIN; Juan Padilla Acad HS; Wichita, KS; (4); 1/4; Art Clb; Computer Clb; Drama Clb; Quiz Bowl; School Musical; School Play; Stage Crew; Ed Nwsp; Intrml Bsktbl; Intrml Ftbl; Lctr Prsh; Our Lady Grace Seminary/Priest.

KEITH, APRIL M; Wichita South HS; Wichita, KS; (2); 134/394; Chorus; KS ST; Bus.

KEITH, SARAH A; Buhler HS; Buhler, KS; (2); Church Yth Grp; FCA; Ofcr Natl FFA Org; Band; Chorus; Church Choir; Mrchg Band; Pep Band; Tennis; High Hon Roll; Ag Ed/Chrch Mnstry.

KEITH, SARAH E; Oswego HS; Oswego, KS; (2); FHA; Quiz Bowl; Var Trk; High Hon Roll; NHS; Grnd Chmpn/1st Art Wrk Cty Fair; Hnrbl Mntn/1st Plc MBL Cmptns; OSU.

KELBLE, JACQUELINE; Shawnee Mission Nw Sr HS; Lenexa, KS; (3); Model UN; SADD; Var Capt Bsktbl; Var Sftbl; Var Vllybl; High Hon Roll; NHS; AAU Bsktbl; Spirit Clb Co-VP.

KELDERHOUSE, MELODY; Goddard HS; Goddard, KS; (3); 15/198; Boy Scts; Library Aide; Quiz Bowl; Scholastic Bowl; Science Clb; Spanish Clb; High Hon Roll; NHS; Ntl Merit SF; Prfct Atten Awd; Sci Olympd.

KELING, HEATHER; Atchison Sr HS; Atchison, KS; (3); Scholastic Bowl; Band; Mrchg Band; Pep Band; Stage Crew; Highland.

KELL, LISA; Lansing HS; Lansing, KS; (3); 43/142; French Clb; Science Clb; Var L Chrldng; Sec French Hon Soc; Hon Roll; NCA All-Amer Chrldr 94-96; USCAA Wnnr 95 & 96; KU; Nrsng; Elem Ed.

KELLENBERGER, GALEN A; Blue Valley HS; Stilwell, KS; (2); Church Yth Grp; Cmnty Wkr; Letterman Clb; VP SADD; Orch; High Hon Roll; Pol Sci Club Sec; KS ST Univ; Pre-Med.

KELLER, ASHLEY; Silver Lake Jr Sr HS; Silver Lake, KS; (3); 11/51; NFL; Spanish Clb; Teachers Aide; Varsity Clb; Band; Drm Mjr(t); Var Trk; JV Vllybl; Hon Roll; KS ST Univ; Animal Sci.

KELLER, BRIAN; Douglass HS; Douglass, KS; (4); 1/43; FCA; HOBY; Sec Letterman Clb; Capt Quiz Bowl; Teachers Aide; Band; Jazz Band; Pep Band; Ed Yrbk; Pres Frsh Cls; KS Hnrs, Tndy Tech Schlrs; Natl Mrt Cmmnd; KS ST U; Med.

KELLER, CURTIS B; Sylvan Unified HS; Hunter, KS; (3); Church Yth Grp; 4-H; Letterman Clb; Math Tm; Quiz Bowl; SADD; Band; Chorus; School Musical; L Bsbl.

KELLER, DALLAS J; Troy HS; Troy, KS; (2); 2/39; Letterman Clb; Natl FFA Org; Pres Frsh Cls; Pres Soph Cls; Capt L Bsktbl; Var L Ftbl; Var L Trk; High Hon Roll; NHS; Amer Leg Bsbl; Ed.

KELLER, ERIK L; Wallace Cty HS; Sharon Springs, KS; (2); Church Yth Grp; Cmnty Wkr; FCA; 4-H; Pep Clb; Varsity Clb; Chorus; Swing Chorus; Var Bsktbl; Var Crs Cntry; Phy Thrpst.

KELLER, JANICE L; Chase Co HS; Cottonwood Falls, KS; (2); Church Yth Grp; Quiz Bowl; Band; Nwsp; Sec Treas Soph Cls; Var Sftbl; High Hon Roll; NHS; Spanish Clb; Chorus; Fncl Dir/VP 96- KAY; Natl Cath Forensics Leag; Jrnlsm Clb Treas 96-.

KELLER, JASON; Rossville HS; Rossville, KS; (4); 10/42; FBLA; Letterman Clb; Rptr Natl FFA Org; Var L Bsktbl; Var L Ftbl; Var L Golf; Cit Awd; Hon Roll; KS ST; Lndscp Dsgn.

KELLER, JENNY; Spring Hill HS; Olathe, KS; (4); 2/98; FCA; Pres 4-H; Pep Clb; Q&S; SADD; Phtg Yrbk; Var L Chrldng; High Hon Roll; NHS; St Schlr; Top 5 4 Yrs; KS St Hrs Shw Crct Qn, Yth Clb Sec/Treas; KS ST U; Anml Sci.

KELLER, MATTHEW; Ingalls Jr Sr HS; Garden City, KS; (2); Letterman Clb; Math Tm; Pep Clb; Quiz Bowl; Scholastic Bowl; Speech Tm; SADD; Varsity Clb; Chorus; School Play.

KELLER, SARAH; Pratt HS; Pratt, KS; (2); Pep Clb; SADD; Band; Chorus; School Musical; Ofcr Stu Cncl; Chrldng; Tennis; Trk; High Hon Roll; Piano.

KELLERMAN, JOSH A; Norton Comm HS; Norton, KS; (3); Church Yth Grp; Cmnty Wkr; Pep Clb; Teachers Aide; Band; Chorus; Jazz Band; Mrchg Band; Orch; Pep Band; All League Team Defense/Hon Mention Ftbl; 5th Pl ST Wrestling Trnmnt USA Natl KS Wrestling Team; Law Enfor.

KELLERMAN, KEVIN E; Iola Sr HS; Iola, KS; (4); Am Leg Boys St; Library Aide; Var Ftbl; Var Trk; High Hon Roll; Prfct Atten Awd; Bwlng Cap; Hntng; Fshng; Allen Cty CC; Plstcs Engnr.

KELLERMAN, ROB R; Anderson Cty Jr Sr HS; Garnett, KS; (2); 1/78; Drama Clb; SADD; Acpl Chr; School Musical; School Play; VP Frsh Cls; Bsktbl; Ftbl; Trk; High Hon Roll; All Leag Ftbl; 2 Sci Acad Awds; KS ST; Eng.

KELLEY, CAROLYN; Trinity Catholic HS; Hutchinson, KS; (3); 2/17; NFL; Band; Drill Tm; Var L Bsktbl; Var L Chrldng; Powder Puff Ftbl; Var L Trk; Var L Vllybl; High Hon Roll; NHS; Catholic Univ Of Amer; Chem.

KELLEY, COURTNEY L; Santa Fe Trail Jr HS; Olathe, KS; (1); 26/345; Debate Tm; Pep Clb; Spanish Clb; Speech Tm; Teachers Aide; Rptr Nwsp; Var Ftbl; Hon Roll; Pres Schlr; Soccer & Trk Voted MVP In Trnmt; KU; Nrs; Dr.

KELLEY, JOANNA J; Mc Pherson HS; Mc Pherson, KS; (4); Church Yth Grp; Cmnty Wkr; Spanish Clb; SADD; Acpl Chr; Chorus; School Musical; Swing Chorus; Trk; Hon Roll; Poetry Wrtng; Piano/Guitar; Music Cmpstn; York Coll; Psychlgy/Music Thrpy.

KELLEY, KRISTIN; Morning Star Acad; Olathe, KS; (4); Church Yth Grp; Church Choir; School Play; Johnson Cty CC Part Time Stu Hnr Roll; Southwest Bapt Acad; Chem.

KELLEY, LEWIS; Rossville HS; Rossville, KS; (4); Am Leg Boys St; FBLA; HOBY; Letterman Clb; NFL; Quiz Bowl; Band; School Musical; Hon Roll; L Crs Cntry; Chrch, Fnrl Hm Piano, Orgnst, Trmpt; Rssvlle Vly Mnr Empl Mnth Vol Awd; KS ST U; Bus Admin.

KELLEY, MICHAEL E; Atchison Sr HS; Atchison, KS; (1); Church Yth Grp; Quiz Bowl; Scholastic Bowl; Church Choir; Treas Frsh Cls; Ofcr Stu Cncl; Mgr Bsktbl; JV Var Ftbl; Mgr(s); L Trk; Nell Smith Ftbl Camp MVP 2 Yrs; Church Jr Deacon; Kelley Family Choir; KS Univ; Sports Jrnlsm.

KELLEY, TIESHA L; Highland Park HS; Topeka, KS; (4); 6/133; Sec Church Yth Grp; Math Clb; Science Clb; Chorus; Rptr Yrbk; VP Jr Cls; Rep Stu Cncl; Church Yth Grp; High Hon Roll; Rep NHS; KS Hon Schlr; 4 Yr Acad Ltr; Blck Stu; KS Univ; Pre Med.

KELLOGG, ALICIA; Lawrence HS; Lawrence, KS; (4); 104/600; German Clb; Intnl Clb; Key Clb; Spanish Clb; Temple Yth Grp; Hon Roll; NHS; Pres Acad Fit Awd; KS Univ; Opto.

KELLY, DAVID S; Mc Louth Schl; Mc Louth, KS; (3); French Clb; School Musical; School Play; Stage Crew; Yrbk; Cit Awd; High Hon Roll; Hon Roll; Ft Hays ST Univ; Comp Pgmng.

KELLY, HEATHER; Thomas More Prep-Marion HS; Hays, KS; (3); 7/69; JCL; Latin Clb; Math Tm; Bsktbl; JV Trk; Var Wt Lftg; High Hon Roll; Acad Awd; NLE Magna Cum Laude; U Of KS; Nursng.

KELLY, RACHEL A; Chaparral HS; Harper, KS; (4); 6/54; FCA; Pep Clb; Chorus; School Musical; Vllybl; High Hon Roll; NHS; St Schlr; Teens As Tchrs; Honr C Awd; KS Jr Acad Of Sci; Wichita St Univ; Nurs.

KELLY, RYAN; Holton HS; Holton, KS; (3); Sec Natl FFA Org; Intrml Bsktbl; Intrml Ftbl; Hon Roll; NHS; Prfct Atten Awd; Mc Pherson Coll.

KELLY, SARA J; Wabaunsee HS; Alma, KS; (2); Church Yth Grp; 4-H; FBLA; Quiz Bowl; Acpl Chr; Band; Church Choir; Pep Band; Stage Crew; JV Crs Cntry; All Amer Schlr; Natl Stus Of America; Dist III Hnr Band; Music.

KELSEY, HOLLY J; Garden Plain Jr Sr HS; Goddard, KS; (3); Red Cross Aide; SADD; School Play; Ed Nwsp; Ed Yrbk; Pom Pon; Wt Lftg; Cit Awd; High Hon Roll; NHS.

KELSEY, MELINDA M; Blue Valley HS; Overland Park, KS; (3); 20/255; Intnl Clb; Mgr(s); Score Keeper; JV Capt Socr; Mgr Vllybl; High Hon Roll; Hon Roll; NHS; Piano; Drawing; Painting.

KELTNER, ERIK J; Manhattan HS; Manhattan, KS; (3); 76/426; Am Leg Boys St; Boy Scts; Church Yth Grp; Socr; Trk; Hon Roll; NHS; Egl Sct; KS ST Univ; Mech Engrg.

KELTY, MARTI; Wamego HS; Wamego, KS; (4); 6/94; Sec Treas FCA; HOBY; Sec SADD; VP Frsh Cls; Rep Soph Cls; Rep Jr Cls; Sec Sr Cls; Pres Stu Cncl; NHS; KS Hnr Schlr; KS ST U; Finance.

KEMMIS, RACHEL M; Skyline Schl; Pratt, KS; (4); 4/30; Pep Clb; SADD; Band; Chorus; Phtg Nwsp; Sec Frsh Cls; Sec Stu Cncl; Cit Awd; Hon Roll; Church Yth Grp; #20 FHA; VP Of Star Events Dist; VP Chptr Mixed Ensbl; Emporia ST Univ; Acctg.

KEMP, KARA; Arkansas City HS; Arkansas City, KS; (4); Am Leg Aux Girls St; Cmnty Wkr; FCA; SADD; Chorus; Rep Sr Cls; Var Chrldng; High Hon Roll; 1st Rnnr Up Miss Ark City Pgnt 95; ACT Scor Schlrshp; Cowely Cty CC; Psych.

KEMP, TRACY D; Blue Valley HS; Overland Park, KS; (4); Cmnty Wkr; FBLA; Mu Alpha Theta; Natl Beta Clb; Spanish Clb; Teachers Aide; Drill Tm; Rep Stu Cncl; High Hon Roll; Jr NHS; KS ST Hon Schlr 96; Acad Schlrsp Awds U Of KS/EMPORIA ST Univ; Washburn Univ/Pittsburg ST Univ; U Of KS; Bus/Acctng.

KEMPKE, MICHAEL; Garden City Sr HS; Garden City, KS; (4); 64/314; Natl FFA Org; Band; Mrchg Band; Pep Band; High Hon Roll; Garden City CC; Farm Mgmt.

KEMPLAY, KELLIE A; Central Heights Sr HS; Rantoul, KS; (2); Art Clb; FCA; FBLA; Girl Scts; Pep Clb; Spanish Clb; VP Frsh Cls; VP Soph Cls; Chrldng; Trk; ASA Sftbl; Emporia; PT/TCHR.

KEMS, BRIANA N; Ottawa HS; Ottawa, KS; (4); 83/138; Church Yth Grp; Cmnty Wkr; FBLA; FTA; Yrbk; Rep Stu Cncl; Chrldng; Gym; Socr; High Hon Roll; All-Star Chrldr Awd; U Of KS; Bus Lawyer.

KENDALL, MEGAN; Turner HS; Kansas City, KS; (4); Pres Church Yth Grp; Pres Thesps; School Musical; School Play; Stage Crew; Bsktbl; JV Sftbl; Prfct Atten Awd; VICE Modrtr Chrstn Yth Fllwship Cabinet Of KS City; Emporia St Univ; Theatr.

KENDALL, PAMELA J; Greensburg HS; Mullinville, KS; (4); Church Yth Grp; Teachers Aide; Band; Drill Tm; Mrchg Band; Pep Band; Sec Jr Cls; Var Bsktbl; Var Trk; Var Vllybl; Dodge City CC; Mid Mngmnt.

KENDRICK, MELISSA; Jackson Heights HS; Whiting, KS; (1); FBLA; FHA; GAA; Pep Clb; Band; Chorus; Mrchg Band; Pep Band; School Musical; School Play; Smmr Sftbl Lg Chmps; KS ST; Bus Law.

KENDRICK, PETER M; Parsons HS; Parsons, KS; (3); Boy Scts; Pep Clb; Spanish Clb; Band; Chorus; Jazz Band; Mrchg Band; Pep Band; Eagle Scout; KS Masonic All ST HS Mrchg Band; Music Co Show Choir; Labette CC; MD.

KENEMORE, KEVIN L; Wellington Sr HS; Wellington, KS; (3); Drama Clb; Library Aide; Chorus; School Play; Variety Show; Wt Lftg; Hon Roll; Comm Theater; Guitar; Amer Stu Travel; Ft Hays; Mass Commnctn.

KENNEDY, CASEY R; Sedan HS; Sedan, KS; (2); 3/34; FHA; Letterman Clb; Natl FFA Org; Quiz Bowl; Spanish Clb; Treas Soph Cls; JV Var Bsbl; JV Var Bsktbl; Hon Roll; Chpt FFA Greenhand Awd/Proficiency Awd; KS ST Univ; Agribus.

KENNEDY, CHARITY; Lakin HS; Lakin, KS; (4); 3/45; Art Clb; Church Yth Grp; 4-H; Quiz Bowl; VP Frsh Cls; Pres Sr Cls; Chrldng; Wt Lftg; NHS; Sec FHA; Livestck Judgng Team; Wichita ST U; Indstrl Engrng.

KENNEDY, CHRISTOPHER; St Marys HS; Emmett, KS; (2); Debate Tm; FBLA; Scholastic Bowl; Mrchg Band; Pep Band; Stage Crew; Pres Soph Cls; Golf; High Hon Roll; NHS; KS ST.

KENNEDY, CHRISTOPHER L; Atchison Co Cmty HS; Huron, KS; (2); Church Yth Grp; Natl FFA Org; Hon Roll; Scndry Schl Tchr.

KENNEDY, DONALD J; Chanute Sr HS; Chanute, KS; (1); Art Clb; Church Yth Grp; Letterman Clb; Varsity Clb; School Play; JV Ftbl; JV Var Trk; Var Wrstlng; High Hon Roll; Arch/Cmptr Graphics.

KENNEDY, JAIMEE R; Great Bend Sr HS; Great Bend, KS; (4); German Clb; Red Cross Aide; Acpl Chr; Chorus; Crs Cntry; Swmmng; High Hon Roll; Hon Roll; NHS; St Schlr; All-Amer Swimming Awd; Schltc Achvmt Awd; Bethany Coll; Elem Ed.

KENNEDY, KAYCEE; Jackson Heights HS; Circleville, KS; (3); 5/44; 4-H; HOBY; Pres Jr Cls; VP Stu Cncl; Var JV Bsktbl; Var JV Vllybl; 4-H Awd; Hon Roll; NHS; Ntl Merit Schol; Fort Hays ST; Nrs Prctnr.

KENNEDY, KHRISTINA; Mulvane Sr HS; Mulvane, KS; (3); 1/134; Church Yth Grp; FCA; SADD; Band; Mrchg Band; Vllybl; High Hon Roll; NHS; Prfct Atten Awd; Pres Acad Fit Awd; Bus.

KENNEDY, LAINE S; Holton HS; Holton, KS; (1); Church Yth Grp; Band; Nwsp; Var Bsktbl; Var Vllybl; High Hon Roll; KAYS; Piano; Med.

KENNEDY, LORI C; Blue Valley HS; Overland Park, KS; (3); 22/252; Art Clb; Church Yth Grp; Band; Mrchg Band; Orch; Pep Band; School Musical; Cit Awd; Hon Roll; NHS; KAYS Tres; Envrnmntl Clb VP; Music.

KENNEDY JR, MARVIN D; Chanute Sr HS; Chanute, KS; (3); Am Leg Boys St; Church Yth Grp; FBLA; Letterman Clb; Varsity Clb; JV Ftbl; Score Keeper; Var Trk; JV Wrstlng; High Hon Roll; Mech Engr.

KENNEDY, MOLLY; Washburn Rural HS; Topeka, KS; (4); 32/295; Cmnty Wkr; HOBY; Ed Nwsp; Pres Frsh Cls; Pres Soph Cls; Pres Stu Cncl; Var Socr; Var Trk; Cit Awd; High Hon Roll; SMU; Intl Law.

KENNEDY, NATASHA D; Junction City HS; Ft Riley, KS; (2); Church Yth Grp; Natl Beta Clb; Quiz Bowl; Teachers Aide; Band; Hon Roll; Troy ST; Law; Nrsng.

KENNEDY, RACHAEL; Madison Jr Sr HS; Madison, KS; (3); 11/26; Pres Church Yth Grp; FBLA; Letterman Clb; Quiz Bowl; Sec Spanish Clb; Phtg Yrbk; Rep Jr Cls; Chrldng; L Trk; Vllybl; St Track 94; Emporia ST U; Nrsng.

KENNEDY, RYE J; Lakin HS; Lakin, KS; (3); 4-H; Quiz Bowl; Pres Jr Cls; JV Ftbl.

KENNEDY, SOPHIE K; Wichita East HS; Wichita, KS; (4); Church Yth Grp; Cmnty Wkr; Spanish Clb; Teachers Aide; JV Bsktbl; High Hon Roll; NHS; Spanish NHS.

KENNEY, CHUCK I; Circle HS; Benton, KS; (2); Boy Scts; Hon Roll; Cmptr Prgrmmng.

KENNEY, PAUL; Hutchinson HS; Hutchinson, KS; (3); Am Leg Boys St; Hon Roll; Prfct Atten Awd; Bible Quizzing; Mid-Amer Nazarene Coll.

KENNEY, TARA C; Hayden HS; Topeka, KS; (2); 40/160; GAA; Pres Intnl Clb; Pep Clb; School Musical; JV Crs Cntry; Var Socr; JV Swmmng; JV Trk; High Hon Roll; NHS.

KENNYHERTZ, JOHNNY C; Shawnee Mission Nw Sr HS; Lenexa, KS; (3); Church Yth Grp; Cmnty Wkr; DECA; Letterman Clb; Office Aide; Varsity Clb; Variety Show; Rep Frsh Cls; Ofcr Stu Cncl; JV Bsktbl; Yng Lf; AAU Jr Olym Wghtlftng Medal; KS Univ; Bus/Fin.

KENT, ARIN C; East HS; Wichita, KS; (4); Debate Tm; German Clb; NFL; Chorus; School Play; Rep Jr Cls; Rep Sr Cls; Rep Stu Cncl; JV Bsktbl; JV Crs Cntry; Tutor; U Of KS.

KENT, EDDIE C; Deerfield HS; Deerfield, KS; (2); Pep Clb; Band; Pep Band; Pres Frsh Cls; VP Soph Cls; Ftbl; Trk; Wt Lftg; Hon Roll; Jr NHS.

KENT, JENNIFER E; Shawnee Mission W Sr HS; Overland Park, KS; (4); 44/365; Girl Scts; Teachers Aide; Band; Mrchg Band; Cit Awd; Hon Roll; NHS; Pres Acad Fit Awd; JAWS Clb Pres; J C Penney Goldn Awd Fnlst; AZ ST U; Elem Ed.

KENT, KATRINA K; Riverton Schl; Galena, KS; (3); 4/61; Church Yth Grp; French Clb; Girl Scts; Math Clb; Scholastic Bowl; Band; Chorus; Church Choir; Mrchg Band; Orch; Pittsburg ST U; Med.

KENTON, MATTHEW; Shawnee Mission S HS; Lenexa, KS; (4); DECA; FCA; Pep Clb; Variety Show; Rep Stu Cncl; Intrml Bsktbl; Var L Trk; Intrml Vllybl; Hon Roll; Church Yth Grp; U Of KS; Mech Eng.

KENWORTHY, CHAD; Frankft HS; Frankfort, KS; (4); 1/30; Am Leg Boys St; SADD; Chorus; School Play; Swing Chorus; Pres Jr Cls; Var L Bsktbl; Var L Ftbl; L Trk; High Hon Roll; 5th St Wrstlng Cls 1-2-3a; KS Hnr Schlr; All Flint Hills Plyr Of Yr Ftbl; All St 1st Tm Offns Ftbl; Educ.

KENYON, DEREK B; Great Bend Sr HS; Great Bend, KS; (2); Church Yth Grp; Acpl Chr; Band; Mrchg Band; Pep Band; Stage Crew; Variety Show; Yrbk; Hon Roll; French Clb; Explorers Cmnctn Post 101.

KENYON, ROBIN R; Wichita Northwest HS; Wichita, KS; (2); Math Tm; Scholastic Bowl; Band; Mrchg Band; Orch; Pep Band; Stage Crew; Rep Frsh Cls; Gym; Hon Roll; Odyssey Of The Mind; Yth Orch Pgm; Wichita Wind Ensemble.

KENYON, WILLIAM E; Otis Bison HS; Otis, KS; (2); Quiz Bowl; Scholastic Bowl; Band; Mrchg Band; Pep Band; Mgr(s); Score Keeper; Cit Awd; Hon Roll.

KEOUGH, LAURA J; Smoky Valley HS; Roxbury, KS; (2); Pres FHA; High Hon Roll; KS ST U; Coll Prof.

KEPFORD, SHANON V; Russell HS; Russell, KS; (1); School Musical; Hon Roll; Nrs.

KEPKA, CARRY; Wilson Jr Sr HS; Dorrance, KS; (4); Church Yth Grp; Rptr Nwsp; Pres Sr Cls; VP Stu Cncl; Capt Chrldng; High Hon Roll; Hon Roll; NHS; 4-H; Model UN; Hnrbl Mntn Natl Jrnlsm Conv; KAY Clb; 4-H Pres; Ft Hays St Univ.

KEPKA, JENNIFER A; Buhler HS; Hutchinson, KS; (2); FCA; Scholastic Bowl; Science Clb; Treas Service Clb; SADD; Band; Chorus; Jazz Band; Rep Frsh Cls; Rep Soph Cls; Lab Band; Committed To Christ; Rennaissance Acad Achvmnt Comm; Politics.

KEPNER, RAECHEL L; Shawnee Heights HS; Topeka, KS; (1); Girl Scts; Hosp Aide; Pep Clb; Orch; High Hon Roll; Prfct Atten Awd; U Of KS; RN.

KERN, JAY M; Washington HS; Washington, KS; (3); Letterman Clb; Natl FFA Org; SADD; Ftbl; Trk; Wt Lftg.

KERN, PETER M; Chase HS; Chase, KS; (3); 3/20; Drama Clb; 4-H; FHA; Letterman Clb; Math Clb; Math Tm; Pep Clb; Quiz Bowl; Science Clb; Spanish Clb; K ST; Industrial Arts.

KERNAL, SOPHIA N; Sumner Acad Of Arts & Science; Kansas City, KS; (1); Church Yth Grp; Cmnty Wkr; Girl Scts; Pep Clb; Spanish Clb; SADD; Chorus; Church Choir; Drill Tm; Score Keeper; MI Univ; Law.

KERNS, CHRISTINA M; Wichita Southeast HS; Wichita, KS; (1); Girl Scts; Orch; Rep Frsh Cls; Hon Roll; Sierra Teens; OWLS Proj Pres; Wichita ST Univ.

KERNS, RIKI L; Palco HS; Zurich, KS; (1); Debate Tm; FHA; GAA; NFL; Pep Clb; Stage Crew; Bsktbl; Hon Roll; Pres Acad Fit Awd.

KERR, JACQUE; Louisburg HS; Louisburg, KS; (4); 14/78; Am Leg Aux Girls St; Bus Profs of Am; Debate Tm; GAA; Letterman Clb; Office Aide; Spanish Clb; SADD; Teachers Aide; Sec Sr Cls; KU; Psych.

KERR, KWES N; Rose Hill HS; Rose Hill, KS; (3); 1/120; Math Tm; Scholastic Bowl; Teachers Aide; Ed Yrbk; JV Bsbl; Var Capt Socr; High Hon Roll; KS ST U; Comp Sci.

KERSEY, LANDON W; Stanton Co HS; Johnson, KS; (2); Church Yth Grp; FCA; 4-H; Pres Frsh Cls; JV Bsktbl; Var L Diving; Var L Trk; Hon Roll; Rock Springs 4-H Ctr Art Prjct Dsplyd 1 Yr; Crs Cntry ST Prtcpnt; ST Track Alternate.

KERSHNER, AUBREY; Dighton HS; Dighton, KS; (4); 11/30; Church Yth Grp; Cmnty Wkr; FCA; HOBY; Speech Tm; Band; Church Choir; Jazz Band; Mrchg Band; Orch.

KERSHNER, ELISE T; Shawnee Mission W Sr HS; Lenexa, KS; (2); 12/418; Church Yth Grp; Cmnty Wkr; Acpl Chr; Chorus; Variety Show; Capt Chrldng; Trk; High Hon Roll; Pres Acad Fit Awd; JAWS; KS ST Univ; Arch Engr.

KERSLEY, MEGAN; Atchison Sr HS; Atchison, KS; (2); Rptr Yrbk; Sec Frsh Cls; VP Soph Cls; JV Chrldng; Mgr(s); JV Vllybl; Mgr Wrstlng; Cit Awd; High Hon Roll; Sci Olympiad; Lunch Of Chmpns; Hlth.

KERSTEN, AUNDRIA L; Immaculata HS; Leavenworth, KS; (3); Hosp Aide; Service Clb; Thesps; Ed Yrbk; Chrldng; Vllybl; High Hon Roll; NHS; Class Awds Spanish Iii English Iireligion Iii; Yrbk Editor Awd; Braodcast Journal.

KESINGER, CASEY L; Lawrence HS; Lawrence, KS; (2); Intrml Ftbl; KS ST Univ; Game Warden.

KESLER, AMBER D; Sabetha HS; Sabetha, KS; (3); 1/80; Church Yth Grp; FCA; FBLA; FHA; Pep Clb; Band; Chorus; Church Choir; Color Guard; Drm Mjr(t); Yth Mnstry.

KESSLER, NIKKI; Mc Louth Schl; Oskaloosa, KS; (3); 7/39; Art Clb; Church Yth Grp; Cmnty Wkr; Dance Clb; Drama Clb; FBLA; FHA; Letterman Clb; NFL; Pep Clb; Johnson Cty CC; Scndry Ed.

KETCH, GARY L; Chase HS; Raymond, KS; (3); Drama Clb; FHA; Letterman Clb; Math Tm; Pep Clb; Quiz Bowl; Spanish Clb; Sec Frsh Cls; Pres Soph Cls; Pres Jr Cls; U Of KS; Pre-Med.

KETTER, SARAH; St Thomas Aquinas HS; Merriam, KS; (3); 61/263; Am Leg Aux Girls St; Church Yth Grp; Office Aide; Var Capt Chrldng; JV Socr; High Hon Roll; Hon Roll; NHS; Prfct Atten Awd; Pres Acad Fit Awd; Horseback Riding; KS ST Univ; Vet Medicine.

KETTER, STACI D; Washburn Rural HS; Topeka, KS; (3); Church Yth Grp; Cmnty Wkr; FBLA; Library Aide; SADD; Flag Corp; Poem Pub; Comm Work Vol; Play Guitar; Baker; RN.

KETTERL, SARAH B; Herndon Schl; Herndon, KS; (4); 1/6; Church Yth Grp; Cmnty Wkr; 4-H; Math Tm; Model UN; Quiz Bowl; Scholastic Bowl; Speech Tm; Teachers Aide; VICA; ST Odyssey Of The Mind; Knwldg Mstr Open; Math Relay Team; Stdnt Of Mo; KACD; 3rd Spch ST; Sterling; Vet Med.

KETTERLING, KINISHA S; Washburn Rural HS; Topeka, KS; (3); #18 in class; Church Yth Grp; FCA; Acpl Chr; Chorus; Church Choir; School Musical; Variety Show; Socr; High Hon Roll; NHS; Regnl & St Vocal Solo Conts; KS Dist Choir Mem; Sr High Rep Chrch NYI; Mid-Amer Nazarene Coll; Music.

KETTLE, ADAM F; Topeka West HS; Topeka, KS; (3); 26/300; Art Clb; Church Yth Grp; French Clb; Math Clb; Science Clb; JV Var Bsbl; Var Ftbl; Var Capt Wrstlng; High Hon Roll; NHS; KS ST U; Engrng.

KETTLE, RYAN D; Topeka West HS; Topeka, KS; (1); French Clb; Intrml Ftbl.

KEY, AUDRA; Campus HS; Wichita, KS; (1); Church Yth Grp; Dance Clb; Debate Tm; Drama Clb; French Clb; GAA; Intnl Clb; NFL; Pep Clb; SADD; Peer Medtn Wrkr; Model; Pittsburgh U; Jrnlsm.

KEYS, CHANTEL E; Blue Valley HS; Stilwell, KS; (3); 14/254; Church Yth Grp; VP Intnl Clb; VP Spanish Clb; Flag Corp; Mrchg Band; Sec Stu Cncl; Capt Trk; High Hon Roll; VP NHS; Pres Acad Fit Awd; Pres Kay Clb KS Assn Yth; Cnslr Outdr Ed Lab; JCCC; Pre-Med.

KHADAVI, ELENA S; Shawnee Mission S Sr HS; Shawnee Mission, KS; (3); Cmnty Wkr; Intnl Clb; Math Clb; Pep Clb; Temple Yth Grp; Band; Mrchg Band; Socr; Trk; High Hon Roll; Piano Cmptns & Awds; KS Univ; Pre-Med.

KHAMMANIVONG, PAULA; Olathe East Sr HS; Olathe, KS; (4); Church Yth Grp; French Clb; Teachers Aide; Church Choir; Chrldng; Powder Puff Ftbl; Vllybl; High Hon Roll; Hon Roll; Chrch Yth Group Sec & VP; HOSA Clb Treas; NABC Yth Of Yr; U Of KS; Nrsng.

KHAN, ABID; Olathe East Sr HS; Overland Park, KS; (3); 1/360; Cmnty Wkr; Debate Tm; Intnl Clb; Math Tm; NFL; Quiz Bowl; Science Clb; Boy Scts; Nwsp; High Hon Roll; Acad Decathalon; Comm Hosp Vol; UMKC; Cardiologist.

KHAN, TARA; Blue Valley Northwest HS; Overland Park, KS; (3); Cmnty Wkr; Hon Roll; Jr NHS; NHS; Sci Knwldge Bowl; U Of MO Kansas City; Med Dr.

KHENSISANA, PHOUTHASACK; Wyandotte HS; Kansas City, KS; (3); 1/256; Chess Clb; Cmnty Wkr; Computer Clb; Teachers Aide; High Hon Roll; Hon Roll; NHS; Ntl Merit Ltr; Cmnty Wk; Cmptr Clb Sec, Treas, VP; HI Pacific U; Bus.

KHOUNVONGSA, SAKHONE; Wyandotte HS; Kansas City, KS; (2); Church Yth Grp; Cmnty Wkr; Intnl Clb; Teachers Aide; Gov Hon Prg Awd; High Hon Roll; Hon Roll; NHS; Prfct Atten Awd; Pres Schlr; Vlntr Tutor.

KHOUNVONGSA, SOUTSADA; Wyandotte HS; Kansas City, KS; (4); 1/200; Intnl Clb; Med Career Clb; Med.

KIBBE, JESSICA H; Osage City HS; Osage City, KS; (3); 3/32; Am Leg Aux Girls St; NFL; Sec Spanish Clb; Rptr Nwsp; Pres Stu Cncl; Var L Sftbl; Var L Vllybl; High Hon Roll; Church Yth Grp; Pep Clb; Natl Frnsc Qlfr; ST Jrnlsm; KS Univ; Tchg.

KIBBE, KARA; Jewell HS; Randall, KS; (1); 1/25; FCA; 4-H; FHA; Speech Tm; SADD; Band; School Play; Chrldng; Vllybl; High Hon Roll.

KIDDER, BETH A; Goodland HS; Goodland, KS; (3); FHA; Office Aide; SADD; Teachers Aide; JV Tennis; AFS Sec 95-; AFS Pres 96-; Elem Ed.

KIEFFER, JARROD C; El Dorado HS; El Dorado, KS; (2); Debate Tm; NFL; Stage Crew; Ftbl; High Hon Roll; Pres Acad Fit Awd; TIP Duke Univ; 3rd Rnr-Up Hoby Awd; Debate Ltrmn; Law Schl; Lwyr.

KIESS, ANDREA S; Wichita South HS; Wichita, KS; (4); 12/292; Church Yth Grp; Debate Tm; Letterman Clb; Library Aide; High Hon Roll; NHS; St Schlr; Campus Life; Friends U; Psych; Span.

KILBURN, AMANDA; Turner HS; Kansas City, KS; (3); Cmnty Wkr; Drama Clb; School Musical; Ofcr Stu Cncl; Chrldng; Hon Roll; Jr NHS; Mark Ecllnc; KS Assn Yth; Pittsburg ST U; Psych.

KILE, TOBIE J; Derby HS; Derby, KS; (2); Church Yth Grp; FCA; Band; Chorus; Church Choir; Mrchg Band; Orch; Variety Show; Cit Awd; High Hon Roll.

KILLINGSWORTH, APRIL; Blue Valley HS; Stilwell, KS; (4); Church Yth Grp; Pres Thesps; Chorus; Drill Tm; School Musical; High Hon Roll; NHS; St Schlr; Drama Clb; Teachers Aide; KS Rgnts Hnr Acad; Supt Awd; Yng Lf; Boston U.

KILLOUGH, KATIE A; Lawrence HS; Lawrence, KS; (3); Church Yth Grp; Cmnty Wkr; Acpl Chr; Church Choir; Golf; High Hon Roll; Pres Acad Fit Awd.

KILMER, JULIE L; Campus HS; Haysville, KS; (3); Church Yth Grp; Chorus; Church Choir; Hon Roll; Chldrns Tchr Chrch; Campus Life Clb; HERO; Butler Comm; RN.

KILPATRICK, BRIANA; Syracuse Jr Sr HS; Syracuse, KS; (2); 1/30; Church Yth Grp; 4-H; Quiz Bowl; Speech Tm; Band; Chorus; School Play; JV Vllybl; High Hon Roll; Syracuse Sngrs; KS ST U; Sec Ed.

KIM, CHONG S; Garden City Sr HS; Garden City, KS; (1); Chess Clb; Socr; Trk; Prfct Atten Awd; Bus.

KIMBALL, AMY B; Manhattan HS; Manhattan, KS; (2); Church Yth Grp; VP Sec 4-H; Spanish Clb; Chorus; JV Tennis; High Hon Roll; NHS; Pre-Med.

KIMBALL, JENNIFER S; Manhattan HS; Manhattan, KS; (2); Art Clb; Church Yth Grp; Cmnty Wkr; 4-H; German Clb; SADD; Varsity Clb; Rptr Nwsp; Intrml JV Bsktbl; Var L Crs Cntry; 2nd Pl ST Fnsh 300 Meter Hurdles; 4th 4oox4; Grnd Chmpn Arts Div/Clthg Buymshp 4-H; Intr Dcrtg/Art/Marine Bio.

KIMBALL, ROSS M; Central Heights Sr HS; Lane, KS; (2); FBLA; Letterman Clb; Science Clb; Spanish Clb; Swing Chorus; JV Bsktbl; Var Ftbl; Var Trk; High Hon Roll; Pittsburg ST; Medicine.

KIMBERLIN, NIKOLE J; Madison Jr Sr HS; Madison, KS; (3); German Clb; Band; Chorus; Jazz Band; Mrchg Band; Pep Band; JV Var Bsktbl; JV Vllybl; Hon Roll; Prfct Atten Awd; Kay-Kayettes; Emporia ST Univ; Dental Asst.

KIMBREL, RYAN; Dodge City HS; Dodge City, KS; (3); Church Yth Grp; Cmnty Wkr; FCA; French Clb; Intnl Clb; Teachers Aide; Mgr Bsktbl; JV Crs Cntry; Var Tennis; NHS; Stu Of Month 95; Ft Hays St Math Relays 1st Pl; Jr Ldrshp Dodge; MIT; Comp Sci.

KIMMEL, REBECCA D; Leavenworth HS; Leavenworth, KS; (3); Church Yth Grp; Acpl Chr; Band; Mrchg Band; Pep Band; Hon Roll; Piano Lsns 5 Yrs; Bsktbl Mgr Equip/Unfrms/Scrkpr; Mus/Art.

KIMMELL, BONNEY; Arkansas City HS; Arkansas City, KS; (4); 31/174; Am Leg Aux Girls St; FCA; Office Aide; VP SADD; Teachers Aide; Yrbk; Rep Soph Cls; Rep Sr Cls; Rep Stu Cncl; High Hon Roll; AFS Sec; Cowley Cty CC; Finance.

KIMMINAU, ASHLEY R; Kapaun-Mt Carmel HS; Wichita, KS; (2); Church Yth Grp; Drama Clb; Science Clb; Chorus; Socr; High Hon Roll; Unsung Hero Awd; CO; Drama.

KIMPLER, CHRISTI; Hutchinson HS; Hutchinson, KS; (3); 8/320; Am Leg Aux Girls St; Debate Tm; Key Clb; NFL; Science Clb; Powder Puff Ftbl; Var Swmmng; High Hon Roll; NHS; Prfct Atten Awd; People To People Stdnt Ambsdr.

KIMZEY, HARMONY G; Independence HS; Independence, KS; (4); 46/139; Cmnty Wkr; FCA; JA; Pep Clb; SADD; Teachers Aide; Chorus; Yrbk; Treas Frsh Cls; Treas Soph Cls; 95 Ftbl Homecoming Queen; 95 Wmn Indpndnc Awd; Top 10 Fnlst Amer Homecoming Queen Comp; Independence Comm Coll; PT.

KINDERKNECHT, BILL J; Thomas More Prep-Marion HS; Hays, KS; (2); Church Yth Grp; Var Ftbl; L Trk; Wt Lftg.

KINDERKNECHT, LEVI A; Wheatland Middle Sr HS; Park, KS; (3); 1/15; Quiz Bowl; Speech Tm; School Play; Pres Frsh Cls; Pres Soph Cls; Pres Jr Cls; Pres Sr Cls; Cit Awd; Art Clb; Regents Hnrs Acad 96; U Of KS; Med.

KINDERKNECHT, WILLIAM; Thomas More Prep-Marian HS; Hays, KS; (2); Church Yth Grp; Scholastic Bowl; Var Ftbl; Var Trk; Hon Roll; KS U; Med.

KINDLER, ZACH T; White Rock HS; Esbon, KS; (3); 3/10; Am Leg Boys St; Church Yth Grp; Cmnty Wkr; 4-H; Speech Tm; Math Tm; Quiz Bowl; Red Cross Aide; SADD; Varsity Clb.

KINDSCHER, LAUREN R; Beloit Jr Sr HS; Beloit, KS; (1); 7/88; Band; Chorus; Drill Tm; Mrchg Band; Orch; Pep Band; Sec Frsh Cls; JV Var Trk; JV L Vllybl; High Hon Roll; Future Med Clb; Crosstire Yth Group; KS Univ; Ped.

KING, AMANDA; St John Jr Sr HS; Saint John, KS; (4); 7/50; VP SADD; School Musical; School Play; Ed Yrbk; Pres Soph Cls; Rep Stu Cncl; Capt Chrldng; L Crs Cntry; Church Yth Grp; FHA; Kayettes; Forensics; Natl His & Govt Awds; U Of KS; Jrnlsm.

KING, ANGELA B; Shawnee Mission W Sr HS; Overland Park, KS; (3); Debate Tm; Spanish Clb; Speech Tm; SADD; Band; Mrchg Band; Pep Band; Stage Crew; Hon Roll; Marching Section Ldr For Band; Talent Identification Pgm; U Of NE Lincoln; Pol Sci.

KING, BECKY A; Iola Sr HS; Iola, KS; (3); 4-H; FBLA; SADD; Band; Mrchg Band; Pep Band; Var Bsktbl; Var Crs Cntry; Hon Roll; NHS; Keyettes.

KING, BRIAN T; Oskaloosa HS; Oskaloosa, KS; (2); FBLA; Letterman Clb; SADD; Jazz Band; Ofcr Bsbl; Bsktbl; Crs Cntry; Ftbl; Trk; Hon Roll; Tns As Tchrs HS Stdnts Tch Yngr Kids Abt Smkng; Frnscs; Wght Lftng; KS Univ; Cvl Engrng.

KING, CALVIN R; Ellis HS; Ellis, KS; (4); 4/40; Natl FFA Org; Treas Frsh Cls; Treas Soph Cls; Treas Jr Cls; Treas Sr Cls; Var Ftbl; Var Wrstlng; NHS; St Schlr; US Army Rsrv Natl Schlr Ath Awd; Fort Hays ST U; Eng Ed.

KING, CAMERON; Atchison Sr HS; Atchison, KS; (4); 12/123; Church Yth Grp; Computer Clb; Letterman Clb; Library Aide; Office Aide; Red Cross Aide; Spanish Clb; Speech Tm; Teachers Aide; Varsity Clb; All-Lg Ftbl 94 & 95; All-Lg Bsbl 95; YMCA Lfgrd; Comms.

KING, DONNIE L; Derby HS; Derby, KS; (2); Computer Clb; Hon Roll; NHS; Comp Pgmng.

KING, DULCINEA D; Council Grove HS; Council Grove, KS; (2); Art Clb; Church Yth Grp; Drama Clb; FCA; FBLA; Key Clb; Math Tm; Quiz Bowl; Scholastic Bowl; SADD; U Of KS; Pre-Med/Med Dctr.

KING, DUSTIN; Holton HS; Holton, KS; (1); Church Yth Grp; Natl FFA Org; Bsktbl; Ftbl; Wt Lftg; Hon Roll; KS ST Univ.

KING, ERIN V; Iola Sr HS; Iola, KS; (3); 2/110; Church Yth Grp; SADD; Chorus; Chrldng; Capt Pom Pon; Tennis; Cit Awd; High Hon Roll; NHS; KAY Pgm Dir/Comm Svc Dir; Govt Ctr Teen Ldrshp; I Dare You Ldrshp Awd; 4 Yr Coll.

KING, JENNIFER; El Dorado HS; El Dorado, KS; (2); Church Yth Grp; Letterman Clb; Spanish Clb; SADD; Ofcr Stu Cncl; JV Var Bsktbl; Var L Swmmng; JV Var Vllybl; Hon Roll; NHS.

KING, JENNIFER E; Hays HS; Hays, KS; (3); Cmnty Wkr; Pep Clb; Acpl Chr; Chorus; School Musical; Stage Crew; Ofcr Soph Cls; Mgr(s); Powder Puff Ftbl; Score Keeper; US Natl Math Awd; Vol Spec Olympics/Devlpmntly Chlngd People; Ft Hays ST Univ; Spec Ed.

KING, JULIA; Wichita North HS; Valley Center, KS; (3); 6/270; Church Yth Grp; Science Clb; Teachers Aide; Band; Mrchg Band; Pep Band; Rep Soph Cls; Rep Jr Cls; Rep Stu Cncl; Var L Socr; 1st Pl ST Fnshr US Inst Peace Essy Cntst; 3rd Pl Reg Fnshr Natl His Day Cntst; Pre-Med.

KING, JUSTIN T; Phillipsburg HS; Phillipsburg, KS; (2); Church Yth Grp; Cmnty Wkr; FBLA; Spanish Clb; Rep Stu Cncl; JV Bsktbl; JV Ftbl; JV Golf; Hon Roll; Knwldge Mster Open; Pharm.

KING, LAURA A; Maize HS; Wichita, KS; (1); SADD; Color Guard; Mrchg Band; Tennis; Hon Roll; Wichita ST; Acctg.

KING, LISA M; Conway Springs HS; Conway Springs, KS; (4); 2/45; Church Yth Grp; Scholastic Bowl; Band; Chorus; Rep Stu Cncl; Var Trk; Var Vllybl; Hon Roll; Ntl Merit SF; MO Southern ST Coll; Bio.

KING, LUCAS; Maranatha Acad; Lenexa, KS; (4); 11/31; Band; Chorus; Mrchg Band; Pep Band; School Play; Ofcr Stu Cncl; Var L Socr; Var L Trk; Hon Roll; NHS; Stu Cncl Chaplain; Tabor Coll; Yth Mnstry.

KING, MARI; Rose Hill HS; Derby, KS; (3); HOBY; Acpl Chr; Jazz Band; School Musical; Yrbk; Rep Stu Cncl; Var Chrldng; Pom Pon; NHS; Church Yth Grp; KAYS; Btlr Yth Ldrshp; Arch.

KING, MERIDETH L; Shawnee Mission S Sr HS; Overland Park, KS; (3); Cmnty Wkr; Intnl Clb; SADD; Teachers Aide; High Hon Roll; Hon Roll; Show Me South Clb; Bus.

KING, NATALIE; Stafford Jr Sr HS; Stafford, KS; (1); Church Yth Grp; FCA; FHA; GAA; Band; Rep Frsh Cls; Rep Stu Cncl; Bsktbl; Trk; Vllybl; Mid-Amer Nazarene Coll; Arch.

KING, TAMARA; Campus HS; Haysville, KS; (4); 42/218; Am Leg Aux Girls St; Church Yth Grp; Girl Scts; Pep Clb; SADD; Teachers Aide; Chorus; Church Choir; School Musical; Swing Chorus; Natural Helpers; Campus Pride; Butler Cty CC; Speech Pthlgst.

KINGERY, SHANNON L; Maize HS; Maize, KS; (4); Spanish Clb; SADD; Hon Roll; NHS.

KINGSBURY, KATIE; Smith Ctr Jr Sr HS; Smith Center, KS; (1); Church Yth Grp; 4-H; FHA; Pep Clb; Quiz Bowl; SADD; Chorus; Flag Corp; Chrldng; Swmmng; KS ST; Lawyer; Tchr.

KINGSBY, JEMEA A; Santa Fe Trail Jr HS; Olathe, KS; (1); Cmnty Wkr; Band; Trk; Cit Awd; High Hon Roll; Pres Acad Fit Awd; Paralegal.

KINKAID, LAURA; Circle HS; Towanda, KS; (1); Church Yth Grp; 4-H; Chorus; Church Choir; School Musical; Chrldng; 4-H Awd; Hon Roll.

KINNAMON, GINA; South Gray HS; Montezuma, KS; (2); Church Yth Grp; Letterman Clb; Pep Clb; Spanish Clb; Teachers Aide; Chorus; Stat Bsktbl; Mgr(s); High Hon Roll; Hon Roll; Chld Psych.

KINSEY, ASHLEY; Leavenworth HS; Leavenworth, KS; (4); Am Leg Aux Girls St; Hosp Aide; SADD; Varsity Clb; Ofcr Sr Cls; JV Stat Bsktbl; Capt L Vllybl; High Hon Roll; NHS; Pres Schlr; Rensselaer Mdl; KS Hnr Schlr; Native Amer Indian Art Cont Wnnr; Psych.

KINSEY, NICOLE M; Troy HS; Troy, KS; (2); Letterman Clb; VP Frsh Cls; Sec Soph Cls; Var L Bsktbl; Var L Crs Cntry; Var L Trk; Var L Vllybl; High Hon Roll; NHS; KS ST Univ; Law.

KINSEY, THERESA D; Wyandotte HS; Kansas City, KS; (3); Church Yth Grp; Chorus; Church Choir; Flag Corp; Mrchg Band; Hon Roll; Grambling St Univ; Comp Prog.

KINSLER, ALLEN; Southeast Of Salina HS; Salina, KS; (4); 1/54; Am Leg Boys St; Church Yth Grp; Pres Science Clb; School Musical; Pres Stu Cncl; L Var Bsktbl; Var Capt Ftbl; High Hon Roll; NHS; St Schlr; U Of KS; Bio; Pre-Med.

KIPPES, JENNIFER A; Blue Valley HS; Overland Park, KS; (3); Intnl Clb; SADD; Hon Roll; NHS; KAYS Sec; Vol Hrtlnd Schl Of Rdng For Hndcpd; Elem/Early Chldhd Ed.

KIPPLEY, MELISSA; Olathe South Sr HS; Olathe, KS; (2); 1/486; Pres Church Yth Grp; FHA; Spanish Clb; Church Choir; Orch; School Musical; High Hon Roll; Pres Acad Fit Awd; Service Clb; Rep Stu Cncl; Olathe Area Yth Symphny & Chamber Orch.

KIRCHGASSNER, AUDRA; Larned HS; Larned, KS; (4); 4/90; Church Yth Grp; Band; Chorus; Flag Corp; Mrchg Band; Pep Band; Powder Puff Ftbl; Sftbl; High Hon Roll; Hon Roll; U Of KS; Law.

KIRCHGASSNER, MELANI; Larned HS; Larned, KS; (4); Am Leg Aux Girls St; Letterman Clb; Varsity Clb; Band; Var Bsktbl; Var Sftbl; Var Vllybl; High Hon Roll; NHS; Prfct Atten Awd; U Of KS; Phrmcy.

KIRCHHOFF, ANNE C; Shawnee Mission E Sr HS; Fairway, KS; (4); GAA; Letterman Clb; Office Aide; Pep Clb; Varsity Clb; Church Choir; Orch; JV Intrml Bsktbl; Capt L Socr; High Hon Roll; Tulane Univ.

KIRCHHOFF, RYAN D; Bishop Miege HS; Fairway, KS; (1); Church Yth Grp; Cmnty Wkr; Letterman Clb; JV Bsbl; Ice Hcky; Var L Socr; Hon Roll.

KIRCHHOFF, TIM; Shawnee Mission S Sr HS; Lenexa, KS; (4); Boy Scts; SADD; Band; Mrchg Band; Capt Chrldng; Tennis; Hon Roll; KS St Univ; Archt.

KIRCHNER, CORY M; Sedan HS; Peru, KS; (2); #16 in class; Letterman Clb; Natl FFA Org; Var JV Bsbl; JV Bsktbl; Ftbl; Var Wt Lftg; Hon Roll; Phys Thrpy.

KIRCHNER, CRYSTAL A; Sedan HS; Sedan, KS; (3); 7/38; FHA; Letterman Clb; Spanish Clb; Teachers Aide; VP Frsh Cls; Var Chrldng; Var Sftbl; JV Vllybl; Hon Roll; Dietician.

KIRCHNER, JOSEPH P; Shawnee Mission W Sr HS; Overland Park, KS; (3); 120/436; Boy Scts; Church Yth Grp; Latin Clb; Pep Clb; Intrml Bsktbl; Var Ftbl; Var Trk; Intrml Wt Lftg; Hon Roll; Shawnee Mssn R&D Frm 1st Pl & Grant Awd Archtctrl Hs Plns; Archtctr.

KIRCHOFF, JEREMY B; Garden City Sr HS; Garden City, KS; (2); Church Yth Grp; Spanish Clb; Band; Church Choir; Mrchg Band; Pep Band; Socr; Var Trk; High Hon Roll; Yth Scoor League Asst Coach; Kansas Bible Camp Vol; Babe Ruth Bsbll.

KIRCHOFF, MARYANNE; Smith Ctr Jr Sr HS; Gaylord, KS; (1); Church Yth Grp; Cmnty Wkr; FHA; Ski Clb; SADD; Band; Chorus; Church Choir; Drill Tm; Jazz Band; Kays; Ft Hays ST U; Engrg.

KIRK, BRENNA; Bucklin Schl; Bucklin, KS; (2); #1 in class; Quiz Bowl; SADD; Band; Church Choir; Mrchg Band; Pep Band; Nwsp; Yrbk; Sec Frsh Cls; Sec Soph Cls; St Track & Speech.

KIRK, CARRIE; Hillcrest Schl; Narka, KS; (4); 6/15; Church Yth Grp; Drama Clb; Natl FFA Org; Band; Chorus; Jazz Band; Swing Chorus; Yrbk; Hon Roll; NHS; Emporia ST U; Scndry Ed.

KIRK, GREG P; Riverton Schl; Riverton, KS; (2); Quiz Bowl; Spanish Clb; Band; Jazz Band; Mrchg Band; Pep Band; Pres Frsh Cls; Wt Lftg; Hon Roll; U MO Rolla; Aero Engrng.

KIRK, JOSIE L; Topeka HS; Topeka, KS; (4); 60/370; Pep Clb; VP Science Clb; Teachers Aide; Capt Drill Tm; Variety Show; Capt Crs Cntry; Capt Diving; Capt Swmmng; High Hon Roll; Hon Roll; Washburn Univ; Vet.

KIRK, KIMBERLY J; Maize HS; Wichita, KS; (2); 1/300; Church Yth Grp; FCA; Q&S; Chorus; Variety Show; Ed Nwsp; High Hon Roll; NHS; Pres Acad Fit Awd; Hosp Aide.

KIRKENDOLL, BRIDGET D; Olathe East Sr HS; Overland Park, KS; (2); Church Yth Grp; French Clb; GAA; Letterman Clb; Math Clb; Pep Clb; Chorus; Drill Tm; VP Soph Cls; VP Jr Cls; Jr All Amer Drll Team Frosh Yr/All Amer Drll Team Soph/Jr Yr; All Amer Dance Co Soph/Jr Yr.

KIRKENDOLL, JAMES M; Andover HS; Andover, KS; (3); 6/156; Church Yth Grp; Acpl Chr; Band; Jazz Band; Pep Band; School Musical; High Hon Roll; NHS; Cmnty Wkr; Mrchg Band; Wichita Wind Ensemble; Reg & St Piano Festival; Piano.

KIRKLAND, JENNIFER; Marysville HS; Marysville, KS; (3); 7/100; Bus Profs of Am; FCA; Letterman Clb; Band; Bsktbl; Sftbl; Var Tennis; Kiwanis Awd; Kayettes Brd; Matmaids Sec; Marysville Yth Coaltn; Phys Thrpy.

KIRKLAND, SABRINA D; Anderson Cty Jr Sr HS; Garnett, KS; (4); 30/77; FHA; Intnl Clb; SADD; Teachers Aide; Band; Jazz Band; Pep Band; Drama Clb; Pep Clb; Quiz Bowl; Tutor; Fornscs Tm Capt; Coffeyville CC; Music Therpst.

KIRKPATRICK, ALEXANDER J; Northeast Magnet HS; Wichita, KS; (4); Am Leg Boys St; JA; Quiz Bowl; Rep Jr Cls; Pres Stu Cncl; Hon Roll; NHS; Cit Awd; High Hon Roll; Pres Acad Fit Awd; Chrch Bsktbl Team; United Way Ctznshp Awd; Top Hum Stu Of Grad Cls; Baker Univ.

KIRKPATRICK, AMANDA; St Paul HS; Walnut, KS; (4); 5/13; Am Leg Aux Girls St; Cmnty Wkr; 4-H; Pep Clb; Speech Tm; Band; Chorus; Pep Band; Phtg Yrbk; Sec Sr Cls; Labett CC; Nrsng.

KIRKPATRICK, JANEL E; Chanute Sr HS; Chanute, KS; (1); Church Yth Grp; Chorus; High Hon Roll; Hon Roll.

KIRKPATRICK, KELLEE JO; Ellinwood Jr Sr HS; Great Bend, KS; (2); Church Yth Grp; Debate Tm; FCA; Speech Tm; Band; Chorus; School Musical; Pres Frsh Cls; High Hon Roll; Art Clb; Mystic Blues Slct Choir; Lawyer.

KIRKPATRICK, KELLY C; Eureka Jr Sr HS; Eureka, KS; (3); Church Yth Grp; FHA; Natl FFA Org; Kayetts; Cottey Coll; Soc Wrk.

KIRKPATRICK, KIMBERLY J; St Paul HS; Walnut, KS; (2); 12/27; Pep Clb; Speech Tm; Sec Soph Cls; JV Sftbl; Hon Roll; Prfct Atten Awd; Labette Cty CC; Nrsng.

KIRKPATRICK, RHONDA L; Caney Valley Jr Sr HS; Havana, KS; (4); 1/75; Church Yth Grp; FHA; Treas Spanish Clb; VP Frsh Cls; Pres Soph Cls; Treas Jr Cls; Treas Sr Cls; Ofcr Stu Cncl; Mgr Ftbl; High Hon Roll; Equus Clb VP; Acctng.

KIRKPATRICK, SHANNA M; Lyndon HS; Lyndon, KS; (4); 13/33; Church Yth Grp; Drama Clb; 4-H; FBLA; FHA; NFL; Speech Tm; Thesps; School Play; Ofcr Sr Cls; U Of KS; Cmptr Sci.

KIRKWOOD, TAMI; Valley Falls HS; Meriden, KS; (4); 8/34; Cmnty Wkr; FHA; Nwsp; Yrbk; Rep Soph Cls; Ofcr Stu Cncl; JV Var Bsktbl; Var Chrldng; Hon Roll; NHS; Emporia ST U; Mrktng Dsgn.

KISBY, BRIAN; Derby HS; Derby, KS; (3); 26/386; Am Leg Boys St; Boy Scts; Church Yth Grp; Key Clb; SADD; Ofcr Frsh Cls; Ofcr Soph Cls; Ofcr Jr Cls; Ofcr Stu Cncl; Mgr(s); Mrt Qlfr; Amer HS Math Exam; Egl/Boy Scts Of Amer; Blue Rbbn Hutchinson CC Indust Tech Expo Brd Drft; Brigham Young Univ.

KISBY, SHERA L; Clifton-Clyde HS; Clifton, KS; (3); VP 4-H; FBLA; Treas Natl FFA Org; Pep Clb; Band; Mrchg Band; Pep Band; Radio Brdcstng.

KISER, DOMINICK L; Salina HS Central; Salina, KS; (1); Band; Mrchg Band; Pep Band; Stat Bsktbl; Intrml Ftbl; Intrml Mgr(s); High Hon Roll; Hon Roll; Bnd Lttr; KS ST Univ Math/Sci Initiative Prgm.

KISSEL, ALEXANDER G; Baster Springs HS; Baxter Springs, KS; (2); Treas Church Yth Grp; Drama Clb; Letterman Clb; Pep Clb; Scholastic Bowl; Science Clb; Band; Chorus; Church Choir; Mrchg Band.

KISSEL, JENNIFER A; Blue Valley HS; Stilwell, KS; (3); 23/255; JCL; Orch; Sec Sr Cls; Rep Stu Cncl; JV Bsktbl; JV Trk; Vllybl; High Hon Roll; Hon Roll; NHS; Pres JCL ST KS; Micrbiolgy.

KISSEL, LAURA J; Anderson Cty Jr Sr HS; Garnett, KS; (3); 1/74; Scholastic Bowl; SADD; Pres Frsh Cls; Ofcr Stu Cncl; Var L Bsktbl; Var L Crs Cntry; High Hon Roll; NHS; Intnl Clb; Pep Clb; Air Force Acad Smr Scientific Smnr; Acad Awds; Octagon Clb; KS Univ; Law.

KISTLER, SANDIE L; Colby Sr HS; Colby, KS; (3); Spanish Clb; KAYS Club.

KISTLER, TAMMY; Udall HS; Udall, KS; (3); Church Yth Grp; Dance Clb; Pep Clb; Band; Mrchg Band; Pep Band; Yrbk; Bsktbl; Chrldng; Sftbl; Radiologist.

KISTNER, ANGIE; Waverly HS; Waverly, KS; (4); 1/21; Capt Quiz Bowl; Ed Nwsp; Pres Stu Cncl; Capt Chrldng; Trk; Vllybl; High Hon Roll; Pres NHS; Prfct Atten Awd; Val; KS Hnr Soc; Gov Schlr; KS St Ldrshp Schlrshp; KS ST U; Mass Comms.

KITCHEN, CURTIS J; Oskaloosa HS; Oskaloosa, KS; (3); Church Yth Grp; FCA; FBLA; Pep Clb; Pres Jr Cls; Var L Bsbl; Var L Bsktbl; Var L Crs Cntry; Cit Awd; NHS; Meterology.

KITE, JARED J; Washburn Rural HS; Topeka, KS; (3); Boy Scts; Computer Clb; Band; Mrchg Band; Pep Band; High Hon Roll; Hon Roll; Shawnee Cty Shrffs Dept Cadet; Washburn Univ.

KITSMILLER, CINDY; Lawrence HS; Lawrence, KS; (4); Bus Profs of Am; DECA; Office Aide; Teachers Aide; High Hon Roll; NHS; Pres Acad Fit Awd; Johnson Cty CC; Bus.

KITTELSON, ELAN; Winfield HS; Winfield, KS; (3); 28/147; Am Leg Boys St; Hon Roll; Perfect Attnd.

KITTLE, EMILY; Augusta Sr HS; Augusta, KS; (4); Church Yth Grp; Band; Mrchg Band; Orch; Bsktbl; Vllybl; Cit Awd; High Hon Roll; NHS; FCA; Athl Trng Pgm; Butler Cty CC; Athl Trng/PT.

KITTRELL, MATT D; Clearwater HS; Clearwater, KS; (2); HOBY; NFL; Stage Crew; Ed Yrbk; Pres Frsh Cls; Pres Soph Cls; JV Bsktbl; L Crs Cntry; L Trk; JV Wrstlng; Baldwin Stud Abroad Pgm Russian Lang; Pro Bsbl; HS Art Tchr.

KIVETT, BAILEY; Halstead HS; Halstead, KS; (2); Cmnty Wkr; Letterman Clb; Spanish Clb; School Play; Yrbk; Bsktbl; Sftbl; Trk; High Hon Roll; NHS; Schltc Art; HS Life Sci Tchr.

KIVETT, LISA; Kinsley HS; Kinsley, KS; (3); Church Yth Grp; Debate Tm; Drama Clb; Spanish Clb; Upward Bound; DCCC Coll Courses; Ed; Law.

KLAMM, STACY; Spring Hill HS; Spring Hill, KS; (3); 4/98; Dance Clb; 4-H; GAA; Spanish Clb; Drill Tm; Sec Soph Cls; Var Pom Pon; Var Sftbl; Cit Awd; High Hon Roll; Crmnl Psych.

KLAPMEYER, RYAN R; Blue Valley HS; Stilwell, KS; (2); Church Yth Grp; Cmnty Wkr; Hosp Aide; Band; Jazz Band; Mrchg Band; Pep Band; Socr; Wrstlng; Hon Roll.

KLASSEN, ANDRA S; Halstead HS; Halstead, KS; (1); Church Yth Grp; German Clb; Sec Frsh Cls; Rep Soph Cls; JV Bsktbl; Var Chrldng; JV Trk; JV Vllybl; Hon Roll; Star Stu; Lifeguard; KS ST Univ; Law; Comp Tech.

KLASSEN, GENEVIEVE M; Ft Scott HS; Fort Scott, KS; (2); 11/200; Band; Chorus; Mrchg Band; Orch; Pep Band; Crs Cntry; Trk; High Hon Roll; Hon Roll; Choir Ensmble; Music Camp; U Of KS; Music Ed.

KLASSEN, HEATHER; Inman Jr Sr HS; Inman, KS; (3); 7/42; Church Yth Grp; Cmnty Wkr; Drama Clb; FHA; German Clb; Math Tm; NFL; Pep Clb; Quiz Bowl; Teachers Aide; Hutchinson JC; Elem Ed.

KLASSEN, HELEN; Lacrosse HS; La Crosse, KS; (1); Art Clb; Drama Clb; Pep Clb; Chorus; Church Choir; Mrchg Band; School Play; VP Frsh Cls; Rep Stu Cncl; Var L Chrldng; Rllr Bldng/Cake Dcrtng/Nls/Hr; Hays Acad Hair Design; Csmtlgst.

KLASSEN, KATIE A; Ft Scott HS; Fort Scott, KS; (3); #1 in class; Church Yth Grp; FCA; Science Clb; Chorus; Var Crs Cntry; JV Sftbl; JV Trk; Vllybl; Hon Roll; NHS; U Of Dallas.

KLASSEN, STEPHANIE; Pratt HS; Pratt, KS; (4); 9/96; Church Yth Grp; 4-H; HOBY; Key Clb; SADD; Teachers Aide; Band; 4-H Awd; High Hon Roll; NHS; KS Music Educators Fstvl Hnr Band 95-96; Wichita ST U; Hlth Svcs.

KLASSEN, WILLIAM; Desoto HS; Olathe, KS; (4); Church Yth Grp; 4-H; Math Tm; Quiz Bowl; Band; Mrchg Band; Pep Band; School Musical; Var Socr; Trk; Natl 4-H Awd; KS ST; Elec Engrng.

KLAUS, JENNIFER; Holcomb HS; Holcomb, KS; (4); 13/41; Drama Clb; French Clb; Spanish Clb; Teachers Aide; Stage Crew; Nwsp; JV Bsktbl; Hon Roll; Forensics 4 Yrs ST Chmpnshps; Washburn; Lgl Asst.

KLAUS, SAYRE; Hays HS; Hays, KS; (4); 25/220; Church Yth Grp; Natl FFA Org; Teachers Aide; Acpl Chr; Chorus; Church Choir; JV Crs Cntry; High Hon Roll; NHS; Ft Hays ST U; Vet Medcn.

KLAUS, STACEY; Thomas More Prep-Marion HS; Hays, KS; (2); Church Yth Grp; Cmnty Wkr; Letterman Clb; Service Clb; Band; Chrldng; Sftbl; High Hon Roll; NHS.

KLAUS, WENDY; Victoria HS; Victoria, KS; (3); 1/30; Church Yth Grp; Varsity Clb; Drill Tm; Yrbk; VP Stu Cncl; Bsktbl; Trk; Vllybl; VP NHS; Dance Clb; Ft Hays; Pharmacy.

KLEIER, TINA M; Gardner-Edgerton HS; Gardner, KS; (2); Church Yth Grp; NFL; Band; Mrchg Band; Pep Band; JV Sftbl; Var Tennis; Mgr Wrstlng; High Hon Roll; Hon Roll; KU; Reg Nurse.

KLEIN, DANIEL; Shawnee Mission E HS; Roeland Park, KS; (4); Am Leg Boys St; Intnl Clb; Model UN; Natl Beta Clb; NFL; Temple Yth Grp; High Hon Roll.

KLEIN, JASON R; Newton Sr HS; Newton, KS; (2); 39/279; Computer Clb; Debate Tm; Key Clb; JV Trk; High Hon Roll; Pres Cssna Arcft Prgrm; Cmptr Ntwrkng Admin.

KLEIN, KRIS; Ulysses HS; Ulysses, KS; (4); 8/93; Am Leg Boys St; FBLA; Library Aide; SADD; Co-Ed Nwsp; Co-Ed Yrbk; Var Golf; NHS.

KLEIN, NIKKI M; Bishop Carroll Catholic HS; Wichita, KS; (3); FCA; SADD; Teachers Aide; Acpl Chr; School Play; Golf; Hon Roll.

KLEIN, PATRICK; St Thomas Aquinas HS; Overland Park, KS; (4); 90/231; Church Yth Grp; Key Clb; Acpl Chr; School Musical; Stage Crew; Variety Show; Hon Roll; Forensics; St Louis Univ; Acctng.

KLEINER, KACHINA S; Riley Cty HS; Manhattan, KS; (2); 4-H; Natl FFA Org; Chorus; 4-H Awd; Ed.

KLEIST, DOROTHY J; Chapman HS; Chapman, KS; (3); 28/143; Pres Church Yth Grp; Drama Clb; French Clb; Girl Scts; Intnl Clb; NFL; Speech Tm; SADD; Thesps; School Play; Intl Exchng Stdnt Russia; Law.

KLEMAN, JAIME L; Baxter Springs HS; Baxter Springs, KS; (3); FCA; FBLA; FHA; GAA; Pep Clb; Rptr Nwsp; Bsktbl; Trk; Hon Roll.

KLEPPER, DEENA M; Great Bend Sr HS; Great Bend, KS; (4); 25/216; Church Yth Grp; German Clb; Hosp Aide; Pep Clb; SADD; Variety Show; Var Mgr(s); High Hon Roll; NHS; St Schlr; Barton CC.

KLIETHERMES, ANGELA D; Wichita Northwest HS; Wichita, KS; (3); VP Bus Profs of Am; Cmnty Wkr; Teachers Aide; Socr; Hon Roll; WSU.

KLIEWER, JOHN P; Hesston HS; Halstead, KS; (1); Church Yth Grp; FCA; FBLA; Band; Chorus; Pep Band; Ftbl; Golf; Wt Lftg; Wrstlng; Ltr Wrstlng; Arch.

KLIMA, CYNTHIA K; Great Bend Sr HS; Great Bend, KS; (3); 41/231; Pres 4-H; German Clb; Band; Mrchg Band; Pep Band; Bsktbl; Var L Golf; Var L Swmmng; Hon Roll; 4-H Cncl Sec; Ger Exch Group; Acctng.

KLIMA, JAKE B; Great Bend Sr HS; Great Bend, KS; (1); 4-H; Band; Mrchg Band; Pep Band; Var L Golf; 4-H Awd; Hon Roll; KS Jr Gold Assoc; FFA.

KLINE, CHAD J; Mc Pherson HS; Mc Pherson, KS; (2); Church Yth Grp; Cmnty Wkr; Letterman Clb; Spanish Clb; SADD; Varsity Clb; School Play; Var Bsbl; Var Bsktbl; Hon Roll.

KLINE, KATHERINE S; Hutchinson HS; Hutchinson, KS; (3); 10/400; Am Leg Aux Girls St; Cmnty Wkr; Science Clb; Speech Tm; Thesps; Chorus; School Musical; Rep Stu Cncl; High Hon Roll; VP Jr NHS.

KLINE, MINDY J; Medicine Lodge HS; Medicine Lodge, KS; (4); 3/54; Church Yth Grp; 4-H; Science Clb; Chorus; School Play; Sec Frsh Cls; Var Vllybl; High Hon Roll; NHS; Pres Acad Fit Awd; KS ST Univ; Elem Ed.

KLINE, SEASON C; Sumner Acad Of Arts & Science; Kansas City, KS; (1); Church Yth Grp; FCA; Orch; Hon Roll; Tutor El Centro Fmly Rsrc Cntr KCK; Nrsng Hme Vstns Chrch; Yth Cncl Org Bus Rt; KS Univ; Soc Wrk/Cnslng.

KLING, JENNIFER; Belleville HS; Belleville, KS; (3); Church Yth Grp; Cmnty Wkr; Drama Clb; 4-H; HOBY; Pep Clb; Science Clb; Spanish Clb; Varsity Clb; Band; Vcl Slst Jz Bnd; Lns Clb ST, Natl Hnr Bnd; KS ST U; Srgcl RN.

KLINGELE, JULIANNE; Leavenworth HS; Leavenworth, KS; (1); FHA; SADD; Teachers Aide; Chorus; Var Chrldng; Hon Roll; DARE Grad, Awd; JA Prjct Bus Awd; Central MO ST U; Scndry Ed.

KLINGENBERG, BRETT; Peabody-Burns Jr Sr HS; Peabody, KS; (1); Church Yth Grp; 4-H; Natl FFA Org; Quiz Bowl; Band; Church Choir; Mrchg Band; Pep Band; School Musical; Bsktbl; KMENC Dist 6 Band; Hi Hnr Band.

KLINGENBERG, ROBERT; Udall HS; Udall, KS; (4); 4/32; Teachers Aide; Band; Mrchg Band; Pep Band; School Play; Bsktbl; Ftbl; Trk; High Hon Roll; Pres Acad Fit Awd; KS Hnrs Schlr 95-96; Trk Discus Schl Recrd & League Chmp 95; Multi Yr Listing; K-ST; Engrng.

KLINKON, CINDY; Northeast HS; Arma, KS; (4); 3/43; Church Yth Grp; Cmnty Wkr; 4-H; Office Aide; Band; Chorus; Drm Mjr(t); Mrchg Band; Pep Band; Ed Yrbk; Pittsburg ST Univ; Phrmcy.

KLOSTER, SHANNON M; Newton Sr HS; Newton, KS; (3); Church Yth Grp; Key Clb; Office Aide; SADD; Chorus; Mgr(s); Var Swmmng; JV Vllybl; Hon Roll; Emporia ST KS.

KLOTZ, CHESTER A; Manhattan HS; Manhattan, KS; (3); #1 in class; Cmnty Wkr; Chorus; Rptr Nwsp; Rptr Yrbk; Intrml Bsktbl; Var L Tennis; Cit Awd; High Hon Roll; NHS; Medicine.

KLUG, ALISHA; Claflin Jr Sr HS; Odin, KS; (1); FHA; Math Tm; Pep Clb; Band; Mrchg Band; Pep Band; Rep Stu Cncl; Bsktbl; Chrldng; Golf; KS U; Pedtrcn.

KLUSENER, WILL C; Maize HS; Maize, KS; (1); Boy Scts; Church Yth Grp; German Clb; Hosp Aide; Band; Church Choir; Jazz Band; Mrchg Band; Pep Band.

KNAPE, KIM A; Ottawa HS; Ottawa, KS; (2); Church Yth Grp; Drama Clb; 4-H; Letterman Clb; Spanish Clb; SADD; Variety Show; Var JV Chrldng; High Hon Roll; Hon Roll; Teenport 2 Yrs; KU; Bus.

KNAPP, ALEX; Olathe South Sr HS; Olathe, KS; (3); #1 in class; Debate Tm; Math Tm; NFL; Quiz Bowl; Speech Tm; High Hon Roll; Hon Roll; Jr NHS; NHS; Pres Acad Fit Awd; Jdg.

KNAPP, DEVIN M; Pittsburg HS; Pittsburg, KS; (2); Library Aide; Spanish Clb; Nwsp; JV Bsktbl; Var Tennis; Pittsburg ST Univ; Ped.

KNAPP, MCKENSY; Shawnee Mission Northwest HS; Shawnee Mission, KS; (4); Church Yth Grp; Cmnty Wkr; Drama Clb; Teachers Aide; Chrldng; Wt Lftg; High Hon Roll; NHS; St Schlr; Yth Ldrshp Tm; Cougars United VP; U Of Pittsburgh; Phys Thrp.

KNAUP, RYAN D; Frontenac Jr Sr HS; Frontenac, KS; (4); 13/35; Math Tm; Pep Clb; Spanish Clb; Teachers Aide; Band; Rep Frsh Cls; Rep Soph Cls; Rep Jr Cls; VP Sr Cls; Rep Stu Cncl; Pittsburg ST; Spch Pthlgy.

KNECHT, JOE E; Paola HS; Paola, KS; (4); Science Clb; Teachers Aide; JV L Bsbl; Var L Wrstlng; Hon Roll; KS ST Univ.

KNEECE, HEATEHR; Leroy HS; Le Roy, KS; (1); 2/17; Church Yth Grp; Bsktbl; Chrldng; Vllybl; Hon Roll.

KNIEP, JAY; Colby Sr HS; Colby, KS; (2); Church Yth Grp; Band; Mrchg Band; Bsktbl; Var L Crs Cntry; Ftbl; JV Golf; Hon Roll; Sci.

KNIERIM, AN DEE; Circle HS; Towanda, KS; (4); 10/99; Church Yth Grp; Drama Clb; Spanish Clb; School Musical; School Play; Yrbk; Mgr(s); High Hon Roll; NHS; Natl Merit Schlr; Rockhurst Coll; Phys Thrpy.

KNIERIM, ANDEE; Circle HS; Towanda, KS; (4); 9/89; Church Yth Grp; Quiz Bowl; Spanish Clb; SADD; Mgr Stage Crew; Ed Yrbk; Lbrn Mgr(s); High Hon Roll; NHS; St Schlr; Pres Schlrshp; Natl Mrt Cmmnd Schlr; Natl Jrnlsm Cmptn Excllnt Awd; Rockhurst Coll; Phys Thrp.

KNIGHT, AMANDA; Lebo Schl; Lebo, KS; (4); 1/27; Am Leg Aux Girls St; 4-H; FBLA; Church Choir; Treas Stu Cncl; Capt L Bsktbl; Capt L Vllybl; NHS; Pres Schlr; Val; Trple Trio; KS ST U; Scndry Ed.

KNIGHT, MONICA R; Blue Valley Northwest HS; Overland Park, KS; (2); Cmnty Wkr; Hosp Aide; Office Aide; Pep Clb; Chorus; School Musical; Hon Roll; Hrsbck Rdng.

KNIGHT, SHANNON; Valley Falls HS; Valley Falls, KS; (3); FBLA; FHA; Yrbk; Rep Frsh Cls; VP Jr Cls; Var Bsktbl; Var Pom Pon; Var Sftbl; Var Vllybl; High Hon Roll.

KNIPP, NATHAN D; Sacred Heart HS; Salina, KS; (2); FBLA; NFL; Quiz Bowl; School Play; Stage Crew; Treas Soph Cls; Treas Jr Cls; Var Bsbl; JV Bsktbl; Var Ftbl; Teen Ambucs VP 2nd Clb In US, Sgt Of Arms; CO Univ; Aeronautical Engr.

KNIPP, REBECCA; Buhler HS; Hutchinson, KS; (4); 10/143; Am Leg Aux Girls St; Pres Church Yth Grp; Chorus; Church Choir; School Musical; School Play; JV Chrldng; High Hon Roll; NHS; KS ST U; Bio.

KNISLEY, ABBY M; Independence HS; Independence, KS; (1); French Clb; L Orch; Sec Frsh Cls; L Stu Cncl; Chrldng; Powder Puff Ftbl; L Var Sftbl; High Hon Roll; KU; Pharm.

KNISLEY III, CAROL R; Independence HS; Independence, KS; (3); 6/146; French Clb; High Hon Roll; NHS; Ku; Elec Engrng.

KNOBBE, MOLLY S; Cimarron HS; Cimarron, KS; (2); 1/50; FCA; Pep Clb; Var Bsktbl; Intrml Powder Puff Ftbl; Var Tennis; Var Trk; High Hon Roll; NHS; Pres Acad Fit Awd; Chsn SW KS All-Area Grls Bsktbl Team; Chsn All League/All Acad League HPL BSKTBL 95-.

KNOBLOCK, SHANA R; Sabetha HS; Sabetha, KS; (4); 8/60; FHA; Pres German Clb; Pep Clb; Band; Chorus; School Musical; Nwsp; Ofcr Stu Cncl; Trk; High Hon Roll; KS ST Univ.

KNOCHE, BRENT; Stafford Jr Sr HS; Stafford, KS; (2); 5/30; Church Yth Grp; Natl FFA Org; VP Frsh Cls; VP Soph Cls; Rep Stu Cncl; Var L Bsktbl; Var L Ftbl; Var L Trk; High Hon Roll; Hon Roll; Completd Ldrshp Course; KU; Accntng.

KNOCKE, RAMONA J; Shawnee Mission NW HS; Shawnee, KS; (4); 35/400; Church Yth Grp; Debate Tm; JA; NFL; Q&S; Speech Tm; Varsity Clb; Nwsp; Golf; High Hon Roll; KS Hon Schlr; Ronald Kean Schlsp Jr Achvmt; Baker Univ; Bus.

KNOEBEL, SARAH D; Blue Valley Northwest HS; Overland Park, KS; (2); Drama Clb; Acpl Chr; Chorus; School Musical; Socr; Vllybl; High Hon Roll; Husky Awd; Frnch, Scl Stds Awd.

KNOLL, KURT; Osborne HS; Osborne, KS; (3); 1/30; Am Leg Boys St; Pres Church Yth Grp; Rep Pres Letterman Clb; Math Tm; Varsity Clb; Rep Frsh Cls; Rep Soph Cls; Sec Stu Cncl; Var Bsbl; Var Ftbl; 3rd Place ST Wrestling 96; 6th Place ST 95; All League 2nd Team Offense Hnrb Mntn Defense Ftbl; Medicine; PE Tchr.

KNOPP, SHANE AUSTIN; Olathe North Sr HS; Lenexa, KS; (4); 42/351; Cmnty Wkr; German Clb; JV Crs Cntry; Var Trk; High Hon Roll; Ntl Merit Ltr; Pres Acad Fit Awd; St Schlr; Var Trk Ltr.

KNOPP, SHAWN M; Buhler HS; Buhler, KS; (2); Church Yth Grp; Cmnty Wkr; Band; Chorus; Church Choir; School Musical; School Play; Mgr Bsktbl; High Hon Roll; Science Clb; Vol Lcl Soup Ktchn; Music Major.

KNOTT, CRYSTAL; Maize HS; Wichita, KS; (3); 1/250; SADD; Var Trk; High Hon Roll; NHS; Pres Acad Fit Awd; Local Gymnastics Regnl Qualifier Level 10; KAYS; Phy Thrpst.

KNOUFT, CARLY; Holton HS; Holton, KS; (4); 9/66; Am Leg Aux Girls St; Church Yth Grp; FHA; HOBY; SADD; Drill Tm; Pres Stu Cncl; Chrldng; Crs Cntry; NHS; KS ST U; Bus.

KNOWLAND, KRISTA M; Topeka West HS; Topeka, KS; (3); French Clb; Pep Clb; Drill Tm; Hon Roll; Chld Thrpy.

KNOWLES, BARBARA; Cheney Jr Sr HS; Cheney, KS; (3); Church Yth Grp; Scholastic Bowl; SADD; School Play; Sec Treas Frsh Cls; Sec Treas Soph Cls; Var Co-Capt Chrldng; JV Vllybl; High Hon Roll; NHS; Pediatrician.

KNOWLES, REBECCA A; Jefferson West HS; Ozawkie, KS; (2); 1/70; Pres FHA; HOBY; Letterman Clb; Sec Scholastic Bowl; Chorus; JV Bsktbl; Var Crs Cntry; Var Trk; High Hon Roll; Prfct Atten Awd.

KNOWLTON, MARGARET L; Liberal HS; Liberal, KS; (2); Church Yth Grp; Debate Tm; FCA; Key Clb; Chorus; School Musical; JV Bsktbl; JV Sftbl; High Hon Roll; NHS; Pub Rltns.

KNOX, MANDY; Atchison Sr HS; Atchison, KS; (4); Debate Tm; DECA; Drama Clb; Quiz Bowl; Treas Spanish Clb; Ed Nwsp; Sec Soph Cls; Rep Stu Cncl; High Hon Roll; NHS; Emporia ST U; Law.

KNUDSON, JODI R; Midway Schl; Bendena, KS; (4); 4-H; Band; Chorus; Drm Mjr(t); School Play; Yrbk; JV Bsktbl; 4-H Awd; Hon Roll; Bio II Strm Tm Ldr.

KNUTSON, ANNA; Salina HS South; Salina, KS; (4); 55/209; Drama Clb; Thesps; Band; Flag Corp; Jazz Band; School Musical; Yrbk; Nwsp; Swmmng; High Hon Roll; KS St Univ; Mus Ed.

KNUTSON, KATHRYN; Olathe South Sr HS; Olathe, KS; (4); Drama Clb; Q&S; Acpl Chr; School Musical; Rptr Ed Yrbk; Ed Lit Mag; Hon Roll; NHS; Pres Acad Fit Awd; Vacatn Bible Schl Mus Thcre; Engl Dept Awd; Augustana Col; Engl.

KOBBEMAN, LIBERTY B; Lincoln Jr Sr HS; Lincoln, KS; (4); 18/32; Church Yth Grp; Drama Clb; FHA; Letterman Clb; Teachers Aide; Chorus; School Musical; School Play; Rptr Yrbk; Hon Roll; Phy Thrpst; Spcl Ed.

KOBISKIE, KELLY; Manhattan HS; Manhattan, KS; (3); Church Yth Grp; FCA; 4-H; Spanish Clb; Teachers Aide; Band; Mrchg Band; Pep Band; Intrml Bsktbl; JV Sftbl; Cty 4-H Amb; 4-H Clb Pres; Piano; Ctznshp Wshngtn Fcs Dlgt; KS ST U.

KOBUSZEWSKI, JOSHUA; Seaman Sr HS; Topeka, KS; (3); Am Leg Boys St; Church Yth Grp; FCA; Letterman Clb; SADD; Ed Nwsp; Var L Bsbl; Var L Bsktbl; Var L Ftbl; Wt Lftg; Coll.

KOCH, AMANDA; Mulvane Sr HS; Wichita, KS; (4); 13/140; FCA; Service Clb; SADD; Teachers Aide; Chorus; Ed Nwsp; Capt Pom Pon; NHS; Pres Acad Fit Awd; Artstc Rollerskating Natl Chmpn; Acctng.

KOCH, CHRISTA L; Pratt HS; Pratt, KS; (2); Mgr(s); Hon Roll; Hlth.

KOCH, JAMIE L; Andover HS; Andover, KS; (4); 37/138; Office Aide; Band; Co-Capt Flag Corp; Mrchg Band; Var Chrldng; Sftbl; Vllybl; Hon Roll; NHS; Library Aide; Studio Art; Sprt Clb; U Of KS; Pre-Med.

KOCH, JOSHUA R; Shawnee Mission W Sr HS; Shawnee Mission, KS; (4); Debate Tm; Ftbl; Wrstlng; High Hon Roll; Pres Schlr; St Schlr; Acad Dcthln; Sci Bwl.

KOCH, JULIE M; Clifton-Clyde HS; Clyde, KS; (3); 6/30; Am Leg Aux Girls St; Church Yth Grp; Pres FBLA; Treas Pep Clb; Speech Tm; Band; Mrchg Band; Pep Band; Stat Bsktbl; Stat Ftbl; 96 2a ST Vlybl Chmpnshp Team; 7th At Natl Ftr Bus Ldrs Of Amer Conf Amer Entrprs Prjct; KS ST Univ; Bus.

KOCH, SARA L; Axtell Schl; Axtell, KS; (2); FCA; FHA; Letterman Clb; Pep Clb; Chorus; School Musical; Var L Bsktbl; Sftbl; Vllybl; Church Yth Grp; KAY Bd; Certfd Nurses Asst; Lincoln Southeast CC; LPN.

KOCI, CHRIS; Jackson Heights HS; Netawaka, KS; (1); 1/41; Chess Clb; Church Yth Grp; FBLA; Pep Clb; Band; Chorus; Mrchg Band; Pep Band; Bsktbl; Ftbl; Bible Quizzing; Jeep Clb; Harvard; Law.

KOCOUREK, MARK A; Blue Valley Northwest HS; Overland Park, KS; (2); Model UN; Socr; Hon Roll; US Naval Acad; Bio.

KOEHLER, ALISON M; Wellington Sr HS; Wellington, KS; (2); Church Yth Grp; Office Aide; SADD; Chorus; Ofcr Stu Cncl; Bsktbl; JV Vllybl; Cit Awd; High Hon Roll; Hon Roll; Lions Clb Awd; Nursng.

KOEHN, AMBER L; Scott City Sr HS; Scott City, KS; (4); 1/76; Band; Flag Corp; Jazz Band; School Musical; Yrbk; Tennis; Gov Hon Prg Awd; High Hon Roll; NHS; Val; Ft Hays ST U.

KOEHN, KAREN; Protection Schl; Protection, KS; (2); Letterman Clb; Pep Clb; Quiz Bowl; Band; Chorus; Pep Band; Stage Crew; Variety Show; Powder Puff Ftbl; Sftbl; OK Univ.

KOEHN, KIMBERLY M; Canton-Galva HS; Galva, KS; (3); 10/48; Church Yth Grp; FBLA; Teachers Aide; Letterman Clb; SADD; Teachers Aide; Band; Flag Corp; Mrchg Band; Pep Band; Ft Hays ST U; Soc Worker.

KOEHN, LANCE; South Gray HS; Montezuma, KS; (4); 2/19; Church Yth Grp; Cmnty Wkr; Letterman Clb; Spanish Clb; Teachers Aide; VP Jr Cls; Pres Sr Cls; Rep Stu Cncl; Var Bsktbl; Var Ftbl; GCTL; Tabor Coll; Mech Engr.

KOEHN, LUKE D; Canton-Galva HS; Canton, KS; (2); 4/35; Church Yth Grp; FBLA; Letterman Clb; Quiz Bowl; SADD; Sec Frsh Cls; Treas Jr Cls; Var L Bsbl; Var L Bsktbl; Var L Ftbl; Engrng.

KOEHN, MICHAEL; South Gray HS; Copeland, KS; (4); 5/19; Letterman Clb; Office Aide; Spanish Clb; Sec Jr Cls; VP Sr Cls; Var Capt Ftbl; Var Capt Wrstlng; Hon Roll; Rural Elec Youth Tour.

KOEHN, SARAH J; Halstead HS; Halstead, KS; (1); Church Yth Grp; Drama Clb; German Clb; Chorus; School Play; High Hon Roll; Pres Acad Fit Awd; Pharm Rsrch.

KOEHN, SARAH J; Dighton HS; Dighton, KS; (4); FCA; Pres 4-H; Quiz Bowl; Pres SADD; Band; Chorus; Vllybl; Hon Roll; NHS; VP Pep Clb; I Dare You Awd; Bethel Col; Lit.

KOEHN, TERRY; South Gray HS; Montezuma, KS; (4); Am Leg Boys St; German Clb; Letterman Clb; Office Aide; Teachers Aide; Band; Pep Band; VP Frsh Cls; Pres Soph Cls; VP Jr Cls; Spartan Schl Of Aeronautics.

KOEHNE, MELISSA B; Andover HS; Wichita, KS; (1); 1/210; Pep Clb; JV Sftbl; Cit Awd; High Hon Roll; Hon Roll; Pres Schlr; KS U; Ed Field.

KOELLING, BONNIE K; Washburn Rural HS; Auburn, KS; (2); Office Aide; Teachers Aide; Band; Mrchg Band; JV Sftbl; Wt Lftg; High Hon Roll.

KOELLING, SHANNA; Quivira Heights HS; Holyrood, KS; (3); 7/26; Letterman Clb; Teachers Aide; Band; JV Var Bsktbl; Var Chrldng; Var Trk; JV Var Vllybl; Hon Roll; Kays Clb; Fine Arts Clb; KS Univ; Med.

KOELSCH, DIANE M; Paola HS; Paola, KS; (4); Church Yth Grp; Drama Clb; Teachers Aide; Chorus; Bsktbl; Hon Roll; Envrnmntl Clb Sec; Emporia ST; Elem Ed.

KOENIG, JOEL F; Wichita East HS; Wichita, KS; (2); Church Yth Grp; Hon Roll; NHS; Japanese Clb; Dr.

KOENIG, STEPHANIE; Sumner Acad Of Arts & Science; Kansas City, KS; (4); Am Leg Aux Girls St; Q&S; SADD; Ed Yrbk; Rep Stu Cncl; Trk; Vllybl; NHS; Acpl Chr; VP Frsh Cls; Natl Achvt Commended Schlr; Peer Hlpr.

KOERNER, KEVIN W; Ness City HS; Ness City, KS; (1); Church Yth Grp; Natl FFA Org; Bsktbl; Ftbl; Trk; Wt Lftg; Cit Awd.

KOERPERICH, ANN; Hiawatha HS; Hiawatha, KS; (1); 20/107; Intnl Clb; Pep Clb; Band; Mrchg Band; Pep Band; Chrldng; Hon Roll.

KOERPERICH, SUZANNE; Hiawatha HS; Hiawatha, KS; (2); Intnl Clb; Pep Clb; Chorus; School Musical; Chrldng.

KOESTER, ANNIE; Conway Springs HS; Conway Springs, KS; (2); Church Yth Grp; Treas Frsh Cls; Treas Soph Cls; Var L Bsktbl; Var L Chrldng; Var Powder Puff Ftbl; Var Sftbl; Var L Trk; Var L Vllybl; Wt Lftg.

KOESTER, BETHANY; Gardner-Edgerton HS; Edgerton, KS; (1); Church Yth Grp; FCA; NFL; Quiz Bowl; Chorus; School Musical; Stage Crew; Var Chrldng; High Hon Roll; Pres Acad Fit Awd; OM St Qlfr.

KOESTER, JENNY; Conway Springs HS; Conway Springs, KS; (4); 4/42; Church Yth Grp; HOBY; Rep Stu Cncl; Bsktbl; Capt Chrldng; Powder Puff Ftbl; Hon Roll; NHS; KS U Hnrs Banquet; All Trnmnt Chrldr; Fall Hmcmng Queen; Wichita ST U; Phys Thrpy.

KOESTER, MARK L; Conway Springs HS; Conway Springs, KS; (3); Quiz Bowl; Bsktbl; Ftbl; High Hon Roll; Hon Roll; Acad & Sci Olympd; Knwldg Mstr Opn.

KOESTER, MICHELLE; Conway Springs HS; Conway Springs, KS; (3); HOBY; VP Jr Cls; Bsktbl; Chrldng; Powder Puff Ftbl; Sftbl; Hon Roll; NHS; Ntl Merit Schol; Prfct Atten Awd.

KOHAKE, GINA K; Maize HS; Wichita, KS; (2); Spanish Clb; Sprt Ed Yrbk; JV Vllybl; USVA Vlybl.

KOHAKE, KIMBERLY S; Nemaha Valley HS; Centralia, KS; (3); Church Yth Grp; Letterman Clb; Quiz Bowl; Sec SADD; Stage Crew; Var L Crs Cntry; Var L Trk; Hon Roll; Pres NHS; KAYS; Jr Schl Svc Sr Sec; Washburn U; RN.

KOHAKE, MICHELLE L; Axtell Schl; Axtell, KS; (2); FCA; FHA; Chorus; School Musical; Sec Frsh Cls; VP Soph Cls; Var Bsktbl; Var Vllybl; High Hon Roll; NHS; KAYS.

KOHAKE, MINDI; Silver Lake Jr Sr HS; Silver Lake, KS; (3); 3/51; NFL; Spanish Clb; Var L Bsktbl; L Capt Pom Pon; Var L Vllybl; Cit Awd; High Hon Roll; VP NHS; Church Yth Grp; Drama Clb; Cath & Natl Forensics League Natl Qualifier; KS Univ; Bus; Acctng.

KOHART, KARA; Syracuse Jr Sr HS; Syracuse, KS; (3); 4/34; Church Yth Grp; Drama Clb; Letterman Clb; Pep Clb; Band; Chorus; Rptr Nwsp; Phtg Yrbk; Var Golf; High Hon Roll; Syracuse Singers; Home Ec Clb Sec; Hutchinson CC; Bus.

KOHLER, JOHN P; Olathe East Sr HS; Overland Park, KS; (2); Boy Scts; Church Yth Grp; Spanish Clb; Yrbk; Stat Ftbl; Intrml Socr; High Hon Roll; Hon Roll; Pres Acad Fit Awd; Pres Schlr; Creighton Univ; Law/Med.

KOHLS, MARK W; Ellsworth HS; Ellsworth, KS; (2); 11/94; Letterman Clb; Band; Mrchg Band; Pep Band; Bsktbl; Ftbl; Golf; High Hon Roll.

KOHLS, MATTHEW; Ellsworth HS; Ellsworth, KS; (4); 1/69; Letterman Clb; Band; VP Frsh Cls; VP Jr Cls; VP Sr Cls; Rep Stu Cncl; Capt Var Bsktbl; Capt Var Ftbl; High Hon Roll; Bausch & Lomb Sci Awd; KS ST; Mech Engrng.

KOHLS, WENDY R; Clearwater HS; Clearwater, KS; (3); Church Yth Grp; Spanish Clb; SADD; Stat Trk; JV Vllybl; Stat Wrstlng; Bus.

KOIRTH, BRANDI L; Thomas More Prep-Marion HS; Hays, KS; (2); 16/85; Rep Frsh Cls; VP Soph Cls; Ofcr Stu Cncl; Trk; Vllybl; Wt Lftg; Hon Roll; Ambassadors; Ft Hays ST U; Bnk Loan Ofcr.

KOLCHINSKY, LEAH M; Shawnee Mission W Sr HS; Lenexa, KS; (3); 50/415; Cmnty Wkr; Teachers Aide; JV Crs Cntry; JV Socr; High Hon Roll; Hon Roll; U Of CA; Math.

KOLLER, CHRISTY A; Moundridge HS; Moundridge, KS; (4); Treas Church Yth Grp; Dance Clb; Debate Tm; FCA; FHA; Library Aide; NFL; Office Aide; Pep Clb; Teachers Aide; Hesston Col; Soc Wrkr.

KOLLHOFF, DAVID; St John's HS; Beloit, KS; (3); Quiz Bowl; Speech Tm; Chorus; Pres Jr Cls; Rep Stu Cncl; Var L Bsktbl; Var Capt Ftbl; Var L Trk; High Hon Roll; NHS; KS Rgnts Hnrs Acad; U KS; Cmptr Engrng.

KOLLHOFF, JOHN; St John's HS; Beloit, KS; (1); Quiz Bowl; Spanish Clb; Speech Tm; School Play; Rep Stu Cncl; Bsktbl; JV Ftbl; Var Trk; Hon Roll; U Of KS; Phys Thrpy.

KOLMAN, KRYSTAL; Hillcrest Schl; Agenda, KS; (3); 2/13; Drama Clb; 4-H; FHA; Letterman Clb; Natl FFA Org; Pep Clb; Quiz Bowl; Speech Tm; Chorus; Drill Tm; Ed.

KOLODY, KRIS A; Ottawa HS; Ottawa, KS; (3); JV Golf; Stu Of Month; Auto CAD; Drafting.

KOLSTAD, ANDREA C; Shawnee Mission W Sr HS; Lenexa, KS; (1); Latin Clb; Letterman Clb; Pep Clb; Acpl Chr; Bsktbl; Var L Trk; Vllybl; Hon Roll; Play Piano; Anesthesiologist.

KOMAREK, STACY; Ellinwood Jr Sr HS; Ellinwood, KS; (1); 2/53; Church Yth Grp; FCA; Band; Chorus; Flag Corp; Pep Band; JV Bsktbl; Var Chrldng; Var Tennis; High Hon Roll.

KOMAZAKI, JUNE; Wichita Collegiate Schl; Wichita, KS; (3); Acpl Chr; Chorus; Variety Show; Phtg Nwsp; JV Golf; Hon Roll; Piano; Dance; Cmnty Svc.

KONDA, KAY L; Spearville Jr Sr HS; Spearville, KS; (2); Band; Mrchg Band; Pep Band; Nwsp; Yrbk; Lit Mag; Elem Ed.

KONEN, KELSEY M; Maize HS; Maize, KS; (1); 90/300; Church Yth Grp; Cmnty Wkr; Office Aide; SADD; Yrbk; Treas Frsh Cls; Ofcr Stu Cncl; DAR Awd; Hon Roll; Pres Schlr; Amer Legion Jr Auxiliary; U Of KS; Sports Medicine.

KONGMANYCHANH, ORN; Wichita East HS; Wichita, KS; (1); Cmnty Wkr; DECA; Hosp Aide; Red Cross Aide; Spanish Clb; Teachers Aide; Nwsp; Rep Stu Cncl; Hon Roll; NHS; DECA VP; Bus Jrnl Sr Sptlght; Wichita ST U; Med Asstnt.

KONRAD, MAST; Central Christian Schl; Hutchinson, KS; (2); High Hon Roll; Cmptr Prgrmng Grp Fndr; Univ Of KS; Cmptr Engr.

KONRADE, KILEY S; Spearville Jr Sr HS; Spearville, KS; (2); Pep Clb; Quiz Bowl; SADD; Band; Chorus; Mrchg Band; Pep Band; Sec Jr Cls; JV Var Bsktbl; Var Sftbl; S W KS Bus Cmptn; Bus.

KONRADE, KIRK M; Spearville Jr Sr HS; Offerle, KS; (3); Letterman Clb; SADD; Teachers Aide; Chorus; Ofcr Stu Cncl; Ofcr Bsbl; Bsktbl; Ftbl; Trk; Wt Lftg.

KONRADE, TRACI; Dodge City HS; Dodge City, KS; (2); Church Yth Grp; Debate Tm; Drama Clb; Girl Scts; Band; Chorus; Color Guard; Flag Corp; Mrchg Band; School Play; Nom Natl Yth Ldrshp Forum Law/Constn; Psych/Law.

KOON, LACEY; Bucklin Schl; Bucklin, KS; (1); 2/39; Church Yth Grp; FCA; Quiz Bowl; Nwsp; Yrbk; Vllybl; High Hon Roll; Serendipity Grls Club.

KOONS, LEANN; Goodland HS; Goodland, KS; (4); 15/72; Cmnty Wkr; Debate Tm; NFL; Drm Mjr(t); Mrchg Band; Orch; Pep Band; School Musical; School Play; Stage Crew; Property Mgnt.

KOOPS, BETH A; Downs HS; Downs, KS; (1); 1/20; FCA; 4-H; FHA; Scholastic Bowl; Band; VP Frsh Cls; Var Vllybl; Cit Awd; High Hon Roll; Pres Acad Fit Awd; Medicine.

KORAN, JESSICA; Manhattan HS; Manhattan, KS; (3); Cmnty Wkr; FCA; Pep Clb; Teachers Aide; Band; Drm Mjr(t); Variety Show; VP Frsh Cls; Score Keeper; JV Var Vllybl; :pre-Med/Radlgst.

KORB, KATRINA; Tonganoxiw HS; Tonganoxie, KS; (2); 1/135; FBLA; Pres FHA; Sec Stu Cncl; Var L Bsktbl; Var L Crs Cntry; Var L Sftbl; High Hon Roll; Kiwanis Awd; Pres Acad Fit Awd; Debate Tm; Vol Local Thriftshop.

KORB, KELLIE; Shawnee Mission Northwest HS; Lenexa, KS; (3); Debate Tm; NFL; Q&S; Pres Sec Thesps; School Musical; School Play; Stage Crew; Ed Nwsp; Hon Roll; NHS; Soph 100 Clb; Awds Feature Wrtng & Page Dsgn Ball ST Jrnlsm Workshps; Awds Outstdng Supprtng Actress.

KORBE, STEPHANIE; Lakin HS; Lakin, KS; (4); 5/48; Am Leg Aux Girls St; Debate Tm; FHA; Pep Clb; Quiz Bowl; Speech Tm; Band; Jazz Band; Mrchg Band; Pep Band; Bnd Dir Awd; Frt Hys ST U; Bus.

KORBER, LORI B; Bern Schl; Bern, KS; (3); Church Yth Grp; Pep Clb; Band; Chorus; Treas Jr Cls; Var Bsktbl; Trk; Vllybl; Hon Roll; NHS; Kayettes World Natl; Schl Svc; Points; K-ST; Med.

KORF, MELISSA L; Oakley HS; Oakley, KS; (3); Church Yth Grp; Cmnty Wkr; Model UN; Teachers Aide; Band; Chorus; Church Choir; Jazz Band; Mrchg Band; Pep Band; Voice Of Democracy Local Champ; Sterling Coll; Ed.

KORINEK, ANDREW S; Ft Scott HS; Fort Scott, KS; (2); 54/178; Church Yth Grp; Band; Pep Band; Golf; Hon Roll; Prfct Atten Awd; Pride Clb; Tiger Paw Awd; Ottawa Univ.

KORTE, CASEY; Hutchinson HS; Hutchinson, KS; (3); Am Leg Boys St; Church Yth Grp; French Clb; Teachers Aide; Varsity Clb; Variety Show; Yrbk; Var Capt Bsktbl; Var Capt Crs Cntry; Var L Golf; Broadcasting; KS ST.

KOSTER, CHRIS J; Great Bend Sr HS; Great Bend, KS; (2); 10/263; Boy Scts; Acpl Chr; Band; Church Choir; Jazz Band; Mrchg Band; Variety Show; Ofcr Bsbl; Ftbl; High Hon Roll; Music/Sci.

KOSTER, LINDSAY; Waconda East HS; Cawker City, KS; (2); Letterman Clb; Varsity Clb; School Play; Sec Soph Cls; Var Sr Cls; Var Chrldng; Var Trk; Var Vllybl; High Hon Roll; NHS.

KOSTMAN, COREY; Troy HS; Troy, KS; (2); 5/40; Natl FFA Org; Varsity Clb; Bsktbl; Ftbl; Cit Awd; High Hon Roll; NHS; Prfct Atten Awd; Cstmzng Trcks; Rstrtn Antique Trctrs; KS ST Univ.

KOSTY, JAMIE L; Field Kindley Mem Sr HS; Coffeyville, KS; (2); Church Yth Grp; German Clb; Ofcr Stu Cncl; Mgr(s); Score Keeper; Hon Roll; Stu Ath Trnr; Phy Thrpst.

KOU, MYVA; Wichita East HS; Wichita, KS; (2); Church Yth Grp; French Clb; Socr; Vllybl; Hon Roll; Otsdng Prfrmnc Prfrmng Arts; Upward Bound Prgm; WSU; Bus.

KOUGH, LINSEY D; Triplains Schl; Russell Springs, KS; (2); Pep Clb; School Play; Yrbk; Var Bsktbl; Var Chrldng; Stat Ftbl; Var Trk; Var Vllybl; NHS; Chorus; All-League Bsbl Hnrb Mntn; St Speech & Drama Festival; Hlth.

KOUYUMDGIEV, JIVKO K; Field Kindley Mem Sr HS; Coffeyville, KS; (4); Cmnty Wkr; German Clb; Office Aide; Bsktbl; Swmmng; Wt Lftg; Swimming Awd; Coffeyville CC; Bus.

KOVEL, DAWN L; Blue Valley Northwest HS; Overland Park, KS; (2); Debate Tm; Teachers Aide; Hon Roll; JV Lttr Debate; Soc Sci Awd; Wrtng Poetry/Shrt Stories; KS Univ; Marriage Cnslr.

KOWALEWICH, STEPHANIE M; Blue Valley HS; Overland Park, KS; (3); Letterman Clb; Drill Tm; Flag Corp; Orch; School Musical; Capt L Chrldng; High Hon Roll; Hon Roll; NHS; Pre-Med.

KRAB, MARIE; Garden City Sr HS; Garden City, KS; (3); Debate Tm; Drama Clb; French Clb; Orch; Ed Nwsp; Score Keeper; Swmmng; SHARE Team Stu Cnslr; Summer Integrated Trip Stud Math/Sci/Soc Stud; Broadcasting; U Of NE Lincoln; Broadcasting.

KRAEMER, KRISTIN L; Ottawa HS; Ottawa, KS; (2); 4-H; Girl Scts; Quiz Bowl; Spanish Clb; Rep Stu Cncl; 4-H Awd; High Hon Roll; GS Silver Awd; Grand Champion Sci Fair Project; Natl 4-H Congress; Sci.

KRAFELS, JENNIFER L; Hutchinson HS; Hutchinson, KS; (3); 36/370; Church Yth Grp; Key Clb; Letterman Clb; Pep Clb; Rptr Yrbk; Var Capt Chrldng; Diving; Swmmng; Tennis; Hon Roll; DARE Rep; Sprt Slthwk Awd.

KRAFT, AMANDA M; Rose Hill HS; Rose Hill, KS; (3); 4-H; FHA; Hosp Aide; Acpl Chr; 4-H Awd; High Hon Roll; Hon Roll; Prfct Atten Awd; Silver Kay Awd Schlstc Art Awds Drawing; KS ST; Vet.

KRAFT, DAMON; Blue Valley HS; Olathe, KS; (3); Teachers Aide; Sprt Ed Nwsp; Var Capt Bsbl; Var Capt Socr; Hon Roll; Amer Legion Bsbl 2 Yrs; All St Soccer; All Sun Cty Bsbl.

KRAFT, LEAH E; Olathe East Sr HS; Overland Park, KS; (2); Acpl Chr; Drill Tm; School Musical; Swing Chorus; Var Pom Pon; Intrml Capt Vllybl; High Hon Roll; Pres Acad Fit Awd; Pres Schlr; Spanish NHS; Drill Tm All Amer; Select Choir 1st Chr Alto; Reg Soloist; KS; Math/Sci/Frgn Lang/Engr.

KRAFVE, KRISTIANNE L; Andover HS; Wichita, KS; (2); Church Yth Grp; Band; Jazz Band; Pep Band; Chrldng; Vllybl; High Hon Roll; Hon Roll; NHS; Karate Brown Belt; U Of WA; Tchr.

KRAGH, KRISTA R; Derby Christian Schl; Clearwater, KS; (2); Church Yth Grp; Drama Clb; Pep Clb; School Play; Yrbk; Vllybl; Cit Awd; Hon Roll; Prfct Atten Awd; Piano; Southern Nazarene U.

KRAMER, BRANDAN; Seaman Sr HS; Topeka, KS; (2); Debate Tm; FBLA; SADD; JV Bsbl; Var L Bsktbl; Var L Ftbl; High Hon Roll; Jr NHS; NHS; Prfct Atten Awd; 1st Team All-Class 5 A Kckr Ftbl; Sprts Med.

KRAMER, DAWN; Jefferson West HS; Meriden, KS; (3); 12/80; Pres VP 4-H; Pres VP FHA; Scholastic Bowl; Band; Chorus; School Play; Pres Sec Stu Cncl; JV Var Sftbl; JV Vllybl; 4-H Awd.

KRAMER, KELLY L; Emporia HS; Emporia, KS; (3); Am Leg Aux Girls St; Cmnty Wkr; FCA; NFL; Orch; Var Sftbl; JV Vllybl; Cit Awd; High Hon Roll; NHS; Piano; Kayettes; Emporia ST Univ; Orthdntstry.

KRAMER, KELLY S; Wichita Co HS; Leoti, KS; (4); 9/56; Pres 4-H; Natl FFA Org; Scholastic Bowl; Teachers Aide; Band; Chorus; Mrchg Band; Pep Band; School Musical; School Play; KS Jr Herford Assoc Treas; Amer Jr Hereford Assoc; Clarendon Col; Animal Prod.

KRAMER, KRISTINE; Elk Valley Jr Sr HS; Longton, KS; (3); 1/20; Am Leg Aux Girls St; FHA; Sec FTA; Band; Yrbk; Sec Jr Cls; Pres Stu Cncl; L Vllybl; High Hon Roll; VP NHS; Bartlesville Wesleyan Coll; Ed.

KRAMER, MARLA; Medicine Lodge HS; Sun City, KS; (3); Church Yth Grp; 4-H; Letterman Clb; Pep Clb; Spanish Clb; Teachers Aide; Chorus; JV Bsktbl; Var Capt Sftbl; Var Vllybl; Butler U; Scndry Ed.

KRAMER, NICOLE R; Lacrosse HS; Bison, KS; (3); 3/30; Drama Clb; French Clb; Pep Clb; Q&S; Scholastic Bowl; Chorus; Drill Tm; School Play; Ed Nwsp; Ed Yrbk.

KRAMER, NIKKI; Lacrosse HS; Bison, KS; (3); 3/30; Drama Clb; French Clb; Q&S; Scholastic Bowl; Speech Tm; SADD; School Play; Ed Nwsp; Ed Yrbk; Chrldng; Psych.

KRAMER, SHAWN J; Hayden HS; Topeka, KS; (2); JV Bsbl; JV Bsktbl; Var L Ftbl; Magna Cum Laude Natl Latin Cont; Comp Sci.

KRAMER, STACIE L; Lawrence HS; Lawrence, KS; (3); Church Yth Grp; FCA; GAA; Office Aide; Teachers Aide; Chorus; Var Bsktbl; Var Capt Crs Cntry; Var Trk; Hon Roll; Ed.

KRAMER, TARA; Hays HS; Hays, KS; (4); 25/205; Pep Clb; Teachers Aide; High Hon Roll; NHS; Pres Acad Fit Awd; KS Hnr Scholar; Fort Hays ST.

KRANZ, ALICIA; Haven HS; Haven, KS; (3); Church Yth Grp; FCA; 4-H; SADD; Band; Church Choir; Chrldng; Mgr(s); High Hon Roll; NHS; Peer Cnslr; Hutchinson JC; Med.

KRANZ, RACHEL A; Holton HS; Denison, KS; (3); 4-H; Letterman Clb; SADD; Chorus; Rep Stu Cncl; Var Bsktbl; Var Sftbl; Var Vllybl; 4-H Awd; Hon Roll.

KRASICK, SARAH; Wyandotte HS; Kansas City, KS; (2); Church Yth Grp; Cmnty Wkr; Drama Clb; FCA; Speech Tm; Church Choir; Mgr Var Bsktbl; Mgr(s); Score Keeper; Trk; J C Penney Goldn Rule Awd; Victoria Tabernacle Hnr Star; Schl Bible Clb; Missns Trip; North Central Bible Coll.

KRASOVEC, HEATHER; Garden City Sr HS; Garden City, KS; (2); French Clb; Teachers Aide; Mgr(s); Trk; Vllybl; High Hon Roll; Prfct Atten Awd; Pres Acad Fit Awd; Chrch Bell Choir; Outstndng Bus Stu 93-94; 4th Pl SW KS Bus Cmptn General Acctng 95; KS ST U; Bus.

KRATOFIL, JOHN; St Thomas Aquinas HS; Overland Park, KS; (3); Am Leg Boys St; Scholastic Bowl; Treas Science Clb; Spanish Clb; Acpl Chr; Ed Nwsp; JV Bsbl; Bsktbl; JV Crs Cntry; High Hon Roll; Dr.

KRATZBERG, AMBER R; Central Heights Sr HS; Richmond, KS; (2); FCA; Pep Clb; Spanish Clb; Swing Chorus; Nwsp; JV Bsktbl; Var Chrldng; Sftbl; Var L Trk; JV Vllybl; II Rtng ST Solo; Coll Of Ozarks; TV Brdcstg.

KRAUS, NICK R; Marion HS; Marion, KS; (2); 1/60; Church Yth Grp; Math Tm; Natl FFA Org; Scholastic Bowl; Band; Jazz Band; Mrchg Band; Pep Band; School Musical; Pres Frsh Cls; FFA Pres; Ag.

KRAUS, TRACEY; Andale HS; Colwich, KS; (3); Church Yth Grp; Cmnty Wkr; Office Aide; JV Bsktbl; Powder Puff Ftbl; JV Vllybl; Gov Hon Prg Awd; High Hon Roll; Hon Roll; Pres Acad Fit Awd; Bd Mem For CYO; KS Newman Coll; Pediatrics.

KRAUSE, ELIZABETH J M; Oskaloosa HS; Perry, KS; (2); Church Yth Grp; Speech Tm; Chorus; Church Choir; Orch; Hon Roll; Choir Reg Trio; Art Show; Emporia ST Univ; Psych.

KRAUSE, MAC; Great Bend Sr HS; Great Bend, KS; (3); Am Leg Boys St; Pep Clb; Acpl Chr; Chorus; School Musical; Variety Show; Rep Soph Cls; VP Jr Cls; JV Bsbl; Bsktbl; Peer Cnslr; Kays Clb; KS St Univ; Eng.

KRAUSHAAR, KAREN E; Baldwin HS; Baldwin City, KS; (4); 2/81; GAA; Math Tm; Teachers Aide; Band; Orch; Trk; Vllybl; Hon Roll; NHS; St Schlr; KS ST Univ; Engrng.

KREBS, HOLLY H; Oskaloosa HS; Mc Louth, KS; (4); 1/45; Sec FBLA; Speech Tm; Band; Chorus; Jazz Band; School Musical; School Play; NHS; Ntl Merit Schol; Val; U Of KS; Music Theory Prof.

KREEGER, JENNIFER; Columbus HS; Galena, KS; (4); 49/97; Church Yth Grp; Cmnty Wkr; Computer Clb; Debate Tm; Drama Clb; FCA; 4-H; FHA; Letterman Clb; Math Tm; Washburn U; Crmnl Jstc.

KREHBIEL, NICHOLAS A; Pratt HS; Pratt, KS; (3); 10/100; Key Clb; Quiz Bowl; Band; Chorus; Pep Band; School Musical; Var L Ftbl; Var L Golf; Hon Roll; NHS; All League Offensve Tackle In Ftbb; Offensve Tackle St Champn Ftbl Team 95; 800 Lb Weightliftng Cls; Pre-Law; Bus; Play Coll Ftbl.

KREHBIEL, NICI; Kingman HS; Kingman, KS; (1); 2/85; FBLA; Band; Mrchg Band; Orch; Chrldng; Trk; Vllybl; Hon Roll; Yth Govt; Med.

KREHBIEL, TONYA M; Moundridge HS; Moundridge, KS; (3); Church Yth Grp; VP Pres 4-H; FHA; Chorus; Church Choir; School Musical; 4-H Awd; 4-H Exch; Hesston Col; Erly Chld Ed.

KREISSLER, JACKIE; Olathe South Sr HS; Olathe, KS; (3); 23/416; Church Yth Grp; German Clb; Hosp Aide; Latin Clb; Band; Drill Tm; High Hon Roll; NHS; Pres Acad Fit Awd; Genetics/Pre-Med.

KRELLER, CHRIS; Victoria HS; Victoria, KS; (2); Letterman Clb; Band; Mrchg Band; Pep Band; Sec Frsh Cls; Bsktbl; Ftbl; Trk; Hon Roll; NHS; Indstrl Tech Club; Knights Taking Chg; Teens As Tchrs; U Of KS; Lawyer.

KRELLER, JENNIFER E; Victoria HS; Victoria, KS; (3); 11/32; Drama Clb; Hist FBLA; Sec FHA; Letterman Clb; SADD; Varsity Clb; School Play; Tennis; Trk; NHS; FHA STAR Sr Creed Mdlst; VFW Oice Of Dmcrcy Dist Wnnr; St Forencisgld Mdl.

KREMEIER, JULIA A; Wichita Heights HS; Wichita, KS; (2); 27/336; Thesps; Band; Jazz Band; Mrchg Band; Pep Band; School Play; Variety Show; Pom Pon; Socr; Hon Roll; Sci Olympd.

KRESS, NICOLE R; Iola Sr HS; Iola, KS; (4); SADD; Chorus; Church Choir; Tennis; Trk; Hon Roll; Kansas Univ; Engrng.

KRETSCHMER, ISA E; Lawrence HS; Lawrence, KS; (2); German Clb; Science Clb; Hon Roll; Comp.

KREUTZER, JAKOB K; Topeka HS; Topeka, KS; (2); German Clb; Var L Socr; Cit Awd; High Hon Roll; Hon Roll.

KREUTZER, KAREN; Trego Comm HS; Wa Keeney, KS; (2); German Clb; Letterman Clb; Pep Clb; SADD; Drill Tm; JV Bsktbl; Var L Chrldng; Var L Golf; Var L Trk; High Hon Roll; Bus.

KREUTZER, KRISTI K; Leavenworth HS; Leavenworth, KS; (3); 81/346; Church Yth Grp; VP Pres DECA; Hosp Aide; Pres Soph Cls; Var Chrldng; JV Socr; Vllybl; High Hon Roll; NHS; Mgr(s); Occu Thpy.

KREUTZER, LINDSEY A; Shawnee Mission N HS; Shawnee Mission, KS; (3); 31/455; Drama Clb; Pep Clb; Thesps; Acpl Chr; Orch; School Musical; School Play; Stage Crew; Hon Roll; NHS; Strolling Strings; Acadltr 3 Yrs.

KRICHIVER, ARI R; Blue Valley Northwest HS; Overland Park, KS; (4); 35/340; Pres Temple Yth Grp; Band; Jazz Band; Mrchg Band; Orch; Pep Band; School Musical; Tennis; Ntl Merit Ltr; Chess Clb; Boston Univ.

KRIER, ANTHONY L; Ashland HS; Ashland, KS; (2); Letterman Clb; VP Frsh Cls; Treas Jr Cls; Var Bsktbl; Var Ftbl; Var Trk; Hon Roll; KU; Phy Thrpst.

KRIER, KARI; Claflin Jr Sr HS; Claflin, KS; (1); 1/23; Church Yth Grp; FHA; Math Tm; Pep Clb; Band; Pres Frsh Cls; Chrldng; JV Golf; JV Vllybl; High Hon Roll; Hnrs Banquet; Med.

KRIER, KELSEY J; Beloit Jr Sr HS; Beloit, KS; (1); 32/93; Church Yth Grp; Cmnty Wkr; Computer Clb; 4-H; FHA; Chorus; Orch; Variety Show; Vllybl; 4-H Awd; Interior Dcrtng.

KRIESEL, DENNIS W; Gardner-Edgerton HS; Olathe, KS; (3); Mgr Am Leg Boys St; Band; Mrchg Band; Pep Band; Treas Jr Cls; High Hon Roll; NHS; Prfct Atten Awd; KS Boys St; Decendant Of Nancy Ward; Pol Sci.

KRIESEL, WENDY A; Gardner-Edgerton HS; Olathe, KS; (2); 1/197; Spanish Clb; Band; Mrchg Band; Orch; Pep Band; High Hon Roll; Asst To Events Mgr OCP-BOS; Natural Helper; Decendents Of Nancy Ward.

KRIESHOK, AARON T; Shawnee Heights Sr HS; Topeka, KS; (2); Science Clb; Band; Jazz Band; Mrchg Band; Pep Band; Socr; Hon Roll; Sci.

KRIGEL, LARA I; Hyman Brand Hebrew Acad; Leawood, KS; (3); Ofcr Stu Cncl; Socr; High Hon Roll; NHS; Fig Skating Jr Freestyle; Bnai Brith Yth Org Pres; Hist/Art/Torah Awds; Finlst Holocaust Essay Cont; History.

KRILEY, AMY M; Stockton HS; Stockton, KS; (4); 4/33; Debate Tm; VP 4-H; Pres FHA; Math Tm; Natl FFA Org; VP Pep Clb; Quiz Bowl; Scholastic Bowl; Rep Band; Jazz Band; CYO; All-Lg Awd Vlybl & Bsktbl; All-St Awd Vlybl; Washburn U; Scl Wrkr.

KRILEY, ISAAC; Ulysses HS; Ulysses, KS; (3); Church Yth Grp; Debate Tm; FBLA; Quiz Bowl; Band; Drm Mjr(t); Mrchg Band; Score Keeper; High Hon Roll; Cmnty Wide Yth Grp Pres; KS Rgnts Hnr Acad Attndnt; Biochem.

KRISTEK, AMANDA L; Campus HS; Wichita, KS; (3); Am Leg Aux Girls St; Church Yth Grp; Science Clb; SADD; Sec Treas Band; Color Guard; Flag Corp; Mrchg Band; Pep Band; Bsktbl; Band Ltr; AP US His; #1 In Regnls For Oboe Solo; Phy Asst.

KRISTEN, KRISTEN; Muncie Christian Schl; Kansas City, KS; (4); 1/8; Chorus; School Play; Yrbk; Pres Jr Cls; Pres Sr Cls; Var Co-Capt Vllybl; Hon Roll; Pres Acad Fit Awd; Val; All Tournament/All Conf Vlybl; ACSI Distnghd Ldrshp Awd; KS Comm Coll; Wildlife Bio.

KRITIKOS, ALEXANDER G; Lyndon HS; Lyndon, KS; (4); 5/34; Church Yth Grp; 4-H; FBLA; Quiz Bowl; Band; Chorus; Church Choir; Mrchg Band; Pep Band; School Play; U Of KS; Cmptr Engrng.

KROEKER, GAIL; Inman Jr Sr HS; Inman, KS; (2); Art Clb; Church Yth Grp; German Clb; Pep Clb; Band; Mrchg Band; Pep Band; Trk; Vllybl; High Hon Roll; Frnscs.

KROGMAN, KELLY L; Holton HS; Holton, KS; (1); GAA; Band; Chorus; Mrchg Band; Stage Crew; Crs Cntry; High Hon Roll; Hon Roll; Marine Bio.

KROGMANN, ALYSIA M; Holton HS; Holton, KS; (2); Letterman Clb; Speech Tm; Varsity Clb; Band; Chorus; Church Choir; Mrchg Band; Pep Band; School Musical; Crs Cntry; Received A I At Regnl Solo & Small Ensemble & A II At St; Baker; Music; Medicine.

KROGMANN, CRYSTAL; Wetmore Schl; Wetmore, KS; (4); 4/17; Am Leg Aux Girls St; Letterman Clb; Pep Clb; Quiz Bowl; Teachers Aide; Band; Chorus; Mrchg Band; Pep Band; School Musical; KS ST U; Accntng.

KROGMANN, JOSH; Sabetha HS; Sabetha, KS; (3); 38/90; Am Leg Boys St; Cmnty Wkr; Debate Tm; Pep Clb; Science Clb; Spanish Clb; Varsity Clb; Church Choir; JV Var Ftbl; Wt Lftg; KS St Univ; Wldlfe Consv.

KROGMANN, RACHEL A; Sabetha HS; Sabetha, KS; (2); Pep Clb; Spanish Clb; Chorus; Trk; Vllybl; Highland CC; Tchng.

KROLL, KELLY M; Pleasant Ridge HS; Easton, KS; (4); 24/64; FBLA; Treas Sr Cls; Hon Roll; FBLA Pres, Reprtr; Pittsburgh ST U; Marine Bio.

KRONE, ANNA; Sterling HS; Sterling, KS; (4); 7/31; Pres 4-H; Pres FHA; Letterman Clb; Pres Science Clb; Sec Treas Sr Cls; Var Capt Bsktbl; L Var Trk; L Var Vllybl; 4-H Awd; Ed NHS; Hutchinson CC; Vet Sci.

KROPP, JOSH M; Goddard HS; Wichita, KS; (2); Debate Tm; Library Aide; Spanish Clb; Yrbk; VP Soph Cls; Var Socr; Hon Roll.

KROUSE, KARYL E; Great Bend Sr HS; Great Bend, KS; (2); 3/263; Hosp Aide; Spanish Clb; Band; Jazz Band; Mrchg Band; JV Tennis; High Hon Roll; Prfct Atten Awd; Church Yth Grp; SADD; Kayettes; Living His Vol Ft Larned Hstrcl Site; KS ST Univ.

KRSTULIC, ANNIE; Shawnee Mission Northwest HS; Shawnee Mission, KS; (4); Cmnty Wkr; Key Clb; Thesps; Crs Cntry; High Hon Roll; Hon Roll; NHS; Ntl Merit SF; St Schlr; Benedictine Coll.

KRUEGER, DONNA L; Wellsville Jr Sr HS; Wellsville, KS; (1); Treas Rep 4-H; 4-H Awd; High Hon Roll; 4-H Ambsdr; Ctznshp Awd; SAC.

KRUEGER, MATTHEW; Sumner Acad Of Arts & Science; Kansas City, KS; (3); Boy Scts; Church Yth Grp; German Clb; Band; Mrchg Band; Orch; Pep Band; JV Crs Cntry; High Hon Roll; NHS; Yth Symphony KS City.

KRUG, KIRSTEN; Garden City Sr HS; Garden City, KS; (4); Pres Church Yth Grp; Math Tm; VP Science Clb; Acpl Chr; Ed Nwsp; Rep Stu Cncl; Var L Tennis; High Hon Roll; Kiwanis Awd; NHS; KS ST.

KRUG, KRISTEN H; Great Bend Sr HS; Great Bend, KS; (1); Church Yth Grp; German Clb; Chorus; Bsktbl; JV Var Sftbl; Vllybl; 4-H Awd; High Hon Roll; Prfct Atten Awd; Pres Acad Fit Awd; Natl Yth Forum ST Letter Winner; Quicksilver Fastpitch Sftbl; MVP Vlybl/Bsktbl 95-; 4 Yr Univ; Med/Ed.

KRUG, MARISSA E; Garden City Sr HS; Garden City, KS; (2); 1/446; Church Yth Grp; Science Clb; Spanish Clb; SADD; Chorus; Church Choir; Sprt Ed Nwsp; Var Tennis; High Hon Roll; Yng Life; Math Relays; Sci Olympd.

KRUGER, JONATHAN; Midland Sda Schl; Overland Park, KS; (1); 1/19; Band; Ed Yrbk; Var Bsktbl; Cit Awd; High Hon Roll.

KRUGER, SHANNON; Silver Lake Jr Sr HS; Silver Lake, KS; (2); 9/70; Church Yth Grp; Letterman Clb; Varsity Clb; Band; Rep Stu Cncl; Var L Bsbl; Var L Bsktbl; Var L Ftbl; High Hon Roll; Hon Roll.

KRULESKI, BRYAN; Garden City Sr HS; Garden City, KS; (2); Church Yth Grp; JV Bsbl; Hon Roll; Prfct Atten Awd; Outstdng Bio Stdnt 95-.

KRUMM, ABE; Smokey Valley HS; Lindsborg, KS; (4); 4-H; Letterman Clb; Q&S; Band; Jazz Band; Orch; Pep Band; Nwsp; Pres Jr Cls; Pres Sr Cls; Quincy Univ; Commnctn.

KRUPICH, BRIAN D; Bishop Miege HS; Shawnee, KS; (1); 9/248; SADD; Nwsp; Ofcr Frsh Cls; Ofcr Soph Cls; Ofcr Bsbl; Bsktbl; High Hon Roll; Coached Midget K Bsbl Team.

KRUSE, JAMIE; Lansing HS; Walnut Bottom, PA; (3); Church Yth Grp; French Clb; Service Clb; Teachers Aide; JV Socr; Var Swmmng; French Hon Soc; High Hon Roll; Hon Roll; Jr NHS; Env Fld.

KRUSE, LANDON K; Washington HS; Greenleaf, KS; (2); Church Yth Grp; FHA; Varsity Clb; Chorus; Var Bsktbl; Var Ftbl; Hon Roll; KS St Univ; Bus.

KRUSE, LAURA M; Olathe North Sr HS; Olathe, KS; (3); Church Yth Grp; Drama Clb; French Clb; Science Clb; Thesps; JV Bsktbl; Var Crs Cntry; JV Socr; High Hon Roll; NHS.

KRUSE, SARA; Little River Jr Sr HS; Little River, KS; (4); 8/22; FHA; Model UN; Spanish Clb; Teachers Aide; Chorus; Rptr Nwsp; Ed Yrbk; Sec Jr Cls; Ofcr Stu Cncl; Capt Chrldng; KS ST U; Mass Comm.

KRUSEMARK, LAURA L; Pratt HS; Pratt, KS; (4); 1/96; Sec 4-H; Pep Clb; Church Yth Grp; Cmnty Wkr; Band; Church Choir; Jazz Band; Mrchg Band; Pep Band; School Musical; KU Hnr Prog; Best Of Class Channel 12; Bethany Col; Art.

KUCHINSKAS, BRANDON M; Bishop Carroll Catholic HS; Wichita, KS; (2); Bsktbl; Crs Cntry; JV Ftbl; Var L Trk; Hon Roll; Prfct Atten Awd; No Schl Demerits 2 Yrs.

KUCHMENT, OLGA; Wichita East HS; Wichita, KS; (2); Cmnty Wkr; Drama Clb; Math Clb; Spanish Clb; School Musical; Hon Roll; NHS; Piano; Guigar; Ceramics; Math Sch L Rutgers Univ; SADD; Chem/Psychtry.

KUEBELBECK, BETH; Basehor Linwood HS; Basehor, KS; (4); Art Clb; Church Yth Grp; Cmnty Wkr; Girl Scts; Q&S; SADD; Band; Drm Mjr(t); School Play; Ed Nwsp; Girl Scout Silver Awd; KS City CC.

KUEBELBECK, MICHAEL; Washington HS; Kansas City, KS; (2); ROTC; Spanish Clb; School Play; Yrbk; Crs Cntry; Swmmng; Trk; Hon Roll; Prfct Atten Awd; Amer Legion ROTC Acad Awd; Eagle Sct Awd; KS Univ; Air Force Ofcr.

KUEKER, RYAN; Concordia Jr Sr HS; Concordia, KS; (3); Am Leg Boys St; Church Yth Grp; Cmnty Wkr; French Clb; Science Clb; SADD; Varsity Clb; Bsktbl; Crs Cntry; Golf; Delegate To Close-Up Washington; AAU Bsktbl Team; KS ST Univ; Med.

KUESER, AMY M; Anderson Cty Jr Sr HS; Richmond, KS; (1); Natl FFA Org; SADD; Chorus; School Musical; Sec Pep Band; Bsktbl; Var Trk; Vllybl; Hon Roll; Medicine.

KUESER, DANNY W; Central Heights Sr HS; Richmond, KS; (1); Boy Scts; Church Yth Grp; Natl FFA Org; Spanish Clb; Varsity Clb; Ofcr Frsh Cls; Bsktbl; Crs Cntry; Powder Puff Ftbl; Trk; Brigham Young Univ.

KUFAHL, ROBIN L; Onaga HS; Wheaton, KS; (2); Church Yth Grp; Pep Clb; Spanish Clb; Phtg Yrbk; Mgr(s); Hon Roll; Kays; K ST; Sports Med/Chldcr.

KUFFLER, AMY D; Douglass HS; Douglass, KS; (4); Drama Clb; Letterman Clb; Office Aide; Speech Tm; Stage Crew; Yrbk; Mgr(s); Hon Roll; Cnslrs Aid; Wichita St Univ; Radiolgy.

KUHLMAN, LES; Manhattan HS; Manhattan, KS; (3); Church Yth Grp; 4-H; Band; Mrchg Band; Pep Band; JV Swmmng; JV Tennis; 4-H Awd; High Hon Roll; NHS; KS ST U; Agronomy.

KUHLMAN, MEGAN; Wallace Cty HS; Sharon Springs, KS; (4); 6/26; Church Yth Grp; FCA; Pres Pep Clb; Band; Chorus; Pres Soph Cls; Pres Jr Cls; Bsktbl; High Hon Roll; NHS; KS Newman Coll; Nrsng.

KUHLMANN, VALERIE D; Olpe Schl; Emporia, KS; (2); Church Yth Grp; GAA; Letterman Clb; Varsity Clb; School Play; Nwsp; JV Var Bsktbl; L Trk; JV Var Vllybl; Hon Roll; KS ST Jrnlsm Cont; Ath Trainer; Rehabilitater.

KUHN, AMY; Coldwater Jr Sr HS; Greensburg, KS; (3); FCA; Letterman Clb; Speech Tm; Band; Chorus; School Musical; Ofcr Stu Cncl; Bsktbl; Trk; NHS.

KUHN, ANGIE M; Hays HS; Hays, KS; (2); Spanish Clb; Orch; School Musical; JV Chrldng; Hon Roll; Fort Hays ST Univ; Tchng.

KUHN, CHRISTY; Seaman Sr HS; Topeka, KS; (3); Office Aide; SADD; Band; Jazz Band; Mrchg Band; Pep Band; Rptr Nwsp; Var L Chrldng; JV Trk; Hon Roll; I Rating At Reg In Piano And Brtne Sax; KS Masonic All St HS Shrine Marchng Bnd; Mus Ed.

KUHN, KRISTI; Thomas More Prep-Marion HS; Victoria, KS; (4); 1/93; Debate Tm; 4-H; HOBY; JCL; Math Tm; Model UN; NFL; Chorus; Nwsp; Rep Jr Cls; Cmnty Swm Tm; Spec Olympcs Vol; Biochem.

KUHN, REBECCA; Sterling HS; Sterling, KS; (4); 1/31; Debate Tm; Pres Drama Clb; Speech Tm; Band; Chorus; School Play; Sec Jr Cls; Hon Roll; Pres NHS; Val; KU; Scl Stds.

KUIPER, KAILI M; Salina HS Central; Salina, KS; (2); Dance Clb; Letterman Clb; SADD; Orch; School Musical; Rep Soph Cls; Mgr(s); Stat Sftbl; Stat Vllybl; High Hon Roll.

KUIPER, MALANI; Salina HS Central; Salina, KS; (4); 1/230; Cmnty Wkr; Letterman Clb; Sec Stu Cncl; Capt Pom Pon; Var Sftbl; Var Capt Vllybl; High Hon Roll; NHS; Pres Acad Fit Awd; Val; Piano; KS Univ; Bio; Pre-Med.

KUJAWA, SUZANNE; Atchison Sr HS; Atchison, KS; (1); Church Yth Grp; Spanish Clb; Band; Church Choir; Mrchg Band; Pep Band; Var L Golf; Intrml Vllybl; High Hon Roll; Hndbl Choir; Rec Fst-Ptch Sftbl; Flute Trio II ST Comp; KS Univ; Rdlgst.

KULICK, JUSTIN M; Washburn Rural HS; Topeka, KS; (3); Yrbk; JV Var Ftbl; Var Wt Lftg; Hon Roll; Univ Of KS.

KUMBERG, LUKE; Skyline Schls; Sawyer, KS; (3); Am Leg Boys St; Church Yth Grp; Pres 4-H; Pep Clb; SADD; Band; Co-Ed Yrbk; Hon Roll; Prfct Atten Awd; Comp Programming; Colby Comm Coll; Phy Thrpst.

KUMER, AUDREY J; Northeast HS; Arma, KS; (3); 2/39; Teachers Aide; Yrbk; Treas Jr Cls; Var L Bsktbl; Var L Sftbl; Var L Vllybl; High Hon Roll; NHS.

KUNANTAEVA, NAILA A; Hillsboro HS; Hillsboro, KS; (2); Church Yth Grp; Library Aide; School Play; Bsktbl; Var Swmmng; Tennis; Cit Awd; High Hon Roll; Hon Roll; Forensics; Play; Kayettes; KS Univ; Heart Surgeon.

KUNC, LAEL; Hillcrest Schl; Cuba, KS; (1); Drama Clb; Speech Tm; Trk; Hon Roll; Pres Acad Fit Awd.

KUNSHEK, SCOTT; Frontenac Jr Sr HS; Frontenac, KS; (2); Boy Scts; Church Yth Grp; Spanish Clb; Yrbk; Ofcr Soph Cls; Ftbl; Wt Lftg; High Hon Roll; Prfct Atten Awd; Eagle Scout; Pittsburg ST U; Bus.

KUNTZ, EMMA E; Topeka HS; Topeka, KS; (3); German Clb; Orch; Var L Tennis; Var L Trk; High Hon Roll; NHS; Russian Club; Natl Merit Sci Awd.

KUNTZ, RUDI P; Topeka HS; Topeka, KS; (2); German Clb; Orch; JV Crs Cntry; JV L Tennis; High Hon Roll; Russian Club.

KURCHE, JONATHAN; Shawnee Mission Nw Sr HS; Lenexa, KS; (3); 26/480; Debate Tm; Drama Clb; Key Clb; NFL; Thesps; School Musical; School Play; Stage Crew; Ed Nwsp; VP Sr Cls; Volntr; Bio.

KURDIAN, MELINEH R; Wichita East HS; Wichita, KS; (4); Pres VP Drama Clb; English Clb; VP French Clb; Pres VP Thesps; School Play; Rep Frsh Cls; Pres Jr Cls; Pres French Hon Soc; Hon Roll; Rep NHS; 11 Yrs Piano; 3 Yrs Guitar; U Of KS.

KURTH, TRAMPAS; Kinsley HS; Kinsley, KS; (3); 1/33; Church Yth Grp; Quiz Bowl; Band; Var Bsktbl; Var Ftbl; Var Trk; High Hon Roll; NHS; Amer Legion Bsbl.

KURTH, TREVOR; Kinsley HS; Kinsley, KS; (2); Quiz Bowl; Ofcr Stu Cncl; Ofcr Bsbl; Bsktbl; Ftbl; Trk; Wt Lftg; Hon Roll; Prfct Atten Awd; Car Restoration; KS ST Univ; Elec Engr.

KURTZ, JUSTIN M; Olathe North Sr HS; Olathe, KS; (3); Church Yth Grp; Cmnty Wkr; Teachers Aide; Acpl Chr; Chorus; Church Choir; Orch; School Musical; Swing Chorus; Variety Show; Aviation Explorers Post VP; Olathe Area Yth Symphny; K-St U Mastr Tchr Smmr Choral Inst; Music.

KURTZ, MELANIE; Eureka Jr Sr HS; Eureka, KS; (4); 1/65; Am Leg Aux Girls St; Chrmn Church Yth Grp; Capt Quiz Bowl; SADD; Teachers Aide; Band; Treas Stu Cncl; Gov Hon Prg Awd; Kiwanis Awd; NHS; Emporia ST U; Sec Math Ed.

KUTILEK, SARAH I; The Learning Alt HS; Wichita, KS; (4); Church Yth Grp; Cmnty Wkr; Hosp Aide; Church Choir; Ed Nwsp; Capt Var Crs Cntry; Gym; Socr; Tennis; Trk; CIT; AWANA Ldr; Bob Jones Univ; Missns.

KUZEMKA, AMY T; Bishop Ward HS; Kansas City, KS; (3); Girl Scts; Library Aide; Pep Clb; Spanish Clb; SADD; Hon Roll; NHS; Peer Mntr; DARE; GIFT Env Clb.

KVASNICKA, MINDY; Hillcrest Schl; Narka, KS; (1); 1/22; Pres Sec 4-H; FHA; Letterman Clb; Natl FFA Org; Drill Tm; Pep Band; Rep Stu Cncl; Bsktbl; Vllybl; 4-H Awd; Cmnty Hero Torchbearer Olympic Torch Relay 96; KS ST U; Tchr.

KWON, SOON YOU; Wichita East HS; Wichita, KS; (2); Church Yth Grp; Debate Tm; Hosp Aide; Math Clb; Orch; Treas Frsh Cls; JV Tennis; French Hon Soc; NHS; French Clb; Wichita Area Girl Sct Sr Bd Dir; Poem Pub GS Clndr Nationwide.

LABARGE, BRANDON; Wichita South HS; Wichita, KS; (3); Band; Jazz Band; Mrchg Band; Orch; Pep Band; Variety Show; Ed Nwsp; Var Tennis; Percusn Advncd Wichita Wnd Ensmbl; All City Bnd; KS Univ; Jrnlsm.

LA BARGE, JOESPH; Hays HS; Hays, KS; (3); Am Leg Boys St; Var L Bsbl; Intrml Bsktbl; Var L Ftbl; Intrml Wt Lftg; High Hon Roll; NHS.

LA BRUE, LYNN N; Goddard HS; Goddard, KS; (2); Church Yth Grp; GAA; Science Clb; Spanish Clb; SADD; Teachers Aide; Varsity Clb; Bsktbl; Vllybl; Hon Roll; Tchr.

LACCHEO, MIKE; Cair Paravel - Latin Schl; Topeka, KS; (2); Teachers Aide; Chorus; School Musical; School Play; Rptr Nwsp; Yrbk; VP Stu Cncl; Var Socr; Hon Roll.

LACHER, CRAIG C; Chanute Sr HS; Eufaula, OK; (3); Am Leg Boys St; Church Yth Grp; Chorus; School Musical; Rep Stu Cncl; Var Bsbl; Var Bsktbl; Var Ftbl; JV Golf; High Hon Roll; OSU; Pol Sci/Law.

LACHKY, JOE B; Blue Valley North HS; Leawood, KS; (2); 33/219; Model UN; Band; Jazz Band; Mrchg Band; Pep Band; Bsktbl; High Hon Roll; Hon Roll.

LACIO, DEREC; Kingman HS; Kingman, KS; (2); 2/80; Church Yth Grp; French Clb; FBLA; Letterman Clb; Quiz Bowl; Varsity Clb; JV Bsktbl; Var Crs Cntry; Trk; High Hon Roll; Hi-Y; Acad All Lg Crss Cntry; Wichita Swim Club; U Of TX; Pre-Med.

LACKEY, ADAM; Highland HS; Highland, KS; (1); Chorus; School Musical; Swing Chorus; Bsktbl; Ftbl; Trk; Hon Roll; KS ST U; Cartoon Illstrtn.

LACKEY, ERIC; Atchison Sr HS; Atchison, KS; (2); Cmnty Wkr; Band; Jazz Band; Mrchg Band; Pep Band; JV Bsbl; JV Bsktbl; JV Var Ftbl; High Hon Roll.

LACKEY, REBECCA; Highland HS; Highland, KS; (4); 8/16; Am Leg Aux Girls St; Girl Scts; Chorus; School Musical; Mgr Nwsp; Mgr Yrbk; Rep Stu Cncl; Var Capt Bsktbl; Var Chrldng; Var Trk; Highland CC; Grphc Dsgn.

LA COSS, JASON; Mulvane Sr HS; Mulvane, KS; (4); 13/146; Thesps; Treas Acpl Chr; School Musical; School Play; Ed Nwsp; Crs Cntry; Trk; Wrstlng; NHS; Pres Acad Fit Awd; Wichita ST U; Aero Engrng.

LACZ, PATRICK W; St Thomas Aquinas HS; Lenexa, KS; (2); Chess Clb; Debate Tm; Math Tm; Model UN; NFL; Science Clb; High Hon Roll; Comp Sci; Software Dsgn.

LADD, ANNA E; Shawnee Mission S Sr HS; Overland Park, KS; (2); Church Yth Grp; Girl Scts; Pep Clb; Teachers Aide; Acpl Chr; Chorus; Church Choir; School Musical; Socr; High Hon Roll; Placd In Reg & St Choral Cmptn.

LADD, MEREDITH S; Shawnee Mission South Sr HS; Overland Park, KS; (2); Church Yth Grp; Girl Scts; Thesps; Acpl Chr; Chorus; Church Choir; Stage Crew; Socr; Cit Awd; Hon Roll.

LADISH, NICK E; Great Bend Sr HS; Great Bend, KS; (3); Drama Clb; Key Clb; Pep Clb; Teachers Aide; Band; Jazz Band; Mrchg Band; Pep Band; Variety Show; Intrml Bsktbl; Mktg.

LADNER, HEATHER; Marysville HS; Marysville, KS; (4); 8/83; Am Leg Aux Girls St; Bus Profs of Am; Letterman Clb; Sec Soph Cls; Rep Jr Cls; VP Sr Cls; Mgr(s); Vllybl; High Hon Roll; Kiwanis Awd; Pittsburg St U; Bio.

LADUSCH, LLOYD G; Holton HS; Holton, KS; (1); Intrml Bsktbl; JV Ftbl.

LA FAY, KELSEY L; Stanton Co HS; Johnson, KS; (2); 1/35; Church Yth Grp; Cmnty Wkr; FBLA; Pep Clb; Teachers Aide; Rptr Nwsp; Rep Frsh Cls; L Bsktbl; L Crs Cntry; L Trk; Air Force Acad; Archtrl Eng.

LA FLASH, MARIA J; Junction City HS; Junction City, KS; (2); 28/228; Dance Clb; Girl Scts; Pep Clb; Teachers Aide; Drill Tm; Pom Pon; High Hon Roll; Jr NHS; KS ST U; Elem Tchre.

LAFORGE, CHRIS R; El Dorado HS; El Dorado, KS; (3); 29/230; Computer Clb; Letterman Clb; Math Clb; Office Aide; Science Clb; Golf; Swmmng; Cit Awd; Hon Roll; Pres Acad Fit Awd; Pre Med/Srgcl.

LAGER, NATHAN; Grinnell HS; Grinnell, KS; (4); 6/14; VP Church Yth Grp; Pres 4-H; HOBY; Scholastic Bowl; Band; Var L Bsktbl; 4-H Awd; Hon Roll; NHS; Prfct Atten Awd; Ftbl All Leag 1st Tm Offns, Hnrb Mntn Defns; K-18 Smmr Bsbl All Star; All St Band; Music European Tour; Emporia ST U; Phys Ed.

LAGGART, DARRIN M; Wichita Southeast HS; Wichita, KS; (2); Church Yth Grp; FCA; Hosp Aide; JV Socr; JV Tennis; Prfct Atten Awd; Bible Clb; KS Univ; Tnns Instr; Phy Thrpst.

LAINCZ, MATTHEW; Atchison Sr HS; Atchison, KS; (4); 14/144; Var Bsbl; Capt Var Bsktbl; Capt Var Ftbl; High Hon Roll; Hon Roll; NHS; Pres Acad Fit Awd; Sprtsmnshp Awd; Ftbl MVP, All-League, All-Area; Bsbl All-League; Bsktbl All-League, All-Area, All-Trny; Pittsburg ST Coll.

LAIR, BRANDON L; Topeka West HS; Topeka, KS; (1); Boy Scts; French Clb; Spanish Clb; Stage Crew; Bsktbl; Ftbl; Swmmng; Wrstlng; Hon Roll; Bsbl Smmr Leag; KSU; Engr.

LAIR, CHRISTINE L; Olathe North Sr HS; Olathe, KS; (3); Pres Art Clb; Acpl Chr; Chorus; School Musical; Variety Show; High Hon Roll; Hon Roll; Northwinds Chorale; 1st Div Rtng Regnl/2nd Div Rtng ST Solo/Ensmble Cmptn For Solo; Johnson Cty CC; Music Ed.

LAIRD, CHRISTOPHER R; Goddard HS; Wichita, KS; (1); Spanish Clb; Teachers Aide; JV Bsbl; Var Ftbl; JV Wrstlng; High Hon Roll; Archery; USAFA; Air Force.

LALL, JONATHAN D; Blue Valley North HS; Overland Park, KS; (2); 69/227; Model UN; Intrml Golf; Hon Roll.

LALLEMAND, JUSTIN L; Girard HS; Girard, KS; (4); 6/69; Boy Scts; Church Yth Grp; Letterman Clb; Science Clb; Spanish Clb; SADD; Varsity Clb; JV Bsbl; Var Bsktbl; Var Ftbl; Pittsburg ST U; Elctrncs Engr.

LAM, DORIS Y; Salina HS Central; Salina, KS; (2); 32/276; Church Yth Grp; Teachers Aide; Band; Mrchg Band; Pep Band; JV Trk; Stat Vllybl; Hon Roll; Atty.

LAM, TRUNG M; Lansing HS; Lansing, KS; (4); 1/148; French Clb; Math Tm; NFL; Scholastic Bowl; Service Clb; Treas Soph Cls; JV Crs Cntry; Var L Trk; French Hon Soc; Gov Hon Prg Awd; Sr Cls Homcmng Attendnt; Natl Latn Examntn-Maxima Cum Laude; Natl Piano Playing Auditions-Natl Roll; U Of KS; Comp Sci; Comp Engrng.

LAMB, ANGELA; Pittsburg HS; Pittsburg, KS; (3); 65/200; Debate Tm; Sec FCA; Rep FHA; VP FTA; Q&S; Spanish Clb; Thesps; Ed Yrbk; Var Golf; Church Yth Grp; Med Explorers Clb Pres; Pittsburg ST Univ; Pre-Med.

LAMB, CHRISTINA; Rock Creek Jr Sr HS; Westmoreland, KS; (2); Church Yth Grp; Library Aide; Math Tm; Scholastic Bowl; SADD; Band; Pep Band; Hon Roll; Quiz Bowl; Wamego Cmnty & All Dist Band; St KS Schlsrshp Testing; Phys Thrpy.

LAMB, DANNY T; Circle HS; El Dorado, KS; (2); SADD; JV Ftbl; Air Frce Acad; Eng.

LAMB, MICHAEL; Seton Home Study Schl; Halstead, KS; (1); 4-H; Church Choir; 4-H Awd; High Hon Roll; Gen Clss Amtr Radio Lcnse; Cmptr Prgrmmng; Piano; Hutchinson Comm Coll; Law Enfce.

LAMB, RACHEL; Seton Home Study Schl; Halstead, KS; (4); 4-H; High Hon Roll; Ntl Merit Ltr; Chrch Organist; Hutchinson CC; Pre-Vet.

LAMB III, ROBERT; Seton Home Study Schl; Halstead, KS; (3); 4-H; High Hon Roll; Gen Clss Amtr Radio Lcnse; Cmptr Prgrmmng; Elctrncs; Hutchinson Comm Coll; Cmptrs.

LAMB, TONYA R; Olathe East Sr HS; Olathe, KS; (2); GAA; Office Aide; SADD; Teachers Aide; Band; Jazz Band; School Play; Var Socr; Prfct Atten Awd; Pres Acad Fit Awd; Sports Medicine.

LAMBERT, ELISE K; Manhattan HS; Manhattan, KS; (3); Cmnty Wkr; Dance Clb; Red Cross Aide; Spanish Clb; SADD; Band; Mrchg Band; Pep Band; JV Bsktbl; Powder Puff Ftbl; Heritage Panal Mbr.

LAMBERT, MELISSA; Silver Lake Jr Sr HS; Silver Lake, KS; (4); 6/50; Debate Tm; FHA; Natl FFA Org; NFL; Chorus; Church Choir; Hon Roll; NHS; Pres Soph Cls; Rep Stu Cncl; KS ST U; Bus Admin.

LAMENDOLA, MARK; Wichita East HS; Wichita, KS; (2); Socr; Hon Roll; Bus Admin.

LAMER, AMANDA; Hays HS; Hays, KS; (3); 7/263; Math Tm; Pep Clb; Red Cross Aide; JV Bsktbl; Var Sftbl; High Hon Roll; Jr NHS; Kiwanis Awd; NHS; Wghtlftg; KS ST; Kinesiology.

LAMIA, ANTHONY J; Quivira Heights HS; Holyrood, KS; (3); Church Yth Grp; Cmnty Wkr; FCA; Letterman Clb; Teachers Aide; Band; Mrchg Band; Pep Band; Stage Crew; Bsktbl.

LAMKEY, MARINA; Kapaun-Mt Carmel HS; Wichita, KS; (4); 7/165; Am Leg Aux Girls St; French Clb; Yrbk; Rep Sr Cls; Ofcr Stu Cncl; Var Capt Chrldng; Sec NHS; Ntl Merit SF; Crimestoppers Pres; Hstry.

LAMME, AMY E; Horton HS; Horton, KS; (3); 11/39; Church Yth Grp; SADD; Band; Drill Tm; Mrchg Band; School Musical; School Play; Chrldng; Hon Roll; Prfct Atten Awd; New Image Vocal/Dance Grp; Emporia ST Univ; Elem Ed.

LAMOND, JAMIE J; Osage City HS; Osage City, KS; (3); Art Clb; Cmnty Wkr; Girl Scts; Pep Clb; Science Clb; Var Golf; Mgr(s); Hon Roll; Commnctn.

LAMOREAUX, CHAYNE; Valley Heights Jr Sr HS; Waterville, KS; (3); 9/30; Cmnty Wkr; FHA; Girl Scts; Speech Tm; Pep Clb; Teachers Aide; Band; Drill Tm; Hon Roll; Dance Clb; Par Law Team; Emporia ST; Engl Tchr.

LAMPE, CHRISTY L; Dodge City HS; Dodge City, KS; (3); Drama Clb; Intnl Clb; Model UN; Speech Tm; Chorus; School Musical; School Play; NHS; Comm Svc; KAYS.

LANCELLOTTI, ANDREA; Spring Hill HS; Spring Hill, KS; (4); 31/97; Am Leg Aux Girls St; 4-H; Letterman Clb; Phtg Nwsp; Phtg Yrbk; Rep Frsh Cls; Stat JV Bsktbl; JV Vllybl; 4-H Awd; Hon Roll; Bstr Clb Vol; Aftr Prm Vol; Johnson Cty CC.

LAND, JENNIFER C; Topeka West HS; Topeka, KS; (4); 39/238; French Clb; Pep Clb; SADD; Drill Tm; Stage Crew; Variety Show; Capt Socr; Tennis; Trk; High Hon Roll; Environmental Clb; KS Univ; Bus; Acctng.

LANDER, NICK; Arkansas City HS; Arkansas City, KS; (3); 5/200; Church Yth Grp; FCA; Sec Scholastic Bowl; Teachers Aide; Orch; Rep Soph Cls; Pres Jr Cls; Pres Stu Cncl; JV Stat Bsktbl; Score Keeper; Hnr Symph; Statistics.

LANDES, JAMIN C; Topeka HS; Topeka, KS; (3); French Clb; Hosp Aide; Pep Clb; Science Clb; Drill Tm; Orch; Variety Show; High Hon Roll; Hon Roll; NHS; Pre-Medicine.

LANDOLL, DARREN; Marysville HS; Marysville, KS; (1); JV Ftbl; Var Trk; JV Wrstlng; High Hon Roll; KU; Med.

LANDON, HEATHER; Garden City Sr HS; Garden City, KS; (4); Church Yth Grp; Cmnty Wkr; Band; L Capt Bsktbl; L Var Trk; L Var Vllybl; High Hon Roll; NHS; Med.

LANDSBAUM, BREE; Maize HS; Wichita, KS; (2); 43/270; Church Yth Grp; Debate Tm; NFL; Spanish Clb; SADD; Chorus; Variety Show; High Hon Roll; NHS; Pres Acad Fit Awd; Chrch Yth Group VP; Vol Comm Svc; Chrch Athl Org Sftbl & Vllybl; Ivy League; Bus Admin.

LANE, CALLIE A; Basehor Linwood HS; Linwood, KS; (2); Trk; Camera & Photo Clb; Math Clb.

LANE, CARRIE; Manhattan HS; Manhattan, KS; (3); Church Yth Grp; Cmnty Wkr; GAA; Math Clb; Office Aide; Pep Clb; Spanish Clb; Teachers Aide; Band; Mrchg Band; KS ST U; Gntc Engnr.

LANE, CARRIE A; Eastern Heights Jr Sr HS; Agra, KS; (2); 3/9; School Play; Sec Frsh Cls; Pres Soph Cls; Ofcr Stu Cncl; Bsktbl; Chrldng; Vllybl; Wt Lftg; Hon Roll; Pep Clb; Vac Bible Schl Hlpr; Day Care Ctr Plnd Act.

LANE, JACOB M; Garden City Sr HS; Garden City, KS; (2); Church Yth Grp; Quiz Bowl; Band; Church Choir; Mrchg Band; Pep Band; Bsktbl; Crs Cntry; Trk; Hon Roll; Yth Grp Band; HS TV Sta Buffalo Brdcstng Syst; 4 Yr Univ; TV Radio/Brd/Law.

LANE, KELLY; Wichita Heights HS; Wichita, KS; (3); Bus Profs of Am; FHA; Girl Scts; Orch; Hon Roll; NHS; Acctng.

LANE, LAURA; Mc Louth Schl; Mc Louth, KS; (1); Art Clb; FHA; Letterman Clb; SADD; Chorus; Crs Cntry; Trk; High Hon Roll; Hon Roll; Smmr Yth Vol KS Hstrcl Msem; I Rtng Indvdl Slo Leg & Regl Lvl 1995; 1st Pl Regl Hist Day Cmptn; Phys Thrpy.

LANE, TINA; Jefferson Co North HS; Winchester, KS; (4); 7/43; FBLA; SADD; Band; Chorus; Flag Corp; Mrchg Band; Pep Band; VP Stu Cncl; JV Var Bsktbl; Var Chrldng; All League DVL Vllybll 2 Yrs; Leavenworth Alla Rea Vllybll; St Track; Ottawa Univ.

LANE, ZECHARIAH L; Cunningham HS; Zenda, KS; (4); Computer Clb; Pep Clb; Science Clb; SADD; JV Ftbl; JV Trk; Hon Roll; U Of AR; Comp Sci.

LANG, ABBY; Burrton Schl; Burrton, KS; (1); 1/30; Church Yth Grp; FCA; Quiz Bowl; Scholastic Bowl; Band; Pep Band; Bsktbl; Trk; Vllybl; Hon Roll.

LANG, ANNE M; Blue Valley HS; Stilwell, KS; (3); Art Clb; Church Yth Grp; Intnl Clb; Chorus; Variety Show; Nwsp; Tennis; Hon Roll; NHS; Envrn Clb Pres; KS Assn Of Yth.

LANG, CATHERINE L; Hill City HS; Hill City, KS; (2); 14/46; Church Yth Grp; Drama Clb; FCA; FHA; Natl FFA Org; NFL; Pres SADD; Band; Chorus; Pep Band; Explorer Scouts Pres/Quarter Master; Elem Ed.

LANG, CHRIS B; Hutchinson HS; Hutchinson, KS; (3); 49/350; Am Leg Boys St; Letterman Clb; Pep Clb; Quiz Bowl; SADD; Teachers Aide; JV Bsktbl; L Var Ftbl; JV Trk; L Var Wt Lftg.

LANG, EMILY; Thomas More Prep-Marian HS; Hays, KS; (2); Rptr Nwsp; JV Capt Chrldng; Hon Roll.

LANG, KYLE; Seaman Sr HS; Topeka, KS; (3); Treas Church Yth Grp; 4-H; Mrchg Band; Pep Band; Golf; Socr; 4-H Awd; Jr NHS; NHS; Pres Acad Fit Awd; Chrch Yth Grp Tres; KS U; Acctng.

LANG, LUKE T; Wellsville Jr Sr HS; Wellsville, KS; (4); 5/55; Am Leg Boys St; Church Yth Grp; Debate Tm; FCA; FBLA; Math Tm; Scholastic Bowl; Band; High Hon Roll; NHS; U Of KS; Med Pract.

LANG, SARA; Lyons HS; Lyons, KS; (1); Church Yth Grp; Dance Clb; FCA; Band; Var Frsh Cls; Ofcr Stu Cncl; Chrldng; Vllybl; Hon Roll; Prfct Atten Awd.

LANG, TIMOTHY A; Washburn Rural HS; Topeka, KS; (2); 15/390; Church Yth Grp; FCA; NFL; SADD; Var Crs Cntry; Var Trk; High Hon Roll; AAU Cross Cntry Natls 27th; AP Claculus; Ministry.

LANGE, ALICIA; Conway Springs HS; Conway Springs, KS; (4); 14/45; Church Yth Grp; Girl Scts; Office Aide; SADD; Teachers Aide; Chorus; Hon Roll; Natl Hnr Roll; All Amer Schlr; Cowley Cty CC; Bus.

LANGE, JENNIFER C; Blue Valley HS; Stilwell, KS; (2); Cmnty Wkr; Latin Clb; Teachers Aide; Ed Yrbk; Bsktbl; Sftbl; Vllybl; Hon Roll; KS Univ; Sports Med.

LANGE, JOCELYN; Miltonvale HS; Miltonvale, KS; (4); 1/7; Capt Quiz Bowl; Pres Sec Stu Cncl; Capt Bsktbl; Gov Hon Prg Awd; NHS; St Schlr; Val; Capt Vllybl; Church Yth Grp; Band; KS Bsktbl Cochs Assn Acad All-St Tem; Hrnb Mntn In Topeka Captl Jornls All St Tem; HS KU Hnr Stu; U Of KS; Phy Therapy.

LANGE, JONATHAN P; Leavenworth HS; Leavenworth, KS; (3); Boy Scts; Church Yth Grp; ROTC; Science Clb; Ski Clb; High Hon Roll; NHS; SADD; Eagle Sct; Vigil Hnr Order Of Arrow BSA; Chem; Vet.

LANGE, KELLY D; Shawnee Mission N HS; Merriam, KS; (1); Pep Clb; Stage Crew; High Hon Roll; Anml Rghts; KU; Jrnlsm.

LANGEROT, NATHAN; Mulvane Sr HS; Mulvane, KS; (3); Sec Church Yth Grp; FCA; HOBY; Q&S; SADD; VP Frsh Cls; Var L Ftbl; Var L Wrstlng; Hon Roll; TEC Rtrt Tm; U Of Notre Dame; Vet.

LANGFORD, CASSIE; Circle HS; Wichita, KS; (2); Church Yth Grp; FHA; Chorus; School Musical; School Play; Variety Show; Sftbl; Hon Roll; PT.

LANGFORD, GABRIEL J; Shawnee Heights Sr HS; Tecumseh, KS; (3); Church Yth Grp; SADD; Hon Roll; Marine Bio; Medicine.

LANGHOFER, JESSICA; Flinthills HS; Cassoday, KS; (4); Am Leg Aux Girls St; Drama Clb; FCA; SADD; Teachers Aide; Band; Chorus; Pep Band; School Musical; Mgr(s); Vernons Schl Csmtlgy; Csmtlgy.

LANGLEY, ERICA E; Blue Valley North HS; Leawood, KS; (2); Church Yth Grp; FCA; Model UN; Chorus; Church Choir; Var L Golf; Hon Roll; Childrens Spcl Needs Ministy Vol.

LANGLEY, MICHAEL J; Louisburg HS; Louisburg, KS; (2); Spanish Clb; JV Bsktbl; High Hon Roll; Hon Roll; Prfct Atten Awd.

LANGREHR, VICTOR L; Great Bend Sr HS; Great Bend, KS; (2); German Clb; Scholastic Bowl; Band; Hon Roll; Pres Acad Fit Awd; Barton Cty CC; Engr.

LANGSTON, JARED P; Quivira Heights HS; Holyrood, KS; (2); Letterman Clb; Band; Mrchg Band; Pep Band; JV Bsktbl; JV Ftbl; JV Tennis; Hon Roll; Hnrb Mntn St Wrd Proc; Comp Anlyst.

LANKARD, JODI L; Independence HS; Independence, KS; (1); Church Yth Grp; 4-H; Pep Clb; Chorus; Trk; 4-H Awd; Hon Roll; 4-H Pres, Prlmntrn, Treas, Rec, Sng Ldr; 4-H Family Of Yr 94-95; Dist Impact Tm & Stu Cncl-Chrch; Cosmetology.

LANNING, TERA J; Field Kindley Mem Sr HS; Coffeyville, KS; (4); French Clb; Chorus; Hon Roll; Coffeyville CC; Sml Bus Mgmt.

LANSING, ERIN; Lansing HS; Leavenworth, KS; (3); Art Clb; 4-H; Pep Clb; JV Bsktbl; Var Chrldng; JV Sftbl; JV Vllybl; Hon Roll; Acrobatics; Horseback Riding; Acctng.

LANTERMAN, CAROLINE M; Salina HS South; Salina, KS; (3); Cmnty Wkr; Math Tm; Quiz Bowl; Teachers Aide; Ofcr Stu Cncl; Phtg Crs Cntry; High Hon Roll; Govt For Teen Ldrshp Clb.

LANZRATH, DARREL E; Remington HS; Newton, KS; (4); Church Yth Grp; VP Letterman Clb; Science Clb; Teachers Aide; Rep Stu Cncl; JV Bsbl; Capt L Ftbl; Var L Trk; Var L Wrstlng; Hon Roll; KS ST; Ag Engrng.

LAPINE, JOHN; Olathe North Sr HS; Olathe, KS; (3); French Clb; Teachers Aide; Nwsp; Yrbk; Ftbl; Trk; Hon Roll; NHS; Pres Acad Fit Awd; Pres Schlr; KS Univ.

LAPLANT, AIMEE; Mulvane Sr HS; Mulvane, KS; (3); Office Aide; SADD; Varsity Clb; Chorus; Bsktbl; Var Chrldng; Var Trk; Var Vllybl; Emporia ST; Elem Ed.

LAPLANT, NICKOLAS; Garden City Sr HS; Garden City, KS; (3); Debate Tm; NFL; Speech Tm; Ftbl; Trk; Wrstlng; NHS; Non Schl Spon Acting.

LARA, DAVID J; Buhler HS; Buhler, KS; (3); Rep Am Leg Boys St; Treas Church Yth Grp; FCA; Letterman Clb; Spanish Clb; SADD; Band; Chorus; Church Choir; Jazz Band; KS All-ST Choir; Summer Choral Inst Hnr Choir; Univ; Vocal Perf Arts; Engrng.

LARA, JENNIFER R; Scott Comm HS; Scott City, KS; (3); 29/75; Hon Roll; VFW; Acctng.

LARKIN, EARNIE G; Goddard HS; Wichita, KS; (4); 47/152; Sprt Ed Nwsp; Var Capt Ftbl; JV Var Trk; Hon Roll; Wichita ST Univ; Atty.

LARKIN II, JAMES L; Oak Grove Baptist Schl; Kansas City, KS; (2); Pres Frsh Cls; Bsktbl; Socr; Hon Roll; Fireman.

LARSEN, HARMONEE; Lincoln Jr Sr HS; Lincoln, KS; (3); Letterman Clb; Pep Clb; Color Guard; Nwsp; Sec Frsh Cls; Sec Jr Cls; Ofcr Stu Cncl; Var L Bsktbl; Var L Chrldng; Var L Sftbl.

LARSEN, HEATHER D; Lincoln Jr Sr HS; Lincoln, KS; (1); Letterman Clb; Pep Clb; School Musical; Var Bsktbl; Var Trk; JV Vllybl; Hon Roll; Hnrbl Mntn All League Bsktbl Team; Penn ST; Archtct.

LARSEN, SHAWNA; Spring Hill HS; Spring Hill, KS; (2); FCA; Scholastic Bowl; Science Clb; SADD; VP Soph Cls; JV Bsktbl; JV Var Vllybl; High Hon Roll; Jr NHS; Pres Acad Fit Awd; 1st Pl Regnls OM 3rd St 94-95.

LARSON, ANDREW; Salina HS Central; Salina, KS; (3); 9/270; Church Yth Grp; Cmnty Wkr; HOBY; Science Clb; SADD; Varsity Clb; Rep Soph Cls; VP Jr Cls; Var Ftbl; Var Capt Trk.

LARSON, BROOKE L; Smoky Valley HS; Lindsborg, KS; (2); Church Yth Grp; FCA; Letterman Clb; Pep Clb; Varsity Clb; Band; Flag Corp; Mrchg Band; Pep Band; Rep Frsh Cls; KAYS; Sftbl; Boys Tennis; U Of KS; Sports Med.

LARSON, DARA R; Derby HS; Derby, KS; (1); Church Yth Grp; ROTC; Band; Church Choir; Drill Tm; Variety Show; Hon Roll; Poems Pub.

LARSON, EMILY; Little River Jr Sr HS; Little River, KS; (4); 2/21; Church Yth Grp; Sec 4-H; Pres German Clb; Math Tm; Band; Phtg Yrbk; Sec Sr Cls; 4-H Awd; High Hon Roll; Pres Schlr; KS Hnrs Schlr; Lvstck Jdgng Tm; Hutchinson CC; Vet.

LARSON, JARED; Riley Cty HS; Riley, KS; (3); Am Leg Boys St; Pres FCA; Pres 4-H; School Play; Pres Frsh Cls; Pres Jr Cls; VP Stu Cncl; Var L Bsktbl; Cit Awd; High Hon Roll; Radio/Tv.

LARSON, KATRINA; Wallace Cnty HS; Sharon Springs, KS; (3); 1/19; Pep Clb; Band; Mrchg Band; Pep Band; Rptr Nwsp; Chrldng; Pom Pon; High Hon Roll; NHS; Bus/Acctng.

LARSON, KATRINE A; Lincoln Jr Sr HS; Tescott, KS; (4); 2/28; Cmnty Wkr; FCA; FHA; Pep Clb; Quiz Bowl; Speech Tm; Teachers Aide; Band; Chorus; Church Choir; Bible Study Group; KS ST U; Music.

LARSON, KRISTI M; Iola Sr HS; Iola, KS; (2); Church Yth Grp; Natl FFA Org; SADD; Band; Chorus; Mrchg Band; Pep Band; JV Crs Cntry; JV Trk; Hon Roll.

LARSON, MATT; Silver Lake Jr Sr HS; Silver Lake, KS; (2); 1/50; Church Yth Grp; NFL; Scholastic Bowl; Band; School Musical; Pres Frsh Cls; Intrml Bsktbl; Intrml Ftbl; High Hon Roll; Cmnty Wkr; Yth Sndy Chrch Song Ldr; Archt Eng.

LARSON, SARAH E; Cunningham HS; Cunningham, KS; (3); Church Yth Grp; Drama Clb; Pep Clb; Quiz Bowl; Science Clb; Speech Tm; SADD; Dance Clb; Hosp Aide; Letterman Clb; CNA; CMA; Musicals; Band; Choir; U Of KS; Nursing.

LARSON, STEPHANIE D; Shawnee Mission E Sr HS; Shawnee Mission, KS; (4); 19/400; French Clb; Girl Scts; Natl Beta Clb; Q&S; Ed Yrbk; French Hon Soc; Hon Roll; NHS; Ntl Merit Ltr; Pres Acad Fit Awd; KS ST Univ.

LARSON, TAMI; Jefferson West HS; Ozawkie, KS; (3); #4 in class; Am Leg Aux Girls St; Spanish Clb; VP Stu Cncl; Var Bsktbl; Var Pom Pon; Var Vllybl; High Hon Roll; NHS; Wt Lftg; Var Sftbl; Lakeside Top Choir; KS Bsktbl Tm Tour To Belgium.

LARSON, TYLER P; Blue Valley North HS; Leawood, KS; (2); Boy Scts; Intnl Clb; Variety Show; JV Bsbl; Var Socr; Wt Lftg; Cit Awd; Hon Roll; Eagle Scout; Bro To 4 Exchnge Stdnts; KS Univ.

LARUE, TIMOTHY V; Leroy HS; Le Roy, KS; (3); Church Yth Grp; HOBY; Quiz Bowl; Band; Chorus; Jazz Band; Mrchg Band; Pep Band; School Musical; Rep Stu Cncl; All St Manc Bnd Cmp 94; I Rtng St Cntst On Vcl Solo 96; II Rtng St Cntst On Tnr Sax Solo 96; Allen Cty Comm Coll.

LA SALLE, ROBERT J; Halstead HS; Mc Pherson, KS; (3); Church Yth Grp; Letterman Clb; Spanish Clb; Intrml Socr; L Wrstlng; Cit Awd; High Hon Roll; Prfct Atten Awd; Tabor Coll; Pre Med.

LASCON, TONY R; Bishop Ward HS; Kansas City, KS; (2); Intrml Bsbl; JV Intrml Ftbl.

LASHINSKI II, ANTHONY F; Derby HS; Derby, KS; (4); CAP; SADD; Orch; Ed Nwsp; Rptr Lit Mag; Rep Frsh Cls; Rep Stu Cncl; Var L Trk; Hon Roll; Pres Acad Fit Awd; U Of KS; Nwsp Jrnlsm.

LASHMET, DEIDRA J; Stanton Co HS; Manter, KS; (3); Boy Scts; Bus Profs of Am; 4-H; FBLA; JA; Office Aide; SADD; Varsity Clb; Band; Mrchg Band; KS ST Univ.

LASITER, MARIE G; Mulvane Sr HS; Wichita, KS; (3); Letterman Clb; SADD; Band; Drm Mjr(t); Yrbk; Var Capt Vllybl; High Hon Roll; Prfct Atten Awd; Teachers Aide; Varsity Clb; Ntl Macy Schlr-MIM-MNRTIES Med; Wichita KS Intrtrbl Warrior Soc Princess 95-96; U Of KS; Cytotechnlgy.

LASSITER, ROBIN; Campus HS; Wichita, KS; (2); Chorus; Chrldng; High Hon Roll; Hon Roll; KS U.

LATHAM, DUSTIN K; Triplains Schl; Winona, KS; (3); 3/18; Church Yth Grp; Cmnty Wkr; Letterman Clb; Ski Clb; School Play; Stage Crew; VP Frsh Cls; Rep Soph Cls; Var Capt Bsktbl; Var Capt Ftbl; All-League Offense-Defense Ftbl.

LATHAM, STEVEN; Wyandotte HS; Kansas City, KS; (3); Chess Clb; Church Yth Grp; Drama Clb; People/People Stu Ambssdr Pgm 93-94; Frnscs Tm; Mrtl Arts; Mulit Yrs Lstd; Aerontcl.

LATHROP, AMANDA L; Shawnee Mission N HS; Shawnee Mission, KS; (2); 128/456; German Clb; GAA; Pep Clb; JV Sftbl; Wt Lftg; Hon Roll; NHS; Multi-Yr Listee; Pittsburg ST.

LATHROP, ANGELA N; Great Bend Sr HS; Ellinwood, KS; (4); Church Yth Grp; Drama Clb; German Clb; SADD; Acpl Chr; Band; Drm Mjr(t); School Play; High Hon Roll; St Schlr; William Jewell; Vcl Prfrmnc.

LATIF, USMAN; Olathe East Sr HS; Olathe, KS; (3); Pres Church Yth Grp; Debate Tm; French Clb; Hosp Aide; Library Aide; Math Clb; Math Tm; School Play; Ed Nwsp; High Hon Roll; U Of MO; Phys.

LATTA, JENNIFER; Smith Ctr Jr Sr HS; Smith Center, KS; (2); Drama Clb; Band; Chorus; School Play; Var Chrldng; JV Vllybl; Hon Roll; Prfct Atten Awd; KAYS; Fort Hays ST U.

LATTA, KRISTA M; Bishop Carroll Catholic HS; Wichita, KS; (2); Chorus; Variety Show; Hon Roll; Play Organ; Sings; Writes Poems/Songs; Prof Vocal.

LATTIMER, DOUGLAS C; Axtell Schl; Axtell, KS; (3); 1/18; Quiz Bowl; School Play; Yrbk; Pres Frsh Cls; VP Stu Cncl; Bsktbl; Ftbl; Trk; High Hon Roll; NHS; Site Base Cncl; Acctng.

LATTIMER, JAMES; Newton Sr HS; Newton, KS; (3); Am Leg Boys St; Dance Clb; Natl FFA Org; Chorus; Hon Roll; FFA Workhorse Awd; Newton FFA Treas; Fruit & Vegetable Prod Ag Proficiency Awd In Entrepeneurship 96; Pratt CC.

LATTY, DAVID I; Caldwell Jr Sr HS; Caldwell, KS; (3); 5/25; Scholastic Bowl; Speech Tm; SADD; Nwsp; Yrbk; Sec Treas Jr Cls; Ftbl; Trk; Wt Lftg; Hon Roll; 2nd Pl Photo St Jrnlsm Cntst; Emporia ST.

LATURNER, MARK A; Galena HS; Galena, KS; (1); 5/75; Church Yth Grp; FCA; FBLA; Scholastic Bowl; Band; Chorus; Mrchg Band; Swimming; Bsktbl.

LATZKE, JENNI; Chapman HS; Woodbine, KS; (4); 15/130; Church Yth Grp; 4-H; Scholastic Bowl; SADD; Teachers Aide; Acpl Chr; Chorus; Church Choir; School Musical; School Play; KS ST U; Mass Commnctn.

LATZKE, MANDY L; Atchison Co Cmty HS; Lancaster, KS; (4); Church Yth Grp; SADD; Chorus; School Musical; Variety Show; Yrbk; Hon Roll; Kays; Vo Tech; Bus.

LAUBER, ALICIA; Yates Ctr HS; Yates Center, KS; (3); Art Clb; Letterman Clb; NFL; Spanish Clb; L Chrldng; L Sftbl; Hon Roll; KAYS VP.

LAUBER, NIKKI R; Wichita East HS; Wichita, KS; (3); 122/337; Hon Roll; WSU; Fash Dsgng.

LAUDERDALE, STACY A; Blue Valley Northwest HS; Shawnee Mission, KS; (4); Debate Tm; 4-H; NFL; Powder Puff Ftbl; High Hon Roll; NHS; Ntl Merit Ltr; St Schlr; Forensics; Rockhurst; Bio.

LAUER, CHRISTOPHER T; Shawnee Mission E Sr HS; Leawood, KS; (2); 9/500; Debate Tm; NFL; Spanish Clb; Speech Tm; Cit Awd; High Hon Roll; Pres Acad Fit Awd; Spanish NHS; Intnl Relations.

LAUFFER, LACI; Protection Schl; Protection, KS; (2); 4/21; Church Yth Grp; Quiz Bowl; Speech Tm; Band; Chorus; Yrbk; JV Bsktbl; Var L Crs Cntry; Var L Trk; High Hon Roll; Kayettes.

LAUFFER, OCTOBER D; Wichita Heights HS; Wichita, KS; (3); 92/250; Am Leg Aux Girls St; Church Yth Grp; Cmnty Wkr; French Clb; Hosp Aide; JA; Pep Clb; Red Cross Aide; SADD; Teachers Aide; Peer Ldrshp Ambassador; Sr LYF Natl Del; KS U; Sports Medicine.

LAUTERS, KAREN; Manhattan HS; Manhattan, KS; (2); Church Yth Grp; JV Chrldng; Hon Roll; KS ST Univ; Law.

LAVA, JANE S; Parsons HS; Parsons, KS; (4); 1/118; Debate Tm; Pres NFL; School Musical; School Play; Pres Soph Cls; Sec Sec Stu Cncl; JV Crs Cntry; Pres NHS; Ntl Merit Ltr; Val; Northwestern U; Engl.

LAVIN, TIMOTHY B; Blue Valley Northwest HS; Overland Park, KS; (2); Church Yth Grp; Latin Clb; Band; Church Choir; Mrchg Band; Ftbl; Wt Lftg; High Hon Roll; Hon Roll.

LA VINE, MARGARET D; Winfield HS; Winfield, KS; (4); Church Yth Grp; Cmnty Wkr; Debate Tm; Drama Clb; Intnl Clb; NFL; Speech Tm; Teachers Aide; Thesps; Acpl Chr; Show-Dance Choir; Southwestern Coll; Mass Commnct.

LAVOIE, MICHELLE M; Sacred Heart HS; Salina, KS; (2); #1 in class; FBLA; Chorus; High Hon Roll; KS ST; Engl.

LAW, ESTHER A; South Haven Schl; Winfield, KS; (1); Church Yth Grp; FCA; Chorus; Church Choir; School Musical; Stage Crew; High Hon Roll; Hon Roll; VBS Tchr; Crim Just.

LAWERENCE, HEATHER; Blue Valley HS; Overland Park, KS; (3); Q&S; SADD; Yrbk; Pres Frsh Cls; Rep Soph Cls; Rep Jr Cls; VP Stu Cncl; Var L Mgr(s); Cit Awd; Hon Roll; 4 Yr Univ; Jrnlsm/Psych.

LAWLESS, VIRGINIA; Kapaun-Mt Carmel HS; Wichita, KS; (3); 10/170; Church Yth Grp; Cmnty Wkr; French Clb; Science Clb; Acpl Chr; Chorus; Church Choir; Stage Crew; High Hon Roll; NHS; Pre Med.

LAWRENCE, CHRIS G; Scott Comm HS; Scott City, KS; (3); Church Yth Grp; Cmnty Wkr; Pres Treas 4-H; Letterman Clb; Natl FFA Org; Varsity Clb; Acpl Chr; Chorus; School Musical; Stage Crew; KS ST U; Comp Sci.

LAWRENCE, CLINTON K; Wellington Sr HS; Wellington, KS; (4); 6/127; Church Yth Grp; Key Clb; Ed Yrbk; Rep Stu Cncl; Var Golf; High Hon Roll; Sec NHS; U Of KS Hnrs Awd; Comp Arts.

LAWRENCE, JOHN W; Desoto HS; Shawnee Mission, KS; (3); Church Yth Grp; Cmnty Wkr; Band; Jazz Band; Mrchg Band; Pep Band; School Musical; Bsktbl; Ftbl; Golf; Fr Clb; Concert Band; KS Univ.

LAWRENCE, KEITH D; Ft Scott HS; Fort Scott, KS; (4); Bus Profs of Am; FTA; Teachers Aide; Ed Nwsp; Ofcr Stu Cncl; Bsktbl; Ftbl; Swmmng; Wt Lftg; Drafting; KU; His Tchr.

LAWRENCE, MELISSA D; Mankato Jr Sr HS; Mankato, KS; (3); Church Yth Grp; Natl FFA Org; Pep Clb; Band; Chorus; Color Guard; Flag Corp; Mrchg Band; Pep Band; Yrbk; Chld Psychlgst.

LAWRIE, KEVIN J; Wichita East HS; Wichita, KS; (2); Church Yth Grp; Chorus; School Musical; Ftbl; Wt Lftg; Hon Roll.

LAWS, LYNNETTE K; Ottawa HS; Ottawa, KS; (2); Bsktbl; Trk; Vllybl; High Hon Roll; Lib Aide.

LAWS, TREVOR; Spring Hill HS; Spring Hill, KS; (2); Church Yth Grp; Scholastic Bowl; Band; Mrchg Band; Pep Band; L Ftbl; Trk; Hon Roll.

LAWSON, CARRIE; Blue Valley HS; Stilwell, KS; (2); JV Socr; Hon Roll; Sftbl; Asst Coach Sccr; KS Univ; Sprts Med/PT.

LAWSON, COLBY; Pratt HS; Pratt, KS; (1); 4-H; FHA; Hosp Aide; Pep Clb; Band; Mrchg Band; Pep Band; Chrldng; Trk; Hon Roll; Obsttrcs/Tchng Yng Chldrn.

LAWSON, KELLY; Shawnee Mission W Sr HS; Lenexa, KS; (4); 14/365; Sec Treas Church Yth Grp; Chorus; Yrbk; VP Soph Cls; VP Jr Cls; VP Stu Cncl; JV Capt Chrldng; High Hon Roll; Hon Roll; NHS; Viking Awd; Prsdntl Schlr Awd; Acad Ftnss Awd; Univ Of KS; Pharm.

LAXSON, ANGELA M; Udall HS; Udall, KS; (2); Church Yth Grp; Dance Clb; Girl Scts; Band; Mrchg Band; Var L Mgr(s); Var L Pom Pon; High Hon Roll; Prfct Atten Awd; Girl Scout Silver Awd.

LAXSON, JESSICA L; Udall HS; Udall, KS; (2); Church Yth Grp; Girl Scts; Var L Chrldng; Var L Pom Pon; JV Vllybl; High Hon Roll; Hon Roll; NHS; Prfct Atten Awd; Computer Clb; Girl Scout Silver Awd.

LAY, ELENA R; Council Grove HS; Alta Vista, KS; (2); FCA; Rptr 4-H; Letterman Clb; Math Tm; Pep Clb; SADD; Band; Mrchg Band; Pep Band; JV Bsktbl; All CVL Track; ST Track; Girls Pep Fastpitch Sftbl Tm; Manhatton Chrstn Coll; Chem.

LAY, JANA E; Neodesha Jr Sr HS; Neodesha, KS; (1); Letterman Clb; Natl FFA Org; L Chrldng; Vllybl; Wt Lftg; Hon Roll; Renaissance Best Eyes; TX A&M; Bus Owner.

LAYMON, CAMERON P; Lyons HS; Lyons, KS; (2); JV Ftbl; Hon Roll; KS U; Electrician.

LAYNE, VALERIE; Stafford Jr Sr HS; Stafford, KS; (4); 3/25; Church Yth Grp; Math Clb; Quiz Bowl; Scholastic Bowl; Science Clb; Teachers Aide; Band; Mrchg Band; Pep Band; Yrbk; KS ST U; Cmptr Sci.

LE, ALAIN I; Blue Valley HS; Overland Park, KS; (2); 15/240; Boy Scts; JCL; Treas Latin Clb; SADD; Lit Mag; Var Bsktbl; Var Crs Cntry; JV Tennis; High Hon Roll; Jr NHS; Tae Kwan Do; Piano; KAYS; Harvard; Dctr.

LE, ANNE G; Blue Vlly HS; Overland Park, KS; (3); Intnl Clb; JCL; Latin Clb; Intrml Bsktbl; JV Socr; Intrml Sftbl; High Hon Roll; Hon Roll; Jr NHS; NHS; U Of MO; Pharm.

LE, DUNG V; Garden City Sr HS; Garden City, KS; (2); Socr.

LE, HUONG D; Wichita East HS; Wichita, KS; (2); Girl Scts; JA; Church Choir; School Play; Hon Roll; Asian Clb; 1kth Annual Asian Fest; Hnrbl Mntn & Merit Achvmnt Awd; KS Univ; Pharm.

LE, LINDA A; Wichita Southeast HS; Wichita, KS; (2); 81/432; Hon Roll; Prfct Atten Awd; Asian Cultrl Org; DECA; Chiroprtcr.

LE, THU THUY T; Wichita North HS; Wichita, KS; (4); SADD; School Play; Nwsp; Ofcr Sr Cls; Bsktbl; Tennis; Nurse.

LE, TIM B; Wichita East HS; Wichita, KS; (4); 20/287; Tnns Ltr; Hnr Roll; WSU; Cmptr Grphc Arts.

LE, TINH H; Garden City Sr HS; Garden City, KS; (4); Teachers Aide; Crim Just.

LEACH, COLBY N; Shawnee Heights HS; Topeka, KS; (1); Service Clb; Spanish Clb; Bsktbl; JV Socr; Var Trk; Hon Roll.

LEACH, MIMI M; Ft Scott HS; Fort Scott, KS; (2); Church Yth Grp; FCA; Pep Clb; Chorus; School Play; Ofcr Soph Cls; Ofcr Stu Cncl; Chrldng; Mgr(s); Powder Puff Ftbl.

LEACH, REBECCA E; Desoto HS; De Soto, KS; (4); Art Clb; SADD; Band; Capt Flag Corp; School Musical; Rptr Nwsp; Stat Vllybl; Cit Awd; Hon Roll; NHS; PRIDE Pgm Mem & Schlsp; Yth For Christ; Presdntl Ed Awd 3 Yrs; Johnson Cty CC; Commercial Art.

LEAHEY, CHRISTINE; Olathe South Sr HS; Olathe, KS; (4); 1/400; Am Leg Aux Girls St; Art Clb; Cmnty Wkr; Computer Clb; Capt Debate Tm; Drama Clb; English Clb; German Clb; Intnl Clb; Latin Clb; Pres SASH; Human Relations Commtte; Cmprtv Lit.

LEARNED, ANDY T; Clearwater HS; Clearwater, KS; (3); Hon Roll; Comp Sci.

LEARNED, TIFFANY L; Newton Sr HS; Newton, KS; (2); Church Yth Grp; Girl Scts; Key Clb; Band; Church Choir; Mrchg Band; Nwsp; Crs Cntry; Socr; U KS; Lbrl Arts.

LEASON, APRIL D; Wichita East HS; Wichita, KS; (3); Q&S; Thesps; Chorus; School Musical; School Play; Phtg Nwsp; Treas Soph Cls; Treas Jr Cls; Church Yth Grp; Drama Clb; KSPA Rgnls 3rs Pl Nwspr Phtgrphy; KSPA ST 2nd Pl Nwspr Phtgrphy; Photojrnlst.

LEATHERWOOD, LISA; Cimarron HS; Cimarron, KS; (3); Church Yth Grp; Pres Sec Natl FFA Org; Pep Clb; Band; Stat Vllybl; High Hon Roll; NHS; Spanish Clb; Jazz Band; Mrchg Band; KS St Limousin Breeders Assn Rptr & VP; Girls III Slalom 1st Pl KS St Water Ski Champs 95; KS ST Univ; Ag Bus.

LE BEAU, JENNIFER; Olathe East Sr HS; Olathe, KS; (3); Cmnty Wkr; Letterman Clb; Pep Clb; Spanish Clb; Teachers Aide; JV Capt Chrldng; Tennis; Trk; Vllybl; Hon Roll; Bowling Schlsp 1987-88; Won 5 Natl Chrldng Titles & 2nd Pl Squad Pro Cheer All Stars.

LECK, KIRK A; Jackson Heights HS; Netawaka, KS; (2); Church Yth Grp; Natl FFA Org; JV L Bsktbl; Var L Crs Cntry; JV Var Ftbl; Var L Trk; Hon Roll; Prfct Atten Awd.

LECLAIR, CURTIS; Clifton-Clyde HS; Clyde, KS; (3); Church Yth Grp; Cmnty Wkr; FBLA; FTA; Letterman Clb; Varsity Clb; Band; VP Sr Cls; Bsktbl; Ftbl; Scndry Ed Math.

LE CLAIRE, NICOLE C; Shawnee Mission Northwest HS; Shawnee Mission, KS; (2); Pep Clb; Drill Tm; JV Gym; JV Trk; High Hon Roll; Yng Life; Dance.

LECLEAR, RACHAEL D; Emporia HS; Emporia, KS; (1); Art Clb; Hosp Aide; Cit Awd; High Hon Roll.

LE CLERCQ, PAUL M; Derby Christian Schl; Wichita, KS; (2); Church Yth Grp; Red Cross Aide; Church Choir; Pres Stu Cncl; Var Bsktbl; Cit Awd; High Hon Roll; Prin Awd Ovrall Bst Stu 9-10th Grd; Nyles-Anderson; Pstrl Stud.

LE COUNT, MIKE A; Hays HS; Hays, KS; (3); NFL; JV L Bsktbl; JV L Crs Cntry; Var L Trk; Hon Roll; NHS; KS ST Univ; Bus/Fin.

LEDERER, BILL; Valley Falls HS; Valley Falls, KS; (4); 7/36; Church Yth Grp; FBLA; FHA; Band; Chorus; Mrchg Band; School Play; Rep Sr Cls; Var Bsbl; Var Bsktbl; U Of KS.

LEDESMA, CHRISTA A; Wellington Sr HS; Wellington, KS; (3); 4/160; Church Yth Grp; Key Clb; Quiz Bowl; Band; Jazz Band; Mrchg Band; School Play; Cmnty Wkr; Drama Clb; Scholastic Bowl; Comm Theatre; All-St Band; Yth Ldr Core.

LEDFORD, TRINA L; Ashland HS; Ashland, KS; (4); 2/25; Sec Treas Church Yth Grp; FCA; Quiz Bowl; Scholastic Bowl; Band; Chorus; Pep Band; Rep Sr Cls; High Hon Roll; NHS; St Cont Trumpet Solo I 94 & 95; Evangel Coll; Missions.

LE DOU, JAY; Colby Sr HS; Colby, KS; (4); 14/97; Debate Tm; Teachers Aide; Ftbl; Trk; Wt Lftg; Hon Roll; ST Dbt/Frnscs; Ottawa Univ; Pre Engrg.

LE DUC, JESSICA A; Clifton-Clyde HS; Clyde, KS; (3); 2/31; Phtg Church Yth Grp; Pres 4-H; Pres Pep Clb; Band; Pres Jr Cls; JV Var Bsktbl; L Trk; Mgr Vllybl; High Hon Roll; NHS; KS ST; Jrnlsm.

LEE, BRANDI R; Atchison Co Cmty HS; Horton, KS; (2); VP Pres 4-H; FBLA; Math Clb; Mu Alpha Theta; Band; Mrchg Band; Pep Band; Bsktbl; Vllybl; 4-H Awd; Kays; Mjrt; Highland JC; Acctng.

LEE, BRANDON D; Central Heights Sr HS; Richmond, KS; (1); 4-H; Letterman Clb; Natl FFA Org; Science Clb; JV Bsktbl; Var L Ftbl; 4-H Awd; High Hon Roll; Prfct Atten Awd; Babe Ruth Bsbl; Natl Sci Merit Awd; All-Amer Schlr Awd.

LEE, BRITTANY L; Derby HS; Derby, KS; (2); Church Yth Grp; Cmnty Wkr; Dance Clb; German Clb; Intnl Clb; Math Clb; Band; Mrchg Band; Pep Band; Ofcr Stu Cncl; Part Of Ntcrckr Ste Chrstms Mtrpltn Blt 6-10th Grds; Part Of Copellia Wichita Ctr Fine Arts 10th Gr; U Of KS; Sci/Bio/Lang.

LEE, BRYAN D; Dodge City HS; Dodge City, KS; (3); Red Cross Aide; SADD; Chorus; Hon Roll; NHS; Sec Of Brd KAYS; U Central OK; Mortuary Sci.

LEE, CHRISTOPHER D; Blue Valley North HS; Leawood, KS; (4); 1/167; VP Debate Tm; VP NFL; Band; Drm Mjr(t); Var Tennis; Gov Hon Prg Awd; High Hon Roll; NHS; Ntl Merit SF; Church Yth Grp; Bausch & Lomb Sci Awd; Pre-Med.

LEE, CLAYTON J; Downtown Law Magnet HS; Wichita, KS; (3); 1/30; Cmnty Wkr; Teachers Aide; Ofcr Stu Cncl; Hon Roll; Washburn; Attorney.

LEE, DONALD; Manhattan HS; Manhattan, KS; (2); Chess Clb; Church Yth Grp; FCA; Hosp Aide; Quiz Bowl; Scholastic Bowl; Spanish Clb; Orch; School Musical; Hon Roll; Play Piano & Violin; Numerous Solo & Ensemble Awds; Trilingual; Mission Trip To Mexico; Hosp Vol; KS Univ; Neuroscience.

LEE, EMILY J; Washburn Rural HS; Topeka, KS; (3); Church Yth Grp; FCA; Teachers Aide; Ed Yrbk; Sec Frsh Cls; Sec Soph Cls; Sec Jr Cls; Bsktbl; Var Tennis; High Hon Roll; All City Stdnt Cncl; Biomed Engrng/Pharm.

LEE, FAITH G; Scott Comm HS; Scott City, KS; (3); Library Aide; Natl FFA Org; Office Aide; Chorus; School Musical; Vllybl; Peer Hlpr Cnslr; Sec Ed.

LEE, KENDRA D; Scott Comm HS; Scott City, KS; (4); 14/77; Sec Frsh Cls; Sec Soph Cls; Sec Stu Cncl; Var Sftbl; Var Vllybl; Wt Lftg; Hon Roll; NHS; Crss Trng; Pratt CC; Tchng.

LEE, KRISSI S; Dodge City HS; Dodge City, KS; (2); SADD; Hon Roll; KAYS; Pittsburg ST U; Med Fld.

LEE, KRISTA M; El Dorado HS; El Dorado, KS; (3); 23/135; FCA; French Clb; Key Clb; Math Clb; NFL; SADD; Mgr Yrbk; Mgr(s); Vllybl; High Hon Roll; KS ST U; Phys Therapy.

LEE, KRISTI; Halstead HS; Halstead, KS; (3); Church Yth Grp; Letterman Clb; Pep Clb; Service Clb; Spanish Clb; Band; Capt Chrldng; Trk; Var Vllybl; High Hon Roll; Pharm.

LEE, LA'TOSHA N; Wichita Southeast HS; Wichita, KS; (2); Teachers Aide; JV Bsktbl; Hon Roll; Prfct Atten Awd; Trng Tmrrws Wmn Today Achvmt Cert; Cmptr Sci/Crmnl Jstc.

LEE, LAKEISHA; Iola Sr HS; Iola, KS; (4); FBLA; Office Aide; Varsity Clb; Nwsp; Yrbk; Sec Frsh Cls; Bsktbl; Chrldng; Sftbl; Trk; All Lge Trqack; Garden City CC; Radlgy Tech.

LEE, MELISSA R; Wyandotte HS; Kansas City, KS; (1); Church Yth Grp; FCA; Acpl Chr; Church Choir; Drill Tm; School Play; Capt Pom Pon; JV Vllybl; Cit Awd; High Hon Roll; Dn Lssns; Piano Lssns.

LEE, REBEKKAH; Miltonvale HS; Miltonvale, KS; (4); 4/8; Drama Clb; Letterman Clb; Pep Clb; Quiz Bowl; School Play; Rptr Nwsp; Phtg Yrbk; Sec Stu Cncl; Chrldng; High Hon Roll; Brown Mackie Coll; Acctg.

LEE, RICKENIA A; Field Kindley Mem Sr HS; Liberty, KS; (2); Church Yth Grp; 4-H; Natl FFA Org; JV Var Bsktbl; Capt Var Vllybl; Wt Lftg; 4-H Awd; Hon Roll; Cofeyville CC.

LEE, SARAH; Ottawa HS; Ottawa, KS; (4); 42/138; Pres Sec Art Clb; Church Yth Grp; FBLA; Ofcr Key Clb; School Play; High Hon Roll; NHS; Natl Eductnl Dev Test Awd; Bethany Coll Skills Day; Art Awds; Frnkln Cty Stu Art Shw Awds; Renaissnc Awd; U Of KS; Art.

LEE, STEPHANIE E; Bishop Miege HS; Shawnee Mission, KS; (4); 1/160; Cmnty Wkr; Ed Yrbk; Lit Mag; Gov Hon Prg Awd; High Hon Roll; NHS; Pres Schlr; Val; Deans Awd Spnsrd By KS ST U Coll Of Engrng For Outstdng Srs In Math & Sci; Tandy Tech Schlr; KS ST U; Engrng.

LEE, SUZANNE M; Blue Valley Northwest HS; Overland Park, KS; (2); Church Yth Grp; Drama Clb; Acpl Chr; Chorus; Church Choir; Orch; School Musical; School Play; Hon Roll; Comm Theater; Musical Theater.

LEE, TATUM; Ness City HS; Ness City, KS; (2); Church Yth Grp; Cmnty Wkr; 4-H; Chorus; VP Frsh Cls; Rep Soph Cls; Var Chrldng; High Hon Roll; Hon Roll; NHS; 4-H Qn; Hnr Choir; Model; KSU; Poly Sci.

LEE, TIFFANY M; Junction City HS; Junction City, KS; (3); Capt Dance Clb; Band; Mrchg Band; School Musical; School Play; Treas Frsh Cls; Ofcr Soph Cls; Ofcr Jr Cls; Ofcr Stu Cncl; Hon Roll; Komomantyns Pres; KS ST; Bus/Theater/Dance.

LEE, TIMOTHY Q; Washington HS; Kansas City, KS; (2); ROTC; Ftbl; Comp Pgrmr.

LEE, TRAVIS; Clay Ctr Cmty HS; Clay Center, KS; (2); Church Yth Grp; 4-H; Rptr Lit Mag; JV Bsktbl; JV Golf; High Hon Roll; Pres Acad Fit Awd; Constrctn Sci.

LEE, TRAVIS T; Field Kindley Mem Sr HS; Liberty, KS; (3); Church Yth Grp; 4-H; Natl FFA Org; Hon Roll; Coffeyville CC.

LEECH, ROBIN L; Great Bend Sr HS; Great Bend, KS; (3); Church Yth Grp; Pep Clb; Teachers Aide; Band; Hon Roll; Elem Ed.

LEEDS, JESSICA A; Emporia HS; Emporia, KS; (2); Art Clb; Church Yth Grp; Dance Clb; FCA; Pep Clb; SADD; Band; Mrchg Band; Pep Band; School Play; Emporia ST U; Art.

LEEKA, JENNIFER A; Kansas City Chrstn Acad; Roeland Park, KS; (4); Church Yth Grp; Letterman Clb; Chorus; Church Choir; School Musical; Ofcr Stu Cncl; L Var Bsktbl; JV Sftbl; L Var Vllybl; DAR Awd; Pres Chrch Yth Grp; Infnt Dev Cntr Vlntrffood Ktchn; Ottawa U; Early Chldhd Spec Ed.

LEEKA, R GRANT; Oak Grove Baptist Schl; Roeland Park, KS; (2); 1/12; Church Yth Grp; Stage Crew; Rep Frsh Cls; Sec Treas Soph Cls; Rep Stu Cncl; JV Var Bsktbl; Var L Socr; High Hon Roll; Hon Roll; Chrstn Character; Engrng.

LEEPER, KATIE; Columbus HS; Columbus, KS; (4); 18/91; Bus Profs of Am; Cmnty Wkr; FHA; Letterman Clb; Math Tm; Drill Tm; Var L Chrldng; Hon Roll; NHS; Church Yth Grp; KAY Clb Pres, VP & Brd Mem; U Of KS.

LEEPER, SETH Z; Protection Schl; Protection, KS; (3); Office Aide; Quiz Bowl; Scholastic Bowl; Speech Tm; Band; Chorus; Mrchg Band; Pep Band; School Musical; School Play; KS Ambassdrs Music; Ntl Yth Ldrshp Forum Nom; Bus.

LEES, CAMMY Y; Derby HS; Derby, KS; (3); 1/384; Cmnty Wkr; Girl Scts; NFL; Scholastic Bowl; Science Clb; Mrchg Band; High Hon Roll; NHS; Odyssey Of Mind; Future Prblm Slvng; Med.

LEEWRIGHT, CHRISTI A; Field Kindley Mem Sr HS; Coffeyville, KS; (3); 1/180; FHA; Math Tm; Natl FFA Org; Pep Clb; Band; Mrchg Band; School Musical; Tennis; High Hon Roll; NHS; Scndry Tchr.

LEFLER, BRIAN; Lansing HS; Lansing, KS; (2); Boy Scts; Band; Drm Mjr(t); Jazz Band; Mrchg Band; Pep Band; Swing Chorus; Socr; Tennis; High Hon Roll.

LEGG, LORI; Olathe South Sr HS; Olathe, KS; (2); 1/468; Church Yth Grp; Cmnty Wkr; GAA; Model UN; Quiz Bowl; Varsity Clb; Capt Drill Tm; Ofcr Stu Cncl; Socr; Cit Awd; Peer Mediation; Homecoming Ct.

LEGGE, TRINA J; Kapun Mt Carmel HS; Wichita, KS; (2); Church Yth Grp; Spanish Clb; SADD; Chorus; Bsktbl; Powder Puff Ftbl; High Hon Roll; Pres Acad Fit Awd; Earth Care Clb; Nom NHS; Natl Engl Merit Awd; Gentcs.

LEGLEITER, JUSTIN; Thomas More Prep-Marion HS; Louisville, KY; (4); #4 in class; Am Leg Boys St; Church Yth Grp; Debate Tm; Math Tm; Model UN; School Musical; L Var Bsktbl; L Var Ftbl; L Var Trk; High Hon Roll; I Dare You Ldrshp Awd; DARE Role Model; Chem.

LEGLEITER, LEAH A; Thomas More Prep-Marion HS; Hays, KS; (3); French Clb; Hosp Aide; Band; Mrchg Band; Pep Band; School Musical; High Hon Roll; Frnscs; Jr Svc Awd; Soph Rlgn Awd; Schl Ambass; Fort Hays ST U.

LEGLEITER, MELISSA L; Thomas More Prep-Marion HS; Hays, KS; (3); 33/77; Church Yth Grp; French Clb; Hosp Aide; School Musical; Yrbk; Vllybl; Hon Roll; Ft Hays St Univ Musical & Madrigal Dinner.

LEGLEITER, PATRICIA L; El Dorado HS; El Dorado, KS; (3); Church Yth Grp; Drama Clb; Girl Scts; Math Clb; NFL; SADD; Thesps; School Musical; JV Crs Cntry; Svrl Strs Pub; Accmpnst Chldrns Chrch Choir/MS Mscls; Bausch & Lomb Sci Awd; CO ST Univ; Chldrns Book Athr.

LE GRAND, LYNETTE M; Leavenworth HS; Leavenworth, KS; (2); 8/389; Church Yth Grp; Debate Tm; Hosp Aide; NFL; SADD; Chorus; School Musical; Sec Soph Cls; High Hon Roll; Doctor/Lwyr.

LEHATTO, ANNE J; Blue Valley Northwest HS; Overland Park, KS; (4); Art Clb; Cmnty Wkr; Hosp Aide; Service Clb; Phtg Yrbk; High Hon Roll; Hon Roll; NHS; St Schlr; Intnl Clb; Deans Schlrshp; Photogrphy Awd; Natl Eng Merit Awd; Univ Of Southern CA; Arch.

LEHMAN, JOSH P; Topeka West HS; Topeka, KS; (3); 77/239; Debate Tm; French Clb; Model UN; NFL; Spanish Clb; Teachers Aide; Jazz Band; Variety Show; Hon Roll; Spirit Clb; Guitars; Washburn; Law; Music.

LEHMAN, LORI R; Sabetha HS; Sabetha, KS; (3); 7/90; FBLA; FHA; Pep Clb; Spanish Clb; Teachers Aide; Chorus; Sec Soph Cls; Pres VP Stu Cncl; Var L Bsktbl; Var L Trk; Snday Schl; Vol At Nrsing Home; KS St Univ; Premed.

LEHMANN, BRIAN T; Sabetha HS; Sabetha, KS; (4); 9/60; Church Yth Grp; FCA; Ofcr Stu Cncl; Var L Bsktbl; Var L Ftbl; Var L Trk; Wt Lftg; Pres NHS; Pres Acad Fit Awd; St Schlr.

LEHMKUHLER, JENNIFER; Dodge City HS; Dodge City, KS; (1); Church Yth Grp; Cmnty Wkr; Phtg Yrbk; High Hon Roll; Dodge City Roundup.

LEI, TAMARA M; Washburn Rural HS; Topeka, KS; (4); 8/400; Math Tm; SADD; Band; Rep Soph Cls; Treas Jr Cls; Treas Sr Cls; Var Powder Puff Ftbl; Var Socr; Var Wt Lftg; High Hon Roll; Govs List; Northwestern U; Bio Engr.

LEICHLITER, STACEY; Decatur Cmty Jr Sr HS; Clayton, KS; (4); 3/35; Am Leg Aux Girls St; Key Clb; Science Clb; Speech Tm; Band; VP Frsh Cls; Treas Soph Cls; Rep Stu Cncl; Var L Vllybl; NHS; KU Hnr Schlr; Gold Awd Sci For Physics, Chem; U Of MO Rolla; Geological Engr.

LEICHTMAN, ALEXANDRA M; Washburn Rural HS; Topeka, KS; (3); 1/400; Debate Tm; French Clb; Letterman Clb; Model UN; NFL; Quiz Bowl; Speech Tm; Var L Socr; High Hon Roll; NHS; Pres Earthbnd Envrmntl Clb; Charter Mem Humn Rghts Clb.

LEIDY, MICHELLE R; Derby Christian Schl; Wichita, KS; (2); 1/15; Church Yth Grp; Church Choir; High Hon Roll; Stdnt Of Month; Optimist Clb; Awd For Highest Grd Avrg In All Classes; Schl Spirit Awd; Rel/Law.

LEIGH, DAVID C; Ft Scott HS; Garland, KS; (3); #1 in class; Pres Computer Clb; Pep Clb; Quiz Bowl; Chorus; School Musical; Mgr(s); High Hon Roll; MIT; Comp Sci.

LEIKAM, SARAH; Victoria HS; Victoria, KS; (1); Dance Clb; FHA; Letterman Clb; Pep Clb; SADD; Chorus; Drill Tm; School Play; Chrldng; Pom Pon; Queen Of Crts Qn 96; Teens As Tchrs; Fort Hays ST U; Med.

LEIKER, BRIAN S; Kapaun-Mt Carmel HS; Wichita, KS; (2); Church Yth Grp; Letterman Clb; Math Clb; Math Tm; Science Clb; Spanish Clb; Varsity Clb; Bsktbl; L Var Crs Cntry; JV Tennis; Engrng.

LEIKER, GERI L; Southeast Saline Schl; Salina, KS; (4); 7/48; Cmnty Wkr; French Clb; Intnl Clb; Math Tm; Pep Clb; Quiz Bowl; Scholastic Bowl; Acpl Chr; Band; Chorus; KS Acpl Chr; Intnl Childrens Choir Festival-Carnegie Hall; Washburn U; Bus Admin; Pre-Law.

LEIKER, JACLYN; Thomas More Prep-Marion HS; Hays, KS; (2); Band; Mrchg Band; Pep Band; Vllybl; Hon Roll.

LEIKER, KINNI; Meade HS; Meade, KS; (4); 6/24; Church Yth Grp; Pep Clb; Spanish Clb; Teachers Aide; Varsity Clb; Acpl Chr; Band; Chorus; Mrchg Band; Pep Band; Kayettes VP; Barton Cty; Elem Ed.

LEIKER, LAURA E; Hoxie HS; Hoxie, KS; (3); 27/42; Church Yth Grp; Debate Tm; VP FHA; Girl Scts; Hosp Aide; Jazz Band; Yrbk; Chrldng; Hon Roll; Girl Scout Gld Awd; Ft Hays State Univ; Soc Work.

KANSAS

LEIKER, RENEE A; Thomas Moore Prep Marian HS; Hays, KS; (4); Church Yth Grp; Chorus; Bsktbl; Wt Lftg; Frosh Cls Rel Awd; Soph Cls Svc Awd; Rel Ed Tchr.

LEIKER, SUZANNE R; Scott Comm HS; Scott City, KS; (3); 12/75; Am Leg Aux Girls St; Church Yth Grp; Band; VP Jr Cls; VP Sr Cls; JV Bsktbl; Var L Trk; Var L Vllybl; Wt Lftg; Hon Roll; Emporia ST Univ; Bus/Acctg.

LEIMER, MEGAN; Mulvane Sr HS; Mulvane, KS; (3); Church Yth Grp; Dance Clb; FCA; Pep Clb; SADD; Chrldng; Pom Pon; Sftbl; Vllybl; High Hon Roll.

LEIS, ERIN M; Thomas More-Marian HS; Hays, KS; (3); 21/70; Church Yth Grp; French Clb; Library Aide; Band; Church Choir; Mrchg Band; Pep Band; Variety Show; Vllybl; Hon Roll; Spec Olympcs Vol; Ambssdrs; Washburn; Chlds Advocate.

LEIS, LESLEY S; Paola HS; Paola, KS; (3); 1/165; Cmnty Wkr; FCA; Math Tm; Q&S; SADD; Ed Yrbk; Ofcr Stu Cncl; Var Bsktbl; Capt Crs Cntry; Var Sftbl; Kent ST; Optmtry.

LEIS, MATTHEW J; Yates Ctr HS; Yates Center, KS; (2); Art Clb; FCA; FHA; Letterman Clb; Pep Clb; SADD; Band; Jazz Band; Mrchg Band; Orch; U Of KS; CAD Arch.

LEIS, PATRICK D; Douglass HS; Douglass, KS; (3); 6/66; Quiz Bowl; Science Clb; Teachers Aide; VP Sr Cls; Crs Cntry; Var Trk; JV Wrstlng; High Hon Roll; NHS; Med Rsrch.

LEIS, PATRICK J; Yates Ctr HS; Yates Center, KS; (3); 1/55; Am Leg Boys St; Church Yth Grp; 4-H; German Clb; Letterman Clb; Natl FFA Org; Office Aide; Quiz Bowl; Scholastic Bowl; Spanish Clb; Engrng.

LEISHMAN, ANNIE; Herington HS; Herington, KS; (3); 1/41; Church Yth Grp; Cmnty Wkr; Dance Clb; Drama Clb; FCA; FHA; HOBY; Letterman Clb; Math Tm; Pep Clb; I Dare You Ldrsp Awd; Otstndng Math Stdnt 95-; Natl Med Ldrsp Forum Nom; Med.

LEITNAKER, MANDY; Ottawa HS; Ottawa, KS; (3); 1/149; Church Yth Grp; Band; School Musical; Swing Chorus; Rep Soph Cls; VP Jr Cls; Co-Capt L Chrldng; Var L Trk; High Hon Roll; NHS.

LEITNER, DENISE G; Blue Valley North HS; Leawood, KS; (4); 6/166; Math Tm; Spanish Clb; VP Treas Temple Yth Grp; Mrchg Band; Pep Band; School Musical; High Hon Roll; Sec NHS; Ntl Merit Ltr; St Schlr; Mentorship Acad Prgm; Tulane Univ Distngd Schlrs Merit Schlsp; Tulane Univ; Physician/Surgeon.

LEITNER, JENNIFER A; Herndon Schl; Herndon, KS; (4); 2/6; 4-H; Model UN; Pep Clb; Quiz Bowl; Speech Tm; Band; Chorus; Pep Band; School Musical; Swing Chorus; Stdnt Rep Site Cncls; Odysy Of Mind 8 Yrs; Coord St Jude's Rsrch Hosp Bike-A-Thon; Ft Hays ST Univ; Bus.

LE MASTER, RICH L; Wellington Sr HS; Wellington, KS; (2); Church Yth Grp; Math Tm; SADD; Rep Soph Cls; JV Bsktbl; Crs Cntry; Cit Awd; High Hon Roll; Hon Roll; Jr NHS; Med.

LEMKE, ELIZABETH D; Oxford HS; Geuda Springs, KS; (4); 5/22; VP Church Yth Grp; FCA; FBLA; NFL; Teachers Aide; Chorus; Mrchg Band; Pep Band; Swing Chorus; Cit Awd; Miss Gueda Springs 95; Local Voice Of Democracy Speech Wnnr; Media Productions; Cowley Cty CC; Brodcst Commctn.

LEMLEY, DONNIE; Peabody-Burns Jr Sr HS; Peabody, KS; (4); Drama Clb; Sec Treas Band; Jazz Band; Mrchg Band; School Musical; VP Jr Cls; Treas Pres Stu Cncl; High Hon Roll; NHS; St Schlr; Marion Cty Hnr Schlr; US Mrne Crps Smpr Fdls Awd Mscl Excl; KS ST U; Instr Msc Ed.

LEMLEY, TABITHA; Weskan Schl; Arapahoe, CO; (1); 1/7; 4-H; Quiz Bowl; Band; Pep Band; 4-H Awd; Hon Roll; Horseback Riding; Horse Cncl; CUCS; Paleontology.

LEMON, JANELL D; Morland Jr Sr HS; Hoxie, KS; (2); 3/12; Church Yth Grp; Band; JV L Bsktbl; Var Chrldng; Var L Crs Cntry; Var L Trk; Hon Roll; NHS; Prfct Atten Awd; Pep Clb; KAYS Natl Svc Dir.

LEMONS, TRACY A; Blue Valley Northwest HS; Overland Park, KS; (3); 130/364; Pep Clb; Phtg Nwsp; Phtg Yrbk; Powder Puff Ftbl; Sftbl; Hon Roll; Env Clb; KAYS Clb.

LENCASTER, ELIZABETH D; Hillsboro HS; Hillsboro, KS; (2); 10/48; Church Yth Grp; HOBY; Chorus; School Musical; School Play; Sec Soph Cls; Trk; Vllybl; Cit Awd; High Hon Roll; Bus Mgmt/Mrktng/Pol Law.

LENHERR, EDWARD; St Marys HS; Saint Marys, KS; (4); 18/50; FCA; Letterman Clb; Pep Clb; VP Sr Cls; Var L Ftbl; High Hon Roll; Hon Roll; NHS; KS ST U; Radio-TV Jrnlsm.

LENHERR, ELIZABETH; St Marys HS; Saint Marys, KS; (2); 10/35; FCA; Letterman Clb; Band; Var L Bsktbl; Var L Sftbl; Var L Vllybl; High Hon Roll; NHS; Pep Clb; Jazz Band; USVBA Vllybl; AAU Bsktbl; Teens As Tchrs; Homcmng Cmmtte.

LENIHAN, JEREMY R; Bishop Miege HS; Overland Park, KS; (1); 79/250; Chorus; School Musical; Intrml Bsbl; Intrml Bsktbl; Intrml Ftbl.

LENNINGTON, KRISSIE S; Lakin HS; Lakin, KS; (2); 1/60; Church Yth Grp; FCA; Band; Church Choir; Jazz Band; Pep Band; Rptr Nwsp; Rptr Yrbk; Rep Frsh Cls; Rep Soph Cls; Med Fld/Neanatal Nrs.

LENTZ, KIMBERLY; Atchison Sr HS; Atchison, KS; (3); 10/101; Church Yth Grp; 4-H; Hosp Aide; Scholastic Bowl; School Play; Treas Soph Cls; Rep Stu Cncl; Mgr(s); 4-H Awd; Hon Roll; KS ST U; Vet.

LENZ, ERICA R; Maize HS; Maize, KS; (3); Art Clb; Spanish Clb; Hon Roll; NHS; KS Assn Yth KAVS; SADD; Frnsc Team/Natl Frnsc; CO; Earth Sci.

LENZ, JENNIFER M; Olathe East Sr HS; Olathe, KS; (3); Drama Clb; French Clb; Hosp Aide; Spanish Clb; Thesps; School Musical; School Play; Stage Crew; Variety Show; Ed Lit Mag; U Of KS; Pre-Med.

LENZ, JOE; Blue Valley HS; Stilwell, KS; (3); Am Leg Boys St; Chorus; Swing Chorus; Variety Show; VP Jr Cls; Rep Stu Cncl; Intrml Bsbl; JV Crs Cntry; Intrml Ftbl; JV Trk; KU.

LEON JR, CARLOS; Shawnee Mission Chrst Schl; Kansas City, MO; (4); Drama Clb; Pep Clb; Spanish Clb; Church Choir; Stage Crew; Var Crs Cntry; Trk; Hon Roll; Chrch Srvnt Of Yr Awd; TX Bapt Col; Bus.

LEONARD, JOSHUA; Sublette HS; Sublette, KS; (1); 1/33; Boy Scts; Church Yth Grp; Bsktbl; Golf; High Hon Roll; Hntng & Fshng; Archery.

LEONARD, KELLY; Shawnee Mission W Sr HS; Lenexa, KS; (4); Pep Clb; Teachers Aide; Variety Show; Var Chrldng; JV Trk; Bd Of Regents Awd; Distngd Schlr Achvmt; U Of KS; Elem Tchr.

LEONARD, TRAVIS; Sublette HS; Sublette, KS; (3); 7/29; Boy Scts; Church Yth Grp; Band; JV Bsktbl; JV Ftbl; Var L Golf; Hon Roll; Prfct Atten Awd; Bsbl, Fishing & Archery; KS ST; Ag.

LEONARD, WENDY; Sublette HS; Sublette, KS; (2); 5/40; Church Yth Grp; Pep Clb; Band; Rep Stu Cncl; JV Var Bsktbl; Var Trk; JV Vllybl; High Hon Roll; NHS; Kays Orgnztn; KS ST U; Phys Thrpy.

LEONE, MARTINO S; Emporia HS; Emporia, KS; (4); 1/285; Church Yth Grp; Debate Tm; Co-Capt FCA; Model UN; NFL; High Hon Roll; NHS; Ntl Merit SF; St Schlr; Clb Sccr Capt; Piano; Brothers & Sisters In Christ; KS ST U; Arch.

LERCH, KARA; Derby HS; Derby, KS; (4); Church Yth Grp; Band; Mrchg Band; Orch; Ofcr Stu Cncl; Mgr Crs Cntry; Hon Roll; NHS; Pres Acad Fit Awd; St Schlr; St Hnr Band; Yth Symphony Hnrs Usher; U Of AR; Music Perfmnc.

LEROY, BILL T; Smoky Valley HS; Lindsborg, KS; (1); Pep Clb; Varsity Clb; JV Bsktbl; Var L Ftbl; Var Trk; High Hon Roll; Hon Roll; Pres Acad Fit Awd; Stdnt Cncl Rep Soph Yr; Sprts Mdcn/Bus.

LE SAGE, PARKER C; Hill City HS; Hill City, KS; (1); Church Yth Grp; Pep Clb; SADD; Band; Chorus; Pep Band; School Musical; JV Crs Cntry; JV Trk; Var L Wrstlng.

LESLIE, SAMANTHA; Shawnee Mission S Sr HS; Shawnee Mission, KS; (2); Intnl Clb; Orch; Rptr Nwsp; Crs Cntry; Trk; Hon Roll; UMKC; Pthlgst.

LESOVSKY, BRANDON; Hillcrest Schl; Cuba, KS; (3); Letterman Clb; Natl FFA Org; Pep Clb; Quiz Bowl; Band; Mrchg Band; Pep Band; L Bus Profs of Am; L Ftbl; L Trk; Hstry Educ.

LESOVSKY, NATHAN; Hillcrest Schl; Cuba, KS; (3); 5/12; Church Yth Grp; FCA; Sec Letterman Clb; Natl FFA Org; Pres Pep Clb; Quiz Bowl; Band; Chorus; Jazz Band; Mrchg Band; Radio/TV Brdcstng.

LESTER, ALISON D; Chanute Sr HS; Chanute, KS; (3); FBLA; GAA; Library Aide; Spanish Clb; Band; Flag Corp; Mrchg Band; JV Tennis; Wt Lftg; Hon Roll.

LETTE, ABRIEL B; Udall HS; Udall, KS; (2); Church Yth Grp; Band; Chorus; Mrchg Band; Stage Crew; Var L Bsktbl; Score Keeper; JV Vllybl; High Hon Roll; Hon Roll; Hnr Str; CBC; Elem Ed.

LETTS, KATY J; Goddard HS; Goddard, KS; (2); Science Clb; Var L Bsktbl; Var L Sftbl; Var L Vllybl; High Hon Roll; 1st Team All-Conf Pitcher-Sftbl.

LEVER, LESTER STAR; Udall HS; Udall, KS; (4); 7/32; Church Yth Grp; Cmnty Wkr; Drama Clb; FCA; NFL; Thesps; Band; Pep Band; School Play; Stage Crew; Roller Blading; Golfing; Skiing; Cowaly Cty CC; Comp Engr.

LEVERING, TOBY; Mulvane Sr HS; Mulvane, KS; (4); 6/144; Am Leg Boys St; Church Yth Grp; Debate Tm; FCA; NFL; Thesps; Jazz Band; Ed Nwsp; High Hon Roll; NHS; KS Assn For Yth Pres 95-96; OK Chrstn U; Yth Mnstry.

LEVERINGTON, HEATHER; Flinthills HS; El Dorado, KS; (3); Church Yth Grp; 4-H; Letterman Clb; Office Aide; SADD; Teachers Aide; Thesps; Band; Pep Band; School Play; Indr Trck; Stdnt Wk; Acctg/Bus.

LEWIS, BENJAMIN; St Thomas Aquinas HS; Bucyrus, KS; (3); Am Leg Boys St; Boy Scts; VP FCA; Rep Jr Cls; Pres Sr Cls; JV Bsbl; JV Bsktbl; Var Golf; Var Socr; Hon Roll.

LEWIS, CATHERINE; Shawnee Mission North HS; Merriam, KS; (3); 5/380; Am Leg Aux Girls St; Hosp Aide; Key Clb; Q&S; Spanish Clb; Yrbk; Var Golf; Var Socr; High Hon Roll; NHS.

LEWIS, DERIK S; Berean Acad; Wichita, KS; (3); Church Yth Grp; Letterman Clb; Chorus; Church Choir; Variety Show; Bsktbl; Socr; Trk; Hon Roll.

LEWIS, HOLLIE J; Riley Cty HS; Riley, KS; (3); 2/50; Rep FHA; Sec Pep Clb; Church Yth Grp; VP FCA; Teachers Aide; Chorus; Flag Corp; Mrchg Band; Yrbk; Treas Sr Cls; Mid-Amer Nazarene Coll; Elem.

LEWIS, J SUMMER; Chaparral HS; Anthony, KS; (3); 1/65; Church Yth Grp; Key Clb; Natl FFA Org; Chorus; Rep Jr Cls; Rep Stu Cncl; Crs Cntry; Trk; High Hon Roll; Jr NHS; Fresh Lge C Cntry Chmp; All Lge C Cntry; 4-H Pres; Premed.

LEWIS, JANE S; Chaparral HS; Anthony, KS; (3); 2/70; Church Yth Grp; Debate Tm; Sec Natl FFA Org; Chorus; Rep Jr Cls; Ofcr Stu Cncl; Crs Cntry; Trk; High Hon Roll; Jr NHS; ST Frmr Dgree FFA; Fr Lgue Chmp Crss Cntry; KU; Onclgy/Pre-Med.

LEWIS, JESSE; Silver Lake Jr Sr HS; Topeka, KS; (2); Debate Tm; FHA; NFL; Pep Clb; Spanish Clb; Teachers Aide; Vllybl; Hon Roll; NHS; Washburn Univ; Corp Tax Law.

LEWIS, JOSH; Blue Valley North HS; Leawood, KS; (3); Am Leg Boys St; Letterman Clb; Model UN; Spanish Clb; L Wrstlng; Hon Roll; NHS; Cmnty Wkr; Pep Clb; Rep Soph Cls; Kauffman Fndtn Entreprep Internshp; Del Overlnd Pk Rotry Fndtn Yth Ldrshp Inst; Optmst Stu Ldrshp Recg; USNA.

LEWIS, LATISHA; Elkhart HS; Elkhart, KS; (2); 2/38; Art Clb; Letterman Clb; Rptr Nwsp; Phtg Yrbk; JV Chrldng; High Hon Roll; NHS; Phys Thpy.

LEWIS, MATT E; Blue Valley Northwest HS; Overland Park, KS; (2); Art Clb; Hon Roll; Envrnmntl Clb VP; Art Garden; Husky Awd; Excllnc Comp Tchnlgy; Schl Garage Sale; MT U; Tchr.

LEWIS, PATTI; Syracuse Jr Sr HS; Syracuse, KS; (2); 5/38; Art Clb; Cmnty Wkr; Drama Clb; 4-H; Letterman Clb; Pep Clb; Quiz Bowl; Scholastic Bowl; Speech Tm; Varsity Clb; Achvt Awd 4-H Discovery Days; Top Nation Hnr Band; 4-H Ldrshp Conf; KSU; Chem.

LEWIS, SHELLY M; Stockton HS; Stockton, KS; (2); FHA; Pep Clb; Quiz Bowl; Rptr Nwsp; Treas Soph Cls; Chrldng; Trk; Vllybl; Wt Lftg; Hon Roll; Accnt.

LEXOW, MATTHEW R; Emporia HS; Emporia, KS; (3); 46/267; Church Yth Grp; Key Clb; Band; Jazz Band; Mrchg Band; Pep Band; Hon Roll; Wildlife & Backpckng Clb; KS ST; Bio.

LI, SHAWN; Wichita Collegiate Schl; Wichita, KS; (3); Chess Clb; JV Tennis; Hon Roll; NHS; U Of TX Austin; Med.

LI, SI-DA; Wichita Collegiate Schl; Wichita, KS; (3); Chess Clb; German Clb; Hosp Aide; Teachers Aide; High Hon Roll; Hon Roll; Jr NHS; NHS; Ntl Merit Ltr; Kum Laude Soc; Univ Of Chicago; Medcn.

LIBEL, BRICE; Wathena Schl; Wathena, KS; (4); 1/36; Cmnty Wkr; Letterman Clb; Treas Math Clb; Quiz Bowl; Treas Science Clb; Band; School Play; Ed Yrbk; Treas Frsh Cls; Treas Soph Cls; Wendy's HS Heisman ST Awd; 3rd KS ST Jrnlsm Cntst Advrtsng; Prins Ldrshp Merit Cert Awd; Bus Admin/Advrtsng.

LIBHART, STEPHANIE; Wichita East HS; Wichita, KS; (3); #10 in class; Church Yth Grp; HOBY; Office Aide; Teachers Aide; Church Choir; School Musical; School Play; Variety Show; Vllybl; High Hon Roll; Jr Assembly; Friends U; Psych.

LICHTENAUER, KELLI; Marais Des Cygnes Valley HS; Melvern, KS; (4); 3/13; Teachers Aide; Varsity Clb; VP Stu Cncl; Var Chrldng; Var Vllybl; St Schlr; U Of KS; Pharm.

LICHTENBERG, TRICIA; St Thomas Aquinas HS; Kansas City, MO; (3); Office Aide; Pep Clb; SADD; Teachers Aide; School Play; Bsktbl; Powder Puff Ftbl; Vllybl; Hon Roll; Psych.

LICHTI, EDITH M; Newton Sr HS; Newton, KS; (1); Cmnty Wkr; German Clb; Quiz Bowl; Acpl Chr; Chorus; Hon Roll; ST Music Fstvl; Hosp Vol; Med.

LICHTI, NOLAN W; Newton Sr HS; Newton, KS; (2); 1/279; Scholastic Bowl; Band; Mrchg Band; JV Crs Cntry; High Hon Roll; Comp Sci.

LICKISS, SARAH; St John Jr Sr HS; Saint John, KS; (2); Church Yth Grp; Dance Clb; FHA; Pep Clb; Spanish Clb; SADD; Band; Chorus; Mrchg Band; Pep Band; Chld Care.

LICKTEIG, ANGELA; Udall HS; Udall, KS; (1); 2/35; Church Yth Grp; Sec 4-H; Band; Mrchg Band; Pep Band; VP Frsh Cls; Bsktbl; Vllybl; 4-H Awd; High Hon Roll; Bio.

LICKTEIG, BRAD; Udall HS; Udall, KS; (3); 1/34; Cmnty Wkr; Drama Clb; Letterman Clb; Math Tm; Speech Tm; SADD; Varsity Clb; School Play; Rptr Nwsp; Var L Bsbl; Comp Engr.

LICKTEIG, CHARLIE C; Anderson Cty Jr Sr HS; Garnett, KS; (3); Church Yth Grp; Natl FFA Org; SADD; Rep Soph Cls; Ofcr Stu Cncl; Ftbl; High Hon Roll.

LICKTEIG, JAMIE; Marmaton Valley Jr Sr HS; Moran, KS; (4); 2/19; FCA; Rptr Natl FFA Org; Ed Nwsp; Phtg Yrbk; Pres Stu Cncl; Var L Bsktbl; Var L Trk; Var Capt Vllybl; High Hon Roll; Sal; KS Hnrs Pgm; Natl Hnr Soc; Allen Cty CC.

LIEBL, MIKE; Fairfield HS; Sylvia, KS; (2); 2/38; SADD; Treas Soph Cls; Var L Bsbl; JV Bsktbl; Var L Ftbl; Var Wt Lftg; Hon Roll; Tech Club; Ath Club.

LIEBSCH, BETSY; Acad Of Mt St Scholastica; Atchison, KS; (4); 2/25; Girl Scts; HOBY; Pres Soph Cls; Pres VP Stu Cncl; Capt Var Bsktbl; Var Capt Chrldng; Capt Socr; Var Capt Vllybl; NHS; Harvard Model Congress.

LIEBSCH, CINDY M; Acad Of Mt St Scholastica; Atchison, KS; (3); 2/30; Girl Scts; VP Sec Service Clb; Speech Tm; Chorus; Pres Stu Cncl; JV Var Bsktbl; Var Socr; JV Var Vllybl; Pep Clb; Drill Tm; Engr.

LIENEKE-NICKLE, SARAH; Shawnee Mission N HS; Westwood, KS; (3); Rep Jr Cls; JV Var Chrldng; JV Var Socr; Intrml Vllybl; Hon Roll; NHS; Accntng.

LIERRO, RENE O; Garden City Sr HS; Garden City, KS; (3); 4/24; Computer Clb; Dance Clb; Latin Clb; Math Clb; Science Clb; Spanish Clb; Ofcr Jr Cls; Ofcr Bsbl; Ftbl; Socr; Albuquerque; Plumber; Policeman.

LIES, MINDY; Mc Pherson HS; Mc Pherson, KS; (2); Church Yth Grp; Q&S; SADD; Teachers Aide; Phtg Yrbk; Treas Soph Cls; Ofcr Jr Cls; JV Sftbl; JV Vllybl; Hon Roll; KAYS; Respite Home Care For Handicapped Children; K-ST; Elem Ed.

LIESWALD, KYRA L; Field Kindley Mem Sr HS; Coffeyville, KS; (3); Church Yth Grp; FCA; Teachers Aide; Band; Church Choir; Pep Band; Yrbk; Bsktbl; Hon Roll; Olivet Nazarene U; Scndry Ed.

LIETZKE, LORI L; Louisburg HS; Bucyrus, KS; (2); Dance Clb; Letterman Clb; Spanish Clb; SADD; Drill Tm; Phtg Yrbk; Var Pom Pon; JV Sftbl; Hon Roll; Outstdng Achvmt In Eng, Sci & Bus; KS Univ; Psychiatrist.

LIEURANCE, TERYN; Wellington Sr HS; Wellington, KS; (3); Church Yth Grp; French Clb; Key Clb; Office Aide; Spanish Clb; SADD; Chorus; Pres Mgr(s); Sftbl; JV Vllybl; U Of KS; Orthodontist.

LIEZERT III, JOHN W; Topeka West HS; Topeka, KS; (2); Debate Tm; French Clb; NFL; Scholastic Bowl; JV Bsbl; Hon Roll.

LIGGATT, SONYA L; Holton HS; Holton, KS; (2); French Clb; Pep Clb; Sec Frsh Cls; Var Chrldng; High Hon Roll; Hon Roll; Pres Acad Fit Awd; Jackson Hghts Schltc Awd Medal; DE Vly League Schltc Awd; Kays; Bus Admin.

LIGGETT, EMILY; Shawnee Mission E Sr HS; Shawnee Mission, KS; (3); 71/409; Church Yth Grp; Cmnty Wkr; Natl Beta Clb; Sec Pep Clb; Q&S; Teachers Aide; Phtg Ed Nwsp; Rep Stu Cncl; Var L Tennis; High Hon Roll; Vol Group Dominican Republic & Habitat For Humanity; Tch Tnns Under Privileged Kids.

LIGGETT, NICHOLE M; Acad Of Mt St Scholastica; Atchison, KS; (4); 14/25; Pep Clb; Teachers Aide; Chorus; Pep Band; Rptr Nwsp; Bsktbl; Mgr(s); Trk; Hon Roll; Harvard Model Congress; Pittsburgh ST Univ; Bio.

LIGHT, CHRISTOPHER W; Leavenworth HS; Fairfax, VA; (3); Art Clb; ROTC; Hon Roll; VA Tech; Tech; Electician.

LIGHTCAP, JUSTIN D; Buhler HS; Hutchinson, KS; (3); FCA; Letterman Clb; Natl FFA Org; SADD; Var L Bsktbl; Var L Ftbl; Var L Trk; Wt Lftg; Hon Roll.

LIGHTNER, CLELL; Chapman HS; Chapman, KS; (3); Am Leg Boys St; SADD; School Play; Stage Crew; Variety Show; JV Var Ftbl; JV Wt Lftg; Hon Roll; Pool; Bsbl/Ftbl/Cmc/Hcky/Bsktbl Crd Cllctng; AFS; NE; Actor/Race Car Drvr.

LIGHTNER, JODI; Inman Jr Sr HS; Inman, KS; (3); 1/38; Sec Art Clb; VP Church Yth Grp; HOBY; Rep Natl FFA Org; Quiz Bowl; Band; Pres Jr Cls; Var Trk; High Hon Roll; NHS.

LIGHTNER, MATTHEW H; Garden City Sr HS; Garden City, KS; (2); Chess Clb; Church Yth Grp; Math Tm; NFL; Science Clb; Treas Frsh Cls; Treas Soph Cls; Treas Jr Cls; Ofcr Stu Cncl; Var Bsktbl; Forensics.

LIGHTNER, OLIVIA; Garden City Sr HS; Garden City, KS; (4); 11/314; Church Yth Grp; Math Tm; Science Clb; SADD; Stat Bsktbl; Var Vllybl; High Hon Roll; Kiwanis Awd; NHS; Pres Acad Fit Awd; Bethel; Acctng.

LIGHTWINE, JAMIE; Desoto HS; De Soto, KS; (4); 33/102; Dance Clb; Office Aide; SADD; Drill Tm; Ofcr Sr Cls; VP Stu Cncl; Var Chrldng; Var Crs Cntry; Pom Pon; Powder Puff Ftbl; All Jrnl Herald Crs Cntry Tm; Kansas City Star Schlr Ath; All ST Crs Cntry/Trck; Fort Hays ST Univ; Elem Ed.

LIGNITZ, KELLIE R; Washburn Rural HS; Topeka, KS; (3); French Clb; Band; Mrchg Band; Orch; Pep Band; School Musical; High Hon Roll; NHS; KS All-St Orch; KS All-Dist Bnd; Topeka Yth Symph; Topeka Yth Wind Ensmbl; Music.

LIGNITZ, LORETTA L; Wamego HS; Manhattan, KS; (1); Swmmng; Bsktbl; Read; Wrtng; KSU.

LIGNT, SHERI R; Clearwater HS; Clearwater, KS; (3); Am Leg Aux Girls St; Cmnty Wkr; HOBY; Letterman Clb; Spanish Clb; SADD; Teachers Aide; Chorus; Nwsp; VP Soph Cls; Pittsburg ST; Exercise Phys.

LIGON, NINA; Wichita South HS; Wichita, KS; (3); Cmnty Wkr; Pep Clb; Chorus; Variety Show; Lit Mag; VP Soph Cls; Pres Jr Cls; Var Chrldng; Var Trk; Cmnty Anti-Drug Coalitions Amer Yth Advsry Cmmtte; Black Awrnes Clb Amanza; South High Gosepl Choir; Engl.

LIKELY, TOMMI; Prairie View Jr Sr HS; Parker, KS; (4); 6/68; VP FBLA; Rep FHA; Letterman Clb; Ed Mgr Yrbk; Ofcr Stu Cncl; Bsktbl; Capt Chrldng; Trk; High Hon Roll; NHS; Hutchinson CC; Phy Asst.

LILES, JOSHUA; Trinity Catholic HS; Hutchinson, KS; (2); Church Yth Grp; Debate Tm; FCA; NFL; School Play; Pres Soph Cls; Capt Ftbl; Trk; Wt Lftg; High Hon Roll; FL ST.

LILLEY, BRIAN S; Silver Lake Jr Sr HS; Silver Lake, KS; (4); 4/46; Debate Tm; NFL; Speech Tm; Crs Cntry; Trk; High Hon Roll; Quiz Bowl; Teachers Aide; Band; Pep Band; Supr Rep At Natl Fornsics Lge Stu; KS St Univ; Bus Mgnt.

LILLICH, CHARLES MORGAN; Council Grove HS; Alta Vista, KS; (2); FCA; SADD; JV Bsktbl; JV Golf; High Hon Roll; Hon Roll; Prfct Atten Awd; Pres Acad Fit Awd; Little Leaague Bsbll Coach; Emporia St Univ; Hstry.

LILLICH, JUSTIN; Turner HS; Kansas City, KS; (3); SADD; Band; Jazz Band; Mrchg Band; Orch; Pep Band; Rep Stu Cncl; Var Golf; Hon Roll.

LILYHORN, AMY; Mc Louth Schl; Lawrence, KS; (3); Pres 4-H; Pres FBLA; HOBY; Pres Band; Jazz Band; School Musical; High Hon Roll; Church Yth Grp; Drama Clb; FHA; KS ST U; Bus.

LIMAYE, RUPALI; Olathe East Sr HS; Olathe, KS; (3); 1/384; Am Leg Aux Girls St; Pres Debate Tm; Pres NFL; Drm Mjr(t); High Hon Roll; Pres NHS; Pres Acad Fit Awd; Cmnty Wkr; English Clb; Letterman Clb; Sr Ofcr For SASH; Yth In Govt; :dare Role Model; U IA; Pol Sci.

LIMBACK, MENDY E; Salina HS Central; Salina, KS; (3); Church Yth Grp; Teachers Aide; Band; Mrchg Band; Orch; Pep Band; JV Golf; Hon Roll; NHS; Breakfast Buddies; Ashby House Shelter Vol; U Of KS.

LIMBEROPOULOS, FANI; Garden City Sr HS; Garden City, KS; (3); 21/309; Am Leg Aux Girls St; Church Yth Grp; CAP; FHA; Latin Clb; Teachers Aide; Acpl Chr; School Musical; Stage Crew; Var Stat Wrstlng; Schl Bible Std Ldr; Med.

LINCK, JAKE; Onaga HS; Havensville, KS; (4); 2/22; Am Leg Boys St; Letterman Clb; Model UN; Quiz Bowl; SADD; Yrbk; VP Stu Cncl; Var Capt Crs Cntry; Pres NHS; Sal; Frgn Exch Stu Greece; KS ST Univ; Comp Sci.

LIND, MIKE; Chanute Sr HS; Chanute, KS; (4); 29/136; Church Yth Grp; Debate Tm; Drama Clb; French Clb; NFL; Thesps; School Musical; High Hon Roll; Hnr Grad; Jr Lions Cl; Jr Rotry; KS ST Univ; Ed.

LINDBERG, PAUL W; Mankato Jr Sr HS; Mankato, KS; (2); Cmnty Wkr; Natl FFA Org; Yrbk; Pres Frsh Cls; Rep Soph Cls; JV Bsktbl; JV Var Golf; Hon Roll; KS ST.

LINDBLAD, TAMME; Hugoton HS; Hugoton, KS; (2); 5/90; Bsktbl; Vllybl; Hon Roll; Pres Acad Fit Awd; All Amer Schlr; U NE Lincoln; Bus Acctng.

LINDBLOOM, AZURE; St Marys HS; Saint Marys, KS; (4); 3/50; FCA; Pres FHA; Capt Drill Tm; Yrbk; Sec Stu Cncl; Golf; Cit Awd; NHS; Cmnty Wkr; VP FBLA; First Luth Chrch; All Rnd Grl Awd; Univ Of KS; Bus/Med.

LINDENBERGER, KREG; Inman Jr Sr HS; Inman, KS; (4); 4/32; Church Yth Grp; Band; Nwsp; Yrbk; Var Bsktbl; Var Ftbl; Var Golf; High Hon Roll; NHS; Teachers Aide; Natl Yng Ldrs Conf WA DC.

LINDENBERGER, LAURA; Olathe South Sr HS; Olathe, KS; (3); Cmnty Wkr; Spanish Clb; Teachers Aide; Yrbk; High Hon Roll; NHS; Pres Acad Fit Awd; Spanish NHS.

LINDER, AMY M; Highland Park HS; Topeka, KS; (3); Church Yth Grp; Cmnty Wkr; JA; Math Clb; Pep Clb; Spanish Clb; SADD; Drill Tm; Pom Pon; Hon Roll; MO Western; Bus Admin.

LINDGREN, DANA M; Smoky Valley HS; Marquette, KS; (2); Church Yth Grp; Cmnty Wkr; Dance Clb; FCA; 4-H; Acpl Chr; Chorus; Church Choir; Mrchg Band; Orch.

LINDGREN, ERIKA R; Newton Sr HS; Newton, KS; (2); 39/300; Church Yth Grp; Hosp Aide; Model UN; Thesps; Acpl Chr; Band; Chorus; School Musical; School Play; Hon Roll; Ballet & Jazz Dance; Music.

LINDGREN, JENNIFER A; Smoky Valley HS; Marquette, KS; (4); 2/68; Church Yth Grp; Cmnty Wkr; Dance Clb; FCA; 4-H; Letterman Clb; Pep Clb; Quiz Bowl; Acpl Chr; Chorus.

LINDQUIST, LISA; Vlly Hts HS; Waterville, KS; (3); 4/31; Am Leg Aux Girls St; Treas Church Yth Grp; 4-H; Sec FHA; Letterman Clb; Model UN; Treas Natl FFA Org; Pep Clb; Scholastic Bowl; Varsity Clb; KS St Univ; Med.

LINDQUIST, TYLER; Little River Jr Sr HS; Windom, KS; (3); Math Tm; Quiz Bowl; Scholastic Bowl; Spanish Clb; Teachers Aide; Hon Roll.

LINDSEY, JASON; Haysville Campus HS; Haysville, KS; (4); 2/211; Am Leg Boys St; Church Yth Grp; Science Clb; SADD; Capt Socr; Gov Hon Prg Awd; NHS; Pres Acad Fit Awd; Sal; St Schlr; Wichita ST U; Aerospace Engrng.

LINDSEY, KATRINA R; Highland Park HS; Topeka, KS; (3); 1/170; Math Clb; Scholastic Bowl; Rep Frsh Cls; Rep Soph Cls; Rep Jr Cls; L Bsktbl; JV Crs Cntry; High Hon Roll; NHS; Mid-Amer Cnsrtm For Eng & Sci Achvt; Upwrd Bnd; Mech Engrng.

LINDSHIELD, BRIAN L; Smoky Valley HS; Lindsborg, KS; (1); Band; Mrchg Band; Pep Band; Var Bsktbl; JV Ftbl; L Tennis; High Hon Roll.

LINDSTEDT, KERI A; Smoky Valley HS; Marquette, KS; (3); Sec Bus Profs of Am; Church Yth Grp; VP Pep Clb; Teachers Aide; Varsity Clb; VP Band; Flag Corp; Mrchg Band; Pep Band; Rep Stu Cncl; Kays VP; KS Univ.

LINGO, TRACY; Basehor Linwood HS; Bonner Springs, KS; (4); 24/121; Co-Capt Dance Clb; FBLA; FHA; GAA; Pep Clb; Spanish Clb; SADD; Teachers Aide; Co-Capt Drill Tm; Co-Capt Pom Pon; U Of KS; Psych.

LININGER, TAMMY; Bucklin Schl; Bucklin, KS; (3); Church Yth Grp; Debate Tm; 4-H; Quiz Bowl; Speech Tm; SADD; Band; Chorus; Var Trk; Hon Roll; Ft Hays; Med.

LINK, KACEY; Central Jr HS; Lawrence, KS; (1); Debate Tm; JA; Acpl Chr; Orch; Rep Stu Cncl; Hon Roll; Yth Symph; Cntrl Jr Hgh Strng Qu; Piano, Viola Lssns; Musicn.

LINK, STEPHANIE; Louisburg HS; Louisburg, KS; (3); Bus Profs of Am; Letterman Clb; Pep Clb; Spanish Clb; Sec Frsh Cls; Sec Soph Cls; Sec Jr Cls; Chrldng; Hon Roll; Excep Attndnce; U Of KS; Elem Ed.

LINKER, JAMIE S; Olathe North Sr HS; Olathe, KS; (4); 29/375; Church Yth Grp; Cmnty Wkr; French Clb; French Hon Soc; High Hon Roll; Hon Roll; NHS; Ntl Merit Ltr; Pres Acad Fit Awd; St Schlr; Stdnt Vol; Johnson Country CC; Ed.

LINKOUS, JAMIE; Wichita Heights HS; Wichita, KS; (3); Bus Profs of Am; Debate Tm; NFL; Speech Tm; Teachers Aide; Nwsp; Yrbk; Hon Roll; Bus.

LINN, ANDREW R; Wichita East HS; Wichita, KS; (3); Office Aide; Hon Roll; Computers.

LINNEBUR, MELISSA A; Andale HS; Colwich, KS; (2); Church Yth Grp; Spanish Clb; Band; Chorus; Mrchg Band; Pep Band; High Hon Roll.

LINTECUM, ROBIN K; Wellington Sr HS; Mayfield, KS; (2); Church Yth Grp; Cmnty Wkr; Math Tm; Natl FFA Org; SADD; Pres Frsh Cls; Rep Soph Cls; Pres Stu Cncl; Hon Roll; Jr NHS; KSU; Bus.

LINTON, TREVOR J; Waconda East HS; Glen Elder, KS; (3); Am Leg Boys St; Library Aide; Math Tm; Speech Tm; Varsity Clb; Band; Pep Band; School Musical; School Play; Variety Show.

LINVILLE, ADAM R; Basehor Linwood HS; Bonner Springs, KS; (2); Art Clb; Church Yth Grp; High Hon Roll; Hon Roll; Gifted Prgm; U Of KS.

LIPKER, CHERYL L; Salina HS South; Salina, KS; (2); Debate Tm; Girl Scts; Hosp Aide; Chorus; School Musical; Variety Show; Drama I; GCTL; K ST; Muscl Thtr.

LIPPERT, MICHELLE; Hays HS; Hays, KS; (1); Church Yth Grp; Girl Scts; Science Clb; Chorus; School Musical; JV L Trk; Hon Roll; Piano; Sftbl/Snw Skiing/Wtrskng/Knee Brdng.

LIPPOLD, MIRANDA; Hiawatha HS; Hiawatha, KS; (1); 26/107; Pep Clb; Science Clb; Band; Mrchg Band; Pep Band; Chrldng; Hon Roll; KAYS; U Of NE; Dentstry.

LIRA, SYLVIA; Wabaunsee HS; Alma, KS; (2); FHA; Math Clb; Spanish Clb; Rptr Nwsp; Rptr Yrbk; Bsktbl; JV Sftbl; Vllybl; Hon Roll; KS U; Zoology/Bio.

LISKOW, MIKE M; Shawnee Mission W Sr HS; Lenexa, KS; (4); Pep Clb; Teachers Aide; Band; Rep Jr Cls; Rep Stu Cncl; JV Ftbl; Stat Swmmng; JV Trk; Intrml Wt Lftg; Hon Roll; Radio/TV 3 Yrs; KS Univ; Music.

LISKOW, SAMANTHA; Shawnee Mission W Sr HS; Lenexa, KS; (3); 5/400; Ed Nwsp; Ed Yrbk; Sec Sr Cls; Crs Cntry; Trk; High Hon Roll; VP NHS; Q&S.

LISTER, DAVID C; Blue Valley North HS; Leawood, KS; (4); 3/166; Band; Jazz Band; Mrchg Band; Orch; Var Capt Socr; High Hon Roll; NHS; Pres Schlr; St Schlr; U Of KS; Bus; Acctng; Pre-Law.

LISTER, FRANCY; Mission Valley HS; Topeka, KS; (4); 6/60; Church Yth Grp; NFL; Q&S; SADD; Ed Yrbk; Cit Awd; High Hon Roll; NHS; Spanish Clb; Teachers Aide; Kays Ofcr; Bio & Bus Awds; Washburn; Bus.

LITTLE, BRIAN; Frankft HS; Frankfort, KS; (4); 1/28; Letterman Clb; Natl FFA Org; Chorus; School Play; Variety Show; Treas Sr Cls; JV Var Bsktbl; JV Var Ftbl; Hon Roll; NHS; KS ST; Criminology.

LITTLE, SAMUEL E; Wellsville Jr Sr HS; Paola, KS; (1); FCA; VP Frsh Cls; JV Bsktbl; JV Var Ftbl; JV Trk; KS Univ.

LITTLEFORD, JAMES A; Field Kindley Mem Sr HS; Coffeyville, KS; (2); FCA; French Clb; Natl FFA Org; Nwsp; Bsktbl; Crs Cntry; Trk; Hon Roll; Horses.

LITTLEJOHN, JENNIFER L; Wichita West HS; Wichita, KS; (4); Office Aide; Orch; Hon Roll; KS Hnr Soc; Exec HS Internship Pgm; Butler CC; Phy Thrpst.

LIU, JUNE; Blue Valley North HS; Leawood, KS; (3); Drama Clb; Treas Intnl Clb; Model UN; Q&S; Science Clb; Teachers Aide; School Play; Phtg Nwsp; Powder Puff Ftbl; JV Var Trk; Acad Dcthln; Sci Olympiad.

LIURANCE, NIKKI; Bishop Carroll Catholic HS; Wichita, KS; (2); Church Yth Grp; SADD; Rptr Nwsp; Chrldng; Mgr(s); Swmmng; KS U; Law.

LIVELY, TIA D; Belle Plaine HS; Belle Plaine, KS; (2); Church Yth Grp; SADD; Chorus; School Musical; School Play; Stage Crew; JV Bsktbl; JV Tennis; Wt Lftg; Hon Roll; KAYS; Madrigals; Stage Prodctn; OK Christian U; Chld Care.

LIVERMAN, CHRIS; Shawnee Mission E Sr HS; Fairway, KS; (2); Church Yth Grp; Cmnty Wkr; Natl Beta Clb; JV Trk; High Hon Roll; Hon Roll; Bass/Guitar; Smmr Sci Inst; Gftd Prgm; Psych.

LIX, JAMIE; Dodge City HS; Wright, KS; (3); 4-H; Band; Mrchg Band; Cit Awd; 4-H Awd; Hon Roll; NHS; KAYS.

LIX, KAREN; Dodge City HS; Wright, KS; (1); Drama Clb; 4-H; NFL; Color Guard; Vllybl; 4-H Awd; Ntl Merit Ltr; Teen Actn Clb.

LIZARDI, MICHAEL; Leavenworth HS; Leavenworth, KS; (3); 63/372; Am Leg Boys St; Bus Profs of Am; Cmnty Wkr; Bsktbl; Mgr(s); Tennis; High Hon Roll; Hon Roll; NHS; Emporia ST; Bus; Acctng.

LLAMAS, SHANNON N; Newton Sr HS; Newton, KS; (2); 32/279; Spanish Clb; Acpl Chr; Chorus; High Hon Roll; U Of KS.

LLANES, TONY D; Chase HS; Chase, KS; (3); 5/13; Church Yth Grp; FHA; Sprt Ed Nwsp; VP Jr Cls; Capt Bsktbl; Var Ftbl; Var Trk; Hon Roll; Hutch Juco; Elec Engr.

LLORENTE, RAFAEL A; St John's Military Schl; Walnut, CA; (3); 3/30; Letterman Clb; NFL; ROTC; Drill Tm; Var L Bsktbl; High Hon Roll; Jr NHS; NHS; Drama Clb; Library Aide; Blue Beret; Acad Achvr; Bus.

LLOYD, JEREMY D; Smoky Valley HS; Lindsborg, KS; (1); Church Yth Grp; Band; Jazz Band; Mrchg Band; Pep Band; Babe Ruth Bsbl; Bsbl; Music.

LLOYD, JESSICA E; Wakefield Schl; Clay Center, KS; (2); FHA; SADD; Band; Sec Soph Cls; Var Sftbl; Var Trk; Var Vllybl; Hon Roll; NHS; Mrchg Band; Photo Club Sec/Treas; U Of WA St Louis; PT.

LLOYD, NATASHA; Valley Falls HS; Valley Falls, KS; (2); #1 in class; 4-H; FHA; Band; Chorus; Pep Band; Var JV Chrldng; Var Pom Pon; Trk; High Hon Roll; Marine Bio.

LOBMEYER, BRIAN H; Pratt HS; Pratt, KS; (3); 3/110; FCA; Scholastic Bowl; SADD; Band; Mrchg Band; Pep Band; JV Tennis; High Hon Roll; JETS Awd; NHS; KS St Univ; Arfcht Eng.

LOCK, ALICIA L; Wallace Cty HS; Wallace, KS; (1); 1/17; Cmnty Wkr; 4-H; Pep Clb; Band; Chorus; Mrchg Band; Pep Band; Sec Frsh Cls; Bsktbl; Vllybl.

LOCK, AMBER N; Hesston HS; Hesston, KS; (1); Dance Clb; Chorus; High Hon Roll; Rssn Acad Awd 95-; Newton Dnc Ctr Jazz Troupe/Ballet; 2 Yr Tap; 3yrs Jazz; 11 Yrs Ballet; Tchrs Dnc Clss.

LOCK, ROSANNA D; Wallace Cty HS; Wallace, KS; (3); 9/19; Cmnty Wkr; Drama Clb; Hosp Aide; Pep Clb; Speech Tm; SADD; Teachers Aide; Band; Chorus; Mrchg Band; Colby CC; Nrsng.

LOCKE, ANDREA N; Paola HS; Paola, KS; (3); 1/100; Drama Clb; FCA; SADD; Band; School Play; Nwsp; Trk; Vllybl; High Hon Roll; NHS; Pittsburg ST; Phy Thrpst.

LOCKE, DESARAE; Atchison Sr HS; Atchison, KS; (3); 7/101; DECA; Rep Stu Cncl; Chrldng; Trk; Hon Roll; NHS; Lnch Chmpns; Pvt Dnce, Piano Lssns; Bus.

LOCKE, GARRATT A; Arkansas City HS; Arkansas City, KS; (2); Church Yth Grp; FCA; 4-H; Natl FFA Org; Band; Ftbl; 4-H Awd; Hon Roll; FFA Awds; Yth Group Awds; KS ST Univ; Ag Operation; Mgmt.

LOCKHART, ADAM D; Atchison Co Cmty HS; Effingham, KS; (3); Letterman Clb; Acpl Chr; Chorus; School Play; Stage Crew; Crs Cntry; Trk; Wt Lftg; Wrstlng; Prfct Atten Awd.

LOCKTON, LINDSAY C; Blue Valley North HS; Leawood, KS; (2); Var Chrldng; Var Tennis; Hon Roll; Young Life.

LOCKWOOD, JOHNEE; Arkansas City HS; Arkansas City, KS; (3); 4-H; 4-H Awd; Hon Roll; NHS; Cowley Cty CC.

LODER, STEPHANIE J; Shawnee Heights Sr HS; Topeka, KS; (4); Teachers Aide; Chorus; Nwsp; Phtg Yrbk; High Hon Roll; Hon Roll; Emporia ST U; Bus Mgmt.

LOEHR, JOHN E; Garden Plain Jr Sr HS; Garden Plain, KS; (2); 8/32; Chess Clb; Red Cross Aide; Scholastic Bowl; Spanish Clb; Band; VP Soph Cls; L Wrstlng; Comp Scis.

LOEHR, ROSE N; Eudora HS; Eudora, KS; (4); 11/48; Church Yth Grp; Cmnty Wkr; Drama Clb; FBLA; GAA; NFL; Office Aide; Pep Clb; SADD; Varsity Clb; Rockhurst; Phys Therapy.

LOEHR, SARAH M; Wichita East HS; Wichita, KS; (3); Cmnty Wkr; Var Golf; Var Sftbl; Var Vllybl; Hon Roll; NHS; German Clb; JA; Intnl Baccalaureate Pgm; Spirit Cabinet-Support Ath Events & Planned 2 Formal & 1 Casual Dances; KS U; Psych; Sports Medicine.

LOEWEN, ADAM R; Lawrence HS; Lawrence, KS; (4); Art Clb; FCA; Key Clb; Teachers Aide; Intrml Capt Bsktbl; Intrml Capt Vllybl; High Hon Roll; Pres Acad Fit Awd; Pres Schlr; Fllwshp Chrstn Stu; Full Schlrshp; Cooper Union; Art.

LOFGREEN, MATTHEW; Norton Comm HS; Norton, KS; (3); 2/60; Am Leg Boys St; 4-H; FHA; Model UN; Pep Clb; Quiz Bowl; Scholastic Bowl; Yrbk; JV Golf; High Hon Roll; KS St; Chem Eng.

LOFTUS, MEGAN; Shawnee Mission N HS; Prairie Village, KS; (3); 100/450; Latin Clb; Q&S; Spanish Clb; Thesps; Orch; Ed Nwsp; Rep Stu Cncl; Hon Roll; NHS; Pres Acad Fit Awd.

LOGAN, AKIBA; Wyandotte HS; Kansas City, KS; (3); Chess Clb; Pep Clb; Q&S; Nwsp; Yrbk; Ed Lit Mag; Hon Roll; NHS; Medcl Careers; KS ST U; Psych.

LOGAN, AMBER; Arkansas City HS; Arkansas City, KS; (4); 1/190; Church Yth Grp; FTA; Office Aide; Service Clb; SADD; Teachers Aide; High Hon Roll; Hon Roll; NHS; Pres Acad Fit Awd; DARE Rl Mdl; Elem Ed.

LOGAN, EMILY L; Nickerson HS; Nickerson, KS; (1); Drama Clb; Quiz Bowl; Scholastic Bowl; Thesps; Chorus; School Play; Var L Sftbl; Vllybl; High Hon Roll; 3rd Pl St His Day Cmptn.

LOGAN, LISA L; Blue Valley North HS; Overland Park, KS; (2); 26/280; Model UN; Thesps; Varsity Clb; Acpl Chr; Band; Drill Tm; Flag Corp; Mrchg Band; School Musical; High Hon Roll; KS Univ; Med.

LOGER, MEGAN C; Clearwater HS; Clearwater, KS; (2); Letterman Clb; Varsity Clb; Bsktbl; Sftbl; Trk; Vllybl; Wt Lftg; High Hon Roll; Vllybll St Champ; Cntrl MO St Univ; Med Sec.

LOHMAN, ERIN M; Leavenworth HS; Leavenworth, KS; (3); Bus Profs of Am; Church Yth Grp; Office Aide; Red Cross Aide; Teachers Aide; Var Swmmng; Pittsburgh ST; Cmptr Tech.

LOHMANN, ROBYN R; Valley Ctr HS; Valley Center, KS; (3); Church Yth Grp; SADD; Stat Bsktbl; Mgr(s); Var Socr; Hon Roll; KS U; Med Fld.

LOHMEYER, LINDSAY L; Olathe East Sr HS; Stilwell, KS; (3); Teachers Aide; Chorus; Church Choir; School Musical; Ofcr Stu Cncl; Hon Roll; NHS; Marine Bio.

LOHMEYER, SCOTT A; Hoisington HS; Hoisington, KS; (2); Church Yth Grp; Letterman Clb; Chorus; Pres Frsh Cls; Var L Bsbl; Var Bsktbl; JV Ftbl; Hon Roll; Lead Yth Forum.

LOHR, JUSTIN; Goodland HS; Goodland, KS; (3); Cmnty Wkr; Pres 4-H; HOBY; Letterman Clb; Var L Crs Cntry; Var L Trk; Cit Awd; 4-H Awd; Shrmn Cty 4-H Ambass; Colby CC; Anml Sci.

LOHRDING, BRIAN; Protection Schl; Coldwater, KS; (4); Church Yth Grp; Scholastic Bowl; Varsity Clb; Pres Frsh Cls; VP Jr Cls; Ofcr Stu Cncl; Bsktbl; Ftbl; High Hon Roll; Pres Acad Fit Awd; Outstndng Math & Sci Stu; All Area Ftbl; 1st Team On Defense-Linebckr; KIOI Classc Bowl; Baylor Schlr; Baylor Univ; His; CIA.

LOHREY, MOLLY; Lacrosse HS; La Crosse, KS; (4); 6/27; Pres 4-H; French Clb; Girl Scts; HOBY; Pep Clb; Band; Chorus; School Play; 4-H Awd; VP NHS; KSU; Arch Engr.

LOLLEY, J. R.; Shawnee Heights Sr HS; Berryton, KS; (2); FBLA; Intrml Bsktbl; JV Golf; High Hon Roll; Hon Roll; Prfct Atten Awd; Spirit Club; Care Co Off; KS ST Univ; Bus Mngmt.

LOLLEY, JEFF; Jefferson West HS; Meriden, KS; (4); 1/62; Boy Scts; Chess Clb; French Clb; FBLA; Letterman Clb; SADD; Teachers Aide; Ofcr Bsbl; Bsktbl; Ftbl; Tns As Tchrs; Elect Engrng.

LOLLIS, TYRICE L; Wichita Southeast HS; Wichita, KS; (3); Bus Profs of Am; Church Yth Grp; Cmnty Wkr; FBLA; Office Aide; Quiz Bowl; Church Choir; Drill Tm; School Musical; Variety Show; St Of KS Legislative Cert Of Recognition As A Page; Best Bus Plan Awd Young Entrepreneurs Of KS; Wichita ST U; Bus.

LOMBARD, JUSTIN W; Blue Valley Northwest HS; Overland Park, KS; (2); Church Yth Grp; Cmnty Wkr; FCA; Bsktbl; Ftbl; Wt Lftg; Hon Roll; Niles Home For Childrn; Helpd Spon A Chld Thru Compssn Intnl; Habitat For Humnty; Talent ID Pgm Duke U; KS Univ; Engr.

LOMIBAO, LOWELL C; Manhattan HS; Manhattan, KS; (3); Spanish Clb; Var Trk; Hon Roll; KU; Phys Thpy.

LOMINSKA, AVERY; Lawrence HS; Lawrence, KS; (3); Science Clb; Service Clb; Teachers Aide; Band; Mrchg Band; Pep Band; JV Socr; Hon Roll; Prfct Atten Awd; Rugby Clb; Music.

LONDON, CARI E; Bishop Carroll Catholic HS; Wichita, KS; (2); Chorus; Hon Roll; KS ST.

LONER, KARA A; Shawnee Mission N HS; Shawnee Mission, KS; (4); 200/450; Art Clb; Cmnty Wkr; Hosp Aide; Library Aide; Natl Beta Clb; Pep Clb; Hon Roll; KS Univ; Med.

LONERGAN, HEATHER M; Wichita East HS; Wichita, KS; (2); Drama Clb; Girl Scts; Spanish Clb; Band; Mrchg Band; Hon Roll; Intl Baccalaureate Prgm; Metropolitan Ballet 9-10th Grd; Vet Med.

LONG, AMBER M; Shawnee Heights Sr HS; Topeka, KS; (2); Hosp Aide; Key Clb; SADD; Band; Hon Roll; Washburn Univ; Nrsng.

LONG, ANGELA; Frankft HS; Frankfort, KS; (3); 4-H; FHA; Pep Clb; Science Clb; Band; Chorus; School Play; VP Jr Cls; High Hon Roll; Show Choir; St Lvl Flt & Vcl Solos; 1st Pl St-Wd Tlnts For Chrst Cmptn; Music.

LONG, BARRETT; El Dorado HS; El Dorado, KS; (4); Am Leg Boys St; Letterman Clb; Varsity Clb; Ed Nwsp; Capt Var Bsbl; Capt Var Bsktbl; Gov Hon Prg Awd; Hon Roll; Washburn Univ.

LONG, BRANDIE J; Kensington Jr Sr HS; Kensington, KS; (3); Church Yth Grp; Library Aide; Pep Clb; Spanish Clb; SADD; Band; Chorus; Mrchg Band; Pep Band; Phtg Yrbk; MO ST Univ; CPA.

LONG, CHARLIE D; Midland Sda Schl; Kansas City, KS; (2); Church Yth Grp; Cmnty Wkr; Drama Clb; Spanish Clb; Band; Sec Stu Cncl; Bsktbl; Cit Awd; Ski Clb; Gym; Washington DC Cngrssnl Yth Ldrsp Cncl; 2 Mssn Trps To Mexico; Dsgn Engr.

LONG, CHRIS D; Ellinwood Jr Sr HS; Ellinwood, KS; (2); Church Yth Grp; Pep Clb; Quiz Bowl; Band; Mrchg Band; Pep Band; High Hon Roll; Hon Roll; FFA Cncl Sentinel 96-97; 2 Schltc Medals; KS ST Univ; Ag Ed.

LONG, COURTNEY S; Blue Valley HS; Overland Park, KS; (2); Church Yth Grp; Band; Church Choir; Mrchg Band; Pep Band; School Musical; JV Trk; Vllybl; High Hon Roll; Hon Roll.

LONG, DAWN M; Campus HS; Wichita, KS; (2); Church Yth Grp; Girl Scts; Science Clb; SADD; Chorus; Church Choir; Orch; Ofcr Stu Cncl; Swmmng; Hon Roll.

LONG, JENNIFER; Prairie View Jr Sr HS; La Cygne, KS; (3); 9/70; VP 4-H; FHA; HOBY; Band; Drm Mjr(t); Jazz Band; Mrchg Band; L Chrldng; Stat Mgr(s); Hon Roll.

LONG, JILL; Jefferson West HS; Meriden, KS; (3); Church Yth Grp; FBLA; Letterman Clb; SADD; Pres Jr Cls; Var Bsktbl; Pom Pon; Trk; Vllybl; NHS; Cmnty Svc Awd; Bus Awd; KS U; Pblc Rltns.

LONG, KEITH W; Topeka West HS; Topeka, KS; (4); 51/257; German Clb; Q&S; Quiz Bowl; Scholastic Bowl; Spanish Clb; Phtg Nwsp; Var Capt Ftbl; Powder Puff Ftbl; Var L Trk; High Hon Roll; Univ Of KS; His.

LONG, KELLY E; Independence HS; Independence, KS; (1); Scholastic Bowl; Band; Chorus; Mrchg Band; Pep Band; School Musical; Hon Roll; Pres Schlr; Kay Clb Points Dir; Univ Of KS; Psychologist.

LONG, LEAH M; Haven HS; Haven, KS; (2); Church Yth Grp; FCA; Letterman Clb; Pep Clb; SADD; Band; Church Choir; Flag Corp; Mrchg Band; Orch.

LONG, LORETTA; Circle HS; El Dorado, KS; (3); Church Yth Grp; Scholastic Bowl; Spanish Clb; SADD; Chorus; Variety Show; Ofcr Stu Cncl; Sftbl; Vllybl; High Hon Roll; Youth Ldrshp Pgm; Natl Hnr Roll; Natl Schlr; OK ST U; Ed.

LONG, MEGAN N; Blue Valley Northwest HS; Overland Park, KS; (2); Cmnty Wkr; Hosp Aide; HOBY; Latin Clb; Varsity Clb; Co-Capt Drill Tm; Flag Corp; Powder Puff Ftbl; High Hon Roll; NHS; Med.

LONG, NATHAN; East HS; Wichita, KS; (3); Boy Scts; Cmnty Wkr; JA; Office Aide; Teachers Aide; Varsity Clb; Orch; Var L Bsbl; JV Bsktbl; Var L Chrldng; Crimnl Jstce.

LONG, NIKKI L; Washington HS; Kansas City, KS; (3); Church Yth Grp; French Clb; Quiz Bowl; Speech Tm; Band; Mrchg Band; Pep Band; Swmmng; High Hon Roll; Hon Roll; Jr DECA; KU Math & Sci Ctr; Law; Mrktg.

LONG, REBECCA M; Topeka West HS; Topeka, KS; (4); #3 in class; Church Yth Grp; English Clb; Girl Scts; Math Clb; Q&S; Scholastic Bowl; Spanish Clb; Stage Crew; Variety Show; Ed Lit Mag; Crtv Wrtng.

LONG, ROBYN; Wichita Northwest HS; Wichita, KS; (4); Am Leg Aux Girls St; Church Yth Grp; Intnl Clb; Chorus; Ed Lit Mag; Pres Stu Cncl; NHS; Cmnty Wkr; School Play; Variety Show; Danforth I Dare You Awd; Ntl Ldrshp Awd; Voted Mst Humorous & Mst Likely To Succeed; Prom Prncss; Baker U; Poltcl Sci.

LONG, SARAH E; Campus HS; Wichita, KS; (2); French Clb; Orch; Diving; Hon Roll.

LONG, SCOTT C; Basehor Linwood HS; Basehor, KS; (2); FBLA; Teachers Aide; Band; Pep Band; High Hon Roll; Lrnd 2 Prgmming Langs; Cmptr Systms Anlyst.

LONGANECKER, KARI L; Olathe East Sr HS; Olathe, KS; (4); Intnl Clb; Office Aide; Teachers Aide.

LONGBERG, CHRISTIE A; Chanute Sr HS; Chanute, KS; (3); Church Yth Grp; FCA; 4-H; Band; Chorus; School Musical; Ofcr Stu Cncl; Hon Roll; NHS; FHA; Nazarene Yth Congress; Prin Ldrshp Team; KSU; Ed.

LONGBERG, MICHELLE L; Chanute Sr HS; Chanute, KS; (4); 4-H; Spanish Clb; Band; Chorus; Drm Mjr(t); Jazz Band; Yrbk; 4-H Awd; Hon Roll; Pres Acad Fit Awd.

LOOMANS, ALYSSA M; Topeka HS; Topeka, KS; (2); Church Yth Grp; Band; Mrchg Band; Pep Band; Hon Roll; Teen Hope; Washburn U; Psych.

LOONEY, AMBER C; Wichita East HS; Wichita, KS; (3); Church Yth Grp; Girl Scts; JV Bsbl; Var Capt Crs Cntry; Var Capt Trk; Hon Roll; NHS; Cmnty Wkr; Church Choir; Japanese Clb; IB Advy Cncl; Natl Art Soc; Arch.

LOONEY, AMBER J; Wichita West HS; Wichita, KS; (2); Church Yth Grp; Cmnty Wkr; Drama Clb; Spanish Clb; Teachers Aide; Chorus; Church Choir; School Musical; School Play; Stage Crew; Vol YESS Prgm; Camp Pride Vol 2 Smmrs Wrkng Hndcppd Kids/Adults; Spec Ed Tchr.

LOOP, BILL; Wellington Sr HS; Wellington, KS; (1); Debate Tm; Pres Stu Cncl; Var Bsktbl; Cit Awd; High Hon Roll; Jr NHS; Lions Awd.

LOPEMAN, JAIME C; Field Kindley Mem Sr HS; Coffeyville, KS; (3); Drama Clb; French Clb; JA; Natl FFA Org; Yrbk; Bsktbl; High Hon Roll; Tomorrows Ldr For Comm.

LOPEZ, JENNIFER M; Kapaun-Mt Carmel HS; Wichita, KS; (4); 23/165; Pres Church Yth Grp; Drama Clb; Sec French Clb; Chorus; School Musical; School Play; Stage Crew; High Hon Roll; NHS; Pres Schlr; U Of Notre Dame; Engl.

LOPEZ, LOREE; Ulysses HS; Ulysses, KS; (2); Church Yth Grp; Spanish Clb; Band; Chorus; Mrchg Band; Pep Band; JV Bsktbl; JV Mgr(s); JV Vllybl; Hon Roll; Med.

LOPEZ, SARA A; Turner HS; Kansas City, KS; (4); 41/200; Church Yth Grp; DECA; Pep Clb; SADD; Varsity Clb; School Musical; Ofcr Stu Cncl; Var Bsktbl; Var Vllybl; Hon Roll; Mark Exccllnc Awd; Vllybl MVP; Bsktbl Hoop Awd; KS City CC; Phys Thrpy.

LORE, KELLI J; Emporia HS; Emporia, KS; (4); 39/280; Pep Clb; Teachers Aide; Variety Show; Rep Jr Cls; Treas Sr Cls; JV L Crs Cntry; Var L Swmmng; Wt Lftg; Cit Awd; High Hon Roll; Black Belt Tae Kwon Do; Emporia ST Univ; Intl Bus.

LOREMAN, AMANDA C; Shawnee Heights HS; Topeka, KS; (1); FTA; Orch; Tennis; Hon Roll; Emporia ST Univ; Elem Schl Tch.

LOREN, DANNY P; Hyman Brand Hebrew Acad; Shawnee Mission, KS; (3); Rptr Frsh Cls; Bsktbl; Socr; High Hon Roll; Hon Roll; NHS; Amer/Wstrn His/Algbr II Awds.

LORENSON, KATE J; Wichita Heights HS; Valley Center, KS; (3); Church Yth Grp; SADD; Chorus; Church Choir; Orch; Var Tennis; Hon Roll; Library Aide; Teachers Aide; School Musical; Bible Clb; Sndy Schl Tchr; Grls Ensmbl; Mid Amer; Educ.

LORENZ, LINDSAY K; KS Schl For The Deaf; Wichita, KS; (2); 3/19; GAA; St Paul Tech; Grphc Dsgn/Art.

LORETT, MELESA; Syracuse Jr Sr HS; Syracuse, KS; (1); Band; Chorus; JV Bsktbl; Var Chrldng; Var Trk; Var Vllybl; High Hon Roll; Law.

LORETTO, MICHAEL; Topeka HS; Topeka, KS; (2); Church Yth Grp; Cmnty Wkr; Acpl Chr; Chorus; Church Choir; School Musical; Variety Show; Var Tennis; High Hon Roll; Hon Roll; St And Dist Hnr Choir.

LOROFF, MANDIE; Troy HS; Troy, KS; (4); Am Leg Aux Girls St; Drama Clb; HOBY; Q&S; Ed Nwsp; Ed Yrbk; Capt Chrldng; Trk; High Hon Roll; NHS; Gftd Prog; KS ST; Gntcs.

LOSIE, MELISSA A; Wichita Southeast HS; Wichita, KS; (2); 44/436; Debate Tm; Girl Scts; NFL; Band; Mrchg Band; Hon Roll; U Of KS; Law.

LOUDERBACK, MIRIAM L; Andover HS; Wichita, KS; (4); 24/138; Church Yth Grp; Cmnty Wkr; HOBY; School Musical; Socr; Vllybl; NHS; Pres Schlr; Spanish NHS; St Schlr; LA Salle Univ Cancun; Bilingual Eng/Span; KS ST Univ; Bus/Span.

LOUDERBAUGH, STACI R; Yates Ctr HS; Yates Center, KS; (3); 723/752; Church Yth Grp; 4-H; FHA; SADD; Teachers Aide; Band; Church Choir; Trk; 4-H Awd; Hon Roll; Elderly At Local Nrsng Home Vol; Med.

LOUDIS, JENNIFER; Salina HS Central; Salina, KS; (4); Church Yth Grp; Cmnty Wkr; HOBY; Quiz Bowl; SADD; School Play; Ed Nwsp; L Var Swmmng; Vllybl; Hon Roll; Charter Pres Teen Tto ABUCS 95-96; Ust Pl SA Rgnl Jrnlsm Cmptn Edtrl Wrtng; Intern TV Station; Commnctns.

LOUIS, MICHELLE A; Sumner Acad Of Arts & Science; Kansas City, KS; (3); 101/148; Cmnty Wkr; Latin Clb; Spanish Clb; Chorus; Church Choir; Phtg Yrbk; Hon Roll; Upward Bound; Drake Univ; Comp Sci.

LOUK, GLENNA D; Hutchinson HS; Hutchinson, KS; (3); 18/325; Church Yth Grp; Acpl Chr; Band; Chorus; Church Choir; Mrchg Band; School Musical; Variety Show; Cit Awd; High Hon Roll; Hutchinson CC; Music.

LOURENTZOS, ANNE E; Lansing HS; Lansing, KS; (3); 48/168; Cmnty Wkr; French Clb; Band; Mrchg Band; Pep Band; Hon Roll; Pre-Med.

LOVE, BETSY; Lebo Schl; Lebo, KS; (1); 1/26; Church Yth Grp; Sec 4-H; FBLA; Band; Pres Frsh Cls; Var Chrldng; Trk; JV Var Vllybl; High Hon Roll; Quiz Bowl; Triple Trio; Coffey Cty Teen Ldrs Sec; Beethvn Soc Pianists; St FBLA-QLFD Natl Cmptn.

LOVE, ETOYA D; F L Schlagle HS; Kansas City, KS; (1); Church Yth Grp; Church Choir; School Musical; Hon Roll; Poetry; Gramblin; Ob/Gyn/Interior Dcrtr.

LOVE, REBEKAH L; Maize HS; Wichita, KS; (1); Church Yth Grp; Cmnty Wkr; FCA; SADD; Thesps; Chorus; Variety Show; Tennis; High Hon Roll; Pres Schlr; Piano Lsns/Perf 10 Yrs; Ftr Prblm Slvng 9th Grd 3rd ST; Wichita ST Univ; PT.

LOVELESS, BRIAN S; Leavenworth HS; Fort Leavenworth, KS; (3); Teachers Aide; JV Bsktbl.

LOVELL, MICHELLE; Olathe East Sr HS; Olathe, KS; (3); Art Clb; Church Yth Grp; Intnl Clb; Letterman Clb; Teachers Aide; Chorus; School Play; Capt Var Chrldng; Var Gym; Powder Puff Ftbl; Mssn Trps/Mexico 96.

LOVELL, SARAH B; Wellington Sr HS; Wellington, KS; (3); Sec Church Yth Grp; 4-H; Key Clb; Band; School Play; Hon Roll; Jr NHS; SADD; Mrchg Band; Pep Band; STARS Yth Grp; Drama.

LOVESEE, JOEL; Kinsley HS; Kinsley, KS; (3); 4/32; Boy Scts; Church Yth Grp; Quiz Bowl; Band; Chorus; Pres Frsh Cls; Capt Var Bsktbl; Capt Var Ftbl; High Hon Roll; Hon Roll; KAY Clb; U Of Denver; Poli Sci.

LOVETT, JENNIFER I; Salina HS South; Salina, KS; (3); Teachers Aide; Chorus; Ofcr Stu Cncl; Vllybl; Hon Roll; Pres Acad Fit Awd; 1st Pl 3-D Art Gen Fed Womens Clb KS; 5 Clb; KS U; Nrs.

LOVETT, NICOLE L; Derby HS; Derby, KS; (1); Contemporary Womens Clb; Drama House Crew; Shop Clb; Child Psycht.

LO VULLO, JAMIE N; Salina HS Central; Salina, KS; (3); Church Yth Grp; Cmnty Wkr; Dance Clb; School Musical; School Play; Variety Show; Yrbk; Rep Frsh Cls; Rep Soph Cls; Rep Jr Cls; NCA All Amer Dancer; Mst Inspirational Player Sftbl; I70 League 2nd Team Catcher; Jr Ldrshp Cncl.

LOWE, ARRAN C; Maize HS; Wichita, KS; (2); Chess Clb; Church Yth Grp; Debate Tm; Drama Clb; NFL; Quiz Bowl; Speech Tm; School Play; Swmmng; NHS; Acad Decathalon; Rice Univ; Math; Statistics.

LOWE, CHANDRA; Olathe North Sr HS; Olathe, KS; (3); Office Aide; Teachers Aide; Nwsp; Hon Roll; U Of KS Coll; Psych.

LOWE, DENNIS A; Wichita South HS; Wichita, KS; (2); 27/436; Chess Clb; Computer Clb; Spanish Clb; Orch; High Hon Roll; Hon Roll; Prfct Atten Awd; Pres Acad Fit Awd; KS ST; Bio/Span.

LOWE, ERIN; Topeka West HS; Topeka, KS; (2); Church Yth Grp; Debate Tm; FCA; German Clb; NFL; Pep Clb; Band; Drm Mjr(t); Jazz Band; Mrchg Band; Bus Admin.

LOWE, KEITH M; Wyandotte HS; Kansas City, KS; (2); Church Yth Grp; Cmnty Wkr; Orch; Ofcr Stu Cncl; High Hon Roll; NHS; Perf Arts Awd; Mus Perf.

LOWE, LINDSEY E; Washburn Rural HS; Topeka, KS; (2); Hosp Aide; SADD; JV Sftbl; Hon Roll.

LOWE, MICHELLE E; Sumner Acad Of Arts & Science; Kansas City, KS; (3); Church Yth Grp; Cmnty Wkr; Drama Clb; JA; Key Clb; Latin Clb; Office Aide; Pep Clb; Spanish Clb; Teachers Aide; Ldrshp 2020; Gospel Choir Pres, VP; Pittsburg ST U; Brdcstng.

LOWEN, JAKE; Nickerson HS; Hutchinson, KS; (3); Debate Tm; French Clb; Ftbl; Pol Sci/Law.

LOWER, CHAD J; Kingman HS; Kingman, KS; (2); Wt Lftg; Hon Roll; Tae Kwon Do; After Schl Job; Learning Electric Guitar; Electrcn.

LOWER, MATTHEW; Humboldt HS; Humboldt, KS; (3); Church Yth Grp; Dance Clb; 4-H; HOBY; Band; Mrchg Band; Rptr Nwsp; Bsktbl; Ftbl; Hon Roll; KS ST U; Cvl Svc.

LOWMAN, ALISA; Eureka Jr Sr HS; Eureka, KS; (4); 5/65; Am Leg Aux Girls St; Speech Tm; Sprt Ed Yrbk; Sec Stu Cncl; Var Bsktbl; Var L Chrldng; Var Golf; Kiwanis Awd; NHS; KS Hnr Schlr; Phys Thrpy.

LOWRANCE, SHARON S; Oskaloosa HS; Ozawkie, KS; (2); Debate Tm; Drama Clb; FHA; NFL; Pep Clb; SADD; Acpl Chr; School Musical; Hon Roll; Prfct Atten Awd; FHA St Bronze; Acad Awd; Emporia ST; Drama Tchr.

LOWRY, MONICA J; Stockton HS; Stockton, KS; (4); 11/33; Pres Church Yth Grp; Debate Tm; Pep Clb; Speech Tm; Band; Chorus; Jazz Band; Mrchg Band; Pep Band; Stage Crew; Voice Of Democracy 1st & 2nd Place; Barton Cty Comm Coll; Ath Trng.

LOWRY, SHANNON; Stockton HS; Stockton, KS; (1); 4/32; Church Yth Grp; Pep Clb; Band; Jazz Band; Mrchg Band; Pep Band; Ofcr Stu Cncl; Var Chrldng; JV Vllybl; Hon Roll.

LOWRY, TIMOTHY A; Washburn Rural HS; Topeka, KS; (4); Church Yth Grp; JA; Natl FFA Org; Ftbl; Trk; Wt Lftg; Wrstlng; Hon Roll; U Of KY; Landscape Arch.

LOZLER, JEFFREY T; Blue Valley North HS; Leawood, KS; (2); Church Yth Grp; Model UN; Pep Clb; SADD; Rep Soph Cls; Intrml Bsktbl; Var Socr; Hon Roll; Optmsm Awd/Recgtn; Rough Riders; Univ Of KS; Dermtlgst.

LU, LINH M; Garden City Sr HS; Garden City, KS; (4); 62/313; Hon Roll; Prfct Atten Awd; Garden City CC; Nursng.

LUBBERS, JASON; Kingman HS; Abbyville, KS; (4); 3/70; Debate Tm; 4-H; NFL; Band; Jazz Band; Mrchg Band; Pep Band; 4-H Awd; Hon Roll; NHS; Wichita ST U; Bus Admin.

LUBBERS, MANDY R; Wichita West HS; Wichita, KS; (2); Hosp Aide; Office Aide; Spanish Clb; Teachers Aide; Hon Roll; Prfct Atten Awd; KS ST; Tchr.

LUBY, JENNIFER W; Olathe South Sr HS; Olathe, KS; (4); Drama Clb; Teachers Aide; Band; Mrchg Band; NHS; Pres Acad Fit Awd; Amer String Tchrs Assn Cmptn Classcl Guitar Natl Fnlst; CO Coll.

LUCAS, ANDREW E; Garden City Sr HS; Garden City, KS; (2); Church Yth Grp; Acpl Chr; Church Choir; VP Frsh Cls; VP Soph Cls; VP Jr Cls; JV Bsbl; High Hon Roll; Hon Roll; Babe Ruth Bsbl; Church Drama; Mid Amer Nazarn Coll; Yth Pstr.

LUCAS, CALEB R; Salina HS South; Salina, KS; (3); Am Leg Boys St; Math Tm; Quiz Bowl; Rptr Ed Nwsp; NHS; Cmnty Wkr; Debate Tm; High Hon Roll; Pres Acad Fit Awd; Yth Task Force Chrprsn; High Scorer Amer HS Math Exam/Amer Invtnl Math Exam; HS Site Cncl; KS ST Univ; Math.

LUCAS, HEATHER M; Clearwater HS; Clearwater, KS; (4); Art Clb; Church Yth Grp; Spanish Clb; SADD; Band; Mrchg Band; Bsktbl; Hon Roll; Best Sr Artist; Butler Cty CC; Art; Theatre; Med.

LUCAS, MICHAEL R; Liberal HS; Liberal, KS; (3); Boy Scts; JV Bsbl; Seward Co CC; Bsbl Tchr.

LUCAS, TROY J; Labette Co HS; Altamont, KS; (3); 18/128; FCA; FBLA; Letterman Clb; Library Aide; JV Bsktbl; Var L Golf; Hon Roll; NHS; Washburn Univ; Bus Mgmt.

LUCAS SWINGLE, MARY; El Dorado HS; El Dorado, KS; (2); 32/183; Debate Tm; NFL; Spanish Clb; Orch; Chrldng; Trk; High Hon Roll; Earth Care Clb.

LUCHSINGER, MINDY M; Solomon Jr Sr HS; Solomon, KS; (2); FHA; SADD; Chorus; JV Bsktbl; JV Vllybl; High Hon Roll.

LUCKE, TYSON J; Chanute Sr HS; Chanute, KS; (2); FCA; Letterman Clb; Varsity Clb; Band; Mrchg Band; Var Bsbl; JV Bsktbl; Hon Roll; Neosho Cty CC.

LUCKEROTH, ACACIA L; Holton HS; Holton, KS; (3); Art Clb; Debate Tm; Drama Clb; Speech Tm; Acpl Chr; Chorus; School Musical; Brdcst Jrnlsm; KS Univ; Nrsng.

LUCKERT, LISA; Brewster Schl; Brewster, KS; (3); 2/10; Am Leg Boys St; Pep Clb; Quiz Bowl; Scholastic Bowl; Band; Pep Band; Ofcr Soph Cls; Ofcr Jr Cls; Ofcr Stu Cncl; Bsktbl; Fort Hays ST U; Acctng.

LUDLUM, BETH A; Uniontown HS; Uniontown, KS; (1); 1/35; Church Yth Grp; FCA; 4-H; Math Tm; Natl FFA Org; Band; Treas Frsh Cls; Var Bsktbl; Var L Trk; JV Vllybl.

LUDLUM, BRANDI; Wamego HS; Wamego, KS; (3); Church Yth Grp; Treas SADD; Band; Pep Band; Rep Stu Cncl; Tennis; Hon Roll; Ntl Merit Ltr; AFS Stu Rep & Sec; KS ST; Bus.

LUEDKE, LINDA MICHELLE; Crest HS; Colony, KS; (2); Math Tm; Natl FFA Org; Chorus; Var Bsktbl; Var Chrldng; Sftbl; Var Vllybl; Hon Roll; GAA; Pep Clb; St Trk High Jump & 4x100 Relay 96; FFA Greenhand Degree.

LUEGER, BRADLEY J; Bailey-Benedict Jr Sr High; Seneca, KS; (1); 2/17; 4-H; Quiz Bowl; Band; Mrchg Band; Pep Band; Intrml Bsktbl; 4-H Awd; High Hon Roll; Hon Roll; Pres Acad Fit Awd; Comp Technician.

LUEGER, KEVIN; Nemaha Valley HS; Seneca, KS; (1); Church Yth Grp; Treas 4-H; Band; Pep Band; Swing Chorus; Bsktbl; Ftbl; Trk; Hon Roll.

LUEGER, MARK; Nemaha Valley HS; Goff, KS; (2); VP Church Yth Grp; Pres 4-H; Band; Mrchg Band; Pep Band; School Play; Pres Frsh Cls; Pres Soph Cls; Intrml Ftbl; Intrml Golf.

LUEGER, SARAH A; Nemaha Valley HS; Seneca, KS; (3); Letterman Clb; SADD; Drill Tm; School Play; Var L Bsktbl; Var Vllybl; High Hon Roll; VP NHS; Quiz Bowl; Scholastic Bowl; KAYS; CYO.

LUEKER, SUZANNE; Junction City HS; Junction City, KS; (4); 14/256; Am Leg Aux Girls St; CAP; Girl Scts; Letterman Clb; Pres Soph Cls; Pres Jr Cls; Chrldng; High Hon Roll; NHS; Ofcr Stu Cncl; U KS; Crmnlgy.

LUETTERS, CRYSTAL; Thomas More Prep-Marion HS; Hays, KS; (4); 2/95; Debate Tm; Hosp Aide; School Musical; School Play; Nwsp; Rptr Soph Cls; Rptr Jr Cls; Rptr Sr Cls; Var Trk; Var Capt Vllybl; Bio.

LUGINBILL, AMANDA D; Newton Sr HS; Newton, KS; (2); Art Clb; Church Yth Grp; German Clb; Model UN; Thesps; Lit Mag; Rep Stu Cncl; JV Var Chrldng; JV Trk; Hon Roll; Mediation Team.

LUJANO, MIGUEL A; Kapaun-Mt Carmel HS; Wichita, KS; (3); Church Yth Grp; Latin Clb; Temple Yth Grp; Amer GI Forum; KS Newman Coll; Comp Prgmr.

LUKE, ERICA K; Blue Valley HS; Olathe, KS; (3); Bsktbl; Hon Roll; KAYS; Prom Comm; Fash Merch.

LUNA, GABE; Maur Hill Prep Schl; Horton, KS; (4); 1/46; Math Clb; Math Tm; Ed Nwsp; Sec Treas Stu Cncl; Var L Bsktbl; JV Ftbl; Var L Trk; High Hon Roll; NHS; Pres Acad Fit Awd; PGA Awd; Spec Plympcs Vol; Notre Dame.

LUNA, JOSHUA J; Maize HS; Maize, KS; (3); Church Yth Grp; French Clb; Spanish Clb; Band; Ftbl; Trk; High Hon Roll; Hon Roll; Fr Awd; 1st Plc Babe Ruth Bsbl Dist Smr League; Earned 2 Coll Credits Chem/Biol.

LUNDBERG, BRETT G; Topeka HS; Topeka, KS; (2); 46/630; Church Yth Grp; Cmnty Wkr; Letterman Clb; Church Choir; Yrbk; Bsktbl; Ftbl; Golf; Wt Lftg; High Hon Roll; Mission Trips To CN & Mexico; Vol Work.

LUNDERMAN, KYNDRA L; Riverton Schl; Riverton, KS; (3); Church Yth Grp; Letterman Clb; Math Tm; Spanish Clb; Chorus; School Play; Ed Yrbk; Sec Jr Cls; Rep Stu Cncl; Hon Roll.

LUNDGREN, JASON; Blue Valley HS; Overland Park, KS; (4); Band; Jazz Band; Mrchg Band; Pep Band; School Musical; Rptr Nwsp; Var Golf; High Hon Roll; Hon Roll; U Of KS; Bus.

LUNDGREN, JENNIFER N; Blue Valley HS; Shawnee Mission, KS; (3); 7/275; Letterman Clb; Spanish Clb; Teachers Aide; Drill Tm; Flag Corp; JV Sftbl; High Hon Roll; NHS; Ed.

LUNT, SARA D; Field Kindley Mem Sr HS; Coffeyville, KS; (3); Dance Clb; French Clb; Drill Tm; Pom Pon; Tennis; Trk; Hon Roll; Jr NHS; NHS; Ntrl Hlprs Prog; KS ST U; Soc Wrk.

LUPHER, DOUG; Linn Schl; Greenleaf, KS; (4); 2/26; Church Yth Grp; FBLA; Scholastic Bowl; Thesps; Varsity Clb; Band; School Play; Ftbl; High Hon Roll; NHS; DARE Role Mdl; Schlr Bwl; Hnr Band; Gftd Prog; FBLA Awds; KS ST U; Engrng.

LUSK, JEREMY A; Wellington Sr HS; Wellington, KS; (2); Math Clb; Spanish Clb; JV Bsktbl; Hon Roll; Prfct Atten Awd.

LUTON, JEFF A; Riverton Schl; Riverton, KS; (2); 1/52; Art Clb; Church Yth Grp; FCA; Letterman Clb; Spanish Clb; Chorus; Trk; Hon Roll; Yoke Fllw; Shw Chr.

LUTSINGER, BEN H; El Dorado HS; El Dorado, KS; (2); JV Var Bsktbl; JV Var Tennis; Syracuse; Tchg/Coach.

LUTTRELL, BRYAN E; Chanute Sr HS; Chanute, KS; (2); French Clb; Library Aide; Ofcr Jr Cls; Bsktbl; Ftbl; Trk; Wt Lftg; Hon Roll; KS Univ; Phy Ed.

LUTTRELL, CURTIS H; Great Bend Sr HS; Great Bend, KS; (3); Church Yth Grp; Band; Jazz Band; Mrchg Band; Variety Show; Var L Crs Cntry; Var L Swmmng; Hon Roll; ST/INTL Lions Bnd.

LUTZ, ASHLEY; Hays HS; Hays, KS; (3); 30/250; Sec Sr Cls; JV Var Chrldng; JV Var Sftbl; Hon Roll; NHS; KSU; Elem Ed.

LUTZ, CHRIS; Eureka Jr Sr HS; Eureka, KS; (2); 10/60; Letterman Clb; Science Clb; Spanish Clb; SADD; Yrbk; Var Bsktbl; Var Ftbl; Trk; Wt Lftg; High Hon Roll; Baseball; Bowling; Notre Dame U; Acctng.

LUTZ, HEATHER; Spearville Jr Sr HS; Wright, KS; (1); Rptr 4-H; Chorus; Sftbl.

LUTZ, JASMINE; Jefferson West HS; Meriden, KS; (3); 18/80; Church Yth Grp; Capt Dance Clb; Pep Clb; Spanish Clb; SADD; Capt Drill Tm; Flag Corp; Sftbl; High Hon Roll; NHS; Lakeside Singers; KU; Psych.

LY, DUY T; Mc Pherson HS; Mc Pherson, KS; (2); French Clb; Scholastic Bowl; JV Socr; Hon Roll.

LY, HIEN H; Highland Park HS; Topeka, KS; (3); #1 in class; Debate Tm; Q&S; Band; Yrbk; VP Jr Cls; Chrldng; Socr; Cit Awd; High Hon Roll; NHS; Upward Bnd; U Of KS.

LY, JENNIFER; Wichita East HS; Wichita, KS; (4); 12/296; Church Yth Grp; Cmnty Wkr; Pres DECA; French Clb; Hosp Aide; VP Latin Clb; Office Aide; Teachers Aide; Hon Roll; NHS; KS Newman Coll; Occup Thrpy.

LYERLA, HEATHER D; Galena HS; Galena, KS; (3); FCA; FHA; Letterman Clb; School Play; Ofcr Jr Cls; Bsktbl; Sftbl; Vllybl; Hon Roll; NHS; Pittsburg ST Univ; Lawyer.

LYMAN, MINDY J; Hutchinson HS; Hutchinson, KS; (1); 1/300; Church Yth Grp; Key Clb; Pep Clb; Bsktbl; JV Sftbl; Vllybl; High Hon Roll.

LYNCH, AMANDA; Burlington HS; Burlington, KS; (1); 9/82; Church Yth Grp; Dance Clb; FBLA; FHA; Chrldng; Vllybl; High Hon Roll; Pres Acad Fit Awd.

LYNCH, KAYTEE A; Council Grove HS; Alta Vista, KS; (2); Art Clb; FBLA; NFL; SADD; Hon Roll; GAS Comm; The Roachies; Keyettes.

LYNCH, NICHOLAS A; Attica Public Schl; Attica, KS; (3); Boy Scts; Scholastic Bowl; Band; School Play; Var Bsbl; JV Bsktbl; High Hon Roll; NHS; Prfct Atten Awd; Eagle Sct; Band KS Ambass Of Music; Pre Med.

LYNCH, TINA M; Santa Fe Trail Jr HS; Olathe, KS; (1); Cmnty Wkr; Office Aide; School Play; Ed Yrbk; Mgr(s); Score Keeper; Hon Roll; Anml Care.

LYND, BROOKE; Trego Comm HS; Ellis, KS; (2); FHA; Letterman Clb; Pep Clb; Science Clb; SADD; JV Var Bsktbl; Var L Chrldng; Mgr(s); Var L Vllybl; Wt Lftg; Kayettes; T-Clb; Frgn Lang Clb; Elem Ed.

LYNN, ANDREW G; Olathe East Sr HS; Olathe, KS; (3); Boy Scts; Church Yth Grp; German Clb; Intnl Clb; Stage Crew; Nwsp; Bsktbl; JV L Ftbl; Hon Roll; Pres Acad Fit Awd; Awded Best Costume In Renaissance Festival; Ski Medal In CO Jr Time Trials; KU; Lawyer.

LYNN, R J; Olathe South Sr HS; Olathe, KS; (3); 131/408; Letterman Clb; Varsity Clb; Ofcr Stu Cncl; JV Bsktbl; Var Ftbl; Var Powder Puff Ftbl; Var Trk; Var Wt Lftg; JV Wrstlng; Hon Roll; Tech Stdnts Assn; TX A&M; Mech Engrng.

LYNN, RYAN; El Dorado HS; El Dorado, KS; (2); Debate Tm; French Clb; NFL; Scholastic Bowl; High Hon Roll; Hon Roll; Elect Engr.

LYNNES, RYAN; Piper HS; Kansas City, KS; (3); 8/90; Am Leg Boys St; Cmnty Wkr; Debate Tm; SADD; Teachers Aide; Rep Stu Cncl; Var L Bsbl; Var L Ftbl; Cit Awd; High Hon Roll; Ftbl All-League & All-KS Kicker 1st Team; Bsbl All-KS Hnrb Mntn; Amer Legion Bsbl; Schlr Ltr; Creighton; Engrng.

LYON, ASHLEY N; Emporia HS; Emporia, KS; (3); 45/289; Church Yth Grp; Cmnty Wkr; FCA; Pep Clb; SADD; Teachers Aide; Drill Tm; Sec Frsh Cls; Rep Soph Cls; Rep Jr Cls; K-1st Grd Sunday Schl Tchr; K-ST; Dieticn.

LYON, MELISSA; Sumner Acad; Kansas City, KS; (4); 56/194; French Clb; Pep Clb; Band; Mrchg Band; Pep Band; Chrldng; French Hon Soc; Hon Roll; NHS; Pres Schlr; Jr Assembly; KS City CC; Ed.

LYONS, DANIEL P; Shawnee Mission W Sr HS; Overland Park, KS; (2); 7/426; Boy Scts; Church Yth Grp; JV Wrstlng; High Hon Roll; 2 Acad Lttrs.

LYONS, JEREMY; Columbus HS; Columbus, KS; (4); FCA; 4-H; Natl FFA Org; Varsity Clb; Chorus; Yrbk; Bsktbl; Ftbl; Wt Lftg; Hon Roll; Chrch Yth Grp; Natl Grd Resrvs; PSU.

LYONS, ZACHARY S; Campus HS; Haysville, KS; (2); JV Bsbl; JV Wrstlng; Frgn Lang Span Ed; Wichita ST U; Engrng.

LYTLE, MATTHEW B; Blue Valley Northwest HS; Overland Park, KS; (3); 1/343; Teachers Aide; High Hon Roll; Stunts Plus Allstar Chrldr; Gym Coach.

MAANUM, ERIK L; Blue Valley Northwest HS; Overland Park, KS; (2); 293/409; Chess Clb; Bsktbl; Ftbl; Wt Lftg; U Of MO.

MAAS, CHRISTA A; Frankft HS; Frankfort, KS; (2); FHA; Quiz Bowl; SADD; Band; Chorus; Color Guard; Flag Corp; Mrchg Band; School Play; Hon Roll; Forensics.

MABRY, BEN M; Halstead HS; Sedgwick, KS; (1); 5/73; Church Yth Grp; Letterman Clb; Spanish Clb; Yrbk; Pres Frsh Cls; Rep Stu Cncl; JV Bsktbl; Var L Ftbl; Var L Trk; High Hon Roll.

MABRY, DOUGLAS; Halsted HS; Sedgwick, KS; (4); 10/53; Debate Tm; German Clb; Letterman Clb; Quiz Bowl; Scholastic Bowl; Teachers Aide; Band; Chorus; Mrchg Band; Pep Band; KAYS; Pittsburgh ST; Math Educ.

MAC ALPINE, MELISSA; Royal Valley HS; Hoyt, KS; (4); 2/54; Am Leg Aux Girls St; SADD; Capt Drill Tm; Pres Frsh Cls; Pres Soph Cls; Pres Jr Cls; Pres Sr Cls; Pres Stu Cncl; Var Bsktbl; Pres NHS; Ntrtnl Advsry Cncl Pres; Ed.

MACAN, VALERIE; Ottawa HS; Ottawa, KS; (3); Key Clb; Spanish Clb; Teachers Aide; Co-Capt Drill Tm; School Play; Variety Show; Powder Puff Ftbl; JV Tennis; Vllybl; High Hon Roll; Bus.

MACE, MEGAN N; Seaman Sr HS; Topeka, KS; (3); Church Yth Grp; Drama Clb; 4-H; Key Clb; Library Aide; NFL; Pep Clb; SADD; Teachers Aide; Thesps; KMEA ST Choir; Dist Choir Natl; Natl Hist Day; Regnl Solo Fest; ST Solo Fest; Baker Univ; Music Perfrmnc.

MACHTLEY, BRIAN J; Blue Valley Northwest HS; Shawnee Mission, KS; (3); Cmnty Wkr; Var L Ftbl; Trk; Wt Lftg; Hon Roll; NHS; Natl Yng Ldrsp Conf 96; Med Fld.

MACIAS, ANGIE T; Kapaun-Mt Carmel HS; Wichita, KS; (2); French Clb; Math Tm; SADD; Var Mgr(s); JV Score Keeper; JV Vllybl; Hon Roll; Marine Bio.

MACIAS, NANCY; Wabaunsee HS; Alma, KS; (4); Latin Clb; Pep Clb; Band; Chorus; Pep Band; Nwsp; Bsktbl; Swmmng; Vllybl; Hon Roll; Folkloric Clb; KAW Voc-Tech; Nrs.

MAC KAMUL, MELINA; South HS; Wichita, KS; (2); 54/302; Church Yth Grp; Debate Tm; NFL; Pep Clb; Q&S; Teachers Aide; Nwsp; Chrldng; Hon Roll.

MAC KAY, ALICIA N; Rose Hill HS; Douglass, KS; (3); Office Aide; Teachers Aide; JV Bsktbl; JV Sftbl; JV Vllybl; Hon Roll; Black Belt In Karate; KS Univ.

MACKEN, JARED G; Maize HS; Wichita, KS; (2); Church Yth Grp; Cmnty Wkr; FCA; Office Aide; Spanish Clb; Hon Roll; NHS; Jr Golf; Guest Stdnt Wichita ST U.

MACKEY, CYNDI L; Olath North HS; Olathe, KS; (4); 23/357; Church Yth Grp; Cmnty Wkr; Letterman Clb; Spanish Clb; Teachers Aide; Varsity Clb; Band; Mgr Lit Mag; Rep Jr Cls; Capt Bsktbl; Dist Schlr; KS Hnr Schlr; Pittsburg St Dean Schlr; KS ST Univ; Bus Admin.

MACKIE, DEIDRA D; Sumner Acad Of Arts & Science; Kansas City, KS; (4); 67/200; French Clb; Pep Clb; Chorus; High Hon Roll; Hon Roll; NHS; De Vry; Acctng; CMA.

MACOUBRIE, KIRBI J; Louisburg HS; Louisburg, KS; (3); Natl FFA Org; Pep Clb; Teachers Aide; Intrml Vllybl; High Hon Roll; Rodeo Team Rep Natl Finals Gillette 95 & Pueblo 96; Ft Scott CC; Chiropractic.

MADDEN, CURTIS M; Wellsville Jr Sr HS; Ottawa, KS; (2); 4-H; FBLA; Intnl Clb; SADD; Band; Mrchg Band; Pep Band; Var L Ftbl; Var L Trk; Wt Lftg; HS Tchr.

MADDEN, DEBORAH; Liberal HS; Liberal, KS; (4); Debate Tm; Drama Clb; HOBY; Sec Rep Key Clb; Chorus; Rep Frsh Cls; Rep Soph Cls; Var Capt Chrldng; Golf; NHS; State Frnscs; KS ST; Bus.

MADDEN, MICHAEL; Hoisington HS; Hoisington, KS; (4); 21/62; Am Leg Boys St; Church Yth Grp; Cmnty Wkr; Letterman Clb; Office Aide; Pep Clb; SADD; Varsity Clb; Chorus; Variety Show; Natrlst Clb; Ath Acad Recog; Barton Cnty CC; Phys Thpy.

MADDEN, RACHAEL L; Atchison Sr HS; Atchison, KS; (1); Church Yth Grp; Spanish Clb; Stage Crew; JV Bsktbl; Hon Roll; VFW Vol; Chrch Bible Schl Vol; U Of KS; Archaeologist.

MADDEN, ROBBY J; Washington HS; Kansas City, KS; (3); Church Yth Grp; FCA; FTA; Letterman Clb; ROTC; VICA; Color Guard; Ftbl; Tennis; Trk; Wrstlng ST Placer; His.

MADDOX, MELISSA A; Rose Hill HS; Andover, KS; (3); 4-H; FHA; Wt Lftg; 4-H Awd; High Hon Roll; Hon Roll; NHS; KS ST Univ; Law/Acctg.

MADDUX, ANDREW T; El Dorado HS; El Dorado, KS; (2); Church Yth Grp; Mrchg Band; Pep Band; JV Bsbl; Var Crs Cntry.

MADDUX, DAISEE M; El Dorado HS; El Dorado, KS; (3); Stat Bsbl; Stat Bsktbl; Crs Cntry; JV Tennis.

MADDUX, ROBERT; El Dorado HS; El Dorado, KS; (4); 13/150; Am Leg Boys St; Letterman Clb; Pep Clb; Mrchg Band; Orch; Pep Band; Pres Sr Cls; Var Crs Cntry; Var Trk; NHS; KS U; Scndry Ed.

MADDY, MATTHEW S; Southeast Saline Schl; Salina, KS; (2); 33/63; Acpl Chr; Band; Chorus; Mrchg Band; Pep Band; Wrstlng; Hon Roll; Mdrgls; Sub ST Vocal Slst.

MADER, LISA M; Kapaun-Mt Carmel HS; Wichita, KS; (3); Church Yth Grp; French Clb; Intrml Bsktbl; Var Golf; High Hon Roll; Art Awd; Regnl Golf Medalist 95; Med.

MADILL, ANGELA; Immaculata HS; Leavenworth, KS; (2); Pres Intnl Clb; Speech Tm; Thesps; Chorus; Church Choir; School Musical; School Play; Rep Stu Cncl; Var Chrldng; NHS; Piano Cmpsr Natl Guild; ST Soloist 1 Rtng; Msnry.

MADISON, ADAM C A; Horton HS; Everest, KS; (2); VP Church Yth Grp; FCA; Natl FFA Org; Pep Clb; SADD; Teachers Aide; Stage Crew; Yrbk; JV Ftbl; Var Wrstlng; Navy Pilot.

MADISON, ARTHUR R; Olathe East Sr HS; Olathe, KS; (4); Band; Mrchg Band; Pep Band; School Musical; Hon Roll; Vo-Tech Schlsp; On Job Nrs Trng; Johnson Cty CC; RN.

MADISON, KAREN; Iola Sr HS; Iola, KS; (4); 16/100; Am Leg Aux Girls St; Church Yth Grp; FCA; FBLA; Letterman Clb; Chorus; Swing Chorus; Var Trk; High Hon Roll; NHS.

MADL, TIFFANY; Baldwin HS; Wellsville, KS; (3); GAA; Letterman Clb; Math Tm; Varsity Clb; Rep Soph Cls; Rep Jr Cls; Ofcr Stu Cncl; JV Var Bsktbl; Var Chrldng; Var Sftbl; Natl Chldrs Assoc All Amrcn.

MADLOCK, SUMMER M; Sumner Acad; Kansas City, KS; (2); Key Clb; Latin Clb; Pep Clb; Quiz Bowl; Spanish Clb; Acpl Chr; Orch; High Hon Roll; NHS; Church Yth Grp; Macy Mnrts Med Prgm; Pre Med.

MADRON, MELISSA S; Caney Valley Jr Sr HS; Wann, OK; (3); 5/73; Church Yth Grp; Cmnty Wkr; FCA; FBLA; GAA; Teachers Aide; Nwsp; Ed Yrbk; Var Capt Chrldng; Trk; KAY Bd Mem; Acctng.

MADSON, DIONE N; Riverton Schl; Galena, KS; (2); Church Yth Grp; Drama Clb; FCA; FHA; Spanish Clb; Band; Orch; Sftbl; Vllybl; High Hon Roll; CBC; Ministry.

MAELZER, BROCK L; Kansas School Of The Deaf; Olathe, KS; (4); Drama Clb; Letterman Clb; Quiz Bowl; Varsity Clb; Ofcr Frsh Cls; Ofcr Soph Cls; Ofcr Jr Cls; Ofcr Stu Cncl; Bsktbl; Val; Deaf All-Amer Ftbl; Deaf All-Amer Bsktbl; KS Schlr Ath; Gallaudet Univ; Acctnt.

MAES, JOSHUA; Heights HS; Kechi, KS; (4); 41/212; Var Swmmng; Hon Roll; NHS; Pres Acad Fit Awd; KS Wesleyan Univ; Psych.

MAESTAS, JONATHAN; Hillcrest Schl; Cuba, KS; (1); Door To Door Mnstry.

MAGEE, CARISSA A; Topeka HS; Topeka, KS; (3); Band; Chorus; Mrchg Band; Pep Band; Sftbl; Vllybl; Hon Roll; Poems Pub; Social Work; Creative Wrtng.

MAGEE, D AMBER; Junction City HS; Ft Knox, KY; (4); 2/256; Band; Rep Jr Cls; Rep Sr Cls; Var Capt Chrldng; Powder Puff Ftbl; Sftbl; Gov Hon Prg Awd; NHS; Pres Schlr; Sal; Ladys Reading Club Scholar; Horseback Riding; KS ST Univ.

MAGERKURTH, STACY; Topeka HS; Topeka, KS; (4); 78/341; Drama Clb; NFL; Speech Tm; Thesps; Acpl Chr; Chorus; Jazz Band; School Musical; School Play; Variety Show; Hnrbl Mtn Topeka Perf Arts Ctr Yng Art Awds Drama; Choir Pres; Natl Qlfr/ST Champ Drmtc Intrptn; De Paul Univ; Acting.

MAGES, PAUL; Spearville Jr Sr HS; Spearville, KS; (3); 3/24; 4-H; Pep Clb; Quiz Bowl; Scholastic Bowl; Speech Tm; Teachers Aide; Chorus; School Play; Rep Stu Cncl; Var Chrldng; Upward Bound; Tx A&M U; Marine Bio.

MAGETTE, AMANDA N; Claflin Jr Sr HS; Claflin, KS; (3); Church Yth Grp; Letterman Clb; Math Tm; Pep Clb; Band; Chorus; Mrchg Band; Pep Band; School Play; Swing Chorus; Church Lector/Cantor; Sftbl Coach.

MAGGARD, JENNY; Marion HS; Lincolnville, KS; (3); 5/41; Church Yth Grp; Band; Var Bsktbl; Var Trk; Var Vllybl; High Hon Roll; Kiwanis Awd; NHS; Ntl Merit Ltr; Pres Acad Fit Awd; Pittsburg Coll; Nrsg/Med Fld.

MAGILL, KELLY A; Piper HS; Kansas City, KS; (3); Treas Drama Clb; FCA; SADD; Chorus; School Musical; Bsktbl; Chrldng; Trk; Hon Roll; NHS; Track/Bsktbl/Theatre/Music/Schlr/Chrldng Ltr; Theatre Clb Treas; Scrub Nurse.

MAGILL, MOLLY; Blue Valley HS; Olsburg, KS; (4); 1/17; Bus Profs of Am; FHA; FTA; Quiz Bowl; SADD; Teachers Aide; Band; Mrchg Band; Pep Band; Stage Crew; KS ST U; Acctng.

MAGINLEY, AMBER; Wabaunsee HS; Paxico, KS; (4); 2/36; 4-H; FHA; HOBY; VP Rep Natl FFA Org; Yrbk; Treas Sr Cls; Var Bsktbl; Var Chrldng; Var Vllybl; Treas Rep NHS; FFA WA Ldrshp Conf Chptr Rep; 4-H Cncl Pres; Cty Fair Queen; KS ST U.

MAGNUSON, BARRY; Smoky Valley HS; Lindsborg, KS; (4); 6/72; Bus Profs of Am; Church Yth Grp; FCA; Letterman Clb; Varsity Clb; Var L Ftbl; High Hon Roll; NHS; St Schlr; Hutchinson CC; Chem.

MAGNUSON, ESTHER; Central Jr HS; Lawrence, KS; (1); Church Yth Grp; 4-H; Band; Orch; Var L Trk; Var Capt Vllybl; High Hon Roll; Cert Achvt Ldrshp, Acad Excl Frm Myr Bob Moody; Ldrshp Tm Capt; Sci Olympd.

MAGNUSSON, KRISTINA; Winfield HS; Winfield, KS; (4); 1/144; VP Bus Profs of Am; Pres Church Yth Grp; Rep Jr Cls; Rep Sr Cls; Cit Awd; Gov Hon Prg Awd; High Hon Roll; NHS; Pres Schlr; Val; Winfield Yth Rally Comm; 1st Pl Interview Cmptn Bus Profs Amer St Ldrshp Conf, Top 12 Nation; Emporia ST Univ; Bus Ed.

MAGSAM, SPRING; Meade HS; Meade, KS; (3); 3/40; 4-H; Girl Scts; HOBY; Letterman Clb; Band; Treas Stu Cncl; Capt Chrldng; Vllybl; High Hon Roll; NHS; Law.

MAGWIRE, LANIE; Wallace Cty HS; Sharon Springs, KS; (2); FCA; Pep Clb; Var Chrldng; Var Pom Pon; JV Vllybl; Hon Roll; Strive For 5; Elem Ed.

MAH, CHRIS; Wichita North HS; Wichita, KS; (4); 30/230; JV Var Bsbl; JV Var Bsktbl; Ftbl; Butler Cty CC; Acctng/Admin.

MAHAN, KELLY; Maize HS; Wichita, KS; (3); Spanish Clb; Teachers Aide; JV Bsktbl; Mgr(s); JV Trk; Wt Lftg; High Hon Roll; Hon Roll; Lttrd Acad 2 Times.

MAHAN, MARK W; Kansas Cty Chrstn HS; Grandview, MO; (3); 5/35; Church Yth Grp; Drama Clb; Teachers Aide; Acpl Chr; Chorus; Church Choir; Bsktbl; High Hon Roll; Hon Roll; Natl Yng Ldrs Conf; NYLC Alumni Rep.

MAHIN, TARA; Jewell HS; Randall, KS; (2); FCA; FHA; Pep Clb; SADD; Band; Flag Corp; Pep Band; Var Chrldng; JV Vllybl; High Hon Roll; Ks U; Med.

MAHON, KRISTA M; Prairie View Jr Sr HS; La Cygne, KS; (2); 8/88; FHA; Quiz Bowl; Spanish Clb; Chorus; Church Choir; Jazz Band; Rep Frsh Cls; Treas Stu Cncl; JV Bsktbl; JV Sftbl; Tchng.

MAHONEY, CURTIS; Russell HS; Russell, KS; (4); 1/66; Am Leg Boys St; Pres Frsh Cls; Pres Soph Cls; Pres Jr Cls; Pres Stu Cncl; DAR Awd; NHS; Ntl Merit SF; Boy Scts; Debate Tm; KS Del US Snt Yth Pgm; KS Del HOBY Wrld Semnr; Eagle Sct; Grgtwn; Intl Law.

MAHONEY, JENNIFER K; Haven HS; Hutchinson, KS; (3); SADD; Band; Chorus; Mrchg Band; Pep Band; School Musical; Variety Show; Var Vllybl; Hon Roll; Wildcat Singers; Hutchinson CC; Bus; Acctng.

MAHONEY, JENNIFER S; Derby HS; Derby, KS; (4); 16/339; Teachers Aide; Co-Ed Yrbk; Rep Jr Cls; Sec Sr Cls; Ofcr Stu Cncl; Capt Pom Pon; JV Sftbl; High Hon Roll; NHS; Pres Acad Fit Awd; KS ST Univ; Bus Admin.

MAHONEY, MICHAEL A; Bishop Miege HS; Overland Park, KS; (3); 18/180; Boy Scts; Tennis; High Hon Roll; Hon Roll; NHS; Amigos De Las Amer; Math; Art.

MAHONEY, RYAN M; Russell HS; Dorrance, KS; (2); Church Yth Grp; CAP; Cmnty Wkr; VP Rep 4-H; Natl FFA Org; Color Guard; JV Wrstlng; 4-H Awd; Stdnt Aircraft Pilot; AF Acad; Pilot.

MAI, HONG T; Wichita East HS; Wichita, KS; (2); Office Aide; Hon Roll; WSU; RN.

MAI, JOEL; Lincoln Jr Sr HS; Lincoln, KS; (3); 5/27; Church Yth Grp; Letterman Clb; Varsity Clb; Bsktbl; Ftbl; Golf; Hon Roll; NHS; Peer Hlpr Grp; Whos Who Bsktbl; Sterling; Arch.

MAI, VI; Garden City Sr HS; Garden City, KS; (3); Latin Clb; Math Tm; High Hon Roll; Hon Roll; Acad Ltrng; US Achvt Acad All Amer Schlr.

MAIDMENT, BEVIN C; Blue Valley Northwest HS; Overland Park, KS; (2); Debate Tm; Teachers Aide; Band; Mrchg Band; High Hon Roll; Hon Roll; Var Ltr In Band; Var Ltr In Debate; Ice Skating; Neonatologist.

MAIER, ANDREA M; Pratt HS; Pratt, KS; (3); Pep Clb; Chorus; School Musical; Mgr(s); Sftbl; Vllybl; Hon Roll; Cmptd KS Jr Acad Sci Excl Rtng; Hnrd Pratt Schlsp Bnqt; Top Stdnt Awd 4 Tms/By Tchr 8 Tms; Ft Hays ST Univ; Sprts Med/PT.

MAILEN, DANA L; Shawnee Heights Sr HS; Topeka, KS; (2); Church Yth Grp; Hosp Aide; Library Aide; Intrml Vllybl; High Hon Roll; Kids Voting KS; Acad Ltr; Jr Olympics Vllybl USVBA; Organized Summer Sftbl; Med Profession.

MAJERLE, SHARON; Olathe South Sr HS; Olathe, KS; (3); 23/408; French Clb; Letterman Clb; Band; Drill Tm; Orch; School Musical; High Hon Roll; Hon Roll; NHS; Pres Acad Fit Awd; Outsdng Bio/Fr Stdnt; KS U; Scndry Ed.

MAK, GREG; Olathe East Sr HS; Overland Park, KS; (4); Church Yth Grp; Orch; Crs Cntry; Trk; Hon Roll.

MALAKNOV, MICHAEL; Blue Valley Northwest HS; Overland Park, KS; (3); German Clb; Intnl Clb; Scientfc Confs; Excl ST Wrtng Exam; ST Math Tm; UMKC; Med.

MALAN, CASEY; Garden City Sr HS; Garden City, KS; (4); Church Yth Grp; Ofcr Bsbl; Bsktbl; Ftbl; High Hon Roll; All WAC Quarterback; All WAC Pitcher; Butler Cty Comm Coll; Bus.

MALAN, DENISE N; Oswego HS; Pittsburg, KS; (2); 1/30; FHA; Math Tm; Quiz Bowl; Band; Pep Band; Treas Frsh Cls; Rep Stu Cncl; Var L Trk; High Hon Roll; NHS; Attnd KS Regnets Hnrs Acad; Art Awds; USAA Awd Wnnr.

MALAN, JENNIFER; Oswego HS; Radley, KS; (3); #1 in class; HOBY; Math Tm; Capt Scholastic Bowl; Band; Chorus; Mrchg Band; Lit Mag; Pres Soph Cls; Var Vllybl; NHS; Gifted Ed Pgm; Pittsburg ST U.

MALARKEY, CHRISTOPHER S; Shawnee Mission E Sr HS; Prairie Village, KS; (2); 146/500; Church Yth Grp; Cmnty Wkr; Model UN; Band; Jazz Band; Pep Band; Intrml Bsktbl; Var Crs Cntry; Var Trk; Hon Roll; Cross Cntry Track; KS ST; Soc Sci.

MALEK, DEVIN; Northern Valley HS; Long Island, KS; (3); 1/16; Pres Church Yth Grp; Cmnty Wkr; HOBY; Model UN; Capt Quiz Bowl; Scholastic Bowl; Spanish Clb; Band; Chorus; Mrchg Band; Natl Yng Ldrs Conf 95; Comm Svc; Purdue; Astrnt.

MALIA, LAURA K; Douglass HS; Douglass, KS; (2); 17/78; Chorus; School Musical; Stage Crew; Variety Show; Hon Roll.

MALICK, TARA L; Blue Valley Northwest HS; Overland Park, KS; (2); Debate Tm; Girl Scts; Hon Roll; Orng Blt Karate; Merit Awd Cmptr Prgmng; Merit Awd His; Law.

MALINAK, ANGELA C; St Thomas Aquinas HS; Overland Park, KS; (4); 184/250; Church Yth Grp; Drama Clb; French Clb; Treas Pres Ski Clb; School Play; Stage Crew; Variety Show; Lit Mag; Var Trk; Hon Roll; Natl Forensics League Sec; NFL Hnr Card Recpnt; U Of KS; BGS Theatre/Film.

MALKIN, BLAIRE; Wichita Collegiate Schl; Wichita, KS; (3); Cmnty Wkr; Debate Tm; Hosp Aide; Quiz Bowl; Scholastic Bowl; VP Temple Yth Grp; Chorus; Ed Lit Mag; JV Capt Sftbl; High Hon Roll; Sunday, Hebrew Schl Tchr; Fay Family Frnch Awd; Litrary Clb.

MALL, BRANDY; Sublette HS; Sublette, KS; (3); Art Clb; Church Yth Grp; Sec Drama Clb; Pres Pep Clb; Varsity Clb; Band; Chorus; Variety Show; Rptr Stu Cncl; NHS; KS U; Med.

MALLON, RHETT E; Olathe South Sr HS; Olathe, KS; (3); Boy Scts; Letterman Clb; Teachers Aide; JV Bsbl; Var Capt Ftbl; Var Trk; Var Capt Wrstlng; Hon Roll; Acctng/Engrng.

MALLORY, BECKY; Jewell HS; Jewell, KS; (4); Drama Clb; Office Aide; Chorus; Church Choir; Yrbk; Var JV Bsktbl; Var Chrldng; Pom Pon; Powder Puff Ftbl; Prfct Atten Awd; St Voclst; NCK Area Voc Schl; Bus.

MALLORY, TIM P; Topeka West HS; Topeka, KS; (3); Cmnty Wkr; French Clb; German Clb; Spanish Clb; SADD; Nwsp; Crs Cntry; Ftbl; Tennis; Hon Roll; Virology.

MALLOW, CHERIE D; Central Heights Sr HS; Rantoul, KS; (3); FCA; FBLA; Letterman Clb; Pep Clb; Spanish Clb; Phtg Yrbk; Chrldng; Trk; High Hon Roll; Church Yth Grp; Labette Cty CC; Grphc Art.

MALM, AMANDA; Valley Falls HS; Valley Falls, KS; (4); 3/36; Pres 4-H; FBLA; FHA; Quiz Bowl; School Play; 4-H Awd; Hon Roll; Treas NHS; Sal; Forensics; KS ST U; Engrng.

MALM, KATIE; Valley Falls HS; Valley Falls, KS; (1); 4-H; FBLA; FHA; School Play; Stage Crew; VP Frsh Cls; Bsktbl; Crs Cntry; Trk; Hon Roll; KS ST U; Engrng.

MALONE, BRIANA L; Seaman Sr HS; Topeka, KS; (3); Drama Clb; English Clb; Key Clb; Office Aide; SADD; Drill Tm; Swmmng.

MALONE, RICCI; Coldwater Jr Sr HS; Coldwater, KS; (2); 2/19; Debate Tm; FCA; FHA; GAA; Girl Scts; Quiz Bowl; Band; Chorus; Pep Band; Tennis; Law.

MALONE, RODNEY S; Mc Pherson HS; Mc Pherson, KS; (3); 14/150; Church Yth Grp; German Clb; Letterman Clb; Math Tm; Bsktbl; Capt L Socr; L Tennis; High Hon Roll; Hon Roll; NHS; Mission Trips Mexico & England; Tchr; Coach.

MALONEY, ADAM R; Protection Schl; Protection, KS; (1); Drama Clb; Quiz Bowl; VP Frsh Cls; Var Bsbl; Var Crs Cntry; Hon Roll; Tulsa OK; Fed Agnt.

MALOTT, NICOLE E; Washburn Rural HS; Topeka, KS; (3); 51/347; Cmnty Wkr; Var L Bsktbl; Var L Socr; Var L Vllybl; High Hon Roll; Ed.

MALSBURY, AMY; Jefferson Co North HS; Oskaloosa, KS; (4); FBLA; FHA; Library Aide; Office Aide; Sec Spanish Clb; SADD; JV Var Chrldng; Hon Roll; Forensics; Tns On Tchrs.

MALTBIA, HANSEL G; Washington HS; Kansas City, KS; (2); Church Yth Grp; Hon Roll; Church Usher Brd; Johnson Cty CC; Electrncs.

MALTHESEN, NOLAN S; Lyons HS; Lyons, KS; (2); 2/72; Church Yth Grp; FCA; Letterman Clb; Math Tm; JV Bsktbl; Var Ftbl; Var Trk; High Hon Roll; NHS; Pres Acad Fit Awd; Astronautical Engr/Chem.

MANDALA, VIVIAN; Goddard HS; Wichita, KS; (3); 33/180; Church Yth Grp; Chorus; Stage Crew; Variety Show; Yrbk; High Hon Roll; Emporia ST U; Art.

MANETH, LISTON; Otis Bison HS; Olmitz, KS; (3); Am Leg Aux Girls St; Church Yth Grp; GAA; SADD; School Play; Ed Rptr Nwsp; JV Vllybl; Hon Roll; KAYS; Sci Olympd; Int Dsgn.

MANGAN, CASSANDRA; Wellington Sr HS; Wellington, KS; (1); 11/178; Church Yth Grp; SADD; Band; Mrchg Band; Bsktbl; Trk; Vllybl; High Hon Roll; Jr NHS; Lions Awd & Plaque Wnnr; Radiologist.

MANGAN, PAUL W; Wellington Sr HS; Wellington, KS; (2); Church Yth Grp; Math Tm; JV Bsbl; Var Bsktbl; JV Var Ftbl; High Hon Roll; Jr NHS; Pres Acad Fit Awd.

MANGELS, ADAM; Ulysses HS; Ulysses, KS; (4); 1/93; Rep FBLA; Library Aide; School Musical; Variety Show; Ed Nwsp; Rptr Yrbk; Rep Stu Cncl; High Hon Roll; Pres NHS; U Of KS; Jrnlsm.

MANGELS, CHRIS; Stanton Co HS; Johnson, KS; (1); Bsktbl; Ftbl; Trk; Hon Roll.

MANGELSDORF, KATHRYN A; Shawnee Mission Northwest HS; Lenexa, KS; (4); 2/402; Cmnty Wkr; Key Clb; Service Clb; Thesps; Orch; School Musical; School Play; Stage Crew; Mgr Vllybl; Gov Hon Prg Awd; U Of KS; Theatre Dsgn.

MANGIMELLI, MOLLY; Acad Of Mt St Scholastica; Atchison, KS; (3); Girl Scts; Pep Clb; Chorus; JV Bsktbl; Var JV Vllybl; High Hon Roll; CYO; SIRCH Clb; Art.

MANGRUM, JASEN R; Shawnee Mission Nw Sr HS; Shawnee Mission, KS; (4); 70/450; Q&S; Sprt Ed Yrbk; Hon Roll; NHS; Pres Schlr; Johnson Cty CC; Jrnlsm.

MANION, LORI L; Maize HS; Wichita, KS; (2); 78/250; FCA; German Clb; Letterman Clb; Chorus; Church Choir; JV Var Bsktbl; Var Socr; JV Sftbl; JV Vllybl; Tabor Wichita ST.

MANION, MICHAEL K; Washburn Rural HS; Topeka, KS; (2); 45/395; JV Bsbl; JV Bsktbl; High Hon Roll; Page At KS House Of Reps; Medicine.

MANN, BRAD A; Riverton Schl; Riverton, KS; (4); 6/60; Am Leg Boys St; FCA; French Clb; FHA; Letterman Clb; Math Clb; Math Tm; Office Aide; Science Clb; Rep Soph Cls; Bsktbl All Conf, All Area, All St, All Trny, MVP; Natl Hnr Soc; KOPE-TV Ath Wk; PE.

MANN, JEFF M; Washburn Rural HS; Topeka, KS; (3); 64/351; Church Yth Grp; Band; Church Choir; Mrchg Band; Pep Band; Intrml Bsktbl; High Hon Roll; Numerous Chrch Choirs & Mission Trips; Bowling; U Of NE; Environmental Engr.

MANN, KALE; Norton Comm HS; Norton, KS; (3); 2/60; Band; Rep Frsh Cls; Rep Soph Cls; VP Jr Cls; VP Stu Cncl; Var L Ftbl; Var L Trk; L Var Wrstlng; High Hon Roll; NHS.

MANNING, CHAD W; Norton Comm HS; Norton, KS; (4); 12/42; DECA; Teachers Aide; Band; Pep Band; Pres Soph Cls; Ofcr Stu Cncl; Var L Ftbl; L Capt Trk; Wrstlng; High Hon Roll; Ft Hays ST Univ; Ecs.

MANNING, DE ANDRE N; Sumner Acad Of Arts & Science; Kansas City, KS; (2); Church Yth Grp; Spanish Clb; Band; Church Choir; Jazz Band; Ftbl; High Hon Roll; Hon Roll; Jr NHS; NHS; Arch Engr.

MANNING, MACKENZIE L; White Rock HS; Burr Oak, KS; (2); 4-H; Quiz Bowl; SADD; Chorus; L Var Bsktbl; L Var Chrldng; Var L Trk; Var L Vllybl; 4-H Awd; Hon Roll; ST Track Meet High Jump 3rd 94-; ST Vocal Solo I Rating 94-; ST Forensics Prose/Solo Act 94-95; Fashion/Modeling.

MANNS, JODI K; Pittsburg HS; Pittsburg, KS; (3); Church Yth Grp; FCA; FHA; Pres Science Clb; Spanish Clb; Church Choir; Bsktbl; Var L Sftbl; JV Var Vllybl; Hon Roll; Pittsburg ST Univ; Sprts Mdcn.

MANOR, MICHAEL E; Garden City Sr HS; Garden City, KS; (2); Computer Clb; Latin Clb; Science Clb; VICA; Band; Mrchg Band; Pep Band; Prin Hnr Roll; Voc Industrial Clbs Of Amer Natl Contestant; Architecture.

MANSHOLT, MONICA M; Wichita Heights HS; Wichita, KS; (2); Church Yth Grp; Cmnty Wkr; FCA; Spanish Clb; Thesps; Orch; School Play; Stage Crew; L Swmmng; High Hon Roll.

MANTHE, JOSEPH H; Leavenworth HS; Leavenworth, KS; (3); 58/370; Church Yth Grp; Acpl Chr; Band; Chorus; Church Choir; Mrchg Band; Pep Band; Ofcr Stu Cncl; JV Var Bsktbl; High Hon Roll; Teens As Tchrs; Acad Ltr; Sports Med; Phy Thrpst.

MANTOOTH, SHANNON M; Caney Valley Jr Sr HS; Caney, KS; (3); Spanish Clb; Phtg Nwsp; Phtg Yrbk; Mgr(s); High Hon Roll; NHS.

MANWARREN, CORTNEY G; Great Bend Sr HS; Great Bend, KS; (1); Church Yth Grp; Pep Clb; Band; Chorus; Pep Band; Variety Show; Bsktbl; JV Sftbl; Vllybl; Hon Roll; Lawyer.

MAPES, MINDY J; Northeast HS; Arma, KS; (1); 1/48; Band; Mrchg Band; Pep Band; JV Bsktbl; JV Chrldng; JV Sftbl; JV Vllybl; High Hon Roll.

MAPES, SHAE B; Newton Sr HS; Newton, KS; (4); Church Yth Grp; Cmnty Wkr; DECA; Letterman Clb; L Bsbl; L Ftbl; Stu Ldrshp Cncl; DARE; Comm Task Force; Allen Cty CC; Vet.

MAR, CATHRYN; Maize HS; Wichita, KS; (1); Church Yth Grp; FCA; Chorus; Church Choir; Variety Show; Bsktbl; Hon Roll.

MAR, CHRISTAN; Maize HS; Wichita, KS; (4); Am Leg Aux Girls St; Church Yth Grp; Q&S; Service Clb; SADD; Thesps; School Play; Nwsp; Hon Roll; NHS; Commnctns.

MARCEAU, TONY C; Wichita North HS; Wichita, KS; (2); Hosp Aide; Office Aide; Hon Roll; NHS; Acad Lttr; Biomed Prog; KS Univ; MD.

MARCELLINO, INGRID S; Mc Pherson HS; Mc Pherson, KS; (4); 87/189; Dance Clb; German Clb; Teachers Aide; Drill Tm; Flag Corp; Bsktbl; Pom Pon; Swmmng; Trk; Hmcmng Attenendant; U KS.

MARCHIN, KATHERINE L; Manhattan HS; Manhattan, KS; (2); Church Yth Grp; Cmnty Wkr; Drama Clb; FCA; Intnl Clb; Science Clb; Thesps; Ofcr Stu Cncl; Socr; High Hon Roll; Eco Ventures Co-Pres.

MARCOTTE, JAROD J; Andale HS; Colwich, KS; (2); Church Yth Grp; Letterman Clb; Spanish Clb; Pres Soph Cls; Rep Stu Cncl; JV Bsktbl; JV Ftbl; L Var Trk; High Hon Roll.

MARCOTTE, KENDRA; Wichita North HS; Wichita, KS; (3).

MARCRUM, HEATHER; Caldwell Jr Sr HS; Caldwell, KS; (1); 1/35; Church Yth Grp; FCA; Math Tm; Quiz Bowl; Scholastic Bowl; Speech Tm; Band; Jazz Band; Mrchg Band; Pep Band; Chem Engr.

MARCUM, LISA M; Washburn Rural HS; Topeka, KS; (4); 97/268; SADD; Band; Vllybl; High Hon Roll; Hon Roll; Washburn Univ; Legal Asstng.

MARDEN, MICHAEL MUSIL; Olathe East Sr HS; Olathe, KS; (2); Debate Tm; NFL; Spanish Clb; Mrchg Band; Ed Yrbk; Pres Frsh Cls; High Hon Roll; Church Yth Grp; Drama Clb; English Clb; Quest; Chosen Tchrs; Ldr Bd; Outsdng His Schlr.

MARGLIN, NICHOLAUS J; Blue Valley HS; Overland Park, KS; (2); JCL; Latin Clb; NFL; School Play; Cit Awd; High Hon Roll; Hon Roll; Forensic St Fstvl; Hghst Grd Latin II; UCLA; Film Dir.

MARGRAVE, BRANDY; J C Harmon HS; Kansas City, KS; (4); Art Clb; Cmnty Wkr; Office Aide; Science Clb; Teachers Aide; High Hon Roll; Hon Roll; NHS; Pres Schlr; Ldrshp; Pres Sr Commily; KCHC CC; Elem Art Tchr.

MARINTZER, JACOB R; Herndon Schl; Herndon, KS; (2); Church Yth Grp; Cmnty Wkr; Letterman Clb; Band; Chorus; Church Choir; Pep Band; School Musical; Swing Chorus; Bsktbl; Bggd Trophy Turkey Sprng 96; Master Anglr Awd Sprng 96.

MARINTZER, JUSTIN G; Herndon Schl; Herndon, KS; (3); Church Yth Grp; Cmnty Wkr; Letterman Clb; Band; Chorus; Church Choir; Pep Band; School Musical; Swing Chorus; Pres Frsh Cls; Hntr; Fshrmn; Fort Hays Univ; Wldlfe Bio.

MARK, LACIE J; Maize HS; Maize, KS; (2); Church Yth Grp; Spanish Clb; Teachers Aide; Band; JV Bsktbl; JV Tennis; High Hon Roll; Hon Roll; NHS; Pres Acad Fit Awd; Acad Ltr; Sports Med/PT.

MARK, TAMMY; Udall HS; Udall, KS; (4); Sec Treas FHA; Speech Tm; Teachers Aide; Band; Pep Band; Cit Awd; High Hon Roll; Hon Roll; KS Newman; Med.

MARKERT, MELISSA; Maranatha Acad; Lenexa, KS; (3); Cmnty Wkr; School Play; Yrbk; Pres Soph Cls; Rep Stu Cncl; Var Chrldng; Var Trk; High Hon Roll; Hon Roll; Pres Acad Fit Awd; Trck Chrstn Chrctr Awd; Mssns Wrk; Multi Yrs Lstd; Dntstry.

MARKHAM, AARON P; Lawrence HS; Lawrence, KS; (2); Boy Scts; Church Yth Grp; Band; Mrchg Band; JV Trk; Hon Roll.

MARKHAM, JOHN; Manhattan HS; Manhattan, KS; (4); Am Leg Boys St; Debate Tm; FCA; Teachers Aide; JV Intrml Bsktbl; L Ftbl; L Trk; Intrml Vllybl; Intrml Wt Lftg; Hon Roll; Vol Frfghtr; Hntng, Fshng; KS ST; Pre-Vet.

MARKLEY, MELINDA; Shawnee Mission N HS; Merriam, KS; (3); Church Yth Grp; Key Clb; Pep Clb; Q&S; Band; Mrchg Band; Rptr Nwsp; Var Socr; Hon Roll; NHS; KU.

MARKLEY, MISTI; Sylvan Unified HS; Lincoln, KS; (4); 2/16; Church Yth Grp; Math Tm; Pep Clb; SADD; Teachers Aide; Band; Chorus; Flag Corp; Mrchg Band; Pep Band; Hutchinson CC; Lndscp Arch.

MARKUS, AUBREY RAELYNNE; Hutchinson HS; Hutchinson, KS; (4); Church Yth Grp; Cmnty Wkr; Pep Clb; Red Cross Aide; Service Clb; Teachers Aide; High Hon Roll; Hon Roll; Cncl Mem HERO Club; Yng Adult Advy Bd Pub Lib 4 Yrs; Kndgtn/1st Grd Tchr Temple Bapt Church; Mc Pherson Coll; Bus Ed/Rel.

MARNETT, JASON; Goddard Jr HS; Goddard, KS; (1); Chess Clb; Teachers Aide; JV Socr; JV Trk; Hon Roll; Prfct Atten Awd; Sci.

MARNEY, COLEEN M; Blue Valley HS; Shawnee Mission, KS; (4); 44/230; Church Yth Grp; Office Aide; Pres SADD; Chorus; Church Choir; School Musical; Hon Roll; NHS; Won By One Chrstn Clb; Johnson Cty CC; Elem Ed.

MAROLF, AMANDA L; Shawnee Heights HS; Berryton, KS; (1); Hosp Aide; Pep Clb; SADD; Jazz Band; Orch; Stage Crew; Variety Show; High Hon Roll; Teach Piano Lessons.

MAROLF, GINA; Seaman Sr HS; Topeka, KS; (3); Debate Tm; English Clb; French Clb; FBLA; Pres FHA; Key Clb; NFL; SADD; High Hon Roll; NHS; CO U Boulder; Law.

MARQUEZ, DANIELLE R; Shawnee Heights HS; Topeka, KS; (1); Rep Frsh Cls; Rep Soph Cls; Ofcr Stu Cncl; High Hon Roll; Dance; Care Co Mem; Spirit Clb; U Of KS.

MARRON, GEORGE L; Bishop Ward HS; Kansas City, KS; (3); 32/103; Yrbk; Var Bsktbl; Var Ftbl; Hon Roll; KS Univ.

MARSELUS, CARRIE B; Shawnee Mission N HS; Overland Park, KS; (4); 64/360; Church Yth Grp; Pep Clb; Spanish Clb; Teachers Aide; Church Choir; Orch; High Hon Roll; Hon Roll; NHS; N Cntrl Bible Col; Elem Ed.

MARSH, AMBER; El Dorado HS; El Dorado, KS; (4); 5/155; Am Leg Aux Girls St; Church Yth Grp; Cmnty Wkr; Debate Tm; Speech Tm; Pres Stu Cncl; Chrldng; Pom Pon; High Hon Roll; NHS; Grinnell Coll; Poltcl Sci.

MARSH, AMY; Waverly HS; Waverly, KS; (4); Cmnty Wkr; Debate Tm; Drama Clb; Pep Clb; Quiz Bowl; Band; Chorus; School Musical; VP Soph Cls; VP Jr Cls; WINGS; KS ST U; Chem Engr.

MARSH, REBECCA; Hiawatha HS; Hiawatha, KS; (4); Pres Church Yth Grp; Sec Drama Clb; Thesps; Capt Drill Tm; School Musical; School Play; Swing Chorus; Capt Pom Pon; Cit Awd; NHS; Ricks Coll; Elem Ed.

MARSHALL, JESSICA; El Dorado HS; El Dorado, KS; (3); 20/150; Church Yth Grp; Debate Tm; NFL; Quiz Bowl; Speech Tm; SADD; Band; School Musical; Hon Roll; KS Rgnts Hons Acad.

MARSHALL, JULIE; Basehor Linwood HS; Basehor, KS; (2); Cmnty Wkr; FBLA; GAA; Quiz Bowl; Spanish Clb; Pres SADD; Chorus; Ed Nwsp; Var Chrldng; Gym; Miami Cty Classic All Acad Team; Acad Excl Awd; Jrnlsm; Pol Sci.

MARSHALL, KEITH L; Galena HS; Galena, KS; (1); Church Yth Grp; FBLA; Scholastic Bowl; JV Bsktbl; Var Crs Cntry; Var L Trk; High Hon Roll; Amateur Ath Union; Babe Ruth Bsbl Lguie; SE KS Grand Prix Rnrs Clb.

MARSHALL, KIMBERLY M; Kapaun-Mt Carmel HS; Wichita, KS; (2); #31 in class; Church Yth Grp; Debate Tm; French Clb; Church Choir; Yrbk; Var Trk; JV Vllybl; High Hon Roll; NHS; Prfct Atten Awd.

MARSHALL, LACI L; El Dorado HS; El Dorado, KS; (3); Church Yth Grp; FCA; Letterman Clb; Office Aide; SADD; Varsity Clb; Church Choir; Intrml Powder Puff Ftbl; Var Swmmng; JV Vllybl; LIFE; KS ST U; Psych.

MARSHALL, NEIL T; Valley Ctr HS; Valley Center, KS; (3); 1/166; Debate Tm; Intnl Clb; Quiz Bowl; Scholastic Bowl; Service Clb; Spanish Clb; Speech Tm; Ed Rptr Nwsp; Crs Cntry; Trk.

MARSHALL, STACY L; Clifton-Clyde HS; Clifton, KS; (3); 16/38; Am Leg Aux Girls St; Church Yth Grp; Drama Clb; 4-H; FBLA; Natl FFA Org; Office Aide; Pep Clb; Speech Tm; Teachers Aide; Vet Med.

MARSHALL, STARLA A; Nickerson HS; Nickerson, KS; (3); Mgr(s); Wrstlng; Nrsng.

MARSHALL, WHITNEY; Shawnee Mission E Sr HS; Shawnee Mission, KS; (2); Math Tm; Band; Mrchg Band; Pep Band; Stage Crew; High Hon Roll; Physics.

MARSTALL, DAVID; Kapaun-Mt Carmel HS; Wichita, KS; (4); Church Yth Grp; Debate Tm; French Clb; NFL; Science Clb; Chorus; Crs Cntry; Trk; High Hon Roll; Ntl Merit Ltr; Marquette Univ; Rlgn Tchr.

MARTELL, BERNADINE T; Lawrence HS; Lawrence, KS; (2); 80/681; Church Yth Grp; Cmnty Wkr; Hosp Aide; Spanish Clb; Chorus; Gov Hon Prg Awd; High Hon Roll; Hon Roll; Flwshp Of Chrstn Stdnts; Excl In Art Awd; 2nd Pl Awd Sci Fair; Music; Vllybl; Bsktbl; Tchng.

MARTEN, BRANDY L; Topeka West HS; Topeka, KS; (3); 4/260; Cmnty Wkr; Drama Clb; Service Clb; VP Spanish Clb; SADD; Drill Tm; School Musical; School Play; Variety Show; JV Bsktbl; Top 1% Cls Frosh; T W Plyr; Nom St Sprtng Actrs; KS Univ; Intl Bus.

MARTEN, TINA; Onaga HS; Onaga, KS; (2); 4/45; Church Yth Grp; Girl Scts; Pep Clb; SADD; Band; Drm Mjr(t); Mrchg Band; Pep Band; Yrbk; Treas Frsh Cls; U Of KS; Psych.

MARTENS, STACY; Winfield HS; Winfield, KS; (2); Church Yth Grp; Pep Clb; Rep Frsh Cls; Rep Stu Cncl; Chrldng; Emporia ST; Chld Care.

MARTIN, ABIGAIL L; Yates Ctr HS; Yates Center, KS; (3); 9/56; FCA; FHA; Letterman Clb; Office Aide; SADD; Band; Chorus; Pres Stu Cncl; Var Bsktbl; Stat Ftbl; Elem Ed.

MARTIN, ADRIAN L; Derby HS; Derby, KS; (3); 68/400; Drama Clb; FCA; SADD; Thesps; Acpl Chr; School Musical; Var L Chrldng; Var L Ftbl; Var Trk; NHS; 3 Times ST Chmpn Drftng Grd Lvl; Dist Choir 94; OK ST U; Archtctr.

MARTIN, AMANDA; Columbus HS; Hallowell, KS; (4); 13/92; VP Art Clb; Bus Profs of Am; Church Yth Grp; Pres FCA; FHA; Sec Sr Cls; Ofcr Stu Cncl; Capt Var Bsktbl; Hon Roll; NHS; Pittsburg ST U; Bus Mgmt.

MARTIN, ANDREA; Winfield HS; Burden, KS; (4); 65/185; Ofcr Am Leg Aux Girls St; Cmnty Wkr; Pres 4-H; Model UN; Drm Mjr(t); Chorus; Church Choir; Chrldng; 4-H Awd; Hon Roll; Cowley Cty 4-H Ambssdr; N Amer Jr Limousin Assn; KS Jr Limousin Assn Treas; Hutchinson CC; Ag.

MARTIN, ANNA M; Onaga HS; Onaga, KS; (2); Church Yth Grp; 4-H; Yrbk; JV L Vllybl; Wt Lftg; Cit Awd; 4-H Awd; High Hon Roll; Hon Roll; Prfct Atten Awd; 95 Silver Mdlst AAU Jr Olympcs Wghtlftng; KS Univ; O/P Thrpy.

MARTIN, APRIL; Conway Springs HS; Conway Springs, KS; (2); 2/56; Church Yth Grp; FHA; HOBY; Band; Ofcr Stu Cncl; Var Bsktbl; Var Trk; Var Vllybl; High Hon Roll; St Bnk Hnrs; 1st Team All League Vllybl, Bsktbl; Cardinalaires; Bus.

MARTIN, BRANDI J; Galena HS; Galena, KS; (2); FHA; Letterman Clb; Bsktbl; Sftbl; Vllybl; Wt Lftg; Hon Roll; NHS; Bowling; Bus.

MARTIN, BRANDON T; Protection Schl; Protection, KS; (2); Debate Tm; Letterman Clb; Speech Tm; Band; Chorus; Mrchg Band; Orch; Pep Band; School Musical; School Play; KS Ambassador Of Music-European Tour; K-101 Classic Bowl; Comp.

MARTIN, BRIE; Shawnee Heights Sr HS; Topeka, KS; (4); Intnl Clb; JA; Pep Clb; SADD; Teachers Aide; Sec Drill Tm; Ed Yrbk; Hon Roll; SAE Clb; All Amer Schlr; KU; Zlgy.

MARTIN, BROOKE E; Wichita Heights HS; Wichita, KS; (4); 35/245; Church Yth Grp; SADD; Chorus; Sec Treas Stu Cncl; Mgr Sftbl; Hon Roll; NHS; Pres Acad Fit Awd; Madrigals; Womens Ensemble; Peer Ldrshp; Wichita ST Univ.

MARTIN, BRYON P; Hartford HS; Neosho Rapids, KS; (2); Letterman Clb; L Var Bsktbl; L Var Ftbl; L Var Trk; High Hon Roll; Hon Roll.

MARTIN, CARESSA; Hugoton HS; Hugoton, KS; (2); 11/89; Church Yth Grp; Cmnty Wkr; Debate Tm; FCA; NFL; Spanish Clb; Pep Band; School Play; NHS; Prfct Atten Awd; Elem Ed.

MARTIN, EREN NALANI; Goddard HS; Goddard, KS; (3); Cmnty Wkr; SADD; Pres Band; School Play; Sec Jr Cls; Sec Sr Cls; Var Tennis; High Hon Roll; NHS; Prfct Atten Awd; Harvard; Marine Bio.

MARTIN, ERIN M; Andale HS; Andale, KS; (1); Church Yth Grp; Quiz Bowl; Spanish Clb; Band; Flag Corp; Mrchg Band; Pep Band; Crs Cntry; Trk; High Hon Roll; Ath Lttr Awd Cross-Cntry; Hnrbl Mention ST Awd HS Hlth-Emporia ST Test; Med.

MARTIN, JENNALEE L; Russell HS; Russell, KS; (1); Dance Clb; Key Clb; Math Tm; SADD; Bsktbl; Trk; Vllybl; Wt Lftg; High Hon Roll; Pres Acad Fit Awd; Finals ST Trck; Sec/Treas Key Club; U Of KS; Math/Bus Accntng.

MARTIN, JESSICA; Trinity Catholic HS; Hutchinson, KS; (3); 1/18; Church Yth Grp; NFL; Band; Drill Tm; Pres Jr Cls; Var Bsktbl; Var Trk; Var Vllybl; High Hon Roll; NHS; Commnctns.

MARTIN, KELLY; Goddard HS; Colwich, KS; (2); Spanish Clb; JV Bsktbl; Chrldng; High Hon Roll; NHS; Homeless Shelter Vol; Spcl Olympics Vol; Dr.

MARTIN, KIM; Blue Valley North HS; Leawood, KS; (4); 7/167; Art Clb; Church Yth Grp; Girl Scts; Model UN; Q&S; Ofcr Spanish Clb; Ed Yrbk; High Hon Roll; Hon Roll; NHS; Duke Univ; Marine Bio.

MARTIN, KIMARIE A; Riverton Schl; Riverton, KS; (3); #3 in class; Math Clb; Science Clb; Band; Orch; Vllybl; Hon Roll.

MARTIN, KIMBERLY; Shawnee Mission Northwest HS; Lenexa, KS; (3); Church Yth Grp; Cmnty Wkr; Dance Clb; Hosp Aide; Letterman Clb; Math Clb; Pep Clb; SADD; Teachers Aide; Varsity Clb; Explrng Chldhd Ofcr; Dvnshr Dncr Rnsnc Fstvl; Dnc Elec Prfrmng Trp; U Of AZ; Dnc Ther.

MARTIN, KRISTA; Leavenworth HS; Leavenworth, KS; (4); 68/350; Bus Profs of Am; Church Yth Grp; Computer Clb; Office Aide; SADD; Teachers Aide; Bsktbl; JV Var Sftbl; JV Vllybl; KS Wt Lftg; KS Mrt Schlr; Bus Profs Of Amer Schlr; Office & Tech Internship Pgm; KS ST U; Ath Trainer.

MARTIN, LINDSAY; Clay Ctr Cmty HS; Clay Center, KS; (4); 15/100; Am Leg Aux Girls St; Church Yth Grp; Science Clb; Band; Chorus; Mrchg Band; Pep Band; Bsktbl; L Chrldng; L Crs Cntry; Mssn Ed Trip; Crmnlgy.

MARTIN, MICHAEL; Clay Ctr Cmty HS; Clay Center, KS; (2); 1/150; Art Clb; Church Yth Grp; Debate Tm; Drama Clb; 4-H; Science Clb; Speech Tm; Thesps; School Play; Golf; St Envirothon Wnnr; St Wildlife Mgmt Habitat Wnnr; U Of KS; Envrnmntl Chem Engrng.

MARTIN, NATHAN; Bucklin Schl; Ford, KS; (3); 2/50; 4-H; Quiz Bowl; Speech Tm; Band; Pep Band; Nwsp; Yrbk; Intrml Bsktbl; Intrml Golf; Cit Awd; Livestck Judgng KS St Chmpn Team; KS ST U; Animal Sci.

MARTIN, PAM; Liberal HS; Liberal, KS; (3); French Clb; FHA; Quiz Bowl; Band; Jazz Band; Mrchg Band; Pep Band; High Hon Roll; Hon Roll; NHS; Awd In Bnd For Solo; KS St Univ; Bus.

MARTIN, PHILLIP; Bucklin Schl; Ford, KS; (1); 4-H; Mrchg Band; Pep Band; Ofcr Frsh Cls; Bsktbl; Golf; 4-H Awd; Jr Babe Ruth Bsbl.

MARTIN, REBEKKA A; Herndon Schl; Herndon, KS; (2); 4-H; Scholastic Bowl; Speech Tm; Chorus; Rep Stu Cncl; Var L Chrldng; 4-H Awd; High Hon Roll; VP Church Yth Grp; Math Tm; Stu Of Month; OK ST Univ Ger By Satellite Hnr Stu; NE Draft Horse & Mule Assn Qn; KS ST; Ag; Vet Sci.

MARTIN, RICHIE; Larned HS; Larned, KS; (2); 14/100; Church Yth Grp; Band; Chorus; Jazz Band; Mrchg Band; Pep Band; Hon Roll; Pre Vet Med.

MARTIN, ROMARTA M; Washington HS; Kansas City, KS; (2); Church Yth Grp; Cmnty Wkr; Dance Clb; Pep Clb; ROTC; Chorus; Church Choir; Bsktbl; Ftbl; Hon Roll; Sunday Schl Sec; U Of AR; Engr.

MARTIN, SHANNON; Shawnee Heights HS; Topeka, KS; (4); Church Yth Grp; Cmnty Wkr; L Debate Tm; HOBY; Spanish Clb; Acpl Chr; Chorus; Band; Church Choir; Pep Band; Gymnstcs Instr; Youth Cncl; Youth Rep To Israel; Youth Rep Worship; Youth Choir; U Of KS; Botany.

MARTIN, SHATOJA; Sumner Acad Of Arts & Science; Kansas City, KS; (3); Treas Key Clb; NFL; Speech Tm; Church Choir; Orch; Ed Yrbk; Ofcr Jr Cls; Hon Roll; NHS; Church Yth Grp; Kansas City Yth Symph; Xavier Univ; Law.

MARTIN, STEVE A; Bishop Miege HS; Roeland Park, KS; (3); 20/200; Church Yth Grp; FCA; 4-H; Letterman Clb; Service Clb; Spanish Clb; Varsity Clb; Jazz Band; Ofcr Bskbl; Bsktbl.

MARTIN, SUSAN A; Manhattan HS; Manhattan, KS; (3); Church Yth Grp; Drama Clb; FCA; French Clb; Intnl Clb; Pep Clb; Quiz Bowl; Church Choir; School Play; Ed Yrbk; Manhattan Nwspr Yth Page Rptr; Piano/Dance/Tennis Lessons; GATE Prgm; Tchng.

MARTIN, TYLER N; Council Grove HS; Council Grove, KS; (3); Church Yth Grp; 4-H; FBLA; Key Clb; Pep Clb; SADD; Band; Chorus; Church Choir; Jazz Band; X Ray Tech.

MARTINEZ, ADRIANNE T; Goodland HS; Goodland, KS; (2); FHA; GAA; SADD; Chorus; Drill Tm; School Musical; JV Chrldng; JV Powder Puff Ftbl; JV Vllybl; Hon Roll; Grph Arts.

MARTINEZ, FELIX; Garden City Sr HS; Garden City, KS; (2); Church Yth Grp; Drama Clb; Crs Cntry; Tennis; Wt Lftg; Hon Roll; Biking; Manhattan Chrstn Coll.

MARTINEZ, MATT J; Hutchinson HS; Hutchinson, KS; (1); Spanish Clb; JV Bsbl; Intrml Ftbl; Intrml Wt Lftg; Hon Roll; Prfct Atten Awd; HIP; Wichita ST U; Mgmt.

MARTINEZ, NICOLE D; Wichita North HS; Wichita, KS; (4); Girl Scts; Spanish Clb; Ofcr Jr Cls; Hon Roll; Prfct Atten Awd; Friends Univ; Radio Tech.

MARTINEZ, ROBERT L; Junction City HS; Fort Riley, KS; (2); 56/257; Church Yth Grp; Computer Clb; ROTC; Color Guard; Drill Tm; Hon Roll; Amer Legion Military Excl; Nssar, Bronze ROTC Medal, Mst Outstndg Cadet; Pres Ftnss Awd; West Point; Med & Military.

MARTINO, LOUIS ANTHONY; Pittsburg HS; Pittsburg, KS; (3); Am Leg Boys St; Church Yth Grp; Q&S; Spanish Clb; Band; Ed Nwsp; Crs Cntry; Trk; High Hon Roll; Debate Tm; Span Natl Exam; U Of KS; Psych; Bus.

MARTIR, JACQUELINE; Topeka HS; Topeka, KS; (2); Model UN; Drill Tm; Swmmng; Tennis; Japanese Clb; Mrktng.

MARTLING, BRIAN W; Maize HS; Wichita, KS; (4); 14/232; Debate Tm; German Clb; Math Tm; NFL; Quiz Bowl; Scholastic Bowl; Speech Tm; Band; Chorus; Mrchg Band; Knowledge Masters Cmptn; Delta Epsilon Phi; Wichita ST U; Aerospace Engr.

MARTZALL, DAVID M; Douglass HS; Douglass, KS; (3); 13/64; Boy Scts; Chess Clb; Pep Clb; Teachers Aide; Band; JV Bsktbl; JV Var Ftbl; JV Wrstlng; High Hon Roll; Hon Roll; Wrtng; Frncs; Actng; K ST; Lawyer.

MARVIL, SUSAN; Olathe East Sr HS; Lenexa, KS; (2); Church Yth Grp; Cmnty Wkr; Dance Clb; Pep Clb; Spanish Clb; Rep Frsh Cls; Chrldng; High Hon Roll; NHS; Spanish NHS; Fshn Mrchndsng Clb; Natl Dance Cmptn; U KS; Med.

MARVIN, SHAWN C; Hoisington HS; Hoisington, KS; (3); Am Leg Boys St; Cmnty Wkr; Letterman Clb; Quiz Bowl; Teachers Aide; Varsity Clb; Chorus; School Musical; Var L Crs Cntry; Var L Trk; Tch Yng Kkds Sprtsmnshp/Tm Play; BCCC; PE.

MARX, DARCIE L; Lenora HS; Clayton, KS; (1); Intnl Clb; Pep Clb; SADD; School Play; Sec Frsh Cls; Hon Roll; Pres Awd For Ed Imprvmnt.

MASON, ADRIANNE; Wyandotte HS; Kansas City, KS; (4); Church Yth Grp; Cmnty Wkr; Computer Clb; Girl Scts; Church Choir; Yrbk; Ofcr Stu Cncl; Hon Roll; Jr NHS; Prfct Atten Awd; Med Careers Clb; KS Hon Schlr; Univ KS Crowell Book Awd; Bible Clb; Donnelly Coll; Nrsng.

MASON, BILLY D; Ashland HS; Ashland, KS; (2); Church Yth Grp; Var Bsktbl; Var Ftbl; Hon Roll; A-Clb; Rodeo; St In Ftbl & Bsktbl Same Yr; Fort Hays St Univ.

MASON, CHRISTINE R; F L Schlagle HS; Kansas City, KS; (3); Art Clb; VP SADD; Ed Lit Mag; Hon Roll; Vet.

MASON, GARIAN D; Wichita Southeast HS; Wichita, KS; (4); Church Yth Grp; Church Choir; Ftbl; Trk; Phy Thrpst.

MASON, JAMIE; Turner HS; Kansas City, KS; (2); Band; Treas Jr Cls; Ofcr Stu Cncl; Chrldng; Cit Awd; High Hon Roll; Hon Roll; NHS; Prfct Atten Awd; Pres Schlr; KU; Plastic Surgery.

MASON, JULIE; Hugoton HS; Hugoton, KS; (2); 1/88; Church Yth Grp; FCA; Spanish Clb; Chorus; Stat L Mgr(s); Hon Roll.

MASON, LA DONNA C; Wichita West HS; Wichita, KS; (3); 33/283; Church Yth Grp; Library Aide; Hon Roll; Jr NHS; Prfct Atten Awd; Hnrble Mtn; KSU; Arch.

MASSEY, MANDY; Eureka Jr Sr HS; Eureka, KS; (4); 9/65; Am Leg Aux Girls St; 4-H; Teachers Aide; Band; Sec Jr Cls; Sec Sr Cls; Rptr Stu Cncl; 4-H Awd; High Hon Roll; NHS; Pittsburg ST; Phrmcy.

MASSEY, MELISSA M; Rose Hill HS; Rose Hill, KS; (3); Church Yth Grp; FHA; Office Aide; Teachers Aide; Bsktbl; Sftbl; Vllybl; Hon Roll; KAYS Club.

MASSEY, REBECCA J; Campus HS; Wichita, KS; (3); Intnl Clb; Science Clb; SADD; Teachers Aide; Chorus; Swing Chorus; Wt Lftg; High Hon Roll.

MASSOTH, REBEKAH L; Cimarron HS; Cimarron, KS; (4); 1/50; Pres 4-H; Band; Chorus; Rep Jr Cls; Ofcr Sr Cls; Var L Tennis; Var L Trk; Pres Schlr; St Schlr; Val; Piano Accompanist To Band & Chorus; St Paino Festival; St Solos & Ensembles; KS ST Univ; Acctng; Piano Perf.

MASTERSON, JEFF D; Washburn Rural HS; Topeka, KS; (2); Boy Scts; Church Yth Grp; Computer Clb; Debate Tm; NFL; Pep Clb; Band; Jazz Band; Mrchg Band; Orch; Pioneer Drum/Bugle Corps; MIT; Physics.

MASTERSON, PARC W; Olathe East Sr HS; Overland Park, KS; (2); Letterman Clb; Teachers Aide; JV Ftbl; Trk; Wt Lftg; Hon Roll; Pres Schlr.

MASUD, FARIHAH M; Wichita East HS; Wichita, KS; (2); Debate Tm; Drama Clb; French Clb; NFL; Socr; French Hon Soc; Hon Roll; Rep NHS; Intnl Baccalaureate Prgm; Pedtrcn/Psychtrst/Wrtr.

MATAS, TIM P; Chapman HS; Abilene, KS; (4); 13/115; Scholastic Bowl; Pres SADD; Chorus; Pres Soph Cls; VP Stu Cncl; Var L Ftbl; Var Trk; Var L Wrstlng; High Hon Roll; NHS; Jr & Sr Mixed Ensmbl; U NE Lincoln; Mech Engr.

MATEJ, ERICA M; Wichita East HS; Wichita, KS; (2); Math Clb; Spanish Clb; SADD; Teachers Aide; Orch; Stat Var Mgr(s); Hon Roll; NHS.

MATHES, ANDREW R; Dodge City HS; Dodge City, KS; (3); Boy Scts; Church Yth Grp; SADD; Band; JV Ftbl; Var Trk; Ntl Merit Ltr; Debate Tm; Model UN; Phtgrphy; Presbytery Of Southern KS Yth Cncl; KAYS; PT.

MATHES, APRYL; Washburn Rural HS; Topeka, KS; (4); 20/292; Dance Clb; English Clb; Library Aide; SADD; Teachers Aide; Band; Capt Drill Tm; Mrchg Band; Pep Band; Variety Show; Hmcmng Queen Candidate; Prom Chm; Spec Olympics Vol; KS ST Univ.

MATHES, TRAVIS L; Hutchinson HS; Hutchinson, KS; (3); Am Leg Boys St; Art Clb; 4-H; Office Aide; Chorus; Ftbl; 4-H Awd; Hon Roll; Slvr Ky Schlstc Art Awd; K-ST.

MATHEW, SELIA; Wichita Northwest HS; Tulsa, OK; (3); Church Yth Grp; Tennis; Wt Lftg; Hon Roll; OK St Tnns Champn 94-95; MO Vly Sectnl Tnns Champn 94; Natl Levl Tnns Playr; Music; Piano; Ballet; Pre-Med.

MATHEWS, KIM M; Blue Valley Northwest HS; Overland Park, KS; (3); Cmnty Wkr; FCA; Latin Clb; Var Bsktbl; Powder Puff Ftbl; JV Swmmng; Wt Lftg; High Hon Roll; Hon Roll; NHS.

MATHEWS, STEPHANIE D; Campus HS; Haysville, KS; (3); SADD; Teachers Aide; Rptr Nwsp; Ofcr Stu Cncl; Bsktbl; Hon Roll.

MATHEY, ANNE N; Blue Valley HS; Leawood, KS; (3); 47/215; Art Clb; Cmnty Wkr; JCL; Latin Clb; Q&S; Ed Nwsp; JV Tennis; High Hon Roll; NHS; Ntl Merit Ltr.

MATHIA, COLLEEN; Immaculata HS; Leavenworth, KS; (4); 9/48; Cmnty Wkr; JA; Red Cross Aide; School Play; Stage Crew; Phtg Yrbk; Co-Capt Chrldng; Sftbl; High Hon Roll; Hon Roll; U Of KS; Speech Pathology.

MATHIAS, JEFF M; Syracuse Jr Sr HS; Syracuse, KS; (2); Acpl Chr; Chorus; Pres Frsh Cls; VP Soph Cls; Ofcr Stu Cncl; JV Var Bsktbl; JV Var Crs Cntry; Var L Golf; Hon Roll; NHS.

MATHIPRAKASAM, MURTHY; Shawnee Mission E Sr HS; Overland Park, KS; (4); Computer Clb; German Clb; Math Clb; Math Tm; Natl Beta Clb; Hon Roll; NHS; Ntl Merit SF; Lcl Engrng Frm Intrnshp; Tutr Clcls, Cmptr Sci; Cmptr Sci.

MATLACK, JUSTIN; Burrton Schl; Burrton, KS; (1); Church Yth Grp; Debate Tm; FCA; Pep Clb; Speech Tm; Band; Mrchg Band; Pep Band; School Musical; Stage Crew.

MATLOCK, MARCI M; Chanute Sr HS; Chanute, KS; (3); Church Yth Grp; FCA; FBLA; GAA; Pep Clb; SADD; Teachers Aide; Varsity Clb; Sftbl; Swmmng; Dntstry.

MATNEY, DENNIS L; Turner HS; Kansas City, KS; (2); Boy Scts; SADD; JV Var Ftbl; Hon Roll; CO Univ; Forestry.

MATSON, DANIEL R; Centralia Schl; Vermillion, KS; (2); Pres 4-H; Letterman Clb; Natl FFA Org; Science Clb; Chorus; School Musical; School Play; Stage Crew; JV Var Ftbl; Var L Trk; FFA Judging Team; FFA Proficiency Awds.

MATTER, KATRINA; Jewell HS; Jewell, KS; (3); Church Yth Grp; Sec FCA; FHA; HOBY; Band; Ed Yrbk; L Chrldng; Var Vllybl; High Hon Roll; NHS; Sterling Coll.

MATTHEWS, BRYAN R; Liberal HS; Liberal, KS; (3); Debate Tm; Stage Crew; Hon Roll; OK ST; Tv Broadcasting.

MATTHEWS, KRISTEN; Garden City Sr HS; Garden City, KS; (2); Debate Tm; SADD; Crs Cntry; Sftbl; Trk; Hon Roll; KS St Univ; Crim Just.

MATTHEWS, NICK R; Clearwater HS; Clearwater, KS; (2); L Ftbl; L Golf; L Trk; Hon Roll; Sports Med.

MATTHEWS, ROBIN; Olathe North Sr HS; Olathe, KS; (3); 50/415; Church Yth Grp; 4-H; Science Clb; Acpl Chr; Church Choir; Orch; School Musical; Variety Show; Ofcr Jr Cls; JV Crs Cntry; Chrch Organist; Gardeners Of Amer Charter Mem Olathe Clb; Environmental Sci; Music.

MATTHIAS, CHAD E; Midway Schl; Atchison, KS; (3); Church Yth Grp; Letterman Clb; Quiz Bowl; JV Ftbl; Hon Roll; NHS.

MATTIX, LILY G; Northern Heights HS; Reading, KS; (4); 6/53; Church Yth Grp; FCA; FHA; Girl Scts; Natl FFA Org; NFL; Pep Clb; Scholastic Bowl; Spanish Clb; Band; Girl Sct Trip England Peak 95; Marine Bio.

MATTOCKS, SHELLEY M; Great Bend Sr HS; Great Bend, KS; (2); 50/263; Church Yth Grp; Girl Scts; Band; Chorus; Mrchg Band; Pep Band; Variety Show; High Hon Roll; Kayettes Org; Girl Scts Silver Awd; Acad & Band Ltrs; Acctng.

MATUS, SHANNA M; Shawnee Mission N HS; Shawnee Mission, KS; (3); Pep Clb; Drill Tm; Var Chrldng; Hon Roll.

MAUCH, JULIE A; Smoky Valley HS; Lindsborg, KS; (1); Bus Profs of Am; Church Yth Grp; FCA; FHA; Pep Clb; Band; Mrchg Band; Pep Band; JV Bsktbl; Vllybl; Lindsborq Swedish Dncrs; KS Univ; Acct.

MAUK, ADAM W; Douglass HS; Rose Hill, KS; (3); 30/65; FCA; Science Clb; Band; Chorus; Jazz Band; Phtg Rptr Yrbk; Rep Stu Cncl; Var Crs Cntry; Var Wrstlng; Hon Roll; Teens As Tchrs; Show Choir; Marine Bio.

MAUNE, JASON D; Syracuse Jr Sr HS; Syracuse, KS; (2); Church Yth Grp; Dance Clb; 4-H; Mrchg Band; VP Soph Cls; Var Bsktbl; Var Ftbl; Var Trk; Bus.

MAUPINS, KAIA D; F L Schlagle HS; Kansas City, KS; (1); Office Aide; Hon Roll; Nrsng Aide; Cosmetology.

MAUS, MONICA; Frontenac Jr Sr HS; Frontenac, KS; (4); 19/38; Am Leg Aux Girls St; FHA; FTA; Girl Scts; Office Aide; Pep Clb; Spanish Clb; Teachers Aide; Rptr Nwsp; Rptr Yrbk; Pittsburg ST U.

MAX, JOSH B; Blue Valley Northwest HS; Overland Park, KS; (1); Temple Yth Grp; JV Crs Cntry; JV Wrstlng; Hon Roll; MD/VET.

MAXEY, KAY R; Andale HS; Andale, KS; (1); Church Yth Grp; Spanish Clb; SADD; Band; Chorus; Mrchg Band; Pep Band; Crs Cntry; Trk; Hon Roll.

MAXIMUK, SARAH L; Blue Valley HS; Overland Park, KS; (4); 20/223; Letterman Clb; Q&S; Ed Yrbk; Capt L Bsktbl; Capt L Socr; Var L Vllybl; Hon Roll; NHS; Pres Schlr; Stu Ath Woman Of The Yr; U Of NE.

MAXON, DAVE A; Blue Valley Northwest HS; Shawnee Mission, KS; (3); Boy Scts; Cmnty Wkr; Band; Mrchg Band; Pep Band; JV Ftbl; Hon Roll; NHS; Egl Sct; Frgn Exch Stdnt Australia; Comm Rgby Tm; TX A&M; Marine Sci.

MAXSON, MICHAEL D; Labette Co HS; Edna, KS; (2); FCA; Letterman Clb; Science Clb; Crs Cntry; Trk; Hon Roll; KS; Med.

MAXWELL, JEFF P; Rose Hill HS; Derby, KS; (3); Church Yth Grp; Cmnty Wkr; Letterman Clb; Varsity Clb; Intrml Bsktbl; JV Var Ftbl; Intrml Vllybl; Hon Roll; Prfct Atten Awd; Lift-A-Thn; CYO Vlybl; PE Instr/Coach/Hist Tchr.

MAXWELL, KEVIN E; Washburn Rural HS; Topeka, KS; (2); FCA; Socr; Hon Roll; U Of KS.

MAXWELL, LAKEISHA S; Washington HS; Kansas City, KS; (2); Hon Roll; Memphis ST; Attrny/Accntng.

MAXWELL, NOAH D; Goddard HS; Wichita, KS; (1); Church Yth Grp; JV Bsbl; JV Bsktbl; High Hon Roll; Pres Schlr.

MAXWELL, STACY R; Topeka West HS; Topeka, KS; (1); Band; Mrchg Band; Orch; Pep Band; Hon Roll; Topeka Yth Wind Ensmbl; Sprt Club; Cvl War Rnctr; Coll/Comm/Fine Arts.

MAY, ADAM; Andover HS; Andover, KS; (3); 4/157; Debate Tm; French Clb; HOBY; NFL; Pres Frsh Cls; Pres Soph Cls; Pres Jr Cls; Rep Stu Cncl; Var L Crs Cntry; Trk.

MAY, APRIL M; Halstead HS; Newton, KS; (3); Model UN; SADD; Orch; School Play; Vllybl; Hon Roll; Washburn Univ; Surgeon.

MAY, DERRICK; Garden Plain Jr Sr HS; Goddard, KS; (4); Chess Clb; Pres Church Yth Grp; Spanish Clb; Pep Band; Treas Soph Cls; Capt L Bsktbl; Hon Roll; Pratt CC; Automotive Tech.

MAY, DUSTIN L; Larned HS; Pawnee Rock, KS; (2); Acpl Chr; Band; Stage Crew; Wt Lftg; Hon Roll; Received Presdntl Acad Ftnns Awd 92; Took Part In Beginnings-Elite Vocal Group Of 8 Singers; Law-Civil Litigations.

MAY, JEREMY; Tipton HS; Tipton, KS; (3); HOBY; Math Tm; Capt Quiz Bowl; Rep Stu Cncl; Var L Bsktbl; Var L Ftbl; Var L Golf; Var L Trk; 4-H Awd; Sec NHS; Schlr Athlete Awd; KS Farm Bureau Ldrshp Seminar; Yth Task Force; Notre Dame; Engrng.

MAY, JEREMY R; Wellington Sr HS; Wellington, KS; (2); Debate Tm; Speech Tm; Var Tennis; JV Wrstlng; High Hon Roll; Hon Roll; Jr NHS.

MAY, JOHN N; Andale HS; Colwich, KS; (1); Church Yth Grp; Cmnty Wkr; Letterman Clb; Quiz Bowl; Scholastic Bowl; Spanish Clb; SADD; Bsktbl; Ftbl; High Hon Roll; Teens/Tchrs; Stock Mrkt Club; Wichita West Urban Bsbl; Twin Rvrs Bsbl; Notre Dame; MD.

MAY, MARTIN P; Lawrence HS; Lawrence, KS; (2); Boy Scts; Church Yth Grp; Science Clb; Band; Jazz Band; Mrchg Band; Orch; Pep Band; Variety Show; Rptr Yrbk; Bio Clb; Sci Olympiad; GATE Pgm; KS Univ; Music; Sci.

MAY, MICHELLE L; Conway Springs HS; Conway Springs, KS; (3); Drama Clb; Office Aide; SADD; Stage Crew; Yrbk; Rep Frsh Cls; Rep Soph Cls; Rep Jr Cls; Rep Sr Cls; Stat Ftbl; ST Bnk Hnrs Dinner For Top 5 Of Cls; Emporia ST Univ; Bus.

MAY, REBEKAH; St Thomas Aquinas HS; Lenexa, KS; (3); Acpl Chr; School Musical; Var Chrldng; Diving; Powder Puff Ftbl; Hon Roll; Show Choir Zero Hr; Fine Arts.

MAY, STEPHANIE S; Great Bend Sr HS; Great Bend, KS; (2); Pep Clb; Spanish Clb; JV Bsktbl; JV Tennis; High Hon Roll; Pres Acad Fit Awd; Kayettes; Shw Qrtr Hrses Natl Lvl; KS Qrtr Hrs Yth Assn Pres; KS Univ; Pre-Med.

MAY, TRACY M; Garden Plain Jr Sr HS; Goddard, KS; (3); 1/34; Treas Church Yth Grp; Red Cross Aide; Scholastic Bowl; Sec Spanish Clb; SADD; Capt Drill Tm; VP Pres Stu Cncl; JV Var Bsktbl; High Hon Roll; NHS; Jr Class Attndt Ftbll Hmcmng; Mdl Of Exc In Offc Practc; Bus Admin.

MAY, TRICIA L; Topeka West HS; Topeka, KS; (4); Pres English Clb; FTA; Q&S; Scholastic Bowl; Teachers Aide; Acpl Chr; Ed Lit Mag; High Hon Roll; NHS; Ntl Merit SF; U Of KS; Engl Educ.

MAYANS, MICHAEL J; Bishop Carroll Catholic HS; Wichita, KS; (2); Church Yth Grp; Quiz Bowl; Spanish Clb; Ofcr Stu Cncl; Crs Cntry; Trk; High Hon Roll.

MAYER, CARI; Marysville HS; Marysville, KS; (4); 9/85; Am Leg Aux Girls St; 4-H; Service Clb; School Play; Yrbk; Treas Stu Cncl; Var L Bsktbl; Var L Trk; High Hon Roll; Church Yth Grp; Twrlr; KS Natl Cath Frnscs Lge Tres; Photo-Pblshd Photos; KS ST U; Bus.

MAYER, TERESA L; Louisburg HS; Louisburg, KS; (3); Letterman Clb; Chorus; Variety Show; Lit Mag; Hon Roll; NHS; Ntl Merit Ltr; U Of KS.

MAYES, KELLEE; Wyandotte HS; Kansas City, KS; (4); #8 in class; Church Yth Grp; Cmnty Wkr; Debate Tm; Drama Clb; Intnl Clb; Pep Clb; Church Choir; Ofcr Sr Cls; Bsktbl; Chrldng; Martin Luther King Edctnl Awd; Vlybl 1st Team All-League, 2nd Team All-Kansan; Lane Coll; Bio.

MAYFIELD, DANNY A; Halstead HS; Halstead, KS; (3); Ofcr Jr Cls; Hon Roll; Stu Of Month Awds; Art Awd Of Excl For Limestone Sculpture; Acad Achvmt Ltr.

MAYFIELD, MARC; Derby HS; Douglass, KS; (4); 5/312; Math Tm; Quiz Bowl; Scholastic Bowl; High Hon Roll; NHS; Pres Schlr; St Schlr; Fnd/Engr Schlrshps KS ST Univ; KS ST Univ.

MAYNARD, DUANE A; Burlington HS; Burlington, KS; (4); 6/80; Church Yth Grp; Scholastic Bowl; Band; Mrchg Band; Pep Band; Golf; High Hon Roll; Hon Roll; NHS; Prfct Atten Awd; Wichita St Univ; Elec Eng.

MAYO, MEGAN D; Garden City Sr HS; Garden City, KS; (2); Church Yth Grp; VP 4-H; Sec FHA; HOBY; VP Key Clb; Band; JV Var Bsktbl; JV Sftbl; 4-H Awd; Gov Hon Prg Awd; KS ST U.

MAYO, SEAN; Washburn Rural HS; Topeka, KS; (4); 21/300; Cmnty Wkr; VP JA; VP SADD; Acpl Chr; School Musical; Treas Stu Cncl; Var Capt Ftbl; Gov Hon Prg Awd; NHS; St Schlr; Outstdng Yth Selected By Area Nwsp; Homcmng King; Srv Awd Selected By Gov & City Cncl; Baylor Univ; Pre-Med.

MAYS, AARON; Topeka HS; Topeka, KS; (3); Am Leg Boys St; JA; Teachers Aide; Thesps; Chorus; School Musical; School Play; Stage Crew; Variety Show; Hon Roll; Bus; Theatre.

MAZOUCH, GREG J; Great Bend Sr HS; Great Bend, KS; (3); Am Leg Boys St; Church Yth Grp; Rep German Clb; Pep Clb; Acpl Chr; Variety Show; VP Stu Cncl; JV Var Bsbl; JV Var Bsktbl; High Hon Roll.

MC ADAM, JUSTIN P; Kapaun-Mt Carmel HS; Wichita, KS; (3); 17/170; Quiz Bowl; Scholastic Bowl; Spanish Clb; Teachers Aide; L Ftbl; L Trk; High Hon Roll; NHS; Prfct Atten Awd; Piano.

MC ADDO, MOLLY R; Topeka HS; Topeka, KS; (3); 17/323; Church Yth Grp; Cmnty Wkr; Dance Clb; Spanish Clb; Church Choir; Drill Tm; Jazz Band; JV Sftbl; High Hon Roll; Hon Roll; Lvl 9 Gymnstcs Reg Prtcpnt; Mscnshp Adtns/Gld Piano 5 Yrs; Pre Med.

MC ADOO, MOLLY; Topeka HS; Topeka, KS; (3); 17/323; Church Yth Grp; Cmnty Wkr; Dance Clb; Spanish Clb; Drill Tm; Jazz Band; Diving; Sftbl; High Hon Roll; Hon Roll; Classical Pianist; Competitive Gymnast; Youngest Chrch Elder; Med.

MC AFEE, BROOKE A; Wamego HS; Belvue, KS; (2); FCA; FHA; Letterman Clb; Pep Clb; Service Clb; Spanish Clb; SADD; Chorus; Bsktbl; Gym; KS ST Univ; Phy Therapy.

MC ALEXANDER, MELYNDE S; Basehor Linwood HS; Basehor, KS; (4); 13/121; Church Yth Grp; Hist FBLA; FTA; Q&S; Treas Service Clb; Nwsp; VP Stu Cncl; High Hon Roll; NHS; Pres Acad Fit Awd; Smr Cmp Vol 4 Yrs; Msns Trp Jamaica; Mst Vlbl Rnchhnd Smr Cmp; Park Coll; Scndry Eng/Lit.

MC ALLISTER, CASEY; Paola HS; Paola, KS; (4); 1/124; Am Leg Aux Girls St; Cmnty Wkr; Drama Clb; Pres FCA; Office Aide; SADD; Band; Chorus; Drill Tm; Mrchg Band; All St Hnrb Mntn Vllybl Plyr 95; Med.

MC ANANY, STEPHANIE C; Shawnee Mission W Sr HS; Overland Park, KS; (2); Intnl Clb; Hon Roll.

MC ANULLA, KEVIN M; Great Bend Sr HS; Great Bend, KS; (4); 24/218; Am Leg Boys St; Boy Scts; Pep Clb; Spanish Clb; School Play; Variety Show; Phtg Yrbk; Pres Sr Cls; Acpl Chr; Eagle Sct; KS Univ; Genetic Engrng.

MC ARTHUR, TROY ALDEN; Jefferson West HS; Meriden, KS; (2); Cmnty Wkr; Letterman Clb; Teachers Aide; Varsity Clb; Var L Bsbl; Var L Ftbl; High Hon Roll.

MC ASEY, VERONICA; Jackson Heights HS; Holton, KS; (2); 1/37; Church Yth Grp; Rptr FBLA; Rptr Nwsp; Yrbk; Pres Frsh Cls; Rep Stu Cncl; JV Bsktbl; L Var Crs Cntry; L JV Trk; Hon Roll; 1st Pl St & Dist FBLA Conts; All Amer Schlr Awd.

MC ATEE, CARRIE; Newton Sr HS; North Newton, KS; (4); Am Leg Aux Girls St; Church Yth Grp; French Clb; Key Clb; Model UN; Band; Chorus; Drill Tm; Nwsp; Hon Roll; KS Hnr Schlr; U KS.

MC BRIDE, ALICIA A; Stockton HS; Stockton, KS; (2); Debate Tm; FHA; Quiz Bowl; Rep Chorus; JV Bsktbl; Var Trk; JV Vllybl; High Hon Roll; Hon Roll; Comp Engr.

MC BRIDE, JENNIFER L; Basehor Linwood HS; Bonner Springs, KS; (2); Hon Roll; Very Intrstd Poetry; Phtgrphy; Wrkng Sml Chldrn; KS U; Tchr/Phtgrphr.

MC BRIDE, JENNIFER R; Central Heights Sr HS; Lane, KS; (1); Pep Clb; Science Clb; Spanish Clb; Chorus; Drill Tm; Swing Chorus; Rptr Nwsp; Intrml Trk; High Hon Roll; Hon Roll; Cetologist/Mar Bio.

MC BURNEY, MEGHAN E; Douglass HS; Douglass, KS; (4); 8/42; Church Yth Grp; FCA; Speech Tm; Teachers Aide; Chorus; Church Choir; Drill Tm; School Musical; Swing Chorus; Variety Show; KS St Univ; Arch.

MC CABE, AUSTIN E; Olathe North Sr HS; Olathe, KS; (2); Ofcr Drama Clb; Spanish Clb; Rep Thesps; Band; Chorus; Mrchg Band; School Musical; School Play; Rptr Nwsp; Hon Roll; Var Lttr Ernd Drama; Best Sppring Actrs Soiuth Pcfc Elctd Pub Rel Offcr Of Next Yrs DC; Elem Ed/Thrtr.

MC CABE, JUSTIN M; Olathe East Sr HS; Olathe, KS; (2); Band; Jazz Band; Mrchg Band; Pep Band; Hon Roll.

MC CABE, SARAH H; Salina HS South; Salina, KS; (2); Teachers Aide; Sftbl; Hon Roll; Stu Cncl Comm; Wrtng; Soc Sci.

MC CAFFREY, MICHAEL; Manhattan HS; Manhattan, KS; (3); 99/426; Treas Am Leg Boys St; Boy Scts; Band; Chorus; Jazz Band; Mrchg Band; Pep Band; School Musical; High Hon Roll; NHS; Soc Fr Presrvtn/Encourgmt Barbrshp Qrtet Singing In Amer; KS ST; Fin.

MC CALLOP, MELISSA A; Wichita South HS; Wichita, KS; (3); Church Yth Grp; DECA; Library Aide; Church Choir; Rptr Yrbk; Treas Jr Cls; Hon Roll; Cntrl Region VP KS DECA; Multi-Yr Listee; WSU; Bus; Acctng; Banking.

MC CALLOP, NICOLE R; Sumner Acad Of Arts & Science; Kansas City, KS; (2); Church Yth Grp; Key Clb; Latin Clb; Pep Clb; Spanish Clb; Band; NHS; Yth Union Dist VP; Aeronautics.

MC CANN, JENNY; Mc Pherson HS; Mc Pherson, KS; (2); Church Yth Grp; Letterman Clb; NFL; SADD; Color Guard; Drill Tm; Ed Yrbk; Ofcr Soph Cls; Var Chrldng; Hon Roll; KAYS; Scndry Ed.

MC CARTY, JUSTIN R; Labette Co HS; Mound Valley, KS; (2); Chess Clb; FCA; Letterman Clb; Pres Frsh Cls; Bsktbl; Ftbl; Trk; Hon Roll.

MC CASKEY, JENNIFER; Mulvane Sr HS; Mulvane, KS; (3); FCA; FHA; Spanish Clb; SADD; Band; Flag Corp; Mrchg Band; Hon Roll; NHS; Prfct Atten Awd; Wichita ST; Elem Educ.

MC CASKEY, MARY; Spring Hill HS; Spring Hill, KS; (3); 12/86; Debate Tm; 4-H; Letterman Clb; SADD; Var L Bsktbl; JV Sftbl; Var Trk; JV Vllybl; Hon Roll; Bsktbl All-Frontier League Hnrb Mntn.

MC CAY, AMANDA S; Williamsburg Schl; Williamsburg, KS; (2); Church Yth Grp; Cmnty Wkr; FCA; Natl FFA Org; Pep Clb; Speech Tm; Teachers Aide; Band; Chorus; Church Choir; Selctd To Play In All Star Eight-Man Ftbl Marchng Band 96; Recvd II At St On Clarinet Solo 95-96; Emporia ST U; Musical Therapy.

MC CHRISTIAN, JACKIE; Arkansas City HS; Arkansas City, KS; (3); FCA; GAA; SADD; Ofcr Soph Cls; Ofcr Jr Cls; Golf; Sftbl; Wt Lftg; Hon Roll; ST Sftbl Chmpnshp Tm; All Ark Vly Sftbl 2nd Tm 2nd Bsmn; Law.

MC CLANAHAN, BRIAN T; Anderson Cty Jr Sr HS; Garnett, KS; (2); Art Clb; Generation Singers; Art Tchr.

MC CLASKEY, MARK T; South Haven Schl; Geuda Springs, KS; (3); Natl FFA Org; Pep Clb; Scholastic Bowl; Speech Tm; Band; Mrchg Band; Pep Band; School Musical; VP Frsh Cls; Pres Soph Cls; Arkansas City Cmnty Band; Cowley Cty Juco; Radio Brdcstng.

MC CLELLAN, KELLIE; Pretty Prairie HS; Pretty Prairie, KS; (4); 1/20; Church Yth Grp; FCA; Quiz Bowl; Chorus; School Play; Bsktbl; Vllybl; Gov Hon Prg Awd; High Hon Roll; Val; Slvr, Brnz & Gld Math Lg Cntst; Natl Eng Mrt Awd; Gld, Slvr & Brnz Htchnsn Comm JC Math Ctst; KS ST U; Mass Comms.

MC CLELLAN, TY A; Glasco HS; Glasco, KS; (2); 1/13; Church Yth Grp; Cmnty Wkr; Quiz Bowl; Pres Frsh Cls; Pres Soph Cls; Ofcr Stu Cncl; L Bsktbl; High Hon Roll; NHS; L Ftbl; DARE Spksmn/Role Mdl; KS ST Univ; Arch.

MC CLINTIC, KRISTEN M; Wichita Southeast HS; Wichita, KS; (2); 73/408; Church Yth Grp; French Clb; SADD; Rep Frsh Cls; Ofcr Stu Cncl; JV Socr; Hon Roll; U Of KS; Neonatal Nrsng.

MC CLINTICK, CHAD; Eureka Jr Sr HS; Eureka, KS; (2); #1 in class; Church Yth Grp; HOBY; Quiz Bowl; Red Cross Aide; Spanish Clb; Chorus; School Play; Rep Stu Cncl; Var Bsktbl; High Hon Roll; U KS.

MC CLINTON, FREDA M; Junction City HS; Junction City, KS; (3); Key Clb; Trk; Wt Lftg; High Hon Roll; Hon Roll; Komomantyns; Abstinence Clb; SWEAT; Early Chldhd Ed.

MC CLOSKEY, BRYAN; Maur Hill Prep Schl; Atchison, KS; (4); 2/46; Boy Scts; Capt Math Tm; School Play; Ed Nwsp; Treas Sr Cls; Var Bsktbl; JV Bsktbl; High Hon Roll; Sec NHS; Pres Acad Fit Awd; U Of KS.

MC CLUER, MEAGAN A; Olathe South Sr HS; Olathe, KS; (4); Art Clb; Pep Clb; Teachers Aide; Drill Tm; Orch; Phtg Nwsp; Phtg Yrbk; Phtg Lit Mag; Pom Pon; Trk; KS Univ.

MC CLURE, ALLISON; Tescott HS; Tescott, KS; (4); 1/13; Am Leg Aux Girls St; Quiz Bowl; Band; Yrbk; Capt L Bsktbl; L Trk; L Capt Vllybl; High Hon Roll; NHS; Val; Fort Hays ST U; Spch Pthlgy.

MC CLURE, ANN; Douglass HS; Douglass, KS; (2); 10/80; Pres FHA; Letterman Clb; Scholastic Bowl; Sec Science Clb; Sec Soph Cls; Chrldng; JV Sftbl; High Hon Roll; Hon Roll; NHS; FHA Dist Pres; Yth Ldrshp Butler; KS ST U.

MC CLURE, CHRISTINA; Perry Lecompton HS; Lecompton, KS; (4); 8/70; Letterman Clb; School Musical; Pres Stu Cncl; Var Bsktbl; Capt Pom Pon; Var Trk; Var Vllybl; Cit Awd; NHS; St Schlr; Hmcmg Queen Cand; Tonganoxie Bsktbl Trnmnt Queen Cand; Emporia ST Univ; Scndry Ed/Eng.

MC CLURE, JESSICA; St Marys HS; Saint Marys, KS; (3); 6/42; FBLA; FHA; Letterman Clb; Library Aide; Pep Clb; Band; Drill Tm; Jazz Band; Mrchg Band; Orch; Emporia ST U.

MC CLURE, JODY; Nickerson HS; Hutchinson, KS; (1); Church Yth Grp; Band; Jazz Band; Mrchg Band; Pep Band; Tennis; Hon Roll; Stdnt Wk; Steel Drum Bnd.

MC CLURE, JOSHUA P; Goddard HS; Clearwater, KS; (1); Church Yth Grp; Band; Mrchg Band; JV Socr; High Hon Roll.

MC CLURE, KATHERINE; Blue Valley HS; Spring Hill, KS; (2); Church Yth Grp; Band; Mrchg Band; Pep Band; Intrml Bsktbl; Hon Roll; Young Life/Wyldlife Vol Ldr; Vol Heartlands Schl Rdng For Hndcpd; PT.

MC CLURE, KEVIN N; Arkansas City HS; Arkansas City, KS; (1); Boy Scts; Church Yth Grp; Socr; Hon Roll.

MC COLLOUGH, LESLEY E; Jewell HS; Randall, KS; (3); 1/15; FHA; Band; Pres Frsh Cls; Sec Soph Cls; Sec Jr Cls; VP Stu Cncl; Chrldng; Vllybl; High Hon Roll; NHS; Pre-Med.

MC COLLUM, JEFFREY A; Gardner-Edgerton HS; Gardner, KS; (3); 9/126; Am Leg Boys St; French Clb; High Hon Roll; Hon Roll; Aerospace Engrng.

MC COMB, AMANDA G; Blue Valley Northwest HS; Leawood, KS; (4); 49/340; Cmnty Wkr; VP German Clb; Service Clb; Stage Crew; Var Golf; High Hon Roll; Hon Roll; NHS; St Schlr; Hiking; Skiing; U Of The South.

MC CONEGHEY, JOHN; Northeast Magnet HS; Wichita, KS; (2); 1/119; Church Yth Grp; Drama Clb; Hosp Aide; Scholastic Bowl; Science Clb; Church Choir; Treas Soph Cls; High Hon Roll; JETS Awd; NHS; NEDC; AHSME Fnlst; Acad, Attendance, Act & Attitude Schl Awds; Medicine.

MC CONNELL, AMY; Atchison Sr HS; Atchison, KS; (3); Spanish Clb; Band; Color Guard; Flag Corp; Mrchg Band; Pep Band; JV Chrldng; Mgr(s); Stat Wrstlng; High Hon Roll; Univ Of KS; Nrsng/PT.

MC CONNELL, RENEE R; Hoisington HS; Hoisington, KS; (2); Pep Clb; SADD; Band; Mrchg Band; Pep Band; School Play; JV Golf; Hon Roll; Forensics Team Mem; Bus.

MC CONNELL, RORY W; Bonner Springs HS; Edwardsville, KS; (3); Church Yth Grp; Acpl Chr; Chorus; Church Choir; Yrbk; L Bsktbl; Capt Var Ftbl; L Trk; Wt Lftg; Cit Awd.

MC COOL, JESSICA; Olathe East Sr HS; Overland Park, KS; (4); 13/305; Church Yth Grp; Debate Tm; HOBY; Spanish Clb; Teachers Aide; Ed Nwsp; High Hon Roll; NHS; Pres Acad Fit Awd; Ozark Chrstn Coll.

MC CORD, DANIEL D; Great Bend Sr HS; Great Bend, KS; (2); Debate Tm; Drama Clb; NFL; Band; Mrchg Band; Pep Band; Ftbl; Hon Roll; X-Ray Tech; Radiology.

MC CORD, SEAN; Olathe North Sr HS; Olathe, KS; (2); Ftbl; Trk; Wt Lftg; Hon Roll.

MC CORD, STACY L; Great Bend Sr HS; Great Bend, KS; (4); Church Yth Grp; Drama Clb; Band; Mrchg Band; Pep Band; Hon Roll; Prfct Atten Awd; Keyettes; Barton Cty CC; Erly Chldhd Ed.

MC CORMACK, AMY L; El Dorado HS; El Dorado, KS; (3); Church Yth Grp; Drama Clb; FCA; Girl Scts; Math Clb; NFL; Scholastic Bowl; SADD; Teachers Aide; Thesps; Best Featured Actress Play; Theatre; Eng.

MC CORMICK, CALI D; Osawatomie HS; Osawatomie, KS; (4); VP Pres Church Yth Grp; Cmnty Wkr; Sec Treas FBLA; Letterman Clb; Pep Clb; Science Clb; Treas Service Clb; Spanish Clb; Teachers Aide; Pres Chorus; Comm Svc; Singing For Beauty Pageants, Ribbon Cuttings & Bsktbl Games; KS ST Univ; Envrnmntl Engrng.

MC CORMICK, KELLY D; Pittsburg HS; Pittsburg, KS; (1); Cmnty Wkr; French Clb; FHA; Girl Scts; Chorus; Intrml Vllybl; High Hon Roll; Future Edctrs Amer Recorder; Small Ensemble & Dist Choir; GSUSA Silver Awd; Pediatrician; Obstetrician.

MC CORMICK, KIMBERLY A; Blue Valley Northwest HS; Overland Park, KS; (4); Cmnty Wkr; Teachers Aide; Sec Varsity Clb; Rep Frsh Cls; Pres Soph Cls; Sec Jr Cls; VP Stu Cncl; Bsktbl; Var Sftbl; JV Vllybl; Emporia ST U; Elem Ed.

MC CORMICK, SALLY L; Otis Bison HS; Timken, KS; (4); 4/25; Church Yth Grp; Quiz Bowl; Band; Chorus; Jazz Band; School Play; Treas Sr Cls; High Hon Roll; Sec Treas NHS; Pres Schlr; Barton Cty CC; Music Ed.

MC CORMICK, WYNDI; Sante Fe Trail HS; Carbondale, KS; (3); FBLA; HOBY; Band; Flag Corp; Mrchg Band; Pep Band; Stage Crew; Hon Roll; Jr Girls Dghtr VFW Pres; 2nd Pl Spnsh I Div Fstvl Fine Arts Cmptn; Belmont U; Art Mgmt.

MC COSKEY, DESIRE M; Great Bend Sr HS; Great Bend, KS; (1); Band; Mrchg Band; Mid Amer Nazarene Coll.

MC COY, AMY J; Osage City HS; Osage City, KS; (3); 6/30; Art Clb; Church Yth Grp; Key Clb; Science Clb; Spanish Clb; Teachers Aide; Ed Yrbk; Ofcr Jr Cls; Ofcr Stu Cncl; Var Sftbl; Bus.

MC COY, AMY LIANE; Blue Valley North HS; Leawood, KS; (3); 27/222; Intnl Clb; Key Clb; Model UN; Chorus; JV Fld Hcky; Var JV Powder Puff Ftbl; Intrml Tennis; High Hon Roll; Hon Roll; Photo; Tae Kwon Do; KS ST U; Crmnl Psych.

MC COY, CHRISTINE M; Augusta Sr HS; Augusta, KS; (4); 14/124; FCA; French Clb; Girl Scts; Scholastic Bowl; Teachers Aide; Band; Drm Mjr(t); Pep Band; Rep Stu Cncl; Mgr Wrstlng; KU Hnr Schlr; KS ST U; Vet Med.

MC COY, JENNIFER; Bishop Carroll Catholic HS; Wichita, KS; (2); 2/250; Church Yth Grp; Scholastic Bowl; Spanish Clb; Band; Mrchg Band; Pep Band; Sal; High Hon Roll.

MC COY, RINA D; Junction City HS; Junction City, KS; (2); #5 in class; Church Yth Grp; Church Choir; Mgr(s); Score Keeper; Stat Trk; Hon Roll; Prfct Atten Awd; Upward Bound; KSU Schol; Acad Lttrwnnr; Howard Univ; Soc Wrk.

MC COY, RYAN M; Santa Fe Trail Jr HS; Olathe, KS; (1); 10/240; Teachers Aide; Rptr Nwsp; L Bsktbl; L Ftbl; L Trk; Hon Roll.

MC COY, SAM; Mulvane Sr HS; Mulvane, KS; (4); 9/144; Treas SADD; VP Thesps; Band; Chorus; Jazz Band; School Musical; Pres Swing Chorus; Rep Stu Cncl; NHS; JV Bsktbl; KS Hnrs Schlr; OK City U; Mscl Thtr Actor.

MC COY, SHEREDY S; Blue Valley HS; Shawnee Mission, KS; (4); 115/230; Var Capt Bsktbl; Var Capt Trk; Var Vllybl; 6th Pl High Jump St Trck; Schl Rcrd Pntathln; Johnson Cty CC.

MC CRACKEN, CHRISTOPHER; Ness City HS; Ness City, KS; (3); 6/37; Church Yth Grp; Band; Mrchg Band; Pep Band; JV Var Bsktbl; Var L Tennis; High Hon Roll; Hon Roll; NHS; Stu Of Month; Bus Admin.

MC CRACKEN, JESSICA D; Andover HS; Andover, KS; (3); Church Yth Grp; Teachers Aide; Band; Mrchg Band; Lit Mag; Hon Roll; Peer Cnslr; Ambssdr; Miami Univ; Tchr.

MC CRARY, GINNY; Goddard HS; Goddard, KS; (4); 15/154; Church Yth Grp; Drama Clb; Band; Mrchg Band; Orch; Pep Band; Yrbk; High Hon Roll; NHS; Girl Scts; Bible Club; KAYS Cncl; Acteens; OK Bapt Univ; Music/Fine Arts.

MC CRAY, KRISTA L; Desoto HS; Shawnee, KS; (3); Church Yth Grp; GAA; SADD; Teachers Aide; JV Bsktbl; Mgr(s); Var L Sftbl; JV Vllybl; Cit Awd; High Hon Roll; KS ST; Childcare.

MC CREADY, JENNIFER M; Chanute Sr HS; Chanute, KS; (2); 43/160; FCA; FTA; Band; Chorus; Jazz Band; Mrchg Band; Pep Band; Vllybl; Pittsburgh ST Univ; Music Ed.

MC CRITE, KATIE; Hayden HS; Topeka, KS; (3); Dance Clb; FBLA; Intnl Clb; Office Aide; Pep Clb; SADD; Yrbk; JV Var Chrldng; Powder Puff Ftbl; JV Var Tennis; SMU; Psych.

MC CUISTION, CLAY D; El Dorado HS; El Dorado, KS; (3); 1/140; Am Leg Boys St; Drama Clb; NFL; Capt Quiz Bowl; Thesps; Chorus; Orch; School Musical; Ed Nwsp; High Hon Roll; St, Natl Jrnlsm Cont; Radio Show; St Frnscs Qulfr; Jrnlsm.

MC CULLEY, CAROL E; Maize HS; Maize, KS; (1); 1/315; Church Yth Grp; School Play; High Hon Roll; Odyssey Of Mind; Knowledge Mstrs.

MC CULLOUGH, ANNA T; Washburn Rural HS; Topeka, KS; (2); 27/380; Debate Tm; Model UN; NFL; Quiz Bowl; Co-Ed Lit Mag; JV Tennis; High Hon Roll; Nom Natl Yth Ldrshp Frm Law/Cnsttn; Nom Natl Yng Ldrs Conf; Harvard; Phlsphy.

MC CULLOUGH, ASHLEY L; Wichita Southeast HS; Wichita, KS; (1); Church Yth Grp; Hosp Aide; Chorus; School Musical; Stage Crew; Co-Ed Yrbk; Skate East; Wichita ST Univ.

MC CULLOUGH, CARI; Manhattan HS; Manhattan, KS; (4); Chess Clb; FCA; 4-H; SADD; Thesps; Bsktbl; Mgr(s); Trk; Hon Roll; Ride & Show Arabian Horses; Ftbl & Soccer Sister Pep Clb; Colby CC; Veterinary Tech.

MC CULLOUGH, CARRIE L; Desoto HS; Shawnee, KS; (4); 17/108; Cmnty Wkr; Band; Mrchg Band; Nwsp; Sec Soph Cls; Sec Jr Cls; Sec Sr Cls; Hon Roll; NHS; Pres Acad Fit Awd; PRIDE Pgm; Acad Ltr; Flute Choir; Johnson Cty CC; Math Field.

MC CULLOUGH, CINDEE D; Iola Sr HS; La Harpe, KS; (3); Church Yth Grp; Drama Clb; FHA; SADD; Church Choir; School Play; Ed Lit Mag; Chrldng; Pom Pon; Hon Roll; Poem Pub; Criminal Justice; Soc Work.

MC CULLOUGH, HUGH R; Washburn Rural HS; Topeka, KS; (3); Chess Clb; Computer Clb; Debate Tm; Model UN; NFL; Speech Tm; Ofcr Sr Cls; High Hon Roll; Hon Roll; Ntl Merit Ltr; KS Univ; Law.

MC CULLOUGH, KIRK; St Thomas Aquinas HS; Leawood, KS; (3); 2/269; Am Leg Boys St; Pres FCA; SADD; Var L Bsktbl; JV Golf; High Hon Roll; JETS Awd; NHS; Ntl Merit Ltr; Church Yth Grp; Male Schlr/Athl Schl Rep; Proj Helpnet Stu Bd Rep.

MC CULLOUGH, SHAWN P; St Thomas Aquinas HS; Shawnee Mission, KS; (4); Am Leg Boys St; Cmnty Wkr; French Clb; Pres Jr Cls; Pres Stu Cncl; Var Capt Socr; Var L Trk; High Hon Roll; Prfct Atten Awd; Stdnt Ldrshp Cls; Clean Team Spksmn; Fclty/Stdnt Actv Plng Comm.

MC CULLUM, TINA A; Great Bend Sr HS; Great Bend, KS; (4); French Clb; Chorus; Hon Roll; Kayettes; Barton Cty Comm Coll; Bus; Acctn.

MC CUNE, AMERICA; Mulvane Sr HS; Mulvane, KS; (4); 16/122; Am Leg Aux Girls St; Church Yth Grp; Capt Debate Tm; FCA; SADD; Pres Thesps; Band; Jazz Band; School Play; Ed Nwsp; Dana Coll; Eng.

MC CUNE, STACI A; Flinthills HS; Cassoday, KS; (2); 2/20; FCA; Pres 4-H; HOBY; Letterman Clb; SADD; Band; Pep Band; Sec Frsh Cls; Sec Soph Cls; Rep Stu Cncl; Peer Helpers.

MC CUNE, STEPHANIE; Flinthills HS; Cassoday, KS; (4); 5/22; Pres VP 4-H; HOBY; Letterman Clb; SADD; Band; Ed Nwsp; VP Pres Stu Cncl; Var Bsktbl; Var Capt Vllybl; NHS; Jr Acad Sci; Soc Range Mgmt; Travel; Colby CC; Agronomy.

MC CURDY, BRADEN R; Wichita Southeast HS; Wichita, KS; (2); Boy Scts; Phtg Yrbk; Hon Roll.

MC CURDY, DOUGLAS J; Olathe East Sr HS; Olathe, KS; (2); Boy Scts; Teachers Aide; JV Socr; Trk; High Hon Roll; Hon Roll; Pres Acad Fit Awd.

MC CURDY, MICHAEL B; Trego Comm HS; Wa Keeney, KS; (2); 14/53; Cmnty Wkr; FHA; Letterman Clb; Science Clb; SADD; JV Ftbl; High Hon Roll; Pres Acad Fit Awd; Kayes; 4 Yr Schl.

MC CURRY, SARA S; Great Bend Sr HS; Great Bend, KS; (2); 35/275; Pep Clb; JV Var Bsktbl; High Hon Roll; Pres Acad Fit Awd; KAY Bd Mbr 94-; KS ST Univ; Optometry/Phrmcy.

MC CUSH, CHRIS S; Lyndon HS; Vassar, KS; (3); Boy Scts; CAP; Ftbl; Trk; Wt Lftg; Aerospace Eng.

MC CUTCHEN, EVA L; Wichita West HS; Wichita, KS; (2); ROTC; Teachers Aide; Chorus; Color Guard; Drill Tm; Sftbl; Vllybl; Mdlng Clb.

MC DANELD, JEN N; Blue Valley HS; Stilwell, KS; (3); Rep Stu Cncl; Bsktbl; Var L Tennis; Var L Trk; Vllybl; High Hon Roll; Plyd Piano 9 Yrs; Otstndng Frosh Bio Stdnt.

MC DANIEL, BENJAMIN R; Newton Sr HS; Newton, KS; (4); Church Yth Grp; Drama Clb; English Clb; Treas Key Clb; Math Clb; Quiz Bowl; VP Thesps; Acpl Chr; Band; Chorus; Chrch Pianist; Lead Trumpet Band; Hutchinson Com Coll; Music Comp.

MC DANIEL, CRYSTAL N; Holton HS; Holton, KS; (1); Dance Clb; Band; Chorus; Mrchg Band; Pep Band; School Musical; Bsktbl; Sftbl; Vllybl; High Hon Roll; Kayette Club.

MC DANIEL, KATHALEEN D; Glasco HS; Delphos, KS; (2); Chorus; KS ST; Child Psych.

MC DANIEL, KRISTI; Pretty Prairie HS; Pretty Prairie, KS; (3); 1/14; Church Yth Grp; FBLA; HOBY; SADD; Teachers Aide; Treas Jr Cls; Ofcr Stu Cncl; Var L Bsktbl; Var L Vllybl; High Hon Roll; Occptnl Thrpy.

MC DANIEL, REGHAN; Lyndon HS; Lyndon, KS; (3); 2/40; Church Yth Grp; Drama Clb; FBLA; VP Pres FHA; Math Tm; NFL; Quiz Bowl; Scholastic Bowl; Speech Tm; SADD; Schl Site Cncl Sec; KS St Univ; Jrnlsm.

MC DANIEL, STEVE; Wichita Northwest HS; Spokane, WA; (3); Church Yth Grp; Cmnty Wkr; Math Clb; Capt Math Tm; Teachers Aide; Var Bsktbl; Var Golf; High Hon Roll; JETS Awd; NHS.

MC DANIELS, HEATHER D; Northeast HS; Arma, KS; (4); 5/45; Teachers Aide; Yrbk; Ofcr Sr Cls; Ofcr Stu Cncl; Chrldng; Pom Pon; Sftbl; High Hon Roll; NHS; Ozark Tech CC; Medcl Recrds.

MC DERMOT, CHRISTY; Washington HS; Kansas City, KS; (3); Bus Profs of Am; DECA; Drama Clb; JA; Key Clb; Pep Clb; Spanish Clb; SADD; Teachers Aide; Nwsp; Quilified St Regnls In DECA For Natls In FL; SMSU.

MC DERMOTT, ALEXA J; Wichita East HS; Wichita, KS; (2); Cmnty Wkr; Teachers Aide; Orch; School Musical; NHS; Ballet Stu; Pvt Violin Stud; Placed On Natl Span Exam Level I & II; Marine Biologist.

MC DERMOTT, CHRISTY; Washington HS; Kansas City, KS; (3); DECA; Key Clb; Pep Clb; Speech Tm; Teachers Aide; Nwsp; Bsktbl; Powder Puff Ftbl; Sftbl; Wt Lftg; DECA Qualified Natls Held In FL; KU; Attorney.

MC DIFFETT, JODY; Wamego HS; Wamego, KS; (4); SADD; Teachers Aide; Sprt Ed Yrbk; Var L Bsktbl; Var L Ftbl; Var Wt Lftg; Cit Awd; Hon Roll; DARE Role Model; KS ST Univ; Rec/Parks Admin.

MC DILL, BRIANA L; Junction City HS; Fort Riley, KS; (3); Pep Clb; Speech Tm; Band; Pep Band; FL Tribe E Creek Indians; Swmng; Hrsbck Riding; Trvlng; U Of W FL; Arch.

MC DONALD, AARON J; Chapman HS; Chapman, KS; (3); 3/110; Church Yth Grp; Letterman Clb; Varsity Clb; Jazz Band; Mrchg Band; Pep Band; Var Crs Cntry; Var Trk; Pres NHS; Pres Schlr; Pre-Med.

MC DONALD, BROOKE R; Mankato Jr Sr HS; Mankato, KS; (2); Church Yth Grp; FHA; Treas Natl FFA Org; Red Cross Aide; Church Choir; Var L Bsktbl; Var L Vllybl; Wt Lftg; High Hon Roll; L Hon Roll; FFA Soph Ldrshp Awd, Frosh Str Grnhnd Awd, Soph 3 Str Gld Mdl St FHA Prlmntry Prcdr Cntst.

MC DONALD, JASON E; Wichita West HS; Wichita, KS; (3); 34/375; Letterman Clb; Varsity Clb; Rep Soph Cls; Rep Jr Cls; Rep Stu Cncl; Var L Mgr(s); JV Score Keeper; Var L Socr; JV Wrstlng; Hon Roll; Natl Schol Congrssnl Yth Ldshp Cncl.

MC DONALD, JENNIFER; Osage City HS; Osage City, KS; (2); 1/52; Debate Tm; Pep Clb; Quiz Bowl; Science Clb; Spanish Clb; Crs Cntry; Gov Hon Prg Awd; High Hon Roll; Kiwanis Awd; Spanish NHS; Aerospc Eng.

MC DONALD, JESSICA; Stockton HS; Stockton, KS; (4); Church Yth Grp; FHA; Pep Clb; School Play; Nwsp; Yrbk; Chrldng; Vllybl; Hon Roll; Teens As Tchrs; Washburn U; Ed.

MC DONALD, KATIE K; Anderson Cty Jr Sr HS; Garnett, KS; (4); 18/79; Drama Clb; SADD; Chorus; School Musical; School Play; Ofcr Stu Cncl; Var Chrldng; Capt L Vllybl; Hon Roll; KS Assoc For Yth VP; Ottawa Univ; Mass Comm.

MC DONALD, KYLE; Greensburg HS; Mullinville, KS; (2); 1/35; Church Yth Grp; 4-H; Band; Pep Band; VP Frsh Cls; JV Bsktbl; JV Ftbl; High Hon Roll; Hon Roll; 4 Yr Coll.

MC DONALD, LACY L; Caldwell Jr Sr HS; Caldwell, KS; (2); Sec Church Yth Grp; Cmnty Wkr; FCA; Letterman Clb; Library Aide; Office Aide; Pep Clb; Red Cross Aide; Speech Tm; SADD; Cert Lfgurd/CPR/FIRST Aide.

MC DONALD, MARY ELIZABAETH; Holton HS; Holton, KS; (1); Scholastic Bowl; Band; Trk; Vllybl; High Hon Roll; Prfct Atten Awd; Mrchg Band; Pep Band; Lady Belles; 1st UMC/SUNDAY Schl.

MC DONALD, MELISSA; Greensburg HS; Mullinville, KS; (4); 1/34; Church Yth Grp; 4-H; FHA; Band; Pres Stu Cncl; Bsktbl; Trk; Vllybl; NHS; Val; KS St Univ; Mech Eng.

MC DONALD, MIKI L; Rolla HS; Rolla, KS; (4); Quiz Bowl; Speech Tm; Band; Ofcr Stu Cncl; Cit Awd; High Hon Roll; NHS; Prfct Atten Awd; FCA; Library Aide; All Lg Qz Bwl Tm; IA ST Chmp Qz Bwl Tm 95-; Danforth I Dare You Awd; Garden City CC; Eng.

MC DONALD, TARA F; Salina HS Central; Salina, KS; (3); Letterman Clb; Teachers Aide; Varsity Clb; Var Sftbl; Var Vllybl; High Hon Roll; Hon Roll; Pres Acad Fit Awd; KS ST U; Tchr.

MC DOWELL, ALICIA D; Gardner-Edgerton HS; Gardner, KS; (2); Am Leg Aux Girls St; Church Yth Grp; 4-H; GAA; Teachers Aide; Band; Mrchg Band; Pep Band; JV Bsktbl; JV Sftbl; Anml Sci.

MC DOWELL, JEREMY M; Baschor Linwood HS; Linwood, KS; (4); 11/120; Church Yth Grp; Debate Tm; FCA; FBLA; Math Clb; Spanish Clb; Teachers Aide; School Play; Var Capt Bsbl; Bsktbl; Johnson Cty CC; Bus Admin.

MC DOWELL, NICKI J; Basehor Linwood HS; Linwood, KS; (2); 1/140; Church Yth Grp; FCA; FBLA; Rep FHA; Math Clb; SADD; Teachers Aide; Rep Stu Cncl; High Hon Roll; Emporia ST Univ; Math Tchr.

MC DUFF, MISTY A; Great Bend Sr HS; Great Bend, KS; (1); French Clb; Pep Clb; Chorus; Variety Show; Socr; Vllybl; Wt Lftg; High Hon Roll; Hon Roll; Kytts Clb; Fresh Rep Pep Clb Bd; Fres Hmcmng Attndnt Ftbll.

MC EACHERN, AMIEE L; Chase Co HS; Cottonwood Falls, KS; (2); FCA; Girl Scts; Pep Clb; Spanish Clb; SADD; Chorus; Bsktbl; Powder Puff Ftbl; Sftbl; Trk; Kay Clb; KS ST; Vet/Police Ofcr.

MC ECRHON, RONALD; Turner HS; Kansas City, KS; (3); 20/230; Cit Awd; Hon Roll; Prfct Atten Awd; TSA; Arctct.

MC ELHENY, STACY D; Hutchinson HS; Hutchinson, KS; (2); Church Yth Grp; Pep Clb; Drill Tm; Pom Pon; JV Sftbl; Cit Awd; Hon Roll; KS Univ; Scndry Ed.

MC ELROY, STEFANIE L; Seaman Sr HS; Topeka, KS; (4); Church Yth Grp; Cmnty Wkr; FHA; Key Clb; Office Aide; Pep Clb; SADD; Teachers Aide; Drill Tm; JV Trk; Washburn U; Erly Chldhd Ed.

MC ENROE, JENNIFER L; Basehor Linwood HS; Basehor, KS; (3); 1/100; FHA; GAA; Hosp Aide; Capt Drill Tm; Ed Yrbk; Pres Stu Cncl; Bsktbl; Capt Pom Pon; Sftbl; Vllybl; Vol; Nom To Prom Princess; KS St Univ; Mass Comm.

MC EUEN, BRIAN S; Washburn Rural HS; Topeka, KS; (3); Drama Clb; Hosp Aide; Intnl Clb; Model UN; Chorus; School Musical; School Play; Stage Crew; Variety Show; JV Wrstlng; Radio/Television.

MC FALL, LACEY L; Greensburg HS; Greensburg, KS; (3); FHA; NFL; Band; Chorus; Pep Band; VP Sr Cls; Ofcr Stu Cncl; Var Bsktbl; Tennis; High Hon Roll; Cmnty Ldrshp Prtnrs.

MC FALL, LINDSEY D; Greensburg HS; Greensburg, KS; (1); Church Yth Grp; FHA; Band; Rep Frsh Cls; Ofcr Stu Cncl; Bsktbl; Trk; Vllybl; Hon Roll; PCL; Arch.

MC GEE, JASMINE A; Salina HS Central; New Cambria, KS; (3); Cmnty Wkr; Debate Tm; NFL; Thesps; Chorus; Orch; School Play; Swing Chorus; Hon Roll; NHS; Comm Theatre; Theatre.

MC GEE, KRESSA R; Wichita North HS; Wichita, KS; (2); Church Yth Grp; Hosp Aide; Office Aide; Chorus; Church Choir; School Musical; Var Bsktbl; Var Trk; Var Vllybl; Hon Roll; Obstetrician.

MC GEE, SANDY L; St Thomas Aquinas HS; Lenexa, KS; (3); 20/260; GAA; Girl Scts; Chorus; JV Sftbl; Vllybl; High Hon Roll; NHS; Horseback Riding Trainer For Girl Scouts; Pre-Med; Bio; Phy Therapy.

MC GEHEE, KRISTEN M; Field Kindley Mem Sr HS; Coffeyville, KS; (3); Art Clb; Spanish Clb; Co-Ed Yrbk; Vllybl; Hon Roll; NHS; Dance Team; Coffeyville CC.

MC GILL, BRENT J; Garden City Sr HS; Garden City, KS; (3); Math Clb; SADD; Yrbk; Pres Soph Cls; Bsktbl; Crs Cntry; Ftbl; High Hon Roll; Hon Roll; NHS; Spon Rd To Clean; U TX Arlngtn; Cmptr Engrng.

MC GINLEY, CASEY J; Topeka West HS; Topeka, KS; (3); 36/239; German Clb; Science Clb; SADD; Drill Tm; Powder Puff Ftbl; Sftbl; Vllybl; High Hon Roll; Hon Roll; Pres Acad Fit Awd; USVBA MVP Sftbl Hnrb Mntn All City; Hnrb Mtn Vllybl; 2nd Team All City; Golden Glove Awd; Meteorology.

MC GINN, AMBER L; Halstead HS; Halstead, KS; (1); Church Yth Grp; Letterman Clb; Spanish Clb; Drill Tm; Bsktbl; Pom Pon; Trk; Vllybl; Hon Roll; Drill Tm & Track Lttrmn; Star Of Mnth; Booster Clb; Kayettes; KS St Univ.

MC GINN, KENDRA; Sedgwick HS; Sedgwick, KS; (2); 2/36; Church Yth Grp; FHA; Letterman Clb; Quiz Bowl; Scholastic Bowl; Var L Bsktbl; High Hon Roll; Physcl Sci, Home Ecs Awds; Wds/Mtls Excl Awd.

MC GINNIS, AVERY; Shawnee Mission Northwest HS; Shawnee Mission, KS; (4); 83/385; Church Yth Grp; VP VICA; Capt Swmmng; Hon Roll; NHS; Fash Careers Pres; Natl VICA Cmptn Cmmrcl Swng 3rd Pl; KS ST U; Fash Mrchndsng.

MC GINNIS, CRYSTALYNNE V; Washington HS; Kansas City, KS; (2); German Clb; Crmnl Law.

MC GINNIS, JENNIFER M; Kingman HS; Kingman, KS; (2); Church Yth Grp; FCA; SADD; Church Choir; JV Bsktbl; Var Trk; JV Vllybl; High Hon Roll; All Leag Trck; CU; Bus.

MC GINNIS, NICOLE M; Basehor Linwood HS; Linwood, KS; (3); Cmnty Wkr; GAA; Library Aide; Office Aide; Science Clb; Teachers Aide; JV Bsktbl; L Sftbl; Intrml Vllybl; Hon Roll; Univ Of KS; Sprts Med.

MC GINNIS, RANDY M; Beloit Jr Sr HS; Beloit, KS; (1); Science Clb; Spanish Clb; Varsity Clb; Chorus; Bsktbl; Ftbl; Trk; Hon Roll.

MC GIVERN, SEAN M; Shawnee Heights HS; Topeka, KS; (1); Quiz Bowl; JV Golf; High Hon Roll.

MC GLOHON, DAVID; Ulysses HS; Ulysses, KS; (3); Am Leg Boys St; Church Yth Grp; VP FCA; School Musical; Swing Chorus; JV Var Bsktbl; Var L Ftbl; Var L Tennis; NHS; ORU; Chemical Engr.

MC GOVERN, TRISHA D; Shawnee Mission S Sr HS; Overland Park, KS; (4); 98/431; Cmnty Wkr; Intnl Clb; Teachers Aide; Orch; School Musical; Variety Show; Crs Cntry; Hon Roll; NHS; KS City Yth Symphony; Natl Hnrs Orch 96; Gold Key, 2 Slvr Key Rgnl Schltc Art Awds; Quartet; St Orch; Boston U; Violin Perfmnc.

MC GOWAN, CARINA; Arkansas City HS; Arkansas City, KS; (1); 4-H; Natl FFA Org; Orch; Vllybl; 4-H Awd; Hon Roll; Vet.

MC GOWN, CAMERON T; Basehor Linwood HS; Tonganoxie, KS; (2); 1/130; Boy Scts; Church Yth Grp; Letterman Clb; Quiz Bowl; Scholastic Bowl; Science Clb; Band; Church Choir; Mrchg Band; Ftbl; Eagle Sct; Engrng & Sci Smmr Inst KS St U; Med.

MC GOWN, KATHLEEN L; Junction City HS; Junction City, KS; (2); Debate Tm; Pep Clb; Scholastic Bowl; Vllybl; Hon Roll.

MC GRANAHAN, JENNIFER; St Marys HS; Saint Marys, KS; (3); 4/45; Am Leg Aux Girls St; FBLA; Pep Clb; Quiz Bowl; Band; Mrchg Band; Orch; Pep Band; Var Chrldng; Var JV Sftbl; KS Regents Hnrs Acad; Swimming; Girls Scots; Acctng.

MC GRATH, EDWARD H; Sumner Acad Of Arts & Science; Kansas City, KS; (3); French Clb; Spanish Clb; JV Ftbl; Var Wrstlng; Hon Roll; KS ST Univ.

MC GRATH, VANESSA A; Bishop Miege HS; Shawnee, KS; (2); 15/245; Hosp Aide; Red Cross Aide; Var L Swmmng; High Hon Roll; PT.

MC GRAW, JESSE L; Olathe South Sr HS; Olathe, KS; (3); Art Clb; Church Yth Grp; Debate Tm; Scholastic Bowl; Science Clb; Lit Mag; Ofcr Bsbl; High Hon Roll; Quiz Bowl; Spanish Clb; The Anti-Humanist Legion Mem; Worldwide Superstar; Wheaton Coll; Fine Arts; Pol Sci.

MC GUFFIN, ANTHONY L; Holton HS; Holton, KS; (1); Scholastic Bowl; Band; Mrchg Band; Pep Band; Bsktbl; Ftbl; Trk; Benedictine Coll.

MC GUIRE, DUSTIN GILKISON; Madison Jr Sr HS; Madison, KS; (4); 9/26; FBLA; Letterman Clb; NFL; Varsity Clb; School Play; Rep Stu Cncl; L Var Bsktbl; L Var Ftbl; L Var Trk; Hon Roll; KS All St Cls A Bsktbl; Ottawa U.

MC GUIRE, ERIN C; Parsons HS; Parsons, KS; (4); 12/120; Church Yth Grp; Sec GAA; SADD; Band; School Play; High Hon Roll; NHS; Pres Acad Fit Awd; KS Lions St Bnd; St Solo Ensmble Fest; Dist Bnd Membr; Pittsburg St Univ; Elem Ed.

MC GUIRE, KERRY J; Gardner-Edgerton HS; Gardner, KS; (3); Church Yth Grp; Drama Clb; Band; Chorus; School Musical; School Play; Stage Crew; Stat Sftbl; Ltr Band, Chorus; U Of KS; Music Ed.

MC GUIRE, LAURA L; Cheney Jr Sr HS; Cheney, KS; (3); 11/44; Church Yth Grp; Band; Jazz Band; Pep Band; Var Trk; Var Vllybl; High Hon Roll; Hon Roll; Jr NHS; NHS; Hutch Jr Col; Vet.

MC GUIRE, MOLLY L; Hays HS; Hays, KS; (3); 40/237; FCA; Pep Clb; Nwsp; Var Bsktbl; Var Trk; Var Vllybl; Hon Roll; Jr NHS; NHS; Pres Acad Fit Awd; All League Vlybl; Bsktbl Hnrbl Mntn; 9th Grd All ST Track.

MC GUIRK, NICK A; Wellington Sr HS; Wellington, KS; (2); Boy Scts; Rep Church Yth Grp; FCA; SADD; Band; Mrchg Band; Var L Crs Cntry; Var L Trk; High Hon Roll; Jr NHS; TX Chrstn U.

MC HENRY, PETER; Midland Sda Schl; Shawnee Mission, KS; (2); Church Yth Grp; Band; Chorus; High Hon Roll; Yth Symphony Of KC.

MC HUGH, ERIN E; Blue Valley Northwest HS; Overland Park, KS; (3); 35/378; Cmnty Wkr; Q&S; Co-Ed Yrbk; Powder Puff Ftbl; Sftbl; High Hon Roll; Hon Roll; NHS.

MC ILVAIN, JOLIE S; Madison Jr Sr HS; Madison, KS; (2); Cmnty Wkr; GAA; Letterman Clb; Pep Clb; Spanish Clb; Rep Band; Chorus; Jazz Band; Mrchg Band; Pep Band; Emporia ST U; Acctng.

MC INTIRE, HALEY D; Southwestern Heights HS; Liberal, KS; (4); 19/37; Church Yth Grp; Drama Clb; French Clb; FHA; Speech Tm; School Musical; School Play; Stage Crew; Prfct Atten; Seward Cty CC; Primary Ed.

MC INTOSH, SARAH E; Wichita Northwest HS; Wichita, KS; (2); 32/360; Debate Tm; Girl Scts; HOBY; Intnl Clb; NFL; Speech Tm; Rep Frsh Cls; Rep Soph Cls; Rep Jr Cls; High Hon Roll; Campus Life; KN St Univ; Debte.

MC INTYRE, JOANNA D; Wichita East HS; Wichita, KS; (2); Girl Scts; Teachers Aide; Office Asst; Pittsburgh ST; RN.

MC INTYRE, SAMANTHA S; Topeka West HS; Topeka, KS; (3); Cmnty Wkr; French Clb; Pep Clb; Pres SADD; Teachers Aide; Band; Mrchg Band; Pep Band; Hon Roll; DARE.

MC IVER, RACHAEL; Fairfield HS; Abbyville, KS; (1); 4-H; Quiz Bowl; Speech Tm; Band; Chorus; Church Choir; Pep Band; School Musical; School Play; Ofcr Frsh Cls; Young Wmn Harmony Barbershop Chorus.

MC KAIG, SARAH; Paola HS; Paola, KS; (4); 1/113; Am Leg Aux Girls St; HOBY; Q&S; Treas SADD; Pres Band; Ed Nwsp; Treas Stu Cncl; Capt Chrldng; Var L Trk; NHS; Brdcst Jrnlsm.

MC KANEY, WADE E; Great Bend Sr HS; Great Bend, KS; (1); Church Yth Grp; German Clb; Band; Jazz Band; Mrchg Band; Pep Band; Variety Show; Stat Bsbl; Bsktbl; Stat Ftbl; Cmptr Engr.

MC KANNA, AUDREY; Ollathe North Sr HS; Olathe, KS; (3); Drama Clb; Spanish Clb; Teachers Aide; Drill Tm; Lit Mag; Rep Soph Cls; Pom Pon; Vllybl; High Hon Roll; Hon Roll; Faraday Soc.

MC KEAN, ANNE C; Washburn Rural HS; Topeka, KS; (2); Church Yth Grp; Debate Tm; Drama Clb; FCA; Spanish Clb; SADD; Powder Puff Ftbl; Cmnty Wkr; High Hon Roll; Pan Amer Stu Forum Fnslt; ESL Chldrn Tutor; Rice Univ; Engr.

MC KEE, JAKE E; Goodland HS; Brewster, KS; (4); Letterman Clb; School Musical; Swing Chorus; Bsktbl; Ftbl; Trk; Hon Roll; Pres Schlr; All-ST Hnrs Ftbl/Bsktbl/Trck; U Of NE Lincoln.

MC KEE, JANEL E; Goodland HS; Goodland, KS; (2); 15/95; Church Yth Grp; Dance Clb; Drama Clb; FHA; GAA; Pep Clb; SADD; Varsity Clb; Acpl Chr; Chorus; Kayettes; U Of NE; Music Perfmnc.

MC KEE, JENNY; Caney Valley Jr Sr HS; Independence, KS; (4); 2/55; Church Yth Grp; FCA; GAA; Band; Drm Mjr(t); Pres Sr Cls; Chrldng; High Hon Roll; NHS; Sal; Pittsburg ST U; Scndry Ed; Eng.

MC KEE, KRISTI; Lansing HS; Lansing, KS; (2); Art Clb; Drama Clb; Office Aide; Chorus; Church Choir; Drill Tm; Swing Chorus; Var Pom Pon; Hon Roll; Pink Rbbn All Amer Nom NCA Dnc Cmp; Perf Arts/Dsny Wrld.

MC KEE, MEGAN; Spearville Jr Sr HS; Spearville, KS; (1); 4-H; Pep Clb; Quiz Bowl; Spanish Clb; Band; Chorus; Church Choir; Mrchg Band; Pep Band; School Play.

MC KEE, MONICA R; Labette Co HS; Edna, KS; (3); 3/133; FCA; FBLA; Letterman Clb; VICA; Chorus; Yrbk; Rep Stu Cncl; Sftbl; Hon Roll; NHS; Lib Clb Stuco Rep & Pres; Natl Young Ldrs Con.

MC KEITHAN, RYAN A; Jefferson West HS; Ozawkie, KS; (1); 1/50; Boy Scts; Chess Clb; Debate Tm; FBLA; Letterman Clb; Varsity Clb; Swing Chorus; Rep Frsh Cls; Var L Bsbl; Var L Bsktbl; Duke Univ; Comp Dsgn.

MC KELVEY, MANDY M; Olathe East Sr HS; Olathe, KS; (2); Church Yth Grp; Dance Clb; Drama Clb; Letterman Clb; Library Aide; Pep Clb; Drill Tm; Chrldng; Socr; Wt Lftg; U Of AR.

MC KENDREE, MEREDITH A; Blue Valley North HS; Overland Park, KS; (2); Church Yth Grp; Latin Clb; Chorus; Hon Roll; Kay Club; Comm Srvc; Med Schl.

MC KENNA, AMY; Jennings Schl; Jennings, KS; (2); 1/3; 4-H; FHA; Natl FFA Org; Pep Clb; Teachers Aide; Band; JV Bsktbl; JV Var Trk; Var Vllybl; Hon Roll; Barton Cty CC; PT/BUS.

MC KENNA, HEATHER R; Solomon Jr Sr HS; Solomon, KS; (3); 6/20; Drama Clb; FHA; Library Aide; Model UN; SADD; Band; Treas Frsh Cls; Var Sftbl; JV Vllybl; Hon Roll; Child Psych.

MC KENNA, SARAH; Jennings Schl; Jennings, KS; (2); 1/3; Church Yth Grp; Cmnty Wkr; 4-H; FHA; Quiz Bowl; Scholastic Bowl; Speech Tm; Teachers Aide; Band; Chorus; U Of KS; Med.

MC KENZIE, ANGIE S; Independence HS; Independence, KS; (1); Church Yth Grp; Church Choir; Hon Roll; Concordia Coll; Elem Ed.

MC KIBBIN, ROCHELLE; Thomas More Prep-Marion HS; Hays, KS; (4); 13/93; Church Yth Grp; FBLA; Model UN; Band; Pep Band; School Musical; Stat Ftbl; Stat Wrstlng; High Hon Roll; Service Awd; KS ST; Bus Admin.

MC KIMIE, ZACHARY B; Blue Valley North HS; Leawood, KS; (2); Church Yth Grp; Model UN; Band; Wrstlng; Hon Roll; Black Belt Tae Kwon Do; Heart Awd; Southern Nazarene Univ.

MC KINDRA, TRACI K; Sumner Acad; Kansas City, KS; (2); Art Clb; Church Yth Grp; Cmnty Wkr; Spanish Clb; Church Choir; Orch; Rep Jr Cls; Sftbl; Hon Roll; NHS; Yth Symphony KS City Sr Orch; Art; Music.

MC KINLEY, NOEL; Olathe North Sr HS; Olathe, KS; (2); Spanish Clb; Chorus; Var L Bsktbl; JV L Socr; Var L Swmmng; Hon Roll; U Of KS; Artist.

MC KINNEY, JERNALE D; Leavenworth HS; Leavenworth, KS; (3); Bsktbl; Ftbl; Trk; Wt Lftg; Spcl Olympics Vol; Bus.

MC KINNEY, KEVIN J; Maize HS; Wichita, KS; (3); Boy Scts; Church Yth Grp; French Clb; Letterman Clb; Office Aide; Chorus; Variety Show; Ftbl; Hon Roll; Eagle Scout.

MC KNAB, DAVID K; Emporia HS; Emporia, KS; (3); Church Yth Grp; FCA; FBLA; Latin Clb; JV Bsktbl; High Hon Roll; NHS; KS Regents Hnrs Acad Stu.

MC KOWN, BRETT; Seaman Sr HS; Topeka, KS; (4); 10/248; Cmnty Wkr; L Debate Tm; NFL; High Hon Roll; Prfct Atten Awd; Gftd Pgm; Comp; Comp Sci.

MC LAIN, ANDREW; Sumner Acad Of Arts & Science; Kansas City, KS; (3); Church Yth Grp; Key Clb; Spanish Clb; Hon Roll; Engr.

MC LAIN, COREY; Trinity Catholic HS; Hutchinson, KS; (4); 2/30; Am Leg Boys St; Hosp Aide; NFL; Sec Stu Cncl; L Capt Ftbl; NHS; St Schlr; Boy Scts; Church Yth Grp; Debate Tm; Dnfrth I Dare You Awd; DARE Rl Mdl; US Natl Ldrshp Mrt Awd; Rockhurst; Phys Thrpy.

MC LAIN, ERIN E; Hutchinson HS; Hutchinson, KS; (2); 3/350; Debate Tm; French Clb; Key Clb; Letterman Clb; NFL; Speech Tm; Teachers Aide; Varsity Clb; High Hon Roll; Prfct Atten Awd; Pol Sci.

MC LAIN, MEREDITH; Blue Valley HS; Overland Park, KS; (4); Am Leg Aux Girls St; Church Yth Grp; Chorus; School Musical; Swing Chorus; Sec Jr Cls; Chrldng; Hon Roll; NHS; Johnson Ctys Jr Miss; Elem Ed.

MC LAIN, PATRICK J; Bishop Carroll Catholic HS; Wichita, KS; (3); Church Yth Grp; FCA; Spanish Clb; Var JV Socr; JV Tennis; VP Of Chrch Yth Grp; KSU.

MC LAREN, TAD J; El Dorado HS; El Dorado, KS; (2); Letterman Clb; Spanish Clb; SADD; Ofcr Bsbl; Ftbl; Powder Puff Ftbl; Wt Lftg; High Hon Roll; Hon Roll; KS Assn Yth.

MC LAUGHLIN, JILL N; Remington HS; Potwin, KS; (3); Letterman Clb; Thesps; Varsity Clb; Ed Yrbk; Var Bsktbl; Hon Roll; CVL Bus Skills Cont 3rd Pl Awd; Butler Cty CC.

MC LAUGHLIN, MARCUS E; Sumner Acad Of Arts & Science; Kansas City, KS; (3); Art Clb; JA; Key Clb; Quiz Bowl; Scholastic Bowl; Spanish Clb; Ftbl; Trk; Wrstlng; Hon Roll; Yth Group Of Black Hlth Care Coalition; Acad Decatholon; U Of KS; His; Art.

MC LEAN, STACY J; Circle HS; Towanda, KS; (3); 1/120; Am Leg Aux Girls St; Dance Clb; Acpl Chr; School Musical; Spanish Clb; SADD; Nwsp; Pom Pon; High Hon Roll; NHS; KS ST Univ; Acctnt.

MC LELLAN, MELINDA; St Thomas Aquinas HS; Lenexa, KS; (4); 15/231; Cmnty Wkr; Var Debate Tm; French Clb; Model UN; Ed Nwsp; Sec Stu Cncl; High Hon Roll; NHS; Ntl Merit Ltr; St Schlr; Rtry Clb Stu Amb To Frnc; Poli Sci.

MC LILLY, BRIANA N; Leavenworth HS; Leavenworth, KS; (2); Dance Clb; NFL; Thesps; Chorus; School Play; Stage Crew; Cit Awd; High Hon Roll; Thespians; U Of KS; Scndry Ed.

MC MAHON, JENNIFER E; Junction City HS; Fort Riley, KS; (1); Church Yth Grp; German Clb; Red Cross Aide; Varsity Clb; Band; Mrchg Band; Pep Band; Sftbl; Tennis; High Hon Roll.

MC MAHON, MELISSA L; Osawatomie HS; Osawatomie, KS; (1); Church Yth Grp; FBLA; Pep Clb; Science Clb; Band; Color Guard; Mrchg Band; Pep Band; Bsktbl; Score Keeper.

MC MAHON, ROBERT E; Junction City HS; Fort Riley, KS; (2); Church Yth Grp; German Clb; JV Bsbl; Var Socr; Var Swmmng; High Hon Roll; Jr NHS; NHS.

MC MANNIS, JOSHUA D; Canton-Galva HS; Canton, KS; (2); Church Yth Grp; FBLA; Letterman Clb; SADD; JV Var Bsktbl; Var L Ftbl; Hon Roll.

MC MANNIS, REBECCA J; Canton-Galva HS; Canton, KS; (3); Church Yth Grp; FBLA; SADD; Teachers Aide; Ed Yrbk; High Hon Roll; NHS; Ath Trnr; Nrsing.

MC MASTER, MARK B; Wichita Southeast HS; Wichita, KS; (4); 8/200; Cmnty Wkr; Debate Tm; Capt Quiz Bowl; Pres Spanish Clb; Chorus; Ed Nwsp; High Hon Roll; Ntl Merit SF; Northwestern U; Jrnlsm.

MC MILLAN, TYCE L; Stanton Co HS; Johnson, KS; (4); 8/32; Church Yth Grp; Drama Clb; Quiz Bowl; Band; Chorus; Pep Band; School Play; Variety Show; Ftbl; NHS; KS ST Univ; Argonomy.

MC MILLIAN, NICHOLAS D; Basehor Linwood HS; Basehor, KS; (3); Church Yth Grp; Cmnty Wkr; Debate Tm; JV Bsktbl; JV Ftbl; High Hon Roll; Hon Roll; Natl Yng Ldrs Conf; Notre Dame/KS Univ; Med Prof.

MC MULLEN, BRANT W; Lawrence HS; Lawrence, KS; (2); Church Yth Grp; Rep Frsh Cls; Rep Soph Cls; Trk; Hon Roll; Pres Acad Fit Awd; CDC Virologist.

MC MULLEN, HEATHER D; El Dorado HS; El Dorado, KS; (2); Debate Tm; Key Clb; Hon Roll; Achvmnt Plus Club; Jrnlsm One; Phtgrphy; Butler; Plstc Srgn/Dr.

MC MURRAY, LORI; Southeast Saline Schl; Salina, KS; (2); 16/63; Sec Art Clb; Drama Clb; NFL; Pep Clb; Varsity Clb; Band; Drill Tm; Mrchg Band; Pep Band; Variety Show; Plys For Elem; Flght Clss; Awds Artstc Ablty; Plt.

MC MURTRY, LISA N; Wichita South HS; Wichita, KS; (2); 1/392; Church Yth Grp; Scholastic Bowl; Orch; JV Socr; Var L Tennis; Hon Roll; Vac Bible Schl Tchr; HOSTS Vol; CYO Vlybl; U Of KS; Biochem.

MC NALLY, ANDREA C; Sumner Acad Of Arts & Science; Kansas City, KS; (3); Rep Debate Tm; Rep Drama Clb; Rep French Clb; Key Clb; Rep NFL; SADD; Rep Thesps; JV Chrldng; French Hon Soc; NHS; Psych/Ed.

MC NALLY, DAVID A; Shawnee Mission North HS; Overland Park, KS; (3); CAP; Cmnty Wkr; Debate Tm; Letterman Clb; NFL; Pep Clb; ROTC; Color Guard; Drill Tm; Sons Amer Revolution Bronze ROTC Medal; Rocky Mt Silver Chanter; Shephard & Sons Young Bagpiper Awd; Criminologist.

MC NALLY, MATTHEW T; St Mary's Colgan HS; Pittsburg, KS; (4); Boy Scts; Debate Tm; Drama Clb; Q&S; Teachers Aide; Ed Mgr Yrbk; L Bsktbl; L Ftbl; L Trk; High Hon Roll; Art Awd; Math Relays; KS ST; Comp Engrng.

MC NALLY, MEGAN; St Mary's Colgan HS; Pittsburg, KS; (1); Debate Tm; NFL; Pep Clb; VP Frsh Cls; JV Bsktbl; Var Chrldng; Var Trk; JV Vllybl; High Hon Roll; Pre-Medicine.

MC NAMEE, ELIZABETH A; Immaculata HS; Leavenworth, KS; (2); Cmnty Wkr; GAA; Math Tm; Spanish Clb; Varsity Clb; JV Var Bsktbl; Intrml JV Vllybl; Hon Roll.

MC NANEY, DE ANN R; Great Bend Sr HS; Great Bend, KS; (4); 16/230; Ofcr Church Yth Grp; Ofcr FCA; Rep Spanish Clb; Band; Flag Corp; Yrbk; JV Bsktbl; Var L Crs Cntry; Var L Trk; High Hon Roll; Mid Amer Naz Coll.

MC NANEY, EVERETTE W; Great Bend Sr HS; Great Bend, KS; (1); Church Yth Grp; FCA; German Clb; Band; Jazz Band; Mrchg Band; Pep Band; Stage Crew; Variety Show; JV Mgr Bsktbl; Cmptr Engr.

MC NARY, ERIN; Oskaloosa HS; Oskaloosa, KS; (2); Art Clb; Church Yth Grp; Debate Tm; Drama Clb; 4-H; FBLA; FHA; Letterman Clb; NFL; Office Aide; Forensics; Forensics Recitale; Tchr.

MC NARY, NIKKI; Jefferson West HS; Meriden, KS; (3); Cmnty Wkr; Drama Clb; FBLA; FHA; Girl Scts; SADD; Teachers Aide; School Play; Stage Crew; Var L Chrldng; Kaw Area Tech Schl; Lgl Asst.

MC NAUGHT, DAVID; Garden City Sr HS; Garden City, KS; (2); Spanish Clb; Ofcr Bsbl; Wt Lftg; Gov Hon Prg Awd; Homcmng Royalty; Intnl Bus.

MC NAUL, JAMES; Buhler HS; Hutchinson, KS; (4); Am Leg Boys St; Church Yth Grp; FCA; Letterman Clb; Teachers Aide; Varsity Clb; Ftbl; Powder Puff Ftbl; Wt Lftg; Wrstlng; All League 2nd Team CTL Wrestling; All League Hnrb Mntn Ftbl & Wrestling; Ftbl; Architecture.

MC NEILL JR, THOMAS A; Maize HS; Wichita, KS; (3); Spanish Clb; Band; Jazz Band; Mrchg Band; Pep Band; Hon Roll; KS U; Engr; Military.

MC NICHOLAS, SHARRON L; Holton HS; Holton, KS; (4); 17/63; 4-H; Teachers Aide; Rptr Nwsp; Yrbk; 4-H Awd; Hon Roll; NHS; U Of KS; Exercise Physiology.

MC NICKLE, JILL; Ashland HS; Ashland, KS; (3); Church Yth Grp; Quiz Bowl; Treas Frsh Cls; Pres Soph Cls; Rep Jr Cls; Pres Sr Cls; Pres Stu Cncl; Var L Bsktbl; Var L Tennis; Var L Trk.

MC NOLTY, LESLIE A; Newton Sr HS; Newton, KS; (2); Model UN; Scholastic Bowl; Thesps; Acpl Chr; Chorus; School Musical; Chrldng; Gym; Swmmng; High Hon Roll; Sci Olympd Team; KS His Day Comp.

MC NOWN, CHRISTOPHER W; Shawnee Heights Sr HS; Topeka, KS; (2); Church Yth Grp; Cmnty Wkr; FBLA; Ski Clb; Band; Pep Band; High Hon Roll; Hon Roll; Swimming, Tnns; Prin List.

MC PARTLIN, MOLLY; St Thomas Aquinas HS; Overland Park, KS; (3); Church Yth Grp; Cmnty Wkr; Socr; High Hon Roll; Hon Roll; Prfct Atten Awd; Show Me Aquinas Clb.

MC PEAKE, JESSICA; Shawnee Mission N HS; Shawnee Mission, KS; (4); 23/474; ROTC; Spanish Clb; Band; Mrchg Band; Bsktbl; Socr; Trk; Vllybl; NHS; Pres Acad Fit Awd; KS ST Univ; Criminology.

MC PEEK, JOSEPH A; Olathe East Sr HS; Olathe, KS; (2); Spanish Clb; Hon Roll; Pres Acad Fit Awd.

MC QUADE, HOLLY M; Hoisington HS; Hoisington, KS; (2); Church Yth Grp; Math Tm; Quiz Bowl; Speech Tm; SADD; High Hon Roll; Hon Roll; Nrsing Home Actvties Asst.

MC QUEEN, MEGAN; Wabaunsee HS; Alma, KS; (1); Church Yth Grp; FHA; Quiz Bowl; Chorus; School Musical; School Play; L Var Trk; Intrml Vllybl; High Hon Roll; GSA Silver Awd.

MC QUILKIN, LISA M; Hayden HS; Topeka, KS; (3); Debate Tm; Chorus; Nwsp; Hon Roll; Debate Ltr; KS ST Univ; Vet.

MC QUILLER, AMBER K; Leavenworth HS; Leavenworth, KS; (2); Church Yth Grp; Church Choir; High Hon Roll; Hon Roll; Upward Bound; NAACP; Acctnt.

MC RAE, JOSH D; Garden City Sr HS; Garden City, KS; (2); Chess Clb; Church Yth Grp; Cmnty Wkr; Science Clb; Teachers Aide; High Hon Roll; Hon Roll; Jr NHS; Prfct Atten Awd; KS ST U; Veterinary Medicine.

MC RALL, SCOTT; Salina HS; Salina, KS; (2); Church Yth Grp; Debate Tm; NFL; Band; Mrchg Band; Pep Band; Nwsp; Golf; Hon Roll; Sci Fld.

MC REYNOLDS, ANGELA D; Ottawa HS; Ottawa, KS; (3); Office Aide; Spanish Clb; SADD; JV Chrldng; Acctng.

MC SHEA, MATTHEW D; Stockton HS; Stockton, KS; (4); 3/33; Church Yth Grp; Cmnty Wkr; HOBY; Math Tm; Quiz Bowl; Band; Pres Stu Cncl; Var L Ftbl; Hon Roll; VP NHS; KAYS VP; KS Hnr Schlr; KU; Engr.

MC VICKER, KELLY; Buhler HS; Hutchinson, KS; (3); Am Leg Aux Girls St; Spanish Clb; Sec Jr Cls; Rep Stu Cncl; Var Bsktbl; Trk; High Hon Roll; NHS; Ntl Merit Ltr; Pres Acad Fit Awd; Mrshl Grad 96; Natl Ldrshp Awd; Span I Hnr Stdnt; Intl Rltns.

MC VICKER, MISSY D; Garden City Sr HS; Garden City, KS; (1); SADD; Orch; Rep Soph Cls; Ofcr Stu Cncl; Chrldng; Gym; High Hon Roll; Hon Roll; United Meth Yth Grp/Sndy Schl; Natl Sci Mrt Awd; Orch First Chr Violinest; KS ST; Pdtrcn/Neontlgst.

MC WHIRT, T CURTIS; Field Kindley Mem Sr HS; S Coffeyville, OK; (4); Office Aide; Quiz Bowl; VP Pres Pep Band; Var Bsktbl; Var Ftbl; Cit Awd; High Hon Roll; NHS; Pres Schlr.

MC WILLIAMS, BRENT J; Washington HS; Kansas City, KS; (2); Drama Clb; Library Aide; Stage Crew; JV Bsbl; JV Crs Cntry; JV Wrstlng; Hon Roll; AIA; Drftg Tech.

MC WILLIAMS, JUSTIN A; Central Heights Sr HS; Richmond, KS; (1); Band; JV Bsktbl; Cmptr Prgmng/Sftwr Wrtr.

MEAD, BEN D; Northwest HS Wichita; Largo, FL; (4); ROTC; Scholastic Bowl; Chorus; Color Guard; Drill Tm; Orch; Variety Show; Var L Trk; Church Yth Grp; Cmnty Wkr; US Mrn Rsrv; Army Rsrv Vol; Mdrgl Sngrs; U Of KS.

MEAD, BETHANY; Skyline Schl; Sawyer, KS; (4); 5/32; Church Yth Grp; Cmnty Wkr; NFL; Pep Clb; SADD; Band; Chorus; Mrchg Band; Pep Band; School Musical; Homecoming Attendant & Queen; KS State; Child Psych.

MEAD, KERRI A; Larned HS; Larned, KS; (2); Church Yth Grp; Debate Tm; Drama Clb; FCA; Scrkpr Scholastic Bowl; Band; Chorus; Church Choir; Jazz Band; 1st Chr Dstrct Band Trmpt; KMEA ST Band Trmpt Grd 10; Solo Chair/Dist Jazz Bnd.

MEAD, SHANDA L; Russell HS; Russell, KS; (1); Cmnty Wkr; Key Clb; SADD; Chorus; School Musical; Stage Crew; Variety Show; High Hon Roll; U Of KS; Nrsng.

MEADOWS, LEVI A; Independence HS; Elk City, KS; (1); Band; Mrchg Band; Pep Band; Bsktbl; Ftbl; His.

MEAGHER, JANINE C; Bishop Miege HS; Westwood, KS; (2); 52/163; Hosp Aide; Quiz Bowl; Pep Band; School Play; Stage Crew; Ed Lit Mag; Sftbl; Hon Roll; Campus Ministry Team Slvr Awd; Spirit Clb; Campus Ministry Team; U Of KS; Neonatoogy Nrs.

MEAKER, BRYCE; Shawnee Mission Northwest Schl; Lake Quivira, KS; (4); 75/393; Art Clb; Computer Clb; Debate Tm; Model UN; Ofcr Jr Cls; Ofcr Sr Cls; Ofcr Stu Cncl; Socr; Wt Lftg; High Hon Roll; Intl Stud Ctr Japanese 4 Yrs; YFU Prgm Schlsp Awd Travel To Japan; KS Univ; Intl Bus.

MEANS, DAVID L; Haven HS; Mount Hope, KS; (3); Band; Jazz Band; Mrchg Band; Orch; Pep Band; JV Bsbl; JV Var Bsktbl; JV Ftbl; High Hon Roll; Pres Acad Fit Awd; KS U.

MEARS, TAMI Z; Nickerson HS; Nickerson, KS; (1); Cmnty Wkr; Debate Tm; Drama Clb; GAA; Girl Scts; Key Clb; NFL; Red Cross Aide; Thesps; Band; SAVE; Vet.

MEARS, TANIA; Nickerson HS; Nickerson, KS; (4); 5/120; Art Clb; Church Yth Grp; Cmnty Wkr; Debate Tm; Drama Clb; French Clb; FHA; HOBY; Key Clb; Library Aide; Big Sister Prog; Stu Agnst Vlnce On Earth; Pres Of Sci Clb; Baylor Univ; Premed.

MECHNIG, DUSTIN C; Anderson Cty Jr Sr HS; Westphalia, KS; (1); Chorus; Bsktbl; JV Ftbl; KS Univ; Lwyr.

MECKFESSEL, SARA J; Larned HS; Garfield, KS; (2); Church Yth Grp; FCA; Intnl Clb; Spanish Clb; Chorus; Crs Cntry; Trk; Stage Crew; Prfct Atten Awd; Dist Choir; Southrn Bapt Acteen Actvtr; Ldrshp America-KS Farm Bureau; Massage Thrpy.

MECOM, JOSH B; Field Kindley Mem Sr HS; Coffeyville, KS; (3); Letterman Clb; Office Aide; Teachers Aide; Varsity Clb; Rep Jr Cls; Ofcr Stu Cncl; JV Intrml Bsktbl; Var Ftbl; Var Trk; Var Wt Lftg; KS Univ; Law.

MEDELLIN, FELICIA R; Bishop Miege HS; Roeland Park, KS; (3); 37/170; Cmnty Wkr; SADD; Yrbk; JV Sftbl; Hon Roll; NHS; Amigos De Las Amercas Vol Paraguay.

MEDER, JAY T; Victoria HS; Pfeifer, KS; (3); 4-H; VICA; Ftbl; 4-H Awd; Hon Roll; NHS; Universal Tech Inst; Auto Tech.

MEDER, RENEE S; Victoria HS; Pfeifer, KS; (2); Church Yth Grp; 4-H; FBLA; FHA; Pep Clb; SADD; Varsity Clb; Var L Bsktbl; Var L Tennis; Cit Awd; FHA; SADD; Natural Sciences.

MEDINA, JAYME; Sublette HS; Sublette, KS; (4); 3/30; Church Yth Grp; Letterman Clb; Sec Frsh Cls; Sec Soph Cls; Sec Jr Cls; Sec Sr Cls; Var Bsktbl; Var Golf; High Hon Roll; Pres NHS; Acctng.

MEDLEY, ELIZABETH A; Goddard HS; Goddard, KS; (1); Church Yth Grp; Office Aide; Teachers Aide; Band; Mrchg Band; Pep Band; JV Socr; JV Var Vllybl; High Hon Roll; Hon Roll; U Of KS.

MEDLOCK, BEN; Dodge City HS; Dodge City, KS; (3); Church Yth Grp; Band; Drm Mjr(t); Mrchg Band; Pep Band; Bsktbl; Trk; Hon Roll; NHS; Stdnt Mnth 96; Fine Arts Stdnt Mnth 96; Assoc Of Yr Dillons 95; Psychgst.

MEDRANO, JOHNNIE A; Maize HS; Wichita, KS; (2); 71/294; Spanish Clb; TX Tech; Surgeon.

MEDRANO, MICHELE; Emporia HS; Emporia, KS; (3); Cmnty Wkr; Dance Clb; FBLA; GAA; Intnl Clb; Letterman Clb; Pep Clb; Service Clb; Teachers Aide; Varsity Clb; NCA All Amer Chrldr, Dancer; Crime Stoppers Sec; U Of KS; Pre-Law.

MEEK, DAWN; Spring Hill HS; Spring Hill, KS; (3); 6/100; Cmnty Wkr; Letterman Clb; SADD; Drill Tm; Rep Frsh Cls; Rep Soph Cls; Rep Jr Cls; Var L Sftbl; High Hon Roll; NHS; Scl Wrkr.

MEEK, JOSH; Louisburg HS; Louisburg, KS; (3); Letterman Clb; Natl FFA Org; Bsktbl; Ftbl; Golf; Wt Lftg; Hon Roll; Auto Mech.

MEEK, MARK; Spring Hill HS; Bucyrus, KS; (3); Am Leg Boys St; 4-H; Letterman Clb; Rep Frsh Cls; Rep Soph Cls; Rep Jr Cls; VP Stu Cncl; Var L Bsbl; JV Bsktbl; Var L Ftbl; All Frontier League 1st Team Offense & Defense Ftbl, 2nd Team DH Bsbl; All Metro Hnrbl Mntn Ftbl Off; Kansas ST Univ; Ag Bus.

MEEKER, MICHAEL W; Wellington Sr HS; Wellington, KS; (2); Church Yth Grp; Math Tm; Natl FFA Org; JV Bsktbl; JV Var Ftbl; Var Trk; Hon Roll; Farming.

MEERPOHL, KELLY J; Holton HS; Holton, KS; (3); 10/76; Am Leg Boys St; Letterman Clb; Band; School Musical; Ofcr Stu Cncl; JV Var Ftbl; JV Var Golf; High Hon Roll; Hon Roll; NHS; St Lions Band; U Of KS; Engrng.

MEESE, SARA; Turner HS; Kansas City, KS; (3); #3 in class; Bus Profs of Am; GAA; Varsity Clb; Var L Bsktbl; Var L Sftbl; Var Vllybl; High Hon Roll; Jr NHS; NHS; Vlybl Hnbl Mntn; Bsbl All Hrn, All KS; Arch.

MEHL, KRISTEN A; Blue Valley Northwest HS; Shawnee Mission, KS; (3); 16/364; Varsity Clb; Powder Puff Ftbl; Score Keeper; Var Socr; High Hon Roll; NHS.

MEHRER, TERRA; Garden City Sr HS; Garden City, KS; (3); Cmnty Wkr; Office Aide; Science Clb; Spanish Clb; Teachers Aide; Band; Mrchg Band; Pep Band; Bsktbl; Marine Bio.

MEIER, AUGUSTINE G; Washburn Rural HS; Topeka, KS; (3); 153/338; Debate Tm; Drama Clb; Band; Mrchg Band; Orch; Pep Band; School Musical; Rep Frsh Cls; Rep Soph Cls; Treas Jr Cls; Band Pres; Glf City 3rd Pl; Stdnt Cncl Treas; Bus.

MEIER, DAVID; Garden City Sr HS; Garden City, KS; (2); 1/462; Boy Scts; Science Clb; Sec Spanish Clb; High Hon Roll; Prfct Atten Awd; Sci Fair Grnd Prz Wnnr; Acad Lttr; Eagle Scout; Eng.

MEIER, HEATH D; Hayden HS; Topeka, KS; (3); Thesps; Acpl Chr; Church Choir; School Musical; L Ftbl; Hon Roll; Law.

MEIER, JESSICA; Thomas More Prep-Marion HS; Hays, KS; (2); Library Aide; Co-Capt JV Chrldng; Hon Roll; Vol Svc Hrs; Bus.

MEIER, KENDRA; Ulysses HS; Ulysses, KS; (2); VP FHA; Band; Mrchg Band; Pep Band; School Musical; Hon Roll.

MEIER, LIZ; Shawnee Mission Northwest HS; Lenexa, KS; (2); 15/459; Math Clb; Pep Clb; JV L Chrldng; Var L Trk; Cit Awd; High Hon Roll; Hon Roll; Pres Acad Fit Awd; Yng Life; Cmpgnrs.

MEIER, STEPHANIE D; Lincoln Jr Sr HS; Lincoln, KS; (1); Hon Roll; Frosh Geometry Clss; KS ST Univ; Author/Chef.

MEIERS, HEATHER; Marysville HS; Blue Rapids, KS; (2); Art Clb; Debate Tm; NFL; High Hon Roll; Hon Roll; Kiwanis Awd; Duke U TIP; St Hstry Day Qlfr; Wrstlng Trnmt Mat Maids; KSU; Archlgst.

MEILI, BILLIE; Lincoln Jr Sr HS; Lincoln, KS; (4); 1/32; Pres Sec Church Yth Grp; Color Guard; Var Trk; Gov Hon Prg Awd; High Hon Roll; VP NHS; Val; Treas Jr Cls; Var Chrldng; Wt Lftg; KAY Clb; KS ST Univ Deans Awd Math/Sci; KS Hon Schlr/Crowell Book Awd; KS ST U; Acctng.

MEINEN, LISA; Baldwin HS; Baldwin City, KS; (4); 18/81; Am Leg Aux Girls St; Church Yth Grp; Debate Tm; Intnl Clb; Letterman Clb; Math Tm; NFL; Teachers Aide; Rep Soph Cls; Sec Jr Cls; Hstry.

MEINHARDT, JANET B; Hayden HS; Topeka, KS; (2); Church Yth Grp; Intnl Clb; Chorus; Yrbk; Hon Roll; Wrtng Poetry/Stories; Piano; Creighton U; Jrnlsm.

MEIS, FREDRICK J; Hill City HS; Hill City, KS; (1); Church Yth Grp; Cmnty Wkr; FCA; Pep Clb; Quiz Bowl; Speech Tm; Bsktbl; Golf; High Hon Roll; KAYS.

MEIS, JAMES; Hays HS; Catharine, KS; (3); 8/237; Ofcr Bsbl; Intrml Bsktbl; Intrml Wt Lftg; High Hon Roll; Prfct Atten Awd; Stdnt Private Pilot; KS St; Elect Eng.

MEISEL, JEFFREY A; Lakin HS; Lakin, KS; (1); 1/50; Church Yth Grp; FCA; 4-H; Quiz Bowl; Band; Pep Band; VP Frsh Cls; JV Bsktbl; Var Crs Cntry; Var Trk.

MEITLER, SCOTT M; Hugoton HS; Hugoton, KS; (2); 11/88; Church Yth Grp; Cmnty Wkr; Drama Clb; Spanish Clb; School Musical; School Play; Stage Crew; Hon Roll; Tchr.

MEIVES, KENT J; Olathe South Sr HS; Olathe, KS; (3); Church Yth Grp; Spanish Clb; Teachers Aide; JV Crs Cntry; JV Socr; JV Trk; High Hon Roll; Hon Roll; NHS; Pres Treas Spanish NHS; Spnsh Hnr Soc Pres & Treas; Spnsh.

MELCHER, JENNIFER; Shawnee Mission Northwest HS; Lenexa, KS; (4); 32/390; Church Yth Grp; Girl Scts; Thesps; Band; Mrchg Band; Pep Band; School Musical; School Play; Stage Crew; Lit Mag; Natl Forensic League; U Of MO Columbia; Tech Theatre.

MELCHER, SARAH E; Ottawa HS; Ottawa, KS; (2); Pres Church Yth Grp; Chorus; School Musical; School Play; Variety Show; Rep Stu Cncl; High Hon Roll; Drama Clb; Church Choir; Show Choir; KSHSAA St Vocal Solo.

MELIA, SARAH; Goodland HS; Goodland, KS; (3); 7/97; VP Church Yth Grp; Sec GAA; Sec SADD; Teachers Aide; Pres Sr Cls; Ofcr Stu Cncl; L Bsktbl; L Trk; L Vllybl; High Hon Roll.

MELLARD, JENNIFER; Meade HS; Meade, KS; (3); 6/42; French Clb; VP Pres Key Clb; Band; Drm Mjr(t); Sec Stu Cncl; Var L Chrldng; Var L Tennis; Cit Awd; High Hon Roll; NHS; Farm Bureau Ldshp Awd; EMT Expl Pres; Pres Awd For Ed Exc; Orgztl Mgnt.

MELLEGAARD, SHELLI R; Olathe East Sr HS; Overland Park, KS; (2); Church Yth Grp; 4-H; GAA; Letterman Clb; Spanish Clb; Band; Chorus; Church Choir; Jazz Band; Mrchg Band; Prin Ldrshp Awrd; QUEST Gifted Prgm; All Sunflwr League Hnrbl Mntn Vlybl.

MELLIES, BRENDA; Ness City HS; Ness City, KS; (2); 1/40; Church Yth Grp; FHA; Math Tm; Pep Clb; Quiz Bowl; Scholastic Bowl; Sec Treas Frsh Cls; VP Soph Cls; Bsktbl; Trk; Med.

MELLON, BRANDY M; North East HS; Arcadia, KS; (2).

MELTON, DRUSILLA E; Wichita Heights HS; Wichita, KS; (2); 1/336; Church Yth Grp; Acpl Chr; Chorus; Variety Show; High Hon Roll; Chr Bible Quiz; Bible Clb; Sunday Schl Tchr; Girls Ensemble; Yth Ensemble; Evangel Coll; Psych/Cnslng.

MELTON, JOHN; Ell-Saline Jr Sr HS; Salina, KS; (3); 3/30; Boy Scts; Church Yth Grp; 4-H; Math Tm; Natl FFA Org; Stat Bsktbl; Stat Ftbl; High Hon Roll; NHS; TX A&M Univ; Civil Chem Engrn.

MELTON, MARCELLA E; Valley Ctr HS; Wichita, KS; (3); Chess Clb; 4-H; Scholastic Bowl; Chorus; School Musical; Hon Roll; Horses; KS ST.

MELTON, MARK R; Beloit Jr Sr HS; Beloit, KS; (1); 15/90; SADD; Rep Frsh Cls; Ofcr Stu Cncl; Var Bsbl; Intrml Bsktbl; High Hon Roll.

MELTON, REBECCA J; Wabaunsee HS; Maple Hill, KS; (2); FHA; Rptr Nwsp; Var L Crs Cntry; Powder Puff Ftbl; Hon Roll; KAYS; KS ST U; Psych.

MELTON, STACIE L; Washington HS; Kansas City, KS; (3); Debate Tm; Drama Clb; NFL; Spanish Clb; Nwsp.

MELTON, STAR T; Wabaunsee HS; Maple Hill, KS; (3); Boy Scts; Stage Crew; Stat Mgr Ftbl; Trk; Wrstlng.

MELVIN, JASON E; Northeast HS; Arma, KS; (1); 22/48; Boy Scts; Church Yth Grp; Cmnty Wkr; 4-H; Library Aide; Red Cross Aide; Band; Stage Crew; Variety Show; Nwsp; Order Of Arrow; Yth Del For ECLA Conf 96; Pres Of Chrch Yth Group 96-97; Photo.

MENDENHALL, SCOTT A; J C Harmon HS; Kansas City, KS; (3); Am Leg Boys St; Chess Clb; NFL; Ftbl; Wt Lftg; Wrstlng; Hon Roll; X Ray Tech.

MENDEZ, JON R; Turner HS; Kansas City, KS; (2); JV Bsktbl; Hon Roll; Jr NHS; Pres Acad Fit Awd.

MENDEZ, MIRANDA; Shawnee Mission N HS; Overland Park, KS; (2); Drama Clb; Pep Clb; Spanish Clb; Thesps; School Play; Stage Crew; Ofcr Stu Cncl; Var Chrldng; Sftbl; Performing Arts.

MENDEZ, NATASHA; Jackson Heights HS; Whiting, KS; (1); Church Yth Grp; FHA; Band; Chorus; Mrchg Band; Pep Band; School Musical; Trk; Vllybl; Hon Roll; KS ST; Tchr/Cnslr.

MENDEZ, REINA M; Wichita East HS; Wichita, KS; (2); Girl Scts; Math Clb; Spanish Clb; SADD; Teachers Aide; High Hon Roll; NHS; Girl Sct Silver Awd; Wichita ST U; Spcl Ed.

MENDEZ, ROCIO; Bishop Ward HS; Kansas City, KS; (2); 10/93; Cmnty Wkr; SADD; Intrml Bsktbl; Hon Roll; NHS; U Of KS; Pre-Med.

MENDOZA, J R; Shawnee Heights Sr HS; Topeka, KS; (3); FBLA; Stage Crew; Rptr Nwsp; Hon Roll; Hispnc Amer Ldrshp Org; Justica Inc Vltr; Church Vlntr; Commnctns.

MENELEY, LANCE D; Jefferson West HS; Meriden, KS; (2); 5/70; Art Clb; Letterman Clb; Pep Clb; Scholastic Bowl; Band; Jazz Band; Pep Band; JV Bsbl; Var L Ftbl; L Wt Lftg; Amer Lgn Amer Awd; Math Tchr/PT.

MENENDEZ, LAURIE E; Blue Valley Northwest HS; Overland Park, KS; (2); Church Yth Grp; Debate Tm; Hosp Aide; Hon Roll; Creative Wrtng; Psych; Eng.

MENG, LAWRENCE; Kingman HS; Murdock, KS; (3); Chrmn Church Yth Grp; Pres Natl FFA Org; SADD; High Hon Roll; NHS; KSU; Crop Spclst.

MENG, RYAN; Garden City Sr HS; Garden City, KS; (3); 49/310; Letterman Clb; Varsity Clb; Bsktbl; Ftbl; Score Keeper; Trk; Wt Lftg; High Hon Roll; Sociolgy.

MENGELKOCH, KRISTEN A; Wichita East HS; Wichita, KS; (2); Drama Clb; Spanish Clb; Thesps; Chorus; School Musical; School Play; Stage Crew; Variety Show; Pres Frsh Cls; Hon Roll; Msc Thtre Wchta, Msc Thtr Yng Pepl Wchta; Vc Lssns; Intl Bcclrt Pgrm; Friends U; Msc Thtre.

MENKE, TONY S; Hartford HS; Neosho Rapids, KS; (3); 1/18; Treas FBLA; Pres Letterman Clb; Capt Quiz Bowl; Scholastic Bowl; Var L Bsktbl; Var Capt Ftbl; Var L Trk; High Hon Roll; NHS.

MENNING, TONY; Lawrence HS; Lawrence, KS; (3); Boy Scts; German Clb; Teachers Aide; High Hon Roll; Ntl Merit Ltr; Eagle Scout; Intnl Bus.

MENSE, JAKE B; Grinnell HS; Grinnell, KS; (2); 2/15; Church Yth Grp; Math Clb; Science Clb; Speech Tm; Band; Chorus; Church Choir; Mrchg Band; Pep Band; School Play.

MERANDO, ANTHONY; Frontenac Jr Sr HS; Pittsburg, KS; (1); Boy Scts; Church Yth Grp; Pep Clb; Quiz Bowl; Scholastic Bowl; Cit Awd; Hon Roll; Ntl Merit Schol; Prfct Atten Awd.

MERCER, BETH; Wichita North HS; Wichita, KS; (3); 1/350; Church Yth Grp; Hosp Aide; Lit Mag; Rep Soph Cls; Rep Jr Cls; NHS; Fllwshp Clb; Natl His Day 3rd City; 31 ACT; KS ST U; Psych/Eng.

MERCER, CHRIS J; El Dorado HS; El Dorado, KS; (3); 14/144; Boy Scts; Scholastic Bowl; Band; Mrchg Band; Pep Band; Ofcr Bsbl; Ftbl; Trk; High Hon Roll; Prfct Atten Awd; BSA Eagle Sct; SW Smnr Schlrshp.

MERCER, JACINDA B; Holton HS; Holton, KS; (1); Art Clb; GAA; Letterman Clb; Pep Clb; Band; Mrchg Band; Pep Band; Var Ftbl; Var Mgr(s); High Hon Roll; Kays; Var Chrldr.

MERCER, JOSHUA; Southwestern Heights HS; Plains, KS; (4); 11/39; Am Leg Boys St; Church Yth Grp; Quiz Bowl; Band; Jazz Band; Pep Band; JV Bsktbl; L Crs Cntry; JV Ftbl; L Tennis; Seward Cty CC; Aerospc Engr.

MERCER, MIKELLE M; Southeast HS; Wichita, KS; (3); 1/345; SADD; Teachers Aide; Orch; Pom Pon; Socr; Vllybl; High Hon Roll; Educ.

MERINO, STEPHANIE J; Bishop Miege HS; Kansas City, MO; (3); 61/170; Church Yth Grp; Pep Clb; High Hon Roll; UMKC; Legal.

MERKEL, KELLY; Highland HS; Robinson, KS; (2); 1/35; Sec Natl FFA Org; Quiz Bowl; Chorus; School Musical; Swing Chorus; Var L Bsktbl; Var L Trk; Var L Vllybl; Hon Roll; NHS.

MERRELL, RUSSEL; Waverly HS; Waverly, KS; (4); 3/22; Church Yth Grp; School Musical; Treas Frsh Cls; Treas Soph Cls; Treas Jr Cls; Treas Sr Cls; Capt L Bsktbl; Capt L Ftbl; Capt L Trk; High Hon Roll; St 3200 M Champ Class 1a 93; Vol Frfghtr; Emporia ST U; Elem Ed.

MERRICK, LIVIA; Macksville HS; Belpre, KS; (1); 4-H; Quiz Bowl; Band; Ofcr Stu Cncl; JV Bsktbl; JV Chrldng; Trk; JV Vllybl; Hon Roll; Church Yth Grp; St Piano Fstvl; Kayette Brd Mem; Med.

MERRILL, TONYA G; Concordia Jr Sr HS; Concordia, KS; (4); 34/98; Debate Tm; Drama Clb; NFL; Quiz Bowl; Science Clb; Spanish Clb; Teachers Aide; Band; Pep Band; CCCC; Corp Law.

MERRILL, TONYA S; Phillipsburg HS; Phillipsburg, KS; (2); Debate Tm; Drama Clb; FHA; Spanish Clb; Speech Tm; SADD; Stage Crew; JV Var Tennis; High Hon Roll; Hon Roll; C Of C Math Stu; Ft Hays Univ; CPA.

MERRIMAN, VICTORIA L; Field Kindley Mem Sr HS; Coffeyville, KS; (4); Debate Tm; Girl Scts; NFL; Spanish Clb; Teachers Aide; Mrchg Band; Stat Sftbl; Hon Roll; Prfct Atten Awd; Girl Sct Gold & Silver Awds; Coffeyville CC; Phys Thpry.

MERRYMAN, ERIK D; Bishop Miege HS; Kansas City, MO; (3); 58/170; Stage Crew; Lit Mag; Var L Ftbl; Wt Lftg; Var L Wrstlng; Hon Roll; Comm Svc Chldrns Mrcy Hosp; KU; Arch/Anthrplgst.

MERSBERG, KERRY L; Field Kindley Mem Sr HS; Dearing, KS; (4); Debate Tm; French Clb; German Clb; NFL; Teachers Aide; Mgr Bsbl; Chrldng; Hon Roll; Treas NHS; Pres Schlr; Coffeyville Comm Coll; Chirprtc.

MERSMAN, KIM M; Anderson Cty Jr Sr HS; Garnett, KS; (1); SADD; Bsktbl; Vllybl; Hon Roll; Prfct Atten Awd; Prin Hnr Roll; Acad Excl Awd In Span; Dog Pound; Photo.

MERSMANN, MOLLY; Eudora HS; Eudora, KS; (3); 5/65; Rep Church Yth Grp; Hist FBLA; Model UN; Scholastic Bowl; SADD; Ed Nwsp; Rptr Yrbk; VP Stu Cncl; High Hon Roll; NHS; Poem Pub 95; KSPA St Jrnlsm Cont 1st Pl News, Headline Wrtng 95, Regnl 95-96, 2nd Pl 96; KS ST Univ; Jrnlsm.

MERTENS, LANCE; South Gray HS; Montezuma, KS; (1); 4-H; Quiz Bowl; Band; Chorus; Pep Band; School Musical; JV Ftbl; Var Trk; Var Wrstlng; DAR Awd.

MERTZ, KATHERINE M; St Thomas Aquinas HS; Overland Park, KS; (4); 29/231; French Clb; Hosp Aide; Pres SADD; Ed Yrbk; Capt Var Swmmng; High Hon Roll; NHS; St Schlr; 1st Pl St Jrnlsm Cont For Layout/Dobule Page Spread; U Of MO-COLUMBIA; Jrnlsm.

MERWIN, BRANDY L; Madison Jr Sr HS; Madison, KS; (2); Drama Clb; School Play; Stage Crew; JV Bsktbl; Hon Roll; Kay-Kayettes; Child Ed.

MERZ, JONATHAN; Lawrence HS; Lawrence, KS; (4); CAP; Band; Jazz Band; Mrchg Band; Pep Band; JV Trk; Tae Kwon Do-Temporary Black Belt; U Of KS; Comp Sci.

MERZ, MICHELLE; Garden City Sr HS; Garden City, KS; (3); Teachers Aide; High Hon Roll; Acctnt.

MESA, JENNIFER L; Garden City Sr HS; Garden City, KS; (1); Church Yth Grp; VP FHA; Band; Bsktbl; Sftbl; Cit Awd; Hon Roll; Pres Acad Fit Awd; KU; Intr Dsgn.

MESEKE, DARRIN R; Wabaunsee HS; Alma, KS; (3); Natl FFA Org; Office Aide; Teachers Aide; Yrbk; Rep Jr Cls; Ofcr Stu Cncl; JV Bsktbl; Ftbl; Hon Roll.

MESERVE, KIMBERLY; Campus HS; Haysville, KS; (4); Am Leg Aux Girls St; Bus Profs of Am; SADD; Teachers Aide; Hon Roll; Cowley County CC; Bus Admin.

MESPLAY, TRACY T; Northeast HS; Arma, KS; (2); 1/45; Scholastic Bowl; Hon Roll; Prfct Atten Awd; Princpl Hnr Roll; Cert Achvmnt Hnrs Eng/Algebra II.

MESSALL, MARY K; Blue Valley Northwest HS; Overland Park, KS; (1); Science Clb; School Play; Stage Crew; Lit Mag; High Hon Roll; Hon Roll; Cmptrs/Philosoph/Sci/His/Sci-Fi/Hist Fic/British Humor/95 Hon Men/KS Voices Wrtng Contest; Physics.

MESSENGER, LAURA; Ulysses HS; Ulysses, KS; (3); Pres Church Yth Grp; FHA; Chorus; Church Choir; School Musical; Var Chrldng; Hon Roll; NHS; Frgn Lang Clb.

MESSENGER, TIFFANY; South Haven Schl; Geuda Springs, KS; (4); 2/15; Church Yth Grp; FCA; FHA; Pep Clb; Scholastic Bowl; Band; Chorus; Drm Mjr(t); Mrchg Band; Orch; Pratt CC; Physthpy.

MESSER, JENNIFER; Olathe North Sr HS; Olathe, KS; (4); 81/331; Spanish Clb; Teachers Aide; Bsktbl; Mgr(s); Sftbl; Vllybl; Hon Roll; Prfct Atten Awd; KS ST Univ; Tchr.

MESSERLY, BRYAN J; Olathe East Sr HS; Overland Park, KS; (2); JV Bsbl; Var Crs Cntry; Var Trk; High Hon Roll; Surgeon.

MESSERLY, JASON; Sublette HS; Sublette, KS; (4); 1/29; Boy Scts; Letterman Clb; Rep Jr Cls; Pres Sr Cls; Var Capt Bsktbl; Var Capt Ftbl; Var Trk; High Hon Roll; VP NHS; Prfct Atten Awd; Natl Hnr Roll; Acctng.

MESSING, JEREMY; Wellington Sr HS; Wellington, KS; (1); JV Bsktbl; Var Tennis; High Hon Roll; Jr NHS.

MESSMAN, MICHELLE; Derby HS; Wichita, KS; (2); Church Yth Grp; Teachers Aide; Chorus; Variety Show; Mgr(s); High Hon Roll; Hon Roll.

MESTER, JESSICA L; Topeka West HS; Topeka, KS; (2); 3/375; Model UN; Pep Clb; Scholastic Bowl; Spanish Clb; Chorus; School Musical; JV L Crs Cntry; High Hon Roll; Math Clb; SADD; Natl Span Exam Lvl 3 ST 1st Pl; Ballet Mdwst Co Ladies Div.

METCALF, CARLA A; Caldwell Jr Sr HS; Caldwell, KS; (4); Church Yth Grp; Cmnty Wkr; Library Aide; Pep Clb; SADD; Teachers Aide; Chorus; School Musical; School Play; Variety Show; Cowley Cty Comm Coll; Soc Work.

METCALF, KELLIE; Spring Hill HS; Spring Hill, KS; (4); FCA; 4-H; VP Letterman Clb; Sec Pep Clb; VP Science Clb; SADD; Band; Drill Tm; Pep Band; Var Bsktbl; Creighton U; Health.

METCALF, SHEA; South Haven Schl; South Haven, KS; (1); Math Tm; Band; Mrchg Band; Pep Band; JV Bsktbl; L Trk; JV Vllybl; High Hon Roll; Hon Roll; Poem Pub By Natl Lib Of Poetry; Cowley Cty Hnr Band; KU Med Schl; Medicine.

METRO, RACHEL D; Great Bend Sr HS; Great Bend, KS; (4); 37/218; Church Yth Grp; GAA; Pep Clb; Spanish Clb; Teachers Aide; Var Capt Bsktbl; Var L Sftbl; Var L Tennis; JV Vllybl; Hon Roll; Gale Yahne Sports Awd; Butler Cty CC.

METTLEN, CORY L; Ellsworth HS; Geneseo, KS; (2); 16/90; Rptr Yrbk; Ftbl; Wt Lftg; Hon Roll.

METZ, GREG D; Winfield HS; Winfield, KS; (4); Am Leg Boys St; Church Yth Grp; VP Soph Cls; Rep Jr Cls; Var Bsktbl; Var Ftbl; High Hon Roll; NHS; Ntl Merit SF.

METZGER, CHRIS A; Olathe East Sr HS; Olathe, KS; (2); Spanish Clb; VICA; Band; Jazz Band; High Hon Roll; Hon Roll; KS Univ.

METZINGER, AMY S; Arkansas City HS; Arkansas City, KS; (2); 16/311; Am Leg Aux Girls St; Church Yth Grp; Cmnty Wkr; FCA; 4-H; GAA; Natl FFA Org; Office Aide; Speech Tm; Church Choir; KS ST Univ; Animal Sci.

METZINGER, JESSICA; Dexter Jr Sr HS; Dexter, KS; (4); 1/11; 4-H; FHA; Math Tm; Band; Mrchg Band; Pep Band; Nwsp; Yrbk; Rep Sr Cls; Vllybl; KS Hnrs Prm; Cowley Cty CC; History.

METZINGER, SHEILA; Arkansas City HS; Arkansas City, KS; (4); 18/178; Am Leg Aux Girls St; Church Yth Grp; 4-H; FHA; Red Cross Aide; Service Clb; SADD; Teachers Aide; Bsktbl; Swmmng; 3 Yrs Lifeguard; Acad Ltr; Cowley Cty CC; Nrs.

MEYER, CARLIE; Ulysses HS; Ulysses, KS; (3); 1/150; Church Yth Grp; FCA; Letterman Clb; Spanish Clb; SADD; Varsity Clb; Chorus; Church Choir; School Musical; Swing Chorus; Frgn Lang Clb; Elem Ed.

MEYER, CASEY L; Washburn Rural HS; Topeka, KS; (2); 15/380; Church Yth Grp; Cmnty Wkr; GAA; Letterman Clb; Ed Yrbk; Var Bsktbl; Var Sftbl; Var Vllybl; High Hon Roll; 25 Vol Hrs; Duke; Bus.

MEYER, CHERYL L; Sabetha HS; Morrill, KS; (3); Pep Clb; Teachers Aide; Band; Flag Corp; Var Vllybl; Stat Var Wrstlng; Pres Acad Fit Awd; Nationally Ranked In Womens Wrestling 3rd In USA 95-96.

MEYER, CHRISTOPHER H; Blue Valley Northwest HS; Overland Park, KS; (2); 119/440; Band; Mrchg Band; Pep Band; Hon Roll; Comp Sci.

MEYER, CORY J; Leroy HS; Westphalia, KS; (4); 3/16; Am Leg Boys St; Church Yth Grp; Math Tm; Office Aide; Teachers Aide; Chorus; School Play; Variety Show; Nwsp; Yrbk; ACCC.

MEYER, DANICA; Pratt HS; Pratt, KS; (2); Pep Clb; SADD; Band; Mrchg Band; Pep Band; JV Chrldng; Hon Roll; Dental.

MEYER, DARREN M; Kapaun-Mt Carmel HS; Wichita, KS; (3); Church Yth Grp; CAP; Teachers Aide; Rep Jr Cls; Var L Wrstlng; High Hon Roll; Mech Eng.

MEYER, ERIKA L; Madison Jr Sr HS; Madison, KS; (2); Band; Mrchg Band; Pep Band; JV Vllybl; Hon Roll; Kay-Kayettes; Emporia St Univ.

MEYER, HEATHER; Hiawatha HS; Hiawatha, KS; (4); 16/101; Am Leg Aux Girls St; Intnl Clb; Library Aide; Pep Clb; Science Clb; Chorus; School Musical; High Hon Roll; NHS; KSU; Elem Ed.

MEYER, JASON; Smith Ctr Jr Sr HS; Smith Center, KS; (3); Am Leg Boys St; Art Clb; Church Yth Grp; Cmnty Wkr; Letterman Clb; Math Clb; Math Tm; Science Clb; SADD; Varsity Clb; Schl Knowldege Master Open Team Mem; St Medalist In Natl Sci Olympiad; Artist Of Yr Awd; U Of NE-KEARNEY; Comp Pgmng.

MEYER, JEFFERY; Wellsville Jr Sr HS; Rantoul, KS; (3); 30/60; Pres Church Yth Grp; FCA; Treas 4-H; FBLA; Var L Ftbl; Var L Trk; Var L Wrstlng; Ottawa Univ; Scndry Ed.

MEYER, JOSHUA; Bern Schl; Bern, KS; (3); Church Yth Grp; Sec Frsh Cls; Pres Soph Cls; VP Jr Cls; VP Sr Cls; JV Bsktbl; Mgr Ftbl; JV Wt Lftg; Cit Awd; High Hon Roll.

MEYER, JOSHUA R; Blue Valley HS; Shawnee Mission, KS; (3); 10/251; Debate Tm; NFL; Speech Tm; Thesps; School Play; Rptr Nwsp; Pres Stu Cncl; High Hon Roll; NHS; Ntl Merit SF; NCTE Wrtng Achva Nom; Natl Frnsictnmt; St Champ In Poetry Intrp; Film.

MEYER, KENNY J; Conway Springs HS; Conway Springs, KS; (2); Church Yth Grp; Ftbl; N Cntrl KS Voc Tech; Farm.

MEYER, KIMBERLY; Wellsville Jr Sr HS; Rantoul, KS; (4); 17/47; Church Yth Grp; Drama Clb; 4-H; FBLA; Intnl Clb; Quiz Bowl; SADD; Band; Mrchg Band; Pep Band; KS St Univ; Aged.

MEYER, LESHA K; Washburn Rural HS; Topeka, KS; (3); 55/351; Office Aide; SADD; JV Socr; JV L Tennis; High Hon Roll; Bus.

MEYER, NATALIE L; Madison Jr Sr HS; Madison, KS; (2); 3/28; Church Yth Grp; Cmnty Wkr; GAA; Girl Scts; Letterman Clb; Math Tm; Pep Clb; Spanish Clb; Varsity Clb; Band; Emporia ST; Elem Ed.

MEYERHOFF, MELISSA; Linn Schl; Palmer, KS; (3); 1/19; VP Art Clb; Pres FBLA; Rptr FHA; HOBY; School Play; Rep Stu Cncl; Var JV Vllybl; High Hon Roll; NHS; Letterman Clb; KS St Bd Ed Tech Fair; KS St Cptl House Rep Pg; KS ST U.

MEYERS, CHARISSA J; Wichita East HS; Wichita, KS; (2); Treas Art Clb; Cmnty Wkr; Drama Clb; English Clb; Spanish Clb; Chorus; School Musical; School Play; Hon Roll; Spanish NHS; Cndt Intnl Bcclrt Dplm; Stdnt Ambssdr Russia/Baltic Rep Co W/People/People; IB Lit Scty Mbr.

MEYERSICK, AMBER B; Goddard HS; Goddard, KS; (3); Math Tm; Office Aide; Pep Clb; Science Clb; Teachers Aide; Varsity Clb; High Hon Roll; Pres Acad Fit Awd; Pres Schlr; Var Vllybl.

MHATRE, MONA V; Washburn Rural HS; Topeka, KS; (2); Library Aide; Spanish Clb; Orch; School Musical; High Hon Roll; Nrsng Home Vol; Tae Kwon Do; Topeka Yth Symphony; Pre-Med; Physician.

MICHAEL, CALE E; Washburn Rural HS; Topeka, KS; (2); Church Yth Grp; Band; Mrchg Band; Pep Band; Wrstlng; High Hon Roll; Hon Roll; Johnson Cty CC; Med; Sci.

MICHAELIS, CARRIE; Wabaunsee HS; Paxico, KS; (4); 1/35; Pres Natl FFA Org; Mgr Yrbk; Pres Jr Cls; Sec Stu Cncl; Var Bsktbl; Var Chrldng; Var Pom Pon; Var Vllybl; High Hon Roll; NHS; KS ST U; Info Sys.

MICHAELIS, ERIN E; Hays HS; Hays, KS; (1); Church Yth Grp; Cmnty Wkr; Pep Clb; Bsktbl; JV Var Sftbl; Vllybl; Hon Roll.

MICHAELIS, KAYLYNN M; St Marys HS; Saint Marys, KS; (2); FCA; VP FBLA; Pep Clb; Band; Jazz Band; Mrchg Band; Var JV Bsktbl; L Var Sftbl; JV Var Vllybl; Hon Roll; USVBA.

MICHAELIS, NATALIE; Hugoton HS; Hugoton, KS; (4); 3/62; Am Leg Aux Girls St; Church Yth Grp; FCA; Teachers Aide; Band; Chorus; Swing Chorus; Ofcr Stu Cncl; Bsktbl; Vllybl; KS Hnr Schlr; All-Amer Schlr; KS St U Outstndg Math & Sci Stu 95-96; KS ST U; Accntng.

MICHAUD, DENNA J; Clifton-Clyde HS; Clyde, KS; (3); Church Yth Grp; FBLA; Pep Clb; Red Cross Aide; Band; Mrchg Band; Pep Band; JV Var Bsktbl; Trk; Wt Lftg; Kayettes Pres; Chiropractor.

MICHEL, CESAR; Liberal HS; Liberal, KS; (4); French Clb; Key Clb; Math Clb; Math Tm; Texas Spanish Clb; VICA; JV Bsktbl; Capt Socr; High Hon Roll; Hon Roll; Teens As Tchrs; Lbrl Area Vo-Tech; Elec Tech.

MICKELSON, NOLAN R; Lyndon HS; Lyndon, KS; (3); 3/37; VP FBLA; Math Tm; NFL; Quiz Bowl; SADD; Band; Mrchg Band; Pep Band; School Play; Pres Stu Cncl; Engrng.

MICKEY, CHAD; Dodge City HS; Dodge City, KS; (2); Boy Scts; Jazz Band; Orch; Pep Band; Socr; Wrstlng; Pit Orch For Musicals & Chamber Orch; Stu Of The Month; Coach Little Kids Soccer Team; KS ST Univ; Auto Engrng.

MIDDLESWART, TERESA; Fowler HS; Fowler, KS; (3); Quiz Bowl; Band; VP Pres Frsh Cls; VP Pres Soph Cls; VP Pres Jr Cls; Bsktbl; Chrldng; Trk; Vllybl; High Hon Roll; Pre-Med.

MIDDLETON, LACY M; Northwest HS Wichita; Wichita, KS; (3); Church Yth Grp; Debate Tm; NFL; Speech Tm; Chorus; Variety Show; Bsktbl; Hon Roll; NHS; Supr Rtng St Piano Fstvl.

MIERAU, SUSANNA; Wichita North HS; Wichita, KS; (4); 1/234; Capt Debate Tm; Capt Scholastic Bowl; Capt Science Clb; Band; Sec Stu Cncl; Capt Golf; Pres NHS; Ntl Merit Schol; St Schlr; Val; Sunday Schl Tchr For Pre Schl; MA Inst Of Tech; Brain Sci.

MIKITISH, JOSEPH M; Leavenworth HS; Fort Leavenworth, KS; (3); Boy Scts; Chess Clb; Church Yth Grp; Computer Clb; JV Var Bsbl; JV Wt Lftg; High Hon Roll; Hon Roll; NHS; Optimist Essay Cont Wnnr; Planned Intnl Dinner At Lawton Chrstn Schl; MT Tech; Comp Sci; Engrng.

MILAM, STACY; Olathe South Sr HS; Olathe, KS; (3); Church Yth Grp; Drama Clb; GAA; Thesps; Varsity Clb; Drill Tm; School Musical; School Play; Stage Crew; Variety Show; Drll Tm Cptn; 3 Poems Pblshd; Dance.

MILAM, STACY N; Junction City HS; Junction City, KS; (1); Rep Stu Cncl; Hon Roll; Med.

MILBURN, MIKE; St Mary's Colgan HS; Pittsburg, KS; (2); Scholastic Bowl; Science Clb; L Stat Bsktbl; Ftbl; Mgr(s); Score Keeper; Wt Lftg; High Hon Roll; Prfct Atten Awd; U Of KS; Metrlgst.

MILBY, SHELLY M; Arkansas City HS; Arkansas City, KS; (3); Church Yth Grp; Band.

MILER, STEPHANIE; Gridley HS; Burlington, KS; (3); Church Yth Grp; Dance Clb; FBLA; FHA; Pep Clb; Band; Chorus; Drill Tm; Pep Band; Soph Cls; II Rtng St M Usic Fstvl Soph Yr; Ed.

MILES, CAROLYN M; Burlingame HS; Burlingame, KS; (1); 7/29; 4-H; Natl FFA Org; Band; Mrchg Band; Stat Bsktbl; Mgr(s); JV Vllybl; 4-H Awd; High Hon Roll; Hon Roll; Grnhse; KAYS; Envrnmntls Club; KS Bckskin Hrse Assc; Natl Barrel Hrse Assc; Amer Bckskn Rgstry Assc; KS ST Univ; Animal Sci.

MILES, LANETTA; Lyons HS; Lyons, KS; (1); Drama Clb; Pep Clb; Chorus; Chrldng; Vllybl.

MILFELD, TYLER; Wichita Collegiate Schl; Wichita, KS; (2); 10/65; Debate Tm; Spanish Clb; Speech Tm; Teachers Aide; Score Keeper; JV Tennis; High Hon Roll; Psych.

MILLAR, JESSICA M; Blue Valley Northwest HS; Overland Park, KS; (4); 10/340; Church Yth Grp; Hosp Aide; Q&S; Ed Yrbk; Var Crs Cntry; Powder Puff Ftbl; Var Trk; High Hon Roll; NHS; Pres Schlr; Rensallear Mrt Schlr; KS Hnrs Schlr; Natl Eng Mrt Awd; OK ST Univ; Bio; Med.

MILLARD, JENNIFER; Ulysses HS; Ulysses, KS; (4); 23/93; FHA; Teachers Aide; Chorus; School Musical; Capt Chrldng; Wt Lftg; High Hon Roll; Effort Awd; Ecology Clb; Elem Ed.

MILLARD, KYLIE M; Topeka HS; Topeka, KS; (2); 38/526; Office Aide; Teachers Aide; Chorus; Drill Tm; Treas Jr Cls; Pom Pon; High Hon Roll; Hon Roll.

MILLE, KENDALL E; Ottawa HS; Ottawa, KS; (3); Hon Roll; Military.

MILLER, AARON; Blue Valley Northwest HS; Overland Park, KS; (3); 37/379; Intnl Clb; Spanish Clb; Nwsp; VP Sr Cls; High Hon Roll; Hon Roll; Jr NHS; NHS; Ntl Merit Ltr; FCA; Intnl Poets Soc; Natl Schlr.

MILLER, ALYSON B; Wichita North HS; Wichita, KS; (4); 1/234; VP Jr Cls; Treas Stu Cncl; Pom Pon; Swmmng; Hon Roll; NHS; Pres Schlr; Val; Clb Swimmer; AZ St Univ; Bus.

MILLER, ANGIE M; Belle Plaine HS; Belle Plaine, KS; (4); 10/60; French Clb; Letterman Clb; Pep Clb; SADD; Teachers Aide; Band; Drm Mjr(t); Jazz Band; Pep Band; Yrbk; KS Newman Univ; Rdlgy Tech.

MILLER, BENJAMIN G; Robert E Clark Jr HS; Bonner Springs, KS; (1); Church Yth Grp; Band; Mrchg Band; Var L Trk; Hon Roll; Fr I Frosh Yr; Fr II Soph Yr; KS ST Univ; Mech Eng.

MILLER, BRANDIE; Andale HS; Colwich, KS; (3); Church Yth Grp; Letterman Clb; Pep Clb; SADD; VP Jr Cls; Var Capt Chrldng; Powder Puff Ftbl; Var L Trk; Var Wt Lftg; Hon Roll; KS ST; Radiology.

MILLER, BREANNA G; Topeka HS; Topeka, KS; (3); Church Yth Grp; Teachers Aide; Acpl Chr; Pres Chorus; School Musical; School Play; VP Sr Cls; Capt Chrldng; Powder Puff Ftbl; Sftbl; Psych.

MILLER, BRENT C; Trinity Catholic HS; Hutchinson, KS; (1); 8/36; Debate Tm; Math Tm; NFL; Pep Clb; Band; Jazz Band; Mrchg Band; Pep Band; JV Bsktbl; Stat Ftbl; Univ Of KS; Tax Lawyer.

MILLER, CARLY J; Douglass HS; Douglass, KS; (2); 6/73; Sec FHA; Science Clb; Teachers Aide; High Hon Roll; Teens As Tchrs; Psych.

MILLER, CASSANDRA R; Garden City Sr HS; Garden City, KS; (2); Church Yth Grp; Cmnty Wkr; Latin Clb; Math Tm; Orch; Ed Yrbk; High Hon Roll; Futr Problm Slvrs; Odyssey Of The Mind; NORWICH Univ; Crim Just.

MILLER, CHARLES J; Plainville HS; Plainville, KS; (4); Church Yth Grp; Drama Clb; Sec Natl FFA Org; Pep Clb; Chorus; School Play; Sec Swing Chorus; Rptr Nwsp; Yrbk; Sec Sr Cls; ST Forensics Qualifier 2 Yrs; FFA Schlstc Awd; Booster Of Yr; Ft Hays ST Univ; Elem Ed.

MILLER, CORY J; Arkansas City HS; Arkansas City, KS; (2); JV Bsktbl; NC; Ag Bus.

MILLER, DARIN R; Garden City Sr HS; Garden City, KS; (1); Church Yth Grp; Debate Tm; Tennis; Hon Roll; Yng Life; Ping Pong; KS Univ; Arch.

MILLER, EMILY M; Bishop Miege HS; Shawnee Mission, KS; (2); 50/163; Service Clb; Color Guard; Yrbk; JV Crs Cntry; JV Socr; JV Tennis; Hon Roll.

MILLER, ERICA O; Topeka West HS; Topeka, KS; (3); Art Clb; Cmnty Wkr; Pep Clb; Spanish Clb; SADD; Swmmng; Tennis; High Hon Roll; Hon Roll; KS U.

MILLER, ERIN L; Olathe North Sr HS; Olathe, KS; (4); 91/351; French Clb; Hosp Aide; Band; Phtg Lit Mag; Sec Frsh Cls; Rep Jr Cls; Bsktbl; Socr; JV Vllybl; French Hon Soc; Schl Site Cncl; St Cld St Univ; Meterlgy.

MILLER, GLENN; Campus HS; Haysville, KS; (3); Boy Scts; Church Yth Grp; SADD; Var L Bsbl; Var Ftbl; Wt Lftg; High Hon Roll; Hon Roll; Arch Class; Auto Class; KS U; Arch Dsgn.

MILLER, JANETTE; Downs HS; Downs, KS; (4); 5/20; FHA; Natl FFA Org; Teachers Aide; Band; Pep Band; Var Capt Bsktbl; Trk; Var Capt Vllybl; High Hon Roll; Pres Acad Fit Awd; Ft Hays ST Univ; Ag Bus Mngmt.

MILLER, JASON R; Leavenworth HS; Springville, UT; (3); Boy Scts; Church Yth Grp; Drama Clb; Thesps; Acpl Chr; Church Choir; School Musical; School Play; Wt Lftg; Jr NHS; Brigham Young Univ; Lrng.

MILLER, JENNIFER; Valley Falls HS; Valley Falls, KS; (1); 5/44; FBLA; Band; Chorus; Pep Band; Bsktbl; Sftbl; Ofcr Bsbl; High Hon Roll; Hon Roll; KAY.

MILLER, JESSICA; Royal Valley HS; Mayetta, KS; (4); 15/54; HOBY; Letterman Clb; SADD; Band; Rptr Co-Ed Nwsp; Var L Bsktbl; Var L Trk; Var L Vllybl; Hon Roll; NHS; Nutrition Advsry Cncl; KS Assn Yth; 1st Team All Leag Vllybl; Emporia ST U; Scndry Educ.

MILLER, JESSICA; Atchison Co Cmty HS; Cummings, KS; (1); Chrldng; Vllybl; Hon Roll; KSU; Amer His Tchr.

MILLER, JODI; Goodland HS; Goodland, KS; (3); 13/82; Teachers Aide; Varsity Clb; Ed Yrbk; Var Crs Cntry; Var Sftbl; JV Vllybl; Hon Roll; Pres Acad Fit Awd; NYLF On Medicine; Phy Therapy.

MILLER, JOIE R; St Xavier's HS; Fort Riley, KS; (2); 4/16; Church Yth Grp; FHA; SADD; School Musical; Intrml Bsktbl; L Var Chrldng; L Var Crs Cntry; L JV Trk; L JV Vllybl; High Hon Roll; Hubbard Tchrs Wkshp Schlsp; Regnl Fnlst Crss Cntry & Trk; St Fnlst Amer Co-Ed Paget & Manhattan Model; Weber ST Univ; Elem Ed.

MILLER, JORDAN L; Anderson Cty Jr Sr HS; Greeley, KS; (1); Pep Clb; Band; Mrchg Band; Pep Band; Vllybl; Hon Roll.

MILLER, JULIE M; Chase HS; Chase, KS; (1); Spanish Clb; Vllybl; Hon Roll; KSU; Microbiology.

MILLER, KATIE; Great Bend Sr HS; Great Bend, KS; (3); Church Yth Grp; Cmnty Wkr; FCA; Pep Clb; Spanish Clb; Teachers Aide; Acpl Chr; Variety Show; Rep Soph Cls; VP Sr Cls; Barton Cty CC; Dntl.

MILLER, KELLI; Atchison Co Cmty HS; Atchison, KS; (4); 2/65; Sec VP Church Yth Grp; Letterman Clb; VP SADD; Drill Tm; Trk; Vllybl; High Hon Roll; NHS; Sal; Natl Yth Ldrshp Forum Med; Benedictine Coll; Med.

MILLER, KELLY; Washburn Rural HS; Topeka, KS; (2); 58/380; Debate Tm; Hosp Aide; SADD; Chorus; Variety Show; Yrbk; JV Chrldng; Var JV Crs Cntry; Powder Puff Ftbl; High Hon Roll; Gymnstcs; U Of NC; Neontlgy.

MILLER, KELLY A; Lawrence HS; Lawrence, KS; (4); 1/525; Rep Soph Cls; Var Socr; Var Vllybl; NHS; Val; KS 6-A Vlybl St Chmpns 94, 95.

MILLER, KELLY L; Derby HS; Derby, KS; (3); 3/384; Lit Mag; Ofcr Stu Cncl; JV Socr; High Hon Roll; Pres NHS; Math Tm; Scholastic Bowl; Envrnmnt Clb; Odyssey Of Mnd; Ftr Prblm Slvrs; KS ST U; Vet Med.

MILLER, LAURA J; Independence HS; Neodesha, KS; (1); Orch; Hon Roll; ELP; Chrstn Mnstry Trng; ST Music Fstvl Scnd Div Awd; Voc Trng; Photo Jrnlst.

MILLER, LISA; Wichita Heights HS; Wichita, KS; (3); Bus Profs of Am; Church Yth Grp; Cmnty Wkr; Dance Clb; FCA; FBLA; JA; Pep Clb; SADD; Teachers Aide; Phy Thrpst.

MILLER, MAGGIE; Blue Valley North HS; Leawood, KS; (4); 69/166; Art Clb; Church Yth Grp; Intnl Clb; Service Clb; Co-Ed Lit Mag; Powder Puff Ftbl; Hon Roll; Optmst Clb Awd Rcpt; Mutli Yr Listee; Pres Combnd Ablty Schol; Truman St Univ.

MILLER, MELANIE J; Northwest HS; Wichita, KS; (3); Cmnty Wkr; Hosp Aide; Ski Clb; JV Socr; High Hon Roll; Hon Roll; Jr NHS; NHS; KS Univ; Neonatolgst.

MILLER, MELISA D; Elwood Schl; Saint Joseph, MO; (4); 3/17; Drama Clb; Quiz Bowl; Band; Mgr Bsktbl; Mgr Trk; Cit Awd; Hon Roll; VP Sec NHS; Pres Frsh Cls; Pres Soph Cls; Math Awd; Sci Awd; MO Western ST Coll.

MILLER, MICHELLE M; Turner HS; Kansas City, KS; (2); Church Yth Grp; Drama Clb; NFL; SADD; Thesps; Ofcr Stu Cncl; Hon Roll; Jr NHS; Bus Profs of Am; School Musical; Job's Daughters Pst Hon Queen/Grnd Bethel Jr Princess; BPA 2nd Pl Vrbl Comm/Extmprns 1/4th Pl; Lawyer.

MILLER, MINDY A; Ottawa HS; Ottawa, KS; (2); Girl Scts; Rep Soph Cls; Mgr(s); Powder Puff Ftbl; Mgr Vllybl; High Hon Roll; Hon Roll; Lettered Froh Yr; Emporia ST Univ; Elem Ed.

MILLER, MORGAN; Downs HS; Downs, KS; (2); FCA; FHA; Natl FFA Org; Pep Clb; Band; Chorus; Mrchg Band; Pep Band; JV Bsktbl; Chrldng; Natl Eng Merit Awd; KS Univ; Sports Med.

MILLER, RACHEAL; Caney Valley Jr Sr HS; Caney, KS; (3); 10/80; Art Clb; FBLA; FHA; Pep Clb; Spanish Clb; Band; Mrchg Band; Pep Band; High Hon Roll; Hon Roll; Coffeyville CC; Nrsng.

MILLER, REESE B; Olathe North Sr HS; Olathe, KS; (4); Computer Clb; Drama Clb; Acpl Chr; School Play; Stage Crew; High Hon Roll; Hon Roll; Dsgn/Edit World Wide Web Hmpg HS; Schlrshp Howard E Payne; JCC; Telecomm.

MILLER, SAM D; Atchison Co Cmty HS; Atchison, KS; (4); 15/61; Treas VP Art Clb; Church Yth Grp; Letterman Clb; Varsity Clb; School Musical; School Play; Stage Crew; L Capt Bsktbl; L Capt Ftbl; Score Keeper; 4a KS Bsktbll Champ Tm; All St 3absktbll Tm; Multi Yr Listee; KS St Univ; Ar.

MILLER, SARA E; Buhler HS; Hutchinson, KS; (3); Cmnty Wkr; FCA; Science Clb; SADD; Band; JV Tennis; High Hon Roll; Church Yth Grp; Intnl Clb; Scholastic Bowl; KS Yth Choir; Wichita Yth Symphny; ST Band.

MILLER, SARAH; Rossville HS; Topeka, KS; (3); #4 in class; 4-H; Scholastic Bowl; Band; Jazz Band; Mrchg Band; Pep Band; School Musical; Sec Frsh Cls; JV Bsktbl; JV Var Sftbl; FBLA; Dist Band Alt Sax; KS U; Med.

MILLER, SARAH E; Mankato Jr Sr HS; Mankato, KS; (3); 1/23; Quiz Bowl; Jazz Band; Pres Frsh Cls; Pres Soph Cls; Pres Jr Cls; Bsktbl; Vllybl; High Hon Roll; NHS; DARE Role Model; KS ST U; Legal Profession.

MILLER, SHAWN M; Jayhawk-Linn Jr Sr HS; Prescott, KS; (4); 2/37; Treas Church Yth Grp; Math Tm; Band; School Play; Var Bsktbl; Var Ftbl; High Hon Roll; Hon Roll; NHS; Sal; U Of KS; Aerospace.

MILLER, STACEY; Garden City Sr HS; Garden City, KS; (4); 37/332; French Clb; Science Clb; Vllybl; High Hon Roll; Hon Roll; NHS; Pres Schlr.

MILLER, STACI; Wichita East HS; Wichita, KS; (4); Debate Tm; Spanish Clb; SADD; Var Sftbl; JV Vllybl; Hon Roll; NHS; Spanish NHS; KU Hnr Schlr; Forensics; Natl Forensics League Sec 93; Psycht.

MILLER, STEPHANIE; El Dorado HS; El Dorado, KS; (4); 4/155; Church Yth Grp; Debate Tm; HOBY; Math Clb; Band; Orch; Ed Nwsp; Var L Tennis; High Hon Roll; NHS; Erth Care Clb Coord; Fll Hmcmng Rylty; KS St Coll Engrng Deans Awd; U KS.

MILLER, STEPHANIE M; Kapaun-Mt Carmel HS; Wichita, KS; (3); Chess Clb; Spanish Clb; High Hon Roll; United Crsdr; Crsdr For Life; KU; Ed.

MILLER, TERI; Centre Jr Sr HS; Lincolnville, KS; (2); FBLA; Letterman Clb; Ofcr Stu Cncl; Chorus; Treas Soph Cls; Rep Stu Cncl; Vllybl; High Hon Roll; Hon Roll; NHS.

MILLER, TODD B; Attica Public Schl; Zenda, KS; (4); 2/24; Church Yth Grp; 4-H; Quiz Bowl; Scholastic Bowl; SADD; Band; School Play; VP Stu Cncl; Bsktbl; 4-H Awd; Fort Hays ST U; Farm Mgmt.

MILLER, TRAVIS M; El Dorado HS; Augusta, KS; (3); Boy Scts; Cmnty Wkr; FCA; Key Clb; Letterman Clb; Library Aide; Spanish Clb; Speech Tm; SADD; Teachers Aide; Butler Cty CC; Paramedic.

MILLER, WILLIAM D; Olathe East Sr HS; Overland Park, KS; (4); Church Yth Grp; Letterman Clb; Pep Clb; Teachers Aide; Chorus; Pres Frsh Cls; Rep Stu Cncl; JV Var Bsktbl; Var Ftbl; JV Var Trk; SASH Mem; North Eastern Chptr Of Johnson Cty NAACP Mem; U Of KS; Chem.

MILLERSHASKI, SANDRA; Ingalls Jr Sr HS; Ingalls, KS; (2); 2/25; Dance Clb; Pres 4-H; Letterman Clb; Band; Chorus; Mrchg Band; School Play; Bsktbl; Trk; NHS; 4-H Cncl Gray Cty Treas; K ST.

MILLIGAN, CHRIS; Saint Thomas Aquinas HS; Overland Park, KS; (3); 13/269; Am Leg Boys St; FBLA; German Clb; Math Tm; JV Socr; Var Tennis; High Hon Roll; JETS Awd; NHS; Ntl Merit Ltr; Comp Sci.

MILLIKAN, ERIN E; Maize HS; Wichita, KS; (1); #353 in class; Chorus; Hon Roll; Local Hosp Vol; Dance Classes; CPA.

MILLISON, SHERRIE K; Basehor Linwood HS; Basehor, KS; (2); FHA; SADD; High Hon Roll; REACH; Tch Gymnstcs; PT.

MILLS, ADAM; Washburn Rural HS; Topeka, KS; (2); #67 in class; Wheatland Cycling Team Mem; KU.

MILLS, CARRIE; Cunningham HS; Cunningham, KS; (1); 1/25; Church Yth Grp; Pep Clb; Science Clb; SADD; Band; Chorus; Mrchg Band; Pep Band; JV Var Bsktbl; Var Powder Puff Ftbl; Sm Schls Essay Cont Div II 1st Pl; Piano Accmpnst; Sub Chrch Pianist; Anml Sci.

MILLS, JASON; Eureka Jr Sr HS; Eureka, KS; (3); Letterman Clb; Quiz Bowl; SADD; Thesps; Orch; VP Stu Cncl; Var Bsbl; Var Crs Cntry; Var Trk; Science Clb; Wichita Wind Ensmbl; KS ST Univ; PHD Music.

MILLS, JENNIFER L; Clearwater HS; Clearwater, KS; (3); 4/90; FCA; Yrbk; VP Frsh Cls; Pres Soph Cls; Pres Jr Cls; Var Bsktbl; Var Vllybl; High Hon Roll; NHS.

MILLS, KATHLEEN S; Newton Sr HS; Newton, KS; (4); 12/213; Church Yth Grp; Am Leg Aux Girls St; Cmnty Wkr; French Clb; FTA; Office Aide; Scholastic Bowl; Chorus; School Musical; Swmmng; KS Honors Schol; Concordia Col; Premed.

MILLS, KRISTINA; Columbus HS; Weir, KS; (3); Drama Clb; FCA; Library Aide; Pep Clb; Acpl Chr; Chorus; Chrldng; Mgr(s); Score Keeper; Pittsburg ST U.

MILLSAP, KYLE; Wichita East HS; Wichita, KS; (3); Band; Chorus; Jazz Band; Mrchg Band; Orch; Pep Band; School Musical; Variety Show; High Hon Roll; Wichita Wind Ensemble & Yth Symphony Orch; Mid KS Jazz Ensemble; Music Perfmnc.

MILROY, DAVID R; Shawnee Mission E Sr HS; Prairie Village, KS; (4); 28/373; Church Yth Grp; Natl Beta Clb; Acpl Chr; Treas Sr Cls; Rep Stu Cncl; Var Stu Cncl; Var Crs Cntry; High Hon Roll; NHS; Pres Schlr; Univ Of KS; PT.

MILUM, JODY N; Minneapolis HS; Minneapolis, KS; (4); 1/40; French Clb; Math Tm; Teachers Aide; Chorus; Sec Frsh Cls; Sec Soph Cls; Sec Jr Cls; Sec Sr Cls; L Trk; L Vllybl; KS ST Univ; Acctng.

MINARD, ROBERT J; El Dorado HS; Leon, KS; (2); Boy Scts; Debate Tm; Scholastic Bowl; Spanish Clb; JV Tennis; High Hon Roll; Hon Roll; Pres Acad Fit Awd; USAF Acad; Comp Pgrmmng.

MINCHER, JESSICA L; Bishop Miege HS; Overland Park, KS; (1); Church Yth Grp; JV Vllybl; High Hon Roll; Red Crss Cert Lifeguard; CMT.

MINDELL, MARA; Topeka HS; Topeka, KS; (3); Thesps; Acpl Chr; School Musical; School Play; Variety Show; Treas Jr Cls; Treas Stu Cncl; Powder Puff Ftbl; NHS; STRAPP.

MINER, ANDY R; Beloit Jr Sr HS; Beloit, KS; (1); Drama Clb; Quiz Bowl; Speech Tm; Band; Mrchg Band; Pep Band; School Play; Stage Crew; Variety Show; High Hon Roll; Atty.

MINGS, JUSTIN B; Lakin HS; Lakin, KS; (2); Red Cross Aide; JV Bsbl; Var Ftbl; Var Wt Lftg; Hon Roll; KS ST; Sprts Trnr.

MINGUS, CHRISTINA A; Meade HS; Meade, KS; (2); Cmnty Wkr; GAA; Letterman Clb; Math Tm; Pep Clb; Band; Mrchg Band; Pep Band; Var Trk; JV Var Vllybl; Kayetts; Dodge City CC; Beautician.

MINK, JESSICA R; Great Bend Sr HS; Great Bend, KS; (3); Key Clb; Band; Church Choir; Drm Mjr(t); Jazz Band; Mrchg Band; Orch; Pep Band; Variety Show; Teachers Aide; Musical Work Horse Awd; KS Lions Band 2 Yrs; Regnl Honor Band 2 Yrs; KS ST Univ; Music Ed.

MINNER, ROD P; Wichita Southeast HS; Wichita, KS; (4); JA; Teachers Aide; Ofcr Bsbl; Bsktbl; Ftbl; Wt Lftg; High Hon Roll; Hon Roll; KS Univ; Chiropractor.

MINOR, CINDY A; Labette Co HS; Oswego, KS; (2); 3/158; Church Yth Grp; FBLA; FHA; SADD; High Hon Roll; KS Assn Yth; Lib Clb; Math & Bus Ind Achvt Awds; Rennaisance.

MINOR, MELANIE M; Wichita Southeast HS; Wichita, KS; (1); 79/455; Library Aide; Span 6 Yrs; High GPA Alg I Frosh Yr; U Of NM; RN/SPAN.

MINOR, TIFFANY E; Andover HS; Andover, KS; (3); 56/176; Church Yth Grp; French Clb; Girl Scts; Teachers Aide; Chorus; School Musical; School Play; Lit Mag; Stat Bsktbl; JV Var Mgr(s); Camp Cnslr; Girl Scout Vol; Campus Life; Letterwmn; Wmns Vcl Ensmbl.

MINTNER, ANNIE M; Bonner Springs HS; Bonner Springs, KS; (3); Cmnty Wkr; Pres Key Clb; Office Aide; SADD; Teachers Aide; Acpl Chr; Band; Church Choir; School Musical; School Play; Johnson County CC; Ed.

MINTSKOVSKY, MICHAEL; Blue Valley Northwest HS; Overland Park, KS; (3); 73/353; Boy Scts; Chess Clb; Computer Clb; Debate Tm; Math Clb; Math Tm; NFL; Pep Clb; Temple Yth Grp; Mgr Socr; 47th Annual AHSME 3rd Pl; Speak/Write Russian; Vlntr; K-ST; Comp Sci.

MIRES, NATHAN E; Blue Valley HS; Olathe, KS; (2); Band; Jazz Band; Mrchg Band; Pep Band; Cit Awd; High Hon Roll; Hon Roll; Ctznshp Awd.

MIROSTAW, JAY; St Thomas Aquinas HS; Shawnee Mission, KS; (3); 65/261; Am Leg Boys St; FCA; Var L Bsktbl; High Hon Roll; Pre-Law.

MIRSAFIAN, SUDABEN; Wichita East HS; Wichita, KS; (2); Rep Debate Tm; Sec Soph Cls; JV Socr; JV Vllybl; Rep French Hon Soc; Rep High Hon Roll; Rep NHS; Rep French Clb; Rep Teachers Aide; Rep Frsh Cls; Natl Forensics League Treas 95-; Natl French Exam 11th Pl 94-95; Gymnastics; Med.

MISER, MOLLY J; Chase Co HS; Cottonwood Falls, KS; (4); 2/37; Church Yth Grp; Cmnty Wkr; VP 4-H; Ed Nwsp; Ed Yrbk; Treas Sr Cls; Capt L Bsktbl; NHS; Sal; St Schlr; KS St Univ.

MISHLER, JUSTIN; Clearwater HS; Clearwater, KS; (3); Boy Scts; Church Yth Grp; 4-H; 4-H Awd; Hon Roll; Prfct Atten Awd; Elctrcl Eng.

MISIEWICZ, ERIN; St Thomas Aquinas HS; Lenexa, KS; (4); Am Leg Aux Girls St; Cmnty Wkr; German Clb; Hosp Aide; Model UN; NFL; Nwsp; Var Capt Crs Cntry; Var Trk; NHS; Spec Ed.

MISRA, SANDEEP; Blue Valley Northwest HS; Shawnee Mission, KS; (4); 45/340; Ed Lit Mag; Capt Socr; JETS Awd; U Of KS; Elec Eng.

MITCHELL, ALICIA; Kapaun-Mt Carmel HS; Wichita, KS; (2); Cmnty Wkr; Girl Scts; Q&S; SADD; Ed Yrbk; Bsktbl; L Trk; JV Vllybl; High Hon Roll; NHS.

MITCHELL, BRIAN; Neodesha Jr Sr HS; Neodesha, KS; (3); 14/65; Am Leg Boys St; Letterman Clb; Math Tm; Natl FFA Org; Pep Clb; Ed Nwsp; Bsktbl; Var Ftbl; Var Tennis; Hon Roll; KS Univ; Med.

MITCHELL, BROOK; Hamilton HS; Hamilton, KS; (3); Church Yth Grp; FCA; FHA; Letterman Clb; Quiz Bowl; Scholastic Bowl; Pres Frsh Cls; Pres Soph Cls; Pres Jr Cls; Var Bsktbl; All Amer Schlr; Emporia U; Envrnmntl Bio.

MITCHELL, DALE B; Maranatha Acad; Shawnee Mission, KS; (3); Church Yth Grp; Pep Clb; Band; Mrchg Band; Pep Band; Treas Jr Cls; JV Bsbl; Var L Socr; Hon Roll; Bus.

MITCHELL, DAVID; Hays HS; Hays, KS; (3); 15/237; Debate Tm; Math Tm; NFL; Speech Tm; Nwsp; JV Bsbl; L JV Crs Cntry; Var L Trk; Jr NHS; Ntl Merit Ltr; U Of KS; Pol Sci.

MITCHELL, DAVID; Valley Falls HS; Valley Falls, KS; (3); Church Yth Grp; FHA; Pep Clb; Teachers Aide; Varsity Clb; Chorus; Bsktbl; Crs Cntry; Trk; Hon Roll; Cedarville Coll; Law Enforcemnt.

MITCHELL, ERIN; Shawnee Mission N HS; Leawood, KS; (4); Church Yth Grp; Office Aide; Pep Clb; Spanish Clb; Chorus; Chrmn Rep Stu Cncl; Var L Chrldng; JV Socr; Hon Roll; Bid To Natls Chrldng 95-96; Johnson Cty CC; Psych.

MITCHELL, GREG; Olathe East Sr HS; Olathe, KS; (2); Computer Clb; Spanish Clb; Band; Ed Nwsp; High Hon Roll; Hon Roll; Ntl Merit Ltr; Pres Schlr; Explorers Post; Dentistry; Medicine.

MITCHELL, GREGORY J; Maize HS; Wichita, KS; (2); Var Bsbl; Var Ftbl; High Hon Roll; Hon Roll; Jr NHS; Prfct Atten Awd; TX Tech; Arch.

MITCHELL, HOLLY; Emporia HS; Emporia, KS; (1); Church Yth Grp; Pep Clb; Chrldng; JV Var Socr; SMILE Club; U Of NC; Sports Med.

MITCHELL, JACOB L; J C Harmon HS; Kansas City, KS; (4); VP Drama Clb; School Play; Co-Ed Nwsp; JV Ftbl; Hon Roll; NHS; Actr Of Yr 94-; Cmmncmnt Spkr; Johnson Cty CC; Advrtsng/Drama.

MITCHELL, JAY; Wellington Sr HS; Wellington, KS; (1); Church Yth Grp; Band; Chorus; Jazz Band; Mrchg Band; Pep Band; Rptr Stu Cncl; Ftbl; Golf; Wrstlng; Rotary Schlr Awd; Outstdng Mscnshp Awd Intl Assn Jazz Edctrs; I Rtng Reg ST Music Fstvl.

MITCHELL, JESSE H; Sabetha HS; Sabetha, KS; (3); 25/84; Church Yth Grp; Cmnty Wkr; FHA; Pep Clb; Spanish Clb; Teachers Aide; Var Golf; Pres Acad Fit Awd; KS U; Comp Programming.

MITCHELL, JULIANN D; Wellington Sr HS; Wellington, KS; (4); 12/122; Church Yth Grp; Cmnty Wkr; Key Clb; Red Cross Aide; Ed Yrbk; Treas Jr Cls; Sec Sr Cls; Rep Stu Cncl; Var Chrldng; Trk; Wichita Gymnstcs Clb 6 Yrs Cmptn; KS Hnr Schlr; NCA All Amer Chrldr; All Amer Spirit Chrldr; KS U.

MITCHELL, KATIE E; Augusta Sr HS; Augusta, KS; (2); Drama Clb; French Clb; Band; Mrchg Band; Pep Band; Stage Crew; High Hon Roll; NHS; Tchr.

MITCHELL, MELISSA A; Louisburg HS; Paola, KS; (2); Church Yth Grp; Spanish Clb; Speech Tm; SADD; Band; Church Choir; Mrchg Band; Pep Band; Wt Lftg; High Hon Roll; Piano; KU; RN.

MITCHELL, MOLLY K; South Haven Schl; South Haven, KS; (1); Church Yth Grp; Drama Clb; FHA; Math Tm; Natl FFA Org; Band; Jazz Band; Mrchg Band; School Play; Pres Frsh Cls; Piano Lsns 1 Rtng All Cntsts; Quiz Bwl Team; Gifted Prgrm; OK ST Univ; Animal Sci.

MITCHENER, AIMEE; Wichita North HS; Wichita, KS; (2); 12/395; French Clb; Band; Mrchg Band; Pep Band; Rptr Nwsp; JV Bsktbl; Hon Roll; Elem Ed.

MITCHUM, PATRICK S; Wichita East HS; Wichita, KS; (2); Boy Scts; Church Yth Grp; Mgr Nwsp; Crs Cntry; Socr; Swmmng; AZ ST Univ.

MITTEL, JESSICA J; Great Bend Sr HS; Great Bend, KS; (4); 20/217; Pep Clb; Swmmng; Hon Roll; NHS; U KS.

MITTS, KYLENE; Olathe South Sr HS; Olathe, KS; (3); 1/425; Church Yth Grp; Spanish Clb; Band; Drill Tm; Stage Crew; JV Sftbl; High Hon Roll; VP NHS; Pres Acad Fit Awd; Spanish NHS; Outstdng Bio, Eng & Span Stu.

MITZEL, DAVID; Corinthian Chrstn Acad; Newton, KS; (3); Art Clb; Church Yth Grp; Drill Tm; School Play; JV Ftbl; JV Wt Lftg; ST Art Comp; Ntl ACE Art Comp; Mid Amer Bible Coll; Crtnst/Art.

MIX, MIKE L; Uniontown HS; Uniontown, KS; (3); #3 in class; Art Clb; VP FCA; Math Clb; Spanish Clb; Rptr Yrbk; High Hon Roll; Hon Roll; NHS; Prfct Atten Awd; Ministry.

MIZE, KEVIN D; Shawnee Mission S Sr HS; Overland Park, KS; (4); Cmnty Wkr; Debate Tm; Natl Beta Clb; L Capt Bsktbl; Var Trk; Wt Lftg; High Hon Roll; Hon Roll; NHS; Pres Acad Fit Awd; 1st, 2nd, 3rd & 4th Yr Schlrshp Pins; Debate & Trk Ltrs; Vanderbilt U; Bus.

MIZNER, KENNY R; White Rock HS; Esbon, KS; (2); 5/14; 4-H; Letterman Clb; Math Tm; Natl FFA Org; Pep Clb; SADD; Varsity Clb; VP Frsh Cls; VP Soph Cls; Var Bsktbl; Ag Mechanics Awd; Livestock & Land Judging; FFA; Hays; Ag.

MOATS, ASHLEY S; Blue Valley HS; Stilwell, KS; (3); 5/252; Intnl Clb; Teachers Aide; Mgr L Bsktbl; Var Mgr(s); JV Trk; JV Capt Vllybl; High Hon Roll; NHS; Olympic Vllybl Teams; NCTE Wrtng Awd; Jr Outstdng Wrtr Awd; Amer His Achvmt Awd; Tiger Pride; Ed.

MOATS, ORIN; Blue Valley HS; Stilwell, KS; (2); JV Bsktbl; JV Socr; JV Trk; Hon Roll.

MOATS, SHANA; Campus HS; Wichita, KS; (4); 30/213; Am Leg Aux Girls St; Cmnty Wkr; Q&S; SADD; Teachers Aide; Orch; Yrbk; High Hon Roll; Hon Roll; Pt 5 Awd; Eng Dlgnce Awd; U KS; Jrnlsm.

MOBERG, KAREN; Olathe South Sr HS; Olathe, KS; (3); Drama Clb; Math Tm; Band; Mrchg Band; Pep Band; School Play; Stat Vllybl; High Hon Roll; NHS; KS ST U; Veterinary Medicine.

MOCK, HEATHER; Goddard Jr HS; Wichita, KS; (1); Band; Mrchg Band; Ed Nwsp; Co-Ed Yrbk; High Hon Roll; Ldr Pck Awd; Elem Ed.

MOCK, JENNIFER L; Nickerson HS; South Hutchinson, KS; (4); Girl Scts; Teachers Aide; Nwsp; Tennis; Wt Lftg; Girl Sct Gold Awd; Lifeguard; Hutchinson CC; Nrsng.

MODICH, MICHAEL R; Independence HS; Independence, KS; (1); Church Yth Grp; Pep Clb; Ofcr Bsbl; Ftbl; Trk; Wt Lftg; Wrstlng; Hon Roll; Pres Acad Fit Awd; Engr/Ftbl/Bsbl Coach.

MODLIN, CHRISTINA R; Paola HS; Paola, KS; (4); Pres Art Clb; Debate Tm; Drama Clb; NFL; Speech Tm; SADD; Teachers Aide; Thesps; High Hon Roll; Hon Roll; KS U; Poly Sci.

MODROW, JUSTIN A; Ellsworth HS; Kanopolis, KS; (2); #43 in class; Intrml Trk; Hon Roll; Prfct Atten Awd; 4-H Clb.

MOEDER, ALISHA; Otis Bison HS; Otis, KS; (1); Church Yth Grp; NFL; SADD; Band; Chorus; Church Choir; School Play; Mgr(s); Trk; Hon Roll; KAYS.

MOEDER, JULIE; Thomas More Prep-Marian HS; Hays, KS; (4); Am Leg Aux Girls St; Debate Tm; HOBY; Math Tm; Model UN; Speech Tm; Chorus; Orch; School Musical; School Play; Ft Hays ST U; Elem Ed.

MOFFITT, AUTUMN; Maize HS; Wichita, KS; (4); Cmnty Wkr; Debate Tm; Drama Clb; FCA; NFL; Science Clb; Service Clb; Spanish Clb; SADD; Thesps; Pittsburgh St Univ.

MOGLE, BRANDY; Basehor Linwood HS; Basehor, KS; (4); 3/124; Cmnty Wkr; Pres 4-H; Sec FBLA; HOBY; Sec Treas Science Clb; Pres Sec Stu Cncl; Mgr(s); 4-H Awd; NHS; Sal; Org Rgnl Lock-In; PRIDE Comm; I Dare You Awd; 4-H Key Awd; U Of KS; Adv.

MOHLER, WENDY; Circle HS; El Dorado, KS; (3); 7/98; Church Yth Grp; Acpl Chr; Band; Church Choir; Flag Corp; School Musical; Ofcr Stu Cncl; Golf; High Hon Roll; NHS; Butler Cty CC; Nrsng.

MOHLMAN, CLAIRE; White Rock HS; Esbon, KS; (2); 3/15; Church Yth Grp; HOBY; Letterman Clb; Math Tm; Quiz Bowl; SADD; Spanish Clb; Var L Bsktbl; Var L Vllybl; High Hon Roll.

MOHR, ERIN C; Wichita West HS; Wichita, KS; (4); Church Yth Grp; FCA; Hosp Aide; Service Clb; Pres SADD; Rep Stu Cncl; Chrldng; Mgr(s); Socr; High Hon Roll; Photo; Wichita ST U; Physician Asst.

MOHWINKLE, RYAN C; Hayden HS; Topeka, KS; (3); Ofcr Bsbl; Ftbl; Tennis; Wt Lftg; Hon Roll; Orthodontist.

MOISE, ROBERT W; Pierson Jr HS; Kansas City, KS; (1); Chorus; Hon Roll; KS Univ.

MOLAMPHY, DAVID R; Wichita East HS; Wichita, KS; (4); 14/278; Pres Church Yth Grp; Cmnty Wkr; Q&S; Yrbk; Rep Stu Cncl; L Bsktbl; L Ftbl; Mgr(s); High Hon Roll; NHS; Wichita Bus Jrnl-Sptlght Srs; KS Shrine Bwl; Crmr Athl Cmps; KS St U; Engrng.

MOLAMPHY, MARK; Wichita East HS; Wichita, KS; (2); Church Yth Grp; Cmnty Wkr; Teachers Aide; Bsktbl; Var L Ftbl; Var Trk; Wt Lftg; Var L Wrstlng; Hon Roll; All Cty Hnrbl Mntn Nose Tckl Ftbl.

MOLGREN, ZACH J; Newton Sr HS; Newton, KS; (4); Church Yth Grp; Hon Roll; Bicycle Rdng; Hutchinson CC; Bus Admin.

MOLL, MATTHEW J; Stockton HS; Stockton, KS; (4); 2/33; Church Yth Grp; Cmnty Wkr; Debate Tm; FHA; Pep Clb; Quiz Bowl; Speech Tm; Band; Jazz Band; Mrchg Band; KS Schlr Awd; Natl Engrng Dsgn Chllng; U Of KS; Med.

MOLLER, HEATHER A; Mankato Jr Sr HS; Mankato, KS; (2); 3/35; Church Yth Grp; VP FHA; Chorus; Swing Chorus; Nwsp; L Trk; Vllybl; High Hon Roll; Hon Roll; Letterman Clb; Forensics; Pre-Med.

MOLLETT, CAROLYN A; Hutchinson HS; Hutchinson, KS; (4); 7/266; Church Yth Grp; Cmnty Wkr; French Clb; GAA; Key Clb; Letterman Clb; Pep Clb; Q&S; Science Clb; Varsity Clb; Young Amer Top 10; Class Top 10; KS Hnr Schlr; UNIV Of KS; Jrnlsm; His.

MOLNAR, MATTY; Bishop Miege HS; Prairie Village, KS; (4); 82/160; Am Leg Boys St; Acpl Chr; Church Choir; School Musical; Variety Show; Rep Stu Cncl; Hon Roll; Church Yth Grp; SADD; Teachers Aide; Music Dept Awd; Chrstn Ldrshp Awd; St Music Cmptns Vocal Super Ratngs; Emporia ST U; Music Ed.

MOLZ, PHILENE; St Thomas Aquinas HS; Overland Park, KS; (1); Cmnty Wkr; German Clb; Hosp Aide; SADD; Drill Tm; Co-Capt Chrldng; Vllybl; High Hon Roll; Jr NHS; Pres Acad Fit Awd; Duke U Math Tlnt Prog; Cincinnati City Bllt; Gold & Slvr Mdls Natl Dnc Cmptn; Notre Dame; Bus.

MOMENT, MARISSA N; Wichita Heights HS; Wichita, KS; (3); Am Leg Aux Girls St; Church Yth Grp; Debate Tm; VP French Clb; NFL; SADD; Var Crs Cntry; Var Tennis; YPT; EHI; Adv/Fshn/Textiles.

MONFORT, ROY; Iola Sr HS; Iola, KS; (3); Am Leg Boys St; 4-H; FBLA; 4-H Awd; Hon Roll; NHS; KS ST U; Criminology.

MONGOLD, CHASITY; Sublette HS; Liberal, KS; (3); 8/31; Teachers Aide; Band; Chorus; Flag Corp; Mrchg Band; Pep Band; School Musical; Var Mgr(s); JV Vllybl; Hon Roll; KAYS; GCTL; AFS.

MONK, KEITH M; Topeka HS; Topeka, KS; (4); Teachers Aide; Band; Jazz Band; Mrchg Band; Pep Band; High Hon Roll; AFS VP; Colby Coll; Lawyer.

MONROE, JENNIFER L; Blue Valley HS; Stilwell, KS; (4); 4/229; Am Leg Aux Girls St; Jazz Band; Mrchg Band; Pep Band; Rptr Stu Cncl; High Hon Roll; VP NHS; St Schlr; Girl Scts; Band; USMC Schlstc Excl Awd; Optmst Ldrshp Awd; KS Regnts Hnrs Acad; KS ST U; Elem Ed.

MONROE, STEPHANIE; Blue Valley HS; Stilwell, KS; (2); 1/282; Church Yth Grp; Band; Mrchg Band; Treas Soph Cls; Treas Jr Cls; Var L Crs Cntry; Var L Trk; High Hon Roll; Church Yth Grp; Pep Band; Prins Cncl; Safe Schls Comm; Peer Cnslr.

MONSER, KRISTIN; Blue Valley HS; Olsburg, KS; (3); 1/33; Treas Church Yth Grp; VP FTA; HOBY; Quiz Bowl; Pres Spanish Clb; Band; Treas Jr Cls; Var Bsktbl; Var Trk; Var Vllybl; Piano Perf; Stu Of Mnth; Washburn U; Acctng.

MONTANDON, CRYSTAL; Central HS; Grenola, KS; (4); 6/28; English Clb; Pep Clb; Band; Chorus; Jazz Band; Pep Band; School Play; Chrldng; Sftbl; Cit Awd; John Phillip Sousa Band Awd; Natl Choral Awd; US Navy.

MONTEE, STACY; Shawnee Mission NW HS; Lenexa, KS; (2); 19/450; Church Yth Grp; Drama Clb; Thesps; Acpl Chr; Drill Tm; Mrchg Band; School Musical; VP Soph Cls; High Hon Roll; Hon Roll; Phys Thpy.

MONTGOMERY, AUDREY L; Hays HS; Hays, KS; (3); Pep Clb; Teachers Aide; Stage Crew; Var Bsktbl; Var Crs Cntry; Var Sftbl; Prfct Atten Awd; KS Univ; Sec Ed.

MONTGOMERY, AUTUMN R; Garden Plain Jr Sr HS; Garden Plain, KS; (3); Chess Clb; Quiz Bowl; Sec Spanish Clb; SADD; Band; Mrchg Band; Pep Band; School Play; Stat Bsktbl.

MONTGOMERY, CAMILLA; Norton Comm HS; Norton, KS; (4); 4/41; Church Yth Grp; Math Tm; Model UN; Pep Clb; Pres SADD; Band; Ofcr Stu Cncl; Pom Pon; Vllybl; Hon Roll; Bible Bowl; Manhattan Chrstn Col; Phys Thpy.

MONTGOMERY, DANNY J; Hays HS; Hays, KS; (3); Var Bsbl; JV Intrml Bsktbl; JV Crs Cntry; Hon Roll; 1st Schl/2nd ST HS Stock Mrkt Game; Law Enfrcmnt/Pol Sci.

MONTGOMERY, ERA L; Garden Plain Jr Sr HS; Garden Plain, KS; (4); 1/30; VP Scholastic Bowl; SADD; Band; Chorus; Co-Capt Drill Tm; Jazz Band; Mrchg Band; Pep Band; Gov Hon Prg Awd; High Hon Roll; Pittsburg ST Univ.

MONTOYA, CHRISTY L; Quivira Heights HS; Holyrood, KS; (2); Nrsng.

MONTY, KELLY J; Hutchinson HS; Nickerson, KS; (3); Debate Tm; Drama Clb; FHA; Quiz Bowl; School Play; Stage Crew; VP Frsh Cls; Mgr(s); JV Tennis; Hon Roll; Dtctv.

MOODY, ERIK B; Protection Schl; Protection, KS; (2); 5/22; Letterman Clb; Band; Mrchg Band; Pep Band; Var L Bsktbl; Var Capt Ftbl; Wt Lftg; Hon Roll.

MOON, AMY; Wichita South HS; Wichita, KS; (3); Boy Scts; Hosp Aide; SADD; Chorus; School Musical; Variety Show; Nwsp; Crs Cntry; Trk; High Hon Roll; Wichita ST Univ; Tchng; Cnslng.

MOON, ERIC W; Burlingame HS; Burlingame, KS; (1); 1/29; Scholastic Bowl; Spanish Clb; Band; Mrchg Band; Pep Band; Pres Frsh Cls; JV Ftbl; Var Trk; Var Wrstlng; High Hon Roll; KS ST Univ; Math; Physics.

MOON, ROSE; Derby HS; Derby, KS; (3); Church Yth Grp; FCA; Acpl Chr; Chorus; Church Choir; School Musical; School Play; Variety Show; Hon Roll; Msn Trp AZ; Sftbl For Ch; Emporia ST Univ; Ed/Tchr.

MOONEY, JENNIFER J; Washington HS; Kansas City, KS; (2); German Clb; SADD; Hon Roll; Acad Ltr 9/10; Psych.

MOONEY, RACHEL M; Minneola Schl; Minneola, KS; (3); Church Yth Grp; Cmnty Wkr; Speech Tm; Chorus; School Musical; Bsktbl; High Hon Roll; Hon Roll; Pres Acad Fit Awd; GAA; Acad Olympics; KS ST Univ; Fashion Mrktg.

MOONEY, TOMMIE; Columbus HS; Columbus, KS; (2); Bus Profs of Am; FCA; FHA; Chorus; School Musical; JV Var Bsktbl; Powder Puff Ftbl; Sftbl; Wt Lftg; Hon Roll; Med.

MOORE, ANDREA V; Hartford HS; Neosho Rapids, KS; (3); 4/18; Drama Clb; Sec FHA; Hosp Aide; Quiz Bowl; SADD; School Play; Sec Stu Cncl; Hon Roll; Forensics; Home Ec Fair; KS Univ; Nrsng.

MOORE, ASHLEY; Blue Valley HS; Leawood, KS; (2); Pres Latin Clb; Rptr Nwsp; JV Chrldng; Hon Roll; Jr Classial League Hnr Soc; Jrnlsm.

MOORE, ASTASIA L; Olathe East Sr HS; Olathe, KS; (2); Drama Clb; Pep Clb; Spanish Clb; Acpl Chr; Church Choir; Drill Tm; School Play; Stage Crew; Swing Chorus; High Hon Roll; Mdlng Hoffman Intl; KS St.

MOORE, AUBREE L; Great Bend Sr HS; Great Bend, KS; (2); Church Yth Grp; FCA; Pep Clb; Spanish Clb; L Var Crs Cntry; L Trk; High Hon Roll; Band; JV Bsktbl; Hon Roll; Church Jr Deacon; Vol AAU Track Coach; Kayettes Club.

MOORE, BRENT N; Olathe South Sr HS; Olathe, KS; (4); 151/367; Church Yth Grp; Cmnty Wkr; Teachers Aide; Band; Mrchg Band; Phtg Nwsp; Phtg Yrbk; Lit Mag; Hon Roll; Lifegrd; Asst Dir Aftr Schl Prgm Schl Yr YMCA; Dsgnd Lndscpng Sr Prjct HS Courtyrd; Bot/Grnhous Asst; Mid Amer Nazarene Coll; Relgn.

MOORE, CHARLES F; Hope HS; Woodbine, KS; (3); FBLA; Scholastic Bowl; Hon Roll.

MOORE, CHRISTINA L; Tonganoxie HS; Tonganoxie, KS; (4); 7/125; Church Yth Grp; FCA; FHA; GAA; Science Clb; Pres Spanish Clb; SADD; Teachers Aide; Pres Soph Cls; Pres Jr Cls; John Danforth I Dare You Awd; All Area & All Trnmt Teams Vllybl & Bsktbl; KS City Star Schlr Ath; Neosho Cty CC.

MOORE II, CLINTON W; Cherryvale HS; Independence, KS; (4); Computer Clb; FHA; Scholastic Bowl; Spanish Clb; Acpl Chr; Band; Chorus; Church Choir; Jazz Band; Mrchg Band; Army Achvmt Medal; Multi Yr Listee; Pittsburg ST KS; Comp Engr.

MOORE, DANIELLE R; Newton Sr HS; Newton, KS; (4); 97/203; Bus Profs of Am; French Clb; Varsity Clb; Stage Crew; Bsktbl; Mgr(s); Score Keeper; Sftbl; Vllybl; Wt Lftg; Var Lttrmn Sftbl 3 Yrs Row; Ft Scott CC; Athltc Trnr.

MOORE, DANNY S; Wichita East HS; Wichita, KS; (2); L Bsbl; Hon Roll.

MOORE, DAWN M; Baldwin HS; Baldwin City, KS; (4); Church Yth Grp; 4-H; FHA; Library Aide; Pep Clb; Mgr(s); Score Keeper; Tennis; Cit Awd; 4-H Awd; Drawing; Universal Tech Inst; Prof CAD.

MOORE, DENNIS W; Olathe North Sr HS; Olathe, KS; (2); Church Yth Grp; Cmnty Wkr; Drama Clb; French Clb; Latin Clb; Math Clb; Math Tm; Quiz Bowl; Science Clb; Thesps; Sevrl Math Awds Incldng Silvr Medl At St Levl; Acad, Dram & Chor Ltrs; Selct Mens Chor Suprr Ratng.

MOORE, DIANE; Frankft HS; Frankfort, KS; (4); Am Leg Aux Girls St; Pres Sec FHA; Girl Scts; Pep Clb; SADD; Band; Chorus; Drm Mjr(t); Mrchg Band; Pep Band; Barton Cty CC; Phys Thrp.

MOORE, EDDIE A; Wichita East HS; Wichita, KS; (2); JV Bsbl; Chef.

MOORE, GREG; Arkansas City HS; Arkansas City, KS; (4); Church Yth Grp; FCA; SADD; Rep Jr Cls; Sec Sr Cls; Var Ftbl; Var Wrstlng; Hon Roll; NHS; US Naval Acad; Engrng.

MOORE, JAMES L; Wellsville Jr Sr HS; Wellsville, KS; (1); FCA; FBLA; Ofcr Frsh Cls; JV Ftbl; Trk; Wt Lftg; Wrstlng.

MOORE, JAVEN D; Sedan HS; Chautauqua, KS; (2); 9/33; Cmnty Wkr; FHA; Letterman Clb; Natl FFA Org; Spanish Clb; Rep Frsh Cls; Pres Soph Cls; JV Bsbl; Var L Bsktbl; Hon Roll; Star Greenhand FFA; Proficency Awd FFA; FFA Ofcrs Reporter/Sentinel; Ag.

MOORE, JENNY; Shawnee Mission East HS; Shawnee Mission, KS; (3); 90/400; Church Yth Grp; Cmnty Wkr; Letterman Clb; Model UN; Natl Beta Clb; Q&S; Varsity Clb; Rptr Nwsp; JV Socr; Var Tennis; K-Life Chrstn Yth Group; Jrnlsm; Advertising.

MOORE, JEREMY L; Halstead HS; Halstead, KS; (3); Church Yth Grp; Chorus; School Musical; Swing Chorus; Var Mgr(s); Var Ftbl; Var Wt Lftg; Law Enfcmnt.

MOORE, JOHN; Muluane HS; Mulvane, KS; (4); 23/133; Mrchg Band; Ftbl; Wrstlng; Hon Roll; KS St Univ; Math.

MOORE, JULIE B; Council Grove HS; Council Grove, KS; (2); Art Clb; FCA; SADD; Chorus; School Musical; Variety Show; Bsktbl; Crs Cntry; Vllybl; High Hon Roll; KS St Univ; Psych.

MOORE, JUSTIN S; Seaman Sr HS; Topeka, KS; (3); 93/300; Church Yth Grp; Cmnty Wkr; Var L Bsbl; Intrml Wt Lftg; Hon Roll; All Centennial League Bsbl; Pre-Dntl.

MOORE, KEVIN; East HS; Wichita, KS; (4); Computer Clb; FBLA; Varsity Clb; Chrldng; Ftbl; Trk; Wt Lftg; Wrstlng; Hon Roll; Barton County CC; Comp Sci.

MOORE, KINSEY M; Manhattan HS; Manhattan, KS; (3); Church Yth Grp; Teachers Aide; JV Vllybl; NHS; Trvlng Sftbl; KS ST U; Early Ed.

MOORE, LEVI T; Ottawa HS; Ottawa, KS; (2); Letterman Clb; Spanish Clb; SADD; VP Frsh Cls; Pres Soph Cls; Var L Bsbl; Var L Tennis; Var L Wrstlng; Hon Roll.

MOORE, LINDSEY M; Blue Valley Northwest HS; Overland Park, KS; (3); Church Yth Grp; Cmnty Wkr; Sec FCA; Teachers Aide; Orch; JV Bsktbl; Powder Puff Ftbl; JV Socr; Hon Roll; NHS; Univ; Sec Ed.

MOORE, MALIA; Hope HS; Woodbine, KS; (4); 1/10; FBLA; Co-Ed Yrbk; Pres Sr Cls; L Var Trk; Var L Vllybl; Gov Hon Prg Awd; High Hon Roll; NHS; Ntl Merit SF; Val; Bausch & Lomb Awd; I Dare You Awd; U Of Rochester.

MOORE, MATTHEW R; Sumner Acad Of Arts & Science; Kansas City, KS; (3); 1/140; German Clb; Teachers Aide; Rptr Nwsp; Capt Var Bsktbl; High Hon Roll; NHS; Ntl Merit Ltr; AAU Bsktbl; Cornell Coll; Medicine.

MOORE, MELISSA; Turner HS; Kansas City, KS; (4); 35/250; Bus Profs of Am; French Clb; SADD; Hon Roll; Prfct Atten Awd; Mrk Of Excl; Jonsn CCC; Chiroprctr.

MOORE, MICHAEL D; Topeka West HS; Topeka, KS; (3); Art Clb; French Clb; Math Clb; KS Univ.

MOORE, MINDIE; Kingman HS; Kingman, KS; (2); FBLA; Model UN; SADD; Sec Frsh Cls; Var Bsktbl; Var L Tennis; Var Trk; Intrml Wt Lftg; High Hon Roll; NHS; Chisholm Trl League Acad All League; Phys Thrpy.

MOORE, MORGAN M; Douglass HS; Douglass, KS; (3); 15/67; Letterman Clb; Varsity Clb; Var L Bsktbl; Var L Ftbl; Hon Roll; KS ST Univ; Wildlife Bio.

MOORE, NICK; Central Christian Schl; Hutchinson, KS; (2); Church Yth Grp; Debate Tm; Nwsp; Ofcr Stu Cncl; Ftbl.

MOORE, PHILIP J; Ashland HS; Ashland, KS; (2); Church Yth Grp; FCA; 4-H; Pres Soph Cls; JV Var Bsktbl; JV Var Ftbl; Hon Roll; Ft Hays ST Univ; Acctng.

MOORE, REBEKAH J; Madison Jr Sr HS; Madison, KS; (2); German Clb; NFL; Spanish Clb; Band; Jazz Band; Mrchg Band; Pep Band; High Hon Roll; Participation In Odyssey Of The Mind; Kayette Clb; U Of KS.

MOORE, RICK; Ottawa HS; Ottawa, KS; (3); FTA; Letterman Clb; Teachers Aide; Chorus; Var Ftbl; Mgr(s); Intrml Wt Lftg; Var Wrstlng; Local Animal Shelter Vol; Pittsburg ST; Scndry Ed; PE.

MOORE, ROLESHA K; Washington HS; Kansas City, KS; (2); Church Yth Grp; Dance Clb; FCA; Pep Clb; Drill Tm; Bsktbl; Vllybl; Hon Roll; Ed.

MOORE, SARA N; Halstead HS; Halstead, KS; (1); Church Yth Grp; German Clb; Chorus; Pep Band; School Musical; Var Trk; JV Vllybl; Hon Roll; Piano 8 Yrs; KS Yth Choir; Music.

MOORE, SHANDRA D; Coldwater Jr Sr HS; Coldwater, KS; (1); Rptr 4-H; Treas FHA; Pep Clb; Band; Chorus; Mrchg Band; Pep Band; School Musical; Variety Show; Trk; 2 Trophies For Horsemanship In 4-H; Photo; Stamps; Post Mistress.

MOORE, TOSHA; Pratt HS; Pratt, KS; (2); Church Yth Grp; Cmnty Wkr; FCA; Hosp Aide; Library Aide; Office Aide; Pep Clb; Ski Clb; SADD; Teachers Aide; Host Vol; Water Skiing; Acad Achvmt Awds; Ob-Gyn; Ob Nrs.

MOORHOUS, JACLYN A; Wheatland Middle Sr HS; Grainfield, KS; (3); 3/15; Sec Treas Church Yth Grp; Pres Sec 4-H; Speech Tm; Band; Chorus; Church Choir; Pep Band; School Play; Sec Frsh Cls; Sec Soph Cls; Ft Hays ST Univ; Office Admin.

MORAN, CHRISTINA M; Shawnee Heights HS; Berryton, KS; (4); 16/240; Key Clb; Pep Clb; Pres SADD; Teachers Aide; Drill Tm; Var L Crs Cntry; Var L Socr; High Hon Roll; Pres Acad Fit Awd; St Schlr; U Of KS.

MORAN, JULIA; Shawnee Mission Nw Sr HS; Shawnee Mission, KS; (3); 16/460; JA; SADD; Band; Intrml Bsktbl; Var L Trk; Var L Vllybl; High Hon Roll; NHS; Yth In Govt; U Of MN; Bus.

MOREAU, ANDREW C; Blue Valley HS; Shawnee Mission, KS; (2); Pres VP 4-H; SADD; 4-H Awd; High Hon Roll; Hon Roll; Black/Veatch Engr Explrs Post; Task Force Agnst Drgs/Alchl; Attndng Natl 4 H Cngrss 96; 4 Yr Coll.

MOREL, BRANDON; Smoky Valley HS; Lindsborg, KS; (3); Bus Profs of Am; Church Yth Grp; FCA; Letterman Clb; Pep Clb; Band; Jazz Band; Mrchg Band; Orch; Pep Band; Univ Of KS; Cmptr Engr/Prgrmng.

MOREL, ERICA C; Smoky Valley HS; Lindsborg, KS; (2); FCA; Sec FHA; Letterman Clb; Pep Clb; Teachers Aide; Band; Pep Band; High Hon Roll; NHS; Cmnty Wkr; KAYS Brd; K ST; Animal Sci.

MOREL, LINDY A; Oakley HS; Oakley, KS; (4); 3/45; Church Yth Grp; Cmnty Wkr; Treas Rep FHA; Teachers Aide; Chorus; Church Choir; VP Frsh Cls; Treas Jr Cls; VP Sr Cls; Rep Stu Cncl; Plnsmn Sngrs; Logan Cty Jr Miss 1st Rnr-Up 96; KS Hnr Stdnt; PEO Stdnt Mnth; Dale Dennis Excl Ed Awd; U Of KS; Hum Bio.

MORELAND, SCOTT G; Blue Valley Northwest HS; Overland Park, KS; (1); School Play; High Hon Roll; Hon Roll; KS Univ; Engr/Arch.

MOREN, BARBIE D; Maize HS; Wichita, KS; (2); Cmnty Wkr; Spanish Clb; SADD; Thesps; Stage Crew; Var Pom Pon; JV Socr; Var Wt Lftg; High Hon Roll; NHS; Phys Therapy.

MORENO, JASON; Garden City Sr HS; Garden City, KS; (4); 37/313; High Hon Roll; Span Stdnt Yr; U Of KS.

MORENO, YANET; Scott Comm HS; Scott City, KS; (3); Chorus; Stage Crew; Bsktbl; Vllybl; TX Tech U.

MORFORD, LACE M; Wallace Cty HS; Sharon Spgs, KS; (2); Church Yth Grp; FCA; Pep Clb; SADD; Teachers Aide; Chorus; JV Var Bsktbl; JV Var Vllybl; Hon Roll; Medcl.

MORGAN, AMANDA; Caney Valley Jr Sr HS; Caney, KS; (2); 4/68; Church Yth Grp; DECA; FCA; School Play; Chrldng; High Hon Roll; NHS; FBLA; GAA; Rep Frsh Cls; Comm Theatre; European Music Tour; St Flute Solo I Rating; Brown; Ct Rptr.

MORGAN, BARRY L; Field Kindley Mem Sr HS; Coffeyville, KS; (4); JA; Hon Roll; Bsktbl; Guitar Playing; On The Job Trng At Coffeyville Tchrs Credit Union; Coffeyville CC; Acctng.

MORGAN, BEN J; Basehor Linwood HS; Tonganoxie, KS; (2); Boy Scts; Church Yth Grp; Letterman Clb; Var Ftbl; Var L Wrstlng; Hon Roll; Eagle Scout.

MORGAN, BRENDA; Peabody-Burns Jr Sr HS; Burns, KS; (4); 2/30; Church Yth Grp; Cmnty Wkr; FCA; Mrchg Band; Treas Soph Cls; Pres Sr Cls; Rep Stu Cncl; Var Capt Bsktbl; High Hon Roll; NHS; PEAK; KS ST U; Int Dsgn.

MORGAN, BRIAN; Leavenworth HS; Leavenworth, KS; (3); Hon Roll; De Vry; Comp.

MORGAN, BRIAN J; Blue Valley North HS; Leawood, KS; (3); 128/230; Model UN; Science Clb; Hon Roll.

MORGAN, CRYSTAL D; Caney Valley Jr Sr HS; Caney, KS; (3); Art Clb; Drama Clb; FCA; Spanish Clb; School Play; Stage Crew; Treas Soph Cls; High Hon Roll; Hon Roll; NHS.

MORGAN, GEORGE C; Blue Valley HS; Overland Park, KS; (2); Debate Tm; Bsktbl; Crs Cntry; Trk; Vllybl; Hon Roll; St Track, Cross Cntry.

MORGAN, JACOB; Olathe South Sr HS; Olathe, KS; (3); Am Leg Boys St; Boy Scts; Church Yth Grp; Band; JV Crs Cntry; Var Trk; Hon Roll; NHS; Pres Acad Fit Awd; Spanish NHS; Bio.

MORGAN, JARED M; Hope HS; Hope, KS; (3); Church Yth Grp; Treas 4-H; FBLA; Rptr Treas Natl FFA Org; SADD; Band; School Play; VP Sr Cls; Var L Bsktbl; Var L Ftbl; Natl 4-H Horsebowl & Western Pleasure Rider; 4-H Cty Awd Plant Sci & Exch Trip Del; KS ST.

MORGAN, JENNIFER; Jackson Heights HS; Soldier, KS; (1); Church Yth Grp; Sec 4-H; FBLA; Pep Clb; Band; Chorus; Mrchg Band; Pep Band; School Musical; Stat Bsktbl.

MORGAN, JENNIFER K; Topeka West HS; Topeka, KS; (3); 38/239; FHA; Hosp Aide; Rep Pep Clb; Rep Spanish Clb; SADD; Teachers Aide; Thesps; Chorus; Drill Tm; School Musical; Gldn Rule Awd Nominee; Emporia St; Tchr.

MORGAN, KATIE; Garnder Edgerton HS; Gardner, KS; (1); Church Yth Grp; Spanish Clb; Var Chrldng; High Hon Roll; Hon Roll; Ftbl & Bsktbl Vrsty Ltrs; KU; Bus.

MORGAN, LILY R; Lawrence HS; Eudora, KS; (3); Drama Clb; Spanish Clb; Thesps; School Musical; Stage Crew; Lit Mag; Hon Roll; NCTE Nom; Mst Impvd Perf Awd Thespians 95-; KS Univ.

MORGAN, MATTHEW; Garden City Sr HS; Garden City, KS; (3); Treas Church Yth Grp; JV Var Bsktbl; Var Tennis; High Hon Roll; Hon Roll; KS ST U; Bus Admin.

MORGAN, MELANIE; Olathe South Sr HS; Olathe, KS; (4); Church Yth Grp; Cmnty Wkr; Dance Clb; FHA; Letterman Clb; Office Aide; Pep Clb; Spanish Clb; Teachers Aide; Drill Tm; Stu Ambssdrs Pgm; KU Almni Hnrs; U Of KU; Dnc.

MORGAN, RACHEL D; Haven HS; Haven, KS; (2); Church Yth Grp; Acpl Chr; Band; Chorus; Flag Corp; School Musical; Variety Show; Ofcr Stu Cncl; Vllybl; Hon Roll; KAYS Clb; Wildcat Singers; Peer Cnslr; Bapt Bible Coll; Music.

MORGAN, RONDA D; Shawnee Heights HS; Topeka, KS; (1); Church Yth Grp; Cmnty Wkr; Drama Clb; 4-H; Hosp Aide; Pep Clb; Science Clb; Church Choir; Jazz Band; Orch; Hlth Care Prof.

MORGAN, RUSTAIN L; Burlington HS; Burlington, KS; (2); Church Yth Grp; Drama Clb; FBLA; NFL; Scholastic Bowl; Thesps; School Play; JV Golf; High Hon Roll; NHS; Wings Prog; KS U; Psych.

MORGAN, STEPHEN M; Blue Valley HS; Overland Park, KS; (2); Church Yth Grp; Bsktbl; Golf; Hon Roll; 4 Yr Univ; Acctng.

MORGAN, THOMAS B; Topeka HS; Topeka, KS; (1); Church Yth Grp; Science Clb; SADD; Band; Chorus; Church Choir; Mrchg Band; Hon Roll; Med.

MORGAN, TRAVIS; Mulvane Sr HS; Mulvane, KS; (3); 1/130; Boy Scts; Pres Church Yth Grp; L Scholastic Bowl; Science Clb; Pres Spanish Clb; SADD; Mgr Nwsp; Rep Stu Cncl; Var Bsbl; High Hon Roll; Bus Admin.

MORIARTY, CORINNE; Trinity Catholic HS; Hutchinson, KS; (2); Rep Soph Cls; Rep Stu Cncl; Var Chrldng; Powder Puff Ftbl; Vllybl; Hon Roll; Dance Clb; Pep Clb; School Play; L Trk; Campus Ministry.

MORIARTY, EMILY F; Washburn Rural HS; Auburn, KS; (2); Spanish Clb; Bsktbl; Sftbl; High Hon Roll; Hon Roll; Photogrphy; KS Univ; Tchr/Acctnt.

MORIARTY, MINDY A; Goddard HS; Wichita, KS; (3); Drama Clb; SADD; Drill Tm; Rep Soph Cls; Rep Jr Cls; Pres Stu Cncl; L Pom Pon; Var Trk; L Vllybl; High Hon Roll; PALS; KAYS; KS ST U.

MORIN, ASHLEE; Seaman Sr HS; Topeka, KS; (3); #74 in class; Church Yth Grp; Cmnty Wkr; FBLA; Hosp Aide; Office Aide; SADD; Teachers Aide; Drill Tm; Chrldng; Hon Roll.

MORLAN, JASON; Coldwater Jr Sr HS; Coldwater, KS; (4); 10/20; Sec Am Leg Boys St; Cmnty Wkr; Pep Clb; Teachers Aide; Band; Chorus; Mrchg Band; Pep Band; School Musical; School Play; EMT; Cnty Fire Fghtr; Dsptchr Sheriffs Ofc; Butler Cnty CC; Admin Of Just.

MORLAND, DEBBIE; Girard HS; Girard, KS; (3); Am Leg Aux Girls St; Pres Church Yth Grp; Drama Clb; Scholastic Bowl; Band; Chorus; Mrchg Band; Swing Chorus; High Hon Roll; Pres NHS; Qlfd Dist/ST Band Contests; Qulfd ST Forensics Contests; Theater Arts.

MORLEY, KRISTEN N; Blue Valley Northwest HS; Overland Park, KS; (1); 3/357; Church Yth Grp; Dance Clb; High Hon Roll.

MORLEY, NANCY; Haviland HS; Haviland, KS; (4); 2/15; Church Yth Grp; HOBY; Band; Rptr Nwsp; Var L Bsktbl; Var L Chrldng; Var L Vllybl; High Hon Roll; Sal; Presdntl Clsrm Yng Amer; Barclay Coll; Pre-Med.

MORRELL, NATALIE S; Beloit Jr Sr HS; Beloit, KS; (1); 1/95; Girl Scts; Spanish Clb; Band; Mrchg Band; Orch; Pep Band; High Hon Roll; Kayettes-Songleader; Intnl Frgn Lang Awd; Pediatrics.

MORRICAL, LEVI S; Salina HS South; Salina, KS; (2); Church Yth Grp; Spanish Clb; Teachers Aide; Tennis; Hon Roll; Prfct Atten Awd; Renssnc Prog; COU; Biolgst.

MORRILL, MONTY M; Natoma HS; Paradise, KS; (1); 3/11; Natl FFA Org; Pres Soph Cls; Var L Bsktbl; Ft Hays ST Univ; Family Ranch.

MORRIS, ADRIA M; Haven HS; Mount Hope, KS; (3); SADD; Chorus; Yrbk; Bsktbl; Chrldng; Sftbl.

MORRIS, CHERIE; Macksville HS; Macksville, KS; (4); 1/21; Am Leg Aux Girls St; Church Yth Grp; Girl Scts; Letterman Clb; Capt Quiz Bowl; Treas Service Clb; Speech Tm; Teachers Aide; Band; Jazz Band; Med.

MORRIS, JACKIE S; Nickerson HS; Nickerson, KS; (3); Church Yth Grp; Spanish Clb; Rptr Nwsp; Phtg Yrbk; JV Var Bsktbl; Var L Crs Cntry; Var L Sftbl; JV Vllybl; Hon Roll; Prfct Atten Awd.

MORRIS, JAMIE; Hugoton HS; Hugoton, KS; (4); SADD; Band; Chorus; Pres Frsh Cls; Treas Soph Cls; Treas Jr Cls; Pres Sr Cls; Pres Stu Cncl; Bsktbl; Vllybl; Pilot.

MORRIS, JAMIE L; Blue Valley North HS; Leawood, KS; (2); Var Golf; Hon Roll.

MORRIS, JESSICA; Topeka HS; Topeka, KS; (2); 8/660; Pres Boy Scts; Church Yth Grp; Band; Mrchg Band; Var Swmmng; High Hon Roll; Eckerd; Marine Bio.

MORRIS, JON; Russell HS; Russell, KS; (1); Church Yth Grp; FCA; Key Clb; Pep Clb; SADD; Bsktbl; Score Keeper; Hon Roll; Prfct Atten Awd; Ft Hays ST Univ; Bus.

MORRIS, JOSHUA P; Salina HS South; Salina, KS; (3); Art Clb; Church Yth Grp; Ftbl; Trk; Wt Lftg; Hon Roll; Pres Acad Fit Awd; Frosh Ath Of The Yr.

MORRIS, JULIE C; Washburn Rural HS; Topeka, KS; (3); Office Aide.

MORRIS, KELLY; Winfield HS; Winfield, KS; (4); 32/177; Bus Profs of Am; Church Yth Grp; Debate Tm; SADD; Varsity Clb; Ofcr Frsh Cls; Ofcr Stu Cncl; Tennis; High Hon Roll; Hon Roll; Southwestern Coll; Bus Ed.

MORRIS, LISA; Leavenworth HS; Leavenworth, KS; (3); #4 in class; Church Yth Grp; School Musical; Swing Chorus; VP Soph Cls; Pres Jr Cls; Var Capt Chrldng; Socr; Cit Awd; High Hon Roll; NHS; Vol & Missionary Work; Pre-Med; Intl Bus.

MORRIS, LISA M; Blue Valley Northwest HS; Overland Park, KS; (2); 12/450; Debate Tm; FCA; NFL; Teachers Aide; Varsity Clb; Orch; Var L Bsktbl; Var L Socr; Var L Vllybl; Intrml Wt Lftg; All East KS League Vlybl 2nd Team; Sun Cntry Vlybl Hnrbl Mention; All East KS League Soccer 2nd Tm.

MORRIS, MANDY M; Blue Valley Northwest HS; Overland Park, KS; (3); Drama Clb; Thesps; Acpl Chr; Chorus; Orch; School Musical; School Play; Stage Crew; Swing Chorus; Variety Show.

MORRIS, MELISSA; Independence HS; Independence, KS; (3); 1/200; Church Yth Grp; French Clb; Pep Clb; Orch; Chrldng; High Hon Roll; NHS; Orthodontist.

MORRIS, ROSALYNN; Plainville HS; Plainville, KS; (4); 13/52; HOBY; VP Rep Natl FFA Org; Pep Clb; Speech Tm; Teachers Aide; Band; Chorus; High Hon Roll; Hon Roll; NHS; Ft Hays ST U; Chem.

MORRIS, SARAH; Lyons HS; Lyons, KS; (4); 3/75; VP Treas Drama Clb; HOBY; Pres NFL; Acpl Chr; Band; Chorus; Rep Stu Cncl; JV Bsktbl; JV Vllybl; High Hon Roll; KS Ambsdr Music European Tour 94; Rice Cty Yth Ldrshp Ambsdr; Stu Cncl Camp 95; KU; Law.

MORRIS, TANDIE L; Campus HS; Wichita, KS; (3); SADD; Chorus; Hon Roll; High Hnrs German II Awd; Wichita ST U; Travel.

MORRIS, TANYA L; Wichita Heights HS; Wichita, KS; (4); 58/212; Band; Church Choir; Mrchg Band; Orch; Pep Band; School Musical; Chess Clb; Church Yth Grp; Pep Clb; Spanish Clb; John P Sousa Bnd Awd; Dist Bnd 2 Yrs; FOCUS Clb; SADD; Emporia St Univ; Elem Ed.

MORRIS, VALERIE L; Washburn Rural HS; Topeka, KS; (2); Church Yth Grp; SADD; Ed Yrbk; High Hon Roll; Hon Roll; Vol Midland Hospic Chld Brvmnt Ctr; KS Univ; Psych.

MORRISON, ANDREW K; Desoto HS; Shawnee Mission, KS; (3); 69/170; Am Leg Boys St; Church Yth Grp; Cmnty Wkr; Drama Clb; French Clb; NFL; Office Aide; Pep Clb; Intrml Quiz Bowl; Speech Tm; Esperanza; Natl Yth Evant Plng Cmte; Stu Of Mnth; Doane Univ; Ed.

MORRISON, BRIDGET R; Newton Sr HS; Newton, KS; (2); Church Yth Grp; French Clb; JV Vllybl; High Hon Roll; Hon Roll; Early Chldhd Dev.

MORRISON, DOUG; St John's Military Schl; Highland, IN; (3); 3/60; Church Yth Grp; Cmnty Wkr; Computer Clb; ROTC; Band; Drill Tm; Mrchg Band; Ftbl; Hon Roll; NHS; Co Commander Hnr Co Awd; Media Clb Pres; Lyman G Linger Schlsp Awd; Military Svc; Comp Tech; Engrng.

MORRISON, JESSICA L; Washington HS; Kansas City, KS; (2); Church Yth Grp; Cmnty Wkr; Drama Clb; Hosp Aide; Thesps; Chorus; Church Choir; School Musical; School Play; Stage Crew; Acad Letter For High GPA; Pitt; Arts Tchr.

MORRISON, KIM M; Scott Comm HS; Scott City, KS; (3); Church Yth Grp; Pep Clb; SADD; Teachers Aide; Band; Mrchg Band; Pep Band; Var L Bsktbl; Var L Vllybl; Hon Roll; Emporia ST Univ; Elem Ed.

MORRISON, MARY E; Louisburg HS; Louisburg, KS; (3); Church Yth Grp; Q&S; Band; Chorus; Church Choir; Color Guard; Mrchg Band; Pep Band; Ed Nwsp; Acad Awd Soc Sci Jr Yr; 1st Pl Rg KSPA News Wrtng Comp; 2 Yrs KS Reg Solo/Ensmbl Music Comp; 4 Yr Univ; Med/Mus/His.

MORRISON, MICHAEL J; Yates Ctr HS; Yates Center, KS; (2); VP 4-H; Rptr Natl FFA Org; Var Bsbl; JV Bsktbl; 4-H Awd; High Hon Roll; NHS; KS ST; Engr.

MORRISON, STACIE J; Blue Valley HS; Stilwell, KS; (2); Key Clb; Band; Mrchg Band; Pep Band; Stage Crew; JV Trk; Hon Roll; Pole Vaulting; KU; Ed.

MORRISON, WILLIAM T; Yates Ctr HS; Yates Center, KS; (3); Art Clb; German Clb; Teachers Aide; Band; Mrchg Band; Pep Band; JV Bsktbl; Var Golf; Hon Roll; Psych.

MORRISSEY, AMANDA A; Wetmore Schl; Wetmore, KS; (3); 1/12; School Musical; School Play; Swing Chorus; Phtg Yrbk; Pres Jr Cls; Rep Stu Cncl; Var Chrldng; Var Vllybl; High Hon Roll; NHS; KS ST; Vet Med.

MORROU, MATTHEW S; Olathe East Sr HS; Olathe, KS; (2); Church Yth Grp; Band; Church Choir; Jazz Band; Mrchg Band; JV Crs Cntry; JV Trk; JV Wrstlng; High Hon Roll; Pres Acad Fit Awd; Eng.

MORROW, CHRISTOPHER T; Newton Sr HS; Newton, KS; (2); Church Yth Grp; Drama Clb; Letterman Clb; Thesps; Chorus; School Play; Var Socr; Perf Arts.

MORROW, LYDIA; Wyandotte HS; Kansas City, KS; (4); 6/110; Church Yth Grp; Cmnty Wkr; Drama Clb; Intnl Clb; Church Choir; Ofcr Jr Cls; Ofcr Sr Cls; Mgr(s); Hon Roll; NHS; KC Alumn; In Rd; Exec Inter; Entrprp Inter; Tlnt Rsrch; Howard; Acctng.

MORROW, STACY; Ottawa HS; Ottawa, KS; (3); 17/149; French Clb; SADD; Bsktbl; JV Vllybl; High Hon Roll; U Of KS; Bus.

MORSE, BRANDON J; Newton Sr HS; Newton, KS; (2); 1/275; Band; Jazz Band; Mrchg Band; Pep Band; High Hon Roll; KS Msnc All-St HS Mrchng Band; KS & Grtr Kansas City Ambs Of Msc Eurpn Tour 96; U Of KS; Mscn.

MORSE, JENNI; Wichita Collegiate Schl; Wichita, KS; (3); VP SADD; Chorus; School Musical; Crs Cntry; Pom Pon; High Hon Roll; Swmmng W/Wcht Swm Clb; SHARP Svc.

MORSE, ROBERT; Royal Valley HS; Mayetta, KS; (3); Church Yth Grp; Pep Clb; SADD; Acpl Chr; Band; Pep Band; School Musical; Variety Show; Ftbl; Trk; Sprtng Clays; Elctrnc Engrng.

MORSE, RYAN; Olathe East Sr HS; Olathe, KS; (2); Boy Scts; Church Yth Grp; Drama Clb; Band; Jazz Band; Mrchg Band; Pep Band; School Play; Ofcr Frsh Cls; Hon Roll; Eagle Scout & Sr Patrol Ldr; Mid-Amer Music Assn Cmptn Jr Virtuoso Frosh; Mid Amer Music Assn Cmptn 96.

MORTER, MATTHEW R; Ft Scott HS; Fort Scott, KS; (3); 40/162; Pep Clb; Hon Roll; NHS; Pittsburg ST Univ; Acctnt.

MORTON, AMY D; Augusta Sr HS; Augusta, KS; (2); Letterman Clb; Spanish Clb; SADD; Nwsp; Yrbk; Sec Frsh Cls; Rep Soph Cls; Bsktbl; Vllybl; Hon Roll; Letrmns Clb; Harvard Univ; Law.

MORTON, CRAIG F; Frankft HS; Frankfort, KS; (4); Church Yth Grp; Letterman Clb; Natl FFA Org; Office Aide; VP Sr Cls; Bsktbl; Ftbl; Hon Roll; Ath Trng.

MORTON, KEVIN; Ottawa HS; Ottawa, KS; (4); Boy Scts; Spanish Clb; Band; Jazz Band; Mrchg Band; Pep Band; Variety Show; Golf; NHS; St Schlr; Chrch Of Chrst; Ottawa Lib Vol; U Of KS; Cmptr Engr.

MORTON, NOAH J; Canton-Galva HS; Canton, KS; (3); 13/41; Am Leg Boys St; Church Yth Grp; FBLA; Letterman Clb; Quiz Bowl; VP SADD; VP Jr Cls; VP Sr Cls; JV Bsktbl; Ftbl; Hutchinson CC; Ath Trainer.

MOSELEY, CHAD; Mankato Jr Sr HS; Mankato, KS; (3); Am Leg Boys St; Quiz Bowl; Band; Chorus; Jazz Band; Swing Chorus; Trk; Hon Roll; Mascot; Grphc Dsgn.

MOSER, EMBER M; Bern Schl; Bern, KS; (3); GAA; Letterman Clb; Pep Clb; Sec Treas SADD; Varsity Clb; Band; Chorus; Drill Tm; Mrchg Band; Pep Band; KS ST U.

MOSES, COREY; Dodge City HS; Dodge City, KS; (3); 10/300; Letterman Clb; Library Aide; SADD; Teachers Aide; Ofcr Bsbl; Ftbl; Wrstlng; Hon Roll.

MOSES, JOHN L; Dodge City HS; Dodge City, KS; (4); 23/295; FCA; Letterman Clb; Library Aide; Office Aide; SADD; Teachers Aide; Ofcr Bsbl; Ftbl; Golf; Wrstlng.

MOSES, LESLIE; Acad Of Mt St Scholastica; Atchison, KS; (4); 1/27; Church Yth Grp; Drama Clb; NFL; Pep Clb; Service Clb; Chorus; Church Choir; Drill Tm; School Play; Stage Crew.

MOSES, LESLIE; MSSA; Topeka, KS; (4); 1/25; NFL; Pep Clb; Band; Chorus; Church Choir; Drill Tm; Mrchg Band; School Musical; School Play; Stage Crew; Valparaiso; Poly Sci.

MOSHER, JOSEPH D; Glasco HS; Glasco, KS; (2); 2/13; Office Aide; Quiz Bowl; Teachers Aide; Band; JV Bsktbl; Var L Ftbl; Var Trk; High Hon Roll; Hon Roll; NHS; U Of KS; Physician.

MOSHER, NATALIE; Robert E Clark Jr HS; Bonner Springs, KS; (1); Church Yth Grp; Cmnty Wkr; FHA; Ski Clb; SADD; Chorus; Church Choir; Chrldng; Hon Roll; Church Yth Grp Adopted Play Grndmthr From Nrsng Hm; KS U Lawrence; Brdcstng/Comm.

MOSHER, SARAH E; KS Schl For The Deaf; Lawrence, KS; (3); 1/14; Office Aide; Capt Scholastic Bowl; School Play; Ed Lit Mag; Pres Soph Cls; Sec Treas Stu Cncl; Var Stat Bsktbl; Var Chrldng; Var Vllybl; High Hon Roll; Jr Natl Assn Of Deaf.

MOSHER, STEPHEN B; Shawnee Heights HS; Topeka, KS; (4); 54/237; Pep Clb; Band; Jazz Band; Mrchg Band; Orch; Pep Band; School Musical; Variety Show; Rptr Yrbk; Hon Roll; DCI Div II World Champ Pioneer Drum, Bugle & Flag Corp 94; Co-Founder & Ed Nwsp; King Of Ct Cand 96; U Of KS; Philosophy.

MOSIER, DUSTIN R; St Marys HS; Maple Hill, KS; (2); Band; Var Bsbl; JV Bsktbl; French Hon Soc; 4-H Awd.

MOSIER, KARLA M; Buhler HS; Hutchinson, KS; (2); Church Yth Grp; FCA; Band; Chorus; Church Choir; Mrchg Band; Pep Band; Hon Roll; Tchrs Choice Awd; Family/Chldrn Thtr Actress.

MOSIMAN, LINDSAY D; Highland Park HS; Topeka, KS; (2); Church Yth Grp; Cmnty Wkr; Dance Clb; German Clb; ROTC; Drill Tm; Chrldng; Pom Pon; High Hon Roll; Pres Acad Fit Awd; AFJROTC Smmr Ldshp Schl; Dnce Tm Acpt; Mtrlgy In Air Frc.

MOSIMAN, MICHELLE; Peabody-Burns Jr Sr HS; Peabody, KS; (1); Church Yth Grp; FCA; Girl Scts; Band; Color Guard; Mrchg Band; Pep Band; Stage Crew; JV Bsktbl; JV Vllybl.

MOSKALEW, MICHELLE N; Kinsley HS; Kinsley, KS; (3); Church Yth Grp; SADD; Var Chrldng; Hon Roll; VFW Ladies Auxiliary Voice Of Democracy Awd 5th Pl In Cls; Dodge City CC; Floral Designer.

MOSS, MICHAEL; Ft Scott HS; Fort Scott, KS; (2); Church Yth Grp; Computer Clb; Debate Tm; FCA; NFL; Scholastic Bowl; Science Clb; High Hon Roll; Ntl Merit Ltr.

MOSS, NEANDA; Atchison Sr HS; Atchison, KS; (4); 13/125; Chess Clb; Church Yth Grp; Band; Church Choir; Mrchg Band; Ofcr Soph Cls; Treas Jr Cls; Sec Sr Cls; Pres Stu Cncl; Var Chrldng; Hmcmng Qn; Emporia ST; Psych.

MOSS, ROBYN E; Bluestem HS; Augusta, KS; (3); Acpl Chr; Band; Chorus; Jazz Band; Mrchg Band; Pep Band; Sec Stu Cncl; Var Crs Cntry; Var Sftbl; Hon Roll; KS Masonic All-St HS Band 1st Char Trumpt 94; Earnd I Ratng On Trumpt Solo At St Cmptn 96; Music Ed.

MOSSETTO, AUDREY; Topeka HS; Topeka, KS; (2); 18/465; Church Yth Grp; Cmnty Wkr; Teachers Aide; Thesps; Flag Corp; High Hon Roll; Bus Admin.

MOTES, KEVIN L; Beloit Jr Sr HS; Scottsville, KS; (2); Church Yth Grp; Cmnty Wkr; 4-H; Natl FFA Org; Var Ftbl; 4-H Awd; Hon Roll; KS ST Univ.

MOTLEY, MOLLY; Garden City Sr HS; Garden City, KS; (3); Church Yth Grp; Band; Chorus; Mrchg Band; Pep Band; High Hon Roll; Prfct Atten Awd; Choir, Band & Acad Ltrs; KS Ambssdrs Of Music; U Of KS; Brdcstng.

MOTT, DUSTIN D; Independence HS; Independence, KS; (1); Band; Mrchg Band; Pep Band; Bsktbl; Score Keeper; Hon Roll; Renaissance Pgm; Penn ST.

MOTT, DWAYNE A; Enterprise Sda Acad; Kansas City, MO; (4); Church Yth Grp; Band; Church Choir; Drill Tm; School Play; Nwsp; Gym; Cit Awd; Hon Roll; Prfct Atten Awd; Whos Who Hnr Stu Nom; Gymnist Of Yr; Pathfinder Clb; Union Coll; Elec Engrng.

MOTT, JEANETTE C; St Marys HS; Belvue, KS; (2); Pres Church Yth Grp; Debate Tm; FCA; Pres FHA; Letterman Clb; Pep Clb; Varsity Clb; Rep Frsh Cls; Rep Soph Cls; Rep Jr Cls; 1st In St In CC & 2 Mile St; 2nd In Natls.

MOTT, JUSTIN; Seaman Sr HS; Topeka, KS; (4); 34/248; Band; Jazz Band; Mrchg Band; Pep Band; Var L Socr; High Hon Roll; KS HS Cchs All Acad Sccr Tm; KMEA Band All St 95; Cmptr Engnr.

MOTTER, JILL; Halstead HS; Halstead, KS; (3); HOBY; Letterman Clb; VP Pep Clb; Spanish Clb; Var L Chrldng; Var L Vllybl; Hon Roll; Commnctns.

MOTTIN, ANGELA; Miltonvale HS; Miltonvale, KS; (4); 1/7; Capt Scholastic Bowl; Yrbk; VP Stu Cncl; Gov Hon Prg Awd; High Hon Roll; NHS; St Schlr; Val; Letterman Clb; Pep Clb; KS Bd Of Regents Schlr; KU Hnrs Schlr; The Brown Mackie Coll; Bus Admn.

MOUNTAIN, SETH; Garden Plain Jr Sr HS; Viola, KS; (3); Letterman Clb; Red Cross Aide; SADD; School Play; Bsktbl; Ftbl; Trk; Wt Lftg; Rep COOP At Farmland Ldrshp Conf At Liberty MO; Jrep REC At Ldrshp Conf Seminar At Steamboat CO; Ft Hays; Comp Graphics.

MOUNTS, CHRIS T; Andale HS; Goddard, KS; (3); 2/68; Debate Tm; School Musical; School Play; VP Sr Cls; JV Bsktbl; Var L Crs Cntry; Var L Ftbl; Var L Trk; High Hon Roll; NHS; Forensics Team ST Champs Qualifier In IDA.

MOURNING, JOSH B; Ottawa HS; Ottawa, KS; (2); Boy Scts; Church Yth Grp; Cmnty Wkr; FCA; SADD; Chorus; School Musical; School Play; Variety Show; Ofcr Bsbl.

MOWERY, KAYLA; Northern Heights HS; Americus, KS; (2); FBLA; SADD; School Musical; Swing Chorus; Co-Capt Chrldng; Trk; Vllybl; Hon Roll; Read; Collect Books; VIP Show Ch Oir; Engl.

MOYER, CHRISTEN; Independence HS; Independence, KS; (1); Debate Tm; Chrldng; Pom Pon; Kays Clb; SCUM; KU; Med.

MOYER, ERIN RENEE; Goddard HS; Wichita, KS; (1); Ed Nwsp; Ed Yrbk; Var Socr; JV Vllybl; High Hon Roll; Ntl Merit Ltr; Pres Awd For Educl Excl.

MOYER, JEREMY; Ulysses HS; Ulysses, KS; (3); Church Yth Grp; FCA; SADD; Ftbl; Score Keeper; Tennis; Trk; Wt Lftg; High Hon Roll; NHS.

MOYER, KATI A; Council Grove HS; Alta Vista, KS; (3); Cmnty Wkr; Drama Clb; VP Girl Scts; Treas Key Clb; Library Aide; Quiz Bowl; Speech Tm; Ofcr SADD; School Play; Ed Yrbk; KS St Univ; Libry Sci.

MOYER, STACY; Shawnee Mission Nw Sr HS; Shawnee Mission, KS; (3); Church Yth Grp; Cmnty Wkr; FCA; GAA; NFL; Pep Clb; Capt Var Chrldng; Hon Roll; NHS; Pres Acad Fit Awd; Synchrnzd Swmmng; Clb For Uniting Beginning Stus; Prom Cmmtte; Elem Educ.

MOYER, STUART A; Olathe East Sr HS; Overland Park, KS; (2); Spanish Clb; Chorus; Var Bsktbl; Hon Roll; KS Univ; Bus.

MUELLER, CHRISTY; Wichita East HS; Wichita, KS; (3); 1/400; Church Yth Grp; Q&S; Chorus; School Musical; Variety Show; Ed Nwsp; Treas Jr Cls; JV Chrldng; Hon Roll; NHS; Vol Tutor; Natl Hnr Soc Exec Cncl Jr Rep; Jrnlsm.

MUELLER, JENNIFER; Linn Schl; Palmer, KS; (4); 7/26; Art Clb; Church Yth Grp; Cmnty Wkr; FBLA; FHA; HOBY; Letterman Clb; Pep Clb; Teachers Aide; Varsity Clb; St Brd Ed Tech Fair; St Vllybl; Cloud Cty CC; Comp Ed.

MUELLER, JODIE L; Shawnee Mission W Sr HS; Lenexa, KS; (1); 2/443; Church Yth Grp; High Hon Roll; Hon Roll; St Pauls UMC Dist Cncl Yth Mnstrs Rep; Chr Nrsry Vol; Ansthslgst.

MUELLER, JOHN ROBERT; Olathe North Sr HS; Olathe, KS; (4); 15/350; Am Leg Boys St; Boy Scts; Church Yth Grp; French Clb; Quiz Bowl; Orch; School Musical; Rep Frsh Cls; French Hon Soc; Gov Hon Prg Awd; Eagle Scout; Chmbr Ensmbls; Gifted Prgm; St Louis Univ; Physician.

MUELLER, JULIE A; Ashland HS; Ashland, KS; (4); 12/24; Church Yth Grp; Cmnty Wkr; Library Aide; Speech Tm; Teachers Aide; Band; Chorus; Church Choir; Orch; Pep Band; Fornscs Semi Fnls; NE Chrstn Coll; Mag Jrnlsm.

MUELLER, RYAN; Hanover Schl; Hanover, KS; (4); 1/23; Church Yth Grp; Letterman Clb; Natl FFA Org; SADD; VP Jr Cls; Rep Stu Cncl; Capt L Bsktbl; Capt L Ftbl; High Hon Roll; Hon Roll; KU Hnr Schlr; All Area BVL Ftbl 2nd Team; KS ST U; Phys Thrpy.

MUGGY, DANA; Manhattan HS; Manhattan, KS; (2); Church Yth Grp; FCA; VP SADD; Chorus; Nwsp; JV Capt Chrldng; Socr; Riley Cty Police Dept Explr; Crmnl Jstc.

MULANAX, MARCY; Rossville HS; Delia, KS; (3); 3/45; Debate Tm; Treas FBLA; HOBY; NFL; Teachers Aide; JV Sftbl; High Hon Roll; Hon Roll; NHS; Frnscs Tm; Htl Mgmt.

MULCAHY, MARTY; Olathe South Sr HS; Olathe, KS; (4); Cmnty Wkr; Debate Tm; Math Clb; Math Tm; Teachers Aide; VP Frsh Cls; Rep Soph Cls; Rep Jr Cls; Treas Stu Cncl; Bsktbl; U Of KS; Cvl Engr.

MULDER, JEFFERY J; Eastern Heights Jr Sr HS; Phillipsburg, KS; (3); Letterman Clb; Speech Tm; Thesps; L Var Ftbl; L Trk; High Hon Roll; Hon Roll; Jr NHS; NHS; Pres Acad Fit Awd; Cadet Law Enfrcmnt Acad; All-Amer Schlr Awd; Natl Hnr Scty VP; KS ST Univ; Elect Engrng.

MULDREW, MELISSA A; Garden City Sr HS; Garden City, KS; (2); Church Yth Grp; Latin Clb; SADD; Stat Wrstlng; Cit Awd; Soph Bus Awd; Chrch Yth Grp; 1st Pl Cty Sci Fr Awd; U NE; Rdlgy.

MULIK, KATHLEEN D; Bishop Miege HS; Roeland Park, KS; (2); Natl Yth Ldrshp Forum Law Consntn Spirit Miege Awd; Vol DARE; Heritage Panel; Promise Proj KA City.

MULL, BRIAN J; Maize HS; Maize, KS; (3); Letterman Clb; Science Clb; Spanish Clb; Varsity Clb; Stage Crew; Ftbl; Trk; Wt Lftg; Hon Roll; Prfct Atten Awd; Martial Arts; KS ST; Horticulture.

MULLEN, JONI; Lawrence HS; Lawrence, KS; (4); German Clb; Hosp Aide; Key Clb; Chorus; Orch; School Musical; Hon Roll; NHS; Pres Acad Fit Awd; Pres Schlr; Exchng Stu To Eutin Germany; Middlebury Coll; German.

MULLEN, ROBERT T; Buhler HS; Hutchinson, KS; (2); FCA; Letterman Clb; Spanish Clb; SADD; Varsity Clb; Chorus; School Musical; Stage Crew; Rep Stu Cncl; JV Bsbl; Civil Engr.

MULLER, JESSE; Ness City HS; Ness City, KS; (3); 1/38; Church Yth Grp; Sec Soph Cls; Var L Bsktbl; Var L Ftbl; Var L Trk; High Hon Roll; NHS.

MULLER, MATT J; Maize HS; Wichita, KS; (3); 38/250; Debate Tm; Letterman Clb; NFL; Science Clb; Band; Jazz Band; Gov Hon Prg Awd; High Hon Roll; Boy Scts; Chess Clb; Knwldg Master; Future Prblm Slvg; KS; Cmptr Sci.

MULLIKIN, ANNETTE M; Osawatomie HS; Osawatomie, KS; (1); Church Yth Grp; Science Clb; Band; Church Choir; Color Guard; Mrchg Band; Pep Band; Mgr(s); JV Tennis; Hon Roll; Kays & Kayettes; Ger Lessons.

MULLIN, JILL; St Thomas Aquinas HS; Overland Park, KS; (3); 13/285; Church Yth Grp; Cmnty Wkr; Math Tm; Yrbk; Vllybl; High Hon Roll; JETS Awd; Piano Dist I Adtns Hnrb Mntn 95, Excllnt Rtng Avila Coll Music Fest 96; Fall Fest High Hnrs 94; Med.

MULLIN, LUELLEN; Eureka Jr Sr HS; Fall River, KS; (3); 1/54; Rep Church Yth Grp; Quiz Bowl; Thesps; Phtg Yrbk; Sec Frsh Cls; Sec Soph Cls; Vllybl; High Hon Roll; NHS; Kayettes Sec, Treas; KS ST U; Engrng.

MULLINIX, DAWN; Burlingame HS; Burlingame, KS; (1); 12/36; FBLA; Science Clb; Band; Stage Crew; Sec Frsh Cls; Bsktbl; Var Trk; Var Vllybl; Hon Roll; Prfct Atten Awd.

MULSOW, AMANDA; Yates Ctr HS; Yates Center, KS; (2); FCA; Sec 4-H; FHA; Letterman Clb; Service Clb; Spanish Clb; SADD; Stat Bsbl; Var Chrldng; Hon Roll; Gymnastics; Lfegrd ARC Certfd; KS ST Univ; Human Eclgy/Sclgy.

MULTHAUP, KAREN; Wichita Collegiate Schl; Goddard, KS; (4); Cmnty Wkr; Hosp Aide; Chorus; School Musical; School Play; Ed Yrbk; JV Tennis; High Hon Roll; Lit Clb Pres; Natl Ltn Exm Cum Laude Awd; Invstmnt Brkr.

MUNDEN, KATY J; Haven HS; Burrton, KS; (2); Church Yth Grp; FCA; Scholastic Bowl; Band; Chorus; Flag Corp; School Musical; Variety Show; Ofcr Stu Cncl; High Hon Roll; KAYS Natl Svc Rep; Bible Stud.

MUNDINGER, MANDY; Baldwin HS; Baldwin City, KS; (4); 10/81; Am Leg Aux Girls St; Church Yth Grp; Cmnty Wkr; Intnl Clb; Letterman Clb; Math Tm; Pep Clb; Science Clb; SADD; Varsity Clb; KAYS; U Of KS; Med.

MUNDINGER, MOLLY; Baldwin HS; Baldwin City, KS; (1); Church Yth Grp; Dance Clb; German Clb; Band; School Musical; Rep Soph Cls; Var L Chrldng; Var L Trk; Vllybl; Hon Roll; Schlrshp Cont, 1st Pl Algebra I.

MUNK, HEATHER; Hays HS; Hays, KS; (4); Pep Clb; Teachers Aide; School Musical; School Play; Nwsp; High Hon Roll; NHS; Ft Hays ST U.

MUNK, MELISSA; Syracuse Jr Sr HS; Syracuse, KS; (4); 1/29; Church Yth Grp; 4-H; HOBY; Quiz Bowl; Band; Var Crs Cntry; 4-H Awd; High Hon Roll; NHS; Pres Schlr; SAE; Danforth I Dare You Awd; 4-H Key Awd; All-Lg Acad Team; Psych.

MUNOZ, MANOLITO M; El Dorado HS; El Dorado, KS; (3); 33/150; Am Leg Boys St; Church Yth Grp; Cmnty Wkr; Spanish Clb; SADD; Varsity Clb; Chorus; Swmmng; High Hon Roll; Jr NHS; Natl Yth Ldrs Conf Nom; Hnrs Regents Acad Nom; KS St Senate Page; KS ST Univ; Occptnl Thrpst.

MUNOZ, REGINA M; Hayden HS; Topeka, KS; (2); Church Yth Grp; Debate Tm; Intnl Clb; NFL; SADD; Church Choir; Trk; Stat Wrstlng; High Hon Roll; NHS; Med.

MUNOZ, ROSANNA C; Shawnee Mission N HS; Merriam, KS; (4); Pep Clb; Spanish Clb; Phtg Yrbk; Rep Frsh Cls; Mgr Trk; High Hon Roll; Hon Roll; NHS; KS Hnr Schlr; Northwest MO ST Univ.

MUNSCH, MONICA R; Thomas More Prep-Marion HS; Hays, KS; (2); 48/85; FTA; SADD; Var L Bsktbl; Var L Trk; Var JV Vllybl; Hon Roll; Frosh-Soph Natural Helpers Org; Faith In Gold Awd Soph; Coaches Bsktbl-Track Awds; Fort Hays Univ; Tchr.

MUNSCH, TAMMY E; Hays HS; Hays, KS; (3); Church Yth Grp; Girl Scts; Hosp Aide; Natl FFA Org; Band; Mrchg Band; Orch; School Musical; High Hon Roll; NHS; Natl FFA Band; Pharmacy.

MUNSEY, KIRSTEN; Emporia HS; Emporia, KS; (3); Am Leg Aux Girls St; Boy Scts; Debate Tm; Drama Clb; Key Clb; Model UN; NFL; Band; Jazz Band; Mrchg Band; Eagle Sct; Emporia ST; Pol Sci.

MUNSON, MICHAEL R; Junction City HS; Junction City, KS; (2); Church Yth Grp; 4-H; Pep Clb; Band; Mrchg Band; Ofcr Soph Cls; Var Bsktbl; Var Ftbl; Var Wt Lftg; 4-H Awd; KS ST Univ.

MUNTZ, CASSANDRA D; Olathe East Sr HS; Olathe, KS; (2); Church Yth Grp; Cmnty Wkr; French Clb; GAA; Letterman Clb; Pep Clb; Varsity Clb; Hist Band; Church Choir; Drill Tm; MANC; Med/Arch Fld.

MUNTZ, CHAD; Olathe East Sr HS; Olathe, KS; (4); 16/306; Cmnty Wkr; French Clb; Letterman Clb; Math Clb; Math Tm; Spanish Clb; Band; Church Choir; Jazz Band; Mrchg Band; Outstdng Band Dedication; KC Yth For Christ; Taught Weekly Cls Local Chrch; Psych; Math.

MURDIE, AVERY S; Jefferson West HS; Meriden, KS; (1); 1/79; Chess Clb; VP Natl FFA Org; Band; Pep Band; School Play; JV Bsktbl; JV Ftbl; High Hon Roll; Various Awds And Hon Through FFA; KS St Univ; Gentic Eng.

MURDOCK, JADA; Spring Hill HS; Spring Hill, KS; (4); 50/100; Am Leg Aux Girls St; Office Aide; Sec Pep Clb; SADD; Teachers Aide; Rep Stu Cncl; Capt Chrldng; Hon Roll; All Star Awd Chrldng; Johnson Cty CC; Law Enfrcmnt.

MURDOCK, RICHARD G; Leavenworth HS; Leavenworth, KS; (3); DECA; Band; Mrchg Band; Orch; Pep Band; Bsktbl; Hon Roll; Leavenworth KS Emergency Prepardness Crew Mem; Hosp Nutritional Svc Attendant; Natl & ST DECA Awds; KS Univ; Advertising; Bus.

MURPHREE, REBEKAH S; Dexter Jr Sr HS; Dexter, KS; (2); Sec Treas Church Yth Grp; Science Clb; Band; Chorus; Church Choir; Mrchg Band; Pep Band; JV Bsbl; JV Vllybl; Hon Roll; Rating II Flute Solo League/Regs Frosh/Soph Yrs; Woodwind Trio Rating II Regs/League Frosh Yr; KS Univ; Music/Band Dir.

MURPHY, AILEEN M; Bishop Ward HS; Kansas City, KS; (3); 2/75; Am Leg Aux Girls St; Church Yth Grp; Cmnty Wkr; 4-H; Quiz Bowl; SADD; Stage Crew; Bsktbl; Crs Cntry; Trk; Teen Adv Cncl; Yth Crt Atty; Stdnt As Tchrs Tutor Mentor Prg; Boston Univ; Soc Wrk.

MURPHY, AUDRA; Olpe Schl; Olpe, KS; (3); 5/33; Church Yth Grp; FBLA; Band; Ofcr Soph Cls; Bsktbl; Var Chrldng; Vllybl; High Hon Roll; Hon Roll; NHS; Emporia St; Sci.

MURPHY, BETHANY; Hays HS; Hays, KS; (3); 1/236; Hosp Aide; NFL; Pres Science Clb; Band; Drm Mjr(t); High Hon Roll; NHS; Church Yth Grp; Speech Tm; Church Choir; I Rating Oboe Solo ST Cntst; Symphny Orch; Ft Hays ST U Woodwind Quintet; Music Therapy.

MURPHY, DARREN; Trego Comm HS; Wa Keeney, KS; (4); 13/46; Debate Tm; Letterman Clb; Science Clb; Spanish Clb; Chorus; School Musical; Bsktbl; Tennis; High Hon Roll; Tennis 95 3-A KS St Trnmt 10th Pl; St Forensics Trnmt Qualfr Informtve Speakng 95; Fort Hays ST U; Bus Mgmt.

MURPHY, JANELLE; West Elk Jr Sr HS; Moline, KS; (4); 7/32; Am Leg Aux Girls St; FCA; FHA; Library Aide; Band; Bsktbl; L Chrldng; Sftbl; L Vllybl; Hon Roll; Cowley Cty CC; Acctng.

MURPHY, JONATHAN D; Immaculata HS; Leavenworth, KS; (3); Boy Scts; Rep Frsh Cls; Rep Soph Cls; Pres Jr Cls; Var L Bsktbl; Var L Crs Cntry; Var L Ftbl; Var L Trk; NHS; Am Leg Boys St; Eagle Sct.

MURPHY, LAURA; Udall HS; Udall, KS; (2); 2/40; 4-H; Math Clb; Quiz Bowl; Scholastic Bowl; Nwsp; Sftbl; Cit Awd; 4-H Awd; High Hon Roll; NHS; KS ST U; Bus/Acctng.

MURPHY, MATTHEW; Blue Valley North HS; Leawood, KS; (3); 44/222; Cmnty Wkr; Math Tm; Model UN; NFL; Pres Quiz Bowl; Hon Roll; NHS; Ntl Merit Ltr; St Champ Emporia St Chem Test; Hnrb Mntn His & Physics; Pol Sci Clb; Amer His, Chem & Calculus AP Test; Harvey Mudd; Chem Engrng.

MURPHY, MELISSA; Circle HS; El Dorado, KS; (4); Spanish Clb; SADD; Acpl Chr; Band; Chorus; Church Choir; Var Tennis; High Hon Roll; Hon Roll; KS St Univ; Bio.

MURPHY, MONICA; Maize HS; Wichita, KS; (4); 42/225; Church Yth Grp; FCA; 4-H; Letterman Clb; Science Clb; Spanish Clb; Pres SADD; Treas Thesps; School Play; Bsktbl; KS ST Univ; Intnl Bus; Span.

MURPHY, PAUL; Nemaha Valley HS; Seneca, KS; (3); Drama Clb; Scholastic Bowl; Speech Tm; Teachers Aide; Band; Mrchg Band; Pep Band; School Play; Swing Chorus; Sec Jr Cls; Mem All ST Masonic Mrchng Bnd 95; Natl Yth Frm Med; Med/Physcn.

MURPHY, TODD; Liberal HS; Liberal, KS; (4); 6/212; Am Leg Boys St; Church Yth Grp; Key Clb; Q&S; Scholastic Bowl; Band; Ed Nwsp; Pres Sr Cls; Var Tennis; Pres NHS; Pepperdine Univ.

MURRAY, AMY L; Ft Scott HS; Fort Scott, KS; (2); Church Yth Grp; FCA; SADD; Band; Mrchg Band; Pep Band; JV Tennis; JV Trk; Wt Lftg; Hon Roll; FSCC; Music Ed; Ministry.

MURRAY, ANNE C; Lawrence HS; Lawrence, KS; (4); 1/550; FCA; Latin Clb; L Bsktbl; L Swmmng; L Vllybl; Cit Awd; Gov Hon Prg Awd; Hon Roll; NHS; Pres Schlr; Dartmouth Coll.

MURRAY, ASHLEY C; Wellington Sr HS; Wellington, KS; (2); Church Yth Grp; Debate Tm; Math Tm; Office Aide; Quiz Bowl; Scholastic Bowl; SADD; Hon Roll; Jr NHS; Prfct Atten Awd.

MURRAY, CODY L; Mankato Jr Sr HS; Mankato, KS; (3); Pres 4-H; Pres Natl FFA Org; Swing Chorus; Sec Frsh Cls; Treas Soph Cls; Rep Jr Cls; JV Var Ftbl; 4-H Awd; Hon Roll; Church Yth Grp; Rcvd Slvr Rcgtn Dscvr Card Schlrshp Awd Arts/Hum 96; I Dare You/Key Awds/4-H 95; Colby CC; Ag Ed.

MURRAY, DEANNE; Shawnee Heights Sr HS; Tecumseh, KS; (2); Church Yth Grp; Capt L Chrldng; Trk; High Hon Roll.

MURRAY, GREG W; Washburn Rural HS; Auburn, KS; (3); Boy Scts; Cmnty Wkr; Teachers Aide; Band; Mrchg Band; Pep Band; School Play; High Hon Roll; Acad Ltr Every Yr; Railroad Explorer Scouts Former Pres; Star Trek Clb; Math.

MURRAY, SEAN P; Great Bend Sr HS; Great Bend, KS; (4); Hon Roll; Taekwondo 2nd Degree Black Belt; KS St Champion; Barton Cty CC; Philosophy.

MURRELL, MATTHEW; Chase Co HS; Cottonwood Falls, KS; (3); Church Yth Grp; Cmnty Wkr; HOBY; Math Tm; Quiz Bowl; Spanish Clb; Chorus; School Musical; School Play; Ofcr Soph Cls; Wichita ST U; Engr.

MURRELL, TERESA; Apostolic Acad; Junction City, KS; (4); #1 in class; Church Yth Grp; Office Aide; Teachers Aide; Church Choir; Phtg Yrbk; Pres Stu Cncl; Cit Awd; High Hon Roll; Prfct Atten Awd; Val; KA ST Univ.

MURRY, BRANDI J; Riverton Schl; Baxter Springs, KS; (1); Church Yth Grp; Cmnty Wkr; Drama Clb; FCA; Letterman Clb; Pep Clb; Band; Jazz Band; Mrchg Band; Orch; Acctng.

MURRY, CARMEN R; Great Bend Sr HS; Great Bend, KS; (3); 29/230; Church Yth Grp; Spanish Clb; Co-Ed Ed Nwsp; Rep Soph Cls; Rep Jr Cls; Sec Stu Cncl; JV Var Bsktbl; JV Var Vllybl; High Hon Roll; NHS; KAY Pres; Slctd Attend Natl Yth Ldrs Camp Washington DC; U Of KS; Jrnlsm/Comm.

MUSALEK, MATTHEW; Hays HS; Hays, KS; (3); Church Yth Grp; Band; Mrchg Band; Treas Orch; Pep Band; Intrml JV Bsktbl; Var L Crs Cntry; Var L Trk; Hon Roll.

MUSEOUSKY, MIKE J; Wichita North HS; Wichita, KS; (2); Pep Clb; JV Var Bsktbl; Var Ftbl; Var Trk; Wt Lftg; High Hon Roll; Hon Roll; Pres Acad Fit Awd; Ath For Abstnc; KS Univ; Bus Mngng/Mrktng.

MUSEOUSKY, NICHOLAS J; Wichita North HS; Wichita, KS; (2); Pep Clb; JV Bsbl; JV Var Bsktbl; JV Var Ftbl; JV Trk; Var Wt Lftg; High Hon Roll; Yth Day Of Caring; Ath Fr Abstnence; Engrng.

MUSEOUSKY, RACHEL; Wichita North HS; Wichita, KS; (2); Yrbk; Ofcr Jr Cls; Swmmng; High Hon Roll; Quill/Scroll Soc; KS Univ.

MUSFELT, ADAM D; Salina HS South; Salina, KS; (3); Hon Roll; Vo-Tech Refrigeration; VICA Mem 1st In St 14th In Nation; Jr Coll; Refrigeration.

MUSICK, DANIELLE; Garden City Sr HS; Garden City, KS; (3); 55/310; Debate Tm; Latin Clb; Acpl Chr; Band; Mrchg Band; Orch; School Musical; Stage Crew; JV Var Chrldng; Var JV Trk; Dist Band/Choir; ST Choir; ACDA.

MUSICK, PAIGE A; Shawnee Mission S Sr HS; Overland Park, KS; (4); 51/413; Cmnty Wkr; DECA; Hosp Aide; Intnl Clb; Pep Clb; High Hon Roll; Hon Roll; NHS; Pres Schlr; KS ST U; Bus.

MUSKOPF, BLAINE; Shawnee Mission West HS; Lenexa, KS; (3); Art Clb; NFL; Q&S; VICA; Yrbk; Hon Roll; Prfct Atten Awd; Pittsburg ST Univ; Grphc Dsgn.

MUSSON, MICAH; Arkansas City HS; Arkansas City, KS; (3); Drama Clb; FCA; SADD; Acpl Chr; Chorus; School Musical; Golf; Sftbl; Hon Roll; VP NHS; 1st Alt Close-Up WA Prgm; Elem Ed.

MUTHUKRISHMAN, ARAVIND; Manhattan HS; Manhattan, KS; (3); 1/500; Chess Clb; Debate Tm; Math Tm; NFL; Capt Quiz Bowl; Capt Scholastic Bowl; Pres Science Clb; Spanish Clb; Teachers Aide; Temple Yth Grp; St KS Schlrshp Tst; Jr Clss Hnrry; MA Inst Of Tech; Engnr.

MYERS, AMANDA K; Frankft HS; Frankfort, KS; (2); Church Yth Grp; Cmnty Wkr; FHA; Spanish Clb; SADD; Chorus; Hon Roll; St Schlr; Rep Frsh Cls; KS Univ; Bus.

MYERS, AMY; Jefferson West HS; Meriden, KS; (3); 3/80; VP FBLA; VP FHA; FTA; Band; Pep Band; Ofcr Stu Cncl; Sftbl; Vllybl; High Hon Roll; NHS; Cmnty Svc Awd; KS ST.

MYERS, BRAD A; Topeka West HS; Topeka, KS; (3); 75/300; French Clb; German Clb; Model UN; Pep Clb; Chorus; School Musical; High Hon Roll; Hon Roll; OK Chrstn.

MYERS, BRADY; Washburn Rural HS; Topeka, KS; (3); 97/369; Church Yth Grp; SADD; Acpl Chr; Chorus; Swing Chorus; Variety Show; JV Ftbl; Var Wt Lftg; Hon Roll; Sumr Bsbl Prgm; IM Bsktbl.

MYERS, DANA M; Jefferson West HS; Meriden, KS; (3); 31/70; Cmnty Wkr; Letterman Clb; Spanish Clb; Band; Chorus; Mrchg Band; Pep Band; Crs Cntry; Trk; Hon Roll.

MYERS, DUSTY K; Topeka HS; Topeka, KS; (2); Dance Clb; Office Aide; Pep Clb; Teachers Aide; Band; Drill Tm; Mrchg Band; Pep Band; Var Socr; JV Tennis.

MYERS, DYLAN T; Dodge City HS; Dodge City, KS; (2); Band; Mrchg Band; Pep Band; JV Bsbl; JV Bsktbl; JV Ftbl; High Hon Roll; Optometry.

MYERS, ERIK V; Great Bend Sr HS; Great Bend, KS; (3); Band; Mrchg Band; Var Swmmng; Barton City CC; Hwy Patrol.

MYERS, JAMIE M; Campus HS; Wichita, KS; (3); Cmnty Wkr; Office Aide; Wt Lftg; Hon Roll; Wtr Ski; Fish; KS ST.

MYERS, JENNIFER; Valley Falls HS; Valley Falls, KS; (1); Rptr Nwsp; Yrbk.

MYERS, JESSICA; Valley Falls HS; Valley Falls, KS; (2); 7/42; Cmnty Wkr; Acpl Chr; Chorus; Rptr Nwsp; Hon Roll; Jrnlsm.

MYERS, MEGAN; Wellington Sr HS; Wellington, KS; (3); 40/180; Church Yth Grp; Cmnty Wkr; Key Clb; Band; Church Choir; Mrchg Band; Crs Cntry; Hon Roll; NHS.

MYERS, MOLLY; Shawnee Heights Sr HS; Topeka, KS; (4); Hosp Aide; JA; Key Clb; Model UN; Teachers Aide; Thesps; Stage Crew; Rptr Yrbk; Hon Roll; Engrng.

MYERS, NATHAN R; Russell HS; Russell, KS; (2); Natl FFA Org; JV Bsktbl; JV Crs Cntry; Hon Roll.

MYERS, ROBERT R; Jefferson West HS; Meriden, KS; (1); 6/73; FBLA; Letterman Clb; Spanish Clb; Chorus; Pres Frsh Cls; Ofcr Stu Cncl; Bsktbl; Ftbl; Trk; Wt Lftg.

MYERS, RYAN D; Newton Sr HS; Newton, KS; (2); Art Clb; Church Yth Grp; French Clb; JV Ftbl; JV Golf; Hon Roll; HS Div Tm Wichita Yth Thndr Hcky Assn Ice Hcky Plyr; U KS Lwrnce; Arch.

MYERS, STEPHANIE L; Atchison Sr HS; Atchison, KS; (1); Dance Clb; French Clb; Red Cross Aide; Band; Mrchg Band; Pep Band; Chrldng; Mgr(s); Pom Pon; Hon Roll; Dncng; Tchng Swmng Lessons 5 Yrs; Benidictin; Nrlgy.

MYERS, VIKKI; Santa Fe Trail HS; Overbrook, KS; (4); Sec VP FBLA; HOBY; Rep Jr Cls; Rep Sr Cls; Ofcr Stu Cncl; L Bsktbl; L Trk; L Vllybl; High Hon Roll; Hist NHS.

MYRAH, DEJA R; Washburn Rural HS; Topeka, KS; (3); French Clb; SADD; Band; Color Guard; Capt Flag Corp; Mrchg Band; Pep Band; School Play; JV Socr; Stand; KS St; Psych.

MYRICK, ERYN M; Topeka HS; Topeka, KS; (2); Dance Clb; Intnl Clb; Model UN; Band; Mrchg Band; Pep Band; High Hon Roll; Pres Schlr; Church Yth Grp; French Clb; Spcl Olympcs Vol; Ballet Lessons.

NAAB, LAWRENCE; Spearville Jr Sr HS; Spearville, KS; (3); HOBY; Pep Clb; Quiz Bowl; Band; Chorus; Pep Band; Ed Nwsp; Ed Yrbk; Ed Lit Mag; Var Bsktbl; St Jrnlsm & Speech Team; Mens Vocal Ensemble; KSU; Elec Engr.

NAAF, JOEL R; Marysville HS; Summerfield, KS; (2); Natl FFA Org; Wrstlng; High Hon Roll; Hon Roll; Multi Yr Listee; KSU.

NAAS, CARMEN; Junction City HS; Junction City, KS; (3); Cit Awd; High Hon Roll; Hon Roll.

NAASZ, MELANIE R; Wichita East HS; Wichita, KS; (2); Debate Tm; GAA; NFL; Band; Mrchg Band; Bsktbl; Hon Roll; Wrtng Poetry; KS Univ; Jrnlsm.

NAFF, MELISSA S; Humboldt HS; Humboldt, KS; (3); 9/63; Natl FFA Org; Ed Nwsp; Yrbk; Trk; Dance Clb; Ot Of Schl Jb; Rdng; Pittsburg ST U; Ped.

NAGLE, BRIAN C; Topeka West HS; Topeka, KS; (4); 34/236; Spanish Clb; Teachers Aide; Var L Bsktbl; JV Ftbl; High Hon Roll; Nom For Natl Hon Soc; INROADS Corp; Barton Cnty Bsktbll And Acad Schol; Barton Cnty CC; Bus.

NAGLE, CRISTINA; Topeka HS; Topeka, KS; (2); #1 in class; Cmnty Wkr; Spanish Clb; Teachers Aide; Varsity Clb; Variety Show; Ed Yrbk; VP Soph Cls; Bsktbl; Var L Chrldng; Var L Swmmng; Mexican Amer Yth Org Treas.

NAILL, ADAM L; Flinthills HS; El Dorado, KS; (4); 1/22; Library Aide; Capt Quiz Bowl; SADD; School Play; Pres Frsh Cls; Pres Soph Cls; NHS; Pres Acad Fit Awd; St Schlr; Val; U Of KS; Humanbio.

NAIRN, SHANA; Stanton Co HS; Johnson, KS; (4); Church Yth Grp; FBLA; Office Aide; Chorus; Golf; Pom Pon; Vllybl; Hon Roll; NHS; Prfct Atten Awd; Scholars; Colby CC; Physthpy Asst.

NANNALLY, DANIEL B; Shawnee Mission W Sr HS; Overland Park, KS; (3); 67/415; Band; Mrchg Band; Pep Band; Hon Roll; Prfct Atten Awd; Band & Acad Ltrs; The KS Of Univ; Bus.

NANNINGA, KATIE L; Axtell Schl; Axtell, KS; (4); Church Yth Grp; Pres Drama Clb; VP 4-H; FHA; Letterman Clb; Teachers Aide; Band; Chorus; School Musical; School Play; Mc Pherson Col; Chld Psych.

NANTZ, NICOLE K; Shawnee Heights HS; Topeka, KS; (1); Cmnty Wkr; GAA; Hosp Aide; Pep Clb; Red Cross Aide; Trk; Vllybl; Wt Lftg; Hon Roll; Pres Acad Fit Awd; KS ST Univ.

NAPIER, AARON N; Wellington Sr HS; Wellington, KS; (3); Church Yth Grp; SADD; Band; Jazz Band; Mrchg Band; Pep Band; High Hon Roll; Jr NHS; Natl Hr Lions Clb Awd Wnnr; Multi Yr Listing; Bus Mgmt.

NAPIER, BRAD C; Oswego HS; Oswego, KS; (1); Pep Clb; Spanish Clb; SADD; Chorus; Var L Ftbl; Var L Trk; Hon Roll; Big Brothers; Tutor; OK Univ.

NAPIER, TRAVIS A; Rossville HS; Rossville, KS; (3); Letterman Clb; Varsity Clb; Var Bsbl; Var Bsktbl; Var Ftbl; Neosho County.

NAPOLITANO, KATRINA E; Great Bend Sr HS; Great Bend, KS; (1); Church Yth Grp; Pep Clb; Band; Chorus; Mrchg Band; Orch; Pep Band; Variety Show; High Hon Roll; Pres Acad Fit Awd; Distngd Schlstc Achvmnt; Amer Music Fndtn; KS ST HS Actvts Assn; Music.

NARAMORE, MEGAN; Northwest HS; Wichita, KS; (3); Cmnty Wkr; Office Aide; Q&S; Teachers Aide; Color Guard; Mrchg Band; Ed Yrbk; Hon Roll; NHS; Sftbl; WSU.

NARINO, JULIAN; Mc Pherson HS; Mc Pherson, KS; (2); Art Clb; German Clb; NFL; Speech Tm; Band; Mrchg Band; Pep Band; School Musical; School Play; Stage Crew; Film Dir/Ed.

NASH, CHAD M; Field Kindley Mem Sr HS; Coffeyville, KS; (3); French Clb; Band; Jazz Band; Var Crs Cntry; Var Diving; Var Swmmng; Var Trk; Hon Roll.

NASH, D RYAN; Labette Co HS; Altamont, KS; (2); Church Yth Grp; FCA; JV Golf; Hon Roll; Individ Achvmnt Awd Math; FL ST Univ; Elem Ed.

NASH, JOSEPH J; Olathe East Sr HS; Olathe, KS; (4); Band; Drm Mjr(t); Jazz Band; Mrchg Band; Orch; Pep Band; School Musical; Variety Show; Hon Roll; Prins Ldrshp Awd; Semper Fidelis Awd/Musical Excl; Southwest MO ST Univ; Politcs.

NASH, KIMBERLY D; Labette Co HS; Altamont, KS; (3); 3/143; Church Yth Grp; FCA; Rep FBLA; VICA; Chorus; School Musical; Swing Chorus; Rep Jr Cls; High Hon Roll; NHS; PKP Dns Schlrshp; St Music Fest I Rtngs; Soc Sci Acad Achvt Awd; Acctng.

NASH, SARA A; Lawrence HS; Lawrence, KS; (4); 52/520; Drama Clb; German Clb; Key Clb; Service Clb; Teachers Aide; Band; Mrchg Band; Pep Band; School Play; Lit Mag; U Of KS; Elem Ed.

NASH, STEPHANIE M; Shawnee Mission Nw Sr HS; Lenexa, KS; (3); 110/460; Am Leg Aux Girls St; Pres Cmnty Wkr; Hist Debate Tm; Girl Scts; Pep Clb; Pres Speech Tm; Pres SADD; Cit Awd; High Hon Roll; Hon Roll; Ms Lenexa 1st Rnnr Up; Houlihans 3 Cheers For Vols 3rd Pl; Cougars Commited To Comm Pres; Psych; Pub Relations.

NASH, TAMMY; Garden City Sr HS; Garden City, KS; (3); 76/357; Church Yth Grp; Dance Clb; 4-H; Natl FFA Org; Teachers Aide; Pom Pon; Wt Lftg; 4-H Awd; High Hon Roll; NHS; Dog Shwmnshp St Chmp; FT ST U; Bus.

NASH, TREVOR; Garden City Sr HS; Garden City, KS; (4); 4-H; Natl FFA Org; 4-H Awd; Little Britches Rodeo; HS Rodeo Tm; Ft Hays ST; Ag Bus.

NATION, ANTONY C; Ottawa HS; Ottawa, KS; (3); L Debate Tm; NFL; Office Aide; L Speech Tm; Teachers Aide; Band; Drm Mjr(t); Jazz Band; Mrchg Band; Pep Band; Amer Legion Bsbl; Drama Production Pgm Designer; Wichita ST Univ; Debate Coach.

NAU, KIMBERLY N; Spearville Jr Sr HS; Spearville, KS; (2); Pep Clb; Vllybl; Hon Roll; Acctng.

NAU, TERRI D; Spearville Jr Sr HS; Spearville, KS; (2); 4-H; Letterman Clb; Pep Clb; Varsity Clb; Band; Drill Tm; Var Bsktbl; Var Sftbl; Var Vllybl; Hon Roll; SW KS Bus Cmptn; Acad Olympics; Organist; Dodge City CC; Accnt.

NAUMAN, ERIC M; Louisburg HS; Louisburg, KS; (2); Church Yth Grp; FCA; Pep Clb; Band; Church Choir; Mrchg Band; Pep Band; Bsktbl; Score Keeper; Wt Lftg; KS Univ; Aerospace.

NAVARRO, SHERYSE; Wichita North HS; Wichita, KS; (4); 31/247; Q&S; Teachers Aide; Phtg Nwsp; Phtg Yrbk; Rep Sr Cls; Var Pom Pon; JV Var Socr; Hon Roll; St Schlr; Cls Clb; Environmental Clb; U Of KS.

NAVINSKY, BRANDON J; Basehor Linwood HS; Basehor, KS; (3); Church Yth Grp; Co-Ed Nwsp; JV Bsbl; Bsktbl; Ftbl; High Hon Roll; Hon Roll; Prfct Atten Awd; Sci Olympiad Reg/ST; Hnrbl Mntn Natl Jrnlsm Conf Advtsng.

NAYLOR, LATICIA; Leavenworth HS; Fort Leavenworth, KS; (4); 113/314; Am Leg Aux Girls St; Cmnty Wkr; FBLA; ROTC; Chorus; Flag Corp; Mrchg Band; Hon Roll; Bus Profs of Am; Church Yth Grp; Yth Cncl NAACP Ust VP; Hampton U; Pre-Med.

NAZIR, SAMIHA Z; Blue Valley HS; Overland Park, KS; (3); Hosp Aide; Intnl Clb; SADD; Hon Roll; KAYS; U Of KS; Med.

NEAD, AMY; Pierson Jr HS; Kansas City, KS; (1); Girl Scts; Rptr Nwsp; Rep Stu Cncl; Hon Roll; Jr NHS; KS ST Univ; Tchr.

NEAL, AHMAD R; Wyandotte HS; Kansas City, KS; (2); Church Yth Grp; Computer Clb; Teachers Aide; Ofcr Bsbl; Bsktbl; Ftbl.

NEAL, AMY M; Kingman HS; Kingman, KS; (3); Church Yth Grp; SADD; Band; Chorus; Mrchg Band; Pep Band; School Musical; NHS.

NEAL, BROOKE; Southwestern Heights HS; Plains, KS; (3); 3/52; Church Yth Grp; HOBY; Band; Chorus; Pep Band; Bsktbl; Crs Cntry; Trk; Hon Roll; NHS; KAYS; Piano; Mstng Sngrs; U Of KS; Med.

NEAL, CYNTHIA J; Gardner-Edgerton HS; Edgerton, KS; (4); Church Yth Grp; Drama Clb; SADD; Thesps; Band; Chorus; Flag Corp; School Musical; Sec Stu Cncl; High Hon Roll; US Stu Cncl Awd; Emporia ST Univ; Nrsng.

NEAL, JAMIE L; Newton Sr HS; Newton, KS; (1); Sec Church Yth Grp; German Clb; Key Clb; Quiz Bowl; School Play; Var Crs Cntry; JV Swmmng; Hon Roll.

NEAL, MICHAEL A; Robert E Clark Jr HS; Bonner Springs, KS; (1); Church Yth Grp; Cmnty Wkr; FHA; Ofcr Bsbl; Ftbl; Wt Lftg; Hon Roll; Summer Rec Prgm Umpire; CCD Tchr Aide Church; JV Awd Bsbl; Wichita ST Univ; Arch.

NEARY, JULIE E; Silver Lake Jr Sr HS; Silver Lake, KS; (3); 17/51; Church Yth Grp; Spanish Clb; Chorus; Phtg Yrbk; JV Var Bsktbl; Var Chrldng; Var Sftbl; JV Var Vllybl; Hon Roll; NHS.

NEBITT, MEGAN M; Chaparral HS; Danville, KS; (3); 9/65; Chorus; School Musical; Var Trk; Intrml Vllybl; High Hon Roll; Hon Roll; NHS; Teens As Tchrs; Select Girls Ensmble; Elem Ed.

NECH, JAMES R; Norton Comm HS; Norton, KS; (3); JV Ftbl; Hon Roll; U Of TX; Law Enforcement.

NECHODOMU, THOMAS D; Golden Plains Middle HS; Rexford, KS; (4); 3/13; Church Yth Grp; Sec Letterman Clb; Quiz Bowl; Speech Tm; Band; Chorus; Church Choir; Pep Band; School Play; Trk; Grace Univ; Pstorl Studs.

NEDDO, FREDERICK A; Chapman HS; Abilene, KS; (3); Art Clb; Church Yth Grp; Latin Clb; Natl FFA Org; NFL; Spanish Clb; SADD; Varsity Clb; Band; Ed Yrbk; KS Univ; Med.

NEECK, CHRIS; Maranatha Acad; Shawnee, KS; (2); Church Yth Grp; Math Tm; Pep Clb; Band; Color Guard; Jazz Band; Mrchg Band; Pep Band; School Play; Variety Show.

NEEDHAM, KELSEY D; Jayhawk-Linn HS; Mound City, KS; (3); 1/50; Am Leg Aux Girls St; Drama Clb; Math Tm; Band; School Play; Sec Frsh Cls; Sec Soph Cls; Pres Jr Cls; High Hon Roll; NHS; Med/Doctor.

NEEDHAM, MICAH H; Independence HS; Independence, KS; (1); Church Yth Grp; Cmnty Wkr; JA; Quiz Bowl; Scholastic Bowl; Ed Yrbk; JV Stat Ftbl; JV Var Tennis; Gov Hon Prg Awd; High Hon Roll; KS ST U Stck Mrkt Gm 2nd Region; Extnd Lrng Prgm; Acad Achvmt Awd; Princeton; Bus/Pol Law.

NEEL, HEATHER N; Wamego HS; Wamego, KS; (2); Church Yth Grp; Dance Clb; FCA; FHA; Service Clb; SADD; Chorus; Church Choir; Drill Tm; VP Frsh Cls; K ST; Psychlgst.

NEELAND, HILLARY D; Great Bend Sr HS; Great Bend, KS; (2); Church Yth Grp; Debate Tm; Rep French Clb; NFL; Acpl Chr; Band; Mrchg Band; Variety Show; JV Sftbl; Hon Roll; Del Farmland Natl Yth Ldrshp Conf; Madrigal Pop Sngrs 96-.

NEELEY, JENNIFER S; Spearville Jr Sr HS; Spearville, KS; (2); Pep Clb; Band; Chorus; Pep Band; Trk; Vllybl; Soc Work.

NEELY, DESMOND S; Washington HS; Kansas City, KS; (3); Chess Clb; Church Yth Grp; FCA; German Clb; Teachers Aide; High Hon Roll; Hon Roll; NHS; JT Prdctn Yth Choir/Drama Team; African Amer Male Ldrshp Acad; Yng Adult Usher Brd Treas.

NEET, AARON T; Riverton Schl; Galena, KS; (4); 8/57; Capt FHA; HOBY; Letterman Clb; Capt Scholastic Bowl; Pres Science Clb; VP Service Clb; Ofcr Stu Cncl; L Trk; Treas NHS; Presdentl Clsrm; NYLF Security/Defns; U S Naval Acad Smmr Engrng Pgm; KS U; Law.

NEFF, DA LAENA; Colley HS; Selden, KS; (3); HOBY; Pep Clb; Spanish Clb; Chorus; Pres Frsh Cls; Sec Soph Cls; JV Var Bsktbl; JV Var Vllybl; Hon Roll; Chrch Srvs; CYO; KS ST U; Schl Cnslr.

NEGRETE, ANGELINA C; Olathe East Sr HS; Olathe, KS; (4); Pep Clb; Spanish Clb; Acpl Chr; Stage Crew; Rep Soph Cls; Sec Stu Cncl; Powder Puff Ftbl; Var Tennis; Prin Ldrshp Awd; Miss Sweet Sicteen 94; JCCC; Bus.

NEIDHART, SAVANNAH J; Prairie View Jr Sr HS; Centerville, KS; (3); 15/67; Church Yth Grp; Pres Math Clb; Quiz Bowl; Capt Scholastic Bowl; Spanish Clb; Teachers Aide; Church Choir; Trk; Hon Roll; Physcs Comp Gld Medl; Pittsbrg St Univ; Med.

NEIHARDT, TRAVIS A; Thomas More Prep-Marion HS; Hays, KS; (3); Quiz Bowl; Stage Crew; Var Ftbl; Hon Roll; Ft Hays St Univ; Sprts Med.

NEILL, COREY A; Atchison Co Cmty HS; Cummings, KS; (2); Pres Church Yth Grp; 4-H; Math Clb; Quiz Bowl; Science Clb; Pres Frsh Cls; Var Bsktbl; Var Ftbl; Var Trk; Var Wt Lftg; FFA Chptr Sentinel; 3a ST Champ 110m High Hurdles; Ag.

NEISES, DAN J; Bishop Carroll Catholic HS; Maize, KS; (3); 21/220; German Clb; NFL; Quiz Bowl; School Play; VP Jr Cls; Pres Sr Cls; Bsktbl; High Hon Roll; NHS; GCTL Mem; CYA Mem.

NEISES, REBECCA; Bishop Carroll Catholic HS; Viola, KS; (4); 8/143; Am Leg Aux Girls St; Church Yth Grp; Pres SADD; Teachers Aide; Rep Jr Cls; Rep Sr Cls; Mgr Ftbl; Powder Puff Ftbl; High Hon Roll; NHS; KS ST U.

NEISWENDER, JAIME; Jackson Heights HS; Circleville, KS; (1); Cmnty Wkr; FHA; Girl Scts; Pep Clb; Chorus; School Musical; Var Mgr(s); Intrml Sftbl; Var Trk; Intrml Vllybl; Kids Of FACE; DARE; Jump Rope For Heart; KS ST; Nrsng.

NEJDL, DANIELLE M; Quinter Jr Sr HS; Quinter, KS; (3); Art Clb; Acpl Chr; Chorus; School Musical; School Play; Yrbk; Crs Cntry; Var Trk; Pres Acad Fit Awd; Q Clb; Colby CCPHYS Ther.

NELLANS, CARRIE; Peabody-Burns Jr Sr HS; Peabody, KS; (3); Church Yth Grp; Drama Clb; FCA; HOBY; Band; Mrchg Band; Ed Yrbk; Crs Cntry; Trk; NHS.

NELSEN, BRANDON M; Salina HS South; Salina, KS; (3); Church Yth Grp; FCA; Ski Clb; Spanish Clb; Teachers Aide; Band; Mrchg Band; Var JV Bsbl; Wt Lftg; Hon Roll; KS ST Univ.

NELSON, ANGELA K; Salina HS Central; Salina, KS; (3); Church Yth Grp; SADD; Teachers Aide; Chorus; Swmmng; 3-D, 2-D Art, Forensics; Music Ltr; KS ST.

NELSON, ANNA M; Elyria Christian Schl; Mc Pherson, KS; (2); Church Yth Grp; Letterman Clb; Spanish Clb; Chorus; Church Choir; School Play; Bsktbl; Score Keeper; Vllybl; Hon Roll.

NELSON, BEN W; Smoky Valley HS; Lindsborg, KS; (1); Cit Awd; High Hon Roll; Hon Roll; Pres Acad Fit Awd.

NELSON, BROOK; Shawnee Mission Nw Sr HS; Shawnee Mission, KS; (4); 7/403; Church Yth Grp; Cmnty Wkr; DECA; English Clb; FTA; Hosp Aide; HOBY; Pres Intnl Clb; Key Clb; Office Aide; Cougars Untd Acts Coord & Pres; Mltpl Hnrs Sci High Lvl; U Of KS; Med.

NELSON, CHAD M; Smoky Valley HS; Lindsborg, KS; (2); Church Yth Grp; Band; Mrchg Band; Pep Band; Pres Frsh Cls; Var Bsktbl; Var L Ftbl; Var L Tennis; High Hon Roll; Hon Roll; Pharm.

NELSON, CHELSIE M; Grinnell HS; Grinnell, KS; (3); Church Yth Grp; Cmnty Wkr; Sec Treas Pep Clb; Band; Chorus; Phtg Rptr Yrbk; Pres Soph Cls; L Chrldng; Mgr(s); Mgr Vllybl; Yth Pride 6 Yrs; Small Choir Ensmbl; Ft Hays ST U; Psych.

NELSON, CHRIS; Lyons HS; Lyons, KS; (3); 6/65; Am Leg Boys St; Church Yth Grp; Quiz Bowl; Band; Jazz Band; Mrchg Band; Pep Band; JV Var Crs Cntry; Var Trk; NHS; MI Chrstn Coll; Bus Mgmt; Acctg.

NELSON, CHRISTOPHER K; Canton-Galva HS; Galva, KS; (2); 2/32; Church Yth Grp; VP FBLA; Letterman Clb; SADD; VP Frsh Cls; Ofcr Bsbl; Bsktbl; Ftbl; Hon Roll; NHS.

NELSON, CRAIG S; Garden City Sr HS; Garden City, KS; (1); JV Bsbl; JV Bsktbl; High Hon Roll; 1st Plc Finney Cnty Sci Fair; NW Kansas Tech Schl Drafting Exh Beginng Pictorial 3rd Plc; Drafting/Cmptrs.

NELSON, DARREN; Little River Jr Sr HS; Windom, KS; (4); 3/21; Treas Church Yth Grp; FCA; Pres 4-H; Math Clb; Math Tm; Spanish Clb; Chorus; School Musical; L Capt Bsktbl; L Capt Ftbl; KS ST U; Mech Engrng.

NELSON, ERIKA L; Shawnee Heights Sr HS; Topeka, KS; (2); Church Yth Grp; Intnl Clb; Band; Church Choir; Mrchg Band; Pep Band; Var L Crs Cntry; Var L Trk; High Hon Roll; Hon Roll; Symphonic Band; Dr Martin Luther Coll; Psych.

NELSON, HEATHER; Blue Valley HS; Olsburg, KS; (1); 1/40; Bus Profs of Am; Sec Church Yth Grp; Sec 4-H; FHA; Acpl Chr; Band; Chorus; Mrchg Band; Pep Band; School Play; BPA Natl Ldrshp Conf 10th In Kybrdng/Prev Plcd 5th; Psych.

NELSON, JAMES L; Salina HS South; Salina, KS; (3); Church Yth Grp; Quiz Bowl; Hon Roll; Sci Olympiad; Math Relays; Cmptr Pgmg Cntst; KS ST Univ Salina; Cmptr Sci.

NELSON, JAMIE L; Dexter Jr Sr HS; Dexter, KS; (2); Rep FHA; Math Tm; Band; Mrchg Band; Pep Band; Rep Frsh Cls; VP Soph Cls; Vllybl.

NELSON, JANELLE; Little River Jr Sr HS; Marquette, KS; (4); Am Leg Aux Girls St; 4-H; German Clb; Math Tm; Band; Chorus; School Musical; School Play; Sec Soph Cls; JV Bsktbl; Homecoming Candidate; ELEM Tchr.

NELSON, JEFFREY H; Eastern Heights Jr Sr HS; Agra, KS; (2); 1/9; FCA; Letterman Clb; School Play; L Bsktbl; L Ftbl; L Trk; Wt Lftg; High Hon Roll; Hon Roll; Prfct Atten Awd; Barton Co CC.

NELSON, JOSH L; Washington HS; Washington, KS; (3); Church Yth Grp; FCA; French Clb; FHA; Letterman Clb; Natl FFA Org; Band; Jazz Band; Mrchg Band; Pep Band; Bible Bowl.

NELSON, JOSHUA D; Smoky Valley HS; Lindsborg, KS; (1); Band; Jazz Band; Mrchg Band; Orch; Pep Band; Variety Show; Ftbl; High Hon Roll; 2nd Chair KMEA Orch/Band Offcr; 1 Ratngs Solos Dist/ST Msc Cntsts; Bckpckng/Skng/Fly Fshng/Mtn Bkn; Ntrlst.

NELSON, LISA C; Bishop Miege HS; Shawnee Mission, KS; (1); 60/245; Var Tennis; High Hon Roll; AZ ST; Ed/Bus.

NELSON, MIKE D; Haven HS; Hutchinson, KS; (3); Acpl Chr; Band; Chorus; Mrchg Band; Pep Band; School Musical; Variety Show; Ftbl; Trk; Wt Lftg; Med.

NELSON, PAUL A; Topeka HS; Topeka, KS; (3); 8/320; Boy Scts; Band; Mrchg Band; Pep Band; High Hon Roll; NHS; Jap Clb Pres; Philsphy Clb; Karate.

NELSON, RENEE S; Wichita Heights HS; Wichita, KS; (3); 92/250; Teachers Aide; Mgr(s); Tennis; Hon Roll; Wichita ST U; Psych.

NELSON, SAMANTHA K; Olathe North Sr HS; Lenexa, KS; (2); Church Yth Grp; Cmnty Wkr; Spanish Clb; Teachers Aide; Chorus; Church Choir; Swmmng; Hon Roll; Fmly-Cnsmr Scis; KS Univ; Tchng.

NELSON, SANDI A; Troy HS; Troy, KS; (3); Letterman Clb; Speech Tm; Band; Sec Treas Stu Cncl; L Var Bsktbl; Var Chrldng; L Trk; L Var Vllybl; High Hon Roll; NHS; Kytts Rep; Dance Team V/Co-Capt; U Of KS; PT.

NELSON, TAMMIE; Southwestern Hghts HS; Kismet, KS; (4); 10/38; 4-H; Natl FFA Org; Pep Clb; SADD; Teachers Aide; Band; Jazz Band; Mrchg Band; Pep Band; JV Bsktbl; All-League Hnrb Mntn & Mst Inspiritational Vllybl 95; Heart Of Determination Vllybl 94; Seward Cty CC; Swine Mgmt.

NELZEN, JOHN A; Hesston HS; Hesston, KS; (2); Boy Scts; Church Yth Grp; FCA; FBLA; German Clb; Model UN; Scholastic Bowl; Band; Chorus; Jazz Band; NRPHSS; Eagle Sct Rank; I Rtng Tenor Saxophone Solo ST Music Fstvl; Scndry Ed/Chem.

NESMITH, ALAINA D; Dodge City HS; Dodge City, KS; (2); Cmnty Wkr; GAA; Hosp Aide; Red Cross Aide; Var JV Trk; JV Vllybl; Hon Roll; KS ST Univ; Anesthesiologist.

NESTER, JEREMY; Marysville HS; Marysville, KS; (3); Am Leg Boys St; 4-H; Teachers Aide; Chorus; Bsktbl; L Tennis; 4-H Awd; KY St Univ.

NETTLES, KATE; Shawnee Mission W Sr HS; Lenexa, KS; (2); 24/436; Church Yth Grp; Acpl Chr; Chorus; Orch; School Musical; JV Gym; JV Trk; High Hon Roll; Hon Roll; Pres Acad Fit Awd; Strolling Strings; KMEA St Orch; Acad Ltrs; U Of KS; Pediatrics.

NEUFELD, BETHANY; Newtan HS; Newton, KS; (4); 103/233; Am Leg Aux Girls St; Bus Profs of Am; Church Yth Grp; Model UN; Natl FFA Org; SADD; Band; Bsktbl; JV Chrldng; Var Gym; KS ST U; Pre-Med.

NEUFELD, JASON A; Moundridge HS; Moundridge, KS; (2); Church Yth Grp; Debate Tm; German Clb; Math Tm; Office Aide; Quiz Bowl; Band; Chorus; Church Choir; Jazz Band; ST Del Champs Frosh Yr; 5th Pl Soph Yr Debate; ST Champs Extemp Forensics Soph Yr; Lawyer.

NEUFELD, JEFF D; Hillsboro HS; Hillsboro, KS; (4); Church Yth Grp; Natl FFA Org; Acpl Chr; Band; Chorus; Jazz Band; Mrchg Band; Pep Band; JV Bsktbl; JV Ftbl; Mc Pherson Cntrl Col; Prfrm Art.

NEUFELD, MICHAEL; Silver Lake Jr Sr HS; Silver Lake, KS; (2); 12/60; Debate Tm; NFL; Band; Chorus; School Musical; Bsktbl; Ftbl; Trk; Hon Roll; NHS; Eng.

NEUMAN, JAMIE L; Garden City Sr HS; Garden City, KS; (2); 1/446; Church Yth Grp; Jazz Band; Mrchg Band; Var L Swmmng; High Hon Roll; DARE Role Model; Acad Ltr; Chrch Pianist; Acctng.

NEVANS, B. J.; Iola Sr HS; Iola, KS; (2); Band; Jazz Band; Mrchg Band; Pep Band; Crs Cntry; Trk; Band Section Ldr; KS Univ; Bio.

NEVE, JENNIFER; Lansing HS; Lansing, KS; (4); Cmnty Wkr; Drama Clb; Hosp Aide; Band; Mrchg Band; Pep Band; Hon Roll; NHS; Pres Schlr; Pittsburg ST Univ; Pre-Med.

NEVELS, BRANDI; Dodge City HS; Dodge City, KS; (3); SADD; Teachers Aide; Var Bsktbl; Var Sftbl; Var Vllybl; Cit Awd; High Hon Roll; NHS; Octagon Club; Brdcstng/Comm Phtgrphy.

NEVES, BRANDI A; Olathe South Sr HS; Olathe, KS; (4); 1/346; Church Yth Grp; Debate Tm; Drama Clb; German Clb; Girl Scts; Math Clb; Ed Yrbk; Gov Hon Prg Awd; High Hon Roll; Hon Roll; Girl Sct Gld Awd; U Of KS; Bus Admin.

NEVILLE, LEVI M; Uniontown HS; Bronson, KS; (2); Math Tm; Spanish Clb; Band; School Play; Var JV Bsktbl; Var JV Ftbl; Var Trk.

NEWBY, DAVID; Caney Valley Jr Sr HS; Coffeyville, KS; (4); 1/53; Pres Church Yth Grp; Treas FCA; Pres 4-H; HOBY; Letterman Clb; Pres Natl FFA Org; Spanish Clb; Teachers Aide; Pres Stu Cncl; L Capt Ftbl; Coffeyville CC; Vet.

NEWCOMB, RACHEL E; Wichita Southeast HS; Wichita, KS; (3); #33 in class; Church Yth Grp; GAA; Band; Mrchg Band; JV Trk; JV Vllybl; Hon Roll; Jr NHS; KUMED; Neonatalogist.

NEWCOMER, CRAIG K; Trego Comm HS; Ogallah, KS; (2); 1/56; Church Yth Grp; Letterman Clb; Math Tm; Natl FFA Org; SADD; JV Bsktbl; Var Ftbl; Var Trk; High Hon Roll; FFA Ofcr; Farm Bureau Ldrshp Camp; Renaissance Acad Excl.

NEWELL, ALICIA A; Maize HS; Wichita, KS; (2); Church Yth Grp; Spanish Clb; SADD; Acpl Chr; Chorus; Variety Show; Cit Awd; Pres Acad Fit Awd; Pres Schlr; Hispanic Yth Ldrshp Pgm; Heritage Panel; Summer League Sftbl-Fast Pitch; KS U; Med.

NEWELL, LUCAS R; Stafford Jr Sr HS; Stafford, KS; (3); 3/25; Teachers Aide; Yrbk; VP Soph Cls; Var Bsktbl; Ftbl; Cit Awd; High Hon Roll; KS St Univ; Agbus.

NEWELL, MARY S; Sacred Heart HS; Salina, KS; (4); 1/23; VP Church Yth Grp; Hosp Aide; Chorus; School Musical; Nwsp; Yrbk; VP Sr Cls; Gov Hon Prg Awd; NHS; Val; Jr Cvtn Pres; Fort Hays ST U; Psych.

NEWELL, SARA; Jefferson West HS; Meriden, KS; (4); 9/62; 4-H; FBLA; Hosp Aide; Natl FFA Org; SADD; Yrbk; Powder Puff Ftbl; 4-H Awd; High Hon Roll; NHS.

NEWKIRK, MELISSA K; Olathe North Sr HS; Olathe, KS; (4); Rep Church Yth Grp; Debate Tm; Sec NFL; Speech Tm; Church Choir; Ed Nwsp; Rep Frsh Cls; High Hon Roll; Hon Roll; Pres Acad Fit Awd; Acad Ltr; Johnson Cty CC; Bio Tchr.

NEWMAN, D J; Wichita Southeast HS; Wichita, KS; (2); DECA; JV Var Mgr(s); JV Var Bsktbl; Morehouse Coll; Commercial Art.

NEWMAN, MISTY S; Rock Creek Jr Sr HS; Saint George, KS; (2); Pep Clb; SADD; Rep Frsh Cls; JV Var Stu Cncl; Var Chrldng; Var Sftbl; Var Trk; Var Vllybl; Hon Roll; In Vllybl Had All League & Hnrb Mntn All St Cls 3a.

NEWMAN, TIM R; Highland Park HS; Topeka, KS; (3); JA; Math Clb; Model UN; Q&S; ROTC; Scholastic Bowl; Spanish Clb; Drill Tm; Yrbk; Tennis.

NEWPORT, HOLLY C; Larned HS; Larned, KS; (2); Natl FFA Org; Band; Pep Band; Var Trk; JV Var Vllybl; Hon Roll; Garden City CC.

NEWPORT, JAMIE; Paola HS; Paola, KS; (4); 22/113; Bus Profs of Am; FCA; FHA; Q&S; SADD; Yrbk; Sec Soph Cls; Pres Jr Cls; Rep Stu Cncl; JV Vllybl; Johnson Cty CC; RN.

NEWPORT, PEGGY S; Desoto HS; De Soto, KS; (4); 52/114; Teachers Aide; Band; Ed Yrbk; Hon Roll; Msn Trp With KS City Yth For Chrst Plnd, Russia 95; Avila Coll; Bus Admin.

NEWTON, AMY D; Independence HS; Independence, KS; (1); Church Yth Grp; Cmnty Wkr; 4-H; Band; Mrchg Band; Pep Band; 4-H Awd; Hon Roll; Photo.

NEWTON, LORI A; Concordia Jr Sr HS; Concordia, KS; (3); 9/102; Church Yth Grp; Drama Clb; French Clb; Quiz Bowl; SADD; Acpl Chr; Band; Pep Band; Hon Roll; NHS; JC; Acctng.

NEWTON, MELISSA A; Hutchinson HS; Hutchinson, KS; (3); Church Yth Grp; Debate Tm; Key Clb; NFL; Pep Clb; Speech Tm; Chorus; Church Choir; Rep Jr Cls; Var Sftbl; Pol Sci.

NEY, HOLLY; Hanston Jr Sr HS; Hanston, KS; (4); 4/13; Church Yth Grp; Speech Tm; Teachers Aide; Band; Chorus; Church Choir; Drill Tm; Mrchg Band; Pep Band; School Play; Ft Hays St Univ; Bus Mgmt.

NEY, JESSICA L; Hoisington HS; Hoisington, KS; (3); Church Yth Grp; Drama Clb; 4-H; SADD; Stage Crew; Treas Jr Cls; JV Var Bsktbl; JV Var Trk; Hon Roll; NHS; K-St; Sci.

NGUON, LE M; Garden City Sr HS; Garden City, KS; (1); Hon Roll; Prfct Atten Awd; Tchng.

NGUYEN, AN V; Wichita East HS; Wichita, KS; (2); UCLA; Arch; Lawyer; Dr.

NGUYEN, ANH; Derby HS; Wichita, KS; (4); 12/316; VP French Clb; NHS; ASAP; Friends U; Psych.

NGUYEN, CINDY; Wichita North HS; Wichita, KS; (4); Cmnty Wkr; Scholastic Bowl; Science Clb; Rep Sr Cls; Rep Stu Cncl; Var Chrldng; JV Socr; Hon Roll; Ldrshp 2000; N HS Rdskn Mo Awd; Friends U; Med.

NGUYEN, DANIELLE; Sabetha HS; Sabetha, KS; (3); Bus Profs of Am; Pep Clb; Teachers Aide; Yrbk; Ofcr Stu Cncl; Bsktbl; Chrldng; Trk; Vllybl; Hon Roll; KS ST; Socl Work.

NGUYEN, HANH-NGOC; Wichita East HS; Wichita, KS; (4); 18/350; Cmnty Wkr; Hnr Roll 92-95; Asian Clb Treas; Wichita ST U; Accntng.

NGUYEN, HIEP T; Garden City Sr HS; Garden City, KS; (3); Garden City CC.

NGUYEN, HIEU D; Wichita East HS; Wichita, KS; (2); High Hon Roll; WSU; Med Dr.

NGUYEN, HUYEN B; Garden City Sr HS; Garden City, KS; (1); Orch; Cit Awd; Prfct Atten Awd; Pres Ed Awds Prgm 8th Grd; Drw Pics; Dr.

NGUYEN, HUYEN B; Chanute Sr HS; Chanute, KS; (3); French Clb; Flag Corp; Orch; French Hon Soc; High Hon Roll; Arlington Univ; Acctng.

NGUYEN, HUYVU T; Manhattan HS; Manhattan, KS; (2); Spanish Clb; Bsktbl; High Hon Roll; Pres Acad Fit Awd; KS ST Univ; Bus.

NGUYEN, JIM C; Southeast HS; Wichita, KS; (3); 10/300; Church Yth Grp; Math Clb; Science Clb; JV Crs Cntry; High Hon Roll; Hon Roll; NHS; U Of KS; Eng.

NGUYEN, KHANH H; Wichita East HS; Wichita, KS; (4); 1/296; Hon Roll; St Schlr; Asian Clb; 95 Wichita HS Ping Pong Trnmt 4th Pl; Wichita ST U.

NGUYEN, KIM K; Salina HS South; Salina, KS; (3); English Clb; JA; Math Clb; Science Clb; Butler Univ; Acctng.

NGUYEN, KIM N; Immaculata HS; Leavenworth, KS; (4); 11/48; Art Clb; Cmnty Wkr; VP JA; Teachers Aide; Rep Frsh Cls; Pres Soph Cls; Ofcr Stu Cncl; JV Tennis; JV Capt Vllybl; High Hon Roll; Natl Math Awd; KS St Univ; Acctng.

NGUYEN, LAN T; Wichita North HS; Wichita, KS; (3); Art Clb; French Clb; Teachers Aide; Hon Roll; Seals SE Asian Ldrshp; Explrs Post Med; WSU; Med.

NGUYEN, NGAN T; Garden City Sr HS; Garden City, KS; (3); 65/375; Church Yth Grp; Key Clb; Science Clb; SADD; Teachers Aide; Nwsp; Rep Stu Cncl; JV Bsktbl; Var L Crs Cntry; L Trk; 300 M Hurdles Track Schl Record; Univ Of KS; Sports Med.

NGUYEN, NHAT M; Wichita East HS; Wichita, KS; (3); Church Yth Grp; French Clb; Teachers Aide; Lit Mag; Hon Roll; Asian Clb; Chrch Yth Grp Ldr; ASVAB Test High Score; Wichita ST U; Professor.

NGUYEN, TAM N; Wichita West HS; Wichita, KS; (2); 1/30; French Clb; Red Cross Aide; SADD; School Play; Yrbk; Bsktbl; Score Keeper; French Hon Soc; High Hon Roll; Hon Roll; Dr.

NGUYEN, THO T; Wichita West HS; Wichita, KS; (2); #3 in class; Church Yth Grp; French Clb; Church Choir; Ofcr Frsh Cls; Ofcr Soph Cls; Hon Roll; Prfct Atten Awd; Vietnamese Clb; KS Univ; Dctr.

NGUYEN, VINCENT T; Sacred Heart HS; Salina, KS; (3); Debate Tm; FBLA; NFL; High Hon Roll; NHS; Jr Cvtn Club; KS U; Med.

NGUYEN, VU A; Wichita East HS; Wichita, KS; (4); Hon Roll; Asian Clb; Wichita ST U; Electronic Engr.

NIBLACK, ELISABETH; Douglass HS; Rose Hill, KS; (2); 19/73; FHA; Mgr(s); Trk; Hon Roll; KS ST; Tchr.

NICHOL, JANA M; Salina HS South; Salina, KS; (3); Dance Clb; Drama Clb; NFL; Thesps; Chorus; Mrchg Band; School Musical; School Play; Swing Chorus; Variety Show; Perf Lovewell Inst For Creative Arts; Performed The Fantasticks Intl Thespian Fstvl 96; Webster Univ; Musical Theatre.

NICHOL, LORI A; Claflin Jr Sr HS; Claflin, KS; (3); 5/23; Treas Pep Clb; Band; Chorus; Mrchg Band; Pep Band; Var Bsktbl; Var Trk; Var Vllybl; Hon Roll; NHS; Barton Cty CC; Acctng.

NICHOLAS, NIKI L; Stanton Co HS; Johnson, KS; (1); Church Yth Grp; Variety Show; Rep Frsh Cls; Var Bsktbl; Var Trk; Var Vllybl; Hon Roll; KAYS.

NICHOLL, KATE A; Liberal HS; Liberal, KS; (3); Band; Chorus; Mrchg Band; School Musical; School Play; Hon Roll; Exch Stu; Psych.

NICHOLS, AUDRA; Wellington Sr HS; Wellington, KS; (1); Church Yth Grp; Debate Tm; SADD; Jazz Band; Mrchg Band; Pep Band; Bsktbl; Sftbl; Tennis; Hon Roll; Church Confrmtn Class Tchr.

NICHOLS, CHARISSA R; Arkansas City HS; Arkansas City, KS; (3); Church Yth Grp; FCA; Chorus; Hon Roll; NHS.

NICHOLS, JARROD L; Sabetha HS; Morrill, KS; (3); Church Yth Grp; 4-H; FHA; Pep Clb; Spanish Clb; Pres Frsh Cls; Pres Soph Cls; Rep Sr Cls; Rptr Stu Cncl; Var L Bsktbl; KS ST Univ; Lndscp Arch.

NICHOLS, JOSH; Wellington Sr HS; Wellington, KS; (3); Church Yth Grp; Mrchg Band; Pep Band; Ofcr Bsbl; Bsktbl; Ftbl; Golf; Cntrl Sts ELCA Convention Rep; ADF Regnls 3 Yrs, St 2 Yrs & 10th Pl 96; Bus; Comp.

NICHOLS, JULIE L; Olathe East Sr HS; Olathe, KS; (2); Letterman Clb; Spanish Clb; Teachers Aide; Orch; Trk; High Hon Roll; Pres Acad Fit Awd; Camp Fire Boys/Grls; Olthe Area Yth Symphny; SASH; Arch Engr.

NICHOLS, MELODY A; Galena HS; Galena, KS; (2); Church Yth Grp; Drama Clb; FCA; Math Clb; SADD; Chorus; Church Choir; School Play; Chrldng; Sftbl; Csmtlgst.

NICHOLS, RYAN; Osborne HS; Alton, KS; (3); 3/40; Am Leg Boys St; Chess Clb; Church Yth Grp; Pres 4-H; Pres FHA; HOBY; Letterman Clb; Math Tm; Natl FFA Org; Quiz Bowl; Stu Of Month; Voc Stu Of Yr; Natl FHA Cmptn Asst Lead Consultnt; KS ST U; Bio.

NICHOLS, VIRGINIA L; Wellington Sr HS; Wellington, KS; (3); Boy Scts; Church Yth Grp; FCA; SADD; Varsity Clb; Band; Chorus; Mrchg Band; Var Tennis; Cit Awd; Bus.

NICHOLSON, SARAH J; Bishop Miege HS; Fairway, KS; (2); 3/163; Cmnty Wkr; Debate Tm; Hosp Aide; NFL; Sec Soph Cls; Rep Jr Cls; Intrml Bsktbl; High Hon Roll; Campus Mnstry Team; Acad Exclnc Awd; Highest GPA Soph Femals; Bio Tchr.

NICKEL, CARLENE K; Hillsboro HS; Hillsboro, KS; (2); 28/49; Church Yth Grp; Chorus; School Musical; Phtg Nwsp; Phtg Yrbk; Bsktbl; Trk; Vllybl; Hon Roll; Bus.

NICKEL, LORI; Olathe North Sr HS; Olathe, KS; (3); Cmnty Wkr; Pep Clb; Spanish Clb; Stage Crew; Chrldng; Gym; JV Socr; Trk; High Hon Roll; Hon Roll; Med/Pedtrcn.

NICKELL, RICHARD DEAN; Lawrence HS; Lawrence, KS; (2); FCA; Rptr Soph Cls; Var Crs Cntry; Cit Awd; High Hon Roll; Prfct Atten Awd; Pres Acad Fit Awd; Pres Schlr; Play Premier Soccer Tm.

NICKERSON, JANELLE L; Highland Park HS; Topeka, KS; (1); 16/150; Cmnty Wkr; Cit Awd; Hon Roll; Langston Univ; Jrnlsm.

NICKOLS, JOEL T; Colby Sr HS; Colby, KS; (2); 56/106; Band; Chorus; Jazz Band; Mrchg Band; Pep Band; School Musical; Variety Show; Ofcr Stu Cncl; AFS Clb; KAYS Clb Stuco Rep; KS ST Univ; Music Ed.

NICKS, JOSH; Lacrosse HS; Rush Center, KS; (3); 5/30; Pres 4-H; Band; Jazz Band; Pep Band; JV Bsktbl; Var L Ftbl; Var L Trk; 4-H Awd; High Hon Roll; NHS; Electronic Engr.

NICKS, MATTHEW L; Maize HS; Maize, KS; (3); Debate Tm; NFL; Science Clb; Speech Tm; Teachers Aide; Chorus; Variety Show; Hon Roll; Cmptr Sys Analyst.

NICOLACE, JUSTIN M; Bishop Miege HS; Overland Park, KS; (3); 2/190; Debate Tm; Teachers Aide; Ofcr Sr Cls; Rep Stu Cncl; Bsktbl; Ftbl; High Hon Roll; NHS; Acad Excl Awd; Nom NCTE Achvmt Awd; Med.

NICOLAY, JASON M; Buhler HS; Hutchinson, KS; (2); FCA; Spanish Clb; SADD; Chorus; Stage Crew; Ftbl; Golf; Wt Lftg; High Hon Roll; Frosh/Soph Sngrs; Male Ensmble; Pre-Med.

NIEBAU, SETH; Louisburg HS; Louisburg, KS; (3); Am Leg Boys St; Math Clb; VICA; Band; Mrchg Band; Pep Band; JV Ftbl; Wt Lftg; High Hon Roll; Hon Roll; Recreation League Soccer; Tech Stu Assoc; Engrng.

NIEDENTHAL, CRISDA B; Russell HS; Russell, KS; (1); 1/100; Church Yth Grp; Key Clb; Math Tm; Natl FFA Org; Band; Mrchg Band; Pep Band; Rep Stu Cncl; JV Trk; High Hon Roll; Tchr.

NIEDENTHAL, JENIFER; Field Kindley Mem Sr HS; Coffeyville, KS; (4); 1/134; Am Leg Aux Girls St; Church Yth Grp; Debate Tm; NFL; Yrbk; Chrldng; Diving; Swmmng; NHS; Val; Pol Sci.

NIEDENTHAL, TROY A; Russell HS; Russell, KS; (3); 1/95; VP FCA; VP Pep Clb; Pres SADD; Band; Rep Stu Cncl; Var L Ftbl; L Var Trk; Var L Wt Lftg; High Hon Roll; NHS; Soph Stu Of Yr; CO ST; Bus Admin.

NIEGSCH, JORDAN; Frontenac Jr Sr HS; Frontenac, KS; (1); 1/50; Art Clb; Pep Clb; Pres Frsh Cls; Rptr Stu Cncl; Ofcr Bsbl; Bsktbl; Ftbl; Wt Lftg; Hon Roll; Prfct Atten Awd.

NIEHAGE, PAULETTA A; Moundridge HS; Moundridge, KS; (4); 1/33; Sec Pres Church Yth Grp; Sec Pres FCA; Rep Treas Pep Clb; Chorus; School Musical; Pres Sr Cls; Var L Bsktbl; Var L Vllybl; Cit Awd; NHS; Bethel Coll.

NIEHAGE, POLLY A; Moundridge HS; Moundridge, KS; (4); 1/33; Pres Sec FCA; Rep Treas Pep Clb; School Musical; Yrbk; Pres Sr Cls; Var L Bsktbl; Var L Vllybl; Cit Awd; NHS; Val; Bethel Col.

NIEHUES, JANEL J; Wetmore Schl; Goff, KS; (2); 5/14; Letterman Clb; Pep Clb; Band; Chorus; Mrchg Band; Pep Band; School Musical; Var Bsktbl; L Trk.

NIELSON, KJERSTEN A; Olathe East Sr HS; Overland Park, KS; (2); Art Clb; Church Yth Grp; German Clb; Intnl Clb; Quiz Bowl; JV Trk; Cit Awd; Pres Acad Fit Awd; Chrprctr/Accpnctrst.

NIEMEYER, JENNIFER L; Yates Ctr HS; Yates Center, KS; (3); Am Leg Aux Girls St; Co-Capt FCA; VP FHA; Letterman Clb; Pep Clb; Pres Jr Cls; Pres Sr Cls; Var L Bsktbl; Var L Trk; Var L Vllybl; All-League Hnrb Mntn Bsktbl; KS Univ; Nrsng.

NIEUWENDAAL, RYAN; Maur Hill Prep Schl; Atchison, KS; (3); #2 in class; Debate Tm; Letterman Clb; Math Tm; NFL; Varsity Clb; Chorus; VP Soph Cls; VP Jr Cls; Socr; NHS.

NIGHTENGALE, NATASHA; South Gray HS; Sublette, KS; (2); Letterman Clb; Teachers Aide; Var Bsktbl; Var Trk; Var Vllybl; Hon Roll; KYAS Sec.

NIGHTINGALE, ALLISON; Holton HS; Holton, KS; (3); 3/85; 4-H; Drill Tm; School Musical; Bsktbl; Chrldng; Sftbl; Vllybl; NHS; KSU.

NIGHTINGALE, MARCIA K; Moundridge HS; Galva, KS; (3); Debate Tm; NFL; Pep Clb; Chorus; School Musical; School Play; Hon Roll; Natl Forensic Lge Sec & VP.

NILGES, THERESA J; Manhattan HS; Manhattan, KS; (2); Church Yth Grp; FTA; Speech Tm; Treas Thesps; Band; Mrchg Band; School Musical; School Play; Stage Crew; High Hon Roll; Drama Stdnt Yr; Best Asst Dir; Best Actress; KA Univ; Theatre/Prof Actress.

NIOCE, AMANDA J; Horton HS; Horton, KS; (4); 13/57; Office Aide; Pep Clb; Yrbk; JV Var Bsktbl; JV Var Vllybl; Cit Awd; Hon Roll; Upward Bnd Senator; U Of KS; Acctng.

NIX, HOLLY N; Moscow HS; Hugoton, KS; (2); 1/9; 4-H; Band; Pep Band; School Play; Ofcr Frsh Cls; Pres Soph Cls; Ofcr Stu Cncl; Chrldng; Var Vllybl; NHS; Russian Frgn Exch Stu; Washburn Univ; Psych.

NIXON, AUDRA P; Parsons HS; Parsons, KS; (2); School Musical; School Play; Stage Crew; Var Chrldng; L Trk; SADD; Sprts Club; Spec Olym Torch Run 9-10 Gde.

NIYAKORN, JERAYU; Wichita South HS; Wichita, KS; (3); 1/394; Hosp Aide; Scholastic Bowl; Sec Frsh Cls; Rep Stu Cncl; L Pom Pon; Var Tennis; High Hon Roll; Girls Acad & Ath Ltrs; ASAIL Clb; Phy.

NKANA, DERICK E; Wichita East HS; Wichita, KS; (3); Church Yth Grp; Computer Clb; 4-H; SADD; Church Choir; Drill Tm; Bsktbl; Socr; Hon Roll; Ntl Merit Ltr; Grambling; Astronomy; Comp Tech.

NOBLE, ANGELA; Dodge City HS; Dodge City, KS; (3); Drama Clb; Band; Drill Tm; Variety Show; Chrldng; High Hon Roll; NHS; Jr Ldrshp Dodge Chosn To Compt In Acad Relys; KAYS; Danc Clss & Cmptns; Can-Can Dancr At Boot Hill; Pittsburg ST U; Pharmacy.

NOBLE, PIPER J; Washington HS; Kansas City, KS; (4); DECA; Pep Clb; Intrml Chrldng; JV Var Sftbl; KCKCC; Addiction Cnslng.

NODGAARD, CATHRINE C; Southeast HS; Wichita, KS; (2); 30/300; Church Yth Grp; Cmnty Wkr; FCA; HOBY; Letterman Clb; Spanish Clb; Varsity Clb; Ed Nwsp; Var L Crs Cntry; Var L Swmmng; KS St Womens Press Assn 3rd Feature Wrtng, Hnrb Mntn Dsgn Layout.

NOE, TY D; Girard HS; Farlington, KS; (4); Church Yth Grp; Natl FFA Org; Spanish Clb; SADD; Band; Mrchg Band; Pep Band; Var L Bsbl; JV Bsktbl; Var L Ftbl; Spartan Schl Aeronautics; Tech.

NOGUERA, ERIKA C; Olathe North Sr HS; Olathe, KS; (2); #1 in class; Church Yth Grp; Drama Clb; Office Aide; Pep Clb; Spanish Clb; Thesps; Acpl Chr; School Musical; School Play; Stage Crew; Drama Clb VP 94-95; Choir Sec 95-96; Bilingl Spnsh & Engl; Nutrition.

NOLAN, SPENCER; Maur Hill Prep Schl; Atchison, KS; (3); 10/74; Church Yth Grp; NFL; Chorus; Rptr Stu Cncl; Var JV Bsktbl; Var Socr; High Hon Roll; Ntl Merit Ltr; Pres Acad Fit Awd; All-Amer Schlr 94-95; Natl Yng Ldrs Conf Washington DC 95.

NOLAND, DAVID W; Holton HS; Mayetta, KS; (4); 24/64; Church Yth Grp; Letterman Clb; Chorus; Capt Var Bsktbl; L JV Crs Cntry; Var L Golf; High Hon Roll; Hon Roll; NHS; Prfct Atten Awd; Pensacola Chrstn Coll; Acctng.

NOLKER, MARK; Shawnee Mission E HS; Prairie Village, KS; (4); 75/475; Q&S; Nwsp; JV Crs Cntry; High Hon Roll; Hon Roll; Japanese; HS TV Station; Gustavus Adolphus; Advertising.

NOLL, ALISHA; Jefferson Co North HS; Winchester, KS; (4); 3/38; FBLA; Letterman Clb; SADD; Band; Flag Corp; Treas Stu Cncl; Var L Chrldng; JV Vllybl; High Hon Roll; Sec NHS; Hgh Hnr Rll; Cmmnty Svcs, Actvts; Pep Bnd; Emporia ST U; Chem Engrng.

NOLL, JESSE; Jefferson Co North HS; Nortonville, KS; (4); 4/37; FBLA; Letterman Clb; SADD; Ed Nwsp; Ed Yrbk; Rep Jr Cls; Treas Stu Cncl; Bsktbl; Trk; Wt Lftg; KS Hnr Schlr Awd; FBLA St VP; FBLA Local Chptr VP; KSU; Arch.

NOLL, JUSTIN; Jefferson Co North HS; Atchison, KS; (3); 2/37; Treas 4-H; FBLA; Letterman Clb; Pep Clb; SADD; Treas Frsh Cls; JV Bsktbl; Var Ftbl; Var Trk; Var Wt Lftg; Lfgrdng; Skiing; Span; Sci.

NOLLER, AIMEE; Shawnee Mission W Sr HS; Lenexa, KS; (4); 25/365; Am Leg Aux Girls St; Cmnty Wkr; Orch; School Musical; Trk; High Hon Roll; NHS; NFL; Quiz Bowl; Teachers Aide; Strllng Strngs; Natl Mrt Commended Schlr; Categories Team; Loyola U-Chicago.

NORDHUS, BRANDON; Nemaha Vlly HS; Seneca, KS; (4); 2/52; Boy Scts; Sec Church Yth Grp; Rep Letterman Clb; Pres Frsh Cls; VP Jr Cls; Pres Sr Cls; Ofcr Bsbl; Var Capt Bsktbl; Var Capt Ftbl; Var Golf; KS St Univ; Acctng.

NORDSTROM, INGA M; Colby Sr HS; Colby, KS; (3); Church Yth Grp; Debate Tm; NFL; Office Aide; Scholastic Bowl; Science Clb; Service Clb; Chorus; School Musical; Swing Chorus; Top Soph Eng Stdnt; All St Choir; Amer Leg Aux Grls St Alt.

NORDYKE, KELSEY; Ulysses HS; Ulysses, KS; (2); Church Yth Grp; Pres 4-H; Natl FFA Org; SADD; Chorus; Bsktbl; Chrldng; 4-H Awd; Hon Roll; FFA Chptr VP; Rodeo Clb Sec; KS ST U; Vet Med.

NOREZ, RODOLFO; Lyons HS; Lyons, KS; (2); Boy Scts; Band; Jazz Band; Mrchg Band; Pep Band; Var Crs Cntry; Ftbl; Var Capt Wrstlng; Hon Roll; Tae Kwon Do; Air Frc Acad; Pilot.

NORMAN, BRETT; Blue Valley HS; Overland Park, KS; (2); Boy Scts; Church Yth Grp; Band; Church Choir; Mrchg Band; Pep Band; School Musical; JV Crs Cntry; JV Trk; High Hon Roll; Certifd CPR/FRST Aid; KS Univ.

NORMAN, MISTY; Rossville HS; Rossville, KS; (3); 1/47; FBLA; Quiz Bowl; Jazz Band; School Musical; Stage Crew; Pres Jr Cls; Mgr(s); High Hon Roll; NHS; Coll Of William & Mary; Sci.

NORMAN, TAMIKA R; J C Harmon HS; Kansas City, KS; (2); Girl Scts; Pep Clb; Band; Church Choir; Drill Tm; Mrchg Band; Sec Frsh Cls; Hon Roll; Prfct Atten Awd; YAC Pgm; Wichita ST Univ; Comp Tech.

NORQUIST, DENISE A; Nickerson HS; Hutchinson, KS; (4); 35/101; Church Yth Grp; FHA; Key Clb; Red Cross Aide; Spanish Clb; Nwsp; Yrbk; Var Bsktbl; Var Sftbl; Var Vllybl; Ft Hays ST Univ; Bus.

NORRIS, ANDREW W; Maize HS; Wichita, KS; (3); 39/242; Chess Clb; German Clb; Library Aide; Scholastic Bowl; High Hon Roll; Hon Roll; NHS; Aiakido; Muay Thai; Comp Sci.

NORRIS, CHAD J; Salina HS South; Salina, KS; (2); Cmnty Wkr; Chorus; Var Swmmng; Var L Trk; Hon Roll; Stdnt Of Wk 95-.

NORRIS, DARA M; Horton HS; Horton, KS; (2); Church Yth Grp; Drama Clb; NFL; Pep Clb; Church Choir; School Musical; School Play; Co-Capt Chrldng; Powder Puff Ftbl; JV Trk; Participated In St Forensics; Best Actress In Character Role Awd; KS ST Univ; Bus; Tchng.

NORRIS, JOSH; Kingman HS; Kingman, KS; (3); Am Leg Boys St; French Clb; Library Aide; SADD; High Hon Roll; Hon Roll; Wichita ST Univ.

NORRIS, MEGAN M; Shawnee Mission N HS; Shawnee Mission, KS; (2); 13/466; Pep Clb; Band; Orch; High Hon Roll; Stdnt ST Ballet; UMKC; Chem.

NORRIS, MICHELE R; Kensington Jr Sr HS; Kensington, KS; (4); Church Yth Grp; Pep Clb; Spanish Clb; SADD; Teachers Aide; Chorus; School Musical; Stage Crew; Phtg Yrbk; Rep Stu Cncl; AC Grphc Dsn Schl; Grphc Desgn.

NORRIS, NIKI; Wichita East HS; Wichita, KS; (2); Rptr Nwsp; Var Sftbl; Var Vllybl; High Hon Roll; Hon Roll; USVB Vlybl; Sftbl; Wichita ST Univ.

NORRIS, TANNER R; Shawnee Heights HS; Topeka, KS; (3); FCA; FBLA; Key Clb; Pep Clb; Teachers Aide; Varsity Clb; Chorus; Rep Frsh Cls; Rep Soph Cls; Rep Sr Cls; Clss Top 5 Pct Acad Awds; Topekas Top Kids TV Feature; Serve Topeka Comm Prjct.

NORSWORTHY, DANA; Meade HS; Meade, KS; (4); 1/26; HOBY; Teachers Aide; Band; Chorus; Rep Frsh Cls; Rep Soph Cls; Pres Jr Cls; Pres Sr Cls; High Hon Roll; NHS; Math, Sci Outstndng Sr KS St U; KU Hnr Stu; Cmptr Engrng.

NORSWORTHY, SHERRY L; Meade HS; Meade, KS; (1); Sec Church Yth Grp; Key Clb; Pep Clb; Quiz Bowl; Band; Chorus; Church Choir; Mrchg Band; Pep Band; School Musical; MANC.

NORTH, ADAM; Ellis HS; Hays, KS; (4); 1/40; Am Leg Boys St; Church Yth Grp; VP Natl FFA Org; Band; L Bsktbl; L Ftbl; Gov Hon Prg Awd; High Hon Roll; St Schlr; Val; U Of KS Hon Prgm; Mid Continent Leag Ldrshp Conf; Fort Hays ST U; Indstrl Tech.

NORTH, BRIAN M; Olathe East Sr HS; Overland Park, KS; (3); 178/360; Cmnty Wkr; Debate Tm; French Clb; Hosp Aide; NFL; School Musical; High Hon Roll; Art Clb; Drama Clb; Math Clb; Yth Crt; Optmsts Mode Lgsltr In Topeka; Stu Tchr At Elem Schl; TX A&M Univ; Comm.

NORTH, CINDY D; Victoria HS; Victoria, KS; (3); Dance Clb; FHA; Letterman Clb; Pep Clb; SADD; Varsity Clb; School Play; Ofcr Stu Cncl; Var Bsktbl; Var Trk; Medicine.

NORTH, DAVID J; Altoona Midway HS; Altoona, KS; (3); 3/30; Scholastic Bowl; SADD; Teachers Aide; Varsity Clb; Band; VP Stu Cncl; L Bsbl; Var Capt Ftbl; Hon Roll; Pres Acad Fit Awd; Pittsburgh ST Univ; Comp Sci.

NORTH, TYLER J; Ellis HS; Ellis, KS; (4); Natl FFA Org; Band; Chorus; Mrchg Band; School Play; Trk; Hon Roll; KMEA Band; FFA Chptr Reporter & St Band; Ft Hays ST Univ; Music Ed.

NORTHERN, SHAWN M; Washington HS; Kansas City, KS; (2); Intrml Mgr Bsktbl; UCLA; Bus.

NORTHRIP, DAVID F; Bishop Miege HS; Shawnee Mission, KS; (1); 38/246; Debate Tm; NFL; Quiz Bowl; Speech Tm; High Hon Roll.

NORTHRUP, ROXANNE M; Andover HS; Andover, KS; (3); French Clb; Teachers Aide; Ed Nwsp; Tennis; High Hon Roll; Hon Roll; Karate; OK ST U; Lawyer.

NORTHUP, SHAUDEL; Goodland HS; Goodland, KS; (3); FHA; Teachers Aide; Treas Frsh Cls; VP Soph Cls; VP Jr Cls; Rep Stu Cncl; Chrldng; Powder Puff Ftbl; Hon Roll; NHS; Kayettes.

NORTON, GWAYAIN; F L Schlagle HS; Kansas City, KS; (4); FHA; HOBY; Office Aide; Teachers Aide; Rep Frsh Cls; Rep Soph Cls; Rep Jr Cls; Ftbl; Optimist Intl Essay 3rd Pl Wnnr; Wichita.

NORTON, HEATHER D; Medicine Lodge HS; Medicine Lodge, KS; (4); 13/54; Drama Clb; Letterman Clb; Pep Clb; SADD; Band; Chorus; Ed Nwsp; Yrbk; Sec Soph Cls; Sec Jr Cls; Miss Tean Scholar; Northwestern OK St Univ; Educ.

NORTON, KATRINA L; Williamsburg Schl; Williamsburg, KS; (4); 3/18; FCA; Speech Tm; Co-Ed Yrbk; Ofcr Frsh Cls; Treas Jr Cls; Ofcr Sr Cls; Treas Stu Cncl; Var Bsktbl; Var Vllybl; NHS; Pittsbrgh St Univ; Soc Wrk.

NORWOOD, CARL A; Ottawa HS; Ottawa, KS; (4); 67/143; Church Yth Grp; FCA; Letterman Clb; Pep Clb; Varsity Clb; Acpl Chr; Chorus; Church Choir; School Musical; Swing Chorus; Pub Natl Poetry Soc; Emporia ST U; Sec Ed.

NOTTINGHAM, ERIN S; Newton Sr HS; Newton, KS; (3); Art Clb; Church Yth Grp; Teachers Aide; Art.

NOTTINGHAM, KENDRA L; Newton Sr HS; Newton, KS; (1); Church Yth Grp; Chorus; Tennis; Elem Ed.

NOUHNLASY, VILAIVONE M; Salina HS South; Salina, KS; (4); Drill Tm; School Play; Stage Crew; Rep Stu Cncl; Intrml Bsktbl; Intrml Socr; Var Trk; Intrml Vllybl; Gov Hon Prg Awd; High Hon Roll; KSU; Acctng.

NOVAK, ABBY; Belleville HS; Belleville, KS; (4); 28/41; Treas Art Clb; Church Yth Grp; VP Drama Clb; Girl Scts; NFL; Teachers Aide; Thesps; Band; Mrchg Band; Pep Band; Qulfd/Part ST Frnscs 96; 12 Scouting Ernd 4 Serv Bars/3 Ldrshp Awrds; Troop Treas 92-; Silver Awrd 92; CCCC; Art Thrpy.

NOWAK, CHRISTINA S; Abilene Baptist Acad; Salina, KS; (4); Church Yth Grp; 4-H; Band; Chorus; Church Choir; School Play; Var Chrldng; JV Var Vllybl; 4-H Awd; Hon Roll; KS ST.

NOWAK, JESSICA A; Blue Valley Northwest HS; Overland Park, KS; (3); Cmnty Wkr; FCA; Latin Clb; Letterman Clb; Spanish Clb; Teachers Aide; Varsity Clb; Capt Var Bsktbl; Var Swmmng; JV Var Vllybl.

NOYES, JAMIE C; Pleasant Ridge HS; Easton, KS; (3); 4-H; Girl Scts; Hosp Aide; Office Aide; Pep Clb; SADD; Band; Pep Band; Mgr(s); 4-H Awd.

NUDSON, LENA M; Southeast HS; Wichita, KS; (3); Cmnty Wkr; Dance Clb; Debate Tm; FCA; JA; SADD; Drill Tm; Orch; Var Pom Pon; Sftbl; Vol At Many Orgnzatns; U Of KS; Flt Nurs.

NUESSEN, AMY; Eureka Jr Sr HS; Eureka, KS; (2); Science Clb; Teachers Aide; Treas Soph Cls; Var Bsktbl; Var Chrldng; Golf; Var Vllybl; High Hon Roll; Pres Acad Fit Awd; Spanish NHS; KS U; Sports Med.

NUGENT, JASON; Cheney Jr Sr HS; Cheney, KS; (3); 1/47; VP Frsh Cls; VP Soph Cls; VP Jr Cls; Rep Stu Cncl; Var L Bsktbl; Var L Ftbl; Var JV Trk; High Hon Roll; NHS; Pres Acad Fit Awd; Pre-Med.

NULTY, MONICA J; Jewell HS; Jewell, KS; (1); FCA; FHA; Pep Clb; Band; Flag Corp; Pep Band; Sec Frsh Cls; Mgr(s); Var Vllybl; Wt Lftg; Inter Dsgn.

NUN, ERIC M; Derby HS; Derby, KS; (2); Var Mgr(s); Var Socr; Hon Roll; NHS.

NUNLEY, TIFFANY; Summer Acad Of Arts/Science; Kansas City, KS; (2); Church Yth Grp; Key Clb; Pep Clb; Acpl Chr; Church Choir; Rptr Nwsp; Rep Jr Cls; Var Chrldng; NHS; KS ST HS Regnl Music Festival 2nd Division Awd Vocal Solo; Pre-Med.

NUSSBAUM, TIM A; Wichita North HS; Wichita, KS; (2); Church Yth Grp; Chorus; School Musical; Rep Stu Cncl; JV Bsbl; Var L Socr; Hon Roll; Pres Acad Fit Awd; Elem Stdnts Helper; Chrch Svc Project & Helped Build Houses.

NUSZ, LINDSAY; Haviland HS; Haviland, KS; (2); 4/16; Church Yth Grp; 4-H; Office Aide; Pep Clb; Scholastic Bowl; Speech Tm; Chorus; School Musical; School Play; Stage Crew; Y Teens Clb; Athltc Trnr.

NUSZ, TIFFANY; Haviland HS; Haviland, KS; (4); 3/16; Church Yth Grp; Chorus; Co-Ed Nwsp; Co-Ed Yrbk; VP Stu Cncl; L Bsktbl; Capt Chrldng; L Vllybl; Hon Roll; 4-H; Y Teens Pres, Devotional Ldr; Friends U; Publctns.

NUTSCH, LEATHAN; Pike Valley HS; Norway, KS; (4); Treas FBLA; Math Tm; Treas Natl FFA Org; Quiz Bowl; Treas Soph Cls; VP Stu Cncl; L Ftbl; L Trk; Hon Roll; VP NHS; FFA Range Mgmt Cntst High Ind Jr Yr/Scnd High Sr Yr; Cloud Cty CC; Mllng Sci/Mngmt.

NUTTER, NANCY L; Smoky Valley HS; Lindsborg, KS; (2); Drama Clb; Letterman Clb; Thesps; Band; Chorus; School Play; Var Trk; High Hon Roll; VP NHS; Church Yth Grp; Conf Cncl Yth Mnstrs Sec; Sci.

NUTZ, ANDREW; Derby HS; Derby, KS; (4); 18/300; Boy Scts; ROTC; Jazz Band; Var Capt Swmmng; DAR Awd; Gov Hon Prg Awd; High Hon Roll; L Pres NHS; Pres Acad Fit Awd; St Schlr; Air Force ROTC 4 Yr Schlrshp Arspc Engr; Red Cross Advncd Water Sfty Cert Lifeguard; US Air Force Acad; Arntcl Engr.

NUZUM, TYLER W; Garden City Sr HS; Garden City, KS; (3); Church Yth Grp; Drama Clb; Church Choir; School Musical; School Play; Yrbk; Ofcr Stu Cncl; Tennis; Hon Roll; Missionary.

NYP, PENNY; Wamego HS; Wamego, KS; (4); 4/86; Rep FCA; FHA; Science Clb; SADD; Treas Soph Cls; Sec Jr Cls; Rep Stu Cncl; JV Bsktbl; JV Vllybl; Hon Roll; Tandy Tech Schlr; Math Dept Plaque Wnnr; Wamego Jr Comm Cncl Sec; U Of KS; Chem Engrng; Bio-Med.

NYSTROM, JARED; Maize HS; Wichita, KS; (3); 64/264; Am Leg Boys St; Church Yth Grp; 4-H; Capt Band; Jazz Band; Mrchg Band; Pep Band; 4-H Awd; Hon Roll; Lions Clb ST Bnd; KS Ambsdrs Tour Bnd; Anthrplgy.

OAKLEAF, GREG J; Atchison Co Cmty HS; Effingham, KS; (3); 1/60; Cmnty Wkr; Letterman Clb; Math Clb; Math Tm; Mu Alpha Theta; Science Clb; Band; Chorus; Mrchg Band; Pep Band; Jr Golf Asst; Cty Fair 4-H Dept Asst; KS Univ; Pharmacist.

OARD, BENJAMIN; Inman Jr Sr HS; Inman, KS; (3); Church Yth Grp; Letterman Clb; Teachers Aide; Band; Mrchg Band; Bsktbl; Ftbl; Trk; Wt Lftg; Hon Roll; KS ST U.

OBERLEY, LUKE A; Ness City HS; Ness City, KS; (3); Church Yth Grp; Letterman Clb; Scholastic Bowl; Phtg Yrbk; L Ftbl; High Hon Roll; Hon Roll; NHS; Pres Soph Cls; Treas Jr Cls; KS ST Univ; Chem.

OBERMEIER, KATRINA K; Osawatomie HS; Osawatomie, KS; (1); Stat Bsktbl; Stat Mgr(s); JV Trk; Intrml Vllybl; Hon Roll; NHS; Vlybl Benefit Trnys.

OBERMEYER, LORI A; Garden City Sr HS; Garden City, KS; (2); Debate Tm; NFL; Speech Tm; Orch; Vllybl; High Hon Roll; Prfct Atten Awd; Garden City Comm Orch & Band; Criminal Psych; Sociology.

OBERMUELLER, ERICA A; Lincoln Jr Sr HS; Lincoln, KS; (2); Church Yth Grp; Cmnty Wkr; Drama Clb; Letterman Clb; Pep Clb; Band; Mrchg Band; Pep Band; Nwsp; Ofcr Soph Cls.

OBERMUELLER, KATE; Wichita Southeast HS; Wichita, KS; (2); Church Yth Grp; Drama Clb; Sec German Clb; School Play; Stage Crew; Rptr Nwsp; Rep Frsh Cls; Rep Soph Cls; JV Socr; High Hon Roll; Stu Ambssdr; Kids Votng KS Alt; Presbytrn Church Stu Minstry Team, Servanthd Team.

OBERST, NICK R; Ft Scott HS; Fort Scott, KS; (3); 1/145; Am Leg Boys St; Letterman Clb; Pep Clb; Stage Crew; Sec Frsh Cls; Var L Bsbl; Var L Ftbl; Wt Lftg; High Hon Roll.

OBERZAN, MEGHAN E; Lawrence HS; Lawrence, KS; (2); Church Yth Grp; Cmnty Wkr; Pep Clb; Chorus; Rptr Phtg Yrbk; JV Chrldng; Cit Awd; Hon Roll; Pres Acad Fit Awd; U Of KS; PT.

OBORNY, CHRISTOPHER; Lacrosse HS; Rush Center, KS; (4); 2/25; Natl FFA Org; Teachers Aide; Sec Jr Cls; Rep Stu Cncl; High Hon Roll; NHS; Prfct Atten Awd; Sal; Golden Hammer Awd Otstdng Wdwrk; KU Alumni Assn Hnr Awd; KS ST Fair Class A FFA 95; Dodge City CC; Ag.

OBORNY, ERICA; Derby HS; Derby, KS; (4); 10/310; Girl Scts; Orch; Var Capt Swmmng; Cit Awd; NHS; Pres Schlr; St Schlr; Church Yth Grp; FCA; SADD; KMEA Dist/ST Orch; Wichita Yth Symphny; Wichita Symphny Hnr Usher; Truman ST; Exercise Sci.

OBORNY, JENNY L; Lacrosse HS; La Crosse, KS; (4); Debate Tm; Drama Clb; 4-H; French Clb; Girl Scts; Pep Clb; SADD; Band; Mrchg Band; Pep Band; Ft Hays ST U; Nrsng.

OBORNY, JEREMY S; Trego Comm HS; Wa Keeney, KS; (2); 1/49; Debate Tm; Drama Clb; NFL; Quiz Bowl; Scholastic Bowl; Science Clb; Speech Tm; Band; Mrchg Band; Pep Band; Top 32 Teams Cath Forensics League Natl Debate Trnmnt; KS Univ; Radiologist.

OBORNY, JOSIAH D; Larned HS; Larned, KS; (2); Art Clb; Church Yth Grp; Acpl Chr; Church Choir; Hon Roll; Great Bend Swim Team; Guitarist; Frmd Own Bnd; KS ST Univ; Archlgy.

OBORNY, LUKE; Lacrosse HS; La Crosse, KS; (3); 7/28; Debate Tm; Pres Drama Clb; HOBY; Q&S; Speech Tm; School Play; Ed Nwsp; Co-Ed Yrbk; Sec Stu Cncl; NHS; 1st Pl St J Rnlsm Infogrphcs; Best Actor Awd; Notre Dame U; Commnctns.

OBORNY, NATHAN J; Great Bend Sr HS; Larned, KS; (4); Church Yth Grp; FCA; Math Tm; Quiz Bowl; Scholastic Bowl; Spanish Clb; Acpl Chr; Church Choir; Crs Cntry; Swmmng; 2 Swim Relay Schl Records; Placed In Boys ST Swim Comptn; Swim Team Extra Curr; U Of KS; Biochem.

O BRIEN, SARA R; Shawnee Mission W Sr HS; Overland Park, KS; (3); 140/411; Church Yth Grp; HOBY; Latin Clb; Teachers Aide; Chorus; Bsktbl; Vllybl; Hon Roll; Schlr Ath Coll Stepping Stone Schlsp; Acad Ltr; U Of KS; Phy Therapy.

O'BRIEN, SHAWN P; Ft Scott HS; Fort Scott, KS; (3); Cmnty Wkr; 4-H; FTA; Chorus; Yrbk; Mgr(s); 4-H Awd; Citizenship WA Focus 4-H; Ft Scott CC; Bus Mgmt.

O BRYAN, JAYME B; Blue Valley North HS; Leawood, KS; (2); FCA; FBLA; Letterman Clb; Varsity Clb; Rep Jr Cls; Ofcr Stu Cncl; Var L Bsktbl; Socr; Cit Awd; Hon Roll; Stdnt Ldrshp Awd 95-; Elite Regl Finalst Model Search 95-; Miss KS Teen USA Del 96-; Notre Dame; Med.

O'BRYANT, CARIE A; Shawnee Mission N HS; Shawnee Mission, KS; (3); Church Yth Grp; GAA; Girl Scts; Ofcr Frsh Cls; Ofcr Soph Cls; Ofcr Jr Cls; Ofcr Sr Cls; Chrldng; Gym; Socr; Tchr Cadet; KS ST Univ; Early Ed.

OCHS, CLIFFIE J; Great Bend Sr HS; Great Bend, KS; (1).

OCHS, E J; Trego Comm HS; Wa Keeney, KS; (2); FHA; Natl FFA Org; Science Clb; SADD; Varsity Clb; Ofcr Soph Cls; Ofcr Bsbl; Ftbl; Trk; Wt Lftg; Fort Hays ST; Crmnl Jstc.

OCHS, ERIC S; Great Bend Sr HS; Great Bend, KS; (3); Church Yth Grp; Drama Clb; Teachers Aide; Band; Mrchg Band; Pep Band; School Play; High Hon Roll; WSU.

OCHS, STEPHANIE A; Triplains Schl; Russell Springs, KS; (2); Church Yth Grp; Letterman Clb; Chorus; School Play; Bsktbl; Trk; Vllybl; 4-H Awd; Hon Roll; 4-H; Kayettes; Jrnsics; Colby CC; Vet Tech.

OCHS, TRACIE; Triplains Schl; Russell Springs, KS; (3); Church Yth Grp; Pres 4-H; Band; School Play; Ed Yrbk; Var Bsktbl; L Chrldng; Var Trk; Var Vllybl; Sec Letterman Clb; Kayettes Points Chrmn; Forensics; Colby CC; PT.

OCKER, TRAVIS A; Hutchinson HS; Hutchinson, KS; (4); Nwsp; Var L Bsbl; Var L Socr; 2nd Team All St Bsbl 96; 1st Team All AR Vly; Ottawa Univ; Ed.

O'CONNELL, JILL R; Shawnee Mission N HS; Shawnee Mission, KS; (3); 20/400; Pep Clb; Red Cross Aide; Spanish Clb; Teachers Aide; Stage Crew; Ofcr Jr Cls; Ofcr Stu Cncl; JV Capt Chrldng; High Hon Roll; NHS; Northwestern Univ; Lawyer.

O'CONNOR, BRIAN; St Thomas Aquinas HS; Gardner, KS; (3); 25/267; Am Leg Boys St; FCA; French Clb; Pres FBLA; Band; School Musical; Tennis; High Hon Roll; Treas NHS; Most Inspirational Tennis Player Soph Yr/Tennis Jr Yr.

O'CONNOR, CHRISTINE; Olathe South Sr HS; Olathe, KS; (3); 23/412; Church Yth Grp; Letterman Clb; Spanish Clb; Teachers Aide; Nwsp; Ed Phtg Yrbk; Ofcr Stu Cncl; Bsktbl; Chrldng; Crs Cntry; Vol KS Schl For Deaf; Horseback Rdg 6 Yrs; St Marys Food Kitchen Vol.

O CONNOR, COREY P; Pratt HS; Pratt, KS; (3); Spanish Clb; Hon Roll; TSA Clb.

O CONNOR, CORINNE L; Blue Vlly NW HS; Shawnee Mission, KS; (3); 1/360; Cmnty Wkr; Q&S; Spanish Clb; Teachers Aide; Rptr Nwsp; Mgr(s); High Hon Roll; NHS.

O'CONNOR, JOHN T; Immaculata HS; Leavenworth, KS; (2); French Clb; Intnl Clb; Quiz Bowl; Science Clb; Var Golf; French Hon Soc; Hon Roll; Candy Stripe Hosp Vol; Stu That Care; KS ST Univ; Veterinarian.

O'DELL, ERIN L; Caney Valley Jr Sr HS; Caney, KS; (3); Treas FBLA; VP GAA; Office Aide; Pres Jr Cls; Ofcr Stu Cncl; Var Bsktbl; Var Chrldng; Var Trk; High Hon Roll; NHS; KS 3a Trk 2nd Pl In 100m & 200m Dash.

ODLE, KEEGAN P; Beloit Jr Sr HS; Glen Elder, KS; (1); 5/90; Letterman Clb; Spanish Clb; SADD; Varsity Clb; Variety Show; Pres Frsh Cls; Rep Stu Cncl; Var Bsbl; JV Ftbl; Var Wt Lftg; Future Med Careers; KS ST Univ; Arch Engrng.

O'DONNELL, ANNIE; Blue Valley HS; Overland Park, KS; (2); Art Clb; Mgr(s); High Hon Roll; Hon Roll; Pres Acad Fit Awd; PETA; WWF; Whale Sponsor.

OEDING, DAWN D; Cunningham HS; Spivey, KS; (3); 4/27; Church Yth Grp; Pep Clb; Quiz Bowl; Science Clb; SADD; Stage Crew; Var Bsktbl; Var Chrldng; Intrml Powder Puff Ftbl; Stat Trk; KS ST U; Bio.

OEHLERT, JENNIFER M; Salina HS South; Salina, KS; (2); Computer Clb; Teachers Aide; Chorus; Intrml Mgr(s); Intrml Score Keeper; JV Trk; High Hon Roll; Hon Roll; KS Univ; Child Care.

OEHLERT, NATHAN J; Lawrence HS; Lawrence, KS; (3); Teachers Aide; Trk; Wrstlng; Photo.

OEHMKE, JESSICA A; Wichita Collegiate Schl; Derby, KS; (3); Cmnty Wkr; Drama Clb; Acpl Chr; School Musical; School Play; Rep Soph Cls; Rep Jr Cls; Sec Sr Cls; Sec Stu Cncl; Tennis; Mrktg; Law; Pol Sci.

OELSCHLAEGER, LYDIA; Lawrence HS; Lawrence, KS; (4); 28/521; Church Yth Grp; FCA; Key Clb; Spanish Clb; Var Capt Crs Cntry; Var Trk; NHS; St Schlr; KS U.

OETINGER, CATHRYN J; Hesston HS; Hesston, KS; (1); 20/84; Church Yth Grp; FCA; FBLA; Band; Church Choir; Jazz Band; Pep Band; L Trk; Vllybl; Hon Roll; Acad Decathlon; Odyssey Of Mind; Gierman Awd Of Excl; U Of KS; Chiropractor.

OFFUTT, NEIL G; Beloit Jr Sr HS; Beloit, KS; (2); 6/68; Science Clb; SADD; Chorus; Orch; Variety Show; Var Bsbl; JV Bsktbl; High Hon Roll; Mens Ensmbl; Dist Choir.

OFFUTT, TRACI L; Coldwater Jr Sr HS; Coldwater, KS; (1); FCA; FHA; Pep Clb; Band; Chorus; Mrchg Band; Pep Band; School Musical; Trk; Hon Roll; Vet Medcn; Wildlf Park & Game.

OGDEN, JEREMY R; Wellington Sr HS; Wellington, KS; (4); Am Leg Boys St; Church Yth Grp; Natl FFA Org; Bsktbl; Hon Roll; Jr NHS; Friends U; Bus Admin.

OGDEN, NATASHA; Wellington Sr HS; Wellington, KS; (1); Church Yth Grp; Debate Tm; Drama Clb; GAA; Letterman Clb; Chorus; JV Bsktbl; High Hon Roll; Jr NHS; Jr Lions Awd; Forensics Stdnt Of Yr; KU; Cnslr.

OGG, DAVID M; Santa Fe Trail Jr HS; Olathe, KS; (1); Teachers Aide; Band; Socr; High Hon Roll; Pres Acad Fit Awd.

OGLE, HAMLIN N; Hoisington HS; Hoisington, KS; (2); Debate Tm; Drama Clb; Speech Tm; SADD; Teachers Aide; Band; Mrchg Band; Pep Band; School Musical; School Play; KS ST U; Vet Med.

OGLE, SHALON L; Salina HS South; Salina, KS; (3); Church Yth Grp; Drama Clb; FHA; Ed Yrbk; High Hon Roll; NHS.

OGLESBY, JAMIE M; Galena HS; Galena, KS; (1); Church Yth Grp; FCA; Band; Chorus; Church Choir; Jazz Band; Mrchg Band; Pep Band; School Play; Chrldng; OK Baptist Univ; Tchr.

OGREN, TRACY J; Immaculata HS; Fort Leavenworth, KS; (2); Church Yth Grp; FCA; L Var Socr; Hon Roll; Acad/Sprts Awd 94-95; Sccr Mst Vble Offnse Awd 94-95; Wght Lftng Awd 95-96.

OH, STACIE; Manhattan HS; Manhattan, KS; (4); 1/420; Spanish Clb; Orch; School Musical; High Hon Roll; NHS; St Schlr; AFS Pres; Sci Olympd; KS Rgnts Hnrs Acad; U KS; Phrmcy.

OHADI, MARYAM C; Northeast Magnet HS; Wichita, KS; (2); Girl Scts; Prfct Atten Awd; Art; Drawng; Cretv Wrtng; Wichita Pub Schls Stu Achvmt Awd For KS Art Cmssn Mural; Art His; Fine Arts.

O'HANLON, JOHN P; Dodge City HS; Dodge City, KS; (3); Church Yth Grp; 4-H; French Clb; NFL; Office Aide; Spanish Clb; SADD; Mgr(s); 4-H Awd; Hon Roll; Photo.

O'HANLON, JOSEPH; Dodge City HS; Dodge City, KS; (1); Church Yth Grp; Debate Tm; 4-H; NFL; Quiz Bowl; 4-H Teen Actvty Clb, VP; Stck Mrkt Clb; Med.

O HARA, ANDY A; St Thomas Aquinas HS; Olathe, KS; (4); 9/232; Am Leg Boys St; FCA; School Musical; School Play; Ed Nwsp; Pres Jr Cls; Rep Sr Cls; Var L Crs Cntry; Var L Trk; NHS; Creighton Univ; Acctng; Ec.

O'HARE, CLINT; Turner HS; Kansas City, KS; (3); 17/250; Bus Profs of Am; Chess Clb; German Clb; Math Clb; Math Tm; Ofcr Stu Cncl; Intrml Bsktbl; Var Trk; Hon Roll; Jr NHS; Bowling; KS U; Comp Sci.

OHL, MARIE; Conway Springs HS; Conway Springs, KS; (3); 7/35; French Clb; FHA; Teachers Aide; Bsktbl; Tennis; Hon Roll; NHS; Bus.

OHLDE, JOLYNN; Linn Schl; Palmer, KS; (4); 4/26; Church Yth Grp; FBLA; Band; Sec Sr Cls; Var L Bsktbl; L Var Trk; Capt Var Vllybl; Cit Awd; High Hon Roll; NHS; KS ST Univ; Pre-Hlth.

OHLDE, THEA C; Smoky Valley HS; Lindsborg, KS; (1); Sec Intnl Clb; Math Tm; NFL; Scholastic Bowl; Thesps; Orch; School Musical; Tennis; Hon Roll; Sci Olympiad 1st, 2nd & 3rd At Regnls & 3rd At St Cmptns; Writers Clb; Lib Clb.

OHLMEIER, CHRISSY; Paola HS; Osawatomie, KS; (3); 24/133; SADD; Teachers Aide; JV Var Bsktbl; JV Var Sftbl; JV Vllybl; Hon Roll; NHS; Kays.

OHLSON, JAMES; Garden City Sr HS; Garden City, KS; (3); Church Yth Grp; Teachers Aide; VICA; Ofcr Bsbl; Golf; Mgr(s); Hon Roll; Garden City CC; Engrng.

O'KEEFFE, SHAUN U; Topeka West HS; Topeka, KS; (4); 37/239; Boy Scts; Pep Clb; Q&S; Spanish Clb; Phtg Yrbk; High Hon Roll; Hon Roll; Pittsburg ST Univ; Air Condit.

OKESON, KENDALL; Winfield HS; Winfield, KS; (4); 15/170; Treas Church Yth Grp; Cmnty Wkr; Debate Tm; French Clb; VP Letterman Clb; Red Cross Aide; Teachers Aide; Ofcr Frsh Cls; Ofcr Soph Cls; Treas Jr Cls; Amer Legion Schl Awd; KS HSAA/WHS Citz Serv Awd; Schlr Ath; Outstdng Sr Boy Schlr Ath Awd; US Air Force; Engrng.

OKORO, CHIMA; Wichita Southeast HS; Wichita, KS; (1); Bus Profs of Am; Spanish Clb; Ofcr Frsh Cls; Bsktbl; Socr; Auto Mechs; KS U; Engrng.

OLBERDING, KELLI K; Hayden HS; Topeka, KS; (2); 1/175; Pres SADD; Church Choir; JV Vllybl; High Hon Roll; NHS; Female Soph Of Yr Hayden Awd; Schlstc Jrnlsm Awd Most Valued Staffer; Acad Ltr.

OLD, JENNIFER; Wabaunsee HS; Alma, KS; (3); Girl Scts; Letterman Clb; Quiz Bowl; School Musical; Ed Yrbk; Powder Puff Ftbl; Var L Trk; JV Vllybl; Mgr Wrstlng; Hon Roll; Univ Of KS; Med.

OLDRIDGE, ABBY; Wellington Sr HS; Wellington, KS; (2); Natl FFA Org; Office Aide; Bsktbl; Vllybl; Jr NHS.

O'LEARY, MARY E; Elk Valley Jr Sr HS; Elk City, KS; (3); 1/25; VP FTA; VP Stu Cncl; Capt Chrldng; Var Sftbl; High Hon Roll; Sec NHS; Math Tm; NFL; Office Aide; Pep Clb; GCTL; Wichita ST; PT.

OLEEN, LORI; Smoky Valley HS; Falun, KS; (4); Church Yth Grp; 4-H; Q&S; Band; Chorus; Nwsp; Co-Ed Yrbk; Sec Jr Cls; VP Stu Cncl; NHS; KS ST Univ; Mass Commnctns.

OLESON, PATRICIA J; Maize HS; Wichita, KS; (3); 1/247; German Clb; Letterman Clb; Office Aide; SADD; Varsity Clb; Var L Bsktbl; L Mgr(s); Var L Sftbl; Stat Vllybl; Wt Lftg; ASA Traveling Sftbl Team; Nrsng.

OLIVER, KATRINA; Campus HS; Haysville, KS; (3); English Clb; Girl Scts; Library Aide; Lit Mag; Hon Roll; Ldrshp Awd For Cretv Wrtg Clb.

OLIVER, TIM; Winfield HS; Winfield, KS; (3); Am Leg Boys St; Church Yth Grp; Cmnty Wkr; FCA; Library Aide; Teachers Aide; Church Choir; JV Bsktbl; JV Socr; Var Trk; Pres Of Chrch Stu Cncl; NYI; Elks Lodge 732 Essay Cont 1st Pl.

OLIVER, TRACE; Ulysses HS; Ulysses, KS; (2); Letterman Clb; VICA; Band; Mrchg Band; Pep Band; Crs Cntry; Hon Roll; KS ST U.

OLIVERIA, LILIA; Colby Sr HS; Colby, KS; (4); Drama Clb; Science Clb; JV Bsktbl; JV Vllybl; High Hon Roll; Recognition Of Top Stu In Chem; Recognition Of A Participate In KS Sci Olympiad 96.

OLMOS, SONIA K; Leavenworth HS; Leavenworth, KS; (3); Cmnty Wkr; Hon Roll; Goodfellows; Spcl Olympics Vol; Emporia ST Univ; Psych.

OLMSTEAD, SARAH; Junction City HS; Junction City, KS; (2); Key Clb; Ofcr Soph Cls; JV Sftbl; Hon Roll; KS U.

OLMSTED, DUSTIN J; Phillipsburg HS; Phillipsburg, KS; (3); FBLA; FHA; Pep Clb; Spanish Clb; SADD; Teachers Aide; Band; Pep Band; JV Bsktbl; Mgr Ftbl; Ft Hays; Comp Sci.

O'LOUGHLIN, THOMAS J; Sedgwick HS; Sedgwick, KS; (3); Varsity Clb; Chorus; School Play; Variety Show; JV Var Bsktbl; L Ftbl; L Trk; Hon Roll.

OLSEN, DAVID S; Salina HS South; Salina, KS; (3); Boy Scts; NFL; Teachers Aide; Orch; School Musical; School Play; Stage Crew; Rep Stu Cncl; Stat Crs Cntry; Mgr(s); Med Explorers; Bethany; Phys Therapy.

OLSEN, JEREMIE M; Lyndon HS; Lyndon, KS; (3); 2/42; Sec FBLA; Quiz Bowl; Pres Sr Cls; Capt Bsbl; Var L Trk; Var L Wt Lftg; NHS; Pres Acad Fit Awd; Church Yth Grp; Cmnty Wkr; KS Snflwr ST Gms Two Gld Mdls; KS ST Wghtlftng 2 A 2nd Plc Hng Cln/8th Ovrl; NSCA 2nd Pl.

OLSEN, LUCRETIA L; Ft Scott HS; Fort Scott, KS; (3); Debate Tm; NFL; Band; Law.

OLSON, ANDREW; Maranatha Acad; Kansas City, MO; (3); 1/49; Chess Clb; Church Yth Grp; Cmnty Wkr; Math Tm; Ed Yrbk; High Hon Roll; Ntl Merit Ltr; Cretv Poetic Wrtngs; Comp Graphics; Comp Programming; Musical Composition & Analysis; Art; Design; Juggln; Comp Sci.

OLSON, COLTARA; Hiawatha HS; Hiawatha, KS; (1); 24/104; Church Yth Grp; Pep Clb; Chorus; Church Choir; School Musical; School Play; Chrldng; Trk; Vllybl; Hon Roll; Tchr.

OLSON, ELIZABETH; Garden City Sr HS; Garden City, KS; (3); Treas Church Yth Grp; Ofcr FHA; Key Clb; Science Clb; Acpl Chr; Sec Jr Cls; Sec Sr Cls; Var Capt Pom Pon; High Hon Roll; NHS; U Of CO Boulder.

OLSON, EZRA R; Concordia Jr Sr HS; Concordia, KS; (3); Boy Scts; Church Yth Grp; Natl FFA Org; Hon Roll; Eagle Sct; Cloud Cty Civil Defense Team & Rural Fire Dept; Southwestern Coll.

OLSON, HEATHER; Rock Creek Jr Sr HS; Saint George, KS; (2); Church Yth Grp; Cmnty Wkr; 4-H; Natl FFA Org; SADD; Band; Mrchg Band; Pep Band; Stage Crew; JV Var Bsktbl; Fort Hays ST U; Accntng.

OLSON, INGRID; Hays HS; Hays, KS; (4); Am Leg Aux Girls St; Debate Tm; NFL; Orch; Ed Nwsp; Pres Sr Cls; Var Capt Chrldng; High Hon Roll; Hist NHS; Church Yth Grp; Vision Dance Team Natl Wnnrs; KS ST U; Scl Sci.

OLSON, MANDY; Atchison Co Cmty HS; Muscotah, KS; (1); Band; Mrchg Band; Pep Band; Chrldng; Sftbl; Muscotan Saddle Club Queen; Rodeo; KS ST Univ; Early Chldhd Ed.

OLSON, SKYLER M; Greeley Co Schl; Tribune, KS; (3); Natl FFA Org; Band; Chorus; Mrchg Band; Pep Band; School Play; Var L Bsktbl; L Trk; Var L Vllybl; Ft Hays ST; Sports Medicine.

OLSON, TAMARA K; Washburn Rural HS; Auburn, KS; (2); 2/400; Church Yth Grp; Cmnty Wkr; Var L Bsktbl; Var L Trk; JV Vllybl; High Hon Roll.

OMENSKI, DOUG M; Bishop Carroll Catholic HS; Wichita, KS; (2); German Clb; Ftbl; Tennis; Wt Lftg; Wrstlng; Hon Roll; KS ST U.

O NEAL, JUDD; Blue Valley HS; Stilwell, KS; (2); Church Yth Grp; Debate Tm; Chorus; School Musical; Hon Roll; U Of MI.

ONEDA, BRUNA; Blue Valley Northwest HS; Overland Park, KS; (4); Intnl Clb; Gym; Wt Lftg; Stdyng Abroad; KS U; Phys Thrpy.

O'NEIL, JACOB T; Blue Valley HS; Overland Park, KS; (3); Am Leg Boys St; Boy Scts; Church Yth Grp; Letterman Clb; SADD; Varsity Clb; Nwsp; Var Ftbl; Wt Lftg; Var Capt Wrstlng; 5th At St Wrestlng 96; 1st KS Freestyle Cup 96; Engrng.

O'NEILL, BRANDON; Spearville Jr Sr HS; Spearville, KS; (1); 4-H; Chorus; Mrchg Band; Orch; Pep Band; Ftbl; Trk; Wt Lftg; 4-H Awd.

O'NEILL, JEANIE; Jefferson Co North HS; Winchester, KS; (1); Church Yth Grp; 4-H; Scholastic Bowl; SADD; Band; Mrchg Band; Pep Band; School Musical; Chrldng; Hon Roll; Med.

O'NEILL, TIFFANY; Dodge City HS; Spearville, KS; (4); Cmnty Wkr; Drama Clb; 4-H; Vllybl; 4-H Awd; Stu Mon & Yr; Acctng.

OPAT, JACLYN M; Smoky Valley HS; Lindsborg, KS; (1); Church Yth Grp; Letterman Clb; Pep Clb; Varsity Clb; Band; Mrchg Band; Pep Band; JV Bsktbl; L Var Trk; L Var Vllybl.

OPAT, JAIME L; Smoky Valley HS; Lindsborg, KS; (3); Church Yth Grp; Letterman Clb; Office Aide; Pep Clb; Teachers Aide; Varsity Clb; Band; Flag Corp; Mrchg Band; Orch.

OPHEIM, SARA A; Campus HS; Haysville, KS; (1); Science Clb; SADD; JV Tennis; Intrml Vllybl; High Hon Roll; Hon Roll; U Of KS; Phys Thrpy.

OPLOTHIK, AMBER; Columbus HS; Baxter Springs, KS; (2); Band; Mrchg Band; Var L Chrldng; Mgr(s); High Hon Roll; NHS.

OPLOTHIK, ASHLEY; Columbus HS; Baxter Springs, KS; (2); Band; Mrchg Band; Var Capt Chrldng; Mgr(s); High Hon Roll; NHS.

OPPERT, CRIS; Manhattan HS; Manhattan, KS; (4); 19/377; Am Leg Boys St; Chess Clb; Science Clb; Spanish Clb; Teachers Aide; Var L Socr; Var L Tennis; Hon Roll; NHS; Pres Acad Fit Awd; St Sci Olympd 2nd Pl, Reg 8 Mdls; KS HS Schl Cchs All Acad Sccr 1st Tm; Optmst Frdm Essay 2nd Pl; Marine Bio.

OPPLIGER, BECKY; Lakin HS; Deerfield, KS; (4); 7/53; Am Leg Aux Girls St; Church Yth Grp; FCA; GAA; HOBY; School Play; Ed Nwsp; Yrbk; Sec Jr Cls; Var Bsktbl; Bio.

ORDONEZ, DORA; Hugoton HS; Hugoton, KS; (2); 11/88; Hon Roll; Spnsh, Engl.

ORNOPIA, DAISY L; Midland Sda Schl; Olathe, KS; (2); Church Yth Grp; Chorus; Ed Yrbk; VP Frsh Cls; Pres Soph Cls; Pres Stu Cncl; Cit Awd; High Hon Roll; Piano; Stu Of Week.

O'ROURKE, COLLEEN M; Saint Thomas Aguinas HS; Lenexa, KS; (4); 63/231; Am Leg Aux Girls St; Church Yth Grp; Cmnty Wkr; French Clb; Girl Scts; Hist Key Clb; Spanish Clb; SADD; NHS; Service Clb; Sci Olympd Co-Capt, Sec; Ed.

OROURKE, KELLY J; Blue Valley Northwest HS; Overland Park, KS; (3); Cmnty Wkr; Girl Scts; Red Cross Aide; Teachers Aide; Chorus; School Musical; School Play; Stage Crew; Lit Mag; High Hon Roll; Outdr Rec Activities; Ed/Psych/Eng.

O'ROURKE, MONICA N; Goddard HS; Goddard, KS; (4); VP Science Clb; SADD; Rep Band; Jazz Band; Mrchg Band; Pep Band; Stage Crew; Phtg Yrbk; NHS; Church Yth Grp; John Philip Souza Outstdng Band Stu; Tabor Coll; Missionary.

OROZCO, MARGARITA J; Ellsworth HS; Kanopolis, KS; (2); Church Yth Grp; Girl Scts; HOBY; Intnl Clb; Quiz Bowl; Band; Chorus; JV Vllybl; High Hon Roll; Spanish NHS; Duke Univ; Ed.

ORR, ANGELA D; Wellington Sr HS; Wellington, KS; (2); Church Yth Grp; Cmnty Wkr; Key Clb; Band; Jazz Band; Mrchg Band; Pep Band; High Hon Roll; Hon Roll; Prfct Atten Awd; Law.

ORR, CARY R; Goddard HS; Wichita, KS; (1); Office Aide; SADD; High Hon Roll; Hon Roll; Nrsing.

ORR, PEYTON J; Kapaun-Mt Carmel HS; Wichita, KS; (3); Pol Discussion Group Mem; Northwestern U; Transportation.

ORRELL, BRIDGET A; Blue Valley Northwest HS; Overland Park, KS; (3); Cmnty Wkr; Debate Tm; German Clb; Intnl Clb; Math Clb; NFL; Scholastic Bowl; Teachers Aide; Var L Golf; Intrml Powder Puff Ftbl; KAYS.

ORRISON, DENISE; Olathe North Sr HS; Olathe, KS; (4); FHA; NFL; Q&S; Spanish Clb; Variety Show; Ed Nwsp; Rep Stu Cncl; Capt Chrldng; Capt Vllybl; High Hon Roll; Johnson Cty CC.

ORTH, ELIZABETH; Larned HS; Larned, KS; (2); Church Yth Grp; Chorus; Rptr Yrbk; Bsktbl; Vllybl; High Hon Roll; Hon Roll; Pres Acad Fit Awd; Optmtrst.

ORTH, JENNIFER; Bishop Ward HS; Kansas City, KS; (4); 4/92; Pep Clb; Ofcr Frsh Cls; Ofcr Soph Cls; Ofcr Jr Cls; Ofcr Sr Cls; Bsktbl; Sftbl; Vllybl; High Hon Roll; NHS; KS Hnr Schlr; Rtry Clb; Capt Vrsty Bsktbl; KS ST; Admin.

ORTIZ, ANDREA; Garden City Sr HS; Garden City, KS; (4); Hosp Aide; Spanish Clb; SADD; Band; Color Guard; Mrchg Band; Mgr Wrstlng; Cit Awd; Office Aide; Teachers Aide; DARE Role Model; Big Brother/Big Sister Pgm Big Sister; Ft Hays ST U; Med.

ORTIZ, DENA; Jefferson West HS; Ozawkie, KS; (3); 16/80; Letterman Clb; SADD; Flag Corp; Yrbk; Bsktbl; Pom Pon; Trk; Vllybl; High Hon Roll; NHS; Hlth Awd; KU; Hlth.

ORTIZ, JIMMY L; Dodge City HS; Dodge City, KS; (2); Quiz Bowl; Band; Mrchg Band; Pep Band; Stage Crew; Coll Clss; Dodge City Cowboy Band; Upward Bound; Genetics; Music.

ORTIZ, SHAWNA M; Turner HS; Kansas City, KS; (2); Art Clb; Latin Clb; Pep Clb; Spanish Clb; SADD; Teachers Aide; Ofcr Stu Cncl; Hon Roll; NHS; LULAC; Pittsburg Univ; Arch.

ORTMAN, SARAH I; Mankato Jr Sr HS; Mankato, KS; (2); 5/31; FHA; HOBY; Quiz Bowl; Band; Chorus; Jazz Band; Swing Chorus; JV Golf; JV Vllybl; Hon Roll; Luther Leag; Vac Bible Schl Music Coord; KS ST Univ; Doctor.

OSBORN, BRETT M; Shawnee Mission E Sr HS; Overland Park, KS; (2); Church Yth Grp; Debate Tm; JV Bsbl; Wt Lftg; High Hon Roll; Hon Roll; ISA; Mexico Missions Trips; All-Schl Awd; K ST; Yth Work; Minister.

OSBORN, JENNIFER R; Anderson Cty Jr Sr HS; Greeley, KS; (1); SADD; Chorus; Hon Roll.

OSBORN, LUCAS; Washburn Rural HS; Topeka, KS; (2); Quiz Bowl; Spanish Clb; SADD; Band; Mrchg Band; Pep Band; School Play; High Hon Roll; KS U; Dctr.

OSBORN, REBECCA; Anderson Cty Jr Sr HS; Garnett, KS; (4); #10 in class; Church Yth Grp; Debate Tm; Intnl Clb; NFL; Pep Clb; SADD; Chorus; Church Choir; Rptr Nwsp; Var Capt Chrldng; KS ST U; Anthropology.

OSBORN, SHANNON; Dodge City HS; Dodge City, KS; (2); SADD; Teachers Aide; Chrldng; KAYS; AZ ST U.

OSBORN, TYSON B; Emporia HS; Emporia, KS; (3); Pep Clb; Intrml Bsktbl; JV Ftbl; Var Golf; High Hon Roll; Pre-Med.

OSBOURN, ELIZABETH J; Olathe East Sr HS; Olathe, KS; (3); 1/340; Drama Clb; Spanish Clb; Thesps; Drill Tm; School Musical; School Play; Stage Crew; NHS; Pres Acad Fit Awd; Spanish NHS.

OSBOURN, ERIN J; Santa Fe Trail Jr HS; Olathe, KS; (1); Drama Clb; Spanish Clb; Drill Tm; School Play; Stage Crew; Trk; High Hon Roll.

OSENBAUGH, JEFF; Hutchinson HS; Hutchinson, KS; (3); Am Leg Boys St; Boy Scts; Church Yth Grp; Var Mgr Bsbl; Var Mgr(s); Hon Roll; Prfct Atten Awd; Eagle Scout Awd With Bronze Plan.

OSGOOD, LAUREN N; Maize HS; Wichita, KS; (3); FCA; Speech Tm; SADD; Teachers Aide; Thesps; Band; Chorus; Church Choir; Mrchg Band; Pep Band; 6 Poems Publshd; KAYS; Chld Psychlgst.

O'SHEA, WINTER; Blue Valley HS; Blaine, KS; (1); Bus Profs of Am; Church Yth Grp; FHA; Natl FFA Org; Band; Chorus; Mrchg Band; Pep Band; Stage Crew; Bsktbl; Trck; KS ST; RN.

OSNER, JASON K; Cunningham HS; Cunningham, KS; (3); 3/24; Pep Clb; Science Clb; Pres SADD; JV Bsktbl; Var L Trk; Hon Roll.

OSNER, WENDY; Conway Springs HS; Conway Springs, KS; (3); 7/33; Church Yth Grp; Rep Stu Cncl; Bsktbl; Co-Capt Pom Pon; Var Tennis; Hon Roll; Bus Mrktg.

OSTERHAUS, ERIC S; Nemaha Valley HS; Seneca, KS; (4); 12/52; Church Yth Grp; Cmnty Wkr; Drama Clb; Letterman Clb; Varsity Clb; School Play; Var Bsbl; Var Bsktbl; High Hon Roll; NHS; 3rd Tm Class 3a KS Bsktbl; 1st Tm All Big Seven Leag; KS ST Univ; Ed/Math.

OSTERHAUS, GRETA L; Wetmore Schl; Wetmore, KS; (2); Letterman Clb; Chorus; School Musical; Ofcr Frsh Cls; Ofcr Soph Cls; Ofcr Jr Cls; Ofcr Stu Cncl; Bsktbl; Trk; Vllybl; Hold 3 Schl Trk Records.

OSTMEYER, DIANA; Trinity Catholic HS; Arlington, KS; (4); 10/32; Am Leg Aux Girls St; Church Yth Grp; Cmnty Wkr; Dance Clb; Drama Clb; Sec 4-H; Girl Scts; Letterman Clb; Math Tm; NFL; Ctznshp WA Fcs Trp; Bib Sis; 4-H Camp Cnslr; KS ST U; Sec Eng Tchr.

OSTMEYER, SARA; Ottawa HS; Ottawa, KS; (3); #26 in class; Letterman Clb; Office Aide; Spanish Clb; Teachers Aide; School Play; Variety Show; Rep Stu Cncl; Intrml Bsktbl; Var L Trk; JV Var Vllybl.

OSTRANDER, GRETCHEN; Jefferson Co North HS; Winchester, KS; (2); #5 in class; Church Yth Grp; FBLA; Band; Flag Corp; Rep Stu Cncl; JV Bsktbl; L JV Trk; JV Vllybl; High Hon Roll; Prfct Atten Awd; U Of KS; Med.

OSTRANDER, MEAGHEN; Jefferson Co North HS; Winchester, KS; (4); 1/38; Am Leg Aux Girls St; Treas Church Yth Grp; FBLA; Letterman Clb; Band; Pres Chorus; Pres Sr Cls; L Var Bsktbl; High Hon Roll; Pres NHS; KS ST U.

OSWALD, JAMIE; Athison Cty Comm HS; Effingham, KS; (2); Letterman Clb; Pep Clb; Band; Chorus; School Play; Variety Show; JV Bsktbl; JV Chrldng; Var Trk; Hon Roll; Cosmtlgy.

OTERO, DEANNA R; Garden City Sr HS; Garden City, KS; (3); Sftbl; Soc Wkr/Cnslr.

OTOOLE, ERIN K; Olathe East Sr HS; Overland Park, KS; (3); Church Yth Grp; French Clb; Acpl Chr; Church Choir; Capt Drill Tm; School Musical; VP Soph Cls; VP Jr Cls; Pres Sr Cls; Powder Puff Ftbl; Spch Thrpy.

OTOOLE, JENNIFER L; Maize HS; Wichita, KS; (1); 1/401; Church Yth Grp; SADD; Chorus; Variety Show; High Hon Roll.

O'TOOLE, LORI; Maize HS; Wichita, KS; (3); 25/242; Letterman Clb; Q&S; SADD; Chorus; Variety Show; Ed Nwsp; Var Crs Cntry; NHS; Church Yth Grp; FCA; KSPA Stu Bd; Governors Stu Task Force For Kids Voting KS; Advertising; Jrnlsm.

OTTEM, LETITIA; Atwood HS; Atwood, KS; (3); 1/49; Girl Scts; Model UN; Scholastic Bowl; Band; VP Frsh Cls; Sec Soph Cls; Sec Jr Cls; Var Chrldng; Var Vllybl; High Hon Roll; Engrng.

OTTENS, VANESSA N; Sumner Acad Of Arts & Science; Kansas City, KS; (1); French Clb; Band; Comm Zoo Vol; Camp Fire; Zoology.

OTTMAN, MATT; Topeka West HS; Topeka, KS; (3); 18/239; Church Yth Grp; Pep Clb; Band; Mrchg Band; Pep Band; L Trk; Hon Roll; KS ST Univ; Elctrnc Engrg.

OTTO, ANDREW M; Washburn Rural HS; Topeka, KS; (3); Jazz Band; Variety Show; High Hon Roll; Hon Roll; Contemporary Instruments; Duke Univ Math & Comprehensive Talent Pgm; Psych; Bio.

OTTO, ANN; Manhattan HS; Manhattan, KS; (3); Church Yth Grp; Debate Tm; Drama Clb; FTA; Natl FFA Org; NFL; SADD; Teachers Aide; Thesps; Ofcr Stu Cncl; Natl Spnsh Exam Top 10; Make Up Crew Plays; Engl Hrs Rdr/Trnr; KS ST U; Ag.

OUDERKIRK, THERESA; Washburn Rural HS; Topeka, KS; (2); Girl Scts; Intnl Clb; Pep Clb; Band; Mrchg Band; Pep Band; Lit Mag; Hon Roll; AFS 96-97; Topeka Yth Wind Ensemble; St Solo Cont; Arch.

OUELLETTE, JAMES C; Washington HS; Washington, KS; (3); Art Clb; Treas Boy Scts; VP Church Yth Grp; French Clb; Letterman Clb; Pep Clb; Scholastic Bowl; Ftbl; Trk; High Hon Roll; Order Arrow; Golden Eagle.

OUSLEY, THERESA; Spring Hill HS; Spring Hill, KS; (4); 15/97; Am Leg Aux Girls St; Letterman Clb; Drill Tm; VP Frsh Cls; Pres Soph Cls; Pres Sr Cls; Rep Stu Cncl; Bsktbl; Crs Cntry; Trk; Bus Mgmt.

OVERBAUGH, STEFANI M; Shawnee Mission E Sr HS; Prairie Village, KS; (2); Church Yth Grp; Drama Clb; Library Aide; Chorus; Church Choir; Hon Roll; U Of KS; Phy Thrpst.

OVERHAUG, JENNIFER E; Lawrence HS; Lawrence, KS; (2); German Clb; SADD; Cit Awd; KS ST.

OVERHOLT, AMANDA; Wichita North HS; Wichita, KS; (2); Church Yth Grp; Teachers Aide; Band; Church Choir; Mrchg Band; JV Chrldng; Cit Awd; Hon Roll; NHS; Pres Acad Fit Awd; Mid Amer Nazarene Coll.

OVERHOLT, AMY; Wichita North HS; Wichita, KS; (3); 1/300; Church Yth Grp; Band; Church Choir; Mrchg Band; Orch; Pep Band; Rep Soph Cls; VP Jr Cls; Treas Stu Cncl; NHS; Mid-Amer Nazarene Col; Bus.

OVERMAM, MONICA; Columbus HS; Columbus, KS; (4); 2/87; Bus Profs of Am; Church Yth Grp; 4-H; Math Tm; Drill Tm; School Musical; Swing Chorus; Variety Show; Rep Jr Cls; Var Chrldng; Tri-M Music Soc; Grls Golf ST Champ Tm; Southwest MO ST Univ.

OVERMAN, CHARITY D; Oswego HS; Oswego, KS; (1); 10/45; Church Yth Grp; FHA; Scholastic Bowl; Rep Stu Cncl; Stat Bsktbl; JV Chrldng; L Mgr(s); JV Vllybl; Hon Roll; Wrtr.

OVERMAN, MONICA S; Columbus HS; Columbus, KS; (4); 2/92; Bus Profs of Am; Treas 4-H; Math Tm; Spanish Clb; Chorus; School Musical; Variety Show; Rep Jr Cls; Var Chrldng; Var L Golf; Dare Role Mod; Mss Clmbus 1st Attndnt; Grls Glf Tm St Chmps 3x; KS U Hnr Schlr; Southwest MO ST U.

OVERMAN, MORGAN; Columbus HS; Columbus, KS; (1); Bus Profs of Am; FCA; 4-H; Chorus; Drill Tm; Sec Frsh Cls; Rep Stu Cncl; Var L Bsktbl; Var L Sftbl; Kays Clb; KU TN; Traveling/Med.

OVERMAN, SUMMER; Chetopa Schl; Welch, OK; (2); 2/19; Church Yth Grp; 4-H; Quiz Bowl; Scholastic Bowl; Band; Chorus; Church Choir; Mrchg Band; Pep Band; Sec Frsh Cls; NEO; Nrsg.

OVERMILLER, MICHELLE R; Smith Ctr Jr Sr HS; Smith Center, KS; (4); Church Yth Grp; Drama Clb; Pres Sec FHA; Pep Clb; Speech Tm; Band; Swing Chorus; Ofcr Stu Cncl; High Hon Roll; Cmnty Wkr; KAYS; Tabor Coll; Bus Admin.

OVERSTAKE, ERIN G; Wichita Southeast HS; Wichita, KS; (2); Church Yth Grp; Drama Clb; SADD; Church Choir; Orch; School Musical; Stage Crew; Socr; Hon Roll; Pres Acad Fit Awd; KS ST; Vet Medicine.

OVERSTREET, ERIC P; Maize HS; Maize, KS; (3); 27/289; Church Yth Grp; Math Tm; SADD; Teachers Aide; Band; Chorus; Mrchg Band; Pep Band; Variety Show; Ftbl; KS Natl Hstry Day 1st 95; KS Natl Hstry Day 2nd 96; Natl Hstry Day KS Rep 95, 96.

OVERSTREET, IRIS M; Goessel HS; Lehigh, KS; (3); 3/25; Band; Chorus; Mrchg Band; Pep Band; School Musical; School Play; Rptr Yrbk; Pres Stu Cncl; Stat Vllybl; High Hon Roll; 1a ST Chmpn Imform Spch 96 ST Forensics; 1 Rtng ST Mus Cntst 94-/Xylophone 94-95 Vocal; Mus Ed.

OVERTIN, CRYSTAL L; Neodesha Jr Sr HS; Neodesha, KS; (1); Band; Chorus; Mrchg Band; Pep Band; Vllybl; Hon Roll; Smmr Sftbl; KS Univ; Elec Engr/Thrpst.

OVERTON, ANDREW; Buhler HS; Buhler, KS; (3); Am Leg Boys St; Boy Scts; Debate Tm; NFL; Band; Jazz Band; Mrchg Band; L Bsbl; Hon Roll; Prfct Atten Awd.

OWEN, EMMA; Eureka Jr Sr HS; Eureka, KS; (3); Am Leg Aux Girls St; Cmnty Wkr; Drama Clb; Quiz Bowl; Thesps; Band; Crs Cntry; High Hon Roll; Kiwanis Awd.

OWEN, JOANNA L; Blue Valley Northwest HS; Overland Park, KS; (4); 125/340; Intnl Clb; Science Clb; Band; Mrchg Band; Pep Band; Hon Roll; Natl Eng Mrt Awd; All Amer Schlr; Environmental Clb; U Of KS; Jrnlst.

OWEN, JOHN ISAAC; Topeka HS; Topeka, KS; (2); 1/450; Letterman Clb; Varsity Clb; Orch; Socr; High Hon Roll; Russian Clb; KS St Hnrs Orch; Eng.

OWEN, MICHAEL R; Field Kindley Mem Sr HS; Coffeyville, KS; (2); FCA; German Clb; School Musical; Rep Stu Cncl; Var L Bsbl; Var L Bsktbl; JV Crs Cntry; JV Ftbl; Hon Roll.

OWEN, NICK; Concordia Jr Sr HS; Concordia, KS; (3); Am Leg Boys St; Art Clb; Church Yth Grp; Sec Treas Drama Clb; NFL; Spanish Clb; Thesps; School Musical; School Play; Stage Crew; Best Supporting Actor 93; Outstdng Perfmnc 94; Outstdng Stu Dir 95; Charter Thespian Mem; TV Media Prod; Scndry Ed; Theater.

OWEN, TINA; Flinthills HS; El Dorado, KS; (3); 4/19; Church Yth Grp; FCA; HOBY; VP Letterman Clb; Pep Clb; SADD; Rep Frsh Cls; Var Capt Chrldng; High Hon Roll; Hon Roll; Butler Cty CC; Drafting.

OWENS, DANIELLE; Wichita West HS; Wichita, KS; (4); 69/263; DECA; French Clb; Office Aide; Teachers Aide; Ofcr Frsh Cls; Ofcr Soph Cls; Mgr(s); Hon Roll; Black Awareness Clb; Hnrb Mntn; Prins Awd.

OWENS, HOLLIE L; Olathe North Sr HS; Olathe, KS; (4); German Clb; SADD; L Bsktbl; Powder Puff Ftbl; Var Socr; Var Vllybl; Hon Roll; Comm Svc; KS ST; Pre-Pharm.

OWENS, JUSTIN; Mulvane Sr HS; Mulvane, KS; (4); 15/142; FCA; Pep Clb; SADD; Teachers Aide; L Ftbl; L Trk; Hon Roll; NHS; Prfct Atten Awd; Pres Acad Fit Awd; Wichita ST U.

OWENS, JUSTIN; Caney Valley Jr Sr HS; Tyro, KS; (4); 5/57; Church Yth Grp; FCA; 4-H; Letterman Clb; Natl FFA Org; Band; Mrchg Band; Pep Band; Ofcr Stu Cncl; Bsktbl; FFA Awds; Independence CC; Ag Eng.

OWENS, MEREDITH Q; Blue Valley Northwest HS; Overland Park, KS; (3); Church Yth Grp; Drama Clb; VP French Clb; Thesps; Band; Church Choir; Mrchg Band; Stage Crew; Hon Roll; NHS; Yth Deacon In Chrch; Bus.

OWENS, MIRANDA; Quivira Heights HS; Bushton, KS; (3); 2/21; Am Leg Aux Girls St; Treas Church Yth Grp; Letterman Clb; School Play; Pres Frsh Cls; Sec Stu Cncl; Co-Capt Bsktbl; Chrldng; Co-Capt Tennis; VP NHS; Psych.

OWENSBY, CRYSTAL D; Shawnee Mission S Sr HS; Overland Park, KS; (3); Church Yth Grp; Debate Tm; DECA; Drama Clb; GAA; Pep Clb; Hon Roll; Politically Active Yth; Forensics; BSA For Law; K-ST; Pre-Law.

OWNBY, MATTHEW D; Olathe South Sr HS; Olathe, KS; (3); Science Clb; High Hon Roll; Ntl Merit Ltr; Sci Olympiad; Maxima Cum Laude Natl Latin Exam Latin I; KS ST; Elec/Chem Engr.

OXANDALE, BRETT; Jackson Heights HS; Wetmore, KS; (3); FBLA; Treas Natl FFA Org; Pep Clb; Var Bsktbl; Var Ftbl; Var Trk; Gov Hon Prg Awd; Ntl Merit Ltr; Prfct Atten Awd; Pres Acad Fit Awd.

OXLER, JASON P; Blue Valley Northwest HS; Shawnee Mission, KS; (3); Band; Jazz Band; Capt Socr; High Hon Roll; NHS.

OXLEY, JACOB P; Haven HS; Haven, KS; (2); Natl FFA Org; Ofcr Bsbl; Span; KS ST Univ; Zoolgy/Vet Sci.

PACHECO, ANGELINA M; Garden City Sr HS; Garden City, KS; (1); Church Yth Grp; Debate Tm; Church Choir; Rep Frsh Cls; Rep Stu Cncl; Law.

PACKARD, BEN; White Rock HS; Burr Oak, KS; (2); 1/16; Letterman Clb; Math Tm; Quiz Bowl; SADD; Bsktbl; Ftbl; Trk; Cit Awd; High Hon Roll; NHS.

PADAVIC, MICHAEL; Shawnee Mission Northwest HS; Shawnee Mission, KS; (4); 17/385; Pep Clb; Q&S; Sprt Ed Yrbk; Var L Bsbl; Var Capt Ftbl; High Hon Roll; NHS; Pres Acad Fit Awd; St Schlr; Ten Mst Influential Srs; All-Journal Herald Defense; Hnrb Mntn All League Defense; Sun Cty & KC Schlr; AZ ST; Arch.

PADEN, ARON; Faith Christian Schl; Osawatomie, KS; (4); Chorus; School Play; Ed Nwsp; Ed Yrbk; Var Bsbl; Bsktbl; Socr; Val; Kite Clb Pres/Ownr; Stunt Kite Flyr; De Vry Tech Schl; Comp Pgmng.

PADEN, DARBY; Atchison Sr HS; Atchison, KS; (3); Church Yth Grp; DECA; Band; Pep Band; Rep Stu Cncl; Bsktbl; Sftbl; Vllybl; High Hon Roll; Hon Roll; Lnchn Chmpns 6x; UMKC; Dntl.

PADEN, JUSTIN; Ellsworth HS; Ellsworth, KS; (2); 13/80; Letterman Clb; Band; Mrchg Band; Pep Band; Ofcr Bsbl; Stat Bsbl; Var Ftbl; Var Tennis; Wt Lftg; Hon Roll; West Point.

PADILLA, LIZ; St John Jr Sr HS; Saint John, KS; (3); Cmnty Wkr; SADD; JV Bsktbl; JV Mgr(s); Var Tennis; Hon Roll; NHS; U Of KS.

PADILLA, PATRICIO J; Hayden HS; Topeka, KS; (3); Cmnty Wkr; FBLA; Intnl Clb; Library Aide; SADD; Sec Soph Cls; Rep Jr Cls; Crs Cntry; Trk; Pres Acad Fit Awd; Intl Bus.

PAFUME, AIMEE C; Wichita East HS; Wichita, KS; (4); Church Yth Grp; Pep Clb; Spanish Clb; Acpl Chr; Chorus; Church Choir; School Play; Variety Show; Swmmng; High Hon Roll.

PAGE, AMANDA J; Maize HS; Wichita, KS; (1); Teachers Aide; Chorus; Variety Show; High Hon Roll.

PAGE, KRISTI; Girard HS; Girard, KS; (4); 1/69; Ofcr Am Leg Aux Girls St; VP Science Clb; Sec Spanish Clb; Pres SADD; Band; Sec Sr Cls; Golf; Sftbl; High Hon Roll; NHS; U KS; Med.

PAGEL, JENNY; Jackson Heights HS; Holton, KS; (1); 4-H; FHA; Pep Clb; Chorus; School Musical; JV Bsktbl; Var JV Mgr(s); Var JV Trk; 4-H Awd; Hon Roll; KAYS; Interior Dsgn.

PAGEL, WILL; Jackson Heights HS; Holton, KS; (3); 15/44; Letterman Clb; Natl FFA Org; Chorus; School Musical; Sec Bsktbl; Var Ftbl; JV Var Mgr(s); Var Wt Lftg; High Hon Roll; Prfct Atten Awd.

PAGENKOPF, CAMBRY L; Skyline Schl; Pratt, KS; (4); 3/31; Church Yth Grp; Cmnty Wkr; Pres 4-H; Pep Clb; Quiz Bowl; SADD; Band; Chorus; Church Choir; Drm Mjr(t); Mission Trip Haiti; Comm Theatre; All League Vlybl Plyr; KS ST Univ; Jrnlsm/Mass Comm.

PAIGE, COURTNEY C; Wichita Southeast HS; Wichita, KS; (1); 159/539; Church Yth Grp; Debate Tm; Drama Clb; NFL; Chorus; Church Choir; Drill Tm; School Musical; School Play; Swing Chorus; Gspl Choir; Atlanta; Law.

PAINE, ALISON M; Olathe East Sr HS; Olathe, KS; (3); 1/360; Church Yth Grp; Intnl Clb; Chorus; Yrbk; Crs Cntry; Trk; High Hon Roll; NHS; Pres Acad Fit Awd; Spanish NHS; U Of KS; BSN.

PAINTER, AMANDA; Circle HS; Towanda, KS; (2); Church Yth Grp; FHA; SADD; Acpl Chr; Chorus; Variety Show; Sec Soph Cls; Capt Jr Cls; Ofcr Stu Cncl; JV Var Bsktbl; KU; Acting.

PAJOR, JENNIFER A; Bishop Carroll Catholic HS; Wichita, KS; (2); Sec Boy Scts; Church Yth Grp; Girl Scts; Red Cross Aide; Rptr Yrbk; Ofcr Frsh Cls; Hon Roll; FCA; Service Clb; SADD; Girl Sct Slvr Awd; Mssn Club; Stdnt Of Mnth; Notre Dame; Marine Bio.

PAK, LISA; Garden City Sr HS; Garden City, KS; (3); 1/347; Cmnty Wkr; Red Cross Aide; Acpl Chr; Chorus; School Musical; Ed Nwsp; Sec Wrstlng; High Hon Roll; Prfct Atten Awd; Natl Yth Ldrshp Conf; Prom Cmmtte; KS ST U; Virolgy.

PALENSKE, JAKE; Seaman Sr HS; Topeka, KS; (4); 95/280; Church Yth Grp; Pres German Clb; Model UN; Office Aide; Quiz Bowl; Teachers Aide; Stage Crew; Ed Nwsp; Hon Roll; Mgr Mgr(s); DARE Role Model; Chldrns Cmnty Theater; KS ST U; Jrnlsm.

PALENSKE, NICOLE; Wabaunsee HS; Alma, KS; (4); 4/35; Pres 4-H; FBLA; Pres FHA; Hist Jr Cls; Ofcr Stu Cncl; Var Bsktbl; Var Powder Puff Ftbl; Var Vllybl; Hon Roll; NHS; KS Hnr Schlr.

PALKOWITSH, CARRIE A; Garden City Sr HS; Garden City, KS; (2); Debate Tm; Speech Tm; Stat Mgr(s); JV Vllybl; High Hon Roll; Frsncs; Lincoln Douglas Debate; Drury Coll; Marine Biol.

PALMER, GARY A; Ft Scott HS; Fort Scott, KS; (3); Am Leg Boys St; Art Clb; Church Yth Grp; Cmnty Wkr; FCA; 4-H; Ed Yrbk; Ofcr Stu Cncl; 4-H Awd; Hon Roll; 4-H Pub Spkng ST Wnnr; KS 4-H Phtgrphy ST Fnlst For ST Wnnr; Prof Phtgrphr.

PALMER, JAMES A; Solomon Jr Sr HS; Solomon, KS; (3); Natl FFA Org; SADD; JV Bsktbl; K ST Salina; Arch.

PALMER, JENNIFER Y; Junction City HS; Milford, KS; (1); 3/409; Girl Scts; JV Swmmng; JV Tennis; Cit Awd; Hon Roll; Jr NHS; Pres Acad Fit Awd; Equines Club; K ST; Air Force/FBI.

PALMER, MEGAN A; Lucus-Luray HS; Lucas, KS; (2); Church Yth Grp; 4-H; Speech Tm; SADD; Band; Chorus; Church Choir; Pep Band; Sec Treas Soph Cls; 4-H Awd; Kays & Kayettes.

PALMER, SECALEY; Golden Plains Middle HS; Rexford, KS; (2); Church Yth Grp; Band; Chorus; VP Frsh Cls; VP Soph Cls; JV Var Bsktbl; Var Chrldng; Var Trk; JV Vllybl; Hon Roll; ST Music 1 Rating In Choir; Marine Bio.

PALMER, TARIN J; Lucus-Luray HS; Luray, KS; (2); Church Yth Grp; Cmnty Wkr; SADD; Var L Bsktbl; Var L Ftbl; Var L Trk; Hon Roll.

PALMER, TERROL; Lucus-Luray HS; Lucas, KS; (3); 2/9; Am Leg Boys St; Quiz Bowl; VP SADD; Pres Soph Cls; Rep Jr Cls; Var Bsktbl; Var Ftbl; Var Golf; High Hon Roll; Hon Roll; KS U; Engrng.

PALMER, TRAVIS; Maize HS; Maize, KS; (2); Teachers Aide; Var Bsbl; Bsktbl; Var JV Ftbl; Var Wt Lftg; Hon Roll; Lettered In Ftbl; Var Bsbl 3rd Pl In St Trnmt; Helped With Cls Float; Ath Player; Coach; Tchr.

PANKRATZ, ADAM T; Lyndon HS; Scranton, KS; (2); FBLA; Scholastic Bowl; Rep Soph Cls; Pres Jr Cls; High Hon Roll; NHS; HS Site Cncl; Ldrshp Osage Cnty; Lit Clb; U Of KS; Med.

PANKRATZ, JASON C; Madison Jr Sr HS; Madison, KS; (3); Boy Scts; Church Yth Grp; FBLA; Letterman Clb; Capt Quiz Bowl; Band; Mrchg Band; Pep Band; Var Bsktbl; Var Capt Ftbl.

PANNING, AMANDA L; Ellinwood Jr Sr HS; Ellinwood, KS; (2); 2/45; Church Yth Grp; Quiz Bowl; Spanish Clb; Band; Sec Soph Cls; VP Jr Cls; Var Crs Cntry; Var Trk; High Hon Roll; NHS.

PANTAZIS, ALETHIA H; Blue Valley North HS; Leawood, KS; (2); Church Yth Grp; JV Bsktbl; Hon Roll; Violin; CPR Certfd; Lifeguard; Medicine.

PANTER, CINDY; Derby HS; Derby, KS; (3); Church Yth Grp; Acpl Chr; Chorus; School Play; Variety Show; Chrldng; Vllybl; Wt Lftg; Hon Roll; Sign Lang Clb Frosh Yr; PT Obsrvtn Hrs; Butler Cty CC; OT.

PANZER, JARROD; Lewis Schl; Lewis, KS; (3); 2/18; Church Yth Grp; FBLA; HOBY; Quiz Bowl; JV Bsktbl; Var Ftbl; Wt Lftg; Hon Roll; NHS; Ntl Merit Schol.

PAPE, MELISSA D; Washington HS; Washington, KS; (4); 2/30; Am Leg Aux Girls St; French Clb; FHA; Band; Var L Bsktbl; Var L Chrldng; Var L Trk; Var L Vllybl; High Hon Roll; NHS; DARE Role Mdl; Homcmng Royalty; KS ST U; Acctng.

PAPES, LATRICIA; Marysville HS; Marysville, KS; (4); 4/83; Am Leg Aux Girls St; Teachers Aide; Band; Mrchg Band; School Musical; Treas Jr Cls; Bsktbl; Var Trk; Var Vllybl; Hon Roll; Tap, Jzz, Ballt Dnc; Sftbll City Rec; UKS; Bus.

PAPISH, ADAM; Frontenac Jr Sr HS; Frontenac, KS; (4); 1/35; Rep Am Leg Boys St; Church Yth Grp; Spanish Clb; Var L Ftbl; Var L Golf; High Hon Roll; Sec NHS; Ntl Merit Schol; St Schlr; Cmmrcl Art.

PAPSDORF, DANIEL A; Berean Acad; Wichita, KS; (3); Church Yth Grp; Speech Tm; VP Jr Cls; Var L Socr; Var L Trk; Hon Roll; Ntl Merit Ltr.

PARACHINI, FLORA L; Morland Jr Sr HS; Morland, KS; (1); 3/10; Cmnty Wkr; Drama Clb; Yrbk; VP Frsh Cls; JV Bsktbl; JV Vllybl; Var Wt Lftg; High Hon Roll; Hon Roll; Ft Hays; Interior Decrtr.

PARADIES, KARRIE; Royal Valley HS; Mayetta, KS; (4); 7/56; FHA; SADD; Teachers Aide; Yrbk; Hon Roll; KS Assn Of Yth.

PARADISE, BRIANNE R; Olathe East Sr HS; Olathe, KS; (2); Cmnty Wkr; Latin Clb; Math Clb; School Play; Nwsp; High Hon Roll; Prfct Atten Awd; Swimming; Dr.

PARCELLS, SHAWN L; Topeka West HS; Topeka, KS; (2); Boy Scts; Church Yth Grp; FCA; German Clb; Hosp Aide; Pep Clb; ROTC; Chorus; Church Choir; Variety Show; Hospital Vol; UMKC; Pathologist.

PARDEE, AMBER R; Washburn Rural HS; Topeka, KS; (2); 31/430; Church Yth Grp; Cmnty Wkr; FCA; French Clb; SADD; Church Choir; Golf; Swmmng; High Hon Roll.

PARDO, AMY; Satanta Jr Sr HS; Satanta, KS; (3); 1/23; Bus Profs of Am; FCA; HOBY; Key Clb; Letterman Clb; Pres Frsh Cls; Treas Soph Cls; Rep Stu Cncl; Var L Bsktbl; Var L Vllybl; KSU.

PARIKH, BIJAL; Wichita East HS; Wichita, KS; (3); Spanish Clb; SADD; Teachers Aide; JV Tennis; High Hon Roll; Spanish NHS; Literary Soc; Bus.

PARILLO, DONATA T; Manhattan HS; Manhattan, KS; (4); 22/386; Church Yth Grp; Cmnty Wkr; French Clb; SADD; Powder Puff Ftbl; JV Sftbl; JV Trk; Kiwanis Awd; NHS; St Schlr; Manhattan Optimist Lasers; U Of KS Crowell Bk Awd; St Of KS Schlsp Tests Placed 14 Times; U Of Notre Dame; Sci; Engrng.

PARISH, GRAHAM R; Sumner Acad Of Arts & Science; Kansas City, KS; (1); Church Yth Grp; Band; Mrchg Band; Pep Band; Rep Soph Cls; Var Bsbl; JV Bsktbl; Var Crs Cntry; Hon Roll; Jr NHS; AAU Silver Medal; Natl Bsbl Trnmnt; All Trnmnt Team Pitcher; All KS Cross Cntry Frosh; PE.

PARKER, AMANDA; Eudora HS; Eudora, KS; (1); Art Clb; FBLA; Pep Clb; Drill Tm; Ofcr Frsh Cls; Chrldng; Mgr(s); Pom Pon; Sftbl; Cit Awd; Chrldng; Envrnmntl Clb; Boston Coll; Med.

PARKER, ANGIE; Buhler HS; Hutchinson, KS; (3); Sec Church Yth Grp; FCA; Sec Treas 4-H; FHA; Q&S; Church Choir; Mgr Nwsp; Treas Frsh Cls; Hon Roll; NHS; Pratt Acad Olympics; Kayettes; Ottawa Univ; CPA.

PARKER, BRAD; Olathe North Sr HS; Olathe, KS; (2); Ftbl; Trk; Wt Lftg; Hon Roll; KU; Surgeon.

PARKER, BRANDON J; Humboldt HS; Iola, KS; (2); Church Yth Grp; Quiz Bowl; Thesps; Band; Chorus; Mrchg Band; Pep Band; School Play; Swing Chorus; Hon Roll; Evangel Coll; Cmptr Prgmng.

PARKER, BRANDY B; Sumner Acad Of Arts & Science; Kansas City, KS; (4); 40/195; Debate Tm; NFL; Q&S; Ed Yrbk; Rep Jr Cls; JV L Bsktbl; JV Var Trk; NHS; Spanish NHS; French Clb; Frnscs; Tutor; U Of KS; Jrnlsm/Intl Rltns.

PARKER, JENNIFER; Ulysses HS; Ulysses, KS; (1); Church Yth Grp; Band; Chorus; Mrchg Band; School Musical; Chrldng.

PARKER, JESSICA M; Olathe East Sr HS; Olathe, KS; (2); Church Yth Grp; Cmnty Wkr; Spanish Clb; Teachers Aide; Chorus; School Musical; Rptr Yrbk; JV Sftbl; Var Tennis; Hon Roll; Bus.

PARKER, JOHN M; Buhler HS; Hutchinson, KS; (2); Church Yth Grp; FCA; French Clb; Band; Jazz Band; Mrchg Band; Pep Band; High Hon Roll; Intern For Yth Pastor; Wichita ST U; Musician.

PARKER, JOSHUA D; Wyandotte HS; Kansas City, KS; (1); Boy Scts; Church Yth Grp; Chorus; JV Bsbl; Bwlng; KU.

PARKER III, PUAL W; Leavenworth HS; Leavenworth, KS; (3); Var L Ftbl; Var Wt Lftg; High Hon Roll; Hon Roll.

PARKER, TONY; Goodland HS; Goodland, KS; (3); 10/97; Church Yth Grp; Letterman Clb; Band; Chorus; Jazz Band; Mrchg Band; Pep Band; Tennis; High Hon Roll; NHS.

PARKES, SAMANTHA D; Shawnee Mission N HS; Overland Park, KS; (3); Church Yth Grp; Thesps; Chorus; Mrchg Band; Orch; School Musical; Stage Crew; High Hon Roll; NHS; Graceland Col; Soc Svcs.

PARKIN, CHRISTOPHER J; Williamsburg Schl; Williamsburg, KS; (2); Band; Mrchg Band; Stage Crew; L Bsktbl; Var L Ftbl; Var L Trk; Phys Thrpy.

PARKS, ASHLEY; Emporia HS; Emporia, KS; (4); 60/300; Am Leg Aux Girls St; Art Clb; Cmnty Wkr; French Clb; Pep Clb; Q&S; Teachers Aide; Nwsp; Var Capt Tennis; High Hon Roll; Pride Ambssdr & Chprsn; Emporia ST U; Elem Ed.

PARKS, CANDY; El Dorado HS; El Dorado, KS; (3); Cmnty Wkr; SADD; Teachers Aide; Varsity Clb; Var Bsktbl; Powder Puff Ftbl; Var Trk; Var Vllybl; Wt Lftg; Pres Acad Fit Awd; Bus Mgmt; Coach.

PARKS, CASEY D; Council Grove HS; Council Grove, KS; (2); Rep Church Yth Grp; Cmnty Wkr; FCA; Letterman Clb; Quiz Bowl; Red Cross Aide; Pres SADD; School Play; VP Pres Stu Cncl; Bsktbl; KS St Univ.

PARKS, HEATHER; Lawrence HS; Lawrence, KS; (4); 521/600; Bus Profs of Am; Office Aide; Pep Clb; SADD; Band; Chorus; Color Guard; Mrchg Band; School Musical; Ntl Merit Ltr; Wichita KS Law Appl BPA 1st Pl 96; BPA Natls Phoenix AZ 96; BPA ST Bus Law 2nd Pl; KS Univ; Soc Work/Law.

PARKS, JENNIFER E; Hoisington HS; Hoisington, KS; (4); Model UN; Pep Clb; SADD; Band; Stu Naturalist Clb; Bethany Coll; Soc Work.

PARKS, JORY D; Wallace Cty HS; Sharon Springs, KS; (2); Sec 4-H; Pep Clb; SADD; Drm Mjr(t); Mrchg Band; Bsktbl; Ftbl; Trk; 4-H Awd; Hon Roll; Amer Legion Bsbl; KS ST Univ; Elec Engrng.

PARKS, MICHAEL; Newton Sr HS; Newton, KS; (3); Am Leg Boys St; Math Clb; SADD; Rep Frsh Cls; JV Bsbl; Var L Ftbl; Var L Tennis; Hon Roll; Sprtsmnshp Boys Bsbl ST Trny A 95; GMI; Intl Bus.

PARMAN, STACI; Seaman Sr HS; Topeka, KS; (4); 4/248; Model UN; Scholastic Bowl; Spanish Clb; SADD; Ed Lit Mag; Hon Roll; NHS; Ntl Merit Ltr; KS Hnrs Schlr; Crtv Wrtng.

PARMENTER, JENNY B; Goddard HS; Goddard, KS; (2); Church Yth Grp; SADD; High Hon Roll; NHS; Tutored Spcl Needs Children.

PARR JR, STEPHEN E; Washburn Rural HS; Topeka, KS; (3); Varsity Clb; Chorus; Church Choir; JV Bsktbl; Var Ftbl; JV Trk; Var Wt Lftg; High Hon Roll; Jr NHS; Prfct Atten Awd.

PARRA, BENJAMIN M; Shawnee Mission N HS; Overland Park, KS; (4); Drama Clb; Pep Clb; Thesps; Band; Mrchg Band; Orch; Pep Band; School Musical; School Play; Stage Crew; Japanese.

PARRISH, JENNIFER L; Northeast HS; Arma, KS; (2); FHA; Band; Mrchg Band; Pep Band; Yrbk; JV Bsktbl; Var L Chrldng; Var L Sftbl; Hon Roll; MO Southern CC; Medcl Fld.

PARRISH, REAGAN; Hutchinson HS; Hutchinson, KS; (4); 54/266; Am Leg Aux Girls St; Pres Pep Clb; Red Cross Aide; Varsity Clb; Ofcr Stu Cncl; Capt Chrldng; Capt Powder Puff Ftbl; Var Tennis; High Hon Roll; NHS; HutchinsonCC; Nrs.

PARROTT, JESSICA L; Buhler HS; Hutchinson, KS; (2); Art Clb; Church Yth Grp; FCA; Letterman Clb; Math Clb; Science Clb; Teachers Aide; Band; Chorus; Church Choir; Tchr Choice Awds; Tlnt Shws; Messiah Coll; Med.

PARRY, MEGAN L; Circle HS; Augusta, KS; (3); FCA; French Clb; Hosp Aide; Letterman Clb; NFL; Teachers Aide; Ofcr Frsh Cls; Ofcr Stu Cncl; Sftbl; Vllybl; Butler Co CC; Teaching.

PARSON, DENISE; Oxford HS; Oxford, KS; (4); 9/21; Church Yth Grp; Drama Clb; FCA; Scholastic Bowl; Spanish Clb; Varsity Clb; School Play; Stage Crew; Trk; Sec NHS; KS ST U; Mech Engrng.

PARSONS, ANDREA R; Southeast HS; Pittsburg, KS; (3); Debate Tm; Service Clb; Nwsp; Chrldng; Mgr(s); Score Keeper; Pittsbrgh St Univ.

PARSONS, BECKY A; Russell HS; Russell, KS; (1); Church Yth Grp; Debate Tm; Key Clb; NFL; Band; Chorus; Mrchg Band; School Musical; JV Var Trk; Hon Roll; Trvl Prof/Acctng.

PARSONS, BROOKE; Abilene HS; Enterprise, KS; (3); FBLA; HOBY; Spanish Clb; VP Frsh Cls; Pres Jr Cls; Hon Roll; NCKL Art Awd.

PARSONS, DANA; Kingman HS; Spivey, KS; (2); Church Yth Grp; FBLA; Spanish Clb; SADD; Yrbk; Treas Stu Cncl; Var Bsktbl; Swmmng; Var Vllybl; NHS; Sprts Med.

PARSONS, TOM D; Quivira Heights HS; Holyrood, KS; (3); 7/22; FCA; Key Clb; NFL; Pep Clb; Varsity Clb; Chorus; Rep Frsh Cls; Rep Soph Cls; Rep Jr Cls; Rep Stu Cncl; Sci; Biologist; Math.

PARTRIDGE, STEFANIE; Wamego HS; Wamego, KS; (4); 3/83; NFL; Speech Tm; School Play; High Hon Roll; Drama Clb; FCA; FHA; Letterman Clb; Science Clb; SADD; KS Hnr Schol; Forensics Natl Qulfr; Wamegs Optimist Essy Wnnr; KS St Univ.

PARVIN, SUSAN E; Shawnee Mission W Sr HS; Overland Park, KS; (3); Pres Intnl Clb; Var L Sftbl; Hon Roll; Acad Ltr; Cmptrs/Bus.

PASEK, APRIL L; Russell HS; Russell, KS; (3); Church Yth Grp; FCA; Pep Clb; SADD; Acpl Chr; Chorus; JV Chrldng; JV Sftbl; High Hon Roll; Primary Ed.

PASEK, CHRISTINA N; Parsons HS; Parsons, KS; (1); 5/148; FBLA; Key Clb; Spanish Clb; Chorus; School Play; Rep Stu Cncl; Var Chrldng; Hon Roll; Pre Med Clb; Extended Lrng Pgm; Sprts Clb.

PASEK, MICHELE; Russel HS; Russell, KS; (4); 23/65; Girl Scts; Chorus; Drill Tm; School Musical; Variety Show; Bsktbl; Winter Sports Qn 96; North Cntrl KS Area Voc Tech.

PASMAN, KATHERINE; Oxford HS; Oxford, KS; (3); 1/28; Drama Clb; HOBY; Scholastic Bowl; Speech Tm; School Play; Ed Nwsp; Phtg Rptr Yrbk; Pres Frsh Cls; Pres Soph Cls; Rep Sr Cls; Phys Thrpy.

PASTOR, AARON; Blue Valley HS; Stilwell, KS; (3); 74/282; Teachers Aide; JV Bsbl; JV Var Ftbl; JV Var Wrstlng; High Hon Roll; Hon Roll; Chrch Charity Wk; Spec Olympcs; Lawn Maintenance Bus Co-Ownr; Med.

PATE, ELISHA; White Rock HS; Esbon, KS; (4); 4/17; Am Leg Aux Girls St; Drama Clb; Letterman Clb; Pep Clb; Quiz Bowl; SADD; Chorus; Yrbk; Treas School Play; JV Bsktbl; NCK Vo-Tech; Clnry Arts.

PATEL, ARCHITA V; Independence HS; Independence, KS; (1); 4-H; French Clb; Pep Clb; Chorus; Orch; Rep Frsh Cls; Ofcr Stu Cncl; Intrml Powder Puff Ftbl; JV Tennis; Hon Roll; Indian Flk Dncng Comp; KU; Bio/Bus.

PATEL, KAVITA N; Independence HS; Independence, KS; (3); 11/270; Pep Clb; Rep Stu Cncl; Bsktbl; Powder Puff Ftbl; Trk; Vllybl; High Hon Roll; NHS; Pres Acad Fit Awd; U Of KS.

PATEL, NISHA; Northeast Magnet HS; Wichita, KS; (4); 11/69; Cmnty Wkr; Office Aide; Ed Yrbk; Sec Jr Cls; VP Sr Cls; Rep Stu Cncl; Hon Roll; Jr NHS; NHS; Prfct Atten Awd; Yth Cncl; Prom Comm; Wichita ST Univ; Pharm.

PATEL, RAKHI; El Dorado HS; El Dorado, KS; (2); 1/200; Cmnty Wkr; Debate Tm; Letterman Clb; Math Clb; NFL; Quiz Bowl; Scholastic Bowl; Spanish Clb; Teachers Aide; Varsity Clb; LIFE; Yth Ldrshp Butler; DARE Role Mdl; El Dorado C Of C Jr Ambssdr Chrmn; Tutor; Kats 4 Kids; Law.

PATEL, ROSHNI I; El Dorado HS; El Dorado, KS; (3); #1 in class; Cmnty Wkr; Math Clb; Quiz Bowl; Spanish Clb; SADD; Varsity Clb; Orch; Ed Nwsp; Tennis; High Hon Roll; Jr Ambssdr Sec; KU; Phy Thrpy.

PATEL, SEJAL R; Southeast HS; Wichita, KS; (3); Church Yth Grp; Cmnty Wkr; Girl Scts; Key Clb; Library Aide; Office Aide; Q&S; Scholastic Bowl; Spanish Clb; Yrbk; Indian Clscl Dance; Vol Aviation Mus; Girl Scouts Gold Awd; U Of San Diego; Pharm/Med Field.

PATES, VALERIE E; Salina HS South; Salina, KS; (2); Artist.

PATRICK, CURTIS W; Smoky Valley HS; Lindsborg, KS; (2); Church Yth Grp; Cmnty Wkr; Letterman Clb; Pep Clb; Varsity Clb; Band; Mrchg Band; Pep Band; Ftbl; Wt Lftg; Mechs.

PATRICK, GREGORY J; Smoky Valley HS; Lindsborg, KS; (1); Church Yth Grp; Cmnty Wkr; Pep Clb; Band; Mrchg Band; Pep Band; Cit Awd; Mechncs.

PATRICK, HEATHER L; Blue Valley Northwest HS; West Palm Bch, FL; (2); Church Yth Grp; English Clb; SADD; Teachers Aide; School Musical; Stage Crew; Swmmng; Hon Roll; Scuba Diving SSCI Scuba License; CPR/LIFE Guard Trng Classes.

PATRICK, KENDRA R; Wyandotte HS; Kansas City, KS; (2); Church Yth Grp; Girl Scts; Band; Church Choir; Mrchg Band; Intrml JV Bsktbl; Hon Roll; 6 Yrs Piano; Rest Mgmt.

PATTERSON, CASSIE; Circle HS; Towanda, KS; (4); 7/90; FCA; Acpl Chr; Mgr Yrbk; Capt Bsktbl; Var Swmmng; Capt Tennis; All Trny Team Lady T Bird Cls Bsktbl; All Ark Vly League Swmng; KS Hnr Schlr.

PATTERSON, CLAYTON S; Chanute Sr HS; Chanute, KS; (3); 1/150; Am Leg Boys St; FBLA; Math Tm; Spanish Clb; SADD; Band; Chorus; Mrchg Band; Pep Band; 4-H Awd; Psych.

PATTERSON, JANEA; St Mary's Colgan HS; Pittsburg, KS; (4); 5/25; Girl Scts; VP NFL; Treas Pep Clb; Q&S; Quiz Bowl; Scholastic Bowl; Ed Yrbk; Treas Frsh Cls; Rep Soph Cls; VP Jr Cls; Univ Of KS; His.

PATTERSON, JEFFREY S; Campus HS; Wichita, KS; (2); Intrml Crs Cntry; Intrml Trk; Elec Eng.

PATTERSON, JENNIFER D; Nickerson HS; South Hutchinson, KS; (4); 10/100; Nwsp; Ed Yrbk; Pres Jr Cls; Pres Sr Cls; Rep Stu Cncl; Var L Bsktbl; Capt Sftbl; Var L Vllybl; NHS; St Schlr; Ran & Lettered Crss Cntry & Trk; Baker U; Mass Commnctn.

PATTERSON, KELSEY; Chaparral HS; Anthony, KS; (2); Debate Tm; FCA; Key Clb; NFL; Chorus; School Play; Rptr Nwsp; Var Chrldng; Church Yth Grp; Pep Clb; Debate Spkr Yr 95; 10 Yr Dnce Stu.

PATTERSON, LATRINA N; Topeka HS; Topeka, KS; (3); Hon Roll; Acad Ltr; Black Stu Union As A Frosh; FL A&M Univ; Bus Admin.

PATTERSON, LISA; Olathe North Sr HS; Olathe, KS; (2); Band; Jazz Band; Pres Stu Cncl; Chrldng; Gym; Sftbl; High Hon Roll; Prfct Atten Awd; Pres Acad Fit Awd.

PATTERSON, MEGAN; Maize HS; Wichita, KS; (3); 52/242; Am Leg Aux Girls St; Church Yth Grp; Science Clb; Spanish Clb; SADD; Acpl Chr; Chorus; Church Choir; Variety Show; Hon Roll; Occptnl Therapy.

PATTERSON, SARA; Olathe North Sr HS; Olathe, KS; (4); 32/351; Hosp Aide; Red Cross Aide; Band; Jazz Band; Pres Stu Cncl; Chrldng; Gym; Hon Roll; NHS; Pres Acad Fit Awd; KS Hnr Schlr; Homcmng Qn; KS ST Univ; Nrsng.

PATTERSON, VALERIE J; Blue Valley HS; Leawood, KS; (2); Church Yth Grp; Cmnty Wkr; JV Sftbl; JV Vllybl; Hon Roll; Young Life; Arch; Criminal Psycht.

PATTON, BRAD S; Buhler HS; Hutchinson, KS; (2); German Clb; SADD; Chorus; Ftbl; Wt Lftg; Hon Roll; U Of KS; Insrnce Sales.

PATTON, GRACE; Peabody-Burns Jr Sr HS; Peabody, KS; (4); 1/29; Church Yth Grp; FCA; 4-H; FHA; Math Tm; Band; Jazz Band; Mrchg Band; Pep Band; School Musical; U Of KS; Math Ed.

PATTON, JARED M; Chapman HS; Abilene, KS; (4); 10/116; Quiz Bowl; Speech Tm; Band; Chorus; Jazz Band; Mrchg Band; Pep Band; School Musical; School Play; High Hon Roll; KS St Univ; Biochem.

PATTON, JAY M; Maize HS; Wichita, KS; (3); Boy Scts; Church Yth Grp; SADD; Teachers Aide; Trk; Hon Roll; Eagle Sct; KS Newman Coll; Ath Trainer.

PATTON, MELISSA S; Anderson Cty Jr Sr HS; Garnett, KS; (1); Art Clb; Dance Clb; Natl FFA Org; Band; Jazz Band; Mrchg Band; Pep Band; Hon Roll; Garnett Saddle Clb; MCKWHA Horse Assn; Rodeo; Star Greenhand Awd; Rptr Greenhand Ofcr; Toe Ballet; Chrch; K ST; Ag.

PATTY, JASON S; El Dorado HS; El Dorado, KS; (4); Letterman Clb; Spanish Clb; SADD; Teachers Aide; Variety Show; Ed Yrbk; Var Bsbl; JV Wrstlng; Hon Roll; Kay Clb; Hnrbl Mntn Shrtstp All AR Vlly Bsbll.

PAUGH, LUTE T; Circle HS; Towanda, KS; (3); JV Var Bsbl; Var Ftbl; Intrml Wt Lftg; Capt Wrstlng; Hon Roll; Butler Cnty CC; Ath/Plt/Scb Dv.

PAUGH, ROBERT R; Olathe North Sr HS; Olathe, KS; (2); Cmnty Wkr; Hon Roll.

PAUL, VINCENT J; Wichita Southeast HS; Wichita, KS; (3); 59/378; Am Leg Boys St; Church Yth Grp; Cmnty Wkr; FCA; Hosp Aide; Letterman Clb; Office Aide; Spanish Clb; Teachers Aide; Rptr Nwsp; Boys ST; SE Ambsdr; KS Univ; Pre Med/Pre Law.

PAULIN, ALLISON A; Derby HS; Derby, KS; (3); French Clb; Girl Scts; SADD; Chorus; Church Choir; Variety Show; High Hon Roll; Piano; Rainbows United Vol; KS ST Univ; Psych.

PAULS, AARON; Inman Jr Sr HS; Inman, KS; (4); 7/32; Band; Mrchg Band; Pep Band; Stage Crew; Trk; High Hon Roll; Cmptr Sci.

PAULS, ANDY; Inman Jr Sr HS; Inman, KS; (2); Church Yth Grp; German Clb; Math Tm; Pep Clb; Band; Mrchg Band; Orch; Pep Band; JV Bsktbl; JV Trk.

PAULY, BRANDON J; Conway Springs HS; Conway Springs, KS; (2); Church Yth Grp; Pres Frsh Cls; Pres Jr Cls; Var Bsktbl; Var Ftbl; Hon Roll; NHS; Pres Acad Fit Awd; KS ST; Animal Sci.

PAULY, ETHAN L; Garden Plain Jr Sr HS; Viola, KS; (2); 4/34; Quiz Bowl; Spanish Clb; SADD; Rptr Nwsp; Phtg Yrbk; Pres Frsh Cls; Treas Soph Cls; L Bsktbl; L Ftbl; L Trk; St Johns CYO; Red Crs; Engrng.

PAULY, GERALD W; Midway Schl; Denton, KS; (2); 1/18; Church Yth Grp; Cmnty Wkr; Quiz Bowl; Band; Mrchg Band; Pep Band; School Play; Stage Crew; Pres Frsh Cls; VP Rep Soph Cls; Med.

PAULY, LETISHA R; Cheney Jr Sr HS; Cheney, KS; (3); 18/42; Church Yth Grp; Chorus; Church Choir; Variety Show; Treas Jr Cls; Bsktbl; Vllybl; Hon Roll; NHS; Prfct Atten Awd; KS Univ; Pre-Med.

PAVKOV, AARON S; Southeast Saline Schl; Assaria, KS; (2); 1/63; Church Yth Grp; Quiz Bowl; Acpl Chr; Band; Church Choir; School Musical; Var L Crs Cntry; Var L Trk; High Hon Roll; NHS; 4th/5th Pl Math Tsts Taken By ST Top HS Indvdls; Crss Cntry Tm 2nd Pl ST Chmpnshps.

PAVLIK, BENJAMIN T; Shawnee Mission W Sr HS; Lenexa, KS; (2); 40/414; Cmnty Wkr; Sec Frsh Cls; Sec Treas Soph Cls; Ofcr Stu Cncl; Bsktbl; Crs Cntry; Golf; Trk; Hon Roll; Pres Acad Fit Awd; Acad Lttr Awd; Stdnt Cncl Exec Bd; Ctlln.

PAWLOSKI, CHRISTINE; Hillsboro HS; Hillsboro, KS; (4); Am Leg Aux Girls St; Church Yth Grp; Cmnty Wkr; Band; Chorus; Drill Tm; Pep Band; Capt Chrldng; High Hon Roll; NHS; KU Hnr Roll; Acad Ltr Wnnr; Kayettes; Butler CC; Accntng.

PAWLOSKI, GREGORY J; Kapaun-Mt Carmel HS; Derby, KS; (4); 14/164; High Hon Roll; Pres Schlr; St Schlr; Advance Placement Prgm; Emory Linquest Hnrs Prgm WSU Schlsp; Josephine Stabler Schlsp WSU; Wichita ST Univ; Cmptr Sci.

PAXSON, ASHLEY; Columbus HS; Columbus, KS; (4); 11/92; FHA; Nwsp; Sec Jr Cls; Var Golf; Mgr Wrstlng; High Hon Roll; Rptr NHS; Math Tm; Spanish Clb; School Musical; Chntlrs Vcl Perf Group; KS Assn Yth Club Wrld Ntn Offcs; Tri-M Msc Hnr Soc VP; U Of KS; Psych.

PAYEUR, CRYSTAL R; Clifton-Clyde HS; Clyde, KS; (3); 4-H; FBLA; Natl FFA Org; NFL; Yrbk; 4-H Awd; Hon Roll; Train Horses; Photo; Geology; Painting; Geology; Equine Mgmt.

PAYEUR, LAURIE; Topeka HS; Topeka, KS; (4); 1/339; Pres German Clb; HOBY; Pres Model UN; Mrchg Band; Orch; School Musical; NHS; Pep Clb; Thesps; Band; KS Hnr Soc; Twr Awd; KMEA St Bnd; Washburn U; Math.

PAYNE, AMANDA D; Labette Co HS; Oswego, KS; (3); FHA; SADD; Cit Awd; Hon Roll; NHS; RT.

PAYNE, ANDY E; Washburn Rural HS; Topeka, KS; (2); 99/400; Var Crs Cntry; Var Golf; Hon Roll; All-City & All-St Crss Cntry; Naval Acad.

PAYNE, CHRISTIE L; Ft Scott HS; Fort Scott, KS; (4); Church Yth Grp; FBLA; SADD; SADD; Teachers Aide; Chorus; Church Choir; Cit Awd; Hon Roll; Ft Scott CC; Ct Rprtng.

PAYNE, DANIEL J; Trinity Acad; Wichita, KS; (4); Church Yth Grp; Cmnty Wkr; Computer Clb; Math Tm; Pep Clb; Band; Pep Band; Ed Nwsp; Rep Jr Cls; Pres Stu Cncl; TX A&M Univ; Comp Eng.

PAYNE, DANIELLE R; Hays HS; Hays, KS; (1); Church Yth Grp; Pep Clb; Stat Bsktbl; JV Chrldng; Sftbl; Wt Lftg; Stat Wrstlng.

PAYNE, ERIC; Salina HS Central; Salina, KS; (3); 25/260; Am Leg Boys St; Church Yth Grp; JA; Letterman Clb; Teachers Aide; Pres Frsh Cls; Pres Soph Cls; Pres Jr Cls; Rep Sr Cls; Pres Stu Cncl; I Dare You Awd; Boys Watson Fnlst Nom; Jr Ldrshp Salina Pgm.

PAYNE, JEAN; Wyandotte HS; Kansas City, KS; (2); Church Yth Grp; Hosp Aide; Church Choir; Ofcr Stu Cncl; JV Chrldng; Var Crs Cntry; JV Trk; High Hon Roll; NHS; Prfct Atten Awd; KU Med; Surgeon.

PAYNE, JOHN DAVID; Ft Scott HS; Fort Scott, KS; (2); Church Yth Grp; FCA; FBLA; Chorus; Church Choir; Golf.

PAYNE, MATTHEW; Turner HS; Kansas City, KS; (3); Chess Clb; French Clb; Band; Mrchg Band; Pep Band; Var Bsbl; NHS; Scuba Diving.

PAYNE, STACEY; Spring Hill HS; Olathe, KS; (3); FHA; Pep Clb; JV Sftbl; JV Vllybl; Hon Roll; Jr NHS; Pres Acad Fit Awd; KU; Fshn Dsgn.

PAYNE, TAUSHA M; Wyandotte HS; Kansas City, KS; (3); Chrldng; High Hon Roll; Hon Roll; Grambling U; Lawyer; Pediatricia.

PEACOCK, ANDREA; Winfield HS; Winfield, KS; (4); Cmnty Wkr; Girl Scts; Acpl Chr; Chorus; School Musical; School Play; Stage Crew; Hon Roll; NHS; Vllybl; Abate; Cowley Cty CC; Phys Thpry.

PEAK, KEVIN; Atchison Sr HS; Atchison, KS; (2); Art Clb; Church Yth Grp; Computer Clb; Scholastic Bowl; Socr; Hon Roll; Comp Prgmr.

PEAK, KYLEE; Atchison Sr HS; Atchison, KS; (2); Church Yth Grp; Spanish Clb; Band; Chorus; Church Choir; Flag Corp; School Musical; Hon Roll; Kytts; Hnr Choir; Nrsng.

PEARCE, JONATHAN; Lawrence HS; Lawrence, KS; (3); Am Leg Boys St; Boy Scts; Church Yth Grp; Debate Tm; JA; NFL; Acpl Chr; Band; Chorus; Church Choir; Perfect Rating At ST Gilde Piano Cmptn; Ec.

PEARCE, MEGAN E; Ft Scott HS; Fort Scott, KS; (3); FCA; Key Clb; Yrbk; Var Tennis; Hon Roll.

PEARON, JANELLE; Valley Ctr HS; Valley Center, KS; (3); 51/162; Art Clb; French Clb; SADD; Drill Tm; School Musical; Rep Frsh Cls; Rep Soph Cls; Ofcr Stu Cncl; Mgr(s); Pom Pon; GCTL; Psych; Soc Work.

PEARSE, MICHELLE J; Eureka Jr Sr HS; Eureka, KS; (3); Spanish Clb; Speech Tm; Band; Chorus; Mrchg Band; Pep Band; School Musical; School Play; Hon Roll; Butler Cty CC; Bus; Comp.

PEARSON, AMY D; Beloit Jr Sr HS; Barnard, KS; (2); Cmnty Wkr; 4-H; Natl FFA Org; SADD; Varsity Clb; Chorus; Orch; Chrldng; 4-H Awd; Hon Roll.

PEARSON, MICHAEL S; Smoky Valley HS; Hutchinson, KS; (2); Cmnty Wkr; Letterman Clb; Pep Clb; Quiz Bowl; Scholastic Bowl; Stage Crew; JV Bsktbl; JV Trk; High Hon Roll; NHS; Var Sci/Math Comptns.

PECK, COREY; Olathe South Sr HS; Olathe, KS; (3); Drama Clb; FHA; Q&S; Science Clb; Ed Yrbk; Lit Mag; Rep Stu Cncl; High Hon Roll; NHS; Pres Acad Fit Awd; KS U; Photographer.

PECK, CRYSTAL L; Sedan HS; Peru, KS; (2); Sec Church Yth Grp; FCA; Rptr FHA; Sec Spanish Clb; Band; VP Chorus; Sec Frsh Cls; Mrchg Band; Pep Band; Variety Show; Stdnt Cncl Co-Chm; Church Praise/Worship Ldr; Lifeline; Wrtr.

PECK, DAVID S; Great Bend Sr HS; Great Bend, KS; (3); Church Yth Grp; FCA; Pep Clb; Spanish Clb; Acpl Chr; Chorus; School Musical; Variety Show; Rep Jr Cls; Ofcr Stu Cncl; KAYS Clb; Explr Scout; Madrgl Pops Sngrs; Prom Comm.

PECK, JUSTIN G; Dighton HS; Dighton, KS; (2); Church Yth Grp; FCA; Pep Clb; SADD; Band; Chorus; Jazz Band; Pep Band; School Musical; Bsktbl.

PECK, KIMBERLY L; Chanute Sr HS; Chanute, KS; (2); Church Yth Grp; FCA; Spanish Clb; Chorus; School Musical; Ofcr Stu Cncl; JV Sftbl; JV Vllybl; Hon Roll; Prncpls Ldrshp Tm; Emporia ST; Ed.

PECKHAM, AMBER M; Canton-Galva HS; Galva, KS; (2); Church Yth Grp; FBLA; Girl Scts; SADD; Chorus; Bsktbl; Vllybl; Wt Lftg; Hon Roll; Elem Ed.

PECKHAM, ANGELA; Seaman Sr HS; Topeka, KS; (4); 1/250; Cmnty Wkr; Pres Drama Clb; FBLA; Treas Pres Chorus; Jazz Band; School Musical; School Play; Jr NHS; NHS; Ntl Merit Ltr.

PECKMAN, ERICA L; Paola HS; Paola, KS; (4); Church Yth Grp; Drama Clb; Library Aide; Q&S; SADD; Teachers Aide; Acpl Chr; Chorus; School Play; Stage Crew; Close-Up Washington DC Pgm; Var Choir Sec; U Of KS; Engl.

PEED, BRANDY L; Turner HS; Kansas City, KS; (2); French Clb; SADD; Teachers Aide; Yrbk; Trk; Vllybl; Hon Roll; Jr NHS; Campfire Boys & Girls; Intnl Order Jobs Dghtrs; Bio.

PEEK, ZACH; Waverly HS; Williamsburg, KS; (4); 1/23; Am Leg Boys St; Pres Sr Cls; Capt Var Ftbl; Trk; Gov Hon Prg Awd; NHS; Prfct Atten Awd; Pres Acad Fit Awd; St Schlr; Val; Ottawa U; Bus.

PEER, CAMMIE M; Blue Valley HS; Overland Park, KS; (3); Church Yth Grp; Church Choir; High Hon Roll; Hon Roll; Prfct Atten Awd; Infnt/Chld/Adlts CNA.

PEER, MELISSA E; Wichita HS NW; Wichita, KS; (2); Church Yth Grp; Band; Mrchg Band; Orch; Pep Band; JV Sftbl; JV Vllybl; Hon Roll; Ch Nrsry Vol; Ch Orch; Advncd Wichita Wind Ensmbl; Wichitas Yth Symphny.

PEINE, JODY S; Central Heights Sr HS; Princeton, KS; (1); Sec 4-H; VP Natl FFA Org; Pep Clb; Service Clb; VP Frsh Cls; JV Bsktbl; Var L Crs Cntry; Var L Pom Pon; Var L Trk; High Hon Roll; KU U; Pdtrc Nrs.

PEINE, MARILYN A; Anderson Cty Jr Sr HS; Greeley, KS; (2); Sec 4-H; Intnl Clb; Sec Natl FFA Org; SADD; VP Soph Cls; 4-H Awd; High Hon Roll; Farmland Yth Ldrsp Conf; Acad Awd; KAY; KJLA; KS ST Univ; Bus.

PEINTNER, BEN P; Spearville Jr Sr HS; Spearville, KS; (2); Church Yth Grp; Letterman Clb; Pep Clb; Quiz Bowl; Scholastic Bowl; Sec Frsh Cls; Var L Bsktbl; Var L Ftbl; High Hon Roll; Prfct Atten Awd.

PEINTNER, KURT R; Spearville Jr Sr HS; Spearville, KS; (3); Letterman Clb; Pep Clb; Quiz Bowl; Band; Pep Band; Stage Crew; Bsktbl; Ftbl; Hon Roll; Hutchinson CC.

PEIRANO, CANDI L; Maize HS; Wichita, KS; (2); 25/350; Church Yth Grp; Letterman Clb; Pep Clb; SADD; Var L Bsktbl; Var L Trk; JV Vllybl; Wt Lftg; High Hon Roll; NHS; Kays Club; Med Prfsn.

PEIRCE, CLAYTON D; Haven HS; Hutchinson, KS; (4); 9/65; Church Yth Grp; FCA; Scholastic Bowl; SADD; Chorus; Rep Frsh Cls; JV Bsktbl; Var L Crs Cntry; Var Mgr(s); Var L Trk; Pomona.

PELCAK, BRIAN G; Junction City HS; Junction City, KS; (1); Drm Mjr(t); Mrchg Band; Pep Band; Rep Frsh Cls; Rep Stu Cncl; JV Socr; JV Tennis; High Hon Roll; Jr NHS; Pres Acad Fit Awd; NU; Engrng.

PELLEGRINI, ANDREA; Udall HS; Udall, KS; (1); Pres 4-H; Band; Mrchg Band; Pep Band; JV Bsktbl; JV Vllybl; 4-H Awd; High Hon Roll; Hon Roll; KS ST; Vet.

PELSMA, ANDREW; Lawrence HS; Lawrence, KS; (3); Am Leg Boys St; Boy Scts; Church Yth Grp; Cmnty Wkr; FCA; Letterman Clb; Varsity Clb; Var Capt Crs Cntry; Var Trk; Hon Roll.

PELTON, DANIEL; Holton HS; Holton, KS; (3); Letterman Clb; Natl FFA Org; Bsktbl; Var Crs Cntry; JV Ftbl; Var Trk.

PELTON, SHANNA L; Pawnee Heights East HS; Burdett, KS; (1); 1/15; Church Yth Grp; 4-H; FBLA; Pep Clb; Band; Chorus; Pep Band; School Musical; School Play; Pres Frsh Cls; Chrstn Trvlng Mime Team; Vol Hstrcl Site; KS ST Univ; Spec Ed Of Deaf.

PELTZER, MICHELLE N; Atchison Co Cmty HS; Lancaster, KS; (3); 4/51; Letterman Clb; Math Clb; Mu Alpha Theta; Band; School Play; JV Bsktbl; Var Capt Vllybl; High Hon Roll; NHS; Prfct Atten Awd; Smmr Fstptch Sftbl.

PELZ, ERIN; Andale HS; Andale, KS; (3); Church Yth Grp; Girl Scts; Letterman Clb; Spanish Clb; SADD; Teachers Aide; Band; Drill Tm; VP Frsh Cls; Var Co-Capt Chrldng; Natl Food Chain Conf Panelist.

PENA, FRANCES; J C Harmon HS; Kansas City, KS; (2); Hon Roll; Lu Lac Clb; Mecha Clb; KS City CC.

PENA, MATT; Bishop Miege HS; Kansas City, MO; (1); Church Yth Grp; Cmnty Wkr; Computer Clb; Debate Tm; English Clb; JA; Spanish Clb; SADD; Band; Cit Awd; Painted Murals Around Comm; Awd From Mayor; KS Univ; Bus/Law/Fshn Dsgnr.

PENA, MONICA M; Salina HS South; Salina, KS; (3); 62/256; Library Aide; JV Mgr(s); Cit Awd; Hon Roll; Prfct Atten Awd; SAVE Clb; Music; Art; U Miami; Lawyer; Pre-Law.

PENCE, KATIE; Wichita Collegiate Schl; Wichita, KS; (4); Cmnty Wkr; Hosp Aide; Chorus; Lit Mag; Mgr(s); Var JV Sftbl; Var Trk; Var JV Vllybl; High Hon Roll; Hon Roll; KS ST; Bio Med Rsrch.

PENCE, MISTY D; Lawrence HS; Lawrence, KS; (3); Debate Tm; NFL; Chrldng; L Mgr Vllybl; Hon Roll; Elem Schl Tutor; U Of KS; Med/Ob-Gyn.

PENDARVIS, TIMOTHY; Junction City HS; Junction City, KS; (2); CAP; HOBY; ROTC; Pres Frsh Cls; Pres Soph Cls; Var L Ftbl; Wt Lftg; Cit Awd; NHS.

PENDERGRASS, JESSE; Buhler HS; Hutchinson, KS; (3); Am Leg Boys St; Cmnty Wkr; Computer Clb; Math Tm; Quiz Bowl; Science Clb; Spanish Clb; SADD; Chorus; School Musical; Pre-Med.

PENDLETON, BEVERLY S; Shawnee Mission E Sr HS; Prairie Village, KS; (2); SADD; Vllybl; Wt Lftg; Hon Roll; Play Sftbl; Vet; Archaeologist.

PENDLLETON, CRYSTAL D; Neodesha Jr Sr HS; Neodesha, KS; (2); Band; Mrchg Band; Pep Band; Hon Roll; FFA.

PENLEY, JONATHAN J; Southeast HS; Wichita, KS; (4); Art Clb; Band; Jazz Band; Mrchg Band; Pep Band; School Musical; Variety Show; Swmmng; High Hon Roll; Pres Schlr; Wichita ST Univ.

PENNER, CARRIE; Hillsboro HS; Hillsboro, KS; (4); 1/45; Church Yth Grp; Band; Chorus; Sec Jr Cls; Sec Sr Cls; JV Var Bsktbl; JV Trk; JV Var Vllybl; High Hon Roll; NHS; I Dare You Awd; Med.

PENNER, CHAD ALLEN; Labette Co HS; Edna, KS; (3); 54/140; Church Yth Grp; FCA; VICA; Acpl Chr; Band; Chorus; Church Choir; Jazz Band; Mrchg Band; Pep Band; KS St Lions Band; Mid Amer Nazarene Clg.

PENNER, ESTHER; Ingalls Jr Sr HS; Ingalls, KS; (2); Church Yth Grp; Dance Clb; Letterman Clb; Pep Clb; Red Cross Aide; Band; Chorus; Bsktbl; Vllybl; High Hon Roll.

PENNER, JESSICA D; Hillsboro HS; Hillsboro, KS; (3); 22/65; Am Leg Aux Girls St; Church Yth Grp; Chorus; School Musical; School Play; Swing Chorus; Phtg Nwsp; Phtg Yrbk; High Hon Roll; Hon Roll; William Jewellcol; Eng.

PENNER, MELVIN E; Topeka HS; Topeka, KS; (2); Hon Roll; Joe Kuberts Schl Of Cartooning.

PENNER, ROBYN P; Berean Acad; Whitewater, KS; (3); Church Yth Grp; Sec 4-H; Letterman Clb; Math Tm; Teachers Aide; Band; Pep Band; Stat Vllybl; High Hon Roll; Hon Roll; Med.

PENNINGTON, AARON; Turner HS; Kansas City, KS; (4); 50/190; Bus Profs of Am; DECA; Q&S; SADD; Varsity Clb; Ed Nwsp; Var Capt Bsbl; Hon Roll; Highland CC.

PENNINGTON, ERIN; Hesston HS; Hesston, KS; (2); Debate Tm; Chorus; High Hon Roll; Hon Roll; Dance Team Co-Capt; Lifeguard.

PENNINGTON, MARCY J; Meade HS; Meade, KS; (2); Church Yth Grp; Letterman Clb; Band; Chorus; Pep Band; Treas Soph Cls; Var L Bsktbl; Var L Tennis; High Hon Roll; Hon Roll; Kyts.

PENNINGTON, SARAH B; Turner HS; Kansas City, KS; (2); 4-H; FTA; German Clb; Quiz Bowl; SADD; Band; Mrchg Band; Pep Band; Nwsp; Jr NHS; U Of KS; Intnl Bus.

PENROD, CURTIS J; Garden City Sr HS; Garden City, KS; (2); Boy Scts; Chess Clb; Church Yth Grp; Debate Tm; Band; Mrchg Band; Pep Band; Crs Cntry; Tennis; Arch.

PENSICK, KELLI J; Hayden HS; Topeka, KS; (2); Intnl Clb; Pep Clb; Crs Cntry; Var Socr; Sftbl; High Hon Roll; NHS.

PENTLIN, THERESA M; Oskaloosa HS; Oskaloosa, KS; (3); 5/65; Sec 4-H; Letterman Clb; Pep Clb; Pres SADD; Teachers Aide; Band; Pep Band; Var Bsktbl; JV Sftbl; Var Vllybl; Tutoring; Colby CC; Pre-Vet Medicine.

PEOPLES, CHRISTOPHER S; Santa Fe Trail Jr HS; Olathe, KS; (1); Orch; High Hon Roll; Ntl Merit Ltr; Yth Symphny; Olathe Babe Ruth Bsbl; Bwlg League.

PEPPLE, WILLIAM D; Lawrence HS; Lawrence, KS; (4); Boy Scts; Drama Clb; Thesps; School Musical; School Play; Stage Crew; Lit Mag; Ofcr Stu Cncl; Ftbl; Trk; Sr Planning Comm; Co-Dir Sr Video; ST MO ST Univ; Mass Media.

PERCHELLET, STEPHEN J; Manhattan HS; Manhattan, KS; (3); Chess Clb; Var L Crs Cntry; Var L Trk; Var L Wrstlng; Hon Roll; NHS; 1st St & 10th Nation Concours Natl De Francais 3b; All-Amer Schlr; KS ST; Dr.

PERCIVAL, LESLEY; Grinnell HS; Grinnell, KS; (2); Church Yth Grp; Cmnty Wkr; Math Clb; Pep Clb; Science Clb; Chorus; Church Choir; Rptr Yrbk; Sec Soph Cls; Var Capt Bsktbl; Colby CC; Interior Dsgn.

PERCIVAL, MITCHELL R; Grinnell HS; Grinnell, KS; (4); 9/16; Church Yth Grp; Math Clb; Science Clb; Speech Tm; Ed Yrbk; Pres Stu Cncl; Var L Crs Cntry; Var Trk; Wt Lftg; Hon Roll; Anouncr Ftball Games; Sec Treas Ofcath Yth Org; Homcomng King 95; Colby CC; Radio Brdcsting.

PERCIVAL, TABITHA D; Wichita Heights HS; Wichita, KS; (4); Spanish Clb; SADD; Hon Roll; Wichita ST U; Lawyer.

PERDUE, ELLEN A; Topeka West HS; Topeka, KS; (2); French Clb; Band; Mrchg Band; Pep Band; High Hon Roll; Hon Roll; 11th In ST KS Natl Fr II Exam; Best Instrumental Music Stu Awd; Bio.

PERDUE, SARAH J; Midway Schl; Denton, KS; (3); 3/24; Church Yth Grp; Cmnty Wkr; Hosp Aide; Letterman Clb; Quiz Bowl; School Play; Ofcr Stu Cncl; Capt Chrldng; Mgr(s); High Hon Roll; Space Camp; Stephens Univ; Premed.

PEREDA, TIMOTHY M; Leavenworth HS; Andrews AFB, MD; (3); Church Yth Grp; Teachers Aide; JV Var Bsktbl; Hon Roll; Jr NHS.

PERESSIN, CHRISTIAN J; Wichita Southeast HS; Wichita, KS; (1); Socr; High Hon Roll; Var Soccer Goal Keeper; Southeast Ambassador.

PEREZ, CABRINA M; Garden City Sr HS; Garden City, KS; (3); FTA; Spanish Clb; Teachers Aide; Sftbl; Hon Roll; DARE Role Model; La Familia Clb.

PEREZ, CARISSA A; Salina HS South; Salina, KS; (2); Swmmng; Vol For Handicapped; Medicine; Anesthesiologist.

PEREZ, DANIELLE; Southeast Saline Schl; Gypsum, KS; (3); 16/56; Church Yth Grp; Pep Clb; Varsity Clb; Band; Chorus; Pep Band; School Musical; Chrldng; Sftbl; Hon Roll; Trumpet Church; Elem Ed Tchr.

PEREZ, TARYN R; Lakin HS; Lakin, KS; (2); Rptr Nwsp; Yrbk; Sec Soph Cls; JV Bsktbl; Var Trk; JV Vllybl; Hon Roll; NHS; Engrng.

PERI JR, CRAIG R; Dexter Jr Sr HS; Dexter, KS; (4); 3/12; Band; Pres Jr Cls; VP Sr Cls; Ofcr Bsbl; Capt Bsktbl; Capt Ftbl; Hon Roll; NHS; Pres Schlr; Cowley Cnty CC; Aeronautics.

PERICA, NICOLE; Bonner Springs HS; Bonner Springs, KS; (3); HOBY; Key Clb; Chorus; School Play; Stage Crew; Ofcr Stu Cncl; Var Chrldng; Tennis; Trk; Church Yth Grp; Acad Decathalon, Dance & Gymnastics; Sci Olympiad; Kayettes; Ecology Clb; KCU; Cnclng.

PERKINS, JENNY; Olathe East Sr HS; Olathe, KS; (3); Cmnty Wkr; Dance Clb; Drama Clb; Pres Math Clb; Spanish Clb; Chorus; Drill Tm; School Musical; School Play; Rep Jr Cls; Natl Yth Ldrshp Forum; Natl Hnr Soc; Law.

PERKINS, KELI; F L Schlagle HS; Kansas City, KS; (1); Drama Clb; Church Choir; Mgr(s); High Hon Roll; Joyce Todd Productions Musical & Drama Act.

PERKINS, KRISTIN E; Maize HS; Wichita, KS; (2); Church Yth Grp; FCA; German Clb; SADD; Teachers Aide; Church Choir; Intrml Tennis; Hon Roll; Acad Ltr; Piano; K ST; PT.

PERKINS, SCOTT R; Ft Scott Christian Heights; Fort Scott, KS; (2); Office Aide; Teachers Aide; Stage Crew.

PERLEBERG, ANA C; Wichita East HS; Wichita, KS; (1); Drama Clb; French Clb; Thesps; Chorus; Church Choir; School Musical; School Play; Variety Show; French Hon Soc; Hon Roll; 15 Eng Crdt Hrs Wichita ST U; Intl Bclrte Prgm; Guitar/Piano Plyr; St Johns Coll; Creative Wrtng.

PERLSTEIN, EMILY H; Blue Valley Northwest HS; Overland Park, KS; (2); Debate Tm; VP Temple Yth Grp; Rptr Nwsp; Hon Roll; Peer Facilitator; Crtv Wrtng.

PERLSTEIN, SARA; Blue Valley Northwest HS; Overland Park, KS; (4); 97/343; Q&S; VP Temple Yth Grp; Ed Nwsp; Rep Stu Cncl; Hon Roll; U Of MO; Jrnlsm.

PERNEY, GWENDOLYN K; Topeka HS; Topeka, KS; (3); French Clb; Model UN; Band; Drill Tm; Variety Show; Powder Puff Ftbl; Swmmng; Vllybl; Hon Roll; NHS; Topeka Yth Wind Ensemble.

PERRIER, MARK; Eureka Jr Sr HS; Eureka, KS; (2); Church Yth Grp; 4-H; Quiz Bowl; Science Clb; Spanish Clb; Band; Mrchg Band; Pep Band; JV Bsktbl; JV Ftbl.

PERRIER, MICHELE; Eureka Jr Sr HS; Eureka, KS; (4); 1/64; 4-H; FHA; Letterman Clb; Natl FFA Org; Nwsp; L Bsktbl; Var L Vllybl; Gov Hon Prg Awd; High Hon Roll; NHS; KS ST U; Bio.

PERRY, BARBARA; Columbus HS; Columbus, KS; (2); Sec Art Clb; Bus Profs of Am; Church Yth Grp; FCA; FHA; Intrml Bsktbl; Var Powder Puff Ftbl; Var Tennis; High Hon Roll; Hon Roll; Prlmntry Prcdr Tm; Bio.

PERRY, JESSICA; Lyons HS; Lyons, KS; (4); Am Leg Aux Girls St; Cmnty Wkr; Ofcr FHA; Office Aide; Pep Clb; Teachers Aide; Chorus; Yrbk; Treas Sr Cls; JV Var Chrldng; Peer Cnslng; Rice Cty Ldrshp; Hutchinson CC; Dntl Hygne.

PERRY, KAMBRIA D; Riley Cty HS; Manhattan, KS; (3); FCA; FBLA; Natl FFA Org; Pep Clb; Band; School Play; Sec Jr Cls; Rep Stu Cncl; NHS; Pres Acad Fit Awd; Mustang Collector; K ST; Acctng.

PERRY, LATASHA R; Washington HS; Kansas City, KS; (2); FCA; Hosp Aide; Pep Clb; Speech Tm; Teachers Aide; Band; Chorus; Mrchg Band; Pep Band; School Musical; Yth Advy Cncl Yth Opprtnts Unltd; Stu Ambssdr Prgm; Real Mag; Practcl Law; Clark; Bus.

PERRY, MANDI; Frankft HS; Frankfort, KS; (4); 8/29; Am Leg Aux Girls St; FHA; GAA; Girl Scts; Letterman Clb; SADD; Teachers Aide; Band; Chorus; Stage Crew; KS U; Med Tech.

PERRY, MATT D; Salina HS South; Salina, KS; (3); Church Yth Grp; FCA; Office Aide; Teachers Aide; Nwsp; Rep Stu Cncl; Var L Crs Cntry; Var L Trk; Hon Roll; Teen Too AMBUCS.

PERRY, PAIGE; Jackson Heights HS; Soldier, KS; (1); FHA; Pep Clb; Chorus; School Musical; Mgr(s); Trk; Vllybl; High Hon Roll; FHA ST Star Event; Track Ltr; Excl Hnr; KS Univ.

PERRY, SCOTT J; Basehor Linwood HS; Linwood, KS; (3); 1/100; FBLA; Math Clb; Scholastic Bowl; Hon Roll; NHS.

PERRY, SHAWN; St Marys HS; Saint Marys, KS; (2); FCA; Drill Tm; Treas Frsh Cls; Bsktbl; Vllybl; High Hon Roll; NHS.

PERRY, SUZANNE; St Mary's Colgan HS; Pittsburg, KS; (4); Pep Clb; Q&S; Ed Yrbk; Sec Stu Cncl; Capt Pom Pon; Vllybl; Hon Roll; Ftbl & Bsktbl Royalty Nom; Attnd Washington Jrnlsm Conf Nom 96; United Natl Ldrshp & Svc Awd Wnnr; Pittsburgh ST Univ; Tchr.

PERSHIN, NEKE N; Neodesha Jr Sr HS; Neodesha, KS; (1); Church Yth Grp; Cmnty Wkr; FTA; Hosp Aide; Pep Clb; Spanish Clb; Bsktbl; Trk; Vllybl; Wt Lftg; Tchr/Bus.

PERSSON, CASEY; Olathe North Sr HS; Olathe, KS; (3); Spanish Clb; Band; Jazz Band; Mrchg Band; Orch; Socr; Swmmng; Tennis; High Hon Roll; NHS; Comp Pgmng-Internet-Comp Assistance; Accepted To KMEA Dist Band; Ensemble To St Music Festival; Comp.

PERSSON, HOLLIE M; Santa Fe Trail Jr HS; Olathe, KS; (1); Church Yth Grp; Chorus; Drill Tm; Orch; High Hon Roll; Pres Schlr; Dance; UMKC; Music.

PESAVENTO, JOHNNA; St Mary's Colgan HS; Pittsburg, KS; (2); 1/41; NFL; Pep Clb; VP Soph Cls; Var L Chrldng; Var L Trk; JV Vllybl; Hon Roll; Bus/Law.

PESCHKA, DARRIN; Wilson Jr Sr HS; Wilson, KS; (4); 4/24; Church Yth Grp; Library Aide; Chorus; Church Choir; School Play; Ed Nwsp; Co-Ed Yrbk; Sec Stu Cncl; JV Bsktbl; Var Chrldng; St HS Jrnslm Awd; U Of KS; Comms.

PESCHKA, KIMBERLY A; Great Bend Sr HS; Great Bend, KS; (4); 2/217; Cmnty Wkr; Acpl Chr; Swing Chorus; Variety Show; Rep Jr Cls; Rep Sr Cls; Gov Hon Prg Awd; High Hon Roll; Sec NHS; Sal; KS Regents Honors Acad; KS Assn For Yth Area VI Pres; Univ Of KS Honor Schlr; KS ST U; Chem.

PESCHKA, RYAN J; Ellsworth HS; Ellsworth, KS; (2); 9/88; Church Yth Grp; Letterman Clb; Varsity Clb; Band; Pep Band; Rptr Phtg Nwsp; JV Bsktbl; JV Crs Cntry; JV Ftbl; Capt Var Golf; Qualified For ST Frosh-Soph Yr Golf; Bsktbl; KJGA; AJGA; JV Scoring; Mngmt.

PETERIE, JASON; El Dorado HS; El Dorado, KS; (2); 18/177; Church Yth Grp; FCA; Letterman Clb; Math Clb; SADD; Band; JV Ftbl; Var L Wrstlng; High Hon Roll; NHS; KAY; Erth Care Clb; KS ST; Genetic Engr.

PETERIE, MEGAN; Wichita Collegiate Schl; Wichita, KS; (2); Church Yth Grp; Cmnty Wkr; FCA; Var JV Bsktbl; Var L Crs Cntry; Trk; High Hon Roll; Natl Frnch Cont 4th Pl; Piano.

PETERMAN, KASIE D; Maize HS; Maize, KS; (2); 121/308; GAA; Vllybl; Cit Awd; Hon Roll; KS Univ; Pediatrics.

PETERS, ANGELA; Kapaun-Mt Carmel HS; Wichita, KS; (3); #3 in class; Church Yth Grp; Cmnty Wkr; Spanish Clb; Teachers Aide; Bsktbl; Sftbl; Tennis; Vllybl; High Hon Roll; NHS; United Crusaders Clb Treas; NHGA; First Tm All ST Class 5a Bsktbl.

PETERS, CHRISTINA; Larned HS; Larned, KS; (4); 2/90; Church Yth Grp; Intnl Clb; Math Tm; Chorus; Sec Soph Cls; Sec Jr Cls; Var Bsktbl; Var Tennis; High Hon Roll; Treas NHS; PAL; All Amer Schlrs Awd; U Of KS; Bio Sci.

PETERS, KELLY D; Chanute Sr HS; Chanute, KS; (2); 1/148; Church Yth Grp; Cmnty Wkr; FCA; French Clb; Band; School Musical; Phtg Yrbk; Tennis; Cit Awd; High Hon Roll; Medicine.

PETERS, MANDY; Emporia HS; Emporia, KS; (2); Church Yth Grp; SADD; JV Bsktbl; Var JV Vllybl; Hon Roll; Kayettes, Sprtn Club; Yth Smnr Prvtn Of Alchl/Drug Abs Teens.

PETERS, MARLA; Hays HS; Hays, KS; (4); 27/211; Pep Clb; Teachers Aide; Mgr Bsbl; Mgr Bsktbl; Var Chrldng; Mgr(s); Score Keeper; High Hon Roll; Jr NHS; NHS; Tchr & Offc Aide; KS ST U; Psych.

PETERS, MEGAN S; Jewell HS; Jewell, KS; (1); FHA; Pep Clb; Band; Mrchg Band; Pep Band; Ofcr Frsh Cls; Hon Roll; Y Teens.

PETERS, PAUL A; Central Heights Sr HS; Richmond, KS; (1); Church Yth Grp; 4-H; Spanish Clb; Ofcr Bsbl; JV Bsktbl; JV Var Ftbl; Socr; Var Trk; Wt Lftg; 4-H Awd; 3rd Pl 15 Yr Babe Ruth Regnl.

PETERS, TODD; Kapaun-Mt Carmel HS; Wichita, KS; (3); 5/190; Drama Clb; French Clb; Q&S; Acpl Chr; School Musical; School Play; Ed Nwsp; Pres Jr Cls; High Hon Roll; NHS.

PETERSEN, SARAH K; Bishop Miege HS; Roeland Park, KS; (4); 64/169; Church Yth Grp; Cmnty Wkr; Acpl Chr; Chorus; School Musical; School Play; Stage Crew; Rptr Frsh Cls; Rptr Soph Cls; Rptr Jr Cls; Amigos De Las Americas Cmnty Svc Wrk Mexico; Theatr.

PETERSILIE, JARED; Ness City HS; Ness City, KS; (4); 6/29; Pres 4-H; Pep Clb; Ofcr Stu Cncl; JV Bsktbl; Tennis; 4-H Awd; High Hon Roll; Pres NHS; I Dare You Ldrshp Awd; Enrgy Smnr Dlgt; Frm Bur Ldrshp Amer Jr Ldr; Ag.

PETERSILIE, LE ANN M; Otis Bison HS; Otis, KS; (2); Church Yth Grp; HOBY; Quiz Bowl; Speech Tm; SADD; Band; High Hon Roll; NHS; Science Clb; Pep Band; Upward Bound Math/Sci Pgm; KAY World Svc Dir.

PETERSON, ANDREW; Solomon Jr Sr HS; Solomon, KS; (4); 1/15; Church Yth Grp; Pres FHA; VP Letterman Clb; VP Natl FFA Org; Capt Quiz Bowl; School Play; Capt Var Bsktbl; Capt Var Ftbl; VP NHS; Val; HS Wrtr Lit Awd; KS ST U; Ag Engrng.

PETERSON, BRENT; Olathe South Sr HS; Olathe, KS; (3); Boy Scts; Church Yth Grp; Teachers Aide; JV Bsktbl; Var Crs Cntry; Var Trk; High Hon Roll; NHS; Pres Acad Fit Awd; Creatve Writng Awd 93-94; Natl Spnsh Exam 10th Pl; Seminary 3 Yrs; BYU; Accntng.

PETERSON, BRIAN K; Junction City HS; Junction City, KS; (3); Am Leg Boys St; Church Yth Grp; CAP; Cmnty Wkr; FCA; Teachers Aide; Ofcr Stu Cncl; Var Golf; Var Capt Socr; Hon Roll; I-70 League All Acad Team; Defensive Soccer Player Of Yr; Bartlesville Wesleyan Coll.

PETERSON, COLETTE; Blue Valley HS; Overland Park, KS; (2); Band; Mrchg Band; Pep Band; Var Sftbl; High Hon Roll; PRIDE; Outstdng Stu Awd; KS ST.

PETERSON, DANIELLE L; Wichita Southeast HS; Wichita, KS; (2); Drama Clb; Thesps; School Musical; Stage Crew; Pom Pon; Intrml Socr; Hon Roll; Pres Acad Fit Awd; All Amer Schlr; Pom-Pon Squad.

PETERSON JR, DAVID W; Stockton HS; Stockton, KS; (2); Church Yth Grp; Cmnty Wkr; Natl FFA Org; All Amer Schlr.

PETERSON, EMILY; Herington HS; Herington, KS; (1); Church Yth Grp; Cmnty Wkr; Dance Clb; Drama Clb; FCA; FHA; Pep Clb; Band; Chorus; Church Choir.

PETERSON, ERIC G; Blue Valley Northwest HS; Overland Park, KS; (4); 43/343; Varsity Clb; Capt L Cmnty Wkr; Var L Trk; High Hon Roll; Hon Roll; NHS; Pres Schlr; St Schlr; Spcl Olympic Vol 2 Yrs; Vanderbilt Univ; Bio; Med Dr.

PETERSON, JAIMIE L; Santa Fe Trail Jr HS; Olathe, KS; (1); Church Yth Grp; Cmnty Wkr; Hosp Aide; Church Choir; Orch; Bsktbl; Hon Roll; Pres Acad Fit Awd; Pres Schlr; Kay Club; Choir Ldrshp Team.

PETERSON, JAMIE; Shawnee Heights Sr HS; Topeka, KS; (3); Church Yth Grp; Sec Pres Key Clb; Model UN; Pep Clb; Band; Stage Crew; Rptr Nwsp; Pom Pon; Hon Roll; Sci Olympiad.

PETERSON, JENNIFER E; Wichita North HS; Wichita, KS; (3); Girl Scts; Teachers Aide; Band; Mrchg Band; Orch; Pep Band; JV Socr; Stat Wrstlng; Hon Roll; MRI-ST Francis Hosp Secrtl Work Vol; Child Care; RN.

PETERSON, JOHN J; Rose Hill HS; Rose Hill, KS; (3); Am Leg Boys St; Church Yth Grp; NFL; Scholastic Bowl; Chorus; School Musical; Treas Sr Cls; Var L Golf; Drama Clb; Quiz Bowl; KAY Clb Pres; Video Yrbk Comp Graphics Designer; Luther Coll; Radio & Television.

PETERSON, JOSH; Spring Hill HS; Olathe, KS; (3); Am Leg Boys St; Letterman Clb; Teachers Aide; Var Ftbl; Var Trk; Wt Lftg; Hon Roll; JCCC; Bus.

PETERSON, JOSH D; Shawnee Mission E Sr HS; Prairie Village, KS; (3); Cmnty Wkr; Dance Clb; Natl Beta Clb; High Hon Roll; NHS; Spanish NHS; Tnns 9th Grd; Cross Cntry 9-10 Grd; SHAPE Habitat For Humanity; KS ST; Vetrnrn.

PETERSON, KASEY; Leroy HS; Le Roy, KS; (3); Church Yth Grp; Chorus; Drill Tm; School Musical; Yrbk; Chrldng; Vllybl; Hon Roll; Emporia ST; Elem Ed.

PETERSON, KIRSTIN; Olathe East Sr HS; Olathe, KS; (4); 1/304; Church Yth Grp; Cmnty Wkr; Hosp Aide; Letterman Clb; Spanish Clb; Chorus; Church Choir; Orch; School Musical; School Play; Truman ST U; Bio.

PETERSON, KRISTA A; Mc Pherson HS; Mc Pherson, KS; (3); JV Bsktbl; JV Var Vllybl; DECA Pres Sr Yr; Mortician/Nrsng.

PETERSON, MATTHEW D; Ft Scott HS; Fort Scott, KS; (3); 98/138; Church Yth Grp; Teachers Aide; Varsity Clb; Ftbl; Trk; Wt Lftg; Wrstlng; Prfct Atten Awd; FSCC.

PETERSON, MEGAN A; Garden City Sr HS; Garden City, KS; (2); Art Clb; Church Yth Grp; Debate Tm; NFL; School Musical; School Play; JV Crs Cntry; Mgr(s); Var Swmmng; Hon Roll; AFS; Best Acress Awd 94-95, 95-96; Manhattan Chrstn Col.

PETERSON, PAIGE E; Hayden HS; Topeka, KS; (2); Church Yth Grp; Debate Tm; VP Frsh Cls; Var Chrldng; JV Sftbl; Hon Roll; KS Univ.

PETERSON, SALLYANN; Spring Hill HS; Spring Hill, KS; (2); Debate Tm; Band; Mrchg Band; Pep Band; Pres Soph Cls; JV Vllybl; Hon Roll.

PETERSON, TANNER J; Smoky Valley HS; Mc Pherson, KS; (2); FCA; Pres 4-H; Letterman Clb; Math Tm; Q&S; Band; Phtg Nwsp; Var Ftbl; High Hon Roll; NHS; Eng/Archtctr.

PETRIE, DAVID E; Valley Ctr HS; Valley Center, KS; (3); 22/162; Spanish Clb; Varsity Clb; Rep Stu Cncl; Var Bsktbl; Var Ftbl; Var Wt Lftg; Hon Roll; NHS; Teens As Tchrs; GCTL; Baker; Pre-Med.

PETRIE, LISA S; Garden City Sr HS; Garden City, KS; (2); 87/500; Hosp Aide; Acpl Chr; Chorus; School Musical; School Play; Stage Crew; High Hon Roll; Piano; St His Day; Stu Intrnshp Srgy; KSU; Med.

PETRIK, DUSTIN; Manhattan HS; Manhattan, KS; (3); 1/500; Am Leg Boys St; Var Debate Tm; NFL; Band; Jazz Band; Mrchg Band; Pep Band; Rep Stu Cncl; Pres NHS; Drm Mjr(t); Schlrs Bowl Ltr Wnnr; Music Ltr Wnnr; Schlrs Bowl/High-Q Var; Genetics.

PETTIGREW, ALLISON M; Wellington Sr HS; Wellington, KS; (3); Church Yth Grp; Band; Jazz Band; Mrchg Band; Rep Stu Cncl; Bsktbl; Hon Roll; Jr NHS; Pres Acad Fit Awd; U Of KS; Med.

PETTIGREW, MELISSA A; Dexter Jr Sr HS; Dexter, KS; (2); Math Tm; Band; Mrchg Band; Bsktbl; Trk; Vllybl; High Hon Roll; UCLA; Med.

PETTY, KRISTEN; Protection Schl; Protection, KS; (2); 1/22; Church Yth Grp; Pep Clb; Quiz Bowl; Scholastic Bowl; Speech Tm; Band; Chorus; Church Choir; Jazz Band; Mrchg Band; Hrsbck Riding; Eastern NM Univ; Bus Ownr.

PETTY, RISA; Lawrence HS; Lawrence, KS; (4); 17/521; Teachers Aide; Ed Yrbk; Var Sftbl; Intrml Vllybl; Intrml Wt Lftg; Hon Roll; NHS; U Of KS.

PETZ, ANGIE RENEE; Lacrosse HS; Mc Cracken, KS; (4); 10/24; HOBY; Q&S; Band; Ed Yrbk; VP Soph Cls; L Capt Bsktbl; L Trk; L Capt Vllybl; High Hon Roll; Sec Treas NHS.

PFANNENSTEIL, DUSTY J; Great Bend Sr HS; Great Bend, KS; (1); Band; Mrchg Band; Pep Band; Intrml Bsbl; Intrml Ftbl; Intrml Mgr(s); High Hon Roll; Prfct Atten Awd; Pres Acad Fit Awd; Using Cmptrs.

PFANNENSTIEL, AMANDA M; Ness City HS; Ness City, KS; (1); Church Yth Grp; VP 4-H; FHA; Pep Clb; Thesps; Chorus; VP Frsh Cls; Golf; Vllybl; Hon Roll; FHA Star Evnts Natl Wnr; KAYS; Sweet Adelines; Elem Ed.

PFANNENSTIEL, AMY; Thomas More Prep-Manan HS; Hays, KS; (4); Church Yth Grp; Cmnty Wkr; Latin Clb; Model UN; School Musical; Stage Crew; Yrbk; Rep Frsh Cls; Chrldng; Hon Roll.

PFANNENSTIEL, CHRIS; Udall HS; Udall, KS; (3); Math Tm; Quiz Bowl; Varsity Clb; Band; Chorus; Mrchg Band; Var Bsbl; Var Bsktbl; Var Capt Ftbl; Cit Awd.

PFANNENSTIEL, LAURA M; Trego Comm HS; Wa Keeney, KS; (3); 14/50; Pres Drama Clb; NFL; Science Clb; Speech Tm; SADD; Band; Treas Jr Cls; Var Tennis; Hon Roll; NHS; KS ST Univ; Bus.

PFANNENSTIEL, LISA; Ellis HS; Hays, KS; (3); Cmnty Wkr; 4-H; FBLA; HOBY; JA; Natl FFA Org; Quiz Bowl; SADD; School Musical; School Play; 4-H Ambsdr/Awds; FFA Greenhand; Kayettes; Ft Hays ST U; Ag Bus.

PFANNENSTIEL, NICK; Silver Lake Jr Sr HS; Silver Lake, KS; (2); 11/62; FHA; Letterman Clb; Pep Clb; Spanish Clb; Speech Tm; Band; Mrchg Band; Phtg Yrbk; Rep Frsh Cls; JV Bsbl; Univ Of KS.

PFANNENSTIEL, SARAH; Goddard HS; Goddard, KS; (3); Church Yth Grp; Cmnty Wkr; German Clb; Pep Clb; Science Clb; Chrldng; Hon Roll; Psych.

PFANNENSTIEL, SARAH M; Udall HS; Udall, KS; (3); Dance Clb; Drama Clb; Math Tm; NFL; Quiz Bowl; Thesps; Chorus; School Play; Stat Bsbl; Stat Ftbl; GCTL.

PFEIFER, BRANDON; Ellis HS; Ellis, KS; (2); Church Yth Grp; Pres 4-H; Treas Natl FFA Org; Pep Clb; Band; Mrchg Band; Pep Band; Var Ftbl; Var Wt Lftg; Var Wrstlng; 2nd Pl KS 3-2-La St Wrstlng; Beloit Tech Schl; Htng Air.

PFEIFER, BRYAN; Marysville HS; Marysville, KS; (3); 51/89; Am Leg Boys St; Letterman Clb; Teachers Aide; Chorus; School Musical; Variety Show; Var Bsktbl; Var Tennis; Hon Roll; Kiwanis Awd.

PFEIFER, JENNIFER; Hays HS; Hays, KS; (3); 54/280; Am Leg Aux Girls St; Church Yth Grp; Hosp Aide; Pep Clb; Nwsp; Chrldng; Sftbl; Tennis; Trk; Hon Roll; Ft Hays ST U; Bus Mgmnt.

PFEIFER, JILL M; Victoria HS; Victoria, KS; (4); 4/25; Sec Treas Church Yth Grp; Treas FBLA; VP FHA; Office Aide; Pres Pep Clb; VP Stu Cncl; Capt Bsktbl; Capt Vllybl; High Hon Roll; NHS; Ft Hays ST U; Agribus.

PFEIFER, LANCE M; Morland Jr Sr HS; Morland, KS; (2); Church Yth Grp; Math Tm; School Play; Stage Crew; Rptr Nwsp; JV Bsktbl; Hon Roll; Alter Boy At Chrch; Restoring Antique Tractors.

PFEIFER, MANDY; Hays HS; Hays, KS; (4); 35/220; Pep Clb; Teachers Aide; Stat Bsktbl; Mgr(s); Powder Puff Ftbl; Score Keeper; Stat Sftbl; Stat Vllybl; Cit Awd; Hon Roll; Ft Hays ST Univ; Elem Ed.

PFEIFF JR, DENNIS; Triplains Schl; Winona, KS; (3); Quiz Bowl; Rep Soph Cls; Ftbl; Hon Roll; NHS; Martial Arts; Role Plyng; Rdng; HI Pacific Univ; Marine Bio.

PFEIFFER, ATTIE J; Douglass HS; Douglass, KS; (2); 12/73; FCA; Service Clb; Band; Flag Corp; Jazz Band; Mrchg Band; Pep Band; Var Sftbl; JV Vllybl; High Hon Roll; Lions Clb St Band, Intnl Band; Wichita St Univ Hnr Band; CSU; Nrsng.

PFEIFLEY, KRISTIN; Manhattan HS; Manhattan, KS; (3); Church Yth Grp; Dance Clb; FCA; FBLA; Pep Clb; Teachers Aide; Varsity Clb; Drill Tm; School Play; Stage Crew; Homcmng Hnry; K-ST; Hotl/Rest Mgmt.

PFLAUM, LINDSAY; Hays HS; Hays, KS; (4); 12/200; Teachers Aide; Drill Tm; Chrldng; Pom Pon; Hon Roll; NHS; Ft Hays ST Univ; Bus Ed.

PHADKE, LEENA D; Olathe East Sr HS; Olathe, KS; (2); Debate Tm; French Clb; Girl Scts; Speech Tm; Chorus; School Play; High Hon Roll; Pres Acad Fit Awd; Piano.

PHAM, DIEN P; Wichita Hghts HS; Wichita, KS; (2); 24/336; Cmnty Wkr; Computer Clb; Latin Clb; Chorus; Yrbk; Bsktbl; Tennis; Cit Awd; Gov Hon Prg Awd; High Hon Roll; Travel; Early Grad; Upward Bound Math & Sci; Wichita ST Univ; Pharmacy.

PHAM, HUY Q; F L Schlagle HS; Kansas City, KS; (4); 30/180; Office Aide; High Hon Roll; Hon Roll; NHS; Outstndng Achv Physics; KS Bd Rgents Prep Crs Awd; Rdng; Mltry Sci; Avtn; Photo; Intl Trvl; Pol; Drftng; U Of KS; Arspc Engr.

PHAM, LINH N; Kapaun-Mt Carmel HS; Wichita, KS; (3); U Of KS; Pre-Med.

PHAM, MAI; Bishop Carroll Catholic HS; Wichita, KS; (2); 1/175; JA; SADD; Pres Soph Cls; Var Pom Pon; Hon Roll.

PHAN, NGOC ANH; Salina HS South; Salina, KS; (3); Cmnty Wkr; JV Tennis; Hon Roll; NHS; KS U.

PHANSIRI, OUDOMPHONE T; J C Harmon HS; Kansas City, KS; (3); Cmnty Wkr; Latin Clb; Quiz Bowl; Scholastic Bowl; Band; KS U Math/Sci Pgm; KS U.

PHANYORAJ, NAPHAPHONE; Garden City Sr HS; Garden City, KS; (1); VP FHA; Nwsp; Bsktbl; JV Sftbl; Cert Hon Svng FHA/HERO VP Achvmt; Sci Merit Awd; Dr.

PHEASANT, MELISSA J; Washburn Rural HS; Topeka, KS; (2); Church Yth Grp; Hosp Aide; Church Choir; Orch; School Musical; High Hon Roll; Yth Symphony; 1 Rating ST Music Comp; Emporia ST; Elem Schl Tchr.

PHELPS, MICHAEL S; Olathe North Sr HS; Olathe, KS; (3); Computer Clb; Math Clb; Math Tm; Science Clb; Teachers Aide; Acpl Chr; Church Choir; Orch; School Musical; JV Wrstlng; Law Enfrcmnt.

PHELPS, NATACHA; Junction City HS; Junction City, KS; (2); Teachers Aide; Drill Tm; Flag Corp; VP Soph Cls; Mgr(s); Pom Pon; High Hon Roll; Grambling; Comp Engrng.

PHILBROOK, BROOKE S; Salina HS South; Salina, KS; (2); Cmnty Wkr; Teachers Aide; Band; Mrchg Band; Pep Band; Hon Roll; NAHRA Pgm Vol; Ft Hays ST U; Phys Therapy.

PHILBROOK, KAMBRA L; Salina HS South; Salina, KS; (3); 27/250; Debate Tm; Letterman Clb; NFL; Pep Clb; Teachers Aide; Orch; School Musical; L Var Chrldng; Hon Roll; NHS; Elem Ed.

PHILHOUR, CHAD; Desoto HS; Shawnee Mission, KS; (4); 32/106; Letterman Clb; Varsity Clb; Ofcr Stu Cncl; Var L Bsbl; Var L Bsktbl; Var L Ftbl; Powder Puff Ftbl; Hon Roll; Pride Pgm; KS Univ; Arch.

PHILIPP, JEREMY; Manhattan HS; Manhattan, KS; (4); 68/388; Church Yth Grp; Cmnty Wkr; FBLA; Spanish Clb; SADD; Nwsp; Tennis; Cit Awd; High Hon Roll; Hon Roll; U KS; Bus Admin.

PHILLIPPI, LAURA; Marysville HS; Marysville, KS; (2); 27/98; Art Clb; Mgr(s); High Hon Roll; Kiwanis Awd; Matmaids; Emporia KS; Sci.

PHILLIPS, AMY; Winfield HS; Winfield, KS; (4); Bus Profs of Am; Church Yth Grp; Office Aide; Teachers Aide; Band; Church Choir; Mrchg Band; Pep Band; Ofcr Stu Cncl; Hon Roll; Cowley; Csmtlgy.

PHILLIPS, ASHLEY E; Shawnee Mission E Sr HS; Shawnee Mission, KS; (2); Teachers Aide; Thesps; Chorus; School Musical; School Play; Stage Crew; Hon Roll; Comm & Prof Theatre KC Area; Choreogrphy; Dance Tchr; Perf Arts.

PHILLIPS, BETTY T; Wichita West HS; Wichita, KS; (2); #13 in class; Hosp Aide; Trk; Hon Roll; Pediatrcn.

PHILLIPS, CHARITY; Labette Co HS; Dennis, KS; (2); 50/160; Church Yth Grp; FCA; Ofcr FBLA; FHA; SADD; Bsktbl; Hon Roll; Violin Chrch Offtry; FBLA Cont; Int Dsgn Coll Schlrshp; Labette Cty Coll; Grphc Art.

PHILLIPS, JENNIFER M; Wichita East HS; Wichita, KS; (4); Church Yth Grp; Cmnty Wkr; Spanish Clb; Band; Chorus; Mrchg Band; Pep Band; School Musical; Kiwanis Awd; NHS; Wheaton Coll.

PHILLIPS, JENNY; Kingman HS; Cheney, KS; (1); Church Yth Grp; FBLA; NFL; School Play; Var Chrldng; Var Golf.

PHILLIPS, JERROD D; Goodland HS; Goodland, KS; (2); 40/87; Church Yth Grp; FHA; Crs Cntry; Ftbl; Golf; Wrstlng; Cit Awd; Arch.

PHILLIPS, JESSICA I; Turner HS; Kansas City, KS; (4); 2/189; Church Yth Grp; Drama Clb; Math Tm; Spanish Clb; Drill Tm; School Play; Rep Stu Cncl; Gov Hon Prg Awd; NHS; Sal; Mssns Trps Jamaica, Plnd, Rssa; Kansas City Yth Chrst Cmp L-Bar-L Rnch Vol Lfgrd; West Point; Med.

PHILLIPS, MINDY; Palco HS; Palco, KS; (3); Art Clb; FHA; Pep Clb; School Play; Stage Crew; Ed Nwsp; Phtg Yrbk; Chrldng; Trk; Vllybl; Athltc Clb; Hays Acad Of Hair Dsgn.

PHILLIPS, NICOLE; Otis Bison HS; Albert, KS; (3); 2/26; HOBY; Letterman Clb; Chorus; School Play; Ed Rptr Nwsp; Var Bsktbl; Var Chrldng; Var Vllybl; High Hon Roll; NHS; SADD Treas/Rep; Dance Cmmtte; KAY Treas/Ldrshp Camp; KSU.

PHILLIPS, SARAH K; Maize HS; Wichita, KS; (2); Cmnty Wkr; French Clb; Science Clb; SADD; Pom Pon; Socr; Hon Roll; NHS; KS Assn Yth Svcs; KS Univ; Bus Mngmnt.

PHILLIPS, STACY; Goddard HS; Goddard, KS; (3); Spanish Clb; Band; Mrchg Band; Pep Band; Sftbl; Tennis; Hon Roll; NHS.

PHILLIPS, TIFFANY L; Pittsburg HS; Pittsburg, KS; (1); JV Bsktbl; Var Chrldng; Var L Crs Cntry; Var L Trk; Intrml Wt Lftg; High Hon Roll; Hon Roll; Pres Acad Fit Awd; Hnrbl Mention All Conf Cross Cntry; All Conf Track; ST Track Qualified; Ftbl Hmcmng Attndnt.

PHILPOT, ROGER J; Norton Comm HS; Norton, KS; (3); Letterman Clb; Natl FFA Org; Pep Clb; SADD; Varsity Clb; Chorus; VP Frsh Cls; VP Soph Cls; Ofcr Bsbl; Bsktbl; All Conf Ftbl; ST Plcr Dscs; Law Enfrcmnt/Bus.

PHILPOTT, BRODY T; Midland Sda Schl; Shawnee Mission, KS; (2); Ski Clb; Band; Cit Awd; Hon Roll; Sthrn Col Of SD.

PHIMSIPRASOM, VONGSAVANH T; Wichita East HS; Wichita, KS; (2); 16/360; Math Tm; Quiz Bowl; Science Clb; Teachers Aide; JV Bsktbl; Var Trk; Cit Awd; Hon Roll; Prfct Atten Awd; Pres Acad Fit Awd; WSU; Elec Eng.

PHIPPS, KENNETH; Remington HS; Whitewater, KS; (3); 8/37; Am Leg Boys St; Scholastic Bowl; Band; School Play; Sec Jr Cls; Rep Stu Cncl; Var Bsktbl; Var L Ftbl; Hon Roll; NHS.

PHIPPS, MATT; Mulvane Sr HS; Mulvane, KS; (3); 2/160; Cmnty Wkr; Letterman Clb; Office Aide; Pep Clb; SADD; Varsity Clb; Band; Drm Mjr(t); Jazz Band; Mrchg Band; Emporia ST U; Bus.

PIATKOWSKI, ROBERT T; Northeast HS; Mulberry, KS; (1); Boy Scts; Band; Chorus; Mrchg Band; Pep Band; Bsktbl; Trk; Wt Lftg; Hon Roll; Prfct Atten Awd.

PIATT, MATT; Thomas More Prep-Marion HS; Victoria, KS; (1); 2/60; Debate Tm; Model UN; Quiz Bowl; Band; Jazz Band; School Musical; School Play; Rptr Nwsp; Hon Roll; Odyssey Of Mind.

PICKELL, BRITT; Pittsburg HS; Pittsburg, KS; (4); 18/160; Am Leg Aux Girls St; Rep L French Clb; Pres Soph Cls; Var L Bsktbl; Var L Crs Cntry; Var L Trk; Var L NHS; Church Yth Grp; Sec FCA; FHA; KRHA; GCTL.

PICKELL, KRISTIN; Pittsburg HS; Pittsburg, KS; (4); 9/160; Treas French Clb; HOBY; Ofcr Stu Cncl; Var Capt Bsktbl; Var Capt Crs Cntry; Var L Trk; Pres NHS; Am Leg Aux Girls St; Church Yth Grp; Treas FCA; KRHA.

PICKENS, CHRISTI; Olathe North Sr HS; Olathe, KS; (4); Church Yth Grp; FBLA; Office Aide; Scholastic Bowl; Spanish Clb; Teachers Aide; Church Choir; School Play; Hon Roll; Pres Acad Fit Awd; Nazarene Coll; Elem Ed.

PICKENS, DONNETA M; Wichita East HS; Wichita, KS; (3); 8/294; Spanish Clb; Teachers Aide; Bsktbl; Socr; High Hon Roll; Blk Ldrshp/Peer Ldrshp; Spirit Cabinet; Ltrd Acad; Hanger Bd; Bio.

PICKERT, ERICA A; Central Heights Sr HS; Richmond, KS; (3); 5/60; Drama Clb; Treas FCA; Sec Treas FBLA; Sec Pep Clb; School Play; Swing Chorus; Yrbk; Pres Soph Cls; Pres Jr Cls; JETS Awd; Psych.

PICKETT, JASON R; Stockton HS; Stockton, KS; (3); Boy Scts; Church Yth Grp; FCA; FTA; Math Tm; Quiz Bowl; Scholastic Bowl; Band; Jazz Band; Mrchg Band; All Amer Schlr; Natl Hnr Rll; Nike Golf Cmp With Pros; KU; Bus Brdcstng.

PICKETT, JENNY L; Goodland HS; Goodland, KS; (3); 34/85; Church Yth Grp; Cmnty Wkr; FHA; SADD; Var Mgr(s); JV Vllybl; Hon Roll; KS Assn Of Yth-Kayettes.

PICKETT, KELLI; Blue Valley Northwest HS; Overland Park, KS; (2); Cmnty Wkr; English Clb; Lit Mag; Cit Awd; High Hon Roll; Enviro Clb Pres; Enviro Stds.

PICKMAN, MICHAEL C; Maur Hill Prep Schl; Atchison, KS; (3); Church Yth Grp; NFL; Teachers Aide; Varsity Clb; Stage Crew; Phtg Rptr Nwsp; Socr; Trk; Hon Roll; Var Soccer Since Frosh Yr; Ottawa Coll; Elem Tchr.

PICOLET, ANGELA M; Council Grove HS; Dwight, KS; (3); Art Clb; FCA; Key Clb; SADD; Band; Mrchg Band; Orch; Pep Band; Var Bsktbl; Var Vllybl; Whos Who In Sports 94-96; KS Univ; Bus; Fin.

PICOLET, KELLY R; Council Grove HS; Dwight, KS; (2); Art Clb; Drama Clb; FBLA; NFL; SADD; Hon Roll; GAS Cmmty; Theocrtc Ministry Schl; Roachies Bnd; Intr Desgn.

PICOW, DAVID H; Shawnee Mission E Sr HS; Shawnee Mission, KS; (3); 164/409; Boy Scts; Church Yth Grp; Drama Clb; Latin Clb; Thesps; School Play; Hon Roll; Eagle Sct; Theatre Ltr.

PIEPENBRING, ERICH B; Shawnee Mission E Sr HS; Prairie Village, KS; (2); Model UN; Bsktbl; Ftbl; Hon Roll; Ctr For Intl Stds Jpns & Geo-Pltcs Stu.

PIERCE, CHARITY S; Liberal HS; Liberal, KS; (4); VP Bus Profs of Am; Debate Tm; FTA; Speech Tm; Gym; Trk; Hon Roll.

PIERCE, COREY S; Gardner-Edgerton HS; Gardner, KS; (2); Spanish Clb; Yrbk; Hon Roll; Jr NHS; KS Univ; Robotic Engrng & Dsgn.

PIERCE, JEFFREY D; Topeka West HS; Topeka, KS; (1); 10/400; Spanish Clb; Ofcr Frsh Cls; Bsktbl; Crs Cntry; High Hon Roll.

PIERCE, KRISTEN KATHLEEN; Topeka West HS; Topeka, KS; (4); 8/270; Spanish Clb; Teachers Aide; Bsktbl; Sftbl; Vllybl; Gov Hon Prg Awd; High Hon Roll; Jr NHS; NHS; Pres Acad Fit Awd; Bsktbll-All St, All League, All Conf, Conf Plyr Of Yr; Garvey Schol; Washburn Univ; Phy Thrpy.

PIERCE, REBECCA M; Campus HS; Haysville, KS; (2); Church Yth Grp; Intnl Clb; SADD; Church Choir; Mgr(s); L Swmmng; Mgr L Wrstlng; High Hon Roll; KS Univ; Acctng.

PIERCE, TONY L; Hayden HS; Topeka, KS; (2); Debate Tm; NFL; Scholastic Bowl; Speech Tm; Nwsp; Hon Roll; NHS; Crtfd Lfgrd; Comm.

PIERSON, BELINDA; Augusta Sr HS; Augusta, KS; (4); 6/125; VP French Clb; Scholastic Bowl; Ofcr Jr Cls; Var Chrldng; Pom Pon; Gov Hon Prg Awd; High Hon Roll; NHS; Ntl Merit Ltr; St Schlr; Wichita ST U; Aerospc Engrng.

PIFER, LINDSEY H; Washington HS; Washington, KS; (3); Am Leg Aux Girls St; French Clb; FHA; Natl FFA Org; Letterman Clb; Pep Clb; Church Yth Grp; Band; School Musical; DAR Awd.

PIGG, SCOTT J; Topeka West HS; Topeka, KS; (3); 10/250; Church Yth Grp; Cmnty Wkr; French Clb; German Clb; Math Clb; Q&S; SADD; Rep Soph Cls; Rep Jr Cls; Rep Stu Cncl; KS Univ; Med.

PIHL, DEREK R; Smoky Valley HS; Lindsborg, KS; (1); Band; Mrchg Band; Pep Band; JV Ftbl; JV L Tennis.

PIKE, JAMIE; Minneola Schl; Minneola, KS; (4); Cmnty Wkr; Teachers Aide; Bsktbl; Ftbl; Trk; Wt Lftg; High Hon Roll; Hon Roll; All-St, All-League & All-Area Ftbl; Dodge City CC; Ag.

PILCHER, BRANDEE D; Hope HS; Hope, KS; (2); Church Yth Grp; FBLA; Natl FFA Org; Pep Clb; Teachers Aide; Band; Chorus; Mrchg Band; Pep Band; Treas Frsh Cls; KS ST Univ; Bus.

PILGER, DREW W; Wallace Cty HS; Wallace, KS; (2); Church Yth Grp; FCA; 4-H; Pep Clb; Quiz Bowl; Chorus; School Musical; Rep Stu Cncl; JV Var Bsktbl; Var L Crs Cntry.

PINAIRE, JESSICA E; Wichita Northwest HS; Wichita, KS; (4); 74/283; Drama Clb; Letterman Clb; Thesps; Varsity Clb; Color Guard; Mrchg Band; School Play; Swmmng; Hon Roll; Piano; Wichita Univ; Bus Admin; Mktg.

PINEDA, MELISSA; Liberal HS; Liberal, KS; (4); 56/212; Office Aide; School Musical; School Play; Hon Roll; Seward Cty Comm Coll; Phy Asst.

PINEO, NIKI; Jayhawk-Linn HS; Mound City, KS; (4); 6/35; Debate Tm; Natl FFA Org; Band; School Play; Pres Stu Cncl; Var Bsktbl; High Hon Roll; Hon Roll; NHS; Math Tm; ST FFA Degree; KS ST Univ; Ag Jrnlsm.

PINICK, MELISSA R; Basehor Linwood HS; Basehor, KS; (3); VP Art Clb; Church Yth Grp; FHA; JV Bsktbl; DAR Awd; High Hon Roll; Hon Roll; Prfct Atten Awd; 2 Poems Pub; Art Awd; KS Univfinterior Dsgn.

PINKHAM, CANDICE; Maryville HS; Marysville, KS; (3); Church Yth Grp; Drama Clb; FHA; Band; Mrchg Band; Pep Band; Stage Crew; Hon Roll; Kayettes 1 Yr; Matmaids; U Of KS; Pre Med.

PINKSTON, JASON; Macksville HS; Seward, KS; (4); 2/24; Letterman Clb; Sec Jr Cls; Ofcr Stu Cncl; Var Capt Bsktbl; Var Capt Ftbl; Trk; High Hon Roll; NHS; KU Schlr; All Lg Hnrb Mntn Ftbl; All Lg 1st Tm Bsktbl; Ft Hays ST U; Agribus.

PINNELL, ALEX E; Blue Valley Northwest HS; Overland Park, KS; (2); 1/400; Boy Scts; Church Yth Grp; Band; Mrchg Band; Pep Band; School Musical; Socr; High Hon Roll.

PINNELL, E ALEXANDER; Blue Valley Northwest HS; Overland Park, KS; (2); 1/400; Boy Scts; Church Yth Grp; Band; Mrchg Band; Pep Band; School Musical; JV Socr; High Hon Roll.

PINSUWAN, RANAI; Thomas More Marian HS; Hays, KS; (3); KU.

PINTAR, ADAM L; Northeast HS; Arcadia, KS; (2); 3/45; Library Aide; Scholastic Bowl; Bsktbl; Trk; High Hon Roll.

PINTER, ANNETTE; Louisburg HS; Louisburg, KS; (4); 17/78; Pres Bus Profs of Am; Cmnty Wkr; FCA; Letterman Clb; Spanish Clb; SADD; Teachers Aide; Stage Crew; Treas Jr Cls; Vllybl; KS ST; Fshn Merchandising.

PINTER, JAMY; Louisburg HS; Louisburg, KS; (3); 18/92; Bus Profs of Am; Cmnty Wkr; Drama Clb; Math Clb; Math Tm; Spanish Clb; SADD; Teachers Aide; Rptr Yrbk; JV Sftbl; 3rd Pl St Bus Prof Entrprnrshp; Duke U; Pre-Law.

PIOTROWSKY, NADIA; Ottawa HS; Ottawa, KS; (3); #1 in class; Treas Church Yth Grp; Pres Treas 4-H; Pres Key Clb; School Musical; Rptr Nwsp; Stu Cncl; L Stat Bsktbl; NHS; Debate Tm; Pres Drama Clb; I Dare You Ldrshp Awd; HOBY Ambssdr Wrld Ldrshp Congrss 95; Dist I Hnrs Choir Alto.

PIQUARD, AMBER L; Neodesha Jr Sr HS; Neodesha, KS; (1); Church Yth Grp; Natl FFA Org; Band; Pep Band; Hon Roll.

PIROTTE, RACHEL D; Bishop Carroll Catholic HS; Wichita, KS; (2); Nwsp; Yrbk; Tennis; High Hon Roll; Hon Roll; Eng/Law.

PISCIOTTA, DONNA T; Shawnee Mssn W HS; Overland Park, KS; (2); Chess Clb; Drama Clb; Spanish Clb; SADD; Thesps; School Musical; School Play; Stage Crew; Lit Mag; High Hon Roll; Bio.

PISHNEY, HOLLY C; Valley Heights Jr Sr HS; Blue Rapids, KS; (3); Am Leg Aux Girls St; Drama Clb; 4-H; FHA; Girl Scts; Letterman Clb; Pep Clb; VICA; Chorus; Pep Band; Cloud Cty CC; Bus Hotel Mgmt.

PITCHER, LEIA; Wichita Collegiate Schl; Wichita, KS; (4); Cmnty Wkr; Quiz Bowl; Scholastic Bowl; Chorus; School Musical; Yrbk; Rep Sr Cls; Ofcr Stu Cncl; Var L Crs Cntry; Var L Trk; Bio Lab Aide.

PITLUCK, MOLLY R; Blue Valley Northwest HS; Overland Park, KS; (2); Debate Tm; Hon Roll; Duke TIP St Hnrs; UCLA; Actng.

PITNER, TIONNA; Atwood HS; Atwood, KS; (2); Church Yth Grp; Girl Scts; HOBY; Natl FFA Org; Church Choir; Rep Soph Cls; Rep Jr Cls; Rep Stu Cncl; Vllybl; Hon Roll; U Of KS; Criminlgy.

PITT, TAMMY C; Yates Ctr HS; Yates Center, KS; (2); Art Clb; Drama Clb; 4-H; FHA; Chorus; Powder Puff Ftbl; Trk; Vllybl; 4-H Awd; Hon Roll; Lv To Be In Plys & Act; Tchr.

PITTMAN, BRANDE J; Turner HS; Kansas City, KS; (2); School Play; Ofcr Stu Cncl; Capt Var Chrldng; Kays; Coll Plan; Frnsc Club; Med.

PITTMAN, REBEKAH A; Maize HS; Wichita, KS; (4); 1/230; Pres French Clb; Chorus; VP Sr Cls; Treas Stu Cncl; Var Capt Socr; Vllybl; Gov Hon Prg Awd; Pres Jr NHS; NHS; Val; Drury Coll; Intl Bus.

PITTS, BRANDON E; Uniontown HS; Redfield, KS; (4); 4-H; FHA; Letterman Clb; Teachers Aide; Band; Jazz Band; Mrchg Band; Pep Band; VP Frsh Cls; Bsktbl; FSCC.

PITTS, DARIN W; Olathe East Sr HS; Shawnee Mission, KS; (4); French Clb; Band; Jazz Band; Mrchg Band; School Musical; Variety Show; Hon Roll; Jr NHS; NHS; Prfct Atten Awd; GMI; Eng.

PITTS, GREGORY A; Junction City HS; Junction City, KS; (2); Pep Clb; Red Cross Aide; Band; Mrchg Band; Pep Band; Diving; Socr; Hon Roll; All Acad Schlsp; KS U; Scndry Ed.

PITTS, JESSICA R; Nickerson HS; Nickerson, KS; (2); Girl Scts; Sec Spanish Clb; Yrbk; Var L Crs Cntry; Var L Trk; Hon Roll; Girl Scouts Silver Awd; SAVE; Psych.

PIVONKA, JEREMY C; Great Bend Sr HS; Great Bend, KS; (1); Church Yth Grp; Spanish Clb; Golf; Hon Roll; Prfct Atten Awd; Acad Awd; Teach Guitar.

PLANK, SAMUEL E; Haven HS; Yoder, KS; (3); Church Yth Grp; Band; Jazz Band; Mrchg Band; Pep Band; JV Bsbl; Debate Tm; Hon Roll; Prfct Atten Awd; Outdoor Act Hunting & Fishing; Bowling; Hutchinson CC; Math.

PLANTE, TABITHA; Hill City HS; Hill City, KS; (3); 4/33; HOBY; Chorus; Color Guard; School Musical; School Play; L Mgr(s); JV Vllybl; Hon Roll; KMEA Hnr Choir; 1st Div St Music Fnlst; Ft Hays ST U; Bus.

PLATT, RYAN M; Blue Valley Northwest HS; Overland Park, KS; (3); Acpl Chr; Chorus; JV Bsbl; Bsktbl; Hon Roll; Brown Univ.

PLATT, SERENA A; Wellington Sr HS; Wellington, KS; (3); 15/164; Church Yth Grp; Girl Scts; Band; JV Var Sftbl; Hon Roll; Jr NHS; Blck Blt Tae Kwon Do; KS U; Crmnl Jstc.

PLATT, STACIE L; Campus HS; Haysville, KS; (3); Am Leg Aux Girls St; Science Clb; Spanish Clb; SADD; Teachers Aide; Var Sftbl; JV Vllybl; High Hon Roll; Hon Roll; Pre Med.

PLEDGE, MOLLY K; Blue Valley Northwest HS; Overland Park, KS; (3); 8/371; FCA; Q&S; Teachers Aide; Varsity Clb; Ed Nwsp; Var Capt Bsktbl; Var Trk; High Hon Roll; NHS.

PLENERT, KATIE A; Hillsboro HS; Hillsboro, KS; (2); 14/49; Church Yth Grp; FCA; Rep Frsh Cls; VP Jr Cls; JV Bsktbl; Intrml Sftbl; Var Trk; JV Vllybl; Hon Roll.

PLENGE, HEATHER; St John Jr Sr HS; Saint John, KS; (4); 8/28; Church Yth Grp; GAA; Office Aide; Pep Clb; Teachers Aide; Band; Pep Band; School Play; Treas Frsh Cls; Ofcr Stu Cncl; Barton Cty CC; Phy Thrpst.

PLESE, SARAH; Shawnee Mission W Sr HS; Overland Park, KS; (4); 29/380; Cmnty Wkr; Spanish Clb; Chorus; JV L Crs Cntry; High Hon Roll; Hon Roll; Pres Acad Fit Awd; KS Hnr Schlr; KS St Univ; Wldlf Bio.

PLETCHER, TYLER W; Great Bend Sr HS; Great Bend, KS; (2); Band; Mrchg Band; Pep Band; U Of UT.

PLEVIAK, ALYSON; Washburn Rural HS; Topeka, KS; (2); 27/400; FCA; Hosp Aide; Office Aide; Pep Clb; SADD; Variety Show; Ed Yrbk; Var Chrldng; Wt Lftg; High Hon Roll.

PLINSKY, MANDY; Ashland HS; Ashland, KS; (4); 1/25; Church Yth Grp; HOBY; Quiz Bowl; Band; School Play; Yrbk; Sec Stu Cncl; Capt Bsktbl; L Trk; High Hon Roll; All St 1st Tm Bsktbl 95; KS Poets Clb; St Medlst Track 92-94; Tabor Coll; Med.

PLOUTZ, ELIZABETH A; Ellsworth HS; Kanopolis, KS; (2); Church Yth Grp; Intnl Clb; Spanish Clb; Rep Frsh Cls; Rep Stu Cncl; JV Bsktbl; JV Vllybl; DAR Awd; Hon Roll; Fort Hays ST Univ; Phy Thrpst.

PLUFF, NATHAN J; J C Harmon HS; Kansas City, KS; (2); Church Yth Grp; Hon Roll; Chrch Bsktbl League.

PLUMB, AMBER L; Blue Valley Northwest HS; Overland Park, KS; (2); Bsktbl; Trk; Vllybl; High Hon Roll.

PLUMB, KELLY A; Olathe North Sr HS; Olathe, KS; (3); Band; Mrchg Band; Orch; Pep Band; School Musical; High Hon Roll; Church Yth Grp; Science Clb; Church Choir; Lit Mag; Yth Symphony; Amer Legion Band; Local Theatre Productions & Orch; Acad Excl Awd; Flute Hnrs Recital; U Of KS; Music.

PLUMMER, JACK; Spring Hill HS; Paola, KS; (2); 4-H; JV Wrstlng; Hon Roll.

PLUMMER, JAMES; Rock Creek Jr Sr HS; Saint George, KS; (2); 3/65; Church Yth Grp; Scholastic Bowl; SADD; Band; Jazz Band; Pep Band; Ftbl; Wrstlng; Hon Roll; NHS; KS ST Univ.

PLUMMER, JENNIFER E; Olathe North Sr HS; Olathe, KS; (3); Church Yth Grp; Pep Clb; Spanish Clb; Band; School Play; Hon Roll; Pres Awd Frosh Yr; U Of KS.

PLUMMER, SCOTT B; Kansas Schl For The Deaf; Paola, KS; (4); 1/17; Boy Scts; Church Yth Grp; Debate Tm; Drama Clb; Quiz Bowl; Speech Tm; School Play; Pres Stu Cncl; Gov Hon Prg Awd; Val; Jr Rational Assoc For The Deaf Clb, Pres; Wildcat Clb; Gallaudet Univ; Meteorologist.

PLUNKETT, KELLY M; Salina HS South; Salina, KS; (3); Band; Mrchg Band; Pep Band; Hon Roll; Comm Vol; Trk Mgr; CYO; KS ST; Med Sci; Sci Field.

POAGE, CORA E; Thomas More Prep-Marion HS; Hays, KS; (1); 27/71; Church Yth Grp; Cmnty Wkr; Drama Clb; Pep Clb; School Musical; School Play; Stage Crew; Var Bsktbl; Var Trk; Var Vllybl; TMP Ambsdrs.

POINTING, TARA M; Smoky Valley HS; Marquette, KS; (3); Church Yth Grp; Cmnty Wkr; Letterman Clb; Pep Clb; Band; Chorus; Church Choir; Flag Corp; Mrchg Band; Pep Band; Comm Choir; Bible Schl Tchr; Swimming Lessons Tchr; Dental Hygiene.

POLLACK, KEVIN A; Blue Valley Northwest HS; Overland Park, KS; (2); 33/450; Band; Ftbl; High Hon Roll; Hon Roll; Vol To Cystic Fibrosis Found; Northwestern Univ; Stck Brkr.

POLLARD, COURTNEY C; Goddard HS; Wichita, KS; (2); Debate Tm; NFL; Science Clb; Spanish Clb; Speech Tm; Chorus; High Hon Roll; Pres Acad Fit Awd; KS ST.

POLLMILLER, MICHELLE; Parsons HS; Parsons, KS; (3); Debate Tm; Speech Tm; Chorus; Orch; School Musical; School Play; Stage Crew; U Of KS; Psych.

POLLOM, MEGAN L; Silver Lake Jr Sr HS; Silver Lake, KS; (3); 16/54; Church Yth Grp; Nwsp; Bsktbl; Crs Cntry; Pom Pon; Sftbl; Trk; Vllybl; NHS; AAU Bsktbl; HS Yth Spnsr Jr HS Yth Grp; Sprts Med.

POLOK, REGINA; Hope HS; Hope, KS; (4); 1/10; Rptr 4-H; Sec FBLA; Scholastic Bowl; Chorus; Yrbk; Pres Jr Cls; Capt Chrldng; Gov Hon Prg Awd; High Hon Roll; NHS; KS Hnr Schlr; Natl Jr Horticultural Assn Jdng Cont 4th Pl Team 93; U Of KS; Bus.

POLSTON, LESLIE A; Pittsburg HS; Pittsburg, KS; (3); #15 in class; Am Leg Aux Girls St; Cmnty Wkr; Treas FCA; Pres FTA; Office Aide; Q&S; Teachers Aide; Co-Ed Yrbk; Rep Frsh Cls; VP Soph Cls; Miss Teen Of KS; Asst & Dancer Of Jody Phillips Dance Co; Pittsburg ST Univ; Elem Ed.

POMATTO, JACQUELYN; St Mary's Colgan HS; Pittsburg, KS; (2); Cmnty Wkr; Math Tm; Pep Clb; Chorus; Sec Soph Cls; Pom Pon; Vllybl; High Hon Roll; Dnc Instrctr.

POMEROY, TROY E; Topeka HS; Topeka, KS; (3); Boy Scts; Sec Spanish Clb; Rep Nwsp; Rep Jr Cls; Treas Sr Cls; Powder Puff Ftbl; Var Trk; High Hon Roll; Church Yth Grp; Bsktbl; Frisbee Clb Pres; City Of Topeka Comm Vol Awd.

POMMIER, JENNIFER D; Northeast HS; Arma, KS; (2); 6/48; Drama Clb; Pep Clb; Scholastic Bowl; Thesps; Band; JV Bsktbl; Var Chrldng; Var Sftbl; Vllybl; High Hon Roll; Jr Ldrshp Crawford Cty; Notre Dame; Interior Decorator.

POMMIER, SYDNEY D; St Mary's Colgan HS; Pittsburg, KS; (4); Drama Clb; Library Aide; Pep Clb; Thesps; School Play; Stage Crew; Var Chrldng; Prfct Atten Awd; Pittsburg ST Univ.

PONGPUT, CHAIYA; Leavenworth HS; Leavenworth, KS; (4); 37/290; Boy Scts; Debate Tm; Intnl Clb; ROTC; School Musical; JV L Tennis; Hon Roll; MA Inst Of Tech; Aero Eng.

POOL, JOSHUA R; Great Bend Sr HS; Great Bend, KS; (2); Church Yth Grp; Teachers Aide; Band; Mrchg Band; Var Crs Cntry; Intrml Socr; Var Trk; Intrml Wt Lftg; Hon Roll; Pres Acad Fit Awd; Yth Missions Wrk; Sound Man Yth Grp Svcs; Managing Tauping Svc Bus; Sthrn CA Coll.

POOL, SARA M; Great Bend Sr HS; Great Bend, KS; (4); Church Yth Grp; Cmnty Wkr; Drama Clb; FHA; Pep Clb; Spanish Clb; SADD; Band; Mrchg Band; Pep Band; Sterling Coll; Early Ed.

POOL, SUZANN M; Morland Jr Sr HS; Penokee, KS; (3); 2/8; Church Yth Grp; Cmnty Wkr; FCA; 4-H; Office Aide; Scholastic Bowl; Speech Tm; Band; Chorus; School Play; Washburn; Pre-Law.

POORE, JENNY; Stockton HS; Woodston, KS; (1); 5/32; Drama Clb; Pres 4-H; Natl FFA Org; NFL; Pep Clb; Band; Jazz Band; Mrchg Band; Pep Band; Stage Crew; KS ST; Sprts Med.

POPE, AMANDA L; Southeast HS; Wichita, KS; (2); Teachers Aide; Hon Roll; Fine Arts.

POPE, THADDAEUS A; Washburn Rural HS; Topeka, KS; (2); Band; Church Choir; Jazz Band; Mrchg Band; Orch; Pep Band; Variety Show; JV Bsktbl; Band Awds; Musician Awds; Arch; Band.

POPELKA, AARON; Belleville HS; Munden, KS; (3); 2/41; Am Leg Boys St; Church Yth Grp; VP Natl FFA Org; Quiz Bowl; Pres Science Clb; Band; Rep Treas Stu Cncl; Var L Ftbl; High Hon Roll; NHS; KS ST Univ; Ag Ec.

POPP, C W; Hoxie HS; Studley, KS; (3); 3/43; Pres Church Yth Grp; Sec Pres Natl FFA Org; Quiz Bowl; Teachers Aide; Band; Jazz Band; School Musical; Wrstlng; High Hon Roll; NHS; KS ST Univ; Mech Engr.

POPP, MIRANDA; Ness City HS; Utica, KS; (2); FHA; Pep Clb; Chorus; JV Var Bsktbl; Vllybl; Wt Lftg; Cit Awd; High Hon Roll; Stu Achvt Awd 94-95; 95 Miss Ness Cty; Psych.

POPPE, TARA; South Gray HS; Montezuma, KS; (1); 1/30; Rptr 4-H; Quiz Bowl; Band; Chorus; Pep Band; Sec Frsh Cls; JV Bsktbl; Vllybl; High Hon Roll; Kay Clb; KS ST U; Vet Med.

POPPELREITER, HEIDI; St Marys HS; Maple Hill, KS; (3); 1/40; FCA; GAA; HOBY; Letterman Clb; Natl FFA Org; Quiz Bowl; Scholastic Bowl; Varsity Clb; Jazz Band; Orch; High 5 Bsktbl Cmp; Hnrb Mntn Bsktbl; MEL Hnrb Mntn Vlybl; MEL All-Lg Vlybl & Sftbl 95; St Qlfr Trck; KS ST U; Athltc Trnr.

POPPERLREITER, HEIDI M; St Marys HS; Maple Hill, KS; (3); 1/48; Cmnty Wkr; FCA; HOBY; Letterman Clb; Math Tm; Natl FFA Org; Pep Clb; Quiz Bowl; Scholastic Bowl; Teachers Aide; Lifeguard; Water Sfty Instr Aide; Ski; PT/ATHLETIC Trnr.

PORBANDARWALA, ALI A; Wichita East HS; Wichita, KS; (3); Cmnty Wkr; Spanish Clb; SADD; Teachers Aide; Band; Mrchg Band; L Swmmng; Hon Roll; Treas NHS; Intl Baccalaureate; WA U St Louis; Med.

PORRAZ, VICTOR M; J C Harmon HS; Kansas City, KS; (2); Band; Chorus; School Play; Stage Crew; Variety Show; Ftbl; Trk; Wrstlng; Hon Roll; Lulac & MECHA Clbs; Ldrshp Pgm; Bus Mgmt.

PORTER, AMY E; Basehor Linwood HS; Tonganoxie, KS; (3); 1/105; Church Yth Grp; Cmnty Wkr; Rep Science Clb; Ed Yrbk; Rep Frsh Cls; Rep Soph Cls; Ofcr Jr Cls; Rep Stu Cncl; JV Sftbl; L Trk; Acad Excl Banquet; Chrch Spcl Music; KSPA Regnl Jrnlsm Cont 2nd & 3rd Pl.

PORTER, AUSTIN L; Manhattan HS; Manhattan, KS; (3); Teachers Aide; School Play; Ftbl; Wt Lftg; Hon Roll; KS ST.

PORTER, BRYCE; Holton HS; Mayetta, KS; (4); 7/69; Am Leg Boys St; 4-H; Library Aide; Natl FFA Org; Teachers Aide; Chorus; L Ftbl; High Hon Roll; NHS; Prfct Atten Awd; KSU; Eng.

PORTER, ELIZABETH; Columbus HS; Galena, KS; (3); 2/100; Rptr 4-H; Pres FHA; Hosp Aide; Math Tm; Mgr(s); Var L Tennis; Var L Trk; High Hon Roll; Sec NHS; Drftng Clb; Offcrs Clb; Deans Schlsp.

PORTER, HOLLY S; Kapaun-Mt Carmel HS; Wichita, KS; (4); Church Yth Grp; SADD; Band; Chorus; Orch; Pep Band; School Musical; Variety Show; Hon Roll; Eclgy Clb; Untd Crsdrs; KS U; Bio.

PORTER, JAMES R; Goodland HS; Goodland, KS; (3); 38/87; Computer Clb; FHA; German Clb; Pep Clb; Band; Jazz Band; Mrchg Band; Orch; Pep Band; Ftbl; Ger Awd; Ft Hays ST Univ; Cmptr Sci.

PORTER, JESSICA L; Holton HS; Mayetta, KS; (1); Church Yth Grp; Cmnty Wkr; Natl FFA Org; Hon Roll; Prfct Atten Awd; KS ST Univ; Ag Bus.

PORTER, LUCAS S; Beloit Jr Sr HS; Glen Elder, KS; (2); Letterman Clb; Pres Natl FFA Org; Capt Quiz Bowl; VP Spanish Clb; SADD; Treas Frsh Cls; Treas Soph Cls; Ofcr Stu Cncl; Var Wrstlng; Hon Roll.

PORTER, MELISSA; Eureka Jr Sr HS; Eureka, KS; (2); 5/65; Letterman Clb; Quiz Bowl; Science Clb; SADD; Band; Bsktbl; Crs Cntry; High Hon Roll; Kiwanis Awd; Spanish NHS; Lions Clb Awd; KS U; Med.

PORTER, NICOLE L; Smoky Valley HS; Lindsborg, KS; (1); Church Yth Grp; FCA; Service Clb; Chorus; Orch; JV Bsktbl; JV Vllybl; Hon Roll; Church Yth Cnsl; KS Assc Yth; Lrng Dsblts Tchr.

POSLADEK, DANICA; Shawnee Mission E HS; Leawood, KS; (2); Natl Beta Clb; Q&S; Drill Tm; Rptr Yrbk; JV Sftbl; High Hon Roll; Hon Roll; Pres Schlr.

POST, CARRIE; Olathe North Sr HS; Olathe, KS; (3); 5/400; Church Yth Grp; Library Aide; Teachers Aide; Rptr Nwsp; High Hon Roll; NHS; KC Zoo Vltr; Eastern Nazarene Coll; Physl Th.

POST, CHRIS; Manhattan HS; Manhattan, KS; (4); 30/480; Church Yth Grp; Spanish Clb; Teachers Aide; Ftbl; Swmmng; Wt Lftg; High Hon Roll; Kiwanis Awd; NHS; U Of OK; Hist.

POST, JANDEE; Peabody-Burns Jr Sr HS; Burns, KS; (2); 5/49; Drama Clb; FCA; 4-H; GAA; NFL; Pep Clb; Spanish Clb; Band; Chorus; Color Guard; Mar Bio.

POST, JENNIFER L; Wichita East HS; Wichita, KS; (3); 4/294; Cmnty Wkr; Spanish Clb; Chorus; School Musical; Variety Show; Var L Chrldng; High Hon Roll; NHS; Spanish NHS; Phy Thrpst.

POST, KATHERINE S; Blue Valley Northwest HS; Overland Park, KS; (2); Debate Tm; NFL; Orch; High Hon Roll; Hon Roll; Future Prblm Slvng St Bowl 2nd Pl; Radiology.

POTTER, AMY N; Pleasant Ridge HS; Easton, KS; (3); 4-H; Natl FFA Org; SADD; Pres Frsh Cls; Sec Jr Cls; Vllybl; Cit Awd; High Hon Roll; Hon Roll; NHS.

POTTER, HEATHER L; Wetmore Schl; Wetmore, KS; (3); Science Clb; Hon Roll.

POTTER, LESLIE F; Olathe North Sr HS; Olathe, KS; (4); 1/350; Drama Clb; Spanish Clb; School Play; Stage Crew; Variety Show; Ed Yrbk; Ed Lit Mag; High Hon Roll; NHS; Pres Acad Fit Awd; Various Wrtng Cont Awds; KU.

POTTER, PERRY G; Marysville HS; Marysville, KS; (2); Art Clb; Boy Scts; Church Yth Grp; Letterman Clb; Band; Mrchg Band; Pep Band; Ftbl; Wt Lftg; Wrstlng; KS ST U.

POTTER, TRAVIS W; Labette Co HS; Coffeyville, KS; (2); Boy Scts; Church Yth Grp; FCA; Letterman Clb; SADD; Church Choir; Var L Crs Cntry; JV Trk; Cit Awd; Hon Roll; Law.

POTTORF, ERIK A; Topeka HS; Topeka, KS; (2); Church Yth Grp; Debate Tm; FCA; FBLA; Model UN; SADD; Band; Jazz Band; Ftbl; Golf; Rodeo Bullriding; KC; Law.

POTTORF, JENNIFER; Seaman Sr HS; Topeka, KS; (4); 6/248; Debate Tm; NFL; Pep Clb; Speech Tm; Treas SADD; Capt Chrldng; High Hon Roll; Prfct Atten Awd; Pres Acad Fit Awd; St Schlr; U KS; Bio.

POTUCEK, RACHEL E; Buhler HS; Hutchinson, KS; (2); Cmnty Wkr; Debate Tm; Intnl Clb; NFL; Science Clb; Spanish Clb; School Play; Stat L Trk; High Hon Roll; Hon Roll; Frnscs Tm; Physics/Lit.

POULSON, BOBBIE D; Muncie Christian Schl; Kansas City, KS; (2); Art Clb; Computer Clb; Debate Tm; Drama Clb; Math Tm; Spanish Clb; Speech Tm; Acpl Chr; Chorus; School Play; Excl Author Awd; Radiologist.

POUND, JACOB; St John Jr Sr HS; Saint John, KS; (3); FCA; Pep Clb; SADD; Band; Var Ftbl; Var Trk; Var Wt Lftg; Var Wrstlng; Hon Roll; Mst Imprvd World His Stu Awd 95-96.

POUND, LACEY J; Southeast Saline Schl; Salina, KS; (3); Church Yth Grp; FHA; Hosp Aide; Office Aide; Pep Clb; Band; Chorus; Church Choir; Flag Corp; Jazz Band; Concert Band; Select Vocal Group; Hutchinson CC; Nrsng.

POUNDS, JAMIE S; Coldwater Jr Sr HS; Coldwater, KS; (1); FCA; FHA; Pep Clb; Chorus; Variety Show; Nwsp; Vllybl; High Hon Roll; Ntl Merit Ltr; Prfct Atten Awd; SW Univ; Animal Spec.

POUPPIRT, SHAWN; Basehor Linwood HS; Basehor, KS; (2); Church Yth Grp; Cmnty Wkr; FBLA; JV Bsktbl; High Hon Roll.

POWELL, AMY; St John's HS; Beloit, KS; (1); 1/16; Boy Scts; Church Yth Grp; Cmnty Wkr; Quiz Bowl; SADD; Band; Pep Band; JV Stat Vllybl; High Hon Roll; Pres Acad Fit Awd; Explorers.

POWELL, BUBBA J; Shawnee Mission W Sr HS; Overland Park, KS; (3); FCA; Teachers Aide; JV Bsbl; Var L Ftbl; JV Wrstlng; Hon Roll; Rotry Clb Yth Ldrshp Inst.

POWELL, CODY E; Minneola Schl; Minneola, KS; (3); 7/23; Acpl Chr; Band; Chorus; Jazz Band; Pep Band; School Musical; Var Bsktbl; Var Trk; Var Vllybl; High Hon Roll; Washburn Univ; Social Work.

POWELL, CORY A; Shawnee Heights Sr HS; Topeka, KS; (3); 2/325; FBLA; Model UN; NFL; Pep Clb; Speech Tm; SADD; Teachers Aide; Chorus; Rep Sr Cls; Capt L Socr; Bus Admin.

POWELL, ERIN E; Caldwell Jr Sr HS; Caldwell, KS; (2); FCA; HOBY; Math Tm; Speech Tm; SADD; Jazz Band; Pep Band; Rep Soph Cls; Var Vllybl; Hon Roll.

POWELL, JASON D; Rose Hill HS; Rose Hill, KS; (4); Debate Tm; Drama Clb; Math Tm; Speech Tm; Thesps; Acpl Chr; School Musical; School Play; Stage Crew; Hon Roll; Friends Univ; Comp Sci.

POWELL, JESSICA L; Junction City HS; Fort Riley, KS; (1); Church Yth Grp; GAA; Hosp Aide; Red Cross Aide; Band; Mrchg Band; JV Var Tennis; High Hon Roll; Plastic Surgery.

POWELL, JULIANA; Kingman HS; Kingman, KS; (3); FBLA; SADD; Teachers Aide; High Hon Roll; NHS; Yth In Govt; Teens Today/Ldrs Tmrrw Cabinet Mbr/VP.

POWELL, JUSTIN K; Newton Sr HS; Newton, KS; (2); Art Clb; Church Yth Grp; Var L Socr; Var L Trk; High Hon Roll; Hon Roll.

POWELL, LARISSA; Eureka Jr Sr HS; Eureka, KS; (3); 1/50; Letterman Clb; Science Clb; Spanish Clb; Bsktbl; Crs Cntry; Ftbl; Vllybl; High Hon Roll; Kiwanis Awd.

POWELL, MARLEY J; Meade HS; Meade, KS; (2); Cmnty Wkr; 4-H; Key Clb; Pep Clb; Band; Pep Band; JV Bsktbl; Var Mgr(s); Trk; Stat Boy Scts; Meade HS Stdnt Trnr; Key Clb Pres 96-; SEY/TLC; Garden City CC; Sprts Med/PT.

POWELL, MYCA J; Shawnee Mission W Sr HS; Overland Park, KS; (4); Pep Clb; Teachers Aide; Hon Roll; Peer Mediator; Stu PTA Mem; Sweetheart Princess; Johnson Cty Comm Coll; Scndry.

POWELL, ROBYN R; Mankato Jr Sr HS; Mankato, KS; (3); 2/26; Church Yth Grp; Natl FFA Org; Pep Clb; Band; Chorus; Church Choir; Flag Corp; Mrchg Band; Pep Band; Swing Chorus; FFA Awds/ST Dgr; FFA WA Ldrshp Conf WA DC; KS ST Univ; Med Tech.

POWELL, STEPHANIE; Bonner Springs HS; Bonner Springs, KS; (3); #13 in class; FTA; Key Clb; Spanish Clb; SADD; Rep Jr Cls; Var Chrldng; Powder Puff Ftbl; Var Sftbl; Var Tennis; Hon Roll; Kaytts Clb; Acad Decthln; Sec Ed Tchr.

POWERS, BENJAMIN C; St Thomas Aquinas HS; Leawood, KS; (2); Boy Scts; Church Yth Grp; Cmnty Wkr; Key Clb; School Play; Pres Soph Cls; Ofcr Stu Cncl; High Hon Roll; Hon Roll; Eagle Scout; Notre Dame; Pre Med.

POWERS, COURTNEY D; Maize HS; Wichita, KS; (1); 1/308; SADD; Chorus; School Musical; Variety Show; High Hon Roll; Regnl/ST Choir Comps 1 Rnkng; Med.

POWERS, JASON W; Douglass HS; Douglass, KS; (4); 5/48; Pres VP 4-H; Band; Jazz Band; JV Wrstlng; 4-H Awd; High Hon Roll; Prfct Atten Awd; Butler Cty CC; Mech Eng.

POWERS, RACHELLE R; Labette Co HS; Altamont, KS; (3); FCA; French Clb; Library Aide; Spanish Clb; SADD; Chorus; School Musical; Mgr(s); Hon Roll; Church Yth Grp; Individual Achvmt In Lang; Emporia ST; Elem Ed.

POWERS, SHANNON R; Douglass HS; Douglass, KS; (2); 15/73; Church Yth Grp; Pres Treas 4-H; Band; Jazz Band; Mrchg Band; Pep Band; Variety Show; Mgr(s); Vllybl; High Hon Roll; Cmptr Pgrmng.

POWNELL, JESSICA L; Newton Sr HS; Newton, KS; (1); Hosp Aide; Treas Key Clb; Model UN; Ed Nwsp; Lit Mag; JV Tennis; JV Trk; High Hon Roll; Forensics ST Chmpnshps Qualifer; News Anchor In Schl TV News Prgm Railer News; Writers Club; Med.

PRACHT, CHRISTINE D; Wichita North HS; Wichita, KS; (2); 13/500; Cmnty Wkr; Latin Clb; Teachers Aide; Rep Frsh Cls; Rep Soph Cls; JV Socr; High Hon Roll.

PRADO, STEVEN M; Sumner Acad; Kansas City, KS; (3); 12/149; Pres Spanish Clb; Var Tennis; High Hon Roll; NHS; Spanish NHS; St KS Natl Span Exam 2nd Pl; Phy Thrpst.

PRALLE, SUZIE; Valley Heights Jr Sr HS; Blue Rapids, KS; (4); 9/27; Church Yth Grp; Debate Tm; Pres 4-H; FHA; Model UN; Rep Natl FFA Org; Chorus; Yrbk; Pres Sr Cls; Chrldng; 2nd Rnnr Up Marshall Cty Jr Miss; KS ST Univ; Psych; Elem Schl.

PRATER, APRIL D; Riverton Schl; Galena, KS; (2); Church Yth Grp; French Clb; FHA; Chorus; Church Choir; Hon Roll.

PRATHER, TODD; Washburn Rural HS; Wakarusa, KS; (4); Boy Scts; Band; Mrchg Band; Pep Band; Socr; Trk; Hon Roll; KS St Univ; Vet.

PRATT, AMANDA E; Turner HS; Kansas City, KS; (2); Am Leg Aux Girls St; Band; Mrchg Band; Pep Band; School Play; Variety Show; Score Keeper; Hon Roll; Prfct Atten Awd.

PREBBLE, KATIE A; Valley Falls HS; Valley Falls, KS; (1); Church Yth Grp; FBLA; GAA; Band; Pep Band; JV Stat Bsktbl; Var Sftbl; Stat Vllybl; Hon Roll; Chorus; OFALT; KAY; Pittsburgh; Tch.

PREBYL, MICHELLE; Marysville HS; Oketo, KS; (2); 2/98; Band; Mrchg Band; Pep Band; JV Tennis; Hon Roll; Kiwanis Awd.

PRECHT, KIMBERLY D; Shawnee Mission N HS; Shawnee Mission, KS; (3); 13/380; Key Clb; Pep Clb; Spanish Clb; Band; Mrchg Band; Orch; Pep Band; School Musical; L Var Swmmng; NHS; Marine Bio/Engr.

PREEDY, BILLIE; Sublette HS; Sublette, KS; (3); 11/31; Church Yth Grp; Cmnty Wkr; Pep Clb; Varsity Clb; Acpl Chr; Band; Chorus; Jazz Band; Pep Band; School Musical.

PREISNER, KENNETH; Ashland HS; Ashland, KS; (2); Teachers Aide; VP Jr Cls; L Var Bsktbl; L Var Ftbl; Hon Roll; Bsktbl All Leag; KBCA Hnrbl Men; All Area Tm Hnrbl Men.

PRENO, DEDE; Shawnee Mission East HS; Overland Park, KS; (4); 90/402; Latin Clb; Math Tm; SADD; JV Bsbl; Intrml Bsktbl; Var Ftbl; Hon Roll; NHS; Pres Acad Fit Awd; Drama Clb; Prins Grad Comm; U Of KS; Psych; Jrnlsm.

PRESCOTT, ANDY L; Manhattan HS; Manhattan, KS; (4); Boy Scts; French Clb; Band; Mrchg Band; Pep Band; Hon Roll; KS St Univ; Acctng.

PRESSGROVE, CINDY L; Topeka West HS; Topeka, KS; (2); Church Yth Grp; Cmnty Wkr; Debate Tm; French Clb; German Clb; NFL; Var L Socr; Vllybl; High Hon Roll; Hon Roll.

PRESSON, AMBER; Blue Valley HS; Stanley, KS; (2); 1/282; Cmnty Wkr; Quiz Bowl; Band; Mrchg Band; Pep Band; School Musical; JV L Crs Cntry; JV L Sftbl; JV L Vllybl; High Hon Roll.

PRESTWOOD, RACHEL A; Sabetha HS; Sabetha, KS; (2); 1/70; Church Yth Grp; Drama Clb; Model UN; Pep Clb; Spanish Clb; Var Bsktbl; Var L Trk; JV Vllybl; High Hon Roll; NHS; KS ST U.

PRETZ, ERIC M; Osawatomie HS; Paola, KS; (1); 4-H; Science Clb; Acpl Chr; Band; Mrchg Band; Pep Band; School Musical; School Play; Stage Crew; Variety Show; Music.

PREUSS, EMILIE; Phillipsburg HS; Stuttgart, KS; (2); Hosp Aide; Pep Clb; Band; Pep Band; Rep Stu Cncl; Bsktbl; Chrldng; Golf; Hon Roll; Pres FHA; K-Hy-S.

PREUSS, KEVIN M; Marysville HS; Marysville, KS; (2); Boy Scts; Drama Clb; 4-H; Natl FFA Org; NFL; 4-H Awd; High Hon Roll; Kiwanis Awd; Band; Mrchg Band; M-ACT; GCTL; Bio.

PREVITERA, JENNY L; Maize HS; Wichita, KS; (3); GAA; Letterman Clb; Science Clb; Spanish Clb; Speech Tm; SADD; Varsity Clb; Chorus; School Musical; Variety Show; KAYS KS Assoc For Yth; Phys Thpy.

PREWITT, KARA; Peabody-Burns Jr Sr HS; Florence, KS; (2); Art Clb; Church Yth Grp; Cmnty Wkr; Chorus; Nwsp; Yrbk; High Hon Roll; Hon Roll; PEAK; KS ST Univ; Comp Analyst.

PREWO, PAUL E; Thomas More Prep-Marion HS; Hays, KS; (2); 37/82; Church Yth Grp; Band; Church Choir; Mrchg Band; Pep Band; School Musical; Bsktbl; JV Ftbl; Golf; Hon Roll; Ft Hays St Univ Math Relays.

PRICE, ADAM B; Bishop Miege HS; Kansas City, MO; (1); 81/245; Church Yth Grp; Cmnty Wkr; High Hon Roll; Hon Roll; Amer Kenpo Karate; UMKC.

PRICE, AMANDA R; Goddard HS; Wichita, KS; (2); Science Clb; Spanish Clb; Rep Soph Cls; High Hon Roll; Hon Roll; Jr NHS; NHS; Current Mem Natl Parks & Conservation Assoc; K STRN; Medicine.

PRICE, COURTNEY J; Wichita Co HS; Leoti, KS; (3); 23/43; Church Yth Grp; Drama Clb; Pep Clb; Varsity Clb; School Play; Var Chrldng; Chrldng St Wrestlng Perfmnce.

PRICE, CRYSTAL; Marysville HS; Marysville, KS; (3); Sec Treas FCA; HOBY; Letterman Clb; SADD; Band; Mrchg Band; Pep Band; VP Jr Cls; Chrldng; Trk; Mtmds; Kytts; Twlr Mrchng Bnd; Benedictine; Ob.

PRICE, CYNTHIA; Perry Lecompton HS; Grantville, KS; (4); 2/70; Drama Clb; 4-H; VP FBLA; Pres Intnl Clb; NFL; Ed Lit Mag; Vllybl; NHS; Pres Schlr; Sal; Emporia St Univ; Indus Psych.

PRICE, GAYLE R; Medicine Lodge HS; Zenda, KS; (2); VP Church Yth Grp; VP 4-H; Letterman Clb; Natl FFA Org; Pep Clb; Science Clb; JV Bsktbl; Var L Sftbl; JV Vllybl; 4-H Awd; OK ST U; Sprts Med/Ath Trnr.

PRICE, JOEL N; Great Bend Sr HS; Great Bend, KS; (3); Am Leg Boys St; Chorus; Intrml Socr; Var Tennis; Hon Roll; Kays Club.

PRICE, JOSH; Seaman Sr HS; Topeka, KS; (3); Office Aide; SADD; Band; Jazz Band; Pep Band; Rep Nwsp; Ofcr Bsbl; JV Bsktbl; Var L Ftbl; High Hon Roll; Scndry Ed.

PRICE, KRISTA M; Great Bend Sr HS; Great Bend, KS; (3); Girl Scts; Acpl Chr; Chorus; Church Choir; Variety Show; Var L Tennis; High Hon Roll; Hon Roll; NHS; Prfct Atten Awd; All Conf Champion For Tnns 94 & 95; Bethany Coll; Med.

PRICE, MONIQUE; Greenburg HS; Mullinville, KS; (1); Church Yth Grp; VP 4-H; Band; Mrchg Band; Pep Band; Shooting Sprts; Lvstck Jdgng; Colby; Vet.

PRICE, RICK J; Dighton HS; Dighton, KS; (3); Church Yth Grp; FCA; Band; Chorus; Pep Band; School Musical; Bsktbl; Ftbl; Golf; Wt Lftg.

PRICE, TREVOR D; Great Bend Sr HS; Great Bend, KS; (4); Am Leg Boys St; Pep Clb; Spanish Clb; Acpl Chr; Stage Crew; Variety Show; Var Capt Crs Cntry; Intrml Socr; Var Capt Trk; Hon Roll; Barton Cty CC; Sports Medicine.

PRIDE, KIM; Manhattan HS; Manhattan, KS; (3); 29/433; Cmnty Wkr; Debate Tm; Intnl Clb; SADD; Thesps; Powder Puff Ftbl; Intrml Sftbl; Hon Roll; NHS; Sprkd/Smmr Awd; Law.

PRIEB, TREVIN S; Canton-Galva HS; Canton, KS; (2); Church Yth Grp; Computer Clb; 4-H; FBLA; Letterman Clb; Math Tm; SADD; Var Ftbl; 4-H Awd; Hon Roll; HS Rodeo.

PRIEST, KELLY; Sabetha HS; Sabetha, KS; (3); #19 in class; Church Yth Grp; Sec 4-H; FBLA; FHA; Natl FFA Org; Church Choir; Var L Bsktbl; Var L Vllybl; 4-H Awd; Prfct Atten Awd; Raise/Shw Limousn Cttle; KS Belles AAU Bsktbl Tm.

PRIEST, KERRY; Sabetha HS; Sabetha, KS; (3); 4/80; Pres Church Yth Grp; Pres 4-H; VP Natl FFA Org; Chorus; Treas Jr Cls; JV Var Bsktbl; JV Var Vllybl; 4-H Awd; High Hon Roll; NHS; Natl FFA Chorus 95; Raise/Shw Limousn Cttle; FFA Lvstck & Mts Jdgng, Pub Spkng; KS ST U; Ag Ed.

PRIEST, NATHAN; Highland HS; Guymon, OK; (4); 11/120; Am Leg Boys St; Debate Tm; Q&S; Capt Quiz Bowl; Swing Chorus; Rep Stu Cncl; Crs Cntry; High Hon Roll; Kiwanis Awd; NHS; KS Regents Acad; OSU; Enviornmental Engrng.

PRINCE, DUSTIN L; Pittsburg HS; Pittsburg, KS; (1); JV Bsbl; JV Ftbl; Wt Lftg; Hon Roll.

PRINCE, JEFF E; Pittsburg HS; Pittsburg, KS; (1); Church Yth Grp; Bsktbl; Ftbl; Var L Golf; Wt Lftg.

PRINCE, JOSEPH M; Blue Valley Northwest HS; Overland Park, KS; (4); Boy Scts; Key Clb; Phtg Nwsp; Gov Hon Prg Awd; Ntl Merit Ltr; IN U.

PRINDS, KARLY A; Blue Vlly HS; Overland Park, KS; (3); 4-H; Girl Scts; Acpl Chr; Chorus; Variety Show; Wt Lftg; 4-H Awd; Hon Roll; Natl Fed Of Blind; Comp.

PRINDS, KELLEY R; Blue Valley HS; Overland Park, KS; (3); 4-H; Intnl Clb; Latin Clb; Sftbl; Vllybl; Hon Roll; Tiger Pride Awds 3 Yrs; Multi Yr Listee; KS Univ; Path.

PRINGLE, KENNETH E; Junction City HS; Junction City, KS; (4); 51/256; FBLA; Intnl Clb; Key Clb; ROTC; SADD; Color Guard; Drill Tm; Rep Soph Cls; Rep Stu Cncl; Hon Roll; AFS; U Of KS; Intnl Bus.

PRITCHARD, JANELLE M; Salina HS South; Salina, KS; (3); French Clb; Hosp Aide; Band; Sftbl; Wt Lftg; Hon Roll; KS ST; Acctnt.

PRO, STEPHAN; Olathe South Sr HS; Olathe, KS; (4); 30/390; Yrbk; Crs Cntry; Socr; Trk; NHS; Pres Acad Fit Awd; St Schlr; Math Clb; Varsity Clb; Band; Kansas City Schlr Ath Spec Mentn; Intnl Lang Awd French; US Army Rsrv Natl Schlr Ath Awd; Wake Forest Univ; Pre Med.

PROBST, MANDY; Protection Schl; Protection, KS; (4); HOBY; Sec Frsh Cls; Pres Soph Cls; Treas Jr Cls; Sec Sr Cls; Pres Stu Cncl; Var Bsktbl; Var Chrldng; Cit Awd; DECA; Kayette Brd 4 Yrs; Dodge City CC; Bus.

PROBUS, THOMAS M; Wichita South HS; Wichita, KS; (1); Socr; Hon Roll.

PROCHASKA, KELLY A; Blue Valley Northwest HS; Overland Park, KS; (1); GAA; Chorus; Intrml Bsktbl; Capt Intrml Socr; Intrml Vllybl; High Hon Roll; Schl PE Awd; Natl Eng Merit Awd; KS Univ; Pediatrician.

PROCK, MELINDA J; Chanute Sr HS; Chanute, KS; (3); Drama Clb; Band; Chorus; Mrchg Band; School Play; Hon Roll; Hrdrssr.

PROCTOR, AMBER A; Washburn Rural HS; Auburn, KS; (2); Debate Tm; Hosp Aide; Lit Mag; High Hon Roll; Pres Acad Fit Awd; Humn Rights Club Sec; AIDS Ed Vol; Cnty Hlth Dept Vol; VA Hosp Vol; Cal ST At Berkley; Botany.

PROCTOR, ERIC A; Goddard HS; Goddard, KS; (1); Var L Bsbl; JV Socr; JV L Wrstlng; Hon Roll; Pres Acad Fit Awd; Wichita ST Univ.

PROFFER, DANIEL; Garden City Sr HS; Garden City, KS; (4); 65/320; Church Yth Grp; DECA; Key Clb; VICA; Acpl Chr; School Musical; School Play; Stage Crew; Ftbl; Wt Lftg; Garden City CC.

PROFFER, DARRICK; Garden City Sr HS; Garden City, KS; (3); Chess Clb; Church Yth Grp; Teachers Aide; Acpl Chr; High Hon Roll; Hon Roll; KS U; Psych.

PROFFER, DAVID; Garden City Sr HS; Garden City, KS; (4); Church Yth Grp; Letterman Clb; Varsity Clb; Acpl Chr; Chorus; School Musical; Stage Crew; Variety Show; Ftbl; L Wrstlng; Wrestlng Fall Guy Schlrshp; Dist Choir 3 Yrs; St Choir 2 Yrs; KS St U Smmr Choral Inst W/Rod Walker; Garden City CC; Music.

PROFFITT, JOSEPH M; Wichita North HS; Wichita, KS; (2); Church Yth Grp; Ftbl; Hon Roll.

PROFFITT, MAGGIE A; Lyons HS; Lyons, KS; (2); Church Yth Grp; Letterman Clb; NFL; Quiz Bowl; Chorus; JV Var Bsktbl; Var Tennis; High Hon Roll; NHS; Pres Acad Fit Awd; Medicine.

PROFITT, AARON; Kansas City Bible Clg High; Overland Park, KS; (3); 1/5; Boy Scts; Math Tm; School Musical; Mgr Nwsp; VP Stu Cncl; Var JV Bsktbl; High Hon Roll; Chorus; Pres Frsh Cls; Pres Soph Cls; Joseph Baldwin Acad; Sci Knwldge Bwl; ACSI Cmptn Mdlst.

PROIETTI, STEPHANIE M; Lawrence HS; Lawrence, KS; (2); Church Yth Grp; Cmnty Wkr; Drama Clb; Office Aide; Spanish Clb; Thesps; Chorus; Church Choir; School Play; Stage Crew; Nrsng Home Vol; Pediatrician.

PROROPIO, KRISTI L; Lyons HS; Lyons, KS; (2); Church Yth Grp; Pep Clb; Spanish Clb; Teachers Aide; Chorus; Vllybl; Hon Roll; Comps.

PROSSER, ELESA J; Pratt HS; Pratt, KS; (3); Pep Clb; SADD; Teachers Aide; Chorus; Stage Crew; Bsktbl; Trk; Vllybl; Hon Roll; Wichita ST Univ Sr Schlr; PT.

PROW, SARA; Olathe South Sr HS; Olathe, KS; (3); Hosp Aide; NFL; Spanish Clb; Drill Tm; School Play; Stage Crew; Powder Puff Ftbl; Hon Roll; NHS; Spanish NHS.

PRUENTE, REBECCA S; Bishop Miege HS; Shawnee Mission, KS; (3); 40/180; Am Leg Aux Girls St; Church Yth Grp; Hosp Aide; Service Clb; SADD; Teachers Aide; Church Choir; Stat Bsktbl; Mgr(s); JV Vllybl; CMT; Substance Awrnss Tm; Nrsng.

PRUESSNER, HOLLY; Atchison Sr HS; Atchison, KS; (1); Hosp Aide; Library Aide; Spanish Clb; Stat Bsktbl; Hon Roll; Univ Of KS; Child Psych.

PRUETT, JANET; Valley Falls HS; Valley Falls, KS; (3); FHA; Band; School Play; Rptr Yrbk; Hon Roll.

PRUETT, MATTHEW M; Holton HS; Holton, KS; (2); 4-H; Model UN; Quiz Bowl; Scholastic Bowl; Acpl Chr; Band; Mrchg Band; Pep Band; School Musical; Nwsp; KS Optimist Yth In Govt Prog.

PRUETT, RHONITA R; Harmon HS; Kansas City, KS; (2); Library Aide; Science Clb.

PRUITT, AMANDA; Victoria HS; Victoria, KS; (2); Letterman Clb; Speech Tm; SADD; Drill Tm; School Play; Var L Chrldng; Var L Tennis; Var L Trk; Hon Roll; NHS.

PRUITT, SONYA D; Chanute Sr HS; Chanute, KS; (1); 4-H; French Clb; Speech Tm; Band; Chorus; Mrchg Band; Stage Crew; Bsktbl; Hon Roll; Notre Dame; Med.

PRUNER, COURTNEY A; Central Heights Sr HS; Princeton, KS; (1); 6/60; Cmnty Wkr; 4-H; Treas Natl FFA Org; Science Clb; Spanish Clb; Band; High Hon Roll; Hon Roll; Mrchg Band; Pep Band; Tae Kwon Do; Dance; DVM.

PRUSA, LORI; Coldwater Jr Sr HS; Coldwater, KS; (3); Church Yth Grp; FBLA; Band; Variety Show; Yrbk; VP Stu Cncl; Crs Cntry; Trk; Vllybl; High Hon Roll; Site Cncl; KS St; Psych.

PRVETT, KELLY F; Dodge City HS; Dodge City, KS; (3); Church Yth Grp; Spanish Clb; SADD; Teachers Aide; Chorus; Sftbl; Vllybl; High Hon Roll; Jr NHS; DARE; KAYS.

PTACEK, JACOB C; Thomas More Prep-Marion HS; Hays, KS; (2); 14/83; Debate Tm; JCL; Model UN; Quiz Bowl; Scholastic Bowl; Speech Tm; Thesps; Church Choir; School Musical; School Play; Engl.

PTACEK, JASON R; Blue Valley HS; Stilwell, KS; (4); 20/230; Debate Tm; Math Tm; NFL; Chorus; School Musical; Cit Awd; High Hon Roll; Hon Roll; NHS; U Of MO Rolla; Biochem Engrng.

PTASNIK, MARK B; Immaculata HS; Leavenworth, KS; (3); 3/47; Am Leg Boys St; Cmnty Wkr; Socr; Trk; Wrstlng; High Hon Roll; NHS; KS Rgnts Hnrs Acad.

PUCHOSIC, SARAH; Mc Pherson HS; Mc Pherson, KS; (1); Art Clb; Church Yth Grp; Band; Chorus; Church Choir; School Musical; Ofcr Stu Cncl; Chrldng; Hon Roll; KS ST U; Fine Arts.

PUCKET, ANNE; Ulysses HS; Ulysses, KS; (3); Church Yth Grp; Debate Tm; FBLA; Hosp Aide; Office Aide; SADD; Band; Mrchg Band; Pep Band; NHS.

PUCKET, CONNIE; Ulysses HS; Ulysses, KS; (2); Church Yth Grp; FHA; Band; Chorus; Church Choir; Flag Corp; Jazz Band; Mrchg Band; Pep Band; School Musical.

PUCKET, MARCIA; Ulysses HS; Ulysses, KS; (4); 1/96; Church Yth Grp; Band; Chorus; Jazz Band; Sec Soph Cls; Sec Jr Cls; Trk; Hon Roll; NHS; All Amer Schlr; Miss SW KS Pgnt Pianist; Helped Build Libry In Africa; Tabor Coll; Music Ed.

PUDERBAUGH, ALLISON L; Baldwin HS; Baldwin City, KS; (3); VP Intnl Clb; Math Tm; Spanish Clb; Mrchg Band; Pep Band; School Musical; Stage Crew; Rep Stu Cncl; Hon Roll; NHS; Dead Bug Prdctns Prdcs Short Films Stdnt Body.

PUETT, LINDSAY; Shawnee Mission Nw Sr HS; Shawnee Mission, KS; (3); Church Yth Grp; Dance Clb; NFL; Speech Tm; Drill Tm; Mrchg Band; Swmmng; High Hon Roll; Hon Roll; NHS; Yng Life; Campaigners; U Of KS.

PUETZ, TIM; St Thomas Aquinas HS; Overland Park, KS; (3); Am Leg Boys St; Boy Scts; Science Clb; Treas SADD; Rptr Nwsp; Crs Cntry; Var Trk; Capt Wrstlng; High Hon Roll; VP NHS; KS Trck&Fld 2 Yrs; Art.

PUFAHL, CHRISTIN M; Wichita Southeast HS; Wichita, KS; (1); Church Yth Grp; Cmnty Wkr; Drama Clb; Teachers Aide; Trk; Vllybl; High Hon Roll; Hon Roll; Jr NHS; KS ST.

PUFAHL, SHANNON; Shawnee Heights Sr HS; Berryton, KS; (2); Yrbk; Ed Frsh Cls; Var Bsktbl; Var Sftbl; Hon Roll; Sftbl 2nd Tm All City; US Natl Jrnlsm Awds; All Amer Schlr; U KS; Ed.

PULEC, JESSICA T; Stockton HS; Stockton, KS; (4); 17/33; FHA; Pep Clb; Band; Jazz Band; Mrchg Band; Pep Band; Sftbl; Trk; Hon Roll; KS ST U; Elem Spcl Ed.

PULKRABEK, DAVID P; Derby HS; Derby, KS; (4); Church Yth Grp; Cmnty Wkr; Hon Roll; NHS; Pres Schlr; Wood Is Good; Heartland Share Pgm Vol; Cowely Cty Comm Coll; Machinist.

PULLIAM, CHRISTINA; Olathe South Sr HS; Olathe, KS; (3); GAA; Letterman Clb; Spanish Clb; Teachers Aide; Yrbk; JV Socr; JV Vllybl; High Hon Roll; NHS; Spanish NHS; KS Univ; Engnr.

PULLIAM, KENDRA M; Clearwater HS; Clearwater, KS; (2); SADD; Chorus; Stat Bsktbl; Stat Crs Cntry; Mgr(s); Score Keeper; JV Var Trk; Hon Roll; Wt Lftg; AVSO Soccer; GCTL; Tchr; Phy Thrpst.

PULS, SETH; Chaparral HS; Mt Pleasant, SC; (3); 1/63; Am Leg Boys St; Debate Tm; Key Clb; Quiz Bowl; Band; Chorus; Mrchg Band; Pep Band; High Hon Roll; NHS; CO Schl Of Mines; Mng Engrg.

PUNSWICK, KEVIN J; Blue Valley North West HS; Overland Park, KS; (4); 39/340; Intnl Clb; Band; Mrchg Band; Orch; Pep Band; Intrml Bsbl; JV Ftbl; Var Capt Swmmng; High Hon Roll; NHS; HS St Swmmng & Dvng Champ 94 & 96; Husky Awd 94; Acad All-Amer 96; Truman ST U; Med.

PURCELL, ELIZABETH; Hayden HS; Topeka, KS; (3); 22/140; Dance Clb; Intnl Clb; Pep Clb; Drill Tm; Pom Pon; High Hon Roll; NHS; Sports Med/PT.

PURCELL, JOHN S; Labette Co HS; Parsons, KS; (4); 67/128; Chess Clb; FCA; 4-H; Letterman Clb; VICA; Rptr Nwsp; Var Bsbl; Var Capt Bsktbl; Hon Roll; William-Jewell; Bus; Tech.

PURKEYPILE, CARRIE; Midland Sda Schl; Lenexa, KS; (2); Church Yth Grp; Hosp Aide; Band; Chorus; Yrbk; Pres Stu Cncl; Bsktbl; Cit Awd; Hon Roll; Natl Choral Awd; Union Coll.

PURTLE, JIM; Kansas City Bible Clg High; Mission, KS; (4); #1 in class; Boy Scts; Band; Pep Band; School Play; Ed Nwsp; VP Stu Cncl; Var Bsktbl; Var Trk; High Hon Roll; Pres Acad Fit Awd; Elec Engr.

PURTLE, LYNETTE; Kansas City Bible Clg High; Mission, KS; (1); 1/11; Church Yth Grp; Pep Clb; Band; Chorus; Church Choir; School Play; Treas Frsh Cls; Capt Var Bsktbl; Var Sftbl; High Hon Roll.

PURVIS, SAMANTHA R; Jayhawk-Linn HS; Mound City, KS; (4); Natl FFA Org; Pep Clb; Spanish Clb; Band; Chorus; Church Choir; Mrchg Band; Pep Band; Ed Yrbk; Ofcr Frsh Cls; Art Clb; Libry Clb; Arts.

PYLE, AMY; Shawnee Mission N HS; Overland Park, KS; (2); Church Yth Grp; Latin Clb; Q&S; Band; Mrchg Band; Pep Band; Nwsp; Ed Yrbk; Rep Frsh Cls; JV Bsktbl.

PYLE, ASHLEY; Dodge City HS; Dodge City, KS; (3); Math Tm; Spanish Clb; SADD; Chorus; Church Choir; Bsktbl; Trk; Vllybl; Cit Awd; NHS; Pre-Med.

PYLE, HEATHER; Pittsburg HS; Pittsburg, KS; (4); FHA; Q&S; Co-Ed Nwsp; Hon Roll; KS ST Univ; Elem Ed.

PYLE, JEFFREY A; Berean Acad; Wichita, KS; (4); Church Yth Grp; Math Tm; Acpl Chr; Band; Chorus; Mrchg Band; St Schlr; KS ST Univ; Ec.

QUACKENBUSH, KIM; Olathe North Sr HS; Olathe, KS; (3); 1/391; Math Tm; Science Clb; Band; Church Choir; Drill Tm; Jazz Band; VP Jr Cls; VP Stu Cncl; High Hon Roll; NHS; Tchng Flute Lessons Dist Band; ST/REG Cmptns Solos; Math Awd; Med.

QUANCY, CONNIE; Burlingame HS; Burlingame, KS; (4); 3/35; Am Leg Aux Girls St; 4-H; Pres FBLA; Letterman Clb; Teachers Aide; Band; L Vllybl; High Hon Roll; NHS; St Schlr; Emporia ST U; Acctng.

QUANDT, ALEXIA L; Valley Ctr HS; Valley Center, KS; (3); 9/167; Spanish Clb; Chorus; School Musical; Var Socr; Hon Roll; Pres Acad Fit Awd; Acad Awd; Soccer Coach For Younger Children; Phy Thrpst.

QUANG, PHILIP; Wichita HS SE; Wichita, KS; (4); Chess Clb; Computer Clb; High Hon Roll; Hon Roll; NHS; KU Alumni Hnr; WSU; Elec Eng.

QUARLES, AARON R; Halstead HS; Burrton, KS; (3); Quiz Bowl; Scholastic Bowl; Treas Frsh Cls; Treas Soph Cls; Var Ftbl; Var Score Keeper; Var Trk; Hon Roll; Hubbard Summer Acad For Future Tchrs 96; KAYS; Glendale CC; Scndry Ed.

QUAST, CRYSTAL A; Hutchinson HS; Hutchinson, KS; (4); 71/216; Church Yth Grp; Cmnty Wkr; Drama Clb; Office Aide; Pep Clb; Science Clb; Service Clb; VICA; Chorus; School Play; Certfd Nrss Aide; Certfd Medication & Rehabilitation Aides; Hutchinson CC; Pre-Med.

QUIGLEY, CHAD A; Thomas More Prep-Marion HS; Hays, KS; (4); Debate Tm; JCL; Model UN; Phtg Yrbk; Var Crs Cntry; Var Ftbl; Var Trk; Hon Roll; Fort Hays ST Univ.

QUIGLEY, ERIN C; Derby HS; Derby, KS; (2); Art Clb; Orch; High Hon Roll; Env Clb.

QUIGLEY, KARI; Cheerryvale HS; Cherryvale, KS; (3); FHA; HOBY; Chorus; Mgr(s); Hon Roll; CHS Jazz Choir; Tri M Sec; Elem Ed.

QUIGLEY, SARAH; Rock Creek Jr Sr HS; Westmoreland, KS; (2); Church Yth Grp; FHA; Pep Clb; SADD; Band; Var JV Bsktbl; Var Trk; Var JV Vllybl; Hon Roll; NHS; Sci Fair Soph Clss Gld Mdl, Top Hnr.

QUINLAN, SARAH A; Faith Bapt Christian Schl; Perry, KS; (2); Church Yth Grp; Teachers Aide; High Hon Roll; Prfct Atten Awd; Northland Bapt Bible Coll; Bio.

QUINN, TERE M; Wyandotte HS; Kansas City, KS; (3); Church Yth Grp; Drama Clb; Q&S; Church Choir; Ed Nwsp; Hon Roll; Oakwood Coll; Soc Work.

QUINT, KENDRA L; Hill City HS; Hill City, KS; (4); 10/40; Church Yth Grp; FHA; Pep Clb; SADD; Teachers Aide; Band; Color Guard; Phtg Nwsp; Rptr Phtg Yrbk; Acctng Stu Mnth; Strs Pub Wrte Teb; NW KS Anthlgy Wrd Prcssng Tm Of Yr; Fort Hays ST U; Elem Ed.

QUINTON, CYNTHIA; Mulvane Sr HS; Mulvane, KS; (4); 25/146; Drama Clb; FHA; Pep Clb; SADD; Teachers Aide; Thesps; Band; Chorus; School Play; Rptr Nwsp; Kay; St Frnscs; Zoology.

RAAB, NICHOLE; Pierson Jr HS; Kansas City, KS; (1); 11/302; Dance Clb; Service Clb; Ofcr Stu Cncl; High Hon Roll; NHS; Pres Acad Fit Awd; Ballet & Jazz; Foster Sister To Childrn Needing Homes For 8 Yrs; Trng In Art, Portrait Sketching; FL ST; Marine Bio; Arts.

RABER, ELIZABETH L; Wichita North HS; Wichita, KS; (4); Art Clb; Dance Clb; Metro Ballet Wichita 14 Yrs; KS Newman; Bus/Dance Tchr.

RADCLIFFE, AMY B; Hill City HS; Hill City, KS; (2); FCA; FHA; Pep Clb; Scholastic Bowl; Chorus; Bsktbl; Var Trk; Var Vllybl; Hon Roll; Church Yth Grp; Kays.

RADEBAUGH, BECKY; Buhler HS; Hutchinson, KS; (4); Cmnty Wkr; Dance Clb; Band; Drill Tm; Pep Band; Hon Roll; Wind Ensmbl Hon Band; Wrtr/Bus Mgr.

RADENBERG, KATRINA D; Hoisington HS; Hoisington, KS; (2); Intnl Clb; Pep Clb; SADD; Band; Mrchg Band; Pep Band; Variety Show; Tennis; High Hon Roll; Univ Of KS.

RADER, COURTNEY R; Bishop Carroll Catholic HS; Wichita, KS; (4); School Play; Mgr(s); Hon Roll; Sec FCA; SADD; Phtg Ed Nwsp; Phtg Ed Yrbk; Rep Soph Cls; Mgr Bsktbl; KS ST; Soc Work.

RADER, KERRI L; Wichita Heights HS; Wichita, KS; (4); 40/242; Church Yth Grp; Quiz Bowl; Scholastic Bowl; Var L Golf; Var L Trk; Hon Roll; NHS; Pres Acad Fit Awd; Pres Schlr; St Schlr; KS ST Univ; Vet.

RADER, NIKKI; Belle Plaine HS; Peck, KS; (4); 23/67; Am Leg Aux Girls St; Rptr Phtg Nwsp; VP Jr Cls; Rep Sr Cls; L Bsktbl; L Chrldng; L Pom Pon; L Trk; L Capt Vllybl; Hon Roll; US Vllybll Assn; KS ST.

RADFORD, KIRA R; Wichita North HS; Wichita, KS; (4); Latin Clb; Red Cross Aide; Science Clb; Teachers Aide; Color Guard; Yrbk; Intrml Bsktbl; Hon Roll; KS Wldlf Fed Yth Cnsrvtnst O Fyr; NEWT; River Watchers; Wichita ST Univ; Marine Bio.

RADKE, RYAN L; Salina HS South; Salina, KS; (3); Church Yth Grp; Cmnty Wkr; Office Aide; Band; Jazz Band; Mrchg Band; Pep Band; Dist Hnr Band.

RADOVICH, PETE J; St Thomas Aquinas HS; Kansas City, MO; (4); 90/241; Church Yth Grp; Hosp Aide; JA; Math Clb; Math Tm; Science Clb; Spanish Clb; Nwsp; JV Ftbl; Var L Tennis; Explrers Hosp Wrk; Stck Mrkt Clb; TX Chrstn Univ; Chem/Pre Med.

RAFFERTY, KATIE E; Bishop Miege HS; Overland Park, KS; (1); 63/258; GAA; Bsktbl; JV Socr; Hon Roll; Soccer.

RAFINER, JENNIFER M; Blue Valley Northwest HS; Overland Park, KS; (4); 104/343; Chess Clb; Office Aide; Var Sftbl; Hon Roll; NHS; Pres Schlr; Vol At Hosp; Pittsburgh St Univ; Premed.

RAGAIN, HEATHER L; Columbus HS; Columbus, KS; (4); 5/90; Math Tm; Band; Mrchg Band; High Hon Roll; PSU; Pediatrician.

RAGAN, KELLY; St Thomas Aquinas HS; Lenexa, KS; (1); Pep Clb; SADD; Capt Chrldng; JV Sftbl; Wt Lftg; Hon Roll.

RAGHAVAN, AMIT; Wichita Collegiate Schl; Wichita, KS; (4); Capt Debate Tm; Hosp Aide; NFL; Scholastic Bowl; Chorus; School Musical; Ed Nwsp; Yrbk; Var L Tennis; High Hon Roll; Natl Latin Exam Awd Summa Cum Laude 93, Maxima Cum Laude 95, Cum Laude 94.

RAGHUNATH, KRISHNA D; Shawnee Mission E Sr HS; Shawnee Msn, KS; (2); Cmnty Wkr; French Clb; Math Clb; Band; Mrchg Band; Pep Band; Hon Roll; Sky Rydres Drum & Bugle Corps Sci Fiction Clb.

RAHBAR, PEDRAM; Goddard Jr HS; Wichita, KS; (2); Chess Clb; Debate Tm; Band; Drm Mjr(t); Mrchg Band; High Hon Roll; Pres Schlr; Univ Of KS; Med.

RAIBURN, JOSHUA; Wichita West HS; Wichita, KS; (3); 27/283; Church Yth Grp; Cmnty Wkr; SADD; Var Capt Bsbl; Var Capt Bsktbl; High Hon Roll; NHS; Prfct Atten Awd; All City Bsbl 1st Tm; All City Bsktbl Hnrbl Mntn Grd.

RAIBURN, PAULA J; Campus HS; Wichita, KS; (3); Am Leg Aux Girls St; SADD; Teachers Aide; Chorus; High Hon Roll; NHS; KS ST U; Vet.

RAINES, JAME C; Hayden HS; Topeka, KS; (3); Boy Scts; Church Yth Grp; Cmnty Wkr; Debate Tm; Var Bsbl; High Hon Roll; Umpire; U Of KS; Human Bio/Pre-Med.

RAINES, NORMAN B; Shawnee Heights Sr HS; Berryton, KS; (2); Boy Scts; Band; Mrchg Band; Pep Band; JV Bsbl; Var L Crs Cntry; Var L Trk; JV Wrstlng; Hon Roll; Prfct Atten Awd.

RAINS, SHANNON L; Ft Scott HS; Fort Scott, KS; (2); Chess Clb; Church Yth Grp; JV Ftbl; High Hon Roll; Hon Roll.

RAINS, SHILOH; Wellington Sr HS; Wellington, KS; (1); 14/184; French Clb; Office Aide; SADD; Mgr(s); High Hon Roll; Jr NHS; NHS; U Of KS; Bus.

RAITT, LUCAS N; Rose Hill HS; Derby, KS; (3); Art Clb; Chorus; Ofcr Bsbl; Bsktbl; Ftbl; Socr; Hon Roll; Gold Key Art Awd.

RAJEWSKI, JUSTIN; Thomas More Prep-Marion HS; Hays, KS; (2); Church Yth Grp; Latin Clb; Band; Jazz Band; Mrchg Band; Pep Band; Ofcr Bsbl; Crs Cntry; High Hon Roll; Robert Brown Band Camp 94 & 95; KS St U Salina ACE Acad Smmr 95; U Of KS.

RALEIGH, HILARY; Little River Jr Sr HS; Windom, KS; (3); 1/27; Church Yth Grp; Spanish Clb; Chorus; School Musical; Pres Soph Cls; VP Jr Cls; Var Bsktbl; Vllybl; High Hon Roll; NHS; Washburn; PT.

RALEIGH, JILL; Concordia Jr Sr HS; Concordia, KS; (4); 14/95; French Clb; Orch; JV Bsktbl; Mgr(s); High Hon Roll; Hon Roll; NHS; Cloud Cty CC; Architecture.

RAMAGLIA, REBECCA D; Olathe South Sr HS; Olathe, KS; (4); 1/345; Q&S; Phtg Nwsp; Phtg Yrbk; Lit Mag; L Vllybl; Gov Hon Prg Awd; NHS; Pres Acad Fit Awd; Spanish NHS; Val; U Of KS; Comm.

RAMCHANDANI, ANJALI; Ulysses HS; Ulysses, KS; (2); Chorus; School Musical; Ed Nwsp; Ed Yrbk; Sec Soph Cls; Rep Stu Cncl; Tennis; High Hon Roll; Drama Clb; Piano Cpmsng, Plyng; Bio.

RAMIAS, CHRISTOPHER J; St John's Military Schl; Phoenix, AZ; (3); Rptr Yrbk; High Hon Roll; ASU; Veterinary Medicine.

RAMIREZ, JOSEPH; Dodge City HS; Dodge City, KS; (2); Temple Yth Grp; Ofcr Bsbl; Bsktbl; Ftbl; Score Keeper; Socr; Wt Lftg.

RAMIREZ, KATIE E; Atchison Sr HS; Atchison, KS; (1); Debate Tm; Chrldng; Hon Roll; Loyola U; Grphc Arts.

RAMIREZ, MIKKI L; Wichita South HS; Wichita, KS; (1); 170/489; Band; Mrchg Band; Pep Band; Prfct Atten Awd.

RAMIREZ, THOMAS C; Maur Hill Prep Schl; Kansas City, MO; (1); Boy Scts; Cmnty Wkr; Office Aide; Chorus; Stage Crew; Hon Roll; Math Achvmt Awd; Line Creek Archaeological Museum Vol; Notre Dame; Archaeology.

RAMIREZ, YESENIA K; Garden City Sr HS; Garden City, KS; (4); FHA; Office Aide; Spanish Clb; Hon Roll; La Familia Clb Sec; Garden City CC; Ed.

RAMSEY, CHAD D; Jewell HS; Randall, KS; (3); Am Leg Boys St; FCA; 4-H; Natl FFA Org; Rep Jr Cls; VP Stu Cncl; Var L Bsktbl; Var L Ftbl; Var L Trk; Hon Roll; Wendys Heisman Nom.

RAMSEY, CRYSTAL R; Chanute Sr HS; Chanute, KS; (3); 12/146; Church Yth Grp; FCA; Spanish Clb; Band; Church Choir; Mrchg Band; Pep Band; JV Sftbl; Var Tennis; JV Vllybl.

RAMSEY, DALLAS J; Louisburg HS; Louisburg, KS; (3); Am Leg Boys St; Church Yth Grp; Letterman Clb; Math Clb; SADD; Band; Drm Mjr(t); Mrchg Band; JV Var Bsktbl; Hon Roll; Soccer; Pittsburg ST Univ; PT.

RAMSEY, DAYLA C; Louisburg HS; Louisburg, KS; (2); Church Yth Grp; Debate Tm; HOBY; Letterman Clb; SADD; Band; School Play; Pom Pon; High Hon Roll; Mrchg Band; Outstndng Acad Achvmnt Sci/Bus; Hnrs Band; Soccer; Law.

RAMSEY, FREDERICO E; J C Harmon HS; Kansas City, KS; (3); Ofcr Soph Cls; Bsktbl; Ftbl; Cit Awd; KS.

RAMSEY, HEATHER D; Buhler HS; Hutchinson, KS; (2); Church Yth Grp; FCA; Band; Chorus; Mrchg Band; Pep Band; SMAD; KSU; Tchng.

RAMSEY, KYLE R; Maize HS; Maize, KS; (2); Nwsp; Hon Roll; KY St Univ.

RAMSEY, REGINA M; Maize HS; Wichita, KS; (1); GAA; School Play; Golf; Hon Roll; Pub Poetry Anthologies; Future Farmers Amer; TX A&M; Vet.

RANDALL, KELLI; Argonia Jr Sr HS; Argonia, KS; (2); 3/25; Church Yth Grp; Scholastic Bowl; Band; VP Frsh Cls; VP Soph Cls; Var Chrldng; JV Vllybl; Hon Roll; Letterman Clb; Speech Tm; League Music Fstvl Piano Solo 1st Pl Frosh-Soph Yrs; JETS.

RANDALL, LAUREN; Horton HS; Horton, KS; (2); 3/80; Church Yth Grp; Cmnty Wkr; Pep Clb; Scholastic Bowl; Drill Tm; School Play; Rep Stu Cncl; High Hon Roll; Hon Roll; NHS; Frnscs; Gftd/Tlntd Class Coll Courses Highland CC; Upward Bnd Math/Sci St Louis Univ; Purdue Univ; Crim Just/Chem.

RANDALL, MIKE; Spring Hill HS; Spring Hill, KS; (3); 1/95; Boy Scts; Chess Clb; Debate Tm; Quiz Bowl; Band; Mrchg Band; Pep Band; High Hon Roll; NHS; KRHA; Engrng.

RANDALL, MILLICENT; Olathe North Sr HS; Olathe, KS; (4); Cmnty Wkr; HOBY; Office Aide; Spanish Clb; Teachers Aide; Chorus; Drill Tm; VP Sr Cls; Pres Stu Cncl; Powder Puff Ftbl; Johnson Cty CC; Med.

RANDALL, SCOTT R; Washburn Rural HS; Topeka, KS; (4); Boy Scts; Debate Tm; Teachers Aide; Band; Jazz Band; Mrchg Band; High Hon Roll; Hon Roll; 1st Chair Trumpet; Section Ldr Band; Bio; Marine Bio; Music.

RANDEL, BETSY J; Baldwin HS; Baldwin City, KS; (4); 11/81; Pep Clb; Band; Mrchg Band; Pep Band; Rptr Nwsp; Yrbk; Sec Treas Frsh Cls; Sec Stu Cncl; Bsktbl; Hon Roll; Sr Indstrl Tech Awd; Pres Ed Awrd Otstdng Acad Achvmt; U Tech Inst; Cmptr Aided Drftng.

RANDEL, KODIE S; Cair Paravel - Latin Schl; Auburn, KS; (3); Church Yth Grp; 4-H; Teachers Aide; Acpl Chr; Band; Chorus; Orch; Socr; Vllybl; 4-H Awd; Johnson Cty CC; Dntl Hygn.

RANDLE, SCHEHERA; Wichita East HS; Wichita, KS; (4); Church Yth Grp; French Clb; Pep Clb; Acpl Chr; Chorus; Church Choir; School Musical; Variety Show; Var L Golf; French Hon Soc; Intnl Bcclrte Dplma; Haysar Brd; CO Coll; Eng.

RANDLES, TONY M; Topeka HS; Topeka, KS; (3); Cmnty Wkr; Letterman Clb; Capt Var Ftbl; Powder Puff Ftbl; JV Trk; Var Wt Lftg; Var Wrstlng; Hon Roll; Six Var Ltrs; AFSCME Union Vol; Pitt ST Univ; Bus Admin.

RANDOLPH, AMY M; Jennings Schl; Jennings, KS; (1); 1/14; Church Yth Grp; 4-H; FHA; Pep Clb; Band; Mrchg Band; Pep Band; Treas Frsh Cls; 4-H Awd; High Hon Roll.

RANDOLPH, BRETT; Goodland HS; Goodland, KS; (1); 4/110; Boy Scts; Church Yth Grp; FHA; Letterman Clb; Pep Clb; SADD; Band; Chorus; Church Choir; Mrchg Band; Biochem.

RANDOLPH, KATRINA D; El Dorado HS; El Dorado, KS; (2); Church Yth Grp; Debate Tm; Drama Clb; French Clb; NFL; School Musical; Pres Frsh Cls; Ofcr Stu Cncl; Ntl Merit Schol; Comm Vol; Harvard; Law.

RANEY, LORI J; Pratt HS; Iuka, KS; (3); Church Yth Grp; Debate Tm; FCA; 4-H; Pep Clb; SADD; Teachers Aide; Church Choir; Stage Crew; Var L Bsktbl; Kys Clb Pres; Whos Who In Sprts; Sci Olmpd Prtcpnt; Sci.

RANEY, WILTON P; Wichita North HS; Wichita, KS; (2); Chess Clb; Spanish Clb; Teachers Aide; Wrstlng; Hon Roll; KS U.

RANGEL, COREY; Wichita East HS; Wichita, KS; (4); Cmnty Wkr; Office Aide; Q&S; Variety Show; Ed Nwsp; Rep Stu Cncl; Hon Roll; KSNW Nws Chnl 3 Intrn; Vaughn Singh Schlrsp; WSU; Brdcst Jrnlsm.

RANK, DANA T; Bishop Ward HS; Kansas City, KS; (2); 19/93; Pep Clb; Rep Frsh Cls; Rep Soph Cls; JV Vllybl; Hon Roll; NHS; Law; Acctng.

RANKER, SOMMER; Ellsworth HS; Ellsworth, KS; (3); 2/67; Sec Church Yth Grp; 4-H; Natl FFA Org; Teachers Aide; Band; Mrchg Band; Pres Soph Cls; JV Var Bsktbl; JV Vllybl; High Hon Roll; Horse Trnr/Shows; Early Grad; Natl FFA Schlrshp; VFW Endwmnt; KS ST U; Animal Sci/Pre-Vet.

RANKIN, JILL K; Maize HS; Wichita, KS; (3); Treas Church Yth Grp; Drama Clb; Hosp Aide; Letterman Clb; Science Clb; Spanish Clb; SADD; Thesps; Color Guard; Stage Crew; KS Assocn For Yth; MVP On JV Scr; KS U; Psych.

RAO, SUMITHRA; Blue Valley Northwest HS; Overland Park, KS; (1); Drama Clb; Acpl Chr; Chorus; High Hon Roll; Hon Roll; Singr; Voc Lessns; Ind Stud Corss From U Of MO World & Medvl His; Artst; Acad Excl In Art Cert 95-96; Pre-Med; Psychitrst; Authr-Rsrch.

RAPLE, BRAD J; Andale HS; Colwich, KS; (2); Church Yth Grp; Letterman Clb; Quiz Bowl; JV Var Wrstlng; Hon Roll.

RAPP, MELISSA NOELLE; Olathe South Sr HS; Olathe, KS; (4); Church Yth Grp; Debate Tm; French Clb; NFL; Band; Color Guard; Mrchg Band; Orch; High Hon Roll; KS Optmst Yth Govt; Show Me South Club; U Of Evansville; Pol Sci/Fr.

RAPP, REBEKAH K; Northeast HS; Arma, KS; (2); 1/47; FHA; NFL; Scholastic Bowl; Co-Ed Nwsp; Val; Pittsburg ST Univ; Acctng.

RAPSON, HILLARY A; Gardner-Edgerton HS; Gardner, KS; (2); Church Yth Grp; Spanish Clb; Hon Roll; Chrch Yth Grp Tecate Mssn Trp; KS City Art Inst; Hallmark.

RASMUSSEN, ERIKA N; Independence HS; Independence, KS; (1); French Clb; NFL; Band; Color Guard; Mrchg Band; Orch; High Hon Roll; Pres Acad Fit Awd; Twirler For Marching Band.

RASSETTE, MATTHEW; Abilene HS; Abilene, KS; (3); 2/150; Am Leg Boys St; CAP; Debate Tm; FBLA; German Clb; NFL; Quiz Bowl; Var L Ftbl; Var L Trk; High Hon Roll; Ec For Ldrs; Prog Spon By Fndtn For Teaching Ec; Vet; Frgn Svc.

RATHBUN, LISA; Ellis HS; Ellis, KS; (4); SADD; Chorus; School Play; Nwsp; Yrbk; Bsktbl; Sftbl; Trk; Vllybl.

RATHBUN, THERESA B; South Haven Schl; Ponca City, OK; (1); FCA; FHA; Pep Clb; Band; Chorus; Church Choir; Mrchg Band; Orch; Pep Band; School Musical; TCU; Chrstn Singer/Missions Fl.

RATHBUN, TIFFANI D; Great Bend Sr HS; Great Bend, KS; (1); Church Yth Grp; FCA; Pep Clb; Chorus; Mrchg Band; Var Mgr(s); Var Swmmng; Stat Vllybl; High Hon Roll; Hon Roll; Grand Canyon U; His/Sec Tchg.

RATLIFF, TONI; Campus HS; Haysville, KS; (3); Church Yth Grp; Debate Tm; HOBY; Church Choir; VP Frsh Cls; VP Soph Cls; VP Jr Cls; Powder Puff Ftbl; Trk; Vllybl; Chrch Yth Grp Teen Ldrshp Cncl; Campus Life Co-Pres; Piano; Cntrl Bible Coll; Pastoral Cnsl.

RATZLAFF, DEIDRA L; Haven HS; Hutchinson, KS; (3); Church Yth Grp; SADD; Chorus; Vllybl; Phys Thrpy.

RAUHUT, ABBY R; Wamego HS; Wamego, KS; (2); Church Yth Grp; FCA; VP FHA; Church Choir; School Musical; JV Var Bsktbl; Var L Tennis; JV Trk; Hon Roll; NHS.

RAULSTON, BRIAN A; Junction City HS; Junction City, KS; (3); Var L Wrstlng; High Hon Roll; Manhattan Tech Ctr; Comp Repair.

RAUSCH, CYNDEE D; Labette Co HS; Parsons, KS; (3); 15/143; Rep Stu Cncl; Intrml Tennis; Church Yth Grp; FHA; SADD; Flag Corp; NHS; Ntl Merit Schol; KAY Brd 2 Yrs/VP 1 Yr; Part Schl Piano Rctls; Pittsburg ST Univ; Acctg.

RAUSCH, ERIC J; Chanute Sr HS; Chanute, KS; (3); FCA; FBLA; FHA; Var L Ftbl; Var L Trk; Hon Roll.

RAUSCH, JENNIFER L; Garden Plain Jr Sr HS; Viola, KS; (3); Church Yth Grp; 4-H; SADD; Var L Bsktbl; Cit Awd; 4-H Awd; Hon Roll; NHS; Drama Clb; Pep Clb; Chisolm Trl Rodeo Queen; Haysvillesddl Clb Rodeo Queen; Colby CC; Equine Sci.

RAUSCH, KRISTINE A; Andale HS; Andale, KS; (1); Church Yth Grp; Drama Clb; Scholastic Bowl; Spanish Clb; SADD; Band; Chorus; Mrchg Band; Pep Band; School Play; KS Univ.

RAUSCH, MELISSA A; Garden Plain Jr Sr HS; Viola, KS; (2); 2/30; Church Yth Grp; Letterman Clb; SADD; Pres Soph Cls; JV Bsktbl; Var Pom Pon; Var Trk; JV Vllybl; High Hon Roll; Quiz Bowl; Forensics.

RAUSCH, SARA L; Wichita Southeast HS; Wichita, KS; (2); #1 in class; Drama Clb; Pom Pon; High Hon Roll; Hon Roll; NHS; Ballet; Gifted Prgm; Modeling; KSU.

RAVIS, LORI N; Blue Valley Northwest HS; Overland Park, KS; (3); Cmnty Wkr; HOBY; Temple Yth Grp; Hon Roll; Bnai Brith Yth Org Cncl Pres.

RAY, BRANDI M; Buhler HS; Hutchinson, KS; (2); Church Yth Grp; FCA; FHA; German Clb; Girl Scts; Letterman Clb; Chorus; JV L Bsktbl; JV L Sftbl; Stat L Vllybl; Tchrs Choice Awd; Ofcr FHA; 1 Star Ratng FHA Star Event Creed; KS Univ; Pedtrcn/HS Tchr.

RAY, DAMIEN T; Circle HS; Towanda, KS; (3); JV Var Bsktbl; Var Trk; Hon Roll.

RAY, DANICA E; Maize HS; Wichita, KS; (2); Church Yth Grp; FCA; French Clb; Band; Church Choir; Mrchg Band; Pep Band; French Hon Soc; High Hon Roll; NHS; Forensics; Flute Ensembles; Music Ed/Performance.

RAY, DIANA L; Medicine Lodge HS; Lake City, KS; (4); 7/54; Church Yth Grp; Pres 4-H; Var Bsktbl; Var Sftbl; Var Vllybl; 4-H Awd; High Hon Roll; Hon Roll; NHS; Prfct Atten Awd; Emporia ST Univ; Elem Ed.

RAY, KYLIE M; Circle HS; Towanda, KS; (2); Church Yth Grp; Dance Clb; FCA; Drill Tm; Yrbk; Golf; Pom Pon; Vllybl; KS St Univ; Bus.

RAY, PRISCILLA; Wyandotte HS; Kansas City, KS; (1); Church Yth Grp; SADD; Church Choir; Chrldng; Hon Roll; Magnet & Entrepreneur Pgm; Cnslr; Soc Work.

RAY, RANDA; Northern Valley HS; Almena, KS; (4); 3/10; Am Leg Aux Girls St; Church Yth Grp; Cmnty Wkr; Dance Clb; Pep Clb; Scholastic Bowl; Spanish Clb; Teachers Aide; Acpl Chr; Band; KSU; Mass Commnctns.

RAY, ROCHEL L; Topeka HS; Topeka, KS; (2); SADD; Vllybl; Hon Roll; Child Day Care.

RAY, SHAWN M; Madison Jr Sr HS; Madison, KS; (2); Boy Scts; Church Yth Grp; Cmnty Wkr; Pep Clb; SADD; Var Ftbl; Var Mgr(s); Var Wt Lftg; Schl Maintenance Work JPA Job Trng 95-96; Flint Hills Voc Schl Emporia Industrial Maintenance; Emporia ST Univ.

RAY, THERESA L; Sumner Acad Of Arts & Science; Kansas City, KS; (3); 27/148; Art Clb; Latin Clb; Spanish Clb; SADD; High Hon Roll; NHS; Ricks Col; Med.

RAYA, RACHEL; Trinity Catholic HS; Hutchinson, KS; (4); Debate Tm; Drama Clb; NFL; SADD; Thesps; School Play; Stage Crew; Yrbk; Church Yth Grp; Office Aide; Hutchinson CC; Early Ed.

RAYMER, KEVIN; Russell HS; Russell, KS; (4); 3/66; Boy Scts; Rep Stu Cncl; Var L Ftbl; Var L Trk; Var L Wt Lftg; Cit Awd; High Hon Roll; NHS; Pres Acad Fit Awd; Sal; KS Hnr Schol; U Of Ks; Phys Thpy.

RAYMOND, BRAD; Anderson Cty Jr Sr HS; Garnett, KS; (2); 3/80; Church Yth Grp; Cmnty Wkr; Pep Clb; SADD; Pres Frsh Cls; Rep Soph Cls; Treas Jr Cls; Ofcr Stu Cncl; L Bsbl; L Ftbl.

RAYMOND, JENNIFER K; Anderson Cty Jr Sr HS; Garnett, KS; (4); 1/80; Church Yth Grp; Cmnty Wkr; Intnl Clb; Pep Clb; Science Clb; Yrbk; Treas Frsh Cls; Treas Soph Cls; Pres Jr Cls; Ofcr Sr Cls; NHS Schlrshp; KS ST U; Phys Thrpy.

RAYMOND, SCOTT; Maranatha Acad; Belton, MO; (3); Chess Clb; Church Yth Grp; Computer Clb; Pep Clb; Band; Jazz Band; Mrchg Band; Pep Band; School Musical; Stage Crew; Several Mission Trips; Sax Solo Best Cls Medal Reg ACSI Fstvl/Digital Photo Best Cls Medal; Electrnc Commnctns.

RAZAFSKY, DAVID S; Blue Valley Northwest HS; Overland Park, KS; (2); 53/409; Church Yth Grp; Temple Yth Grp; Band; Mrchg Band; Pep Band; Mgr(s); Socr; Hon Roll; KS Univ Mdcl Ctr Vol; Mayors Christmas Tree Vol; Med/Sprts Med.

RAZAK, DESIREE D; Holton HS; Holton, KS; (3); Q&S; Teachers Aide; Nwsp; Yrbk; Hon Roll; Kayettes; Art; Pittsburg ST U; Bus; Mgmt.

READ, MEGAN L; Wichita East HS; Wichita, KS; (4); 2/256; Church Yth Grp; Cmnty Wkr; Debate Tm; Pres NFL; Speech Tm; Teachers Aide; Church Choir; Capt L Socr; High Hon Roll; NHS; Ntl Dbt; William Jewell; Chem.

READINGER, JENNIFER; Ft Scott HS; Pittsburg, KS; (4); Letterman Clb; Pep Clb; Spanish Clb; JV Var Bsktbl; JV Var Chrldng; JV Var Crs Cntry; Var Sftbl; JV Var Vllybl; High Hon Roll; NHS; Physcs Clb; Hstry Clb; Labetta CC; Rdlgy.

READMAN, LUCAS M; Maranatha Acad; Olathe, KS; (4); Church Yth Grp; School Play; Stage Crew; Ed Yrbk; Var Bsktbl; Var Socr; Traveled With Intnl Soccer USA To Europe Playing Soccer; Schl Vol; Sterling Coll.

REAMER, ERIC; Rossville HS; Delia, KS; (3); 7/47; FBLA; Letterman Clb; Quiz Bowl; Stage Crew; Rep Stu Cncl; JV Bsktbl; Capt Crs Cntry; Var Trk; High Hon Roll; Prfct Atten Awd; Cmptr Sci.

REARDON, TRISTIN D; Victoria HS; Victoria, KS; (2); Math Tm; Pep Clb; SADD; Chorus; JV Tennis; High Hon Roll; Hon Roll; NHS; Elem Ed.

REBANT, NICHOLAS A; Atchison Sr HS; Atchison, KS; (2); Church Yth Grp; JV Var Bsktbl; JV Ftbl; Wt Lftg; Hon Roll; Superstar Awd Fr; Acctng.

REBECK, NICHOLAS; Bishop Ward HS; Kansas City, KS; (1); 1/120; Cmnty Wkr; Var L Socr; Var L Trk; JV Wrstlng; High Hon Roll; KCMO Michael Forbes CCVI Trolley Run 2nd Pl; Engl Dept Outstdng Frosh Stu Awd Engl II.

REBER, KELLEY; Chaparral HS; Anthony, KS; (2); Dance Clb; FCA; Key Clb; Pep Clb; Ski Clb; Chorus; Nwsp; Yrbk; Chrldng; Hon Roll; KS ST U; Nrsng.

RECTOR, COLLEEN; Hugoton HS; Hugoton, KS; (4); 6/64; Church Yth Grp; Pres FCA; Ofcr Stu Cncl; Vllybl; Hon Roll; NHS; Emporia ST U; Bus Ed.

RECTOR, TIMOTHY S; Stanton Co HS; Johnson, KS; (3); 3/35; Church Yth Grp; FBLA; Scholastic Bowl; Band; Chorus; Jazz Band; Mrchg Band; Pep Band; School Play; Variety Show.

REDBURN, TODD E; Blue Valley North HS; Leawood, KS; (2); Church Yth Grp; Model UN; JV Socr; Intrml Trk; Intrml Wt Lftg; Hon Roll; Prfct Atten Awd; KS U; Hist.

REDD, CHRISTY; Frontenac Jr Sr HS; Frontenac, KS; (4); 3/35; Drama Clb; Pep Clb; Scholastic Bowl; Spanish Clb; Band; Flag Corp; School Play; Hon Roll; Pres NHS; Sec Stu Cncl; Stu Of Mnth; St Msc Fest; Pittsburg ST U; Bio.

REDDIG, ROBERT T; Bishop Miege HS; Kansas City, MO; (3); 2/170; Am Leg Boys St; Boy Scts; Capt Quiz Bowl; VP Science Clb; Ftbl; JV Wrstlng; High Hon Roll; Hon Roll; NHS; Eagle Scout; U Of MO Sci/Math/Tech Inst.

REDDING, HEATHER R; Sumner Acad Of Arts & Science; Kansas City, KS; (3); 2/150; Cmnty Wkr; Key Clb; Latin Clb; Library Aide; Spanish Clb; Chorus; High Hon Roll; NHS; Ntl Merit Ltr; Spanish NHS.

REDDY, MADHAVI P; Thomas More Prep-Marion HS; Hill City, KS; (4); 43/98; Drama Clb; French Clb; Library Aide; Speech Tm; Nwsp; Crs Cntry; Trk; Hon Roll; Ambassadors; Pres Awd For Outstdng Edcl Imprvmnt; U Of KS; Psych.

REDEKER, JAMIE; Olpe Schl; Olpe, KS; (2); 25/26; Cmnty Wkr; Sec Soph Cls; Var Bsktbl; Var Trk; Var Vllybl; High Hon Roll.

REDEKER, TRAVIS; Olpe Schl; Olpe, KS; (3); 1/26; Cmnty Wkr; Scholastic Bowl; Ofcr Stu Cncl; Var Bsktbl; Var Ftbl; Trk; High Hon Roll.

REDETZKE, BRANDON L; Cimarron HS; Cimarron, KS; (4); Am Leg Boys St; Church Yth Grp; Letterman Clb; Red Cross Aide; Teachers Aide; Band; Pres VP Stu Cncl; Bsktbl; Crs Cntry; Ftbl; Nrsng.

REDFERN, DAVID; Maranatha Acad; Kansas City, MO; (3); 3/50; Chess Clb; Church Yth Grp; Intrml Tennis; Var Trk; High Hon Roll; Hon Roll; Ntl Merit Ltr; Nom US Natl Math Awd; Mech Engr.

REDING, STACEY; Wabaunsee HS; Alma, KS; (1); Church Yth Grp; FBLA; Quiz Bowl; Bsktbl; JV Sftbl; Trk; Vllybl; Hon Roll.

REECE, ADAM; Udall HS; Udall, KS; (2); Quiz Bowl; High Hon Roll; Prfct Atten Awd; Nrsng Hm Vstr; Chrch Ldrshp Cmp.

REECE, CORY K; Pawnee Heights East HS; Burdett, KS; (1); 3/15; Speech Tm; VP Frsh Cls; Var Bsktbl; Var Ftbl; Hon Roll; KS ST Univ; Phy Thrpst.

REED, ALICIA M; Great Bend Sr HS; Great Bend, KS; (3); 1/315; Cmnty Wkr; Debate Tm; Math Tm; Pres NFL; Scholastic Bowl; Rep Spanish Clb; Speech Tm; Golf; High Hon Roll; NHS; Amer Lgn Ortrcl 4th Pl ST; VFW Voice Of Democracy Spch 5th Pl; U KS; Engrng Physics.

REED, ALLISHA; Wichita East HS; Wichita, KS; (2); 44/339; Teachers Aide; Church Choir; Hon Roll; SSBS; Pedtrc.

REED, AMANDA; Spring Hill HS; Olathe, KS; (2); Church Yth Grp; Debate Tm; FCA; 4-H; NFL; Band; Mrchg Band; Pep Band; JV Bsktbl; JV Sftbl; San Diego ST; Sprts Med.

REED, BARRY L; Circle HS; Towanda, KS; (2); 4/125; Drama Clb; Math Clb; Math Tm; Q&S; Quiz Bowl; Scholastic Bowl; Spanish Clb; Acpl Chr; Orch; School Musical; Pre-Law; Math.

REED, BECKY; Mc Pherson HS; Mc Pherson, KS; (4); 16/280; Debate Tm; DECA; NFL; SADD; Teachers Aide; Thesps; Jazz Band; Mrchg Band; Pep Band; School Musical; Washburn Univ; Lwyr.

REED, CODY; Syracuse Jr Sr HS; Syracuse, KS; (3); 1/36; Letterman Clb; Library Aide; Chorus; Intrml Bsktbl; Var Ftbl; Var Golf; Cit Awd; High Hon Roll; KS ST U; Dntl.

REED, DAVID W; Newton Sr HS; Newton, KS; (1); Boy Scts; Church Yth Grp; Chorus; Trk; Brigham Young Univ; Zoology.

REED, ERIN C; Garden City Sr HS; Garden City, KS; (3); Church Yth Grp; Acpl Chr; Chorus; Rep Jr Cls; Rep Stu Cncl; Bsktbl; Sftbl; Vllybl; DARE; KS ST Univ; Psych.

REED, HEATHER D; Lawrence HS; Lawrence, KS; (2); Church Yth Grp; Cmnty Wkr; Debate Tm; JA; Teachers Aide; Chorus; Chrldng; High Hon Roll; Hon Roll; Baker Univ; Span; Bus.

REED JR, JOSEPH M; Blue Valley HS; Stilwell, KS; (2); Boy Scts; Latin Clb; JV Var Swmmng; Var Trk; Fbr Opt.

REED, KARA R; Caldwell Jr Sr HS; Caldwell, KS; (3); Drama Clb; Pep Clb; Speech Tm; SADD; Band; Chorus; Mrchg Band; Pep Band; School Play; Stage Crew; Acadmc Ltr.

REED, KATIE M; Erie HS; Erie, KS; (4); 4/41; Church Yth Grp; Pres Drama Clb; Pres 4-H; Scholastic Bowl; Science Clb; Sec Spanish Clb; Church Choir; Hon Roll; NHS; St Schlr; KS Hnr Schlr; Outstdng Stu In Math & Sci; CNC Acad All Conf Team; Labette CC; Engrng.

REED, KERI A; Salina HS South; Salina, KS; (3); Church Yth Grp; Teachers Aide; Band; Hon Roll; NHS; Chrch Yth Elder; Key Rexall Pharm Clerk; KS ST Univ; Acctng.

REED, MARCI N; Shawnee Mission W Sr HS; Lenexa, KS; (2); 81/426; Church Yth Grp; Cmnty Wkr; German Clb; GAA; NFL; Pep Clb; Speech Tm; Teachers Aide; Hon Roll; U Of KS; Tchr; Child Dev.

REED, MATT; Ft Scott HS; Fort Scott, KS; (2); Church Yth Grp; Cmnty Wkr; French Clb; Wrstlng.

REED, MISCHELLE M; Goddard HS; Wichita, KS; (2); Debate Tm; NFL; Chorus; Hon Roll.

REED, NICHOLAS; Olathe South Sr HS; Olathe, KS; (3); Teachers Aide; Band; Stage Crew; Phtg Nwsp; Phtg Yrbk; Phtg Lit Mag; Rep Soph Cls; Rep Jr Cls; Intrml Bsktbl; High Hon Roll; Gold Key Awd Art Cmptn; Mrktg; Advertising.

REED, PHILIP; Derby HS; Derby, KS; (3); Church Yth Grp; FCA; Acpl Chr; Chorus; Church Choir; Ofcr Stu Cncl; JV Var Ftbl; Var Trk; Var Wrstlng; High Hon Roll; ST Musical Fstvl Mxd Ensmbl I Ratg; 2nd Tm All Leag Lnbckr; PT.

REED, RAYMOND J; Shawnee Mission Northwest HS; Shawnee, KS; (4); Pres Pep Clb; Teachers Aide; Thesps; School Musical; School Play; Stage Crew; Variety Show; VP Frsh Cls; VP Soph Cls; Rep Jr Cls; Outstndng Stu 93; Bst Actr 94; Bst Spprtng Actr 95; Amer Acad Drmtc Arts; Actr.

REED, REBECCA K; Shawnee Heights HS; Berryton, KS; (3); Church Yth Grp; Cmnty Wkr; FCA; 4-H; Intnl Clb; JA; Office Aide; Science Clb; SADD; Teachers Aide.

REED, SCOTT A; Basehor Linwood HS; Bonner Springs, KS; (4); #1 in class; Boy Scts; Math Clb; Scholastic Bowl; School Play; Ed Nwsp; High Hon Roll; Ntl Merit SF; Prfct Atten Awd; St Schlr; Val; KS Brd Of Regnts Hnrs Acad; FBLA Natl Conf; KS St U; Scndry Gftd Ed.

REED, SHAUNE C; Galena HS; Galena, KS; (2); 17/43; Church Yth Grp; Cmnty Wkr; Temple Yth Grp; High Hon Roll; Hon Roll; MO Southern Coll; Lawyer/Tchr.

REED, TYSHIA R; Wichita West HS; Wichita, KS; (2); Church Choir; Drill Tm; Ofcr Soph Cls; Bsktbl; Hon Roll; Career Pathways; Wichita ST Univ; Med Doctor.

REEDER, ADDRIENNE M; Iola Sr HS; Iola, KS; (2); SADD; Band; Mrchg Band; Pep Band; Stage Crew; Capt Trk; JV Vllybl; Hon Roll; Sftbl; KS Univ; Ath.

REEDER, SARIAH N; Garden City Sr HS; Garden City, KS; (2); Church Yth Grp; Bsktbl; Score Keeper; Trk; Vllybl; Wt Lftg.

REEDY, ERIK; Topeka West HS; Topeka, KS; (3); 1/240; HOBY; Math Clb; Quiz Bowl; Service Clb; Spanish Clb; Rep Frsh Cls; Rep Soph Cls; Rep Jr Cls; High Hon Roll.

REEL, AMY R; Onaga HS; Blaine, KS; (3); Pep Clb; Spanish Clb; Chorus; Drill Tm; School Play; Sftbl; Trk; Vllybl; Hon Roll; Prfct Atten Awd; Dentistry; Orthodontics.

REESE, CHRISTOPHER REAGAN; St John's Military Schl; Prior Lake, MN; (3); 3/30; Chess Clb; Cmnty Wkr; VP Computer Clb; Math Clb; Quiz Bowl; ROTC; Scholastic Bowl; Science Clb; Ski Clb; Teachers Aide; Natl Sojourners Awd; Rifle Team Captain; Biking; Running; Reading; Pharmacy.

REESE, MONICA; Goddard HS; Goddard, KS; (4); 11/152; German Clb; NFL; SADD; Thesps; Chorus; Jazz Band; School Musical; Tennis; NHS; Bible Clb; Friends U; Msc/Theatre Ed.

REESE, REBECCA A; Hill City HS; Hill City, KS; (4); 10/35; VP FHA; Sec Pep Clb; SADD; Teachers Aide; Chorus; Stage Crew; Treas Sr Cls; Bsktbl; Chrldng; Mgr(s); KAYS Pres; Explrs VP & Pres; US Marine Corps Schol Awd; U Of KN; Grphcdsgn.

REEVES, CHRISTY M; Parsons HS; Parsons, KS; (1); 26/148; Sftbl; Vllybl; Hon Roll; Sprts Clb.

REEVES, JESSICA E; St Thomas Aquinas HS; Olathe, KS; (4); 33/231; French Clb; NFL; SADD; School Play; Yrbk; High Hon Roll; Hon Roll; NHS; Pres Schlr; St Schlr; NW MO ST Univ; Scndry Ed.

REEVES, KURT J; Goddard HS; Wichita, KS; (1); Church Yth Grp; Crs Cntry; Trk; High Hon Roll; Pres Acad Fit Awd; Crss Cntry & Trk Frosh St; Crss Cntry Record; Trk Record; Acctnt; CPA.

REEVES, SAMUEL M; Columbus HS; Columbus, KS; (3); VICA; Hon Roll.

REEVES, SHANA M; Northeast Magnet HS; Wichita, KS; (4); CAP; Cmnty Wkr; Girl Scts; Hosp Aide; Teachers Aide; Variety Show; Prfct Atten Awd; Achieving Women In Sci Tech & Math; Outstndg Comm Svc; KS Jr Acad Of Sci Reg & St Finals; Wichita ST Univ; Aero Engr.

REEVES, SHANNON L; Piper HS; Kansas City, KS; (4); 24/84; Church Yth Grp; Debate Tm; FCA; Mu Alpha Theta; Spanish Clb; SADD; Teachers Aide; Chorus; Ed Nwsp; Vllybl; KC CC Acad Schol, Schlr Lttr; Bioclb; Stu Of Mnth; KSPA St Jrnlsm 1st; Engl Lit Perf Cert; KC CC.

REEVES, TIFFANY L; Northeast Magnet HS; Wichita, KS; (3); Cmnty Wkr; Red Cross Aide; Chorus; Variety Show; Sec Soph Cls; Ofcr Stu Cncl; Hon Roll; Prfct Atten Awd; Wichita River Festival Prairie Schooner Mate 96; Reg & St Sci Olympiad; Exec HS Internship; Bryn Mawr; Archaeology; Med Anth.

REGAN, FELICIA M; Santa Fe Trail Jr HS; Olathe, KS; (1); Teachers Aide; Ed Co-Ed Yrbk; Ofcr Stu Cncl; Bsktbl; Trk; Vllybl; Hon Roll; Was Recognized For PE & Yrb At Acad Awds; San Diego U; Oceanographer.

REGAN, JAMES P; Blue Valley Northwest HS; Overland Park, KS; (3); Teachers Aide; Band; Mrchg Band; Orch; Pep Band; Socr; Hon Roll; People To People Stdnt Ambsdr Europe 96; Aviation Club; Aviaon/Bus.

REGAN, KATIE; St Thomas Aquines HS; Shawnee Mission, KS; (2); Chrldng; Powder Puff Ftbl; Spirit Clb; Tchr.

REGENSBERG, AMANDA A; Liberal HS; Liberal, KS; (3); Debate Tm; French Clb; German Clb; NFL; Science Clb; Speech Tm; Band; Mrchg Band; Pep Band; Sftbl; Competitive Forensics; KS State; Vet Med.

REGIER, CARLIN; Hillsboro HS; Hillsboro, KS; (2); 4/50; Church Yth Grp; Chorus; School Musical; School Play; Sec Soph Cls; JV Vllybl; High Hon Roll.

REGIER, ERICA; Liberal HS; Liberal, KS; (3); Art Clb; Church Yth Grp; Band; Mrchg Band; Pep Band; Pratt St Univ; Art.

REGIER, KIM A; Newton Sr HS; Newton, KS; (4); Church Yth Grp; Dance Clb; German Clb; Library Aide; Office Aide; Varsity Clb; Drill Tm; Mgr(s); Pom Pon; Swmmng; DARE; DARE Mentor; KS St Univ; Elem Ed.

REGNIER, JASON C; Salina HS Central; Salina, KS; (2); Debate Tm; Band; Mrchg Band; Pep Band; Hon Roll; Frnscs.

REH, WADE; Inman Jr Sr HS; Inman, KS; (4); 8/29; Natl FFA Org; Teachers Aide; VP Frsh Cls; VP Soph Cls; High Hon Roll; Treas NHS; Natl Yth Ldrshp Conf; FFA Equine Sci Dist & Anml Spclty; OK ST U; Animal Sci.

REICHEL, CHRISTINA M; Shawnee Mission N HS; Overland Park, KS; (2); 168/463; Cmnty Wkr; Drama Clb; GAA; Hosp Aide; Pep Clb; Drill Tm; Stage Crew; JV Mgr(s); Hon Roll; Score Keeper; VFW Ladies Aux Jr Grls Unit St Asst Cndctrss & Lcl Sec Treas; JCCC; Phrmcst.

REICHENBERGER, JULIE M; Andale HS; Mount Hope, KS; (1); Church Yth Grp; SADD; Flag Corp; Pep Band; Treas Frsh Cls; Var L Crs Cntry; Var L Trk; 4-H Awd; High Hon Roll; Pres Acad Fit Awd; Wichita ST.

REICHENBERGER, MARCY A; Andale HS; Mount Hope, KS; (4); 3/65; Church Yth Grp; 4-H; SADD; Band; Church Choir; Flag Corp; Cit Awd; High Hon Roll; NHS; Pres Acad Fit Awd; Wllc Schlr; Physcs & Home Ec Awds; Wichita ST U; Engrng.

REICHLE, HEATHER M; Topeka HS; Topeka, KS; (2); Dance Clb; Debate Tm; Drama Clb; Pep Clb; Drill Tm; Yrbk; High Hon Roll; Hon Roll; Eutopia Club.

REID, AMY; Goddard HS; Wichita, KS; (3); Church Yth Grp; Science Clb; VP SADD; Chorus; Church Choir; Variety Show; Var Chrldng; Trk; High Hon Roll; NHS; Bible Clb; Spirit Clb; Ft Hays ST; Phy Thrpst.

REID, ERIN N; Leavenworth HS; Leavenworth, KS; (2); 8/423; Cmnty Wkr; Pres Debate Tm; Pres NFL; School Play; Rptr Nwsp; Rep Stu Cncl; L JV Tennis; High Hon Roll; NHS; Math Tm; Close-Up Clb Sec; Tlnt Identification Pgm Duke Univ; Theatre; Pol Sci.

REID, KRISTEN; Maize HS; Wichita, KS; (1); Var Chrldng; Hon Roll; KS Univ; Bus/Advrtsmnt.

REID, NICOLE B; Maize HS; Wichita, KS; (3); Church Yth Grp; Debate Tm; Letterman Clb; NFL; Science Clb; Service Clb; Spanish Clb; SADD; Bus Admin.

REIF, PATRICIA L; Kapaun-Mt Carmel HS; Wichita, KS; (4); 26/164; Drama Clb; Office Aide; SADD; School Musical; JV Sftbl; Var Vllybl; High Hon Roll; NHS; Pres Schlr; Wichita ST Univ; Bus.

REIF, TAMMY; Great Bend Sr HS; Great Bend, KS; (4); 25/228; Am Leg Aux Girls St; Sec VP 4-H; German Clb; Math Tm; Pep Clb; SADD; Varsity Clb; Band; Mrchg Band; Pep Band; Kayettes Finance Drctr; Emporia U; Tchr.

REILLY, DIANE CARLEEN; Leavenworth HS; Leavenworth, KS; (4); 5/289; Church Yth Grp; SADD; Band; Rep Jr Cls; Var Chrldng; Powder Puff Ftbl; High Hon Roll; NHS; Mrchg Band; Pep Band; Goodfellows; Earth Clb; KS Hnr Schlr; U Of KS.

REILLY, KIT L; Blue Valley Northwest HS; Overland Park, KS; (3); Wrstlng; Hon Roll; Ntl Merit Ltr; Yoga; Tai Chi; U Of CA San Diego.

REILLY, MATT; Blue Valley Northwest HS; Overland Park, KS; (2); 1/500; Debate Tm; Latin Clb; Band; Mrchg Band; Pep Band; High Hon Roll.

REIMER, BROCK C; Olathe East Sr HS; Olathe, KS; (2); Church Yth Grp; Spanish Clb; Chorus; High Hon Roll; Hon Roll; Pres Schlr; Lndscpe Arch.

REIMER, BROOKE; Cimarron HS; Cimarron, KS; (4); Pep Clb; Spanish Clb; Band; Mrchg Band; Pep Band; Nwsp; Phtg Rptr Yrbk; Var Capt Chrldng; Powder Puff Ftbl; JV Vllybl; Fort Hays ST; Soclgy.

REIMER, KARISSA; Wichita West HS; Wichita, KS; (4); 4/250; Pres Stu Cncl; Ofcr Pom Pon; Var Socr; Cit Awd; Gov Hon Prg Awd; NHS; Prfct Atten Awd; Pres Schlr; St Schlr; Hosp Aide; Trail Blazer Awd; Wichita ST Univ; Pre-Med.

REIMER, KELLY; Newton Sr HS; Newton, KS; (4); 12/220; Cmnty Wkr; French Clb; Hosp Aide; Chorus; Orch; Ofcr Soph Cls; Ofcr Jr Cls; Ofcr Stu Cncl; Capt Pom Pon; High Hon Roll; KU Freshmn Honor Schol; KS Univ; Bus.

REIMER, LORI B; Newton Sr HS; Newton, KS; (2); Church Yth Grp; School Musical; School Play; Capt Bsktbl; JV Sftbl; Var Trk; JV Vllybl; High Hon Roll; 1st Pl St-Wide Lvl II Frnch Poetry Cont KS Wesleyan U; Elem Ed.

REIMER, NAOMI M; Clearwater HS; Wichita, KS; (3); Am Leg Aux Girls St; Church Yth Grp; Intnl Clb; Letterman Clb; SADD; Chorus; Ed Nwsp; Yrbk; Ofcr Jr Cls; Bsktbl; Brdcst/Jrnlsm.

REIMER, TYLER G; Sedgwick HS; Sedgwick, KS; (3); 7/35; Am Leg Boys St; Boy Scts; FCA; Letterman Clb; Pep Clb; Quiz Bowl; Acpl Chr; Chorus; Pep Band; School Musical; 1 Rating St Vocal Cont; Emporia ST U; Primary Ed.

REIMER, VANCE D; Meade HS; Meade, KS; (2); 2/20; Church Yth Grp; Key Clb; Letterman Clb; Math Tm; Pep Clb; Band; Chorus; Mrchg Band; Pep Band; School Musical; Grace Univ; Arch.

REINBOLD, PAM; Solomon Jr Sr HS; New Cambria, KS; (3); #1 in class; Dance Clb; 4-H; Model UN; Quiz Bowl; SADD; Drill Tm; Pep Band; Var Bsktbl; High Hon Roll; Spanish NHS.

REINERT, ANDREW M; Herington HS; Herington, KS; (2); Church Yth Grp; Drama Clb; FCA; FHA; Math Tm; Pep Clb; Quiz Bowl; Science Clb; JV Ftbl; High Hon Roll.

REINERT, CARRIE; Herington HS; Herington, KS; (3); 1/45; Lbrn FHA; HOBY; Math Tm; Quiz Bowl; Rep Stu Cncl; High Hon Roll; NHS; Pres Acad Fit Awd; Church Yth Grp; Drama Clb; KS Mn St Stu Advy Bd; Dcknsn Co Yth Tsk Frc; Outstndg For Lng Stu/Yr 94; KS ST U; Jrnlsm.

REINERT, CHAD A; Ness City HS; Ness City, KS; (1); Church Yth Grp; Natl FFA Org; Wt Lftg; High Hon Roll; Ft Hays ST Univ; Cmptr Prgrmr.

REINERT, JEFFERY J; Dodge City HS; Ensign, KS; (1); Church Yth Grp; Band; Mrchg Band; L Bsbl; L Bsktbl; L Ftbl; L Wt Lftg; Hon Roll; KS Univ; Eng/Ag/Med.

REINERT, JENNY L; Newton Sr HS; Walton, KS; (3); Thesps; Chorus; High Hon Roll; Emporia ST; Acctg.

REINERT, TARA; Wabaunsee HS; Ness City, KS; (3); Church Yth Grp; FHA; Band; Chorus; Pep Band; School Musical; Trk; Vllybl; High Hon Roll; NHS; Girl Scout Silver Awd; Wartburg Coll.

REINHARD, ELIZABETH M; St Marys HS; Maple Hill, KS; (3); 4/50; FBLA; Pep Clb; Drill Tm; Golf; High Hon Roll; Med Field.

REINHARDT, AMY M; Otis Bison HS; Bison, KS; (3); 6/35; Church Yth Grp; Cmnty Wkr; 4-H; Letterman Clb; Pep Clb; Speech Tm; SADD; Varsity Clb; Acpl Chr; Band; St Trk 2 Yrs; Yth For Music; St Forensics; Occptnl Therapy.

REINHARDT, ELIZABETH; Otis Bison HS; Bison, KS; (3); 7/26; Am Leg Aux Girls St; Church Yth Grp; Cmnty Wkr; Drama Clb; 4-H; Letterman Clb; Pep Clb; Speech Tm; SADD; Varsity Clb; Yth For Music; Stafford All Trnmt Team; All Area & All League Hnrb Mntn; KS ST Univ.

REINHART, MARY B; Topeka HS; Topeka, KS; (2); Church Yth Grp; Cmnty Wkr; Drama Clb; Spanish Clb; Thesps; Acpl Chr; Chorus; Church Choir; Drill Tm; Variety Show; Hospatality Chm Of Local Yth Drama Grp.

REINKE, BRIEN; Maranatha Acad; Shawnee Mission, KS; (4); 5/32; Church Yth Grp; Pep Clb; Chorus; School Musical; VP Stu Cncl; Var Capt Bsktbl; Var Chrldng; Trk; High Hon Roll; NHS; Pres Ed Awd; Coll Of The Ozarks; Med Tech.

REINKE, DAREN; Maranatha Acad; Shawnee Mission, KS; (2); 4/49; Chess Clb; Church Yth Grp; Math Tm; Chorus; Bsktbl; Trk; High Hon Roll; Astronmcl Engrng.

REINSTATLER, AMANDA L; Derby HS; Wichita, KS; (1); Drama Clb; SADD; Thesps; Chorus; School Musical; School Play; Stage Crew; Variety Show; Hon Roll; Drama Ltr; Good Conduct Certs; UCLA; Law.

REINSTATLER, KELLY A; Derby HS; Wichita, KS; (3); Cmnty Wkr; Teachers Aide; Chorus; Stage Crew; Variety Show; Cit Awd; Hon Roll; KAY Clb Sec & Treas; WSU; Elem Ed.

REISCHMANN, ANNE L; Bishop Carroll Catholic HS; Wichita, KS; (2); Hon Roll; Cath Yth Org; KS ST Univ; Vet.

REISINGER, JAMIE; Washington HS; Kansas City, KS; (4); DECA; French Clb; Key Clb; Pep Clb; Teachers Aide; JV Chrldng; Kansas City KS CC.

REISINGER, TOMMIE; Washington HS; Kansas City, KS; (4); 6/222; DECA; French Clb; Key Clb; Pep Clb; SADD; Teachers Aide; Var JV Chrldng; French Hon Soc; High Hon Roll; NHS; Peer Ldr; Role Mdl; Kansas City CC.

REISMAN, CHRISTINA M; Bishop Carroll Catholic HS; Wichita, KS; (3); Church Yth Grp; Girl Scts; Service Clb; Spanish Clb; JV Tennis; High Hon Roll; NHS; Vol At Hosp; Diet.

REIST, TABITHA; Highland HS; Highland, KS; (4); 2/16; Church Yth Grp; Letterman Clb; Band; Chorus; Mrchg Band; Pep Band; School Musical; School Play; Swing Chorus; Nwsp.

REIST, THATCHER; Highland HS; Highland, KS; (2); Church Yth Grp; Letterman Clb; Quiz Bowl; Band; Chorus; School Musical; Swing Chorus; Pres Frsh Cls; L Bsktbl; L Ftbl.

REISWIG, SHANNON L; Manhattan HS; Manhattan, KS; (3); Church Yth Grp; SADD; Teachers Aide; Hon Roll; Eqstrn Shw Jmpng; KS ST U; Eqn Sci/Vet.

REITER, CHRIS; Olathe South Sr HS; Olathe, KS; (4); Church Yth Grp; Teachers Aide; JV Var Ftbl; Hon Roll; NHS; Pres Schlr; Play Rugby For Olathe Tm 11th-12th Grds; Johnson Cty CC; Sci.

REITER, DAVID M; Halstead HS; Halstead, KS; (3); Pres Letterman Clb; Pres Varsity Clb; Acpl Chr; Chorus; VP Soph Cls; Var Capt Ftbl; L Tennis; High Hon Roll; Hon Roll; NHS; Slow Pitch Sftbl; Acad Dcthln ST 2nd Pl; Pub Rltns.

REITZ, ALICIA; Wellington Sr HS; Wellington, KS; (3); Church Yth Grp; Drama Clb; 4-H; Chorus; Church Choir; School Play; 4-H Awd; Hon Roll.

REITZ, JASON D; Goodland HS; Goodland, KS; (2); Church Yth Grp; Debate Tm; Math Tm; Band; Mrchg Band; Pep Band; Phtg Yrbk; JV Bsktbl; Var Trk; Hon Roll.

RELPH, BENJAMIN W; Kapaun-Mt Carmel HS; Wichita, KS; (3); Boy Scts; Church Yth Grp; JV Trk; Hon Roll.

REMIGIO, JEFF A; Dodge City HS; Dodge City, KS; (3); Var Bsbl; Amer Legion Bsbl.

REMLEY, SAMUEL H; Blue Valley Northwest HS; Overland Park, KS; (2); 1/410; Ski Clb; Band; Mrchg Band; Pep Band; High Hon Roll; IA.

REMPEL, JODI M; Hesston HS; Hesston, KS; (3); 27/60; Church Yth Grp; FCA; Teachers Aide; Chorus; Church Choir; Var L Bsktbl; Var L Trk; Var L Vllybl; High Hon Roll; Acad Ltr Soph/Jr Yrs; Sngr; Nrsng.

REMPEL, SARAH M; Newton Sr HS; Newton, KS; (2); 1/250; Church Yth Grp; German Clb; Model UN; Orch; Lit Mag; Var L Crs Cntry; Var Socr; JV Tennis; High Hon Roll; Jr NHS; Congress Bundestag Exchng Schlrshp 1 Yr Germany; KMEA Dist Orch; Music.

RENARD, CHRIS S; Wichita South HS; Wichita, KS; (2); Church Yth Grp; Var L Ftbl; Wt Lftg; JV Wrstlng; High Hon Roll; Hon Roll; Prfct Atten Awd.

RENFRO, COURTNEY; Mulvane Sr HS; Derby, KS; (4); SADD; Teachers Aide; Bsktbl; Chrldng; Vllybl; Hon Roll; Pres Acad Fit Awd; Cowley Cty CC; Mrktng.

RENFRO, KRISTEN; Gardner-Edgerton HS; Gardner, KS; (1); Var Chrldng; High Hon Roll; Hon Roll; Emporia ST U; Tchr.

RENICH, ANDREW J; Halstead HS; Halstead, KS; (2); Church Yth Grp; German Clb; Letterman Clb; JV Var Bsktbl; JV Var Ftbl; Var L Trk; High Hon Roll.

RENICH, DANIEL B; Halstead HS; Halstead, KS; (4); 5/53; Letterman Clb; Spanish Clb; Chorus; Ed Nwsp; L Ftbl; L Trk; High Hon Roll; NHS; Wichita ST Univ; Elec Engrng.

RENN, BEN; Wellington Sr HS; Wellington, KS; (1); Church Yth Grp; FCA; Office Aide; SADD; JV Bsbl; JV Bsktbl; Wt Lftg; High Hon Roll; Pres Jr NHS; Yth Bsktbl & Bsbl Ofcl; U Of KS.

RENNE, FRANCES A; Wyandotte HS; Kansas City, KS; (1); Capt Crs Cntry; Capt Trk; Perfect Attendance; Dr.

RENNEKE, RICHARD; Hayden HS; Topeka, KS; (4); 3/110; Debate Tm; Intnl Clb; Quiz Bowl; Socr; High Hon Roll; NHS; St Schlr; KS ST U; Nuclear Engr.

RENNER, JESSI L; Lyndon HS; Lyndon, KS; (3); Library Aide; Quiz Bowl; Rptr Nwsp; Hon Roll; Culture Club; Future Business Ldrs Of Amer; Future Homemakers Of Amer; Emporia ST Univ.

RENNER, TIM; Goodland HS; Goodland, KS; (1); 25/98; Computer Clb; Chorus; Stage Crew; High Hon Roll; Martial Arts; Space Camp Schlsp; UCLA.

RENN-SCANLAN, AMBRIEL N; Hayden HS; Topeka, KS; (2); Cmnty Wkr; Debate Tm; NFL; Speech Tm; Thesps; School Musical; School Play; JV Tennis; Cit Awd; High Hon Roll; Comm Theatre Actedin; Cath Forensics League Mem & Qualifier; Teen Advs; Commnctn; Pre-Law; Applied Arts.

RENO, JOSHUA D; Maranatha Acad; Linwood, KS; (4); Church Yth Grp; Cmnty Wkr; Treas 4-H; Teachers Aide; School Musical; School Play; Ed Yrbk; 4-H Awd; Hon Roll; Mid Amer Nazarene Coll; Bus Adm.

RENYER, CINDY R; Sabetha HS; Sabetha, KS; (3); 13/80; FHA; Pep Clb; Spanish Clb; VP Jr Cls; Rep Stu Cncl; Var Bsktbl; Var Trk; Var Vllybl; High Hon Roll; Hon Roll; Bus/Ed.

RENZ, DANA S; Axtell Schl; Summerfield, KS; (2); Band; Chorus; Pep Band; School Play; Rep Frsh Cls; Sec Soph Cls; Rep Jr Cls; JV Vllybl; Hon Roll; Kays; Cloud CC; Elem Tchr.

REPP, PHILIP; Northeast Magnet HS; Wichita, KS; (3); 11/100; CAP; Science Clb; Hon Roll; JETS Awd; Sut Achvmt; Gold & Bronze KS Sci Olympiad; KS Univ; Arch Engrng.

RESER, BENJAMIN; Topeka HS; Topeka, KS; (4); Boy Scts; Debate Tm; Model UN; NFL; Science Clb; Teachers Aide; NHS; Ntl Merit Ltr; Pres Acad Fit Awd; St Schlr; Muscular Dystrophy Assn Vol; KS ST Univ; Comp Sci.

RESER, KATIE; Topeka West HS; Topeka, KS; (1); Art Clb; German Clb; JV Tennis; JV Trk; Hon Roll; U Of KS; Med.

RESNICK, ALISON P; Shawnee Mission E Sr HS; Shawnee Mission, KS; (4); 132/408; Q&S; Temple Yth Grp; Phtg Nwsp; JV Var Swmmng; JV Var Tennis; Var Trk; Hon Roll; NHS; Bd Of Ed Hnrs; Pblshd Wrtr; U Of CO-BOULDER; Jrnlsm.

RETHMAN, JASON; Onaga HS; Corning, KS; (3); Church Yth Grp; VP Pres 4-H; Natl FFA Org; Quiz Bowl; Spanish Clb; SADD; Band; Jazz Band; Orch; Pep Band; Dist & St Solo Level I Ratngs; Northeast KS Dist Hnrs Jazz Band; KS ST U; Ag Tech.

RETTELE, REGINA L; Sabetha HS; Wetmore, KS; (3); 8/88; Am Leg Aux Girls St; Church Yth Grp; FCA; FBLA; FHA; German Clb; Letterman Clb; Pep Clb; Quiz Bowl; Band; All Lge Hon Bsktbll; All Lge Hon.

RETZLAFF, KRISTINA; Bishop Carroll Catholic HS; Wichita, KS; (3); Cmnty Wkr; HOBY; SADD; Band; Jazz Band; School Musical; Rep Frsh Cls; VP Soph Cls; Sec Jr Cls; Church Yth Grp; Crime Stoppers; Boston Coll; Law.

REUBER, TRISHA; Atwood HS; Ludell, KS; (2); Art Clb; Rep Church Yth Grp; Girl Scts; Letterman Clb; Rep Natl FFA Org; Ski Clb; Flag Corp; Nwsp; Rep Frsh Cls; Rep Stu Cncl.

REUTER, COURTNEY A; Maize HS; Raleigh, NC; (2); Church Yth Grp; Girl Scts; Letterman Clb; Spanish Clb; SADD; JV Crs Cntry; Var Mgr(s); JV Socr; JV Vllybl; High Hon Roll; CSF; U Of NC.

REUTER, KIMBERLY M; Maize HS; Wichita, KS; (1); Church Yth Grp; Hosp Aide; Science Clb; SADD; Crs Cntry; High Hon Roll; Natl Sci Olympiad Gld & 2 Brnz Mdls; Kays.

REWERTS, SHANNON C; Stafford Jr Sr HS; Stafford, KS; (4); 9/24; FCA; Phtg Yrbk; Pres Frsh Cls; Rep Soph Cls; Pres Jr Cls; VP Sr Cls; Capt Bsktbl; Crs Cntry; Trk; Cit Awd; Bd Of Regents Awd; Dodge City CC; Scndry Ed.

REXER, STACEY; Seaman Sr HS; Topeka, KS; (3); Church Yth Grp; Drama Clb; French Clb; SADD; Chorus; Church Choir; School Musical; Lit Mag; NHS; Yth Spnsr For Jr HS Yth Grp; Chrstn Mssns.

REYBURN, WAYNE; Marysville HS; Marysville, KS; (4); FCA; Letterman Clb; Band; Sec Stu Cncl; Ofcr Bsbl; Var L Bsktbl; Var L Trk; Hon Roll; Kiwanis Awd; NHS; 3rd In St Bsktbl 95 & 96; Pnscla Chrstn Coll; Pre-Med.

REYES, CHRISTINA M; Bishop Miege HS; Kansas City, MO; (2); 74/163; Cmnty Wkr; Hon Roll; Comm Vlybl Leag; El Centro Grd Schl Tutor; KS ST; Pediatrcn.

REYNOLDS, BETHANY A; Jefferson West HS; Meriden, KS; (3); 25/85; Church Yth Grp; Cmnty Wkr; Dance Clb; FBLA; FHA; Letterman Clb; Pep Clb; SADD; Teachers Aide; Drill Tm; KS State; Interior Dsgn.

REYNOLDS, DOUGLAS CORY; Ellsworth HS; Ellsworth, KS; (1); 5/75; NFL; Bsktbl; Mgr(s); Tennis; High Hon Roll; Hon Roll; Rep Frsh Cls; Forensics Ltr; U Of KS.

REYNOLDS, JULIE; Columbus HS; Columbus, KS; (3); Church Yth Grp; FHA; Math Tm; Spanish Clb; Church Choir; School Musical; Hon Roll; NHS; Tri M Music Hnr Soc; Chanteliers.

REYNOLDS, KRISTY L; Emporia HS; Emporia, KS; (3); FBLA; Pep Clb; Hon Roll; Bus/Med.

REYNOLDS, LISA M; Wellington Sr HS; Wellington, KS; (2); Church Yth Grp; Key Clb; SADD; Ofcr Stu Cncl; Crs Cntry; Hon Roll; Jr NHS; Pub 4 Poems; Elem Ed.

REYNOLDS, MATT W; Anderson Cty Jr Sr HS; Greeley, KS; (1); SADD; Band; JV Ftbl; JV Trk; JV Wrstlng; Comp Animation.

REYNOLDS, SALENA M; El Dorado HS; El Dorado, KS; (2); Church Yth Grp; Debate Tm; Letterman Clb; Band; Flag Corp; Mrchg Band; Sftbl; Vllybl; High Hon Roll; Prfct Atten Awd.

REYNOLDS, STEPHANIE R; Blue Valley Northwest HS; Overland Park, KS; (2); Church Yth Grp; Chorus; Church Choir; Rptr Nwsp; Bsktbl; JV Crs Cntry; JV Sftbl; Hon Roll; KS Univ; Brdcstng Jrnslm.

REZAC, CINDY; St Marys HS; Saint Marys, KS; (2); 1/50; FCA; Pres 4-H; Rep Natl FFA Org; Pep Clb; Band; JV Bsktbl; High Hon Roll; NHS; Natl Jr Angus Assn; Cty 4-H Cncl Secy; KS ST U; Microbio.

RHEA, NICOLE J; Lenora HS; Lenora, KS; (2); Cmnty Wkr; Intnl Clb; Pep Clb; SADD; Nwsp; Yrbk; Trk; Hon Roll; Yth Grp; Colby Col; Phy Thrpy.

RHEEM, AMY; Wichita Collegiate Schl; Wichita, KS; (3); French Clb; Letterman Clb; SADD; Chorus; School Musical; School Play; VP Frsh Cls; VP Soph Cls; VP Jr Cls; Var L Bsktbl; Tom Boettger Awd; MVP Bsktbl; Ath Of Month; All-St Tnns; Hnrb Mntn All-St Bsktbl & Sftbl.

RHOADS, ANN; Topeka West HS; Topeka, KS; (3); 4/238; Science Clb; Band; Var Capt Socr; JV Sftbl; Var Tennis; High Hon Roll; NHS; Ntl Merit Ltr; Pres Acad Fit Awd; Pres Schlr; U Of KS; Medicine.

RHOADS, BETH; Olathe North Sr HS; Olathe, KS; (2); Sec French Clb; GAA; Latin Clb; Teachers Aide; L Vllybl; High Hon Roll; Pres Acad Fit Awd; Knowledge Master Open; 1st Pl Short Story Div Wrtng Conf Inc Wrtng Cont; Pediatrician; Pediatric Surgeon.

RHOADS, JANETT G; Manhattan HS; Manhattan, KS; (4); French Clb; SADD; Teachers Aide; Intrml Bsktbl; Powder Puff Ftbl; Var L Socr; JV Trk; Intrml Vllybl; High Hon Roll; Kiwanis Awd; KS ST; Engrng.

RHOBACK, KRISTIE; Blue Valley North HS; Leawood, KS; (4); 23/167; Am Leg Aux Girls St; FBLA; VP Intnl Clb; JA; Pres Sec Key Clb; Q&S; Spanish Clb; Ed Lit Mag; NHS; Cmnty Wkr; Hstry.

RHODES, BETHANIE I; Northeast HS; Arma, KS; (2); 13/48; Band; Mrchg Band; Ed Yrbk; Var Golf; Hon Roll; Pittsburg ST Univ; PT.

RHODES, ERICA L; South Barber HS; Kiowa, KS; (2); Church Yth Grp; Girl Scts; Pep Clb; Chorus; Drm Mjr(t); Pep Band; School Musical; Var Socr; Var Tennis; JV Wt Lftg; Wichita Univ.

RHODES, ERIN M; Louisburg HS; Louisburg, KS; (2); 1/98; Letterman Clb; Math Clb; Spanish Clb; Chorus; JV Sftbl; Var L Vllybl; High Hon Roll; MAST; Peer Tutor; Hon Frontier Leag Vlybl; Ed.

RHODES, JENNIFER R; Turner HS; Kansas City, KS; (1); Bus Profs of Am; HOBY; Math Clb; Math Tm; SADD; Chorus; Var JV Bsktbl; JV Chrldng; Var JV Vllybl; High Hon Roll; Camp Fire Boys & Girls Of Amer; KS City Native Amer Indian Clb; Anthropology.

RHODES, LAURA J; Lawrence HS; Lawrence, KS; (2); FCA; Letterman Clb; Chorus; Orch; Var Bsktbl; Chrldng; JV Vllybl; Cit Awd; High Hon Roll; Pres Acad Fit Awd; ARCHT/DSNG.

RHODES, SARA; Argonia Jr Sr HS; Argonia, KS; (2); 5/25; Letterman Clb; Scholastic Bowl; Speech Tm; Band; Stage Crew; JV Var Bsktbl; Var Trk; JV Var Vllybl; Hon Roll; Prfct Atten Awd; Frosh Class Atndnt Hmcmng; KS ST Univ; Vet.

RHODUS, LINDSAY; Basehar-Linwood HS; Bonner Springs, KS; (1); Church Yth Grp; Pep Clb; SADD; Chrldng; Powder Puff Ftbl; High Hon Roll; Pres Acad Fit Awd; NCA All Amer; Yr Round Hnr Roll; Local Hosp Vol; UMKC; Dentistry.

RHONE, ALANA R; Topeka West HS; Topeka, KS; (3); 54/240; Spanish Clb; Ntl Merit Ltr; Spirit Club; Peer Helper; Tea Party; Univ Of KS; Comm/Psychology.

RHYNERSON, ARICA; Prairie View Jr Sr HS; La Cygne, KS; (3); 9/90; FCA; Letterman Clb; Phtg Yrbk; Pres Stu Cncl; Var Bsktbl; Var Sftbl; Var Capt Vllybl; Wt Lftg; High Hon Roll; NHS; USVBA Jr Olympic Vllybl Team; Hnrb Mntn For Poem Pub; Pittsburg ST Univ; Ed.

RIAHI, RICHELLE; Shawnee Mission West HS; Lenexa, KS; (3); Church Yth Grp; Hosp Aide; VP Intnl Clb; Office Aide; SADD; Teachers Aide; Hon Roll; Exploring Chldhd; JAWS; Pittsburgh ST.

RIBELIN, KIM; Valley Falls HS; Valley Falls, KS; (3); Church Yth Grp; FHA; Band; Mrchg Band; Pep Band; School Play; Nwsp; Bsktbl; High Hon Roll; NHS.

RICE, AUTUMN L; Council Grove HS; White City, KS; (2); Church Yth Grp; FHA; SADD; Band; Chorus; Pep Band; Var Chrldng; JV Vllybl; Var Wt Lftg; High Hon Roll; Radiol Tech.

RICE, BRANDON L; Maize HS; Wichita, KS; (1); Boy Scts; Church Yth Grp; Drama Clb; Thesps; Hon Roll; Scuba Diving; Coin Collecting; Univ Of PR Mayaguez; Pre Med.

RICE, CHRIS; Wilson Jr Sr HS; Wilson, KS; (3); 6/18; Am Leg Boys St; Church Yth Grp; Model UN; Science Clb; Speech Tm; School Play; Sec Jr Cls; Var JV Bsktbl; Var JV Ftbl; Var Trk; KS ST-SALINA; Oceanography.

RICE, CYNTHIA; Inman Jr Sr HS; Inman, KS; (4); 6/30; Church Yth Grp; 4-H; Pres FHA; NFL; Pep Clb; Ed Nwsp; Ed Yrbk; Trk; High Hon Roll; NHS; Washburn U.

RICE, ERIN L; Maize HS; Wichita, KS; (1); Var Pom Pon; Hon Roll; Phtjrnlsm Phtgrphr Nwspr/Yrbk.

RICE, JANET M; Washburn Rural HS; Topeka, KS; (3); Hosp Aide; Model UN; NFL; SADD; Band; Mrchg Band; Pep Band; Rptr Nwsp; Var L Golf; Var L Sftbl; Topeka Yth Wind Ensmbl 3 Yrs; ST Solo Fstvl I Rtng 96; All City 1st Tm Ptchr.

RICE, JESSICA; Winfield HS; Winfield, KS; (1); Church Yth Grp; Pep Clb; Chorus; Chrldng; Hon Roll.

RICE, KAREN J; Washburn Rural HS; Topeka, KS; (4); 5/272; Debate Tm; VP French Clb; Hosp Aide; Model UN; NFL; Quiz Bowl; SADD; Band; Mrchg Band; Pep Band; U Of NE Kearney; PT.

RICE, KRISTEN; Manhattan HS; Manhattan, KS; (4); Cmnty Wkr; French Clb; Pep Clb; Rep SADD; VP Thesps; School Play; Stage Crew; JV Var Tennis; JV Trk; Hon Roll; Experimntl Theatre Wkshp; Medcl Explrs; Meml Hosp Aux; Alcohol Advsry Brd; Amnsty Intl; Crowell Bk Awd; KU; Med.

RICE, MARK A; Olathe South Sr HS; Olathe, KS; (4); 1/386; Math Clb; Quiz Bowl; Pres Science Clb; Rep Stu Cncl; Var Bsbl; Gov Hon Prg Awd; High Hon Roll; NHS; Ntl Merit SF; Chem Engrng.

RICE, MELISSA; Pittsburg HS; Pittsburg, KS; (4); 13/165; Am Leg Aux Girls St; Cmnty Wkr; FTA; Library Aide; Spanish Clb; Teachers Aide; Band; Pep Band; Pres Sr Cls; Ofcr Stu Cncl; Pittsburg ST U; Poli Sci.

RICE, MISTY D; Yates Ctr HS; Iola, KS; (2); Art Clb; FHA; Letterman Clb; Spanish Clb; SADD; Var Sftbl; Var L Trk; JV Vllybl; Hon Roll; Criminology.

RICE, SCOTT A; Marais Des Cygnes Valley HS; Melvern, KS; (3); 3/23; Letterman Clb; Natl FFA Org; Yrbk; Pres Frsh Cls; Pres Soph Cls; Pres Jr Cls; Pres Sr Cls; Rep Stu Cncl; Bsktbl; Ftbl.

RICH, LARA; Protection Schl; Protection, KS; (3); 2/16; Church Yth Grp; Pres 4-H; Treas Letterman Clb; Pep Clb; Scholastic Bowl; Speech Tm; Band; Chorus; Bsktbl; High Hon Roll; KS Ambssdrs Of Music Tour Of Europe; Acad Olympics; Math.

RICH, ROBERT C; Elkhart HS; Elkhart, KS; (3); Letterman Clb; Band; Mrchg Band; Pep Band; School Musical; Ofcr Stu Cncl; JV Bsbl; JV Bsktbl; Var Ftbl; Var Golf; Natural Hlpr.

RICH, SARA A; Ottawa HS; Williamsburg, KS; (2); 1/200; Church Yth Grp; Drama Clb; Scholastic Bowl; Spanish Clb; Stage Crew; High Hon Roll; KS St Univ; Cosmo.

RICHARD, LAURA; Osage City HS; Osage City, KS; (3); 2/30; Church Yth Grp; Debate Tm; Pep Clb; Science Clb; Pres Jr Cls; Rep Stu Cncl; Var Chrldng; Var Golf; High Hon Roll; Kiwanis Awd; Forensics Team; Kay Clb; NFL; Loyola; Bus.

RICHARD, REBECCA; St John's HS; Beloit, KS; (4); 1/13; Hosp Aide; SADD; Chorus; Gov Hon Prg Awd; High Hon Roll; NHS; Pres Acad Fit Awd; St Schlr; Val; Pep Clb; Spec Olym Coach; KS ST Univ; Soc Wrkr.

RICHARD, TWINKIE; Wyandotte HS; Kansas City, KS; (3); Quiz Bowl; Scholastic Bowl; Teachers Aide; Mrchg Band; Yrbk; Ofcr Jr Cls; Ofcr Bsbl; Golf; Sftbl; Tennis.

RICHARDS, CASSIDY; Rose Hill HS; Rose Hill, KS; (4); 1/106; Am Leg Aux Girls St; FCA; SADD; Teachers Aide; Acpl Chr; Var L Bsktbl; Var L Vllybl; High Hon Roll; NHS; St Schlr; U Of KS; Med.

RICHARDS, ERIC L; Trego Comm HS; Wa Keeney, KS; (2); 1/49; Letterman Clb; Math Tm; Treas Soph Cls; L Bsktbl; L Ftbl; L Trk; High Hon Roll; Wakeeney Lions Clb; Schlstc Achvmt; 4th Plc Fort Hays ST Univ Math Rlys; Hnrbl Mtn Qrtrbck Midcntl Lg; Fort Hays ST Univ; Arch.

RICHARDS, HEATHER C; Blue Valley North HS; Leawood, KS; (2); Model UN; Yrbk; High Hon Roll; Amer Yth Ballet Co.

RICHARDS, LAURA D; Ottawa HS; Ottawa, KS; (4); Cmnty Wkr; French Clb; FTA; SADD; Band; Mrchg Band; Pep Band; Co-Ed Yrbk; Rep Stu Cncl; High Hon Roll; REC VP; Tnprt; Neosho CCC; Bus.

RICHARDS, LINDSAY L; Hoisington HS; Hoisington, KS; (3); Debate Tm; Intnl Clb; Pep Clb; SADD; Teachers Aide; Band; Mrchg Band; Pep Band; Variety Show; Nwsp; K ST U; Pre-Vet Med.

RICHARDS, ZAC M; Andale HS; Colwich, KS; (1); Debate Tm; Spanish Clb; JV Bsktbl; JV Ftbl; L Trk; Hon Roll; Spcl Schlsp Tests; Triple Jump St; Slam Dunk Cont 2nd Pl; Arch.

RICHARDSON, CINDY A; Bishop Miege HS; Shawnee Mission, KS; (4); 24/160; Pres Soph Cls; Pres Jr Cls; Pres Sr Cls; Var Crs Cntry; Var Trk; Cit Awd; NHS; Cmnty Wkr; Teachers Aide; Phtg Nwsp; Hmcmng Queen; Aquinos Awd; Pr Hlprs; U Of MO At Columbia; Psych.

RICHARDSON, JON R; Nickerson HS; Hutchinson, KS; (1); Math Tm; Quiz Bowl; Band; Mrchg Band; Pep Band; Ftbl; Wt Lftg; L Var Wrstlng; High Hon Roll; Trng Pilots Lic; Lttrd Var Schlrs Bwl; Pilot.

RICHARDSON, KARI D; Riverton Schl; Riverton, KS; (3); Church Yth Grp; FCA; Spanish Clb; Chorus; School Musical; School Play; Stage Crew; Swing Chorus; Hon Roll; Ntl Merit Ltr; Pittsburg ST U.

RICHARDSON, KERI; Lakin HS; Lakin, KS; (3); Cmnty Wkr; Dance Clb; FHA; Pep Clb; Chorus; Chrldng; Hon Roll; NHS; KS ST; Soc Svcs.

RICHARDSON, LAYNE; Nemaha Valley HS; Seneca, KS; (3); Drama Clb; Var Quiz Bowl; Scholastic Bowl; Treas Band; Treas Mrchg Band; Treas Pep Band; School Play; Phtg Yrbk; Treas Soph Cls; Stat Bsktbl; KS ST U; Arch.

RICHARDSON, MELANIE; Clearwater HS; Clearwater, KS; (4); Sec Church Yth Grp; Math Tm; Scholastic Bowl; SADD; Ed Phtg Yrbk; Rep Stu Cncl; NHS; St Schlr; Val; Smmr Leag Sftbl; Elem Ed.

RICHARDSON, SHANNON L; Olathe East Sr HS; Olathe, KS; (2); Church Yth Grp; Spanish Clb; Chorus; Church Choir; Drill Tm; Hon Roll; Yth Mission Trips; Competitive Dancing.

RICHARDSON, TONI; Dexter Jr Sr HS; Dexter, KS; (4); 4/11; Church Yth Grp; HOBY; Math Tm; SADD; Band; Co-Capt Bsktbl; Co-Capt Chrldng; Capt Vllybl; NHS; Emporia ST Univ; Elem Ed.

RICHES, MIKE B; Washburn Rural HS; Topeka, KS; (3); 15/375; Boy Scts; Church Yth Grp; French Clb; Chorus; School Musical; School Play; Variety Show; High Hon Roll; NHS; This Generation Shw Choir; Brigham Young U; Pre-Med.

RICHEY, TARESSA L; Caney Valley Jr Sr HS; Caney, KS; (2); Church Yth Grp; FCA; FBLA; GAA; JV Var Bsktbl; JV Var Sftbl; High Hon Roll; Hon Roll; NHS; Piano Gold Medals At St Cmptn.

RICHLING, SHELBY P; Horton HS; Horton, KS; (3); 9/39; Boy Scts; Natl FFA Org; Band; Mrchg Band; Pep Band; L Golf; Wt Lftg; Capt L Wrstlng; Hon Roll; KS St Univ; Soil Consvtn.

RICHMEIER, STEPHANIE R; Morland Jr Sr HS; Morland, KS; (2); 1/10; Church Yth Grp; Scholastic Bowl; Band; School Play; Rep Stu Cncl; Bsktbl; Sftbl; Vllybl; High Hon Roll; NHS.

RICHMOND, BECKY S; Newton Sr HS; Newton, KS; (4); 17/217; Church Yth Grp; Capt Bsktbl; Var Vllybl; High Hon Roll; NHS; Pres Schlr; St Schlr; KS St Outstdng Math & Sci Awd; KS Hnrs Schlrs; KS Bsktbl Acad All-St; U Of KS.

RICHTER, LEAH M; Topeka West HS; Topeka, KS; (2); Art Clb; French Clb; Pep Clb; Color Guard; Orch; School Musical; Variety Show; Hon Roll; Topeka Symphny Yth Orch 2 Yrs; NE; Bus.

RICHTER, MELINDA; Jackson Heights HS; Holton, KS; (3); FBLA; FHA; Library Aide; Hon Roll.

RICKE, BENJAMIN J; Nickerson HS; Hutchinson, KS; (1); Church Yth Grp; Band; Jazz Band; Mrchg Band; Pep Band; VP Frsh Cls; Bsktbl; Var L Crs Cntry; Var L Trk; High Hon Roll; CPR Prfsnl Rscr Cert; Swm Instr/Red Crs Lfgd YMCA.

RICKE, DAVID A; Great Bend Sr HS; Great Bend, KS; (3); Boy Scts; Church Yth Grp; Cmnty Wkr; Debate Tm; Drama Clb; German Clb; Hosp Aide; Library Aide; NFL; Pep Clb; Notre Dame; Law/Med.

RICKE, KARISSA; Wellington Sr HS; Wellington, KS; (1); 7/200; Church Yth Grp; Office Aide; SADD; Yrbk; Var Chrldng; Hon Roll; Jr NHS; Rotary Awd; Princess Nom.

RICKE, KELSI L; Wellington Sr HS; Wellington, KS; (3); 15/161; Church Yth Grp; Office Aide; VP Stu Cncl; Bsktbl; Sftbl; Vllybl; Cit Awd; High Hon Roll; Jr NHS.

RICKE, TERI A; Kingman HS; Kingman, KS; (3); Church Yth Grp; Natl FFA Org; Spanish Clb; SADD; Stage Crew; Bsktbl; Vllybl; Wt Lftg; High Hon Roll; Hon Roll; Teens Today Ldrs Tomorrow; Vet.

RICKEL, MEGAN; St Mary's Colgan HS; Pittsburg, KS; (1); NFL; Pep Clb; Chrldng; Vllybl; Hon Roll.

RICKER, DIRK S; Ellinwood Jr Sr HS; Raymond, KS; (2); 3/47; Hist Treas Church Yth Grp; Debate Tm; FCA; Band; Chorus; School Musical; Rep Stu Cncl; JV Ftbl; High Hon Roll; NHS; Wht Bwl Yth Cmmtte; Chrch Srvnt Trps; Engrng.

RICKER, SUZANNE; Chaparral HS; Anthony, KS; (3); Church Yth Grp; FCA; 4-H; HOBY; Key Clb; Teachers Aide; Chorus; Mgr(s); 4-H Awd; Hon Roll; Key Clb Dir & Publc Rels; 4-H Rptr & Outstndng Wrtng Awd; Fine Arts.

RICKETTS, AMANDA M; Ottawa HS; Ottawa, KS; (4); 1/143; Church Yth Grp; FTA; Spanish Clb; Church Choir; Rep Stu Cncl; Gov Hon Prg Awd; High Hon Roll; NHS; Pres Schlr; Val; Evangel Col; Elem Ed.

RICKLEFS, BETH; Shawnee Heights Sr HS; Topeka, KS; (4); Dance Clb; FBLA; Intnl Clb; SADD; Ed Yrbk; Hon Roll; Natl Jrnlsm Schlrs Awd; Amer Schlrs Awd; Jobs Dghtr; KS ST.

RICKLEFS, DANIELLE M; Wichita Hts Sr HS; Wichita, KS; (4); 100/230; Spanish Clb; SADD; Thesps; Band; Color Guard; Flag Corp; Mrchg Band; Orch; Pep Band; Trk; Multi Yr Listee; MO Wstrn St Col; Mus Ed.

RICKLEFS, TRENTON; Manhattan HS; Manhattan, KS; (3); 141/426; Am Leg Boys St; Chess Clb; Science Clb; Teachers Aide; Band; Mrchg Band; Hon Roll; NHS; Black Belt In Tae Kwon Do; Coastal Stud Clb-Selected To Go On Trip To NC To Stud Coast; IM Bsktbl; KS ST U; Chemical Engrng.

RICKLEY, JACKIE L; Salina HS South; Salina, KS; (4); Church Yth Grp; Pres Pep Clb; Church Choir; Ed Yrbk; Mgr Bsbl; Stat Bsktbl; Hon Roll; Yth Bwln Lge House Rep Sec Treas; Pratt CC; Acctng.

RICKS, KIZZIE T; Lawrence HS; Lawrence, KS; (2); German Clb; GAA; Library Aide; Quiz Bowl; Orch; Rep Stu Cncl; Sec Bsktbl; Var Trk; Cit Awd; Hon Roll; Blck Stdnt Union Pres 9th; Natl Merit Awd; Obstrics/Prentl Care.

RICO, VICTORIA M; Wellington Sr HS; Wellington, KS; (3); Cmnty Wkr; SADD; Chorus; Phtg Yrbk; Stat Mgr(s); Stat Score Keeper; Stat Vllybl; Hon Roll; Jr NHS; Jr High Ensemble; Wellington High Singers; KAY Clb; Telecommnctns; Psych.

RIDDER, AMY; Kapaun-Mt Carmel HS; Wichita, KS; (2); Var Bsktbl; Var Chrldng; Var Sftbl; JV Tennis; JV Vllybl; Hon Roll; Med Nurse, EMT.

RIDDLE, JENNIFER; St Mary's Colgan HS; Pittsburg, KS; (3); 1/50; Cmnty Wkr; Pep Clb; Quiz Bowl; School Play; Pres Soph Cls; Rep Jr Cls; VP Stu Cncl; Var JV Bsktbl; Var Sftbl; Var JV Vllybl; Prom Chm; KS Jr Acad Of Sci & CNC League Sci Fair; Arch.

RIDDLE, LUCAS A; Ottawa HS; Ottawa, KS; (3); Boy Scts; Church Yth Grp; Letterman Clb; Spanish Clb; Color Guard; Ftbl; High Hon Roll; Hon Roll; KS Army Natl Guard; KU; Electronics.

RIDENOUR, BOBBI J; Robert E Clark Jr HS; Bonner Springs, KS; (1); Teachers Aide; Band; Chorus; School Musical; Vllybl; Cit Awd; Hon Roll; Prfct Atten Awd; Ldrs Bd Pres; Dist 1 HS Solos; KS Univ; Music.

RIDER, JARED; Valley Falls HS; Valley Falls, KS; (2); Drama Clb; FBLA; FHA; Band; Pep Band; Var Bsbl; Var Bsktbl; Var Crs Cntry; Ftbl; FL ST.

RIDER, TYLER; Ness City HS; Ness City, KS; (1); Church Yth Grp; Natl FFA Org; Quiz Bowl; Scholastic Bowl; JV Ftbl; Wt Lftg; Pres Acad Fit Awd; KS ST U; Ag.

RIDGWAY, AMY M; El Dorado HS; El Dorado, KS; (2); Church Yth Grp; Math Clb; NFL; SADD; Teachers Aide; Orch; Powder Puff Ftbl; High Hon Roll; Jr Ambassador; Co-Mem Chamber Of Commerce; KS Univ; Cosmotologist; Tchr.

RIDLEY, BRADLEE D; Manhattan HS; Manhattan, KS; (3); KS ST Univ.

RIEBEL, BRADLEY W; Iola Sr HS; La Harpe, KS; (3); Var Bsktbl; Crs Cntry; Hon Roll; Involved In Amer Legion Bsbl; KS U; Comp Sci.

RIEDEL, SUNNE; Derby HS; Derby, KS; (2); 43/441; Rep Soph Cls; Rep Stu Cncl; Var Chrldng; Var Sftbl; High Hon Roll; Prfct Atten Awd; Pres Acad Fit Awd; All Amer Chlrdr; Stu Co Chair Of Natl Stu Cncl Conf; U Of KS; Med.

RIEDESEL, AMY; Shawnee Heights HS; Berryton, KS; (4); 20/229; Debate Tm; Hosp Aide; SADD; High Hon Roll; Kiwanis Awd; NHS; St Schlr; Teachers Aide; Socr; Pres SAE; Wstrdg Mall Fshn Pnl 93-94; Ltts/Mdl Debate/Acad; KS ST U; Elem Ed.

RIEGEL, AMY; St John Jr Sr HS; Saint John, KS; (1); Pep Clb; Band; Flag Corp; Mrchg Band; Pep Band; Bsktbl; Trk; Vllybl; Wt Lftg; Hon Roll; Vlybl Sub ST Runner Ups.

RIEGEL, CHAMBRE; Bucklin Schl; Ford, KS; (2); FCA; Speech Tm; Band; Chorus; Pres Soph Cls; Var Bsktbl; Capt Chrldng; Trk; Var Vllybl; High Hon Roll.

RIFFEL, BRANDON J; Desoto HS; De Soto, KS; (4); Cmnty Wkr; Letterman Clb; Math Clb; Spanish Clb; Teachers Aide; Acpl Chr; Band; Chorus; Church Choir; Mrchg Band; Pittsburg U KS; Comp Info.

RIFFEL, JACKIE; Chapman HS; Hope, KS; (2); NFL; SADD; Chorus; School Play; Treas Soph Cls; Var Chrldng; High Hon Roll; Prfct Atten Awd; KS U.

RIGGS, JASON L; Desoto HS; De Soto, KS; (3); 33/165; Church Yth Grp; Chorus; Mrchg Band; School Musical; Rep Soph Cls; L Var Bsktbl; L Capt Ftbl; L Var Trk; NHS; Cmnty Wkr; AutoCAD Wrk; Ump Ltl Leag, Babe Ruth; Engrng.

RIGGS, JOZETTE A; Labette Co HS; Altamont, KS; (4); French Clb; FHA; SADD; Chorus; School Musical; Cit Awd; Hon Roll; NHS; FHA VP; Tchng.

RIGGS, SHEILA; Clearwater HS; Clearwater, KS; (3); SADD; Phtg Yrbk; JV Bsktbl; Swmmng; JV Vllybl; Hon Roll; Tackwondo.

RILEY, AMANDA R; Blue Valley Northwest HS; Overland Park, KS; (2); 23/418; Cmnty Wkr; Var L Debate Tm; Pres Pep Clb; High Hon Roll; Hon Roll; Peer Tutoring; Vol Elem Schl Envrnmntl Clb; Psych.

RILEY, AMY; Garden City Sr HS; Garden City, KS; (3); Church Yth Grp; Band; Chorus; Color Guard; School Musical; Rep Jr Cls; Chrldng; High Hon Roll; NHS; Mrchg Band; Piano Perfomer/Accompianist; KS ST Univ; Ath Trainer.

RILEY, CHRISTY; Nemaha Valley HS; Seneca, KS; (3); Scholastic Bowl; Speech Tm; SADD; Drill Tm; School Play; Yrbk; Treas Stu Cncl; Var L Chrldng; Var L Trk; NHS; 3a ST Jrnlsm Contest 2nd Pl; Gen Sci/Bio/Keybrdg/Bus Math/Wrld Geog Acad Achvmt Awds; KS ST U; Acctg.

RILEY, ERIN J; Hartford HS; Emporia, KS; (2); Church Yth Grp; FHA; Letterman Clb; Pep Clb; Var L Chrldng; Var L Trk; Var L Vllybl; High Hon Roll; Hon Roll.

RILEY, ERINN; F L Schlagle HS; Kansas City, KS; (3); Am Leg Aux Girls St; Church Yth Grp; Cmnty Wkr; Pep Clb; SADD; Acpl Chr; Ofcr Jr Cls; Hon Roll; NHS; Mgr(s); Banner Line; Wichita ST; Bus.

RILEY, HEATHER S; Bishop Ward HS; Kansas City, KS; (2); Drama Clb; Girl Scts; School Musical; School Play; Stage Crew; High Hon Roll; NHS; Slvr Grl Sct Awd.

RILEY, JACOB; South Gray HS; Montezuma, KS; (4); 3/30; Band; Chorus; Pep Band; Rep Frsh Cls; JV Ftbl; Var Wrstlng; DAR Awd; 4-H Awd; Hon Roll; Prfct Atten Awd; CO.

RILEY, JONNIEGH; Norwich HS; Norwich, KS; (4); Am Leg Aux Girls St; Scholastic Bowl; Speech Tm; Chorus; Ed Yrbk; Var L Chrldng; Var L Trk; Var L Vllybl; Hon Roll; Church Yth Grp; Smmr Acad For Ftr Tchrs At Emporia St Univ; KS ST U; Sec Eng Ed.

RILEY, KENDRA; Dexter Jr Sr HS; Dexter, KS; (2); 1/15; Sec 4-H; Math Tm; Band; Pres Soph Cls; Ofcr Stu Cncl; Bsktbl; Vllybl; High Hon Roll; NHS; Sftbl; KS Rgnts Hnrs Acad.

RILEY, MARIAN L; Wichita Co HS; Leoti, KS; (3); 3/42; Church Yth Grp; Girl Scts; Pep Clb; Teachers Aide; Band; Mrchg Band; Pep Band; Hon Roll; Vol; Emporia; Med Record Keeping.

RILEY, MARK W; Rose Hill HS; Rose Hill, KS; (4); Vllybl; High Hon Roll; Hon Roll; Music/Guitar/Piano; Ambassador Univ; Fnrl Dir/Emblm.

RILEY, MARY R; Anderson Cty Jr Sr HS; Garnett, KS; (1); Church Yth Grp; Hist 4-H; Natl FFA Org; Band; Chorus; Church Choir; Mrchg Band; Orch; Pep Band; Rep Frsh Cls; FFA Greenhand Pres; KS ST Univ.

RILEY, RISHUAN A; Sumner Acad Of Arts & Science; Kansas City, KS; (3); Art Clb; Cmnty Wkr; French Clb; JA; Chorus; Variety Show; Bsktbl; Ftbl; Hon Roll; Black Hlth Care Coalition Yth Ldrshp Grp; Writing/Prdcnt/Prfrmnce Rap Song/Music; Cal Arts Inst; Graphic Dsgn.

RIMBO, DONNA J; Blue Valley HS; Overland Park, KS; (2); Church Yth Grp; Cmnty Wkr; FCA; Letterman Clb; Teachers Aide; Chorus; School Musical; Swing Chorus; Hon Roll; WYLDLIFE Ldrshp; Missions Trips; ICTHUS Ldrshp.

RINEHART, ANNE M; Colby Sr HS; Colby, KS; (4); Church Yth Grp; Girl Scts; Natl FFA Org; Spanish Clb; SADD; Ofcr Stu Cncl; Girl Sct Gold Awd; Red Rock CC; Intl Cmptr Engrng.

RINER, JENNIFER; West HS; Wichita, KS; (4); French Clb; Pep Clb; Teachers Aide; Chrldng; Hon Roll; Butler Coll; Dental.

RING, MATTHEW J; Lawrence HS; Lawrence, KS; (3); FCA; JA; Model UN; Office Aide; Ed Nwsp; Lit Mag; Ofcr Bsbl; Bsktbl; JV Capt Socr; High Hon Roll.

RINGER, NICOLE; Concordia Jr Sr HS; Concordia, KS; (3); Church Yth Grp; Drama Clb; 4-H; NFL; Office Aide; Science Clb; Spanish Clb; Varsity Clb; Band; Mrchg Band; Xerox Awd Wnnr; TEAMS Comp Spon By JETS Natl Comp Fnlst 96; All League Acad/Ath Awd Wnnr; KS ST Univ; Vet Med.

RINGEY, SEAN D; Clearwater HS; Clearwater, KS; (2); Forensics Team Mem; Recipient Of 2nd Div Regnl Speech & Drama Awd.

RINGWALD, AMY; Iola Sr HS; Iola, KS; (3); 1/117; Pres Church Yth Grp; HOBY; Sec Frsh Cls; Treas Stu Cncl; L Var Bsktbl; L Var Vllybl; High Hon Roll; NHS; FBLA; Letterman Clb; Kayettes Clb Pblcty Dir; Art Cmptn; Natl Fed Msc Clbs Piano Cmptn; U Of KS.

RINGWALD, CHRISTOPHER; Quivira Heights HS; Ellinwood, KS; (4); 1/24; Am Leg Boys St; Church Yth Grp; FCA; Treas Frsh Cls; Treas Soph Cls; Treas Jr Cls; Treas Sr Cls; Var Capt Ftbl; JV Var Golf; Gov Hon Prg Awd; KS ST Univ; Mech Engrng.

RINGWALD, JUSTIN R; Quivira Heights HS; Ellinwood, KS; (1); Church Yth Grp; NFL; Pep Clb; Speech Tm; Band; Jazz Band; Mrchg Band; Pep Band; School Play; Variety Show; Peer Cnslr; KS Assn For Yth; KS ST Univ; Mech Engr.

RINNGLER, NICHOLAS E; Sylvan Unified HS; Sylvan Grove, KS; (2); Church Yth Grp; Band; Chorus; School Musical; Ofcr Bsbl; Bsktbl; Ftbl; Wt Lftg; High Hon Roll; NHS.

RION, JIMMY D; Southeast HS; Weir, KS; (4); 3/52; Computer Clb; Debate Tm; Capt Quiz Bowl; Capt Scholastic Bowl; Rep Nwsp; Pres Jr Cls; VP Stu Cncl; High Hon Roll; NHS; Ntl Merit SF; Tulane U; Wrtr.

RIOS, ADRIANA; Wyandotte HS; Kansas City, KS; (3); Chess Clb; Pres Intnl Clb; School Musical; High Hon Roll; Hon Roll; NHS; Jr Hlth Careers Opportunity Pgm; Stu As Tchrs Vol; LULAC; Rockhurst Coll; Lib Arts; Sci.

RIPLEY, MATT R; Minneola Schl; Dodge City, KS; (3); Speech Tm; Band; Jazz Band; Pep Band; Bsktbl; Golf; Hon Roll; Boy Scts; Church Yth Grp; Cmnty Wkr; Festival Of The Winds Hnr Brd 96; Biking Across KS; 1st Pl Schl For Essay Writing Contest 95; KS ST Univ; Bus Mgmnt.

RIPPE, BRENDA S; Herndon Schl; Ludell, KS; (2); Pres Church Yth Grp; Band; Chorus; Church Choir; Ofcr Frsh Cls; Ofcr Soph Cls; Var L Bsktbl; Var L Chrldng; Var L Trk; High Hon Roll; KS Okyssey Of The Mind; Soc Work.

RIPPE, SHANA R; Sabetha HS; Fairview, KS; (4); 2/62; FBLA; FHA; VP German Clb; Capt Quiz Bowl; Band; Jazz Band; Mrchg Band; Pep Band; JV Vllybl; High Hon Roll; KAYS; Quiz Bowl Tm Plcd Meets/St Qlfd; 1st Pl Bus Law/Engl Bus Cont; U KS; Acctng.

RISCOE, AMY L; Blue Valley Northwest HS; Overland Park, KS; (3); Dance Clb; Pep Clb; Color Guard; Drill Tm; Mrchg Band; Yrbk; Var Powder Puff Ftbl; JV Socr; Hon Roll.

RITGERALD, LISA M; Olathe North Sr HS; Olathe, KS; (4); 29/351; Intnl Clb; Spanish Clb; Acpl Chr; Yrbk; High Hon Roll; Hon Roll; Kiwanis Awd; NHS; Ntl Merit Ltr; Spanish NHS; All Dist Schlr, Natl Hnrs Soc, Span Natlhnr Soc, KS Almni Schlr; Baker U; Bus Mrktng.

RITTER, CHRYSTAL M; Caney Valley Jr Sr HS; Niotaze, KS; (1); Band; Color Guard; Mrchg Band; Pep Band; School Musical; Trk; High Hon Roll; Hon Roll; Prfct Atten Awd; Swimming; Sports; Animals; CCC; Animal Trnr/Psych.

RITTER, DUSTIN K; Hoisington HS; Hoisington, KS; (4); Cmnty Wkr; Letterman Clb; Pep Clb; SADD; Teachers Aide; Var Ftbl; Var Golf; Var Wt Lftg; Var Capt Wrstlng; Barton County CC; Bio.

RITTER, MISTI K; Junction City HS; Fort Bragg, NC; (1); Church Yth Grp; CAP; Debate Tm; Red Cross Aide; Acpl Chr; Church Choir; Hon Roll; Pep Clb; Stage Crew; Teens As Tchrs; Abstinence Clb; True Love Waits.

RITZKE, COURTNEY D; Kensington Jr Sr HS; Kensington, KS; (3); 3/22; Am Leg Aux Girls St; Sec Church Yth Grp; Cmnty Wkr; JA; Letterman Clb; Math Tm; Pep Clb; Quiz Bowl; Scholastic Bowl; Pres SADD; Regl, St Vcl, Trio & Qu I Ratngs; Sprstmanshp Awd 94, 95; Chrch Orgnst; KS ST U; Bus Adm.

RIVAS, JAVIER N; Garden City Sr HS; Garden City, KS; (2); Art Clb; Bus Profs of Am; CAP; Computer Clb; Ofcr Soph Cls; Bsktbl; Ftbl; Wt Lftg.

RIVERA, ERIKA; Hayden HS; Tecumseh, KS; (3); 12/150; FBLA; Office Aide; JV Bsktbl; Var Capt Sftbl; Var Tennis; JV Vllybl; High Hon Roll; Hon Roll; NHS; Chicanos Unidos.

RIVERA, JENNIFER A; Junction City HS; Junction City, KS; (3); 12/270; Am Leg Aux Girls St; SADD; Ed Nwsp; Ofcr Jr Cls; High Hon Roll; Hon Roll; NHS; Ltrd Acad 3 Yrs; Emporia ST U; Elem Ed.

RIVERS, DENISE; Wichita North HS; Wichita, KS; (4); Bus Profs of Am; Teachers Aide; High Hon Roll; NHS; Vol Ronald Mc Donald Hse.

RIVERS, LANA E; Smoky Valley HS; Smolan, KS; (1); FHA; JV Vllybl; High Hon Roll; KS Assn Of Yth Svcs.

RIWGER, DEREK I; Clearwater HS; Peck, KS; (2); Scholastic Bowl; Hon Roll; Cmptr Prgrmmr.

RIXON, SHAWN; St John Jr Sr HS; Saint John, KS; (2); Church Yth Grp; 4-H; Pep Clb; Quiz Bowl; Band; Mrchg Band; Pep Band; School Play; Pres Frsh Cls; VP Soph Cls; KS ST.

ROACH, JAIME M; Yates Ctr HS; Piqua, KS; (3); Key Clb; SADD; Chorus; High Hon Roll; JETS Awd; Cit Awd; Kays Clb; Stu & Tchr Awds Art; Vet Medicine; Art.

ROACH, ROBERT E; Newton Sr HS; Newton, KS; (2); Church Yth Grp; Letterman Clb; Pep Clb; Teachers Aide; Acpl Chr; Band; Chorus; Church Choir; Jazz Band; Mrchg Band; Music Clb VP; Newton HS Olympic Ensemble.

ROADY, CHRISTOPHER R; Lawrence HS; Lawrence, KS; (2); Spanish Clb; Thesps; School Play; Stage Crew; Cit Awd; Jr NHS; U KS; Theatre.

ROBB, HEATHER; Arkansas City HS; Arkansas City, KS; (3); 31/210; Am Leg Aux Girls St; Cmnty Wkr; FCA; JA; Letterman Clb; VP Frsh Cls; Pres Soph Cls; Rep Jr Cls; Var Golf; High Hon Roll; Ath Of Wk Golf Awd; Dstngshd Schlstc Achvmt Awd; Acad Achvmt Awd; Law/Psych.

ROBB, JENNI L; Washburn Rural HS; Wakarusa, KS; (2); SADD; Chorus; Variety Show; Socr; U Of KS.

ROBBEN, JACKIE; Mc Pherson HS; Mc Pherson, KS; (4); 15/180; Spanish Clb; Sftbl; Hon Roll; NHS; Pres Acad Fit Awd; St Schlr; Art Clb; German Clb; SADD; Teachers Aide; Ku Hnr Schlr; Kayettes; Prom Queen Attendent; Outstndng Acad Achvmnt Pres Awd; KS ST Univ; Architecture.

ROBBEN, LESLIE; Thomas More Prep-Marion HS; Hays, KS; (3); French Clb; Trk; High Hon Roll; NHS; Pres Acad Fit Awd; Ft Hays ST U.

ROBBEN, RAELYNN D; Bishop Carroll Catholic HS; Wichita, KS; (2); SADD; Chorus; School Musical; JV Var Bsktbl; Vllybl; Hon Roll; Bus.

ROBEN, MELANIE; Ellsworth HS; Ellsworth, KS; (2); 29/90; Church Yth Grp; Letterman Clb; NFL; Band; Chorus; Mrchg Band; School Play; Chrldng; Trk; Hon Roll; Kayetts; Comm/Drama.

ROBERDS, MISTY L; Lacrosse HS; La Crosse, KS; (3); 7/30; Pep Clb; Band; Chorus; Jazz Band; Mrchg Band; Pep Band; VP Soph Cls; Var L Chrldng; Hon Roll; NHS; Southwestern U; CPA.

ROBERSON, IISH SHAA G; Bern Schl; Seneca, KS; (4); Church Yth Grp; Cmnty Wkr; Hosp Aide; Letterman Clb; Pep Clb; SADD; Varsity Clb; Chorus; Phtg Yrbk; Rep Soph Cls; KS ST U; Nrsng.

ROBERTS, AMY L; Liberal HS; Liberal, KS; (2); Girl Scts; Hon Roll; 1st Degree Black Belt Tae Kwon Do; 3rd Pl Jr Olympics For Tae Kwon Do; 2nd Pl St IA Go Cart Racing; U NC; Genetic Cnslng.

ROBERTS, BRIAN; Newton Sr HS; Newton, KS; (3); Am Leg Boys St; Boy Scts; Church Yth Grp; Band; Mrchg Band; Var L Ftbl; Wt Lftg; Cit Awd; Hon Roll; Eagle Scout Awd.

ROBERTS, CAMI E; Wichita Southeast HS; Wichita, KS; (2); 63/436; Girl Scts; Acpl Chr; Band; Mrchg Band; Pep Band; Variety Show; Wichita ST U; Msc Ed.

ROBERTS, ELISABETH A; Lakin HS; Lakin, KS; (2); 1/70; Church Yth Grp; Quiz Bowl; Band; Church Choir; Pep Band; School Play; Stage Crew; JV Bsktbl; High Hon Roll; NHS.

ROBERTS, JAMES C; Solomon Jr Sr HS; Solomon, KS; (2); FHA; Quiz Bowl; JV Bsktbl; Hon Roll; Emporia St Schlsp Bio 1st Pl League & St Hnrb Mntn; U Of KS; Surgeon.

ROBERTS, JENNIFER L; Gardner-Edgerton HS; Gardner, KS; (1); Church Yth Grp; Debate Tm; Library Aide; NFL; Hon Roll.

ROBERTS, JOEL M; Palco HS; Palco, KS; (2); JV Stat Bsktbl; JV Wt Lftg; Hnrb Mntn List; Provisional Ltr Var Bsktbl; Live Commnctn Jr Cont 1st Pl; Goodland Voc Tech; Telecommnctn.

ROBERTS, JUNNAE; Ashland HS; Ashland, KS; (2); School Play; Sec Treas Frsh Cls; Sec Soph Cls; Var JV Bsktbl; Var Chrldng; Var Crs Cntry; Var Powder Puff Ftbl; Var Sftbl; Var Trk; Hon Roll.

ROBERTS, KRISTIN E; Bishop Carroll Catholic HS; Wichita, KS; (1); French Clb; JV Socr; Vllybl.

ROBERTS, MACKENZIE M; Olathe North Sr HS; Olathe, KS; (2); Drama Clb; Teachers Aide; Thesps; Chorus; School Play; High Hon Roll; Pres Schlr; Faraday Soc Sci Group-Chem Demostration; Sci Olympiad; U Of KS.

ROBERTS, MELANIE M; Lawrence HS; Lawrence, KS; (3); Bus Profs of Am; Pep Clb; Swmmng; Adptn Club; Univ Of KS; Bus Admin.

ROBERTS, REBECCA J; Dighton HS; Shields, KS; (4); 1/30; 4-H; Quiz Bowl; Scholastic Bowl; SADD; Cit Awd; Gov Hon Prg Awd; High Hon Roll; NHS; Pres Schlr; Val; Southwestern; Pre Phy Therapy.

ROBERTS, SAMANTHA M; Newton Sr HS; Newton, KS; (4); Bsktbl; Trk; Vllybl; All-Area & All-League Bsktbl; St Qualifier Trk; Butler Cty CC; Scndry Ed.

ROBERTS, SHELLY; Atchison Sr HS; Atchison, KS; (3); 1/100; HOBY; School Play; VP Frsh Cls; Pres Soph Cls; Rep Stu Cncl; Var Chrldng; Stat Ftbl; JV Capt Vllybl; High Hon Roll; NHS; Natl Yng Ldrshp Conf Wshngtn DC; Sci Cmptn.

ROBERTS, STEPHANIE J; Dighton HS; Shields, KS; (1); 1/27; 4-H; Quiz Bowl; Scholastic Bowl; Ofcr Frsh Cls; 4-H Awd; High Hon Roll; Showing Horses; Raising Foster Puppies For KS Specialty Dog Svc In Washington DC.

ROBERTS, STROTHER E; Manhattan HS; Manhattan, KS; (3); 1/433; Am Leg Boys St; Debate Tm; Scholastic Bowl; Rep Stu Cncl; Hon Roll; ST Chmpnshp High Q Team; KS ST Univ; His.

ROBERTS, TRAVIS; Burlingame HS; Burlingame, KS; (1); Band; School Play; JV Bsktbl; Track.

ROBERTSON, AMANDA J; Lawrence HS; Lawrence, KS; (2); Chorus; Hon Roll; Vol Wrk Big Bros/Big Sis Douglas Cnty; KU; Elem Schl Tchr/Intr Dsgn.

ROBERTSON, AMY M; Burlington HS; Burlington, KS; (3); 3/83; FBLA; FHA; Scholastic Bowl; Band; Rep Stu Cncl; JV Chrldng; High Hon Roll; NHS; Drama Clb; Jazz Band; Bnd Cncl Treas, VP; Natl Hist Day.

ROBERTSON, ERIN; Shawnee Mission West HS; Lenexa, KS; (3); 39/421; Church Yth Grp; Cmnty Wkr; Q&S; Band; Mrchg Band; Ed Yrbk; Var Capt Chrldng; Var L Gym; Cit Awd; High Hon Roll; Miss Lenexa 2nd Rnnr Up 96; Spcl Olympics Vol; Organized Organ Donor Awareness At Schl.

ROBERTSON, JAMES J; Andover HS; Andover, KS; (3); 5/163; Band; Mrchg Band; Pep Band; Treas Stu Cncl; L Mgr(s); Capt L Socr; High Hon Roll; Hon Roll; NHS; Engrng.

ROBERTSON, KIESHA D; Arkansas City HS; Arkansas City, KS; (2); FHA; SADD; OSU; Psycht.

ROBERTSON, KIMBERLY C; Shawnee Mission W Sr HS; Lenexa, KS; (2); 24/414; Church Yth Grp; Cmnty Wkr; ROTC; SADD; Church Choir; Color Guard; Drill Tm; School Musical; High Hon Roll; Flag Corp; NJROTC Drl Tm Cmndr; Comm Theatre; PHD.

ROBERTSON, MARLINA D; Shawnee Heights HS; Topeka, KS; (3); Intnl Clb; Pep Clb; SADD; Chorus; High Hon Roll; Hon Roll; Prfct Atten Awd; Tchr Aide; Acad Ltrs; U Of KS; Bus.

ROBERTSON, MICHELLE L; Independence HS; Elk City, KS; (3); Church Yth Grp; CAP; FCA; Pep Clb; SADD; Chorus; Church Choir; Nwsp; Yrbk; Hon Roll; KSU; Jrnlsm; His; Music.

ROBERTSON, NICOLE M; Hayden HS; Topeka, KS; (3); 32/134; Church Yth Grp; Hosp Aide; Intnl Clb; NFL; Band; Drill Tm; JV Crs Cntry; JV Socr; JV Trk; Hon Roll; 334 Hrs Local Hosp Vol Regntn; Down Hill Skiing; U KS; Med.

ROBINSON, AMANDA; Shawnee Mission E Sr HS; Shawnee Mission, KS; (4); Cmnty Wkr; Hosp Aide; Office Aide; Pep Clb; SADD; Teachers Aide; Varsity Clb; JV Chrldng; Var Swmmng; Hon Roll; Univ Of AZ; Edu.

ROBINSON, AMBER N; Independence HS; Independence, KS; (1); SADD; Band; Chorus; Color Guard; Mrchg Band; Pep Band; School Musical; Rep Frsh Cls; Ofcr Stu Cncl; Vllybl; Baton Twirler For Marching Band; Kay Clb; KU; Pediatrician.

ROBINSON, BETSY; Valley Ctr HS; Valley Center, KS; (4); 24/135; HOBY; VP SADD; VP Chorus; Pres Stu Cncl; Capt Bsktbl; Capt Socr; Capt Vllybl; NHS; Church Yth Grp; Hosp Aide; KS ST U; Poltcl Sci.

ROBINSON, CARL; Basehor Linwood HS; Linwood, KS; (4); 5/120; French Clb; Pres FBLA; Math Clb; Math Tm; Q&S; Quiz Bowl; Scholastic Bowl; Science Clb; Teachers Aide; Nwsp; KS U; Comp Engr.

ROBINSON, CARRIE; Weskan Schl; Weskan, KS; (1); Church Yth Grp; FCA; Pep Clb; Scholastic Bowl; Band; Chorus; Church Choir; Pep Band; Nwsp; Yrbk; Commnctns.

ROBINSON, CRYSTAL M; Field Kindley Mem Sr HS; Independence, KS; (2); Cmnty Wkr; Dance Clb; French Clb; Mgr Bsbl; Gym; Pom Pon; Hon Roll; Prfct Atten Awd; KS St Univ; Chiro.

ROBINSON, CYNTHIA L; Sumner Acad Of Arts & Science; Kansas City, KS; (3); French Clb; JA; Latin Clb; Pep Clb; Rep Stu Cncl; Intrml JV Bsktbl; JV Var Sftbl; French Hon Soc; Hon Roll; NHS; KS ST U.

ROBINSON, ELIZABETH A; Chanute Sr HS; Chanute, KS; (2); 1/100; Art Clb; French Clb; Varsity Clb; VP Jr Cls; JV Tennis; JV Var Trk; High Hon Roll; Hon Roll.

ROBINSON, JILL D; Dodge City HS; Dodge City, KS; (2); Church Yth Grp; Intnl Clb; SADD; Mgr Nwsp; Socr; Cit Awd; High Hon Roll; Jrnlsm Ed Assn Super Wrtng Awd 95; Peer Helpers.

ROBINSON, JUSTIN R; Washburn Rural HS; Melvern, KS; (2); Church Yth Grp; Band; Mrchg Band; Pep Band; High Hon Roll; Hon Roll; Washburn Univ; Bus Ownr.

ROBINSON, KELLY; Manhattan HS; Manhattan, KS; (4); 112/365; SADD; Teachers Aide; Stage Crew; Var L Bsktbl; Var L Vllybl; Hon Roll; NHS; KS ST U.

ROBINSON, KIRSTEN J; Gardner-Edgerton HS; Edgerton, KS; (2); Church Yth Grp; Cmnty Wkr; 4-H; Hosp Aide; Sftbl; 2nd Pl KS ST Art Cntst; 3rd Pl Acad Pntln Envrnmntl/Geography Quiz; Nrsng.

ROBINSON, LACIE L; Eastern Heights Jr Sr HS; Phillipsburg, KS; (1); 1/9; VP 4-H; Natl FFA Org; Band; Chorus; Pres Frsh Cls; Ofcr Stu Cncl; Var L Bsktbl; Var L Chrldng; L Trk; L Vllybl; KS Horse Quiz Bowl 2nd Pl; Hippology 1st Pl Team/3rd Ind.

ROBINSON, MAKISHA; Washington HS; Kansas City, KS; (4); FTA; Key Clb; Office Aide; Teachers Aide; Chorus; Emporia ST Univ; Day Care.

ROBINSON, MEGAN; Field Kindley Mem Sr HS; Independence, KS; (3); 8/172; Cmnty Wkr; FCA; Band; Yrbk; Var Chrldng; JV Sftbl; Hon Roll; NHS; Ntv Amer Clb Pres; USAA Natl Awd; KS ST U; Engrng.

ROBINSON, MIKE; Great Bend Sr HS; Great Bend, KS; (3); Spanish Clb; Var Bsbl; Var Ftbl; Hon Roll; Prfct Atten Awd; Barton County CC.

ROBINSON, MISTY D; Independence HS; Independence, KS; (1); French Clb; Chorus; School Musical; JV Vllybl; Cit Awd; Hon Roll; NHS; Pres Acad Fit Awd; PUPPS; Neelah Deb; Washburn Univ; Intl Lawyr.

ROBINSON, NATASHA L; Oswego HS; Oswego, KS; (2); Art Clb; Cmnty Wkr; FHA; Pep Clb; Pres Frsh Cls; Stat Bsktbl; Stat Vllybl; Hon Roll; NHS; Smr Cls At LCC; OK ST Univ; Psych.

ROBINSON, RASHIDA R; Washington HS; Kansas City, KS; (1); Church Yth Grp; Debate Tm; FCA; FTA; Girl Scts; Office Aide; Quiz Bowl; Church Choir; Orch; Bsktbl; Harvard; Lawyer.

ROBINSON, SEAN M; Blue Valley Northwest HS; Overland Park, KS; (4); 164/340; Boy Scts; Church Yth Grp; FCA; SADD; Teachers Aide; Band; Mrchg Band; Orch; Pep Band; School Musical; KMEA Dist Band; Band Mgr; Wichita ST; Music Ed.

ROBINSON, SHARON; Ingalls Jr Sr HS; Ingalls, KS; (3); Church Yth Grp; Dance Clb; Letterman Clb; Pep Clb; Speech Tm; SADD; Band; Chorus; Drill Tm; Mrchg Band; Garden City CC; Socl Wrk.

ROBINSON, TAMARA A; Topeka West HS; Topeka, KS; (1); Church Yth Grp; Cmnty Wkr; Dance Clb; FBLA; Pep Clb; Speech Tm; Chorus; Church Choir; Trk; Cit Awd.

ROBINSON, VANASSA N; Sumner Acad Of Arts & Science; Kansas City, KS; (3); Church Yth Grp; Key Clb; Latin Clb; Spanish Clb; Church Choir; Orch; Hon Roll; Ctznshp Awd; Ltr In Orch; Pre-Med; Comp Scis.

ROBINSON, WESI; Lawrence HS; Lawrence, KS; (3); Cmnty Wkr; 4-H; FTA; Key Clb; Math Clb; Natl Beta Clb; Pres Frsh Cls; High Hon Roll; Kiwanis Awd; Engrng.

ROBISON, JENNIFER L; Sumner Acad Of Arts & Science; Kansas City, KS; (4); Art Clb; Spanish Clb; Chorus; Recived An IB Diploma In Art-Dsgn-Acad Hnr; KCKCC; Arts.

ROBISON, JOSHUA; Maize HS; Wichita, KS; (1); Church Yth Grp; Hon Roll; Future Prblm Solvers; Odyssey Of Mind.

ROBISON, LACEY D; Silver Lake Jr Sr HS; Silver Lake, KS; (4); 23/50; GAA; Pep Clb; Teachers Aide; Acpl Chr; Swing Chorus; Var Bsktbl; Var Crs Cntry; Var Sftbl; Var Trk; Var Vllybl; Emporia ST Univ; Elem Ed.

ROBISON, MICHAELA J; Colby Sr HS; Colby, KS; (2); French Clb; Service Clb; Band; Mrchg Band; Pep Band; Intrml Vllybl; High Hon Roll; Lions Clb ST Bnd.

ROBL, LISA; Ellinwood Jr Sr HS; Hudson, KS; (1); Church Yth Grp; Dance Clb; FCA; Quiz Bowl; Scholastic Bowl; Spanish Clb; Band; Chorus; Church Choir; Flag Corp.

ROBSON, ANDY C; Ellsworth HS; Ellsworth, KS; (2); Church Yth Grp; Letterman Clb; Band; Mrchg Band; Pep Band; JV Var Ftbl; JV L Golf; Var L Wrstlng; Hon Roll.

ROBSON, JENNY; Sublette HS; Sublette, KS; (3); 1/32; Church Yth Grp; Letterman Clb; Pep Clb; Band; Pep Band; Pres Frsh Cls; Pres Soph Cls; Pres Jr Cls; Bsktbl; Powder Puff Ftbl; GCTL; Med.

ROBSON, STEPHANIE M; Wichita East HS; Wichita, KS; (2); 66/339; Math Clb; Spanish Clb; SADD; Teachers Aide; Band; Mrchg Band; Pep Band; School Musical; All City Band/Wichita Wind Ensbl/Regnl Solo/Ensbl Festvl/ST Solo/Ensbl Festvl; U Of KS; Bus Profsnl/Musician.

ROBY, ALLISON; Shawnee Heights Sr HS; Topeka, KS; (4); Key Clb; Model UN; Pep Clb; Capt Drill Tm; School Musical; Stage Crew; Rptr Nwsp; High Hon Roll; Band; Variety Show; Stu Actn Ed VP; KS Hnr Schlr; KS U; Elem Ed.

ROCHA, NICHOLAS P; Bishop Miege HS; Kansas City, MO; (3); Church Yth Grp; Cmnty Wkr; Dance Clb; Pep Clb; Spanish Clb; SADD; School Play; Rep Frsh Cls; VP Sr Cls; Hon Roll; Mexican Folklore Dance Group; Camp Anytown Del; NCLR Conf Yth Ldrshp Rep; Phy Thrpst.

ROCHE, KAREN A; Shawnee Mission S Sr HS; Overland Park, KS; (4); Church Yth Grp; Teachers Aide; Intrml Bsktbl; Intrml Ftbl; Hon Roll; Pres Acad Fit Awd; U Of KS; Acctng.

ROCHFORD, CHRIS P; Pratt HS; Pratt, KS; (3); Church Yth Grp; Debate Tm; Sec 4-H; Intnl Clb; NFL; Quiz Bowl; Scholastic Bowl; Chorus; School Musical; Variety Show; Rotary Club Stdnt Of Month; GATE; KS ST Univ.

ROCK, AMBER N; Hope HS; Hope, KS; (2); Church Yth Grp; FBLA; Natl FFA Org; SADD; Band; Ofcr Stu Cncl; Bsktbl; Cit Awd; High Hon Roll; NHS.

ROCK, SARA E; Olathe East HS; Lenexa, KS; (3); Dance Clb; Library Aide; Spanish Clb; Gym; Trk; Wt Lftg; Cit Awd; Hon Roll; NHS; PT.

ROCKERS, AARON C; Paola HS; Paola, KS; (4); 7/98; FCA; Teachers Aide; Var Bsbl; Var Bsktbl; Var Ftbl; High Hon Roll; NHS; Winter Homcomng King; KS Hnr St Schol; KS Univ; Radiobrdcstng.

ROCKERS, AMY R; Anderson Cty Jr Sr HS; Greeley, KS; (2); Cmnty Wkr; Intnl Clb; Office Aide; Pep Clb; SADD; Varsity Clb; Chorus; Rptr Frsh Cls; Var Bsktbl; Var JV Vllybl; KS U; Medcl.

ROCKERS, DUSTIN J; Anderson Cty Jr Sr HS; Garnett, KS; (3); Natl FFA Org; SADD; Teachers Aide; JV Bsktbl; Intrml Vllybl; Intrml Wt Lftg; Hon Roll; Acad Awd In Acctng; KS St Univ; Cvl Eng.

ROCKERS, MELANIE L; Anderson Cty Jr Sr HS; Garnett, KS; (1); Natl FFA Org; Pep Clb; Band; Mrchg Band; Pep Band; Hon Roll; KS ST Univ:vet/Mortuary Sci.

ROCKERS, NATHAN A; Paola HS; Paola, KS; (4); 1/98; VP FCA; Acpl Chr; Rptr Nwsp; Rep Sr Cls; Var Bsbl; Var Capt Bsktbl; Var Capt Ftbl; Gov Hon Prg Awd; NHS; Val; KS St Schol; U Of KS; Med.

ROCKERS, SARAH M; Anderson Cty Jr Sr HS; Greeley, KS; (1); Pep Clb; SADD; High Hon Roll; Rcvd Slvr Card Rnsnc Prgm; Pediatric Srgn.

ROCKERS, SENNETT M; Anderson Cty Jr Sr HS; Greeley, KS; (2); Drama Clb; Intnl Clb; Quiz Bowl; Chorus; School Musical; School Play; Swing Chorus; JV Golf; High Hon Roll; Hon Roll; One Act Plays; Theatre Arts.

ROCKWELL, MISHA R; Salina HS South; Salina, KS; (3); Cmnty Wkr; Pep Clb; Teachers Aide; Orch; School Musical; School Play; Stage Crew; Mgr(s); Mgr Tennis; Hon Roll; Kiwanis Vol; U KS; Bus.

RODABAUGH, RACHEL J; Leavenworth HS; Leavenworth, KS; (3); Drama Clb; Teachers Aide; Mgr Bsktbl; JV Mgr Tennis; Mgr Trk; Mgr Trk; High Hon Roll; Bwlng 9 Yrs; Goodfellows 94-; KS City CC; Scndry Schl Tchr.

RODE, DANIELLE; St Thomas Aquinas HS; Shawnee Mission, KS; (4); 3/241; German Clb; Socr; High Hon Roll; Hon Roll; NHS; St Schlr; Comm Svc; Univ Of San Diego; Psych.

RODEALD, ERIN; Lawrence HS; Lawrence, KS; (4); 1/492; Am Leg Aux Girls St; Debate Tm; Hosp Aide; Key Clb; Acpl Chr; Band; Var Chrldng; Gov Hon Prg Awd; NHS; Val; UMKC; Med Schl.

RODECKER, JARED M; Blue Valley Northwest HS; Overland Park, KS; (4); 1/350.

RODEHORST, AARON M; Downs HS; Downs, KS; (2); 1/17; Natl FFA Org; Spanish Clb; Chorus; Pres Frsh Cls; Ofcr Soph Cls; Bsktbl; Ftbl; Trk; High Hon Roll; NHS; K ST; Bus/Ed.

RODENBAUGH, AARON; Sumner Acad Of Arts & Science; Kansas City, KS; (4); 67/192; French Clb; Pep Clb; Speech Tm; Orch; Ed Lit Mag; JV Wrstlng; NHS; Comp Sci.

RODERICK, JEREMY B; Garden City Sr HS; Garden City, KS; (1); Church Yth Grp; Chorus; Church Choir; Var Crs Cntry; Var Trk; High Hon Roll; Prfct Atten Awd; 2nd On Natl Latin Exm Slvr Mdl; Srgry.

RODEWALD, ERIN; Lawrence HS; Lawrence, KS; (4); 1/623; Am Leg Aux Girls St; Debate Tm; Hosp Aide; Key Clb; Acpl Chr; Band; Yrbk; Rep Stu Cncl; Var Capt Chrldng; NHS; KS Hnr Schlr.

RODGERS, BRET J; Topeka West HS; Topeka, KS; (4); Church Yth Grp; Hon Roll; Outstndng Intgrtd Comp Achvmnt Awd; Washburn Univ; Comp Sci.

RODGERS, MISTY; Hugoton HS; Hugoton, KS; (3); 6/74; Church Yth Grp; 4-H; Band; Chorus; Nwsp; Yrbk; Chrldng; Crs Cntry; Mgr(s); Sftbl; Vocal Ensemble & Solo Awds; Commnctns.

RODGERS, SADIE A; Lyndon HS; Lyndon, KS; (3); Art Clb; Church Yth Grp; Drama Clb; Nwsp; Lit Mag; Rptr Stu Cncl; JV Bsktbl; JV Vllybl; Hon Roll; Prk/Rec Smmr Art Clss Tchr; KS U; Photo.

RODHAIR, MATT E; Blue Valley Northwest HS; Overland Park, KS; (1); Church Yth Grp; Ftbl; Golf; Wt Lftg; Hon Roll; Snow/Water Skiing; Reading.

RODRICKS, J K; St Thomas Aquinas HS; Olathe, KS; (3); 97/260; Cmnty Wkr; Acpl Chr; School Musical; School Play; Hon Roll; Prfct Atten Awd; Teens For Life Treas & Rep.

RODRIGUEZ, CLAUDIA; Garden City Sr HS; Garden City, KS; (1); Band; Mrchg Band; Pep Band; School Musical.

RODRIGUEZ, GABE M; Garden City Sr HS; Waterloo, IA; (1); Debate Tm; Sprts Med.

RODRIGUEZ, MICHELLE L; Newton Sr HS; Newton, KS; (1); Church Yth Grp; Spanish Clb; Hon Roll; Zoo.

RODRIGUEZ, RENEE F; Wichita East HS; Wichita, KS; (2); Church Yth Grp; Pep Clb; Teachers Aide; High Hon Roll; NHS; Hanger Bd; Spirit Cabinet.

RODRIGUEZ, RICHARD A; Topeka West HS; Topeka, KS; (3); Art Clb; Cmnty Wkr; Nwsp; Lit Mag; Hon Roll; Mayo Clb~wnnr 2 Awds Best Of Show & Judges Awds Art; 1st Pl Wnnr Congrssnl Art Cmptn; KC Art Inst; Art.

RODRIGUEZ, SOCORRO M; Wichita North HS; Wichita, KS; (3); 1/395; Church Yth Grp; Dance Clb; FBLA; Latin Clb; Office Aide; Intrml Pom Pon; Intrml Wt Lftg; Hon Roll; Received Unsung Hero Awd From Breakfest Optimist Clb Of Wichita 96; Wichita ST U.

RODROCK, CHERI J; Wichita Co HS; Leoti, KS; (3); 3/40; Art Clb; Church Yth Grp; Cmnty Wkr; NFL; Pep Clb; Science Clb; Teachers Aide; Mrchg Band; Pep Band; Yrbk; Colby CC; Lab Tech.

RODVELT, JENNIFER; Horton HS; Horton, KS; (4); 11/60; Drama Clb; VP FHA; Quiz Bowl; School Musical; School Play; Stage Crew; High Hon Roll; NHS; Pres Acad Fit Awd; Acctng.

ROE, CHARISSA A; Russell HS; Russell, KS; (1); Church Yth Grp; Girl Scts; SADD; Band; Chorus; Mrchg Band; Orch; Pep Band; Lit Mag; Mgr(s); RCT; Band Booster Clb.

ROE, LINDSAY A; Logan HS; Logan, KS; (2); 2/12; Church Yth Grp; Pep Clb; Scholastic Bowl; Band; Chorus; Mrchg Band; Pep Band; Rep Frsh Cls; VP Soph Cls; Rep Stu Cncl; KAY; KS Univ; Nrsng/Schl Cnslr.

ROE, SCOTT R; Hays HS; Hays, KS; (2); Cmnty Wkr; Natl FFA Org; JV Ftbl; Wt Lftg; Hon Roll; Kiwanis Awd; FFA Greenhand Degree; NCK Vo Tech; Mechnc/Autobody.

ROE, SEAN M; Derby HS; Derby, KS; (2); Boy Scts; Scholastic Bowl; Band; Church Choir; Mrchg Band; Hon Roll; NHS; Derby Swim Clb; Wichita Fencing Acad.

ROE, SONDRA A; Hays HS; Hays, KS; (3); 28/224; 4-H; Natl FFA Org; Chorus; Powder Puff Ftbl; High Hon Roll; NHS; Pt.

ROECKER, TRESSA T; Newton Sr HS; Newton, KS; (2); Art Clb; Church Yth Grp; Girl Scts; SADD; Vllybl; High Hon Roll; Hon Roll; Cabana Patrol; Phys Ed Tchr.

ROEDER, KATIE J; Frankft HS; Frankfort, KS; (2); Cmnty Wkr; FHA; GAA; SADD; Chorus; Drill Tm; Pres Frsh Cls; Treas Jr Cls; JV Var Bsktbl; JV Vllybl; KS ST; Child Psych.

ROEDER, MARCIA L; Frankft HS; Frankfort, KS; (1); Cmnty Wkr; Drama Clb; 4-H; FHA; GAA; Letterman Clb; Speech Tm; Chorus; School Play; Pres Frsh Cls; Stu Of Mnth; Yth Ctr; KS U; Med.

ROEDER, TIM; Frankft HS; Frankfort, KS; (4); 11/29; Boy Scts; Pres 4-H; VP Natl FFA Org; SADD; Ofcr Stu Cncl; Bsktbl; Hon Roll; NHS; Pres Schlr; BSA Eagle Sct Awd; FFA 1st In Dist & 4th In St Dairy Foods Judging 95; Natl FFA Schlsp; NE MO; Vet Medicine.

ROEHL, JOSH K; Ottawa HS; Ottawa, KS; (2); Ftbl; Trk; Wrstlng; Hon Roll; Sept Soph Stu Mnth 95.

ROEMISCH, LARISA E; Andover HS; Andover, KS; (4); 1/143; Scholastic Bowl; Jazz Band; Pep Band; Mgr Nwsp; Socr; Sftbl; Gov Hon Prg Awd; NHS; Pres Acad Fit Awd; Val; KU; Bio.

ROENBAUGH, KATIE; Macksville HS; Haviland, KS; (2); 1/25; Quiz Bowl; School Play; Ofcr Soph Cls; Bsktbl; Chrldng; Trk; Vllybl; High Hon Roll; Forensics; Piano.

ROENNE, RITA K; Downtown Law Magnet HS; Wichita, KS; (4); 7/32; Pres Church Yth Grp; Debate Tm; Church Choir; Mrchg Band; Pep Band; Nwsp; Yrbk; Pres Sr Cls; Cit Awd; Hon Roll; Vol Wrk Dist Crt Jdge; Overall Outstdng Magnet/Law Stdnt Awd; Ottawa U; Bus.

ROENNIGKE, MARK L; St Thomas Aquinas HS; Shawnee Mission, KS; (4); 42/240; Art Clb; Spanish Clb; Ofcr Bsbl; JV Var Socr; High Hon Roll; NHS; Pres Acad Fit Awd; U MO Kansas City; Bio.

ROEPKA, ALLEN H; Nickerson HS; Hutchinson, KS; (1); French Clb; Ftbl; Golf; High Hon Roll; Hon Roll; Engr.

ROGERS, AMBER D; Wichita North HS; Wichita, KS; (3); Band; Mrchg Band; Pep Band; Heston Coll; RN.

ROGERS, ANDREA; Wichita Heights HS; Wichita, KS; (4); 50/242; Church Yth Grp; Cmnty Wkr; Debate Tm; NFL; Q&S; Teachers Aide; Ed Nwsp; Var L Socr; Hon Roll; NHS; VP Press Club; Ofcr Natl Forensic League; OK Chrstn Univ; Mass Commctns.

ROGERS, ANGIE; Oskaloosa HS; Ozawkie, KS; (4); Pep Clb; SADD; Band; Church Choir; Drill Tm; Pep Band; Nwsp; Yrbk; Bsktbl; Capt Chrldng; U Of KS; Elem Ed.

ROGERS, ASHLEY; Seaman Sr HS; Topeka, KS; (4); Cmnty Wkr; FHA; Hosp Aide; Spanish Clb; Sec SADD; Ed Yrbk; Hon Roll; Prfct Atten Awd; Pres Acad Fit Awd; Library Aide; Optmst Essy Comp; U Of KS; Soc Wel.

ROGERS, BRIAN; Southeast Of Saline HS; Salina, KS; (3); 5/54; Am Leg Boys St; Art Clb; Church Yth Grp; Cmnty Wkr; 4-H; FHA; Letterman Clb; Math Tm; Pep Clb; Science Clb; KS ST-SALINE; Aviation.

ROGERS, DALLIS; Dodge City HS; Dodge City, KS; (1); Church Yth Grp; Letterman Clb; Band; Mrchg Band; Pep Band; JV Bsbl; JV Bsktbl; Var Capt Socr; Jr Olympcs Rcqtbl; Old Mexico Hm Bldg Mssn Trp; KS Univ; Med.

ROGERS, FRANNIE; Lebo Schl; Lebo, KS; (3); 6/29; Church Yth Grp; Cmnty Wkr; Rptr 4-H; Ed FBLA; HOBY; VP Sec Natl FFA Org; Quiz Bowl; Band; Chorus; Pep Band; Agri-Sci Rsrch.

ROGERS, JENNIFER; Berean Acad; Wichita, KS; (3); Church Yth Grp; Letterman Clb; Teachers Aide; Chorus; Church Choir; JV Var Vllybl; Hon Roll; His.

ROGERS, JOHN; Bucklin Schl; Bucklin, KS; (1); 6/39; Church Yth Grp; FCA; Quiz Bowl; Band; Ftbl; Trk; Wt Lftg; Hon Roll; Archaeology.

ROGERS, KIMBERLY G; Leavenworth HS; Leavenworth, KS; (3); Cmnty Wkr; Debate Tm; Cit Awd; Hon Roll; 1st Lt In Pol Explr; Lttr Debate.

ROGERS, MELISSA; Arkansas City HS; Arkansas City, KS; (3); Church Yth Grp; SADD; Teachers Aide; Var Capt Chrldng; JV Tennis; Hon Roll; Pres Acad Fit Awd.

ROGERS, NATE; Blue Valley HS; Overland Park, KS; (4); Am Leg Boys St; Church Yth Grp; Band; Jazz Band; Pep Band; Variety Show; L Ftbl; L Wt Lftg; L Wrstlng; Hon Roll; Guitar; Chrch Yth Music Rep; Guitar; Music; Bus.

ROGERS, REBECCA E; Field Kindley Mem Sr HS; Coffeyville, KS; (3); 5/250; Pres Drama Clb; Teachers Aide; Pres Thesps; Band; Chorus; Church Choir; Jazz Band; Mrchg Band; Pep Band; School Play; Show Choir; Friends Univ; Music; Drama.

ROGERS, REBEKAH E; Derby Christian Schl; Belle Plaine, KS; (3); 4/8; Church Yth Grp; Cmnty Wkr; Drama Clb; 4-H; School Play; Variety Show; 4-H Awd; Hon Roll; Prfct Atten Awd; Pepperdine; Scientist.

ROGERS, SARAH E; Newton Sr HS; Newton, KS; (4); Sec Pres Boy Scts; Church Yth Grp; Teachers Aide; Orch; Crs Cntry; Hon Roll; NHS; Pres Schlr; 4-H; Trk; KS Hnr Schlr; OM; Wichita ST U; Spcl Ed/Music.

ROGERS, TARA J; Pratt HS; Dodge City, KS; (4); 100/257; Art Clb; Church Yth Grp; Cmnty Wkr; Intnl Clb; Office Aide; Teachers Aide; Ofcr Stu Cncl; High Hon Roll; Hon Roll; Pres Schlr; Kay Club; FORT Hays U; Bus.

ROGERS, TARA M; Newton Sr HS; Newton, KS; (3); Art Clb; Latin Clb; Spanish Clb; Socr; Sisters & Brothers 4 Life; Hosp Vol.

ROGERS, TRACY L; Rossville HS; Delia, KS; (3); Bsktbl; Sftbl; Trk; Wt Lftg; Hon Roll; Washburn Univ.

ROGERS, TRISHA M; Maize HS; Wichita, KS; (3); Art Clb; Church Yth Grp; Spanish Clb; Band; Mrchg Band; Pep Band; Intrml JV Tennis; Hon Roll; NHS; Dietician/Ntrtnst.

ROGERS, VIRGINIA; Bucklin Schl; Bucklin, KS; (4); Am Leg Aux Girls St; Church Yth Grp; Quiz Bowl; Spanish Clb; SADD; DAR Awd; Hon Roll; Cntra Coll; Acctng.

ROGGE, FRED T; Washington HS; Washington, KS; (2); Math Tm; Treas Natl FFA Org; Hon Roll.

ROGGE, MICHELLE A; Riley Cty HS; Riley, KS; (3); 1/50; Cmnty Wkr; FCA; FBLA; Treas FHA; Girl Scts; Treas Pep Clb; Band; Color Guard; Mrchg Band; Pep Band; Travel.

ROHLING, MEGAN L; Norton Comm HS; Prairie View, KS; (3); Drama Clb; Pep Clb; Band; Chorus; Orch; Pep Band; Stat Vllybl; Hon Roll; Emporia ST Univ; Scndry Tchng.

ROHLING, RYAN M; Northern Valley HS; Prairie View, KS; (1); Natl FFA Org; Quiz Bowl; Scholastic Bowl; Chorus; VP Frsh Cls; JV L Ftbl; Hon Roll; League Acad Cmptn.

ROHLMEIER, JESUSITA A; Washburn Rural HS; Topeka, KS; (3); Church Yth Grp; Teachers Aide; Band; Mrchg Band; Pep Band; Washburn U; Early Childhd Ed.

ROHLMEIER, MICHEAL R; Washburn Rural HS; Topeka, KS; (2); 138/380; Church Yth Grp; NFL; Band; Mrchg Band; Pep Band; JV Ftbl; Washburn U; Law.

ROHN, MITCH; Colby Sr HS; Colby, KS; (3); Church Yth Grp; Nwsp; Rep Frsh Cls; Rep Soph Cls; Rep Jr Cls; Var L Bsktbl; Var L Golf; Hon Roll; NHS.

ROHR, AARON; Thomas More Prep-Marion HS; Hays, KS; (3); 2/92; Bsktbl; Ftbl; Trk; High Hon Roll; NHS; Prfct Atten Awd; Pres Acad Fit Awd; KS U; Psych.

ROHR, REBECCA L; Thomas More Prep-Marion HS; Hays, KS; (2); 4-H; Hon Roll; Karate; Chem Engrng; Genetics.

ROJAS, RAYMIE M; Garden City Sr HS; Garden City, KS; (1); 1/32; High Hon Roll; Prfct Atten Awd; U Of KS; Med.

ROLAND, KRISTEN A; Wichita Northwest HS; Wichita, KS; (2); 1/392; Orch; JV Socr; High Hon Roll; Hon Roll; Pres Acad Fitness Awd; Piano 8 Yrs; Outstdng Achvmnt Sci Awd 96; Chem.

ROLEY, SHANTINA R; Leavenworth HS; Fort Leavenworth, KS; (3); Church Yth Grp; Cmnty Wkr; Intnl Clb; ROTC; Spanish Clb; SADD; Band; Color Guard; Mrchg Band; Pep Band; Goodfellows; U Of MO Kansas City; OB-GYN.

ROLFE, AARON D; Topeka West HS; Topeka, KS; (1); Church Yth Grp; Cmnty Wkr; French Clb; JA; Pep Clb; SADD; JV Bsktbl; Var L Swmmng; Hon Roll; Rcgntn Outstndng Cmnty Svc Pres Awd; AAU Bsktbl; Chrch Wk Cmps; Hbt Hmnty; Chrch Bells; Law.

ROLFE, HILLARY M; Topeka HS; Topeka, KS; (2); 4-H; Flag Corp; Orch; 4-H Awd; High Hon Roll; Hon Roll; NHS; Intl Ord Rainbow For Girls; Akido; Soccer; Psychiatrist/PT.

ROLFE, TERA; Abilene HS; Abilene, KS; (4); Spanish Clb; Band; Chorus; Pep Band; School Musical; Powder Puff Ftbl; Var Sftbl; Var Tennis; Hon Roll; Spanish NHS; Jr Optimist Awd; Butler CC; Phys Ed.

ROLFS, DANIEL B; Quivira Heights HS; Geneseo, KS; (2); 6/20; Church Yth Grp; 4-H; Letterman Clb; Varsity Clb; Band; Mrchg Band; Pep Band; School Musical; School Play; Rep Soph Cls; OK; Meteorology.

ROLING, STEPHANIE M; St Thomas Aquinas HS; Kansas City, MO; (4); 65/231; Cmnty Wkr; Hosp Aide; SADD; JV Crs Cntry; Intrml JV Socr; Hon Roll; Dance; U Of KS; Chld Psych.

ROLLINGS, CHRISTY; Wichita South HS; Wichita, KS; (3); 62/353; Cmnty Wkr; Hosp Aide; Acpl Chr; Chorus; School Musical; Variety Show; Var Chrldng; Var Gym; Cit Awd; Hon Roll; UCLA; Med.

ROLO, STACY; Ness City HS; Ness City, KS; (3); 4/38; Church Yth Grp; Cmnty Wkr; 4-H; Sec FHA; Speech Tm; VP Thesps; Band; Pres Jr Cls; Var L Tennis; High Hon Roll; Dstnghsd Schlstc Achvt; Stu Achvt Awd; KAYS; Washburn U; Acctng.

ROLO, WILLIE K; Ness City HS; Ness City, KS; (1); Thesps; Band; Mrchg Band; Pep Band; JV Tennis; Hon Roll; Kays; Ft Hays ST; Cmptr Prgrmmng.

ROLOFF, R RYAN; Atchison Co Cmty HS; Atchison, KS; (2); 4-H; FBLA; Library Aide; Math Clb; Math Tm; Natl FFA Org; NFL; SADD; Band; Chorus; Knowledge Bowl; Kays; K ST Manhattan; Ag Rltd Bus.

ROLPH, JONATHAN D; Wichita Collegiate Schl; Wichita, KS; (3); Church Yth Grp; FCA; Chorus; School Musical; School Play; Stage Crew; Variety Show; Yrbk; Pres Soph Cls; Pres Jr Cls; Video Magazine; Video Yrbk; Stu Ministry Team.

ROMAIN, ERICA G; Shawnee Mission W Sr HS; Overland Park, KS; (3); VP Latin Clb; Pep Clb; Spanish Clb; SADD; JV Swmmng; Hon Roll; Librns Wrtrs Comptn Wnnr; KS Jr Clsscl League Sec; Pre-Med.

ROMBECK, TERRY M; Belle Plaine HS; Belle Plaine, KS; (3); 1/65; Quiz Bowl; Band; Jazz Band; Mrchg Band; Pep Band; Nwsp; Rep Stu Cncl; L Bsbl; 4-H Awd; High Hon Roll; Dist Bnd Orch; Dist Jazz Bnd; Wichita Wnd Ensmble; Mus Ed.

ROME, MINDY M; Thomas More Prep-Marion HS; Hays, KS; (1); 34/72; Rep Frsh Cls; Var Bsktbl; Var Crs Cntry; Var Trk; JV Vllybl; Hon Roll.

ROME, SARAH G; Russell HS; Russell, KS; (2); Church Yth Grp; Sec Natl FFA Org; Band; Mrchg Band; Pep Band; JV Sftbl; Intrml Wt Lftg; Hon Roll; Annl Poetry Pblctn Edtr; Band Booster Club Advrtsg Head; Prtcptd Reg Music Fstvl; Ft Hays ST; Nrsg.

ROMERO, RACHEL D; Wichita East HS; Wichita, KS; (2); #45 in class; Church Yth Grp; Teachers Aide; Hon Roll; Bus/Span.

ROMIG, MATT D; Wichita Heights HS; Wichita, KS; (4); 1/250; Church Yth Grp; Quiz Bowl; Spanish Clb; Var L Bsbl; Var L Ftbl; Intrml Wt Lftg; Hon Roll; NHS; Ntl Merit SF; Val; AP Schlr W/Hnr; Exch Stu Budapest Hungary 2xs; AHSME Scrd Hgh; Prtcptd AIME 2xs; Engrng.

RONDEAU, GAVIN O; Great Bend Sr HS; Great Bend, KS; (1); Church Yth Grp; Scholastic Bowl; Spanish Clb; Band; Mrchg Band; Pep Band; Var L Swmmng; High Hon Roll; 1st Degree Black Belt Taekwondo.

RONNAU, BENJAMIN J; Wabaunsee HS; Alma, KS; (3); Boy Scts; Church Yth Grp; Cmnty Wkr; FBLA; Letterman Clb; Quiz Bowl; SADD; Pres Stu Cncl; Var L Bsbl; Var L Ftbl; St Sftbll; Air Frce Acad; Cvl Eng.

RONNEBAUM, ROBIN L; Axtell Schl; Axtell, KS; (3); 3/21; FCA; Letterman Clb; Pep Clb; Quiz Bowl; Band; Chorus; School Musical; Yrbk; Treas Frsh Cls; VP Jr Cls; KS ST U; Med.

RONNEBAUM, SARAH L; Nemaha Valley HS; Seneca, KS; (3); 7/48; Sec Treas Church Yth Grp; Letterman Clb; SADD; Band; Chorus; VP Soph Cls; JV Var Trk; Var L Vllybl; Hon Roll; Jazz Band; KAYS VP/TREAS/ASST Prgm Mgr; 4 Yr Coll; Marine Bio.

RONNEBAUM, SARAH M; Nemaha Valley HS; Baileyville, KS; (2); Church Yth Grp; Letterman Clb; Scholastic Bowl; Band; Pep Band; Phtg Yrbk; VP Frsh Cls; Bsktbl; High Hon Roll; NHS; KAY Bd Mem; Grinnell; Med Rsrch.

ROOT, JUANA; Highland Park HS; Topeka, KS; (4); 35/160; Church Yth Grp; Cmnty Wkr; Office Aide; Pep Clb; Q&S; Spanish Clb; Teachers Aide; Flag Corp; Rptr Nwsp; Phtg Rptr Yrbk; Nationwide Art Cont; Jrnlsm Camp; MAYO Clb VP; Military; Marine.

ROPP, AMANDA L; Ft Scott HS; Fort Scott, KS; (3); Am Leg Aux Girls St; Art Clb; Letterman Clb; Pep Clb; Science Clb; Chorus; Orch; Ofcr Stu Cncl; Wt Lftg; Hon Roll; Forgn Lang Clb; Slct Ensmble; Florida Col; Bio.

RORABACK, JAMES M; Smoky Valley HS; Lindsborg, KS; (1); Band; Pep Band; High Hon Roll; Mech.

RORABACK, RACHEL S; Smoky Valley HS; Lindsborg, KS; (3); 12/59; Church Yth Grp; FCA; Scholastic Bowl; Chorus; Orch; High Hon Roll; Site Cncl; Wrtrs Club; Frnscs; Music Perf.

ROSCHE, RYAN D; Blue Valley Northwest HS; Overland Park, KS; (1); Intrml Bsktbl; Intrml Ftbl; High Hon Roll; Hon Roll; KS ST; Archtecture.

ROSE, AMY; Erie HS; Erie, KS; (4); 11/42; Church Yth Grp; Drama Clb; FCA; NFL; VP SADD; Sec Stu Cncl; Chrldng; Trk; Cit Awd; DAR Awd; KAYS; Frgn Lang Clb; U Of CO; Advrtsng.

ROSE, ANNIE E; Topeka West HS; Topeka, KS; (2); 66/282; Church Yth Grp; French Clb; Pep Clb; Spanish Clb; SADD; Church Choir; Drill Tm; Chrldng; Tennis; High Hon Roll; Classical Ballet.

ROSE, BENJAMIN W; Salina HS Central; Salina, KS; (2); 21/300; JV Bsktbl; JV Ftbl; Hon Roll.

ROSE, BRIAN; Jefferson West HS; Meriden, KS; (3); 17/83; Art Clb; Letterman Clb; Var JV Ftbl; Var Trk; High Hon Roll; Hon Roll; NHS.

ROSE, CHRIS A; Baldwin HS; Baldwin City, KS; (3); Letterman Clb; Pep Clb; Bsktbl; Mgr(s); Hon Roll; Kansas ST; Phys Edu.

ROSE, JARED A; Lyons HS; Lyons, KS; (2); VP Church Yth Grp; FCA; Math Tm; Pep Clb; Quiz Bowl; Scholastic Bowl; Acpl Chr; Chorus; Pres Soph Cls; L Bsbl; Schlrshp Banquet; Vocal Solos.

ROSE, JENNIFER A; Olathe East Sr HS; Olathe, KS; (2); Church Yth Grp; Drama Clb; Letterman Clb; Acpl Chr; Chorus; Orch; School Play; Hon Roll; Silver Strings Putnam City; OK Yth Symphony; 1 Rating All ST Music Fest Large Ensemble; Music Ed.

ROSE, LAURA; Lawrence HS; Lawrence, KS; (3); Cmnty Wkr; Debate Tm; Sec Drama Clb; NFL; Thesps; School Play; Rep Stu Cncl; Hon Roll; Church Yth Grp; Spanish Clb; Part Lcl Art Shows 5 Yrs; Won Best Actress Awrd Thspn Troupe.

ROSE, RICHARD; Learenworth HS; Fort Leavenworth, KS; (4); ROTC; Teachers Aide; Band; Orch; Pep Band; School Musical; KS ST U; Aeronautical Sci.

ROSEBROOK, JENNIFER; Lincoln Jr Sr HS; Lincoln, KS; (1); 4-H; FHA; Science Clb; Band; Chorus; Church Choir; Mrchg Band; Pep Band; School Musical; School Play; Colby CC; Vet Asst.

ROSEL, ANGELA; Washburn Rural HS; Topeka, KS; (4); 76/268; Church Yth Grp; Dance Clb; Office Aide; Spanish Clb; SADD; Variety Show; Yrbk; Chrldng; Swmmng; High Hon Roll; Powder Puff Ftblf; KS U.

ROSEL, PAUL D; Washburn Rural HS; Topeka, KS; (2); 148/356; Boy Scts; Church Yth Grp; Bsktbl; Ftbl; Wt Lftg; Hon Roll; U Of KS.

ROSENBERG, ELI H; Hyman Brand Hebrew Acad; Overland Park, KS; (3); 6/18; Boy Scts; Varsity Clb; Orch; Nwsp; Phtg Ed Yrbk; Var Bsktbl; Var Socr; Sftbl; High Hon Roll; Hon Roll; Play Violin; Comm Svc; Lib Awd; Washington Univ; MD.

ROSENGARTEN, COREY R; Bern Schl; Bern, KS; (3); Drama Clb; Letterman Clb; Scholastic Bowl; Band; Chorus; Mrchg Band; Pep Band; Rep Frsh Cls; Var L Bsktbl; Var L Ftbl; Wendys Heisman HS Candidate; KSU; Bus.

ROSS, ALLISON; Arkansas City HS; Arkansas City, KS; (2); Church Yth Grp; FCA; Jazz Band; Yrbk; Rep Soph Cls; Ofcr Stu Cncl; Var L Golf; High Hon Roll; NHS; Pres Acad Fit Awd.

ROSS, BRANDON M; Maize HS; Wichita, KS; (3); Debate Tm; NFL; Band; Jazz Band; Mrchg Band; Pep Band; Hon Roll; Prfct Atten Awd; KS ST U; Music Perfmnc.

ROSS, CODY E; Oswego HS; Chetopa, KS; (1); 4-H; Natl FFA Org; 4-H Awd; Hon Roll; LCC; Ag Tech.

ROSS, HALEY; Dodge City HS; Dodge City, KS; (2); 4-H; NFL; Band; Chorus; Mrchg Band; Pep Band; School Musical; Nwsp; Cit Awd; High Hon Roll; Madrigals; KS Ambassadors Of Music Chorus/Band; Boot Hill Repertory Co Prfrmr; Wichita ST U; Fine Arts.

ROSS, JASON; Thomas More Prep-Marion HS; Hays, KS; (3); 11/69; Pep Clb; Quiz Bowl; Scholastic Bowl; High Hon Roll.

ROSS, JASON; Silver Lake Jr Sr HS; Silver Lake, KS; (1); JA; Letterman Clb; Band; Mrchg Band; Var L Bsbl; JV Bsktbl; Var L Ftbl; Cit Awd; Hon Roll.

ROSS, KAREN M; Lawrence HS; Lawrence, KS; (2); VP Rep 4-H; Band; Chorus; Mrchg Band; Pep Band; Variety Show; Ofcr Stu Cncl; Bsktbl; JV Socr; Trk.

ROSS, KATY L; Blue Valley HS; Leawood, KS; (2); Church Yth Grp; Hon Roll; Yth Grp Vol; Multi Yr Listee; Med.

ROSS, KORI K; Oswego HS; Chetopa, KS; (3); Am Leg Aux Girls St; 4-H; Sec Soph Cls; Sec Jr Cls; Treas Sr Cls; Var L Bsktbl; Var L Sftbl; Var L Vllybl; Hon Roll; NHS; LCC; Spch Pthlgy.

ROSS, KRISTY D; Wichita Collegiate Schl; Wichita, KS; (4); Church Yth Grp; Var Pom Pon; Var Sftbl; Var Vllybl; High Hon Roll; Wichita Natl Dance Team; Vanderbilt U.

ROSS, MICHELLE; Blue Valley Northwest HS; Leawood, KS; (4); 1/343; Rep Am Leg Aux Girls St; Debate Tm; Rep Soph Cls; Pres Jr Cls; Rep Sr Cls; JV Capt Socr; High Hon Roll; NHS; Ntl Merit Ltr; St Schlr; Ldrshp Cttn Awd; Ynglfe Jr Ldr; Law.

ROSSI, ADRIAN; Northwest HS; Wichita, KS; (4); 58/334; Cmnty Wkr; Office Aide; Teachers Aide; Stage Crew; Hon Roll; NHS; Natl Art Hon Soc; Phtgrphy; Pottery; Emporia ST Univ; Elem Ed.

ROSSON, MONICA J; Labette Co HS; Edna, KS; (2); 9/158; FCA; FBLA; Bsktbl; Sftbl; Vllybl; High Hon Roll.

ROTE, CASEY L; Spring Hill HS; Spring Hill, KS; (1); Church Yth Grp; Chorus; Church Choir; Var Chrldng; Hon Roll; Wrtng.

ROTERT, LESLIE I; Galena HS; Galena, KS; (3); Church Yth Grp; Natl FFA Org; JV Bsktbl; JV Sftbl; Var Vllybl; Hon Roll; Prfct Atten Awd; Pittsburg ST Univ; Rdlgst.

ROTH, BRIAN D; Dodge City HS; Dodge City, KS; (3); Am Leg Boys St; Church Yth Grp; Cmnty Wkr; FCA; Band; JV Bsbl; Bsktbl; Var Ftbl; Var Trk; Hon Roll; Pr Cnslr.

ROTH, JUSTIN R; Blue Valley Northwest HS; Overland Park, KS; (2); Letterman Clb; Varsity Clb; JV Var Ftbl; Var Trk; High Hon Roll; Hon Roll; Recrtnl Bsbl/Bsktbl; Dsgng/Instllng Car Audio Sys; Comptng Audio Shws; KS ST Univ; Mech/Arch Engrng.

ROTH, ROBIN; Wabaunsee HS; Paxico, KS; (3); 1/50; FBLA; Capt Scholastic Bowl; Varsity Clb; Band; School Play; Powder Puff Ftbl; Var Tennis; High Hon Roll; Pres NHS; KS ST U; Biochem Engrng.

ROTHCHILD, ERIN; St John's HS; Beloit, KS; (2); Church Yth Grp; Drama Clb; Pep Clb; Quiz Bowl; Speech Tm; SADD; Band; Chorus; Pep Band; School Play; EMT Explrs; Tchr.

ROTHS, SCOTT A; Conway Springs HS; Conway Springs, KS; (3); Church Yth Grp; Treas Natl Beta Clb; Quiz Bowl; Science Clb; Band; Mrchg Band; Var L Tennis; Hon Roll.

ROTTINGHASUS, JARED M; Nemaha Valley HS; Seneca, KS; (3); 5/47; Church Yth Grp; Cmnty Wkr; 4-H; JA; Letterman Clb; Quiz Bowl; Scholastic Bowl; Spanish Clb; Band; Mrchg Band; KS Univ; Med.

ROTTINGHAUS, CHARLES A; Wetmore Schl; Wetmore, KS; (4); 1/15; Pres Letterman Clb; Capt Quiz Bowl; Capt Scholastic Bowl; School Musical; School Play; VP Pres Jr Cls; Pres Sr Cls; Var Capt Bsktbl; St Schlr; Val; KS St Univ; Premed.

ROTTINGHAUS, JARED; Nemaha Valley HS; Seneca, KS; (3); Church Yth Grp; Cmnty Wkr; 4-H; Letterman Clb; Quiz Bowl; Scholastic Bowl; Band; Treas Jr Cls; JV Bsktbl; JV Golf; KS U; Med Fld.

ROTTINGHAUS, JESSICA; Hiawatha HS; Hiawatha, KS; (4); 7/101; Am Leg Aux Girls St; Intnl Clb; Pep Clb; Rep Frsh Cls; Chrldng; Vllybl; Hon Roll; NHS; Key Clb; Library Aide; Bio Clb Pres; KAYS VP, Sec; Jr Prom Cmmtte; Rockhurst Coll; Phys Thrpy.

ROTTINGHAUS, KATIE R; Bishop Ward HS; Kansas City, KS; (2); 3/100; Cmnty Wkr; Pep Clb; SADD; Bsktbl; Trk; L Var Vllybl; High Hon Roll; NHS; Stage Crew; Powder Puff Ftbl; Peer Cnslng; GIFT.

ROTTINGHAUS, MICHAEL; Rock Creek Jr Sr HS; Westmoreland, KS; (4); 2/55; Am Leg Boys St; Cmnty Wkr; Letterman Clb; Math Tm; Pep Clb; Quiz Bowl; Teachers Aide; Band; Church Choir; Pep Band; Acad All St; 1st Tm Bsktbl; Putnam Schlr KSU; Dirs Schlr Benedictine; KSU; Bio.

ROTTINGHAUS, REBECCA A; Bailey-Benedict Jr Sr High; Seneca, KS; (2); 3/20; Church Yth Grp; Treas FBLA; Treas FHA; Pep Clb; Scholastic Bowl; Band; Church Choir; Mrchg Band; Pep Band; Sec Frsh Cls; KS St Univ.

ROUSE, JASON; Wichita East HS; Wichita, KS; (4); HERO; Hnrb Mntn; Stu Cncl; Wichita Area Tech Coll.

ROUSH, CHASITY; Stafford Jr Sr HS; Stafford, KS; (1); Church Yth Grp; FHA; Pep Clb; Band; Chorus; Pep Band; JV Bsktbl; Var Chrldng; Var Trk; JV Vllybl; KS ST U; Law.

ROUSH, CHRISTINA M; Shawnee Mission N HS; Shawnee, KS; (4); 115/346; Key Clb; Teachers Aide; Orch; Vllybl; Hon Roll; Acad Ltr; Act Ltrs; Mc Pherson; Scndry Ed.

ROUSH, KELLY; Stafford Jr Sr HS; Stafford, KS; (3); Cmnty Wkr; Band; Chorus; Mrchg Band; Pep Band; Rep Frsh Cls; Rep Jr Cls; Stat Bsktbl; Stat Ftbl; Hon Roll; Chi Bd Trd Cmmdty Chllng 95; Hutchinson CC; Chld Psych.

ROUSH, MICHAEL; Jackson Heights HS; Holton, KS; (2); Church Yth Grp; 4-H; Natl FFA Org; Pep Clb; JV Bsktbl; JV Ftbl; 4-H Awd; High Hon Roll; FFA Grnhnd Awd.

ROUSH, T J; Wichita Collegiate Schl; Wichita, KS; (4); Boy Scts; Church Yth Grp; Debate Tm; Acpl Chr; School Musical; Var L Bsbl; Mgr(s); Var Score Keeper; High Hon Roll; Hon Roll; Eagle Scout; Northwestern Univ.

ROUTON, AMANDA D; Garden City Sr HS; Garden City, KS; (1); Church Yth Grp; Teachers Aide; Orch; Nwsp; Var Bsktbl; Score Keeper; Wt Lftg; High Hon Roll; Farm Bureau Ldrsp Amer 96; Writing; Marine Biologist.

ROVENSTINE, ERIC C; Goddard HS; Wichita, KS; (2); Boy Scts; Church Yth Grp; Teachers Aide; Band; Jazz Band; Mrchg Band; Orch; Pep Band; Crs Cntry; Trk; VFW Essay Awd; Mid Amer Nazarene Coll; Mtrlgy.

ROW, JOHN A; Fredonia HS; Fredonia, KS; (3); Church Yth Grp; Science Clb; Band; Jazz Band; Mrchg Band; Pep Band; Hon Roll; Prfct Atten Awd; 3rd Pl Arch Drafting; Mech Engr.

ROWAN, ELIZABETH; Topeka West HS; Topeka, KS; (2); Pep Clb; Spanish Clb; Chorus; Church Choir; Drill Tm; Ofcr Soph Cls; Mgr(s); Swmmng; Hon Roll; SADD; Washburn; Soc Svcs.

ROWE, STEPHANIE; Udall HS; Udall, KS; (1); Band; Mrchg Band; Pep Band; JV Bsktbl; Var Chrldng; Prfct Atten Awd; 5 Clb; Cowley Cty CC.

ROWE, TYLER R; Wichita Collegiate Schl; Wichita, KS; (3); Debate Tm; School Musical; School Play; Ofcr Bsbl; Wt Lftg; High Hon Roll; Video Magazine; NYU; Film; Native Amer Stud.

ROWE, WAYNE DOUGLAS; Midland Sda Schl; Belton, MO; (1); Church Yth Grp; Office Aide; Bsktbl; Score Keeper; Socr; Hon Roll; Med.

ROWLAND, COURTNEY; Wichita Collegiate Schl; Wichita, KS; (3); Cmnty Wkr; Debate Tm; High Hon Roll.

ROWLAND, JOHN K; Sumner Acad Of Arts & Science; Kansas City, KS; (3); Chess Clb; Church Yth Grp; JCL; Key Clb; VP Latin Clb; Church Choir; Stage Crew; Trk; Hon Roll; Prfct Atten Awd.

ROWLETT, SADIE; Paola HS; Paola, KS; (4); 10/94; Q&S; VP Science Clb; Ed Nwsp; Sec Frsh Cls; Sec Soph Cls; Pres Sec Stu Cncl; Var Capt Chrldng; Var Capt Sftbl; Var Vllybl; NHS; KS U; Scndry Ed.

ROWLEY, BECKY L; Osage City HS; Osage City, KS; (3); 1/28; Church Yth Grp; Office Aide; Pep Clb; Teachers Aide; Hon Roll; Kiwanis Awd; Horseback Riding.

ROY, JENNI N; Stockton HS; Stockton, KS; (3); Church Yth Grp; FHA; JA; Pep Clb; Rptr Phtg Nwsp; Ed Phtg Yrbk; High Hon Roll; Hon Roll; KAY Clb; Natl Engrng Design Awd; NCK; RN.

ROYAL, ROBIN; Enterprise Sda Acad; Sedgwick, KS; (3); 3/30; Church Yth Grp; Cmnty Wkr; Office Aide; Acpl Chr; Band; Gym; Cit Awd; High Hon Roll; Prfct Atten Awd; Hon Roll.

ROYER, REBECCA; St Marys HS; Saint Marys, KS; (3); 6/42; Am Leg Aux Girls St; Debate Tm; Sec FBLA; Scholastic Bowl; Band; Drill Tm; Var L Golf; French Hon Soc; High Hon Roll; NHS; KS ST; Bus Mgmt.

ROZENBERG, ERIKA R; Shawnee Mission S Sr HS; Shawnee Mission, KS; (3); Teachers Aide; Co-Capt Drill Tm; Co-Capt Chrldng; Var Sftbl; High Hon Roll; Hon Roll; NHS; Psych.

ROZENFELD, BELLA H; Blue Valley Northwest HS; Overland Park, KS; (3); Cmnty Wkr; Debate Tm; Math Clb; Temple Yth Grp; High Hon Roll; Hon Roll; Pres Acad Fit Awd; Vol In Camp; Vol In Hosp; Premed.

ROZENFELD, IZABELLA; Blue Valley Northwest HS; Overland Park, KS; (3); UMKC Med Schl; Pre-Med.

RUBASH, CALEB G; Junction City HS; Dwight, KS; (2); Boy Scts; French Clb; Pep Clb; Band; Mrchg Band; Stage Crew; JV Var Socr; Hon Roll; YMCA Soccer Coach; KSU; Firefighter; EMT.

RUBIN, SARAH E; Blue Valley Northwest HS; Overland Park, KS; (3); Cmnty Wkr; Chrldng; Powder Puff Ftbl; Socr; Hon Roll; NHS; Ntl Merit Ltr; Psych.

RUBIO, JAMMIE; Manhattan HS; Manhattan, KS; (3); Spanish Clb; Thesps; Chorus; School Musical; School Play; Stage Crew; Swing Chorus; Intrml Var Chrldng; High Hon Roll; Hon Roll; Northwestern IL; Chld Psych.

RUBLE, ANGIE K; Great Bend Sr HS; Great Bend, KS; (2); FCA; German Clb; Girl Scts; Pep Clb; Spanish Clb; Acpl Chr; Variety Show; Var L Golf; Hon Roll; Jobs Dghtrs; KAYS Kayettes; KS Univ; Pharmcst.

RUBLE, JEFF P; Great Bend Sr HS; Great Bend, KS; (2); Church Yth Grp; Pep Clb; Teachers Aide; JV Bsbl; Bsktbl; JV Ftbl; Kays Clb; KS ST U; Arch.

RUBOTTOM, ERIC; Wabaunsee HS; Alma, KS; (2); Boy Scts; FBLA; Letterman Clb; Quiz Bowl; JV Stat Bsktbl; Var Crs Cntry; Var L Tennis; JV Trk; High Hon Roll; NHS; K-ST; Arch.

RUBY, LISA M; Wichita North HS; Wichita, KS; (2); Church Yth Grp; Cmnty Wkr; English Clb; Office Aide; Spanish Clb; Teachers Aide; Socr; High Hon Roll; Hon Roll; Play Clarinet 5 Yrs; Rdng Bks.

RUCKER, BRADLEY L; Attica Public Schl; Sharon, KS; (3); Church Yth Grp; Cmnty Wkr; Quiz Bowl; Var Bsbl; JV Bsktbl; Ftbl; Trk; Wt Lftg.

RUCKER, CHRISTINA M; Newton Sr HS; Newton, KS; (1); Church Yth Grp; Debate Tm; Girl Scts; Quiz Bowl; SADD; Varsity Clb; JV Golf; Var L Socr; High Hon Roll; Prfct Atten Awd; Premier Soccer Clubmach V Team; 4 Yr Coll.

RUCKER, SANDRA M; Shawnee Mission N HS; Shawnee Mission, KS; (3); 19/394; Pep Clb; Q&S; Thesps; Band; Drm Mjr(t); Mrchg Band; Pep Band; School Musical; School Play; Stage Crew.

RUCKER, SHAUN; Peabody-Burns Jr Sr HS; Peabody, KS; (2); 1/41; Natl FFA Org; Quiz Bowl; VP Frsh Cls; Var JV Bsktbl; Var JV Ftbl; High Hon Roll; Natl Mrt Sci Awd.

RUDE, DEZERAE; Burlington HS; Burlington, KS; (1); Natl FFA Org; Var Bsktbl; Var Chrldng; Var Pom Pon; Var Trk; Var Vllybl; Uncontrollable Energy Dance Team; WINGS; Presdntl Sprts Awd Pres Clinton; Horse Back Riding; Vet.

RUDER, CORI L; Thomas More Prep-Marion HS; Hays, KS; (3); 35/77; Church Yth Grp; 4-H; French Clb; SADD; Variety Show; Sftbl; Vllybl; Wt Lftg; Cit Awd; 4-H Awd; Ambassadors; Natural Helpers; Teens As Tchrs; Art; Bus; Zoology.

RUDER, DAVID J; Trego Comm HS; Wa Keeney, KS; (3); 17/56; Boy Scts; Scholastic Bowl; Science Clb; SADD; Teachers Aide; Varsity Clb; Band; Mrchg Band; Sec Soph Cls; VP Jr Cls; GATE Prgm; Invtd Natl Yth Ldrshp Forum On Med; U Of KS; Pre-Med.

RUDKIN, CHRISTOPHER C; Belle Plaine HS; Belle Plaine, KS; (3); Church Yth Grp; Band; Jazz Band; School Play; Stage Crew; Hon Roll; Mrchg Band; Pep Band; School Musical; JV Trk; DCYM Rep, CCYM Alt; E Asian Culture, Hstry, Phlsphy; U KS; Perf Arts.

RUDMAN, NICHOLAS K; Trinity Catholic HS; Hutchinson, KS; (4); 11/28; Am Leg Boys St; Debate Tm; NFL; Yrbk; VP Soph Cls; Rep Jr Cls; Pres Stu Cncl; Var L Ftbl; High Hon Roll; JV Bsktbl; Benedictine Col; Mass Comm.

RUDOLPH, WENDY; Centre Jr Sr HS; Marion, KS; (3); Church Yth Grp; Letterman Clb; Treas Pep Clb; SADD; Chorus; Pep Band; School Play; Rptr Nwsp; Ed Yrbk; Sec Stu Cncl; Schltc Achvmt Awd; Phy Thrpst; Sports Med.

RUEB, SARAH; Spearville Jr Sr HS; Spearville, KS; (4); 4/15; HOBY; Quiz Bowl; Band; Chorus; Nwsp; Yrbk; VP Jr Cls; Ofcr Stu Cncl; Hon Roll; Art Clb; HOBY Cnslr; St Jrnlsm; Fort Hays St Art Awd; KS ST U; Int Dsgn.

RUEDEBUSCH, KELLY M; Wichita Southeast HS; Wichita, KS; (2); Church Yth Grp; Cmnty Wkr; Chorus; Variety Show; Bsktbl; Trk; Vllybl; Hon Roll; NHS.

RUELAS, ARTHUR R; Washburn Rural HS; Topeka, KS; (3); Church Yth Grp; Drama Clb; FCA; Library Aide; Band; Mrchg Band; Pep Band; High Hon Roll; Hon Roll; Guitar, Singing; Poems; Drawing; Destiny Coll; Lit.

RUES, RYAN P; Anderson Cty Jr Sr HS; Garnett, KS; (1); Boy Scts; Speech Tm; Band; JV Bsktbl; JV Ftbl; Wt Lftg; Hon Roll.

RUFF, CHARLISS L; Hanston Jr Sr HS; Hanston, KS; (3); 3/7; Church Yth Grp; Cmnty Wkr; Pres 4-H; Ofcr Natl FFA Org; Pep Clb; Speech Tm; Teachers Aide; School Play; Ed Nwsp; Yrbk; Livestock Judging & Showing; Initiated & Conducted Livestock Judging Cont & Show; Livestock.

RUFF, COLIN A; Blue Vlly HS; Stilwell, KS; (2); Band; Jazz Band; Mrchg Band; Pep Band; School Musical; JV Bsbl; High Hon Roll; KS All St Jazz Bnd; Rotary All Star Jazz Bnd.

RUGG, SANDRA A; Anderson Cty Jr Sr HS; Garnett, KS; (1); Pep Clb; SADD; Chorus; School Musical; Var L Vllybl; Hon Roll; Octagon, Kay Clb; Marine Bio.

RUGGERO, MELISSA; Ft Scott Christian Heights; Fort Scott, KS; (4); 1/140; Debate Tm; HOBY; Key Clb; NFL; Scholastic Bowl; Service Clb; Band; Sec Sr Cls; NHS; St Schlr; Prsdntl Clssrm Ldrshp Sem; Poli Actn Club VP; Bnd Stu Drctr; Washburn U; Psych.

RUGGIERO, MARY J; Smoky Valley HS; Lindsborg, KS; (1); Art Clb; Church Yth Grp; Cmnty Wkr; Drama Clb; FCA; Speech Tm; Band; Pep Band; School Play; Bsktbl; KAYS; KS ST U; Tchr.

RUGGLES, CARRIE E; Wichita East HS; Wichita, KS; (2); Church Yth Grp; Drama Clb; French Clb; Chorus; Church Choir; School Musical; School Play; Variety Show; JV Socr; French Hon Soc; U Of KS; Advertising.

RUGGLES, LILLIAN C; Wichita East HS; Wichita, KS; (4); Pres Church Yth Grp; French Clb; Hosp Aide; Chorus; Church Choir; School Musical; Variety Show; French Hon Soc; Hon Roll; NHS; Amer Cancer Soc Vol.

RUHNKE, CHRIS J; Northeast Magnet HS; Wichita, KS; (2); 33/125; Boy Scts; Church Yth Grp; Cmnty Wkr; Science Clb; Yrbk; Swmmng; Hon Roll; Prfct Atten Awd; Friends Univ; Zoo Keeper.

RUHNKE, CHRISTOPHER D; Derby HS; Derby, KS; (3); 66/432; Pres Church Yth Grp; Drama Clb; FCA; Quiz Bowl; SADD; Thesps; School Play; Stage Crew; Co-Ed Yrbk; Tennis; Prms Kprs; Adv.

RUHNKE, JACEY; Atchison Sr HS; Atchison, KS; (2); Church Yth Grp; French Clb; Office Aide; Band; Mrchg Band; Pep Band; Rptr Yrbk; Rep Stu Cncl; JV Chrldng; Intrml Socr; Superstar Awd; Lunch Of Chmpn Awd; KSU.

RUIZ, ELISHA; Bishop Miege HS; Kansas City, MO; (2); Church Yth Grp; Pep Clb; Spanish Clb; SADD; Rep Jr Cls; Hon Roll; Campus Ministry Team; Dsgn; Art.

RUIZ, VERONICA; Dodge City HS; Dodge City, KS; (1); Chrldng; Psychology.

RUKAVINA, KRISTY L; Blue Valley HS; Stilwell, KS; (2); Church Yth Grp; Cmnty Wkr; Debate Tm; Orch; School Musical; Bsktbl; Var JV Socr; Hon Roll; KS Music Edctrs Assn Hnrs Orch; Soph Cls Rep Parents Clb Schl Orch; Stanford; Chmcl Engrng.

RULE, KRISTI; Linn Schl; Linn, KS; (3); Art Clb; FBLA; Thesps; School Play; Sec Soph Cls; Sec Jr Cls; Hon Roll; NHS; KS Muzzleloaders Assn Mem & Republican Vly Ofcr.

RULLMAN, LAURA; Wathena Schl; Wathena, KS; (4); 5/37; Church Yth Grp; VP 4-H; Math Clb; Natl FFA Org; Chrmn Science Clb; Band; School Play; Mgr Nwsp; Var Vllybl; NHS; Sterling Coll.

RUMBACK, CARA M; Grinnell HS; Oakley, KS; (4); 3/15; Pres Math Clb; Pep Clb; Pres Science Clb; Band; Chorus; Pep Band; School Play; VP Frsh Cls; Sec Soph Cls; VP Sr Cls; 3rd Pl St Smll Schls Essy; 2nd Pl Msnc Ldg Essy; Barton Cty CC; Grphc Dsgn.

RUMBACK, HAYLEY N; Wichita Northwest HS; Wichita, KS; (2); 1/380; Debate Tm; NFL; Speech Tm; School Play; Rep Frsh Cls; Treas Soph Cls; Rep Jr Cls; High Hon Roll; United Way Of Plains Vol Wrk; Frnscs Tm; Acad/Stdnt Govt/Debate/Frnscs Ltrs; Psych/Pre-Law.

RUMISEK, JAY D; Wichita Collegiate Schl; Wichita, KS; (3); Church Yth Grp; Band; Chorus; Church Choir; Jazz Band; Pep Band; School Musical; Variety Show; Nwsp; Var Tennis; Summer Coll Architecture; Ldrshp Conf; Formed A Rock Band Cut A Demo Of Original Music.

RUNDLE, ANNE C; St Thomas Aquinas HS; Shawnee Mission, KS; (4); 26/231; Am Leg Aux Girls St; Cmnty Wkr; Hosp Aide; Key Clb; SADD; Co-Ed Yrbk; JV Swmmng; High Hon Roll; NHS; Pep Clb; Score 4 AP Engl; N E MO ST U.

RUNDLE, JEFF; Royal Valley HS; Hoyt, KS; (2); 1/70; Church Yth Grp; HOBY; Letterman Clb; Model UN; Quiz Bowl; Band; Nwsp; Var Bsktbl; Var Ftbl; Pres Acad Fit Awd; Law/Pol Sci.

RUNNEBAUM, NIKKI; Nemaha Valley HS; Seneca, KS; (4); 7/51; SADD; Sec Frsh Cls; Pres Soph Cls; Rep Jr Cls; Rep Sr Cls; Var Capt Bsktbl; Var Trk; Var Capt Vllybl; VP NHS; Prfct Atten Awd; Emporia ST U; Scndry Educ.

RUNNION, SABASTIN J; El Dorado HS; El Dorado, KS; (2); Var Trk; High Hon Roll; Hon Roll; Ntl Merit Ltr; Phy Thrpst; Comp, Elec Engrng.

RUNYON, MICHELLE; Olathe South Sr HS; Olathe, KS; (4); Church Yth Grp; Teachers Aide; Chorus; Church Choir; Drill Tm; Stat Bsktbl; Var Socr; Hon Roll; NHS; Var Soccer Tm Co-Capt; Mid-Amer Nazarene Coll.

RUPERT, CHELSIE R; Salina HS South; Salina, KS; (4); Teachers Aide; Orch; Hon Roll; Bus Clb; KS ST U; Acctng.

RUPERT, CHRISTINE M; Bishop Ward HS; Kansas City, KS; (1); Vllybl; Hon Roll.

RUPP, JAMIE; Hoisington HS; Hoisington, KS; (4); 14/62; HOBY; Letterman Clb; Model UN; Rep Soph Cls; Rep Sr Cls; Bsktbl; Chrldng; Vllybl; High Hon Roll; NHS; All Lg Vlybl, All Area Hnrbl Mntn; Fort Hays ST U.

RUPP, MITCHELL C; Thomas More Prep-Marion HS; Hays, KS; (2); 13/85; Debate Tm; NFL; Band; Chorus; Mrchg Band; Pep Band; School Musical; School Play; Swing Chorus; Ed Nwsp.

RUS, MARIDETH; St Thomas Aquinas HS; Overland Park, KS; (2); 1/281; FCA; Key Clb; Swmmng; High Hon Roll; KC Swim Acad; JV Natl Fnlst JETS Cntst; ST Swim 100 Yd Brstrk 8th Jpl.

RUSCHE, MICHAEL J; Bailey-Benedict Jr Sr High; Baileyville, KS; (2); Church Yth Grp; Yrbk; JV Bsktbl; Var Wt Lftg; Hon Roll; Prfct Atten Awd; KS ST U; Sftwr Dsgnr.

RUSCO, RYAN R; Argonia Jr Sr HS; Argonia, KS; (3); Church Yth Grp; Letterman Clb; Band; Rep Stu Cncl; Var Capt Bsktbl; Hon Roll; Prfct Atten Awd.

RUSH, CAYLA; Brewster USD #314; Brewster, KS; (1); Quiz Bowl; Scholastic Bowl; Band; Chorus; Flag Corp; Mrchg Band; Pep Band; Var L Bsktbl; Var Chrldng; Var L Trk.

RUSH, CHRIS A; Bishop Miege HS; Kansas City, MO; (1); 3/245; Cmnty Wkr; French Clb; Science Clb; Bsktbl; JV Socr; Var L Tennis; High Hon Roll.

RUSH, DAVID W; Ellinwood Jr Sr HS; Ellinwood, KS; (2); Church Yth Grp; Debate Tm; Quiz Bowl; Spanish Clb; Band; Mrchg Band; Pep Band; Stage Crew; Bsktbl; JV Var Ftbl.

RUSK, CHRISTINE N; Buhler HS; Hutchinson, KS; (2); Cmnty Wkr; Spanish Clb; SADD; Chorus; Hon Roll; Help With Sunday Schl Clss; SMAD; Dr.

RUSSELL, BRADLEY; Garden City Sr HS; Garden City, KS; (3); Church Yth Grp; French Clb; FTA; Office Aide; Teachers Aide; Ofcr Bsbl; Ftbl; Mgr(s); Wt Lftg; High Hon Roll; Dr.

RUSSELL, CHRISTINA; Uniontown HS; Redfield, KS; (2); Church Yth Grp; FCA; Math Clb; Spanish Clb; Band; Mrchg Band; Pep Band; Phtg Nwsp; Ofcr Soph Cls; JV Bsktbl; Pittsburg ST U; Prof Photo.

RUSSELL, DARCY; Rose Hill HS; Douglass, KS; (4); 11/103; Debate Tm; HOBY; VP Jr Cls; Sec Stu Cncl; Var Sftbl; Var Vllybl; Wt Lftg; Hon Roll; Treas NHS; Am Leg Aux Girls St; 3rd Pl St Voice Of Democracy Cont; KAYS Clb; Sftbl St Chmpns; Med.

RUSSELL, EMILY D; Junction City HS; Junction City, KS; (1); Church Yth Grp; Cmnty Wkr; Dance Clb; Drama Clb; Library Aide; Band; Church Choir; School Play; Trk; High Hon Roll; Winter Homcmng Princess; Peer Mediator; Teen Actively Promoting Abstinence Clb; KS St Univ.

RUSSELL, JENNIFER J; Basehor Linwood HS; Bonner Springs, KS; (2); FHA; SADD; VP Soph Cls; High Hon Roll; Hon Roll; Outstdng Achvmnts Fr Class Accent/Ldrshp; Summer League Sftbl; St Marys Coll; Elem Ed.

RUSSELL, KRISTIE L; Emporia HS; Emporia, KS; (3); Church Yth Grp; Pres Girl Scts; Key Clb; Chorus; Church Choir; Cit Awd; Hon Roll; ESU; Elem Ed.

RUSSELL, LISA; Udall HS; Udall, KS; (3); 28/31; Church Yth Grp; SADD; Mgr(s); High Hon Roll; Hon Roll; Emporia ST Univ.

RUSSELL, REBECCA A; Louisburg HS; Louisburg, KS; (4); 10/80; Cmnty Wkr; Drama Clb; French Clb; FTA; NFL; School Play; Stage Crew; Hon Roll; NHS; Pres Awd At Grad; Mst Imprvd Forensics Novice 93-94; Theatr For Yng America Intrnshp; U Of KS; Theatr.

RUSSELL, REBECCA L; Derby HS; Derby, KS; (1); Church Yth Grp; SADD; Teachers Aide; Band; Mrchg Band; Pep Band; Hon Roll; KAY Clb; Env Clb; KS Univ; Peds Med.

RUSSEN, BRANDON K; Wallace Cty HS; Sharon Spgs, KS; (2); Boy Scts; Church Yth Grp; FCA; Pep Clb; JV Var Bsktbl; Var L Ftbl; Var L Trk; Hon Roll; All Lg Ftbl; Outstndng Schltc Achvt 95, 96.

RUSSIN, LAURA A; Eureka Jr Sr HS; Eureka, KS; (2); 6/60; Church Yth Grp; 4-H; FHA; Science Clb; SADD; Band; Mrchg Band; Pep Band; School Play; Stage Crew; Schl Achvmnt Awds; Kayettes; Emporia ST Univ; Bio.

RUST, KATHERINE; Ft Scott HS; Fort Scott, KS; (4); 23/130; Am Leg Aux Girls St; FCA; Key Clb; Science Clb; Chorus; Church Choir; Var Bsktbl; Var Chrldng; Capt Var Sftbl; Capt Vllybl; Speech Pathology.

RUTHERFORD, DUSTY D; Labette Co HS; Edna, KS; (2); Church Yth Grp; Band; Jazz Band; Mrchg Band; Pep Band; Ftbl.

RUTHERFORD, MICHELE; Campus HS; Haysville, KS; (1); SADD; Acpl Chr; Chorus; School Musical; Ofcr Stu Cncl; Chrldng; Cit Awd; High Hon Roll; Natl Title Holdng Dance Cos; Intl Ordr Rainbow For Girls Several St Grand Ofcs.

RUTLEDGE, DUSTIN L; Wellsville Jr Sr HS; Wellsville, KS; (1); FCA; FBLA; Band; Mrchg Band; Pep Band; JV Bsktbl; JV Var Ftbl; Intrml Wt Lftg; Hon Roll.

RUTLEDGE, ELIZABETH; Highland Park HS; Topeka, KS; (4); 31/136; Q&S; Red Cross Aide; ROTC; Church Choir; Mrchg Band; Pep Band; Nwsp; Ofcr Sr Cls; Socr; Hon Roll; Chrch Yth Grp; Washburn U; Mass Media.

RUTLEDGE, MEGHAN L; Wellington Sr HS; Wellington, KS; (3); 2/160; Church Yth Grp; Debate Tm; Key Clb; SADD; Band; Jazz Band; Mrchg Band; Sftbl; High Hon Roll; Jr NHS; Conf Cncl Yth Mnstry Yth Svc Fnd Chrprsn; Dist Cncl Yth Mnstry Sec.

RUTLER, TRACY; Piper HS; Kansas City, KS; (3); 15/90; Drama Clb; French Clb; NFL; Science Clb; SADD; Chorus; Drill Tm; Rptr Nwsp; High Hon Roll; Jr NHS; Drll Tm Cap & All Amer 2x; Thtr Clb VP; Frnscs St Fest 1st Div Rtng; KS U; Acting.

RUTTGEN, CARA J; Labette Co HS; Parsons, KS; (2); FBLA; SADD; Cit Awd; High Hon Roll; Hon Roll; Summer Cls Fo Finish HS; Nrsng/Acctg.

RYAN, AARON; Campus HS; Wichita, KS; (4); 21/213; Am Leg Boys St; Church Yth Grp; Cmnty Wkr; Debate Tm; JV Ftbl; JV Trk; High Hon Roll; NHS; Pres Schlr; St Schlr; Spotlight On Srs 95; Peer Helping Group; Wichita ST Univ; Phy Asst.

RYAN, ALLISON; Clay Ctr Cmty HS; Clay Center, KS; (3); 1/100; VP Church Yth Grp; SADD; Chorus; Capt Pres Drill Tm; Phtg Yrbk; VP Stu Cncl; L Chrldng; L Vllybl; Hon Roll; NHS; U Of NC; Mus Ed.

RYAN, ASHLEY; Blue Valley HS; Overland Park, KS; (3); 105/215; Church Yth Grp; German Clb; Office Aide; Q&S; Ed Nwsp; Treas Frsh Cls; VP Soph Cls; Rep Jr Cls; Bsktbl; Var Mgr(s); KS St Univ; Jrnlsm.

RYAN, CRAIG A; Prairie View Jr Sr HS; La Cygne, KS; (2); 1/70; Church Yth Grp; Cmnty Wkr; FCA; FHA; Letterman Clb; Math Clb; Math Tm; Quiz Bowl; Scholastic Bowl; Spanish Clb.

RYAN, DOUGLAS; Shawnee Mission Nw Sr HS; Shawnee Mission, KS; (4); 86/400; Debate Tm; Scholastic Bowl; Science Clb; Band; Church Choir; Mrchg Band; Pep Band; Socr; Hon Roll; NHS; KS St Univ; Natl Forest.

RYAN, ELSIE M; Marion HS; Marion, KS; (2); Debate Tm; Drama Clb; Library Aide; School Musical; School Play; Hon Roll; KS St Uinv; Psych.

RYAN, JANA M; Olathe East Sr HS; Olathe, KS; (2); Church Yth Grp; Cmnty Wkr; Acpl Chr; Chorus; Var Swmmng; Hon Roll.

RYAN, JENNIFER N; Immaculata HS; Lansing, KS; (2); Hosp Aide; Intnl Clb; Varsity Clb; Acpl Chr; Chorus; Church Choir; School Musical; JV Bsktbl; Var Chrldng; Hon Roll; Music Awd 95-96; Comp Awd 94-95; VBS Music Tchr; Lansing Elem Smmr Schl Camp Vlntr; Music.

RYAN, KATIE; Kapaun-Mt Carmel HS; Wichita, KS; (3); 26/170; Hosp Aide; Spanish Clb; SADD; Rep Frsh Cls; Treas Soph Cls; Rep Jr Cls; Treas Sr Cls; Crs Cntry; Socr; High Hon Roll; Mission Clb VP/PRES; United Crsdrs; Crsdrs For Life Ofcr; Creighton Univ; Pre-Med/OT.

RYAN, KATIE A; Shawnee Mission W Sr HS; Shawnee Mission, KS; (4); 28/337; Bsktbl; Diving; High Hon Roll; NHS; KS Hnrs Schlr; Scl Stds Stu Mnth; Pres Acad Awd; U Of KS.

RYAN, MINDA L; Piper HS; Kansas City, KS; (4); Cmnty Wkr; Drama Clb; FCA; French Clb; NFL; Science Clb; SADD; School Musical; School Play; Variety Show; Jr Assmbly; Home Ec Club; Frnscs; Johnson Cty CC.

RYAN, PATRICIA L; Oakley HS; Colby, KS; (4); 6/45; Church Yth Grp; FHA; Speech Tm; Teachers Aide; Thesps; Chorus; Pep Band; Yrbk; Rep Soph Cls; Rep Sr Cls; KS Newman Coll; Nrsng.

RYAN, SHANNON R; Salina HS South; Salina, KS; (4); Church Yth Grp; SADD; Orch; Phtg Nwsp; Ed Yrbk; JV Tennis; Hon Roll; NHS; Valparaiso; His.

RYFF, MANDY; Centre Jr Sr HS; Ramona, KS; (3); 3/16; Treas Church Yth Grp; FBLA; VP FHA; Girl Scts; Letterman Clb; Quiz Bowl; SADD; Band; Hon Roll; NHS.

RYMER II, BRETT M; Washington HS; Kansas City, KS; (2); Dance Clb; Spanish Clb; JV Var Bsbl; JV Crs Cntry; Ftbl; Var Swmmng; High Hon Roll; Prfct Atten Awd; Peer Ldr; Role Model; Wldlf/Game Prsrvtn.

RYS, TOMEK P; Manhattan HS; Manhattan, KS; (3); Boy Scts; Chess Clb; JV Wrstlng; High Hon Roll; Hon Roll; NHS; Bsktbl; Mtrcrs; Snwbrdng; K ST; Mech Engr.

RZIHA, DAVID; Centre Jr Sr HS; Tampa, KS; (2); 2/26; Letterman Clb; Natl FFA Org; Scholastic Bowl; Speech Tm; Varsity Clb; Ftbl; Trk; Wt Lftg; Hon Roll.

SAATHOFF, CHRISTOPHER; Valley Falls HS; Valley Falls, KS; (4); 5/35; Cmnty Wkr; FBLA; FHA; Band; Pep Band; VP Sr Cls; Capt Var Ftbl; Var Trk; Var Wt Lftg; High Hon Roll; Schlstc All Amer; KS ST U; Engrng.

SAATHOFF, SHAWNA; Valley Falls HS; Valley Falls, KS; (3); 1/40; Nwsp; Band; Rep Soph Cls; Sec Stu Cncl; Bsktbl; Chrldng; Pom Pon; Trk; High Hon Roll; NHS.

SACHEN, LAURA S; Sumner Acad Of Arts & Science; Kansas City, KS; (3); 11/148; FCA; Sec VP German Clb; VP Pres Key Clb; SADD; Nwsp; VP Frsh Cls; Ofcr Jr Cls; Ofcr Stu Cncl; Bsktbl; Vllybl; Grmn Natl Hnrs Scty; KS ST Rep Trip To Japan; Pre-Med Sci.

SACHSE, MEGAN A; Pleasant Ridge HS; Easton, KS; (3); Sec 4-H; Natl FFA Org; SADD; School Play; Co-Ed Yrbk; Hon Roll; NHS; Hum Club; Psych.

SACKET, SUSAN E; Maize HS; Kenosha, WI; (4); Ski Clb; Church Yth Grp; Cmnty Wkr; FBLA; Hosp Aide; Spanish Clb; SADD; Orch; Swmmng; High Hon Roll; U Of WI Parkside; Acctg.

SACKSCHEWSKY, MEGAN R; Independence HS; Independence, KS; (1); Church Yth Grp; GAA; Letterman Clb; Bsktbl; Crs Cntry; Trk; Hon Roll; Pres Acad Fit Awd; K ST; Vet.

SADE, MATT; Udall HS; Udall, KS; (4); Cmnty Wkr; Math Tm; Teachers Aide; Stat Ftbl; L Trk; Gov Hon Prg Awd; High Hon Roll; Pres Schlr; Span Tutor For Soph Span Cls; Cowley Co CC; Engrng.

SADE, NIKKI; Udall HS; Udall, KS; (2); Church Yth Grp; Dance Clb; Math Tm; Scholastic Bowl; Band; Mrchg Band; Bsktbl; Sftbl; Trk; Vllybl.

SADOWSKY, ARICA; Little River Jr Sr HS; Little River, KS; (1); Church Yth Grp; FHA; Pep Clb; Quiz Bowl; Chorus; School Musical; Chrldng.

SAGE, SHANNON M; Burlingame HS; Burlingame, KS; (1); 9/29; Spanish Clb; Band; Hon Roll.

SAGER, BRAD; Shawnee Mission Northwest HS; Shawnee Mission, KS; (2); 124/454; JA; Q&S; SADD; Ed Nwsp; Crs Cntry; Hon Roll; CUBS VP; Corporate Jrnlsm.

SAGER, LINDSAY; Marmaton Valley Jr Sr HS; Moran, KS; (1); 3/38; Church Yth Grp; Drama Clb; FCA; 4-H; FHA; Math Clb; Math Tm; Pep Clb; Band; Pep Band.

SAGHIR, MOHAMMED K; Blue Valley Northwest HS; Overland Park, KS; (3); 1/370; Pres Chess Clb; Cmnty Wkr; Scholastic Bowl; High Hon Roll; NHS; Ntl Merit Ltr; Bausch And Lomb Hnry Sci Awd.

SAHLFELD, AMANDA; St John's HS; Beloit, KS; (1); Church Yth Grp; Drama Clb; GAA; Pep Clb; Quiz Bowl; Scholastic Bowl; Speech Tm; Chorus; School Musical; School Play.

SAHNI, PRIYA; Blue Valley Northwest HS; Overland Park, KS; (1); Church Yth Grp; Chorus; Church Choir; Orch; High Hon Roll; Chrch Bell Choir; Regnl Msc Fest/Excl Violin Solo/Strng Ensmbl; Acad Excl Span I; Johnson CC; PT/MSC Thpst/Tchr.

SAINDON, CRISTINA; Rose Hill HS; Rose Hill, KS; (3); Cmnty Wkr; FHA; Band; Jazz Band; Mrchg Band; Orch; Pep Band; School Musical; High Hon Roll; Prfct Atten Awd; Peer Helpers; Wichita Wing Ensemble; Elem Stdnt Math/Sci Tutor; KS ST Univ; Vet Med.

ST CLAIR, JESSICA; Valley Ctr HS; Valley Center, KS; (2); Church Yth Grp; Cmnty Wkr; Drama Clb; HOBY; Office Aide; Pep Clb; Service Clb; SADD; Acpl Chr; Band; Teens As Tchrs Agnst Tobacco Prvntn; Mck Trial; Vly Players; KS Univ; Bus/Law.

ST MARTIN, FAITH E; Maize HS; Wichita, KS; (2); 62/298; Church Yth Grp; English Clb; French Clb; Office Aide; Science Clb; Spanish Clb; Teachers Aide; Thesps; Acpl Chr; Band; Notre Dame; Ob-Gyn; Soc Work.

ST PETER, GENNY; Maize HS; Wichita, KS; (2); Letterman Clb; Q&S; Science Clb; SADD; Chorus; Variety Show; Yrbk; Pom Pon; High Hon Roll; Hon Roll; Harlequins; KAYS.

ST ROMAIN, THERESA L; Wichita East HS; Wichita, KS; (2); Drama Clb; French Clb; SADD; Thesps; Chorus; School Musical; School Play; Variety Show; French Hon Soc; High Hon Roll; Literary Soc; Coll; Lbrl Arts.

SALAZAR, NICOLES D; Maize HS; Wichita, KS; (1); Drama Clb; SADD; Chorus; Variety Show; Var JV Tennis; Hon Roll; KAYS Sec; Harlaquins.

SALIGER, CHRISTINA; Chaparral HS; Harper, KS; (4); 9/64; Pep Clb; Scholastic Bowl; Band; Flag Corp; Mrchg Band; Pep Band; Nwsp; Yrbk; Var Chrldng; Var Tennis; Renaissance Card Holder; Chaparral Hnr C; Hutchinson CC; Comp Sci.

SALINAS, YOLANDA R; Shawnee Mission N HS; Merriam, KS; (2); 12/446; Church Yth Grp; Debate Tm; NFL; Pep Clb; Spanish Clb; Trk; High Hon Roll; Lge Of Unted Latn Amer Ctzns; Acadlttr Frshmn; Lettrd In Forensics Soph Yr; Psych.

SALISBURY, JENNY M; Augusta Sr HS; Augusta, KS; (3); Church Yth Grp; Girl Scts; Spanish Clb; Band; Mrchg Band; Pep Band; High Hon Roll; Grl Sct Slvr Awd 93; KS Sr Grl Scts Trp To Mexico 96; Elem Ed.

SALL, MATTHEW P; Shawnee Mission S Sr HS; Overland Park, KS; (4); 41/413; High Hon Roll; NHS; Pres Schlr; St Schlr; KS St Univ; Chem Eng.

SALMANS JR, GARY; El Dorado HS; El Dorado, KS; (3); 45/141; Am Leg Boys St; Boy Scts; Letterman Clb; Math Clb; NFL; Teachers Aide; Yrbk; Ftbl; Var Trk; Var Capt Wrstlng; Cntrl MO ST; Scndry Ed.

SALMANS, JASON O; Hanston Jr Sr HS; Hanston, KS; (4); 2/13; Boy Scts; Church Yth Grp; Quiz Bowl; VP Frsh Cls; Sec Stu Cncl; Capt Bsktbl; Capt Ftbl; L Trk; Cit Awd; Hon Roll; Baylor U.

SALMANS, JENNIFER J; Dodge City HS; Dodge City, KS; (4); 33/254; Church Yth Grp; FCA; SADD; Teachers Aide; Capt L Bsktbl; Capt L Vllybl; Cit Awd; High Hon Roll; NHS; Pres Schlr; DARE Role Model; Octagon Clb; Garden City CC; Phy Thrpst.

SALMON, DIANA; Fowler HS; Fowler, KS; (2); Church Yth Grp; 4-H; Math Tm; Quiz Bowl; Band; Chorus; Mrchg Band; Pep Band; Pres Frsh Cls; Pres Soph Cls; Dist Hnr Choir; St Music Cont; KAY Bd Mem; Meade Co 4-H Cncl Sec.

SALMON, EMILY A; Blue Valley Northwest HS; Shawnee Mission, KS; (1); Church Yth Grp; Math Tm; Service Clb; Orch; School Musical; Trk; High Hon Roll; Oustdng Ger Stdnt Of Yr; Yth Symphony KS City Asst Prin; Schl Orch Section Leader; U Of KS.

SALMON, PATRICIA J; Olathe North Sr HS; Olathe, KS; (4); 62/351; Pres Art Clb; Church Yth Grp; Teachers Aide; Band; Mrchg Band; Variety Show; High Hon Roll; NHS; Schlstc 3 Gld Kys, 2 Hnrbl Mntns; KS City Art Inst; Art Educ.

SALMON, TARA J; Santa Fe Trail Jr HS; Olathe, KS; (1); Church Yth Grp; Drama Clb; Band; Stage Crew; High Hon Roll; Hon Roll; Pres Schlr; Engl Acad Awd; Raider Of Qrtr.

SALOF, SUZANNE M; Shawnee Mission W Sr HS; Lenexa, KS; (4); 57/352; Art Clb; Church Yth Grp; Pep Clb; Hon Roll; Natl Arts Hnr Soc; San Diego ST Univ; Bio.

SALOGA, TERI; Skyline Schl; Coats, KS; (2); Hosp Aide; Pep Clb; SADD; Chorus; School Play; Yrbk; Rep Soph Cls; Rep Stu Cncl; Bsktbl; Chrldng; U Of KS; Med.

SALTER, JAIMEE; Mc Pherson HS; Mc Pherson, KS; (4); 2/187; Art Clb; Church Yth Grp; German Clb; Math Tm; Teachers Aide; Ofcr Frsh Cls; Co-Capt Var Bsktbl; Powder Puff Ftbl; Var Trk; Co-Capt Var Vllybl; M Club; William Jewell Coll.

SALVAY, RACHEL A; Shawnee Mission E Sr HS; Shawnee Mission, KS; (2); Cmnty Wkr; Girl Scts; Intnl Clb; Temple Yth Grp; Hon Roll; Explorers Group; Architectural Engr.

SALVIA, DARRELL; Blue Valley HS; Overland Park, KS; (3); Church Yth Grp; Dance Clb; Drama Clb; SADD; Chorus; Church Choir; School Musical; School Play; Swing Chorus; Variety Show; K-ST; Acctng.

SALVONI, RYAN L; Olathe East Sr HS; Olathe, KS; (4); Church Yth Grp; FCA; Letterman Clb; Teachers Aide; Sec Frsh Cls; JV Bsbl; Var L Ftbl; Var L Trk; Var L Wt Lftg; Hon Roll; OK St Univ; Arch.

SAMPAT, BRENDA; Washburn Rural HS; Topeka, KS; (2); 20/430; Debate Tm; Drama Clb; Ofcr French Clb; Intnl Clb; Model UN; SADD; Orch; High Hon Roll; Human Rghts Clb; Earthbnd Env Clb; Fornscs; Nrsng Hms Vol; HOPE Cnnctn Hmlss Ctr.

SAMPLES, SHAUNTELLE L; Topeka HS; Topeka, KS; (2); Church Yth Grp; Cmnty Wkr; JA; Library Aide; Office Aide; Drill Tm; Orch; JV Chrldng; Hon Roll; STRAPP; BSU; KS ST Univ; Soc Wrk.

SAMPSON, BILL J; Ft Scott HS; Fort Scott, KS; (3); Var Wrstlng; Hon Roll.

SAMUEL, JEREMY C; Nickerson HS; Hutchinson, KS; (3); 24/108; Church Yth Grp; FCA; Library Aide; Scholastic Bowl; Band; Jazz Band; Mrchg Band; Pep Band; Hon Roll; Prfct Atten Awd; Natl His Day; Pilot Telecommnctn Project; Aerospace Engrng.

SAMUELS, BRETT M; Olpe Schl; Olpe, KS; (3); 10/31; Church Yth Grp; Cmnty Wkr; 4-H; FBLA; Science Clb; Church Choir; Ofcr Stu Cncl; Bsktbl; Crs Cntry; Trk; Amer Legion Bsbl Team; Coll; Own Bus.

SAMUELSON, EMILY; Seaman Sr HS; Topeka, KS; (2); Drama Clb; Pep Clb; SADD; Teachers Aide; Stage Crew; JV Chrldng; Hon Roll; KS ST.

SANCHEZ, DAVID F; Manhattan HS; Lubbock, TX; (1); Band; Mrchg Band; JV Socr; High Hon Roll; Hon Roll.

SANCHEZ, ELISA M; Bishop Ward HS; Kansas City, KS; (2); 27/93; Pep Clb; SADD; Hon Roll; Drawng; Music; Dncng.

SANCHEZ, LUIS; Manhattan HS; Manhattan, KS; (3); Chess Clb; Debate Tm; NFL; Band; Mrchg Band; Pep Band; Socr; Tennis; High Hon Roll; NHS; Bus.

SANCHEZ, NORMA; Rolla HS; Rolla, KS; (3); 8/17; FCA; Band; Pep Band; Ed Nwsp; Ed Yrbk; JV Var Bsktbl; Sftbl; Trk; Vllybl; Seward Cty CC.

SANCHEZ, SUSANA; Olathe South Sr HS; Olathe, KS; (3); #1 in class; Cmnty Wkr; Q&S; Spanish Clb; Yrbk; Lit Mag; High Hon Roll; NHS; Pres Acad Fit Awd; Spanish NHS; SASH Chprsn; U Of KS; Medcl Phy.

SANDALL, JANA C; Goddard HS; Goddard, KS; (1); 5/200; Hosp Aide; Ed Nwsp; Ed Yrbk; Pres Stu Cncl; JV Bsktbl; Var Capt Socr; JV Vllybl; Cit Awd; High Hon Roll; Pres Acad Fit Awd.

SANDBOTHE, APRIL; Neodesha Jr Sr HS; Neodesha, KS; (3); 1/60; Pres Church Yth Grp; Sec FHA; Natl FFA Org; NFL; Sec Jr Cls; Capt Chrldng; Var Pom Pon; JV Vllybl; High Hon Roll; NHS.

SANDBULTE, TOM; Winfield HS; Winfield, KS; (4); Am Leg Boys St; Church Yth Grp; Scholastic Bowl; Spanish Clb; Speech Tm; Ftbl; Golf; High Hon Roll; NHS; Pres Acad Fit Awd; KS St Univ; Bus Admin.

SANDEFUR, JOSH L; Wichita South HS; Wichita, KS; (3); Chorus; Orch; Variety Show; KS ST HS Solo Festival I Rating; KS Ambassadors Of Music Mem.

SANDER, CURTIS; Thomas More Prep-Marion HS; Hays, KS; (3); 1/69; Church Yth Grp; Math Tm; Band; Mrchg Band; Pep Band; JV Crs Cntry; Mgr Trk; High Hon Roll; Ntl Merit Ltr; Presdntl Awd Schlrshp; Bus.

SANDER, LORA L; Great Bend Sr HS; Great Bend, KS; (3); Hosp Aide; JA; Letterman Clb; Library Aide; Pep Clb; Spanish Clb; Teachers Aide; Varsity Clb; Var L Sftbl; JV Vllybl; Selected To Western Ath All Conf Team Sftbl; Chosen To Go To Natl Yth Ldrshp Forum On Medicine; Med.

SANDERHOLM, ERIC; Olathe North Sr HS; Olathe, KS; (2); VP Church Yth Grp; Band; Jazz Band; Mrchg Band; High Hon Roll; Pres Schlr; Office Aide; Quiz Bowl; Scholastic Bowl; Teachers Aide; Outstdng Band Mem 94-95; Outstdng Musician In Jazz Presented By IAJE; Acad Ltr For 95-96; KU; Pre-Med; Vet Medicine.

SANDERS, ARIA L; J C Harmon HS; Kansas City, KS; (3); English Clb; Hosp Aide; Math Clb; NFL; Spanish Clb; Acpl Chr; Church Choir; Drill Tm; Variety Show; Yrbk; Study Of Dead.

SANDERS, COREY L; Liberal HS; Liberal, KS; (3); Church Yth Grp; Teachers Aide; Chorus; Church Choir; JV Var Bsktbl; JV Var Ftbl; JV Var Trk; JV Var Wt Lftg; Prfct Atten Awd; U Of NE; Hlth Care.

SANDERS, JENNIFER S; Buhler HS; Hutchinson, KS; (2); FCA; Hosp Aide; Science Clb; Spanish Clb; Band; Mrchg Band; Yrbk; Swmmng; Wt Lftg; Intr Dsgnr.

SANDERS, JESSICA; Washburn Rural HS; Topeka, KS; (4); 135/272; Church Yth Grp; GAA; Letterman Clb; Teachers Aide; Chorus; Church Choir; School Musical; Variety Show; Powder Puff Ftbl; Socr; Tnns St Trnmt & Ltr; All City Soccer Team Capt & Ltr; Winter Royalty Sq; KS ST Univ; Acctng.

SANDERS, KRISTINA; Leavenworth HS; Leavenworth, KS; (2); Var L Bsktbl; Var L Vllybl; Hon Roll.

SANDERS, NICHOLAS E; Turner HS; Kansas City, KS; (3); 32/252; Am Leg Boys St; Bus Profs of Am; Science Clb; SADD; Rep Sr Cls; Rep Stu Cncl; L Crs Cntry; Var L Socr; Var L Trk; Hon Roll; U Of KS; Pediatrics.

SANDERS, PHILLIP A; Washburn Rural HS; Topeka, KS; (3); 85/351; Church Yth Grp; Hist 4-H; Office Aide; Mgr Bsktbl; Mgr Trk; 4-H Awd; High Hon Roll; Hon Roll; Acad Lttr 9th Grd Yr; Sprts Lttr Bsktbl Trck 2; Olympica Pen Cllctng; Ed/Bus.

SANDERS, SAMUEL S; Maize HS; Wichita, KS; (4); Stock Mrkt Game 1st Regnl/2nd ST; Math/Sci Olympcs Comp; Butler Cty CC; Cmptr Prgmmng.

SANDERSON, JAY L; Douglass HS; Douglass, KS; (2); Letterman Clb; Quiz Bowl; Science Clb; Speech Tm; Var Bsbl; JV Bsktbl; JV Ftbl; Cit Awd; High Hon Roll; NHS; TV Jrnlsm.

SANDERSON, MATT; Spring Hill HS; Olathe, KS; (3); 14/96; Letterman Clb; Pep Clb; SADD; Varsity Clb; Var L Bsbl; JV Bsktbl; Cit Awd; Hon Roll; Jr NHS; Pres Acad Fit Awd.

SANDMANN, TONYIA; Marysville HS; Frankfort, KS; (4); Am Leg Aux Girls St; Band; Drm Mjr(t); Sec Frsh Cls; Rep Soph Cls; VP Jr Cls; Rep Stu Cncl; Var Bsktbl; Var Tennis; High Hon Roll; KS St U; Bus.

SANDOMIRSKY, MARIANNA; Blue Valley Northwest HS; Overland Park, KS; (4); 100/350; Art Clb; Cmnty Wkr; French Clb; Hosp Aide; Quiz Bowl; Varsity Clb; Powder Puff Ftbl; Var Tennis; Pres Schlr; St Schlr; Natl Schltc Art Awd; WA Univ; Medicine.

SANDOVAL, ANGELICA V; Turner HS; Kansas City, KS; (4); 10/190; Art Clb; Dance Clb; Spanish Clb; SADD; Drill Tm; Wrstlng; Hon Roll; NHS; Schlstc Art Awd Slvr Key & Hnrb Mntn; Wrstlng Mgr; Kansas City Art Inst; Pntng.

SANDOVAL, CINTHIA; Ulysses HS; Ulysses, KS; (4); 13/93; Church Yth Grp; FBLA; Band; Flag Corp; Treas Sr Cls; Ofcr Stu Cncl; Var Chrldng; Vllybl; Hon Roll; NHS; HALO Pres; Hmcmng Queen 95-96; Frgn Lang Clb VP; Dodge City CC; Intl Bus.

SANDOVAL, LINDA; Ulysses HS; Ulysses, KS; (3); Church Yth Grp; FHA; Spanish Clb; SADD; Band; Flag Corp; Mrchg Band; Ofcr Jr Cls; Chrldng; Wt Lftg; FHA; SADD; HALO; STUCO; Bnd Flte Solo Awds; Sec.

SANDOVAL, LYDIA; Stafford Jr Sr HS; Stafford, KS; (2); Church Yth Grp; Band; Pep Band; Sec Soph Cls; Var Bsktbl; Var Chrldng; JV Vllybl; Frnscs; Math Sci Rlys; Chorale.

SANDOVAL, MICHAEL; Stafford Jr Sr HS; Stafford, KS; (1); Church Yth Grp; Natl FFA Org; JV Var Ftbl; JV Var Trk; Var Wrstlng; High Hon Roll; Hon Roll; Prfct Atten Awd.

SANDS, RIAN A; Blue Valley HS; Olathe, KS; (3); Q&S; Quiz Bowl; VP Service Clb; Ed Nwsp; Cit Awd; Hon Roll; NHS; Pres Acad Fit Awd; Museum Sci.

SANDS, SCOTT E; Girard HS; Girard, KS; (4); French Clb; Science Clb; SADD; Teachers Aide; Band; Mrchg Band; Pep Band; Ftbl; Trk; Wt Lftg; Pittsburg ST Univ; Auto Tech.

SANFORD, MOLLY D; Marmaton Valley Jr Sr HS; Moran, KS; (4); 3/29; Math Tm; Scholastic Bowl; Chorus; Capt Flag Corp; Mrchg Band; Capt JV Chrldng; High Hon Roll; NHS; Cmnty Wkr; Pep Clb; VFW Essay Cntst Wnnr; Vlntr Hum Soc, Legsltv Wrk Anml Rghts; UKS-LAWRENCE; Neurlgy.

SANKEY, ERIC D; Salina HS South; Salina, KS; (2); Band; Mrchg Band; Pep Band; Hon Roll; KS ST Univ; Chem Engrng.

SANKO, CASSIE L; Spearville Jr Sr HS; Spearville, KS; (3); Rptr 4-H; Library Aide; Pep Clb; Band; Chorus; Mrchg Band; Pep Band; School Play; Nwsp; Yrbk; Ft Hays ST Univ; Lib Sci/Eng.

SANNEMAN, LINDSAY; Clay Ctr Cmty HS; Clay Center, KS; (2); Church Yth Grp; Band; Drill Tm; Jazz Band; Mrchg Band; Pep Band; Tennis; High Hon Roll; Baton Twirler.

SANNES, MATTHEW R; Blue Valley HS; Overland Park, KS; (2); Church Yth Grp; Band; Church Choir; Mrchg Band; Pep Band; Intrml Bsktbl; JV Ftbl; JV L Wrstlng; Hon Roll; Peer Mediator; JCCC; Meteorologist.

SANO, PENNY; Manhattan HS; Manhattan, KS; (1); Church Yth Grp; 4-H; Chorus; Chrldng; Cit Awd; 4-H Awd; Hon Roll; Dance; Tribe Schl Pgm.

SAN ROMAN, SALVADOR L; Wichita North HS; Wichita, KS; (3); Library Aide; Office Aide; Teachers Aide; Wrstlng.

SAN ROMANI, HEATHER L; Rose Hill HS; Rose Hill, KS; (3); Church Yth Grp; FHA; SADD; Chorus; Church Choir; Variety Show; Vllybl; Hon Roll; NHS; KAYS; Peer Helpers.

SANSON, TANYA L; Blue Valley HS; Overland Park, KS; (2); Church Yth Grp; GAA; Latin Clb; Teachers Aide; Mgr(s); Score Keeper; Sftbl; Mgr Vllybl; Hon Roll; Rec Actvts; KU; Law.

SANTELLI, TAMARA; Blue Valley Northwest HS; Overland Park, KS; (3); 1/350; HOBY; Pep Clb; Orch; Treas Frsh Cls; Treas Soph Cls; Treas Jr Cls; Mgr Ftbl; JV Socr; High Hon Roll; KS City Yth Symphny; Heartlands Schl Riding Vol; Dist & St Orch; Zoology.

SANTELLI, TANARA S; Blue Valley Northwest HS; Overland Park, KS; (3); 1/350; HOBY; Orch; Treas Frsh Cls; Treas Soph Cls; Treas Jr Cls; Pres Sr Cls; Mgr(s); JV Socr; High Hon Roll; NHS; Yth Symphony Of KS City; Music Ed.

SANTIAGO, MARISOL; Wichita Northwest HS; Wichita, KS; (3); Chorus; Variety Show; Hon Roll; KS Newman; Med.

SANTIMANO, DAVINIA; Lansing HS; Lansing, KS; (3); Art Clb; Drama Clb; NFL; Science Clb; Thesps; Chorus; Nwsp; Capt Pom Pon; Tennis; Hon Roll; Kayettes; U Of KS.

SAPP, MICHELLE; Pierson Jr HS; Kansas City, KS; (1); Art Clb; Computer Clb; Girl Scts; JA; Ed Nwsp; Stat Bsktbl; Hon Roll; Jr NHS; KU; Pedtrc Psych.

SARE, JUSTIN E; Osawatomie HS; Rantoul, KS; (2); Art Clb; Church Yth Grp; Quiz Bowl; Science Clb; Teachers Aide; Acpl Chr; Swing Chorus; Phtg Yrbk; VP Jr Cls; Var Bsbl; Grphc Dsgnr.

SARFANI, ASIF; Washburn Rural HS; Topeka, KS; (2); Bus Profs of Am; Debate Tm; Trk; High Hon Roll; Hon Roll; Aga Khan Hlth Bd; Attnd ESSI K-State Univ; Chem; Nuclear Engrng.

SARGEANT, AIMEE; Mulvane Sr HS; Wichita, KS; (3); Church Yth Grp; SADD; Band; Bsktbl; Pom Pon; Trk; Vllybl; Dance Clb; NHS; KS U; Psych.

SASSAMAN, ACACIA; Garden City Sr HS; Garden City, KS; (3); JV Bsktbl; JV Vllybl.

SATTERFIELD, SHAWNA M; Great Bend Sr HS; Great Bend, KS; (3); Pep Clb; Intrml Bsktbl; Intrml Vllybl; Hon Roll; Barton Co CC; CPA.

SATTERLEE, MIKE; Peabody-Burns Jr Sr HS; Peabody, KS; (3); 8/32; Church Yth Grp; FCA; Natl FFA Org; Pres Rep Jr Cls; Capt L Bsktbl; Capt L Ftbl; Var L Trk; Hon Roll; NHS; Teachers Aide; Elem Ed.

SATTLER, ANGELA L; Herndon Schl; Herndon, KS; (2); Church Yth Grp; Pep Clb; Speech Tm; Band; Chorus; Church Choir; Rep Stu Cncl; Var Chrldng; JV Var Vllybl; High Hon Roll; Odyssey Of The Mind; Bsktbl Acad Awd; Bus; Nutrition.

SAUBER, TAMMIE; Southwestern Hgts HS; Liberal, KS; (4); 9/33; Church Yth Grp; HOBY; Teachers Aide; Band; Cit Awd; Hon Roll; Pres Acad Fit Awd; 4-H; Mrchg Band; Pep Band; Athl Trnr; KAY Clb; Ldrshp Amer; Paralgl.

SAUBER, TERESA; Southwestern Heights HS; Liberal, KS; (2); HOBY; Teachers Aide; Chorus; Bsktbl; Chrldng; Cit Awd; Hon Roll; NHS; Kays Clb; Ldrshp Amer; Northwestern Coll; Elem Tchr.

SAUBLE, MARYANN; Newton Sr HS; Newton, KS; (2); French Clb; Stage Crew; Hon Roll.

SAUDER, CHRIS; Midland Sda Schl; Lenexa, KS; (2); 1/20; Chorus; Treas Soph Cls; JV Var Bsktbl; Cit Awd; High Hon Roll.

SAUER, SHERI; Ransom Jr Sr HS; Brownell, KS; (3); Church Yth Grp; Drama Clb; FCA; Letterman Clb; Pep Clb; Band; Chorus; Yrbk; Var Trk; Hon Roll; Chem.

SAUERWEIN, AARON; Newton Sr HS; Newton, KS; (3); 10/250; Am Leg Boys St; Church Yth Grp; Chorus; Bsktbl; Var Tennis; High Hon Roll; NHS; Univ Of KS; Opt.

SAUERWEIN, ANGIE R; Ft Scott HS; Fort Scott, KS; (4); 1/130; NFL; Quiz Bowl; Teachers Aide; Orch; Golf; Gov Hon Prg Awd; High Hon Roll; NHS; St Schlr; Val; Pittsburgh St Univ; Comm.

SAULET, SEASON J; Bishop Miege HS; Overland Park, KS; (3); Art Clb; Hon Roll; WIN Club 9th Grd; Univ Of Appalachain; Fshn Dsgn.

SAUNDERS, KEVIN G; Shawnee Mission N HS; Shawnee, KS; (2); Drama Clb; JV Golf; JV Socr; Environment Sci.

SAUNDERS, LORI L; Olathe East Sr HS; Olathe, KS; (2); Church Yth Grp; Dance Clb; Spanish Clb; Teachers Aide; Acpl Chr; Chorus; School Musical; School Play; Variety Show; Mgr(s); SASH Mem & Exec Bd; Natl Dance Cmptn Team Champ; Mid Amer Nazarene Coll; Medicn.

SAVAGE, JENNIFER M; Marion HS; Florence, KS; (2); Church Yth Grp; Cmnty Wkr; Teachers Aide; Thesps; Band; School Musical; Stage Crew; Yrbk; Stat Mgr(s); High Hon Roll; Nrsg Hm Vol; Kds Clb TA; U Of KS; Erly Chld Ed/Psy.

SAVAGE, MEGAN L; Blue Valley Northwest HS; Overland Park, KS; (2); Pep Clb; Varsity Clb; Band; Drill Tm; Mrchg Band; Trk; Hon Roll; Received All Amer Drill Team At Camp; Drill Team Co-Capt; St In 400m Dash As Soph.

SAVAGE, OCTAVIA J; Washington HS; Des Moines, IA; (3); Drama Clb; Hosp Aide; Spanish Clb; School Play; Mgr(s); Powder Puff Ftbl; Hon Roll; NHS; Prfct Atten Awd; Bst Actrs Awd 95-; Pr Ldr; Cmptrs.

SAVERINO, ROBERT C; Maur Hill Prep Schl; Saint Joseph, MO; (1); Boy Scts; Church Yth Grp; Debate Tm; Speech Tm; School Play; Bsktbl; Tennis; Wt Lftg; Hon Roll.

SAVILLE, BEN R; Washburn Rural HS; Topeka, KS; (3); 8/336; Boy Scts; Church Yth Grp; Band; Orch; Socr; Trk; Wrstlng; NHS; Jazz Band; Mrchg Band; 1st Chair Trombone 95-96 KS All-St Orch; Soccer 2nd Highest Goal In KS St; Trombone Perfmnc.

SAVILLE, TABITHA; Olathe North Sr HS; Olathe, KS; (3); French Clb; Hosp Aide; Office Aide; Pep Clb; Teachers Aide; Varsity Clb; Drill Tm; Flag Corp; Mrchg Band; Nwsp; Pre-Med.

SAWATZKY, MELISSA; Little River Jr Sr HS; Windom, KS; (1); 1/30; Church Yth Grp; FHA; Quiz Bowl; Scholastic Bowl; Band; Mrchg Band; Pep Band; JV Bsktbl; Stat Vllybl; Hon Roll.

SAWYER, KASEY J; Oxford HS; Oxford, KS; (4); 1/24; Drama Clb; School Play; VP Pres Stu Cncl; JV Var Bsktbl; Var Crs Cntry; Var Trk; Gov Hon Prg Awd; High Hon Roll; NHS; Val; Butler Cty CC; Scndry Ed.

SAXTON, SUZANNE; Shawnee Mission W Sr HS; Lenexa, KS; (4); Q&S; Varsity Clb; Chorus; Yrbk; Var L Swmmng; Hon Roll; St Schlr; JAWS; Fshn Careers I, II; Prom Crt; KU; TV Brdcst.

SAYE, WILLIS R; Ft Scott HS; Fort Scott, KS; (2); Computer Clb; JV Trk; Natural Helpers; Peer Mediations; Writer.

SAYEED, ALMAS; Wichita East HS; Wichita, KS; (3); Cmnty Wkr; Debate Tm; NFL; Q&S; Scholastic Bowl; Spanish Clb; Speech Tm; Ed Nwsp; Pres Frsh Cls; Treas Soph Cls; Intnl Baccalaureate Stu; Natl Forensics League Pres; Comm Svc; Biochem; Philosophy.

SAYER, DESDA L; Smoky Valley HS; Lindsborg, KS; (3); NFL; VP Frsh Cls; Pres Stu Cncl; Intrml JV Bsktbl; JV Socr; Hon Roll; U Of WA; Archtctr/Lndscp.

SAYERS, LISA; Peabody-Burns Jr Sr HS; Florence, KS; (2); 6/40; Church Yth Grp; Pres 4-H; Math Tm; JV Bsktbl; L Trk; JV Var Vllybl; 4-H Awd; High Hon Roll; Wichita St Univ; Eng.

SAYLOR, ADAM L; Topeka West HS; Topeka, KS; (3); Cmnty Wkr; French Clb; German Clb; Letterman Clb; Math Clb; Pep Clb; Q&S; SADD; Thesps; Varsity Clb; TV Prod Crew.

SAYLOR, LINDSAY L; Sabetha HS; Sabetha, KS; (2); 11/64; Church Yth Grp; Pep Clb; Spanish Clb; Teachers Aide; JV Bsktbl; Var L Crs Cntry; Var L Trk; Hon Roll; NHS; Pres Acad Fit Awd; Kays Club.

SCADUTO, MIKE H; Blue Valley Northwest HS; Leawood, KS; (2); Diving; Mgr(s); Hon Roll.

SCAFER, LIS; Jackson Heights HS; Soldier, KS; (4); Church Yth Grp; Pres FHA; School Musical; School Play; Nwsp; Yrbk; Capt Chrldng; Vllybl; NHS; KS ST U.

SCALZI, FRANCESCA; Garden City Sr HS; Garden City, KS; (4); 14/334; Pres Drama Clb; English Clb; Girl Scts; JCL; VP Latin Clb; Model UN; NFL; Capt Quiz Bowl; Scholastic Bowl; Science Clb; Brotherhood Of The Card; KS ST U; Tech Theater.

SCANLON, KAREN A; Trego Comm HS; Wa Keeney, KS; (2); 16/49; Church Yth Grp; Drama Clb; FHA; Letterman Clb; NFL; Pep Clb; Science Clb; SADD; Band; Drill Tm; Ft Hays ST Univ.

SCANLON, LUKE C; El Dorado HS; El Dorado, KS; (3); Letterman Clb; SADD; Band; Mrchg Band; JV Bsbl; Bsktbl; JV L Crs Cntry; Hon Roll; Earth Care Club; KAY; Butler Cty CC; Bio Sci.

SCHAAFF, ALISON M; Aguinas HS; Overland Park, KS; (4); Drama Clb; Key Clb; SADD; Yrbk; Treas Soph Cls; Sec Jr Cls; L Tennis; High Hon Roll; Hon Roll; NHS; KS St Univ; Art.

SCHACHTNER, DANIEL R; Riverton Schl; Riverton, KS; (3); Church Yth Grp; French Clb; Letterman Clb; Band; Chorus; Jazz Band; Mrchg Band; Orch; Pep Band; School Musical; Pittsburg ST U; Scndry Ed.

SCHADE, JANICE K; Olpe Schl; Olpe, KS; (2); Church Yth Grp; Treas 4-H; Ed FBLA; HOBY; School Play; Treas Jr Cls; Var L Bsktbl; JV Vllybl; 4-H Awd; Hon Roll; FBLA Nwsltr Pub; Eagle Creek Saddle Clb; Chrch Soloist; Surgeon.

SCHAEFER, JEREMY T; Marysville HS; Bremen, KS; (4); Church Yth Grp; FCA; Letterman Clb; Band; Mrchg Band; Pep Band; L Var Bsktbl; Var L Trk; Hon Roll; Coached Pee Wee Bsbl; KS ST Univ.

SCHAEFER, KATHARINE; Immaculata HS; Leavenworth, KS; (2); Intnl Clb; Quiz Bowl; Ski Clb; Teachers Aide; Pres Frsh Cls; Rep Stu Cncl; High Hon Roll; Tp Grd Awd Grd 11 Bio/Tech/Mrlty Grd 9; Ovrl Ave Awd; Tp Grd Awd Wrld His/Kybrdng/Cmptr Appl/Eng 10; Queens U; Veterinarian.

SCHAEFER, LINDSEY R; Wichita South HS; Wichita, KS; (3); 13/294; Cmnty Wkr; Office Aide; Acpl Chr; Chorus; Church Choir; Variety Show; High Hon Roll; Hon Roll; NHS; KS Ambsdrs Of Music European Tour 95; Meteorolgy.

SCHAFER, NICOLE E; Topeka HS; Topeka, KS; (4); Cmnty Wkr; Debate Tm; German Clb; Girl Scts; Intnl Clb; Model UN; NFL; Speech Tm; Chorus; Variety Show; Vol Awd Of Topeka; Fort Hays St Univ; Engl.

SCHAFER, RYAN D; Salina HS South; Salina, KS; (3); Church Yth Grp; Teachers Aide; Band; Mrchg Band; JV Var Ftbl; JV Var Golf; Var L Trk; Hon Roll; NHS; KS ST Univ; Scndry Ed.

SCHAFFER, JEFF; Dodge City HS; Dodge City, KS; (3); Am Leg Boys St; Boy Scts; Church Yth Grp; Church Choir; Trk; Hon Roll; KS St Squire Of Yr; Eagle Sct.

SCHAID, LAURA L; Independence HS; Independence, KS; (1); Church Yth Grp; French Clb; NFL; Band; Mrchg Band; Pep Band; Tennis; Hon Roll; Prfct Atten Awd; Natl Forensic Lge Degree Of Merit; Awd Reg Mus Fest 2nd Div Awd; Kay Clb; Psych.

SCHAKE, DAWN M; El Dorado HS; El Dorado, KS; (3); 34/144; Church Yth Grp; FTA; Letterman Clb; Office Aide; SADD; Teachers Aide; Varsity Clb; JV Var Bsktbl; Intrml Powder Puff Ftbl; Var Sftbl; Sftbl All League Hnrbl Mention/First Team; Hubbard Summer Acad Future Tchrs Awd; PE.

SCHAMBER, JOHN J; Palco HS; Damar, KS; (1); 2/11; Debate Tm; Letterman Clb; Quiz Bowl; Speech Tm; VP Frsh Cls; Bsktbl; Ftbl; Trk; Wt Lftg; Hon Roll; Vet.

SCHANTZ, WENDY; Shawnee Mission North Schl; Shawnee Mission, KS; (2); 24/416; Church Yth Grp; Letterman Clb; Pep Clb; Q&S; Treas Chorus; Ed Yrbk; JV Co-Capt Chrldng; High Hon Roll; Habitat For Humanity Vol.

SCHAPER, ALBERT K; Independence Bible Schl; Parsons, KS; (3); 5/8; Church Yth Grp; Chorus; Church Choir; Pres Soph Cls; Pres Jr Cls; Rep Stu Cncl; Hon Roll; Prfct Atten Awd; Select Choir; Male Quartet.

SCHATZ, SARAH L; Central HS; Salina, KS; (2); Sec Debate Tm; Drama Clb; Sec Thesps; Band; Jazz Band; High Hon Roll.

SCHAUB, JEANA L; Northeast HS; Arcadia, KS; (2); 6/45; 4-H; HOBY; Library Aide; Nwsp; Yrbk; Ofcr Stu Cncl; Var L Bsktbl; Var L Sftbl; Hon Roll; Cmnty Wkr; Soph Homecoming Queen Cnddt; FHA Jr Ilstrd Tlk Rgnl Wnr; Pittsburg ST Univ.

SCHAVEE, SHANNON L; Leavenworth HS; Leavenworth, KS; (3); Hosp Aide; Band; Mrchg Band; Pep Band; JV Var Crs Cntry; JV Socr; High Hon Roll; Pre-Med.

SCHAWE, KELBY; Dodge City HS; Dodge City, KS; (3); Am Leg Boys St; Church Yth Grp; Model UN; Office Aide; Spanish Clb; School Play; Hon Roll; NHS; Columbia Squires Ofcr; Jr Ldrshp Dodge.

SCHEAHRER, ERIN K; Eudora HS; Eudora, KS; (4); 8/42; Church Yth Grp; Pres Spanish Clb; Band; Jazz Band; Mrchg Band; Pep Band; Hon Roll; Jr NHS; Environmental Clb; U Of KS; Nrsng.

SCHEEF, KATIE A; Jewell HS; Jewell, KS; (4); 5/15; Pres Church Yth Grp; FCA; Treas SADD; Sec Frsh Cls; Treas Soph Cls; Sec Jr Cls; Sec Sr Cls; Sec Stu Cncl; Var Bsktbl; Hon Roll; Teens As Tchrs; STUCO Ldrshp Camp; Hubbard Sumr Acad Fut Tchrs; Butler Co CC; Elem/Spec Ed.

SCHEER, JENNY L; Garden Plain Jr Sr HS; Garden Plain, KS; (3); Church Yth Grp; Letterman Clb; Spanish Clb; SADD; Chorus; Drill Tm; Rep Stu Cncl; Var Capt Pom Pon; Trk; Hon Roll; Red Cross; Pittsburg; Pre-Med.

SCHEERER, JONATHAN R; Shawnee Mission E Sr HS; Leawood, KS; (3); Church Yth Grp; Math Tm; Natl Beta Clb; Sec Frsh Cls; JV Capt Socr; High Hon Roll; NHS; Rugby Team; Art Awds Recipient.

SCHEETZ, JARED L; Lenora HS; New Almelo, KS; (4); 4/7; Church Yth Grp; Pep Clb; Ofcr Sr Cls; Ofcr Stu Cncl; Bsktbl; Ftbl; Golf; Trk; High Hon Roll; Hnrbl Men Pntr & Rnng Bck; Soph Clss Pres; All Leg Pntr; Altrnt Shrn Bwl & By St Ftbl Tm; Dodge City CC; Farm Mgmt.

SCHEFFLER, DANIEL R; Newton Sr HS; Newton, KS; (1); SADD; Rptr Yrbk; Lit Mag; Bsktbl; Ftbl; JV Trk.

SCHEFFLER, MELISSA V; Newton Sr HS; Newton, KS; (2); 22/279; Key Clb; SADD; Chorus; Ed Lit Mag; High Hon Roll; Eclipse Clb; Weebok Stu; Writers Anonymous Clb; U Of Notre Dame; Biochem.

SCHEIBE, KATHIE; Basehor Linwood HS; Basehor, KS; (4); 4/120; Debate Tm; FBLA; Pres Math Clb; NFL; Q&S; Mrchg Band; Ed Nwsp; Ofcr Stu Cncl; Mgr Trk; NHS; Photo St Jrnlsm Cont 1st Pl; U Of KS; Jrnlsm.

SCHEIBNER, BRIAN C; Olathe East Sr HS; Olathe, KS; (3); Boy Scts; Computer Clb; Drama Clb; Thesps; Band; Mrchg Band; Pep Band; School Musical; School Play; Stage Crew; Eagle Scout Awd; Coll Of Ozarks; News Brdcstng.

SCHEILKE, JUSTIN; Colby Sr HS; Colby, KS; (4); 3/100; Am Leg Boys St; Boy Scts; Science Clb; Spanish Clb; Nwsp; High Hon Roll; NHS; Pres Acad Fit Awd; Pres Thomas Cnty Sheriff Explrs; KS St Univ; Fin.

SCHELL, SHANDA R; Ulysses HS; Ulysses, KS; (3); L Debate Tm; FBLA; VP NFL; SADD; VP Jr Cls; Var Trk; L Vllybl; Lawyer.

SCHELLMAN, KELLY A; Lawrence HS; Lawrence, KS; (2); Church Yth Grp; Spanish Clb; Teachers Aide; Thesps; Chorus; School Play; Stage Crew; Variety Show; Rep Stu Cncl; Hon Roll; Intnl Thespian Soc Mem; Yth Theatre; Musical Theatre.

SCHEMM, CRYSTAL A; Smith Ctr Jr Sr HS; Smith Center, KS; (4); 8/42; Pres Church Yth Grp; VP FHA; VP SADD; Band; Chorus; Drm Mjr(t); Mrchg Band; Pep Band; Cit Awd; High Hon Roll; KAYS-TREAS Frosh, Sec & Membership Coord Jr Yr; UNE Kearney; Psych; Crmnl Jstce.

SCHENCK, ELIZABETH J; Independence Bible Schl; Altamont, KS; (2); 2/14; Church Yth Grp; Teachers Aide; Band; Chorus; Church Choir; Orch; School Musical; School Play; Yrbk; Ofcr Frsh Cls; Music Club; Church Music Prgm; Pittsburgh ST Univ; Music Tchr.

SCHENIDER, JENNIFER L; Otis Bison HS; Olmitz, KS; (2); #1 in class; Church Yth Grp; Quiz Bowl; SADD; Band; Jazz Band; Mrchg Band; VP Frsh Cls; JV Vllybl; High Hon Roll; Cmnty Wkr; Frnscs; Music Ed.

SCHEOPNER, KENDRA D; Goodland HS; Goodland, KS; (4); Church Yth Grp; GAA; Math Tm; Scholastic Bowl; Swing Chorus; Capt Powder Puff Ftbl; Var L Trk; Var L Vllybl; Wt Lftg; Kiwanis Awd; Fastpitch Sftbl; Cloud Cty CC; Advertising.

SCHEPMANN, JILL A; Salina HS South; Salina, KS; (4); 11/220; GAA; NFL; Ed Nwsp; Rep Frsh Cls; VP Soph Cls; VP Jr Cls; Rep Sr Cls; Rep Stu Cncl; JV Bsktbl; Powder Puff Ftbl; U Of KS; Archaeologist.

SCHERER, ANGELA; Lansing HS; Lansing, KS; (3); 8/140; Cmnty Wkr; Drama Clb; FTA; Science Clb; Spanish Clb; Thesps; Swing Chorus; Chrldng; High Hon Roll; NHS; Emporia ST U; Early Chldhd Ed.

SCHERER, MICHAEL H; Atchison Co Cmty HS; Atchison, KS; (2); Church Yth Grp; Letterman Clb; Math Clb; Math Tm; Natl FFA Org; Quiz Bowl; Pres Soph Cls; Pres Jr Cls; Ofcr Stu Cncl; JV Bsktbl; KS ST; Tchr.

SCHERER, REBECCA R; Atchison Co Cmty HS; Lancaster, KS; (2); Church Yth Grp; FBLA; Pep Clb; Quiz Bowl; SADD; Band; Chorus; Mrchg Band; Pep Band; High Hon Roll; KS Assn Yth; KMEA Dist I Hnr Bnd; Gifted Ed Prgm.

SCHERRER, DAVID; Olathe North Sr HS; Olathe, KS; (3); Church Yth Grp; German Clb; Band; Jazz Band; Mrchg Band; Pep Band; Variety Show; Var Bsktbl; JV Tennis; Hon Roll; Art Achvmt Awd.

SCHERTZ, SUSAN; Triplains Schl; Monument, KS; (4); 2/8; Church Yth Grp; Pres Letterman Clb; Pres Pep Clb; Quiz Bowl; Band; Chorus; Mrchg Band; Pep Band; School Play; Yrbk; Hnrbl Mntn All League Vlybl; All ST Bsktbl Acad Tm; Pres Ed Awd; Colby CC; Pre-Phrmcy.

SCHETTLER, JAYME; Great Bend Sr HS; Great Bend, KS; (3); 7/239; Church Yth Grp; Cmnty Wkr; French Clb; Pep Clb; Service Clb; Spanish Clb; Varsity Clb; Var L Bsktbl; Capt L Tennis; High Hon Roll.

SCHEUERMAN, ANDREA L; Maize HS; Wichita, KS; (3); Church Yth Grp; Drama Clb; FCA; Q&S; Teachers Aide; Thesps; School Play; Stage Crew; Nwsp; Hon Roll; KS ST Univ; Spcl Ed; Phy Thrpy.

SCHIEBER, BRANDI A; Derby HS; Derby, KS; (1); Church Yth Grp; Rep Frsh Cls; Rep Stu Cncl; Bsktbl; High Hon Roll; Optom.

SCHIELD, CHRISSY; St Francis Cmnty HS; Saint Francis, KS; (3); Art Clb; Church Yth Grp; FHA; German Clb; Q&S; Teachers Aide; Chorus; School Musical; School Play; Co-Ed Yrbk; TV Brdcstng.

SCHIELDS, CRYSTAL; Goodland HS; Goodland, KS; (3); 1/85; Church Yth Grp; FHA; GAA; HOBY; Pres Service Clb; School Musical; Swing Chorus; Var Bsktbl; Var Crs Cntry; Var Trk; Mission Trips Africa & MX; Oral Roberts U.

SCHIERER, ERIC; Kapaun-Mt Carmel HS; Wichita, KS; (3); Quiz Bowl; High Hon Roll; Hon Roll; Pol Discussion Group.

SCHIERLING, DEVIN; Inman Jr Sr HS; Inman, KS; (2); 12/49; Church Yth Grp; Pres 4-H; Treas Natl FFA Org; NFL; Pep Clb; Spanish Clb; Band; Mrchg Band; Pep Band; Rep Frsh Cls.

SCHIERMAN, ALEXIS; Paola HS; Paola, KS; (3); 1/175; Drama Clb; FCA; Math Tm; Pep Clb; Quiz Bowl; Scholastic Bowl; Science Clb; SADD; Band; Drm Mjr(t).

SCHIFFELBEIN, MATT; Seaman Sr HS; Topeka, KS; (3); Church Yth Grp; Math Clb; SADD; Band; Jazz Band; Mrchg Band; L Ftbl; L Wrstlng; High Hon Roll; NHS; Topeka Yth Wnd Ensm; Topeka Yth Jazz Wrkshp.

SCHILLING, NICOLE; Garden City Sr HS; Garden City, KS; (3); 1/400; Church Yth Grp; Drama Clb; FHA; Quiz Bowl; Science Clb; Service Clb; Band; School Play; Ed Lit Mag; High Hon Roll; Envrnmtl Engrng.

SCHILLING, NICOLE M; Shawnee Heights Sr HS; Topeka, KS; (3); Pres FBLA; Nwsp; Ed Yrbk; Rep Stu Cncl; Tennis; High Hon Roll; Hon Roll; 2 Acad Lttrs; Tnns Lttr; U Of KS; Spch Path.

SCHILTZ, CORY M; Grinnell HS; Menlo, KS; (2); Band; Golf; Wt Lftg.

SCHINDLER, JENNIFER L; Madison Jr Sr HS; Madison, KS; (4); 8/27; Drama Clb; FBLA; Band; Chorus; Drm Mjr(t); Jazz Band; Mrchg Band; School Play; Treas Jr Cls; Pres Sr Cls; Emporia ST U; Dramatic Arts.

SCHINDLER, JOHN M; Colby Sr HS; Colby, KS; (3); Spanish Clb; Bsktbl; Ftbl; Hon Roll; Bsbl; Bus Mgmt; Acctng.

SCHINSTOCK, RYAN; Trinity Catholic HS; Hutchinson, KS; (4); 3/27; Am Leg Boys St; Teachers Aide; Sec Jr Cls; Var L Ftbl; Var L Tennis; Var L Trk; Cit Awd; High Hon Roll; NHS; Sal; Hutchinson CC; Comp Graphics.

SCHIPPERS, REBECCA; Thomas More Prep-Marion HS; Hays, KS; (2); Church Yth Grp; HOBY; Scholastic Bowl; Band; School Musical; Stage Crew; Rptr Nwsp; Var Chrldng; High Hon Roll; Schl Ambsdr.

SCHIPPERT, DAVID; Great Bend Sr HS; Great Bend, KS; (4); 2/300; Am Leg Boys St; VP Sr Cls; JV Bsktbl; JV L Ftbl; Gov Hon Prg Awd; High Hon Roll; NHS; Sal; Pres Acad Fit Awd; Pep Clb; Natl Hnr Soc Pres Local Chapter; Ger Clb Treas; Natl DECA Cont; U Of KS.

SCHIRK, LYNN; St Mary's Colgan HS; Pittsburg, KS; (3); 10/52; Debate Tm; JA; NFL; Pep Clb; Science Clb; Thesps; Drill Tm; School Musical; School Play; Chrldng; Theatrics; Fr.

SCHIRMER, SARAH; Jackson Heights HS; Circleville, KS; (1); FHA; Band; Chorus; Church Choir; Pep Band; School Musical; Trk; Vllybl; Hon Roll; Clarinet Choir; KS U Lawrence; Tchng.

SCHLAMADINGER, LINDA N; Wichita East HS; Shawnee, KS; (4); Intnl Clb; Johnson Cty CC; Intl Bnkng.

SCHLEHUBER, SHARON M; Hillsboro HS; Hillsboro, KS; (3); Chorus; School Musical; School Play; Phtg Yrbk; Tennis; Trk; High Hon Roll; Hon Roll; Acctng; Info Systems.

SCHLEPP, JESSICA; Salina HS South; Salina, KS; (4); Am Leg Aux Girls St; Church Yth Grp; Cmnty Wkr; Mrchg Band; Pep Band; Var L Crs Cntry; Var L Mgr(s); Var L Trk; NHS; Pres Acad Fit Awd; Bible Quizzing; Chrch Vllybl Tm; Mid-America Nazarene Coll.

SCHLESENER, LINDY; Hope HS; Hope, KS; (1); Sec Church Yth Grp; FBLA; Pep Clb; Quiz Bowl; SADD; Band; Chorus; JV Bsktbl; JV Vllybl; High Hon Roll; KS ST U; Bus Admin.

SCHLEY, JENNIFER; Wabaunsee HS; Paxico, KS; (3); Church Yth Grp; FBLA; FHA; Chorus; School Musical; Powder Puff Ftbl; Computer Clb; Vllybl; High Hon Roll; NHS; Emporia ST; Elem Tchr.

SCHLICK, JESSICA; Colby Sr HS; Colby, KS; (3); 1/100; Church Yth Grp; Drama Clb; HOBY; Scholastic Bowl; Pres Service Clb; Chorus; School Musical; High Hon Roll; NHS; KS All-St Chr Altnt 94-95; Outstndng Chem Stu 95; 96 St Sci Olymp Tm; Elem Ed.

SCHLINK, BRYAN S; Highland Park HS; Topeka, KS; (1); Church Yth Grp; ROTC; L Golf; Cit Awd; Hon Roll; Arch/Bldg Engr.

SCHLODDER, PAMELA D; Holton HS; Holton, KS; (1); Natl FFA Org; VP Frsh Cls; Bsktbl; JV Var Sftbl; Vllybl; High Hon Roll.

SCHLOEMER, BRANDON; Ulysses HS; Ulysses, KS; (3); FBLA; SADD; Pres Frsh Cls; Ofcr Stu Cncl; Ofcr Bsbl; Bsktbl; Ftbl; High Hon Roll; NHS; Frgn Lang Clb; ACT; KS Music Edctrs Assn Hnr Band.

SCHLYER, AMANDA S; Hays HS; Ellis, KS; (1); Hosp Aide; NFL; Hon Roll.

SCHMANKE, KEITH S; Wabaunsee HS; Alma, KS; (4); 15/35; Church Yth Grp; Letterman Clb; Stage Crew; Bsktbl; Ftbl; Trk; Hon Roll; Lifeguard; KS ST Univ; Arch Engr.

SCHMELZLE, WILLIAM; Valley Falls HS; Valley Falls, KS; (4); 6/32; Cmnty Wkr; Quiz Bowl; School Play; Swing Chorus; Ed Yrbk; Sec Jr Cls; High Hon Roll; NHS; Drama Clb; FBLA; Horatio Alger & All-Amer Schlr; KS Assn For Yth; Bethany Coll; Elem Ed.

SCHMERSEY, KELLY L; Shawnee Heights Sr HS; Berryton, KS; (2); Church Yth Grp; Debate Tm; SADD; Band; Chorus; Church Choir; Mrchg Band; Pep Band; Tennis; Hon Roll.

SCHMIDR, DEREK A; Garden City Sr HS; Garden City, KS; (2); JV Var Ftbl; Wt Lftg; Bus.

SCHMIDT, ALISON; Thomas More Prep-Marian HS; Hays, KS; (3); 16/69; Debate Tm; 4-H; Math Tm; Flag Corp; Rptr Nwsp; Crs Cntry; Trk; 4-H Awd; High Hon Roll; Forensic Tech.

SCHMIDT, AMBER R; Ingalls Jr Sr HS; Ingalls, KS; (2); 4-H; Math Tm; Pep Clb; Speech Tm; SADD; Varsity Clb; Chorus; School Play; VP Soph Cls; Bsktbl; Dodge City CC.

SCHMIDT, ANGELA M; Newton Sr HS; Newton, KS; (1); Church Yth Grp; Quiz Bowl; Scholastic Bowl; SADD; Teachers Aide; High Hon Roll; Hon Roll; Eclps Clb; Knwldg Mstr; U Of KS; Law/Med.

SCHMIDT, ANN; Thomas More Prep-Marion HS; Hays, KS; (1); 4-H; Var Crs Cntry; Var Trk; 4-H Awd; Hon Roll; Ft Hays Coll.

SCHMIDT, BRAD F; Hays HS; Hays, KS; (3); Var Ftbl; Wt Lftg; Hon Roll; Ft Hays ST.

SCHMIDT, BRANDON P; Mc Pherson HS; Mc Pherson, KS; (3); Church Yth Grp; Letterman Clb; Office Aide; Spanish Clb; Varsity Clb; Band; Jazz Band; Mrchg Band; Pep Band; JV Bsbl; NE; Engrng.

SCHMIDT, CARISSA S; Blue Valley HS; Overland Park, KS; (2); Cmnty Wkr; Var L Bsktbl; Var L Vllybl; Cit Awd; Hon Roll; PT/SPORTS Trng.

SCHMIDT, CARRIE M; Newton Sr HS; Newton, KS; (4); Pres Church Yth Grp; Capt Debate Tm; Drama Clb; Capt NFL; Office Aide; Speech Tm; Teachers Aide; Mgr(s); Var Socr; JV Tennis; Site Cncl Rep; St Debate Ranked 96; Church Yth Group Pres; Washburn Univ; Speech Commnctns.

SCHMIDT, DEREK A; Garden City Sr HS; Garden City, KS; (2); JV Ftbl; KS ST U; Comm/Bus.

SCHMIDT, GENTRY A; Greensburg HS; Greensburg, KS; (3); 1/27; Church Yth Grp; Chorus; Ofcr Soph Cls; Ofcr Jr Cls; Ofcr Stu Cncl; Var L Bsktbl; Var L Trk; Var L Vllybl; High Hon Roll; Hon Roll; Bus.

SCHMIDT, HEIDI; Ellis HS; Ellis, KS; (2); Church Yth Grp; FHA; HOBY; JV Var Bsktbl; Var Chrldng; JV Var Vllybl; Hon Roll.

SCHMIDT, JACKIE; Victoria HS; Victoria, KS; (3); Church Yth Grp; FHA; Letterman Clb; Pep Clb; SADD; Band; Drill Tm; Mrchg Band; Pep Band; School Play; Rcrtnl Sftbl; Fort Hays ST; Psych.

SCHMIDT, JANELL; Thomas More Prep-Marion HS; Hays, KS; (2); 4-H; Flag Corp; Nwsp; Crs Cntry; Trk; 4-H Awd; Hon Roll.

SCHMIDT, JASON; Augusta Sr HS; Augusta, KS; (4); Chess Clb; Church Yth Grp; German Clb; Office Aide; SADD; Band; Mrchg Band; Pep Band; High Hon Roll; NHS; KS Univ; Orthopaedic Surgeon.

SCHMIDT, JESSICA D; Moundridge HS; Moundridge, KS; (2); FCA; FHA; Pep Clb; Chorus; School Musical; Bsktbl; Vllybl; Hon Roll; KAY; Art Awds.

SCHMIDT, JODY; Peabody-Burns Jr Sr HS; Peabody, KS; (3); Church Yth Grp; 4-H; Band; Chorus; School Musical; High Hon Roll; NHS; Teachers Aide; Mrchg Band; Dance Stu; Frnsc.

SCHMIDT, JOSHEUA J; Kinsley HS; Kinsley, KS; (3); Rep Stu Cncl; L Var Ftbl; L Var Wrstlng; Hon Roll; Pratt Comm Coll; Lineman.

SCHMIDT, JUSTA L; Shawnee Heights Sr HS; Berryton, KS; (1); Church Yth Grp; Hosp Aide; Intnl Clb; Model UN; Pep Clb; Drill Tm; JV Chrldng; High Hon Roll; Photojrnlst/Jrnlst.

SCHMIDT, KACY MYREE; Manhattan HS; Manhattan, KS; (4); Church Yth Grp; Cmnty Wkr; FCA; Spanish Clb; SADD; Bsktbl; JV Vllybl; Wt Lftg; Hon Roll; NHS; Washburn; Chiropractic Practice.

SCHMIDT, KENDRA L; Haven HS; Haven, KS; (2); 1/65; Debate Tm; NFL; Scholastic Bowl; Band; Pres Soph Cls; Pres Jr Cls; Rep Stu Cncl; Sftbl; Vllybl; High Hon Roll; KAYS; NFL; Lttr Sftbl/Band/Acads; Arspc Med/Mtrlgy.

SCHMIDT, KEVIN C; Shawnee Mission N HS; Shawnee, KS; (2); Church Yth Grp; Pep Clb; Band; Stage Crew; Var L Socr; Var L Trk; High Hon Roll; Hon Roll; Acad Lttr.

SCHMIDT, KRISTY; Fairfield HS; Arlington, KS; (1); 1/45; Church Yth Grp; 4-H; Quiz Bowl; Speech Tm; SADD; Rptr Yrbk; Pres Frsh Cls; Rep Stu Cncl; High Hon Roll; Cmnty Wkr; Yth Prevention Team; Schl Mascot; KSPA ST Contest 1st Place Cutline Wrtng; U Of KS; Bus Admin; Mrktg.

SCHMIDT, LUKE; Peabody-Burns Jr Sr HS; Peabody, KS; (1); Church Yth Grp; 4-H; Quiz Bowl; Band; School Musical; JV Bsktbl; JV Crs Cntry; JV Trk; High Hon Roll; Mrchg Band; Bsbl.

SCHMIDT, MANDI; Atwood HS; Ludell, KS; (2); 1/25; Chess Clb; Church Yth Grp; Cmnty Wkr; VP 4-H; Rptr Natl FFA Org; Scholastic Bowl; Spanish Clb; Church Choir; Pres Soph Cls; Rptr Stu Cncl; FFA Chptr Newsletter, Rptr & Writer; KS ST U.

SCHMIDT, RYAN D; Olpe Schl; Olpe, KS; (4); 15/28; Boy Scts; Church Yth Grp; Drama Clb; Letterman Clb; Scholastic Bowl; Science Clb; Speech Tm; Band; Chorus; Jazz Band; Cmnty Fstvl Cmmtte; Emporia ST U; Engrng.

SCHMIDT, SAMANTHA M; Lawrence HS; Lawrence, KS; (3); Debate Tm; DECA; Hosp Aide; Spanish Clb; School Play; Rep Stu Cncl; JV Tennis; Stu Advy Bd; 1st At St With A Learn & Earn Project Through DECA; KS Univ; Nrsng.

SCHMIDT, SCOTT; Lacrosse HS; La Crosse, KS; (3); 8/28; Natl FFA Org; SADD; Band; Pres Frsh Cls; Capt Bsktbl; Var Ftbl; Var Trk; Var Wt Lftg; High Hon Roll; NHS; Chiropractic.

SCHMIDT, TRAVIS J; Thomas More Prep-Marion HS; Victoria, KS; (2); Cmnty Wkr; Letterman Clb; Spanish Clb; Teachers Aide; Nwsp; Pres Soph Cls; JV Var Ftbl; JV Wt Lftg; Cit Awd; Hon Roll; K ST; Arch Dsgn.

SCHMIDT, TY M; Ellis HS; Ellis, KS; (4); 8/39; Church Yth Grp; VP Pres Frsh Cls; VP Pres Soph Cls; VP Pres Jr Cls; Ofcr Stu Cncl; Var Crs Cntry; Var L Ftbl; JV Var Golf; JV Var Trk; Var Wrstlng; FFA; Barton Cnty CC.

SCHMIDTBERGER, SHANNON; Shawnee Heights Sr HS; Topeka, KS; (2); Debate Tm; FBLA; Hosp Aide; Pep Clb; SADD; Nwsp; JV Trk; Hon Roll; Pres Acad Fit Awd; U KS; Phys Thrpy.

SCHMIDTDBERGER, NICHOLE L; Victoria HS; Victoria, KS; (2); Church Yth Grp; 4-H; FHA; Math Tm; Sec Soph Cls; Powder Puff Ftbl; Vllybl; 4-H Awd; Hon Roll; NHS; 4-H Reserve Grand Champ; CYO Sec; Jr Cls VP; Ft Hays ST Univ; Law; Legal Sec.

SCHMIEDING, THOMAS B; Turner HS; Kansas City, KS; (2); 4-H; Band; Jazz Band; Mrchg Band; Pep Band; Crs Cntry; Trk; 4-H Awd; High Hon Roll; Hon Roll; TSA; Reflections Photography Awd; General Motors Awd Recycling.

SCHMITT, CHRIS C; Olathe East Sr HS; Overland Park, KS; (4); French Clb; Teachers Aide; Ofcr Frsh Cls; Ofcr Soph Cls; Ofcr Stu Cncl; Socr; Hon Roll; KS ST Univ; Bus Mrktng.

SCHMITT, JARED L; Downs HS; Cawker City, KS; (1); Church Yth Grp; Band; Mrchg Band; Pep Band; Pres Frsh Cls; JV Bsktbl; Var Golf; High Hon Roll; St Golf Meet 10th Pl; KU.

SCHMITT, LISA; Tipton HS; Tipton, KS; (2); Drama Clb; 4-H; Pep Clb; Band; Chorus; VP Soph Cls; JV Bsktbl; Var Trk; JV Vllybl; Hon Roll.

SCHMITT, SHERYL; Topeka HS; Topeka, KS; (4); 8/354; Church Yth Grp; Cmnty Wkr; French Clb; Teachers Aide; Bsktbl; Crs Cntry; Trk; High Hon Roll; NHS; Sal; Teens & Talent Super Rating; Bartlesville Wesleyan; Ministry.

SCHMITZ, AMY M; Marysville HS; Marysville, KS; (2); Drama Clb; Hon Roll; Keyettes; KS St Univ; Bus.

SCHMITZ, JAKE A; Marysville HS; Marysville, KS; (2); Church Yth Grp; Cmnty Wkr; FCA; Band; Var JV Bsktbl; JV Wt Lftg; Hon Roll; Kays Sec; Pharmacy.

SCHMITZ, JASON C; Bailey-Benedict Jr Sr High; Baileyville, KS; (3); 1/13; Am Leg Boys St; Church Yth Grp; Pres FBLA; Scholastic Bowl; Pres Stu Cncl; Var Ftbl; Var Trk; Cit Awd; High Hon Roll; Pres Acad Fit Awd; Pharm.

SCHMITZ, MIKAYLA; St John's HS; Beloit, KS; (1); 3/16; Pep Clb; Quiz Bowl; Red Cross Aide; Speech Tm; Sec Frsh Cls; Trk; High Hon Roll; Hon Roll; Pres Acad Fit Awd.

SCHMITZ, MIKE; Jackson Heights HS; Holton, KS; (2); 1/40; FBLA; Scholastic Bowl; Pres Band; School Musical; VP Soph Cls; JV Bsktbl; Var L Crs Cntry; L Trk; High Hon Roll; Prfct Atten Awd; Hnr Band; 1st Pl Bus Math & Intrdctn To Bus & 2nd Pl Bus Calculations Dist FBLA Conts.

SCHMITZ, RYAN C; Bailey-Benedict Jr Sr High; Baileyville, KS; (2); 1/18; Math Tm; Quiz Bowl; Rptr Yrbk; Rep Stu Cncl; Bsktbl; High Hon Roll; Prfct Atten Awd; KS ST U; Engrng.

SCHMOTZER, TAI A; Burlington HS; Burlington, KS; (3); Church Yth Grp; Drama Clb; FBLA; Model UN; Scholastic Bowl; Thesps; Band; Mrchg Band; School Play; Yth & Bus Treas, Pres Elect; Pre-Med.

SCHNEE, LEE; Washburn Rural HS; Topeka, KS; (4); 2/272; Debate Tm; Hosp Aide; Math Tm; Quiz Bowl; Science Clb; Intrml Bsktbl; NHS; St Schlr; Natl Merit Cmnd Stu; U Of KS; Bio/Med.

SCHNEIDER, AMANDA C; Lincoln Jr Sr HS; Lincoln, KS; (3); Church Yth Grp; Debate Tm; Drama Clb; Letterman Clb; Pep Clb; SADD; Phtg Ed Nwsp; VP Stu Cncl; Bsktbl; Hon Roll; KAY Clb; Ftbl & Bsbl Mgr; Ft Hays ST Univ; Sports Medicine.

SCHNEIDER, AMANDA J; Basehor Linwood HS; Bonner Springs, KS; (3); 13/98; Church Yth Grp; 4-H; Teachers Aide; Band; Church Choir; Pep Band; JV Vllybl; 4-H Awd; High Hon Roll; Hon Roll; Vet Medicine; Criminal Justice.

SCHNEIDER, DANIEL; Blue Valley Northwest HS; Overland Park, KS; (3); Church Yth Grp; SADD; Teachers Aide; Ofcr Bsbl; Bsktbl; Ftbl; Wt Lftg; Hon Roll; Eng.

SCHNEIDER, JEFF D; Trego Comm HS; Wa Keeney, KS; (2); 28/49; FHA; Letterman Clb; Science Clb; SADD; Sec Jr Cls; Bsktbl; Ftbl; Golf; Wt Lftg; Hon Roll; Kays Clb; Jr Prom Svr; Woodwkg; Acctg.

SCHNEIDER, JEFF T; Otis Bison HS; Olmitz, KS; (3); 1/26; Band; Chorus; Jazz Band; School Play; VP Frsh Cls; Treas Sr Cls; Rptr Stu Cncl; Var Bsktbl; Var Ftbl; NHS; KAY Clb Pres; KAY Area V Pres.

SCHNEIDER, JULIE M; Andale HS; Goddard, KS; (2); Letterman Clb; Spanish Clb; SADD; Varsity Clb; Var Crs Cntry; Var Trk; High Hon Roll; Hon Roll; Ft Hays Univ; Graphic Dsgn.

SCHNEIDER, KINSEY S; Greeley Co Schl; Tribune, KS; (3); Drama Clb; Letterman Clb; Pep Clb; Scholastic Bowl; Band; Yrbk; Var L Bsktbl; Var L Crs Cntry; High Hon Roll; Church Yth Grp; 4 Yr Schl; Med.

SCHNEIDER, KRISTI; Ness City HS; Ness City, KS; (3); Art Clb; Cmnty Wkr; Computer Clb; FHA; German Clb; Pep Clb; Chorus; JV Tennis; Hon Roll; Prfct Atten Awd.

SCHNEIDER, MONTE; Trego Comm HS; Wa Keeney, KS; (4); 6/46; Church Yth Grp; Pres Science Clb; Chorus; School Play; Var Bsktbl; Var Ftbl; NHS; Letterman Clb; SADD; School Musical; All A Hnr Roll; Mst Outstndg Male Jr Athl; 1st Team All-League Hnrs Bsktbl & Ftbl; Fort Hays ST U; Pharmcy.

SCHNEIDER, NATHAN M; Holton HS; Holton, KS; (1); Art Clb; Cmnty Wkr; Band; Mrchg Band; Pep Band; Hon Roll; Fed Jr Duck Stamp Dsgn; League Art Show; KS Univ; Sketching; Commrcl Art.

SCHNEIDER, NICHOLE M; Great Bend Sr HS; Great Bend, KS; (4); Church Yth Grp; Cmnty Wkr; FCA; German Clb; Math Tm; Pep Clb; Teachers Aide; Chorus; Variety Show; Chrldng; KS St Univ; Archt.

SCHNEIDER, TAMMY; Goddard HS; Goddard, KS; (3); 1/180; Key Clb; Science Clb; Spanish Clb; Band; Mrchg Band; Yrbk; Bsktbl; Vllybl; High Hon Roll; NHS; All Conf Bsktbl 95-; All ST Hnrbl Mntl Bsktbl 95-; Bus.

SCHNEIDER, TAMRA L; Jefferson Co North HS; Nortonville, KS; (4); Art Clb; Church Yth Grp; Treas FHA; Library Aide; SADD; Rptr Nwsp; Phtg Yrbk; Trk; Hon Roll; NHS; Teen Tchr; Washburn U; Elem Ed.

SCHNELLBACHER, GEORGE J; Topeka West HS; Topeka, KS; (3); Pep Clb; Spanish Clb; JV Bsbl; JV Bsktbl; Capt Ftbl; Mgr Powder Puff Ftbl; JV Trk; Capt Wt Lftg; Hon Roll; Pres Of Woodcrfts Clb; Pres Of Weightlftrs Clb; Nuclr Eng.

SCHNELLBACHER, NICOLE M; Hayden HS; Topeka, KS; (3); Ed Yrbk; JV Chrldng; JV Tennis; High Hon Roll; Hon Roll; Prom Cmte; U Of KS; Arch.

SCHNELLER, GEORGE F; Bishop Carroll Catholic HS; Wichita, KS; (3); 3/200; Church Yth Grp; Cmnty Wkr; FCA; Letterman Clb; Spanish Clb; Varsity Clb; Var Bsbl; Var Bsktbl; Var Ftbl; Intrml Wt Lftg.

SCHNELLER, STEVE J; Bishop Carroll Catholic HS; Wichita, KS; (2); Church Yth Grp; Cmnty Wkr; Letterman Clb; Spanish Clb; Varsity Clb; Var Golf; Intrml Wt Lftg; Hon Roll.

SCHNEPP, JESSICA; Olathe East Sr HS; Olathe, KS; (4); 40/300; Pres Church Yth Grp; German Clb; Pres VP Girl Scts; Intnl Clb; Science Clb; Pep Band; Church Choir; Mrchg Band; Orch; Pep Band; Sci Olympd; KS ST; Biochem.

SCHNEWEIS, LAURA J; Bishop Ward HS; Kansas City, KS; (2); Church Yth Grp; Drama Clb; Pep Clb; Red Cross Aide; SADD; School Musical; School Play; Stage Crew; JV Chrldng; Crs Cntry; Jr Dance & Assembly; Acctng.

SCHNEWEIS, RACHEL L; Lawrence HS; Lawrence, KS; (3); Church Yth Grp; VP FTA; Spanish Clb; Teachers Aide; Stage Crew; Kay Clb; Gov Teen Ldrshp; Tchr.

SCHOEN, CHARLES W; Moundridge HS; Moundridge, KS; (4); Debate Tm; Drama Clb; Speech Tm; Ftbl; Carpentry; Fundraising; Fishing; Running; Biking; Weight Lifting.

SCHOENBERGER, JACQUELINE B; Bishop Miege HS; Shawnee, KS; (2); Pep Clb; Chorus; Church Choir; School Musical; School Play; Stage Crew; Variety Show; Spirit Miege Awd; CMT; JCCC; Med Fld.

SCHOENDALLER, AMY L; Victoria HS; Walker, KS; (3); Dance Clb; FHA; Letterman Clb; Pep Clb; SADD; Varsity Clb; Drill Tm; Var Bsktbl; Powder Puff Ftbl; Var Tennis; Ft Hays St Univ; Int Dsgn.

SCHOENEBECK, CASEY; Maize HS; Wichita, KS; (2); Cmnty Wkr; Debate Tm; German Clb; NFL; Chorus; Variety Show; Wrstlng; Cit Awd; High Hon Roll; KS ST Univ; DVM.

SCHOENECKER, KRISTEN; Sedgwick HS; Sedgwick, KS; (4); 1/28; Am Leg Aux Girls St; Sec Frsh Cls; Pres Soph Cls; Pres Jr Cls; Sec Sr Cls; Rep Stu Cncl; High Hon Roll; NHS; Pres Acad Fit Awd; Val; St & Othr Awds Art Class; St & Othr Cmptns Piano; KS ST U; Arch.

SCHOENHOFER, TRACY M; St Paul HS; Saint Paul, KS; (4); 4/13; Art Clb; Church Yth Grp; Letterman Clb; Varsity Clb; Church Choir; Ofcr Soph Cls; Ofcr Sr Cls; Var Capt Bsbl; Var Capt Bsktbl; Var Capt Ftbl; Acctng.

SCHOENTHALER, AMY L; Ellis HS; Ellis, KS; (4); 14/40; FHA; Pep Clb; SADD; Chorus; School Play; Phtg Yrbk; Sec Sr Cls; Hon Roll; Prfct Atten Awd; Jr Princess; FHSU; Phy Therapy.

SCHOEPFLIN, TRACY; Baldwin HS; Baldwin City, KS; (4); 9/81; Am Leg Aux Girls St; Pres FHA; Math Tm; Pep Clb; Teachers Aide; Chorus; School Play; Nwsp; Yrbk; Rep Jr Cls; Homcmng Qn; Cntrl MO ST U; Acctng.

SCHOLSSESR, DANI; Goodland HS; Goodland, KS; (3); 20/82; Art Clb; 4-H; FHA; GAA; SADD; Bsktbl; Powder Puff Ftbl; Vllybl; Wt Lftg; High Hon Roll; Pittburg ST Univ; Graphic Dsgn.

SCHOLZ, CHRISTOPHER R; Shawnee Mission N HS; Shawnee, KS; (3); German Clb; Pep Clb; Varsity Clb; Ftbl; Trk; NHS; Acctng.

SCHOLZ, CRAIG K; Troy HS; Atchison, KS; (4); Letterman Clb; Teachers Aide; Varsity Clb; Sec Soph Cls; Var Bsktbl; Var Ftbl; Prfct Atten Awd; MO Westrn St Col.

SCHOLZ, ERICA M; Midway Schl; Huron, KS; (3); Var Bsktbl; Var Trk; Var Vllybl; Hon Roll; Highland Jr Coll.

SCHOLZ, RENEE; Troy HS; Atchison, KS; (3); 2/27; Drama Clb; HOBY; School Play; Pres Soph Cls; Pres Jr Cls; VP Stu Cncl; Bsktbl; Chrldng; Var Vllybl; High Hon Roll; Med.

SCHOOLCRAFT, KARIE D; Fredonia HS; Fredonia, KS; (3); Church Yth Grp; Dance Clb; FCA; FHA; Pep Clb; Science Clb; Spanish Clb; Band; Chorus; Drill Tm; All Amer Team Awd NCA; Camp Ldrshp Awd NCA Danz; U Of KS; Bus; Dance.

SCHOOLEY, TYREL; Central Schl Of Burden; Latham, KS; (4); Church Yth Grp; Math Tm; Natl FFA Org; NFL; Teachers Aide; Varsity Clb; School Play; Var Bsbl; Var Ftbl; Var Wrstlng; Cowely Cnty CC; Mth Tchr.

SCHOONOVER, BRADLEY P; Santa Fe Trail Jr HS; Olathe, KS; (1); Debate Tm; Speech Tm; Teachers Aide; Intrml Bsktbl; Intrml Ftbl; JV Swmmng; Intrml Trk; Intrml Wt Lftg; Optmst Intnl Ortrcl Cntst; U Of KS; Atty.

SCHOPPER, JENNIFER A; Emporia HS; Emporia, KS; (3); Church Yth Grp; Debate Tm; Drama Clb; NFL; Thesps; School Play; Sec 4-H; SADD; Teachers Aide; Band; Jr Bd; Elem Ed/Theatre.

SCHRADER, BETH M; Mc Louth Schl; Mc Louth, KS; (2); 7/54; Church Yth Grp; FBLA; FHA; Pep Clb; Spanish Clb; SADD; Varsity Clb; Var Bsktbl; Var Vllybl; Hon Roll.

SCHRADER, THERESA M; Wichita North HS; Wichita, KS; (4); Bus Profs of Am; Church Yth Grp; Red Cross Aide; Chorus; Church Choir; Orch; School Musical; Variety Show; Natl Cmptn Bus Prof Of Amer 2nd Pl; Wichita ST; Bus.

SCHRAG, BRAD; Inman Jr Sr HS; Inman, KS; (2); Church Yth Grp; Math Clb; Pep Clb; Spanish Clb; Acpl Chr; Band; Chorus; Mrchg Band; Pep Band; Bsktbl; Biked Acrss KS 4 Times; Comp Sci.

SCHRAG, PAULA S; Haven HS; Hutchinson, KS; (4); 13/69; Church Yth Grp; Hosp Aide; Band; Mrchg Band; Pep Band; Variety Show; Rep Sr Cls; Rep Stu Cncl; JV Vllybl; High Hon Roll; Bethany Coll; Acctng.

SCHRAG, RACHEL S; Berean Acad; Hesston, KS; (4); 3/30; VP Church Yth Grp; Letterman Clb; Band; Chorus; Church Choir; Pep Band; Co-Ed Nwsp; Score Keeper; Tennis; High Hon Roll; Chrstn Actn Treas; KS Hnrs Stu; Moody Bible Inst; Mus.

SCHRAMM, MARGARET; Shawnee Mission N HS; Shawnee Mission, KS; (3); 30/380; Church Yth Grp; French Clb; Orch; Lit Mag; Rep Frsh Cls; Rep Soph Cls; Rep Jr Cls; Intrml Crs Cntry; JV Tennis; JV Trk; Art.

SCHRANT, KIMBERLY D; Wellington Sr HS; Wellington, KS; (3); Church Yth Grp; SADD; Chorus; Var Sftbl; JV Vllybl; High Hon Roll; Hon Roll; Jr NHS; NHS; KS Newman; Occptnl Thrpy.

SCHRATTER, AMANDA; Schlagle HS; Kansas City, KS; (4); 7/180; Chess Clb; Math Clb; Q&S; Science Clb; Band; Mrchg Band; Pep Band; Ed Pres Yrbk; High Hon Roll; NHS; Phi Beta Kappa; Excllnc Schlrshp Awd; Sci Olympd; Plsh-Am Ctzns Clb/Yth Mtvtnl Svc Pgm Schlrshps; KS City U.

SCHREFFLER, TERESA M; Anderson Cty Jr Sr HS; Garnett, KS; (1); 6/110; Cmnty Wkr; French Clb; Intnl Clb; Math Clb; Pep Clb; Quiz Bowl; Scholastic Bowl; SADD; French Hon Soc; High Hon Roll; Math And Forgn Lang Awds; Schol Bowl Tm; Law.

SCHREIBER, BURT D; St Thomas Aquinas HS; Overland Park, KS; (2); Cmnty Wkr; Var Bsbl; Intrml Bsktbl; Var L Socr; Intrml Wt Lftg; Cit Awd; Hon Roll; Pres Acad Fit Awd; KS ST Select ODP Sccr 5 Yrs; Engr.

SCHREIBER, JULEE; Claflin Jr Sr HS; Beaver, KS; (1); FHA; Pep Clb; Band; Mrchg Band; Pep Band; Ofcr Frsh Cls; Bsktbl; Chrldng; Golf; Vllybl.

SCHREIBER, MATT; Jackson Heights HS; Soldier, KS; (1); 4-H; Natl FFA Org; Pep Clb; Chorus; School Musical; Rep Frsh Cls; Rep Stu Cncl; Bsktbl; Ftbl; Sftbl; Ag Engr.

SCHREINER, TORY A; Olpe Schl; Olpe, KS; (3); 6/30; Church Yth Grp; Drama Clb; FBLA; Office Aide; Spanish Clb; Band; Chorus; Pep Band; School Play; Yrbk; Emporia ST U.

SCHREMMER, JAMES A; Claflin Jr Sr HS; Claflin, KS; (4); 5/27; Pres Letterman Clb; Rep Stu Cncl; Var Capt Bsktbl; Var Capt Ftbl; Var L Gym; Hon Roll; NHS; Church Yth Grp; Cmnty Wkr; Math Tm; Lettermans Club Honor Sr Ath; Acad Letter 4 Yrs; Barton Cnty CC; Ed.

SCHREPEL, JACKIE; Lansing HS; Lansing, KS; (4); 27/143; French Clb; Teachers Aide; Chorus; Swing Chorus; Ofcr Stu Cncl; French Hon Soc; High Hon Roll; Pres Schlr; Acad Ltr; Choir & Stu Cncl Outstndg Schlstc Achvt; Kayettes, Brd; Kansas City CC; Elem Ed.

SCHRICK, CORY; Jefferson Co North HS; Nortonville, KS; (3); 1/42; FBLA; Letterman Clb; Band; Capt Bsktbl; Var Ftbl; Intrml Wt Lftg; Hon Roll; NHS; Prfct Atten Awd; Pres Acad Fit Awd; KS St U; Arch.

SCHRICK, RAYMOND J; Maur Hill Prep Schl; Atchison, KS; (1); Chorus; Pres Frsh Cls; Capt Bsktbl; Var Pom Pon; Var Trk; Hon Roll; JV Forensic.

SCHROCK, HOLLY; Golden Plains HS; Selden, KS; (2); Art Clb; Church Yth Grp; Dance Clb; Spanish Clb; Speech Tm; Chorus; Nwsp; Chrldng; Vllybl.

SCHROCK, TERESA; Fairfield HS; Arlington, KS; (2); Church Yth Grp; SADD; Chorus; Church Choir; Phtg Yrbk; Treas Frsh Cls; Treas Jr Cls; JV Vllybl; Cit Awd; High Hon Roll; KS ST Univ; Landscape Arch.

SCHROEDER, AMY D; Newton Sr HS; Newton, KS; (2); 21/272; Church Yth Grp; French Clb; Key Clb; Chorus; JV Chrldng; Var Socr; Mgr Vllybl; Hon Roll; KS ST U; Psych.

SCHROEDER, BONNIE; Central Christian Schl; Buhler, KS; (1); Church Yth Grp; Teachers Aide; Var Bsktbl; Var Chrldng; Var Trk; JV Vllybl; Hon Roll; Tabor Coll; Phys Ed.

SCHROEDER, CHAD E; Newton Sr HS; Newton, KS; (1); Art Clb; Church Yth Grp; German Clb; JV Socr; High Hon Roll.

SCHROEDER, CHARITY; Inman Jr Sr HS; Inman, KS; (2); 14/44; Church Yth Grp; FHA; NFL; Pep Clb; Spanish Clb; Band; Chorus; Pep Band; Chrldng; High Hon Roll.

SCHROEDER, DANA; Rose Hill HS; Rose Hill, KS; (4); 1/105; Church Yth Grp; Pres SADD; Ed Yrbk; Ofcr Stu Cncl; Var Co-Capt Chrldng; Pom Pon; Cit Awd; High Hon Roll; NHS; St Schlr; UKS; Pre-Med.

SCHROEDER, DARIC L; Washburn Rural HS; Topeka, KS; (2); Church Yth Grp; Band; Church Choir; Jazz Band; Mrchg Band; Pep Band; High Hon Roll; Hon Roll.

SCHROEDER, ERIC M; Great Bend Sr HS; Great Bend, KS; (2); Church Yth Grp; Variety Show; Intrml Bsktbl; Var Ftbl; L Trk; Wt Lftg; Hon Roll; KS ST U; Dentistry.

SCHROEDER, HEATH; Hugoton HS; Hugoton, KS; (3); 3/67; Church Yth Grp; Debate Tm; FCA; 4-H; Quiz Bowl; Spanish Clb; Band; Jazz Band; Mrchg Band; Pep Band; KU; Bio.

SCHROEDER, KURSTAN; Tipton HS; Tipton, KS; (3); Treas Sec 4-H; Math Tm; Quiz Bowl; Speech Tm; Band; Chorus; Church Choir; Mrchg Band; Pep Band; School Play; KSU; Arntcl Engr.

SCHROEDER, LAURA; Colby Sr HS; Colby, KS; (4); Am Leg Aux Girls St; FHA; Library Aide; Office Aide; Teachers Aide; Band; Hon Roll; Psych.

SCHROEDER, MENDY; Liberal HS; Claremore, OK; (4); 28/212; Church Yth Grp; GAA; Q&S; Teachers Aide; Varsity Clb; Band; Mrchg Band; Nwsp; Bsktbl; Mgr(s); Dodge City CC; Scndry Ed.

SCHROEDER, RAYLENE M; Wichita South HS; Wichita, KS; (4); Debate Tm; NFL; Teachers Aide; VICA; Hon Roll; Acad Ltr; Wichita ST U; Phys Thrpy.

SCHUBARTH, MICHELE S; Emporia HS; Emporia, KS; (3); 106/265; Church Yth Grp; 4-H; Chorus; Stage Crew; Cit Awd; Hon Roll; Vol Local Zoo; Trng/Riding Hrses; Equine Studies/Wldlf Mngmnt.

SCHUCKMAN, STACY; Lacrosse HS; La Crosse, KS; (4); 13/25; Drama Clb; Pep Clb; Q&S; Band; Yrbk; Bsktbl; Vllybl; High Hon Roll; Hon Roll; NHS; Homcmng Qn 95-96; Hutchinson CC; Soc Work.

SCHUELE, NICK A; Maur Hill Prep Schl; Atchison, KS; (1); Chorus; JV Bsktbl; JV Ftbl; Hon Roll.

SCHUESSLER, RON E; Hanover Schl; Hanover, KS; (3); 7/17; Treas Church Yth Grp; Debate Tm; 4-H; FBLA; Natl FFA Org; SADD; Teachers Aide; Pres Frsh Cls; Treas Soph Cls; VP Jr Cls; KS St Univ.

SCHUETZ, CHAD M; Holton HS; Holton, KS; (1); Chorus; Mrchg Band; School Musical; Sec Frsh Cls; Bsktbl; JV Ftbl; JV Var Trk; High Hon Roll; Pep Band.

SCHUETZ, HEATHER E; Field Kindley Mem Sr HS; Coffeyville, KS; (3); Church Yth Grp; French Clb; Yrbk; Var Chrldng; High Hon Roll; NHS; Psych.

SCHUETZ, MATTHEW S; Horton HS; Powhattan, KS; (3); Rptr Phtg Yrbk; Var L Bsktbl; Var L Golf; Hon Roll.

SCHULER, JACOB J; Goddard HS; Wichita, KS; (1); Debate Tm; L Ftbl; Wrstlng; Arch.

SCHULTE, CODY L; Spearville Jr Sr HS; Spearville, KS; (3); Art Clb; Drama Clb; Pep Clb; Speech Tm; Band; Chorus; Drm Mjr(t); Mrchg Band; Pep Band; School Play; Mus Ed.

SCHULTES, ADRIENE; Silver Lake Jr Sr HS; Topeka, KS; (3); 3/52; Debate Tm; NFL; Speech Tm; School Musical; Swing Chorus; Var Chrldng; Var Pom Pon; JV Var Vllybl; High Hon Roll; NHS.

SCHULTHEISS, MARSHA D; Mc Pherson HS; Mc Pherson, KS; (3); Church Yth Grp; Teachers Aide; Yrbk; Tennis; Cit Awd; Hon Roll; Photography Hnrbl; Fshn Mdl Dillards 95; Fshn Dsgnr.

SCHULTZ, BETSY; Troy HS; Troy, KS; (1); 4-H; Pep Clb; Band; Pep Band; VP Frsh Cls; Var L Chrldng; Trk; JV Vllybl; Hon Roll; KS ST U; Vet Med.

SCHULTZ, BRIC R; Wichita Collegiate Schl; Wichita, KS; (3); Drama Clb; Letterman Clb; Varsity Clb; School Musical; School Play; Bsktbl; Crs Cntry; Trk; Hon Roll; Ath Of Month 96; Madrigals Comm Svc Awd Violin/Piano; Cmptr Sci.

SCHULTZ, CHERYL A; Pittsburg HS; Pittsburg, KS; (1); Church Yth Grp; Band; Chorus; Mrchg Band; Pep Band; School Musical; School Play; KS U; Math.

SCHULTZ, JODI D; Hope HS; Hope, KS; (2); Church Yth Grp; FBLA; Natl FFA Org; SADD; Pep Band; Bsktbl; Trk; Vllybl; High Hon Roll; NHS.

SCHULTZ, MELISSA D; Great Bend Sr HS; Great Bend, KS; (2); Spanish Clb; Color Guard; Mrchg Band; Pep Band; JV Mgr(s); Var JV Tennis; High Hon Roll; Hon Roll; Prfct Atten Awd; Drama Clb; Kayetes; KS Assn For Yth; Envrnmnt Clb; Univ Of KS; Radiology.

SCHULTZ, NICK J; Blue Valley Northwest HS; Overland Park, KS; (2); Church Yth Grp; FCA; Red Cross Aide; Teachers Aide; Varsity Clb; JV Bsbl; JV Bsktbl; Var Ftbl; Wt Lftg; High Hon Roll; Ftbl Tm ST.

SCHULTZ, TIM; Pretty Prairie HS; Pretty Prairie, KS; (4); 3/21; VP Church Yth Grp; VP Computer Clb; Band; Chorus; Yrbk; Rep Soph Cls; Rep Sr Cls; Capt Bsktbl; Var Ftbl; Var Trk; KS ST U; Comp Engrng.

SCHULTZW, CASSIE; Nickerson HS; Hutchinson, KS; (4); 27/100; Key Clb; Office Aide; Spanish Clb; Teachers Aide; Yrbk; Sec Soph Cls; Sec Jr Cls; Rep Sr Cls; Rep Stu Cncl; Bsktbl; Ashcraft Pharm Schlsp; Coca-Cola Bottling Schlsp; Hutchinson Comm Jr Coll; Nrsng.

SCHULZ, AMBER V; Central Heights Sr HS; Rantoul, KS; (3); Drama Clb; FBLA; Letterman Clb; Pep Clb; VP Band; Mrchg Band; Pep Band; Sec Swing Chorus; Pom Pon; Vllybl; Received I Rating At Regnl Music Festival In Vocal Music; Emporia ST U; Ed.

SCHULZ, ANGELA; St Thomas Aquinas HS; Lenexa, KS; (1); Sec Frsh Cls; Chrldng; Hon Roll; Piano.

SCHULZ, AUBREY L; Thomas More Prep-Marion HS; Hays, KS; (2); 5/85; Debate Tm; High Hon Roll; Hon Roll; Neo Gea Envrnmntl Clb; Rel Outstdng Acad Achvmnt Awd; Natl Pro-Life March Washington DC; Nrsng/Physcns Asst.

SCHULZ, KATIE; Holton HS; Holton, KS; (3); VP 4-H; Natl FFA Org; Band; Var Chrldng; Var Vllybl; 4-H Awd; Hon Roll; NHS; Prfct Atten Awd; Kays Treas; KS ST; Vet Med.

SCHULZ, MICHELLE; Lincoln Jr Sr HS; Hunter, KS; (1); 1/60; Church Yth Grp; Cmnty Wkr; Debate Tm; Drama Clb; FHA; Letterman Clb; Ofcr Frsh Cls; Bsktbl; Trk; Vllybl; AAU Bsktbl Team Mem; Pediatrics.

SCHULZE, AMBER N; Norton Comm HS; Norton, KS; (4); 15/43; Sec Drama Clb; VP 4-H; VP Pep Clb; School Play; VP Sr Cls; 4-H Awd; Hon Roll; Pres Acad Fit Awd; Pres Schlr; Church Yth Grp; Ldrshp Amer Camp Farm Bureau; Parks Jr Coll; Bus/Acctg.

SCHUMACHER JR, DANIEL J; Manhattan HS; Manhattan, KS; (3); 248/426; Boy Scts; Science Clb; Teachers Aide; VICA; Hon Roll; Auto Tech.

SCHUMACHER, JOHANNA I; Topeka HS; Topeka, KS; (3); 22/324; Cmnty Wkr; Model UN; NFL; School Play; Variety Show; Sec Frsh Cls; Sec Soph Cls; Sec Jr Cls; Sec Stu Cncl; High Hon Roll; Russian & Ecology Clbs.

SCHUMACHER, JOSHUA J; Lakin HS; Lakin, KS; (3); Band; Jazz Band; Pep Band; Ofcr Bsbl; Ftbl; Trk; Wt Lftg; Cit Awd; Hon Roll; TX A&M; Music.

SCHUMAKER, SHEILA I; St Marys HS; Saint Marys, KS; (2); Am Leg Aux Girls St; FBLA; FHA; Pep Clb; JV Bsktbl; Var Crs Cntry; JV Sftbl; Hon Roll.

SCHURLE, AMANDA; Manhattan HS; Manhattan, KS; (3); 1/500; Church Yth Grp; Cmnty Wkr; FCA; 4-H; French Clb; Hosp Aide; Band; Variety Show; Ofcr Stu Cncl; Intrml Bsktbl; Med Explrs Pst Pres Elct; SHARE Vol; Mnhttn Mrlns Swim Team; KS U; Bio.

SCHUTTE, EMILY; Olathe North Sr HS; Olathe, KS; (3); 46/400; Am Leg Aux Girls St; Art Clb; Cmnty Wkr; Boy Scts; Ofcr French Clb; Intnl Clb; Thesps; School Play; Stage Crew; Lit Mag; Faraday Soc Chem Grp; SASH Humanities Comm; Intnl Stud.

SCHUTTE, KATHLEEN M; Washington HS; Kansas City, KS; (3); Teachers Aide; Stage Crew; JV Sftbl; JV Vllybl; Hon Roll; NHS; Write Poetry.

SCHUTZ, EMILY A; Blue Valley HS; Overland Park, KS; (2); GAA; Band; Mrchg Band; Pep Band; JV Var Trk; Hon Roll; Pres Acad Fit Awd; UW Madison; Phy Thrpst; Pharm.

SCHWAKOPF, PETER A; Blue Valley Northwest HS; Overland Park, KS; (3); JV Bsbl; JV Capt Socr; KS Schl; Bus.

SCHWART, JENNY; Olathe South Sr HS; Olathe, KS; (4); 29/400; Church Yth Grp; Ofcr Stu Cncl; Var Capt Bsktbl; Var L Sftbl; JV Var Vllybl; High Hon Roll; Hon Roll; NHS; Pres Acad Fit Awd; St Schlr; Mid America Nazarene Coll.

SCHWARTZ, AUDREY A; Dighton HS; Alamota, KS; (1); Drama Clb; 4-H; GAA; Chorus; School Play; Nwsp; Yrbk; Score Keeper; Trk; Vllybl; KS ST Univ; Vet; Sec.

SCHWARTZ, MARY; Blue Valley North HS; Leawood, KS; (3); HOBY; Band; Treas Frsh Cls; Treas Soph Cls; Treas Jr Cls; Rep Stu Cncl; Var L Chrldng; JV Sftbl; JV Tennis; High Hon Roll; Inner Delta; Stu Based Ldrshp; Stu Ambsdrs.

SCHWARTZ, NICOLE; Atchison Sr HS; Atchison, KS; (3); 8/101; Church Yth Grp; Quiz Bowl; Jazz Band; Pep Band; School Play; Var L Trk; NHS; United Meth Israel Stu Tour, UN/DC Tour KS East Conf; KS Regents Hnrs Acad; Baker; Educ.

SCHWARTZ, SARAH; Manhattan HS; Manhattan, KS; (4); Church Yth Grp; FCA; Hosp Aide; Letterman Clb; Ftbl; Trk; Hon Roll; Kiwanis Awd; Radeo Club Sec/Treas; KS ST Univ; Amnl Sci/Indstry.

SCHWARZ, KELLI; Halstead HS; Sedgwick, KS; (2); Treas 4-H; German Clb; Library Aide; Pep Clb; Mgr Vllybl; Mgr Wrstlng; Cit Awd; 4-H Awd; Hon Roll; 4-H Ambsdr; KS ST; Chld Psych/Soc Wrkr.

SCHWARZE, THOMAS A; Marysville HS; Marysville, KS; (4); Art Clb; Boy Scts; Church Yth Grp; FCA; Band; Jazz Band; Mrchg Band; Pep Band; Phtg Nwsp; Co-Ed Yrbk; Jrnlsm.

SCHWARZER, AMANDA B; Atchison Co Cmty HS; Muscotah, KS; (4); FBLA; Letterman Clb; Teachers Aide; Yrbk; Ofcr Stu Cncl; Bsktbl; Trk; Vllybl; High Hon Roll; NHS; ASA Cls A Sftbl; Emporia ST; Sec Ed; Coaching.

SCHWENN, STEVEN J; Emporia HS; Emporia, KS; (3); Am Leg Boys St; Boy Scts; Pep Clb; SADD; Chorus; Rep Jr Cls; JV Ftbl; JV Golf; Var Capt Swmmng; High Hon Roll; Eagle Sct; Vigil Mem Order Of The Arrow; Emporia ST Univ; Law.

SCHWERDTFEGER, KAMI; Skyline Schl; Pratt, KS; (3); 2/19; 4-H; HOBY; Pep Clb; Quiz Bowl; Band; School Musical; School Play; Nwsp; Rptr Frsh Cls; Sec Jr Cls; Mass Cmmnctns.

SCHWERDTFEGER, RYAN D; Wellington Sr HS; Wellington, KS; (2); Boy Scts; Church Yth Grp; Natl FFA Org; Office Aide; SADD; Crs Cntry; Trk; Hon Roll; Archery Club; City Park Vol; Hutchison Jaco; Nvl Nclr Pwr.

SCHWERMAN, AARON; St John's HS; Beloit, KS; (2); Church Yth Grp; Drama Clb; Quiz Bowl; Speech Tm; SADD; School Play; Ofcr Bsbl; Bsktbl; Ftbl; Var Trk.

SCHWERMAN, RACHEL S; Jewell HS; Jewell, KS; (1); FCA; Natl FFA Org; Pep Clb; Band; Flag Corp; Mrchg Band; Pep Band; School Musical; Var Bsktbl; Var Trk.

SCHWERTFEGER, JENNIFER; Mc Pherson HS; Mc Pherson, KS; (1); Church Yth Grp; Girl Scts; SADD; Chorus; JV Co-Capt Chrldng; Hon Roll; Law.

SCHWIETERMAN, LUCIE; Garden City Sr HS; Garden City, KS; (3); Church Yth Grp; Cmnty Wkr; Debate Tm; Science Clb; Speech Tm; Teachers Aide; Band; Var Golf; Hon Roll; Office Aide; Music Fstvls & Recitals Piano; Ntl Yth Ldrshp; Cmnty Svc; KSU; Bus.

SCHWIND, CORY J; Goddard HS; Goddard, KS; (1); Computer Clb; Math Tm; Spanish Clb; Speech Tm; High Hon Roll; Hon Roll; Pres Acad Fit Awd; Engr.

SCHWINDT, AARON L; Washburn Rural HS; Topeka, KS; (3); 37/380; JA; Band; Mrchg Band; Ofcr Bsbl; Ftbl; Trk; Wt Lftg; High Hon Roll; KU.

SCHWINDT, BRANDON J; Ness City HS; Ness City, KS; (3); Ofcr Bsbl; JV Bsktbl; JV Var Ftbl; Trk; Wt Lftg; Wrstlng; FFA.

SCHWINDT, JOEL D; Smoky Valley HS; Lindsborg, KS; (4); 15/75; Pres Treas Church Yth Grp; Drama Clb; FCA; Quiz Bowl; Speech Tm; Thesps; Acpl Chr; Band; Chorus; Church Choir; Wrtrs Clb Pblshng; KHSAA St Forensics Chmpnshp Fnlst; Music.

SCHYLER, JASON S; Russell HS; Russell, KS; (1); Church Yth Grp; Natl FFA Org; SADD; Chorus; Church Choir; JV Ftbl; Hon Roll; U Of NE Lincoln.

SCIANDRA, MICHAEL; Valley Hgts Jr/Sr HS; Waterville, KS; (4); 3/26; Model UN; Natl FFA Org; Rptr Nwsp; Mgr Yrbk; Rep Stu Cncl; High Hon Roll; Sec Treas NHS; KS FFA Ag Nwswrtng 4th; Peer Tutor; KS Univ Hnr Schol; Ft Hays St Univ; Comm.

SCIMECA, NICK S; Northeast HS; Arcadia, KS; (2); 5/46; Scholastic Bowl; Rptr Yrbk; Var L Crs Cntry; Var L Trk; Hon Roll; Rec Motocross; Water Skiing; Auto/Go Kart Racing; Pittsburg ST Univ.

SCOGGINS, PARKER J; Parsons HS; Parsons, KS; (3); #10 in class; Church Yth Grp; Cmnty Wkr; FCA; Key Clb; Spanish Clb; SADD; Teachers Aide; Var Bsbl; Var Wt Lftg; Var Wrstlng; Med.

SCORE, JENNIFER E; Junction City HS; Junction City, KS; (1); Church Yth Grp; Drama Clb; Band; Pep Band; Stage Crew; Vet.

SCOTT, AMANDA; Andover HS; Andover, KS; (1); 41/208; Church Yth Grp; Pep Clb; Chorus; Chrldng; Hon Roll.

SCOTT, CHANTRY C; Stanton Co HS; Johnson, KS; (4); 4/34; Art Clb; Pres Church Yth Grp; FCA; Teachers Aide; Band; Mrchg Band; Pres Jr Cls; Var Bsktbl; Var Ftbl; Var Trk; KS Univ; Bus.

SCOTT, ERIC T; Olathe East Sr HS; Olathe, KS; (3); High Hon Roll; Hon Roll; TSA Reporter; Comp Sci.

SCOTT, JAIME; Bucklin Schl; Bucklin, KS; (4); 6/18; Am Leg Aux Girls St; FCA; Pep Clb; Speech Tm; Band; Chorus; Pep Band; Co-Ed Nwsp; Yrbk; Pres Jr Cls; Serendipity Girls Clb Pres, Sec; Ft Hays ST U; Elem Ed.

SCOTT, JENNIFER; Newton Sr HS; Newton, KS; (4); Am Leg Aux Girls St; Key Clb; Chorus; Sec Frsh Cls; Rep Soph Cls; Sec Jr Cls; Rep Sr Cls; Ofcr Stu Cncl; High Hon Roll; NHS; S Nazarene U; Occptnl Thrpy.

SCOTT, JENNIFER L; Topeka HS; Topeka, KS; (3); 143/32; Boy Scts; Church Yth Grp; Cmnty Wkr; Teachers Aide; Stage Crew; Hon Roll; Zoo Explorer; Explorer Of The Month; Marine Bio.

SCOTT, JENNIFER S; Manhattan HS; Manhattan, KS; (3); Church Yth Grp; 4-H; Quiz Bowl; Scholastic Bowl; SADD; Color Guard; Ed Nwsp; Rep Stu Cncl; High Hon Roll; NHS; Baker Univ; Pre-Medicine.

SCOTT, JENNY M; Blue Valley HS; Bucyrus, KS; (3); Church Yth Grp; JCL; Latin Clb; High Hon Roll; Hon Roll; NHS.

SCOTT, JIMMICA M; Bishop Ward HS; Kansas City, KS; (3); Debate Tm; French Clb; Library Aide; Office Aide; Teachers Aide; Mrchg Band; Vllybl; Hon Roll; Yth Advy Cncl; Accntnt/Bus Mngmt.

SCOTT, JOSH; Blue Vlly HS; Manhattan, KS; (3); Am Leg Boys St; FHA; Natl FFA Org; Pep Clb; Band; Mrchg Band; Bsktbl; Ftbl; Trk; High Hon Roll; KS St Univ; Eng.

SCOTT, KELLY J; Washburn Rural HS; Topeka, KS; (3); Debate Tm; NFL; Teachers Aide; Stat Bsktbl; JV Socr; Wt Lftg; High Hon Roll; Hon Roll; Teens As Teachers; Peer Mediation; Washburn Univ; Elem Ed.

SCOTT, LAUREY M; Canton-Galva HS; Canton, KS; (2); FBLA; SADD; Chorus; Church Choir; Rep Soph Cls; Rep Stu Cncl; High Hon Roll; Hon Roll; Comp.

SCOTT, LEAH D; Wichita North HS; Wichita, KS; (2); Pep Clb; Teachers Aide; Chorus; School Musical; Variety Show; Var Swmmng; Var Vllybl; High Hon Roll; Hon Roll; Speed Skating; USVBA Vllybl; Lawyer.

SCOTT, MELISSA L; Hill City HS; Hill City, KS; (4); 2/35; FHA; Natl FFA Org; NFL; Pep Clb; SADD; School Musical; School Play; High Hon Roll; Pres Schlr; St Schlr; Fort Hays ST U; Spec Educ.

SCOTT, MELODY; Jubilee HS; Newton, KS; (3); Church Yth Grp; Drama Clb; Chorus; Church Choir; School Musical; School Play; Yrbk; Var Bsktbl; Intrml Vllybl; Hon Roll; Northland Bapt Bible Coll.

SCOTT, MIKE; Marysville HS; Oketo, KS; (4); 2/82; Church Yth Grp; Pres 4-H; Letterman Clb; VP Natl FFA Org; Pres Frsh Cls; Var Bsbl; Var L Ftbl; 4-H Awd; High Hon Roll; Kiwanis Awd; Ft Hays ST U; Gen Ag.

SCOTT, MIKE P; Shawnee Mission W Sr HS; Overland Park, KS; (2); 148/426; Hon Roll; Metal Tech; Metallurgy; Welding; MIT; Comp.

SCOTT, NICOLE A; Decatur Cmty Jr Sr HS; Oberlin, KS; (3); Church Yth Grp; Cmnty Wkr; Girl Scts; Office Aide; Science Clb; Spanish Clb; Chorus; School Musical; Hon Roll; NHS; Bus.

SCOTT, SARAH; St Mary's Colgan HS; Pittsburg, KS; (2); 1/40; Debate Tm; HOBY; Math Tm; NFL; Pep Clb; Scholastic Bowl; Speech Tm; Acpl Chr; Chorus; High Hon Roll; KS Regnts Schlr; Corps De Ballet Cecchetti Dance Syllabus; Univ CO; Psych/Phil/Law.

SCOTT, SARAH R; Blue Valley HS; Stilwell, KS; (3); 1/200; Treas Sr Cls; Var L Bsktbl; Var L Socr; Var L Tennis; JV Vllybl; High Hon Roll; Hon Roll; NHS; Hnrb Mntn All EKL Bskbl 96; Jr Class Swthrt Prncss 96; Harvard Bk Awd; Med.

SCOTT, SHELLEY I; Maize HS; Maize, KS; (3); 37/300; Science Clb; Spanish Clb; SADD; Varsity Clb; Chorus; Variety Show; Hon Roll; U Of KS; Elem Ed.

SCOTT, SHILOH; Ne Kansas Area Voc-Tech School; Atchison, KS; (4); 44/115; Hist Bus Profs of Am; Quiz Bowl; Capt Color Guard; Capt Flag Corp; School Play; Ofcr Stu Cncl; L JV Chrldng; Hon Roll; Office Aide; Teachers Aide; Sec Kayettes; Phys/Mentally Chllngd Camp Cnslr; 2nd Pl Chptr Yrbk; 3rd Pl Job/Appl Intvw Bus Prof Amer; NEKA Vo-Tech; Data Prcsng.

SCOTT, TROY; Eureka Jr Sr HS; Piedmont, KS; (3); Am Leg Boys St; 4-H; Natl FFA Org; SADD; Teachers Aide; Rptr Lit Mag; Intrml Var Bsktbl; L Var Ftbl; Var Wt Lftg; JV L Wrstlng; FFA Awds; Spcl Olympics & Handicapped Vol; Outdoor Act; Carpenter; Wildlife.

SCOVILLE, JAMI J; Salina HS South; Salina, KS; (3); Teachers Aide; Band; Mrchg Band; Pep Band; School Musical; Bsktbl; Crs Cntry; Trk; Cit Awd; High Hon Roll; DARE Rep; Teen Too Ambucs; Crs Cntry/Trck Ltr; Ft Hays ST.

SCRIBNER, ELIZABETH; Highland Park HS; Topeka, KS; (3); Debate Tm; Drama Clb; English Clb; Intnl Clb; Library Aide; Model UN; NFL; Office Aide; Pep Clb; SADD; Teens Hope; Gardne City CC; Phtojrnlsm.

SCRIVENER, CHRIS Z; Ft Scott HS; Fort Scott, KS; (3); 85/138; Church Yth Grp; Science Clb; Spanish Clb; JV Bsbl; Crs Cntry; JV Trk; Hon Roll; Natrl Hlprs; UTI.

SCROGGINS, MARLISHA Y; Washington HS; Kansas City, KS; (3); GAA; Office Aide; Varsity Clb; Band; Var Bsktbl; Var Trk; Vllybl; Hon Roll; Jr NHS; NHS; PEER; Acad Ltr; Vet Med.

SCROGGS III, WILLIAM A; Derby HS; Derby, KS; (2); Scholastic Bowl; Hon Roll; NHS; Wichita Jaycees; Derby Optimist B-B Gun Shooting Team 14th Pl Nationals; Eng.

SCULLY, JEFFREY A; Garden City Sr HS; Garden City, KS; (1); Boy Scts; Mgr(s); Tennis; Prfct Atten Awd; Span Pealzs Sct Ranch Staff; Comp Prgmr.

SEABAUGH, SARA N; Blue Valley North HS; Leawood, KS; (2); Church Yth Grp; Cmnty Wkr; FCA; Hosp Aide; Model UN; Pep Clb; Science Clb; Orch; Yrbk; JV Capt Bsktbl; Hlth Care.

SEACAT, MICHELLE; Dodge City HS; Dodge City, KS; (1); Church Yth Grp; Treas 4-H; Band; Mrchg Band; Pep Band; Bsktbl; Hon Roll; Fine Arts Stu Of Month 95; KS ST; Engl.

SEALS, TYRNELL A; Wichita South HS; Wichita, KS; (4); Teachers Aide; Wichita ST Univ; Art.

SEARCY, JESSICA; Olathe South Sr HS; Olathe, KS; (4); Cmnty Wkr; Drama Clb; German Clb; Letterman Clb; Spanish Clb; Chorus; Crs Cntry; Intrml L Trk; High Hon Roll; Hon Roll; Johnson Cnty CC; FBI Agnt.

SEARLE, SHELLY D; Lyons HS; Lyons, KS; (2); Art Clb; Dance Clb; FCA; Pep Clb; Spanish Clb; Drill Tm; Sec Frsh Cls; Var Chrldng; Var Pom Pon; JV Tennis; KU; Hygnst.

SEARLE, TYLER O; Great Bend Sr HS; Great Bend, KS; (4); Church Yth Grp; Cmnty Wkr; FCA; Pep Clb; Acpl Chr; Swing Chorus; Rep Stu Cncl; Var L Bsbl; Cit Awd; Hon Roll; Tabor Coll; Bio; Ed.

SEARS, C J; Mc Pherson HS; Mc Pherson, KS; (4); 12/194; Debate Tm; Math Tm; NFL; Science Clb; Var Bsktbl; Var Tennis; NHS; German Clb; Varsity Clb; Band; Teens As Tchrs; Homecoming King; Mid-Amer Nazerene Coll; Acctng.

SEARS, MEGAN R; Erie HS; Erie, KS; (2); Church Yth Grp; FCA; 4-H; HOBY; Natl FFA Org; Church Choir; VP Frsh Cls; VP Soph Cls; Sec Jr Cls; Rep Stu Cncl.

SEARS, SARAH; Olathe South Sr HS; Olathe, KS; (4); FHA; Math Clb; Band; Mrchg Band; Orch; School Musical; Cit Awd; NHS; Pres Acad Fit Awd; St Schlr.

SEASTROM, CRYSTAL L; Burlingame HS; Burlingame, KS; (3); FHA; Girl Scts; Office Aide; Spanish Clb; Band; Mrchg Band; Pep Band; School Play; Yrbk; Stat Bsktbl; Slvr Awd Grl Scts; KU.

SEASTROM, DAVID W; Burlingame HS; Burlingame, KS; (3); 11/32; Am Leg Boys St; Church Yth Grp; CAP; Var FBLA; Letterman Clb; Science Clb; Spanish Clb; Band; Chorus; Drm Mjr(t); Natl Math Awd 95; KS Univ; Sprts Med/PT.

SEAVER, KRISTOPHER M; Washington HS; Kansas City, KS; (3); Church Yth Grp; Cmnty Wkr; Office Aide; Hon Roll; Sr High Senate Chrch; RLDS Wrld Yth Conf Corp.

SEAWOOD, OCTAVIA; Wyandotte HS; Kansas City, KS; (4); 12/198; Cmnty Wkr; 4-H; Office Aide; Q&S; Drill Tm; Rptr Yrbk; Ofcr Jr Cls; Ofcr Sr Cls; High Hon Roll; Hon Roll; Washburn U; Chem.

SEBA, AMBER; Larned HS; Larned, KS; (2); 1/102; Church Yth Grp; Band; Chorus; Church Choir; Mrchg Band; JV Vllybl; High Hon Roll; Les Chanttes.

SEBELIUS, EDWARD K; Topeka HS; Topeka, KS; (1); Debate Tm; Drama Clb; Model UN; NFL; Thesps; Bsktbl; Ftbl; L Tennis; High Hon Roll; KS Kids Vote.

SEBES, KAREN; Hanston Jr Sr HS; Hanston, KS; (4); 1/13; Church Yth Grp; Pres 4-H; VP Natl FFA Org; Pres Stu Cncl; Var L Bsktbl; Intrml Sftbl; Var L Trk; Var L Vllybl; St Schlr; Val; Acctng.

SEDIVY, HEIDI; Linn Schl; Barnes, KS; (2); 1/23; 4-H; FBLA; Letterman Clb; Thesps; School Play; JV Var Bsktbl; Var Chrldng; Var Trk; High Hon Roll; NHS; Bus.

SEDLAK, SARAH; Jefferson Co North HS; Winchester, KS; (3); 2/36; 4-H; FBLA; SADD; Band; VP Jr Cls; High Hon Roll; NHS; Pres Acad Fit Awd; Church Yth Grp; VP FHA; Btn Twrlr; Cty 4-H Grnd Champ In Fshn Rvw & Cnstrctn; Washburn; Psych.

SEDLOCK, KIRSTEN; Leavenworth HS; Leavenworth, KS; (2); Church Yth Grp; JV Var Crs Cntry; JV Var Trk; Hon Roll; KS ST Univ.

SEEBECK, MARIA; Lansing HS; Leavenworth, KS; (2); Acpl Chr; Band; Chorus; Church Choir; Mrchg Band; Pep Band; Lit Mag; VP Soph Cls; Trk; Hon Roll; KS Assoc For Yth Grls Soph Rep; Schl Stu Of Mnth Prog; Engl.

SEEFELDT, GILLIAN; Pretty Prairie HS; Pretty Prairie, KS; (4); Am Leg Aux Girls St; Church Yth Grp; Drama Clb; NFL; Office Aide; Quiz Bowl; Speech Tm; Teachers Aide; Band; Chorus; Vol Firefghtr; Hutchinson CC; Fire Sci.

SEEGER, KARA N; Ottawa HS; Ottawa, KS; (3); 1/146; Key Clb; Band; Mrchg Band; Pep Band; High Hon Roll; NHS; Mssns.

SEEGER, KATIE N; Topeka HS; Topeka, KS; (2); Cmnty Wkr; French Clb; NFL; JV Vllybl; Hon Roll; Mntn Bike Rdng.

SEELY, JAMES A; Junction City HS; Junction City, KS; (1); Scholastic Bowl; Band; Mrchg Band; Pep Band; Crs Cntry; High Hon Roll; Jr NHS; Pres Acad Fit Awd; Comm Band; Eng.

SEEM, STEPHANIE; Blue Valley North HS; Shawnee Mission, KS; (4); Cmnty Wkr; Thesps; Color Guard; School Play; Stage Crew; Swing Chorus; Crs Cntry; Hon Roll; Kiwanis Awd; NHS; Westminster.

SEEMAN, JAMIE E; Sumner Acad Of Arts & Science; Kansas City, KS; (3); Art Clb; Cmnty Wkr; Latin Clb; Spanish Clb; Sec Thesps; Chorus; School Play; Stage Crew; High Hon Roll; NHS; Dsgn/Sw Cstums/Fshns Wm; Dir Ply Sr Yr; Fshn Dsgn.

SEEMAN, TIFFANY; Bishop Ward HS; Kansas City, KS; (4); 3/92; Drama Clb; Pep Clb; Capt Drill Tm; School Play; Co-Ed Nwsp; Rep Soph Cls; Pres Sec Stu Cncl; Var JV Sftbl; NHS; St Schlr; KS Acad Decathlon Team; Natl Stu Cncl Delg Tulsa OK Summer 95; Universal Dance Asst Dance Star; Law.

SEEMATTER, JUSTINE; Frankft HS; Frankfort, KS; (4); Am Leg Aux Girls St; Teachers Aide; Band; Flag Corp; Yrbk; VP Soph Cls; Var L Crs Cntry; Var L Trk; Vllybl; Hon Roll; All Amer Schlr 2xs; Manhattan Area Tech Ctr; Bus.

SEGENHAGEN, RACHEL; Holton HS; Holton, KS; (4); 4/65; Natl FFA Org; Teachers Aide; High Hon Roll; Hon Roll.

SEGER, LAURA M; Blue Valley North HS; Overland Park, KS; (1); Girl Scts; Math Tm; Band; School Musical; Bsktbl; Trk; Vllybl; High Hon Roll; KS Cty Yth Smphny.

SEGLIE, SARAH; St Mary's Colgan HS; Pittsburg, KS; (3); Treas NFL; Pep Clb; Yrbk; Treas Frsh Cls; Treas Soph Cls; Pom Pon; Trk; Vllybl; High Hon Roll.

SEGLIE, SCOTT; Leavenworth HS; Leavenworth, KS; (4); Am Leg Boys St; Boy Scts; Church Yth Grp; SADD; Ofcr Jr Cls; Ofcr Sr Cls; Capt Socr; High Hon Roll; NHS; St Schlr; BSA Eagle Sct; Gdfllws; Prom & Hmcmnt Cts; KS ST U; Info Systms Mgmt.

SEGRIST, SARAH; Shawnee Heights HS; Berryton, KS; (3); FBLA; Intnl Clb; Pep Clb; Chorus; Var Co-Capt Chrldng; Hon Roll; Care Co Fcltr.

SEHNERT, SHANE L; St John's Military Schl; Plano, TX; (2); ROTC; Acpl Chr; Band; Chorus; Church Choir; School Musical; Hon Roll; Prfct Atten Awd; Psych.

SEHORN, ERIN; Olathe East Sr HS; Olathe, KS; (4); 29/304; Dance Clb; French Clb; FHA; Pep Clb; Teachers Aide; Drill Tm; Lit Mag; High Hon Roll; Hon Roll; Pres Acad Fit Awd; Histy, Engl, Art Excllnc; Dstngshd Schlstc Achvt; Acad Schlrshp Achvt; All Dist Schlr; KU; Bus.

SEIB, KRISTIN J; Ness City HS; Ness City, KS; (1); Church Yth Grp; Sec FHA; Pep Clb; Band; Mrchg Band; Pep Band; JV Bsktbl; JV Golf; Var Sftbl; JV Vllybl; Dist V Hnr Bnd Sax 3 Yrs; Dist ST Natl FHA Star Evt; Sum Lfe Grd; Bus.

SEIB, NICK L; Ness City HS; Ness City, KS; (3); Boy Scts; Pep Clb; Ed Yrbk; Var L Bsktbl; Var L Tennis; Var L Trk; Hon Roll; Fort Hays ST Univ.

SEIBEL, DEDRA B; Mc Pherson HS; Mc Pherson, KS; (4); 33/180; Am Leg Aux Girls St; Church Yth Grp; Var Debate Tm; Pres French Clb; HOBY; Red Cross Aide; Science Clb; Pres VP Service Clb; Var Speech Tm; SADD; VFW Voice Of Democracy 2nd In St; Miss Ldrshp; US Rep To Soroptimist Intnl Yth Forum; U Of KS; Environmental Stud.

SEICHEPINE, JOSH; Olathe East Sr HS; Overland Park, KS; (3); Art Clb; Church Yth Grp; Teachers Aide; Band; Hon Roll; Bsktbl Lg Non Schl; Chrch Sprt Act; Wrtng; Schlstc Art Awd Art Stdnt Yr; Graceland Coll; Arts.

SEILER, AMANDA J; Fredonia HS; Fredonia, KS; (4); 9/72; FCA; FHA; Pep Clb; Science Clb; SADD; Band; Chorus; Capt Drill Tm; Mrchg Band; Pep Band; KS Assn For Yth VP, Stu Cncl Rep; Independence CC; Csmtlgy.

SEILER, STEPHANIE A; Wichita West HS; Wichita, KS; (3); 54/245; Girl Scts; Spanish Clb; Teachers Aide; Band; Church Choir; Drm Mjr(t); Mrchg Band; Pep Band; Prfct Atten Awd; Wichita St Univ; Phys Thpy.

SEIPP, KELLY L; Olathe East Sr HS; Overland Park, KS; (2); Spanish Clb; Rptr Yrbk; Hon Roll; Elem Ed.

SEITTER, ANITA C; Liberal HS; Liberal, KS; (2); FCA; FTA; Teachers Aide; Chorus; Variety Show; Vllybl; Hon Roll; Lubbock Chrstn Univ.

SEITZ, MEREDITH; Manhatton HS; Manhattan, KS; (1); Church Yth Grp; FBLA; Pep Clb; Chorus; Chrldng; Swmmng; Hon Roll.

SEITZ, ROBIN; St Marys HS; Saint Marys, KS; (4); Am Leg Boys St; Boy Scts; Debate Tm; Pres FBLA; Quiz Bowl; Band; Chorus; School Musical; High Hon Roll; Pres NHS; KS ST U; Engrng Law.

SEITZ, SAMANTHA; Shawnee Mission N HS; Olathe, KS; (3); Art Clb; Drama Clb; Latin Clb; Treas Pep Clb; Thesps; School Musical; School Play; Stage Crew; Ultimate Frisbee; UMKC; Med Field.

SEKAVEC, DANIEL A; Ness City HS; Ness City, KS; (2); Math Tm; Natl FFA Org; Pep Clb; Scholastic Bowl; Thesps; JV Bsktbl; Var L Ftbl; Var L Golf; Wt Lftg; Hon Roll; Kays.

SELK, LOU ANNA; Wellington Sr HS; Wellington, KS; (1); Office Aide; Vllybl; High Hon Roll; Hon Roll; Jr NHS; KAY; K ST; Lwyr.

SELLAND, JASON D; Horton HS; Everest, KS; (3); 5/39; Pres Church Yth Grp; Natl FFA Org; Band; Mrchg Band; Pep Band; Ftbl; Trk; Wrstlng; High Hon Roll; Hon Roll; KS St Lions Band.

SELLENS, JENNIFER A; Ottawa HS; Ottawa, KS; (3); Cmnty Wkr; Girl Scts; Key Clb; Spanish Clb; SADD; Tennis; High Hon Roll; Hon Roll; NHS; Pres Acad Fit Awd; Horseback Rider; KS ST Univ; Vet Medicine.

SELLEY, NIKKI; Seaman Sr HS; Topeka, KS; (4); Church Yth Grp; Dance Clb; Key Clb; SADD; Lbrn Chorus; Church Choir; Co-Capt Drill Tm; School Musical; Var Crs Cntry; Var Trk; KS ST.

SELTZER, MARY KATHRYN; Manhattan HS; Manhattan, KS; (4); FBLA; Pep Clb; Q&S; SADD; Teachers Aide; Ed Yrbk; Pres Jr Cls; Pres Sr Cls; Intrml Bsktbl; Var L Golf; Drctr Cls Play; Chrprsn Prom Cmmtte; Homcmng Honorary; Sub Deb Scl Org; Poltcl Vlntr; KS ST U; Jrnlsm.

SEMMEL, KIM L; Lyons HS; Lyons, KS; (2); Church Yth Grp; NFL; Band; Jazz Band; Mrchg Band; Rep Stu Cncl; Var L Chrldng; Var JV Tennis; High Hon Roll; NHS; OU; Meteorology.

SENKBEIL, NIKKI; Garden City Sr HS; Garden City, KS; (4); Dance Clb; French Clb; FHA; Office Aide; Pep Clb; Chorus; Drill Tm; School Play; Stage Crew; Phtg Yrbk; Modeling; Dance Team; Var Dance Team Capt; Pageant & Won Miss SW Teen; Miss Garden City & SW KS Pagnt; Barton Cty CC; Fshn Merchandsn.

SENN, CATHERINE M; Holton HS; Holton, KS; (1); Church Yth Grp; Band; Mrchg Band; Pep Band; Hon Roll; Natls Bible Qzzng; Kndgtn Tchr.

SERNA, HAYDEE; Wichita North HS; Wichita, KS; (3); 10/243; Cmnty Wkr; Teachers Aide; Hon Roll; Acad Lttr; Wichita St Univ.

SERRANO, MARCO G; St Thomas Aquinas HS; Overland Park, KS; (4); 5/231; Church Yth Grp; VP Math Clb; Quiz Bowl; Spanish Clb; Nwsp; Crs Cntry; Natl Hispanic Schlr; KS Hnrs Schlr; Hstry.

SERVEN, JEFFREY W; Shawnee Mission S Sr HS; Lenexa, KS; (2); Pep Clb; JV Ftbl; Wt Lftg; Var L Wrstlng; Hon Roll; Weight Lift; Golf; KSU; Arch Engr/Law Enfrcmnt.

SESTRIC, RYAN M; Shawnee Mission N HS; Overland Park, KS; (1); ROTC; Teachers Aide; School Play; Stage Crew; Tae Kwondo Instr Black Belt; K ST; Drama.

SETCHELL, SHELLEY R; Cair Paravel - Latin Schl; Topeka, KS; (3); Teachers Aide; Acpl Chr; Chorus; School Musical; School Play; Stage Crew; Nwsp; Yrbk; Rep Soph Cls; Hon Roll.

SETO, CINDY; Junction City HS; Junction City, KS; (4); Key Clb; Quiz Bowl; Band; Mrchg Band; Rep Jr Cls; Rep Sr Cls; Rep Stu Cncl; JV Tennis; Hon Roll; NHS; Amer Field Svc; U Of KS; Phys Therapy.

SETZKORN, RYAN H; Udall HS; Rock, KS; (2); Math Tm; Band; Mrchg Band; Pep Band; School Play; JV Bsktbl; Var Ftbl; Var Trk; High Hon Roll; Hon Roll; KS ST Univ.

SEVERIN, JEFF; Hiawatha HS; Robinson, KS; (3); 1/115; Am Leg Boys St; FCA; Science Clb; Teachers Aide; Chorus; School Musical; Pres Rep Stu Cncl; Bsktbl; Var L Tennis; Hon Roll; U Of KS; Med.

SEVERIN, STACEY A; Derby HS; Derby, KS; (4); 2/342; Church Yth Grp; High Hon Roll; NHS; Ntl Merit SF; Pres Schlr; Sal; Horseback Riding; Envrnmnt Clb; KSU; Vet.

SEVIER, COURTNEY B; Wichita East HS; Wichita, KS; (2); Church Yth Grp; Chorus; Variety Show; Tennis; Jr Assmbly Clb; Piano Lessons.

SEWELL, JACOB A; Beloit Jr Sr HS; Beloit, KS; (4); 9/53; Pres Church Yth Grp; Drama Clb; Capt Quiz Bowl; Spanish Clb; Treas Band; Orch; NHS; Ntl Merit SF; U Chicago.

SEXTON, JENNIFER; Erie HS; Walnut, KS; (2); 10/51; Treas Drama Clb; Spanish Clb; Thesps; School Play; JV Chrldng; KAYS; Arch.

SEYB, KECIA; Stanton Co HS; Johnson, KS; (1); Church Yth Grp; Band; Mrchg Band; Pep Band; Sec Frsh Cls; JV Bsktbl; Var Chrldng; Var Crs Cntry; Trk; JV Vllybl; Southwest KS Bus Cmptn Ust Pl Keybrdng 96; Stanford U; Bus.

SEYB, RHETT C; Stanton Co HS; Johnson, KS; (4); Church Yth Grp; Var L Bsktbl; Var L Crs Cntry; Var L Golf; Hon Roll; NHS; Prfct Atten Awd; ST Chmpnshp Cross Cntry Tm 94-95/Glf Tm 94-95; All ST Glf Mdlst 95-; May Stdnt Of Month; Acctng Awd; Southwestern Coll.

SHADE, TRAVIS; Garden City Sr HS; Garden City, KS; (3); Debate Tm; 4-H; Intrml Stat Bsktbl; 4-H Awd; Hon Roll; Med.

SHAFF, ANN A; Cedar Vale HS; Cedar Vale, KS; (3); Church Yth Grp; FHA; Letterman Clb; Scholastic Bowl; Drm Mjr(t); Pres Sr Cls; Pres Stu Cncl; Cit Awd; NHS; SADD; Miss Cedar Vale Sr; Lions Clb Hnr Stu; BYU; Comp Sci; Buis Admin.

SHAFFER, BRANDON; Horton HS; Horton, KS; (2); 20/80; Boy Scts; Speech Tm; School Play; Ofcr Stu Cncl; Bsktbl; Ftbl; Trk; High Hon Roll; Teachers Aide; Hon Roll; ST Forensics IDA 5th Pl Mdl; ST Trk Tm; Air Force Acad.

SHAFFER, BRANDY L; Louisburg HS; Louisburg, KS; (3); Debate Tm; Speech Tm; Chorus; Drill Tm; JV Sftbl; High Hon Roll; Hon Roll; Prfct Atten Awd; Lcl Recycling Ctr Vol; U Of KS; Law.

SHAFFER, K ERIC; Clearwater HS; Conway Springs, KS; (3); Guitar; KSU; Prof Bounty Hunter.

SHAFFER, LESLEY D; Louisburg HS; Paola, KS; (2); Spanish Clb; Chorus; Hon Roll; Lawyer.

SHAFFER, SHAYLA D; Northeast HS; Mulberry, KS; (3); 3/40; Office Aide; Band; Chorus; Yrbk; Pres Jr Cls; L Chrldng; JV Sftbl; JV Vllybl; Hon Roll; NHS; PSU.

SHAH, AALI M; Wichita Collegiate Schl; Wichita, KS; (4); Chess Clb; Debate Tm; Scholastic Bowl; High Hon Roll; Ntl Merit Ltr; Karate; Univ Of KS; Pre-Med.

SHAH, RAJVEE M; Shawnee Mission E Sr HS; Lenexa, KS; (4); 10/410; Cmnty Wkr; Hosp Aide; Spanish Clb; Teachers Aide; Chrmn Stu Cncl; Var L Tennis; High Hon Roll; NHS; Ntl Merit Schol; Intnl Baccalaureate Diploma Grad; U Of MO; Med.

SHAHAN, TENNILLE; Udall HS; Udall, KS; (3); Church Yth Grp; Cmnty Wkr; FHA; Letterman Clb; Service Clb; Band; Mrchg Band; Pep Band; Stage Crew; Bsktbl; Sftbl Mst Insprtnl 94; FHA Stuco Rep; 1st Pl Dist Engl Essay Cmptn; Emporia; Ed.

SHAIN, KARI ANN; Buhler HS; Buhler, KS; (4); 23/138; Church Yth Grp; Pres Natl FFA Org; SADD; Teachers Aide; Band; Mrchg Band; Pep Band; Intrml Bsktbl; Mgr(s); Powder Puff Ftbl; Dekalb Agrcltrl Acmplshmnt Awd; Tchrs Choice Awd 95; Bible Schl Nrsry 92-; Mc Pherson Coll; Elem Ed.

SHALLENBURGER, CANDICE D; Baxter Springs HS; Baxter Springs, KS; (1); Girl Scts; Pep Clb; Band; Chorus; Mrchg Band; Rep Stu Cncl; Var Chrldng; Trk; High Hon Roll; Pres Schlr; Par Law.

SHALLUE, CAROL A; Derby HS; Wichita, KS; (3); Art Clb; VP Pres Church Yth Grp; High Hon Roll; Hon Roll; Ntl Merit Ltr; Prfct Atten Awd; Pres Acad Fit Awd; Env Clb; Arch.

SHAN, DAVID W; Blue Valley Northwest HS; Overland Park, KS; (3); 28/364; Cmnty Wkr; German Clb; Intnl Clb; Math Clb; Math Tm; Science Clb; Band; Mrchg Band; Hon Roll; JETS Awd; Eng.

SHANE, CHRISTOPHER T; Salina HS South; Salina, KS; (4); 9/225; Boy Scts; Quiz Bowl; Orch; School Musical; JV Bsktbl; L Crs Cntry; NHS; Ntl Merit SF; KS ST U; Math.

SHANEYFELT, ASHLEY J; Blue Valley Northwest HS; Overland Park, KS; (3); 80/364; Church Yth Grp; Cmnty Wkr; Debate Tm; Teachers Aide; Hon Roll; NHS; Ntl Merit Ltr; All Amer Schlr; Mexico Mission Trip.

SHANK, JENNIFER; Hays HS; Hays, KS; (3); 23/237; Pep Clb; Nwsp; Rep Frsh Cls; Rep Jr Cls; Ofcr Stu Cncl; JV Vllybl; NHS; Ft Hays ST Univ.

SHANKER, SHALINI; Paola HS; Osawatomie, KS; (1); Cmnty Wkr; SADD; High Hon Roll; Opthalmologist.

SHARMA, MONICA D; Kapaun-Mt Carmel HS; Wichita, KS; (1); Spanish Clb; Crs Cntry; Trk; Hon Roll; Tae Kwon Do; KU; Doctor/Tchr.

SHARON, RICHARD H; Wichita East HS; Wichita, KS; (3); Cmnty Wkr; Debate Tm; Hosp Aide; Chorus; Wt Lftg; Wrstlng; High Hon Roll; Hon Roll; Jr NHS; NHS; Judo; Kenpo Karate; Medicine.

SHARP, AIMEE; Concordia Jr Sr HS; Concordia, KS; (4); 25/106; Am Leg Aux Girls St; Debate Tm; Girl Scts; Spanish Clb; Speech Tm; Teachers Aide; Band; Rptr Nwsp; 4-H Awd; Hon Roll; Ft Hays ST U; Pblc Rels.

SHARP, EMILY; Rossville HS; Rossville, KS; (3); Pres FBLA; Letterman Clb; NFL; Drill Tm; Drm Mjr(t); Pres Frsh Cls; Pres Soph Cls; Co-Capt Jr Cls; NHS; Regents Hnr Acad 95; KS ST U; Med.

SHARP, HEATHER M; Lawrence HS; Lawrence, KS; (3); 36/584; Church Yth Grp; Red Cross Aide; Band; Drm Mjr(t); Ed Nwsp; Var Swmmng; NHS; Cmnty Wkr; Girl Scts; Letterman Clb; Presdntl Classroom Schlr; All-Dist & All-St Clarinet Player; Yth In Local Govt Treas.

SHARP, JEREMY L; Derby HS; Derby, KS; (2); Math Tm; Scholastic Bowl; 4-H Awd; High Hon Roll; NHS; Hutchinson CC Indus Arts Expo Medl For Wdwrking; KS St Univ; Eng.

SHARP, JONATHAN A; Olathe South Sr HS; Olathe, KS; (3); Varsity Clb; Ftbl; Wt Lftg; Wrstlng; Cit Awd; Hon Roll; JCCC; Sales Rep.

SHARP, JUSTIN; Newton Sr HS; Newton, KS; (3); Am Leg Boys St; Boy Scts; Band; Jazz Band; Mrchg Band; Pep Band; Ftbl; Trk; Wt Lftg; Wrstlng; Future Edctrs Amer; Eagle Sct 96; Arch Engrng.

SHARP, KRISTI; Dighton HS; Dighton, KS; (4); 13/30; Am Leg Aux Girls St; FCA; Band; Jazz Band; Yrbk; Sec Soph Cls; Pres Jr Cls; Ofcr Stu Cncl; Hon Roll; NHS; Fort Hays ST U; Rdlgy.

SHARP, TABITHA; Circle HS; El Dorado, KS; (4); 11/90; Am Leg Aux Girls St; Office Aide; Spanish Clb; SADD; Acpl Chr; Chorus; Church Choir; Variety Show; High Hon Roll; Hon Roll; Washburn U; Law.

SHAVER, ASHLEY B; Washburn Rural HS; Topeka, KS; (3); Cmnty Wkr; Pep Clb; Hon Roll; KS ST U; Eng.

SHAVER, JESSICA A; Goddard HS; Wichita, KS; (2); Church Yth Grp; Debate Tm; GAA; JA; Thesps; Acpl Chr; School Musical; Variety Show; Socr; High Hon Roll; Juliard NY; Cmpsr Msc/Psych.

SHAVER, MISTI; Atchison Sr HS; Atchison, KS; (2); 6/130; Church Yth Grp; Letterman Clb; Pep Clb; Spanish Clb; Var Bsktbl; Var Vllybl; High Hon Roll; Hon Roll; Jr NHS.

SHAW, AMY L; Wellington Sr HS; Wellington, KS; (4); 12/125; Am Leg Aux Girls St; Church Yth Grp; Key Clb; Library Aide; Math Clb; Quiz Bowl; Red Cross Aide; Scholastic Bowl; SADD; Band; Natl Yth Ldrshp Frm Med; Sci Olympd 3rd Pl; KS ST U; Bio.

SHAW, APRIL D; Wichita West HS; Wichita, KS; (2); Hosp Aide; Office Aide; Teachers Aide; Band; Mrchg Band; Pep Band; Mgr Trk; Hon Roll; NHS; Forensic Pathlgy.

SHAW, BRANDON W; Holton HS; Holton, KS; (1); Natl FFA Org; Golf; KS ST U; Comp Programming.

SHAW, GRETCHEN; Kingman HS; Penalosa, KS; (3); French Clb; FBLA; Library Aide; Natl FFA Org; SADD; Rep Stu Cncl; Var Capt Chrldng; Sftbl; Vllybl; Hon Roll; Teens Today Ldrs Tomorrow; Yth & Govt; Prom Decorating Comm; KS ST.

SHAW, KELLY; Ashland HS; Ashland, KS; (4); 2/24; Church Yth Grp; Quiz Bowl; Pep Band; School Play; Yrbk; Pres Jr Cls; Pres Sr Cls; Var Bsktbl; Var Tennis; Var Trk; KS ST Univ; Acctg.

SHAW, LINN; Wellington Sr HS; Wellington, KS; (1); 1/160; Church Yth Grp; Math Tm; Office Aide; Quiz Bowl; Scholastic Bowl; SADD; Rep Stu Cncl; JV Bsbl; Var Bsktbl; Var Crs Cntry; Rotary Awd.

SHAW, SUE E; Caney Valley Jr Sr HS; Caney, KS; (1); Church Yth Grp; Natl FFA Org; Var L Trk; Hon Roll; OK St Univ; Anml Sci.

SHAW, TASHA; Golden Plains HS; Selden, KS; (2); Art Clb; Church Yth Grp; Spanish Clb; Speech Tm; Band; Chorus; Chrldng; Vllybl; Wt Lftg; Hon Roll; Stu Cncl; Colby CC; FBI.

SHAY, JENIFER; Winfield HS; Winfield, KS; (3); Church Yth Grp; Teachers Aide; Band; Rptr Nwsp; Rep Frsh Cls; Rep Soph Cls; Ofcr Stu Cncl; Chrldng; Swmmng; Hon Roll; U KS.

SHEA, LESLI D; Smoky Valley HS; Lindsborg, KS; (3); Pep Clb; Band; Mrchg Band; Pep Band; Trk; Hon Roll; Wichita ST; Physcns Asst.

SHEAFFER, KATY L; Central Heights Sr HS; Richmond, KS; (4); Church Yth Grp; Pep Clb; Science Clb; Spanish Clb; Teachers Aide; Band; Mrchg Band; Pep Band; Mgr(s); JV Vllybl; 1st Pl Intermed Physics Tst KU Eng; 3rd Pl Bridge Bldg Cntst KU; Emporia ST Univ; Elem Ed/Sp Ed.

SHEAN, BECKY J; Spearville Jr Sr HS; Spearville, KS; (2); Pep Clb; Band; Chorus; Chrldng; Vllybl; Hon Roll; NHS.

SHEAR, LISA; Hesston HS; Hesston, KS; (4); NFL; Acpl Chr; Chorus; School Musical; School Play; Stage Crew; Variety Show; High Hon Roll; Ntl Merit SF; Odyssey Of The Mind; Mt Holyoke Coll.

SHEARBURN, SHANNA M; El Dorado HS; El Dorado, KS; (3); Church Yth Grp; VP Pres FCA; SADD; Chorus; Stage Crew; Stat Bsktbl; Mgr(s); Powder Puff Ftbl; Mgr Swmmng; Hon Roll.

SHEEDY, CHRISTIAN L; Yates Ctr HS; Yates Center, KS; (3); Boy Scts; Letterman Clb; Band; Mrchg Band; Pep Band; JV Bsktbl; JV Ftbl; Var Trk; Hon Roll; Marines.

SHEEDY, CORY; Northwest HS; Wichita, KS; (2); 79/357; Band; Mrchg Band; Pep Band; High Hon Roll; Advanced Wichita Wind Ensemble.

SHEETS, BEAU W; Colby Sr HS; Colby, KS; (2); Church Yth Grp; 4-H; Bsktbl; Ftbl; Trk; 4-H Awd; High Hon Roll; Hon Roll; Outstnd Geom Stu Of Yr; Outstnd Advalg Stu Of Yr; Eng.

SHEETS, LINDSEY D; Rolla HS; Rolla, KS; (4); 3/13; Church Yth Grp; FCA; Letterman Clb; Quiz Bowl; Scholastic Bowl; Band; Mrchg Band; Pep Band; Nwsp; Pres Frsh Cls; KS ST Univ; Mech Engrng.

SHEETS, TAMMY; Douglass HS; Douglass, KS; (2); 2/73; Church Yth Grp; Letterman Clb; Varsity Clb; Band; Color Guard; Flag Corp; Jazz Band; Mrchg Band; Pep Band; Variety Show; Teens Of Tchrs; D-Club; Cowley Cnty CC; CPA.

SHEFFIELD, ANGIE M; Olathe East Sr HS; Olathe, KS; (2); Church Yth Grp; Dance Clb; Letterman Clb; Pep Clb; Teachers Aide; Drill Tm; Yrbk; Socr; Vllybl; Hon Roll.

SHELDON, JONI; Sylvan Unified HS; Lincoln, KS; (4); 1/15; Pres Church Yth Grp; Capt Dance Clb; 4-H; Pep Clb; Quiz Bowl; SADD; Teachers Aide; Band; Chorus; Church Choir; K ST Deans Awd; KU Hnr Stdnt; Govs Schlr; KS ST Univ; Scl Work.

SHELEY, LISA M; Wabaunsee HS; Paxico, KS; (3); Church Yth Grp; Nwsp; Ofcr Stu Cncl; Var Bsktbl; Var Chrldng; Var Sftbl; Var Trk; Var Vllybl; Hon Roll; NHS.

SHELOR, BRENT; Spring Hill HS; Olathe, KS; (4); 7/95; Am Leg Boys St; Art Clb; Chess Clb; Debate Tm; NFL; Pep Clb; Quiz Bowl; Science Clb; Spanish Clb; JV Bsktbl; KS ST U; Comp Prgmng.

SHELTON, MICHAEL J; Lawrence HS; Lawrence, KS; (2); Chess Clb; Church Yth Grp; FCA; Chorus; Intrml Bsktbl; Intrml Trk; Gov Hon Prg Awd; Hon Roll; Pres Acad Fit Awd.

SHEPARD, JEREMY W; Ottawa HS; Ottawa, KS; (3); 13/200; Am Leg Boys St; FCA; Letterman Clb; Varsity Clb; JV Bsktbl; Var L Ftbl; Var L Trk; Var L Wrstlng; High Hon Roll; NHS; Notre Dame; Crmnl Jstc.

SHEPERD, JAMES; Shawnee Mission N HS; Shawnee Mission, KS; (4); 1/360; Boy Scts; Chess Clb; German Clb; Pep Clb; Q&S; Nwsp; Ed Yrbk; Var L Swmmng; Trk; Gov Hon Prg Awd; Univ Of KS; Jrnlsm/Med.

SHEPHERD, BRADY; Olathe East Sr HS; Olathe, KS; (3); VP Drama Clb; French Clb; Thesps; School Musical; Rptr Phtg Nwsp; Trk; High Hon Roll; Teachers Aide; Chorus; Church Choir; K ST Univ Summer Choral Inst Hnr Choir; SWACDA; ST Hnr Choir; Bus.

SHEPHERD, CASSANDRA D; Central Heights Sr HS; Richmond, KS; (1); 4-H; Natl FFA Org; Band; Mrchg Band; Pep Band; High Hon Roll; Hon Roll; KS ST Univ.

SHEPHERD, JENNIFER I; Maize HS; Wichita, KS; (3); Spanish Clb; SADD; Band; Chorus; Color Guard; Pep Band; School Musical; Variety Show; Hon Roll; Prfct Atten Awd; Study Music Ed; Music Ed.

SHEPHERD, JENNY; Goddard HS; Goddard, KS; (3); Science Clb; Service Clb; Spanish Clb; SADD; School Play; Var Bsktbl; Var Sftbl; Var Vllybl; High Hon Roll; NHS; NHS Act Dir; Pre-Med.

SHEPHERD, JOSEPH; Ellis HS; Ellis, KS; (3); Am Leg Boys St; Church Yth Grp; Math Tm; Speech Tm; SADD; Pres Frsh Cls; Pres Soph Cls; Pres Stu Cncl; High Hon Roll; NHS; Discover Card Tribute Awd 2nd Pl St; Duet Acting 3rd Pl St; FFA St Speaking Cont 7th Pl; Medicine.

SHEPHERD, MICHAEL; Ellis HS; Ellis, KS; (2); 1/40; Math Tm; Natl FFA Org; Band; Chorus; Pres Frsh Cls; Pres Soph Cls; Bsktbl; Ftbl; Trk; High Hon Roll; St Piano Cont I Rating.

SHEPHERD, MOLLY; Frankft HS; Frankfort, KS; (3); FHA; SADD; Band; Chorus; School Play; Hon Roll; Pres Acad Fit Awd; Piano Accmpnst; Dist Hnr Bnd; Lgn Trmptr; Bethany; Music.

SHEPHERD, SARA; Emporia HS; Emporia, KS; (2); Art Clb; Church Yth Grp; Debate Tm; 4-H; Phtg Yrbk; Rep Soph Cls; JV Chrldng; Var Crs Cntry; Var Swmmng; Hon Roll; Ballet Midwest Co Dancer.

SHERARD III, RONALD E; Plainville HS; Plainville, KS; (4); 9/54; Band; Jazz Band; Mrchg Band; Pep Band; School Play; Stage Crew; Rep Stu Cncl; Golf; Hon Roll; NHS; Type II ROTC Air Force Schlsp; U Of MO Rolla; Civil Engrng.

SHERIDAN, BROOKE; Shawnee Mission E Sr HS; Prairie Village, KS; (4); SADD; Ofcr Soph Cls; Ofcr Jr Cls; Ofcr Sr Cls; Chrldng; Crs Cntry; Hon Roll; NHS; SHARE; U Of AZ.

SHERMAN, DENAE H; Coldwater Jr Sr HS; Coldwater, KS; (1); Church Yth Grp; FCA; FHA; Girl Scts; Band; Chorus; Church Choir; Mrchg Band; School Musical; Variety Show.

SHERMAN, GEORGE J; Goddard HS; Goddard, KS; (3); Science Clb; Ftbl; Hon Roll.

SHERMAN, MEGHAN; Coldwater Jr Sr HS; Coldwater, KS; (3); 3/14; Church Yth Grp; Drama Clb; FCA; FHA; Letterman Clb; Pep Clb; Band; Chorus; Mrchg Band; Pep Band; KS St Univ; Optom.

SHERMOEN, JESSICA A; Topeka HS; Topeka, KS; (2); 32/423; Dance Clb; Hosp Aide; Pep Clb; SADD; High Hon Roll; Hon Roll; Natl Yth Svc Day Hnre 95-; Hills Vet Eexplorer Post; Prof Animal Trainer.

SHERRER, LISA K; Olathe North Sr HS; Olathe, KS; (4); Church Yth Grp; Drama Clb; Spanish Clb; School Play; Stage Crew; Yrbk; Socr; Trk; Hon Roll; Chrch Yty Grp Cncl; Multi Yr Listing; JCCC; Intr Dsgn.

SHERRILL, BRIAN K; Kapaun-Mt Carmel HS; Derby, KS; (1); Church Yth Grp.

SHERWOOD, JEFFREY E; Independence HS; Independence, KS; (4); 2/160; Am Leg Boys St; French Clb; NFL; Quiz Bowl; High Hon Roll; NHS; Pres Acad Fit Awd; Sal; St Schlr; KS Regents Hnrs Acad; Army ROTC Schlsp; VFW Endowment Awd; Pittsburg ST U; Bio.

SHERWOOD, JENNIFER A; Circle HS; El Dorado, KS; (2); Math Tm; SADD; Chorus; School Musical; Variety Show; Bsktbl; Golf; Cit Awd; High Hon Roll; Hon Roll; KS ST; Bus.

SHEWELL, MAXINE; Turner HS; Kansas City, KS; (3); 29/224; Chorus; Yrbk; Hon Roll; Jr NHS.

SHIELDS, AIMEE R; Chanute Sr HS; Chanute, KS; (2); Church Yth Grp; Debate Tm; Drama Clb; FCA; NFL; School Play; Stage Crew; Chorus; JV Trk; Hon Roll; Regnls Debate & Forensics; St Speech Festival I Rating; Mst Outstdng Female Awd; Pol Sci.

SHIELDS, BRAD M; Smoky Valley HS; Lindsborg, KS; (1); Math Tm; Band; Mrchg Band; Pep Band; Bsktbl; High Hon Roll; Hon Roll; Golf; Art/Sci.

SHIELDS, JONATHAN A; Shawnee Mission N HS; Overland Park, KS; (3); Band; Mrchg Band; Orch; School Musical; Score Keeper; Submission Staff; UT; Arch.

SHIELDS, KATHERINE A; Bonner Springs HS; Bonner Springs, KS; (4); 7/150; FHA; SADD; High Hon Roll; Hon Roll; NHS; KU Hnr Schlr; Dwight D Eisenhower Veterans Hosp Vol; VFW Mem Of Ladies Auxiliary 6401; KS City CC; Elem Ed.

SHIELDS, TERA L; Wichita South HS; Wichita, KS; (4); 32/292; Church Yth Grp; Teachers Aide; Band; Church Choir; Drill Tm; Mrchg Band; Orch; Pep Band; School Musical; Variety Show; Intl Org Of Rainbow For Grls; KS Univ; Pharm.

SHIELDS, TYLER; Labette Co HS; Oswego, KS; (2); HOBY; Band; Chorus; Mrchg Band; School Musical; Var Crs Cntry; Var Trk; High Hon Roll; Mu Alpha Theta; Jazz Band; HOBY 96; Yth Rep Chrch Fin Comm; Law/Crtv Wrtng.

SHIK, SARAH J; Blue Valley Northwest HS; Overland Park, KS; (3); Var Debate Tm; Hosp Aide; Model UN; NFL; Scholastic Bowl; VP Sec Temple Yth Grp; Hon Roll; NHS; Acad Decathalon Fine Arts; Forensics Squad; Wrtng/Soc Sci.

SHIMANEK, BRIAN L; Wichita Co HS; Leoti, KS; (3); Jazz Band; Mrchg Band; Pep Band; School Play; Var Bsktbl; Var Ftbl; JV Golf; Wt Lftg; Debate Tm; Hon Roll; KS ST; Acctng.

SHIMER, ANDY L; Wellington Sr HS; Wellington, KS; (4); 17/125; Am Leg Boys St; Church Yth Grp; Cmnty Wkr; Key Clb; Red Cross Aide; Rep Stu Cncl; JV Var Ftbl; Var Trk; High Hon Roll; Hon Roll; KS ST Univ; Arch.

SHIMER, ELIZABETH A; Wellington Sr HS; Wellington, KS; (3); 12/180; Church Yth Grp; Key Clb; Varsity Clb; Chorus; Var Chrldng; Var Trk; JV Vllybl; High Hon Roll; Hon Roll; NHS; Piano Cmptn I Rtng St, Rgnl; Tri St I Rtng; KS ST U; Med.

SHINDLEY, LESLIE D; Dighton HS; Dighton, KS; (1); 3/35; Drama Clb; Scholastic Bowl; Band; Sec Frsh Cls; High Hon Roll; Hon Roll; Recog WKEA Art Show Chm Art Dept; Fort Hays ST; Cmpt Anlyst.

SHIPLEY, MARILEIGH M; Dodge City HS; Dodge City, KS; (3); Church Yth Grp; SADD; Teachers Aide; Rep Stu Cncl; Cit Awd; High Hon Roll; Treas NHS; Prfct Atten Awd; Peer Hlprs; All-Amer Schlr; Intl Frgn Lang Awd; Emporia ST Univ; Pdtrcs PT.

SHIPMAN, AMY; El Dorado HS; El Dorado, KS; (3); 7/144; 4-H; NFL; SADD; Varsity Clb; Rep Frsh Cls; Rep Soph Cls; Rep Jr Cls; Sec Stu Cncl; Stat Bsbl; Var Capt Chrldng; Butler Co CC SW Hnrs Prog; KS Regnts Hnr Acad Nmnee; KSHSAA Stu Cncl Conf Dlgt; KS St Univ; Pdtrcn.

SHIPMAN, CHANCE; Blue Valley HS; Overland Park, KS; (2); Debate Tm; Intnl Clb; Spanish Clb; Rep Soph Cls; JV Crs Cntry; JV Tennis; Hon Roll; Spanish NHS; U Of MI; Architecture.

SHIPPERS, BECKY L; Thomas More Prep Marian HS; Hays, KS; (2); 1/85; Church Yth Grp; Scholastic Bowl; Band; School Musical; Stage Crew; Rptr Nwsp; Var Chrldng; High Hon Roll; KS Regents Hnrs Acad; TMP-MARIAN Ambassador.

SHIPPY, SELENA L; Attica Public Schl; Sharon, KS; (3); 5/15; HOBY; Quiz Bowl; Scholastic Bowl; School Play; Sec Treas Jr Cls; Var Bsktbl; Var Trk; Var Vllybl; High Hon Roll; Hon Roll.

SHIPPY, SUZANN; Attica Public Schl; Sharon, KS; (2); Speech Tm; School Play; Rptr Nwsp; Phtg Yrbk; JV Bsktbl; Var Chrldng; Var L Trk; JV Vllybl; Hon Roll; Prfct Atten Awd.

SHIRE, CARRIE E; Independence HS; Independence, KS; (3); 7/150; Am Leg Aux Girls St; School Musical; Swing Chorus; Rep Frsh Cls; Rep Soph Cls; Rep Jr Cls; Pres Stu Cncl; Tennis; Trk; NHS; KS Univ; Intl Comm/Bus.

SHIRES, NATHAN L; St John's Military Schl; Littleton, CO; (2); Chess Clb; Church Yth Grp; Cmnty Wkr; 4-H; ROTC; Trk; 4-H Awd; Hon Roll; Exchng Stu To Japan.

SHIRK, ABBY M; Great Bend Sr HS; Great Bend, KS; (2); 10/263; Church Yth Grp; FCA; Pep Clb; Spanish Clb; SADD; Acpl Chr; Chorus; Variety Show; L Var Crs Cntry; L Var Trk; Amer Red Cross Cert Lfgrd; KS ST Univ.

SHOAF, AMANDA R; Wichita Collegiate Schl; Wichita, KS; (3); SADD; Acpl Chr; Chorus; Drill Tm; School Musical; School Play; Golf; Pom Pon; Tennis; Hon Roll; Mscls; Piano 12 Yrs; Psych.

SHOAF, LAURA K; Wichita North HS; Wichita, KS; (2); Acpl Chr; Band; Chorus; Mrchg Band; Pep Band; Rep Frsh Cls; Rep Soph Cls; Rep Stu Cncl; Hon Roll; Hlth Advy Bd; KS U; Psych Or Pediatrics.

SHOCK, MALINDA C; Campus HS; Wichita, KS; (3); French Clb; Pep Clb; SADD; Teachers Aide; Ofcr Stu Cncl; U Of KS; Crdlgy.

SHOCKEY, MIKE G; Manhattan HS; Manhattan, KS; (4); Boy Scts; Spanish Clb; Hon Roll.

SHOCKEY, TAVI L; Leavenworth HS; Leavenworth, KS; (1); SADD; Chorus; Chrldng; High Hon Roll; Hon Roll.

SHOEMAKER, DANELLE; St John's HS; Beloit, KS; (3); 1/12; Drama Clb; Quiz Bowl; Rep Frsh Cls; Pres Soph Cls; VP Stu Cncl; Chrldng; Stat Ftbl; High Hon Roll; NHS; Pep Clb; Spirit Awd; KS Regents Hnrs Acad; Med.

SHOEMAKER, GARRETT; Lebo Schl; Lebo, KS; (3); Am Leg Boys St; Boy Scts; 4-H; Natl FFA Org; Ofcr Stu Cncl; Var Ftbl; Var Trk; Intrml Wt Lftg; Hon Roll; NHS; Comm Theater.

SHOEMAKER, SHANNA A; Williamsburg Schl; Williamsburg, KS; (4); 2/18; Church Yth Grp; FCA; Natl FFA Org; Band; Chorus; Mrchg Band; School Play; Ed Yrbk; Bsktbl; Trk; St Champion High Jumper; Salutatorian Of Grad Cls; Co-Ed Of Yrbk; KS U; Bus.

SHOMIN, ANGELA; Bishop Ward HS; Kansas City, KS; (2); 1/99; Drama Clb; Pep Clb; SADD; School Musical; School Play; Stage Crew; Swing Chorus; Rep Soph Cls; Intrml JV Chrldng; Var Trk; Tutor; Vlntr El Centro Yth Advsry Cncl; Air Force Acad; Aeronautics.

SHOOK, COURTNEY D; Wichita Heights HS; Wichita, KS; (4); 1/1; Church Yth Grp; Drama Clb; Intnl Clb; Scholastic Bowl; Spanish Clb; Thesps; School Play; Stage Crew; Mgr(s); High Hon Roll; KS St Univ; Theatr.

SHOREMAN, JENNIFER M; St Thomas Aquinas HS; Leawood, KS; (3); 2/261; FBLA; Hosp Aide; Math Clb; NFL; Var L Pom Pon; High Hon Roll; NHS; FCA; French Clb; Key Clb; KS Regents Hnrs Acad; Natl Hnr Conf Delgtn; Milwaukee Ballet Schol; Med.

SHORNEY, DARCI J; Olathe North Sr HS; Olathe, KS; (3); Church Yth Grp; German Clb; Key Clb; Office Aide; Q&S; Acpl Chr; Chorus; Rptr Nwsp; Hon Roll; Pres Acad Fit Awd; Law.

SHOROCK, TOM; Great Bend Sr HS; Great Bend, KS; (3); Am Leg Boys St; Boy Scts; Debate Tm; German Clb; NFL; Quiz Bowl; Speech Tm; Orch; Hon Roll.

SHORT, ALLISON; Mulvane Sr HS; Mulvane, KS; (4); Church Yth Grp; SADD; Teachers Aide; Chorus; Church Choir; School Play; Stage Crew; Swing Chorus; Hon Roll; Prfct Atten Awd; Church Assn Yth Cncl Rcdng Sec; Church Yth Cncl; Otstdng Esprit De Corps Awd; OK Bapt U; Intrprsnl/Pub Comm.

SHOUP, JOSHUA D; Larned HS; Larned, KS; (2); Boy Scts; Church Yth Grp; Band; Jazz Band; Mrchg Band; Pep Band; Rep Soph Cls; Rep Jr Cls; Ofcr Stu Cncl; L Bsbl; LDS Seminary; Brigham Yng Univ.

SHOUP, STEFANIE; Arkansas City HS; Arkansas City, KS; (4); 5/170; Church Yth Grp; Drama Clb; FCA; SADD; Band; Mrchg Band; Pep Band; School Play; Bsktbl; Sftbl; Frnscs/Acad/Bsktbl Lttrmn; KS ST Univ; Env Engrng.

SHOUP, TRISHA; Arkansas City HS; Arkansas City, KS; (2); Drama Clb; FCA; SADD; Orch; Bsktbl; Trk; High Hon Roll; Hon Roll; NHS; Univ Of KS; Arch Engrng.

SHOWALTER, AMBER J; Ottawa HS; Ottawa, KS; (4); 50/150; 4-H; French Clb; Key Clb; SADD; Teachers Aide; Band; Jazz Band; Mrchg Band; Orch; Pep Band; Explorer; Ottawa Univ; Bio; Pre-Med.

SHOWALTER, KATE; Shawnee Mission West HS; Lenexa, KS; (3); 131/421; Debate Tm; DECA; Latin Clb; Letterman Clb; NFL; Stage Crew; Ofcr Stu Cncl; Var Chrldng; Mgr(s); Hon Roll; Red Crss Certfd Lifeguard, CPR & 1st Aid; Art Pub; Cotillion Clb; KS ST Univ.

SHRINER, BRIAN P; Shawnee Mission W Sr HS; Overland Park, KS; (4); 52/356; Hosp Aide; Hon Roll; U Of KS; Pre-Med.

SHROUF, DANIELLE L; Junction City HS; Junction City, KS; (4); 44/244; Teachers Aide; Hon Roll; Jr Comm; Sr Comm; Radiolgy Tech.

SHROYER, ASHLEY; Sterling HS; Sterling, KS; (2); 3/38; Church Yth Grp; Debate Tm; HOBY; VP Sec Science Clb; Speech Tm; Band; Rptr Yrbk; Rep Stu Cncl; Var L Chrldng; High Hon Roll; MCAA Oration Chmpn Forensics 96; Prncpl Hnr Stu; Pre-Med.

SHROYER, JASON D; Wichita North HS; Wichita, KS; (2); Hon Roll; Pub Poetry Schl Lit Mgzn; Phtgrphy; Antique Car Rfrbshng; U Of AR; Med Field.

SHUFELBERGER, SHAUN S; Hayden HS; Topeka, KS; (2); JV Bsktbl; Var L Golf; Hon Roll.

SHULL, ANDREA K; Dighton HS; Newton, KS; (4); Rep Sr Cls; Rep Stu Cncl; Var L Trk; Var L Vllybl; Hon Roll; Pres Schlr; Colby CC; Horse Prdctn/Mngmt.

SHULL, MEGAN J; Dighton HS; Dighton, KS; (2); Church Yth Grp; Drama Clb; HOBY; Pep Clb; Speech Tm; SADD; Band; Chorus; Jazz Band; Mrchg Band; World Ldrshp Cncl Ambssdr HOBY 96; KS ST Univ; Psychlgy.

SHULL, PRESTON C; Sedan HS; Wichita, KS; (2); FHA; NFL; Spanish Clb; Thesps; School Play; Wichita St Univ; Arts.

SHULTZ, ERIN R; Dodge City HS; Dodge City, KS; (3); Church Yth Grp; Band; Mrchg Band; Lit Mag; Hon Roll; NHS; Hlth Sci.

SHULTZ, JENNIFER L; Goddard HS; Wichita, KS; (1); Church Yth Grp; Cmnty Wkr; Drama Clb; Office Aide; School Play; Stage Crew; Equestrian Evnts; Author.

SHUM, JUSTIN; Marysville HS; Marysville, KS; (3); 40/89; Am Leg Boys St; Bus Profs of Am; FCA; Letterman Clb; Jazz Band; School Play; VP Stu Cncl; L Var Trk; High Hon Roll; Prfct Atten Awd; KS ST Univ.

SHUMAN, MELISSA J; Colby Sr HS; Colby, KS; (2); Spanish Clb; Band; Mrchg Band; Pep Band; Hon Roll; Chrch & Museum Vol; Chrch Mssn Ed Tour.

SHURLEY, KORTNEY E; Wichita North HS; Wichita, KS; (3); Bus Profs of Am; Teachers Aide; JV Socr; Hon Roll; Sec.

SHURTZ, LINDSEY A; Ness City HS; Ness City, KS; (1); Church Yth Grp; VP FHA; Pep Clb; Chorus; Church Choir; Chrldng; Golf; Vllybl; Hon Roll; Miss Teen Ness Cty 95; FFA Natl Gold Medalist 96; Law.

SICKLER, CHRISTOPHER P P; Olathe East Sr HS; Overland Park, KS; (2); Socr; High Hon Roll; Hon Roll; Pres Acad Fit Awd; Comp Sci.

SICKLER, KIMBERLY A; Olathe East Sr HS; Overland Park, KS; (3); Am Leg Aux Girls St; Cmnty Wkr; Treas Debate Tm; French Clb; German Clb; Intnl Clb; Treas NFL; Spanish Clb; Variety Show; Rep Jr Cls; Intl Bus/Law.

SIDMAN, AMANDA L; Norton Comm HS; Norton, KS; (3); Cmnty Wkr; FHA; Hosp Aide; Model UN; Pep Clb; SADD; Band; Jazz Band; Mrchg Band; Pep Band; KAYS.

SIEBERT, ELIZABETH A; Hoisington HS; Hoisington, KS; (3); Debate Tm; Speech Tm; Band; Mgr Bsktbl; JV Golf; JV Sftbl; JV Trk; Hon Roll; Church Yth Grp; Girl Scts; Frgn Exchg Stdnt 95; Congrsnl Yth Ldrshp Cncl; U Of KS; Law.

SIEBERT, WES; Salina HS Central; Salina, KS; (4); Am Leg Boys St; Debate Tm; JA; Letterman Clb; NFL; Teachers Aide; Cit Awd; Hon Roll; NHS; Forensics; Stu Congress; Natl Eng Mrt Awd; KS Univ; Surgeon.

SIEFKES, MELISSA; St John Jr Sr HS; Hudson, KS; (3); 1/43; Church Yth Grp; Pep Clb; School Musical; Ofcr Stu Cncl; Stat Bsktbl; Crs Cntry; Trk; 4-H Awd; High Hon Roll; NHS; KS ST U; Elem Ed.

SIEGELE, CAM S; Shawnee Mission W Sr HS; Overland Park, KS; (2); 147/400; Pep Clb; JV Bsbl; Hon Roll; NASA NSTA 96 Rgnl Wnr; Engrng.

SIEGERT, STACEY J; Shawnee Mission Northwest HS; Lenexa, KS; (4); Cmnty Wkr; Drama Clb; Hosp Aide; Pep Clb; Thesps; School Musical; School Play; Stage Crew; Hon Roll; Thespian Off 94-95; VP 95-; Jr/Sr Rep Spirit Club; KS Univ; Theatre/Film.

SIEGLE, DANA S; Rock Creek Jr Sr HS; Westmoreland, KS; (2); 12/72; Am Leg Aux Girls St; Church Yth Grp; FHA; SADD; Var Bsktbl; Mgr(s); Var L Sftbl; Var L Trk; Var Vllybl; High Hon Roll; USUBA Rockies Sftbl Tm; Summer League Bsktbl; KS ST Univ; Law/Med.

SIEGRIST, CHESLEY R; Bishop Carroll Catholic HS; Wichita, KS; (4); Church Yth Grp; Red Cross Aide; Ski Clb; Sndy Schl Tchr; KS Newman Univ; Bus.

SIEKER, MICHELLE R; Chase HS; Chase, KS; (1); FHA; Math Tm; Quiz Bowl; Spanish Clb; Band; Pep Band; VP Frsh Cls; Rep Soph Cls; JV L Bsktbl; Mgr(s); Pharmacist.

SIEMENS, DAILA D; Meade HS; Meade, KS; (1); 5/35; Church Yth Grp; Scholastic Bowl; Chorus; Church Choir; School Musical; Sec Frsh Cls; Sec Soph Cls; Var L Tennis; High Hon Roll; Pres Schlr; Grace Univ.

SIEMERS, ELLA; Chapman HS; Chapman, KS; (4); 19/108; Office Aide; Red Cross Aide; SADD; Phtg Nwsp; Ed Pres Yrbk; Mgr(s); Cit Awd; High Hon Roll; Hon Roll; NHS; Sr Mixed Ensmbl; Ft Hays ST Univ; Comm.

SIEMILLER, BRANDY L; Lucas Luray HS; Luray, KS; (4); 2/4; Letterman Clb; VP Pep Clb; SADD; Band; Chorus; School Play; VP Sr Cls; L Bsktbl; NHS; Sal; Ft Hays ST U; Wildlife Bio.

SIEMSEN, CODY L; Colby Sr HS; Colby, KS; (4); 10/82; Pres Church Yth Grp; SADD; Teachers Aide; Drill Tm; Drm Mjr(t); Ed Yrbk; Chrldng; Golf; NHS; AFS Pres; Colby CC; Elem Ed.

SIGLE, MINDY; Maize HS; Wichita, KS; (3); 34/295; NFL; Q&S; Spanish Clb; SADD; Band; Mrchg Band; Ed Yrbk; Var Golf; Hon Roll; NHS; Recreational Swim Team; U Of KS; Jrnlsm.

SIGLER, JEREMY D; Chanute Sr HS; Chanute, KS; (2); FCA; Spanish Clb; JV Bsktbl; Intrml Ftbl; High Hon Roll; Amer Legion Bsbl; Natural Hlprs; KS Univ.

SIKES, CHELSEA C; Clifton-Clyde HS; Clyde, KS; (3); Drama Clb; NFL; Mrchg Band; Pep Band; School Play; Yrbk; Lit Mag; Hon Roll; KS St Univ; Psych.

SIKES, TERESA; Wellington Sr HS; Wellington, KS; (4); 5/122; Church Yth Grp; Drama Clb; Key Clb; Band; Chorus; Drm Mjr(t); Swing Chorus; Bsktbl; L Capt Socr; NHS; York Coll; Bus.

SILHAN, FRED R; Centre Jr Sr HS; Marion, KS; (2); Letterman Clb; Natl FFA Org; VP Pep Clb; School Play; VP Frsh Cls; VP Soph Cls; Var L Ftbl; Trk; Wt Lftg; NHS.

SILLS, JAKE D; Garden City Sr HS; Garden City, KS; (3); 100/450; Church Yth Grp; FCA; Letterman Clb; Teachers Aide; Varsity Clb; Var L Bsktbl; Var L Ftbl; Score Keeper; Var L Trk; Wt Lftg; All ST Ftbl/Bsktbl; 2nd Pl ST Track Meet Javlin; KS ST; Sprts Med.

SILSBY, CHRISTOPHER; Topeka HS; Topeka, KS; (2); #1 in class; NFL; Scholastic Bowl; Thesps; Acpl Chr; Orch; School Musical; High Hon Roll; Boy Scts; Drama Clb; Math Tm; ASHME Exam; Natl Fornsc Leag Natl Trnmnt; Spirit, Svc & Coop Awd.

SILVIS, RHONDA R; Marmaton Valley Jr Sr HS; Gas, KS; (2); Church Yth Grp; Spanish Clb; Chorus; Cit Awd; Hon Roll; Art; Hnrb Mntn Citywide Amer Legion Essay Cont; Hawaii Pacific; Photo; Florist.

SIMLER, CHERI L; Wichita West HS; Wichita, KS; (4); 32/246; Church Yth Grp; French Clb; Acpl Chr; Chorus; Variety Show; Nwsp; Lit Mag; Ofcr Frsh Cls; Hon Roll; Prfct Atten Awd; Frnch Clb; JROTC Clb Vol.

SIMMONS, ADIENNE D; Riverton Schl; Galena, KS; (4); 3/57; Am Leg Aux Girls St; Math Clb; Scholastic Bowl; VP Sec Science Clb; VP Spanish Clb; Orch; VP Sr Cls; Pres Stu Cncl; Var Capt Bsktbl; Var Capt Chrldng; Vanderbilt U; Sec Ed.

SIMMONS, BRANDIE M; Great Bend Sr HS; Great Bend, KS; (3); German Clb; Hosp Aide; Pep Clb; Acpl Chr; Band; Chorus; Capt Color Guard; Mrchg Band; Pep Band; Hon Roll; Kayettes; Capt Of HS Flag Team; 4 Yr Coll; Archtctr/Drftng.

SIMMONS, LABRIAL T; Wyandotte HS; Kansas City, KS; (1); Spanish Clb; Chorus; Drill Tm; Nwsp; Swmmng; Vllybl; Cit Awd; High Hon Roll; Hon Roll; Baker Univ.

SIMMONS, MICAELA; Leavenworth HS; Leavenworth, KS; (2); 6/390; VP Church Yth Grp; Cmnty Wkr; Drama Clb; HOBY; Letterman Clb; Quiz Bowl; ROTC; SADD; Thesps; Acpl Chr; All ST Choir; Chldrns Choir; Chrch Vctn Bible Schl Msc Dir; Mdwstrn Msc Cmps Outstdng Fmle Vclst; Educl Admin.

SIMON, AMANDA L; Clearwater HS; Clearwater, KS; (2); Letterman Clb; Spanish Clb; SADD; Treas Frsh Cls; Treas Soph Cls; L Trk; JV Vllybl; L Wt Lftg; Stat Wt Lftg; NHS.

SIMON, AMY; Syracuse Jr Sr HS; Syracuse, KS; (1); Church Yth Grp; Pep Clb; Band; Chorus; Mrchg Band; Pep Band; Bsktbl; Chrldng; Vllybl; Hon Roll; KU; Dental Hygn.

SIMON, ANNE M; Andale HS; Colwich, KS; (3); Art Clb; Church Yth Grp; Spanish Clb; Varsity Clb; Rep Frsh Cls; JV Bsktbl; Var Powder Puff Ftbl; JV Var Trk; Var Vllybl; High Hon Roll; KS ST; Hlth.

SIMON, DANIEL J; Andale HS; Andale, KS; (2); Spanish Clb; Band; Mrchg Band; Pep Band; JV Bsktbl; JV Ftbl; Intrml Wt Lftg; High Hon Roll; NHS; KS ST; Engr.

SIMON, JASON; Leroy HS; Le Roy, KS; (3); Am Leg Boys St; 4-H; Quiz Bowl; Band; Drm Mjr(t); Mrchg Band; Pep Band; Bsktbl; Trk; Hon Roll.

SIMON, JERAD L; Leroy HS; Le Roy, KS; (3); 3/20; Am Leg Boys St; 4-H; Quiz Bowl; Bsktbl; Trk; High Hon Roll; Natl Young Ldrs Conf; Comp Engrng.

SIMON, JEREMY R; Leavenworth HS; Leavenworth, KS; (3); Letterman Clb; Office Aide; Spanish Clb; Varsity Clb; Variety Show; Var Bsktbl; Var Diving; Var Ftbl; Var Socr; Var Swmmng; All City Newcomer Of The Yr, All Dist Defensive MVP, All City Linebacker 95; Univ Of KS; Pharmacy.

SIMON, MEGAN T; Bishop Miege HS; Overland Park, KS; (2); 11/200; Pep Clb; Service Clb; SADD; Varsity Clb; Chorus; Drill Tm; Swmmng; High Hon Roll.

SIMON, MELODY A; Wichita North HS; Wichita, KS; (2); French Clb; GAA; Letterman Clb; Swmmng; Hon Roll; Stdnt Of Month.

SIMON, NATHAN J; Andale HS; Mount Hope, KS; (1); Chess Clb; Quiz Bowl; Scholastic Bowl; SADD; Band; Mrchg Band; Orch; Pep Band; Bsktbl; Crs Cntry.

SIMON, STEVEN A; Northeast HS; Arma, KS; (2); 4/45; Scholastic Bowl; Band; Mrchg Band; Pep Band; VP Frsh Cls; Rep Stu Cncl; JV Var Bsbl; JV Bsktbl; JV Var Ftbl; Var Trk; Pittsburg St Univ; Tech.

SIMON, SUZANNE C; Northeast HS; Arma, KS; (2); 11/45; HOBY; Band; Mrchg Band; Pep Band; School Play; Stage Crew; Yrbk; Rep Stu Cncl; JV Var Bsktbl; JV Chrldng; Pittsburgh St Univ; Zoolgy.

SIMONCIC, STEFANIE J; Southeast HS; Cherokee, KS; (3); Pres Church Yth Grp; Band; Capt Drill Tm; Chrldng; Pom Pon; Trk; Hon Roll; NHS.

SIMONE, ANTHONY J; Bishop Miege HS; Kansas City, MO; (4); 47/160; Debate Tm; NFL; Pep Clb; Teachers Aide; Var Trk; High Hon Roll; Hon Roll; Peer Helper; Guitar/Band; KS U; Opthamology.

SIMONEAU, CARRIE L; Concordia Jr Sr HS; Concordia, KS; (4); FBLA; Letterman Clb; Thesps; Acpl Chr; VP Sr Cls; Pom Pon; Trk; Cit Awd; NHS; Miss KS Natl Teenager; KS ST Univ; Archtctr.

SIMONEAU, JENNIFER D; Palco HS; Damar, KS; (3); Treas 4-H; Pres Letterman Clb; Model UN; VP Natl FFA Org; Band; Sec Frsh Cls; Sec Soph Cls; VP Jr Cls; VP Sr Cls; Var L Bsktbl; KS U; Pre-Med.

SIMONEAU, WESTON; Hays HS; Hays, KS; (3); 22/242; Var Bsktbl; Var Ftbl; Var Golf; High Hon Roll; NHS.

SIMONICH, JACKSON L; Lawrence HS; Lawrence, KS; (2); Cmnty Wkr; Spanish Clb; Acpl Chr; Variety Show; High Hon Roll; Hon Roll; Pres Schlr; Lawrence HS Bike Club; K-State Engrng Schl; Chem Engr.

SIMONS, CORY; Bishop Carroll Catholic HS; Wichita, KS; (2); Church Yth Grp; High Hon Roll; Hon Roll.

SIMONS, JOSH J; Jayhawk-Linn HS; Mound City, KS; (4); 5/37; Art Clb; Band; Mrchg Band; Pep Band; Treas Sr Cls; Var Capt Bsktbl; Var Capt Ftbl; Wt Lftg; High Hon Roll; Pittsburg ST U; Plastics Engr.

SIMONS, JOSHUA; Paola HS; Paola, KS; (4); 16/113; Am Leg Boys St; Church Yth Grp; FCA; Office Aide; Church Choir; High Hon Roll; Hon Roll; NHS; St Schlr; Boys St Cnslr 96; Safe Schls Comm; Speaker Drug Reduction Pgm & Rotry Clb; Emporia ST U; Math Tchr.

SIMPLER, DEBBIE D; Derby HS; Derby, KS; (3); 79/368; GAA; Key Clb; Teachers Aide; Varsity Clb; Var L Sftbl; Var L Vllybl; Wt Lftg; Hon Roll.

SIMPSON, ANGIE; Shawnee Mission Nw HS; Shawnee Mission, KS; (4); 36/417; Drama Clb; Q&S; Science Clb; Teachers Aide; Thesps; School Musical; School Play; Nwsp; High Hon Roll; NHS; Guitar; Music Theory; Johnson Cty CC; Jrnlsm.

SIMPSON, COURTNEY A; Blue Valley HS; Stanley, KS; (2); 67/276; Debate Tm; Intnl Clb; NFL; Chorus; Hon Roll; Div I Rating At CMSU Span Cmptn; 1st Pl Span Quiz Bowl; Solo At Regnl Choir Cmptn; Frgn Lang; Scndry Ed.

SIMPSON, DONALD J; Ft Scott HS; Garland, KS; (3); Church Yth Grp; FCA; Band; Chorus; Mrchg Band; Orch; Pep Band; School Musical; Swing Chorus; Hon Roll; All St Choir 2 Yrs.

SIMPSON, ERIN; Shawnee Mission Nw Sr HS; Lenexa, KS; (3); 2/465; Debate Tm; Pres Intnl Clb; JA; Key Clb; Model UN; NFL; Speech Tm; Pres SADD; JV Tennis; High Hon Roll; Compttr NFL Natn Finls 96; 3rd KS St Debt Trnmt; Authr Of Natl Qualfyng Stu Congrss Legsltn; Pol Sci; Frgn Relations.

SIMPSON, KATHERINE; Garden City Sr HS; Garden City, KS; (3); 15/331; Art Clb; Church Yth Grp; Red Cross Aide; VICA; Band; Mrchg Band; Pep Band; High Hon Roll; Jr NHS; Prfct Atten Awd; Numerous Art Wi Awds; Med.

SIMPSON, KELLY C; Topeka West HS; Topeka, KS; (4); 44/254; Church Yth Grp; Pep Clb; Capt Drill Tm; School Musical; Variety Show; Rep Sr Cls; Capt Chrldng; Hon Roll; NHS; Bus Awd; 96 Yng Arts Awd In Dnce; KS St Univ; Human Ecolgy.

SIMPSON, MANDY L; Wellington Sr HS; Wellington, KS; (3); 56/175; Church Yth Grp; Chrldng; High Hon Roll; Hon Roll; Jr NHS; All Amer Chrldr Awd 94-95; Frnch Awd 94; KS U; Nrsng.

SIMPSON, NEIL; Garden City Sr HS; Garden City, KS; (3); German Clb; Office Aide; Var Bsbl; Hon Roll; Odyssy Mnd; Mrktng.

SIMPSON, SUMMER; Stafford Jr Sr HS; Stafford, KS; (4); 2/20; FHA; Office Aide; Spanish Clb; School Play; Rep Soph Cls; Sec Sr Cls; Var L Bsktbl; Var L Trk; Var L Vllybl; Wt Lftg; CPL All Leag Vllybl, Bsktbl 2 Yrs; Cntrl Prairie Leag Hnr Stu 2 Yrs; 2a St 100m Hurdle Champ; Pratt CC; Sports Med.

SIMPSON, T J; Highland HS; Highland, KS; (1); 2/24; Church Yth Grp; 4-H; Natl FFA Org; School Musical; Treas Frsh Cls; Var JV Bsktbl; Chrldng; Trk; Var JV Vllybl; Hon Roll; KS ST U.

SIMS, ANGELA J; Sumner Acad Of Arts & Science; Kansas City, KS; (1); Cmnty Wkr; JCL; Latin Clb; Pep Clb; Spanish Clb; Chorus; Church Choir; Drill Tm; Rep Soph Cls; Hon Roll; Bus Admin.

SIMS, BENJAMIN J; Salina HS South; Salina, KS; (2); Chorus; Ofcr Bsbl; Ftbl; Hon Roll; Renaissance Clb; Babe Ruth Bsbl All Star Team; KS ST.

SIMS, CHANICE R; Wyandotte HS; Kansas City, KS; (2); Church Yth Grp; Dance Clb; Drama Clb; Girl Scts; Pep Clb; Acpl Chr; Church Choir; Drill Tm; School Musical; School Play; Comm Svcs; Rank 1st In Dist Vocal Festival; Clarke U; Fashion Designer.

SIMS, JARED O; Meade HS; Meade, KS; (1); Church Yth Grp; Pep Clb; Quiz Bowl; Band; Mrchg Band; Pep Band; Var Bsktbl; Var Crs Cntry; Var Trk; Cit Awd.

SIMS, JEFFREY L; Sumner Acad Of Arts & Science; Kansas City, KS; (3); Church Yth Grp; FCA; Latin Clb; Spanish Clb; Church Choir; Orch; Rep Soph Cls; Intrml Bsktbl; Var Ftbl; Hon Roll; Black & Weatch Engrng Explorers Mem; Univ Of Southern CA; Arch Engr.

SIMS, LAUREL R; Buhler HS; Buhler, KS; (2); Church Yth Grp; FCA; Letterman Clb; Spanish Clb; Band; Mgr(s); JV Var Tennis; High Hon Roll; Pres Acad Fit Awd; JV Bsktbl; Denver Svc Project Participant; Play Clarinet In Chrch Praise Band; Rel.

SIMS, NEELY N; Blue Valley Northwest HS; Leawood, KS; (4); 127/345; Cmnty Wkr; Pep Clb; SADD; Acpl Chr; Chorus; Stage Crew; Var L Chrldng; Golf; Powder Puff Ftbl; JV Socr; Amer Ath Achvmnt Awd; Baker Univ; Ed.

SIMS, PARKS; Pierson Jr HS; Kansas City, KS; (1); Church Yth Grp; Cmnty Wkr; Church Choir; School Play; Rptr Nwsp; Rep Stu Cncl; Trk; Cit Awd; Drama Clb; Spanish Clb; Stdnt Ldrshp Team; Blck His Mnth Dir 96; Law/Bus.

SIMS, ROBYNN M; Buhler HS; Buhler, KS; (2); Church Yth Grp; FCA; Letterman Clb; Q&S; Band; Rptr Nwsp; JV Bsktbl; Mgr(s); JV Vllybl; High Hon Roll; Chrch Nwsltr Rptr; Denver Comm Svc Project; Praise Band Chrch; Chrstn Univ; Jrnlst.

SIMS, SENA M; Meade HS; Meade, KS; (3); Church Yth Grp; Library Aide; Pep Clb; Spanish Clb; Band; Chorus; Mrchg Band; Pep Band; School Musical; Yrbk; Kayettes; M-Clb; Ambassador Univ; Sec Ed.

SINCLAIR, AARON; Atchison Sr HS; Atchison, KS; (4); 3/125; Am Leg Boys St; Boy Scts; Church Yth Grp; French Clb; Ed Yrbk; JV Bsktbl; Stat Ftbl; Var Socr; High Hon Roll; NHS; Kayettes; Bsktbl Coach 7th-8th Grd Tm; Eagle By Sct; Med.

SINCLAIR, MEGAN A; Kapaun-Mt Carmel HS; Wichita, KS; (1); Drama Clb; French Clb; School Play; Stage Crew; High Hon Roll; Jr NHS; Dnc/Blt/Jz; Cmptv Dnc Co; Wake Forest; Corp Atty.

SINGER, ERICH K; Hayden HS; Topeka, KS; (2); Debate Tm; NFL; Ftbl; Wrstlng; Hon Roll; NHS; Tchng.

SINGER, MICHAEL A; Topeka HS; Topeka, KS; (3); Teachers Aide; Var Ftbl; JV Trk; Hon Roll; KS ST.

SINGER, NICHOLAS R; Goddard HS; Wichita, KS; (2); Church Yth Grp; Debate Tm; Chorus; School Play; Golf; Hon Roll; Mdrgl Chr.

SINGLETON, JACQUELYN; Gardner-Edgerton HS; Edgerton, KS; (4); 2/110; Church Yth Grp; FCA; Pep Clb; Spanish Clb; Teachers Aide; School Musical; Rep Frsh Cls; Sec Soph Cls; VP Jr Cls; Treas Stu Cncl; Ntrl Hlprs; Washburn In Topeka; Scndry Ed.

SINGLETON, JESSICA; Gardner-Edgerton HS; Edgerton, KS; (4); 1/109; Am Leg Aux Girls St; Church Yth Grp; HOBY; Pres Frsh Cls; VP Soph Cls; Sec Jr Cls; Pres Sr Cls; L Var Crs Cntry; NHS; St Schlr; Yth Ldr Core; Nrsng.

SINGMASTER, NICOLE R; Ft Scott HS; Arcadia, KS; (2); Church Yth Grp; FCA; Pep Clb; Chorus; Church Choir; School Musical; Hon Roll; Church Yth Grp Pres 2 Yrs; Wmns Ensmbl; Frosh Mixed Ensmbl; Pittsburg ST.

SINNETT, STASHA; Southeast Saline Schl; Assaria, KS; (1); Chrldng; Univ Of NE; Bus.

SIPP, STEPHANIE C; Emporia HS; Emporia, KS; (3); 40/270; Church Yth Grp; GAA; Office Aide; Varsity Clb; Var Diving; Var Capt Gym; Var Wt Lftg; Cit Awd; High Hon Roll; Pres Acad Fit Awd; Gymnstcs Coach Mdwst Gym; Yth Ldr Indpndnt Lvng.

SIROKY, CHEREE; South HS; Wichita, KS; (1); Church Yth Grp; Dance Clb; Chorus; Rep Frsh Cls; Chrldng; Pom Pon; High Hon Roll.

SIS, KATHRYN; Atwood HS; Atwood, KS; (3); Sec Church Yth Grp; 4-H; Hosp Aide; Band; Church Choir; Swing Chorus; Capt Chrldng; Var Trk; Var Vllybl; Hon Roll; U NE Lincoln; Dental Hygnst.

SISEL, ERIK M; Blue Valley Northwest HS; Overland Park, KS; (2); 102/409; Var Bsbl; JV Bsktbl; Hon Roll; NHS.

SISK, CHERYL ANN; Campus HS; Haysville, KS; (4); 80/219; Computer Clb; Dance Clb; Science Clb; SADD; Teachers Aide; Band; Drill Tm; Mrchg Band; Pep Band; Pom Pon; Multi Yr Listing; Wichita ST U; Bio.

SISK, ERIN; Olathe South Sr HS; Olathe, KS; (3); 1/416; Church Yth Grp; Drama Clb; French Clb; Letterman Clb; Service Clb; Teachers Aide; Pres Sec Acpl Chr; Church Choir; Cit Awd; High Hon Roll.

SISNEY, BROCK G; Ft Scott HS; Arcadia, KS; (3); Pep Clb; Am Leg Aux Girls St; Hon Roll; Prfct Atten Awd; Pittsburg ST; Bus Mgmt.

SISSON, ADAM F; Spearville Jr Sr HS; Spearville, KS; (2); Pep Clb; Quiz Bowl; Scholastic Bowl; Acpl Chr; Band; Chorus; School Play; VP Soph Cls; High Hon Roll; NHS; Dodge City CC; Bio.

SISSON, KENNETH E; Derby HS; Derby, KS; (3); 49/387; Cmnty Wkr; ROTC; Service Clb; Crs Cntry; Trk; High Hon Roll; Hon Roll; NHS; KS Rgnts Hon Acad; Word Odessy Of The Mind; Var Crs Cntry/Trck/3 Tm Ltrd Crs Cntry/2 Tm Ltr Trch; IA ST; Genetics.

SISSON, STEVEN B; Derby HS; Derby, KS; (1); Debate Tm; ROTC; Scholastic Bowl; Speech Tm; Hon Roll; Natl Sci Mrt & Natl Svc & Ldrshp Awds; Sapphire Rating In Natl Forensics League; MI; Phy Asst.

SIVILS, TYSON J; Oxford HS; Geuda Springs, KS; (2); FCA; Varsity Clb; Ofcr Bsbl; Bsktbl; Ftbl; Hon Roll; NHS; Hnrable Mntn Ptchr; Walter Johnson Leag Chmpns.

SIZELOVE, JAMES; Shawnee Mission S Sr HS; Overland Park, KS; (4); Hon Roll; Ntl Merit Ltr; Art; Piano; U Of KS.

SJOGREN, STACY D; Derby Christian Schl; Tucson, AZ; (3); Church Yth Grp; Teachers Aide; Church Choir; Yrbk; Bsktbl; Vllybl; Hon Roll; Bible Clb; Southwestern Bible Coll; Tchr.

SKACH, CHRISTAL; Goddard HS; Wichita, KS; (4); 1/145; Church Yth Grp; Q&S; Science Clb; Ed Nwsp; Ed Yrbk; Var L Bsktbl; Capt L Vllybl; Pres NHS; Sal; Key Clb; Natl Sci Olympiad Sci Of Fitness Cont 9th Pl; KS Newman Coll; Nrsng.

SKAGGS, CARA; Derby HS; Derby, KS; (3); Church Yth Grp; FCA; NFL; SADD; Acpl Chr; Variety Show; Rep Jr Cls; Chrldng; Hon Roll; NHS; Dance Studio 10 Yrs; Pittsburg ST Univ; PT.

SKAGGS, TONYA; Derby HS; Derby, KS; (2); Church Yth Grp; Chorus; Variety Show; JV Var Chrldng; JV Var Gym; JV Var Socr; Hon Roll; Hockey; Vet.

SKEA, MATT; Faith Christian Schl; Ottawa, KS; (2); Church Yth Grp; Bsktbl; Socr; Hon Roll; Prfct Atten Awd.

SKELTON, APRYL C; Halstead HS; Newton, KS; (3); Art Clb; Church Yth Grp; Cmnty Wkr; German Clb; SADD; Chorus; School Musical; Stage Crew; Yrbk; Mgr(s); Bio; Zoology.

SKILES, MONICA L; Maize HS; Wichita, KS; (3); Church Yth Grp; Spanish Clb; SADD; Hon Roll; NHS.

SKILLEN, MATTHEW G; Maize HS; Wichita, KS; (2); 98/291; Drama Clb; Thesps; Band; Jazz Band; Pep Band; School Play; Stage Crew; Ice Hcky; Awd Bst Spprtng Actor In Family Man; Active In Karate Clss/On Wichita Jr Thndr Trvlng Ice Hcky Tm; Law Enfrcmnt/Music.

SKILLMAN, SHANNON K; Burlington HS; New Strawn, KS; (3); Pres FHA; Girl Scts; Teachers Aide; JV Trk; Cit Awd; High Hon Roll; Hon Roll; NHS; Emporia St Univ; Tchng.

SKINNER, KATIE A; St Thomas Aquinas HS; Olathe, KS; (4); 13/231; Hosp Aide; Key Clb; Pep Clb; SADD; Ed Nwsp; Var L Tennis; JV Trk; NHS; Pres Schlr; St Schlr; Natl Foreign Lang Awd; St Mary Coll; Premed.

SKINNER, KATRINA; Garden City Sr HS; Garden City, KS; (4); 24/324; Church Yth Grp; Debate Tm; NFL; Service Clb; Speech Tm; Thesps; Band; Flag Corp; Kiwanis Awd; NHS; Manhattan Chrstn; Chrstn Svc.

SKINNER, ROSLYN D; Lawrence HS; Lawrence, KS; (2); 4-H; Teachers Aide; Nwsp; Rep Frsh Cls; Rep Soph Cls; Ofcr Stu Cncl; Capt Chrldng; Pom Pon; 4-H Awd; Hon Roll; Intnl Dance Troupe; U Of GA; Advertisingk.

SKINNER, WILLIAM E; Wichita East HS; Wichita, KS; (3); Church Yth Grp; Debate Tm; Church Choir; Back Acad; Urban League; Church Bsktbl; Banston Univ; Navy.

SKINTA, MATTHEW D; Andover HS; Andover, KS; (3); 35/156; Church Yth Grp; German Clb; Band; Mrchg Band; Hon Roll; Sci Olympd; Vet Asst; Prevet.

SKJONSBY, BRITT S; Blue Valley Northwest HS; Overland Park, KS; (3); Church Yth Grp; Math Clb; Varsity Clb; Lit Mag; Powder Puff Ftbl; Socr; Trk; Vllybl; Hon Roll; Ntl Merit Ltr; Cmnty Svc Spec Olympics; Multi Yr Listee; Psych.

SKOLAUT, ANGELA C; Great Bend Sr HS; Great Bend, KS; (4); Church Yth Grp; German Clb; Intnl Clb; Pep Clb; SADD; Acpl Chr; Band; Chorus; Church Choir; Mrchg Band; Cllgrphy; City Band; Lcnsd Amtr Radio Oprtr; Barton Cty CC; Elem Ed.

SKOLAUT, PAUL J; Trinity Catholic HS; Hutchinson, KS; (1); Debate Tm; Math Tm; NFL; Speech Tm; Jazz Band; Pep Band; Pres Frsh Cls; JV Bsktbl; JV Tennis; High Hon Roll.

SLACK, AMANDA K; Rose Hill HS; Rose Hill, KS; (3); FHA; Hosp Aide; SADD; L Mgr(s); Var L Sftbl; JV Vllybl; Hon Roll; 3 Acad Ltrs; Peer Helpers 3 Yrs; Wichita ST Univ; Phy Therapy.

SLACK, MELISSA B; Pittsburg HS; Pittsburg, KS; (3); Q&S; Mgr Yrbk; Var Crs Cntry; Var Trk; Pittsburg ST Univ.

SLAGLE, ANDREA; Ness City HS; Ness City, KS; (3); 2/38; Church Yth Grp; Pep Clb; Quiz Bowl; Speech Tm; Band; Chorus; School Musical; JV Vllybl; High Hon Roll; NHS; KAYS Pt Drctr; CNA; Connie Belin/Jacqueline N Blank Intl Ctr Gftd Educ Tlnt Dvlpmnt; NRPHSS; Med.

SLAGLE, MELISSA; Ness City HS; Ness City, KS; (1); Church Yth Grp; NFL; Pep Clb; Thesps; JV Bsktbl; JV Trk; JV Vllybl; High Hon Roll; Kay Club; Tchr.

SLATER, JEREMY S; Olpe Schl; Olpe, KS; (3); Boy Scts; Cmnty Wkr; Quiz Bowl; Scholastic Bowl; Nwsp; Yrbk; Treas Sr Cls; JV Var Ftbl; High Hon Roll; Hon Roll; KS St Jrnlsm Cont-1st Editrl; Drama-Schl Play; Stu Colmnst-Empor Gazztt; Natl HS Novelist Comp Fnlst; Jrnlsm; Creative Wrtng.

SLATER, JOSEPH L; Jefferson West HS; Meriden, KS; (3); 33/75; Treas Drama Clb; Pep Clb; Speech Tm; Thesps; Acpl Chr; Band; Chorus; Jazz Band; Mrchg Band; Pep Band; Dist Bnd; Topeka Yth Wind Ensmble; Forensics; KS Univ; Mus Ed.

SLATES, MELISSA M; Wichita South HS; Wichita, KS; (1); Asian Clb; Art.

SLATTERY, ALESHA M; Dodge City HS; Dodge City, KS; (2); Teachers Aide; Band; Mrchg Band; Pep Band; Hon Roll; Frosh Bsktbl; KS Univ; Psych.

SLAUGHTER, CASEY; Maize HS; Wichita, KS; (3); 30/246; Cmnty Wkr; Office Aide; Spanish Clb; Teachers Aide; JV Ftbl; High Hon Roll; Hon Roll; NHS; Govnrs Task Force Kids Voting; Yth Bwlng Coach Vol; Names Dsplyd Ntl Bldg Hall Of Fame 2 300 Games 96.

SLAVEN JR, RONALD D; Arkansas City HS; Arkansas City, KS; (2); Boy Scts; Church Yth Grp; Debate Tm; NFL; SADD; Temple Yth Grp; JV Crs Cntry; High Hon Roll; Hon Roll; Prfct Atten Awd; Order Of Arrow; Nom Candidate Otstndng Stdnt In Comm; Excels Wrtng Assessmnt Skills; Brigham Yng Univ; Cmptrs.

SLAYMAN, JOHN; Osawatomie HS; Osawatomie, KS; (4); Band; Chorus; Mrchg Band; Orch; Pep Band; School Musical; Stage Crew; Variety Show; Var Ftbl; Wt Lftg; Electronic Engr.

SLAYTON, DAVID N; Derby HS; Derby, KS; (4); 151/341; Church Yth Grp; FCA; Var L Bsktbl; Hon Roll; Chrch Mission Trips Yth, VBS Helper, Yth Worship Ldr; Jr Olympic Try-Outs Mens Vllybl; WWAAHSS; Butler Cty CC; Acctng; CPA.

SLECHTA, EMILIE M; Ellsworth HS; Ellsworth, KS; (2); 19/90; Church Yth Grp; Natl FFA Org; Varsity Clb; Band; Mrchg Band; Pep Band; Crs Cntry; Mgr(s); Trk; High Hon Roll; KS ST Univ; Tchng.

SLEDER, MATT; Goddard HS; Goddard, KS; (3); Church Yth Grp; FCA; JV Bsbl; Var Ftbl; Wt Lftg; Var Wrstlng; Hon Roll; NHS; All ST Wrstlr; Bus.

SLEICHTER, JILL M; Abilene HS; Abilene, KS; (3); 5/115; Am Leg Aux Girls St; Church Yth Grp; FBLA; German Clb; Quiz Bowl; Chorus; School Musical; Ofcr Stu Cncl; Var L Trk; High Hon Roll; OT/GERMAN.

SLEPICKA, KEVIN R; Santa Fe Trail Jr HS; Olathe, KS; (1); Boy Scts; Drama Clb; Teachers Aide; Band; Jazz Band; Mrchg Band; School Play; Variety Show; Sec Treas Stu Cncl; Hon Roll; Cmptr Sci.

SLEPICKA, KIRSTIN E; Olathe North Sr HS; Olathe, KS; (4); 51/375; Latin Clb; Band; Color Guard; Mrchg Band; Lit Mag; Ofcr Frsh Cls; Ofcr Soph Cls; Ofcr Jr Cls; Ofcr Sr Cls; Bsktbl; KS St Univ; Bus.

SLIPKE, CHERYL M; Downs HS; Cawker City, KS; (3); VP FHA; Co-Capt Drill Tm; Ed Yrbk; JV Bsktbl; Var Crs Cntry; High Hon Roll; NHS; Sec Soph Cls; Sec Jr Cls; KS ST Univ; Tchng/Elem.

SLOAN, EMILY A; Blue Valley North HS; Leawood, KS; (2); Orch; Var Trk; Var Vllybl; High Hon Roll; KAYS Clb Pres; St Orch 1st Violin; Super Rating Piano; All Sun Cntry Trk & 2nd Team Vllybl.

SLOAN, J; Horton HS; Powhattan, KS; (3); 1/47; 4-H; HOBY; Quiz Bowl; Teachers Aide; School Play; Pres Soph Cls; Pres Jr Cls; Golf; High Hon Roll; NHS; Scndry Educ.

SLOAN, JAMES C; Horton HS; Powhattan, KS; (3); 1/37; Am Leg Boys St; 4-H; HOBY; Scholastic Bowl; School Play; Pres Soph Cls; Pres Jr Cls; JV L Golf; Cit Awd; NHS.

SLOAN, MAHOGANY D; Wyandotte HS; Kansas City, KS; (2); Church Yth Grp; Cmnty Wkr; Drama Clb; Chorus; Church Choir; Drill Tm; Ofcr Soph Cls; Pom Pon; Vllybl; Hon Roll.

SLOBOJAN, BOBBIE; St Marys HS; Saint Marys, KS; (2); FBLA; Pep Clb; Drill Tm; Var Chrldng; JV Vllybl; High Hon Roll; Mar Bio.

SLOUS, JASON D; Hoisington HS; Hoisington, KS; (3); Am Leg Boys St; Ofcr Bsbl; Capt Ftbl; Wt Lftg; High Hon Roll; NHS; Hnrb Mntn All-St Mid Linebacker Ftbl; All-League Mid Linebacker Ftbl; All-Area Mid Linebacker Ftbl; Wharton U; Investment Banking.

SLOYER, NIKKI; Kapaun-Mt Carmel HS; Derby, KS; (3); Cmnty Wkr; Hosp Aide; Teachers Aide; Chorus; Var Chrldng; JV Sftbl; Vllybl; Med.

SLY, DEBORAH L; Olathe North Sr HS; Olathe, KS; (2); Church Yth Grp; Dance Clb; Ofcr Drama Clb; Pep Clb; Spanish Clb; Thesps; Acpl Chr; Chorus; School Musical; School Play; Cert Of Hnr Outstdng Achvmt In Thetr; Best Ovrll Renssnc Festvl Partcpnt 95; St Solo & Ensmbl Festvl.

SMAIL, EMILY S; Washburn Rural HS; Auburn, KS; (3); 150/400; Church Yth Grp; Spanish Clb; SADD; Chorus; Church Choir; Variety Show; Hon Roll; Sftbl; Sun Schl Tchr; Emporia; Tchr.

SMAJDA, JON M; Shawnee Mission W Sr HS; Lenexa, KS; (2); Yrbk; Var L Crs Cntry; Var L Trk; High Hon Roll; Acad Lttr.

SMALL, CHRISTOPHER M; Junction City HS; Junction City, KS; (2); Church Yth Grp; Cmnty Wkr; Quiz Bowl; Band; Mrchg Band; Pep Band; Nwsp; Var Bsbl; Var Bsktbl; Var Ftbl; KS Rgnts Hnrs Acad; KS Univ; Sprts Med.

SMALL, DUSTIN A; Chapman HS; Junction City, KS; (3); 3/100; Cmnty Wkr; SADD; Stage Crew; Treas Frsh Cls; Treas Soph Cls; Treas Jr Cls; Treas Sr Cls; Rep Stu Cncl; Var Bsktbl; Var Ftbl; Hi Y Treas; KS ST Univ; Engrng.

SMALLEY, CARY S; St Thomas Aquinas HS; Leawood, KS; (3); Boy Scts; Church Yth Grp; Debate Tm; FBLA; NFL; Ski Clb; Spanish Clb; High Hon Roll; NHS; Phy; Pre-Med.

SMARSH, SARAH; Kingman HS; Murdock, KS; (2); 1/80; Rptr FBLA; SADD; School Play; Treas Soph Cls; JV Bsktbl; Var L Chrldng; Var L Trk; High Hon Roll; NHS; Art Clb; Teens Today Ldrs Tmrrw; 1st Pl Bus & Intro To Bus Comms St FBLA Conf; Bd Of Rgnts Hnrs Acad; Wrtng.

SMART, AMANDA L; Leavenworth HS; Leavenworth, KS; (1); Band; Mrchg Band; Pep Band; Rep Frsh Cls; High Hon Roll; Goodfellows; Frosh Hnr Band Acad/Band Lttr; ST Solos II Rating/Regnl Solos I Rating; 4 Yr Univ; Pub Rltns/Music Perf.

SMART, BRYAN W; Burlingame HS; Burlingame, KS; (4); 8/36; Am Leg Boys St; Church Yth Grp; FBLA; Letterman Clb; Varsity Clb; Band; Chorus; Jazz Band; Mrchg Band; Pep Band; Masonic Band; Neosho Cty CC; Sports Med.

SMART JR, JOHN W; Wichita Southeast HS; Wichita, KS; (3); Church Yth Grp; Cmnty Wkr; Office Aide; Chorus; JV Bsbl; JV Var Bsktbl; High Hon Roll; Jr NHS; NHS; Black Awareness; Gospel Choir; PT.

SMELTZER JR, ROGER W; Andover HS; Wichita, KS; (4); Boy Scts; Church Yth Grp; Debate Tm; FCA; Model UN; NFL; Spanish Clb; SADD; Ofcr Bsbl; Ftbl; Eagle Sct; Frgn Lang Stu In Quito Ecuador 95-96; Yth Group & Span Clb Pres; CPA; Lawyer.

SMIESHEK, GINGER; Paola HS; Paola, KS; (3); 13/138; Drama Clb; HOBY; Scholastic Bowl; Thesps; Band; Chorus; Flag Corp; Orch; Chrldng; NHS; KS ST U; Chem Engrng.

SMILEY, JERRY; Columbus HS; Scammon, KS; (1); Church Yth Grp; FCA; Var Bsbl; JV Bsktbl; High Hon Roll; PSU; Sprts/Math.

SMILEY, MATTHEW A; Emporia HS; Emporia, KS; (3); FCA; Teachers Aide; Var Bsbl; JV Bsktbl; Var Ftbl; Var Socr; Hon Roll; Mst Admrd Stdnts In Class.

SMILOR, MATTHEW W; Blue Valley North HS; Overland Park, KS; (2); Church Yth Grp; Model UN; School Musical; School Play; Golf; Wrstlng; Hon Roll; Bus.

SMITH, AARON C; Gardner-Edgerton HS; Edgerton, KS; (3); Band; Church Choir; Mrchg Band; Orch; Pep Band; School Musical; High Hon Roll; St Orch; Natl Orch; Div I Rtng Trombone Solo; Mus Perf.

SMITH, ADRIENNE M; Ellinwood Jr Sr HS; Ellinwood, KS; (3); 1/46; Am Leg Aux Girls St; Church Yth Grp; Dance Clb; Pres Debate Tm; FCA; Quiz Bowl; VP Spanish Clb; Band; Chorus; Drill Tm; U Of KS.

SMITH, ALLISON L; Shawnee Mission E Sr HS; Shawnee Mission, KS; (2); Cmnty Wkr; Natl Beta Clb; Nwsp; Ed Yrbk; Hon Roll; NHS; Pres Acad Fit Awd; Russian Scholar Awd 3 Times; Russian/Bio.

SMITH, AMANDA; Shawnee Mission Northwest HS; Shawnee Mission, KS; (3); Church Yth Grp; Cmnty Wkr; Intnl Clb; Pep Clb; Capt Var Chrldng; Hon Roll; NHS; CUBS Pres; Prom Cmmtte; Shawnee Mission Cotilln.

SMITH, AMBER F; Humboldt HS; Humboldt, KS; (3); Drama Clb; Quiz Bowl; Band; Chorus; Mrchg Band; Pep Band; School Play; JV Vllybl; KS Lions St Band; KS Snt Page; Early Elem Ed.

SMITH, ANDREA D; Wyandotte HS; Kansas City, KS; (2); Office Aide; Ofcr Soph Cls; Bsktbl; High Hon Roll; Acad Excl In Phy Sci; K-ST; Psychologist.

SMITH, ANDREA R; Pittsburg HS; Pittsburg, KS; (4); 21/187; Church Yth Grp; Cmnty Wkr; DECA; FTA; Pep Clb; Teachers Aide; Chrldng; Sftbl; Hon Roll; Pittsburg ST U; Comp Info Sys.

SMITH, ANDREW M; Kingman HS; Kingman, KS; (3); 30/85; FBLA; Ski Clb; Teachers Aide; Ofcr Bsbl; JV Var Bsktbl; Ftbl; Sftbl; High Hon Roll; Hon Roll; Pres Acad Fit Awd; Wtrski; KS ST U; Engrng.

SMITH, ANDREW T; Liberal HS; Liberal, KS; (3); Boy Scts; Church Yth Grp; French Clb; FTA; VP Key Clb; Band; JV Intrml Bsktbl; JV Intrml Ftbl; JV Tennis; Prfct Atten Awd; Ft Hays ST U; Comp Sci.

SMITH, APRIL E; Campus HS; Haysville, KS; (1); Church Yth Grp; Band; Mrchg Band; VP Frsh Cls; Ofcr Stu Cncl; Bsktbl; Pom Pon; High Hon Roll; Cmps Pride; Cmps Life; Spec Olympics Vol.

SMITH, ASHANTI S; Topeka HS; Topeka, KS; (2); Office Aide; Teachers Aide; Hon Roll; St Francis Vol; STRAPP Mem; Washburn Univ; RN.

SMITH, AUDREY L; Kingman HS; Kingman, KS; (1); Church Yth Grp; FBLA; Girl Scts; SADD; Band; Chorus; Mrchg Band; Pep Band; VP Frsh Cls; Rep Stu Cncl; Eagle Hnr Roll.

SMITH, BECKY A; Lawrence HS; Lawrence, KS; (2); Church Yth Grp; Letterman Clb; Band; Chorus; Mrchg Band; Pep Band; Stat Bsktbl; Mgr(s); Cit Awd; Hon Roll; Stu Vol Of Yr; Stu Of Month; KS Univ; Sports Med.

SMITH, BRADLEY H; Smoky Valley HS; Lindsborg, KS; (2); Boy Scts; Letterman Clb; Teachers Aide; Varsity Clb; Band; Mrchg Band; Pep Band; Var Ftbl; Hon Roll; Natl & KS HS Rodeo Assns; Lvstck Ind.

SMITH, BREA M; Belle Plaine HS; Belle Plaine, KS; (3); Drama Clb; Math Tm; Scholastic Bowl; Spanish Clb; School Musical; Nwsp; NHS; French Clb; Math Clb; Quiz Bowl; Bronze Trade/Tech Stud Discover Card Tribute Awd 96; Belle Plaine Emerg Svcs Cadet Prgm Pres 2 Yrs; Johnson Cty CC; Paramedic.

SMITH, BRENT L; Wichita South HS; Wichita, KS; (1); Church Yth Grp; Band; Mrchg Band; Pep Band; OK Univ; Air Force.

SMITH, BRETT T; Garden City Sr HS; Garden City, KS; (1); Boy Scts; Pres Church Yth Grp; Cmnty Wkr; French Clb; Bsktbl; Wt Lftg; High Hon Roll; Brigham Young Univ.

SMITH, BRIAN; Peabody-Burns Jr Sr HS; Peabody, KS; (2); 1/30; Boy Scts; Quiz Bowl; Scholastic Bowl; Var Golf; JV Mgr(s); High Hon Roll; Hon Roll; Pres Acad Fit Awd; Pres Schlr; Heart Amer Schlr Awd 94 & 95; ACT 30; KU; Comp Sci.

SMITH, BROOKE A; Emporia HS; Emporia, KS; (3); Church Yth Grp; FCA; Sec Latin Clb; SADD; Varsity Clb; Bsktbl; Socr; High Hon Roll; Hon Roll; TS A&M Galveston; Marine Bio.

SMITH, BRYCE S; Louisburg HS; Louisburg, KS; (3); Am Leg Boys St; Letterman Clb; Office Aide; SADD; Sec Soph Cls; VP Jr Cls; Treas Stu Cncl; Ofcr Bsbl; Bsktbl; Ftbl; All Leag Hnrs Ftbl/Bsbl/Bsktbl.

SMITH, CAREY; Perry Lecompton HS; Perry, KS; (4); 24/90; Drama Clb; HOBY; VP Pres Pep Clb; Band; Mrchg Band; Pep Band; Mgr Stage Crew; Var L Bsktbl; Var L Trk; Var L Vllybl; KS ST U; Anml Sci.

SMITH, CARRIE; Hutchinson HS; Hutchinson, KS; (4); Dance Clb; Key Clb; Pep Clb; Teachers Aide; Chorus; Drill Tm; Nwsp; Powder Puff Ftbl; Vllybl; High Hon Roll; Hutchinson CC; Criminology.

SMITH, CARRIE A; Shawnee Mission N HS; Roeland Park, KS; (2); Pep Clb; Johnson Cnty CC; Engl.

SMITH, CHASIDY N; Hutchinson HS; Hutchinson, KS; (1); Church Yth Grp; High Hon Roll; Music; Band Instr.

SMITH, CHRIS J; Junction City HS; Junction City, KS; (1); Var Wrstlng; Hon Roll; Pres Acad Fit Awd; Went To St In Wrestling; Acad & Ath Ltr.

SMITH, CHRIS S; Maize HS; Wichita, KS; (2); Teachers Aide; Golf; Hon Roll; Wichita Tech Coll; Arcrft Engr.

SMITH, CHRISTAL; Goddard HS; Wichita, KS; (4); 1/145; Church Yth Grp; Q&S; Science Clb; SADD; Ed Yrbk; Bsktbl; Co-Capt Vllybl; Pres NHS; Sal; High Hon Roll; Sci Olympiad Team Natls; KS Newman Coll; Nrsng.

SMITH, CHRISTOPHER M; Shawnee Mission W Sr HS; Overland Park, KS; (3); 190/420; Art Clb; Latin Clb; Teachers Aide; Varsity Clb; Ftbl; Trk; Wrstlng; Hon Roll; Best Of Show, Grand Awd & 1st Pl Awd In Rsrch & Dev Forum For Wood Tech; Tchng; Phy Sports Medicine.

SMITH, CINDY; Sublette HS; Sublette, KS; (3); HOBY; Varsity Clb; Pres Band; Jazz Band; Pep Band; Var Capt Bsktbl; Var Trk; Var Vllybl; Hon Roll; NHS; TX A&M; Acctng.

SMITH, CRISTINA R; Oskaloosa HS; Oskaloosa, KS; (2); Church Yth Grp; FBLA; NFL; SADD; JV Bsktbl; JV Chrldng; Sftbl; Vllybl; Hon Roll; Pres Acad Fit Awd; Rcvd Acad Exclnc Awrd Recog Schlstc Achvmnt 95-; 5th Pl Awrd FBLA ST Prin/Proc Test; KS Univ; Med Fld/Biochem.

SMITH, CYNTHIA; Mulvane Sr HS; Mulvane, KS; (3); 15/131; Pres Church Yth Grp; VP FCA; SADD; Band; Chorus; Rep Stu Cncl; High Hon Roll; NHS; Prfct Atten Awd; Sndy Schl Tchr.

SMITH, DAIRA C; F L Schlagle HS; Kansas City, KS; (1); Church Yth Grp; Chorus; Church Choir; Variety Show; Bsktbl; Vllybl.

SMITH, DANIEL R; Wichita Heights HS; Wichita, KS; (4); Boy Scts; French Clb; Science Clb; Band; Mrchg Band; Crs Cntry; Trk; Hon Roll; Eagle Sct; KS ST Univ; Elec Engrng.

SMITH, DEANNA; Sumner Acad Of Arts & Science; Kansas City, KS; (3); Church Yth Grp; Sec Debate Tm; Drama Clb; FCA; Pres German Clb; Hosp Aide; Sec NFL; Pep Clb; Thesps; School Play.

SMITH, DEIDRA M; Emporia HS; Emporia, KS; (3); Am Leg Aux Girls St; Art Clb; Church Yth Grp; Cmnty Wkr; FCA; Girl Scts; Hosp Aide; Latin Clb; Office Aide; Pep Clb; Emporia ST U; Elem Ed.

SMITH, DIANA M; South Haven Schl; South Haven, KS; (2); 2/24; Church Yth Grp; FCA; Letterman Clb; Math Tm; Natl FFA Org; Pep Clb; Quiz Bowl; Scholastic Bowl; Band; Mrchg Band; KS ST Univ; Pre-Med.

SMITH, ERIKA; Sedgwick HS; Sedgwick, KS; (4); 4/24; FCA; Letterman Clb; Office Aide; Chorus; School Musical; Ed Yrbk; VP Sr Cls; Var L Vllybl; High Hon Roll; NHS; Wichita ST U; Bus Mgmt.

SMITH, GREG M; Emporia HS; Emporia, KS; (4); Boy Scts; Church Yth Grp; Cmnty Wkr; Latin Clb; Pep Clb; SADD; Socr; Tennis; Wrstlng; Hon Roll; Emporia ST U; Bus Mngmt.

SMITH, HILARY; Holton HS; Holton, KS; (2); FHA; Letterman Clb; Band; Drill Tm; Mrchg Band; Pep Band; Pres Soph Cls; Chrldng; Crs Cntry; Acad Ltr; KSU; Crmnl Jstc.

SMITH, HOLLY; Central Christian Schl; Hutchinson, KS; (2); 6/23; Church Yth Grp; FCA; FHA; Girl Scts; Pep Clb; Band; Chorus; Pep Band; School Musical; Variety Show.

SMITH, JACILYN L; Goodland HS; Goodland, KS; (3); 28/82; Church Yth Grp; Dance Clb; FHA; Library Aide; Office Aide; SADD; Drill Tm; Hon Roll; Johnson Cty CC; Dolphin Trnr.

SMITH, JACLYN R; Bishop Miege HS; Kansas City, MO; (3); 36/170; SADD; Phtg Nwsp; Rep Soph Cls; JV Sftbl; JV Swmmng; Var Tennis; High Hon Roll; NHS; Lifeguard; Bus Admin.

SMITH, JACOB N; Emporia HS; Emporia, KS; (2); Debate Tm; Var L Trk; High Hon Roll; Wildlife & Backpacking Clb; Medicine.

SMITH, JACQUE L; Oak Grove Baptist Schl; Bonner Springs, KS; (3); 2/12; Church Yth Grp; Office Aide; Pep Clb; Chorus; Church Choir; School Play; Pres Jr Cls; Bsktbl; Co-Capt Chrldng; Score Keeper; Camp Cook; Awana Wrkr; Math Ed.

SMITH, JAMES L; Sumner Acad Of Arts & Science; Basehor, KS; (3); Latin Clb; Spanish Clb; Orch; Ftbl; Wt Lftg; High Hon Roll; Hon Roll; Jr NHS; NHS; Pharm/Physician.

SMITH, JANE; Washington HS; Kansas City, KS; (2); Office Aide; Pep Clb; SADD; Teachers Aide; Pres Soph Cls; Ofcr Stu Cncl; Var Chrldng; Sftbl; Trk; High Hon Roll; Peerldr; George Washington; Pedtrcn.

SMITH, JENNIFER L; Wellington Sr HS; Wellington, KS; (2); 1/180; VP Church Yth Grp; SADD; Chorus; School Play; Yrbk; Rep Frsh Cls; Rep Soph Cls; Ofcr Stu Cncl; Vllybl; High Hon Roll; Wllngtn Hi Sngrs; Lions Clb Awd; Rtrn Awd; Knght Bt Nws Co Anchr; Arts.

SMITH, JEREMI A; Erie HS; Erie, KS; (4); 1/50; Art Clb; FCA; NFL; School Play; Nwsp; Yrbk; Treas Frsh Cls; Rep Jr Cls; Rep Sr Cls; Rep Stu Cncl; KS Assn For Yth; Target; Gftd Pgm; U KS At Lawrence; Adv.

SMITH, JEREMY M; Haven HS; Hutchinson, KS; (4); Church Yth Grp; Chorus; School Musical; Variety Show; Var Bsbl; Var Ftbl; High Hon Roll; NHS; Hutchinson Comm Jr Coll; Engrng.

SMITH, JON R; Rose Hill HS; Rose Hill, KS; (3); Cmnty Wkr; FCA; Pres Soph Cls; Rep Stu Cncl; JV Bsbl; JV Var Bsktbl; Var L Ftbl; Var L Trk; High Hon Roll; NHS; Acad Ltr; SILT Team Mem; St Trk Meet Participant; All League 2nd Team Offensive Guard For Ftbl 95; Engrng.

SMITH, JORDAN; Wichita West HS; Wichita, KS; (3); 14/283; Church Yth Grp; Orch; Ofcr Stu Cncl; Var Capt Chrldng; Socr; Hon Roll; NHS; Prfct Atten Awd; Abilene Chrstn U; Elem Ed.

SMITH, JORDAN R; Blue Valley Northwest HS; Overland Park, KS; (2); Cmnty Wkr; Hon Roll; Comm Sprts Act/Tms.

SMITH, JOSH C; Larned HS; Larned, KS; (4); Am Leg Boys St; Church Yth Grp; Teachers Aide; Acpl Chr; Pres Jr Cls; Ofcr Stu Cncl; Ofcr Bsbl; Ftbl; Golf; Tennis; N Centrl KS Vo Tech; Elec.

SMITH, JULIE G; Ft Scott HS; Fort Scott, KS; (4); 17/127; Church Yth Grp; Pres FCA; Letterman Clb; Pep Clb; SADD; Teachers Aide; Chorus; School Musical; VP Pres Jr Cls; Pres Sr Cls; Natl Hist And Govt Awd Recpt; Summr Choral Inst; SW Baptist Univ; Engl.

SMITH, KARLA; Jackson Heights HS; Whiting, KS; (3); 4-H; FHA; Band; Mrchg Band; Pep Band; Chrldng; Crs Cntry; Trk; Hon Roll; Prfct Atten Awd; Highland CC; Legal Sec.

SMITH, KEISHA; Liberal HS; Liberal, KS; (4); Debate Tm; French Clb; FHA; NFL; Q&S; Speech Tm; School Musical; Variety Show; Rptr Nwsp; Black Stu Union Pres; Jackson ST Univ; Mass Commnctn.

SMITH, KELLI C; Washburn Rural HS; Topeka, KS; (2); 20/380; SADD; Chorus; Orch; School Musical; Variety Show; JV Bsktbl; JV Sftbl; High Hon Roll.

SMITH, KRISTI; Kansas City Chrstn Acad; Kansas City, KS; (3); Church Yth Grp; Cmnty Wkr; Office Aide; Thesps; Church Choir; Yrbk; Rep Stu Cncl; Capt Var Gym; Var L Trk; Hon Roll; NCA Best Chrldr 96; NCA-UCA Pro-Cheer All Stars Natl Chmpns 96; Sports Med.

SMITH, KRISTINE M; Salina HS South; Salina, KS; (3); Church Yth Grp; Pep Clb; SADD; Mrchg Band; Pep Band; Hon Roll; Sons Of The Amer Legion Awd Frosh Yr; Salina KS ST Univ; Comp Engr.

SMITH, KRISTY L; Wichita Heights HS; Wichita, KS; (4); Chess Clb; Debate Tm; Spanish Clb; Teachers Aide; Band; Church Choir; Mrchg Band; Hon Roll; NHS; Pres Acad Fit Awd.

SMITH, KYE; Washburn Rural HS; Topeka, KS; (2); JV Var Bsktbl; JV Var Socr; High Hon Roll; Hon Roll; KS U; Arch.

SMITH, KYLE; Kansas City Christian Schl; Overland Park, KS; (3); Cmnty Wkr; Debate Tm; Math Tm; Band; Pep Band; Rep Jr Cls; Socr; High Hon Roll; Hon Roll; NHS; Mem Of KS City Yth Smphny As 1st Trmpt; Engrng.

SMITH, KYLE C; Lawrence HS; Lawrence, KS; (3); School Play; Stage Crew; Ftbl; Hon Roll; Pres Schlr; Tae Kwon Do; Small Animal Vet.

SMITH, KYLIE J; Dighton HS; Dighton, KS; (3); Church Yth Grp; FCA; Library Aide; SADD; Chorus; School Musical; School Play; Rptr Nwsp; JV Golf; Stat Wrstlng; Spirit Clb; Criminology.

SMITH, LACEY N; Independence HS; Independence, KS; (2); Ofcr Stu Cncl; Bsktbl; Hon Roll; U Of KS.

SMITH, LAURA; Nrthrn Hghts HS; Reading, KS; (3); Art Clb; Church Yth Grp; GAA; Girl Scts; JA; Pep Clb; Sec Jr Cls; VP Sr Cls; Chrldng; Vllybl; Wght Lftng; KS U.

SMITH, LINDSEY E; Lawrence HS; Lawrence, KS; (3); Cmnty Wkr; French Clb; Hosp Aide; Latin Clb; Variety Show; Ofcr Jr Cls; JV Tennis; Hon Roll; NHS; Pres Acad Fit Awd; Horseback Riding Cmptvly; Cum Laude Natl Latin Exam; KS Univ; PT.

SMITH, LIZ; St Thomas Aquinas HS; Lenexa, KS; (4); Var Chrldng; Var Crs Cntry; Var Capt Trk; Johnson Co CC; Elem Ed.

SMITH, MARIO D; Wichita South HS; Wichita, KS; (1); Church Yth Grp; Cmnty Wkr; Church Choir; Drill Tm; Nwsp; Yrbk; Ftbl; Hon Roll.

SMITH, MARK M; Blue Valley Northwest HS; Overland Park, KS; (1); Boy Scts; Church Yth Grp; Debate Tm; NFL; Science Clb; Hon Roll; Gftd Enrichment Pgm; Odyssey Of The Mind; Duke Univ TIP For HS Stdnts; MIT; Biochemical Engrng; Rsrch.

SMITH, MARTIN; Burrton Schl; Burrton, KS; (2); 3/27; FCA; Math Tm; Scholastic Bowl; Var Bsktbl; Var Crs Cntry; Var Trk; High Hon Roll; Hon Roll.

SMITH, MATT; Protection Schl; Protection, KS; (3); 2/17; Letterman Clb; Chorus; Pres Rep Jr Cls; VP Stu Cncl; Var L Bsktbl; Var L Ftbl; Var L Trk; High Hon Roll; Hon Roll; NHS; Bsbl All-Star Tm; Sclgy.

SMITH, MEGHAN E; Blue Valley North HS; Leawood, KS; (2); Church Yth Grp; Cmnty Wkr; FCA; Model UN; Pep Clb; JV Tennis; Hon Roll; Young Life; KAYS Club; KS ST Univ; Soc Wrkr.

SMITH, MELANIE; Junction City HS; Fort Riley, KS; (3); Drama Clb; Pep Clb; Teachers Aide; Chorus; School Musical; School Play; Ofcr Jr Cls; Chrldng; Diving; Swmmng; Lifeguard; Fun Sports; Brigham Young Univ; Elem Ed.

SMITH, MELANIE; Pittsburg HS; Pittsburg, KS; (4); Cmnty Wkr; Sec French Clb; FHA; NFL; Q&S; Spanish Clb; Chorus; Phtg Nwsp; JV Bsktbl; High Hon Roll; Med Explorers Treas; Future Edctrs Of Amer.

SMITH, MELINDA M; Olathe East Sr HS; Olathe, KS; (2); 2/1000; Office Aide; Teachers Aide; Chorus; High Hon Roll; Hon Roll; Dsng.

SMITH, MELISSA K; Hartford HS; Neosho Rapids, KS; (3); 2/18; FBLA; Quiz Bowl; SADD; Chorus; School Play; High Hon Roll; Hon Roll; NHS; St Music Conts Ii Rank Vocal Solo; Lyon Cty League Schlrshp Conts 2nd Pl Lit XI, 3rd Pl Spnsh I; Marine Bio.

SMITH, MELODY J; Olathe South Sr HS; Olathe, KS; (4); Church Yth Grp; Cmnty Wkr; Latin Clb; Teachers Aide; Chorus; Church Choir; Ofcr Stu Cncl; High Hon Roll; Bible Quizzing; Wnnr White Rose Essay Cont; Mid-Amer Nazarene Coll; Eng.

SMITH, MICHAEL; Pawnee Hghts HS; Lewis, KS; (3); Var Ftbl; Var Trk; Acad Olympics; KS ST; PT.

SMITH, MICHAEL D; St Thomas Aquinas HS; Lenexa, KS; (3); Quiz Bowl; VP Science Clb; Spanish Clb; Hist SADD; Var Crs Cntry; Var Capt Trk; Var Wrstlng; High Hon Roll; Hist NHS; Prfct Atten Awd; Teens For Life; Clean Team; Film Club; March For Life; Vol Mid-Amer Gms For Dsble; Bsktbl Coach Vol.

SMITH, MICHAEL D; Blue Valley Northwest HS; Overland Park, KS; (2); Boy Scts; Church Yth Grp; Math Tm; Stage Crew; Pres Frsh Cls; JV Bsktbl; JV Socr; Var Trk; High Hon Roll; Hon Roll; Chrstn Alt Band; Yth Ministry; Sports Med.

SMITH, MINDY L; Buhler HS; Buhler, KS; (2); FCA; GAA; Thesps; Band; Chorus; Pep Band; School Musical; Variety Show; Trk; Vllybl.

SMITH, MIRANDA M; Maize HS; Wichita, KS; (3); 64/246; Drama Clb; Science Clb; Spanish Clb; SADD; Thesps; School Play; Variety Show; JV Chrldng; Hon Roll; Ray Club; KS ST Univ; Int Dsgn.

SMITH, NICHOLAS; Junction City HS; Fort Riley, KS; (3); 25/400; Am Leg Boys St; German Clb; Ofcr Bsbl; Bsktbl; JV Crs Cntry; JV Golf; High Hon Roll; Pres Acad Fit Awd; Bwlng; Cmptr Repair.

SMITH, NICK B; Gardner Edgerton-Antioch HS; Gardner, KS; (3); Letterman Clb; Varsity Clb; Stage Crew; JV Bsbl; Var L Ftbl; High Hon Roll; Hon Roll; US Naval Acad; Aerospc; Engr.

SMITH, NICK D; Shawnee Heights Sr HS; Topeka, KS; (2); Pep Clb; Science Clb; JV Bsbl; JV Bsktbl; JV Ftbl; JV Golf; High Hon Roll; KS ST; Engrng.

SMITH, PATRICIA G; J C Harmon HS; Kansas City, KS; (2); Church Yth Grp; GAA; Church Choir; JV Bsktbl; JV Chrldng; Var Trk; Hon Roll; Prfct Atten Awd; Aerobics.

SMITH, REBECCA L; Eastern Heights Jr Sr HS; Agra, KS; (3); Girl Scts; Letterman Clb; Pep Clb; Varsity Clb; Chorus; Stage Crew; JV Var Bsktbl; JV Var Vllybl; Hon Roll; K ST; Bus/Acctg.

SMITH, RICHARD B; Kapaun-Mt Carmel HS; Wichita, KS; (3); 15/175; Church Yth Grp; Spanish Clb; Var L Ftbl; Intrml Wt Lftg; JV Wrstlng; High Hon Roll; Pres NHS; United Crusaders; Crusaders For Life; Ftbl Ltrmn 2 Yrs; Arch.

SMITH, ROBYN N; Campus HS; Haysville, KS; (3); Church Yth Grp; Dance Clb; Science Clb; SADD; Varsity Clb; Acpl Chr; Chorus; Drill Tm; Nwsp; Treas Frsh Cls; OK U; Jrnlsm.

SMITH, RYAN D; F L Schlagle HS; Kansas City, KS; (3); Church Yth Grp; Cmnty Wkr; Drama Clb; French Clb; SADD; Chorus; Church Choir; School Musical; Variety Show; Ofcr Soph Cls; Yth Grp VP; Schlagle Gspl Choir Pres; Pub Schl Adm.

SMITH, RYAN W; Shawnee Heights HS; Topeka, KS; (2); Church Yth Grp; FBLA; Bsktbl; JV Ftbl; Pub Lit Mag; Acad Mdl Phys Conditioning.

SMITH, SANDRA K; Douglass HS; Douglass, KS; (4); 26/100; Church Yth Grp; Teachers Aide; Mgr(s); Mgr Sftbl; High Hon Roll; Hon Roll; Crafts; Art 1st Pl Cntrl Plains League Jewelry Art Show; Butler CC; Arts.

SMITH, SARAH; Garden City Sr HS; Garden City, KS; (3); 42/400; Church Yth Grp; Band; Capt Color Guard; Mrchg Band; Pep Band; Hon Roll; U KS; Med.

SMITH, SCHOEN; Shawnee Mission S Sr HS; Overland Park, KS; (4); 28/413; Debate Tm; FCA; Intnl Clb; Pep Clb; Var Crs Cntry; JV Trk; Intrml Vllybl; Hon Roll; NHS; St Schlr; SHOC Vol Wk; Stdnt Radio/TV Pgrm KSMS; Law Explorers; U Of Notre Dame; Fin.

SMITH, SEGEN; Manhattan HS; Manhattan, KS; (4); 1/388; Sec Am Leg Aux Girls St; Pres French Clb; Church Choir; Orch; School Musical; Swing Chorus; Variety Show; Ofcr Stu Cncl; High Hon Roll; Pres NHS; KS Regnts Hnrs Acad; Crrnt Tchr Suzuki Violin Stu; Med.

SMITH, SETH; Wichita Southeast HS; Rose Hill, KS; (2); 34/443; Art Clb; Church Yth Grp; FCA; Var Bsbl; Var Socr; Hon Roll; Yth Group Ldr; Schltc Art Awd; Jr Assembly; Yth Ministry; Fine Arts.

SMITH, SHANE; Jetmore HS; Jetmore, KS; (4); 3/15; Church Yth Grp; Cmnty Wkr; 4-H; Natl FFA Org; Scholastic Bowl; Stage Crew; Sec Treas Frsh Cls; Pres Soph Cls; VP Jr Cls; Pres Sr Cls; FFA Stuco Rep/Treas/Sec; J-Clb Pres; 4th Pl ST Bsktbl Trnmnt 95; Best Male Ath Awd Track 95; Fort Hays ST Univ; Bus.

SMITH, SHANNON; Liberal HS; Liberal, KS; (1); Church Yth Grp; Pep Clb; Church Choir; JV Chrldng; Hon Roll; Piano Lssns; Top 10 Prcnt Frosh Clss; Pharm.

SMITH, SHAUNNA M; Burlington HS; Strawn, KS; (2); Chess Clb; VP FHA; Church Choir; Treas Frsh Cls; VP Jr Cls; Rep Stu Cncl; Trk; Vllybl; High Hon Roll; NHS; Acteens; Piano, Voice Lessons; KU; Ped.

SMITH, SHERRIE M; Wichita West HS; Wichita, KS; (2); 47/431; Office Aide; Pep Clb; Chrldng; Hon Roll; Soc Worker.

SMITH, STEPHANIE; Blue Valley North HS; Overland Park, KS; (4); Church Yth Grp; Cmnty Wkr; FCA; Pep Clb; Ofcr Spanish Clb; Ed Yrbk; JV Crs Cntry; Gym; Var Trk; Hon Roll; KS St Univ; Jrnlsm.

SMITH, STEPHANIE ELLEN; Mulvane Sr HS; Mulvane, KS; (3); 13/131; Church Yth Grp; VP FHA; Library Aide; Pep Clb; SADD; Rptr Nwsp; JV Sftbl; JV Vllybl; Hon Roll; NHS; Lead Horses For Disabled Chldrn; Nrsng Hm Vlntr; Psych.

SMITH, STEPHEN L; Independence HS; Elk City, KS; (3); Boy Scts; Spanish Clb; Chorus; School Musical; Hon Roll; Sct Of The Yr Awd; Linguistics.

SMITH, SUSAN D; Wichita Heights HS; Wichita, KS; (3); 83/250; Art Clb; Church Yth Grp; Cmnty Wkr; Pep Clb; Red Cross Aide; SADD; Teachers Aide; Orch; KS Newman Univ; Chiro.

SMITH, TAMMIE LEA; Skyline Schl; Haviland, KS; (4); Church Yth Grp; FHA; Pep Clb; SADD; Teachers Aide; Acpl Chr; Band; Mrchg Band; Pep Band; Variety Show; Hmcmng Queen Ftbll; St Mus Vocal Solo; St Jrnlsm; Pratt CC; Grphc Desgn.

SMITH, TERESA; Enterprise Sda Acad; Topeka, KS; (2); Church Yth Grp; Band; Chorus; Rep Soph Cls; Gym; High Hon Roll; Union Col.

SMITH, TERRA S; Dodge City HS; Dodge City, KS; (1); Debate Tm; Girl Scts; Orch; Nwsp; Lawyer.

SMITH, TIA M; Shawnee Mission S Sr HS; Shawnee Mission, KS; (3); Teachers Aide; Band; Mrchg Band; JV Sftbl; High Hon Roll; NHS; Schol Achv Awd; Amigos; Med.

SMITH, TRACY; Ellsworth HS; Ellsworth, KS; (3); Church Yth Grp; Band; Mrchg Band; Pep Band; Stage Crew; Phtg Yrbk; Var Chrldng; Reg & St Jrnlsm Cntsts 1st Pl; Jrnlsm.

SMITH, TRAVIS W; Haven HS; Hutchinson, KS; (3); Church Yth Grp; NFL; Chorus; School Musical; Variety Show; Treas Sr Cls; Var Bsbl; Var Bsktbl; High Hon Roll; NHS; Sports Broadcaster.

SMITH, TRISHA A; Labette Co HS; Oswego, KS; (2); Library Aide; Pep Clb; SADD; Chorus; JV Sftbl; Hon Roll; KAY; Soundsations; Music Co; U Of KS; Radiologist.

SMITH, TYLER L; Russell HS; Russell, KS; (2); Church Yth Grp; Band; Chorus; Jazz Band; Mrchg Band; Pep Band; ST Street Singers.

SMITHA, ERIN; Mission Valley HS; Harveyville, KS; (4); 1/61; Q&S; Capt Quiz Bowl; School Play; Var Capt Sftbl; Gov Hon Prg Awd; Kiwanis Awd; NHS; Pres Schlr; St Schlr; Val; Topeka Capital Journal All ST Acad Team Hnrb Mntn; All-League Acad Ath; Eng Dept Awd; KS ST U; Kinesiology.

SMITHYMAN, MIKE L; Blue Valley Northwest HS; Overland Park, KS; (2); Latin Clb; Tennis; Hon Roll.

SMOLL, JENNIFER; Dodge City HS; Dodge City, KS; (3); Church Yth Grp; Debate Tm; HOBY; NFL; Pep Clb; Band; Color Guard; Pres Jr Cls; JV Tennis; NHS; Jrblsp Dodge; Schltc Achvt Awd; Peer Helper; Bus.

SMOTHERS, JESSICA M; F L Schlagle HS; Kansas City, KS; (3); #30 in class; Church Yth Grp; Pep Clb; Spanish Clb; SADD; Teachers Aide; Chorus; Church Choir; High Hon Roll; Hon Roll; NHS; UM Kansas City.

SNAPP, DAVID A; Shawnee Mission N HS; Mission, KS; (2); Church Yth Grp; Cmnty Wkr; Debate Tm; Key Clb; Letterman Clb; Library Aide; NFL; Speech Tm; Acpl Chr; Nwsp; Warner Pacific; Yth Speaker; Law.

SNAPP, WILLIAM; Mankato Jr Sr HS; Mankato, KS; (3); 12/28; Church Yth Grp; Band; Church Choir; Jazz Band; Mrchg Band; Orch; Pep Band; Bsktbl; Ftbl; Golf.

SNAVELY, ABBY; Salina HS South; Salina, KS; (3); 6/256; Church Yth Grp; FCA; HOBY; Math Tm; Teachers Aide; JV Bsktbl; Var L Trk; Var L Vllybl; Intrml Wt Lftg; High Hon Roll; Teen Too Ambucs.

SNELL, JUSTIN R; Northeast Magnet HS; Wichita, KS; (1); Quiz Bowl; Church Choir; JV Bsktbl; Hon Roll; Hoop It Up MVP & All Star Team; Chrch Drummer; Bsktbl; NBA; Auto Mechanic.

SNELLER, KELLY; Atchison Sr HS; Atchison, KS; (1); Church Yth Grp; Computer Clb; Debate Tm; Rep Stu Cncl; Intrml Socr; JV Vllybl; High Hon Roll; Hon Roll; Law/Psych.

SNETHEN, SCOTT A; Ottawa HS; Ottawa, KS; (3); Cmnty Wkr; Ofcr Bsbl; Bsktbl; Ftbl; Hon Roll; Tm Port; 95 Best Dfnsv Plyr Awd Amer Lgn Bsbl; Comm Art/Grphc Dsgn.

SNIDER, ERIC; Kapaun-Mt Carmel HS; Wichita, KS; (3); Church Yth Grp; Q&S; Ed Nwsp; Rep Soph Cls; Treas Jr Cls; Treas Sr Cls; High Hon Roll; NHS; Grt Chef Awd; Jrnlsm.

SNODGRASS, APRIL D; Shawnee Mission W Sr HS; Olathe, KS; (1); Teachers Aide; RN.

SNODGRASS, ERIN S; Blue Valley HS; Stilwell, KS; (3); SADD; Co-Capt Chrldng; Hon Roll; KS Univ; Nrsng.

SNOKE, ELIZABETH; Larned HS; Larned, KS; (2); 16/102; Church Yth Grp; Debate Tm; Drama Clb; French Clb; Letterman Clb; Red Cross Aide; Spanish Clb; Hon Roll; Vet.

SNOW JR, LONNIE; Wyandotte HS; Kansas City, KS; (1); Boy Scts; Cmnty Wkr; Ftbl; Tennis; Hon Roll; Recreation Ctr Bsktbl & Sftbl; KS U; Engrng.

SNOW, STACY M; Eudora HS; Eudora, KS; (3); FBLA; FHA; Spanish Clb; Teachers Aide; High Hon Roll; Hon Roll; Jr NHS; Bus; Comps.

SNOWDEN, TARA J; Olathe East Sr HS; Olathe, KS; (2); Church Yth Grp; Library Aide; Office Aide; Am Leg Boys St; Teachers Aide; Chorus; School Musical; Hon Roll; Kay Clb; Harding U.

SNOWER, ANDREA M; Shawnee Mission E Sr HS; Leawood, KS; (2); Pres Temple Yth Grp; Band; Mrchg Band; Orch; Pep Band; Hon Roll; Espirit De Corps Ldrshp Awd 94-5 & 95-96; 1 Rating At St Solo Music Cmptn; Elem Ed; Tchr.

SNYDER, ALISHA; Conway Springs HS; Viola, KS; (4); 7/44; Church Yth Grp; Natl Beta Clb; Pep Clb; Red Cross Aide; Scholastic Bowl; Teachers Aide; Band; Chorus; Jazz Band; Mrchg Band; Pittsburg ST U; Nrsng.

SNYDER, BREANNA K; Blue Valley Northwest HS; Overland Park, KS; (4); Church Yth Grp; FCA; Key Clb; Office Aide; Teachers Aide; Varsity Clb; Mgr(s); Var Powder Puff Ftbl; Stat Sftbl; Stat Vllybl; KAYS; U Of KS; Marine Bio.

SNYDER, CODY E; Washburn Rural HS; Auburn, KS; (3); JV Var Bsktbl; Var Capt Ftbl; Var L Trk; High Hon Roll; Hon Roll; City Ftbl Player Of Week; All-St Hnrb Mntn; 2nd Team All-City.

SNYDER, COREY M; Topeka West HS; Topeka, KS; (3); 24/239; Cmnty Wkr; German Clb; NFL; Q&S; Quiz Bowl; SADD; Treas Stu Cncl; Var L Bsbl; Var Capt Socr; NHS; Phys Thpy.

SNYDER, ERIN L; Ft Scott HS; Fort Scott, KS; (3); Letterman Clb; Church Choir; Ofcr Stu Cncl; JV Crs Cntry; Var Sftbl; Hon Roll; NHS; Frgn Language & Natural Helpers Clb; Choir Ensemble.

SNYDER, HOLLY E; Blue Valley HS; Overland Park, KS; (3); 20/220; Church Yth Grp; Debate Tm; German Clb; Model UN; NFL; Science Clb; Speech Tm; Varsity Clb; Chrldng; Powder Puff Ftbl; St Debate 5th Pl Finish; St Forensics Qualifer In Extemoporaneous Speaking; Bus; Law.

SNYDER, JESSICA; Rossville HS; Rossville, KS; (3); 7/46; FBLA; Teachers Aide; JV Bsktbl; JV Sftbl; JV Var Vllybl; Intrml Wt Lftg; High Hon Roll; Hon Roll; NHS; KS ST U; Accntng.

SNYDER, QUINTON E; Blue Valley HS; Stilwell, KS; (3); Teachers Aide; Band; Jazz Band; Mrchg Band; Pep Band; Mgr Bsktbl; Hon Roll; NHS; KS ST Univ; Vet Med.

SNYDER, TISHA M; Augusta Sr HS; Augusta, KS; (3); Church Yth Grp; Cmnty Wkr; Debate Tm; French Clb; Socr; Soccer Coach; Hiking; KS Univ; Defense Lawyer.

SNYDER, VENUS M; Mankato Jr Sr HS; Formoso, KS; (3); Art Clb; Drama Clb; HOBY; JA; Letterman Clb; Natl FFA Org; Pep Clb; Band; Chorus; Drm Mjr(t); ST VFW Art Comp 1st; Cty VFW Art Comp 1st; Bst Of Shw Area Art Comp; Otis Art Schl; Mdrn Artst.

SNYDER, ZACHARY R; Lawrence HS; Lawrence, KS; (2); Chorus; Hon Roll; Water Gardening Job; Mowing Bus; Envrnmntlst.

SOCTT, CARMEN; Louisburg HS; Louisburg, KS; (2); Spanish Clb; Drill Tm; Yrbk; JV Sftbl; JV Vllybl; Hon Roll; Phtgrphy; MAST.

SOETAERT, CHRIS C; Gardner-Edgerton HS; Spring Hill, KS; (3); Quiz Bowl; Band; Mrchg Band; Pep Band; JV Bsktbl; Var Tennis; Hon Roll.

SOETAERT, LIBBY L; Gardner-Edgerton HS; Spring Hill, KS; (2); Spanish Clb; Band; Mrchg Band; Pep Band; High Hon Roll; Hon Roll; Prfct Atten Awd.

SOETAERT, THEODORE J; Bishop Miege HS; Shawnee, KS; (1); Church Yth Grp; Office Aide; Ftbl; Wt Lftg; High Hon Roll; KU Notre Dame; Med Schl.

SOHM, JEREMY T; Otis Bison HS; Otis, KS; (2); Church Yth Grp; Pep Clb; SADD; Chorus; Church Choir; JV Ftbl; Hon Roll.

SOHM, VICKI L; Great Bend Sr HS; Great Bend, KS; (4); Girl Scts; Pep Clb; Spanish Clb; SADD; Acpl Chr; Band; Variety Show; Sec Treas Stu Cncl; Chrldng; Hon Roll; Magna Cum Laude; Girl Sct Silver Awd; US Navy; Psych.

SOJKA, CANDICE; Wichita West HS; Wichita, KS; (4); 42/272; Am Leg Aux Girls St; GAA; Pep Clb; SADD; Thesps; Band; Mrchg Band; Pep Band; School Play; Rep Soph Cls; Peer Mediation; Schl Cmmtte Chrprsn; Spotlight Srs; KSU; Bio.

SOLEIMANI, ALI; Olathe South Sr HS; Olathe, KS; (3); 1/400; French Clb; Math Tm; Quiz Bowl; Science Clb; Yrbk; High Hon Roll; NHS; Ntl Merit SF; Cmnty Wkr; FHA; Dartmouth Outstdng Scholar Book Awd; Outstdng Soph Of Yr 95; Outstdng Jr KCATM Math Cmptn 96.

SOLKO, KRISTAL ELAINE; Herndon Schl; Herndon, KS; (3); Chess Clb; Cmnty Wkr; Library Aide; Model UN; Quiz Bowl; Speech Tm; Teachers Aide; Band; Chorus; Pep Band; Odyssey Of Mind; Site Cncl; Pride Comm; Goodland Vo Tech; Exec Sec.

SOLLY, CLARE; Pittsburg HS; Pittsburg, KS; (3); 7/300; Church Yth Grp; Sec Treas Drama Clb; VP NFL; Q&S; Thesps; Band; Mrchg Band; School Musical; School Play; Sierra Svc Prjct; Phi Kappa Phi Jr Hnrs Awd; Jrnlsm.

SOLOMON, CASEY; Wichita West HS; Wichita, KS; (1); JV Var Chrldng.

SOLOMON, ERIN M; Yates Ctr HS; Yates Center, KS; (2); Sec Church Yth Grp; Cmnty Wkr; Pres 4-H; FHA; Sec Treas German Clb; Scholastic Bowl; Ed Nwsp; Sec Treas Frsh Cls; Sec Treas Soph Cls; Mgr(s); Del To Farm Bureau Ldrshp Amer 96; Competed In STARTS Events At Natl FHA Convention In Wash DC; KS ST U; 4-H Extension Agent.

SOLON, KATIE; Desoto HS; Shawnee Mission, KS; (3); Am Leg Aux Girls St; Cmnty Wkr; Math Clb; Math Tm; Pep Clb; Spanish Clb; SADD; Teachers Aide; Rptr Nwsp; Yrbk; PRIDE; TRENDS; Baker U; Bus.

SOMMER, ALEXANDER H; Olathe East Sr HS; Olathe, KS; (3); French Clb; Orch; Crs Cntry; Trk; 1st ST Ensemble Orch 96; Yth Ct; Kuork ST; Med/Mltry.

SOMMER, JACLYN M; Washburn Rural HS; Topeka, KS; (2); Spanish Clb; Speech Tm; Teachers Aide; JV Var Bsktbl; Var L Trk; Var L Vllybl; High Hon Roll.

SOMMER, THOMAS; Olathe North Sr HS; Olathe, KS; (3); German Clb; Var L Crs Cntry; JV L Wrstlng; High Hon Roll.

SONG, JACK G; Blue Valley Northwest HS; Overland Park, KS; (3); Chess Clb; Band; Mrchg Band; Orch; High Hon Roll; Hon Roll; NHS; U IL-IRBAN; Engrng.

SONNIER, JAIMIE L; Blue Valley Northwest HS; Overland Park, KS; (3); Church Yth Grp; Debate Tm; Chorus; Church Choir; Hon Roll; Human Video Drama Club; Pltcl Sci Club; Chld Psych.

SONS, ERIKA; Central Christian Schl; Hutchinson, KS; (2); Church Yth Grp; Debate Tm; Nwsp; Var Bsktbl; Vllybl; Hon Roll; Sydneys Schl; Csmtlgy.

SORELL, JOSHUA J; Clifton-Clyde HS; Clyde, KS; (3); FBLA; Natl FFA Org; Band; Ftbl; High Hon Roll; Hon Roll; KSU; Cmptr Engrng.

SORENSEN, CARRIE; Buhler HS; Hutchinson, KS; (3); Pres FHA; Chorus; Stat Bsktbl; Mgr(s); Score Keeper; Stat Sftbl; Stat Vllybl; Hon Roll; Hutchinson CC; Pdtrcn.

SORENSEN, KYLE S; Blue Valley Northwest HS; Overland Park, KS; (4); Art Clb; Cmnty Wkr; Letterman Clb; Pep Clb; Var Crs Cntry; JV Wrstlng; NHS; Natl Optmst Clb Ldrshp Awd; Natl Art Hnr Soc; Natl Schlstcs Art Cmptn Slvr Key.

SORENSEN, TARA; Bishop Miege HS; Shawnee, KS; (2); Cmnty Wkr; Drama Clb; French Clb; Hosp Aide; Pep Clb; Service Clb; SADD; Teachers Aide; Acpl Chr; Chorus; Svc Awd; Schlsp Ti KU Music Camp; Dr; Music.

SORG, AMANDA L; Kapaun-Mt Carmel HS; Wichita, KS; (2); Church Yth Grp; Chorus; Church Choir; Nwsp; JV Bsktbl; JV Sftbl; JV Vllybl; Hon Roll; NHS; Yth Prvntn Team; Peer Listening Grp; Sec/Treas Cath Yth Org; Pre Med/Pre Vet.

SORIA, SONIA; Shawnee Heights Sr HS; Topeka, KS; (4); 87/229; Am Leg Aux Girls St; Debate Tm; Model UN; NFL; Church Choir; Mrchg Band; Co-Ed Lit Mag; Chrldng; Crs Cntry; Hon Roll; Legistre Intrn; Poltcl Sci.

SOSA, GILBERT M; Dodge City HS; Dodge City, KS; (3); Debate Tm; Latin Clb; Pep Clb; Ofcr Jr Cls; Socr; Wt Lftg; Hon Roll; Law Schl.

SOSINSKI, KRISTEN A; Sumner Acad Of Arts & Science; Kansas City, KS; (2); Art Clb; French Clb; Chorus; Bsktbl; JV Tennis; French Hon Soc; High Hon Roll; Hon Roll; NHS; Photo.

SOUKUP, ABBY L; Ellsworth HS; Ellsworth, KS; (3); 10/76; Church Yth Grp; Band; Chorus; Drm Mjr(t); Mrchg Band; Pep Band; Intrml Golf; High Hon Roll; Hon Roll; Kayettes; KS ST Univ; Psych.

SOUKUP, CHRISTINA; Wilson Jr Sr HS; Wilson, KS; (4); 2/24; Treas Church Yth Grp; Cmnty Wkr; Pres Rptr Natl FFA Org; Bsktbl; Chrldng; Trk; Vllybl; Cit Awd; NHS; Pres Schlr; ST FFA Degree; KS ST Brd Regents Cert; KS ST Deans Awd Engrg; Colby Comm Coll; Pharmacy.

SOUKUP, LAURA; Lakin HS; Lakin, KS; (3); 1/61; Am Leg Aux Girls St; Art Clb; Church Yth Grp; Quiz Bowl; Chorus; Sec Frsh Cls; VP Soph Cls; Rep VP Stu Cncl; Chrldng; High Hon Roll; Gold Key Awd At Sw KS Schltc Art Show In Textiles & Jewelry; Lakin KS PRIDE Comm; Nrsng.

SOUKUP, RENEE; Hanston Jr Sr HS; Hanston, KS; (2); 1/16; 4-H; HOBY; Quiz Bowl; Speech Tm; Band; Chorus; Church Choir; L Var Chrldng; L Var Trk; Hon Roll; Nrs.

SOURK, GRANT; Hiawatha HS; Hiawatha, KS; (4); Am Leg Boys St; 4-H; HOBY; Letterman Clb; Natl FFA Org; Scholastic Bowl; Ofcr Stu Cncl; Bsktbl; Trk; 4-H Awd; Washburn U; Pre Law.

SOUTER, TRACIE L; Derby HS; Derby, KS; (3); 18/384; Church Yth Grp; Scholastic Bowl; VP Science Clb; SADD; Orch; Mgr Bsbl; Hon Roll; NHS; Teachers Aide; Church Choir; Env Clb Sec; Natl Wthr Svc Intrn; U Of KS; Mtrlgy.

SOUTHARD, AMY; Lansing HS; Lansing, KS; (2); French Clb; Hosp Aide; Band; Pep Band; Var Tennis; JV Trk.

SOUTHER, STACEY; Pittsburg HS; Havelock, NC; (4); Pep Clb; Q&S; Thesps; School Play; Stage Crew; Nwsp; Yrbk; Photo Awd; Photo Jrnlsm.

SOUTHERLAND, LEVI; Gardner-Edgerton HS; Gardner, KS; (3); 40/120; Church Yth Grp; Spanish Clb; Var L Ftbl; Var L Trk; Intrml Wt Lftg; Var L Wrstlng; Hon Roll; Haskell Indian JC; Athl Trnr.

SOUTHERLNAD, STACEY; Campus HS; Haysville, KS; (4); 35/200; Debate Tm; NFL; Office Aide; Q&S; Science Clb; SADD; Teachers Aide; Orch; Yrbk; JV Var Chrldng; Campus Pride; Ft Hays ST Univ; PT.

SOVA, BECKY L; Andale HS; Maize, KS; (1); Church Yth Grp; English Clb; Spanish Clb; Band; Mrchg Band; Pep Band; School Musical; School Play; High Hon Roll; Hon Roll; Prins Hon Roll.

SOWDER, LINDSAY; Eureka Jr Sr HS; Toronto, KS; (2); 5/65; 4-H; FHA; Letterman Clb; Natl FFA Org; SADD; Band; Var L Bsktbl; Var L Trk; Var L Vllybl; High Hon Roll; Elem Grls Bsktbl Team Coach; 4-H Awd; Frng Lang Clb.

SOWERS, REBECCA; Salina HS South; Salina, KS; (4); 71/217; Sec Church Yth Grp; Cmnty Wkr; Chorus; Church Choir; School Musical; Variety Show; Rptr Nwsp; Rptr Yrbk; Hon Roll; Mid America Nazarene Coll; Engl.

SOWERS, WADE R; Scott Comm HS; Scott City, KS; (4); 26/87; Church Yth Grp; Natl FFA Org; Teachers Aide; Var Trk; Hon Roll; ST FFA Prfncy Awd; Ag Mgmt.

SPACHEK, STACY A; Kapaun-Mt Carmel HS; Wichita, KS; (1); GAA; Spanish Clb; SADD; Bsktbl; JV Sftbl; Hon Roll.

SPAENY, RYAN; Hutchinson HS; Hutchinson, KS; (3); Am Leg Boys St; Var L Bsbl; Var L Bsktbl; Var L Socr; Hon Roll; Acad Excl Awd; Super Salthawk Awd.

SPANGENBERG, MELISSA; St John Jr Sr HS; Hudson, KS; (4); 3/28; Pep Clb; VP SADD; Band; Jazz Band; Pep Band; School Musical; School Play; Stage Crew; NHS.

SPANGENBERG, NICOLE; El Dorado HS; El Dorado, KS; (2); Letterman Clb; Spanish Clb; SADD; Chorus; JV Chrldng; Trk; High Hon Roll; NHS; Pr Cnslng; Earth Care Clb.

SPANGLER, MELANI N; Santa Fe Trail Jr HS; Olathe, KS; (1); Spanish Clb; High Hon Roll; Acad Excl Awd For Span; U Of KS.

SPANIER, JILL; Garden City Sr HS; Garden City, KS; (4); Church Yth Grp; Band; Nwsp; Mgr Bsktbl; JV Vllybl; High Hon Roll; Pres Schlr; Outstndg Accntng Stu; GCCC; Bus.

SPARE, KEIV D; Parsons HS; Parsons, KS; (4); Am Leg Boys St; Church Yth Grp; Debate Tm; Drama Clb; Key Clb; Letterman Clb; Math Tm; NFL; Office Aide; Spanish Clb; Natl Forensics League Natl Tourn; Spch Tm St Champ; Debte Tm St 3rd; KS St Univ; Cvl Eng.

SPARE, MICHELLE; Dodge City HS; Dodge City, KS; (2); Church Yth Grp; Dance Clb; SADD; Band; Mrchg Band; Pep Band; Photography; Fort Hays; Elem Ed.

SPARKS, ALISON; Olathe South Sr HS; Olathe, KS; (4); 21/390; Church Yth Grp; Band; Yrbk; Sec Jr Cls; Ofcr Stu Cncl; Var Bsktbl; Var Chrldng; Var Trk; High Hon Roll; NHS; Ne MO Truman ST U; Bio.

SPARKS, JACOB W; Independence HS; Independence, KS; (1); 41/200; Church Yth Grp; Var Tennis.

SPARKS, JENNIFER; Campus HS; Wichita, KS; (4); 12/219; Pres Intnl Clb; Pres Scholastic Bowl; SADD; Rep Frsh Cls; Rep Sr Cls; JV Crs Cntry; Var Sftbl; High Hon Roll; NHS; Pres Acad Fit Awd; KS Hnr Schlr; Army ROTC Schlsp; IL Inst Tech; Civil Engrng.

SPARKS, KANDIC; Mc Louth Schl; Mc Louth, KS; (3); 7/42; Art Clb; VP FBLA; FHA; Pep Clb; SADD; Varsity Clb; Phtg Yrbk; Rep Jr Cls; Rep Stu Cncl; Var Chrldng; Var CC Of KS; Arch.

SPARKS, LAURA N; Iola Sr HS; Iola, KS; (3); 1/111; Am Leg Aux Girls St; Church Yth Grp; FBLA; SADD; Chorus; Church Choir; Crs Cntry; Trk; Vllybl; High Hon Roll; Kayette Sec; NHS Sec; Pharm.

SPARKS, NICOLE R; Wichita Northwest HS; Wichita, KS; (3); Church Yth Grp; Cmnty Wkr; Intnl Clb; Band; Chorus; Church Choir; Mrchg Band; Pep Band; Variety Show; Ofcr Jr Cls; Involved Widely Church Act; WSU; PT.

SPARTAN, ANASTASIA; Bonner Springs HS; Bonner Springs, KS; (1); JV Chrldng; Hon Roll.

SPAULDING, CHE TIANA; Hayden HS; Topeka, KS; (4); 40/110; Church Yth Grp; Cmnty Wkr; GAA; Teachers Aide; Chorus; Sftbl; Hon Roll; Faith In Action Yth For Christ; Lvg Dream Awrd; Who's Who Among Amer HS Stdnts; Drake U; Brdcst News Sprtscstr.

SPAYDE, MISTI; Ness City HS; Ness City, KS; (4); Church Yth Grp; Drama Clb; Pep Clb; Speech Tm; Thesps; Chorus; School Play; Vllybl; Cit Awd; Hon Roll; U Of KS; Accounting.

SPEAKE, STEPHANIE M; Midland Sda Schl; Olathe, KS; (2); Church Yth Grp; Chorus; Hon Roll; K ST.

SPEARS, DEANNA; Lucus-Luray HS; Lucas, KS; (1); Church Yth Grp; Drama Clb; 4-H; Pep Clb; Quiz Bowl; SADD; Band; Chorus; Pep Band; School Play.

SPECHT, DAVID P; Topeka HS; Topeka, KS; (3); Varsity Clb; JV Crs Cntry; Var Ftbl; Var Tennis; Hon Roll; Russian Clb; Frisbee Clb; KS ST; Arch; Sports Med.

SPECTOR, GAIL; Shawnee Mission S Sr HS; Shawnee Mission, KS; (4); Intnl Clb; Pep Clb; Q&S; Temple Yth Grp; Ed Yrbk; Cit Awd; Hon Roll; NHS; Ntl Merit Ltr; Pres Acad Fit Awd; Grinnell Col; Premed.

SPEER, ALISSA L; Maize HS; Overbrook, KS; (2); Cmnty Wkr; Band; Chorus; Color Guard; Mrchg Band; Pep Band; Stage Crew; Variety Show; Poetry Pub; KS Governors Acad 96; KS Co-Ed Pageant 97; Vet; Commercial Art.

SPEER, JAMIE; Wellsville Jr Sr HS; Wellsville, KS; (4); 14/47; FCA; Pres FBLA; VP Stu Cncl; Var Co-Capt Chrldng; Hon Roll; VP NHS; KAYS Pres; Johnson County CC; Dntl Hygne.

SPEER, KASEY L; Dodge City HS; Dodge City, KS; (1); Cmnty Wkr; Teachers Aide; Tennis; KS Univ; Law.

SPEER, SONYA; Atchison Co Cmty HS; Horton, KS; (3); 14/48; Church Yth Grp; Chorus; School Musical; Hon Roll; KAYS; Lttrd Chorus; Cmptrs.

SPEFSLAGE, BONNIE J; Wetmore Schl; Goff, KS; (2); Letterman Clb; Pep Clb; Quiz Bowl; Service Clb; Band; Chorus; Stage Crew; JV Var Bsktbl; Var L Vllybl; High Hon Roll; KS ST Univ; Fam Prctc Physn.

SPELLMAN, JENNIFER N; Ellsworth HS; Kanopolis, KS; (3); Band; Chorus; Mrchg Band; Hon Roll; Kayettes; Ft Hays ST Univ; Peds.

SPELLMAN, LISA RENEE; Ellsworth HS; Kanopolis, KS; (1); 4-H; SADD; Acpl Chr; Chorus; Mgr Vllybl; Hon Roll; Fort Hays St Univ; Sec Math Tch.

SPELLMEIER, ARLINDA K; Sabetha HS; Sabetha, KS; (2); Drama Clb; Pres 4-H; FHA; Letterman Clb; Natl FFA Org; Pep Clb; Spanish Clb; Speech Tm; Sftbl; Trk; KS ST Univ; Phys Thpy.

SPELLMEIER, BRYN R; Sabetha HS; Fairview, KS; (2); Pep Clb; Spanish Clb; Rep Stu Cncl; JV Bsktbl; JV Vllybl; High Hon Roll; Hon Roll; NHS; KAYS; Prom Srvr.

SPELLMEIER, LUKE R; Sabetha HS; Sabetha, KS; (3); Boy Scts; Church Yth Grp; Cmnty Wkr; FBLA; Letterman Clb; Pep Clb; Intrml Bsktbl; L Ftbl; L Trk; Intrml Wt Lftg; KS ST Univ.

SPELLMEIER, STACEY; Royal Valley HS; Hoyt, KS; (4); 5/53; Letterman Clb; SADD; Band; Co-Capt Drill Tm; Jazz Band; Treas Stu Cncl; JV Bsktbl; Var Capt Crs Cntry; NHS; Pres Schlr; Yth Advsry Clb; KS ST; Cvl Engrng.

SPENCER, ANDREA; Jackson Heights HS; Circleville, KS; (3); 1/40; Church Yth Grp; FCA; Pres FHA; Sec Natl FFA Org; VP Jr Cls; Treas Stu Cncl; JV Vllybl; High Hon Roll; Pres NHS; Prfct Atten Awd; KAYS Pres; Washburn.

SPENCER, ANDREW E; Ft Scott HS; Fort Scott, KS; (3); Church Yth Grp; Debate Tm; NFL; Quiz Bowl; Hon Roll; Ntl Merit SF.

SPENCER, BROOKLYN M; Chanute Sr HS; Thayer, KS; (2); 1/143; Church Yth Grp; Cmnty Wkr; FCA; Letterman Clb; Math Tm; Spanish Clb; Pres Frsh Cls; Ofcr Stu Cncl; JV Bsktbl; Var Sftbl; Tech Awd.

SPENCER, DANIEL; Immaculata HS; Leavenworth, KS; (3); 5/48; HOBY; Math Clb; Math Tm; Quiz Bowl; Scholastic Bowl; Science Clb; Spanish Clb; JV Bsktbl; Var Tennis; High Hon Roll; Spnsh, Bio & Engl Awds; Stus Who Care; Immaculata Boys Actn Clb; Bus Admin.

SPENCER, JANELLE; Topeka HS; Topeka, KS; (2); Chorus; Yrbk; High Hon Roll; Hon Roll; Drawng; Paintng; Wrtng; KS ST Univ; Engr.

SPENCER, JOSH D; Scott Comm HS; Scott City, KS; (3); Natl FFA Org; Teachers Aide; Ofcr Bsbl; Bsktbl; Crs Cntry; Ftbl; Golf; Wt Lftg; Hon Roll; KS ST Univ.

SPENCER, KENDALL W; Wichita East HS; Wichita, KS; (3); Boy Scts; Pres Church Yth Grp; Acpl Chr; Chorus; Church Choir; School Musical; Variety Show; Hon Roll; Ger Natl Hnr Soc; Boy Scout Hnr Camping Soc; Dougleas Express; USAF Acad; Chem.

SPENCER, MARIE; Manhattan HS; Manhattan, KS; (4); Art Clb; Church Yth Grp; Cmnty Wkr; 4-H; Drill Tm; Stage Crew; Rep Stu Cncl; JV Chrldng; Var Capt Crs Cntry; JV Sftbl; Ricks JC; Fine Arts Ed.

SPENCER, RACHEL K; Meade HS; Meade, KS; (2); Sec 4-H; Letterman Clb; Pep Clb; Quiz Bowl; Band; Chorus; Mrchg Band; Pep Band; School Musical; Pres Frsh Cls.

SPENCER, SARA; Central Christian Schl; Buhler, KS; (4); Church Yth Grp; Chorus; School Musical; School Play; Rptr Nwsp; Phtg Rptr Yrbk; Rep Soph Cls; Rep Stu Cncl; Bsktbl; Hon Roll; Anderson Univ; Music Perfmnc.

SPERRY, ANGELA C; Wichita Heights HS; Wichita, KS; (2); 32/375; Church Yth Grp; Cmnty Wkr; Hosp Aide; Spanish Clb; Chorus; Church Choir; Variety Show; High Hon Roll; Pre-Med.

SPERRY, MARGO R; Olathe East Sr HS; Olathe, KS; (4); 49/280; Am Leg Aux Girls St; Debate Tm; NFL; Speech Tm; Lit Mag; Ofcr Jr Cls; Bsktbl; Ofcr Stu Cncl; Bsktbl; High Hon Roll; Comm.

SPEXARTH, ADAM P; Andale HS; Colwich, KS; (2); Debate Tm; Drama Clb; Spanish Clb; Chorus; School Musical; JV Bsktbl; JV Ftbl; High Hon Roll; NHS.

SPEXARTH, ELIZABETH M; Andale HS; Colwich, KS; (1); SADD; Church Yth Grp; Band; Chorus; Mrchg Band; Pep Band; School Musical; School Play; Hon Roll.

SPICER, AMBER; Hays HS; Hays, KS; (4); 18/209; Pres Church Yth Grp; Pres Pep Clb; Red Cross Aide; Band; Orch; Ofcr Stu Cncl; L Sftbl; L Vllybl; High Hon Roll; NHS; Attndg Schl Morocco Africa.

SPICER, CURTIS; Clay Ctr Cmty HS; Clay Center, KS; (2); 1/120; Church Yth Grp; Debate Tm; 4-H; Band; Ftbl; 4-H Awd; High Hon Roll; Pres Acad Fit Awd; Stu Pilot; Midget Race Car Driver; KS ST Univ; Engr.

SPICHER, COREY N; Beloit Jr Sr HS; Beloit, KS; (1); SADD; Chorus; School Musical; Ofcr Bsbl; Ftbl; MI Univ; Dr Pro Ftbl.

SPIEGEL, PATRICIA; Wichita East HS; Wichita, KS; (4); VP FTA; Teachers Aide; Ofcr Frsh Cls; Ofcr Soph Cls; Ofcr Jr Cls; Ofcr Sr Cls; Pom Pon; Hon Roll; Acad Decath Tm; Duane Wallace Yth Ventrue Grnt Cmmtee; Cowely Cnty CC; Bus Admin.

SPIEGELBERG, MATTHEW C; Blue Valley Northwest HS; Overland Park, KS; (2); 32/409; Var L Bsbl; Intrml Bsktbl; High Hon Roll; Hon Roll.

SPIES, ROBERT J; Trego Comm HS; Wa Keeney, KS; (3); Letterman Clb; Natl FFA Org; Science Clb; Teachers Aide; Rep Soph Cls; Capt Ftbl; Var Trk; Var Wt Lftg; High Hon Roll; Var Bsktbl; ST Track/Field 1st/4th Pl Soph Yr LJ/3RD Pl Jr Yr; Elem Ed.

SPIESS, JEFFREY A; Basehor Linwood HS; Bonner Springs, KS; (3); Church Yth Grp; FBLA; Science Clb; Teachers Aide; Intrml Bsktbl; L Crs Cntry; Intrml Golf; High Hon Roll; Hon Roll; JETS Awd; Johnson Cnty CC; Bus.

SPIESS, KRYSTI R; Acad Of Mt St Scholastica; Overland Park, KS; (4); Drama Clb; Intnl Clb; Pep Clb; Stage Crew; Nwsp; Rep Soph Cls; Rep Jr Cls; Rep Sr Cls; Rep Stu Cncl; Socr; Schlstca Awd; Amer Lgn God/Cntry Awd; U Of KS.

SPIGARELLI, GINA S; Pittsburg HS; Pittsburg, KS; (2); Dance Clb; Teachers Aide; Pom Pon; Hon Roll; Pres Acad Fit Awd; Art; Comp Graph; PSU.

SPIGLE, ERIK R; Ottawa HS; Ottawa, KS; (3); 21/149; Am Leg Boys St; Church Yth Grp; FCA; Teachers Aide; Varsity Clb; Crs Cntry; Trk; High Hon Roll; Hon Roll; NHS; Evangel Coll; Comp Sci.

SPIKER, DEANNE M; Wetmore Schl; Wetmore, KS; (2); Letterman Clb; Band; Chorus; School Musical; Var L Bsktbl; Var L Trk; Var L Vllybl; Hon Roll; Prfct Atten Awd; KAYS Treas; Vet.

SPILMAN, SKIP A; Chanute Sr HS; Chanute, KS; (3); Am Leg Boys St; Computer Clb; Math Clb; Math Tm; Office Aide; Science Clb; Spanish Clb; Teachers Aide; VP Stu Cncl; Score Keeper; 96 Pittsburg ST Math Relays 4th In Programming 95 2nd Place; Schl Medals In Math & Tech Ed; Aeronautical Engr.

SPILMAN, WENDY S; Chanute Sr HS; Chanute, KS; (1); 37/170; English Clb; FCA; Spanish Clb; JV Bsktbl; JV Sftbl; JV Vllybl; Hon Roll.

SPINDLE, REGAN; Olathe South Sr HS; Olathe, KS; (3); Church Yth Grp; Q&S; Band; Mrchg Band; Yrbk; Lit Mag; Bsktbl; Cit Awd; High Hon Roll; NHS; Mid Amer Nazarene Coll.

SPIRES, AMY A; Circle HS; Towanda, KS; (4); 29/91; Church Yth Grp; Drama Clb; VP FCA; French Clb; FHA; Math Clb; Natl FFA Org; Scholastic Bowl; SADD; Teachers Aide; Bethany Coll; Bus.

SPITZENGEL, JEANNIE; Career Opportunity Center; Kansas City, KS; (3); Cmnty Wkr; Teachers Aide; School Play; 1st Pl 12th Grd Lit Career Opportunity Ctr PTA Reflections Contest; KS Univ; PT.

SPOHN, BARBARA; White City HS; White City, KS; (1); 1/22; Church Yth Grp; Dance Clb; 4-H; Scholastic Bowl; Speech Tm; Band; School Play; Bsktbl; 4-H Awd; High Hon Roll.

SPOHN, DARLENE R; Liberal HS; Liberal, KS; (3); Church Yth Grp; Drama Clb; FTA; Key Clb; Thesps; Chorus; Church Choir; School Musical; High Hon Roll; NHS; Penn ST; Meterolgy.

SPOHN, JESSICA; Fredonia HS; Fredonia, KS; (3); VP FHA; Var L Bsktbl; Var Chrldng; Var L Golf; Var L Trk; High Hon Roll; Pres Acad Fit Awd; Church Yth Grp; Debate Tm; FCA; Gymnstcs; Bsktbl All-Acad Team; Hnrb Mntn All-Lg Bsktbl Team; KS U; Phy Ther.

SPOKES, PETER A; Blue Valley North HS; Overland Park, KS; (2); 1/200; Church Yth Grp; Cmnty Wkr; FCA; Model UN; Church Choir; JV Golf; High Hon Roll; 7th Pl 2nd In Schl On Level 3 Natl Span Exam; Young Life Ldrshp Vol; Stanford; Bus; Arch.

SPOONER, JERALD; Turner HS; Kansas City, KS; (3); Bus Profs of Am; Chess Clb; German Clb; Hon Roll; Jr NHS; Peer Cnslr; Bowling; U Of KS; Bus.

SPORTSMAN, ANDREA E; Sumner Acad Of Arts & Science; Kansas City, KS; (1); Pep Clb; Band; Mrchg Band; Pep Band; Chrldng; High Hon Roll; Piano Lessons At UMKC; Phys Therapy.

SPOTTS, JULIE L; Blue Valley Northwest HS; Overland Park, KS; (3); Church Yth Grp; Chorus; Church Choir; Mrchg Band; Stat Bsbl; Powder Puff Ftbl; Trk; Vllybl; Hon Roll; NHS.

SPRADLING, SHELBY; Ness City HS; Ness City, KS; (2); FHA; Pep Clb; Thesps; Band; Var Chrldng; JV Vllybl; High Hon Roll; NHS; KS Assn For Yth Rep 94-95, Brd 95-96.

SPRAGUE, ALI N; Labette Co HS; Parsons, KS; (2); 1/167; Church Yth Grp; FCA; FBLA; Letterman Clb; Yrbk; Var L Bsktbl; Var L Sftbl; Var L Vllybl; Cit Awd; High Hon Roll; Paramedics Clb.

SPRAGUE, APRIL R; Leavenworth HS; Leavenworth, KS; (3); Church Yth Grp; Cmnty Wkr; JV Sftbl; High Hon Roll; Hon Roll; NHS; U Of KS; Soc Wrrkr.

SPRAGUE, REBECCA M; Yates Ctr HS; Yates Center, KS; (3); Cmnty Wkr; Treas FHA; Letterman Clb; NFL; Red Cross Aide; Speech Tm; Teachers Aide; Variety Show; Treas Yrbk; Hon Roll; ST For Star Evnts; Treas 2 Yrs KAYS; Bus Mgmt.

SPRANG, ANGIE; Atchison Co Cmty HS; Effingham, KS; (3); 7/55; Church Yth Grp; VP 4-H; Rptr Natl FFA Org; Drill Tm; School Play; Ed Nwsp; Sec Jr Cls; Var Chrldng; High Hon Roll; NHS; KS ST U; Bus Mgmt.

SPRATLIN, BETSY L; Shawnee Mission S Sr HS; Overland Park, KS; (2); Natl Beta Clb; NFL; Sec Pep Clb; SADD; VP Soph Cls; Rep Stu Cncl; JV Socr; High Hon Roll; Pres Acad Fit Awd; Show Me South Publicity.

SPRATLIN, SAMUEL J; Junction City HS; Junction City, KS; (2); Cmnty Wkr; Pep Clb; Quiz Bowl; Scholastic Bowl; Nwsp; Ofcr Soph Cls; Ftbl; Wt Lftg; Wrstlng; 4-H Awd.

SPRESSER, SARAH; Jennings Schl; Dresden, KS; (3); VP Pres FHA; Quiz Bowl; Scholastic Bowl; Speech Tm; Teachers Aide; Chorus; Sec Frsh Cls; Sec Soph Cls; Sec Jr Cls; Sec Stu Cncl; CNA; Colby CC; Chldcare.

SPRINGER, ADAM; Iola Sr HS; Iola, KS; (3); 1/115; Am Leg Boys St; Church Yth Grp; Letterman Clb; SADD; Band; JV Bsktbl; Capt Crs Cntry; Trk; High Hon Roll; Rep NHS; Eng.

SPRINGER, MICHAEL; Neodesha Jr Sr HS; Independence, KS; (4); 1/41; 4-H; HOBY; Math Clb; Math Tm; Natl FFA Org; Teachers Aide; Sec Soph Cls; Pres Jr Cls; Pres Stu Cncl; Cit Awd; FFA Natl Fnlst Fd Grn Prdctn, Chptr Pres, Dist Star Grnhnd; KS ST U; Ag Ecs.

SPRINKLE, LORETTA J; Shawnee Mission E Sr HS; Prairie Village, KS; (2); Church Yth Grp; Pep Clb; Chrldng; Hon Roll; Johnson County CC; Scl Wrk.

SPROCK, ANDREW; Hays HS; Hays, KS; (3); 32/235; Church Yth Grp; Cmnty Wkr; FCA; Band; L Ftbl; L Swmmng; L Tennis; Wt Lftg; High Hon Roll; NHS; Nmntd For Wendys HS Heisman; Yth Ldr Cre Through Amer Bapt Ch; Vpres Natl Hnr Soc.

SPRUNGER, PETER H; Newton Sr HS; Newton, KS; (2); 39/279; Chess Clb; Math Clb; Model UN; Quiz Bowl; Scholastic Bowl; Diving; Golf; High Hon Roll; Mrktng.

SPUDIC, IVAN M; Bishop Ward HS; Kansas City, KS; (2); 11/93; Socr; High Hon Roll; U Of KS; Comp Engrng.

SPURLOCK, JEDIAH; Wichita West HS; Wichita, KS; (3); #26 in class; Church Yth Grp; Girl Scts; Thesps; Treas Acpl Chr; Lbrn Orch; School Musical; School Play; Stage Crew; Hon Roll; NHS; YPT; Peer Mediation; Southern Univ; Music; Fine Arts.

SQUIRE, ELIZABETH; Arkansas City HS; Arkansas City, KS; (3); Cmnty Wkr; SADD; Teachers Aide; Rep Jr Cls; Tennis; High Hon Roll; Pres Schlr; Psych.

SQUIRES, ANDREA M; Lawrence HS; Lawrence, KS; (3); Cmnty Wkr; Spanish Clb; Ed Yrbk; Hon Roll; NHS; Pres Acad Fit Awd; Jrnlsm; Psych.

SQUIRES, NICK; Bucklin Schl; Bucklin, KS; (2); 2/27; Boy Scts; HOBY; Scholastic Bowl; Band; Chorus; Mrchg Band; Pep Band; Mgr Ftbl; Mgr(s); Cit Awd.

SQUIRES, STEVE G; Salina HS South; Salina, KS; (2); Church Yth Grp; Ofcr Bsbl; Bsktbl; Ftbl; KS Univ; Bus.

SRAMEK, ANDY J; Cheylin Jr Sr HS; Mc Donald, KS; (2); 5/8; Church Yth Grp; 4-H; Natl FFA Org; Mgr Bsktbl; Var Ftbl; Var Trk; Var Wt Lftg; High Hon Roll; NHS; Emporia St Geog Test 3rd In Cls & Hnrb Mntn St.

SRAMEK, PAULA; Shawnee Mission W Sr HS; Overland Park, KS; (3); 121/415; Cmnty Wkr; Library Aide; Q&S; Speech Tm; Yrbk; Intrml Sftbl; JV Vllybl; Hon Roll; Photo Asst Ed For Yrbk; Psych.

SRRIEN, RANELLE; Lincoln Jr Sr HS; Lincoln, KS; (2); 3/36; Church Yth Grp; 4-H; Letterman Clb; Pep Clb; Quiz Bowl; VP Soph Cls; JV Vllybl; 4-H Awd; High Hon Roll; NHS; Taught Vacation Bible Schl 2 Yrs; KY ST; Elem Tchr.

STAAB, DANA D; Larned HS; Topeka, KS; (3); Letterman Clb; Red Cross Aide; Teachers Aide; Varsity Clb; Acpl Chr; Var Sftbl; High Hon Roll; Hon Roll; Occupational Therapy.

STAAB, JAYE; Ellis HS; Ellis, KS; (4); 8/42; FHA; SADD; Ed Phtg Yrbk; Sec Soph Cls; Capt Chrldng; Var Cit Awd; High Hon Roll; Church Yth Grp; Drama Clb; Office Aide; MCL Ldrshp Conf; Site Bs Cncl; Acad Brnz Awd; Grls St Dlgt; Awd Excllnc Comm Disorders; Fort Hays ST U; Speech.

STAAB, KATHRYN; Thomas More Prep-Marion HS; Hays, KS; (3); 12/69; JCL; Latin Clb; Math Tm; Speech Tm; Var JV Trk; High Hon Roll; Ntl Merit Schol; Natl Yng Ldrs Conf.

STAAB, MOLLY; Larned HS; Larned, KS; (4); 7/90; Church Yth Grp; Cmnty Wkr; Spanish Clb; Teachers Aide; Chorus; Rep Stu Cncl; Var Chrldng; JV Vllybl; High Hon Roll; NHS; PAL; Vol Tutor; KS ST U; Bus.

STAATS, SHALEAH L; Greensburg HS; Greensburg, KS; (3); Church Yth Grp; FHA; Chorus; School Musical; Rep Stu Cncl; Hon Roll; Bus Mgmt.

STACY, KEVIN C; Arkansas City HS; Arkansas City, KS; (4); 7/170; Drama Clb; Band; Chorus; School Musical; School Play; Cit Awd; High Hon Roll; NHS; SADD; Mrchg Band; Musical Theatre; SAGE; I Rating Vocal Solos ST Cont; U Of KS; Psychiatrist.

STAEDTLER, HAYLER; Mc Pherson HS; Mc Pherson, KS; (3); Art Clb; Letterman Clb; Pep Clb; Chrldng; Hon Roll; Wnng Sprt Trphy In Chrldng Comp At Rs Hl95; Art.

STAFFORD, APRIL N; Maize HS; Wichita, KS; (1); Church Yth Grp; SADD; Hon Roll; Psych.

STAFFORD, COURTNEY A; Blue Valley Northwest HS; Overland Park, KS; (4); 50/342; Cmnty Wkr; Intnl Clb; Key Clb; Service Clb; Chorus; School Musical; High Hon Roll; NHS; Pres Schlr; U Of KS; Med.

STAFFORD, JILL; Hill City HS; Hill City, KS; (4); 5/35; Church Yth Grp; Cmnty Wkr; Capt FCA; 4-H; FHA; VP Natl FFA Org; Pep Clb; Scholastic Bowl; Service Clb; SADD; DARE Role Model; Homecoming Queen; Dawson Place Svc Accmpnst; KS ST U; CPA.

STAFFORD, KASEY N; Northeast HS; Arma, KS; (3); 7/40; Ed Yrbk; VP Jr Cls; JV Bsktbl; JV Sftbl; JV Vllybl; High Hon Roll; Hon Roll; Pres NHS; Chorus; Regnls 2nd Pl Jrnlsm; FL ST; Law.

STAFFORD, MARCELL E; Wyandotte HS; Kansas City, KS; (1); Boy Scts; Hon Roll; Prfct Atten Awd; Comp Engrng.

STAFFORD, MATTHEW W; Parsons HS; Parsons, KS; (4); 4/120; Pres FCA; Pres Key Clb; Ed Yrbk; Sec Frsh Cls; Var Capt Bsbl; Var Bsktbl; Var Ftbl; Cit Awd; Hon Roll; Kiwanis Awd; Cntrl MS ST Univ; Bus Mgmt.

STAGGS, BRETT G; Blue Valley Northwest HS; Overland Park, KS; (3); Boy Scts; Chess Clb; Church Yth Grp; German Clb; Key Clb; SADD; Band; Nwsp; Socr; Hon Roll; Sci Olympian 1st Pl Awd; Eagle Scout 95; Univ Of KS; Bus.

STAGL, MIKE J; Kapaun-Mt Carmel HS; Wichita, KS; (4); Q&S; Band; Yrbk; Univ Of ND; Airline Pilot.

STAHL, MATTHEW T; Thomas More Prep-Marion HS; Pittsburgh, PA; (1); Church Yth Grp; Hon Roll; Resdnt Frshmn Rep Ambssdr Clb.

STAIB, NICHOLAS L; Haven HS; Hutchinson, KS; (3); Church Yth Grp; 4-H; Band; Jazz Band; Mrchg Band; Pep Band; JV Bsbl; Hon Roll; Municipal Band; Hutchinson CC; Prof Pilot.

STAIERT, ANGIE; Manhattan HS; Manhattan, KS; (4); 216/388; Am Leg Aux Girls St; Pres Church Yth Grp; Cmnty Wkr; FBLA; Hosp Aide; Pres SADD; Teachers Aide; Chorus; Hon Roll; KS St Bus Wk; St Lgsltre Zero Tlrnce Spkr; Teens As Tchrs; Highland CC; Bus.

STAIR, JAKKI; Independence HS; Independence, KS; (1); Church Yth Grp; French Clb; Pep Clb; Chrldng; Sftbl; Hon Roll.

STALEY, CHRISTOPHER D; Frankft HS; Frankfort, KS; (2); Letterman Clb; Natl FFA Org; Chorus; Ftbl; Mgr(s); Score Keeper; Trk; Wt Lftg; High Hon Roll; Hon Roll; Hunting; Reading; Fishing; Univ Of NE; Electronics.

STALEY, JUSTINA; Sublette HS; Sublette, KS; (3); 6/31; Letterman Clb; Pep Clb; Ofcr Stu Cncl; Bsktbl; Vllybl; Hon Roll; NHS; Gov Ctr Feen Ldrshp; US Natl Ldrshp Mrt Awd; Washburn; Law.

STALEY, NICOLE; Grace Chrstn Acad; Wellington, KS; (4); Am Leg Aux Girls St; Church Yth Grp; Teachers Aide; Chorus; Church Choir; School Musical; School Play; Capt Bsktbl; Capt Chrldng; Capt Vllybl; Calvary Bible Coll; Tchr.

STALLBAUMER, KRISTIN L; Axtell Schl; Axtell, KS; (2); Church Yth Grp; Pep Clb; Band; Chorus; Mrchg Band; Pep Band; School Musical; JV Var Bsktbl; JV Vllybl; High Hon Roll; KAYS Clb; Child Care.

STALLBAUMER, LAURA; Frankft HS; Frankfort, KS; (4); 1/29; Am Leg Aux Girls St; SADD; Chorus; School Play; VP Frsh Cls; Bsktbl; Trk; Vllybl; High Hon Roll; NHS; Med.

STALLBAUMER, MELISSA SUE; Paola HS; Paola, KS; (2); 1/140; FCA; SADD; Teachers Aide; Yrbk; Rep Soph Cls; Sftbl; Vllybl; High Hon Roll; PT/SPCH Pthlgy.

STALLBAUMER, SARA; Frankft HS; Frankfort, KS; (4); 13/29; Am Leg Aux Girls St; FHA; Am Leg Boys St; SADD; Hon Roll; NHS; FHA Mmbrshp Chrmn, Stuco Rep; Acctng.

STALLBAUMER, TRAVIS E; Bailey-Benedict Jr Sr High; Seneca, KS; (4); 1/7; Church Yth Grp; Letterman Clb; Quiz Bowl; Scholastic Bowl; Varsity Clb; School Play; Phtg Yrbk; VP Frsh Cls; VP Soph Cls; VP Jr Cls; Stu Tchr; KS Sts Outstndng Math & Sci Stu; Army Schlr Athl Awd; KS ST U; Hlth.

STALLMAN, BRETT; Spring Hill HS; Spring Hill, KS; (4); Chess Clb; Pep Clb; Scholastic Bowl; Band; High Hon Roll; Hon Roll; NHS; Pres Acad Fit Awd; St Schlr; KSU; Comp Sci.

STAMM, JENNIFER L; Cair Paravel - Latin Schl; Tecumseh, KS; (3); Church Yth Grp; Teachers Aide; Chorus; Orch; Bsktbl; Vllybl.

STAMM, MICHAEL J; Washington HS; Washington, KS; (4); Pres Church Yth Grp; Pres Treas 4-H; Natl FFA Org; Band; Jazz Band; Var L Crs Cntry; Var L Trk; 4-H Awd; High Hon Roll; NHS; Lead Trombone In Dist 3 Hnr Jazz Band; KS ST Univ.

KANSAS

STAMMER, KARYN D; Oswego HS; Oswego, KS; (2); Church Yth Grp; FHA; Letterman Clb; Pep Clb; Speech Tm; Acpl Chr; Chorus; Church Choir; School Musical; Ofcr Frsh Cls; Bus Stu Of Yr.

STAMPER, BONNIE; Arkansas City HS; Arkansas City, KS; (2); Church Yth Grp; FCA; Hosp Aide; Band; Mrchg Band; School Musical; Rep Stu Cncl; JV Var Crs Cntry; Sftbl; JV Var Trk.

STAMPS, NICOLE M; Independence HS; Independence, KS; (1); Debate Tm; Library Aide; Color Guard; Flag Corp; Stage Crew; Mgr Vllybl; Hon Roll; Kay's KS Acc Of Yth; Marching Band; ICC; Doctor.

STAND, JEANA; Cimarron HS; Cimarron, KS; (3); 21/58; Art Clb; Church Yth Grp; Cmnty Wkr; FCA; Pep Clb; Spanish Clb; Teachers Aide; Varsity Clb; Band; Chorus; Mid Amer Nazarene Col; Dntstry.

STANDARD, JANNIA Q; Leavenworth HS; Leavenworth, KS; (3); Church Yth Grp; Teachers Aide; Church Choir; Hon Roll; RN.

STANDAU, ERIN; Wichita West HS; Wichita, KS; (4); 53/271; Am Leg Aux Girls St; Debate Tm; FTA; Office Aide; Teachers Aide; Orch; Hon Roll; Hnrbl Mntn; 3 Str For HERO St Cmptn; U Of KS; Soc Wrkr.

STANDLEY, STEPHANIE L; Beloit Jr Sr HS; Beloit, KS; (2); 1/60; Church Yth Grp; Science Clb; Spanish Clb; Chorus; Orch; JV Var Bsktbl; JV Vllybl; High Hon Roll; NHS.

STANFIELD, ISAAC W; Campus HS; Haysville, KS; (2); Church Yth Grp; Scholastic Bowl; Science Clb; SADD; Band; Church Choir; Jazz Band; Mrchg Band; Pep Band; JV Var Tennis.

STANFIELD, MELISSA L; Topeka HS; Topeka, KS; (4); 25/334; Cmnty Wkr; Debate Tm; Letterman Clb; Model UN; NFL; School Musical; Variety Show; JV Socr; JV Tennis; NHS; TX Christian Univ; Law; Pol Sci.

STANFIELD, SHANAN L; Maize HS; Wichita, KS; (3); Band; Mrchg Band; Pep Band; JV Var Tennis; Hon Roll; KAYS; KS ST Univ; Accntng/Bus.

STANFORD, ROMAR; Crest HS; Colony, KS; (4); Church Yth Grp; FCA; FHA; Quiz Bowl; Chorus; Hon Roll; Allen Cty CC.

STANGA, JOHN P; Wichita East HS; Wichita, KS; (4); Church Yth Grp; Cmnty Wkr; Quiz Bowl; Science Clb; Hon Roll; Ntl Merit SF; KU Alumni Assn KS Hnr Schlr; IB Diploma; Co Author Pblshd Book; Bio.

STANGE, NATHAN; Wichita NW HS; Wichita, KS; (3); Am Leg Boys St; Scholastic Bowl; Ed Nwsp; Lit Mag; VP Frsh Cls; Rep Soph Cls; Pres Jr Cls; VP Stu Cncl; Hon Roll; Ntl Merit Ltr; Hnrs Cls; Engl.

STANLEY, DAVID; Augusta Sr HS; Augusta, KS; (3); 1/160; Am Leg Boys St; Office Aide; Scholastic Bowl; Band; Mrchg Band; Pep Band; High Hon Roll; NHS; League Bowling; Vet Aide; KS ST; Vet.

STANLEY, ERIN E; Leavenworth HS; Leavenworth, KS; (1); Church Yth Grp; Cmnty Wkr; Drama Clb; JA; Service Clb; Thesps; Chorus; School Play; Stage Crew; High Hon Roll.

STANLEY, GARRET B; Dodge City HS; Dodge City, KS; (3); Band; JV Crs Cntry; JV Ftbl; JV Wrstlng; Hon Roll; KS ST; Pre-Med.

STANLEY, JOSEPH B; Field Kindley Mem Sr HS; Coffeyville, KS; (2); JV Bsbl.

STANLEY, MATTHEW; Dodge City HS; Dodge City, KS; (2); Church Yth Grp; Teachers Aide; JV Bsktbl; JV Ftbl; Wt Lftg; High Hon Roll; Hon Roll; Stdnt Of Mnth.

STANLEY, SKYE R; Campus HS; Haysville, KS; (3); Science Clb; SADD; NHS.

STANSBURY, DANIEL K; Northeast HS; Mulberry, KS; (1); 26/48; Cmnty Wkr; Chorus; Stdnt Wk; Educ.

STANSBURY, KEVIN; Hesston HS; Hesston, KS; (3); Church Yth Grp; Cmnty Wkr; Key Clb; Letterman Clb; Teachers Aide; Varsity Clb; Acpl Chr; Chorus; Church Choir; Color Guard; St Trk; Hutchinson JC; Law Enforcement.

STANTON, ERRICA; Troy HS; Troy, KS; (3); Drama Clb; Natl FFA Org; Pep Clb; Chorus; School Musical; Stage Crew; JV Score Keeper; JV Vllybl; Hon Roll; Oceanography; Animal Sci.

STAPLETON, JANELLE; Coldwater Jr Sr HS; Mullinville, KS; (3); FCA; FHA; Letterman Clb; Office Aide; Pep Clb; Chorus; School Musical; Swing Chorus; Variety Show; Yrbk; Pedtrc Nrse.

STAPP, TREVOR; Holcomb HS; Holcomb, KS; (2); Sec Soph Cls; Pres Jr Cls; Var L Bsktbl; Var L Ftbl; Var L Trk; High Hon Roll; NHS; Ntl Merit Ltr.

STARK, BREANNE; Bishop Ward HS; Kansas City, KS; (3); JCL; Pep Clb; Varsity Clb; Ofcr Jr Cls; Chrldng; Sftbl; Johnson Cty CC; Dntl Hygnst.

STARK, IAN; Southeast HS; Weir, KS; (4); 17/56; Science Clb; Hon Roll; JETS Awd; Pittsburg ST Univ; Cmprt Prgm.

STARK, JOSH T; Rose Hill HS; Rose Hill, KS; (3); Debate Tm; Math Tm; Scholastic Bowl; Spanish Clb; Teachers Aide; Varsity Clb; Band; Drm Mjr(t); Yrbk; Ofcr Bsbl; Var Soccer Capt; Spcl Hnrs For Best Sportsmanship; Several Trng Camps BB & Soc Participant; KS Univ; Engrng.

STARK, LEVI J; Campus HS; Wichita, KS; (3); 5/206; FHA; German Clb; Intnl Clb; Teachers Aide; Var Ftbl; Powder Puff Ftbl; Var Trk; Var Wt Lftg; High Hon Roll; NHS.

STARKEY, JEFFREY A; Colby Sr HS; Colby, KS; (2); Church Yth Grp; Chess Clb; Band; Chorus; Jazz Band; Mrchg Band; Pep Band; Var Bsktbl; Var Crs Cntry; JV Golf.

STARNES, JOHN THOMAS; Wichita West HS; Wichita, KS; (3); Church Yth Grp; Cmnty Wkr; Debate Tm; NFL; Scholastic Bowl; Golf; Wrstlng; Hon Roll; NHS.

STARNS, NICOLE; Thomas More Prep-Marion HS; Hays, KS; (1); Drama Clb; French Clb; School Musical; School Play; Rep Frsh Cls; Ofcr Stu Cncl; JV Chrldng; Trk; Vllybl; High Hon Roll; Ambs; Frnscs.

STATEN, SARAH; Blue Valley HS; Stilwell, KS; (4); 26/244; Boy Scts; Church Yth Grp; Cmnty Wkr; 4-H; Teachers Aide; 4-H Awd; Hon Roll; NHS; Prfct Atten Awd; ST FHA/HERO Treas; Johnson Cty 4-H Ambsdr; Presdntl Excl In Ed Awd; KS ST U; Constr Sci/Mgmt.

STAUDACHER, VICKIE S; Wichita North HS; Wichita, KS; (3); Girl Scts; Intnl Clb; Pep Clb; Band; Chorus; Drill Tm; Mrchg Band; School Musical; Ofcr Jr Cls; Pom Pon; Girl Scouts Gold Awd; Pom/Chrldng Cmptn Awds; Multi Yr Listing; WSU; Bio/Zoology.

STAUFFER, BECKY; Washburn Rural HS; Topeka, KS; (3); 4/357; Church Yth Grp; Dance Clb; SADD; Variety Show; Ed Yrbk; Ofcr Sr Cls; Chrldng; Powder Puff Ftbl; Tennis; High Hon Roll; KS U; Bus Commnctn.

STAUFFER, ELISHA; Wichita Northwest HS; Wichita, KS; (2); #1 in class; Church Yth Grp; Drama Clb; Math Tm; Church Choir; Stage Crew; Variety Show; Var Chrldng; High Hon Roll; Hon Roll.

STAUFFER, ISAAC; Northeast Magnet HS; Wichita, KS; (4); #1 in class; VP Church Yth Grp; JA; Capt Quiz Bowl; Science Clb; Rep Frsh Cls; Treas Jr Cls; Rep Sr Cls; Treas Stu Cncl; Gov Hon Prg Awd; High Hon Roll; KS ST Univ; Engr.

STAUFFER, NANCY MAGDALENE; El Dorado HS; El Dorado, KS; (2); Debate Tm; Drama Clb; Math Clb; NFL; Scholastic Bowl; Band; Stage Crew; Var Swmmng; High Hon Roll; NHS; ST Qlfr His Day Cmptn; Cosmlgy.

STAUTH, TARA K; Cimarron HS; Cimarron, KS; (4); 6/49; Church Yth Grp; FCA; GAA; Pep Clb; Teachers Aide; Band; Yrbk; Bsktbl; Trk; Vllybl; Ft Hays State Univ; Spch Thrpy.

STEARNS, JOSEPH M; Wellington Sr HS; Wellington, KS; (3); 9/165; Church Yth Grp; Acpl Chr; Chorus; Pres Frsh Cls; Var Bsbl; JV Bsktbl; Var Ftbl; Hon Roll; NHS.

STEARS, BENJAMIN; Olathe North Sr HS; Olathe, KS; (3); 1/350; Debate Tm; Drama Clb; HOBY; NFL; Speech Tm; Thesps; Acpl Chr; Chorus; School Musical; School Play; KS Music Edctrs Assn All St Choir; IN Chptr Natl Socty Fund Raising Exec Yth Achvt Awd; U Of NE; Law.

STEC, WADE T; Sylvan Unified HS; Sylvan Grove, KS; (3); 7/19; Am Leg Boys St; Quiz Bowl; Scholastic Bowl; SADD; VP Jr Cls; Var L Golf; Hon Roll; NHS; Masonic Essay Cntst Wnr; 4 Yr Coll; Rdlgy.

STECKLEIN, KAREN; Sylvan Unified HS; Sylvan Grove, KS; (3); Am Leg Aux Girls St; Pep Clb; Chorus; Treas Jr Cls; Var L Bsktbl; Capt Chrldng; Var L Sftbl; Var L Vllybl; High Hon Roll; NHS; Kayette Clb.

STEEBY, WILLIAM; Watlena HS; Wathena, KS; (3); Am Leg Boys St; Natl FFA Org; VICA; Treas Frsh Cls; Treas Jr Cls; Hon Roll.

STEELE, EMILY S; Yates Ctr HS; Yates Center, KS; (2); Drama Clb; Letterman Clb; NFL; Office Aide; Pep Clb; Spanish Clb; Speech Tm; SADD; Bsktbl; Mgr(s); KAYS Rec Dir; Bus.

STEELE, JORDAN R; Goodland HS; Goodland, KS; (3); 30/82; Church Yth Grp; Cmnty Wkr; FHA; Chorus; Ftbl; Hon Roll; Fort Hay ST; Engrng.

STEELE JR, KENNETH; Junction City HS; Junction City, KS; (3); German Clb; SADD; Stat Bsktbl; KS Univ; Legal, Admin Prsnl.

STEELE, KEVIN D; Blue Valley Northwest HS; Overland Park, KS; (4); 1/347; Quiz Bowl; Scholastic Bowl; High Hon Roll; NHS; Ntl Merit SF; Pres Schlr; St Schlr; Participated In The Resident Hnrs Pgm U Of Southern CA; Taught Supplemental Chem Cls In Med-Cor USC; Univ Southern CA; Pub Policy.

STEELE, LESLIE; Jefferson West HS; Meriden, KS; (4); 7/58; Letterman Clb; SADD; School Play; Crs Cntry; Trk; High Hon Roll; Hon Roll; NHS; U KS; Art Ed.

STEELE, MANDY K; Yates Ctr HS; Yates Center, KS; (3); 13/52; Hon Roll; KAYS Pres 95-; Allen Cty CC; Elem Ed.

STEFEK, JESSICA R; Ellsworth HS; Ellsworth, KS; (1); #5 in class; Church Yth Grp; Letterman Clb; Natl FFA Org; Band; Mrchg Band; School Play; Var L Crs Cntry; Var Trk; High Hon Roll.

STEFFAN, AMANDA; Chase HS; Chase, KS; (2); Church Yth Grp; Cmnty Wkr; Drama Clb; FHA; Letterman Clb; Pep Clb; Spanish Clb; Varsity Clb; Band; Chorus; Fort Hays ST; Tchr.

STEFFEN, TYSON M; Pawnee Heights East HS; Burdett, KS; (1); Church Yth Grp; VP 4-H; Quiz Bowl; Band; Chorus; Mrchg Band; Pep Band; School Musical; Treas Frsh Cls; JV Bsktbl; KS ST Univ.

STEGEMAN, MICHELLE M; Louisburg HS; Louisburg, KS; (2); 1/105; Sec Pres Art Clb; Capt Bus Profs of Am; Debate Tm; FCA; Math Clb; Math Tm; SADD; Trk; High Hon Roll; Prfct Atten Awd; Tech Stu Assoc; St 1st Plc Fnlst; Natl Part; Art Exc Art Merit Awd; Math.

STEGMAN, REBECCA A; Lincoln Jr Sr HS; Lincoln, KS; (4); 12/30; Church Yth Grp; Cmnty Wkr; Girl Scts; Letterman Clb; Office Aide; Pep Clb; SADD; Band; Chorus; Church Choir; KS Assn Yth Club Pres; Ft Hays ST Univ; Graphic Dsgn.

STEGNER, DAN; Ellsworth HS; Kanopolis, KS; (4); 1/67; Pres Church Yth Grp; Cmnty Wkr; Intnl Clb; Office Aide; Cit Awd; High Hon Roll; Prfct Atten Awd; St Schlr; Barton Comm Coll; Chem.

STEICHEN, LAUREL M; Manhattan HS; Manhattan, KS; (2); Science Clb; Spanish Clb; Acpl Chr; Church Choir; School Musical; Var L Socr; JV Tennis; High Hon Roll; NHS; Yth Soccr Coach; Giftd Smmr Schl Tchng; Multi St Fld Bio Cls.

STEIN, HEATHER L; Council Grove HS; Alta Vista, KS; (2); FCA; FHA; SADD; Bsktbl; Vllybl; Hon Roll; Grnd Vlly St Univ; Phys Thpy.

STEIN, KRISTAN; Campus HS; Haysville, KS; (4); 47/198; Cmnty Wkr; French Clb; Q&S; SADD; Teachers Aide; Ed Yrbk; Sec Sr Cls; Ofcr Stu Cncl; Var L Chrldng; Var L Swmmng; Campus Pride Pres; Wichita Bus Journal Spotlighten Srs; KS ST U Schlsp; KS ST U; Jrnlsm.

STEIN, MICHAEL W; Halstead HS; Halstead, KS; (3); Teachers Aide; Varsity Clb; Var Golf; High Hon Roll; Hon Roll; Woodwrkng; Stdnt Of Mnth Awd 2 Mnths; KS ST; Engrng.

STEIN, PHILLIP; Olathe East Sr HS; Overland Park, KS; (3); Am Leg Boys St; Church Yth Grp; Debate Tm; NFL; Thesps; Acpl Chr; Rep Pres Stu Cncl; High Hon Roll; NHS; Pres Acad Fit Awd; Presbyn Yth Ldrshp Cncl; Ambassador Natl Ldrshp Camp; Pre-Law.

STEINBRINK, ERIN M; Madison Jr Sr HS; Madison, KS; (3); Am Leg Aux Girls St; FBLA; German Clb; Letterman Clb; Quiz Bowl; Band; Chorus; Jazz Band; Mrchg Band; Pep Band; Summer League Bsktbl; Sunday Schl & Chrch Act; League Schlsp Test Participant.

STEINBROCK, JUSTIN J; Clifton-Clyde HS; Clifton, KS; (3); 12/31; Boy Scts; Cmnty Wkr; Drama Clb; FBLA; FHA; Letterman Clb; Natl FFA Org; NFL; Spanish Clb; Speech Tm; K ST.

STEINER, CASEY J; Riley Cty HS; Manhattan, KS; (3); Treas FCA; Treas FBLA; Math Tm; Pres Pep Clb; Treas SADD; Treas Stu Cncl; Var L Bsktbl; Var L Ftbl; High Hon Roll; Treas NHS; Natl Qlfr Bus Clctns; FBLA; KS ST U; Arch Eng.

STEINER, CINDY A; Great Bend Sr HS; Great Bend, KS; (2); Church Yth Grp; Girl Scts; Pep Clb; Spanish Clb; Teachers Aide; JV Chrldng; High Hon Roll; Prfct Atten Awd; Keyette Brd; Env Clb Brd; Fort Hays St Univ; Bus.

STEINER, KEVIN J; Centre Jr Sr HS; Lincolnville, KS; (2); Letterman Clb; Pep Clb; Varsity Clb; School Play; Ofcr Jr Cls; Bsktbl; Ftbl; Trk; Wt Lftg; His Tchr & Coaching.

STEINERT, ANDY; Hoisington HS; Hoisington, KS; (4); 17/62; Am Leg Boys St; Church Yth Grp; Letterman Clb; Math Tm; Varsity Clb; Var Bsbl; JV Bsktbl; Var Ftbl; Var Wt Lftg; Hon Roll; KS ST Univ; Ag.

STEINERT, MICHAEL; Hoisington HS; Hoisington, KS; (4); 12/62; Am Leg Boys St; Church Yth Grp; Letterman Clb; Math Tm; Varsity Clb; Var L Bsbl; JV Bsktbl; Var L Ftbl; Var Wt Lftg; Hon Roll; KS ST U.

STEINFORT, JOHN; Valley Heights Jr Sr HS; Blue Rapids, KS; (4); 1/28; Am Leg Boys St; Church Yth Grp; HOBY; Natl FFA Org; Band; Rep Pres Stu Cncl; Capt L Bsktbl; Capt L Ftbl; Hon Roll; NHS; Rrl Elec Coop Ldrshp Smnr; Hab For Hum Vol; Vet Med.

STEINKE, CORY; Olpe Schl; Olpe, KS; (4); 3/26; Cmnty Wkr; Quiz Bowl; Teachers Aide; VP Jr Cls; Rep Stu Cncl; Var Capt Bsktbl; Var Capt Ftbl; Cit Awd; High Hon Roll; Prfct Atten Awd; Optmst Ldrshp Awd; Wash DC Ldrshp Awd; Co-Fndr Olpe Lgn Bsbl 95; Emporia St U; Engrng.

STEINKE, SCOTT W; Olpe Schl; Olpe, KS; (2); 8/26; Cmnty Wkr; Var Bsbl; JV Bsktbl; JV Ftbl; Var Trk; Hon Roll.

STEINKUHLER, SARA; Emporia HS; Emporia, KS; (3); 48/289; Church Yth Grp; Sec FCA; FBLA; Pep Clb; Teachers Aide; Chorus; Ofcr Jr Cls; Rep Stu Cncl; Var Chrldng; Var Gym; Kayettes; Dnce Tm; Bus Admin.

STEINLAGE, RENEE; Centralia Schl; Corning, KS; (2); 6/26; 4-H; FHA; Natl FFA Org; Chorus; School Musical; Yrbk; VP Frsh Cls; Sftbl; Trk; Hon Roll.

STEINMAN, RANDEL L; Chanute Sr HS; Humboldt, KS; (3); 43/143; Art Clb; Church Yth Grp; FCA; 4-H; FBLA; Pep Clb; Band; Jazz Band; Mrchg Band; Pep Band; 4-H Ambassador & Jr Clb Ldr; Natural Helper; Page For KS House Of Reps; KS ST Univ.

STEINMETZ, DEANNA M; Immaculata HS; Bonner Springs, KS; (2); Church Yth Grp; GAA; Hosp Aide; Intnl Clb; NFL; Thesps; School Play; Rep Frsh Cls; Rep Soph Cls; Rep Jr Cls; Stdnts Who Care; Bio/His.

STEINMETZ, JAROD M; Sumner Acad Of Arts & Science; Kansas City, KS; (3); Art Clb; Key Clb; Spanish Clb; Chorus; High Hon Roll; Hon Roll; NHS; KS City KS CC.

STEJSKAL, DUSTIN A; Greensburg HS; Greensburg, KS; (3); Debate Tm; Letterman Clb; VP Frsh Cls; Pres Soph Cls; VP Jr Cls; Pres Sr Cls; Pres VP Stu Cncl; Var Bsktbl; Var Trk; Hon Roll; 9 Hrs Coll Credits; U Of KS; Pre Law/Bus.

STELLJES, SPENCER H; Derby HS; Derby, KS; (1); Acpl Chr; Chorus; Rep Frsh Cls; VP Soph Cls; Ofcr Stu Cncl; JV Crs Cntry; JV Golf; Gov Hon Prg Awd; Hon Roll; Pres Acad Fit Awd; Pgd Cpto Sntr Frnd; U Of KS; Crdvsclr Srgn.

STENSON, REBECCA; Andover HS; Andover, KS; (2); 31/167; Church Yth Grp; SADD; Band; Mrchg Band; High Hon Roll.

STEPHEN, DENICIA; Turner HS; Kansas City, KS; (3); 36/260; Bus Profs of Am; Spanish Clb; Vol Wrk Wth Foster Kids; Interpretng.

STEPHENS, BRADY A; Emporia HS; Emporia, KS; (3); FBLA; Pep Clb; Teachers Aide; JV Bsktbl; Var Cit Awd; High Hon Roll; Hon Roll; Prfct Atten Awd; Pres Acad Fit Awd; KS ST U; Civil Engr.

STEPHENS, CLINT; Eureka Jr Sr HS; Severy, KS; (2); 10/63; 4-H; FHA; Quiz Bowl; Science Clb; Spanish Clb; Yrbk; Stat Bsktbl; JV Golf; High Hon Roll.

STEPHENS JR, DONALD E; Northeast HS; Arcadia, KS; (4); 7/40; Am Leg Boys St; Art Clb; Library Aide; Band; Mrchg Band; Pep Band; Wt Lftg; Hon Roll; NHS; Prfct Atten Awd; St Music Festival Tenor-Sax Solo Receiving I Ratings Gold Medals; Pittsburg ST Univ; Elec Engr.

STEPHENS, EMELIA M; Lawrence HS; Lawrence, KS; (4); 96/520; Pres Church Yth Grp; Key Clb; NFL; Orch; Stat Bsktbl; Mgr(s); Stat Vllybl; NHS; Debate Tm; French Clb; Pres Awd Educl Excl; Dstngshd Schlr; U Of KS; Crmnlst FBI.

STEPHENS, ERIN M; Wichita North HS; Wichita, KS; (2); Church Yth Grp; Library Aide; Yrbk; Var Sftbl; Vllybl; Hon Roll; Marine Biology.

STEPHENS, J MICHAELA; Council Grove HS; Alta Vista, KS; (3); FHA; Natl FFA Org; SADD; School Play; Hon Roll; Tchng.

STEPHENS, JASON; Lewis Schl; Garfield, KS; (3); 6/20; Am Leg Boys St; Teachers Aide; Band; Chorus; Mrchg Band; Pep Band; School Musical; School Play; Var L Bsktbl; Var L Ftbl; Hutchinson CC; Criminal Justc.

STEPHENS, LYNE; Ashland HS; Ashland, KS; (4); 10/25; Church Yth Grp; 4-H; Quiz Bowl; Speech Tm; Teachers Aide; Band; Chorus; Jazz Band; Pep Band; Ofcr Stu Cncl; Non Resident Trustee Schlrshp Western ST Coll CO Schlrshp; Bryan Allison Mem Schlrshp; Western ST Coll Of CO; His.

STEPHENS, MELISSA M; Ozark Adventist Acad; Olathe, KS; (4); 11/52; Church Yth Grp; Drama Clb; Band; Chorus; School Play; Yrbk; Pres Soph Cls; Sec Sr Cls; Ftbl; Socr.

STEPHENS, RYAN M; Shawnee Mission South HS; Lenexa, KS; (3); Boy Scts; Church Yth Grp; Cmnty Wkr; Letterman Clb; Scholastic Bowl; Crs Cntry; Ftbl; Trk; High Hon Roll; NHS; Brigham Young Univ.

STEPHENS, SARAH; Wichita Heights HS; Wichita, KS; (4); Bus Profs of Am; Church Yth Grp; Cmnty Wkr; Pep Clb; Spanish Clb; SADD; Band; Mrchg Band; Var Tennis; United Way Vol, Dwayne L Wallace Cmte Vice Chm, Yth Day Crng Plnng Cmte; Wichita ST U; Law.

STEPHENS, STARR R; St Mary's Colgan HS; Arcadia, KS; (3); Pep Clb; Hon Roll; Pittsburg ST Univ; Med Field.

STEPHENS, SUSAN L; Field Kindley Mem Sr HS; Coffeyville, KS; (1); German Clb; Letterman Clb; Var Swmmng; High Hon Roll.

STEPHENS, TIMOTHY; Lawrence HS; Lawrence, KS; (3); 1/650; Pres FCA; VP Science Clb; Treas Pres Key Clb; Church Choir; Orch; JV Trk; Hon Roll; NHS; Ntl Merit Ltr; Prfct Atten Awd; Med.

STEPHENSEN, BRETT; Leavenworth HS; Leavenworth, KS; (3); Art Clb; Boy Scts; Church Yth Grp; German Clb; Ski Clb; Band; Rptr Yrbk; Socr; Tennis; Wrstlng; Weber St Univ; Advtsng.

STEPHENSON, ANTHONY D; Atchison Sr HS; Atchison, KS; (1); Cmnty Wkr; Letterman Clb; Spanish Clb; Band; Mrchg Band; Pep Band; School Musical; Socr; Hon Roll; KY U.

STEPHENSON, CARRIE E; Shawnee Mission E Sr HS; Shawnee Mission, KS; (3); Church Yth Grp; Cmnty Wkr; Dance Clb; Hosp Aide; Natl Beta Clb; Pep Clb; Service Clb; High Hon Roll; NHS; SHARE Chprsn; Pre-Prof Stu St Ballet Of MO.

STEPHENSON, CHARLES D; Central Heights Sr HS; Rantoul, KS; (2); Art Clb; Church Yth Grp; FCA; Letterman Clb; Natl FFA Org; Quiz Bowl; Science Clb; Band; Jazz Band; Mrchg Band; Level I & II Future Astronaut Trng.

STEPHENSON, JULIE A; Frontenac Jr Sr HS; Frontenac, KS; (4); 10/36; Cmnty Wkr; Drama Clb; FTA; Office Aide; Pep Clb; Spanish Clb; Band; Flag Corp; Mrchg Band; Pep Band; Pittsburg ST Univ; Scndry Ed.

STEPHENSON, TRAVIS J; Mc Pherson HS; Mc Pherson, KS; (1); Church Yth Grp; CAP; Math Tm; Quiz Bowl; Science Clb; Orch; JV Golf; High Hon Roll; Oddsy Of Mind; Sci Olympd; Dist Orch; Air Force Acad; Arntcs.

STEPPS, TRAVIS U; Ft Scott HS; Fort Scott, KS; (3); Am Leg Boys St; Church Yth Grp; Cmnty Wkr; Letterman Clb; Office Aide; Pep Clb; Service Clb; Church Choir; Stage Crew; Variety Show; Neosha Vly Yth Dept 1st VP; Primary Sndy Schl Instr; Pittsburg ST U; Scndry Instr.

STERLING, SCOTT M; Shawnee Heights Sr HS; Berryton, KS; (2); Church Yth Grp; FCA; Bsktbl; Var L Golf; High Hon Roll; St Golf Tourn 4th Pl; AAV Bsbl Natls In Memphis & Columbus; Engr.

STETLER, ELIZABETH; Kansas City Christian Schl; Shawnee Mission, KS; (4); Church Yth Grp; Debate Tm; Math Tm; Speech Tm; Teachers Aide; Varsity Clb; Rptr Yrbk; Pres Frsh Cls; VP Soph Cls; Ofcr Jr Cls; Ldrshp Schol Nom; Templeton Awd Nom; KS St Univ; Arch.

STETZLER, JENNIFER L; Blue Vlly HS; Shawnee Mission, KS; (3); Sec Drama Clb; Thesps; Chorus; School Musical; School Play; Hon Roll; NHS; Wellesley Bk Awd For Ldshp And Schol; Perf Arts.

STEUBER, JENNY; Turner HS; De Soto, KS; (3); SADD; Chorus; Hon Roll; Mentorshp; DECA; KAYS; KU; Children.

STEUBER, KRISTINA R; Maize HS; Wichita, KS; (1); Church Yth Grp; Cmnty Wkr; Hosp Aide; Hon Roll; Pres Schlr; ELCA Cntrl St Synod Cncl Yth Rep.

STEUVER, KENDRA; Wichita West HS; Wichita, KS; (3); 20/300; Am Leg Aux Girls St; Teachers Aide; Pres Jr Cls; Pres Sr Cls; Capt Socr; Vllybl; Hon Roll; NHS; Scndry Ed.

STEVE, CYNTHIA; Pleasant Ridge HS; Leavenworth, KS; (4); 1/64; Pres 4-H; Pres FBLA; Natl FFA Org; Capt Scholastic Bowl; VP SADD; Pres Frsh Cls; Pres Soph Cls; Var L Trk; Var Capt Vllybl; NHS; Emporia ST U; Bus Ed Tchr.

STEVEN, ARON D; Maize HS; Wichita, KS; (2); Spanish Clb; JV Socr; Hon Roll; Ntl Merit Ltr; Bus.

STEVENS, ANGIE; Nickerson HS; Hutchinson, KS; (2); Church Yth Grp; FCA; FHA; Science Clb; Spanish Clb; Acpl Chr; Chorus; Drill Tm; Chrldng; Pom Pon; Peer Cnslr; KS U; Psych.

STEVENS, BRENT C; Maize HS; Wichita, KS; (1); Church Yth Grp; JV Socr; Wt Lftg; Hon Roll; Eng.

STEVENS, BRETT R; Ft Scott HS; Ft Scott, KS; (2); Boy Scts; Chess Clb; Eagle Sct; Ft Scott Natl Histrc Site.

STEVENS, CHRIS J; Campus HS; Wichita, KS; (2); Church Yth Grp; Library Aide; Pep Clb; Science Clb; Band; Mrchg Band; Pep Band; JV Bsbl; Score Keeper; High Hon Roll; Arch.

STEVENS, CURTIS L; Scott Comm HS; Scott City, KS; (3); Am Leg Boys St; Church Yth Grp; Cmnty Wkr; Debate Tm; 4-H; Speech Tm; SADD; Pres Frsh Cls; Pres Soph Cls; Pres Jr Cls; Peer Cnslr; Stu Congress; Lawyer.

STEVENS, JENNIFER D; Lacrosse HS; La Crosse, KS; (3); 4/28; Drama Clb; Q&S; Pres Band; Rep Chorus; Mrchg Band; Yrbk; Sec Treas Sr Cls; High Hon Roll; NHS; Prfct Atten Awd; Bus.

STEVENS, JENNIFER R; Chanute Sr HS; Forsyth, IL; (2); Chorus; JV Bsktbl; JV Mgr(s); Hon Roll; Flwshp Chrstn Ath; Schlstc Hon Roll; Prncpls Ldrshp Team.

STEVENS, JONELLE; Ashland HS; Ashland, KS; (3); 7/14; Sec 4-H; HOBY; Quiz Bowl; Speech Tm; School Play; Phtg Rptr Yrbk; Treas Soph Cls; JV Bsktbl; JV Var Tennis; Hon Roll; EMT; Hutchison CC; Paramedic.

STEVENS, KENDRA; Oxford HS; Oxford, KS; (3); 5/30; Church Yth Grp; VP FBLA; Varsity Clb; JV Bsktbl; Var Chrldng; Var Trk; Var Vllybl; High Hon Roll; Hon Roll; NHS; VP Kayettes.

STEVENS, KRISTY L; Jayhawk-Linn HS; Mound City, KS; (3); Debate Tm; GAA; Rptr Pres Natl FFA Org; Chorus; Nwsp; Bsktbl; Trk; Vllybl; Hon Roll.

STEVENS, MELISSA F; Maize HS; Wichita, KS; (4); Hosp Aide; NFL; Science Clb; Spanish Clb; SADD; Chorus; Variety Show; JV Bsktbl; JV Var Socr; Hon Roll.

STEVENS, MICHAEL; Marmaton Valley Jr Sr HS; Kincaid, KS; (2); 2/35; Church Yth Grp; Natl FFA Org; Pep Clb; Golf; Wt Lftg; High Hon Roll; Hon Roll; Tech Stu Assoc; Ag Edu.

STEVENS, SARAH C; Shawnee Mission N HS; Overland Park, KS; (3); Church Yth Grp; Pep Clb; Orch; Var L Trk; Dance Clb; NHS; Strllng Strngs; 2nd Chair St Orch Cmptn; Emporia ST U; Spec Ed.

STEVENS, SETH L; Downs HS; Downs, KS; (1); FCA; FHA; Quiz Bowl; Scholastic Bowl; Band; Pep Band; JV L Bsktbl; JV Ftbl; Var L Golf; High Hon Roll; U Of KS; Bus Mgmt.

STEVENS, STEPHANIE; Erie HS; Erie, KS; (1); 6/42; FCA; Spanish Clb; Sec Frsh Cls; Chrldng; Sftbl; Hon Roll; Emporia ST U; Speech Pthlgst.

STEVENS, ZACH; Olathe North Sr HS; Olathe, KS; (3); Church Yth Grp; Drama Clb; Letterman Clb; Teachers Aide; Varsity Clb; School Play; Ftbl; Trk; Wt Lftg; Wrstlng; Mission Trips To Mexico; KV.

STEVENSEN, PAULA S; Olpe Schl; Olpe, KS; (3); Church Yth Grp; Teachers Aide; Band; Chorus; Church Choir; Mrchg Band; Pep Band; School Play; Stage Crew; JV Bsktbl; Photo Yrbk, Nwsp; Piano Tchr; Med.

STEVENSON, CHRISTOPHER M; Shawnee Mission North HS; Shawnee Mission, KS; (4); Church Yth Grp; Hosp Aide; Math Tm; Pep Clb; Spanish Clb; Teachers Aide; Var Bsbl; Var Socr; High Hon Roll; NHS; Southern Nazarene U; Sports Med.

STEVENSON, KEITH R; Great Bend Sr HS; Great Bend, KS; (4); 140/243; Spanish Clb; Ftbl; Var Wt Lftg; Var Wrstlng; Kiwanis Awd; Dodge City CC; Engrng.

STEVENSON, ROBERT A; Shawnee Mission E Sr HS; Shawnee Mission, KS; (2); Church Yth Grp; Model UN; Var Ice Hcky; High Hon Roll.

STEVENSON, SCHAEFFER A; Washington HS; Kansas City, KS; (3); Band; Jazz Band; Mrchg Band; Pep Band; Intrml Ftbl; High Hon Roll; Hon Roll; DECA; Langston Univ; Eng.

STEWART, AARON M; Manhattan HS; Manhattan, KS; (3); L Ftbl; Wt Lftg; L Wrstlng; Fort Hays ST; Cchng.

STEWART, ALISON N; Wichita Southeast HS; Wichita, KS; (1); Church Yth Grp; GAA; Var Socr; World Geo Awd; KS Univ; Dermatologist.

STEWART, BRADY L; Yates Ctr HS; Yates Center, KS; (2); Art Clb; FCA; Letterman Clb; Ofcr Bsbl; Ftbl; Wt Lftg; Hon Roll.

STEWART, BRIAN R; Uniontown HS; Bronson, KS; (3); FHA; Natl FFA Org; Bsktbl; Pittsburgh ST Univ.

STEWART, CHAD R; Blue Valley Northwest HS; Overland Park, KS; (1); Church Yth Grp; Ofcr Bsbl; Bsktbl; Mgr(s); Stat Vllybl; Hon Roll.

STEWART, CHRISSY; Marmaton Valley Jr Sr HS; Iola, KS; (1); 6/40; Church Yth Grp; Drama Clb; 4-H; FHA; Natl FFA Org; Pep Clb; Quiz Bowl; Band; Flag Corp; Mrchg Band; KS ST; Sports Med.

STEWART, COURTNEY D; Blue Valley Northwest HS; Overland Park, KS; (3); 1/360; Church Yth Grp; Debate Tm; Band; Mrchg Band; Pep Band; Sftbl; Vllybl; High Hon Roll; NHS; EKL Sftbl Hnrbl Mntn; Sun Cntry Hnrbl Mntn Sftbl.

STEWART, DANIEL RYAN; Garden City Sr HS; Garden City, KS; (4); Chess Clb; Computer Clb; Spanish Clb; Hon Roll; Cmptr Sci.

STEWART, DHON D; Wichita East HS; Wichita, KS; (3); 25/250; 4-H; 4-H Awd; Hon Roll; Prfct Atten Awd; Vet Tech.

STEWART, JACQUE S; Cheney Jr Sr HS; Cheney, KS; (4); Church Yth Grp; Drama Clb; Band; Mrchg Band; Pep Band; School Play; Stat Bsktbl; Pres Acad Fit Awd; Highland Comm Coll; Commercial.

STEWART, JARED; Wellington Sr HS; Wellington, KS; (1); Church Yth Grp; Band; Pep Band; Var Tennis; ST Solo Band; Reg Tennis.

STEWART, JASON; Pleasant Ridge HS; Leavenworth, KS; (4); 28/61; VP 4-H; Letterman Clb; Rptr Natl FFA Org; Spanish Clb; Teachers Aide; Sec Sr Cls; Var Capt Ftbl; Trk; Wt Lftg; Wrstlng; Hum Clb; Homcmng King; KS ST; Ag.

STEWART, JENNIFER R; Bishop Carroll Catholic HS; Wichita, KS; (3); 13/181; Hosp Aide; Teachers Aide; High Hon Roll; NHS; Golden Eagle Acad Achvmt Awd.

STEWART, JEREMY; Wellington Sr HS; Wellington, KS; (1); Church Yth Grp; Var Tennis.

STEWART, JOHN; Wichita Collegiate Schl; Wichita, KS; (2); Drama Clb; Quiz Bowl; Scholastic Bowl; JV Tennis; High Hon Roll; Literary Clb; Biochem.

STEWART, JONAS; Leavenworth HS; Leavenworth, KS; (3); Am Leg Boys St; VP Drama Clb; Teachers Aide; Thesps; School Musical; School Play; Stage Crew; Rep Jr Cls; Pres Stu Cncl; Hon Roll; Washburn Univ Law Cmp; KSHSAA Stuco Wrkshp; KS St Univ; Law.

STEWART, KATHRYN V; Shawnee Mission N HS; Merriam, KS; (3); 19/450; Latin Clb; Mrchg Band; Orch; School Musical; Phtg Nwsp; High Hon Roll; Ntl Merit SF; Sec Of Amnsty Intl; Stolling Strng; KILE Fand Clb; KU; Math.

STEWART, KELLY A; Lawrence HS; Lawrence, KS; (4); 43/521; Key Clb; Band; Mrchg Band; Rep Stu Cncl; Var Capt Swmmng; High Hon Roll; NHS; Prfct Atten Awd; Pres Acad Fit Awd; Pres Schlr; Comm Svc; Sr Planning Comm; Private Clb Swimming; U Of KS; Bio; Pre-Med.

STEWART, KENDA R; Beloit Jr Sr HS; Hunter, KS; (4); #1 in class; Pres Treas Church Yth Grp; Pres VP 4-H; German Clb; Ed Yrbk; VP Stu Cncl; Stat L Bsktbl; 4-H Awd; Gov Hon Prg Awd; NHS; St Schlr; Teens As Tchrs; KS ST Univ; Physician.

STEWART, KRISHA L; Beloit Jr Sr HS; Hunter, KS; (2); Sec Church Yth Grp; 4-H; French Clb; Quiz Bowl; Scholastic Bowl; Spanish Clb; Speech Tm; Stage Crew; Treas Frsh Cls; Rep Stu Cncl; KS Univ; Psychlgy.

STEWART, LISA; Leavenworth HS; Fort Leavenworth, KS; (2); Stage Crew; JV Crs Cntry; Var JV Trk; High Hon Roll; Hon Roll; Publc Rltns.

STEWART, MANDI; Hutchinson HS; Hutchinson, KS; (3); Church Yth Grp; Office Aide; Thesps; Band; Church Choir; Mrchg Band; Pep Band; School Musical; School Play; Stage Crew; Dist Band 95; Chrch Yth Cncl 95-; Creatv Reflectns Phtgrphy Rep 96; Southwest Bapt Univ; Elem Ed.

STEWART, MIKE; Spring Hill HS; Olathe, KS; (4); 8/98; Letterman Clb; Pep Clb; Science Clb; VP Frsh Cls; VP Jr Cls; Treas Stu Cncl; Var Capt Bsbl; Var L Bsktbl; JV Ftbl; High Hon Roll; NW MO ST U; Adv.

STEWART, STEPHANIE; Minneapolis HS; Minneapolis, KS; (4); 1/38; Am Leg Aux Girls St; French Clb; Quiz Bowl; Church Choir; School Musical; School Play; Rep Jr Cls; Rep Stu Cncl; Capt Chrldng; NHS; KS Rgnts Hnrs Acad; Law.

STICH, DELORES K; Thayer HS; Thayer, KS; (4); Office Aide; Science Clb; Teachers Aide; L Bsbl; Mgr(s); Trk; Universal Tech Inst; Comp Drftn.

STICKNEY, BETH; Medicine Lodge HS; Medicine Lodge, KS; (3); 4/55; Church Yth Grp; Drama Clb; HOBY; Letterman Clb; Library Aide; Pep Clb; Science Clb; Band; Chorus; Mrchg Band; Prtt Acad Olympcs; All Tnrmnt Chrldng Sqd; Bsktbl Hmcmng Rylty.

STIDHAM, ELIZABETH L; Turner HS; Kansas City, KS; (4); 39/192; Computer Clb; Library Aide; Q&S; Teachers Aide; VICA; Chorus; Nwsp; Lit Mag; Desktop Pblshng.

STIEBEN, SAMANTHA; Glasco HS; Glasco, KS; (1); Church Yth Grp; Band; Chorus; Mrchg Band; Pep Band; Var Chrldng; Hon Roll; City Pool Lifegrd; KS ST U.

STIFFLER, ROBERT M; Salina HS South; Salina, KS; (2); Hon Roll; Pres Acad Fit Awd; Summer Bsbl; KS Univ; CPA.

STIFTER, TINA M; Anderson Cty Jr Sr HS; Greeley, KS; (1); Drama Clb; Intnl Clb; Scholastic Bowl; SADD; Chorus; School Musical; Stage Crew; Mgr(s); High Hon Roll; Hon Roll; KS Assn Yth Kay Club; Tutored Schls Tutrng Prgm; Non Schl Spnsrd Smmr Sftbl.

STIGGE, REBECCA H; Winfield HS; Winfield, KS; (4); 1/177; Church Yth Grp; Debate Tm; Drama Clb; Scholastic Bowl; Speech Tm; Orch; Rptr Nwsp; Trk; High Hon Roll; NHS.

STILES, CALLIE S; Jefferson West HS; Meriden, KS; (3); 37/90; Church Yth Grp; 4-H; FTA; Hosp Aide; Natl FFA Org; Spanish Clb; Band; Chorus; Pep Band; Crs Cntry; Grange; Baker Univ; Nrsng.

STILES, NICK; Spring Hill HS; Spring Hill, KS; (3); 4-H; Office Aide; Band; Mrchg Band; Pep Band; JV Bsktbl; Hon Roll; Prfct Atten Awd; JCCC.

STILLWELL, JONATHAN A; Beloit Jr Sr HS; Beloit, KS; (1); Church Yth Grp; Chorus; Bsktbl; High Hon Roll; KS ST Univ.

STILSON, AMY; Wichita East HS; Wichita, KS; (3); Cmnty Wkr; Hosp Aide; Quiz Bowl; Spanish Clb; SADD; Orch; Var L Crs Cntry; Var L Trk; High Hon Roll; Sec NHS; Natl Cncl Tchrs Of Engl.

STILTNER, REBECCA D; Basehor Linwood HS; Linwood, KS; (3); 34/100; Church Yth Grp; Debate Tm; NFL; Band; Mrchg Band; Pep Band; School Play; Stage Crew; Stat Bsktbl; Mgr(s); Cnslr.

STILWELL, AMANDA; Maize HS; Wichita, KS; (4); Church Yth Grp; SADD; Band; Chorus; Mrchg Band; Pep Band; School Musical; Variety Show; Capt Pom Pon; Hon Roll; KAYS; Choir Ltr; Band Ltr; Pom Pon Ltr; 1 Rating Regnl Cmptn In Flute Solo 95-96; Butler CC; Nrsng.

STILWELL, JOHN; Shawnee Mission E Sr HS; Shawnee Mission, KS; (4); Math Clb; Math Tm; Model UN; Natl Beta Clb; Capt L Crs Cntry; L Trk; High Hon Roll; Hon Roll; JETS Awd; NHS; KS Hnr Schol; KS St Univ; Eng.

STIMAC, CHRISTIE K; Wetmore Schl; Wetmore, KS; (2); Sec Treas Church Yth Grp; Letterman Clb; Pep Clb; Teachers Aide; JV Var Bsktbl; Vllybl; Hon Roll; KS St Univ; Nurs.

STIMATZE, ALAN; USD 494 Syracuse HS; Syracuse, KS; (4); 7/29; Art Clb; Boy Scts; FHA; Office Aide; Teachers Aide; Yrbk; Intrml Capt Bsktbl; Ftbl; Hon Roll; Universal Tech Inst; Auto Mech.

STIMEC, BRANDY M; Pierson Jr HS; Kansas City, KS; (1); Cmnty Wkr; Dance Clb; GAA; Intnl Clb; Pep Clb; SADD; Drill Tm; L Pom Pon; JV Var Trk; High Hon Roll; NE ST U; Law.

STINEMETZ, DEANNA; Garden City Sr HS; Garden City, KS; (3); 45/356; Church Yth Grp; Band; Chorus; Church Choir; Mrchg Band; Pep Band; Hon Roll; Prfct Atten Awd; Gymnstcs; KS Ambsdr Msc; Dist 5 Chr; Wrld Msc Fstvl; Reg & St Msc Fest; Prom Comm; Emproia St U; Scndry Ed.

STINEMETZ, JENNIFER R; Pawnee Heights East HS; Burdett, KS; (1); Church Yth Grp; 4-H; Band; Chorus; Pep Band; School Musical; Sec Frsh Cls; JV Bsktbl; JV Vllybl; Hon Roll; Acad Olympics 6th Pl In Eng I; Piano Lessons; Sterling Coll; Pre-Schl Tchr.

STINEMETZ, TERESA A; Hanston Jr Sr HS; Hanston, KS; (4); 5/13; Church Yth Grp; FCA; Office Aide; Speech Tm; Band; Chorus; Church Choir; School Play; Rptr Nwsp; Rptr Yrbk; Miss Teen KS Schol; VFW Essay Cntst 2nd; Tabor Col; Bus Admin.

STINNETT, JOHN; Arkansas City HS; Arkansas City, KS; (3); 6/189; Boy Scts; Church Yth Grp; Band; Jazz Band; Mrchg Band; Pep Band; JV Bsbl; High Hon Roll; NHS; FCA; Eagle Sct.

STINSON, ELIZABETH; Shawnee Mssn E HS; Shawnee Mission, KS; (4); Church Yth Grp; Office Aide; Pep Clb; SADD; Teachers Aide; Church Choir; Rep Frsh Cls; Rep Soph Cls; Rep Jr Cls; Crs Cntry; Heralder; Sweetheart Queen; U Of KS; Earlyeduc.

STITES, ROBERT E C; Prairie View Jr Sr HS; La Cygne, KS; (2); 10/80; FBLA; Math Clb; JV Bsbl; JV Bsktbl.

STITH, BRIANNE L; Blue Valley Northwest HS; Overland Park, KS; (2); Church Yth Grp; Hosp Aide; Band; Church Choir; Orch; Yrbk; Hon Roll; Vol Heartland Schl Of Riding For Disabld People; Cnsl Trout Lake Camp MN; Med.

STOCK, DUSTIN W; Olathe East Sr HS; Lenexa, KS; (2); Debate Tm; NFL; Spanish Clb; Hon Roll; KS U; Law; Bus.

STOCKHAM, LISA; Garden City Sr HS; Garden City, KS; (3); Teachers Aide; Nwsp; Var Tennis; Hon Roll; Art Awds ST Lvl; Lit Publ Poem Publ; Red Cross Svcs; KS U; Psych/Engl Lit.

STOCKMAN, NATHAN; Goddard HS; Goddard, KS; (4); 7/158; Church Yth Grp; Math Tm; Science Clb; Spanish Clb; Thesps; Band; Jazz Band; Var Tennis; NHS; Pres Schlr; Gvrnrs Cncl For Tn Ldrshp; Tns As Tchrs; KS ST U; Chmcl Engrng.

STOCKTON, AMY K; Shawnee Mission Nw Sr HS; Shawnee Mission, KS; (3); Drill Tm; Mrchg Band; Ed Yrbk; Ofcr Frsh Cls; Ofcr Stu Cncl; Hon Roll; Fshn; Tap, Ballet, Jazz; U Of CO Boulder.

STOCKWELL, JIM R; Ness City HS; Ness City, KS; (3); Church Yth Grp; Letterman Clb; Rep Frsh Cls; Rep Soph Cls; Rep Jr Cls; JV L Bsktbl; Var L Ftbl; Var L Trk; Var L Wt Lftg; High Hon Roll; Powerlifting Champ; Outstdng Male Hvywght Lifter; Bigger/Faster/Stronger Mag All-Sectnl Team; Sports Med/PT.

STOCKWELL, SARAH; Burlington HS; Burlington, KS; (1); FBLA; Pep Clb; Thesps; Band; School Play; Sec Frsh Cls; Var Chrldng; Var Pom Pon; High Hon Roll; Pres Acad Fit Awd; Piano; Lifegrd; KS U; Law.

STOERMANN, LINDSEY A; Louisburg HS; Louisburg, KS; (2); Spanish Clb; Band; Mrchg Band; Pep Band; Hon Roll.

STOFFER, JENNIFER; Chapman HS; Abilene, KS; (4); 18/115; Church Yth Grp; Pres 4-H; Natl FFA Org; Chorus; Church Choir; Var L Vllybl; High Hon Roll; NHS; SADD; Teachers Aide; DARE; Teen Tchr; Tabor Coll; Elem Ed.

STOHS, AMBER; Marysville HS; Marysville, KS; (4); Am Leg Aux Girls St; Pres FCA; Sec Letterman Clb; Ed Yrbk; Sec Stu Cls; Var Bsktbl; Var Trk; Var Vllybl; Hon Roll; Kiwanis Awd; AAU Jr Olympian; 4 A St Rnnr Up Track 95; Kayettes Brd; KSU; Kinesiology.

STOHS, GINNY; Hanover Schl; Hanover, KS; (3); 1/16; Church Yth Grp; FBLA; FHA; Band; Chorus; Yrbk; Treas Jr Cls; Co-Capt Chrldng; Vllybl; NHS; KS ST U; Psych.

STOHS, GREG S; Wamego HS; Wamego, KS; (3); 25/122; Church Yth Grp; Science Clb; VICA; JV Capt Bsktbl; Trk; Cit Awd; Hon Roll; Prfct Atten Awd; Wood Working; Architecture; KS ST Univ; Archtctrl Dsgn.

STOKER, MATT; Olathe North Sr HS; Olathe, KS; (4); FCA; Spanish Clb; Teachers Aide; Var L Ftbl; Var Trk; Hon Roll; U Of KS; Chiropractor.

STOLL, CHRISTINE; Northern Heights HS; Americus, KS; (2); Pep Clb; Quiz Bowl; Science Clb; Mrchg Band; Pep Band; School Musical; Var Chrldng; Var Vllybl; High Hon Roll; Band; Emporia ST U; Engrng.

STONE, ADRIANNE; Wakefield Schl; Clay Center, KS; (1); School Play; Ed Nwsp; Rep Stu Cncl; Var Chrldng; JV Vllybl; Hon Roll; Forensics Tm.

STONE, ANDREW L; Manhattan HS; Manhattan, KS; (3); Church Yth Grp; 4-H; School Play; Rep Stu Cncl; JV Bsbl; PE.

STONE, BEN E; Emporia HS; Emporia, KS; (2); Boy Scts; FCA; Bsktbl; Socr; Trk; Hon Roll; God & Cntry; KS U; Pharmacy.

STONE, BENJAMIN H; Horton HS; Horton, KS; (4); 2/61; Cmnty Wkr; Band; Pres Frsh Cls; Rep Stu Cncl; Var L Ftbl; Var L Trk; Cit Awd; Pres NHS; Pres Acad Fit Awd; Sal; US Army Reserve Natl Schlr/Ath Awd; Sno-Ball King; Schl Record Holder Triple Jump; KS ST Univ; Pre-Med.

STONE, ERIC; Topeka West HS; Topeka, KS; (4); 17/254; Cmnty Wkr; English Clb; French Clb; Q&S; Teachers Aide; Thesps; Nwsp; Lit Mag; JV Bsktbl; L Socr; All St Acad For Sccr; Publshed Essy In REAL Natl Magzne; Fitness Awd; KU; Jrnlsm.

STONE, HOLLIE; White Rock HS; Burr Oak, KS; (3); Am Leg Aux Girls St; Church Yth Grp; Letterman Clb; Math Tm; Quiz Bowl; Scholastic Bowl; SADD; Band; Chorus; Church Choir; Piano; Music.

STONE, JEFF R; Sabetha HS; Sabetha, KS; (2); Quiz Bowl; Spanish Clb; JV Var Golf; Hon Roll; NHS; Prfct Atten Awd; Bus Clb.

STONE, JESSICA; Olathe East Sr HS; Olathe, KS; (2); Church Yth Grp; Drama Clb; French Clb; Band; Drill Tm; Vllybl; Hon Roll; Natl Fr Awd; Amer Dance-Drill Team Schl Achvmts Awds; Pediatric Nrsng.

STONE, KELLI L; F L Schlagle HS; Kansas City, KS; (1); Church Yth Grp; Drama Clb; 4-H; Library Aide; Pep Clb; SADD; Orch; Chrldng; Golf; 4-H Awd; Schl Television Production; U Of KS; Phy Thrpst.

STONE, MICHELLE L; Northeast Magnet HS; Wichita, KS; (3); Girl Scts; SADD; Chorus; Variety Show; Sec Frsh Cls; Pres Soph Cls; Rep Stu Cncl; L Vllybl; Intnl Clb; JA; Intnl Order Of Jobs Dghtrs; HS Stu Ambassador; U Of KS; Geneticcs.

STONEY, ELIZABETH A; Herndon Schl; Herndon, KS; (3); Model UN; Quiz Bowl; Speech Tm; Chorus; Phtg Yrbk; JV Stat Bsktbl; High Hon Roll; Odyssey Of Mind 12th Pl Wrld Fnls; Ft Hays ST Univ; Soc Wrk.

STOPPEL, CHRISTOPHER; Sublette HS; Sublette, KS; (3); #4 in class; Boy Scts; Church Yth Grp; Letterman Clb; Rep Stu Cncl; Ftbl; Hon Roll; NHS; Eagle Sct; K-ST.

STOPPEL, CHRISTOPHER A; Washington HS; Washington, KS; (3); Boy Scts; Pres Church Yth Grp; Pres FHA; Band; Jazz Band; Var Bsktbl; Var Ftbl; Var Golf; High Hon Roll; NHS; Bidi Ball Coach; U Of KS.

STOREY, ANTHONY D; Junction City HS; Junction City, KS; (2); Math Clb; Band; Intrml Bsktbl; Var Cit Awd; High Hon Roll; Hon Roll; NHS; Ntl Merit Ltr; Prfct Atten Awd.

STOREY, URAINA P; Northeast Magnet HS; Wichita, KS; (1); Church Yth Grp; Cmnty Wkr; Dance Clb; Girl Scts; Acpl Chr; Chorus; Church Choir; Drill Tm; Variety Show; Nwsp; Washburn; Lawyer.

STORK, BRYAN; Manhattan HS; Manhattan, KS; (4); 20/388; Am Leg Boys St; Church Yth Grp; Cmnty Wkr; 4-H; Quiz Bowl; Scholastic Bowl; Spanish Clb; 4-H Awd; High Hon Roll; NHS; KSU Jr Crew; Natl 4h Congress; I Dare You Awd; KSU; Med.

STOS, DANAH L; Hoisington HS; Hoisington, KS; (4); 5/62; Church Yth Grp; Office Aide; Pep Clb; Teachers Aide; Chorus; Var L Chrldng; Var L Tennis; High Hon Roll; Hon Roll; NHS; KS Hnr Schlr; Barton Cnty CC; Bus/Acctg.

STOS, SHAWN M; Great Bend Sr HS; Great Bend, KS; (3); 7/230; Office Aide; Pep Clb; Spanish Clb; Vllybl; High Hon Roll; Hon Roll; Kayettes; Acctng/Bus.

STOTLER, DAN W; Iola Sr HS; Iola, KS; (3); Church Yth Grp; Treas FBLA; SADD; Drm Mjr(t); Ed Lit Mag; VP Soph Cls; Ofcr Jr Cls; Treas Stu Cncl; Hon Roll; Art Clb; Ft Scott CC; Bus Mgmt/Tch.

STOUGHTON, JASON A; Ft Scott HS; Fort Scott, KS; (3); #1 in class; Debate Tm; NFL; Treas Frsh Cls; Hon Roll; NHS.

STOUT, MELISSA; Glasco HS; Glasco, KS; (4); 2/9; VP Church Yth Grp; Hosp Aide; Office Aide; Scholastic Bowl; Band; Chorus; Mrchg Band; Yrbk; NHS; Sal; Ft Hays St Univ; Nrsing.

STOUT, MICHELLE; Bucklin Schl; Ford, KS; (1); Church Yth Grp; NFL; Speech Tm; Band; Chorus; Mrchg Band; Pep Band; Sec Frsh Cls; Vllybl; Hon Roll.

STOUTENBOROUGH, JAMES W; Louisburg HS; Louisburg, KS; (3); 6/95; Am Leg Boys St; Debate Tm; Sec Treas Latin Clb; Math Clb; Spanish Clb; School Play; Pres Jr Cls; High Hon Roll; NHS; Math Tm; TSA; Engrng.

STOVALL, JEREMIAH; Maur Hill Prep Schl; Tampa, FL; (2); 1/60; Computer Clb; Math Clb; Math Tm; Orch; Ofcr Bsbl; Socr; High Hon Roll; Hon Roll; Ntl Merit Ltr; Pres Schlr; Brdr Cncl; Schl Amb; Med.

STOVER, ELIZABETH E; Quinter Jr Sr HS; Quinter, KS; (3); 1/28; Church Yth Grp; FHA; Quiz Bowl; Band; Chorus; Rptr Jr Cls; Crs Cntry; Trk; Cit Awd; NHS.

STOVER, SARAH; Quinter Jr Sr HS; Quinter, KS; (4); 1/24; Sec Pres Church Yth Grp; FCA; VP FHA; Letterman Clb; Chorus; School Musical; Pres Sr Cls; Capt L Chrldng; L Trk; NHS; Mc Pherson Coll; Ed Admin.

KANSAS

STOVER, SHILOAH; Colby Sr HS; Colby, KS; (3); Am Leg Boys St; Church Yth Grp; Spanish Clb; SADD; Teachers Aide; Var L Bsktbl; Var L Crs Cntry; Var L Golf; Hon Roll; KS Univ; PT.

STOVER, TYLER W; Caldwell Jr Sr HS; Wellington, KS; (3); Church Yth Grp; SADD; Teachers Aide; Stage Crew; Phtg Rptr Yrbk; Ftbl; Wt Lftg; Wrstlng; Hon Roll; Stu Of Month; Emporia ST.

STOWELL, SHELLY; Louisburg HS; Louisburg, KS; (4); Am Leg Aux Girls St; Debate Tm; Letterman Clb; Spanish Clb; Teachers Aide; School Musical; School Play; Variety Show; Jr NHS; NHS; Crmnl Frnsc Pthlgst.

STRADER, MERIDITH A; Wellington Sr HS; Wellington, KS; (2); Key Clb; Chorus; Church Choir; School Play; Yrbk; Rep Frsh Cls; Rep Soph Cls; Mgr(s); Cit Awd; Hon Roll; Chrch Hndbll Choir; Schl News Blltn Rptr & Anchr; Jrnlsm.

STRAHM, BENJAMIN J; Sabetha HS; Sabetha, KS; (2); FCA; Pep Clb; Spanish Clb; L Ftbl; L Trk.

STRAHM, JEREMIAH D; Sabetha HS; Sabetha, KS; (2); 8/60; Pep Clb; VP Spanish Clb; Church Choir; JV Bsktbl; Var Ftbl; Var Trk; JV Wrstlng; High Hon Roll; Hon Roll; NHS; KAY Mbr; Eng.

STRAHM, MARTHA J; Bern Schl; Bern, KS; (3); Letterman Clb; Pep Clb; SADD; Band; Chorus; Drill Tm; Mrchg Band; Pep Band; School Play; Sec Frsh Cls; Emporia ST Univ; Med Tech.

STRAHM, TRAVIS; Sabetha HS; Sabetha, KS; (3); Art Clb; Church Yth Grp; Pres 4-H; FBLA; Sec Natl FFA Org; Pep Clb; Spanish Clb; 4-H Awd; High Hon Roll; NHS; Natl FFA Awds; N Amer Limousin Jr Assn; KS ST U; Ag Engrng.

STRAIN, JENNIFER L; Chanute Sr HS; Chanute, KS; (3); 7/150; Church Yth Grp; FCA; French Clb; FHA; GAA; Spanish Clb; Varsity Clb; Chorus; Church Choir; School Musical; Prin Ldrshp Tm; Rotary Ldrshp Conf; PT.

STRAIN, MEGAN D; St John Jr Sr HS; Saint John, KS; (3); Church Yth Grp; Pep Clb; SADD; Band; Flag Corp; Pep Band; JV Tennis; High Hon Roll; Hon Roll; Barton Cty CC; Elem Ed.

STRAIT, JENNIFER; Kingman HS; Kingman, KS; (2); 1/72; Church Yth Grp; FCA; Quiz Bowl; Scholastic Bowl; Band; Yrbk; Bsktbl; Tennis; High Hon Roll; NHS; Washburn U; Law.

STRALEY, MIKE; Spring Hill HS; Spring Hill, KS; (3); Am Leg Boys St; Wt Lftg; Hon Roll; Johnson Cty CC.

STRAMEL, BERT J; Colby Sr HS; Colby, KS; (2); Church Yth Grp; FCA; 4-H; Natl FFA Org; Band; Mrchg Band; Pep Band; L Ftbl; Trk; L Wt Lftg; 4-H Pres, Awd Cty Ldrshp.

STRAND, STEVE; Leavenworth HS; Leavenworth, KS; (2); Boy Scts; Church Yth Grp; Math Clb; Math Tm; Pep Clb; Ski Clb; Band; Church Choir; Mrchg Band; Pep Band.

STRANGE, ERIN B; Pleasant Ridge HS; Leavenworth, KS; (4); Debate Tm; Natl FFA Org; NFL; SADD; School Musical; School Play; Ed Nwsp; 4-H Awd; 4-H; Drill Tm; I Dare You Ldrshp Awd; Natl Art Hnr Soc; KS City Art Inst.

STRANO, JODI; Leavenworth HS; Leavenworth, KS; (4); 1/314; Church Yth Grp; Math Tm; SADD; Teachers Aide; Var L Bsktbl; Var L Swmmng; Var L Vllybl; Cit Awd; High Hon Roll; NHS; Navy ROTC Schlrshp 4 Yrs; Army ROTC Schlrshp 4 Yrs; U Of Notre Dame; Chem Engrng.

STRATEMEIER, MATT; Neodesha Jr Sr HS; Neodesha, KS; (3); 4/75; Am Leg Boys St; VP Church Yth Grp; Drama Clb; Spanish Clb; Drm Mjr(t); Pep Band; School Play; Stage Crew; L Tennis; NHS; KS Univ; Corp Law.

STRATHMAN, DANA; Axtell Schl; Axtell, KS; (2); 1/15; FCA; Pep Clb; Varsity Clb; Chorus; VP Frsh Cls; Bsktbl; Trk; Vllybl; High Hon Roll; NHS.

STRATHMAN, JANELLE; Nemaha Valley HS; Seneca, KS; (4); 3/52; Church Yth Grp; HOBY; NFL; Quiz Bowl; SADD; Band; School Play; High Hon Roll; NHS; KS Assn For Yth Area I Pres 94-95; Teen Tchr; Benedictine; Med.

STRATHMAN, TRAVIS J; Nemaha Valley HS; Seneca, KS; (3); Letterman Clb; VP Jr Cls; VP Sr Cls; JV Var Bsktbl; JV Var Ftbl; Trk; Hon Roll; NHS; Prfct Atten Awd; Ldrshp Awd Nom; St Trk Patricipant; Fin Analyst; Mgr.

STRATMAN, AMBER L; Palco HS; Palco, KS; (2); 3/12; Church Yth Grp; Letterman Clb; Speech Tm; Chorus; Pep Band; School Play; Treas Soph Cls; Var Trk; Var Vllybl; Hon Roll; Washburn Univ.

STRATMAN, ELIZABETH; Yates Ctr HS; Yates Center, KS; (4); 5/34; Am Leg Aux Girls St; FCA; FHA; VP Stu Cncl; Capt Var Bsktbl; Stat Ftbl; Var Powder Puff Ftbl; Var Capt Sftbl; Var Capt Vllybl; NHS; KS Newman Coll; Scndry Engl Ed.

STRATMAN, JOSH E; Yates Ctr HS; Yates Center, KS; (2); FCA; Rep Frsh Cls; VP Soph Cls; VP Jr Cls; Rep Stu Cncl; JV Bsbl; Var L Bsktbl; Var L Ftbl; High Hon Roll; NHS.

STRATMANN, CHAD E; Quivira Heights HS; Geneseo, KS; (2); Church Yth Grp; 4-H; Natl FFA Org; JV Var Bsktbl; JV Ftbl; L Var Trk; Hon Roll.

STRAW, SHELLIE; Protection Schl; Protection, KS; (1); Key Clb; Letterman Clb; Pep Clb; Quiz Bowl; Scholastic Bowl; Band; Chorus; Mrchg Band; Pep Band; School Musical; TBA; Tchr; Police Ofcr.

STRAWDER, JASON L; Leroy HS; Le Roy, KS; (3); Var Bsktbl; Var Ftbl; Var Trk; Hon Roll.

STRECKER, JESSICA; Trego Comm HS; Wa Keeney, KS; (2); Church Yth Grp; Dance Clb; Debate Tm; Drama Clb; FHA; German Clb; Math Tm; NFL; Pep Clb; Science Clb; Tch Dance; Kays/Kayette Org; FHA Treas; CYO Sec; FLC VP; Qualfd Natls Dclmtn; 4th Pl ST Debate; KS U; Bus/Advrtsng/Admin.

STRECKER, SHAWNA L; Dodge City HS; Dodge City, KS; (3); Church Yth Grp; Library Aide; Band; Crs Cntry; Hon Dplma; Wichita ST Univ; OT/PT.

STREFF, TIMOTHY J; Bishop Miege HS; Shawnee, KS; (1); 8/250; JV Crs Cntry; JV Trk; High Hon Roll.

STREMEL, ANGIE Y; Hartford HS; Reading, KS; (2); Church Yth Grp; 4-H; Letterman Clb; Pep Clb; Acpl Chr; Band; Chorus; Church Choir; Pep Band; School Musical; KS ST; Music.

STREMEL, KARA; Thomas More Prep-Marion HS; Hays, KS; (3); 8/80; Natl FFA Org; Band; VP Frsh Cls; Treas Soph Cls; Var L Bsktbl; Var L Vllybl; Cit Awd; 4-H Awd; High Hon Roll; Acctng.

STREVEY, HOLLIE; Norton Comm HS; Clayton, KS; (3); Church Yth Grp; 4-H; Band; Pres Frsh Cls; Pres Soph Cls; Pres Jr Cls; JV Var Bsktbl; Var Capt Chrldng; Var JV Vllybl; NHS.

STRICKLAND, STACEY; Hugoton HS; Hugoton, KS; (2); 4/80; Church Yth Grp; Spanish Clb; Band; Church Choir; Mrchg Band; Pep Band; Cit Awd; Hon Roll; NHS; Prfct Atten Awd; Chrch Choir; Yth Grp; Chldrns Choir Asst.

STRICKLAND, TANDI J; Hoisington HS; Hoisington, KS; (3); Office Aide; Pep Clb; SADD; Teachers Aide; Varsity Clb; Band; Chorus; Mrchg Band; Pep Band; School Musical; Barton Cty Comm Coll; Elem Ed.

STRNAD, JILL E; Goodland HS; Brewster, KS; (3); 5/85; FHA; GAA; SADD; Chorus; School Musical; Var Crs Cntry; JV Tennis; Trk; NHS; Natl Yng Ldrs Conf 11.

STROADE, KIM; Pretty Prairie HS; Pretty Prairie, KS; (4); 1/22; Pres Church Yth Grp; Chorus; School Play; Pres Frsh Cls; Pres Soph Cls; Pres Stu Cncl; Var Bsktbl; Var Vllybl; High Hon Roll; Natl Eng Mrt Awd; KS ST U; Ntrtn.

STROBEL, HEATHER M; Larned HS; Larned, KS; (2); 11/110; Band; Mrchg Band; Pep Band; KS Ambassador Of Music Europe Tour; Ft Hays ST Univ; Astronomer.

STROBLE, JOANNA K; Leavenworth HS; Leavenworth, KS; (3); Secrtrl.

STROBLE, MICHAEL R; Kapaun-Mt Carmel HS; Wichita, KS; (3); Church Yth Grp; Varsity Clb; Ofcr Frsh Cls; Ofcr Soph Cls; Ofcr Stu Cncl; Bsktbl; Golf; Coached Boys Bsktbl YMCA; Bus; Law; Pol Sci.

STRODA, KIMBERLY L; Hope HS; Hope, KS; (4); 4/12; FBLA; Natl FFA Org; Office Aide; SADD; Pres Stu Cncl; Bsktbl; Sftbl; Vllybl; Hon Roll; NHS; Fall Homcmng Queen; Vllybl Eisenhower League Hnrbl Mntn; Neosho Cty CC.

STROEDE, JOHN; Ellsworth HS; Kanopolis, KS; (4); 3/70; Letterman Clb; Quiz Bowl; Teachers Aide; Var Bsktbl; Var Ftbl; Var Tennis; Hon Roll; Ntl Merit Ltr; Prfct Atten Awd; St Schlr; KS ST U; Mech Engrng.

STROHL, CHERI; Cunningham HS; Cunningham, KS; (2); 1/21; Church Yth Grp; Letterman Clb; Pep Clb; Quiz Bowl; Science Clb; Spanish Clb; SADD; Stage Crew; VP Frsh Cls; Rptr Stu Cncl; Acad Olympcs.

STROHM, BOBBY L; Bishop Miege HS; Kansas City, MO; (1); 54/245; Var Wrstlng; High Hon Roll.

STROHM, DANIEL; Augusta Sr HS; Augusta, KS; (3); 15/147; Am Leg Boys St; Debate Tm; Scholastic Bowl; Spanish Clb; Band; Ofcr Stu Cncl; JV Golf; Var Socr; High Hon Roll; NHS; U Of KS.

STROHMEYER, BRIE; Manhattan HS; Manhattan, KS; (2); Church Yth Grp; Cmnty Wkr; Dance Clb; FCA; French Clb; FBLA; Pep Clb; Rep Stu Cncl; Chrldng; High Hon Roll; Miss KS Amer Teen 94; Acad Awd Wnnr Natls Miss Amer Teen; Intl Bus.

STROLE, DYLAN G; Lawrence HS; Lawrence, KS; (4); Church Yth Grp; DECA; Office Aide; Teachers Aide; Trk; Prfct Atten Awd; Johnson Cnty CC; Bus Admin.

STROME, MINDY; Herrington HS; Herington, KS; (2); Dance Clb; FCA; FHA; Q&S; Band; Drm Mjr(t); Mrchg Band; School Musical; VP Frsh Cls; Rep Stu Cncl; KS ST U; Pediatrc Physiolgist.

STRONG, AMY B; Olathe East Sr HS; Olathe, KS; (3); 16/368; Church Yth Grp; Band; Drm Mjr(t); School Musical; High Hon Roll; NHS; Pres Acad Fit Awd; Spanish NHS; Cmnty Wkr; Spanish Clb; Yth Ct; SASH; Brigham Young Univ; Nrs.

STRONG, LINDSAY; Atchison Sr HS; Atchison, KS; (3); Band; Drm Mjr(t); Jazz Band; Mrchg Band; School Play; Pres Jr Cls; Rep Stu Cncl; Var Chrldng; Var Trk; Hon Roll; St Band; Regents Hnr Acad.

STROOT, AARON M; Bishop Carroll Catholic HS; Wichita, KS; (1); French Clb; Hon Roll; Notre Dame.

STROTHMAN, BRENT W; Wellington Sr HS; Wellington, KS; (4); 1/120; Am Leg Boys St; Church Yth Grp; HOBY; Band; Jazz Band; Ofcr Stu Cncl; Bsktbl; JV Ftbl; JV Tennis; Cit Awd; KS ST U; Arch Engrng.

STROTHMAN, SARA; Kingman HS; Kingman, KS; (4); 35/70; FBLA; SADD; School Play; Yrbk; Ofcr Stu Cncl; Bsktbl; Chrldng; Sftbl; Tennis; Hon Roll; Teens Today Leaders Tomorrow; KS ST U; Scndry Ed.

STROTHMAN, TARA C; Wellington Sr HS; Wellington, KS; (3); Key Clb; Band; Yrbk; Var Bsktbl; Var Sftbl; Vllybl; High Hon Roll; Jr NHS; NHS; Sftbl 1st Tm All Leag Pitcher Awd.

STROTHMAN, TRACIE; Wellington Sr HS; Wellington, KS; (3); Church Yth Grp; Office Aide; Ofcr Frsh Cls; Ofcr Stu Cncl; Bsktbl; Sftbl; Vllybl; High Hon Roll; Jr NHS; Lions Awd.

STROUD, BRAD; Frontenac Jr Sr HS; Frontenac, KS; (1); Church Yth Grp; Pep Clb; Ofcr Bsbl; Bsktbl; Ftbl; High Hon Roll; Hon Roll; Smmr Bsbl Team.

STROUP JR, RAYMOND L; Wabaunsee HS; Mc Farland, KS; (4); Quiz Bowl; Acpl Chr; Chorus; Church Choir; School Musical; School Play; Swing Chorus; Variety Show; Toured England With KS Festival Chours 96; KS ST Univ; Vocal Performance.

STRUBE, GREG; Horton HS; Horton, KS; (3); 13/39; Natl FFA Org; Office Aide; Yrbk; Bsktbl; Ftbl; Score Keeper; Wt Lftg; Hon Roll; Ntl Merit Ltr; Prfct Atten Awd; KS ST; Ag.

STRUBLE, CHRISTA L; Wellington Sr HS; Wellington, KS; (2); Chorus; Chrldng; High Hon Roll; Jr NHS; Nrsng.

STRUEMPH, JEREMY H; St Marys HS; Rossville, KS; (2); Debate Tm; FCA; VP FBLA; Letterman Clb; Spanish Clb; Speech Tm; Rep Soph Cls; Rep Stu Cncl; Var Crs Cntry; Var Wrstlng; K ST; Engr.

STRUNK, ROGER F; Halstead HS; Halstead, KS; (2); Hon Roll; KS ST U; Arch.

STRUNK, TAMMY A; Goddard HS; Goddard, KS; (2); Science Clb; Teachers Aide; JV Var Bsktbl; Var JV Mgr(s); High Hon Roll; Hon Roll; NHS; Friends U; Interior Design; Nrs.

STRUNK, WENDI M; Topeka HS; Topeka, KS; (3); Art Clb; Church Yth Grp; Cmnty Wkr; Library Aide; Spanish Clb; Teachers Aide; Chrldng; High Hon Roll; Indep Living 5 Awds; Spec Olympics Coach/Vol; Outstndng Vol Awd; Univ Of KS; Med.

STRYKER, TRAVIS E; Topeka HS; Topeka, KS; (2); Boy Scts; Rep Church Yth Grp; Spanish Clb; Chorus; Church Choir; Variety Show; JV Crs Cntry; Hon Roll; Bus Ed Dept Awd; KS Univ; Pediatrician.

STUART, JESSE A; Manhattan HS; Manhattan, KS; (1); Band; Jazz Band; Mrchg Band; Pep Band; Hon Roll; Table Tnns; KS ST Univ; Engrng.

STUART, LISA M; Washington HS; Kansas City, KS; (2); Teachers Aide; Stage Crew; VP Stu Cncl; JV Bsktbl; Var Mgr(s); JV Var Sftbl; Hon Roll; Schltc Art & Writing Awds Regional 95 Gold Key 96, Silver Key; Peer Ldr; Non Violence Mediator.

STUART, MORGAN; Bucklin Schl; Ford, KS; (1); Church Yth Grp; FCA; SADD; Band; Pep Band; JV Bsktbl; Trk; JV Vllybl; Hon Roll; Serendipity.

STUART, RYAN C; Herington HS; Herington, KS; (2); 1/60; Church Yth Grp; Cmnty Wkr; FCA; FHA; Pres Stu Cncl; Capt Bsbl; Var Bsktbl; Var Golf; High Hon Roll; NHS; Acctng; Ed.

STUART, TYSON B; Wichita Southeast HS; Wichita, KS; (2); Art Clb; JA; SADD; Band; Jazz Band; Pep Band; School Play; JV Bsktbl; Hon Roll; NHS; Stdnt Minstr Yth Group; Activ Miss Wrkr Church; Nom Natl Yth Ldrshp Conf; Duke Univ; Anesthsiolgy/Premed.

STUBBS, JAY R; Kingman HS; Kingman, KS; (1); Church Yth Grp; Ftbl; Hon Roll.

STUBBS, KEITH A; Kingman HS; Kingman, KS; (3); Church Yth Grp; FCA; FBLA; Library Aide; Spanish Clb; Teachers Aide; Rep Stu Cncl; JV Bsktbl; JV Var Tennis; High Hon Roll; Wlkng; Cmptr Sci.

STUBBY, JARED; Frederic Remington HS; Newton, KS; (3); Am Leg Boys St; Boy Scts; Church Yth Grp; Letterman Clb; Math Tm; Band; Jazz Band; Mrchg Band; Pep Band; School Play; Engrng.

STUBY, MONICA; Seaman Sr HS; Topeka, KS; (3); Debate Tm; Drama Clb; VP 4-H; FBLA; NFL; Speech Tm; High Hon Roll; NHS; Pres Acad Fit Awd.

STUCK, KELLY; Atchison Co Cmty HS; Lancaster, KS; (2); FBLA; Pep Clb; Service Clb; Band; Jazz Band; Mrchg Band; Pep Band; Trk; High Hon Roll; Hon Roll; Writers Clb; Animal Field.

STUCKEY, KRISTEEN M; Wichita East HS; Wichita, KS; (2); Church Yth Grp; Hon Roll; Wichita Schl Sys Vol Ofc Work; Sec.

STUCKY, BRIAN J; Moundridge HS; Moundridge, KS; (2); Church Yth Grp; Debate Tm; NFL; Quiz Bowl; Speech Tm; Band; Chorus; Jazz Band; Mrchg Band; Pep Band; St Frncs 2nd; St Quiz Bowl 4th; St Debate 5th; Schl Math Cntst 2nd; Bethel Col.

STUCKY, CHRISTOPHER M; Ness City HS; Ness City, KS; (1); 27/42; Church Yth Grp; Cmnty Wkr; Pep Clb; Service Clb; Band; Mrchg Band; Pep Band; School Play; Ftbl; Golf; Ed.

STUCKY, COLLIN J; Newton Sr HS; Newton, KS; (1); JV Bsktbl; High Hon Roll.

STUCKY, KATIE; Inman Jr Sr HS; Inman, KS; (2); Church Yth Grp; Rep VP 4-H; Sec Natl FFA Org; Pep Clb; Band; Chorus; Pep Band; School Musical; Vllybl; High Hon Roll; KS ST U.

STUCKY, RUSSELL; Ness City HS; Ness City, KS; (4); 3/29; Am Leg Boys St; Boy Scts; Church Yth Grp; Math Tm; Quiz Bowl; Scholastic Bowl; Thesps; School Play; Yrbk; Rep Stu Cncl; KAY; KU; Arsp Engr.

STUCKY, SHELESE; Hesston HS; Moundridge, KS; (3); Church Yth Grp; FCA; 4-H; Acpl Chr; Chorus; School Musical; Variety Show; Var L Bsktbl; Var L Vllybl; High Hon Roll.

STUDE, CHRISTI; Claflin Jr Sr HS; Ellinwood, KS; (3); Pep Clb; Teachers Aide; Varsity Clb; Chorus; School Musical; School Play; Swing Chorus; Yrbk; Var Chrldng; Tennis; Barten Cty CC; Bus.

STUDE, TRAVIS J; El Dorado HS; El Dorado, KS; (2); Church Yth Grp; Cmnty Wkr; Letterman Clb; NFL; SADD; Orch; Var L Swmmng; Hon Roll; NBC Baseball Champ Scrkeeper; Comm Swmng.

STUDER, JENNY; Wathena Schl; Wathena, KS; (4); 17/36; Art Clb; Cmnty Wkr; Letterman Clb; Math Clb; NFL; Red Cross Aide; Science Clb; Varsity Clb; Band; Chorus; Highland CC; Bus Mgmt.

STUDT, NICK L; Olathe East Sr HS; Lenexa, KS; (4); Art Clb; Boy Scts; Spanish Clb; Trk; High Hon Roll; Hon Roll; NHS; BSA Eagle Sct; Tech Svc Clb; U Of KS; Comp Engrng.

STUDT, RYAN T; Olathe East Sr HS; Lenexa, KS; (2); Boy Scts; Debate Tm; Stage Crew; JV Ftbl; High Hon Roll; Hon Roll; QUEST; Pediatrician.

STUEVE, ANN; Hiawatha HS; Hiawatha, KS; (3); 1/113; HOBY; Quiz Bowl; Band; Flag Corp; Treas Stu Cncl; Var L Bsktbl; Var L Crs Cntry; Var L Trk; Hon Roll; NHS; KS Rgnts Hnrs Acad; Cmnty Swm Tm; Piano; U Of KS; Pharm.

STUEVE, LEA; Olpe Schl; Olpe, KS; (4); 2/27; Church Yth Grp; FBLA; Scholastic Bowl; Chorus; Pres Frsh Cls; VP Soph Cls; Pres Stu Cncl; Var L Vllybl; 4-H Awd; Sal; Natl 4-H Ambssdr.

STUEVER, AMBER; Conway Springs HS; Conway Springs, KS; (3); 1/40; Church Yth Grp; Rep SADD; Drill Tm; School Play; Ed Nwsp; Pres VP Stu Cncl; Var Tennis; Hon Roll; NHS; Pres Schlr; Jrnlsm.

STUEWE, ELIZABETH; Wabaunsee HS; Maple Hill, KS; (2); VP Church Yth Grp; FBLA; FHA; Band; Mrchg Band; Pep Band; Ofcr Frsh Cls; VP Soph Cls; JV Var Bsktbl; Var Sftbl.

STUEWE, KRISTIE; Wabaunsee HS; Maple Hill, KS; (2); Church Yth Grp; FBLA; FHA; Band; Pep Band; VP Frsh Cls; Pres Soph Cls; JV Bsktbl; Sftbl; Vllybl; Sci Mrt Awds; Kayettes.

STUEWE, MELISSA; Wabaunsee HS; Alma, KS; (2); Sec Church Yth Grp; FBLA; VP FHA; Natl FFA Org; Treas Soph Cls; Rep Stu Cncl; Bsktbl; Powder Puff Ftbl; Vllybl; Hon Roll.

STUEWE, RYAN; Wichita HS NW; Wichita, KS; (3); Art Clb; Debate Tm; Intnl Clb; Lit Mag; Hon Roll; NHS; Natl Art Hnrs Soc; Natl Eng Merit Awd; Awd Vis Arts; Regnl Schlstc Art Comp; Reed Coll; Hum/Cultural Stud.

STUHLMAN, BECKY; Shawnee Mission N HS; Shawnee Mission, KS; (3); Pep Clb; Spanish Clb; JV Var Chrldng; Hon Roll; NCA All Amer Chrldr; KS ST Univ.

STUHLSATZ, JAMIE J; Conway Springs HS; Mayfield, KS; (3); Church Yth Grp; FHA; Office Aide; SADD; Chorus; Phtg Ed Yrbk; Powder Puff Ftbl; Score Keeper; Tennis; Hon Roll; Ldrshp Bd Mbr FHA.

STUHLSATZ, JOSHUA M; Garden Plain Jr Sr HS; Garden Plain, KS; (3); Church Yth Grp; Hon Roll; SADD; Prfct Atten Awd; 4 Wheeling.

STUHLSATZ, KRISTI M; Garden Plain Jr Sr HS; Garden Plain, KS; (2); Church Yth Grp; GAA; Letterman Clb; SADD; Varsity Clb; Drill Tm; Rptr Nwsp; Yrbk; Rep Soph Cls; VP Jr Cls.

STUHLSATZ, SCOTT A; Garden Plain Jr Sr HS; Garden Plain, KS; (3); 11/36; Church Yth Grp; Red Cross Aide; SADD; Varsity Clb; Acpl Chr; Chorus; School Musical; Rep Frsh Cls; Rep Soph Cls; Intrml Bsbl.

STUHLSATZ, WILLIAM J; Wichita Northeast Magnet HS; Wichita, KS; (3); 6/99; Var Capt Socr; Hon Roll.

STUKEY, SARA; Great Bend Sr HS; Great Bend, KS; (4); 36/246; Pres Girl Scts; Pep Clb; Spanish Clb; SADD; Band; Color Guard; Tennis; High Hon Roll; NHS; Church Yth Grp; Kayettes Bd Mem; Barton Cty CC; Acctng.

STULTS, AMBER; Ottawa HS; Ottawa, KS; (3); Church Yth Grp; Dance Clb; Variety Show; High Hon Roll; NHS; Teenport; O Club; Bio.

STUMBAUGH, STEPHANY A; Washburn Rural HS; Topeka, KS; (3); 145/351; Art Clb; SADD; Yrbk; Lit Mag; Hon Roll; Artwrk Inclded In HS Lit Mag; Al Collins Schl; Comp Grphcs.

STUMP, JAMI; Valley Heights Jr Sr HS; Blue Rapids, KS; (4); 10/27; Debate Tm; Pres 4-H; VP Natl FFA Org; Speech Tm; Nwsp; Ed Yrbk; VP Frsh Cls; Rep Stu Cncl; Var Bsktbl; Var Vllybl; KS ST Univ; Ag Jrnlsm.

STUMPFF, ANNETTE M; Wellsville Jr Sr HS; Edgerton, KS; (2); FBLA; Yrbk; JV Bsktbl; Var L Crs Cntry; Var L Trk; Cit Awd; High Hon Roll; Hon Roll; NHS; Ntl Merit Ltr; Ag Sci; Horse Trainer; Helped Comm To Raise Money To Restore Old Schl House.

STUMPS, AUSTIN T; Derby HS; Derby, KS; (1); Orch; Score Keeper; Wt Lftg; JV Wrstlng; KS Univ.

STUNKEL, MELISSA; Larned HS; Larned, KS; (4); 8/85; Cmnty Wkr; Band; Flag Corp; Mrchg Band; Pep Band; Yrbk; High Hon Roll; NHS; Pres Schlr; Hutchinson CC; Med.

STURDEVANT, ELIZABETH; Garden City Sr HS; Garden City, KS; (4); 29/315; Church Yth Grp; Chorus; Church Choir; High Hon Roll; NHS; DECA; Mid-Amer Nazarene Coll; Nrsng.

STURGELL, AMANDA L; Wichita East HS; Wichita, KS; (2); Church Yth Grp; Chrldng; Trk; Hon Roll; Treas Sr Hgh Yth Grp; Plyng Piano; Physcl Thrpst.

STURGIS, AMANDA K; Riverton Schl; Columbus, KS; (2); Art Clb; Drama Clb; FHA; Letterman Clb; Chorus; School Musical; School Play; Stage Crew; Rptr Yrbk; Pres Soph Cls; Pittsburg ST Univ.

STURGIS, MATT A; Riverton Schl; Columbus, KS; (3); FHA; Letterman Clb; Math Tm; Pep Clb; VICA; Bsktbl; Ftbl; Trk; Wt Lftg; Hon Roll; Sprts Med.

STUTEVILLE, SHAMMARA; Leavenworth HS; Leavenworth, KS; (3); Intnl Clb; ROTC; Drill Tm; Trk; Hon Roll; Intl Frgn Lang Awds; Acad Ltr Jr Yr; Jr Rsrv Ofcrs Trng Corps Cert Cmndtn; Johnson Cty CC; Culinary Arts.

STUTHIET, JAINA; Manhattan HS; Manhattan, KS; (4); 108/354; Nwsp; Yrbk; Hon Roll; Kiwanis Awd; Environment; Animals; Helping Endangered Animals; KS ST U; Wildlife Bio.

STUTZ, CHRISTY; Jefferson Co North HS; Nortonville, KS; (3); 15/35; Church Yth Grp; FBLA; FHA; HOBY; SADD; Teachers Aide; Church Choir; Rep Jr Cls; Var Trk; Hon Roll; Dist E FHA Sec; FBLA; Acctng.

SU, JOEY; Blue Valley Northwest HS; Overland Park, KS; (4); 4/343; Chess Clb; Cmnty Wkr; Debate Tm; Model UN; NFL; Varsity Clb; Orch; JV Var Trk; Gov Hon Prg Awd; High Hon Roll; U Of KS; Comp Sci.

SUAREZ, JOEL; Washburn Rural HS; Topeka, KS; (3); Bsktbl; Ftbl; Hon Roll.

SUBELKA, ADAM; Mc Louth Schl; Mc Louth, KS; (3); 10/35; Drama Clb; FHA; Letterman Clb; Pep Clb; Quiz Bowl; Ski Clb; Spanish Clb; SADD; Teachers Aide; Varsity Clb; Washburn Univ; Broadcast Tech.

SUCHY, MELISSA; Emporia HS; Emporia, KS; (4); 1/285; Church Yth Grp; Treas Girl Scts; Hosp Aide; Pep Clb; Service Clb; Treas SADD; Teachers Aide; Treas Band; Mrchg Band; Pep Band; SMILE; Emporia ST U; Pre-Med/Pdtrcn.

SUDBECK, ALISHA D; Seaman Sr HS; Topeka, KS; (3); FHA; Hosp Aide; Spanish Clb; SADD; High Hon Roll; Hon Roll; Prfct Atten Awd; KS St Univ; Nrsing.

SUDDARTH, RANDY D; Yates Ctr HS; Yates Center, KS; (3); Art Clb; Church Yth Grp; FCA; 4-H; Letterman Clb; Natl FFA Org; Spanish Clb; Varsity Clb; Band; Mrchg Band; Natural Hlprs; Allen Cnty CC.

SUDERMAN, RYAN; Hillsboro HS; Marion, KS; (2); 5/49; Church Yth Grp; 4-H; Pres Frsh Cls; Bsktbl; Ftbl; Wt Lftg; 4-H Awd; High Hon Roll; Peer Cnslr.

SUDERMAN, TAMARA R; Lawrence HS; Lawrence, KS; (4); 17/630; Cmnty Wkr; Drama Clb; JA; Model UN; Quiz Bowl; Scholastic Bowl; Science Clb; Spanish Clb; Thesps; Acpl Chr; Rsrch Sci Inst MIT; Amn Intl Pres 95-96; Lab Asst KS U; Life Sci.

SUELLENTROP, JULIE; Bishop Carroll Catholic HS; Colwich, KS; (4); 30/130; Church Yth Grp; FCA; SADD; Varsity Clb; Ed Nwsp; Intrml Bsktbl; Mgr(s); Capt Powder Puff Ftbl; Var L Tennis; High Hon Roll; KS ST Univ.

SUELTER, EMILY; Sacred Heart Jr-Sr HS; Brookville, KS; (4); 2/22; Am Leg Aux Girls St; Pep Clb; Quiz Bowl; Teachers Aide; School Musical; School Musical; Ed Yrbk; Var L Tennis; High Hon Roll; NHS; Benedictine Coll; Sociology.

SUELTER, JESSICA G; Great Bend Sr HS; Great Bend, KS; (3); Church Yth Grp; DECA; Drama Clb; Pep Clb; Spanish Clb; Chorus; Stage Crew; Hon Roll; Prfct Atten Awd.

SUFFAL, DEANNA M; Marmaton Valley Jr Sr HS; La Harpe, KS; (2); Drama Clb; FBLA; Math Tm; NFL; Acpl Chr; Band; Chorus; School Musical; School Play; Hon Roll; Music.

SUFFRON, AMY J; Ottawa HS; Ottawa, KS; (4); 71/144; French Clb; FBLA; FTA; Pep Clb; SADD; Teachers Aide; VICA; Powder Puff Ftbl; Hon Roll; Pres Acad Fit Awd.

SUGHART, SALLY; Oskaloosa HS; Oskaloosa, KS; (4); #1 in class; Am Leg Aux Girls St; FBLA; Jazz Band; Pres Frsh Cls; Treas Sr Cls; Var Bsktbl; Var Sftbl; Var Vllybl; Pres NHS; Val; Prncpl Hnr Stu; Homcmng Qn 95; Top Art Stu 94-95; Liberty U; Phys Thrpy.

SUH, EUN S; Manhattan HS; Manhattan, KS; (4); Debate Tm; NFL; Scholastic Bowl; Rep Thesps; School Play; Swing Chorus; St Schlr; Sci Olympd 1st In St Rocks, Minrls & Fossls Catgry 96; Stream Team 2 Natl Confs; Wide Horzns Natr Pgm; KS ST U; Bio; Environ Sci.

SUH, SU J; Wichita Southeast HS; Wichita, KS; (3); Art Clb; Church Yth Grp; Cmnty Wkr; FCA; Pres Intnl Clb; SADD; School Musical; JV Socr; JV Tennis; Traditional Korean Dance; Korean Schl Tchr; Nrsng.

SUKONTARARS, CYNTHIA J; Junction City HS; Fort Riley, KS; (3); CAP; Chorus; Hon Roll; KS ST Univ; Vet.

SULLINS, JENNIFER M; Olathe North Sr HS; Olathe, KS; (3); Band; Mrchg Band; Socr; High Hon Roll; Hon Roll; Comm Svc; Meteorology.

SULLIVAN, ANNA M; Field Kindley Mem Sr HS; Coffeyville, KS; (3); Church Yth Grp; 4-H; German Clb; Natl FFA Org; Acpl Chr; Mrchg Band; School Musical; 4-H Awd; Hon Roll; Art Clb; Highest Praise Touring Choir; Phy Thrpst; Music.

SULLIVAN, GRANT; Ulysses HS; Ulysses, KS; (2); 1/101; Church Yth Grp; Cmnty Wkr; Debate Tm; Crs Cntry; Golf; High Hon Roll; Squires; Piano; U Of KS; Med.

SULLIVAN, JONATHAN; Shawnee Mission N HS; Shawnee Mission, KS; (4); 11/370; Pres Chess Clb; JCL; Pep Clb; Band; Jazz Band; Mrchg Band; School Musical; Capt Swmmng; VP NHS; St Schlr; Quincy U; Elem Ed.

SULLIVAN, KATY J; Lakin HS; Lakin, KS; (2); Church Yth Grp; FCA; 4-H; Band; Pep Band; Stage Crew; Nwsp; Yrbk; Pres Frsh Cls; JV Bsktbl; Tchr.

SULLIVAN, KELLY; Wichita Northwest HS; Wichita, KS; (2); Church Yth Grp; Intnl Clb; Math Clb; Q&S; Scholastic Bowl; Orch; Rptr Nwsp; Rep Soph Cls; Rep Jr Cls; High Hon Roll; Wichita Yty Symphony; Wichita Symphony Usher; Jrnlsm.

SULLIVAN, PATRICIA A; Sumner Acad Of Arts & Science; Kansas City, KS; (4); Drama Clb; Key Clb; Latin Clb; NFL; Pep Clb; Spanish Clb; SADD; Thesps; School Play; High Hon Roll; U Of KS; Ed.

SULLIVAN, RYAN; Hillsboro HS; Hillsboro, KS; (4); 7/45; Pres Church Yth Grp; School Musical; Pres Sr Cls; Var Capt Ftbl; High Hon Roll; NHS; Band; Chorus; Church Choir; Mrchg Band; Peer Cnslr/Mediator; Hmcmng King; Danforth Awd; Madrigal; Ftbl All Area & All Leag; Multiple Yr Listing; Tabor Coll; Acctng.

SULLIVAN, SARAH D; Derby HS; Derby, KS; (1); Drama Clb; Hosp Aide; Lit Mag; Mgr(s); Vllybl; Hon Roll; Poetry Wrtng; Wichita ST Univ; Dctr/Mar Bio.

SULLIVAN, TONYA L; Great Bend Sr HS; Great Bend, KS; (2); Girl Scts; Teachers Aide; Art.

SULTZER, ERIK M; Hays HS; Hays, KS; (2); JV Bsbl; JV Ftbl; Wt Lftg; Hon Roll; Arch Engr.

SULZMAN, CARRIE L; Colby Sr HS; Colby, KS; (3); Church Yth Grp; FCA; Spanish Clb; SADD; Yrbk; JV Var Bsktbl; JV Tennis; CCC; Peditrician.

SUMMERS, JENNIFER A; Shawnee Mission W Sr HS; Lenexa, KS; (2); Drama Clb; Library Aide; NFL; Pep Clb; Speech Tm; Thesps; School Musical; School Play; Stage Crew; Hon Roll; JAWS; U Of KS.

SUMMERS, TRACI J; Great Bend Sr HS; Great Bend, KS; (2); French Clb; Pep Clb; Service Clb; Chorus; Variety Show; All WAC Swmng.

SUMMERSON, COURTNEY D; St Thomas Aquinas HS; Overland Park, KS; (4); 24/231; Dance Clb; Key Clb; SADD; Sec Drill Tm; Powder Puff Ftbl; JV Tennis; NHS; Union Bays Search For Inspiration Fnlst; KS ST U.

SUMNER, ASHLEIGH L; Leavenworth HS; Leavenworth, KS; (1); Church Yth Grp; Drama Clb; Girl Scts; Ski Clb; Chorus; School Musical; Rep Frsh Cls; Var Crs Cntry; Var Swmmng; Hon Roll; 3rd Best Runner In Crss Cntry; KS U; Pediatrician.

SUMNER, CYNTHIA R; Anderson Cty Jr Sr HS; Garnett, KS; (2); Intnl Clb; Pep Clb; SADD; Sec Soph Cls; JV Var Bsktbl; JV Vllybl; High Hon Roll; Acad Awd Family & Consumer Scis & Lang Arts; Ed.

SUMNERS, JOHN Q; Rock Creek Jr Sr HS; Westmoreland, KS; (3); 1/45; Bus Profs of Am; Church Yth Grp; Cmnty Wkr; 4-H; HOBY; Letterman Clb; Math Tm; Quiz Bowl; Scholastic Bowl; Var L Bsbl; Acad All Team Frosh Soph Jr Yr; KS ST U; CPA.

SUMP, AUTUMN; Blue Valley HS; Randolph, KS; (2); 1/30; Church Yth Grp; FHA; Band; Chorus; VP Soph Cls; Bsktbl; Vllybl; Wt Lftg; High Hon Roll; NHS; Fort Hays St U; Interior Dcrtng.

SUMPTER, JUSTIN T; Silver Lake Jr Sr HS; Silver Lake, KS; (3); #21 in class; Debate Tm; HOBY; Key Clb; Scholastic Bowl; Rep Soph Cls; Capt Var Bsbl; Capt Var Bsktbl; High Hon Roll; Hon Roll; Pres Acad Fit Awd.

SUMPTER, MATTHEW; Kansas City Bible Clg High; Overland Park, KS; (2); 1/12; Boy Scts; Church Yth Grp; Computer Clb; Math Tm; Band; Treas Frsh Cls; Rep Soph Cls; Var Bsktbl; Hon Roll.

SUN, JIMMY; Rockhurst HS; Fairway, KS; (3); 2/199; Debate Tm; Drama Clb; Math Tm; NFL; Quiz Bowl; Scholastic Bowl; Service Clb; Spanish Clb; Speech Tm; Variety Show; PRIMO; Northwestern Univ; Med.

SUNDAHL, KRIS; Great Bend Sr HS; Great Bend, KS; (3); Rep Am Leg Boys St; Church Yth Grp; Cmnty Wkr; FCA; Letterman Clb; Pep Clb; Spanish Clb; Varsity Clb; Nwsp; JV Var Bsbl; All-Star Selection For Ftbl & Bsktbl; Broadcasting.

SUNDBLAD, LAURA M; Bishop Miege HS; Kansas City, MO; (1); Debate Tm; Girl Scts; NFL; School Musical; School Play; Crs Cntry; High Hon Roll; Outdr Clb; Cmps Minstry Tm; MOU; MD.

SUNG, VENUS J; Pleasant Ridge HS; Leavenworth, KS; (3); 5/30; Art Clb; Church Yth Grp; Cmnty Wkr; SADD; Drill Tm; School Musical; Sec Frsh Cls; Sec Soph Cls; Sec Stu Cncl; L Capt Chrldng; Med.

SUNLEY, ALICIA; Garden City Sr HS; Garden City, KS; (3); Church Yth Grp; Key Clb; Pres Spanish Clb; SADD; Acpl Chr; Wt Lftg; Hon Roll; NHS; Peer Hlprs Pgm; DARE Role Model.

SUPER, NICOLE; Sumner Acad HS; Kansas City, KS; (1); Church Yth Grp; Debate Tm; NFL; Pep Clb; Spanish Clb; Chorus; Drill Tm; Intrml Chrldng; Hon Roll; KS U; Ansthslgy.

SUPERNOIS, KRISTI M; Newton Sr HS; Newton, KS; (2); 29/272; Railer Conductors; Hutchinson Coll; Schl Cnslr.

SUPON, JAMI R; Wellington Sr HS; Wellington, KS; (2); Girl Scts; Stat Bsktbl; Stat Sftbl; Hon Roll; Jr NHS; KAY Club; Pre-Med.

SURMEIER, DARRELL P; Colby Sr HS; Colby, KS; (2); Church Yth Grp; Letterman Clb; L Bsktbl; Stat Ftbl; Stat Mgr(s); Intrml Score Keeper; Var Trk; Intrml Wt Lftg; High Hon Roll; Hon Roll; Eng Hnrs Cls; Amer Legion Bsbl; Colby CC; Sports Medicine.

SUTHER, AUDREA; Rock Creek Jr Sr HS; Blaine, KS; (4); 4/51; Church Yth Grp; Sec Rptr Natl FFA Org; Jazz Band; High Hon Roll; Kiwanis Awd; NHS; St Schlr; Cmnty Wkr; Math Tm; Pep Clb; Bausch/Lomb Sci Awd; KS St Univ Deans Awd; KS St Outstndng Sr Math/Sci; Ks St U; Bio/Resrch.

SUTHER, CHRISTOPHE; Maur Hill Prep Schl; Atchison, KS; (4); 10/47; Am Leg Boys St; Drama Clb; HOBY; Thesps; Ed Yrbk; Pres Frsh Cls; Pres Soph Cls; Var L Bsbl; Var L Ftbl; Var L Tennis; KS U.

SUTHERLAND, MISTY; Belle Plaine HS; Peck, KS; (3); NFL; Quiz Bowl; Spanish Clb; Speech Tm; Band; School Musical; School Play; Var Capt Chrldng; Vllybl; Hon Roll; WA Jrnlsm Conf; Channel 3 Television Sta Internship; U Of MO Columbia; Sportscstng.

SUTTER, CARRIE; Pratt HS; Pratt, KS; (2); Church Yth Grp; Drama Clb; FCA; NFL; Pep Clb; Service Clb; Hist SADD; Rep Soph Cls; Var Chrldng; NHS; Hastings; Elem Ed.

SUTTERFIELD, AMBER R; Washburn Rural HS; Wakarusa, KS; (2); Chorus; Church Choir; Orch; Stage Crew; Lit Mag; Tennis; High Hon Roll; Play Guitar; Wrt Msc; Epdmlgy/Paralegal.

SUTTON, AARON M; South Haven Schl; South Haven, KS; (1); FCA; Math Tm; Natl FFA Org; Band; School Play; Rep Stu Cncl; Ftbl; Trk; Hon Roll; KS Univ; PT.

SUTTON, BETHANY A; Ness City HS; Ness City, KS; (2); Church Yth Grp; Hosp Aide; NFL; Pep Clb; Thesps; Band; School Play; JV Chrldng; Tennis; Hon Roll; Nurse.

SUTTON, JACOB A; Shawnee Heights HS; Berryton, KS; (4); 72/236; Teachers Aide; Wrstlng; Hon Roll; Elctrncs/Psych.

SUTTON, NIKI; Ness City HS; Ness City, KS; (3); GAA; HOBY; Math Tm; Pep Clb; VP Soph Cls; Sec Stu Cncl; Var L Tennis; Hon Roll; NHS; Church Yth Grp; Kays; KS St; Phrmcy.

SUTTON, STEPHANIE; Lyons HS; Lyons, KS; (4); 7/68; Letterman Clb; Pep Clb; Band; Chorus; Pep Band; Var Capt Chrldng; L Pom Pon; Tennis; Hon Roll; KS Hnrs Stdnt; KS ST U; Psych.

SUTTON, TIFFANY; Arkansas City HS; Arkansas City, KS; (3); 1/180; Am Leg Aux Girls St; Drama Clb; Scholastic Bowl; Orch; School Musical; School Play; VP Jr Cls; Tennis; High Hon Roll; NHS; Amer Fld Svc; Usherettes; Jr Ldrshp Ark City 96; Pittsburg ST U; Pre-Med.

SVATY, SETH; Ellsworth HS; Ellsworth, KS; (4); 1/65; Church Yth Grp; Band; Chorus; School Play; Pres Stu Cncl; DAR Awd; High Hon Roll; Debate Tm; Pres 4-H; Natl FFA Org; Voice Of Democracy Awd; Forensics Team; Xerox Awd Humanities, Scl Sci; Sterling Coll; Firefighter.

SVOBODA, ANDREW; Quivira Heights HS; Holyrood, KS; (2); 3/17; Band; Pep Band; Sec Treas Frsh Cls; Sec Treas Soph Cls; JV Ftbl; High Hon Roll; Art Project Recognition At Hays HS Art Show; KAYS Awd; Hutchinson CC; Agricultural.

SVOBODA, ANTHONY; Blue Vlly N HS; Overland Park, KS; (3); Am Leg Boys St; Boy Scts; Church Yth Grp; Spanish Clb; Band; Jazz Band; Pep Band; Var Capt Chrldng; Var Ftbl; Var Trk; Eagle Sct; Med.

SWAFFAR, MITZI N; Blue Valley Northwest HS; Overland Park, KS; (1); Church Yth Grp; Debate Tm; Crs Cntry; Trk; Hon Roll; Peer Facilitator Ldrshp Pgm; KU; MD; Psycht.

SWAFFORD, AMBER; Central Heights Sr HS; Princeton, KS; (3); 6/60; FCA; FBLA; Letterman Clb; Science Clb; Spanish Clb; Drill Tm; School Play; Vllybl; High Hon Roll; NHS; His.

SWAFFORD, MICHELLE; Sumner Acad Of Arts & Science; Kansas City, KS; (4); 51/195; Am Leg Aux Girls St; Debate Tm; NFL; Q&S; Band; Orch; Rptr Nwsp; High Hon Roll; NHS; Pres Schlr; Frnscs Tm; Pr Cnslr; Drake U; Jrnlsm.

SWAIN, EMILY F; Topeka HS; Topeka, KS; (4); Debate Tm; Drill Tm; Orch; School Musical; Variety Show; Nwsp; Phtg Yrbk; Phtg Lit Mag; Tennis; High Hon Roll; Orch Ltr.

SWALLEY, ERIC D; Council Grove HS; Council Grove, KS; (2).

SWANEY, DEVEN L; Riverton Schl; Galena, KS; (1); FHA; Hosp Aide; Science Clb; Rep Band; Rep Orch; Pres Frsh Cls; Ofcr Stu Cncl; JV Sftbl; High Hon Roll; KAYS Bd Mem; Stu Activity Cncl; Graphic Artist; Neonatology.

SWANEY, KARA P; Riverton Schl; Galena, KS; (4); 17/57; Art Clb; FHA; Letterman Clb; Science Clb; Orch; Co-Capt Chrldng; Hon Roll; NHS; Trk; Wt Lftg; Shw Choir; KAYS; Pittsburgh ST U.

SWANN, KIMBERLY; Rock Creek Jr Sr HS; Wamego, KS; (4); Dance Clb; Debate Tm; Drama Clb; Pep Clb; SADD; Teachers Aide; Chorus; School Musical; Nwsp; Yrbk; K ST; Tchng.

SWANSON, ASHLEY A; Wallace Cty HS; Sharon Spgs, KS; (1); Church Yth Grp; FCA; Quiz Bowl; Scholastic Bowl; SADD; Band; Bsktbl; Trk; Vllybl; Hon Roll; Harvard; Jrnlsm.

SWANSON, IAN E; Smoky Valley HS; Lindsborg, KS; (1); Art Clb; Boy Scts; Dance Clb; Drama Clb; English Clb; NFL; Quiz Bowl; Scholastic Bowl; Science Clb; Thesps; 2nd ST Erth Sci ST Sci Olypd; 6th ST Imprmt Duet Actng Frnscs; Leag Champ Imprmptv Team; Bettany Coll; Ordnd Mnstr Luth.

SWANSON, MEGAN M; Lawrence HS; Lawrence, KS; (2); Art Clb; Letterman Clb; Band; Stage Crew; JV Bsktbl; JV Sftbl; JV Trk; JV Vllybl; Intrml Wt Lftg; High Hon Roll; Horseback Riding; Sculpting; Fine Arts.

SWANSON, MICHAEL A; Pleasant Ridge HS; Leavenworth, KS; (3); FCA; Stage Crew; Rptr Nwsp; JV Var Ftbl; Hon Roll; Prfct Atten Awd.

SWANWICK, DANIEL L; Ft Scott HS; Fort Scott, KS; (4); 1/131; Pres Key Clb; Capt Scholastic Bowl; Pres Soph Cls; Var L Ftbl; Var L Tennis; Ntl Merit SF; St Schlr; Val; Am Leg Boys St; Church Yth Grp; All St Acad Team; Robert Byrd Schlsp; St Choir, 3 Yr Medalist; Duke Univ; Math; Linguistics.

SWART, STEVEN; Eureka Jr Sr HS; Eureka, KS; (4); Am Leg Boys St; Letterman Clb; Quiz Bowl; Science Clb; Spanish Clb; SADD; VP Stu Cncl; Ftbl; High Hon Roll; NHS; KS ST U; Chem.

SWART, STEVEN C; Wichita West HS; Wichita, KS; (4); Mgr Var Ftbl; Unsung Hero Optmst Clb Awd; UNLV; Scnrdy Ed.

SWARTLEY, ANDRE B; Hesston HS; Hesston, KS; (3); Drama Clb; NFL; Chorus; Jazz Band; Orch; School Musical; School Play; Variety Show; Tennis; Hon Roll; Eastern Mennonite U.

SWARTZ, REBEKAH; Wellington Sr HS; Wellington, KS; (1); Church Yth Grp; Office Aide; Church Choir; Hon Roll; Jr NHS.

SWARTZ, RIAN; Weskan Schl; Weskan, KS; (4); 1/6; Math Tm; Pep Clb; Quiz Bowl; Band; Chorus; Stage Crew; Var Capt Bsktbl; Var Capt Ftbl; Trk; Hon Roll; KS Wesleyan U; Crmnl Jstc.

SWARTZ, SHELLY J; Downs HS; Downs, KS; (1); Church Yth Grp; Ofcr Frsh Cls; High Hon Roll; Hon Roll; Beautician.

SWARTZ, VALORIE; Downs HS; Downs, KS; (4); 12/18; Church Yth Grp; Chorus; School Play; Stage Crew; Rptr Nwsp; Yrbk; Hon Roll; Beloit Vo-Tech; Exec Secy.

SWEANEY, JOSHUA C; Cedar Vale HS; Cedar Vale, KS; (2); 1/20; Church Yth Grp; FCA; Letterman Clb; Quiz Bowl; Scholastic Bowl; SADD; Band; Jazz Band; Mrchg Band; Pep Band; Amtr Trpshtng Assn; Pittsburgh ST U; Med.

SWEARENGIN, LEIGH M; Parsons HS; Parsons, KS; (2); 19/138; Treas VP Church Yth Grp; Hosp Aide; Key Clb; Pep Clb; Science Clb; SADD; JV Var Chrldng; High Hon Roll; Hon Roll; NHS; U Of KS; Pre-Med.

SWEENEY, KELLY S; Parsons HS; Parsons, KS; (3); 1/110; Hosp Aide; Treas Key Clb; Treas Pep Clb; Scholastic Bowl; Sec SADD; Ed Yrbk; Pres Frsh Cls; Capt Chrldng; High Hon Roll; VP NHS; Pre-Med; Pediatrician.

SWENSON, JENNIFER; Beloit Jr Sr HS; Beloit, KS; (3); 1/63; HOBY; Rep Frsh Cls; Rep Soph Cls; Rep Jr Cls; Sec Stu Cncl; Var L Bsktbl; Var L Crs Cntry; Var L Trk; High Hon Roll; NHS; Presdntl Clsrm Schlr; 2nd Pl St Ntl Spnsh Test; U Of KS; Elem Ed.

SWETT, CHRIS A; Olathe East Sr HS; Olathe, KS; (2); Letterman Clb; Teachers Aide; Chorus; Ftbl; JV Trk; Wt Lftg; Hon Roll; Bsbl; Police Officer.

SWICK, CHRISTOPHER E; Mc Pherson HS; Mc Pherson, KS; (2); Rptr Nwsp; Intrml Bsbl; Intrml Ftbl; Cit Awd; Hon Roll; Creative Drawing; Media Brdcstng.

SWIFT, BROOKS D; Shawnee Heights HS; Topeka, KS; (2); Church Yth Grp; Pep Clb; Science Clb; Varsity Clb; Phtg Nwsp; Phtg Yrbk; Var Chrldng; Var Ftbl; Wt Lftg; Hon Roll.

SWIFT, JEREMY L; Blue Valley HS; Overland Park, KS; (4); Am Leg Boys St; Cmnty Wkr; Teachers Aide; Ed Lit Mag; Pres Sr Cls; Ofcr Bsbl; Var Trk; Var Wrstlng; Hon Roll; Pittsburg ST U; Intl Bus.

SWIFT, TANNER J; Circle HS; Benton, KS; (2); 4-H; Letterman Clb; VP SADD; School Musical; School Play; VP Soph Cls; Church Yth Grp; Cmnty Wkr; Acpl Chr; Band; Yth Ldrshp Btlr, 96-97 Slctd At Dlgt; Btlr Cty 4-H Ambsdr; Stu Rl Mdl DARE Prgm; Mtrlgst.

SWINDALL, ANDY D; Shawnee Heights Sr HS; Tecumseh, KS; (2); Boy Scts; Church Yth Grp; JA; Trk; Hon Roll; U Of AL; Sls.

SWINGLE, EMILY; Attica Public Schl; Zenda, KS; (3); 1/16; Scholastic Bowl; School Play; Yrbk; VP Jr Cls; Var Chrldng; Var Vllybl; High Hon Roll; NHS; Ntl Merit Ltr; Prfct Atten Awd; Lifeguard; First Rspndr; Natl Cngrsnl Yth Ldr; Washburn U; KBI Agent.

SWINGLE, MARNIE L; Blue Valley Northwest HS; Plano, TX; (2); Key Clb; Math Tm; Var Swmmng; High Hon Roll; Hon Roll; NHS; Perf Scr KS Wrtng Asgnmt; Swmmng ST Fnlst Top 6; PT.

SWINGLE, MARTA L; Blue Valley Northwest HS; Overland Park, KS; (2); Var Swmmng; Hon Roll; Hunter-Jumper Equestrian; Vet.

SWIRCZYNSKI, SARAH L; Blue Vlly HS; Stilwell, KS; (3); 51/251; Am Leg Aux Girls St; Church Yth Grp; Debate Tm; Q&S; Orch; Ed Nwsp; Hon Roll; NHS; Yng Life; Vlntr Wyld Life Ldr.

SWISHER, KEIR G; Smoky Valley HS; Lindsborg, KS; (3); 8/59; Church Yth Grp; Cmnty Wkr; FCA; Letterman Clb; Pep Clb; Varsity Clb; Band; Orch; Pep Band; Variety Show; Sports Medicine.

SYMES, RYAN J; Emporia HS; Emporia, KS; (3); 1/267; Am Leg Boys St; Church Yth Grp; FCA; FBLA; Letterman Clb; SADD; JV Bsbl; Var L Bsktbl; Wt Lftg; Cit Awd; KS ST Univ; Bus Admin.

SYMES, STEPHANIE; Emporia HS; Emporia, KS; (4); 19/285; Am Leg Aux Girls St; Treas Frsh Cls; Rep Soph Cls; Sec VP Stu Cncl; Capt Var Chrldng; Cit Awd; DAR Awd; High Hon Roll; NHS; Kytt Sec, VP/PRES; Emprns Drg Awrnss Bd; MLK Jr Ldrshp Awd; KS ST U; Bus.

SYMMONDS, A BROOKE; Emporia HS; Emporia, KS; (3); 20/267; Church Yth Grp; FBLA; Intrml Bsktbl; Intrml Wt Lftg; High Hon Roll; Hon Roll.

SYMONDS, LONI D; Circle HS; Benton, KS; (2); FHA; SADD; Chorus; School Musical; Stage Crew; Rptr Nwsp; Stat Var Bsktbl; Var Mgr(s); JV Sftbl; Hon Roll; 1 Of Top 10 Nwsp Articles Of The Yr; Bus; Tchng.

SYRING, MORGAN P; Council Grove HS; Alta Vista, KS; (3); FCA; 4-H; SADD; JV Bsktbl; Var L Crs Cntry; Var L Trk; Hon Roll; NHS; Kayettes; KS U.

SZETO, ALEXANDER M; Blue Vlly NW HS; Shawnee Mission, KS; (4); 30/340; Chess Clb; Debate Tm; NFL; Scholastic Bowl; Band; Jazz Band; Mrchg Band; Pep Band; Var Capt Swmmng; Hon Roll; Mntrshp Acad Prog; Acad All Amer Boys Swimming; Truman St Univ; Labor Rltns.

KANSAS

SZETO, STEPHEN B; Blue Valley Northwest HS; Overland Park, KS; (2); Chess Clb; Orch; Var Swmmng; Var Tennis; High Hon Roll; DECA; Pres Nulti-Cltrl Club; ST Chmpnshp Swim Team; Prncpl Hon Roll; Harvard Univ; Biochem.

SZEWCZYK, LINDSAY M; Blue Valley Northwest HS; Overland Park, KS; (3); GAA; Varsity Clb; Rep Frsh Cls; Rep Soph Cls; Rep Stu Cncl; Var Bsktbl; Var Sftbl; JV Vllybl; Hon Roll; Powder Puff Ftbl; Peer Tutoring Disable Chldrn; Peer Facilitating Prgm; U Of KS.

SZUWALSKI, CODY; Holton HS; Holton, KS; (3); 8/80; Model UN; Quiz Bowl; Scholastic Bowl; Rep Stu Cncl; Bsktbl; Trk; High Hon Roll; NHS; Amer Legn Bsbl; Karate; Chem.

TABIN, PATRICK; Junction City HS; Fort Riley, KS; (1); 1/409; Boy Scts; Church Yth Grp; ROTC; JV Socr; High Hon Roll; Acad Ltr; VFW Awd; JROTC Acad Excl Awd.

TACHA, BECKY L; Meade HS; Meade, KS; (1); 6/32; Pep Clb; Band; Chorus; Mrchg Band; Pep Band; School Musical; JV Bsktbl; High Hon Roll; Hon Roll; Kayettes; Fort Hays ST Math Relays; Ed.

TACKLING, SEBASTIAN M; Manhattan HS; Manhattan, KS; (2); Chess Clb; Church Yth Grp; FBLA; Band; Mrchg Band; Orch; Tennis; High Hon Roll; Jr NHS; Pres Acad Fit Awd; Elem Music Ed.

TADDIKEN, TAWNYA; Clay Ctr Cmty HS; Clifton, KS; (3); Church Yth Grp; Debate Tm; Drama Clb; 4-H; HOBY; Science Clb; Teachers Aide; School Play; Golf; Wrstlng; Sr Acolyte St Pauls Epis Church; Cty 4-H Wnnr; Pre-Law.

TADLOCK, BRIAN D; Cimmaron Jr Sr HS; Cimarron, KS; (4); Debate Tm; Letterman Clb; Library Aide; Quiz Bowl; Scholastic Bowl; Spanish Clb; Speech Tm; Teachers Aide; Varsity Clb; Nwsp; Kirkwood Comm Clg; Acctng & Fin.

TAGGART, KELLI J; Shawnee Hghts HS; Wakarusa, KS; (4); 69/260; Cmnty Wkr; 4-H; FBLA; Office Aide; Pep Clb; SADD; Teachers Aide; Varsity Clb; Mrchg Band; L Var Bsktbl; KS ST Univ; Bus.

TAGGART, LACY A; Russell HS; Bunker Hill, KS; (2); SADD; Chorus; JV Var Bsktbl; Var Mgr(s); JV Vllybl; Hon Roll; Kay Club; Elem Ed.

TAKAHASHI, TAIGA; Washburn Rural HS; Topeka, KS; (3); 9/351; Boy Scts; Pres Debate Tm; NFL; Band; Pres Jr Cls; Pres Sr Cls; Intrml Bsktbl; JV Var Trk; NHS; Ntl Merit Ltr.

TAKEGUCHI, TERENCE H; Blue Valley North HS; Leawood, KS; (2); Boy Scts; Church Yth Grp; Model UN; Pep Clb; Band; Mrchg Band; School Musical; Socr; JV Trk; Hon Roll; Inner Delta.

TAKEMOTO, MICHELLE; Manhattan HS; Manhattan, KS; (3); Cmnty Wkr; FBLA; VP SADD; Acpl Chr; School Musical; Swing Chorus; Rep Jr Cls; L Chrldng; DAR Awd; Hon Roll; SADD Clb Fall Hnry; Clb Cnsl Rep, Cmmtte; KU.

TAKUSAGAWA, KEN; Lawrence HS; Lawrence, KS; (4); 1/623; Sec Key Clb; Model UN; Capt Scholastic Bowl; Pres Science Clb; Band; Chorus; Treas Soph Cls; Comp Prgmr; Standford U; Comp Sci.

TALBOTT, MARK D; Smoky Valley HS; Lindsborg, KS; (2); Church Yth Grp; Cmnty Wkr; FCA; Letterman Clb; Pep Clb; SADD; Teachers Aide; Band; Bsktbl; Ftbl; Mntr Stdnts Jr High; Bethany Coll; Tchr.

TALBOTT, TRACI L; Smoky Valley HS; Lindsborg, KS; (2); Church Yth Grp; Cmnty Wkr; FCA; SADD; Varsity Clb; Band; Orch; Bsktbl; Tennis; High Hon Roll; Crmstprs Bd; Hnrbl Mntn All League Bsktbl; KS ST; Attrny/Tchr.

TALCOTT, MICHELLE; Olathe North Sr HS; Olathe, KS; (2); Drama Clb; Office Aide; Pep Clb; Spanish Clb; Chorus; School Play; Hon Roll; Figure Skating; Hnrs Eng; Presdntl Acad Awd; Vet.

TALCOTT, SHELLY R; Halstead HS; Halstead, KS; (4); Cit Awd; Hon Roll; Art Awds; Actng; Washburn U; Anthrplgy.

TALIB, HINA; Blue Valley North HS; Leawood, KS; (3); 1/232; Debate Tm; Hosp Aide; Model UN; NFL; Q&S; Nwsp; Rep Frsh Cls; Gov Hon Prg Awd; High Hon Roll; NHS; Bausch & Lomb Sci Awd; Soc Women Engrs Awd; Natl Teams Fnlst Mem 96; Medicine.

TALLENT, CHRISTOPHER M; Shawnee Mission West HS; Lenexa, KS; (3); Cmnty Wkr; DECA; Ed Nwsp; JV Bsbl; Crs Cntry; Hon Roll; Conflict Resolution Mediator-Peer Helper; Bus; Acctng; Fin Ec.

TALLEY, JOSHUA G; Topeka West HS; Topeka, KS; (3); 14/240; French Clb; Math Clb; Band; Mrchg Band; Orch; Pep Band; School Musical; Var Trk; French Hon Soc; High Hon Roll; Soc Rep Frnch Clb 95-/Pres 96-; Tuba Sec Ldr 95-/Band Pres 96-; Acoustic Engr.

TALLMAN, JAMIE R; Neodesha Jr Sr HS; Neodesha, KS; (1); 1/100; Church Yth Grp; Math Tm; Natl FFA Org; Spanish Clb; Ofcr Stu Cncl; Ofcr Bsbl; Ftbl; Wt Lftg; High Hon Roll; Rotary Club Awd; Keith Hersh Schlr Awd.

TALLY, KEITH P; Madison Jr Sr HS; Madison, KS; (3); Boy Scts; Church Yth Grp; Band; Chorus; Church Choir; Mrchg Band; Pep Band; School Play; JV Var Bsktbl; L Var Ftbl; Crpntr.

TANG, ALICE; Shawnee Mission N HS; Overland Park, KS; (3); French Clb; Pep Clb; Phtg Yrbk; Var Tennis; High Hon Roll; NHS; WA Univ; Med.

TANGNEY, JAMIE L; Bishop Carroll Catholic HS; Wichita, KS; (2); Intrml Bsktbl; JV Var Sftbl; JV Vllybl; High Hon Roll; Hon Roll.

TANKING, JOSH P; Jackson Heights HS; Wetmore, KS; (3); FCA; Pres Sec Natl FFA Org; VP Pep Clb; Yrbk; VP Stu Cncl; Var L Bsktbl; Var L Crs Cntry; Var L Ftbl; Var L Trk; Wt Lftg; KS ST; Pblc Rltns.

TANKING, MACY; St Marys HS; Saint Marys, KS; (3); FCA; Band; Pres Frsh Cls; Rep Jr Cls; Ofcr Stu Cncl; Var Bsktbl; Var Sftbl; Var Trk; Var Vllybl; High Hon Roll.

TANNINI, EDDIE P; Chapman HS; Chapman, KS; (3); Am Leg Boys St; Boy Scts; VP Bus Profs of Am; Church Yth Grp; Pep Band; JV Bsktbl; JV Ftbl; High Hon Roll; NHS; Prfct Atten Awd; U Of CA Berekley; Engrng.

TAPPY, KEVIN M; Blue Valley Northwest HS; Overland Park, KS; (2); Church Yth Grp; Debate Tm; Hon Roll; Sprts Crd Cllctr; KS U; Entrepnr.

TARDIFF, REBECCA G; Shawnee Heights HS; Topeka, KS; (1); Church Yth Grp; Cmnty Wkr; Chorus; Bsktbl; High Hon Roll; City Bsbl League; Sunday Schl Tchr Asst; Piano; Sci.

TARPLEY, MATT B; Garden City Sr HS; Garden City, KS; (2); Computer Clb; High Hon Roll; Hon Roll; Rlr Hcky.

TARWATER, CRYSTAL; Pierson Jr HS; Kansas City, KS; (1); Art Clb; Cit Awd; Hon Roll; Jr NHS; Prfct Atten Awd; Pres Schlr; Art/Math.

TARWATER, SARAH; Baldwin HS; Baldwin City, KS; (3); FHA; Nrsng/Med Asst.

TASHKOFF, REBECCA E; F L Schlagle HS; Kansas City, KS; (4); 2/190; Drama Clb; French Clb; Q&S; Pres Thesps; School Play; Stage Crew; NHS; SADD; School Musical; Ed Nwsp; VSD 500 Jrnlst Of Yr; Emporia St Univ; Actress.

TASSET, DANA M; Spearville Jr Sr HS; Spearville, KS; (3); 9/27; Dance Clb; Pep Clb; Quiz Bowl; Speech Tm; Band; Chorus; Church Choir; Drill Tm; Mrchg Band; Pep Band; Organist; Song Ldr; Tchr.

TATE, ANDREA; Central USD 462; Latham, KS; (1); Church Yth Grp; 4-H; Band; Pep Band; JV Bsktbl; Var Chrldng; JV Sftbl; JV Vllybl; 4-H Awd; High Hon Roll; KS ST U; Vet.

TATE, KIMBERLY D; Shawnee Mission N HS; Merriam, KS; (4); Latin Clb; Office Aide; Pep Clb; Teachers Aide; Sftbl; NHS; Categories; 4 Yr Acad Ltr; Prsdntl Hnr Awd; Baylor U; Pre Bio/Heart Srgn.

TATE, SHANAE N; Acad Of Mt St Scholastica; Atchison, KS; (3); Church Yth Grp; Girl Scts; NFL; Chorus; Ed Nwsp; Pres Soph Cls; Pres Jr Cls; Hon Roll; NHS; Cmnty Wkr; Stdnt Pilot; George Washington U; Intl Affrs.

TATE, SHAWN; Winfield HS; Winfield, KS; (3); Am Leg Boys St; JV Crs Cntry; Hon Roll; NHS; Prfct Atten Awd; SW CC.

TATRO, MEGHANN; Mc Pherson HS; Mc Pherson, KS; (3); 32/191; Art Clb; Dance Clb; DECA; French Clb; Key Clb; Chorus; Var Drill Tm; Flag Corp; Stage Crew; Var Chrldng; Brdcst Jrnlsm.

TATRO, MIKE; Winfield HS; Winfield, KS; (4); Am Leg Boys St; Boy Scts; Church Yth Grp; French Clb; Scholastic Bowl; Band; Jazz Band; Crs Cntry; Trk; NHS; U Of KS; Chem Eng.

TAUL, KELLY K; Baldwin HS; Baldwin City, KS; (4); 22/77; Art Clb; Sec 4-H; Treas Hist FHA; NFL; Sec Treas Acpl Chr; School Musical; School Play; Cit Awd; 4-H Awd; Hon Roll; Dist & St Voclst; HS Best Feml Voclst 95-96; Fornscs Best Exprncd Comptr 95-96; HS Best Actrss 95-96; Baker Univ; Phy & Occptnl Thrpy.

TAUSSIG, JACOB S; Manhattan HS; Manhattan, KS; (3); Church Yth Grp; Cmnty Wkr; FCA; Bsktbl; Crs Cntry; Wt Lftg; KS ST Univ.

TAVERNER, JAIME F; Udall HS; Udall, KS; (2); Church Yth Grp; Spanish Clb; Band; Chorus; Mrchg Band; Pep Band; Stage Crew; Var Sftbl; Cit Awd; Hon Roll; Schl Bible Stdy; Hamline U; Art.

TAYLOR, ALLISON M; F L Schlagle HS; Kansas City, KS; (1); High Hon Roll; Hon Roll; Poetry/Art.

TAYLOR, AMANDA E; Blue Valley HS; Stilwell, KS; (2); Church Yth Grp; Var Crs Cntry; Var Trk; High Hon Roll; Hon Roll.

TAYLOR, AMANDA L; Washington HS; Kansas City, KS; (2); 10/245; Church Yth Grp; 4-H; Q&S; Quiz Bowl; ROTC; SADD; Flag Corp; Nwsp; Yrbk; JV Sftbl; Tank Engr.

TAYLOR, ANGELA M; Sacred Heart HS; Salina, KS; (3); 1/38; Am Leg Aux Girls St; Pres FBLA; Pep Clb; Quiz Bowl; Sec Sr Cls; JV Bsktbl; Var Chrldng; Var Vllybl; NHS; JV Sftbl; Jr Cvtn VP/PRES; Wichita ST Diet/Pre-Optmtry.

TAYLOR, ARON; Parsons HS; Parsons, KS; (4); 5/120; Q&S; Spanish Clb; Teachers Aide; Ed Nwsp; JV Var Bsbl; High Hon Roll; Hon Roll; NHS; Pres Schlr; Acad Awd, Acad Achvmt; Amer Legion Bsbl; Sr Babe Ruth Bsbl; Pittsburg ST Univ; TV-RADIO.

TAYLOR, CORTNEY L; Labette Co HS; Edna, KS; (2); 28/158; FCA; FBLA; Natl FFA Org; Bsktbl; Sftbl; Vllybl; Hon Roll; Ag Ed.

TAYLOR, CURTIS R; Olathe South Sr HS; Olathe, KS; (3); Sec Church Yth Grp; Teachers Aide; Varsity Clb; Chorus; Ftbl; Var Golf; Attnd Washington DC Natl Ldrsp Conf; Accntng.

TAYLOR, DENISE E; Burlingame HS; Burlingame, KS; (4); 10/36; FBLA; Girl Scts; VP Natl FFA Org; Teachers Aide; Band; Mrchg Band; Pep Band; JV Vllybl; High Hon Roll; Hon Roll; Gold Awd Girl Scts; KS ST; Nrsng.

TAYLOR, JE TAIME L; Washington HS; Kansas City, KS; (2); Debate Tm; FCA; NFL; Speech Tm; Church Choir; Orch; Var Bsktbl; Var Trk; Var Vllybl; Hon Roll; Close Up Clb; KU; Law.

TAYLOR, JENNIFER; Mc Pherson HS; Mc Pherson, KS; (3); 15/180; Church Yth Grp; Debate Tm; Drama Clb; 4-H; German Clb; NFL; Q&S; Quiz Bowl; Scholastic Bowl; KS Hnrs Rgnts Acad.

TAYLOR, JESSIE; Larned HS; Larned, KS; (4); 14/90; Latin Clb; Spanish Clb; Acpl Chr; Band; Chorus; Flag Corp; Swing Chorus; Sec Jr Cls; Sec Sr Cls; Chrldng; Cowley Cty CC; Deaf Educ.

TAYLOR, JOHNNA K; Louisburg HS; Louisburg, KS; (3); Church Yth Grp; FCA; Letterman Clb; Spanish Clb; Varsity Clb; Nwsp; Sec Frsh Cls; Sec Stu Cncl; JV Bsktbl; Var Sftbl; Excptnl Atndnc Frosh, Soph, Jr Yr; Scrd Tp 5% On KS Assmnt Tsts; Pittsburg U; His Tchr.

TAYLOR, KENYA T; Turner HS; Kansas City, KS; (2); Cmnty Wkr; GAA; Intnl Clb; JA; Spanish Clb; Teachers Aide; VP Jr Cls; Var Bsktbl; Var Trk; Var Vllybl; Frgn Lang.

TAYLOR, LATOYA; Sumner Acad Of Arts & Science; Kansas City, KS; (4); 73/192; Art Clb; JA; Key Clb; Latin Clb; Pep Clb; Spanish Clb; Church Choir; Ofcr Frsh Cls; Ofcr Jr Cls; Bsktbl; Xavier U Of New Orleans; Bio.

TAYLOR, LYDIA D; Bluestem HS; Augusta, KS; (3); Math Tm; Scholastic Bowl; Ed Nwsp; Lit Mag; Hon Roll; Ntl Merit Ltr; Wrk Publshd Local/Natl Litry Publctns; Creative Wrtng/Jrnlsm.

TAYLOR, LYNDSAY E; Washburn Rural HS; Topeka, KS; (3); Sec Latin Clb; Band; Phtg Nwsp; Phtg Yrbk; Phtg Lit Mag; JV Mgr(s); High Hon Roll; Hon Roll; Mrchg Band; School Musical; Teens As Tchrs; Peer Mediation; Johnson Cnty CC.

TAYLOR, MICHELLE; Newton Sr HS; Newton, KS; (4); French Clb; Key Clb; Teachers Aide; Mgr Bsktbl; L Pom Pon; JV Var Sftbl; JV Vllybl; Cit Awd; Hon Roll; Pres Schlr; Optmist Schlsp; KS ST U; Bus Comm.

TAYLOR, MIRANDA N; Dodge City HS; Dodge City, KS; (3); GAA; SADD; Teachers Aide; Varsity Clb; Var Bsktbl; Var Sftbl; Var Tennis; DAR Awd; Hon Roll.

TAYLOR, NOVA D; Salina HS South; Salina, KS; (3); Church Yth Grp; Dance Clb; Debate Tm; FCA; FHA; Pep Clb; Var Chrldng; Pom Pon; Hon Roll; Sons Of Amer Revolution; Comm.

TAYLOR, RACHEL; Mulvane Sr HS; Mulvane, KS; (3); Church Yth Grp; FCA; SADD; Teachers Aide; Thesps; Band; Mrchg Band; Var Chrldng; Var Trk; Cit Awd; KSU.

TAYLOR, ROCHELLE M; Immaculata HS; Orlando, FL; (2); JA; Chorus; School Musical; High Hon Roll; Hon Roll; Prfct Atten Awd; All-Amer Schlr; Intl Frgn Lang Awd; Dsgn Art Awds; Med Fld.

TAYLOR, RUSSELL J; Desoto HS; Shawnee Mission, KS; (3); 6/180; Am Leg Boys St; NFL; VP Thesps; Band; School Musical; School Play; High Hon Roll; NHS; Pres Acad Fit Awd; Cmnty Wkr; TRENDS; Baker Univ; Med Sci.

TAYLOR, SHAWN L; Shawnee Heights Sr HS; Berryton, KS; (2); JV Bsbl; Intrml Bsktbl; JV Var Socr; Pres Acad Fit Awd; Vlybl; Coaching Yth Soccer; Engr.

TAYLOR, TANYA N; Wyandotte HS; Kansas City, KS; (2); Hon Roll; Magnet Hnr; Yth Amng Frnds Clb; Oprtn Brghtsd Cmnty Srvc; Bus Law.

TAYLOR, TARA N; Neodesha Jr Sr HS; El Dorado, KS; (1); FHA; Spanish Clb; High Hon Roll; Hon Roll; Emporia U; Mntl Thrpsts.

TAYLOR, TARYN N; Garden City Sr HS; Garden City, KS; (2); Church Yth Grp; Dance Clb; FCA; Chorus; Church Choir; High Hon Roll; Acad Lttr; Tchr.

TAYLOR, TORI D; Ellsworth HS; Geneseo, KS; (1); 18/80; Church Yth Grp; Pep Clb; Chorus; Mgr(s); Hon Roll.

TAYLOR, WHITNEY A; Wichita Southeast HS; Wichita, KS; (1); JV Socr; JV Trk; Hon Roll.

TEACH, JARED G; Seaman Sr HS; Topeka, KS; (3); 73/283; Church Yth Grp; FBLA; FHA; Pres Sr Cls; Rep Stu Cncl; Var Bsbl; Var Bsktbl; Var Socr; High Hon Roll; Hon Roll.

TEAGUE, DANIELLE E; Bishop Miege HS; Kansas City, MO; (3); Church Yth Grp; Cmnty Wkr; French Clb; Pep Clb; Chorus; Church Choir; Var Capt Chrldng; High Hon Roll; Hon Roll; NHS; Missions Trips To Mexico/China; Yth For Christ; Stunts Plus Comptv Chrldng; Engrng.

TEDDER, TAYLOR D; Stanton Co HS; Manter, KS; (1); Bsktbl; Ftbl; Trk; Wt Lftg; Hon Roll.

TEEGARDEN, MOLLY; Kingman HS; Kingman, KS; (1); FBLA; Acpl Chr; Band; Pres Frsh Cls; Rep Stu Cncl; Var L Chrldng; Intrml Vllybl; High Hon Roll; Renssnce Brd Mem; Yth/Govt.

TEEL, LOGAN I; Liberal HS; Liberal, KS; (3); Quiz Bowl; Jr NHS; Physcs.

TEEL, TOBY E; Horton HS; Horton, KS; (3); JV Bsktbl; JV Ftbl; Var Wrstlng; High Hon Roll; Hon Roll; Drafting.

TEETZEN, DANELLE; Garden City Sr HS; Garden City, KS; (4); 9/330; Church Yth Grp; Cmnty Wkr; Orch; High Hon Roll; NHS; Prfct Atten Awd.

TEETZEN, MICALA; Garden City Sr HS; Garden City, KS; (4); 6/330; Church Yth Grp; Cmnty Wkr; Orch; High Hon Roll; NHS; Prfct Atten Awd.

TEGTMEIER, GINELL M; Hanover Schl; Hanover, KS; (3); 5/16; Am Leg Aux Girls St; VP FBLA; Sec FHA; Chorus; Co-Ed Yrbk; Sec Stu Cncl; Var Bsktbl; Var Vllybl; High Hon Roll; Pres NHS; Bus Mgmt.

TEIG, MATTHEW J; Blue Valley HS; Overland Park, KS; (3); 1/250; Church Yth Grp; Cmnty Wkr; Band; Mrchg Band; Pep Band; JV Socr; Var Trk; High Hon Roll; NHS; Rensselaer Medal Top Jr Math/Sci; Columb Ia U Book Awd; 4th Pl KS 5a St Track Meet 4x800 Relay.

TEMPLE, BENJAMIN D; Blue Valley Northwest HS; Overland Park, KS; (4); Chess Clb; Quiz Bowl; Band; Jazz Band; Mrchg Band; Orch; Pep Band; School Musical; Variety Show; Hon Roll; Natl Eng Mrt Awd; Film Distributed In 8 Countries; Editor At Local ABC Affiliate Network; UCLA Film Schl; Film.

TEMPLE, JEFF B; Topeka HS; Topeka, KS; (2); German Clb; Band; Jazz Band; Mrchg Band; Pep Band; School Musical; Hon Roll.

TEMPLE, MANDY L; Blue Valley HS; Stanley, KS; (2); High Hon Roll; Hon Roll; Sgn Lang; KS U; Tchr Of Df.

TEMPLE, MIKE W; Salina HS South; Salina, KS; (4); Church Yth Grp; FCA; NFL; Chorus; Variety Show; Rep Frsh Cls; Rep Soph Cls; Rep Jr Cls; Bsktbl; JV L Crs Cntry; Ambucs Pres Of Socls Comm.

TEMPLETON, ALISHA; Olathe South Sr HS; Olathe, KS; (4); Letterman Clb; Pep Clb; Treas Spanish Clb; Teachers Aide; Variety Show; L Bsktbl; L Chrldng; Var Trk; High Hon Roll; Pres Acad Fit Awd.

TEMPLIN, MELISSA; Northwest HS; Wichita, KS; (4); 1/334; HOBY; Band; Chorus; Church Choir; Orch; Sec Soph Cls; Var Chrldng; Var Swmmng; NHS; St Schlr; All Amer Stu; Wichita ST U; Ed.

TENBRINK, TRAVIS M; Topeka West HS; Topeka, KS; (2); Church Yth Grp; Debate Tm; Pep Clb; L Var Socr; L Var Trk; Hon Roll; Lfgrd; KS ST Univ; Forestry.

TENCLEVE, KRISTY M; Wellington Sr HS; Wellington, KS; (4); 18/120; Am Leg Aux Girls St; Church Yth Grp; Library Aide; Red Cross Aide; Pres Frsh Cls; Ofcr Soph Cls; Ofcr Jr Cls; VP Sr Cls; Pres Stu Cncl; Bsktbl; 2nd Runnr Up Miss TEEN KS 93; KSU; Nrs.

TENEBHN, JENNIFER M; Shawnee Mission N HS; Shawnee Mission, KS; (3); 95/425; Key Clb; Pep Clb; Socr; Wt Lftg; Hon Roll; Ntl Merit Ltr; Tap/Ballet Lssns; JCCC; Nurse.

TENNANT, JUSTEN K; Canton-Galva HS; Canton, KS; (3); FBLA; SADD; Ofcr Bsbl; Bsktbl; KS ST; Arch.

TENNISSEN, CARRIE M; Shawnee Mission Northwest HS; Olathe, KS; (4); 85/475; Debate Tm; Intnl Clb; NFL; Q&S; Ed Yrbk; Golf; Hon Roll; NHS; Creighton Univ; Bio.

TEPAVCEVIC, SLADANA; Manhattan HS; Manhattan, KS; (4); Intnl Clb; SADD; Chorus; School Musical; Swing Chorus; Variety Show; Kiwanis Awd; Ballet, Jazz, Tap Dance; KS ST U; Bus.

TERHUNE, CHRIS R; Dighton HS; Dighton, KS; (1); Debate Tm; Drama Clb; French Clb; Speech Tm; School Play; Wt Lftg; Hon Roll; Garden City CC; Disel Techn.

TERHUNE, EMILY R; Bishop Carroll HS; Wichita, KS; (4); Church Yth Grp; Cmnty Wkr; German Clb; SADD; Cit Awd; Hon Roll; Pres Acad Fit Awd; U Of KS; Bus.

TERHUNE, MICHAEL D; Conway Springs HS; Conway Springs, KS; (3); Church Yth Grp; Drama Clb; Bsktbl; Ftbl; Powder Puff Ftbl; Trk; Wt Lftg; 8 Ball Pool; Hunting; Marines.

TERNES, MARTHA; Neodesha Jr Sr HS; Neodesha, KS; (1); Church Yth Grp; Drama Clb; FHA; Math Tm; Natl FFA Org; NFL; School Musical; School Play; Ofcr Frsh Cls; JV Bsktbl.

TERRONEZ, STEPHANIE D; Campus HS; Haysville, KS; (2); Computer Clb; Intnl Clb; SADD; Hon Roll; Washburn Univ; Lwyr.

TERRY, KELLY R; Nemaha Valley HS; Seneca, KS; (3); Church Yth Grp; Speech Tm; Band; Chorus; Mrchg Band; Pep Band; Hon Roll; Nrsg Hm Vol; Nrsg.

TERRY, SHAWN H; Great Bend Sr HS; Great Bend, KS; (4); 50/220; Letterman Clb; Band; Mrchg Band; Bsktbl; Ftbl; Trk; High Hon Roll; Hon Roll; St Track Cmptn; Ftbl & Bsktbl Camps; Town Sftbl, Bsbl & Bsktbl; Cub Scts; Phys Thrpy.

TERRY, SUSAN L; Goodland HS; Goodland, KS; (4); 8/85; Church Yth Grp; Cmnty Wkr; Pep Clb; Band; Mrchg Band; Pep Band; High Hon Roll; Hon Roll; Pres Acad Fit Awd; Colby CC; Psych.

TESTORFF, JENNIFER; Ottawa HS; Ottawa, KS; (4); 1/143; Am Leg Aux Girls St; Church Yth Grp; Key Clb; Treas Band; Chorus; Drm Mjr(t); School Musical; NHS; St Schlr; FCA; Natl Amer Bapt Yth Peer Ldr; Drake U; Music.

TETER, ANGELA M; Central Heights Sr HS; Richmond, KS; (1); Treas 4-H; Natl FFA Org; Science Clb; Drill Tm; Treas Frsh Cls; JV Bsktbl; Var Sftbl; 4-H Awd; High Hon Roll; Prfct Atten Awd; Livestock Judging; Barrel Racing Quarter Horses; KS ST; Vet.

TETER, LESLIE A; Wichita East HS; Wichita, KS; (2); German Clb; Orch; Wichita ST Univ; Violinist.

TEVIS, KATHY E; Spring Hill HS; Spring Hill, KS; (1); Church Yth Grp; Cmnty Wkr; Scholastic Bowl; Chorus; School Musical; JV Sftbl; High Hon Roll; Missn Trip Mexico; Mid-America Nazarene Coll.

THACH, EMILY; Burrton Schl; Burrton, KS; (2); 5/32; Key Clb; Scholastic Bowl; Band; Chorus; Nwsp; Yrbk; Ofcr Stu Cncl; Bsktbl; Trk; Vllybl; KS U; Bus.

THACKER, CHASTITY L; Russell HS; Russell, KS; (2); Cmnty Wkr; FCA; Key Clb; Math Tm; Pep Clb; SADD; Chorus; Ofcr Frsh Cls; Ofcr Jr Cls; Cit Awd.

THACKER, TAVI M; Russell HS; Russell, KS; (2); Pep Clb; Chorus; Hon Roll; Pres Acad Fit Awd; Jrnlsm; Cmptr; KU; Cmptr Graphics.

THAETE, AARON M; Claflin Jr Sr HS; Claflin, KS; (3); Pres 4-H; Letterman Clb; Library Aide; Pep Clb; Ed Yrbk; Ftbl; Mgr(s); 4-H Awd; Hon Roll; NHS.

THAI, BINH; Larned HS; Larned, KS; (3); #1 in class; Cmnty Wkr; Scholastic Bowl; Treas Spanish Clb; Teachers Aide; Phtg Yrbk; Tennis; High Hon Roll; NHS; KS Regents Hnrs Acad Stu.

THALMANN, DAMIAN D; Hoisington HS; Hoisington, KS; (2); Am Leg Boys St; Boy Scts; Band; Chorus; JV Bsbl; Stat Bsktbl; Stat Ftbl; Var Mgr(s); Var Score Keeper; Hon Roll; Barton Cnty CC; Cmptr Animatn.

THALMANN, DREW E; Cheney Jr Sr HS; Haven, KS; (3); Band; Chorus; Mrchg Band; Pep Band; Rep Soph Cls; Rep Jr Cls; Var L Bsktbl; Var L Ftbl; Var L Trk; Hon Roll; Ag.

THALMANN, SHERRY A; Cheney Jr Sr HS; Haven, KS; (2); 4/48; Band; Chorus; Jazz Band; Mrchg Band; Pep Band; Pres Frsh Cls; Pres Soph Cls; Var L Bsktbl; Var L Trk; Var L Vllybl.

THARP, AMY; Indian Trail Jr HS; Olathe, KS; (2); Service Clb; Spanish Clb; Varsity Clb; Drill Tm; Rep Soph Cls; JV Bsktbl; JV Crs Cntry; JV Trk; High Hon Roll; Letterman Clb; Pres Ed Awds Pgm-Outstndg Acad Achvmt; Cougar Of The Yr; Distngd Schlstc Achvmt; Phy Thrpst.

THATCHER, SABRINA L; Triplains Schl; Winona, KS; (2); 5/16; Church Yth Grp; 4-H; Quiz Bowl; Speech Tm; Band; Chorus; Orch; School Play; Kayettes; Paraed.

THAYER, ELIZABETH; Campus HS; Wichita, KS; (4); 4/213; Am Leg Aux Girls St; Drama Clb; Girl Scts; Intnl Clb; Red Cross Aide; SADD; Chorus; Orch; High Hon Roll; Treas NHS; Vcl Solo-Rgnl, St 1 Rtng; Emporia St U; Math.

THAYER, KELLY R; Wichita East HS; Wichita, KS; (3); Bus Profs of Am; Office Aide; Pep Clb; Band; School Play; High Hon Roll; Hon Roll; Pres Acad Fit Awd.

THAYER, ROBBY; Campus HS; Wichita, KS; (2); FTA; Varsity Clb; Var Golf; Var Capt Wrstlng; High Hon Roll; NHS; Stdnts As Tchrs; Wrstlng ST Cmptr; 2nd Tm AVL Wrstlng; Arch.

THEDINGER, TYSON; St Thomas Aquinas HS; Overland Park, KS; (4); Am Leg Boys St; Boy Scts; Debate Tm; FCA; Library Aide; Office Aide; Quiz Bowl; Science Clb; Teachers Aide; School Play; Pepperdine Univ; Med.

THEEL, BRIAN K; Emporia HS; Emporia, KS; (2); Boy Scts; Treas Church Yth Grp; Key Clb; Band; Mrchg Band; Pep Band; Swmmng; Cit Awd; Hon Roll; Wildlife & Backpacking Clb; Psych.

THEIS, MEGAN R; Spearville Jr Sr HS; Wright, KS; (2); Church Yth Grp; Cmnty Wkr; Letterman Clb; Quiz Bowl; Spanish Clb; Chorus; Rep Stu Cncl; High Hon Roll; Hon Roll; NHS; Bus; Ed.

THESING, ERICA C; St Thomas Aquinas HS; Leawood, KS; (3); Church Yth Grp; Cmnty Wkr; Ed Nwsp; High Hon Roll; Ntl Merit Ltr; NHS; Peer Minister; Showing Arabian Horses.

THEURER, TY C; Wellington Sr HS; South Haven, KS; (3); 15/165; Am Leg Boys St; Church Yth Grp; Pres 4-H; HOBY; Math Tm; VP Natl FFA Org; Band; Jazz Band; Mrchg Band; Pep Band; Wshngtn Ldr Conf; KS ST U; Feed Sci.

THIBAULT, GABE; Osborne HS; Osborne, KS; (3); 5/32; 4-H; FHA; Natl FFA Org; Scholastic Bowl; Bsktbl; Ftbl; Golf; High Hon Roll; NHS; Pres Acad Fit Awd; KS ST Univ.

THIBAULT, JASON P; Shawnee Heights Sr HS; Topeka, KS; (3); Church Yth Grp; NFL; Hon Roll; KS Regents Hnr Acad 96; KS Museum Of His Vol 95; U Of KS.

THIBAULT, JEREMY R; Garden City Sr HS; Garden City, KS; (3); Computer Clb; Spanish Clb; Var Golf; Hon Roll; KS St Univ.

THIBAULT, JOSH; Garden City Sr HS; Garden City, KS; (4); 76/351; Pres VP Computer Clb; NFL; Quiz Bowl; Science Clb; VICA; Nwsp; Hon Roll; Prfct Atten Awd; KS ST U; Comp Sci.

THIBODEAUX, CHRISTOPHER J; Olathe South Sr HS; Olathe, KS; (3); Math Clb; VICA; High Hon Roll; Jr NHS; Pres Schlr; Prtcptd Sci Olympiad; Lttrd Acad Hnrs Three Times; KS ST Univ; Archtctrl Engr.

THIELENHAUS, ERIK W; Otis Bison HS; Bison, KS; (2); Church Yth Grp; Cmnty Wkr; 4-H; Key Clb; SADD; Chorus; School Play; Variety Show; Ofcr Frsh Cls; Ofcr Soph Cls; Fort Hays ST; Pharm.

THIEME, JUSTINA M; Kingman HS; Zenda, KS; (2); Church Yth Grp; 4-H; Band; Mrchg Band; Pep Band; Vllybl; Hon Roll; CPA.

THIES, ABBY; Wichita East HS; Wichita, KS; (4); 1/347; Church Yth Grp; Acpl Chr; High Hon Roll; NHS; Ntl Merit SF; VP Spanish NHS; Val; JA; Spanish Clb; SADD; Literary Soc; Natl Art Hnr Soc; Humane Soc Vlntr; Baylor U; Intl Rltns.

THIESSEN, KATHRYN J; Inman Jr Sr HS; Inman, KS; (2); 15/50; 4-H; German Clb; Pep Clb; Speech Tm; Teachers Aide; Band; Chorus; Mrchg Band; Pep Band; School Musical; Scndry Eng Tchr.

THIESSEN, PATRICK R; Hutchinson HS; Hutchinson, KS; (3); 4/360; Am Leg Boys St; Debate Tm; Key Clb; NFL; Quiz Bowl; Speech Tm; Pres Sr Cls; JV Bsbl; Var Crs Cntry; Pres NHS; Frgn Diplomat.

THILL, SUMMER; Lyndon HS; Lyndon, KS; (4); 1/34; Drama Clb; Treas FBLA; FHA; Office Aide; Co-Capt Quiz Bowl; SADD; Band; Chorus; Mrchg Band; Pep Band; KU Hnr Awd; US Army Rsrv Natl Schlr/Ath Awd; U Of KS; Pre Med Studies.

THIMESCH, AMY; Kingman HS; Kingman, KS; (3); Church Yth Grp; FCA; FBLA; Q&S; SADD; Ed Yrbk; High Hon Roll; NHS; KS Rgnts Hnrs Acad 96; Teens Tdy Ldrs Tmrrw.

THIRAKUL, KATRINA V; Garden City Sr HS; Garden City, KS; (1); Orch; Vllybl; All-Amer Schlr; Wichita ST Univ; Pediatrician.

THOLEN, KARA R; Anderson Cty Jr Sr HS; Garnett, KS; (1); Drama Clb; 4-H; Intnl Clb; Pep Clb; Scholastic Bowl; SADD; Chorus; School Musical; Swing Chorus; Hist Frsh Cls; Environmental Engr.

THOLEN, LISA; Iola Sr HS; Iola, KS; (4); 1/94; Bus Profs of Am; Church Yth Grp; Cmnty Wkr; Drama Clb; FBLA; Letterman Clb; Library Aide; NFL; Office Aide; Spanish Clb; KS Rgnts Hnrs Acad; Farm Bureau & Rotary Ldrshp Camps; Ft Hays ST U; Zoology.

THOMAS, ANNA M; Bishop Carroll Catholic HS; Wichita, KS; (3); 12/167; Spanish Clb; JV Crs Cntry; JV Socr; Var L Trk; High Hon Roll; NHS.

THOMAS, AUBREE J; Cimarron HS; Cimarron, KS; (4); 9/49; Pep Clb; Spanish Clb; Band; Mrchg Band; Var JV Tennis; Trk; Hon Roll; NHS; Pres Acad Fit Awd; St Schlr; Dodge City CC; Nrsng.

THOMAS, DREW A; Hays HS; Hays, KS; (1); Debate Tm; Pres 4-H; Model UN; NFL; 4-H Awd; Hon Roll; Fornscs Tm; Debate Novc Of Yr; Novc NFL All Tm Pt Ldr; MI ST; Lwyr/Debate Tchr.

THOMAS, ERICH C; Bishop Miege HS; Overland Park, KS; (1); 67/274; Trk; Wrstlng; Hon Roll; KU.

THOMAS, ERIKA D; El Dorado HS; El Dorado, KS; (3); Church Yth Grp; FCA; Chorus; Church Choir; Ofcr Frsh Cls; Ofcr Soph Cls; Ofcr Jr Cls; Bsktbl; Vllybl; Hon Roll.

THOMAS, HEATHER M; Olathe East Sr HS; Olathe, KS; (3); Bus Profs of Am; English Clb; FBLA; JCL; Math Clb; Math Tm; Scholastic Bowl; SADD; Jr NHS; NHS; Math, Algebra, Soc Stud & Natl Hnrs Awd; KU; Bus.

THOMAS, JAYME L; Horton HS; Horton, KS; (2); Spanish Clb; JV Bsktbl; JV Vllybl; DECA; Intl Frgn Lang Awd; KS ST Univ; Bus.

THOMAS, JENNIFER; Augusta Sr HS; Augusta, KS; (4); 7/133; Co-Ed Ofcr Am Leg Aux Girls St; FCA; VP Spanish Clb; Sec Varsity Clb; Ofcr Stu Cncl; Var Capt Bsktbl; Var Tennis; Var Capt Vllybl; High Hon Roll; NHS; Brown Belt Karate; Butler Cty CC; Law.

THOMAS, JENNIFER M; Topeka HS; Topeka, KS; (4); 140/345; German Clb; Girl Scts; Office Aide; Teachers Aide; Band; Mrchg Band; Pep Band; Powder Puff Ftbl; Hon Roll; All Amer Schlr; Emporia St Univ; Engl.

THOMAS, JEREMIAH C; Lawrence HS; Lawrence, KS; (2); Church Yth Grp; Office Aide; Chorus; Rptr Nwsp; Fllwshp Chrstn Stdnts Slct Chorale; Rec Bsktbl & Sccr Tm Asstnt Cch; Bus.

THOMAS, JEREMIAH J; Salina HS Central; Salina, KS; (2); 16/258; JV Crs Cntry; JV Trk; Hon Roll; KS ST; Arch; Mech Engrng.

THOMAS, JESSICA J; Council Grove HS; Alta Vista, KS; (3); Art Clb; VP Church Yth Grp; Pres Drama Clb; FCA; Sec 4-H; NFL; Speech Tm; Ofcr SADD; Chorus; School Musical; Jrnlsm Excllnc Awd; Summer Sftbl; Jrnlsm.

THOMAS, JODI; Marion HS; Marion, KS; (4); 14/56; Church Yth Grp; Cmnty Wkr; Debate Tm; Drama Clb; English Clb; FHA; HOBY; NFL; Pep Clb; Spanish Clb; Fll Hmcmng Qn; All Lge 2nd Tm 3xs; KS ST U.

THOMAS, JODIE; Buhler HS; Hutchinson, KS; (4); Church Yth Grp; NFL; Q&S; Co-Ed Nwsp; Mgr Bsktbl; Var L Crs Cntry; Mgr(s); Var L Trk; High Hon Roll; Hon Roll; Soc Sci Dept Awd; U Of MO; Mtlrgcl Eng.

THOMAS, JONATHAN; Olathe South Sr HS; Olathe, KS; (3); Pres Church Yth Grp; Cmnty Wkr; Debate Tm; NFL; Spanish Clb; Thesps; Chorus; Church Choir; School Musical; School Play; Mission Trips To Africa Arizpna& Manhattan; Barbershop Quartet Ntnl Recognition; Ministry/Music.

THOMAS, JULIE L; Bishop Miege HS; Overland Park, KS; (4); 60/171; GAA; Hosp Aide; Teachers Aide; Rptr Yrbk; Bsktbl; Sftbl; Trk; Vllybl; Hon Roll; KS Vlybl Plyr Of Yr; Jov All Amer Clb Div 95; PT.

THOMAS, KELLY C; Wyandotte HS; Kansas City, KS; (2); Cit Awd; Med.

THOMAS, KYLE; Troy HS; Troy, KS; (2); 4-H; Natl FFA Org; Rep Frsh Cls; Rep Stu Cncl; Var Bsktbl; Var Ftbl; Hon Roll; NHS; Prfct Atten Awd; Ath Trnr.

THOMAS, LACEY R; Troy HS; Troy, KS; (4); 11/35; Am Leg Aux Girls St; Church Yth Grp; Drama Clb; Letterman Clb; Pep Clb; Q&S; Teachers Aide; Band; Chorus; Pep Band; MO W St Col; RN.

THOMAS, LAUREN A; St Thomas Aquinas HS; Kansas City, MO; (3); 60/300; VP French Clb; Hist FBLA; SADD; Phtg Yrbk; Intrml Socr; Var Tennis; Intrml Trk; High Hon Roll; Hon Roll; NHS.

THOMAS, MARK A; Meade HS; Meade, KS; (2); Church Yth Grp; Key Clb; Letterman Clb; Pep Clb; Band; Chorus; Mrchg Band; Pep Band; School Musical; Var Bsktbl; Rec Cmmssn Bsbl.

THOMAS, MATTHEW; Leavenworth HS; Leavenworth, KS; (4); Am Leg Boys St; Boy Scts; Church Yth Grp; Debate Tm; SADD; Rep Stu Cncl; Var Crs Cntry; Var Golf; High Hon Roll; NHS; Eagle Sct; U Of KS.

THOMAS, MENDY L; Moundridge HS; Moundridge, KS; (4); VP French Clb; Rep FHA; Pep Clb; Teachers Aide; Chorus; School Musical; Ofcr Stu Cncl; Stat Bsktbl; Mgr(s); Hon Roll; Pittsburg ST U; Sociology.

THOMAS, MICHAEL; Leavenworth HS; Leavenworth, KS; (4); Am Leg Boys St; Boy Scts; Debate Tm; NFL; SADD; Rep Stu Cncl; Var Crs Cntry; Var Trk; High Hon Roll; NHS; Eagle Sct; KS ST U; Cmptr Sci.

THOMAS, SETH A; Field Kindley Mem Sr HS; Coffeyville, KS; (3); 1/170; Church Yth Grp; FCA; Band; Mrchg Band; Bsktbl; Crs Cntry; Trk; High Hon Roll; Sec NHS; Arch Eng.

THOMAS, TABITHA D; Field Kindley Mem Sr HS; Coffeyville, KS; (3); Natl FFA Org; Spanish Clb; Teachers Aide; Chorus; High Hon Roll; NHS; Pres Schlr; Pittsburg St Univ; Bnkng.

THOMASON, BETHANEY L; Leavenworth HS; Leavenworth, KS; (2); Cmnty Wkr; ROTC; Chorus; Hon Roll; Pittsburg ST; Nrsng.

THOMASON, REBECCA L; Topeka West HS; Topeka, KS; (3); 19/239; Church Yth Grp; French Clb; Office Aide; Chorus; Drill Tm; Variety Show; JV Sftbl; JV L Tennis; High Hon Roll; Hon Roll; White Rose; K-ST; Psych.

THOMASSON, SCOTT A; Thomas More Prep-Marion HS; Hays, KS; (2); 43/71; 4-H; French Clb; JV Ftbl; JV Trk; Var Wt Lftg; 4-H Awd; Hon Roll.

THOMPSON, AMY E; Beloit Jr Sr HS; Beloit, KS; (2); 4-H; FHA; Red Cross Aide; Spanish Clb; Chorus; Variety Show; JV Vllybl; High Hon Roll; Hon Roll; NHS; 4-H Clb VP; KS ST; Vet Asstnt.

THOMPSON, ANNETTE C; Goddard HS; Goddard, KS; (3); Drama Clb; Hosp Aide; Office Aide; Spanish Clb; SADD; Teachers Aide; Variety Show; Mgr(s); Hon Roll; 5th In Acad Olympics; Acctng/Law.

THOMPSON, AUDREY J; South Barber HS; Kiowa, KS; (3); 2/25; Am Leg Aux Girls St; Church Yth Grp; Scholastic Bowl; SADD; Chorus; VP Stu Cncl; Capt Chrldng; Var L Vllybl; High Hon Roll; NHS; Kayettes Rep & Hstrn; Chambers Singers, Pop Choir & Girls Ensmbl; GGPL All Leag Vllybl; Acad Exclnc Awd; Sec Math Ed.

THOMPSON, CARRIE; Osborne HS; Osborne, KS; (4); 1/24; Am Leg Aux Girls St; Church Yth Grp; FHA; GAA; Letterman Clb; Pep Clb; Quiz Bowl; Band; Mrchg Band; Pep Band; Stdnt Mo; KS ST U; Exrcs Sci.

THOMPSON, CHANDRA F; Newton Sr HS; Newton, KS; (4); VP Church Yth Grp; FTA; Model UN; Office Aide; Acpl Chr; Chorus; Church Choir; Orch; School Musical; School Play; Stu Mediation Team; Ltr Music-Solo At St Vocal Group 1st; Brother-Sisters For Life; Baker; Music Ed.

THOMPSON, DOUGLAS; Shawnee Mission S Sr HS; Overland Park, KS; (3); 67/448; Church Yth Grp; HOBY; Office Aide; Varsity Clb; Pres Frsh Cls; Pres Soph Cls; Pres Jr Cls; Bsktbl; Socr; Trk; Overland Park Rotary Clb Yth Ldrshp Smnr; KSMS Schl Radio Sta DJ; U Of KS.

THOMPSON, ERIN E; Blue Valley HS; Overland Park, KS; (2); Church Yth Grp; Hosp Aide; Letterman Clb; SADD; Acpl Chr; Chorus; School Musical; Variety Show; JV Bsktbl; High Hon Roll; Law.

THOMPSON, GABE I; Neodesha Jr Sr HS; Neodesha, KS; (1); Boy Scts; Math Clb; Math Tm; Band; Mrchg Band; Pep Band; Var L Trk; Wt Lftg; Hon Roll; Yth Soccer League.

THOMPSON, GREG L; Haven HS; Hutchinson, KS; (2); Art Clb; French Clb; Math Clb; Natl FFA Org; JV Var Bsbl; JV Bsktbl; JV Var Ftbl; Hon Roll.

THOMPSON, JAIME M; Olathe North Sr HS; Olathe, KS; (4); Drama Clb; Pep Clb; Band; Color Guard; Drill Tm; Mrchg Band; School Play; Chrldng; Gym; Pom Pon; Johnson Cty CC; Pre-Law.

THOMPSON, JASMINE E; Wichita East HS; Wichita, KS; (3); Debate Tm; Teachers Aide; VP Sr Cls; JV Bsktbl; Hon Roll; Gospel Choir; Ger NHS; U Of KS.

THOMPSON, JESSICA L; Olathe East Sr HS; Overland Park, KS; (3); Pres Q&S; Band; Capt Drill Tm; Jazz Band; Rep Frsh Cls; JV Bsktbl; JV Sftbl; NHS; Pres Schlr; French Clb; Fr Cultrl Exchng Stdnt/Host; Yth Symphny.

THOMPSON, JESSICA L; Wichita East HS; Wichita, KS; (2); Band; Pep Band; JV Bsktbl; Var Trk; Hon Roll; Gosepl Choir; Orthopedic Surgeon.

THOMPSON, JILL R; Northeast HS; Arcadia, KS; (1); 17/52; JV Bsktbl; JV Sftbl; JV Var Vllybl; Pittsburg St U.

THOMPSON, KARA A; Newton Sr HS; Newton, KS; (2); Pres Church Yth Grp; Girl Scts; Service Clb; Acpl Chr; Chorus; Church Choir; Orch; School Musical; Variety Show; Mgr(s); Sis & Bro 4 Life; I Rtng Rgnl Solo/Ens Cello Solo; Sr Ldrshp Awd Grl Sct; Music Perf.

THOMPSON, KEILAH A; Garden City Sr HS; Garden City, KS; (2); Debate Tm; NFL; Band; Mrchg Band; Pep Band; High Hon Roll; Ntl Merit Ltr.

THOMPSON, KIMBERLY D; Russell HS; Russell, KS; (2); Drama Clb; Pep Clb; Spanish Clb; Band; Chorus; Mrchg Band; Pep Band; School Musical; School Play; Hon Roll.

THOMPSON, KYM R; Leavenworth HS; Leavenworth, KS; (3); Church Yth Grp; Cmnty Wkr; Drama Clb; Church Choir; Mgr(s); Hon Roll; Mission Trips; Spcl Olympics Vol; Missionary; Hlth Care.

THOMPSON, LAURA L; Burlingame HS; Burlingame, KS; (2); 1/33; Pres Girl Scts; Natl FFA Org; Quiz Bowl; Scholastic Bowl; Sec Frsh Cls; Treas Jr Cls; JV Vllybl; High Hon Roll; NHS; Ntl Merit Ltr.

THOMPSON, LUKE; Maranatha Acad; Overland Park, KS; (4); Chess Clb; Pep Clb; Teachers Aide; Chorus; School Musical; Pres Stu Cncl; High Hon Roll; Hon Roll; NHS; Ntl Merit Ltr; UMKC; Ed.

THOMPSON, MAGGIE H; Washburn Rural HS; Topeka, KS; (3); 77/338; Cmnty Wkr; French Clb; Girl Scts; Ed Nwsp; High Hon Roll; NHS; Cert Recognition Governor For Vol Svc; Gold Awd.

THOMPSON, MATTHEW R; Dexter Jr Sr HS; Arkansas City, KS; (3); Church Yth Grp; VP Treas 4-H; Math Tm; Ofcr Bsbl; Var L Bsktbl; 4-H Awd; Hon Roll; Bsktbll Most Imprvd Plyr; S Cntrl Border League Hnrbl Mntn, Tourn Hnrrl; KS Schl Span Hnrbl Mntn; Cowley Cnty CC; Drftng.

THOMPSON, MINDI; Great Bend Sr HS; Great Bend, KS; (4); 1/217; Am Leg Aux Girls St; Spanish Clb; Orch; Rep Sr Cls; High Hon Roll; VP NHS; Val; Drama Clb; Pep Clb; Variety Show; Natl Merit Commended Stu; DARE; Peer Cnslr; U Of KS; Pre-Med.

THOMPSON, PHILLIP M; Goodland HS; Goodland, KS; (4); 28/74; Am Leg Boys St; Treas DECA; FHA; Hon Roll; DECA Natls 94-96; DECA Natls Top 10 Natl Fr Entrprs Prjct 96; FHA Mbr Yr 93; Devry; Elec Tech.

THOMPSON, SARAH; Campus HS; Haysville, KS; (4); 11/198; Church Yth Grp; SADD; Pres Chorus; Church Choir; Orch; High Hon Roll; NHS; Pres Acad Fit Awd; St Schlr; Yth Ldrshp Cncl; Ouachita Bapt U; Missions.

THOMPSON, SKYE D; Maize HS; Wichita, KS; (1); Chorus; Variety Show; Vllybl; Hon Roll; Pres Acad Fit Awd; Choir Letter; KS ST Univ; PT.

THOMPSON, STEVEN K; Southeast KS Spec Ed Coop; Galena, KS; (2); 1/55; Church Yth Grp; Quiz Bowl; Scholastic Bowl; Pres Frsh Cls; VP Soph Cls; Rep Stu Cncl; Var JV Bsbl; Var JV Ftbl; Wt Lftg; High Hon Roll; U KS; Med.

THOMPSON, TAMMY M; Shawnee Heights HS; Tecumseh, KS; (1); Church Yth Grp; Dance Clb; Spanish Clb; SADD; Drill Tm; Var Pom Pon; Care Co; Spirit Club; K ST Univ; Chldrn.

THOMPSON, THOMAS A; Protection Schl; Protection, KS; (2); 10/20; Letterman Clb; Band; Mrchg Band; Pep Band; Stage Crew; Treas Frsh Cls; JV Bsktbl; Var Ftbl; Wt Lftg; Hon Roll; Garden City CC; Cmptr Pgrmr.

THOMPSON, TONY P; Beloit Jr Sr HS; Beloit, KS; (2); Letterman Clb; Variety Show; Pres Soph Cls; Rep Stu Cncl; L Var Bsktbl; L Var Ftbl; L Var Trk; St Discus Champ Cls 3-A; 3rd Pl Shot-Put.

THOMPSON, TRINA M; Horton HS; Horton, KS; (2); 34/85; Church Yth Grp; Trk; Wt Lftg; Hon Roll; Prfct Atten Awd; Highland CC.

THOMPSON, WESLEY; Southeast HS; Weir, KS; (3); Debate Tm; HOBY; Letterman Clb; Math Tm; Quiz Bowl; Science Clb; Varsity Clb; VP Jr Cls; JV Bsbl; Stat Bsktbl; Rgnl Sci Fair Grnd Champ; Gftd Prog; Kay Rep; KU; Med.

THOMSEN, JEREMY L; Madison Jr Sr HS; Madison, KS; (3); 5/28; Boy Scts; Cmnty Wkr; Letterman Clb; Math Tm; Varsity Clb; Band; Mrchg Band; Pep Band; School Play; Stage Crew; Stugo VP; KS ST Univ; Vet.

THOMSON, ELIZABETH C; Pittsburg HS; Pittsburg, KS; (3); 60/250; Letterman Clb; Spanish Clb; Varsity Clb; JV Bsktbl; Var Trk; JV Vllybl; DAR Awd; Hon Roll; Dance; U Of KS; Arch.

THOMSON, MELISSA A; Shawnee Mission W Sr HS; Lenexa, KS; (3); 11/440; Cmnty Wkr; Q&S; Teachers Aide; Ed Nwsp; High Hon Roll; NHS; Acad Ltr; Jrnlsm.

THONEN, KAREN; Jackson Heights HS; Circleville, KS; (3); FBLA; FHA; Office Aide; Chorus; High Hon Roll; Hon Roll; Prfct Atten Awd.

THONI, CHRISTI T; Shawnee Mission N HS; Shawnee, KS; (2); 51/521; Church Yth Grp; Dance Clb; Pep Clb; Drill Tm; Mrchg Band; Socr; High Hon Roll; Hon Roll; Dance Troupe.

THORNBURG, ALYSSA K; Hayden HS; Topeka, KS; (2); Cmnty Wkr; Intnl Clb; NFL; Quiz Bowl; SADD; JV Crs Cntry; JV Trk; Cit Awd; High Hon Roll; NHS; Piano; Kenyon Coll; Med.

THORNBURG, ERIC; Ulysses HS; Ulysses, KS; (3); Boy Scts; Church Yth Grp; Var JV Ftbl; Var JV Trk; Wt Lftg; High Hon Roll; Jr NHS; NHS; Engrng.

THORNBURY, MICHELLE; Spring Hill HS; Olathe, KS; (4); 4/104; Am Leg Aux Girls St; Pres NFL; Chorus; Orch; School Musical; School Play; Rep Stu Cncl; Var Chrldng; NHS; KSHAA St Debate Chmps 96; Pittsburgh St Hnrs Coll.

THORNTON, ADAM; Jackson Heights HS; Whiting, KS; (1); 1/37; Church Yth Grp; FBLA; Pep Clb; School Musical; Pres Frsh Cls; Bsktbl; Ftbl; Hon Roll.

THORNTON, BRANDI A; Meade HS; Meade, KS; (2); 4/20; Drama Clb; French Clb; HOBY; Quiz Bowl; Pep Band; School Musical; Treas Frsh Cls; Treas Jr Cls; L Tennis; Cit Awd; PT.

THORNTON, CHARLIE; Chanute Sr HS; Chanute, KS; (3); 20/140; Boy Scts; Library Aide; Spanish Clb; JV Var Bsbl; Hon Roll; Amer Legion Bsbl; Comp Scis.

THORNTON, JENNIFER; Hiawatha HS; Hiawatha, KS; (3); 4/100; Church Yth Grp; Cmnty Wkr; Jazz Band; Mrchg Band; Pep Band; Var L Tennis; High Hon Roll; NHS; ST Lions Bnd; Intl Lions Bnd; Brd Chmbr/Cmmrc.

THORNTON, MATTHEW H; Haven HS; Burrton, KS; (3); 6/80; Am Leg Boys St; Debate Tm; NFL; Speech Tm; Chorus; Drm Mjr(t); Jazz Band; Ed Nwsp; Pres Jr Cls; High Hon Roll.

THORNTON, MICKEY; Oakley HS; Oakley, KS; (3); Debate Tm; HOBY; Model UN; Scholastic Bowl; Speech Tm; Band; School Play; Var JV Bsktbl; High Hon Roll; Hon Roll; Prchng; HOBY Alt; Pr Mdtr; Natl Hnrs Soc; Mnstry.

THORNTON, REBEKAH; Jackson Heights HS; Whiting, KS; (4); 6/38; Church Yth Grp; FBLA; HOBY; Model UN; SADD; Church Choir; School Musical; Vllybl; NHS; HOBY Jr Cnslr; FBLA St Pres; KS ST U; Mrktng.

THORNTON, SHAUN A; Quivira Heights HS; Lorraine, KS; (3); Church Yth Grp; Cmnty Wkr; Teachers Aide; School Play; Stage Crew; Ed Nwsp; Yrbk; Stat Trk; Hon Roll; Childrens Miracle Network; Muscular Distrophy Fundraiser; Ft Hays ST; Comp Graphics.

THRASHER, BRIAN; St John Jr Sr HS; Saint John, KS; (1); Church Yth Grp; Treas Rep 4-H; Band; Church Choir; Jazz Band; Mrchg Band; Pep Band; School Musical; Bsktbl; L Crs Cntry; Bus.

THRASHER, DARREN; St John Jr Sr HS; Saint John, KS; (3); Church Yth Grp; Cmnty Wkr; Treas 4-H; Pep Clb; Quiz Bowl; Ofcr SADD; Pres VP Band; Church Choir; Jazz Band; Mrchg Band; KMEA Hnr Band; KAYS Bd Mem; Distngd Schltc Achvmt Awd; Engrng.

THULL, ANDREW; Newton Sr HS; North Newton, KS; (3); 16/260; Am Leg Boys St; Church Yth Grp; Cmnty Wkr; French Clb; Math Clb; Science Clb; Teachers Aide; Ftbl; High Hon Roll; NHS; We Back Our Kids Awd Nom; KS ST Univ.

THUMMEL, MEGAN; Dodge City HS; Dodge City, KS; (2); Church Yth Grp; Girl Scts; Intnl Clb; Rptr Yrbk; Socr; JETS Awd.

THUMMEL, SARAH M; Andale HS; Goddard, KS; (2); Spanish Clb; Band; Drill Tm; Mrchg Band; Pep Band; Var Pom Pon; High Hon Roll; Hon Roll; U Of KS.

THUNBERG, MEGAN M; Maize HS; Wichita, KS; (1); Hosp Aide; SADD; JV Var Tennis; Hon Roll.

THURMAN, TRAVIS R; Arkansas City HS; Arkansas City, KS; (1); Church Yth Grp; Tennis.

THURMON, SHANNON M; El Dorado HS; El Dorado, KS; (2); 5/200; Church Yth Grp; Debate Tm; FCA; NFL; Band; Mrchg Band; Pep Band; Var Diving; Powder Puff Ftbl; JV Sftbl; City Band; Emporia ST U; Scndry Ed/Math.

THURSTON, JESSI A; Hillsboro HS; Hillsboro, KS; (3); Church Yth Grp; Band; Jazz Band; Mrchg Band; Pep Band; School Play; Stage Crew; VP Sr Cls; JV Bsktbl; Var Crs Cntry; Emporia ST; Soc Work.

TIBBETTS, MEGAN; Emporia HS; Emporia, KS; (2); Cmnty Wkr; Dance Clb; Debate Tm; FCA; NFL; Red Cross Aide; SADD; Varsity Clb; Drill Tm; Orch; Comm Hero Olympic Torch Bearer; Pres Of Frosh & Soph Bd.

TICE, CAROL R; Beloit Jr Sr HS; Beloit, KS; (1); Band; Chorus; Drm Mjr(t); Mrchg Band; Orch; Variety Show; Chrldng; Trk; Hon Roll; Kytts Dir Of Music; Emporia ST Univ; Elem Ed/Music.

TICE, CHRISTY; Greeley Co Schl; Tribune, KS; (3); 7/17; HOBY; SADD; High Hon Roll; Hon Roll; NHS; Prfct Atten Awd; STUCO; Peer Hlprs; KS U; Med.

TICKEL, JAEMA L; Rose Hill HS; Rose Hill, KS; (3); Hosp Aide; Library Aide; Office Aide; Teachers Aide; JV Bsktbl; JV Var Mgr(s); JV Var Score Keeper; JV Sftbl; Hon Roll; Mercy Hosp Vol Of Yr Awd; Tchr/Cnslr.

TIDEMANN, BRIA; Valley Ctr HS; Valley Center, KS; (3); 66/162; Church Yth Grp; Letterman Clb; Teachers Aide; Church Choir; Chrldng; Powder Puff Ftbl; Socr; Hon Roll; Bethany Coll; Elem Ed.

TIEBEN, ANDY C; Dodge City HS; Wright, KS; (1); Church Yth Grp; JV Golf; Var Wrstlng; St Wrestling Champ As Frosh; Comp Prmng.

TIEGREEN, JOSHUA A; Ft Scott HS; Fort Scott, KS; (3); Church Yth Grp; FBLA; Latin Clb; Letterman Clb; NFL; Scholastic Bowl; Ed Yrbk; Var Tennis; High Hon Roll; NHS; Bus.

TIEKING, JASON N; Concordia Jr Sr HS; Concordia, KS; (3); Am Leg Boys St; Church Yth Grp; Cmnty Wkr; Science Clb; Spanish Clb; Band; Mrchg Band; Pep Band; Stage Crew; JV Bsktbl; All League For Acads & Ath Var Ltr; Hosp Vol; Tnns Clb; Ed; Hlth; PE; Recreation.

TIEMANN, CHERYL; Chanute Sr HS; Chanute, KS; (4); Art Clb; 4-H; French Clb; FBLA; Quiz Bowl; Teachers Aide; Acpl Chr; 4-H Awd; Hon Roll; Spch Pthlgy.

TIEMEYER, ROBYN; Sedgwick HS; Sedgwick, KS; (1); Sec Frsh Cls; High Hon Roll; Heart Of Amer Schlrshp Tsts; Med.

TIESMEYER, LACEY; Kingman HS; Kingman, KS; (3); Church Yth Grp; Sec VP 4-H; Rep FBLA; Natl FFA Org; Office Aide; Red Cross Aide; Spanish Clb; SADD; School Play; Phtg Rptr Yrbk; Snow & Water Skiing; Recreation Sftbl; Acad All Leag; 5th Pl St FBLA Cont Bus Commnctns; KS ST U; Vet.

TIESZEN, BRIAN E; Wellington Sr HS; Wellington, KS; (3); Library Aide; Prfct Attndnc; Bethel Coll.

TIGERSTROM, PAUL A; Pierson Jr HS; Kansas City, KS; (1); Hon Roll; Wrtr.

TILFORD, EVA J; F L Schlagle HS; Kansas City, KS; (1); 2/340; French Clb; Yrbk; Mgr(s); High Hon Roll; Acctg.

TILLERY, KACY M; Piper HS; Kansas City, KS; (4); 22/86; Cmnty Wkr; Pres GAA; Office Aide; Spanish Clb; SADD; Teachers Aide; Var Bsktbl; Var Sftbl; Var Vllybl; High Hon Roll; All Kansan Team Bsktbl; All Kaw Vly Leag Bsktbl; KS City KS CC; PT.

TILLETT, JAMIE; Augusta Sr HS; Augusta, KS; (4); Am Leg Aux Girls St; FCA; Letterman Clb; Treas Soph Cls; Rep Stu Cncl; Bsktbl; Capt Var Crs Cntry; Var L Trk; Pres High Hon Roll; NHS; U KS; Nrsng.

TILLEY, AMY; Frankft HS; Frankfort, KS; (4); 1/28; Am Leg Aux Girls St; School Play; Variety Show; Yrbk; Pres Soph Cls; Sec Treas Stu Cncl; L Bsktbl; L Vllybl; High Hon Roll; NHS; All Amer Schlr; Msnc Ldg Awd; Hmcmng Qn; KS ST U; Med.

TILLEY, JOSEPH R; Frankft HS; Frankfort, KS; (1); Art Clb; Church Yth Grp; Cmnty Wkr; Letterman Clb; SADD; Treas Frsh Cls; JV Capt Bsktbl; JV Ftbl; L Trk; Cit Awd; KS ST Univ; PT.

TILLEY, MIKE; Frankft HS; Frankfort, KS; (4); 5/29; Am Leg Boys St; Boy Scts; Letterman Clb; Scholastic Bowl; SADD; Chorus; Ftbl; Wt Lftg; High Hon Roll; Hon Roll; KS ST U; Med.

TILLOTSON, TIFFANY; Wichita Northwest HS; Wichita, KS; (3); Church Yth Grp; Intnl Clb; Rep Jr Cls; Ofcr Stu Cncl; Hon Roll; Jr NHS; NHS; HERO Club; OK Bapt Univ; Pre-Med.

TIMBERLAKE, EMILY A; Shawnee Mission N HS; Shawnee Mission, KS; (3); Church Yth Grp; Pep Clb; Spanish Clb; Band; Mrchg Band; Pep Band; Yrbk; Ofcr Frsh Cls; Swmmng; Hon Roll; KS ST Univ; Elem Ed.

TIMBERLAKE, MATTHEW A; Manhattan HS; Manhattan, KS; (3); Drama Clb; Thesps; School Musical; School Play; VP Soph Cls; Var Swmmng; U Of KS; Theatr.

TIMM, ALLAN J; White City HS; White City, KS; (2); Band; Jazz Band; Mrchg Band; Orch; Pep Band; Pres Frsh Cls; Var L Bsktbl; Var L Ftbl; Var Wt Lftg; Hon Roll.

TIMM, MELISSA; Atwood HS; Ludell, KS; (2); Church Yth Grp; Natl FFA Org; Ski Clb; Spanish Clb; Church Choir; Flag Corp; JV Bsktbl; Var Powder Puff Ftbl; Var Trk; JV Vllybl; Keyboarding & Spnsh Awds.

TIMS, JESSICA S; Northeast HS; Arma, KS; (1); 12/56; Dance Clb; Drama Clb; FHA; Chorus; Rep Stu Cncl; Var Chrldng; Sftbl; Vllybl; Hon Roll; KS House Of Reps Page; UCA JV All-Star Chrldr; Marched In Houston Thanksgvng Parade; Pittsburg ST U; Tchng; Med.

TINDAL, DARRELL; Northwest HS; Wichita, KS; (3); Boy Scts; Church Yth Grp; JA; Teachers Aide; Stage Crew; Hon Roll; St Jr Acad Scie Supr Achvmnt Awd 1993; Jr Acad Sci Top 5 Awd Dist 1992, 1993; Oarzk Chrstn Coll; Entrprnr.

TINDLE, BETH M; Blue Valley Northwest HS; Overland Park, KS; (1); 33/360; GAA; JV Bsktbl; JV Socr; JV Vllybl; High Hon Roll; Fast Pitch Sftbl; Soccer Goalkeeper.

TINKLER, SANDRA M; Smoky Valley HS; Lindsborg, KS; (1); Church Yth Grp; Drama Clb; NFL; Thesps; Band; Mrchg Band; Pep Band; School Play; Tennis; Hon Roll; Med.

TINSLEY, HEATHER D; Belle Plaine HS; Belle Plaine, KS; (4); 4/70; Letterman Clb; SADD; School Musical; Ofcr Stu Cncl; Bsktbl; Pom Pon; Cit Awd; High Hon Roll; NHS; Pres Acad Fit Awd; Wichita ST U; Intl Bus.

TIPTON, CHERILYN M; Oak Grove Baptist Schl; Kansas City, KS; (3); Church Yth Grp; Letterman Clb; Pres Pep Clb; Chorus; School Musical; Yrbk; Var Bsktbl; Var Chrldng; Mgr Vllybl; Hon Roll; Mssns Trip; U Of KS; Med.

TISCHHAUSER, CARYL L; Council Grove HS; Council Grove, KS; (3); Church Yth Grp; 4-H; Chorus; Stage Crew; Ofcr Frsh Cls; Ofcr Soph Cls; Sftbl; Vllybl; Wt Lftg; Hon Roll; KS ST; Hlth.

TISDALE, JILL A; Lawrence HS; Lawrence, KS; (2); Drama Clb; Spanish Clb; Thesps; Acpl Chr; Chorus; Chrldng; Tennis; Cit Awd; DAR Awd; Pres Ed Awd; Music Masters Awd; Mustang Mrt Awd; UC Berkley; Art Historian.

TOBIA, ALEX L; Maize HS; Wichita, KS; (3); Art Clb; Acpl Chr; Chorus; School Musical; Variety Show; Crs Cntry; Trk; Hon Roll; KS U; Chemical Engrng.

TOBIAS, AARON; Lyons HS; Lyons, KS; (3); 1/65; Am Leg Boys St; Capt Scholastic Bowl; Band; Rep Stu Cncl; Var L Ftbl; High Hon Roll; NHS; Bronze Congressional Awd; Rice Cty Yth Ldrshp Grp; Yth Appointee To Rice Cty Strategic Plan Oversight; U Of KS; Aerospace Engrng.

TOBIN, JOSHUA J; Goddard HS; Wichita, KS; (1); Office Aide; Band; Mrchg Band; Orch; Hon Roll; Prde Drmlne; ST Bnd Fstvl 1st Rtng; ST Solo/Ensmble Fstvl 1st Rtng; Drmmr; Cmpng; Bkng; Hacky Sack; Music.

TOBY, MICHAEL A; Nemaha Valley HS; Seneca, KS; (3); Quiz Bowl; JV Golf; High Hon Roll; Prfct Atten Awd; Pres Acad Fit Awd; Babe Ruth St Qualifers; Geog Acad Achvmt Awd; KS ST Univ.

TODD, DALLAS D; Atchison Co Cmty HS; Effingham, KS; (2); Church Yth Grp; Letterman Clb; Math Clb; Science Clb; Nwsp; VP Soph Cls; VP Jr Cls; Intrml Bsbl; Var Bsktbl; Var Ftbl.

TODD, DAVID C; Wichita North HS; Wichita, KS; (4); Church Yth Grp; Band; Mrchg Band; Pep Band; Socr; Hon Roll; AC 77 Clb Soccer Team Mem; SEP Pgm Mem 96; WSU HCOP Pgm Mem; Wichita ST; Phy Therapy.

TODD, NICHOLE; Washington HS; Kansas City, KS; (3); 15/234; Drama Clb; Ofcr ROTC; Spanish Clb; Stage Crew; Ed Yrbk; Treas Jr Cls; Pres Stu Cncl; NHS; Ed.

TODD, PATRICK N; El Dorado HS; El Dorado, KS; (3); 26/144; Am Leg Boys St; Boy Scts; Debate Tm; Letterman Clb; VP NFL; Office Aide; Spanish Clb; Speech Tm; SADD; Teachers Aide; Peer Cnslr; All St Swmmng 3 Yrs; Stqlfr Cross Cntry.

TOEBBEN, SETH; Lawrence HS; Lawrence, KS; (3); 130/600; Am Leg Boys St; Church Yth Grp; Debate Tm; Drama Clb; Acpl Chr; School Play; VP Frsh Cls; Rep Stu Cncl; JV Socr; Hon Roll.

TOLAND, THOMAS J; Cimarron HS; Cimarron, KS; (2); Ftbl; Wt Lftg; Archaeologist.

TOLBERT, NOEL E; Newton Sr HS; Newton, KS; (4); Teachers Aide; JV Bsbl; JV Intrml Bsktbl; Var L Socr; Hon Roll; Wichita ST U.

TOLEFREE, NICOLE D; Wyandotte HS; Kansas City, KS; (3); Church Yth Grp; Church Choir; Hon Roll; Jr NHS; Yth Mtvtn Prgm; KS Univ.

TOLLE, KELLY; Northeast Magnet HS; Wichita, KS; (2); 1/115; Math Tm; Quiz Bowl; Scholastic Bowl; Teachers Aide; Band; School Musical; Variety Show; Ed Yrbk; Hon Roll; NHS; A Awd; KSHSAA St Piano Fest; Achieving Women Of Math & Sci.

TOLLEFSON, AMANDA; Silver Lake Jr Sr HS; Silver Lake, KS; (1); 4/52; Church Yth Grp; FHA; Band; Chorus; Sec Church Yth Grp; Bsktbl; Var Pom Pon; Var JV Sftbl; JV Vllybl; Hon Roll.

TOLLEFSON, DRAKE G; Hayden HS; Topeka, KS; (2); Church Yth Grp; Band; Mrchg Band; JV Bsktbl; JV Crs Cntry; Var Trk; Gov Hon Prg Awd; High Hon Roll; Hon Roll; JA; JUCO; Med/Bus.

TOLLEFSON, MATT; Silver Lake Jr Sr HS; Silver Lake, KS; (4); 1/41; Band; VP Soph Cls; VP Jr Cls; VP Sr Cls; Ftbl; Trk; Cit Awd; Gov Hon Prg Awd; Pres NHS; Val; Capital Journal All-St Acad Team Hnrbl Mntn; Mem Of Local & Natl Pontiac-Oakland Car Clb; KS Hnrs Awd; KS ST Univ; Civil Engrng.

TOLLETT, BARBIE J; Hartford HS; Hartford, KS; (2); 2/45; Church Yth Grp; 4-H; FBLA; FHA; Letterman Clb; Quiz Bowl; Speech Tm; SADD; Pres Frsh Cls; Pres Soph Cls; FBLA Pres; Whos Who In KS FBLA; Acad Lttr; Baker Univ; Bus Admin.

TOLSON, JERRID; Ottawa HS; Ottawa, KS; (2); Letterman Clb; Var L Ftbl; Var L Trk; High Hon Roll; Hon Roll; Ottawa Babe Ruth Bsbl All-Star; Auburn Univ; Engrng.

TOMASICH, NICK; Shawnee Mission Northwest HS; Shawnee, KS; (4); 80/398; Am Leg Boys St; Boy Scts; Model UN; Band; Mrchg Band; Pep Band; Mgr L Trk; Hon Roll; NHS; Jazz Band; Yth/Govt; Env Ed Pgm; Johnson Cty CC.

TOMES, GARY G; Wichita East HS; Wichita, KS; (4); 94/296; Boy Scts; JA; Office Aide; Science Clb; Teachers Aide; Ofcr Bsbl; Chrldng; Ftbl; Swmmng; Wt Lftg; All Amer Yell Ldr; Wichita All Star Chrldng Sqd; KU; Chem Engr.

TOMLINSON, GREGORY P; Shawnee Mssn NW HS; Lenexa, KS; (4); 101/420; Teachers Aide; Var Bsbl; Bsktbl; Hon Roll; NHS; Kansas ST Univ.

TOMMER, SARAH E; F L Schlagle HS; Kansas City, KS; (1); 1/300; Church Yth Grp; SADD; Ofcr Frsh Cls; Ofcr Stu Cncl; JV Var Bsktbl; JV Var Vllybl; High Hon Roll; Summer Swim Team; AAU Bsktbl; Outstdng Yth Awd Camp Fire.

TONEY, RAEGAN; Lansing HS; Leavenworth, KS; (3); 50/150; Church Yth Grp; Drama Clb; French Clb; NFL; Science Clb; Thesps; Band; Mrchg Band; School Play; Yrbk.

TONGIER, BRIAN C; Lawrence HS; Lawrence, KS; (4); 38/521; Boy Scts; Cmnty Wkr; Latin Clb; Model UN; Scholastic Bowl; Science Clb; Acpl Chr; Chorus; Crs Cntry; High Hon Roll; Eagle Sct; U Of MN; Soc Sci.

TONN, RAMEE; Wichita West HS; Wichita, KS; (3); 35/230; Dance Clb; Pep Clb; Drill Tm; Rep Frsh Cls; Rep Soph Cls; Rep Jr Cls; Var L Chrldng; Var L Pom Pon; JV Socr; Hon Roll; U Of KS; Sports Medicine.

TOOLEY, NANCY L; Central Heights Sr HS; Richmond, KS; (3); 2/56; Church Yth Grp; Letterman Clb; Teachers Aide; Mrchg Band; Pep Band; Var Bsktbl; L Trk; Var Vllybl; High Hon Roll; NHS.

TOOMBS, JEROME A; Sumner Acad Of Arts & Science; Kansas City, KS; (2); Boy Scts; Cmnty Wkr; Debate Tm; German Clb; Latin Clb; JV Bsbl; JV Ftbl; High Hon Roll; Hon Roll; Jr NHS; KS ST Univ; Arch Engr.

TOPHAM, MELISSA; Peabody-Burns Jr Sr HS; Peabody, KS; (4); 7/33; Sec Church Yth Grp; Pres FCA; HOBY; Teachers Aide; Band; Mrchg Band; Pep Band; School Musical; Nwsp; Var L Bsktbl; Vlybl All Lg Hnrbl Mntn; Marion Cty Hnr Schlr; Sterling Coll; Mass Comms.

TORBETT, AMANDA L; Independence HS; Independence, KS; (1); Pep Clb; Orch; Rep Frsh Cls; Ofcr Stu Cncl; JV Bsktbl; Powder Puff Ftbl; JV Sftbl; Var Tennis; High Hon Roll; Sun Schl Tchr; Strng Ensmbl; Art Cmptn Awds.

TORRES, CARRIE M; Kinsley HS; Kinsley, KS; (4); 6/36; Debate Tm; Drama Clb; Band; School Play; VP Frsh Cls; Var JV Bsktbl; NHS; KS W Conf Cncl Yth Mnstrs; Jrsdctnl Cmnty Crrctns Bd Dist; U Of KS; Law.

TORRES, JACLYN R; Garden City Sr HS; Garden City, KS; (2); Church Yth Grp; French Clb; Girl Scts; Teachers Aide; Band; Mrchg Band; Pep Band; Bsktbl; High Hon Roll; U Of KS; Arch.

TORREY, BENJAMIN A; Minneola Schl; Minneola, KS; (3); 4-H; Quiz Bowl; Yrbk; Lit Mag; Golf; Cit Awd; 4-H Awd; KQHYA St Wide Orgnztn Pblc Rltns, Wrt/Pblsh Monthly Artcls; 8th Pl Wrld AQHA Yth Assn Imprtu Spkng; Horse Trnr.

TORREY, BETH; Minneola Schl; Minneola, KS; (1); Church Yth Grp; Band; Jazz Band; Pep Band; Rptr Nwsp; Vllybl; 4-H Awd; KQHYA Brd Dir; Vet.

TOSH, KRISTI A; Field Kindley Mem Sr HS; Coffeyville, KS; (4); Church Yth Grp; FCA; JA; Spanish Clb; Ed Nwsp; Ofcr Stu Cncl; Mgr(s); Sftbl; Hon Roll; NHS; Sftbl-All SEK Hnrb Mntn; Jr Achvmt-1st Pl Essay Cont; Cowley Cty CC; Crmnl Justice.

TOTH, JENNIFER M; Turner HS; Overland Park, KS; (4); 3/190; Spanish Clb; SADD; Drill Tm; Yrbk; Lit Mag; Sec Stu Cncl; High Hon Roll; NHS; Pres Acad Fit Awd; Bus Profs of Am; Tlntd & Gftd Pgm; Cntrl MO ST U; Psych.

TOVAR, MELISSA; Augusta Sr HS; Augusta, KS; (3); Am Leg Aux Girls St; Dance Clb; Drama Clb; FCA; Latin Clb; NFL; Spanish Clb; Speech Tm; Chorus; Drill Tm; Wrtng Poetry; Working With Children; Comm Theater Plays; ASA Umpire; Vol Peer To SMH Stdnts; U Of KS; Ed.

TOWELL, KATY D; Goddard HS; Wichita, KS; (1); Church Yth Grp; Church Choir; Orch; High Hon Roll; Wichita ST Univ; Grphc Dsgn.

TOWNER, KARI R; Paola HS; Paola, KS; (4); 33/150; Art Clb; Cmnty Wkr; Drama Clb; Teachers Aide; Chorus; Nwsp; High Hon Roll; Hon Roll; Prfct Atten Awd; Art Clb VP; Johnson Cnty CC.

TOWNSEND, CRAIG; Goodland HS; Goodland, KS; (2); 12/91; Church Yth Grp; FHA; HOBY; Letterman Clb; Pep Clb; Quiz Bowl; Scholastic Bowl; SADD; Band; Jazz Band; Amer Lgn Bsbl; K ST; Engrng.

TOWNSLEY, CHAD M; Manhattan HS; Manhattan, KS; (2); Church Yth Grp; Church Choir; Hon Roll; Cmmrcl Plt.

TOY, DARANY K; Wichita Heights HS; Wichita, KS; (2); Hon Roll; Ntl Merit Ltr; Prfct Atten Awd; Spanish NHS.

TRA, FRANK; Bishop Carroll Catholic HS; Wichita, KS; (3); Church Yth Grp; Cmnty Wkr; Drama Clb; School Play; Wrstlng; Hon Roll; Optometry.

TRACKWELL, MELANIE J; Larned HS; Garfield, KS; (3); Am Leg Aux Girls St; Church Yth Grp; Acpl Chr; Church Choir; Mrchg Band; Pep Band; Hon Roll; Pres Acad Fit Awd; Air Force ROTC; Optomotrist.

TRACY, LIZ A; Syracuse Jr Sr HS; Syracuse, KS; (2); Church Yth Grp; Cmnty Wkr; Drama Clb; Letterman Clb; Quiz Bowl; Speech Tm; Chorus; School Play; JV Golf; Hon Roll.

TRACY, MATT T; Riverton Schl; Riverton, KS; (3); Church Yth Grp; FCA; Band; Mrchg Band; Pep Band; School Musical; School Play; Stage Crew; Stat Bsktbl; Golf; Med.

TRACY, SHANE T; Hutchinson HS; Hutchinson, KS; (2); #18 in class; Boy Scts; SADD; Band; Mrchg Band; Pep Band; High Hon Roll; Prfct Atten Awd; Super Salthawk Awd; Crmnlstcs.

TRAFFAS, STEPHANIE; Wichita West HS; Wichita, KS; (1); 26/435; Pep Clb; Var Chrldng; Var Pom Pon; Var Socr; Intrml Vllybl; Hon Roll; Frosh Cls Clb; Frosh Hmcmng Princess; U Of KS.

TRAMELL, CARRIE J; Leavenworth HS; Leavenworth, KS; (4); Mgr Bsktbl; Mgr Sftbl; Intrml Vllybl; Goodfellows; Sftbl & Bsktbl Mgr; KS Univ; Phy Thrpst.

TRAMMELL, BRENT; Olathe East Sr HS; Olathe, KS; (3); Variety Show; Hon Roll; Electric Guitar; Electric Bass Guitar; Acoustic Classical; Music Perfmnc.

TRAMPOSH, LAUREN C; Bishop Miege HS; Shawnee, KS; (1); GAA; Stage Crew; Sftbl; Vllybl; Hon Roll; Pres Acad Fit Awd; KU; TV Broadcasting; Rptr.

TRAN, DIEN; Wichita West HS; Wichita, KS; (3); French Clb; Intnl Clb; Quiz Bowl; Scholastic Bowl; Teachers Aide; Trk; Wrstlng; High Hon Roll; Hon Roll; NHS; NCCJ Heritage Panel; Wichita St Univ; Physcn.

TRAN, HUYEN-TRAM N; Wichita West HS; Lawrence, KS; (1); 5/270; Art Clb; Church Yth Grp; Cmnty Wkr; FTA; Intnl Clb; Key Clb; Red Cross Aide; Science Clb; Spanish Clb; SADD; Asian Clb Pres; Sci Olympiad; Presdntl Awd; UMKC Schl Of Dentistry.

TRAN, MICHAEL; Kapaun-Mt Carmel HS; Derby, KS; (3); 4/162; Cmnty Wkr; Debate Tm; Service Clb; Crs Cntry; High Hon Roll; NHS; Ntl Merit Ltr; Pres Acad Fit Awd; KS ST Outstdng Sr Math/Sci; Yale U; Law.

TRAN, OSCAR N; Wichita Southeast HS; Wichita, KS; (2); Church Yth Grp; Cmnty Wkr; Ed Nwsp; Hon Roll.

TRAN, THUY B; Bishop Carroll Catholic HS; Wichita, KS; (3); FCA; Red Cross Aide; SADD; Teachers Aide; Chorus; Church Choir; School Musical; Nwsp; Var Crs Cntry; Var Trk; SEALS Mem; Cardiovascular Surgeon.

TRAN, VINHAN H; Garden City Sr HS; Garden City, KS; (2); Church Yth Grp; Debate Tm; Drama Clb; NFL; Quiz Bowl; Speech Tm; Acpl Chr; Church Choir; School Play; High Hon Roll.

TRAPP, ANDREA; Herington HS; Herington, KS; (2); Church Yth Grp; Drama Clb; FCA; 4-H; FHA; Letterman Clb; Math Tm; Pep Clb; Band; Chorus; Dickinson Cty Yth Tsk Frc; Peer Cnslr; KSU; Bio.

TRAPP, ANDREW; Hoisington HS; Susank, KS; (4); 12/62; Am Leg Boys St; Letterman Clb; Model UN; NFL; SADD; Chorus; School Play; L Bsbl; Hon Roll; Ntl Merit Ltr; Natl Mrt Commended Schlr; Fort Hays ST U.

TRAXEL, KIMBERLY; Junction City HS; Junction City, KS; (4); 2/256; Am Leg Aux Girls St; Church Yth Grp; FCA; Teachers Aide; Church Choir; Ofcr Jr Cls; Ofcr Sr Cls; High Hon Roll; Hon Roll; Treas NHS; KS ST U; Acctng.

TREAKLE, PAMELA L; Shawnee Mission W Sr HS; Overland Park, KS; (4); Cmnty Wkr; SADD; Hon Roll; NHS; Pres Acad Fit Awd; Cmp Fire; Belmont U Nashville; Music Bus.

TREDER, STEPHEN L; Dodge City HS; Dodge City, KS; (4); 12/254; Boy Scts; Band; Jazz Band; Mrchg Band; Pep Band; Cit Awd; High Hon Roll; NHS; Pres Acad Fit Awd; St Schlr; Eagle Scout/Vigil Hon/Order Of Arrow BSA; Bethany Coll; Pre-Med/Music.

TREECE, AKYA R; Field Kindley Mem Sr HS; Coffeyville, KS; (2); 78/163; Church Yth Grp; Cmnty Wkr; Debate Tm; French Clb; German Clb; NFL; Var Mgr(s); Var Trk; Hon Roll; Var Vllybl; Red Cross HIV/AIDS Licensed Instr; Spellman; OB GYN.

TREFZ, LYNN A; Rose Hill HS; Rose Hill, KS; (2); Church Yth Grp; Orch; Bsktbl; Trk; High Hon Roll; Pres Acad Fit Awd; Wchta Yth Symphny; KS ST Univ; Mscn/Chmst.

TREGEMBA, ANGELA D; Shawnee Heights HS; Topeka, KS; (3); FBLA; Model UN; Pep Clb; Band; Mrchg Band; Orch; High Hon Roll; Hon Roll; Optmtry.

TREIBER, JOE P; Labette Co HS; Dennis, KS; (2); FCA; Natl FFA Org; Ftbl; Trk; PSU; Ftbl.

TRENT, JESSICA A; Wichita East HS; Wichita, KS; (2); Church Yth Grp; Cmnty Wkr; Hosp Aide; Letterman Clb; Spanish Clb; Band; Church Choir; Mrchg Band; All-ST Music Band; Lions Clb ST/INTL Band; Intl Baccalaureate Prgm; Doc/Med Schl.

TRETHEWAY, ANGELA J; Derby HS; Derby, KS; (3); FCA; Key Clb; Library Aide; Office Aide; SADD; Chorus; Church Choir; School Play; Variety Show; Socr; KS ST U; Bus.

TREVINO, CRYSTAL H; Garden City Sr HS; Garden City, KS; (1); French Clb; FHA; Spanish Clb; Orch; Bsktbl; Sftbl; Cit Awd; Hon Roll; Summer Sftbl; Chrch; Sci.

TRIANA, MONICA R; Wichita Heights HS; Wichita, KS; (2); #23 in class; Church Yth Grp; Cmnty Wkr; Pep Clb; Teachers Aide; Ofcr Stu Cncl; Chrldng; Mgr(s); High Hon Roll; Peer Mediator; KS U; Med Stud.

TRICK, JESSI; Derby HS; Derby, KS; (2); VP Church Yth Grp; Key Clb; Pep Clb; SADD; Chorus; Church Choir; School Musical; Yrbk; Ofcr Stu Cncl; JV Var Chrldng; DECA; KAYS; Friends U; Bus/Advrtsng.

TRIEBEL, JUSTIN A; Labette Co HS; Coffeyville, KS; (2); 22/160; Cmnty Wkr; 4-H; FHA; Natl FFA Org; VICA; L Wrstlng; High Hon Roll; Hon Roll; Renaissance Org; HS Horse Judging Competiting In St Cmptn; Showing Horses Placing Top 5 In St; KS ST Univ; Vo-Ag Instr.

TRIMBLE, STEPHANIE L; Field Kindley Mem Sr HS; Dearing, KS; (1); Church Yth Grp; French Clb; Rptr Nwsp; Rep Frsh Cls; Trk; French Hon Soc; Acctnt.

TRIMMELL, HOLLY M; Wichita West HS; Wichita, KS; (2); Teachers Aide; Nwsp; Ofcr Frsh Cls; Ofcr Soph Cls; Hon Roll; Penn ST; Law/Crmnl Prsctng Aty.

TRIMMER, JUSTIN L; Topeka HS; Topeka, KS; (2); Band; Mrchg Band; Pep Band; Hon Roll; Bwlng; Hlpd Bld Race Car For Stck Car Rcng/Pit Crew 2 Yrs; KS Univ; Math.

TRIMMER, KYLE; Winfield HS; Winfield, KS; (4); 14/177; Church Yth Grp; Dance Clb; Debate Tm; HOBY; NFL; VP Frsh Cls; Pres Soph Cls; Pres VP Stu Cncl; Swmmng; NHS; TX Chrstn U; Educ.

TRINKA, AMBER N; Hoisington HS; Hoisington, KS; (3); Church Yth Grp; GAA; Office Aide; Pep Clb; Quiz Bowl; SADD; Teachers Aide; Temple Yth Grp; Band; Chorus; Dental Asst; Dental Hygiene.

TRIPLETT, ANGELA; Pratt HS; Pratt, KS; (3); Rep Church Yth Grp; Cmnty Wkr; FCA; Pres Pep Clb; Hist SADD; Chorus; Ed Yrbk; Sec Jr Cls; High Hon Roll; Sec NHS; Rotry Stu Of Month; Asst Dir Of Chrch Childrens Choir.

TRIPP, ADAM T; Clearwater HS; Clearwater, KS; (3); 4/65; Am Leg Boys St; Math Tm; Scholastic Bowl; Science Clb; Band; School Musical; Yrbk; High Hon Roll; NHS; NYLC; Comp Sci; Acctng.

TRISLER, NATHAN C; Field Kindley Mem Sr HS; Coffeyville, KS; (2); French Clb; Math Tm; Scholastic Bowl; Hon Roll; Sci Fair Wnnr.

TRITSCH, AMANDA J; Olathe East Sr HS; Olathe, KS; (2); Pep Clb; Spanish Clb; Teachers Aide; JV Bsktbl; JV Sftbl; JV Tennis; Var Trk; High Hon Roll; Hon Roll; Pres Acad Fit Awd; Cmptv Sftbl; Sports Med.

TROEGER, MEGAN A; Lincoln Jr Sr HS; Beverly, KS; (2); Debate Tm; Drama Clb; FHA; Hosp Aide; Letterman Clb; Pep Clb; Speech Tm; Mrchg Band; Pep Band; Hon Roll; KS U; Bus Admin.

TROLLOPE, KARI; Independence HS; Independence, KS; (3); 50/150; FTA; JA; Pep Clb; Co-Capt Var Chrldng; Hon Roll; U Of Akron; Human Resources.

TROMBLA, BRET; El Dorado HS; El Dorado, KS; (4); 28/170; Am Leg Aux Girls St; Letterman Clb; Spanish Clb; Sec SADD; Var L Crs Cntry; Powder Puff Ftbl; Var L Trk; JV Vllybl; Hon Roll; Treas NHS; NEMA Engl Awd; Butler County CC; Phys Thrpy.

TROMBOLD, JOHN M; Blue Valley North HS; Leawood, KS; (2); Boy Scts; Church Yth Grp; Model UN; JV Bsbl; Var L Swmmng; Hon Roll; Eagle Scout; Mtrlgy/Med.

TRONSGARD, AARON C; Dodge City HS; Dodge City, KS; (1); Pres Church Yth Grp; Ftbl; JV Trk.

TROST, MATT; Seaman Sr HS; Topeka, KS; (3); Boy Scts; Church Yth Grp; Letterman Clb; Library Aide; Teachers Aide; Phtg Nwsp; Phtg Yrbk; Swmmng; Trk; High Hon Roll; Sldr Twnshp Fire Dept Cdt Chf Cdts; Eagle Sct-Jyhwk Area Cncl; City Topeka Fire Dept Cdt; Johnson Cty CC; Paramedc.

TROTTER, ANNIE S; Blue Valley Northwest HS; Overland Park, KS; (3); Drill Tm; Pom Pon; High Hon Roll; Fshn Mrchnd.

TROTTER, TERA R; Wichita East HS; Wichita, KS; (3); Chorus; School Play; Variety Show; Nwsp; Yrbk; Chrldng; Trk; Wt Lftg; Hon Roll; Pres Acad Fit Awd; Butler Cty CC; Sign Lang Intrp.

TROUT, REBECCA E; Blue Valley Northwest HS; Leawood, KS; (4); 1/345; Treas German Clb; Band; Mrchg Band; Orch; Var Crs Cntry; Var Capt Socr; JV Tennis; Gov Hon Prg Awd; High Hon Roll; NHS; Johnson Cty Diversion Bd Mem; Jim Thompson Schlsp; All KS Acad 1st Team Soccer; Wesleyan Univ.

TROWBRIDGE, AMY S; Basehor Linwood HS; Basehor, KS; (3); FCA; 4-H; French Clb; Latin Clb; Chorus; School Play; High Hon Roll; Hon Roll; Office Aide; Pep Clb; Chmbr Sngrs; Wmns Ensmbl.

TROWBRIDGE, ANDREA M; Shawnee Heights Sr HS; Topeka, KS; (2); SADD; Band; Flag Corp; Mrchg Band; Pep Band; Stage Crew; High Hon Roll; Explorer Scout Treas; Acad Ltr; 2 Acad Medals; Tchr; Vet.

TROWBRIDGE, JULIE A; Wichita West HS; Wichita, KS; (2); Chorus; Bsktbl; Hon Roll; Prfct Atten Awd; Wichita ST Univ; Tchng.

TROYER, SHANE M; Shawnee Mission N HS; Merriam, KS; (1); Church Yth Grp; Pep Clb; Band; Jazz Band; Mrchg Band; Pep Band; Rep Stu Cncl; Socr; Tennis; High Hon Roll; Teens Alive Natl Yth Org K C Chap; Law/Arch.

TRUDE, JENNIFER A; Eastern Heights Jr Sr HS; Kirwin, KS; (2); Church Yth Grp; 4-H; Letterman Clb; Pep Clb; Sec Soph Cls; Trk; Vllybl; 4-H Awd; Hon Roll; Prfct Atten Awd.

TRUMBLE, GRADY; Clay Ctr Cmty HS; Clay Center, KS; (4); 1/99; FHA; Pres Church Yth Grp; Cmnty Wkr; VP Pres FBLA; Pres Frsh Cls; Pres Soph Cls; Rep Sr Cls; Var Capt Bsbl; JV Bsktbl; Var L Ftbl; KS ST U; Engrng.

TRUMBULL, AMY C; Ottawa HS; Rantoul, KS; (3); JV Trk; Hon Roll; Stu Naturalist; AZ; Bio.

TRUNECEK, JILL; Goddard HS; Wichita, KS; (3); Church Yth Grp; Hosp Aide; Pep Clb; Science Clb; Spanish Clb; Band; Church Choir; High Hon Roll; NHS; U Of KS; Pre-Med.

TRUPP, SARAH E; Robert E Clark Jr HS; Bonner Springs, KS; (1); Church Yth Grp; Cmnty Wkr; Letterman Clb; Teachers Aide; Trk; Vllybl; Hon Roll; Lake Forest Swm Tm; Johnson Cty CC; Archlgst/Egypt.

TRUTA, BETH D; Shawnee Mission W Sr HS; Lenexa, KS; (2); 84/450; Treas Stu Cncl; Chrldng; Swmmng; Hon Roll; 4 Yr Coll; Bus.

TRUTA, BRYAN A; Bishop Miege HS; Overland Park, KS; (3); 33/184; Boy Scts; Hosp Aide; NFL; Quiz Bowl; Scholastic Bowl; Pres Stu Cncl; High Hon Roll; NHS; Church Yth Grp; Cmnty Wkr; Awd 1000 Schlsp Exec Wmn Intl; Slctd Attnd KU Rgnts Hnrs Prgm Smmr 96; U Of KS; Jrnlsm/Brdcstng.

TRYEE, TRENIECE C; Topeka HS; Topeka, KS; (2); Church Yth Grp; Cmnty Wkr; Dance Clb; Hosp Aide; JA; Church Choir; Flag Corp; School Play; Stage Crew; Mgr Bsktbl; BSU; STRAPP; Tuskegee Univ; Nrsng.

TRYON, JENNY; Washburn Rural HS; Topeka, KS; (2); Band; Mrchg Band; Pep Band; Variety Show; Yrbk; Var Chrldng; High Hon Roll; Piano; Gym; KS ST U; Intrr Dsgn.

TSCHANNEN, KRISTIN M; Olathe East Sr HS; Olathe, KS; (2); Chorus; Capt Drill Tm; Orch; School Musical; Var L Tennis; High Hon Roll; Hon Roll; Pres Acad Fit Awd; Olathe Area Yth Symphony; Cmptn Dance Team; European Tour Olathe Intergenerational Chorus.

TSEN, KARL; Manhattan HS; Manhattan, KS; (3); Am Leg Boys St; Dance Clb; German Clb; Intnl Clb; NFL; Quiz Bowl; Scholastic Bowl; High Hon Roll; Hon Roll; NHS; NFL Degree Of Distinction; Medicine.

TUBBS, KERRY C; Washburn Rural HS; Topeka, KS; (3); Church Yth Grp; Nwsp; Var L Bsbl; Intrml Bsktbl; JV Socr; Var Wt Lftg; High Hon Roll; Hon Roll; Pub Relations; Jrnlsm.

TUBBS, LEAH; Wichita West HS; Wichita, KS; (4); 2/250; GAA; ROTC; Varsity Clb; Chorus; Chrldng; Trk; Vllybl; Gov Hon Prg Awd; High Hon Roll; NHS; Wichita ST Univ; Engr.

TUCK, CORY D; Jefferson West HS; Hoyt, KS; (1); 1/90; Chess Clb; Debate Tm; Math Tm; Quiz Bowl; Scholastic Bowl; Var Bsbl; JV Bsktbl; Var Crs Cntry; High Hon Roll; Prfct Atten Awd; Pt.

TUCK, KRIS; Royal Valley HS; Meriden, KS; (4); Cmnty Wkr; Library Aide; SADD; Teachers Aide; Varsity Clb; Band; Rep Stu Cncl; Var Capt Bsktbl; Var Capt Ftbl; Var Wt Lftg; KU; Engrng.

TUCKER, AMORY B; Independence HS; Independence, KS; (1); Band; Mrchg Band; Orch; Pep Band; Intrml Vllybl; High Hon Roll; St Mus Awd II Div Awd; Acad Lttr Awd For Outs Acad Achv; IHS Fresh Awd.

TUCKER, CARA; Wichita Heights HS; Wichita, KS; (3); 9/250; Church Yth Grp; Debate Tm; Hosp Aide; NFL; Spanish Clb; High Hon Roll; NHS; Spanish NHS; Eclgy Clb; KS ST U; Bus Admin.

TUCKER, HEIDI M; Salina HS South; Salina, KS; (3); Church Yth Grp; Teachers Aide; Band; Chorus; Jazz Band; Mrchg Band; Orch; Pep Band; School Musical; Hon Roll; Speech Pathologist.

TUCKER, JAIME S; Labette Co HS; Parsons, KS; (4); SADD; Chorus; Rep Soph Cls; Rep Sr Cls; Tennis; NHS; FHA; Library Aide; Hon Roll; Sigma Mu Music Clb; UKS.

TUCKER, JESSE N; Wheatland Middle Sr HS; Gove, KS; (4); 2/16; Quiz Bowl; Rptr Phtg Nwsp; Pres Frsh Cls; Pres VP Stu Cncl; Bsktbl; Crs Cntry; Tennis; Hon Roll; Prfct Atten Awd; Sal; KS ST U.

TUCKER, JORDAN T; Kingman HS; Kingman, KS; (2); Church Yth Grp; Cmnty Wkr; Letterman Clb; Science Clb; SADD; Varsity Clb; Band; Jazz Band; Mrchg Band; Pep Band; Eagle Sct; Duke Univ TIPS Pgm; Hi-Y Guitarist St Hnr; U Of KS; Pre-Med.

TUCKER, JULIA E; Blue Valley Northwest HS; Overland Park, KS; (2); Band; Mrchg Band; JV Chrldng; Hon Roll; Movie Producer.

TUCKER, JUNILDA M; Circle HS; El Dorado, KS; (3); FCA; FHA; Pep Clb; SADD; Teachers Aide; Chorus; Variety Show; Var Mgr(s); JV Sftbl; JV Vllybl; HOTT; Butler Cnty Col.

TUCKER, KELLY J; Cimarron HS; Cimarron, KS; (3); Church Yth Grp; FCA; Pep Clb; Spanish Clb; SADD; Teachers Aide; Band; Pep Band; Pres Soph Cls; JV Var Bsktbl; Med Field.

TUCKER, LACEY; Oskaloosa HS; Ozawkie, KS; (4); 1/47; Am Leg Aux Girls St; FBLA; Sec Soph Cls; VP Sr Cls; Bsktbl; Golf; High Hon Roll; NHS; St Schlr; Val; U Of KS; Nrsng.

TUCKER, SABRINA N; Scott Comm HS; Scott City, KS; (4); 11/77; Debate Tm; HOBY; NFL; School Play; Rep Stu Cncl; Hon Roll; Pres Acad Fit Awd; Drama Clb; Office Aide; Teachers Aide; HOBY Cnslr; Stu Cngrss; All St Dbt; All St Frnscs; KS ST U; Bus Admin.

TUCKER, SARA; Shawnee Mission N HS; Shawnee Msn, KS; (4); 68/326; Q&S; Spanish Clb; Thesps; Acpl Chr; School Musical; Stage Crew; Rptr Yrbk; Mgr Gym; Hon Roll; NHS; U Of KS; Law.

TUCKER, SHELLY; Stanton Co HS; Johnson, KS; (1); Church Yth Grp; Cmnty Wkr; Variety Show; JV Bsktbl; Var L Chrldng; JV Vllybl; Hon Roll; Elem Tchr.

TUCKER, TAMMY L; Washburn Rural HS; Topeka, KS; (3); Church Yth Grp; FCA; Band; CAP; Pep Band; High Hon Roll; Hon Roll; KS ST Hon Band Clinic 2 Yrs; Topeka Yth Wind Ensmbl; Topeka Symphony Yth Orch; Washburn Univ; Mus Ed.

TUCKWOOD, TRACY L; Wichita East HS; Wichita, KS; (3); 14/337; Church Yth Grp; Band; Chorus; Church Choir; Mrchg Band; Orch; School Musical; Gym; Trk; Hon Roll; Mission Work Throughout The US; Music Ed.

TUEL, JESSE C; Lawrence HS; Lawrence, KS; (3); Church Yth Grp; Teachers Aide; Acpl Chr; Band; Mrchg Band; Variety Show; JV Var Bsktbl; JV L Crs Cntry; Hon Roll; Prfct Atten Awd; Hnr Choir.

TUMBLESON, MEA; Lyndon HS; Lyndon, KS; (3); Church Yth Grp; FBLA; FHA; Chorus; Nwsp; Yrbk; Bsktbl; Chrldng; Pom Pon; Wt Lftg.

TUNISON, CHRIS D; Washburn Rural HS; Topeka, KS; (3); Boy Scts; Chess Clb; Church Yth Grp; Debate Tm; NFL; Hon Roll; U Of KS.

TUNNELL, CHRISTINE; Kapaun-Mt Carmel HS; Wichita, KS; (3); 5/170; Q&S; Spanish Clb; Ed Nwsp; JV Bsktbl; Var Sftbl; Var Vllybl; High Hon Roll; Pre-Med.

TUNNELL, RUSS R; Riverton Schl; Baxter Springs, KS; (3); Art Clb; 4-H; Natl FFA Org; Mgr(s); 4-H Awd; Hon Roll; Speech; Meterology & Astronomy; Human & Biological Sci; Radiology; Nuclear Medicine.

TUPPER, GAREN; Otis Bison HS; Bison, KS; (3); Am Leg Boys St; Church Yth Grp; 4-H; Letterman Clb; Pep Clb; Capt Quiz Bowl; Capt Scholastic Bowl; Rep SADD; Band; Chorus.

TURLEY, SHARNELL R; Scott Comm HS; Marienthal, KS; (3); 17/75; Cmnty Wkr; Pep Clb; Band; Mrchg Band; Pep Band; Chrldng; Hon Roll; Frgn Stud Club; U Of KS; Rdlgy.

TURLEY, TIM E; Coldwater Jr Sr HS; Coldwater, KS; (3); Church Yth Grp; Cmnty Wkr; Letterman Clb; Math Tm; Pep Clb; Varsity Clb; Acpl Chr; Band; Chorus; Mrchg Band.

TURLEY, TONY G; Scott Comm HS; Scott City, KS; (4); Library Aide; Natl FFA Org; Teachers Aide; Ftbl; Wt Lftg; Wrstlng; Hon Roll; Hnrb Mntn Ftbl 2nd Team Defense ST; 2nd Team League Ftbl; Fort Hays ST Univ; Sports Med.

TURNBAUGH, CARRIE; Lawrence HS; Lawrence, KS; (4); Church Yth Grp; JA; Teachers Aide; Ofcr Sr Cls; Ofcr Stu Cncl; Var Chrldng; Hon Roll; Prfct Atten Awd; Emporia ST U; Elem Ed.

TURNBOW, STUART D; Ellsworth HS; Geneseo, KS; (2); 11/75; Church Yth Grp; Band; Chorus; Mrchg Band; Pep Band; Cit Awd; High Hon Roll; Hon Roll.

TURNBULL, STACI L; Burlingame HS; Eskridge, KS; (2); 8/33; Rptr VP 4-H; Pep Clb; Spanish Clb; Band; Chorus; Mrchg Band; Pep Band; School Play; Rptr Nwsp; Rep Soph Cls; KS St Univ; Pharm.

TURNBULL, VALERIE; Pittsburg HS; Pittsburg, KS; (3); 11/200; Am Leg Aux Girls St; Church Yth Grp; FTA; Treas Q&S; Spanish Clb; Teachers Aide; Mgr Nwsp; Var Capt Chrldng; High Hon Roll; Pittsburgh ST Univ; Pharmacy.

TURNER, BRANDI N; Labette Co HS; Hallowell, KS; (3); 27/146; French Clb; Spanish Clb; SADD; Chorus; School Musical; School Play; Stage Crew; Intrml JV Chrldng; High Hon Roll; NHS; U Of ME; Anstslgst/Crmnl Psych.

TURNER, BRIAN T; Wichita Northwest HS; Wichita, KS; (4); 41/367; Treas DECA; Capt Quiz Bowl; Var Capt Ftbl; Var Wrstlng; Hon Roll; NHS; KS ST; Bus Mrtkg.

TURNER, CLINT A; Chanute Sr HS; Chanute, KS; (2); FCA; Chorus; Jazz Band; School Musical; JV Bsbl; Intrml Bsktbl; Var Chrldng; Var Mgr(s); High Hon Roll; Hon Roll.

TURNER, CODY J; Larned HS; Larned, KS; (3); Acpl Chr; Trk; KS State Univsch Of Tech; Pil.

TURNER, CRYSTAL; Wyandotte HS; Kansas City, KS; (3); Chess Clb; Chorus; High Hon Roll; Hon Roll; NHS; Gspl Chr; Comm.

TURNER, DAVID B; Circle HS; Towanda, KS; (1); Church Yth Grp; 4-H; 4-H Awd; Hon Roll; KS U; Arch.

TURNER, DENA R; Wyandotte HS; Kansas City, KS; (2); Cmnty Wkr; Rep Soph Cls; Pres Stu Cncl; Hon Roll; NHS; STLICO Pres 95-97; Outstdng STLICO Worker Awd; Lib Arts; Sculpture.

TURNER, JERRI L; Valley Ctr HS; Valley Center, KS; (3); 11/166; Drama Clb; Spanish Clb; SADD; Rep Soph Cls; L Pom Pon; JV Socr; High Hon Roll; Pittsburg ST; Pre-Med; Dr.

TURNER, LAURIE A; Blue Valley HS; Stilwell, KS; (3); Chorus; Hon Roll; U Of MO.

TURNER, ROLAND D; Eureka Jr Sr HS; Eureka, KS; (3); Am Leg Boys St; Boy Scts; Church Yth Grp; Debate Tm; Drama Clb; FHA; Letterman Clb; Quiz Bowl; Science Clb; Spanish Clb.

TURNER, SONIA D; Chanute Sr HS; Chanute, KS; (2); Church Yth Grp; Cmnty Wkr; FCA; Spanish Clb; Chorus; Church Choir; School Musical; Sec Frsh Cls; Ofcr Stu Cncl; Bsktbl; Track St Champ; Princple Ldshp Tm; MI St Univ; Prem.

TURNER, STEPHANIE M; Emporia HS; Emporia, KS; (3); Pres Church Yth Grp; Cmnty Wkr; Debate Tm; FCA; Key Clb; SADD; Chorus; Var L Swmmng; Cit Awd; High Hon Roll; Wildlife & Backpacking Clb; Emporia ST U; Bio; Radiology; Ed.

TURNEY, ROSS D; Basehor Linwood HS; Bonner Springs, KS; (2); 6/143; Cmnty Wkr; Debate Tm; HOBY; NFL; Quiz Bowl; Science Clb; Treas Frsh Cls; Rep Soph Cls; Var L Bsbl; JV Bsktbl; Natl Yng Ldrs Conf.

TURNQUIST, SHUSTEN; Shusten Turnquist HS; Salina, KS; (2); 30/278; Debate Tm; NFL; Sec Frsh Cls; Rep Soph Cls; Ofcr Stu Cncl; Chrldng; Swmmng; Tennis; Hon Roll; KS U.

TURVEY, MICHAEL WILLIAM; Lawrence HS; Lawrence, KS; (3); Am Leg Boys St; Church Yth Grp; JA; Spanish Clb; Hon Roll; NHS; Prfct Atten Awd; Cmptr Engr.

TURVEY, PAUL; Lawrence HS; Lawrence, KS; (4); Am Leg Boys St; Church Yth Grp; JA; Rep Stu Cncl; L Bsktbl; Hon Roll; NHS; Pres Acad Fit Awd; Yth In Lcl Govt Rep On Douglas Cnty Plnng Comm; KS Mock Trial; KS Univ; Bus.

TURYBURY, CARTER S; Goddard HS; Wichita, KS; (2); Boy Scts; Church Yth Grp; Library Aide; Science Clb; Spanish Clb; SADD; Socr; Trk; High Hon Roll; Eagle Sct; Comp Sci.

TURYBURY, WESLEY; Goddard HS; Wichita, KS; (4); 1/150; Boy Scts; Science Clb; Bsktbl; Socr; Trk; High Hon Roll; NHS; Ntl Merit Ltr; Val; Eagle Sct; OK ST Univ; Chem Engr.

TUSH, BENJAMIN R; Anderson Cty Jr Sr HS; Garnett, KS; (2); Church Yth Grp; Drama Clb; Pep Clb; Science Clb; Thesps; Band; Jazz Band; Mrchg Band; Pep Band; Stage Crew; KS Masonic All ST Mrchng Band; Dist Hnr Band 1st Chair; ST Fornscs; Music Ed/Perfmng Arts.

TUTTLE, ELETHA J; Washington HS; Kansas City, KS; (3); French Clb; Key Clb; Pep Clb; Mrchg Band; Orch; Pep Band; Chrldng; Powder Puff Ftbl; Sftbl; High Hon Roll; DECA; Spcl Ed Elem Tchr.

TUTTLE, EVAN G; Quinter Jr Sr HS; Collyer, KS; (4); 6/24; Pres FCA; Sec Natl FFA Org; Speech Tm; Pres Stu Cncl; Crs Cntry; Cit Awd; High Hon Roll; NHS; Pres Acad Fit Awd; KS ST U; Theatre.

TUTTLE, KYLE L; Wellington Sr HS; Wellington, KS; (2); 80/182; Chorus; Bsktbl; Sftbl; Vllybl; Hon Roll; Prfct Atten Awd; Kays Sec; Sign Lang.

TWADDLE, KELLY; Desoto HS; Olathe, KS; (4); 2/110; Am Leg Aux Girls St; Math Tm; Service Clb; Rptr Nwsp; Ed Yrbk; High Hon Roll; NHS; Pres Acad Fit Awd; Church Yth Grp; SADD; KU Hnr Schlr; PRIDE Pgm; KS Schlstc Press Assn Stu Brd; Acad Ltr & Bar; KSU; Engr.

TWIGG, NICOLE; Derby HS; Derby, KS; (3); FCA; Key Clb; Service Clb; SADD; Ed Yrbk; Lit Mag; Var L Crs Cntry; Var L Trk; High Hon Roll; NHS; Pittsburg ST; Engrng/Jrnlsm.

TYLER, KENDRAH; Sumner Acad Of Arts & Science; Kansas City, KS; (3); 75/140; Drama Clb; Key Clb; Latin Clb; Pep Clb; Spanish Clb; SADD; Band; Drill Tm; Mrchg Band; Pep Band; Pol Sci; Corp Lawyer.

TYNER, HAYLEY; Topeka HS; Topeka, KS; (2); Girl Scts; Office Aide; Chorus; Vllybl; High Hon Roll; Horseback Riding; KS ST Univ.

TYSON, AMANDA I; Marais Des Cygnes Valley HS; Melvern, KS; (3); 1/26; Am Leg Aux Girls St; Church Yth Grp; Cmnty Wkr; Quiz Bowl; School Musical; School Play; Rptr Frsh Cls; JV Bsktbl; JV Vllybl; High Hon Roll; Forensics; U Of New Orleans; Ed.

UBEL, KATHERINE A; Manhattan HS; Manhattan, KS; (3); Church Yth Grp; FBLA; Pep Clb; Spanish Clb; Teachers Aide; Golf; Var Mgr(s); Score Keeper; Hon Roll; Ntl Merit Ltr; SADD; KS St Uinv; Prepharm.

UDLAND, KYLE A; Maize HS; Wichita, KS; (4); Church Yth Grp; Math Tm; Spanish Clb; Yrbk; Bsktbl; Hon Roll; NHS; KA Regents Schlr; KS St Univ; Eng.

UDLAND, MATTHEW H; Maize HS; Wichita, KS; (1); Church Yth Grp; Acpl Chr; Band; Chorus; Church Choir; Mrchg Band; Pep Band; School Musical; Variety Show; Hon Roll; Band Ltr; 1 Rtng Regnl & St Cmptns Trombone & Vocal Solos; KS Drug-Free Tae Kwon Do Demonstrn Tm.

UHL, KATHERINE E; Garden City Sr HS; Garden City, KS; (2); Church Yth Grp; Debate Tm; NFL; JV Chrldng; Var Am Leg Aux Girls St; High Hon Roll; Stdnt Cngrss; Novice Debate Tm Of Yr Awd; Outstdng Hon Geog Stdnt Awd.

UHLRICH, JILL S; Chase Co HS; Cottonwood Falls, KS; (2); Quiz Bowl; Spanish Clb; Band; Ed Nwsp; Chrldng; Vllybl; High Hon Roll; NHS; Math Tm; Pep Band; KAYS Sec & Treas; U Of KS; Tchr; Nrs.

UHLS, DUSTIN M; Sedan HS; Sedan, KS; (2); 4/33; Church Yth Grp; Cmnty Wkr; Ofcr FHA; Natl FFA Org; Quiz Bowl; Scholastic Bowl; Spanish Clb; Teachers Aide; High Hon Roll; Hon Roll; FFA Ofcr; Natl Hnr Soc; Gftd Cls.

UKENA, HEATHER M; Manhattan HS; Manhattan, KS; (2); SADD; Chorus; Powder Puff Ftbl; Hon Roll; Stream/Coastal Studies.

UKENA, JAMIE K; Rock Creek Jr Sr HS; Saint George, KS; (3); 16/42; Pep Clb; FHA; Office Aide; SADD; Teachers Aide; Band; Mrchg Band; Pep Band; Phtg Rptr Yrbk; Score Keeper; KS ST Univ; Acctng.

ULBRICH, LISA; Sedgwick HS; Valley Center, KS; (1); Church Yth Grp; 4-H; Band; Mrchg Band; Pep Band; JV Bsktbl; JV Vllybl; 4-H Awd; High Hon Roll.

ULBRICH, TENESSA; Sedgwick HS; Valley Center, KS; (3); Church Yth Grp; 4-H; FHA; Letterman Clb; SADD; Band; Jazz Band; Mrchg Band; Pep Band; School Musical; Kays Clb; Wichita ST U; Prmry Ed.

ULLMER, JANELL M; Junction City HS; Milford, KS; (2); Pep Clb; Spanish Clb; Band; Flag Corp; Mrchg Band; Ofcr Soph Cls; Vllybl; High Hon Roll; KS Univ; Bus.

ULSH, AMBER L; Olathe East Sr HS; Olathe, KS; (2); Church Yth Grp; Dance Clb; Pep Clb; Spanish Clb; Chorus; Rep Frsh Cls; Chrldng; Powder Puff Ftbl; Trk; Vllybl; UCA All Star Chrldr Frosh Yr; Dancing; Outstdng Span/Life Sci Awd Frosh Yr; Frosh/Soph Yr Acad Awds; KS Univ.

UMBEHR, JARED J; Wabaunsee HS; Alma, KS; (3); Var Ftbl; KS ST U.

UMBERGER, AMY; Pawnee Heights HS; Rozel, KS; (4); Am Leg Aux Girls St; 4-H; FBLA; Quiz Bowl; Nwsp; Sec Sr Cls; Bsktbl; Vllybl; DAR Awd; Hon Roll; KS ST U; Phys Thpry.

UMMEL, STACI D; Great Bend Sr HS; Great Bend, KS; (3); 36/230; Library Aide; Pep Clb; Sec Treas Spanish Clb; Nwsp; Bsktbl; Tennis; High Hon Roll; Kayettes; Bus Mgmt.

UMSTEAD, RANDY; Olathe South Sr HS; Olathe, KS; (3); Church Yth Grp; Capt Debate Tm; NFL; Acpl Chr; Chorus; Church Choir; High Hon Roll; NHS; Drama Clb; Letterman Clb; Soloist KS All-ST Chorus 95; Soloist Choral Fest Of Netherlands; Mnstr Of Music.

UN, KUM H; Junction City HS; Junction City, KS; (1); Church Yth Grp; Church Choir; Bsktbl; Mgr(s); Swmmng; Vllybl; High Hon Roll; Dr.

UNDERWOOD, BROOKE; Atchison Sr HS; Atchison, KS; (4); 6/123; Office Aide; VP Pres Spanish Clb; Rptr Nwsp; Rptr Yrbk; Rep Stu Cncl; Var L Chrldng; High Hon Roll; Hon Roll; NHS; KS ST U.

UNDERWOOD, CHIRSTOPHER E; Wichita South HS; Wichita, KS; (4); 9/292; Church Yth Grp; Cmnty Wkr; Swmmng; Trk; High Hon Roll; Hon Roll; NHS; Prfct Atten Awd; Pres Acad Fit Awd; Pres Schlr; Pres Of Campus Life; VP Of Stu-Led Bible Study; Southwestern Assembly Of God.

UNDERWOOD, ERIC; Jefferson Co North HS; Valley Falls, KS; (4); Church Yth Grp; 4-H; FBLA; Letterman Clb; Office Aide; SADD; Pres Frsh Cls; Rep Soph Cls; VP Jr Cls; VP Sr Cls; Team KS Plyr At Intl Bsktbl Trnmnt Belgium; KS St Trck & Fld Chmpnshps Qulfr 94-95; KS ST U; Bus.

UNDERWOOD, MELISSA; Ft Scott HS; Garland, KS; (3); Debate Tm; Pep Clb; SADD; Chorus; Chrldng; Vllybl.

UNDERWOOD, MELODY; White Rock HS; Burr Oak, KS; (4); 12/17; Am Leg Aux Girls St; Letterman Clb; Natl FFA Org; Ed Yrbk; Bsktbl; Trk; Vllybl; 4-H Awd; Hon Roll; Prfct Atten Awd; SADD VP; Sweetheart Qn; Cloud Cty CC; Spcl Ed.

UNDERWOOD, NICK; Larned HS; Larned, KS; (2); 3/120; Church Yth Grp; Quiz Bowl; Spanish Clb; Ofcr Stu Cncl; Var Golf; High Hon Roll; Prfct Atten Awd; AZ ST.

UNDERWOOD, TAMMY; Sedan HS; Sedan, KS; (1); 12/33; Sec FHA; Letterman Clb; VP Natl Beta Clb; Spanish Clb; Chorus; Cit Awd; Pep Clb; School Musical; Ofcr Frsh Cls; Ofcr Stu Cncl; Law.

UNG, NELSON; Wichita Heights HS; Wichita, KS; (3); 49/250; Am Leg Boys St; Debate Tm; NFL; Spanish Clb; JV Ftbl; Var L Socr; Var L Tennis; High Hon Roll; Hon Roll; NHS; Clb Soccer; Spcl Olympics Bsktbl Referee; Clb Tnns; KS Univ; Biomedical.

UNGEHEUER, ABRA; Jayhawk-Linn HS; Centerville, KS; (4); 11/35; Am Leg Aux Girls St; Church Yth Grp; Cmnty Wkr; Debate Tm; Drama Clb; Pres 4-H; Natl FFA Org; Teachers Aide; Band; School Play; Dist/Chptr Pres FFF; Jayhawk-Linn Hmntrn Awd; Tutor Jr Hgh Stdnts; KS ST U; Ag/Jrnlsm.

UNGER, LYNETTE; Circle HS; Towanda, KS; (3); Hosp Aide; Spanish Clb; Var Speech Tm; Pres SADD; Flag Corp; School Play; Rep Frsh Cls; Rep Soph Cls; Pres Jr Cls; Var L Crs Cntry; Poltcl Sci.

UNGLES, ABBY; Andale HS; Colwich, KS; (1); Church Yth Grp; Cmnty Wkr; Band; Mrchg Band; Pep Band; Bsktbl; Sftbl; Tennis; Vllybl; Hon Roll; KS U; Phys Therapy.

UNION, STARLA J; Wyandotte HS; Kansas City, KS; (1); GAA; Bsktbl; Trk; Vllybl; Grambling; Bus Admin.

UNREIN, CHAD W; Maize HS; Wichita, KS; (3); 1/285; Debate Tm; Math Tm; NFL; Spanish Clb; SADD; Var L Tennis; High Hon Roll; NHS; Prfct Atten Awd; Pres Acad Fit Awd; Qlfd Natl His Day; 4.o GPA.

UNREIN, SHANE W; Maize HS; Wichita, KS; (3); 1/250; Cmnty Wkr; Debate Tm; NFL; Spanish Clb; SADD; Var L Tennis; High Hon Roll; NHS; Natl His Day Grp Proj; U Of KS.

UNRUH, AMANDA; South Gray HS; Montezuma, KS; (4); 4/19; English Clb; Quiz Bowl; Spanish Clb; Teachers Aide; Ed Yrbk; Hon Roll; Prfct Atten Awd; KS ST Univ.

UNRUH, ANTHONY; Field Kindley Mem Sr HS; Coffeyville, KS; (3); 14/178; Church Yth Grp; HOBY; JA; Spanish Clb; Nwsp; High Hon Roll; Hon Roll; NHS; Prfct Atten Awd; Notre Dame; Comp Sci.

UNRUH, ARIANA L; Hesston HS; Hesston, KS; (1); Church Yth Grp; FCA; Chorus; Church Choir; Rep Frsh Cls; Ofcr Stu Cncl; Bsktbl; JV Trk; Vllybl; High Hon Roll.

UNRUH, COREE; Bucklin Schl; Bucklin, KS; (3); Church Yth Grp; Debate Tm; FCA; Quiz Bowl; Speech Tm; SADD; Thesps; Chorus; High Hon Roll; Hon Roll; All Lgue Schlrs Bowl; ST Dbte/Speech Cmpetr; KS ST Univ; Pol Sci/Soc Wrk.

UNRUH, ISLEY; Vlly Ctr HS; Sedgwick, KS; (2); Art Clb; Scholastic Bowl; Spanish Clb; Wt Lftg; Wrstlng; High Hon Roll; Chem.

UNRUH, JAMIE L; UPN HS; Weskan, KS; (3); 1/1; Treas Art Clb; Debate Tm; Math Tm; Pep Clb; Scholastic Bowl; Pep Band; Stage Crew; Pres Jr Cls; JV Chrldng; Wt Lftg; Photo Class; Hsts Goodland Elk Ldg; Poem Pub; Cmpltd 10-12th Grds In 8 Mnths; CO Inst Art; Photo/Visual Arts.

UNRUH, JAY R; Berean Acad; Peabody, KS; (3); Church Yth Grp; Letterman Clb; Quiz Bowl; VP Band; Pep Band; Var Crs Cntry; Var Trk; High Hon Roll; NHS; St Band 95; Dist Band 94-95; Medicine.

UNRUH, JULIE I; Canton-Galva HS; Galva, KS; (3); 10/48; VP Church Yth Grp; FBLA; SADD; Band; Ofcr Stu Cncl; Vllybl; Hon Roll; Bethel Coll; Nrsng.

UNRUH, KORY W; Meade HS; Meade, KS; (4); 2/26; Church Yth Grp; Chorus; School Musical; Pres Stu Cncl; Capt Var Bsktbl; Var L Ftbl; Var L Tennis; High Hon Roll; NHS; Sal; Taber Coll; Ag.

UNRUH, KRAIG; South Gray HS; Montezuma, KS; (3); Church Yth Grp; Letterman Clb; Quiz Bowl; Spanish Clb; Chorus; Pres Frsh Cls; JV Bsktbl; Ftbl; Wt Lftg; High Hon Roll; Aeronautics.

UNRUH, KRISTA L; Council Grove HS; Alta Vista, KS; (4); 1/77; FCA; Treas Sec 4-H; Key Clb; Natl FFA Org; SADD; Yrbk; Treas Sr Cls; JV Var Bsktbl; JV Var Vllybl; NHS; Hnrs Regents Pgm; KS ST Univ; Elem Ed.

UNRUH, MATT; Burrton Schl; Burrton, KS; (3); Letterman Clb; Scholastic Bowl; Band; Chorus; Pep Band; School Musical; Var Ftbl; Var Golf; Hon Roll.

UNRUH, ROBYN; Hillsboro HS; Durham, KS; (3); 10/65; Church Yth Grp; Chorus; School Musical; Nwsp; Yrbk; Sec Sr Cls; Chrldng; Tennis; High Hon Roll; NHS; Occptnl Thrpst.

UNRUH, SHANNON; Hillsboro HS; Hillsboro, KS; (4); 6/45; Band; Chorus; School Musical; Ed Nwsp; Ed Yrbk; Var Tennis; High Hon Roll; NHS; 1st Rtng St Piano Cmptn; Tabor Coll; Acctng.

UNRUH, STACIE; Quinter Jr Sr HS; Quinter, KS; (2); FCA; Letterman Clb; Band; Flag Corp; School Musical; Yrbk; Var L Chrldng; JV Golf; JV Vllybl; High Hon Roll; Lab Tech.

UNRUH, VANESSA; Chaparral HS; Harper, KS; (2); Sec Church Yth Grp; Debate Tm; Drama Clb; Key Clb; Chorus; School Play; Rptr Nwsp; Rptr Yrbk; Var Chrldng; NHS; Hesston; Brdcst Jrnlsm.

UNRUH, WELLS R; Anderson Cty Jr Sr HS; Garnett, KS; (1); German Clb; Chorus; Yrbk; JV Bsktbl; Var Ftbl; Pres Acad Fit Awd; Drawing; Art; Rollerblading; Comp; KU; Bus Acctng.

UPHAM, KENDRA; White City HS; White City, KS; (4); 1/10; Am Leg Aux Girls St; Scholastic Bowl; Band; Chorus; School Play; Yrbk; Pres Jr Cls; Pres Sr Cls; High Hon Roll; NHS; Hrtlnd Vcs; Washburn U.

UPHAUS, SARA; Seaman Sr HS; Topeka, KS; (3); FBLA; German Clb; Key Clb; SADD; Band; Mrchg Band; Pep Band; High Hon Roll; Hon Roll; Prfct Atten Awd; KS ST.

UPLINGER, KARA A; Great Bend Sr HS; Great Bend, KS; (4); 30/230; L Drama Clb; Office Aide; Service Clb; Spanish Clb; SADD; L Orch; School Play; Stage Crew; Variety Show; Var Swmmng; St Gymnst; Dance; KS Rgnts Schlr; WSU Msc Schlrshp; St Swmmng; Asst Dir Theatre; Wichita ST U; Msc.

URBAN, AMANDA; Lucas-Luray HS; Lucas, KS; (1); Church Yth Grp; Pep Clb; Speech Tm; SADD; Band; Chorus; Pep Band; School Play; L Bsktbl; Var Vllybl; Phys Thrpy.

URBAN, ANN; Lucus-Luray HS; Lucas, KS; (3); 1/7; Church Yth Grp; Girl Scts; Pep Clb; SADD; School Play; Ofcr Jr Cls; Var Bsktbl; Var Vllybl; Hon Roll; NHS; KS ST U; Vet Med.

URBAN, JEFFREY; Maur Hill Prep Schl; Atchison, KS; (3); 4-H; Math Tm; Stage Crew; Bsktbl; Ftbl; Golf; Wt Lftg; High Hon Roll; Pres Acad Fit Awd.

URBAN, JENNIFER L; Shawnee Heights HS; Topeka, KS; (4); #37 in class; Church Yth Grp; Intnl Clb; Model UN; SADD; Teachers Aide; Church Choir; Stage Crew; Variety Show; High Hon Roll; Pres Schlr; U Of KS; Eng.

URBAN, KRISTEN; Otis Bison HS; Bison, KS; (4); 1/25; Pep Clb; Band; Chorus; Jazz Band; Pep Band; Pres Sr Cls; Var L Vllybl; High Hon Roll; NHS; Val; Fort Hays ST U; Music.

URBANO, NICK A; Wichita East HS; Wichita, KS; (2); Church Yth Grp; Office Aide; Hangar Bd; KS ST; Arch.

URBAUER, SARA; Frankft HS; Frankfort, KS; (3); Church Yth Grp; FHA; Girl Scts; Letterman Clb; Sec SADD; Chorus; Var L Chrldng; JV Vllybl; Hon Roll; Pres Acad Fit Awd; KS ST Univ; Med/Obgyn.

URCZYK, KYLIE F; Olathe East Sr HS; Olathe, KS; (3); 1/374; French Clb; Hosp Aide; Latin Clb; Phtg Rptr Yrbk; High Hon Roll; NHS; Pres Acad Fit Awd; Hoffman Intnl Modelingt Schl; Fash Merch Club; Fmly/Cnsmr Sci Club.

URQUILLA, MARIO; Manhattan HS; Manhattan, KS; (2); Boy Scts; Chess Clb; Church Yth Grp; Drama Clb; FTA; Math Tm; Treas SADD; Thesps; Band; Intrml Bsktbl; Acctg.

URTON, SHERRY L; El Dorado HS; El Dorado, KS; (2); Drama Clb; Thesps; Band; Flag Corp; Mrchg Band; Pep Band; School Musical; School Play; Stage Crew.

USHER, LETITIA L; Newton Sr HS; Newton, KS; (4); Art Clb; Key Clb; Office Aide; Chorus; JV Var Bsktbl; JV Vllybl; Hon Roll; NHS; KS ST U; Veterinary Medicine.

USSARY, JOSHUA L; Olathe East Sr HS; Olathe, KS; (2); Band; Mrchg Band; Nwsp; Rep Stu Cncl; High Hon Roll; Hon Roll.

UTHE, JESSICA; Ingalls Jr Sr HS; Pierceville, KS; (3); SADD; Chorus; Drill Tm; Rep Jr Cls; VP Sr Cls; Rep Stu Cncl; Bsktbl; Chrldng; Hon Roll; NHS; KS Univ; Phys Therapy.

UTHE, JESSICA A; Ingalls Jr Sr HS; Garden City, KS; (3); Speech Tm; SADD; Pres Chorus; Yrbk; Rep Jr Cls; VP Sr Cls; Rep Stu Cncl; Var Bsktbl; Var Chrldng; Pres NHS; I-Club Pres; KS U; Phys Thrpy.

VACA, JENNIFER M; Sumner Acad Of Arts & Science; Kansas City, KS; (3); #33 in class; French Clb; JA; Chorus; Rep Frsh Cls; Rep Soph Cls; Rep Stu Cncl; JV Var Bsktbl; French Hon Soc; High Hon Roll; NHS; Pittsbrgh St Univ; Nurs.

VACHAL, JANE A; Garden City Sr HS; Garden City, KS; (3); Hosp Aide; Latin Clb; Band; Color Guard; Mrchg Band; Pep Band; Stage Crew; Co-Ed Nwsp; High Hon Roll; Hon Roll; Magna Cum Laude Natl Latin Exam Latin II; 2nd Pl Fnny Co Sci Fair Trad Ctgry.

VACHON, JESSE D; Ft Scott HS; Fort Scott, KS; (2); JV Bsktbl; JV Var Ftbl; Var Trk; Cit Awd; DAR Awd; High Hon Roll.

VACHON, KATY L; Ft Scott HS; Fort Scott, KS; (4); 1/135; Letterman Clb; School Musical; Phtg Yrbk; Ofcr Stu Cncl; Var Chrldng; Var Tennis; Gov Hon Prg Awd; Sec Treas NHS; Val; His Clb VP; PRIDE; Physics Clb; U Of KS.

VAGUE, DAN W; Ellsworth HS; Ellsworth, KS; (2); 1/80; VP Church Yth Grp; Letterman Clb; Natl FFA Org; Band; Mrchg Band; Pep Band; VP Frsh Cls; JV Bsktbl; Var Ftbl; Var Trk; Aca Hnr Awd; Ag Ed.

VAIL, AMY E; Lawrence HS; Lawrence, KS; (4); 181/566; Church Yth Grp; Treas Sec 4-H; Library Aide; Office Aide; Spanish Clb; Teachers Aide; Var Vllybl; Hon Roll; NHS; Pres Acad Fit Awd; KS Univ; Pediatrician; Obstetri.

VAIL, BECKY; Girard HS; Girard, KS; (4); JV Sftbl; High Hon Roll; Hon Roll; Pittsburgh ST Univ.

VAIL, SAM L; Labette Co HS; Altamont, KS; (3); Var Ftbl; JV Trk; Var Wrstlng.

VAILLE, MANDY J; Blue Valley Northwest HS; Overland Park, KS; (2); Hosp Aide; Vllybl; High Hon Roll; Hon Roll; Peer Facltng; MS Tutor; U Of K; Elem Schl Tchr.

VALDEZ, MATT; Thomas More Prep-Marion HS; Hays, KS; (1); 1/80; Computer Clb; Debate Tm; Latin Clb; Model UN; NFL; Scholastic Bowl; School Musical; School Play; Trk; High Hon Roll; Theatr.

VALENCIA, ROBERTO A; Enterprise Sda Acad; Enterprise, KS; (4); SADD; School Play; Phtg Nwsp; Phtg Yrbk; Ofcr Jr Cls; Pres Sr Cls; Rep Stu Cncl; Intrml Bsktbl; Intrml Ftbl; Intrml Gym; Union Coll.

VALENTIN, MITZI T; Shawnee Mission W Sr HS; Overland Park, KS; (3); Cmnty Wkr; FCA; Hosp Aide; Bsktbl; Sftbl; Var Tennis; Var Trk; Hon Roll; NC.

VALIGURA, CHRISTEL; Jefferson West HS; Meriden, KS; (3); 8/83; Church Yth Grp; French Clb; Library Aide; Office Aide; Band; Jazz Band; Yrbk; Mgr(s); High Hon Roll; NHS; Early Ed.

VALKENAAR, JILL; Augusta Sr HS; Augusta, KS; (4); 23/129; VP Art Clb; Church Yth Grp; Cmnty Wkr; Treas FCA; Letterman Clb; Library Aide; Office Aide; Spanish Clb; Teachers Aide; Varsity Clb; ST Vlybl/Trck; NHS Fin Comm; Prin Hnr Roll; Schlstc Art Gld Key Awd; Schlrshps Ath Bstr/Vlybl/Lions C; Butler Cty CC; Scndry Ed.

VALLE, JOSE A; Newton Sr HS; Newton, KS; (3); Am Leg Boys St; Debate Tm; French Clb; Teachers Aide; Pres Jr Cls; Pres Stu Cncl; JV Bsktbl; JV Socr.

VALLEJOS, CESAR DANIEL; Shawnee Mission E Sr HS; Prairie Village, KS; (2); Cmnty Wkr; Pep Clb; SADD; Orch; Ofcr Bsbl; Wt Lftg; Hon Roll; Drama Clb; Stage Crew; Ftbl; Peer Mdtr; DARE; Star Team; U Of KS; Tchr.

VAN, CUONG V; Wichita North HS; Wichita, KS; (1); #36 in class; Cit Awd; Hon Roll; Sci Olympiad; Penn ST; Mgmt Informtn Sys Mgr.

VAN ALLEN, TAMMY; Wallace Cty HS; Sharon Springs, KS; (3); 5/20; FCA; Pep Clb; SADD; School Musical; Nwsp; Yrbk; Bsktbl; Vllybl; High Hon Roll; NHS; Emporia St Univ; Sec Ed.

VAN BLARICUM, JAY P; Pratt HS; Pratt, KS; (3); Boy Scts; French Clb; Band; Chorus; School Musical; Pres Stu Cncl; Crs Cntry; Ftbl; Golf; NHS; Compose & Perform Piano, Choral & Rock Music In Chrch, Schl Choir & Band.

VAN BUREN, KATHERINE M; Washington HS; Kansas City, KS; (3); 36/247; Church Yth Grp; Drama Clb; FCA; French Clb; German Clb; Library Aide; Quiz Bowl; ROTC; Science Clb; SADD; Pre-Med.

VANBUSKIRK, MONICA; St Thomas Aquinas HS; Olathe, KS; (2); Debate Tm; FBLA; NFL; Quiz Bowl; Acpl Chr; Band; Chorus; Variety Show; Socr; Hon Roll; Roller Blading; Psych; Fine Arts.

VANCE, CHRIS L; Sumner Acad Of Arts & Science; Kansas City, KS; (2); Spanish Clb; JV Ftbl; High Hon Roll; NHS; Spanish NHS.

VANCE, STEVE R; Dighton HS; Dighton, KS; (2); Church Yth Grp; FCA; Scholastic Bowl; Speech Tm; Rep SADD; Band; VP Jr Cls; Var Crs Cntry; Var Trk; High Hon Roll; Math.

VANDECREEK, ROB; Chapman HS; Enterprise, KS; (4); 38/109; 4-H; Natl FFA Org; SADD; Teachers Aide; School Musical; L Bsktbl; L Ftbl; L Golf; Hon Roll; Turf Mgmt.

VAN DENABEELE, MATT E; Gardner-Edgerton HS; Kansas City, KS; (2); Band; Mrchg Band; Orch; Pep Band; School Musical; JV Bsktbl; JV Crs Cntry; JV Golf; High Hon Roll; Summer Bsktbl League; KS U.

VANDEPUTTE, MATTHEW K; J C Harmon HS; Kansas City, KS; (1); Band; Mrchg Band; Pep Band; Cit Awd; Hon Roll; Prfct Atten Awd; KS Univ; Engr.

VANDERBOGART, LEE A; Lawrence HS; Lawrence, KS; (2); Drama Clb; School Play; Ed Yrbk; Socr; Jr Players 2 Ltrs; Hnrs Drama; Photo-1st Pl Awd; U Of KS; Art.

VANDER HAMM, LAURA D; St Marys HS; Hutchinson, KS; (2); Church Yth Grp; Quiz Bowl; Band; Chorus; Mrchg Band; Pep Band; Pres Frsh Cls; Powder Puff Ftbl; High Hon Roll; Cnslng.

VAN DER WEGE, EMMY L; South Barber HS; Hardtner, KS; (2); FHA; GAA; Letterman Clb; SADD; Band; Chorus; Church Choir; Mrchg Band; Pep Band; Sec Frsh Cls; Kayettes Pres.

VANDERWEIDE, DERRICK; Atchison Sr HS; Atchison, KS; (4); 13/123; Am Leg Boys St; Teachers Aide; Var L Ftbl; L Var Wrstlng; High Hon Roll; Hon Roll; HIP Lnchn Chmps; USA Kids Wrstlng St Qulfr; North Cntrl KS Area Voc Tech.

VANDERWIEDE, JOSHUA; Atchison Sr HS; Atchison, KS; (1); Computer Clb; JV Bsbl; Ftbl; L Var Wrstlng; High Hon Roll; Smmr Pgm Asst Girls Sftbl Coach; Sacred Heart Chrch Life Mem; Atchison Kids Wrstlng Club St Qualifier.

VAN DYKE, HEATHER; Lansing HS; Leavenworth, KS; (3); Drama Clb; FCA; NFL; Science Clb; Thesps; Chrldng; Trk; NHS; Church Yth Grp; Debate Tm; Natl Chrldrs Assn All-Amer Chrldr 94/96; Miss Teen KS 1st Rnr-Up Pub Spkng 95; Intl Frgn Lang Awd.

VANDYNE, BLAIR T; Blue Valley North HS; Leawood, KS; (2); 22/250; Model UN; JV Bsktbl; JV Mgr(s); High Hon Roll; NHS; Hrnbl Mntn Chem.

VAN DYNE, SANDRA J; Shawnee Heights Sr HS; Topeka, KS; (3); Sec Church Yth Grp; FTA; Intnl Clb; Pep Clb; Service Clb; SADD; High Hon Roll; High Hnrs Awd For Acad, Math, Home Ec; Mid Amer Nazarene Col; Elem Tch.

VANEK, JENNIFER ANN; Thomas More Prep-Marian HS; Hays, KS; (4); 9/87; Church Yth Grp; Cmnty Wkr; Model UN; Chorus; School Musical; Var Co-Capt Chrldng; Intrml Vllybl; High Hon Roll; Hon Roll; Ambassadors; Liturgy Commission; Amer Legion Awd; Ft Hays ST Univ; Pharmacy.

VANEK, JESSICA M; Thomas More Prep-Marion HS; Hays, KS; (2); 18/85; Latin Clb; JV Var Bsktbl; Var L Crs Cntry; Var L Trk; High Hon Roll; Hon Roll; Trck 3rd 400 M 3rd 4x400 Relay ST Trck Meet; Sprts Med/Optmtry.

VAN EREM, JOHN P; Blue Valley Northwest HS; Overland Park, KS; (1); Hon Roll.

VAN FLEET, JASON; Winfield HS; Winfield, KS; (4); Church Yth Grp; FCA; Library Aide; SADD; Rep Stu Cncl; Socr; Swmmng; Trk; Hon Roll; NHS; 1st Tm AVL Socr; ST Qlfr Swmmng 3 Yrs/Trck 4 Yrs/Pole Vltng 2nd; KS Boys ST Del; Distngshd Ath; CCCC; Bus Mngmt/Cmptrs.

VAN FOSSEN, CHRISTY; Independence HS; Independence, KS; (3); #5 in class; French Clb; Girl Scts; HOBY; Chorus; School Musical; Rep Frsh Cls; Treas Jr Cls; Rep Jr Cls; JV Tennis; High Hon Roll; Dance Ballet, Tap, Jazz & Tchr; KU; Bus Mgmt.

VANG, JUDY T; J C Harmon HS; Kansas City, KS; (2); Church Yth Grp; Key Clb; Chorus; Church Choir; Ed Lit Mag; Hon Roll; Ocmp Sci; Pediatrician.

VAN GAASBEEK, AMBER K; Clifton-Clyde HS; Clyde, KS; (3); FBLA; Booster Clb; Kayetts; KS St Univ; Elem Ed.

VAN GIESON, KASIE; Norwich HS; Norwich, KS; (3); 3/20; Church Yth Grp; HOBY; Quiz Bowl; VP SADD; Drm Mjr(t); School Play; Variety Show; Sec Jr Cls; Var Vllybl; High Hon Roll; York Coll.

VAN GOETHEN, SARAH; Olathe East Sr HS; Olathe, KS; (2); Pep Clb; Spanish Clb; Band; Chorus; Drill Tm; School Play; Sftbl; High Hon Roll; Drill Tm; Hnr For 3.8/Abve GPA.

VAN HORN, KARI; Ottawa HS; Ottawa, KS; (3); 1/180; Am Leg Aux Girls St; Pres FCA; Drill Tm; Rep Jr Cls; Var L Chrldng; Trk; DAR Awd; High Hon Roll; Pres NHS; Library Aide; Tnprt; O Club; Prom Coord; Washburn; Soc Wrk/Chld Law.

VAN HOUTAN, ANDY D; Oskaloosa HS; Ozawkie, KS; (3); SADD; Ofcr Bsbl; Bsktbl; Ftbl; Wt Lftg; Hon Roll; Lgn Bsebll; Bus Mgnt.

VANICE IV, KAER P; Midland Sda Schl; Linwood, KS; (1); Chorus; Hon Roll; U Of KS At Lawrence; Law/Drama.

VAN KIRK, LISA M; Pleasanton HS; Pleasanton, KS; (3); Church Yth Grp; Cmnty Wkr; FHA; Intnl Clb; Library Aide; Natl FFA Org; Spanish Clb; Band; Chorus; Church Choir; Ft Scott CC; Nrs.

VANKOTEN, TRAVIS S; Phillipsburg HS; Phillipsburg, KS; (3); Church Yth Grp; Quiz Bowl; Band; Mrchg Band; Pep Band; Rptr Nwsp; Rep Jr Cls; JV Var Bsktbl; Var L Ftbl; Var L Trk; Ft Hays ST U.

VAN LEEUWEN, KALE H; St Paul HS; Saint Paul, KS; (2); 13/25; Art Clb; Chess Clb; Drama Clb; Quiz Bowl; Scholastic Bowl; Band; School Musical; School Play; Hon Roll; St Act Participant 2 Yrs.

VAN METER, LISA; Mc Pherson HS; Mc Pherson, KS; (4); 12/196; Am Leg Aux Girls St; Church Yth Grp; Cmnty Wkr; French Clb; Math Tm; VP Sec NFL; NHS; Debate Tm; Letterman Clb; Quiz Bowl; KS Hns Schlr; Natl Frnsc Leag Natl Qlfr Stu Cngrss Hs Of Rep; KSHSAA Cls 5 A St Chmpnshp Debate/Frns; KS ST U; Acctng.

VAN METER, PATRICK J; Shawnee Mission E Sr HS; Leawood, KS; (3); JV Bsktbl; JV Tennis; NHS.

VANN, CASSIE A; Lakin HS; Lakin, KS; (2); FCA; Band; Chorus; Jazz Band; Pep Band; School Play; JV Bsktbl; Var Sftbl; Var Trk; JV Vllybl; Fine Arts Coll; Sing.

VANNAMAN, BROOK; Wichita Northwest HS; Valley Center, KS; (4); Am Leg Aux Girls St; Church Yth Grp; Chorus; Ofcr Stu Cncl; Var Bsktbl; Var Swmmng; Var Vllybl; Hon Roll; Drama Clb; Intnl Clb; GCTL Pres; Tns HOPE; WSU; Phy Asst.

VANNAMAN, JOSEPH R; Shawnee Mission S Sr HS; Shawnee Mission, KS; (4); Band; Mrchg Band; JV Socr; Swmmng; Trk; Hon Roll.

VANNOSTER, KERI D; Independence HS; Independence, KS; (2); 66/189; Church Yth Grp; FCA; Pep Clb; SADD; Band; Mrchg Band; Orch; Pep Band; JV Bsktbl; Hon Roll.

VAN NOVER, STACEY L; Wichita South HS; Wichita, KS; (3); 22/294; Chorus; School Musical; Hon Roll; NHS; Wichita St Univ; Bus.

VANOVERSCHELDE, HANNA R; Olathe East Sr HS; Overland Park, KS; (2); Church Yth Grp; Office Aide; Pep Clb; Spanish Clb; Treas Soph Cls; Pres Jr Cls; JV Chrldng; JV Socr; High Hon Roll; Hon Roll.

VANOVERSCHELDE, RILEY B; Olathe East Sr HS; Overland Park, KS; (3); Church Yth Grp; Cmnty Wkr; Debate Tm; Math Clb; Spanish Clb; Teachers Aide; Varsity Clb; Var L Socr; High Hon Roll; Hon Roll; Truman ST; Elec Engrng.

VAN PELT, CARRIE; Wellington Sr HS; Wellington, KS; (1); JA; SADD; Chorus; Intrml Bsktbl; Intrml Vllybl; High Hon Roll; Hon Roll; Jr NHS; KS Univ.

VAN SICKLE, AMY R; Emporia HS; Emporia, KS; (3); 13/259; Pres VP Church Yth Grp; Cmnty Wkr; FBLA; Pep Clb; Teachers Aide; Orch; JV Sftbl; Cit Awd; High Hon Roll; NHS; SMILE Pres & Sec; BASIC Co-Head; DARE Role Model; Emporia ST Univ; Fr; Math; Music.

VAN SICKLE, JEANA; Wichita East HS; Wichita, KS; (3); 66/337; Church Yth Grp; Cmnty Wkr; JV Chrldng; Golf; Hon Roll; NHS; Deacon 1st Presbyn Chrch; Care Coordination Team; Teen Hope AIDS Ed For Elem Stdnts.

VAN SICKLE, JOHN C; Topeka HS; Topeka, KS; (2); 12/600; Model UN; NFL; Thesps; Acpl Chr; School Musical; Variety Show; Socr; Tennis; High Hon Roll; St Champ Duet Actng.

VAN TUYL, JANET; Cair Paravel - Latin Schl; Topeka, KS; (4); 1/15; Church Yth Grp; Drama Clb; Chorus; School Play; Rptr Nwsp; Yrbk; Rptr Frsh Cls; Capt Chrldng; Var Vllybl; Hon Roll; Smmr Wk Grp.

VANTUYL, SHANNA; Perry Lecompton HS; Perry, KS; (3); Letterman Clb; Varsity Clb; Sec Treas Frsh Cls; Sec Treas Soph Cls; Sec Treas Jr Cls; Var Chrldng; Var Pom Pon; Var Sftbl; Hon Roll; Kaw Vly All League 2nd Team Sftbl; Psych.

VAN VLACK, AMANDA; Prairie View Jr Sr HS; La Cygne, KS; (2); 18/98; FHA; Drill Tm; Bsktbl; Score Keeper; Trk; Vllybl; Wt Lftg; High Hon Roll; Hon Roll; Nrsng.

VAN WINKLE, CHRISTINE N; Field Kindley Mem Sr HS; Coffeyville, KS; (3); Church Yth Grp; 4-H; Natl FFA Org; 4-H Awd; Hon Roll; NHS; KS ST U; Ag Sci.

VARDIJAN, ANA; Robert E Clark Jr HS; Edwardsville, KS; (1); Art Clb; High Hon Roll; Hon Roll; KS Univ; Bus/Acctg/Law Schl.

VARDY, AMY M; Arkansas City HS; Arkansas City, KS; (4); Teachers Aide; Socr; Hon Roll; Pres Schlr; Cowley Cty CC.

VARGAS, LAURA; Liberal HS; Liberal, KS; (3); Church Yth Grp; Cmnty Wkr; Chorus; Church Choir; Bsktbl; Vlybl; K U; Tchr.

VARGHESE, MARTIN D; Blue Vlly HS NW; Overland Park, KS; (3); Debate Tm; Intnl Clb; Yrbk; Hon Roll; NHS; St Yrbk Fnlst; MADD Essay Cont Fnlst; Teen HIV Cnslr; Poli.

VARLEY, AMBER; Wichita South HS; Wichita, KS; (3); 10/320; Church Yth Grp; FHA; HOBY; Red Cross Aide; SADD; Mgr(s); Powder Puff Ftbl; High Hon Roll; NHS; YPSA.

VARNER, LISA; Holton HS; Denison, KS; (4); 1/66; Church Yth Grp; VP 4-H; FHA; Band; School Musical; Pres Jr Cls; JV Vllybl; Pres NHS; 2nd Pl Ntl Bible Quiz 94; St Piano Fstvl I Rtng; Grace Coll; Piano Perf.

VARNER, STEPHEN; Holton HS; Denison, KS; (2); Church Yth Grp; 4-H; Band; Chorus; Church Choir; Mrchg Band; Pep Band; School Musical.

VARNEY, AMY; Shawnee Heights HS; Tecumseh, KS; (2); Cmnty Wkr; SADD; Chorus; Yrbk; Rep Soph Cls; Ofcr Stu Cncl; Var L Chrldng; Var L Socr; Hon Roll; Amer Diabetes Assn Cmp Cnslr; Ed/Tchr.

VARNEY, BRENT R; Shawnee Hgts HS; Tecumseh, KS; (3); SADD; Teachers Aide; Acpl Chr; Var L Bsbl; Var L Bsktbl; Var L Ftbl; Hon Roll; Cmnty Wkr; Letterman Clb; Chorus; Acad Awd Algebra II/AMER His; Bsktbl Hnrbl Mntn Cty/Lg; Natl NBC Bsbl Chmpn 93-94; Sci/Engr/Cmptrs.

VARVEL, SCOTT D; Leroy HS; Le Roy, KS; (2); Church Yth Grp; Quiz Bowl; Scholastic Bowl; Band; Pep Band; Hon Roll; Musician.

VASEL, HEIDI J; Northeast Magnet HS; Wichita, KS; (2); 15/113; Church Yth Grp; Cmnty Wkr; 4-H; Library Aide; Service Clb; Chorus; Church Choir; Vllybl; High Hon Roll; NHS; Sci & Math Awd; Prncpls List; Schlrath Awd; Bio.

VASQUEZ, CHRISSY M; Blue Valley North HS; Leawood, KS; (2); Church Yth Grp; Hosp Aide; Model UN; Band; Mrchg Band; Pep Band; School Musical; Capt L Golf; Hon Roll; Kays Club; AZ ST U; Bus/Pre-Med/Golf.

VAUGHN, CARA; Oxford HS; Oxford, KS; (1); Varsity Clb; Rep Frsh Cls; Chrldng; Crs Cntry; Trk; Kayettes Frosh Rep.

VAUGHN, CDRIC D; Wichita South HS; Wichita, KS; (1); Clark Univ; Busmktng.

VAUGHN, DEREK S; Colby Sr HS; Colby, KS; (3); 4-H; Nwsp; Fld Hcky; Wrstlng; 4-H Awd; All Area Ftbl Tm; Wrstlng St Qlfr; I Dr You Awd; Sprts Med.

VAUGHN, ERIC; Waverly HS; Waverly, KS; (3); 3/15; Band; Chorus; Pep Band; School Musical; JV Bsktbl; Var Ftbl; High Hon Roll; NHS; Prfct Atten Awd; Cmnty Wkr; Frnscs Tm, Brnz Mdl; Msns Acad Awd; Nwcmr Drama Awd; Cmptr Sci.

VAUGHN, JENNIFER L; Lawrence HS; Jefferson City, MO; (2); Church Yth Grp; FCA; Latin Clb; Teachers Aide; Rep Stu Cncl; Tennis; High Hon Roll; Pres Acad Fit Awd; Ntnly Rnkd Tns Plyr.

VAVRICKA, CHRIS V; Ness City HS; Ness City, KS; (3); Var L Bsktbl; Var L Ftbl; Var L Trk; High Hon Roll; NHS; Bus Mgmt.

VAWTER, AMANDA J; Topeka West HS; Topeka, KS; (3); French Clb; Pep Clb; SADD; Bsktbl; Sftbl; Vllybl; French Hon Soc; Hon Roll; Sftbl Ltrs, All-City, All-League; Bsktbl Ltrs; Vlybl Ltrs, All-League, All-City Hnrb Mntn.

VAZQUEZ, FELICITA; Junction City HS; Fort Riley, KS; (3); Pep Clb; JV Bsktbl; Var Chrldng; Hon Roll; Dance; Schl Act; CA; Med.

VAZQUEZ, JAMES P; Sumner Acad Of Arts And Sci; Kansas City, KS; (4); 36/197; Pres Art Clb; Cmnty Wkr; L Socr; High Hon Roll; NHS; Ntl Merit SF; Spanish NHS; Spanish Clb; Intrml Ftbl; Hon Roll; Natl Hispnc Schlr; MADD; Hrt Of Amrca Shkspr Fstvl Pstr Cnts Wnr 1st Pl 95 & 96; Cooper Union; Grphc Dsgn Artst.

VEEDER, BETH M; Wichita East HS; Wichita, KS; (2); Debate Tm; Pom Pon; Wichita St Univ; Bus.

VEERHUSEN, CALIE M; Herington HS; Herington, KS; (1); 2/40; Church Yth Grp; Cmnty Wkr; FHA; Quiz Bowl; Band; Mrchg Band; Pep Band; Treas Frsh Cls; JV Bsktbl; High Hon Roll; Arch.

VEESART, LAUREL L; Garden City Sr HS; Garden City, KS; (1); Church Yth Grp; Girl Scts; Hosp Aide; Speech Tm; Chorus; Church Choir; School Play; Hon Roll; KS ST; Tchng.

VEGA, AMOS; Salina HS South; Salina, KS; (2); Debate Tm; Letterman Clb; NFL; Teachers Aide; JV Trk; High Hon Roll; Guitarist In Area Bands; U Of KS.

VEGA, DEBORAH S; Wichita Southeast HS; Wichita, KS; (2); Church Yth Grp; Spanish Clb; Chorus; Church Choir; Cmptr Sci/Law.

VEGA, MICHAEL A; Washington HS; Kansas City, KS; (4); ROTC; Teachers Aide; Hon Roll; 2 Schlrshp Awds K Louie & Victor Lerner Traveling All Star League; Wichita St; Bus Admin.

VEH, SAMANTHA J; Shawnee Mission N HS; Overland Park, KS; (4); 32/360; Drama Clb; Key Clb; Pep Clb; High Hon Roll; Hon Roll; NHS; Baker Univ; Intl Bus.

VELADOR, APRIL C; Hays HS; Hays, KS; (2); Dance Clb; Drama Clb; Thesps; School Play; Stage Crew; Cit Awd; Hon Roll; Prfct Atten Awd; Martial Arts; Gallery Openings; Studio Asst Visual Arts; Actress/FBI.

VELASCO, MARC J; Shawnee Heights HS; Topeka, KS; (1); Math Tm; Quiz Bowl; Orch; School Musical; School Play; JV Socr; VP Hon Roll.

VELASQUEZ, EVELINA; Ulysses HS; Ulysses, KS; (4); 1/96; Debate Tm; FBLA; Letterman Clb; Library Aide; NFL; Spanish Clb; SADD; Ofcr Stu Cncl; High Hon Roll; NHS; Our Lady Of Lk U; Bus.

VENERABLE, JENNIFER; Sumner Acad; Kansas City, KS; (1); Dance Clb; NFL; Pep Clb; Spanish Clb; Chorus; JV Chrldng; Hon Roll; Duke; Dance.

VENHAUS, STEPHANIE; Maize HS; Wichita, KS; (2); Teachers Aide; High Hon Roll; Hon Roll; NHS; Pres Acad Fit Awd; Aca Ltr; Peer Tutor; Bus.

VENKATESH, NINA; Blue Valley Northwest HS; Leawood, KS; (3); Art Clb; Debate Tm; Drama Clb; French Clb; Hosp Aide; Intnl Clb; NFL; Speech Tm; Temple Yth Grp; Stage Crew; Natl Hnr Soc; Alliance Francouis Ambssdr; Jr Natl Hnr Soc; Hnr Rll; WHO Projectthrough UN; Columbia Univ; Pol Sci.

VENTERS, CASEY L; Dighton HS; Dighton, KS; (1); Drama Clb; FCA; Letterman Clb; Pep Clb; Speech Tm; Band; Church Choir; Jazz Band; Mrchg Band; Pep Band.

VERBECK, VALERIE J; Attica Public Schl; Attica, KS; (3); 3/17; Church Yth Grp; Cmnty Wkr; NFL; Quiz Bowl; Scholastic Bowl; Band; Chorus; Pep Band; JV Bsktbl; High Hon Roll; Lead Church Play; Top Stdnt Math; Pratt Acad Olumpics; Emporia ST; Acctng/RN.

VERCIO, MICHAEL; Enterprise Sda Acad; Wichita, KS; (3); Model UN; Office Aide; Co-Ed Nwsp; VP Stu Cncl; Intrml Bsktbl; Intrml Vllybl; High Hon Roll; Union Coll; Physics.

VERING, KENDRA; St John's HS; Beloit, KS; (4); 3/14; Church Yth Grp; HOBY; Pep Clb; Quiz Bowl; Speech Tm; SADD; Chorus; Yrbk; Pres Soph Cls; VP Jr Cls; Danforth I Dare You Awd; Homcmng Qn; Xray Tech.

VERMILLION, CHRIS A; Liberal HS; Liberal, KS; (3); French Clb; Crs Cntry; Trk; Wt Lftg; Jr NHS; NHS; Bus.

VERNON, ANGIE; Dodge City HS; Dodge City, KS; (2); SADD; Teachers Aide; Yrbk; JV Chrldng; KAYS; Upwrd Bound Pgm; Edctnl Tlnt Srch Pgm; WV U; Dance.

VERNON, PAUL R; Maize HS; Wichita, KS; (2); 1/290; Debate Tm; Math Tm; NFL; Scholastic Bowl; SADD; JV Golf; High Hon Roll; NHS; Prfct Atten Awd; U Of KS.

VERNON, TREY L; Ft Scott HS; Fort Scott, KS; (2); Pep Clb; Chorus; School Musical; JV Bsktbl; Var Crs Cntry; Intrml Ftbl; Var Trk.

VERSAW, LEA ANNE R; Olathe North Sr HS; Olathe, KS; (4); 100/357; Church Yth Grp; Dance Clb; FCA; Pep Clb; Spanish Clb; Teachers Aide; Band; Chorus; Drill Tm; Mrchg Band; Fshn Clb/Shw Mdl; KS ST Univ; Elem Ed.

VERSAW, MARIANNE L; Olathe North Sr HS; Olathe, KS; (1); Church Yth Grp; Cmnty Wkr; Dance Clb; FCA; Letterman Clb; Pep Clb; Spanish Clb; Teachers Aide; Band; Chorus; Fshn Clb/Shws; Southwest MO ST Univ; Nrsng.

VERTZ, KELLY R; Turner HS; Kansas City, KS; (4); #12 in class; FBLA; Science Clb; SADD; Teachers Aide; Yrbk; Ofcr Stu Cncl; Cit Awd; VP NHS; Prfct Atten Awd; St Schlr; Top 10%; Kansas City CC; Bus.

VESPESTAD, HEATHER L; Lawrence HS; Lawrence, KS; (3); Church Yth Grp; Office Aide; Teachers Aide; Bsktbl; Sftbl; Tennis; Cit Awd; High Hon Roll; Prfct Atten Awd; Bell Choir; Psych.

VESTER, CANDACE S; Wyandotte HS; Kansas City, KS; (1); Church Yth Grp; Dental.

VETTER, GERICA L; Beloit Jr Sr HS; Beloit, KS; (2); Church Yth Grp; Letterman Clb; Spanish Clb; SADD; Chorus; Orch; Sec Soph Cls; JV Intrml Bsktbl; Mgr(s); JV Vllybl; Ftr Med Careers; Comm Orch.

VEVERKA, KARA; Pratt HS; Pratt, KS; (4); 23/96; FHA; Hosp Aide; Library Aide; Office Aide; Pep Clb; SADD; Chorus; Yrbk; Ofcr Stu Cncl; Var Chrldng; U Of KS; Psych.

VICKNAIR, ASHLEY; Derby HS; Derby, KS; (3); Church Yth Grp; Dance Clb; Teachers Aide; Drill Tm; Bsktbl; Chrldng; Socr; Vllybl; Hon Roll.

VIERGETS, AARON; Goodland HS; Goodland, KS; (3); Am Leg Boys St; Math Tm; Natl FFA Org; Band; Chorus; School Musical; Cit Awd; 4-H Awd; Hon Roll; NHS; 4 Yr Coll; Ecologist.

VIERTHALER, BETH; Spearville Jr Sr HS; Spearville, KS; (1); 4-H; Pep Clb; Quiz Bowl; Band; Chorus; Drill Tm; School Play; Rep Stu Cncl; JV Trk; Hon Roll; KSU.

VIERTHALER, JESSE; Cunningham HS; Isabel, KS; (1); 9/25; Church Yth Grp; Pep Clb; Quiz Bowl; Scholastic Bowl; Science Clb; SADD; Church Choir; Stage Crew; JV Bsktbl; Var Mgr(s); KS U; Med.

VIERTHALER, KATHERINE; Spearville Jr Sr HS; Spearville, KS; (3); Quiz Bowl; Band; Chorus; School Play; Ed Lit Mag; Pres Jr Cls; Var Bsktbl; Var Trk; Var Vllybl; Hon Roll; KSU; Vet.

VIESCAS, RENEE L; Claflin Jr Sr HS; Ellsworth, KS; (3); Church Yth Grp; FHA; Pep Clb; Quiz Bowl; Scholastic Bowl; Speech Tm; School Play; Ed Yrbk; Var L Tennis; Hon Roll; Frnscs; 1st Pl ST/REGNL Jrnlsm; Jrnlsm/Graphic Dsgn.

VIEUX, ALEXANDER N; Garden City Sr HS; Garden City, KS; (4); French Clb; Latin Clb; Quiz Bowl; Scholastic Bowl; Science Clb; Band; Church Choir; Jazz Band; Mrchg Band; Orch; Ryu Kyu Kempo Karate Blue Belt; Ft Hays ST Univ; Elec Engrng.

VIEUX, ANDREA R; Lawrence HS; Lawrence, KS; (2); Church Yth Grp; Office Aide; Spanish Clb; Teachers Aide; Pres Soph Cls; Treas Stu Cncl; Var L Bsktbl; Var L Swmmng; Cit Awd; High Hon Roll; U Of KS; Med.

VIEYRA, MIGUEL; Marysville HS; Marysville, KS; (1); Band; Jazz Band; Mrchg Band; Pep Band; Stage Crew; Var Tennis; Var Wrstlng; High Hon Roll; Kiwanis Awd; Pres Acad Fit Awd; GCTL; Marysville Yth Coalition.

VIGNERY, CURTIS J; Desoto HS; De Soto, KS; (3); Var L Bsbl; Var L Bsktbl; Var L Ftbl; Wt Lftg; Hon Roll; Pres Acad Fit Awd; 3 Yr Ltr Wnnr In Bsktbl; 3 Yr Ltr Wnnr Bsbl; Shawnee Herald All-Area Team Ftbl & Bsktbl.

VILLAMANA, MOLLY; Decatur Cmty Jr Sr HS; Oberlin, KS; (4); 2/37; Am Leg Aux Girls St; Church Yth Grp; Cmnty Wkr; Drama Clb; Hosp Aide; Key Clb; Letterman Clb; Science Clb; Spanish Clb; Speech Tm; Kytts Bd Mem; Asstns; Attrny.

VILLAREAL JR, MICHAEL D; Wellington Sr HS; Wellington, KS; (4); 9/121; Am Leg Boys St; Math Tm; Scholastic Bowl; High Hon Roll; MA Inst Of Tech; Physics.

VILLARREAL, SALLIE A; Thomas More Prep-Marion HS; Grand Prairie, TX; (2); Spanish Clb; Band; Mrchg Band; Pep Band; JV Co-Capt Bsktbl; JV Capt Sftbl; JV Vllybl; Hon Roll; TX Chrstn U.

VILLEGAS, AMIE L; Hayden HS; Topeka, KS; (2); Intnl Clb; Spanish Clb; Intrml Bsktbl; Var JV Sftbl; Var JV Vllybl; Intrml Wt Lftg; High Hon Roll; Hon Roll; Work-A-Thon.

VINCIGUERRA, ANDY; Shawnee Mission Northwest HS; Lenexa, KS; (3); 60/425; Teachers Aide; Var Bsbl; Hon Roll; NHS; Northwestern U.

VINER, LINDSAY A; Oskaloosa HS; Oskaloosa, KS; (3); 1/78; Church Yth Grp; Cmnty Wkr; VP FBLA; FHA; Letterman Clb; Pep Clb; SADD; Sec Soph Cls; L Pom Pon; Cit Awd; Outstdng Span & Bus Stu; Optometry; Bio.

VINEYARD, AMY; Independence HS; Independence, KS; (1); Girl Scts; Library Aide; Quiz Bowl; Scholastic Bowl; Band; Mrchg Band; Pep Band; Stage Crew; Trk; Rating Reg Bnd Fstvl Frnch Horn; K ST; Bnd Dir/Surgeon.

VINSONHALER, JASON S; Seaman Sr HS; Topeka, KS; (3); 55/265; Church Yth Grp; FCA; FBLA; Key Clb; Natl FFA Org; Church Choir; Ofcr Bsbl; Ftbl; Wt Lftg; Hon Roll; GMI; Mech Engr.

VIN ZANT, EMILY; Kapaun-Mt Carmel HS; Wichita, KS; (3); Dance Clb; French Clb; Pep Clb; Q&S; Yrbk; Ofcr Frsh Cls; Ofcr Soph Cls; Ofcr Jr Cls; Ofcr Sr Cls; Ofcr Stu Cncl.

VIN ZANT, KATHARINE R; Derby HS; Derby, KS; (3); Church Yth Grp; Drama Clb; Thesps; Band; School Play; Stage Crew; High Hon Roll; NHS; Prfct Atten Awd.

VISALLI, JERICA; Columbus HS; Columbus, KS; (3); 11/98; Church Yth Grp; Math Tm; Pep Clb; Spanish Clb; Band; Jazz Band; Mrchg Band; Pep Band; High Hon Roll; Hon Roll; Tri-M Hnrs Soc; Kay Club; Drafting Club; OK Univ Of Sci/Arts.

VISSER, GREG; Centralia Schl; Goff, KS; (4); 15/23; VP 4-H; Stage Crew; Rptr Nwsp; Wt Lftg; 4-H Awd; Hon Roll; FFA; NCK Vo-Tech; Ag Mechanic.

VITT, JESSICA; Erie HS; Erie, KS; (4); 13/43; Church Yth Grp; FCA; Pep Clb; Service Clb; SADD; Ed Nwsp; Ed Yrbk; Var JV Chrldng; Var L Pom Pon; Var L Trk; KAYS; NCA All Amer Chrldr; Pittsburg ST U; Elem Ed.

VITZTUM, JO ANN; Thomas More Prep-Marion HS; Hays, KS; (4); 9/97; Model UN; Band; VP Frsh Cls; Pres Soph Cls; Pres Jr Cls; Pres Stu Cncl; Cit Awd; DAR Awd; High Hon Roll; Bio Sci.

VIX, KARIE L; Olathe East Sr HS; Olathe, KS; (2); 1/416; Church Yth Grp; Math Clb; Spanish Clb; Chorus; Drill Tm; School Musical; Treas Stu Cncl; L Bsktbl; High Hon Roll; Spanish NHS; Dist Hnr Choir; Voc Ensmbl I Rating ST Select Ensmbl Soph Outstdng Musician Awd; Archtctrl Engr.

VO, TRINH; Wichita East HS; Wichita, KS; (2); #34 in class; Band; Church Choir; School Musical; Socr; Hon Roll; Bible Clb; Wichita ST Univ; Aerospace Eng.

VOBORIL, HEIDI; White Rock HS; Esbon, KS; (3); 4/7; Letterman Clb; Pep Clb; Speech Tm; SADD; Sec Frsh Cls; Sec Soph Cls; Sec Jr Cls; Var L Bsbl; Var L Chrldng; Var L Vllybl; Cosmetologist.

VOBORIL, MLADA A; Bishop Carroll Catholic HS; Wichita, KS; (3); 1/170; Church Yth Grp; Debate Tm; Scholastic Bowl; Spanish Clb; School Musical; School Play; Sec Sr Cls; High Hon Roll; NHS; Ntl Merit Ltr; Sndy Schl Aide; Scndry Edctn.

VOCASEK, ANDREW; Dodge City HS; Dodge City, KS; (4); 14/250; Church Yth Grp; Drama Clb; Speech Tm; SADD; School Musical; School Play; Nwsp; High Hon Roll; NHS; Pres Acad Fit Awd; KS ST U; Theatre.

VOGEL, ADRIAN L; Cimarron HS; Cimarron, KS; (2); Boy Scts; 4-H; Treas Natl FFA Org; Band; Pep Band; Ftbl; Trk; Wt Lftg; 4-H Awd; Hon Roll; Ft Hays ST Univ; Bus Admin.

VOGEL, ALICIA D; Cimarron HS; Cimarron, KS; (3); 4-H; Girl Scts; Pep Clb; Acpl Chr; Band; Chorus; Mrchg Band; Pep Band; School Play; Stage Crew; Ft Hays Univ; Radiologist.

VOGEL, BRIAN J; Bishop Carroll Catholic HS; Wichita, KS; (2); Ftbl; Wt Lftg; Hon Roll; USMC.

VOGEL, JOSHUA E; Spearville Jr Sr HS; Wright, KS; (2); 5/30; Church Yth Grp; Quiz Bowl; Teachers Aide; Chorus; Var L Ftbl; Var L Trk; Wt Lftg; High Hon Roll; Hon Roll; NHS; Bslb-Summer League; Pittsburg ST; Comp Sci.

VOGEL, KRISTIN; Phillipsburg HS; Phillipsburg, KS; (2); Quiz Bowl; Band; Yrbk; Pres Soph Cls; Var JV Bsktbl; Chrldng; Var L Trk; Var L Vllybl; High Hon Roll; NFL; Kays Clb; Gifted Pgm.

VOGEL, KRISTY L; Dodge City HS; Dodge City, KS; (3); Church Yth Grp; Red Cross Aide; SADD; Band; Mrchg Band; Pep Band; Stage Crew; Hon Roll; NHS; Vol Work; Emporia ST Univ; Mech Engrng.

VOGEL, LINDSAY; Manhattan HS; Manhattan, KS; (3); Am Leg Aux Girls St; Pep Clb; Sec Frsh Cls; Sec Soph Cls; Sec Jr Cls; Var Chrldng; JV Var Tennis; Hon Roll; Sec NHS; KS ST Univ; Bus; Fin; Pre-Law.

VOGEL, SHERRIE L; Shawnee Heights Sr HS; Tecumseh, KS; (2); Sec SADD; Color Guard; Hon Roll.

VOGT, TRESSA A; Campus HS; Haysville, KS; (4); 6/199; Boy Scts; Girl Scts; VP Intnl Clb; Science Clb; Teachers Aide; Band; Chorus; Mrchg Band; Pep Band; School Musical; KS Hnr Schlr; Brd Of Regents Awd; Girl Sct Gold Awd; Wichita ST U.

VOGTS, ANGIE M; Sublette HS; Sublette, KS; (3); 19/29; Chorus; School Musical; JV Vllybl; Prfct Atten Awd; Amer Field Serv; Gov Cntr Teen Ldrshp; KS Assn Youth; Brown Mackey; Exec Sec.

VOGTS, LANA J; Canton-Galva HS; Canton, KS; (2); #4 in class; Sec FBLA; SADD; Band; Yrbk; Sec Soph Cls; Rep Stu Cncl; JV Capt Bsktbl; JV Vllybl; High Hon Roll; NHS; Fort Hays ST.

VOGTS, VALECIA L; Flinthills HS; Rosalia, KS; (3); 3/20; 4-H; Letterman Clb; Quiz Bowl; SADD; Nwsp; Sec Frsh Cls; Sec Soph Cls; Sec Jr Cls; Rep Stu Cncl; Var Bsktbl.

VOLDEN, MANDY; Elkhart HS; Elkhart, KS; (3); 20/32; Natl FFA Org; Office Aide; JV Bsktbl; JV Chrldng; JV Trk; Hon Roll; Ft Hays CC; Mgnt.

VOLK, JENNIFER; Tonganoxie HS; Tonganoxie, KS; (4); 25/120; Church Yth Grp; 4-H; Natl FFA Org; Science Clb; SADD; 4-H Awd; High Hon Roll; NHS; Pres Acad Fit Awd; NE St Dary Quiz Bowl Tem 92 & 95-96; Northst NE HS Rod Clb Sec; NE St Holstn Assn Rptr 95 & VP 96; KS ST U; Animal Scis.

VOLK, JULIE A; Haven HS; Hutchinson, KS; (2); FCA; FHA; Hosp Aide; Band; Mrchg Band; Pep Band; High Hon Roll; Art Cls Frosh Yr Had Spcl Project To Paint Mural For Prom; Point Loma; Art.

VOLK, LISA; Circle HS; El Dorado, KS; (4); 1/90; FHA; Quiz Bowl; Spanish Clb; SADD; Pres Frsh Cls; VP Soph Cls; Pres Stu Cncl; Cit Awd; High Hon Roll; NHS; U AR; Nrsng.

VOLLERTSEN, LESLIE D; Norton Comm HS; Norton, KS; (3); Church Yth Grp; Sec Natl FFA Org; SADD; Teachers Aide; Var L Bsktbl; Var L Pom Pon; Var L Vllybl; High Hon Roll; NHS; Var Trk; Washington DC Ldrshp Conf Schol; KS Assoc For Yth Treas; KS St Univ; Animal Sci.

VOLMER, MONICA D; Field Kindley Mem Sr HS; Coffeyville, KS; (3); French Clb; Nwsp; Pom Pon; High Hon Roll; NHS; Pittsburg ST Univ; Nrsng.

VOLTS, STACY L; Basehor Linwood HS; Linwood, KS; (3); Science Clb; SADD; Stat Bsktbl; High Hon Roll; Hon Roll; Lawyer.

VON FANGE, JILL; Lincoln Jr Sr HS; Lincoln, KS; (1); Treas Church Yth Grp; Treas Pres 4-H; FHA; Letterman Clb; Acpl Chr; Band; Chorus; School Play; Sec Frsh Cls; JV Var Bsktbl; Tchng/Music.

VONGPHRACHANH, KAN; Turner HS; Kansas City, KS; (4); Art Clb; FBLA; VICA; Hon Roll; U Of KS; Medcl Technlgy.

VONGTHEVA, PANITHA; Emporia HS; Emporia, KS; (3); French Clb; Cit Awd; High Hon Roll; Hon Roll; Emporia ST U; Med Asst/Pre Med.

VONGVILATH, AMY; Liberal HS; Russellville, AR; (2); Church Yth Grp; Cmnty Wkr; Natl Beta Clb; Spanish Clb; Teachers Aide; Church Choir; Ofcr Bsbl; Sftbl; Vllybl; Hon Roll.

VON KNORRING, ANGIE; Spring Hill HS; Spring Hill, KS; (4); 51/98; Am Leg Aux Girls St; Church Yth Grp; Dance Clb; Debate Tm; Drama Clb; FCA; Letterman Clb; NFL; Pep Clb; SADD; Drill Tm Capt; JCCC; Cosmetology.

VON LINTEL, AMY; Shawnee Mission E Sr HS; Shawnee Mission, KS; (3); 7/400; French Clb; Pres Natl Beta Clb; Q&S; Rptr Yrbk; Chrldng; Tennis; Trk; French Hon Soc; High Hon Roll; Hon Roll; SHARE; Habtat For Humnty; Histry.

VON LINTEL, MANDI; Goodland HS; Goodland, KS; (3); Church Yth Grp; Debate Tm; FHA; Spanish Clb; Teachers Aide; JV Tennis; JV Vllybl; Cit Awd; Hon Roll; AFS Jr Rep; Engrng.

VON SCHRILTZ, AMANDA E; Washburn Rural HS; Topeka, KS; (2); 63/380; Band; Jazz Band; Mrchg Band; Orch; Pep Band; Mgr Mgr(s); Sftbl; Vllybl; High Hon Roll; Jr NHS; YMCA Vlybl; Ken Berry League Sftbl; KS ST; Sports Med/PT.

VON WEDELL, TRACY; Columbus HS; Columbus, KS; (3); 16/95; Art Clb; Bus Profs of Am; FHA; Drill Tm; Nwsp; JV Chrldng; JV Golf; JV Tennis; Intrml Wt Lftg; Hon Roll; Natl Yng Ldrs Conf Almni; Pittsburg ST Univ; Vet Sci.

VOORHEES, AMANDA J; Maize HS; Maize, KS; (2); 192/300; Hosp Aide; SADD; Chorus; School Musical; Variety Show; Wesley Med Ctr Vol; Surgeon.

VOOS, SCOTT A; Manhattan HS; Manhattan, KS; (3); Am Leg Boys St; FCA; Letterman Clb; Science Clb; Spanish Clb; SADD; Teachers Aide; Varsity Clb; Rep Stu Cncl; L Bsbl; Law Enfcmnt.

VORAK, NATALIE L; Bishop Carroll Catholic HS; Wichita, KS; (2); 4/200; Church Yth Grp; Drama Clb; Letterman Clb; Acpl Chr; Church Choir; School Musical; Variety Show; Ofcr Jr Cls; High Hon Roll; Hon Roll; Select Womens Choir; High Rating At St Vocal Music Cont; Span Awd; Musical Therapy.

VOSBURG, JEREMY W; Sedgwick HS; Sedgwick, KS; (3); 7/40; Am Leg Boys St; Letterman Clb; Quiz Bowl; Variety Show; Rep Nwsp; Rep Yrbk; Var Bsktbl; Var Trk; High Hon Roll; Hon Roll; Med.

VOSBURG, SU ANN; Sedgwick HS; Sedgwick, KS; (2); 3/40; FHA; Letterman Clb; Band; School Musical; Rep Stu Cncl; Chrldng; Vllybl; High Hon Roll; NHS; Kays.

VOSS, MONICA G; Cheney Jr Sr HS; Cheney, KS; (2); 1/50; Church Yth Grp; Band; Chorus; Rep Frsh Cls; Rep Soph Cls; JV Bsktbl; Var L Trk; JV Var Vllybl; High Hon Roll; Pres Acad Fit Awd; Girls Glee Clb.

VOTH, AMANDAD; Independence HS; Independence, KS; (2); French Clb; SADD; Chorus; School Play; Rep Soph Cls; Var L Chrldng; Dance.

VOTH, KRISTINA L; Arkansas City HS; Arkansas City, KS; (4); FHA; SADD; Teachers Aide; Hon Roll; NHS; Ntl Merit Ltr; Pres Awd For Educl Excllnc; Cowley Cty CC; Acctng.

VOTRUBA, JULIE A; Buhler HS; Hutchinson, KS; (2); Debate Tm; Hosp Aide; Letterman Clb; Spanish Clb; Varsity Clb; Chorus; Stage Crew; Chrldng; Hon Roll; Law/Med.

VOUGHT, KATHERN J; Hope HS; Hope, KS; (3); Church Yth Grp; FBLA; FHA; GAA; Natl FFA Org; NFL; SADD; Band; Chorus; Jazz Band; Chem Awd; UBMS Prog; Mrne Bio.

VRANA, AMANDA; Inman Jr Sr HS; Windom, KS; (2); Art Clb; 4-H; Pep Clb; School Play; Nwsp; Yrbk; Chrldng; Vllybl; Hon Roll; Church Yth Grp; Mltpl Sclrss Rd A Thn; Hutchinson CC; Law.

VRATIL, ANDREW J; Blue Valley Northwest HS; Overland Park, KS; (2); Math Tm; Scholastic Bowl; Spanish Clb; Varsity Clb; Band; Mrchg Band; Ftbl; Socr; Trk; Wt Lftg; KSHSAA Excel; Duke TIP Prog.

VRBAS, ERIK; Atwood HS; Atwood, KS; (4); Boy Scts; Church Yth Grp; 4-H; Letterman Clb; Natl FFA Org; Ski Clb; SADD; Varsity Clb; School Play; Rep Stu Cncl; Garden City CC; Forestry.

VSETECKA, EMILY D; Great Bend Sr HS; Great Bend, KS; (4); 40/230; Pep Clb; Spanish Clb; SADD; Mrchg Band; Pep Band; JV Bsktbl; Vllybl; Hon Roll; Ballet; Mdrn Dncr; Barton Cty CC; Engrng.

VU, DUY; Garden City Sr HS; Garden City, KS; (4); 1/334; Am Leg Aux Girls St; Chess Clb; FHA; German Clb; Hosp Aide; JCL; Latin Clb; Math Tm; Science Clb; SADD; DARE Role Mdl; SE Asian Clb Pres & Sec; Crmstpprs; Dstngshd Schlstc Achvt Awd; U Of KS; Bio.

VU, HOANG T; Wichita East HS; Wichita, KS; (4); 4/337; Boy Scts; Church Yth Grp; Cmnty Wkr; English Clb; French Clb; Library Aide; Science Clb; Service Clb; Church Choir; Ofcr Stu Cncl; Future Amer Awd; Mst Outstndng Stu Awd; Star Employee; Wichita ST U; Med.

VU, JOHN KHANG N; Wichita Northwest HS; Wichita, KS; (4); 1/339; Am Leg Boys St; Cmnty Wkr; Computer Clb; FTA; Sec Intnl Clb; Pres Math Clb; Capt Math Tm; Capt Quiz Bowl; Capt Scholastic Bowl; Capt Science Clb.

VU, JULIE K; Heights HS; Wichita, KS; (4); 12/242; Cmnty Wkr; Red Cross Aide; Sec SADD; Rptr Nwsp; VP Jr Cls; VP Sr Cls; Rep Stu Cncl; Var Socr; Var Tennis; NHS; Peer Ldr; Peer Mdtr; USD 259 Dist N Cncl Rep; Kansas Univ; Bio.

VU, NGA T; Southeast HS; Wichita, KS; (4); #1 in class; Treas Spanish Clb; Orch; Treas Frsh Cls; JV Tennis; Gov Hon Prg Awd; NHS; Pres Schlr; St Schlr; Val; Piano; Tandy Tech Schlr; Advncd Plcmnt Distgnd Schlr; Wichita ST Univ.

VULGAMORE, JARROD L; Cheney Jr Sr HS; Cheney, KS; (2); Drama Clb; Quiz Bowl; Scholastic Bowl; Band; Church Choir; Jazz Band; Mrchg Band; Pep Band; School Play; Stat Bsktbl; Bus.

VYZOUREK, JOE; Atwood HS; Atwood, KS; (4); 13/39; Church Yth Grp; Letterman Clb; Natl FFA Org; Speech Tm; Varsity Clb; Band; Mrchg Band; Orch; Pep Band; Stage Crew; Disc Jockey Svcs To Chrch, Schl & Cmnty; Colby CC; Mass Commnctns.

WACKER, AUDRA; Sylvan Unified HS; Lincoln, KS; (4); 3/15; Pres Church Yth Grp; Pres 4-H; Teachers Aide; Band; Mgr(s); Stat Trk; 4-H Awd; Hon Roll; NHS; Pep Clb; Cloud Cty CC.

WACKER, CARISA; Greensburg HS; Greensburg, KS; (3); 6/29; FHA; Spanish Clb; Teachers Aide; Chorus; Rep Frsh Cls; Rep Soph Cls; Rep Jr Cls; Rep Sr Cls; Bsktbl; Trk; Vlybl All League/All Area/All ST; Bsktbl All League; Psych.

WACKERLY, MELISSA; Wellsville Jr Sr HS; Wellsville, KS; (3); 5/50; Debate Tm; FCA; FBLA; Intnl Clb; SADD; Vllybl; High Hon Roll; Hon Roll; NHS; KAYS; U Of Puget Sound; Bus/Math.

WADDELL, LISA A; Field Kindley Memrl HS; Coffeyville, KS; (4); 10/150; Cmnty Wkr; Debate Tm; French Clb; NFL; Nwsp; Chrldng; High Hon Roll; NHS; Pres Schlr; CCC JC; Law.

WADDY, JAMI M; Wyandotte HS; Kansas City, KS; (4); Cmnty Wkr; Drama Clb; Hosp Aide; Office Aide; Thesps; Church Choir; Flag Corp; Stage Crew; Ofcr Sr Cls; Ofcr Stu Cncl; KS ST U; Psych.

WADE, AMBER R; Galena HS; Galena, KS; (1); Church Yth Grp; FCA; FBLA; SADD; Band; Jazz Band; Mrchg Band; Pep Band; School Play; Pres Frsh Cls; Schlstc Achvmnt Awd; Ozark Chrstn Coll; Elem Educ.

WADE, BRADLEY; Prairie View Jr Sr HS; La Cygne, KS; (3); 1/67; Am Leg Boys St; FCA; School Musical; Pres Sr Cls; VP Stu Cncl; Var JV Bsktbl; Var Crs Cntry; Var Trk; High Hon Roll; NHS; Nrsng.

WADE, ISAAC I; Galena HS; Galena, KS; (2); Church Yth Grp; FCA; FBLA; FHA; Scholastic Bowl; SADD; Acpl Chr; Chorus; Church Choir; School Musical; Comm Theater; Vcl Theater; Coll Dramas/Musicals; Drama/Musical Vocal.

WADE, PAULA; Olathe South Sr HS; Olathe, KS; (3); Letterman Clb; Q&S; Mrchg Band; Pep Band; Rptr Nwsp; Yrbk; Swmmng; Cit Awd; Hon Roll; Pres Acad Fit Awd; Flute Tchr; KSPA Jrnlsm St Cmptn Qualifier; Embryology; Genetics; Jrnlsm.

WADEL, AUTUME L; Greensburg HS; Greensburg, KS; (1); Church Yth Grp; FHA; Chorus; School Musical; Vllybl; Hon Roll; Smmr Rec Sftbl; Rdng; Biking.

WADKINS, JENNY; Seaman Sr HS; Topeka, KS; (2); 52/297; Cmnty Wkr; FHA; Pep Clb; Spanish Clb; SADD; Teachers Aide; Chrldng; Powder Puff Ftbl; Hon Roll; Emporia ST; Elem Tchr.

WAGGONER, ASHLEY; Shawnee Mission E Sr HS; Leawood, KS; (2); Drama Clb; GAA; Natl Beta Clb; School Play; Capt Sftbl; High Hon Roll; Hon Roll; NHS; Promise Prjct Yth Cncl/Endwmnt Comm.

WAGGONER, JEROD L; Beloit Jr Sr HS; Glen Elder, KS; (2); Cmnty Wkr; Letterman Clb; Spanish Clb; Band; Mrchg Band; Orch; Variety Show; JV Var Bsktbl; Var Ftbl; Wt Lftg; His Clb.

WAGGONER, SCOTT; Bishop Ward HS; Bonner Springs, KS; (2); 7/93; Pep Band; Rep Frsh Cls; Rep Soph Cls; JV Ftbl; L Swmmng; JV Wrstlng; High Hon Roll; NHS; Med.

WAGHER, LANA; Ingalls Jr Sr HS; Pierceville, KS; (3); 3/23; Church Yth Grp; Pep Clb; Chorus; Drill Tm; Pres Soph Cls; Pres Jr Cls; Pres Sr Cls; VP Sec Stu Cncl; Cit Awd; NHS.

WAGNER, ANDREA; Garden City Sr HS; Garden City, KS; (4); 64/313; VP FHA; Teachers Aide; Band; Mrchg Band; Pep Band; Chrldng; Pom Pon; Hon Roll; NHS; HERO Mem; Spch Pthlgy.

WAGNER, BECKY M; El Dorado HS; El Dorado, KS; (2); Cmnty Wkr; FCA; Math Clb; Math Tm; Spanish Clb; SADD; JV Crs Cntry; JV Trk; High Hon Roll; Prfct Atten Awd; Earth Care Club; KAY; Psych.

WAGNER, CHANDI; Maize HS; Wichita, KS; (2); 1/300; Church Yth Grp; FCA; Math Tm; NFL; Spanish Clb; Chorus; High Hon Roll; NHS; Letterman Clb; Scholastic Bowl; Planning Panel Intl Yth Cnvntn; Pres Schl Bible Stu Chaos; Prtcpnt Intl Ftr Prblm Slvng Comp.

WAGNER, DENISE A; Wichita East HS; Wichita, KS; (3); VP Art Clb; Church Yth Grp; Pres French Clb; Hosp Aide; Science Clb; VP SADD; Trk; French Hon Soc; Hon Roll; NHS; 200 Hrs Comm Svc; Leathercraft; Tree Climbing; Acad Ltr; Natl Ar Thnr Soc VP.

WAGNER, GREG; Silver Lake Jr Sr HS; Lyndon, KS; (3); Quiz Bowl; Teachers Aide; Chorus; Treas Frsh Cls; Bsktbl; Fld Hcky; JV Trk; Wt Lftg; Cit Awd; Hon Roll; KS ST Univ.

WAGNER, JESSICA A; Kensington Jr Sr HS; Franklin, NE; (3); 6/22; Natl FFA Org; Teachers Aide; Phtg Yrbk; JV Var Bsktbl; JV Golf; Pom Pon; JV Var Sftbl; JV Vllybl; Hon Roll; NHS; Ft Hays ST U; Sec Ed.

WAGNER, JILL M; Larned HS; Garfield, KS; (2); 25/106; Church Yth Grp; Band; Chorus; Mrchg Band; Pep Band; JV Bsktbl; JV Vllybl; Hon Roll; Case Worker; Soc Worker.

WAGNER, JULIA D; Shawnee Mission N HS; Shawnee Mission, KS; (3); Debate Tm; Latin Clb; NFL; Thesps; Chorus; School Musical; School Play; Stage Crew; High Hon Roll; Natl Latin Exam Silver Mdl; U Of KS; Exprmntl Psych.

WAGNER, KENT; Garden City Sr HS; Garden City, KS; (4); Church Yth Grp; Debate Tm; Teachers Aide; Thesps; Acpl Chr; Chorus; School Musical; School Play; Swing Chorus; Phtg Nwsp; Stu Brd Of Directors Fidlty St Bnk; Manhattan Chrstn Col; Yth Mnstr.

WAGNER, LAURA; Maranatha Acad; Shawnee Mission, KS; (3); Band; Chorus; Color Guard; Mrchg Band; Orch; Pep Band; School Musical; School Play; Var Chrldng; NHS; U Of KS; Speech Pathology.

WAGNER, SHELBYE L; Wichita East HS; Wichita, KS; (2); Drama Clb; Spanish Clb; Thesps; Chorus; School Musical; School Play; Variety Show; Swmmng; Hon Roll; Intl Baccalaureate Dlpm.

WAGNER, STEPHANIE A; Winfield HS; Winfield, KS; (3); Model UN; Variety Clb; JV Var Golf; Var Trk; JV Var Vllybl; High Hon Roll; Hon Roll; NHS; Jr Prom Plng Comm; Intrct Clb; Pre-Dnstry.

WAGNER, TERRI; Frankft HS; Frankfort, KS; (4); Band; Chorus; Drill Tm; Flag Corp; School Play; Yrbk; Bsktbl; Var Trk; Var Vllybl; High Hon Roll; SADD; FHA.

WAGNER, TIFFANY; Burlington HS; Burlington, KS; (1); FBLA; Pep Clb; Band; Chrldng; Pom Pon; Vllybl; Hon Roll; Pres Acad Fit Awd.

WAGONER, BOBBY L; Quinter Jr Sr HS; Quinter, KS; (3); 6/30; Debate Tm; FCA; Math Tm; Natl FFA Org; Pep Clb; Quiz Bowl; Scholastic Bowl; Speech Tm; Sec Jr Cls; High Hon Roll; FFA ST Parlmntry Proc Team; 99% Math/Lang 96% Rdng Natl CTBS Test; Hnr Mntn ST Schlsp Test; Bus.

WAGONER, BRANDY L; Pomona HS; Pomona, KS; (3); FBLA; Rptr FHA; Letterman Clb; Nwsp; Phtg Yrbk; VP Jr Cls; Ofcr Stu Cncl; JV Bsktbl; L Trk; Var L Vllybl; Hon Roll; KS; Pre-Med; Bus Admin.

WAGSTAFF, JEFFREY S; St John's Military Schl; Granada Hills, CA; (2); Quiz Bowl; ROTC; Spanish Clb; Teachers Aide; Varsity Clb; Color Guard; Ofcr Bsbl; Bsktbl; Trk; Wt Lftg; U Of AZ; Attorney; Animator.

WAHLE, JAIME L; St Xavier's HS; Junction City, KS; (2); SADD; Sec Frsh Cls; Var Bsktbl; Var Capt Chrldng; Var Crs Cntry; JV Trk; Var Vllybl; Wt Lftg; Hon Roll; NHS; Cloud Cty CC; Phy Ed.

WAHLGREN, CHAD A; Salina HS South; Salina, KS; (3); 6/250; Pres Church Yth Grp; Pres FCA; Chorus; Ofcr Stu Cncl; JV Bsktbl; Var Capt Crs Cntry; Var Trk; Cit Awd; Hon Roll; NHS; Grad Of Jr Ldrshp Salina; Cls Rep; U Of KS; Graphic Dsgn.

WAHLMEIER, JOSHUA A; Trego Comm HS; Wa Keeney, KS; (2); 16/54; Church Yth Grp; Debate Tm; Drama Clb; German Clb; Science Clb; Band; Ofcr Jr Cls; Bsktbl; Golf; High Hon Roll; Ft Hays ST; Crmnlgy.

WAINSCOTT, CIERRA N; Olathe East Sr HS; Olathe, KS; (2); Office Aide; Teachers Aide; Band; Swmmng; Hon Roll; KU; Nrsing Schl.

WAIT, ALI; Sublette HS; Sublette, KS; (2); Church Yth Grp; CAP; Pep Clb; Band; Chorus; Mrchg Band; Pep Band; School Musical; High Hon Roll; NHS; Med.

WAKEFIELD, CRISTA D; Mankato Jr Sr HS; Mankato, KS; (3); Cmnty Wkr; Office Aide; Teachers Aide; Yrbk; Mgr(s); Trk; Hon Roll; Amer Sign Lang; Johnson Cty CC; Sign Lang Intp.

WALDO, MICHELLE M; Hayden HS; Grantville, KS; (3); Hosp Aide; Intnl Clb; JV Tennis; Hon Roll.

WALDREN, MATT; Lewis Schl; Lewis, KS; (4); 3/17; Am Leg Boys St; Boy Scts; FBLA; Quiz Bowl; Scholastic Bowl; Pres Stu Cncl; Ftbl; Cit Awd; NHS; Prfct Atten Awd; US Yth Senate Pgm 96; Knox Coll; Coll Prof.

WALDREN, STEVE; Olathe North Sr HS; Olathe, KS; (3); Art Clb; Hon Roll; Natl Art Hon Soc.

WALDRON, STEVE C; Ft Scott HS; Fort Scott, KS; (2); 1/184; Computer Clb; Quiz Bowl; Chorus; Ftbl; High Hon Roll; Prfct Atten Awd.

WALDSCHMIDT, MINDY; Ellis HS; Ellis, KS; (4); Ed Yrbk; Sec Stu Cncl; Capt Bsktbl; Co-Capt Chrldng; Var Sftbl; Capt Vllybl; Church Yth Grp; FHA; SADD; Band; Hutchinson CC; Mar Bio.

WALGREN, JASMINE; Junction City HS; Junction City, KS; (3); Pep Clb; Chorus; HI Pacific Univ; Writer.

WALKER, ADAM; Rock Creek Jr Sr HS; Manhattan, KS; (1); 1/70; Church Yth Grp; 4-H; Math Tm; Service Clb; Pres Frsh Cls; Bsktbl; Ftbl; Trk; Wt Lftg; 4-H Awd; Acad/Ath Awd Mid-East Leag; GPA Above 3.5; KS ST.

WALKER, BEN; Hutchinson HS; Hutchinson, KS; (3); 4/350; Am Leg Boys St; VP Debate Tm; Pres French Clb; NFL; Var L Socr; High Hon Roll; NHS; Key Clb; Pep Clb; Science Clb; Boys Nation Del; 5th Pl Natl Forensics League Debate Trnmt; Natl Qualifier Frgn Extemporeaneous Spkng; Pol Sci.

WALKER, BRIAN L; Washington HS; Washington, KS; (2); Letterman Clb; School Play; Pres Frsh Cls; Pres Soph Cls; Pres Jr Cls; Rep Stu Cncl; Stat Bsktbl; Var L Ftbl; L Trk; Boy Scts; Frnscs ST Chmps; KS; Med.

WALKER, CHRIS; Stockton HS; Stockton, KS; (3); Band; Chorus; Jazz Band; Mrchg Band; Pep Band; Var Capt Bsbl; Var L Ftbl; Wt Lftg; Var L Wrstlng; Hon Roll; Washburn; Tchng/Coaching.

WALKER, DAMIAN; Wellington Sr HS; Wellington, KS; (1); 17/182; Church Yth Grp; Scholastic Bowl; Bsktbl; High Hon Roll; Jr NHS; Rotary Awd; Nom Lions Awd; Dctr.

WALKER, DANIELLE D; Turner HS; Kansas City, KS; (2); Church Yth Grp; Drama Clb; Band; Drill Tm; School Musical; Ofcr Stu Cncl; Hon Roll; Jr NHS; NHS; Prfct Atten Awd; KS Univ; Pre-Med.

WALKER, FELICIA; Jefferson West HS; Meriden, KS; (2); 22/72; Computer Clb; FTA; Letterman Clb; Pep Clb; Band; Chorus; Jazz Band; Mrchg Band; Pep Band; Bsktbl; Vet.

WALKER, GARY D; Mc Louth Schl; Mc Louth, KS; (2); FBLA; FHA; Varsity Clb; Pres Frsh Cls; Pres Soph Cls; Treas Stu Cncl; Var Ftbl; High Hon Roll; NHS; Pres Acad Fit Awd; Cnstrctn/Engr/Bus.

WALKER, JENNIFER; Basehor Linwood HS; Basehor, KS; (4); 24/124; FBLA; GAA; Q&S; VICA; Nwsp; Yrbk; Bsktbl; Crs Cntry; High Hon Roll; Hon Roll; KS City.

WALKER, JO VANNA S; Parsons HS; Parsons, KS; (3); Drama Clb; FHA; FTA; Quiz Bowl; Red Cross Aide; Service Clb; Thesps; School Musical; School Play; Stage Crew; Cornell Col; Ed.

WALKER, JOEL; Chaparral HS; Anthony, KS; (1); Boy Scts; Church Yth Grp; 4-H; Key Clb; JV Var Bsktbl; Tennis; Hon Roll; Pres Acad Fit Awd; Ftr Frmrs Of America; KS U Kansas City; Math.

WALKER, KRISTA L; Wichita North HS; Wichita, KS; (4); 25/250; Church Yth Grp; Cmnty Wkr; Q&S; Chorus; Church Choir; School Musical; Mgr Nwsp; Mgr(s); High Hon Roll; NHS; Sterling Univ; Premed.

WALKER, LISA M; Wichita Southeast HS; Wichita, KS; (2); Church Yth Grp; Girl Scts; Band; Chorus; Chrldng; Pom Pon; High Hon Roll; Hon Roll; NHS.

WALKER, MICHAEL J; Beloit Jr Sr HS; Simpson, KS; (2); 4-H; Spanish Clb; Band; Mrchg Band; Pep Band; JV Bsktbl; High Hon Roll; FFA; KS; Law.

WALKER, STACEE; Wyandotte HS; Kansas City, KS; (3); Chess Clb; Cmnty Wkr; Pep Clb; Orch; Hon Roll; KS U; Pediatric Nurse.

WALKER, STEVEN W; Wichita Heights HS; Wichita, KS; (3); Boy Scts; Church Yth Grp; Chorus; Church Choir; Drill Tm; Bsktbl; Hon Roll; Wichita St Univ; Comp Tech.

WALKER, SUSAN M; Hope HS; Hope, KS; (3); Debate Tm; FBLA; FHA; Spanish Clb; Teachers Aide; Band; Chorus; Mrchg Band; Pep Band; JV Var Vllybl.

WALKER, TIFFANY; Wyandotte HS; Kansas City, KS; (4); 2/188; Church Yth Grp; 4-H; Office Aide; Pep Clb; Acpl Chr; Chorus; Rep Sr Cls; Var Chrldng; High Hon Roll; Pres NHS; PEER; Teen Hope; Washburn U; Bus Admin.

WALKER, TRACEE M; Wyandotte HS; Kansas City, KS; (3); Chess Clb; Ofcr Pep Clb; Teachers Aide; Orch; Hon Roll; Med Careers Club; Bus/Entrprnrshp Magnet Prgm; RN.

WALKER, ZACH; Shawnee Mission E Sr HS; Shawnee Msn, KS; (3); Church Yth Grp; Natl Beta Clb; Q&S; Pres Spanish Clb; Pep Band; Yrbk; JV Var Crs Cntry; JV Trk; Hon Roll; NHS; Drums In Chrch Band; Parks Cleanup & Ronald Mc Donald House Vol; Notre Dame; Bus; Philosophy.

WALL, GWEN M; Shawnee Mission E Sr HS; Shawnee Mission, KS; (4); Cmnty Wkr; Hon Roll; Emporia ST U.

WALL, JAMI; South Gray HS; Montezuma, KS; (4); 1/19; HOBY; Quiz Bowl; Band; Church Choir; Pres Stu Cncl; Var Capt Bsktbl; Var Capt Vllybl; NHS; St Schlr; Church Yth Grp; KS Rgnts Hnrs Acad; U Of KS; Pharmacy.

WALL, JENNY; Hillsboro HS; Hillsboro, KS; (3); 4/63; Church Yth Grp; Scholastic Bowl; Band; Chorus; School Play; Rptr Nwsp; Rptr Yrbk; L Var Crs Cntry; L Var Trk; High Hon Roll.

WALL, LISA M; Conway Springs HS; Conway Springs, KS; (2); 1/60; Church Yth Grp; Band; Chorus; Church Choir; Mrchg Band; Pep Band; School Play; Phtg Nwsp; Bsktbl; L Var Pom Pon; I Rtng ST Piano Cntst; 2nd Pl Nwspr Phtgrphy ST Cntst; 4th Pl Girls Javlin ST Trck Meet; Nrsng.

WALL, MICHAEL; South Gray HS; Montezuma, KS; (3); Church Yth Grp; Cmnty Wkr; Letterman Clb; Spanish Clb; Band; Chorus; Pep Band.

WALLACE, BEAU R; Chase Co HS; Cottonwood Fall, KS; (2); Church Yth Grp; Cmnty Wkr; Spanish Clb; Band; Chorus; Mrchg Band; Pep Band; Var L Ftbl; Mgr(s); Cit Awd; KS ST Univ; Law.

WALLACE, JODIE E; Wellington Sr HS; Wellington, KS; (3); 9/161; Church Yth Grp; Office Aide; SADD; Yrbk; Pres Jr Cls; VP Stu Cncl; Bsktbl; Crs Cntry; Mgr(s); Trk.

WALLACE, KARA G; Dighton HS; Dighton, KS; (3); Church Yth Grp; FCA; 4-H; Pep Clb; Scholastic Bowl; Speech Tm; SADD; Acpl Chr; Band; Chorus; KS ST Univ; Optometry.

WALLACE, KATHERINE A; Shawnee Mission Northwest HS; Lenexa, KS; (4); Church Yth Grp; English Clb; Q&S; Band; Church Choir; Jazz Band; Mrchg Band; School Musical; Ed Lit Mag; High Hon Roll; Drum Corps; Sterling Coll; El Ed.

WALLACE, LINDSAY R; Garden City Sr HS; Garden City, KS; (3); 1/306; Dance Clb; Drill Tm; Rep Frsh Cls; VP Soph Cls; Pres Jr Cls; Stat L Bsktbl; Capt Pom Pon; High Hon Roll; JETS Awd; Score Keeper; Acad Lttrs; Dance Capt & Lttr; Arch.

WALLACE, MELANIE D; Anderson Cty Jr Sr HS; Garnett, KS; (3); Intnl Clb; Var Capt Chrldng; High Hon Roll; Octagon Clb; KAY Clb; Math/Bus/Lang Arts Acad Awds; Baker Univ; Acctnt/Math Engr.

WALLACE, MICHAEL P; Olathe South Sr HS; Olathe, KS; (3); Boy Scts; Church Yth Grp; Cmnty Wkr; Drama Clb; Letterman Clb; Spanish Clb; Varsity Clb; Band; Church Choir; Mrchg Band; US Naval Sea Cadets; Rode In MS 150 Mile Bike Ride; Aerospace Engrng; Navy-Pilot.

WALLACE, SAMANTHA A; Northeast HS; Arcadia, KS; (1); 11/53; Cmnty Wkr; Band; Chorus; Flag Corp; Chrldng; Mgr(s); Hon Roll; Prfct Atten Awd.

WALLACE, STEPHANIE L; Blue Valley Northwest HS; Overland Park, KS; (2); 1/400; Band; Mrchg Band; Lit Mag; Treas Jr Cls; Intrml Vllybl; High Hon Roll.

WALLACE, SYDNEY N; Blue Valley Northwest HS; Overland Park, KS; (3); Cmnty Wkr; Debate Tm; NFL; Rptr Nwsp; Rep Stu Cncl; Intrml Capt Socr; Hon Roll; Hist NHS; Ntl Merit Ltr; KS Stdnt Cncl Camp; Pre Law.

WALLACE, WENDY A; Douglass HS; Douglass, KS; (3); 1/67; Quiz Bowl; Mgr Yrbk; High Hon Roll; Ntl Merit Ltr; Med Schl.

WALLER, LAURA A; Shawnee Heights Sr HS; Tecumseh, KS; (2); VP Pres Church Yth Grp; Debate Tm; Girl Scts; Hosp Aide; Intnl Clb; Pep Clb; SADD; JV Var Trk; Prfct Atten Awd; Pres Acad Fit Awd; Acad Tlntd Pgm; Topeka Rescue Mission Vol; KS Univ; Radiologic Technician.

WALLERT, RENA J; Ellsworth HS; Ellsworth, KS; (2); Chorus; School Play; High Hon Roll; Hon Roll; Kayettes; CNA At Nrsng Home.

WALLGREN, MANDY; Phillipsburg HS; Phillipsburg, KS; (4); 18/56; Am Leg Aux Girls St; Church Yth Grp; Debate Tm; Drama Clb; Key Clb; SADD; Teachers Aide; Acpl Chr; Nwsp; Ed Yrbk; Amndmnt Slct Sngng Grp; Fort Hays.

WALLING, CAROLINE; Wichita Collegiate Schl; Wichita, KS; (3); Cmnty Wkr; Debate Tm; Science Clb; Teachers Aide; Ed Yrbk; Var L Sftbl; Var L Tennis; High Hon Roll.

WALSH, ANDRIA; Bishop Carroll Catholic HS; Wichita, KS; (1); Spanish Clb; JV Chrldng; High Hon Roll; Golden Eagle Acad Awd; Piano; Med.

WALSH, DIANA C; Shawnee Mission North HS; Merriam, KS; (1); 28/553; Art Clb; German Clb; Pep Clb; Bsktbl; Hon Roll.

WALSH, JULIE; St Marys HS; Emmett, KS; (2); Cmnty Wkr; FCA; FBLA; Pep Clb; Band; JV Bsktbl; Golf; Score Keeper; High Hon Roll; Hon Roll; Hlth Care.

WALSH, LAUREL L; Wichita Collegiate Schl; Wichita, KS; (3); Cmnty Wkr; SADD; Thesps; Chorus; School Musical; Pres Frsh Cls; Var Bsktbl; Var Tennis; High Hon Roll; Hon Roll; I Dare You Ldshp Awd; Bst Fml Vclst Awd At UCS; 3yr Madrigal Choir Ptcpt; Eng.

WALSHIRE, JAMES D; Silver Lake Jr Sr HS; Silver Lake, KS; (4); 21/48; Chorus; Var Bsbl; JV Var Bsktbl; JV Var Ftbl; Hon Roll; School Musical; Cit Awd; Bsktbl Hnrbl Mntn All League/All Trnmnt Tm; Bsbl ST Trnmnt/2nd Pl ST/ST Chmpns; Amer Legion Bsbl; Cloud Cty CC; Bus.

WALSHIRE, JASON M; Shawnee Heights Sr HS; Topeka, KS; (2); Cmnty Wkr; JA; Pep Clb; Stage Crew; High Hon Roll; KS Univ; Arch Drftng.

WALSTON, SHELLY M; Maize HS; Wichita, KS; (3); 22/256; VP Church Yth Grp; Sec French Clb; NFL; SADD; Band; Mrchg Band; Pep Band; High Hon Roll; Hon Roll; NHS; Ed.

WALSWORTH, HOLLIE P; Humboldt HS; Humboldt, KS; (3); 21/60; Drama Clb; FHA; Natl FFA Org; NFL; School Play; Stage Crew; Variety Show; Phtg Nwsp; Phtg Yrbk; Pres Frsh Cls; Sec Ed.

WALTER, ANDREW; Hays HS; Catharine, KS; (4); 39/209; Natl FFA Org; Hon Roll; NHS; Ntl Merit Ltr; FFA Sentinel; Ft Hays ST Univ; Ind Tech.

WALTER, BRIAN L; Washington HS; Washington, KS; (2); FCA; FHA; Letterman Clb; School Play; Pres Frsh Cls; Pres Soph Cls; Rep Stu Cncl; Var L Ftbl; L Trk; Boy Scts; Chammps; Med.

WALTER, CRYSTAL D; Waconda East HS; Cawker City, KS; (4); 3/20; FHA; Varsity Clb; Capt Drill Tm; Sec Sr Cls; Var Capt Bsktbl; Var Trk; Var Capt Vllybl; Cit Awd; High Hon Roll; VP NHS; Cath Yth Org Pres; St Track Mt Ptcpt; KS St Univ; Sprts Med.

WALTER, ELIZABETH; Mc Pherson HS; Mc Pherson, KS; (4); Art Clb; Church Yth Grp; French Clb; FHA; Hosp Aide; Library Aide; Office Aide; Science Clb; VP Spanish Clb; SADD; Pratt CC; Bio/Pre Med.

WALTER, JULIE; Thomas More Prep-Marion HS; Hays, KS; (1); Debate Tm; Latin Clb; School Musical; Rep Frsh Cls; Ofcr Stu Cncl; JV Chrldng; Sftbl; Vllybl; High Hon Roll.

WALTER, LYNN; Central Christian Schl; Hutchinson, KS; (3); 1/14; Church Yth Grp; Quiz Bowl; Chorus; Treas Jr Cls; Rep Stu Cncl; Var Bsktbl; Var Ftbl; Var Trk; High Hon Roll; Bausch/Lomb Sci Awd.

WALTER, TARA; Circle HS; El Dorado, KS; (4); 18/90; Am Leg Aux Girls St; Pres FCA; Pres FHA; Library Aide; Pres Spanish Clb; SADD; Teachers Aide; Rep Stu Cncl; Stat Bsktbl; Var Tennis; Emporia ST U; Elem Educ.

WALTER, TIFFANY; St John's HS; Beloit, KS; (2); Sec Church Yth Grp; Drama Clb; HOBY; Sec Pep Clb; Quiz Bowl; Scholastic Bowl; Speech Tm; SADD; Chorus; School Play; Phys Thrpy.

WALTERS, BENJAMIN D; Ottawa HS; Ottawa, KS; (3); Boy Scts; Church Yth Grp; Cmnty Wkr; Library Aide; Chorus; Hon Roll; Pres Schlr; Emporia ST U.

WALTERS, BLAKE N; Centralia Schl; Centralia, KS; (2); Boy Scts; Church Yth Grp; Letterman Clb; Science Clb; Chorus; Ofcr Soph Cls; JV Var Bsktbl; Var Crs Cntry; JV Ftbl; Trk; Fulfilling Eagle Sct Proj; Athletic Trnr.

WALTERS, H ALIENE; Wichita South HS; Wichita, KS; (2); Hosp Aide; NFL; Office Aide; Chorus; Variety Show; High Hon Roll; Hon Roll; Lifeguard Prdatt Pub Pool; Love To Swim; U Of KS; OB.

WALTERS, HEATHER; Olathe East Sr HS; Olathe, KS; (3); 94/400; Cmnty Wkr; French Clb; Acpl Chr; Chorus; School Play; Swing Chorus; Sftbl; Vllybl; Hon Roll; Pres Acad Fit Awd; Pittsburgh ST Univ; Med.

WALTERS, JANELL; Thomas More Prep-Marion HS; Hays, KS; (4); 6/93; Cmnty Wkr; Math Tm; Stage Crew; Co-Capt Bsktbl; Trk; Vllybl; High Hon Roll; NHS; Ambsdrs; Neo-Gea; KS U; Psych.

WALTERS, JODY; Thomas More Prep-Marion HS; Hays, KS; (4); 15/98; Cmnty Wkr; VP FBLA; Math Tm; NFL; Church Choir; School Musical; Mgr(s); Hon Roll; Pres Schlr; St Schlr; U Of KS.

WALTERS, LUKE W; Russell HS; Russell, KS; (1); Church Yth Grp; Capt Quiz Bowl; School Musical; VP Frsh Cls; Rep Stu Cncl; Bsktbl; JV Tennis; High Hon Roll; Chorus; Math Relay Team 1st Prblm Slvng; Rgnl ST Sci Olympd 3rd ST Srfn The Net.

WALTERS, TIFFANY A; Emporia HS; Emporia, KS; (4); 41/273; Debate Tm; Girl Scts; NFL; Band; Drm Mjr(t); Mrchg Band; Pep Band; Var Trk; NHS; Pres Acad Fit Awd; Emporia ST Univ; Pre-Medicine.

WALTMAN, JENNIFER L; Circle HS; Augusta, KS; (3); 12/108; Am Leg Aux Girls St; 4-H; FHA; SADD; Acpl Chr; Rptr Yrbk; Mgr(s); Tennis; 4-H Awd; High Hon Roll; Butler Cty CC.

WALTNER, JEANNETTE K; Moundridge HS; Moundridge, KS; (2); Church Yth Grp; FCA; 4-H; Pep Clb; Band; Chorus; Mrchg Band; Pep Band; School Musical; Sec Frsh Cls; Bethel Coll.

WALTON, AUDRA A; Nickerson HS; South Hutchinson, KS; (4); 63/97; Library Aide; Office Aide; Teachers Aide; JV Powder Puff Ftbl; JV Vllybl; Dental Careers Acad Topeka.

WALTON, DONOVAN; Mankato Jr Sr HS; Mankato, KS; (4); Church Yth Grp; Natl FFA Org; Band; Var L Bsktbl; Var L Ftbl; Var L Golf; Wt Lftg; Hon Roll; NHS; Prfct Atten Awd; NHS Chptr Pres 95-96; KS Ambassadors Of Music European Tour Mem 96; KS ST Univ; Hlth.

WALTON, JENNIFER L; Humboldt HS; Humboldt, KS; (2); 18/55; FHA; Chorus; Swing Chorus; Phtg Nwsp; Phtg Yrbk; Rep Stu Cncl; L Golf; High Hon Roll; Hon Roll; Letterman Clb; KAY Mem & Bd Mem; Piano; Violin; Soc.

WALTRIP, EMILY; St Mary's Colgan HS; Pittsburg, KS; (2); Letterman Clb; Math Tm; Pep Clb; Chorus; Var Bsktbl; Score Keeper; Var Sftbl; Var Vllybl; Hon Roll; Pres Acad Fit Awd; KU.

WALZ, MELLISA B; Leavenworth HS; Smithville, MO; (4); 68/326; Church Yth Grp; Teachers Aide; Acpl Chr; Chorus; Rep Frsh Cls; Mgr(s); High Hon Roll; Goodfellows; Vol Spec Olympcs; Mascot; Maple Wood Coll; Ed.

WAMBOLD, PATRICK C; Garden City Sr HS; Garden City, KS; (3); Cmnty Wkr; Debate Tm; Band; Church Choir; Jazz Band; Mrchg Band; Orch; Pep Band; School Play; Hon Roll; Vol Crp Wlk; Bwlng Big Brthr/Big Sister; Dist Jazz Bnd; Dist Bnd; Lions Bnd Cmp; Masonic Bnd Cmp; K U; Sci/Medical.

WAMMACK, JESSE S; Riverton Schl; Galena, KS; (2); Library Aide; Math Clb; Math Tm; Ofcr Bsbl; Bsktbl; Golf; Hon Roll.

WAMPLER, ANNIE; Oskaloosa HS; Oskaloosa, KS; (2); 16/72; Church Yth Grp; FBLA; FHA; Girl Scts; Letterman Clb; SADD; JV Var Chrldng; JV Vllybl; High Hon Roll; Hon Roll; Swimming Lessons Instr Asst; Silver Awd In Girl Scouts.

WAN, SHENG; Lawrence HS; Lawrence, KS; (3); Intnl Clb; Key Clb; Library Aide; Orch; Hon Roll; Lawrence Memrl Hosp Vol 95-96; Northwestern; Pre-Med; Medicine.

WANER, KATIE I; Wichita North HS; Wichita, KS; (2); Church Yth Grp; Dance Clb; Drama Clb; Office Aide; Church Choir; Hon Roll; Rehma Bible Trng Ctr; Tchr.

WANG, EDWARD K; Lawrence HS; Lawrence, KS; (4); Cmnty Wkr; JA; Latin Clb; Chorus; Orch; School Musical; Rep Frsh Cls; VP Soph Cls; Pres Jr Cls; Pres Sr Cls; Magna Cum Laude Natl Latin Exam; Natl Current Events Tm; Northwestern Univ; Elec Engr.

WANG, GE; Shawnee Mission S Sr HS; Lenexa, KS; (4); 13/430; Church Yth Grp; Debate Tm; Math Clb; NFL; Quiz Bowl; Science Clb; Jazz Band; Trk; High Hon Roll; Ntl Merit SF; Music Recording & Composite; Film.

WANG, JOLINE; St Xavier's HS; Junction City, KS; (2); #1 in class; Church Yth Grp; German Clb; Math Clb; SADD; VP Frsh Cls; Sec Soph Cls; Var Bsktbl; Var Crs Cntry; High Hon Roll; 7th Pl Eco Meet; Harvard U; Law.

WANG, LUKE Y; Shawnee Mission E Sr HS; Shawnee Mission, KS; (4); 1/402; French Clb; Model UN; Pep Clb; Capt Quiz Bowl; Capt Scholastic Bowl; Orch; School Musical; JV Trk; Hon Roll; St Schlr.

WANGERIN, LUCAS M; Eastern Heights Jr Sr HS; Agra, KS; (1); Boy Scts; Drama Clb; Scholastic Bowl; Band; Chorus; Pep Band; School Play; Var L Bsktbl; Var L Ftbl; High Hon Roll.

WANGERIN, NICOLE K; Kensington Jr Sr HS; Kensington, KS; (3); 11/22; Church Yth Grp; Girl Scts; Letterman Clb; Library Aide; Natl FFA Org; Pep Clb; Spanish Clb; Speech Tm; SADD; Band; Kays Sec; Ft Hays; Prim Ed.

WANGSGARD, ALYSSIA M; Maize HS; Wichita, KS; (2); French Clb; Science Clb; SADD; High Hon Roll; Hon Roll; NHS; Kays; Wichita ST Univ.

WANKLYN, KEVIN; Lakin HS; Lakin, KS; (4); 1/42; Am Leg Boys St; Quiz Bowl; Band; VP Sr Cls; VP Stu Cncl; Var Golf; Cit Awd; Gov Hon Prg Awd; VP NHS; St Schlr; KS ST Univ; Engr.

WANTOCH, SARAH M; Shawnee Mission N HS; Shawnee Mission, KS; (3); 1/429; Hosp Aide; Q&S; Orch; School Musical; JV Crs Cntry; JV Trk; NHS; Harvard/Radcliff/Dartmouth/Coll Bks Awd; USAMTS.

WAPELHORST, JOSEPH P; Great Bend Sr HS; Great Bend, KS; (3); Church Yth Grp; German Clb; Pep Clb; Chorus; Ofcr Bsbl; High Hon Roll; Hon Roll; KAYS Club; Attnd 96 Natl Yth Ldrshp Forum Med; KS Univ; Pharm.

WAPELHORST, MICHELLE L; Bishop Carroll Catholic HS; Colwich, KS; (3); 6/170; VP Church Yth Grp; Cmnty Wkr; SADD; Teachers Aide; L Chorus; School Musical; Var L Tennis; High Hon Roll; Hon Roll; VP NHS; Natl Ldrshp Forum On Medicine Nom; Page US House Of Reps Nom; Little League Bsbl Statscn.

WARD, AMANDA R; Shawnee Heights HS; Topeka, KS; (1); Church Yth Grp; Pep Clb; Chorus; Drill Tm; Capt Chrldng; Trk; High Hon Roll; Pres Acad Fit Awd; Bus Hnrs; Soc Stud Hnrs; Acad Medal; Emporia ST Univ; Medicine.

WARD, CLINTON E; Galena HS; Galena, KS; (1); Letterman Clb; VP Frsh Cls; Var Bsbl; Var Ftbl; Wt Lftg; Hon Roll; A Hnr Roll.

WARD, ELISA; Pratt HS; Pratt, KS; (3); 1/97; Cmnty Wkr; Drama Clb; FCA; FHA; Key Clb; NFL; Pep Clb; Quiz Bowl; Scholastic Bowl; Speech Tm; U Of KS; Pre-Med/Chem.

WARD, HEATHER; Jewell HS; Jewell, KS; (4); 5/15; Church Yth Grp; VP FCA; FHA; FTA; Library Aide; Office Aide; Sec Pep Clb; SADD; Rptr Yrbk; Rep Jr Cls; KS St Univ.

WARD, JOSEPH; Wilson Jr Sr HS; Wilson, KS; (4); 9/24; Am Leg Boys St; German Clb; Math Tm; Varsity Clb; Phtg Nwsp; Phtg Yrbk; VP Sr Cls; Treas Stu Cncl; Ofcr Bsbl; Capt Bsktbl; Hmcmng Roylty; King Ctrs; Bsktbl King; Ger Exch Stu; U Of KS; Phys Thrpy.

WARD, JOSHUA; Mulvane Sr HS; Mulvane, KS; (3); 12/135; Scholastic Bowl; Band; Mrchg Band; Ed Nwsp; Mgr Bsbl; Mgr Ftbl; Var L Mgr(s); NHS; Frgn Lang Std.

WARD, JOSHUA J; Beloit Jr Sr HS; Beloit, KS; (2); Drama Clb; NFL; Spanish Clb; School Musical; School Play; Stage Crew; JV Ftbl; JV Golf; High Hon Roll; Hon Roll; Marine Bio.

WARD, LOUIS; Washington HS; Kansas City, KS; (3); Letterman Clb; Varsity Clb; Orch; School Musical; Stat Bsktbl; Var L Ftbl; L Var Mgr(s); L Var Trk; Hon Roll; All Conf Ftbl; Acad Ltr Wnnr; PE.

WARD, MEREDITH NICOLE; Kingman HS; Kingman, KS; (3); 1/85; Cmnty Wkr; FCA; FBLA; Pres SADD; Church Choir; Lit Mag; Var Crs Cntry; NHS; Ntl Merit Schol; St Schlr; Univ Of KS.

WARD, ROBYN; Syracuse Jr Sr HS; Syracuse, KS; (3); 5/34; Drama Clb; 4-H; Letterman Clb; Pep Clb; Chorus; Drm Mjr(t); School Play; Var Chrldng; Var Golf; NHS; Natl I Dare You Awd; KS ST; Vcl Msc Ed.

WARD, SARAH; Paola HS; Paola, KS; (4); 12/120; Am Leg Aux Girls St; FCA; 4-H; Yrbk; Rep Stu Cncl; Var Capt Bsktbl; Var Sftbl; Var Vllybl; High Hon Roll; NHS.

WARD, SHAWN; Garden City Sr HS; Garden City, KS; (2); 1/450; French Clb; Letterman Clb; Math Tm; Var Bsbl; JV Bsktbl; Gov Hon Prg Awd; Hnrs Bio Stdnt Yr; PE Stdnt Yr.

WARD, STEPHANIE E; Bishop Ward HS; Kansas City, KS; (1); 28/115; Cmnty Wkr; Girl Scts; Pep Clb; Chrldng; Vllybl; Hon Roll; Grl Scts Slvr Awd Pin; AAU Vlybl 3 Yrs Sttr/Pssr; Asst Coach Yth Vlybl; KU; Med/Bus.

WARDEN, SHANNON; Olathe East Sr HS; Olathe, KS; (4); 18/300; FHA; Teachers Aide; Lbrn Band; Mrchg Band; Pep Band; Ed Yrbk; Gym; High Hon Roll; Hon Roll; NHS; Southwest MO ST U.

WARE, ERICA M; Ottawa HS; Lawrence, KS; (3); Art Clb; Church Yth Grp; French Clb; SADD; Chorus; Variety Show; High Hon Roll; Hon Roll; Pres Acad Fit Awd; 3rd Pl Ribbon In Art Cmptn; Art; Music; Interior Dsgn; Chef.

WARE, KATHLEEN A; Bishop Carroll Catholic HS; Wichita, KS; (3); Spanish Clb; SADD; Hon Roll; Math.

WARINNER, TINA G; St Thomas Aquinas HS; Overland Park, KS; (2); 1/281; German Clb; Sec Math Clb; Math Tm; Mu Alpha Theta; Quiz Bowl; Science Clb; JV Var Trk; Var Vllybl; High Hon Roll; Prfct Atten Awd; USAV Jr Olympic Vlybl Plyr Setter 3 Yrs; Outstdng Rsrch Awd KS Univ Med Ctr 95; Bio Chem/Med Rsrch.

WARKENTINE, LUCAS ALAN; Emporia HS; Emporia, KS; (3); Var L Ftbl; Var L Trk; Intrml Wt Lftg; Hon Roll.

WARLICK, CHARITY; Kapaun-Mt Carmel HS; Wichita, KS; (3); Church Yth Grp; French Clb; Hosp Aide; JA; Mgr Nwsp; Pres Frsh Cls; Rep Soph Cls; Rep Jr Cls; Rep Sr Cls.

WARNER, BRANDON K; Otis Bison HS; Bison, KS; (3); Boy Scts; Quiz Bowl; Band; Jazz Band; Pep Band; Nwsp; Yrbk; Ftbl; Hon Roll; Amer Leg Cadet Law Enforcement Acad.

WARNER, JEREMY M; Great Bend Sr HS; Great Bend, KS; (1); Bsktbl; Crs Cntry; Trk; High Hon Roll.

WARNER, KEVIN; Ulysses HS; Ulysses, KS; (3); Am Leg Boys St; Boy Scts; Letterman Clb; SADD; School Musical; Ofcr Bsbl; Ftbl; Mgr(s); Wt Lftg; High Hon Roll.

WARNER, SARAH J; Stanton Co HS; Johnson, KS; (1); Church Yth Grp; Band; Chorus; Church Choir; Mrchg Band; Pep Band; School Play; Variety Show; Yrbk; Chrldng; Hnr Choir; Outstdng Stdnt Frosh Choir; Baptist Bible Coll; Mus.

WARNER, SHAROL A; Wichita East HS; Wichita, KS; (3); #5 in class; Church Yth Grp; Girl Scts; High Hon Roll; NHS; Girl Scts Gold & Silver Awds; Med.

WARNKEN, ERIK J; Great Bend Sr HS; Great Bend, KS; (1); Band; Mrchg Band; Pep Band; Hon Roll; KAYS Clb; Comm Svc Vol-Helped Pilot Clb Mem; KS ST Univ; Comp Sci.

WARREN, BRITTA; Goodland HS; Goodland, KS; (1); 1/90; Church Yth Grp; FHA; German Clb; GAA; SADD; JV Bsktbl; JV Vllybl; Hon Roll; AFS Clb.

WARREN, CHRIS A; Wichita Southeast HS; Wichita, KS; (2); Church Yth Grp; FCA; Socr; Bible Stud; Acctng.

WARREN, CLINTON S; Blue Valley HS; Overland Park, KS; (2); Church Yth Grp; Cmnty Wkr; Hosp Aide; Office Aide; Treas Frsh Cls; Pres Soph Cls; Rep Jr Cls; Var Trk; Hon Roll; Chorus; Engrng Pgm Purdue Univ; Young Life.

WARREN, EMILY; Goodland HS; Goodland, KS; (4); 16/85; Am Leg Aux Girls St; Church Yth Grp; Debate Tm; FHA; German Clb; GAA; SADD; Stage Crew; Yrbk; Sec Frsh Cls; Smmr Exchng Stu 95; U Of KS; Ger.

WARREN, JENNIFER A; Salina HS Central; Salina, KS; (3); Church Yth Grp; Band; Church Choir; Mrchg Band; Pep Band; School Musical; Swing Chorus; NHS; Pres Acad Fit Awd; High Hon Roll; VP For Unted Peers For Chrst; Bethany Col; Elem Ed.

WARREN, JESSE L; Manhattan HS; Manhattan, KS; (2); Church Yth Grp; Intrml Bsktbl; JV Ftbl; Var Trk; Intrml Wt Lftg; Cit Awd; Hon Roll; Pres Acad Fit Awd; KS St Univ; Vet.

WARREN, JESSICA J; Beloit Jr Sr HS; Beloit, KS; (2); Church Yth Grp; Dance Clb; Spanish Clb; SADD; JV Bsktbl; Var Crs Cntry; High Hon Roll; Hon Roll.

WARREN, JULIE; Columbus HS; Chetopa, KS; (3); Bus Profs of Am; Church Yth Grp; Computer Clb; Dance Clb; FCA; Math Tm; Pep Clb; Service Clb; Spanish Clb; Church Choir; HS Internet Clb; Sundy Schl Tchr; KU; Engl Ed.

WARREN, PUANANI; Bonner Springs HS; Kansas City, KS; (2); Pep Clb; Orch; Chrldng; High Hon Roll; Var Mock Trial As Attorney; Washburn; Attorney.

WARREN, SVONNE; Leavenworth HS; Leavenworth, KS; (2); 121/389; ROTC; Drill Tm; JV Bsktbl; JV Vllybl; Hon Roll; Good Fellows; Cadet Of Month; 1st Pl ROTC Phys Fitness; 2nd Pl Drill Rifle ROTC; Grambling ST Univ; PT.

WARREN, WILLAIM; Campus HS; Wichita, KS; (2); Drama Clb; Quiz Bowl; Scholastic Bowl; Thesps; School Musical; School Play; Stage Crew; Variety Show; Zoology.

WARRINGTON, DAWN M; Haven HS; Hutchinson, KS; (3); Church Yth Grp; Girl Scts; Band; Chorus; Church Choir; Variety Show; Yrbk; Chrldng; Vllybl; Hon Roll; Northwestern; Cmptr Grphcs.

WARTA, TARA N; Colby Sr HS; Colby, KS; (2); 13/111; Church Yth Grp; FCA; GAA; Spanish Clb; Yrbk; Bsktbl; Score Keeper; Computer Clb; Tennis; Trk; Colby CC.

WARTICK, MACKENZIE; Circle HS; El Dorado, KS; (3); 24/97; Church Yth Grp; FCA; 4-H; FHA; SADD; Acpl Chr; Chorus; Variety Show; Horse Shwng Wstrn Plsr Natl Chmp, Wrld Chmp Yth Hltr Mares; KS Jr Paint Hrs Clb Pres; Butler Cty Jr CC; Tchr.

WARTICK, MC KENZIE L; Circle HS; El Dorado, KS; (3); Church Yth Grp; FCA; 4-H; FHA; Pres SADD; Acpl Chr; Chorus; Church Choir; Variety Show; Sec Frsh Cls; St Track Meet; St 4-H Horse; KU Relays Track Meet Qualifier; Butler Cty JC.

WASHBURN, JENNIFER D; Derby HS; Derby, KS; (4); Church Yth Grp; FCA; Ed Nwsp; Sftbl; Capt Tennis; Hon Roll; NHS; DECA; KA ST U; Adv.

WASHBURN, RYAN; Norton Comm HS; Norton, KS; (3); Natl FFA Org; Pep Clb; Band; Jazz Band; Mrchg Band; Pep Band; Var Ftbl; JV Trk; Wt Lftg; Var Wrstlng; KS St Univ; Mech Eng.

WASHER, MARY; Hayden HS; Topeka, KS; (4); Art Clb; Intnl Clb; Pep Clb; Var Chrldng; Var Swmmng; VP NHS; Pres Schlr; KS ST Univ; Pre-Med; Radiology.

WASHINGTON, BEONCA; Wichita Heights HS; Kechi, KS; (4); 15/294; Am Leg Aux Girls St; Church Yth Grp; Chorus; Church Choir; Ofcr Soph Cls; Ofcr Jr Cls; Ofcr Stu Cncl; High Hon Roll; NHS; Btn Twrlr; KS U; Pharm.

WASHINGTON, CORNELIUS D; Wichita Southeast HS; Wichita, KS; (3); Church Yth Grp; Church Choir; Nwsp; VP Jr Cls; Pres Sr Cls; JV Bsktbl; Blck Male Ldrshp Prgm; Blck Awrness Clb; Archtct.

WASINGER, AMBER D; Ness City HS; Ness City, KS; (3); Pep Clb; Thesps; Phtg Yrbk; Sec Frsh Cls; Rep Stu Cncl; Var L Vllybl; Hon Roll; KS Univ; Nrsng Anethesist.

WASINGER, LAURA; St John's HS; Beloit, KS; (4); 2/13; Church Yth Grp; Cmnty Wkr; Pep Clb; Quiz Bowl; SADD; Teachers Aide; Band; Chorus; Church Choir; Pep Band; Ft Hays St U Bronze Awd; Ft Hays St U Awd Of Excllnc Bus; Fort Hays ST U; Bus.

WASINGER, NICK P; Wichita East HS; Wichita, KS; (2); Drama Clb; French Clb; Thesps; Chorus; School Musical; School Play; Stage Crew; Variety Show; JV Socr; French Hon Soc; Intnl Baccalaureate Prgm; Umpiring Little League; Astronaut/Areonautical Engr.

WASINGER, SARAH; Victoria HS; Victoria, KS; (1); 2/35; Church Yth Grp; GAA; Letterman Clb; Pep Clb; Band; Chorus; JV Bsktbl; Var Chrldng; Var Trk; JV Vllybl; Notre Dame; Phy Thrpst; Nurse.

WASSENBERG, RUSSELL; Marysville HS; Home, KS; (3); 8/90; Drama Clb; Natl FFA Org; School Play; Wrstlng; Hon Roll; Kiwanis Awd; KS ST; Pre-Vet.

WASSINGER, SUZANN N; Ness City HS; Ness City, KS; (3); 10/39; Church Yth Grp; Cmnty Wkr; Treas Pep Clb; Acpl Chr; Chorus; Church Choir; JV Var Bsktbl; JV Var Vllybl; High Hon Roll; NHS; Kay Clu Hstrn-Comm Svc Chm/Pres Sr Yr; KS ST Univ; Elem Ed.

WASSON, ABBY S; Wichita East HS; Wichita, KS; (2); Church Yth Grp; Pep Clb; Chorus; School Musical; Variety Show; Chrldng; Gym; Hon Roll; Lttr Wnnr Gymnstcs; PT.

WATERMAN, KRISTY; Atwood HS; Atwood, KS; (3); Church Yth Grp; Hosp Aide; Model UN; Scholastic Bowl; Spanish Clb; Speech Tm; Chorus; Church Choir; School Play; High Hon Roll; Navy Hnrs Pgm Cert Of Achvmt; Creative Wrtng Awds; Concordia Coll; Bus Mgmt.

WATERS, AMBER N; Lawrence HS; Lawrence, KS; (2); Orch; Stage Crew; Hon Roll; Art Exhbt To Rep Lawrence Publc Schls 96; Elem Ed.

WATERS, ANDREW; Blue Valley Northwest HS; Overland Park, KS; (1); 213/355; Boy Scts; Church Yth Grp; CAP; Cmnty Wkr; Band; Church Choir; Color Guard; Mrchg Band; Pep Band; Ftbl; Chrch Lead Acolyte.

WATERS, JOCELYN NICCI; Campus HS; Haysville, KS; (3); Church Yth Grp; Girl Scts; Intnl Clb; NFL; Spanish Clb; SADD; Teachers Aide; Nwsp; Hon Roll; Girl Scout Gold & Silver Awds; CIT Pgm; Creative Wrtng Clb; Pre-Law.

WATERS, SHANNON M; Blue Valley HS; Olathe, KS; (4); Church Yth Grp; Teachers Aide; Hon Roll; NHS; Pres Schlr; Natl Art Hnr Scty; Kansas City Art Inst; Photo.

WATERS, STEVEN J; Salina HS South; Salina, KS; (3); Boy Scts; Debate Tm; Var L Crs Cntry; L Mgr(s); Var L Swmmng; Hon Roll; NHS; Pres Acad Fit Awd; BSA Order Of Arrow Fnds Awd; Univ Of KS; Vet Med.

WATKINS, CASSE; Ellinwood Jr Sr HS; Ellinwood, KS; (3); Dance Clb; FCA; Spanish Clb; Teachers Aide; JV Var Bsktbl; Var Chrldng; Var Pom Pon; Tennis; High Hon Roll; Pres Acad Fit Awd; Tennis 7th Pl Singles, 8th Pl Doubles; Tap & Jazz Dance; Ed.

WATKINS, MINDY L; Emporia HS; Hartford, KS; (3); FCA; Teachers Aide; Ofcr Sr Cls; Var Capt Bsktbl; Var Capt Sftbl; Wt Lftg; High Hon Roll; Prfct Atten Awd; Pres Acad Fit Awd; St Schlr; Triple A Renaissance Awd; DARE; KS Belles AAU Natl Bsktbl Tm; Jr Olympic Fstvl All Str Tm; Prof Bsktbl Plyr.

WATKINS, MISTY; Columbus HS; Columbus, KS; (3); VP Bus Profs of Am; Pep Clb; Band; Mrchg Band; Pep Band; Var Tennis; Hon Roll; NHS; KAY Clb Secy; Masonic HS Band; 9 Yrs Piano; 6 Yrs Flute.

WATKINS, TIFFANY A; Anderson Cty Jr Sr HS; Garnett, KS; (1); Cmnty Wkr; 4-H; Pep Clb; Band; Mrchg Band; Pep Band; JV Chrldng; JV Crs Cntry; Hon Roll; Adventures In Missions-Missonary Trip To MX; Saddle Clb; Boot-N-Spur; Comp Technologist.

WATKINS, TRACY L; Galena HS; Galena, KS; (1); GAA; Letterman Clb; Varsity Clb; Bsktbl; Sftbl; Vllybl; Wt Lftg; KS Univ; Phy Thrpst.

WATKINS, ZACH; Jackson Heights HS; Whiting, KS; (4); Church Yth Grp; Cmnty Wkr; FCA; Pep Clb; SADD; Teachers Aide; Varsity Clb; Band; Chorus; Church Choir; 1st Team 2a All St Bsktbl/DVL, 1st Team N E KS All Star; KSU; Phys Thrpy.

WATSON, CANDACE M; Northeast Magnet HS; Peck, KS; (4); 14/60; Church Yth Grp; Cmnty Wkr; Office Aide; Pres Sr Cls; Ofcr Stu Cncl; Sci Achvmt Awd; Achieving Women Sci & Tech; Sci P Tech Diploma; Cowley Cty CC; Meteorology.

WATSON, CHRISTY L; El Dorado HS; El Dorado, KS; (4); 49/250; Church Yth Grp; Cmnty Wkr; Letterman Clb; SADD; Teachers Aide; Orch; Swmmng; Hon Roll; Soccer Tchr & Referee; Chamber Orch; Tchr.

WATSON, CURT; Central Heights Sr HS; Princeton, KS; (3); FBLA; Natl FFA Org; Pep Clb; Science Clb; Spanish Clb; Ftbl; High Hon Roll; Hon Roll; Prfct Atten Awd.

WATSON, JESSICA A; Salina HS South; Salina, KS; (2); Church Yth Grp; FCA; L Bsktbl; L Sftbl; L Vllybl; Hon Roll; Pres Acad Fit Awd.

WATSON, KAREN L; Manhattan HS; Manhattan, KS; (2); Art Clb; Hon Roll; Martial Arts; Sharron Washington Dance Studio; KS ST; Comic/Crtnst.

WATSON, KRISTEN; Topeka West HS; Topeka, KS; (3); Church Yth Grp; Cmnty Wkr; VP French Clb; Pep Clb; Acpl Chr; Chorus; Color Guard; School Musical; Variety Show; Lit Mag.

WATSON, MATTHEW K; Sublette HS; Sublette, KS; (3); 15/38; Church Yth Grp; Cmnty Wkr; Bsktbl; Golf; Garden City CC; Physicist.

WATSON, MICHAEL; Kansas Schl For The Deaf; Topeka, KS; (2); Church Yth Grp; Cmnty Wkr; Bsktbl; Ftbl; Trk; Wildcat Clb; Arch.

WATSON, NAUDIA T; Washington HS; Kansas City, KS; (3); 5/250; Library Aide; Pep Clb; ROTC; VP Jr Cls; VP Sr Cls; High Hon Roll; NHS; Peer; Peer Support; Ldrshp 2020; DARE; Teen Hope; Law.

WATSON, SHAWN M; Clearwater HS; Peck, KS; (2); Church Yth Grp; Cmnty Wkr; Stage Crew; Score Keeper; Wt Lftg.

WATSON, STEVEN C; Central Heights Sr HS; Princeton, KS; (3); FBLA; Math Clb; Science Clb; Spanish Clb; Ftbl; Hon Roll; Prfct Atten Awd; KS ST U.

WATSON, THOMAS; Hillsboro HS; Hillsboro, KS; (4); 25/45; Church Yth Grp; Natl FFA Org; Ofcr Stu Cncl; JV Golf; JV Wrstlng; KS ST U; Agribusiness.

WATSON III, VIRGIL; Arkansas City HS; Arkansas City, KS; (4); FCA; Hosp Aide; Var Bsbl; Var Capt Bsktbl; Hon Roll; Pres Schlr; 1st Team All Ark Vly 2nd Baseman; 2nd Team Class 5a 2nd Baseman; KS Ath Bsbl Conf All Star Selection; Hutchinson Clg; Engrng.

WATTERSON, ANN M; Olathe North Sr HS; Olathe, KS; (4); French Clb; Var Chrldng; High Hon Roll; NHS; Pres Acad Fit Awd; St Schlr; Truman ST Univ.

WATTON, MICHELLE; Derby HS; Derby, KS; (4); 23/342; Church Yth Grp; Thesps; Rptr Yrbk; Treas Stu Cncl; Capt L Bsktbl; Var L Trk; L Capt Vllybl; Hon Roll; NHS; St Schlr; Derby Female Ath Of Yr 96; Ft Hays ST Univ; Info Netwrkng.

WATTS, ARON R; Wellington Sr HS; Wellington, KS; (4); 8/118; Capt Bsbl; Capt Bsktbl; High Hon Roll; NHS; KS U Hnr Schlr.

WATTS, DANA; Syracuse Jr Sr HS; Syracuse, KS; (4); 1/29; Rptr Church Yth Grp; Pres 4-H; Quiz Bowl; Speech Tm; Chorus; Var L Crs Cntry; High Hon Roll; VP NHS; Cmnty Wkr; VP Sec Drama Clb; Gftd Pgm; Syracuse Sngrs; IM Bsktbl; Eng.

WATTS, JESSICA L; Lyndon HS; Quenemo, KS; (2); Art Clb; 4-H; FBLA; SADD; Band; Mrchg Band; Pep Band; Stage Crew; Phtg Yrbk; Rep Soph Cls; USVBA; ISE Vllybl Trnmnt; Comm Arts.

WATTS, KARI; Syracuse Jr Sr HS; Syracuse, KS; (1); 5/34; Church Yth Grp; Cmnty Wkr; 4-H; Letterman Clb; NFL; Pep Clb; Band; Chorus; Flag Corp; Mrchg Band; Bstkbl Tnrmnt 1st Pl; Fst Ptch Sftbl St 9th Pl; Educ.

WATTS, SHEILA A; Independence HS; Independence, KS; (1); Church Yth Grp; Hon Roll; Pres Acad Fit Awd; BYUART.

WATTS, TYSON M; Chanute Sr HS; Chanute, KS; (3); 24/146; 4-H; Hon Roll; NHS; KS St Univ; Anml Sci.

WATTS, WADE H; Chase Co HS; Cottonwood Falls, KS; (3); Art Clb; Cmnty Wkr; School Musical; Stage Crew; Ed Nwsp; JV Var Golf; Bus Clb; Jrnlsm Clb; Teen Ldrshp Org.

WATTSON, CASEY A; Wichita East HS; Wichita, KS; (2); 13/425; Church Yth Grp; Cmnty Wkr; JV Bsbl; Bsktbl; Cit Awd; Hon Roll; 2nd In St Natl Spnsh Exam Fresh Yr; Eng.

WAUGH, BRIDGET K; Labette Co HS; Coffeyville, KS; (2); FCA; FBLA; Letterman Clb; Ofcr Frsh Cls; Rep Stu Cncl; Var L Crs Cntry; Bsktbl; Var L Trk; 4-H Awd; High Hon Roll; 2nd Pl St Trk Meet; Sek Crss Cntry Champ 94-95; OK ST Univ; Radiology.

WAUGH, CHRISTINA; Dighton HS; Dighton, KS; (2); Church Yth Grp; Pep Clb; SADD; Band; Chorus; Mrchg Band; School Musical; School Play; Chrldng; High Hon Roll; Regnl Hnr Band 2 Yrs; Forensics; Law.

WAUGH, VERONICA; Dighton HS; Dighton, KS; (4); Church Yth Grp; Hosp Aide; Pep Clb; Chorus; School Musical; Chrldng; Mgr(s); Trk; Wt Lftg; Hon Roll; Fort Hays ST U; Nrsng.

WAWRZYNAIK, NATHANIAL I; Caney Valley Jr Sr HS; Independence, KS; (1); JV Bsbl; JV Ftbl; Hon Roll; Prfct Atten Awd.

WAY, ADRIAN N; Topeka HS; Topeka, KS; (2); 43/800; Pep Clb; Teachers Aide; JV Socr; High Hon Roll; JV Sccr Frosh/Soph Yrs; Bus.

WAY, KRISTEN N; Maize HS; Wichita, KS; (2); 119/281; Art Clb; Drama Clb; SADD; Teachers Aide; Hon Roll; Kays; Elem Ed.

WAYMASTER, TROY L; Russell HS; Bunker Hill, KS; (4); 18/68; Am Leg Boys St; Cmnty Wkr; Debate Tm; Drama Clb; 4-H; German Clb; Model UN; Quiz Bowl; Spanish Clb; SADD; KAY Clb Rep/Pres; Jr Cnslr Stdnt Cncl Cmp ST KS; Schl Trp Europe; U Of KS; Intl Lawyer.

WAYNE, JAKE; Wichita Collegiate Schl; Wichita, KS; (2); Scholastic Bowl; Chorus; Var L Crs Cntry; Var L Trk; High Hon Roll.

WEAST, LOGAN; Blue Valley HS; Shawnee Mission, KS; (2); Boy Scts; Church Yth Grp; Debate Tm; JCL; Latin Clb; NFL; Quiz Bowl; Orch; School Musical; High Hon Roll; Art Awds German, Latin; KMEA St Fstvl Orchstra; 2nd Pl St OM Cmptn.

WEATHERFORD, JUSTIN; Atchison Sr HS; Atchison, KS; (4); Math Tm; Science Clb; JV Bsbl; High Hon Roll; Hon Roll.

WEAVER, DAVID; Shawnee Mission East HS; Prairie Village, KS; (3); 10/413; Chess Clb; Natl Beta Clb; Q&S; Orch; Nwsp; French Hon Soc; High Hon Roll; NHS; Quiz Bowl; Tae Kwon Do Black Belt; Habita For Humanity.

WEAVER, DOUG; Wichita North HS; Wichita, KS; (3); Bus Profs of Am; Church Yth Grp; Band; Church Choir; Jazz Band; Mrchg Band; Pep Band; Var L Bsbl; JV Bsktbl; Var L Ftbl; Habitat For Hum; Wichita ST U; Bus.

WEAVER, JACQUELYN R; Sumner Acad Of Arts & Science; Kansas City, KS; (1); Pep Clb; Orch; Hon Roll; Pep Club Ofcr; Elem Ed.

WEAVER, JENNIFER; Lansing HS; Lansing, KS; (4); 2/145; Am Leg Aux Girls St; Red Cross Aide; Ed Yrbk; JV Chrldng; Var Powder Puff Ftbl; Trk; Pres French Hon Soc; High Hon Roll; Pres NHS; Pres Acad Fit Awd; Jrnlsm/Pblctn Staffs; U Of KS; Jrnlsm/Econ.

WEAVER, MARIA K; Glasco HS; Aurora, KS; (2); Chorus; Ofcr Soph Cls; Bsktbl; Chrldng; Vllybl; Hon Roll; NHS; KS ST Univ; Acctng.

WEAVER, MELINDA; Fairfield HS; Arlington, KS; (3); 3/35; Quiz Bowl; Chorus; School Play; Yrbk; Mgr(s); Cit Awd; High Hon Roll; Hon Roll; NHS; Pres Acad Fit Awd; Acad Lttr; KS Univ; Jrnlsm.

WEAVER, TAMMI; Garden City Sr HS; Garden City, KS; (3); 27/306; Var L Bsktbl; Var L Sftbl; Hon Roll; Prfct Atten Awd; Pres Acad Fit Awd; All Western Athl Conf Hnrb Mntn Bsktbl; All Western Athl Conf 1st Team Sftbl; Athl Trnr.

WEAVERLING, BRYAN D; Salina HS South; Salina, KS; (3); Drama Clb; Hosp Aide; Teachers Aide; Band; School Musical; JV Bsbl; Capt Ftbl; JV Golf; Hon Roll; KS ST Univ.

WEBB, JARED; Spring Hill HS; Olathe, KS; (4); Am Leg Boys St; Church Yth Grp; Letterman Clb; Ofcr Stu Cncl; Bsktbl; Ftbl; Trk; Hon Roll; Fort Hays ST U; Engr.

WEBB, JEFFERY A; Muncie Christian Schl; Kansas City, KS; (3); 1/12; Bus Profs of Am; Church Yth Grp; Drama Clb; Letterman Clb; Chorus; School Musical; School Play; Stage Crew; Phtg Rptr Yrbk; Pres Frsh Cls; Chrstn Patriot Awd; Sprtsmnshp Awd Soccer; Schlstc Achvr Awd; Page KS ST Senate; Cmpng; Scoutng; Swim; Cntrl Coll; Elec/Mech Engrng.

WEBB, JUSTUS; Leavenworth HS; Leavenworth, KS; (4); Am Leg Aux Girls St; Drama Clb; Thesps; School Play; Stage Crew; Pres Frsh Cls; JV Vllybl; Sec Wrstlng; High Hon Roll; Hon Roll; Coll Of Ozarks; Poli Sci.

WEBB, MICHAEL; Cheney Jr Sr HS; Cheney, KS; (3); 6/48; Cmnty Wkr; Acpl Chr; School Musical; Swing Chorus; Variety Show; JV Var Bsktbl; High Hon Roll; NHS; Pres Acad Fit Awd; Pres Schlr; Naval Acad Smmr Smnr; Amer Red Cross Dnr; KS Natl Math Cont; Sgn Lang Intrprtr; Natl Yth Ldrshp; US Naval Acad Annapolis; Engr.

WEBB, NATALIE; Highland HS; Highland, KS; (1); Church Yth Grp; Natl FFA Org; Pep Clb; Chorus; School Musical; Swing Chorus; Rep Frsh Cls; Bsktbl; Chrldng; Trk; Piano.

WEBB, ROBERT L; Garden City Sr HS; Garden City, KS; (2); Church Yth Grp; Office Aide; Teachers Aide; Var Bsktbl; Var Ftbl; Var Trk; Wt Lftg; Hon Roll; Prfct Atten Awd; AZ ST Univ; Bus Mgmt/Cnslng.

WEBB, STEPHANIE F; Buhler HS; Hutchinson, KS; (4); VP Church Yth Grp; Debate Tm; FCA; Hosp Aide; Spanish Clb; SADD; Chorus; Church Choir; School Musical; JV Tennis; Bible Quizzing; Mid Amer Nazarene Coll.

WEBBER, TARAN J; Pleasant Ridge HS; Leavenworth, KS; (3); Natl FFA Org; Trk; High Hon Roll; Hon Roll; Northwest Voc Tech; Mechanic.

WEBER, AARON C; Shawnee Mission North HS; Overland Park, KS; (4); 178/430; L Debate Tm; DECA; JA; NFL; Pep Clb; Teachers Aide; Varsity Clb; Mgr Nwsp; L Bsbl; Bsktbl; DECA 1st In KS Entrepreneurship Paper; Ftbl Ltr; KS ST; Mrktg Mgmt.

WEBER, ANNETTE L; Yates Ctr HS; Yates Center, KS; (3); Band; Church Choir; Drm Mjr(t); Mrchg Band; Pep Band; Trk; Hon Roll.

WEBER, BARBARA A; Northwest HS; Colwich, KS; (3); Am Leg Aux Girls St; Church Yth Grp; NFL; SADD; Thesps; School Play; Vllybl; Hon Roll; Debate Tm; Office Aide; Teens As Tchrs; Lang Clb; Butler CCC; PE.

WEBER, BETH A; Blue Valley HS; Overland Park, KS; (2); JV Tennis; High Hon Roll; Hon Roll; Dnc Cls.

WEBER, CAROLYN; St John's HS; Beloit, KS; (2); Math Tm; Pep Clb; Speech Tm; SADD; Chorus; Mgr(s); Score Keeper; Stat Vllybl; Hon Roll; NHS; Hays U; Sec.

WEBER, DAVID R; Shawnee Heights HS; Berryton, KS; (2); FBLA; Pep Clb; Bsktbl; JV Socr; Dr; Medicine.

WEBER, DEREK; St Mary's Colgan HS; Pittsburg, KS; (1); JV Bsbl; JV Bsktbl; JV Ftbl; High Hon Roll.

WEBER, DUSTIN; Wathena Schl; Wathena, KS; (4); Cmnty Wkr; Math Clb; Natl FFA Org; Science Clb; Spanish Clb; Varsity Clb; Church Choir; School Musical; School Play; Stage Crew; ST Qualifier Chorus Jr/Sr Yrs; KS ST Univ; Park/Rec Admin.

WEBER, ETHAN W; Northwest HS; Wichita, KS; (3); 75/325; Church Yth Grp; Teachers Aide; Band; Mrchg Band; Pep Band; JV Socr; VP Of Cessna; Tm Capt Of Sccr Tm In AYSO; Comp Sci.

WEBER, HAYLEY; Louisburg HS; Paola, KS; (3); Letterman Clb; Math Clb; Spanish Clb; Band; Mrchg Band; Pep Band; JV Vllybl; High Hon Roll; Hon Roll; NHS; A-Team; Explorer Post; KS ST Univ.

WEBER, HEIDI; Wichita North HS; Wichita, KS; (3); 1/25; Church Yth Grp; German Clb; Hosp Aide; HOBY; Pep Clb; Teachers Aide; Thesps; Chorus; School Musical; High Hon Roll; Friends Univ; Elem Ed.

WEBER, JAMES R; Baldwin HS; Baldwin City, KS; (4); 13/83; Boy Scts; Letterman Clb; Math Tm; Quiz Bowl; Band; Jazz Band; Mrchg Band; Pep Band; JV Bsktbl; JV Ftbl; CO Schl Of Mns; Engrng.

WEBER, JASON P; Trego Comm HS; Wa Keeney, KS; (2); 1/50; Treas Church Yth Grp; Debate Tm; Letterman Clb; Math Tm; Band; Rep Frsh Cls; Rep Soph Cls; JV Bsktbl; Var L Trk; High Hon Roll; Lions Clb Schlr; Dist Hnr Band.

WEBER, JENNIFER; Shawnee Mission W Sr HS; Shawnee Mission, KS; (3); 43/415; Pres Church Yth Grp; Cmnty Wkr; HOBY; Pres Spanish Clb; Treas Soph Cls; Pres Jr Cls; Ofcr Stu Cncl; Var Socr; High Hon Roll; Pres Acad Fit Awd; Acad Ltr; Young Lf; Bus Admin.

WEBER, LARRY H; Campus HS; Haysville, KS; (3); 30/200; Am Leg Boys St; Var L Socr; Hon Roll; KS Newman Col.

WEBER, MICHAEL; Salina HS Central; Salina, KS; (3); Band; Jazz Band; Mrchg Band; Orch; Pep Band; School Musical; School Play; Stage Crew; Hon Roll; Dist & St Band; I Ratings St Music Festival; City Band; Musical Ed.

WEBER, WARD D; Olathe East Sr HS; Olathe, KS; (2); 186/409; Boy Scts; Teachers Aide; Hon Roll; 2 Bands Of My Own; Johnson County CC; Music.

WEBSTER, AARON C; Bishop Miege HS; Shawnee Mission, KS; (3); Pep Clb; Spanish Clb; Rep Sr Cls; Rep Stu Cncl; Intrml Bsktbl; JV Socr; Var Tennis; High Hon Roll; NHS; Natl Gold Plus Tm Tennis.

WEBSTER, AMY L; Olathe East Sr HS; Olathe, KS; (3); Church Yth Grp; Spanish Clb; Church Choir; Bsktbl; Var Crs Cntry; Var Capt Trk; Hon Roll; Prfct Atten Awd; KS ST.

WEBSTER, BRITY; Winfield HS; Winfield, KS; (2); Pep Clb; Spanish Clb; SADD; Band; Jazz Band; Mrchg Band; Var Golf; Mgr(s); Var Sftbl; High Hon Roll; Law.

WEBSTER, CYNDEE M; Blue Valley HS; Fostoria, KS; (4); 3/17; FHA; SADD; Band; Pep Band; Treas Sr Cls; VP Stu Cncl; Bsktbl; Trk; Vllybl; Hon Roll; Cloud Cty CC; Acctng.

WEBSTER, JUSTIN; Pratt HS; Pratt, KS; (4); 35/100; Church Yth Grp; Debate Tm; Drama Clb; FCA; NFL; Speech Tm; Teachers Aide; Band; Mrchg Band; Pep Band; Univ Of KS; Law.

WEBSTER, KARISA L; Waconda East HS; Cawker City, KS; (4); 1/20; Drill Tm; Ed Nwsp; Ed Yrbk; Ofcr Stu Cncl; Trk; Vllybl; Gov Hon Prg Awd; Pres NHS; St Schlr; Val; KS ST U; Hlth.

WEDAN, ASHLEY M; Wichita North HS; Wichita, KS; (2); Church Yth Grp; Cmnty Wkr; French Clb; Pep Clb; Chorus; Hon Roll; Ntl Merit Ltr; Chrch Vacation Bible Schl Tchr.

WEDDING, RAVEN D; Labette Co HS; Parsons, KS; (1); FCA; FBLA; GAA; Girl Scts; Red Cross Aide; Spanish Clb; Intrml Bsktbl; Intrml Sftbl; Intrml Tnk; Intrml Vllybl; AAU Trck Tm; Paramedcs Club; Northwestern Law Schl; Corp Law.

WEDEL, ANGIE; Lyons HS; Lyons, KS; (4); 4/70; Sec Treas Pep Clb; Ed Nwsp; Ed Yrbk; Rep Stu Cncl; Var Chrldng; JV Tennis; Pres Acad Fit Awd; St Schlr; Cmnty Wkr; Dance Clb; Lionaires Spcl Perf Choir; Yth Ldrshp Rice Co; Hutchinson CC; RN.

WEDEL, EMILY N; Canton-Galva HS; Canton, KS; (2); FBLA; Letterman Clb; Band; Pep Band; SADD; JV Bsktbl; Var Trk; Emporia.

WEDEL, JOHN J; Topeka West HS; Topeka, KS; (2); Cmnty Wkr; Debate Tm; NFL; Thesps; Chorus; School Play; Trk; Hon Roll; Church Yth Grp; Model UN; MAYO Ofcr & VP; Page For Rep & Senators Every Yr; Law.

WEDEL, KIMBERLY R; Newton Sr HS; Newton, KS; (2); 22/279; Art Clb; Treas Church Yth Grp; Girl Scts; Model UN; Band; Color Guard; Mrchg Band; Pep Band; High Hon Roll; 11 Yrs Ballet, 4 Yrs Modern; 5 Yrs Church Yth Bell Choir; Music Clb.

WEDEL, RACHEL A; Leavenworth HS; Leavenworth, KS; (3); 4-H; Hosp Aide; Office Aide; Teachers Aide; Tennis; 4-H Awd; Hon Roll; AKC Dog Shows; Leavenworth Cty 4-H Dog Group Pres; Local Essay Cont Wnnr; KS Univ; Jrnlsm.

WEDEL, REBECCA; Mc Pherson HS; Mc Pherson, KS; (3); Art Clb; German Clb; Flag Corp; Yrbk; Chrldng; Pom Pon; Trk; Hon Roll; Pres Acad Fit Awd; JEA KSPA Natl Jrnlsm Awd, Excllnt Awd; Cty Art Awds Svrl 1st & Hnrb Mntns; KS ST U; Vet Med.

WEDEL, STEPH R; Moundridge HS; Moundridge, KS; (3); Church Yth Grp; Pep Clb; Band; Chorus; Church Choir; Jazz Band; Pep Band; Ofcr Jr Cls; Ofcr Sr Cls; Ofcr Stu Cncl.

WEDMAN, KYLE R; Chaparral HS; Danville, KS; (1); Key Clb; L Bsktbl; L Ftbl; L Var Tennis; Hon Roll.

WEED, JENNIFER; Liberal HS; Liberal, KS; (2); Church Yth Grp; Drama Clb; French Clb; Thesps; Acpl Chr; Chorus; School Play; Variety Show; JV Vllybl; High Hon Roll; CU; TV News Broadcasting.

WEEGE, COY; Baldwin HS; Baldwin City, KS; (4); 7/80; Rep Letterman Clb; Math Tm; Band; Ofcr Bsbl; Var Capt Ftbl; Var Capt Trk; Var Capt Wrstlng; High Hon Roll; NHS; Prep Clb; KS Hnrs Schlr; Natl Chrldng Assn All-Amer; NCA/UCA Chrldng Champs; U/KS; Mech Engrng.

WEEKS, ALISA; Burlington HS; Strawn, KS; (1); Dance Clb; Pep Clb; Var Chrldng; Var Pom Pon; Hon Roll; PRADD; NCA All Amer Chrldng; NCA All Amer Dnce; Starfire Dnce Co; KS U; Prfrmng Arts.

WEEKS, CORTNEY P; Salina HS South; Salina, KS; (3); Boy Scts; Church Yth Grp; Cmnty Wkr; Teachers Aide; Ofcr Stu Cncl; JV Var Trk; JV Wrstlng; Hon Roll; Mountain Biking.

WEEKS, JENNIFER L; Ransom Jr Sr HS; Brownell, KS; (3); 2/11; Pres FCA; Speech Tm; Varsity Clb; Pep Band; Sec Stu Cncl; Var L Bsktbl; Var L Trk; Var L Vllybl; High Hon Roll; Church Yth Grp; Kayettes; Ft Hays ST; Acctng/Bus Ed.

WEEKS, JENNIFER M; Ellsworth HS; Ellsworth, KS; (2); Church Yth Grp; Math Tm; Band; Mrchg Band; Pep Band; Stat Crs Cntry; Hon Roll; Intnl Clb; Pep Clb; Stat Bsktbl; U Of KS; Child Ed.

WEEMS, AMANDA S; Cimarron HS; Cimarron, KS; (2); FHA; Library Aide; Pep Clb; Teachers Aide; Chorus; Tennis; Hon Roll; Fort Hays ST Univ; Medicine.

WEGELE, MICHAEL P; Trego Comm HS; Wa Keeney, KS; (2); Boy Scts; Church Yth Grp; Drama Clb; Science Clb; SADD; Band; Mrchg Band; Pep Band; Mgr(s); Wt Lftg; KS Assn Yth.

WEGENG, COURTNEY A; Kapaun-Mt Carmel HS; Wichita, KS; (3); Church Yth Grp; Drama Clb; JA; Thesps; School Play; Stage Crew; Var JV Golf; JV Sftbl; Tae Kwon Do Jr Olympic Gold Medalist In Sparring; U Of KS; Theatre; Elem Ed.

WEGNER, ERIN M; Beloit Jr Sr HS; Beloit, KS; (1); 1/90; Band; Mrchg Band; Orch; Bsktbl; L Trk; Vllybl; High Hon Roll; Pres Acad Fit Awd; FHA; SADD; 3rd Pl St Span Cont; Kayettes; Improvisional Troupe.

WEGNER, LEAH; Desoto HS; De Soto, KS; (4); 2/111; Am Leg Aux Girls St; Drill Tm; Rep Stu Cncl; Var Chrldng; Var Crs Cntry; Var Swmmng; Var Trk; High Hon Roll; NHS; Pres Acad Fit Awd; Madrigal Select Choir; League, Reg & St Music Fests; Baker U; Intl Bus.

WEHKAMP, BRIAN; Ingalls Jr Sr HS; Ingalls, KS; (4); 3/15; Church Yth Grp; Cmnty Wkr; Letterman Clb; Office Aide; Pep Clb; SADD; Church Choir; Bsktbl; Cit Awd; Hon Roll; Dodge City CC; Diesel Tech.

WEHNER, KATIE J; St Marys HS; Saint Marys, KS; (2); Church Yth Grp; Pep Clb; Spanish Clb; Band; Jazz Band; Mrchg Band; Orch; Pep Band; Hon Roll.

WEI, LEI; Lawrence HS; Lawrence, KS; (3); Chess Clb; DECA; Intnl Clb; JA; Latin Clb; Var L Swmmng; Var Trk; Hon Roll; NHS; Prfct Atten Awd; Maxima Cum Laude Awd Latim Exam 96; Plcd 1st Fin/Credit Exam DECA Career Dev Conf 96; KU; Intl Bus/Premed.

WEIBLE, KERRY; Valley Ctr HS; Wichita, KS; (4); 2/136; French Clb; Letterman Clb; Science Clb; Band; Rep Sr Cls; Rep Stu Cncl; Capt Chrldng; JETS Awd; NHS; Sal; Wichita ST Univ.

WEIBLE, STACY; Valley Ctr HS; Wichita, KS; (4); 9/137; Art Clb; VP Science Clb; Band; Mrchg Band; Pep Band; Chrldng; Sftbl; Hon Roll; Mgr(s); Powder Puff Ftbl; KS Hnr Schlr; His Club; Wichita ST Univ.

WEIDE, STEVEN W; Arkansas City HS; Arkansas City, KS; (3); Am Leg Boys St; Pres Church Yth Grp; FCA; Acpl Chr; Band; Chorus; Church Choir; Mrchg Band; Pep Band; Inner Discovery Retreat Team; K-St.

WEIDNER, DANIEL R; Wichita East HS; Wichita, KS; (2); Church Yth Grp; Debate Tm; Orch; JV Socr; High Hon Roll; Hon Roll; Soccer Coach For AYSO Vol; Low Alliance Car & Bicycle Clb Sec; Bus Admin; Acctng.

WEIDNER, NICK L; Wichita South HS; Wichita, KS; (1); JV Bsbl; Intrml Ftbl; Mgr(s); Hon Roll; Pres Acad Fit Awd; U Of KS.

WEIGANT, DAVID; Campus HS; Haysville, KS; (3); Church Yth Grp; L Debate Tm; Hist Drama Clb; Sec NFL; L Scholastic Bowl; L Speech Tm; Thesps; School Play; Stage Crew; L Mgr(s); Outstdng Dist Natl Frnscs Lgue; KS ST Thspn Bd; Asst Prprty Mstr Wrld Prmr Jane Eyre Ctr For Arts; Tech Thtre.

WEIGEL, APRIL M; Russell HS; Gorham, KS; (1); FCA; Key Clb; Letterman Clb; Pep Clb; Red Cross Aide; SADD; Chorus; Drm Mjr(t); Rep Stu Cncl; Sftbl; KS Univ; Tchr/Cosmotology.

WEIGEL, BRUCE; Trego Comm HS; Wa Keeney, KS; (3); 4/48; Science Clb; SADD; Teachers Aide; Band; Mrchg Band; Pep Band; JV Bsktbl; High Hon Roll; Hon Roll; Ft Hays ST U; Acctng.

WEIGEL, JENNIFER A; Bishop Miege HS; Kansas City, KS; (1); Pep Clb; SADD; JV Bsktbl; Var L Socr; Vllybl; Hon Roll; AAU Bsktbl; Premier Soccer.

WEIGEL, NATALIE A; Shawnee Mission S Sr HS; Overland Park, KS; (3); 44/465; Church Yth Grp; Ofcr Intnl Clb; Pep Clb; Yrbk; Bsktbl; L Capt Crs Cntry; L Capt Trk; High Hon Roll; NHS; Ntl Merit Ltr; U Of MO; Pre-Med; Phy Therapy.

WEIGEL, SETH C; Maranatha Acad; Stilwell, KS; (3); Church Yth Grp; Pep Clb; Acpl Chr; Chorus; Church Choir; School Musical; Intrml Ftbl; JV Var Socr; High Hon Roll; Hon Roll; Yell Leading; Roller Hockey; Washburn U Of Topeka; Bus Law.

WEIGLE, AMY L; Ness City HS; Ness City, KS; (3); 16/37; Church Yth Grp; Pep Clb; Stage Crew; Yrbk; Rep Stu Cncl; Var Bsktbl; Sftbl; Var Trk; Vllybl; Hon Roll; Bio.

WEILERT, CLINT; Thomas More Prep-Marion HS; Hays, KS; (1); Debate Tm; 4-H; Quiz Bowl; Scholastic Bowl; 4-H Awd; High Hon Roll.

WEILERT, SARAH; Thomas More Prep-Marion HS; Hays, KS; (3); 16/76; Am Leg Aux Girls St; Dance Clb; 4-H; Hosp Aide; Church Choir; Flag Corp; School Musical; 4-H Awd; High Hon Roll; Hon Roll; Tutor.

WEINMAN JR, JON M; Phillipsburg HS; Phillipsburg, KS; (2); Church Yth Grp; JV Bsktbl; Capt JV Ftbl; Wt Lftg; JV Wrstlng; High Hon Roll; Hon Roll; Amer Lgn Bsbll.

WEINMANN, ERIC R; Atchison Sr HS; Atchison, KS; (3).

WEINMANN, MARJORIE B; Acad Of Mt St Scholastica; Atchison, KS; (3); Drama Clb; Pep Clb; Band; Church Choir; Drill Tm; School Play; Stage Crew; Variety Show; Mgr(s); KS ST U; Music Prfmnc.

WEIR, J SCOTT; Trinity Catholic HS; Halstead, KS; (2); 1/35; Church Yth Grp; Cmnty Wkr; Debate Tm; Drama Clb; Math Tm; NFL; Quiz Bowl; Scholastic Bowl; Spanish Clb; School Play; Berkley U; Genrl Pract.

WEIR, JEFFREY S; Trinity HS; Halstead, KS; (2); Debate Tm; School Play; High Hon Roll; Drama Clb; NFL; Quiz Bowl; Scholastic Bowl; Spanish Clb; Speech Tm; VP Frsh Cls; Booster Clb; Notre Dame; Medicine; His.

WEIR, JESSICA; Trinity Catholic HS; Halstead, KS; (4); #7 in class; Am Leg Aux Girls St; Church Yth Grp; Cmnty Wkr; Debate Tm; Hosp Aide; NFL; Church Choir; Ed Nwsp; High Hon Roll; Hon Roll; Keyettes; Writing Poetry Pub Anthology Of Poetry By Young Americans 95; Emporia ST U; Comm.

WEIS, CHRISTOPHER R; Southeast HS; Wichita, KS; (3); Boy Scts; Church Yth Grp; Temple Yth Grp; Wt Lftg; Wrstlng; Hon Roll; Prof Airling Plt.

WEISBROD, KRISTEN J; Manhattan HS; Manhattan, KS; (3); FCA; FBLA; SADD; Chorus; Church Choir; Color Guard; Mrchg Band; School Play; JV Mgr(s); Score Keeper; CO ST U; District Attorney.

WEISER, LYNZEE; Garden City Sr HS; Garden City, KS; (4); 62/315; Bus Profs of Am; Teachers Aide; Band; Color Guard; Flag Corp; Mrchg Band; Score Keeper; Hon Roll; Prfct Atten Awd; Butler Cty CC; Bus.

WEISER, RYAN J; Sacred Heart HS; Salina, KS; (4); FBLA; Var Bsktbl; Var L Crs Cntry; Var L Golf; High Hon Roll; NHS; Ntl Merit Ltr; Prfct Atten Awd; Pres Acad Fit Awd; KS ST; Bus.

WEISS, DEBORAH; Shawnee Mission E Sr HS; Shawnee Mission, KS; (4); 10/398; Model UN; Q&S; Orch; School Musical; Ed Nwsp; Ed Yrbk; French Hon Soc; NHS; Ntl Merit Ltr; St Schlr; 280 Hours Of CC; IB Diploma Rcpt; All St Fest Orch; Yale Univ; Amerstuds.

WEITER, DANA E; Topeka West HS; Topeka, KS; (2); Church Yth Grp; French Clb; Pep Clb; Church Choir; Hon Roll; Intl Bus.

WEITZE, SHANE C; Bishop Ward HS; Kansas City, KS; (3); 19/75; Office Aide; SADD; Var Bsbl; Intrml Bsktbl; Hon Roll; Peer Cnslng; Conflict Resolution; U Of MO.

WEIXELMAN, JENIFER; Kapaun-Mt Carmel HS; Wichita, KS; (3); Church Yth Grp; French Clb; SADD; Chorus; Rep Jr Cls; Rep Sr Cls; JV Crs Cntry; JV Socr; NHS; Piano; Physicians Asst.

WELBORN, NICOLE R; Jefferson West HS; Meriden, KS; (2); 7/70; Church Yth Grp; Cmnty Wkr; FTA; Letterman Clb; Rptr Natl FFA Org; Pres Frsh Cls; Sftbl; Vllybl; High Hon Roll; Hon Roll; Acad Hon In Forgn Lang, Math, Engl, Hlth; Marine Bio.

WELCH, ERIC A; Salina HS Central; Salina, KS; (3); Church Yth Grp; Math Tm; Band; Jazz Band; Mrchg Band; Pep Band; School Musical; Mgr Bsktbl; JV Var Mgr(s); Hon Roll; KS St Univ; Comp Sci.

WELCH, MARY; Hayden HS; Topeka, KS; (3); 13/140; Cmnty Wkr; HOBY; Band; Drill Tm; Jazz Band; School Musical; Lit Mag; High Hon Roll; NHS; Pro-Life Grp Pres; Natl Pro-Life Mrch Wshngtn DC 96; Strwrs & FTF Assn; Zoolgy.

WELCH, TERRI; Olathe South Sr HS; Olathe, KS; (3); Pres Treas Church Yth Grp; Teachers Aide; Band; Drm Mjr(t); Mrchg Band; Phtg Yrbk; JV Tennis; High Hon Roll; NHS; Pres Acad Fit Awd.

WELLBROCK, CURTIS W; Victoria HS; Victoria, KS; (4); 14/30; Letterman Clb; Math Tm; SADD; Varsity Clb; Chorus; Ftbl; Wt Lftg; Hon Roll; NHS; Prfct Atten Awd; Bst Proj Awd W KS Tech Edu Fair; 2nd Pl Prob Solv Comptn Tech Fair; Salina Area Vocschl; Auto Bdy.

WELLER, TIFFANY; Arkansas City HS; Arkansas City, KS; (2); Debate Tm; FCA; NFL; Band; Mrchg Band; Var JV Chrldng; Var Pom Pon; High Hon Roll; Hon Roll; Pres Acad Fit Awd; Gymnstcs Cmptn; 1st Chair Sr Band Fresh/Soph; Roadrunner Cls All Trnmt Squad Awd; OK ST U; Psych.

WELLS, BRADLEY J; Riverton Schl; Columbus, KS; (3); Church Yth Grp; FCA; Sec 4-H; FHA; VP Band; Chorus; Church Choir; Jazz Band; School Musical; Pres Soph Cls; Ldrs Of Pack; Pitt ST; Sec Ed.

WELLS, BYRON M; Cheney Jr Sr HS; Cheney, KS; (3); JV Bsktbl; JV Var Ftbl; Hon Roll; NHS; KS St Univ; Ag.

WELLS, JOHN; Blue Valley Northwest HS; Overland Park, KS; (1); JV Ftbl; JV Tennis; Intrml Wt Lftg; High Hon Roll.

WELLS, MICHAEL A; Salina HS South; Salina, KS; (4); Boy Scts; Drama Clb; Speech Tm; School Play; Stage Crew; Yrbk; Shrff Dept Explors; KS ST U; Cmptr Sci.

WELLS, RENEE L; Olathe North Sr HS; Olathe, KS; (3); Art Clb; Church Yth Grp; French Clb; Sec Acpl Chr; Chorus; Church Choir; Swing Chorus; Variety Show; Teachers Aide; Ntl Merit Ltr; Northwinds 2 Yrs; Piano Trophy; Lancaster Bible Coll.

WELLS, SAM; Riley Cty HS; Manhattan, KS; (2); Church Yth Grp; FCA; Girl Scts; Pep Clb; Band; Chorus; Mrchg Band; Pep Band; School Play; Var Capt Chrldng; AFS Frgn Exchng Stu; St Music Fest; KS St Univ; Crim Law.

WELLS, VALLEY A; Paola HS; Paola, KS; (4); Chess Clb; Church Yth Grp; Debate Tm; Drama Clb; Chorus; Church Choir; School Musical; Stage Crew; Tennis; Johnson Cty CC; Vcl Mus Ed.

WELSH, TOMMY; Spring Hill HS; Spring Hill, KS; (1); Scholastic Bowl; SADD; Orch; Bsktbl; Ftbl; Var Trk; Hon Roll; Schlr Bowl; Odyssey Of The Mind; Knowledge Master Open; Psych.

WELTA, BONNIE; Andale HS; Andale, KS; (2); Church Yth Grp; Dance Clb; English Clb; 4-H; Spanish Clb; Rep Frsh Cls; Rep Soph Cls; Intrml JV Bsktbl; Var Chrldng; Intrml Vllybl; KS ST U; Ed.

WELTHA, CASEY N; Mc Louth Schl; Mc Louth, KS; (2); Chess Clb; VP FBLA; Quiz Bowl; Band; Mrchg Band; Pep Band; Bsktbl; Ftbl; Trk; Wt Lftg.

WELTMER, JEFF W; Shawnee Mission Nw Sr HS; Shawnee Mission, KS; (3); 128/460; Intrml Bsktbl; Intrml Ftbl; JV Socr; Intrml Trk; Hon Roll; NHS; Acctng; Sports Admin.

WELTMER, MELODY R; Plainville HS; Plainville, KS; (4); 2/54; Church Yth Grp; FHA; Band; Chorus; Church Choir; Trk; Vllybl; High Hon Roll; NHS; Sal; KS Hons Prgm; Red Cross Blood Dnr; Mid America Nazarene Coll; Nrsg.

WELTON, MELANEE B; Caney Valley Jr Sr HS; Caney, KS; (3); 3/70; Church Yth Grp; FCA; GAA; JA; Letterman Clb; NFL; Office Aide; Spanish Clb; Chorus; School Musical; Future Ldrs Of Tomorrow.

WELTY, MALANEE; Maize HS; Wichita, KS; (4); 37/239; Q&S; Spanish Clb; Thesps; Chorus; Variety Show; Ed Phtg Yrbk; L Trk; Capt L Vllybl; Hon Roll; NHS; AAU 1st Pl Natl Heptahlon 95; 2nd Pl AAU Natl High Jump 94; 1st Team All-League Vllybl 95; Wichita ST Univ; Ath Trng.

WELTY, MELLANEE D; Maize HS; Wichita, KS; (4); 37/239; Church Yth Grp; Key Clb; Letterman Clb; Q&S; Science Clb; Spanish Clb; SADD; Thesps; Varsity Clb; Chorus; MO Vally Mst Outs Ath; Wichita St Univ.

WENDELL, AMANDA; St John's HS; Beloit, KS; (2); 1/10; Church Yth Grp; Math Tm; Quiz Bowl; SADD; Sec Frsh Cls; Treas Soph Cls; Var L Trk; High Hon Roll; NHS; Acad Ltr Awd; Finance.

WENDLING, TESSA; Halstead HS; Halstead, KS; (4); 1/52; Am Leg Aux Girls St; VP Sec 4-H; Sec Treas German Clb; Band; School Musical; Rep Stu Cncl; Var L Bsktbl; Var L Chrldng; Var L Vllybl; Sec JETS Awd; KS Assn For Yth Pres; Cath Yth Org Sec Commnctns; KS ST U; Bus.

WENDT, CARRIE A; Russell HS; Russell, KS; (3); 33/88; Am Leg Aux Girls St; Church Yth Grp; Cmnty Wkr; SADD; Band; Mrchg Band; Var L Chrldng; Var L Tennis; Hon Roll; Prfct Atten Awd.

WENDT, KELLY; Salina HS South; Salina, KS; (4); 1/225; Am Leg Aux Girls St; Teachers Aide; Orch; JV Sftbl; Var L Vllybl; High Hon Roll; Pres NHS; Bausch & Lomb Sci Awd; Best Rep Girl Cls; KU; Chem Engr.

WENDT, MELISSA L; Salina HS South; Salina, KS; (4); 72/217; Cmnty Wkr; Letterman Clb; Library Aide; Teachers Aide; Chorus; School Musical; Stage Crew; Variety Show; Hon Roll; Lettered In Vocal; Crafting; Multi-Yr Listee; KS ST Manhattan; Pub Reltns.

WENDT, SHANNA A; Derby HS; Derby, KS; (4); 22/384; ROTC; High Hon Roll; Hon Roll; NHS; Ntl Merit Schol; Ger Hnrs; 1st Pl KMTA Piano Comp; ROTC Acad Excl/Ldrshp Awds; Cornell Coll; Jrnlsm/Nvlst/Art.

WENGER, MELISSA D; Horton HS; Horton, KS; (2); Church Yth Grp; Drama Clb; FCA; Pep Clb; SADD; Teachers Aide; Band; Mrchg Band; Pep Band; Sftbl; Washburn U; Acctng/Chem.

WENIGER, ROBBI; Kingman HS; Kingman, KS; (3); 1/85; Church Yth Grp; Cmnty Wkr; FCA; FBLA; Red Cross Aide; Service Clb; Spanish Clb; VP SADD; Teachers Aide; Rep Stu Cncl; Yth In Govt; Girls Sftbl Coach; Chisholm Trl Acad All League; Chld Psych.

WENKE, PAT R; Washburn Rural HS; Topeka, KS; (3); 10/350; Debate Tm; Math Tm; Var L Ftbl; Var L Trk; Wt Lftg; High Hon Roll; Ntl Merit Ltr; Comp Prgmr; Comp Sci.

WENNDT, ELIZABETH K; Independence HS; Independence, KS; (1); Church Yth Grp; Church Choir; Preschl & Kndgtn Tchr; Acad Ltr; Chorus In Comm Musical; Preschl Tchr.

WENRICH, ERIC; Garden City Sr HS; Garden City, KS; (3); Church Yth Grp; Math Tm; School Musical; School Play; Wt Lftg; High Hon Roll; Ntl Merit Ltr; Prfct Atten Awd; Ping Pong Clb; Engrng.

WENTZ, ERIK L; Northern Valley HS; Almena, KS; (2); Natl FFA Org; NFL; Quiz Bowl; Scholastic Bowl; Spanish Clb; Band; Jazz Band; Mrchg Band; Pep Band; VP Jr Cls; KS ST Univ Manhattan; Agrnmy.

WENZ, AMY R; Quivira Heights HS; Holyrood, KS; (2); #1 in class; Bus Profs of Am; Church Yth Grp; Cmnty Wkr; FCA; Letterman Clb; Pep Clb; Chorus; Vllybl; High Hon Roll; Prfct Atten Awd; Bus.

WERNER, RYAN D; Spearville Jr Sr HS; Spearville, KS; (3); 2/26; Cmnty Wkr; Math Tm; Quiz Bowl; Speech Tm; Rep Stu Cncl; Ofcr Bsbl; Var Capt Ftbl; High Hon Roll; VP Pres NHS; Pres Acad Fit Awd; Champion KS Rural Electric Cooperatives Cont; U Of KS; Bus; Acctng.

WERNER, WYATT; Garden City Sr HS; Garden City, KS; (3); Intnl Clb; High Hon Roll; Prfct Atten Awd.

WERRING, ANDREW; Maur Hill Prep Schl; Atchison, KS; (2); 6/50; Boy Scts; Church Yth Grp; Letterman Clb; Chorus; VP Frsh Cls; VP Soph Cls; Bsktbl; Ftbl; Golf; Hon Roll.

WERTENBERGER, LISA; Thomas More Prep-Marion HS; Hays, KS; (3); 22/77; School Musical; Variety Show; Capt Chrldng; Svc Awd; Ambssdr; GAG; Neo Gea; Ft Hays St Univ; Spch Path.

WERTH, BECKY L; Trego Comm HS; Ellis, KS; (3); Church Yth Grp; 4-H; FHA; Sec Natl FFA Org; SADD; Band; Mrchg Band; Pep Band; 4-H Awd; High Hon Roll; KS Jr Livestock Assn Dir; KAY Clb Fresh Rep & Points Chm; Colby CC; Ag; Bus.

WERTH, CLINTON; Thomas More Prep-Marion HS; Hays, KS; (2); 6/73; Quiz Bowl; Var L Ftbl; Var L Wrstlng; Hon Roll; Mchncl Engrng.

WERTH, DARRELL L; Quinter Jr Sr HS; Quinter, KS; (2); 1/28; FCA; Math Tm; Sec Frsh Cls; Rep Soph Cls; VP Jr Cls; Var L Ftbl; Var L Trk; Cit Awd; High Hon Roll; NHS; KS Regents Hnrs Acad; Engrng.

WERTH, NATHAN J; Campus HS; Wichita, KS; (3); High Hon Roll; NHS.

WERTIN, MINNIE; Spring Hill HS; Olathe, KS; (3); Art Clb; Stage Crew; Hon Roll; Frnsc Tm; Mar Bio.

WESLEY, DANIEL S; Turner HS; Kansas City, KS; (4); Computer Clb; Boy Scts; Math Tm; Quiz Bowl; Band; Jazz Band; Mrchg Band; Pep Band; Nwsp; Var Bsbl; KCKCC Pres Hnr Roll; Chrch Yth Grp; U Of KS; Cmptr Tech.

WESLEY, RACHEL A; Elyria Christian Schl; Mc Pherson, KS; (2); Church Yth Grp; Cmnty Wkr; School Play; Phtg Rptr Yrbk; Var L Bsktbl; Var L Sftbl; Hon Roll; Piano; Lead Role In Play; Nom Natl Schlr/Invited To Natl Young Ldrs Conf.

WESLEY, ROSALIE; Halstead HS; Burrton, KS; (2); 1/70; Quiz Bowl; Spanish Clb; Drill Tm; School Musical; VP Soph Cls; VP Jr Cls; Var Bsktbl; Var Trk; JV Vllybl; High Hon Roll; Vcl Solo; Attnded KS Rgnts Hnrs Acad; Crdlgst.

WESLEY, TONI M; Medicine Lodge HS; Lake City, KS; (3); 18/53; Pres 4-H; Girl Scts; Pres Natl FFA Org; NFL; Ed Nwsp; Ed Yrbk; Vllybl; High Hon Roll; NHS; Danforth Awd; KS ST Univ; Ag.

WESSEL, MICHELLE E; Marion HS; Marion, KS; (2); Church Yth Grp; Pep Clb; Teachers Aide; Band; Jazz Band; Mrchg Band; School Musical; School Play; Sec Frsh Cls; Sec Soph Cls; Band Clb VP; League Hnr Band; KSU; Pre-Med.

WESSEL, PATRICIA; Holton HS; Holton, KS; (2); Band; Mrchg Band; Pep Band; Mgr(s); High Hon Roll; Hon Roll; Prfct Atten Awd; Lttrlds Clb; Elem Ed.

WESSLING, NATALIE A; Beloit Jr Sr HS; Beloit, KS; (2); 1/56; Art Clb; Church Yth Grp; Letterman Clb; Drill Tm; Orch; Ofcr Stu Cncl; Var L Chrldng; Capt Pom Pon; High Hon Roll; NHS; CPR & Lfgrdng Cert; Cmnty Svc; KS ST U; Marine Bio.

WEST, ALLISON; Shawnee Mission W Sr HS; Shawnee, KS; (2); 3/430; Band; Mrchg Band; Pep Band; Var Sftbl; JV Vllybl; Intrml Wt Lftg; High Hon Roll; Pr Mdtrs.

WEST, AMANDA; Pratt HS; Pratt, KS; (3); FHA; Pep Clb; Chorus; School Musical; Chrldng; Hon Roll.

WEST, CHRISTINA S; Wichita South HS; Wichita, KS; (4); 8/292; Church Yth Grp; Scholastic Bowl; Thesps; Chorus; Orch; Variety Show; Sec Stu Cncl; NHS; Chess Clb; Cmnty Wkr; Sci Olympd; Titanantics Set Crw; U Of KS; Chem Engrng.

WEST, DESMOND D; Sumner Acad Of Arts & Science; Kansas City, KS; (4); Boy Scts; Cmnty Wkr; German Clb; Key Clb; Var Ftbl; Socr; Trk; Civil Engr.

WEST, JACOB A; Pierson Jr HS; Kansas City, KS; (1); Art Clb; Boy Scts; Model UN; Ed Nwsp; Rep Soph Cls; Ofcr Stu Cncl; JV Crs Cntry; Intrml Wt Lftg; Cit Awd; High Hon Roll; Trnmnt Archry 3-D Shoots; Pitt ST.

WEST, MATT; Derby HS; Derby, KS; (3); Bus Profs of Am; FCA; Var Ftbl; JV Socr; JV Trk; Hon Roll; Emporia St Univ; Scndry Ed.

WEST, VENESSA; Wichita West HS; Wichita, KS; (3); 32/283; Church Yth Grp; German Clb; Office Aide; Drill Tm; Flag Corp; Sftbl; Hon Roll; Prfct Atten Awd; Multi-Yr Listee; Wichita ST; Tchng Cmptrs/Bus.

WESTERVELT, KELLY; Columbus HS; Columbus, KS; (4); 1/92; Pres Art Clb; VP FHA; HOBY; Math Tm; Var Sftbl; Hon Roll; VP NHS; KS Assn For Yth Pres; Govs Schlr; Stu Cncl VP; Pittsburg ST U.

WESTFAHL, ALLISON; Haven HS; Haven, KS; (3); 1/90; Pres Church Yth Grp; Pres 4-H; HOBY; NFL; School Musical; Swing Chorus; Var L Vllybl; 4-H Awd; High Hon Roll; FCA; Peer Cnslr; IDA Fornsc St Chmpn 95; NY U; Perfmng Arts.

WESTFAHL, NICHOLAS A; Maize HS; Wichita, KS; (2); 1/290; Debate Tm; Math Tm; NFL; JV Capt Socr; Var Wrstlng; High Hon Roll; NHS; M Club; Sci Olympd.

WESTFAHL, TIM J; Maize HS; Wichita, KS; (1); 1/300; Math Tm; High Hon Roll; Stock Mrkt.

WESTFALL, MICHELLE M; Wallace Cty HS; Sharon Springs, KS; (1); Church Yth Grp; Cmnty Wkr; Dance Clb; Drama Clb; English Clb; FCA; 4-H; Letterman Clb; Office Aide; Pep Clb; OK Panhandle ST Univ; Music.

WESTHOFF, BRANDON; Arkansas City HS; Arkansas City, KS; (2); Church Yth Grp; FCA; Band; Church Choir; Jazz Band; Mrchg Band; Pep Band; Ofcr Bsbl; Socr; Cit Awd; Bowling; Band Frosh/Soph Class Rep; Hnr Bnd ST On Solos; Dentist.

WESTHOFF, MEGAN; St Mary's Colgan HS; Pittsburg, KS; (3); 5/50; Pep Clb; Scholastic Bowl; Science Clb; School Play; Stage Crew; High Hon Roll; NHS; Comm Theatre; Our Lady Of Lourdes Choir/Rel Act; Pittsburg ST U; Law/Theatr.

WESTMARK, KERI L; Shawnee Mission South HS; Overland Park, KS; (3); Church Yth Grp; Cmnty Wkr; Drama Clb; FCA; SADD; Band; Church Choir; Orch; Jr NHS; NHS; CODE; Yth Group Cncl; Bell Choir; Mid-Amer Nazarene Coll; Soc Sci.

WESTON, JAY A; Beloit Jr Sr HS; Beloit, KS; (1); 15/89; Church Yth Grp; Natl FFA Org; JV Ftbl; High Hon Roll; Prfct Atten Awd.

WESTON, STACY; Marmaton Valley Jr Sr HS; Moran, KS; (2); Church Yth Grp; FCA; Treas FHA; Natl FFA Org; Q&S; Rep Frsh Cls; Rep Soph Cls; Ofcr Stu Cncl; JV Var Bsktbl; JV Vllybl.

WESTON, TIFFANY J; Arkansas City HS; Arkansas City, KS; (4); 11/172; Drama Clb; SADD; Band; School Musical; School Play; High Hon Roll; NHS; Church Yth Grp; Cmnty Wkr; FCA; KU Hnr Stu; OK ST U; Zlgy.

WESTOVER, JOSHUA M; Junction City HS; Fort Riley, KS; (1); Hon Roll; Marine Biologist.

WESTPHAL, KRISTYN; Shawnee Mission E HS; Shawnee Mission, KS; (3); 47/483; German Clb; Natl Beta Clb; Q&S; Acpl Chr; Chorus; School Musical; Rptr Nwsp; High Hon Roll; NHS; Ntl Merit Ltr; Tutr Of Engl As 2nd Lang; Germn Interp.

WETMORE, TRENT; Neodesha Jr Sr HS; Neodesha, KS; (4); 9/43; Cmnty Wkr; FHA; Pep Clb; VP Frsh Cls; VP Soph Cls; VP Jr Cls; Treas Sr Cls; Rep Stu Cncl; Var Capt Bsbl; Var Capt Ftbl; Multi Yr Listee; KS ST Univ; Chemical Engr.

WETSCHENSKY, TRACY L; Piper HS; Kansas City, KS; (3); Cmnty Wkr; French Clb; GAA; JA; SADD; Nwsp; Intrml Swmmng; Var Vllybl; High Hon Roll; NHS; U Of KS; Dr.

WETTA, BRIAN J; Andale HS; Andale, KS; (3); 1/65; Treas Church Yth Grp; 4-H; Letterman Clb; Quiz Bowl; Scholastic Bowl; Spanish Clb; Rep Frsh Cls; Rep Soph Cls; Pres Stu Cncl; JV Var Ftbl; Sedgwick Cty Meat Identification Team Mem; Ed.

WETTA, JEFF; Wellington Sr HS; Wellington, KS; (3); Church Yth Grp; Ftbl; Golf; Hon Roll.

WETTERER, AMBER; Olathe North Sr HS; Olathe, KS; (3); Art Clb; Church Yth Grp; 4-H; German Clb; Hosp Aide; SADD; Teachers Aide; Chorus; Rptr Frsh Cls; Rptr Soph Cls; William Jewell; Sclgy Psych.

WEWERS, CARRIE M; Hayden HS; Topeka, KS; (2); Intnl Clb; Spanish Clb; Yrbk; JV Bsktbl; Intrml Score Keeper; JV Trk; JV Var Vllybl; Hon Roll; NHS; Yrbk Section Ed; Jr Ofcr At Large Natl Hnrs Soc.

WEYGANDT, TRAVIS; Enterprise Sda Acad; Enterprise, KS; (1); Band; Bsktbl; Ftbl; Sftbl; Vllybl; Hon Roll.

WEYHRAUCH, KATHERINE A; Topeka HS; Topeka, KS; (1); 5/500; Chorus; Church Choir; Drill Tm; Orch; School Musical; Chrldng; Hon Roll; Ballett Cls & Perfmnc; Music; Voice.

WEYRAUCH, RYAN W; El Dorado HS; El Dorado, KS; (2); Spanish Clb; SADD; Ofcr Bsbl; Bsktbl; Golf; High Hon Roll; Natl Engl Merit Awd; Butler Cnty CC.

WHALEY, LARR S; Tonganoxie HS; Leavenworth, KS; (4); 17/127; FBLA; FHA; Letterman Clb; SADD; L Crs Cntry; L Trk; Hon Roll; Acctng.

WHEARTY, JENNY E; Andover HS; Andover, KS; (4); 6/143; Letterman Clb; Prfct Atten Awd; Pres Acad Fit Awd; Sal; Mgr Bsbl; Mgr Ftbl; Mgr Wrstlng; Wichita St Univ; Acctng.

WHEAT, ROSANN; Hamilton HS; Eureka, KS; (2); Church Yth Grp; Debate Tm; FBLA; FHA; Quiz Bowl; Scholastic Bowl; VP Frsh Cls; Var Chrldng; Var Vllybl; Hon Roll; Washburn U; Law.

WHEELER, ANDREW; Atchison Sr HS; Atchison, KS; (4); Am Leg Boys St; Church Yth Grp; Office Aide; Pep Clb; SADD; Band; Jazz Band; Mrchg Band; Pep Band; Rep Frsh Cls; Butler Cnty CC.

WHEELER, DEATRA; Jackson Heights HS; Circleville, KS; (1); Church Yth Grp; Pep Clb; Chorus; Stage Crew; Bsktbl; Vllybl; Hon Roll; Prfct Atten Awd; Pres Lit Exclnce Awd; Natl Authors Regstry Hnrb Mntn.

WHEELER, DERRIC S; Topeka HS; Topeka, KS; (3); Math Clb; Science Clb; Teachers Aide; Varsity Clb; Stage Crew; JV Intrml Bsktbl; Var Capt Ftbl; Var L Trk; Var L Wrstlng; Cit Awd; STRAPP; MSIP; NE At Kearney; Archtctr.

WHEELER, JAIME; Jackson Heights HS; Wetmore, KS; (4); 1/38; Church Yth Grp; Drama Clb; FCA; FBLA; FHA; Sec Natl FFA Org; Pep Clb; Teachers Aide; Chorus; School Musical; All Amer Schlr; Ft Hays ST U; Nursing.

WHEELER, MAX M; Riverton Schl; Baxter Springs, KS; (2); Church Yth Grp; Speech Tm; School Musical; School Play; Stage Crew; JV Bsbl; Bsktbl; Hon Roll; Stu Actvty Cncl; Arch.

WHETSTONE, SHAUN E; Labette Co HS; Parsons, KS; (4); Natl FFA Org; Treas VICA; Indvdl Achvmt Awd 95-; Vica Skls Olympc 3rd Plc Extmprns Spkng 95; Ford Ast Prgm; OK ST Univ; Ford Tech.

WHILES, TIFFANY D; Shawnee Mission E Sr HS; Fairway, KS; (4); Art Clb; Cmnty Wkr; Dance Clb; Intnl Clb; Pep Clb; SADD; Teachers Aide; Orch; Lit Mag; Hon Roll; Art Awds; Vrs Lit Awds/Hnrs; Violin Perf; Bllt-Jazz Dnc; Acad Lttr; U Of Tampa; Lang Arts.

WHISLER, CHERYL D; Washington HS; Kansas City, KS; (2); German Clb; Spanish Clb; SADD; Chorus; Flag Corp; High Hon Roll; Hon Roll; KS Univ; Vet Med/Law.

WHITAKER, JASON M; Wetmore Schl; Goff, KS; (2); Letterman Clb; Pep Clb; Chorus; School Musical; School Play; Mgr Bsktbl; Golf; High Hon Roll; Wetmore Comm Connection Television Chief Operator; Sound Sensations; KS ST Univ; Comp Engrng.

WHITAKER, JOLYN D; Dodge City HS; Dodge City, KS; (3); Church Yth Grp; Office Aide; SADD; Mrchg Band; High Hon Roll; NHS; Prfct Atten Awd; Cmnty Wkr; Band; Jazz Band; I Rating Regnl Solo Cntst; Dist Hnr Bnd; Dodge City Cowboy Bnd; Dodge City CC; Psych.

WHITE, AARON R; Minneola Schl; Kingsdown, KS; (4); 1/12; FCA; Var L Bsktbl; Var L Crs Cntry; Var L Trk; Cit Awd; Gov Hon Prg Awd; High Hon Roll; Pres Acad Fit Awd; St Schlr; Val; Sterling Coll; Anml Sci/Ag Bus.

WHITE, ALISA M; Wellington Sr HS; Wellington, KS; (3); Bus Profs of Am; Dance Clb; SADD; Drill Tm; School Play; Rep Jr Cls; Rep Stu Cncl; Mgr(s); Pom Pon; High Hon Roll; KS ST U.

WHITE, AMANDA; Circle HS; Towanda, KS; (2); Church Yth Grp; FCA; SADD; Chorus; Variety Show; Yrbk; Chrldng; Pom Pon; Hon Roll; Quill/Scrll Awd; Med.

WHITE, ANDREA D; Medicine Lodge HS; Medicine Lodge, KS; (4); 14/54; Church Yth Grp; Office Aide; Pep Clb; Science Clb; Band; Chorus; Mrchg Band; Pep Band; Swing Chorus; Rep Frsh Cls; Sterling Coll; Elem Ed.

WHITE, ANDREW; Inman Jr Sr HS; Inman, KS; (2); Math Tm; Natl FFA Org; Quiz Bowl; JV Bsktbl; Var Ftbl; Hon Roll.

WHITE, ANDY; Lewis Schl; Lewis, KS; (2); 3/16; Pres FBLA; Quiz Bowl; Band; Chorus; School Musical; Pres Frsh Cls; Ofcr Soph Cls; Treas Jr Cls; Var L Bsktbl; Var L Ftbl; Entrprnr.

WHITE, BECKY; Elkhart HS; Richfield, KS; (4); 10/30; Church Yth Grp; Teachers Aide; Varsity Clb; Chorus; Yrbk; Sec Jr Cls; Pres Sr Cls; VP Stu Cncl; Var Capt Chrldng; Cit Awd; Sprtsmnshp Awd; Ftbl Hmcmng Qn 95; Dodge City CC; Elem Ed.

WHITE, BRANDY R; Wallace Cty HS; Sharon Springs, KS; (1); Girl Scts; Ofcr Bsbl; Bsktbl; Sftbl; Trk; Vllybl; Pol Ofcr.

WHITE, BRIAN C; Argonia Jr Sr HS; Argonia, KS; (3); Church Yth Grp; Letterman Clb; Quiz Bowl; Band; Ftbl; Hon Roll.

WHITE, CALLIE; Topeka West HS; Topeka, KS; (4); 51/243; Church Yth Grp; Cmnty Wkr; French Clb; Q&S; Stage Crew; Ed Yrbk; Powder Puff Ftbl; Capt Socr; Hon Roll; NHS; KCYF; Univ Of KS; Nrsng; Jrnlsm.

WHITE, CLINT R; Olathe South Sr HS; Olathe, KS; (2); Boy Scts; Science Clb; Chorus; Hon Roll; Pres Acad Fit Awd; Eng Expl Post; Eagle Sct; Lcl St Lvl Sci Olympd Ptcpt; KS St Univ; Eng.

WHITE, DAVID M; Olathe East Sr HS; Overland Park, KS; (2); Boy Scts; Church Yth Grp; Spanish Clb; JV Wrstlng; Hon Roll; USAF Acad; Engrng.

WHITE, DONJE E; Hayden HS; Topeka, KS; (2); Church Yth Grp; Intnl Clb; Yrbk; Bsktbl; Var L Sftbl; Var L Vllybl; 1AV Jr Olympc Vlybl Tm 6 Yrs; ASA Jr Olympc Sftbl Tm 11 Yrs, St Chmpns, Natl Tournament; Lfgrd; Sprts Med.

WHITE, GREGORY T; Robert E Clark Jr HS; Edwardsville, KS; (1); Hon Roll; KS CC; Arch.

WHITE, HEATHER L; Sumner Acad Of Arts & Science; Kansas City, KS; (4); 75/200; Cmnty Wkr; Key Clb; Pep Clb; Spanish Clb; SADD; Drill Tm; High Hon Roll; NHS; Spanish NHS; KCK Brd Of Ed Outstndg Vlntr Awd; KS ST U; Scl Wrk.

WHITE, JACQUIE; Kinsley HS; Kinsley, KS; (2); 1/42; Sec Church Yth Grp; Debate Tm; Quiz Bowl; School Musical; School Play; Pres Frsh Cls; Pres Soph Cls; Bsktbl; Chrldng; High Hon Roll; KS Newman; Brdcstng.

WHITE, JEFF; Lincoln Jr Sr HS; Lincoln, KS; (4); 5/31; Church Yth Grp; Letterman Clb; Library Aide; Pep Clb; Quiz Bowl; Scholastic Bowl; Chorus; Church Choir; School Musical; School Play; Ft Hays ST U; Ag Tech Mngmt.

WHITE, JEFFREY D; Independence HS; Independence, KS; (2); French Clb; Pep Clb; Quiz Bowl; Scholastic Bowl; Teachers Aide; Ofcr Bsbl; Hon Roll; Indpndnc CC; CPU Prgmng.

WHITE, JESSICA; Olathe East Sr HS; Olathe, KS; (3); Letterman Clb; Teachers Aide; Bsktbl; Capt Chrldng; Powder Puff Ftbl; Sftbl; Trk; Vllybl; Wt Lftg; Hon Roll; Johnson Cty CC; Phy Thrpst.

WHITE, JESSICA L; Eudora HS; Eudora, KS; (4); 4-H; FBLA; Spanish Clb; SADD; Varsity Clb; Phtg Nwsp; Phtg Yrbk; Chrldng; Crs Cntry; Mgr(s); U Of KS; Magazine Advertising.

WHITE, JOSH; Seaman Sr HS; Topeka, KS; (4); 17/250; Cmnty Wkr; Key Clb; Rep Jr Cls; Sec Stu Cncl; Capt Var Bsbl; Intrml Bsktbl; Capt Var Ftbl; Var Wt Lftg; High Hon Roll; St Schlr; Homcmng King; KS Alumni Hnr Schlr; Air Force Acad; Pre-Med.

WHITE, JOSHUA A; Wichita Heights HS; Wichita, KS; (2); 72/330; Church Yth Grp; Cmnty Wkr; Office Aide; Teachers Aide; Acpl Chr; Variety Show; Socr; Trk; Hon Roll; Prfct Atten Awd; Frosh/Soph Var Sccr; Cnslng/Tchng.

WHITE, KATIE; Little River Jr Sr HS; Little River, KS; (2); Church Yth Grp; FHA; German Clb; GAA; Math Tm; Pep Clb; Stage Crew; Bsktbl; High Hon Roll; Hon Roll; KS HS Rodeo Tm; KS ST U; Vet Sci.

WHITE, KELLY A; Mc Louth Schl; Lawrence, KS; (2); Art Clb; Church Yth Grp; FHA; Pep Clb; Spanish Clb; Band; Mrchg Band; Pep Band; School Musical; Intrml Bsktbl; Art Awd Best Art I/II Stdnt 95-Schl Yr; Comm Art.

WHITE, MARILYN L; Derby HS; Wichita, KS; (1); Cmnty Wkr; NFL; ROTC; Varsity Clb; Drill Tm; Score Keeper; Trk; Wrstlng; Hon Roll; Mrs Teen KS ST Fnlst; Yale/Harvard; Doctor/Chld Psych.

WHITE, NATALIE C; Emporia HS; Emporia, KS; (2); 115/400; FCA; Key Clb; Pep Clb; Orch; JV Diving; Var Golf; Cit Awd; Hon Roll; Peer Mediation; Soph Bd; Kayette Bd; Emporia ST Univ; Elem Ed.

WHITE, NIKKI; Lansing HS; Leavenworth, KS; (2); Church Yth Grp; Drama Clb; Sftbl; Hon Roll; Georgetown U; Lawyer.

WHITE, RYAN M; Medicine Lodge HS; Medicine Lodge, KS; (2); 12/56; Boy Scts; Church Yth Grp; Cmnty Wkr; Library Aide; Natl FFA Org; Pep Clb; Science Clb; Band; Mrchg Band; Orch; HS Rodeo.

WHITE, SARA L; Shawnee Mission S Sr HS; Overland Park, KS; (3); 37/450; Intnl Clb; JCL; Latin Clb; Pep Clb; SADD; Rptr Nwsp; Trk; High Hon Roll.

WHITE, SETH; Emporia HS; Emporia, KS; (4); 17/283; Am Leg Boys St; Pep Clb; Varsity Clb; JV Trk; JV Wrstlng; Cit Awd; High Hon Roll; Pres Schlr; St Schlr; KS St Univ; Mech Eng.

WHITE, STEPHANIE; Argonia Jr Sr HS; Argonia, KS; (4); 2/16; Quiz Bowl; Band; Chorus; Bsktbl; Vllybl; Hon Roll; Sal; St Schlr; Church Yth Grp; Cmnty Wkr; Multi Yr Listee; ST Music Fest 3 Yrs; ST Quiz Bowl Meet 96; Northwestern OK ST Univ; PHD.

WHITE, VENESSA; Peabody-Burns Jr Sr HS; Peabody, KS; (3); 11/28; Church Yth Grp; Dance Clb; Band; Flag Corp; Mrchg Band; Pep Band; VP Jr Cls; JV Var Bsktbl; Var Sftbl; JV Var Vllybl; Lift Weights; Vet.

WHITE, WENDY LYNN; Clearwater HS; Clearwater, KS; (2); Church Yth Grp; SADD; Chorus; Mgr(s); Hon Roll; Tae Kwon Do; Kytts.

WHITE, ZACHARY K; Oskaloosa HS; Oskaloosa, KS; (2); FBLA; Letterman Clb; Quiz Bowl; Scholastic Bowl; Varsity Clb; Jazz Band; JV Bsktbl; Var L Ftbl; L Trk; High Hon Roll; Prlmntry Prcdrs Team Won ST FBLA Contest; Local Chptr Prlmntrn FBLA; Med.

WHITED, CARMEN B; Sumner Acad Of Arts & Science; Kansas City, KS; (4); 10/190; Church Yth Grp; Pep Clb; Quiz Bowl; Spanish Clb; SADD; Acpl Chr; High Hon Roll; NHS; Spanish NHS; Stu As Tchrs Tutoring Pgm; KSKCC.

WHITEHEAD, KRISTEN M; Northeast HS; Arma, KS; (1); 9/58; FHA; Office Aide; Band; Ofcr Stu Cncl; Bsktbl; Chrldng; Sftbl; Var Vllybl; Hon Roll; Pittsburg ST Univ; Dntl Hygnst.

WHITEHILL, JORDAN L; Maize HS; Wichita, KS; (3); 56/350; Letterman Clb; SADD; Teachers Aide; Rptr Nwsp; Var L Socr; Var L Tennis; Hon Roll; Chem.

WHITEMAN, LAURA; Kansas City Christian Schl; Olathe, KS; (3); Hosp Aide; Teachers Aide; Chorus; Yrbk; Ofcr Frsh Cls; VP Jr Cls; Capt Vllybl; High Hon Roll; VP NHS; Church Yth Grp; Lydia Awd Recognizing Excl Of Character & Svc; Occptnl Therapy.

WHITESIDE, LIANNE A; Olathe East Sr HS; Olathe, KS; (2); 87/409; Debate Tm; Girl Scts; Spanish Clb; Chorus; Yrbk; Stat Vllybl; Hon Roll; Pres Schlr; Girl Sct Silver Awd; Powell Gardens Vol; KS City Renaissance Festival Benefit KS Art Inst Vol; Bus; Frgn Lang.

WHITESIDE, MISTY M; El Dorado HS; El Dorado, KS; (3); 55/170; Band; Mrchg Band; Orch; Var Sftbl; Var Swmmng; Var Vllybl; Hon Roll; Prfct Atten Awd; Zoolgy.

WHITESIDE, S S; Wichita Collegiate Schl; Wichita, KS; (3); Art Clb; Cmnty Wkr; Science Clb; Drill Tm; School Musical; Pom Pon; Sftbl; High Hon Roll; Art Stu Of Yr 95-96; Ind Schls Of Southwest Art Festvl Stu Planning & Exectng Comm; Spcl Olympics Vol; Medcn; Sports Medcn; Phys Therpy.

WHITMER, ZACK L; Wichita Northwest HS; Wichita, KS; (2); #1 in class; Bsktbl; Var Socr; High Hon Roll; Hon Roll; Sci Awd; U Of KS.

WHITMORE, DANA A; Bishop Miege HS; Fairway, KS; (1); 14/245; SADD; Bsktbl; Score Keeper; Socr; Vllybl; High Hon Roll; Spirit Clb.

WHITMORE, TARA L; Axtell Schl; Axtell, KS; (2); Natl FFA Org; Pep Clb; Band; Chorus; Sec Soph Cls; VP Jr Cls; Mgr Bsktbl; JV Vllybl; Hon Roll; Kays Grndprnts; U Of NE; Law/Psych.

WHITNEY, AMY L; Chase Co HS; Elmdale, KS; (3); Church Yth Grp; 4-H; Spanish Clb; Chorus; Nwsp; Bsktbl; 4-H Awd; Hon Roll; NHS; Jrnlsm Clb.

WHITNEY, CHARLES N; Russell HS; Russell, KS; (1); Key Clb; Natl FFA Org; JV Var Ftbl; L Var Trk; L Var Wrstlng; High Hon Roll; KS ST; Dentist.

WHITNEY, CRYSTAL N; Russell HS; Russell, KS; (2); 24/83; Dance Clb; FCA; German Clb; Key Clb; Letterman Clb; Math Tm; Pep Clb; Rep SADD; Band; Chorus; Teens As Tchrs; K-ST; CPA.

WHITSON, JOSH G; Circle HS; Benton, KS; (3); 34/140; Church Yth Grp; Cmnty Wkr; FCA; Letterman Clb; Office Aide; Quiz Bowl; SADD; Teachers Aide; Varsity Clb; Band; WSU; Phys Ed.

WHITTEMORE, LUKE A; Lawrence HS; Lawrence, KS; (3); 1/621; Boy Scts; Debate Tm; Drama Clb; Sec Treas Model UN; Thesps; Acpl Chr; School Play; High Hon Roll; NHS; German Clb; Lawrence Aquahawks Comm Swim Team; Sign Lang Clb Treas; Mammoth Clb; US Naval Acad; Engrng.

WHITTINGTON, DEVON; Washington HS; Kansas City, KS; (1); Pep Clb; ROTC; Chorus; Chrldng; Swmmng; Hon Roll; Psych.

WHITTLE, JENNIFER S; Blue Valley Northwest HS; Pittsburg, KS; (4); 70/350; Church Yth Grp; Cmnty Wkr; Service Clb; Church Choir; Orch; Ed Lit Mag; NHS; Msc/Acad Schlrshp To PSU; Hndbls At Chrch; Pittsburg ST U; Dr.

WHITTREDGE, BENJAMIN L; Buhler HS; Hutchinson, KS; (3); Church Yth Grp; Debate Tm; Science Clb; Band; Jazz Band; Orch; Swmmng; High Hon Roll; NHS; SMAD; Medicine.

WICHMANN, JOHN-PAUL; Shawnee Mission Nw Sr HS; Shawnee, KS; (3); Bus Profs of Am; Church Yth Grp; Cmnty Wkr; Letterman Clb; Var Capt Ftbl; Var Wt Lftg; Wrstlng; Received 2nd Pl At DECA St Trnmt.

WICK, JENIFER M; Labette Co HS; Coffeyville, KS; (1); Church Yth Grp; Chorus; School Musical; Hon Roll; Harding Univ.

WICKSTRUM, ANGELA K; Manhattan HS; Manhattan, KS; (4); Church Yth Grp; Cmnty Wkr; FCA; Hosp Aide; Office Aide; Spanish Clb; Teachers Aide; Church Choir; Cit Awd; Hon Roll; Amer Fld Svc Ofcr; Pres Schlsp Awd MCC; Vol Nrsng Hm; Manhattan Chrstn Cll; Mssnry Dr.

WICKSTRUM, GABE A; Manhattan HS; Manhattan, KS; (2); Boy Scts; Church Yth Grp; Chorus; Church Choir; Tennis; Wrstlng; High Hon Roll; Hon Roll; Spanish NHS; Amer Field Svc; Mid-Amer Nazarene Coll.

WICKSTRUM, JASON R; Shawnee Heights Sr HS; Topeka, KS; (4); Intnl Clb; VP Sr Cls; JV Wrstlng; High Hon Roll; Prfct Atten Awd; GAPP; KS U.

WIDCHAM, AMANDA; Fredonia HS; Fredonia, KS; (2); Art Clb; Church Yth Grp; FCA; FHA; Pep Clb; Science Clb; Pres Soph Cls; Var Chrldng; Var L Golf; High Hon Roll; Lifeguard; Ballet; Gymnstcs; CU.

WIDNER, MEGAN; Columbus HS; Scammon, KS; (2); Art Clb; Bus Profs of Am; Church Yth Grp; FHA; Bsktbl; Powder Puff Ftbl; Wt Lftg; Hon Roll; Bsktbll Mgr; Yth Ara Soccr; Bus.

WIEBE, BROOKE J; Bishop Carroll Catholic HS; Wichita, KS; (3); Cmnty Wkr; German Clb; Girl Scts; Hon Roll; Pro Life Club; Chasity Club; Cath Yths Actn; Law.

WIEBE, JENNIFER D; Newton Sr HS; Newton, KS; (2); Art Clb; Church Yth Grp; German Clb; Orch; JV Vllybl.

WIEBE, LEEANN E; Eastern Heights Jr Sr HS; Kirwin, KS; (1); 3/9; Church Yth Grp; FCA; GAA; Pep Clb; Varsity Clb; Band; Chorus; Mrchg Band; Pep Band; School Play; Chrch; Kays Clb; M Clb; Indstrl Arts Awd; Vet.

WIEBKE, LACIE D; Lincoln Jr Sr HS; Lincoln, KS; (4); 9/32; Pep Clb; SADD; Teachers Aide; Band; Mrchg Band; Pep Band; Stage Crew; Nwsp; Bsktbl; Sftbl; Kay Clb; Bethany Coll; PE.

WIEDEMAN, HEATHER; Hays HS; Hays, KS; (3); High Hon Roll; Hon Roll; Escort At Grad Due To Good Attdnc; Ft Hays ST; Bus/Math.

WIEDMER, JILL L; Troy HS; Troy, KS; (3); Drama Clb; Letterman Clb; VP Pres Natl FFA Org; Varsity Clb; Stage Crew; Pres Frsh Cls; VP Pres Soph Cls; Sec Treas Jr Cls; Ofcr Stu Cncl; Var Bsktbl; MO W St Col; Nrsng.

WIEDNER, JENNIFER; Turner HS; Kansas City, KS; (4); 17/200; Bus Profs of Am; VP DECA; FTA; Q&S; SADD; Nwsp; Ofcr Stu Cncl; High Hon Roll; NHS; Pres Schlr; KS U; Tchr.

WIEDOWER, SARAH; Wellington Sr HS; Wellington, KS; (1); Office Aide; Band; Mrchg Band; Ofcr Frsh Cls; Chrldng; Cit Awd; High Hon Roll; Jr NHS; Outstdng Schlstc Attnmnt Rotary Clb; Dance Comptns Awds; UCA All ST Chrldr; U Of KS; Law.

WIELAND, COLEENA M; Colby Sr HS; Colby, KS; (4); Debate Tm; Office Aide; Red Cross Aide; Science Clb; Spanish Clb; Teachers Aide; Varsity Clb; Band; Chorus; Mrchg Band; Multi Yr Listee; Cross Cntry/Track Schlsp; Colby CC; Elem Ed.

WIELAND, KAREN E; Colby Sr HS; Colby, KS; (3); French Clb; Science Clb; Nwsp; Bsktbl; Chrldng; Golf; Tennis; Trk; Hon Roll; NHS; KS ST Univ; Bus/Med.

WIEMERS, APRIL; Washington HS; Washington, KS; (3); Am Leg Aux Girls St; Church Yth Grp; FHA; Band; School Musical; School Play; Chrldng; Golf; High Hon Roll; Hon Roll; KS ST U; Med.

WIEMEYER, MEGAN R; Maize HS; Wichita, KS; (2); Church Yth Grp; FCA; German Clb; SADD; Chorus; Variety Show; High Hon Roll; Hon Roll; NHS; Pres Acad Fit Awd; Friends Univ; Tchg.

WIENCK, COLLEEN; Blue Valley HS; Blue Rapids, KS; (2); FHA; Natl FFA Org; Band; Chorus; Bsktbl; Vllybl; High Hon Roll; NHS; Pres Acad Fit Awd; Dist FHA Pres; 4-H Styl Revue Champ.

WIENS, ANDREW S; Meade HS; Meade, KS; (2); Boy Scts; Church Yth Grp; Key Clb; Pep Clb; Quiz Bowl; Band; Pep Band; Rep Stu Cncl; Var Bsktbl; Var Crs Cntry.

WIENS, KATIE; Inman Jr Sr HS; Inman, KS; (3); 4/36; Pres Art Clb; Am Leg Aux Girls St; Church Yth Grp; Cmnty Wkr; FCA; German Clb; NFL; Pep Clb; Varsity Clb; Band; Psych.

WIENS, KATIE; Great Bend Sr HS; Great Bend, KS; (4); Cmnty Wkr; Pep Clb; SADD; Acpl Chr; Chorus; Church Choir; Variety Show; Nwsp; Yrbk; Trk; Barton Cnty CC.

WIENS, TIMOTHY B; Newton Sr HS; Newton, KS; (4); 35/201; Church Yth Grp; French Clb; Mrchg Band; Pep Band; Var Capt Swmmng; Hon Roll; Chrch Yth Grp Co-Pres; Le Tourneau Univ; Mech Eng.

WIER, AMY L; Goddard HS; Clearwater, KS; (2); Sec Church Yth Grp; Science Clb; Spanish Clb; Chorus; High Hon Roll; Hon Roll; KAYS Clb; Vol For Bld Drve; Intr Decrtr.

WIER, BRANDON; Olathe North Sr HS; Olathe, KS; (3); 1/350; Cmnty Wkr; FCA; Letterman Clb; Varsity Clb; Ofcr Stu Cncl; Ofcr Bsbl; Bsktbl; Ftbl; Cit Awd; High Hon Roll; 1st Team All Sunflower League Fooball; 1st Team All Sun Country Football; Alir Force Acad; Chem Eng.

WIERENGA, PAMELA R; Maranatha Acad; Parkville, MO; (3); Chorus; Nwsp; JV Vllybl; High Hon Roll; Editor Schl Nespr 94-95; ACSI; Truman Univ; Tchr.

WIERICK, MADELINE C; Campus HS; Haysville, KS; (3); Art Clb; Bus Profs of Am; Drama Clb; FBLA; Thesps; Rep Soph Cls; KS ST U; Geophysics.

WIESNER, REBECCA A; Salina HS Central; Salina, KS; (4); 99/248; Church Yth Grp; Drama Clb; Teachers Aide; Thesps; Band; Chorus; Orch; School Musical; Mgr(s); Mgr Trk; Natl Yng Ldrs Conf; KS Wesleyan U.

WIETERS, RYAN; Linn Schl; Barnes, KS; (2); Art Clb; Cmnty Wkr; Drama Clb; FBLA; Letterman Clb; Thesps; School Play; Pres Frsh Cls; Stat Ftbl; Mgr(s); Drama Bst Actr 95; Scnd Div Awd Duet Actng; FBLA Sls Prsntn 95; 9th Pl ST Cntst; KS ST U.

WIGGINS, MOLLY E; Blue Valley North HS; Leawood, KS; (2); 1/227; Church Yth Grp; FCA; Chorus; School Musical; VP Soph Cls; Rep Jr Cls; JV Crs Cntry; Var L Trk; High Hon Roll; Rep Frsh Cls; Young Life; Pre Med.

WIGNER, JAIME; Garden City Sr HS; Garden City, KS; (4); Ed Nwsp; JV Chrldng; Washburn U; Psych.

WIGNER, LORI A; Garden City Sr HS; Garden City, KS; (2); Yrbk; Hon Roll; Washburn Univ; Acctg.

WIKOFF, BERGIN; Lyons HS; Lyons, KS; (2); Church Yth Grp; Cmnty Wkr; Letterman Clb; Pep Clb; JV Bsktbl; Var Crs Cntry; Var Trk; High Hon Roll; FCA; Spanish Clb; Stucco 9th/10th Grad; Rod/Gun Club 10th Grad; Schlsp Banquet 10th Grad; Baton CC; Marine Bio.

WILBUR, JENNIFER A; Wichita Co HS; Leoti, KS; (4); 5/56; Band; Flag Corp; Yrbk; Var Bsktbl; Var Chrldng; Var Trk; Var Vllybl; High Hon Roll; Jr NHS; NHS; 3 I Rtngs ST/REG Piano Cntst; Fl Sprts Hmcmng Qn; Acad Ofcr Yrbk Clb; KS ST Univ; Acctng.

WILBURN, MINDIE A; Horton HS; Horton, KS; (3); 17/39; 4-H; FHA; Pep Clb; Band; Chorus; Church Choir; Mrchg Band; Pep Band; Ofcr Stu Cncl; 4-H Awd; Page For St Rep; Dist Office In FHA; Ldrshp Awd; Radiology Tech.

WILBURN, SHAYNE L; Ft Scott HS; Fort Scott, KS; (2); Art Clb; Prfct Atten Awd; Guitar; Graphics Dsgnr; Musican.

WILCUTT, SHANE; Olathe East Sr HS; Overland Park, KS; (3); 34/400; Am Leg Boys St; Debate Tm; NFL; Spanish Clb; Teachers Aide; Jazz Band; Mrchg Band; Pep Band; High Hon Roll; Pres Schlr; Pres Of 95-96 Debate Team; Span Clb; U Of KS.

WILD, BECKY A; St Marys HS; Maple Hill, KS; (2); Church Yth Grp; FCA; Letterman Clb; Pep Clb; Jazz Band; Mrchg Band; Pep Band; Var L Bsktbl; Var L Golf; Var L Sftbl; Sports Thrpy.

WILDEMAN, JONI; Jennings Schl; Jennings, KS; (3); 1/13; Church Yth Grp; FHA; Natl FFA Org; Quiz Bowl; Band; Pep Band; VP Frsh Cls; VP Soph Cls; VP Jr Cls; VP Sr Cls; Frosh, Soph & Jr Outstdng Track Ath Of Yr; Chiropratics.

WILDEN, JASON J; Shawnee Heights HS; Topeka, KS; (1); Debate Tm; NFL; Speech Tm; Band; Mrchg Band; Pep Band; Socr; High Hon Roll; Hon Roll; Pres Acad Fit Awd; Top 5 Fnsh Empirical Sci Fair; MIT; Physcst.

WILDER, KARLA J; Clay County Comm HS; Clay Center, KS; (4); 16/95; Church Yth Grp; FHA; Band; Chorus; Stat Trk; Stat Vllybl; Hon Roll; NHS; Pittsburg ST U; Acctng.

WILES, KEVIN M; Enterprise Sda Acad; Falcon, MO; (3); Church Yth Grp; Gym; Boys Clb Pres; Amer His/Math Tchr.

WILEY, DAVID; Independence HS; Independence, KS; (3); Am Leg Boys St; Church Yth Grp; FCA; Spanish Clb; Var JV Golf; PUPPS; KS U; Bus Admin.

WILEY, WESLEY P; Gardner-Edgerton HS; Gardner, KS; (2); Church Yth Grp; Spanish Clb; Band; Mrchg Band; Pep Band; Ftbl; Wt Lftg; Wrstlng; Hon Roll; Natural Helpers; Mid-Amer Naz Coll; Sports Med.

WILFONG, MICHAEL J; Douglass HS; Douglass, KS; (4); 10/43; Boy Scts; Pres Church Yth Grp; Band; Jazz Band; Var Bsbl; Var Capt Crs Cntry; High Hon Roll; NHS; FCA; Mrchg Band; Deacon At Oakview Chrstn Chrch; Butler Cty CC; Arch; Engrng.

WILHITE, JULIE A; Baldwin HS; Baldwin City, KS; (4); 5/78; Church Yth Grp; Cmnty Wkr; 4-H; Intnl Clb; Math Tm; Acpl Chr; Chorus; Church Choir; School Musical; Rep Stu Cncl; Old Castle Dance Grp; Pittsburg ST Univ; PT.

WILHITE, VANESSA A; Wichita Hghts HS; Wichita, KS; (2); 51/336; Band; Mrchg Band; Hon Roll; Wichita ST; Phy Thrpst.

WILHM, BRENNA N; Washburn Rural HS; Topeka, KS; (3); Cmnty Wkr; Science Clb; Spanish Clb; Orch; School Musical; Variety Show; High Hon Roll; Hon Roll; Jr NHS; NHS; Concertmasters Of KMEA St Orch, Topeka Yth Symphony 3 Yrs & Washburn Rural HS Orch 2 Yrs; Violin Perfmnc; Genetics Bio.

WILKEN, AMBER K; Scott Comm HS; Scott City, KS; (3); Pep Clb; SADD; Teachers Aide; Band; Mrchg Band; Pep Band; L Chrldng; JV Tennis; Hon Roll; Frgn Stds Clb; KU; Pharmcy.

WILKEN, LISA R; Lakin HS; Lakin, KS; (2); Cmnty Wkr; 4-H; Rptr Nwsp; Rptr Yrbk; VP Soph Cls; JV Bsktbl; Stat Trk; JV Vllybl; High Hon Roll; NHS; Bio Awd; Spnsh Awd.

WILKENING, JAMI; Ulysses HS; Ulysses, KS; (4); Cmnty Wkr; FCA; Sec FBLA; Letterman Clb; Library Aide; Teachers Aide; Band; Jazz Band; Pep Band; Capt Bsktbl; Butler Cty CC; Bus.

WILKENS, ADENA; Linn Schl; Clifton, KS; (3); VP Church Yth Grp; Hist FBLA; Pres FHA; Thesps; Chorus; Pres Jr Cls; Vllybl; High Hon Roll; Hon Roll; NHS; Cmptr.

WILKERSON, BECKY; Thomas More Prep-Marion HS; Hays, KS; (2); Var Bsktbl; Var Sftbl; JV Capt Vllybl; High Hon Roll; Pres Acad Fit Awd; KS U; Bus.

WILKERSON, JENNIFER L; Beloit Jr Sr HS; Beloit, KS; (2); Cmnty Wkr; FHA; Chorus; Variety Show; Yrbk; Hon Roll; Hnr Chptr FHA VP/AWDS; Nrsng Home Vol; Kayettes; KS ST; Acctng.

WILKERSON, SHAWN; Stanton Cnty HS; Manter, KS; (4); 1/34; Scholastic Bowl; Yrbk; Var Bsktbl; Var Crs Cntry; Var Pom Pon; Gov Hon Prg Awd; High Hon Roll; NHS; St Schlr; Val; U Of KS; Fine Arts.

WILKEY, HOLLY; South Haven Schl; Braman, OK; (3); Drama Clb; FCA; Letterman Clb; Math Tm; Natl FFA Org; Spanish Clb; Band; Pep Band; School Play; Yrbk; Ftbl Hmcmng Qn 95; OK ST U; Intr Dsgn.

WILKEY, LYNAE L; South Haven Schl; Braman, OK; (1); Church Yth Grp; FCA; FHA; Math Tm; Natl FFA Org; Pep Clb; Band; Jazz Band; Mrchg Band; Pep Band; OK ST U; Interior Design.

WILKINSON, ERICA D; Dighton HS; Shields, KS; (1); JV Bsktbl; Hon Roll; One-Act Play; Ath Trng.

WILKINSON, STEPHANIE; Wichita East HS; Wichita, KS; (2); Cmnty Wkr; French Clb; Q&S; Orch; School Play; Nwsp; French Hon Soc; Hon Roll; Rep NHS; KS Univ; Psych; Eng.

WILL, JAMIN D; Burlingame HS; Burlingame, KS; (1); 3/29; Church Yth Grp; Pep Clb; Band; Mrchg Band; Pep Band; School Musical; School Play; VP Frsh Cls; VP Soph Cls; Var Bsbl; Greenhouse; Queen Of Courts Attnt Frosh; Math.

WILL, JENNIFER L; Burlingame HS; Burlingame, KS; (3); Am Leg Aux Girls St; Church Yth Grp; FBLA; Letterman Clb; Pep Clb; Band; Chorus; Jazz Band; Pep Band; School Musical; Hmcmng Attndnt; Kays; Emporia ST U.

WILL, LINDSEY N; Wichita Collegiate Schl; Wellington, KS; (3); Church Yth Grp; Cmnty Wkr; SADD; Teachers Aide; Bsktbl; Trk; Vllybl; High Hon Roll; Prfct Atten Awd; Unsung Hero Optmst Club; Bio.

WILL, STEPHEN M; Riley HS; Manhattan, KS; (4); German Clb; SADD; Ed Yrbk; Rep Stu Cncl; Var Swmmng; JV Var Tennis; Wt Lftg; Hon Roll; NHS; Delta Epilon Phi; U Of TX Arlington; Arch.

WILLARD, DANIEL E; Wichita South HS; Wichita, KS; (4); Band; Jazz Band; Mrchg Band; Orch; Pep Band; School Musical; NHS; Mid Amer Nazarene Coll; Chem.

WILLARD, LINNZI R; Liberal HS; Liberal, KS; (2); Church Yth Grp; Chorus; Church Choir; Hon Roll; U Of CO; Brdcstng.

WILLEMS, LINDSEY; Protection Schl; Protection, KS; (3); Letterman Clb; Pep Clb; Band; Chorus; Color Guard; Pep Band; Bsktbl; Chrldng; Vllybl; NHS; Kayetts.

WILLEY, MEGAN E; Parsons HS; Parsons, KS; (3); 3/115; Cmnty Wkr; Treas Key Clb; Pep Clb; SADD; Orch; JV Bsktbl; Var Sftbl; Var Vllybl; High Hon Roll; Sec NHS; KS ST U; Bus Mrktng.

WILLHITE, KATHERINE L; Lawrence HS; Lawrence, KS; (2); Band; Chorus; Mrchg Band; School Play; Nwsp; Chrldng; Trk; Retirement Hm Wk; Church Act.

WILLHITE, RYAN M; El Dorado HS; El Dorado, KS; (2); Quiz Bowl; Scholastic Bowl; Ed Nwsp; High Hon Roll; NHS; Prfct Atten Awd; Earth Care Clb; Bsbl Statistician; Bus Admin/Mrktng.

WILLHOITE, CHRIS J; Olathe South Sr HS; Olathe, KS; (3); 20/410; Boy Scts; Church Yth Grp; Letterman Clb; Math Tm; Varsity Clb; Treas Soph Cls; Treas Jr Cls; Treas Stu Cncl; L Bsbl; Var Ftbl; I Dare You Ldrshp Awd; Eagle Sct; Arch Chem Engrng.

WILLIAMS, AARON K; Liberal HS; Liberal, KS; (3); Var Bsbl; Var Bsktbl; Var Ftbl; Cit Awd; High Hon Roll; NHS.

WILLIAMS, AMIE; Colby Sr HS; Colby, KS; (3); Dance Clb; Debate Tm; Office Aide; Spanish Clb; Teachers Aide; Drill Tm; Bsktbl; Chrldng; Crs Cntry; Pom Pon; KS ST; Commnctns.

WILLIAMS, AMOS D; Bluestem HS; El Dorado, KS; (4); 9/68; FCA; FTA; Teachers Aide; Ofcr Stu Cncl; Var Bsbl; Var Capt Bsktbl; Var Capt Ftbl; Var Wt Lftg; High Hon Roll; NHS; Independence CC; Ath Trainer.

WILLIAMS, AMY; Stafford Jr Sr HS; Stafford, KS; (3); 2/24; Band; Chorus; Pep Band; School Musical; School Play; High Hon Roll; Hon Roll; Church Yth Grp; Mrchg Band; Vllybl; Forensics; KS Yth Choir; Band Secy & Treas; Drama Professer.

WILLIAMS, AMY M; Salina HS South; Salina, KS; (2); Drama Clb; Pres Pep Clb; Thesps; Stage Crew; Hon Roll; Phys Thrpst.

WILLIAMS, ASHLEY S; Derby HS; Derby, KS; (4); Band; Mrchg Band; High Hon Roll; Hon Roll; Prfct Atten Awd; Pres Acad Fit Awd; Ft Hays St Univ; Comp Sci.

WILLIAMS, AUBREE B; Maize HS; Maize, KS; (3); 65/258; Drama Clb; SADD; Teachers Aide; Thesps; Acpl Chr; Band; Chorus; Drm Mjr(t); Mrchg Band; Pep Band; OK City U; Music Thtr.

WILLIAMS, BETHANY R; Garden City Sr HS; Garden City, KS; (2); Church Yth Grp; Church Choir; Hon Roll; Ottawa.

WILLIAMS, BRANDIS A; Turner HS; Kansas City, KS; (2); Church Yth Grp; Dance Clb; Girl Scts; Library Aide; Pep Clb; Red Cross Aide; Science Clb; SADD; Teachers Aide; Band; Zoo Sea Lions Vol; Internship With Dolphin At Worlds Of Fun; U Of HI; Marine Mammals.

WILLIAMS, BRIAN; Ness City HS; Ness City, KS; (4); 8/29; Pres Church Yth Grp; Pres 4-H; Natl FFA Org; School Play; Bsktbl; Co-Capt Ftbl; L Tennis; Cit Awd; NHS; Am Leg Boys St; YABA Pres; Poetry Contest Semi Finalist; Barton Cty CC; Acctnt.

WILLIAMS, CARLA; Augusta Sr HS; Augusta, KS; (4); 17/124; Drama Clb; French Clb; Office Aide; Sec SADD; School Play; Stage Crew; Co-Ed Nwsp; Co-Ed Yrbk; High Hon Roll; NHS; U Of KS; Psych.

WILLIAMS, CARLA R; Derby HS; Derby, KS; (1); Wichita ST U; Chldrns Thrpst.

WILLIAMS, CLARENCE DAVID; Blue Valley Northwest HS; Overland Park, KS; (2); Debate Tm; NFL; Spanish Clb; High Hon Roll; Hon Roll; Dr.

WILLIAMS, CLINTON DANIEL; Leroy HS; Le Roy, KS; (3); Am Leg Boys St; 4-H; Quiz Bowl; JV Bsktbl; Var L Ftbl; Var L Trk; High Hon Roll; Prfct Atten Awd; Office Aide; Engrng.

WILLIAMS, CYNTHIA; Turner HS; Kansas City, KS; (3); 20/200; Church Yth Grp; Math Clb; Chorus; Rptr Nwsp; Lit Mag; High Hon Roll; Hon Roll; Mark Of Excllnc Awd; KS ST U; Vet Med.

WILLIAMS, DEBORAH L; Hamilton HS; Hamilton, KS; (3); 1/8; Church Yth Grp; Cmnty Wkr; Scholastic Bowl; Band; School Musical; Yrbk; Treas Jr Cls; High Hon Roll; Hon Roll; Tied For 6th On League Schltc Team In Amer His; 6th Pl Lit II; Bapt Bible Coll; Missions.

WILLIAMS, DEENA; Kapaun-Mt Carmel HS; Wichita, KS; (3); Cmnty Wkr; Q&S; Spanish Clb; Teachers Aide; Chorus; Orch; Yrbk; Hon Roll; Reg And St Mus Fest; KSPA Reg Andst Jrnlsm Contst; Wichita Symph Yth Orch; Comm.

WILLIAMS, DUSTIN W; Horton HS; Horton, KS; (2); 20/85; Treas Church Yth Grp; Drama Clb; FCA; Treas FHA; SADD; Band; Jazz Band; Pep Band; School Musical; School Play; KS ST; Cmptr Sci.

WILLIAMS, DUSTY A; Syracuse Jr Sr HS; Syracuse, KS; (2); Bus Profs of Am; Ofcr Frsh Cls; Ofcr Soph Cls; Ofcr Jr Cls; Ofcr Sr Cls; Bsktbl; Ftbl; Industrilants Clb; Ftbl Hnrs Awd; Ranching & Feedyard Mgmt.

WILLIAMS, HAROLD T; Ness City HS; Ness City, KS; (2); Church Yth Grp; 4-H; Pep Clb; Ofcr Bsbl; Bsktbl; Tennis; Wt Lftg; 4-H Awd; Hon Roll.

WILLIAMS, JACQUELINE M; Washington HS; Kansas City, KS; (3); Church Yth Grp; Girl Scts; Hon Roll; Nrsng.

WILLIAMS, JAMIE J; Coldwater Jr Sr HS; Coldwater, KS; (1); FHA; GAA; Pep Clb; Band; Chorus; Mrchg Band; Pep Band; Variety Show; Var Trk; Var Vllybl.

WILLIAMS, JAMIE L; Canton-Galva HS; Galva, KS; (3); 1/44; Church Yth Grp; Hist Ed FBLA; Office Aide; SADD; Band; Co-Ed Nwsp; Co-Capt Jr Cls; High Hon Roll; VP NHS; Cntrl Dist Sec Treas Of KCYF.

WILLIAMS, JENNY; Wathena Schl; Wathena, KS; (3); 1/40; Church Yth Grp; Letterman Clb; Math Clb; Science Clb; Band; Chorus; Pep Band; Yrbk; Treas Soph Cls; Rep Stu Cncl; Bus Clb; Schlstc Achvt Awd; Law.

WILLIAMS, JESSICA E; Wichita North HS; Wichita, KS; (2); Teachers Aide; Church Choir; Socr; BASE Club; Nmw Rccs Club; WSU; Dr.

WILLIAMS, JOE L; Salina HS Central; Salina, KS; (2); Teachers Aide; Ofcr Bsbl; Bsktbl; Ftbl; Hon Roll; Amer Legion Bsbl.

WILLIAMS, JONATHAN; Manhattan HS; Manhattan, KS; (3); 1/450; Church Yth Grp; Cmnty Wkr; Debate Tm; NFL; Quiz Bowl; Speech Tm; Chorus; High Hon Roll; NHS; Barbershop Quartet.

WILLIAMS, JOSEPH T; Hope HS; Woodbine, KS; (3); Boy Scts; Cmnty Wkr; FBLA; Teachers Aide; Band; Rptr Nwsp; Ofcr Bsbl; Bsktbl; Ftbl; Trk; Luth Yth Fllwshp; Manhatton Tech Coll; Cmptr Repr.

WILLIAMS, JOY L; Basehor Linwood HS; Basehor, KS; (2); Church Yth Grp; FHA; Office Aide; SADD; Bsktbl; JV Trk; High Hon Roll; Pres Acad Fit Awd; KCKCC; Acctng.

WILLIAMS, JULIE L; Topeka HS; Topeka, KS; (1); Band; Chorus; Pep Band; Chrldng; Tennis; High Hon Roll.

WILLIAMS, JUSTIN R; Blue Valley HS; Overland Park, KS; (2); German Clb; Letterman Clb; Quiz Bowl; Varsity Clb; Ed Nwsp; Var Ftbl; Var Wrstlng; Hon Roll; Jrnlsm.

WILLIAMS, KATHARINE M; Wichita North HS; Wichita, KS; (3); Q&S; Phtg Nwsp; Ed Yrbk; Pres Soph Cls; Rep Stu Cncl; Var Pom Pon; Var L Socr; Var L Tennis; Hon Roll; NHS; Drug & Alcohol Resistance Ed HS Role Model; Stu Cncl Exec Bd; Jrnlsm.

WILLIAMS, KATHRYN M; Desoto HS; Lenexa, KS; (3); Church Yth Grp; Cmnty Wkr; French Clb; Band; Cit Awd; Hon Roll; NHS; Pres Acad Fit Awd; Mrchg Band; Pep Band; PRIDE; TRENDA; KS Univ.

WILLIAMS, KATHY L; Rolla HS; Rolla, KS; (4); 5/14; Church Yth Grp; Drama Clb; FCA; Hosp Aide; Letterman Clb; Pep Clb; Scholastic Bowl; Speech Tm; Band; Chorus; KS Certfd Nurses Aide & EMT; Seward Cty Comm Coll; Nrsng.

WILLIAMS, KELLEY; Derby HS; Derby, KS; (3); 1/450; Church Yth Grp; FCA; HOBY; SADD; Orch; Treas Stu Cncl; Var L Bsktbl; Var L Swmmng; High Hon Roll; NHS; Yth Symphny Orch Wichita; Spcl Olympc Swim Tm Coach; Piano; Wichita ST U; Chem.

WILLIAMS, KENNETH B; Ness City HS; Ness City, KS; (2); Church Yth Grp; Bsktbl; Ftbl; Trk; 4-H Awd.

WILLIAMS, KRISTA L; Rose Hill HS; Rose Hill, KS; (3); #1 in class; Intnl Clb; Teachers Aide; Thesps; Acpl Chr; Chorus; School Musical; School Play; High Hon Roll; Hon Roll; Prfct Atten Awd; Vol Untd Way; Treas Thespians; Dist Hnrs Choir; U Of KS; Pre-Med.

WILLIAMS, KRISTAL M; Wellington Sr HS; Wellington, KS; (2); Church Yth Grp; Chorus; Church Choir; Vllybl; Hon Roll; Jr NHS; YPD Chrch Pres; Spellman Atlanta GA; Acctng.

WILLIAMS, KRISTEN; Shawnee Mission E Sr HS; Shawnee Mission, KS; (3); Natl Beta Clb; Pep Clb; Chrldng; Trk; High Hon Roll; NHS; Stu Ambsdr; SHARE; DARE Rep; Baker U; Elem Ed.

WILLIAMS, LINDA; Girard HS; Girard, KS; (4); Am Leg Aux Girls St; Debate Tm; Drama Clb; Pres VP FHA; SADD; Chorus; School Musical; School Play; Yrbk; Ofcr Stu Cncl; Kayettes Dir Of Schl Svcs & Wrld Svcs; Chld Psych.

WILLIAMS, MARIA E; Russell HS; Russell, KS; (3); Debate Tm; Model UN; VP Pres NFL; Quiz Bowl; Band; School Musical; Swing Chorus; Pres Jr Cls; Rep Pres Stu Cncl; NHS; Participated In KS Ambassadors Of Music 96 European Tour.

WILLIAMS, MARIANNE C; Maize HS; Wichita, KS; (3); Church Yth Grp; Drama Clb; Spanish Clb; SADD; Teachers Aide; Thesps; Chorus; Church Choir; School Play; Variety Show; Healthcare.

WILLIAMS, MARK H; Junction City HS; Junction City, KS; (1); Church Yth Grp; High Hon Roll; Jr NHS; Arch/Drafting.

WILLIAMS, MATT; Holton HS; Mayetta, KS; (3); Letterman Clb; Model UN; Scholastic Bowl; Band; Chorus; Pep Band; Pres Soph Cls; Pres Jr Cls; Var Bsktbl; Var Golf.

WILLIAMS, MATTHEW M; Campus HS; Haysville, KS; (2); Church Yth Grp; Science Clb; Church Choir; Intrml Bsktbl; Var Trk; Hon Roll; Msn Wrk; Umprd Ltl League Bsbl; Taught VBS 4 Yrs; Oauchita; Yth Mnstrs.

WILLIAMS, MELISSA A; Independence HS; Independence, KS; (1); Church Yth Grp; Cmnty Wkr; French Clb; Chorus; Flag Corp; Mrchg Band; Tennis; Trk; Hon Roll; AZ ST Univ.

WILLIAMS, PAMELA D; Salina HS South; Salina, KS; (4); 43/209; Drama Clb; Thesps; Band; Chorus; Jazz Band; Mrchg Band; School Musical; Variety Show; Hon Roll; NHS; KS ST U.

WILLIAMS, PHILIP; Holton HS; Holton, KS; (1); Church Yth Grp; Letterman Clb; Acpl Chr; Chorus; School Musical; Bsktbl; JV Ftbl; Var Golf; High Hon Roll; Hon Roll; KS Jr Golf; KU; Architecture.

WILLIAMS, QUANITA; Jewell HS; Jewell, KS; (4); 7/15; Am Leg Aux Girls St; Church Yth Grp; FCA; FHA; Pep Clb; SADD; Chorus; Cloud Cty CC; Trvl/Trsm.

WILLIAMS, RENEE A; Caldwell Jr Sr HS; Caldwell, KS; (2); 3/32; Treas Church Yth Grp; 4-H; Library Aide; Pep Clb; SADD; Band; Jazz Band; Mrchg Band; Pep Band; School Play; Tap/Jazz/Ballet Dance Stdnt 13yrs/Tchr 2 Yrs; Swim; KSU.

WILLIAMS II, RODERICK M; Derby HS; Derby, KS; (3); 32/368; Church Yth Grp; ROTC; Band; Church Choir; Mrchg Band; Var Trk; NHS; Gftd Prgm; KRHA; Morehouse; Engrng.

WILLIAMS, SAMANTHA A; Colby Sr HS; Colby, KS; (2); Debate Tm; Drama Clb; Rep French Clb; Thesps; Chorus; Drill Tm; School Play; Variety Show; Chrldng; Hon Roll; Forensics Tm Duet Actng 5/6/3rd Pl Medaled; Psych.

WILLIAMS, SARAH D; Ellis HS; Ellis, KS; (3); Pres FHA; Speech Tm; Sec SADD; Band; Drm Mjr(t); Var L Bsktbl; Var L Trk; Var L Vllybl; NHS; Church Yth Grp; NTV Sons/Dghtrs KS; 1ST 5S Essay Cntst; Vol Ellis RR Museum; Pdtrcn.

WILLIAMS, SHANNA; Riley Cty HS; Leonardville, KS; (1); FCA; FHA; Pep Clb; School Play; Var Chrldng; Hon Roll; Pres Acad Fit Awd.

WILLIAMS, STACEY L; Canton Galva HS; Galva, KS; (4); 3/29; Church Yth Grp; FBLA; Capt Quiz Bowl; Teachers Aide; Band; Mrchg Band; Pep Band; Yrbk; VP Soph Cls; High Hon Roll; Bethany Coll; Pre-Pharmacy.

WILLIAMS, STEPHANIE; Burlington HS; Burlington, KS; (4); 6/78; Am Leg Aux Girls St; Drama Clb; FBLA; Hosp Aide; NFL; Teachers Aide; Thesps; Rep Band; Mrchg Band; Pep Band; Frgn Lang Clb Sec; Natl Yth Ldrshp Conf; U Of PA; Med.

WILLIAMS, TIFFANY H; Shawnee Heights Sr HS; Topeka, KS; (3); SADD; Hon Roll; High Hnrs In His, Span & Eng; Washburn Univ; Law.

WILLIAMS, TIMIKA; Junction City HS; Fort Riley, KS; (1); Church Yth Grp; Cmnty Wkr; Key Clb; Chorus; Church Choir; Bsktbl; High Hon Roll; Jr NHS; Mem Of Top 5 Frosh Cls; Acad Ltr & Lamp Of Knowledge Pin; Pediatrician.

WILLIAMS, TRACY L; Trego Comm HS; Wa Keeney, KS; (2); Cmnty Wkr; Debate Tm; Drama Clb; FHA; GAA; NFL; Pep Clb; Science Clb; SADD; Teachers Aide; Hrses; Johns Hopkins; Pre-Med.

WILLIAMS, TRAVIS; Washurn Rural HS; Topeka, KS; (2); Computer Clb; Hon Roll; KS St Univ; Comp Prog.

WILLIAMS, TRISHA A; Parsons HS; Parsons, KS; (1); Church Yth Grp; Chorus; Sftbl; Vllybl; Wt Lftg; KS U.

WILLIAMSON, ANDREW R; Blue Valley Northwest HS; Overland Park, KS; (1); High Hon Roll; Hon Roll; KS Univ; Eng.

WILLIAMSON, JENNI L; Meade HS; Meade, KS; (1); 14/25; Cmnty Wkr; Pep Clb; Band; Mrchg Band; Pep Band; JV Bsktbl; JV Wt Lftg; Hon Roll; Ftr Astrnt Trng Prgm Lvl II; Kayettes; Pittsburg ST Univ; Dntstry.

WILLIAMSON, KRISTY; Hayden HS; Topeka, KS; (4); 7/110; Cmnty Wkr; Intnl Clb; Office Aide; Teachers Aide; Ed Yrbk; Swmmng; High Hon Roll; NHS; St Schlr; U Of IA; Clinical Lab Sci.

WILLIAMSON, MATT K; Blue Valley Northwest HS; Overland Park, KS; (1); Church Yth Grp; Diving; Hon Roll; Rec Bsbl; Golf; Weight Lifting; U Of CO Oregon; Bus/Med.

WILLIAMSON, SARA; Rose Hill HS; Rose Hill, KS; (4); 6/101; Am Leg Aux Girls St; Church Yth Grp; FCA; FHA; Girl Scts; Intnl Clb; Office Aide; SADD; VP Stu Cncl; High Hon Roll; Red Cross Lifeguard; Prins Ldrshp Awd; KS ST U; Nutrition.

WILLIAMSON, ZACHARY D; Baxter Springs HS; Baxter Springs, KS; (1); Scholastic Bowl; Band; Chorus; Mrchg Band; Pep Band; School Musical; JV Bsbl; Intrml Bsktbl; JV Ftbl; High Hon Roll; WINGS; Parliamntry Law; Sr Ctzns Day; U Of KS.

WILLICH, KERRY M; Horton HS; Horton, KS; (4); 6/60; Church Yth Grp; School Play; Pres Soph Cls; Pres Jr Cls; Bsktbl; Trk; Vllybl; Hon Roll; NHS; St Schlr; KS ST U; Finance.

WILLIG, TERRI J; Campus HS; Wichita, KS; (3); Church Yth Grp; Library Aide; Office Aide; Science Clb; SADD; Acpl Chr; Chorus; Church Choir; Swing Chorus; Variety Show; Pvt Voice Lessons; KS Newman Coll; Elem Tchr.

WILLINGHAM, ROBERT D; Washington HS; Kansas City, KS; (3); German Clb; Teachers Aide; Ofcr Stu Cncl; Bsktbl; NHS; Tulane; Civil Engrng.

WILLIS, ABBY B; Hoisington HS; Hoisington, KS; (3); Church Yth Grp; Debate Tm; Speech Tm; SADD; Band; School Play; Hon Roll; NHS; Outstdng Debater Awd; Outstdng Forensicator Awd.

WILLIS, CHAD W; Maize HS; Maize, KS; (1); Cmnty Wkr; Debate Tm; French Clb; NFL; L Ftbl; Hon Roll.

WILLIS, MICHELLE; Olathe North Sr HS; Olathe, KS; (3); 83/393; Church Yth Grp; German Clb; Pep Clb; Band; Mrchg Band; Var Capt Chrldng; Hon Roll; NHS; Mid America Nazarene Coll.

WILLMAN, JENNIFER J; Blue Valley Northwest HS; Overland Park, KS; (1); 33/355; Debate Tm; NFL; Acpl Chr; JV Var Socr; Vllybl; High Hon Roll; VP Frsh Cls; Pres Soph Cls; KC Comm Svc.

WILLMON, ANNA S; Bonner Springs HS; Bonner Springs, KS; (3); Spanish Clb; Band; Mrchg Band; Pep Band; JV Sftbl; JV Vllybl; High Hon Roll; NHS; Sec Of Kyts; Rtry Clb Awd For Bus; Emporia ST U; Elem Ed.

WILLMS, SHEILA; Little River Jr Sr HS; Little River, KS; (4); 1/21; Am Leg Aux Girls St; Church Yth Grp; Math Tm; Quiz Bowl; Chorus; School Musical; School Play; Yrbk; High Hon Roll; Val; KS ST U; Engr.

WILLS, AMBER L; Conway Springs HS; Conway Springs, KS; (2); FHA; Scholastic Bowl; Nwsp; Hon Roll; Beta Club.

WILLSON, JENNIFER; Udall HS; Udall, KS; (3); Church Yth Grp; School Play; VP Frsh Cls; Pres Jr Cls; Pres Sr Cls; Bsktbl; Chrldng; Sftbl; Vllybl; NHS; GCTL; Girls Sct Silver Awd; Southwestern; Elem Ed.

WILLT, AMY; Maranatha Acad; Lenexa, KS; (1); Church Yth Grp; Math Tm; Var Socr; JV Vllybl; High Hon Roll; PT.

WILLT, BEN; Maranatha Acad; Lenexa, KS; (3); 5/50; Church Yth Grp; Ski Clb; Band; Jazz Band; Mrchg Band; Pep Band; School Musical; Var Socr; High Hon Roll; NHS; Aerospace Engr.

WILSEY, JESSICA L; Independence HS; Independence, KS; (2); French Clb; SADD; Chorus; School Musical; Swing Chorus; Dist Chr 2 Yrs; KS Assoc For Yth Fin Dir; Peers Undrstndng Peer Prob; Extnd Lrng Prog; Psych.

WILSLEF, JACKIE; Valley Falls HS; Valley Falls, KS; (4); 11/31; Cmnty Wkr; Library Aide; Teachers Aide; Drill Tm; Nwsp; Yrbk; Ofcr Stu Cncl; Chrldng; Trk; Hon Roll; Highland CC.

WILSON, ADAM M; Caney Valley Jr Sr HS; Caney, KS; (2); Wt Lftg; Hon Roll; Outdoor Sports; Archery; Wildlife Conservation.

WILSON, ANDREA D; Kansas City Chrstn Acad; Overland Park, KS; (4); 6/35; Church Yth Grp; Office Aide; Teachers Aide; Chorus; Sec Jr Cls; Sec Sr Cls; Rep Stu Cncl; High Hon Roll; Pres NHS; School Play; KS City Yth For Christ Vol Vocal Musician; Cedarville Coll; Eng Ed; Bible.

WILSON, ANICA M; Colby Sr HS; Colby, KS; (2); Church Yth Grp; Cmnty Wkr; Science Clb; Service Clb; Chorus; Rptr Nwsp; Hon Roll; Music.

WILSON, ASHLEY; Salina HS Central; Salina, KS; (2); Teachers Aide; Var L Bsktbl; Var L Chrldng; Var L Sftbl; Var L Tennis; High Hon Roll; Hon Roll; Pres Acad Fit Awd; Lttrd In Tnns; Law.

WILSON, BRIAN N; Wyandotte HS; Kansas City, KS; (2); Bsktbl; Ftbl.

WILSON, CELINA; Lebo Schl; Lebo, KS; (4); 3/25; VP FBLA; Church Yth Grp; Cmnty Wkr; HOBY; Quiz Bowl; SADD; Church Choir; Nwsp; Treas Frsh Cls; Treas Soph Cls; KS Anthrplgcl Soc.

WILSON, CHLOE B; Haven HS; Yoder, KS; (2); Church Yth Grp; FCA; Quiz Bowl; Chorus; Church Choir; Vllybl; High Hon Roll; Hon Roll.

WILSON, CORY; Maur Hill Prep Schl; Atchison, KS; (3); VP Soph Cls; Var JV Bsktbl; Var JV Ftbl; Var Tennis; High Hon Roll; Hon Roll.

WILSON, DENNIS; Gardner-Edgerton HS; Gardner, KS; (4); 40/121; Chorus; Church Choir; School Musical; Stage Crew; L Ftbl; L Golf; L Wrstlng; Hon Roll; Southwestern Coll.

WILSON, DONALD J; Washington HS; Kansas City, KS; (3); DECA; Latin Clb; Quiz Bowl; Spanish Clb; Hon Roll; NHS.

WILSON, ERIN; Glasco HS; Glasco, KS; (4); 1/9; Church Yth Grp; Quiz Bowl; Band; Chorus; Drm Mjr(t); Yrbk; Rep Stu Cncl; Var Chrldng; NHS; Val; Cloud County CC; Bus.

WILSON, GLENDA K; Elkhart HS; Elkhart, KS; (3); 3/35; Letterman Clb; Red Cross Aide; Teachers Aide; School Musical; School Play; Stage Crew; Nwsp; Yrbk; Treas Jr Cls; Pres Stu Cncl; AZ ST U; Phys Therapy.

WILSON, HEATHER D; Maize HS; Wichita, KS; (3); 82/243; Drama Clb; Office Aide; SADD; Treas Thesps; School Play; Stage Crew; JV Capt Chrldng; Socr; Hon Roll; KAYS; KS ST; 2nd Grd Tchr.

WILSON, HEATHER D; Topeka HS; Topeka, KS; (3); 40/323; Art Clb; Church Yth Grp; Cmnty Wkr; French Clb; Letterman Clb; Pep Clb; Acpl Chr; Lit Mag; Powder Puff Ftbl; Cit Awd; Teen Pages A Survival Guide, Teen Cncl Mem 4 Yrs & Now Pub; Jobs Dghtrs Honrd Qn; 10 Yr Comm Svc Vol; Pittsburg ST; Commnctn; Engrng.

WILSON, JANET L; Shawnee Mission S Sr HS; Overland Park, KS; (3); Cmnty Wkr; FTA; Intnl Clb; Latin Clb; Pep Clb; SADD; Var Chrldng; Co-Capt Pom Pon; Trk; Hon Roll; Pep Club Exec; Peer Cnslng Sec; Multi-Yr Listee; U Of KS; Cnslng.

WILSON, JENNIFER; Rock Creek Jr Sr HS; Wamego, KS; (4); 5/51; Church Yth Grp; FBLA; Sec FHA; Pep Clb; SADD; Teachers Aide; Band; Ofcr Stu Cncl; Golf; High Hon Roll; Prom & Grad Cmmttes; KS ST U.

WILSON, JIANA; Ulysses HS; Ulysses, KS; (3); 8/150; Church Yth Grp; 4-H; FHA; SADD; Rptr Nwsp; Phtg Yrbk; Rep Stu Cncl; Var Chrldng; 4-H Awd; Natl Schlrshp & Ldrshp Awds.

WILSON, JIMMIE E; Burlingame HS; Carbondale, KS; (2); 21/32; Church Yth Grp; Computer Clb; FBLA; Pep Clb; Spanish Clb; JV Bsktbl; JV Ftbl; Var Trk; Hon Roll; Summer Bsbl; Lawn Mowing Bus Partner; Raises Limousin Cattle With Parents; KS ST U; Arch Dsgn.

WILSON, JOSH; Jackson Heights HS; Netawaka, KS; (1); Boy Scts; FBLA; Pep Clb; Scholastic Bowl; Band; Chorus; Mrchg Band; Pep Band; School Musical; Stage Crew; KS ST; Elec Engr.

WILSON, JUSTIN; Waconda East HS; Cawker City, KS; (4); 10/18; Church Yth Grp; Cmnty Wkr; Drama Clb; HOBY; Letterman Clb; Pep Clb; Quiz Bowl; Scholastic Bowl; Speech Tm; Varsity Clb; Upwrd Bnd Math & Sci; HOBY Jr Cnslr 95; Phy Ther.

WILSON, KRISTIE L; Marysville HS; Marysville, KS; (2); Letterman Clb; Library Aide; Rep Stu Cncl; JV Var Bsktbl; Var Trk; Var Vllybl; Hon Roll; Kiwanis Awd; U Of NE; Bus.

WILSON, KRISTTYN D; Central Heights Sr HS; Rantoul, KS; (1); GAA; Science Clb; Spanish Clb; Band; Mrchg Band; Pep Band; JV Bsktbl; JV Vllybl; High Hon Roll; Swimming; Vllybl; Sftbl.

WILSON, KYLA; Park Hill HS; Kansas City, KS; (4); 70/532; Intnl Clb; Band; Nwsp; Trk; Vllybl; High Hon Roll; Hon Roll; NHS; Harvard Univ; Comm/Jrnlsm.

WILSON, KYLE A; Field Kindley HS; Coffeyville, KS; (3); #1 in class; Church Yth Grp; Debate Tm; Speech Tm; School Play; Rep Soph Cls; Tennis; High Hon Roll.

WILSON, MARI D; Campus HS; Haysville, KS; (3); Church Yth Grp; Girl Scts; Intnl Clb; SADD; Ofcr Stu Cncl; High Hon Roll; Hon Roll; NHS; Silver Awd For Girl Scts; Gold Awd For Girl Scts.

WILSON, MATT; Olathe South Sr HS; Olathe, KS; (3); Church Yth Grp; Math Clb; Spanish Clb; High Hon Roll; Hon Roll; NHS; Ntl Merit Ltr; Pres Acad Fit Awd; Spanish NHS; Teachers Aide; Harding Univ; Intl Bus.

WILSON, MELISSA; Garden City Sr HS; Garden City, KS; (3); Church Yth Grp; Cmnty Wkr; Red Cross Aide; Ed Nwsp; Rptr Yrbk; Stat Bsktbl; Var Tennis; Hon Roll; U Of KS; Jrnlsm.

WILSON, MELISSA R; Manhattan HS; Manhattan, KS; (3); Art Clb; Cmnty Wkr; Pep Clb; Teachers Aide; Thesps; School Play; Stage Crew; Yrbk; Ofcr Jr Cls; Ofcr Stu Cncl.

WILSON, NATHAN S; El Dorado HS; El Dorado, KS; (2); Letterman Clb; Band; Pep Band; Crs Cntry; Trk; Hon Roll; Frnscs.

WILSON, REBECCA; Jackson Heights HS; Circleville, KS; (4); 4/40; FBLA; FHA; Scholastic Bowl; Band; VP Frsh Cls; VP Soph Cls; Pres Jr Cls; Pres Sr Cls; Sec Stu Cncl; NHS; KS Hnrs Pgm; Brown Mackie Coll; Bus.

WILSON, REBECCA L; Beloit Jr Sr HS; Beloit, KS; (2); Church Yth Grp; Spanish Clb; Chorus; Orch; Swing Chorus; Ofcr Stu Cncl; Vllybl; Hon Roll; Cmnty Wkr; Variety Show; Beloit Comm Orch; Future Medical Careers Clb; Bethany Coll; Speech Thrpst.

WILSON, ROCHELLE; Anderson Cty Jr Sr HS; Garnett, KS; (2); Intnl Clb; Pep Clb; SADD; Var Bsktbl; JV Vllybl; Wt Lftg; Hon Roll; Kay Club; Octagon; Emporia ST Univ; Tchr.

WILSON, RYAN D; Marysville HS; Marysville, KS; (3); Sec Art Clb; Drama Clb; NFL; Quiz Bowl; Scholastic Bowl; SADD; Stage Crew; Nwsp; Var Crs Cntry; Kiwanis Awd; Ftre Artcls Author; Pntng/Drwng; Cmptrs; Crtve Wrtng/Jrnlsm.

WILSON, SARA; Olathe North Sr HS; Olathe, KS; (3); Drama Clb; HOBY; Teachers Aide; Band; Mrchg Band; School Musical; Ed Yrbk; High Hon Roll; Jr NHS; 3rd Pl Wrtrs Inc Cntst; 1st Pl Dist & 2nd Pl Rgnl Band Cntsts; Med.

WILSON, SARAH; Abilene HS; Abilene, KS; (3); Church Yth Grp; FCA; Natl FFA Org; Ofcr Stu Cncl; JV Bsktbl; Chrldng; Var Crs Cntry; Var Trk; Wt Lftg; Hon Roll; 6-7 Grd Coach Rec Bsktbl Tm; 4-H Bsktbl Tm Coach; U Of KS; Psych.

WILSON, STEVEN A; Olathe South Sr HS; Olathe, KS; (3); Letterman Clb; Var Trk; Intrml Wt Lftg; JV Wrstlng; High Hon Roll; Hon Roll; Electronics.

WILSON, TARA; Norwich HS; Norwich, KS; (3); Church Yth Grp; FCA; SADD; Band; Flag Corp; Mrchg Band; Pep Band; School Play; Treas Jr Cls; Var L Bsktbl; Kayettes 95-; Kayettes Sec 96-; KS ST Univ; Ed.

WILSON, ZABRINA D; South Haven Schl; Geuda Springs, KS; (2); 3/19; Chorus; Ed Frsh Cls; JV Bsktbl; Hon Roll; NHS; Stu Of Mnth; Cowley Cnty CC; Acctng.

WILTSE, AMY L; Ft Scott HS; Fort Scott, KS; (3); Debate Tm; French Clb; Latin Clb; Library Aide; NFL; Var Crs Cntry; Var Trk; Hon Roll; NHS; Pres Acad Fit Awd; Tiger Paw Awd; Graceland Coll; Scndry Ed His.

WILTSE, JONATHAN C; Labette Co HS; Parsons, KS; (2); Spanish Clb; SADD; Nwsp; Cit Awd; Hon Roll; Reniassance Pgm; Individual Achvmt Awds; Jrnlsm.

WIMBERLY, AMY; Peabody-Burns Jr Sr HS; Burns, KS; (2); Church Yth Grp; 4-H; FHA; Band; Chorus; Church Choir; Mrchg Band; Pep Band; School Musical; School Play; Church Orch; 4-H Music Contests; Sr Citizens; Amer Coll; Fash Dsgn/Atty.

WINANS, CHRISTIE; Olathe East Sr HS; Olathe, KS; (2); 25/409; French Clb; Letterman Clb; Math Clb; Var L Bsktbl; Var L Vllybl; High Hon Roll; Hon Roll; AAW Bsktbl 79 KS Miracles; MO Vly Reg Chmps 96; Panther Of Mnth 94/Sem 95; Panther Pride Awd 95.

WINANS, JAMES R; St John's Military Schl; Plano, TX; (2); Church Yth Grp; Drama Clb; ROTC; Band; Mrchg Band; School Play; High Hon Roll; Prfct Atten Awd; All Band Awd To St Johns Military Schl 95-96; All Region For KS Fr Horn 95; Psych.

WINANS, JENNIFER A; Newton Sr HS; Newton, KS; (2); #1 in class; Key Clb; Model UN; Treas SADD; Sec Frsh Cls; Pres Soph Cls; JV Intrml Bsktbl; JV Var Sftbl; JV Tennis; Hon Roll; Med.

WINANS, JENNY REBECCA; Leavenworth HS; Leavenworth, KS; (2); Church Yth Grp; Debate Tm; Drama Clb; Acpl Chr; School Musical; Co-Ed Nwsp; VP Frsh Cls; Chrldng; Crs Cntry; High Hon Roll; Goodfellows-Comm Svc Group; Chrch Elder-1st Presbyn Chrch Of Leavenworth; Theology; Music.

WINCHELL, HOPE N; Axtell Schl; Axtell, KS; (4); 6/15; Church Yth Grp; Cmnty Wkr; Dance Clb; FCA; FHA; Letterman Clb; Pep Clb; Scholastic Bowl; Spanish Clb; Teachers Aide; Kays & Kay Bd; St Trk & Vllybl; Doane; Pre-Med.

WINDHOLZ, JACQUE L; Russell HS; Gorham, KS; (1); Church Yth Grp; 4-H; German Clb; Key Clb; SADD; Chorus; JV Bsktbl; Var L Sftbl; JV L Vllybl; 4-H Awd; KS ST Univ; Phys Therapy.

WINDHOLZ, KEVIN N; Quinter Jr Sr HS; Quinter, KS; (3); Drama Clb; Teachers Aide; School Musical; School Play; Nwsp; Yrbk; Ofcr Stu Cncl; Crs Cntry; Trk; High Hon Roll; Ft Hays ST Univ; Brdcst Jrnlsm.

WINDHOLZ, MARK; Hays HS; Hays, KS; (4); High Hon Roll; NHS; Prfct Atten Awd; KS Hwy Patrol Trng Ctr-Cadet Law Enforcement Acad; Ft Hays ST U; Law Enforcement.

WINDHOLZ, SARAH J; Trego Comm HS; Ogallah, KS; (3); 3/48; Church Yth Grp; Drama Clb; VP 4-H; FHA; Pep Clb; Science Clb; Spanish Clb; Band; Pep Band; Rep Soph Cls; Bausch/Lomb Sci Awd; Lions Club Awd; Med Dr.

WINDLER, JENNIFER D; Shawnee Mission S Sr HS; Shawnee Mission, KS; (3); 61/465; Hosp Aide; Intnl Clb; Pep Clb; Color Guard; Intrml Crs Cntry; High Hon Roll; Hon Roll; NHS; Co-Capt Color Guard; Marine Sci.

WINDSOR, SUSIE E; Gardner-Edgerton HS; Gardner, KS; (3); 13/126; Am Leg Aux Girls St; FCA; NFL; Spanish Clb; Band; Drm Mjr(t); School Musical; School Play; VP Stu Cncl; NHS; Stdnt Rep Dist Drug Advsry Comm; Stdnt Cncl Natl Awrd; Natl Acad Exclnc Awrd; Emporia Univ; Eng/Scndry.

WINEGARNER, GINGER R; Wichita East HS; Wichita, KS; (4); Church Yth Grp; Cmnty Wkr; Sec Treas DECA; Pep Clb; Band; Mrchg Band; Pep Band; Sftbl; Hon Roll; NHS; Brown Mackie Univ; Bus Admin.

WINEINGER, NICOLE E; Holcomb HS; Holcomb, KS; (4); 8/41; Office Aide; Pep Clb; Spanish Clb; Band; Jazz Band; Mrchg Band; Pep Band; Bsktbl; Hon Roll; Fidelity St Bank Stu Bd Of Dir Sec 95-96; Pittsburg ST Univ; Accntg.

WINES, CLARK A; Liberal HS; Liberal, KS; (2); Boy Scts; Acpl Chr; Band; Chorus; Mrchg Band; Pep Band; School Musical; Swing Chorus; Jr NHS; Red Skin Singers; Unsung Hero; U Of OK; Music; Psych.

WING, ELIZABETH; Bishop Ward HS; Kansas City, KS; (4); 6/92; Pep Clb; VP Soph Cls; VP Jr Cls; VP Sr Cls; Rep Stu Cncl; JV Bsktbl; JV Sftbl; Hon Roll; NHS; St Schlr; Coach YMCA Yth Boys Team Bsktbl; Bus.

WING, EMILY; Turner HS; Kansas City, KS; (3); #1 in class; Church Yth Grp; Math Tm; Quiz Bowl; Band; Church Choir; Jazz Band; Mrchg Band; Hon Roll; NHS; Pres Acad Fit Awd; KSU; Engr.

WINGEBACH, BERNARD J; Northeast HS; Arma, KS; (2); 12/55; Cmnty Wkr; Letterman Clb; Varsity Clb; Band; Mrchg Band; Pep Band; School Musical; JV Bsbl; Intrml Bsktbl; Hon Roll; Pittsburg ST U; Engrng.

WINGERT, EMILY; Shawnee Mission N Sr HS; Mission, KS; (3); 30/380; Model UN; Pep Clb; Spanish Clb; Rep Stu Cncl; Var Co-Capt Chrldng; JV Co-Capt Sftbl; High Hon Roll; NHS; Church Yth Grp; Math Tm; USSR-KS Exch Stu; Miss Teen Of KS Fnlst; U Of KS; Pre-Med.

WINKEL, DOUG J; Waconda East HS; Glen Elder, KS; (3); 1/22; Letterman Clb; Math Tm; Nwsp; Yrbk; Sec Soph Cls; L Golf; High Hon Roll; NHS; City Of Glen Elder Worker; KS ST Univ; Engrng.

WINKLE, JESSICA N; El Dorado HS; El Dorado, KS; (2); Church Yth Grp; Debate Tm; Girl Scts; NFL; SADD; Chorus; Powder Puff Ftbl; Hon Roll; Kay Clb; Earth Care Clb; BCCC; Lawyr.

WINKLER, RACHAEL C; Wichita East HS; Wichita, KS; (2); Girl Scts; Math Clb; Spanish Clb; SADD; Teachers Aide; Var Mgr(s); Stat JV Sftbl; Vllybl; Hon Roll; NHS.

WINN, MICHELE; Shawnee Mission E Sr HS; Prairie Village, KS; (2); 127/500; Church Yth Grp; Natl Beta Clb; Q&S; Thesps; School Musical; School Play; Ed Yrbk; Hon Roll; Pres Acad Fit Awd.

WINRIGHT, KYLE; Lakin HS; Lakin, KS; (3); 1/69; Am Leg Boys St; Church Yth Grp; FCA; HOBY; Pres Frsh Cls; JV Stat Bsktbl; Var Capt Ftbl; Var L Trk; Intrml Wt Lftg; Cit Awd; Bus Mgmt.

WINSLOW, MELINDA; Central Of Burden Jr Sr HS; Winfield, KS; (4); 1/26; Girl Scts; Math Tm; Speech Tm; Sec Stu Cncl; L Chrldng; Gov Hon Prg Awd; High Hon Roll; NHS; Val; FCA; KU Hnrs Pgm; VFW Voice Of Democracy Wnnr; Emporia ST U; Law.

WINSLOW, NATALIE C; Shawnee Mission Nw Sr HS; Shawnee Mission, KS; (3); Acpl Chr; Chorus; Stage Crew; Phtg Nwsp; Phtg Yrbk; Lit Mag; Hon Roll; NHS; Ofcr Church Yth Grp; Intnl Clb; Founder Of The Philosophy Clb; Environmental Clb.

WINSTON, KIZZY M; Topeka HS; Topeka, KS; (4); Church Yth Grp; Cmnty Wkr; Debate Tm; Office Aide; Teachers Aide; Church Choir; Mgr(s); Hon Roll; STRAPP Vp; Pre-Med; Pediatrician.

WINTER, AMY; Olathe East Sr HS; Olathe, KS; (4); Church Yth Grp; Cmnty Wkr; 4-H; French Clb; FHA; Office Aide; 4-H Awd; Hon Roll; Bsktbl 92-93; Church Yng Women Medallion; YMCA Day Care; BYU; Elem Ed.

WINTER, ANGELA S; Russell HS; Russell, KS; (1); Key Clb; SADD; Chorus; Chrldng; Hon Roll; Ft Hays; Psycht; Soc Work.

WINTER, APRIL; Silver Lake Jr Sr HS; Silver Lake, KS; (2); 7/65; Church Yth Grp; Dance Clb; VP FHA; Pep Clb; Scholastic Bowl; Varsity Clb; Band; Chorus; Drill Tm; Pep Band; St Champion In Var Sftbl.

WINTER, JARED M; Andale HS; Colwich, KS; (1); Church Yth Grp; 4-H; SADD; Intrml Bsktbl; Intrml Ftbl; Intrml Wt Lftg; 4-H Awd; Hon Roll.

WINTER, KIMBERLY A; Hillsboro HS; Hillsboro, KS; (4); 12/52; Band; Chorus; Drm Mjr(t); School Musical; School Play; VP Frsh Cls; Pres Jr Cls; Var Vllybl; High Hon Roll; St Schlr; St Vllybl 2nd; Neosho Cnty CC; Spch Path.

WINTER, KRISTA; Hillsboro HS; Hillsboro, KS; (1); Church Yth Grp; 4-H; Natl FFA Org; Quiz Bowl; Chorus; Church Choir; School Musical; JV Bsktbl; Vllybl; 4-H Awd.

WINTER, KRISTEN A; Shawnee Mission West HS; Lenexa, KS; (3); 91/398; Cmnty Wkr; DECA; FCA; Socr; Tennis; Hon Roll; Jr NHS; NHS; Young Life; CO Univ Boulder; Bus.

WINTER, MIT; Washburn Rural HS; Topeka, KS; (3); 10/336; SADD; JV Bsbl; Capt L Bsktbl; High Hon Roll.

WINTERBERG, RUSSELL T; Shawnee Mission South HS; Overland Park, KS; (3); Drama Clb; Latin Clb; School Play; Stage Crew; JV Crs Cntry; Var Trk; Hon Roll; DECA; Ft Hays ST; Ed; Bus.

WINTER-FOSS, MELISSA A; Trinity Catholic HS; Nickerson, KS; (1); 3/36; Cmnty Wkr; Debate Tm; Pres 4-H; Band; JV Var Bsktbl; Powder Puff Ftbl; JV Var Tennis; JV Var Trk; Wt Lftg; High Hon Roll.

WINTERRINGER, DAWN D; Washington HS; Kansas City, KS; (3); #12 in class; Cmnty Wkr; Drama Clb; Key Clb; Pep Clb; ROTC; SADD; Teachers Aide; Chorus; School Play; Sftbl; Resrv Ofcrs Awd, Air Force Assn Awd ROTC; Harvard; Corp Law.

WINTERS, EMILY S; Frankft HS; Frankfort, KS; (3); Am Leg Aux Girls St; Church Yth Grp; Girl Scts; Pep Clb; SADD; Varsity Clb; Stage Crew; Var Capt Bsktbl; Var Crs Cntry; L Mgr(s); K ST; Drafting; Legal Asst.

WINTERS, TRAVIS L; Horton HS; Everest, KS; (3); Library Aide; Ftbl; Hon Roll; Nashville Auto/Dsl; Auto Mech.

WINTERSCHEIDT, BLAKE D; Lyndon HS; Lyndon, KS; (3); 11/40; Church Yth Grp; French Clb; FBLA; FHA; Library Aide; Teachers Aide; Capt Bsktbl; Capt Ftbl; Hon Roll; Prfct Atten Awd; All Area & All League Ftbl; All Area All League & All ST Bsktbl; Ftbl; Sports Medicine.

WINTJEN, CARA R; Caney Valley Jr Sr HS; Caney, KS; (2); Church Yth Grp; FCA; 4-H; FHA; Hon Roll; Coffeyville JC.

WINZENRIED, ADAM M; Blue Valley HS; Olathe, KS; (3); Am Leg Boys St; Debate Tm; German Clb; NFL; Q&S; Ed Nwsp; Socr; JV Trk; Hon Roll; NHS; U Of KS.

WIRT, JOHN G; Santa Fe Trail Jr HS; Olathe, KS; (1); Band; Jazz Band; Mrchg Band; Hon Roll.

WIRTHS, JAMIE L; Wichita North HS; Wichita, KS; (2); Church Yth Grp; GAA; Var Sftbl; Var Vllybl; Hon Roll; Pres Acad Fit Awd; All City 2nd Tm Sftbl; Making Blankets For Hmls With Yth Grp; PT.

WIRTZ, BRIAN; Maranatha Acad; Olathe, KS; (3); CAP; HOBY; Letterman Clb; Red Cross Aide; Ski Clb; Varsity Clb; Band; Mrchg Band; Orch; School Musical; Top 6 Male Semifnlst HOBY 95; Pilot.

WISE, BRETT N; El Dorado HS; El Dorado, KS; (2); Earth Care; Butler Cty CC; Tchr.

WISE, JESSI M; Ellsworth HS; Ellsworth, KS; (1); 1/50; Church Yth Grp; Band; Mrchg Band; Pep Band; School Play; Pres Frsh Cls; Var Chrldng; JV Trk; Vllybl; Cit Awd; Kayettes; Hon Bnqt; :ks Univ; PA.

WISE, LESLIE D; Emporia HS; Emporia, KS; (4); 4-H; Letterman Clb; Office Aide; SADD; Varsity Clb; JV Bsktbl; Var L Vllybl; Cit Awd; 4-H Awd; Hon Roll; Jr Cls Bd; KS ST; Bus; Comps.

WISE, STEPHEN R; Wichita North HS; Wichita, KS; (2); Debate Tm; Drama Clb; Thesps; School Play; Var Crs Cntry; Var Swmmng; JV Tennis; Law/Med.

WISHALL, PAUL; St Mary's Colgan HS; Pittsburg, KS; (4); Cmnty Wkr; Debate Tm; NFL; Scholastic Bowl; Science Clb; JV Ftbl; High Hon Roll; Hon Roll; NHS.

WISHALL, ROSE; St Mary's Colgan HS; Pittsburg, KS; (4); 1/24; Cmnty Wkr; Debate Tm; Girl Scts; Pep Clb; Scholastic Bowl; School Play; Treas Sr Cls; NHS; St Schlr; Val; K ST.

WISKE, JOLINDA; Medicine Lodge HS; Medicine Lodge, KS; (4); 3/54; 4-H; Natl FFA Org; Pep Clb; Band; Mrchg Band; Pep Band; High Hon Roll; NHS; Pres Acad Fit Awd; St Schlr; KS ST Univ; Ag Ec.

WISLEF, MANDY; Valley Falls HS; Valley Falls, KS; (2); Dance Clb; Drama Clb; FHA; Pep Clb; Band; Chorus; Drill Tm; Jazz Band; Mrchg Band; Pep Band; KAY Spksprsn; KS U.

WISMER, KRISTIN; Maranatha Acad; Lenexa, KS; (3); 3/48; Church Yth Grp; Cmnty Wkr; Math Tm; School Musical; School Play; Ofcr Jr Cls; Chrldng; Socr; High Hon Roll; NHS.

WISNER, JEREMIAH B; Burrton Schl; Burrton, KS; (2); 5/30; Church Yth Grp; FCA; Math Tm; Scholastic Bowl; Ed Rptr Nwsp; Yrbk; L Var Bsktbl; L Var Crs Cntry; L Var Trk; Hon Roll; Tchr; Coach.

WISSINK, JEREMY R; Garden City Sr HS; Garden City, KS; (2); Chess Clb; Church Yth Grp; Math Tm; Orch; High Hon Roll; OM; Outstdng Soph Stdnt Math/Sci/Bus; Grace Univ.

WISSLER, KELLIE; Lawrence HS; Lawrence, KS; (4); Bus Profs of Am; Church Yth Grp; JA; Teachers Aide; Varsity Clb; Band; Chorus; Church Choir; Flag Corp; Mrchg Band; GCTL/FYI Drug Prvntn Prgm; Clrgrd/Flag Corps Sctn Ldr; Bus Profs Amer VP; Dplmt Torch Awd; Johnson Cty; Soc Worker.

WISWELL, AMBER; Sublette HS; Sublette, KS; (2); Church Yth Grp; Band; Rep Stu Cncl; Var Bsktbl; Var Sftbl; Var Vllybl; High Hon Roll; NHS.

WITHERS, STEPHANIE; Blue Valley Northwest HS; Overland Park, KS; (2); Church Yth Grp; Cmnty Wkr; Var L Bsktbl; Intrml Vllybl; High Hon Roll; Gold Medallion; Brigham Young Univ; Acctng; Bus.

WITHRODER, ELIZABETH A; Halstead HS; Halstead, KS; (1); Dance Clb; 4-H; Letterman Clb; Pep Clb; Spanish Clb; Drill Tm; L Pom Pon; Intrml Powder Puff Ftbl; L Trk; Intrml Vllybl; Kayettes; KS ST Univ; Vet Med.

WITT, JENNIFER; Louisburg HS; Paola, KS; (3); #1 in class; Am Leg Aux Girls St; Dance Clb; Drama Clb; FCA; Letterman Clb; Sec Math Clb; Office Aide; Quiz Bowl; Scholastic Bowl; Band; Yth Action Coalition; KS Regens Hnrs Acad; GATE Pgm; Bio; Chem.

WITT, KARI; Junction City HS; Junction City, KS; (3); 9/275; Am Leg Aux Girls St; Church Yth Grp; FCA; Girl Scts; HOBY; Pep Clb; Red Cross Aide; Service Clb; Teachers Aide; Chorus; DARE Role Model; KS ST; Educ.

WITT, MARCUS; Kansas City Bible Clg High; Overland Park, KS; (2); Boy Scts; Church Yth Grp; Computer Clb; Band; JV Bsktbl; Hon Roll.

WITTE, AMBER L; Andale HS; Colwich, KS; (1); Church Yth Grp; Cmnty Wkr; Girl Scts; Spanish Clb; SADD; Chorus; High Hon Roll; Emporia St Univ Schlrs Awd Cls Div & St Div; Teens As Tchrs; Military; Bio Engr.

WITTENBORN, GRANT; Olathe South Sr HS; Olathe, KS; (3); Boy Scts; Church Yth Grp; Cmnty Wkr; Letterman Clb; Teachers Aide; Mrchg Band; Var Stat Bsbl; Var Mgr Bsktbl; Var Mgr Ftbl; KS Dlgte Natl Yth Ldshp Conf; Stuambssdr; Aero Eng; AZ St Univ.

WITTER, NICOLE R; Wichita Southeast HS; Wichita, KS; (2); High Hon Roll; Piano; Psych.

WITTLUHN, BRENT; Halstead HS; Sedgwick, KS; (4); Letterman Clb; Varsity Clb; Pres Frsh Cls; L Ftbl; L Trk; Cit Awd; Hon Roll; Emporia ST Univ; Bio/Cmptrs.

WITTMAN, HEATHER L; Victoria HS; Victoria, KS; (4); FBLA; FHA; Letterman Clb; Model UN; Pep Clb; SADD; Chorus; Drill Tm; Ed Lit Mag; Sec Jr Cls; FBLA Pres; SADD Sec/Treas; FHA Sec/Treas; Ltrmns Clb VP; Dance Tm Capt; Ft Hays ST Univ; Bus Mgmt.

WITTUM, REBECCA L; Caldwell Jr Sr HS; Medford, OK; (2); 3/30; Church Yth Grp; Drama Clb; FCA; Pep Clb; Speech Tm; SADD; Teachers Aide; School Play; Sec Treas Frsh Cls; Sec Treas Soph Cls; Hnrs Prgm; Wrote For Local Nwspr; Bus/Sec.

WITTWER, SANDON J; Sabetha HS; Salem, NE; (3); Boy Scts; Chess Clb; Church Yth Grp; FCA; 4-H; Pep Clb; Spanish Clb; JV Bsktbl; Var L Ftbl; L Var Trk; KS ST Univ.

WITTY, AMANDA; Wakefield Schl; Wakefield, KS; (4); 1/31; Church Yth Grp; FHA; HOBY; Quiz Bowl; SADD; Band; Chorus; School Play; Yrbk; VP Frsh Cls; KS ST U; Pre-Phrmcy.

WOELZLEIN, ELISA M; Herington HS; Herington, KS; (3); Church Yth Grp; Drama Clb; FHA; Math Tm; Pep Clb; Teachers Aide; Band; Mrchg Band; Pep Band; Treas Jr Cls; Interior Dsgnr.

WOERNER, BUCK; White Rock HS; Burr Oak, KS; (4); 3/18; Church Yth Grp; Letterman Clb; Math Tm; Natl FFA Org; Quiz Bowl; Speech Tm; Chorus; VP Jr Cls; Var Ftbl; Var Trk; Natl Lnd Judging Comp; Fort Hays St Univ; Crim Just.

WOHLENHAUS, SARA; Garden City Sr HS; Garden City, KS; (3); CAP; Cmnty Wkr; Red Cross Aide; Thesps; Stage Crew; High Hon Roll; Prfct Atten Awd; CAP Clr Grd; Comm Frst Aide Instr; Amer Red Crs Yth Grp Pres; U Of MT; Bus.

WOHLER, KENLY A; Southeast HS; Wichita, KS; (4); GAA; Letterman Clb; Spanish Clb; SADD; Teachers Aide; Varsity Clb; JV Bsktbl; JV Mgr(s); JV Score Keeper; Capt L Sftbl; Debutante In Local Filipino Cultural Org; WSU; Phy Therapy.

WOHLER, MARY L; Bishop Miege HS; Prairie Village, KS; (3); 7/170; Cmnty Wkr; Spanish Clb; SADD; Teachers Aide; Phtg Nwsp; Phtg Yrbk; Rep Jr Cls; Rep Sr Cls; Stat Socr; JV Sftbl; Stu Ath Trnr; Vol Wrk Mexico Amigos De Las Amer; PT.

WOHLER, NICOLE M; Maize HS; Wichita, KS; (2); Church Yth Grp; Debate Tm; Spanish Clb; Hon Roll; Law.

WOHLFORT-BARNES, ALEXA; South East Of Saline HS; Assaria, KS; (3); Church Yth Grp; HOBY; Speech Tm; Varsity Clb; Band; Chorus; Jazz Band; Mrchg Band; Orch; Ed Yrbk; Lovewell Inst Crtv Arts; Hnr & Dist Band; Keynote Spkr Pediatric Cancer Soc; Music Thrpy.

WOHLGEMUTH, AMY; Seaman Sr HS; Topeka, KS; (4); 6/248; Hosp Aide; Band; Chorus; Rep Soph Cls; VP Jr Cls; Sec Sr Cls; Var Co-Capt Chrldng; Cit Awd; High Hon Roll; VP NHS; Site Cncl; Mid Amer Nazarene Coll; Elem Ed.

WOHLGEMUTH, BRYAN; Lansing HS; Leavenworth, KS; (3); 25/142; Am Leg Boys St; Var Ftbl; Wt Lftg; Hon Roll; Prfct Atten Awd; Kays, Svc Org; Took 4 Coll Courses During HS; Comp Sci.

WOHLGEMUTH, DEREK; Atchison Sr HS; Atchison, KS; (2); 1/115; Church Yth Grp; Cmnty Wkr; Spanish Clb; JV Bsbl; Bsktbl; Hon Roll; Prfct Atten Awd; Lnch Of Champs; Dwnhll Skiing; Bus.

WOHLGEMUTH, LINDSEY; Remington HS; Benton, KS; (4); Am Leg Aux Girls St; FHA; Teachers Aide; Band; Mrchg Band; Pep Band; Variety Show; Co-Capt Pom Pon; Hon Roll; KS ST U; Ag Bus.

WOHLGEMUTH, STACI; Seaman Sr HS; Topeka, KS; (4); 4/272; Church Yth Grp; Hosp Aide; Treas Band; Ed Yrbk; Rep Soph Cls; Treas Jr Cls; Treas Sr Cls; Trk; Vllybl; High Hon Roll; Sm Ensmbl; Washburn; Frnsc Sci.

WOIRHAYE, DAVID; Blue Valley HS; Stilwell, KS; (2); Church Yth Grp; Band; Jazz Band; Mrchg Band; Pep Band; School Musical; Intrml Bsbl; JV Golf; JV Socr; Hon Roll; JV Soccer Co-Capt; Band Section Ldr; Outstdng Musicianship Awds; KS Univ; Musician; Eng.

WOIRHAYE, JEFF C; Blue Valley HS; Stilwell, KS; (3); Am Leg Boys St; Church Yth Grp; Band; Jazz Band; Mrchg Band; Pep Band; JV Bsbl; Var Socr; Hon Roll; NHS; Section Ldr Band; Rotry Camp Interprize; Engr.

WOJTKIEWICZ, NATHAN E; Shawnee Mission N HS; Overland Park, KS; (3); 11/929; DECA; Spanish Clb; Sec Jr Cls; Treas Stu Cncl; Var Capt Socr; High Hon Roll; NHS; Engrg.

WOLAK, LUKAS; Goodland HS; Goodland, KS; (1); Church Yth Grp; Chorus; JV Ftbl; JV Trk; JV Wrstlng; Cit Awd; High Hon Roll; NHS.

WOLF, CURTIS; Thomas More Prep-Marion HS; Hays, KS; (1); JCL; Latin Clb; Bsktbl; Trk; High Hon Roll; Natl Latin Exam Magna Cum Laude.

WOLF, JAMIE; Burlingame HS; Burlingame, KS; (2); 5/34; Girl Scts; Hosp Aide; Quiz Bowl; Band; Chorus; Jazz Band; Mrchg Band; Pep Band; School Play; Pres Frsh Cls; Envrnmntl Clb; Microbio.

WOLF, JESSICA M; Derby HS; Derby, KS; (3); #10 in class; Drama Clb; Girl Scts; Math Tm; Scholastic Bowl; Band; Mrchg Band; Stage Crew; High Hon Roll; NHS; Ntl Merit Ltr; Grd Schl Tutor; Math/Cmptr Sci.

WOLF, KRISTIN M; Bishop Miege HS; Overland Park, KS; (2); Church Yth Grp; Intrml Mgr Bsktbl; Var Sftbl; Intrml Mgr Vllybl; Hon Roll; Sprts Thpy.

WOLF, KYLE P; Grinnell HS; Grinnell, KS; (4); 8/14; Church Yth Grp; Quiz Bowl; Speech Tm; Chorus; Church Choir; Var Capt Bsktbl; Var Capt Ftbl; Var Capt Trk; Cit Awd; Hon Roll; Played In KS 8 Man All-Star Ftbl Game; 4th In St Forensics Cmptn; 4 Time K-18 All-Star Bsbl; Ft Hays ST Univ; His.

WOLF, MATTHEW D; Great Bend Sr HS; Pawnee Rock, KS; (4); Quiz Bowl; Spanish Clb; Teachers Aide; Band; Jazz Band; Mrchg Band; Pep Band; Variety Show; Bsktbl; Tennis; Bethany Coll Art Awds; Barton; Psych.

WOLF, SHENA; Wabaunsee HS; Alma, KS; (1); Girl Scts; Quiz Bowl; Scholastic Bowl; Chorus; Orch; School Musical; School Play; High Hon Roll.

WOLFE, DAVID R; Topeka HS; Topeka, KS; (2); Boy Scts; Church Yth Grp; Debate Tm; Model UN; NFL; Speech Tm; Hon Roll; Russian Club.

WOLFE, ELSIE A; Solomon Jr Sr HS; Solomon, KS; (4); FHA; Library Aide; Office Aide; Red Cross Aide; SADD; Teachers Aide; JV Vllybl; Wt Lftg; Cit Awd; Hon Roll; Salina Area Voc-Tech; Dntl Asst.

WOLFE, TARA K; Lawrence HS; Lawrence, KS; (3); Nwsp; Lit Mag; Tennis; Hon Roll; Photo; Creative Wrtng; U Of KS; Bus.

WOLFF, AARON; Caldwell Jr Sr HS; Caldwell, KS; (4); 1/23; Pres Church Yth Grp; Capt FCA; 4-H; HOBY; Capt Scholastic Bowl; SADD; Teachers Aide; School Play; Pres Jr Cls; Pres Sr Cls; KS U Hnr Schlr; Wendys Hsmn Awd St Fnlst; Cleveland Chrprctc; Med.

WOLFF, BRANDON M; Maize HS; Wichita, KS; (3); Church Yth Grp; Cmnty Wkr; Office Aide; SADD; Teachers Aide; Var L Bsktbl; Mst Insprtnl Plyr Awd; Hrt Of Amer Bsktbl Cmp; Friends U At Wichita.

WOLFF, JEREMY M; Derby HS; Derby, KS; (2); 1/440; Quiz Bowl; Scholastic Bowl; Science Clb; Band; Mrchg Band; Orch; Pep Band; High Hon Roll; Hon Roll; NHS; Odyssey Of Mind; Future Prblm Slvng; Natl Yng Ldrs Conf Nom; PHYSICS/ASTRONOMY.

WOLFF, SARAH A; Junction City HS; Junction City, KS; (2); Church Yth Grp; Band; Church Choir; Mrchg Band; Pep Band; Hon Roll; Manhattan Chrstn Coll; Teen Wrk.

WOLFING, RACHELLE L; Elwood Schl; Wathena, KS; (3); Pep Clb; Band; Chorus; Bsktbl; Chrldng; Trk; VP Frsh Cls; Sec Soph Cls; VP Jr Cls; Business.

WOLFRAM, KATHRYN; Liberal HS; Liberal, KS; (4); Am Leg Aux Girls St; Church Yth Grp; FCA; Quiz Bowl; Varsity Clb; Band; Church Choir; Mrchg Band; Pep Band; Co-Ed Lit Mag.

WOLKEN, AMANDA J; Shawnee Mission N HS; Shawnee Mission, KS; (3); 24/460; Key Clb; Pep Clb; Spanish Clb; Thesps; School Musical; School Play; Stage Crew; Rep Soph Cls; Capt Sftbl; Vllybl; Span/Intl Rel.

WOLKENFELD, DANIEL; Kansas City Bible Clg High; Overland Park, KS; (2); Hist Boy Scts; Chess Clb; Church Yth Grp; Math Tm; Band; Chorus; Treas Soph Cls; Trk; Hon Roll; Arch.

WOLLENBERG, JENNY; Hanover Schl; Hanover, KS; (3); 1/16; Am Leg Aux Girls St; VP Pres Drama Clb; Capt Scholastic Bowl; Band; School Play; VP Sr Cls; JV Var Vllybl; High Hon Roll; Sec NHS; FBLA; ST Speech Champ 96; 6th In ST Speech 95; Washington Cnty Jr Miss 2nd Runner-Up; Bethany Coll; Atty.

WOLLIN, LYNN; Seaman Sr HS; Topeka, KS; (4); 5/248; Drama Clb; English Clb; Pres Math Clb; Mu Alpha Theta; VP Spanish Clb; SADD; Flag Corp; School Musical; Tennis; NHS; Natl Engl Merit Awd; Intl Ordr Jobs Dghtrs Hnrd Qn Of Bethel 58; KS ST U; Phys Thrpy.

WOLTERS, DAYNA R; Turner HS; Leavenworth, KS; (4); Bus Profs of Am; Band; Mrchg Band; Sftbl; High Hon Roll; Hon Roll; NHS; Pres Acad Fit Awd; Yth Enrichment Schlsp; Pep Band; KS City CC; Med Tech.

WOMACK, LYNNETTE A; Wichita Heights HS; Wichita, KS; (2); 14/349; Bus Profs of Am; Cmnty Wkr; Debate Tm; HOBY; NFL; Speech Tm; Rep Frsh Cls; VP Soph Cls; High Hon Roll; Bus Prof Of Amer Natl; NFL Natls; HOBY Ambssdr.

WOMACK, MELISSA R; Sumner Acad Of Arts & Science; Kansas City, KS; (3); Church Yth Grp; Cmnty Wkr; French Clb; Hosp Aide; Latin Clb; Church Choir; Orch; Sec Stu Cncl; Hon Roll; Emporia ST U; Eng.

WOMELDORFF, MATT C; Parsons HS; Parsons, KS; (4); 48/119; Church Yth Grp; FCA; NFL; Office Aide; Pep Clb; Spanish Clb; Speech Tm; SADD; Acpl Chr; Band; Coffeyville CC; Sec Ed.

WONDRA, TRACIE R; Great Bend Sr HS; Great Bend, KS; (3); Church Yth Grp; Pep Clb; Spanish Clb; Var Bsktbl; Var Sftbl; JV Vllybl; Wt Lftg; Hon Roll; All WAC; Barton Cnty CC.

WONG, JAMES N; Junction City HS; Junction City, KS; (1); Church Yth Grp; Band; Church Choir; Mrchg Band; Pep Band; School Musical; School Play; High Hon Roll.

WOO, JAMIE; Wichita North HS; Wichita, KS; (4); 10/247; Am Leg Aux Girls St; Hosp Aide; Office Aide; Rep Stu Cncl; Var Socr; High Hon Roll; NHS; Sal; Pres S E Asian Ldrshp; Heritage Panel; KS Regents Hnr Acad; Friends U; Med.

WOOD, AMANDA; Valley Falls HS; Meriden, KS; (3); Church Yth Grp; FHA; Band; Chorus; Church Choir; Swing Chorus; JV Chrldng; Var Crs Cntry; Var Sftbl; JV Vllybl; Ltrd Vlybl/Crs Cntry/Sftbl/Bnd; Highland CC; Vet Med.

WOOD, AMANDA L; Chapman HS; Wakefield, KS; (3); Church Yth Grp; SADD; Teachers Aide; Pep Band; School Play; Ofcr Frsh Cls; Ofcr Soph Cls; Crs Cntry; Mgr(s); Trk; RN.

WOOD, CAROLYN; Manhattan HS; Manhattan, KS; (4); 18/388; French Clb; Orch; Pres Frsh Cls; Rep Stu Cncl; Var L Socr; Hon Roll; NHS; Church Yth Grp; SADD; Church Choir; Var Soccer MVP 95; All-St Hnrs Orch 94, 95 & 96; St Music Fest Violin Solo Super Ratng 93, 94 & 95; U Of KS; Cellular Bio.

WOOD, CHRIS L; Wichita Southeast HS; Wichita, KS; (1); Church Yth Grp; French Clb; ROTC; Band; Mrchg Band; Pep Band; Hon Roll; Hnr Guard ROTC; Ldrshp Dev Camp ROTC; Wichita ST U; Military Scis.

WOOD, DALLAS; Seaman Sr HS; Topeka, KS; (3); 35/300; FBLA; Natl FFA Org; SADD; Teachers Aide; High Hon Roll; Prfct Atten Awd; KSU; Scndry Ed.

WOOD, HESTER R; Stockton HS; Stockton, KS; (4); 8/32; Church Yth Grp; Cmnty Wkr; FHA; Library Aide; Pep Clb; Band; Drill Tm; Jazz Band; Mrchg Band; Pep Band; U Of KS; Optometry.

WOOD, KATY S; Turner HS; Kansas City, KS; (2); GAA; Band; Capt Chrldng; Var Sftbl; Var Vllybl; High Hon Roll; NHS; Math Clb; Math Tm; Quiz Bowl; Top 3 Ntn Yamaha Elec Fstvl; 10th Pl ST Spelling Bee; 4.0 GPA; U Of KS; Med Prof.

WOOD, MARIETTA; Troy HS; Atchison, KS; (4); 4-H; Pep Clb; Var L Chrldng; Trk; JV Vllybl; High Hon Roll; Prfct Atten Awd; KS ST U; Vet Med.

WOOD, ROBERT C; Washburn Rural HS; Topeka, KS; (3); Church Yth Grp; FCA; Quiz Bowl; Scholastic Bowl; Spanish Clb; JV Bsbl; JV Var Ftbl; JV Var Trk; Hon Roll; MVP Ftbl Frosh & Soph; Tennyson Reyes Memrl Awd; Purdue Univ; Frgn His; Span.

WOOD, SHAUNA D; Field Kindley Mem Sr HS; Coffeyville, KS; (4); 18/138; Church Yth Grp; Spanish Clb; Teachers Aide; Chorus; Flag Corp; High Hon Roll; NHS; Prfct Atten Awd; Pres Acad Fit Awd; Pres Schlr; Military.

WOOD, STEPHANIE R; Northeast HS; Mulberry, KS; (1); 21/48; Span I; Art I; Pittsburg St Univ.

WOOD, TIM A; Blue Valley Northwest HS; Stilwell, KS; (3); 21/420; Cmnty Wkr; Pep Clb; JV Bsbl; Intrml Bsktbl; Intrml Socr; High Hon Roll; NHS; Medicine.

WOOD, TRAVIS E; Northeast HS; Arma, KS; (1); 10/43; Band; Var Bsbl; JV Bsktbl; JV Ftbl; Wt Lftg; Hon Roll; Prfct Atten Awd.

WOOD, WILLIAM M; Blue Valley North HS; Overland Park, KS; (2); Letterman Clb; Tennis; Hon Roll.

WOODARO, CHRISTINA M; Bishop Carroll Catholic HS; Colwich, KS; (2); GAA; JV Var Bsktbl; Var Trk; High Hon Roll.

WOODBURY, BRENDAN S; Shawnee Mission E Sr HS; Shawnee Mission, KS; (3); Cmnty Wkr; Debate Tm; Hosp Aide; Math Tm; Model UN; NFL; Pep Clb; Q&S; Service Clb; Ed Nwsp; Mock Trial; Natl Ldrshp Forum On Law/Constitutn.

WOODBURY, DEEDRA M; Trinity Catholic HS; Hutchinson, KS; (1); Debate Tm; Math Tm; NFL; Office Aide; Pep Clb; Band; Mrchg Band; Pep Band; JV Var Bsktbl; JV Var Trk.

WOODBURY, JOEY A; Seaman Sr HS; Topeka, KS; (3); Church Yth Grp; FBLA; Pep Clb; Teachers Aide; Phtg Nwsp; Phtg Yrbk; Rptr Stu Cncl; Var L Ftbl; Wrstlng; Hon Roll; Military.

WOODFORD, JENNIFER; Manhattan HS; Manhattan, KS; (4); 38/365; FCA; FBLA; Pep Clb; Spanish Clb; Band; Mrchg Band; Pep Band; Powder Puff Ftbl; Hon Roll; NHS; KS ST U; Acctng.

WOODS, ANGELA A; El Dorado HS; El Dorado, KS; (3); Church Yth Grp; FCA; Letterman Clb; SADD; Band; School Play; Mgr Bsbl; Stat Bsktbl; Mgr(s); Powder Puff Ftbl; Treas For Fellowship Of Chstn Ath; LIFE Member; KAY; U Of KS; Bio.

WOODS, ANGELA R; Field Kindley Mem Sr HS; Coffeyville, KS; (3); Spanish Clb; Hon Roll; Child Care; KS Univ; Clinical Psychlgy.

WOODS, BRANDI K; Wyandotte HS; Kansas City, KS; (3); 8/243; Treas VICA; High Hon Roll; NHS; Creative Wrtr REAL Mag; Dedicated Tutor Awd M E Pearson Elem Schl; Nom Jabberwock Contest; Kansas City KS JC; Acctg.

WOODS, CAMILLE; Mulvane Sr HS; Mulvane, KS; (2); 10/170; Church Yth Grp; Girl Scts; Thesps; Chorus; School Musical; School Play; JV Var Chrldng; Cit Awd; Hon Roll; Pres Acad Fit Awd; Outstndg Keybrdng Stu; U Of KS; Med.

WOODS, DEREK W; Manhattan HS; Manhattan, KS; (3); Teachers Aide; Nwsp; Yrbk; Hon Roll; Wdwrkng; KS ST Univ; Comms Field.

WOODS, JAMES; Wyandotte HS; Kansas City, KS; (3); Boy Scts; Church Yth Grp; Drama Clb; JV Bsbl; JV Crs Cntry; High Hon Roll; Hon Roll; NHS; Robotic Engr.

WOODS, KATRICE L; Dodge City HS; Dodge City, KS; (2); Girl Scts; Chorus; JV Bsktbl; JV Sftbl.

WOODS, MELISSA; Sublette HS; Sublette, KS; (2); 10/41; Cmnty Wkr; Pep Clb; Band; Mrchg Band; Pep Band; Rep Stu Cncl; Powder Puff Ftbl; Trk; Vllybl; Hon Roll; AFS Stu Cncl Rep; Govs Ctr For Teen Ldrshp; KS Assn For Yth; Mrkt Rsrch.

WOODS, MISTI L; Elkhart HS; Elkhart, KS; (4); 4/32; Church Yth Grp; FCA; Letterman Clb; Scholastic Bowl; Varsity Clb; Var L Bsktbl; Var L Vllybl; Hon Roll; NHS; Prfct Atten Awd; KS ST Univ; PT.

WOODS, ROBERT; Ellsworth HS; Ellsworth, KS; (4); #32 in class; Natl FFA Org; Teachers Aide; Intrml Mgr Ftbl; Hon Roll; Prfct Atten Awd; Crops Ed Awd; Hutch CC; Crop Counsultant.

WOODS, TESA; Cimarron HS; Cimarron, KS; (2); Church Yth Grp; Cmnty Wkr; FCA; Pep Clb; Drill Tm; JV Chrldng; Sftbl; Hon Roll; NHS; Prfct Atten Awd.

WOODSON, CHRISTINA N; Wyandotte HS; Kansas City, KS; (3); 51/200; Pep Clb; Ofcr Jr Cls; Ofcr Sr Cls; Ofcr Stu Cncl; U Of KS; Nrsng.

WOODSON, JENNY L; Uniontown HS; Uniontown, KS; (3); Art Clb; FHA; Library Aide; Natl FFA Org; Chorus; Hon Roll; NHS; Prfct Atten Awd; Schol Achv Awd For US Hstry; Schol Achv Awd For Psych; KS KMEA Dist II Hnrs Chorus.

WOODSON, JEREMY M; Washburn Rural HS; Topeka, KS; (2); Church Yth Grp; Orch; High Hon Roll; Kckbxng; Fighter Pilot.

WOODWARD, ANNE; Kapaun-Mt Carmel HS; Wichita, KS; (4); 11/167; French Clb; Office Aide; Thesps; Acpl Chr; School Musical; School Play; Stage Crew; High Hon Roll; NHS; Pres Schlr; KS Hnr Schlr; Natl His/Govt Awd; KS ST Univ; His.

WOODWARD, HOLLEY; Wichita South HS; Wichita, KS; (4); 13/292; Church Yth Grp; Pep Clb; SADD; Teachers Aide; Thesps; Chorus; Drill Tm; School Musical; Variety Show; VP Frsh Cls; UDA All-Star Danc Tem; Natl Schlr Ath; Natl Chrldr Perfmnc In Macys Thanksgiving Parade; Friends Univ; Pre-Med.

WOODWARD, JACKIE; Manhattan HS; Manhattan, KS; (4); Cmnty Wkr; FBLA; Office Aide; SADD; Teachers Aide; JV Mgr(s); JV Trk; JV Vllybl; High Hon Roll; Hon Roll; VP Of Rodeo Clb; KS St Univ; Mgnt.

WOODY, NATHAN R; El Dorado HS; El Dorado, KS; (3); Am Leg Boys St; Church Yth Grp; Debate Tm; Quiz Bowl; Scholastic Bowl; Band; Mrchg Band; Var L Ftbl; Var L Wrstlng; Ntl Merit SF; Amer Math Cmpttns Schl Wnnr; KS ST Sci/Engr Smmr Inst; Ftre Astrnt Trng Prgm; KS ST Univ; Nclr Engr.

WOOLARD, JOSH D; Lewis Schl; Lewis, KS; (3); 1/17; Boy Scts; FBLA; Quiz Bowl; Band; Chorus; Pep Band; School Musical; School Play; Ofcr Frsh Cls; Ofcr Soph Cls; Natl Eng Merit Awd; Ad Altare Deis; MIT Boston; Comp Engr.

WOOLBRIGHT, THOMAS B; Southeast HS; Cherokee, KS; (4); 1/58; Scholastic Bowl; Science Clb; Nwsp; Ofcr Frsh Cls; Ofcr Soph Cls; Hon Roll; NHS; Ntl Merit SF; Pres Acad Fit Awd; St Schlr; Multi Yr Listing; U Of KS.

WOOLFOLK, TYLER R; Protection Schl; Protection, KS; (1); Letterman Clb; Band; Mrchg Band; Pep Band; Bsktbl; Ftbl; Wt Lftg; Hon Roll; Val; KSU; Strength Coach.

WOOLS, JENNY; Crest HS; Colony, KS; (1); Church Yth Grp; Drama Clb; Pres 4-H; FHA; Hosp Aide; School Play; Chrldng; Crs Cntry; 4-H Awd; High Hon Roll.

WOOLSEY, JENNIFER D; Wichita South HS; Wichita, KS; (1); Hosp Aide; Spanish Clb; Band; Mrchg Band; Pep Band; Hon Roll.

WOOLSEY, TUCKER; Decatur Cmty Jr Sr HS; Oberlin, KS; (3); Am Leg Boys St; Church Yth Grp; Letterman Clb; Pres Sr Cls; Ofcr Stu Cncl; Var L Ftbl; Var L Golf; Wt Lftg; Var L Wrstlng; Hon Roll; TACT.

WOOLSONCROFT, BETH; Centralia Schl; Centralia, KS; (4); 5/23; VP Sec 4-H; Sec Treas Letterman Clb; Sec Treas Science Clb; Chorus; Pres Jr Cls; Sec Treas Sr Cls; Var L Bsktbl; Var L Vllybl; Hon Roll; NHS; Hmcmng Queen; Natl Mrt Awds Ldrshp & Eng; Hnrb Mntn All-Lg Vllybl; KS ST; Comp Sci.

WOOLSONCROFT, TIARA D; Salina HS South; Salina, KS; (3); Cmnty Wkr; Dance Clb; NFL; Orch; School Musical; Sec Jr Cls; Rep Stu Cncl; Chrldng; Pom Pon; Pep Clb; Radiology.

WORCESTER, JAKE D; Hill City HS; Hill City, KS; (4); 1/35; Church Yth Grp; FCA; Natl FFA Org; Pep Clb; SADD; Pres Stu Cncl; Var L Bsktbl; Var Capt Crs Cntry; Var L Golf; Cit Awd; US Marine Corp Math/Sci Awd; Dane Hansen Ldr Of Tomorrow; Dist FFA VP; KS ST Univ; Ag Commnctn.

WORK, IAN M; Quinter Jr Sr HS; Quinter, KS; (2); 4/30; FCA; Letterman Clb; Band; School Musical; VP Soph Cls; Rep Stu Cncl; Var L Trk; High Hon Roll; NHS; HS Math Tchr.

WORLEY, JOHN; Atchison Sr HS; Atchison, KS; (3); 14/101; Hon Roll; Bio Olympc Tm 95.

WORRALL, CASEY M; Lansing HS; Leavenworth, KS; (4); 20/160; Am Leg Boys St; Cmnty Wkr; Key Clb; Letterman Clb; Office Aide; Pep Clb; Teachers Aide; Varsity Clb; Var Bsbl; Var Bsktbl; Bowling; Golf; Vol Work; Hunt; Fish; Skeet; KS Univ Lawrence; Sports Med.

WORTHAM, TAMARIR M; J C Harmon HS; Kansas City, KS; (3); Church Yth Grp; GAA; Teachers Aide; Acpl Chr; Church Choir; School Musical; JV Vllybl; High Hon Roll; Grambling U.

WORTHEN, HOLLY M; Mc Pherson HS; Mc Pherson, KS; (2); 1/200; Art Clb; Church Yth Grp; Cmnty Wkr; NFL; Quiz Bowl; Scholastic Bowl; Science Clb; Spanish Clb; Band; Chorus; Prsbytrn Yth Cncl; Sun Schl Tchr.

WORTHEN, JENNIFER A; Campus HS; Wichita, KS; (2); VP Science Clb; SADD; Band; Yrbk; Pom Pon; JV Sftbl; Vllybl; Hon Roll; NHS; Drill Tm; Bowling KS Top Ten; KS ST Univ; Psych/Law.

WORTHINGTON, JASON E; Louisburg HS; Bucyrus, KS; (2); Math Clb; Natl FFA Org; Varsity Clb; Intrml Bsktbl; L Ftbl; L Wrstlng; Hon Roll; Tech Stu Assn Treas; N Cntrl KS Voc Tech; Ag Bus.

WOYDZIAK, AMBER; Lyons HS; Lyons, KS; (2); 13/74; Church Yth Grp; Cmnty Wkr; Dance Clb; FCA; Pep Clb; Chorus; Variety Show; Var Chrldng; Hon Roll; NHS; ST Cntst Vcl Soloist; Slctd Lionaire Vcl Grp; KS ST Univ; Elem Tchr.

WOYDZIAK, FRANK E; Bishop Carroll Catholic HS; Wichita, KS; (2); Var Bsbl; JV Bsktbl; Wt Lftg; Bus.

WOYDZIAK, NATHAN; Hoisington HS; Hoisington, KS; (4); 1/65; Am Leg Boys St; Model UN; SADD; Pres Sr Cls; Capt Bsktbl; Cit Awd; Gov Hon Prg Awd; VP NHS; Val; Ath Drctrs Aide; KS ST U; Chem Engrng.

WRAY, MEGAN M; Kapaun-Mt Carmel HS; Wichita, KS; (1); Trk.

WRECKE, GARRETT A; Shawnee Mission W Sr HS; Overland Park, KS; (2); Teachers Aide; JV Bsbl; Var L Bsktbl; JV Ftbl; Hon Roll.

WREN, SABRINA M; Turner HS; Kansas City, KS; (4); Teachers Aide; Band; Chorus; Church Choir; Mrchg Band; Pep Band; School Musical; School Play; Stage Crew; Scuba Dvng; Kansas City CC; Trnsltr.

WRENCH, KRYSTAL D; Hoisington HS; Hoisington, KS; (2); Church Yth Grp; Drama Clb; Intnl Clb; NFL; Quiz Bowl; SADD; Rptr Nwsp; Yrbk; Score Keeper; Wt Lftg; Psych.

WRIGHT, AMY L; Cherryvale HS; Cherryvale, KS; (4); 13/38; FCA; FBLA; FHA; Ofcr Stu Cncl; Hon Roll; Independence CC.

WRIGHT, ANNA M; Burlingame HS; Burlingame, KS; (2); 3/33; Quiz Bowl; Spanish Clb; Chorus; School Musical; L Bsktbl; JV Var Trk; L Vllybl; Cit Awd; Hon Roll; RAY Clb; Ed.

WRIGHT, CHELSEA R; Wellsville Jr Sr HS; Wellsville, KS; (1); Church Yth Grp; Drama Clb; FCA; FBLA; Chorus; Church Choir; Vllybl; Hon Roll; Kays Club.

WRIGHT, DAMON R; Washburn Rural HS; Topeka, KS; (4); 68/298; FBLA; JA; Letterman Clb; SADD; Teachers Aide; Varsity Clb; Rep Soph Cls; Rep Sr Cls; Rep Stu Cncl; Ofcr Bsbl; Natl Yng Ldrs Conf Mmbr; INROADS Intern; Multi Yr Listee; KS Univ; Bus Mgnt.

WRIGHT, DEBORAH A; Canton-Galva HS; Canton, KS; (2); FBLA; Math Tm; SADD; Band; Chorus; Mrchg Band; Pep Band; JV Var Trk; JV Vllybl; Hon Roll; Vocal Soloist 1 Regnl Ltr Soph; Hnrs Choir; Fort Hays ST Univ; Lwyer/Tchr.

WRIGHT, DEREK; Triplains Schl; Wallace, KS; (3); 5/10; Letterman Clb; Phtg Yrbk; Var Capt Bsktbl; Var Capt Ftbl; Var Trk; Hon Roll; NHS; St Track Meet 3rd Pl.

WRIGHT, DUSTIN J; Seaman Sr HS; Topeka, KS; (4); Church Yth Grp; Hosp Aide; Office Aide; Spanish Clb; SADD; Wrstlng; Hon Roll; Jr NHS; Township Fire Dept Cadet Pgm; KS U.

WRIGHT, GARY E; Bishop Miege HS; Overland Park, KS; (4); 14/170; French Clb; Teachers Aide; Wrstlng; High Hon Roll; U Of KS; Pre-Med.

WRIGHT, GINA; Pawnee Heights HS; Burdett, KS; (4); Am Leg Aux Girls St; Church Yth Grp; FBLA; Library Aide; Speech Tm; Band; Chorus; Mrchg Band; Pep Band; School Musical; IVCK Vo Tech; Secrtrl.

WRIGHT, GINNY; Wichita South HS; Wichita, KS; (2); Church Yth Grp; Q&S; Thesps; School Musical; School Play; Stage Crew; Ed Nwsp; Treas Jr Cls; JV Tennis; Ntl Merit Ltr; SHAB Sec; Mass Comm.

WRIGHT, GREG; Kansas City Bible Clg High; Overland Park, KS; (4); 1/5; Church Yth Grp; Math Clb; Scholastic Bowl; Church Choir; Pep Band; Yrbk; Pres Stu Cncl; Var Capt Bsktbl; High Hon Roll; Pres Acad Fit Awd; Kansas City Coll; Bus Admin.

WRIGHT, JENNIFER M; Blue Valley HS; Leawood, KS; (2); Church Yth Grp; Cmnty Wkr; Girl Scts; Orch; School Musical; High Hon Roll; Hon Roll; Kansas City Yth Symphny Cellist; Private Cello Instr; Church Cello Plyr; Music Bus.

WRIGHT, JEREMIAH C; Shawnee Mission W Sr HS; Overland Park, KS; (2); Bsktbl; Intrml Wt Lftg; Hon Roll.

WRIGHT, JEREMY W; Manhattan HS; Manhattan, KS; (3); FBLA; Science Clb; Teachers Aide; Var L Socr; Hon Roll; SADD; TRIBE; Johnson Cty CC; Mrktg; Dsgn.

WRIGHT, SHAWNA; Hutchinson HS; Hutchinson, KS; (4); 16/255; Am Leg Aux Girls St; Church Yth Grp; Debate Tm; NFL; Quiz Bowl; Scholastic Bowl; Speech Tm; Ed Lit Mag; NHS; St Schlr; Ftre Prblm Slvng; Hi-Q; KS Hnrs Rgnts Acad; U KS.

WRIGHT, STACEY L; Maize HS; Maize, KS; (3); Church Yth Grp; Debate Tm; Drama Clb; NFL; Office Aide; Pep Clb; Science Clb; Spanish Clb; Speech Tm; SADD; Partners In Ldrshp Project; Chrch Yth Group Pres; Hutchinson CC; Elem Ed.

WRISTEN, ELIZABETH A; St Thomas Aquinas HS; Shawnee Mission, KS; (4); 70/231; Debate Tm; Nwsp; Co-Ed Lit Mag; Crs Cntry; L Mgr(s); L Var Trk; High Hon Roll; NHS; Hosp Aide; Spanish Clb; Rotary Yth Camp Delg; US Rowing; U Of KS; Envrmntl Sci.

WROTH, ANDREW L; Highland Park HS; Topeka, KS; (3); Phtg Yrbk; Var Chrldng; High Hon Roll; KS U.

WRY, HEATHER A; Turner HS; Kansas City, KS; (4); 4/200; Cmnty Wkr; JA; Math Tm; NFL; Quiz Bowl; Science Clb; SADD; Teachers Aide; Drill Tm; Pres Frsh Cls; KS U; Med.

WU, RICHARD S; Blue Valley Northwest HS; Overland Park, KS; (3); Socr; Tae Kwon Doe Qualified For Natls 3 Times; Bus.

WUERFELE, SANDY R; Atchison Sr HS; Atchison, KS; (4); French Clb; Library Aide; Band; Pep Band; KS St Univ; Acctng.

WUERTZ, SARAH L; Central Heights Sr HS; Richmond, KS; (1); Church Yth Grp; FCA; 4-H; Letterman Clb; Pep Clb; Science Clb; Spanish Clb; Varsity Clb; Band; Mrchg Band.

WULF, TRAVIS C; Cimarron HS; Cimarron, KS; (2); Church Yth Grp; Letterman Clb; Natl FFA Org; Band; Var L Ftbl; L Wrstlng; Hon Roll; NHS; Pittsburgh St Univ; Auto.

WULLENSCHNEIDE, WILLIAM D; Burlingame HS; Scranton, KS; (2); 20/33; Natl FFA Org; Hon Roll; Industrial Design.

WUNDERLY, JENNIFER; Ft Scott HS; Fort Scott, KS; (2); 1/180; Natl FFA Org; Acpl Chr; Chorus; Bsktbl; Powder Puff Ftbl; Sftbl; High Hon Roll; Hon Roll.

WURTH, JOHN; Kapaun-Mt Carmel HS; Andover, KS; (3); Church Yth Grp; French Clb; Hosp Aide; Bsktbl; Crs Cntry; Trk; High Hon Roll; KS Univ; Psychlgy.

WURTZ, KRISTIN R; Wamego HS; Wamego, KS; (3); FHA; Office Aide; SADD; Bsktbl; Var L Tennis; Vllybl; High Hon Roll; Hon Roll; CCCC; Pediatric Nrs.

WURTZ, NICHOLE N; Goodland HS; Goodland, KS; (2); Church Yth Grp; FHA; Chorus; Drill Tm; School Musical; Bsktbl; Golf; Powder Puff Ftbl; Vllybl; Hon Roll; KU; Pediatrician.

WYATT, AMANDA L; Sumner Acad Of Arts & Science; Kansas City, KS; (4); Church Yth Grp; Pep Clb; Spanish Clb; Band; Chorus; Church Choir; Drm Mjr(t); Mrchg Band; Pep Band; Hon Roll; KCKCC; Span Ed.

WYATT, COY M; Glasco HS; Glasco, KS; (2); Church Yth Grp; Bsktbl; Ftbl; Trk; Wt Lftg; Hon Roll.

WYATT, JAYME L; Topeka HS; Topeka, KS; (2); 104/450; Hosp Aide; JA; Tennis; Hon Roll; Origami Clb; Sewing; Explorers; KS ST Univ; Elem Ed.

WYATT, KRISTINA; Manhattan HS; Manhattan, KS; (3); Cmnty Wkr; Pep Clb; Red Cross Aide; Spanish Clb; Intrml Bsktbl; Intrml Powder Puff Ftbl; Hon Roll; Jr NHS; NHS; KS ST U; Rdlgy.

WYCOFF, LAURA; Wichita West HS; Wichita, KS; (4); 15/271; Sec Soph Cls; Pres Jr Cls; Pres Sr Cls; Var L Crs Cntry; Capt L Socr; Var Trk; VP NHS; KS Hnr Schlr; KS Newman Coll Sccr Schlrshp; KS Newman Coll.

WYER, BRANDI D; Maize HS; Wichita, KS; (1); FCA; SADD; Teachers Aide; Bsktbl; Var Sftbl; Vllybl; Hon Roll; Pres Acad Fit Awd; Hooligans Fstptch Sftbl Summer Trvlng Tm; CTL Outfldr Hnrbl Mntn; Swmng Lsns Tchr; Chld Psych.

WYLER, ANDREW; Olathe North Sr HS; Olathe, KS; (3); Office Aide; Teachers Aide; Acpl Chr; Socr; Playng Own Band; De Paul Univ; Comm.

WYLIE, SAMUEL J; Wellington Sr HS; Wellington, KS; (3); Church Yth Grp; FCA; Natl FFA Org; SADD; Church Choir; Wrstlng; Hon Roll; Helped With Toys For Tots; Helped Operation Holliday; Pet Ministry For Nrsng Home Attendants.

WYNKOOP, YVONNE; Valley Falls HS; Valley Falls, KS; (2); Cmnty Wkr; FHA; Pep Clb; Chorus; Pep Clb; Nwsp; Yrbk; JV Bsktbl; JV Var Trk; JV Vllybl; KS U; Comp.

WYNN, CLINT P; Sumner Acad Of Arts & Science; Kansas City, KS; (3); Art Clb; Bus Profs of Am; FBLA; JA; Latin Clb; Office Aide; Spanish Clb; Thesps; Church Choir; Variety Show; WANA Pblshrs Asst Dir; Cmptr Sci.

WYRICK, APRIL L; Gardner-Edgerton HS; Edgerton, KS; (1); Church Yth Grp; Band; Chorus; Mrchg Band; School Play; Stage Crew; Hon Roll; Vac Bbl Schl Tchr Preschl; UCLA; Psych.

WYRICK, ERIN; Southwestern Heights HS; Kismet, KS; (4); 6/38; Am Leg Aux Girls St; Church Yth Grp; Band; Chorus; Drm Mjr(t); Jazz Band; Mrchg Band; Pep Band; JV Bsktbl; JV Chrldng; KS Lns St Hnr Bnd; KS Msc Ed Dist 5 HS Hnr Bnd, St HS Fest Bnd; Music Ed.

WYRICK, LORETTA R; Emporia HS; Emporia, KS; (3); 1/350; Church Yth Grp; NFL; Pep Clb; Q&S; Service Clb; Chorus; Ed Nwsp; Rep Jr Cls; Rep Sr Cls; High Hon Roll; SMILE Treas; Steering Comm For Renaissance Pgm; Commnctn.

WYRILL, COURTNEY; West Smith Cty HS; Kensington, KS; (4); 2/26; Am Leg Aux Girls St; Letterman Clb; Math Tm; Pep Clb; Quiz Bowl; Speech Tm; VP SADD; Band; Drill Tm; Yrbk; KS U; Crmnl Jstc.

WYRILL, JESSICA A; Eastern Heights Jr Sr HS; Kirwin, KS; (3); 3/13; Church Yth Grp; Letterman Clb; Pep Clb; Band; Chorus; Pep Band; Rptr Ed Nwsp; Rptr Yrbk; Ofcr Stu Cncl; JV Var Vllybl; 4 Yr Coll; Grphc Dsgn/Comm Art.

WYSONG, DAVID J; Sabetha HS; Sabetha, KS; (3); 1/90; Church Yth Grp; FHA; Pep Clb; Ofcr Bsbl; Ftbl; Golf; High Hon Roll; NHS; Pres Acad Fit Awd; Spanish Clb.

WYSS, DIANE; Southeast HS; Wichita, KS; (3); Teachers Aide; Wichita St Univ; Med.

XIONG, PANG I; J C Harmon HS; Kansas City, KS; (2); French Clb; GAA; Key Clb; Scholastic Bowl; Bsktbl; Hon Roll; Edctnl Tlnt Srch; Upward Bound; Comp Grphcs Artst.

YADAV, ANUPAMA S; Shawnee Mission S Sr HS; Shawnee Mission, KS; (4); 50/480; Drama Clb; Intnl Clb; Orch; Yrbk; Sec NHS; Debate Tm; NFL; Crs Cntry; Natl Mrt Cmmnd; Frnscs Secy, St, Dist Natl; Indpndt Stdy; Lttr; Psych.

YA DULLAH, AKILAH F; Shawnee Mission W Sr HS; Overland Park, KS; (2); Pep Clb; Acpl Chr; Rptr Nwsp; Pres Frsh Cls; Pres Soph Cls; Pres Jr Cls; Var Trk; Cit Awd; High Hon Roll; Prfct Atten Awd; JAWS; Camping Connctn; Dnce Tm; KS St Univ; Botny.

YAMBOT, JOVE F; Olathe East Sr HS; Olathe, KS; (3); Boy Scts; Spanish Clb; Band; Jazz Band; Mrchg Band; Pep Band; Variety Show; JV Tennis; High Hon Roll; DECA; KS Music Edctr Assn Dist I Hnr Bnd; Elctrcl Eng.

YANG, CAROLYN B; Blue Valley Northwest HS; Overland Park, KS; (2); Hosp Aide; Intnl Clb; Orch; Lit Mag; High Hon Roll; Hon Roll; Sci Knowledge Bowl Team; KAYS Clb; Piano; Yth Symphony Of KS City; Med.

YANG, JINGRONG; Manhattan HS; Manhattan, KS; (4); 45/470; Debate Tm; French Clb; Quiz Bowl; Scholastic Bowl; Speech Tm; Teachers Aide; Orch; School Musical; Swmmng; Hon Roll; AFS; Piano; KS ST U; Med.

YANG, SUDY R; Bishop Carroll Catholic HS; Wichita, KS; (3); JV Tennis; Bus.

YANG, XAO; Wyandotte HS; Kansas City, KS; (4); 24/200; Chess Clb; Church Yth Grp; Computer Clb; Intnl Clb; Ofcr Sr Cls; Hon Roll; NHS; Prfct Atten Awd; De Vry; Comp.

YARBROUGH, STEPHEN M; Shawnee Mission E Sr HS; Shawnee Mission, KS; (2); Church Yth Grp; Key Clb; Church Choir; School Musical; School Play; Hon Roll.

YARDLEY, KATHERINE M; Garden City Sr HS; Garden City, KS; (2); French Clb; Band; Mrchg Band; Pep Band; PA St Univ.

YARGER, THERESA A; Hiawatha HS; Hiawatha, KS; (4); Cmnty Wkr; Letterman Clb; Pep Clb; Teachers Aide; Band; Mrchg Band; Pep Band; School Musical; L Mgr(s); Score Keeper; NEK Jr Miss Scnd Rnnr-Up; Kay Clb Comm Ldr; Emporia ST Univ; Elem Ed.

YARMER, TIMOTHY M; Otis Bison HS; Albert, KS; (1); Church Yth Grp; SADD; Band; Chorus; Church Choir; Mrchg Band; Pep Band; Trk; High Hon Roll; Prfct Atten Awd.

YARNALL, ALISHA R; El Dorado HS; El Dorado, KS; (4); Church Yth Grp; FCA; Math Clb; Science Clb; Spanish Clb; SADD; Varsity Clb; Band; Drill Tm; Orch; K ST; Lwyr.

YARNELL, AMY M; Eastern Heights Jr Sr HS; Agra, KS; (1); 2/9; Church Yth Grp; FCA; Letterman Clb; Pep Clb; Speech Tm; Band; Chorus; Mrchg Band; Pep Band; School Play; Ray Clb; ST Speech/Drama Gold Medal.

YARNELL, BETHANY A; Wichita East HS; Wichita, KS; (3); Church Yth Grp; Debate Tm; Band; Mrchg Band; Pep Band; Hon Roll; NHS; Ntl Merit Ltr; Vol Meonnonite Housing; Intl Bcclrt Prgm; Pre-Law.

YASUHARA, KELLI D; Shawnee Mission S Sr HS; Shawnee Mission, KS; (3); 123/447; Church Yth Grp; Intnl Clb; Pep Clb; NHS; Heart/Hand Svc Projects; Schlrshp Pin; Rsrch/Dvlpmnt Awd Of Distinction; Psych/Chrstn Cnslng.

YATES, JILL R; Northeast HS; Arma, KS; (1); 14/48; Cmnty Wkr; Drama Clb; Spanish Clb; Band; Mrchg Band; Pep Band; Hon Roll; Prfct Atten Awd; 1 Rtng Regnl Frnscs; 2 Rtng ST Frnscs; Chrldr 96-; Law.

YATES, KEVIN J; Blue Valley Northwest HS; Overland Park, KS; (4); Boy Scts; Hosp Aide; Varsity Clb; Band; Mrchg Band; Pep Band; Wrstlng; Hon Roll; Prfct Atten Awd; Johnson Co CC.

YAU, MICHAEL F; Bishop Miege HS; Kansas City, KS; (2); 39/163; Cmnty Wkr; French Clb; Pep Clb; Pep Band; School Musical; School Play; Stage Crew; High Hon Roll.

YAU, RANI; Blue Valley Northwest HS; Overland Park, KS; (3); Cmnty Wkr; Intnl Clb; Math Clb; Spanish Clb; SADD; Teachers Aide; Orch; Var Tennis; High Hon Roll; NHS; Ice Skating; Piano; Violin.

YAUSSI, AMY M; Horton HS; Hiawatha, KS; (4); 18/57; Rptr FHA; Scholastic Bowl; Band; Mrchg Band; Pep Band; Yrbk; High Hon Roll; Hon Roll; Prfct Atten Awd; MO Western ST Coll; Elem Ed.

YAVORNITZKY, VALERIE N; St Thomas Aquinas HS; Overland Park, KS; (3); Cmnty Wkr; Debate Tm; French Clb; German Clb; Hosp Aide; Key Clb; Golf; High Hon Roll; Natl Yth Ldshp Forum On Law And Const; Indpnt Writer; U Of KS; Poli Sci.

YBARRA, ADAM L; Wellington Sr HS; Wellington, KS; (3); Church Yth Grp; JV Bsbl; Hon Roll; U Of Notre Dame; Elec Engrng.

YEAGER, ANNA; Rock Creek Jr Sr HS; Saint George, KS; (4); FHA; Natl FFA Org; Pep Clb; Band; Pep Band; Bsktbl; Chrldng; Vllybl; Wt Lftg; Queen Of Crts; KSU; Ag.

YEAROUT, JESSIE C; Andover HS; Andover, KS; (3); 30/156; Hon Roll.

YEAROUT, SHAILA; Wellington Sr HS; Wellington, KS; (1); 14/171; SADD; Chorus; Hon Roll; Spcl Olympics Gymnastics/Track/Field.

YEH, SUSAN; Topeka HS; Topeka, KS; (4); Cmnty Wkr; Pres VP Model UN; VP NFL; Capt Quiz Bowl; Orch; Ed Lit Mag; L Tennis; VP NHS; Ntl Merit SF; Debate Tm; NCTE Achvt Awd-Wrtng; AP Schlr W/Dstnctn.

YEINGST, FEATHER A; Great Bend Sr HS; Great Bend, KS; (3); Cmnty Wkr; German Clb; L Acpl Chr; L Band; Mrchg Band; Pep Band; High Hon Roll; Treas NHS; Variety Show; Kayettes Holly Sales Dir; City Band; Schlrs Bowl; AP Classes; Ger Exch; Bus Admin/Ger.

YERKE, SHANNON M; Sacred Heart HS; Salina, KS; (1); Cmnty Wkr; FBLA; JA; Pep Clb; Spanish Clb; Phtg Yrbk; JV Var Mgr(s); Var Sftbl; JV Vllybl; Hon Roll; Jr Civitian; Bible Schl Helpe; Comm Svc; KS ST; Bus Mgmt.

YESKE, CARRIE N; Topeka West HS; Topeka, KS; (3); 37/250; Cmnty Wkr; French Clb; Hosp Aide; Letterman Clb; Pep Clb; SADD; L Stat Bsktbl; Mgr(s); Hon Roll; NHS; Multi Yr Listee; KS St Univ; Elem Ed.

YESKE, NATALIE A; Topeka West HS; Topeka, KS; (3); 41/239; Art Clb; Pep Clb; Spanish Clb; SADD; Orch; L Var Crs Cntry; Var L Trk; Hon Roll; White Rose; Keyboarding & ICA Bus Awds; KS Univ; Arch Engrng.

YETSCHKE, KENDRA D; Great Bend Sr HS; Great Bend, KS; (3); 4-H; Office Aide; Pep Clb; Teachers Aide; Band; Color Guard; Flag Corp; Mrchg Band; Hon Roll; Kayette Clb; Marine Bio/Pathology.

YEUNG, KENNY; Manhattan HS; Manhattan, KS; (3); Cmnty Wkr; Church Yth Grp; French Clb; FBLA; Rep Soph Cls; High Hon Roll; NHS; Prfct Atten Awd; PACA; TSA; U Of KS; Med.

YIP, RAYMOND C; Campus HS; Wichita, KS; (4); Boy Scts; Bus Profs of Am; German Clb; Intnl Clb; Scholastic Bowl; Science Clb; Rep Stu Cncl; Golf; High Hon Roll; Hon Roll; Wichita ST Univ.

YOACHIM, COLLIN D; Arkansas City HS; Arkansas City, KS; (2); VICA; Rep Frsh Cls; Rep Stu Cncl; Var Bsbl; Var Socr; Hon Roll; NE.

YOACHIM, MARYE E; Arkansas City HS; Arkansas City, KS; (1); Rep Frsh Cls; Ofcr Stu Cncl; JV Chrldng; Var Trk; Hon Roll; KSU.

YOCKEY, JENNIFER; Campus HS; Haysville, KS; (3); 14/200; Church Yth Grp; Cmnty Wkr; Intnl Clb; SADD; Teachers Aide; Treas Soph Cls; Treas Jr Cls; VP Stu Cncl; Mgr(s); Powder Puff Ftbl; Catholic Yth Org Chprsn Of Pgm/Sec/Pres; Camus Life; Arch/Tchg.

YODER, ANDREW L; Nickerson HS; South Hutchinson, KS; (4); Teachers Aide; Yrbk; Bsktbl; Hon Roll; Univ Of KS; Aerosp Engr.

YODER, CHRISTOPHER C; Haven HS; Hutchinson, KS; (2); Church Yth Grp; FCA; Band; Jazz Band; Mrchg Band; Pep Band; Debate Tm; Regnl & St Piano Cmptns I Rtngs; Bus.

YOKUM, AMY M; Wichita East HS; Wichita, KS; (2); Church Yth Grp; JA; Pep Clb; Spanish Clb; Teachers Aide; Varsity Clb; Nwsp; Var L Sftbl; Var L Vllybl; Hon Roll; USVBA; Teach Swimming; Sports Medicine.

YOKUM, GLENNA M; Iola Sr HS; Iola, KS; (3); 1/150; SADD; Var Bsktbl; Var L Trk; Var L Vllybl; Cit Awd; High Hon Roll; NHS; Prfct Atten Awd; Pres Acad Fit Awd.

YOKUM, LORRIE; Iola Sr HS; Iola, KS; (4); 6/100; Spanish Clb; SADD; Teachers Aide; Var Capt Bsktbl; Var Capt Tennis; Var L Trk; Rep NHS; KS Hnr Schlr; All Acad Trn Tm; Imgs Wrtng Clb.

YORK, CHRISTOPHER; St Thomas Aquinas HS; Overland Park, KS; (3); 27/263; Var L Crs Cntry; Var L Trk; Var L Wrstlng; High Hon Roll; NHS; Prfct Atten Awd; Engr.

YORK, ELIZABETH; Louisburg HS; Bucyrus, KS; (4); 1/78; VP Am Leg Aux Girls St; Capt Dance Clb; Debate Tm; Sec FCA; HOBY; Letterman Clb; Treas Spanish Clb; Treas SADD; School Play; VP NHS; Dance.

YORK, JULIE E; Blue Valley Northwest HS; Overland Park, KS; (3); JV Var Bsktbl; Var Vllybl; High Hon Roll; Pres Acad Fit Awd.

YORK, LOGAN M; Louisburg HS; Bucyrus, KS; (4); Boy Scts; Church Yth Grp; Letterman Clb; Natl FFA Org; Spanish Clb; Band; Mrchg Band; Pep Band; Var Bsbl; Var Ftbl; Eagle Sct; KS ST U.

YORKE, RUTH C; Blue Valley Northwest HS; Overland Park, KS; (3); Church Yth Grp; Cmnty Wkr; Drama Clb; Chorus; Church Choir; Variety Show; Bsktbl; Crs Cntry; Trk; High Hon Roll; Forensics Team.

YOST, ECHO D; Otis Bison HS; Bison, KS; (2); Church Yth Grp; 4-H; SADD; Band; Chorus; Sec Soph Cls; Var Bsktbl; Var Trk; JV Vllybl; High Hon Roll; ST Forensics; ST Trk; Bst Of Show Sci Fair Proj.

YOST, KRISTAL K; Dighton HS; Dighton, KS; (1); Chorus; Trk; Vllybl; Wt Lftg; Hon Roll.

YOST, SUMMER H; Otis Bison HS; Bison, KS; (1); Church Yth Grp; 4-H; Speech Tm; Band; Chorus; Jazz Band; Bsktbl; 4-H Awd; Hon Roll; Pep Clb; AAU Bsktbl; U Of KS; Pre Med.

YOTHPHOY, SONAKHONE T; Wyandotte HS; Kansas City, KS; (2); Hon Roll; NHS.

YOULE, BROOKE E; Winfield HS; Winfield, KS; (3); Am Leg Aux Girls St; Church Yth Grp; Pep Clb; SADD; Orch; Rep Frsh Cls; Rep Soph Cls; Pres Sr Cls; Sec Stu Cncl; Var Bsktbl.

YOUNG, ABBY; Kingman HS; Kingman, KS; (2); Church Yth Grp; French Clb; Treas FBLA; HOBY; Natl FFA Org; SADD; Acpl Chr; Chorus; School Play; VP Frsh Cls; Teens Today Ldrs Tomorrow Cabnt Mem; Yth In Govt; Rodeo Clb.

YOUNG, CHRISTINA M; Washington HS; Kansas City, KS; (3); Dance Clb; Debate Tm; Drama Clb; Girl Scts; JA; Key Clb; Library Aide; Office Aide; Pep Clb; Varsity Clb.

YOUNG, ERICA; Southeast Saline Schl; Salina, KS; (4); 11/48; HOBY; Teachers Aide; Acpl Chr; Chorus; School Musical; School Play; Ed Nwsp; Ed Lit Mag; High Hon Roll; NHS; U Of KS; Psycht.

YOUNG, ERIN; Olathe East Sr HS; Olathe, KS; (3); Cmnty Wkr; NFL; Acpl Chr; School Musical; Var Socr; NHS; Debate Tm; GAA; Letterman Clb; Pep Clb; Outstdng Svc Vol Awd96; DARE Role Model; Olathe Intrgenrtnl Choir/Humn/Cvl Rghts Awds; KS Univ; Orthpdc Srgn.

YOUNG, HOLLY; Atchison Co Cmty HS; Effingham, KS; (4); 1/58; Church Yth Grp; Cmnty Wkr; Dance Clb; Drama Clb; Pres 4-H; Sec FBLA; GAA; Letterman Clb; Math Clb; Mu Alpha Theta; Cty 4-H Ambsdr; Hmcmng Qn Cand; NE Dist FFA Rprtr; KS ST U; Ag.

YOUNG, JENNIFER; Kansas City Bible Clg High; Shawnee Mission, KS; (1); Church Yth Grp; Drama Clb; Pep Clb; Chorus; Church Choir; Orch; Sec Frsh Cls; Var Bsktbl; Var JV Vllybl; Hon Roll; Violin; Stu Of Mnth; Lawyer.

YOUNG, JENNIFER; Shawnee Mission E Sr HS; Leawood, KS; (3); 1/485; Cmnty Wkr; Dance Clb; HOBY; Math Tm; Chrmn Natl Beta Clb; Phtg Rptr Nwsp; JV Chrldng; Vllybl; French Hon Soc; High Hon Roll; U Of MO Kansas City HS Sci, Math, Tech Inst; Adopt-A-Clssrm; Engrng.

YOUNG, JENNIFER M; Arkansas City HS; Arkansas City, KS; (2); FCA; SADD; Orch; Vllybl; Hon Roll; Wichita ST U; Dnstry.

YOUNG, JESSICA; Spring Hill HS; Spring Hill, KS; (3); 2/99; Church Yth Grp; Cmnty Wkr; Pep Clb; Science Clb; SADD; Band; School Musical; High Hon Roll; NHS; Dance Team; U Of KS; Med.

YOUNG, JONI L; Haven HS; Burrton, KS; (3); FHA; Model UN; NFL; Band; Chorus; Jazz Band; School Musical; Var Bsktbl; Var Crs Cntry; Hon Roll; HS ST Piano Fstvl 1st Rtng; KS ST.

YOUNG, KAILA R; Derby HS; Derby, KS; (2); 1/450; HOBY; Math Tm; Scholastic Bowl; Ofcr Stu Cncl; Stat Bsktbl; High Hon Roll; NHS; Church Yth Grp; Cmnty Wkr; Ofcr Frsh Cls; Kay Club Sec/Pts Dir 2 Yrs 10th/11th; Outstdng Frosh Stuco Awd; GTC Prgm/OM/FPS/STCK Mrkt; 4 Yr Coll; Math/Engrng.

YOUNG, KATHERINE E; Topeka HS; Topeka, KS; (4); 29/340; Teachers Aide; Band; Jazz Band; Mrchg Band; Orch; Pep Band; High Hon Roll; Natl Achvt Fnlst; KS Masonic All St HS Marchng Band; KSU; Psych.

YOUNG, KATIE; Bishop Carroll Catholic HS; Wichita, KS; (4); Church Yth Grp; French Clb; SADD; Varsity Clb; Band; Mrchg Band; Chrldng; Socr; Governors Cncl Of Teen Ldrs; Natl Chrldng Tryouts.

YOUNG, MALISSA A; Olathe North Sr HS; Olathe, KS; (3); 23/389; Church Yth Grp; Acpl Chr; Chorus; Mrchg Band; Swing Chorus; Stat Wrstlng; Hon Roll; NHS; Math Tm; Teachers Aide; Chem Demonstrations Team; HOPE Worldwide Walk-A-Thons & Comm Projects; Piano; U Of MO; Pharmaceuticals.

YOUNG, MICHAEL; Lawrence HS; Lawrence, KS; (3); Am Leg Boys St; Debate Tm; German Clb; NFL; Acpl Chr; Orch; School Musical; Variety Show; Sec Stu Cncl; High Hon Roll; Natl Yth Ldrshp Conf Nom; HS Rep On City Cmssn; Div I Music; KS ST HS Act Assn; U Of KS; Lawyer; Pub Servant.

YOUNG, NIKKI J; Lyndon HS; Lyndon, KS; (3); Cmnty Wkr; Drama Clb; FBLA; Pres FHA; Office Aide; SADD; Band; Pep Band; Stage Crew; Rptr Nwsp; Washburn U; Psych.

YOUNG, SARA D; Turner HS; Kansas City, KS; (2); French Clb; Math Clb; Math Tm; Co-Capt Drill Tm; Cit Awd; Hon Roll; Jr NHS; Prfct Atten Awd; Pres Acad Fit Awd; Pres Schlr; Drill Team Capt; Jr Cls Rep; Wichita ST Univ.

YOUNG, VANESSA M; Blue Valley Northwest HS; Overland Park, KS; (3); Office Aide; Hon Roll.

YOUNG, YASHAUNA C; Junction City HS; Junction City, KS; (2); Church Yth Grp; Cmnty Wkr; Pep Clb; ROTC; Teachers Aide; Chorus; Church Choir; School Musical; School Play; Stage Crew; KS St Univ Upward Bound Sec; KS St Univ; Bus Mgnt.

YOUNGBLOOD, KENNEY L; Galena HS; Galena, KS; (3); Cmnty Wkr; Ftbl; Trk; Wt Lftg; Cit Awd; Hon Roll; NHS; PSU; Comp Operator; Arch.

YOUNGER, CASEY L; Basehor Linwood HS; Tonganoxie, KS; (3); Debate Tm; FBLA; FHA; GAA; NFL; SADD; Sec Jr Cls; Vllybl; High Hon Roll; Dbtc VP; Ftre Hmmkrs Of Amer VP PR; Prom Comm/Hmcmng Floats; Cert Of Merit Effrt/Achvmnt/Ptntl Alg; Johnson Cty CC; Bus Mgmt.

YOUNGGREN, SUMMER; Uniontown HS; Uniontown, KS; (3); FHA; HOBY; Math Clb; Math Tm; Spanish Clb; Phtg Yrbk; Ofcr Jr Cls; L Vllybl; High Hon Roll; NHS; Vlntr Fort Scott Natl Hstrc Site.

YOUNGSTROM, WHITNEY A; Olathe East Sr HS; Overland Park, KS; (3); Drama Clb; Letterman Clb; Spanish Clb; Teachers Aide; Thesps; Varsity Clb; Band; Mrchg Band; School Play; Yrbk; Comm Svc; Chm Of YMCA Teen Adv Cnsl; Engrng.

YOUNKER, NICHOLAS E; Ellinwood Jr Sr HS; Ellinwood, KS; (2); 6/45; Chess Clb; Church Yth Grp; Debate Tm; FCA; Latin Clb; Quiz Bowl; Speech Tm; School Musical; VP Frsh Cls; VP Soph Cls; Lgl Stud.

YOURDON, JOEL L; Wichita Heights HS; Wichita, KS; (2); 68/316; Church Yth Grp; French Clb; Letterman Clb; Varsity Clb; Chorus; Church Choir; Variety Show; Crs Cntry; Trk; Alg II & Pre Calc Acad Achvt 95-96; Piano Cmptn St II Ratng, Reg I Ratng; Math.

YU, STEPHANIE Y; Shawnee Mission S Sr HS; Overland Park, KS; (4); 1/451; Pres Cmnty Wkr; Pres Intnl Clb; Pres Science Clb; Pres Service Clb; Pres Orch; Rep Stu Cncl; Swmmng; French Hon Soc; High Hon Roll; Val; Ymha Ntl Piano Cmptn St Wnnr 4xs; W Cntrldv 2nd Pl 95-96; Slst W/Tpka Symphny, Slng Symphny, Ovrnld Pk; Yale U; Bio.

YUNK, JILL; Manhattan HS; Manhattan, KS; (4); 1/377; Am Leg Aux Girls St; HOBY; Rptr Pep Clb; Orch; School Play; Sec Rptr Stu Cncl; Var L Golf; Hon Roll; Treas NHS; FCA; Sci Olympd; KU Hnrs Prog; KS ST U; Med.

YUONG, NGUYEN X; Wichita Southeast HS; Wichita, KS; (2); #1 in class; Math Tm; Science Clb; Teachers Aide; High Hon Roll; Hon Roll; NHS; Prfct Atten Awd; U Of KS; Pharmacist.

YUST, RICHARD D; Haven HS; Haven, KS; (2); Debate Tm; NFL; Varsity Clb; Chorus; Pep Band; JV Ftbl; JV Tennis; High Hon Roll; Var Wrstlng; Hon Roll; Forensic Team; Nom US Natl Math Awd; KS ST Univ; Lang/Meteorlgy.

YUTZY, CARRIE N; Haven HS; Haven, KS; (4); Dance Clb; Stage Crew; Nwsp; Pres Soph Cls; Rep Stu Cncl; Var Vllybl; Pres Schlr; USC.

ZAGER, TONY J; Circle HS; El Dorado, KS; (3); Church Yth Grp; SADD; Band; Chorus; VP Frsh Cls; VP Soph Cls; VP Stu Cncl; Bsktbl; Crs Cntry; Golf; KS ST U; Tchng.

ZAINALI, AREZO; Liberal HS; Liberal, KS; (3); Church Yth Grp; Cmnty Wkr; FCA; French Clb; Hosp Aide; HOBY; Key Clb; Quiz Bowl; Science Clb; Thesps; Med.

ZAJIC, DEAN; St John Jr Sr HS; Saint John, KS; (3); 13/46; Am Leg Boys St; FHA; Quiz Bowl; SADD; School Musical; School Play; Pres Jr Cls; VP Sr Cls; Pres Stu Cncl; JV Bsktbl.

ZAMAN, DOUG E; Osawatomie HS; Osawatomie, KS; (1); JV Bsbl; Var Bsktbl; Wt Lftg; High Hon Roll.

ZAMORA, LAURIE; J C Harmon HS; Kansas City, KS; (3); Drama Clb; Q&S; Stage Crew; Co-Ed Nwsp; Hon Roll; DECA; LULAC; Scndry Ed.

ZAMRZLA, ERIN L; Sylvan Unified HS; Sylvan Grove, KS; (2); Church Yth Grp; Pres 4-H; Quiz Bowl; Band; Chorus; Sec Frsh Cls; Sec Soph Cls; Var L Bsktbl; Var L Trk; NHS; KS Assc Yth Treas; Gov Cntr Teen Ldrshp; Baton Twrlng.

ZARCHAN, ADAM M; Kapaun-Mt Carmel HS; Wichita, KS; (4); 8/170; Spanish Clb; Socr; High Hon Roll; St Schlr; KS Hnr Schlr; Wichita ST U; Sports Medicine.

ZARTER, C RYAN; Shawnee Mission Nw Sr HS; Shawnee, KS; (4); 11/396; Boy Scts; Church Yth Grp; Science Clb; Service Clb; Mrchg Band; Co-Capt Ice Hcky; Ntl Merit SF; Cmnty Wkr; Math Tm; Teachers Aide; Snow Skiing; Guitar.

ZEBELL-MANN, SAVANNAH R; Derby Christian Schl; Wichita, KS; (2); Church Yth Grp; Teachers Aide; School Play; Rptr Nwsp; VP Frsh Cls; Ofcr Stu Cncl; High Hon Roll; Hon Roll; Sci Fair Grand Prz Wnnr; Personal Comps; Internet; Med; Comps; Bus.

ZEDRICK, ANN M; Kingman HS; Kingman, KS; (3); 21/80; Church Yth Grp; Drama Clb; FCA; FBLA; Natl FFA Org; Office Aide; SADD; Stage Crew; Ed Yrbk; Vllybl; CYO Bd 3 Yrs; Emporia Univ; PT.

ZEHNEDER, SARAH B; Smoky Valley HS; Lindsborg, KS; (2); Church Yth Grp; Drama Clb; FHA; Pep Clb; Orch; School Musical; School Play; Chrldng; Hon Roll; KAY 2 Yr Ofcr; Section Ldr Orchestra; Jrnlsm.

ZEHNER, JENNIFER L; Gardner-Edgerton HS; Edgerton, KS; (2); Drama Clb; French Clb; Band; Mrchg Band; Pep Band; Stage Crew; Hon Roll; Animals; OK Univ; Meteorology.

ZEIT, NATHAN; Hiawatha HS; Fairview, KS; (3); 26/100; Am Leg Boys St; 4-H; Scholastic Bowl; Treas Stu Cncl; JV Ftbl; Hon Roll; KS ST Univ; Ag.

ZELFER, AMBER L; Wheatland Middle Sr HS; Grainfield, KS; (4); 6/16; Art Clb; FHA; Chorus; Church Choir; Phtg Nwsp; Phtg Yrbk; Treas Jr Cls; Ofcr Sr Cls; Ofcr Stu Cncl; Var Capt Bsktbl; 6th Dist Fed Wmns Ctznshp Wrtng Awd; Colby CC; Phys Thrpst.

ZELL, DEVIN T; Burlington HS; Burlington, KS; (4); 4/86; Drama Clb; FBLA; Model UN; Quiz Bowl; Scholastic Bowl; Thesps; School Musical; School Play; Stage Crew; Yrbk; U Of KS; Graphic Dsgn.

ZELLER, BERNADETTE; Royal Valley HS; Mayetta, KS; (3); 1/60; Church Yth Grp; Cmnty Wkr; Drama Clb; Letterman Clb; Pep Clb; Scholastic Bowl; SADD; Band; Chorus; Church Choir; KS Rgnst Hon Acad At Pttsbrgh Stuniv; KS St Eng And Sci Smmr Inst; Multi Yr Listee; Elem Ed.

ZELLER, LISA; Olpe Schl; Olpe, KS; (2); 4-H; FBLA; Quiz Bowl; 4-H Awd; Riding; Swimming; K-St Univ; Bio.

ZELLER, MARGIE; Desoto HS; Shawnee Mission, KS; (4); Church Yth Grp; Cmnty Wkr; Drama Clb; NFL; Office Aide; Spanish Clb; SADD; Thesps; Chorus; Flag Corp; Pittsburg ST Univ; Ed.

ZELLERS, CORY D; Topeka HS; Topeka, KS; (4); Church Yth Grp; Band; Jazz Band; Mrchg Band; Pep Band; Variety Show; KS Regents Curriculum Awd; Coleman Hawkin Jazz Awd; Outstdng Sr Jazz Musician; Emporia ST Univ; Music Ed.

ZELLERS, KYLIE E; Topeka HS; Topeka, KS; (2); Church Yth Grp; Cmnty Wkr; Pep Clb; Band; Mrchg Band; Pep Band; Hon Roll; Teens HOPE AIDS Ed Group; Preschl Tchr.

ZEMAITIS, TAMRA D; Washington HS; Kansas City, KS; (2); Drama Clb; Spanish Clb; Chorus; Stage Crew; Entrtnmnt Indstry.

ZEMAN, JUDY F; Ellsworth HS; Ellsworth, KS; (1); 12/75; Nwsp; Ofcr Frsh Cls; Hon Roll; KS ST U; Scndry Tchr; Tchng.

ZENS, KELLY A; Wellington Sr HS; Wellington, KS; (3); 19/185; Church Yth Grp; Key Clb; Red Cross Aide; SADD; Band; Mrchg Band; Jr NHS; NHS; Lfegrdng; Swm Tm.

ZERGER, SCOTT A; Hutchinson HS; Hutchinson, KS; (4); 11/255; Am Leg Boys St; Church Yth Grp; French Clb; Pep Clb; Speech Tm; Rep Jr Cls; Rep Sr Cls; Var L Ftbl; Var L Trk; JV Wrstlng; Hutchinson CC.

ZHANG, JINGYUAN; Shawnee Mission E Sr HS; Overland Park, KS; (2); 60/470; Chorus; Hon Roll; One Yr Schlsp Pin 96; Piano; Drawing; Painting; Singing.

ZHAO, NAN; Wichita Northwest HS; Wichita, KS; (2); 1/380; Debate Tm; Intnl Clb; Math Clb; NFL; Speech Tm; VP Soph Cls; Hon Roll; Photo; Japanese; Engrng.

ZICKEFOOSE, ANNE M; Shawnee Mission E Sr HS; Shawnee Mission, KS; (4); 153/373; Cmnty Wkr; Debate Tm; Math Clb; Service Clb; Varsity Clb; Variety Show; Var Chrldng; Hon Roll; NHS; Pres Acad Fit Awd; Amigos De Las Americas; Amer Cncl For Intl Stud; Jr League Cotillion Mem; KS Univ.

ZIEGENHORN, TIFFANY; Olathe South Sr HS; Olathe, KS; (3); Church Yth Grp; Pres 4-H; Spanish Clb; Band; Color Guard; Flag Corp; Mrchg Band; Pep Band; 4-H Awd; Hon Roll; Japan Exch Stdnt; KS ST Univ; Geophyslgy/Tchng.

ZIEGLER, ELLEN; Hoxie HS; Hoxie, KS; (3); Church Yth Grp; Debate Tm; Quiz Bowl; Band; Chorus; Jazz Band; Pep Band; School Musical; High Hon Roll; NHS; John Philip Sousa Awd Wnr.

ZIEGLER, HOLLY R; Trego Comm HS; Collyer, KS; (3); Church Yth Grp; Drama Clb; 4-H; FHA; German Clb; Science Clb; SADD; Band; Pep Band.

ZIEGLER, JENNY L; Girard HS; Girard, KS; (4); 1/69; Pres Church Yth Grp; Rep French Clb; FHA; Girl Scts; Math Tm; Scholastic Bowl; Science Clb; Rep Spanish Clb; SADD; Teachers Aide; KA ST Univ; Arch Eng.

ZIEGLER, LEAH; Ellis HS; Ellis, KS; (1); Church Yth Grp; Band; Chorus; Pep Band; Sec Frsh Cls; Ofcr Stu Cncl; Chrldng; Trk; Cit Awd; Hon Roll; Kayettes; Piano; KU; Pre-Med.

ZIEGLER, MITZI M; Great Bend Sr HS; Great Bend, KS; (3); Pep Clb; Band; Flag Corp; Trk; Vllybl; Wt Lftg; Hon Roll; Kayettes.

ZILLHART, TIERNEY E; Ottawa HS; Ottawa, KS; (2); Band; Mrchg Band; JV Capt Chrldng; Powder Puff Ftbl; Vllybl; Hon Roll; Prelaw.

ZILLMANN, MICHELLE D; Chase Cnty HS; Strong City, KS; (3); 4/40; Spanish Clb; Band; Ed Nwsp; Ofcr Stu Cncl; Mgr Bsktbl; L Mgr(s); L Sftbl; Vllybl; High Hon Roll; NHS; Voiced; KAY Clb; KSU; Bus Admin.

ZIMEMRMAN, PATRICIA L; Piper HS; Kansas City, KS; (3); Church Yth Grp; Cmnty Wkr; French Clb; GAA; Math Tm; Office Aide; Chorus; Co-Ed Yrbk; Rep Sr Cls; Var Mgr(s); U Of KS; Optom.

ZIMMERLI, BEN; Pierson Jr HS; Kansas City, KS; (1); Nwsp; Yrbk; Jr NHS.

ZIMMERMAN, ANDREW; Arkansas City HS; Arkansas City, KS; (3); 38/189; Scholastic Bowl; Teachers Aide; Orch; Hon Roll; ST Solo/Ensmbl Contest; Dist Six Hnrs Orch; Winfield Regnl Symphony; Mus Ed.

ZIMMERMAN, ANGELA C; Dodge City HS; Dodge City, KS; (2); French Clb; HOBY; Band; Drill Tm; Mrchg Band; Ofcr Stu Cncl; Capt Pom Pon; Hon Roll; KS St Univ; Brcst Jrnlsm.

ZIMMERMAN, AUDREY M; Larned HS; Larned, KS; (3); Am Leg Aux Girls St; Sec Treas Church Yth Grp; Letterman Clb; Office Aide; Teachers Aide; Acpl Chr; Chorus; Bsktbl; Var Tennis; Hon Roll; Tennis Instr; Barton Cty CC; Elem Educ.

ZIMMERMAN, CARLY A; Andover HS; Wichita, KS; (4); 1/145; Scholastic Bowl; Phtg Yrbk; VP Sr Cls; Gov Hon Prg Awd; High Hon Roll; Pres NHS; Pres Acad Fit Awd; St Schlr; Val; Btlr Cty Yth Ldrshp; U Of KS; Psych.

ZIMMERMAN, CRYSTAL R; Wichita South HS; Wichita, KS; (2); 1/350; Church Yth Grp; Cmnty Wkr; Chorus; Church Choir; School Musical; Stage Crew; Variety Show; Sec Frsh Cls; Var Pom Pon; Crime Stoppers; Play Piano; Kelley Elem Mentor Chldrn; Music/Psych.

ZIMMERMAN, HEATHER A; Protection Schl; Protection, KS; (2); Scholastic Bowl; Band; Chorus; Pep Band; School Musical; Yrbk; Sec Treas Frsh Cls; Bsktbl; Vllybl; High Hon Roll; Univ Of KS; PT.

ZIMMERMAN, JOSEPH M; Stafford Jr Sr HS; Stafford, KS; (4); 4/20; Boy Scts; Church Yth Grp; Pep Clb; Quiz Bowl; Scholastic Bowl; Science Clb; Teachers Aide; Treas Sr Cls; Crs Cntry; Ntl Merit Schol; Emporia ST Univ; Soc; Fam Stud.

ZIMMERMAN, KELLI; Jefferson West HS; Ozawkie, KS; (2); 11/65; Chess Clb; Pep Clb; Chorus; Var L Chrldng; Powder Puff Ftbl; Var Trk; Stat Vllybl; Wt Lftg; High Hon Roll; KSU; Dietcn.

ZIMMERMAN, KISHA; Douglass HS; Rose Hill, KS; (4); 16/48; Am Leg Aux Girls St; Church Yth Grp; Cmnty Wkr; FCA; FHA; Intnl Clb; NFL; Office Aide; Science Clb; Chorus; Grls St; Wichita ST; Spch Pthlgy.

ZIMMERMAN, LANCE A; Greensburg HS; Mullinville, KS; (3); 2/27; Am Leg Boys St; Chrmn Church Yth Grp; Capt Debate Tm; Pep Clb; Band; Chorus; Church Choir; Mrchg Band; Pep Band; Pres Jr Cls; Ft Hays ST Univ; CPA.

ZIMMERMAN, MELISSA; Arkansas City HS; Arkansas City, KS; (4); 10/171; Church Yth Grp; FCA; Office Aide; SADD; Sftbl; Vllybl; High Hon Roll; NHS; Yth Amer Bowling Alliance Ark City League Sec; AYABA Jr Travel League Sec; Cowley Cty CC; CPA.

ZIMMERMAN, MELISSA L; Council Grove HS; Council Grove, KS; (3); 13/80; FCA; FBLA; FHA; Girl Scts; SADD; Chorus; School Musical; School Play; Nwsp; High Hon Roll; Completed 12 Hrs Coll Courses; KS ST U; Elem Ed.

ZIMMERMAN, MICKEY E; Pratt HS; Pratt, KS; (3); Am Leg Boys St; Church Yth Grp; FCA; Pres Treas 4-H; JV Golf; 4-H Awd; Hon Roll; KS ST U; Comp Sci.

ZIMMERMAN, MISSY A; Galena HS; Galena, KS; (2); Sec Church Yth Grp; Sec FHA; GAA; Letterman Clb; Math Tm; Scholastic Bowl; Spanish Clb; SADD; Chorus; Church Choir; Pittsburg ST Univ.

ZIMMERMAN, NICHOLAS J; Pratt HS; Pratt, KS; (4); 19/95; Church Yth Grp; Cmnty Wkr; FCA; Treas 4-H; JV Golf; 4-H Awd; Hon Roll; Kiwanis Awd; St Schlr; Ctzshp Smnr To UN; Ft Hays St Univ; Elem Ed.

ZIMMERMAN, NIKAELA J; Lacrosse HS; La Crosse, KS; (4); 3/28; French Clb; Quiz Bowl; Band; Jazz Band; Mrchg Band; Pep Band; School Play; VP Sr Cls; Ofcr Stu Cncl; NHS; Stu Taking A Responsible Stand Sec, Treas; U Of KS; Psych.

ZIMMERMAN, TARA; Douglass HS; Douglass, KS; (2); 7/73; Cmnty Wkr; Drama Clb; FCA; Chorus; School Musical; Ofcr Stu Cncl; Mgr Crs Cntry; Mgr Sftbl; High Hon Roll; Church Yth Grp; Teens As Tchrs.

ZINK, RYAN L; Quivira Heights HS; Bushton, KS; (2); Red Cross Aide; Band; Chorus; Pep Band; Rep Frsh Cls; JV Bsktbl; Var Ftbl; L Golf; Hon Roll; Kays Bd Mem.

ZINK, SARAH M; Great Bend Sr HS; Great Bend, KS; (2); 56/263; Cmnty Wkr; Pep Clb; Spanish Clb; Chorus; Variety Show; Stat Bsktbl; JV Chrldng; JV Tennis; Hon Roll; Prfct Atten Awd.

ZINN, JESSICA M; Wichita East HS; Wichita, KS; (3); Church Yth Grp; Teachers Aide; Sec Frsh Cls; Sec Soph Cls; JV Var Pom Pon; Hnrb Mntn; Jr Assembly; Hangar Bd Dance Comm; Baker; Elem Ed.

ZOGELMAN, LISA D; Marion HS; Florence, KS; (3); Church Yth Grp; Pep Clb; Teachers Aide; Band; Chorus; Drm Mjr(t); Flag Corp; Jazz Band; Mrchg Band; Pep Band; Pianist.

ZOHNER, JUSTIN J; Hill City HS; Penokee, KS; (3); Church Yth Grp; Cmnty Wkr; FCA; Natl FFA Org; Quiz Bowl; SADD; Band; Pep Band.

ZOOK, L. CHAD; Columbus HS; Columbus, KS; (3); 1/110; Bus Profs of Am; Math Tm; Lit Mag; Ofcr Stu Cncl; High Hon Roll; Treas NHS; Bus Prof Amer KS Assn St VP.

ZSUZSICS, ALLEN J; Lincoln Jr Sr HS; Lincoln, KS; (1); Church Yth Grp; Letterman Clb; Quiz Bowl; Band; Mrchg Band; Pep Band; Ftbl; Trk; Wrstlng; Hon Roll; KS U; Pro Ftbl; Team Mgr.

ZUERCHER, AMBER H; Berean Acad; Whitewater, KS; (3); Church Yth Grp; 4-H; Letterman Clb; Library Aide; Math Tm; Teachers Aide; Varsity Clb; Band; Church Choir; Pep Band; Acctng; Missions.

ZULKOSKI, PAIGE; Caldwell Jr Sr HS; Caldwell, KS; (2); Church Yth Grp; FCA; Pep Clb; SADD; Teachers Aide; Band; Mrchg Band; Pep Band; Rep Jr Cls; Var Bsktbl; Kayettes.

ZUMBRUNN, BRENDA; Atchison Sr HS; Atchison, KS; (4); 1/123; Church Yth Grp; Cmnty Wkr; Hosp Aide; Band; Mrchg Band; Pep Band; Var Capt Tennis; High Hon Roll; Sec NHS; Office Aide; All St Marching Band; NWMSU Sci Olympd; Coll Of St Mary; Med.

ZWEYGARDT, AMY; St Francis Cmnty HS; Saint Francis, KS; (4); 2/27; Church Yth Grp; FHA; Natl FFA Org; Office Aide; Pep Clb; Q&S; Scholastic Bowl; Teachers Aide; Chorus; Co-Ed Yrbk; All Acad Tm Oberlin Bsketball Tourn; Honor Grd; Mccook CC; Accounting.

ZWICK, ELIZABETH A; Lyons HS; Lyons, KS; (2); Church Yth Grp; Debate Tm; FCA; 4-H; Pep Clb; Chorus; Golf; 4-H Awd; Hon Roll.

ZWILLENBERG, JONATHAN G; Shawnee Mission E Sr HS; Leawood, KS; (3); Intnl Clb; Pep Clb; Temple Yth Grp; Tennis; Hon Roll.

OKLAHOMA

ABBOTT, ANGELA F; North Intemediate HS; Broken Arrow, OK; (1); Church Yth Grp; JCL; Latin Clb; Chorus; Swmmng; Hon Roll; Jr NHS; OK Hnr Soc; ST Latin Drvtvs Tst 5th Pl; Brigham Young Univ; Hum Rsrc.

ABBOTT, BRETT; Latta Sr HS; Stonewall, OK; (2); 1/50; Church Yth Grp; VP Drama Clb; Letterman Clb; Co-Capt Quiz Bowl; Co-Capt Scholastic Bowl; VP Speech Tm; VP Thesps; School Play; Mgr Stage Crew; Var Chrldng; OK Blood Inst Vol; OK Bptst; Dntst.

ABBOTT, BRYAN; Wagoner Sr HS; Hulbert, OK; (2); Church Yth Grp; 4-H; Socr; Hon Roll; NHS; Teens For Chrst; NSU.

ABBOTT, CRYSTAL; Calera HS; Calera, OK; (3); 1/37; Rep Natl FFA Org; Ed Yrbk; Sec Treas Frsh Cls; Pres Soph Cls; VP Jr Cls; Sec Treas Stu Cncl; Chrldng; High Hon Roll; NHS; Ntl Merit Ltr; Upward Bound Math-Sci Soc Chprsn; Southeastern OK ST U; Dietics.

ABBOTT, ERIC R; Morris HS; Morris, OK; (4); 6/72; Church Yth Grp; Letterman Clb; Office Aide; Quiz Bowl; Scholastic Bowl; Teachers Aide; Thesps; Band; Church Choir; Jazz Band; OSU; Comp Grphcs.

ABBOTT, TINA M; Morris HS; Morris, OK; (3); Church Yth Grp; FHA; Teachers Aide; Band; Mrchg Band; Pep Band; High Hon Roll; NHS.

ABDULLAH, IBN Z; Spiro HS; Spiro, OK; (1); FCA; SADD; Nwsp; Yrbk; Ofcr Bsbl; Bsktbl; Ftbl; Score Keeper; Trk; Wt Lftg; Georgetown; Bsktbl Plyr.

ABEL, AARON J; B T Washington HS; Tulsa, OK; (1); Boy Scts; Church Yth Grp; JV Var Socr; Baylor; Med.

ABEL, ANGELA D; Wagoner Sr HS; Wagoner, OK; (3); 34/138; Church Yth Grp; Cmnty Wkr; Teachers Aide; Yrbk; Hon Roll; Prom Comm; Make A Difrnc Day; Northeastrn ST Univ; RN.

ABELS, ERIN; Tahlequah Sr HS; Tahlequah, OK; (4); 28/251; Church Yth Grp; Science Clb; Service Clb; SADD; Teachers Aide; Chorus; Sec Frsh Cls; Rep Stu Cncl; NHS; ORU Math Acad; Rotary Yth Ldrshp Awd; Elem Ed.

ABERCROMBIE, BRIAN M; Edmond North HS; Edmond, OK; (3); 1/348; Computer Clb; Mu Alpha Theta; ROTC; Service Clb; Band; High Hon Roll; NHS; Ntl Merit SF; Prfct Atten Awd; Air Force Assn Medal Natl Awd; Military Order Of World Wars Medal Natl Awd; Distngd Cadet Awd; OK U; Comp Engrng.

ABINGTON, SARAH E; South Intermediate HS; Broken Arrow, OK; (1); Pres Church Yth Grp; Band; Color Guard; Mrchg Band; Ofcr Stu Cncl; High Hon Roll; Jr NHS; Outstdng Hnrs Geometry/Physicalsci/Eng I; OK Hnr Soc.

ABLES, ANNA C; Choctaw HS; Midwest City, OK; (3); #29 in class; Office Aide; High Hon Roll; Hon Roll; Jr NHS; NHS; Pres Acad Fit Awd; Cmptv Dncr Nmrs Awds Rglnny & Ntnlly; Dance Instr; Northwestern; Bus.

ABLES, HIEDI B; Walters HS; Walters, OK; (2); 4/57; Sec Art Clb; FHA; HOBY; Quiz Bowl; Scholastic Bowl; SADD; Teachers Aide; High Hon Roll; Hon Roll; NHS; Vrsty Acad Tm; Acad Trnmt Chmpn; Georgetown U; Crmnl Law.

ABODE, PHILIP J; Stillwater Sr HS; Stillwater, OK; (3); 1/360; Am Leg Boys St; Church Yth Grp; FCA; Key Clb; Latin Clb; Mu Alpha Theta; Natl Beta Clb; Science Clb; Yrbk; Rep Stu Cncl; Natl Macy Schlr; Amer Leg Cert Of Schl Awd; Natl Latin Exam Magna Cumlaude; Med.

ABRAHAM, ROBBIE; Yukon Middle HS; Yukon, OK; (2); Church Yth Grp; JA; Scholastic Bowl; Spanish Clb; High Hon Roll; NHS; Ntl Merit Ltr; Renaissance Cmmtte.

ABRAMIAN, JARED R; Ponca City Sr HS; Ponca City, OK; (4); Church Yth Grp; Cmnty Wkr; Hosp Aide; Letterman Clb; Orch; Var Capt Swmmng; Hon Roll; Jr NHS; NHS; OSU; Pre-Med.

ABRAMS, AMBER M; Barnsdall Jr Sr HS; Barnsdall, OK; (4); 5/36; Cmnty Wkr; Drama Clb; FHA; Library Aide; Office Aide; Pep Clb; Quiz Bowl; Spanish Clb; SADD; Teachers Aide; NSU; Comms.

ABRAMS, JESSICA L; Pawhuska HS; Pawhuska, OK; (3); 20/90; Am Leg Aux Girls St; FCA; 4-H; FBLA; Key Clb; Office Aide; Pep Clb; Science Clb; Spanish Clb; Teachers Aide.

ABRAMS, SUSAN; Pawhuska HS; Pawhuska, OK; (4); 16/85; Church Yth Grp; FBLA; Key Clb; Letterman Clb; Math Clb; Mu Alpha Theta; Science Clb; Spanish Clb; Teachers Aide; VICA; Ntv Amer Stdnt Assn; Peer Hlprs; NOC; Cmptr Sci.

ABSHER, APRIL; Wetumka Jr Sr HS; Wetumka, OK; (3); Church Yth Grp; 4-H; Library Aide; Natl FFA Org; Spanish Clb; Band; Church Choir; Flag Corp; Mrchg Band; Pep Band; Vo Tech Natl Hnr Soc Awd; HOSA; Blood Drive Vol; RN.

ABSHIRE, DARREN J; Velma Alma HS; Duncan, OK; (3); Quiz Bowl; SADD; Band; Jazz Band; Mrchg Band; L Ftbl; Wt Lftg; Hon Roll; NHS.

ABULJEDAYAL, FAHAD E; Star Spencer HS; Spencer, OK; (4); 21/122; Church Yth Grp; Drama Clb; FBLA; JA; Library Aide; Math Clb; Spanish Clb; Teachers Aide; Band; Church Choir; 95-96 FBLA Sprng St Ldrshp Conf 2nd Pl Bus Procdres; Metro-Tech Voc Ctr Ambssdr; OSU Tech; Bus Admin.

ACKERMAN, CHRIS J; Gore HS; Gore, OK; (2); Ftbl; Wt Lftg; Hon Roll; OK Hnr Soc.

ACKERSON, SCOTT; Tonkawa Jr Sr HS; Tonkawa, OK; (3); Church Yth Grp; Cmnty Wkr; Letterman Clb; Library Aide; Quiz Bowl; Scholastic Bowl; Teachers Aide; Chorus; Church Choir; School Play; Lfgrd; Swmng Tchr; Red Crss Distr Aid Grp; Emory; Med.

ACKLEY, MARKA D; Jenks HS; Jenks, OK; (3); Art Clb; French Clb; FHA; Key Clb; Pep Clb; Quiz Bowl; Science Clb; Spanish Clb; Teachers Aide; Ed Yrbk; Arch.

ACOSTA JR, RAUL J; Anadarko HS; Anadarko, OK; (4); 37/107; Art Clb; French Clb; Wrstlng; Hon Roll; Yth Art Cmptn Wtrclr 1st Pl; Art Cmpnt Jr Ind 1st Pl Drwng, Bst Shw-Albstr Sclptr; Jr Art Fstvl 2nd Pl; Art.

ACRE, AMY L; Canton HS; Canton, OK; (4); 11/45; Pres 4-H; Hist FHA; VP Natl FFA Org; Band; Church Choir; Mrchg Band; Pep Band; School Play; Nwsp; Cit Awd; Natl FFA Schlsp; Meth Chrch Yth Group Mission Trips; Southwest ST U; Dietetic Tech.

ACRE, EMALEE J; Canton HS; Canton, OK; (2); 9/38; Pres Church Yth Grp; VP Sec 4-H; FHA; Sec VP Natl FFA Org; Spanish Clb; SADD; Capt Band; Church Choir; Capt Color Guard; Capt Flag Corp; Rainbow Grand Rep KS, Grand Choir & Worthy Adv; Northwestern; Yth Minister.

ACREE, ERIC; Seminole Jr Sr HS; Maud, OK; (1); Church Yth Grp; Ofcr Bsbl; Bsktbl; Ftbl; High Hon Roll; OU.

ACREE, SARA; South Intermediate HS; Broken Arrow, OK; (1); Girl Scts; Hon Roll; Jr NHS; Pres Schlr; St Schlr; Bus Awd Typng Skls; Surgery.

ADAIR, BOBBIE J; Okmulgee HS; Okmulgee, OK; (4); Church Yth Grp; Cmnty Wkr; Spanish Clb; Chorus; Church Choir; Lit Mag; Hon Roll; OHS Hnr Choir Otsdng Achvmnt 95-; Fam Of Faith Coll; Mus/Eng.

ADAIR, MATT D; Western Heights Sr HS; Oklahoma City, OK; (1); 1/220; Church Yth Grp; Wt Lftg; Hon Roll; Jr NHS; Pres Acad Fit Awd; Outstdng Bio Stdnt.

ADAM, JEREMY; Midwest City HS; Midwest City, OK; (4); 23/419; FCA; FBLA; Spanish Clb; French Hon Soc; Hon Roll; Jr NHS; NHS; Prfct Atten Awd; Spanish NHS; Val; U Of OK Hnrs Awd; Vlntr OK Memrl Hosp; Svc Prjct FHA; U Of OK; Law.

ADAMS, ALISHA R; North Intemediate HS; Broken Arrow, OK; (1); Church Yth Grp; Drama Clb; Spanish Clb; Band; Color Guard; Mrchg Band; Hon Roll; Jr NHS; Dntl Asst.

ADAMS, ALLEN D; Madill HS; Madill, OK; (1); Natl FFA Org; Band; JV Bsbl; JV Bsktbl; JV Ftbl; JV Trk; S Eastern; Htng/Air.

ADAMS, AMANDA; Kingston HS; Kingston, OK; (2); 4/73; Spanish Clb; Phtg Band; Hist Jazz Band; Pep Band; Rep Soph Cls; Trk; Hon Roll; NHS; Ntl Merit Schol; Prfct Atten Awd; All-Amer Schlr; U Of OK; Law/Music.

ADAMS, ANGI; Medford Schl; Medford, OK; (4); 11/22; FCA; FHA; Letterman Clb; Library Aide; Natl FFA Org; Pep Clb; Varsity Clb; Capt Bsktbl; Capt Sftbl; High Hon Roll; Homecoming Queen; OK ST U; Med.

ADAMS, ASHLEY M; Putnam City North HS; Oklahoma City, OK; (1); Church Yth Grp; Cmnty Wkr; FCA; Hosp Aide; Ofcr Frsh Cls; JV Tennis; Hon Roll; 3d-Dont Do Drugs; Outstdng Span I Stu Awd; Med.

ADAMS, BARBARA D; Shawnee Sr HS; Shawnee, OK; (2); Church Yth Grp; Drama Clb; Latin Clb; Varsity Clb; Band; School Play; Crs Cntry; Trk; Wt Lftg; Hon Roll; OU; Dr.

ADAMS, CHRISTINE M; Bray-Doyle HS; Osnabrock, ND; (2); Church Yth Grp; Office Aide; Teachers Aide; Chorus; Church Choir; School Play; Stage Crew; Hon Roll; NHS; OK Hnrs Soc; Vet.

ADAMS, DANIELLE; Comanche HS; Hastings, OK; (1); Church Yth Grp; SADD; Band; Mrchg Band; High Hon Roll.

ADAMS, DAVID; Indianola HS; Mcalester, OK; (1); 3/35; Church Yth Grp; 4-H; Natl FFA Org; Quiz Bowl; Yrbk; 4-H Awd.

ADAMS, DAVID L; Broken Arrow Sr HS; Broken Arrow, OK; (4); Am Leg Boys St; Church Yth Grp; Band; Mrchg Band; Jr NHS; NHS.

ADAMS, DUSTIN; Wister Schl; Wister, OK; (4); 11/21; Am Leg Boys St; Church Yth Grp; Quiz Bowl; Science Clb; Speech Tm; Teachers Aide; School Play; Rptr Jr Cls; Rptr Sr Cls; Capt Var Bsbl; Carl Albert ST Coll; Scndry Ed.

ADAMS, ERICA L; Putnam City West HS; Bethany, OK; (3); Church Yth Grp; FCA; French Clb; Girl Scts; Band; Church Choir; Mrchg Band; Orch; Pep Band; School Musical; OK ST Univ.

ADAMS, JAMIE; Coweta HS; Coweta, OK; (3); VP Church Yth Grp; Cmnty Wkr; FCA; FBLA; Church Choir; Yrbk; Bsktbl; Var Chrldng; Hon Roll; Jr NHS; Mst Outstndng Non Officer Awd Coweta FBLA Chptr; Chrch Camp Cnslr; U Cntrl OK; Family Dev.

ADAMS, JAMIE; Preston Schl; Beggs, OK; (3); Sec Jr Cls; Var Bsktbl; Var Sftbl; High Hon Roll; NHS.

ADAMS, JENNIFER D; Wilson HS; Healdton, OK; (4); 5/29; Church Yth Grp; FHA; Teachers Aide; Chorus; Ed Nwsp; Yrbk; Rep Frsh Cls; Rep Soph Cls; Rep Jr Cls; Pres Stu Cncl; Murray ST Coll; Pre-Law.

ADAMS, JENNIFER L; Wagoner Sr HS; Wagoner, OK; (3); 9/131; Am Leg Aux Girls St; Church Yth Grp; FBLA; FHA; Quiz Bowl; School Play; Hist Frsh Cls; Sec Soph Cls; Sec VP Stu Cncl; Var Socr; Frgn Lang Club.

ADAMS, JOHN R; Woodward HS; Woodward, OK; (2); Natl FFA Org; Wt Lftg; Hon Roll; Prfct Atten Awd; Hons Pgm; Northwestern OK ST.

ADAMS, JUSTIN; Nathan Hale HS; Tulsa, OK; (2); Hon Roll; Tulsa Univ; Comp Eng.

ADAMS, KARA M; Buffalo Jr Sr HS; Buffalo, OK; (3); Church Yth Grp; Hist 4-H; Hosp Aide; Band; Chorus; Drm Mjr(t); Jazz Band; Mrchg Band; Pep Band; Sec Jr Cls; Show Choir; Tulsa U; Nrsng.

ADAMS, KAREN D; Sapulpa Sr HS; Tulsa, OK; (4); 46/285; Church Yth Grp; FHA; Science Clb; Nwsp; Treas Wrstlng; Hon Roll; NHS; Pres Acad Fit Awd; Spanish NHS; Tulsa JC; Psych.

ADAMS, KERRI B; Putnam City North HS; Oklahoma City, OK; (4); 32/436; Cmnty Wkr; French Clb; Hosp Aide; Key Clb; SADD; JV Var Vllybl; Jr NHS; NHS; Pres Schlr; St Schlr; U Of OK.

ADAMS, LEAH M; Westmoore HS; Oklahoma City, OK; (1); Church Yth Grp; Drama Clb; Chorus; Sooner St Games 2 Medals Figure Sktng; Piano 5 Yrs; Schl Choir Soloist; OK U; Perfmng Arts.

ADAMS, LEIGH; Canton HS; Canton, OK; (3); 1/30; Church Yth Grp; Rep FCA; Quiz Bowl; Pres Spanish Clb; VP SADD; Pres Soph Cls; Pres Jr Cls; Rep Stu Cncl; Trk; High Hon Roll; NHS; Val; U Of OK; Phrmcy.

ADAMS, LONNIE; Indianola HS; Mcalester, OK; (2); FHA; Natl Beta Clb; Sec Soph Cls; Var Bsktbl; Hon Roll; Ntl Merit Ltr; Med.

ADAMS, M JAMES; Durant HS; Durant, OK; (2); Church Yth Grp; Debate Tm; Prfct Atten Awd; OK U; Med.

ADAMS, MAHEISHA; Guthrie Sr HS; Guthrie, OK; (3); 24/220; Drama Clb; Mu Alpha Theta; SADD; Trk; Cit Awd; Hon Roll; Jr NHS; NHS; Ntl Merit Ltr; U Of OK; Pre-Med.

ADAMS, MELISSA M; Union Sr HS; Tulsa, OK; (3); 47/741; Church Yth Grp; Key Clb; Spanish Clb; Swmmng; High Hon Roll; Hon Roll; NHS; Pres Acad Fit Awd; Spanish NHS; Natl Hnr Soc Soph Rep, VP; U Tulsa.

ADAMS, MICHAL; Coweta HS; Coweta, OK; (4); Capt FHA; HOBY; Ofcr Yrbk; Rep Jr Cls; Sec Sr Cls; Rep Stu Cncl; Capt Stu Cncl; Cit Awd; High Hon Roll; Church Yth Grp; Ms Fall Fstvl Schlrshp Pgnt Wnnr; U Of OK; Poltcl Sci.

ADAMS, NICOLE L; Capitol Hill HS; Oklahoma City, OK; (3); Pep Clb; Sec Spanish Clb; Chorus; Church Choir; Pres Soph Cls; VP Jr Cls; Swmmng; NHS; Received Smith Coll Book Awd; Pediatric Medicine.

ADAMS, NINA; Mustang HS; Yukon, OK; (2); Office Aide; Teachers Aide; Varsity Clb; Chorus; Trk; COCDA Awd; Dist/ST Solo Cntst Supr Awds.

ADAMS, SAMUEL J; Dickson HS; Ardmore, OK; (2); Church Yth Grp; Drama Clb; Spanish Clb; SADD; Chorus; Church Choir; School Musical; School Play; Hon Roll; Pres Acad Fit Awd.

ADAMS, SARAH J; Southeast HS; Oklahoma City, OK; (1); Church Yth Grp; ROTC; SADD; Hon Roll.

ADAMS, SHANNON; Texhoma HS; Texhoma, OK; (2); Church Yth Grp; GAA; Pep Clb; School Play; Var Bsktbl; Var Chrldng; High Hon Roll; Hon Roll; NHS; Child Counselor.

ADAMS, STACEY C; Jenks HS; Tulsa, OK; (4); 105/517; Church Yth Grp; French Clb; German Clb; Acpl Chr; Band; Chorus; Church Choir; Jazz Band; Mrchg Band; Orch; Truman ST U; Bus Admin.

ADAMS, STEPHANIE L; Wilson HS; Healdton, OK; (3); Church Yth Grp; GAA; Natl Beta Clb; JV Var Bsktbl; Chrldng; Sftbl; Wt Lftg; Hon Roll; Ntl Merit Ltr; Lincoln; Dr.

ADAMS, T'NIKA; Millwood HS; Oklahoma City, OK; (3); FBLA; ROTC; Spanish Clb; Chorus; Drill Tm; Hon Roll; Phys Thrpst.

ADAMS, TIFFANY A; Mustang HS; Yukon, OK; (2); 30/403; JV Vllybl; NHS; Pilot.

ADAMS, TONI M; Eisenhower Sr HS; Lawton, OK; (4); Library Aide; Teachers Aide; Band; Mrchg Band; Pep Band; School Play; Hon Roll; Jr NHS; NHS; Gymnastics; Cameron Univ; Elem Ed.

ADAMS HALVORSO, JENNIFER; Harrah HS; Harrah, OK; (2); 77/153; GAA; Bsktbl; Mgr(s); Sftbl; Trk; Hon Roll; Cameron Univ.

ADAY, SUNDEE; Shawnee Sr HS; Shawnee, OK; (4); 31/272; Am Leg Aux Girls St; Cmnty Wkr; FCA; Spanish Clb; Nwsp; Rep Stu Cncl; Chrldng; High Hon Roll; NHS; Page For Sen Brad Henry; Big Bro/Big Sis Jr Bd VP; Tri-Hi-Y Hstrn; OK U; Med.

ADCOCK, CLIFTON J; Quinton Jr Sr HS; Quinton, OK; (3); Art Clb; Natl FFA Org; Ofcr Bsbl; Bsktbl; Ftbl; Trk; Wt Lftg; Hon Roll; Bio Awd.

ADENIGBA, JIMMY; B T Washington HS; Tulsa, OK; (2); Computer Clb; French Clb; Cal Tech; Comp Sci.

ADESINA, ORE-OFE O; West Middle HS; Norman, OK; (1); Church Yth Grp; Bsktbl; Hon Roll.

ADKINS, ALICIA M; Moore HS; Oklahoma City, OK; (4); 170/526; Church Yth Grp; Debate Tm; Phtg DECA; German Clb; Hosp Aide; Treas Mu Alpha Theta; NFL; Scholastic Bowl; Church Choir; Var Swmmng; Fllwshp Chrstn Stdnts Pres; Fire Christ VP; Jr Engrng Tech Soc Rptr; U Of Central OK; Frnsc Sci.

ADKINS, JOHNATHAN M; Wellston Schl; Wellston, OK; (3); Church Yth Grp; FCA; FHA; Spanish Clb; SADD; Teachers Aide; Phtg Yrbk; Var Bsbl; Var Bsktbl; Var Capt Ftbl.

ADKINS, MELINDA; Chisholm Sr HS; Enid, OK; (3); FCA; Spanish Clb; Chorus; Rep Frsh Cls; Rep Jr Cls; Ofcr Stu Cncl; Bsktbl; Sftbl; Trk; NHS; Dance Cmmttes; OK ST U; Bus.

ADKINS, RACHEL; Okeene Jr Sr HS; Okeene, OK; (4); 5/27; Church Yth Grp; Pres Drama Clb; VP FHA; Teachers Aide; School Play; Stage Crew; Yrbk; Rep Stu Cncl; High Hon Roll; NHS; Southwestern OK ST; Psych.

ADKINS, TERRA L; Wellston Schl; Wellston, OK; (2); Church Yth Grp; FCA; FHA; Spanish Clb; SADD; Church Choir; Stat Mgr Bsbl; Var Bsktbl; Mgr Ftbl; Mgr(s).

ADLER, STEPHANIE A; Putnam City North HS; Oklahoma City, OK; (1); VP Sec French Clb; Hosp Aide; Rep Temple Yth Grp; Horseback Riding.

ADMIRE, BOBBIE K; Morris HS; Morris, OK; (4); Church Yth Grp; 4-H; Hist FHA; Natl FFA Org; Teachers Aide; Var Bsktbl; Var Sftbl; Var Trk; 4-H Awd; All-Conf Fastpitch Sftbl 95; Attnd OSU Acad Of Environmental Sci 94; OSU Okmulgee; Elem Ed.

AEBI, KEVIN L; Pond Creek-Hunter Schl; Pond Creek, OK; (2); Church Yth Grp; FCA; Natl FFA Org; Var Bsbl; Var Ftbl; Wt Lftg; Hon Roll; NHS; Northwestern; Phy Thrpst.

AEBI, KYLE L; Pond Creek-Hunter Schl; Pond Creek, OK; (2); Church Yth Grp; FCA; Treas Natl FFA Org; Var Bsbl; Var Ftbl; Wt Lftg; Hon Roll; NHS; Prfct Atten Awd; Northwestern; Commnctn; Vet.

AEBISCHER, CHAD E; Westmore HS; Oklahoma City, OK; (1); Church Yth Grp; Drama Clb; FCA; French Clb; Quiz Bowl; Scholastic Bowl; School Play; Rep Stu Cncl; Bsktbl; Ftbl; Weightlifting; Drawing.

AFFENTRANGER, MIKE; Prague HS; Prague, OK; (4); 11/70; Church Yth Grp; FCA; HOBY; Key Clb; Scholastic Bowl; Teachers Aide; Ofcr Stu Cncl; Var Crs Cntry; Var Ftbl; Var Trk; Banc Frst Stu Brd Dir; OK ST U; Acctng.

AGEE, PHILLIP J; Henryetta Sr HS; Henryetta, OK; (3); FCA; Office Aide; Phtg Yrbk; Golf; Hon Roll.

AGENT, MANDILYN C; Union Intermediate HS; Broken Arrow, OK; (2); 108/800; Key Clb; Nwsp; Yrbk; NHS; Athtlc Sprts Trnr; U Of AZ Tucson; Sprts Med.

AGENT, MELISSA R; Union Sr HS; Broken Arrow, OK; (4); 44/629; Drama Clb; French Clb; FBLA; Intnl Clb; Key Clb; School Play; Rptr Stu Cncl; Hon Roll; NHS; Pres Acad Fit Awd; Tulsa JC Courses; OK ST U; Med.

AGNEW, HULING W; Caney Valley HS; Ramona, OK; (3); Rep Frsh Cls; Rep Soph Cls; Rep Jr Cls; Ofcr Stu Cncl; Ftbl; Tulsa JC.

AGNEW, JOSHUA D; Velma Alma HS; Loco, OK; (2); Church Yth Grp.

AGNEW, NICOLE C; Pauls Valley HS; Pauls Valley, OK; (3); Key Clb; Bsktbl; Tennis; Dancing; Edmnd Univ.

AGUILERA, ALENE; Shawnee Sr HS; Shawnee, OK; (2); Debate Tm; Spanish Clb; Ofcr Stu Cncl; High Hon Roll; Jr NHS.

AGUILERA, ANDREA; Shawnee Sr HS; Shawnee, OK; (3); Library Aide; Spanish Clb; Ofcr Stu Cncl; High Hon Roll; Big Brothers/Big Sisters Jr Bd; KS U; Span.

AGUIRRE, EDWARD; Madill HS; Madill, OK; (2); VP Frsh Cls; Hon Roll; Stu Cncl; Bus.

AHDUNKO, AUNANE Y; Hinton HS; Hinton, OK; (2); FHA; SADD; Var Bsktbl; Var Trk; Cit Awd; High Hon Roll; Hon Roll; NHS; Val; Acad Team; Art Contests; SWOSU Swim Meet; U Of OK; Hlth Field.

AHL, KELLY A; Memorial HS; Tulsa, OK; (2); French Clb; Intnl Clb; Key Clb; Library Aide; Var Socr; High Hon Roll; Hon Roll; Team Capt Clb Sccr Team Blitz United; NC At Chapel Hill.

AHLBORN, RACHAEL; Owasso Sr HS; Owasso, OK; (2); 9/400; Church Yth Grp; Debate Tm; Drama Clb; English Clb; FCA; Office Aide; Science Clb; Service Clb; Spanish Clb; Temple Yth Grp; BYU.

AHLDEN, STACIE; Wanette HS; Wanette, OK; (4); 1/20; FBLA; FHA; VP Sr Cls; Pres Stu Cncl; Var Capt Bsktbl; Var Sftbl; NHS; Val; Lf Guide Pr Cnslr; Acad Tm Cap; OK ST U; Med.

AHLEFELD, KELSEA; Mustang HS; Yukon, OK; (1); Church Yth Grp; FCA; GAA; Hosp Aide; Spanish Clb; Varsity Clb; Drill Tm; Rep Stu Cncl; Chrldng; Powder Puff Ftbl; Stu Cncl Rep; Int Decorator.

AHMAD, AISHA; Union Sr HS; Tulsa, OK; (3); 7/741; Cmnty Wkr; Key Clb; Library Aide; Rep Frsh Cls; Jr NHS; NHS; Pres Acad Fit Awd; Renaissance Clb; Acad Ltr; Tulsa Yth Ct; Law.

AHMAD, NABEEL; Western Heights Sr HS; Oklahoma City, OK; (1); 19/206; Band; Mrchg Band; Pep Band; U Of OK; Sprts Med.

AHMAD, TARIQ; Western Heights Sr HS; Oklahoma City, OK; (3); 44/177; French Clb; Math Clb; Teachers Aide; Band; Jazz Band; Mrchg Band; Orch; Pep Band; Hon Roll; U Of MI; Sprts Med.

AHMADIFAR, SHOKOOH; Putnam City HS; Warr Acres, OK; (1); Church Yth Grp; Cmnty Wkr; Hosp Aide; Key Clb; Spanish Clb; Hon Roll; NHS; NCU; Neurosurgeon.

AHMED, NATASHA R; Owasso Sr HS; Owasso, OK; (4); 5/296; Art Clb; Drama Clb; FTA; Spanish Clb; Teachers Aide; Ed Nwsp; Ofcr Stu Cncl; Trk; High Hon Roll; NHS; Hip Hop Dance Class; OK ST Univ; Bio Med Engr.

AHREND, MATT D; North Intemediate HS; Broken Arrow, OK; (2); Church Yth Grp; JV Bsktbl; Hon Roll; Jr NHS; NHS.

AHREND, T S; Ada HS; Ada, OK; (4); Church Yth Grp; Drama Clb; FCA; French Clb; School Play; Yrbk; Var Tennis; Hon Roll; U Of OK.

AHRENS, SHELI J; Colcord Schl; Colcord, OK; (2); Church Yth Grp; FBLA; GAA; Math Tm; Quiz Bowl; Sec Frsh Cls; Bsktbl; Chrldng; Score Keeper; Trk; :law.

AICHELE, ADAM; Stillwater Sr HS; Stillwater, OK; (4); 37/350; Am Leg Boys St; Boy Scts; Key Clb; Latin Clb; Mu Alpha Theta; Natl Beta Clb; VP Science Clb; Jazz Band; Mrchg Band; NHS; Eagle Sct; OSU; Mech Engr.

AICHELE, CLINT PHILIP; Stillwater Jr HS; Stillwater, OK; (1); #1 in class; Boy Scts; Cmnty Wkr; Letterman Clb; Band; Mrchg Band; Var Crs Cntry; Var Trk; Var Wrstlng; Cit Awd; High Hon Roll; BSA Life Scout; Rotary Clb Stdnt Month 95.

AICHELE, MATTHEW D; Union Intermediate HS; Broken Arrow, OK; (1); Boy Scts; Church Yth Grp; FCA; Mrchg Band; Pep Band; Nwsp; Yrbk; High Hon Roll; NHS; Acad Tm; Yng Astronauts Pres; Acad Rsrce Cntr; Cncl Freshmn Pres.

AILEY, JACOB T; Pryor Sr HS; Pryor, OK; (2); Boy Scts; Church Yth Grp; English Clb; SADD; School Play; Ftbl; Socr; Wt Lftg; Wrstlng; Cit Awd.

AINOOSON, JEFF; Jarman Jr HS; Oklahoma City, OK; (1); Church Yth Grp; Spanish Clb; Bsktbl; Jr NHS; Prfct Atten Awd.

AINOOSON, RICHARD; Midwest City HS; Oklahoma City, OK; (2); Church Yth Grp; Spanish Clb; Var Bsktbl; Wt Lftg; Jr NHS; Prfct Atten Awd.

AINSWORTH, WANDA J; Central Jr HS; Lawton, OK; (1); Mgnt; Comp Applctns; Bus Mgnt.

AIRINGTON, AMY J; Edmond Memorial HS; Edmond, OK; (2); Church Yth Grp; FCA; HOBY; Spanish Clb; Variety Show; Pom Pon; Trk; High Hon Roll; NHS; Pres Acad Fit Awd; OK Indian Hnr Soc; NCA All Amer Pom; ASC All Amer Pom; NCA Golden Star Ldrshp Awd; OK Univ.

AIRINGTON, ASHLEY R; Central Mid-HS; Norman, OK; (2); Drama Clb; Pres Girl Scts; Model UN; L Band; Mrchg Band; Sec Orch; High Hon Roll; NHS; High Hon Roll; Pres Awd Eductnl Exccllnc; Acad Excllnc Awds Sci, Alg II, Wrld Hstry; Cadette Sctng Silver Awd; Chem Engr.

AIRINGTON, MISTY D; Velma Alma HS; Ratliff City, OK; (1); 4-H; SADD; Band; Mrchg Band; Pep Band; JV Bsktbl; JV Chrldng; Trk; Hon Roll; OU.

AISHMAN, AMANDA; Spiro HS; Spiro, OK; (2); Drama Clb; Math Clb; Natl FFA Org; Quiz Bowl; Band; Var Chrldng; High Hon Roll; NHS; OSU; Applied & Animal Scis.

AISHMAN, SAMANTHA; Spiro HS; Spiro, OK; (3); 8/89; Church Yth Grp; FCA; Math Clb; Spanish Clb; Mrchg Band; Pep Band; Rptr Nwsp; Hon Roll; NHS; FHA; OK Hnr Soc; NE ST U; Scndry Ed Eng Tchr.

AITSON, CANDICE T; Riverside Indian Schl; Carnegie, OK; (3); Cmnty Wkr; FCA; Science Clb; Church Yth Grp; Drama Clb; Library Aide; Spanish Clb; Chorus; Church Choir; Phtg Yrbk; OK Fed Of Indian Women; Close-Up; TX Yth & Govt; Future Indian Lawyers Amer; Minority Achievers.

AKER, NATHAN A; Westmore HS; Oklahoma City, OK; (2); Office Aide; Cit Awd; Hon Roll; NHS; Pres Acad Fit Awd; Masonic Awd; 4th Pl SWOSU Drafting Cont; OK Univ; Arch.

AKERMAN, KRISTEN; Ada HS; Konawa, OK; (4); 20/136; Rep DECA; Spanish Clb; Capt Color Guard; Mrchg Band; High Hon Roll; Jr NHS; NHS; Spanish NHS; JOM Stu Yr 92-93; Psych Clb; E Cntrl U; Deaf Instr.

AKERS, SAMANTHA; Southeast HS; Oklahoma City, OK; (2); 1/273; Church Yth Grp; Drama Clb; FCA; School Play; Treas Soph Cls; Pres Stu Cncl; Var Chrldng; High Hon Roll; Acad Decthln; OK Bapt U.

AKERS, TRACEY L; Del City HS; Del City, OK; (1); Pres Church Yth Grp; Spanish Clb; Chorus; Church Choir; Var Sftbl; Var Wt Lftg; High Hon Roll; Hon Roll; Jr NHS; NHS; OSA; CPA.

AKINS, JAMIE; Holdenville HS; Holdenville, OK; (3); FBLA; FHA; Office Aide; Quiz Bowl; Band; Mrchg Band; Hon Roll; NHS.

ALACHKAR, WAEL F; Union Sr HS; Tulsa, OK; (3); Ofcr Jr Cls; Swmmng; Honor Alg II; Med Schl.

ALAJAJI, SYLVIA A; Union Sr HS; Tulsa, OK; (3); 2/741; Church Yth Grp; French Clb; Hosp Aide; VP Intnl Clb; Key Clb; Quiz Bowl; Orch; Cit Awd; High Hon Roll; Pres Acad Fit Awd; Tri-M; Jr Clss Brd; Piano; Med.

ALANIZ, ANGELICA; Ringwood HS; Ringwood, OK; (2); Church Yth Grp; FCA; FHA; Pep Clb; Quiz Bowl; School Play; Var Chrldng; NHS; Hon Roll; GATE Stdnt Cncl Rep; Attend OK Prin Sci Schlrs; B-Clb.

ALARCON, MARICELA H; Northeast HS; Oklahoma City, OK; (3); 5/120; Church Yth Grp; FBLA; Model UN; Red Cross Aide; Science Clb; Vllybl; Gov Hon Prg Awd; High Hon Roll; Jr NHS; NHS; Otsdng Frosh Bio Med Sci Prgm; Exec Wmn Intl Schlrshp Prgm Fnlst; Explorer Med Post; OK City CC; Nrs.

ALARID, JOSEPH C; U S Grant HS; Oklahoma City, OK; (2); FCA; Letterman Clb; Office Aide; L Bsbl; L Ftbl; L Wt Lftg; L Wrstlng; Hon Roll; Wrstlng Hmecmg Escort; Mst Imprvd Stdnt Engl Dept; Sports Med.

ALBARRAN, DAWNA R; Blanchard Jr Sr HS; Blanchard, OK; (3); 6/61; Am Leg Aux Girls St; VP Computer Clb; Treas Mu Alpha Theta; Pres Latin Clb; Church Choir; Yrbk; NHS; Rep Soph Cls; Sec Jr Cls; Ofcr Stu Cncl; ESE Hnr Stdnts Span; Sndy Schl Tchr; Gifted/Tlntd.

ALBEE, A B; Choctaw HS; Choctaw, OK; (4); 36/308; Pres Key Clb; Sec SADD; Sec Soph Cls; Sec Jr Cls; Sec Stu Cncl; Mgr Ftbl; Powder Puff Ftbl; Jr NHS; NHS; Girl Of Month; Key Clbbr Of Month; U Of OK; Phrmcy.

ALBEE, BROOKE; Choctaw HS; Choctaw, OK; (4); 38/298; Key Clb; Sec Soph Cls; Sec Jr Cls; Sec Stu Cncl; Mgr(s); Powder Puff Ftbl; Jr NHS; Kiwanis Awd; NHS; St Schlr; U Of OK; Med.

ALBEE, RYAN D; Choctaw HS; Choctaw, OK; (2); Letterman Clb; Office Aide; JV Bsbl; L Var Bsktbl; L Var Ftbl; High Hon Roll; Jr NHS; Pres Acad Fit Awd; Val; OK; Math.

ALBERS, BRANDON E; Midwest City HS; Oklahoma City, OK; (4); Church Yth Grp; Drama Clb; FCA; FTA; Spanish Clb; SADD; Band; Chorus; Church Choir; Jazz Band; Prince Of RIOF Bible Clb; Rose ST Schlsp; Music Choir Royalty; U Of Cntrl OK; Music; Drama Ed.

ALBERTER, KATHRYN; Central Mid-HS; Norman, OK; (1); Chorus; Crs Cntry; Trk; Hon Roll; RN.

ALBIN, LACY L; Walters HS; Walters, OK; (2); Church Yth Grp; FCA; Letterman Clb; Quiz Bowl; Scholastic Bowl; Band; Church Choir; Jazz Band; Mrchg Band; Pep Band; Rtry Awd; Band Dirs Awd; Hrtcltr.

ALBRECHT, KENNETH G; Norman Sr HS; Norman, OK; (4); 257/657; Ofcr CAP; Debate Tm; Treas German Clb; Latin Clb; Math Clb; Model UN; NFL; Capt Scholastic Bowl; Rep Jr Cls; Ofcr Stu Cncl; Med Explorers Post 931 Sec 95-96 & Sgt At Arms 94-95; U Of OK; Ec.

ALBRIGHT, BRANDY G; Choctaw HS; Choctaw, OK; (4); 12/305; Key Clb; Scholastic Bowl; Science Clb; Band; Mrchg Band; Pep Band; High Hon Roll; NHS; Pres Acad Fit Awd; Hnr Band; Natl Sci Mrt Awd; U Of OK; Zoology.

ALBRIGHT, BRYN L; Indiahoma Schl; Indiahoma, OK; (1); Church Yth Grp; FCA; GAA; Yrbk; VP Frsh Cls; Rptr Stu Cncl; Bsktbl; Sftbl; Hon Roll; NHS.

ALBRIGHT, JUSTIN T; Mc Alester HS; Mcalester, OK; (4); 14/215; Church Yth Grp; Cmnty Wkr; Science Clb; Spanish Clb; Bsktbl; Hon Roll; NHS; Chem Clb; Pysics Clb; U Of OK; Podiatry.

ALBRIGHT, RYAN S; Maysville Jr Sr HS; Lindsay, OK; (2); 1/32; Church Yth Grp; FCA; Key Clb; Natl FFA Org; School Play; VP Frsh Cls; Sec Soph Cls; Bsktbl; Ftbl; Trk; OK Univ; Engrng.

ALBRITTON, ANGELA B; Vinita HS; Vinita, OK; (3); 1/100; Church Yth Grp; German Clb; Quiz Bowl; Spanish Clb; Pres Soph Cls; Treas Stu Cncl; Hon Roll; NHS; OK ST Univ; Bus.

ALCANTARA, RAQUEL; Moore HS; Moore, OK; (4); 50/525; Church Yth Grp; FCA; Latin Clb; Office Aide; Teachers Aide; Crs Cntry; Trk; Cit Awd; Jr NHS; Pres NHS; Escort; OU Ldrshp Awd; Racquetball; Charleston Southern U; Nrsng.

ALCORN, JESSICA R; Westmoore HS; Oklahoma City, OK; (3); Spanish Clb; Chorus; Yrbk; Hon Roll; NHS; Schol Tm; Tchr Class Chrch; Stu Forclnr Env; Belmonst Univ; Mus Bus.

ALDRICH, AMBER K; Luther HS; Luther, OK; (4); 9/45; Sec FHA; Spanish Clb; Teachers Aide; Varsity Clb; Pres Band; Rep Stu Cncl; Var Bsktbl; Var Capt Chrldng; Hon Roll; Pres Schlr; Rose ST Coll; Rdlgy Tech.

ALDRICH, ASHLEY N; Putnam City HS; Oklahoma City, OK; (4); 1/345; Cmnty Wkr; FCA; French Clb; Key Clb; Ofcr Stu Cncl; Var Bsktbl; Var Crs Cntry; Var Capt Socr; Var Trk; JV Vllybl; Oral Roberts U; Med.

ALDRICH, JASON; Fargo Schl; Gage, OK; (4); 2/22; Natl Beta Clb; Natl FFA Org; Quiz Bowl; Ofcr Bsbl; DAR Awd; Hon Roll; Pres Acad Fit Awd; Val; OK U, OK St U Almni Hnr Soc; OSU; Engrng.

ALDRIDGE, BROOKE L; Wakita Schl; Manchester, OK; (1); Church Yth Grp; FCA; FHA; Band; Bsktbl; Chrldng; Sftbl; Hon Roll.

ALDRIDGE, GLENDA; Ripley HS; Ripley, OK; (4); 2/34; Church Yth Grp; FBLA; FHA; Spanish Clb; Rep Frsh Cls; Rep Soph Cls; Treas Jr Cls; High Hon Roll; Prfct Atten Awd; Sal; Hlth Occs Studnts Of Amer-Pres; Nrsng.

ALDRIDGE, JEREMIAH; Chelsea HS; Big Cabin, OK; (4); FHA; Quiz Bowl; Band; Jazz Band; Mrchg Band; Pep Band; Hon Roll; Tae Kwon Do; Concert Band; Band Cncl VP; Northeastern ST U; Med.

ALDRIDGE, KIMBERLI R; Yukon Middle HS; Yukon, OK; (2); Church Yth Grp; Treas FHA; Mgr Bsktbl; Mgr Ftbl; Golf; NHS; 3-D; HS Heroes; Pre-Med; Pediatrics.

ALDRIDGE, NALANI D; Mooreland Jr Sr HS; Mooreland, OK; (1); Church Yth Grp; FHA; Speech Tm; Hon Roll; Started Bible Stud In Schl.

ALDRIDGE, STEPHEN; Wakita Schl; Manchester, OK; (4); Am Leg Boys St; Church Yth Grp; FCA; Pep Clb; Band; Mrchg Band; Pep Band; School Play; Pres Soph Cls; Var Bsbl.

ALEMAN, CHRISTINA; Moore HS; Moore, OK; (3); FCA; Spanish Clb; Band; Color Guard; Mrchg Band; Nwsp; JV Bsktbl; Var Wt Lftg; Multcltrl Stu Assn; OK ST U; Ed.

ALEMAO, TINA S; Northeast HS; Yukon, OK; (4); 24/125; Church Yth Grp; Cmnty Wkr; FCA; FBLA; Girl Scts; Math Clb; Mu Alpha Theta; Office Aide; Science Clb; Spanish Clb; Ftbl Homcmng Qn 95-96; Miss Yukn Ten USA 94-95; Eng Awd Of Jr Cls 94-95; Span Awd Of Yr 94-96; Langston U; Phys Therapy.

ALENE, KELLI; Westmoore HS; Oklahoma City, OK; (4); 40/610; Church Yth Grp; FBLA; Latin Clb; Teachers Aide; Church Choir; Variety Show; Chrldng; Cit Awd; ST Champ Chrldng; Sci Fair 3rd Pl; Prins Hnr Roll; Drama/Debate Class; Natl Chmpshp Dance; OK City CC; CPA.

ALEXANDER, ASHLEY K; Union Intermediate HS; Tulsa, OK; (2); 71/800; Cmnty Wkr; Chorus; Church Choir; School Musical; Variety Show; High Hon Roll; Jr NHS; NHS; Pres Acad Fit Awd; Cmnty Theatre Grp; Super Rtngs St Vocal Cont; Vocal Music.

ALEXANDER JR, BARRY C; Life Christian HS; Norman, OK; (3); 3/17; Church Yth Grp; VP Soph Cls; Var JV Bsktbl; Var Ftbl; Var Trk; Hon Roll; Teachers Aide; Ofsnv Plyr Of Yr Bsktbl 95-; Outstndg Eng Stdnt 94-95; Wrld Hist 94-95; Anatomy Stndt 95-.

ALEXANDER, BEAU D; North Intemediate HS; Broken Arrow, OK; (2); Thesps; Wt Lftg; Wrstlng; High Hon Roll; Env Conscious; Rdng; Excell Math/Sci; OSU; Wildlf Ecolgy.

ALEXANDER, BEN C; Bartlesville Sr HS; Bartlesville, OK; (1); Boy Scts; Church Yth Grp; Band; Mrchg Band; Hon Roll; Eagle Sct 96; Staff Boy Scout Camp Cherokee Grove OK; Chptr Chief Ordr Arrow; OK ST U.

ALEXANDER, BRIAN; Ardmore HS; Ardmore, OK; (4); 47/173; Boy Scts; Church Yth Grp; Science Clb; Teachers Aide; Band; Chorus; Church Choir; Drm Mjr(t); Mrchg Band; School Musical; Eagle & Explr Scout; OK ST U; Vet.

ALEXANDER, CHAD M; Latta Sr HS; Ada, OK; (3); Church Yth Grp; FCA; Varsity Clb; Rep Frsh Cls; Var Bsbl; JV Bsktbl; Hon Roll; NHS; Masonic Awd; Arch.

ALEXANDER, CRYSTAL G; Sapulpa Sr HS; Sapulpa, OK; (2); Church Yth Grp; French Clb; Science Clb; Chorus; Color Guard; Flag Corp; Rptr Phtg Nwsp; French Hon Soc; High Hon Roll; Hon Roll; Legan Sec; Acctnt.

ALEXANDER, DAVID A; B T Washington HS; Tulsa, OK; (3); Computer Clb; VP Debate Tm; NFL; Speech Tm; Pres Temple Yth Grp; Jazz Band; NHS; TV Anchor Local Tulsa Public Schls Channel; Bus.

ALEXANDER, DIANA; Hinton HS; Hinton, OK; (4); 3/30; Church Yth Grp; FCA; Sec FHA; Quiz Bowl; SADD; Teachers Aide; Band; Chorus; Rep Sr Cls; Cit Awd; OK Music Ed Assn All St Chorus; Southwestern OK ST U; Music.

ALEXANDER, JENNIFER; Alex Public Schls; Alex, OK; (4); 1/21; Am Leg Aux Girls St; Church Yth Grp; Ofcr FCA; Pres FBLA; Scholastic Bowl; Spanish Clb; Treas Jr Cls; Sec Sr Cls; Var Capt Bsktbl; Val; OK HS Hnr Socty; Pastors Asst; Masonic Lodge Stu Of Today; Oklahoma City U; Poltcl Sci.

ALEXANDER, JENNIFER M; Byng Sr HS; Ada, OK; (2); Church Yth Grp; FBLA; Natl Beta Clb; Spanish Clb; Chorus; High Hon Roll; Hon Roll; Math/Sci/Cmptr Club; U Of OK; PT.

ALEXANDER, JEREMY L; Union Intermediate HS; Tulsa, OK; (2); Church Yth Grp; FCA; Intnl Clb; Math Clb; Spanish Clb; Var Socr; Intrml Wt Lftg; Hon Roll; Pres Acad Fit Awd; Pres Schlr; OK Olympc Dvlpmnt Sccr Pgm; Adv Sccr CmpMVP; Acctng.

ALEXANDER, JERRY K; Wynnewood HS; Wynnewood, OK; (2); Natl FFA Org; Office Aide; Law Enf.

ALEXANDER, MATTHEW D; Putnam City North HS; Oklahoma City, OK; (1); FCA; Quiz Bowl; Spanish Clb; Band; Mrchg Band; Pep Band; Rep Stu Cncl.

ALEXANDER, MICHELLE A; Hinton HS; Hinton, OK; (2); Church Yth Grp; Co-Capt FCA; FHA; SADD; Var Bsktbl; Var Crs Cntry; Var Powder Puff Ftbl; Var Trk; Hon Roll; NHS; NE St Univ; Psych.

ALEXANDER, MIKE; Choctaw HS; Choctaw, OK; (4); Band; Chorus; Mrchg Band; Pep Band; School Musical; Swing Chorus; Variety Show; Hon Roll; U Of Central OK; Music.

ALEXANDER, NICOLE; Woodward HS; Woodward, OK; (1); Church Yth Grp; Cmnty Wkr; Dance Clb; French Clb; Pep Clb; Mgr(s); High Hon Roll; Hon Roll; Kiwanis Awd; St Schlr; Amer Kids ST Champ Dance; Golden W Awds; Acad Letterman; U Of OK; Radiology.

ALEXANDER, RACHEL L; Heavener HS; Heavener, OK; (1); 1/102; Church Yth Grp; French Clb; Scholastic Bowl; Pres Frsh Cls; Var L Sftbl; High Hon Roll; NHS; Carl Albert ST Coll; Pharm.

ALEXANDER, SCOTT R; Edmond Memorial HS; Edmond, OK; (3); Church Yth Grp; Cmnty Wkr; Key Clb; Spanish Clb; Chorus; Church Choir; School Musical; School Play; Variety Show; Rptr Nwsp; Washington Jrnlsm Conf Delegate 96; 2nd Pl Feature Wrtng OIPA; Super Rating Dist Vocal Soloist; Commnctn; Psych.

ALEXANDER, SHANE H; Byng Sr HS; Ada, OK; (4); 14/70; Band; Mrchg Band; Orch; Pep Band; School Musical; Hon Roll; East Cntrl Univ.

ALEXANDER, SHEA N; Midwest City HS; Midwest City, OK; (3); 28/364; Church Yth Grp; FBLA; Spanish Clb; Yrbk; OK ST Univ; Humanities.

ALEXANDER, VESHAWNA; Central HS; Tulsa, OK; (4); 20/178; Art Clb; Church Yth Grp; FCA; FHA; FTA; GAA; JA; Office Aide; Spanish Clb; Teachers Aide; Prnthd; Comm Arts; UCT; Med.

ALFERS, KERI E; Catoosa HS; Catoosa, OK; (2); Church Yth Grp; FCA; Girl Scts; Intnl Clb; School Play; Stage Crew; Yrbk; Wt Lftg; Fmly/Frnds, Hvng Fn.

ALFORD, PHILLIP A; Caney Jr Sr HS; Caddo, OK; (3); Natl FFA Org; Ofcr Frsh Cls; Pres Soph Cls; Ofcr Bsbl; Bsktbl; Panhandle ST.

ALGEO, CHRISTIE; Blanchard Jr Sr HS; Blanchard, OK; (2); FHA; Sec Natl FFA Org; Pres Soph Cls; Jr NHS; Sec NHS; ESE; Dallas Bapt Univ; Pol Sci.

ALLEE, DALLAS; Depew HS; Depew, OK; (4); 7/47; Church Yth Grp; Drama Clb; HOBY; Pep Clb; Spanish Clb; VP Soph Cls; Treas Jr Cls; Sec Rep Sr Cls; Var Bsktbl.

ALLEN, ALLYSA; Garber Sr HS; Garber, OK; (3); Church Yth Grp; FCA; 4-H; FHA; Office Aide; Pep Clb; Quiz Bowl; Scholastic Bowl; School Play; Var Bsktbl.

ALLEN, AMANDA B; Choctaw HS; Choctaw, OK; (3); 1/332; Church Yth Grp; Cmnty Wkr; German Clb; Key Clb; Band; Mrchg Band; School Musical; Hon Roll; Pres Acad Fit Awd; Hnr Bnd; Purdue U; Aeronautcl Engrng.

ALLEN, AMANDA F; Muldrow HS; Muldrow, OK; (2); Church Yth Grp; Debate Tm; Drama Clb; Science Clb; Cit Awd; Gov Hon Prg Awd; High Hon Roll; Hon Roll; NHS; Pres Schlr; OU; Music.

ALLEN, AMBER D; El Reno Sr HS; El Reno, OK; (1); Office Aide; Hon Roll; NHS; Intnl Order Rainbow Girls; Bowling 5 Yrs.

ALLEN, ANGELA; Edmond Santa Fe HS; Edmond, OK; (4); Art Clb; Church Yth Grp; HOBY; Quiz Bowl; Science Clb; Spanish Clb; SADD; Nwsp; Ofcr Sr Cls; NHS; Mdevl Clb VP; Afro-Amer Multi-Cltrl Clb; Multi-Cltrl Soc Awd Of Excllnc; Art Hist.

ALLEN, ANGELA L; Pona City HS; Ponca City, OK; (3); Spanish Clb; Ofcr Jr Cls; Hon Roll; NHS; Natl Young Ldrs Nom; Paralegal; Vet.

ALLEN, ANNISHA L; Choctaw HS; Midwest City, OK; (2); German Clb; GAA; Varsity Clb; JV Var Bsktbl; JV Var Socr; Var Trk; Outstdng Soph; Most Ath; Bus Mngmt.

ALLEN, BECCA; Collinsville HS; Collinsville, OK; (2); Church Yth Grp; Chorus; Chrldng; Socr; Trk; Cit Awd; Enrolled In Vo-Tech Pre-Schl Child Dev; Southern Nazerene; Pre-Schl Ed.

ALLEN, BEN; Blackwell HS; Blackwell, OK; (1); Band; Jazz Band; Mrchg Band; Pep Band; High Hon Roll; Hon Roll; OSU; Aerospace.

ALLEN, CARRIE; Claremore Sr HS; Claremore, OK; (2); 1/250; Church Yth Grp; GAA; Treas Frsh Cls; Ofcr Stu Cncl; Var Chrldng; Var Gym; Trk; High Hon Roll; Prfct Atten Awd; Math Awd; All Amer Schlr.

ALLEN, CHRISTINA; Liberty Acad; Shawnee, OK; (1); Church Yth Grp; Cmnty Wkr; Var Bsktbl; Chrldng; Hon Roll; Bsktbl Awd; Notre Dame.

ALLEN, CRAIG R; Yukon HS; Yukon, OK; (4); 20/396; Church Yth Grp; Cmnty Wkr; Spanish Clb; Var L Ftbl; Wt Lftg; NHS; Pres Acad Fit Awd; Ftbll All Conf Tm; Marine Schol; Amer Leg Schlr; OK St Univ; Arch Dsgn.

ALLEN, DANIEL; Perry Sr HS; Perry, OK; (4); 20/73; FCA; FBLA; FHA; Natl FFA Org; Office Aide; Spanish Clb; Ofcr Bsbl; Var Capt Ftbl; Var Capt Wrstlng; Bsbl All Area, All Conf 94-95; Ftbl All Area, All Dist 95; Wrstlng All Area; Physcs.

ALLEN, DUSTIN; Perkins-Tryon HS; Perkins, OK; (2); Church Yth Grp; Cmnty Wkr; FCA; FHA; Intnl Clb; Key Clb; Letterman Clb; Spanish Clb; Ofcr Bsbl; Bsktbl.

ALLEN, DUSTIN J; Bishop Kelley HS; Broken Arrow, OK; (1); Debate Tm; JA; High Hon Roll; Hon Roll; Duke Univ Talent Identification Prgm; U Of NC; Med Doctor.

ALLEN, GLENDA F; Arkoma Jr Sr HS; Arkoma, OK; (1); Scholastic Bowl; RN.

ALLEN, HEATHER D; Porter Consolidated Schls; Porter, OK; (3); FCA; Letterman Clb; Spanish Clb; SADD; Acpl Chr; Yrbk; Rep Stu Cncl; Var L Chrldng; Hon Roll; NHS; Marine Bio.

ALLEN, JACLYN; Moore HS; Norman, OK; (4); 1/525; Church Yth Grp; Pres French Clb; VP Science Clb; Band; Mrchg Band; School Musical; School Play; NHS; Val; Am Leg Aux Girls St; 12 Yrs Piano.

ALLEN, JAKE L; Porter Jr Sr HS; Porter, OK; (2); Chess Clb; Natl FFA Org; L Bsbl; L Ftbl; L Wt Lftg; FFA St & Natl Conv Nom; Air Force.

ALLEN, JAMES R; Union Sr HS; Tulsa, OK; (4); 26/619; French Clb; Band; Mrchg Band; Cit Awd; High Hon Roll; Jr NHS; NHS; Ntl Merit Schol; Pres Schlr; Prcsn Ensmbl; Prcssv Arts Intrnt Soc Conv 1995; Schlstca; Natl Mrt Fnlst; U Of IL Urbana; Elec Engnrng.

ALLEN, JENNIFER M; South Intermediate HS; Broken Arrow, OK; (1); Drama Clb; School Play; Bsktbl; Hon Roll; NHS; Theatre.

ALLEN, JEREMY D; Yukon Middle HS; Yukon, OK; (2); Church Yth Grp; FCA; Church Choir; Hon Roll; NHS; Nat His Awd; Govt Awd; Amer Govt Awd 94-95; Engr.

ALLEN, JOHN W; Westmoore HS; Oklahoma City, OK; (4); 289/610; Boy Scts; JCL; Scholastic Bowl; Science Clb; Thesps; Chorus; Church Choir; Ntl Merit SF; Chess Clb; Drama Clb; Bst Math Paper St OJAS Cmptn; Wupr Rtng Dist Solo & Ensmbl Cntst; OK U; Chem Engrng.

ALLEN, JONATHAN; Deer Creek HS; Edmond, OK; (4); 4/76; Am Leg Boys St; Boy Scts; Science Clb; Band; Jazz Band; Ftbl; Wrstlng; Hon Roll; NHS; Church Yth Grp; Eagle Sct Awd; CO Coll.

ALLEN, JONATHAN A; B T Washington HS; Tulsa, OK; (1); Boy Scts; Church Yth Grp; Socr; Hon Roll; Chinese Clb.

ALLEN, KASEY; Claremore Sr HS; Claremore, OK; (3); #1 in class; Spanish Clb; SADD; Drm Mjr(t); Jazz Band; School Musical; Rep Stu Cncl; NHS; Prfct Atten Awd; Band; High Hon Roll; All Amer Schlr; All Dist Concert Band; Part Time Job; Music Educ.

ALLEN, KATHY; Crowder Schl; Indianola, OK; (4); 5/40; FHA; Teachers Aide; Treas Stu Cncl; Var Bsktbl; Hon Roll; Eastern OK ST Coll; Psych/Soc.

ALLEN, KELSEY J; Spiro HS; Spiro, OK; (2); Cmnty Wkr; FCA; Natl FFA Org; Red Cross Aide; Church Choir; Var Bsktbl; Var Sftbl; Hon Roll; NHS; Ntl Merit Ltr; FFA Ldrshp Camp; Lfgrd; Vol Lcl Pool Tchng Lssns; AR U; PT/ASST.

ALLEN, KERRY E; Tahlequah Jr HS; Tahlequah, OK; (1); Girl Scts; Service Clb; Chorus; Tennis; Hon Roll; Jr NHS; Piano.

ALLEN, KEVIN L; Muldrow HS; Muldrow, OK; (2); Natl Beta Clb; Spanish Clb; Ftbl; Trk; Wt Lftg; Hon Roll; Deer Hunting; Fishing; Westark CC; Bus/Mrktng.

ALLEN, KRISTY N; Wilburton Sr HS; Wilburton, OK; (3); 3/92; Church Yth Grp; Cmnty Wkr; FBLA; Ed Yrbk; Pres Frsh Cls; VP Soph Cls; Pres Jr Cls; Rep Stu Cncl; NHS; Ntl Merit Schol; FBLA Comm Svc Project 1st Pl St Report Wnnr; NSU Tahlequah; Bus Admin.

ALLEN, LARRY W; Broken Bow HS; Broken Bow, OK; (3); Spanish Clb; FFA; Research.

ALLEN, LINDY M; Owasso Sr HS; Owasso, OK; (2); 165/432; Church Yth Grp; Csmtlgy.

ALLEN, MARANDA D; Will Rogers HS; Tulsa, OK; (4); Key Clb; Varsity Clb; Chorus; Church Choir; School Musical; Yrbk; Pres Frsh Cls; Pres Soph Cls; Var Bsbl; Var Bsktbl; ORU Music Solo Awd; Hnr Chorus Awds; Athtlc Awds; Acad Awds; AR U; Music.

ALLEN, MISSY L; Memorial HS; Tulsa, OK; (2); 1/250; Church Yth Grp; Key Clb; Pep Clb; Red Cross Aide; Spanish Clb; Chorus; Sec Soph Cls; Chrmn Jr Cls; Rep Stu Cncl; Var L Swmmng; His; Law.

ALLEN, NICOLE J; Midwest City HS; Midwest City, OK; (2); 187/473; Spanish Clb; Band; Mrchg Band; Pep Band; Hon Roll; U Of OK; Sci.

ALLEN, ROBYN; Moore HS; Norman, OK; (3); Church Yth Grp; Cmnty Wkr; Drama Clb; French Clb; Rptr Science Clb; Church Choir; Flag Corp; School Musical; School Play; Stage Crew; Pblc Lib Teen Adv Bd.

ALLEN, RYAN; Enid Sr HS; Enid, OK; (4); 18/430; Am Leg Boys St; Spanish Clb; Varsity Clb; Swing Chorus; Pres Stu Cncl; Bsktbl; Capt Ftbl; L Trk; Cit Awd; NHS; Ftbl, Super Prep, Blue Chp, All Amer, All Mdlnds, All St, All Bwl, Spr Big 12 1st Tm; OK U; Med.

ALLEN, SCOTT E; North Intemediate HS; Broken Arrow, OK; (1); Boy Scts; Math Clb; Hon Roll; Explorer Law Enfrcmnt; Acad Tm; OK Close-Up Prgm 96.

ALLEN, SHELLY D; Putnam City North HS; Oklahoma City, OK; (4); FCA; Spanish Clb; Mgr Yrbk; Rep Stu Cncl; Var Sftbl; Wrstlng; Hon Roll; NHS; Homecoming Queen; S Nazarene Univ; Ath Trng.

ALLEN, STEFANIE; Owasso Sr HS; Collinsville, OK; (2); Church Yth Grp; English Clb; FCA; Office Aide; Science Clb; VICA; Yrbk; Chrldng; High Hon Roll; St Schlr; Natl Sci Merit Awd; All Amer Schlr; OK ST U; Phys Thrpy.

ALLEN, TIMOTHY; Edmond Memorial HS; Edmond, OK; (4); Church Yth Grp; FCA; HOBY; Key Clb; SADD; School Musical; School Play; Rep Jr Cls; Rep Stu Cncl; Kiwanis Awd; Bus.

ALLEN, TRAVIS D; Central Schl; Sallisaw, OK; (3); Stage Crew; Cmnty Wkr; Pep Clb; Quiz Bowl; Scholastic Bowl; VP Soph Cls; Pres Jr Cls; Rep Stu Cncl; Var Bsktbl; Var Ftbl.

ALLEN, TYRONE G; Edmond North HS; Edmond, OK; (3); Art Clb; Church Yth Grp; Computer Clb; Dance Clb; Drama Clb; FCA; FTA; SADD; Band; Chorus; OK Christian Sci/Arts; Tchr.

ALLEN, ZACHARY S; Choctaw HS; Oklahoma City, OK; (2); Psych.

ALLES JR, RODNEY NEAL; Mc Alester HS; Mcalester, OK; (3); 1/215; Am Leg Boys St; Quiz Bowl; Science Clb; Spanish Clb; Ofcr Stu Cncl; Var L Golf; High Hon Roll; Jr NHS; NHS; U Of OK; Pre-Medicine.

ALLI, ADAM S; Heritage Hall Schl; Oklahoma City, OK; (2); Cmnty Wkr; Debate Tm; Rep French Clb; Mu Alpha Theta; NFL; Varsity Clb; Chorus; Treas Jr Cls; Rep Stu Cncl; L Var Bsktbl; Otstdng Soph Awd; Physician.

ALLISON, APRIL D; Bartlesville Sr HS; Bartlesville, OK; (1); Church Yth Grp; FBLA; JV Var Sftbl; High Hon Roll; Prfct Atten Awd; OK HS Hnr Soc.

ALLISON, BECKY; Afton HS; Afton, OK; (3); 1/36; Church Yth Grp; FCA; Teachers Aide; Yrbk; Rep Frsh Cls; Rep Soph Cls; VP Pres Stu Cncl; Chrldng; Hon Roll; NHS; U Of OK.

ALLISON, BECKY D; Afton HS; Vinita, OK; (3); 1/36; Church Yth Grp; FCA; Office Aide; Red Cross Aide; Teachers Aide; Yrbk; Rep Frsh Cls; Rep Soph Cls; VP Pres Stu Cncl; Chrldng; U Of OK.

ALLISON, BRANDI; Washington HS; Washington, OK; (1); Church Yth Grp; Cmnty Wkr; FCA; GAA; Pep Clb; Var Bsktbl; Var Sftbl; Var Trk; Var Powder Puff Ftbl; Cnslr For Hanicapped Children At Summer Camp; Little League Umpire-ASA.

ALLISON, BROOKE; Panama HS; Panama, OK; (2); Church Yth Grp; Quiz Bowl; SADD; Ofcr Frsh Cls; Ofcr Soph Cls; Ofcr Stu Cncl; Chrldng; Score Keeper; NHS; OU; Psych.

ALLISON, MARGARET E; Lawton Sr HS; Lawton, OK; (2); Church Yth Grp; French Clb; Chorus; Church Choir; Rep Stu Cncl; OK ST U; Vet.

ALLISON, MELISSA; Midwest City HS; Midwest City, OK; (2); 49/501; FCA; Spanish Clb; Yrbk; Mgr(s); Var Socr; Var Sftbl; Var Trk; Var Cit Awd; High Hon Roll; Hon Roll; OSU.

ALLISON, ROBBIE; Alex Jr Sr HS; Alex, OK; (3); 1/32; Am Leg Aux Girls St; Church Yth Grp; FCA; Rptr Natl FFA Org; VP Jr Cls; Var Bsktbl; Var Chrldng; Var Sftbl; Var Trk; Piano.

ALLISON, RORY J; Seminole Jr Sr HS; Seminole, OK; (2); FCA; French Clb; Math Clb; Natl FFA Org; Rep Stu Cncl; Var Ftbl; Var Trk; Var Wt Lftg; Hon Roll; Univ Of OK; Pharm.

ALLISON, SUSAN L; Cushing HS; Cushing, OK; (2); 11/175; Church Yth Grp; Cmnty Wkr; 4-H; FHA; Hosp Aide; Math Clb; Spanish Clb; Teachers Aide; Chorus; Church Choir; Gold Card Awd; Outstndg Typst; Var Schlr; Weatherford; Pharmcy.

ALLISON, WHITNEY; Bartlesville Sr HS; Bartlesville, OK; (3); 42/446; Spanish Clb; Chorus; School Musical; Pom Pon; High Hon Roll; Jr NHS; NHS; Prfct Atten Awd; Spanish NHS; All Dist Hnr Choir 3 Yrs; Dist Sci Fair 1st Pl OK St Sci Fr; All Amer Schlr; Intl Frgn Lang Awd; U Of OK; Medcl.

ALLISS, TAMMERA J; Enid Sr HS; Enid, OK; (3); Church Yth Grp; Drama Clb; Girl Scts; Letterman Clb; Pep Clb; Speech Tm; Church Choir; Stage Crew; Nwsp; Rep Soph Cls; OK St Univ Paleontology Acad; Elem Ed.

ALLRED, EDWARD; Midwest City HS; Oklahoma City, OK; (2); 28/488; Band; Mrchg Band; Jr NHS; Prfct Atten Awd.

ALLRED, MICHAEL B; Roland Sr HS; Roland, OK; (3); JV Bsktbl; Ftbl; Wt Lftg; Bio.

ALLRED, TIMOTHY; U S Grant HS; Oklahoma City, OK; (4); 12/183; FBLA; Rep Nwsp; VP Soph Cls; VP Jr Cls; Pres Stu Cncl; High Hon Roll; NHS; Pres Schlr; Drama Clb; FCA; OASC St Dist 8 Pres; Rotry Yth Ldrshp Awd; U Of OK; Law.

ALMON, TANYA A; Marietta HS; Marietta, OK; (3); Speech Tm; Stage Crew; Jrnlsm.

ALMY, ONALEE R; Cushing HS; Cushing, OK; (2); VP FHA; Spanish Clb; High Hon Roll; Hon Roll; NHS; Mascot; OK ST U; Tchng.

ALPHIN, CRYSTAL L; Poteau HS; Poteau, OK; (3); Office Aide; Var Bsktbl; Var Powder Puff Ftbl; Var Sftbl; Hon Roll; Jr NHS; NHS; Prom Cmte; Phy Thpry.

ALSBAUGH, JENNIFER; Commerce HS; Miami, OK; (1); Church Yth Grp; FCA; Scholastic Bowl; Science Clb; SADD; Church Choir; Bsktbl; Chrldng; Trk; High Hon Roll; 1st Pl OK Art Cond Native Amer Stu.

ALSPAUGH, CANDICE; Union Intermediate HS; Broken Arrow, OK; (1); Church Yth Grp; Debate Tm; Drama Clb; FCA; Math Clb; Spanish Clb; Rep Frsh Cls; Rep Stu Cncl; JV Chrldng; Hon Roll; OK Univ; Scndry Ed.

ALSTON, JASON W; Okemah HS; Okemah, OK; (4); Am Leg Boys St; Boy Scts; VP FBLA; Pep Clb; Rptr Phtg Nwsp; Sec Jr Cls; Var Bsbl; Var Ftbl; Hon Roll; Quiz Bowl; Jrnlsm Awds; U Of OK; Comms.

ALTA, STEVEN A; West Mid HS; Norman, OK; (1); CAP; Cmnty Wkr; Color Guard; Socr; All Star Soccer; 1st Aid & CPR Cert-Amer Red Cross; U Of OK; Arch; Military.

ALTENDORF, JAMES M; Union Intermediate HS; Tulsa, OK; (2); Boy Scts; Church Yth Grp; Church Choir; Hon Roll; Eagle Sct.

ALTHOUSE, TRIXIE M; Will Rogers HS; Tulsa, OK; (2); Debate Tm; Mrchg Band; Socr; Hon Roll; CODE; Cncrt Band; TU; Tchr.

ALTMAN, BRYAN; Kingfisher HS; Kingfisher, OK; (1); Debate Tm; NFL; Quiz Bowl; Speech Tm; Bsktbl; Golf; Hon Roll; U NE Lincoln; Engr.

ALTOM, DONISE N; Blair Schl; Blair, OK; (4); Church Yth Grp; FCA; Treas Natl Beta Clb; Natl FFA Org; School Play; Nwsp; Yrbk; Sec Sr Cls; VP Stu Cncl; Capt Chrldng; All St Chrldr; SE OK ST U; Engl.

ALTOM, NICKI; Blair Schl; Blair, OK; (4); 4/30; Chorus; School Play; Yrbk; Sec Sr Cls; VP Stu Cncl; Capt Chrldng; High Hon Roll; NHS; FFA Rprtr; Beta Clb Treas.

ALVARADO, ROGER D; Temple Jr Sr HS; Temple, OK; (2); Church Yth Grp; Ofcr Soph Cls; Ofcr Bsbl; Bsktbl; Crs Cntry; Ftbl; Trk; Hon Roll.

ALVEY, JAMES; Pond Creek-Hunter Schl; Hunter, OK; (4); 4/30; VP Church Yth Grp; VP English Clb; Natl FFA Org; Capt Quiz Bowl; ROTC; School Play; Bsktbl; Crs Cntry; Ftbl; Hon Roll; Southwestern OK ST U Smmr Sci, Math Acad; OK ST U; Army Ofcr.

AMBROSE, BREE; Union Intermediate HS; Tulsa, OK; (2); 194/800; Church Yth Grp; Key Clb; Spanish Clb; Church Choir; School Play; Hon Roll; Charles Page Math Test; Church Drama Team, Ldrshp Team; Mission Trips; ORU; Drama.

AMBROSE, DAVID; Checotah HS; Checotah, OK; (4); Am Leg Boys St; FCA; Teachers Aide; VP Soph Cls; Sec Treas Jr Cls; Pres Sr Cls; Ofcr Stu Cncl; Bsktbl; Ftbl; Hon Roll.

AMBROSI, LEO A; Edmond Memorial HS; Edmond, OK; (3); Cmnty Wkr; Drama Clb; German Clb; Science Clb; School Play; Rep Stu Cncl; Socr; NHS; OK St Fnlst & Natl DECA Fnlst 95-96; 3rd Pl Food Mrktng OK St DECA CDC 95-96; FLMM; OK U; Mrktng.

AMEN, LACY M; Putnam City West HS; Oklahoma City, OK; (4); 16/270; Pres Church Yth Grp; Intnl Clb; Teachers Aide; Phtg Ed Yrbk; Capt Crs Cntry; Var Trk; Jr NHS; NHS; Grad 4.30 GPR; Outstdng Photo Stdnt; U Of Cntrl OK; CPA.

AMENDT, MARK; Noble HS; Noble, OK; (3); 1/167; Church Yth Grp; Model UN; Mu Alpha Theta; Scholastic Bowl; Band; Drm Mjr(t); Jazz Band; Mrchg Band; JV Var Bsktbl; High Hon Roll.

AMES, GUY C; Putnam City North HS; Oklahoma City, OK; (2); Church Yth Grp; JA; Church Choir; Intrml Bsktbl; JV Socr; OK Univ.

AMEY, BROOKE L; Ripley HS; Stillwater, OK; (1); Debate Tm; FCA; FHA; Math Clb; Natl FFA Org; Science Clb; Spanish Clb; Bsktbl; High Hon Roll; Prfct Atten Awd; Tulsa Univ; Law.

AMMONS, TRINA; Cushing HS; Cushing, OK; (2); 38/159; Spanish Clb; Teachers Aide; Chrldng; High Hon Roll; Hon Roll; NHS; Pres Schlr.

ANDEREGG, ERIC; Vinita HS; Vinita, OK; (2); Church Yth Grp; Math Clb; Spanish Clb; Teachers Aide; Band; Mrchg Band; Pep Band; Hon Roll.

ANDERS, RYAN THOMAS; Wright Christian Acad; Tulsa, OK; (4); 13/38; Rptr Yrbk; Sanford Univ; Grphc Dsgn.

ANDERSON, AARON R; Locust Grove HS; Locust Grove, OK; (2); Church Yth Grp; German Clb; Quiz Bowl; VICA; High Hon Roll; Hon Roll; TU; Cmptrs.

ANDERSON, ADRIAN; Star Spencer HS; Spencer, OK; (3); Var L Bsktbl; Var L Crs Cntry; Ldrshp Bsktbl 95-96; MVP Crs Cntry Trck 95-96; Ldrshp Crs Cntry Trck 94-95; Electrnc Engrng.

ANDERSON, ALLISON; Bartlesville Sr HS; Bartlesville, OK; (4); Church Yth Grp; 4-H; Spanish Clb; Chorus; Church Choir; School Play; Cit Awd; 4-H Awd; High Hon Roll; NHS; MD Bus Ldrs Conf Awd; St Gardng/Hortclte Wnnr; Denvr 4-H Ldrsp & Ctznsp Washingtn Focus Trips Wnnr; Abilene Christian U; Bus Mgmt.

ANDERSON, AMANDA; Empire Schl; Duncan, OK; (2); Church Yth Grp; Cmnty Wkr; FHA; Pep Clb; Chorus; Pres Frsh Cls; Hon Roll; Vol Free Comm Hlth Care Clnc.

ANDERSON, AMANDA; Hilldale HS; Muskogee, OK; (4); 4/78; Art Clb; Sec Computer Clb; Drama Clb; Pres Key Clb; Pres Mu Alpha Theta; Science Clb; Spanish Clb; SADD; Yrbk; VP NHS; Connors St Coll; Art.

ANDERSON, AMANDA; Smithville Sr HS; Smithville, OK; (2); FHA; GAA; Quiz Bowl; Scholastic Bowl; Church Choir; Rep Soph Cls; Bsktbl; High Hon Roll; Hon Roll; NHS; Stdnt Of Yr 95-; OK ST U; Interior Dsgnr.

ANDERSON, AMY J; Carney Schl; Carney, OK; (1); Church Yth Grp; Cmnty Wkr; FHA; Ofcr Soph Cls; Cit Awd; Hon Roll; Prfct Atten Awd; OSU; Vet Asst.

ANDERSON, ANDRE L; Mc Alester HS; Krebs, OK; (3); Boy Scts; DECA; VP FCA; Spanish Clb; Ofcr Stu Cncl; JV Var Ftbl; Trk; Wt Lftg; Hon Roll; NHS; Indian Clb; Cmptr Tech.

ANDERSON, ANGELA; Western Heights Sr HS; Oklahoma City, OK; (3); Church Yth Grp; Cmnty Wkr; FCA; Key Clb; Chorus; School Musical; School Play; Stage Crew; DAR Awd; NHS; Ldrshp Ed Apprenticeship Pgm Pres; Stu Cncl; OK ST Univ.

ANDERSON, ASHLEY; Westmoore HS; Moore, OK; (3); Spanish Clb; Bsktbl; OK Univ; Law.

ANDERSON, ASHLEY M; Dale Sr HS; Shawnee, OK; (1); Drama Clb; Natl FFA Org; Hon Roll; Wrtng Poetry.

ANDERSON, BECKY R; Foyil Schl; Foyil, OK; (2); Chrldng; Sing.

ANDERSON, BRADLEY; Norman Sr HS; Norman, OK; (4); 111/677; Spanish Clb; Swing Chorus; Pres Frsh Cls; Hist Soph Cls; Pres Jr Cls; Hist Sr Cls; Ofcr Stu Cncl; Var Bsbl; Var Bsktbl; Var Ftbl; FCA; Who In Sprts; Univ Of OK.

ANDERSON, BRANDON C; Union Sr HS; Broken Arrow, OK; (4); 15/616; Church Yth Grp; Jazz Band; Mrchg Band; Orch; Nwsp; Yrbk; Hon Roll; NHS; Ntl Merit Ltr; Spanish NHS; OK ST U; Mech Engrng.

ANDERSON, BRANDY; Catoosa HS; Catoosa, OK; (2); Church Yth Grp; FCA; Spanish Clb; School Play; Rep Stu Cncl; JV Bsktbl; Var Chrldng; Var Trk; Hon Roll; Chrldng Awds; Track Awds.

ANDERSON, CAMERON; Ponca City Sr HS; Ponca City, OK; (4); 88/358; Am Leg Boys St; Boy Scts; English Clb; Spanish Clb; SADD; Teachers Aide; Church Choir; Ftbl, Bsktbl, Trk; Afrcn Amer Clb VP; Bus.

ANDERSON, CHAD; Westmoore HS; Oklahoma City, OK; (3); 15/615; Church Yth Grp; FCA; Spanish Clb; Nwsp; Var Bsbl; Wt Lftg; Hon Roll; NHS; Debate Tm; Jr NHS; Schlstc Tm; Future Jrnlsts Of Amer; Intro Law Awd; U Of OK.

ANDERSON, CHET; Moore HS; Moore, OK; (2); Boy Scts; Church Yth Grp; Swmmng; Hon Roll; Comp Info Systs.

ANDERSON, CLIFFORD W; Tishomingo HS; Tishomingo, OK; (2); Boy Scts; Church Yth Grp; CAP; Quiz Bowl; Band; Chorus; Mrchg Band; Crs Cntry; Hon Roll; OK Hnr Soc; Ministry.

ANDERSON, CODEE; Spiro HS; Spiro, OK; (4); 8/92; Art Clb; FBLA; Math Clb; Natl FFA Org; Var Trk; Hon Roll; NHS; Pres Schlr; OK HS Hnr Soc; Stu Of Today; FFATOP Slsmn; E OK St Col; Pre-Vet.

ANDERSON, CORY A; Walters HS; Walters, OK; (2); 3/57; Art Clb; Church Yth Grp; FCA; HOBY; Ftbl; Wt Lftg; Gov Hon Prg Awd; High Hon Roll; Hon Roll; Pres Hnr Roll; Var Acad Team; Arch Engrng.

ANDERSON, DONDE R; Oklahoma Sch Of Science & Math; Broken Arrow, OK; (2); French Clb; VP Math Clb; Band; Rep Stu Cncl; Hon Roll; NHS; Pres Acad Fit Awd; Mrchg Band; Pep Band; Acad Team; Outstdng Hnrs Alg II Stdnts/Fr I/II Stdnts.

ANDERSON, DONNA M; Northeast HS; Oklahoma City, OK; (3); FBLA; Science Clb; Orch; Mgr Vllybl; Hon Roll; OK Yth Symphny; Oklahoma City CC.

ANDERSON, ELIZABETH R; Tahlequah Jr HS; Cookson, OK; (1); Band; Mrchg Band; Jr NHS; Med.

ANDERSON, EMILY H; Cameron Schl; Cameron, OK; (1); Church Yth Grp; FCA; 4-H; FHA; Pep Clb; Quiz Bowl; JV Var Bsktbl; JV Var Sftbl; Hon Roll; Newcomer Awed Sftbl.

ANDERSON, EMILY M; Stillwater Sr HS; Stillwater, OK; (3); Drama Clb; French Clb; Key Clb; Thesps; School Musical; School Play; Stage Crew; Hon Roll; NHS; Pres Chrch Yth Grp; Crtv Wrtng.

ANDERSON, ERICA J; Jenks HS; Jenks, OK; (4); 114/475; DECA; FHA; Key Clb.

ANDERSON, HEATHER DAWN; Waukomis HS; Waukomis, OK; (3); Math Tm; Scholastic Bowl; Spanish Clb; Sec Jr Cls; Hon Roll; NHS; Southwestern OK ST U; Phrmcy.

ANDERSON, IRA B; Choctaw HS; Choctaw, OK; (3); Church Yth Grp; Office Aide; Spanish Clb; SADD; Teachers Aide; JV Bsbl; Wt Lftg; High Hon Roll; Hon Roll.

ANDERSON, JANNA; Pauls Valley HS; Pauls Valley, OK; (3); 7/113; Pres Church Yth Grp; Treas FCA; Pres FHA; Pres FTA; HOBY; Sec Spanish Clb; Ed Yrbk; Cit Awd; Hon Roll; NHS; Poetry Publshd Anthology; Americas Natl Teen Pgnt Fnlst; U Of Tulsa; Law.

ANDERSON, JARROD D; Shawnee Sr HS; Shawnee, OK; (1); Church Yth Grp; FCA; Spanish Clb; Church Choir; JV Bsbl; JV Bsktbl; Hon Roll; OBU.

ANDERSON, JENNIFER; Liberty Acad; Tecumseh, OK; (1); Church Yth Grp; FCA; Lit Mag; Rep Frsh Cls; Ofcr Stu Cncl; Bsktbl; Chrldng; Hon Roll; OK U; Sprts Med.

ANDERSON, JEREMY M; South Coffeyville Schl; S Coffeyville, OK; (1); Quiz Bowl; JV Bsbl; JV Bsktbl; JV Ftbl; OK ST Univ.

ANDERSON, JILL K; Stillwater Sr HS; Stillwater, OK; (4); 33/344; 4-H; Hosp Aide; Latin Clb; Treas Natl Beta Clb; Spanish Clb; Chorus; 4-H Awd; Kiwanis Awd; NHS; Pres Acad Fit Awd; Elk Teenager Of Yr; St 4-H Record Bk Wnnr; OK ST Univ; Med.

ANDERSON, JONATHAN L; Commerce HS; Commerce, OK; (1); Church Yth Grp; Debate Tm; Letterman Clb; Quiz Bowl; Science Clb; Spanish Clb; SADD; Band; Mrchg Band; Pep Band; OK ST U; Arch.

ANDERSON, KAILEE A; Walters HS; Walters, OK; (3); FCA; FHA; GAA; Letterman Clb; Office Aide; SADD; Varsity Clb; Ed Yrbk; Bsktbl; Sftbl; Southwestern OK; Med.

ANDERSON, KARA E; Broken Arrow Sr HS; Broken Arrow, OK; (3); 96/868; Church Yth Grp; Band; Church Choir; Mrchg Band; Pep Band; High Hon Roll; Hon Roll; Jr NHS; NHS; Pres Acad Fit Awd; Chrstns Action Pres 10th Grd; First Lieutenant Mrchng Bnd 11th Grd; U Of Tulsa; Sprts Med.

ANDERSON, KAREN; Stigler HS; Stigler, OK; (4); 14/73; Church Yth Grp; Pep Clb; SADD; Church Choir; Rep Sr Cls; Var Bsktbl; Var Sftbl; Hon Roll; Jr NHS; NHS; 4-H Cty Pres; Sub Dist FFA Rec Ldr; Connors ST Coll; Elem Ed.

ANDERSON, KATHRYN L; Union Sr HS; Tulsa, OK; (3); 1/750; Hosp Aide; Key Clb; Spanish Clb; Rptr Jr Cls; Jr NHS; NHS; Pres Acad Fit Awd; Spanish NHS; Renaissnce; Acad Resrce Ctr Cncl; Drug Free Yth.

ANDERSON, KEITH A; Bartlesville Mid HS; Bartlesville, OK; (2); 1/481; Church Yth Grp; Ofcr Spanish Clb; Pres Stu Cncl; Bsktbl; Var L Socr; High Hon Roll; NHS; Ofcr FBLA; Chorus; Ftbl; Civitan Stdnt Of Yr Awd; US Stdnt Cncl Awd; Dist Hnr Choir.

ANDERSON, KELLIE; Ponca City Sr HS; Ponca City, OK; (1); Church Yth Grp; FCA; Pep Clb; SADD; Chorus; Church Choir; School Musical; Bsktbl; Chrldng; Hon Roll.

ANDERSON, KENNY; Cookson Hills Chrn Schl; Kansas, OK; (2); Church Yth Grp; FCA; Church Choir; Pres Frsh Cls; Rep Soph Cls; Rep Stu Cncl; Var Bsbl; Var Capt Bsktbl; Var Socr; Cit Awd; U Of OK; Physcn.

ANDERSON, KIMBERLY; Union Intermediate HS; Broken Arrow, OK; (2); Church Yth Grp; FCA; GAA; HOBY; Office Aide; Bsktbl; JV Socr; High Hon Roll; Jr NHS; NHS; DFV VP UN Intrmdt; Ambssdr Wrld Ldrshp Cngrs OK HOBY; MD.

ANDERSON, KRISTY; Adair HS; Adair, OK; (2); Church Yth Grp; FCA; Science Clb; Church Choir; JV Bsktbl; High Hon Roll; Pres Acad Fit Awd; KS U; Phys Thrpy.

ANDERSON, LAURA L; Putnam City West HS; Bethany, OK; (4); 34/270; Church Yth Grp; FCA; French Clb; Intnl Clb; JCL; Rep Stu Cncl; Bsktbl; Jr NHS; NHS; St Schlr; Comm Head Of Housing Comm For OK Stu Cncl St Convention; Bartlesville Wesleyan; Math.

ANDERSON, LEAL; Prague HS; Paden, OK; (4); 11/69; Am Leg Boys St; Church Yth Grp; Cmnty Wkr; Key Clb; Natl FFA Org; Scholastic Bowl; Church Choir; Rep Frsh Cls; Ofcr Soph Cls; VP Jr Cls; OU; Mrktng.

ANDERSON, LINCOLN R; Hilldale HS; Muskogee, OK; (2); CAP; Science Clb; Chorus; Ftbl; US Air Force/Vetry Med.

ANDERSON, LUCAS; Shawnee Sr HS; Shawnee, OK; (4); 10/262; French Clb; Latin Clb; Math Clb; Quiz Bowl; Scholastic Bowl; Science Clb; Cit Awd; NHS; Natl Yth Ldrshp Frm Med; U Of OK; Pre-Med.

ANDERSON, LUKE J; Snyder HS; Snyder, OK; (2); 1/42; Church Yth Grp; Speech Tm; Rep Stu Cncl; Intrml Wrstlng; High Hon Roll; Hon Roll; NHS; St Hnr Soc; St Placer Wrstlng; Acad Team FFA; Law.

ANDERSON, MICHAEL P; Altus Sr HS; Jefferson City, MO; (2); French Clb; Band; Mrchg Band; Pep Band; School Musical; Hon Roll; Jr NHS; St Louis Univ; Cmptr Sci.

ANDERSON, MICHELLE M; Del City HS; Del City, OK; (3); 34/424; Church Yth Grp; Band; Chorus; Church Choir; Mrchg Band; Jr NHS; NHS; Forfrount Ministries; UM; Ceramic Engr.

ANDERSON, MICHELLE R; Mustang HS; Mustang, OK; (3); Chorus; Color Guard; Flag Corp; Var Pom Pon; Var Powder Puff Ftbl; Hon Roll; Winterguard; Nite Express Drum & Bugle Corp; OK U; Eng Tchr; Bus.

ANDERSON, NATHAN; Coleman Schl; Coleman, OK; (3); 1/18; Church Yth Grp; FCA; 4-H; Quiz Bowl; Pres Frsh Cls; Pres Soph Cls; Pres Jr Cls; High Hon Roll; Hon Roll; NHS; OK Chrstn U; Chem Engr.

ANDERSON, NIKKI; Clinton HS; Clinton, OK; (3); Church Yth Grp; FBLA; VP Spanish Clb; SADD; Band; Color Guard; Flag Corp; Mrchg Band; Pep Band; Var Chrldng; Southwestern; Cnslng.

ANDERSON, RACHEL C; Vicotry Chrstn HS; Tulsa, OK; (4); 17/62; Teachers Aide; Acpl Chr; Phtg Yrbk; Mgr(s); Socr; Sftbl; Swmmng; High Hon Roll; Hon Roll; NHS; USAA Natl Ldr Awd & Natl Schlr Awd; Malone Col.

ANDERSON, RHONDA; Tuttle HS; Tuttle, OK; (1); 1/101; FHA; GAA; Girl Scts; Bsktbl; Chrldng; High Hon Roll; Girl Scout Silver Awd; Chldrns Phys Thrpst.

ANDERSON, ROMI L; Sayre HS; Sayre, OK; (2); FCA; SADD; Band; Chorus; Mrchg Band; Chrldng; All Star Chrldr UCA; Southwestern ST U; Spch Pthlgy.

ANDERSON, RUSSELL C; Moore HS; Moore, OK; (4); 98/520; Church Yth Grp; FCA; Office Aide; Spanish Clb; Rep Stu Cncl; JV Bsbl; Hon Roll; NHS; Pres Acad Fit Awd; German Clb; Play Guitar Chrstn Cntry Band; OK Cty CC; Frnsc Sci/Scndy Ed.

ANDERSON, SAMUEL; Millwood HS; Oklahoma City, OK; (3); Cmnty Wkr; FCA; ROTC; Ftbl; Hon Roll; W Point; Dctr.

ANDERSON, SHAWNA D; Will Rogers HS; Tulsa, OK; (2); Red Cross Aide; Teachers Aide; School Musical; School Play; Rep Stu Cncl; High Hon Roll; Hon Roll; Participated In Will Rogers Round Up Show & Was Miss Rogers Soph Attendant; Law; Attorney; Physiology.

ANDERSON, SONJA J; Edmond Memorial HS; Edmond, OK; (4); French Clb; FHA; Sec Key Clb; SADD; Chorus; Orch; School Musical; NHS; 1st Chrstn; Prvt Violin Lsns 6 Yrs; Orch Rylty; U Of Cntrl OK; Early Chldhd Ed.

ANDERSON, STEPHEN; Altus Sr HS; Altus, OK; (4); 8/232; Am Leg Boys St; Church Yth Grp; Band; VP Jr Cls; VP Stu Cncl; Var Bsktbl; Var Golf; Var Capt Socr; Var Capt Swmmng; NHS; US Air Force Acad; Pilot.

ANDERSON, TERRENCE; Stillwater Sr HS; Stillwater, OK; (4); 10/350; Am Leg Boys St; Boy Scts; Pres Church Yth Grp; Drama Clb; FCA; VP Latin Clb; Natl Beta Clb; Capt Quiz Bowl; Science Clb; Varsity Clb; Med.

ANDERSON, WENDY; Broken Bow HS; Broken Bow, OK; (4); 11/140; Dance Clb; Drama Clb; Spanish Clb; School Musical; Rep Frsh Cls; Chrldng; Hon Roll; Jr NHS; NHS; Pres Acad Fit Awd; Carl Albert Coll.

ANDERSON, WHITNEY A; Owasso Sr HS; Owasso, OK; (2); 72/432.

ANDERSON, WHITNEY L; Piedmont HS; Piedmont, OK; (3); CAP; Scholastic Bowl; SADD; Band; Flag Corp; Pep Band; Tennis; Pres Acad Fit Awd; NHS; Mrchg Band; Natl Indian Hon Soc; Ntve Amer Clb, Pres, Vp, Rep; U Of OK; Nurs.

ANDERSON, ZACHARY D; Cushing HS; Cushing, OK; (4); 12/156; Church Yth Grp; Math Clb; Quiz Bowl; Science Clb; Spanish Clb; Speech Tm; Band; Jazz Band; Mrchg Band; Pep Band; OK Hnr Soc; Tomorrows Ldrs; OK U; Aeronautcl Engrng.

ANDERSON, ZACHARY T; Union Intermediate HS; Broken Arrow, OK; (2); Boy Scts; Pres Church Yth Grp; Treas FCA; Letterman Clb; Spanish Clb; Varsity Clb; Church Choir; JV Bsktbl; JV Ftbl; L Var Trk; DFY; Pr Mdtn; Brigham Young U.

ANDREWS, BRADLEY; Muldrow HS; Muldrow, OK; (3); 4/100; Math Clb; Natl Beta Clb; Science Clb; Spanish Clb; Speech Tm; Var Golf; High Hon Roll; Hon Roll; NHS; Elec Engr.

ANDREWS, HILARY K; Edmond Memorial HS; Edmond, OK; (3); 120/500; Church Yth Grp; Spanish Clb; Band; Drm Mjr(t); Jazz Band; Mrchg Band; Pep Band; School Musical; Chrldng; Hon Roll.

ANDREWS, KEVIN; Ada HS; Ada, OK; (3); FCA; Stage Crew; Yrbk; Var L Ftbl; Score Keeper; Trk; Wt Lftg; Hon Roll.

ANDREWS, MELISSA; Claremore Sr HS; Claremore, OK; (4); 1/231; Hosp Aide; Math Clb; Office Aide; Science Clb; Spanish Clb; Ed Yrbk; Gym; High Hon Roll; NHS; Val; OK ST U; Pre-Med.

ANDREWS, MISTY; Stuart Sr HS; Haywood, OK; (4); 6/28; Church Yth Grp; FCA; FHA; Yrbk; Bsktbl; Sftbl; High Hon Roll; NHS; Ntl Merit Ltr; Pres Schlr; Schlstc Tm; Natl Sci Merit Awd Wnnr; Sr Ath Awd; Estrn OK ST Coll; Elem Ed.

ANDRIS, COLBY; Blanche Thomas Jr Sr HS; Sentinel, OK; (3); Church Yth Grp; Natl Beta Clb; Var Bsbl; Gov Hon Prg Awd; Hon Roll; NHS; OU; Med.

ANDRUS, MATTHEW J; Westmoore HS; Oklahoma City, OK; (4); 15/610; VP German Clb; Quiz Bowl; Scholastic Bowl; Science Clb; Jr NHS; NHS; St Schlr; Val; Schlstc Lttr; OK St Univ; Elec Eng.

ANGALA, JENIFER; Midwest City HS; Midwest City, OK; (4); 27/390; 4-H; Sec FHA; Key Clb; Pep Clb; Var Capt Socr; 4-H Awd; Gov Hon Prg Awd; NHS; Pres Schlr; Val; Rose ST Coll; Tchr.

ANGLE, SHANNON; Burlington Schl; Amorita, OK; (2); 1/16; Dance Clb; HOBY; Natl FFA Org; Quiz Bowl; Band; School Play; Rep Frsh Cls; Rep Soph Cls; Bsktbl; High Hon Roll; Natl Kids Rnnr Up; OK FFA St Spch Cont 4th FFA Opportnts; Natl Hstry Day; OK ST U; Commnctns.

ANGLEN, BOBBIE A; Muldrow HS; Muldrow, OK; (4); 40/98; FHA; Office Aide; Spanish Clb; Band; Mrchg Band; Pres Frsh Cls; Var L Bsktbl; Var L Sftbl; Var L Trk; Hon Roll; Sr Superlative; Bsktbl Homcomng Qn.

ANGLEY, SHAUN M; Putnam City North HS; Oklahoma City, OK; (3); Church Yth Grp; FCA; German Clb; Stage Crew; JV Bsbl; Var Ftbl; Var Swmmng; Hon Roll; Jr NHS; NHS; Engrng.

ANGOLANO, JOSHUA D; Oologah HS; Claremore, OK; (3); Boy Scts; Band; Jazz Band; Mrchg Band; Hon Roll; Cliff Littler Boy Sct Awd; Boys Scts 1st Pl Sailing Regatta; Comp Sci.

ANKROM, SHANNON; Seiling Schl; Seiling, OK; (2); Art Clb; Church Yth Grp; FCA; FHA; Letterman Clb; Natl Beta Clb; Band; Flag Corp; Ofcr Stu Cncl; Bsktbl.

ANNESLEY, LEESA B; Sulphur HS; Sulphur, OK; (2); Church Yth Grp; FHA; Band; Chorus; Co-Capt Color Guard; Flag Corp; Mrchg Band; Pep Band; School Musical; Stage Crew; OK Univ; Phy Therapy.

ANNO, SARAH; Ponca City Sr HS; Ponca City, OK; (2); Church Yth Grp; Cmnty Wkr; FCA; Chorus; Var L Chrldng; Trk; Hon Roll; Piano; Ballet.

ANTHAMATTEN, BROOKE M; Bishop Kelley HS; Tulsa, OK; (2); Key Clb; Pep Clb; Spanish Clb; Yrbk; Hon Roll.

ANTHIS, JENNIFER; Mulhall Orlando HS; Mulhall, OK; (4); 8/22; Church Yth Grp; FCA; German Clb; Library Aide; Speech Tm; SADD; Band; Church Choir; Nwsp; Yrbk; Dallas Chrstn Coll Teenage Choir; U Of Cntrl OK; Early Chldhd Ed.

ANTHONY, JENNY M; Westmoore HS; Oklahoma City, OK; (4); Sftbl.

ANTHONY, ROBERT D; Del City HS; Del City, OK; (2); VICA; Band; Mrchg Band; Hon Roll; NHS; OU; Constructior Techlgy.

ANTHONY, SHELLIE; Norman Sr HS; Norman, OK; (3); Church Yth Grp; Sec Drama Clb; Girl Scts; Red Cross Aide; Spanish Clb; Rep Stage Crew; JV Var Chrldng; Var Sftbl; High Hon Roll; NHS; Scndry Ed.

ANTWINE, LA TASHA; Preston Schl; Okmulgee, OK; (2); Church Choir; School Play; Rep Soph Cls; Hon Roll; Prfct Atten Awd; Amer Hnr Soc; Phys Thpy.

APPLE, BRIAN K; Muskogee HS; Muskogee, OK; (2); Church Yth Grp; Stage Crew; Socr; Hon Roll; OK Univ; Ped Srgn.

APPLEBY, DARREN K; John Marshall HS; Oklahoma City, OK; (4); Drama Clb; German Clb; Letterman Clb; Yrbk; Ofcr Bsbl; Golf; Swmmng.

APPLEGATE, BEAU; Eufaula Sr HS; Eufaula, OK; (4); 12/75; Math Tm; Quiz Bowl; Band; Church Choir; Jazz Band; Mrchg Band; Pep Band; Hon Roll; NHS; U Of OK; Engrng.

APPLEGATE, MELISSA L; Muskogee HS; Muskogee, OK; (1); Church Yth Grp; English Clb; ROTC; Color Guard; Drill Tm; Cit Awd; NHS; OK ST Univ; Aerospace Tech.

APPLEGATE, PRIACILLA; Tahlequah Sr HS; Hulbert, OK; (4); 17/443; Treas FBLA; Pep Clb; Hon Roll; Jr NHS; NHS; Ntl Merit Ltr; Pres Acad Fit Awd; Indian Heritage Clb; Homcmng Ct; NSU; Bus Admin.

APPLEGATE, RAYMOND G; Will Rogers HS; Tulsa, OK; (4); 51/197; German Clb; JA; Teachers Aide; Soc Studs Dept Awd; Forgn Lang Dept Awd; Schl Svc Awd; NE St Univ; Bus.

APPLESETH, ANDREA K; Putnam City HS; Oklahoma City, OK; (2); Church Yth Grp; German Clb; 3-D; Med.

ARAGON, SANTOS; Little Axe Sr HS; Newalla, OK; (3); Science Clb; Spanish Clb; Sec Stu Cncl; Hon Roll; NHS; Show Choir; US Marine Corps.

ARAGON, TRINA; Turpin Schl; Turpin, OK; (3); Drama Clb; FCA; FHA; NFL; Speech Tm; School Play; Var Chrldng; Hon Roll; Speech Tm Offcr; FHA Hstrn.

ARAMBULA, ELIANA M; Southeast HS; Oklahoma City, OK; (3); Church Yth Grp; Pres FCA; FBLA; HOBY; Rptr Yrbk; Hist Stu Cncl; Var Bsktbl; Var Sftbl; Kiwanis Awd; NHS; Show Choir; Tchr; His.

ARAMBULA, TEASHA D; Moore HS; Oklahoma City, OK; (3); Church Yth Grp; Hosp Aide; Model UN; Office Aide; Chorus; Church Choir; Hon Roll; Jr NHS; NHS; DECA; OJT; Play Piano 10 Yrs; OSU; Vet; Music Or Sci Tchr.

ARBUCKLE, NICOLE R; Norman Sr HS; Norman, OK; (4); 117/600; French Clb; Rep Soph Cls; French Hon Soc; Hon Roll; NHS; U Of OK Norman.

ARBUCKLE, SARAH; West Middle HS; Norman, OK; (1); FCA; JCL; Latin Clb; Var Stu Cncl; Bsktbl; Chrldng; Socr; Cit Awd; Hon Roll; Whos Who At West; OK Hnr Soc.

ARCHER, ASHLEY N; Harrah HS; Harrah, OK; (3); 17/150; Church Yth Grp; Cmnty Wkr; Drama Clb; Spanish Clb; SADD; Teachers Aide; Acpl Chr; Chorus; School Musical; Ofcr Frsh Cls; Marketing.

ARCHER, GRAEME; Chickasha Jr HS; Chickasha, OK; (1); DECA; Jr NHS; Roller Hockey; Harvard; Phy.

ARCHER, JON A; West Mid HS; Norman, OK; (3); Church Yth Grp; Orch; Pres Acad Fit Awd; OK Univ; Comp Eng.

ARCHER, SUSIE L; Tahlequah Sr HS; Tahlequah, OK; (3); Science Clb; Chorus; Orch; JV Crs Cntry; Hon Roll; Jr NHS; NHS; Bausch & Lomb Sci Awd; U Of AR; Chem Engr.

ARCHULETA, MELISHA G; Hartshorne Sr HS; San Juan Pueblo, NM; (2); Teachers Aide; Hon Roll; NSU; Pedtrcn.

ARDLE, JACKIE; Owasso Sr HS; Owasso, OK; (3); 99/387; Church Yth Grp; FCA; French Clb; FTA; JA; Library Aide; Office Aide; Var Crs Cntry; Var Trk; Hon Roll; Sci Merit Awd; TAG; DFY; Ozark Christian Coll; Psych.

ARDUINE, CHERI; Noble HS; Norman, OK; (4); Drama Clb; Mu Alpha Theta; Spanish Clb; SADD; Teachers Aide; Thesps; Chorus; School Play; Nwsp; Yrbk; U Of OK; Elem Ed.

AREA, DAVID S; Union Sr HS; Tulsa, OK; (3); 24/741; FCA; FBLA; Spanish Clb; Ofcr Bsbl; Bsktbl; Hon Roll; Jr NHS; NHS; Spanish NHS; DECA; Renaissance; Bus Mgmt.

ARENA, DYLAN A; B T Washington HS; Tulsa, OK; (3); Spanish Clb; NHS; Ntl Merit Ltr; Pres Acad Fit Awd; 1st Dan Blck Belt; Accptd ST Arts Inst Poetry.

ARGO, AARON V; Spiro HS; Spiro, OK; (2); Art Clb; Bsktbl; U Of AR; Lawyer; Artist.

ARGO, JIMMY; Hollis Jr Sr HS; Hollis, OK; (3); 2/55; Am Leg Boys St; 4-H; Math Tm; Band; L Bsktbl; L Trk; Gov Hon Prg Awd; High Hon Roll; Mrchg Band; Acad Team; All Amer Schlr; Atnd SWIM; Engrng.

ARGO, SALLI J; Caney Jr Sr HS; Atoka, OK; (2); Church Yth Grp; FHA; GAA; Letterman Clb; Varsity Clb; Church Choir; School Play; Yrbk; Sec Soph Cls; Var Bsktbl; Perfect Attdnc For 10 Yrs; Voted Most Friendly In Schl; Southeastern OK ST Univ.

ARINGTON, ANTHONY A; Putnam City West HS; Bethany, OK; (2); JV Bsbl; JV Var Ftbl; NHS; HOSA Sentinel.

ARKUCKLE, JANEEN L; Putnam City West HS; Bethany, OK; (4); 1/275; Cmnty Wkr; French Clb; Band; Lit Mag; Jr NHS; NHS; St Schlr; Val; NHS Pres; Bio Clb Sec; OK Blood Inst Vol; OK U; Microbio; Pre-Med.

ARMENTA, CESAR A; Southeast HS; Oklahoma City, OK; (1); Art Clb; Church Yth Grp; VICA; JV Bsktbl; High Hon Roll; Law.

ARMENTROUT, RYAN; Watonga HS; Watonga, OK; (1); 1/70; Boy Scts; FCA; FBLA; FHA; Quiz Bowl; Mrchg Band; Treas Soph Cls; Ftbl; Wrstlng; Hon Roll; Comm Thtr Prdctn; Blaine Cty Law Day Essy 2nd Pl; Smmr Sci Acad.

ARMER, MARCIE D; Woodward HS; Woodward, OK; (1); Church Yth Grp; Drama Clb; German Clb; School Play; Trk; High Hon Roll.

ARMITAGE, JUSTIN M; Meeker HS; Meeker, OK; (3); Sec Cmnty Wkr; Debate Tm; 4-H; Natl FFA Org; Scholastic Bowl; Bsktbl; Wt Lftg; 4-H Awd; Natl Ldrshp Awd 95; Octagon Cmnty Svc Org; OSU; Ag Econ.

ARMSTRONG, DAMIEN; Seiling Schl; Seiling, OK; (4); 7/40; VP Church Yth Grp; FCA; FBLA; Letterman Clb; Band; Chorus; Rep Soph Cls; Rep Jr Cls; Rep Sr Cls; Capt Var Ftbl; Ftbl St Fnlst 95; OSU; Hotel/Restaurant Mgmt.

ARMSTRONG, DIRK; Guthrie Sr HS; Guthrie, OK; (4); 56/167; Church Yth Grp; FCA; VP Natl FFA Org; Spanish Clb; VICA; Var L Ftbl; OK Panhandle ST Univ; Ag Ed.

ARMSTRONG, DOUG C; Choctaw HS; Choctaw, OK; (2); JV Bsbl; JV Bsktbl; Jr NHS; Val.

ARMSTRONG, JAN B; Boise City HS; Boise City, OK; (3); Church Yth Grp; FCA; FHA; German Clb; Band; Rep Jr Cls; Rep Stu Cncl; Chrldng; Hon Roll; NHS; Gymnastics; 5 Sts Hnr Band.

ARMSTRONG, JASON; Lone Wolf Schl; Lone Wolf, OK; (2); FHA; Spanish Clb; Bsktbl; Trk; Wt Lftg; Cmnty Wkr; Cit Awd; Hon Roll; Chrstn Ldshp Awd.

ARMSTRONG, JEFF; Westmoore HS; Oklahoma City, OK; (4); 122/627; Church Yth Grp; JV Var Bsbl; Hon Roll; Pres Acad Fit Awd; SE OK St Univ; Sprts Med.

ARMSTRONG, JEREMY; Ada HS; Ada, OK; (3); Var Tennis; Hon Roll; Jr NHS; East Cntrl Univ Ada.

ARMSTRONG, JUDY F; Cordell Sr HS; Bessie, OK; (2); Rptr Church Yth Grp; Girl Scts; Natl FFA Org; Rptr Spanish Clb; Band; Mrchg Band; High Hon Roll; Hon Roll; Write Poems/Stories; Comm Svc Acts; SWOSU; Ownr Gallery.

ARMSTRONG, LINDSEY; Holdenville Jr HS; Holdenville, OK; (1); Church Yth Grp; Girl Scts; Teachers Aide; Band; Mrchg Band; Yrbk; Ofcr Stu Cncl; Hon Roll.

ARMSTRONG, MANDY L; Bixby Sr HS; Broken Arrow, OK; (1); Drama Clb; Speech Tm; School Play.

ARMSTRONG, MARIE A; Fairland Jr Sr HS; Fairland, OK; (1); Church Yth Grp; Trk; Hon Roll; Prfct Atten Awd; Natl Hnr Roll; Keybrding I Awd; Ricks Col; Marine Bio.

ARMSTRONG, MICHELLE; Empire Schl; Duncan, OK; (2); FBLA; FHA; SADD; Rptr Nwsp; Pres Soph Cls; Rep Stu Cncl; Pom Pon; Cit Awd; Kiwanis Awd; NHS; Med.

ARMSTRONG, MONICA A; Cushing HS; Cushing, OK; (1); Church Yth Grp; Drama Clb; FCA; Office Aide; Teachers Aide; Stage Crew; Hon Roll; NHS.

ARMSTRONG, SARAH R; Bishop Kelley HS; Tulsa, OK; (2); Drama Clb; French Clb; Hon Roll; Fashion; Media.

ARNALL, KEISA; Miami Sr HS; Miami, OK; (2); 24/250; Drama Clb; GAA; Varsity Clb; School Play; Ofcr Stu Cncl; Var Chrldng; Var Gym; High Hon Roll; Hon Roll; NHS; OSU; Law.

ARNETT, ERIC; Will Rogers HS; Tulsa, OK; (4); 29/200; German Clb; Wt Lftg; High Hon Roll; Hon Roll; NHS; OK ST U; Pre Med.

ARNETT, JAMES W; Henryetta Sr HS; Henryetta, OK; (2); Church Yth Grp; Chorus; School Musical; School Play; Rep Soph Cls; JV Ftbl; Var Trk; Var Wt Lftg; Guitar; Singer & Song Writer; Cartoonist; OK Chrstn U Sci/Arts; Arts.

ARNEY, AYLA; Moore HS; Oklahoma City, OK; (4); Art Clb; FBLA; Phtg Yrbk; NHS; Piano Tchr; Ttr; Chrch Pianist; Jrnlsm Awd; MSA; Svc Pin NHS; U OK.

ARNMSTRONG, TOMMY; Jay HS; Jay, OK; (3); Am Leg Boys St; Pep Clb; Quiz Bowl; VP Jr Cls; Ftbl; Wt Lftg; Wrstlng; NHS; OK ST; Pre Med.

ARNOLD, APRIL D; Charles Page HS; Sand Springs, OK; (4); 2/342; FCA; VP Key Clb; Capt Color Guard; Rep Stu Cncl; Cit Awd; High Hon Roll; NHS; Ntl Merit Ltr; Pres Acad Fit Awd; Val; 1st Pl ST Sci Engr Schlrshp; Coca Cola Fnlst Schlrshp; 2nd Pl ST Amer Legion Ortrcl; U Of Tulsa; Pol Sci/Intl Law.

ARNOLD, CHRISTY D; Morris HS; Okmulgee, OK; (1); Art Clb; Computer Clb; English Clb; GAA; Math Clb; Pep Clb; Science Clb; Acpl Chr; Band; Mrchg Band; OSU; Med Sec.

ARNOLD, CINDY; Berryhill Jr HS; Sand Springs, OK; (2); FHA; Service Clb; Spanish Clb; High Hon Roll; NHS; Val; OSU.

ARNOLD, KASY R; Colcord Schl; Colcord, OK; (4); 8/42; Church Yth Grp; FBLA; FHA; GAA; Teachers Aide; Church Choir; Ofcr Stu Cncl; Var Bsktbl; Hon Roll; Hosp Aide; Northeastern ST; Dntl Hygnst.

ARNOLD, KRISTA L; Ponca City Middle HS; Ponca City, OK; (1); Church Yth Grp; High Hon Roll; Hon Roll; OK ST Univ; Sci; Math Field.

ARNOLD, LAKEYC L; Muskogee HS; Muskogee, OK; (4); FBLA; Office Aide; Church Choir; Prfct Atten Awd; Scndry Tchr.

ARNOLD, MARY; Vinita HS; Vinita, OK; (4); 1/74; Am Leg Aux Girls St; Pres 4-H; VP Math Clb; Spanish Clb; Teachers Aide; Ed Yrbk; High Hon Roll; NHS; Val; Rec Yty Tour Wnnr 96; Jr Lion; Sr Rotarian; U Of OK; Med.

ARNOLD, NICKI L; Muskogee HS; Fort Gibson, OK; (3); FCA; French Clb; GAA; Hosp Aide; Math Clb; Office Aide; Pep Clb; JV Bsktbl; Var Socr; Var Sftbl; Med.

ARNOLD, SARA; Braman Schl; Blackwell, OK; (1); Church Yth Grp; FCA; Var Trk; High Hon Roll; NHS.

ARNOLD, SHERRY; Kingston HS; Kingston, OK; (1); Church Yth Grp; Computer Clb; Drama Clb; FCA; GAA; Girl Scts; Natl FFA Org; Chorus; Drill Tm; Flag Corp; Piano.

ARNOLD, TINA; Sayre HS; Sayre, OK; (4); 20/48; Am Leg Aux Girls St; FHA; Pep Clb; SADD; Band; Jazz Band; Nwsp; Rep Frsh Cls; Sec Sr Cls; High Hon Roll; Amer Lgn; FHA Pres & Sub-Dist Pblc Rels Offcr; Southwestern U; Math/Phys Ed.

ARNOLD, TOMI-LYNN; Tishomingo HS; Milburn, OK; (3); Natl FFA Org; Teachers Aide; Flag Corp; Yrbk; High Hon Roll; NHS; CO ST Univ.

ARPELAR, ERIC R; Mc Alester HS; Mcalester, OK; (3); 26/350; Church Yth Grp; Natl FFA Org; Spanish Clb; Acpl Chr; Band; Chorus; TSA 1st Pl Speech Hnrs; Indian Ed Ranked Rptr; Haskell Indian Nation Coll.

ARRINGTON, ANDREA; Booker T Washington HS; Tulsa, OK; (4); 29/264; Drama Clb; HOBY; Letterman Clb; Red Cross Aide; Varsity Clb; Rep Sr Cls; Rep Stu Cncl; Var Swmmng; Hon Roll; NHS; Yth & Govt Sec; Yng Demcrts Sec; Chinese Clb; Knox Coll; Scndry Educ.

ARRINGTON, KARA; Shawnee Sr HS; Shawnee, OK; (3); Church Yth Grp; Band; Drm Mjr(t); Mrchg Band; Pep Band; Chrldng; Hon Roll; Band Cncl; Big Bros/Big Sistrs Jr Brd.

ARRIOLA, JAMES F; Southeast HS; Yukon, OK; (2); Church Yth Grp; Office Aide; Scholastic Bowl; Teachers Aide; VICA; Golf; Hon Roll; News 101 Film & Edit Stories About Schl & Comm & Submit To Local News Channel; Video Editor.

ARROIKA, C W B; Indianola HS; Mcalester, OK; (2); VP Soph Cls; Var Bsktbl; Hon Roll; Greenhand FFA Awd; FFA Rprtr/Proficiency Awds; OSU.

ARROWOOD, JIMMY; Berryhill Jr HS; Tulsa, OK; (2); VP Computer Clb; FBLA; HOBY; Mu Alpha Theta; Quiz Bowl; Rep Stu Cncl; Var Bsbl; Wt Lftg; High Hon Roll; NHS; U Of Tulsa.

ARROYAVE, CLAUDIA; Claremore Sr HS; Claremore, OK; (4); Am Leg Aux Girls St; Church Yth Grp; Chorus; Yrbk; Sec Soph Cls; VP Sr Cls; Ofcr Stu Cncl; Pres Hon Roll; Prfct Atten Awd; Val; Med.

ARROYO, E CISCO; Wilburton Sr HS; Wilburton, OK; (1); Am Leg Boys St; Boy Scts; CAP; Ofcr Bsbl; Ftbl; Hon Roll; U Of Miami; Aero.

ARSTINGSTALL, CRAIG E; Midwest City HS; Midwest City, OK; (2); Var Ftbl; Var Wt Lftg; Hon Roll; Jr NHS; NHS; Prfct Atten Awd; Chrch Usher; OK ST; Law Enfrcmt.

OKLAHOMA

ARTER, CALEB; Oklahoma Bible Acad; Enid, OK; (3); Church Yth Grp; Cmnty Wkr; FCA; Chorus; Church Choir; VP Frsh Cls; VP Soph Cls; Rep Stu Cncl; Var L Bsktbl; Var L Socr.

ARTERBERRY, AARON; Ft Gibson HS; Fort Gibson, OK; (4); 4/132; Am Leg Boys St; Pres FCA; VP Math Clb; VP Science Clb; School Musical; Sprt Ed Nwsp; Ed Yrbk; Rep Stu Cncl; Socr; High Hon Roll; Oct Stu Mo; Bst Prsnlty; U Of AR; Med.

ARTHUR, CRYSTAL L; Byng Sr HS; Ada, OK; (2); Church Yth Grp; FCA; Math Clb; Natl Beta Clb; Science Clb; Chorus; Church Choir; Ofcr Stu Cncl; Hon Roll; Jr NHS; Schl Tchr/Psychtrst.

ARTHUR, JEFF; Edmond North HS; Edmond, OK; (3); 1/400; Am Leg Boys St; Boy Scts; Church Yth Grp; Cmnty Wkr; Mu Alpha Theta; ROTC; NHS; Ntl Merit Ltr; French Clb; Band; Song Of The Amer Revolution; Order Of The Daedalians Awd.

ARTHURS, RYAN; Kingfisher HS; Kingfisher, OK; (3); 1/110; Church Yth Grp; FCA; Key Clb; Quiz Bowl; Scholastic Bowl; Science Clb; Spanish Clb; Var Capt Bsktbl; Var Golf; High Hon Roll; Outstndng Chem & Bio Awds; Med.

ARTRE, ERIN; Comanche HS; Duncan, OK; (1); Church Yth Grp; German Clb; Hon Roll.

ARVIZO III, TEODORO; Oklahoma Schl Of Science; Stillwater, OK; (4); Hosp Aide; Latin Clb; Math Clb; Math Tm; Office Aide; Science Clb; Spanish Clb; Rep Soph Cls; Hon Roll; Natl Hspnc Schlrs Rcgntn Pgm; Mntrshp; MIT; Cmptr Engrng.

ARY, RAYMOND; Chandler HS; Chandler, OK; (4); 1/69; Am Leg Boys St; Pres Church Yth Grp; Natl FFA Org; Spanish Clb; Teachers Aide; Rep Stu Cncl; Trk; Hon Roll; NHS; Val; Tech Stu Assn Chptr Pres, Treas, Rprtr; OK ST U; Wildlife Mgmt.

ARYIKU, RHODA A; Westmoore HS; Oklahoma City, OK; (1); Church Yth Grp; Cmnty Wkr; Ofcr Frsh Cls; Rep Stu Cncl; Mgr(s); Tennis; Cit Awd; Hon Roll; Jr NHS; FCA; Spirit Club; Peer Hlpr; U Of OK; OB/GYN Dr.

ASAL, ELAINE M; Putnam City North HS; Oklahoma City, OK; (1); Church Yth Grp; Girl Scts; Hosp Aide; JCL; Key Clb; Latin Clb; Hon Roll; Law.

ASAVAMONCHAI, BRENT; Enid Sr HS; Enid, OK; (4); 18/412; Am Leg Boys St; Debate Tm; Drama Clb; FCA; Sec Math Clb; Speech Tm; JV Bsbl; JV Bsktbl; Var Bsbl; NHS; OK ST U; Engrng.

ASBELL, RICHARD W; Charles Page HS; Sand Springs, OK; (2); Bus Degree.

ASBILL, MATT J; Tahlequah Sr HS; Park Hill, OK; (2); Church Yth Grp; Chorus; JV Bsbl; Bsktbl; JV Var Ftbl; Jr NHS; NHS; Reg Sci Fair; CCNLL All Star Tm.

ASH, JEREMY B; Sapulpa Sr HS; Sapulpa, OK; (2); Debate Tm; Speech Tm; Acad Team; Art.

ASH, KEVIN; Westmoore HS; Oklahoma City, OK; (3); Church Yth Grp.

ASH, MISTY D; Catoosa HS; Tulsa, OK; (3); FCA; French Clb; Var Socr; Var Trk; Hon Roll; All-Dist Soccer; ST Soccer Champions 96; Trk Silver Medals Hurdles; Miss Hustle.

ASH, SHAMONE; Macarthur Sr HS; Lawton, OK; (4); Church Yth Grp; Cmnty Wkr; Hosp Aide; Science Clb; Spanish Clb; SADD; VICA; Acpl Chr; Chorus; Church Choir; Pres Xinds Phi Delta Kappa Inc 94-95; Jr Ldrshp OK Part 95-; Langston Univ; PT.

ASHBRENER, JULIE A; Wagoner Sr HS; Wagoner, OK; (3); FBLA; FHA; Sec Jr Cls; Rep Stu Cncl; Hon Roll; NHS; Frgnlang Clb Sec; Prom Cmte; OK St Univ; Math.

ASHBY, ERRYN; Edmond North HS; Edmond, OK; (2); 1/450; Cmnty Wkr; FCA; JA; Letterman Clb; Mu Alpha Theta; Spanish Clb; Rep Stu Cncl; Chrldng; Jr NHS; NHS; Nom Edmond Chmbr Comm Ldrshp Pgm; Frosh Nom Stdnt Of Yr; Multi-Yr Listee; OK ST U; Vet Med.

ASHBY, TROY; Enid Sr HS; Enid, OK; (4); 8/412; FCA; Letterman Clb; Rptr Math Clb; Varsity Clb; Chorus; Var L Bsbl; Var Trk; High Hon Roll; NHS; Church Yth Grp; We The People Team St Champs; U Of Cntrl OK; Bus Mgmt; Lawyer.

ASHBY, TYLER; Edmond North HS; Edmond, OK; (3); 1/350; Cmnty Wkr; French Clb; Letterman Clb; Mu Alpha Theta; Jr NHS; NHS; Soph Stdnt Of Yr Nom; Jr Stdnt Of Yr Nom; Nom Natl Yth Ldrshp Forum Of Med; U Of OK; Med Opthmlgy/Rdlgy.

ASHE, TONIA; Boynton Schl; Taft, OK; (3); Church Yth Grp; Debate Tm; Hosp Aide; Natl FFA Org; Quiz Bowl; Scholastic Bowl; Science Clb; Varsity Clb; Church Choir; VP Frsh Cls; Natl Vocl Tech Hnr Soc; Wendys HS Heiman Nom; Greenhand FFA Dgr; U Of OK; PT.

ASHFORD, BOBBI JEAN; Kiefer Jr Sr HS; Kiefer, OK; (2); FCA; Natl Beta Clb; Pres Frsh Cls; Ofcr Stu Cncl; Stat Bsbl; Var Bsktbl; Mgr(s); Hon Roll; Tulsa U; Psych.

ASHFORD, ROBBIE R; Blackwell HS; Blackwell, OK; (4); 7/112; Church Yth Grp; FCA; FBLA; HOBY; Letterman Clb; Pep Clb; Spanish Clb; Speech Tm; Chorus; School Musical.

ASHLEY, JERI L; Paoli HS; Paoli, OK; (4); 12/20; Church Yth Grp; FHA; Library Aide; Teachers Aide; Church Choir; Yrbk; Ofcr Jr Cls; Ofcr Sr Cls; Bsktbl; Cit Awd; Stndt Yr 94-95; Bible Study Ldr; E Cntrl Univ; Exclnt Wrtr.

ASHLEY, LYNNE; Paoli HS; Paoli, OK; (4); 11/20; Church Yth Grp; Library Aide; Church Choir; Yrbk; Ofcr Jr Cls; Ofcr Sr Cls; Cit Awd; Hon Roll; Stu Yr 94-95; Engl Tchr.

ASHLEY, SHANNON R; Ninnekah HS; Ninnekah, OK; (2); 3/45; 4-H; Model UN; Natl FFA Org; Spanish Clb; High Hon Roll; Hon Roll; OK Hon Soc 2 Yrs; Natl Lgn Merit Awd FFA 95-; ; Ffa Chptr Sec 96-; Lvstck Shwng/Jdgng Tms; OK ST Univ; Vet/Ag Ed Instr.

ASHLEY, TARA; Ada HS; Ada, OK; (3); Spanish Clb; Var JV Bsktbl; High Hon Roll; NHS; Spanish NHS.

ASHLOCK, BRIAN; Laverne Jr Sr HS; Laverne, OK; (3); 1/42; Boy Scts; Debate Tm; Natl Beta Clb; Natl FFA Org; Scholastic Bowl; Hon Roll; Jr NHS; NHS; Comps; Pre-Law.

ASHLOCK, LEON A; Graham Schl; Henryetta, OK; (4); 4/14; FHA; Nwsp; Yrbk; VP Sr Cls; Var Capt Bsktbl; Hon Roll; Prfct Atten Awd; Bsktbl All Str/All Conf; Hnrbl Mntn All ST Bsktbl; Natl Sclr Ath Awd; East Cntrl Univ; Coach.

ASHWORTH, AMBER M; Union Sr HS; Broken Arrow, OK; (3); 390/673; Church Yth Grp; Spanish Clb; Teachers Aide; Color Guard; Nrs Aide; Tulsa JC; ER Nrs; Nrsng.

ASHWORTH, RACHEL; Mt St Marys HS; Oklahoma City, OK; (2); 6/78; VP FCA; Hist French Clb; Service Clb; Sec Frsh Cls; Hist Jr Cls; Rptr Stu Cncl; L Bsktbl; L Vllybl; Cit Awd; High Hon Roll; REPS; Intr Dcrtng.

ASKINS, LINDSEY B; Westmoore HS; Oklahoma City, OK; (3); Church Yth Grp; Hosp Aide; JCL; Latin Clb; Chorus; Church Choir; School Musical; Natl Jr Classical League Latin Hnr Soc; OK ST U.

ASKINS, TREVOR B; Bartlesville Mid HS; Bartlesville, OK; (2); Art Clb; Church Yth Grp; Band; Chorus; Mrchg Band; Crs Cntry; Hon Roll; Jr NHS; Msc.

ASPER, KRISTINA; Mustang HS; Mustang, OK; (4); 1/347; Church Yth Grp; FBLA; Rptr FHA; Key Clb; Spanish Clb; Powder Puff Ftbl; High Hon Roll; NHS; Val; U Of SCI & Arts; Pre-Law.

ASTON, AMBER R; Sayre HS; Sayre, OK; (2); Church Yth Grp; Cmnty Wkr; Pharm.

ASTON, JO E; Woodland HS; Fairfax, OK; (3); Office Aide; Spanish Clb; Church Choir; School Musical; School Play; Nwsp; Yrbk; Rep Stu Cncl; Hon Roll; Pres NHS; Northeast OS ST; Inter Dsgn.

ATCHISON, MELANIE; Mustang HS; Yukon, OK; (2); Church Yth Grp; Cmnty Wkr; FCA; Ofcr Soph Cls; Trk; Hon Roll; NHS; OU.

ATHA, DAWN; Cheyenne HS; Cheyenne, OK; (4); 1/19; Church Yth Grp; 4-H; FHA; Chorus; Stage Crew; 4-H Awd; NHS; Val; Sec Frsh Cls; Sec Soph Cls; OK Bptst U.

ATHAY, TAI T; Putnam City West HS; Bethany, OK; (1); Drama Clb; Socr; Mock Trial; Midwife.

ATHERTON, SALLY E; B T Washington HS; Tulsa, OK; (3); Art Clb; Church Yth Grp; Intnl Clb; ROTC; Chorus; Church Choir; Jr NHS; NHS; Fncng Team; Amer Lgn Acad Excllnc Mdl & Awd; Psych.

ATKINS, CASEY L; Woodward HS; Woodward, OK; (1); German Clb; Band; Jazz Band; Mrchg Band; Pep Band; Sec Frsh Cls; Northwestern OSU.

ATKINSON, STACI; Blair Schl; Mangum, OK; (4); 2/30; HOBY; Sec Natl Beta Clb; Natl FFA Org; Yrbk; VP Frsh Cls; Sec Jr Cls; High Hon Roll; NHS; Sal; All Amer Schlr; Ntl Hnr Roll; U Of OK; Med.

ATTALLA, MEREDITH S; South Intermediate HS; Broken Arrow, OK; (1); Intnl Clb; Spanish Clb; Teachers Aide; Cit Awd; High Hon Roll; Jr NHS.

ATTEBERRY, ANNA; Coleman Schl; Coleman, OK; (1); 1/15; Church Yth Grp; FCA; Quiz Bowl; High Hon Roll; Val; Stu Today Awd; Sthwstrn OK ST U; Psych.

ATTERBURY, JENNIFER; Midwest City HS; Midwest City, OK; (3); 1/390; Church Yth Grp; DECA; FCA; FHA; Pep Clb; Yrbk; Sec Stu Cncl; NHS; 4 0 Clb; OK Bapt U; Nrsng.

ATUKPAWU, GRACE; Norman Sr HS; Norman, OK; (3); 1/799; Church Yth Grp; Cmnty Wkr; Pres French Clb; FBLA; Hosp Aide; JA; Math Clb; Mu Alpha Theta; Service Clb; Rep Frsh Cls; Tomorrows Ldrs; Rtry Yth Ldshp Awd; Chrch Aclyte; Harvard Univ; Med.

ATWELL, CONAN C; Duncan HS; Stillwater, OK; (2); Church Yth Grp; FBLA; Science Clb; Crs Cntry; Ftbl; Trk; Hon Roll; NHS; OK Univ; Med Field; Radiologic.

ATWOOD, BRIAN B; Union Intermediate HS; Broken Arrow, OK; (2); Boy Scts; Band; Swmmng; Hon Roll; NHS; Eagle Scout.

ATWOOD, NICK C; Shawnee Sr HS; Shawnee, OK; (3); Cmnty Wkr; FCA; French Clb; Library Aide; Office Aide; Scholastic Bowl; Teachers Aide; L Bsktbl; Intrml Vllybl; Hon Roll; Senate & House Of Reps Page; Big Brothers & Big Sisters Org.

AULAKH, KANWALJIT S; Enid Sr HS; Enid, OK; (2); 16/431; Hosp Aide; Quiz Bowl; Scholastic Bowl; Band; Jazz Band; Mrchg Band; High Hon Roll; Hon Roll; Jr NHS; NHS; Biogntcs/Biochem.

AULD, APRIL L; Shawnee Sr HS; Shawnee, OK; (2); Church Yth Grp; Spanish Clb; Hon Roll; Pub In Bk Of Poetry.

AUST, CHERYL; East Central HS; Tulsa, OK; (1); Church Yth Grp; SADD; Ofcr Frsh Cls; Chrldng; Gym; Hon Roll; Pedtrcn.

AUSTIN, AMBER Q; El Reno Sr HS; El Reno, OK; (3); 28/195; Church Yth Grp; FCA; Math Clb; Natl FFA Org; Red Cross Aide; Science Clb; Rep Jr Cls; Bsktbl; Vllybl; NHS; Central Coll-Mc Pherson KS.

AUSTIN, ANGELA R; Muskogee HS; Muskogee, OK; (3); 5/286; VP Church Yth Grp; Scholastic Bowl; Sec Science Clb; Spanish Clb; Sec Church Choir; Cit Awd; High Hon Roll; Hon Roll; Jr NHS; NHS; Minorities In Medicine Natl Macy Schlr; OK Hnr Soc; Outstdng Yth Of Yr 93-94; Washington Univ; Pre-Medicine.

AUSTIN, CANDY; Hinton HS; Geary, OK; (1); Church Yth Grp; FCA; GAA; Bsktbl; Chrldng; Crs Cntry; Powder Puff Ftbl; Score Keeper; Sftbl; Trk; OK ST U; Occptnl Thrpy.

AUSTIN, CAROLYN; Midwest City HS; Midwest City, OK; (2); German Clb; Band; Mrchg Band; Capt Chrldng; NHS; Best All-Around Frosh; Chrch Yth Group; Ed; Frgn Lang.

AUSTIN, CHRIS L; Mustang HS; Yukon, OK; (3); Church Yth Grp; FBLA; Math Clb; Quiz Bowl; Science Clb; Teachers Aide; Hon Roll; NHS; Archt.

AUSTIN, DREW A; Choctaw HS; Choctaw, OK; (2); Church Yth Grp; JV Bsktbl; Var L Golf; Cit Awd; Gov Hon Prg Awd; High Hon Roll; Jr NHS; NHS; Pres Acad Fit Awd; Val.

AUSTIN, JAIME D; Putnam City North HS; Oklahoma City, OK; (1); Church Yth Grp; PEAK.

AUSTIN, KARA; Boswell Sr HS; Boswell, OK; (1); Church Yth Grp; FCA; FHA; GAA; Key Clb; Rep Frsh Cls; Bsktbl; Chrldng; 4-H Awd; High Hon Roll; Piano; Sngng; Rdng; Sthestrn OK ST U.

AUSTIN, KATHERINE Z; Marlow HS; Marlow, OK; (3); 2/100; Church Yth Grp; FCA; Band; Drm Mjr(t); Flag Corp; Jazz Band; Rep Stu Cncl; High Hon Roll; Sal; All Regnl SWOBDA Hnr Band 3 Yrs; OK Bapt All-ST Yth Choir/Orch 3 Yrs; Howard Payne Univ.

AUSTIN, RACHEL M; Choctaw HS; Choctaw, OK; (2); Church Yth Grp; Yrbk; Chrldng; Pom Pon; Hon Roll; Pres Acad Fit Awd; U Of Cntrl OK; Psych.

AUSTIN, SARA; Tishomingo HS; Tishomingo, OK; (2); FHA; GAA; Letterman Clb; Yrbk; Pres Soph Cls; Rep VP Stu Cncl; Bsktbl; Sftbl; High Hon Roll; Southern OK ST U; Spch Thrpy.

AUSTIN, STACEY J; Mustang HS; Mustang, OK; (2); 75/365; FCA; Spanish Clb; Rptr Yrbk; Rep Frsh Cls; Rep Soph Cls; Stat Bsbl; Stat Bsktbl; Stat Ftbl; Hon Roll; NHS; Ftbl Water Girl; Bsbl & Bsktbl Stat Girl; Page For Senator Bill Gustafson; Criminologist.

AUSTIN, WILLIAM A; Choctaw HS; Choctaw, OK; (2); Church Yth Grp; JV Bsktbl; Var L Golf; High Hon Roll; Jr NHS; NHS; Pres Acad Fit Awd; Val.

AUTREY, SAMANTHA; Springer HS; Springer, OK; (3); FBLA; Library Aide; Office Aide; Teachers Aide; Ed Yrbk; Ofcr Stu Cncl; Cit Awd; High Hon Roll; Enrld Art Instr Schls; Psych.

AUTRY, JULIE M; Cordell Sr HS; Cordell, OK; (3); Art Clb; Church Yth Grp; FCA; FHA; Pep Clb; Spanish Clb; SADD; High Hon Roll; Hon Roll; NHS.

AVANTS, CARMELA; Carnegie Jr HS; Carnegie, OK; (3); 2/60; Art Clb; Church Yth Grp; Scholastic Bowl; Treas Stu Cncl; Var Bsktbl; Chrldng; Var Sftbl; Var Trk; Hon Roll; St Schlr; Outstndng Jr & Art Stdnt; OK ST U; FBI Agent.

AVERY, AERIAL A; Eisenhower Sr HS; Lawton, OK; (2); Church Yth Grp; Intnl Clb; Church Choir; Ftbl; Wt Lftg; High Hon Roll; Hon Roll; Jr NHS; NHS; Prfct Atten Awd; Afrcn Amer Essay Cont Wnnr; GATE; Tae Kwon Do; Duke; Pre Med.

AVERY, LAUREN K; Bishop Mcguinness HS; Oklahoma City, OK; (4); 5/158; FCA; Spanish Clb; SADD; Rep Frsh Cls; Rep Soph Cls; Sec Jr Cls; Ofcr Stu Cncl; Var Crs Cntry; Treas NHS; Ntl Merit SF; Art Hstry.

AVERYT, AMANDA D; Clinton HS; Clinton, OK; (2); 4-H; FBLA; Bsktbl; Hon Roll; St Schlr; OK ST Univ; Law.

AVINGTON, CORNESHIA; Central HS; Tulsa, OK; (3); Dance Clb; Chorus; School Musical; Variety Show; JV Bsktbl; Var Chrldng; Powder Puff Ftbl; Var Trk; Cit Awd; Hon Roll; Brdcstng.

AXSOM, ANDREW G; Bishop Kelley HS; Broken Arrow, OK; (3); Am Leg Boys St; Boy Scts; Debate Tm; Key Clb; NFL; Quiz Bowl; High Hon Roll; NHS; Sons Of The Amer Revolution Citizenship Awd; ST Champion Acad Decathlon; Law.

AXSOM, CALEB J; South Intermediate HS; Broken Arrow, OK; (1); Church Yth Grp; Bsktbl Tm Salv Army Bys/Grls Clb; All-Star Bsktbl Bys/Grls Clb; Sprts Med.

AXSOM, MONICA L; Bishop Kelley HS; Broken Arrow, OK; (1); Cmnty Wkr; Latin Clb; Pep Clb; Hon Roll; Pharmacist; Early Chldhd Dev.

AXTON, AMBER; Stillwater Sr HS; Stillwater, OK; (2); Church Yth Grp; FCA; Rep Soph Cls; Ofcr Stu Cncl; Var Chrldng; Hon Roll; Pres Acad Fit Awd; Masonic Awd; OK ST Univ.

AXTON, CHRISTY; Battiest Jr Sr HS; Pickens, OK; (1); Church Yth Grp; Rptr FHA; JA; Speech Tm; Rptr Nwsp; Sftbl; Hon Roll; Sal; Medcl.

AYCOX, TERRY; Hennessey HS; Hennessey, OK; (4); 2/54; Am Leg Boys St; Church Yth Grp; Quiz Bowl; Scholastic Bowl; Nwsp; Pres Soph Cls; Var Bsbl; High Hon Roll; NHS; Sal; AZ U; Astrnmy.

AYERS, KEN; Wilson HS; Wilson, OK; (2); 2/44; Computer Clb; Natl Beta Clb; Quiz Bowl; Spanish Clb; Hon Roll; NHS; Pres Acad Fit Awd; Upward Bound Math & Sci; OK Schl Sci & Math; Harvard.

AYERS, MELISSA; Piedmont HS; Piedmont, OK; (4); 7/75; Church Yth Grp; Cmnty Wkr; FBLA; Office Aide; Capt Color Guard; Mrchg Band; Pep Band; NHS; Prfct Atten Awd; Pres Acad Fit Awd; Redlands CC; Offc Admin & Tech.

AYERS, SARA; North Intemediate HS; Broken Arrow, OK; (1); Church Yth Grp; Chrldng; Wt Lftg; Hon Roll; 5 Yrs Of Dance; TJC; Dentist.

AYERS, SCOTT; Heritage Hall Schl; Oklahoma City, OK; (4); Church Yth Grp; Drama Clb; Mu Alpha Theta; Chorus; School Play; VP Sr Cls; Var Capt Bsktbl; Pres French Hon Soc; Hon Roll; Pres NHS; TX Chrstn U.

AYLWARD, JULIE; Watonga HS; Watonga, OK; (1); Church Yth Grp; FCA; FBLA; Band; Pres Frsh Cls; Ofcr Stu Cncl; Bsktbl; Trk; Hon Roll; Quiz Bowl; Hnrs Engl.

AYRES, ASHLEY; Madill HS; Madill, OK; (1); FCA; FBLA; Bsktbl; Chrldng; Crs Cntry; Trk; Hon Roll; GATE; OU; Coach.

AYRES, STEPHANIE; Midwest City HS; Tinker Afb, OK; (3); 90/386; Church Yth Grp; Spanish Clb; Band; Color Guard; Mrchg Band; Orch; Pep Band; Swmmng; L Trk; Hon Roll.

AZBELL, CHRISTOPHER; Tecumseh HS; Tecumseh, OK; (4); 3/140; Am Leg Boys St; Boy Scts; Church Yth Grp; Treas FCA; VP Math Clb; Lbrn Mu Alpha Theta; Natl Beta Clb; Office Aide; Scholastic Bowl; Science Clb; Stu Of Month; Acad Ltrmn Jckt; OSU For Minority Schlrshp; OK ST U; Envrmntl Sci.

AZIERE, PENNY N; Union Intermediate HS; Tulsa, OK; (2); French Clb; Girl Scts; Key Clb; Quiz Bowl; Color Guard; School Musical; Rptr Nwsp; Phtg Yrbk; High Hon Roll; NHS; Girl Sct Silvr Awd; Law.

AZLIN, LISA; Christian Heritage Acad; Oklahoma City, OK; (2); Church Yth Grp; Church Choir; High Hon Roll; Hon Roll; Prfct Atten Awd; Yth Cncl Chrch Pres; WA & CO Mission Trips; OK Cntrl U; Elem Ed.

BABB, KARA; Shawnee Sr HS; Shawnee, OK; (3); Church Yth Grp; Cmnty Wkr; Dance Clb; Drama Clb; FCA; HOBY; NFL; Office Aide; Service Clb; Ski Clb; Tae Kwon Do; Piano; HOBY; Poli Sci.

BABB, MEGAN R; Cushing HS; Cushing, OK; (1); 10/190; Pep Band; Chrldng; High Hon Roll.

BABCOCK, DERIC; Lone Grove HS; Ardmore, OK; (2); Boy Scts; Church Yth Grp; German Clb; Quiz Bowl; Rptr Nwsp; Var JV Trk; Var JV Wt Lftg; High Hon Roll; NHS.

BABER, MANDI; Texhoma HS; Texhoma, OK; (1); Pep Clb; Band; Sec Frsh Cls; Var Bsktbl; Var Chrldng; Trk; Cit Awd; Hon Roll; Prfct Atten Awd.

BABIONE, MOLLY B; Altus Sr HS; Altus, OK; (3); Church Yth Grp; Drama Clb; FCA; GAA; Chorus; School Musical; Ed Nwsp; Rep Soph Cls; Rep Jr Cls; Sec Stu Cncl; Video Yrbk; OK ST Univ; Jrnlsm.

BABIONE, RENEE M; Midwest City HS; Midwest City, OK; (2); 199/501; Church Yth Grp; Dance Clb; French Clb; Ed Yrbk; Judo Blue Belt; Arch.

BABONJO, SIA N; Southeast HS; Oklahoma City, OK; (1); JA; SADD; Chorus; Trk; Hon Roll; Spelman Coll; Med.

BACH, DAVID M; Westmoore HS; Oklahoma City, OK; (3); NHS; OU; Meterologist.

BACHHOFER, DUSTIN K; Marietta HS; Marietta, OK; (3); Church Yth Grp; FBLA; Natl FFA Org; JV Bsbl; Accts Pay/Rec Clerk; Admnstrtv Asstnt; Cmptr Repair.

BACIGALUPI, FORREST V; Norman Sr HS; Norman, OK; (4); Art Clb; Cmnty Wkr; Drama Clb; VP French Clb; Mu Alpha Theta; NFL; School Musical; School Play; Rep Frsh Cls; French Hon Soc; Hspnc Mrt, Commended Schlrs; Tomorrows Ldrs; WA U; Genetics.

BACKWATER, AMY J; Jay HS; Salina, OK; (2); Church Yth Grp; Hon Roll; NHS; IDFY; OK ST Univ; Hospitality Svcs.

BACKWATER, MICAH Q; Pryor Sr HS; Pryor, OK; (4); 33/150; Church Yth Grp; Debate Tm; Drama Clb; FCA; German Clb; Math Clb; Mu Alpha Theta; NFL; Speech Tm; Hon Roll; U Of Tulsa; Bus Mgmt.

BACON, CODY; Claremore Sr HS; Claremore, OK; (3); 11/268; Boy Scts; Church Yth Grp; FCA; Math Clb; Scholastic Bowl; Science Clb; SADD; Rep Jr Cls; Hon Roll; NHS; Mech Engrng.

BACON, HOLLY M; Claremore Sr HS; Claremore, OK; (1); 1/281; Church Yth Grp; Dance Clb; French Clb; Girl Scts; Speech Tm; Yrbk; Score Keeper; French Hon Soc; High Hon Roll; Silver Awrd Girl Scouts 96; OK HS Hnr Soc 95-; Matmaid Wrstlg Tm; FL ST.

BACON, MILES; Claremore Sr HS; Claremore, OK; (3); 1/237; Church Yth Grp; Pres German Clb; Library Aide; Pres Math Clb; Pres Science Clb; Church Choir; Treas Jr Cls; Hon Roll; NHS; Med.

BACU, C J; Durant HS; Durant, OK; (3); 50/200; FCA; Letterman Clb; Yrbk; Rep Frsh Cls; Rep Soph Cls; Ofcr Stu Cncl; Var L Bsbl; Var L Ftbl; Hon Roll; FL ST; Medical Field.

BAERISWY, PAMELA J; Wilson HS; Ardmore, OK; (3); 4-H; SADD; Band; Sftbl; Vol Spec Olympcs; Peds/Dntl Asst.

BAETHKE, MISSY A; Owasso Sr HS; Owasso, OK; (2); 42/451; Office Aide; Teachers Aide; Hon Roll; Ntl Merit Schol; Prfct Atten Awd; OK Univ; Acctng.

BAGBY, SARAH; Will Rogers HS; Tulsa, OK; (1); Cmnty Wkr; English Clb; Girl Scts; Hosp Aide; Key Clb; Spanish Clb; Swmmng; Tennis; High Hon Roll; Hon Roll; Earned Girl Scout Silver Awd; Marine Biologist.

BAGGITT, CHARLES E; Enid Sr HS; Enid, OK; (2); 268/430; Church Yth Grp; Band; Church Choir; Mrchg Band; Electronics; Coast Guard.

BAGINSKI, JENNIFER A; Bartlesville Sr HS; Bartlesville, OK; (3); 154/450; Band; Mrchg Band; Pep Band; Hon Roll; U Of OK; Meteorolgy.

BAGWELL, JESSICA C; Union Sr HS; Broken Arrow, OK; (3); 27/741; Quiz Bowl; Spanish Clb; NHS; Pres Acad Fit Awd; Spanish NHS; Acad Rsrc Ctr; Renaissance.

BAGWELL, MONICA S; Trinity Christian Schl; Tulsa, OK; (3); Church Yth Grp; Orch; Bsktbl; Mgr(s); Socr; Vllybl; Hon Roll; Mech Engr.

BAHLINGER, ERIN E; Bishop Kelley HS; Tulsa, OK; (4); Cmnty Wkr; Drama Clb; Hosp Aide; Speech Tm; Chorus; School Play; Stage Crew; Bsktbl; Cit Awd; Hon Roll; Schl Mascot; Drama/Spch Ed.

BAILEY, BILL; Anadarko HS; Anadarko, OK; (4); 6/107; Am Leg Boys St; FCA; FBLA; Sec Natl FFA Org; Rep Stu Cncl; Var Bsbl; Gov Hon Prg Awd; High Hon Roll; NHS; Pres Acad Fit Awd; OK ST U; Vet.

BAILEY, BRIAN B; Edmond Memorial HS; Edmond, OK; (1); 80/437; Spanish Clb; Bsktbl; Hon Roll; Jr NHS; Pres Acad Fit Awd; Farm; Church Confirmation; Sports Med.

BAILEY, BRYAN; Holdenville HS; Wewoka, OK; (3); Capt Quiz Bowl; Scholastic Bowl; Ofcr Stu Cncl; Var Bsbl; Var Bsktbl; Var Crs Cntry; High Hon Roll; Jr NHS; NHS; Prfct Atten Awd; S W OK ST; Phrmcy.

BAILEY, CINDY L; Dover Schl; Dover, OK; (1); FCA; Ed Natl FFA Org; Chorus; Pres Frsh Cls; Var Chrldng; High Hon Roll; Chrch Act; Vocal Lessons; Redlands CC; Sec.

BAILEY, JALYN; Cushing HS; Cushing, OK; (2); #1 in class; Church Yth Grp; 4-H; Quiz Bowl; Spanish Clb; Rep Band; Jazz Band; Mrchg Band; Pep Band; Var Tennis; High Hon Roll; OSU; Bio.

BAILEY, JENIFER M; Casady Schl; Oklahoma City, OK; (4); Pres Art Clb; Church Yth Grp; Cmnty Wkr; Dance Clb; Drama Clb; FCA; Sec French Clb; GAA; Pep Clb; SADD; John R Cook Awd; Natl Fr Awd Regn; Natl Fr Awd Natn; OKU.

BAILEY, JILL; Paden HS; Paden, OK; (4); 1/20; Church Yth Grp; 4-H; FHA; SADD; JV Var Bsktbl; Cit Awd; 4-H Awd; High Hon Roll; NHS; Val; Seminol JC; Erly Chldhd Dev.

BAILEY, KELLI A; Bartlesville Mid HS; Bartlesville, OK; (2); JA; Office Aide; Spanish Clb; Hon Roll.

BAILEY, KENDRIC; Coweta HS; Coweta, OK; (4); Am Leg Boys St; Capt Scholastic Bowl; Pres Science Clb; Band; Jazz Band; Nwsp; Rep Stu Cncl; Jr NHS; NHS; U Of OK; Engrng.

BAILEY, MEAGAN; Holdenville HS; Wewoka, OK; (3); 1/80; HOBY; Pres Natl Beta Clb; Scholastic Bowl; Band; Drm Mjr(t); VP Jr Cls; Ofcr Stu Cncl; Var Bsktbl; Var Trk; High Hon Roll; TX A&M; Optmtry.

BAILEY, MISTY; Panama HS; Panama, OK; (2); Quiz Bowl; Band; Drm Mjr(t); Sec Soph Cls; Hon Roll; NHS; Pres Acad Fit Awd; Med.

BAILEY, ROBERT; Eufaula Sr HS; Eufaula, OK; (2); Church Yth Grp; Natl FFA Org; Rep Frsh Cls; Var Ftbl; Var Wt Lftg; Hon Roll; NHS; OK Honor Socty; Stu Of Today Awd.

BAILEY, STEPHANIE; Chisholm Sr HS; Carrier, OK; (4); 10/70; FCA; Natl FFA Org; Rptr Nwsp; Ed Yrbk; Rep Sr Cls; Ofcr Stu Cncl; Sftbl; Hon Roll; NHS; Sthwstrn OK ST; Medcl Fld.

BAIN, JARED; Ponca City Sr HS; Ponca City, OK; (4); Church Yth Grp; Cmnty Wkr; Treas Natl FFA Org; Variety Show; Hon Roll; NE OK A&M Univ; Ag Ed.

BAKER, AMBER M; Ponca City Middle HS; Ponca City, OK; (1); Church Yth Grp; Hon Roll.

BAKER, ANGELA M; Tuttle HS; Tuttle, OK; (3); FHA; GAA; Spanish Clb; Ofcr Stu Cncl; Bsktbl; Crs Cntry; OK ST Univ; Elem Educ.

BAKER, AUDREY; Chelsea HS; Chelsea, OK; (4); 2/95; FBLA; FHA; Chorus; High Hon Roll; NHS; Sal; TSA Pres; Multiple Yr Listing.

BAKER, AUTUMN; Keifer Public Schl; Sapulpa, OK; (2); FCA; GAA; Bsktbl; Chrldng; Sftbl; Wt Lftg; Cit Awd.

BAKER, BETHANY; Cimarron Christian Acad; Mannford, OK; (3); Church Yth Grp; Cmnty Wkr; Teachers Aide; Chorus; Church Choir; School Play; Stage Crew; Var Bsktbl; Var Sftbl; Cit Awd; Equstrn Rdng; Piano.

BAKER, BILL J; Tahlequah Sr HS; Tahlequah, OK; (2); Wrstlng; U Of AR; Arch.

BAKER, BRADLEY A; Union Intermediate HS; Tulsa, OK; (2); CAP; German Clb; Hon Roll; NHS; Aviation Explrs; Aerontcl Engr.

BAKER, BRICE; Cheyenne HS; Cheyenne, OK; (3); Church Yth Grp; FCA; VP Frsh Cls; VP Soph Cls; VP Jr Cls; Var Bsbl; Var Bsktbl; Cit Awd; Hon Roll; Prfct Atten Awd; OSU.

BAKER, BROOKE; Victory Christian Schl; Jenks, OK; (2); Teachers Aide; Acpl Chr; Chorus; Var Chrldng; High Hon Roll; Jr NHS; NHS; Natl Finals Soloist.

BAKER, CARRIE A; El Reno Sr HS; Yukon, OK; (3); 55/195; Church Yth Grp; Key Clb; Speech Tm; Teachers Aide; School Play; Stage Crew; Nwsp; Cit Awd; Hon Roll; Comm Ldshp Class; U Of Cntrl OK; Mgnt Inf Systms.

BAKER, CASSY; Hulbert Jr Sr HS; Tahlequah, OK; (2); Church Yth Grp; 4-H; Chorus; Sec Soph Cls; Bsktbl; Sftbl; Trk; Hon Roll; Jr NHS; Prfct Atten Awd; Phys Thrpy.

BAKER, CELENA R; Putnam City West HS; Oklahoma City, OK; (2); Church Yth Grp; HOBY; Intnl Clb; Treas Frsh Cls; Treas Soph Cls; JV Sftbl; Wrstlng; NHS; Spanish Clb; SADD; OASC St Convention Comm Head; Gftd & Tlntd; OK ST U; Mrktg; Advertising.

BAKER, DANNY; Little Axe Sr HS; Newalla, OK; (2); Math Clb; Quiz Bowl; Scholastic Bowl; Science Clb; Band; Pep Band; Rep Stu Cncl; Ftbl; Trk; Wt Lftg; MIT; Mech Engr.

BAKER, DAVID M; Antlers Sr HS; Antlers, OK; (3); 3/65; Am Leg Boys St; Church Yth Grp; FCA; Quiz Bowl; School Play; Var Bsbl; Var Fld Hcky; Sprt Ed Cit Awd; Gov Hon Prg Awd; High Hon Roll; OK Hnr Soc Awd; Duke Univ Tlnt ID Prgm High Scorer Math Awd; Schl Orgnzd Drug Free Prgm Stdnt Cncl; Sprts Med/Orthscpc Surgeon.

BAKER, ELIESE; Cordell Sr HS; Cordell, OK; (4); Church Yth Grp; Cmnty Wkr; FHA; Pep Clb; Teachers Aide; Chorus; Church Choir; Variety Show; Sec Treas Frsh Cls; Sec Treas Soph Cls.

BAKER, JAMES E; Purcell HS; Purcell, OK; (3); Hosp Aide; Var JV Bsktbl; JV Ftbl; High Hon Roll; Hon Roll; Pres Acad Fit Awd.

BAKER, JAY; Sapulpa Sr HS; Sapulpa, OK; (3); 13/300; Church Yth Grp; VP FBLA; Sec Key Clb; JV Bsbl; Var Ftbl; Var Wrstlng; High Hon Roll; NHS; Pres Acad Fit Awd; Spanish NHS; Chftn Mnth 1995 & 1996; Acad Hnr Bnqt 1995 & 1996; Elctrcl Engr.

BAKER, JENNIFER; Talihina Sr HS; Wister, OK; (4); 1/36; Rep Am Leg Aux Girls St; FCA; Speech Tm; VP Sr Cls; Capt Bsktbl; Var Sftbl; Var Trk; Hon Roll; Val; Natl FFA Org; Local FFA Chptr Pres; Bsktbl Coach.

BAKER, JOHN D; Claremore Sr HS; Claremore, OK; (3); Natl FFA Org; Prfct Atten Awd; Precision Mach Shop Vo-Tech.

BAKER, JULIE D; Moore HS; Norman, OK; (3); 13/530; French Clb; Office Aide; Scholastic Bowl; Science Clb; Chorus; Trk; Jr NHS; NHS; Peer Cnslr; NHS Sec; U Of OK; Bio Chem.

BAKER, KELLEY D; Cashion HS; Cashion, OK; (1); Church Yth Grp; FCA; Church Choir; Bsktbl; High Hon Roll; Swimming; Sftbl; Reading; Arch.

BAKER, KYLE; Bartlesville Sr HS; Bartlesville, OK; (3); Church Yth Grp; FCA; JA; Rptr Nwsp; Rptr Lit Mag; OK Bapt U.

BAKER, LOWELL L; Enid Sr HS; Enid, OK; (2); Boy Scts; Church Yth Grp; Cmnty Wkr; Quiz Bowl; Scholastic Bowl; High Hon Roll; Hon Roll; JETS Awd; Jr NHS; NHS; PADT Cert Open Wtr Scuba Dvr; Ham Radio Oper.

BAKER, MATTHEW E; Western Heights Sr HS; Oklahoma City, OK; (3); Church Yth Grp; Cmnty Wkr; FCA; FBLA; FHA; Key Clb; Teachers Aide; Acpl Chr; Chorus; Church Choir; Chrch Yth Pres; SMU; Music Composer.

BAKER, MELISSA; Aline-Cleo Jr Sr HS; Cleo Springs, OK; (1); 1/22; Church Yth Grp; FCA; Pep Clb; Band; VP Frsh Cls; Var Bsktbl; Var Sftbl; Jr NHS; NHS; Pres Acad Fit Awd; N W Hnr & Red Carpet Hnr Bands.

BAKER, MISHA L; Union Intermediate HS; Broken Arrow, OK; (1); Key Clb; Office Aide; Band; Pep Band; Swmmng; High Hon Roll; NHS; Guitar; Dance; Perf Arts; Choreography.

BAKER, MISTY D; Tishomingo HS; Denver, CO; (4); Art Clb; Computer Clb; Office Aide; Spanish Clb; Teachers Aide; Hon Roll; NHS; Pres Acad Fit Awd; Cit Awd; Top Ten Percent Voc-Tech Fshn Dsgn; EMT.

BAKER, NICHOLAS K; Sapulpa Sr HS; Sapulpa, OK; (3); #6 in class; Church Yth Grp; FCA; Ofcr Bsbl; Bsktbl; High Hon Roll; Hon Roll; NHS; Prfct Atten Awd; Pres Acad Fit Awd.

BAKER, RHONDA S; Yukon Middle HS; Yukon, OK; (3); Church Yth Grp; FCA; Nwsp; Yrbk; Hon Roll; Southwestern OK ST U; Cmptrs.

BAKER, SETH; Oklahoma Christian Schl; Edmond, OK; (4); 9/36; Am Leg Boys St; Church Yth Grp; Drama Clb; FCA; Stage Crew; VP Frsh Cls; VP Soph Cls; Pres Jr Cls; Pres Sr Cls; Ftbl; Lake Forest; Phys Ther.

BAKER, STEPHEN; Seminole Jr Sr HS; Seminole, OK; (3); Am Leg Boys St; Church Yth Grp; Cmnty Wkr; French Clb; Letterman Clb; Math Clb; SADD; Varsity Clb; Band; Church Choir; Crimeology.

BAKER, SUMMER; Reydon HS; Durham, OK; (2); 2/13; Cmnty Wkr; FHA; Library Aide; Varsity Clb; Chorus; School Musical; Rptr Nwsp; Var L Bsktbl; JV L Trk; High Hon Roll; SWIM Rep; GATE Stu; St Cmptn Choir; Med; Secretarial Records.

BAKER, TY L; Oologah HS; Claremore, OK; (2); 10/90; Church Yth Grp; Cmnty Wkr; FCA; Intnl Clb; Science Clb; SADD; Rep Frsh Cls; Sec Soph Cls; Rep Stu Cncl; L Var Bsbl; Med.

BAKER, WREN J; Valliant HS; Valliant, OK; (4); 11/88; Church Yth Grp; FCA; French Clb; Pres FHA; Office Aide; Q&S; Quiz Bowl; Spanish Clb; Stage Crew; Co-Capt Yrbk; Southeastern OK ST U.

BAKEWELL, DANIEL J; Lindsay HS; Lindsay, OK; (2); #1 in class; VP Art Clb; Church Yth Grp; FCA; Math Clb; Math Tm; Quiz Bowl; Scholastic Bowl; SADD; Yrbk; Rep Stu Cncl.

BALDERAS, CHRISTOPHER W; Tipton Jr Sr HS; Tipton, OK; (2); Church Yth Grp; Science Clb; Band; Church Choir; Mrchg Band; Pep Band; Hon Roll; NHS.

BALDERAS, MICHELLE; Tipton Jr Sr HS; Tipton, OK; (3); 8/29; Church Yth Grp; Band; Pres Frsh Cls; Pres Soph Cls; Pres Jr Cls; Hon Roll; Jr NHS; NHS; Prfct Atten Awd; WOSC; Comp Sci.

BALDRIDGE, JASON; White Oak Jr-Sr HS; Vinita, OK; (1); 1/14; Science Clb; VP Frsh Cls; Var Bsbl; Var Bsktbl; Var Ftbl; High Hon Roll; NHS; Pres Awd For Edctnl Excl; Comp Pgmng.

BALDRIDGE, ROY; White Oak Jr-Sr HS; Vinita, OK; (4); 4/25; Math Tm; Quiz Bowl; Science Clb; VP Sr Cls; Var Bsbl; Var Bsktbl; Var Ftbl; Hon Roll; Ftbl 8 Man All-St; Commnctns.

BALDWIN, AMBER; Empire Schl; Duncan, OK; (2); Church Yth Grp; Science Clb; Chorus; Church Choir; School Musical.

BALDWIN, BRETT A; Lawton Sr HS; Lawton, OK; (2); Boy Scts; Church Yth Grp; FCA; HOBY; Key Clb; Quiz Bowl; Pres Spanish Clb; Var Socr; High Hon Roll; NHS; Pre-Med.

BALDWIN, DANIEL; Blackwell HS; Blackwell, OK; (3); Drama Clb; Speech Tm; Band; Jazz Band; Mrchg Band; Pep Band; School Musical; Stage Crew; JV Bsbl; Hon Roll; Band NOC Hnr, Ltr; Amer Leg Bsbl; Northwestern ST Coll; Music.

BALDWIN, DENISE; Lawton Sr HS; Lawton, OK; (3); Spanish Clb; Chrldng; Hon Roll; Co-Ed Cmptn Squad.

BALDWIN, DENNIS; Douglass HS; Oklahoma City, OK; (2); Ftbl; Golf; Wrstlng; High Hon Roll; Dist Perf Awds/Myr Yth Emplyment 95; Cert Achvmt Math 95; Acad Achvmt 95; Cert Achvmt JTPA 95; Elec/Mech Engrng.

BALDWIN, KATHY S; Owasso Sr HS; Owasso, OK; (4); 25/357; Church Yth Grp; FCA; Office Aide; Spanish Clb; VICA; Crs Cntry; Trk; High Hon Roll; NHS; Temple Yth Grp; 9th Grd Most Imprvd Cross Cntry Rnnr; Yth Alive Bible Study.

BALDWIN, KELLY; Wilburton Jr HS; Wilburton, OK; (1); Church Yth Grp; Cmnty Wkr; Pres Stu Cncl; Bsktbl; Hon Roll; NHS; Prfct Atten Awd; Southwestern OK ST U.

BALDWIN, KIANA; Mc Lain Career Acad; Tulsa, OK; (4); DECA; Rep Stu Cncl; Zeno; Jackson ST Univ; Cmptr Sci.

BALDWIN, KRISTIN; Holdenville Jr HS; Holdenville, OK; (1); Church Yth Grp; Office Aide; Band; Chorus; Church Choir; Mrchg Band; Pep Band; Rep Frsh Cls; JV Chrldng; Hon Roll.

BALDWIN-DICKSON, JENNIFER; Tahlequah Sr HS; Tahlequah, OK; (4); 34/241; Drama Clb; French Clb; Office Aide; School Play; Rptr Nwsp; Ed Lit Mag; High Hon Roll; Hon Roll; All-Am Schlrs; Natl Hnr Rll; Erskn Fllw & GA Cert Mrt; Northeastern ST U; Elem Ed.

BALES, MENDI L; Panola HS; Red Oak, OK; (2); Drama Clb; Natl FFA Org; Chorus; School Play; Sec Soph Cls; Ofcr Stu Cncl; Bsktbl; Sftbl; Hon Roll; St Acad Champs Var Bsktbl; St Quarterfinalist Var Bsktbl; HS Math Tchr; Coach.

BALES, MISSY; Chisholm Sr HS; Enid, OK; (2); 1/100; Church Yth Grp; FCA; VP FHA; Scholastic Bowl; Spanish Clb; Chorus; Rep Soph Cls; Var Chrldng; Hon Roll; OK ST U; Pre-Med.

BALES, THOMAS B; Ponca City Middle HS; Ponca City, OK; (1); Church Yth Grp; Pep Clb; Chorus; Nwsp; Yrbk; Bsktbl; Chrldng; Ftbl; High Hon Roll; NHS; OK ST; Pediatrcn.

BALES, TIM; Kellyville Sr HS; Kellyville, OK; (4); 37/65; Office Aide; Pres VP VICA; Pres Soph Cls; Ofcr Bsbl; Chrldng; Ftbl; Wrstlng; Law Enforcement 95 St Champ, 4th Pl In Natls 95; Rose ST Coll; Criminal Justice.

BALL, ALLYNN B; Sapulpa Sr HS; Sapulpa, OK; (3); Church Yth Grp; Key Clb; Math Clb; Science Clb; Spanish Clb; Band; Mrchg Band; Nwsp; Yrbk; Socr; Mst Otstdng Eng Stdnt 9th Grd; OK Univ.

BALL, CORI M; Capitol Hill HS; Oklahoma City, OK; (3); Drama Clb; Office Aide; Pep Clb; School Play; Stage Crew; Bsktbl; Mgr(s); Sftbl; Hon Roll; Camp Fire Boys & Clb; Theatre.

BALL, MICHAEL H; Putnam City North HS; Oklahoma City, OK; (2); Church Yth Grp; Key Clb; ROTC; Band; Drill Tm; Mrchg Band; OK Univ; PT.

BALL, ROBERT B; Bartlesville Mid HS; Bartlesville, OK; (2); Church Yth Grp; HOBY; Letterman Clb; VP Chorus; JV Bsbl; JV Bsktbl; Var Ftbl; Hon Roll; Pres Acad Fit Awd; DARE Rep; Music Ed.

BALL, TAMINA A; John Marshall HS; Oklahoma City, OK; (1); Church Yth Grp; Drama Clb; Spanish Clb; School Musical; School Play; Stage Crew; High Hon Roll; Started A Bible Stud At Chrch.

BALLARD, AMANDA B; Pauls Valley HS; Pauls Valley, OK; (1); Church Yth Grp; GAA; Natl FFA Org; Bsktbl; Trk; Hon Roll; East Cntrl Univ; Phy Thrpst.

BALLARD, GREG A; Healdton HS; Ringling, OK; (2); Church Yth Grp; 4-H; Stage Crew; L Bsktbl; L Golf; Capt L Trk; Hon Roll; NHS; Pres Schlr; Industrial Arts Awd.

BALLARD, JEREMY; North Intemediate HS; Broken Arrow, OK; (1); Church Yth Grp; JV Bsbl; Bsktbl; Ftbl; Wt Lftg; Hon Roll; Jr NHS; NHS; Ltl League Umpire; Electrician Asst; OU; Sports Med.

BALLARD, KATE; Pryor Sr HS; Pryor, OK; (3); Church Yth Grp; FHA; German Clb; Chorus; School Musical; Rep Frsh Cls; Rep Soph Cls; Rep Stu Cncl; Stat Bsktbl; Stat Mgr(s); Northeastern ST Univ; Psych.

BALLARD, MATTHEW E; Trinity Christian Schl; Tulsa, OK; (3); 7/12; Church Yth Grp; Speech Tm; Church Choir; School Musical; School Play; VP Jr Cls; L Bsktbl; L Golf; L Socr; Hon Roll; Bob Jones Univ.

BALLARD, MICHELLE; Claremore Sr HS; Claremore, OK; (2); Church Yth Grp; Spanish Clb; Teachers Aide; High Hon Roll; Prfct Atten Awd.

BALLARD, MICHELLE R; Muskogee HS; Muskogee, OK; (3); Church Yth Grp; Computer Clb; FBLA; JCL; Latin Clb; Office Aide; Hon Roll; Jr NHS; NHS; OK Hnr Soc; Octgn Clb; Eclgy Clb; OU; Optmety.

BALLARD, ROBBY D; Meeker HS; Meeker, OK; (2); Cit Awd; High Hon Roll; Prfct Atten Awd; EMT.

BALLARD, SHAUNA R; Checotah HS; Council Hill, OK; (4); 19/90; Office Aide; Teachers Aide; Band; Color Guard; Mrchg Band; Ed Yrbk; High Hon Roll; Hon Roll; Joint Enrllmt Connors St Coll 95-96; Connors ST Coll; Bus Accntg.

BALLENGER, TERESA; North Intemediate HS; Gore, OK; (3); Church Yth Grp; FTA; Acpl Chr; Church Choir; High Hon Roll; Hon Roll; Jr NHS; NHS; Pres Acad Fit Awd; NSU; Ed.

BALLEW, JAIME; Collinsville HS; Collinsville, OK; (4); 22/102; Cmnty Wkr; Office Aide; Spanish Clb; Cit Awd; High Hon Roll; All Amer Schlr At Large; Natl Ldrshp & Svc Awds; US Natl Ldrshp Mrt Awd; E Central U; Cnslng.

BALLEW, JOHN C; Macarthur Sr HS; Lawton, OK; (4); 2/160; French Clb; Office Aide; High Hon Roll; Jr NHS; Pres Acad Fit Awd; Sal; St Schlr; Univ Of OK; Comp.

BALLEW, RICKY J; Western Heights Sr HS; Oklahoma City, OK; (2); Boy Scts; Cmnty Wkr; ROTC; Spanish Clb; SADD; Teachers Aide; AFJROTC Drll Tm, Saber Tm Ldr, Clr Grd, Mrtrs Achvt Awd; NJROTC Drll Tm, Clr Grd, NCO Chrg, Exemp; TX A&M; Elec Engrng.

BALTHROP, COURTNEY D; Yukon Middle HS; Oklahoma City, OK; (1); Church Yth Grp; FCA; FHA; Spanish Clb; Church Choir; Hon Roll.

BALTIERRA, FRED S; Indiahoma Schl; Indiahoma, OK; (2); Church Yth Grp; FCA; Rep Frsh Cls; VP Soph Cls; JV Bsktbl; High Hon Roll; Hon Roll; NHS; OK Hnr Soc; Natl Young Ldrs Conf Cand; Inter Schltc Cont Ger 2nd Pl; USF; Surgeon.

BAN, TRACY; El Reno Sr HS; Yukon, OK; (4); 25/173; Cmnty Wkr; Key Clb; Math Clb; Science Clb; Bsktbl; Crs Cntry; Tennis; High Hon Roll; Hon Roll; Kiwanis Awd; OU.

BANDY, JOHN; Amber Pocasset Jr Sr HS; Tuttle, OK; (2); Church Yth Grp; Computer Clb; Math Clb; Science Clb; Spanish Clb; School Play; High Hon Roll; NHS; Mascot; Visual Effects Art.

BANDY, LINDSEY B; Verden HS; Anadarko, OK; (1); Church Yth Grp; Sec Treas FHA; Scholastic Bowl; Science Clb; Church Choir; Bsktbl; Sftbl; High Hon Roll; Hon Roll; Pres Acad Fit Awd; OK HS Hnr Soc; FCA; Tch Presch Bible Schl; OK Univ; Legal/Med Fld.

BANDY, SHEA; Comanche HS; Comanche, OK; (4); Am Leg Boys St; Art Clb; German Clb; Office Aide; Science Clb; Ofcr Bsbl; Ftbl; Trk; Wt Lftg; NHS; Medcl Tech.

BANGURA, OSMONDA; B T Washington HS; Tulsa, OK; (3); Church Yth Grp; French Clb; Rep Jr Cls; VP Stu Cncl; Trk; OK St Univ; Premed.

BANIS, MARY C; Claremore Sr HS; Claremore, OK; (1); Church Yth Grp; Band; Mrchg Band; OK Univ; Tchng.

BANK, WHITNEY; Elk City HS; Elk City, OK; (4); 9/130; Computer Clb; Key Clb; Letterman Clb; Math Clb; Office Aide; Pep Clb; Science Clb; Spanish Clb; Band; Mrchg Band; OK U.

BANKS, ANGIE; Blanche Thomas Jr Sr HS; Sentinel, OK; (4); 4/28; Church Yth Grp; 4-H; Pres Treas FHA; Pres Natl Beta Clb; Quiz Bowl; Teachers Aide; VP Frsh Cls; Sec Soph Cls; Pres Jr Cls; Pres Stu Cncl; OK St Univ; Bus.

BANKS, CHANTRY S; Hammon Schl; Hammon, OK; (2); Church Yth Grp; HOBY; Quiz Bowl; Speech Tm; Chorus; Pres Frsh Cls; Rep Soph Cls; Cit Awd; High Hon Roll; OK City U; Theatre.

BANKS, J R; White Oak Jr-Sr HS; Chelsea, OK; (4); 2/24; Math Clb; Quiz Bowl; Science Clb; Sec Soph Cls; Pres Sr Cls; Var Ftbl; Hon Roll; NHS; Sal; Meteorlgy.

BANKS, KATHY; Sapulpa Sr HS; Sapulpa, OK; (3); Church Yth Grp; Dance Clb; GAA; Sec Key Clb; Letterman Clb; VP Natl FFA Org; Science Clb; Teachers Aide; Sec Jr Cls; Bsktbl; OK ST U; Elem Tchr.

BANKS, KRISTEN M; Durant HS; Durant, OK; (2); Church Yth Grp; Drama Clb; 4-H; Chorus; Variety Show; JV Var Bsktbl; Hon Roll; Southeastern OK; Bus/Fshn Dsgn.

BANKS, LISA M; Mc Loud HS; Mc Loud, OK; (3); 52/135; Library Aide; Phtg Yrbk; Sftbl; Hon Roll; Elem Tchr.

BANKS, MARRI; Checotah HS; Checotah, OK; (3); 7/120; FBLA; HOBY; SADD; Pres Frsh Cls; Sec Stu Cncl; Var JV Bsktbl; Var JV Chrldng; High Hon Roll; NHS; Pres Schlr; Rebekkas Plgrmg Ambass; Psychnlgy.

BANNING, LAURISA A; Stillwater Sr HS; Stillwater, OK; (2); Church Yth Grp; French Clb; Key Clb; Band; Church Choir; Mrchg Band; Pep Band; Dancing, Tap & Ballet; TX Chrstn Univ.

BANNING, RANDY L; Shawnee Sr HS; Shawnee, OK; (3); Church Yth Grp; FCA; Ftbl; Socr; Hon Roll.

BANTA, JANA N; Pauls Valley HS; Pauls Valley, OK; (2); Church Yth Grp; Debate Tm; FBLA; FHA; Rep Key Clb; Natl FFA Org; Sec Spanish Clb; Speech Tm; SADD; Hon Roll; Funniest In Class Frosh; OK ST Univ; Mass Comm.

BANUELOS, ARTURO; Thomas Jr Sr HS; Thomas, OK; (3); 26/38; Chess Clb; Church Yth Grp; FCA; HOBY; Letterman Clb; Quiz Bowl; Speech Tm; Band; Church Choir; Mrchg Band; Clark U; Music Bus.

BARBEE, CLAY; Foyil Schl; Claremore, OK; (3); Church Yth Grp; Key Clb; Church Choir; School Play; Yrbk; Bsktbl; Socr; Hon Roll; Rogers St; Sci.

BARBER, JENNIFER A; Yukon Middle HS; Yukon, OK; (3); 77/407; FCA; FHA; Hosp Aide; Teachers Aide; Sftbl; Cit Awd; NHS; OK ST; Interior Design.

BARBOUR, SARAH J; Edmond Memorial HS; Edmond, OK; (2); 1/415; FCA; Math Clb; Mu Alpha Theta; Spanish Clb; Phtg Nwsp; JV Vllybl; High Hon Roll; NHS; Pres Schlr; Yng Life; Pre-Med.

BARBY, ASHLEA; Laverne Jr Sr HS; Laverne, OK; (3); 1/37; Am Leg Aux Girls St; Natl Beta Clb; Natl FFA Org; Sec Jr Cls; Var Bsktbl; High Hon Roll; NHS; 4-H; Letterman Clb; Treas Frsh Cls; FFA Pres/Swthrt; All ST Trck/Crs Cntry; Acad Tm; Amer Lgn Schl Awd.

BARDIN, JASON W; Davis HS; Davis, OK; (3); 15/80; Debate Tm; Drama Clb; 4-H; Speech Tm; School Musical; School Play; Nwsp; Rep Frsh Cls; Stat Score Keeper; Cit Awd; Acad Tm; OK ST U; Recrtn Wrkr.

BARDIN, JEREMY J; Tishomingo HS; Milburn, OK; (3); Church Yth Grp; FCA; Letterman Clb; Varsity Clb; Band; Mrchg Band; Pep Band; JV Bsbl; Var L Bsktbl; Var L Crs Cntry; IA A&M Univ; Oceangrphy.

BARE, DOUG; Gracemont HS; Gracemont, OK; (2); Ofcr Bsbl; Bus Profs of Am; Trk; Hon Roll; Prfct Atten Awd; Acad Tm.

BARE, GREGORY A; Owasso Sr HS; Claremore, OK; (3); 56/405; Church Yth Grp; Var Capt Tennis; Hon Roll; U Of Tulsa; Pre-Med.

BAREFOOT, AMY S; Putnam City West HS; Bethany, OK; (2); Cmnty Wkr; Drama Clb; Office Aide; Red Cross Aide; Spanish Clb; SADD; Teachers Aide; School Musical; School Play; Stage Crew; Tap Dncng 10 Yrs.

BAREFOOT, BETH A; Putnam City West HS; Bethany, OK; (4); 37/285; Art Clb; Cmnty Wkr; French Clb; German Clb; Red Cross Aide; Scholastic Bowl; SADD; Band; Swmmng; NHS; NHS VP; Bio Clb VP; U Of OK; Anthropology.

BAREFOOT, BRIAN S; Blanchard Jr Sr HS; Blanchard, OK; (2); Church Yth Grp; Cmnty Wkr; FCA; Office Aide; Teachers Aide; Ofcr Bsbl; Bsktbl; Score Keeper; Wt Lftg; OK City U; Law; Bus.

BARENTINE, DUSTIN L; Pocola HS; Pocola, OK; (3); FBLA; Quiz Bowl; Band; Jazz Band; Mrchg Band; Bsktbl; Golf; Mgr(s); Trk; Wt Lftg; U Of AR.

BARESEL, MARY T; Edmond Memorial HS; Edmond, OK; (1); High Hon Roll; Hon Roll; TAEKWONDO Red Belt; OK HS Hnr Soc; Pres Ed Awds Prgm.

BARGAS, KEVIN E; Mc Alester HS; Mcalester, OK; (4); 17/206; Quiz Bowl; Spanish Clb; Jazz Band; Mrchg Band; Rptr Nwsp; Cit Awd; NHS; Church Yth Grp; Band; Pep Band; OK Hon Soc; Superior Rated Trombone Solo OK ST Cntst; Southeastern OK All-Dist Band 3 Yrs; Eastern OK ST Coll; Entrprnrs.

BARKER, AMANDA D; Clinton HS; Clinton, OK; (4); 40/88; Church Yth Grp; FCA; FBLA; FHA; FTA; Spanish Clb; Teachers Aide; Chorus; Treas Sr Cls; Chrmn Stu Cncl; USAD; Bus.

BARKER, BLAKE; Ft Towson HS; Fort Towson, OK; (2); 5/35; Church Yth Grp; FCA; Quiz Bowl; VP Frsh Cls; Var Bsbl; Stat Bsktbl; Tech Stu Assoc Treas.

BARKER, JENNY; Waynoka HS; Waynoka, OK; (4); Church Yth Grp; Cmnty Wkr; HOBY; Library Aide; Pep Clb; Stage Crew; Bsktbl; Hon Roll; Val; All Amer Schlrs; Engr.

BARKER, JOSHUA R; Noble HS; Noble, OK; (3); 28/164; Church Yth Grp; FCA; Mu Alpha Theta; SADD; JV Bsktbl; Hon Roll.

BARKER, JULIANNE; Waynoka HS; Waynoka, OK; (1); Church Yth Grp; Natl FFA Org; Pep Clb; Sec Frsh Cls; 4-H Awd; Hon Roll; Pres Acad Fit Awd; OSU.

BARKER, KASH; Pawhuska HS; Pawhuska, OK; (3); 1/95; Am Leg Boys St; FBLA; Key Clb; Mu Alpha Theta; Quiz Bowl; Science Clb; Spanish Clb; Band; Mrchg Band; Ofcr Stu Cncl; FBLA Rprtr; ST Hnr Soc; U Of OK; Engrng/Med.

BARKER, MATT; Yukon HS; Yukon, OK; (4); 99/435; Am Leg Boys St; Church Yth Grp; Natl FFA Org; Office Aide; Ofcr Stu Cncl; Wrstlng; Pres Acad Fit Awd; Natl Yth Ldrshp Frm Def Intlgnc & Dplmcy; Mar Rsrvs; OK ST U; Pre-Vet.

BARKER, STEPHANIE; Jenks HS; Tulsa, OK; (3); Art Clb; Church Yth Grp; Cmnty Wkr; French Clb; FHA; Latin Clb; Mu Alpha Theta; Red Cross Aide; Pres Science Clb; Teachers Aide; Acad Tm; Natl Art Hnr Soc; BYU.

BARKLEY, ANNIE M; Velma Alma HS; Duncan, OK; (3); SADD; Chorus; School Play; Ed Nwsp; Hon Roll; NHS; All Amer Schlr.

BARKLEY, KELLENE; Collinsville HS; Collinsville, OK; (4); 13/104; Church Yth Grp; FCA; Bsktbl; Chrldng; Trk; Capt Vllybl; NHS; Intl Frgn Lang Awd; OK HS Hnr Soc; TU; Psych.

BARKLEY, MICHELLE R; Collinsville HS; Collinsville, OK; (2); Church Yth Grp; Cmnty Wkr; Hosp Aide; Spanish Clb; Chorus; Church Choir; Rptr Nwsp; Var Bsktbl; Var Score Keeper; JV Vllybl; Sftbl; Vo-Tech Prgm; PT.

BARKLEY, SHANNON; Bartlesville Mid HS; Bartlesville, OK; (2); 88/481; Office Aide; Chorus; Tennis; Hon Roll; NHS; OU; Hrtcltrst.

BARKUS, EBONI; Bowlegs Schl; Seminole, OK; (1); Natl FFA Org; Bsktbl; Sftbl; Hon Roll; Upward Bound Seminole St Coll; OSU; Dentist.

BARLOW, ED L; Tahlequah Jr HS; Tahlequah, OK; (1); Church Yth Grp; Band; Mrchg Band; Pep Band; JV Bsktbl; Pres Acad Fit Awd; Voted KWG Annual Jr HS Coronation.

BARNABY, JACQLYN L; Skiatook HS; Skiatook, OK; (4); 13/107; FCA; French Clb; Red Cross Aide; Teachers Aide; Chorus; School Musical; School Play; Nwsp; High Hon Roll; Hon Roll; Ftbl Hmcmng Qn 95; Cncrrnt Enrllmnt; OK U; Brdcst Jrnlsm.

BARNARD, JA NAE; Fairview HS; Fairview, OK; (3); Church Yth Grp; Natl FFA Org; Office Aide; Chorus; Church Choir; Rep Stu Cncl; Intrml Bsktbl; Hon Roll; NHS; OK ST U; Horticulture.

BARNARD, SUSAN; Leedey Schl; Leedey, OK; (4); 1/20; Church Yth Grp; Sec FCA; Pres 4-H; Pres FBLA; Sec FHA; Hosp Aide; HOBY; Quiz Bowl; Spanish Clb; SADD; Miss Leedy HS & Miss Dewe Cty; Outstndng Svc Awd; OK Chrstn U; Phys Thrpy.

BARNAS, JOSEPH; Deer Creek HS; Edmond, OK; (4); 8/68; Church Yth Grp; Cmnty Wkr; Science Clb; Teachers Aide; School Play; Stage Crew; Ofcr Bsbl; Hon Roll; NHS; Jr Rotarian; Guitar; OK ST U; Phys Thrpy.

BARNES, BRANDON L; Sapulpa Sr HS; Sapulpa, OK; (2); Church Yth Grp; Debate Tm; Speech Tm; Band; Drm Mjr(t); Jazz Band; Mrchg Band; Stage Crew; Tae Kwon Do; Music.

BARNES, BRANDON W; Union Intermediate HS; Tulsa, OK; (2); Boy Scts; Church Yth Grp; Speech Tm; Hon Roll; NHS.

BARNES, BRENT R; Edmond Santa Fe HS; Edmond, OK; (3); 55/279; Church Yth Grp; FCA; Office Aide; SADD; Ofcr Stu Cncl; Var Bsbl; Var Ftbl; Cit Awd; NHS.

BARNES, BROOKE; Jenks HS; Tulsa, OK; (2); Church Yth Grp; DECA; FCA; Varsity Clb; Rep Stu Cncl; Var Chrldng; Fresh, Soph Homcmng; NCA Chmpnshps Dallas TX; Hnrs Engl; Fresh Voted Mst Schl Spirited; U AR; Jrnlsm.

BARNES, CALISTA A; Southeast HS; Oklahoma City, OK; (3); 3/100; Church Yth Grp; Drama Clb; FCA; FBLA; Model UN; Office Aide; Pep Clb; ROTC; Spanish Clb; Church Choir; OK Hlth & Sci Ctr Acad; Southwestrn Smmr Sci Acad; OBU; Medcl.

BARNES, CAMERON; Bartlesville Mid HS; Bartlesville, OK; (2); Art Clb; Boy Scts; Church Yth Grp; Band; Mrchg Band; Pep Band; Stage Crew; JV Bsbl; Hon Roll; Prfct Atten Awd; All-Dist Bnd; OK Univ; Hstry.

BARNES, CARRIE A; Catoosa HS; Catoosa, OK; (4); 14/136; Drama Clb; FCA; FHA; Office Aide; Pep Clb; Stage Crew; Treas Soph Cls; Rptr Sr Cls; JV Var Bsktbl; Var Trk; 3rd St FHA HERO Cmptn; Most Outstndng Stu Chld Dev; Northwestern OK ST U; Chldhd.

BARNES, CHAD A; John Marshall HS; Oklahoma City, OK; (4); 8/160; FBLA; German Clb; ROTC; High Hon Roll; Acad Decath; Rose St Coll Acad Cmptn, Wlrd Hist & Amer Govt 1st Pl, & Econ 2nd Pl; OK Trnmnt Chmpns; U Of Central OK; Jrnlsm.

BARNES, CHRIS; Bartlesville Mid HS; Bartlesville, OK; (4); 30/460; Boy Scts; Church Yth Grp; Office Aide; Band; Mrchg Band; Orch; Pep Band; Rep Stu Cncl; Var Bsbl; Var Ftbl; U Of OK; Environ Eng.

BARNES, CHRISTINA R; Choctaw HS; Mc Loud, OK; (3); Church Yth Grp; FCA; Crs Cntry; Socr; Hon Roll; Jr NHS; NHS; Ntl Merit SF; Pres Acad Fit Awd.

BARNES, CHRISTOPHER D; Ponca City Sr HS; Ponca City, OK; (3); German Clb; Ofcr Stu Cncl; Bsktbl; Crs Cntry; Trk; Wt Lftg; High Hon Roll; Hon Roll; Vlntr Ponca City Humane Soc; Northern OK Coll; Law Enfrcmnt.

BARNES, GLEN; Empire Schl; Comanche, OK; (3); Church Yth Grp; Natl FFA Org; JV Wrstlng; Hon Roll; Huntng & Fishng.

BARNES, HEATHER; Lawton Christian Schl; Lawton, OK; (2); 1/13; Church Yth Grp; Gov Hon Prg Awd; High Hon Roll; Pres Acad Fit Awd; Quiz Bowl; Chorus; School Musical; Therptc Horsbck Ridng & STITCHES Vols; Chrc Clown Troup & Puppt Tem; 2 Missn Tripto Romania & Mexico.

BARNES, JASON; Gans Public Schl; Gans, OK; (3); Church Yth Grp; Library Aide; Natl FFA Org; Pres Frsh Cls; VP Stu Cncl; Intrml Bsbl; Var Treas Bsktbl; High Hon Roll; Hon Roll; Sal; Accntng.

BARNES, JENNIFER; Tomlinson Jr HS; Lawton, OK; (1); Church Yth Grp; FCA; Spanish Clb; Orch; Var Bsktbl; Var Sftbl; Var Trk; High Hon Roll; Jr NHS; NHS; Med.

BARNES, JEREMY O; Panola HS; Red Oak, OK; (3); Math Tm; Hon Roll; 2 US Math Awds; OSU Tech; Mech Engr.

BARNES, KANITA L; Classen Schl; Oklahoma City, OK; (2); Hosp Aide; Mu Alpha Theta; Spanish Clb; Band; Jazz Band; Pep Band; School Musical; Hon Roll; NHS; NW Hnr Bnd; All City Bnd; Flute Solo Cntst Superior Rating; Bio.

BARNES, KELLIE; Newcastle HS; Newcastle, OK; (2); 11/89; Church Yth Grp; FBLA; Quiz Bowl; Scholastic Bowl; Band; Chorus; Rep Stu Cncl; Hon Roll; NHS; OK St Geog Bee; Aviation.

BARNES, LINDSAY J; Southeast HS; Oklahoma City, OK; (2); FCA; ROTC; Spanish Clb; Chorus; Color Guard; Rep Stu Cncl; JV Var Bsktbl; Var Chrldng; Mgr(s); Var Sftbl; OU; Med; Military.

BARNES, LUCAS K; Bishop Mcguinness HS; Edmond, OK; (3); Art Clb; Church Yth Grp; Cmnty Wkr; Drama Clb; Science Clb; Var Socr; JV Wrstlng; Art; Engl.

BARNES, MARCI; Purcell HS; Purcell, OK; (4); 5/74; Church Yth Grp; FHA; Hosp Aide; HOBY; Pres Key Clb; Spanish Clb; Pres Frsh Cls; Hon Roll; NHS; Pres Acad Fit Awd; Mock Trial; Hstry Ed.

BARNES, MARK A; Lindsay HS; Lindsay, OK; (1); 15/75; FHA; Pres Frsh Cls; Ftbl; Wt Lftg; Hon Roll; Guitar; Fishing; Acctng.

BARNES, MICHAEL G; Ada HS; Ada, OK; (3); Church Yth Grp; Phtg Yrbk; Wrstlng; High Hon Roll; NHS; Mr Hustle 93-; Multi Yr Listee; Who's Who In Sports 95-; E Central Univ; Crmnl Juste.

BARNES, MISSY; Memorial HS; Edmond, OK; (3); 79/400; Cmnty Wkr; FCA; Hosp Aide; Spanish Clb; Chorus; Sec Frsh Cls; Ofcr Stu Cncl; JV Chrldng; High Hon Roll; Hon Roll; U Of TX; Heart Surgeon.

BARNES, NATHAN; Hobart HS; Hobart, OK; (1); Capt Wrstlng; Hon Roll; Prfct Atten Awd; Pres Acad Fit Awd.

BARNES, NATHAN B; Union Intermediate HS; Tulsa, OK; (1); Church Yth Grp; Band; Church Choir; Jazz Band; Orch; Pep Band; MIDI; Music Composition & Instruments; ORU; Music Composition.

BARNES, NOAH; Porter Jr Sr HS; Porter, OK; (3); Math Clb; Natl Beta Clb; Office Aide; Quiz Bowl; Science Clb; Band; Mrchg Band; NHS; Med.

BARNES, RACHEL; Stigler HS; Stigler, OK; (3); 23/86; Art Clb; FHA; Spanish Clb; SADD; Band; Color Guard; Rep Soph Cls; NHS; I Dare You Ldrshp Awd; Northeastern; Psych.

BARNES, ROBERT S; Broken Arrow Sr HS; Coweta, OK; (4); Debate Tm; English Clb; NFL; Speech Tm; Temple Yth Grp; Band; Mrchg Band; Ntl Merit SF; Indian Stdys; Taekwondo; Debt Cmp; Hrvrd Smmr Schl, Fld Archlgy Israel; Hbrw Tchr; Rbbnc Mntrshp; U Of Chicago; Intl Finance.

BARNES, ROBYN; Comanche HS; Comanche, OK; (2); Chorus; High Hon Roll; Completed Coll Lvl Ger I, II; HS Tchr.

BARNES, SARAH D; Colegio Int Punta Carden HS; Broken Arrow, OK; (3); Church Yth Grp; Spanish Clb; Chorus; Church Choir; Chrstn Stu Union; Gftd Prog; Baylor Univ; Phy Thrpy.

BARNES, STEVEN L; Sallisaw HS; Sallisaw, OK; (3); 8/142; French Clb; Spanish Clb; Cit Awd; High Hon Roll; Hon Roll; NHS; Law.

BARNES JR, THOMAS; Mc Loud HS; Mc Loud, OK; (4); Church Yth Grp; Computer Clb; Quiz Bowl; Scholastic Bowl; Varsity Clb; Var Socr; High Hon Roll; Hon Roll; Jr NHS; NHS.

BARNETT, AMBER R; Duncan HS; Marlow, OK; (2); FBLA; Key Clb.

BARNETT, AMY; Stigler HS; Stigler, OK; (4); Natl FFA Org; Office Aide; SADD; Teachers Aide; Hon Roll; Natl FFA Org; St FFA Degree Recipient; Connors ST Coll; Acctng; Bus.

BARNETT, ASHLEY; Choctaw HS; Sparks, OK; (4); GAA; Varsity Clb; Ed Yrbk; Capt Chrldng; Gym; Trk; Wt Lftg; High Hon Roll; Hon Roll; Prfct Atten Awd; All St & All Star Chrldr; U OK; Fshn Mrchndsng.

BARNETT, BRANDIE; Davis HS; Davis, OK; (4); 10/54; Am Leg Aux Girls St; Art Clb; Drama Clb; FHA; Key Clb; Library Aide; Office Aide; Spanish Clb; Speech Tm; SADD; Spch Qn 95-96; Spch VP; NBTA 3 St Chmpn 95-96; Multi Yr Listing; Psch Pthlgy.

BARNETT, CHARLA M; Bray-Doyle HS; Marlow, OK; (2); Church Yth Grp; Drama Clb; FCA; FHA; Speech Tm; SADD; Church Choir; School Play; Stage Crew; Variety Show; FHA ST Off; Stdnt Of Month; Family/Consum Sci Ed.

BARNETT, CHRIS; Vanoss Schl; Stratford, OK; (1); 1/45; Church Yth Grp; Quiz Bowl; Scholastic Bowl; Gov Hon Prg Awd; High Hon Roll; Val; Flyers For Chrst.

BARNETT, ELIZABETH J; Putnam City HS; Oklahoma City, OK; (3); 5/340; Church Yth Grp; JCL; Key Clb; Latin Clb; Quiz Bowl; Scholastic Bowl; VP Science Clb; Band; Mrchg Band; Orch; Putnam City Mock Trial Team; Mrchng Band Auxiliary Percussion Section Ldr.

BARNETT, HAYLEY; Durant HS; Durant, OK; (4); 3/250; Church Yth Grp; Office Aide; Chorus; Variety Show; Ed Yrbk; VP Jr Cls; VP Sr Cls; Rep Stu Cncl; Bsktbl; Var Chrldng; OK Hnr Soc; Natl Hnr Soc; Annual Qn; Ftbl Homcmng Atten; Spirit Ldr Of Yr; Mst Outstndng Chrldr; Friendliest; U Of OK; Nrsng.

BARNETT, JENNIFER; Frederick HS; Frederick, OK; (4); 1/80; Dance Clb; FCA; Pres FHA; Treas Speech Tm; Yrbk; Pres Stu Cncl; Sftbl; NHS; Val; OK Hnr Soc.

BARNETT, KIM; Roland Sr HS; Roland, OK; (1); Sec Treas FHA; Band; Mrchg Band; Capt Chrldng; Cit Awd; Hon Roll; Flute Duet Supr Rtng 1995 & Excllnt Rtng 1996; Sftbl 1st Base, Mst Dedctd Plyr & Bst Tag Team 1995; OSU; Law.

BARNETT, MANDI M; Alva HS; Alva, OK; (2); Church Yth Grp; French Clb; FHA; FTA; Teachers Aide; Chorus; Swmmng; Tennis; Bbl Bwl Tm; Yth Grp Chrty Vol; Harding U; Arch.

BARNETT, MICHELLE L; Ponca City Sr HS; Ponca City, OK; (4); Debate Tm; NFL; Spanish Clb; Mgr(s); Var Sftbl; High Hon Roll; Pres Acad Fit Awd; OSU.

BARNETT, MINNIE J; Okmulgee HS; Okmulgee, OK; (4); Church Yth Grp; FCA; French Clb; Office Aide; Pep Clb; Science Clb; Teachers Aide; Chorus; Church Choir; Ed Nwsp; SW MO St Univ; Advtsng.

BARNETT, ROBERT; Kingfisher HS; Kingfisher, OK; (3); #8 in class; Am Leg Boys St; Key Clb; Sec Stu Cncl; Var L Ftbl; High Hon Roll; Hon Roll; Jr NHS; NHS; Prfct Atten Awd; Church Yth Grp; Chem Engnr.

BARNETT II, RONALD; Vanoss Schl; Stratford, OK; (2); Church Yth Grp; Library Aide; Quiz Bowl; Scholastic Bowl; Trk; Cit Awd; High Hon Roll; NHS; Cmptr Prgrmmng; Cmptrs.

BARNETT, RYAN C; Edmond Memorial HS; Oklahoma City, OK; (3); 102/371; Church Yth Grp; FCA; Spanish Clb; Golf; Hon Roll; Jr NHS; U Of OK; Bus Mgmt.

BARNETT, TRE J; Mustang HS; Yukon, OK; (1); Church Yth Grp; Hosp Aide; Natl FFA Org; Ofcr Frsh Cls; Ftbl; FFA Awds; Sheep Shwng Rbns; OSU; Ag.

BARNETTE, JENNY; Clinton HS; Clinton, OK; (2); 16/150; Church Yth Grp; FHA; Key Clb; Spanish Clb; Hon Roll; NHS; Engrng.

BARNEY, LISA; Pauls Valley HS; Pauls Valley, OK; (2); Church Yth Grp; French Clb; GAA; Sec Key Clb; Natl Beta Clb; Varsity Clb; Church Choir; Var Tennis; High Hon Roll; NHS; GATE Hnrs Clss; Mck Trl; Stdnt Yr Dmcrcy, Alg I 94-95.

BARNHART, ALICIA D; Pauls Valley HS; Rotonda West, FL; (2); Quiz Bowl; Scholastic Bowl; Ofcr Stu Cncl; High Hon Roll; Acad Team; Natl Sci Mrt Awds; US Bus Ed Awds; All Amer Schlrs Natl Hnr Roll; Jrnlsm.

BARNHART, CANDICE; Jay HS; Jay, OK; (4); 2/94; Pres FBLA; Natl Beta Clb; Rptr Stu Cncl; Chrldng; Hon Roll; Ofcr NHS; Sal; Intl Drug Free Yth; OSU; Arch.

BARNHART, MARLO A; South Coffeyville Schl; S Coffeyville, OK; (2); Sec FHA; Yrbk; JV Bsktbl; Hon Roll.

BARNHILL, VALERIE M; Central Mid-HS; Norman, OK; (3); Church Yth Grp; FCA; French Clb; Teachers Aide; Chorus; Church Choir; Ofcr Stu Cncl; French Hon Soc; Hon Roll; Pres Acad Fit Awd; Piano Supers At St 2 Yrs In Row.

BARR, CARLA F; Broken Arrow Sr HS; Broken Arrow, OK; (3); Art Clb; Church Yth Grp; Spanish Clb; Hon Roll; NHS; Pres Acad Fit Awd; OK Hon Soc; 1st Plc In Schl PTA Rflctns Cont; Fine Arts.

BARR, CHRISTY; El Reno Sr HS; Yukon, OK; (3); 14/196; Am Leg Aux Girls St; Church Yth Grp; FCA; Key Clb; Color Guard; School Play; Stat Bsktbl; Tennis; High Hon Roll; Renaissnce; Math & Sci Clb; Envrmntl Clb; Law.

BARR, DAWN; Blair Schl; Altus, OK; (3); Cmnty Wkr; Hosp Aide; Natl Beta Clb; Quiz Bowl; Band; Chorus; School Play; VP Jr Cls; Hon Roll; NHS.

BARR, NIKKIA N; Southeast HS; Oklahoma City, OK; (1); Computer Clb; FBLA; Mrchg Band; Pep Band; Rep Frsh Cls; Rep Stu Cncl; Chrldng; High Hon Roll; Hon Roll; NHS; Upward Bnd Prgm; OK Univ; Psychtrst.

BARRETT, ASHLI D; Putnam City West HS; Oklahoma City, OK; (3); Church Yth Grp; FCA; Spanish Clb; Var L Bsktbl; 3-D Club; CIA; Var Sftbl Ltrd 3 Yrs; PE/SPRTS Ed.

BARRETT, ERIN; Coweta HS; Coweta, OK; (2); SADD; Yrbk; Sec Soph Cls; Var Chrldng; High Hon Roll; Jr NHS; NHS; 1st Pl Typng Awd TJC Offc Sklls Chllng; Cmptr Systs Anlyst.

BARRETT, JAMIE; Owasso Sr HS; Owasso, OK; (3); 126/357; Church Yth Grp; Pres 4-H; Natl FFA Org; Red Cross Aide; VICA; Cit Awd; 4-H Awd; Hon Roll; Horses; OK ST U; Med.

BARRETT, JON; Liberty Acad; Mc Loud, OK; (1); Q&S; Var JV Bsktbl; Ntl Merit Ltr.

BARRETT, LEANN R; Mannford HS; Mannford, OK; (2); 40/113; Church Yth Grp; Spanish Clb; SADD; Chorus; Co-Ed Yrbk; Rep Stu Cncl; Chrldng; Hon Roll; Jr Miss Striper City Pageant 94-; OK ST Univ; Elem Ed.

BARRETT, LUKE L; Sulphur HS; Sulphur, OK; (3); English Clb; Key Clb; Letterman Clb; Quiz Bowl; Scholastic Bowl; Science Clb; Band; Mrchg Band; Orch.

BARRETT, SHERITA; Star Spencer HS; Oklahoma City, OK; (4); 1/122; Am Leg Aux Girls St; Church Yth Grp; Library Aide; Pep Clb; Scholastic Bowl; Co-Ed Nwsp; Kiwanis Awd; Pres Acad Fit Awd; Val; Voted Most Likely To Succed& Most Studious Sr Cls; OK City U.

BARRETT, TAMI; Holdenville Jr HS; Holdenville, OK; (1); Church Yth Grp; Scholastic Bowl; Band; Church Choir; Mrchg Band; High Hon Roll; NHS; Prfct Atten Awd.

BARRETT, TERESA A; Claremore Sr HS; Claremore, OK; (2); Church Yth Grp; Spanish Clb; Church Choir; High Hon Roll; Hon Roll; Prfct Atten Awd; Native Amer Clb; JOM Claremore Intertribal Yth Cncl; OK U; Psych.

BARRICK, ELISE; Holdenville HS; Holdenville, OK; (2); Church Yth Grp; Drama Clb; FCA; Natl Beta Clb; Scholastic Bowl; Science Clb; Band; Church Choir; Color Guard; School Play; Gymnastics; Forestry Jdng; OSU 3rd Annual Smmr Wrtng Prjct; OSU.

BARRON, AMANDA; Canadian Schl; Eufaula, OK; (2); 6/35; 4-H; Var Bsktbl; Stat Sftbl; Hon Roll; Crmnlgy.

BARRON, KATHLEEN E; Edmond Memorial HS; Edmond, OK; (2); Church Yth Grp; Debate Tm; Key Clb; Spanish Clb; NHS.

BARRON, ROBERT; Oologah HS; Talala, OK; (3); 13/130; Am Leg Boys St; Church Yth Grp; FCA; HOBY; Pres Frsh Cls; Pres Jr Cls; Treas Stu Cncl; Var Bsbl; Var Ftbl; NHS; Baker U; Law.

BARRON, TIMOTHY N; Bishop Kelley HS; Tulsa, OK; (2); Cmnty Wkr; JV Bsbl; Cit Awd; Hon Roll; Prfct Atten Awd; Sports Med.

BARROS, BRYAN M; Woodward HS; Woodward, OK; (4); 36/172; Art Clb; Church Yth Grp; Cmnty Wkr; FCA; Letterman Clb; SADD; Varsity Clb; Band; Church Choir; Mrchg Band; Congressional Yth Ldrshp Awd; Natl Ath Endorsement; OK City Univ; Graphic Arts.

BARSALEAU, JANA; Christian Heritage Acad; Oklahoma City, OK; (2); Church Yth Grp; FCA; Chorus; Church Choir; Vllybl; High Hon Roll; Hon Roll; Pres Acad Fit Awd; 5th Pl OK Hstry Rose St Coll HS Schlstc Cont; OK Bapt U; Poly Sci.

BART, PHILLIP H; Ardmore HS; Ardmore, OK; (3); 62/202; Chorus; Hon Roll; Show Choir 1 Yr; AUTO Tech.

BARTEE, SARAH; Classen Schl; Oklahoma City, OK; (3); Letterman Clb; Mu Alpha Theta; Spanish Clb; Varsity Clb; Stage Crew; Variety Show; Tennis; Vllybl; High Hon Roll; Hon Roll; Piano.

BARTEL, JON; Fairview HS; Fairview, OK; (1); 1/78; Church Yth Grp; FCA; Band; Church Choir; Mrchg Band; Pep Band; Bsktbl; Ftbl; High Hon Roll; TSA Sgt Arms; Bus.

BARTEL, JUSTIN W; Balko Public Schl; Balko, OK; (2); Boy Scts; Yrbk; Ftbl; Trk; High Hon Roll; NHS; Val; Eagle Sct; ROTC; Cmptr Prgrmng.

BARTEN, JESSICA S; Elk City HS; Elk City, OK; (4); 11/144; Church Yth Grp; Pres FHA; Teachers Aide; Pres VICA; High Hon Roll; NHS; Pres Schlr; St Schlr; Southwestern OK ST U; Art Ed.

BARTER, JENNIFER I; Muldrow HS; Muldrow, OK; (3); 4-H; FHA; Spanish Clb; JV Bsktbl; Sftbl; 4-H Awd; Hon Roll; NHS; Natl FFA Org; Band; Cmptrs; Span Queen Attndnt; Westlark; LPN/TCHNG.

BARTHEL, ALICIA D; Hinton HS; Hinton, OK; (2); Church Yth Grp; FCA; FHA; GAA; Key Clb; SADD; Acpl Chr; Chorus; Bsktbl; Powder Puff Ftbl; Upward Bound.

BARTHOLOMEW, CATHERINE R; Chattanooga Schl; Chattanooga, OK; (1); 1/25; Church Yth Grp; Var Bsktbl; JV Chrldng; Var Sftbl; Hon Roll; NHS; Val; Jrnlsm Staff Mem; Actress.

BARTLETT, BRUCE; Altus Sr HS; Altus, OK; (4); Am Leg Boys St; Church Yth Grp; Cmnty Wkr; FCA; Letterman Clb; Office Aide; Chorus; Yrbk; VP Frsh Cls; Ofcr Stu Cncl; Ftbl Acad St Chmpn; OK Coaches Assn All Star Tm, All Dist, Offnsv Linemn Of Yr, Down Undr Austrla Ftbl; OK ST; Sports Med.

BARTLETT, JONATHAN L; Union Sr HS; Tulsa, OK; (4); 6/600; Church Yth Grp; Cmnty Wkr; FCA; Var Ftbl; Var Co-Capt Tennis; High Hon Roll; Jr NHS; NHS; Ntl Merit SF; Pres Acad Fit Awd; Sr Of Mo; OK Bapt Univ Schlsp; ST Regents Schlsp; Mr Union Fnlst; Sci Bowl Ntls; OK Bapt U; Mnstry/Cmptr Sci.

BARTLETT, LEAH B; Duncan HS; Duncan, OK; (1); Church Yth Grp; Cmnty Wkr; FBLA; Key Clb; SADD; Chorus; Chrmn Frsh Cls; Hon Roll; Church Yth Ctr Vol; Lucky Cir Club; OK Univ; Psych/Bus.

BARTLEY, TRICIA L; Metro Christian Acad; Tulsa, OK; (2); Church Yth Grp; Church Choir; Rptr Nwsp; Stat Bsktbl; Vllybl; High Hon Roll; Hon Roll; NHS; Sftbl.

BARTMANN, JESSICA; Cascia Hall Prep School; Tulsa, OK; (4); Church Yth Grp; Pep Clb; Chorus; School Musical; Stat Bsbl; Var Co-Capt Chrldng; Hon Roll; Miss Teen OK Mrit Finalist 93-95; Miss OK Hosptlty 95; Baker U; Bus Mgmt.

BARTON, GARY C; Harrah HS; Harrah, OK; (3); #1 in class; Church Yth Grp; FCA; SADD; Var L Bsbl; Var L Bsktbl; High Hon Roll; Jr NHS; NHS.

BARTON, JENNIFER; Mustang HS; Mustang, OK; (4); Band; Color Guard; Jazz Band; Mrchg Band; Pep Band; Ed Lit Mag; Wntrgrd Capt; Crtv Wrtng; Msc Hist.

BARTON, KELLY; Stuart Sr HS; Mcalester, OK; (4); 2/29; FCA; 4-H; FHA; Intnl Clb; Quiz Bowl; Teachers Aide; Nwsp; Ed Yrbk; Rep Frsh Cls; VP Stu Cncl; OK ST U; Bus Admin.

BARTON, MELISSA S; Afton HS; Afton, OK; (3); Church Yth Grp; FHA; Speech Tm; Band; Ofcr Jr Cls; Hon Roll; Prfct Atten Awd; NEO; Nrsng.

BARTON, SARA L; East Central HS; Tulsa, OK; (2); Cmnty Wkr; Girl Scts; Key Clb; Pep Clb; Red Cross Aide; Science Clb; Spanish Clb; Rptr Nwsp; Phtg Yrbk; Rep Jr Cls; Drug Free Yth; Girl Sct Slvr Awd; Elem Ed.

BARTON, STACEY; Miami Sr HS; Miami, OK; (4); 22/131; Chess Clb; Cmnty Wkr; FCA; Teachers Aide; Chorus; Yrbk; Var Capt Bsbl; Chrldng; Var Capt Ftbl; Wt Lftg; Scndry Ed.

BARTRAM, CHRISTY; Sequoyah HS; Claremore, OK; (4); 5/79; Am Leg Aux Girls St; Pres FCA; Band; Phtg Yrbk; VP Stu Cncl; Var L Bsktbl; Ftbl; Var L Trk; High Hon Roll; Pres NHS; Stu Cncl Rep, Hist & Pblcty Mgr; SW MO ST U; Sprts Med.

BARWICK, APRIL N; Pond Creek-Hunter Schl; Pond Creek, OK; (2); Pep Clb; Bsktbl; Sftbl; Phys Therapy.

BASAS, STEVE M; Union Intermediate HS; Tulsa, OK; (2); CAP; German Clb; Speech Tm; Orch; NHS; Military Acad; Military.

BASE, TONYA M; Union Intermediate HS; Tulsa, OK; (2); Color Guard; Hon Roll; NHS; Psych.

BASHAW, MISTY M; Sayre HS; Sayre, OK; (1); Church Yth Grp; Sec FHA; GAA; Pep Clb; Band; Mrchg Band; Bsktbl; Sftbl; Hon Roll; Prfct Atten Awd; OK ST Univ; Bsktbl & Sftbl.

BASINGER, MANDI M; Checotah HS; Checotah, OK; (3); 9/115; Church Yth Grp; FBLA; FHA; High Hon Roll; NHS; Ntl Merit Ltr; OK Hnr Soc; Top 10 Pct Frosh/Soph/Jr Yr; Bus Admin.

BASINGER, STEPHANIE D; Jay HS; Eucha, OK; (3); FCA; FHA; Natl Beta Clb; Science Clb; Chorus; Nwsp; Hon Roll; NHS; Fthrs Of Many Clrs Indn Club; Itnl Drug Free Yth; Dr.

BASKETT, ANGIE D; Putnam City North HS; Oklahoma City, OK; (2); Church Yth Grp; Dance Clb; Drama Clb; Pep Clb; Drill Tm; Variety Show; Pom Pon; Hon Roll; NHS.

BASS, AMY; Norman Sr HS; Norman, OK; (3); 1/800; Pres DECA; Girl Scts; Math Clb; Natl FFA Org; Spanish Clb; Var L Bsktbl; High Hon Roll; Hon Roll; Jr NHS; NHS; U Of OK; Pharm.

BASS, EMILY; Oklahoma Christian Schl; Edmond, OK; (3); 2/50; Church Yth Grp; Cmnty Wkr; FCA; Math Tm; Church Choir; Sec Treas Jr Cls; Var Co-Capt Chrldng; Var Pom Pon; Var Powder Puff Ftbl; Var Socr; His Clb; St Champs Chrldng & Pom Pn; U OK; Engr.

BASS, JACOB; Kingfisher HS; Kingfisher, OK; (2); Quiz Bowl; Band; Jazz Band; Mrchg Band; Pep Band; Hon Roll.

BASS, JERIMY M; Durant HS; Durant, OK; (3); FBLA; Pep Clb; Drug Free Yth; Natl Geo Soc 91; Southeastern OK St Univ; Bus.

BASS, KIM; Vinita HS; Vinita, OK; (2); Church Yth Grp; FCA; FHA; Math Clb; Science Clb; Spanish Clb; Chrldng; Gym; Hon Roll; Northeastern ST U; Tchr.

BASSANDEH, AUTUM; Brink Jr HS; Moore, OK; (1); Chorus; Mgr Nwsp; Jr NHS.

BASSETT, ALISHA M; Edmond Memorial HS; Edmond, OK; (4); 48/352; Church Yth Grp; Band; Chorus; Church Choir; Mrchg Band; Orch; Pep Band; NHS; U Of Cntrl OK; Music Ed.

BASSETT, F SCOTT; Union Sr HS; Tulsa, OK; (4); 82/629; Church Yth Grp; FCA; Intnl Clb; Mu Alpha Theta; Spanish Clb; Teachers Aide; Church Choir; NHS; Prfct Atten Awd; Acstc Guitar; Bst Male Sci Stu Awd; Bio.

BASSITY, LEAH R; Verden HS; Chickasha, OK; (2); Scholastic Bowl; Spanish Clb; Nwsp; Yrbk; Rep Frsh Cls; Sec Soph Cls; Var Bsktbl; Cit Awd; High Hon Roll; NHS; Mck Trl; Stdnt Mo; Int Dsgn.

BASTERI, RYAN C; Union Sr HS; Tulsa, OK; (3); #110 in class; FCA; Spanish Clb; Var JV Bsktbl; High Hon Roll; NHS; Law Enfrcmt.

BATCHELOR, ANNA K; Sallisaw HS; Sallisaw, OK; (3); Sec Art Clb; Church Yth Grp; Drama Clb; FCA; Sec Math Clb; Pep Clb; Science Clb; Spanish Clb; Church Choir; School Play; St Hnr Soc; Reg Spch Cntst Qlfr; NCA Cheer Cmp All Amer Nom; Nrsng.

BATCHELOR, CHAD E; Valliant HS; Broken Bow, OK; (1); 11/90; Pres 4-H; Natl FFA Org; Quiz Bowl; School Play; Rep Stu Cncl; Bsktbl; Ftbl; Cit Awd; 4-H Awd; Hon Roll; Certfd Lifeguard; Trained In CPR; Music King; Voted Frosh Cls Smartest Boy; Se Dist 4-H Ofcr; OSU; Vet.

BATCHELOR, TONYA D; Union Intermediate HS; Tulsa, OK; (1); Church Yth Grp; Sftbl; Hon Roll; Stnfrd; Clmbia; Ped.

BATDORF, RICK; Pawhuska HS; Pawhuska, OK; (4); Am Leg Boys St; Boy Scts; FCA; Mu Alpha Theta; Spanish Clb; Band; Rep Stu Cncl; Ofcr Bsbl; Bsktbl; Ftbl; Engrng.

BATEMAN, PAULA K; Will Rogers HS; Tulsa, OK; (1).

BATES, BECKY; Davenport Jr Sr HS; Davenport, OK; (4); 4/31; Pres Pep Clb; Rptr Nwsp; Pres Frsh Cls; VP Soph Cls; Pres Jr Cls; Pres Stu Cncl; L Bsktbl; Var L Sftbl; Prfct Atten Awd; I Dare You Awd; Army Rsrv Schl Athl Awd; Kommotion; Cnslr.

BATES, BLANE; Wellston Schl; Wellston, OK; (2); Church Yth Grp; Quiz Bowl; VP Frsh Cls; Pres Soph Cls; Hon Roll; Jr NHS; NHS; OSU.

BATES, COURTNEY; Empire Schl; Comanche, OK; (2); Church Yth Grp; Scholastic Bowl; Science Clb; Chorus; Church Choir; OSU.

BATES, CRYSTAL A; Byng Sr HS; Ada, OK; (2); Church Yth Grp; Drama Clb; French Clb; Scholastic Bowl; Speech Tm; Thesps; Chorus; School Play; Stage Crew; Ofcr Stu Cncl; Distinct Impact On Comm; Southern Nazarene U; Yth Pastor.

BATES, DUSTIN L; Bartlesville Mid HS; Bartlesville, OK; (1); Church Yth Grp; Letterman Clb; Gym; Hon Roll; NHS; Lang Arts Awd; Acad All-Amer Team Awd; OK Univ; Dr Of Medicine.

BATES, EMILY; Elk City Jr HS; Elk City, OK; (1); Church Yth Grp; 4-H; GAA; Phtg Rptr Yrbk; Bsktbl; Crs Cntry; Trk; Hon Roll.

BATES, EMILY; Edmond North HS; Edmond, OK; (2); Church Yth Grp; FCA; Mu Alpha Theta; SADD; Church Choir; VP Frsh Cls; Ofcr Stu Cncl; Var L Crs Cntry; Var L Trk; Cit Awd; Rgstrd Dietician.

BATES, HEATHER J; El Reno Sr HS; El Reno, OK; (2); 27/232; Cmnty Wkr; SADD; Treas Soph Cls; Pom Pon; Cit Awd; High Hon Roll; Renaissance; Grad With 5 Schl Ltrs; Southwestern OK ST U.

BATES II, JERRY; Tuttle HS; Tuttle, OK; (4); Am Leg Boys St; Quiz Bowl; Scholastic Bowl; Spanish Clb; Var L Bsbl; Var L Ftbl; Mgr(s); Var L Wrstlng; Hon Roll; NHS; USAO.

BATES, JOHN C; Western Hts HS; Oklahoma City, OK; (4); 21/169; Boy Scts; FCA; French Clb; Var Letterman Clb; Rptr VICA; Rptr Nwsp; Bsktbl; Var Crs Cntry; Var Socr; Var Wt Lftg; Eagle Sct 95; Srvstr All-Amer Voctnl Stu Awd 96; Outstndng Ldr NW Dist VICA 95; OK City CC; Auto Svc.

BATES, MARIA C; Western Heights Sr HS; Oklahoma City, OK; (2); #1 in class; French Clb; Letterman Clb; Pres Frsh Cls; Rep Soph Cls; Rep Stu Cncl; JV Bsktbl; Var Socr; Var Sftbl; High Hon Roll; Hon Roll; LEAP Bd Of Dirs Chair.

BATHE, CHRISTIE L; Midwest City HS; Midwest City, OK; (2); 82/473; FCA; Spanish Clb; Teachers Aide; Bsktbl; Sftbl; Trk; NHS; Prfct Atten Awd; Outstdng Yth Awd; DECA; UCLA; Phy Thrpst.

BATHE, WINTER; Midwest City HS; Midwest City, OK; (3); Drama Clb; VP German Clb; VP Key Clb; School Play; Rptr Frsh Cls; Rptr Soph Cls; Capt Chrldng; Sftbl; Jr NHS; NHS; OU; Med.

BATSON, JEANEAU; Coweta HS; Redbird, OK; (4); 1/153; SADD; Band; Jazz Band; Mrchg Band; Orch; Rptr Soph Cls; Jr NHS; NHS; Val; 2 Yrs All St Band; De Paul U; Music Ed.

BATTESE, TAMARA; Apache HS; Apache, OK; (2); Band; Mrchg Band; JV Bsktbl; Var Chrldng; JV Swmmng; Native Amer Clb.

BATTLE, KIMBERLY D; Chandler HS; Chandler, OK; (3); 30/87; Church Yth Grp; Cmnty Wkr; FCA; Girl Scts; Church Choir; Drill Tm; Ed Yrbk; Var Bsktbl; Var Sftbl; Cit Awd; Young Chrstn Ambassdrs; U Of Cntrl OK; Child Psych.

BATTLE, MINDY E; Claremore Sr HS; Claremore, OK; (2); Church Yth Grp; Cmnty Wkr; FCA; GAA; Office Aide; Spanish Clb; SADD; Trk; High Hon Roll; Hon Roll; Vol Mission; Ldrshp Cls/Slctd Stu Body Ldrs; Acad Bst Bio I Stu.

BAUER, CARL; Ft Towson HS; Fort Towson, OK; (3); 3/36; Am Leg Boys St; FHA; Co-Capt Quiz Bowl; Nwsp; Ofcr Bsbl; Bsktbl; Hon Roll; NHS; SOSU.

BAUER, GREG; Jenks HS; Tulsa, OK; (4); 36/520; FCA; Math Tm; Office Aide; Teachers Aide; Var L Bsbl; Var L Ftbl; Gov Hon Prg Awd; High Hon Roll; Hon Roll; Jr NHS; NHS; USA Bsbl Team Mem; OK Bsbl Player Of Yr; Wichita ST U; Orthopdc Surgn.

BAUER, KATIE R; Putnam City North HS; Oklahoma City, OK; (3); Church Yth Grp; Cmnty Wkr; DECA; FCA; Key Clb; Pep Clb; Spanish Clb; SADD; Chorus; Church Choir; 3-D; CAWS; Panther PALS; Piano; OU.

BAUGHMAN II, JEFFREY L; Central Mid-HS; Norman, OK; (2); Latin Clb; Mu Alpha Theta; Band; Jazz Band; Mrchg Band; Yrbk; Treas Soph Cls; Gov Hon Prg Awd; High Hon Roll; NHS; Johns Hopkins Univ; Med.

BAUMANN, AMY; Midwest City HS; Midwest City, OK; (2); 25/488; FHA; German Clb; Pep Clb; Rep Stu Cncl; Bsktbl; Trk; Wt Lftg; 4-H Awd; Hon Roll; NHS; Outstndng Female Bsktbl Player, All Conf, Trnmt, Invtnl Trnmt Top Offnsv Bsktbl Plyr; SNU.

BAUMANN, PAUL M; Mangum Sr HS; Mangum, OK; (3); 3/46; Quiz Bowl; Scholastic Bowl; Band; Mrchg Band; Pres Stu Cncl; Var Bsktbl; Var Ftbl; Hon Roll; NHS; Stu Today Awd; OK ST Univ; Civil Engrg.

BAUMWART, CHAD; Clinton HS; Clinton, OK; (4); 11/99; Church Yth Grp; FCA; Letterman Clb; Natl FFA Org; Office Aide; Spanish Clb; SADD; Varsity Clb; Capt Ftbl; Capt Socr; OSU; Vet.

BAUMWART, JENNI; El Reno Sr HS; El Reno, OK; (3); Art Clb; Church Yth Grp; FCA; FHA; Key Clb; Math Clb; Science Clb; High Hon Roll; Hon Roll; Kiwanis Awd.

BAXTER, ASHLEY D; Enid Sr HS; Enid, OK; (3); 41/415; Church Yth Grp; Cmnty Wkr; Pres FHA; Drill Tm; Nwsp; Rep Stu Cncl; Pom Pon; Hon Roll; Jr NHS; NHS.

BAXTER, BRIAN; Liberty Acad; Shawnee, OK; (1); Ofcr Stu Cncl; Bsktbl; Trk; Vllybl; High Hon Roll; Ntl Merit Ltr; Prfct Atten Awd.

BAXTER, ELIZABETH M; South Intermediate HS; Broken Arrow, OK; (1); 1/610; Church Yth Grp; Girl Scts; Acpl Chr; Band; Church Choir; Gov Hon Prg Awd; High Hon Roll; Spanish Clb; Mrchg Band; Pep Band; Outstdng Frosh Acad Excl Frgn Lang/Sci/Soc Stud/Lang Arts/Math; Acad Tm 1st Pl Abl Conf; Harvard; Med.

BAXTER, ROBBY J; Caddo HS; Caddo, OK; (1); Chorus; Hon Roll; NHS; All-Amer Schlr Directory.

BAXTER, WILLIAM K; Muldrow HS; Muldrow, OK; (1); Natl Beta Clb; Speech Tm; Band; Mrchg Band; Pep Band; Hon Roll; Prfct Atten Awd; U Of AR.

BAY, T J; Oklahoma Sch Of Science & Math; Chandler, OK; (4); Math Tm; Quiz Bowl; Acpl Chr; Chorus; Ofcr Soph Cls; High Hon Roll; NHS; St Schlr; TEAMTS; Physics.

BAY, THOMAS; OK Schl Of Sci/Math; Chandler, OK; (4); Math Tm; Quiz Bowl; Chorus; School Play; Treas Soph Cls; Bsktbl; Vllybl; High Hon Roll; NHS; St Schlr; Northwestern Univ; Physics.

BAYLESS, SUSAN C; Union Sr HS; Tulsa, OK; (3); 72/741; DECA; FCA; FBLA; Spanish Clb; Pom Pon; Cit Awd; Hon Roll; Jr NHS; NHS; Pres Schlr; NCA Danz All Amer; OK U; Phys Thrpy.

BAYS, EMILY E; Alva HS; Alva, OK; (3); 8/75; Church Yth Grp; Cmnty Wkr; Debate Tm; 4-H; Key Clb; NFL; Office Aide; Speech Tm; Band; Chorus; YFU Schlsp Wnnr Of Exch Trip To Japan; Natl 4-H Wnnr To Purdue U Vet Summer Wkshp; Jrnlsm; Medicine.

BAZILLE, BLAKE; Central HS; Tulsa, OK; (3); 10/175; Cmnty Wkr; German Clb; Band; Mrchg Band; Rptr Nwsp; Yrbk; Cit Awd; High Hon Roll; Hon Roll; Jr NHS; Indian Hlth Cr Rsrc Ctr Vol Yr; Tulsa U; Med.

BEACH, CARISSA; Muskogee HS; Muskogee, OK; (1); 102/481; Chorus; Church Choir; Hon Roll; OK ST Univ; Acctng.

BEACH, LAURA A; Union Sr HS; Tulsa, OK; (3); 37/741; Hist Church Yth Grp; German Clb; Key Clb; Band; Jazz Band; Jazz Band; High Hon Roll; Jr NHS; NHS; Music.

BEADLE, MYRIA L; Rush Springs HS; Rush Springs, OK; (3); 15/55; Church Yth Grp; FCA; 4-H; Letterman Clb; Spanish Clb; Band; Chorus; Church Choir; Mrchg Band; Pep Band; YAB; All Dist Sftbl 95; St Gregory; Radiology.

BEAIRD, DANA M; Healdton HS; Fox, OK; (3); Church Yth Grp; FCA; GAA; Office Aide; Teachers Aide; Band; Color Guard; Flag Corp; Jazz Band; Mrchg Band; Math Achvmt Awd; SOSU Upward Bound Math & Sci; Tchr.

BEAL, APRIL; Stigler HS; Whitefield, OK; (1); Church Yth Grp; FCA; FHA; Pep Clb; SADD; Ofcr Bsbl; Hon Roll; NHS; Ntl Merit Ltr; Gifted/Talented; OU; Acctg/Law.

BEAL, BILLIE J; Tupelo Jr Sr HS; Centrahoma, OK; (2); 1/25; Church Yth Grp; Cmnty Wkr; JA; Scholastic Bowl; Band; Chorus; Church Choir; Pres Soph Cls; Pres Jr Cls; Pres Stu Cncl; Upward Bound Math/Sci Prgm 2 Yrs; E Cntrl Univ.

BEAL JR, DWIGHT H; Midwest City HS; Charleston Afb, SC; (3); Church Yth Grp; Math Clb; Science Clb; Spanish Clb; Band; Church Choir; Jazz Band; Rep Stu Cncl; Var Bsktbl; Ftbl; Royal Ambassadors; OSU; Elec Engr.

BEALL, KRISTIN J; North Intemediate HS; Broken Arrow, OK; (2); Cmnty Wkr; FHA; Office Aide; Treating Abused Children.

BEALL, SUSAN; Midwest City HS; Midwest City, OK; (4); 38/419; Band; Mrchg Band; Orch; School Musical; Hon Roll; Pres Acad Fit Awd; Val; OK Bapt All St Orch; CODA All Rgn Hnr Bnd; All St Hnr Bnd Alt; OK ST U; Vet Med.

BEAM, JACQUELINE E; North Intemediate HS; Broken Arrow, OK; (1); Church Yth Grp; Cmnty Wkr; Band; Color Guard; Mrchg Band; Pep Band; Hon Roll; Jr NHS; First Bapt Church Yth Choir; OSU; Int Dctr.

BEAM, KATHERAN; Broken Arrow Sr HS; Broken Arrow, OK; (3); 22/921; Church Yth Grp; HOBY; Thesps; Acpl Chr; Church Choir; School Musical; School Play; Stage Crew; Swing Chorus; Variety Show; Campfire Boys & Girls; Law.

BEAM, LAURA N; Edmond Memorial HS; Edmond, OK; (2); 1/408; Church Yth Grp; FCA; HOBY; Spanish Clb; VP Frsh Cls; Pres Soph Cls; Ofcr Stu Cncl; Var Crs Cntry; Var Socr; Jr NHS; OK HS Hnr Soc; Comm Ldrsp Rep; Pres Outstdng Acad Achvmt Awd.

BEAM, SHARON K; Harrah HS; Harrah, OK; (3); 10/153; Church Yth Grp; FHA; Office Aide; Hon Roll; NHS; Art Stdnt; Art Awds 2nd Pl Rose ST Coll Schlstc Cntst/Gld/Silvr Medls Drwngs Cntst.

BEAMS, AUDREY E; Union Sr HS; Tulsa, OK; (3); 55/741; Church Yth Grp; FCA; FBLA; Spanish Clb; Rep Frsh Cls; Rep Soph Cls; Rep Jr Cls; Var Chrldng; Cit Awd; Hon Roll; 2nd Pl Natl Champ Chrldng Squad; Symph Set; KS U; Phy Ther.

BEAN, AMY; Claremore Sr HS; Claremore, OK; (4); Church Yth Grp; Cmnty Wkr; FHA; Spanish Clb; Flag Corp; Gym; Pom Pon; Powder Puff Ftbl; Tennis; Trk; Vet Medicine; Phy Thrpst.

BEAN, ANDIE; Dickson HS; Ardmore, OK; (3); Church Yth Grp; Cmnty Wkr; FCA; FHA; German Clb; GAA; Key Clb; Office Aide; SADD; Teachers Aide; Ftbl Homcmng Ct; Miss Teen Pageant 95-96; FHA Sweetheart, New Mem Of Yr 94-95; Cert Achvmt Ger; Med Field.

BEAN, JESSI R; Madill HS; Madill, OK; (2); FCA; 4-H; Letterman Clb; Natl FFA Org; Var Bsktbl; Sftbl; 4-H Awd; Hon Roll; NHS; Prfct Atten Awd; Shwng Pigs; Bsktbl Hmcmng Candt; TX Tech; Sprts Med.

BEAN, RACHEL L; Choctaw HS; Choctaw, OK; (3); Church Yth Grp; FCA; Church Choir; Bsktbl; Trk; Hon Roll; Jr NHS; House Of Reps Page; Model.

BEAR, ALICIA R; Dustin Schl; Dustin, OK; (3); FHA; School Play; Yrbk; Bsktbl; Sftbl; Hon Roll; Yrbk Awd; Amer Hist Awd; Zoologist.

BEARD, ANGELEIGH; Midwest City HS; Midwest City, OK; (4); 73/413; Pres Church Yth Grp; Cmnty Wkr; Sec FCA; Key Clb; Speech Tm; Varsity Clb; Church Choir; Rep Soph Cls; Rep Stu Cncl; Crs Cntry; Missions Bosnia 95; Oklahoma City U; Relgn.

BEARD, CORTNEY; Bridge Creek HS; Blanchard, OK; (1); Church Yth Grp; FCA; Spanish Clb; Chorus; Chrldng; Hon Roll; OK Chrstn Bilde Bowl; OK ST Univ; Nrsng/Pediatrics.

BEARD, LAUREN; Miami Sr HS; Miami, OK; (4); 10/121; Am Leg Aux Girls St; Church Yth Grp; Pres Band; Drm Mjr(t); Mrchg Band; High Hon Roll; Hon Roll; Treas NHS; Ldrshp Awd; All-St Band 95 & 96; Dist Methdst Yth Sec; U Of OK; Pharmcy.

BEARD, LINDSI R; Alva HS; Alva, OK; (2); Church Yth Grp; Key Clb; Spanish Clb; Chorus; Var Crs Cntry; Hon Roll; NHS; FCA; JV Bsktbl; OK Hnr Soc; Schlrshp Chrstn Serv Ldrshp Camp.

BEARD, REBEKAH A; Burns Flat-Dill City HS; Midwest City, OK; (4); 4-H; FHA; GAA; Sec Pep Clb; Chorus; Church Choir; School Musical; School Play; Stage Crew; JV Var Bsktbl; Outstdng Jr Vocalist; Guitar; Skateboarding; Composing; Pharmaceutical.

BEARD, SHAE; Bridge Creek HS; Blanchard, OK; (3); Church Yth Grp; Drama Clb; FCA; Hosp Aide; Spanish Clb; SADD; School Play; Ofcr Stu Cncl; Chrldng; Homcmng Attndnt; OK ST U; Spcl Ed.

BEARDEN, MICHELLE; Kingston HS; Kingston, OK; (1); Church Yth Grp; FCA; Sec FHA; Spanish Clb; Ofcr Stu Cncl; JV Sftbl; Hon Roll; Fshn Dsgn.

BEARDEN, PIPER; Garber Sr HS; Garber, OK; (2); 4-H; FHA; HOBY; Var Bsktbl; Var Chrldng; Var Sftbl; Hon Roll; NHS; Pres Acad Fit Awd; Twirling Corp; Razzle Dazzle Pom Squad; YMCA Sftbl Coach.

BEARE, MINDY M; Hartshorne Sr HS; Hartshorne, OK; (2); Church Yth Grp; FCA; GAA; Letterman Clb; Math Tm; Natl FFA Org; Office Aide; Band; Church Choir; Mrchg Band; OK U; Law.

BEASLEY, HEATHER L; Ruff HS; Fitzhugh, OK; (4); 9/23; Church Yth Grp; 4-H; Natl Beta Clb; Scholastic Bowl; Teachers Aide; Varsity Clb; Nwsp; Yrbk; VP Jr Cls; Var L Bsktbl; E Cntrl Univ; Scndry Art Ed.

BEASLEY, HOLLY; Ruff HS; Fitzhugh, OK; (2); 3/17; Church Yth Grp; 4-H; Natl Beta Clb; Scholastic Bowl; Varsity Clb; Sec Frsh Cls; Sec Soph Cls; Capt Bsktbl; 4-H Awd; Gov Hon Prg Awd; OSU; Vet.

BEASLEY, JOHN J; Putnam City West HS; Bethany, OK; (2); 9/42; Boy Scts; Computer Clb; JA; Rep Soph Cls; JV Bsbl; JV Chrldng; JV Socr; Hon Roll; Prfct Atten Awd; Jr Achvmt Awd Bethany Masonic Lodge 529; OK City Univ; Bio; Philosophy.

BEASLEY, RANDA; Tuttle HS; Tuttle, OK; (1); 1/101; FHA; Girl Scts; Bsktbl; Chrldng; Score Keeper; Hon Roll; Hostess At Governors Christmas Open House; SWOSU; Med; ER Dr.

BEASON, RITCHIE; Lexington HS; Lexington, OK; (3); Church Yth Grp; FCA; Ofcr Bsbl; Bsktbl; Ftbl; Amer Legion Bsbl; ECU; Tchr.

BEATLEY, KRISTI M; Sulphur HS; Sulphur, OK; (1); Church Yth Grp; Band; Color Guard; Mrchg Band; Hon Roll; NHS; E Cntrl Univ; Pdtry.

BEATTY, MEREDITH; Mc Alester HS; Mcalester, OK; (1); Church Yth Grp; Chrldng; Var Pom Pon; Hon Roll.

BEAUCHAMP, CASEY; Arapaho Schl; Arapaho, OK; (4); 3/15; Church Yth Grp; 4-H; Yrbk; VP Rptr Stu Cncl; Var Bsktbl; Cit Awd; High Hon Roll; Hon Roll; Amer Legion Ctznsp Awd; SWOSU; Pre-Law.

BEAULIEU, GEOFF; Bartlesville Mid HS; Bartlesville, OK; (2); 61/481; Church Yth Grp; Cmnty Wkr; Rep Frsh Cls; Var Bsbl; JV Bsktbl; Ftbl; Wt Lftg; Cit Awd; High Hon Roll; Hon Roll.

BEAVEN, MONICA D; Catoosa HS; Claremore, OK; (3); Intnl Clb; Band; Hon Roll; 2nd Degree Black Belt Tae Kwon Do; Intnl Clb Act Coord; OSU; Massuese.

BEAVER, ANDREA; Collinsville HS; Collinsville, OK; (3); Church Yth Grp; FCA; Chorus; Chrldng; Tennis; Hon Roll; NHS; OU; Meterology.

BEAVER, BROOKE; Hilldale HS; Muskogee, OK; (3); 7/101; Drama Clb; FCA; Pres FHA; German Clb; Key Clb; Math Clb; Mu Alpha Theta; Sec Science Clb; Yrbk; Rep Stu Cncl; U Of AR; Jrnlsm.

BEAVER, DUSTIN L; Washington HS; Washington, OK; (1); Boy Scts; Church Yth Grp; Cmnty Wkr; 4-H; Natl FFA Org; 4-H Awd; Hon Roll; Prfct Atten Awd; OK ST U; Animal Sci.

BEAVER, JASON; Bethany HS; Bethany, OK; (3); Church Yth Grp; Var L Bsbl; Var L Bsktbl; Hon Roll; Amer Leg Bsbl; OK ST U; Gen Stds.

BEAVER, VANESSA; Pocola HS; Arkoma, OK; (2); FCA; VP Frsh Cls; Var Bsktbl; Var Chrldng; Gym; Sftbl; Hon Roll; Prfct Atten Awd; Gifted/Talented; Carl Albert.

BEAVERS, DANIEL C; Putnam City North HS; Oklahoma City, OK; (3); Am Leg Boys St; Church Yth Grp; FCA; JCL; Latin Clb; Office Aide; Pep Clb; Orch; Cit Awd; Hon Roll; Bicycle Racing; VP Latin Club; Oncology.

BEAVERS, JOSH J; Preston Schl; Okmulgee, OK; (1); Church Yth Grp; Quiz Bowl; Scholastic Bowl; High Hon Roll; Hon Roll; NHS; Tulsa U; Archaeology.

BEBEE, BRANDY D; Warner HS; Warner, OK; (1); Hon Roll; Upward Bound; Tsa La Gi Trail Of Tears Awd For Acad; Psych.

BEBEE, TAMMY D; Warner HS; Warner, OK; (3); Church Yth Grp; FCA; Spanish Clb; Powder Puff Ftbl; Sftbl; Hon Roll; Cmptr Lit Awd; US Achvmt Acad Awd; Nom Cong Yth Ldrshp Cncl; Conners ST Coll; Chld Dev.

BEBERMEYER, RACHEL; Victory Christian Schl; Tulsa, OK; (1); Color Guard; Rep Frsh Cls; Chrldng; Jr NHS.

BECANNEN, JACOB J; Edmond Memorial HS; Edmond, OK; (3); Church Yth Grp; FCA; Spanish Clb; SADD; Acpl Chr; Chorus; Church Choir; School Musical; School Play; Stage Crew; Battle Of Bands Wnnr; Act II Prfrmnc Trp; Oklahoma City U; Music.

BECERRA, FABIAN A; Southeast HS; Oklahoma City, OK; (2); FBLA; ROTC; Socr; High Hon Roll; NHS; GPA 3.78.

BECK, ALISA R; Jay HS; Jay, OK; (4); Church Yth Grp; FCA; FHA; German Clb; Natl Beta Clb; Office Aide; Pep Clb; Temple Yth Grp; Chorus; Church Choir; ST Vcl Cntsts; Ricks Coll; Music Prfrmnce.

BECK, BRIAN S; Enid Sr HS; Enid, OK; (2); 122/431; Church Yth Grp; Letterman Clb; Speech Tm; Teachers Aide; Band; Drm Mjr(t); Jazz Band; Mrchg Band; Pep Band; School Play.

BECK, CODY J; Jay HS; Spavinaw, OK; (3); FCA; Var Bsktbl; Hon Roll; Boys St.

BECK, JENNIFER; Holdenville HS; Atwood, OK; (4); 6/80; Church Yth Grp; Cmnty Wkr; Pres FCA; Natl Beta Clb; Scholastic Bowl; Science Clb; Acpl Chr; Chorus; Church Choir; Treas Stu Cncl; St FFA Chorus, Degree; St Profcncy Awd Oil Crop Prdctn; OK ST U; Animal Sci.

BECK, KENNETH A; Atoka HS; Stringtown, OK; (3); 1/89; Pres Church Yth Grp; Debate Tm; FCA; Natl FFA Org; Quiz Bowl; Scholastic Bowl; Speech Tm; SADD; Church Choir; School Play; Mock Trial Best Prosctng Atty; Pol Sci-Pre Law.

BECK, LISA M; Choctaw HS; Choctaw, OK; (3); 17/350; JV Bsktbl; Var Mgr(s); Var Score Keeper; Var Sftbl; Var Trk; Hon Roll; Jr NHS; Prfct Atten Awd; Sci Stu Mon; Outstndng Fresh Sprts Plyr; All Around Best Athl; U OK; Med.

BECK, RYAN; Fairview HS; Fairview, OK; (1); Church Yth Grp; Cmnty Wkr; FCA; Band; Mrchg Band; Pep Band; Var Bsbl; Var Bsktbl; Var Ftbl; High Hon Roll; Stu Mnth; OKU.

BECKER, AARON; Miami Sr HS; Miami, OK; (4); 10/121; Cmnty Wkr; Quiz Bowl; Scholastic Bowl; Teachers Aide; Band; Jazz Band; Mrchg Band; Pep Band; Golf; High Hon Roll; Martl Arts; All Amer Schlr; US Natl Ldrshp Mrt Awd; U OK; Meteorlgy.

BECKER, CRYSTAL; Okeene Jr Sr HS; Isabella, OK; (2); 2/35; Church Yth Grp; FHA; Pres Frsh Cls; Pres Soph Cls; Rep Stu Cncl; Chrldng; Gym; Trk; High Hon Roll; NHS; All Star Chrldr; U Of OK.

BECKER, DOUGLAS; Midwest City HS; Midwest City, OK; (3); Church Yth Grp; French Clb; FHA; Key Clb; Office Aide; SADD; Ofcr Bsbl; Golf.

BECKER, JOHN R; Enid Sr HS; Enid, OK; (2); 161/412; Boy Scts; Church Yth Grp; Band; Mrchg Band; Pep Band; Golf; Hon Roll; NHS; Eagle Scout; Northwest Hnr Band; Red Carpet Hnr Band; U Of AZ; Cmptr Eng.

BECKER, KERRY; Coweta HS; Coweta, OK; (3); Church Yth Grp; Cmnty Wkr; SADD; Band; Church Choir; Mrchg Band; Chrldng; Jr NHS; NHS; OP Hnr Soc; NSU; Tching.

BECKER, TARYN; Little Axe Sr HS; Newalla, OK; (4); Church Yth Grp; Spanish Clb; Teachers Aide; Band; Hon Roll; NHS; Htl Mgmt.

BECKHAM, CHAD; Cimarron Public Schl; Lahoma, OK; (1); 1/23; Church Yth Grp; Natl FFA Org; Scholastic Bowl; Science Clb; Band; Church Choir; Mrchg Band; Pep Band; High Hon Roll; Hon Roll; Camp Cnslr; Purdue; Arspc Engr.

BECKHAM, GREGG; Maysville Jr Sr HS; Maysville, OK; (2); 4-H; Natl FFA Org; Scholastic Bowl; Rptr Frsh Cls; 4-H Awd; High Hon Roll; NHS; Prfct Atten Awd; GATE Prgm; Outstndng Stdnt Chem/World His; Zoology.

BECKHAM, MIKE C; Putnam City North HS; Oklahoma City, OK; (2); German Clb; Bsktbl; Trk; Hon Roll; OK City Bombing Vol; Big Brother; OK Univ; Sprts Med.

BECKMAN, KARI A; Elgin HS; Lawton, OK; (2); Office Aide; Indian Hrtg Clb.

BECKTOLD, TAMBER L; Luther HS; Luther, OK; (4); 11/51; Art Clb; Church Yth Grp; Cmnty Wkr; Debate Tm; Spanish Clb; Teachers Aide; Band; Yrbk; Cit Awd; Hon Roll; OK ST U; Elem Ed.

BEDA, STEPHANIE N; Weatherford HS; Weatherford, OK; (3); 5/120; Church Yth Grp; FCA; Natl FFA Org; Rep Stu Cncl; Var L Bsktbl; Var L Crs Cntry; Ftbl; Var L Trk; High Hon Roll; Jr NHS.

BEEBE, AMANDA C; Nathan Hale HS; Tulsa, OK; (4); 21/203; Church Yth Grp; Cmnty Wkr; English Clb; Red Cross Aide; Spanish Clb; Teachers Aide; Church Choir; Ofcr Stu Cncl; High Hon Roll; NHS; Ecology Clb Pres 2 Yrs; Chrch Yth Grp Rep; U Tulsa; Commnctns.

BEEBE, JOSEPH; Enid Sr HS; Enid, OK; (2); 91/435; Church Yth Grp; Band; Jazz Band; Mrchg Band; Hon Roll; Jr NHS; NHS; Prfct Atten Awd.

BEEBY, MATT; Fairview HS; Fairview, OK; (4); 1/55; Am Leg Boys St; Church Yth Grp; FCA; Quiz Bowl; Pres Band; Mrchg Band; Pres Sr Cls; Var L Bsbl; Var L Bsktbl; Var L Ftbl; NOC Acad Bowl All Star; Outstnndg Stu Algebra, Hstry, Algebra III, French I, Calculus, French II; OK ST U; Arch.

BEEKMANN, MARTHA; Owasso Sr HS; Owasso, OK; (2); 1/451; Cmnty Wkr; English Clb; Library Aide; Math Tm; Office Aide; Quiz Bowl; Science Clb; Teachers Aide; Ofcr Stu Cncl; Cit Awd; Yng Repblcns Club; His Club; Great Books; Cardiovascular Surgeon.

BEEL, AMY; Westmoore HS; Oklahoma City, OK; (4); Am Leg Aux Girls St; Church Yth Grp; Cmnty Wkr; Debate Tm; FCA; Library Aide; Office Aide; Pep Clb; Teachers Aide; Mgr Bsbl; U Of OK.

BEEMAN, CASSIDY A; Choctaw HS; Oklahoma City, OK; (4); 1/313; FCA; Key Clb; Treas SADD; JV Var Bsktbl; Tennis; Hon Roll; Jr NHS; NHS; Pres Acad Fit Awd; All Amer Schlr; U Of OK; Engrng.

BEENE, AMY L; Mc Loud HS; Mc Loud, OK; (3); FTA; Rep Hist Natl FFA Org; Stat Bsktbl; Hon Roll; OK ST Univ; Phy Thrpst.

BEENE, BRANDON; Commanche Sr HS; Comanche, OK; (4); 12/60; Cmnty Wkr; Natl FFA Org; Teachers Aide; Var Bsbl; L Ftbl; High Hon Roll; Hon Roll; NHS; Prfct Atten Awd; Seminole ST Coll; Crmnl Juste.

BEENE, CHRIS; Stigler HS; Stigler, OK; (1); Boy Scts; SADD; JV Bsktbl; Hon Roll; Pres Acad Fit Awd; OK ST U; Vet.

BEENE, STEPHANIE A; Haskell HS; Haskell, OK; (1); Church Yth Grp; FHA; Band; Mrchg Band; Pep Band; Intrml Chrldng; Hon Roll; Tulsa JC; Dntl Hygnst.

BEESE, AARON; Newcastle HS; Newcastle, OK; (2); 1/80; Am Leg Boys St; Church Yth Grp; Model UN; Quiz Bowl; Scholastic Bowl; Science Clb; Var Bsktbl; High Hon Roll; NHS; Arch.

BEESLEY, CHAD M; Webster HS; Tulsa, OK; (2); Church Yth Grp; FBLA; Key Clb; Band; Drm Mjr(t); Mrchg Band; Pres Frsh Cls; Sec Soph Cls; JV Bsbl; NHS; Stanford; Coach; Sports Mgmt.

BEESLEY, LACY J; Minco HS; Minco, OK; (3); Church Yth Grp; Cmnty Wkr; FCA; FBLA; FHA; Girl Scts; Natl FFA Org; SADD; Church Choir; Art Clb; SW; Bus.

BEESON, CARRIE J; Sayre HS; Sayre, OK; (3); 7/54; Am Leg Aux Girls St; Church Yth Grp; Sec Natl FFA Org; Scholastic Bowl; Chorus; Rptr Phtg Yrbk; Sec Frsh Cls; Rep Stu Cncl; High Hon Roll; Pep Clb; Acctng; Bookkeeping.

BEESON, JAIME; Edmond Memorial HS; Edmond, OK; (4); 54/322; FCA; Office Aide; Spanish Clb; Mgr(s); Hon Roll; U Of Central OK.

BEESON, JEDD E; Duncan HS; Duncan, OK; (2); Church Yth Grp; FCA; Letterman Clb; Var Bsbl; Var Bsktbl.

BEHRENS, KATIE E; Putnam City North HS; Oklahoma City, OK; (2); 112/490; Church Yth Grp; Drama Clb; Key Clb; SADD; Chorus; Church Choir; School Play; Stage Crew; High Hon Roll; NHS; OCU; Musical Ther.

BEHRENS, KOURTNI; Dickson HS; Ardmore, OK; (1); Church Yth Grp; English Clb; FCA; FHA; Math Clb; Natl FFA Org; Spanish Clb; SADD; VP Frsh Cls; Chrldng; FFA Sentinel; Hs Stu Cncl; OSU; Agrcltrl Ed Tchr.

BEIKMANN, DEANNE M; El Reno Sr HS; El Reno, OK; (2); 47/227; Pres Art Clb; VP Church Yth Grp; Drama Clb; Library Aide; Thesps; School Play; Stage Crew; Cit Awd; French Hon Soc; Hon Roll; Cncordia; Drama; Art; Early Chldh.

BEISLEY, DUSTIN; Dewey HS; Dewey, OK; (3); Natl FFA Org; Teachers Aide; VP Soph Cls; Ofcr Stu Cncl; Var L Ftbl; Var L Trk; Var L Wt Lftg; Hon Roll; NHS; Pres Acad Fit Awd; OK ST; Educ.

BEISTLE, ADRIENNA N; Pauls Valley HS; Pauls Valley, OK; (1); French Clb; Band; Mrchg Band; Ofcr Frsh Cls; Tennis; Photo; E Cntrl Univ; Lawyer; X-Ray Tech.

BEITTENMILLER, NATHAN C; Ardmore HS; Ardmore, OK; (3); 17/202; French Clb; Mu Alpha Theta; Quiz Bowl; Science Clb; Teachers Aide; Orch; Hon Roll; NHS; Comp Sys Analysis; Chem Engrng.

BEJCEK, STACI L; Oologah HS; Oologah, OK; (3); 12/120; Am Leg Aux Girls St; Pres Church Yth Grp; Debate Tm; Drama Clb; Pres NFL; School Play; Stage Crew; Variety Show; Hon Roll; NHS; Southeastern ST Univ; Math/His.

BELDEN, SARAH A; Broken Arrow Sr HS; Broken Arrow, OK; (3); Church Yth Grp; Drama Clb; Intnl Clb; Teachers Aide; Acpl Chr; Church Choir; School Musical; Yrbk; Rep Stu Cncl; Hon Roll; Poetry & Wrtng Awds; Multi-Yr Listee; SBU; Sports Medicine.

BELK, DENISE M; Sapulpa Sr HS; Sapulpa, OK; (2); 33/350; School Play; Rep Frsh Cls; Rep Soph Cls; Sec Jr Cls; Rep Stu Cncl; Mgr Var Bsktbl; High Hon Roll; Jr NHS; Pres Acad Fit Awd; Church Yth Grp; Kiwanis Soph Of Yr-OK/TX; OK ST Univ; Ed/Sprts Med.

BELL, AMANDA; Apache HS; Apache, OK; (2); Church Yth Grp; HOBY; Natl FFA Org; VP Band; VP Mrchg Band; VP Pep Band; Var Chrldng; Score Keeper; Hon Roll; OSU; Bus Tchr.

BELL, ANDREA; Oklahoma Christian Schl; Jones, OK; (3); 2/48; Church Yth Grp; Debate Tm; Drama Clb; Scholastic Bowl; Speech Tm; Teachers Aide; School Play; Var Socr; Var Sftbl; TX A&M.

BELL, BETHANY; Wright Christian Acad; Tulsa, OK; (3); Church Yth Grp; Sec Soph Cls; Var Chrldng; Var Tennis; Pepperdine; Advertising.

BELL, CLEVELAND; Star Spencer HS; Midwest City, OK; (1); FBLA; HOBY; ROTC; Color Guard; Drill Tm; DAR Awd; Dghtrs Of Fndrs & Patriots Of Amer; Outstndng JROTC Perfmnc Awd; FL A&M U; Comp Tech.

BELL, FREDERICK; Central HS; Tulsa, OK; (4); Office Aide; VICA; Hon Roll; Natl Vo Tech Hnr Soc; OSU.

BELL, JAMES; Midwest City HS; Midwest City, OK; (4); 94/412; Am Leg Boys St; FCA; French Clb; FHA; Office Aide; Teachers Aide; Rep Stu Cncl; Ofcr Bsbl; Ftbl; Hon Roll; All-Conf Ftbl 92-95; All-Conf Bsbl 93-94 & 94-95; Snblt Clssc 94-95; All-Dist Ftbl 95; Crmnl Jstc.

BELL, JAMIE; Douglass HS; Oklahoma City, OK; (4); 9/116; Bus Profs of Am; Church Yth Grp; Computer Clb; English Clb; FBLA; Library Aide; ROTC; Church Choir; Drill Tm; Ofcr Stu Cncl.

BELL, JULIE A; Catoosa HS; Tulsa, OK; (4); 48/126; Office Aide; Teachers Aide; Rptr Nwsp; Co-Ed Yrbk; Ofcr Bsbl; Sftbl; Hon Roll; St Hnr Scty; Bst Offnsve Sftbll Player; Tulsa Jc; Ed.

BELL, JUSTIN W; Thomas A Edison HS; Tulsa, OK; (4); 4/178; Church Yth Grp; Latin Clb; Office Aide; Pep Clb; Spanish Clb; Teachers Aide; Rep Frsh Cls; Rep Soph Cls; Rep Jr Cls; Rep Sr Cls; OK ST U; Bus.

BELL, KRISTINA E; Catoosa HS; Tulsa, OK; (2); FCA; GAA; Spanish Clb; Yrbk; Sftbl; Best Def Playr; Paralegl.

BELL, LACI A; Cameron Schl; Cameron, OK; (2); 4/35; FCA; FHA; GAA; Quiz Bowl; Ofcr Frsh Cls; Ofcr Soph Cls; Bsktbl; Sftbl; Vllybl; Hon Roll; Connors; Neurosurgeon.

BELL, LORI; Catoosa HS; Catoosa, OK; (3); Church Yth Grp; Intnl Clb; Spanish Clb; Nwsp; Sec Frsh Cls; Sec Jr Cls; Chrldng; Gym; Score Keeper; Homcmng Attendant Soph; OK ST; Television Broadcastng.

BELL, MARY R; Morris HS; Okmulgee, OK; (3); 1/65; Girl Scts; Pep Clb; Band; Mrchg Band; School Play; Hon Roll; NHS; Prfct Atten Awd; OK Hemophilia Soc Vol; Marine Bio.

BELL, MEGHAN M; Olive Jr Sr HS; Bristow, OK; (2); 1/36; Art Clb; Church Yth Grp; Scholastic Bowl; Science Clb; Speech Tm; Rep Frsh Cls; Rep Soph Cls; Bsktbl; Cit Awd; Hon Roll.

BELL, NINA N; Lawton Sr HS; Lawton, OK; (3); Drama Clb; Chorus; School Play; Rep Stu Cncl; Hon Roll; Prfct Atten Awd; Won Best Actress Awd; Psych.

BELL, PRISCILLA K; Hobart HS; Hobart, OK; (3); FHA; FTA; Hosp Aide; Library Aide; Teachers Aide; NHS; RN.

BELL, PRISCILLA M; El Reno Sr HS; El Reno, OK; (2); Church Yth Grp; FHA; Natl FFA Org; Hon Roll; Renaissance; 2 Yr CC; Psych.

BELL, SARA; Mangum Sr HS; Mangum, OK; (1); 3/53; Church Yth Grp; VP Frsh Cls; JV Bsktbl; Chrldng; Sftbl; Trk; Hon Roll; NHS.

BELL, SHAREESE; Chisholm Sr HS; Enid, OK; (2); Church Yth Grp; Cmnty Wkr; FCA; GAA; Spanish Clb; VP Soph Cls; Var Bsktbl; Var Crs Cntry; Trk; Wt Lftg; Barrel Racing; OSU; Vet.

BELLAMY, HEATHER C; Yukon Middle HS; Yukon, OK; (2); Church Yth Grp; Debate Tm; FHA; Speech Tm; Drill Tm; Var Pom Pon; Powder Puff Ftbl; High Hon Roll; Jr NHS; NHS; 3d Don'T Do Drugs; PT.

BELLER, JOSHUA; Coalgate HS; Coalgate, OK; (4); 2/43; Am Leg Boys St; Church Yth Grp; Cmnty Wkr; FCA; FBLA; Natl FFA Org; Office Aide; Teachers Aide; Rptr Nwsp; VP Jr Cls; Acad Athl Awd; U Tulsa.

BELLETTINI, B J; Coalgate HS; Coalgate, OK; (4); 1/43; Am Leg Boys St; FCA; Natl FFA Org; Cit Awd; High Hon Roll; Jr NHS; NHS; Val; Boy Scts; Church Yth Grp; Stu Mon, Today, Athl Acad Awds; OSU; Med.

BELLINGER, BRAD S; Bethany HS; Oklahoma City, OK; (4); 27/81; Church Yth Grp; FCA; Rep Sr Cls; Rep Stu Cncl; Var Bsbl; Var Bsktbl; JV Tennis; Var Vllybl; Hon Roll; Pres Acad Fit Awd; OK ST Univ; Mech Eng.

BELLISARIO, MARYANN C; Choctaw HS; Oklahoma City, OK; (3); 15/250; Church Yth Grp; Drama Clb; Key Clb; Stage Crew; Hon Roll; Jr NHS.

BELLON, JOSH J; Altus Sr HS; Altus, OK; (2); Art Clb; Church Yth Grp; Drama Clb; Hon Roll; WOSC; Art; Eng.

BELONCIK, APRIL E; Chandler HS; Chandler, OK; (3); 7/79; Am Leg Aux Girls St; Girl Scts; Spanish Clb; Teachers Aide; Chorus; School Musical; Variety Show; Ofcr Frsh Cls; Pres Jr Cls; Rep Stu Cncl; Dance; NA; Nrsng.

BELSHE, CHASITY D; Tecumseh HS; Tecumseh, OK; (3); #3 in class; Pres French Clb; FHA; Teachers Aide; JV Bsktbl; Var Sftbl; High Hon Roll; Hon Roll; Jr NHS; NHS; Cornell Univ; Vet.

BELTER, CARRIE; Claremore Sr HS; Claremore, OK; (2); #1 in class; Church Yth Grp; Debate Tm; Drama Clb; French Clb; Quiz Bowl; Speech Tm; Var Gym; Hon Roll; NHS; Acad Ltr Acad Bwl; 2nd Pl Conf Acad Bwl.

BELTER, STEPHEN L; Claremore Sr HS; Claremore, OK; (4); Boy Scts; Church Yth Grp; Debate Tm; German Clb; NFL; Speech Tm; NHS; Yth For Understndg Intl Exch Pgm; Boston U; Commnctns.

BELTON, KESHA L; Boynton Schl; Boynton, OK; (3); Church Yth Grp; FHA; Natl FFA Org; VICA; Bsktbl; Chrldng; Sftbl; 4-H Awd; Hon Roll; Upwrd Bnd Pgm Bacone Coll; Air Force.

BELVIN, RACHAEL; Balko Public Schl; Balko, OK; (4); 1/19; Am Leg Aux Girls St; FHA; Pep Clb; Band; Chorus; Church Choir; Pep Band; Bsktbl; Chrldng; NHS; Med.

BEN, MOE M; Clayton Jr Sr HS; Clayton, OK; (3); Church Yth Grp; Band; Band 5 Yrs; Rdng Olympcs Wnnr 2 Yrs; Med Field.

BENANZER, JULIE M; Putnam City HS; Oklahoma City, OK; (2); Art Clb; Church Yth Grp; FCA; GAA; Spanish Clb; Teachers Aide; Varsity Clb; Var Socr; Hon Roll; 3-D; PT.

BENCH, JAMI B; Guthrie Sr HS; Guthrie, OK; (4); 27/167; VP Spanish Clb; SADD; Ed Yrbk; Prfct Atten Awd; Stdnt Infrmtn Serv; U Of Cntrl OK; Early Child Ed.

BENDER, EMILY D; Putnam City North HS; Oklahoma City, OK; (3); 5/497; Spanish Clb; Acpl Chr; Pres Church Choir; School Musical; Swing Chorus; Cit Awd; High Hon Roll; Sec NHS; OMEA All-ST Chorus; Smith Coll Bk Awd; Grd Schl Stu Mentor.

BENDER, LACI; Perry Sr HS; Perry, OK; (3); 12/93; FCA; German Clb; Nwsp; Bsktbl; Powder Puff Ftbl; Sftbl; Trk; Hon Roll; NHS; All Amer Schlr; Speech Path.

BENDER, SYLVIA L; Central Mid-HS; Norman, OK; (2); Art Clb; Drama Clb; French Clb; School Play; Stage Crew; Hon Roll; Model Cngrss; Frnch II Poetry 1st; U Of WI; Lib Arts.

BENEAR, SASHA N; Putnam City West HS; Warr Acres, OK; (3); 43/303; Church Yth Grp; Band; Chorus; School Play; Hnrd U Of OK HS Acad Achvtms Math, Art, Swmmng; Math.

BENEDICT, CHAD; Ada HS; Ada, OK; (4); 3/187; Church Yth Grp; Cmnty Wkr; Debate Tm; HOBY; Math Clb; Mu Alpha Theta; NFL; Science Clb; Spanish Clb; Speech Tm; Mck Trl Outstndng Atty; SE OK HOBY Clb Pres; Rice U; Law.

BENEFIELD, CLENT; Howe Public Schl; Howe, OK; (2); 8/25; Church Yth Grp; Natl FFA Org; SADD; Yrbk; Pres Soph Cls; Var Bsbl; Var Bsktbl; Trk; Wt Lftg; Hon Roll; Forestry Jdgng; Soil Cnsrvtn; Land Capability; Forestry Bio.

BENEFIELD, JEFF; Western Heights Sr HS; Mustang, OK; (4); Church Yth Grp; Cmnty Wkr; DECA; FCA; Letterman Clb; Math Clb; Teachers Aide; Varsity Clb; Chorus; Church Choir; Outstdng Male Ath; OK Chrstn.

BENES, KILEY T; Pawnee HS; Pawnee, OK; (3); 7/70; Church Yth Grp; Computer Clb; Math Tm; Bsktbl; Golf; Cit Awd; High Hon Roll; Prfct Atten Awd; Comp Sci.

BENGS, MORGAN; Kingfisher HS; Kingfisher, OK; (2); Church Yth Grp; Cmnty Wkr; FCA; Quiz Bowl; Scholastic Bowl; JV Ftbl; Var Wrstlng; High Hon Roll; NHS; Sci.

BENGTSON, KASEY L; Vinita HS; Vinita, OK; (2); Church Yth Grp; Spanish Clb; Band; Chorus; Trk; Hon Roll; Rodeo; WY U; Acctng.

BENITEZ, MARILYN C; Eisenhower Sr HS; Lawton, OK; (3); 1/485; Model UN; Chorus; School Musical; School Play; L Swmmng; High Hon Roll; Hon Roll; Jr NHS; NHS; Prfct Atten Awd; Jr Ldrshp Lawton; Aim-Hi Team; Med Explorers Treas; U Of OK; Pediatrician.

BENJAMIN, ALICIA M; Lomega HS; Kingfisher, OK; (2); 2/14; Rep 4-H; GAA; Rep Stu Cncl; JV Bsktbl; NHS; Prfct Atten Awd; OK Hnr Soc; Supr Hnr Rl; Humanities Awd; Adventist Coll; Marine Bio.

BENJAMIN, LORETTA J; Checotah HS; Council Hill, OK; (3); FBLA; FHA; Var Chrldng; Trk; High Hon Roll; Natl Math Awd; HOSA; Natl Voc Tech Hnr Soc; OK Univ; Med Field.

BENNER, MISTY D; Webster HS; Tulsa, OK; (3); Sec DECA; FBLA; Key Clb; Sec Frsh Cls; Treas Sr Cls; Ofcr Stu Cncl; Var Score Keeper; JV Trk; High Hon Roll; Hon Roll.

BENNETT, ALECIA M; Will Rogers HS; Tulsa, OK; (3); DECA; Key Clb; Rep Stu Cncl; Med Field.

BENNETT, ANGELA N; Harrah HS; Harrah, OK; (4); 24/91; FCA; SADD; Pres Sr Cls; Rep Stu Cncl; Var Co-Capt Bsktbl; Tennis; Hon Roll; Church Yth Grp; French Clb; Whos Who In Sports; US Army Reserve Natl Schlr Ath Awd; Mid Amer Bible Coll; Behvrl Sci.

BENNETT, ASHLEY D; Healdton HS; Healdton, OK; (2); Treas Jr Cls; Var Bsktbl; Var Chrldng; Var Golf; Cit Awd; High Hon Roll; NHS; Pres Acad Fit Awd; Pres Schlr; St Schlr; Ophmlgy/Coll Prof.

BENNETT, CARL D; Lawton Sr HS; Lawton, OK; (2); Var Tennis; High Hon Roll; Jr NHS; NHS; Ntl Merit Ltr; Bowling; Acad Clb; Renaissance Acad Achvmnt Awd; Med.

BENNETT, CASEY P; Putnam City North HS; Oklahoma City, OK; (3); FCA; Ofcr Bsbl; Bsktbl; Ftbl; Wt Lftg; Cit Awd.

BENNETT, CHRIS D; Shawnee Sr HS; Shawnee, OK; (1); FCA; Var L Ftbl; Var L Wrstlng; High Hon Roll; OK ST Univ; Sports Med.

BENNETT, CODY L; Shawnee Sr HS; Shawnee, OK; (3); FCA; L Ftbl; L Wrstlng; Hon Roll; NHS; ECU; Sprts Med/Sci Tchr.

BENNETT, JAMILA K; B T Washington HS; Tulsa, OK; (4); 69/264; FBLA; Pep Clb; Drm Mjr(t); School Musical; School Play; Sec Sr Cls; Var Trk; Hon Roll; NHS; Howard U; Bio.

BENNETT, JULIANNA A; Sapulpa Sr HS; Sapulpa, OK; (3); 1/250; Debate Tm; Key Clb; Natl FFA Org; NFL; Science Clb; Speech Tm; Flag Corp; Mrchg Band; High Hon Roll; NHS; OSU; Vet.

BENNETT, MATTHEW; Poteau HS; Poteau, OK; (4); Am Leg Boys St; Pres Frsh Cls; Pres Sr Cls; Rep Stu Cncl; Var Ftbl; Var Trk; Capt Var Wrstlng; OSU; Engrng.

BENNETT, MICHELLE; Jarman Jr HS; Midwest City, OK; (1); Letterman Clb; Pep Clb; Spanish Clb; Var Chrldng; Var Trk; Var Vllybl; Wt Lftg; NHS; OU; Phy Ther.

BENNETT, SHERRY; Durant HS; Durant, OK; (3); Spanish Clb; Chorus; Church Choir; Drill Tm; Nwsp; VP Soph Cls; Rep Stu Cncl; High Hon Roll; All St Chorus.

BENNETT, T J; Mustang HS; Yukon, OK; (4); 150/350; Am Leg Boys St; FCA; Spanish Clb; Var L Ftbl; Capt Powder Puff Ftbl; Var L Trk; Ftbl All Dist Offnsv Lineman 95-96; Ftbl Hmcmng Crt 95; Engrng.

BENNETT, TIMIA J; Union Sr HS; Tulsa, OK; (2); Library Aide; Rep Stu Cncl; Hon Roll; Trs Afro-Amer Soc; Mem For Lang Clb; Bus Mgmt.

BENNETT-WILLIAMSON, LAURA S; Putnam City North HS; Oklahoma City, OK; (4); Drama Clb; French Clb; JA; Library Aide; NFL; School Play; Hon Roll; NHS; Ntl Merit SF; OK ST U; Med.

BENSCH, CHERYL; Laverne Jr Sr HS; Logan, OK; (3); #1 in class; Church Yth Grp; 4-H; FHA; Natl Beta Clb; Chorus; Flag Corp; School Play; Pres Jr Cls; Rep Stu Cncl; Trk; Bible Clb Pres 96-97; Sr Cls Pres 96-97; OK Girl St; Apost Faith Bible Clg; Intr Dsg.

BENSCH, JEANNE; Seiling Schl; Seiling, OK; (4); 2/34; Church Yth Grp; Drama Clb; FCA; FBLA; Pres Natl Beta Clb; Office Aide; Band; School Musical; Pres Sr Cls; NHS; OSU.

BENSCH, RACHELLE; Seiling Schl; Fairview, OK; (4); 4/34; VP Church Yth Grp; Sec Natl Beta Clb; Speech Tm; Teachers Aide; Flag Corp; Sec Sr Cls; Capt Chrldng; NHS; Rainbow Grand Offcr; NWOSU; Phys Thrpy.

BENSCH, RHONDA; Seiling Schl; Chester, OK; (2); FCA; FHA; Letterman Clb; Band; Chorus; Bsktbl; Var Cit Awd; Hon Roll; NHS; Mar Bio.

BENSON, TIFFANY; Woodward HS; Woodward, OK; (1); FCA; Pep Clb; Bsktbl; Mgr(s); Trk; High Hon Roll; Hon Roll; Ntl Merit Ltr; OK Hnr Soc; Wrtng Wood Winner.

BENTLEY, AMBER; Hobart HS; Hobart, OK; (2); 10/90; Church Yth Grp; FCA; 4-H; GAA; Natl FFA Org; Rep Stu Cncl; Var Bsktbl; Var Sftbl; Hon Roll; NHS; OK ST U.

BENTLEY, AMY; Coyle Public Schl; Coyle, OK; (3); 1/25; Am Leg Aux Girls St; FHA; German Clb; Hosp Aide; Natl FFA Org; Ed Yrbk; Var Capt Bsktbl; Gov Hon Prg Awd; High Hon Roll; NHS.

BENTLEY, JASON; Piedmont HS; Piedmont, OK; (2); HOBY; Band; Rptr Frsh Cls; Rep Stu Cncl; JV Var Bsktbl; JV Var Ftbl; Hnr Band Tri-ST; People To People Stndt Ambssdr/Australia/New Zealand.

BENTLEY, JULIA; Edmond Memorial HS; Edmond, OK; (2); FCA; Key Clb; Science Clb; Spanish Clb; Chorus; JV Chrldng; Var L Sftbl; L Trk; Intrml Wt Lftg; Hon Roll; 1st Pl St Overall Grp & Ensmbl-Vcl Msc; Cert Instr Smkng Prvntn Tchr Elem Stus; Piano; OK Hnr Soc.

BENTLEY, JUSTIN D; Pond Creek-Hunter Schl; Pond Creek, OK; (3); FCA; Rptr 4-H; Natl FFA Org; Pep Clb; Ofcr Frsh Cls; Sec Soph Cls; Rptr Jr Cls; Var Bsbl; Var Ftbl; Var Wt Lftg.

BENTLEY, MELISSA D; Altus Sr HS; Altus, OK; (4); French Clb; Scholastic Bowl; Chorus; High Hon Roll; OK Hnr Soc; U Of Tulsa; Cnslng.

BENTLEY, MISTY L; Hartshorne Sr HS; Hartshorne, OK; (3); Church Yth Grp; FHA; Hon Roll; OK Univ; Law.

BENTLEY, SHACOY R; Buffalo Jr Sr HS; Buffalo, OK; (1); Church Yth Grp; Pep Clb; Chorus; Var Chrldng; Interdnmnl Yth Grp Chrstn Action; Cnslr Abused/Troubled Kids.

BENTLEY, TRACEE; Claremore Sr HS; Claremore, OK; (4); #1 in class; Hosp Aide; Scholastic Bowl; School Play; Hon Roll; NHS; Val; Brdcstng.

BENTLEY, WILLARD S; Southeast HS; Oklahoma City, OK; (1); Art Clb; Chess Clb; Church Yth Grp; FCA; JA; Gov Hon Prg Awd; High GPA Hnr Rl; OK Univ; Coll Prof/Coach/Tchr.

BENTON, KEISHA D; Healdton HS; Healdton, OK; (2); Church Yth Grp; FCA; FHA; Library Aide; Office Aide; Teachers Aide; Chorus; Church Choir; Trk; OK Bapt U.

BENTON, PAIGE C; Edmond Memorial HS; Edmond, OK; (3); Church Yth Grp; FCA; Red Cross Aide; Spanish Clb; SADD; Nwsp; Yrbk; Ofcr Frsh Cls; Ofcr Jr Cls; Trk; Envrnmntl Engr.

BENTON, TONY; Jarman Jr HS; Tinker Afb, OK; (1); Spanish Clb; Band; Sec Frsh Cls; Ofcr Bsbl; Cit Awd; Jr NHS; All-Rgn Hnr Bnd 1st Chr; All-Dist Hnr Bnd; Duke U; Band.

BEOTTLER, AMARA; Hennessey HS; Hennessey, OK; (3); 1/62; Church Yth Grp; HOBY; Quiz Bowl; Scholastic Bowl; Band; Church Choir; Drm Mjr(t); Pres Jr Cls; NHS; Sthrn Nzrne U; Elem Ed.

BERG, JOSH; Adair HS; Adair, OK; (3); FCA; Natl FFA Org; Science Clb; Teachers Aide; Pres Frsh Cls; Pres Soph Cls; Pres Jr Cls; Rep Stu Cncl; Var Bsbl; Var Bsktbl; OK U.

BERG, KAREN; Okeene Jr Sr HS; Okeene, OK; (4); 9/26; Am Leg Aux Girls St; Drama Clb; FHA; Speech Tm; SADD; Band; Hon Roll; Kiwanis Awd; Prfct Atten Awd; S Nazarene U; Med.

BERG, SABRINA; Timberlake Schl; Helena, OK; (4); 6/24; Am Leg Aux Girls St; FCA; FHA; VP Sr Cls; Var Bsktbl; Var Chrldng; Var Sftbl; Hon Roll; NHS; Bsktbl Awds; Nrthwstrn OK ST U; Psych.

BERGER, KARISSA; Moore HS; Oklahoma City, OK; (2); Church Yth Grp; FCA; SADD; Teachers Aide; Chorus; Church Choir; School Play; Variety Show; Chrldng; Trk; OU; Medcl.

BERGERON, VIKKI; Empire Schl; Duncan, OK; (2); Church Yth Grp; Cmnty Wkr; FBLA; FHA; Hosp Aide; Rep Soph Cls; Rep Stu Cncl; Var Bsktbl; Hon Roll; NHS; Natl Govt & His Awd; Natl Math Awd; Jet Skiing & Camping; U Of OK; Bio; Cardiologist.

BERGIN, JENNIFER; Yukon Middle HS; Yukon, OK; (2); Dance Clb; FHA; Pep Clb; SADD; Pom Pon; Hon Roll; NHS; All-Amer Schlrs; NHS.

BERGIN, LAURA E; Putnam City North HS; Oklahoma City, OK; (4); 128/464; Church Yth Grp; FCA; French Clb; Key Clb; Office Aide; SADD; Pom Pon; DAR Awd; NHS; OK Bapt Univ; His; Coll Prof.

BERGLAN, THAJA D; Choctaw HS; Choctaw, OK; (4); 21/305; Church Yth Grp; FCA; Key Clb; Office Aide; Spanish Clb; Yrbk; Bsktbl; Hon Roll; Jr NHS; NHS; U Of OK; Phys Thrp.

BERGMAN, JESSICA; Edmond North HS; Edmond, OK; (3); 20/360; Church Yth Grp; Cmnty Wkr; Drama Clb; FCA; Key Clb; Mu Alpha Theta; VP Natl Beta Clb; Pep Clb; Service Clb; Spanish Clb; Tap, Jazz, Ballet & Lyrical Dance.

BERGMANN, JAKE R; Putnam City HS; Oklahoma City, OK; (3); 21/363; Church Yth Grp; FCA; FBLA; Letterman Clb; Ski Clb; Ofcr Bsbl; Bsktbl; High Hon Roll; Hon Roll; NHS; Sprts Med/Orthdntcs.

BERGMEIER, GRETCHEN; Piedmont HS; Piedmont, OK; (2); Chorus; VP Pres Frsh Cls; Pres Soph Cls; Rep Stu Cncl; Stat Bsktbl; Var L Chrldng; Var L Sftbl; High Hon Roll; Hon Roll; NHS.

BERGNER, MELISSA; Midwest City HS; Tinker Afb, OK; (3); 45/405; French Clb; FHA; SADD; Ofcr Jr Cls; Mgr(s); Vllybl; Jr NHS; NHS; CONS Rptr; OK Dance Mstrs Assn; FL ST U; Marine Bio.

BERGREN, ALLISON D; Edmond Memorial HS; Edmond, OK; (2); 1/408; French Clb; Chorus; Church Choir; School Musical; NHS.

BERGREN, LYNSEY L; Edmond Memorial HS; Edmond, OK; (2); 61/408; Dance Clb; FCA; Spanish Clb; Chorus; Variety Show; Pom Pon; NHS; All Amrcn Dncr; One Mnth Dnce Schol To Edge Perf Arts Cntr; Asst Dncetchr; Intr Dsgn.

BERGREN, STEVEN M; Edmond Memorial HS; Edmond, OK; (4); 7/322; Church Yth Grp; Spanish Clb; Chorus; Church Choir; School Musical; School Play; Stage Crew; Swing Chorus; Variety Show; NHS; OK ST U; Elec Engrng.

BERKEY, TAMARA; Moyers Public Schl; Moyers, OK; (1); 2/20; 4-H; Spanish Clb; VP Frsh Cls; Var Bsktbl; Var Chrldng; Var Trk; 4-H Awd; Hon Roll; Prfct Atten Awd; USAA; SOSU.

BERKOWITZ, AARON M; B T Washington HS; Tulsa, OK; (1); Temple Yth Grp; Jr NHS; MIT; Physcst.

BERKOWITZ, STEVEN M; Norman Sr HS; Norman, OK; (4); 1/672; Boy Scts; Debate Tm; Model UN; Mu Alpha Theta; NFL; Spanish Clb; Ofcr Stu Cncl; Hon Roll; NHS; Ntl Merit SF; Boys Scts Order Arrow; Poly Sci.

BERNABE, BERENICE A; Douglass HS; Oklahoma City, OK; (2); Latin Clb; Socr; Sftbl; Prfct Atten Awd.

BERNAL, GABRIEL; Will Rogers HS; Tulsa, OK; (2); Cmnty Wkr; Key Clb; Rep Soph Cls; Rep Stu Cncl; JV Ftbl; Hon Roll; CO ST U; Bus.

BERNARD, JESSICA R; Christian Heritage Acad; Moore, OK; (2); Church Yth Grp; Office Aide; Chorus; School Play; Yrbk; Sec Jr Cls; Var Tennis; Var Vllybl; Hon Roll; Page For OK House Of Rep; Missions Trips To Belize Mexico Yganda Zambia; Chrstn Character Awds; U Of OK; Jrnlsm.

BERNARD, TONI; Hollis Jr Sr HS; Hollis, OK; (4); 10/57; Church Yth Grp; FBLA; Letterman Clb; Teachers Aide; School Play; Rptr Nwsp; Sec Stu Cncl; Capt Bsktbl; Mgr Ftbl; Var Sftbl.

BERNHART, ANKE; Stillwater Sr HS; Stillwater, OK; (3); 54/363; Pres German Clb; Hosp Aide; Mu Alpha Theta; Natl Beta Clb; Teachers Aide; Chorus; Score Keeper; High Hon Roll; Hon Roll; NHS; Sci Careers Clb VP; TOG Sec; TABS; OSU; Ped Srgry.

BERNS, ASHLEY B; Shawnee Sr HS; Shawnee, OK; (1); High Hon Roll; Kiwanis Awd; Prfct Atten Awd; Pep Clb; Tutor; Lions Clb Awd; Nrsng.

BERRONG, MARISSA; Clinton HS; Clinton, OK; (3); Church Yth Grp; FCA; Spanish Clb; Treas Stu Cncl; Chrldng; Hon Roll; Show Choir; Jazz Choir; Adv Chorus.

BERRY, COURTNEY; Waurika Sr HS; Waurika, OK; (4); 1/35; Pres Church Yth Grp; Hosp Aide; HOBY; Natl Beta Clb; Pres Band; School Musical; Pres Stu Cncl; Chrldng; Sec NHS; Val; Nrthestrn ST U; Vision Sci.

BERRY, ELIZABETH; Sapulpa Jr HS; Sapulpa, OK; (1); Church Yth Grp; Dance Clb; FHA; Drill Tm; Ofcr Stu Cncl; Chrldng; Golf; Score Keeper; Tennis; French Hon Soc.

BERRY, JULIE B; Union Intermediate HS; Tulsa, OK; (2); Girl Scts; Office Aide; Spanish Clb; Teachers Aide; Band; JV Sftbl; Clrnt/Gtr/Piano; Med Fld.

BERRY, MELANIE; Wetumka Jr Sr HS; Wetumka, OK; (2); 1/47; Cmnty Wkr; GAA; Treas Key Clb; Quiz Bowl; Band; Flag Corp; Pres Frsh Cls; Rep Soph Cls; JV Bsktbl; Trk; St Hnr Socty; OK ST U; Elem Tchr.

BERRY, TINA M; Wapanucka Schl; Wapanucka, OK; (3); 4-H; Rptr Frsh Cls; Rptr Jr Cls; 4-H Awd; Hon Roll; NHS; Ntl Merit Ltr; Drama Clb; GAA; Quiz Bowl; E Cntrl Univ Currclm Meet 3rdpl Nwsprp Ed/2nd Pl Bus Math; SE OK ST Univ Currclm Meet 4th Span I; Video Prod.

BERRYHILL, NICOLE M; Weleetka Sr HS; Okemah, OK; (3); FHA; Spanish Clb; Band; Mrchg Band; Stage Crew; JV Bsktbl; Sftbl; Hon Roll; NHS; Native Amer Club; Rdgrphc Tech.

BERRYMAN, AMY; Tulsa Memorial HS; Tulsa, OK; (4); 4/250; Am Leg Aux Girls St; Church Yth Grp; Pres German Clb; Pres Girl Scts; Pres Key Clb; Band; Chorus; Capt Swmmng; High Hon Roll; Sec NHS; Phys Thrpy.

BERRYMAN, SHANNON; Ada HS; Ada, OK; (3); Mu Alpha Theta; SADD; Church Choir; Pres Jr Cls; Rep Stu Cncl; JV Var Bsktbl; JV Var Sftbl; Var Trk; NHS; Spanish NHS; Interact; ADAPT; Psych Clb; Law.

BERTALOTTO, CHAD B; Union Sr HS; Tulsa, OK; (4); 93/632; NHS; Rnssnc; OK U; Cnmtgrphy.

BERTOLASIO, LESLIE M; Yukon HS; Yukon, OK; (3); Dance Clb; Pep Clb; School Play; Lit Mag; Var Tennis; Hon Roll; NHS; Ntl Merit Ltr; League Sftbl; Prof Model; Multi-Yr Listee; Pre-Med.

BERTONE, AMANDA B; Mc Alester HS; Mcalester, OK; (2); Spanish Clb; Chorus; Ofcr Stu Cncl; Var Tennis; Trk; Cutting Horse Shows; Med; Tchng.

BERTSCH, JAMES D; Bethel HS; Shawnee, OK; (1); 1/83; FCA; Spanish Clb; Ftbl; Wt Lftg; High Hon Roll; OK Hon Soc; NCAA Stu Ath Awd; OK; Pdtrcn.

BERUMEN, LESLIE A; Putnam City West HS; Oklahoma City, OK; (3); Church Yth Grp; Cmnty Wkr; FCA; Ofcr Frsh Cls; Bsktbl; Vllybl; DECA Bus Mgmnt; Southern Nazarene Univ; Acctnt.

BESS, LARRISHA G; Lawton Sr HS; Lawton, OK; (3); ROTC; Teachers Aide; Band; Church Choir; Drill Tm; Mrchg Band; Pep Band; School Musical; Ntl Merit Ltr; Band Letter/Bars; Military/Air Force.

BEST, BECKY J; Putnam City West HS; Oklahoma City, OK; (2); Church Yth Grp; Drama Clb; Red Cross Aide; Thesps; Chorus; Orch; School Musical; School Play; Rep Soph Cls; NHS; OKC Univ; Dance; Mgmt; Perf.

BEST, JAMES A; Plainview HS; Ardmore, OK; (3); 35/83; Art Clb; Latin Clb; Office Aide; Hon Roll; Nolan Ryan Bsbl Cards; Soccer; Made Video About Kennedy Assination For Amer His Cls; U Of OK; Meteorology.

BEST, JOHANNA K; Claremore Sr HS; Claremore, OK; (1); Church Yth Grp; Girl Scts; Quiz Bowl; Chorus; Church Choir; School Musical; Stage Crew; High Hon Roll; Jr NHS; Dist Hnr Choir; Chicago Univ; Pediatrician.

BETANCOURT, RAUL C; Ardmore HS; Ardmore, OK; (3); Church Yth Grp; Spanish Clb; Var L Tennis; Natl Schlr Congrssnl Yth Ldrshp Cncl; 2 Doubles ST Champ Tennis; Chem Engr.

BETTNECOURT, ALISA K; Homeschl; Choctaw, OK; (4).

BEVERAGE, AMY; Christian Heritage Acad; Oklahoma City, OK; (2); Church Yth Grp; Chorus; School Play; Rep Soph Cls; JV Vllybl; High Hon Roll; Homcmng Attend; Med.

BEVERLY, TIFFIANY; North Intemediate HS; Broken Arrow, OK; (1); French Clb; Band; Mrchg Band; Pep Band; Hon Roll; Prfct Atten Awd; Law.

BEVERS, TANYA; Byng Sr HS; Ada, OK; (4); 2/71; VP Computer Clb; Treas FHA; Natl FFA Org; Spanish Clb; Yrbk; Rep Stu Cncl; Hon Roll; Jr NHS; NHS; Prfct Atten Awd; OK ST U; Zoology.

BEZANSON, MICHAEL C; Sapulpa Sr HS; Sapulpa, OK; (3); 14/299; Church Yth Grp; Cmnty Wkr; FCA; Key Clb; Letterman Clb; Math Clb; Science Clb; Teachers Aide; Band; Mrchg Band.

BEZDEK, AMBER N; West Jr HS; Oklahoma City, OK; (1); Drama Clb; French Clb; Office Aide; Teachers Aide; Chrldng; Gym; Mgr(s); Cit Awd; French Hon Soc; Hon Roll; OK Univ; Med.

BHAKTA, NIRAL; Ardmore HS; Ardmore, OK; (4); 21/167; Drama Clb; Math Clb; Office Aide; Science Clb; Spanish Clb; Teachers Aide; School Play; Stage Crew; JV Bsbl; Var Mgr(s); OK Univ; Pre-Pharmacy.

BHATTI, EDMOND S; El Reno Sr HS; El Reno, OK; (3); FTA; SADD; Hon Roll; NHS; Engrng; Comp.

BIARD, MATTHEW R; Claremore Sr HS; Claremore, OK; (1); Boy Scts; Church Yth Grp; Quiz Bowl; Speech Tm; High Hon Roll; Hon Roll; Cardiologist.

BIAUCHAMP, JOHN D; Union Intermediate HS; Broken Arrow, OK; (1); Jazz Band; Guitarist.

BIBEE, AMY; Stigler HS; Stigler, OK; (2); Church Yth Grp; FCA; Speech Tm; SADD; Band; Pres Frsh Cls; Chrldng; Cit Awd; Hon Roll; Twirlng; OU; Law.

BIBLE, CHRIS; Bluejacket Schl; Vinita, OK; (4); Church Yth Grp; Rep FHA; VP Natl FFA Org; Band; Rep Stu Cncl; Bsktbl; Hon Roll; NHS; Prfct Atten Awd; NEO; Bus Admin.

BIBLE, MICHELLE D; Miami Sr HS; Miami, OK; (3); Church Yth Grp; Band; Church Choir; Mrchg Band; Hon Roll; IICOT Pow-Wow Princess; HS Indian Clb VP; OK Univ; Nrsng.

BIBLE, MORAN A; Frontier Public Schl; Red Rock, OK; (2); Art Clb; Church Yth Grp; Debate Tm; Teachers Aide; Ofcr Bsbl; Bsktbl; Trk; Wt Lftg; Cit Awd; Hon Roll; Peer Helper-Tutored Elem & Jr High Stdnts; Cls A St Champion Bsktbl Of OK 96; Comp Technician; Comp Engr.

BIBY, BRANDY L; Wakita Schl; Wakita, OK; (2); 1/14; Church Yth Grp; Rep Stu Cncl; Bsktbl; Chrldng; Crs Cntry; Sftbl; Trk; Cit Awd; NHS; Pres Acad Fit Awd; Univ Of AZ; Pre Law.

BIBY, STONY; Wakita Schl; Nash, OK; (4); 2/14; VP FCA; Sec Natl FFA Org; Capt Quiz Bowl; Capt Scholastic Bowl; VP Soph Cls; Pres Jr Cls; Pres Stu Cncl; Var Bsbl; Var Bsktbl; Co-Capt Var Ftbl; Acad All ST; OSU; Elec Engr.

BICKERSTAFF, KATHRYN; Claremore Sr HS; Claremore, OK; (4); 1/241; Church Yth Grp; Bsktbl; Crs Cntry; Gym; Socr; Trk; High Hon Roll; NHS; Pres Acad Fit Awd; Val; OK Hist, Eng, Geog & Alg I Cert Awd; Outstndng Tm Mem Plq; Ltr C Awds Bsktbl, Track & Eng; Elks Awd; Rogers ST Coll; Bus.

BICKNELL, TRISHA; Holdenville HS; Holdenville, OK; (3); Church Yth Grp; Drama Clb; FCA; Teachers Aide; Bsktbl; Chrldng; Crs Cntry; Trk; High Hon Roll; Hon Roll; Stu Cncl; Tulsa U; Pre-Law.

BIELLI, JENNIFER L; North Intermediate HS; Broken Arrow, OK; (1); FHA; Stat Wt Lftg; Law Class; Comm Sftbl; Pub Dfndr Law Schl/Dist Atty.

BIERS, ANDREA K; Stillwater Sr HS; Stillwater, OK; (2); Church Yth Grp; German Clb; Natl Beta Clb; L Band; Mrchg Band; Pep Band; 4-H Awd; Hon Roll; Pres Acad Fit Awd; Cmpttve Hrsbck Rdng; OK ST Univ; Arch Engr.

BIFFLE, BEAU; Sapulpa Sr HS; Sand Springs, OK; (2); 6/280; Boy Scts; Natl FFA Org; Band; Mrchg Band; High Hon Roll; Pres Acad Fit Awd; St Schlr.

BIFFLE, BRANDON K; Varnum Jr Sr HS; Seminole, OK; (3); Church Yth Grp; 4-H; Teachers Aide; Sec Soph Cls; Ofcr Bsbl; Bsktbl; Trk; 4-H Awd; MOST Imprvd Bsbl 2 Yr; Most Imprvd Bsktbl 1 Yr; Algebra Awd; OK Univ; Chrprctr.

BIFFLE, CHRISTIE; Comanche HS; Comanche, OK; (3); Church Yth Grp; Science Clb; SADD; Teachers Aide; Chorus; Yrbk; Sec Jr Cls; Hon Roll; NHS; Amer Kids 2 Yrs; East Cntrl Univ; Elem Ed.

BIFFLE, LORI R; Velma Alma HS; Velma, OK; (2); Band; Sftbl; High Hon Roll; OK Hnr Soc.

BIFFLE, R T; Velma-Alma Jr Sr HS; Velma, OK; (3); Church Yth Grp; Cmnty Wkr; FCA; JA; Pres Natl FFA Org; Quiz Bowl; Pres SADD; Ed Nwsp; Pres Stu Cncl; JV Bsktbl; US Achvmnt Acad; Natl Merit Awd; NAS; OK St Univ.

BIFFLE, ROBERT T; Velma Alma HS; Velma, OK; (3); Church Yth Grp; Pres SADD; Ed Nwsp; Pres Stu Cncl; High Hon Roll; Jr NHS; NHS; Ntl Merit Schol; Prfct Atten Awd; Natl H Nr Soc Sci Mrt Awd; SADD Pres; OSU.

BIGBEAR, WILLIAM; Perkins-Tryon HS; Perkins, OK; (2); Intnl Clb; Ofcr Soph Cls; Ftbl; Trk; Wt Lftg; Nat Amer Biolgcl Sci Prgm OK ST U; OK ST U; Engr.

BIGGERS, TIFFANY D; Western Heights Sr HS; Oklahoma City, OK; (2); French Clb; Hon Roll; OSU; Phy Thrpst.

BIGGERSTAFF, AMY; Medford Schl; Medford, OK; (4); 1/22; Art Clb; Church Yth Grp; FCA; FHA; Natl FFA Org; Pep Clb; Spanish Clb; Teachers Aide; Chorus; Pres Frsh Cls; OK Hnr Soc; OK ST U; Phy.

BIGGERSTAFF, LORI; Medford Schl; Medford, OK; (2); 1/16; Church Yth Grp; FCA; GAA; Natl FFA Org; Pep Clb; Sec Frsh Cls; Pres Soph Cls; Var Bsktbl; Var Sftbl; Var Trk; OK Hnr Soc; OSU.

BIGGERT, MEAGEN L; El Reno Sr HS; El Reno, OK; (2); Hon Roll; Boston U; Psych.

BIGGS, PATRICK; Perry Sr HS; Perry, OK; (3); 21/120; Church Yth Grp; Natl FFA Org; Var Bsbl; Var Ftbl; Var Lftg; Jr NHS; NHS; AA/AAA Amer Legion Bsbl; OK Jr Herford Assn; Amer Intl Jr Charolais Assn; Langston U; Phys Thrpy.

BIGHAM, CINDI A; Durant HS; Durant, OK; (2); Chorus; Tennis; Hon Roll; OK ST Univ; Vet Med.

BIGHEART, LYNSEY A; Enid Sr HS; Enid, OK; (2); 16/391; Church Yth Grp; FCA; GAA; Hosp Aide; Pep Clb; Quiz Bowl; Scholastic Bowl; Nwsp; VP Frsh Cls; VP Soph Cls; Stu Of Today; Dr.

BIGPOND, AMY; Mounds Schl; Sapulpa, OK; (4); 14/42; Natl Beta Clb; Office Aide; School Play; Phtg Yrbk; Ofcr Stu Cncl; Bsktbl; Sftbl; Cit Awd; Hon Roll; NHS; U Of OK; X Ray Tech.

BILBREY, AMANDA; Putnam City North HS; Oklahoma City, OK; (2); 10/435; Church Yth Grp; Church Choir; Rep Orch; NHS; Chrch Orch; OK Yth Symphony; Putnam City Slvr Strngs; Music/Mrktg.

BILBREY, LEVI; Empire Schl; Duncan, OK; (1); Church Yth Grp; FBLA; Spanish Clb; SADD; Hon Roll; NHS; Ntl Merit Ltr; Comp Sci.

BILBY, DARRAH; Nathan Hale HS; Tulsa, OK; (4); Church Yth Grp; DECA; FCA; GAA; Key Clb; Office Aide; Pep Clb; Teachers Aide; Varsity Clb; Chorus.

BILES, MICHAEL; Elgin HS; Elgin, OK; (3); Am Leg Boys St; Boy Scts; Church Yth Grp; Dance Clb; FCA; Chorus; Church Choir; Yrbk; Rep Jr Cls; VP Sr Cls.

BILLEN, CASEY J; Deer Creek HS; Edmond, OK; (3); 68/103; Art Clb; Boy Scts; Church Yth Grp; Drama Clb; Science Clb; SADD; Band; Church Choir; Stage Crew; Ofcr Bsbl; Electronics; Comp Pgmng.

BILLINGS, KENDRA R; Wister Schl; Poteau, OK; (3); Church Yth Grp; FCA; FHA; Office Aide; Yrbk; Ofcr Jr Cls; Bsktbl; Sftbl; High Hon Roll; NHS; Carl Albert ST Coll; Med.

BILLINGS, SOMMER A; East Central HS; Tulsa, OK; (2); Church Yth Grp; Cmnty Wkr; Key Clb; Spanish Clb; Nwsp; Vllybl; High Hon Roll; NHS; Ecology Clb Pres; Pianist; OK Chrstn Univ Of Sci; Lawyer.

BILLINGS, STACY R; Okemah HS; Okemah, OK; (3); 12/70; Natl Beta Clb; Science Clb; SADD; Thesps; Chorus; Church Choir; School Play; Yrbk; Cit Awd; Life Leaders; PT.

BILLINGSLEA, CRYSTAL; Westmoore HS; Oklahoma City, OK; (1); Church Yth Grp; Drama Clb; Spanish Clb; Teachers Aide; School Play; Hon Roll; Jr NHS; Drama Awd; Pres Hnr Roll; OK Univ; Med/PT/PEDS.

BILLS, JOSH; Tupelo Jr Sr HS; Tupelo, OK; (1); Quiz Bowl; VP Frsh Cls; Var Bsbl; Var Bsktbl; Prfct Atten Awd.

BILYEU, HEATHER; Cyril Jr Sr HS; Cyril, OK; (3); Church Yth Grp; FHA; Natl FFA Org; Rep Frsh Cls; Sec Soph Cls; Sec Jr Cls; Chrldng; Hon Roll; NHS; Bus.

BILYEU, JASON N; Union Intermediate HS; Tulsa, OK; (2); Church Yth Grp; Band; Church Choir; Jazz Band; Mrchg Band; School Musical; High Hon Roll; NHS; Pres Acad Fit Awd; Outstndng Soloist Jazz Bnd.

BILYEU, TIFFANY L; Dibble Jr Sr HS; Lindsay, OK; (4); 4/32; Office Aide; SADD; VP Jr Cls; VP Sr Cls; VP Stu Cncl; Intrml Var Bsktbl; Capt Chrldng; Var Crs Cntry; Intrml Var Trk; Intrml Var Vllybl; Nrs.

BINGHAM, NICK G; Edmond Memorial HS; Edmond, OK; (3); Church Yth Grp; Hon Roll; NHS; Prfct Atten Awd; Drafting; ACAD.

BINGHAM, RACHEL D; Hobart HS; Hobart, OK; (3); 19/60; Church Yth Grp; FCA; FTA; Hosp Aide; Office Aide; Teachers Aide; Rptr Yrbk; Rep Stu Cncl; Mgr(s); Hon Roll; Radiolgy.

BINGHAM, TONNYA S; Geary Jr Sr HS; Geary, OK; (1); FHA; GAA; Natl Beta Clb; Natl FFA Org; Rep Frsh Cls; JV Var Bsktbl; JV Var Sftbl; Hon Roll; St Schlr; OU.

BINGHAM, WARREN D; Westmoore HS; Oklahoma City, OK; (2); Church Yth Grp; French Clb; Wt Lftg; Ply Drums; Campus Mnstry 1st Priority; Fireman/Musician.

BINGMAN, ANNIE E; Sapulpa Sr HS; Sapulpa, OK; (3); Dance Clb; Science Clb; Drill Tm; VP Frsh Cls; VP Soph Cls; Rep Jr Cls; Rep Sr Cls; Pres Stu Cncl; Pom Pon; Hon Roll; Hmcmng Attndnt; Pom Pon Sqd Capt; OK U; Ed.

BIRDSELL, JAMIE; Mc Loud HS; Harrah, OK; (4); Am Leg Aux Girls St; Church Yth Grp; Drama Clb; Speech Tm; Thesps; Band; Chorus; Mrchg Band; School Play; Stage Crew; NFL; U Of Ozarks.

BIRDSHEAD, JENNFER; Apache HS; Apache, OK; (2); Church Yth Grp; FHA; Hon Roll; NHS; Art; Native Amer Clb; Schltc Meets.

BIRDSONG, TAMARA L; Washington HS; Norman, OK; (2); Church Yth Grp; English Clb; FHA; Scholastic Bowl; Spanish Clb; Chorus; Church Choir; School Musical; High Hon Roll; Spanish NHS; Piano; Homeless & Chrch Act Vol; Singing Concerts; U Of OK; Pediatrician; Music.

BIRDTAIL, DEREK; Porum HS; Porum, OK; (2); 6/23; FHA; Library Aide; Hon Roll; Ntl Merit Ltr; Title IX Parent Comm Stdnt Rep; Indian Club Rprtr.

BIRDWELL, ASHLEY; Stillwater Sr HS; Stillwater, OK; (2); Church Yth Grp; Cmnty Wkr; Dance Clb; FCA; JCL; Latin Clb; Natl Beta Clb; Chorus; School Musical; Pres Frsh Cls; Comm Theater; Vcl Ensmlbs Supr Ratgs; Rotary Stdnt Of Mnth.

BIRDWELL, NICOLE; Elk City Jr HS; Elk City, OK; (1); Church Yth Grp; Band; Jazz Band; Yrbk; Hon Roll; Jr Actors Guild; Piano.

BIRK, BRAIN S; Tuttle HS; Tuttle, OK; (3); 3/90; Math Tm; Quiz Bowl; Scholastic Bowl; Spanish Clb; Wt Lftg; Wrstlng; High Hon Roll; NHS; Pres Acad Fit Awd; Duke U TIP Mem; Placing 3rd In St Wide Schltc Cmptn; U Of OK; Comp Sci.

BIRK, BRIAN S; Tuttle HS; Tuttle, OK; (4); 3/183; Math Tm; Office Aide; Quiz Bowl; Scholastic Bowl; Spanish Clb; Wrstlng; High Hon Roll; NHS; Pres Acad Fit Awd; Val; Talent ID Pgm Duke Univ; ST Acad Cmptn 3rd; OU; Comp Engrng Sci.

BIRKENFELD, KYLE E; Pryor Sr HS; Pryor, OK; (2); Church Yth Grp; Church Choir; Stage Crew; Crs Cntry; Trk; Hon Roll; 95-96 Crss Cntry Awd.

BIRNBAUM, JENNY S; Union Intermediate HS; Tulsa, OK; (2); 3/850; Church Yth Grp; Cmnty Wkr; Key Clb; Library Aide; Scholastic Bowl; High Hon Roll; Jr NHS; NHS; Acad Ltr; Stu Mon; Top 10 St Fnlst OK Aim Hi M Ath Cmptn; Zoology.

BIRSUL, DEREK G; Edmond Memorial HS; Edmond, OK; (2); Cmnty Wkr; German Clb; JV Bsktbl; JV Ftbl; Trk; Hon Roll.

BISCHOFF, CARRIE L; Edmond North HS; Edmond, OK; (2); 192/420; Church Yth Grp; FCA; Var Chrldng; Var Trk; Qualfd & Comptd In Indr Natls For Var Trk, 3rd Pl; Girls All St Indr Trk Wnnr:1st Pl Long Jump; Engrng; Marine Bio.

BISCHOFF, MELISSA A; Edmond North HS; Edmond, OK; (3); 52/348; Church Yth Grp; French Clb; Band; Var Trk; Jr NHS; NHS; Mu Alpha Theta; Var Track Indoor Natls; Var Track Outdoor ST Meet.

BISCOE, BRANDI P; Putnam City North HS; Oklahoma City, OK; (3); Cmnty Wkr; French Clb; Scholastic Bowl; Ofcr Stu Cncl; Pom Pon; Cit Awd; NHS; PEAK; OSCA; Big Bro/Big Sisters Prgm; Bio Med Eng.

BISHLINE, SERENA L; South Intermediate HS; Broken Arrow, OK; (1); Church Yth Grp; Intnl Clb; Chorus.

BISHOP, CARRIE; Cement Jr Sr HS; Chickasha, OK; (3); 1/20; Sec FHA; HOBY; Natl FFA Org; Scholastic Bowl; Sec Frsh Cls; Rptr Soph Cls; Sec Jr Cls; High Hon Roll; NHS; Psycht.

BISHOP, CHRIS I; Del City HS; Del City, OK; (2); Debate Tm; Drama Clb; Library Aide; Office Aide; Speech Tm; School Play; Rep Frsh Cls; JV Bsbl; JV Ftbl; JV Wt Lftg; FL ST U.

BISHOP, DEANNA M; Cameron Schl; Cameron, OK; (2); Church Yth Grp; FHA; Carl Albert ST Coll; Sec.

BISHOP, EMMA J; Putnam City HS; Oklahoma City, OK; (2); Drama Clb; German Clb; Chorus; Rep Stu Cncl; Hon Roll; Prfct Atten Awd; Intl Ordr Rnbw Grls/Wrthy Adv 95-/Grnd Rep IA 96-; U Cntrl OK HS Schlstc Trnmnt 95; PEAK GATE.

BISHOP, FOHNTA; Braman Schl; Braman, OK; (4); Pres FHA; Natl FFA Org; Office Aide; Teachers Aide; Yrbk; Treas Jr Cls; Mgr Bsktbl; Hon Roll; NHS; ST FFA Degree; Connors ST Coll; Vet Med.

BISHOP, SHELLI J; Marlow HS; Marlow, OK; (4); 17/96; Art Clb; FCA; FTA; Office Aide; SADD; Teachers Aide; Bsktbl; Chrldng; Score Keeper; Sftbl; Mentor/Mediator Pgm; Tchr Cadets; East Cntrl Univ; Nrs.

BISHOP, STACY J; Dewey HS; Dewey, OK; (1); Church Yth Grp; Hosp Aide; Spanish Clb; Rep Stu Cncl; Hon Roll; Pres Acad Fit Awd; Acad Bowl Tm; Drama Club; Vlybl; Swmng.

BISHOP, THOMAS C; Broken Arrow Sr HS; Broken Arrow, OK; (3); Church Yth Grp; Drama Clb; Latin Clb; Thesps; Acpl Chr; School Musical; Voice/Mscl Thtr.

BISWELL, JENNIFER; Claremore Sr HS; Claremore, OK; (4); 1/241; Church Yth Grp; Math Clb; Science Clb; Spanish Clb; Ed Nwsp; Ofcr Stu Cncl; NHS; 1st & 3rd Pl OK Intrschlstc Press Assn St Cntst 95; Lcl Wnnr Optmst Club Essay Cntst 95; OK Bptst U; Elem Ed.

BIVINS, JAMIE ANN; Milburn Schl; Tishomingo, OK; (3); 4-H; Natl FFA Org; Chorus; Yrbk; Rep Stu Cncl; JV Var Bsktbl; 4-H Awd; Hon Roll; NHS; Quiz Bowl; Singing With Bnd; Murray ST Coll; Vet.

BJURSTROM, AMANDA K; Stillwater Sr HS; Stillwater, OK; (3); Key Clb; Letterman Clb; Natl Beta Clb; Spanish Clb; Nwsp; Swmmng; High Hon Roll; NHS; Stdnt Of Mnth.

BLACHLY, MELANIE D; Ft Gibson HS; Fort Gibson, OK; (3); Church Yth Grp; Cmnty Wkr; French Clb; Math Tm; Scholastic Bowl; Sec Spanish Clb; SADD; Teachers Aide; Hon Roll; NHS; OK Univ; Pediatrcn.

BLACK, AMBER L; Asher Schl; Asher, OK; (2); Church Yth Grp; Cmnty Wkr; 4-H; FHA; School Play; Ofcr Frsh Cls; Bsktbl; Sftbl; 4-H Awd; OBU; Child Care.

BLACK, BENJAMIN A; Wright Christian Acad; Tulsa, OK; (1); Church Yth Grp; Key Clb; School Musical; School Play; Pres Frsh Cls; Var Bsbl; High Hon Roll; Hon Roll.

BLACK, IAN; Pawhuska HS; Bartlesville, OK; (4); 3/87; Am Leg Boys St; Church Yth Grp; Key Clb; Jazz Band; Yrbk; Ftbl; Wrstlng; NHS; Sal; St Schlr; Nrthrn OK Coll; Law Enfrcmnt.

BLACK, JAMIE L; North Intemediate HS; Broken Arrow, OK; (2); Church Yth Grp; Library Aide; Acpl Chr; Hon Roll; NHS; OK Hon Soc; Chrstns Action; Harding Univ.

BLACK, JASON R; Mustang HS; Mustang, OK; (4); 106/350; Church Yth Grp; Cmnty Wkr; FCA; FHA; Letterman Clb; Office Aide; Red Cross Aide; Spanish Clb; Teachers Aide; Varsity Clb; Rcvd OBU Chrch Voc Schlsp; Cls Reg Chmpn 3200m Run 95; Certfd Lfgrd; Pianist 10 Yrs Pvt Lssns; OK Bapt U; Mnstry.

BLACK, KYLENE; Turner Schl; Burneyville, OK; (3); 1/17; FHA; Natl Beta Clb; Quiz Bowl; Ed Yrbk; Treas Jr Cls; Capt Chrldng; High Hon Roll; NHS; Prfct Atten Awd; Val.

BLACK, LUKE L; Locust Grove HS; Locust Grove, OK; (3); Church Yth Grp; Cmnty Wkr; Drama Clb; JV Var Bsbl; JV Ftbl; Hon Roll; Flwshp Of Chrstn Stdnts; Cmpttve Shtng Sprts; Play Guitar; Southwestern OK; Phrmcst.

BLACK, NATHAN; Sperry Sr HS; Tulsa, OK; (4); Am Leg Boys St; Church Yth Grp; Pres 4-H; Pres FBLA; Lbrn Office Aide; Scholastic Bowl; Spanish Clb; Pres VICA; Chorus; Church Choir; Royal Rangrs; Oral Roberts U; Intl Bus.

BLACK, RICHARD A; Miami Sr HS; Miami, OK; (3); 30/179; Am Leg Boys St; Church Yth Grp; Debate Tm; Drama Clb; FCA; NFL; Red Cross Aide; Phtg Yrbk; Rep Frsh Cls; Rep Soph Cls; CO ST Coll; Pediatrics.

BLACK, SABER R; Bartlesville Sr HS; Bartlesville, OK; (1); Art Clb; FHA; Crtv Wrtng; Storm Chasing; Meteorology.

BLACK, SARA M; Ardmore HS; Ardmore, OK; (3); Church Yth Grp; Drama Clb; French Clb; Latin Clb; Science Clb; School Play; Stage Crew; Rep Jr Cls; Hon Roll; NHS; Outstndng Stu OSU Alumni; U Of OK; Nuclear Medicine.

BLACK, SARAH A; Bartlesville Mid HS; Bartlesville, OK; (3); 78/447; Church Yth Grp; FCA; Color Guard; Sec Mrchg Band; L Var Crs Cntry; L Var Trk; Hon Roll; Jr NHS; Sign Lang Cls; St Champ Time Trial Cycling Team; Deaf Interpreter.

BLACK, TRINA D; Strother Jr Sr HS; Seminole, OK; (1); 1/30; Church Yth Grp; FHA; Church Choir; Rep Frsh Cls; Rep Stu Cncl; Mgr(s); High Hon Roll; Pres Acad Fit Awd; Natl Sci Mrt Awd; Intrschlstc Mt Tm; Law.

BLACKBURN, CHRIS D; Wilson HS; Wilson, OK; (2); 5/44; Boy Scts; Natl Beta Clb; Quiz Bowl; Scholastic Bowl; JV Band; Chorus; Hon Roll; Eagle Scout.

BLACKBURN, JUSTIN; Empire Schl; Duncan, OK; (2); Church Yth Grp; FCA; 4-H; FBLA; Letterman Clb; Natl FFA Org; SADD; Rep Soph Cls; Ofcr Bsbl; Ftbl.

BLACKBURN, SAWYER; Ponca City Sr HS; Ponca City, OK; (4); Church Yth Grp; Cmnty Wkr; FCA; Office Aide; Spanish Clb; Teachers Aide; Bsktbl; Tennis; Hon Roll.

BLACKBURN, TARA K; Pauls Valley HS; Pauls Valley, OK; (1); Sec Treas Church Yth Grp; Cmnty Wkr; Girl Scts; Pep Clb; Thesps; Band; Chorus; Church Choir; School Musical; High Hon Roll; Girl Sct Silver Awd; Stu Dance Instrctr; Dance Co Cmptn Team; OK City U; Music Perf.

BLACKETER, AMY; Braman Schl; Braman, OK; (2); 2/15; Drama Clb; FHA; GAA; Quiz Bowl; Speech Tm; Teachers Aide; School Play; Stage Crew; Variety Show; Phtg Ed Yrbk.

BLACKFORD, LUCINDA; Salina HS; Salina, OK; (4); 4/47; Am Leg Aux Girls St; FCA; Office Aide; Yrbk; Sec Sr Cls; Treas Stu Cncl; Var Chrldng; High Hon Roll; NHS; Sal; Rogers ST Coll; Spcl Ed.

BLACKHAM, ASHLEY N; Durant HS; Durant, OK; (3); Band Reporter; Var Girls Sccr Tm Capt; All Dist Concert Bnd; U Of OK; Pre Mdcn.

BLACKMAN, CARA; Cascia Hall Prep School; Tulsa, OK; (3); Pep Clb; Spanish Clb; Chorus; Yrbk; Var Chrldng; Hon Roll; NHS; Amer Heart Assn Sweetheart; Habitat For Humanity; Tulsa Philharmonic Symphony Sct; Parent Child Ctr Vol.

BLACKMON, BRANDON J; Harrah HS; Harrah, OK; (1); FCA; Frgn Lang Clb; ORU; Sci; Astronomy.

BLACKMORE, ANDREA L; Union Intermediate HS; Tulsa, OK; (2); 54/800; Spanish Clb; Mrchg Band; Var Swmmng; Vet.

BLACKSTON, WILLIAM; Wetumka Jr Sr HS; Wetumka, OK; (2); Computer Clb; German Clb; Key Clb; Natl FFA Org; Quiz Bowl; Band; High Hon Roll; Hon Roll; E Central U; Quantum Physics.

BLACKWELL, MARLA; Cheyenne HS; Cheyenne, OK; (3); Church Yth Grp; FHA; Quiz Bowl; Chorus; Drm Mjr(t); Sec Stu Cncl; Var Bsktbl; Var Sftbl; NHS.

BLAD, BRIAN; Edmond Memorial HS; Edmond, OK; (3); 1/370; Church Yth Grp; Math Clb; Spanish Clb; Church Choir; Rep Stu Cncl; Cit Awd; Hon Roll; NHS; Pres Acad Fit Awd; St Schlr; Med.

BLAIN, JASON W; Geary Jr Sr HS; Geary, OK; (4); Church Yth Grp; Natl FFA Org; Band; Var L Bsktbl; Var L Ftbl; Var Trk.

BLAIR, APRIL D; Choctaw HS; Choctaw, OK; (2); Church Yth Grp; Hon Roll; Jr NHS.

BLAIR, CARISSA M; Moore HS; Norman, OK; (3); 35/550; Church Yth Grp; FCA; French Clb; JA; Science Clb; Church Choir; Bsktbl; NHS; 4.0 GPA Recognition; Art Achvmt Awd; Hnrs Soc Svc Medal; U Of OK; Bus; Acctng.

BLAIR, CHRISTY; Perkins-Tryon HS; Perkins, OK; (4); 7/71; FCA; FHA; Intnl Clb; Band; Mrchg Band; NHS; OK Hnr Soc; Amer Red Cross Explorer Post; Concurrent Enrollment At OK ST U; OK ST U; Acctng.

BLAIR, ERIC; East Central HS; Tulsa, OK; (4); 7/209; Am Leg Boys St; Church Yth Grp; FCA; Ofcr Soph Cls; Ofcr Jr Cls; Var Capt Ftbl; Computer Clb; Cit Awd; High Hon Roll; NHS; Ed.

BLAIR, KIM; Noble HS; Noble, OK; (3); 1/180; Church Yth Grp; Mu Alpha Theta; Sec SADD; VP Band; Jazz Band; Mrchg Band; Ofcr Stu Cncl; Hon Roll; Jr NHS; NHS; OK Bapt Univ; Missions.

BLAIR, LISA; Kingfisher HS; Kingfisher, OK; (1); FCA; Quiz Bowl; JV Bsktbl; Chrldng; Var Golf; Hon Roll; Jr NHS; NHS; Piano; All Amer Chrldr & Schlr; Law.

BLAIR, LONNIE; Capitol Hill HS; Oklahoma City, OK; (4); 7/151; Drama Clb; FBLA; Science Clb; Spanish Clb; School Play; Yrbk; Sec Stu Cncl; Var Bsbl; Hon Roll; NHS; Jr Rtrn; Top Pre-AP Gmtry Stu; Bst Spprtng Actr; U Of OK; Astrnmy.

BLAIR, MARIA L; Tomlinson Jr HS; Lawton, OK; (1); Church Yth Grp; Sec FHA; Key Clb; Pep Clb; School Play; Rep Frsh Cls; Cit Awd; Kiwanis Awd; NHS; Pres Acad Fit Awd; TX A&M; Bus Mgmt/Law.

BLAIR, MATT; Berryhill Sr HS; Tulsa, OK; (4); 6/52; Church Yth Grp; FCA; HOBY; Yrbk; VP Sr Cls; Rep Stu Cncl; Var L Bsbl; Var Ftbl; Sal; Hillsdale Free Will Bapt Coll.

BLAIR, MICHELLE; Moore HS; Moore, OK; (3); 138/525; Church Yth Grp; Cmnty Wkr; FCA; Letterman Clb; Varsity Clb; Sec Jr Cls; Var Socr; Jr Sr Prom Org; Grls Var Tm Cap; CORE Stndt Cncl; Educ.

BLAIR, MIKELYN S; Muldrow HS; Muldrow, OK; (4); FCA; 4-H; Letterman Clb; Yrbk; Bsktbl; Var Capt Chrldng; Var Sftbl; Var Trk; Var Vllybl; High Hon Roll; Most Outstdng Bus Cmnctns Stdnt Awd 95-.

BLAIR, NIKKI L; Edmond Memorial HS; Edmond, OK; (3); Am Leg Aux Girls St; Church Yth Grp; Cmnty Wkr; French Clb; Nwsp; Vllybl; Hon Roll; NHS; OKC Force Jr Olympic Vllybll Clb; Stanford Univ; Jrnlsm.

BLAIR, RYAN M; Midwest City HS; Midwest City, OK; (2); 73/473; Pres Church Yth Grp; German Clb; Pep Clb; Science Clb; Spanish Clb; Drill Tm; Yrbk; VP Soph Cls; Hon Roll; NHS; Stu Ath Trainer; Sports Medicine.

BLAIR, SARAH K; Broken Arrow Sr HS; Broken Arrow, OK; (4); 100/1000; Church Yth Grp; Spanish Clb; Orch; Hon Roll; Jr NHS; NHS; Pres Acad Fit Awd; TU; Ed.

BLAIR, SHANNA M; Weatherford HS; Weatherford, OK; (3); Natl FFA Org; Bsktbl; Trk; Hon Roll; NHS; U Of OK Acad Achvt Cert; OK HS Rodeo Assn Rodeo; Southwstrn OK ST U; Phys Thrp.

BLAIS, NATHAN M; Putnam Cityt West HS; Bethany, OK; (1); Church Yth Grp; Scholastic Bowl; Golf; Hon Roll; All Amer Schlr; St Gregorys; Meteorology.

BLAKE, LINDSAY; Newcastle HS; Norman, OK; (4); #1 in class; Church Yth Grp; FCA; FBLA; Office Aide; Pep Clb; Science Clb; Teachers Aide; Cit Awd; High Hon Roll; NHS; Bus.

BLAKEMORE, LAURA A; Bartlesville Mid HS; Bartlesville, OK; (2); 58/481; Church Yth Grp; Chorus; Ofcr Stu Cncl; Co-Capt JV Chrldng; Hon Roll; Prfct Atten Awd; OSU; Nrsng.

BLAKESLEY, ROBIN R; Indiahoma Schl; Indiahoma, OK; (4); 3/13; Church Yth Grp; FHA; Girl Scts; Letterman Clb; Natl FFA Org; Office Aide; Teachers Aide; Yrbk; Pres Frsh Cls; Pres Soph Cls; Cameron U; Nursing.

BLAKLEY, ABBEY V; Pioneer Jr Sr HS; Douglas, OK; (3); 4/50; Church Yth Grp; Rptr FHA; Pres Natl Beta Clb; Band; Co-Capt Flag Corp; Cit Awd; High Hon Roll; NHS; Ntl Merit Ltr; Quiz Bowl; Comm Thtr; Archdscs Owanoma City Yth Advy Bd Rep; Pioneer HS Hero; Pol/Intl Affrs.

BLAKNEY, BONNIE; Coleman Schl; Kenefic, OK; (2); 1/10; Church Yth Grp; FCA; Quiz Bowl; Pres Frsh Cls; Rptr Soph Cls; Bsktbl; Hon Roll; Val; SOSU.

BLALACK, BRANDY D; Stillwater Jr HS; Stillwater, OK; (1); Tae Kwon Do; Pms Pubpttry; OK ST U; Psych.

BLALOCK, DANIEL E; Will Rogers HS; Tulsa, OK; (2); ROTC; Var Ftbl; JV Wt Lftg; JV Wrstlng; All Nations Indian Yth Pres; Rogers Indian Clb Mem; Champion Indian Fancy Dancer; U Of FL; Surgeon.

BLANCHE, JOSH; Tuttle HS; Chickasha, OK; (3); Church Yth Grp; FCA; Letterman Clb; Varsity Clb; Ofcr Bsbl; Bsktbl; Trk; OK ST HS Trk 6th In 100 Meters; OSU; Surgeon.

BLANCHETT JR, JOHN O; Rush Springs HS; Rush Springs, OK; (2); Boy Scts; Church Yth Grp; Math Tm; Band; Chorus; Church Choir; Mrchg Band; Stage Crew; Variety Show; Var Bsbl; Acad Team; OK His Stu Of Yr; Music Theory; OU.

BLANCHETTE, ALLISON M; Putnam City West HS; Oklahoma City, OK; (4); 66/270; Art Clb; Drama Clb; School Play; Stage Crew; Socr; Trk; High Hon Roll; Hon Roll; NHS; OK ST U; Pre-Med.

BLAND, FRANCES J; Mannford HS; Mannford, OK; (2); 6/113; Drama Clb; Girl Scts; Speech Tm; Band; Color Guard; Jazz Band; Mrchg Band; School Play; NHS; Legislative Page House Of Rep OKC.

BLAND, GILLIAN; Chisholm Sr HS; Enid, OK; (1); Church Yth Grp; FHA; GAA; Spanish Clb; Rep Stu Cncl; Bsktbl; Crs Cntry; Sftbl; Trk; Hon Roll; Church Praise/Wrshp Tm; OSU; Acctnt/Ind Bus.

BLANKENSHIP, BRANDI; Kiefer Jr Sr HS; Kiefer, OK; (4); #1 in class; FCA; Natl Beta Clb; Teachers Aide; Phtg Yrbk; Rep Sr Cls; Ofcr Stu Cncl; Capt Bsktbl; Capt Sftbl; High Hon Roll; Val; Tulsa JC; Lib Sci.

BLANKENSHIP, DOYLE; Kiowa Jr-Sr HS; Wardville, OK; (4); 1/23; Am Leg Boys St; Church Yth Grp; Pres Sr Cls; Treas Stu Cncl; Var Bsktbl; High Hon Roll; St Schlr; Val; FFA VP; Elks Awd; OK ST U; Scndry Ed; Math.

BLANKENSHIP, JOHNNY D; Kiowa Jr-Sr HS; Wardville, OK; (3); 1/34; Church Yth Grp; 4-H; Natl FFA Org; Quiz Bowl; School Play; Nwsp; VP Soph Cls; Rep Jr Cls; Sec Stu Cncl; Bsktbl.

BLANKENSHIP, KEVIN; Quinton Jr Sr HS; Quinton, OK; (2); Church Yth Grp; FCA; Quiz Bowl; Band; Church Choir; Trk; High Hon Roll; ACE.

BLANKENSHIP, LEANNA; Bartlesville Mid HS; Bartlesville, OK; (3); Art Clb; Treas Boy Scts; Girl Scts; Spanish Clb; Var L Socr; Jr NHS; NHS; Girl Sct Silver & Gold Awds; PTP Ambassador Australia & New Zealand.

BLANKENSHIP, MARIA N; Southeast HS; Oklahoma City, OK; (1); FBLA; Swmmng; OK Univ; Nrs.

BLANKINSHIP, KATIE; Cache HS; Cache, OK; (3); #2 in class; Church Yth Grp; Natl Beta Clb; Color Guard; Drm Mjr(t); Nwsp; Yrbk; Sec Frsh Cls; Bsktbl; Chrldng; NHS; OK ST Univ; Law Enfrmnt/Med.

BLANTON, ASHLI; Comanche HS; Comanche, OK; (3); Natl FFA Org; VP Science Clb; Pres Frsh Cls; Pres Soph Cls; Pres Jr Cls; Sec Stu Cncl; Bsktbl; Golf; Sftbl; NHS; East Central.

BLANTON, BRIAN D; Afton HS; Afton, OK; (2); FCA; Sec Soph Cls; Var L Bsbl; Var L Bsktbl; Var L Ftbl; Lucky 7 Hnrb Mntn All Conf In Bsbl; OK Univ; Pe.

BLANTON, JENNY; Oklahoma Bible Acad; Enid, OK; (1); Church Yth Grp; Band; Mrchg Band; Chrldng; Gym; Hon Roll; NHS.

BLANTON, KIMBER; Edmond North HS; Edmond, OK; (3); 47/371; Am Leg Aux Girls St; Church Yth Grp; FCA; Mu Alpha Theta; NFL; SADD; Rptr Nwsp; Rep Jr Cls; Var Chrldng; High Hon Roll; Stu Of Yr; Swthrt; MS ST U; Pblc Rels.

BLASCHKE, EMILY; Heritage Hall Schl; Oklahoma City, OK; (3); Cmnty Wkr; VP Debate Tm; Drama Clb; FCA; Letterman Clb; VP NFL; Pep Clb; Rep Spanish Clb; School Musical; School Play; Rotary Yth Ldrshp Conf Rep; Star Discussn Ldr 2 Yrs; Intnl Bus.

BLASCHKE, SAMANTHA; Casady Schl; Oklahoma City, OK; (2); Cmnty Wkr; German Clb; Pep Clb; Acpl Chr; Chorus; Ftbl; Med.

BLATCHFORD, CRISTY D; Wagoner Sr HS; Wagoner, OK; (3); Church Yth Grp; Hon Roll; NHS; Acctng.

BLAYLOCK, DANILE G; Pocola HS; Pocola, OK; (3); Band; Jazz Band; Mrchg Band; Pep Band; School Musical; Bsktbl; Trk.

BLAYLOCK, ERIN S; Poteau HS; Howe, OK; (2); 77/198; Church Yth Grp; Pres 4-H; FHA; Ed Natl FFA Org; Church Choir; 4-H Awd; FFA Rptr; Show Registered Maine Anjoe Cows; Carl Albert; Med; Dntl Asst.

BLAYLOCK, PAT; Waukomis HS; Waukomis, OK; (1); 4/42; FCA; Quiz Bowl; Scholastic Bowl; Var Ftbl; Var Trk; Hon Roll; NHS; OK.

BLAYLOCK, TONYA L; Grove HS; Grove, OK; (3); Church Yth Grp; FCA; FHA; GAA; Key Clb; Letterman Clb; Office Aide; Band; Chorus; Mrchg Band; Early Chldhd Ed.

BLEDSOE, NICOLAS; Bluejacket Schl; Bluejacket, OK; (2); Natl FFA Org; Var Bsktbl; Var Ftbl; High Hon Roll; Hon Roll; Jr NHS; NHS; Prfct Atten Awd.

BLEHM, MATTHEW S; Muskogee HS; Muskogee, OK; (4); 57/303; Church Yth Grp; Computer Clb; Science Clb; Band; Mrchg Band; Orch; Pep Band; Stage Crew; Hon Roll; NHS; Yale Sci & Engrng Awd; Rose Hulman Inst Of Tech.

BLEVINS, ANTHONY; Goodwell Public Schl; Guymon, OK; (3); Church Yth Grp; Band; Mrchg Band; Bsktbl; Ftbl; Golf; Tennis; Prfct Atten Awd; Pres Acad Fit Awd.

BLEVINS, CYNTHIA M; Tahlequah Jr HS; Tahlequah, OK; (1); Church Yth Grp; FCA; Church Choir; Wt Lftg; Hon Roll; Tulsa Univ; Vet Asst.

BLEVINS, JOSEPH; Moore HS; Moore, OK; (4); Latin Clb; Variety Show; NHS; Med.

BLEVINS, LYNDSEY A; Vinita HS; Vinita, OK; (2); 3/100; FCA; GAA; Math Clb; Service Clb; Spanish Clb; Speech Tm; Chorus; Bsktbl; Golf; Trk; All Conf In Golf; Environmental Clb; Schl Mascot; TX A&M; Vet.

BLEVINS, ROBIN; Sasakwa Schl; Sasakwa, OK; (2); 3/16; FHA; GAA; Library Aide; Quiz Bowl; Drill Tm; Pres Soph Cls; Ofcr Stu Cncl; Bsktbl; Sftbl; Hon Roll; Murray ST Coll; Law.

BLEWETT, JUSTIN E; South Intermediate HS; Broken Arrow, OK; (1); Boy Scts; Spanish Clb; Band; Mrchg Band; Hon Roll; Pres Acad Fit Awd; Band; KS U; Child Psych.

BLICKENSTAFF, LAURA M; Putnam City North HS; Oklahoma City, OK; (4); Science Clb; Spanish Clb; SADD; Nwsp; Crs Cntry; NHS; CAWS Pres; OK St Univ.

BLISH, SAMANTHA A; Union Intermediate HS; Tulsa, OK; (2); FCA; Hosp Aide; Pep Clb; Spanish Clb; Var JV Chrldng; JV Socr; Peer Mediatn; FL U; Medcl.

BLISS, DANNA D; Sallisaw HS; Sallisaw, OK; (2); Drama Clb; FCA; GAA; Math Clb; Science Clb; Spanish Clb; Speech Tm; School Play; Stage Crew; Var L Trk; Ballet; Swim; Horseback Riding; Acctng; Bus.

BLISSITT II, CARL F; Eisenhower Sr HS; Fort Sill, OK; (3); Cmnty Wkr; Key Clb; Red Cross Aide; JV Var Bsktbl; JV Ftbl; High Hon Roll; Hon Roll; NHS; Prfct Atten Awd; Gifted/Talented.

BLIZZARD, APRIL L; Fairland Jr Sr HS; Fairland, OK; (1); Church Yth Grp; GAA; Chorus; JV Var Bsktbl; JV Var Sftbl; Var Trk; Hon Roll; Prfct Atten Awd; U Of AZ; Tchr; Coach.

BLOM, ABBY; Oologah-Talala HS; Claremore, OK; (3); 5/107; Hosp Aide; NFL; Speech Tm; Band; Chorus; Orch; Rep Frsh Cls; Sec Jr Cls; Ntl Merit SF; St Schlr; Qualified ST Speech; Instrumental & Vocal Conts Super Ratings; OK ST Univ; Photo; Nrsng.

BLOM, JAMI C; Oologah HS; Claremore, OK; (3); 1/108; Church Yth Grp; FCA; Intnl Clb; Band; Church Choir; Jazz Band; Mrchg Band; Hon Roll; NHS; Ntl Merit Ltr; Acctng.

BLOODWORTH, JENNIFER; Hugo HS; Hugo, OK; (4); 5/100; Art Clb; Computer Clb; Scholastic Bowl; Science Clb; Speech Tm; Teachers Aide; Mrchg Band; Yrbk; Sec Treas Sr Cls; Hon Roll; FEX Spkng Gld Mdl; East Central U; Law.

BLOOMER, MARIE; Newkirk HS; Newkirk, OK; (3); Spanish Clb; VICA; Band; Mrchg Band; Orch; Pep Band; School Musical; Socr; High Hon Roll; NHS; Archt.

BLOSE, JONATHAN M; Macarthur Sr HS; Lawton, OK; (3); Church Yth Grp; FCA; HOBY; Office Aide; Quiz Bowl; Science Clb; Acpl Chr; Pres Stu Cncl; Var Tennis; High Hon Roll; Church; Dentistry.

BLOUCH, JAYSON PATRICK; Will Rogers HS; Tulsa, OK; (2); Var Ftbl; Penn ST.

BLOUNT, JARRED L; Velma Alma HS; Velma, OK; (1); Quiz Bowl; Band; Mrchg Band.

BLOUNT, JUSTIN L; Velma Alma HS; Velma, OK; (1); Cmnty Wkr; Quiz Bowl; Hon Roll.

BLOW, ANDREA L; Westmoore HS; Oklahoma City, OK; (3); 3/6; Church Yth Grp; Spanish Clb; Church Choir; Ed Nwsp; Ed Yrbk; Sec NHS; Pres Acad Fit Awd; Scholastic Bowl; Golf; High Hon Roll; Bible Quiz; Dist Fine Arts Writingcatgry; Southwestern Assembly Of God.

BLOXHAM, CINDI L; Spiro HS; Spiro, OK; (2); FCA; HOBY; Math Clb; Natl FFA Org; Band; Color Guard; Var Bsktbl; Var Sftbl; NHS; 8-Undr Sftbl Coach; OSU; Lwyr.

BLOXSOM, BRANDI; Hulbert Jr Sr HS; Hulbert, OK; (2); GAA; Var Bsktbl; Sftbl; Trk; High Hon Roll; Jr NHS; NHS.

BLUINES, ABIGAIL E; Midwest City HS; Midwest City, OK; (2); 60/491; German Clb; Rptr Yrbk; Rep Stu Cncl; JV Sftbl; JV Vllybl; Hon Roll; Jr NHS; NHS; Prfct Atten Awd; FL ST; Math/Sci.

BLUMA, DANIELLE; Perry Sr HS; Perry, OK; (2); Church Yth Grp; FCA; Band; Jazz Band; Mrchg Band; Pep Band; Bsktbl; Pom Pon; Cit Awd; Hon Roll.

BLUNK, HOLLY R; Union Sr HS; Tulsa, OK; (3); Church Yth Grp; Orch; NHS; Tri M; DFY; Rnssnce; Ed.

BLUNT, CODI; Millwood HS; Oklahoma City, OK; (2); Church Yth Grp; GAA; ROTC; Chorus; Church Choir; Drill Tm; Bsktbl; Crs Cntry; Trk; Hon Roll.

BLUNT, MARIAH; Collinsville HS; Collinsville, OK; (4); 8/104; Cmnty Wkr; FCA; HOBY; Office Aide; Yrbk; VP Frsh Cls; VP Soph Cls; Sec Sr Cls; Rep Stu Cncl; Bsktbl; Chrmn Angel Free 2 Yrs; Southwestern U; Phrmcy.

BOARDMAN, MARY FRANCES; Stillwater Sr HS; Stillwater, OK; (2); Church Yth Grp; Drama Clb; German Clb; JCL; Latin Clb; Natl Beta Clb; School Musical; School Play; Stage Crew; Hon Roll; Field Stud Acad; TOG Clb.

BOATMAN, ALICIA A; Muldrow HS; Muldrow, OK; (1); Church Yth Grp; FHA; Pep Clb; Cit Awd; Hon Roll; Prfct Atten Awd; Val; FHA Dists/Subdists 1st Pl Wnnr; YACTS; Bsktbl; Cmptr Rcptnst.

BOATMAN, JANA; Mustang HS; Mustang, OK; (4); 67/365; Cmnty Wkr; Natl FFA Org; Red Cross Aide; Spanish Clb; Teachers Aide; Bsktbl; Sftbl; Hon Roll; NHS; Oklahoma City U; Bio.

BOATRIGHT, ADINA N; Roland Sr HS; Fort Smith, AR; (3); 1/105; Church Yth Grp; FCA; Quiz Bowl; Pres Spanish Clb; Yrbk; Rep Frsh Cls; L Bsktbl; Var Trk; High Hon Roll; NHS; Hnrs Club; Westark CC; Cmptr Sci.

BOATRIGHT, CARI P; Will Rogers HS; Tulsa, OK; (2); Church Yth Grp; VP English Clb; French Clb; HOBY; Quiz Bowl; School Play; Lit Mag; Tennis; High Hon Roll; Hon Roll; Biol.

BOATSMAN, JUSTIN; Cache HS; Cache, OK; (2); #1 in class; Art Clb; Church Yth Grp; Natl Beta Clb; Science Clb; High Hon Roll; NHS; Prfct Atten Awd; Wghtlftng; OK ST U; Medicine.

BOBIER, BRIAN; Midwest City HS; Midwest City, OK; (4); 77/417; Am Leg Boys St; Ofcr Sr Cls; Ofcr Stu Cncl; NHS; Athl Trng.

BOBO, CARRIE D; Deer Creek HS; Edmond, OK; (1); Church Yth Grp; Cmnty Wkr; Debate Tm; High Hon Roll.

BOBROVICZ, TODD A; Velma HS; Duncan, OK; (2); Boy Scts; Church Yth Grp; FCA; FBLA; Letterman Clb; Office Aide; SADD; Var Bsktbl; Var Crs Cntry; Var Trk; Southwestern OK ST; Pharm.

BOCKELMAN, AMBER L; Southeast HS; Oklahoma City, OK; (2); FCA; Natl FFA Org; Chorus; Ed Yrbk; Mgr Ftbl; Capt Swmmng; Hon Roll; Jr NHS; OK ST U; Vet Med.

BOCOCK, DARLA A; Boise City HS; Boise City, OK; (2); 10/40; 4-H; GAA; Natl FFA Org; Crs Cntry; Trk; 4-H Awd; Hon Roll; NHS; St Crss Cntry Qualifier; Mst Tlntd; Relay St Champs Cls A; OK ST Univ; Vet Tech.

BODENHAMER, ALISSHA G; Bartlesville Sr HS; Bartlesville, OK; (4); 32/412; Church Yth Grp; Cmnty Wkr; FHA; Service Clb; Cit Awd; High Hon Roll; NHS; Spanish NHS; FBLA; Spanish Clb; Pres Sci Explr Post; AP Schlr Awd; Univ Of MO Rolla; Engr.

BODENHAMER, ANDREW; Bartlesville Mid HS; Bartlesville, OK; (1); 1/450; Church Yth Grp; FHA; Spanish Clb; Band; Mrchg Band; Cit Awd; High Hon Roll; Washington Cty Yth Ct.

BODINE, ADAM; Ada HS; Ada, OK; (4); Am Leg Boys St; Am Leg Aux Girls St; Band; Jazz Band; Mrchg Band; Pep Band; Hon Roll; U AR; Music.

BOECKMAN, ANDREW; Okeene Jr Sr HS; Hitchcock, OK; (2); 11/36; Natl FFA Org; Var Bsbl; Var Bsktbl; Var Ftbl; Hon Roll; Kiwanis Awd; Prfct Atten Awd; FFA Ofcr 95-96.

BOECKMAN, ANTHONY A; Oklahoma Sch Of Science & Math; Medford, OK; (3); Computer Clb; Library Aide; Quiz Bowl; Scholastic Bowl; School Play.

BOECKMAN, DREW; Medford Schl; Medford, OK; (3); OK Schl Math And Sci.

BOECKMAN, ERIN; Fairview HS; Cleo Springs, OK; (1); 1/77; FHA; Speech Tm; High Hon Roll; Hon Roll.

BOECKMAN, KIM; Woodward HS; Woodward, OK; (2); 1/250; Church Yth Grp; German Clb; High Hon Roll; NHS; Delta Epsilon Phi; Acad Lttrmn; OK Hnr Soc; Optmtrst.

BOECKMAN, SHELLY C; Enid Sr HS; Enid, OK; (3); Church Yth Grp; Dance Clb; Teachers Aide; Color Guard; Drill Tm; Mrchg Band; High Hon Roll; Hon Roll; Jr NHS; NHS; Drill/Dance Tm Capt; Tap Dncng Best Imprvmt/Most Achvmt; OSU; Stdnt Cnslr.

BOESE, CHAD M; Enid Sr HS; Enid, OK; (4); Church Yth Grp; Office Aide; Bsktbl; Hon Roll; Jr NHS; NHS; Pres Acad Fit Awd; Ltl League Bsbl Umpire/Ftbl/Bsktbl Referee YMCA; Sprts Mrktg.

BOGARD, MEDINA; Savanna HS; Mcalester, OK; (4); 2/49; Church Yth Grp; FCA; GAA; Science Clb; Capt Var Bsktbl; Var Trk; Cit Awd; Hon Roll; NHS; Prfct Atten Awd; All St Trck; S Nazarene Univ; Elem Ed.

BOGART, BRENDA; Oologah-Talala HS; Oologah, OK; (1); Church Yth Grp; GAA; SADD; Chorus; Church Choir; Capt Chrldng; Trk; Wt Lftg; High Hon Roll; Hon Roll; Psych.

BOGHETICH, APRIL; Heritage Hall Schl; Oklahoma City, OK; (3); Cmnty Wkr; Science Clb; Service Clb; School Play; Phtg Rep Yrbk; Capt JV Chrldng; Sftbl; French Hon Soc; NHS; Slctd Sr Pr Ldr.

BOGIE, LAUREN; Jenks HS; Tulsa, OK; (1); 148/641; Office Aide; JV Chrldng; Trk; Hon Roll; Scuba Diving.

BOGLE, JAMIE M; Duncan HS; Duncan, OK; (2); Church Yth Grp; Key Clb; Spanish Clb; Band; Flag Corp; High Hon Roll; NHS; Chrch Co-Ed Sftbl Team.

BOGLE, REBECCA C; Ninnekah HS; Ninnekah, OK; (4); Church Yth Grp; FHA; Library Aide; Treas Science Clb; Spanish Clb; Nwsp; Yrbk; Hon Roll; USAO; Ultrasound Tech.

BOGLE, RONNIE; Ninnekah HS; Ninnekah, OK; (3); Church Yth Grp; FHA; Spanish Clb; VICA; Rptr Nwsp; Hon Roll; OSU Tech; Engrng.

BOHANNAN, AMANDA; Fox Sr HS; Fox, OK; (2); Church Yth Grp; FCA; Pep Clb; Rep Soph Cls; Var Bsktbl; Var Chrldng; NHS; Ntl Merit Ltr; Sal; ECU; Dntl Hygnst.

BOHANNON, CHRYSTAL R; Charles Page HS; Sand Springs, OK; (3); Church Yth Grp; French Clb; Band; Church Choir; Jazz Band; Mrchg Band; Pep Band; Hon Roll; Prfct Atten Awd; 3 Time Mmbr All Dist Hnr Band Alto Sxphne; Psych/Thrpst.

BOKIES, SUSAN L; Durant HS; Durant, OK; (3); 12/150; Am Leg Aux Girls St; Church Yth Grp; Cmnty Wkr; FCA; French Clb; Key Clb; Math Clb; Pep Clb; Scholastic Bowl; Science Clb; St Vocal Solo & Ensembles 1st Div; All Dist Choir & Band; Div II Dist Bassoon Solo; Piano Cont; Southeastern OK Univ; Pre-Law.

BOKKER, FEATHER C; El Reno Sr HS; El Reno, OK; (2); 15/256; Church Yth Grp; FTA; Key Clb; SADD; Varsity Clb; JV Bsktbl; JV Crs Cntry; Cit Awd; Hon Roll.

BOLAND, NICKI I; Choctaw HS; Choctaw, OK; (4); 1/304; Church Yth Grp; Spanish Clb; Chorus; Jr NHS; NHS; St Schlr; All St Chorus; Vocal Jazz Grp; U Of Cntrl OK; Music Ed.

BOLAY, ROBYN; Perry Sr HS; Perry, OK; (4); 30/63; 4-H; FBLA; German Clb; Office Aide; Band; Chorus; JV Bsktbl; Var Sftbl; Adv Vocal Music; OK Kids ST Finalist; Ewe Lead ST Champ 93/95; Intnl Bus.

BOLDEN, LATOSHIA A; U S Grant HS; Oklahoma City, OK; (4); 16/183; FBLA; Pep Clb; Rep Soph Cls; Treas Jr Cls; Pres Sr Cls; Ofcr Stu Cncl; High Hon Roll; NHS; Explrs Banking Post Treas; Hi-Lion Of Lions OKC Downtown Clb; MI ST U; Acctnt.

BOLDING, HOLLY; Ft Towson HS; Sawyer, OK; (3); Capt FCA; 4-H; FHA; Sec Frsh Cls; Sec Soph Cls; Sec Jr Cls; Sec Stu Cncl; Var Co-Capt Bsktbl; Var Sftbl; Hon Roll; Northeastern ST U; Acctng.

BOLDING, KATIE L; Edmond Memorial HS; Edmond, OK; (3); Church Yth Grp; Pep Clb; Spanish Clb; Chorus; Church Choir; School Musical; Swing Chorus; Variety Show; Music; Opera Singer.

BOLDING, TIYA; Blanchard Jr Sr HS; Blanchard, OK; (1); Pep Clb; Var Bsktbl; Var Chrldng; Hon Roll; Pres Acad Fit Awd; OSU.

BOLES, TERESA K; Ponca City Sr HS; Ponca City, OK; (4); 12/358; Church Yth Grp; FCA; Spanish Clb; Band; Mrchg Band; Var Capt Bsktbl; Trk; High Hon Roll; NHS; U Of OK.

BOLEY, DANIEL; U S Grant HS; Haileyville, OK; (4); FCA; Ofcr Bsbl; Bsktbl; Ftbl; Wt Lftg; Hon Roll; Arch Engr.

BOLIEN, KRISTY D; Mc Alester HS; Krebs, OK; (3); Art Clb; Church Yth Grp; Cmnty Wkr; Drama Clb; French Clb; Hosp Aide; Red Cross Aide; VICA; Pres Acad Fit Awd; HOSA; CPR Cert; Basic Microbiology; Death & Dying; Mentlly & Phys Challngd Chldrn.

BOLIN, MELISSA; Vian HS; Vian, OK; (3); 10/58; FHA; Service Clb; Spanish Clb; Drill Tm; Var Co-Capt Chrldng; Gym; Hon Roll; Indian Clb; D-Fy; Obstetrics.

BOLING, BECKY L; Valliant HS; Hugo, OK; (1); 7/89; Church Yth Grp; FHA; Chorus; Church Choir; Stat Bsktbl; Var Trk; Hon Roll; St Schlr.

BOLLES, MELISSA M; Wilson HS; Wilson, OK; (3); 9/43; Teachers Aide; Band; Flag Corp; Mrchg Band; Bsktbl; Chrldng; Sftbl; Hon Roll; U Of OK; Cmptr/Bus Mngmnt.

BOLLING, AMANDA K; Choctaw HS; Choctaw, OK; (3); Art Clb; Drama Clb; Girl Scts; Office Aide; Chorus; Tennis; Med/Sci.

BOLLING, JAMIE C; Muskogee HS; Muskogee, OK; (4); Church Yth Grp; JCL; Chorus; Church Choir; High Hon Roll; NHS; OK Hon Soc; Latn Hon Soc; DECA; NSU; Psych.

BOLLINGER, CRYSTAL; Turpin Schl; Hardesty, OK; (3); 12/27; Church Yth Grp; Letterman Clb; Library Aide; Chorus; Variety Show; Yrbk; High Hon Roll; Hon Roll; Infrml Geometry Acad Awd; Intnl Prblms Acad Awd.

BOLSTEAD, JASON T; Stillwater Sr HS; Stillwater, OK; (2); 1/450; FCA; Natl Beta Clb; JV Bsbl; JV Ftbl; Var Wrstlng; High Hon Roll; Prfct Atten Awd; Pres Acad Fit Awd; Pres Schlr; Bus.

BOLSTER, TAMMY M; Meeker HS; Chandler, OK; (1); FHA; Comp Tech.

BOLT, KRISTA; Midwest City HS; Midwest City, OK; (3); 14/384; DECA; Pep Clb; Spanish Clb; Yrbk; Ofcr Soph Cls; Ofcr Jr Cls; Bsktbl; Mgr(s); NHS; Spanish NHS.

BOLT, MATT T; Edmond Memorial HS; Edmond, OK; (2); 1/408; Boy Scts; Church Yth Grp; Spanish Clb; Band; Mrchg Band; JV Bsbl; JV Ftbl; High Hon Roll; NHS; Prfct Atten Awd; U Of OK; Phys Sci.

BOLTE, KARL E; Mc Alester HS; Mcalester, OK; (2); Church Yth Grp; Cmnty Wkr; Quiz Bowl; Band; Chorus; Jazz Band; School Musical; High Hon Roll; St Schlr; Water Sprts; OK ST Univ.

BOLTON, KRYSTAL; Grandfield Jr Sr HS; Grandfield, OK; (3); 4/27; Church Yth Grp; FHA; Pep Clb; Pres Frsh Cls; Bsktbl; High Hon Roll; NHS; Acctng.

BOLTON, ROBERT M; Bethany HS; Bethany, OK; (2); Church Yth Grp; FCA; HOBY; Library Aide; Chorus; VP Jr Cls; Var Bsktbl; Cit Awd; High Hon Roll; NHS.

BOLZLE, SETH R; B T Washington HS; Tulsa, OK; (4); 23/264; Drama Clb; VP German Clb; Church Choir; Capt Golf; Hon Roll; NHS; St Schlr; Natl Merit Hnr; Nom OK All ST Schlsp Prgm Hnr; CO Coll.

BOMAN, AUDREY A; Commerce HS; Commerce, OK; (1); Science Clb; SADD; Band; Mrchg Band; Pep Band; Ofcr Frsh Cls; Ofcr Stu Cncl; Hon Roll; Band; Stdnt Cncl; NE OK Univ; Elem Tchr.

BOMBACH, ROGER; Beaver HS; Beaver, OK; (3); 7/34; Church Yth Grp; FCA; Varsity Clb; Chorus; Yrbk; Var L Bsbl; Var L Bsktbl; Var L Ftbl; Var L Trk; Hon Roll; All Conf Bsktbl; All Dist Hnrb Mntn Ftbl; Medicine.

BOMHOFF, LOUIE G; El Reno Sr HS; El Reno, OK; (3); Boy Scts; Church Yth Grp; Cmnty Wkr; Natl FFA Org; Scholastic Bowl; Stage Crew; Variety Show; Stat Bsktbl; Mgr(s); Score Keeper; De Molay Ofcs; Cmptr Tm 2 Yrs; U Of OK; Med.

BOND, KELSI; Canton HS; Canton, OK; (2); FHA; SADD; Pres Frsh Cls; VP Soph Cls; Bsktbl; Crs Cntry; Trk; Cit Awd; Hon Roll; Rep NHS; Stu Of Today Awd; Qrtr Fnlst 2a Bsktbl 94-95; 3200 M Rly St Champs 94-95; Phy Ther.

BOND, MARY E; Stillwater Sr HS; Stillwater, OK; (3); #77 in class; Church Yth Grp; Cmnty Wkr; Debate Tm; Drama Clb; FCA; French Clb; Natl Beta Clb; NFL; Pep Clb; Science Clb; Schlrs Diploma 96; Frosh Eng Comp I; OSU; Pre-Med.

BOND, MIKE; Broken Bow HS; Broken Bow, OK; (4); 8/146; Church Yth Grp; FCA; Golf; Hon Roll; Kiwanis Awd; NHS.

BOND, SHERRY; Carl Albert HS; Midwest City, OK; (3); 1/220; Cmnty Wkr; French Clb; Hosp Aide; Key Clb; SADD; Band; Jazz Band; Mrchg Band; Hon Roll; Jr NHS; Outstndng Frnch I Stu Awd; Soph Of Yr; Page For OK Hse Of Reps; TX A&M; Elem Ed/Frnch.

BOND, SOLOMON A; Edmond North HS; Edmond, OK; (4); 91/339; Art Clb; Mu Alpha Theta; Quiz Bowl; Var L Bsktbl; Var L Trk; Ntl Merit SF; Multicltrl Clb; Med Research.

BOND, TARA; Garber Sr HS; Enid, OK; (1); FCA; Natl FFA Org; Bsktbl; Sftbl; Hon Roll; Pres Acad Fit Awd; OK ST Univ; Bsktbl Coach.

BONDS, DAYSHA D; Altus Sr HS; Altus, OK; (3); Church Yth Grp; Sec FCA; Church Choir; School Musical; Pres Frsh Cls; Pres Soph Cls; Sec Pres Stu Cncl; Chrldng; Hon Roll; NHS; Acad All Star; OK Univ; Chld Psychlgst.

BONE, AMY; Turner Schl; Marietta, OK; (1); Church Yth Grp; 4-H; FHA; Natl Beta Clb; Pep Clb; JV Bsktbl; Hon Roll; Eng; Ed.

BONE, CORY M; Wilson HS; Wilson, OK; (4); Am Leg Boys St; Boy Scts; Church Yth Grp; Ftbl; Wt Lftg; Hon Roll; Amer Red Crss CPR Cert.

BONE, JACOB; Spiro HS; Spiro, OK; (3); FCA; FBLA; Teachers Aide; Varsity Clb; Var Bsbl; Var Golf; Hon Roll; NHS; Phy.

BONHAM, AMANDA G; Ponca City Middle HS; Ponca City, OK; (2); Church Yth Grp; Dance Clb; High Hon Roll; Hon Roll; Elem Ed.

BONHAM, BRANDI ELAINE; Northeast HS; Oklahoma City, OK; (3); Art Clb; FBLA; Science Clb; Cit Awd; Hon Roll; Cit Clb; Bio-Med Sci Pgm; Jr Judge Of ST Wide Invention Conv; OSU Tech; Nrsng.

BONHAM, NATALIE D; Bartlesville Mid HS; Bartlesville, OK; (2); 113/481; FHA; JA; Quiz Bowl; Golf; Hon Roll; OSU; Vet.

BONNER, BYRON; Brink Jr HS; Oklahoma City, OK; (1); Rep Stu Cncl; Bsktbl; Ftbl; FL ST; Art.

BONNETT, RACHEL C; Enid Sr HS; Enid, OK; (3); 10/435; Church Yth Grp; Spanish Clb; Band; Church Choir; Mrchg Band; Orch; Pep Band; High Hon Roll; Hon Roll; Jr NHS; Fiesta Bowl Natl Pagent Of Bnds; Big Bros/Big Sisters.

BONSER, SHAD; Cheyenne HS; Cheyenne, OK; (4); Natl FFA Org; Band; Mrchg Band; Capt Bsbl; Var Bsktbl; Wt Lftg; Hon Roll; Red Lands CC; Cmmrcl Art.

BOOHER, RYAN; Ada HS; Ada, OK; (3); Church Yth Grp; Scholastic Bowl; Church Choir; Bsktbl; High Hon Roll; Jr NHS; NHS; Stu Of Today.

BOOKER, CRAIG T; Edmond North HS; Edmond, OK; (3); Church Yth Grp; Mu Alpha Theta; Office Aide; VICA; Hon Roll; Stu Of Mnth Soph Yr.

BOONE, AMY; Clinton HS; Clinton, OK; (2); Church Yth Grp; FCA; FHA; Ofcr Stu Cncl; Var Bsktbl; Var Socr; High Hon Roll; NHS.

BOONE, JENNY; Macarthur Jr HS; Lawton, OK; (1); Church Yth Grp; FCA; Pep Clb; Science Clb; Var Chrldng; Hon Roll; NHS; Marine Blgst.

BOONE, KERI; Merritt Schl; Elk City, OK; (1); Church Yth Grp; FCA; Natl FFA Org; SADD; Chorus; Ofcr Stu Cncl; Chrldng; Cit Awd; NHS; Sal; Phys Thrp.

BOONE, KIMBERLE D; Edmond Santa Fe HS; Edmond, OK; (4); 11/209; Cmnty Wkr; Orch; JV Var Bsktbl; Var JV Socr; Var Trk; High Hon Roll; Jr NHS; NHS; Pres Acad Fit Awd; Pres Schlr; OK Yth Orch Mem; N Cntrl Hnrs Orch Mem; Orch Cncl Jr & Sr Rep; Sciencing On Saturday Vol; OK ST Univ; Mrktg.

BOONE, RUSSELL A; Union Intermediate HS; Tulsa, OK; (2); Band; Pres Acad Fit Awd; Elec/Elec Engr.

BOONE, SUMMER M; Mannford HS; Mannford, OK; (4); FCA; NFL; Science Clb; Spanish Clb; SADD; Teachers Aide; VP Sr Cls; Pres Stu Cncl; Golf; NHS; Stu Of Yr; Masonic Ldgs Stu Of Today; U OK; Occuptnl Thrpy.

BOOSAMRA, SHANNON R; Turner Schl; Burneyville, OK; (2); FHA; Child Daycare.

BOOTH, RYAN; Hugo HS; Hugo, OK; (4); 35/127; Am Leg Boys St; Church Yth Grp; FCA; Natl FFA Org; Spanish Clb; Varsity Clb; VICA; Church Choir; Rep Stu Cncl; Var Co-Capt Ftbl; Yth Evangelism Conf Rep; Church Usher; Radiologist.

BOOTHE, ASHLEY C; Bishop Mcguinness HS; Oklahoma City, OK; (3); 33/144; Church Yth Grp; FCA; Pep Clb; Var Crs Cntry; Var Trk; NHS; Spanish NHS; Kairos Retreat Ldr; Frosh Cls Rep For Mc Guiness Olympics.

BORAY, VIVEK N; Union Sr HS; Broken Arrow, OK; (4); 16/669; Boy Scts; Church Yth Grp; CAP; Dance Clb; 4-H; French Clb; FTA; JCL; Mu Alpha Theta; Office Aide; Climate Cntrl Inst; Climate Spc.

BORDEN, JESSICA; Hinton HS; Hinton, OK; (3); 8/25; Church Yth Grp; FCA; Sec Treas FHA; Key Clb; SADD; Teachers Aide; Acpl Chr; Chorus; Church Choir; School Musical; OSU Okmulgee; Jewelery Tech.

BOREN, JARED; Tahlequah Sr HS; Tahlequah, OK; (4); 10/251; Math Clb; Spanish Clb; Jr NHS; NHS; Pres Acad Fit Awd; Martial Arts; Wght Lftng; Northeastern ST U; FBI.

BORGELT, TESSA Y; Mc Alester HS; Mcalester, OK; (4); Church Yth Grp; Math Clb; Office Aide; Treas Science Clb; Chorus; School Musical.

BORK, SISSY M; Harrah HS; Mc Loud, OK; (3); 32/163; Art Clb; Cmnty Wkr; FHA; Pep Clb; Spanish Clb; SADD; Chrldng; Pom Pon; Cit Awd; High Hon Roll; Eng III Acad Awd; Home Ec III Awd; U Of OK; Commercial Photogrphr.

BORNMANN, SUZANNE; Boswell Sr HS; Boswell, OK; (3); 1/35; Sec FCA; Sec Key Clb; Natl FFA Org; Yrbk; Sec Jr Cls; Cit Awd; High Hon Roll; NHS; Masonic Awd; Southwestern OK ST U.

BORRSON, BEVERLY; Chandler HS; Wellston, OK; (3); Church Yth Grp; FCA; FHA; Spanish Clb; Band; Mrchg Band; Rep Jr Cls; Bsktbl; Sftbl; NHS; NEMA; Med.

BORUM, COURTNEY ANN; Moore HS; Moore, OK; (4); Mgr(s); Trk; Wt Lftg; Achvmt Awds; OSU; Nrsng.

BORUM, NICKI R; Arkoma Jr Sr HS; Arkoma, OK; (4); 2/30; Church Yth Grp; FCA; FBLA; FHA; GAA; Scholastic Bowl; Yrbk; Sec Frsh Cls; Pres Soph Cls; VP Jr Cls; Westark Ft Smith.

BOSCH, TABITHA L; Moore HS; Oklahoma City, OK; (2); Office Aide; Pep Clb; Scholastic Bowl; Hon Roll; Jr NHS; NHS; OU; Math Tchr.

BOSS, DARBYE; Eufaula Sr HS; Eufaula, OK; (4); 14/73; FHA; Math Clb; Science Clb; Teachers Aide; Cit Awd; Hon Roll; NHS; Pres Acad Fit Awd; Yearbook Clb; Connors; Phy Asst.

BOSTIAN, LAURA B; Bixby Sr HS; Bixby, OK; (4); 14/189; Church Yth Grp; FCA; German Clb; SADD; Ofcr Stu Cncl; Socr; High Hon Roll; Jr NHS; NHS; Sal; Acad All ST Nom 96; All Dist 11th/12th Sccr; OK ST Univ.

BOSTIC, HEIDI E; Guthrie Sr HS; Guthrie, OK; (1); 19/308; Church Yth Grp; Lbrn Chorus; Church Choir; School Musical; Variety Show; Vol Mental/Phys Handicap; Music.

BOSTIC, TARYN L; Hugo HS; Hugo, OK; (3); Spanish Clb; Ofcr Stu Cncl; OU; Law.

BOSTICK, ROBERT NEIL; Broken Bow HS; Broken Bow, OK; (4); 2/150; Am Leg Boys St; Drama Clb; Capt Quiz Bowl; Science Clb; Spanish Clb; School Musical; NHS; Ntl Merit SF; St Schlr; Intl Frgn Lang Awd; U Tulsa; Comp Sci.

BOSTON, ERIC W; Woodward HS; Woodward, OK; (1); Art Clb; Church Yth Grp; FCA; Letterman Clb; Red Cross Aide; Spanish Clb; Ftbl; Wt Lftg; Prfct Atten Awd; Rose St Univ; Phy Thrpy.

BOTT, KIMBERLY A; Putnam City North HS; Oklahoma City, OK; (4); 90/490; Church Yth Grp; Hosp Aide; Orch; U Cntrl OK; Nrsng.

BOTTOM, BRIAN; Cordell Jr HS; Cordell, OK; (3); Am Leg Boys St; Church Yth Grp; Letterman Clb; Spanish Clb; Band; Chorus; Mrchg Band; Yrbk; VP Frsh Cls; Rep Soph Cls; Bst All Arnd Athlte; Bst All Arnd Male Stu; OK St Senate Page; Optmtry.

BOTTOM, BROOKE R; Altus Sr HS; Altus, OK; (3); 1/275; Church Yth Grp; Cmnty Wkr; Hosp Aide; Spanish Clb; Teachers Aide; Ed Nwsp; Ed Yrbk; High Hon Roll; JETS Awd; Sec Jr NHS; Jr Engrng Tech Soc; Schltc Team Sec; Tech Stu Assn Sec, Tres & Pres; Acad Decthln; Modl Congrss Delgt; Southwestern OK ST U; Medcn.

BOTTS, AMANDA J; Drummond Schl; Waukomis, OK; (4); Pres VICA; Rep Sr Cls; Church Yth Grp; French Clb; Bsktbl; Sftbl; Trk; Hon Roll; Jr NHS; NHS; Cmmptncy Cert Camera Oprtr, Offset Pltmkng/Prs Oprtr, Paste Up Artist, Electrnc Imgr.

BOUAKADAKIS, AUTUMN E; Bishop Kelley HS; Tulsa, OK; (1); Pep Clb; Red Cross Aide; Rep Frsh Cls; Pom Pon; Hon Roll; Fresh Cls Brd Pres; Music.

BOUCHER, KRISTIE; Claremore Sr HS; Claremore, OK; (4); Art Clb; Drama Clb; German Clb; Quiz Bowl; Science Clb; Rep Stu Cncl; Hon Roll; NHS; Guitar, Piano & Organ; BSA Explorers; OK ST Univ; His Prof.

BOUDREAUX, JODY M; North Intemediate HS; Broken Arrow, OK; (1); Bsktbl.

BOUGOUBA, MELISSA H; North Intemediate HS; Broken Arrow, OK; (1); Band; Mrchg Band; Pep Band; OK ST U; Vet.

BOUNDS, CLIFF; Owasso Sr HS; Owasso, OK; (2); 100/420; Church Yth Grp; FCA; Library Aide; Teachers Aide; Var Bsktbl; Var Golf; High Hon Roll; Prof Golf.

BOUNDS, DOUG; Elk City Jr HS; Elk City, OK; (3); Church Yth Grp; Drama Clb; FCA; Natl FFA Org; Pep Clb; Spanish Clb; Teachers Aide; Stage Crew; Var Ftbl; Var Golf; OK ST Univ; Animal Sci.

BOUNDS, STACEY R; Ninnekah HS; Rush Springs, OK; (3); Church Yth Grp; FBLA; FHA; Spanish Clb; High Hon Roll; Comp Bus Applications Cls Mst Achieved Stu; Chem I, Eng II & III Awds; Bus.

BOURGEOIS, ANNIE; Owasso Sr HS; Owasso, OK; (3); Church Yth Grp; FCA; FHA; Intnl Clb; Spanish Clb; SADD; Ofcr Jr Cls; Rep Stu Cncl; Chrldng; Hon Roll; Teen Actn Grp; Cmp Entrprse-Ldrshp Cmp; U OK.

BOURISAW, ERIN C; Choctaw HS; Choctaw, OK; (3); 1/330; Church Yth Grp; Cmnty Wkr; Key Clb; Chorus; Church Choir; Color Guard; Treas Jr Cls; High Hon Roll; Jr NHS; Val; Piano.

BOURISAW, TIFFANY; Choctaw Jr HS; Choctaw, OK; (1); 1/216; Church Yth Grp; Band; Church Choir; High Hon Roll; Jr NHS; Piano.

BOUSE, SARAH K; Edmond Memorial HS; Edmond, OK; (1); Church Yth Grp; Cmnty Wkr; Spanish Clb; SADD; Rep Stu Cncl; Hon Roll.

BOUTWELL, LORETTA A; Shawnee Sr HS; Shawnee, OK; (4); French Clb; Chorus; Church Choir; Dirs Awd Choir; Pre-Vet.

BOW, KRISSIE; Caddo HS; Kenefic, OK; (3); 7/26; Church Yth Grp; Rptr FHA; Chorus; Church Choir; Rptr Jr Cls; Var Capt Chrldng; Hon Roll; NHS; Multi Yr Listing; Marine Bio.

BOWDEN, LEAH F; Claremore Sr HS; Claremore, OK; (1); French Clb; Band; Mrchg Band; Pep Band; High Hon Roll; OK HS Hnr Soc; OK Dressage Soc; US Dressage Fed; OK ST Univ; Veterinary Medcn.

BOWEN, AMANDA J; Catoosa HS; Tulsa, OK; (1); Hon Roll.

BOWEN, ASHLEY; Idabel HS; Idabel, OK; (2); Art Clb; Rptr Church Yth Grp; FCA; FBLA; Science Clb; Yrbk; Sec Frsh Cls; Sec Soph Cls; Ofcr Stu Cncl; Co-Capt Chrldng; NCA All Amer Chrldr.

BOWEN, ASHLEY; Kremlin Jr Sr HS; Enid, OK; (2); 1/22; Boy Scts; HOBY; Quiz Bowl; Band; L Bsbl; Capt Var Ftbl; High Hon Roll; JETS Awd; Ntl Merit Ltr; Pres Acad Fit Awd; U OK; Petroleum Engrng.

BOWEN, BARBARA M; Mc Lain Career Acad; Tulsa, OK; (2); Hon Roll; Hlth Tech; EMSA Lcl Amblnc Svc; Tutoring Elem Stdnts; Tulsa U; Psych.

BOWEN, BRANDI; Madill HS; Kingston, OK; (1); Church Yth Grp; FBLA; FHA; Quiz Bowl; SADD; Band; School Musical; Ofcr Stu Cncl; Hon Roll; Pres Acad Fit Awd; Stanford; Physcn.

BOWEN, EVERICK K; Northeast HS; Oklahoma City, OK; (2); Church Yth Grp; Capt Bsbl; Var Ftbl; Hon Roll; Htlh Careers II Stu Of Month; NE; Sports Med.

BOWEN, KEILA J; Healdton HS; Wilson, OK; (2); 4-H; Band; Chorus; Church Choir; Jazz Band; Mrchg Band; Rep Stu Cncl; Cit Awd; Hon Roll; Pres Schlr; Tulsa Univ; Marine Bio.

BOWEN, KIMBERLY D; Indianola HS; Mcalester, OK; (3); 4-H; FHA; JV Bsktbl; Prfct Atten Awd; FHA Outstndng Mbr; ADAPT; Little Buddies; SE OK St Univ; Comp Prog.

BOWEN, NANCY; Drumright HS; Drumright, OK; (3); 5/44; Art Clb; 4-H; HOBY; Math Tm; Rptr Natl FFA Org; Spanish Clb; Speech Tm; Score Keeper; 4-H Awd; High Hon Roll; Amer Jr Paint Horse Assn; Miss Creek Cty 95-96; Livestock Exhibits; Crop Judging Tm; :agronomy/Bus.

BOWEN, NONIQUE; Star Spencer HS; Oklahoma City, OK; (2); Computer Clb; FBLA; Teachers Aide; High Hon Roll; U Of N TX; Bus/Cmptr Tech.

BOWEN, OLIVER E; Jenks HS; Jenks, OK; (4); Math Tm; Natl FFA Org; Hon Roll; Ntl Merit SF.

BOWER, LAURA A; Metro Christian Acad; Tulsa, OK; (2); Church Yth Grp; Key Clb; Spanish Clb; Chorus; Church Choir; School Musical; High Hon Roll; NHS; Outstdng Wrtr; Best Span Stdnt; Best Poet; Crtv Wrtg.

BOWER, MICHAEL A; Ninnekah HS; Chickasha, OK; (3); Hist FBLA; Science Clb; VICA; Hon Roll; Natl His/Govt Awd; U Of TX Arlington; Acctg.

BOWERS, AUTUMN N; Calumet Schl; Calumet, OK; (3); Church Yth Grp; FCA; 4-H; FHA; Letterman Clb; Teachers Aide; School Play; Yrbk; JV Var Bsktbl; JV Vllybl; Psych.

BOWERS, BILLY; Canton HS; Longdale, OK; (3); Model UN; Spanish Clb; SADD; Rep Frsh Cls; L Trk; L Wt Lftg; NW OK ST Rgnls Wght Meet/Area 3rd Pl; OK ST Wght Meet/4th Pl In ST.

BOWERS, COLBY J; Duncan HS; Duncan, OK; (2); Church Yth Grp; Letterman Clb; SADD; Yrbk; Pres Jr Cls; Ofcr Stu Cncl; Ofcr Bsbl; Stu Cncl Ambassador; World Changers.

BOWERS, SHAWN L; Blanchard Jr Sr HS; Blanchard, OK; (4); 13/71; Church Yth Grp; Computer Clb; Math Clb; Mu Alpha Theta; Office Aide; Band; Mrchg Band; Cit Awd; Hon Roll; NHS; USAO; Acctng.

BOWERSOCK, R BLAKE; Bartlesville Sr HS; Bartlesville, OK; (3); Church Yth Grp; Pres FBLA; VP German Clb; HOBY; Chorus; Ofcr Stu Cncl; High Hon Roll; Jr NHS; Kiwanis Awd; NHS; Intnl Bus.

BOWERSOCK, RICHARD B; Bartlesville Sr HS; Bartlesville, OK; (3); 21/485; Church Yth Grp; Pres FBLA; VP German Clb; HOBY; Chorus; Sec Stu Cncl; Cit Awd; High Hon Roll; Jr NHS; Kiwanis Awd; Pol Sci/Ec.

BOWIE, JESSICA R; Shawnee Sr HS; Shawnee, OK; (2); 36/295; Church Yth Grp; DECA; Spanish Clb; Chorus; Var Socr; High Hon Roll; Ldrshp Shawnee; OK Bapt Univ.

BOWLAN, MARK S; Shawnee Sr HS; Shawnee, OK; (1); Church Yth Grp; FCA; Spanish Clb; Church Choir; JV Bsktbl; High Hon Roll; Piano 5 Yrs.

BOWLER, DONDRANEA; Millwood HS; Oklahoma City, OK; (4); Church Yth Grp; Office Aide; Band; Chorus; Church Choir; Drm Mjr(t); Mrchg Band; Hon Roll; NHS; Med.

BOWLES, AMANDA L; Union Intermediate HS; Tulsa, OK; (1); 18/866; Var Debate Tm; Key Clb; VP Math Clb; NFL; Capt Quiz Bowl; High Hon Roll; NHS; Church Choir; Chnse Lang Awd; Drug Free Yth; Frgn Lang Club.

BOWLES, REBEKAH G; Asher Schl; Asher, OK; (3); Church Yth Grp; Drama Clb; FHA; Church Choir; School Musical; School Play; Rptr Nwsp; Sec VP Frsh Cls; Ofcr Soph Cls; Hon Roll; FHA Offcr Reptr, Hist; E Cntrl Univ; Home Ec Tchr.

BOWLES, STEPHANIE R; Bartlesville Sr HS; Bartlesville, OK; (1); Church Yth Grp; Pom Pon; Hon Roll; Studied Ballet 12 Yrs; Dance/Tchng.

BOWLES, TIFFANY; Daniel Webster HS; Tulsa, OK; (1); Church Yth Grp; Pres Frsh Cls; Rep Stu Cncl; Var Chrldng; High Hon Roll.

BOWLIN, ALANA; Carnegie HS; Mountain View, OK; (4); Church Yth Grp; Sec Sr Cls; Pres Stu Cncl; Bsktbl; Chrldng; NHS; Val.

BOWLIN, ALLANA; Carnegie Jr HS; Mountain View, OK; (4); 2/50; Church Yth Grp; Quiz Bowl; Teachers Aide; Var Chrldng; Var Trk; NHS; Pres Acad Fit Awd; Rep Frsh Cls; Treas Soph Cls; Pres Jr Cls; OK ST U.

BOWLIN, DESIREE T; North Intemediate HS; Broken Arrow, OK; (1); Church Yth Grp; Dance Clb; Drama Clb; Office Aide; Spanish Clb; Chorus; Church Choir; Rep Stu Cncl; High Hon Roll; Hon Roll; OK Hnr Scty; Rhema Bible Col; Yth Pastr.

BOWLIN, JASON T; Sapulpa Sr HS; Sapulpa, OK; (2); Church Yth Grp.

BOWMAN, AMANDA J; East Central HS; Tulsa, OK; (3); Key Clb; Spanish Clb; Yrbk; Var Socr; Hon Roll; NHS; Amer Indian Clb; DFY; TX A&M; Bio; Oceanography.

BOWMAN, BENJAMIN J; Deer Creek HS; Edmond, OK; (2); Boy Scts; Church Yth Grp; Drama Clb; HOBY; Pres Frsh Cls; Ofcr Soph Cls; Ofcr Jr Cls; Ftbl; Wrstlng; NHS; Eagle Sct; Dentist.

BOWMAN, BROCK J; Tecumseh HS; Shawnee, OK; (3); Spanish Clb; Acpl Chr; Band; Chorus; Mrchg Band; Orch; Pep Band; School Play; ECOCDA Hnr Choir; Band Cncl.

BOWMAN, CHRIS C; Owasso Sr HS; Owasso, OK; (3); 45/400; Band; Mrchg Band; Hon Roll; NHS; Demolays; Frnch Clb; Dead General Soc; Aero Eng.

BOWMAN, ELISHA; Holdenville HS; Holdenville, OK; (4); 1/74; Church Yth Grp; FBLA; Natl Beta Clb; Sec VP Natl FFA Org; Science Clb; Band; Mrchg Band; Phtg Yrbk; Hon Roll; NHS; OK ST Univ; Ag Econ; Acctng.

BOWMAN, KENT; Deer Creek HS; Edmond, OK; (4); 33/66; Am Leg Boys St; Boy Scts; Church Yth Grp; Cmnty Wkr; Pres Jr Cls; Ofcr Sr Cls; Pres Stu Cncl; JV Var Ftbl; Var Capt Wrstlng; Cit Awd; Wendys Natl Hsmn Awd; Rgnl Schl Athl Of Yr; Mr Deer Crk; Sprts Med.

BOWMAN, LAURA; Seminole Jr Sr HS; Seminole, OK; (2); Debate Tm; French Clb; Math Clb; NFL; Speech Tm; Stage Crew; Mock Trial; Model Congress.

BOWMAN, SEAN M; Union Intermediate HS; Tulsa, OK; (2); 108/800; NHS; Yng Astronauts; OK Aeronautics Acad; Astronaut.

BOWSHER, NIKKI; Cache HS; Cache, OK; (4); Art Clb; Hosp Aide; Science Clb; Band; Chorus; Flag Corp; Jazz Band; VP Frsh Cls; High Hon Roll; NHS; Univ Of OK; RN/MUSIC.

BOWZER, JOANNA L; Putnam City West HS; Bethany, OK; (1); Church Yth Grp; Drama Clb; JCL; School Musical; Treas Frsh Cls; Treas Soph Cls; Ofcr Bsbl; Bsktbl; Ftbl; Sftbl; Ath Trainer For Olympic Handball Trials 96; Orthopedics.

BOX, JAMIE; Keota Schl; Keota, OK; (3); 1/47; Church Yth Grp; FHA; German Clb; HOBY; NFL; Pep Clb; Pres Soph Cls; Treas Stu Cncl; Cit Awd; Hon Roll; OU; Med.

BOX, LINDSEY; Stigler HS; Stigler, OK; (1); Church Yth Grp; Drama Clb; FCA; SADD; Acad Team; GATE; Oral Roberts U.

BOX, MATTHEW; Indianola HS; Mcalester, OK; (2); Natl Beta Clb; Bsktbl; Spanish NHS.

BOY, MARANDA; Pryor Jr HS; Chouteau, OK; (2); Church Yth Grp; Sec Debate Tm; German Clb; Sec Natl FFA Org; NFL; Spanish Clb; Sec Speech Tm; School Play; High Hon Roll; Jr NHS; 3rd Pl Tri-St Fair 94; Reg Semi-Fnlst Spch/Dbt 94 & 95; Grnd Champ Mrkt Lamb & 2nd Pl Tulsa St Fair 95; TX A&M U; Anml Sci.

BOYATTIA, TIFFANY S; Muskogee HS; Muskogee, OK; (3); Church Yth Grp; Cmnty Wkr; Spanish Clb; SADD; Swing Chorus; Cit Awd; Hon Roll; NHS; Pres Schlr; Acpl Chr; Childrens Ministry Tchr; Boughers Against Illegal Drugs Chpln; Schlst Achvmnt Acad Awd; OK Univ; Pre Med.

BOYCE, J WILFORD H; Bartlesville Sr HS; Bartlesville, OK; (3); 67/441; Church Yth Grp; FCA; Letterman Clb; Varsity Clb; Chorus; Rep Soph Cls; Rep Jr Cls; VP Stu Cncl; Var L Ftbl; Hon Roll; K Life Youth Grp/Bible Stud; Cnslr Skys Limit Innr City Yth Camp; Dentistry/Psych.

BOYD, ANDREA I; Mustang HS; Yukon, OK; (3); Church Yth Grp; Band; Chorus; Church Choir; Color Guard; Drm Mjr(t); Mrchg Band; Var Socr; Var Trk; Hon Roll; Drum Mjr 96-; Var Band/Choir; Wntrgrd; Music.

BOYD, BARRY B; Midwest City HS; Oklahoma City, OK; (2); 130/473; DECA; Library Aide; Quiz Bowl; Scholastic Bowl; Spanish Clb; Stage Crew; Ftbl; Mgr(s); Cit Awd; High Hon Roll; Ftbl Equip Mgr 10th Grd; Comp Cert Occup Slsprsn; Moorehouse; Dctr/Lwyr/Frnsc Spe.

BOYD, CARRIE; Mannford HS; Sand Springs, OK; (2); Church Yth Grp; Phtgrphy.

BOYD, EBONY C; Northwest Classen HS; Oklahoma City, OK; (3); Sec German Clb; Office Aide; ROTC; Chorus; Hon Roll; Data Entry Speclst.

BOYD, JEREMY D; Central Schl; Sallisaw, OK; (3); Cmnty Wkr; Ftbl; Wt Lftg; Hon Roll; Hnrs Govt; Spec Olympcs Vol; EMT.

BOYD, KATIE; Okemah HS; Okemah, OK; (2); 12/70; VP FHA; Natl Beta Clb; Scholastic Bowl; Thesps; Sec Band; School Play; Hon Roll; Church Yth Grp; 4-H; Key Clb; GATE Pgm; Model Congress; Chrch Pianist; Law.

BOYD, KIMBERLY D; Fairland Jr Sr HS; Miami, OK; (1); Church Yth Grp; Pep Clb; Chorus; Church Choir; Ofcr Frsh Cls; Bsktbl; Sftbl; Trk; Pres Acad Fit Awd; Sftbl Hnrbl Mntn; NEO; Coach; Cosmetologist.

BOYD, MICHAEL T; South Intermediate HS; Broken Arrow, OK; (1); Quiz Bowl; Band; Mrchg Band; Pep Band; Rep Stu Cncl; Hon Roll; St Schlr; Chrstn Stu U; USAF Acad; Cmmrcl Airln Pilot.

BOYD, SHEILA; Tipton Jr Sr HS; Tipton, OK; (4); 4/17; Pres VP FHA; HOBY; Rptr Sec Natl FFA Org; Sec Frsh Cls; Sec Soph Cls; Sec Jr Cls; Sec Sr Cls; VP Stu Cncl; Capt Bsktbl; Chrldng; 1st Pl Voice Of Dmcrcy Essay; Gld Mdl FHA Star Evnts; Ms Tipton Amb; Wstrn OK ST Coll; Elem Ed.

BOYD, TOLIN BEX; Blackwell HS; Blackwell, OK; (2); 1/126; Church Yth Grp; FCA; Letterman Clb; VP Frsh Cls; Pres Soph Cls; Ofcr Stu Cncl; Var L Bsktbl; Var L Tennis; High Hon Roll; ST Hnr Scty.

BOYDSTON, LAURA M; El Reno Sr HS; El Reno, OK; (4); Church Yth Grp; Debate Tm; Band; Chorus; Church Choir; Ed Yrbk; Cit Awd; High Hon Roll; Pres Acad Fit Awd; Stu Choir Dir; Redland JC; Elem Ed.

BOYER, AMY N; Westmoore HS; Oklahoma City, OK; (2); Church Yth Grp; Spanish Clb; Chrldng; Trk; NHS.

BOYER, FRANKLIN; Senior HS; Mcalester, OK; (4); Am Leg Boys St; Computer Clb; Debate Tm; Hosp Aide; ROTC; Speech Tm; Thesps; Band; Phtg Yrbk; Rep Jr Cls; Pedtrcn.

BOYER, JACOB; Keyes HS; Keyes, OK; (3); HOBY; Quiz Bowl; Pres Frsh Cls; Sec Soph Cls; VP Jr Cls; Ofcr Bsbl; High Hon Roll; NHS; Comp Prgmng.

BOYER, JEFF T; Durant HS; Durant, OK; (3); DECA; FCA; Letterman Clb; Varsity Clb; Wrstlng; Hon Roll; DECA Clb Ofcr; OK ST Univ Stilwater; Mrktg.

BOYER, SARAH; Stillwater Sr HS; Stillwater, OK; (4); 77/344; Debate Tm; FBLA; FHA; Latin Clb; Natl Beta Clb; Natl FFA Org; NFL; Speech Tm; Teachers Aide; Rep Yrbk; FFA Greenhand Awd; OK ST U; Agrcltrl Commnctn.

BOYER, STEPHANIE B; Norman Sr HS; Norman, OK; (3); 1/799; Pres Girl Scts; Latin Clb; Treas Mu Alpha Theta; Spanish Clb; High Hon Roll; NHS; Ntl Merit Ltr; Ballt & Modrn Danc; Atten OK Summr Arts Inst For Modrn Danc & OU Summr Acad For Hlth Sci Careers.

BOYER, TAWNYA M; Putnam City HS; Oklahoma City, OK; (2); Church Yth Grp; FCA; FBLA; Letterman Clb; Math Tm; Spanish Clb; Vllybl; Cit Awd; High Hon Roll; NHS; Outdoors; Reading; Music; PT.

BOYETTE, SUSAN M; Arkoma Jr Sr HS; Spiro, OK; (2); FCA; FHA; Office Aide; Chorus; NHS.

BOYLAN, RAMAR; Deer Creek HS; Oklahoma City, OK; (4); 7/66; Science Clb; Band; Var Bsktbl; Hon Roll; NHS; Pres Acad Fit Awd; Bsktbl Tournament MVP 96; Little All City Offnsv Bsktbl Plyr Of Game 96; Coca-Cola Acad Schlrsp Wnnr; OK City Univ; Cmptr Techlgy.

BOYLES, BRANDON M; Ripley HS; Ripley, OK; (1); 2/53; Math Clb; Natl FFA Org; Quiz Bowl; Science Clb; Ofcr Bsbl; High Hon Roll; NHS; OK ST Univ.

BOZARTH, CHRIS; Welch Jr Sr HS; Welch, OK; (2); 1/23; Church Yth Grp; FCA; HOBY; Quiz Bowl; Rep Frsh Cls; Ftbl; Cit Awd; Hon Roll; NHS; Pres Soph Cls; Page OK St Senate; Brown Belt Karate; Northeastern ST U; Elem Educ.

BOZARTH, JOSHUA; Seiling Schl; Seiling, OK; (3); 1/37; FCA; VP FBLA; Letterman Clb; Natl Beta Clb; Scholastic Bowl; School Musical; Ed Yrbk; Var Bsktbl; Var Ftbl; NHS; OSU; Comp Sci.

BOZARTH, TIFFANY M; Yukon Middle HS; Yukon, OK; (2); French Clb; FHA; Phtg Nwsp; Phtg Yrbk; Sftbl; Wrstlng; High Hon Roll; NHS; 3d Dont Do Drugs; Phys Thrpy.

BOZONE, SHERI J; Webster HS; Tulsa, OK; (1); Drama Clb; Hosp Aide; Ofcr Soph Cls; High Hon Roll; Teen Miss Dnce OK; Dncr.

BRACK, CHAD; Comanche HS; Duncan, OK; (4); 1/61; German Clb; Natl FFA Org; VP Soph Cls; Sec Jr Cls; Sec Sr Cls; Wrstlng; NHS; Pres Acad Fit Awd; Val; Natl Engl Merit Awd; All-Amer Schlr; Natl Ldrshp/Svc Awd; OK ST U; Chem Engrng.

BRACK, JOSH; Hinton HS; Hinton, OK; (4); 2/29; Am Leg Boys St; Church Yth Grp; FCA; Var L Wrstlng; Sal; Wrstlng St Qlfr & 3rd Pl St; Athl Of Week Prep; SW OK ST U; Phrmcy.

BRACKETT, BRANDI; Collinsville HS; Collinsville, OK; (3); Church Yth Grp; FCA; FHA; Spanish Clb; Chorus; Stage Crew; High Hon Roll; Hon Roll; Ntl Merit Ltr; OSU; Acctng.

BRADDOCK, KEVIN; Ada HS; Ada, OK; (3); Church Yth Grp; FCA; French Clb; Math Clb; Mu Alpha Theta; Chorus; Church Choir; Pres Frsh Cls; Ofcr Stu Cncl; Var Bsktbl; Interschltc Meets; OK U; Engrng.

BRADEN, APRIL; Afton HS; Afton, OK; (2); 2/38; Church Yth Grp; Hist FHA; Ofcr Soph Cls; Trk; High Hon Roll; Hon Roll; NHS; Pres Acad Fit Awd; Val; OCCP; U OK; Law.

BRADEN, CHRIS D; El Reno Sr HS; El Reno, OK; (3); Boy Scts; FCA; FHA; JV Ftbl; Var Trk; JV Wrstlng; Hon Roll.

BRADFORD, JANTZ; Hollis Jr Sr HS; Hollis, OK; (4); 17/58; Am Leg Boys St; Church Yth Grp; Letterman Clb; Office Aide; Teachers Aide; School Play; Var Capt Ftbl; Wt Lftg; Hon Roll; All-St Ftbl 95.

BRADFORD, JOSEPH I; Waynoka HS; Waynoka, OK; (2); Church Yth Grp; Cmnty Wkr; FCA; FHA; Letterman Clb; Pep Clb; Church Choir; L Bsbl; JV L Bsktbl; Stat Ftbl; Bsbl Best Glove 95; Bsktbl Mst Imprvd 95; Northwestern ST Univ; Tchr.

BRADFORD, KATY; Edmond Memorial HS; Edmond, OK; (2); 1/449; Church Yth Grp; Key Clb; Spanish Clb; JV Chrldng; Hon Roll; NHS; Chrldng Capt.

BRADFORD, KERI; Sperry Sr HS; Sperry, OK; (3); 6/76; FCA; HOBY; Var Chrldng; Tennis; Pres NHS; Ntl Merit Ltr; Church Yth Grp; Cmnty Wkr; Dance Clb; GATE Hnr Course; United Ways Outfront Ldrshp Pgm Alumni; Natl Ldrshp & Svc Awds; U Tulsa; Psych.

BRADFORD, MATTHEW D; Waynoka HS; Waynoka, OK; (1); FCA; FHA; Pep Clb; Pres Frsh Cls; L Bsktbl; Cit Awd; Hon Roll; Art Stu Spclzng Fantasy Art; Msnc Lodge Stu Today Awd; OK ST Univ; Art Spcl Efcts.

BRADFORD, MELISSA R; Alva HS; Alva, OK; (1); Church Yth Grp; FHA; Band; Mrchg Band; Pep Band; Nwsp; Socr; Pedtrc Nrs.

BRADLEY, AMANDA M; Latta Sr HS; Ada, OK; (3); Church Yth Grp; Pres Drama Clb; FHA; Girl Scts; Hosp Aide; Pep Clb; Speech Tm; Acpl Chr; School Play; Sftbl; Rotary Ldrshp Awrd; East Central Univ.

BRADLEY, GWENDOLYN D; Dickson HS; Ardmore, OK; (3); 24/76; Key Clb; Band; Mrchg Band; Nrsg Cmp Rockhurst Coll Kansas City MO; Tishomingo Assmbly Gd Yth Grp Frstrtrs; East Cntrl Univ; Nrsg.

BRADLEY, JORDAN R; Muskogee HS; Muskogee, OK; (3); Cmnty Wkr; Hosp Aide; JCL; Key Clb; Latin Clb; Service Clb; Var Tennis; Hon Roll; Jr NHS; NHS; Law.

BRADLEY, LEIGH; Edmond North HS; Edmond, OK; (3); FCA; SADD; Rep Stu Cncl; Chrldng; Pom Pon; Hon Roll; NHS.

BRADLEY, SARAH; Watts HS; Watts, OK; (1); Hon Roll.

BRADSHAW, KELLY; Madill HS; Madill, OK; (2); FCA; 4-H; FBLA; Natl FFA Org; Treas Frsh Cls; Treas Soph Cls; Ofcr Stu Cncl; Stat Bsktbl; Var Sftbl; Hon Roll; OSU; Vet.

BRADSHAW, MONICA K; Westmoore HS; Oklahoma City, OK; (3); GAA; Varsity Clb; Sftbl; Hon Roll; Zoolgy Acad Excl Awd 96; Multi Yr Listee; Vet Med/Elem Ed.

BRADT, STACY R; Buffalo Jr Sr HS; Buffalo, OK; (3); Letterman Clb; Pep Clb; Band; Jazz Band; Mrchg Band; Pep Band; Chrldng; Sftbl; Hon Roll; Phy Thrpst.

BRADY, JENNIFER B; Stonewall Jr-Sr HS; Stonewall, OK; (4); 6/23; Am Leg Aux Girls St; GAA; Natl FFA Org; Ofcr Jr Cls; Ofcr Sr Cls; Bsktbl; Cit Awd; Hon Roll; NHS; Prfct Atten Awd; Murray ST; Nrsng.

BRADY, JENNIFER L; Durant HS; Durant, OK; (2); DECA; Spanish Clb; Chorus; Ed Yrbk; Rep Frsh Cls; Rep Soph Cls; Sec Jr Cls; Ofcr Stu Cncl; Var Chrldng; High Hon Roll; Drug Free Yth; Annual Queen; Sthestrn OK ST Univ; Per Med.

BRADY, MICHAEL; Midwest City HS; Midwest City, OK; (4); 15/390; Church Choir; Var Bsktbl; Var Wt Lftg; Cit Awd; 4-H Awd; Hon Roll; NHS; Prfct Atten Awd.

BRADY, ROSEMARIE; Douglass HS; Oklahoma City, OK; (2); Art Clb; Spanish Clb; Hon Roll.

BRADY, SHANNON; Comanche HS; Comanche, OK; (3); Art Clb; FHA; Hosp Aide; Science Clb; SADD; Nwsp; Yrbk; Hon Roll; NHS; OK Hnr Soc; All Amer Schlr; USBEA.

BRAGG, JONATHAN P; Deer Creek HS; Edmond, OK; (2); Church Yth Grp; Cmnty Wkr; Debate Tm; FBLA; Science Clb; Band; Mrchg Band; Sec Soph Cls; JV Bsbl; Var Crs Cntry; Guitgarist Chrch Yth Bnd; 2 Mission Trips Honduras; 6th Pl ST Intrdctn Bus Cmptn; Mock Trial Team; Pepperdine; Pre Law.

BRAGGS, CHRIS J; John Marshall HS; Oklahoma City, OK; (3); ROTC; Stage Crew; Var Bsbl; Var Ftbl; OK Univ; Prof Bsbl; Lawyer.

BRAKEFIELD, VANCE; Chelsea HS; Chelsea, OK; (3); 11/68; Church Yth Grp; FCA; Band; Chorus; Jazz Band; Mrchg Band; Pep Band; Bsktbl; Hon Roll; NHS; U Of Tulsa; Accntng.

BRAKEY, JULIE A; Union Intermediate HS; Tulsa, OK; (1); Church Yth Grp; Dance Clb; FCA; Chorus; Drill Tm; Pom Pon; Hon Roll; Jr NHS; NHS.

BRAKHAGE, JASON G; Edmond Santa Fe HS; Edmond, OK; (3); Church Yth Grp; Cmnty Wkr; Church Choir; Var L Ftbl; Var L Trk; NHS; Acad Ltr; OK ST Univ; Med/Neurosurgeon.

BRALEY, ABIGAIL R; Del City HS; Del City, OK; (3); 14/437; Church Yth Grp; Band; Chorus; Church Choir; Pep Band; Hon Roll; NHS; Prfct Atten Awd; U Of Central OK; Accnt/Bus Ed.

BRAME, LORI A; Christian Heritage Acad; Del City, OK; (2); Church Yth Grp; FCA; Teachers Aide; Acpl Chr; Chorus; Church Choir; Var L Bsktbl; Var L Vllybl; Hon Roll; AAU Bsktbl; Tchng; Phy Thrpst.

BRAMLETT, ERIC; Jenks HS; Jenks, OK; (3); Church Yth Grp; Mu Alpha Theta; Ofcr Stu Cncl; Wt Lftg; Hon Roll; Asian Amer Soc; Mock Trial Comp Best Trial Atty 96.

BRAMLETT, RAVEN; El Reno Sr HS; El Reno, OK; (3); Church Yth Grp; FHA; Math Clb; Office Aide; Science Clb; Hon Roll; NHS; Redlands CC; Bus.

BRAMMER, ALEXANDER L; Southeast HS; Oklahoma City, OK; (1); Chess Clb; Church Yth Grp; Computer Clb; Scholastic Bowl; Teachers Aide; Band; Stage Crew; Gov Hon Prg Awd; High Hon Roll; Jr NHS; Page For St Rep Cert; 1st Pl Essay Cont Rep Womens Assn; Comp Pgmng.

BRAMMER, DAVID A; Macarthur Sr HS; Lawton, OK; (3); HOBY; Yrbk; Var Bsbl; Hon Roll; Prfct Atten Awd; YABA Bowling.

BRANAM, CHRISTIE; Mc Alester HS; Mcalester, OK; (4); 10/217; Am Leg Aux Girls St; Science Clb; Spanish Clb; Pres Stu Cncl; Chrldng; Cit Awd; High Hon Roll; NHS; Office Aide; Pep Clb; Hosp Explrs Pres; OK Hnr Soc; Ntl Sci Olympd; OK ST U; Med.

BRANCH, AMANDA; Pawhuska HS; Barnsdall, OK; (2); 1/90; Church Yth Grp; Debate Tm; Key Clb; NFL; Speech Tm; High Hon Roll; Kiwanis Awd; NHS; Spch Thrpy/Rel Ed.

BRANCH, DEANNE; Mustang HS; Mustang, OK; (2); 46/403; Church Yth Grp; Quiz Bowl; Scholastic Bowl; Church Choir; Hon Roll; NHS; Sunday Schl Tchr; Tchr.

BRANCH, JULIE Y; Will Rogers HS; Tulsa, OK; (3); 4/250; Church Yth Grp; Pres French Clb; Hosp Aide; Key Clb; Scholastic Bowl; Pres Sec Stu Cncl; NHS; Cmnty Wkr; Church Choir; High Hon Roll; Cir Frnds Grp Of Stdnts Interacting With Handicapped Stdnts; Rodeo Clb Sec; CODE Clss Pres; U Of Tulsa; Pre-Med/Pediatrcn.

BRANCH, MISTY M; Healdton HS; Ringling, OK; (2); Church Yth Grp; Chorus; Ofcr Frsh Cls; Ofcr Soph Cls; Ofcr Jr Cls; Chrldng; Sftbl; Hon Roll; NHS; Pres Acad Fit Awd; Hmcmng Ct; SW; Med.

BRANCH IV, TOMMY P; Nathan Hale HS; Tulsa, OK; (3); Boy Scts; Church Yth Grp; Drama Clb; Jazz Band; School Play; Stage Crew; Rptr Nwsp; JV Bsktbl; Musician.

BRANDENBERGER, JACKSON B; Deer Creek HS; Edmond, OK; (2); Cmnty Wkr; Science Clb; SADD; Stage Crew; Var L Bsbl; Var L Bsktbl; Hon Roll; Pres Acad Fit Awd.

BRANDENBERGER, ROSANNA; Deer Creek HS; Edmond, OK; (4); 1/66; Art Clb; VP French Clb; FBLA; Science Clb; SADD; Rep Jr Cls; Treas Sr Cls; High Hon Roll; Sec NHS; Val; Stage Prod; U Of Denver; Librl Arts.

BRANDENBURG, TIFFANY M; Tomlinson Jr HS; Lawton, OK; (1); 4-H; FHA; Office Aide; Spanish Clb; Teachers Aide; Band; Chorus; School Play; Cit Awd; 4-H Awd; Zoology.

BRANDES, JOHN; Norman Sr HS; Norman, OK; (2); Church Yth Grp; FCA; Mu Alpha Theta; Spanish Clb; Rep Stu Cncl; JV Bsktbl; High Hon Roll; NHS; Pres Acad Fit Awd; St Schlr; HS Heroes.

BRANDON, MIRANDA C; Shawnee Sr HS; Shawnee, OK; (1); Phtg Yrbk; MA Coll Of Art; Photo; Artist.

BRANDT, JAMES; Okemah HS; Okemah, OK; (2); 1/75; 4-H; Quiz Bowl; Science Clb; Band; Jazz Band; Mrchg Band; Pep Band; School Play; 4-H Awd; High Hon Roll; OSU Okmulgee; Advrtsng.

BRANECKY, SARAH; Moore HS; Newalla, OK; (4); 36/537; Church Yth Grp; Yrbk; Jr NHS; NHS; Val; U Of Cntrl OK; Elem Ed.

BRANHAM, ANGELA; Carnegie HS; Carnegie, OK; (3); Church Yth Grp; FHA; Chorus; Swing Chorus; Yrbk; Chrldng; Sftbl; Cit Awd; Hon Roll; Prfct Atten Awd; Multi Yr Listee; Southwestern OK ST U; PT.

BRANHAM, JOY C; Muskogee HS; Muskogee, OK; (1); Hon Roll; NHS; Art; Supt Christmas Card Design Contst; Art Schl; Art.

BRANKEL, LESLIE; Claremore Sr HS; Claremore, OK; (3); Church Yth Grp; FCA; Red Cross Aide; SADD; Band; Church Choir; Jazz Band; Mrchg Band; School Musical; Golf; Elks Awd.

BRANNAN, JAMIE; Big Pasture HS; Randlett, OK; (3); Church Yth Grp; 4-H; Key Clb; Chorus; School Musical; Rptr Nwsp; Yrbk; Var Bsktbl; Var Chrldng; Var Crs Cntry; I Dare You Awd; 4-H St Proj Schlrshp; OK St U Anml Sci Brtchr Mem Achvt Awd; OK ST U.

BRANNON, ASHLEY; Ft Gibson HS; Fort Gibson, OK; (1); Church Yth Grp; FCA; SADD; Band; Chorus; Mrchg Band; Chrldng; Hon Roll; Pres Schlr; Cckls Dnc Acad; Photo.

BRANNON, ROYAL S; Oklahoma Christian Acad; Forest Park, OK; (2); Church Yth Grp; Church Choir; Drill Tm; Bsktbl.

BRANSCUM, LARRA; Seminole Jr Sr HS; Seminole, OK; (3); Church Yth Grp; FHA; GAA; Math Clb; Spanish Clb; Bsktbl; Trk; High Hon Roll; Gifted & Talented Pgm; U Of OK; Med.

BRANSCUM, MARSHALL; Seminole Jr Sr HS; Seminole, OK; (3); Church Yth Grp; Math Clb; Quiz Bowl; Spanish Clb; Chorus; Rep Stu Cncl; Bsktbl; Tennis; High Hon Roll; NHS; Gifted & Talented Pgm; Med.

BRANSCUM MUNCY, ROBIN; Red Oak Schl; Wister, OK; (3); FHA; GAA; Spanish Clb; Var Bsktbl; Var Sftbl; High Hon Roll; Hon Roll; NHS; Elem Tchr.

BRANTLEY, STEVEN; Del City HS; Del City, OK; (3); 1/490; Debate Tm; Ofcr Bsbl; Hon Roll; NHS.

BRANTLEY, THOMAS; Milburn Schl; Milburn, OK; (3); Debate Tm; FBLA; HOBY; Quiz Bowl; Scholastic Bowl; Teachers Aide; Rep Stu Cncl; Var Bsbl; High Hon Roll; NHS; Med.

BRASEL, MATTHEU; Collinsville HS; Collinsville, OK; (3); Church Yth Grp; FCA; Var Bsbl; Var Ftbl; L Wt Lftg; Hon Roll; OU; Acctng.

BRASHEAR, CARL W; Stilwell HS; Stilwell, OK; (2); Church Yth Grp; Key Clb; Math Clb; Natl Beta Clb; Scholastic Bowl; Science Clb; Spanish Clb; Band; Jazz Band; Pep Band; OK Univ.

BRASHEARS, ANGELA; Weatherford HS; Weatherford, OK; (3); Church Yth Grp; Pres 4-H; Spanish Clb; Band; Color Guard; JV Var Socr; Cit Awd; 4-H Awd; Kiwanis Awd; FCA; OK ST Univ; Bus Mgmt.

BRASHER, STACY; Edmond North HS; Edmond, OK; (2); 1/490; Church Yth Grp; Cmnty Wkr; Dance Clb; HOBY; Letterman Clb; Varsity Clb; Ed Nwsp; Ofcr Frsh Cls; Ofcr Soph Cls; Var L Sftbl; Amer Legion Aux Mem & Schl Mascot; TEENLINE Vol; Nom Frosh Stu Of Yr; Stu Of Month 94-96.

BRASHERS, CHRIS; Chelsea HS; Chelsea, OK; (3); 16/65; Church Yth Grp; Spanish Clb; Band; Jazz Band; Mrchg Band; JV Var Bsktbl; JV Ftbl; Hon Roll; Pres Acad Fit Awd.

BRASHERS, KEVIN; Wyandotte Jr Sr HS; Miami, OK; (4); 1/36; Church Yth Grp; FCA; FHA; Letterman Clb; Math Tm; Quiz Bowl; Red Cross Aide; Teachers Aide; Varsity Clb; Yrbk; Tech Stdnts Assn; Chldrn Amer Rvltn; NEO A&M; PT.

BRASHIER, AMANDA; Porum HS; Porum, OK; (1); FHA; Rptr Nwsp; Rptr Stu Cncl; Horse Back Riding; Swim; Roller Skate; Comp.

BRASSFIELD, REBECCA E; Davis HS; Davis, OK; (1); Art Clb; Church Yth Grp; 4-H; French Clb; Cit Awd; Hon Roll; OK St Univ; Vet.

BRASSFIELD, TIFFANY; Mc Loud HS; Newalla, OK; (3); Church Yth Grp; FBLA; FHA; Band; Color Guard; Mrchg Band; Orch; Pep Band; Hon Roll; NHS; OK Hnr Soc; OK Chrstn U.

BRASUELL, SHANNON L; Oklahoma Sch Of Science & Math; Shawnee, OK; (3); Cmnty Wkr; Drama Clb; Science Clb; Pres Band; Jazz Band; JETS Awd; NHS; Ntl Merit SF; OBU Hnr Bd; East Cntrl All Dist Hnr Band; Engr Team; Dartmouth Coll; Chem.

BRATCHER, JAMES; Thackerville HS; Thackerville, OK; (3); Am Leg Boys St; FHA; Natl FFA Org; Quiz Bowl; VICA; Sec Soph Cls; Sec Jr Cls; Hon Roll; FFA Pres 95-96, Sec 94-95, Star Chptr Farmr 94-95.

BRATCHER, MICHAEL; Thackerville HS; Thackerville, OK; (2); 1/25; Church Yth Grp; Quiz Bowl; Scholastic Bowl; Ed Nwsp; Phtg Yrbk; Rep Stu Cncl; Mgr(s); High Hon Roll; Chrch Rprtr & Librn; OK Hnr Soc; Away Bsktbl Games Bkkpr; Jrnlsm.

BRAUCHI, KATHY J; Sayre HS; Sayre, OK; (3); 18/50; Church Yth Grp; GAA; Pep Clb; Band; Chorus; Mrchg Band; Pep Band; Var Bsktbl; Var Sftbl; Cit Awd; Stu Of Today/Schlstc Achv; Southwestern OK ST Univ; Med.

BRAUN, JUSTIN; Mt St Marys HS; Oklahoma City, OK; (2); FCA; Key Clb; Varsity Clb; Var Bsbl; Var Capt Bsktbl; High Hon Roll; NHS.

BRAWLEY, SHAWN L; Lone Grove HS; Ardmore, OK; (2); Church Yth Grp; Spanish Clb; Bsktbl; Var Trk; Cit Awd; Hon Roll; OK U.

BRAWNER, PATRICK W; Dover Schl; Dover, OK; (3); Church Yth Grp; FCA; Letterman Clb; Var JV Ftbl; Hon Roll; NHS; Ntl Merit Ltr; OK ST U; Engrng.

BRAY, ALLISON C; Edmond North HS; Edmond, OK; (1); 211/456; Church Yth Grp; Cmnty Wkr; Spanish Clb; JV Bsktbl; Var Sftbl; Var Trk; Cit Awd; Prfct Atten Awd; Coffee Crk Rdng Ctr Handcpd Vol; PT.

BRAY, AMBER; Washington HS; Purcell, OK; (3); Church Yth Grp; FCA; FHA; GAA; Girl Scts; Pep Clb; Band; Pep Band; Chrldng; Powder Puff Ftbl; OK U; Eng Lit.

BRAY, ANGELIA L; Wilson HS; Wilson, OK; (2); 13/50; FCA; Natl Beta Clb; Var Bsktbl; Var Sftbl; Hon Roll; OU; Phy Therapy.

BRAY, JASON; Cashion HS; Cashion, OK; (4); Church Yth Grp; Cmnty Wkr; Letterman Clb; SADD; Varsity Clb; VP Frsh Cls; Ofcr Bsbl; Bsktbl; Cit Awd; DAR Awd; Masonic Awd.

BRAY, JENNIFER M; Midwest City HS; Midwest City, OK; (2); FHA; Hosp Aide; Key Clb; Ofcr Soph Cls; Var Vllybl; RN/PDTRCN.

BRAY, JOELEEN; Bixby Sr HS; Broken Arrow, OK; (1); Art Clb; Church Yth Grp; FCA; GAA; SADD; Rep Frsh Cls; Bsktbl; Score Keeper; Trk; Wt Lftg; Hnrb Mntn Essay Awd; 16 Trk Medals; Hnrb Mntns In Drawings & Oil Pastels; UCLA; Marine Bio.

BRAZIL, MARY E; Cashion HS; Cashion, OK; (3); Church Yth Grp; FCA; FHA; Girl Scts; Spanish Clb; Band; Chorus; Church Choir; Tennis; Chrch Drama Grp; U Of OK.

BRAZIL, RODNEY; Hobart HS; Hobart, OK; (2); 6/80; Church Yth Grp; Rptr 4-H; Natl FFA Org; Jazz Band; Mrchg Band; School Play; Rptr Nwsp; Rptr Soph Cls; Ofcr Stu Cncl; High Hon Roll.

BREDING, NICHOLE KATHERINE; Westmoore HS; Oklahoma City, OK; (4); 52/610; Church Yth Grp; FCA; FHA; Spanish Clb; Phtg Yrbk; Rep Stu Cncl; Var Bsktbl; Capt Tennis; NHS; Val; All St Tnns Team; Southern Nazarene Univ; Elem Ed.

BREEDLOVE, NICOLE; Roland Sr HS; Roland, OK; (1); Church Yth Grp; FHA; Speech Tm; Band; Mrchg Band; Pep Band; Nwsp; Rep Frsh Cls; Chrldng; Sftbl.

BREEZE, E CAROL; Ryan Schl; Ryan, OK; (4); 2/25; VP FHA; Natl Beta Clb; Rptr Nwsp; Pres Jr Cls; Capt Bsktbl; Chrldng; High Hon Roll; Hon Roll; NHS; Sal; Served As A Page At The OK House Of Rep; The Masonic Lodge Awd; Southwestern OK ST; Soc Work.

BREEZE, ELIZABETH CAROL; Ryan Schl; Ryan, OK; (4); 2/25; Church Yth Grp; VP FHA; Scholastic Bowl; Rptr Nwsp; Pres Jr Cls; Capt Bsktbl; Cit Awd; High Hon Roll; NHS; Sal; House Of Reps Page; Southwestern OK ST U; Soc Wrk.

BREHM, JASON; Clinton HS; Clinton, OK; (4); Drama Clb; FHA; Key Clb; Library Aide; Science Clb; Spanish Clb; Hon Roll; Key Clb Pres; SWOSU; Phrmcy.

BRENDLE, ALICE A; Mangum Sr HS; Mangum, OK; (2); HOBY; Variety Show; Rep Frsh Cls; Var Bsktbl; Var Chrldng; Var Sftbl; High Hon Roll; NHS.

BRENNAN, GINGER A; Quinton Jr Sr HS; Quinton, OK; (3); Church Yth Grp; 4-H; Natl FFA Org; Band; Church Choir; Color Guard; Drill Tm; Mrchg Band; Var Bsktbl; Var Chrldng; Bio I Awd; Home Ec I Awd; Prin Hnr Rl; Super Hnr Rl; Eastern Coll; RN.

BRENNAN, JOSEPH B; Elgin HS; Elgin, OK; (4); 16/74; Band; Pep Band; School Musical; Cameron Univ; Comp Sci.

BRENNAN, NADIA; Maud HS; Maud, OK; (4); FHA; Pep Clb; Band; Flag Corp; Sec Soph Cls; Sec Jr Cls; Bsktbl; Chrldng; Sftbl; Trk; Jr Miss Seminole Nation OK, Miss Seminole Nation OK; Comp Sci.

BRENNAN, TARAH L; Union Sr HS; Broken Arrow, OK; (3); 121/800; Church Yth Grp; Cmnty Wkr; Drama Clb; Key Clb; Mu Alpha Theta; NFL; Office Aide; Speech Tm; Teachers Aide; Thesps; Renssnce Clb; Nrsng Hm Aide; Oral Roberts U; Ed.

BRENNER, RACHEL M; Midwest City HS; Midwest City, OK; (2); 112/441; FHA; German Clb; Chorus; L Mgr(s); Score Keeper; Socr; Hon Roll; U Of Cntrl OK; Sports Mdcn.

BRESHEARS, JODI; Union City Schl; Mustang, OK; (1); 1/47; FHA; Bsktbl; High Hon Roll; Treas Frsh Cls.

BRESHEARS, MICHELLE; Woodward HS; Woodward, OK; (1); German Clb; Hosp Aide; Quiz Bowl; Scholastic Bowl; High Hon Roll; NHS.

BRESHEARS, WENDY; Union City Schl; Mustang, OK; (4); 1/24; VP FHA; Math Clb; Office Aide; Scholastic Bowl; Science Clb; Yrbk; Rep Jr Cls; VP Sr Cls; Sec Stu Cncl; Val; OSU; Interior Dsgn.

BRETT, LAURA K; B T Washington HS; Tulsa, OK; (3); Debate Tm; Letterman Clb; Spanish Clb; Speech Tm; Tennis; Hon Roll.

BREVETTI, MICHELLE C; Deer Creek HS; Edmond, OK; (2); Church Yth Grp; Science Clb; JV Bsktbl; Chrldng; Crs Cntry; Socr; Sftbl; Hon Roll; NHS; School Play; Hnrbl Mntn All Amnd Scr Tm 95-96; Scr All Trnmnt & Ofnsv Plyr; Hnrbl Mntn OK 95-96 Scr Tm.

BREVILLE, HOPE L; Kellyville Sr HS; Kellyville, OK; (2); ROTC; Band; Color Guard; Drill Tm; Mrchg Band; Pep Band; High Hon Roll; Hon Roll; Raider Pltn; Rifle Team; Marine Bio.

BREWER, ANGELA R; Pauls Valley HS; Pauls Valley, OK; (2); French Clb; Key Clb; Tennis; High Hon Roll; NHS; Mck Trial Tm Timekpr.

BREWER, CARISSA D; Muldrow HS; Muldrow, OK; (1); Spanish Clb; Band; Jazz Band; Mrchg Band; FHA; Westark.

BREWER, DA COLE NICHELLE; Del City HS; Oklahoma City, OK; (2); Church Yth Grp; GAA; Office Aide; ROTC; Spanish Clb; Teachers Aide; Drill Tm; Ofcr Frsh Cls; Ofcr Soph Cls; Bsktbl; Mst Likely To Succeed Frosh; Frosh Bsktbl Qn; Span II Clb Pres; Wichita ST Univ; Law.

BREWER, DAVID; Mc Loud HS; Newalla, OK; (3); Church Yth Grp; Cmnty Wkr; FBLA; FTA; Scholastic Bowl; Science Clb; Spanish Clb; Band; Jazz Band; Mrchg Band; OK Christian; Law Enfrcmt.

BREWER, JENNIFER L; Bartlesville Sr HS; Bartlesville, OK; (1); Church Yth Grp; Band; Trk; Vllybl; High Hon Roll; Hon Roll.

BREWER, KERI; Woodward HS; Woodward, OK; (1); 40/180; Art Clb; Church Yth Grp; Cmnty Wkr; FCA; GAA; Pep Clb; JV Chrldng; JV Socr; JV Wt Lftg; Hon Roll; OSU; Med.

BREWER, LAURA K; Enid Sr HS; Enid, OK; (3); FHA; Orch; High Hon Roll; Hon Roll; Jr NHS; NHS; Enid Strolling Strings; U Of KY; Law.

BREWER, LINDSEY; Muskogee HS; Muskogee, OK; (3); 1/370; Pres Church Yth Grp; Cmnty Wkr; FCA; JCL; Latin Clb; School Musical; Sec Frsh Cls; Var L Chrldng; Socr; High Hon Roll; Ecology Clb Cnsrvtnst; Delphic Lit Soc; OK Hnr Soc; TX Tech; Jrnlsm.

BREWER, LUKE; Mc Loud HS; Choctaw, OK; (2); 7/155; Church Yth Grp; FBLA; Band; Mrchg Band; Pep Band; Socr; High Hon Roll; NHS; Rec Soccer 11 Yrs; Clssc Sccr 1 Yr; OK Chrstn Univ; Med.

BREWER, SARAH E; Oologah HS; Claremore, OK; (3); 19/107; Chorus; High Hon Roll; Hon Roll; Pub 3 Poems; Intnl Soc Of Poets Poets Of Yr Nom 96; Read; Wrte Shrt Stories/Poetry; Anthrplgy/Crtve Wrtng.

BREWER, STACEY L; Sayre HS; Sayre, OK; (2); FHA; Pep Clb; SADD; Key Clb; Jazz Band; Mrchg Band; Pep Band; Southwestern Jr Coll; Grdschl.

BREWER, STEFANIE; Washington HS; Washington, OK; (1); Church Yth Grp; Pep Clb; Chrldng; Prfct Atten Awd; OU; Phys Thrpy.

BREWER, STEVEN; Caney Valley HS; Ochelata, OK; (2); Church Yth Grp; Varsity Clb; Band; Church Choir; Jazz Band; Mrchg Band; Orch; Bsktbl; Ftbl; Golf; Tulsa Philhrmnc Yth Symph; MEOBDA Hnr Band/Jazz Band; NEOBDA Hnr Band 3 Yrs; Music.

BREWER, SUMMER D; Sapulpa Sr HS; Sapulpa, OK; (4); 60/273; Art Clb; Science Clb; SADD; Teachers Aide; Co-Ed Yrbk; Hon Roll; Pres Acad Fit Awd; Acad Lttr 95; Acad Bar 96; Awd Of Merit In Art 95; U Of Sci/Arts Of OK; Bus.

BREWER, ZACHARY W; Trinity Christian Schl; Tulsa, OK; (4); FCA; School Musical; School Play; Pres Soph Cls; Var Bsktbl; Var Socr; High Hon Roll; Prfct Atten Awd; Congressional Yth Ldrshp Cncl; OK ST; Bio.

BREWER-SMITHSON, JULIE A; Ponca City Sr HS; Edmond, OK; (3); 122/347; Church Yth Grp; Hon Roll.

BREWSTER, GEOFFREY S; Dale Sr HS; Shawnee, OK; (1); 1/43; Church Yth Grp; Quiz Bowl; SADD; Band; Drm Mjr(t); Jazz Band; Ofcr Stu Cncl; JV Bsktbl; Hon Roll; Jr NHS; Life Guides Peer Helper Orgn; U Of MI; Pre-Med.

BREWSTER, MELISSA; Wagoner Sr HS; Wagoner, OK; (4); 16/138; Am Leg Aux Girls St; Hist FCA; FBLA; Phtg Ed Yrbk; Hist Jr Cls; VP Sr Cls; Trk; NHS; Teachers Aide; Natl Engl Mrt Awd; Jr Attndt Ftbl Hmcmng; Sr Attndt Wrstlng Hmcmg; OK ST U; Mrktng.

BREZINA, CRISTY A; Enid Sr HS; Enid, OK; (2); 111/431; Library Aide; Hon Roll; Jr NHS; NHS; Nurs.

BRIANS, MILLAY C; Oklahoma Sch Of Science & Math; Norman, OK; (3); Cmnty Wkr; FCA; JA; Red Cross Aide; Varsity Clb; Band; Chorus; Drm Mjr(t); Mrchg Band; Orch; Engrng.

BRIANS, MONICA; Will Rogers HS; Tulsa, OK; (1); Debate Tm; Spanish Clb; Hon Roll; TJC; Bus/Mngmt.

BRIANT, CRYSTAL L; Cresent Acad; Edmond, OK; (2); Church Yth Grp; Drama Clb; English Clb; Science Clb; Co-Ed Nwsp; Co-Ed Yrbk; High Hon Roll; Drama/Sci/Speech/Jrnlsm/Wld His Awds; U Of Central OK; Eng/Wld His.

BRICE, SARAH; Little Axe Sr HS; Newalla, OK; (2); Church Yth Grp; Church Choir; Ed Yrbk; Var Crs Cntry; Var Trk; Hon Roll; Jr NHS; NHS; OU; Jrnlsm.

BRICKER, MELISSA A; Ponca City Sr HS; Ponca City, OK; (2); 4-H; Chorus; Ofcr Frsh Cls; Ofcr Soph Cls; Cit Awd; Pioneer Tech Ctr; Cmptrs.

BRIDEN, DAVID N; Southeast HS; Oklahoma City, OK; (1); Boy Scts; Chess Clb; Church Yth Grp; JA; ROTC; Ftbl; Wrstlng; High Hon Roll.

BRIDENSTINE, CHRIS A; Madill HS; Kingston, OK; (2); Cmnty Wkr; FCA; Var Ftbl; Var Golf; Var Wrstlng; Hon Roll; OK ST Univ; Vet Med.

BRIDGEMAN, JESSI; Madill HS; Lebanon, OK; (1); Church Yth Grp; Spanish Clb; Bsktbl; Sftbl; Trk; Hon Roll; Sci.

BRIDGES, BRAD; Shawnee Sr HS; Shawnee, OK; (2); JV Bsbl; Intrml Ftbl; High Hon Roll; Engrng.

BRIDGES, BRANDON K; Roland Sr HS; Roland, OK; (2); Church Yth Grp; 4-H; Sec Natl FFA Org; Teachers Aide; 4-H Awd; Hon Roll; Prfct Atten Awd.

BRIDGES, CAREY; Chandler HS; Chandler, OK; (3); 1/78; Church Yth Grp; FCA; FHA; Spanish Clb; Rptr Phtg Yrbk; Pres Frsh Cls; VP Jr Cls; Rep Stu Cncl; Capt Bsktbl; Var Trk; Outstndng Engl I & Bio I Stu 94; Outstndng Typing I & Wrld Hstry Stu 95; Bsktbl Offnsv Plyr Of Yr; OK ST U.

BRIDGES, CHRISTOPHER K; Chandler HS; Chandler, OK; (3); #17 in class; Am Leg Boys St; Art Clb; Church Yth Grp; FCA; Teachers Aide; Rep Soph Cls; Rep Jr Cls; Ofcr Stu Cncl; Bsktbl; Ftbl.

BRIDGEWATER, RACHEL E; Union Intermediate HS; Broken Arrow, OK; (2); Boy Scts; Church Yth Grp; Cmnty Wkr; Girl Scts; Spanish Clb; Band; Oral Roberts Univ; Nrs.

BRIDSONG, JEFFERY D; Union Sr HS; Tulsa, OK; (4); 49/632; FCA; Var Bsbl; High Hon Roll; NHS; Pres Acad Fit Awd; Lang Arts Awd; Renaissance; Comp Educ Awd; Acad Ltr Awds; Stu Of Month Awds; Math.

BRIGANCE, KIMBERLY M; Panola HS; Panola, OK; (3); 2/25; Natl FFA Org; School Musical; VP Frsh Cls; VP Soph Cls; Pres Jr Cls; Bsktbl; Sftbl; Hon Roll; Prfct Atten Awd; Page In Captl For St Rep; St Acad CHAMP Bsktbll Tm; EOSC.

BRIGGS, ANGELA M; Tecumseh HS; Tecumseh, OK; (3); Band; Chorus; Mrchg Band; Orch; Hon Roll; Band Medals.

BRIGGS, JOSETTE; Midwest City HS; Oklahoma City, OK; (3); 1/386; Sec Church Yth Grp; DECA; Spanish Clb; Mrchg Band; Pep Band; Ed Yrbk; Jr NHS; NHS; Pres Acad Fit Awd; Biomedcl Engrng.

BRIGGS, SARAH J; Noble HS; Lexington, OK; (2); 18/168; Church Yth Grp; Spanish Clb; School Play; Phtg Stage Crew; Sec Soph Cls; JV Var Chrldng; Hon Roll; NHS; Dance 10 Yrs; OU; Rsrch Scientist.

BRIGHT, DARRYL ROCKY; Booker T Washington Sr HS; Tulsa, OK; (3); Cmnty Wkr; Letterman Clb; Jazz Band; Yrbk; Bsktbl; Ftbl; Wt Lftg; Jr NHS; Pres Acad Fit Awd; Who's Who Amer Athls; Vol Salvation Army; Boys & Girls Clb; Chmpnshp Bsktbl Tm; Sprts Med.

BRIGHT, TAMMY L; Cushing HS; Cushing, OK; (4); 1/156; JA; Math Clb; Sec Science Clb; Spanish Clb; Speech Tm; School Musical; NHS; Val; OK HS Hnr Soc; Natl Yth Ldrshp Frm Med; OK ST U; Ophthlmlgy.

BRIIX, ANGELA M; Harrah HS; Harrah, OK; (2); 14/160; Church Yth Grp; Drama Clb; Sec FCA; GAA; Sec Treas SADD; Varsity Clb; JV Hosp Aide; Var Crs Cntry; Var Socr; Var Sftbl.

BRIJALBA, CATHY; Cache HS; Cache, OK; (3); 16/65; Church Yth Grp; FCA; FHA; Natl Beta Clb; Science Clb; Teachers Aide; VP Frsh Cls; VP Soph Cls; VP Jr Cls; Var Bsktbl; TX Tech; Medcl.

BRILLIANT, CAROLYN R; Coweta HS; Porter, OK; (3); FBLA; FHA; Nwsp; Treas Stu Cncl; Hon Roll; NHS; OSU; Pre-Med; Pediatrician.

BRIMER, AMY; Plainview HS; Ardmore, OK; (4); 2/80; FCA; Latin Clb; Natl Beta Clb; Quiz Bowl; SADD; Lit Mag; Trk; High Hon Roll; NHS; Pres Acad Fit Awd; OK ST U.

BRING, CELESTE M; Oaks Mission Jr Sr HS; Twin Oaks, OK; (3); Band; Hon Roll.

BRINKER, JAMES A; Union Intermediate HS; Tulsa, OK; (2); Church Yth Grp; FCA; JV Socr; Hon Roll; Jr NHS; Pres Acad Fit Awd; Honorary Eng Awd.

BRINKLEY, DONNA M; Elk City Jr HS; Elk City, OK; (1); High Hon Roll; Jr NHS; Pres Acad Fit Awd.

BRINKLEY, JOSEPH G; Haworth Sr HS; Haworth, OK; (3); Natl FFA Org; Office Aide; Quiz Bowl; Chorus; High Hon Roll; Hon Roll; Jr NHS; NHS; Prfct Atten Awd; Sal; Tm Roping/Pl Comp.

BRIONES, PATTY A; Altus Sr HS; Altus, OK; (3); Church Yth Grp; Spanish Clb; Band; Church Choir; Color Guard; Mrchg Band; Hon Roll; Cameron Univ; Psych.

BRISCH, MEGAN; Edmond North HS; Edmond, OK; (3); 1/350; Pres German Clb; JCL; Sec Latin Clb; Mu Alpha Theta; Church Choir; Orch; School Musical; NHS; Prfct Atten Awd; OK Hnr Soc; Chem.

BRISCOE, LEA A; Olive Jr Sr HS; Mannford, OK; (3); 5/35; 4-H; Natl FFA Org; Speech Tm; Teachers Aide; Sec Frsh Cls; Hon Roll; PT.

BRISSEY, RODNEY G; Union Intermediate HS; Tulsa, OK; (2); Band; Color Guard; Jazz Band; Mrchg Band; Pep Band; Hon Roll; NHS; OK U; Med.

BRISTLE, MELANIE L; Owasso Sr HS; Owasso, OK; (3); 51/432; Church Yth Grp; Dance Clb; FCA; Yrbk; High Hon Roll; NHS; OK ST Univ.

BRISTOL, SHAE; Grace Chrn Acad; Oklahoma City, OK; (3); 1/24; Church Yth Grp; Library Aide; VP Frsh Cls; Capt Chrldng; Powder Puff Ftbl; Cit Awd; High Hon Roll; Prfct Atten Awd; Pres Acad Fit Awd; Piano; Fac Awd Gen Excl.

BRISTOW, BRIAN; Holdenville HS; Wewoka, OK; (2); 10/80; Church Yth Grp; Chorus; Bsktbl; Wt Lftg; Hon Roll; Elec Engr.

BRITTON, ABBEY; Leedey Schl; Leedey, OK; (4); 1/20; Church Yth Grp; Pres FCA; FBLA; VP FHA; VP Spanish Clb; Mgr Yrbk; Treas Stu Cncl; Co-Capt Chrldng; NHS; Sal; Singing; Piano; Tae Kwon Do; Cntrl Bapt Coll; Music.

BRITTON, JARED G; Owasso Sr HS; Owasso, OK; (4); Church Yth Grp; Varsity Clb; Bsktbl; OSU; Business.

BRIXEY, AMY; Jay HS; Jay, OK; (2); Church Yth Grp; FCA; Pep Clb; Band; Chorus; Church Choir; Mrchg Band; Rptr Yrbk; Chrldng; Sftbl; Cmptr Bus Tech.

BRIXEY, CORI; Grove HS; Jay, OK; (1); Church Yth Grp; Band; Mrchg Band; Chrldng; Tennis; Ntl Merit Ltr; AR U; Accntng.

BRIXEY, MANDY H; Moore HS; Moore, OK; (4); 175/549; JA; Library Aide; Office Aide; Spanish Clb; Church Choir; Multicltrl Stdnt Assn 10/12; Rcvd Mdl Cncrt Choir 12; Rose ST; Dental Hygnst.

BROADBENT, KANDRA M; Hammon Schl; Hammon, OK; (3); Sec Treas FHA; SADD; Stage Crew; Sec Frsh Cls; Sec Soph Cls; Sec Jr Cls; Hon Roll; SNOWU; Pre-Med.

BROADFOOT, BECKY; Heritage Hall Schl; Oklahoma City, OK; (4); 1/48; Church Yth Grp; FCA; Letterman Clb; Mu Alpha Theta; Pep Clb; Spanish Clb; Chorus; Pres Stu Cncl; Fld Hcky; NHS; OK Yth Rep; Engrng.

BROCHU, MEGAN; Chisholm Sr HS; Enid, OK; (1); 10/91; Church Yth Grp; Band; Chorus; Color Guard; Ofcr Frsh Cls; Hon Roll; NHS; Day Care.

BROCK, CRYSTAL; Berryhill Jr HS; Tulsa, OK; (3); Church Yth Grp; Mu Alpha Theta; Office Aide; VICA; Band; Mrchg Band; Pom Pon; NHS; Pres Acad Fit Awd; Val; OK Hnr Soc; OK Univ; Phy Thrpst; Sports Med.

BROCK, CRYSTAL M; Crescent Schl; Crescent, OK; (2); Church Yth Grp; FCA; FHA; SADD; Jazz Band; Pep Band; Var Sftbl; Var Trk; Hon Roll; Pres Acad Fit Awd; OK Bapt U; Hm Ecs Tchr.

BROCK, DEIDRA; Hinton HS; Hinton, OK; (1); 1/50; Church Yth Grp; FCA; Key Clb; SADD; Chorus; Ofcr Frsh Cls; Ofcr Stu Cncl; Bsktbl; Chrldng; Gym; All-Amer Chrldng; Sprts Med.

BROCK, JOHN; Empire Schl; Comanche, OK; (3); 8/36; Computer Clb; FBLA; HOBY; Key Clb; Natl FFA Org; Nwsp; Yrbk; Ofcr Bsbl; Hon Roll; Kiwanis Awd; Butte MT; Fire Sci.

BROCK, JOSH; Macomb Schl; Macomb, OK; (1); FBLA; Natl FFA Org; Band; School Musical; Pres Frsh Cls; Ofcr Stu Cncl; Hon Roll; NHS; Pres Acad Fit Awd; Val.

BROCK, JULIE L; Heritage Hall Schl; Oklahoma City, OK; (2); Art Clb; Church Yth Grp; Pep Clb; Service Clb; Spanish Clb; JV Fld Hcky; Hon Roll; Spanish NHS; Cmnty Wkr; Art Awd; Ballet/Toe/Jazz Lssns.

BROCK, MELODY L; Crescent Schl; Crescent, OK; (2); Church Yth Grp; FHA; SADD; Band; Jazz Band; Mrchg Band; Pep Band; JV Sftbl; Var Trk; Cit Awd; OK ST Univ.

BROCK, SAMANTHA Y; El Reno Sr HS; El Reno, OK; (2); Hon Roll; Renaissance Awd; OK Univ; Pediatrician.

BROCKHUYSEN, CHARLOTTE L; Edmond Memorial HS; Edmond, OK; (3); Cmnty Wkr; French Clb; Key Clb; Science Clb; Stage Crew; Var Trk; French Hon Soc; High Hon Roll; Jr NHS; NHS.

BROCKMAN, MELANIE; Choctaw HS; Choctaw, OK; (4); 1/313; Pres Church Yth Grp; FTA; Key Clb; Spanish Clb; SADD; Nwsp; Golf; Sftbl; Pres NHS; Val; Benedictine Coll; Math.

BRODA, DANIEL; Putnam City West HS; Bethany, OK; (3); Church Yth Grp; Debate Tm; Band; Mrchg Band; Crs Cntry; Trk.

BRODERICK, BRYAN; Madill HS; Madill, OK; (3); Am Leg Boys St; Church Yth Grp; FCA; Ofcr Stu Cncl; Ofcr Bsbl; Ftbl; Wt Lftg; Hon Roll.

BRODERICK, KATIE; Berryhill Jr HS; Tulsa, OK; (1); Band; Jazz Band; Mrchg Band; JV Bsktbl; Hon Roll.

BROGDON, NICOLE; Madill HS; Durant, OK; (3); Church Yth Grp; SADD; Church Choir; School Play; Co-Ed Nwsp; Yrbk; Rep Soph Cls; Chrldng; High Hon Roll; Ntl Merit Ltr; OK Baptist U; Phys Thrp.

BROOKE, JULIE; Yukon HS; Yukon, OK; (4); 29/398; Church Yth Grp; Cmnty Wkr; Office Aide; Spanish Clb; SADD; Stu Ath Trainer; 3d; Outstdng Geometry Stu; Southwestern OK ST Univ.

BROOKFELT, KIMBERLY R; Wister Schl; Wister, OK; (2); FHA; Spanish Clb; Nwsp; Yrbk; Rep Soph Cls; Ofcr Stu Cncl; Co-Capt Chrldng; Hon Roll; Drawing Art Awds; Carl Albert; PT.

BROOKS, AISHA L; John Marshall HS; Oklahoma City, OK; (1); Church Yth Grp; Chorus; Church Choir; Drill Tm; Hon Roll; UCO; Acctng/Bus Mgmt.

BROOKS, APRIL; Millwood HS; Oklahoma City, OK; (3); Church Yth Grp; Cmnty Wkr; French Clb; Library Aide; Chorus; Ofcr Stu Cncl; Chrldng; Hon Roll; Mrchg Band; Jr Princess; Clark Atlanta U; Med.

BROOKS, COURTNEY D; Midwest City HS; Choctaw, OK; (2); 61/486; German Clb; Band; Jazz Band; Mrchg Band; Jr NHS; Brrl Rc; U Cntrl OK HS Schlstc Tourn 1st Pl; OK Tourn Acad Chmpns Cert Rcgntn; OK ST U; Equine Vet.

BROOKS, ERIKA; Muskogee HS; Muskogee, OK; (3); Church Yth Grp; JCL; Key Clb; Latin Clb; Office Aide; Church Choir; School Musical; Ofcr Stu Cncl; Tennis; High Hon Roll; OK ST Univ.

BROOKS, JACKIE; Wetumka Jr Sr HS; Wetumka, OK; (3); 5/30; Church Yth Grp; Library Aide; Pres Natl FFA Org; Sec Jr Cls; Sftbl; Hon Roll; NHS; OSU; Brdcstng.

BROOKS, JASON E; Sayre HS; Sayre, OK; (3); 13/48; Natl FFA Org; Pres Frsh Cls; Var L Bsbl; Var L Bsktbl; Var L Ftbl; L Wt Lftg; High Hon Roll; Sunbowl Bsbl Clsc Jr Invtn; Bsbl Sooner ST Gms Jr; Prp Plyr Wk Ftbl; Prp Ath Wk Bsbl.

BROOKS, KRISTI K; Sayre HS; Sayre, OK; (2); 12/65; Natl FFA Org; Scholastic Bowl; Band; Mrchg Band; Pep Band; High Hon Roll; Hon Roll; Mst Imprvd In Band 94-95; Outstdng Achvmt At Mind Games Cmptn; Tech Stdnts Of Amer Treas 2 Yrs; OU; Eng.

BROOKS, LISA; Goodwell Public Schl; Goodwell, OK; (2); Church Yth Grp; FCA; Letterman Clb; Var Bsktbl; Var Crs Cntry; Var Trk; High Hon Roll; Jr NHS; Ntl Merit Ltr; OSU; Rdlgy.

BROOKS, LUKE; Beaver HS; Beaver, OK; (4); 4/34; Quiz Bowl; Co-Ed Yrbk; Pres Sr Cls; Var Ftbl; Var Trk; High Hon Roll; NHS; Southwestern OK ST U.

BROOKS, MICHAEL L; Del City HS; Oklahoma City, OK; (4).

BROOKS, TAMMY; Bokoshe Schl; Bokoshe, OK; (4); 1/19; Sec Treas 4-H; FHA; Natl FFA Org; Teachers Aide; Var Bsktbl; Capt Sftbl; 4-H Awd; Hon Roll; NHS; Prfct Atten Awd; Carl Albert ST Coll; Pre-Vet.

BROOKS, TERRENCE D; John Marshall HS; Oklahoma City, OK; (3); Church Yth Grp; Drama Clb; Math Clb; Science Clb; SADD; School Play; Yrbk; Cit Awd; Hon Roll; Val; Rose ST Univ; Dir; Producer.

BROOKSHER, JEANA; Central Mid-HS; Norman, OK; (1); Church Yth Grp; FCA; French Clb; Teachers Aide; Chrldng; Gym; Trk; Cit Awd; Hon Roll.

BROOKSHIRE, JENNIFER; Hinton HS; Hinton, OK; (3); 1/28; Sec FCA; French Clb; HOBY; Key Clb; SADD; VP Jr Cls; Var Capt Chrldng; Kiwanis Awd; NHS; St Schlr; Stu Cncl Tres.

BROOKSHIRE, KELLI; Oklahoma Christian Schl; Oklahoma City, OK; (2); Church Yth Grp; Cmnty Wkr; Math Tm; Office Aide; Scholastic Bowl; Church Choir; Nwsp; Bsktbl; Powder Puff Ftbl; Sftbl; Duke U TIP; UGA; Med.

BROOM, WILLIAM M; Norman Sr HS; Norman, OK; (3); U Of OK; Bus.

BROOMFIELD, BRANDI N; Enid Sr HS; Enid, OK; (3); Church Yth Grp; FCA; Pep Clb; Spanish Clb; Orch; School Musical; Ofcr Jr Cls; Sec Stu Cncl; JV Bsktbl; Capt Chrldng.

BROSS, DAISI; Kingfisher HS; Kingfisher, OK; (1); Church Yth Grp; Spanish Clb; School Play; Hon Roll; Heart Srgn.

BROSS, JESSY L; Edmond Memorial HS; Edmond, OK; (3); 1/400; Cmnty Wkr; FCA; Key Clb; Letterman Clb; Spanish Clb; Variety Show; Ofcr Stu Cncl; Pom Pon; NHS; Val.

BROSSIA, NICHOLI N; Classen Schl; Oklahoma City, OK; (3); Math Clb; Mu Alpha Theta; Varsity Clb; Band; Mrchg Band; Var Crs Cntry; Var Socr; Cit Awd; Hon Roll; NHS; U Of OK.

BROTHERS, KO QUEECE M; Guthrie Sr HS; Guthrie, OK; (3); 75/274; Church Yth Grp; French Clb; FBLA; SADD; Church Choir; Stat Bsktbl; Trk; Heritage Clb; 94-95 Kinsminette Ct 4 Qn Grand Palace; Spcl Olympcs Vol; Grambling U; Comp Prgmr.

BROUGHTON, AMANDA L; Ardmore HS; Ardmore, OK; (3); 1/148; Church Yth Grp; French Clb; Math Clb; Mu Alpha Theta; Science Clb; Chorus; School Musical; School Play; Tennis; High Hon Roll.

BROWN, ABIGAIL; Southeast HS; Oklahoma City, OK; (3); 1/150; Chess Clb; Church Yth Grp; Drama Clb; FCA; Math Clb; Model UN; Pep Clb; Thesps; Band; Chorus; OU; Bus.

BROWN, ADRIANNE S; Owasso Sr HS; Claremore, OK; (4); 16/304; Intnl Clb; Math Tm; Scholastic Bowl; Chorus; Tennis; High Hon Roll; NHS; St Schlr; Library Aide; Office Aide; Natl Schlr 95, 96; Tutor 4 Yrs; TJC.

BROWN, ALEE E; Heritage Hall Schl; Oklahoma City, OK; (4); Church Yth Grp; FCA; Mu Alpha Theta; Pep Clb; Spanish Clb; Chorus; Spanish NHS; Showing/Riding Quarter Horses; Quarter Horse Shows Multiple All Around Chmpn; Univ Of North TX.

BROWN, ALISHA B; Rush Springs HS; Rush Springs, OK; (3); 5/40; Sec Soph Cls; Treas Jr Cls; Bsktbl; Sftbl; Wt Lftg; High Hon Roll; Hon Roll; Jr NHS; NHS; Jrnlsm.

BROWN, AMANDA; Stilwell HS; Bunch, OK; (3); Pep Clb; VICA; Var Chrldng; D-FY; Indian Heritage Clb; RN.

BROWN, AMANDA; Idabel HS; Idabel, OK; (2); Church Yth Grp; Dance Clb; FCA; FBLA; Girl Scts; Library Aide; Chorus; Color Guard; Flag Corp; School Musical; FBLA Natl Test; Gold Awd Girl Scouts; After Schl Tutoring By Stdnts; Math-St Curr Cont; Nrsng; Anesthesia.

BROWN, AMBER D; Altus Sr HS; Altus, OK; (4); 45/250; Church Yth Grp; Cmnty Wkr; Spanish Clb; School Musical; Yrbk; Ofcr Stu Cncl; Chrldng; Powder Puff Ftbl; High Hon Roll; NHS; Miss Natl Tengr Pagnt; KAY Clb Pres, VP& Tres; Var Chor Rep; Lions, Span, Kay Clbs & Chrldng Schlsps; Western OK ST Coll; Soc Work.

BROWN, AMY; Edmond North HS; Edmond, OK; (2); 1/450; Hist Key Clb; Mu Alpha Theta; Science Clb; Spanish Clb; Chorus; Kiwanis Awd; NHS; Acad Letter; Summr Sci Acad At Cameron Univ/Rose ST Coll; TX A/M; Marine Bio.

BROWN, ANTHONY; Grandfield Jr Sr HS; Grandfield, OK; (3); 16/27; Church Yth Grp; FHA; HOBY; Var Bsbl; Var Bsktbl; Var Ftbl; Var Trk; Prfct Atten Awd; Midwestern ST U; Bus Mgmt.

BROWN, ASHLEY; Paden HS; Stroud, OK; (2); 1/20; FHA; HOBY; Math Tm; Natl Beta Clb; Science Clb; Pres Soph Cls; Var Bsktbl; High Hon Roll; Hon Roll; NHS; Beta VP 95-; Stdnt Cncl 94-95; OBU; Psych.

BROWN, BENJAMIN J; B T Washington HS; Tulsa, OK; (1); Jr NHS.

BROWN, BETH; Houston Homan Jr HS; Eufaula, OK; (1); Art Clb; Chorus; Bsktbl; Sftbl; Hon Roll; Jr NHS; Acdmc Tm Mem; Rnbow Grl.

BROWN, BRANDI M; Henryetta Sr HS; Dewar, OK; (2); Church Yth Grp; FCA; GAA; Var L Sftbl; Hon Roll.

BROWN, BRANDY J; Durant HS; Durant, OK; (1); Church Yth Grp; Drama Clb; Yrbk; Ofcr Soph Cls; Intrml Tennis; Hon Roll; SOSU; DA.

BROWN, BRAVIS S; Tahlequah Sr HS; Tahlequah, OK; (3); Am Leg Boys St; Church Yth Grp; Debate Tm; German Clb; Spanish Clb; Crs Cntry; Ftbl; Socr; Tennis; Wt Lftg; Algebra Awd; Water Sports; Fishing; Northeastern ST; Lawyer.

BROWN, CARLI; Sayre HS; Sayre, OK; (2); Church Yth Grp; FCA; Chorus; Pres Frsh Cls; Sec Soph Cls; Pres Stu Cncl; Bsktbl; Sftbl; Hon Roll; Red Crss Certfd Lifeguard; OU.

BROWN, CARMELL L; Muskogee HS; Muskogee, OK; (1); Computer Clb; FHA; Cit Awd; Hon Roll; VA Hosp Vol; Northeastern U; Comp Sci.

BROWN, CAROL; Santa Fe HS; Edmond, OK; (4); 33/209; Church Yth Grp; Office Aide; Spanish Clb; SADD; Bsktbl; NHS; OK ST U.

BROWN, CEDRIC D; Choctaw HS; Midwest City, OK; (4); 42/313; Office Aide; Bsktbl; Hon Roll; NHS; Bstkbl Outstndng Jr Awd; Cmptr Engrng.

BROWN, CHANDRA N; Noble HS; Noble, OK; (3); Mu Alpha Theta; Pres Spanish Clb; Sec Jr Cls; Rep Stu Cncl; Var Bsktbl; Var Sftbl; Hon Roll; NHS; Art Clb; FBLA; Outstdng Girl Ath 93-94; Fast-Pitch All-Star.

BROWN, CHARLES; Norman Sr HS; Norman, OK; (4); 75/670; Pres VP Church Yth Grp; Pres VP French Clb; HOBY; Mu Alpha Theta; Spanish Clb; Chorus; Church Choir; Swing Chorus; Variety Show; Treas Frsh Cls; OK Hnr Soc; Ft Chrstn Chrch Yth Grp Pres, VP; U Of OK; Music Ed.

BROWN, CIARA KAISHA; Union Sr HS; Tulsa, OK; (4); 139/629; Church Yth Grp; Dance Clb; Drama Clb; HOBY; Intnl Clb; NFL; Pres Soph Cls; Gov Hon Prg Awd; NHS; Pres Schlr; Red Crs Yth Yr; Native Amer IEP Hnrs Stu; Clark Theatre Tulsa; ORU; Theatre.

BROWN, COURTNEY S; Liberty HS; Mounds, OK; (3); 4-H; GAA; Red Cross Aide; Ofcr Sr Cls; Bsktbl; Socr; Sftbl; NHS; Prfct Atten Awd; Vo-Tech Hnr Soc; CPR Crftd; Vet.

BROWN, CRYSTAL M; Colbert Jr Sr HS; Cartwright, OK; (3); FHA; Library Aide; Office Aide; Teachers Aide; Chorus; Nwsp; JV Var Bsktbl; Hon Roll; Air Force.

BROWN, DAVID; Paoli HS; Paoli, OK; (4); 9/22; Teachers Aide; VP Jr Cls; VP Sr Cls; Var Bsbl; Capt Bsktbl; High Hon Roll; NHS; Ntl Merit Schol.

BROWN, DENVER C; Union Intermediate HS; Tulsa, OK; (2); 149/800; Boy Scts; Intnl Clb; Math Clb; Band; Mrchg Band; High Hon Roll; NHS; Vlntr Hosp Thrgh Explr Scts; OK U; Phy.

BROWN, DONNA R; Dibble Jr Sr HS; Blanchard, OK; (2); FHA; GAA; Spanish Clb; Rep Frsh Cls; Var Sftbl; Ada East Cntrl Univ; Psych.

BROWN, ERIC; Bixby Sr HS; Bixby, OK; (4); Church Yth Grp; Quiz Bowl; Scholastic Bowl; Band; Jazz Band; Stage Crew; Hon Roll; Jr NHS; NHS; Pres Acad Fit Awd; U Of OK; Med.

BROWN, ERNESTINE L; Westmoore HS; Oklahoma City, OK; (3); 152/656; Church Yth Grp; Chorus; Church Choir; School Musical; Variety Show; Ofcr Stu Cncl; Mus Prodctns; U Of OK; Mus Ed.

BROWN, GRETE D; Bartlesville Sr HS; Bartlesville, OK; (1); Church Yth Grp; Girl Scts; Chorus; Church Choir; High Hon Roll; NHS; Pres Acad Fit Awd; OK HS Hnr Soc; Inner-Chrch Bsktbl League.

BROWN, HEATHER R; Claremore Sr HS; Claremore, OK; (3); 81/260; Band; Jazz Band; Mrchg Band; Pep Band; Swing Chorus; JV Bsktbl; JV Sftbl; High Hon Roll; Hon Roll; Water Skiing; Hosp Pharm Thrgh Hlth Shdw Prgm Vol; Fnrl Dir/PT.

BROWN, JADE; Moss Schl; Holdenville, OK; (3); 1/20; Church Yth Grp; FCA; Natl FFA Org; School Play; Pres Frsh Cls; Treas Stu Cncl; Var Bsktbl; Var Sftbl; Hon Roll; Prfct Atten Awd; East Cntrl Univ.

BROWN II, JAMES D; Owasso Sr HS; Owasso, OK; (3); Church Yth Grp; JV Var Bsbl; Acad Exc Awd; U Of OK; Metrolgy.

BROWN, JAMIE R; Skiatook HS; Skiatook, OK; (1); Church Choir; Jr NHS; Yth Alive; Northeastern OK.

BROWN, JASON; New Lima Jr Sr HS; Wewoka, OK; (1); Chess Clb; Scholastic Bowl; Pres Frsh Cls; Var Bsbl; JV Var Bsktbl; Hon Roll; OU.

BROWN, JEANETTE N; Union Intermediate HS; Tulsa, OK; (2); 121/800; Natl FFA Org; Teachers Aide; Cit Awd; Hon Roll; Zoolgst.

BROWN, JENNIFER L; Tipton Jr Sr HS; Tipton, OK; (2); 4/40; FHA; Natl FFA Org; Band; Rptr Nwsp; Rep Frsh Cls; Rep Soph Cls; Ofcr Stu Cncl; Var Bsktbl; Var Chrldng; Var Sftbl; Msnc Stndt Today Awd; FHA Sec 96-; Hd Chrldt 96-; Southwestern Univ; Bus.

BROWN, JENNIFER N; Durant HS; Durant, OK; (2); Band; Drm Mjr(t); Jazz Band; Mrchg Band; Pep Band; Variety Show; Cit Awd; Hon Roll; Prfct Atten Awd; Feature Twirler.

BROWN, JENNIFER R; Putnam City West HS; Oklahoma City, OK; (3); Intnl Clb; Hist Pep Clb; Spanish Clb; Socr; Hon Roll; NHS; GATE; Med Clb; U Of OK; Pre-Med.

BROWN, JESSICA M; Perkins-Tryon HS; Perkins, OK; (3); FCA; FHA; Intnl Clb; Natl FFA Org; Spanish Clb; Bsktbl; Sftbl; Trk; Hon Roll; Pub In Brimestone Schl Mag.

BROWN, JILL R; Putnam City North HS; Oklahoma City, OK; (3); Key Clb; Spanish Clb; Hon Roll; NHS; Big Brother/Big Sister Prgm; Pres Envir Club; GATE Prgm.

BROWN, JOEY J; Union Intermediate HS; Tulsa, OK; (2); 90/800; VP Church Yth Grp; FCA; Spanish Clb; Rep Stu Cncl; Var Chrldng; Var Trk; Hon Roll; Miss Redskin Homcmng Attend; St Track Meet Silver Medalist; Amer Natl Teenager Schlrshp Pageant Fnlst; Marine Bio.

BROWN, JOHN; Will Rogers HS; Tulsa, OK; (4); #27 in class; Boy Scts; JA; VICA; Band; Mrchg Band; Socr; Hon Roll; NHS; Ntl Merit Schol; Pres Ed Awd; OSU; Elec.

BROWN, JOSH C; Foyil Schl; Claremore, OK; (3); Church Yth Grp; Drama Clb; Church Choir; School Play; Variety Show; Ofcr Stu Cncl; Bsktbl; Ftbl; Trk; Hon Roll; Spcl Of The Yr; Cls B-4 Player Of The Yr; Most Points In Rogers Cty Season By A Soph; Tchr; PE.

BROWN, JOSHUA E; Oklahoma Bible Acad; Enid, OK; (2); Church Yth Grp; Cmnty Wkr; Math Tm; Acpl Chr; Chorus; Church Choir; High Hon Roll; Chemical Engr; Nuclear Engr.

BROWN, JOSHUA E; Enid Sr HS; Enid, OK; (2); 169/432; Band; Mrchg Band; Ftbl; Wt Lftg; Hon Roll; Draw; AZ ST; Sports.

BROWN, KARI; Turner Schl; Marietta, OK; (2); 1/28; Natl Beta Clb; Natl FFA Org; Pep Clb; Speech Tm; Pres Frsh Cls; Var L Bsktbl; Var L Sftbl; High Hon Roll; E Central U; Coaching.

BROWN, KATHRYN M; Purcell HS; Purcell, OK; (3); 7/95; Church Yth Grp; FBLA; FHA; Letterman Clb; Library Aide; Spanish Clb; SADD; High Hon Roll; Hon Roll; St Schlr; Southwestern OK ST; Lib Sci.

BROWN, KATINA S; Mc Alester HS; Mcalester, OK; (2); Church Yth Grp; Spanish Clb; Mrchg Band; Bsktbl; Vllybl; Hon Roll; Nrsng.

BROWN, KELLI; Bixby Sr HS; Bixby, OK; (2); Cmnty Wkr; German Clb; VP Stu Cncl; Sftbl; High Hon Roll; Jr NHS; Pres Acad Fit Awd.

BROWN, KENDRA; Sulphur HS; Sulphur, OK; (4); 17/95; FCA; 4-H; FHA; Key Clb; Office Aide; Teachers Aide; Stage Crew; Yrbk; Rep Soph Cls; Rep Stu Cncl; Bulldog Breakfst Bunch Ldr; East Central U; Bus Mgmt.

BROWN, KERI; Ketchum HS; Ketchum, OK; (3); 5/41; FHA; Science Clb; SADD; Sec Frsh Cls; Rep Soph Cls; Rep Jr Cls; Pres Stu Cncl; Sftbl; Trk; Hon Roll; U Of AR; Sports Med.

BROWN, KRISTAL; Comanche HS; Comanche, OK; (2); Teachers Aide; Chorus; Hon Roll; Actv Chrch Yth Grp Ray Of Hope Comanche; Pharm.

BROWN, KRISTEN; Cordell Sr HS; Cordell, OK; (2); Church Yth Grp; Library Aide; Scholastic Bowl; Spanish Clb; Var Bsktbl; Var Chrldng; Var Sftbl; Hon Roll; NHS; Ftbl Hmcmng Soph Cand; SWIM Cntst Kybrdng 2nd Pl; Math Tchr.

BROWN, LACI; Arapaho Schl; Arapaho, OK; (2); 5/28; Church Yth Grp; 4-H; FHA; HOBY; Teachers Aide; Varsity Clb; Church Choir; Var Bsktbl; 4-H Awd; High Hon Roll; OK Bapt U.

BROWN, LAUREN; Yale Jr Sr HS; Yale, OK; (3); 8/50; HOBY; Natl Beta Clb; Teachers Aide; Rep Nwsp; Rep Lit Mag; Pres Frsh Cls; Rep Stu Cncl; JV Bsktbl; High Hon Roll; Jr NHS; Poetry Pubs; Enrld In Schl GR Prgm; OK ST U; Creative Wrtng Prof.

BROWN, LESTER M; Midwest City HS; Midwest City, OK; (2); Church Yth Grp; Cmnty Wkr; School Play; JV Bsbl; JV Var Bsktbl; JV Ftbl; High Hon Roll; Hon Roll; Prfct Atten Awd; Pres Acad Fit Awd; USAF Acad; Med/Doc.

BROWN, LINDA R; Mt St Marys HS; Mustang, OK; (3); Chorus; Church Choir; L Mgr(s); Hon Roll; NHS; Stu Pilot; Airline Pilot.

BROWN, LISA; Putnam City HS; Oklahoma City, OK; (3); 53/360; Church Yth Grp; FCA; Key Clb; Spanish Clb; Church Choir; Drill Tm; School Musical; Rep Stu Cncl; Chrldng; Pom Pon; FCA MVP Of Wk; Deca Chpln; OK Bapt U; Med.

BROWN, LISA J; Southeast HS; Oklahoma City, OK; (2); ROTC; Color Guard; Drill Tm; Stage Crew; Hon Roll; OU; Model/Cop.

BROWN, LISA M; Pauls Valley HS; Pauls Valley, OK; (1); Chorus; Hon Roll.

BROWN, LORI R; Mustang HS; Oklahoma City, OK; (2); Church Yth Grp; Cmnty Wkr; French Clb; Chorus; Hon Roll; NHS; BSA Med Explrs Clb Anatomy/Phsy Spec Awd; Schl Sci Proj 2nd Pl Tm; Wtrskiing; OU; Med.

BROWN, MARK L; West Middle HS; Norman, OK; (2); Hon Roll; Pres Acad Fit Awd; Graphic Arts; Guitar.

BROWN, MARQUITTA; Mid-Del Christian Schl; Oklahoma City, OK; (2); 1/18; Church Yth Grp; Cmnty Wkr; Church Choir; Rep Soph Cls; High Hon Roll; All-Amer Schlr Engl & Math; Yth Achvr; Natl Engl Merit Awd; Natl Ldrshp/Svc Awd; Medcl Resrch.

BROWN, MARY K; Pocola HS; Pocola, OK; (2); Debate Tm; FBLA; FHA; Color Guard; Drill Tm; Flag Corp; Mrchg Band; High Hon Roll; Hon Roll; West AR; Law.

BROWN, MARY L; Clyde Boyd Jr HS; Sand Springs, OK; (1); Church Yth Grp; Cmnty Wkr; Band; Mrchg Band; Pep Band; Rptr Nwsp; Builders Clb; Bus.

BROWN, MATTHEW; Western Area Voc Tech Schl; Oklahoma City, OK; (4); Am Leg Boys St; Boy Scts; Church Yth Grp; Cmnty Wkr; FCA; Pep Clb; Chorus; Church Choir; School Musical; School Play; Reg & Dist Hnr Choir; Ensmbl 3 Sup Rtngs; St Solo Stup; 3200m Conf Chmp, 1600 M 6th Pl Reg; Med Asstnt.

BROWN, MEGAN; Northwest Classen HS; Oklahoma City, OK; (4); 2/200; Am Leg Aux Girls St; Church Yth Grp; Cmnty Wkr; Key Clb; Mu Alpha Theta; Crs Cntry; Socr; High Hon Roll; Pres NHS; Sal; Schl Dance Team The Company 3rd Lt; Bio.

BROWN, MELAINE; Grove HS; Grove, OK; (2); 1/150; Church Yth Grp; Key Clb; Spanish Clb; Band; Jazz Band; Mrchg Band; Sec Soph Cls; Var Chrldng; High Hon Roll; NHS.

BROWN, MEREDITH; Copan HS; Dewey, OK; (3); 8/36; 4-H; Natl FFA Org; Speech Tm; Band; Color Guard; Flag Corp; Mgr(s); Trk; 4-H Awd; Prfct Atten Awd; OK St Univ.

BROWN, MICHAEL D; Edmond North HS; Edmond, OK; (4); 73/330; Math Clb; Mu Alpha Theta; Band; Jazz Band; Mrchg Band; Pep Band; Hon Roll; NHS; U Of OK.

BROWN, MICHAEL J; Cashion HS; Kingfisher, OK; (3); FBLA; FHA; Natl FFA Org; Scholastic Bowl; Spanish Clb; Band; Pep Band; Phtg Yrbk; Tennis; High Hon Roll; Natn Hnr Scty; US Achvmnt Acad; Uco.

BROWN, MITCHEAL; Achille Schl; Bokchito, OK; (2); Church Yth Grp; Natl FFA Org; High Hon Roll; Hon Roll; NHS.

BROWN, NAOMI R; Ripley HS; Stillwater, OK; (1); FHA; Science Clb; Ofcr Soph Cls; Hon Roll; Fshn Dsgn; Art; OSU; Fshn Dsgn.

BROWN, NICHOLAS W; Elgin HS; Elgin, OK; (3); Natl FFA Org; Varsity Clb; Ftbl; Hon Roll; Cameron Univ.

BROWN, NICOLE E; South Intermediate HS; Broken Arrow, OK; (1); Church Yth Grp; Debate Tm; German Clb; Hosp Aide; Library Aide; Scholastic Bowl; Ofcr Stu Cncl; NHS; Ntl Merit Schol; OSU; Engrng.

BROWN, PHILLIP R; Bixby Sr HS; Bixby, OK; (1); Church Yth Grp; FCA; Ofcr Soph Cls; Var Bsbl; Var Bsktbl; Hon Roll; Prfct Atten Awd; OSU; Vet.

BROWN, PHOEBE; Charles Page HS; Tulsa, OK; (3); 1/365; Am Leg Aux Girls St; Church Yth Grp; Cmnty Wkr; FCA; Letterman Clb; Service Clb; Spanish Clb; Varsity Clb; Nwsp; Ed Phtg Yrbk; Stu Mentor; Sam Sung Schlsp; Tulsa Univ; Chem Engr.

BROWN, RACHEL; U S Grant HS; Oklahoma City, OK; (3); 21/243; Church Yth Grp; Cmnty Wkr; FCA; SADD; Ofcr Sr Cls; Gym; Tennis; High Hon Roll; NHS; Rep-At-Large TAD/SADD; PT.

BROWN, RACHEL J; Deer Creek HS; Oklahoma City, OK; (1); 1/100; Chrldng; Hon Roll; NHS; U Of CO.

BROWN, RANA; Maysville Jr Sr HS; Maysville, OK; (3); 2/27; FHA; VP Key Clb; Scholastic Bowl; VP Sec Stu Cncl; Bsktbl; Chrldng; Trk; Hon Roll; VP NHS; Big 8 All-Cnfrnc/All-Trny/All-State Spcl Rcgntn; Stu Today 95-; Spiritual Aims Awd; E Cntrl Univ; Telecom Wrkr.

BROWN, RANDY; Thackerville HS; Thackerville, OK; (4); 1/20; Church Yth Grp; Library Aide; Math Clb; Natl FFA Org; Office Aide; Scholastic Bowl; Science Clb; Spanish Clb; Pres Sr Cls; Pres Stu Cncl; Wldlf Bio.

BROWN, RICKI LEA; Putnam City West HS; Oklahoma City, OK; (3); 29/300; Church Yth Grp; French Clb; FBLA; Pres Frsh Cls; Rep Stu Cncl; Cit Awd; NHS; Chrch Choir Ensemble; Yth Group Ldrshp Cncl; OK ST U; Ed.

BROWN, RONALD E; Rock Creek Jr Sr HS; Bokchito, OK; (2); 12/44; Church Yth Grp; Natl FFA Org.

BROWN, RONNIE A; Velma Alma HS; Ratliff City, OK; (4); 6/50; Church Yth Grp; FCA; SADD; Pep Band; Rptr Nwsp; Sec Yrbk; VP Soph Cls; Sec Jr Cls; Rep Stu Cncl; Var Capt Bsbl; SOSU; Athl Trnr.

BROWN, RYAN; Edmond North HS; Edmond, OK; (4); 1/330; Am Leg Boys St; Art Clb; Quiz Bowl; Scholastic Bowl; Band; Mrchg Band; Phtg Yrbk; NHS; Ntl Merit Ltr; Quartz Mtn Art Inst Photo; Photo-Jrnlsm.

BROWN, SAM; Arapaho Schl; Arapaho, OK; (4); Am Leg Boys St; Church Yth Grp; Natl FFA Org; Chorus; Church Choir; Sec Frsh Cls; VP Jr Cls; VP Sr Cls; Var Capt Bsbl; Var Bsktbl; OK Bptst U.

BROWN, SETH; Owasso Sr HS; Owasso, OK; (3); 28/400; Church Yth Grp; Ofcr Bsbl; NHS.

BROWN, SHALONDA J; John Marshall HS; Oklahoma City, OK; (2); Drama Clb; FBLA; GAA; Band; Flag Corp; Mrchg Band; Var Sftbl; High Hon Roll; Hon Roll; Pres Acad Fit Awd; Medical Brnch Of TX; Pedtrcn.

BROWN, SHANDA; Madill HS; Madill, OK; (2); 10/100; FCA; Treas FBLA; FHA; Sec Frsh Cls; Sec Soph Cls; Sec Jr Cls; Var Sftbl; Hon Roll; NHS; Church Yth Grp; Wrstlng Hmcmng Queen Soph Yr; East Central Univ.

BROWN, SHELLY; Lawton Sr HS; Lawton, OK; (2); Cmnty Wkr; FHA; JA; Stage Crew; Var Bsktbl; Hon Roll; Jr NHS; Ntl Merit Ltr; Pres Awd Excl; Natl Hnr Rll; Cameron U.

BROWN, STACEY R; Healdton HS; Healdton, OK; (2); Quiz Bowl; Band; Drm Mjr(t); Jazz Band; Mrchg Band; Sec Soph Cls; Bsktbl; Sftbl; High Hon Roll; Pres Acad Fit Awd; Natl Young Ldrs; OK ST Univ; Math; Dntst.

BROWN, STEPHANIE; Edmond North HS; Edmond, OK; (4); Key Clb; Sec Treas Latin Clb; Mu Alpha Theta; Chorus; JV Crs Cntry; NHS; Pres Acad Fit Awd; JCL; SADD; Prfct Atten Awd; Accompniast For HS Choir; Eng Fora Day Awd; Yth For Christ; OK St Univ; Indus Eng.

BROWN, STEPHEN; Douglass HS; Oklahoma City, OK; (4); Am Leg Boys St; Church Yth Grp; FBLA; Bsktbl; Ftbl; Wt Lftg; Hon Roll; NHS; NAACP Yth Cncl; Stu Athls Acad Mentorng Pgm Tutor; Mass Lector; Bus Admin.

BROWN, STEVEN D; Corn Bible Acad; Bessie, OK; (2); 4-H; Chorus; Bsktbl; Pres Acad Fit Awd.

BROWN, TABITHA M; Enid Sr HS; Enid, OK; (2); Office Aide; Nwsp; Rep Soph Cls; Gym; Wt Lftg; Rsptry Thrpst.

BROWN, TAMMI; Piedmont HS; Piedmont, OK; (2); Church Yth Grp; Dance Clb; Letterman Clb; SADD; Band; Mrchg Band; Chrldng; Hon Roll; SADD Bd; Chrldr; NCA All Amer Chrldr; OK U.

BROWN, TIFFANY; Northeast HS; Oklahoma City, OK; (2); Church Yth Grp; FHA; GAA; Pep Clb; Chorus; Church Choir; Sec Frsh Cls; Var JV Chrldng; OCAST Awd; Pol Sci/Attrny.

BROWN, TIM P; Duncan HS; Duncan, OK; (4); Bus Profs of Am; Church Yth Grp; Cmnty Wkr; DECA; FCA; French Clb; FBLA; Office Aide; SADD; Teachers Aide; Duncan HS Ldshp; Cameron Univ; Acctng.

BROWN, TODD; Dale Sr HS; Mc Loud, OK; (2); 1/53; Church Yth Grp; Quiz Bowl; Scholastic Bowl; Spanish Clb; Var Bsbl; High Hon Roll; Jr NHS; NHS; Ntl Merit Ltr; OK.

BROWN, TOMMY R; Ringling HS; Ringling, OK; (3); 9/40; Boy Scts; Church Yth Grp; FCA; 4-H; Natl FFA Org; SADD; Band; Church Choir; Drm Mjr(t); Mrchg Band; Chrch Band Dir & Sngr; Phy Ther.

BROWN, TRACI R; Bixby Sr HS; Bixby, OK; (4); FCA; Spanish Clb; Rep Frsh Cls; Var Bsktbl; Var Socr; Var Sftbl; DAR Awd; Hon Roll; Jr NHS; Church Yth Grp; Hnrb Mntn All Conf Sftbl & Soccer; All Conf Jr Sftbl; OU; Phy Thrpst.

BROWN, TYRA; Del City HS; Oklahoma City, OK; (4); Sec Church Yth Grp; Hosp Aide; Treas Spanish Clb; VP SADD; Teachers Aide; Church Choir; Drill Tm; School Play; Pres NHS; Cmnty Wkr; Multicltr Cncl Pres; Howard Univ; Psych/Prfmng Arts.

BROWN, WENDY M; Wellston Schl; Wellston, OK; (4); Church Yth Grp; 4-H; FHA; Girl Scts; Office Aide; Pep Clb; Scholastic Bowl; Band; Mgr Bsktbl; Mgr(s); Prelaw.

BROWN, WILLIE R; Hollis Jr Sr HS; Hollis, OK; (2); Natl FFA Org; Band; Jazz Band; Mrchg Band; Ofcr Bsbl; Ftbl; Mgr(s); Wt Lftg; Hon Roll; OSU; Cmptr Sci.

BROWN, ZACHERY R; East Central HS; Tulsa, OK; (2); Spanish Clb; Yrbk; Capt Var Socr; High Hon Roll; Hon Roll; NHS.

BROWNELL, DAVID J; Union Sr HS; Tulsa, OK; (3); Church Yth Grp; CAP; Band; Mrchg Band; Vllybl; Bapt Bible Coll; Pastor/Msnry.

BROWNING, APRIL M; Little Axe Sr HS; Mc Loud, OK; (4); Drama Clb; Teachers Aide; Yrbk; Rep Frsh Cls; VP Soph Cls; VP Jr Cls; Rep Stu Cncl; Sftbl; Hon Roll; Jr NHS; Chrch Choir; OK ST U; Law Enf.

BROWNING, DEANE B; Western Heights Sr HS; Oklahoma City, OK; (1); 1/215; Chrldng; Cit Awd; High Hon Roll; Jr NHS; Ntl Merit Ltr; Natl Sci Merit Awd; Outs Bio I Stu; Outs Engl I Stu; OK St Univ; Plst Surg.

BROWNING, JUANITA L; Muldrow HS; Muldrow, OK; (2); FHA; Pep Clb; SADD; Hon Roll; OSU; Active News Reporting.

BROWNING, LORI; Valliant HS; Valliant, OK; (4); French Clb; FHA; Library Aide; Yrbk; Treas Jr Cls; Treas Sr Cls; Rep Stu Cncl; Var Chrldng; Hon Roll; NHS; SE OK ST U; Bus.

BROWNING, MICHAEL E; B T Washington HS; Tulsa, OK; (3); Boy Scts; Church Yth Grp; Drama Clb; French Clb; School Play; Eagle Scout Awd; U Of OK; Atmosphere Sci.

BROWNLEE, MELISSA R; Ardmore HS; Ardmore, OK; (3); Drama Clb; JA; Latin Clb; Band; Mrchg Band; Pep Band; Rptr Phtg Nwsp; Rptr Phtg Yrbk; Hon Roll; Prfct Atten Awd.

BROWNLEE, PATRICK; Okeene Jr Sr HS; Okeene, OK; (4); 1/26; Am Leg Boys St; Church Yth Grp; FCA; Letterman Clb; Rep Frsh Cls; Pres Soph Cls; Var Bsbl; Capt Bsktbl; Cit Awd; High Hon Roll.

BROYLES, AMY K; Shattuck Jr Sr HS; Shattuck, OK; (4); 1/23; FHA; Pep Clb; Teachers Aide; Chorus; Nwsp; Mgr Yrbk; Cit Awd; Art Clb; NHS; Pres Acad Fit Awd; NW OK ST Univ.

BROYLES, KATI; Newkirk HS; Newkirk, OK; (3); Church Yth Grp; Band; Jazz Band; Pep Band; Ofcr Stu Cncl; Var Bsktbl; Var Trk; NHS; STEPP Up.

BRUCE, AMANDA L; Rock Creek Jr Sr HS; Bokchito, OK; (2); 9/45; Church Yth Grp; FCA; FHA; Church Choir; Sec Frsh Cls; Var Bsktbl; Var Sftbl; Hon Roll; Prfct Atten Awd; Chrch Bell Choir; OU; Marine Bio.

BRUCE, BOB; Cache HS; Cache, OK; (2); Chess Clb; FCA; Natl Beta Clb; Church Choir; High Hon Roll.

BRUCE, C TYANNE; Chickasha HS; Chickasha, OK; (2); Cmnty Wkr; VP Frsh Cls; Var Bsktbl; Var Chrldng; Var Sftbl; High Hon Roll; Jr NHS; Mock Trial Tm.

BRUCE, TERRI L; Woodward HS; Woodward, OK; (3); Drama Clb; Pep Clb; Band; Mrchg Band; Pep Band; Stage Crew.

BRUCKNER, KYLIE D; Skiatook HS; Skiatook, OK; (3); FCA; FBLA; Office Aide; Yrbk; VP Stu Cncl; Chrldng; Trk; High Hon Roll; Hon Roll; NHS; US Sts Bus Ed Awd Wnnr; FBLA Plrmntry; OK Univ.

BRUEHL, DAVID M; Del City HS; Midwest City, OK; (1); Art Clb; Church Yth Grp; Hon Roll; Varior Arts Shows Awds; Semi Prof Comic Artist; Graphic Art.

BRUMBELOW, SHONDRA B; Capitol Hill HS; Oklahoma City, OK; (3); 1/150; Cmnty Wkr; Hosp Aide; Letterman Clb; Office Aide; Pep Clb; Varsity Clb; Rep Soph Cls; Rep Jr Cls; Rep Stu Cncl; Var JV Bsktbl; Campfire Boys & Girls; Marshal; Lawyer.

BRUMLEY, ADRIAN M; Putnam City North HS; Oklahoma City, OK; (2); 92/490; Church Yth Grp; Drama Clb; NFL; Chorus; Church Choir; School Musical; School Play; Ofcr Stu Cncl; Cit Awd; Hon Roll; SALT Chrch Yth Cncl; CCYM Choir; U Of WI; Medicine; Pediatrician.

BRUMLEY, CANDI D; Broken Arrow Sr HS; Broken Arrow, OK; (3); Church Yth Grp; Cmnty Wkr; FTA; Hosp Aide; Office Aide; Var L Socr; Hon Roll; Cat Tracks Tutoring Pgm; Poetry & Short Stories Awds; Tulsa JC; Elem Ed.

BRUMLEY, CHARLI T; Ninnekah HS; Ninnekah, OK; (2); FCA; Rep FHA; Girl Scts; Model UN; Natl FFA Org; Red Cross Aide; Rep Stu Cncl; JV Var Bsktbl; Var Crs Cntry; Red Cross Lifgrd; Cpr Standard First Aid Trning; Law Enfcmnt.

BRUMLEY, HEATHER; Jenks HS; Jenks, OK; (4); 118/458; Church Yth Grp; Science Clb; Teachers Aide; Thesps; Chorus; Church Choir; School Musical; Yrbk; Ofcr Stu Cncl; Hon Roll; OK All-St Hnr Choir; 2 Musicals With Comm Theater; U Of OK; Jrnlsm.

BRUMLEY, JO DAWN; Kellyville Sr HS; Kellyville, OK; (1); French Clb; Rep Frsh Cls; Var Chrldng; NEO; Med.

BRUMLEY, SARAH; Tipton Jr Sr HS; Tipton, OK; (3); 5/27; Church Yth Grp; FHA; HOBY; Band; Drm Mjr(t); Mrchg Band; Var Bsktbl; High Hon Roll; Jr NHS; NHS; OK Grls St 96; WOSC; Physcl Thrpst.

BRUMMERT, MICHAEL; Collinsville HS; Collinsville, OK; (4); Church Yth Grp; FCA; Quiz Bowl; Ski Clb; Var L Ftbl; Var L Trk; Var L Vllybl; High Hon Roll; Pres Acad Fit Awd; S W OK St U; Phrmcy.

BRUNDIDGE, ASHLEY; Latta Sr HS; Ada, OK; (3); 1/45; Church Yth Grp; Cmnty Wkr; FCA; FHA; GAA; Teachers Aide; Rptr Nwsp; Rep Frsh Cls; Rep Soph Cls; VP Jr Cls; Pharmacist.

BRUNE, KRYSTA; Canton HS; Canton, OK; (4); 3/44; Am Leg Aux Girls St; Church Yth Grp; FCA; Spanish Clb; SADD; Band; Flag Corp; School Play; Yrbk; NHS; Pres FHA; Treas FCA; Most Likely To Succeed; OSU Stillwater; Comp Sci.

BRUNE, SHAYNA; Canton HS; Canton, OK; (2); 3/39; Church Yth Grp; FCA; FHA; Spanish Clb; SADD; Rep Stu Cncl; Bsktbl; Crs Cntry; Hon Roll; NHS; OSU; Dntstry.

BRUNER, AMY L; Achille Schl; Hendrix, OK; (3); FBLA; FHA; Var Bsktbl; Var Sftbl; Hon Roll; NHS; Bus Ed.

BRUNER, BRANDON J; Healdton HS; Healdton, OK; (3); 3/40; Cmnty Wkr; FCA; Scholastic Bowl; SADD; Rep Frsh Cls; Rep Soph Cls; Rep Jr Cls; Pres Sr Cls; Pres Stu Cncl; JV Var Bsbl.

BRUNER, CARDELIA N; Star Spencer HS; Spencer, OK; (1); Band; Jazz Band; Mrchg Band; Pep Band; Jrnlsm.

BRUNER, CHRISTOPHER TERRON; Holland Hall Schl; Bixby, OK; (3); Church Yth Grp; Cmnty Wkr; Spanish Clb; Ofcr Bsbl; Var Bsktbl; Socr; Hon Roll; Pres Acad Fit Awd; Martial Arts; Weight Lifting; U Of Tulsa; Bus.

BRUNER JR, DANNY R; Yukon HS; Yukon, OK; (2); Quiz Bowl; JV Bsbl; Hon Roll; NHS; OSU.

BRUNER, JAKE; Healdton HS; Healdton, OK; (2); 15/40; FCA; SADD; Rep Frsh Cls; Rep Soph Cls; JV Var Bsbl; JV Var Bsktbl; Var Ftbl; JV Golf; JV Trk; Hon Roll.

BRUNER, MELISSA; Union Intermediate HS; Tulsa, OK; (1); Church Yth Grp; FCA; GAA; Model UN; Office Aide; Spanish Clb; Treas Frsh Cls; Chrldng; Hon Roll; DFY; OK Univ; Sprts Trnr.

BRUNER, SUZANNE; Sasakwa Schl; Sasakwa, OK; (2); 7/22; Teachers Aide; Chorus; Sec Stu Cncl; Intrschlstc Meets; Midwestern ST U; Pharm.

BRUNGARDT, CARRIE; Edmond North HS; Edmond, OK; (3); Dance Clb; Key Clb; Mu Alpha Theta; Spanish Clb; Band; Ed Yrbk; JV Socr; High Hon Roll; Hon Roll; NHS; Math/Pblshng.

BRUNING, ELIZABETH; Guthrie Sr HS; Coyle, OK; (3); 9/250; Church Yth Grp; 4-H; Mu Alpha Theta; Spanish Clb; SADD; JV Crs Cntry; Trk; NHS.

BRUNK JR, ROGER D; Roland Sr HS; Roland, OK; (3); FCA; Spanish Clb; Varsity Clb; Nwsp; Yrbk; Pres Frsh Cls; Rep Jr Cls; Rep Stu Cncl; Var Bsbl; Var Bsktbl.

BRUNKEN, BROOKE; Garber Sr HS; Garber, OK; (3); 4/37; VP Church Yth Grp; FCA; FHA; School Play; Capt Bsktbl; High Hon Roll; NHS; Prfct Atten Awd; Basic Lifesaving; CPR; First Aid; U Of OK.

BRUNKEN, JENNIFER; Midwest City HS; Midwest City, OK; (2); 46/488; Church Yth Grp; FHA; Quiz Bowl; Chorus; Yrbk; Sftbl; Jr NHS; NHS; OK Ctr For Advcmnt Sci & Tech; OK U; Law.

BRUNNER, STACIE R; Woodward HS; Woodward, OK; (1); FHA; Band; Mrchg Band; Hon Roll; Sftbl; Swimming; Med.

BRUNS, BARRY A; Pawnee HS; Pawnee, OK; (3); Church Yth Grp; Cmnty Wkr; FCA; 4-H; Teachers Aide; Phtg Yrbk; Var Bsbl; Var Capt Bsktbl; Var L Ftbl; Cit Awd; Sun Surf Slam Tour HI Bsktbl; Amer Legn Bsbl 2 Yr; All-Star Plyr Babe Ruth St Trnmnt.

BRUNSWICK, SHANA L; Caney Jr Sr HS; Caney, OK; (4); 4/17; FBLA; FHA; Teachers Aide; Sec Sr Cls; Var Capt Sftbl; Hon Roll; Kiamichi Vo-Tech; LPN.

BRUSTER, BOBBY; Madill HS; Madill, OK; (3); FCA; 4-H; Natl FFA Org; SADD; Var L Bsbl; Var L Bsktbl; Var Crs Cntry; JV Ftbl; 4-H Awd; Hon Roll; Chem.

BRUSVEEN, MICHELLE R; Tahlequah Sr HS; Tahlequah, OK; (2); Church Yth Grp; Band; Mrchg Band; Jr NHS; NHS.

BRUTON, HAROLD P; Sapulpa Sr HS; Sapulpa, OK; (4); 83/290; Church Yth Grp; Cmnty Wkr; Band; Mrchg Band; Intrml Vllybl; Hon Roll; Prfct Atten Awd; FCA; Library Aide; JV Bsbl; All-Region Band; All-St Band; Tulsa Univ Hnr Band; Band Dirs Awd 96; East Cntrl Univ; Comp Sci.

BRYAN, CHRISTINE L; Union Intermediate HS; Broken Arrow, OK; (1); Church Yth Grp; FCA; Church Choir; Hon Roll; Jr NHS; Dance; Lifeguard.

BRYAN, JENNIFER; Holdenville HS; Holdenville, OK; (4); 10/75; Scholastic Bowl; Band; Chorus; Flag Corp; Hon Roll; NHS; Church Yth Grp; Natl Beta Clb; Office Aide; Color Guard; All Dist Band; OK ST All Star Mrchng Band; All Dist Choir; E Cntrl Univ; PT.

BRYAN, JOHN S; Edmond Santa Fe HS; Edmond, OK; (3); Church Yth Grp; Cmnty Wkr; Letterman Clb; Quiz Bowl; Scholastic Bowl; Service Clb; Teachers Aide; L Orch; Sec Jr Cls; L Swmmng; Drury Coll Awd; Mst Imprvd Swimmer; OK Hnr Soc; OK Yth Orch; Acad Team Mem; VP Orch Cncl; Acad Ltr; U Of OK; Navy ROTC.

BRYAN, KYLEE R; Elk City HS; Elk City, OK; (3); Computer Clb; FHA; Pep Clb; Spanish Clb; Teachers Aide; Bsktbl; Hon Roll; Elem Ed.

BRYAN, LANCE; Sayre HS; Sayre, OK; (4); 1/43; Am Leg Boys St; Cmnty Wkr; Debate Tm; Natl FFA Org; Scholastic Bowl; Speech Tm; Rptr Nwsp; Rep Frsh Cls; Pres Soph Cls; Pres Jr Cls; Amer Lgn Ortrcl Cntst Champ 95; Rotary Yth Ldrshp Awd; All-Amer Schlr.

BRYAN, MELISSA; Goodwell Public Schl; Goodwell, OK; (3); Church Yth Grp; FCA; Girl Scts; HOBY; Letterman Clb; Pres Band; Chorus; Sec Treas Stu Cncl; Var Bsktbl; Hon Roll; Med.

BRYANT, AARON C; Owasso Sr HS; Owasso, OK; (3); 34/356; Church Yth Grp; FCA; Ski Clb; Teachers Aide; Ofcr Stu Cncl; High Hon Roll; Jr NHS; NHS; Prfct Atten Awd; Pres Acad Fit Awd; Tech Stdnts Assoc; Foreign Exch Clb; Acctng.

BRYANT, AMANDA; Porum HS; Porum, OK; (1); Church Yth Grp; FCA; 4-H; FHA; GAA; Natl FFA Org; Ofcr Frsh Cls; Bsktbl; Cit Awd; NHS.

BRYANT, ANNA M; Bridge Creek HS; Blanchard, OK; (3); Drama Clb; Chorus; School Play; Singer.

BRYANT, BEAU; Okemah HS; Okemah, OK; (4); 10/47; Am Leg Boys St; Church Yth Grp; Drama Clb; Office Aide; School Play; Ofcr Stu Cncl; Ofcr Bsbl; Cit Awd; High Hon Roll; Math.

BRYANT, BRANDON E; Southeast HS; Choctaw, OK; (2); Band; Church Choir; Jazz Band; Mrchg Band; Pep Band; School Musical; Bsktbl; Cit Awd; High Hon Roll; Hon Roll; Drum Capt; Elec Engrng.

BRYANT, JANNELLE; Stigler HS; Porum, OK; (3); Church Yth Grp; FCA; FHA; SADD; Band; Color Guard; Rptr Nwsp; Hon Roll; NHS; Prfct Atten Awd; Northeastern; Med.

BRYANT, JODY; Laverne Jr Sr HS; Laverne, OK; (4); Church Yth Grp; Cmnty Wkr; 4-H; FHA; Letterman Clb; Natl Beta Clb; Natl FFA Org; Office Aide; Speech Tm; Rptr Frsh Cls; OK HS Schl Rodeo & Northwest Rodeo Assn Champion Header; Panhandle ST Univ.

BRYANT, JOE; Stigler HS; Porum, OK; (1); Church Yth Grp; FCA; Natl FFA Org; Scholastic Bowl; Band; Mrchg Band; Rep Frsh Cls; JV Bsbl; Hon Roll; NHS.

BRYANT, KENZI L; Putnam City West HS; Bethany, OK; (3); Church Yth Grp; GAA; Church Choir; School Play; Vllybl; Cnslrs Aide; Var Vllybl MVP; Southwestern OK ST Univ.

BRYANT, KRYSTAL M; Stigler HS; Stigler, OK; (3); Church Yth Grp; FHA; Pep Clb; SADD; Church Choir; Hon Roll; Carl Albert; RN.

BRYANT, KYLA L; Eldorado Schl; Eldorado, OK; (1); 5/13; 4-H; FHA; Natl FFA Org; Pep Clb; Bsktbl; Chrldng; Hon Roll; Ntl Merit Ltr; FFA Beef Awd; Most Ath Awd; OSU; Speech Pathology.

BRYANT, LAURA; Porum HS; Porum, OK; (3); FCA; 4-H; FHA; Yrbk; Rptr Jr Cls; Bsktbl; Sftbl; Hon Roll; Ntl Merit Ltr.

BRYANT, MEGAN K; Stigler HS; Kinta, OK; (3); Church Yth Grp; FCA; 4-H.

BRYANT, MISTY; Anadarko HS; Anadarko, OK; (3); 46/121; DECA; FCA; FHA; Spanish Clb; SADD; Rep Jr Cls; JV Var Bsktbl; Powder Puff Ftbl; Hon Roll; Redlands CC; Phy Therapy.

BRYANT, MISTY R; South Intermediate HS; Broken Arrow, OK; (1); Church Yth Grp; FCA; Band; Church Choir; Mrchg Band; Pep Band; Hnrs His; OK Bapt; Attorney.

BRYANT, NICOLE L; Charles Page HS; Sand Springs, OK; (3); Church Yth Grp; FCA; Key Clb; Spanish Clb; High Hon Roll; Hon Roll; Jr NHS; NHS; Prfct Atten Awd; Pres Acad Fit Awd; OK ST Univ; Vet Med.

BRYANT, ROBERT C; Eisenhower Sr HS; Lawton, OK; (3); Art Clb; Mgr Nwsp; High Hon Roll; Hon Roll; Jr NHS; NHS; Japanese Culture/Lang; Cmptrs; 4 Yr Coll; Cmptr Sci-Tech.

BRYANT, TABITHA L; Moyers Public Schl; Antlers, OK; (2); Church Yth Grp; Quiz Bowl; School Play; Stage Crew; Hon Roll; OK Hnr Soc; Hosp Ward Clerk; ECU; Rsrch.

BRYANT, ZAC R; Santa Fe HS; Edmond, OK; (3); Cmnty Wkr; Debate Tm; FCA; Letterman Clb; SADD; Varsity Clb; JV L Bsbl; Var L Ftbl; Var L Trk; JV L Wrstlng.

BRYCE, HEATHER J; Panola HS; Wilburton, OK; (2); Church Yth Grp; FHA; Natl FFA Org; Sec Frsh Cls; JV Var Bsktbl; Var Sftbl; Cit Awd; High Hon Roll; NHS; Prfct Atten Awd; 1st In Kybrdng Literacy At Carl Albert St Col Cir Cont; Med.

BRYCE, STACEY D; Owasso Sr HS; Owasso, OK; (3); 45/357; Church Yth Grp; Cmnty Wkr; Drama Clb; French Clb; Office Aide; Chorus; Church Choir; Rep Soph Cls; Rep Jr Cls; Rep Sr Cls; Hnrs Cert U Of OK.

BRYER, AMANDA M; Woodward HS; Woodward, OK; (2); Cit Awd; Hon Roll; NWOSU; Nrs/Cmptr Pgmr.

BUCHANAN, ADAM; Stillwater Sr HS; Stillwater, OK; (3); Church Yth Grp; Key Clb; Latin Clb; School Play; Phtg Ed Nwsp; Phtg Ed Yrbk; Intrml Bsktbl; High Hon Roll; NHS; Ntl Merit Ltr; OK ST Univ; Engrng.

BUCHANAN, ASHLEY A; South Intermediate HS; Broken Arrow, OK; (1); Church Yth Grp; Intnl Clb; Band; Mrchg Band; Pep Band; Var Trk; High Hon Roll; Jr NHS; Superior Rtngs ST/DIST Solo/Ensmbl Contest; All Dist Band 96; OK ST Univ; Ed.

BUCHANAN, CHRISTY L; Sapulpa Sr HS; Sapulpa, OK; (2); Church Yth Grp; Chorus; Church Choir; Mdls Solo/Ensmbl Choir; Psych.

BUCHANAN, CLINT L; Kellyville Sr HS; Kellyville, OK; (2); Phtg Rptr Nwsp; Sec Soph Cls; Var Bsbl; Var Bsktbl; Hon Roll; Pres Acad Fit Awd; Ldrshp Awd; Medcl.

BUCHANAN, CRISTIN L; Soper Schl; Soper, OK; (3); Computer Clb; 4-H; FHA; GAA; Natl FFA Org; Pep Clb; Ofcr Jr Cls; FFA Awds; PJC; Nrsng.

BUCHANAN, JENNIFER J; Glenpool HS; Glenpool, OK; (1); Church Yth Grp; Cmnty Wkr; Teachers Aide; Acpl Chr; Chorus; Swing Chorus; Mgr(s); Powder Puff Ftbl; Vllybl; Hon Roll; Slctd Prfm NHS Banquet/Chmbr Cmrc Banquet/VFW Mem Dedication; Page ST Capital; 4 Yr Coll; Theater.

BUCHANAN, JERI DAWN; Clayton Jr Sr HS; Clayton, OK; (2); Church Yth Grp; 4-H; FBLA; Band; Rep Stu Cncl; Var Bsktbl; Var Sftbl; Hon Roll; NHS; Pres Acad Fit Awd; Southeastern ST Univ.

BUCHANAN, KASEY; Clinton HS; Clinton, OK; (3); Church Yth Grp; FCA; FBLA; Rep FHA; Chorus; Yrbk; Rep Stu Cncl; Hon Roll; NHS; OK Christian Coll; Med.

BUCHANAN, MERRICK A; Union Intermediate HS; Tulsa, OK; (2); Church Yth Grp; FCA; FBLA; Spanish Clb; Gym; High Hon Roll; Hon Roll; NHS; Pres Acad Fit Awd; DFY; Chrstn Flwshp Lunch; USGF Regnl Champ; Sports Thrpst.

BUCHANAN, MOLLY; Pawnee HS; Pawnee, OK; (4); 6/56; Church Yth Grp; 4-H; Natl Beta Clb; Treas Natl FFA Org; Pep Clb; Var Co-Capt Chrldng; Hon Roll; Prfct Atten Awd; Pres Acad Fit Awd; OK ST Univ; Ag Ec.

BUCHANAN, SHARLA; Hilldale HS; Muskogee, OK; (3); Church Yth Grp; FCA; German Clb; Mu Alpha Theta; Science Clb; Church Choir; Bsktbl; Chrldng; Trk; High Hon Roll; Northeastern ST U; Acctg.

BUCHANAN, STEPHANIE R; Dickson HS; Ardmore, OK; (3); Church Yth Grp; FHA; German Clb; Key Clb; Library Aide; Sec SADD; Teachers Aide; Yrbk; Rep Stu Cncl; Hon Roll.

BUCHANAN, TANNA; Berryhill Sr HS; Tulsa, OK; (3); 1/78; Mu Alpha Theta; Teachers Aide; Ofcr Yrbk; Rep Stu Cncl; Bsktbl; Powder Puff Ftbl; NHS; Sal; Peds.

BUCHER, ASHLEY R; Heritage Hall Schl; Oklahoma City, OK; (2); VP Debate Tm; NFL; Pep Clb; Spanish Clb; Chorus; JV Fld Hcky; High Hon Roll; Hon Roll; Jr NHS; Spanish NHS; Piano; Voice Lessons; Pre-Law.

BUCHNER, ELIZABETH D; B T Washington HS; Tulsa, OK; (2); Church Yth Grp; Drama Clb; French Clb; Girl Scts; High Hon Roll; NHS.

BUCK, KAREN; Eufaula Sr HS; Eufaula, OK; (3); Art Clb; FHA; Chorus; Variety Show; Hon Roll; NHS; Prfct Atten Awd; Natl Math Awd; All Amer Schlr; Natl Stu Ldrshp/Svc Awd.

BUCKALOO, BOBBY J; Kingston HS; Kingston, OK; (3); Quiz Bowl; Ftbl; OU; Med.

BUCK-KAUFFMAN, LARA; Stillwater Sr HS; Stillwater, OK; (2); Drama Clb; German Clb; School Musical; Bsktbl; TOG HS Sorority; Eng/Actrss.

BUCKLEY, JAY E; Edmond Memorial HS; Edmond, OK; (4); 140/322; Church Yth Grp; Cmnty Wkr; FCA; Letterman Clb; Office Aide; Spanish Clb; Varsity Clb; Ofcr Bsbl; Bsktbl; Invit Natl Jrnlsm Conf; Edmond Memrl All Sprts King; OK St Univ.

BUCKLEY, STEPHANIE; Midwest City HS; Midwest City, OK; (3); 340/370; Pres Church Yth Grp; FCA; German Clb; Pep Clb; SADD; VP Soph Cls; Chrldng; Pom Pon; Hon Roll.

BUCKMASTER, CHAD; Noble HS; Noble, OK; (2); Church Yth Grp; Library Aide; Math Clb; Mu Alpha Theta; Band; Mrchg Band; Orch; Pep Band; Rptr Nwsp; Hon Roll; Odyssy Mind; Untd Meth Yth Fllwshp.

BUCKMINSTER, PENNY; Oklahoma Bible Acad; Lahoma, OK; (3); FCA; Teachers Aide; Chorus; Sec Jr Cls; Var Vllybl; High Hon Roll; Hon Roll; NHS; Distngd Chrstn HS Stu Awd 95-96.

BUCKNER, ALICIA A; Stillwater Sr HS; Stillwater, OK; (2); FBLA; German Clb; Band; Mrchg Band; Pep Band; School Musical; VP Frsh Cls; Var Chrldng; Var Pom Pon; High Hon Roll; OK Hnr Scty.

BUCKNER, MICHELLE; Okeene Jr Sr HS; Okeene, OK; (1); 1/30; FHA; Band; Mrchg Band; Pep Band; High Hon Roll.

BUDDE, ANNIKA; Westmoore HS; Oklahoma City, OK; (3); French Clb; Scholastic Bowl; Ger Exch Stu; Piano 7 Yrs; Lawyer/Law Enfor.

BUDNIK, JAMES E; Union Intermediate HS; Tulsa, OK; (2); JV Bsbl; JV Var Crs Cntry; Var Trk; Hon Roll; Bus.

BUENDIA, ADRIAN; Wewoka HS; Wewoka, OK; (4); 1/51; Am Leg Boys St; Boy Scts; Office Aide; Jazz Band; VP Frsh Cls; Rep Stu Cncl; Var Ftbl; Var Wt Lftg; NHS; Sal; Piano Perf; U Of OK; Med.

BUESING, BETH A; Blackwell HS; Blackwell, OK; (4); 22/110; Church Yth Grp; Pep Clb; Spanish Clb; Chorus; Hon Roll; N OK Col; Physthpy.

BUESING, KARA J; Blackwell HS; Blackwell, OK; (4); 16/110; Church Yth Grp; Spanish Clb; Chorus; Hon Roll; NHS; St Hnr Soc; N OK Col.

BUETTNER, JENNIFER; West Middle HS; Norman, OK; (2); Church Yth Grp; FCA; Latin Clb; Red Cross Aide; Ed Rptr Yrbk; Rep Soph Cls; Ofcr Stu Cncl; Chrldng; Hon Roll; Pres Acad Fit Awd; Yng Lf; U Of OK; Med.

BUFORD, CRYSTAL; Heavener HS; Heavener, OK; (4); 12/86; Church Yth Grp; French Clb; Quiz Bowl; Spanish Clb; Band; Church Choir; Drm Mjr(t); Mrchg Band; NHS; John Philip Sousa Awd; Hardin Simmons U; Band Dir.

BUFTON, ANGELIA M; Ponca City Sr HS; Ponca City, OK; (4); Church Yth Grp; FCA; French Clb; GAA; Teachers Aide; Varsity Clb; Chorus; Church Choir; Rep Stu Cncl; L Bsktbl; Attitude Awd; ST Slct Soccer Tm; All Dist 94-; OK Chrstn.

BUHER, CATHY; Nathan Hale HS; Tulsa, OK; (1); JV Vllybl; Hon Roll.

BUI, BE THANH; U S Grant HS; Oklahoma City, OK; (4); Math Clb; Ofcr Stu Cncl; 4-H Awd; NHS; Natl Math Awd; Sci Awd; Asian Club; OK City CC.

BUI, CA THANH; U S Grant HS; Oklahoma City, OK; (4); #16 in class; JA; Math Clb; Math Tm; 4-H Awd; High Hon Roll; Hon Roll; Jr NHS; NHS; Ntl Merit Ltr.

BUI, KIM C; Western Heights Sr HS; Oklahoma City, OK; (2); Computer Clb; French Clb; FBLA; FHA; Yrbk; LEAP; FBLA; CTA; Pediatrician.

BUI, TOM V; Putnam City West HS; Bethany, OK; (2); Church Yth Grp; FCA; Chorus; JV Ftbl; Var Tennis; Var L Wrstlng; OK ST Univ.

BUI, TUAN-ANH TRA; U S Grant HS; Oklahoma City, OK; (4); 9/180; VP FBLA; High Hon Roll; Hon Roll; Asian Clb Pres; Natl Hnr Soc Treas; U Of OK; Med.

BUKENHOFER, ANNE J; Heavener HS; Heavener, OK; (1); JV Bsktbl; Var JV Sftbl; Var JV Trk; High Hon Roll; Hon Roll; Val; OK HS Hnr Soc; Carl Albert ST Coll; Vet.

BULLARD, CHAD; Durant HS; Durant, OK; (4); 52/185; FCA; Treas FBLA; Rep Frsh Cls; Rep Soph Cls; VP Jr Cls; VP Rep Stu Cncl; L Bsktbl; L Ftbl; Trk; Hon Roll; Page For OK ST Senate; Spcl Olympics-Organize Trk Meet; Little Dribblers Coach; OK ST U; Bus Admin.

BULLARD, CLINTON; Hilldale HS; Muskogee, OK; (1); Church Yth Grp; 4-H; Band; Mrchg Band; Ofcr Bsbl; Bsktbl; Ftbl; Hon Roll; OU.

BULLARD, JAMIE M; Stigler HS; Stigler, OK; (3); Am Leg Boys St; Church Yth Grp; Drama Clb; FCA; 4-H; Math Clb; Natl FFA Org; Pep Clb; Quiz Bowl; Speech Tm; Northeastern ST Univ.

BULLARD, JOSHUA L; Stigler HS; Stigler, OK; (3); SADD; Ftbl; Trk; Wt Lftg; Natl Mrt Sci Awd.

BULLEIGH, ADAM L; South Intermediate HS; Broken Arrow, OK; (1); Church Yth Grp; Red Cross Aide; VP Stu Cncl; Cit Awd; Gov Hon Prg Awd; High Hon Roll; Hon Roll; Hnr Frosh Boy Yr 95-; Harvard Law; Prsctng Attrny.

BULLER, ALISHA; Mc Alester HS; Mcalester, OK; (1); Church Yth Grp; GAA; Varsity Clb; Chrldng; All Amer.

BULLIS, BETH; Hennessey HS; Hennessey, OK; (1); Natl FFA Org; Quiz Bowl; Nwsp; Pres Frsh Cls; Rep Stu Cncl; Hon Roll; Marine Bio.

BULLOCK, MICHELLE; Empire Schl; Duncan, OK; (4); #3 in class; Rptr Debate Tm; Rptr Drama Clb; FBLA; FHA; Key Clb; Rptr Speech Tm; Pres SADD; School Play; Hon Roll; NHS; U Of Sci & Arts; Elem Tchr.

BULLOCK, PATTI; Braggs Schl; Braggs, OK; (1); 2/20; Church Yth Grp; Dance Clb; GAA; Rep Stu Cncl; Bsktbl; High Hon Roll; Sal; Black Belt Karate.

BULLS, JAMES T; Boise City HS; Boise City, OK; (3); 4/32; Church Yth Grp; Office Aide; Band; Pep Band; Hon Roll; NHS; OK Hnr Soc.

BUMBARGER, JENNIFER A; Mc Alester HS; Mcalester, OK; (3); 56/208; Church Yth Grp; Office Aide; Teachers Aide; Band; Church Choir; Color Guard; Mrchg Band; Pep Band; Var Chrldng; Hon Roll; Grl Scts; Elem Schl Tchr.

BUMGARDNER, RYAN W; Guthrie Sr HS; Guthrie, OK; (1); Art Clb; Band; Mrchg Band; All Reg Band Cmptn 5th Pl.

BUMGARNER, BRADLEY; Will Rogers HS; Tulsa, OK; (3); 1/231; Church Yth Grp; FCA; French Clb; HOBY; JA; Key Clb; Teachers Aide; VP Soph Cls; Rep Jr Cls; Rep Stu Cncl; Acad Bwl; Mech Engrng.

BUMGARNER, NANCY; Eufaula Sr HS; Eufaula, OK; (3); Church Yth Grp; Spanish Clb; Teachers Aide; Chorus; Church Choir; Yrbk; Hon Roll; NHS; OK Hnr Soc.

BUMPASS, ANDREA M; Union Sr HS; Tulsa, OK; (3); 17/741; Church Yth Grp; FBLA; Spanish Clb; Hon Roll; NHS; Drug Free Yth; S Nazarene U; Bus Mgmt.

BUMPERS, AMBER; Stigler HS; Stigler, OK; (1); Pep Clb; Chrldng; Sftbl; Hon Roll.

BUN, LISA; Putnam City North HS; Oklahoma City, OK; (4); Library Aide; Variety Show; Hon Roll; Stu Dir DECA Fshn Show 95; Art Inst Of Phila; Fshn Dsgn.

BUNCH, AMANDA J; Lindsay HS; Lindsay, OK; (1); Natl FFA Org; Chorus; School Musical; Bsktbl; Chrldng; Sftbl; Trk; 4-H Awd; Hon Roll; Chickasha.

BUNCH, ANGELA E; Spiro HS; Spiro, OK; (2); Church Yth Grp; FCA; FHA; Trk; Hon Roll; FHA Hstrn; U Of AR; X-Ray Tech.

BUNCH, JULIE D; Oologah HS; Oologah, OK; (3); 9/104; Church Yth Grp; Cmnty Wkr; FCA; Sftbl; Tennis; Cit Awd; High Hon Roll; NHS; Prfct Atten Awd.

BUNCH, PORSHA; Edmond North HS; Spencer, OK; (3); Church Yth Grp; Mu Alpha Theta; Spanish Clb; Ofcr Stu Cncl; Var Chrldng; Var Pom Pon; Var Trk; Hon Roll; NHS; Pres Acad Fit Awd; All Amer Nom NCA Danz; Miss Fashionetta Pageant; Top Gun Funk Winner NCA Danz; U Of OK; Bio/Pre-Med.

BUNCH, STEPHANIE M; Ardmore HS; Wilson, OK; (3); 69/202; Church Yth Grp; Cmnty Wkr; Drama Clb; 4-H; German Clb; Natl Beta Clb; Office Aide; Spanish Clb; Teachers Aide; Church Choir; Algebra I Awd; Engl III Awd; Ger Awd; Falls Creek Chldrns Camp/Cnslr; Peagasus Skydiving Schl; Baylor Univ; Pre-Med.

BUNN, LAURA V; Putnam City North HS; Yukon, OK; (2); 4-H; Key Clb; Spanish Clb; SADD; Chorus; Stat Bsktbl; U Of OK; Denistry.

BURAU, M SCOTT; Union Intermediate HS; Tulsa, OK; (2); 8/800; FBLA; Spanish Clb; NHS; Yng Republicans Clb.

BURBA, CHRISTOPHER M; Union Sr HS; Tulsa, OK; (4); 67/629; Church Yth Grp; Mu Alpha Theta; Spanish Clb; Band; Church Choir; High Hon Roll; Jr NHS; Prfct Atten Awd; Mssn Trps To Mexico; Lnch Bible Study; MO Sthrn ST Coll; Chem.

BURCH, ASHLEY D; Catoosa HS; Tulsa, OK; (3); French Clb; FBLA; Intnl Clb; Rep Stu Cncl; JV Sftbl; Hon Roll; St Schlr; OU; Phy Therapy; Acctng.

BURCH, FELICIA; Sperry Sr HS; Sperry, OK; (4); 27/65; Am Leg Aux Girls St; Cmnty Wkr; Key Clb; Pep Clb; Spanish Clb; SADD; Band; Chorus; Flag Corp; Mrchg Band; Northeastern St U; Ed.

BURCH, JONATHAN R; Bishop Mcguinness HS; Edmond, OK; (4); French Clb; JCL; Latin Clb; Ski Clb; JV Ftbl; Var L Socr; NHS; Pres Schlr; OK U; Med.

BURCH, KARA L; Dickson HS; Ardmore, OK; (2).

BURCH, LAURA J; Enid Sr HS; Enid, OK; (2); Church Yth Grp; Church Choir; Rptr Nwsp; High Hon Roll; Hon Roll; MI ST Univ; Radiologist.

BURCH, MICAH; Blanchard Jr Sr HS; Blanchard, OK; (2); 1/80; Spanish Clb; Band; Ftbl; Trk; Wt Lftg; Jr NHS; NHS.

BURCHAM, PATRICK; Mangum Jr HS; Mangum, OK; (1); Natl FFA Org; Scholastic Bowl; Band; Jazz Band; Mrchg Band; Pep Band; High Hon Roll; NHS; Sal; St Schlr.

BURD, JAMIE; Texhoma HS; Texhoma, OK; (4); 4/25; Church Yth Grp; Cmnty Wkr; 4-H; GAA; Natl FFA Org; Pep Clb; Quiz Bowl; Teachers Aide; Varsity Clb; School Play; MO Sthrn ST Coll; Med.

BURD, JAMIE G; Stillwater Sr HS; Stillwater, OK; (3); Mu Alpha Theta; Spanish Clb; Hon Roll; NHS.

BURDEN, ALLISON; Jenks HS; Broken Arrow, OK; (4); FCA; Key Clb; Jazz Band; Pep Clb; VP Service Clb; Teachers Aide; Ofcr Stu Cncl; Chrldng; Powder Puff Ftbl; Cit Awd; Assisteens; Southern Methodist U.

BURDEN, ERIN; Mustang HS; Yukon, OK; (3); 1/400; French Clb; FBLA; Key Clb; Teachers Aide; High Hon Roll; NHS; Numeros Indvdl Cls Awds; 1st Pl Local & 2nd Pl Reg Sci Fairs; OU.

BURDEN, SONYA; Bowleg Schl; Seminole, OK; (4); Church Yth Grp; Math Clb; Quiz Bowl; Teachers Aide; Rptr Nwsp; Rptr Yrbk; VP Jr Cls; Rep Stu Cncl; L Bsktbl; L Sftbl; Rose ST; Lab Tech.

BURDEN, VANCE; Clinton HS; Clinton, OK; (1); FHA; Hon Roll; Clinton Family Dev Assn.

BURDETT, MARIAH N; Moore HS; Moore, OK; (3); Church Yth Grp; Girl Scts; Office Aide; Spanish Clb; SADD; Teachers Aide; Chorus; Church Choir; Mgr(s); Jr NHS; Attnd Smmr Sci Acad MSC/OSU; Yth Advy Bd Chrch; Psych.

BURDICK, KENDRA; Panama HS; Panama, OK; (4); FHA; German Clb; Quiz Bowl; SADD; Nwsp; Yrbk; Cit Awd; High Hon Roll; Hon Roll; NHS; FHA Rprtr; Phy Ther.

BURGE, KRISTI; Ardmore HS; Ardmore, OK; (4); 2/170; Church Yth Grp; FCA; Pres Mu Alpha Theta; Science Clb; Rep Stu Cncl; Co-Ed Chrldng; Pres NHS; Prfct Atten Awd; Sal; Leaflets Study Clb VP; SE OK St Univ; Elem Ed.

BURGE, MICAH; Crowder Schl; Blocker, OK; (2); Natl FFA Org; Var Bsbl; Var Bsktbl; Hon Roll; NHS; Prfct Atten Awd; OK Hnr Soc.

BURGER, ANGILEE; Broken Arrow Sr HS; Broken Arrow, OK; (3); Varsity Clb; Ed Yrbk; Var L Bsktbl; Var L Chrldng; Var L Sftbl; Var L Trk; Var L Vllybl; High Hon Roll; Sec NHS; Prfct Atten Awd; Yth Grp; Kayettes; JUCO; Grphc Dsgn.

BURGESS, BECKY; Berryhill Jr HS; Tulsa, OK; (1); Church Yth Grp; FCA; FHA; Spanish Clb; Rep Soph Cls; Chrldng; Gym; Powder Puff Ftbl; Sftbl; Trk; Dncng; Serteens.

BURGESS, JENNIFER L; Oilton HS; Jennings, OK; (2); Church Yth Grp; Natl FFA Org; Hon Roll; Hnr Soc; Accntg.

BURGESS, JESSICA D; Antlers Sr HS; Antlers, OK; (2); Church Yth Grp; FBLA; Yrbk; Rptr Frsh Cls; Sec Soph Cls; Tennis; Hon Roll; Jr NHS; Homcmng Attendant; BAD Mem; SE OK ST Univ.

BURGESS, MANDY; Berryhill Jr HS; Tulsa, OK; (4); 1/51; Treas FBLA; Sec FHA; Pres Mu Alpha Theta; VP Spanish Clb; Band; School Play; Sec Treas Soph Cls; Sec Pres Stu Cncl; Var Capt Chrldng; Sal; Bus Admin.

BURGESS, MARLA; Southeast HS; Oklahoma City, OK; (4); 1/75; Church Yth Grp; Cmnty Wkr; FCA; SADD; Ed Yrbk; High Hon Roll; NHS; Val; Art Clb; Office Aide; PTSA; Natl Voc Tech Hnr Soc; Peer Mediatr; OK ST U; Hlth.

BURGESS, NICOLE; Sharon Mutual Jr Sr HS; Vici, OK; (4); 2/21; Church Yth Grp; FCA; Pres FBLA; Hist FHA; HOBY; Letterman Clb; L Bsbl; L Chrldng; Hon Roll; Sal; OK ST U; Bus Admin.

BURGESS, STACEY; East Central HS; Tulsa, OK; (4); 3/209; Church Yth Grp; FCA; HOBY; Red Cross Aide; Spanish Clb; Treas Stu Cncl; High Hon Roll; NHS; Drug Free Yth Pres; Yth Vol; Crdnls For Chrst.

BURGESS, STEPHANIE; Carl Albert HS; Midwest City, OK; (4); 1/239; FCA; Key Clb; Rep Stu Cncl; Capt Chrldng; Capt Trk; Hon Roll; NHS; Pres Acad Fit Awd; St Schlr; Val; Bst Female Chrldr In Natn; Ftbl Hmcmng Prncss; U Of OK; Zoolgy.

BURGESS, TAMMY L; Caddo HS; Durant, OK; (3); FHA; Drill Tm; School Play; Bsktbl; Sftbl; Hon Roll; SOSU; Psych.

BURGESS, TESSA; Boswell Sr HS; Boswell, OK; (1); 3/30; Church Yth Grp; Pres Frsh Cls; High Hon Roll; NHS; Optometrist.

BURHALTER, ELLA; Lone Grove HS; Lone Grove, OK; (4); Key Clb; Math Clb; Math Tm; Natl Beta Clb; VP Natl FFA Org; Office Aide; Quiz Bowl; Science Clb; Band; Sec Jr Cls; Intl Sci & Engrng Fair 4 Yrs; OSU; Envrnmntl Hlth.

BURK, BILLY C; Catoosa HS; Tulsa, OK; (3); 2/150; Boy Scts; Church Yth Grp; FCA; Pres French Clb; FBLA; Rptr Nwsp; Ed Yrbk; Ofcr Stu Cncl; Treas NHS; Debate Tm; OK Hnrs Soc; Cmptr Sci.

BURK, CANDICE A; Geronimo Jr Sr HS; Geronimo, OK; (3); Church Yth Grp; FHA; Math Clb; Natl FFA Org; Office Aide; Science Clb; Church Choir; Sec Jr Cls; High Hon Roll; Hon Roll; Cameron U-Lawton KS.

BURK, JOHN W; Frontier Public Schl; Marland, OK; (3); 3/30; Cmnty Wkr; 4-H; French Clb; Treas Jr Cls; Var L Bsktbl; Cit Awd; High Hon Roll; Hon Roll; NHS; Var Trk; OK St Hnr Soc; Outstdng Algegra & Eng Stu.

BURK, RONNY A; Geronimo Jr Sr HS; Lawton, OK; (3); Math Clb; Natl FFA Org; Ofcr Jr Cls; Ofcr Stu Cncl; Var Bsktbl; Hon Roll; Univ O Tulsa.

BURK, TRACY; Collinsville HS; Collinsville, OK; (3); Natl FFA Org; Hon Roll; NHS; FFA Chptr Rprtr 94-95, 95-96; OSU; Ag.

BURKE, AMANDA; Edmond North HS; Edmond, OK; (1); 55/484; Cmnty Wkr; Spanish Clb; Sec Acpl Chr; Chrldng; 1st Tremaine Natl Dance Cmptn; Fnlst LA Underground Dance Schlrshp; 1st LA Danceforce Cmptn; OK ST U; Law.

BURKE, CHRISTINA L; Wilson HS; Wilson, OK; (2); Church Yth Grp; FCA; Natl Beta Clb; Teachers Aide; Bsktbl; High Hon Roll; Hon Roll; Prfct Atten Awd.

BURKE, KEELY K; Bishop Mcguinness HS; Oklahoma City, OK; (3); 38/140; Art Clb; Church Yth Grp; Drama Clb; FCA; Pep Clb; Pres Spanish Clb; Varsity Clb; Rep Sr Cls; Ofcr Stu Cncl; JV Bsktbl; Piano.

BURKE, SUMMER; Canadian Schl; Eufaula, OK; (2); 1/30; Church Yth Grp; 4-H; Quiz Bowl; Scholastic Bowl; VP Frsh Cls; VP Soph Cls; Var L Bsktbl; Var L Sftbl; 4-H Awd; High Hon Roll; OK Hnr Soc; U Of OK; Ansthtst.

BURKETT, BRIDGET A; East Central HS; Tulsa, OK; (3); Girl Scts; Key Clb; Mrchg Band; School Play; Yrbk; Hon Roll; NHS; NHS VP; Jrnlsm.

BURKETT, NICHOLAS C; Edmond Memorial HS; Edmond, OK; (2); Spanish Clb; Ofcr Stu Cncl; JV Bsbl; Hon Roll; U Of OK; Dentistry.

BURKETT, TRAVIS D; Drumright HS; Drumright, OK; (1); 1/80; FCA; Quiz Bowl; VP Frsh Cls; JV Bsktbl; Var Ftbl; Var Socr; High Hon Roll; Jr NHS; Pres Acad Fit Awd; St Schlr.

BURKHART, DAVID M; Del City HS; Oklahoma City, OK; (2); School Play; Trk; Wrstlng; Hon Roll; All Star Cast Awd Regnl Spch Trnmnt; OK Univ.

BURKHART, JAMIE; Madill HS; Madill, OK; (2); Church Yth Grp; Chorus; School Musical; School Play; Show Choir; HS Boys Quartet; All-St Bapt Yth Choir; OK Bapt Univ; Music; Minister.

BURKHART, JOLEEN L; Enid Sr HS; Enid, OK; (2); 146/463; NFL; Speech Tm; Chorus; School Musical; School Play; Stage Crew; Nwsp; Ofcr Frsh Cls; Hon Roll; Jr NHS; Horseback Riding; Pleasure Barrel Racing; Northwestern Ok ST; Vet.

BURKHART, NICKOLETT; Union Intermediate HS; Tulsa, OK; (2); 118/800; Hosp Aide; Hon Roll; Jr NHS; Pres Schlr; Bus/Adv.

BURKHART, WENDY M; Choctaw HS; Choctaw, OK; (4); Treas FBLA; Rptr Frsh Cls; Pom Pon; Hon Roll; Jr NHS; Swmmng; Tennis; Rose ST.

BURKS, KELEA T; Enid Sr HS; Enid, OK; (2); #137 in class; Church Yth Grp; ROTC; Spanish Clb; Orch; Mgr Bsktbl; Hon Roll; NHS.

BURKS, MINDY; Oklahoma Christian Schl; Edmond, OK; (2); Church Yth Grp; Cmnty Wkr; FCA; GAA; Pep Clb; Spanish Clb; Church Choir; Rep Frsh Cls; Pres Soph Cls; Rep Stu Cncl; Page To OK St Senate; Vol OK Spec Olympcs; Med.

BURKS, RANDA; Broken Bow HS; Broken Bow, OK; (3); 3/150; Cmnty Wkr; Sec Drama Clb; FCA; School Musical; Bsktbl; Sftbl; Trk; NHS; Sec Science Clb; Speech Tm; OK ST U; Bus Law.

BURKS, RONDA; Broken Bow HS; Broken Bow, OK; (3); Drama Clb; FCA; Science Clb; Speech Tm; School Play; Bsktbl; Sftbl; Trk; Hon Roll; NHS; Corp Law.

BURLEIGH, AKILAH; Casady Schl; Oklahoma City, OK; (4); Art Clb; Sec Church Yth Grp; VP Dance Clb; HOBY; Intnl Clb; Pep Clb; Spanish Clb; Lit Mag; Hon Roll; Chrch Yth Usher Brd VP & Secy; Dance Co & Tchr; U Of OK.

BURLESON, JORDON L; Edmond Santa Fe HS; Edmond, OK; (2); Church Yth Grp; FHA; Key Clb; Latin Clb; Scholastic Bowl; Spanish Clb; World His Hnrs Awd; Acad Ltr; Archaeology; OK Univ.

BURLIE, JUSTIN A; Wakita Schl; Wakita, OK; (1); FHA; Band; Mrchg Band; Pep Band; Stage Crew; Video Tech Bsktbl Games; Comm.

BURNESS, JESSIE C; Bartlesville Sr HS; Bartlesville, OK; (3); 1/493; Cmnty Wkr; French Clb; Bsktbl; Socr; High Hon Roll; NHS; Rtry Stdnt Mo; Med.

BURNETT, ALYSSA A; Carl Albert HS; Midwest City, OK; (2); 27/270; Pres Art Clb; French Clb; Girl Scts; Hosp Aide; Library Aide; Science Clb; School Play; Cit Awd; NHS; Dept Awd Cmmnctns/Drm/Phys Sci/Amer His; OCAST Sci/Girl Sct Slvr Awds; Pharm.

BURNETT, BRANDY; Oktana HS; Oktaha, OK; (4); 8/43; Natl FFA Org; Spanish Clb; SADD; VICA; Chorus; Yrbk; Sec Soph Cls; High Hon Roll; NHS; Pres Schlr; HOSA Lcl Sec; Span Excel Awd; Connors St Col; RN.

BURNETT, JAKE R; Owasso Sr HS; Owasso, OK; (2); Church Yth Grp; FCA; Letterman Clb; JV Bsbl; Var Bsktbl; High Hon Roll; Stdnt Of Mnth; Top Stdnt Sci; Top Stdnt Eco Hlth Gym.

BURNETT, JOHN C; Union Sr HS; Tulsa, OK; (3); 16/740; Boy Scts; Church Yth Grp; FCA; Pres Math Clb; Math Tm; Spanish Clb; Varsity Clb; JV Var Bsbl; High Hon Roll; Hon Roll; Chem Engrng.

BURNETT, KATHRYN S; B T Washington HS; Tulsa, OK; (4); 26/262; Church Yth Grp; Drama Clb; Spanish Clb; Teachers Aide; Church Choir; Var Chrldng; NHS; OK ST Univ; Elem Ed.

BURNETT, LORA; Mc Loud HS; Mc Loud, OK; (3); Pres FTA; High Hon Roll; NHS; Arthurian Order Of Avalon; Engl Tchr.

BURNETT, MATTHEW D; Luther HS; Luther, OK; (3); Scholastic Bowl; SADD; Band; Mrchg Band; Pep Band; School Musical; School Play; Stage Crew; JV Var Ftbl; Var Trk; Envrnmntl Clb; Arch Engr.

BURNETT, ROBYN M; Claremore Sr HS; Claremore, OK; (3); 66/268; Church Yth Grp; Cmnty Wkr; FCA; GAA; SADD; Varsity Clb; JV Var Bsktbl; JV Var Sftbl; Cit Awd; Hon Roll; Hnrbl Mtn Bsktbl; Explrs Grp Clrmr Reg Med Ctr; PT.

BURNETT, SHAWNA R; Hydro Jr Sr HS; Hydro, OK; (3); 6/24; Church Yth Grp; Drama Clb; FHA; Spanish Clb; Church Choir; School Musical; School Play; Stage Crew; Rep Stu Cncl; SW OK St Univ.

BURNETT, WESLEY; Kingston HS; Kingston, OK; (3); 1/75; Church Yth Grp; FCA; Bsktbl; Golf; High Hon Roll; Hon Roll; NHS; Prfct Atten Awd.

BURNEY, BRIAN; Moore HS; Moore, OK; (2); 32/500; Band; Church Choir; Mrchg Band; High Hon Roll; Jr NHS; Bands Of America SE Regnls; Solo/Ensmble Music Cont; Med.

BURNHAM, J RUSSELL; Stillwater Jr HS; Stillwater, OK; (1); Church Yth Grp; Cmnty Wkr; Hosp Aide; Library Aide; VP Frsh Cls; Rep Soph Cls; Intrml Bsbl; Var Bsktbl; High Hon Roll; Pres Acad Fit Awd; YMCA Vol; Explrng Optns.

BURNS, AMANDA M; Healdton HS; Wilson, OK; (2); 4-H; Quiz Bowl; Band; Jazz Band; Mrchg Band; High Hon Roll; Pres Acad Fit Awd; Drama Clb; Speech Tm; Chorus; Tutor In Algebra I; OSSM Semi Fnlst; Karate; Zoologist.

BURNS, AMANDA V; Bixby Sr HS; Bixby, OK; (1); 1/230; Church Yth Grp; Hon Roll; Pres Acad Fit Awd; Baylor; Medicine.

BURNS, AMY; Tonkawa Jr Sr HS; Tonkawa, OK; (3); Am Leg Aux Girls St; Pres Church Yth Grp; FCA; GAA; Teachers Aide; Yrbk; VP Soph Cls; Bsktbl; Sftbl; High Hon Roll; Delg Natl Stu Cncl Conv; U Of OK; Phys Thrpy.

BURNS, ASHLEY; Claremore Sr HS; Claremore, OK; (2); Spanish Clb; Teachers Aide; Var Chrldng; High Hon Roll; Ntl Merit Schol; Northeastern ST; Optometry.

BURNS, BAYLEY A; Edmond Memorial HS; Edmond, OK; (2); Church Yth Grp; FCA; JV Bsktbl; Var Sftbl.

BURNS, BRANDON K; Geary Jr Sr HS; Geary, OK; (2); Natl Beta Clb; Natl FFA Org; Stage Crew; Wt Lftg; JETS Awd; NHS; Sal.

BURNS, BROOKE A; Cushing HS; Cushing, OK; (1); Spanish Clb; Bsktbl; Chrldng; Sftbl; High Hon Roll; Hon Roll.

BURNS, CARRIE E; Calvin Public Schl; Calvin, OK; (3); FHA; VP Frsh Cls; JV Bsktbl; JV Sftbl; Upward Bound Pgm; Bus.

BURNS, COURTNEY M; El Reno Sr HS; Calumet, OK; (2); 47/225; 4-H; Natl FFA Org; JV Bsktbl; JV Vllybl; High Hon Roll; Hon Roll; Close Up; Ag Bus.

BURNS, DAVID J; Altus Sr HS; Altus, OK; (3); Am Leg Boys St; Model UN; Office Aide; Ofcr Jr Cls; Treas Stu Cncl; Var Capt Ftbl; Powder Puff Ftbl; L Trk; Wt Lftg; Hon Roll; Acad All Star; Supt Hnr Roll; OK ST; Law.

BURNS, HALEE; Claremore Sr HS; Claremore, OK; (1); JV Chrldng; JV Score Keeper; Northeastern ST U; Nws Rptr.

BURNS, JOHN W; Shawnee Sr HS; Shawnee, OK; (2); Latin Clb; Letterman Clb; Varsity Clb; Ftbl; Socr; Hon Roll.

BURNS, JOSHUA; Edmond Memorial HS; Edmond, OK; (3); #1 in class; Pres Church Yth Grp; Debate Tm; Pres German Clb; HOBY; VP Mu Alpha Theta; VP NFL; Co-Capt Quiz Bowl; Co-Capt Scholastic Bowl; Band; Mrchg Band; Poly Sci.

BURNS, LAUREN E; West Middle HS; Norman, OK; (1); Church Yth Grp; Drama Clb; Thesps; Chorus; Church Choir; Hon Roll; Child Care.

BURNS, MATHEW; Midwest City HS; Del City, OK; (4); Church Yth Grp; DECA; FHA; Hon Roll; NHS; OK ST U.

BURNS, MICHEAL W; Cascia Hall Prep School; Tulsa, OK; (3); Art Clb; Boy Scts; Computer Clb; Library Aide; Math Clb; Math Tm; Pep Clb; Teachers Aide; Pep Band; School Musical; Co-Sysop Cmptr Bulletin Bd Sys; Art Achvmt Awds OK ST Fair; 1st Plc Math Cts Tulsa Diocese; Cmptr Sci.

BURNS, SCOTT; Jenks HS; Tulsa, OK; (4); 1/540; Church Yth Grp; Mu Alpha Theta; Treas Science Clb; Orch; Pres NHS; Ntl Merit Schol; Val; Acad Tm Cap; Mem Of OK All Str Dlgtn To Pnsnic Acad Chalng; Tlsa Yth Symph Violst; OK ST U; Med Dr.

BURNSED, RACHEL M; Fletcher Jr Sr HS; Fletcher, OK; (3); 1/28; Church Yth Grp; 4-H; FHA; Chorus; Church Choir; Var 4-H Awd; High Hon Roll; Prfct Atten Awd; Val; TSA VP & Treas; Acad Tm Capt & 1st Pl Dist, Conf & Rgn; Schubert Music Fstvl & NFMF Super Rtngs; OK ST U; Vet.

BURNSIDE, JASON G; Mc Alester HS; Mcalester, OK; (2); 5/200; Church Yth Grp; High Hon Roll; Hon Roll; NHS; Love Old Cars & Trucks.

BURPO, LACI; Kingfisher HS; Kingfisher, OK; (2); 1/96; Church Yth Grp; FCA; Spanish Clb; Hon Roll; Pres Acad Fit Awd; OK Hnr Soc; Pdtrcs.

BURPO, SHANE H; Oilton HS; Oilton, OK; (2); JV Var Bsbl; Hon Roll.

BURRESS, AMBER; Pawhuska HS; Pawhuska, OK; (3); FBLA; Office Aide; Band; Mrchg Band; Pep Band; Hon Roll; NHS.

BURRIGHT, JOHN W; Edmond North HS; Edmond, OK; (4); 126/330; Church Yth Grp; Cmnty Wkr; FCA; Var Capt Wrstlng; FFA; Jr Rotarian; Adams ST Coll; Bus.

BURRIS, ALESHA R; Webbers Falls Schl; Webbers Falls, OK; (3); Church Yth Grp; 4-H; Spanish Clb; Bsktbl; Score Keeper; Sftbl; Vllybl; Hon Roll; Prfct Atten Awd; Nrsing.

BURRIS, COREY; Fairland Jr Sr HS; Fairland, OK; (4); 3/40; FHA; Red Cross Aide; Jazz Band; Sec Frsh Cls; Var Bsbl; Var Capt Ftbl; Var Wt Lftg; High Hon Roll; Hon Roll; NHS; NEO A&M Coll; Brdcstng.

BURRIS, CORINNE L; American HS; Oklahoma City, OK; (3); DECA; Hon Roll; Jr NHS; Cit Awd; Fsh Inst Of Dsgn Mrch; Fsh Mrch.

BURRIS, JENNIFER; Mc Loud HS; Mc Loud, OK; (4); 16/108; Church Yth Grp; 4-H; FBLA; FHA; FTA; Library Aide; Natl FFA Org; 4-H Awd; High Hon Roll; Hon Roll; Stu Cncld; OK Hnr Soc; FFA; UCO; Nrs.

BURRIS, KATHRYN L; Union Intermediate HS; Tulsa, OK; (2); FBLA; Key Clb; Spanish Clb; Swmmng; Cit Awd; High Hon Roll; Hon Roll; Jr NHS; Pres Acad Fit Awd; USS Swim Tm 8 Yrs; Sci/Bio.

BURRIS, LORI; Plainview HS; Ardmore, OK; (1); Church Yth Grp; Rep Stu Cncl; JV Chrldng; Var Trk; Hon Roll; Jr NHS; UCO; Comp Sci.

BURRIS, MARY E; Union Intermediate HS; Tulsa, OK; (2); FBLA; Spanish Clb; Swmmng; Cit Awd; Gov Hon Prg Awd; High Hon Roll; Hon Roll; Jr NHS; NHS; Pres Acad Fit Awd; Bus Stdnt Of Yr; Marine Bio.

BURRIS, MATTHEW D; Okmulgee HS; Okmulgee, OK; (2); Band; Mrchg Band; Pep Band.

BURRIS, MELISSA C; Olive Jr Sr HS; Jennings, OK; (2); Church Yth Grp; Drama Clb; Natl FFA Org; NFL; Scholastic Bowl; Speech Tm; Thesps; Chorus; VP Soph Cls; Hon Roll; OK ST U.

BURRIS, RAINESHA; Douglass HS; Oklahoma City, OK; (3); FBLA; Orch; Ed Yrbk; VP Frsh Cls; Pres Jr Cls; VP Stu Cncl; Hon Roll; Pride; Close Up; I Dare You Ldrshp Awd; Pre Law.

BURROUGHS, BRENDA C; Harrah HS; Harrah, OK; (1); 78/178; Church Yth Grp; FCA; FHA; Cit Awd; Hon Roll; Tech Ed Assn; Bus Tech; Frnch I; Elem Tchr.

BURROUGHS, MATTHEW; Union Intermediate HS; Tulsa, OK; (2); 17/800; Key Clb; Spanish Clb; Teachers Aide; Rep Stu Cncl; Var Tennis; High Hon Roll; NHS; Tulsa Sr Leag Bsbl All Star Tm 93-95; Acad Tm.

BURROW, JUSTIN; Mustang HS; Oklahoma City, OK; (3); Church Yth Grp; FCA; Church Choir; Pres Stu Cncl; Var Crs Cntry; Var Golf; Hon Roll; OK St Inventors Cmptn 1st Pl; US Champion Trampoline; OSU; Bus Mgmt; Prof Golf.

BURROWS, DEREK R; Northeast HS; Oklahoma City, OK; (3); 37/480; Church Yth Grp; Computer Clb; Drama Clb; Quiz Bowl; ROTC; Band; Variety Show; Socr; Hon Roll.

BURT, BRANDON W; Christian Heritage Acad; Oklahoma City, OK; (2); Church Yth Grp; Chorus; Var Bsbl; JV Bsktbl; JV Ftbl; JV Golf; JV Wt Lftg; Hon Roll; Bus.

BURTON, AMBER; Woodward HS; Woodward, OK; (2); German Clb; Model UN; Quiz Bowl; Speech Tm; School Play; French Hon Soc; Hon Roll.

BURTON, ANGIE D; Madill HS; Madill, OK; (2); Art Clb; Church Yth Grp; FCA; FBLA; FHA; Color Guard; Drill Tm; Hon Roll; NHS; Ntl Merit Ltr; Campfire Boys/Girls; Prlmntry Prcdr Team; Southeastern; Tchr.

BURTON, CRYSTAL; Woodward HS; Woodward, OK; (3); Church Yth Grp; German Clb; Letterman Clb; Model UN; Quiz Bowl; Scholastic Bowl; Acpl Chr; Chorus; Church Choir; School Musical; Woodward Arts Theater Productions; OK ST Univ; Eng Lit.

BURTON, KASEY; Waynoka HS; Waynoka, OK; (3); FCA; FHA; HOBY; Pep Clb; Quiz Bowl; Scholastic Bowl; Ofcr Soph Cls; Sftbl; Trk; Hon Roll; Tae Kwon Do; U Of OK; Drama.

BURTON, KRIS A; Edmond North HS; Edmond, OK; (2); 29/420; Boy Scts; Church Yth Grp; Cmnty Wkr; Pres ROTC; Band; Color Guard; Mrchg Band; Orch; JV L Crs Cntry; Var L Trk; ROTC Sharpest Cadet, Military Order Of World Wars Medal & Prin Awd; Eagle Sct; Us Coast Guard Acad; Marine Sci.

BURTON, KRIS D; Hugo HS; Hugo, OK; (3); Var Ftbl.

BURTON, KRISTY; Shawnee Sr HS; Shawnee, OK; (3); 13/282; Church Yth Grp; FCA; Treas French Clb; Pep Clb; Scholastic Bowl; High Hon Roll; Big Brothers/Big Sisters; Tri-Hi-Y; Dance 11 Yrs; OU; Acctng.

BURTON, NATHAN K; South Intermediate HS; Broken Arrow, OK; (1); Church Yth Grp; Cmnty Wkr; Acpl Chr; Band; Chorus; Church Choir; Mrchg Band; Pep Band; Madrigal Choir; OK Free Wheel 96; Appalachia Svc Prjct 96; U Of CO Boulder; Archaeolgy.

BUSBY, EVAN; Okemah HS; Okemah, OK; (3); Key Clb; Science Clb; SADD; Bsktbl; Hon Roll; OK ST U; Vet.

BUSBY, SHAWN R; Mannford HS; Mannford, OK; (3); FCA; Ftbl; Wt Lftg; Wrstlng; OK St Univ; Jrnlsm.

BUSBY, TROY E; Okemah HS; Okemah, OK; (3); 8/66; Am Leg Boys St; Key Clb; Science Clb; SADD; Bsktbl; Hon Roll; NHS; OK ST Univ; Vet.

BUSCH, CHRISTINA; Metro Christian Acad; Tulsa, OK; (4); 10/61; Church Yth Grp; Pep Clb; Chorus; School Musical; Rep Stu Cncl; Var Capt Chrldng; NHS; Stu Tchr; Oral Roberts Univ; Mus Tchr.

BUSCH, JENNIFER; Wellston Schl; Wellston, OK; (1); Church Yth Grp; FHA; Spanish Clb; JV Bsktbl; Hon Roll; Jr NHS; Johnson & Wales; Culinary Chef.

BUSCHE, AMBER; Ada HS; Ada, OK; (4); 7/162; Am Leg Aux Girls St; Hosp Aide; Mu Alpha Theta; VP Spanish Clb; Sec Pres Chorus; Swing Chorus; High Hon Roll; Sec NHS; Spanish NHS; Interact VP, Pres; Allst Chorus 95; U Of IL; Math.

BUSCHE, CHRIS M; Deer Creek HS; Edmond, OK; (2); Science Clb; Spanish Clb; Art Cls Awd; Phtgrphy; U Of Cntrl OK; Arch/Lndscpng.

BUSE, JENNIFER; Mt St Marys HS; Oklahoma City, OK; (4); 3/64; Cmnty Wkr; JA; Sec Key Clb; Pep Clb; Service Clb; SADD; Teachers Aide; JV Var Vllybl; Intrml Wt Lftg; Cit Awd; Outstdng Sr Grl; Benedictine Coll; Sclgy/Span.

BUSER, ALICIA; Senior HS; Chickasha, OK; (2); Church Yth Grp; FCA; Spanish Clb; SADD; Swing Chorus; Rep Jr Cls; Var Chrldng; Socr; Jr NHS.

BUSEY, THOMAS; Ft Gibson HS; Fort Gibson, OK; (1); Hosp Aide; Intrml Bsktbl; Hon Roll; NHS; Tae Kwn Do; Acadmc Tm.

BUSH, BRIAN; Altus Sr HS; Altus, OK; (4); 14/239; Am Leg Boys St; Church Yth Grp; FCA; Natl FFA Org; School Musical; Pres Stu Cncl; Jr NHS; NHS; Model UN; Office Aide; US Sen Yth Pgm; Jackson Cty Yng Rep Pres; Harding U; Pltcl Sci.

BUSH, LYNZI J; Ardmore HS; Ardmore, OK; (3); 41/167; Computer Clb; DECA; Drama Clb; Math Clb; Mu Alpha Theta; Science Clb; Spanish Clb; Drill Tm; High Hon Roll; Ardmore Ltl Theatre; Denver Mission Trip; Financial Inst; OK ST U.

BUSH, RYAN P; Charles Page HS; Sand Springs, OK; (3); 113/389; Church Yth Grp; Math Tm; Varsity Clb; Socr; Cit Awd; Hon Roll; Prfct Atten Awd; OU; Phy Thrpst.

BUSHNELL, AMANDA; Pond Creek-Hunter Schl; Hunter, OK; (2); FCA; GAA; Yrbk; L Bsktbl; L Crs Cntry; L Trk; Hon Roll; NHS; OK ST Univ; Med Field.

BUSS, BRITTON; Seminole Jr Sr HS; Seminole, OK; (3); Church Yth Grp; FCA; Math Clb; Church Choir; Var Tennis; Hon Roll; NHS.

BUSSE, BRIAN M; Putnam City North HS; Oklahoma City, OK; (2); NHS; OSU Stillwater; Tchr; Coach.

BUSSE, DONALD; Stigler HS; Stigler, OK; (4); 8/73; Am Leg Boys St; Boy Scts; Band; Mrchg Band; Ftbl; Wt Lftg; High Hon Roll; Hon Roll; Prfct Atten Awd; Connor ST Coll; Comp Sci.

BUSSEY, JEREMY B; Erick Jr Sr HS; Erick, OK; (4); 1/20; Am Leg Boys St; Church Yth Grp; Scholastic Bowl; Spanish Clb; VP Frsh Cls; VP Soph Cls; Pres Jr Cls; Pres Sr Cls; Ofcr Bsbl; Bsktbl; S W OK Sayre; Scndry Sci Ed.

BUTCHER, JENNIFER J; Pauls Valley HS; Pauls Valley, OK; (3); Church Yth Grp; FHA; Speech Tm; Chorus; Hon Roll.

BUTCHER, LINDSAY J; West Middle HS; Norman, OK; (1); Dance Clb; Hon Roll; All-Star Comp Pom Natl ASC Champs; Duke Univ; Rdlgst.

BUTCHER, MELODY; Collinsville HS; Collinsville, OK; (4); 5/105; Pres Church Yth Grp; FCA; Rptr Chorus; Rep Jr Cls; Sec Sr Cls; Sec Stu Cncl; Capt Var Chrldng; Capt Var Vllybl; NHS; Ntl Merit Ltr; All St Vlybl Plyr; Outfrnt IV Ldrshp Pgm; Untd Way Vol; U OK; Optmtry.

BUTCHER, SCOTT L; Vinita HS; Vinita, OK; (2); Debate Tm; NFL; Spanish Clb; Speech Tm; Chorus; Co-Ed Yrbk; Rptr Stu Cncl; Trk; Hon Roll; NHS; Tsa-La-Gi Trail Of Tears Awd Excl Acad/Music; Lawyer.

BUTHMAN, GUS H; Enid Sr HS; Enid, OK; (2); Boy Scts; Cmnty Wkr; Drama Clb.

BUTLER, CHEVONNE; Chisholm Sr HS; Enid, OK; (1); Church Yth Grp; Band; Drill Tm; Mrchg Band; Hon Roll; NHS; Modeling; Piano Perfs & Recitals; OK Chrstn U; Med.

BUTLER, CLARENCE A; U S Grant HS; Oklahoma City, OK; (1).

BUTLER, COLBY; Fox Sr HS; Fox, OK; (4); 4/20; Computer Clb; Natl FFA Org; Office Aide; Quiz Bowl; Science Clb; Varsity Clb; Pres Frsh Cls; Ofcr Bsbl; Ftbl; Wt Lftg; Chem Awd; ECU; Med.

BUTLER JR, EVERTT A; Wilson HS; Wilson, OK; (4); 12/29; German Clb; Quiz Bowl; Band; Mrchg Band; Pep Band; Yrbk; Cit Awd; High Hon Roll; Hon Roll; Presdntl Ed Awd; Masonic Lodge Schlsp; Southeastern OK ST Univ.

BUTLER, GIL T; Elgin HS; Cyril, OK; (2); Church Yth Grp; Natl FFA Org; Teachers Aide; Band; Mrchg Band; Pep Band; Rep Frsh Cls; Hon Roll; FFA Prfcncy Awd Soil/Water Mgmt 2 Yrs/Cereal Grain Prdctn; OK ST Univ; Agri-Bus.

BUTLER, GREG; Metro Christian Acad; Broken Arrow, OK; (4); Church Yth Grp; Key Clb; Spanish Clb; Teachers Aide; Var Capt Golf; High Hon Roll; Hon Roll; U OK; Bus.

BUTLER, JEFFERY; Carnegie HS; Carnegie, OK; (4); 8/48; Natl FFA Org; Office Aide; Teachers Aide; High Hon Roll; Hon Roll; Prfct Atten Awd; Pres Acad Fit Awd; Rodeo Teamroper; SWOSU; Bus.

BUTLER, JENNIFER S; Will Rogers HS; Tulsa, OK; (2); Church Yth Grp; Debate Tm; Drama Clb; Hosp Aide; School Play; Ofcr Frsh Cls; Ofcr Soph Cls; Hon Roll; Queen 9th Grd; Psych.

BUTLER, JUNE A; East Central HS; Tulsa, OK; (3); FCA; French Clb; Key Clb; Acpl Chr; Chorus; Trk; Hon Roll; Kiwanis Awd; NHS; VIP; Jr Cls Bd; You Me Rtrt; Law.

BUTLER, KEMILY C; Northeast HS; Oklahoma City, OK; (2); FBLA; Chorus; JV Var Bsktbl; JV Trk; High Hon Roll; Hon Roll; U Of Cntrl OK; Phy Thrpst.

BUTLER, KERI; Jones HS; Jones, OK; (4); Church Yth Grp; FCA; FBLA; FHA; VP Key Clb; Office Aide; Science Clb; VP Jr Cls; Pres Stu Cncl; Capt Bsktbl; OK ST U; Mrktg.

BUTLER, KIMBERLY A; Bishop Kelley HS; Tulsa, OK; (2); Church Yth Grp; Cmnty Wkr; Red Cross Aide; Service Clb; Chorus; School Musical; Rep Soph Cls; High Hon Roll; Hon Roll; Env Club; Smmr Arts; Tulsa Yth Ct; Outfrnt Ldrshp Prog; Save The Manatee Club; Grnpc.

BUTLER, KRISTEN; Nathan Hale HS; Tulsa, OK; (1); FBLA; Hosp Aide; VP Frsh Cls; JV Chrldng; Hon Roll.

BUTLER, KRISTI; Millwood HS; Oklahoma City, OK; (3); Office Aide; High Hon Roll; Hon Roll; Ntl Merit Ltr; Central ST U; Bus.

BUTLER, MELODY B; Stigler HS; Stigler, OK; (3); Drama Clb; Pep Clb; Speech Tm; SADD; Chorus; Church Choir; School Play; Hon Roll; Prfct Atten Awd; Competetive Choral Mem; Northeastern Univ; Elem Ed.

BUTLER, MICHAEL; Moore HS; Oklahoma City, OK; (4); 13/525; Church Yth Grp; Pres FCA; Red Cross Aide; Spanish Clb; Rep Stu Cncl; Intrml JV Bsktbl; Rptr NHS; Val; Masonic Awd; Jr Announcer; OK Baptist U; Ministry.

BUTLER, MICHELE S; Walters HS; Randlett, OK; (1); FHA; Letterman Clb; Spanish Clb; Sftbl; Hon Roll; NHS.

BUTLER, SCOTT B; Oklahoma Sch Of Science & Math; Tonkawa, OK; (3); Boy Scts; Letterman Clb; Quiz Bowl; Scholastic Bowl; Varsity Clb; JV Bsbl; Var L Ftbl; Var L Trk; Var L Wrstlng; High Hon Roll; Eagle Sct; US Air Force Acad; Arntcl Engr.

BUTLER, ZACHARY C; West Middle HS; Norman, OK; (2); Boy Scts; Cmnty Wkr; Yrbk; Lit Mag; Cit Awd; High Hon Roll; NHS; Pres Schlr; U Of OK; Eng.

BUTNER, CHRISTINA; Muskogee HS; Muskogee, OK; (3); 3/400; Treas Church Yth Grp; Hosp Aide; HOBY; Key Clb; VP Science Clb; Spanish Clb; Ofcr Soph Cls; Ofcr Jr Cls; Ofcr Stu Cncl; JV Bsktbl.

BUTNER, RHETT; Wewoka HS; Wewoka, OK; (4); 1/51; Am Leg Boys St; Chess Clb; FCA; Quiz Bowl; Science Clb; Ed Nwsp; Bsktbl; Ftbl; NHS; Val; OU; Law.

BUTTRESS, AMANDA J; Tahlequah Jr HS; Tahlequah, OK; (1); Girl Scts; Office Aide; Band; Mrchg Band; VP Frsh Cls; JV Sftbl; Jr NHS; Pres Acad Fit Awd; Northeastern ST Univ; PT.

BUTTRESS, KELLY L; Spiro HS; Spiro, OK; (2); Drama Clb; FBLA; FHA; Teachers Aide; Cit Awd; Outs FHA Mmbr; OK Baptst Univ; Audiolgy.

BUTTS, ADAM; Union Intermediate HS; Tulsa, OK; (2); 136/800; Debate Tm; FCA; Key Clb; Speech Tm; Intrml JV Ftbl; Natl Hnr Soc; Tchr.

BUTTS, RYAN KIRK; Edmond North HS; Edmond, OK; (4); 30/330; Church Yth Grp; Pres FCA; Key Clb; Mu Alpha Theta; Spanish Clb; Rep Stu Cncl; Golf; Trk; NHS; OK Hnr Soc; Bill Nicklas Mem Golf Fdn Adv Bd; Univ OK Pres Ldrshp Cls; U Of OK; Biochem/Premed.

BUTTS, TIFFANY; Cascia Hall Prep School; Tulsa, OK; (3); Hosp Aide; Chorus; School Musical; School Play; Chrldng; Powder Puff Ftbl; Hon Roll; NHS; KU; Arch Engr.

BUXTON, JUSTIN K; Duke Schl; Duke, OK; (3); 4-H; Natl FFA Org; 4-H Awd; SWIM; Lcl/Dist FFA Judging Cntsts; Frmng; OSU; Vet/Ag Tchr.

BUZZARD, SAMUEL R; Duncan HS; Duncan, OK; (2); 101/309; Chorus; JV Bsktbl; JV Trk; Hon Roll; Comm Theatre; Amer Kids; Engr/Jrnlsm.

BUZZARD, SUSAN R; Stilwell HS; Stilwell, OK; (3); Art Clb; Natl Beta Clb; Office Aide; Spanish Clb; Teachers Aide; Orch; Hon Roll; Kiwanis Awd; Drug Free Yth; North Eastern ST Univ; Law.

BYARD, DANIEL J; Moore HS; Oklahoma City, OK; (3); Hosp Aide; Quiz Bowl; Science Clb; Spanish Clb; Rep Stu Cncl; JV Capt Socr; Jr NHS; DECA; NHS; U Of OK; Fisheries Bio.

BYARS, COREY D; Beggs HS; Beggs, OK; (4); 4/49; Church Yth Grp; Computer Clb; Natl FFA Org; Sec Sr Cls; Ofcr Stu Cncl; JV Bsktbl; Var Ftbl; Wt Lftg; Cit Awd; High Hon Roll; Tulsa CC; Engrng.

BYARS, ROSE M; Blair Schl; Blair, OK; (3); Church Yth Grp; 4-H; Natl Beta Clb; Quiz Bowl; L Chrldng; Hon Roll; Pres Acad Fit Awd; Chrch Drama Team.

BYER, MELISSA L; Edmond Memorial HS; Edmond, OK; (3); 54/371; Church Yth Grp; Spanish Clb; Chorus; Church Choir; School Musical; Swing Chorus; Variety Show; High Hon Roll; Hon Roll; NHS; U Cntrl OK; Tchng.

BYERLEY, ASHLEE J; Edmond North HS; Edmond, OK; (2); Church Yth Grp; VP Mu Alpha Theta; Red Cross Aide; Orch; Phtg Nwsp; Phtg Yrbk; Crs Cntry; Socr; Pres Jr NHS; NHS; Srgn.

BYERLY, ALISHA; Holdenville HS; Holdenville, OK; (2); Church Yth Grp; FCA; Chorus; Ofcr Stu Cncl; Chrldng; Trk; Work With Disabled Children.

BYERLY, DEREK W; Tecumseh HS; Tecumseh, OK; (2); 10/140; Scholastic Bowl; JV Var Bsbl; JV Bsktbl; Intrml Vllybl; High Hon Roll; Hon Roll; NHS; Pres Acad Fit Awd; Tecumseh HS Ath Awd/Ltr; Otsdng Stdnt/Ath GPA 4.0; Engr/Prfsnl Bsbl.

BYERS, KAYCIE; Roff HS; Roff, OK; (1); 1/33; Natl Beta Clb; Chorus; Var Bsktbl; Var Sftbl; High Hon Roll; Ntl Sci Merit Awd Nom; Pol Sci.

BYFORD, LORI; Stratford Schl; Stratford, OK; (4); 1/47; VP FHA; Office Aide; Yrbk; Pres Sr Cls; Rep Stu Cncl; Cit Awd; High Hon Roll; Pres Acad Fit Awd; Val; Masonic Lodge Stu Today Awd; Acctng.

BYNUM, AMY M; Ardmore HS; Springer, OK; (3); 10/200; Church Yth Grp; Cmnty Wkr; Dance Clb; Drama Clb; Library Aide; Math Clb; Mu Alpha Theta; Treas Science Clb; Spanish Clb; Teachers Aide; Smmr Med Acad OU Hlth Sci Cntr 96; Med Dr.

BYNUM, CASEY; Jones HS; Jones, OK; (3); 1/80; FCA; Scholastic Bowl; Pres Jr Cls; Var L Bsbl; Var L Bsktbl; Var L Ftbl; High Hon Roll; NHS; Smmr Bsbl; Daily OK Prep Bsbl Ath Of Wk; OK ST Univ.

BYNUM, JASON E; Latta Sr HS; Ada, OK; (2); Boy Scts; Drama Clb; Quiz Bowl; Scholastic Bowl; Speech Tm; Hon Roll; Pres Acad Fit Awd; Rdng/Plyng Drums.

BYNUM, LEZLIE; Tahlequah Sr HS; Park Hill, OK; (4); 67/251; Am Leg Aux Girls St; Church Yth Grp; FCA; GAA; Office Aide; Science Clb; Speech Tm; Church Choir; Rep Frsh Cls; Sec Soph Cls.

BYNUM, MELANIE D; Choctaw HS; Oklahoma City, OK; (3); 53/333; Church Yth Grp; Key Clb; Church Choir; School Play; Stage Crew; Ed Yrbk; Vllybl; High Hon Roll; Hon Roll; Yrbk Excl; Chrstn Hnr Soc; Vlybl Bst Chrstn Att, Sprtsmnshp 94-95; CO Coll; Med.

BYNUM, ROBYN L; Union Intermediate HS; Tulsa, OK; (2); FBLA; Spanish Clb; School Play; Hon Roll; Amer Legion Auxillary; Psycht.

BYRD, JASON; Plainview HS; Ardmore, OK; (2); 7/72; Band; Jazz Band; Mrchg Band; Cit Awd; Hon Roll; NHS; Pres Acad Fit Awd; Univ OK; Dermatlgst.

BYRD, NECIA R; Wagoner Sr HS; Wagoner, OK; (2); Church Yth Grp; FCA; FBLA; Ofcr Frsh Cls; Socr; Sftbl; Hon Roll; NHS; Prfct Atten Awd; Pres Acad Fit Awd; Sprtndnts Hnr Rll; OK ST U; Elem Tchr.

BYRD, STARLYN E; B T Washington HS; Tulsa, OK; (4); Church Yth Grp; Cmnty Wkr; Office Aide; Spanish Clb; Teachers Aide; Rep Jr Cls; Var Chrldng; Alpha Kappa Xinos; Sec Of Afro Amer Socty; U Of AR; Engl.

BYRUM, RACHEL L; Will Rogers HS; Tulsa, OK; (2); Church Yth Grp; Drama Clb; FHA; ROTC; Drill Tm; School Musical; School Play; Sec Jr Cls; Bsktbl; Chrldng; Elem Ed.

BYTE, GARY; Guthrie Sr HS; Guthrie, OK; (4); 1/173; FBLA; Mu Alpha Theta; Quiz Bowl; Band; Mrchg Band; NHS; Val; OSU; Comp Sci.

BYUS, KIMBERLY; Mc Loud HS; Mc Loud, OK; (3); 11/129; Church Yth Grp; FCA; FBLA; Mgr(s); Socr; Hon Roll; NHS; OK Hnr Soc; OK U; Phys Thrpy.

CABANISS, SARAH; Arapaho Schl; Arapaho, OK; (3); 3/30; Church Yth Grp; Pres 4-H; FHA; HOBY; Teachers Aide; Pres Frsh Cls; Pres Soph Cls; Pres Jr Cls; Var Bsktbl; Capt Chrldng; Stu Of Today Awd; Showing Lvstck-Mrkst Lambs; Outstndng Showman Awds; OK ST U; Preschl Educ.

CABELLO, CLAUDIA I; Southeast HS; Oklahoma City, OK; (1); Bus Profs of Am; FBLA; Spanish Clb; Church Choir; UCO; Bus Admin.

CABLE, MATTHEW G; Pauls Valley HS; Pauls Valley, OK; (1); FCA; 4-H; Natl FFA Org; Intrml Bsbl; Intrml Bsktbl; Intrml Wt Lftg; High Hon Roll; Hon Roll; Phi Phi Pi Spirit Clb; OSU; Vet.

CADDELL, KRISTEN N; West Middle HS; Norman, OK; (1); Church Yth Grp; JCL; Latin Clb; Cit Awd; Teen Vol Clb.

CADENHEAD, JILL; Seminole Jr Sr HS; Seminole, OK; (2); Church Yth Grp; FCA; Math Clb; Chrldng; Tennis; High Hon Roll.

CADION, AMANDA S; Bishop Kelley HS; Tulsa, OK; (1); FCA; Pres Latin Clb; Rep Frsh Cls; Rep Stu Cncl; Bsktbl; L Var Sftbl; L Var Trk; Hon Roll; Cmnty Wkr; JV Score Keeper; Cthcr/IF/OF-ASA 16 Undr Metro A Sftbl; Sftbl/Bsktbl Yth Clnc Trnr/Cnslr; Jr Clscl League; Stock Brkr.

CAFFEY, BRENT; Spiro HS; Keota, OK; (4); 12/91; Am Leg Boys St; Art Clb; Math Clb; Natl FFA Org; Quiz Bowl; Spanish Clb; High Hon Roll; NHS; St Schlr; Carl Albert ST Coll.

CAGLE, DONALD B; B T Washington HS; Tulsa, OK; (4); 42/264; French Clb; ROTC; Color Guard; Hon Roll; NHS; Amer Lgn Schlstc Excllnc Awd; Acad Ltr With Bar; U Of OK; Math Tchr.

CAGLE, MANDI J; El Reno Sr HS; El Reno, OK; (3); 74/175; FHA; JA; Library Aide; Natl FFA Org; Office Aide; Teachers Aide; VICA; Cit Awd; Hon Roll; Prfct Atten Awd; Vlybl; Tulsa U; Acctng.

CAHALAN, DAN; Edmond North HS; Edmond, OK; (4); 30/333; Church Yth Grp; French Clb; Treas Math Clb; Treas Mu Alpha Theta; Band; Drm Mjr(t); Jazz Band; Mrchg Band; Orch; Pep Band; OK ST Univ; Elec Engr.

CAHLIK, LINDSAY A; Westmoore HS; Oklahoma City, OK; (2); Church Yth Grp; Drama Clb; German Clb; Church Choir; School Musical; Rep Frsh Cls; Jr NHS; NHS; Pres Acad Fit Awd; Ofcr Stu Cncl; Piano Grd Lvl 5; Natl Guild Of Piano Tchrs/Superior Rtng; OK Christian U Of Sci/Arts.

CAIN, CASSIE D; Duncan HS; Duncan, OK; (2); FBLA; Key Clb; JV Golf; High Hon Roll; Hon Roll; NHS; SADD; OK Univ; Med.

CAIN, DEE DEE; Crowder Schl; Mcalester, OK; (2); Ofcr Soph Cls; Bsktbl; Sftbl; Hon Roll; NHS; OK Hnr Soc; FHA; OK U; Ortho Srgn.

CAIN, KERI; Norman Sr HS; Norman, OK; (3); 1/900; Cmnty Wkr; Debate Tm; HOBY; Mu Alpha Theta; NFL; Cit Awd; Hon Roll; Pres Acad Fit Awd; Church Yth Grp; FCA; Tmrrws Ldrs; Habitat For Hmnty; Cty Litrcy Proj; Hist.

CAIN, RYAN J; Edmond Memorial HS; Edmond, OK; (3).

CAINE, NICHOLE D; Ponca City Sr HS; Ponca City, OK; (3); 101/438; Church Yth Grp; Cmnty Wkr; Dance Clb; Letterman Clb; Spanish Clb; Orch; Hon Roll; Kiwanis Awd.

CAISSIE, BETH; Colcord Schl; Colcord, OK; (3); Church Yth Grp; Band; Nwsp; Rptr Jr Cls; NHS; Ntl Merit Ltr.

CALAHAN, AMIE; Eufaula Sr HS; Eufaula, OK; (4); 19/73; Dance Clb; FBLA; FHA; Math Clb; Office Aide; Teachers Aide; Acpl Chr; Color Guard; Drill Tm; Mrchg Band; East Cntrl U.

CALAWAY, MELISSA; Mt St Marys HS; Oklahoma City, OK; (4); Cmnty Wkr; Pres FCA; Capt L Bsktbl; Var L Sftbl; Var L Tennis; Var L Trk; High Hon Roll; NHS; All St Sftbl; Little All City Bsktbl; Regnl Qualifier Tnns; OSU; Exercise Physiology.

CALDERWOOD, LECHELLE; Putnam City West HS; Oklahoma City, OK; (3); 19/321; Am Leg Aux Girls St; Cmnty Wkr; English Clb; FCA; HOBY; Boy Scts; Scholastic Bowl; Spanish Clb; SADD; Ed Yrbk; Natl Yng Ldrs Conf In DC; OK Stu Cncl Assn Del Chrmn; Natl Stu Cncl Assn Del; Barnard; Jrnlsm.

CALDWELL, APRIL M; Blanchard Jr Sr HS; Blanchard, OK; (2); Church Yth Grp; Computer Clb; FHA; Church Choir; Chrmn Soph Cls; Hon Roll; NHS.

CALDWELL, BRANDI C; Preston Schl; Okmulgee, OK; (1); Girl Scts; Speech Tm; Acpl Chr; Variety Show; Score Keeper; Wt Lftg; Cit Awd; Hon Roll; Prfct Atten Awd; Pres Schlr; OSU; Marine Biologist.

CALDWELL, CARRIE; Woodward HS; Woodward, OK; (2); FCA; German Clb; Key Clb; Letterman Clb; Pep Clb; Phtg Rptr Yrbk; Ofcr Soph Cls; Rep Stu Cncl; Bsktbl; Hon Roll; OK Hnr Soc; 4 Yr U; Peds/PT.

CALDWELL, CINDI L; Deer Creek HS; Edmond, OK; (2); 41/103; Church Yth Grp; Hosp Aide; Science Clb; Band; Color Guard; Flag Corp; Socr; Civil Engrng.

CALDWELL, CRISTA; Jarman Jr HS; Midwest City, OK; (1); Church Yth Grp; Drama Clb; Spanish Clb; School Play; Chrldng; Gym; Vllybl; Hon Roll; Jr NHS; 4.0 Clb.

CALDWELL, DAWNETTA G; Idabel HS; Idabel, OK; (3); 1/95; Sec Church Yth Grp; FBLA; Color Guard; Pres Sr Cls; Sec Rep Stu Cncl; Var Chrldng; Sec NHS; Val; Debate Tm; FTA; Best Chrstn Exmpl 2 Yrs; Nom/Attnd Rotary Yth Ldrshp Assn Camp; Attnd Smmr Sci Inst; Southeastern OK ST Univ; Math.

CALDWELL, EDWARD T; Choctaw HS; Choctaw, OK; (4); Boy Scts; Church Yth Grp; Varsity Clb; Var Bsktbl; Var Crs Cntry; Var Ftbl; Var Socr; Var Trk; Hon Roll; St Gregorys; Bus.

CALDWELL, JAMIE D; Yukon Middle HS; Yukon, OK; (3); Church Yth Grp; FHA; Spanish Clb; High Hon Roll; NHS; 3-D; OK ST Univ; Bus.

CALDWELL, JASON; Pawhuska HS; Pawhuska, OK; (2); Key Clb; JV Bsktbl; JV Var Crs Cntry; Var Trk; High Hon Roll; OK ST U; Chem.

CALDWELL, JEFF T; Deer Creek HS; Guthrie, OK; (4); Church Yth Grp; FBLA; Science Clb; Spanish Clb; Band; Church Choir; Mrchg Band; Stage Crew; Stat Bsbl; Stat Socr; Martial Arts; Poetry; U Of Cntrl OK; Bus; Phy Thrpst.

CALDWELL JR, JOE; Okmulgee HS; Okmulgee, OK; (2); FCA; Var L Bsbl; Var L Ftbl; Wt Lftg; Var L Wrstlng; Hon Roll; Ntl Merit Ltr; Phy Thrpy.

CALDWELL, JOSHUA; Yukon HS; Yukon, OK; (4); Church Yth Grp; Cmnty Wkr; Natl FFA Org; Chorus; Church Choir; Ofcr Bsbl; Bsktbl; Ftbl; Trk; High Hon Roll; FFA Rptr; Breed Champion Shorthorn Steer OKC Spring Fair; OSU; Vet.

CALDWELL, KRISSY R; Elk City HS; Elk City, OK; (3); Church Yth Grp; Computer Clb; FHA; Pep Clb; Spanish Clb; SADD; Mrchg Band; Pep Band; High Hon Roll; Hon Roll; Southwestern OK ST U; Phy.

CALDWELL, KYLE; Watonga HS; Watonga, OK; (3); 1/60; Am Leg Boys St; HOBY; Quiz Bowl; Band; VP Jr Cls; Pres Stu Cncl; Var L Bsktbl; Var L Ftbl; Var L Trk; NHS; OK Cadet Lawman Acad; Class 2a Fltbl ST Chmpns 93-94; ST Acad Bowl Chmpns Class 2a 96.

CALDWELL, MICAH; Woodward HS; Woodward, OK; (3); Drama Clb; German Clb; Key Clb; Letterman Clb; Model UN; Red Cross Aide; Band; Orch; School Play; St Schlr; OK ST Univ Almn Schlr; Prof Orch Perf; Nmrs Superior/Hnr Band Awds; OK ST Univ; Cmptr Sci/Comm.

CALDWELL, MINDY D; Yukon Middle HS; Yukon, OK; (2); FHA; Quiz Bowl; Spanish Clb; JV Crs Cntry; Mgr(s); JV Trk; High Hon Roll; SWOSU; Phrmcst.

CALDWELL, RANDALL K; El Reno Sr HS; El Reno, OK; (4); FHA; Natl Beta Clb; Ftbl; Wt Lftg; Wrstlng; High Hon Roll; Hon Roll; Num Wrstlng Awds; MO Vly; Elem Ed.

CALDWELL, TERRA J; Union Intermediate HS; Tulsa, OK; (1); Drama Clb; Chorus; School Play; Stage Crew; Sftbl; Hon Roll; Jr NHS; Prfct Atten Awd; Pres Acad Fit Awd; UCLA.

CALDWELL, TISEE M; Amber Pocasset Jr Sr HS; Pocasset, OK; (4); Church Yth Grp; FCA; Science Clb; Spanish Clb; Church Choir; Sec Frsh Cls; Pres Soph Cls; Pres Jr Cls; Bsktbl; Chrldng; Masonic Awd; Carl Alberts St Coll; Phys Ther.

CALDWELL, VICTORIA; Moyers Public Schl; Antlers, OK; (1); FCA; 4-H; Var Bsktbl; Var Chrldng; Var Crs Cntry.

CALEY, ANGELA; Mangum Sr HS; Mangum, OK; (3); 2/46; Pres Church Yth Grp; VP FBLA; HOBY; Sec Band; Co-Capt Flag Corp; Pres Frsh Cls; Pres Soph Cls; Treas Stu Cncl; Var Chrldng; NHS; Frshmn Ftbl Qn; Oral Roberts U.

CALFEE, EVELYN; Lawton Sr HS; Lawton, OK; (4); Sec Computer Clb; Sec French Clb; Key Clb; Library Aide; Office Aide; Band; Mrchg Band; School Musical; School Play; Stage Crew; Stdnt Mnth; Rec Svrl Schlrshps PLUS; Pub Collage Lit Mag; Cameron Univ; Tech Theatre/Psyc.

CALHOUN, MISTY C; Okay Jr Sr HS; Lawton, OK; (3); 20/500; Church Yth Grp; Key Clb; Library Aide; Drm Mjr(t); Flag Corp; School Musical; School Play; High Hon Roll; Jr NHS; NHS; Competed Ms Teen Of OK; Fine Arts/Brdcstng.

CALHOUN, TAMMY; Broken Bow HS; Broken Bow, OK; (3); Art Clb; Cmnty Wkr; Quiz Bowl; Science Clb; Spanish Clb; High Hon Roll; Hon Roll; NHS; Pres Schlr; East TN St U; Math/Cmptr Sci.

CALICCHIO, JODI; Jenks HS; Jenks, OK; (1); Co-Capt Chrldng; Arch.

CALICO, AMANDA E; Union Intermediate HS; Broken Arrow, OK; (2); Band; School Play; Tchnlgy Stdnts Assn; Yng Astrnts; Rnglng Schl Of Art; Anmtn.

CALKIN, BRENT W; John Marshall HS; Oklahoma City, OK; (2); Church Yth Grp; Cmnty Wkr; Office Aide; Chorus; Church Choir; Stage Crew; VP Frsh Cls; OK City Univ; Jrnlsm/Mass Comm.

CALL, JOSHUA C; Edison HS; Tulsa, OK; (4); 45/178; Am Leg Boys St; Church Yth Grp; French Clb; FTA; Latin Clb; Ed Yrbk; Var L Wrstlng; Hon Roll; Fencing; KS U; Pre-Law.

CALLAGHAN, MICHAEL M; West Middle HS; Norman, OK; (1); Church Yth Grp; FCA; Letterman Clb; L Bsbl; Capt Ftbl; Powder Puff Ftbl; Yng Life.

CALLAHAN, BLAKE; Frederick HS; Frederick, OK; (3); 8/50; Am Leg Boys St; Church Yth Grp; FBLA; Treas Soph Cls; Var Bsbl; High Hon Roll; Hon Roll; Jr NHS; NHS; St Bus Calculations 3rd Pl FBLA.

CALLAHAN, CRYSTAL M; Anadarko HS; Anadarko, OK; (3); DECA; FBLA; Sec FHA; Natl FFA Org; Nwsp; Rep Soph Cls; Rep Jr Cls; Ofcr Stu Cncl; Var Tennis; Jr NHS; Stu Of Month; FFA Washington DC Ldrshp Conf 96; Southwestern OK ST Univ; Med.

CALLAHAN, MICHAEL; Apache HS; Apache, OK; (4); 2/37; Office Aide; Pres Jr Cls; Rep Stu Cncl; Bsktbl; Ftbl; High Hon Roll; Hon Roll; NHS; Sal; AISES; U OKFMECH Engr.

CALLAN, CHRISTINE M; Metro Christian Acad; Tulsa, OK; (3); Church Yth Grp; FCA; Girl Scts; Office Aide; Red Cross Aide; School Play; Bsktbl; Tennis; Hon Roll; Pres Acad Fit Awd; St Champ Tns; Natl Yng Ldr; U Of DC; Pre-Med.

CALLAN, SUSAN M; Choctaw HS; Choctaw, OK; (2); FTA; German Clb; Key Clb; After Schl Tutor; Pres Awd For Educl Excl; OK ST Univ; Elem Ed.

CALLAWAY, AMY; Ponca City Sr HS; Ponca City, OK; (4); 43/340; FCA; Spanish Clb; SADD; Ed Yrbk; L Ftbl; L Golf; High Hon Roll; NHS; Pres Acad Fit Awd; St Schlr; Hd Ftbl Trnr; Natl Mcy & OK Acad Schlrs; OK ST U; Med.

CALLEN, TERESITA; Marietta HS; Marietta, OK; (4); 7/53; FHA; Quiz Bowl; Spanish Clb; Teachers Aide; Yrbk; Vllybl; Hon Roll; Lions Clb Stu Of Month 96; Southeastern OK ST U; Crmnlgy.

CALLENDAR, STEVEN; Durant HS; Durant, OK; (4); 35/190; Church Yth Grp; FCA; Letterman Clb; Office Aide; Varsity Clb; VICA; Variety Show; Rep Stu Cncl; Var L Bsbl; Var Capt Ftbl; U Of OK.

CALLIES, MARTI; Little Axe Sr HS; Norman, OK; (2); Church Yth Grp; Drama Clb; Band; Chorus; Church Choir; Mrchg Band; School Musical; School Play; Sec Treas Stu Cncl; Hon Roll; Southern Nazarene U; Ed.

CALLIS, SARAH; Berryhill Jr HS; Tulsa, OK; (1); Church Yth Grp; FCA; Church Choir; Yrbk; Pres Stu Cncl; Hon Roll; Camp Fire Horizon; Serteens; Living Christmas Tree; Marine Bio.

CALVARESE, JUSTIN; Bixby Sr HS; Tulsa, OK; (4); 1/179; Math Tm; Teachers Aide; Pres Band; Jazz Band; Mrchg Band; Rep Stu Cncl; High Hon Roll; NHS; Ntl Merit Ltr; Val; Acad Team; Comp Challenge Team; OK ST Univ; Civil Engr.

CALVERT, DERRICK; Kiefer Jr Sr HS; Sapulpa, OK; (1); FCA; Ofcr Bsbl; Bsktbl; Hon Roll; Sal; KS U; Bsktbl.

CALVERT, KELLY A; Washington HS; Purcell, OK; (3); 1/50; FCA; FBLA; Bsktbl; Powder Puff Ftbl; Sftbl; Hon Roll; NHS; Guitar.

CALVERT, LA DONNA; Cheyenne HS; Durham, OK; (3); Church Yth Grp; 4-H; FHA; German Clb; Band; Mrchg Band; Pep Band; Cit Awd; High Hon Roll; Ntl Merit Schol; Outstndng Yng Mohair Producer 94; Acad Tm; Panhandle ST U; Acctng.

CALVERT, MAYGAN S; Atoka HS; Atoka, OK; (3); 20/120; Church Yth Grp; Computer Clb; FBLA; Sec Natl FFA Org; Science Clb; Teachers Aide; 4-H Awd; High Hon Roll; Hon Roll; Prfct Atten Awd; OK U; Med.

CALVERT, MELANIE; Houston Homan Jr HS; Eufaula, OK; (1); Church Yth Grp; Cmnty Wkr; FHA; JA; Natl FFA Org; Quiz Bowl; Spanish Clb; Chorus; School Musical; Yrbk; VP Natl Hnr Soc Team; FFA Sweetheart.

CALVERT, RHONDA L; Colcord Schl; Watts, OK; (4); 1/45; FBLA; FHA; Spanish Clb; Church Choir; Ed Yrbk; Pres Soph Cls; Pres Jr Cls; VP Sr Cls; High Hon Roll; NHS; FBLA & FHA Pres; CSU Okmulgee; Comp Sys Tech.

CALVERT, THOMAS S; Washington HS; Purcell, OK; (1); Church Yth Grp; Natl FFA Org; Prfct Atten Awd.

CALVIN, SHAWN; Broken Bow HS; Broken Bow, OK; (4); 1/145; Am Leg Boys St; FCA; Quiz Bowl; Science Clb; Band; Church Choir; JV Bsbl; Var Bsktbl; Wt Lftg; Hon Roll; Piano, Trumbone & Drums; Singing; Miss Broken Bow Pgnts Technical Crew; U Of OK; Genetic Engr.

CALVIN, SIMON A; Union Intermediate HS; Broken Arrow, OK; (1); Church Yth Grp; Spanish Clb; Rep Stu Cncl; Hon Roll; NHS; ARC Gftd Pgm & Stu Cncl Publicity Chm; Young Astronauts Historian; Novelist; Comp Prgmr.

CALVIN, TERESA; Hugo HS; Hugo, OK; (2); JV Var Bsktbl; Var Trk; Var Bsktbll Mst Imprvd Plyr; Trck Wrkmnshp Awd; E TX ST Coll; Cmptr Pgrmmr.

CAMACHO, ELIZABETH; Midwest City HS; Midwest City, OK; (4); 2/419; FCA; VP Key Clb; SADD; School Musical; Nwsp; VP Sr Cls; Kiwanis Awd; Pres NHS; Val; High Hon Roll; Sprt Cncl Secy, VP; Nws 101 Reprtr; Jr Rtrn; U MO; Brdcst Jrnlsm.

CAMERON, CAMBRA; Elk City HS; Elk City, OK; (3); Church Yth Grp; SADD; Band; Rep Chorus; Flag Corp; Mrchg Band; Rep Frsh Cls; High Hon Roll; NHS; Pres Acad Fit Awd; St Hnr Soc; Show Choir; Natl Mrt Commended; Lubbock Chrstn U.

CAMERON, CARLTON L; Lindsay HS; Lindsay, OK; (1); Church Yth Grp; Bsktbl; Ftbl.

CAMERON, DAVID A; Deer Creek HS; Edmond, OK; (2); 9/106; Boy Scts; Quiz Bowl; Band; Jazz Band; Mrchg Band; Orch; Pep Band; Hon Roll; NHS; Engr.

CAMP, HEATHER D; Checotah HS; Checotah, OK; (3); 2/120; Am Leg Aux Girls St; Natl FFA Org; Quiz Bowl; Chorus; Ofcr Stu Cncl; Bsktbl; High Hon Roll; NHS; Church Yth Grp; Debate Tm; Natl Frat Fo Sut Mscns; OK FFA Chrs; E OK Hnr Chr; Tulsa Univ; Hstry.

CAMP, KENNY J; Putnam City HS; Oklahoma City, OK; (3); 7/360; Church Yth Grp; Key Clb; Office Aide; Science Clb; Spanish Clb; NHS; Acad Team; Mock Trial; G/T Pgm; Oklahoma City U; Ed.

CAMP, KRISSIE A; Morris HS; Okmulgee, OK; (3); Church Yth Grp; 4-H; Teachers Aide; Chorus; Church Choir; Variety Show; Var Chrldng; 4-H Awd; Hon Roll; Choir Metals; Bible Bowl; Ozark Chrstn; Phycoligist.

CAMP, TRENTON A; Okeene Jr Sr HS; Okeene, OK; (3); 14/28; Rptr Nwsp; Hon Roll; Kiwanis Awd; Prfct Atten Awd; Southwestern Univ; Comp Pgmng.

CAMPBELL, ADRIAN; Pond Creek-Hunter Schl; Hunter, OK; (2); 1/30; Pres Church Yth Grp; Quiz Bowl; Band; Mrchg Band; Pres Frsh Cls; Ftbl; Trk; High Hon Roll; NHS.

CAMPBELL, ALISHA; Thomas Jr Sr HS; Thomas, OK; (2); Church Yth Grp; Cmnty Wkr; FHA; Chorus; Tennis; High Hon Roll; Hon Roll; NHS; All Amer Schlr; U Of CO; Scndry Schl Eng Tchr.

CAMPBELL, ANDY B; Enid Sr HS; Enid, OK; (2); Boy Scts; Church Yth Grp; Quiz Bowl; Scholastic Bowl; Band; Jazz Band; Mrchg Band; Pep Band; Bsktbl; Trk.

CAMPBELL, BRANDY N; Moore HS; Moore, OK; (3); 8/550; Church Yth Grp; Office Aide; Spanish Clb; Varsity Clb; JV Bsktbl; Var Trk; Jr NHS; NHS; Pres Acad Fit Awd; Scndry Ed Math.

CAMPBELL, BREANNA; Stillwater Jr HS; Joplin, MO; (1); Church Yth Grp; FCA; Natl Beta Clb; Nwsp; Yrbk; Chrldng; High Hon Roll; Hon Roll; Pres Acad Fit Awd; 3rd Pl Edtrl OK Intrschlstc Press Assn; Phy Ther.

CAMPBELL, BROCK; Perry Sr HS; Perry, OK; (4); 11/66; FCA; German Clb; Band; Jazz Band; Mrchg Band; Pep Band; Rep Stu Cncl; Golf; Hon Roll; NHS; Hnr Band 2 Yrs; OSU; Music Ed.

CAMPBELL, CHRIS A; Stillwater Sr HS; Stillwater, OK; (2); Church Yth Grp; Cmnty Wkr; FCA; Library Aide; Treas Math Clb; Mu Alpha Theta; Natl Beta Clb; JV Var Bsktbl; Golf; High Hon Roll; U Of AZ.

CAMPBELL, CHRISTOPHER; Union Intermediate HS; Broken Arrow, OK; (2); Boy Scts; Church Yth Grp; Pres FCA; Teachers Aide; Chorus; Church Choir; School Musical; School Play; Rep Frsh Cls; Rep Soph Cls; BSA Eagle Sct, Ordr Arrow, Pine Tree, Natl Heroism Awd; All Amer Schlrs; Baylor; Bus.

CAMPBELL, CLINTON J; Putnam City West HS; Oklahoma City, OK; (2); 1/380; Church Yth Grp; FCA; German Clb; Scholastic Bowl; Rep Soph Cls; NHS; All-Amer Schlr; Chrch Yth Group Sec; Outstdng Hnrs Eng II Stu; Comp Sci.

CAMPBELL, CRYSTAL; Tuttle HS; Tuttle, OK; (4); 4/87; Am Leg Aux Girls St; Church Yth Grp; Natl FFA Org; Sec Spanish Clb; Sec Jr Cls; VP Sr Cls; Var Chrldng; NHS; Val; 3 Yr St Chmpn Chrldr.

CAMPBELL, CRYSTAL L; Okemah HS; Okemah, OK; (4); 29/55; 4-H; FHA; Library Aide; SADD; Band; Jazz Band; Mrchg Band; 4-H Awd; Hon Roll; Prfct Atten Awd; Keywanettes; OSU; Graphic Dsgn.

CAMPBELL, CRYSTAL Z; West Middle HS; Norman, OK; (2); Cmnty Wkr; Spanish Clb; NHS; Pres Schlr; Med Explorers-NRH; All Shades Of Brown Clb; Teen Vols.

CAMPBELL, DAX; Dale Sr HS; Shawnee, OK; (4); 5/49; Natl FFA Org; Quiz Bowl; Scholastic Bowl; Ofcr Stu Cncl; Ofcr Bsbl; Bsktbl; OK ST U; Chem Engrng.

CAMPBELL, GINA; Ninnekah HS; Ninnekah, OK; (4); 8/38; Model UN; VP Science Clb; Spanish Clb; Ed Nwsp; Yrbk; VP Frsh Cls; VP Soph Cls; VP Jr Cls; Treas Sr Cls; Hon Roll; Pres Envrnmntl Yth Awd; Engl Awd 3 Yrs; East Cntrl U.

CAMPBELL, HEATHER; Putnam City West HS; Oklahoma City, OK; (4); 90/278; Am Leg Aux Girls St; Church Yth Grp; DECA; VP Pep Clb; Chorus; Church Choir; Stu To Stu; Chrstn In Action; 1 Voice Ensmbl Church; OK Baptist U.

CAMPBELL, HOLLEY J; Sapulpa Sr HS; Sapulpa, OK; (2); Church Yth Grp; Cmnty Wkr; Debate Tm; FCA; French Clb; NFL; Speech Tm; Teachers Aide; School Musical; School Play; Prins Cncl; Prins Hnr Roll; Otstdng His Stdnt; Johns Hopkins Univ; Neurosrgn.

CAMPBELL, IVY M; Nathan Hale HS; Tulsa, OK; (1); Sec VP Art Clb; Church Yth Grp; Cmnty Wkr; Co-Ed Nwsp; Hon Roll; Wrtng; Rprtng; Wrtr.

CAMPBELL, JAIME L; Latta Sr HS; Ada, OK; (2); 4-H; FHA; Pep Clb; Speech Tm; Chorus; 4-H Awd; Hon Roll.

CAMPBELL, JANNA A; Canton HS; Longdale, OK; (1); Church Yth Grp; FCA; FHA; Scholastic Bowl; SADD; Church Choir; School Musical; Pres Frsh Cls; High Hon Roll; Hon Roll; Musical Achvmt Awds; U Of OK; Psych.

CAMPBELL, JASON D; Enid Sr HS; Galveston, TX; (2); Boy Scts; Band; Mrchg Band; Pep Band; Ftbl.

CAMPBELL, JENNIFER; Clinton HS; Clinton, OK; (2); FHA; Var Chrldng; Hon Roll; NHS; Gymnstcs; OSU; Tchr.

CAMPBELL, JEREMIAH D; Sayre HS; Sayre, OK; (3); 12/60; Am Leg Boys St; 4-H; Natl FFA Org; Speech Tm; Var Ftbl; Var Wt Lftg; 4-H Awd; Hon Roll; Bareback Rodeo Riding; Team Roper; OSU; Ag.

CAMPBELL, JESSE; Tuttle HS; Tuttle, OK; (1); Church Yth Grp; Natl FFA Org; Intrml Ftbl; Intrml Wt Lftg.

CAMPBELL, JOEL K; B T Washington HS; Tulsa, OK; (3); Church Yth Grp; Spanish Clb; Teachers Aide; L Socr; L Swmmng; Jr NHS.

CAMPBELL, JUDD; Kingfisher HS; Kingfisher, OK; (4); 8/96; Quiz Bowl; Nwsp; Ed Yrbk; VP Frsh Cls; VP Soph Cls; VP Jr Cls; Ofcr Sr Cls; Rep Stu Cncl; Hon Roll; NHS; Scholastic Tm; Spanish Clb VP; U Of Cntrl OK; Dentistry.

CAMPBELL, KACI D; Broken Arrow Sr HS; Broken Arrow, OK; (3); Hosp Aide; Spanish Clb; Hon Roll; Jr NHS; Prfct Atten Awd; HOSA; KS Univ; Med.

CAMPBELL, KECIA S; Southeast HS; Oklahoma City, OK; (2); FCA; Natl FFA Org; ROTC; Scholastic Bowl; Mgr(s); Sftbl; High Hon Roll; Val; FFA Grnhnd Qz 2nd Pl 95; Ktty Hwk Air Soc Cmmndr; Flaw.

CAMPBELL, KELLY; Claremore Sr HS; Claremore, OK; (2); Church Yth Grp; FHA; Church Choir; Nwsp; Hon Roll; NHS; Medicine.

CAMPBELL, KELLY D; Stonewall Jr-Sr HS; Clarita, OK; (4); #5 in class; Natl FFA Org; Office Aide; Rep Sr Cls; Rep Stu Cncl; Capt Bsbl; Capt Bsktbl; High Hon Roll; Jr NHS; NHS; Murray St Col; Ag Bus.

CAMPBELL, KRISTIN M; Christian Heritage Acad; Oklahoma City, OK; (2); Church Yth Grp; Chrldng; Gym; Vllybl; Pres Acad Fit Awd; 16th Pl Indvdl SCORE Natls 95-96; All St Chrldr 94-95 95-96; Office Aid 95-96; V Non Music Natl Chmpns; OK ST U; Sales.

CAMPBELL, MARKUS D; Cordell Sr HS; Cordell, OK; (1); FHA; Ofcr Bsbl; Ftbl; Wt Lftg; Wrstlng; Hon Roll; NHS.

CAMPBELL, MELANIE; Del City HS; Del City, OK; (3); Church Yth Grp; FCA; Acpl Chr; Chorus; Swing Chorus; Var Chrldng; Var Pom Pon; Jr NHS; NHS; Prfct Atten Awd; Vocal Music Hall Fame; Del Aires VP; OK Univ.

CAMPBELL, MELINDA; Lawton Sr HS; Lawton, OK; (4); 118/323; Key Clb; Spanish Clb; Band; Mrchg Band; Pep Band; Chrldng; Hon Roll; Pres Acad Fit Awd; Tchr Cadets; Cameron Univ; Spec Ed.

CAMPBELL, MICHAEL; Turner Schl; Overbrook, OK; (4); 1/21; Church Yth Grp; Natl Beta Clb; Natl FFA Org; Teachers Aide; VICA; Hon Roll; NHS; Prfct Atten Awd; Val; OSU; Dsl Svc Tech.

CAMPBELL, PATRICK A; Pond Creek-Hunter Schl; Hunter, OK; (2); Church Yth Grp; Natl Beta Clb; Quiz Bowl; Band; Mrchg Band; Pres Frsh Cls; L Ftbl; L Trk; High Hon Roll; NHS; Comp Eng.

CAMPBELL, RACHEL L; Westmoore HS; Oklahoma City, OK; (3); Church Yth Grp; GAA; Swmmng; Hon Roll; Jr NHS; NHS; OU; Sports Medicine.

CAMPBELL, REBECCA A; Byng Sr HS; Fitzhugh, OK; (3); Church Yth Grp; Cmnty Wkr; FCA; GAA; Quiz Bowl; Scholastic Bowl; Chorus; Church Choir; School Musical; Rptr Nwsp; Doctor.

CAMPBELL, SHAWN B; Putnam City North HS; Oklahoma City, OK; (4); 198/436; Church Yth Grp; FCA; Var Bsktbl; Rose ST JC; Fin.

CAMPBELL, STACY; Putnam City West HS; Bethany, OK; (1); Church Yth Grp; Drama Clb; Church Choir; Ed Nwsp; Capt Chrldng; Hon Roll.

CAMPBELL, TIM; Okemah HS; Okemah, OK; (2); 16/75; Chess Clb; Church Yth Grp; Cmnty Wkr; Debate Tm; 4-H; FHA; Key Clb; Natl FFA Org; Quiz Bowl; Science Clb; Ranch Mgmt.

CAMPBELL, TORI L; Thomas Jr Sr HS; Custer City, OK; (1); Church Yth Grp; 4-H; FHA; Chorus; 4-H Awd; PT.

CAMPOS, MARCUS S; Central HS; Tulsa, OK; (3); Church Yth Grp; Intnl Clb; Var Socr; Var Swmmng; 4-H Awd; High Hon Roll; Hon Roll; OK ST; Civil Eng.

CAMREN, TARA; Fairview HS; Fairview, OK; (1); Church Yth Grp; FHA; GAA; Intrml Bsktbl; High Hon Roll; Educ.

CANADA, HALEY S; Harrah HS; Harrah, OK; (2); 1/168; Art Clb; Church Yth Grp; FCA; GAA; Letterman Clb; Pep Clb; SADD; Varsity Clb; Ed Jr Cls; Var L Socr; USSA Awd Wnnr; Schlrs Clb; Career Skills Awd; Architectural Engrng.

CANADA, JUSTIN; Central Mid-HS; Norman, OK; (1); Church Yth Grp; Treas FCA; Model UN; Treas Mu Alpha Theta; Hon Roll; OK Hon Soc; Meterologist.

CANADA, SABRINA A; Dickson HS; Ardmore, OK; (3); 6/76; Church Yth Grp; Key Clb; Teachers Aide; Band; Church Choir; Mrchg Band; High Hon Roll; Hon Roll; NHS; Prfct Atten Awd; RN.

CANADAY, STACIA K; Bethany HS; Oklahoma City, OK; (3); 1/83; Am Leg Aux Girls St; Church Yth Grp; Cmnty Wkr; Pres Key Clb; Office Aide; Service Clb; Spanish Clb; Teachers Aide; Church Choir; Ed Yrbk; 3 Yrs Yth Alive 1 Yr VP; 4 Wks OK ST Univ Plntlgy Acad; 3 Wks U Of OK Geosci Acad; Plntlgy.

CANADY, BENETTE; John Marshall HS; Oklahoma City, OK; (3); School Play; Stage Crew; Yrbk; Chrldng; Tennis; Cit Awd; Hon Roll; TX Southern.

CANADY, CRYSTAL M; Webster HS; Tulsa, OK; (3); FBLA; Key Clb; Red Cross Aide; Hon Roll; Prfct Atten Awd; Tulsa Jr Coll; Data Entry.

CANADY, TRAVIS; Dewey HS; Bartlesville, OK; (4); 16/88; Church Yth Grp; FCA; Teachers Aide; Church Choir; Ftbl; Golf; Sftbl; Trk; Wt Lftg; Hon Roll; Ozrk Chrstn Coll Hghst Praise; Ozark Chrstn Coll; Psych.

CANARY, MISTY; Little Axe Sr HS; Norman, OK; (2); Church Yth Grp; Chorus; Church Choir; Swing Chorus; L Var Sftbl; Hon Roll; NHS; Music Thrpy.

CANDALL, JONATHAN; Lawton Christian Schl; Fort Sill, OK; (2); Church Yth Grp; Cmnty Wkr; Band; Jazz Band; Mrchg Band; Var Tennis; Cit Awd; Hon Roll; Jr NHS.

CANNING, JASON; Guthrie Sr HS; Guthrie, OK; (3); Am Leg Boys St; FCA; French Clb; Mu Alpha Theta; Natl FFA Org; Temple Yth Grp; Var Bsbl; NHS; Criminal Law.

CANNING, JEREMY; Guthrie Sr HS; Guthrie, OK; (3); French Clb; Mu Alpha Theta; Band; Mrchg Band; Pep Band; Socr; Hon Roll; OK ST U Alumni Assn Hnr Schlr; De Molay; OK U.

CANNON, ALICIA; Cordell Sr HS; Cordell, OK; (4); 10/50; Stu City Cncl Mayor; Miss CORDELL HS 95-; Southwestern OK ST Univ; Phar.

CANNON, BRIDGET; Washington HS; Blanchard, OK; (3); 1/50; FCA; FBLA; Sec FHA; Sec Treas Pep Clb; Pres Band; VP Frsh Cls; Treas Jr Cls; VP Stu Cncl; Trk; VP NHS; Supt Hnr Rl; U Of OK; Pre-Law.

CANNON, CASEY; Antlers Sr HS; Atoka, OK; (1); Church Yth Grp; Debate Tm; Natl FFA Org; Quiz Bowl; Spanish Clb; Church Choir; Bsktbl; High Hon Roll; Hon Roll; Val; OK ST U; Aqtc Mcrblgst.

CANNON, CLENDON; Comanche HS; Comanche, OK; (4); 1/60; Art Clb; Science Clb; SADD; Var Bsbl; Var Bsktbl; Var Golf; High Hon Roll; JETS Awd; NHS; Val; Engrng.

CANOE, CAROL; Madill HS; Madill, OK; (3); Church Yth Grp; FCA; Rptr FHA; SADD; Band; Ofcr Stu Cncl; Hon Roll; NHS; Chcksw Ntn Exec Dist Yth Cncl; ECU.

CANTON, DOUG B; North Intemediate HS; Broken Arrow, OK; (2); Art Clb; Church Yth Grp; JV Bsktbl; JV Golf; FL ST Univ.

CANTRELL, ALLISON M; Stillwater Sr HS; Stillwater, OK; (3); Cmnty Wkr; FHA; Natl FFA Org; Var Socr; Hon Roll; Peer Advocate; Spcl Olympic Vol; Little League Coach; OK ST Univ; Spec Ed.

CANTRELL, BRIANNA; Stigler HS; Stigler, OK; (3); Church Yth Grp; FHA; SADD; Band; Color Guard; Mrchg Band; Rptr Nwsp; FCA; 4-H; Library Aide; Northeastern Tahlequah; Educ.

CANTRELL, JEREMY; Stigler HS; Stigler, OK; (2); 17/111; 4-H; HOBY; Natl FFA Org; Band; Mrchg Band; Var Bsbl; JV Bsktbl; Ftbl; Hon Roll; NHS; Star Grnhnd Awd FFA; Showmanship Awd FFA; All Dist Band; OK ST U.

CANTRELL, SARAH N; North Intemediate HS; Broken Arrow, OK; (1); FHA; Cosmo.

CANTRELL, SHANNA R; El Reno Sr HS; El Reno, OK; (2); Vet.

CANTRELL, SOMERLYN; Ada HS; Ada, OK; (4); 37/163; Am Leg Aux Girls St; Church Yth Grp; Cmnty Wkr; DECA; FCA; Letterman Clb; Pep Clb; Q&S; Scholastic Bowl; Spanish Clb; Wshngtn Jrnlsm Conf; KTEN TV Rprtr; Ada Evng Nws Stff Wrtr; U Tulsa; Advrtsng.

CANTRELL JR, ZEDDIE L; Bristow HS; Bristow, OK; (2); Church Yth Grp; Cmnty Wkr; FCA; HOBY; Natl FFA Org; Church Choir; Pres Frsh Cls; Rep Soph Cls; Pres Rep Stu Cncl; Ftbl; OK Hnrs Scty; FFA ST Spch Qlfr.

CANTU, DAVID ISAAC; Bartlesville Sr HS; Bartlesville, OK; (4); 86/426; Am Leg Boys St; Boy Scts; Church Yth Grp; Cmnty Wkr; FBLA; Sec Treas Science Clb; Pres Spanish Clb; Teachers Aide; Acpl Chr; Sec Treas Chorus; Rtry Stu Of Mnth; OK Boys St; Cty Yth Ct Head Jdg; Intl Bus.

CANTWELL, BEN; Moore HS; Moore, OK; (4); 4/505; Am Leg Boys St; Church Yth Grp; Cmnty Wkr; FCA; German Clb; Model UN; Science Clb; Ftbl; Hon Roll; NHS; Schlr Athl Of Yr 95-96; Masonc Stu Of Today 95; OK ST U; Mech Engr.

CANTWELL, JAMI N; Elmore City Jr Sr HS; Elmore City, OK; (2); 1/50; High Hon Roll; Hon Roll; U Of OK; Meteor.

CANTWELL, LINDSAY R; Elmore City Jr Sr HS; Elmore City, OK; (2); Bsktbl; Trk; Hon Roll; NHS; Prfct Atten Awd; U Of OK.

CAPERS, RACHEL R; Pauls Valley HS; Pauls Valley, OK; (2); 1/107; Church Yth Grp; FHA; Key Clb; Scholastic Bowl; Acpl Chr; Chorus; School Musical; School Play; Stage Crew; High Hon Roll; Mock Trial Team; OK Hnr Soc; Partial Schlsp OK Chrstn.

CAPEZZA, RICK A; Owasso Sr HS; Owasso, OK; (2); 38/432; VP Church Yth Grp; FCA; French Clb; SADD; Var Ftbl; Var Wt Lftg; High Hon Roll; NHS; Drg Free Yth; Frgn Exch Clb; Choice Bible Study; Ed.

CAPPS, JINA; Valliant HS; Millerton, OK; (2); #11 in class; 4-H; Natl FFA Org; Pep Clb; VP Soph Cls; JV Bsktbl.

CAPPS, JUDY; Braggs Schl; Gore, OK; (3); 5/16; Nwsp; Yrbk; Var Sftbl; Hon Roll; Connors ST Coll; Nrs.

CARAM, DUSTIN; Midwest City HS; Midwest City, OK; (2); 51/488; FCA; German Clb; Ofcr Bsbl; Ftbl; Hon Roll; Prfct Atten Awd; Plyr GA ST Chmpns.

CARD, LISA A; John Marshall HS; Oklahoma City, OK; (2); Orch; School Musical; Sftbl; Tennis; High Hon Roll; Hon Roll; Strolling Strings; Childhood Ed.

CARDEN, LISA; Claremore Sr HS; Claremore, OK; (3); Church Yth Grp; Girl Scts; Hosp Aide; Band; Jazz Band; Mrchg Band; Pep Band; Hon Roll; NHS; Prfct Atten Awd.

CARDENAS, LUCIA; Capitol Hill HS; Oklahoma City, OK; (4); ROTC; Spanish Clb; Color Guard; Hon Roll; Co Cmmndr.

CARDER, TONYA L; Picher-Cardin HS; Picher, OK; (3); Church Yth Grp; FHA; GAA; Math Clb; Science Clb; JV Bsktbl; Var Sftbl; NHS.

CARDNER, RACHEL; Tonkawa Jr Sr HS; Tonkawa, OK; (3); Am Leg Aux Girls St; Natl FFA Org; School Play; Yrbk; Rep Stu Cncl; Hon Roll; Jr NHS; NHS; Pres Acad Fit Awd; Church Yth Grp; Ext Stud Pgm; Acad Ltrmn; Ftbl Mgr; Northern OK Coll; Ag.

CARDWELL, ALISHA; Ft Gibson HS; Fort Gibson, OK; (3); 3/150; Church Yth Grp; CAP; Debate Tm; French Clb; Speech Tm; SADD; Band; Chorus; Color Guard; School Musical; U Of Central OK.

CAREY, CRYSTAL; Guthrie Sr HS; Guthrie, OK; (3); Church Yth Grp; 4-H; Hosp Aide; Sec Key Clb; Mu Alpha Theta; Sec Science Clb; SADD; Co-Ed Nwsp; 4-H Awd; VP NHS.

CAREY, DUSTIN J; Mc Alester HS; Krebs, OK; (2); Spanish Clb; Var Trk; Var Wrstlng; Hon Roll; Sci/Tech Awd; OSU Okmulgee; Diesel Mech.

CAREY, JO BETH; Eufaula Sr HS; Stidham, OK; (2); 4-H; Natl FFA Org; High Hon Roll; NHS; Val; Bio & Eng Outstndng Stu; Pres Educ Awds; Northeastern U; Pharm.

CAREY, MICHAEL; Mid-Del Christian Schl; Del City, OK; (2); 2/16; Treas Soph Cls; Treas Stu Cncl; Socr; Tennis; Cit Awd; Ntl Merit Ltr.

CARGIL, CURTIS E; Kellyville Sr HS; Bristow, OK; (2); Quiz Bowl; JV Var Bsbl; JV Var Bsktbl; JV Var Ftbl; Hon Roll; Connors; Basbl Schlsp Sports Md.

CARIKER, AMI L; Central Schl; Sallisaw, OK; (3); Art Clb; Drama Clb; Pep Clb; Spanish Clb; Speech Tm; Varsity Clb; Nwsp; Yrbk; Chrldng; Hon Roll; Hrsebck Rdng Clb; Phtgrphy; Span Clb Queen 95-; Photo Jrnlst.

CARIKER, EMILY; Stigler HS; Stigler, OK; (1); Church Yth Grp; FCA; FHA; SADD; Church Choir; Var Bsktbl; High Hon Roll; NHS; TX A&M; Law.

CARLBERG, DEVIN; Shawnee Sr HS; Shawnee, OK; (2); Boy Scts; Quiz Bowl; Scholastic Bowl; Band; Jazz Band; Mrchg Band; Pep Band; High Hon Roll; Jr NHS; Piano.

CARLILE, MICHAEL C; Tahlequah Sr HS; Tahlequah, OK; (3); Church Yth Grp; Computer Clb; Quiz Bowl; Teachers Aide; Northeastern ST U; Comp Prgmr.

CARLILE, TESSA L; Bethel HS; Tecumseh, OK; (1); Church Yth Grp; Office Aide; Spanish Clb; Bsktbl; Sftbl; Hon Roll; NHS.

CARLISLE, GREG B; Midwest City HS; Oklahoma City, OK; (3); 140/359; Hosp Aide; Office Aide; Phtg Yrbk; Wt Lftg; Hon Roll; Prfct Atten Awd; Unix Script Pgmng; Web Page Dsgn; FL Inst Of Tech; Comp.

CARLOCK, ASHLEY G; Putnam City West HS; Oklahoma City, OK; (3); 50/300; Art Clb; Church Yth Grp; Cmnty Wkr; Drama Clb; FCA; French Clb; Office Aide; Science Clb; Church Choir; Stage Crew; 3rd Pl OK St Trk Meet; St Champions 94-95; Mst Imprvd; Tiger Awds.

CARLOCK, JULIA L; Parker Middle HS; Mcalester, OK; (2); Band; Color Guard; Flag Corp; Mrchg Band; Yrbk; Bsktbl; Tennis; Cit Awd; Hon Roll; Piano.

CARLOZZI, BRIAN M; Stillwater Sr HS; Stillwater, OK; (3); Church Yth Grp; FCA; Teachers Aide; Nwsp; Ofcr Bsbl; Bsktbl; Crs Cntry; Ftbl; OSU.

CARLSON, CRYSTAL C; Shawnee Sr HS; Shawnee, OK; (2); Church Yth Grp; GAA; Bsktbl; Hon Roll; OBU.

CARLSON, GREGORY; Claremore Sr HS; Claremore, OK; (4); 23/241; Am Leg Boys St; French Clb; Math Clb; Scholastic Bowl; Science Clb; Crs Cntry; Ftbl; Trk; Wrstlng; NHS; Balfour Awd Amer Hstry; OK ST U; Engrng.

CARLSON, MATT E; Sayre HS; Sweetwater, OK; (3); Church Yth Grp; Hon Roll.

CARLTON, ANDRE M; John Marshall HS; Oklahoma City, OK; (1); Boy Scts; Pep Clb; SADD; Band; JV Bsktbl.

CARLTON, JOHN R; Mc Alester HS; Mcalester, OK; (4); 20/200; Art Clb; Church Yth Grp; Drama Clb; Office Aide; Quiz Bowl; Scholastic Bowl; Science Clb; Speech Tm; Ed Nwsp; High Hon Roll; Eastern OK Stcoll; Pre Med.

CARLTON, JOSHUA J; Guthrie Sr HS; Guthrie, OK; (1); Church Yth Grp; Band; Mrchg Band; Pep Band; JV Bsbl; Coach.

CARLTON, TRACY; Guthrie Sr HS; Guthrie, OK; (4); Am Leg Aux Girls St; Church Yth Grp; VP SADD; Pres Band; Church Choir; Drm Mjr(t); Mrchg Band; Pep Band; School Musical; Golf; Sthwstrn OK ST U; Nrsng.

CARLTON, WILLIAM; Ketchum HS; Tonopah, NV; (4); 4/31; Art Clb; Boy Scts; Church Yth Grp; HOBY; Quiz Bowl; Scholastic Bowl; Science Clb; Spanish Clb; Teachers Aide; Yrbk; U OK; Med.

CARLTON, WILLIAM; Ketchum HS; Langley, OK; (4); 4/31; Art Clb; Boy Scts; Church Yth Grp; HOBY; Quiz Bowl; Scholastic Bowl; Science Clb; Spanish Clb; Teachers Aide; Yrbk; U Of OK; Med.

CARMACK, CAREN A; Heavener HS; Heavener, OK; (1); Church Yth Grp; French Clb; FHA; Hosp Aide; Hon Roll.

CARMAN, TEYLOR N; Jenks HS; Tulsa, OK; (4); DECA; FCA; Church Choir; Rep Sr Cls; Chrldng; Hon Roll; Church Yth Grp; Cmnty Wkr; Office Aide; Pep Clb; DECA Ofcr; Mission Trips; Assisteens League; Symphony Set; OK ST Univ.

CARMAN, ZAC; Charles Page HS; Sand Springs, OK; (2); 1/385; Church Yth Grp; Debate Tm; Key Clb; NFL; Quiz Bowl; Spanish Clb; Speech Tm; Hon Roll; NHS; Yth & Govt; Sgt At Arms; Engrng.

CARMER, ALEXIS R; South Intermediate HS; Broken Arrow, OK; (1); 1/1100; Church Yth Grp; Acpl Chr; Chorus; Gov Hon Prg Awd; High Hon Roll; Hon Roll; Super OK St Solo & Ensemble; Chrstn Stu Union VP; Acad Tm Lttr; MA Inst Of Tech; Physics.

CARMICHAEL, ROBERT E; Oklahoma Bible Acad; Enid, OK; (3); Church Yth Grp; Cmnty Wkr; Church Choir; Yth Cncl At First Bapt Chrch; Nrsng Admin.

CARMICHEAL, BRANDON V; North Intemediate HS; Broken Arrow, OK; (1); Church Yth Grp; Drama Clb; French Clb; Thesps; Ofcr Stu Cncl; Bsktbl; Ftbl; MI.

CARNAGEY, KARA; Ft Gibson HS; Fort Gibson, OK; (2); 3/194; VP Church Yth Grp; VP French Clb; VP SADD; Band; Ofcr Stu Cncl; Bsktbl; Socr; High Hon Roll; Pres Acad Fit Awd; Spanish NHS; Cvl War Renctr; OK Indian Hnr Soc; Natl Piano Gld; OK U; Med.

CARNER, DOUG; Kiefer Jr Sr HS; Kiefer, OK; (3); FCA; Natl Beta Clb; Band; VP Frsh Cls; Treas Soph Cls; Bsktbl; Ftbl; Hon Roll; NHS; Prfct Atten Awd; Multi Yr Listing.

CARNER, STEPHANIE L; Glenpool HS; Glenpool, OK; (2); Church Yth Grp; Drama Clb; Chorus; Church Choir; School Play; VP Frsh Cls; Chrldng; High Hon Roll; Jr NHS; NHS; Warrior Singers Show Choir; Various Music Awds Super & Excl; Med.

CAROLINA, NKECHI; Butner Schl; Wewoka, OK; (4); 4/22; Church Yth Grp; Cmnty Wkr; 4-H; FHA; Quiz Bowl; Scholastic Bowl; Pres Jr Cls; VP Sr Cls; VP Stu Cncl; Bsktbl; Homcmng Qn; Miss BHS; Annual King; U Of Central OK; Pediatrcs.

CAROLINA, RICHARD; Butner Schl; Wewoka, OK; (2); 1/20; Church Yth Grp; Cmnty Wkr; 4-H; Quiz Bowl; Pres Frsh Cls; Bsktbl; Ftbl; High Hon Roll; Hon Roll; NHS; OK Hnr Soc; Law.

CARON, STACY L; Eisenhower Sr HS; Lawton, OK; (3); Church Yth Grp; Cmnty Wkr; Pep Clb; Chorus; Church Choir; Hon Roll; Prfct Atten Awd; Child Psych.

CAROTHERS, SHANNON; Midwest City HS; Midwest City, OK; (3); 51/384; Church Yth Grp; Girl Scts; SADD; Church Choir; Rep Stu Cncl; Bsktbl; Trk; High Hon Roll; Jr NHS; Prfct Atten Awd; Thnksgvng & Chrstms Needy Family Adptn Clb; Intl Mrktng.

CAROTHERS, TREY A; Snyder HS; Indiahoma, OK; (2); Church Yth Grp; 4-H; Natl FFA Org; Band; Wt Lftg; Wrstlng; 4-H Awd; Hon Roll; Cameron Univ.

CARPENTER, BARRY; Clinton HS; Clinton, OK; (1); 5/170; Church Yth Grp; Bsktbl; Golf; Score Keeper; Hon Roll; NHS.

CARPENTER, CARRIE S; Booker T Washington HS; Tulsa, OK; (3); Art Clb; French Clb; Var L Swmmng; NHS; Natl Art Hon Soc; Site-Base/Shrd Dcsn Mkng Cncl Mmbr; Brigham Young Univ; Engr.

CARPENTER, CATHERINE E; Guthrie Sr HS; Guthrie, OK; (1); #37 in class; Bus Profs of Am; Cmnty Wkr; Tennis; Hon Roll; Jr NHS; NASA Math & Sci Camp OSU; Senate Page OK St; AZ ST Univ; Phy Thrpst.

CARPENTER, DAVID G; Owasso Sr HS; Owasso, OK; (2); Boy Scts; Church Yth Grp; FCA; SADD; JV Ftbl; Wt Lftg; De Molay; Snow Skiing; U Of AR; Arch.

CARPENTER, DOUGLAS; Claremore Sr HS; Claremore, OK; (3); 1/268; Church Yth Grp; Math Clb; Science Clb; Var Socr; High Hon Roll; NHS; OM.

CARPENTER, JENNIFER; Blair Schl; Blair, OK; (3); 3/37; Church Yth Grp; Cmnty Wkr; Natl Beta Clb; Quiz Bowl; Red Cross Aide; School Play; High Hon Roll; Jr NHS.

CARPENTER, KIERRA B; Stonewall Jr-Sr HS; Stonewall, OK; (2); 2/30; Church Yth Grp; Sec FBLA; Pres Soph Cls; Var Bsktbl; Var Sftbl; High Hon Roll; NHS; Val; FCA; Natl FFA Org; All Around Girl; All Area 3rd Team In Bsktbl; Star Greenhand Awd; East Cntrl Univ; PE Coach.

CARPENTER, LAURA A; Bethel HS; Mc Loud, OK; (1); 10/83; Church Yth Grp; Quiz Bowl; Scholastic Bowl; Band; Chorus; Jazz Band; Mrchg Band; High Hon Roll; Show Choir; Presdntl Recognition; OK HS Hnr Soc; U Of OK; Meteorologist.

CARPENTER, LAURA L; Bartlesville Sr HS; Bartlesville, OK; (4); 12/420; Chrmn Church Yth Grp; FCA; Sec French Clb; Service Clb; Band; Mrchg Band; Pep Band; Capt Chrldng; French Hon Soc; High Hon Roll; Chrysalis Emmaus Cmmty Events; Phillips Gynstic Inst; See You At The Pole Evnt; OK Baptist Univ.

CARPENTER, MARSHA R; Drummond Schl; Douglas, OK; (4); 11/22; Yrbk; FHA; Natl FFA Org; Quiz Bowl; SADD; Treas Soph Cls; Stat Bsktbl; Stat Sftbl; Cit Awd; High Hon Roll; NW OK ST Univ; Travel Agent.

CARPENTER, MELODI; Midwest City HS; Oklahoma City, OK; (2); 51/501; Church Yth Grp; GAA; Band; Chorus; Church Choir; Drill Tm; School Play; Ofcr Frsh Cls; Ofcr Soph Cls; Rep Stu Cncl; Med.

CARPENTER, NICOLE; Clinton HS; Clinton, OK; (3); 5/120; Church Yth Grp; FCA; FBLA; FHA; Spanish Clb; Hon Roll; NHS; Ntl Merit Ltr; OSU; Accntg.

CARPENTER, RACHELLE D; Christian Heritage Acad; Oklahoma City, OK; (2); Church Yth Grp; FCA; Spanish Clb; Ed Yrbk; Var Vllybl; Cit Awd; High Hon Roll; Jr NHS; OSU; Jrnlsm/Radio/TV/BRDCSTNG.

CARPENTER, SHAWNA; Sulphur HS; Sulphur, OK; (3); Art Clb; Church Yth Grp; FCA; Spanish Clb; Rep Frsh Cls; Sec Soph Cls; Sec Jr Cls; JV Bsktbl; Var Chrldng; JV Trk; Ftbl Homecoming Queen 95-; E Coll Univ; Nrsng.

CARR, ADAM; Newcastle HS; Newcastle, OK; (3); Church Yth Grp; Math Tm; Model UN; Quiz Bowl; Science Clb; Hon Roll; NHS; Ntl Merit Ltr; Mock Trial; OK ST U; Vet Sci.

CARR, AMY L; Midwest City HS; Midwest City, OK; (3); FHA; German Clb; Pep Clb; VICA; Ofcr Soph Cls; Mgr(s); Jr NHS; Pres Acad Fit Awd; Rose ST Coll; Child Related.

CARR, DAVID; Bowlegs Schl; Bowlegs, OK; (4); 4/26; Natl Beta Clb; Quiz Bowl; Band; Mrchg Band; Pep Band; VP Jr Cls; Pres Sr Cls; Hon Roll; NHS; Beta Club Pres; Military.

CARR, JAMIE; Bartlesville Sr HS; Bartlesville, OK; (3); Sftbl; Hon Roll; Phys Thrpy.

CARR, JAMIE L; Harrah HS; Harrah, OK; (3); 52/153; Church Choir; French Clb; Chorus; Trk; 3rd Rnnr Up Miss Harrah Pgnt; Church Bsktbl; St Vcl, Piano Super Rtng; Piano Lssns 9 Yrs; UCO; Music.

CARR, JUSTIN G; Colcord Schl; Colcord, OK; (2); Geolgy.

CARR, NATHAN D; Christian Heritage Acad; Oklahoma City, OK; (2); Church Yth Grp; Hosp Aide; Chorus; Church Choir; Ofcr Soph Cls; Tennis; Hon Roll; Med Dr.

CARR, ROSALIND R; Western Heights Sr HS; Oklahoma City, OK; (2); #39 in class; Church Yth Grp; FCA; Spanish Clb; Chorus; Church Choir; School Musical; Ofcr Stu Cncl; Chrldng; Hon Roll; Jr NHS; Received Outstdng In Show Choir; Washington U.

CARR, SHYLA D; Arapaho Schl; Arapaho, OK; (3); 9/23; Church Yth Grp; Pres FHA; Letterman Clb; Scholastic Bowl; Teachers Aide; Varsity Clb; Rep Stu Cncl; Var Bsktbl; Var Chrldng; Prfct Atten Awd; Leading Rebnd Awd In Basktbl; Leading Fld Goal % Awd In Bsktbl; Phys Thpy.

CARRELL, DANIEAL G; Dickson HS; Ardmore, OK; (4); Church Yth Grp; Cmnty Wkr; FCA; FHA; Key Clb; SADD; Teachers Aide; Color Guard; Sec Frsh Cls; Sec Soph Cls; OSU; Med/Law.

CARRERAS, CATHERINE; Eisenhower Sr HS; Lawton, OK; (3); #88 in class; Ofcr Jr Cls; Ofcr Stu Cncl; Hon Roll; Jr NHS; NHS; Nrsng.

CARRIGAN, AMANDA; Foyil Schl; Claremore, OK; (1); FHA; GAA; Pep Clb; Quiz Bowl; Rep Frsh Cls; Chrldng; Mgr(s); Score Keeper; Trk; OK Union.

CARR-LALLI, BENJAMIN D; Mc Alester HS; Mcalester, OK; (4); Am Leg Boys St; Boy Scts; FCA; Letterman Clb; Office Aide; Ofcr Bsbl; Ftbl; Wt Lftg; Hon Roll; Eagle Sct; All-Dist & All-Area Ftbl Teams; Eastern OK ST Coll; Pre-Med.

CARROLL, ADAM M; Dickson HS; Ardmore, OK; (3); 3/90; Spanish Clb; SADD; VICA; Band; Mrchg Band; Pep Band; High Hon Roll; NHS; Prfct Atten Awd; AMA; Ama; GNC; Engrng.

CARROLL, CHASITY; Fox Sr HS; Healdton, OK; (1); Church Yth Grp; FCA; 4-H; FHA; Band; Mrchg Band; Sftbl; Jr NHS; Pres Acad Fit Awd; Archery; OK; Vet.

CARROLL, CHRISTOPHER S; Cashion HS; Cashion, OK; (2); FCA; FBLA; Natl FFA Org; Bsktbl; Hon Roll; FFA St Champn In Gen Ag Spech Cont & Parlmntry Procdr Tem Pres; OK ST Univ; Tchr; Minister.

CARROLL, HOLLY; Chickasha HS; Chickasha, OK; (1); Church Yth Grp; Science Clb; Spanish Clb; Chorus; Church Choir; Sec Frsh Cls; JV Bsktbl; Chrldng; Var Socr; Hon Roll; Outstdng Girl In Mixed Chorus 93-95; All Dist Soccer 96; Psych.

CARROLL, JAMIE; B T Washington HS; Tulsa, OK; (2); Flag Corp; Sftbl; Lawyer.

CARROLL, JAYME; Miami Sr HS; Miami, OK; (3); Church Yth Grp; FCA; GAA; Letterman Clb; Natl FFA Org; Teachers Aide; Sec Jr Cls; Bsktbl; Score Keeper; Hon Roll; Stdnt Cncl Mem; FFA Cmptv Spkng; NEO A&M Coll; Optmtry.

CARROLL, JENNEFER T; Lone Grove HS; Lone Grove, OK; (2); Speech Tm; Hon Roll; Fishing; Horse Bck Rdg; SOSU; Vet Sci.

CARROLL, JENNIFER; Cashion HS; Cashion, OK; (4); 7/34; Church Yth Grp; Cmnty Wkr; FCA; VP Sec 4-H; Rep FBLA; Girl Scts; Pres Rep Natl FFA Org; VP Pep Clb; Spanish Clb; Speech Tm; ST FFA Deg; Hnr Schlr Acad Achvmnt Awd OSU Alumni Assn.

CARROLL, MIKE L; Claremore Sr HS; Claremore, OK; (2); Computer Clb; Hon Roll; U Of KS; Cmptr Sci.

CARROLL, TOM L; Oaks Mission Jr Sr HS; Inola, OK; (4); Church Yth Grp; FCA; FBLA; Letterman Clb; Natl FFA Org; Office Aide; Teachers Aide; Nwsp; Yrbk; Sec Sr Cls; North Eastern ST U; Wldlf Mngt.

CARRUTH, RONNIE; Union City Schl; Union City, OK; (4); 4/24; Math Clb; Natl FFA Org; Quiz Bowl; Scholastic Bowl; Science Clb; Teachers Aide; Bsktbl; Hon Roll; NHS; Ntl Merit Ltr; OK Hnr Soc; Yth Alv; OK ST U; Vet Med.

CARSON, CHRISTI B; Fargo Schl; Fargo, OK; (3); 5/15; Natl FFA Org; Rptr Science Clb; Spanish Clb; Yrbk; Rptr Jr Cls; Bsktbl; Mgr(s); Sftbl; Trk; Hon Roll; Southwestern OK ST Univ; RN.

CARSON, CHRISTOPHER C; Heritage Hall Schl; Edmond, OK; (2); Boy Scts; Cmnty Wkr; French Clb; Letterman Clb; JV Bsktbl; Var L Socr.

CARSON, DARRIN; Okemah HS; Castle, OK; (3); 15/65; Am Leg Boys St; Art Clb; Church Yth Grp; Science Clb; Spanish Clb; Band; Church Choir; Drm Mjr(t); Mrchg Band; Var Bsbl; Rose St Col; Sprts Med.

CARSON, KYLIE; Turpin Schl; Turpin, OK; (2); FCA; Quiz Bowl; Pres Frsh Cls; Pres Soph Cls; Sec Stu Cncl; Var Bsktbl; Var Sftbl; Var Trk; Hon Roll; NHS; W TX A&M U; Vet; Dr.

CARSON, SHENNA C; Union Intermediate HS; Tulsa, OK; (2); Church Yth Grp; FCA; Band; Pep Band; Ofcr Soph Cls; Trk; Cit Awd; Hon Roll; Chrch Yth Grp; ORU.

CARSON, THOMAS J; Ada HS; Ada, OK; (4); 83/170; Church Yth Grp; Rptr Nwsp; Rptr Lit Mag; Var Ftbl; Var Trk; Hon Roll; E Central U; Yth Mnstry.

CART, CORY D; Binger-Oney HS; Binger, OK; (3); 1/40; Church Yth Grp; 4-H; Natl Beta Clb; Pres Natl FFA Org; Office Aide; Ed Nwsp; Stat Bsktbl; Hon Roll; NHS; Val; OK Quarter Horse Yth Assn Pres; OK ST Univ.

CARTER, ANDREW S; Yukon Middle HS; Yukon, OK; (3); Church Yth Grp; FCA; Church Choir; VP Stu Cncl; Var Ftbl; Var Wt Lftg; NHS; OK Univ; Bus.

CARTER, BRANDON; Afton HS; Afton, OK; (3); 3/39; Quiz Bowl; Teachers Aide; Pres Frsh Cls; Pres Soph Cls; VP Jr Cls; Var Bsbl; Var Bsktbl; Var Ftbl; Var Trk; Var Wt Lftg; Northeastern ST U; Optmtry.

CARTER, BRITTANY; Moore HS; Moore, OK; (3); Art Clb; Church Yth Grp; Cmnty Wkr; Thesps; School Play; Trk; Dancer; U CO; Lwyr.

CARTER, CARA J; Haskell HS; Haskell, OK; (4); Teachers Aide; Band; Color Guard; Flag Corp; Mrchg Band; Pep Band; Hon Roll; Connors ST Coll; Spcl Ed.

CARTER, CATRECE D; Geary Jr Sr HS; Geary, OK; (2); 4/25; FHA; GAA; Band; Yrbk; Bsktbl; Wt Lftg; Hon Roll; LPN.

CARTER, CHAD M; B T Washington HS; Tulsa, OK; (4); 70/280; German Clb; Library Aide; Quiz Bowl; VICA; Stage Crew; Phtg Yrbk; Cit Awd; Natl Voc Hnr Soc Mem 2nd Yr; Vo Stu Org Photographer; Head Photographer C/O 96 Prodctn 1 Slide Show; U Ctr At Tulsa; Bus Admin.

CARTER, CHRISTI L; Meeker HS; Chandler, OK; (2); Art Clb; ROTC; Spanish Clb; Color Guard; Drill Tm; Bsktbl; Sftbl; Vllybl; High Hon Roll; Hon Roll; Art.

CARTER, CORBY; Wagoner Sr HS; Hulbert, OK; (4); VP 4-H; Pres FBLA; Teachers Aide; Var L Ftbl; Var L Socr; Intrml Wt Lftg; 4-H Awd; Hon Roll; NHS; Street Hockey Co-Capt; OK U; Med.

CARTER, CORY R; Cushing HS; Cushing, OK; (1); Church Yth Grp; JV Bsbl; JV Ftbl; Wt Lftg; High Hon Roll; Hon Roll; NHS; Sprts Med.

CARTER, DANESA D; Buffalo Jr Sr HS; Buffalo, OK; (3); Church Yth Grp; 4-H; FBLA; Band; Chorus; Jazz Band; Mrchg Band; Pep Band; Sec Frsh Cls; Cit Awd; Amer Schlr; Natl Band Awd; Phillips Univ; Music Ther.

CARTER, JACQUELINE; Midwest City HS; Midwest City, OK; (4); 22/419; FCA; Rptr FHA; HOBY; SADD; Church Choir; Ofcr Sr Cls; Vllybl; High Hon Roll; Pres Acad Fit Awd; Val; African Amer Alliance Sec; Midwest City Stomp Team Capt; U Of TX; Cardiolgy.

CARTER, JEREMY; Broken Arrow Sr HS; Broken Arrow, OK; (2); CAP; Band; Jazz Band; Mrchg Band; Pep Band; School Musical; School Play; Ofcr Stu Cncl; Pres Acad Fit Awd; Flying Aircraft; U Of AZ; Military Aviator.

CARTER, JEREMY L; Central Schl; Sallisaw, OK; (3); Art Clb; Church Yth Grp; Computer Clb; Pep Clb; Spanish Clb; Yrbk; Ofcr Jr Cls; Ftbl; Wt Lftg; Author; Stand Up Comedy; Poet; Arts Coll; Actor; Author; Animatr.

CARTER, JERRY L; Mustang HS; Yukon, OK; (1); FCA; Hon Roll; NHS; OK ST Univ; Lwyr.

CARTER, JESSICA J; Westmoore HS; Oklahoma City, OK; (3); Church Yth Grp; Cmnty Wkr; Band; Church Choir; Govt Class Pres 11th Grd; Art Cntst 3rd Pl; Sndy Sch/Tch 1st/2nd Grd Kids; Southern Nazerine Univ; His.

CARTER, JIMMY D; Madill HS; Madill, OK; (2); Art Clb; Church Yth Grp; FCA; SADD; Ofcr Jr Cls; Ofcr Bsbl; Bsktbl; Ftbl; Score Keeper; Trk; NEO; Eng.

CARTER, JOHN W; Velma Alma HS; Velma, OK; (2); Church Yth Grp; FCA; Natl FFA Org; JV Var Bsktbl; High Hon Roll; Hon Roll; Law.

CARTER, JOSH L; Butler Jr Sr HS; Hammon, OK; (4); Natl FFA Org; VP Sr Cls; Cit Awd; Hon Roll; NHS.

CARTER, JULIA D; Grandfield Jr Sr HS; Grandfield, OK; (1); Church Yth Grp; Cmnty Wkr; FHA; Pep Clb; Church Choir; Bsktbl; Sftbl; Trk; Howard Univ; Tchr.

CARTER, KACEY L; Moyers Public Schl; Finley, OK; (3); 2/15; Church Yth Grp; Cmnty Wkr; 4-H; Office Aide; SADD; Church Choir; Pres Jr Cls; Var Bsktbl; 4-H Awd; Hon Roll; Olkmogee; Sec.

CARTER, KERRIE L; Stonewall Jr-Sr HS; Stonewall, OK; (2); Church Yth Grp; Pep Clb; Scholastic Bowl; Var Chrldng; Hon Roll; Elem Ed.

CARTER, KIMBERLY J; Moore HS; Moore, OK; (3); #16 in class; Church Yth Grp; FHA; Office Aide; Teachers Aide; Chorus; Hon Roll; Nursng.

CARTER, LINDSAY R; Catoosa HS; Tulsa, OK; (1); Dance Clb; Pep Clb; Spanish Clb; Drill Tm; Yrbk; Bsktbl; Chrldng; Crs Cntry; Gym; Socr.

CARTER, MATTHEW J; Stonewall Jr-Sr HS; Stonewall, OK; (2); 5/30; Church Yth Grp; FCA; 4-H; Natl FFA Org; Scholastic Bowl; Var Bsbl; Var Bsktbl; Hon Roll; Masonic/All Rnd Fresh Boy Awds.

CARTER, MISTY R; Noble HS; Noble, OK; (3); French Clb; FHA; Mu Alpha Theta; Band; Chorus; Mrchg Band; Phtg Yrbk; Hon Roll; Jr NHS; NHS; OK Univ.

CARTER, NANCY L; Roland Sr HS; Roland, OK; (3); Speech Tm; Chorus; High Hon Roll; Poetry; Acad Cont; Adolesent Psych.

CARTER, NICK W; Choctaw HS; Midwest City, OK; (2); Office Aide; Var Bsktbl; Var Ftbl; Var Golf; Var Wt Lftg; Hon Roll; Jr NHS; East Cntrl U; Bus.

CARTER, REGINA; Rattan Sr HS; Finley, OK; (4); 3/32; 4-H; French Clb; FHA; Office Aide; Nwsp; High Hon Roll; Hon Roll; NHS; Trinity Vly CC; Sec.

CARTER, ROSE; Cheyenne HS; Cheyenne, OK; (4); 10/19; Church Yth Grp; FBLA; FHA; Band; Flag Corp; Mrchg Band; Chrldng; Sftbl; Hon Roll; Prfct Atten Awd; Hnr Band 94-96; 101 Clssc Bwl 95; Bus Mgmt.

CARTER, RYAN; El Reno Sr HS; El Reno, OK; (3).

CARTER, SHANON; Wynnewood HS; Wynnewood, OK; (3); 4/60; Pres FHA; Speech Tm; Teachers Aide; VP Jr Cls; High Hon Roll; NHS; Psych.

CARTER, SHERIDA R; Mc Lain Career Acad; Tulsa, OK; (4); Church Yth Grp; Teachers Aide; High Hon Roll; Nurses Aid.

CARTER, VALERIE; Hulbert Jr Sr HS; Hulbert, OK; (1); Church Yth Grp; 4-H; Chorus; Stage Crew; Gov Hon Prg Awd; High Hon Roll; Hon Roll; Jr NHS; Prfct Atten Awd; GATE; Tlnt Srch; Acad Tm; NSU; Zoology.

CARTER, WESLEY R; Muskogee HS; Muskogee, OK; (2); Church Yth Grp; High Hon Roll; Chrch Drama Team; U Of OK.

CARTMILL, CASEY L; Cushing HS; Cushing, OK; (3); Church Yth Grp; Cmnty Wkr; Debate Tm; Drama Clb; Math Clb; Quiz Bowl; Spanish Clb; Speech Tm; School Musical; School Play.

CARTWRIGHT, ALLISON L; Tahlequah Jr HS; Tahlequah, OK; (1); Church Yth Grp; Girl Scts; Band; Color Guard; Jr NHS; Pres Awd Educl Exclnc; OK Jr Acad Sci; Tri-ST Hnr Band.

CARVER, BRANDON K; Elgin HS; Elgin, OK; (1); Natl FFA Org; Ofcr Bsbl; Bsktbl; Ftbl; Wt Lftg; High Hon Roll.

CARVER, JEB S; Sapulpa Sr HS; Sapulpa, OK; (3); 48/300; Church Yth Grp; Math Clb; Scholastic Bowl; Science Clb; Spanish Clb; Band; Jazz Band; Mrchg Band; Orch; Hon Roll; U Of OK.

CARVER, LESLIE E; Apache HS; Apache, OK; (2); Church Yth Grp; Drama Clb; FHA; Thesps; School Play; Stage Crew; Sec Frsh Cls; Sec Soph Cls; Ofcr Stu Cncl; Southwestern OK ST U; Acctng.

CARY, ANGELA; Westmoore HS; Oklahoma City, OK; (4); 8/622; Am Leg Aux Girls St; FCA; Q&S; Yrbk; Rep Stu Cncl; Var L Crs Cntry; Var L Trk; NHS; Val; FJA; Advrtsng.

CARY, BRANDON H; Hollis Jr Sr HS; Hollis, OK; (2); 1/70; Church Yth Grp; Drama Clb; Natl FFA Org; Quiz Bowl; Speech Tm; VP Frsh Cls; VP Soph Cls; L Bsbl; Intrml Ftbl; NHS.

CARY, DUSTIN; Ardmore HS; Ardmore, OK; (4); Art Clb; FCA; Latin Clb; Ofcr Bsbl; Ftbl; Wt Lftg; Wrstlng; U Of Central OK; Ed.

CASBURN, ELIZABETH A; Edmond North HS; Edmond, OK; (3); #50 in class; French Clb; Mu Alpha Theta; Rep Stu Cncl; Var Socr; Var Sftbl; JV Vllybl; NHS; Sun Clb; Smmr Rec Sftbl Tm; Soccer Mst Imprvd Awd 2 Yrs.

CASE, BRAD; Midwest City HS; Midwest City, OK; (3); 136/384; Church Yth Grp; Office Aide; Var L Socr; Jr NHS; All Mid St Sccr Team.

CASE, CARRIE; Seiling Schl; Fairview, OK; (4); Art Clb; FCA; FBLA; FHA; Letterman Clb; Band; School Play; Phtg Yrbk; Rep Soph Cls; Rep Stu Cncl; OK ST U.

CASE, DAVID J; Clayton Jr Sr HS; Clayton, OK; (4); Debate Tm; Drama Clb; NFL; Speech Tm; Teachers Aide; Band; Chorus; Mrchg Band; Pep Band; School Play; Tour Europe Amer Music Ambassador; USAA Band, Eng & Amer Schlr Awds; Southeastern Univ; Music.

CASE, GRANT S; Mustang HS; Mustang, OK; (3); Am Leg Boys St; FBLA; Quiz Bowl; Scholastic Bowl; L Mgr(s); NHS; Natl Jr Acad Of Scis Del.

CASE, JEREMY D; Union Intermediate HS; Tulsa, OK; (2); FCA; Var Crs Cntry; Var Trk; High Hon Roll; Jr NHS; NHS; Pres Acad Fit Awd; Church Yth Grp; JCL; Chorus; 5 Time USA Trck & Fld All-Amer; 3 Time AAU X-Cntry & Trck & Fld All-Amer; All-St X-Cntry 1995; Psych.

CASEY, BRADLEY; Kiowa Jr-Sr HS; Kiowa, OK; (4); 3/23; Church Yth Grp; Natl FFA Org; Sec Rep Frsh Cls; Pres Jr Cls; Pres Stu Cncl; Bsktbl; Pres Acad Fit Awd; Sal; Rep Soph Cls; OK ST FFA Sec; Japanese Ag Exchnge Stdnt; OK Farmers Sr Advy Cncl; OSU; Ag Ed/Ag Econ.

CASEY, MELISSA; Tecumseh HS; Shawnee, OK; (3); 5/143; Church Yth Grp; FCA; French Clb; HOBY; Natl Beta Clb; SADD; VP Jr Cls; Sec Stu Cncl; Mgr(s); NHS; Cls Pres; VFW Awd; Amer Legion Awd; Top Ten; OK Baptist U; Phys Thrpy.

CASEY, MIKE; Collinsville HS; Collinsville, OK; (4); 17/100; Church Yth Grp; Spanish Clb; Hon Roll; Tulsa JC; Bus.

CASH, KEVIN M; Union Intermediate HS; Tulsa, OK; (1); Church Yth Grp; French Clb; Math Clb; Orch; Ofcr Stu Cncl; High Hon Roll; NHS; Hon Roll; Snpsrd Spd Sktr Trmntr Brngs; ARC GATE Prgm; Yng Astrnts Club; Duke U.

CASH, RACHEL A; Pauls Valley HS; Pauls Valley, OK; (1); Church Yth Grp; 4-H; Pep Clb; Hon Roll; FFA; Arabian & Quater Hores Trng & Showing; OK ST U; Equine Vet Med.

CASILLAS, RICKY D; Skiatook HS; Avant, OK; (2); Church Yth Grp; Ofcr Bsbl; Bsktbl; Ftbl; Hon Roll; OK ST Univ; Avtn Main Tech.

CASPER, ERIC D; Edmond North HS; Edmond, OK; (2); 45/420; Church Yth Grp; FCA; Band; Drm Mjr(t); Jazz Band; Mrchg Band; Pep Band; Rep Stu Cncl; Swmmng; Jr NHS; Outstdng Trmbone Soloist UCO Music Fstvl; Lfgrd; Leading Actor Natl Telvsd Chrstn Play; Pre Med/Dr.

CASS, MILTON B; Pawhuska HS; Pawhuska, OK; (3); Church Yth Grp; FCA; Natl FFA Org; VICA; Var Bsbl; Var Ftbl; Var Wt Lftg; Var Wrstlng; Hon Roll; NASA; Petroleum Engr.

CASSAVAUGH, FELICIA; Asher Schl; Byars, OK; (1); Church Yth Grp; FHA; School Play; Rptr Nwsp; Capt Pom Pon; Var Sftbl; Hon Roll; Actrss.

CASSIDAY, MELISSA; Crescent Schl; Crescent, OK; (3); 5/50; Church Yth Grp; CAP; FCA; FHA; Natl Beta Clb; SADD; Chorus; Hon Roll; Pres Acad Fit Awd; Yrbk.

CASTEEL, ANTONIA; Rock Creek Jr Sr HS; Bokchito, OK; (3); 2/36; FCA; FHA; Natl FFA Org; Spanish Clb; Teachers Aide; Chorus; School Musical; High Hon Roll; NHS; Pres Acad Fit Awd; SOSU; Psych.

CASTILLO, AMY E; Frontier Public Schl; Red Rock, OK; (2); Band; Chorus; School Musical; Cit Awd; High Hon Roll; NHS; Tri-ST Hnr Choir; Prin Awd Johnson O'Malley Fndtn.

CASTILLO, JUSTIN D; Memorial HS; Tulsa, OK; (2); Key Clb; Red Cross Aide; Science Clb; Spanish Clb; Sec Jr Cls; Swmmng; Hon Roll; Acad Tm; Columbia; Nvlst.

CASTLE, BROOK; Clinton HS; Crawford, OK; (4); 28/99; Church Yth Grp; DECA; FCA; Natl FFA Org; Ofcr Stu Cncl; Var Bsktbl; Hon Roll; 4-H; GAA; Library Aide; US Army Rsrv Natl Schlr/Ath Awd; 96 Sprts Chlng Intl Switzerland Bsktbl Tour; Bsktbl Schlrshp; OK Panhandle ST U; Bus Admin.

CASTLE, SHERRI L; Oklahoma Sch Of Science & Math; Del City, OK; (3); Church Yth Grp; FCA; Scholastic Bowl; Drm Mjr(t); Flag Corp; Orch; Rep Stu Cncl; JV Var Sftbl; NHS; Pres Acad Fit Awd; Aerosp Engrng.

CASTLE, VICTORIA; New Lima Jr Sr HS; Seminole, OK; (2); #1 in class; Church Yth Grp; Quiz Bowl; Church Choir; Rep Stu Cncl; JV Var Bsktbl; Hon Roll; OK Hnr Socty; U Of OK; Phys Thrpst.

CASTLEBERRY, JOHN E; Keota Schl; Keota, OK; (2); Natl FFA Org; Ofcr Soph Cls; Var L Ftbl; Comp Tech; Surgeon.

CASTLEBERRY, WOODROW S; Mill Creek Schl; Mill Creek, OK; (3); Church Yth Grp; Varsity Clb; Ofcr Bsbl; Bsktbl; Hon Roll.

CASTNER, CHRISTY L; Mustang HS; Yukon, OK; (3); Church Yth Grp; FCA; Acpl Chr; Rep Soph Cls; Rep Jr Cls; Treas Sr Cls; Ofcr Stu Cncl; Chrldng; Powder Puff Ftbl; Hon Roll; FBC Yth Cncl; Var Chrldng Co-Capt; Renaissance Acad Awd; OK Bapt Univ; Scndry Ed.

CASTRO, AMY; Mt St Marys HS; Norman, OK; (2); 1/78; Pres FCA; Treas Frsh Cls; VP Soph Cls; Pres Jr Cls; JV Bsktbl; Var L Mgr(s); Var L Tennis; Var L Vllybl; High Hon Roll; Hon Roll; 4 Yr U; Elem Ed.

CASTROP, CASEY D; El Reno Sr HS; El Reno, OK; (2); Church Yth Grp; Cmnty Wkr; Spanish Clb; Golf; Cit Awd; Hon Roll.

CASWELL, JOSEPH F; Macarthur Sr HS; Lawton, OK; (3); 4/272; Church Yth Grp; FCA; French Clb; German Clb; Quiz Bowl; Science Clb; Var L Socr; High Hon Roll; Jr NHS; Ntl Merit Ltr; U Of VA; Bio-Chem/Pre-Med.

CATER, ANGELA; Macomb Schl; Macomb, OK; (4); 2/20; FBLA; Sec Frsh Cls; Sec Soph Cls; Sec Jr Cls; Sec Sr Cls; Rep Stu Cncl; Var Capt Bsktbl; Var Capt Sftbl; High Hon Roll; Sal; T-Ball Cch; OK Hist 2nd Pl Awd; All Star Bsktbl; Saint Gregorys Catholic Coll.

CATES, LESLEY; Stuart Sr HS; Haywood, OK; (4); 7/30; Am Leg Aux Girls St; Church Yth Grp; Sec FCA; Rptr Nwsp; Yrbk; VP Frsh Cls; Pres Soph Cls; Pres Sr Cls; Pres Stu Cncl; Hon Roll; First United Bnk Jr Brd VP; Natl Sci Mrt Awd; E Cntrl OK U; Bus Admin.

CATES, WILL; Beaver HS; Beaver, OK; (1); Church Yth Grp; Quiz Bowl; Chorus; Sec Frsh Cls; Var Bsbl; JV Bsktbl; JV Ftbl; Hon Roll; Tennis; Track.

CATHEY, LUCAS U; Mustang HS; Mustang, OK; (1); Cmnty Wkr; Debate Tm; FCA; Science Clb; Spanish Clb; Teachers Aide; Yrbk; OSU; Vet Med.

CATLETT, KENDI; Clinton HS; Clinton, OK; (2); Church Yth Grp; FCA; FHA; Chorus; Renassance Acad Prgrm.

CATLETT, MICHELLE A; Claremore Sr HS; Claremore, OK; (2); Boy Scts; Church Yth Grp; Cmnty Wkr; Drama Clb; Hosp Aide; Office Aide; Speech Tm; Pres SADD; Teachers Aide; School Musical; Var Bsbl Batgirl; DARE Role Model Spkr; Surgeon.

CATLETT, MONICA; Clinton HS; Clinton, OK; (3); Church Yth Grp; Drama Clb; FHA; GAA; Hosp Aide; Key Clb; Chorus; School Play; Yrbk; Socr; Piano; U Of OK; Dntstry.

CATLIN, AMY C; Buffalo Jr Sr HS; Buffalo, OK; (1); Church Yth Grp; Cmnty Wkr; 4-H; Key Clb; Band; Chorus; L Sftbl; 4-H Awd; Hon Roll; Mrchg Band; FFA; Show Choir.

CATLIN, JENNIFER; Buffalo Jr Sr HS; Buffalo, OK; (3); FCA; Pres 4-H; HOBY; Band; Chorus; Yrbk; Sftbl; Trk; NHS; Church Yth Grp; Show Choir.

CATON, AMANDA; Oologah Talala HS; Oologah, OK; (1); Chorus; Var Chrldng; Var Socr; Var Trk; High Hon Roll; Opthomologist.

CATON, ELIZABETH T; Latta Sr HS; Ada, OK; (3); Am Leg Aux Girls St; Church Yth Grp; Cmnty Wkr; FCA; GAA; Office Aide; Quiz Bowl; Rep Frsh Cls; Rep Jr Cls; Var Bsktbl; KADA Prep Player Of The Yr Bsktbl; Horseback Riding; Natl Hnr Soc Schlsp Nom; E Central; Speech Pathology.

CAUDLE, MATTHEW D; Union Intermediate HS; Tulsa, OK; (2); Church Yth Grp; Key Clb; Spanish Clb; Hon Roll; NHS; Taekwon Do; MO; Broadcast Jrnlsm.

CAUGHMAN, ANNIE; Tahlequah Sr HS; Tahlequah, OK; (2); Church Yth Grp; Cmnty Wkr; Wt Lftg; Matt Maid; Spirt Club; Model; U Of CO; Psychrst.

CAUGHMAN, DARAH; Pawhuska HS; Pawhuska, OK; (2); 5/85; Church Yth Grp; Cmnty Wkr; FCA; GAA; Key Clb; Pep Clb; Acpl Chr; Chorus; Church Choir; Rep Frsh Cls.

CAUGHMAN, JERRY W; Sallisaw HS; Sallisaw, OK; (1); Church Yth Grp; FCA; Math Clb; Science Clb; Rptr Frsh Cls; Ftbl; Golf; Trk; Wt Lftg; Hon Roll; Octagon Clb; OU; Optometrist.

CAUGHRON, CHRISTY; Nathan Hale HS; Tulsa, OK; (3); Church Yth Grp; Math Clb; Chorus; Church Choir; Var Co-Capt Chrldng; Var Crs Cntry; Trk; High Hon Roll; Jr NHS; NHS; OK ST; Med.

CAUTHON, CARY L; Ponca City Sr HS; Ponca City, OK; (4); Office Aide; Hon Roll; Med Ctr Lab Phlebotamist; Outstdng Stu Awd Family Living; Northern OK Coll; Med; Psych.

CAVALLI, CIRILO A; Bishop Kelley HS; Tulsa, OK; (1); JV Var Ice Hcky; Var Socr; Hon Roll; Spanish NHS; Engrng.

CAVENDER, BETHANY; Idabel HS; Idabel, OK; (1); 9/135; Church Yth Grp; 4-H; FHA; Pep Clb; Chorus; Var Chrldng; 4-H Awd; High Hon Roll; Hon Roll; Jr NHS; Se OK Horse Judging Team, Numerous Hi Pt Titles & Awds; Ne OK JC; Elem Ed.

CAVER, BRANDY M; Guthrie Sr HS; Guthrie, OK; (1); 37/308; Art Clb; Church Yth Grp; Chorus; Church Choir; Art Awds; Dallas Art Inst.

CAVES, MELISSA N; Sallisaw HS; Sallisaw, OK; (1); Art Clb; Church Yth Grp; Computer Clb; Drama Clb; Speech Tm; School Play; Stage Crew; Hon Roll; NE ST U; Sec.

CAVIN, ASHLEY; Tonkawa Jr Sr HS; Tonkawa, OK; (1); Church Yth Grp; FCA; Rep Frsh Cls; Var L Chrldng; High Hon Roll; Hon Roll; U Of AR; Mgmt.

CAVIN, AUTUMN C; Grace Lane Home Schl; Tahlequah, OK; (4); Church Yth Grp; Dance Clb; Thesps; Church Choir; School Play; Swmmng; Tennis; Prfct Atten Awd; Oral Roberts U; Drama/TV/FLM.

CAVIN, DAVID J; Tonkawa Jr Sr HS; Tonkawa, OK; (3); Church Yth Grp; Teachers Aide; Rep Stu Cncl; Var L Ftbl; Var L Wrstlng; Hon Roll; NHS; OK ST Univ.

CAVIN, JENNIFER; Grace Lane HS; Tahlequah, OK; (4); Church Yth Grp; Church Choir; Two Chrch Yth Cncls; NE St Univ; Erly Chld Dvlp.

CAVIN, MANDI; Wakita Schl; Wakita, OK; (3); 1/15; Church Yth Grp; Rptr FCA; Pres FHA; Letterman Clb; Pep Clb; Band; Ed Nwsp; Bsktbl; High Hon Roll; NHS; OSU; Vet Medicine.

CAVNER, HILLARY J; Union Sr HS; Broken Arrow, OK; (4); 72/629; Office Aide; Hon Roll; Jr NHS; NHS; Rollerblading; Big Family Org; Med.

CAVNEY, CHRISTINA R; Rush Springs HS; Rush Springs, OK; (3); Church Yth Grp; Model UN; Spanish Clb; Hon Roll; ST Inter Schlstc Meet; Yth Alive Sec; SW Assmbls Of God U; Cnslng.

CAYOT, ERIC; Okeene Jr Sr HS; Okeene, OK; (4); Am Leg Boys St; Church Yth Grp; FCA; Letterman Clb; Swing Chorus; Yrbk; Bsktbl; Ftbl; Trk; Hon Roll; Cls A All Star, K101 Plyr Game, Dist A2 Off Bck Of Yr, Jumbo Foods Off/Def Plyr Game, Co-Capt Ftbl; Southwestern ST; Engrng.

CAYTON, LATONIA F; Boise City HS; Boise City, OK; (1); Church Yth Grp; FCA; FHA; GAA; JV Bsktbl; Trk; OK ST U.

CAYTON, LYNNIE-ROSE; Midwest City HS; Midwest City, OK; (4); 17/387; Treas Art Clb; FHA; Hon Roll; Acad Var Awd; Rose ST Coll; Art.

CAYWOOD, CHRISTOPHER A; Mid-Del Christian Schl; Del City, OK; (2); Boy Scts; Church Yth Grp; ROTC; Teachers Aide; Band; Chorus; Church Choir; School Musical; School Play; Score Keeper; Yth Cnslr; Church Yth Grp Contact; Pgmr Syst Analyst/Interprtr.

CAZZELLE, HEATHER; Ripley HS; Stillwater, OK; (4); 18/33; FCA; Girl Scts; Library Aide; Math Clb; Office Aide; Science Clb; Teachers Aide; Sec Soph Cls; Sec Jr Cls; Treas Sr Cls; Homcmng Qn 96; Cimmarron Vly All Conf Sftbl 96; OK ST Univ; Nrsng.

CCROWDER, GINGER; Cherokee Jr Sr HS; Cherokee, OK; (1); 5/30; Church Yth Grp; FCA; NFL; Scholastic Bowl; Speech Tm; Sec Frsh Cls; Var Bsktbl; Var Chrldng; Var Trk; Hon Roll; All St Bapt Yth Choir; U OK.

CECIL, JULIAN D; Snyder HS; Mountain Park, OK; (3); 4/41; Church Yth Grp; Band; Mrchg Band; Pep Band; VP Jr Cls; Var Bsbl; Var JV Bsktbl; Var Ftbl; Var Trk; Var Wt Lftg; U Of OK; Comp Prgmr.

CEDARS, MICHELLE L; Choctaw HS; Choctaw, OK; (3); 44/313; Church Yth Grp; High Hon Roll; Hon Roll; NHS; Rose St Col; Eng.

CEDERBLOM, JASON L; Afton HS; Afton, OK; (3); Phtg Yrbk; VP Jr Cls; VP Stu Cncl; Var Bsktbl; Var L Ftbl; Var L Trk; Ntl Merit Ltr; NEO; Comp Programming.

CERDA, AARON M; Del City HS; Oklahoma City, OK; (2); Church Yth Grp; Spanish Clb; Socr; Wt Lftg; Jr NHS; Native Amer Clb.

CERMAK, AMY M; Mustang HS; Mustang, OK; (2); 49/350; Band; Jazz Band; Mrchg Band; Pep Band; Vllybl; Hon Roll; NHS; ST Fair Hnr Band; OCU; Music/Sci.

CERVANTES, SHARLA; Dover Schl; Dover, OK; (2); 1/14; Dance Clb; HOBY; Scholastic Bowl; Pres Soph Cls; Bsktbl; Trk; Vllybl; High Hon Roll; Hon Roll; NHS; OK ST U; Ed.

CESARIO, ANASTASIA; Claremore Sr HS; Claremore, OK; (2); Church Yth Grp; Girl Scts; Hosp Aide; Scholastic Bowl; Band; Church Choir; Mrchg Band; Pep Band; High Hon Roll; Jr NHS; Dance/Ballet/Mod.

CESARIO, ANNA L; Claremore Sr HS; Claremore, OK; (2); 1/272; Girl Scts; Hosp Aide; Quiz Bowl; Band; Mrchg Band; Pep Band; High Hon Roll; Jr NHS; NHS.

CESARIO, ANTHONY; Claremore Sr HS; Claremore, OK; (4); 72/286; Church Yth Grp; Quiz Bowl; Scholastic Bowl; Band; Church Choir; Jazz Band; Mrchg Band; Orch; Pep Band; School Musical; U Of OK; Music Cmpstn/Ed.

CHACKO, CELIN; Yukon Middle HS; Yukon, OK; (2); Church Yth Grp; FHA; Hosp Aide; Quiz Bowl; Scholastic Bowl; Spanish Clb; Hon Roll; US Sntr David L Boren Awd; Outstndng Achvmnt Awd; Pre-Med.

CHACON, MARIA C; Central Mid-HS; Norman, OK; (3); Band; Orch; Phtg Yrbk; Amer Kids; Native Amer Clb; Sec Tchr.

CHADWICK, CHRISHA D; Edmond Santa Fe HS; Edmond, OK; (3); Church Yth Grp; FCA; SADD; Yrbk; NHS.

CHADWICK, JILLIAN; Sulpjur HS; Sand Springs, OK; (3); 2/76; Church Yth Grp; Cmnty Wkr; FCA; HOBY; Key Clb; Spanish Clb; Teachers Aide; Rep Frsh Cls; Rep Soph Cls; Rep Stu Cncl; OK U; Med.

CHAFFIN, AMANDA; Seminole Jr Sr HS; Seminole, OK; (2); Church Yth Grp; Debate Tm; Speech Tm; Chorus; Church Choir; High Hon Roll; Hon Roll; Pres Acad Fit Awd; OK ST U.

CHAFFIN, DAVID P; Davis HS; Davis, OK; (3); Church Yth Grp; 4-H; FBLA; Key Clb; Natl FFA Org; Chorus; School Musical; Yrbk; Rep Frsh Cls; All-Amer Schlr; Nom Natl Young Ldrs Conf; OK Bapt Univ; Psych.

CHAINAKUL, WEERA; Oklahoma Sch Of Science & Math; Shawnee, OK; (4); Boy Scts; Latin Clb; Math Clb; Quiz Bowl; Scholastic Bowl; Science Clb; Ofcr Jr Cls; Ofcr Sr Cls; Ofcr Stu Cncl; Socr; Eagle Scout; Rice Univ; Elect Eng.

CHAISON, REBECCA M; Tonkawa Jr Sr HS; Tonkawa, OK; (4); 11/36; Band; Chorus; Flag Corp; Mrchg Band; School Musical; Stage Crew; Treas Sr Cls; High Hon Roll; Hon Roll; NHS; Northern OK Coll.

CHAKRABART, KAUSHIK; Idabel HS; Idabel, OK; (4); 4/110; Am Leg Boys St; FBLA; Library Aide; Office Aide; Quiz Bowl; Science Clb; Sec Sr Cls; Rep Stu Cncl; Bsktbl; Var Golf; Outstndng Acad Achvts; U Of OK Geosciences Acad; U Of OK; Envrnmntl Sci.

CHALAKEE, SHEILA K; Eufaula Sr HS; Eufaula, OK; (3); 9/100; Drama Clb; Speech Tm; Band; Mrchg Band; School Play; Rptr Yrbk; Var Swmmng; Hon Roll; NHS; St Schlr; Paralegal.

CHALLIS, TRISHA L; Ponca City Sr HS; Ponca City, OK; (3); 151/371; Drama Clb; NFL; Spanish Clb; Speech Tm; Thesps; Chorus; School Play; Hon Roll; Orch; Tae Kwon Do; Spirit Ofcr NFL; Theatre; Ed.

CHALONER, ALL; El Reno Sr HS; El Reno, OK; (2); Church Yth Grp; 4-H; Natl FFA Org; Chrldng; Sftbl; Hon Roll; NHS; Psych.

CHALOUPEK, AMBER L; Owasso Sr HS; Owasso, OK; (4); 61/296; Church Yth Grp; FCA; FHA; Hist FTA; GAA; Office Aide; Teachers Aide; VICA; Ofcr Stu Cncl; Var Capt Bsktbl; Tulsa World Awd For Acad Excel; OHS Female Ath Of Yr 95-; US Army Reserve Scholar/Ath Awd; U Of OK.

CHAMBERLAIN, BROOK L; South Intermediate HS; Broken Arrow, OK; (1); Church Yth Grp; French Clb; Office Aide; Hon Roll; Pres Schlr; Modeling; St Gftd Pgm.

CHAMBERS, BRANDON; Oologah HS; Claremore, OK; (4); 3/100; Am Leg Boys St; Teachers Aide; Jazz Band; Mrchg Band; Var Ftbl; Capt Swmmng; Hon Roll; NHS; Sal; OK Sgt-At-Arms Sns Amer Lgn; Natl Yng Ldrs Conf Wshngtn DC.

CHAMBERS, CORY J; Ardmore HS; Ardmore, OK; (3); Am Leg Boys St; Boy Scts; Church Yth Grp; FHA; Hosp Aide; Latin Clb; Math Clb; Mu Alpha Theta; Red Cross Aide; Ski Clb; Lifeguard; OSU.

CHAMBERS, DEENA; Ripley HS; Ripley, OK; (3); 10/41; Church Yth Grp; FBLA; HOBY; Teachers Aide; VP Band; Ofcr Jr Cls; Sec Stu Cncl; Mgr(s); Hon Roll; NHS; Piano; Clog.

CHAMBERS, ERICA; Lone Grove HS; Lone Grove, OK; (4); 4/77; Capt Debate Tm; Treas Key Clb; Sec Math Clb; Model UN; Natl Beta Clb; NFL; Sec Science Clb; Speech Tm; Band; School Musical; U Of OK; Mrn Bio.

CHAMBERS, GREGORY S; West Middle HS; Norman, OK; (1); Church Yth Grp; Var Bsktbl; Hon Roll.

CHAMBERS, JAMIE N; B T Washington HS; Tulsa, OK; (4); 47/264; French Clb; Office Aide; Rptr Stu Cncl; Capt Crs Cntry; Capt Trk; Hon Roll; Jr NHS; NHS; U Tulsa; Phys Thrpy.

CHAMBERS, MANDI; Achille Schl; Achille, OK; (4); 1/30; Church Yth Grp; FHA; Library Aide; Acpl Chr; Chorus; Ofcr Soph Cls; Ofcr Jr Cls; Ofcr Sr Cls; Chrldng; Sftbl; Southeasern OK ST U; Pre-Med.

CHAMBERS, SEAN; Central HS; Tulsa, OK; (1); High Hon Roll; Hon Roll; Hnrs.

CHAMBERS, TREVOR; Pond Creek-Hunter Schl; Pond Creek, OK; (3); Church Yth Grp; Sec Frsh Cls; Sec Soph Cls; Pres Jr Cls; Rep Stu Cncl; Var Bsbl; Var Bsktbl; Var Ftbl; High Hon Roll; NHS; Bus.

CHAMPION III, JOE; Big Pasture HS; Devol, OK; (3); 4-H; Church Choir; School Musical; Nwsp; Yrbk; Mgr Bsktbl; Cit Awd; 4-H Awd; Hon Roll; Southeastern ST.

CHAMPLAIN, TAMARKIA; Ponca City Sr HS; Ponca City, OK; (3); Debate Tm; FCA; Office Aide; VP Soph Cls; Ofcr Bsbl; Var Chrldng; Gym; Hon Roll; NHS; NSU; Pre-Med.

CHAN, ERIC Y; Putnam City North HS; Oklahoma City, OK; (2); Cmnty Wkr; French Clb; Science Clb; Spanish Clb; Cit Awd; Kiwanis Awd; NHS; Piano Dist Achvmt/Music Fstvl/ST Cmptn Awds; PEAK.

CHAN, HUI-MIN; Edmond North HS; Edmond, OK; (3); 1/379; Boy Scts; Cmnty Wkr; French Clb; Treas Key Clb; Latin Clb; Mu Alpha Theta; ROTC; SADD; Drill Tm; NHS; Amnesty Intnl; Ballet; U Of CA Berkeley; Pre-Med/Vet.

CHAN, SHUI S; Moore HS; Moore, OK; (2); Art Clb; Church Yth Grp; Trk; Vllybl; Frgn Exchng Stu; U Of Hong Kong.

CHANCE, CASSIE M; Wakita Schl; Nash, OK; (2); 5/16; Church Yth Grp; 4-H; Natl FFA Org; Pep Clb; Thesps; Chorus; Church Choir; School Play; Rptr Nwsp; 4-H Awd; OK Bapt All ST Choir; OK ST FFA Choir; Soc Wrk.

CHANCE, JASON W; Enid Sr HS; Enid, OK; (3); Quiz Bowl; Spanish Clb; Band; Mrchg Band; High Hon Roll; Hon Roll; Jr NHS; NHS; Ntl Merit Ltr; Math Clb; Mock Trial; Pol Soc; U Of OK; Pol Sci/Law/Govt.

CHANCE, KYLENE D; Shattuck Jr Sr HS; Shattuck, OK; (3); Church Yth Grp; Cmnty Wkr; FCA; Hist FHA; Letterman Clb; Pep Clb; Teachers Aide; Rep Chorus; Rptr Nwsp; Ed Yrbk; Bwlng ST Chmpn; UCO; Child Psychgst.

CHANCE, SHAWNA L; Billings HS; Billings, OK; (4); 2/15; Band; Jazz Band; Mrchg Band; Pep Band; Rep Sr Cls; High Hon Roll; Sal; Church Yth Grp; 4-H; Outstndng Woodwind Musician; All Amer Hl Fm Band Hnrs; Northwestern OSU Alva; Music.

CHANCELLOR, BRANDY; Clinton HS; Clinton, OK; (1); Church Yth Grp; FHA; Key Clb; Chorus; High Hon Roll; OK Chrstn U; Chem.

CHANCELLOR, EVAN G; Shawnee Sr HS; Shawnee, OK; (1); Boy Scts; Church Yth Grp; French Clb; Intnl Clb; Band; Church Choir; Mrchg Band; Crs Cntry; Trk; Jr NHS; Tae Kwon Do/Hapkido.

CHANCELLOR, KATRINA G; Salina HS; Salina, OK; (2); 4-H; FTA; GAA; Letterman Clb; Natl FFA Org; Bsktbl; Sftbl; High Hon Roll; NHS; St Hnr Soc.

CHANCELLOR, MELISSA; Dewey HS; Bartlesville, OK; (3); 6/90; Church Yth Grp; Hosp Aide; Quiz Bowl; Band; Chorus; Jazz Band; Co-Ed Yrbk; Gov Hon Prg Awd; NHS; Pres Acad Fit Awd; OK ST Hnr Soc; Pharmacy/Music.

CHANCELLOR, MELISSA S; Dewey HS; Dewey, OK; (3); 6/100; Hosp Aide; Quiz Bowl; Red Cross Aide; Band; Chorus; Jazz Band; Co-Ed Yrbk; NHS; Pres Acad Fit Awd; St Schlr; Chem Engr.

CHANCELLOR, MISTI; Moore HS; Moore, OK; (4); 22/549; Church Yth Grp; Model UN; Quiz Bowl; Scholastic Bowl; Band; Chorus; Church Choir; Mrchg Band; NHS; Val; OK City CC; Comp Programming.

CHANCELLOR, RUBY; Apache HS; Tishomingo, OK; (1); 3/56; Debate Tm; FHA; Natl FFA Org; Quiz Bowl; Scholastic Bowl; Intrml Powder Puff Ftbl; High Hon Roll; Hon Roll; NHS; Elem Tchng.

CHANDLER, AMBER; Vanoss Schl; Ada, OK; (3); Pres 4-H; FBLA; Library Aide; Office Aide; Teachers Aide; Sec Frsh Cls; Pres Soph Cls; Sec Jr Cls; Var JV Bsktbl; Var JV Trk.

CHANDLER, AMY; North Intemediate HS; Broken Arrow, OK; (1); Church Yth Grp; French Clb; Band; Church Choir; Mrchg Band; Pep Band; High Hon Roll; Jr NHS; Chrstns In Action; OK Hnr Soc; Tulsa U; Music Ed.

CHANDLER, ANGELA B; Newcastle HS; Newcastle, OK; (3); 19/92; Church Yth Grp; GAA; Pep Clb; Hist Science Clb; VP Spanish Clb; Bsktbl; Sftbl; Hon Roll; NHS; Teachers Aide; Pres Stdnt Cncl.

CHANDLER, BRANDON K; Vanoss Schl; Ada, OK; (3); VP 4-H; FBLA; Natl FFA Org; Bsktbl; Hon Roll; NHS; Pres Acad Fit Awd.

CHANDLER, DARLA J; Muldrow HS; Muldrow, OK; (4); Cmnty Wkr; FHA; Science Clb; Service Clb; Spanish Clb; Speech Tm; Chorus; School Musical; School Play; Nwsp; Photo Of Yrbk; Westark; Nrsng.

CHANDLER, JOSEPH A; Muldrow HS; Muldrow, OK; (3); Chess Clb; Cmnty Wkr; Drama Clb; 4-H; FHA; Math Clb; Model UN; Natl Beta Clb; NFL; Office Aide; U Of OK; Chem Engr; MD.

CHANDLER, KERRI; Amber Pocasset Jr Sr HS; Pocasset, OK; (2); Church Yth Grp; FCA; Natl FFA Org; Speech Tm; VP Frsh Cls; Pres Soph Cls; Bsktbl; High Hon Roll; Prfct Atten Awd.

CHANDLER, LACI D; Boswell Sr HS; Boswell, OK; (3); 4-H; FBLA; FHA; Key Clb; Teachers Aide; Nwsp; Yrbk; Hon Roll; SOSU Durant.

CHANDLER, LISHA; Moore HS; Moore, OK; (3); French Clb; Office Aide; Science Clb; Rptr Stu Cncl; Mgr Ftbl; Mgr(s); Mgr Trk; Mgr Wrstlng; Hon Roll; Jr NHS; OU; Med.

CHANDLER, SIMONE R; Moore HS; Oklahoma City, OK; (4); 110/595; Art Clb; French Clb; Office Aide; SADD; Wt Lftg; Cit Awd; Hon Roll; Jr NHS; NHS; OK City CC; Jrnlsm; Broadcstng.

CHANDLER, ZECHARIAH J; Broken Arrow Sr HS; Broken Arrow, OK; (3); Church Yth Grp; Computer Clb; Band; Church Choir; Jazz Band; Mrchg Band; Pep Band; Gftd Prog; OK Univ; Med Eng.

CHANEY, CHAUNDRA M; Booker T Washington HS; Tulsa, OK; (3); GAA; Office Aide; Spanish Clb; Teachers Aide; Powder Puff Ftbl; Trk; Jr NHS; KS U; Crmnl Law.

CHANG, AMY; Putnam City North HS; Oklahoma City, OK; (1); Art Clb; Cmnty Wkr; Intnl Clb; Key Clb; Spanish Clb; Variety Show; High Hon Roll; Dance Ballet, Tap, Jazz & Chinese Cultural Dance; Asian Soc.

CHANG, AMY I; Cascia Hall Prep School; Tulsa, OK; (4); Pres Church Yth Grp; Cmnty Wkr; Pep Clb; Spanish Clb; Acpl Chr; Chorus; Church Choir; Ed Yrbk; Var Vllybl; Hon Roll; Piano; VP Chinese Lang Club; Habitat For Humanity; IN U Bloomington; Bus Admin.

CHANG, BILL; Edmond North HS; Edmond, OK; (4); 28/330; VP Church Yth Grp; Pres German Clb; JA; Key Clb; Math Clb; Mu Alpha Theta; Church Choir; Tennis; High Hon Roll; NHS; Natl Olymp Chem Awd; U Of OK; Dentist.

CHANG, PANG; Union Intermediate HS; Tulsa, OK; (2); Church Yth Grp; FBLA; High Hon Roll; NHS; Pres Acad Fit Awd; Frgn Lang Clb; Psych/Soc.

CHANG, YI; Oklahoma Sch Of Science & Math; Oklahoma City, OK; (2); Pres Art Clb; Key Clb; Quiz Bowl; Band; Color Guard; Nwsp; Ed Yrbk; Tennis; NHS; Biochem/Pre-Med.

CHANSOMBATH, SOUTSAKHO S; Westmoore HS; Oklahoma City, OK; (3); French Clb; FBLA; Key Clb; Office Aide; Jr NHS; NHS; Asian Club; SEC; U Of OK.

CHAPELLE, DEBBIE; Chandler HS; Chandler, OK; (4); 4/71; Church Yth Grp; FCA; Spanish Clb; Sec Frsh Cls; Sec Treas Stu Cncl; Var Capt Bsktbl; Var Score Keeper; Var Trk; Hon Roll; NHS; St Hnr Soc; OK Baptist U; HPER K-12.

CHAPLIN, JAMIE; Hobart HS; Hobart, OK; (2); 11/82; Church Yth Grp; 4-H; FHA; Natl FFA Org; Sec Frsh Cls; Sec Soph Cls; Rep Stu Cncl; Var Bsktbl; Hon Roll; NHS.

CHAPLIN, REBEKAH E; Cherokee Jr Sr HS; Cherokee, OK; (3); 14/32; Church Yth Grp; Girl Scts; Library Aide; Scholastic Bowl; Spanish Clb; Band; Mrchg Band; Hon Roll; Rotry Yth Ldrshhp Awd; Pre-Med; Psychiatry.

CHAPMAN, CHRISTINA; Bridge Creek HS; Newcastle, OK; (2); 9/72; Church Yth Grp; Drama Clb; FCA; Quiz Bowl; Spanish Clb; SADD; Thesps; School Play; High Hon Roll; Hon Roll; U OK; Med.

CHAPMAN, LA TASHA; Clinton HS; Clinton, OK; (2); 27/139; FHA; Thesps; Band; Hon Roll; Comm Theatre; SW OK St U; Phrmcst.

CHAPPELL, BRADLEY P; Metro Christian Acad; Tulsa, OK; (2); 1/80; Chess Clb; Church Yth Grp; French Clb; HOBY; Orch; JV Var Bsktbl; High Hon Roll; NHS; Prfct Atten Awd; Harvard; Pre-Med/Bus Admin.

CHAPPELL, SHAWNA K; Oologah HS; Oologah, OK; (2); Church Yth Grp; Natl FFA Org; JV Chrldng; Greenhand In Ag; Star Chptr Farmer In Ag; Bible Quiz Bolw With Chrch; Marine Biologist; Zoologist.

CHAPPELLE, DEBBIE; Chandler HS; Chandler, OK; (4); 4/69; Church Yth Grp; FCA; Spanish Clb; Band; Mrchg Band; Rep Frsh Cls; Sec Stu Cncl; Var Capt Bsktbl; Var Trk; NHS; St Hnr Soc; Ntl Hnr Roll; Ntl Engl Mrt; OK Baptist U; Phys Ed.

CHARBENEAU, KELLY; Mt St Marys HS; Oklahoma City, OK; (2); 15/67; Church Yth Grp; GAA; Pres Frsh Cls; VP Stu Cncl; JV Var Bsktbl; Var Tennis; Var Vllybl; High Hon Roll; Hon Roll; NHS; JV Bsktbl Tm Capt 10th Grd; Pol Sci.

CHARLES, BECKY E; Western Heights Sr HS; Mustang, OK; (3); 13/167; Church Yth Grp; FCA; Key Clb; Chorus; School Musical; Swing Chorus; VP Soph Cls; High Hon Roll; Hon Roll; NHS; Natl Hstry/Govt Awd; Stu Cncl Rep; Church Yth Grp Cmnty Svc; Oklahoma City U; Engl Ed.

CHARLES, ELIJAH J; Claremore Sr HS; Claremore, OK; (2); Church Yth Grp; Natl FFA Org; Band; Church Choir; School Musical; School Play; Ftbl; Hon Roll; Rogers St Col; Comp Syst Anlst.

CHARLES, JARROD; Sequoyah HS; Claremore, OK; (3); Church Yth Grp; Cmnty Wkr; Drama Clb; English Clb; FCA; HOBY; Church Choir; Pres Frsh Cls; Pres Soph Cls; Pres Jr Cls; FCA VP; Chrch Yth Cncl; Track St Qulfr 300 Hurdles; Psych.

CHARLES, SHANE G; Vinita HS; Vinita, OK; (2); Boy Scts; Natl FFA Org; Spanish Clb; Var Bsbl; Hon Roll; Golf; Flying; NE ST Univ; Aviation.

CHARLTON, MICHAEL W; Union Sr HS; Tulsa, OK; (3); 80/800; Church Yth Grp; Key Clb; Var Quiz Bowl; Var Scholastic Bowl; Spanish Clb; Chorus; Church Choir; Orch; School Musical; Hon Roll; Teenage Rep Pres, Sec; Rflctns Wrtng Cont St Fnlst; Stu Mnth; Tri-M.

CHARMASSON, ALICIA; Woodward HS; Woodward, OK; (1); Church Yth Grp; Dance Clb; FCA; Pep Clb; Bsktbl; JV Chrldng; Hon Roll; OSU; Coach.

CHARMASSON, CHRIS; Fargo Schl; Woodward, OK; (4); 3/21; Am Leg Boys St; FCA; Letterman Clb; Natl Beta Clb; Natl FFA Org; Quiz Bowl; Scholastic Bowl; Science Clb; Spanish Clb; Pres Stu Cncl; Vet.

CHARMASSON, KEITH; Fargo Schl; Woodward, OK; (3); 1/16; FCA; Natl Beta Clb; Natl FFA Org; Quiz Bowl; Science Clb; Spanish Clb; Ofcr Bsbl; Bsktbl; Hon Roll; OK ST U; Vet Sci.

CHAROONSAK, ERIC; Moore HS; Moore, OK; (3); Band; Jr NHS; U Of OK; Elctrnc Engrng.

CHASE, KELSEY; Westmoore HS; Oklahoma City, OK; (4); 26/610; Boy Scts; Key Clb; Spanish Clb; Hon Roll; NHS; Val; Hosp Vol; YMCA Vol; OK St Univ; Bio Systm Eng.

CHASTAIN, BRIAN; Wetumka Jr Sr HS; Wetumka, OK; (3); 1/28; FCA; German Clb; Key Clb; Natl FFA Org; Yrbk; Var Bsbl; Var Bsktbl; Var Ftbl; Var Golf; Var Trk; U Of OK; Sprts Med.

CHASTAIN, CHRISTINA R; Ringling HS; Ringling, OK; (2); Band; Mrchg Band; Careers Cls & Awd; U OK; Med.

CHASTAIN, MINDY S; Coalgate HS; Coalgate, OK; (3); 2/48; Church Yth Grp; Dance Clb; Library Aide; Quiz Bowl; Yrbk; VP Frsh Cls; VP Soph Cls; Var Bsktbl; Var Sftbl; High Hon Roll.

CHASTAIN, SARAH; Preston Schl; Okmulgee, OK; (3); 4-H; Yrbk; Rptr Soph Cls; Rptr Jr Cls; High Hon Roll; NHS; Prfct Atten Awd; Pres Acad Fit Awd; Top 10 Pct Cls; High GPA 3 Yrs; Vet.

CHASTEEN, BREANNA M; Union Intermediate HS; Tulsa, OK; (2); Church Yth Grp; FCA; GAA; Intnl Clb; Math Clb; Pep Clb; Spanish Clb; Teachers Aide; Bsktbl; Hon Roll; Drug Free Yth; Sprt Comm; Jrnlsn/Brdcst/Wrtng.

CHATHAM, JACI; Turpin Schl; Turpin, OK; (4); 5/42; Am Leg Aux Girls St; VP Church Yth Grp; Cmnty Wkr; HOBY; Pres SADD; Sec Sr Cls; Pres VP Stu Cncl; Capt Chrldng; FCA; Letterman Clb; Natl Chrldrs Assn; Two Tms All Amer Chrldr 93-; OK Jr Olympcs; US Trck/Fld Assn; Hsmn St Wnnr 95; U Of OK; Sprts Med.

CHATMAN, JANELLE R; Muskogee HS; Muskogee, OK; (1); 55/481; Church Choir; High Hon Roll; OK Univ; Phys Thpy.

CHATMAN, TIMOTHY J; Broken Arrow Sr HS; Broken Arrow, OK; (4); Church Yth Grp; Computer Clb; Intnl Clb; Spanish Clb; Teachers Aide; Var Socr; High Hon Roll; Hon Roll; Jr NHS; NHS; Hampden-Sydney Coll; His/Span.

CHATMON, TONNETTA; B T Washington HS; Tulsa, OK; (2); Cmnty Wkr; Spanish Clb; Teachers Aide; Ofcr Stu Cncl; Xinos Alpha Kappa Chptr; Phy Thrpst; Pharmacist.

CHAU, BINH C; East Central HS; Tulsa, OK; (4); 4/209; Art Clb; Church Yth Grp; FCA; Math Clb; Pres Science Clb; Spanish Clb; Var Tennis; Hon Roll; NHS; Acad Bowl; Peer Mediation; OK U; Pre-Med.

CHAU, LINH M; East Central HS; Tulsa, OK; (4); 10/209; French Clb; Math Clb; Mu Alpha Theta; VICA; High Hon Roll; NHS; HOSA Stf Offcr; Med Asst; U Of OK; Pre-Med.

CHAVES, EILEEN A; Union Intermediate HS; Broken Arrow, OK; (1); 1/896; Church Yth Grp; Scholastic Bowl; High Hon Roll; NHS; Young Astrnts Club; Church's Handbell Choir; Piano 3 Yrs; Oxford; Pre Med.

CHAVEZ, SHANNA; Coalgate HS; Coalgate, OK; (2); 12/57; FBLA; Quiz Bowl; Flag Corp; Hon Roll; NHS; Lawyer.

CHAVEZ, TIFFANY G; Noble HS; Noble, OK; (2); 21/170; Church Yth Grp; FHA; GAA; Mu Alpha Theta; Sec Spanish Clb; Teachers Aide; Rep Stu Cncl; Var Chrldng; Var Crs Cntry; Cit Awd; Pres Educ Awrd Outstndg Acad Achvmnt; Univ Of OK; Tchr/Phys Thrpst.

CHEARY, SHALLYN; Glencoe Public Schl; Glencoe, OK; (1); French Clb; Ofcr Stu Cncl; JV Var Bsktbl; Var JV Sftbl; Hon Roll; Intl Frgn Lang Awd; Stu Of Month 95.

CHEATHAM, DANA L; Haskell HS; Haskell, OK; (3); Hon Roll; NHS; Jr Chmber Of Cmmrc; OK U; Nrsng.

CHEATHAM, JAMIE L; Haskell HS; Haskell, OK; (1); Hon Roll.

CHEATWOOD, ANDREW; Choctaw HS; Harrah, OK; (4); 19/302; Key Clb; Quiz Bowl; Scholastic Bowl; Nwsp; Yrbk; Ofcr Stu Cncl; Tennis; Cit Awd; High Hon Roll; Jr NHS; U Of Southern CA; Intnl Reltns.

CHEATWOOD, G ANDREW; Choctaw HS; Harrah, OK; (4); 17/320; Cmnty Wkr; Key Clb; Library Aide; Office Aide; Quiz Bowl; Scholastic Bowl; School Play; Variety Show; Nwsp; Yrbk; U Of Sthrn CA; Cinema.

CHEATWOOD, JEREMY S; Butner Schl; Wewoka, OK; (3); 1/20; Am Leg Boys St; Pres Frsh Cls; Pres Soph Cls; Pres Jr Cls; Pres Sr Cls; Var Bsbl; Var Ftbl; High Hon Roll; Jr NHS; NHS; Massive Commnctn.

CHEEK, LISA BRITTANY; Tahlequah Jr HS; Tahlequah, OK; (1); Office Aide; Band; Color Guard; Flag Corp; Mrchg Band; Hon Roll; Jr NHS; Pres Schlr; RISE Prgm; Mntrshp Prgm; Marine Bio.

CHEEK, TIFFANY K; Jenks HS; Tulsa, OK; (4); 65/475; DECA; FCA; FHA; Office Aide; Pep Clb; Spanish Clb; Teachers Aide; Hon Roll; Ntl Merit Ltr; Prfct Atten Awd; Spirit Comm Ofcr; Ct Cuties Ofcr; U Of OK; Psych; Jrnlsm.

CHELENZA, NICOLE A; Eisenhower Sr HS; Lawton, OK; (4); 20/396; Cmnty Wkr; Drama Clb; Intnl Clb; JV Bsktbl; High Hon Roll; Jr NHS; NHS; Cameron; Chem.

CHEN, BEST; Edmond North HS; Edmond, OK; (3); 1/390; Church Yth Grp; Cmnty Wkr; German Clb; Hosp Aide; Math Clb; Mu Alpha Theta; Quiz Bowl; Orch; Cit Awd; Hon Roll; Natl Sci Merit Awds; Asia Soc OK Awd Excl; US Achvmt Acad; All Amer Scholar; Pre Med.

CHEN, CHIH-WEI; Putnam City West HS; Oklahoma City, OK; (3); Var Crs Cntry; JV Socr; Wrstlng 96-; NHS 96-; OU; Math.

CHEN, HSIAO-LING; Union Sr HS; Broken Arrow, OK; (4); 70/616; Sec Treas Intnl Clb; Key Clb; Spanish Clb; Teachers Aide; Hist Stu Cncl; Capt Var Tennis; High Hon Roll; Hon Roll; Pres NHS; Spanish NHS; Renaissance Secy; Stu Of Month; Yng Democrats; U Of Tulsa; Commnctns.

CHEN, VICTOR; Edmond Memorial HS; Edmond, OK; (4); 1/335; Am Leg Boys St; Church Yth Grp; Computer Clb; JA; Rptr Yrbk; Rep Stu Cncl; JV Bsktbl; High Hon Roll; VP NHS; Val; U Of PA; Mech Engr.

CHENEY, LISA M; Choctaw HS; Midwest City, OK; (3); Spanish Clb; Band; Chorus; NHS; U Of MI; Med.

CHENNAULT, RASHELL; Comanche HS; Comanche, OK; (3); Art Clb; Church Yth Grp; FHA; German Clb; Office Aide; Science Clb; Teachers Aide; Church Choir; Hon Roll; NHS; TX Bible Coll; Tchr.

CHENOWETH, AARON; Okemah HS; Okemah, OK; (4); 7/46; Am Leg Boys St; Church Yth Grp; Natl Beta Clb; Rptr Nwsp; JV Socr; High Hon Roll; Hon Roll; NHS; Engl Lit.

CHERRY, ANGEL A; Okmulgee HS; Okmulgee, OK; (3); 4/126; Church Yth Grp; Cmnty Wkr; FBLA; Math Clb; Pep Clb; Scholastic Bowl; Science Clb; Spanish Clb; Chorus; Church Choir; Sndry Schl Sec; Physcl Thrpy.

CHERRY, LEANN; Stigler HS; Stigler, OK; (1); JV Bsktbl.

CHERRY, SHAWNA N; Muldrow HS; Muldrow, OK; (3); Church Yth Grp; GAA; Spanish Clb; Band; Jazz Band; Mrchg Band; Bsktbl; Capt Sftbl; Trk; MVP In Bsktbl 95-96; MVP In Sftbl 95-96; Most Imprvd In Bsktbl 94-95.

CHESNEY, ROBERT B; Central HS; Tulsa, OK; (2); Church Yth Grp; ROTC.

CHESSER, MELANIE; Kingston HS; Kingston, OK; (1); Church Yth Grp; FCA; FHA; Spanish Clb; Church Choir; Sec Frsh Cls; JV Var Bsktbl; Var Sftbl; Hon Roll; 4 Yr Coll.

CHESSER, NICOLE M; Altus Sr HS; Altus, OK; (2); Var Church Yth Grp; Drama Clb; Red Cross Aide; Spanish Clb; Yrbk; Hon Roll; Photograper; TSA Mem; SCA Mem; CO ST Univ; Meteorologist.

CHESTNUT, SHANE A; Cushing HS; Cushing, OK; (1); 14/190; OSU; Chem Engr.

CHETEER, SHAUNDA U; Spiro HS; Spiro, OK; (2); Church Yth Grp; FHA; FTA; Library Aide; Office Aide; Teachers Aide; Order Of Eastern Star Yth Div; ULAR; Bus Mgmt; Fin.

CHEUNG, CYNTHIA; Bartlesville Mid HS; Bartlesville, OK; (3); VP Science Clb; Orch; High Hon Roll; NHS; Spanish NHS; All-St Orch; Dist & St Sci Fair; Paleontology.

CHEUNG, KELVIN T; Bartlesville Mid HS; Bartlesville, OK; (3); #1 in class; Debate Tm; High Hon Roll; Jr NHS; Prfct Atten Awd.

CHEVES, CLAUDIA; Pawhuska HS; Pawhuska, OK; (2); 1/100; FCA; VP Frsh Cls; VP Soph Cls; Ofcr Stu Cncl; Var Bsktbl; Var Sftbl; Hon Roll; NHS; Pres Acad Fit Awd; FBLA; Acad Ltrmn; Rodeo.

CHEW, KELLI N; Bishop Kelley HS; Tulsa, OK; (2); Art Clb; FCA; French Clb; GAA; Bsktbl; Socr; Hon Roll; Multi-Yr Listee; FL ST; Fashion Industry.

CHEW, JERIN A; West Middle HS; Norman, OK; (3); Church Yth Grp; Cmnty Wkr; FCA; GAA; Ofcr Stu Cncl; Var L Trk; Var L Vllybl; Hon Roll; Norman HS Sprts Med Trnr; HS Heros Awd; Med.

CHEYNET, RENAY; Edmond Memorial HS; Edmond, OK; (4); 76/322; Church Yth Grp; FBLA; Ed Yrbk; Francis Tuttle Vo Tech Accntg Serv Stdnt Of Yr 95-; Advanced Plcment Courses; OK ST; CPA.

CHIDESTER, LANNA L; Jenks HS; Jenks, OK; (3); Art Clb; Pres VP CAP; DECA; Sec French Clb; Math Tm; Teachers Aide; Lit Mag; Hon Roll; Drug Free Yth; Tulsa Dist United Meth Yth Cncl Sr High Rep.

CHILDERS, AMY; Tuttle HS; Tuttle, OK; (2); 1/60; Church Yth Grp; Natl FFA Org; Hon Roll; NHS; Rose ST Typing I HS Schlst Contes 3rd Pl; Hnr Soc Awd; FFA Public Speaking Contest.

CHILDERS, COURTNEY M; Putnam City West HS; Bethany, OK; (4); 118/270; Church Yth Grp; Drama Clb; JCL; Latin Clb; SADD; Thesps; Chorus; Church Choir; School Play; Stage Crew; Univ Of OK; Law.

CHILDERS, STACEY ALENE; Thomas A Edison HS; Tulsa, OK; (4); 17/178; Pres FTA; Phtg Yrbk; Ofcr Stu Cncl; Sftbl; Hon Roll; Kiwanis Awd; Pres NHS; Pres Schlr; St Schlr; Key Clb; 13 Yrs Camp Fire Wottelo Recipient; U Cntrl OK; Elem Ed.

CHILDERS, WAYNE J; Blackwell HS; Blackwell, OK; (2); Church Yth Grp; FCA; Spanish Clb; Var Bsbl; Hon Roll; NHS.

CHILDERS, WILEY; Blackwell HS; Blackwell, OK; (4); 22/120; Am Leg Boys St; Church Yth Grp; FCA; Letterman Clb; Spanish Clb; Ofcr Bsbl; Hon Roll; Maroon Sprt Rnnr-Up; OK St U; Elec Engrng.

CHILDRESS, CHRISTOPHER D; Caney Jr Sr HS; Caney, OK; (2); 4/35; Church Yth Grp; Quiz Bowl; Scholastic Bowl; Hon Roll; DAV Post 80 Hnr Guard; 1st Pl Div II Southeastern Elec Acad Bowl 95; 20th Annl Ivtn Schltc Cont Awds; MIT; Physics.

CHILDRESS, JILL; Mound Jr Sr HS; Sapulpa, OK; (4); 5/41; Natl Beta Clb; Office Aide; Band; Mrchg Band; School Play; Hon Roll; NHS; Haskell INU; Radiology.

CHILDRESS, MELANIE C; Coweta HS; Coweta, OK; (2); 1/88; SADD; School Play; Var Powder Puff Ftbl; Var Sftbl; Hon Roll; NHS; Frgn Lang Clb; Tsa-La-Gi Awd Of Excl.

CHILDRESS, MIRANDA J; Mounds Schl; Sapulpa, OK; (4); 5/41; Natl Beta Clb; Office Aide; Band; Mrchg Band; School Play; Hon Roll; NHS; Haskell INU; Radiology.

CHILDS, CURTIS W; Mc Lain Career Acad; Tulsa, OK; (3); #3 in class; Computer Clb; French Clb; Teachers Aide; Nwsp; Yrbk; Bsktbl; Cit Awd; Gov Hon Prg Awd; Hon Roll; Sons Of Amer Revalution; Hnr Soc.

CHILDS, DEREK M; Bishop Kelley HS; Broken Arrow, OK; (1); Mtrlgy.

CHILDS, SHELLY M; Edmond North HS; Edmond, OK; (1); Church Yth Grp; Drama Clb; School Play; Wt Lftg.

CHILES, KEISHA M; Douglass HS; Oklahoma City, OK; (2); Computer Clb; Chorus; High Hon Roll; Hon Roll.

CHILSON, DAWN A; Mangum Sr HS; Mangum, OK; (3); 8/40; FBLA; FHA; Score Keeper; Hon Roll; NHS; Air Force Acad; Air Force.

CHILTON, SAMANTHA; Wynnewood HS; Wynnewood, OK; (1); 1/58; Church Yth Grp; Dance Clb; Girl Scts; Scholastic Bowl; Band; Jazz Band; Mrchg Band; Pep Band; High Hon Roll.

CHIN, MICHELLE; Jenks HS; Tulsa, OK; (4); 101/552; DECA; FCA; Key Clb; Math Clb; Mu Alpha Theta; Teachers Aide; Ofcr Stu Cncl; Var Capt Bsktbl; Capt Powder Puff Ftbl; Hon Roll; Acad Ltr & Medal; Pres Ed Awd; Hnrb Mntn All Metro Bsktbl; Young Life; Spirit Comm Ofcr; Symphony Set; OK ST Univ; Bio.

CHIODO, KARA C; Norman Sr HS; Norman, OK; (4); 1/678; JCL; Latin Clb; Model UN; Pres Mu Alpha Theta; Spanish Clb; Lit Mag; Rep Stu Cncl; NHS; Ntl Merit SF; Pres Acad Fit Awd; Earth Clb Pres; Explrs; Octgn.

CHISUM, HELEN A; Shattuck Jr Sr HS; Shattuck, OK; (3); Church Yth Grp; 4-H; FHA; Pep Clb; Chorus; School Play; L Sftbl; Vllybl; 4-H Awd; Hon Roll; Outs Writer Awd For Jr Class; Chld Cnslr.

CHITWOOD, MICHAEL; Guthrie Sr HS; Guthrie, OK; (3); Boy Scts; FCA; ROTC; Band; Mrchg Band; ROTC Rifle Team Capt; OK ST Univ.

CHITWOOD, TRACI L; Hugo HS; Hugo, OK; (3); Church Yth Grp; Computer Clb; Drama Clb; Rptr Natl FFA Org; Spanish Clb; Drill Tm; Ofcr Stu Cncl; Score Keeper; Hon Roll; Natl FFA Horse Prfcncy 95/96, Volntrsm Achvt Awds 96; Murray ST Coll; Phys Thrpy.

CHOAT, JAMIE R; Enid Sr HS; Enid, OK; (2); Church Yth Grp; Speech Tm; Band; Chorus; Mrchg Band; School Musical; School Play; Stage Crew; Variety Show; Ed Nwsp; Dntl Asst.

CHOAT, KASEY D; Harrah HS; Harrah, OK; (3); FBLA; Bsktbl; Hon Roll; NHS; Credit Union Yth Apprntcshp Prgm; Rose ST.

CHOAT, RENA; Calumet Schl; Calumet, OK; (1); Cmnty Wkr; FCA; Letterman Clb; Chorus; Ofcr Frsh Cls; Intrml Bsbl; JV Var Bsktbl; Intrml Gym; JV Var Sftbl; Intrml Vllybl; OK Univ.

CHOATE, KAY; Hennessey HS; Hennessey, OK; (3); 5/64; Church Yth Grp; FCA; Chorus; Church Choir; VP Frsh Cls; Stat Bsbl; Var Capt Chrldng; High Hon Roll; Hon Roll; NHS; NW OK ST U; Elem Ed.

CHOATE, KEITH; Battiest Jr Sr HS; Pickens, OK; (2); Scholastic Bowl; High Hon Roll; Hon Roll; NHS; Val; Natl Hnr Roll; OK Hnr Soc; SE OK ST U; Law.

CHOATE, LANCE; Battiest Jr Sr HS; Pickens, OK; (1); Scholastic Bowl; Hon Roll; Comm Art.

CHOATE, YASMINDA; OK Schl Of Sci & Math; Sasakwa, OK; (3); FHA; HOBY; Quiz Bowl; School Play; Yrbk; Lit Mag; Rep Soph Cls; Capt Powder Puff Ftbl; Sftbl; Vllybl; Tae Kwon Do.

CHOBA, BRUCE T; Putnam City West HS; Oklahoma City, OK; (4); Church Yth Grp; Teachers Aide; Jr NHS; Seattle Pacific U; Med.

CHOWN, BENJAMIN; Enid Sr HS; Enid, OK; (2); 22/450; Boy Scts; Church Yth Grp; CAP; Natl FFA Org; JV Wrstlng; Hon Roll; NHS; Piano; Sunday Schl Tchr; Outstdng Yth Ministry Awd; USAFA; Military Pilot; USAF.

CHRIS, TIFFANY; Nathan Hale HS; Tulsa, OK; (1); Church Yth Grp; FCA; Teachers Aide; Yrbk; Chrldng; Gym; Wt Lftg; Hon Roll; OSU; Vet.

CHRISMAN, JASON; Choctaw HS; Choctaw, OK; (4); 85/305; Letterman Clb; Crs Cntry; Socr; Wrstlng; Rose St Coll Sci Awd; Rose ST; Bus Admin.

CHRISMAN, JOHNATHAN W; Putnam City HS; Oklahoma City, OK; (1); Church Yth Grp; Ftbl; Wt Lftg; Wrstlng; Mar Biolgst.

CHRISMON, CALEB; Cyril Jr Sr HS; Cyril, OK; (4); 4/28; Math Clb; Rep Soph Cls; VP Jr Cls; Var Bsbl; Var Capt Bsktbl; Var Capt Ftbl; High Hon Roll; NHS; Acad All Conf; U Of OK; Phys Thrp.

CHRISMON, SYBIL; Cyril Jr Sr HS; Cyril, OK; (1); 4-H; FHA; School Play; Ofcr Frsh Cls; Ofcr Stu Cncl; Bsktbl; Sftbl; Trk; High Hon Roll; Jr NHS.

CHRISTEL, CAROLYN M; B T Washington HS; Tulsa, OK; (4); 11/259; Drama Clb; Teachers Aide; Chorus; Church Choir; School Musical; School Play; Var Golf; NHS; Chinse Clb; China & Taiwan Govts Delg; Lewis & Clark; Zoolgy.

CHRISTEN JR, FARRELL G; Western Heights Sr HS; Oklahoma City, OK; (1); English Clb; Spanish Clb; Wt Lftg; Hon Roll; Art; Comps.

CHRISTENSEN, ADAM; Seiling Schl; Seiling, OK; (2); Computer Clb; FCA; Letterman Clb; School Play; Yrbk; Ofcr Bsbl; Bsktbl; Ftbl; DAR Awd; Hon Roll; OCU; Bus.

CHRISTENSEN, CARA; Muskogee HS; Muskogee, OK; (3); 25/343; JCL; Sec Key Clb; Var Bsktbl; Var Sftbl; High Hon Roll; NHS; Muskogee HS Human Relations Cncl; Ecology Clb Mem; Muskogee Phoenix/Boatmens Bk IV All Sftbl Team.

CHRISTENSEN, CASEY D; Thomas Jr Sr HS; Thomas, OK; (1); Church Yth Grp; FCA; 4-H; Natl FFA Org; Bsktbl; Sftbl; Hon Roll; Ag Tchr.

CHRISTENSEN, COREY; Midwest City HS; Midwest City, OK; (3); 10/400; Church Yth Grp; Math Clb; Band; Jazz Band; Mrchg Band; Rep Stu Cncl; Var Tennis; JV Wrstlng; High Hon Roll; Hon Roll; Page St Rep 96; Northeastern ST U; Optometrist.

CHRISTENSEN, H L; Putnam City North HS; Oklahoma City, OK; (1); 147/547; Stage Crew; Cit Awd; Hon Roll; Bus Awd Prsnl Fin; Law Enforcement.

CHRISTENSEN, KATHRYN M; Bartlesville Mid HS; Bartlesville, OK; (2); Church Yth Grp; FCA; Pep Clb; Science Clb; Church Choir; Rptr Yrbk; Hon Roll; US Chrch Spnsrd Mission Wrk; Interior Dsgn.

CHRISTENSEN, KAYLI; Thomas Jr Sr HS; Thomas, OK; (1); Church Yth Grp; FCA; Band; Chorus; Church Choir; Mrchg Band; School Musical; Treas Frsh Cls; Bsktbl; Sftbl.

CHRISTENSEN, KELLY; Thomas Jr Sr HS; Thomas, OK; (3); 1/40; 4-H; GAA; JA; Natl FFA Org; Bsktbl; 4-H Awd; High Hon Roll; NHS; Ntl Merit Ltr; Val; Rodeo; O'Connors JC; Equine Sci.

CHRISTENSEN, ROBERT; Midwest City HS; Midwest City, OK; (3); Church Yth Grp; FHA; German Clb; Key Clb; Quiz Bowl; SADD; Ofcr Soph Cls; Tennis; Wrstlng; NHS.

CHRISTIAN, BRYAN R; Fox Sr HS; Healdton, OK; (3); Chess Clb; FCA; 4-H; Quiz Bowl; Pres Stu Cncl; Var Ftbl; Wt Lftg; Hon Roll; Voc Ag; Med.

CHRISTIAN, CALEB M; Stonewall Jr-Sr HS; Stonewall, OK; (3); Boy Scts; Church Yth Grp; FCA; 4-H; Natl FFA Org; Pep Clb; Pres Frsh Cls; VP Soph Cls; Ofcr Bsbl; Bsktbl; FFA Shwmnsp Awds/Rsrve Breed Trophies Wth Anmls; Top Slsprsn Blue/Gld Sausage Lvestck Slctns.

CHRISTIAN, CHAD D; Hominy HS; Hominy, OK; (2); 4/80; Church Yth Grp; VP FCA; Teachers Aide; Ofcr Bsbl; Bsktbl; Ftbl; Trk; Wt Lftg; High Hon Roll; Hon Roll; Math.

CHRISTIAN, DERRICK G; Enid Sr HS; Enid, OK; (2); Art Clb; Cmnty Wkr; Drama Clb; French Clb; Quiz Bowl; Scholastic Bowl; Speech Tm; Teachers Aide; School Play; Stage Crew; Arts & Sci.

CHRISTIAN, JOSHUA; Stonewall Jr-Sr HS; Stonewall, OK; (4); 11/23; Boy Scts; Natl FFA Org; Office Aide; Chorus; Rep Jr Cls; Rep Sr Cls; L Bsbl; L Bsktbl; Hon Roll; Amrcnsm Awd; Stdnt Tdy Msnc Ldg; Outstdng Music Stdnt; Stdnt Mo; Str Chptr Frmr FFA; Sntnl FFA 2 Yrs; Eastern ST Coll; Ag Ed.

CHRISTIAN, ROBERT A; Morris HS; Okmulgee, OK; (1); Church Yth Grp; Church Choir; Hon Roll; U Of Tulsa; Ansthlgst.

CHRISTIAN, STEPHANIE; Burns Flat-Dill City Jshs; Dill City, OK; (4); 7/38; Am Leg Aux Girls St; Church Yth Grp; FHA; German Clb; Varsity Clb; Sec Frsh Cls; Rep Soph Cls; Sec Jr Cls; Co-Capt Bsktbl; Hon Roll; FHA Sub Dist VP; OK Hstry Day; OK ST U; Engrng.

CHRISTIAN, TIFFANY B; Byng Sr HS; Ada, OK; (3); Church Yth Grp; Pres FCA; FBLA; Sec Natl Beta Clb; Spanish Clb; Teachers Aide; Church Choir; Sec Soph Cls; Sec Jr Cls; Capt Chrldng; Natl Yth Ldrshp On Law Nom; All Amer Chrldr Nom; E Cntrl U; Developmental Psych.

CHRISTIAN, TRISH M; Stonewall Jr-Sr HS; Stonewall, OK; (2); FBLA; German Clb; Mgr GAA; Varsity Clb; Sec Frsh Cls; Rep Soph Cls; Chrldng; Hon Roll; NHS; Natl Sci Mrt Awd; Acctng.

CHRISTIE, RACHEL L; Lindsay HS; Lindsay, OK; (1); Art Clb; Scholastic Bowl; Chorus; Hon Roll; Algebra I Class Awd; Gen Phys Sci Class Awd; OK His Class Awd; Art Class Awd; OK Hnr Soc; Psychiatrist.

CHRISTINE, KIMBERLY J; Edmond North HS; Edmond, OK; (2); Drama Clb; Key Clb; Spanish Clb; Band; Mrchg Band; Yrbk; Rep Stu Cncl; JV Chrldng; JV Crs Cntry; JV Trk; ENHS Recycling Pgm Founder; Sci & Recycling Awd 95-96; Rutgers-Cook Coll; Envrnmnt Sci.

CHRISTMAN, BRANDY; Kiowa Jr-Sr HS; Pittsburg, OK; (3); Church Yth Grp; Drama Clb; 4-H; FHA; Natl FFA Org; School Play; VP Frsh Cls; VP Soph Cls; VP Jr Cls; Bsktbl; Wilburton; Psych.

CHRISTMAN, CHRISTINA A; North Intemediate HS; Broken Arrow, OK; (2); Art Clb; Church Yth Grp; Church Choir; Yrbk; Hon Roll; Chrstns In Action; Sci Fctn Bk Clb; John Brown Univ; Bio.

CHRISTMAN, STACEY L; Eisenhower Sr HS; Lawton, OK; (4); 71/386; Chorus; High Hon Roll; Hon Roll; NHS; Pres Acad Fit Awd; GATE; Cameron; Bio/Pre-Med.

CHRISTY, BRANDON D; Mc Loud HS; Shawnee, OK; (2); Church Yth Grp; FCA; FBLA; HOBY; Pres Stu Cncl; Var Ftbl; Wt Lftg; High Hon Roll; NHS; Var Bsktbl Team Acad ST Champ 4a GPA 3.73; Med Prof.

CHRONISTER, JUSTIN; Davis HS; Davis, OK; (2); 1/55; Church Yth Grp; Quiz Bowl; Scholastic Bowl; Church Choir; VP Soph Cls; Ftbl; Wt Lftg; Hon Roll; NHS; OK ST U; Crmnl Jstce.

CHRONISTER, RANDY L; Charles Page HS; Sapulpa, OK; (1); Pres Church Yth Grp; VP Cmnty Wkr; Pres Drama Clb; Thesps; Chorus; School Musical; Ed Phtg Nwsp; Cit Awd; Hon Roll; Pres Acad Fit Awd; Masonic Ldg Stdnt Of Yr 95-; Regnl Sci Fair 1st Pl; ST Sci Fair 4th Pl; OK ST Eastrn Dist Hnr Choir; U Of Tulsa; Srgcl Dr/Tchr/Actor.

CHU, LE ANNA E; Westmoore HS; Oklahoma City, OK; (3); 46/615; Church Yth Grp; Yrbk; Gym; Swmmng; Hon Roll; TX A&M.

CHUBBEE, FRANK C; Hugo HS; Hugo, OK; (2); Computer Clb; Hon Roll; Pres Acad Fit Awd; Taekwondo Red Blt.

CHUNESTUDEY, MICHELLE; Westville HS; Westville, OK; (1); JV Chrldng; JV Vllybl; D-Fy; Northeastern ST U; Eng Tchr.

CHUNG, PHUOC H; Southeast HS; Oklahoma City, OK; (2); Chess Clb; Math Clb; Science Clb; High Hon Roll; Prfct Atten Awd; OK U; Engrng.

CHUNG, TONY NGOC; Union Intermediate HS; Tulsa, OK; (1); NHS; Frgn Lang Clb; UC At Berkeley; Chem Engrng.

CHURCH, JESSICA; Bristow HS; Bristow, OK; (3); Church Yth Grp; Pep Clb; Chorus; Church Choir; School Musical; School Play; VP Frsh Cls; Ofcr Stu Cncl; Chrldng; Hon Roll; Southern Nazarene.

CHURCH II, JOEL D; Anadarko HS; Anadarko, OK; (3); DECA; FBLA; SADD; Teachers Aide; Thesps; Yrbk; NHS; Pres Acad Fit Awd; Tech Stu Assn St Pres; Eagle Sct; OK City Univ; Bus; Mrktng.

CIAH, MICHAEL; Choctaw HS; Spencer, OK; (3); 1/325; Am Leg Boys St; Math Tm; Quiz Bowl; Cit Awd; Jr NHS; NHS; Pres Acad Fit Awd; Val; German Clb; Scholastic Bowl; Key Club Pres; Arch.

CICH, MICHAEL; Choctaw HS; Spencer, OK; (3); 1/386; Cmnty Wkr; Key Clb; Quiz Bowl; Cit Awd; Hon Roll; Jr NHS; NHS; Prfct Atten Awd; Pres Acad Fit Awd; Val; Soccer; Writng.

CINNAMON, KRISTI; Garber Sr HS; Garber, OK; (1); 1/28; Sec Church Yth Grp; FCA; Pres Natl FFA Org; Scholastic Bowl; Pres Frsh Cls; Ofcr Stu Cncl; Var Bsktbl; High Hon Roll; Val; Clss Fvtre; 4-H Pst Pres; Mstu Mnth; FFA Otstndng Lvstck Jdge 96; OK U; Med.

CIRGENSKI, LISA; Central HS; Tulsa, OK; (4); 16/177; Teachers Aide; Yrbk; High Hon Roll; NHS; Cntrl Chiefs Coll Bnd Stu; OSU; Chldcare.

CISCO, JAMIE; Ft Cobb-Broxton HS; Ft Cobb, OK; (2); FHA; Med.

CISKOWSKI, AMANDA M; Bishop Kelley HS; Tulsa, OK; (4); 5/150; Quiz Bowl; Chorus; Church Choir; Var Crs Cntry; High Hon Roll; NHS; Ntl Merit SF; St Schlr; Church Yth Grp; French Clb; Natl Hispanic Schlr; Chrch Mscl; Anchor Clb Hstrn, Pres; OSU; Mech Engr.

CISNEROS, MAYRA I; U S Grant HS; Oklahoma City, OK; (1); Church Yth Grp; Hon Roll; Latino Clb Treas; Law.

CLABORN, ANDREA D; Soper Schl; Soper, OK; (3); FCA; 4-H; FHA; Pres Frsh Cls; VP Soph Cls; Bsktbl; Crs Cntry; Trk; High Hon Roll; Ntl Merit Ltr; Sthestrn OK ST U; CPA.

CLABORN, JENNIFER; Panama HS; Panama, OK; (2); Quiz Bowl; Rep Band; Drm Mjr(t); Mrchg Band; Rep Soph Cls; Rep Stu Cncl; High Hon Roll; Jr NHS; NHS; Nrsng.

CLABORN, JON; Pond Creek-Hunter Schl; Pond Creek, OK; (4); Am Leg Boys St; English Clb; FCA; Natl Beta Clb; Spanish Clb; Rep Stu Cncl; Var Capt Bsktbl; Var Capt Ftbl; Cit Awd; VP NHS.

CLABORN, RONALD; Panama HS; Panama, OK; (2); 5/50; Ftbl; Wt Lftg; Cit Awd; Hon Roll; NHS; Pres Acad Fit Awd; Pres Schlr; TN U; Elec Engr.

CLABORN, RYAN C; Chattanooga Schl; Chattanooga, OK; (3); 1/20; HOBY; Natl FFA Org; VP Frsh Cls; VP Soph Cls; Pres Jr Cls; VP Stu Cncl; Var Bsbl; Var Bsktbl; Hon Roll; NHS; Hnrbl Mntn St Bsbl Tm 95-96; Cameron U; Bio.

CLABORN, SHANE L; Empire Schl; Duncan, OK; (2); FCA; Letterman Clb; Natl FFA Org; Ofcr Bsbl; Ftbl; Wrstlng; High Hon Roll; NHS; Pres Acad Fit Awd; OK U; Tchr.

CLABORN, TRACY; Rock Creek Jr Sr HS; Durant, OK; (2); 4/38; FCA; FHA; Pres Soph Cls; Rep Stu Cncl; Var Chrldng; Hon Roll; SOSU.

CLAFLIN, CORY; Burlington Public Schls; Byron, OK; (4); 2/8; HOBY; Natl FFA Org; Scholastic Bowl; Band; Chorus; Sec Frsh Cls; Sec Soph Cls; Sec Jr Cls; Sec Sr Cls; Sec Stu Cncl; Tae Kwon Do; Natl Honor Roll; OK ST U; Elec Engrng.

CLAMPET, LACEY; Marietta HS; Marietta, OK; (3); Debate Tm; Pres 4-H; Pres VP FHA; Speech Tm; Chorus; Church Choir; School Musical; Swing Chorus; Chrldng; 4-H Awd; OK ST U; Public Rel.

CLAMPET, TIMOTHY J; Haworth Sr HS; Haworth, OK; (2); Church Yth Grp; Natl FFA Org; VICA; Hon Roll; NHS; Rdng Hrs & Str Rpng.

CLAMPITT, CRYSTAL L; South Intermediate HS; Broken Arrow, OK; (1); Co-Ed Yrbk; High Hon Roll; U AR; Chem Engr.

CLAMPITT, RACHEL M; Wynnewood HS; Wynnewood, OK; (1); Church Yth Grp; Drama Clb; FHA; SADD; Band; Color Guard; Flag Corp; Mrchg Band; Pep Band; High Hon Roll; OK Hnr Soc; SCOBDA; GATE; E Cntrl Univ; Ped.

CLANTON, LISA; Charles Page HS; Sand Springs, OK; (4); 9/340; Am Leg Aux Girls St; Rptr FCA; Pres Key Clb; Chorus; School Musical; Rptr Lit Mag; Capt Chrldng; Cit Awd; DAR Awd; Kiwanis Awd; Page St Senate; Phi Delta Kappa Stu Yr; HERFF Junes Prncpls Ldrshp Schlr; OK Bapt U.

CLAPPER, AMANDA B; Union Intermediate HS; Broken Arrow, OK; (2); Church Yth Grp; Debate Tm; Drama Clb; Speech Tm; SADD; Chorus; School Play; Stage Crew; Yrbk; Rep Stu Cncl; VP Frsh Cls; Brdcstng.

CLARDY, DUSTIN A; Valliant HS; Idabel, OK; (1); 4-H; Natl FFA Org; Bsktbl; Ftbl; Cit Awd; 4-H Awd; OK St Univ; Wldlf Bio.

CLARK, ALYSON L; Memorial HS; Tulsa, OK; (2); FCA; Latin Clb; Pep Clb; Ofcr Soph Cls; Ofcr Stu Cncl; Var Chrldng; Swmmng; High Hon Roll; Hon Roll; Mst Sprtd Awd For Pom Pon; Sprts Med.

CLARK, AMBER; Collinsville HS; Collinsville, OK; (3); Nwsp; Bsktbl; Socr; Roger St; Nrsng.

CLARK, ASHLEY; Moore HS; Moore, OK; (4); 20/500; Am Leg Aux Girls St; Dance Clb; FCA; NFL; Spanish Clb; Rep Stu Cncl; Var Socr; NHS; Val; OK City U; FBI.

CLARK, AUSTON W; Midwest City HS; Midwest City, OK; (3); Dance Clb; Drama Clb; Thesps; Varsity Clb; Acpl Chr; Band; Chorus; School Musical; School Play; Stage Crew; Outstndng Dfnsv Inside Linbckr, Wrstlng/Weightlifting Awds; Straight A Clb 94-95; Actng/Vcl Awds.

CLARK, BRENT; Wellston Schl; Wellston, OK; (3); VP FCA; FHA; Spanish Clb; SADD; Yrbk; VP Jr Cls; Var Bsbl; Var Bsktbl; Var Ftbl; Hon Roll; U Of OK.

CLARK, CHAD A; Okay Jr Sr HS; Wagoner, OK; (2); Spanish Clb; Pres Soph Cls; Ofcr Stu Cncl; Var JV Bsbl; Var JV Bsktbl; High Hon Roll; Hon Roll; NHS.

CLARK, CHARIYA; North Intermediate HS; Broken Arrow, OK; (3); Church Yth Grp; Red Cross Aide; Spanish Clb; Church Choir; Drill Tm; Chrldng; Trk; Stomp Squad; Howard U; OB-GYN; Dr.

CLARK, CHRISTY; Turner Schl; Overbrook, OK; (2); Church Yth Grp; Natl Beta Clb; Pep Clb; Pres Soph Cls; Hon Roll.

CLARK, COLT; Cookson Hills Chrn Schl; Kansas, OK; (2); 2/16; Church Yth Grp; Chorus; School Musical; School Play; Stage Crew; Rep Soph Cls; Rep Stu Cncl; Var Capt Bsktbl; Var Capt Socr; High Hon Roll; Tulsa Hawks AAU Bsktbl Team 3 Yrs; OK St Scoring Ldr In Bsktbl; Anesthesiologist.

CLARK, CORY A; Miami Sr HS; Wyandotte, OK; (2); Church Yth Grp; FCA; Natl FFA Org; Chorus; Church Choir; Ftbl; Golf; Wt Lftg; Gov Hon Prg Awd; High Hon Roll; Kiwanis Clb Stu Of Yr 95-96; FFA Treas; OK ST U; Vet Med.

CLARK, COURTNEY; Carney Schl; Carney, OK; (1); 2/20; Church Yth Grp; 4-H; Natl FFA Org; Sec Frsh Cls; Bsktbl; Trk; High Hon Roll; Hon Roll; OSU.

CLARK, DANIEL L; Mustang HS; Mustang, OK; (2); 179/510; Bus Profs of Am; Band; Drill Tm; Jazz Band; Mrchg Band; Orch; Pep Band; School Musical; Hon Roll; St Sci Fair 2nd; Sci.

CLARK, GEORGE R; Durant HS; Durant, OK; (2); Band; Jazz Band; Variety Show; Acad Tm.

CLARK, GINNY; Sapulpa Sr HS; Sapulpa, OK; (2); Pres Church Yth Grp; Drama Clb; FHA; Chorus; Church Choir; School Musical; School Play; Ed Rptr Nwsp; Ed Phtg Yrbk; Hon Roll; MI ST; Law.

CLARK, JENNIFER; Durant HS; Durant, OK; (4); Church Yth Grp; Drama Clb; FBLA; Key Clb; Swmmng; Hon Roll; Intl Order Rainbow Girls; Calculus Clb; Acctng.

CLARK, JESSICA A; Hollis Jr Sr HS; Gould, OK; (3); Computer Clb; FHA; GAA; Office Aide; Rptr Nwsp; Intrml Chrldng; Intrml Trk; Intrml JV Vllybl; UIL Speech; UIL Poetry & Rdng; Arts; Crafts; Phy Thrpst.

CLARK, JILL; Family Of Faith HS; Shawnee, OK; (3); Church Yth Grp; Quiz Bowl; Scholastic Bowl; Church Choir; School Musical; School Play; Yrbk; Lit Mag; High Hon Roll; Span/Eng/World His Schlstc Awds; Pre Algebra Tutor; Frgn Langs.

CLARK, JODY S; Dale Sr HS; Shawnee, OK; (3); 6/58; Church Yth Grp; FCA; GAA; JA; Letterman Clb; Pep Clb; SADD; Varsity Clb; Capt Bsktbl; Hon Roll; OK Bapt Univ.

CLARK, JOSEPH M; Carney Schl; Carney, OK; (3); German Clb; Mu Alpha Theta; High Hon Roll; Hon Roll; Jr NHS; OK HS Hnr Scty; Awds Lang Arts/Grk Mythlgy/Amer His; Prin/Supt Hnr Roll; OSU; Tchr.

CLARK, JOSHUA A; Wright Christian Acad; Tulsa, OK; (3); 4/30; Church Yth Grp; Key Clb; School Musical; School Play; Ofcr Bsbl; High Hon Roll; Key Club Project Comm Chm; Home Club Treas; LT Governor Div 15n; Chrch Sftbl League; Bus Mngmt.

CLARK, JUDY; Prue Schl; Osage, OK; (4); 1/24; FCA; 4-H; German Clb; Pres Jr Cls; Pres Sr Cls; Bsktbl; Sftbl; Cit Awd; High Hon Roll; Val; U Cntrl OK; RN.

CLARK, JUDY L; Checotah HS; Checotah, OK; (2); Band; Mrchg Band; Pep Band; High Hon Roll; NHS; OK Hon Soc; Vet.

CLARK, JUSTIN D; Cushing HS; Cushing, OK; (3); Math Clb; Pep Clb; Science Clb; Spanish Clb; Chorus; JV Bsktbl; High Hon Roll; Hon Roll; NHS; Engrng.

CLARK, KARI A; Shattuck Jr Sr HS; Shattuck, OK; (3); FCA; FHA; Letterman Clb; Natl FFA Org; Pep Clb; Chorus; Rep Stu Cncl; JV Bsktbl; Var Sftbl; Hon Roll; RN.

CLARK, KIM; Durant HS; Durant, OK; (3); Church Yth Grp; Debate Tm; VP Drama Clb; Pres Key Clb; Chorus; Church Choir; School Play; St Schlr; High Hon Roll; SOSU Shksprn Fstvl Team Thtr; Hnr Show Choir; OU; Publc Rltns.

CLARK, KIRSTEN; Morris HS; Okmulgee, OK; (2); Office Aide; Teachers Aide; School Play; Rptr Nwsp; Rep Stu Cncl; Var Chrldng; JV Trk; Mgr Wrstlng; Hon Roll; CA ST; Phy.

CLARK, KYLE S; Bishop Mcguinness HS; Oklahoma City, OK; (4); VP Spanish Clb; SADD; Pres Frsh Cls; Pres Soph Cls; Pres Stu Cncl; JV Var Ftbl; High Hon Roll; NHS; Spanish NHS; Exch Clb Achvmt Awd Stu Achiever Of The Yr; Thurgood Marshall Schlr; OSU; MLK Celebration Fndr & Org; OK ST Univ; Bio; Family Dr.

CLARK, LAUREN; B T Washington HS; Sand Springs, OK; (3); Art Clb; Cmnty Wkr; Red Cross Aide; Service Clb; Teachers Aide; Camp Fire; Ldrshp Cmp Cnslr; Chinese Clb.

CLARK, LIISA O; B T Washington HS; Tulsa, OK; (4); Art Clb; Church Yth Grp; German Clb; Red Cross Aide; Spanish Clb; Varsity Clb; Var Socr; Var Tennis; Var Trk; High Hon Roll; Piano; Young Democrats Clb; Cornell Univ.

CLARK, LORI; Texhoma HS; Texhoma, OK; (1); Church Yth Grp; Pep Clb; Band; JV Var Bsktbl; JV Var Chrldng; Hon Roll.

CLARK, MARANDA A; Enid Sr HS; Waukomis, OK; (3); Church Yth Grp; Dance Clb; Band; Color Guard; Mrchg Band; Rptr Nwsp; Pom Pon; Hon Roll; Prfct Atten Awd; Peer Mediator; Southern Nazarene U; Tch/Cnslr.

CLARK, MARIE; Poteau HS; Poteau, OK; (4); 10/150; Am Leg Aux Girls St; Church Yth Grp; Band; Color Guard; Drm Mjr(t); Flag Corp; Mrchg Band; Sec Frsh Cls; Sec Soph Cls; Rep Stu Cncl; OU; Hlth.

CLARK, MICHAEL C; Claremore Sr HS; Chouteau, OK; (1); 4-H; Natl FFA Org; Ofcr Bsbl; Trk; 4-H Awd; High Hon Roll; Hon Roll; OSU; Vet.

CLARK, MICHAEL S; Midwest City HS; Midwest City, OK; (3); Boy Scts; Church Yth Grp; Letterman Clb; Socr; Hon Roll; Medicine.

CLARK, MISSY; Shawnee Sr HS; Shawnee, OK; (3); Church Yth Grp; Cmnty Wkr; Pep Clb; Scholastic Bowl; Service Clb; Spanish Clb; Yrbk; VP Soph Cls; Chrldng; Hon Roll; U OK.

CLARK, MISTY; Davenport Jr Sr HS; Davenport, OK; (1); Pep Clb; Var Chrldng; Var JV Sftbl; Var Trk; Hon Roll; KOMMOTION; Wlcmng Cmmtte Chrmn; OK U; Med.

CLARK, RYAN J; Duncan HS; Duncan, OK; (4); 67/215; Church Yth Grp; FCA; French Clb; Letterman Clb; Office Aide; Rptr Nwsp; Rptr Yrbk; Var L Bsbl; Var L Bsktbl; Var L Ftbl; Hlth Careers Club; All-Conf & All-St Hnrb Mntn Bsbl; SW OK ST; Rdlgc Tech.

CLARK, RYAN K; Claremore Sr HS; Claremore, OK; (3); 45/265; Boy Scts; Church Yth Grp; Cmnty Wkr; FCA; Letterman Clb; Library Aide; Church Choir; Var L Bsktbl; Var L Crs Cntry; Var L Ftbl; OK ST Univ; Phy Thrpst.

CLARK, SARAH; Woodward HS; Woodward, OK; (1); Art Clb; Church Yth Grp; Cmnty Wkr; Hosp Aide; Pep Clb; Chorus; School Musical; Cit Awd; High Hon Roll; St Schlr; Acad Lttrmn; Artisns Leag Spec Awd; Arch.

CLARK, SHAWNA; Minco HS; Minco, OK; (4); Church Yth Grp; FCA; FHA; GAA; Pep Clb; Teachers Aide; Band; Church Choir; Jazz Band; Mrchg Band; Redlands CC; Nrs.

CLARK, TANISHA D; Kingspark Baptist Acad; Oklahoma City, OK; (3); Bsktbl; Sftbl; Vllybl; Hon Roll; Soc Work.

CLARK, TRACY L; Claremore Sr HS; Chouteau, OK; (3); Teachers Aide; Rptr Yrbk; Hon Roll; 3rd Place Yrbk Wrtng From Northeastern ST Univ; Rogers ST; Lawyer; Soc Svcs.

CLARK, TRAVIS; Moore Pub Schls; Oklahoma City, OK; (1); Church Yth Grp; JV Socr; Olympic Dev Pgm Soccer Team For OK 95; Alt 96.

CLARK, TRAVIS J; Woodward HS; Woodward, OK; (1); Pres Frsh Cls; JV Ftbl; JV Trk; Var Wt Lftg.

CLARK-GILLUM, SHARLA; Panama HS; Spiro, OK; (3); FHA; Scholastic Bowl; Var Bsktbl; Var Chrldng; High Hon Roll; Hon Roll; NHS; Acctng.

CLARKSON, MATTHEW; John Marshall HS; Oklahoma City, OK; (4); 17/178; Am Leg Boys St; VP FBLA; Letterman Clb; Office Aide; Quiz Bowl; Yrbk; Capt L Bsbl; Score Keeper; High Hon Roll; NHS; MYF Pres.

CLARKSON, RACHEL B; South Intermediate HS; Broken Arrow, OK; (2); Dance Clb; French Clb; Intnl Clb; Band; Color Guard; Drill Tm; Mrchg Band; Pom Pon; Hon Roll; NHS; OK Perf Arts; OK ST Univ Stillwater.

CLARO, CANDACE A; Bishop Mcguinness HS; Oklahoma City, OK; (4); 63/153; Church Yth Grp; FCA; Pep Clb; SADD; Rep Frsh Cls; Rep Soph Cls; Rep Jr Cls; Treas Stu Cncl; Var L Bsktbl; Var L Chrldng; FCA VP & Pres; Hnry Pres Schlrshp; U Of OK.

CLARY, DIANA; Moore HS; Moore, OK; (3); 100/670; Band; Color Guard; Flag Corp; Mrchg Band; Pep Band; Jr NHS; NHS; Scndry Ed.

CLARY, JENNIFER K; Putnam City North HS; Oklahoma City, OK; (4); Church Yth Grp; Library Aide; Chorus; NHS; Russian Clb; Odyssey Of Mind St Champions; Russian.

CLASBY, CHARITY E; Pawnee HS; Pawnee, OK; (2); Hon Roll; Prfct Atten Awd; Rcvd Invit To Beta Club; Cndt Rep OK 96 Ssn Natl Yng Ldrs Conf; WA Univ; Arch/Grphc Comm.

CLASBY, CHRISTOPHER M; Edmond North HS; Edmond, OK; (2); Church Yth Grp; Cmnty Wkr; Debate Tm; FCA; Office Aide; Spanish Clb; Bsktbl; Ftbl; Tennis; Regnls Tnns 2nd Pl 94-95.

CLAUNCH, ANDREA L; South Intermediate HS; Broken Arrow, OK; (1); French Clb; Acpl Chr; French Hon Soc; Hon Roll; Jr NHS; Pres Acad Fit Awd; TJC; Psych.

CLAWSON, JENNIFER; Woodward HS; Woodward, OK; (3); Church Yth Grp; Cmnty Wkr; FCA; Natl Beta Clb; Spanish Clb; SADD; JV Bsktbl; JV Sftbl; High Hon Roll; NHS; Presdntl Acad Fitness Awd; Southwestern OK ST U; Phrmcy.

CLAXTON, TARA M; Union Intermediate HS; Tulsa, OK; (2); Art Clb; Dance Clb; French Clb; Hosp Aide; Ofcr Drill Tm; Hon Roll; Pres Acad Fit Awd; CA I Love Dance Assn Dncr; OK 1st Mdrn Dance Assn Prfrmr; Coll Of The Arts; Dance.

CLAY, BRIAN C; Heritage Hall Schl; Oklahoma City, OK; (2); Art Clb; Letterman Clb; Mu Alpha Theta; Pres Spanish Clb; Chorus; Rep Soph Cls; Pres Jr Cls; Rep Stu Cncl; Var Bsbl; Var Crs Cntry; Prtcpte In Smmr Prgm U Of OK Med Schl.

CLAY, CAROLINE; Roland Sr HS; Roland, OK; (4); 12/89; Art Clb; Cmnty Wkr; FCA; Library Aide; Spanish Clb; SADD; Band; Color Guard; Pres Jr Cls; Rep Stu Cncl; All-Star Chrldr-London Trip; 95-96 Ftbl Homcmng Attndnt; Amer Horse Shows Assn Huntr Jumprs; CO ST U; Vet Med.

CLAY, ELIZABETH D; Christian Heritage Acad; Del City, OK; (3); 9/40; Church Yth Grp; Chorus; Church Choir; Ofcr Stu Cncl; Var JV Bsktbl; Hon Roll.

CLAY, KIMBERLY A; Will Rogers HS; Tulsa, OK; (2); Church Yth Grp; Spanish Clb; Church Choir; Hon Roll; Tulsa JC; Nurse.

CLAY, MARCELLO D; Lawton Sr HS; Lawton, OK; (2); Bsktbl; JV Crs Cntry; Var Trk; Hon Roll.

CLAY, SARAH; Ardmore HS; Ardmore, OK; (2); 14/243; Latin Clb; Mu Alpha Theta; Science Clb; Rep Soph Cls; Chrldng; Pom Pon; Tennis; High Hon Roll; Hon Roll; Jr NHS.

CLAYBURN, TIMOTHY R; Poteau HS; Poteau, OK; (3); Church Yth Grp; Cmnty Wkr; Drama Clb; Speech Tm; SADD; Thesps; Chorus; School Musical; School Play; Stage Crew; Interlochen Arts Camp; Interlochen Arts Acad; OK Summer Arts Inst; Theatre Arts; Actor.

CLAYTON, ANDRE D; Mc Lain Career Acad; Tulsa, OK; (4); Letterman Clb; Math Clb; ROTC; Science Clb; Bsktbl; Ftbl; Trk; Wt Lftg; Wrstlng; Hon Roll; Acctng; Bus Mgmt.

CLAYTON, KAYLEE D; Dale Sr HS; Shawnee, OK; (2); 19/48; FHA; Spanish Clb; SADD; Band; Mrchg Band; Dale Yth Christ; OK Univ; Med.

CLAYTON, LACY; Putnam City West HS; Bethany, OK; (1); Church Yth Grp; Stage Crew; Rep Stu Cncl; JV Chrldng.

CLAYTON, SARA; Frederick HS; Frederick, OK; (1); Church Yth Grp; FHA; Girl Scts; Varsity Clb; Band; Chorus; Church Choir; Drill Tm; Flag Corp; Jazz Band; OK ST U; Interior Dsgn.

CLAYTOR, DAVID M; Mc Loud HS; Newalla, OK; (1); Letterman Clb; Natl FFA Org; Bsktbl; Ftbl; Wt Lftg; High Hon Roll; NHS; OSU; Agronimist.

CLEAVER, COURTNEY; Edmond North HS; Edmond, OK; (3); #1 in class; Drama Clb; French Clb; Mu Alpha Theta; School Play; Stage Crew; French Hon Soc; NHS; St Schlr; SUN Clb; Acad Ltr & Bar; U Of OK; Medicine.

CLEEK, KARI; Guthrie Sr HS; Guthrie, OK; (4); 8/150; Church Yth Grp; FCA; HOBY; Mu Alpha Theta; Office Aide; SADD; Church Choir; School Play; Stage Crew; Ed Phtg Yrbk; U Of Cntrl OK; Deaf Ed.

CLEM, MYKEL; Leedey Schl; Camargo, OK; (3); 6/14; Church Yth Grp; FCA; Ofcr FBLA; FHA; HOBY; Spanish Clb; SADD; Yrbk; Treas Frsh Cls; Chrldng; OK Bapt Univ.

CLEMENS, ANGELA M; Mannford HS; Terlton, OK; (3); Church Yth Grp; Cmnty Wkr; Science Clb; Spanish Clb; SADD; Teachers Aide; Band; Jazz Band; Mrchg Band; Orch; Pyhs Sci Cert Of Awd Frosh Yr; Amer His Metal Awd Soph Yr; Scndry Eng Ed; His.

CLEMENT, ADRIENNE S; Bishop Mcguinness HS; Edmond, OK; (4); 2/158; Cmnty Wkr; Sec French Clb; Pres German Clb; SADD; Rep Stu Cncl; French Hon Soc; Pres NHS; Ntl Merit SF; Sal; High Hon Roll; German Hnr Soc; Art Stds; Piano Stds; Intl Rltns.

CLEMENT, SANDY L; Noble HS; Noble, OK; (3); FCA; FHA; Key Clb; Office Aide; SADD; Teachers Aide; Rep Stu Cncl; Var Chrldng; Hon Roll; NHS; Girls JV/VAR Bsktbl Tm Ath Trnr; Ftbl Head Ath Trnr; OK Univ; Early Chldhd Dev.

CLEMENTS, APRIL S; Heavener HS; Heavener, OK; (1); 35/101; Band; Color Guard; Flag Corp; Mrchg Band; Carl Albert ST Coll; Vet.

CLEMENTS, COY R; Mc Alester HS; Mcalester, OK; (2); Art Clb; Boy Scts; Church Yth Grp; Cmnty Wkr; Science Clb; Spanish Clb; Varsity Clb; Mrchg Band; Ofcr Bsbl; Ftbl.

CLEMENTS, JERRY D; Bray-Doyle HS; Marlow, OK; (3); 5/34; Am Leg Boys St; Drama Clb; Science Clb; Ofcr Bsbl; Bsktbl; Ftbl; High Hon Roll; Hon Roll; NHS; Prfct Atten Awd; OK Hon Roll; All Dist Newcomer Yr Ftbl/Area Ftbl; 3rd Team All Area Bsktbl/All Tournmt Team Bsktbl; OSU; Math.

CLEMENTS, JO ANN; Edmond Memorial HS; Edmond, OK; (3); Church Yth Grp; Cmnty Wkr; FCA; FHA; Spanish Clb; SADD; Chorus; NHS; Free Medical Clinic Spon By Integris Health Vol; 1st United Meth Chrch Yth Pgm; Bus Admin & Engrng.

CLEMENTS, NICK H; Lindsay HS; Lindsay, OK; (1); 12/70; Art Clb; Church Yth Grp; FCA; Letterman Clb; Var Bsbl; JV Ftbl; Var Wt Lftg; High Hon Roll; Hon Roll; U Of OK.

CLEMENTS, OBIE; Apache HS; Apache, OK; (1); Art Clb; Science Clb; Band; Mrchg Band; Pep Band; Hon Roll; JETS Awd; Tech Stdnt Assn; ST Fnlst Awd 8th Pl Eng Grphc Anlys II; ST Fnlst Awd 6th Pl Rsrch/Dsgn II; Cameron Univ.

CLEMMONS, MICHAEL; Millwood HS; Oklahoma City, OK; (3); Cmnty Wkr; Office Aide; Band; Mrchg Band; School Musical; Ofcr Bsbl; Trk; Wt Lftg; Cit Awd; Hon Roll; Wichita ST; Comp Pgm.

CLEMONS, AARON K; Will Rogers HS; Tulsa, OK; (3); Church Yth Grp; Debate Tm; English Clb; FCA; Quiz Bowl; Church Choir; Ofcr Stu Cncl; Hon Roll; Jr NHS; French Clb; Yth Group Ldr; Rodeo Clb; Cntrl Bapt Coll; Yth Minister.

CLEMONS, MELISSA R; South Intermediate HS; Broken Arrow, OK; (1); Church Yth Grp; Band; Flag Corp; Hon Roll.

CLEVELAND, CASSIE; Shawnee Sr HS; Shawnee, OK; (2); 9/325; Church Yth Grp; Cmnty Wkr; FCA; GAA; Sec Latin Clb; Math Clb; Pep Clb; Scholastic Bowl; Treas Soph Cls; Ofcr Stu Cncl; Tri-Hi-Y; Poltcl Cmpgning; St Capital Pg; Miami U; Poltcl Sci.

CLEVELAND, DUSTIN; Metro Christian Acad; Tulsa, OK; (2); Chrldng; Trk; Wt Lftg; Delta Demolay; Best Entry Art Awd; Skateboarding; Gymnastics.

CLEVELAND, HYLARY L; Sapulpa Sr HS; Sapulpa, OK; (2); Spanish Clb; Flag Corp; Mrchg Band; Nwsp; Hon Roll; Spanish NHS; Sci-Spcl Awds, Grds & Work Ethic; TCC; Dr Of Psych.

CLEVELAND, MAGAN L; Sharon Mutual Jr Sr HS; Mutual, OK; (2); Sec Church Yth Grp; FCA; FHA; Natl FFA Org; Varsity Clb; Pres Frsh Cls; Treas Jr Cls; Var Bsktbl; Stat Ftbl; L Sftbl.

CLEVELAND, MISTY D; Jay HS; Jay, OK; (4); FCA; FHA; Natl Beta Clb; Pep Clb; Chorus; Powder Puff Ftbl; Hon Roll; NHS; Ricks Coll; Elem Ed.

CLEVENGER, AMY B; Mustang HS; Mustang, OK; (4); 50/350; Cmnty Wkr; Hist Debate Tm; Pres Drama Clb; FHA; Model UN; NFL; VP Speech Tm; SADD; Teachers Aide; Thesps; NEMA Nmntn; All-Star Rgnl Cast Mmbr; Rgnl One-Act Play Comp; Grad Acad Achv Hhs Hon/Drama Hon; Northeastern ST Univ; PT.

CLEVERING, KAREN; Lawton Sr HS; Lawton, OK; (3); Church Yth Grp; HOBY; Band; Mrchg Band; Var L Swmmng; High Hon Roll.

CLICK, C J; Putnam City North HS; Oklahoma City, OK; (4); Am Leg Boys St; Church Yth Grp; Cmnty Wkr; FCA; Spanish Clb; Church Choir; Orch; School Musical; School Play; Stage Crew; LDI Ldrshp Retreat; St Stu Cncl Cnvntn; Basic & Advncnd Ldrshp Retreats; U Of OK; Psycht.

CLICK, RUSSELL; Shawnee Sr HS; Shawnee, OK; (3); 9/300; FCA; Var Ftbl.

CLIFFORD, ERIN; Tomlinson Jr HS; Lawton, OK; (1); Sec Church Yth Grp; Treas FHA; Hosp Aide; Nwsp; High Hon Roll; Jr NHS; NHS; Southwest OK Iris Soc; Nursry Hlpr; Jrnlsm.

CLIFTON, AMY; Lone Grove HS; Ardmore, OK; (3); VP Church Yth Grp; FHA; Cit Awd; U Of OK.

CLIFTON, JAMES M; Chisholm Sr HS; Enid, OK; (2); Church Yth Grp; Cmnty Wkr; Speech Tm; Prfct Atten Awd; OK ST Univ; Comps/Crtng.

CLIFTON, JEREMY; Chisholm Sr HS; Enid, OK; (4); 31/68; Boy Scts; Church Yth Grp; FHA; Church Choir; JV Bsktbl; Var Capt Crs Cntry; Var Mgr Trk; Hon Roll; NHS; Prfct Atten Awd; TX Chrstn U; Fitnss Promtion.

CLIFTON, KIMBERLY A; Webster HS; Tulsa, OK; (3); 4/140; FTA; Library Aide; Math Tm; Pres Spanish Clb; School Play; Ofcr Sr Cls; Rptr Stu Cncl; Capt Var Crs Cntry; Var L Trk; Hon Roll; Wrtng/Rdng Rsrch; Lstng Music; Eng/Bus.

CLIFTON, REBECCA A; Owasso Sr HS; Owasso, OK; (3); Church Yth Grp; Cmnty Wkr; French Clb; Sec VP Service Clb; Band; Mrchg Band; Pep Band; High Hon Roll; Hon Roll; NHS; Camp Fire Ofcr-Sec 2 Yrs, VP 1 Yr Tulsa Cncl; All St Band; Natl Mrt Commended Stu.

CLINE, AMBER C; Jenks HS; Tulsa, OK; (4); 197/475; Church Yth Grp; Cmnty Wkr; DECA; FCA; Pres FHA; Rep Stu Cncl; Mgr(s); Score Keeper; Stat Wrstlng; Hon Roll; Miss JHS Fnlst; 1st Pl DECA St Cmptn & Top 10 Natl Cmptn; OK ST Univ; Family Relations.

CLINE, CRYSTAL; Hartshorne Sr HS; Hartshorne, OK; (2); Cmnty Wkr; FCA; Office Aide; Pep Clb; Teachers Aide; Chorus; School Play; Chrldng; Swmmng; Hon Roll.

CLINE, JUSTIN S; Okmulgee HS; Okmulgee, OK; (2); Church Yth Grp; Cmnty Wkr; FCA; Library Aide; SADD; Rep Frsh Cls; Rep Stu Cncl; JV Bsktbl; Golf; High Hon Roll; Rdng; Stud Rel; Philosophy; Attorney At Law.

CLINGMAN, SARAH; Medford Schl; Medford, OK; (4); 5/22; Sec Church Yth Grp; FCA; FHA; School Play; Yrbk; Rep Jr Cls; Rep Sr Cls; Ofcr Stu Cncl; High Hon Roll; NHS; OU.

CLINTON, BOBBY; Carnegie Jr HS; Carnegie, OK; (3); Am Leg Boys St; Drama Clb; NFL; Quiz Bowl; Scholastic Bowl; Spanish Clb; Speech Tm; Pres Acad Fit Awd; OK Stu Congress Sen.

CLINTON, CLAUDIA; Northeast HS; Oklahoma City, OK; (4); Am Leg Aux Girls St; French Clb; FBLA; Mu Alpha Theta; Science Clb; Orch; Capt Var Chrldng; Var Tennis; High Hon Roll; Sec NHS; Stu Mentor Polk Elem Schl; Jr Rotarian Clb 29; Friends Book Sale 95 Vol; Hendrix Coll; Dental.

CLOAR, NATHAN; Mustang HS; Mustang, OK; (4); 34/347; Am Leg Boys St; Church Yth Grp; Cmnty Wkr; FCA; FBLA; JA; Letterman Clb; Spanish Clb; Varsity Clb; Rep Soph Cls; KQCVS, KNTL FCA MVP Of Wk; 1st Tm Metro All Conf, All St Hnrb Mntn, Schlr Athl Awd; OK Bapt U; Bio.

CLODI, LAUREN K; Union Intermediate HS; Tulsa, OK; (2); French Clb; Chorus; School Musical; Hon Roll; Jr NHS; U IL; Music Thrpy.

CLONCE, CHRISTOPHER; Choctaw HS; Choctaw, OK; (4); Quiz Bowl; Scholastic Bowl; SADD; Varsity Clb; Ftbl; Golf; Trk; Wt Lftg; Jr NHS; NHS; People To People Stu Amb 96; OK U.

CLONTS, ANGIE; Paden HS; Paden, OK; (3); Church Yth Grp; Natl Beta Clb; Teachers Aide; Church Choir; Phtg Yrbk; Pres Jr Cls; High Hon Roll; Hon Roll; Natl Hnr Roll.

CLOPTON, KELI; Gore HS; Gore, OK; (4); Church Yth Grp; FHA; Office Aide; Church Choir; Phtg Yrbk; Sec Jr Cls; Var Bsktbl; Capt Chrldng; Hon Roll; NHS; Cnnrs St Coll Intrschlstc Mt Envrnmntl Sci 2nd Pl 95; Eng III, Gmtry, Envrnmntl Sci Otstndng Achvt Awd; Northeastern ST U; Bus Admin.

CLOUD, CRISTIN A; Canton HS; Canton, OK; (2); Church Yth Grp; FHA; SADD; Band; Mrchg Band; Pep Band; Rep Stu Cncl; SWOSU.

CLOUD, GWENDOLYN J; Edmond Memorial HS; Edmond, OK; (3); 1/392; Church Yth Grp; Chorus; Orch; High Hon Roll; NHS; Zoology.

CLOUD, KERI L; Edmond North HS; Edmond, OK; (3); 38/348; Cmnty Wkr; Math Clb; Mu Alpha Theta; Quiz Bowl; Scholastic Bowl; Chorus; Smith Coll Book Awd; Outstdng Fr Stdnt 3 Yrs; Univ Of Cntrl OK; Tch Fr.

CLOUD, MICAH; Tomlinson Jr HS; Lawton, OK; (1); Church Yth Grp; FCA; FHA; Pep Clb; Ofcr Stu Cncl; Chrldng; Hon Roll; Jr NHS; OK U; Educ.

CLOUGH, KRISTIN; Kingfisher HS; Kingfisher, OK; (1); Church Yth Grp; FCA; Office Aide; Chorus; Church Choir; Sec Frsh Cls; Mgr(s); Cit Awd; Hon Roll; NHS; UCO.

CLOUSE, MATTHEW; Grove HS; Grove, OK; (3); #8 in class; FCA; HOBY; Key Clb; Pres Frsh Cls; VP Jr Cls; Var L Bsbl; Var L Bsktbl; Var L Ftbl; Wt Lftg; Cit Awd; 1st Meth Chrch; U OK; Pre-Med.

CLOUSE, MATTHEW A; Muskogee HS; Muskogee, OK; (3); Church Yth Grp; German Clb; Spanish Clb; SADD; Band; Chorus; Church Choir; Mrchg Band; Orch; Pep Band; Teens For Christ; RAID; Ltr In Choir; OBU; Music Minister.

CLOVER, NIKKI; Wakita Schl; Wakita, OK; (4); 3/14; Church Yth Grp; FCA; Treas FHA; Pep Clb; Teachers Aide; Band; Church Choir; High Hon Roll; Hon Roll; NHS; Knowledge Mstr; Hon Bnds; NW OK ST Univ; Elem Ed.

CLUBB, ALICIA; Silo HS; Durant, OK; (3); Church Yth Grp; Mu Alpha Theta; School Musical; Hon Roll; NHS; 1st Pl Sci Fair; 1st Pl St Engrng Fair.

CLUBB, ALLISON; Silo HS; Durant, OK; (3); Church Yth Grp; Mu Alpha Theta; Teachers Aide; School Musical; High Hon Roll; NHS; 1st Pl Sci Fair; Southeastern; Comp Applications.

CLUBB, BRIAN N; Norman Sr HS; Norman, OK; (3); Band; Mrchg Band; Orch; Hon Roll; Pres Educl Exclnc Awd; Ctzn Bee 1st Pl; St Hnr Soc; Engr.

CLUBB, JULIE; Silo HS; Durant, OK; (2); Church Yth Grp; FHA; Mu Alpha Theta; School Musical; Sec Frsh Cls; High Hon Roll; NHS; 1st Pl St Engrng Fair; 3rd Pl Sci Fair; GATE.

CLUCK, CRYSTAL M; Kingston HS; Kingston, OK; (2); Church Yth Grp; Band; Jazz Band; Mrchg Band; Rptr Nwsp; VP Jr Cls; Stat Mgr(s); Score Keeper; Hon Roll; PT.

CLYMER, CASEY; Westmoore HS; Oklahoma City, OK; (1); Church Yth Grp; GAA; Office Aide; Pep Clb; Teachers Aide; Rep Frsh Cls; Chrldng; Sftbl; Cit Awd; Hon Roll.

CLYMER, ELOISE K; Erick Jr Sr HS; Erick, OK; (3); 1/30; Church Yth Grp; Girl Scts; Red Cross Aide; Spanish Clb; Church Choir; Phtg Rptr Yrbk; Cit Awd; High Hon Roll; NHS; Best Of Fair Local Sci Fair; OK City U; Psych.

CLYNE, TONYA; Edmond Memorial HS; Edmond, OK; (3); 1/400; Church Yth Grp; FCA; Sec French Clb; Red Cross Aide; SADD; Rep Stu Cncl; Diving; Swmmng; High Hon Roll; NHS.

CLYTUS, MARK; Douglass HS; Oklahoma City, OK; (4); 6/116; Am Leg Boys St; Boy Scts; Church Yth Grp; Cmnty Wkr; Computer Clb; FBLA; German Clb; HOBY; JA; Library Aide; OK Soc Prfsnl Engrs Engng For Day; OK Acad Schlr; OKAMP-SMET; JROTC; Pres Ed Awds Prgm; Acad Achvmnt; OK ST Univ; Chem Eng/Pre-Med.

COACHMAN, JANA; Braggs Schl; Braggs, OK; (3); Computer Clb; Varsity Clb; Rptr Nwsp; Yrbk; VP Frsh Cls; Sec Soph Cls; VP Jr Cls; Bsktbl; Chrldng; Var Sftbl; Grad Singer.

COAKLEY, MATTHEW R; Edmond Santa Fe HS; Edmond, OK; (3); 39/283; Am Leg Boys St; Science Clb; Rep Hist Spanish Clb; JV Bsbl; Var JV Golf; NHS.

COATES, ELIZABETH A; Jay HS; Jay, OK; (2); FCA; Natl Beta Clb; Chorus; Rep Soph Cls; Rep Stu Cncl; Hon Roll; NHS; NSU.

COATES, JEFF D; Mustang HS; Yukon, OK; (3); Am Leg Boys St; Church Yth Grp; FCA; Office Aide; SADD; Ofcr Stu Cncl; JV Var Bsktbl; Hon Roll; NHS; OK Bapt Univ; Med Field.

COATES, MICHAEL P; Owasso Sr HS; Owasso, OK; (2); Church Yth Grp; English Clb; FCA; Science Clb; Ofcr Bsbl; Bsktbl; Wt Lftg; Tulsa Rowing Club; Great Books Club.

COATES, MINDY; Broken Arrow Sr HS; Broken Arrow, OK; (4); 30/921; Sec DECA; VP French Clb; Band; Color Guard; Ed Nwsp; Rep Stu Cncl; Ofcr Stu Cncl; Chrldng; Sec NHS; Msnc Ldg Stu Of Yr; Webster U; Adv.

COATNEY, MITCH; Ponca City Sr HS; Ponca City, OK; (4).

COATS, DANA; Freedom Schl; Freedom, OK; (2); Cmnty Wkr; Yrbk; Var Bsktbl; Hon Roll; NHS.

COATS, DENA R; Ponca City Sr HS; Ponca City, OK; (4); Church Yth Grp; Cmnty Wkr; Dance Clb; DECA; Office Aide; Spanish Clb; Chorus; Drill Tm; Variety Show; Ed Nwsp; Supt Hnr Roll; Panic Bd; Rotry Speaker; NOC; Bus Admin.

COATS, JOHN C; Yukon HS; Yukon, OK; (3); Rep Stu Cncl; High Hon Roll; Pres Acad Fit Awd; Renaissance Mem; Pre-Med.

COATS, JOSHUA D; John Marshall HS; Oklahoma City, OK; (2); 1/300; Church Yth Grp; FCA; HOBY; Var L Ftbl; Var L Golf; Var L Socr; Var L Tennis; High Hon Roll; NHS; Pres Schlr; GAPP Clb; Architecture.

COATS, PATSY; Claremore Sr HS; Claremore, OK; (2); Church Yth Grp; Yrbk; NHS; Pediatrician.

COBB, BRYANNA; Ponca City Mid-HS; Ponca City, OK; (1); Church Yth Grp; Chorus; JV Chrldng; High Hon Roll; Bil Span & Eng; Lttr Chrldng & Acad; Northwestern; Drama.

COBB, CHRIS K; Nathan Hale HS; Tulsa, OK; (1); Art Clb; Wt Lftg; Cit Awd; Hon Roll; Tennis; Animated Art; Animated Artist; Drafting.

COBB, ESTER E; Bishop Mcguinness HS; Oklahoma City, OK; (3); 5/137; Pres Pep Clb; Bsktbl; JV Var Chrldng; JV Var Crs Cntry; Smith Bk Awd; English Hunt Seat Equitation; Vet Med.

COBB, JENNIFER M; Stillwater Sr HS; Stillwater, OK; (3); 46/350; FCA; Sec French Clb; Key Clb; Sec Mu Alpha Theta; Natl Beta Clb; Office Aide; Science Clb; Rptr Nwsp; Var Bsktbl; Var Sftbl; Amer HS Math Exam Cert Of Mrt; OK ST Univ; Engrng.

COBB, MELISSA; Noble HS; Noble, OK; (4); Church Yth Grp; Cmnty Wkr; FCA; Model UN; Mu Alpha Theta; SADD; Chrldng; Var Crs Cntry; Var Trk; Hon Roll; U Of OK; CPA.

COBB, PATRICIA; Victory Christian Schl; Tulsa, OK; (2); Church Yth Grp; Drama Clb; FCA; Spanish Clb; School Play; Var Swmmng; JV Vllybl; High Hon Roll; NHS; Pres Acad Fit Awd; OK U; Phys Thrp.

COBB, SAMUEL A; Nathan Hale HS; Tulsa, OK; (2); Teachers Aide; School Play; Bsktbl; Wt Lftg; Cit Awd; High Hon Roll; Jr NHS; NHS; Crss Cntry; Tnns; Medicine; Med Rsrch.

COBB, SARAH E; Enid Sr HS; Enid, OK; (4); #20 in class; JA; Band; Chorus; Mrchg Band; Orch; Pep Band; Ofcr Stu Cncl; High Hon Roll; Jr NHS; NHS; SW OK St Univ; Pharm.

COBB, TAMI J; Oklahoma Bible Acad; Enid, OK; (4); Church Yth Grp; Debate Tm; FCA; French Clb; Speech Tm; Chorus; School Play; Sec Sr Cls; NHS; Drama Clb; OSU; Phy Thrpy.

COBLE, ANGELA; Sapulpa Sr HS; Sapulpa, OK; (2); Dance Clb; Spanish Clb; Chorus; Drill Tm; Pom Pon; High Hon Roll; Ntl Merit Ltr; Prfct Atten Awd; Pres Acad Fit Awd; Spanish NHS; Dance Masters Amer Solo & Grps Lines Awds.

COBLE, KIMBERLY; Spiro HS; Spiro, OK; (3); Rptr Drama Clb; FCA; Pres FHA; HOBY; Quiz Bowl; Spanish Clb; School Play; Rep Jr Cls; Chrldng; NHS; Phys Thrpy.

COBLE, KYLEE; Spiro HS; Spiro, OK; (3); 6/90; Church Yth Grp; FCA; VP FHA; Math Clb; Quiz Bowl; Yrbk; Pres Frsh Cls; Pres Soph Cls; Rptr Jr Cls; Sec Sr Cls; OK Hnrs Soc; Northeastern ST Coll; Cmnctns.

COBOURN, TERI; Claremore Sr HS; Claremore, OK; (3); Debate Tm; German Clb; NFL; Science Clb; Gym; Hon Roll; NHS; Foreign Exchange Stdnt Germany 96-; Congress Bundestag Schlsp.

COCANNOUER, ANGELA; Tuttle HS; Blanchard, OK; (4); 5/72; FHA; Rep Sr Cls; Ofcr Stu Cncl; Chrldng; Gym; High Hon Roll; Hon Roll; NHS; Sal; St Schlr.

COCANOUGHER, KRISTINA R; Perkins-Tryon HS; Perkins, OK; (1); Church Yth Grp; FHA; Intnl Clb; Office Aide; Quiz Bowl; Band; Chorus; Church Choir; Mrchg Band; Pep Band; Perf Cncrts Austria; OK His Awd; Culinary; Univ Of KY; Culinary.

COCHERAN, JUSTIN; Cyril Jr Sr HS; Cyril, OK; (1); 1/43; Church Yth Grp; Drama Clb; Scholastic Bowl; School Play; Pres Frsh Cls; Ofcr Stu Cncl; L Bsbl; Bsktbl; L Ftbl; Hon Roll; OK Hrtg Schlrshp; Mscn Awd.

COCHERAN, RHONDA R; Amber Pocasset Jr Sr HS; Chickasha, OK; (2); Church Yth Grp; FCA; Spanish Clb; Mgr(s); Socr; Sftbl; OK City CC; Paramedic.

COCHNAUER, HEATHER M; Choctaw HS; Choctaw, OK; (4); 14/304; German Clb; JV Bsktbl; Tennis; High Hon Roll; Hon Roll; Jr NHS; NHS; Pres Acad Fit Awd; OK U.

COCHRAN, CAREDY; Timberlake Schl; Jet, OK; (3); 1/24; Church Yth Grp; FCA; Rep FHA; Pres Chorus; Rep Frsh Cls; Treas Jr Cls; Var Bsktbl; High Hon Roll; Natl Engl Mrt Awd; All Amer Schlr; OK Hnr Soc; OSU; Bus Mgmt.

COCHRAN, CARRIE; Bridge Creek HS; Blanchard, OK; (4); Am Leg Aux Girls St; Church Yth Grp; FCA; Science Clb; Spanish Clb; Acpl Chr; Chorus; Church Choir; Rep Stu Cncl; Hon Roll; SW Baptist U; Poli Sci.

COCHRAN, COURTNEY; Timberlake Schl; Jet, OK; (1); Church Yth Grp; FCA; FHA; Quiz Bowl; Chorus; Sec Frsh Cls; Var Bsktbl; Var Chrldng; Hon Roll; NHS; FHA/STAR Evnt Sub-Dist & Dist Wnnr Jr Job Intrvw; YMCA Vlybl; OSU; Vet Med.

COCHRAN, ELANNA J; Checotah HS; Checotah, OK; (2); 5/110; Art Clb; Church Yth Grp; Cmnty Wkr; GAA; Bsktbl; Sftbl; Hon Roll; NHS; Top 10 Prcnt 91-; Hnr C His/Photo/Dsgn 95-; Hnr C Art I 95-; OK Univ; Pedtrcn/Obstrcn.

COCHRAN, HILLARY; Little Axe Sr HS; Norman, OK; (2); 1/100; Hosp Aide; Scholastic Bowl; Crs Cntry; Trk; Cit Awd; Hon Roll; Jr NHS; NHS; Prfct Atten Awd; Amer Leg Awd; Msnc Awd.

COCHRAN, KATY D; East Central HS; Tulsa, OK; (3); 16/212; Church Yth Grp; ROTC; Chorus; Church Choir; Color Guard; Drill Tm; Treas Frsh Cls; Pres Soph Cls; Pres Jr Cls; JV Sftbl; E Cntrl JROTC Battalion Commander; Dghtrs Of Founders/Patriots Of Amer Awd; Military Order World Wars.

COCHRANE, SCOTT; Perry Sr HS; Perry, OK; (2); Church Yth Grp; Capt Var Ftbl; Score Keeper; Wt Lftg; Cit Awd; High Hon Roll; Hon Roll; Jr NHS; NHS; Pres Acad Fit Awd; Chrch Mission Trips; N E OK ST U; Optometrist.

COCHRANE, SHASTA D; Pocola HS; Pocola, OK; (4); 2/45; FCA; FBLA; Hosp Aide; Capt Quiz Bowl; Rep Stu Cncl; Capt Chrldng; VP NHS; Pres Acad Fit Awd; Sal; St Schlr; Westark CC; CIS.

COCKERHAM, CHARLINA E; Dibble HS; Blanchard, OK; (3); 4/50; Dance Clb; Office Aide; Scholastic Bowl; Teachers Aide; Ed Yrbk; Pres Soph Cls; Chrldng; High Hon Roll; Hon Roll; Pres Schlr; Sci; Medicine.

COCKRALL, JASON; Roland Sr HS; Muldrow, OK; (4); 1/82; Cmnty Wkr; Debate Tm; Library Aide; Quiz Bowl; Spanish Clb; Speech Tm; Ed Nwsp; Sec Treas Stu Cncl; Hon Roll.

COCKRELL, AMBER D; Colcord Schl; Colcord, OK; (1); Rep Frsh Cls; High Hon Roll; Pres Acad Fit Awd; Singing, Have Been In Many Music Shows & Tlnt Conts; Phys Thrpy.

CODOPONY, DALLAS; Apache HS; Apache, OK; (2); Scholastic Bowl; Var Bsbl; Var Bsktbl; Var Ftbl; Hon Roll; NHS; Pres Acad Fit Awd.

CODY, MI ANGEL C; Muskogee HS; Muskogee, OK; (3); 29/343; Cmnty Wkr; JCL; Latin Clb; Cit Awd; Hon Roll; Jr NHS; NHS; Pres Acad Fit Awd; St Schlr; Ecology Clb; Cmnty Awd Human Rights 94; RAID; Emory U; Philosophy.

COE, MELISSA; Glencoe Public Schl; Glencoe, OK; (3); 5/30; Church Yth Grp; FCA; Natl FFA Org; Pep Clb; Sec Treas Frsh Cls; Pres Soph Cls; VP Jr Cls; Bsktbl; Sftbl; Trk; 2nd/3rd Pl FFA Speech Conts, Greenhand/Chptr Degrees; Phys Sci, Bio, Engl I, II Awds; FSU; Psych.

COE, NAKITA D; Hydro Jr Sr HS; Hydro, OK; (4); 2/20; Church Yth Grp; Drama Clb; 4-H; School Play; VP Frsh Cls; Sec Soph Cls; Pres Jr Cls; 4-H Awd; NHS; Sal; OK ST U; Ag.

COEN, WENDY; Goodwell Public Schl; Goodwell, OK; (2); 3/8; Church Yth Grp; FCA; Letterman Clb; Pres Soph Cls; Ofcr Stu Cncl; Golf; Hon Roll; Ntl Merit Ltr; Outstndng Scl Stds Stu; OK ST U; Vet.

COFER, SHARA; Anadarko HS; Anadarko, OK; (4); FCA; Natl FFA Org; Ed Nwsp; Pres Sr Cls; Rep Stu Cncl; Var Bsktbl; Var Sftbl; NHS; Pres Acad Fit Awd; Chrldng; OK Hnr Soc; U Of Cntrl OK; Bus Comm.

COFFEY, ILENA; Wynnewood HS; Wynnewood, OK; (1); 1/65; Church Yth Grp; JV Bsktbl; JV Chrldng; Hon Roll; OK Hnr Soc; Duke U; Jrnlsm.

COFFEY, JENNIFER A; Idabel HS; Idabel, OK; (1); Church Yth Grp; Debate Tm; Drama Clb; Quiz Bowl; Science Clb; Band; High Hon Roll; Jr NHS; NHS; Chorus.

COFFEY, JOSIE; Collinsville HS; Collinsville, OK; (2); Church Yth Grp; 4-H; Chorus; Chrldng; 4-H Awd; Certfd Ath Trnr Ftbl; Certfd Ath Trnr.

COFFEY, JULIE J; Elk City HS; Elk City, OK; (3); Am Leg Aux Girls St; Church Yth Grp; FCA; Math Clb; Pep Clb; Science Clb; Spanish Clb; SADD; Rep Band; Sec Church Choir; Chem I, Outstndng Brass Band Membr Awds.

COFFEY, TERRENCE; Okarche HS; Okarche, OK; (3); 1/36; Church Yth Grp; Cmnty Wkr; HOBY; Natl Beta Clb; Quiz Bowl; Scholastic Bowl; Spanish Clb; Pres Frsh Cls; Sec Jr Cls; Cit Awd; DARE; OK ST U; Med.

COFFIN, BREANNE R; Choctaw HS; Nicoma Park, OK; (3); Church Yth Grp; Drama Clb; Band; Chorus; Color Guard; Outstndng Color Guard Solo & Ensemble OK St Champ Med 96; U Of Cntrl OK; Nrsng.

COFFMAN, KIM D; Metro Christian Acad; Tulsa, OK; (3); 1/50; Am Leg Aux Girls St; Church Yth Grp; Teachers Aide; Yrbk; Pres Jr Cls; Sec Stu Cncl; Var Co-Capt Bsktbl; Var Chrldng; High Hon Roll; NHS; Frosh/Soph/Jr Cls Hncmg Attndnt; Rep Natl Yng Ldrs Conf; Exec Ofc ST Auditor/Inspctr OK Girls ST.

COFFMAN, NATASHA J; Colcord Schl; Colcord, OK; (1); Church Yth Grp; FHA; Hon Roll; Prfct Atten Awd.

COFFMAN, RONNA M; Mc Loud HS; Mc Loud, OK; (1); Debate Tm; Drama Clb; Hosp Aide; Speech Tm; School Play; Stage Crew; High Hon Roll; OU; Teen Cnslr.

COGBURN, AMANDA R; Edmond Memorial HS; Edmond, OK; (2); 70/401; Church Yth Grp; FCA; Red Cross Aide; VP Spanish Clb; Ed Yrbk; Powder Puff Ftbl; NHS; Pres Schlr; Yng Life.

COGBURN, REBECCA; Wapanucka Schl; Wapanucka, OK; (2); 4-H; Natl FFA Org; Quiz Bowl; Sec Frsh Cls; Ofcr Stu Cncl; Bsktbl; Hon Roll; East Central; Elem Tchr.

COGER, KIMBERLY; Claremore Sr HS; Claremore, OK; (4); 1/241; Boy Scts; Pres German Clb; Quiz Bowl; Scholastic Bowl; Sec Science Clb; Teachers Aide; Ed Yrbk; Rep Stu Cncl; High Hon Roll; Hon Roll; Tulsa Zoo Teen Trng; Wldlf Bio.

COGGINS, JOY K; Nathan Hale HS; Tulsa, OK; (2); Church Yth Grp; FCA; Socr; Cit Awd; Hon Roll; Pres Schlr; Excllnc Awds Eng, Hist, Alb I, Span & Bio; MI ST; Med.

COGHILL, ANTHONY; Foyil Schl; Claremore, OK; (4); 1/28; Pres VP FBLA; Quiz Bowl; Rptr VICA; Rep Jr Cls; Pres Sr Cls; Var Bsbl; JV Bsktbl; High Hon Roll; Hon Roll; NHS; Mr Will Rogers Personality Awd; OSU; Engr.

COHEA, JAMIE; Edmond North HS; Edmond, OK; (3); 1/348; Church Yth Grp; Drama Clb; French Clb; Key Clb; Mu Alpha Theta; Band; School Musical; Sec Sr Cls; Pom Pon; NHS.

COHEN, LLOYD C; Okmulgee HS; Okmulgee, OK; (3); Boy Scts; Church Yth Grp; Science Clb; Spanish Clb; Varsity Clb; Yrbk; Var Ftbl; Var Trk; Var Wrstlng; Stat Hon Roll; OSU; Comp Field Or Law.

COIBION, MARCIE; Liberty HS; Mounds, OK; (2); 1/35; Church Yth Grp; FCA; VP Frsh Cls; Sec Soph Cls; Rep Sec Stu Cncl; Var Bsktbl; Var Socr; High Hon Roll; NHS; Prfct Atten Awd; Elem Ed.

COKE, KARI M; Owasso Sr HS; Owasso, OK; (4); Church Yth Grp; FCA; Ed Yrbk; Chrldng; Pom Pon; High Hon Roll; NHS; Pharm.

COKE, TROY; Altus Sr HS; Altus, OK; (4); 4/240; Am Leg Boys St; FCA; Quiz Bowl; Chorus; Pres Sr Cls; Var L Bsbl; Var L Bsktbl; Var L Score Keeper; High Hon Roll; NHS; All Dist, St Ftbl; Acad Bsktbl, Bsbl, All Sprts Awds 94-95; Sprtsmnshp Awds Bskbl 92-93, 94-95, Bsbl 92-9; OU; Med.

COKER, AMANDA; Spiro HS; Keota, OK; (2); FCA; Natl FFA Org; Band; Drm Mjr(t); Mrchg Band; Pep Band; Yrbk; Sftbl; Hon Roll; NHS; Spirit Of Amer Natl Hnr Bnd; Law.

COKER, AMY; Westmoore HS; Oklahoma City, OK; (3); Church Yth Grp; Library Aide; Office Aide; Q&S; Teachers Aide; School Play; Ed Nwsp; Ed Yrbk; Rep Stu Cncl; NHS; OU; Speech Pathologist; Psych.

COKER, CANDI M; Mc Loud HS; Shawnee, OK; (2); Church Yth Grp; Cmnty Wkr; Scholastic Bowl; High Hon Roll; Hon Roll; NHS; St Gregorys Coll; Art & Photo.

COKER, FRANCES Y; Woodward HS; Woodward, OK; (2); Church Yth Grp; Band; Color Guard; Flag Corp; Mrchg Band.

COKER, JAMES M; Tuttle HS; Tuttle, OK; (3); 3/110; Church Yth Grp; Capt Quiz Bowl; Scholastic Bowl; Band; Mrchg Band; High Hon Roll; NHS; Bausch/Lamb Sci Awd; Yth Amer; Ateams.

COKER, KASSIE L; Erick Jr Sr HS; Reydon, OK; (2); 3/20; Church Yth Grp; Library Aide; Natl FFA Org; Sec Stu Cncl; High Hon Roll; NHS; TSA; OU.

COKER, MATT; Anadarko HS; Anadarko, OK; (3); 12/124; Church Yth Grp; FCA; French Clb; Letterman Clb; Office Aide; Quiz Bowl; Teachers Aide; Ofcr Stu Cncl; JV Bsbl; JV Bsktbl; Sports Medicine; Therapy.

COKER, MELISSA; Midwest City HS; Del City, OK; (2); 50/988; Church Yth Grp; French Clb; SADD; Chorus; Church Choir; Chrldng; High Hon Roll; Jr NHS; Hstry, Hnrs Engl & Phys Sci Outstndg Achvt; ECOCDA Dist Hnr Choir; OK All-St Bapt Yth Choir; Med.

COKER, NICOLE; Reydon HS; Reydon, OK; (3); Cmnty Wkr; 4-H; GAA; Quiz Bowl; Sec Soph Cls; Sec Jr Cls; Bsktbl; Var Trk; Cit Awd; 4-H Awd; OK U; Envir Engrng.

COKER, R J; Cheyenne HS; Cheyenne, OK; (3); Church Yth Grp; FCA; Natl FFA Org; Sec Soph Cls; Sec Jr Cls; Var Bsbl; Var Bsktbl; SWOSU; Bio.

COKER, ROBIN A; Clayton Jr Sr HS; Clayton, OK; (3); Church Yth Grp; Computer Clb; French Clb; FBLA; FHA; Teachers Aide; Ed Nwsp; Pres Stu Cncl; Var Chrldng; Hon Roll; Natl Yth Ldrshp Conf; Southeastern St Univ; Pre-Med.

COLAW, PATRICK; Bartlesville Sr HS; Bartlesville, OK; (4); Church Yth Grp; Cmnty Wkr; FCA; FHA; JA; Letterman Clb; Spanish Clb; Varsity Clb; Church Choir; Rep Soph Cls; John Wesley Awd; Rtry Yth Ldshp Awd; OK St Univ.

COLBERT, CASEY J; Mustang HS; Yukon, OK; (2); Church Yth Grp; FCA; VP Frsh Cls; Pres Jr Cls; Ofcr Stu Cncl; Ofcr Bsbl; Var Bsktbl; Var Ftbl; Hon Roll.

COLBERT, JORDAN T; Mangum Sr HS; Mangum, OK; (3); 3/45; Church Yth Grp; Treas Jr Cls; JV Var Bsktbl; Wt Lftg; Cit Awd; High Hon Roll; Hon Roll; Jr NHS; NHS; Trck/Fld; All Amer Schlr; US Mltry Acad; Hrt Srgn/Crdlgs.

COLBERT, LA SHELL M; Northeast HS; Oklahoma City, OK; (3); Church Yth Grp; FBLA; Pep Clb; Chorus; Church Choir; Mgr(s); Score Keeper; Hon Roll; Ntl Merit Schol.

COLBERT, LA TOYA D; Mc Lain Career Acad; Tulsa, OK; (3); Church Yth Grp; ROTC; Flag Corp; Mrchg Band; Hon Roll; Nrsng/Pediatrician.

COLBURN, JAMES E; Tahlequah Sr HS; Tahlequah, OK; (3); 64/251; Am Leg Boys St; Cmnty Wkr; FCA; Letterman Clb; Quiz Bowl; Science Clb; Varsity Clb; L Var Ftbl; L Var Wt Lftg.

COLBURN, LINDSEY M; Shawnee Sr HS; Shawnee, OK; (2); Church Yth Grp; Latin Clb; Scholastic Bowl; Ofcr Stu Cncl; Bsktbl.

COLBY, NICOLE; Grove HS; Grove, OK; (3); Boy Scts; FCA; FHA; Rptr Nwsp; JV Var Chrldng; Trk; Hon Roll; NHS; US Chrldr Achvmnt Awds 96; Lwyr.

COLDWATER, LAFE; Forgan Schl; Forgan, OK; (4); 1/9; Am Leg Boys St; 4-H; Key Clb; Quiz Bowl; Pres Sr Cls; VP Stu Cncl; 4-H Awd; High Hon Roll; NHS; Pres Acad Fit Awd; Amer Kids Perf Grp; OK ST U; Sprts Med.

COLDWELL, KATHRYN J; B T Washington HS; Tulsa, OK; (4); 43/264; Church Yth Grp; French Clb; NFL; Pep Clb; Ed Yrbk; Hist Stu Cncl; Var Golf; NHS; Boy Scts; Speech Tm; Camp Fire Boys & Girls VP; SAIL; Natl Yth Advsry Cabnt; Intl Bus Mgmt.

COLDWELL, SARAH J; B T Washington HS; Tulsa, OK; (2); Boy Scts; Church Yth Grp; Treas Service Clb; Orch; Hist Soph Cls; JV Bsktbl; NHS; Cmnty Wkr; Pep Clb; School Musical; Camp Fire CIT; Russian Clb Treas; Natl Yth Svc Awd.

COLE, ANDREA L; Porum HS; Porum, OK; (3); FHA; Pep Clb; Chrldng; Hon Roll; E OK ST Coll; Comp Tech.

COLE, ANDREA S; South Intermediate HS; Broken Arrow, OK; (1); Church Yth Grp; Girl Scts; Band; Church Choir; Mrchg Band; High Hon Roll; Jr NHS; Pres Acad Fit Awd; Girl Sct Silvr Awd; Church Handbell Choir.

COLE, APRIL M; West Moore HS; Oklahoma City, OK; (2); Church Yth Grp; Library Aide; Pep Clb; Swmmng; Hon Roll; Cnslng; Soc Svcs.

COLE, CARISA R; Locust Grove HS; Rose, OK; (3); 31/109; Church Yth Grp; Band; Color Guard; Jazz Band; Mrchg Band; Pep Band.

COLE, CECIL L; Star Spencer HS; Midwest City, OK; (3); Varsity Clb; Band; Mrchg Band; Pep Band; VP Jr Cls; Bsktbl; Crs Cntry; Trk; Cit Awd; Hon Roll.

COLE, CHANDRA; Antlers Sr HS; Antlers, OK; (2); 13/86; 4-H; Quiz Bowl; Var Bsktbl; Hon Roll; S Eastern OK ST; Aviation.

COLE, CRYSTAL M; Antlers Sr HS; Antlers, OK; (2); 4-H; School Musical; Hon Roll; Med.

COLE, DANIELLE E; Preston Schl; Okmulgee, OK; (3); Art Clb; Church Yth Grp; GAA; Hosp Aide; Office Aide; Scholastic Bowl; Teachers Aide; Chorus; Bsktbl; Mgr(s); OK HIV/AIDS Awrns Pstr Cntst; Elctrnc Acad OSU Okmulgee; OK ST U; Ansthslgst.

COLE, JOLENNDA M; Bethany HS; Oklahoma City, OK; (4); 20/81; Church Yth Grp; Cmnty Wkr; Debate Tm; Drama Clb; Key Clb; Letterman Clb; Office Aide; SADD; School Musical; School Play; CCYM Meth Conf; Regnl Wnnr 3rd Pl Essay; OK Hnr Soc; Cntrl Meth; Psych.

COLE, JOSHUA R; Webster HS; Tulsa, OK; (3); FBLA; Yrbk; Ofcr Stu Cncl; Bsktbl; Trk; Hon Roll; NHS; Ntl Merit Ltr; Natl Engl Merit Awd Lttr; Afrcn Amer Stu Assoc; SW TX St Univ; Bus Admin.

COLE, KAREN; Coweta HS; Coweta, OK; (2); Church Yth Grp; Cmnty Wkr; FCA; SADD; Yrbk; Rep Stu Cncl; Var Chrldng.

COLE, KENNETH C; Union Intermediate HS; Tulsa, OK; (2); 350/800; Boy Scts; German Clb; Quiz Bowl; Scholastic Bowl; Band; Chorus; Pep Band; Swmmng; Fencing Clb; Med.

COLE, KENNY; Claremore Sr HS; Claremore, OK; (4); 17/236; Office Aide; Teachers Aide; JV Bsktbl; Var Capt Golf; Hon Roll; Wichita ST; Advertsng.

COLE, KRISTA; Idabe HS; Lexington, OK; (3); Church Yth Grp; Cmnty Wkr; Drama Clb; FCA; FBLA; GAA; Church Choir; Color Guard; Flag Corp; Stage Crew; Church Drama, Band; Miss IHS Cont; OCCC; Emergency Rm Nurse.

COLE, LEANDRA BERRY; Edmond North HS; Edmond, OK; (3); Cmnty Wkr; Dance Clb; JCL; Pres Latin Clb; Mu Alpha Theta; Varsity Clb; Orch; Vllybl; Hon Roll; NHS; Ice & Roller Hockey; Swimming, Line Dancing; U Of Cntrl OK; Vet; Chem Engr.

COLE, MELISSA S; Checotah HS; Checotah, OK; (2); French Clb; Library Aide; Pep Clb; Scholastic Bowl; Flag Corp; Sftbl; Hon Roll; Outstdng Stdnt Prtcptn Acctg; Lwyr.

COLE, RACHEL D; Haileyville Schl; Alderson, OK; (2); Church Yth Grp; FHA; Art; Child Care; Nursery Care; Child Care.

COLE, RON C; Del City HS; Del City, OK; (3); Church Yth Grp; Cmnty Wkr; Debate Tm; FCA; Office Aide; Teachers Aide; Church Choir; Rep Stu Cncl; Var Bsktbl; Var L Ftbl; CSU Cmp; Notre Dame; Bus.

COLE, RYAN; Silo HS; Durant, OK; (4); Am Leg Boys St; English Clb; Math Clb; Mu Alpha Theta; Natl FFA Org; Office Aide; Teachers Aide; Nwsp; Treas Sr Cls; Capt Bsktbl; Southeastern OK ST U; Ed.

COLE, SHACHRISTA L; Blanchard Jr Sr HS; Blanchard, OK; (2); Church Yth Grp; Computer Clb; FHA; Prfct Atten Awd; Hillsdale Baptist Coll.

COLE, SHIRLETTE T; Haskell HS; Haskell, OK; (2); Church Yth Grp; Band; Church Choir; Jazz Band; Mrchg Band; Pep Band; Rep Stu Cncl; Intrml Bsktbl; Outsdng Stdnt Cncl Repr Awd; Cert Top Stdnt Soc Stud I; VP Ushr Bd Estsd Frst Bapt Chrch; U Of TN; Psych.

COLEMAN, ADAM J; Bixby Sr HS; Broken Arrow, OK; (1); Church Yth Grp; JV Bsktbl; Var Golf; Hon Roll; Jr NHS; Stu Of Month.

COLEMAN, AMANDA; Midwest City HS; Midwest City, OK; (2); 1/480; Church Yth Grp; Ofcr DECA; Ofcr FHA; Co-Capt Treas German Clb; Key Clb; Church Choir; Ofcr Soph Cls; Ofcr Stu Cncl; Pom Pon; Hon Roll.

COLEMAN, ANDRA; Bixby Sr HS; Broken Arrow, OK; (4); 1/179; Pres Church Yth Grp; Cmnty Wkr; FCA; Pres French Clb; FHA; Quiz Bowl; Hon Roll; Jr NHS; NHS; Val; Piano Radio Performance; U Of OK; Eng; Wrtng.

COLEMAN, CHRISTINE; Douglass HS; Oklahoma City, OK; (2); Church Choir; JV Var Bsktbl; Var Vllybl; High Hon Roll; Hon Roll; Georgetown; Pediatrician.

COLEMAN, KATHERINE; Midwest City HS; Midwest City, OK; (4); 6/419; Am Leg Aux Girls St; FCA; Pres FHA; German Clb; HOBY; Scholastic Bowl; Sec SADD; Ed Nwsp; Var Capt Pom Pon; Rptr NHS; TX Christian U; Jrnlsm.

COLEMAN, KELLY A; Valliant HS; Valliant, OK; (4); 24/80; Church Yth Grp; FCA; 4-H; GAA; SADD; Chorus; Sftbl; Trk; NHS; Southern AR U; Nrsng.

COLEMAN, LACEY; Idabel HS; Idabel, OK; (1); Church Yth Grp; FBLA; Chorus; Yrbk; Chrldng; Ntl Merit Ltr; Prfct Atten Awd; OK Univ; Law.

COLEMAN, MATTHEW D; Mustang HS; Mustang, OK; (3); Church Yth Grp; Teachers Aide; Band; Color Guard; Jazz Band; Mrchg Band; Orch; Pep Band; Hon Roll; All ST Band Snare Drum.

COLEMAN, MIA; Millwood HS; Oklahoma City, OK; (3); Pres FBLA; Office Aide; Teachers Aide; Band; Chorus; Mrchg Band; Rep Jr Cls; Sec Stu Cncl; Mgr(s); Hon Roll.

COLEMAN, MICHAEL; Manford HS; Terlton, OK; (4); 2/110; Am Leg Boys St; Church Yth Grp; FCA; Letterman Clb; Spanish Clb; Bsktbl; Crs Cntry; High Hon Roll; NHS; Sal; OK ST U; Mechanical Engrng.

COLEMAN, SHAUNA M; Harrah HS; Harrah, OK; (2); 24/160; Church Yth Grp; Church Choir; Sftbl; Tennis; Cit Awd; Hon Roll; Pres Acad Fit Awd; OK Bapt Univ.

COLEMAN, SHETRA J; Coyle Public Schl; Coyle, OK; (3); 4-H; Pep Clb; Church Choir; Bsktbl; Hon Roll; Sal; Sci/Math Awd; Hnry Stdnt Awd; Langston U; Pre-Med.

COLEMAN, STACEY M; Lawton Sr HS; Lawton, OK; (3); Drill Tm; Orch.

COLEMAN, STACIA R; Union Sr HS; Tulsa, OK; (3); 76/783; Church Yth Grp; FHA; Speech Tm; Teachers Aide; Color Guard; Mrchg Band; High Hon Roll; Jr NHS; NHS; Pres Schlr; Wntr Grd; Wlkng W/Chldrn; Natl Chmpn Clr Grd 94; Yng Dems; Duke U; Med.

COLEMAN, STEVEN Z; Woodward HS; Woodward, OK; (1); French Clb; Ftbl; Wt Lftg; Hon Roll; Southwestern ST U.

COLEMAN, TIFFANY L; Del City HS; Oklahoma City, OK; (2); Art Clb; Church Yth Grp; Teachers Aide; Chorus; School Play; Swing Chorus; Ofcr Stu Cncl; Cit Awd; Hon Roll; NHS; Forgn Exch; OU; Psych.

COLES, JAMIE L; Luther HS; Luther, OK; (4); 3/56; Debate Tm; Drama Clb; FBLA; FHA; Letterman Clb; NFL; Speech Tm; Acpl Chr; School Play; Hon Roll; US Army Rsrvst; Cert Nrs Aid; Emrgncy Med Tech; RN/EMT.

COLES, MEGHAN; Claremore Sr HS; Claremore, OK; (3); 1/250; Math Clb; Spanish Clb; Pres Jr Cls; Ofcr Stu Cncl; Var Socr; Var Trk; Hon Roll; NHS.

COLEY, AMY B; Choctaw HS; Choctaw, OK; (3); 70/313; Church Yth Grp; Cmnty Wkr; FCA; Key Clb; Chorus; Church Choir; Pres Soph Cls; Sec Jr Cls; Rep Sr Cls; Socr; Yth Traveling Drama & Praise Team; OBU; Ed; Cnslng.

COLEY, JONATHAN; Bethany Christian Acad; Mustang, OK; (1); Church Yth Grp; Debate Tm; School Play; Bsktbl; Hon Roll; Ministry.

COLEY, STARLA M; Panola HS; Red Oak, OK; (4); 5/16; VP FHA; German Clb; Speech Tm; School Play; Yrbk; Var Bsktbl; Var Sftbl; Hon Roll; Amer Legion & Schlr Athl Awds; Bacone Coll; Elem Ed.

COLLETT, SHERRI; Weleetka Sr HS; Henryetta, OK; (3); FHA; Science Clb; Spanish Clb; Band; Rptr Nwsp; Psych.

COLLEY, TESSA L; Catoosa HS; Tulsa, OK; (3); 3/150; Rptr Spanish Clb; Rptr Nwsp; Treas Jr Cls; Rep Stu Cncl; High Hon Roll; Hon Roll; Jr NHS; NHS; Pres Acad Fit Awd; Office Skills Challenge Schlsp 1st Pl In Bus Law At TJC; Miss Will Rogers Of Catoosa; Tulsa Univ.

COLLIER, AMY; Mc Loud HS; Mc Loud, OK; (4); 5/108; Church Yth Grp; Scholastic Bowl; Band; Capt Color Guard; Jazz Band; Mrchg Band; Rep Stu Cncl; High Hon Roll; Hon Roll; NHS; GATE; Acad Ltr Jckt; Peer Tutor; Stu Of Mnth; U Of OK; Psych.

COLLIER, ANGIE; Drumright HS; Drumright, OK; (4); 3/43; Church Yth Grp; Cmnty Wkr; Computer Clb; Drama Clb; FCA; Math Clb; Office Aide; Scholastic Bowl; Science Clb; Spanish Clb; Hall Of Fame; Stu Of Mnth; Vtd Mst Lkly To Sccd; OK ST U.

COLLIER, ANNINA SOFIA; Norman Sr HS; Norman, OK; (4); 1/600; Hist Latin Clb; Model UN; Pres Band; NHS; Val; Octagon Clb Treas; Med Expl Post 901 Vp; John Phillip Sousa Bnd Awd; St Spndt Awd For Arts Exc; U Of OK; Mus Arts.

COLLIER, BRYAN E; Mc Loud HS; Mc Loud, OK; (1); Church Yth Grp; Cmnty Wkr; Band; Mrchg Band; Pep Band; Var L Socr; Wt Lftg; Hon Roll; Drum Line Awd; Law Enfrcmnt.

COLLINGS, KENDALL A; Ardmore HS; Ardmore, OK; (4); 40/190; Art Clb; Church Yth Grp; FCA; French Clb; Library Aide; Math Clb; Office Aide; Tennis; High Hon Roll; Jr NHS; U Of OK; Fine Arts.

COLLINS, AMANDA S; Carney Schl; Chandler, OK; (1); Rep FHA; Cit Awd; Hon Roll; OSU; Zoologist.

COLLINS, ANDREA; Watonga HS; Watonga, OK; (4); 9/56; FCA; Pres FBLA; Band; Jazz Band; Mrchg Band; Chrldng; Crs Cntry; Score Keeper; Trk; Hon Roll; Chisholm Trl Vo-Tech; Bus.

COLLINS, ANGIE M; Skiatook HS; Skiatook, OK; (3); Church Yth Grp; FCA; Yrbk; Ofcr Stu Cncl; Bsktbl; Mgr(s); Powder Puff Ftbl; Socr; Sftbl; Vllybl; Elem Ed.

COLLINS, ANTHONY R; Union Sr HS; Tulsa, OK; (3); Key Clb; Speech Tm; VP Frsh Cls; Pres Soph Cls; Pres Jr Cls; Hon Roll; NHS; Ntl Merit Ltr; Pres Schlr; Teepee Crw; Jrnlsm.

COLLINS, BILLY J; Muldrow HS; Muldrow, OK; (2); Church Yth Grp; Hosp Aide; Natl Beta Clb; Science Clb; Spanish Clb; Band; Church Choir; JV Bsktbl; JV Trk; Hon Roll.

COLLINS, BRADLEY; Haileyville Schl; Mcalester, OK; (4); FCA; 4-H; FBLA; Ofcr Stu Cncl; Var Capt Bsktbl; Wt Lftg; Cit Awd; High Hon Roll; Prfct Atten Awd; Yrbk Kng; Crrclm Cont Spllng, Dmcrcy, Eng; EOSC; Med.

COLLINS, CAMISHA N; Star Spencer HS; Spencer, OK; (2); Church Yth Grp; Band; Mrchg Band; Pep Band; Tennis; Hon Roll; NHS; Central ST Univ; Pedtrcn.

COLLINS, CARA K; Bartlesville Sr HS; Bartlesville, OK; (4); 171/426; Art Clb; JA; Hon Roll; Environ Clb; MO Southern St Coll; Business.

COLLINS, CINDY S; Brink Jr HS; Oklahoma City, OK; (1); Church Yth Grp; Cmnty Wkr; Office Aide; Teachers Aide; School Musical; School Play; Stage Crew; Cit Awd; Hon Roll; Org Schl Cook-Out; U Of OK; Law.

COLLINS, CRYSTA; Central Schl; Marlow, OK; (2); Church Yth Grp; Ed Yrbk; JV Var Bsktbl; JV Var Chrldng; Cit Awd; Hon Roll; Ad.

COLLINS, CRYSTAL M; Will Rogers HS; Tulsa, OK; (3); DECA; ROTC; Socr; Vllybl; DAR Awd; High Hon Roll; Hon Roll; NE St Univ; Bus.

COLLINS, JAMES; Moore HS; Moore, OK; (4); Boy Scts; French Clb; Natl FFA Org; Quiz Bowl; Science Clb; Swmmng; Eagle Sct; Floriculture Tm; CO ST; Forestry.

COLLINS, JULIE; Holdenville Jr HS; Holdenville, OK; (1); Math Tm; Natl FFA Org; Scholastic Bowl; Ofcr Stu Cncl; Bsktbl; Chrldng; Trk; Pres Acad Fit Awd; High Hon Roll; NHS; Law.

COLLINS, KAREN R; Mannford HS; Sand Springs, OK; (4); 11/89; Church Yth Grp; Office Aide; Science Clb; Spanish Clb; SADD; Teachers Aide; NHS; Prfct Atten Awd; Tutor; OK Hnr Soc; Tulsa JC; Math Tchr; Math.

COLLINS, KATIE; Santa Fe HS; Edmond, OK; (4); Church Yth Grp; Dance Clb; FCA; Key Clb; Office Aide; Pep Clb; Science Clb; Spanish Clb; VP SADD; Variety Show; Sr All-Star Pom Squad; All-City Pom Squad; Wolf Pack Spirit Org; TX Chrstn Univ; Broadcasting.

COLLINS, KERI; Frederick HS; Frederick, OK; (2); 9/85; Church Yth Grp; Dance Clb; FCA; FHA; GAA; Letterman Clb; Math Clb; Drill Tm; Treas Soph Cls; Var Bsktbl; Phrmcy.

COLLINS, KRISTI; Union City Schl; Union City, OK; (4); Am Leg Aux Girls St; Art Clb; FHA; Math Clb; Natl FFA Org; Science Clb; Teachers Aide; Yrbk; Rep Stu Cncl; Hon Roll; Acctng.

COLLINS, KRYSTAL; Boynton Schl; Boynton, OK; (1); Church Yth Grp; Cmnty Wkr; 4-H; Quiz Bowl; Scholastic Bowl; Teachers Aide; Band; Hon Roll; Pres Schlr; Pres Chrch Yth Grp; Attny.

COLLINS, LAURA J; Okmulgee HS; Okmulgee, OK; (2); 10/150; Church Yth Grp; Dance Clb; Hosp Aide; Office Aide; Band; Color Guard; Mrchg Band; Pep Band; Score Keeper; Hon Roll; Piano; Northeastern ST Univ.

COLLINS, MENDY M; Noble HS; Noble, OK; (4); 10/147; Model UN; Mu Alpha Theta; Ed Nwsp; VP Stu Cncl; Co-Capt Bsktbl; Cit Awd; NHS; Pres Acad Fit Awd; Intl Order Jobs Dghtrs; Intl Ordr Rainbow Girls; U Of OK; Jrnlsm.

COLLINS, RANADA L; Southeast HS; Oklahoma City, OK; (2); Chess Clb; Drama Clb; FBLA; Pep Clb; ROTC; Ofcr Soph Cls; Rep Stu Cncl; Bsktbl; Sftbl; Trk; Optmtry.

COLLINS, RYAN; Grace Fellowship Christian Sch; Bixby, OK; (2); Church Yth Grp; Cmnty Wkr; FCA; Spanish Clb; Ofcr Jr Cls; Bsktbl; Socr; Vllybl; Cit Awd; Gov Hon Prg Awd; All ST Sccr 94-95; All ST Sccr/Bsktbl 95-; Faithfl Srvt Awd 94-95; Shld Awd 95-; Arch.

COLLINS, SARA J; Chattanooga Schl; Faxon, OK; (1); Church Yth Grp; Cmnty Wkr; Natl FFA Org; Pep Clb; Quiz Bowl; Hon Roll; FFA Lgn Mrt Awd; Cameron Univ; Neonatology.

COLLINS, SARAH K; Ponca City Sr HS; Ponca City, OK; (4); Church Yth Grp; Spanish Clb; SADD; Teachers Aide; Chorus; Drill Tm; Ed Yrbk; DAR Awd; Hmrm Pres, VP, Sec; Rotarian Of Wk; Panic Brd; OK St Univ; Psych.

COLLINS, STEPHANIE; Clinton HS; Clinton, OK; (3); Church Yth Grp; Acpl Chr; Chorus; Church Choir; Bsktbl; Mgr(s); Socr; Hon Roll; Prfct Atten Awd; St Schlr; OU; Med.

COLLINS, TANESHA L; South Intermediate HS; Broken Arrow, OK; (2); Chorus; Bsktbl; JV Vllybl; Hon Roll; Span/Math.

COLLINS, TARYN; Mustang HS; Yukon, OK; (1); 1/532; Church Yth Grp; FCA; GAA; Rep Frsh Cls; Ofcr Stu Cncl; Bsktbl; Chrldng; Powder Puff Ftbl; Trk; High Hon Roll; Tip In Club; OSU; Engr.

COLLUM, CLAYTON D; Shawnee Sr HS; Shawnee, OK; (2); 22/400; Church Yth Grp; Acpl Chr; Church Choir; Tennis; High Hon Roll; Chapel Ringers; Pre-Med/Dermtlgy.

COLLYAR, JANIE L; Brink Jr HS; Moore, OK; (1); Church Yth Grp; Cmnty Wkr; Hosp Aide; Red Cross Aide; SADD; Hon Roll; Outstdng Accomplshmnt Awd In Scintfc & Technlgcl Discvry From OCAST; Chem Awd; U Of OK Med Schl; Phy; MD.

COLMAN, SKYLER D; Central Jr HS; Lawton, OK; (1); JV Wrstlng; Hon Roll; L Jr NHS; OK Kart Assn 1st Pl For 14-15 Advancd Forms, Sparrng & Wepns; KS St Natl Champn 14-15 Advancd Forms.

COLOMBIN, JACK B; Okmulgee HS; Okmulgee, OK; (3); 10/300; Am Leg Boys St; Church Yth Grp; Ofcr Bsbl; Ftbl; Golf; Wrstlng; NHS; OSU; Vet Sci.

COLOMBIN, SHAVLIN A; Claremore Sr HS; Claremore, OK; (1); Church Yth Grp; Drama Clb; Speech Tm; Church Choir; School Play; Stage Crew; Ozark Chrstn Coll; Bibical.

COLSON, LISHA R; Newkirk HS; Newkirk, OK; (3); 4/40; Am Leg Aux Girls St; Cmnty Wkr; FCA; Hosp Aide; Band; Rep Stu Cncl; JV Sftbl; Cit Awd; High Hon Roll; NHS; STEEP; U Of Cntrl OK; Nrsng.

COLSTON, TIFFANY; Marietta HS; Marietta, OK; (2); Church Yth Grp; Dance Clb; 4-H; FHA; Speech Tm; School Play; 4-H Awd; High Hon Roll; Hon Roll; Cty 4-H Hll Fm Awd; OK U.

COLVIN, CIA; Adair HS; Big Cabin, OK; (4); 1/61; Art Clb; FCA; FHA; Quiz Bowl; Science Clb; Rep Stu Cncl; Trk; Hon Roll; Pres Acad Fit Awd; Val; OSU; Finance.

COLVIN, MEGAN S; Chickasha HS; Chickasha, OK; (1); Church Yth Grp; French Clb; Band; Church Choir; Mrchg Band; Pep Band; NHS; Bio.

COLWELL, JILL D; Blackwell HS; Blackwell, OK; (3); 1/125; Am Leg Aux Girls St; Church Yth Grp; FCA; Sec FHA; Letterman Clb; Rptr Natl FFA Org; Pep Clb; Teachers Aide; Treas Stu Cncl; Mgr Bsbl; OK St Hnr Soc; Rotry Yth Ldrshp Awd Conf Del.

COMBS, CHAD; Comanche HS; Comanche, OK; (2); 1/97; Church Yth Grp; Natl FFA Org; Quiz Bowl; Var Bsktbl; Var Ftbl; Var Golf; High Hon Roll; Hon Roll; NHS; Outstndng Frosh Boy; Msnc Awd; OK ST U; Bio.

COMBS, ISAAC D; Tahlequah Sr HS; Park Hill, OK; (3); Chess Clb; German Clb; Science Clb; SADD; Chorus; L Bsktbl; JV Var Tennis; Pres Acad Fit Awd.

COMBS, JOSHUA T; Charles Page HS; Sand Springs, OK; (2); 31/381; Church Yth Grp; Drama Clb; FCA; School Play; JV Bsbl; JV Bsktbl; High Hon Roll; Hon Roll; Jr NHS; NHS; CAST Spkr 95; U Of NC.

COMBS, KELLI L; Charles Page HS; Sand Springs, OK; (2); 9/385; Spanish Clb; High Hon Roll; NHS; Prfct Atten Awd; Anchor Clb; Play Piano; Compete In Horse Shows.

COMBS, KELLY L; Putnam City North HS; Oklahoma City, OK; (4); Church Yth Grp; Cmnty Wkr; Drama Clb; Hosp Aide; Key Clb; Library Aide; Spanish Clb; SADD; Chorus; School Musical; Natl Acad Of His & Govt; Natl Acad Acad; OK ST U; Phys Therapy.

COMBS, STANLEY CHAD; Comanche HS; Comanche, OK; (2); 1/97; Church Yth Grp; Natl FFA Org; Bsktbl; Ftbl; Golf; Wt Lftg; Hon Roll; NHS; Ntl Merit Ltr; Outstdng Frosh & Soph Boy; OK ST U.

COMBS, TIFFANY; Chandler HS; Chandler, OK; (1); Church Yth Grp; Rptr FHA; GAA; Girl Scts; Scholastic Bowl; VP Frsh Cls; JV Bsktbl; JV Chrldng; JV Sftbl; Var Trk; 2nd Pl FHA Star Events Interprsnl Commnctn; Dance; Speaker To 1st Grd Chldrn About Strangrs, Fire, Sfty; Child Psych.

COMBS, TRAVIS; Pryor Jr HS; Pryor, OK; (1); 1/179; Church Yth Grp; Quiz Bowl; Band; Jazz Band; Mrchg Band; Orch; Pep Band; High Hon Roll; NHS; Pres Acad Fit Awd; Tulsa U; Acctng.

COMER, LEA; El Reno Sr HS; Calumet, OK; (3); 1/220; Church Yth Grp; Cmnty Wkr; FCA; FTA; Key Clb; Math Tm; Quiz Bowl; Scholastic Bowl; Spanish Clb; Chorus; Most Outstdng Stdnt 9th Grd; Superior Rtng ST Show Choir Comp/Schl Div Comp; OU; Hlth Field.

COMER, RHEANNA; Gans Public Schl; Gans, OK; (2); FHA; Library Aide; Hon Roll; RN.

COMINGDEER, JENNIFER L; Deer Creek HS; Edmond, OK; (3); Cmnty Wkr; Letterman Clb; Science Clb; Teachers Aide; Treas Yrbk; Rep Stu Cncl; Var Bsktbl; Socr; Trk; NHS.

COMPSTON, DAVID S; Bartlesville Mid HS; Bartlesville, OK; (2); 22/481; Church Yth Grp; Spanish Clb; Church Choir; JV Var Bsbl; Var Ftbl; High Hon Roll; NHS; Ntl Merit Ltr; Pres Acad Fit Awd; Pres Schlr; Lang Arts Awd; All Amer Schlr; OK ST U; Ag Engr.

COMPTON, BRIAN R; Deer Creek HS; Guthrie, OK; (3); 47/97; FCA; Science Clb; Stage Crew; Yrbk; Bsktbl; JV Var Ftbl; Var L Socr; Var L Wrstlng; Kinesiology.

COMPTON, DUSTAN; Mc Alester HS; Mcalester, OK; (4); 26/216; Am Leg Boys St; Boy Scts; Church Yth Grp; FCA; Office Aide; Pres Science Clb; Sec Treas Sr Cls; Var Ftbl; Trk; Cit Awd; OSU; Envrnmntl Engrng.

COMPTON, JOHNNA; Ada HS; Ada, OK; (3); Church Yth Grp; FCA; French Clb; Service Clb; Band; Church Choir; Mrchg Band; Pep Band; High Hon Roll; NHS; Outstndng Frshmn Bandsmn 93-94; All Dist Band 94; Asbry Meth Untd Meth Yth Fllwshp Sec; East Cntrl U; Psych.

CONARD, CASEY L; Oologah HS; Talala, OK; (3); Church Yth Grp; Cmnty Wkr; VP Intnl Clb; SADD; Hon Roll; NHS.

CONATSER, MINDY A; North Intemediate HS; Broken Arrow, OK; (1); Orch; Pres Schlr; OK Hon Soc; Lit Awd; Prins Hon Rl.

CONAWAY, BRANDI; Moore HS; Moore, OK; (4); 145/525; Church Yth Grp; 4-H; Sec Natl FFA Org; Band; 4-H Awd; Prfct Atten Awd; Eastern OK ST; Ag Educ.

CONAWAY, JASON M; Edmond Santa Fe HS; Edmond, OK; (3); FCA; SADD; Church Choir; School Play; Bsktbl; Ftbl; Trk.

CONAWAY, SANDRA D; Little Axe HS; Tecumseh, OK; (3); Art Clb; Library Aide; Teachers Aide; Band; JV Var Chrldng; Writing Poetry.

CONAWAY, SETH; Edmond North HS; Edmond, OK; (3); 52/380; Cmnty Wkr; FCA; Letterman Clb; Mu Alpha Theta; Varsity Clb; Var Bsktbl; Var Socr; Var Trk; Hon Roll; NHS; Engr.

CONDENI, CHRISTINE A; Union Sr HS; Broken Arrow, OK; (3); 47/741; Spanish Clb; Socr; Cit Awd; Hon Roll; NHS; Spanish NHS; OH Nrthrn U; Phrmcy.

CONDIT, AMI; Parker Middle HS; Mcalester, OK; (2); 1/180; Church Yth Grp; HOBY; Quiz Bowl; Spanish Clb; Band; School Musical; Yrbk; Sec Stu Cncl; Cit Awd; High Hon Roll; U Of N TX Denton; Opthlmlgy.

CONE, SHARLA; Tahlequah Sr HS; Park Hill, OK; (2); German Clb; Service Clb; SADD; Chorus; Chrldng; High Hon Roll; NHS; St Schlr; Kiwanis Soph Of Yr; Columbia Coll; Brdcst Jrnlsm.

CONFER, JENNIFER R; Bridge Creek HS; Tuttle, OK; (3); Drama Clb; Science Clb; Spanish Clb; SADD; Bsktbl; Chrldng; Wt Lftg.

CONKINS, MARIE K; Claremore Sr HS; Claremore, OK; (3); Teachers Aide; Chorus; Gym; High Hon Roll; Hon Roll; Prfct Atten Awd.

CONKLIN, SARAH L; Union Sr HS; Tulsa, OK; (4); 19/650; Church Yth Grp; French Clb; Intnl Clb; Key Clb; Pep Clb; Teachers Aide; High Hon Roll; Jr NHS; NHS; Pres Acad Fit Awd; OK ST U; Hist Prof.

CONLEY, CATHERINE M; Emerson Jr HS; Enid, OK; (1); Church Yth Grp; Chorus; Yrbk; Hon Roll; Turn Arnd Achvt Awd; Psych.

CONLEY, DUSTIN; Mc Loud HS; Mc Loud, OK; (4); 20/102; Church Yth Grp; Cmnty Wkr; FCA; FBLA; Teachers Aide; Var Bsbl; Var Bsktbl; Var Ftbl; Hon Roll; Natl Hon Roll; Mid America Bible Coll; Comp.

CONLEY, JIMMY E; Dale Sr HS; Shawnee, OK; (1); Church Yth Grp; Band; Jazz Band; Mrchg Band; Pep Band; East Cntrl U Hnr Band.

CONLEY, PATRICIA A; Enid Sr HS; Enid, OK; (3); Church Yth Grp; FHA; Teachers Aide; Orch; School Play; Rep Stu Cncl; Var Cit Awd; OSU; Psych.

CONLY, BRYCE; Claremore Sr HS; Claremore, OK; (3); 19/240; Church Yth Grp; Teachers Aide; Varsity Clb; Ofcr Bsbl; Bsktbl; Gym; Tennis; Hon Roll; NHS; Ntl Merit Ltr; Elks Clb Awd; OK ST U.

CONNELLY, BLAKE A; Ponca City Sr HS; Ponca City, OK; (3); Library Aide; Office Aide; Science Clb; Teachers Aide; Pres Soph Cls; VP Jr Cls; Wt Lftg; Cit Awd; Hon Roll; CO Univ; Chem.

CONNELLY, JACOB R; Mannford HS; Mannford, OK; (3); FCA; Letterman Clb; SADD; Varsity Clb; Hist VICA; Ofcr Bsbl; Ftbl; Trk; Hon Roll; Prfct Atten Awd.

CONNELLY, JEREMY L; Del City HS; Del City, OK; (3); Church Yth Grp; Latin Clb; Letterman Clb; Ftbl; Wrstlng; Cit Awd; Hon Roll; OK ST Univ; Vet Medicine.

CONNELLY, JOLYNN; Geary Jr Sr HS; Geary, OK; (1); Church Yth Grp; FHA; Band; Mrchg Band; JV Bsktbl; Var Chrldng; Var JV Sftbl; Hon Roll; OK ST U; Phycologist.

CONNER, BYRON; Newkirk HS; Newkirk, OK; (4); #9 in class; Am Leg Boys St; Scholastic Bowl; Band; Chorus; Church Choir; Var L Bsktbl; Var L Ftbl; NHS; STEPP Up; Eagle Sct; SCION Sci Clb.

CONNER, JASON; Tuttle HS; Tuttle, OK; (4); 33/86; Boy Scts; Church Yth Grp; FCA; Pres Natl Beta Clb; Spanish Clb; Speech Tm; SADD; Teachers Aide; Ofcr Stu Cncl; Hon Roll; Raising & Showing Chmpn Berkshire Hogs; Mchnsts.

CONNER, JENNIFER A; Dewey HS; Dewey, OK; (4); 9/75; Church Yth Grp; Drama Clb; FCA; FHA; Spanish Clb; Ofcr Stu Cncl; Var Capt Bsktbl; Var Sftbl; Var Trk; NHS; All Conf 95-96 Var Bsktbl; MVP 95-96 Varbsktbl; Lady Dogger Chosen By Coaches; Northern OK Coll; Scndry Ed.

CONNER, MISSY; Garber Sr HS; Fairmont, OK; (3); 2/48; Church Yth Grp; Cmnty Wkr; FCA; 4-H; HOBY; Teachers Aide; Band; Mrchg Band; Yrbk; Sec Jr Cls; All Star Chrldr Trvld London Eng Lord Mayors Parade 95; Presdntl Clsrm Stu; NW Dist Of OK Pres 4-H; OK ST U; Elem Educ.

CONNER, SHAUNA L; Durant HS; Durant, OK; (2); Church Yth Grp; Key Clb; Chorus; Drill Tm; Mrchg Band; Variety Show; Hon Roll; Southeastern OK ST; Crmnl Psy.

CONNER, SHEA; Ponca City Mid HS; Ponca City, OK; (1); Church Yth Grp; Cmnty Wkr; Hist Stu Cncl; Capt Chrldng; Hon Roll; Nrsng.

CONRAD, ACIE; Spiro HS; Spiro, OK; (2); FCA; Math Clb; Natl FFA Org; Ftbl; High Hon Roll; Greenhand Awd.

CONRAD, AMANDA D; Pocola HS; Pocola, OK; (2); FCA; FBLA; Hosp Aide; Band; Mrchg Band; Nwsp; Yrbk; VP Soph Cls; Bsktbl; Golf; Motorcross; Westark; Vetrnrn.

CONRAD, JOY R; Union Intermediate HS; Tulsa, OK; (2); 28/800; Band; Mrchg Band; Pep Band; High Hon Roll; Hon Roll; Jr NHS; NHS; Various Stu Of Month Awds; Stu Of Yr; DFY; ROTUS Clb Hstrn; Tulsa U; Indstrl Engrng.

CONRAD, MICHAEL; Union Sr HS; Tulsa, OK; (3); 228/731; Boy Scts; Church Yth Grp; Band; Mrchg Band; Pep Band; Hon Roll; NHS; Tri-M Msc Hnr Soc; Rnssnc Hnr Soc; Jr Of Yr Bnd 95-96; Msc.

CONRAD, SARAH V; Guthrie Sr HS; Guthrie, OK; (1); 1/310; VP FBLA; Hosp Aide; SADD; Band; Mrchg Band; Pep Band; Yrbk; Pres Frsh Cls; Pres Soph Cls; Ofcr Stu Cncl; Top Ten Of Class; Band Rylty.

CONRAD, SHANNON L; Spiro HS; Spiro, OK; (4); 20/89; FCA; FBLA; Hosp Aide; Math Clb; Natl FFA Org; Pres Spanish Clb; Teachers Aide; Pres Band; Capt Color Guard; Capt Flag Corp; Band Sweetheart; Natl Frgn Lang Awd; Acad Schlshp; Carl Albert St Coll; Dental Hyg.

CONREY, BRIANNA; Stillwater Jr HS; Stillwater, OK; (1); Church Yth Grp; Math Tm; Orch; High Hon Roll; Pres Acad Fit Awd; Cellst For Orch At OK Summr Arts Inst; North Cntrl Hnrs Orch; Outstdng 9th Gradr In Stillwater Orch.

CONREY, KEEGAN J; Bishop Kelley HS; Tulsa, OK; (1); Church Yth Grp; FCA; Key Clb; Bsktbl; Var Score Keeper; Hon Roll; Mens Rel Forum; AAU Bsktbl.

CONROY, PATRICIA C; Broken Arrow Sr HS; Broken Arrow, OK; (3); Church Yth Grp; Spanish Clb; Nwsp; JV Socr; Hon Roll; OK Univ; Jrnlsm.

CONSTIEN, CARI; Clinton HS; Clinton, OK; (2); 1/138; VP Church Yth Grp; FCA; FBLA; HOBY; Spanish Clb; Sec Frsh Cls; Rep Stu Cncl; Var L Bsktbl; Var L Golf; NHS; Phys Thpry.

CONSTIEN, SARAH C; El Reno Sr HS; El Reno, OK; (4); 49/163; Church Yth Grp; FTA; Key Clb; Letterman Clb; Math Clb; Office Aide; Science Clb; Var Chrldng; Hon Roll; BPW Grl Of Mnth; V Dance Tm; Mc Pherson Coll; Intr Dsgn.

CONSTIEN, STEVEN; Collinsville HS; Sperry, OK; (3); HOBY; Band; Jazz Band; High Hon Roll; NHS; Elec Engr.

CONVERSE, GREG; Dickson HS; Irving, TX; (3); 2/70; Treas FCA; Key Clb; VP Spanish Clb; Rep SADD; Teachers Aide; Band; Mrchg Band; Ed Yrbk; Cit Awd; High Hon Roll; U Of N TX; Med.

CONWAY, DEANNA L; Stillwater Sr HS; Stillwater, OK; (3); Girl Scts; Mu Alpha Theta; Spanish Clb; Co-Ed Nwsp; Var L Socr; Hon Roll; NHS.

CONWAY, LINDSAY BREE; Jenks HS; Tulsa, OK; (1); Church Yth Grp; FCA; Chrldng; Hon Roll; Comm Thtr Show Skng; NCA Natls 4th; OK Univ.

CONWAY, LISA A; Lone Grove HS; Lone Grove, OK; (2); Church Yth Grp; 4-H; Natl Beta Clb; Natl FFA Org; Spanish Clb; Church Choir; 4-H Awd; Hon Roll; I Dare You Awd 4-H; Star Grnhnd FFA; Star Chptr Frmr FFA; OK ST Univ; Ag Comm.

CONWAY, MELISSA A; Perry Sr HS; Stillwater, OK; (3); Church Yth Grp; 4-H; Pres Natl FFA Org; Band; Mrchg Band; Pep Band; 4-H Awd; Hon Roll; Jr NHS; NHS; Northern OK Coll.

COOK, ALEXANDRA B; Bartlesville Mid HS; Bartlesville, OK; (2); French Clb; FHA; Orch; Hon Roll; Suzuki Strolling Strings; Ens Club; Mscl Rsrch Soc Hnr.

COOK, AMBER; Laverne Jr Sr HS; Laverne, OK; (2); 1/48; Church Yth Grp; Natl Beta Clb; Chorus; Ofcr Stu Cncl; Var Chrldng; Var Golf; Var Sftbl; High Hon Roll; NHS.

COOK, AMY S; Westmoore HS; Oklahoma City, OK; (3); 63/650; Church Yth Grp; Sec FCA; Office Aide; Spanish Clb; Rep Stu Cncl; Mgr(s); NHS; Stdnt Ath Trnr Allsprts; OK ST U; Acctng.

COOK, BRIAN; Eufaula Sr HS; Eufaula, OK; (4); 11/73; Church Yth Grp; Math Clb; Office Aide; Science Clb; Teachers Aide; Phtg Yrbk; Var L Ftbl; Wt Lftg; Hon Roll; Blue Blt Karate; Connors ST Coll; Medcl Prof.

COOK, CANDICE L; Cordell Sr HS; Cordell, OK; (1); 5/52; 4-H; FHA; Natl FFA Org; Pep Clb; JV Bsktbl; JV Sftbl; Hon Roll; NHS; Sal; OSU; Tchr.

COOK, CHRISTOPHER RYAN; Putnam City North HS; Oklahoma City, OK; (3); 16/485; Am Leg Boys St; Pres FCA; Key Clb; Spanish Clb; Rep Stu Cncl; Var Ftbl; NHS; Church Yth Grp; Science Clb; SADD; Sr Cncl; Hnr Show Choir 9-12th Grd; Total Ath; Univ Of OK; Pre-Med.

COOK, COLLEEN M; Putnam City West HS; Bethany, OK; (3); Church Yth Grp; GAA; Pep Clb; Science Clb; Spanish Clb; Varsity Clb; Ofcr Stu Cncl; Var Capt Socr; JV Sftbl; Swmmng.

COOK, CRYSTAL; Cordell Sr HS; Cordell, OK; (3); 4-H; HOBY; VP Natl FFA Org; Pres Frsh Cls; Var Bsktbl; Var Chrldng; Var Sftbl; High Hon Roll; NHS; Presdntl Clsrm Schlr; OSU.

COOK, DUSTIN T; Claremore Sr HS; Claremore, OK; (2); JV Bsbl; JV Ftbl; High Hon Roll; MIT; Nuclear Engr.

COOK, JAMEY; Foyil Schl; Foyil, OK; (2); 1/42; Math Tm; Quiz Bowl; Rep Frsh Cls; Sec Soph Cls; Var Bsktbl; Var Sftbl; High Hon Roll; Sal; Rogers Univ; Bus.

COOK, JENNIFER L; Mustang HS; Mustang, OK; (4); 22/310; Sec French Clb; Treas FBLA; FHA; JA; Teachers Aide; High Hon Roll; NHS; U Of OK; Acctng.

COOK, JENNIFER R; Stillwater Sr HS; Stillwater, OK; (3); Church Yth Grp; Key Clb; Library Aide; Spanish Clb; Chorus; St Schlr.

COOK, JOCELYN; Wilburton Jr HS; Wilburton, OK; (1); Church Yth Grp; Speech Tm; Bsktbl; Chrldng; Trk; Hon Roll.

COOK, JOE; Moore HS; Moore, OK; (4); 74/525; French Clb; Office Aide; Band; Drm Mjr(t); Flag Corp; Mrchg Band; Orch; Pep Band; School Musical; Jr NHS; NHS; OK U; Music Ed.

COOK, KATHERINE A; Bishop Mcguinness HS; Dallas, TX; (3); Cmnty Wkr; FCA; French Clb; Office Aide; Pep Clb; Chorus; Crs Cntry; Hon Roll; NHS; Pres Of Choir; Show Dance Choir; Elem Ed.

COOK, KELLY; Anadarko HS; Anadarko, OK; (4); 17/110; Church Yth Grp; FCA; FBLA; GAA; HOBY; Office Aide; SADD; Teachers Aide; Nwsp; VP Soph Cls; Natl Engl Mrt Awd; U Of OK; Phys Thrpy.

COOK, KIMBERLY J; Clayton Jr Sr HS; Tuskahoma, OK; (2); Church Yth Grp; FHA; Ofcr Soph Cls; Sftbl; Hon Roll; Stu Of Today Math Awd; Estrn OK ST Coll; Nrsng.

COOK, KRIS E; Byng Sr HS; Ada, OK; (3); Church Yth Grp; Spanish Clb; Teachers Aide; Comp.

COOK, LANCE C; Heritage Hall Schl; Oklahoma City, OK; (2); Cmnty Wkr; Debate Tm; French Clb; Math Clb; NFL; Science Clb; Speech Tm; Chorus; Stat Vllybl; Hon Roll; Stdnt Ambsdr.

COOK, LUCETTA J; Del City HS; Oklahoma City, OK; (2); Church Yth Grp; Pep Clb; ROTC; Chorus; Color Guard; Drill Tm; School Musical; School Play; Swing Chorus; Rifle Tm; Military.

COOK, MELISSA; Tuttle HS; Tuttle, OK; (3); 38/110; Boy Scts; Church Yth Grp; Cmnty Wkr; GAA; Church Choir; Bsktbl; Var Mgr(s); JV Var Sftbl; Hon Roll; Prfct Atten Awd; Law Enfrcmnt.

COOK, MISTY N; Union Intermediate HS; Tulsa, OK; (2); Church Yth Grp; FCA; Hosp Aide; Key Clb; Spanish Clb; Teachers Aide; Band; Church Choir; Hon Roll; NHS; NSU; Scndry Ed.

COOK, PEPPER N; Woodward HS; Woodward, OK; (3); Computer Clb; FBLA; Pep Clb; Art Clb Treas.

COOK, PRINCETTA D; Northwest Classen HS; Tulsa, OK; (4); Girl Scts; Office Aide; Scholastic Bowl; Vllybl; Hon Roll; Johnson C Smith; Career Eng.

COOK, RHONDA; Mc Loud HS; Shawnee, OK; (4); 6/110; Church Yth Grp; Sec FCA; FBLA; FHA; Pres Frsh Cls; VP Soph Cls; Capt Bsktbl; Hon Roll; Jr NHS; NHS; Acad Ltr Jacket; Engrng.

COOK, ROBERT; Alex Jr Sr HS; Alex, OK; (4); Church Yth Grp; FCA; FHA; Teachers Aide; Sec Jr Cls; Capt Bsbl; Capt Bsktbl; Hon Roll; Acad Achvt Awds 93, 94, 95; TSA 1 Yr; Parli Pro Team; Bethany; Chiroprctc.

COOK, RYAN; Spiro HS; Spiro, OK; (4); 9/90; Math Clb; Rptr Jr Cls; VP Sr Cls; JV Bsbl; Bsktbl; Cit Awd; High Hon Roll; Hon Roll; Rep NHS; Prfct Atten Awd; Stu Of Month; Westark CC; Phys Therapy.

COOK, SANDRA R; Mc Loud HS; Mc Loud, OK; (2); Band; Jazz Band; Mrchg Band; Pep Band; School Musical; School Play; Hon Roll; NHS; Prfct Atten Awd.

COOK, SARA E; Elgin HS; Lawton, OK; (4); 15/76; FCA; FHA; Natl FFA Org; Office Aide; Teachers Aide; Bsktbl; Score Keeper; Sftbl; Trk; Vllybl; Southwestern OK ST Univ; Bio.

COOK, TRICIA; Moore HS; Moore, OK; (4); Am Leg Aux Girls St; Church Yth Grp; Drama Clb; German Clb; Thesps; Acpl Chr; Chorus; School Musical; School Play; Stage Crew; CP Fnd Vol; Show & Hndbll Choirs; U Of Cntrl OK; Educ.

COOK, TYLER; Bishop Mcguinness HS; Oklahoma City, OK; (2); FCA; Office Aide; Pep Clb; Spanish Clb; SADD; Chrldng; Swmmng; Hospice Vol; Olympc Rep.

COOKS, MELANIE J; John Marshall HS; Oklahoma City, OK; (3); 16/147; Band; Church Choir; Mrchg Band; Pep Band; Pom Pon; Trk; High Hon Roll; Hon Roll; NHS; Prfct Atten Awd; Outstndng Socl Stds; St Hnr Soc; OCCC; Occptnl Thrpy.

COOKSON, BRENT; Hilldale HS; Muskogee, OK; (1); Church Yth Grp; Math Clb; Band; Mrchg Band; Trk; High Hon Roll; OK Schlrshp Cmptn Cty Level; Soccer Referee; Recreational Soccer; OK ST U; Mechncl Engr.

COONCE, TRAVIS L; Owasso Sr HS; Owasso, OK; (2); Church Yth Grp; FCA; Chorus; Ftbl; Wt Lftg; High Hon Roll.

COONS, JUSTIN A; Catoosa HS; Tulsa, OK; (2); 3/180; Church Yth Grp; Drama Clb; FCA; French Clb; Ofcr Stu Cncl; Var Bsktbl; Ftbl; Trk; Wt Lftg; High Hon Roll; Chiropractor.

COONTS, SARAH M; Putnam City West HS; Oklahoma City, OK; (3); German Clb; JCL; Band; Color Guard; Drill Tm; Hon Roll; NHS; OK ST U; Arch Eng.

COOPER, AARON; Eufaula Sr HS; Eufaula, OK; (4); 1/75; Church Yth Grp; Quiz Bowl; Band; Jazz Band; Rep Soph Cls; Rep Jr Cls; Pres Stu Cncl; High Hon Roll; NHS; Val; Georgetown U; Poly Sci.

COOPER, ADAM; Okemah HS; Okemah, OK; (1); Library Aide; Natl FFA Org; Ftbl; Trk; Wt Lftg; Cit Awd; Hon Roll; Pres Acad Fit Awd; OU.

COOPER, APRIL; Hulbert Jr Sr HS; Tahlequah, OK; (4); 2/40; Am Leg Aux Girls St; Drama Clb; 4-H; FBLA; German Clb; Letterman Clb; Library Aide; Teachers Aide; Rep Sr Cls; Ofcr Stu Cncl; Law.

COOPER, APRIL; Barnsdall Jr Sr HS; Barnsdall, OK; (4); FHA; SADD; Chorus; Nwsp; Rep Jr Cls; Chrldng; Powder Puff Ftbl; Indian Clb; NE St Univ; Chld Psych.

COOPER, CASEY M; Kellyville Sr HS; Sapulpa, OK; (4); Church Yth Grp; Library Aide; Office Aide; Band; Color Guard; Nwsp; Chrldng; Hon Roll; Tulsa Junica Col; Humn Reltns.

COOPER, CHRISSY L; Cushing HS; Cushing, OK; (3); 12/144; Church Yth Grp; FCA; Math Clb; Science Clb; Spanish Clb; Yrbk; Var JV Bsktbl; Capt Chrldng; Hon Roll; NHS; OSU; Educ.

COOPER, CHRISTY; Depew HS; Depew, OK; (1); 10/51; 4-H; Natl FFA Org; Quiz Bowl; Band; Cit Awd; 4-H Awd; Hon Roll; Ntl Merit Ltr; Prfct Atten Awd; Publc Speakng; Marine Bio.

COOPER, CLAYTON E; Poteau HS; Poteau, OK; (3); Am Leg Boys St; Church Yth Grp; FCA; Rep Frsh Cls; Var Bsktbl; Cit Awd; High Hon Roll; NHS; Oceanographer.

COOPER, CLINT A; Ada HS; Ada, OK; (3); Church Yth Grp; Pres 4-H; SADD; Band; Jazz Band; Mrchg Band; Bsktbl; Ftbl; Trk; 4-H Awd; ECU; Law; Mass Commnctn.

COOPER, COURTNEY E; Union Intermediate HS; Broken Arrow, OK; (1); Hosp Aide; Teachers Aide; School Play; Var Golf; DAR Awd; Hon Roll; NHS; Grl Scts Grd K-7th; Hosp Vol; VVC Prtcpnt.

COOPER, DANIELLE; Mangum Jr HS; Mangum, OK; (1); Church Yth Grp; FHA; Band; Flag Corp; Mrchg Band; Orch; Hon Roll; NHS.

COOPER, DESMOND; Del City HS; Oklahoma City, OK; (3); Drama Clb; ROTC; Chorus; School Play; Treas Soph Cls; Treas Jr Cls; JV Ftbl; Wrstlng; 4th St Drm Trnmnt; Actor.

COOPER, JENNIFER L; Tecumseh HS; Tecumseh, OK; (3); 17/175; Church Yth Grp; FCA; GAA; Natl Beta Clb; SADD; Sec Jr Cls; Ofcr Stu Cncl; Bsktbl; Sftbl; High Hon Roll; OBU All Trnmnt Tm, All Reg Sftbl; Bsktbl All Conf; OK Baptist U; Bus.

COOPER, KENDRA L; Frontier Public Schl; Marland, OK; (3); Art Clb; Drama Clb; FHA; Natl FFA Org; Pep Clb; Spanish Clb; School Play; Stage Crew; Hon Roll; FHA Ofcr, Rptr; FFA Awd; OSU; RN; Surgical RN.

COOPER, LESLEY; Bartlesville Mid HS; Bartlesville, OK; (2); Church Yth Grp; French Clb; FBLA; Ofcr Stu Cncl; Bsktbl; Trk; Vllybl; High Hon Roll; Jr NHS; Prfct Atten Awd.

COOPER, LESLIE R; Putnam City West HS; Oklahoma City, OK; (2); Debate Tm; Intnl Clb; Science Clb; Spanish Clb; Band; Mrchg Band; Pep Band; School Musical; Stat Bsktbl; JV Var Mgr(s); Alt Piccolo In CODA Hnr Band; I Rating In St & Dist Solo Conts; Psych; Music.

COOPER, LINDSAY D; Westmoore HS; Oklahoma City, OK; (2); Church Yth Grp; Dance Clb; Hon Roll; Sftbl Co-Ed; OK City CC; Elem Tchr.

COOPER, LU WELLA DAWN; Sallisaw HS; Sallisaw, OK; (2); Church Yth Grp; Cmnty Wkr; FHA; Church Choir; Hon Roll; Stu Of Tdy; Sftbl Chrch League; Chrch Drama; Vlybl Chrch League; Cnclr For Yth Chrch Cmp; Lwyr.

COOPER, MELISSA S; Classen Schl; Oklahoma City, OK; (2); Mu Alpha Theta; VP Soph Cls; Capt Chrldng; Var Vllybl; Hon Roll; NHS; Cvl Engr.

COOPER, NICHOLAS; Depew HS; Depew, OK; (3); Church Yth Grp; Debate Tm; Pep Clb; Scholastic Bowl; Spanish Clb; Rep Jr Cls; Sec Treas Stu Cncl; Bsktbl; Ftbl; Trk; St OK Cert Lgsltv Rcgntn; Intl Sco Poets Conv Semi Fnlst; Ptry Pblshd; Baylor U.

COOPER, NICHOLAS; Nathan Hale HS; Tulsa, OK; (3); Spanish Clb; Varsity Clb; Ed Yrbk; VP Sr Cls; Bsktbl; Var Golf; Var Capt Ice Hcky; High Hon Roll; Hon Roll; NHS; In-Ln Hcky.

COOPER, RICKY; U S Grant HS; Oklahoma City, OK; (1); JV Bsbl.

COOPER, STACY; Oklahoma City Christian Acad; Oklahoma City, OK; (4); Hosp Aide; Yrbk; VP Jr Cls; Sec Sr Cls; Hon Roll; Rose ST Coll; Nrsng.

COOPER, TIMOTHY W; Bethel HS; Mc Loud, OK; (2); Church Yth Grp; Ftbl; Trk; Wt Lftg; Wrstlng; High Hon Roll; Hon Roll; NHS; Prfct Atten Awd.

COOPER, TONIA M; Muskogee HS; Muskogee, OK; (2); Church Yth Grp; ROTC; SADD; Church Choir; Swmmng; Conners ST Coll; Mass Comm.

COOPER, VICKIE D; Kellyville Sr HS; Sapulpa, OK; (3); Pep Clb; Teachers Aide; Chrldng; Tchr.

COOTS, AUBREY; Moore HS; Norman, OK; (3); 175/650; Cmnty Wkr; FCA; French Clb; GAA; Letterman Clb; Office Aide; L Bsktbl; Var L Sftbl; NHS; Pres Acad Fit Awd; Fstptch Mid St Conf; Slw Ptch All City; Bio, Alg Otstndng Achvt; U OK; Bio.

COPE, JAIME L; North Intemediate HS; Broken Arrow, OK; (2); Hon Roll; Tap Dancing; Ballet; Jazz Dancing; Tulsa U; Pediatrician.

COPE, JONAS; Varnum Jr Sr HS; Seminole, OK; (1); Quiz Bowl; Scholastic Bowl; Acad Team Capt; Digipen; Cmptr Tech.

COPELAND, ANGELA DAWN; Moore HS; Moore, OK; (3); 6/650; Ofcr Boy Scts; French Clb; Science Clb; Rptr Nwsp; Ed Yrbk; High Hon Roll; Ofcr Hist NHS; Mgr Bsktbl; Mgr Ftbl; Mgr Wrstlng; Spch/Debate Club; Peer Cnslr; Dist/Regnl Sci Fairs 1st Pl; NASA Awd; Duke; Cmptr Sci.

COPELAND, ANITA M; Putnam City West HS; Bethany, OK; (4); 26/278; Church Yth Grp; Office Aide; Sec Band; Church Choir; Mrchg Band; Orch; School Musical; Hon Roll; Jr NHS; NHS; All-St Orch; Northwest OK Nazarene Dist Rep; Deaf Ed Mentorship & Internship; Southern Nazarene U; Fr Horn.

COPELAND, ERIN; Medford Schl; Medford, OK; (4); 11/22; FCA; VP Rep FHA; Natl FFA Org; Pep Clb; Chorus; Yrbk; Hon Roll; OSU.

COPELAND, KIMBERLY; Lone Grove HS; Ardmore, OK; (2); Pep Clb; Chorus; JV Var Chrldng; JV Trk; Hon Roll; Psych.

COPELAND, KRISTIE; Vanoss Schl; Roff, OK; (3); Library Aide; Natl FFA Org; Scholastic Bowl; Hon Roll; Army; Acctg.

COPELAND, KRISTOPHER D; Sallisaw HS; Sallisaw, OK; (3); Church Yth Grp; Science Clb; Spanish Clb; Church Choir; School Play; Hon Roll; NHS; Prfct Atten Awd.

COPELAND, ROXANNA J; Choctaw HS; Choctaw, OK; (3); Church Yth Grp; FCA; Key Clb; Band; Mrchg Band; Pep Band; Hillsdale Free Will Bapt Coll.

COPELAND, STEPHANIE D; Tomlinson Jr HS; Lawton, OK; (1); FHA; FCA; Stu Cncl Rep; Stomp Team Capt; Langston; Law.

COPELIN, CHAD E; West Middle HS; Norman, OK; (1); Church Yth Grp; FCA; Variety Show; High Hon Roll; Hon Roll; Young Life; Spcl Olpymics Vol; Music.

COPPENBARGER, HEIDI B; Davis HS; Davis, OK; (1); Art Clb; Church Yth Grp; Key Clb; Natl FFA Org; Church Choir; Rep Frsh Cls; Var Sftbl; High Hon Roll; OK Hon Soc; OK ST Univ.

COPPER, APRIL D; Barnsdall Jr Sr HS; Barnsdall, OK; (4); FHA; SADD; Chorus; Yrbk; Rep Jr Cls; Chrldng; Powder Puff Ftbl; Indian Clb; Potpourri; Northeastern ST U; Chld Psych.

COPS, ANGELA R; Westmoore HS; Oklahoma City, OK; (3); Church Yth Grp; Cmnty Wkr; Quiz Bowl; Scholastic Bowl; Science Clb; Spanish Clb; Chorus; Jr NHS; NHS; Pres Schlr; Acad Excl In Careers; Pre-Med/Peds.

COPS, STACY L; West Jr HS; Oklahoma City, OK; (1); Spanish Clb; Chorus; Jr NHS; OK ST U; Vet.

CORBETT, SUMMER; Edmond North HS; Edmond, OK; (3); 41/348; French Clb; Mu Alpha Theta; Chorus; Rep Orch; School Musical; Stage Crew; Gov Hon Prg Awd; Sun Club; Hrsbck Rdng; Guitar; Jujitsu; Arntcl Sci/Psych.

CORBIN, LINDSAY; Arapaho Schl; Weatherford, OK; (2); Pep Clb; Chorus; School Musical; Sec Frsh Cls; L Var Chrldng; Gov Hon Prg Awd; High Hon Roll; Southwestern OK ST Univ.

CORBIN, RYAN; Ponca City Sr HS; Ponca City, OK; (4); Church Yth Grp; Cmnty Wkr; FCA; Spanish Clb; Orch; Ed Yrbk; JV Crs Cntry; Var Socr; High Hon Roll; NHS; Rotarian Mon; OK Boys St; OU; Mech Engr.

CORDER, TRACEY L; Edmond Memorial HS; Edmond, OK; (3); Boy Scts; Church Yth Grp; French Clb; Band; Jazz Band; Mrchg Band; Pep Band; U Of Cntrl OK; Chem.

CORDIAL, URSULA L; Lone Grove HS; Lone Grove, OK; (4); 44/77; Math Clb; Natl Beta Clb; Science Clb; Spanish Clb; Hon Roll; NHS; Cameron Univ; Psych.

CORDRAY, AMANDA L; Edmond Memorial HS; Edmond, OK; (2); Church Yth Grp; FCA; GAA; Spanish Clb; SADD; Varsity Clb; Bsktbl; Sftbl; High Hon Roll; Hon Roll; Med.

CORKEN, CANDACE N; Edmond North HS; Edmond, OK; (4); 110/330; Church Yth Grp; Cmnty Wkr; FCA; Pep Clb; Spanish Clb; SADD; Varsity Clb; Acpl Chr; Chorus; Church Choir; OK ST U; Music.

CORLETT, MELISSA; Pryor Jr HS; Pryor, OK; (1); Church Yth Grp; FCA; Var Bsktbl; Var Crs Cntry; Var Trk; Cit Awd; Hon Roll; Pres Acad Fit Awd.

CORLEW, JULIA R; Union Sr HS; Tulsa, OK; (3); 35/741; Church Yth Grp; Chorus; Church Choir; Intrml Vllybl; High Hon Roll; Hon Roll; NHS; Spanish NHS; D-F Y Drug Free Yth:usc; Elem Ed.

CORLEY, LINDA D; Union Intermediate HS; Tulsa, OK; (2); Church Yth Grp; Spanish Clb; Bsktbl; Score Keeper; L Sftbl; Hon Roll; Jr NHS; NHS; Drug Free Yth; YABA; Tulsa U; Advertsng.

CORMAN, BRANDI; Foyil Schl; Claremore, OK; (1); Pep Clb; Var Chrldng; Hon Roll; Stu Today Awd; OSU; Restauranter.

CORMANY, APRIL M; Wayne Public Schl; Wayne, OK; (2); Art Clb; Church Yth Grp; FHA; Pep Clb; SADD; Band; Jazz Band; Mrchg Band; Var Bsktbl; RN.

CORMIER, ANDREW J; Edmond Memorial HS; Edmond, OK; (2); FCA; Spanish Clb; JV Bsktbl; Bio.

CORN, SERAI L; Wagoner Sr HS; Wagoner, OK; (3); FBLA; FHA; Teachers Aide; JV Bsktbl; JV Var Trk; High Hon Roll; Hon Roll; FHA Prlmntrn 94-95/VP95-; Ath Trnr 94-95; Northeastern ST UNIV; Acctng.

CORNEJO, CAMERON M; Woodward HS; Woodward, OK; (1); Boy Scts; Church Yth Grp; Drama Clb; Band; Mrchg Band; School Play; Hon Roll; Vctn Bible Schl Hlpr; Chldrns Hse Vol; Clsc Bowl Hon Bnd; OK Univ; Astrnmy.

CORNELISON, GARRETT; Shawnee Sr HS; Shawnee, OK; (3); Church Yth Grp; Latin Clb; Math Clb; Quiz Bowl; Scholastic Bowl; Science Clb; Teachers Aide; Church Choir; Rptr Nwsp; High Hon Roll; Wkly Column Local Newppr; OK St U; Engrng.

CORNETT, DREW A; Union Intermediate HS; Tulsa, OK; (2); Key Clb; Spanish Clb; Swmmng; Hon Roll; NHS; Pres Awd Ed Exc; 4 Yr Coll; Brdcst Jrnlsm.

CORNISH, MELINDA S; Clayton Jr Sr HS; Nashoba, OK; (2); Church Yth Grp; 4-H; FHA; Chorus; Church Choir; Jazz Band; Hon Roll; NHS; Phys Therapy; Bus.

CORNWELL, JASON W; Bixby Sr HS; Bixby, OK; (1); FCA; German Clb; Rep Frsh Cls; Ofcr Bsbl; Bsktbl; Ftbl; Cit Awd; High Hon Roll; Jr NHS; Church Yth Grp; Tulsa Engrng Challenge 2nd Pl; Mechncl Engrng.

CORNWELL, JOHN; Duncan HS; Duncan, OK; (3); Church Yth Grp; Hon Roll; FFA Achvmt Awd; Outstdng Horticulture Stu FFA; Intl Affair Seminar NY/WA.

CORNWELL, SEAN; Oklahoma Bible Acad; Enid, OK; (2); Church Yth Grp; FCA; Scholastic Bowl; Chorus; Ofcr Bsbl; Bsktbl; Trk; High Hon Roll; VP Jr NHS; Prfct Atten Awd; Poem Selected By Natl Lib Poetry; Math & Bible Awds.

CORNWELL, SONIA; Preston Schl; Okmulgee, OK; (3); 6/36; Church Choir; Bsktbl; Sftbl; Trk; Hon Roll; USA Today All Amer Bkstbll Tm; NAMES Nom; Bus Admin.

CORP, HEATHER; Comanche HS; Comanche, OK; (3); #3 in class; Pep Clb; Science Clb; SADD; Nwsp; Yrbk; Sec Frsh Cls; Sec Jr Cls; Ofcr Stu Cncl; Bsktbl; Chrldng; OSU; Phys Thrpst.

CORP, KEITH; Comanche HS; Comanche, OK; (2); Ofcr Bsbl; Bsktbl; Ftbl; Wt Lftg; Hon Roll; Ntl Merit Ltr; OSU; Engr.

CORR, MELODI K; Alva HS; Alva, OK; (2); Church Yth Grp; Drama Clb; FCA; FHA; NFL; Speech Tm; Stage Crew; Variety Show; Hon Roll; NHS; NWOSU.

CORRICK, CANDACE; Chandler HS; Chandler, OK; (3); Church Yth Grp; Cmnty Wkr; VP FHA; Girl Scts; Spanish Clb; Chorus; Church Choir; School Musical; Ofcr Stu Cncl.

CORWIN, JILL E; Macarthur Sr HS; Lawton, OK; (3); 19/263; Church Yth Grp; Cmnty Wkr; FCA; Drm Mjr(t); Ofcr Stu Cncl; Var Sftbl; Swmmng; High Hon Roll; NHS; Pres Schlr; U Of OK; Nrsng.

COSETTI, SARINA; Coyle Public Schl; Guthrie, OK; (4); 3/17; FHA; Nwsp; Yrbk; Gym; High Hon Roll; NHS; Cit Awd; All Amrcn Schol Awd; US Natl Ldshp Svc Awd; U Of Cent OK; Fash Desgn.

COSNER, KENZIE; Roland Sr HS; Roland, OK; (1); Office Aide; Color Guard; Rep Stu Cncl; Var Bsktbl; Var Chrldng; Var Sftbl; Hon Roll.

COSPER, CHRISTIE D; Mustang HS; Yukon, OK; (3); Church Yth Grp; FBLA; Acpl Chr; Chorus; Swing Chorus; Cit Awd; Hon Roll; All OK Music Edctrs ST Choir; 10th Pl FBLA ST Sprg Cnvntn; OK Bapt Univ; Bus/Music.

COSSEY, KIMBERLY; Shawnee Sr HS; Shawnee, OK; (4); 1/300; Church Yth Grp; Latin Clb; Letterman Clb; Teachers Aide; Church Choir; Stage Crew; High Hon Roll; NHS; Ntl Merit Ltr; Hndbl Choir; Aud Ensmbl.

COSSEY, LORI D; Putnam City West HS; Bethany, OK; (4); 48/278; FCA; Teachers Aide; Var Capt Bsktbl; Var Capt Sftbl; NHS; Army Rsrvs Schlr/Athlt Awd Wnnr; Hmcmng Queen; Med Clb; Chrprctc.

COSTELLO, DENA L; Del City HS; Oklahoma City, OK; (2); Church Yth Grp; French Clb; Band; Yrbk; Tennis; Hon Roll; Matmaids; Peer Mediator; OK ST U; Jrnlsm.

COSTEPHENS, CHANDA; Midwest City HS; Del City, OK; (4); 55/410; Cmnty Wkr; DECA; FHA; Key Clb; Yrbk; Rep Stu Cncl; Jr NHS; NHS; Prfct Atten Awd; Pres Acad Fit Awd; U Of OK; Commnctns.

COSTIGAN, KENDALL; Charles Page HS; Sand Springs, OK; (3); FCA; French Clb; Office Aide; Pep Clb; Rep Soph Cls; Var Chrldng; High Hon Roll; Hon Roll; NHS; Prfct Atten Awd; OK ST U; Med.

COSTILOE, JOSEPH; Southeast HS; Oklahoma City, OK; (1); Boy Scts; Church Yth Grp; ROTC; Band; Chorus; Church Choir; Jazz Band; School Musical; School Play; Nwsp; Ktty Hwk Air Soc; Air Force Acad; Pilot.

COTHERN, AMANDA; Ft Gibson HS; Fort Gibson, OK; (3); 5/137; Church Yth Grp; Rep FCA; FHA; Spanish Clb; Sec SADD; Band; Color Guard; Mrchg Band; Socr; High Hon Roll.

COTHRAN, THOMAS L; Will Rogers HS; Tulsa, OK; (2); Church Yth Grp; Ofcr Jr Cls; JV Var Bsbl; High Hon Roll; Jr NHS; Pres Acad Fit Awd; Masonic Awd; Dent.

COTTLE, ROBERT; Pawhuska HS; Pawhuska, OK; (4); 12/87; Am Leg Boys St; FCA; FTA; Key Clb; Mu Alpha Theta; Var L Bsbl; Var L Ftbl; Var L Wt Lftg; High Hon Roll; NHS; Chem Clb; U Cntrl OK; Elem Ed.

COTTON, GINA; Yukon Mid HS; Yukon, OK; (3); Drama Clb; School Play; Stage Crew; U Of Cntrl OK; His Tchr; Prof.

COTTON, HEATHER E; Union Intermediate HS; Broken Arrow, OK; (2); Church Yth Grp; FCA; Girl Scts; Key Clb; Science Clb; Spanish Clb; Band; Church Choir; Rptr Nwsp; Rptr Phtg Yrbk; Chrch Msn Vol; Girl Scout Slv Awd.

COTTON, M'KAYLA D; Westmoore HS; Oklahoma City, OK; (4); 54/610; Rep Sr Cls; Var Bsktbl; Var L Sftbl; Hon Roll; NHS; Val; Sftbl; Slw/Fast Pitch Var Letterman; OK ST Univ; Bus.

COTTRELL, RYAN; Davis HS; Davis, OK; (2); Church Yth Grp; Letterman Clb; Natl FFA Org; L Ftbl; L Wt Lftg; High Hon Roll; Hon Roll; Jr NHS; NHS; OK U; Med.

COTTRELL, TERAH; Quinton Jr Sr HS; Quinton, OK; (1); 1/45; Church Yth Grp; FCA; FHA; Quiz Bowl; Pres Frsh Cls; Bsktbl; Chrldng; High Hon Roll; Sing.

COUCH, AMANDA R; Heavener HS; Wister, OK; (1); Church Yth Grp; Bsktbl; Sftbl; Tech Stu Assoc VP; Carl Albert Stcol.

COUCH, CHRISTI L; Union Intermediate HS; Broken Arrow, OK; (2); 12/800; Church Yth Grp; French Clb; Band; Church Choir; Intrml Tennis; High Hon Roll; Jr NHS; NHS; USC; D-Fy Drug Free Youth; OK U; Jrnlsm.

COUCH, JAMES A; Stigler HS; Stigler, OK; (3); Am Leg Boys St; Church Yth Grp; Natl FFA Org; SADD; VICA; Band; Hon Roll; Anml Sci.

COUCH, MISTY C; Vinita HS; Vinita, OK; (3); Debate Tm; Math Clb; NFL; Office Aide; Science Clb; Spanish Clb; Speech Tm; Hon Roll; NHS; Environ Clb; Law.

COUGHRAN, JESSICA R; Westmoore HS; Oklahoma City, OK; (1); 35/309; Church Yth Grp; Chorus; Jr NHS; Pres Acad Fit Awd; Peer Helper.

COULSON, AMANDA J; Byng Sr HS; Ada, OK; (2); 15/100; VP Art Clb; Church Yth Grp; Drama Clb; FBLA; Math Clb; Science Clb; Spanish Clb; Speech Tm; School Play; Stage Crew.

COULSON, GARYN L; Bishop Kelley HS; Sperry, OK; (1); Cmnty Wkr; Speech Tm; Hon Roll; Skateboarding; Caring For Animals At Animal Care Clinic; Harmon Sci Ctr Vol; OSU; Vet.

COULTER, AMBER K; Choctaw HS; Choctaw, OK; (4); #1 in class; Am Leg Aux Girls St; VP Key Clb; VP SADD; Ed Nwsp; Ed Yrbk; Pres Stu Cncl; Var Capt Pom Pon; Pres Jr NHS; Kiwanis Awd; Val; Stu Rptr; Masonic Awd; Rotary Youth Ldrshp Awd; Acad Awd; Natl Youth Ldrs Conf; Girl Of Mnth; Chem Awd; U Of OK; Meteorology.

COULTER, ERIC A; Union Sr HS; Tulsa, OK; (3); 19/741; German Clb; Intnl Clb; Quiz Bowl; Church Choir; Orch; JV L Socr; Var L Swmmng; NHS; Pres Schlr.

COULTER, JAMIE M; Spiro HS; Spiro, OK; (3); Church Yth Grp; FHA; Office Aide; Teachers Aide; Chorus; Church Choir.

COURKAMP, KARI; Mc Loud HS; Mc Loud, OK; (3); 1/140; Church Yth Grp; FCA; FBLA; FHA; VP Jr Cls; Sec Bsktbl; Mgr Ftbl; High Hon Roll; NHS; 4th Pl 45th Intl Sci & Engrng Fair; Btncl Soc 2nd Pl 46th Intl Sci & Engrng Fair.

COUROULEAU, TREVOR P; Putnam City HS; Oklahoma City, OK; (2); 3/364; Church Yth Grp; German Clb; Spanish Clb; Band; Church Choir; Mrchg Band; Orch; School Musical; NHS; Prfct Atten Awd; Span I Cert Hnr; Linguistics.

COURSEY II, TERRY; Shawnee Sr HS; Shawnee, OK; (2); 2/350; Church Yth Grp; Drama Clb; Latin Clb; Band; Church Choir; Jazz Band; Mrchg Band; Pep Band; High Hon Roll; NHS; Med.

COURTNEY, CAREY; Davenport Jr Sr HS; Davenport, OK; (3); 1/33; Library Aide; Pep Clb; Spanish Clb; Pres Frsh Cls; Pres Soph Cls; Bsktbl; Mgr(s); High Hon Roll; NHS; U Cntrl OK; Med.

COURTNEY, JENNIFER; Haworth Jr HS; Idabel, OK; (2); Pres Sec Art Clb; Drama Clb; FHA; Office Aide; Speech Tm; Chorus; Pres Frsh Cls; Hon Roll; NHS; Ntl Merit Ltr; Paris JC; Gemologist.

COURTURE, GINA F; Olustee Schl; Olustee, OK; (2); 1/18; HOBY; Pres Frsh Cls; Pres Soph Cls; Rep Stu Cncl; Var Bsktbl; Capt Chrldng; Hon Roll; Boy Scts; Church Yth Grp; Hosp Aide; Sr Ctzn Cntr Vol; Pres/Rprtr Tech Assoc; Pres His Club; Dntstry.

COUSINS, TAMMY R; Morrison Public Schl; Morrison, OK; (3); FCA; FBLA; Rep FHA; Spanish Clb; Ed Nwsp; Yrbk; JV Bsktbl; Var Chrldng; Vllybl; Hon Roll; MEA Hnr Schlr; Natl His/Geo Rcgntn; Univ Of OK Acad Hnr; OK ST Univ; Med.

COVEL, DEANA; Westmoore HS; Moore, OK; (3); 11/615; Library Aide; Spanish Clb; Chorus; Mrchg Band; Gov Hon Prg Awd; High Hon Roll; Jr NHS; NHS; 10th-11th Yth & Govt; 10th-11th On Election Comm; 11th Treasures; Co-Head Pit Crew; U Of Cntrl OK; Scndry Ed.

COVERSTONE, JODY; Silo HS; Durant, OK; (4); Church Yth Grp; GAA; Sec Math Clb; Sec Mu Alpha Theta; Natl FFA Org; Office Aide; Teachers Aide; Church Choir; Yrbk; Sec Soph Cls; Grayson Co Coll; RN.

COVEY, ANJANETTE L; Del City HS; Oklahoma City, OK; (3); German Clb; Pep Clb; Chorus; Mat Maid Wrestling.

COVEY, MARIA; Lone Grove HS; Healdton, OK; (3); 11/98; Am Leg Aux Girls St; Math Tm; VP Jr Cls; Ofcr Stu Cncl; Sftbl; Hon Roll; NHS; Jr Mem Wmns Am Lgn Aux; Natl Ldrshp Conf; E Central U; Spec Ed.

COWAN, AMY J; Balko Public Schl; Balko, OK; (2); FCA; FHA; Pep Clb; Band; Pep Band; Rep Soph Cls; Bsktbl; Hon Roll; NHS; Cmnty Wkr; Teen Eldrly Support; Panhandle ST Univ.

COWAN, CAMMI K; Hominy HS; Ralston, OK; (2); 8/79; Church Yth Grp; FHA; Teachers Aide; Sec Soph Cls; Sec Stu Cncl; Tennis; High Hon Roll; Hon Roll; Harmon's Club; Indian Club; Johnson O'Malley Head Ldy Dncr 132 USAA Awd Prgrm; Pdtrcn.

COWAN, CHAD D; Velma Alma HS; Duncan, OK; (2); Natl FFA Org; SADD; VP Soph Cls; Var Bsktbl; High Hon Roll; Hon Roll; NHS.

COWAN, JAMIE R; Muskogee HS; Muskogee, OK; (3); 48/400; Cmnty Wkr; Hosp Aide; JCL; VP Sec Key Clb; Latin Clb; Natl FFA Org; High Hon Roll; Hon Roll; NHS; Ecology Club; RAID; Teens For Christ; Connors ST Coll; PT/AG.

COWAN, JONATHAN B; Union Sr HS; Tulsa, OK; (3); 30/705; Boy Scts; Church Yth Grp; Spanish Clb; Teachers Aide; Var L Swmmng; High Hon Roll; NHS; Pres Acad Fit Awd; BSA Eagle Sct, Gld, Slvr & Brnz Plms; Swmmng All St & Conf; Wtr Polo; Triathlete.

COWAN, KACEY; Okemah HS; Okemah, OK; (3); 3/85; Natl Beta Clb; Natl FFA Org; Science Clb; Speech Tm; SADD; Var Bsktbl; JV Chrldng; Var Trk; NHS; Sal; Keywanettes; OU; Med.

COWAN, NATASHA D; Locust Grove HS; Locust Grove, OK; (3); Church Yth Grp; German Clb; Speech Tm; Treas Soph Cls; Treas Jr Cls; Gov Hon Prg Awd; High Hon Roll; Hon Roll; NHS; OK U; Pharmcy.

COWAN, REGINA L; Pryor Sr HS; Pryor, OK; (4); 39/145; Art Clb; Cmnty Wkr; Sec FHA; Office Aide; Chorus; School Musical; Yrbk; NHS; Top Eng Awd; Recipient Of Frosh Mrt Schlsp From Rogers Univ; Rogers Univ; Graphics Tech.

COWAN, THOMAS M; Cordell Sr HS; Cordell, OK; (2); Church Yth Grp; Cmnty Wkr; Quiz Bowl; Band; Jazz Band; Mrchg Band; Pep Band; Pres Soph Cls; High Hon Roll; Prfct Atten Awd; MIT; Cmptr Engr.

COWARD, TERESA; Tahlequah Sr HS; Tahlequah, OK; (4); 21/243; VP Science Clb; Band; Color Guard; Drm Mjr(t); Mrchg Band; Pep Band; Hon Roll; NHS; Ntl Merit Ltr; Northeastern ST U; Medcl.

COWDEN, KATY A; Bishop Mcguinness HS; Oklahoma City, OK; (2); 35/167; Church Yth Grp; FCA; German Clb; HOBY; Pep Clb; SADD; JV Var Bsktbl; Var Chrldng; Var Trk; NHS; Ger Clb Sec/Treas; Sprts Mdcn.

COWELL, JULIE; Jenks Public Schls; Tulsa, OK; (1); Church Yth Grp; FCA; Church Choir; Chrldng; Hon Roll; Natl Guild Of Piano Tchrs; Hyechka Music Socty; Trojans For Christ; Nursing.

COWGER, DEANA; Edmond North HS; Edmond, OK; (3); 56/348; Cmnty Wkr; Key Clb; ROTC; Drill Tm; Vllybl; NHS; Prfct Atten Awd; AFJROTC Meritourous Svc Awd & The Perfmnc Awd.

COWHERD, ZACHARY M; Mc Alester HS; Mcalester, OK; (2); Church Yth Grp; Debate Tm; ROTC; Speech Tm; Band; Mrchg Band; Stage Crew; Hon Roll; Hnr Rl 94-; Red Cross Cert Lfe Guard; Cmptr Sci.

COWIN, CARRA; Grove HS; Grove, OK; (4); 5/107; Am Leg Aux Girls St; Church Yth Grp; Band; Chorus; Church Choir; Jazz Band; Ofcr Stu Cncl; Hon Roll; NHS; Cmnty Wkr; All St Chorus; Elem Ed.

COWLES, ALONZO D; Midwest City HS; Midwest City, OK; (3); Church Yth Grp; Spanish Clb; Acpl Chr; Band; Chorus; Church Choir; Jazz Band; Mrchg Band; Ofcr Jr Cls; Afrcn Amer Allnc; Ambssdrs Chldrn/Yth Cncrt Choir; Psych.

COWLEY, KRISTY L; Enid Sr HS; Enid, OK; (3); 59/445; Church Yth Grp; Cmnty Wkr; Pres FBLA; Girl Scts; Yrbk; Ofcr Stu Cncl; Bsktbl; Hon Roll; Jr NHS; NHS; 7th Pl St Pblc Spkng FBLA; OK ST U; Bus.

COWLEY, PHILLIP D; Morrison Public Schl; Morrison, OK; (3); 7/34; Am Leg Boys St; Church Yth Grp; Cmnty Wkr; FCA; FBLA; Pres Natl FFA Org; Office Aide; Spanish Clb; Band; Jazz Band; Outstdng Soph FFA; Outstdng Jr FFA Mem; Horse Prfncy Awd; Washington DC Ldrsp Conf 95; OK ST Univ; Ag Bus.

COWLING, JAMES D; Choctaw HS; Choctaw, OK; (2); Church Yth Grp; JV Golf; JV Wt Lftg; Hon Roll; Rose ST; Sci Fld.

COX, ADAM R; Edmond Memorial HS; Edmond, OK; (3); 1/371; Spanish Clb; Golf; Hon Roll; NHS.

COX, AMY B; Choctaw HS; Midwest City, OK; (3); 26/360; FCA; Key Clb; SADD; Yrbk; Var L Crs Cntry; Var L Socr; Gov Hon Prg Awd; Ntl Merit Ltr; Pres Acad Fit Awd; Natl Acad Of Achvt Math & Jrnlsm Awds; St Hnr Soc; Mass Commnctns.

COX, BEN; West Middle HS; Norman, OK; (1); Church Yth Grp; Cmnty Wkr; FCA; Letterman Clb; Church Choir; Rep Frsh Cls; Rep Stu Cncl; JV L Ftbl; Var L Trk; Cit Awd; HS Heros; Dist & Exch Comm; Yth Sports Camp Cnslr; Fmly Dev Stu Of Yr; All Conf Ftbl Hnrb Mntn; U Of OK; Bus Commnctns; Fin.

COX, BOBBY D; Dale Sr HS; Shawnee, OK; (1); 3/44; Band; Jazz Band; Mrchg Band; Pep Band; Hon Roll; Jr NHS; NHS.

COX, BRANDI; Cherokee Jr Sr HS; Cherokee, OK; (3); Church Yth Grp; Drama Clb; FHA; Spanish Clb; Speech Tm; Church Choir; Ofcr Jr Cls; High Hon Roll; NHS; Yth Grp VP; FHA Rptr; Piano; Spch Sec; CPA.

COX, BRIAN E; Madill HS; Madill, OK; (2); Church Yth Grp; FCA; 4-H; Quiz Bowl; Band; Church Choir; Jazz Band; Mrchg Band; Pep Band; Southeastern OK ST U; Music.

COX, CASEY D; Vinita HS; Vinita, OK; (3); 17/95; Church Yth Grp; German Clb; Speech Tm; Teachers Aide; Band; Mrchg Band; Pep Band; High Hon Roll; Jr NHS; NHS; Plays Keyboards For Yth Worship Svcs; Chrch Play Assist; Chrstn Coll.

COX, CASEY S; Tuttle HS; Tuttle, OK; (2); Church Yth Grp; 4-H; Key Clb; Natl FFA Org; Spanish Clb; Church Choir; Pres Frsh Cls; Pres Soph Cls; Hist Stu Cncl; Ftbl; 4-H St Ambassador, Dist Rptr & Cty Hall Of Fame Wnnr; OSU; Ministry.

COX, CASI; Newcastle HS; Newcastle, OK; (2); 17/89; Church Yth Grp; GAA; Letterman Clb; Science Clb; Var Bsktbl; Var Chrldng; Var Sftbl; Var Trk; Hon Roll; Alg I Awd; All Conf Bsktbl.

COX, CHRIS; Moore HS; Moore, OK; (4); Am Leg Boys St; Bus Profs of Am; Church Yth Grp; FBLA; Math Clb; Office Aide; Spanish Clb; Crs Cntry; Tennis; Trk; OK U; Engr.

COX, CHRISTOPHER L; Coalgate HS; Coalgate, OK; (3); Key Clb; Ofcr Bsbl; Bsktbl; Socr; Hon Roll; Prfct Atten Awd; OSU; Bsktbl/Math/Cmptr Arts.

COX, CURTIS R; Northeast HS; Oklahoma City, OK; (3); Am Leg Boys St; FBLA; Model UN; Science Clb; Var Bsbl; Var Golf; High Hon Roll; NHS; Med Explorer Pres; Dean Mc Gee Eye Inst Vol; Pre-Med.

COX, DONALD CODY; Ponca City Sr HS; Ponca City, OK; (4); Church Yth Grp; Cmnty Wkr; Teachers Aide; Hon Roll; Hmrm Pres 10th Grd; OSU; Anml Sci.

COX, EMILY; Eisenhower Sr HS; Lawton, OK; (3); Church Yth Grp; Cmnty Wkr; FCA; HOBY; Key Clb; Letterman Clb; Church Choir; Drill Tm; Rep Frsh Cls; Rep Soph Cls; U Of OK; Speech Pthlgy.

COX, HARRELL A; Webster HS; Tulsa, OK; (3); Letterman Clb; Varsity Clb; Var Bsktbl; Var Ftbl; Var Trk; Hon Roll; Jr NHS; NHS; Pres Acad Fit Awd; Natl African Amer Stu Assn Pres; Engrng.

COX, JAMIE; Hominy HS; Hominy, OK; (4); 7/59; FCA; FHA; Scholastic Bowl; School Play; Ofcr Jr Cls; Bsktbl; Chrldng; Sftbl; Trk; St Schlr; Rogers ST Coll; Court Rprtng.

COX, JARED J; Bartlesville Mid HS; Bartlesville, OK; (2); 147/452; Ride & Work On Honda 4-Wheeler; OK ST U; Electrncs Engr Tech.

COX, JASON; Elk City Jr HS; Elk City, OK; (1); Church Yth Grp; Letterman Clb; Band; Church Choir; Jazz Band; Orch; VP Frsh Cls; Ftbl; Tennis; Prfct Atten Awd.

COX, JASON; Keyes HS; Texhoma, OK; (3); 4/10; FCA; Nwsp; Rep Frsh Cls; Sec Soph Cls; Rep Jr Cls; Var Bsktbl; High Hon Roll; NHS.

COX, JENNIFER L; Madill HS; Madill, OK; (2); Church Yth Grp; Drama Clb; FCA; Hosp Aide; JV Bsktbl; JV Sftbl; Var Trk; Hon Roll; NHS; Actens; So OK Curr Cont 3rd Pl Bio; OK Bapt Univ; Dr; Med Rsrch.

COX, JESSICA L; Pocola HS; Pocola, OK; (2); FCA; FHA; Scholastic Bowl; JV Var Bsktbl; Var Chrldng; Var Sftbl; Hon Roll; 1st Plc CASC Schlstc Meet $300 Tuition CASC; CASC; Med Fld.

COX, JONATHAN G; Woodward HS; Woodward, OK; (1); 1/236; Church Yth Grp; FCA; German Clb; Letterman Clb; Pep Clb; Bsktbl; High Hon Roll; Kiwanis Awd; OK Hnr Soc; TSA; Mock Trial Tm St Runner Up 95; U Of KS; Law.

COX, JULIE; Putnam City North HS; Oklahoma City, OK; (3); Church Yth Grp; Key Clb; Spanish Clb; Hon Roll; NHS; GATE; Stu To Stu; 3d.

COX, KELLY S; Bridge Creek HS; Tuttle, OK; (3); Drama Clb; Scholastic Bowl; Spanish Clb; SADD; School Play; Treas Jr Cls; Chrldng; High Hon Roll; NHS; Pres Acad Fit Awd; Hnrs Engl; Hnrs OK Hstry, Span I &II, Home Ec; OK Cty Univ; Bus Admin.

COX, KELSEY; Woodward HS; Woodward, OK; (2); Church Yth Grp; Key Clb; Band; Stage Crew; JV Bsktbl; Var Sftbl; Var Trk; High Hon Roll; Puppet Team; Southern Nazarene U; PT.

COX, KENDRA F; Lawton Sr HS; Lawton, OK; (2); Band; Var Bsktbl; Mgr(s); Var Vllybl; Trk; High Hon Roll; Hon Roll; Clark Atlanta Univ.

COX, KESHA; Newcastle HS; Newcastle, OK; (3); 1/92; Acpl Chr; Band; Chorus; Flag Corp; Jazz Band; Mrchg Band; Orch; Pep Band; School Musical; Swing Chorus; Supr Vcl St Cntst I; Excllnt Vcl St Cntst II; OCU; Msc Perf.

COX, MARCY L; Bishop Kelley HS; Broken Arrow, OK; (1); Church Yth Grp; Latin Clb; Pep Clb; School Play; Ofcr Stu Cncl; High Hon Roll; Dncng; Play Rec Sftbl.

COX, MARISA; Madill HS; Madill, OK; (4); 1/70; Church Yth Grp; FCA; Pres FBLA; Pres FHA; Sec Sr Cls; Treas Stu Cncl; Chrldng; Sftbl; High Hon Roll; NHS; SE OK St Univ; Premed.

COX, MATTHEW R; Bixby Sr HS; Bixby, OK; (3); 1/210; Boy Scts; Church Yth Grp; FCA; Spanish Clb; High Hon Roll; Jr NHS; NHS; Pres Acad Fit Awd; Acad Bowl JV & Var Capt; His Clb.

COX, MIKE J; Bartlesville Sr HS; Bartlesville, OK; (4); 1/394; Church Yth Grp; Spanish Clb; Var Ftbl; Intrml Vllybl; Intrml Wt Lftg; High Hon Roll; NHS; Ntl Merit SF; Spanish NHS; Soccer; USVA Vllybl; Med.

COX, RICHARD K; Lone Grove HS; Lone Grove, OK; (2); Church Yth Grp; FCA; Math Clb; Acpl Chr; Chorus; Church Choir; School Musical; School Play; Swing Chorus; Var Bsbl.

COX, ROBIN; Collinsville HS; Collinsville, OK; (3); 2/106; FCA; Office Aide; Chorus; Yrbk; Treas Jr Cls; Rep Stu Cncl; Var Tennis; Var JV Vllybl; Hon Roll; NHS; U Of OK; Pharmcy.

COX, RUSELL; Wynnewood HS; Pauls Valley, OK; (3); Teachers Aide; Band; Jazz Band; Mrchg Band; Pep Band; NHS.

COX, SARAH; Luther HS; Luther, OK; (3); 2/40; Church Yth Grp; FCA; Band; Mrchg Band; Pep Band; Bsktbl; Trk; High Hon Roll; Hon Roll; NHS; Rose ST U Schlstc Meet; OSU.

COX, STEVEN B; B T Washington HS; Tulsa, OK; (4); 58/264; Boy Scts; French Clb; JCL; Latin Clb; Teachers Aide; NHS; Eagle Sct; Acad Ltr; UT Austin; Mgmt Info Sys.

COX, T J; Cushing HS; Cushing, OK; (1); Speech Tm; Band; Mrchg Band; Ftbl; Wt Lftg; Wrstlng; High Hon Roll; Pres Acad Fit Awd; OK Bapt Univ & NW Regnl Hnr Band; U Of MI; Pharmaceautical Chem.

COX, TAMMY; Choctaw Jr HS; Midwest City, OK; (1); Church Yth Grp; FCA; Library Aide; Ofcr Stu Cncl; Tennis; Hon Roll; Jr NHS; Schl Mascot; Brdcstng; Southern Nazarene U; Med.

COX, TIFFANY D; Union Sr HS; Broken Arrow, OK; (3); 87/741; Dance Clb; FBLA; FHA; Spanish Clb; Drill Tm; Hon Roll; Jr NHS; NHS; Dance/Ballet/Tp/Jzz/Acrbtcs/Mscl Thtr/Tchr/Chrgrphr; NY U; Dance.

COX, TRACEY; Marietta HS; Overbrook, OK; (3); #1 in class; Church Yth Grp; 4-H; VP FHA; Quiz Bowl; Church Choir; Stage Crew; Gov Hon Prg Awd; Hon Roll; NHS; OK ST U.

COX, TRACEY; Tuttle HS; Tuttle, OK; (3); 1/96; Church Yth Grp; 4-H; HOBY; Key Clb; Spanish Clb; Rep Jr Cls; Var L Wrstlng; 4-H Awd; High Hon Roll; NHS; 4-H Dist Secy, St Ambassador & Cty Hall Of Fame; OK ST U; Bus/Poltcl Sci.

COX, WILLIE D; Valliant HS; Valliant, OK; (4); 28/86; FCA; Var Bsbl; Intrml Bsktbl; Var L Ftbl; Var Wt Lftg; Hon Roll; NHS; Ntl Merit Ltr; Southeastern OK ST Univ.

COXSEY, DAVID L; Durant HS; Durant, OK; (2); Drama Clb; Speech Tm; School Play; Rptr Nwsp; Hon Roll; Indian Stdnt Of Yr Soph; World Hist Curr 3rd Plc; Natl Hist Awd; OK Univ; Comic Book Wrtr.

COY, ANDREA M; Sapulpa Sr HS; Sapulpa, OK; (2); Church Yth Grp; Band; Chorus; Mrchg Band; Orch; Nwsp; Hon Roll; Pvt Voice Lessons.

COY, BRYAN N; Edmond North HS; Edmond, OK; (3); Church Yth Grp; FCA; Red Cross Aide; SADD; Teachers Aide; Var L Bsbl; JV Bsktbl; Var L Ftbl; Hon Roll; NHS; Red Crs Vol OK City Bombing April 95.

COY, JAMEY J; Hammon Schl; Hammon, OK; (2); Church Yth Grp; FCA; 4-H; GAA; Letterman Clb; Pep Clb; Spanish Clb; Bsktbl; Chrldng; Sftbl; Hall Of Fame; Southwestern OK; Acctg.

COY, LIBBIE M; Skiatook HS; Skiatook, OK; (2); Church Yth Grp; FBLA; FHA; Natl FFA Org; Band; Mrchg Band; Hon Roll; Homcmng Candidate; Elem Tchr.

COYNER, ARON; North Intemediate HS; Broken Arrow, OK; (1); Quiz Bowl; Scholastic Bowl; Spanish Clb; Acpl Chr; Hon Roll; Jr NHS; OK St Hnr Soc; Lcl Paper Rprtr; Astrophyscst.

COZEE, JAMIANNE; Southeast HS; Oklahoma City, OK; (1); Chess Clb; VICA; High Hon Roll; Hon Roll; Most Outstdng Span Stdnt; Most Outstdng Cmptr Stdnt; Wrtng Essays; Lawyer.

COZENS, STEVEN; Mustang HS; Yukon, OK; (4); 23/357; Am Leg Boys St; Church Yth Grp; FCA; Office Aide; Ofcr Stu Cncl; Ofcr Bsbl; Bsktbl; High Hon Roll; NHS; Bus.

CRABBS, LESLIE; Chisholm Sr HS; Enid, OK; (4); 6/70; Natl FFA Org; Office Aide; Band; Var Chrldng; Var Trk; High Hon Roll; NHS; Pres Acad Fit Awd; FFA Sweetheart; S W OK ST U; Vet.

CRABBS, SHANNON; Chisholm Sr HS; Enid, OK; (1); FHA; Spanish Clb; High Hon Roll; Jr NHS; Motocross Rcng.

CRABTREE, CECIL; Eufaula Sr HS; Eufaula, OK; (4); 6/78; Drama Clb; FBLA; HOBY; Band; Drm Mjr(t); Pres Frsh Cls; Sec Stu Cncl; Hon Roll; NHS; Music Ed.

CRABTREE, CORY; Seminole Jr Sr HS; Seminole, OK; (4); 10/82; Church Yth Grp; Scholastic Bowl; Band; Church Choir; Mrchg Band; Orch; Pep Band; Rptr Nwsp; Rptr Yrbk; Hon Roll; OK Assm God Chrchs Bible Quiz Cmptn 2nd Pl St; Seminole JC; Acctng.

CRABTREE, MICHELE R; Mustang HS; Yukon, OK; (3); 112/386; Church Yth Grp; FCA; GAA; JA; Varsity Clb; Rep Frsh Cls; Rep Soph Cls; Rep Stu Cncl; Var JV Bsktbl; Var Golf; Ed Elem/Pre-Law.

CRABTREE, RACHEAL A; Western Heights Sr HS; Oklahoma City, OK; (3); #1 in class; Church Yth Grp; Spanish Clb; Band; Flag Corp; Tennis; High Hon Roll; NHS; Multi-Yr Listee; U Of OK; Phys Therapy.

CRABTREE, TAMI; Boise City HS; Boise City, OK; (1); 10/35; Church Yth Grp; FHA; GAA; Letterman Clb; Sec Frsh Cls; Var L Bsktbl; Var Chrldng; Var L Trk; Hon Roll; UCO; Loan Ofcr.

CRADDOCK, AMIE K; Durant HS; Durant, OK; (2); Intrml Tennis; HOSA; OU.

CRADDOCK, CHRIS A; Union Intermediate HS; Tulsa, OK; (2); Church Yth Grp; FCA; Church Choir; Rep Frsh Cls; Hon Roll; 100 Hrs Attendance In Chrch Sunday Schl; AT In Cultural Lit; MD; Botany.

CRADDOCK, KEISHA N; Ninnekah HS; Ninnekah, OK; (2); Church Yth Grp; FCA; Natl FFA Org; VP Rep Stu Cncl; L Bsktbl; Hon Roll.

CRADDOCK, MATTHEW; Ninnekah HS; Ninnekah, OK; (4); Church Yth Grp; FCA; Office Aide; Science Clb; Ofcr Sr Cls; L Bsktbl; Hon Roll; Prfct Atten Awd.

CRAFT, CARLIE D; Henryetta Sr HS; Henryetta, OK; (2); 16/110; FCA; FHA; JV L Bsktbl; Mgr(s); Var L Sftbl; Var L Trk; Hon Roll; Northeastern ST; PT.

CRAFT, CLINT; Stigler HS; Lequire, OK; (2); Church Yth Grp; 4-H; Natl FFA Org; SADD; Var Ftbl; Var Trk; Var Wt Lftg; 4-H Awd; Hon Roll; Prfct Atten Awd; Le Quire Bapt Chrch; Rcrtn Ofcr 4-H; Ftbl Coach.

CRAFT, JAMES R; Westmoore HS; Oklahoma City, OK; (3); Am Leg Boys St; Boy Scts; Church Yth Grp; VICA; Band; Mrchg Band; Phtg Yrbk; Prfct Atten Awd; Eagle Sct; OK ST U; Elec Engrng.

CRAFT, LACI R; Velma Alma HS; Velma, OK; (2); FHA; Office Aide; Teachers Aide; Chorus; High Hon Roll; Acctng.

CRAFT, MELLOY T; Douglass HS; Oklahoma City, OK; (2); Band; Mrchg Band; Hon Roll; Lawyer.

CRAFT, TABITHA; Trinity Christian Schl; Broken Arrow, OK; (3); 1/12; Church Yth Grp; Drama Clb; Office Aide; Pep Clb; Church Choir; School Play; Rep Yrbk; Chrldng; Socr; Vllybl; 9 Yrs Pno; John Brwon U; Spch.

CRAGAR, GENE W; Tahlequah Sr HS; Tahlequah, OK; (2); Var Wrstlng; Hon Roll; NHS; OK ST U.

CRAGER, ELIZABETH A; Muskogee HS; Muskogee, OK; (3); 3/450; Church Yth Grp; FBLA; Hosp Aide; Spanish Clb; Chorus; Ofcr Frsh Cls; High Hon Roll; Jr NHS; NHS; Pres Acad Fit Awd; Nazaren Bible Quizzing; Chem Physcs; Suprntndntns Hnr Banquet; S Nazarene Univ; Premed.

CRAIG, BRIAN; Central HS; Tulsa, OK; (4); Chess Clb; Church Yth Grp; Band; Church Choir; Jazz Band; Pep Band; NHS; Tulsa U.

CRAIG, CHERYL D; Wister Schl; Wister, OK; (3); High Hon Roll; Hon Roll; NHS; Sal; Eastern OK ST Coll.

CRAIG, CORIENE; Miami Sr HS; Miami, OK; (3); HOBY; NFL; Rep Jr Cls; VP Stu Cncl; Var Bsktbl; Var Capt Sftbl; High Hon Roll; NHS; FCA; Mock Trial; OU; Poly Sci.

CRAIG, DANIEL R; Shawnee Sr HS; Shawnee, OK; (1); Church Yth Grp; FCA; Frosh Ftbl/Bsbl; U Of AR.

CRAIG, HAROLD D; Northeast HS; Oklahoma City, OK; (3); Church Yth Grp; FBLA; Band; Church Choir; Mrchg Band; Pep Band.

CRAIG, JERRY PAUL; Duncan HS; Duncan, OK; (4); 50/220; FCA; Key Clb; Letterman Clb; Spanish Clb; SADD; Variety Show; Phtg Rptr Nwsp; Yrbk; Bsktbl; Tennis; Hlth Careers Clb Pres; Key Clb; OPIA Jrnlsm Awds; OK Univ Norman; Optometry.

CRAIG, JOSEPH D; Stilwell HS; Stilwell, OK; (2); Church Yth Grp; Natl Beta Clb; JV Bsbl; JV Bsktbl; Wt Lftg; High Hon Roll; Hon Roll; Spanish NHS; D-FY; Northeastern ST U.

CRAIG, JOSHUA E; Yukon Middle HS; Yukon, OK; (3); Church Yth Grp; Canadian Cty Sheriffs Dept Explorer Post; Marine Bio.

CRAIG, SHELLY; Hulbert Jr Sr HS; Hulbert, OK; (3); Church Yth Grp; Pres Frsh Cls; Ofcr Soph Cls; Rep Jr Cls; Bsktbl; Chrldng; Sftbl; NHS.

CRAIG, STEPHANIE A; Noble HS; Noble, OK; (4); 1/158; Dance Clb; French Clb; Pres Mu Alpha Theta; Scholastic Bowl; VP SADD; Ed Yrbk; Ntl Merit SF; U Of OK; Elec Engrng.

CRAIG, TONI; Whitesboro Schl; Whitesboro, OK; (1); FHA; GAA; Var Bsktbl; Hon Roll; Phys Ed.

CRAIG, ZAC; Seminole Jr Sr HS; Seminole, OK; (4); 5/90; Am Leg Boys St; FCA; Math Clb; Math Tm; Science Clb; Spanish Clb; SADD; VICA; Chorus; Church Choir; Tulsa; Bus.

CRAIGHEAD, LINDSEY N; Sharon Mutual Jr Sr HS; Woodward, OK; (4); 3/24; FCA; Chorus; Yrbk; VP Frsh Cls; Treas Jr Cls; Bsktbl; Chrldng; Hon Roll; NHS; Miss Sharon Mutual; SW OK St Univ; Fin.

CRAIN, CHRISTIE D; Bixby Sr HS; Bixby, OK; (1); Chorus; OK ST Univ; Law; Interior Dsgn.

CRAIN, CHRISTOPHER; Union Sr HS; Broken Arrow, OK; (4); 30/630; Church Yth Grp; FCA; Office Aide; Spanish Clb; Ofcr Jr Cls; Ofcr Sr Cls; Rep Stu Cncl; Var Golf; High Hon Roll; Hon Roll; Tee Pee Crew; Abilene Chrstn U.

CRAIN, LEIGH N; Union Intermediate HS; Broken Arrow, OK; (2); 38/800; Cmnty Wkr; FCA; Key Clb; Spanish Clb; Var Sftbl; Hon Roll; NHS; Prfct Atten Awd; Acad Tm; Hosp Vol Wrkr; Med.

CRAIN, TIMOTHY; Fargo Schl; Fargo, OK; (4); 1/21; FCA; Rep Natl Beta Clb; Treas Natl FFA Org; Sec Sr Cls; Ofcr Bsbl; Bsktbl; St Schlr; Val; Quiz Bowl; OK Air Natl Guard; Southwestern OK St U; Elec Eng.

CRALL, STACI; Bartlesville Sr HS; Bartlesville, OK; (1); Church Yth Grp; Drama Clb; Science Clb; Hon Roll; Tchr.

CRAM, ANANDA S; Tishomingo HS; Tishomingo, OK; (2); Rep Frsh Cls; Rep Soph Cls; Rep Jr Cls; High Hon Roll; Hon Roll; Ntl Merit Schol; St Schlr; 4-H; FHA; Anatomy/Physlgy Awd Hon Cls; OSAI Qrtz Mtn; OU Fall Sat Cls Schlrshp; OU; Med Field; Dance.

CRANE, JOLETTA A; Tecumseh HS; Tecumseh, OK; (3); Church Yth Grp; Scholastic Bowl; Spanish Clb; Teachers Aide; Temple Yth Grp; Band; Chorus; Mrchg Band; School Musical; NHS.

CRANE, SHAWNA T; East Central HS; Tulsa, OK; (3); Church Yth Grp; Bsktbl; Hon Roll; Tulsa U; Bus Cmptrs.

CRANK, ERIN E; Sperry Sr HS; Sperry, OK; (3); Church Yth Grp; 4-H; FHA; GAA; Office Aide; Spanish Clb; Varsity Clb; JV Bsktbl; Sftbl; Trk; U Of Tulsa; Sprts Med.

CRANKE, ANGELA M; Jenks HS; Tulsa, OK; (3); Cmnty Wkr; FBLA; Ballet; Clinical Psych.

CRANMER, AMY; Oklahoma Christian Schl; Edmond, OK; (4); 5/37; Am Leg Aux Girls St; Debate Tm; HOBY; School Play; Nwsp; Yrbk; Ofcr Stu Cncl; Chrldng; Pom Pon; DAR Awd; Girls St Lt Gov; Girls Nation Sentr; Poltcl Sci.

CRAPARATTA, JASON W; Pioneer Jr Sr HS; Enid, OK; (3); Church Yth Grp; Computer Clb; Quiz Bowl; Scholastic Bowl; Band; School Play; Rep Frsh Cls; JV Var Ftbl; High Hon Roll; Hon Roll; OK ST U.

CRASE, LARENIA V; Gans Public Schl; Muldrow, OK; (3); Church Yth Grp; FHA; Chorus; Church Choir; Rep Frsh Cls; Bus/Cmptr Tech.

CRAVENS, BROOKE A; Salina HS; Salina, OK; (1); School Play; Ofcr Frsh Cls; Hon Roll; NHS; OU; Ct Rptr; CPA; Office Mgr.

CRAWFORD, ALYSON; Vanoss Schl; Ada, OK; (3); FCA; 4-H; Natl FFA Org; JA; Varsity Clb; Ofcr Frsh Cls; Bsktbl; Sftbl; Trk; Cit Awd; Natl MN Bsktbl Ingenious Games Wnnr; Coach.

CRAWFORD, AMANDA; Putnam City West HS; Oklahoma City, OK; (4); 1/270; Pres Art Clb; Hosp Aide; Scholastic Bowl; Sftbl; Cit Awd; Sec NHS; Val; 8 Yrs Piano; 1st Pl SWOSU On-Site Watercolor Cmptn; 2nd Pl U Of Cntrl OK Acrylic Painting; U Of OK; Art.

CRAWFORD, AMY; Silo HS; Durant, OK; (3); Sec FHA; Teachers Aide; Chorus; School Musical; Ofcr Frsh Cls; Sec Soph Cls; Ofcr Jr Cls; Capt Chrldng; 4-H; Wt Lftg; Carnival Qn 2 Yrs; Bst All Arnd; Southeastern OK U; Tchng.

CRAWFORD, ANGELA; B T Washington HS; Tulsa, OK; (4); Church Yth Grp; Cmnty Wkr; FBLA; Office Aide; Pep Clb; ROTC; Spanish Clb; Nwsp; Rptr Yrbk; Rep Soph Cls; Mock Trl Best Wtns/Outstdng Tm Mbr; Southwest MO ST U; Bus Mgmt.

CRAWFORD, CHESNEY; Woodward HS; Woodward, OK; (2); Cmnty Wkr; German Clb; Pep Clb; Rep Soph Cls; Ofcr Stu Cncl; Chrldng; High Hon Roll; NHS.

CRAWFORD, CHRISTIE; Clinton HS; Clinton, OK; (3); 16/120; Church Yth Grp; 4-H; Library Aide; Quiz Bowl; Ofcr Stu Cncl; Cit Awd; 4-H Awd; Hon Roll; Pres Schlr.

CRAWFORD, CHRISTOPHER; Union Intermediate HS; Tulsa, OK; (2); 207/800; Hon Roll; NHS.

CRAWFORD, CRYSTAL D; Claremore Sr HS; Claremore, OK; (2); German Clb; Chorus; School Musical; Hon Roll; Superior Rtng Ger Comp; Wrtng/Prfrmng Skit; Trng Bus Dept; 2 For Singing Duet In Ger; Singing.

CRAWFORD, JAMIE; Grove HS; Grove, OK; (3); 16/170; FCA; Spanish Clb; Band; Mrchg Band; Bsktbl; Sftbl; Trk; Hon Roll; NHS; Ed.

CRAWFORD, JASON I; Thomas Jr Sr HS; Custer City, OK; (3); Boy Scts; Natl FFA Org; Science Clb; Rep Frsh Cls; Var Bsbl; JV Bsktbl; Cit Awd; Hon Roll; NHS; Ntl Merit Ltr; Egle Sct Awd Wth 3 Palms; SW OK ST Univ; Cmptr Sci.

CRAWFORD, JOHN S; Union Intermediate HS; Tulsa, OK; (2); Church Yth Grp; FCA; Intrml Ftbl; NHS; Stu Of Month; Math Hnr Awd; TJC; Engrng.

CRAWFORD, KATIA; Charles Page HS; Sand Springs, OK; (1); Church Yth Grp; FCA; Church Choir; Rep Stu Cncl; Bsktbl; Chrldng; Trk; High Hon Roll; African Amer Stdnt Union VP; Sunday Schl/Yth Dept Chr Sec; Dntstry.

CRAWFORD, MARSHALL E; Locust Grove HS; Locust Grove, OK; (2); Church Yth Grp; Ftbl; Hon Roll; Vo Tech Training; VICA & TSA Clbs; OK Bapt Univ.

CRAWFORD, MECHELL; Braggs Schl; Gore, OK; (2); 4/26; Church Yth Grp; GAA; SADD; Church Choir; JV Bsktbl; Var Sftbl; Hon Roll; Northeastern ST U; Bone Specl.

CRAWFORD, MELISSA; Anadarko HS; Anadarko, OK; (3); 3/115; Pres 4-H; FBLA; HOBY; Spanish Clb; Chorus; School Musical; Rptr Yrbk; Rep Stu Cncl; 4-H Awd; NHS; Psych.

CRAWFORD, SALINA; Amber Pocasset Jr Sr HS; Pocasset, OK; (4); 1/29; FCA; Science Clb; Spanish Clb; VP Soph Cls; VP Jr Cls; JV Var Bsktbl; Var Sftbl; High Hon Roll; VP NHS; Danforth I Dare You Ldrshp Awd; U Of Cntrl OK; Spch Pthlgy.

CRAWFORD, TAMI D; Shawnee Sr HS; Shawnee, OK; (4); 99/268; FBLA; FHA; Band; Church Choir; Color Guard; Flag Corp; Mrchg Band; Var Bsktbl; Hon Roll; Jr NHS; Cnclr At Camp Cirriron; All Stars Camp At OU 95; Co-Capt Of Color Guard At Norphlet HS 94; OSU; Leisure Therapy.

CRAYK, JODIE R; Henryetta Sr HS; Henryetta, OK; (3); FCA; FHA; Library Aide; Office Aide; Band; Mrchg Band; Pep Band; Var Bsktbl; Var Sftbl; High Hon Roll; Sports Med.

CREAMER, SETH G; Cashion HS; Cashion, OK; (1); Church Yth Grp; Quiz Bowl; Band; Mrchg Band; Pep Band; Tech Stdnt Assn.

CREASY, RYAN W; Cascia Hall Prep School; Tulsa, OK; (1); Chess Clb; Church Yth Grp; Cmnty Wkr; Spanish Clb; Speech Tm; Tennis; Hon Roll; Stanford; Surgeon.

CREECH, CHARLOTTE K; Sallisaw HS; Sallisaw, OK; (2); Church Yth Grp; Spanish Clb; Band; Mrchg Band; Hon Roll; Pres Acad Fit Awd; St Hnr Soc; John Brown Univ.

CREEL, CRYSTAL; Antlers Sr HS; Snow, OK; (3); 10/75; Drama Clb; HOBY; SADD; Teachers Aide; Band; Flag Corp; Mrchg Band; Orch; Pep Band; School Play; Mgr Ftbl Tm; Upward Bound Pgm; All Dist Sympronic Band; Southeastern OK ST U; Pre-Med.

CRELLY, MARTI J; Fairview HS; Isabella, OK; (4); 21/57; Church Yth Grp; FHA; Natl FFA Org; Office Aide; Teachers Aide; Phtg Yrbk; High Hon Roll; Hon Roll; NHS.

CREMER, FIORELLA R; El Reno Sr HS; El Reno, OK; (2); Church Yth Grp; FCA; Latin Clb; Spanish Clb; Teachers Aide; Sftbl; Trk; High Hon Roll; Hon Roll; Span Clb Pres; OU; Pediatric Surgeon.

CRENSHAW, JASON A; Indianola HS; Mcalester, OK; (3); 9/30; Boy Scts; Chess Clb; Church Yth Grp; Cmnty Wkr; 4-H; FHA; Library Aide; Natl FFA Org; Varsity Clb; Pres Frsh Cls; Natl Wild Turkey Fed; North Amer Hunting Clb; NRA; Carl Albert; Wildlife Mgr; Forst.

CRESTCITELLI, JENNIFER E; Bishop Kelley HS; Broken Arrow, OK; (3); Church Yth Grp; Drama Clb; NFL; Speech Tm; School Play; Peer Hlprs; Kairos; Search; Psych.

CREWS, LISA; Westmoore HS; Oklahoma City, OK; (3); Church Yth Grp; Cmnty Wkr; FCA; Hosp Aide; Office Aide; Teachers Aide; Jr NHS; NHS; Lttr Var Trng Ftbl/Bsktbl/Sftbl; OU; Comm.

CRICK, CEBOE; Crescent Schl; Crescent, OK; (3); Church Yth Grp; Cmnty Wkr; FHA; Natl Beta Clb; Pep Clb; Red Cross Aide; Band; Jazz Band; Mrchg Band; Pep Band; Wichita ST JC.

CRICKS, CHRISTEL; Macarthur Sr HS; Lawton, OK; (4); 30/260; Art Clb; Church Yth Grp; FCA; 4-H; FHA; Hosp Aide; Office Aide; ROTC; Science Clb; Spanish Clb; JROTC Rifle Tm Co-Capt 2 Yrs; Comm Svc Awd; Cntrl MO ST Univ; Pre-Med/Phy.

CRIESFORRIBS, DESIREE L; Ponca City Middle HS; Ponca City, OK; (1); Var Bsktbl; JV Sftbl; High Hon Roll; Hon Roll; OK Univ; Arch/Engr.

CRIM, SUMMER C; Putnam City North HS; Oklahoma City, OK; (3); Church Yth Grp; FCA; Library Aide; Church Choir; Var Crs Cntry; Var Socr; Cit Awd; Hon Roll; NHS; Mission Trip Nepal; Lead Worship Bible Stud; Guitar; Singing; Art; Outdoor Act.

CRIM, TANESSA; Choctaw Jr HS; Choctaw, OK; (2); 1/350; JV Trk; High Hon Roll; Jr NHS; Pres Acad Fit Awd; Val; Environmental Clb.

CRIPPEN, LAURA; Miami Sr HS; Miami, OK; (3); 42/190; Church Yth Grp; Band; Pep Band; Ofcr Stu Cncl; Var Chrldng; Hon Roll; Jr NHS; NHS; Secondary Educ.

CRIPPS, KATHY L; Ponca City Sr HS; Ponca City, OK; (3); 7/384; Church Yth Grp; Band; Chorus; Church Choir; Mrchg Band; Orch; High Hon Roll; Hon Roll; NHS; 9th Grd Yth Alive Pres; 11th Grd Band Squad Ldr; Southwest Bapt U; Music.

CRIPPS, SHELLY; Stuart Sr HS; Stuart, OK; (3); 6/28; FHA; Scholastic Bowl; Rep Nwsp; Supt Hnr Roll; 3rd Pl Spnsh I ECU 96.

CRISP, ADAM D; Charles Page HS; Sand Springs, OK; (3); 71/371; Church Yth Grp; FCA; Key Clb; Letterman Clb; Office Aide; Spanish Clb; Teachers Aide; Varsity Clb; Chorus; Church Choir; Stage Choir Qn Escort 96; Charles Page HS Coronation Atten 94; Cntrl Jr HS Soccer; OK Dist Player 95; Med Dr.

CRISPIN-STEVENS, LUZ-AMOR; Southeast HS; Oklahoma City, OK; (4); 5/65; Am Leg Aux Girls St; Cmnty Wkr; FCA; French Clb; German Clb; Office Aide; Ed Nwsp; Ed Yrbk; Var L Chrldng; Capt L Socr; Hnrs Outstndng Acad Achvt HS; St Of OK Awd Page OK House Of Rep; 12 30 Clb; Intl Bus.

CRISSUP, CHRISTY M; Coyle Public Schl; Coyle, OK; (2); Art Clb; English Clb; FHA; German Clb; GAA; Natl FFA Org; Pep Clb.

CRISSUP, LANDON G; Norman Sr HS; Norman, OK; (4); 1/672; Church Yth Grp; FCA; NFL; Service Clb; Spanish Clb; SADD; Thesps; Chorus; Church Choir; School Musical; Lions Clb & Rotary Clb Stu Of Mnth; Chrch Ensmbl; U Of OK Cert Outstndng HS Perf; IN U-Bloomington; Vcl Perf.

CROCHET, LINDSAY C; Union Intermediate HS; Tulsa, OK; (2); Church Yth Grp; Girl Scts; Key Clb; Band; Jazz Band; Mrchg Band; Pep Band; High Hon Roll; NHS; Girl Sct Silver Awd.

CROFFORD, ZACHARY A; Holland Hall Schl; Tulsa, OK; (4); Math Clb; Acpl Chr; Jazz Band; School Play; Stage Crew; Lit Mag; JV Ftbl; Ntl Merit SF; Thesps; Chorus; Boy Scts Arts Entrtnmnt Explr Pst; Rl Plyng Clb; Art Evnts Ushr.

CROFT, JONATHAN; Moore HS; Moore, OK; (4); 181/549; Am Leg Boys St; Church Yth Grp; Cmnty Wkr; French Clb; Hosp Aide; JCL; Latin Clb; Swmmng; Cntrl Bible Coll; Pastor.

CROLEY, AMANDA J; Stilwell HS; Stilwell, OK; (2); GAA; Natl Beta Clb; Spanish Clb; Var Bsktbl; Trk; Wt Lftg; High Hon Roll; NHS.

CROMPTON, BARBRA J; Union Intermediate HS; Tulsa, OK; (1); 22/866; Band; Jazz Band; Mrchg Band; Pep Band; High Hon Roll; NHS; Comptv Soccer; Cndystrpng St Francis Hosp 2 Yrs; Excl His Awd; Spr Rtng SS Bnd Fstvl; TX A&M Univ; Med.

CROMWELL, JEREMY D; Owasso Sr HS; Owasso, OK; (4); VICA; High Hon Roll; Tulsa JC; Bus.

CRONCH, LINDSAY E; Edmond North HS; Edmond, OK; (2); #1 in class; Cmnty Wkr; Key Clb; Mu Alpha Theta; SADD; Chorus; Cit Awd; High Hon Roll; Hon Roll; Jr NHS; NHS; People To People Stu Ambdr; Duke Tip ST Math Awd; Piano/Ice Skating Lessons Superior Awds; Univ Of CO Boulden; Elem Tchr.

CRONE, DARRELL A; Mustang HS; Mustang, OK; (3); Science Clb; Jazz Band; Mrchg Band; Rep Jr Cls; Crs Cntry; Socr; Med Field.

CRONE, TRACY; Crowder Schl; Crowder, OK; (4); 3/40; FHA; Chorus; East Cntrl U; Radiology Tech.

CRONEMILLER, MISTY; Midwest City HS; Midwest City, OK; (4); 16/416; Sec Drama Clb; FHA; Pres Key Clb; Library Aide; Spanish Clb; SADD; Teachers Aide; School Musical; School Play; Stage Crew; Cmnty Svc Awd; Presdntl Acad Awd; Acad Ltr Jackt; OK ST U; Bio.

CRONINGER, ANGIE; Bartlesville Sr HS; Bartlesville, OK; (4); 85/400; Church Yth Grp; FBLA; Office Aide; Service Clb; Spanish Clb; Band; Pom Pon; Tennis; Hon Roll; NHS; Mesa ST Coll.

CRONINGER, JENNY; Bartlesville Mid HS; Bartlesville, OK; (2); Church Yth Grp; Office Aide; Spanish Clb; Co-Capt Pom Pon; High Hon Roll; Hon Roll; Jr NHS.

CRONISTER, BENJAMIN D; Crescent Schl; Crescent, OK; (2); FTA; Band; Jazz Band; Mrchg Band; Pep Band; Ofcr Bsbl; Bsktbl; Ftbl; Wt Lftg; Hon Roll; OK ST Univ.

CRONISTER, DAVID; Crescent Schl; Crescent, OK; (2); FHA; Band; Jazz Band; Mrchg Band; Pep Band; JV Bsbl; JV Bsktbl; Var Ftbl; Hon Roll; Pres Acad Fit Awd; OK ST; Vet.

CROOK, ELIZABETH D; B T Washington HS; Tulsa, OK; (4); 20/264; Var L Tennis; High Hon Roll; Hon Roll; Jr NHS; NHS; Yth Choir All Souls Unitarian Church; Yng Democrats; Amer Red Crs; Cornell Univ.

CROOK, TRACI K; Velma Alma HS; Velma, OK; (1); FCA; GAA; SADD; Chorus; Ofcr Stu Cncl; Bsktbl; Hon Roll.

CROOKS, CHRISTNA A; Pawhuska HS; Pawhuska, OK; (2); Spanish Clb; Teachers Aide; Band; Mrchg Band; Pep Band; High Hon Roll; Outstdng 8th Grd Girl Band; Mid-East OK Hon Band; Elem Tchr.

CROOKS, JUSTIN R; Putnam City North HS; Oklahoma City, OK; (3); 19/474; JCL; Latin Clb; Spanish Clb; Teachers Aide; Var Golf; High Hon Roll; Jr NHS; NHS; Pres Schlr; Personal Ftnss Bus Awd; Fin Adv.

CROSBY, ANDREW K; Del City HS; Midwest City, OK; (3); Art Clb; Church Yth Grp; Cmnty Wkr; Drama Clb; Science Clb; Church Choir; Stage Crew; Hon Roll; Tae Kwon Do; Chrch Yth Act; Music; Whitman Coll; Marine Biologist.

CROSBY, SHARESE N; Mc Lain Career Acad; Tulsa, OK; (3); Church Yth Grp; ROTC; Hon Roll; Phy Thrpst.

CROSIER, ASHLEY R; Deer Creek HS; Edmond, OK; (3); Science Clb; School Play; Powder Puff Ftbl; JV Var Socr; OSU.

CROSLEY, JULIE D; Putnam City North HS; Oklahoma City, OK; (2); Church Yth Grp; FCA; Orch; Socr; Hon Roll; NHS; 3-D, Dont Do Drugs; Lifeguard Trng Cert; 1st Aid & CPR.

CROSLIN, JENNIFER A; Midwest City HS; Midwest City, OK; (3); FHA; ROTC; Dep Commndr Delayed Enlstmnt Prgm US Air Force; Radar Specst AWACS Air Force.

OKLAHOMA

CROSS, ANDREW N; Stillwater Sr HS; Stillwater, OK; (4); Office Aide; Nwsp; L Crs Cntry; L Trk; Hon Roll; Pres Acad Fit Awd; Var Schlr; Rnnr Of Wk Crs Cntry; OK St Univ; Arch.

CROSS, CHRISTOPHER B; Fletcher Jr Sr HS; Fletcher, OK; (4); 1/35; Rep Church Yth Grp; Cmnty Wkr; Pres Computer Clb; Capt FCA; 4-H; FHA; HOBY; Natl FFA Org; Capt Quiz Bowl; Capt Scholastic Bowl; OK St Comp Aided Drftng/Dsgn St Chmpn; Tech Stu Assn Wrttn Tech St Chmpn; Wendys Heisman Awd Wnnr OK; OK ST U; Biosystems Engrng.

CROSS, DEVIN; Chandler HS; Chandler, OK; (3); 13/87; Church Yth Grp; FCA; GAA; Girl Scts; Natl FFA Org; Spanish Clb; Sec Jr Cls; Bsktbl; Var L Sftbl; Hon Roll.

CROSS, JOHNATHAN W; Fletcher Jr Sr HS; Fletcher, OK; (1); 1/39; Church Yth Grp; Pres Cmnty Wkr; Computer Clb; FCA; 4-H; Capt Scholastic Bowl; Science Clb; Church Choir; Orch; Co-Ed Nwsp; St Natl Geography Bee Fnlst; St Spllng Bee Fnlst; OK Geography Water Awrnss Poster Cont Wnnr; OK ST U; Aerospc Engrng.

CROSS, JUSTIN E; Stillwater Sr HS; Stillwater, OK; (2); Drama Clb; Thesps; CSU; Wildlife Mngmt/Cmptr Engr.

CROSS, RYAN; Broken Arrow Sr HS; Broken Arrow, OK; (4); 1/921; Am Leg Boys St; Church Yth Grp; VP French Clb; Quiz Bowl; Church Choir; Var L Swmmng; Treas NHS; Ntl Merit Ltr; Prfct Atten Awd; Val; OK U; Bus.

CROSSE, CHERYL A; Lawton Sr HS; Lawton, OK; (2); Band; Chorus; Color Guard; Mrchg Band; Pep Band; Stage Crew; Sftbl; Hon Roll; Band Ltr; MI ST; Vet.

CROSSLAND, JAMIE B; North Intemediate HS; Broken Arrow, OK; (2); Hon Roll; AZ ST U; Biolgst.

CROSSLAND, MICHAEL D; Grandfield Jr Sr HS; Grandfield, OK; (2); 10/26; Church Yth Grp; Natl FFA Org; Church Choir; Stage Crew; Pres Frsh Cls; Ofcr Stu Cncl; Var Ftbl; Wt Lftg; Hon Roll; Prfct Atten Awd; Tech Stud Assc; Pres Frosh/Soph; Star Grnhnd Awd Frosh; Spclty Anml Prod/Wldlf Mngmt Prfc; OSU; Wildlife Bio.

CROSSWHITE, SHANNON; Crescent Schl; Crescent, OK; (4); 6/35; Church Yth Grp; Natl Beta Clb; Office Aide; Band; Rep Frsh Cls; Ofcr Stu Cncl; High Hon Roll; Hon Roll; NHS; Pres Acad Fit Awd; Pilot.

CROSSWY, KARA K; Bixby Sr HS; Bixby, OK; (1); Natl FFA Org; Quiz Bowl; Chrldng; Socr; Hon Roll; Jr NHS; Pres Acad Fit Awd; OK U; Surgeon.

CROUCH, CHRIS M; West Middle HS; Norman, OK; (1); Drama Clb; Spanish Clb; School Play; High Hon Roll; Teen Vol; Music; Creative Writing.

CROUCH, CURTIS R; Chandler HS; Chandler, OK; (4); 17/65; Boy Scts; Office Aide; Spanish Clb; Band; Mrchg Band; SE Univ; Aviation.

CROUCH, SUSAN B; Heritage Chrstn Home Schl; Tecumseh, OK; (1); CAP; 4-H; Stage Crew; Vllybl; 4-H Awd; Hon Roll; 4-H Sec; 1st Pl Dist Vllybl Team.

CROW, ANDREA; Marlow HS; Marlow, OK; (3); 8/105; Church Yth Grp; SADD; Band; Drm Mjr(t); Jazz Band; Mrchg Band; Yrbk; Var Trk; High Hon Roll; NHS; Travelled To England With OK Bapt All-St Choir & Orch 94-95; U Of OK.

CROW, GRETCHEN; Stilwell HS; Stilwell, OK; (3); Church Yth Grp; FBLA; Natl Beta Clb; Spanish Clb; Speech Tm; Capt Color Guard; School Musical; Rptr Nwsp; Chrldng; Hon Roll; Poetry, Story Wrtng; Northeastern ST U; Jrnlsm.

CROW, JAMIE; Walters HS; Walters, OK; (3); Church Yth Grp; FHA; Scholastic Bowl; Chorus; School Musical; School Play; High Hon Roll; Hon Roll; All-Amer Schlr Awd; Southwestern OK ST U.

CROW, JENNIFER; Washita Heights Schl; Corn, OK; (4); 1/12; Church Yth Grp; FHA; German Clb; GAA; Teachers Aide; Band; School Play; Yrbk; Pres Frsh Cls; Pres Soph Cls; Natl Bsktbll Tnrmnt MVP & All-Amer Tm 2 Yrs; OK St U; Pre-Med.

CROWDIS, CASEY E; Duncan HS; Duncan, OK; (2); Boy Scts; Bsktbl; Hon Roll; NHS; Chrch Yth Cncl, Jesus Video Project, Yth Ministry & Sftbl Team; Vllybl; OK ST Univ.

CROWDIS, NATALIE A; Duncan HS; Duncan, OK; (1); Church Yth Grp; Key Clb; Spanish Clb; DAR Awd; Hon Roll; Lucky Circle Clb; Chrch Act; High Impact Arobics Ftns & Nutrition.

CROWE, AMBER N; Putnam City West HS; Bethany, OK; (2); Church Yth Grp; Intnl Clb; Pep Clb; Spanish Clb; Acpl Chr; Church Choir; Var Chrldng; Mexico Missionary; Cmnty Hlpr; Mat Maid; Rhema Univ; Mnstry/Vcl.

CROWE, CHRISTY E; Union Intermediate HS; Broken Arrow, OK; (1); Church Yth Grp; FCA; Spanish Clb; Drill Tm; Ofcr Frsh Cls; Hon Roll; Jr NHS; NHS; Dnc Clss; Intr Dscn.

CROWELL, HEATHER; Union Sr HS; Tulsa, OK; (3); Treas 4-H; FBLA; Teachers Aide; Cit Awd; 4-H Awd; HERO Clb Tulsa Technlgy Clss Pres, Campus VP; Cty Fair Fashn Show/4-H Fashn Revue Cmmntr/Coord/Modl; TX Wesleyan; Fashn Dsgn.

CRUICKSHANK, KRISTEN R; Cascia Hall Prep School; Owasso, OK; (1); Cmnty Wkr; Drama Clb; Office Aide; Teachers Aide; Church Choir; School Play; Swmmng; High Hon Roll; Slvr Hnr Rll; Otstndng Schvmnt Awd Hist I, Span, Bio, Spch I, Hist II, Nw Tstmnt, Grmmr; Law.

CRULL, CRYSTAL; Pauls Valley HS; Pauls Valley, OK; (4); 35/31; French Clb; FHA; Key Clb; Office Aide; SADD; Teachers Aide; Var Chrldng; Trk; Cit Awd; High Hon Roll; Ftbl Homcmng Qn 96; Voted Bst All Around Of Sr Cls; Miss Panther.

CRUM, WANDA C; Mc Lain Career Acad; Tulsa, OK; (4); Church Yth Grp; FTA; Nwsp; Cit Awd; Hon Roll; Kiwanis Awd; NHS; Prfct Atten Awd; Eng Awd; Prin Hnr Roll; OU; Jrnlsm.

CRUMB, RHONDA L; Tipton Jr Sr HS; Tipton, OK; (2); 2/36; Hist FHA; Quiz Bowl; VP Science Clb; Band; Mrchg Band; Bsktbl; Mgr(s); Cit Awd; Hon Roll; Jr NHS; OK Chrstn; Law Or Comp.

CRUMMETT, JILL M; Stillwater Sr HS; Stillwater, OK; (2); Church Yth Grp; Spanish Clb; Teachers Aide; Northern OK Coll; Engrng.

CRUMP, DAVID D; Putnam City West HS; Bethany, OK; (2); School Play; JV Ftbl; Var Trk; Art/Math/Sci; OU; Arch.

CRUMP, MELISSA G; Putnam City West HS; Bethany, OK; (3); 57/300; Drama Clb; French Clb; Intnl Clb; Stage Crew; Trk; NHS; Soc Sci.

CRUSE, BRANDI A; Velma Alma HS; Duncan, OK; (4); FCA; SADD; Teachers Aide; Rep Stu Cncl; Var Bsktbl; Var Crs Cntry; Var Trk; Hon Roll; NHS; Pres Acad Fit Awd; Southeastern.

CRUSE, JAMMIE; Heavener HS; Howe, OK; (4); 4/86; FBLA; Treas FHA; Office Aide; Science Clb; Spanish Clb; Hon Roll; NHS; Sal; Carl Albert ST Coll; Bus Ed.

CRUTCHER, CHARMAINE R; Eisenhower Sr HS; Lawton, OK; (3); Church Yth Grp; Cmnty Wkr; Drama Clb; FCA; Key Clb; Library Aide; Pep Clb; Chorus; Church Choir; School Musical; Teen Crt; Chrch Dancing & Chrldng; WA U; Law.

CRUTCHFIELD, ANDREA; Memorial HS; Tulsa, OK; (4); 8/250; French Clb; Intnl Clb; Pep Clb; Teachers Aide; Sec Soph Cls; Rep Stu Cncl; Capt Chrldng; Powder Puff Ftbl; Swmmng; High Hon Roll; Gamma Sigma; Intl Awds Physics & French.

CRUTCHFIELD, CALEB; Choctaw Jr HS; Choctaw, OK; (1); Church Yth Grp; FCA; Bsktbl; Ftbl; Trk; High Hon Roll; Jr NHS; Arch.

CRUTCHMER, MATT; Edmond Memorial HS; Edmond, OK; (4); #1 in class; Am Leg Boys St; Church Yth Grp; Pres FCA; Math Clb; Mu Alpha Theta; Science Clb; Spanish Clb; L Trk; High Hon Roll; NHS; Spr Fns Edmnd Mem HS Ldr.

CRUTENFIELD, AMY; Edmond Memorial HS; Edmond, OK; (1); 1/431; Church Yth Grp; FCA; Spanish Clb; SADD; Chorus; Variety Show; Chrldng; Hon Roll; Ed.

CRUZN, LAFE C; Chisholm Sr HS; Enid, OK; (2); Chess Clb; Church Yth Grp; FCA; Church Choir; Jazz Band; Ofcr Bsbl; Bsktbl; Ftbl; Wt Lftg; Hon Roll; Sprts Med.

CUBLE, DENOTRIN R; Spiro HS; Fort Smith, AR; (3); Church Yth Grp; FCA; FHA; GAA; Nwsp; VP Frsh Cls; VP Soph Cls; JV Var Bsktbl; Co-Capt Chrldng; Var Trk; OSU; Pediatrican.

CUDJOE, JAMILLA; Millwood HS; Oklahoma City, OK; (3); Church Yth Grp; FHA; VICA; Bus Adm.

CUELLAR, CRYSTAL; Carney Schl; Carney, OK; (3); 5/22; Church Yth Grp; FCA; HOBY; Natl FFA Org; Quiz Bowl; Spanish Clb; Yrbk; Pres Frsh Cls; Rep Stu Cncl; Hon Roll; OK ST U; Bus.

CUERVO, MARTA; Nathan Hale HS; Tulsa, OK; (3); Church Yth Grp; Cmnty Wkr; Drama Clb; FCA; French Clb; Key Clb; Office Aide; Golf; Vllybl; Comp Challnge; 3rd Pl Runway Model In S W Regn; Guitar; Accntng.

CULBERT, LASHELL M; Northeast HS; Oklahoma City, OK; (3); Church Yth Grp; FBLA; Pep Clb; Chorus; Church Choir; Mgr(s); Score Keeper; Hon Roll; Ntl Merit Schol; Lawyer.

CULBERT, STEPHEN; Moore HS; Moore, OK; (4); 25/600; Boy Scts; Hist German Clb; Model UN; Pres Mu Alpha Theta; Capt Quiz Bowl; Science Clb; Band; NHS; Ntl Merit SF; Val; Outstndg Govt Stu; Eagle Sct; OK ST U; Paleontlgy.

CULIE, EDDIE; Locust Grove HS; Hulbert, OK; (2); Ftbl; Wrstlng.

CULLEN, LAURA; Mustang HS; Mustang, OK; (2); Spanish Clb; SADD; Teachers Aide; Chorus; NHS; U Of OK; Cnslr/Scndry Eng Tchr.

CULLEY, LELA; Mason HS; Okemah, OK; (3); GAA; HOBY; Sec Frsh Cls; VP Soph Cls; Rep Stu Cncl; Bsktbl; Sftbl; Trk; Vllybl; Cit Awd; Pres Indian Club; Hmcmng Queen 95, 96; Comp.

CULLEY, TARSHA; Holdenville HS; Holdenville, OK; (2); 12/85; Church Yth Grp; Drama Clb; Band; Chorus; Church Choir; Mrchg Band; School Play; Hon Roll; Interschltc Team; Nurse.

CULLISON, BRIAN T; Ponca City Sr HS; Ponca City, OK; (3); #60 in class; Spanish Clb; Socr; Hon Roll; Jr NHS; Ntl Merit Ltr; Pres Acad Fit Awd; Fin; Stock Market.

CULLISON, LESLEE D; El Reno Sr HS; El Reno, OK; (4); 31/161; Church Yth Grp; FTA; Treas Key Clb; Math Clb; Science Clb; Band; Drm Mjr(t); Mrchg Band; Nwsp; Yrbk; OK City U; RN.

CULLISON, STEPHANIE H; Owasso Sr HS; Owasso, OK; (4); 96/296; Church Yth Grp; Office Aide; Science Clb; SADD; Band; Mrchg Band; Pep Band; Ofcr Stu Cncl; Prfct Atten Awd; 2 Yrs All Region Bnd; Bnd Part OMEA 95-96; Part Univ AR 4 Yrs Pl Top Bnd; Univ Of Tulsa; Grphc Dsgn.

CULLOM, ERICA; Union Intermediate HS; Tulsa, OK; (1); FCA; Hist Math Clb; Office Aide; Spanish Clb; Pres VP Stu Cncl; Bsktbl; JV Capt Chrldng; Hon Roll; NHS; Drug Free Yth; Afrcn Amer Soc Clb; Child Psych.

CULVER, BENJAMIN; Pawhuska HS; Pawhuska, OK; (3); 1/100; Boy Scts; Church Yth Grp; Computer Clb; FCA; FBLA; HOBY; Key Clb; Quiz Bowl; Science Clb; Spanish Clb; Rotary Yth Ldr Awd; BSA Order Arrow, Section Sec; KU; Med.

CULVER, WHIT; Pawhuska HS; Pawhuska, OK; (3); 1/110; Am Leg Boys St; Boy Scts; Pres Church Yth Grp; FCA; Pres FBLA; Key Clb; Quiz Bowl; Science Clb; Spanish Clb; Teachers Aide; Rotary Youth Ldr Awd; Boy Scouts Of Amer; Eagle Scout; OK ST; Law.

CUMMINGS, CARRIE E; Sapulpa Sr HS; Sapulpa, OK; (4); 5/279; Pres Church Yth Grp; Math Clb; Science Clb; SADD; High Hon Roll; NHS; Prfct Atten Awd; Pres Schlr; OK Hnr Soc; U Of OK; Intl Rel.

CUMMINGS, CHRISTOPHER A; Union Sr HS; Tulsa, OK; (4); 67/632; Church Yth Grp; Cmnty Wkr; FCA; Intnl Clb; Key Clb; Spanish Clb; Teachers Aide; Band; Yrbk; Rep Jr Cls; Mech Engrng.

CUMMINGS, JARROD K; Claremore Sr HS; Claremore, OK; (1); Church Yth Grp; Socr; Hon Roll; Chrch Mssnry Wrk; 4-Yr Univ.

CUMMINGS, KIM; Ardmore HS; Ardmore, OK; (1); Chrldng; Golf; Hon Roll; Jr NHS.

CUMMINGS, KIMBERLEY R; Del City HS; Del City, OK; (2); Intrml Bsktbl; Var Vllybl; Hon Roll; NHS; Law.

CUMMINS, AMANDA S; Colbert Jr Sr HS; Colbert, OK; (3); Computer Clb; FHA; Phtg Yrbk; Cit Awd; Prfct Atten Awd; VICA Club; TSA; Southeastern OK ST Univ; Cmpr.

CUMMINS, BOBBY A; Bartlesville Mid HS; Bartlesville, OK; (2); Church Yth Grp; Letterman Clb; Ofcr Jr Cls; JV Var Ftbl; Var Wrstlng; Hon Roll; Bartlesville Mid-HS Ath Ltr Awd; Cert Of Achvmt DARE; Cert Of Awd Acad Excl; OK ST Univ; Surgeon; Engr.

CUMMINS, CLARISHA; Warner HS; Warner, OK; (4); VP FCA; Yrbk; Ofcr Stu Cncl; Capt Bsktbl; Var Chrldng; Capt Crs Cntry; Capt Sftbl; High Hon Roll; NHS; Hmcmng Attndt; Connors ST; Pre-Med/Dctr.

CUMMINS, MARY E; West Middle HS; Norman, OK; (2); Church Yth Grp; FCA; Mu Alpha Theta; Spanish Clb; Chorus; Church Choir; Ofcr Stu Cncl; Trk; High Hon Roll; Hon Roll; Choir Ltr; Snow Choir; SWASS; OK Hnr Soc; Yng Life; COCDA; Pres Awd Ed Excl Vol; Ldrshp Acad; OK Univ; OT.

CUMPSTON, KELLY L; Mc Loud HS; Mc Loud, OK; (1); Church Yth Grp; FCA; GAA; Pep Clb; Variety Show; JV Bsktbl; JV Chrldng; JV Mgr(s); JV Score Keeper; Intrml Sftbl; OSU.

CUNDIFF, BRETT S; Colcord Schl; Colcord, OK; (4); 4/42; Church Yth Grp; FBLA; FHA; Treas Frsh Cls; Rep Soph Cls; VP Jr Cls; Var L Bsbl; Co-Capt Bsktbl; Var L Ftbl; Var Trk; Northeastern ST U.

CUNG, NGO H; Westmoore HS; Oklahoma City, OK; (4); 35/610; Church Yth Grp; Cmnty Wkr; French Clb; Math Tm; Science Clb; Intrml Bsktbl; Intrml Swmmng; JV Tennis; Cit Awd; Hon Roll; OK Del DOE HS Hnr Rsrch Pgrmsandia Lab; NSF Yng Schlrs Pgrm; 1st Plc OK ST Sci/Engr Fair 96; OK ST Univ; Pre Med.

CUNNINGHAM, CARA M; Westmoore HS; Oklahoma City, OK; (4); 232/610; DECA; Hist Drama Clb; Sec School Musical; Mgr School Play; Stage Crew; Mgr Variety Show; Ofcr Stu Cncl; PRIDE; Mrktg Ed-Top Stu 1st Yr; Southwestern OK ST U; Pharmcy.

CUNNINGHAM, CHRISTIN D; Putnam City North HS; Oklahoma City, OK; (1); Church Yth Grp; Girl Scts; Chorus; Church Choir; Vllybl; PEAD 3d Childrens Ministry; OK ST; Ministry; Perf Arts.

CUNNINGHAM, CHRISTOPHER; Guthrie Sr HS; Arcadia, OK; (4); 53/253; FCA; French Clb; FBLA; FHA; Natl FFA Org; Ofcr Sr Cls; Var Bsbl; Capt Ftbl; Var Wt Lftg; Panhandle ST U.

CUNNINGHAM, CHRISTOPHER C; Eisenhoser HS; Lawton, OK; (4); Church Yth Grp; FHA; Science Clb; SADD; VICA; School Play; Rep Soph Cls; Rep Jr Cls; Rep Sr Cls; JV Bsbl; Mechanic.

CUNNINGHAM, CHRISTOPHER K; Jenks HS; Jenks, OK; (4); 169/540; Cmnty Wkr; FCA; Natl FFA Org; Office Aide; Teachers Aide; Hon Roll; Prfct Atten Awd; Tulsa Jr Coll; Bio.

CUNNINGHAM, COLE; Stillwater Sr HS; Stillwater, OK; (2); Boy Scts; School Musical; Bus.

CUNNINGHAM, ERIN R; Ponca City Sr HS; Ponca City, OK; (4); 56/338; Church Yth Grp; FCA; Pep Clb; Spanish Clb; SADD; Teachers Aide; Chorus; JV Var Bsktbl; High Hon Roll; Hon Roll; Schl Geography Awd; Sch Geometry Awd; Multi Yr Listee; Dodge City CC; Educ.

CUNNINGHAM, JENNIFER D; Hartshorne Sr HS; Hartshorne, OK; (4); 7/45; Sec Church Yth Grp; Library Aide; Teachers Aide; Ed Nwsp; Ofcr Stu Cncl; Bsktbl; Sftbl; Hon Roll; All-Amer Schlr; OK Hnr Soc; Outstdng Plyr Kiamichi All-Star Sftbl; Eastern OK ST Coll; Optometry.

CUNNINGHAM, JOHN L; Memorial HS; Tulsa, OK; (2); Church Yth Grp; Bsktbl; Crs Cntry; Socr; Wt Lftg; High Hon Roll; Hon Roll; KS Univ; Mech Engr.

CUNNINGHAM, LEWIS; Plainview HS; Springer, OK; (3); 2/87; Am Leg Boys St; Church Yth Grp; FCA; 4-H; Latin Clb; Math Clb; Mu Alpha Theta; Natl Beta Clb; Quiz Bowl; Science Clb; OK ST Univ; Ag Ec.

CUNNINGHAM, MINDY R; Duncan HS; Duncan, OK; (3); 9/259; Hosp Aide; Sec Key Clb; Pres Spanish Clb; SADD; Rep Sr Cls; JV Tennis; High Hon Roll; NHS; Pres Acad Fit Awd; Pre-Medicine.

CUNNINGHAM, RHONDA; Anadarko HS; Anadarko, OK; (4); 15/104; Am Leg Aux Girls St; Church Yth Grp; FCA; Sec FBLA; Office Aide; Spanish Clb; Church Choir; Ed Yrbk; Treas Soph Cls; Rep Sr Cls; Octagon Clb VP; U Of OK; Mrktng.

CUNNINGHAM III, ROBERT; Midwest City HS; Midwest City, OK; (2); 15/488; Church Yth Grp; FCA; Letterman Clb; Spanish Clb; SADD; Varsity Clb; Ofcr Bsbl; Ftbl; Wt Lftg; Cit Awd; Water Skiing; Motorcycle Racing Circuit.

CUNNINGHAM, STACEY; Newcastle HS; Newcastle, OK; (2); Art Clb; FBLA; Spanish Clb; Chrldng; Hon Roll; NHS; Summer Sci Camp; Med.

CUNNINGHAM, SUSAN J; Fletcher Jr Sr HS; Fletcher, OK; (3); HOBY; Yrbk; Rep Jr Cls; Rep Stu Cncl; Chrldng; Vllybl; Amer Legion Voice Demcrcy Essay Wnnr; Amer Legion Masonic Toptimist Clb Outstndng Stu Awds.

CUNNINGHAM, TIFFANY D; John Marshall HS; Oklahoma City, OK; (3); Church Yth Grp; Dance Clb; DECA; French Clb; Varsity Clb; Chorus; Church Choir; Chrldng; High Hon Roll; Hon Roll; DECA VP; Outstdng Stu Of Yr Awd In Mrktg Pgm; Mrktg.

CUPP, DUSTIN W; Putnam City North HS; Oklahoma City, OK; (2); Church Yth Grp; Spanish Clb; Rep Frsh Cls; JV Var Bsbl; JV Bsktbl; JV Ftbl; Hon Roll; NHS; Clay Culver Awd; Outstdng Anatomy & Physiology Stu; Think Ink Wrtng Awd.

CUPP, KITTY R; Putnam City North HS; Edmond, OK; (4); 21/2; Church Yth Grp; Drama Clb; Pres Rep Key Clb; Treas Science Clb; Ofcr Stu Cncl; Pom Pon; Kiwanis Awd; NHS; PEAK Gifted/Talented; Panther Pals Grp Ldr Stdnts To Kids; OK Bapt Univ.

CUPPS, COURTNEY; Sapulpa Sr HS; Sapulpa, OK; (2); 54/349; Band; Color Guard; Flag Corp; Mrchg Band; Hon Roll; Spanish NHS; Band Aid; OSU; Vet.

CURRAN, DEVIN M; Enid Sr HS; Enid, OK; (2); 16/520; FCA; Quiz Bowl; Scholastic Bowl; Spanish Clb; Lit Mag; Rep Soph Cls; Ftbl; Trk; High Hon Roll; NHS.

CURRAN, LAURA; Midwest City HS; Oklahoma City, OK; (3); FBLA; FHA; Color Guard; Drill Tm; Nwsp; Nrsng.

CURREN, GERALD; Tecumseh HS; Tecumseh, OK; (4); 16/128; Pres 4-H; Mu Alpha Theta; Natl Beta Clb; Treas Natl FFA Org; VP Science Clb; SADD; Ed Nwsp; Rptr Sr Cls; Cit Awd; 4-H Awd; Life Guides 2 Yrs; St Gregorys Coll; Dentstry.

CURREN, GINGER Y; Pond Creek-Hunter Schl; Pond Creek, OK; (3); Drama Clb; Pep Clb; School Musical; School Play; Hon Roll; Alt Delg HOBY Fndtn; Psych.

CURRIN, BRANDI; Okmulgee HS; Okmulgee, OK; (2); Church Yth Grp; Science Clb; Bsktbl; Mgr(s); Trk; Hon Roll; Ntl Merit Ltr; U Of Cntrl OK; Lgl Sec.

CURRY, ANITA L; Cherokee Jr Sr HS; Cherokee, OK; (3); Debate Tm; Drama Clb; FHA; Spanish Clb; Teachers Aide; Chorus; School Musical; School Play; Variety Show; Rptr Nwsp; Outs Acad Achv; Publshed Authr; Zoolgy.

CURRY, BRANDON; Ardmore HS; Ardmore, OK; (4); 2/173; Am Leg Boys St; FCA; Mu Alpha Theta; Science Clb; VP Spanish Clb; Hon Roll; NHS; Ntl Merit SF; Ofcr Bsbl; Crs Cntry; OU.

CURRY, CHRISTOPHER S; Jay HS; Eucha, OK; (3); FCA; Natl Beta Clb; High Hon Roll; NHS; Martial Arts; Scuba Dvr; Golf.

CURRY, JENNIFER; Lawton Sr HS; Lawton, OK; (3); Church Yth Grp; FCA; Chorus; Cit Awd; High Hon Roll; Jr NHS; NHS; Rep OK Miss Teen Amer Prgm San Diego CA; Prvt Violin/Piano Lessons; OK Chrstn; OT.

CURRY, JOY M; Westmoore HS; Oklahoma City, OK; (1); 1/350; Church Yth Grp; VP French Clb; Rep Stu Cncl; Chrldng; Cit Awd; Jr NHS; Masonic Awd; Pres Educ Awd Edctnl Excellence; Med.

CURRY, KARRIE D; Norman Sr HS; Norman, OK; (4); Church Yth Grp; Cmnty Wkr; FCA; GAA; JA; Letterman Clb; Red Cross Aide; Spanish Clb; SADD; Varsity Clb; Young Life; TX Chrstn Univ; Sports Psych.

CURRY, MICHELLE; Cookson Hills Chrn Schl; Kansas, OK; (4); 1/7; Chorus; Var Capt Bsktbl; Var Trk; Var Capt Vllybl; High Hon Roll; Val; Piano; Bartlesville Wesleyan Coll.

CURRY, RYAN G; Catoosa HS; Catoosa, OK; (3); 15/150; Am Leg Boys St; French Clb; Bsktbl; Ftbl; Socr; High Hon Roll; Hon Roll; NHS; Prfct Atten Awd; OK City Univ; Med.

CURRY, RYAN J; John Marshall HS; Oklahoma City, OK; (2); Church Yth Grp; Drama Clb; ROTC; School Musical; School Play; Stage Crew; Hon Roll.

CURRY, SAMMI B; Jay HS; Jay, OK; (4); 25/96; FHA; Mu Alpha Theta; Natl Beta Clb; Natl FFA Org; Rptr Sr Cls; Hon Roll; NHS; Indian Club VP; I-Dfy; Peer Cncl; Northeastern ST Univ; Acct.

CURTIS, AUSTIN M; Muskogee HS; Muskogee, OK; (2); 11/467; French Clb; Var Sftbl; High Hon Roll; RAID; OK Hnr Scty 2 Yrs; Dlphc Club; Rookie Sftbl Plyr Of Yr 95; All Dist Sftbl Plyr 94-95; OK Univ; PT.

CURTIS, CHRISTOPHER H; Pauls Valley HS; Pauls Valley, OK; (2); #1 in class; Pres Church Yth Grp; Scholastic Bowl; Spanish Clb; Band; Church Choir; Mrchg Band; School Musical; High Hon Roll; NHS; Pres Acad Fit Awd.

CURTIS, DALLAS; El Reno Sr HS; El Reno, OK; (4); 10/176; Am Leg Boys St; JA; Variety Show; Bsktbl; Ftbl; Cit Awd; Hon Roll; NHS; Stu Advsry Cncl Vice Chm; All Big City Ftbl; Math & Sci Clb Pres; Northeastern ST U OK.

CURTIS, JAIME; Guymon Sr HS; Guymon, OK; (2); Church Yth Grp; FCA; French Clb; Chorus; Chrldng.

CURTIS, JUSTINA A; Stillwater Sr HS; Stillwater, OK; (2); #85 in class; Natl FFA Org; Hon Roll; Pub Spkng; Var Schlr; Pres Ed Awds Prgm; TX A&M Univ; Mar Bio/Zoology.

CURTIS, KELLI; Guymon Sr HS; Guymon, OK; (2); Church Yth Grp; FCA; French Clb; GAA; Letterman Clb; Chorus; Bsktbl; Chrldng; Crs Cntry; Trk; Masonic Stu Of Today.

CURTIS, LACIE J; Shawnee Sr HS; Shawnee, OK; (3); Art Clb; Dance Clb; Drama Clb; French Clb; FHA; Thesps; Band; Mrchg Band; School Musical; School Play; DECA 2 Outstdng Awds; St Genasians; 1st Pl Radio Drama Awd; TV; Radio Broadcasting.

CURTIS, MARK; Blanche Thomas Jr Sr HS; Sentinel, OK; (4); 1/28; Church Yth Grp; Natl Beta Clb; Scholastic Bowl; Teachers Aide; Capt Bsktbl; Hon Roll; NHS; Pres Acad Fit Awd; Val; St Schlr; Southwestern ST OK Univ.

CURTIS, MISTY; Bridge Creek HS; Tuttle, OK; (3); 1/73; FCA; HOBY; Spanish Clb; Sec Frsh Cls; VP Soph Cls; Treas Stu Cncl; Var Bsktbl; High Hon Roll; Sec NHS; Prfct Atten Awd; Phys Thrpy.

CUSACK, JILLIAN; Jarman Jr HS; Moore, OK; (1); Drama Clb; German Clb; Girl Scts; Quiz Bowl; Scholastic Bowl; Treas Spanish Clb; Golf; Jr NHS; GSA Slvr Awd.

CUSHMAN, ROYANNA; Seminole Jr Sr HS; Seminole, OK; (4); 6/90; French Clb; FHA; Math Clb; Math Tm; NFL; Quiz Bowl; Science Clb; Nwsp; Kiwanis Awd; NHS; East Cntrl U Of OK; Chldhd Ed.

CUSIMANO, JOEL V; Sallisaw HS; Sallisaw, OK; (2); Natl FFA Org; Spanish Clb; Cit Awd; Hon Roll; Jr NHS; NHS; OK HS Rodeo Assn; Natl HS Rodeo Assn; Amer Qrtr Hrs Yth Assn.

CUSKEY, JUSTIN; Ripley HS; Perkins, OK; (4); 6/31; FBLA; HOBY; Math Clb; Natl FFA Org; Quiz Bowl; Scholastic Bowl; Spanish Clb; Mgr(s); Hon Roll; NHS; OSU; Bus.

CUSTER, DOUGLAS; Aline-Cleo Jr Sr HS; Aline, OK; (2); Natl FFA Org; VICA; Var JV Bsktbl; JV Golf; Cit Awd; Hon Roll; NHS; Prfct Atten Awd; Attends Barber Coll During Summers; NW OK ST Univ; Law Enforcmnt.

CUSTER, J W; Cushing HS; Cushing, OK; (2); 12/160; Church Yth Grp; Cmnty Wkr; FCA; Math Clb; Natl FFA Org; L Bsbl; Bsktbl; L Ftbl; L Wt Lftg; High Hon Roll.

CUTARAN, KATHREENA; Midwest City HS; Oklahoma City, OK; (2); 32/501; Church Yth Grp; French Clb; Letterman Clb; Pep Clb; Band; Church Choir; Mrchg Band; Pep Band; Rptr Nwsp; Ed Yrbk; 4.0 Schlstc Clb; Acad Achvt Awd; Band Wind Emsmbl; Notre Dame.

CUTHBERTSON, KATHERINE; Midwest City HS; Midwest City, OK; (3); 1/400; German Clb; Spanish Clb; SADD; Teachers Aide; Ofcr Jr Cls; Mgr Bsbl; Var Chrldng; Mgr Ftbl; Jr NHS; NHS; U Of OK; Med.

CUTHRIELL, APRIL; Choctaw HS; Nicoma Park, OK; (3); FHA; School Play; Prfct Atten Awd; Jr Mem Of Sooner Beagle Clb & Heartland Beagle Clb Of OK; Child Dev.

CYNTHIA, TAYLOR V; Muldrow HS; Muldrow, OK; (4); Art Clb; FHA; GAA; Pep Clb; Varsity Clb; Nwsp; Trk; Vllybl; Hon Roll; Contestant Jr Miss Pageant; HS Beauty.

CYPERT, JACKIE; Putnam City HS; Warr Acres, OK; (3); 41/327; Church Yth Grp; Var FCA; Science Clb; Teachers Aide; VP Jr Cls; Ofcr Stu Cncl; Var L Bsktbl; Var L Ftbl; Hon Roll; DECCA; 3-D; Indstrl Engr.

CYPERT, KELSIE; South Intermediate HS; Broken Arrow, OK; (1); Church Yth Grp; Church Choir; Intrml Bsktbl; Intrml JV Vllybl; Tulsa Clb Vllybl; Sports Med.

CYPERT, LEROY D; Tahlequah Sr HS; Tahlequah, OK; (3); Church Yth Grp; FHA; SADD; VICA; Chorus; VP SADD; Drug Free/Safe Schl Advsry Cncl; Okmulgee Tech; Culinary Chef.

CZARNECKI, JOE C; Mustang HS; Yukon, OK; (3); High Hon Roll; Southwestern OK ST; Pharm.

DAFFORN, ROBIN L; East Central HS; Tulsa, OK; (3); French Clb; Key Clb; School Play; Var Tennis; Hon Roll; NHS; U Of CA; Pub Rltns/Brdcstng.

DAFT, AMANDA M; Fletcher Jr Sr HS; Fletcher, OK; (2); 2/44; Church Yth Grp; FCA; Office Aide; Pep Clb; Band; Chorus; Yrbk; Bsktbl; Chrldng; Ofcr Bsbl; Cameron; Dentist.

DAGGETT, HEIDI L; Leedey Schl; Leedey, OK; (3); Church Yth Grp; Drama Clb; FHA; Chorus; Hon Roll; SW ST Univ Of OK; Mrktng/PR.

DAHLGREN, CHAD; Tuttle HS; Tuttle, OK; (4); 9/77; Church Yth Grp; Scholastic Bowl; Varsity Clb; Var Bsktbl; Cit Awd; Hon Roll; NHS; FL Inst Of Tech; Cmptr Engr.

DAHLGREN, ERIC; Tuttle HS; Tuttle, OK; (1); Church Yth Grp; Natl FFA Org; Bsktbl; Ftbl; Trk.

DAHLGREN, RYAN W; Davis HS; Davis, OK; (1); Art Clb; Key Clb; Quiz Bowl; Spanish Clb; Comp; Bks.

DAHR, MONA; Heritage Hall Schl; Oklahoma City, OK; (2); Debate Tm; HOBY; Mu Alpha Theta; NFL; Spanish Clb; Ed Lit Mag; Rep Stu Cncl; L Fld Hcky; High Hon Roll; Spanish NHS.

DAILEY, MICHAEL; Glenpool HS; Glenpool, OK; (3); 2/125; Math Tm; Capt Quiz Bowl; Spanish Clb; Teachers Aide; Sec Chorus; Rep Frsh Cls; Pres Soph Cls; Treas Jr Cls; Pres Stu Cncl; Pres NHS; Tech Stdnt Assn VP; Pre-Med.

DAILY, JOSHUA; Locust Grove HS; Locust Grove, OK; (4); 1/89; German Clb; HOBY; Math Clb; Office Aide; Quiz Bowl; Yrbk; Treas Stu Cncl; Var Capt Bsktbl; NHS; Val; OK ST U.

DAILY, MINDI J; Newcastle HS; Norman, OK; (3); Art Clb; Church Yth Grp; Spanish Clb; Ed Yrbk; Hon Roll.

DAKE, EMILY; Bridge Creek HS; Newcastle, OK; (2); 1/72; Church Yth Grp; Drama Clb; FCA; Sec FBLA; HOBY; Rep Soph Cls; Rep Stu Cncl; Var Bsktbl; High Hon Roll.

DALE, JONATHAN; Webster HS; Tulsa, OK; (4); Am Leg Boys St; Art Clb; Church Yth Grp; ROTC; Science Clb; VICA; Stage Crew; Hon Roll; NHS; Southern Nazarene U; Comp Tech.

DALE, MISSY A; Western Heights Sr HS; Oklahoma City, OK; (3); Church Yth Grp; Cmnty Wkr; Key Clb; Chorus; Ofcr Jr Cls; Sec Stu Cncl; Socr; Sftbl; Hon Roll; Bsktbl; Matmaid; OK ST U; Phys Thrpy.

D'ALESANDRO, ANDREA; Coweta HS; Coweta, OK; (2); Rptr Nwsp; Rep Stu Cncl; Var Chrldng; Hon Roll; NHS; Tgr Awd Ldrshp; Lttr Chrldng/Stdnt Cncl.

DALLAL, MONIQUE; Bishop Mcguinness HS; Oklahoma City, OK; (4); Treas Am Leg Aux Girls St; VP Church Yth Grp; Capt Dance Clb; Rep Frsh Cls; Rep Soph Cls; Rep Jr Cls; Rep Sr Cls; DAR Awd; Sec NHS; Spanish NHS; Chrch Chr Tr; Lcl Dnc, Vcl Studios.

DALLEY, CHANCE C; Davis HS; Davis, OK; (2); Natl FFA Org; Var Ftbl; JV Trk; Var Wt Lftg; Cit Awd; High Hon Roll; Hon Roll; OK Univ; Pro Ftbl.

DALLY, CHRIS; Deer Creek-Lamont Jr Sr HS; Lamont, OK; (4); 3/13; Am Leg Boys St; FCA; Ed Yrbk; Pres Frsh Cls; Sec Soph Cls; VP Stu Cncl; Capt Bsktbl; Hon Roll; NHS; St Schlr; Grad Honorary Escrt 95; Alg I & II Stu Of Yr; All-Conf Bsktbl Team; OK ST U.

DALRYMPLE, ERIN; Duncan HS; Duncan, OK; (4); 7/215; Am Leg Aux Girls St; Church Yth Grp; Debate Tm; Spanish Clb; SADD; Band; NHS; St Schlr; SAVE; YDYR; U OK.

DALRYMPLE, SHANNON; Eufaula Sr HS; Eufaula, OK; (3); Church Yth Grp; Acpl Chr; Chorus; Church Choir; School Musical; School Play; Ofcr Jr Cls; Bsktbl; Hon Roll; NHS; SW Assmbls God U; Bus.

DALTON, ANNE; Bethany HS; Oklahoma City, OK; (1); Church Yth Grp; FCA; Pep Clb; Chorus; Church Choir; Swing Chorus; Ofcr Frsh Cls; Ofcr Soph Cls; Bsktbl; Chrldng; Southern Nazarene U; Pre Med.

DALTON, DEREK W; Durant HS; Durant, OK; (1); Church Yth Grp; Computer Clb; Acpl Chr; Band; Chorus; Church Choir; Mrchg Band; Pep Band; Yrbk; Tennis; OK ST Univ; Cmptr Engr.

DALTON, JENNIFER R; Howe Public Schl; Howe, OK; (2); FBLA; FHA; GAA; SADD; Yrbk; Ofcr Frsh Cls; Sec Soph Cls; Var Bsktbl; Chrldng; Var Sftbl; Talent Search; CASC; Rn/Cmptrs.

DALY, JENNIFER; Blackwell HS; Blackwell, OK; (1); 1/122; Church Yth Grp; Band; Mrchg Band; Pep Band; Hon Roll; All Amer Schlr.

D'AMICO, MARY S; Choctaw HS; Midwest City, OK; (4); Church Yth Grp; FCA; GAA; Pep Clb; Spanish Clb; Chorus; Ed Nwsp; Rep Stu Cncl; Var Vllybl; High Hon Roll; Hnrs Eng Cls; OK His Highest Achvmt Awd; Scndry Elem Tchr.

DAMON, LORINDA L; Enid Sr HS; Enid, OK; (3); 175/475; DECA; Drama Clb; French Clb; ROTC; Speech Tm; Band; Color Guard; Drm Mjr(t); Yrbk; Pres Jr NHS; Life Clb; OK ST Univ; Military.

DAMRON, KRISTI L; Durant HS; Durant, OK; (1); Church Yth Grp; Acpl Chr; Chorus; Church Choir; Yrbk; Tennis; OK Univ; Pre-Med.

DAMRON, KYLE; Durant HS; Durant, OK; (4); 2/180; Church Yth Grp; FCA; Chorus; Hon Roll; Kiwanis Awd; NHS; Pres Acad Fit Awd; Pres Schlr; Sal; Key Clb; All-St Choir; OK Bapt Univ; Chrch Music.

DAMRON, MARGARET A; Guthrie Sr HS; Guthrie, OK; (1); 56/297; Church Yth Grp; Letterman Clb; Math Clb; Office Aide; Spanish Clb; Varsity Clb; Ofcr Frsh Cls; Ofcr Stu Cncl; Var L Socr; Var Sftbl; Tutor Children; Umpire Local Sports; AR Univ; Dr; Engr.

DAN, DERRICK A; Checotah HS; Checotah, OK; (2); Var Ftbl; Var Trk; OK ST Univ; Dr.

DANCY, JONATHAN B; Christian Heritage Acad; Oklahoma City, OK; (3); Church Yth Grp; FCA; Chorus; Rep Stu Cncl; Var L Ftbl; Var Wt Lftg; Hon Roll; TX A&M; Pre Law; Pre Med.

DANE, BUFFY R; Union Intermediate HS; Tulsa, OK; (2); 128/800; Church Yth Grp; FCA; Office Aide; Chorus; Church Choir; School Musical; School Play; Var L Vllybl; Wt Lftg; Hon Roll; Wrtng; USC.

DANG, DAO A; Putnam City West HS; Oklahoma City, OK; (3); 1/30; Art Clb; Church Yth Grp; Computer Clb; English Clb; JCL; Math Clb; Science Clb; Spanish Clb; Ofcr Jr Cls; Socr; Stud Physiology & Bio; OK U; Med Tech.

DANGOTT, LAURA; Henryetta Sr HS; Henryetta, OK; (1); Church Yth Grp; 4-H; FHA; Letterman Clb; JV Var Tennis; High Hon Roll; Pres Awd Edctnl Excl; Var Athl Awd; OK U; Mtrlgy.

DANIEL, BROOKE; Claremore Sr HS; Claremore, OK; (2); Church Yth Grp; Sec Frsh Cls; Sec Soph Cls; Var JV Bsktbl; Var JV Socr; High Hon Roll; Hon Roll; Dancing; Swmmng; Homecmng Atten Ftbl, Bsktbl.

DANIEL, DUANE; Stonewall Jr-Sr HS; Stonewall, OK; (2); FFA; Acctng.

DANIEL, JACLYN A; Snyder HS; Mountain Park, OK; (3); 17/41; Church Yth Grp; Cmnty Wkr; FCA; Library Aide; Band; Mrchg Band; Pep Band; Yrbk; Short-Grass Hnr Band 3 Yrs.

DANIEL, JASON M; Cascia Hall Prep School; Tulsa, OK; (2); Art Clb; Cmnty Wkr; Drama Clb; German Clb; Pep Clb; Acpl Chr; Chorus; Pep Band; School Musical; School Play.

DANIEL, JASON R; Oologah HS; Claremore, OK; (4); 24/100; FCA; SADD; Var Bsbl; Var Ftbl; Hon Roll; Jr NHS; NHS; Ntl Merit Ltr; Wetland Preservation Pgm; OK ST Univ; Bus.

DANIEL, JEREMY; Pawhuska HS; Pawhuska, OK; (3); Am Leg Boys St; 4-H; FBLA; Quiz Bowl; Science Clb; Spanish Clb; Band; 4-H Awd; High Hon Roll; Hon Roll.

DANIEL, JULIE; Newcastle HS; Newcastle, OK; (2); FBLA; Model UN; Quiz Bowl; Scholastic Bowl; Science Clb; Spanish Clb; Band; Mrchg Band; Pep Band; NHS; Mock Trial; OK ST U; Vet.

DANIEL, LENA; Lawton Sr HS; Fort Sill, OK; (3); FCA; Key Clb; Spanish Clb; Band; Ofcr Stu Cncl; Capt L Chrldng; JV Socr; High Hon Roll; NHS; Pres Acad Fit Awd; U TX; Optmtry.

DANIEL, LISA; Talihina Sr HS; Albion, OK; (4); 2/38; Am Leg Aux Girls St; Church Yth Grp; Sec VP FHA; HOBY; Natl FFA Org; Speech Tm; Ed Yrbk; Var Sftbl; Hon Roll; Eastern OK ST Coll; Hist.

DANIEL, RYAN; Blanchard Jr Sr HS; Blanchard, OK; (2); 12/82; FCA; Mu Alpha Theta; Office Aide; Spanish Clb; VP Soph Cls; Var Bsbl; Var Bsktbl; Var Ftbl; Jr NHS; NHS; U Of OK.

DANIEL, STACY; Milburn Schl; Milburn, OK; (3); 4-H; Co-Ed Yrbk; VP Frsh Cls; Pres Soph Cls; Rep Jr Cls; Rep Stu Cncl; 4-H Awd; Hon Roll; Murray ST; Tchr.

DANIELS, AMY; Edmond Santa Fe HS; Edmond, OK; (4); Art Clb; Key Clb; Science Clb; Spanish Clb; Bus Profs of Am; Bsktbl; Crs Cntry; Socr; Trk; NHS; His Day Dist Wnnr; Governors Commendation; St Gregorys; Phy Therapy.

DANIELS, BRANDON J; Salina HS; Salina, OK; (1); Letterman Clb; Natl FFA Org; Ftbl; Wt Lftg; Car Racing; Hunting & Fishing; Engr.

DANIELS, CARA; Ardmore HS; Ardmore, OK; (1); Church Yth Grp; FCA; Church Choir; Chrldng; Sftbl; Hon Roll.

DANIELS, ERIC R; Haskell HS; Haskell, OK; (2); Church Yth Grp; Drama Clb; Library Aide; Spanish Clb; Pres Frsh Cls; Ofcr Soph Cls; Var Bsbl; JV Bsktbl; Hon Roll; Prfct Atten Awd; Bsbl Tm St Playoff Wnnrs; Upward Bnd; Engl Cert; Vet.

DANIELS, JERAMIE K; Velma Alma HS; Duncan, OK; (3); FCA; 4-H; Letterman Clb; Natl FFA Org; SADD; Teachers Aide; Band; Jazz Band; Mrchg Band; School Musical; Wrtng.

DANIELS, L KEITH; Del City HS; Del City, OK; (2); Boy Scts; Church Yth Grp; Debate Tm; Quiz Bowl; Speech Tm; Chorus; School Play; Rep Stu Cncl; Eagle Sct; Rose ST Coll; Criminal Law.

DANIELS, LAURA K; Union Intermediate HS; Tulsa, OK; (2); Church Yth Grp; German Clb; Hosp Aide; Pep Clb; SADD; Chorus; School Musical; Hon Roll; Jr NHS; NHS; Boston U; Drama.

DANIELS, NICKIE T; Eldorado Schl; Eldorado, OK; (2); Church Yth Grp; FHA; Pep Clb; Scholastic Bowl; Rptr Nwsp; Rptr Yrbk; Bsktbl; Prfct Atten Awd; Star Events 3rd Pl; Wrtng Achvmt Awds; SWOSU; Comp Prgmr.

DANIELS, ROBERT G; Enid Sr HS; Enid, OK; (3); 113/445; Pres FCA; Letterman Clb; Teachers Aide; Varsity Clb; L Ftbl; L Trk; Wt Lftg; Hon Roll; NHS; Prfct Atten Awd.

DANIELS, VIOLA A; Northeast HS; Oklahoma City, OK; (2); Church Yth Grp; Band; Chorus; Church Choir; Mrchg Band; Mgr(s); Vllybl; Bio-Med Hlth Career Pgm; Participant Summer Acad; Participant In Acad Photo, Elecrons, Physics UCO; Nrs Anesthetist.

DANKER, ADAM W; Edmond North HS; Edmond, OK; (3); Var Bsktbl; Engr.

DANKER, CRYSTAL; Wellston Schl; Wellston, OK; (4); 1/42; Pres Sec FHA; German Clb; Pres Frsh Cls; VP Soph Cls; Pres Jr Cls; Pres Sr Cls; Rep Stu Cncl; High Hon Roll; Pres NHS; Val; Nrsng.

DANKER, EMILY; Wellston Schl; Wellston, OK; (4); 4/43; FCA; FHA; SADD; Teachers Aide; Yrbk; Bsktbl; Sftbl; Hon Roll; NHS; U Of Cntrl OK; Pedtrcn.

DANKER, MELANIE; Wellston Schl; Chandler, OK; (2); FCA; SADD; Bsktbl; Sftbl.

DANNENBERG, PETER O; Elgin HS; Elgin, OK; (2); 19/35; Art Clb; Boy Scts; HOBY; Band; Mrchg Band; Hon Roll; Law.

DANSKIN, AMANDA J; Noble HS; Noble, OK; (2); 1/200; Art Clb; Church Yth Grp; Spanish Clb; Chorus; Rep Stu Cncl; Var Chrldng; Hon Roll; NHS; Pres Schlr; Otstng Soph Girl; Music Theatre.

DAO, DAVID T; Oklahoma Sch Of Science & Math; Yukon, OK; (3); Boy Scts; Debate Tm; Treas French Clb; NFL; Speech Tm; Orch; NHS; Ntl Merit Ltr; Renaissance Cmmtte Pres; SADD Pres; Pre-Med.

DARBISON, KRIS J; Byng Sr HS; Ada, OK; (2); Church Yth Grp; Computer Clb; FCA; FBLA; Math Clb; Office Aide; Science Clb; Varsity Clb; Chorus; JV Capt Bsktbl; Sftbl Umpiring; East Central U Ada OK; PE Cch.

DARBY, SABRINA P; B T Washington HS; Tulsa, OK; (3); Drama Clb; JCL; Latin Clb; Pres Temple Yth Grp; School Musical; School Play; Hon Roll; Jr NHS; NHS; Pres Acad Fit Awd.

DARDEN, JASON R; Vanoss Schl; Ada, OK; (2); Art Clb; Church Yth Grp; FCA; FBLA; Scholastic Bowl; VICA; Ofcr Bsbl; High Hon Roll; Prfct Atten Awd; Northeastern Univ; Marine Bio.

DARDEN, TONI; Valliant HS; Valliant, OK; (4); Cmnty Wkr; GAA; Natl FFA Org; Band; Mrchg Band; Bsktbl; Hon Roll; NHS.

DARK, JESSICA R; North Intemediate HS; Broken Arrow, OK; (2); Church Yth Grp; Cmnty Wkr; Science Clb; VP Spanish Clb; Mgr(s); High Hon Roll; NHS.

DARK, RENEE; Lone Grove HS; Lone Grove, OK; (4); 2/75; Office Aide; Science Clb; Chorus; Bsktbl; Chrldng; Sftbl; High Hon Roll; NHS; Pres Acad Fit Awd; Bus.

DARKIS, NATASHA N; Star Spencer HS; Midwest City, OK; (2); Drama Clb; Band; Color Guard; Capt Flag Corp; School Play; Bsktbl; JV Tennis; JV Var Vllybl; Hon Roll; LAW Schl.

DARLING, CASSONDRA; Comanche HS; Comanche, OK; (3); 1/66; Church Yth Grp; Quiz Bowl; Scholastic Bowl; Treas SADD; Church Choir; Co-Ed Nwsp; High Hon Roll; NHS; Vlntr Lcl Nrsng Ctr; Acctnt.

DARLING, JASON; Comanche HS; Comanche, OK; (1); Church Yth Grp; SADD; Acpl Chr; Band; Drill Tm; Church Choir; Jazz Band; Pep Band; Hon Roll.

DARLING, KENNAH A; Velma Alma HS; Velma, OK; (3); FHA; Office Aide; Band; Mrchg Band; Yrbk; High Hon Roll; Twirler; East Cntrl Univ; Acctng.

DARNEAL, FANCI; Panama HS; Panama, OK; (2); FHA; GAA; Natl FFA Org; Speech Tm; Sec Frsh Cls; Bsktbl; Sftbl; Hon Roll; Jr NHS; NHS; OSU; Vet.

DARNEAL, KELLY; Spiro HS; Spiro, OK; (4); 3/90; Am Leg Aux Girls St; Church Yth Grp; VP Natl FFA Org; Mgr Nwsp; Rep Sr Cls; Treas Stu Cncl; Var Bsktbl; Var Sftbl; NHS; Prfct Atten Awd; Carl Albert ST Coll; Ed.

DARNOLD, SHANE E; Charles Page HS; Sand Springs, OK; (2); Drama Clb; Acpl Chr; Chorus; School Musical; School Play; Stage Crew; Nwsp; Trk; Hon Roll; A Cut Above In Vocal Music Awd; Stage Crew Mem Of Yr Awd; Best Supporting Actor Awd In Schl Musical.

DARTER, SARA J; Velma Alma HS; Duncan, OK; (2); Church Yth Grp; FCA; SADD; Sec Soph Cls; Var Bsktbl; Var Chrldng; Var Sftbl; Var Trk; NHS; Photo.

DASHNER, BRITTANI R; South Intermediate HS; Broken Arrow, OK; (2); Church Yth Grp; Key Clb; Library Aide; Acpl Chr; Chorus; Mgr(s); Hon Roll; OSU.

DASHTI, LOTUS; Wynnewood HS; Pauls Valley, OK; (2); 1/40; GAA; Letterman Clb; Bsktbl; Chrldng; High Hon Roll; Hon Roll; Sftbl; CPA.

DATIN, KATIE L; Guthrie Sr HS; Guthrie, OK; (1); Church Yth Grp; Spanish Clb; Band; Mrchg Band; Jr NHS; Elem Tchr.

DAUB, ABBY; Cherokee Jr Sr HS; Cherokee, OK; (2); Church Yth Grp; FCA; FHA; NFL; Speech Tm; Var Bsktbl; Var Chrldng; Gym; Var Sftbl; NHS; Stu Of Today; OK U; Phys Thrpy.

DAUBENECK, SUSAN L; Owasso Sr HS; Oakley, CA; (2); 34/432; Church Yth Grp; Drama Clb; English Clb; FCA; French Clb; NFL; Science Clb; Speech Tm; Stage Crew; NHS; U Of CA Berkeley.

DAUGHERTY, HEATHER; Fairland Jr Sr HS; Fairland, OK; (4); 5/38; Church Yth Grp; FHA; Teachers Aide; Nwsp; Yrbk; Treas Jr Cls; Chrldng; Hon Roll; NHS; Prfct Atten Awd; MO Sthrn St Coll; Bus.

DAUGHERTY, SAMANTHA; Watts HS; Colcord, OK; (2); Math Clb; Natl Beta Clb; Natl FFA Org; Sec Frsh Cls; Var Bsktbl; Mgr(s); High Hon Roll; NHS; Harvard; Bus.

DAUGHHETEE, ANDREW; Freedom Schl; Freedom, OK; (4); Am Leg Boys St; FCA; Letterman Clb; Natl FFA Org; School Play; Yrbk; Ofcr Sr Cls; Bsktbl; Ftbl; Wt Lftg.

DAVENPORT, AMY L; Harrah HS; Harrah, OK; (3); 29/153; Drama Clb; FHA; Office Aide; Spanish Clb; SADD; JV Chrldng; Hon Roll; Future Homemakers Of Amer Awd; U Of OK; Photo.

DAVENPORT, JILLIAN W; Paoli HS; Paoli, OK; (2); 1/30; English Clb; FHA; Capt Math Tm; Scholastic Bowl; Band; Var Bsktbl; Cit Awd; High Hon Roll; NHS; Pres Acad Fit Awd; Flute Solo; Chair Piccolo; Capt Math; Harvard Univ; Lawyer.

DAVENPORT, MARIE; Paden HS; Paden, OK; (2); Church Yth Grp; VP 4-H; FHA; Capt Chrldng; 4-H Awd.

DAVEY, CHRISTOPHER P; Mustang HS; Yukon, OK; (4); CAP; Spanish Clb; Intrml Tennis; OSU Tech; Acctng.

DAVEY, KRYSTAL D; Choctaw HS; Choctaw, OK; (4); 47/303; Am Leg Aux Girls St; Red Cross Aide; JV Var Bsktbl; JV Var Sftbl; Var Trk; DAR Awd; Hon Roll; Jr NHS; NHS; Pres Acad Fit Awd; Jr Olympcs Natl Trmnt Sftbll; Crowder Coll; Med.

DAVIDSON, ANDREW N; Pauls Valley HS; Pauls Valley, OK; (4); 1/83; Sec French Clb; VP Sr Cls; Treas Stu Cncl; Var Ftbl; Var Tennis; NHS; St Schlr; Val; Pi Phi Pi; Chrstn Warriors; Oral Roberts U; Pharm.

DAVIDSON, DUSTIN; Elgin HS; Lawton, OK; (3); Church Yth Grp; FCA; Natl FFA Org; SADD; L Bsbl; L Bsktbl; L Ftbl; L Wt Lftg; High Hon Roll; NHS.

DAVIDSON, GREGORY C; Olney Schl; Coalgate, OK; (1); 1/14; Scholastic Bowl; Treas Frsh Cls; High Hon Roll; Hon Roll; Elks Lodge Per Essay Cntst Wnnr; Page OK Hse Rep; Three Mdls Amer Govt Local U; U Of OK; Law.

DAVIDSON, HEATHER; Hugo HS; Hugo, OK; (4); 5/101; Cmnty Wkr; Sec Computer Clb; HOBY; Math Clb; Science Clb; Pres Spanish Clb; Sec Soph Cls; Rep Stu Cncl; Pres NHS; U OK; CPA.

DAVIDSON, JOSH; Moore HS; Moore, OK; (3); 200/566; FCA; Office Aide; Spanish Clb; Pres Jr Cls; Rep Stu Cncl; Var Capt Golf.

DAVIDSON, KRYSTAL; Perry Sr HS; Perry, OK; (2); Church Yth Grp; Dance Clb; Drama Clb; Girl Scts; Band; Church Choir; Jazz Band; Mrchg Band; Jr NHS; NHS; OK Bapt Youth Choir; Falls Creek Orch 95; Instrumental Music Ed.

DAVIDSON, KYLIE; Choctaw HS; Choctaw, OK; (2); Church Yth Grp; Key Clb; Scholastic Bowl; SADD; Ofcr Frsh Cls; Chrldng; Powder Puff Ftbl; Hon Roll; Jr NHS; OSU; Bus; Acctng.

DAVIDSON, REBECCA L; Duncan HS; Duncan, OK; (4); 48/214; FHA; Office Aide; Teachers Aide; Band; Mrchg Band; Hon Roll; Prfct Atten Awd; Outstndg Achvmt In Word Processing; Dir Awd In Band; 1st Pl Keyboarding II At SW Inter Schltc Meet; USAO; Bus.

DAVIDSON, SCOTT J; Edmond North HS; Edmond, OK; (4); FCA; French Clb; Hosp Aide; Office Aide; SADD; JV Bsbl; Var Bsktbl; NHS; Pres Acad Fit Awd; Univ Cntrl OK; PT.

DAVIDSON, STACEY; Latta Sr HS; Ada, OK; (4); 1/51; Church Yth Grp; Cmnty Wkr; FCA; HOBY; Letterman Clb; Office Aide; Capt Quiz Bowl; Teachers Aide; Varsity Clb; Pres VICA; Karate St Champ; OK ST U; Bus.

DAVIDSON, TAMMY; Westmoore HS; Oklahoma City, OK; (4); 68/610; Church Yth Grp; Debate Tm; Drama Clb; FCA; French Clb; School Musical; School Play; Cit Awd; NHS; Library Aide; Masonic Stu Of Today Awd; U Of Cntrl OK; Psych.

DAVIDSON, TIFFANY A; Cleveland Sr HS; Cleveland, OK; (1); Church Yth Grp; FCA; GAA; Tennis; High Hon Roll; Hon Roll; Hnrs Eng Awd; OK ST Univ; Tchr.

DAVIDSON, WILL; Merritt Schl; Carter, OK; (1); Chorus; Acad Tm; FFA; Scuba Diving; Hnr Choir.

DAVIE, KELLY; Kremlin Jr Sr HS; Enid, OK; (2); FCA; GAA; L Bsktbl; L Sftbl; Hon Roll; Prfct Atten Awd; Sprts Med.

DAVIE, MANDY D; Elk City Jr HS; Elk City, OK; (1); Office Aide; Jr NHS; Southeastern OK ST Univ; PT.

DAVIS, ADRIENNE D; Union Sr HS; Broken Arrow, OK; (4); 52/629; Dance Clb; Debate Tm; Am Leg Aux Girls St; FBLA; Drill Tm; Rep Sr Cls; High Hon Roll; Hon Roll; NHS; Pres Acad Fit Awd; U Of OK; Med.

DAVIS, ALISON M; Woodward HS; Woodward, OK; (3); Church Yth Grp; FCA; FTA; GAA; Letterman Clb; Pep Clb; Bsktbl; Powder Puff Ftbl; Socr; Hon Roll; OSU Alumni Schol.

DAVIS, ALLISON; Westmoore HS; Oklahoma City, OK; (3); Church Yth Grp; Pep Clb; Variety Show; Sec Frsh Cls; Rep Soph Cls; Rep Jr Cls; Rep Sr Cls; Rep Stu Cncl; Var Capt Chrldng; Cit Awd; 3rd Pl 10k Run; Rose ST; Nutrition.

DAVIS, AMANDA; Chelsea HS; Chelsea, OK; (4); 5/60; Dance Clb; FCA; FBLA; Spanish Clb; Teachers Aide; Varsity Clb; Rep Frsh Cls; Rep Soph Cls; Rep Jr Cls; Rptr Sr Cls; Spcl Ed.

DAVIS, AMANDA L; Elmore City Jr Sr HS; Wynnewood, OK; (3); 4-H; Chorus; 4-H Awd; Bsktbl Ltr; Attnd Schltc Meets In Music, Algebra & His At E Cntrl Univ; Cosmetologist.

DAVIS, AMANDA M; Muskogee HS; Muskogee, OK; (4); 45/303; Church Yth Grp; DECA; French Clb; FHA; High Hon Roll; Jr NHS; NHS; RAID; Chrch Drdama Team; Cntrl Bible Coll; Chrch Ministr.

DAVIS, AMBER L; Blanchard Jr Sr HS; Blanchard, OK; (3); Church Yth Grp; Computer Clb; FCA; FHA; GAA; Letterman Clb; Pep Clb; Teachers Aide; Bsktbl; Var Sftbl; Southwestern Univ; Scndry Tchr.

DAVIS, AMBER L; Charles Page HS; Sand Springs, OK; (1); GAA; Letterman Clb; Office Aide; Bsktbl; Sftbl; Trk; His Awd; ST Univ; Elem Tchr; Sftbl Coach.

DAVIS, AMBER S; Eufaula Sr HS; Stidham, OK; (2); FHA; Spanish Clb; Band; Mrchg Band; Hon Roll; Pres Acad Fit Awd; OK Senate/Hse Of Rep Srvd As Page.

DAVIS, AMY C; Owasso Sr HS; Owasso, OK; (4); 64/296; Church Yth Grp; Office Aide; VICA; Hon Roll; Tulsa JC; Elem Educ.

DAVIS, ANDREA D; Eisenhower Sr HS; Lawton, OK; (3); Computer Clb; FHA; Hon Roll; Admin Asst.

DAVIS, ANNA; Grace Fellowship Christian Sch; Bixby, OK; (2); 2/35; Church Yth Grp; Cmnty Wkr; Pres Soph Cls; Treas Stu Cncl; Var Bsktbl; Var Capt Chrldng; Var Crs Cntry; Var Socr; Var Vllybl; Hon Roll; Shield Awd; Sprts Med.

DAVIS, ASHLEY M; Metro Christian Acad; Broken Arrow, OK; (3); Church Yth Grp; French Clb; Teachers Aide; School Play; Rep Frsh Cls; Hist Sr Cls; Rep Stu Cncl; JV Var Chrldng; Socr; High Hon Roll; All Star Chrldng Tulsa Twstrs; Chrldng Coach; TU; Eng Ed.

DAVIS, BARRY J; Minco Jr Sr HS; Minco, OK; (3); 1/33; FCA; Pres Frsh Cls; VP Soph Cls; Ftbl; Wt Lftg; Cit Awd; Hon Roll; NHS; Sal; U Of OK; Pharm.

DAVIS, BRANDEE A; Velma Alma HS; Countyline, OK; (2); FHA; SADD; Hon Roll; OK Hnr Soc; US Bus Ed Awd; Mssg Thrp.

DAVIS, BRANDON S; Edmond North HS; Edmond, OK; (3); 89/420; Boy Scts; Tennis; Jr NHS; NHS; Eagle Sct; U Of OK; Arch.

DAVIS, BRANDY L; Enid Sr HS; Enid, OK; (3); Church Yth Grp; Letterman Clb; Spanish Clb; Speech Tm; Band; Mrchg Band; Pep Band; School Play; Stage Crew; Mgr Bsktbl; Northwestern OK ST Univ; BCA.

DAVIS, BRION L; Tipton Jr Sr HS; Tipton, OK; (3); Letterman Clb; Quiz Bowl; Varsity Clb; Church Choir; Var Bsbl; Var Bsktbl; Capt Ftbl; Hon Roll; NHS; Prfct Atten Awd; All Dist Defnsive Back; Nom For Wash Ldshp Conf; Multi Yr Listee; OK Univ; Eng.

DAVIS, BRITTANY N; Hominy HS; Hominy, OK; (2); 16/78; FHA; GAA; Treas Jr Cls; Var Bsktbl; Var Sftbl; Hon Roll; Kiwanis Awd; Prfct Atten Awd; Creative Wrtng Awd; Sftbl Outstdng Infielder; Soph Cls VP; Connors ST Coll.

DAVIS, CANDICE N; Muskogee HS; Muskogee, OK; (2); Church Yth Grp; French Clb; Chorus; Hon Roll; NHS; Teens For Chrst; Rghrs Agnst Illgl Drgs; Yth Vlntr Corps; Baylor U; Mssnry.

DAVIS, CATHERINE L; Will Rogers HS; Tulsa, OK; (2); Pres German Clb; ROTC; Teachers Aide; Orch; Sec Frsh Cls; Sec Soph Cls; DAR Awd; Hon Roll; US Army Rec Cmmnd Awd; U AR; Med Rsrch.

DAVIS, CHRIS M; Meeker HS; Shawnee, OK; (2); 4/74; Quiz Bowl; Scholastic Bowl; High Hon Roll; Prfct Atten Awd; Pres Acad Fit Awd; St Schlr.

DAVIS, CHRISTIE L; Mc Alester HS; Mcalester, OK; (4); 9/216; DECA; Office Aide; Teachers Aide; Band; Chorus; Mrchg Band; Orch; Pep Band; School Musical; School Play; Music Prfrmnce.

DAVIS, CHRISTINA D; Great Plains Avt-Comanche; Lawton, OK; (3); Church Yth Grp; FBLA; FHA; Church Choir; High Hon Roll; Jr NHS; African-Amer Clb; Upward Bound; I Psi I Step Team; U Of AL; Acctng.

DAVIS, DAVID R; Nathan Hale HS; Tulsa, OK; (3); Church Yth Grp; FCA; Ofcr Bsbl; Var Ftbl; Var Score Keeper; Var Wt Lftg; Var Wrstlng; Hon Roll; Fishing; Playing The Guitar.

DAVIS, DAWN C; Hobart HS; Hobart, OK; (2); Church Yth Grp; Band; Mrchg Band; Pep Band; Phtg Ed Yrbk; Yth Alive Mem; FFA; Bus Mgmt.

DAVIS, DEVIN; Strother Jr Sr HS; Seminole, OK; (4); 4-H; FHA; Natl FFA Org; Red Cross Aide; School Musical; School Play; Rep Stu Cncl; L Bsbl; Capt Ftbl; L Tennis; NASA; Outstdng FFA Mmbr; OK ST Snte Cttn Of Cngrtltns; Seminole ST Coll; Ag Ed.

DAVIS, DIERRA; Hobart HS; Roosevelt, OK; (2); FCA; 4-H; FHA; Pres Frsh Cls; Rep Soph Cls; Rep Stu Cncl; Bsktbl; Var Chrldng; Mgr(s); Var Sftbl; OK Hnr Socty.

DAVIS, ELISA; Shawnee Sr HS; Shawnee, OK; (3); Church Yth Grp; French Clb; Hosp Aide; Art, Piano Lessons.

DAVIS, ERIC; Edmond North HS; Edmond, OK; (4); 40/331; Boy Scts; Church Yth Grp; French Clb; Mu Alpha Theta; ROTC; SADD; Wrstlng; NHS; Prfct Atten Awd; St Schlr; Eagle Scout; U Of OK; Aerospace Engr.

DAVIS, ERIN C; Olustee Schl; Olustee, OK; (3); Church Yth Grp; Chorus; Var Bsktbl; Chrldng; Sftbl; Cit Awd; High Hon Roll; Hon Roll; NHS; Sal; Historical Clb; Med.

DAVIS, ERIN G; Norman Sr HS; Norman, OK; (3); 173/789; FCA; Office Aide; Spanish Clb; Rep Soph Cls; Mgr(s); Hon Roll; Pres Schlr; U Of OK; Fshn Industry.

DAVIS, ERIN N; Edmond Memorial HS; Edmond, OK; (2); Church Yth Grp; FCA; Spanish Clb; Var Bsktbl; Hon Roll; NHS; OK Univ Abilene.

DAVIS, GUYLA; Foyil Schl; Claremore, OK; (3); 1/32; Sec Drama Clb; Rptr FBLA; Pres FHA; Quiz Bowl; Ed Yrbk; Sec Treas Jr Cls; Var Bsktbl; Var Trk; Hon Roll; Math Tm; Homcmng Crt; JOM Tutor; Med.

DAVIS, HEATH T; Webster HS; Tulsa, OK; (2); 9/250; DECA; FBLA; Key Clb; School Play; Rptr Frsh Cls; VP Soph Cls; Hist Stu Cncl; Var Ftbl; Var Wt Lftg; Var Wrstlng.

DAVIS, HEATHER; Hobart HS; Hobart, OK; (2); Church Yth Grp; FHA; FTA; Hon Roll; NHS.

DAVIS, JASON; Lawton Sr HS; Lawton, OK; (4); 22/349; Church Yth Grp; German Clb; Quiz Bowl; Chorus; Church Choir; Hon Roll; NHS; Tchr Cadets; Greenville Coll; Music Prod.

DAVIS, JENNIFER; Claremore Sr HS; Claremore, OK; (4); 1/240; Art Clb; Debate Tm; Drama Clb; Math Clb; Mu Alpha Theta; NFL; Science Clb; Speech Tm; NHS; Val; Carnegie Mellon U; Biomedcl Eng.

DAVIS, JENNIFER; Woodward HS; Woodward, OK; (3); 4-H; Sec German Clb; Letterman Clb; Model UN; Quiz Bowl; Band; Mrchg Band; Hon Roll; Sec NHS; TSA St Rptr; Ger-Amer Partnership Pgm Exch Stu; Rotry Yth Ldrshp Awd; U Of OK; Astronaut.

DAVIS, JENNIFER M; Yukon HS; Yukon, OK; (4); 138/398; Church Yth Grp; FCA; Pep Clb; Acpl Chr; Band; Chorus; Church Choir; Mrchg Band; Hon Roll; Prfct Atten Awd; Show Choir; OK Bptst U; Elem Ed.

DAVIS, JENNY E; Checotah HS; Checotah, OK; (2); 1/107; Debate Tm; Treas FHA; Natl FFA Org; Pep Clb; Speech Tm; Acpl Chr; Chorus; High Hon Roll; NHS; St Schlr; Jrnlsm/Wrtng.

DAVIS, JEREMY; Ninnekah HS; Ninnekah, OK; (4); USAO.

DAVIS, JEREMY; Edmond North HS; Edmond, OK; (2); 49/420; Boy Scts; French Clb; Key Clb; Mu Alpha Theta; NHS; Eagle Scout; Physician/Anesthesiology.

DAVIS, JESSICA; Wynnewood HS; Wynnewood, OK; (1); 9/58; GAA; Band; Church Choir; Color Guard; Flag Corp; Golf; Sftbl; Wt Lftg; Hon Roll; East Central Univ; PT.

DAVIS, JESSICA B; Turpin Schl; Turpin, OK; (4); 24/42; Church Yth Grp; Drama Clb; FCA; Letterman Clb; Office Aide; Pep Clb; Speech Tm; SADD; Varsity Clb; Acpl Chr; Southwestern OK ST U; Psych.

DAVIS, JESSICA D; Putnam City West HS; Bethany, OK; (2); #16 in class; Cmnty Wkr; GAA; Hosp Aide; JA; JV Var Bsktbl; Var Socr; Var Sftbl; Hon Roll; NHS; Neo-Natal/ICU Nurse.

DAVIS, JESSIKA; Comanche HS; Comanche, OK; (3); Art Clb; Church Yth Grp; Speech Tm; School Play; Nwsp; Phtg Yrbk; High Hon Roll; NHS; Masonic Awd; Outstndng Stu; U Of NM; Photo.

DAVIS, JOHN; Grace Fellowship Christian Sch; Bixby, OK; (4); 2/22; Co-Ed Yrbk; Rep Frsh Cls; Pres Soph Cls; Pres Jr Cls; Pres Stu Cncl; Var Capt Bsktbl; Var Capt Socr; Hon Roll; NHS; Sal; Pg AL ST Snt; Air Force Acad; Arosp Eng.

DAVIS, JOVONA M; Fox Sr HS; Countyline, OK; (3); Sec FHA; Pep Clb; SADD; Bsktbl; Sftbl; Hon Roll; NHS; All Amer Schlr; US Army.

DAVIS, JUSTIN M; Edmond Memorial HS; Edmond, OK; (2); Church Yth Grp; Band; Jazz Band; Mrchg Band; Orch; School Musical; Variety Show; Golf; Hon Roll; Dr; Pediatrician.

DAVIS, K ROXANNE; Catoosa HS; Claremore, OK; (3); 14/172; FCA; Spanish Clb; Teachers Aide; Nwsp; Ofcr Jr Cls; Capt Chrldng; Pom Pon; L Socr; High Hon Roll; NHS; Interior Dsgn.

DAVIS, KARINA; Guthrie Sr HS; Guthrie, OK; (3); 1/250; Church Yth Grp; French Clb; Mu Alpha Theta; Sec SADD; Band; Flag Corp; School Musical; Hist Stu Cncl; NHS; St Schlr; All-St Orch; PSYCH.

DAVIS, KATHRYN M; Putnam City Original HS; Oklahoma City, OK; (3); 50/364; Church Yth Grp; Drama Clb; NFL; Hist Orch; Silver Strngs Putnam City Librn; Music Ed.

DAVIS, KELLY; Marlow HS; Marlow, OK; (4); 37/99; Am Leg Boys St; Church Yth Grp; Church Choir; Teachers Aide; Var L Tennis; Var L Wrstlng; Hon Roll; U Cntrl OK; Med.

DAVIS, KENYA; Will Rogers HS; Tulsa, OK; (4); 13/210; Church Yth Grp; Key Clb; Office Aide; Spanish Clb; Teachers Aide; Church Choir; School Play; Rptr Phtg Yrbk; Var L Bsktbl; High Hon Roll; USSA All-Amer Schlrs 95-96; Jackson St Univ; Bus Admin.

DAVIS, KEVIN; Westmoore HS; Oklahoma City, OK; (4); 28/610; French Clb; FBLA; Quiz Bowl; Scholastic Bowl; Hon Roll; St Schlr; Val; Schlstc Lttrmn; Martial Arts; Oklahoma City CC; Cmptr Sci.

DAVIS, KIM; Mustang HS; Yukon, OK; (3); 65/40; Boy Scts; Church Yth Grp; FCA; Spanish Clb; Band; JV Bsktbl; Hon Roll; NHS; Botany/Zoology Awd; Acad Ltr; Bowling.

DAVIS, KRISTON; Grandfield Jr Sr HS; Grandfield, OK; (1); 3/21; Church Yth Grp; FCA; FHA; Natl FFA Org; Pep Clb; Quiz Bowl; Sec Frsh Cls; Hon Roll; Kiwanis Awd; Nrsng.

DAVIS, LATRICE S; Capitol Hill HS; Oklahoma City, OK; (3); Science Clb; Chorus; Church Choir; Mrchg Band; Ofcr Stu Cncl; Bsktbl; Mgr(s); Score Keeper; Trk; Hon Roll; TSU; Cmptr Sci.

DAVIS, LAUREN; Jenks HS; Tulsa, OK; (1); Church Yth Grp; Dance Clb; FCA; SADD; School Play; Ofcr Stu Cncl; Chrldng; Crs Cntry; Trk; Wt Lftg; Southern Meth Univ; Sports.

DAVIS, LAURIE; Blair Schl; Blair, OK; (3); Church Yth Grp; FCA; Natl Beta Clb; Natl FFA Org; Quiz Bowl; SADD; School Play; Sec Frsh Cls; Sec Soph Cls; Pres Jr Cls; Dstngshd Athl Awd By Marine Corps.

DAVIS, LAURIE D; Pioneer Jr Sr HS; Enid, OK; (2); Church Yth Grp; FHA; Library Aide; Pep Clb; Church Choir; Nwsp; Bsktbl; Trk; Vllybl; Hon Roll; Evangel; Elem Tchr.

DAVIS, LEAH E; Putnam City North HS; Oklahoma City, OK; (2); Church Yth Grp; Chorus; Church Choir; Orch; High Hon Roll; NHS; Show Choir; All-ST Orch; OK Yth Sypmhony; Mus.

DAVIS, LESLEA; Hobart HS; Hobart, OK; (3); Church Yth Grp; FCA; 4-H; FTA; Girl Scts; HOBY; Spanish Clb; Teachers Aide; School Play; Treas Jr Cls; FFA; OK ST U; Optometry.

DAVIS, LESLEY; Dale Sr HS; Shawnee, OK; (2); 1/49; Church Yth Grp; FCA; Scholastic Bowl; Spanish Clb; VP Soph Cls; Bsktbl; Sftbl; High Hon Roll; Jr NHS; NHS; Piano; OK St Univ; Law.

DAVIS, LESLIE T; Tahlequah Sr HS; Tahlequah, OK; (4); 49/251; Teachers Aide; Band; Var L Sftbl; NHS; OK Slow Pitch Sftbl Coach Assn All St 96; MVP Tahlequah HS Slow Pitch Sftbl 96; All Trnmt Pitcher; NE St Univ; Elem Ed Tchr.

DAVIS, LORI; Boswell Sr HS; Boswell, OK; (3); 1/33; FHA; Pres Key Clb; Chorus; Ed Nwsp; Yrbk; Pres Soph Cls; Pres Jr Cls; Ofcr Stu Cncl; High Hon Roll; Pres Acad Fit Awd; Curriculum; Natl Yng Ldrs Conf WA DC; Stu Mon; Bus.

DAVIS, MANDY J; Heavener HS; Heavener, OK; (4); 16/89; Church Yth Grp; Drama Clb; French Clb; FHA; GAA; Letterman Clb; Office Aide; Teachers Aide; Rep Soph Cls; Rep Jr Cls; 2nd Rnnr Up Heavener Jr Miss Pgnt; Carl Albert ST Coll; Elem Educ.

DAVIS, MELISSA N; Christian Heritage Acad; Oklahoma City, OK; (2); Church Yth Grp; Hon Roll; Prfct Atten Awd; Cross Stitching; Camping; Sftbl; Legal/Human Resources.

DAVIS, MILENA; Heavener HS; Heavener, OK; (2); Debate Tm; Drama Clb; French Clb; FBLA; Key Clb; Quiz Bowl; Science Clb; Speech Tm; Thesps; School Play; TSA Reporter; Drug Free Clb; U OK; Med.

DAVIS, MISTY; Vanoss Schl; Ada, OK; (2); Church Yth Grp; FBLA; Red Cross Aide; Quiz Bowl; Band; Drill Tm; Mrchg Band; Pep Band; VP Frsh Cls; Chrldng.

DAVIS, MONICA; Covington Douglas HS; Marshall, OK; (4); 1/28; Church Yth Grp; Pres FHA; HOBY; Pres Spanish Clb; Teachers Aide; Band; Drm Mjr(t); Mrchg Band; Pep Band; School Play; OK Hnr Soc; OSU.

DAVIS, NATHAN; Dewey HS; Dewey, OK; (1); 8/97; Church Yth Grp; Cmnty Wkr; FHA; Bsktbl; JV Ftbl; Mgr(s); JV Trk; JV Wt Lftg; Hon Roll; Pres Acad Fit Awd; GATE Math/Soc Studies; People To People Stdnt Ambsdr Untd Kingdom/Ireland; OK St Legislature Page; NE ST U OK.

DAVIS, NEAL; Durant HS; Durant, OK; (3); Key Clb; Cit Awd; DECA; Comp Prgmr.

DAVIS, NICK; Spiro HS; Spiro, OK; (2); 1/100; FCA; FBLA; Math Clb; Model UN; Quiz Bowl; Scholastic Bowl; Spanish Clb; Pres Frsh Cls; Rep Soph Cls; NHS; Cmptr Sci/Cmptr Prgmr.

DAVIS, QUANNAH; Wilson Schl; Henryetta, OK; (1); Natl FFA Org; Speech Tm; Ofcr Frsh Cls; Bsktbl; Qlfd St Speech.

DAVIS, RACHEL R; Snyder HS; Mountain Park, OK; (2); Sec Church Yth Grp; Cmnty Wkr; FHA; Red Cross Aide; Band; Ed Yrbk; Sec Stu Cncl; Chrldng; High Hon Roll; NHS; OK ST Univ; MBA.

DAVIS, REBEKAH; Liberty Acad; Shawnee, OK; (2); Church Yth Grp; Chorus; Church Choir; School Musical; Stage Crew; Cit Awd; Hon Roll; Prfct Atten Awd; Chapel Clb; Educ.

DAVIS, RODNEY E; Velma Alma HS; Foster, OK; (4); 1/44; Church Yth Grp; FCA; Scholastic Bowl; Church Choir; Sec Soph Cls; VP Jr Cls; L Ftbl; Var Golf; L Trk; Var Wt Lftg; Southwestern OK ST U; Engl.

DAVIS, ROXANNE; Catoosa HS; Claremore, OK; (3); 14/170; Church Yth Grp; Spanish Clb; Teachers Aide; Sec Jr Cls; Rep Stu Cncl; Capt Chrldng; Socr; Trk; Wt Lftg; High Hon Roll; Interior Design/Bus Mngmt.

DAVIS, SARAH M; Putnam City West HS; Bethany, OK; (1); Church Yth Grp; CAP; Scholastic Bowl; Chorus; Hon Roll; Pilot Stu; Recieved Billy Mitchell Awd; Aerospace Ed & Ldrshp; Air Force Pilot.

DAVIS, SENA; Varnum Jr Sr HS; Seminole, OK; (4); FCA; Sec FHA; Pep Clb; Rptr Jr Cls; Capt Bsktbl; Socr; Capt Sftbl; Trk; Jr Yr Homcmng Qn; All Amer Schlr; Bacone; Nrs.

DAVIS, STACEY; Central HS; Tulsa, OK; (3); Hist Stu Cncl; Mgr(s); Swmmng; Hon Roll; NHS; Prfct Atten Awd; Native Amer Stu Assn; Lunch Buddy W/Mark Twain Elem Stu; NSU Talequah.

DAVIS, STACI; Marietta HS; Marietta, OK; (2); 1/76; Church Yth Grp; FHA; GAA; Chorus; Bsktbl; High Hon Roll; OK Hnr Soc.

DAVIS, STEPHANIE A; Hulbert Jr Sr HS; Hulbert, OK; (3); 11/39; FBLA; GAA; Spanish Clb; Bsktbl; Hon Roll; NHS; Ctznshp Awd; 4-H Clb; Washington Univ; Psych.

DAVIS, STEVEN E; Claremore Sr HS; Claremore, OK; (3); 89/231; Hon Roll; Duke Univ Talent Search Pgm; Comp Sci; Engrng.

DAVIS, TANISHA K; Lone Grove HS; Ardmore, OK; (2); Church Yth Grp; FHA; Math Clb; Science Clb; Nwsp; Hon Roll; NHS; OU; Crim Psych.

DAVIS, TERRY M; Salina HS; Spavinaw, OK; (4); Math Tm; Teachers Aide; Var Bsktbl; High Hon Roll; Hon Roll; NHS; NSU.

DAVIS, TIFFANY; East Central HS; Tulsa, OK; (4); 68/209; Church Yth Grp; FCA; French Clb; Key Clb; Pep Clb; Teachers Aide; Phtg Yrbk; Rep Sr Cls; Var Chrldng; Hon Roll; NE OK A&M Coll; Enviro Sci.

DAVIS, TIFFANY M; Catoosa HS; Catoosa, OK; (4); 11/135; Drama Clb; Pres FHA; Phtg Intnl Clb; Office Aide; Red Cross Aide; Rep Spanish Clb; Rep Speech Tm; Varsity Clb; Color Guard; School Play; Winterguard St Champion; 3rd Pl At St For FHA; Speech Awd; Tulsa Univ; Pediatric Nrs.

DAVIS, TRACY; Putnam City West HS; Oklahoma City, OK; (4); 41/285; Church Yth Grp; Spanish Clb; Orch; NHS; CIA; Stdnt To Stdnt; GATE; Tch 3rd Grd Sunday Schl; Tutoring; Yth Choir; Gymnstcs Coach; Cnslrs Aide; OK Bapt U; Math Ed.

DAVIS, TRESSA K; South Coffeyville Schl; S Coffeyville, OK; (1); JV Var Bsktbl; Var Chrldng; Var Sftbl; Hon Roll; Prfct Atten Awd; Pittsburg ST; Anstslgst.

DAVISON, DUSTIN S; Choctaw HS; Oklahoma City, OK; (4); FTA; Acpl Chr; Chorus; Stage Crew; Swing Chorus; Variety Show; Cit Awd; Outstdng Bass Awd; St Choir; U Of Cntrl OK; Music Tchr.

DAVISSON, BO; Chisholm Sr HS; Enid, OK; (2); Chess Clb; FCA; Ftbl; Trk; Wt Lftg; High Hon Roll; Hon Roll; NHS; OK ST U; Vet Med.

DAWES, TRAVIS W; Stillwater Jr HS; Stillwater, OK; (1); Church Yth Grp; Natl FFA Org; Hon Roll; FFA Star Greenhand Awd; Natl HS Rodeo Assn; OK HS Rodeo Assn; Panhandle ST OK; PRCA.

DAWSON, CANDACE; Putnam City North HS; Oklahoma City, OK; (2); Church Yth Grp; Pom Pon; Cit Awd; Hon Roll; Pom Pon Sec/Treas; Wetherford; Pharm.

DAWSON, DIANE R; Putnam City HS; Oklahoma City, OK; (3); 25/360; Church Yth Grp; Cmnty Wkr; Hosp Aide; Library Aide; Office Aide; Spanish Clb; Teachers Aide; Nwsp; Rep Stu Cncl; Cit Awd; Siloan Masonic Ldg Otsdng Yng Ldr; Univ Of AR; Elem Ed.

DAWSON, HOLLY; Union City Schl; Union City, OK; (3); FHA; HOBY; Natl FFA Org; VP Jr Cls; Ofcr Stu Cncl; JV Bsktbl; Score Keeper; Hon Roll; NHS; Prfct Atten Awd; Msnc Stu Of Yr; U Of OK; Med.

DAWSON, JAMES JUSTIN; Carl Albert HS; Midwest City, OK; (4); 1/245; Am Leg Boys St; Key Clb; School Musical; Phtg Yrbk; Sec Jr Cls; Treas Sr Cls; Var Bsbl; NHS; Val; Rtry Yth Ldrshp Awd; OK ST U; Mech Engrng.

DAWSON, MARISHA; Douglass HS; Oklahoma City, OK; (3); Church Yth Grp; Pep Clb; ROTC; Drm Mjr(t); Mrchg Band; Sec Stu Cncl; Chrldng; Capt Pom Pon; Trk; Cit Awd; HOSA; Schl Gospel Choir; Comm Work; OK ST Univ; Nrsng.

DAWSON, WILLIAM A; Seminole Jr Sr HS; Seminole, OK; (3); Debate Tm; Drama Clb; French Clb; Math Clb; Speech Tm; Church Choir; Treas Jr Cls; Rep Stu Cncl; Tennis; Hon Roll; Acctng.

DAY, JAIME; Elmore City-Pernell HS; Elmore City, OK; (4); 6/35; Church Yth Grp; FCA; 4-H; Key Clb; Natl FFA Org; Pep Clb; Teachers Aide; Variety Show; Rep Stu Cncl; Capt Bsktbl; St 4-H Proj Area Wnnr; All-Conf Bsktbl; UCA Capts Of Amer Chrldr In Macys Parade; Hillsdale Coll; Bus.

DAY, JASON B; Choctaw HS; Choctaw, OK; (4); 106/320; Drama Clb; School Play; Stage Crew; Jr NHS; Rose ST Coll; Atmospheric Sci.

DAY, JENICE L; Union Sr HS; Coweta, OK; (3); 87/741; FBLA; Office Aide; Spanish Clb; Chorus; Hon Roll; Jr NHS; NHS; Pres Schlr; Spanish NHS; Bus Mgmt.

DAY, JENNIFER C; Plainview HS; Ardmore, OK; (4); FHA; Natl Beta Clb; Drill Tm; High Hon Roll; Hon Roll; NHS; Pres Schlr; All Amer Schlr; OK East Cntrl Univ; Bus; Law.

DAY, JENNY; Roland Sr HS; Roland, OK; (4); FCA; Teachers Aide; Color Guard; Flag Corp; Rep Frsh Cls; Bsktbl; Chrldng; Sftbl; Hon Roll; Hmcmng Qn; Hnrs Clb Pres; Carl Albert ST Coll.

DAY, JULIE B; Edmond Memorial HS; Edmond, OK; (2); Church Yth Grp; Key Clb; Spanish Clb; Band; Church Choir; Mrchg Band; Variety Show; Cit Awd; High Hon Roll; NHS; OK ST Univ; Elem Ed.

DAY, KORIN M; Union Intermediate HS; Broken Arrow, OK; (2); French Clb; Chorus; Hon Roll; NHS; Mdlng.

DAY, KRISTEN; Ponca Ctiy Sr HS; Ponca City, OK; (4); 2/364; Am Leg Aux Girls St; Math Tm; Spanish Clb; Band; Capt Flag Corp; Orch; Rep Stu Cncl; High Hon Roll; Hon Roll; NHS; Med Rsrch.

DAY, MAGGIE L; Poteau HS; Poteau, OK; (4); 27/145; Ed Nwsp; Ed Yrbk; High Hon Roll; Jr NHS; Intern At The Poteau Daily News & Sun; Adult Lit Tutor; Multi-Yr Listee; Westark CC; Commnctns; Wrtr.

DAY, MALCOLM T; Stillwater Sr HS; Stillwater, OK; (3); Church Yth Grp; Church Choir.

DAY, MELISSA R; Wagoner Sr HS; Wagoner, OK; (2); French Clb; Band; Mrchg Band; Tchng.

DAY, REBECCA; Moore HS; Moore, OK; (4); 55/530; Am Leg Aux Girls St; Church Yth Grp; Band; Drm Mjr(t); Mrchg Band; School Musical; NHS; OK ST U.

DAY, RONNELL; Antlers Sr HS; Antlers, OK; (3); Am Leg Aux Girls St; Church Yth Grp; FBLA; FHA; SADD; Treas Soph Cls; Rep Jr Cls; Var JV Bsktbl; Var Sftbl; Hon Roll; BAD; Soph & Jr Homcmng Attend; Tahlequah N E ST U; Med.

DAY, SETH; Apache HS; Apache, OK; (2); 1/54; Pres Frsh Cls; Pres Soph Cls; Pres Jr Cls; VP Stu Cncl; Var L Ftbl; High Hon Roll; NHS; Ntl Merit Ltr; Reg Fnlst Tulsa Wrlds Ctzn Bee; OK ST U; Law.

DAYTON, BRANDI D; Macarthur Sr HS; Lawton, OK; (4); Church Yth Grp; Drama Clb; FCA; FHA; Hosp Aide; Science Clb; School Musical; School Play; Stage Crew; Hon Roll; Kywnntts; Hosp Vol; Cameron U; Elem Ed.

DAYTON, CARRIE; Pond Creek-Hunter Schl; Pond Creek, OK; (4); Am Leg Aux Girls St; English Clb; FCA; Band; School Play; Sec Jr Cls; Ofcr Stu Cncl; Bsktbl; Sftbl; Trk; U Of Cntrl OK; Psych.

DAYTON, KEVIN; Pond Creek-Hunter Schl; Pond Creek, OK; (4); 10/29; Am Leg Boys St; Church Yth Grp; FCA; School Play; Rep Frsh Cls; Rep VP Soph Cls; Rep Jr Cls; Rep Sr Cls; Rep Stu Cncl; L Bsbl; Natl Engl Merit Awd Wnnr; Vol Audio/Video Controller 1st Bapt Church; Brdcstng.

DAYTON, SANDRA; Pond Creek-Hunter Schl; Pond Creek, OK; (2); 1/33; FCA; HOBY; Band; Mrchg Band; Pep Band; Sec Frsh Cls; Var JV Bsktbl; Var Sftbl; NHS; OK Hnr Soc.

DEACON, BRENT K; North Intemediate HS; Broken Arrow, OK; (1); Arts; Musician.

DEAKINS, BRANT W; Deer Creek HS; Edmond, OK; (2); Drama Clb; Science Clb; School Play; Stage Crew; Var Wrstlng; OK ST Univ.

DEAL, DAVID J; Lindsay HS; Lindsay, OK; (4); Church Yth Grp; FCA; FHA; Office Aide; Rep Stu Cncl; Var Ftbl; JV Trk; Hon Roll; OSU Tech; Biomed Technician.

DEAL, EMILY; Midwest City HS; Oklahoma City, OK; (3); Church Yth Grp; FCA; French Clb; FHA; SADD; Rptr Nwsp; Rep Soph Cls; VP Jr Cls; Rep Stu Cncl; Stat Wrstlng; PROMISE; Sprt Cncl; U Of Cntrl OK; Brdcst Jrnlsm.

DEAL, LISA E; Putnam City West HS; Oklahoma City, OK; (4); Drama Clb; French Clb; NFL; Teachers Aide; Thesps; School Musical; School Play; Stage Crew; Rep Sr Cls; Hon Roll; OK City CC; Med Trnscript.

DEAL, TOBY L; Stillwater Sr HS; Stillwater, OK; (4); 100/400; FCA; Yrbk; Ofcr Bsbl; Hon Roll; Jr NHS; Prfct Atten Awd; Duke Math/Sci Hnr; OK ST U; Psycht.

DEAN, ALISHA; Moore HS; Moore, OK; (4); 51/549; Church Yth Grp; Latin Clb; Model UN; Science Clb; Spanish Clb; SADD; Hon Roll; NHS; U Central OK; Elem Ed.

DEAN, ANDREA; Mc Loud HS; Mc Loud, OK; (3); #1 in class; Church Yth Grp; Band; Drm Mjr(t); Jazz Band; Mrchg Band; Pep Band; Socr; High Hon Roll; NHS; OK Hnr Soc; Hnr Schlr Acad Achvmnt Awd.

DEAN, ANTHONY; Morrison Public Schl; Morrison, OK; (4); 8/37; Rep FBLA; Natl FFA Org; Office Aide; Spanish Clb; Teachers Aide; Rptr Jr Cls; Rep Stu Cncl; Var L Ftbl; OSU; Pre-Med.

DEAN, EBONY; Okmulgee HS; Okmulgee, OK; (1); Church Yth Grp; GAA; Pep Clb; Band; Chorus; Church Choir; Mrchg Band; Pep Band; FCA; Spanish Clb; Therapist/Acctng.

DEAN, ERICA R; Mc Alester HS; Mcalester, OK; (3); #5 in class; French Clb; Band; Mrchg Band; Sec Frsh Cls; Chrldng; Wt Lftg; Hon Roll; OK Hon Soc; OSSAA Acad Achvmnt Awd Chrldng 96; OK ST Univ; Sprt Sci/Hlth.

DEAN, GREGORY M; Union Intermediate HS; Tulsa, OK; (2); Church Yth Grp; FCA; Spanish Clb; Ofcr Stu Cncl; Bsktbl; Ftbl; Hon Roll; NHS; Sprts Med Dctr.

DEAN, JENNIFER; Edmond North HS; Edmond, OK; (4); Church Yth Grp; Math Clb; Mu Alpha Theta; Office Aide; Spanish Clb; Hon Roll; Slng Tm; Bllt; OK ST U; Biochem/Dctr.

DEAN, JENNIFER D; North Intemediate HS; Frankston, TX; (1); Church Yth Grp; Cmnty Wkr; Library Aide; Natl FFA Org; Speech Tm; Hon Roll; Jr NHS; TX A&M; Veterinarian/Msnry.

DEAN, STEPHANIE; Hilldale HS; Muskogee, OK; (1); Church Yth Grp; German Clb; High Hon Roll; Hon Roll; Teens For Christ; Ed.

DEAN, STEPHEN M; Putnam North HS; Oklahoma City, OK; (3); Chess Clb; Spanish Clb; Cit Awd; Hon Roll; Emory Riddle; Comp Engr.

DEANS, ANGELA M; Cushing HS; Cushing, OK; (3); Art Clb; Church Yth Grp; Math Tm; Office Aide; Science Clb; Spanish Clb; Teachers Aide; Hon Roll; Prfct Atten Awd; Spanish NHS; Var Schlr.

DEARDORFF, MAX T; B T Washington HS; Tulsa, OK; (2); Computer Clb; German Clb; Scholastic Bowl; NHS; Natl Span Exam 2nd Pl ST; Philosopher.

DEARMAN, CALLIE; Claremore Sr HS; Claremore, OK; (2); Church Yth Grp; French Clb; VP FHA; Hosp Aide; Church Choir; Prfct Atten Awd; Native Amer Clb; Phys Thrpy.

DEARMAN, PATRICK; Porum HS; Porum, OK; (1); 2/35; Church Yth Grp; FCA; FHA; Quiz Bowl; Pres Frsh Cls; High Hon Roll; Pres Acad Fit Awd; Sal; Masonic Awd.

DEASON, BRANDY; Westmoore HS; Oklahoma City, OK; (3); French Clb; Chorus; Bsktbl; NHS; Stdnts For Cleaner Environment; Medicine.

DEASON, HANNAH R; Wright Christian Acad; Sand Springs, OK; (3); Key Clb; Rep Soph Cls; Rep Jr Cls; Hon Roll; Homecoming Attendant; Tulsa Univ; PT.

DEASON, JUSTIN; West Middle HS; Norman, OK; (1); Cmnty Wkr; FCA; French Clb; Red Cross Aide; Ofcr Bsbl; Bsktbl; Ftbl; Wt Lftg; Wrstlng; French Hon Soc; Acquired Cmnty Trng Svcs; Athltc Trnr.

DEASON, MICHAEL J; Okay Jr Sr HS; Okay, OK; (1); 9/42; Art Clb; Church Yth Grp; Church Choir; Ofcr Bsbl; Bsktbl; Cit Awd; Hon Roll; Chrch; Upward Bound Pgm; Baylor U; OB-GYN.

DEATHERAGE, MARY E; Choctaw HS; Choctaw, OK; (4); 33/313; NHS; Ntl Merit Ltr; Pres Acad Fit Awd; OK ST U; Vet.

DEATON, BRANDY L; Pauls Valley HS; Pauls Valley, OK; (1); Church Yth Grp; Girl Scts; Band; Chorus; Flag Corp; School Musical; School Play; Stage Crew; Ofcr Bsbl; Bsktbl; OK ST; OT Asst.

DE BAUD III, JOSEPH E; U S Grant HS; Oklahoma City, OK; (1); JV Var Bsbl; Intrml Bsktbl.

DE BEQUE, JASON; Prue Schl; Osage, OK; (4); 4/26; Drama Clb; German Clb; Letterman Clb; Office Aide; Scholastic Bowl; Varsity Clb; Nwsp; Yrbk; Ftbl; Wt Lftg; Panhandle St Univ; Engl Lit.

DE BOARD, EMILY M; Blackwell HS; Blackwell, OK; (2); Church Yth Grp; FCA; FHA; Letterman Clb; Pep Clb; Red Cross Aide; Var Bsktbl; Var Sftbl; Var Trk; Hon Roll.

DE BOARD, HOLLY S; Edmond Memorial HS; Edmond, OK; (2); 30/408; Church Yth Grp; Spanish Clb; Band; Mrchg Band; Rptr Nwsp; Hon Roll; NHS; Pres Acad Fit Awd; Sign Lang; Abilene Chrstnuniv; Law.

DE BOER, MELINDA R; Stillwater Jr HS; Stillwater, OK; (1); Band; Color Guard; Mrchg Band; Pep Band; Rep Stu Cncl; Swmmng; High Hon Roll; Pres Acad Fit Awd; Hon Letter Band; Notre Dance; His/Anthrplgy.

DE BOSE, ANDREA D; Mc Lain Career Acad; Tulsa, OK; (2); Girl Scts; Hosp Aide; Bsktbl; Vllybl; Hon Roll; Prfct Atten Awd.

DEBOUSE, PAUL; Star Spencer HS; Spencer, OK; (4); Am Leg Boys St; Church Yth Grp; Quiz Bowl; Scholastic Bowl; Band; Church Choir; Mrchg Band; Pep Band; NHS; Pres Acad Fit Awd; Scndry Educ.

DE BUSK II, RONALD CRAIG; Inola Sr HS; Broken Arrow, OK; (4); Church Yth Grp; FCA; Spanish Clb; Teachers Aide; Church Choir; School Musical; Variety Show; L Bsbl; High Hon Roll; Hon Roll; Mr Bsbl; Received An Invitation To US Bsbl Team Going To Europe & Participate; Northeastern OK A&M; Psych.

DE CAMP, NICKOLAS; Depew HS; Stroud, OK; (1); Sec Treas Frsh Cls; Var Bsbl; JV Bsktbl; Var Ftbl; Wt Lftg; Prfct Atten Awd.

DECH, STACI R; Westmoore HS; Oklahoma City, OK; (3); Church Yth Grp; Spanish Clb; Band; Mrchg Band; Pep Band; Swmmng; Hon Roll; RN.

DECK, JARED; Thomas Jr Sr HS; Thomas, OK; (2); 1/42; Church Yth Grp; FCA; HOBY; NFL; Chorus; Rep Frsh Cls; Bsktbl; Trk; High Hon Roll; Western OK Hnr Choir; Acad Team; OK City Univ; PE/SPEC Ed.

DECK, REBECCA; Lone Grove HS; Ardmore, OK; (4); #6 in class; Am Leg Aux Girls St; Church Yth Grp; FHA; Science Clb; Chorus; Color Guard; Natl Hnr Soc; OK Chrstn U Sci/Arts.

DECK, RUSSELL L; Putnam City North HS; Oklahoma City, OK; (3); FCA; Var Bsbl; NHS.

DECKARD, KIMBERLY; Dewar Jr-Sr HS; Dewar, OK; (1); 1/43; Church Yth Grp; FHA; Quiz Bowl; Church Choir; Bsktbl; Chrldng; Sftbl; High Hon Roll; Prfct Atten Awd; Val.

DECKARD, SETH; Grove HS; Jay, OK; (2); CAP; FBLA; Nwsp; Intrml Bsbl; Hon Roll; NHS; USAF Acad; Pilot.

DECKER, AMY; Edmond North HS; Edmond, OK; (4); 68/339; Church Yth Grp; Math Clb; Mu Alpha Theta; SADD; Orch; Bsktbl; Prfct Atten Awd.

DECKER, AMY L; Oologah HS; Oologah, OK; (3); Science Clb; Hon Roll; Vol Wrk At Tall Grass Prairie.

DECKER, MICHAEL G; Enid Sr HS; Enid, OK; (2); Church Yth Grp; French Clb; Chorus; School Musical; School Play; Ofcr Stu Cncl; Ftbl; Socr; Cit Awd; High Hon Roll; OK U; Law.

DE DEYNE, JAMIE L; Bishop Kelley HS; Tulsa, OK; (2); Cmnty Wkr; Pep Clb; Spanish Clb; High Hon Roll; STARS; Sci.

DEEN, ARON; Choctaw HS; Choctaw, OK; (2); 23/396; Chorus; Swing Chorus; Wrstlng; High Hon Roll; Hon Roll; Jr NHS; Genetics.

DEEN, BEAU A; West Middle HS; Norman, OK; (3); Am Leg Boys St; Church Yth Grp; FCA; Letterman Clb; Math Clb; Science Clb; Chorus; Variety Show; Ftbl; Wt Lftg; Natl Yth Forum Intelligence, Diplomacy & Democracy; Naval Acad; Pilot.

DEEN, CARL A; Choctaw HS; Choctaw, OK; (2); Chorus; Swing Chorus; Intrml Golf; Var Wrstlng; High Hon Roll; Hon Roll; Jr NHS; NHS; Wk/Hlp Train Thrghbrd Hrs.

DEERING, BUCK; Yale Jr Sr HS; Yale, OK; (3); 2/35; Church Yth Grp; Natl FFA Org; Cit Awd; High Hon Roll; NHS; OK ST U; Bus.

DEERINWATER, CODY; Hulbert Jr Sr HS; Tahlequah, OK; (1); FHA; Girl Scts; Chorus; Chrldng; High Hon Roll; Hon Roll; Jr NHS; Kiwanis Awd; Archeology.

DEES, NATHAN; Rattan Sr HS; Rattan, OK; (4); 4/30; Church Yth Grp; FCA; French Clb; Rptr Nwsp; Ed Yrbk; Pres Frsh Cls; Pres Soph Cls; Pres Jr Cls; Hon Roll; Sal; Law.

DE FALCO, RICHARD C; Tishomingo HS; Milburn, OK; (4); 17/56; 4-H; Office Aide; Quiz Bowl; Ofcr Stu Cncl; Var Bsbl; Var Bsktbl; Var Trk; Hon Roll; Natl Chmpn Inline Speed Sktr, Intl Chmpn Inline Roller Speed Sktr; GATE; Se OK ST U; Bus.

DE FATTA, KATHERINE M; Bishop Kelley HS; Tulsa, OK; (3); Spanish Clb; Hon Roll; Yth Grp; Svc Prgm.

DE FOREST, KALA; Anadarko HS; Anadarko, OK; (1); Chorus; Chrldng; Hon Roll.

DE FRANCO, JENNIFER JANE; Edmond Santa Fe HS; Edmond, OK; (3); 28/285; Library Aide; Chorus; Church Choir; Mrchg Band; Pep Band; School Musical; School Play; Stage Crew; NHS; Church Yth Grp; Tri-M Music Hnrs Soc; U Of Cntrl OK; Tchng.

DE GASE, KIM; Daniel Webster HS; Tulsa, OK; (3); DECA; FBLA; FTA; Key Clb; Office Aide; Pep Clb; Yrbk; VP Frsh Cls; Sec Soph Cls; VP Jr Cls; OK ST U; Elem Ed.

DE GIUSTI, TARA GIOVANNA; Tuttle HS; Tuttle, OK; (4); 9/77; Am Leg Aux Girls St; FCA; Natl FFA Org; SADD; VP Jr Cls; Capt Bsktbl; Trk; Hon Roll; NHS; Church Yth Grp; Mss Tuttle; U Of OK.

DE GRAFFENREID, JAIME; Del City HS; Oklahoma City, OK; (3); Chorus; Pom Pon; NHS; Dance.

DE GRAFFENREID II, MICHAEL T; Del City HS; Oklahoma City, OK; (4); 9/374; Am Leg Boys St; Boy Scts; Co-Ed Yrbk; Ofcr Stu Cncl; Jr NHS; NHS; Jr Rotarian; Acad Ltr Jacket; Eagle Scout.

DE HART, SUMMER; Chickasha HS; Chickasha, OK; (4); 12/147; Am Leg Aux Girls St; Church Yth Grp; Spanish Clb; SADD; Acpl Chr; Chorus; Ofcr Stu Cncl; Chrldng; Tennis; Hon Roll; Appaloosa Horse Clb Natl Yth Brd Of Dirs; OK ST U; Hstry.

DEIBLER, SHANNON R; Norman Sr HS; Norman, OK; (3); Church Yth Grp; Cmnty Wkr; DECA; Office Aide; Pep Clb; Teachers Aide; Chorus; Cit Awd; Norman Optimist Clb; Page At St Capitol; OK Univ; Law.

DEIS, PATRICIA D; Sapulpa Sr HS; Sapulpa, OK; (4); 93/313; Art Clb; FHA; SADD; Teachers Aide; Ed Yrbk; Prin Cncl; USAO; Art.

DEISIGNE, AMY D; Choctaw HS; Choctaw, OK; (3); Church Yth Grp; Key Clb; Bsktbl; Crs Cntry; Mgr(s); Socr; Tennis; Hon Roll; Jr NHS; NHS; OSU.

DEITER, ASHLEY; Westmoore HS; Moore, OK; (2); Hosp Aide; Pep Clb; Teachers Aide; Chrldng; Gym; Trk; Hon Roll; Jr NHS; Flwshp Chrstn Aths; Bus.

DEITER, MELISSA; Westmoore HS; Oklahoma City, OK; (4); Church Yth Grp; FCA; FHA; Library Aide; Office Aide; Red Cross Aide; Spanish Clb; Rep Frsh Cls; Rep Soph Cls; Rep Jr Cls; Hmcmng Attndnt; Chrch Bsktbl Lg; Vctn Bible Schl Tchr; OK ST U; Sec Ed.

DELA CRUZ, BRIAN; Midwest City Hs; Midwest City, OK; (4); Spanish Clb; Band; Mrchg Band; NHS; Prfct Atten Awd; Pres Acad Fit Awd; Spanish NHS; Val; UOK; Med.

DE LANCEY, JANEE M; Westmoore HS; Oklahoma City, OK; (1); 19/600; Church Yth Grp; Drama Clb; Spanish Clb; Pres Chorus; School Play; Golf; NHS; Acad Team 4th Pl Spnsh; Julliard; Theatr.

DELANEY, SCOTT; Bartlesville Sr HS; Bartlesville, OK; (1); Church Yth Grp; FBLA; Spanish Clb; Golf; Hon Roll; Prfct Atten Awd.

DELAY, TRISHA; Turpin Schl; Liberal, KS; (1); Art Clb; FCA; GAA; Letterman Clb; Pep Clb; Chorus; Bsktbl; Chrldng; Sftbl; Trk; Phy Ther.

DE LEON, NOAH D; Erick Jr Sr HS; Erick, OK; (1); Church Yth Grp; FHA; Quiz Bowl; Scholastic Bowl; Sec Treas Frsh Cls; Ofcr Bsbl; Wt Lftg; High Hon Roll; Hon Roll; TSA; U Of OK.

DELLEGAR, SHAWN; Inola Sr HS; Inola, OK; (4); 1/79; Pres FCA; Pres Science Clb; Pres Frsh Cls; VP Soph Cls; Pres Sr Cls; VP Stu Cncl; Ftbl; Golf; Hon Roll; Pres NHS; Scuba Diving; Vlybl; U Of Tulsa; Biochem/Pre-Med.

DE LONG, HAYLEE J; Sapulpa Sr HS; Sapulpa, OK; (3); 9/289; Dance Clb; French Clb; Drill Tm; Mrchg Band; VP Stu Cncl; Socr; French Hon Soc; High Hon Roll; NHS; Prfct Atten Awd; OK ST Univ; Pre Med.

DELONG, MICHAEL L; Choctaw HS; Midwest City, OK; (3); Boy Scts; Spanish Clb; Var Bsbl; Chem Awds; OU; Pilot.

DELONG, SHAWN K; Hominy HS; Hominy, OK; (2); 2/79; Church Yth Grp; FCA; Teachers Aide; VP Frsh Cls; Var Bsbl; Var Bsktbl; JV Ftbl; Var Trk; Var Wt Lftg; Cit Awd; Hunting; Fishing; Tech Ed Awd; Wildlife Mgmt.

DELOZIER, CHAD D; Latta Sr HS; Ada, OK; (4); 3/52; FCA; Math Clb; Natl FFA Org; Scholastic Bowl; Sec Soph Cls; VP Sr Cls; Var Bsbl; Jr NHS; NHS; Sal; E Centrl Univ; Mech Eng.

DELPHINE, LE ROL; Choctaw HS; Midwest City, OK; (2); Fr Scolarity By Mail; Fr Pharmacy U; Pharmacy.

DELSIGNE, AMY D; Choctaw HS; Choctaw, OK; (3); FCA; Key Clb; Chrldng; Crs Cntry; Powder Puff Ftbl; Socr; High Hon Roll; Hon Roll; NHS; OBU; Math.

DELTPLAIN, CUSTY J; Pauls Valley HS; Pauls Valley, OK; (2); Boy Scts; Church Yth Grp; FCA; Natl FFA Org; Spanish Clb; Varsity Clb; Bsktbl; Ftbl; Trk; Wt Lftg.

DELUCCA, JORGE A; Midwest City HS; Midwest City, OK; (3); 118/364; Boy Scts; ROTC; Spanish Clb; Hon Roll; Spanish NHS; Univ Of FL Gainsville; Arch.

DEMAREE, BRUCE A; Bluejacket Schl; Vinita, OK; (3); 2/20; Church Yth Grp; Computer Clb; JA; Quiz Bowl; Science Clb; Rep Frsh Cls; Sec Soph Cls; Rep Stu Cncl; Crs Cntry; Ftbl; Cadet Of Internation Aerospace Acad At OK City Univ ASTEC; Amer Legion Outstndg Awqd Of Excl Stdnts; Med; Aerospace Sci.

DEMEL, MELISSA; Miami Sr HS; Miami, OK; (4); 35/125; Chess Clb; Church Yth Grp; Cmnty Wkr; Debate Tm; Drama Clb; Library Aide; NFL; Red Cross Aide; Speech Tm; Thesps; 4th Pl Dance Olympus Natl Fnlsts; Dance Mstrs OK Best Overall Sr Duo; 7th 3a St Speech Fnlst; OSU; Theater Arts.

DEMEL, TIFFANY; Miami Sr HS; Miami, OK; (2); 54/225; Church Yth Grp; Cmnty Wkr; Debate Tm; Drama Clb; FCA; NFL; Speech Tm; Crs Cntry; Trk; Hon Roll; Red Ribbon Cmmtte; Envrnmnt Clb; Pittsburg ST U; HS Engl Tchr.

DEMETIES, LEAH F; Eisenhower Jr HS; Lawton, OK; (4); 1/386; Church Yth Grp; Drama Clb; FHA; HOBY; VP Intnl Clb; Library Aide; Model UN; Capt Quiz Bowl; Nwsp; Acad Decath; GT Clb; SAVE; Engl.

DEMOSS, AMANDA; Stillwater Sr HS; Stillwater, OK; (1); Church Yth Grp; Dance Clb; FCA; Pep Clb; Spanish Clb; Nwsp; Yrbk; Ofcr Frsh Cls; Chrldng; Trk.

DE MOSS, LORA R; Canton HS; Longdale, OK; (2); #11 in class; Natl FFA Org; Band.

DEMPSEY, TIECE; Northeast HS; Oklahoma City, OK; (3); 7/100; HOBY; Science Clb; VP Frsh Cls; Pres Soph Cls; JV Chrldng; Mgr(s); High Hon Roll; NHS; Coll Club; Prom Comm Chrmn; Kodak Ldrshp Awd; KS U; Med.

DE NEUI, LUKE A; Broken Arrow Sr HS; Broken Arrow, OK; (4); Church Yth Grp; Church Choir; Natl Voc Tech Hnr Soc; Church Outstdng Teen Awd; Tulsa JC; Music.

DENHAM, SHELLY D; Lone Grove HS; Lone Grove, OK; (3); 31/100; Church Yth Grp; FHA; Speech Tm; Chorus; School Musical; School Play; Variety Show; High Hon Roll; Hon Roll; NHS; Miss Lone Grove 96; Med/Cntry Sngr.

DENHAM, TAMARA E; Eisenhower Jr HS; Lawton, OK; (1); Church Yth Grp; CAP; FCA; FHA; Key Clb; Office Aide; Speech Tm; Church Choir; Bsktbl; Sftbl; Tchr; Drama.

DENISON, CHRISTY; Marietta HS; Marietta, OK; (1); Church Yth Grp; Debate Tm; Drama Clb; FHA; Girl Scts; Speech Tm; Hon Roll; Author.

DENMAN, HEATHER; Elgin HS; Lawton, OK; (2); 2/85; Pres Church Yth Grp; FCA; HOBY; Var Crs Cntry; JV Var Trk; High Hon Roll; Jr NHS; NHS; Pres Acad Fit Awd; Sec Frsh Cls; Acad Ltr 2 Yrs; St Wide United Meth Yth Choir; Stu Cncl Pres 96-97; Marine Bio.

DENMAN, MISTY D; Bartlesville Sr HS; Bartlesville, OK; (3); 59/444; Cmnty Wkr; FHA; High Hon Roll; Hon Roll; Jr NHS; NHS; Prfct Atten Awd; 1st Pl Dist Sci Fair; Ger Natl Hon Soc; OK Ctr Advncmnt Sci/Tech Awd; OU; Elem Ed.

DENNEHY, ZACHARY P; Muskogee HS; Muskogee, OK; (2); Church Yth Grp; JCL; Latin Clb; Service Clb; Golf; Tennis; High Hon Roll; Hon Roll; NHS; OK Hnr Soc; Eclgy Clb.

DENNIS, CARLYE R; Claremore Sr HS; Greenville, KY; (1); Church Yth Grp; Ofcr Bsbl; Hon Roll; Claremore Humane Soc Vol; Pre-Vet.

DENNIS, CHRIS S; Skiatook HS; Skiatook, OK; (3); Church Yth Grp; Drama Clb; FBLA; Library Aide; Teachers Aide; Ed Nwsp; Jr NHS; HS Anthology Ambrotos.

DENNIS, CHRISTOPHER D; Pauls Valley HS; Pauls Valley, OK; (1); Church Yth Grp; Natl FFA Org; Ftbl; Tennis; Wt Lftg; Wrstlng; High Hon Roll; Hon Roll; Pi Phi Pi; OK ST Hnr Soc 96; TX A&M; Vet.

DENNIS, JEREMY P; Del City HS; Del City, OK; (2); Church Yth Grp; FCA; Chorus; Church Choir; Orch; School Musical; Cit Awd; Jr NHS; NHS; Mst Outstdng Alg II Stdnt 95-; Pres Ed Awds Pgm Cert Outstdng Acad Achvmnt; Excl Awd Lang Arts; OBU; Music.

DENNIS, KARLA; Pawnee HS; Pawnee, OK; (4); 1/60; HOBY; Yrbk; Ofcr Jr Cls; Ofcr Sr Cls; Bsktbl; Chrldng; Trk; Cit Awd; Hon Roll; Val; Masonic Stu Of Today; OK ST U.

DENNIS, KERI; Hobart HS; Hobart, OK; (1); 6/100; Church Yth Grp; FCA; FHA; Rptr Frsh Cls; Rep Stu Cncl; Stat Bsktbl; Mgr(s); Score Keeper; Sftbl; Southwestern OK ST U.

DENNIS, KRISTIN A; Cushing HS; Cushing, OK; (2); 1/156; Math Clb; Science Clb; Spanish Clb; Mgr Bsktbl; Hon Roll; NHS; OK Hnr Soc; Var Schlr; Envrnmnt & Rcyclng; OK ST U; Biolgcl Scintst.

DENNIS, LIBBY A; Oologah HS; Claremore, OK; (3); FCA; GAA; Office Aide; Science Clb; SADD; Chorus; Var Bsktbl; Var Powder Puff Ftbl; Var Socr; Wt Lftg.

DENNIS, MATTHEW C; Nathan Hale HS; Tulsa, OK; (2); Multi Yr Listee; Cmptr Actvts; Art; Animation Artist/Cartnst.

DENNISON, SARAH L; Deer Creek HS; Edmond, OK; (3); 48/96; Cmnty Wkr; FCA; FBLA; Quiz Bowl; Scholastic Bowl; Science Clb; Spanish Clb; Teachers Aide; Sec Soph Cls; Mgr(s); Law Enforcement.

DENNY, KYLE; Bluejacket Schl; Bluejacket, OK; (1); #1 in class; FHA; Quiz Bowl; Rep Stu Cncl; Var Bsktbl; High Hon Roll.

DENSMORE, SARAH ANN; Putnam City West HS; Oklahoma City, OK; (4); 1/278; Drama Clb; German Clb; Thesps; Orch; School Musical; School Play; NHS; St Schlr; Val; Silver Strings; Yth & Govt VP & Attorney Gen; Hendrix Coll; Theatre Arts.

DENSON, JOHN; Wapanucka Schl; Wapanucka, OK; (1); Church Yth Grp; 4-H; Natl FFA Org; Quiz Bowl; L Bsbl; L Bsktbl; High Hon Roll.

DENT, LEE B; Will Rogers HS; Tulsa, OK; (3); Teachers Aide; Var Tennis; Cit Awd; Hon Roll; NHS; Nrsng; Pediatrics.

DENT, RICHARD J; Bishop Kelley HS; Tulsa, OK; (2); Church Yth Grp; Cmnty Wkr; JV Bsbl; Hon Roll; Amer Legion All-Star Team Starting Pitcher; Mission Trip To TN; KS U; Medicine.

DENTON, CHRISTY L; Nathan Hale HS; Tulsa, OK; (4); Church Yth Grp; Office Aide; ROTC; Teachers Aide; Spon Jr HS Chrldng Pom Squad 2 Yrs; Nrsng/Dr.

DENTON, KENNY S; Mc Loud HS; Mc Loud, OK; (2); 5/120; FCA; Letterman Clb; Ofcr Bsbl; Ftbl; Wt Lftg; Cit Awd; Hon Roll; NHS.

DEPASSE, EUGINA; Coalgate HS; Coalgate, OK; (2); 10/60; Church Yth Grp; Band; Mrchg Band; Pep Band; Pres Frsh Cls; Pres Soph Cls; Hon Roll; Jr NHS; NHS.

DE PAULO, NATHAN G; Olive Jr Sr HS; Jennings, OK; (3); Debate Tm; FBLA; Quiz Bowl; Scholastic Bowl; Speech Tm; Rep VICA; NHS; Teachers Aide; School Play; Natl VICA Ldrshp Conf Voting Del OK Rep; Close-Up Fndtn Stud Wkshp; Speech & Debate Medal Wnnr; Comp Prgmr; Aerospace Dsgn.

DE PRIEST, LELIA; U S Grant HS; Oklahoma City, OK; (2); Church Yth Grp; Cmnty Wkr; FCA; Church Choir; Ofcr Stu Cncl; JV Var Chrldng; Gym; HS Bus Ed Awd Wnnr 96; Dance; Church Yth Cncl.

DEPUY, DEBRA A; Hooker Jr-Sr HS; Hooker, OK; (4); 1/37; Church Yth Grp; Treas FHA; Scholastic Bowl; Chorus; Sec Treas Frsh Cls; Sec Treas Soph Cls; Sec Treas Jr Cls; Sec Treas Sr Cls; Sec NHS; Val; OK Baptist U; Religion.

DERAMO, JULIE; Oologah HS; Talala, OK; (2); Church Yth Grp; Var Chrldng; Var Gym; Hon Roll.

DERBY, DON B; Owasso Sr HS; Owasso, OK; (4); 94/425; Cmnty Wkr; Spanish Clb; Mrchg Band; Pep Band; Tennis; High Hon Roll; Hon Roll; Prfct Atten Awd; VFW Spch Cntst Post Wnnr; Nashville Cnty Shwdwn St Wnnr; Asst Tenniscoach; Camp Cnslr; U Of Tulsa; Eng.

DERICHSWEILER, KERI A; Memorial HS; Tulsa, OK; (2); French Clb; Key Clb; Speech Tm; Hon Roll; 2 Yr Coll.

DERR, ERIK R; Bartlesville Mid HS; Bartlesville, OK; (2); 142/950; Boy Scts; Church Yth Grp; Pres German Clb; Capt Scholastic Bowl; Band; Drm Mjr(t); DAR Awd; Hon Roll; NHS; Natl Hnr Roll; Bio Chem.

DERRICK, CASSANDRA; Muskogee HS; Muskogee, OK; (2); #45 in class; JCL; Latin Clb; High Hon Roll; NHS; Latin Hon Soc; Eclgy Club; Youth Vol Corps; Physcn.

DERRICK, CHRISTINE M; Star Spencer HS; Spencer, OK; (3); Library Aide; Spanish Clb; Band; Mrchg Band; High Hon Roll; NHS; Distngd Jr Trphy; Outstdng Jr Acad Trphy; Outstdng Musical Perfmnc Plaque; Archaeologist.

DERRICK, ZACK; Oklahoma Union Schl; Bartlesville, OK; (4); 12/46; Math Tm; Natl FFA Org; Quiz Bowl; Science Clb; Teachers Aide; High Hon Roll; Hon Roll; NHS; Prfct Atten Awd; St Champ FFA Swpstks; Natl Qlftyng St Cntst; Murray St Col High Wldng; OK St Univ; Forestry.

DERRYBERRY, PAIGE; Westmoore HS; Oklahoma City, OK; (4); 39/610; FCA; School Musical; Variety Show; Pres Frsh Cls; Rep Stu Cncl; Co-Capt Chrldng; NHS; Val; All St Chrldr; NCS Staff; U Of OK.

DESAI, SHIMA; Midwest City HS; Midwest City, OK; (2); Drama Clb; Letterman Clb; Spanish Clb; Band; Mrchg Band; Powder Puff Ftbl; Tennis; Cit Awd; Hon Roll; Jr NHS; Tnns Plyr Of Yr; Spnsh Clb Treas; 4.0 Clb; OK U; Phys Thrpy.

DESCHAMPS-BRALY, JORDAN; Ada HS; Ada, OK; (3); Church Yth Grp; Math Clb; Mu Alpha Theta; Scholastic Bowl; Spanish Clb; JV Bsktbl; Var Trk; High Hon Roll; NHS; Spanish NHS; Stu Plts License; Piano Cmptn 3 Supers; Gftd/Tlntd Pgm; OU; Med.

DE SHAZO, DARIN; U S Grant HS; Oklahoma City, OK; (4); 1/183; Church Yth Grp; Cmnty Wkr; Science Clb; Church Choir; Jr NHS; NHS; Val; Chrch Bus Mnstry; Awana Clb; Jr Marshal Cls 95 Baccalaureate; U OK; Elec Engr.

DE SPAIN, JENNIFER; Edmond North HS; Edmond, OK; (3); 17/367; Church Yth Grp; French Clb; Key Clb; Mu Alpha Theta; SADD; Bsktbl; Var Tennis; Hon Roll; NHS; Pres Acad Fit Awd.

DESPAIN, STEVE M; Stilwell HS; Stilwell, OK; (2); Natl Beta Clb; Quiz Bowl; Spanish Clb; Band; Jazz Band; Mrchg Band; Pep Band; Stat Bsktbl; Powder Puff Ftbl; Gov Hon Prg Awd; Marching Band Drum Section Ldr; D-Fy Bd Mem Frosh Yr; U Of OK; Sports Medicine.

DETRICH, JANE A; Bishop Kelley HS; Tulsa, OK; (1); Boy Scts; Pep Clb; Rep Frsh Cls; Rep Stu Cncl; JV Trk; JV Vllybl; High Hon Roll; Classical Bk Clb.

DEUUALL, MELISSA R; Mid-Del Christian Schl; Oklahoma City, OK; (3); 5/19; Church Yth Grp; Cmnty Wkr; Yrbk; Rep Jr Cls; Ofcr Stu Cncl; Co-Capt Chrldng; Tennis; Hon Roll; Ntl Merit Ltr; Rose ST Coll; Nursng.

DEUVALL, MELISSA; Mid-Del Christian Schl; Oklahoma City, OK; (3); Church Yth Grp; Church Choir; Yrbk; Rep Jr Cls; Ofcr Stu Cncl; Chrldng; Tennis; Hon Roll; Ntl Merit Ltr; OK U; Nrsng.

DE VANE, MELANIE; El Reno Sr HS; El Reno, OK; (3); #10 in class; Church Yth Grp; Key Clb; Math Clb; Science Clb; Chorus; Swing Chorus; Vllybl; Cit Awd; Hon Roll; Kiwanis Awd; Comm.

DEVEREAUX, JACEY; Stratford Schl; Pauls Valley, OK; (3); 5/40; FCA; FBLA; FHA; Quiz Bowl; Pres Jr Cls; Var Bsktbl; Var Chrldng; Var Sftbl; Var Trk; Hon Roll; U Of OK; Meterology.

DEVINE, BETH S; Woodward HS; Woodward, OK; (1); Drama Clb; Hon Roll; OK Univ; Comm.

DEVITT, LAURA A; Lawton Sr HS; Lawton, OK; (3); Girl Scts; Stage Crew; L Swmmng; Hon Roll; Horseback Riding; Vet Med.

DEVLIN, SHALA; Perry Sr HS; Perry, OK; (3); 1/110; Church Yth Grp; FBLA; FHA; German Clb; Band; Ed Nwsp; VP Frsh Cls; Cit Awd; High Hon Roll; Jr NHS; Mat Maids.

DEVOL, MARGARET R; Duncan HS; Duncan, OK; (2); FBLA; High Hon Roll; NHS; OK Hnr Soc.

DEVOLL, SARAH; Enid Sr HS; Enid, OK; (2); Church Yth Grp; French Clb; GAA; Chrldng; Trk; Hon Roll; Jr NHS; NHS.

DEWBERRY, KATIE L; Metro Christian Acad; Tulsa, OK; (3); Pep Clb; Treas Frsh Cls; Rep Stu Cncl; US House Rep Page Pgm; OK ST Senate Page; Natl Law Week With Former Pres Ford; Law.

DEWEY, DENNIS; Bridge Creek HS; Blanchard, OK; (2); Art Clb; Math Clb; Scholastic Bowl; Spanish Clb; Yrbk; Cit Awd; Hon Roll; NHS; Pres Acad Fit Awd; St Drwng Cnt Gvs Cmmndtn 1st Pl Ovrll; U Sci/Arts OK Blk/Wht Drwng Cnt 1st Pl; Yrbk/Spn Clb Dsgr/Art; U SCI/ARTS OK; Cmmrcl Artst.

DE WITT, AMANDA L; Pocola HS; Pocola, OK; (2); Girl Scts; Band; Chorus; Mrchg Band; Pep Band; Hon Roll; Prfct Atten Awd; St Schlr; OK Hnr Scty; Swmmng/Wrtng; Westark CC; Med/Tchng.

DE WITT, AMY; Braman Schl; Braman, OK; (2); 1/14; FCA; HOBY; Natl FFA Org; Speech Tm; School Play; Pres Frsh Cls; Var Bsktbl; Var Chrldng; High Hon Roll; NHS; PT.

DE WOLF, KRISTY; Wilson Schl; Okmulgee, OK; (4); 2/16; Rptr Natl FFA Org; Pres Speech Tm; School Play; Nwsp; Yrbk; Co-Capt Frsh Cls; Rptr Soph Cls; Co-Capt Jr Cls; Capt Sr Cls; High Hon Roll; Jrnlsm.

DEWWALT, TROY; El Reno Sr HS; El Reno, OK; (2); 15/220; Church Yth Grp; Ofcr Bsbl; Bsktbl.

DEYALSINGH, CALIA C; Ardmore HS; Ardmore, OK; (3); 12/198; Church Yth Grp; French Clb; Math Clb; Mu Alpha Theta; Science Clb; Mrchg Band; Trk; Hon Roll; Jr NHS; NHS; Leaflets Stud Clb; U Of OK; Law.

DEYOE, TARA; Victory Christian Schl; Tulsa, OK; (3); Church Yth Grp; Intnl Clb; Spanish Clb; Teachers Aide; School Musical; Ofcr Frsh Cls; Ofcr Soph Cls; Ofcr Jr Cls; Ofcr Stu Cncl; Sftbl; ORU; Psych.

DE YONG, HAVEN; Shawnee Sr HS; Shawnee, OK; (3); Church Yth Grp; FCA; Pep Clb; Scholastic Bowl; Spanish Clb; Church Choir; Stage Crew; Sec Jr Cls; Var Chrldng; High Hon Roll; Tri Hi Y; TAD; Big Brothers/Big Sisters Jr Brd; Optometry.

DEYWATER, LARRY W; Tecumseh HS; Shawnee, OK; (2); Ldrshp; Fed Bur Of Invest.

DHIMMAR, MARIE F; Cushing HS; Cushing, OK; (4); 1/140; Art Clb; Church Yth Grp; English Clb; Hosp Aide; Library Aide; Math Clb; Math Tm; Quiz Bowl; Science Clb; Spanish Clb; OU; Acctng.

DIAL, BRIAN; Deer Creek HS; Edmond, OK; (2); 9/103; Church Yth Grp; Cmnty Wkr; Science Clb; Nwsp; Yrbk; Var Bsbl; JV Wrstlng; High Hon Roll; Hon Roll; NHS; Poem Pblshd Tmrrws Dream Natl Lbry Of Ptry; Amer Lgn Bsbl; OK Hnr Scty.

DIAZ, CARMEN; Moore HS; Moore, OK; (4); Dance Clb; Church Choir; Jazz Band; Mrchg Band; Orch; Jr NHS; NHS; Jr Escrt 95; OK ST U; Vet Med.

DIAZ, NICOLE; Moore HS; Oklahoma City, OK; (2); JA; Scholastic Bowl; Var Swmmng; Jr NHS; U Of S CA; Med.

DIBBLE, DEANNA R; Western Heights Sr HS; Oklahoma City, OK; (2); 12/200; FCA; Spanish Clb; Chorus; Hon Roll; NHS; Ntl Merit Ltr; Piano; Reading; OK Univ; Med/Ed.

DIBELLO, JOSEPH P; Edmond Memorial HS; Edmond, OK; (4); 67/335; Key Clb; Spanish Clb; Temple Yth Grp; Chorus; School Musical; School Play; Swing Chorus; Variety Show; NHS; Pres Acad Fit Awd; OK ST U; Theatr Ed.

DICK, CHAD M; South Coffeyville Schl; S Coffeyville, OK; (1); 2/30; Rep Frsh Cls; Var Bsbl; Var Bsktbl; Cit Awd; High Hon Roll; MVP Bsbl Frosh Yr.

DICK, DEIDRA L; Cordell Sr HS; Bessie, OK; (1); Church Yth Grp; Cmnty Wkr; 4-H; FHA; Natl FFA Org; Quiz Bowl; Scholastic Bowl; Speech Tm; School Musical; Bsktbl; Mem Teen Ldrs; AAU Bsktbl Team; GATE; OK Univ.

DICKELMAN, JENNIFER L; West Middle HS; Norman, OK; (2); Office Aide; Band; Mrchg Band; Pep Band; Hon Roll; Pres Schlr; Teen Vol Pgm; Bus.

DICKENS, KRYSTAL; Glencoe Public Schl; Glencoe, OK; (1); 1/40; Church Yth Grp; 4-H; FHA; Quiz Bowl; Scholastic Bowl; Bsktbl; Chrldng; Sftbl; High Hon Roll; Stu Of Mnth; OK ST; Phys Thrpy.

DICKERSON, ANGEL D; Velma Alma HS; Velma, OK; (3); FCA; SADD; Teachers Aide; Band; Mrchg Band; School Play; Bsktbl; Sftbl; Trk; Wt Lftg; Cameron U; Schl Cnslr.

DICKERSON, MARC J; Bartlesville Mid HS; Bartlesville, OK; (2); Boy Scts; Church Yth Grp; Office Aide; Science Clb; Chorus; Hon Roll; Prfct Atten Awd.

DICKERSON, TODD; Butner Schl; Cromwell, OK; (4); 2/22; Bsktbl; High Hon Roll; Hon Roll; NHS; Bsktbl Small East All-St, 2 Time East Cntrl Conf Plyr Of Yr; Seminole JC.

DICKEY, BRANDOLYN C; Enid Sr HS; Enid, OK; (3); Church Yth Grp; Cmnty Wkr; Scholastic Bowl; Science Clb; Service Clb; Spanish Clb; VICA; Ed Nwsp; NHS; Constitution Team; Mock Trial; Pol Soc; Ob & Gyn Dr.

DICKEY, CYRSTAL M; Choctaw HS; Choctaw, OK; (3); 1/340; Am Leg Aux Girls St; Church Yth Grp; FCA; Key Clb; Quiz Bowl; Ed Yrbk; Treas Soph Cls; VP Jr Cls; VP Jr NHS; VP NHS; Univ Of OK; Pre Med/Phsy.

DICKEY, GINNY; Henryetta Sr HS; Henryetta, OK; (2); Church Yth Grp; FCA; FHA; Hosp Aide; Office Aide; Band; Church Choir; Mrchg Band; Pep Band; Tennis; Ped.

DICKEY, RENNETTA P; Alva HS; Alva, OK; (1); Band; Mrchg Band; Pep Band; Hon Roll; OK Univ; RN.

DICKINSON, ANN MARIE; Jenks HS; Jenks, OK; (2); 230/618; VP Church Yth Grp; Natl FFA Org; Chorus; Church Choir; Ofcr Stu Cncl; Trk; Wt Lftg; Hon Roll; Landscape Dsgn.

DICKINSON, GREG P; Edmond Memorial HS; Edmond, OK; (1); 130/490; Church Yth Grp; Dance Clb; FCA; Letterman Clb; Rep Frsh Cls; Ofcr Bsbl; Wt Lftg; Wrstlng; Hon Roll; NHS; Sports Medicine; Law.

DICKINSON, JONI E; Pauls Valley HS; Pauls Valley, OK; (2); Church Yth Grp; FCA; Key Clb; Pep Clb; Ofcr Frsh Cls; Bsktbl; Chrldng; Trk; Hon Roll; Pres Acad Fit Awd; OU; Marine Bio.

DICKSON, AMANDA J; Ponca City Sr HS; Ponca City, OK; (2); 67/460; Office Aide; Acpl Chr; Chorus; School Play; Ofcr Stu Cncl; Score Keeper; Tennis; High Hon Roll; Hon Roll; NHS; Camp Sea World 96; Fl ST Univ; Marine Bio.

DICKSON, CORA K; Checotah HS; Checotah, OK; (3); #24 in class; Art Clb; FBLA; Hon Roll; U Of Ctrl OK; Art.

DICKSON, JAMIE; Boswell Sr HS; Boswell, OK; (2); 2/40; FCA; Church Choir; High Hon Roll; Hon Roll; NHS; Pres Acad Fit Awd; Key Clb; Var Bsbl; Var Bsktbl; Natl Engl Soc; Natl Govt & Hstry; Acad Bwl; OBU; Frgn Mssn.

DICKSON, RYAN; Waukomis HS; Waukomis, OK; (3); Church Yth Grp; FCA; Quiz Bowl; Pres Frsh Cls; VP Jr Cls; JV Bsbl; Var Bsktbl; Var Ftbl; Var Trk; Hon Roll.

DIEDE, LAURA; Berryhill Jr HS; Tulsa, OK; (2); Church Yth Grp; Hosp Aide; Mu Alpha Theta; Service Clb; Spanish Clb; Teachers Aide; Yrbk; NHS; Pres Acad Fit Awd; Val; Pre-Med.

DIEDRICH, KRISTIE L; Heavener HS; Heavener, OK; (3); Church Yth Grp; Spanish Clb; Band; Chorus; Mrchg Band; FCS; Drug Free Clb; Cosmotologist.

DIEHL, ALLYSON L; Mustang HS; Mustang, OK; (4); Chess Clb; Cmnty Wkr; Sec Key Clb; Math Clb; Science Clb; Spanish Clb; Pres SADD; Chorus; Hon Roll; Kiwanis Awd; HS Hero Amer Lung Soc; Phy Thrpst.

DIEHL, TIMOTHY K; Bartlesville Mid HS; Bartlesville, OK; (2); 26/458; Boy Scts; Church Yth Grp; German Clb; Quiz Bowl; Rep Stu Cncl; JV Var Ftbl; Hon Roll; Jr NHS; NHS; Eagle Scout; CO Schl Of Mines; Engrng; Bus.

DIEL, CASH; Perkins-Tryon HS; Perkins, OK; (3); 1/75; Church Yth Grp; 4-H; FHA; Intnl Clb; Key Clb; Phtg Yrbk; JV Var Bsktbl; Wt Lftg; Var Wrstlng; 4-H Awd; OK St Univ; Agecon.

DIEL, KRISTEN K; Alva HS; Alva, OK; (2); Church Yth Grp; FHA; Key Clb; Band; Chorus; Church Choir; Jazz Band; Mrchg Band; Pep Band; Wt Lftg; Jazz, Ballet & Tap Dance.

DIEPENBROCK, AMANDA L; Edmond Memorial HS; Edmond, OK; (3); 49/371; Church Yth Grp; FHA; Key Clb; Spanish Clb; Chorus; School Musical; School Play; Variety Show; Hon Roll; NHS; All Amrcn Schol; U Of OK Hnrs Foracad Achv; Acctng.

DIES, AMIE D; Buffalo Jr Sr HS; Buffalo, OK; (3); Church Yth Grp; FCA; FBLA; Natl FFA Org; Band; Chorus; Church Choir; Mrchg Band; Swing Chorus; VP Jr Cls; OSU.

DIES, CARISSA E; Buffalo Jr Sr HS; Buffalo, OK; (1); Church Yth Grp; Cmnty Wkr; Pep Clb; Chorus; School Play; Sec Frsh Cls; Rep Stu Cncl; JV Bsktbl; JV Sftbl; JV Trk.

DIES, MARTHA J; Apache HS; Apache, OK; (2); FHA; Band; Mrchg Band; Pep Band; Ofcr Stu Cncl; Powder Puff Ftbl; Hon Roll; St Schlr; Med.

DIESSELHORST, MATT; Fairview HS; Fairview, OK; (2); Church Yth Grp; FCA; Quiz Bowl; Ofcr Stu Cncl; Var Bsbl; Var Bsktbl; Var Ftbl; High Hon Roll; NHS; Pres Acad Fit Awd; Outstndng Algebra II Stu.

DIETRICH, MINDY; Carnegie Jr HS; Carnegie, OK; (3); 6/56; VP Church Yth Grp; Office Aide; Pep Clb; Quiz Bowl; Teachers Aide; Ed Yrbk; Ofcr Soph Cls; Treas Jr Cls; Ofcr Sr Cls; Ofcr Stu Cncl; OK ST U; Elem Ed.

DIETZ, AMANDA; Bartlesville Mid HS; Bartlesville, OK; (2); 1/481; Church Yth Grp; FBLA; Spanish Clb; Ofcr Stu Cncl; Var Socr; High Hon Roll; Jr NHS; Prfct Atten Awd; Natl His/Govt Awd; Acad Exclnce Awd 2 Yrs; Intl Foreign Lang Awd.

DIETZEL, MATTHEW; Wagoner Sr HS; Wagoner, OK; (4); 17/130; Am Leg Boys St; FCA; FBLA; Ftbl; 4-H Awd; High Hon Roll; NHS; OSU; Med.

DILBECK, ANN MARIE; Jay HS; Jay, OK; (2); Church Yth Grp; FHA; Natl Beta Clb; Natl FFA Org; Pep Clb; Church Choir; Yrbk; Ofcr Soph Cls; Rep Stu Cncl; I-DFY; Peer Cnslr; FOMC; NEO; Obstretics.

DILBECK, JULIE A; Porter Jr Sr HS; Porter, OK; (2); Church Yth Grp; FCA; 4-H; Pres FHA; Treas Natl FFA Org; SADD; Pres Soph Cls; Ofcr Stu Cncl; Score Keeper; 4-H Awd; Natl Sci Mrt Awd; TU; Law.

DILBECK, SCOTT J; Wilburton Sr HS; Wilburton, OK; (3); Church Yth Grp; FCA; Office Aide; Varsity Clb; Nwsp; Bsktbl; Hon Roll; Ntl Merit Ltr; U Of OK; Attorney.

DILDINE, ALISHA; Woodward HS; Woodward, OK; (3); Art Clb; FBLA; FHA; Letterman Clb; Spanish Clb; Rep Frsh Cls; High Hon Roll; Hon Roll; Medicine.

DILL, BENJAMIN; Broken Arrow Sr HS; Broken Arrow, OK; (4); 7/921; Am Leg Boys St; Boy Scts; Debate Tm; French Clb; NFL; Office Aide; Speech Tm; Hon Roll; Jr NHS; NHS; Acad All-St; Prfct SAT Score; OK ST U; Scndry Ed.

DILLAHUNTY, CARMEN D; Putnam City North HS; Oklahoma City, OK; (3); 70/489; FBLA; Spanish Clb; SADD; Band; Mrchg Band; Ofcr Soph Cls; Bsktbl; Sftbl; Trk; Jr NHS; Rdng; Swimming; Comp Sci.

DILLAHUNTY, NATALIE N; Ponca City Middle HS; Ponca City, OK; (2); Church Yth Grp; Debate Tm; Drama Clb; 4-H; Pep Clb; Orch; Lit Mag; Trk; High Hon Roll.

DILLAMAN, PHILLIP M; Madill HS; Madill, OK; (2); Church Yth Grp; Cmnty Wkr; FCA; SADD; Bsktbl; Crs Cntry; Golf; Trk; Wt Lftg; Hon Roll.

DILLARD, SHANNON M; Idabel HS; Idabel, OK; (2); FCA; JV Var Bsktbl; Sftbl; Hon Roll; Cert Outstndng Stu Amer His.

DILLEY, MOLLY; Moore HS; Moore, OK; (4); Drama Clb; FCA; Spanish Clb; SADD; L Bsktbl; Var Golf; Powder Puff Ftbl; Eng II & Amer Hist Schlstc Achvt Awds.

DILLIN, AMANDA; Empire Schl; Yukon, OK; (1); Church Yth Grp; Cmnty Wkr; Sec Debate Tm; Drama Clb; Quiz Bowl; Sec Spanish Clb; Speech Tm; Chorus; NHS; Spanish NHS; Dance; OK U; Bus/Dance.

DILLINGER, DONNA; Midwest City HS; Oklahoma City, OK; (2); 1/489; French Clb; Band; Mrchg Band; Pep Band; Nwsp; Yrbk; High Hon Roll; Jr NHS; NHS; Prfct Atten Awd.

DILLINGHAM, CHRISIE S; Marlow HS; Marlow, OK; (4); 11/99; FCA; FTA; Office Aide; SADD; Teachers Aide; Drill Tm; Rptr Nwsp; Rptr Yrbk; Hon Roll; NHS; Tchr Cadet; E Cntrl Univ; Acctng; Bus.

DILLON, MICHELLE; Carl Albert HS; Midwest City, OK; (3); Church Yth Grp; FCA; Key Clb; Chorus; Variety Show; Var Crs Cntry; Score Keeper; NHS; Spirit Of OK All Star Chrldng; BSA Explorers Post 2002 Med; All Amer Schlr; Pre-Natal Nrsng.

DILLON, STEVEN D; Warner HS; Warner, OK; (1); 1/70; Cmnty Wkr; FHA; Office Aide; Red Cross Aide; Spanish Clb; Phtg Yrbk; High Hon Roll; Val; St Hnr Soc.

DILLS, LISA; Lexington HS; Maysville, OK; (4); 1/69; Hosp Aide; HOBY; Intnl Clb; Mu Alpha Theta; Jazz Band; NHS; Val; Cmnty Wkr; Spanish Clb; Band; Natl FFA Chrs, St Frmr Dgr; Acad All-St; U OK; Phrmcy.

DILLSAVER, MATTHEW J; B T Washington HS; Tulsa, OK; (2); Cmnty Wkr; Spanish Clb; Socr; Hon Roll; NHS.

DILTS, EMILY; Stillwater Jr HS; Stillwater, OK; (1); Key Clb; Office Aide; Thesps; School Play; Ofcr Stu Cncl; JV Tennis; JV Trk; Columbia; Corp Lawyer.

DI MAYO, DOMINIC V; Thackerville HS; Thackerville, OK; (2); 4/31; Quiz Bowl; Scholastic Bowl; Rptr Nwsp; Pres Soph Cls; Var Bsktbl; Var Ftbl; High Hon Roll; Hon Roll; Prfct Atten Awd.

DIMITROV, ALEXANDER S; Western Heights Sr HS; Oklahoma City, OK; (4); Church Yth Grp; Letterman Clb; Scholastic Bowl; Socr; Hon Roll; Pres Schlr; All Amer Tae Kwon Do/Karate Trnmnt; Univ Of Cntrl OK.

DIMMER, KATHLEEN L; Choctaw HS; Choctaw, OK; (2); Church Yth Grp; Debate Tm; Girl Scts; Hosp Aide; Chorus; Church Choir; Ofcr Soph Cls; High Hon Roll; Jr NHS; Sal; St Gregory; Optometry.

DIMON, RACHEL R; Owasso Sr HS; Owasso, OK; (2); Church Yth Grp; Cmnty Wkr; FCA; Office Aide; Band; Mrchg Band; Hon Roll; Jrnlsm.

DINH, CUONG H; Western Heights Sr HS; Oklahoma City, OK; (1); #1 in class.

DINH, THANH D; Putnam City HS; Oklahoma City, OK; (1); Church Yth Grp; Church Choir; Dentistry.

DINH, THIEN D; Putnam City HS; Oklahoma City, OK; (1); Church Yth Grp; Church Choir; Tennis; Hon Roll; Med.

DINKINS, LAMAR E; B T Washington HS; Tulsa, OK; (3); Variety Show; Var Trk; Atten Tulsa Tech Ctr.

DINSE, PIPER; Kingston HS; Kingston, OK; (1); Church Yth Grp; FCA; FHA; GAA; Spanish Clb; Ofcr Stu Cncl; JV Bsktbl; Var Sftbl; High Hon Roll; Hon Roll; Golden Bat Awd In Sftbl; Outstndng Bio & Eng I Stu; Southeastern Univ.

DINSMORE, DUSTIN A; Charles Page HS; San Bruno, CA; (2); 1/385; Church Yth Grp; FCA; Key Clb; Sec Spanish Clb; SADD; Church Choir; Sec Jr Cls; L Bsktbl; Var Socr; Cit Awd; Acad Lttr; Brdcst Jrnlsm/Eng.

DINSMORE, LESLIE M; Pryor Sr HS; Pryor, OK; (4); 15/148; Church Yth Grp; FBLA; Treas German Clb; Pres Mu Alpha Theta; Chorus; Ed Yrbk; Var Socr; Wrstlng; Hon Roll; NHS; OK ST U; Music Bus.

DIRICKSON, KELLEY; Chelsea HS; Chelsea, OK; (4); 11/60; Am Leg Aux Girls St; Church Yth Grp; FCA; Office Aide; Sec Spanish Clb; Teachers Aide; Chorus; Swing Chorus; Yrbk; Sec Frsh Cls; Sen, Hse Rep OK Page; OK ST; Spch Pthlgy.

DIRICKSON, LANDON; Metro Christian Acad; Tulsa, OK; (3); Chess Clb; FCA; Var Bsbl; JV Bsktbl; Var Crs Cntry; JV Wt Lftg; Cit Awd; Gov Hon Prg Awd; High Hon Roll; Hon Roll; Snblt Clssc Cmp 10th Grd; Chrch Yth Grp; OK ST Univ; Engl/Writer.

DIRICKSON, MEGAN; Collinsville HS; Collinsville, OK; (4); 2/104; Am Leg Aux Girls St; Sec FCA; Office Aide; Quiz Bowl; Chorus; School Musical; School Play; Ed Yrbk; Treas Frsh Cls; Treas Jr Cls; Voted Mrs Cardinal Sr Class; Hmcmng Qn; Salvation Army Angel Tree; U Of Tulsa; Pre-Med.

DISBROW, JEREMY C; Tulsa Tech Center-Peoria; Sand Springs, OK; (3); Spanish Clb; VICA; Band; Mrchg Band; Stage Crew; Ofcr Bsbl; JV Ftbl; Prfct Atten Awd; Sec Tulsa Vo-Tech; OSU; Electronics.

DISCHINGER, LORI M; Elgin HS; Elgin, OK; (2); 4-H; Natl FFA Org; 4-H Awd; High Hon Roll; Hon Roll; Jr NHS; NHS; Prfct Atten Awd; Comanche Co 4-H Mdl Hrse Club Pres; FFA Otdr Rec Awd; US His/Eng/Zoology Pins; Animal/Equine Sci.

DISE, LORI L; Tahlequah Sr HS; Tahlequah, OK; (3); German Clb; Science Clb; SADD; Acpl Chr; Chorus; Rep Frsh Cls; Golf; Trk; Jr NHS; NE ST U; PHD Psych.

DISMUKE, VALERIE S; Sapulpa Sr HS; Jenks, OK; (3); 6/300; Church Yth Grp; Spanish Clb; Band; Mrchg Band; High Hon Roll; Hon Roll; Jr NHS; NHS; Pres Acad Fit Awd; Spanish NHS; Bus.

DITTFUTH, RYAN W; Union Intermediate HS; Broken Arrow, OK; (2); 58/800; Church Yth Grp; FCA; German Clb; JV Bsbl; JV Bsktbl; High Hon Roll; NHS; DFY; Engr.

DITTMAR, TENA L; Choctaw HS; Choctaw, OK; (3); Drama Clb; Chorus; Church Choir; School Play; Hon Roll; Prfct Atten Awd; HOSA; OU Health Ctr; Med.

DITTO, LAURIE N; Ardmore HS; Ardmore, OK; (3); #31 in class; Art Clb; French Clb; Math Clb; Mu Alpha Theta; Science Clb; Spanish Clb; Chorus; School Musical; Tennis; Hon Roll; Music Dist Contest Recd 1; Fr Acad Awd; Schlr Ath Awd; Arch.

DIVINE, ASHLEY; Shawnee Sr HS; Shawnee, OK; (1); FCA; Capt Chrldng; JV Sftbl; Trk; High Hon Roll; OSU.

DIXON, CARRIE E; Duncan HS; Duncan, OK; (4); 35/214; Church Yth Grp; Cmnty Wkr; FBLA; Key Clb; Letterman Clb; Office Aide; SADD; Yrbk; Chrldng; NHS; Rotry Stu Of Month; US Chrldr Achvmt Awd; U Of OK; Elem Ed.

DIXON, CHASITY; Canute HS; Canute, OK; (3); 3/22; Church Yth Grp; GAA; VP Jr Cls; Bsktbl; Crs Cntry; Sftbl; Hon Roll; OK U; Law.

DIXON, CHERINA; Vinita HS; Vinita, OK; (2); FCA; Spanish Clb; Chorus; Chrldng; Trk; Hon Roll; Envrnmntl Clb; Talequah U; Sprts Med.

DIXON, DEANNA; Watts HS; Watts, OK; (4); Computer Clb; 4-H; Hosp Aide; Math Clb; Natl Beta Clb; Office Aide; Pep Clb; Phtg Nwsp; Ed Yrbk; Bsktbl; Bus.

DIXON, DEREK; Putram City North HS; Oklahoma City, OK; (4); 199/451; Boy Scts; Science Clb; Spanish Clb; Rep Stu Cncl; Trk; Eagle Sct; U Of Cntrl OK; Optmtrst.

DIXON, DINAH L; Hominy HS; Hominy, OK; (2); 5/79; FHA; Intrml Bsktbl; Intrml Trk; High Hon Roll; Hon Roll; OK HS Hnr Soc; OK Univ; Envrnmntl Engr.

DIXON, HEATHER D; Wakita Schl; Wakita, OK; (3); Church Yth Grp; Hist VP FHA; Band; Mrchg Band; Pep Band; Sftbl; High Hon Roll; Hon Roll; NHS; FCA; Cncrt Bnd ST; Outstdng Band In Clss 2 Yrs; U Of Sci/Arts Of OK; Vet.

DIXON, JASON B; West Middle HS; Norman, OK; (1); Church Yth Grp; FCA; JV Bsktbl; JV Var Golf.

DIXON, JENNEFER; Wynnewood HS; Wynnewood, OK; (4); 8/60; FHA; SADD; Teachers Aide; Band; Jazz Band; Mrchg Band; Hon Roll; Superior I Rating Flute Solo ST Solo/Ensemble Festival 96; East Cntrl Univ; Music.

DIXON, JULIE A; Bethel HS; Shawnee, OK; (1); Library Aide; Band; Mrchg Band; Pep Band; Hon Roll.

DIXON, KATHARINE LEIGH; Wynnewood HS; Wynnewood, OK; (3); 1/73; Letterman Clb; Scholastic Bowl; Teachers Aide; Chorus; Pres Frsh Cls; VP Soph Cls; Chrldng; Golf; Hon Roll; NHS; OK Hnr Soc; Acad Team; Gifted/Talented; East Cntrl Univ; Psych.

DIXON, LA TOISHA D; Mc Lain Career Acad; Tulsa, OK; (2); Church Yth Grp; Key Clb; Red Cross Aide; ROTC; Ofcr Stu Cncl; Golf; High Hon Roll; NHS; Hlth Acad 2000; Hlth Explrs; Bus/Fshn Dsgnr.

DIXON, LYNSEY A; Blackwell HS; Blackwell, OK; (2); Church Yth Grp; FCA; FHA; Hosp Aide; Letterman Clb; JV Bsktbl; Var Sftbl; Var Trk; Hon Roll; U Of Cntrl OK; Sports Medicine.

DIXON, ROBERT C; Ripley HS; Stillwater, OK; (1); Cmnty Wkr; FHA; Library Aide; Spanish Clb; Teachers Aide; Temple Yth Grp; Capt Socr; De Molay; Rollerblading; Pony Of Amer Clb; OK ST Univ; Chef; Bsktbl Playr.

DIXON, STACY; Shawnee Sr HS; Shawnee, OK; (4); Spanish Clb; Rptr Nwsp; High Hon Roll; NHS; Jrnlsm.

DIXON, WES; Dewey HS; Bartlesville, OK; (1); Quiz Bowl; Hon Roll; Pres Acad Fit Awd; St Schlr.

DO, HONG-QUYEN T; Union Sr HS; Tulsa, OK; (4); 95/629; Church Yth Grp; Intnl Clb; Key Clb; Church Choir; Hon Roll; NHS; Chem Acad Achvt Awd 94; Wrld Hstry Acad Achvt Awd 95; NHS 94 & 95; Tulsa JC; Nursng.

DO, LAM-DIEN T; Union Sr HS; Tulsa, OK; (3); 87/741; Church Yth Grp; Intnl Clb; Key Clb; Church Choir; Hon Roll; NHS; Stu Of Month 94-95; Math & Scl Stds Awds 95; Pres Awd For Edctnl Excl 95; ORU; Elec Engrng.

DO, PHUONG; Muskogee HS; Muskogee, OK; (3); 2/300; VP Church Yth Grp; Cmnty Wkr; Hosp Aide; JCL; Key Clb; Latin Clb; Chorus; Pres Soph Cls; High Hon Roll; NHS; Eclgy Clb Sec; Notre Dame; Med.

DO, THUY; Muskogee HS; Muskogee, OK; (4); 5/303; Church Yth Grp; Hosp Aide; Treas JCL; VP Treas Key Clb; Pres Soph Cls; Pres Jr Cls; Ofcr Sr Cls; High Hon Roll; NHS; All Amer Schlr; AZ ST U; Bus.

DOAN, CHRISTINA; East Central HS; Tulsa, OK; (4); 1/209; French Clb; Math Clb; Mu Alpha Theta; VICA; Trk; French Hon Soc; Hon Roll; Val; U Of OK; Med.

DOAN, JOHN T; Oklahoma Sch Of Science & Math; Ardmore, OK; (3); Church Yth Grp; Computer Clb; Dance Clb; French Clb; JCL; Latin Clb; Library Aide; Math Clb; Math Tm; Mu Alpha Theta; Field Of Med.

DOAN, PHUONG T; Norman Sr HS; Norman, OK; (3); Intrml Bsktbl; Hon Roll.

DOAN, SON; Westmoore HS; Oklahoma City, OK; (4); 50/600; JCL; Latin Clb; Office Aide; Band; Mrchg Band; Pep Band; NHS; Val; Univ Schlrshp; U Of OK.

DOAN, TOM; Oklahoma Sch Of Science & Math; Ardmore, OK; (4); HOBY; Pres Latin Clb; Pres Mu Alpha Theta; Capt Scholastic Bowl; Rep Soph Cls; Capt Ftbl; Capt Vllybl; Gov Hon Prg Awd; NHS; Pres Schlr; Tutts Gap Neural Resrch; OU Hlth Sci Ctr Cardiac Resrch; Dartmouth Coll; Med.

DOBBINS, CARRIE; South Intermediate HS; Broken Arrow, OK; (1); Church Yth Grp; JV Chrldng; Intrml Wt Lftg.

DOBBINS, CRYSTAL D; Thomas Jr Sr HS; Thomas, OK; (3); FCA; FHA; GAA; Spanish Clb; Band; Mrchg Band; Pep Band; Var Bsktbl; Var Sftbl; Var Trk; Bus.

DOBBS, ELLIOTT F; Edmond North HS; Edmond, OK; (1); Church Yth Grp; Cmnty Wkr; Orch; Mission Trip SD; TV Station Weather Dept Worker; U Of OK; Meteorology.

DOBBS, JENNIFER E; Charles Page HS; Sand Springs, OK; (3); 5/385; FTA; Spanish Clb; Band; Jazz Band; Mrchg Band; High Hon Roll; NHS; Ntl Merit Ltr; All ST Band/Tulsa Yth Symphny Prin Trmbnst; OK ST Univ; Prof Musician.

DOBBS, MATTHEW H; Bridge Creek HS; Blanchard, OK; (1); 1/75; Church Yth Grp; Quiz Bowl; Scholastic Bowl; Band; Jazz Band; Mrchg Band; Pep Band; High Hon Roll; Sci Acad OK ST Regents Hghr Educ; Aerospace Engr.

DOBRINSKI, AMBER D; Okeene Jr Sr HS; Okeene, OK; (2); Church Yth Grp; Debate Tm; Drama Clb; FCA; Library Aide; Office Aide; Scholastic Bowl; Speech Tm; Band; Chorus; UCLA.

DOBSON, JASON W; Depew HS; Depew, OK; (2); Cmnty Wkr; Drama Clb; Spanish Clb; Band; Stage Crew; Ofcr Stu Cncl; Cit Awd; NHS; Vol Frfghtr; Prdntl Sprt Cmmnty Awd; OK ST U-Stillwater; Frfghtng.

DOBSON, KRISTIN; Sapulpa Jr HS; Sapulpa, OK; (1); Church Yth Grp; Pep Clb; Thesps; Band; School Musical; School Play; Rep Frsh Cls; Ofcr Stu Cncl; Chrldng; Tennis; Frosh Band Attndnt; NSU; Ansthlgy.

DOBSON, MELANIE R; Broken Arrow Sr HS; Broken Arrow, OK; (3); Church Yth Grp; Cmnty Wkr; FCA; Science Clb; Spanish Clb; Teachers Aide; JV Bsktbl; Var Sftbl; Cit Awd; Ntl Merit Ltr; 4 Yr U; Zxercise Sci.

DOCKUM, BETH; Oklahoma Christian Schl; Edmond, OK; (1); Church Yth Grp; Debate Tm; Drama Clb; FCA; Speech Tm; VP Frsh Cls; Bsktbl; High Hon Roll.

DOCKUM, KENT; Oklahoma Christian Schl; Edmond, OK; (3); Church Yth Grp; Computer Clb; Debate Tm; FCA; Math Tm; Science Clb; VP Jr Cls; Rep Stu Cncl; Bsktbl; Cit Awd.

DODD, LAURA M; Trinity Christian Schl; Tulsa, OK; (2); Church Yth Grp; Pep Clb; Church Choir; Var Bsktbl; JV Vllybl; Hon Roll; Missionary Intern Trng For Evangelism.

DODD, MELISSA; Trinity Christian Schl; Tulsa, OK; (3); Church Yth Grp; Pep Clb; Chorus; Church Choir; School Musical; School Play; Stage Crew; Rptr Nwsp; Sec Frsh Cls; Var Bsktbl; Msnry Intern Trng Evnglsm Tm; Guid Cnslng.

DODGE, JENNIFER; Henryetta Sr HS; Henryetta, OK; (3); 2/95; HOBY; School Musical; Yrbk; Rep Stu Cncl; Var Golf; High Hon Roll; NHS; Pres Acad Fit Awd; JA; Letterman Clb; OK Hon Soc; GATE Cls; Acad Tm; Drug Free Yth; OK ST Univ; Vet Med.

DODSON, AMY; Dickson HS; Ardmore, OK; (2); 4-H; Hosp Aide; HOBY; Key Clb; Spanish Clb; SADD; Band; Drm Mjr(t); Mrchg Band; Bsktbl; OK ST 2 Baton Chmpn; Natl Baton Assn Twirler HS Bnd Twirler; Govt/His Awd; Ardmorite Blue Rbn Schlr; Murray; Tchr.

DODSON, BRAYDON H; Edmond Memorial HS; Edmond, OK; (3); 119/371; FCA; Key Clb; VICA; Ag.

DODSON, KRISTEN M; Wagoner Sr HS; Wagoner, OK; (4); 4/133; VP Bus Profs of Am; FCA; FBLA; Office Aide; Spanish Clb; SADD; School Musical; Rep Frsh Cls; Pres Soph Cls; Rep Jr Cls; NW St Univ; Med.

DODSON, MARSHELL; Elgin HS; Medicine Park, OK; (2); Church Yth Grp; Office Aide; Blue Chip Stdnt Great Plains Area Vo Tech; Who's Who Frosh Cls 95; Airforce.

DODSON, RYAN; Washingtn HS; Washington, OK; (4); Am Leg Boys St; Church Yth Grp; FCA; Teachers Aide; Church Choir; VP Frsh Cls; Rep Soph Cls; Sec Treas Jr Cls; Rep Sr Cls; Ofcr Stu Cncl; OK City Area Schlr Athl Awd; OK Coaches Assn All St Ftbltm Clss A; Ed.

DODSON, SERENA L; Charles Page HS; Tulsa, OK; (4); Cmnty Wkr; Debate Tm; Drama Clb; English Clb; Treas FCA; French Clb; Sec Key Clb; Pep Clb; Acpl Chr; Chorus; Writers Niche Co-Fndr; U Of AL Tuscaloosa; Psych.

DOE, RYAN A; Bartlesville Sr HS; Bartlesville, OK; (4); Boy Scts; Church Yth Grp; VP FCA; FBLA; Spanish Clb; Chorus; Church Choir; Rep Jr Cls; Var Trk; Hon Roll; Eagle Scout; OSU Acad Hnr Schlr; Rtry Stu Of Mnth 96; TX A&M; Food Engrng.

DOERN, JOHNA; Edmond North HS; Edmond, OK; (3); 104/348; Drama Clb; FCA; JA; Key Clb; Mu Alpha Theta; Spanish Clb; SADD; School Musical; School Play; Rep Stu Cncl; Vol Tchrs Asstnt Inner City Elem Schl; OK ST Univ; Child Psych.

DOIRON, MICHAEL J; Duncan HS; Duncan, OK; (2); Varsity Clb; Var L Bsktbl; Var L Ftbl; Var L Trk; High Hon Roll; Hon Roll; NHS; Pres Acad Fit Awd.

DOLAN, KEELY; Stratford Schl; Stratford, OK; (2); Church Yth Grp; FBLA; FHA; Scholastic Bowl; Science Clb; Ofcr Stu Cncl; Sftbl; Hon Roll; OK Bapt U.

DOLIAN, NUNE G; Checotah HS; Checotah, OK; (4); FBLA; Spanish Clb; High Hon Roll; NHS; Med.

DOLIN, BRYAN; Shawnee Sr HS; Shawnee, OK; (2); Drama Clb; Quiz Bowl; Spanish Clb; School Play; Wt Lftg; High Hon Roll; Hon Roll; Drama.

DOLLARHIDE, TRACI; Glencoe Public Schl; Glencoe, OK; (1); 2/40; French Clb; Sec Frsh Cls; Bsktbl; Chrldng; Sftbl; High Hon Roll; NHS; Prfct Atten Awd; Sal; Chrch Christ; OK ST U; Phys Thrpy.

DOLLINS, KATHY; Shawnee Sr HS; Shawnee, OK; (4); 126/264; Church Yth Grp; FCA; GAA; Office Aide; Spanish Clb; Band; Chorus; Mrchg Band; Var L Bsktbl; Var L Ftbl; OK St Yth Ldr Pres; Bowling League Pres; FFA; Northeastern ST U; Sports Med.

DOMINGUEZ, MARY; Mt St Marys HS; Oklahoma City, OK; (2); 1/78; Church Yth Grp; Sec Soph Cls; JV Var Vllybl; High Hon Roll; Kiwanis Awd; NHS; Ballet; Keywanettes.

DONAHO, KEVIN W; Carl Albert HS; Midwest City, OK; (4); 85/250; Key Clb; Var Ftbl; Var Trk; Var Wt Lftg; High Hon Roll; Hon Roll; Prfct Atten Awd; Pres Acad Fit Awd; Northwestern OK ST U; Ed.

DONAHUE, MATTHEW; Union Sr HS; Broken Arrow, OK; (4); Art Clb; Boy Scts; FBLA; Eagle Sct; OK ST Univ; Engrng.

DONALDSON, BREANNA; Battiest Jr Sr HS; Bethel, OK; (3); FHA; Scholastic Bowl; Chorus; Ed Nwsp; Yrbk; Rptr Jr Cls; Sftbl; St Judes Chldrns Rsrch Hosp Bike A Thon Sponsr.

DONALDSON, CELESTE; Mustang HS; Mustang, OK; (2); 1/380; Church Yth Grp; FHA; Key Clb; Office Aide; Spanish Clb; SADD; Var Bsktbl; Var Ftbl; Powder Puff Ftbl; Socr; Srvd Page ST Senate Sntr Bill Gustafson; PT/ATH Trnng.

DONALDSON, STACY D; Putnam City HS; Warr Acres, OK; (2); Church Yth Grp; Office Aide; Teachers Aide; Church Choir; Color Guard; Mrchg Band; Ed Yrbk; Ofcr Stu Cncl; Hon Roll; NHS; 3-D Pgm; Freed-Hardman; Tchr Of Blnd/Df.

DONALDSON, TRACY C; Putnam City HS; Warr Acres, OK; (2); Church Yth Grp; German Clb; Color Guard; Yrbk; 3-D Dont Do Drugs; Jrnlsm/Brdcstng.

DONATHAN, BARBARA M; Christian Heritage Acad; Oklahoma City, OK; (2); Church Yth Grp; Teachers Aide; Chorus; Church Choir; Vllybl; Mission Trip To Mexico.

DONATHAN, KRISTY; Panama HS; Panama, OK; (3); FCA; Sec FHA; VP German Clb; Sec Natl FFA Org; SADD; Yrbk; Pres Frsh Cls; Pres Soph Cls; VP Jr Cls; Sftbl; Bsktbl All-Conf, Connors Trnmt MVP, All-Cty Team, USA All-Star Team Belgium; Sftbl All-Cty Team.

DONEHUE, JASON S; Enid Sr HS; Enid, OK; (4); Church Yth Grp; Cmnty Wkr; FCA; Library Aide; Math Clb; Spanish Clb; Teachers Aide; Band; Mrchg Band; Pep Band; OK ST Rgnts Awrd; Bible Club; Pol Soc; Top Acct Stdnt; OK ST Univ; Engr.

DONEY, MISTY A; Drummond Schl; Enid, OK; (2); 2/27; FHA; HOBY; Scholastic Bowl; Band; VP Stu Cncl; Chrldng; Sftbl; High Hon Roll; Quiz Bowl; NHS; Natl Ldrshp & Svc Awds; All-Amer Schlr.

DONMOYER, TIMOTHY R; Edmond Memorial HS; Oklahoma City, OK; (4); 182/322; Key Clb; Office Aide; Ofcr Stu Cncl; Prfct Atten Awd; Tuttle Voc-Tech.

DONNELL, STEPHANIE; Duncan HS; Duncan, OK; (4); 7/215; Church Yth Grp; Cmnty Wkr; Letterman Clb; Scholastic Bowl; Rep Frsh Cls; Sftbl; High Hon Roll; Kiwanis Awd; NHS; Pres Schlr; SWOSU; Pre-Med; Chem.

DONNELLY, RYAN PATRICK; Elgin HS; Elgin, OK; (3); Natl FFA Org; JV Bsbl; L Ftbl; Var Wt Lftg; Hon Roll; Jr NHS; NHS; Cmnty Wkr; Office Aide; Teachers Aide; FFA Welding Tm Pl 1st ST OK; FFA Show Steer Sevl Awds; Elgin Ftbl Lineman Of Yr Awd; OK ST Univ.

DONOVAN, BETH; Perkins-Tryon HS; Wellston, OK; (1); Church Yth Grp; Cmnty Wkr; Hosp Aide; Cmnty Vol; Penn ST Coll; Art Tchr.

DOOLEY, CRYSTAL; Afton HS; Afton, OK; (4); 2/19; FCA; Natl FFA Org; Pres Sr Cls; Capt Bsktbl; Chrldng; Trk; NHS; Sal; Stu Of Today Masonic Awd; Ottawa Cty Comm Partnerships Rptr; NE OK A&M Coll.

DOOLEY, SHAUN E; Cushing HS; Cushing, OK; (2); 18/150; Boy Scts; Church Yth Grp; Hon Roll.

DOOLEY, ZACHARY; Tuttle HS; Tuttle, OK; (1); 1/100; Church Yth Grp; Math Tm; Scholastic Bowl; Ofcr Bsbl; Ftbl; Wrstlng; High Hon Roll; JETS Awd; Engrng.

DORAN, JOSHUA; Hilldale HS; Muskogee, OK; (2); 1/107; Boy Scts; Spanish Clb; Bsktbl; Var Ftbl; Wt Lftg; High Hon Roll.

DORJISURUNG, OCHIRKHU; Enid Sr HS; Enid, OK; (2); 9/431; Pres Spanish Clb; Varsity Clb; Yrbk; Pres Stu Cncl; Chrldng; Ftbl; Cit Awd; High Hon Roll; Prfct Atten Awd; Pres Acad Fit Awd; Bus.

DORMER, KEVIN J; Edmond Memorial HS; Edmond, OK; (2); Church Yth Grp; Band; Drm Mjr(t); Jazz Band; Mrchg Band; Pep Band; Variety Show; Hon Roll; NHS; USAF Acad; Pilot/Aerontcl Engr.

DORN, RICKI J; Will Rogers HS; Tulsa, OK; (2); 8/319; Cmnty Wkr; FHA; German Clb; Pres Girl Scts; Key Clb; Scholastic Bowl; Hon Roll; St Johns Hosp Med Explorer Post Mem; Hellenic Soc Yth Involvement Awd Recipient 95; U Of OK; Phy.

DOROTEO, ANGELICA M; Capitol Hill HS; Oklahoma City, OK; (3); Church Yth Grp; Cmnty Wkr; Dance Clb; GAA; Girl Scts; Latin Clb; School Musical; Stage Crew; Variety Show; Rep Jr Cls; Trvlng Dance Prefrmd UN Tel Conf; Miss OK City/Miss Langston; Great Cncl Of Schl; Exec Schl Bd; Langston Univ; PT.

DOROUGH, MONICA L; Moore HS; Oklahoma City, OK; (4); 72/549; DECA; Office Aide; Rptr Soph Cls; Ofcr Stu Cncl; Powder Puff Ftbl; Var L Socr; NHS; Mst Lkly Sccd; OK ST U; Psych.

DORR, LORI J; Tahlequah Sr HS; Tahlequah, OK; (3); Church Yth Grp; GAA; Office Aide; Pep Clb; Science Clb; SADD; Teachers Aide; JV Var Bsktbl; JV Var Sftbl; Cit Awd; St Patrick Hosp Schl.

DORRANCE, DANIEL O; Deer Creek HS; Edmond, OK; (2); Boy Scts; Church Yth Grp; Letterman Clb; Science Clb; School Play; Treas Soph Cls; Ftbl; Wrstlng; NHS; Xmas In April.

DORRIS, JENNIE; Owasso Sr HS; Owasso, OK; (2); Church Yth Grp; FCA; Band; Nwsp; Yrbk; High Hon Roll; NHS; Mrchg Band; Camp Fire; Odyssy Of Mind; Teen Actn Grp; Comm Jrnlsm.

DORRIS, KRIS; Chickasha Jr HS; Chickasha, OK; (1); Church Yth Grp; Latin Clb; Chorus; Church Choir; Swmmng; Tennis; Hon Roll; Jr NHS; Tri St Vocal Solo Awd Super; Tri St Vocal Ensemble Awd Super; Natl Jr Classical League Latin Hnr Soc; U Of OK; Phy Thrpst.

DORSEY, MICHAEL B; Claremore Sr HS; Claremore, OK; (3); #39 in class; Church Yth Grp; Quiz Bowl; Band; Jazz Band; Mrchg Band; Pep Band; Ofcr Bsbl; Ftbl; High Hon Roll; Hon Roll; Cmptr Sci.

DORTCH, CHELSEA; Collinsville HS; Owasso, OK; (4); 3/96; FCA; Sprt Ed Yrbk; Ofcr Frsh Cls; Ofcr Soph Cls; Ofcr Jr Cls; Ofcr Stu Cncl; Capt Bsktbl; Capt Sftbl; High Hon Roll; NHS; NCLC; OK Senate Page; OK U.

DORTON, ANGELA M; Carl Albert HS; Tinker Afb, OK; (4); 85/239; Cmnty Wkr; JV Bsktbl; Intrml Powder Puff Ftbl; JV Socr; JV Var Sftbl; Var Vllybl; Hon Roll; Rose ST Coll; Bus.

DORTON, DAVID; Grandfield Jr Sr HS; Grandfield, OK; (4); 3/23; Church Yth Grp; HOBY; Natl FFA Org; Quiz Bowl; Yrbk; Rep Sr Cls; Treas Stu Cncl; Co-Capt Ftbl; High Hon Roll; Kiwanis Awd.

DOSHIER, SARAH D; Shawnee Sr HS; Shawnee, OK; (4); 23/269; VP French Clb; Teachers Aide; Band; Mrchg Band; Ofcr Stu Cncl; NHS; Pres Acad Fit Awd; Brd Of Dir Big Brother Big Sisters; Fnlst N Amer Poetry Cont; SHOC; OK ST U; Engl.

DOSS, ANNETTE; Macomb Schl; Macomb, OK; (2); FBLA; FHA; Rep Stu Cncl; JV Bsktbl; JV Sftbl; Hon Roll; Nrsng.

DOSS, CARISSA A; Putnam City North HS; Oklahoma City, OK; (4); 193/436; Church Yth Grp; Church Choir; Vllybl; NHS; U Of Central OK; Med.

DOSS, ERIN R; Putnam City North HS; Oklahoma City, OK; (1); 68/541; Church Yth Grp; Cmnty Wkr; FCA; Chorus; Church Choir; Vllybl; 3 Yr Cocda; Dentistry/Med.

DOSS, JAMES; Claremore Sr HS; Claremore, OK; (2); Quiz Bowl; Ftbl; Wt Lftg; Wrstlng; High Hon Roll; NHS; Ntl Merit Schol; Prfct Atten Awd; Ped Srgn.

DOSS, JESSICA N; Midwest City HS; Midwest City, OK; (2); 73/473; Church Yth Grp; FCA; French Clb; Pep Clb; SADD; Church Choir; Jr NHS; NHS; OK Hnr Soc; OK ST Univ; Pediatrcn.

DOSS, SAMUEL Z; Olive Jr Sr HS; Bristow, OK; (2); 3/40; 4-H; Band; Ofcr Bsbl; Cit Awd; High Hon Roll.

DOSSEY, AARON; Midwest City HS; Midwest City, OK; (4); 32/419; Debate Tm; Letterman Clb; Quiz Bowl; Scholastic Bowl; Band; Jazz Band; Mrchg Band; Orch; Pep Band; Cit Awd; Cllcts, Raises Inscts; OK ST U; Biochem.

DOTSON, ADRIAN; Muskogee HS; Muskogee, OK; (2); Pres Church Yth Grp; FBLA; JCL; Latin Clb; Church Choir; Nwsp; Yrbk; Hon Roll; NHS; Black His Clb; Ecology; Teen For Christ; Morehouse Atlanta; Pharmacist.

DOTSON, ANDREA L; Poteau HS; Poteau, OK; (3); Sec Art Clb; French Clb; Band; Color Guard; Drm Mjr(t); Mrchg Band; Rep Stu Cncl; Hon Roll; Jr NHS; NHS; Psychlgy/Crmnl Law.

DOTSON, AUTUMN L; Southeast HS; Oklahoma City, OK; (1); Church Yth Grp; Computer Clb; Drama Clb; JA; Band; Stage Crew; JV Bsktbl; Var Tennis; Hon Roll; Ntl Merit Ltr; Langston; Cmptr Pgm Analyst.

DOTSON, EMILY L; Choctaw HS; Midwest City, OK; (4); 19/320; Model UN; ROTC; Ed Nwsp; Yrbk; Rep Stu Cncl; Capt Chrldng; Var Sftbl; Var JV Vllybl; Jr NHS; NHS; YMCA Metro Teen Cncl; OK U; FBI.

DOTSON, STEPHANIE; Panama HS; Spiro, OK; (4); 3/50; Spanish Clb; Sec Frsh Cls; Sec Soph Cls; Sec Jr Cls; Bsktbl; Sftbl; Swmmng; High Hon Roll; NHS; Horseback Rdng; Westark CC; Phys Thrpst Asst.

DOTSON, TUCKER D; Pioneer Jr Sr HS; Enid, OK; (2); 15/60; Church Yth Grp; FCA; Natl Beta Clb; Natl FFA Org; VP Soph Cls; Var L Bsbl; L Bsktbl; Var L Ftbl; Var Wt Lftg; Hon Roll; All Dist Acad Tm 96; Vet Med/Ag.

DOTSON, WESLEY; Broken Arrow Sr HS; Broken Arrow, OK; (4); 93/921; Am Leg Boys St; German Clb; Speech Tm; Band; Jazz Band; Mrchg Band; Pep Band; Hon Roll; Jr NHS; NHS; Ntl Merit SF; Paintball Field Vol Ref & Team; OU; Psych.

DOTTER, KATHRYN; Clinton HS; Clinton, OK; (4); Math Clb; Science Clb; Band; Mrchg Band; Ed Nwsp; NHS; High Hon Roll; Pep Band; Office Aide; Bausch & Lomb Sci Awd; I Dare You Awd; Regents Schlr Awd 96; U Of OK; Meteorology.

DOTY, GARRETT; Lone Grove HS; Ardmore, OK; (2); Church Yth Grp; Math Clb; Acpl Chr; Band; Chorus; Mrchg Band; Pep Band; Variety Show; Hon Roll; Southeastern OK ST Univ; PT.

DOTY, MAHTAB R; Lexington HS; Lexington, OK; (2); Drama Clb; JA; Band; Mrchg Band; School Play; Var Sftbl; High Hon Roll; Gftd/Tlntd Pgm 11 Yrs; Psych.

DOTY, MC KENZIE L; Sulphur HS; Sulphur, OK; (4); 14/100; 4-H; Key Clb; Natl FFA Org; Office Aide; Speech Tm; Teachers Aide; NHS; FFA Pres, VP & Sec; St FFA Degree; Murray ST; Ag Bus.

DOUBET, JESSICA M; Wagoner Sr HS; Wagoner, OK; (2); Cmnty Wkr; FBLA; Girl Scts; Spanish Clb; Hon Roll; Frgn Lang Club; NSU.

DOUD, TONYA S; Aline-Cleo Jr Sr HS; Ringwood, OK; (4); 4-H; Natl FFA Org; Pep Clb; Yrbk; St FFA Degree; Alva Vo-Tech; Interpreter.

DOUGET, MICHAEL C; Union Intermediate HS; Tulsa, OK; (2); 128/800; Church Yth Grp; FCA; Key Clb; Spanish Clb; JV Crs Cntry; Var Trk; High Hon Roll; Hon Roll; Chrmn NHS; Page OK St House Rep; Soph Stu Mon; Natl Hnr Soc Fundraiser Cmmtte; Med.

DOUGHTY, BRIAN; Perry Sr HS; Perry, OK; (3); FCA; German Clb; School Play; Rep Nwsp; Rep Stu Cncl; Var Bsbl; Var Bsktbl; Hon Roll; Jr NHS; NHS.

DOUGHTY, CARRIE A; Newcastle HS; Newcastle, OK; (3); 29/93; Art Clb; Church Yth Grp; FBLA; FHA; Science Clb; Chorus; Church Choir; School Musical; Ofcr Stu Cncl; Hon Roll; SNU; Cnslng.

DOUGHTY, LACY A; Putnam City North HS; Oklahoma City, OK; (2); Church Yth Grp; Dance Clb; FCA; Key Clb; Letterman Clb; Sec Spanish Clb; Ofcr Stu Cncl; Swmmng; Trk; Hon Roll; U Of OK; Med.

DOUGHTY HANKINS, JENNIFER; Amber Pocasset Jr Sr HS; Chickasha, OK; (4); 4/26; Church Yth Grp; FBLA; FHA; Spanish Clb; Ofcr Frsh Cls; Bsktbl; Sftbl; Vllybl; Hon Roll; NHS; Canadian Vly Vo-Tech; Comp Bus.

DOUGLAS, ALISA; Mason HS; Okemah, OK; (3); 4-H; HOBY; Spanish Clb; Pres Frsh Cls; Pres Soph Cls; Pres Stu Cncl; Capt Var Bsktbl; NHS; St Hnr Soc; Indian Yth Clb Sec; Graphc Dsgn.

DOUGLAS, AMANDA D; Choctaw HS; Choctaw, OK; (2); Hosp Aide; Acpl Chr; School Musical; Swing Chorus; Variety Show; Rep Frsh Cls; High Hon Roll; Jr NHS; Pres Schlr; Sal; OK Bapt U; Med.

DOUGLAS, APRIL; Westmoore HS; Oklahoma City, OK; (3); 5/620; Church Yth Grp; French Clb; Key Clb; Scholastic Bowl; Teachers Aide; Church Choir; Phtg Yrbk; Rep Stu Cncl; Stat Bsktbl; High Hon Roll; OK ST Univ; Intl Bus.

DOUGLAS, ASHLEY; Ada HS; Ada, OK; (4); 19/165; Church Yth Grp; Ofcr FCA; Mu Alpha Theta; Science Clb; Spanish Clb; SADD; Ed Nwsp; Capt Tennis; VP NHS; VP Spanish NHS; OK Bptst.

DOUGLAS, CHAD A; Pawnee HS; Pawnee, OK; (3); Church Yth Grp; 4-H; Quiz Bowl; Scholastic Bowl; Band; Mrchg Band; Pres Jr Cls; Var Ftbl; Var Golf; Var Wrstlng; 94-95 Natl Beta Club Harris Ldrshp Awd; U Of OK; Med.

DOUGLAS, CHAQUISE; U S Grant HS; Oklahoma City, OK; (2); Drama Clb; Chrldng; Gym; Urban League; RN.

DOUGLAS, D M; Clinton HS; Clinton, OK; (3); 1/150; Key Clb; Library Aide; Chorus; Ofcr Stu Cncl; Var Bsktbl; Var Chrldng; Var Mgr(s); Var Trk; NHS; Val.

DOUGLAS, HOLLY R; Seminole Jr Sr HS; Seminole, OK; (2); 4-H; FHA; Girl Scts; Hon Roll; Prfct Atten Awd; OK U; Phys Thrpst.

DOUGLAS, KARA R; Choctaw HS; Choctaw, OK; (2); Sec Church Yth Grp; FCA; German Clb; Key Clb; Bsktbl; Sftbl; Cit Awd; Hon Roll; Jr NHS; Sprts Thrpst.

DOUGLAS, LISA; Miami Sr HS; Miami, OK; (2); Math Tm; Natl FFA Org; Speech Tm; Hon Roll; NHS; FFA Spchs; Shw Ctl; Lvstck Jdg; Northeastern OK A&M Coll.

DOUGLAS, PAUL T; Lawton Sr HS; Lawton, OK; (2); Boy Scts; Hon Roll; Rnsnce Acad Awd; Cmptr Tech.

DOUGLAS, ROBERT L; Inola Sr HS; Inola, OK; (2); Computer Clb; Natl FFA Org; Rogers ST Coll; Phrmcy.

DOUGLASS, SARA; Broken Arrow Sr HS; Broken Arrow, OK; (3); FHA; Office Aide; Teachers Aide; Var Chrldng; Wt Lftg; High Hon Roll; Hon Roll; USA Gymnastics All Around Champ; All Amer Chrldr 2 Yrs.

DOUTHIT, ALAN R; Union Sr HS; Broken Arrow, OK; (3); 58/742; Church Yth Grp; Spanish Clb; Intrml Bsktbl; Hon Roll; NHS; Hosp Vol; Smmr Lg Bsbl; OK U; Med.

DOUTHIT, SHAWNA D; Owasso Sr HS; Collinsville, OK; (2); FCA; GAA; JV Bsktbl; JV Sftbl; High Hon Roll; Hon Roll.

DOVE, JAHNNA R; Duncan HS; Duncan, OK; (2); Church Yth Grp; Girl Scts; Band; Church Choir; Mrchg Band; Hon Roll; NHS; Art.

DOVE, RACHEL J; Fletcher Jr Sr HS; Fletcher, OK; (1); #5 in class; Chorus; Variety Show; Hon Roll.

DOVELL, JAMES D; Sayre HS; Cheyenne, OK; (3); 2/47; Am Leg Boys St; Scholastic Bowl; Science Clb; Capt Var Ftbl; Wt Lftg; High Hon Roll; Jr NHS; NHS; Ntl Merit Ltr; St Schlr; OK ST Univ; Forestry; Agronomy.

DOWELL, CHANDEE; Claremore Sr HS; Claremore, OK; (4); 23/230; Cmnty Wkr; Drama Clb; NFL; Speech Tm; SADD; High Hon Roll; Hon Roll; NHS; Yng Democrts Of OK Rogers Cty VP; Rogers U; Optmtry.

DOWELL, JESSICA; Claremore Sr HS; Claremore, OK; (4); Am Leg Aux Girls St; Drama Clb; NFL; Speech Tm; SADD; DAR Awd; NHS; Natl Ldrshp Svc Awd; Yng Dmcrts OK Co Pres; Prsthtcs.

DOWELL, MIKE; Woodward HS; Woodward, OK; (3); Church Yth Grp; German Clb; Key Clb; Letterman Clb; High Hon Roll; Hon Roll; NHS; Amer His Awd; Natl Ger Hnr Soc; Rotary Ctznshp Conf.

DOWLER, JULIE; Laverne Jr Sr HS; Laverne, OK; (3); 1/30; Church Yth Grp; Drama Clb; FHA; Natl Beta Clb; Band; Chorus; Rep Stu Cncl; Capt Chrldng; Var Sftbl; Acctng.

DOWLING, JOSH; Westmoore HS; Moore, OK; (3); French Clb; Key Clb; Swmmng; NHS; Red Cross Vol; Work With Handicapped; Ballet, Dance & Fine Arts; U Of AZ; Pharmacy; Drama.

DOWLING, MELISSA K; Westmoore HS; Oklahoma City, OK; (2); Spanish Clb; Band; Color Guard; Mrchg Band; School Musical; High Hon Roll; Jr NHS; NHS; Hon Roll; Jr Rep Band Cncl; FCA/JIM Thorpe Assn Vol; Perf Bands Of Amer Natl Contest Chgo 96; U Of OK; Educ/Med.

DOWLING, MICHELLE L; Alva HS; Alva, OK; (3); 18/65; Debate Tm; Key Clb; NFL; Speech Tm; Teachers Aide; Thesps; Band; School Play; Stage Crew; Hon Roll; U Of Sci & Arts Of OK; Soclgy.

DOWNEN, DREW A; Southwest Covenant Schl; Oklahoma City, OK; (1); Church Yth Grp; Var Ftbl; Hon Roll; Prfct Atten Awd.

DOWNEY, GINA; Konawa Sr HS; Konawa, OK; (4); FHA; HOBY; Natl Beta Clb; Band; Drm Mjr(t); Mrchg Band; Ofcr Sr Cls; Pres Stu Cncl; High Hon Roll; Hon Roll; Meth Church; Northeastern U; Nursing.

DOWNEY, JENNIFER D; Velma Alma HS; Velma, OK; (3); FBLA; FHA; Nwsp; Yrbk; Bsktbl; High Hon Roll; Ntl Merit Ltr; OK Hnr Soc; Acctng.

DOWNING, ALYSSA; Medford Schl; Medford, OK; (3); 3/18; Church Yth Grp; FCA; Sec FHA; Rep Stu Cncl; Var Chrldng; Hon Roll; NHS; OU.

DOWNING, BOBBY G; Jay HS; Jay, OK; (3); Natl Beta Clb; Natl FFA Org; Quiz Bowl; Hon Roll; Ntl Merit Ltr; Frshm Wldr Hgh Ind.

DOWNING, BRIAN A; Yukon HS; Yukon, OK; (3); Boy Scts; Teachers Aide; JV Bsbl; Var Ftbl; Var Trk; Hon Roll; U Of OK; Med.

DOWNING, JEREMY; Medford Schl; Medford, OK; (4); 7/22; Church Yth Grp; FCA; FHA; Natl FFA Org; Pep Clb; Spanish Clb; Band; Chorus; Church Choir; Ofcr Stu Cncl; St FFA Dgr Ag-Bus, Pub Spkng Awd; CPR Cert; Southern Naz U; Bus Adm.

DOWNING, LAURA K; Enid Sr HS; Enid, OK; (3); Church Yth Grp; FCA; Office Aide; Pep Clb; Chorus; JV Bsktbl; Var Trk; Hon Roll; Child Psychiatrist.

DOWNING, RACINE N; Jay HS; Jay, OK; (2); 4-H; FHA; Natl Beta Clb; Natl FFA Org; 4-H Awd; NEO; Vet.

DOWNS, ALANA; Woodward HS; Sharon, OK; (1); Cmnty Wkr; Pep Clb; High Hon Roll; Kiwanis Awd; Gymnastics; Phy.

DOWNS, BRIAN S; Tahlequah Sr HS; Tahlequah, OK; (2); OK St Univ; Brdcst Jrnlsm.

DOWNS, CHARLOTTE; Durant HS; Durant, OK; (3); Church Yth Grp; Drama Clb; FCA; 4-H; Key Clb; Speech Tm; Chorus; Church Choir; Drill Tm; School Musical; OK Shksprn Fstvl; Music.

DOWNS, CHE; Liberty Acad; Shawnee, OK; (1); 4/30; FCA; Math Tm; Var Bsktbl; Cit Awd; High Hon Roll; OK U.

DOWNS, KASI S; Collinsville HS; Collinsville, OK; (2); Church Yth Grp; Chorus; Hon Roll; Prfct Atten Awd; Acting.

DOWNS, LORISSA; Sharon Mutual Jr Sr HS; Sharon, OK; (3); 6/18; Sec Jr Cls; Var Chrldng; Hon Roll; Vlntr Planned Parenthood, Colonial Manor Nrsng Home; Dermatology.

DOWNS, SAMANTHA; Fairland Jr Sr HS; Fairland, OK; (4); 1/34; Church Yth Grp; FHA; Pres Jr Cls; Pres Sr Cls; Var Capt Bsktbl; Var Trk; Hon Roll; NHS; Prfct Atten Awd; Val; NE OK A&M.

DOWNUM, DAVID; Miami Sr HS; Miami, OK; (3); 1/160; Art Clb; Boy Scts; Church Yth Grp; 4-H; Chorus; Bsktbl; Tennis; 4-H Awd; High Hon Roll; Jr NHS; Ricks Coll.

DOWTY, AMANDA D; Woodward HS; Woodward, OK; (3); Pres Church Yth Grp; CAP; FCA; Letterman Clb; Red Cross Aide; Spanish Clb; Chorus; Church Choir; School Musical; Stage Crew; Cltrl Exchnge Club; OK ST Univ; Avtn Mgmt.

DOYLE, ASHLEY K; Edmond Memorial HS; Edmond, OK; (2); 1/400; Spanish Clb; Teachers Aide; Drill Tm; High Hon Roll; Pres Schlr; Purdue U; Math.

DOYLE, CASEY; Westville HS; Stilwell, OK; (3); Church Yth Grp; FCA; 4-H; FBLA; HOBY; Math Clb; Hist Natl FFA Org; Science Clb; L Bsbl; L Bsktbl; Sprts Intl Belguim Bsktbl Tour 95.

DOYLE, CHENAYA; Jay HS; Spavinaw, OK; (3); FCA; Pep Clb; Speech Tm; Rptr Yrbk; Rep Soph Cls; Rep Stu Cncl; Hon Roll; NHS; Wrtng Poetry; Engl Awd Wrtng Stories.

DOYLE, RACHAEL L; Heavener HS; Heavener, OK; (1); Church Yth Grp; Debate Tm; Drama Clb; FHA; Key Clb; Spanish Clb; Church Choir; Stage Crew; Hon Roll; OK ST Hnr Scty; CASC.

DOZIER, KRISTY; Metro Christian Acad; Tulsa, OK; (4); Church Yth Grp; FCA; French Clb; Key Clb; Office Aide; Service Clb; Chorus; Church Choir; School Musical; Rep Soph Cls; Symph/Ony Set; OK Bapt U; Nrsng.

DRAHOS, ABBY; South Intermediate HS; Broken Arrow, OK; (2); Church Yth Grp; FCA; Acpl Chr; Hon Roll; Oral Roberts U; Pre-Law.

DRAKE, CORIE L; Ponca City Sr HS; Ponca City, OK; (3); Chorus; Rptr Nwsp; High Hon Roll; Hon Roll; Pres Acad Fit Awd; Fran/Co Sr Dncrs; OK Twstrs Rlr Hckry; Pre-Calc Awd; OK ST Univ; Pre-Med.

DRAKE, MINDY; Waynoka HS; Waynoka, OK; (4); 1/23; Sec FCA; Sec Pres FHA; Rptr Pep Clb; Teachers Aide; Pres Jr Cls; Capt Var Bsktbl; Sftbl; Sec Hon Roll; NHS; Val; All Amer Schlr; OK Hnr Soc; OSU Stu Ldrshp Conf; NWOSU; Ed.

DRAKE, TABBETHA; Davis HS; Davis, OK; (3); Debate Tm; Drama Clb; 4-H; HOBY; Key Clb; Model UN; Quiz Bowl; Spanish Clb; Speech Tm; Chorus.

DRAKE, TAMMY L; East Central HS; Tulsa, OK; (1); Cmnty Wkr; Drama Clb; Key Clb; Chorus; Church Choir; School Play; Swmmng; Tennis; Vllybl; Hon Roll; OU; Phys Ther.

DRAKE, WILLIAM D; Skiatook HS; Skiatook, OK; (1); Scholastic Bowl; JV Bsbl; JV Bsktbl; Hon Roll; NHS; OK U.

DRAPER, JENNY; Central Mid-HS; Norman, OK; (1); Church Yth Grp; FCA; Church Choir; Hon Roll; Church Yth Prgm Pres; Church Soloist; Piano/Voice Recitals; Jr League Vol For Homeless Shelter; U Of OK.

DRAPER, MELANIE; Claremore Sr HS; Claremore, OK; (2); Office Aide; Teachers Aide; Chrldng; High Hon Roll; Ntl Merit Ltr; Prfct Atten Awd; U Of AR; Pharmacy.

DRAPER, NATHANIEL A; Meeker HS; Meeker, OK; (3); Chess Clb; Science Clb; Band; Jazz Band; Orch; Pep Band; Patntng Invention; Comptr Sci.

DRAWBAUGH, TINA R; Byng Sr HS; Ada, OK; (2); 25/120; Church Yth Grp; Cmnty Wkr; FHA; Office Aide; Spanish Clb; Teachers Aide; Chorus; Ofcr Soph Cls; Cit Awd; Hon Roll; Osdutstdng FHA Stu; Citizenship Awd Trphy; Will Attend Washington DC Nov 96; Law.

DRAY, ASHLEY; Bartlesville Mid HS; Bartlesville, OK; (2); 88/481; Art Clb; Church Yth Grp; JA; Hon Roll; Jr NHS; Natl Hnr Roll; Intl Frgn Lang Awd; Outstdng Acad Achvmt Awd.

DRENNAN, MATTHEW P; Velma Alma Jr Sr HS; Lindsay, OK; (4); 16/35; Natl FFA Org; Scholastic Bowl; Teachers Aide; Ftbl; Attnd Conference On Law & Constition In Wash DC; OK ST Univ; Law.

DRESHER, MATTHEW J; Union Sr HS; Tulsa, OK; (3); 63/741; Church Yth Grp; FCA; Varsity Clb; Rep Stu Cncl; Var Socr; Hon Roll; NHS; Pres Schlr; Spanish NHS; St Olympic Devlpmnt Tm; Drug Free Yth Orgnztn; Hurricane Ftbl Clb Capt; U Of Evansville; Med.

DRESSEL, NAKIA C; Jay HS; Jay, OK; (2); FCA; FBLA; Natl Beta Clb; Science Clb; Pres Frsh Cls; NHS; IDFY; LSU; Pdtrcn.

DRESSEN, AMY S; Ponca City Middle HS; Ponca City, OK; (1); Church Yth Grp; Band; Jazz Band; Mrchg Band; Orch; Hon Roll; Spec Mnstry.

DRESSER, JON C; Union Intermediate HS; Tulsa, OK; (2); Var Diving; Hon Roll; NHS; 1st Pl ST Art Comp 10th Grd UCO; 2 Acad Lttrs; 1 Ath Lttr; Art Dir Motion Pics.

DRESSLER, BRENT A; Union Intermediate HS; Broken Arrow, OK; (1); Church Yth Grp; FCA; Orch; JV Ftbl; JV Mgr(s); Var Trk; High Hon Roll; NHS; Letterman Clb; Var Wt Lftg; Tulsa Yth Phlhmrnc Orch; GATE Cncl Class Rep; Young Astrnauts/Drug Free Yth; Young Repblcns; MI Univ; Sprts Med/Music.

DREW, JASON W; Broken Arrow Sr HS; Tulsa, OK; (3); FBLA; Science Clb; Stage Crew; Lit Mag; JV Golf; Hon Roll; Comp Sys Analayst.

DREW, NICHOLE C; Carney Schl; Carney, OK; (3); FCA; FHA; FTA; GAA; Quiz Bowl; Scholastic Bowl; Rep Stu Cncl; Bsktbl; Chrldng; Sftbl; OSU; Psych.

DRIGGERS, AMANDA M; Union Intermediate HS; Tulsa, OK; (1); Church Yth Grp; Dance Clb; FCA; French Clb; Chorus; Church Choir; Drill Tm; School Musical; High Hon Roll; NHS; Lang Arts Awd; Musical Theatre; Jrnlsm.

DRIGGERS, KIMBERLY J; Union Sr HS; Tulsa, OK; (4); 69/669; English Clb; FHA; German Clb; Intnl Clb; Ski Clb; Mrchg Band; Swmmng; Tennis; Wt Lftg; High Hon Roll; Piano & Guitar; Poetry Cmptns; U Of CO-BOULDER; Dietetics.

DRIGGERS, RYAN A; Mustang HS; Yukon, OK; (3); 62/385; Church Yth Grp; FCA; Band; Ofcr Bsbl; Bsktbl; Psych.

DRILL, JASON J; North Intemediate HS; Tulsa, OK; (1); FCA; Spanish Clb; JV Ftbl; JV Wt Lftg.

DRINKARD, SAMMY; Hugo HS; Hugo, OK; (3); Am Leg Boys St; Math Clb; Rep Sec Natl FFA Org; Science Clb; Spanish Clb; VICA; Ofcr Stu Cncl; Hon Roll; NHS; OK Hnr Soc; Murray ST; Vet.

DRISKILL, HEATHER; Wagoner Sr HS; Wagoner, OK; (3); Am Leg Aux Girls St; Cmnty Wkr; FBLA; FHA; Hosp Aide; HOBY; Red Cross Aide; Phtg Ed Yrbk; Sec Frsh Cls; Pres Soph Cls; U Of AR; Law.

DRISKILL, ROBERT M; Mustang HS; Yukon, OK; (4); 71/360; Church Yth Grp; FCA; Office Aide; Spanish Clb; Teachers Aide; Rep Nwsp; Ed Lit Mag; Hon Roll; NTCE Poetry Writng Awd; 96 Rose St Coll Writng Cmptn Hnrb Mntn; U Of OK.

DRISKILL, RYAN; Thomas Jr Sr HS; Thomas, OK; (4); 2/32; Church Yth Grp; FCA; Hosp Aide; Ofcr Stu Cncl; Ofcr Bsbl; Bsktbl; Ftbl; Cit Awd; Hon Roll; Sal; TX Tech; Phys Thrpy.

DRISKILL, SARAH B; North Intemediate HS; Broken Arrow, OK; (2); Church Yth Grp; French Clb; Band; Church Choir; Mrchg Band; Pep Band; Jr NHS; NHS; Pres Acad Fit Awd; Pres Schlr; OBU; Elem Ed; Bus; Music.

DRIVER, LAKEISSA M; Macarthur Sr HS; Lawton, OK; (3); Cmnty Wkr; Hosp Aide; HOBY; Library Aide; VP Acpl Chr; Church Choir; School Musical; School Play; Hon Roll; Jr NHS; HOSA; Natl Vo-Tech Hnr Soc; Natl Ldrshp & Svc Awd; Cameron Univ; Nrsng.

DROBINKO, LARA A; Owasso Sr HS; Owasso, OK; (4); 25/298; Church Yth Grp; Cmnty Wkr; FCA; Ed Nwsp; Ed Yrbk; Ofcr Sr Cls; High Hon Roll; NHS; French Clb; Hon Roll; TAG; TAR; Spec Olympics Coach; PT.

DROESCHER, JOHN; Central Mid-HS; Norman, OK; (1); Church Yth Grp; FCA; Spanish Clb; Hon Roll; FCA; All Amer Schlr; Cmptr Sys Analyst.

DROKE, JENNIFER G; Union Intermediate HS; Tulsa, OK; (1); School Play; NHS; NYU.

DROLL, JULIE L; Bristow HS; Bristow, OK; (4); #1 in class; Church Yth Grp; Pep Clb; Quiz Bowl; Band; Rep Jr Cls; Rep Sr Cls; NHS; Ntl Merit SF; Val; Stu Active Cmnty Svc; OU.

DRUMELLER, CRYSTAL; Muskogee HS; Muskogee, OK; (3); 8/350; Am Leg Aux Girls St; Church Yth Grp; Cmnty Wkr; GAA; Hosp Aide; JCL; Key Clb; Office Aide; Varsity Clb; Band; Octgn Club Sec; Delphic Lit Soc; U Of OK; Med.

DRUMMOND, BECKY; Lone Grove HS; Ardmore, OK; (3); 4/99; Math Clb; Natl Beta Clb; Science Clb; Spanish Clb; Chorus; Rptr Nwsp; Bsktbl; Hon Roll; NHS; All Amer Schlr; Aim-Hi Math Tm; Geom & Engl Awds; Nrsng.

DRUMMOND, MATT D; Indianola HS; Mcalester, OK; (2); FHA; Natl FFA Org; Rep Stu Cncl; Var Bsbl; Var Bsktbl; Hon Roll.

DRURY, DAYNA L; Velma Alma HS; Countyline, OK; (2); Sec FHA; Girl Scts; Rptr Nwsp; Cit Awd; Prfct Atten Awd; Pres Acad Fit Awd.

DRYDEN, NICOLE L; Walters HS; Walters, OK; (1); 29/68; FHA; GAA; Bsktbl; Sftbl; Cit Awd; OSU.

DU, HAI T; Westmoore HS; Oklahoma City, OK; (4); 72/635; DECA; French Clb; Quiz Bowl; Scholastic Bowl; Science Clb; Band; Mrchg Band; Jr NHS; NHS; Asian Amer Assn; OK ST Univ; Aerospace Engr.

DUARTE, CHAD A; Claremore Sr HS; Claremore, OK; (1); Church Yth Grp; Hon Roll; FFA Top Slsmn; Hntng; Fshng; Rogers ST Coll.

DUARTE, RONALD I; Pauls Valley HS; Pauls Valley, OK; (3); Art Clb; Var Bsktbl.

DUBBERLY, JESSE L; Norman Sr HS; Norman, OK; (3); 125/799; Cmnty Wkr; Model UN; VP Mu Alpha Theta; Orch; Rep Stu Cncl; JV Var Ftbl; Var JV Trk; High Hon Roll; NHS; OK St Legislature Page 92-96; Natl Ldrshp & Svc Awd; His Stu Of Yr 95-96; All-Amer Schlr.

DUBIE, CHRISTINA; Booker T Washington HS; Tulsa, OK; (3); Art Clb; HOBY; NFL; Spanish Clb; Rep Stu Cncl; Var L Chrldng; NHS; Jazz Choir; Acad Ltr; Native Amer Clb Treas.

DU BOIS, JENNIFER R; Sapulpa Sr HS; Sapulpa, OK; (2); Church Yth Grp; Cmnty Wkr; Computer Clb; FBLA; Spanish Clb; Band; Chorus; Church Choir; Rptr Phtg Nwsp; Hon Roll; Highest Hnrs Solo Singing; OU; Phys Thrpy.

DUCHENEAUX, CARRIE E; Tipton Jr Sr HS; Tipton, OK; (3); 1/28; FHA; GAA; Pep Clb; Band; Mrchg Band; Pep Band; Var Bsktbl; Intrml Wt Lftg; Cit Awd; High Hon Roll; 1st Pl In Jr Div Of Local Art Show; 2nd Pl In Regnl Sci Fair Jr Div 94; Hnrs Awd By Univ Of OK; Murray ST; Vet Asst.

DUCK, STEFANIE M; Union Intermediate HS; Tulsa, OK; (2); Spanish Clb; Teachers Aide; Socr; Swmmng; Vet Sci.

DUDGEON, CARISSA L; Cordell Sr HS; Cordell, OK; (3); Library Aide; Pep Clb; Teachers Aide; High Hon Roll; Hon Roll; Southwestern OK ST U; Ansthsl.

DUDGEON, CHERRIE; Cordell Sr HS; Corn, OK; (2); Girl Scts; Spanish Clb; SADD; Band; Chorus; School Play; Hon Roll.

DUEA, MATTHEW J; Yukon Middle HS; Yukon, OK; (2); Church Yth Grp; Band; Mrchg Band; Pep Band; Gov Hon Prg Awd; High Hon Roll; Hon Roll; NHS; Section Ldr In Marching Band.

DUFF, SARAH R; Nathan Hale HS; Tulsa, OK; (3); FTA; Chorus; Ed Nwsp; Var Socr; High Hon Roll; Hon Roll; NHS; Show Choir; Pre-Law.

DUFFEL, BRADLEY; Mustang HS; Yukon, OK; (4); 1/350; Am Leg Boys St; Church Yth Grp; FCA; JA; Scholastic Bowl; Chorus; Var Bsktbl; Hon Roll; NHS; Val.

DUFFY, KACY; Watonga HS; Watonga, OK; (3); FBLA; Band; Mrchg Band; Pep Band; Treas Frsh Cls; Var Bsktbl; Var Chrldng; Var Trk; NHS; OK ST U.

DUGGAN, KARIN; U S Grant HS; Oklahoma City, OK; (2); Dance Clb; FCA; School Musical; Rep Frsh Cls; Ofcr Stu Cncl; Var Chrldng; High Hon Roll; NHS.

DUGGER, ASHLEY; Canton HS; Canton, OK; (2); 1/45; HOBY; Scholastic Bowl; Spanish Clb; VP SADD; Pres Soph Cls; Sec Stu Cncl; Var L Bsktbl; NHS; Church Yth Grp; FHA; Natl Hstry Day 2nd Pl Wnnr; Thoburn Hstry Awd-OK Otstndng Hstry Stu; OK U; Envrnmntl Sci.

DUGGER, LEXIE; Pioneer Jr Sr HS; Enid, OK; (1); Band; Mrchg Band; Ofcr Stu Cncl; Chrldng; Hon Roll; Rnbw; OK ST U.

DUGGER, STACIE L; Stilwell HS; Stilwell, OK; (2); Drama Clb; Spanish Clb; High Hon Roll; Indian Heritage; RN.

DUHON, NATALIE D; John Marshall HS; Oklahoma City, OK; (2); Mgr(s); Co-Capt Pom Pon; JV Sftbl; Hon Roll; Mem Upwrd Bnd; Gramling; Atty.

DUKE, CORBYN; Yukon Middle HS; Yukon, OK; (2); 12/400; Church Yth Grp; Ofcr Bsbl; Bsktbl; Ftbl; High Hon Roll; Jr NHS; NHS; Renaissance Club; Amer Legion Bsbl Tm; OK ST Univ.

DUKESHERER, GARY D; Putnam City West HS; Bethany, OK; (4); 28/302; Drama Clb; JCL; VP Latin Clb; VP Band; Drm Mjr(t); Mrchg Band; School Musical; School Play; Ofcr Stu Cncl; NHS; Camp Oustdng Drum Major; Outstdng Tuba Soloist; Outstdng Frosh, Soph & Jr Schl Band; OU.

DULANEY, JOHN; Turpin Schl; Turpin, OK; (3); 2/36; Pres Drama Clb; Pres FCA; NFL; Pres Speech Tm; VP SADD; Acpl Chr; Chorus; Church Choir; School Musical; School Play; Dramtc Interp St Chmp; Humorous Duet Reg Chmp; Dramtc Duet St Rnnr Up; Ftbl/Trk Titles; Wstrn Hnr Choir; Oklahoma City U; Thelogy.

DULIN, MICHAEL; Hinton HS; Hinton, OK; (3); #2 in class; Church Yth Grp; FCA; Scholastic Bowl; Chorus; School Musical; L Bsktbl; Var L Ftbl; L Trk; Gov Hon Prg Awd; High Hon Roll.

DUMLER, ERIC; Texhoma HS; Texhoma, OK; (1); Church Yth Grp; JV Bsktbl; Var Ftbl; Hon Roll; OK ST U.

DUNAFAN, JOANNA L; Hartshorne Sr HS; Hartshorne, OK; (2); FHA; Pep Clb; Color Guard; Cit Awd; Carlbert JC; Phy Thrpst.

DUNAGAN, JESSICA; Bowlegs Schl; Bowlegs, OK; (4); 1/25; Church Yth Grp; FCA; FHA; Natl Beta Clb; Quiz Bowl; Band; Drm Mjr(t); Var Bsktbl; NHS; Val; Peer Tutor; Vol Nrsng Home; Seminole JC; Nursing.

DUNAGAN, TASHA R; Guthrie Sr HS; Guthrie, OK; (1); Church Yth Grp; Cmnty Wkr; Red Cross Aide; ROTC; Color Guard; Cit Awd; High Hon Roll; Hon Roll; Best Military Appearance ROTC; Ldrshp; Stdnt Cncl Pres 8th Grd; Pol Sci.

DUNAVANT, JAMIE; Claremore Sr HS; Claremore, OK; (3); 4/268; Church Yth Grp; Cmnty Wkr; Teachers Aide; Bsktbl; Trk; Hon Roll; NHS; Ntl Merit Ltr; Pres Acad Fit Awd; Rsptry Thrpy.

DUNAWAY, JOEY A; Bishop Mcguinness HS; Oklahoma City, OK; (2); 40/167; Church Yth Grp; FCA; Var L Ftbl; Var L Trk; Wt Lftg; Var L Wrstlng; NHS.

DUNAWAY, MONICA R; Eisenhower Sr HS; Lawton, OK; (3); Church Yth Grp; Cmnty Wkr; French Clb; FBLA; Treas Intnl Clb; Chorus; Church Choir; High Hon Roll; Hon Roll; NHS; Great Plains Area Vo-Tech Hnr Soc; GATE; 2 Yr Recipient Of Acad Ltr; Bus Admin.

DUNBAR, AMANDA J; Choctaw HS; Midwest City, OK; (4); 28/311; Church Yth Grp; Drama Clb; FCA; Girl Scts; Key Clb; SADD; Teachers Aide; Mrchg Band; Orch; NHS; OK St Hnr Soc; U Of OK; Phys Thrp.

DUNBAR, DEIDRA A; Kellyville Sr HS; Kellyville, OK; (3); Church Yth Grp; 4-H; VP Natl FFA Org; Sec Jr Cls; Var Bsktbl; Hon Roll; NHS; Pres Acad Fit Awd; FFA Awrds; Outstndg Ldrshp Awrd; Alpha Pi; OK ST Univ; Vet Med.

DUNCAN, ANGIE N; Collinsville HS; Collinsville, OK; (2); Church Yth Grp; Rptr Band; Drm Mjr(t); Jazz Band; Mrchg Band; School Play; Hon Roll; NHS; Prfct Atten Awd; Sftbl; Amer Musical Fnd-Bnd Hnrs; S Nazarene Univ; Med.

DUNCAN, BRANDI; Cameron Schl; Cameron, OK; (2); Church Yth Grp; FHA; Natl FFA Org; Quiz Bowl; Church Choir; Yrbk; High Hon Roll; Hon Roll; 4-H; Scholastic Bowl; Kids On Blck Pupptr Prog; St Hnr Soc.

DUNCAN, BRIAN E; Claremore Sr HS; Claremore, OK; (2); Boy Scts; Band; Mrchg Band; Pep Band; Rptr Yrbk; Hon Roll.

DUNCAN, CHARLES R; Fletcher Jr Sr HS; Fletcher, OK; (4); 5/31; Church Yth Grp; Pres Natl FFA Org; Co-Capt Quiz Bowl; Teachers Aide; VICA; Sec Frsh Cls; Ofcr Soph Cls; VP Jr Cls; Var Bsbl; Var Bsktbl; Natl Vo Tech Hnr Soc; N E OK U; Vet.

DUNCAN, DENISE A; Altus Sr HS; Altus, OK; (2); Church Yth Grp; Cmnty Wkr; Spanish Clb; Drill Tm; Var L Crs Cntry; Var L Sftbl; Var L Tennis; NHS; Ntl Merit Ltr; Val; Acad All-Star; OU; Med.

DUNCAN, JENNIFER; Piedmont HS; Bethany, OK; (4); 1/79; Am Leg Aux Girls St; Cmnty Wkr; VP Frsh Cls; Rep Soph Cls; Pres Jr Cls; VP Sr Cls; Rep Stu Cncl; Capt Chrldng; Pres NHS; NCAA All Amer Chrldr 2xs; U OK; Psych.

DUNCAN, JENNIFER R; Kiowa Jr-Sr HS; Kiowa, OK; (2); Church Yth Grp; 4-H; Natl FFA Org; Speech Tm; Yrbk; Rptr Frsh Cls; Rptr Soph Cls; Hon Roll; Yth Alive; ECU Ada; Elem Tchr.

DUNCAN, KAMI; Chandler HS; Chandler, OK; (3); #1 in class; Church Yth Grp; Treas FHA; Girl Scts; Thesps; School Musical; School Play; NHS; FHA N Dist Sub-Dist 5 VP, 3 Star Natl Rtng Prlmntry Prcdr, Stu Cncl Rep.

DUNCAN, MATT; Tecumseh HS; Tecumseh, OK; (1); Boy Scts; Church Yth Grp; Band; Chorus; Church Choir; Jazz Band; Mrchg Band; Orch; Pep Band; Variety Show; OK Univ; Pediatric Neurosurgn.

DUNCAN, RACHEL; Okemah HS; Okemah, OK; (4); Am Leg Aux Girls St; Church Yth Grp; Drama Clb; Key Clb; Office Aide; Science Clb; Thesps; Ofcr Stu Cncl; Var Bsktbl; Gym; Stu Mnth; Chrldr All Conf, All Star; BSKTBL OBU All Trnmnt Tm, All Conf 1st Tm; E Cntrl U; Optmtry.

DUNCAN, SHANNA D; Eufaula Sr HS; Eufaula, OK; (2); Church Yth Grp; Cmnty Wkr; Sec Natl FFA Org; Ed Yrbk; Hon Roll; FFA Star Greenhand; TSA Pres; Connors ST Coll; Med.

DUNCAN, TASSIE; New Lima Jr Sr HS; Seminole, OK; (2); Rep Frsh Cls; Rep Soph Cls; Rep Stu Cncl; Var Chrldng; Hon Roll; NHS; Pres Schlr.

DUNCIL, DAVID J; Will Rogers HS; Tulsa, OK; (2); ROTC.

DUNGY, DAN A; Oklahoma Christian Schl; Oklahoma City, OK; (4); 18/36; Church Yth Grp; Computer Clb; Debate Tm; Drama Clb; Office Aide; Chorus; Church Choir; School Play; Bsktbl; Ftbl; Tae Kwon Do; U Of Cntrl OK; Criminal Justic.

DUNHAM, DAVID P; Cascia Hall Prep School; Tulsa, OK; (3); 3/85; Church Yth Grp; FCA; FBLA; Math Tm; Pres Spanish Clb; Varsity Clb; School Play; Ed Yrbk; Bsktbl; Crs Cntry; Med.

DUNHAM, ERIK C; Ponca City Sr HS; Ponca City, OK; (3); 18/400; Am Leg Boys St; Drama Clb; French Clb; NFL; Speech Tm; School Play; Stage Crew; Rep Stu Cncl; High Hon Roll; Hon Roll; Comm Thtr Tech/Actng; Washington U; Chem Eng.

DUNHAM, ERIN L; Stillwater Sr HS; Stillwater, OK; (2); Church Yth Grp; FCA; Spanish Clb; Acpl Chr; Chorus; School Musical; School Play; Hon Roll; Pres Acad Fit Awd; Mission Projects Jamaica, Belanes & Poland; Missionary.

DUNHAM, JEREMY; Okmulgee HS; Okmulgee, OK; (4); Varsity Clb; Nwsp; Yrbk; VP Sr Cls; Bsktbl; Tennis; St, Reg, Natlly Ranked Tennis 5 Yrs; OU; Phys Thrpy.

DUNHAM, STEPHANIE R; Union Intermediate HS; Tulsa, OK; (2); 108/800; German Clb; Girl Scts; Chorus; School Musical; High Hon Roll; NHS.

DUNIGAN, KATIE E; Webster HS; Tulsa, OK; (2); Church Yth Grp; Cmnty Wkr; Key Clb; Sec Soph Cls; Golf; High Hon Roll; Hon Roll; Jr NHS; Cycling; Frosh Homcng Attendant; Womens Shelter Vol.

DUNKELGOD, BLAKE N; Edmond North HS; Edmond, OK; (2); 96/420; Boy Scts; Church Yth Grp; Drama Clb; HOBY; Letterman Clb; Office Aide; Varsity Clb; Ftbl; Wt Lftg; NHS; Duke Univ; Pre-Med.

DUNKIN, JAMES W; Chisholm Sr HS; Enid, OK; (2); Chess Clb; Cmnty Wkr; FCA; Spanish Clb; Ftbl; Wt Lftg; Roller Hockey; Auto Mechanics; Bus; Auto Mechanics.

DUNLAP, BRIANNE K; Putnam City West HS; Oklahoma City, OK; (2); Phtg Nwsp; Phtg Yrbk; Art Phtgrphy.

DUNLAP, MISTY D; Choctaw HS; Choctaw, OK; (2); Dance Clb; Library Aide; Hon Roll; Nrsng.

DUNLAP, URSULA; Glenpool HS; Glenpool, OK; (4); 4/115; Art Clb; Spanish Clb; High Hon Roll; Ayn Rand Insts Anthem Essy Cont 1st Pl; Amnsty Intl; Concrrntly Enrolled Tulsa Jr Coll; Engl.

DUNN, AARON L; Charles Page HS; Sand Springs, OK; (1); High Hon Roll; Hon Roll; Acad Ltr 4 0 Or Hghr 3 Yrs; Bus.

DUNN, ALICIA A; Charles Page HS; Sand Springs, OK; (3); Church Yth Grp; French Clb; FTA; JA; Church Choir; Hon Roll; Pres Acad Fit Awd.

DUNN, AMANDA S; Miami Sr HS; Miami, OK; (3); #17 in class; Church Yth Grp; Drama Clb; Office Aide; Speech Tm; Church Choir; School Musical; School Play; High Hon Roll; Hon Roll; NHS; U Of OK; Outs Acad Achv Hnr; USNLMA; Jrnlsm; Mass Comm.

DUNN, BRODY; Garber Sr HS; Garber, OK; (2); FCA; Letterman Clb; Band; Mrchg Band; Rep Frsh Cls; Ofcr Bsbl; Ftbl; High Hon Roll; Hon Roll; NHS; Engrng.

DUNN, BRUCE L; Cushing HS; Cushing, OK; (2); 8/149; Cmnty Wkr; Natl FFA Org; Spanish Clb; Teachers Aide; Cit Awd; High Hon Roll; Prfct Atten Awd; Amateur Trapshooting Assn; Hunting; Fishing; OSU; Turf Mgmt.

DUNN, CHAD; Little Axe Sr HS; Newalla, OK; (4); 40/90; FHA; Library Aide; Capt Model UN; JV Capt Quiz Bowl; Scholastic Bowl; Teachers Aide; Co-Ed Nwsp; JETS Awd; His Clb; Civil War Reenacter; Jrnlsm; Print Media.

DUNN, ELISABETH; Perry Sr HS; Perry, OK; (4); 4/70; Church Yth Grp; Cmnty Wkr; FCA; FHA; Chorus; Church Choir; School Musical; Sec Jr Cls; Hon Roll; NHS; Northern OK Coll; Ed.

DUNN, GRACE M; Bixby Sr HS; Leonard, OK; (4); 21/179; French Clb; FHA; VICA; High Hon Roll; NHS; Natl Voc Tech Hnr Soc; Natl Sci Mrt Awd; Avila; Chem.

DUNN, JERA; Perry Sr HS; Perry, OK; (4); 6/66; Pres Church Yth Grp; FCA; FHA; Band; Chorus; Pres Church Choir; Drm Mjr(t); Treas Jr Cls; Rep Stu Cncl; NHS; Lions Clb Rep; FBC Stu Dir; Northern OK Coll; Psych.

DUNN, JOHN S; Union Sr HS; Broken Arrow, OK; (3); 79/741; Boy Scts; Church Yth Grp; Mu Alpha Theta; Band; Nwsp; Yrbk; Hon Roll; Jr NHS; NHS; Pres Ed Awd; Sci Fair 1st Pl Earth/Spce Scis; Kingdom Seekers Church Ldrshp Pgm; U Of OK; Med.

DUNN, KELLIE; Laverne Jr Sr HS; Gate, OK; (4); 11/33; Am Leg Aux Girls St; Church Yth Grp; FHA; Letterman Clb; Natl Beta Clb; Chorus; School Play; Treas Stu Cncl; Chrldng; Hon Roll; Bible Club; Northwestern OK ST U; Sci.

DUNN, KIMBERLY C; Webster HS; Tulsa, OK; (3); Church Yth Grp; High Hon Roll; NHS; Ntl Merit SF; HOSA; Tulsa Univ; Pre-Med; Dr.

DUNN, KONYA; Laverne Jr Sr HS; Gate, OK; (2); 10/43; Church Yth Grp; Drama Clb; Natl Beta Clb; Band; Drm Mjr(t); Flag Corp; Pres Stu Cncl; Chrldng; Sftbl; Hon Roll.

DUNN, SHANNON D; Bethany HS; Oklahoma City, OK; (2); Church Yth Grp; Key Clb; Spanish Clb; Chorus; Church Choir; Treas Jr Cls; Hist Stu Cncl; High Hon Roll; Hon Roll; NHS; People To People Stdnt Ambsdr; Gov Cmndtn; OK Hnr Soc; Musical Ed.

DUNN, TAMMY R; Yukon HS; Yukon, OK; (4); Church Yth Grp; Band; Church Choir; Color Guard; Mrchg Band; School Musical; Rep Frsh Cls; Ofcr Soph Cls; Ofcr Jr Cls; Ofcr Sr Cls; OK City CC; Offc Admin.

DUONG, PHUONG-CHI T; Union Sr HS; Tulsa, OK; (3); #120 in class; Church Yth Grp; FBLA; FHA; Hosp Aide; HOBY; Red Cross Aide; Orch; Sec Frsh Cls; Sec Jr Cls; VP Stu Cncl; Outstndng Stu Cncl Offcr 94-95; Baylor U; Phy Ther.

DUPREE, PATRICIA J; Colbert Jr Sr HS; Colbert, OK; (3); Church Yth Grp; FCA; VP 4-H; Sec Natl FFA Org; Spanish Clb; Teachers Aide; School Play; JV Bsktbl; 4-H Awd; Hon Roll; Tech Stdnt Assn; PT.

DUPUY, LESLIE A; Mc Alester HS; Mcalester, OK; (4); 30/193; French Clb; Office Aide; Red Cross Aide; Pom Pon; Hon Roll; OK HS Hnr Soc; Lunch Buddy Pgrm Elem Stdnts; Otstdng Frnch II Stdnt; LA ST Univ; Theatre.

DURANT, WILLIAM B; Putnam City HS; Warr Acres, OK; (4); 12/345; Church Yth Grp; FCA; German Clb; Key Clb; Ofcr Stu Cncl; Var Capt Golf; Cit Awd; Hon Roll; NHS; St Schlr; Voted All Arnd Sr Boy/Fclty; Nom Pirateer Awd; Awded Most Optmstc/Chrfl Sr Sprltv; OK ST Univ; Civil Engr.

DURANT, ZACK D; Eisenhower Sr HS; Lawton, OK; (4); 12/386; Church Yth Grp; VP Treas Drama Clb; Key Clb; Chorus; School Play; Pres Soph Cls; Pres Jr Cls; Pres Stu Cncl; High Hon Roll; NHS; NYU; Thtr.

DURBIN, LAURA E; Waukomis HS; Waukomis, OK; (2); Church Yth Grp; FCA; Pres Pep Clb; Pres Soph Cls; Var L Bsktbl; Var L Sftbl; Var L Trk; Hon Roll; TX A&M; Law.

DURBIN, NIKKI J; Central Jr HS; Lawton, OK; (1); FHA; Band; Mrchg Band; Pep Band; Hon Roll; U Of CA; Psych.

DUREN, STEPHANIE K; Drumright HS; Drumright, OK; (2); FCA; GAA; Science Clb; Spanish Clb; Varsity Clb; Pres Frsh Cls; Pres Soph Cls; JV Var Bsktbl; Var Capt Chrldng; Var Sftbl; Frshmn Ftbll Homecoming Crt; Soph Bsktbll Homecoming Crt; OSU; Mortician.

DURFEY, CRYSTAL; Timberlake Schl; Cherokee, OK; (2); #1 in class; FCA; FHA; Chorus; Rep Frsh Cls; Sec Treas Soph Cls; Bsktbl; Mgr(s); Score Keeper; High Hon Roll.

DURGIN, DANA; Tomlinson Jr HS; Lawton, OK; (1); FCA; FHA; Pep Clb; School Play; Ofcr Stu Cncl; Bsktbl; Var Chrldng; Var Tennis; Hon Roll; Gym/Tumblng; Scndry Ed.

DURHAM, CARA G; Enid Sr HS; Enid, OK; (2); 8/441; Speech Tm; Band; Mrchg Band; School Play; Stage Crew; High Hon Roll; Jr NHS; NHS; Univ Of OK; Bus Mgmt/Acctg.

DURR, KELSEY; Waller Jr HS; Enid, OK; (1); Church Yth Grp; Dance Clb; FCA; Band; Chrldng; Hon Roll; Jr NHS; KS U; Phys Thrpy.

DURRILL, KATIE; Edmond North HS; Edmond, OK; (3); Church Yth Grp; FCA; Letterman Clb; Spanish Clb; SADD; Ofcr Jr Cls; Ofcr Sr Cls; Ofcr Stu Cncl; Chrldng; Trk; Kanakomo & Kickapoo Princess 96.

DURYEA, JASON A; Cleveland Sr HS; Cleveland, OK; (3); 5/77; Am Leg Boys St; Quiz Bowl; Scholastic Bowl; Band; Chorus; Color Guard; Mrchg Band; Pep Band; Socr; NHS; Aero Eng.

DUSENBERRY, BROOKE N; Mc Alester HS; Mcalester, OK; (3); #2 in class; Church Yth Grp; Science Clb; Spanish Clb; Jazz Band; Mrchg Band; Golf; Jr NHS; Pres Acad Fit Awd; St Schlr; U Of OK; Pre Med.

DUTTON, COURTNEY; Westmoore HS; Oklahoma City, OK; (3); Church Yth Grp; FCA; School Musical; School Play; Pom Pon; NHS; 95-96 Wrestling Jr Homcmng Ct; 2nd Pl With Pom Squad At NCA HS Natls; Won HS Pom Pon St Cmptn; Baylor; Law.

DUTTON, REBECCA; Okmulgee HS; Okmulgee, OK; (3); 19/121; Church Yth Grp; FCA; Var Bsktbl; Hon Roll; NHS; Nrs.

DUTTON, TIFFANY L; Union Intermediate HS; Tulsa, OK; (2); 63/800; Church Yth Grp; Office Aide; Spanish Clb; Color Guard; Var Tennis; JV Vllybl; Hon Roll; NHS; Drug Free Yth.

DUTY, AMANDA; Bridge Creek HS; Tuttle, OK; (2); Church Yth Grp; Cmnty Wkr; GAA; Spanish Clb; Church Choir; Co-Capt Frsh Cls; Capt Soph Cls; JV Bsktbl; Var Sftbl; Hon Roll.

DUTY, DARREN R; Muldrow HS; Muldrow, OK; (1); Chess.

DUTY, SONJA; Hobart HS; Hobart, OK; (2); Church Yth Grp; Girl Scts; Speech Tm; Band; Drm Mjr(t); Jazz Band; Mrchg Band; Pep Band; School Play; Yrbk.

DUVALL, AMY; East Central HS; Tulsa, OK; (3); Red Cross Aide; Sec Science Clb; Pres Spanish Clb; Rep Jr Cls; Rep Stu Cncl; Co-Capt Var Chrldng; High Hon Roll; Kiwanis Awd; NHS.

DUVALL, HEATHER; Sallisaw HS; Sallisaw, OK; (3); Art Clb; Church Yth Grp; FHA; Girl Scts; Science Clb; Spanish Clb; VP Jr Cls; Powder Puff Ftbl; Hon Roll; NHS; Indian Clb; FHA Champ; Acctng.

DUVALL, JEREMY; Liberty Acad; Shawnee, OK; (3); Church Yth Grp; Cmnty Wkr; Dance Clb; Drama Clb; Chorus; School Musical; Yrbk; Rep Soph Cls; Bsktbl; High Hon Roll; Mr Dance Of OK 95; Mr Dance Of America 4th Rnnr-Up 96, Natl Fnlst 96; KAD; Julliard; Perf Arts.

DVORAK, KENDRA L; Pawnee HS; Pawnee, OK; (4); 20/60; Church Yth Grp; FCA; 4-H; Pres Natl FFA Org; Pep Clb; Teachers Aide; Band; Church Choir; Color Guard; Flag Corp; OK Bptist All St Yth Choir; Chrchdrama Grp; U Of Cntrl OK; Elem Ed.

DVORAK, TIMOTHY C; Pawnee HS; Pawnee, OK; (2); Church Yth Grp; FCA; 4-H; Natl FFA Org; Band; Church Choir; Mrchg Band; Pep Band; Ofcr Bsbl; Bsktbl; Chrch Drama Group; Criminal Justice; Hwy Patrol.

DYCHE, JENNIFER; Chisholm Sr HS; Carrier, OK; (3); FCA; FHA; GAA; Office Aide; Varsity Clb; Rep Stu Cncl; Var Bsktbl; Var Crs Cntry; Var Sftbl; Var Trk; OSU.

DYE, ANGELA; Southeast HS; Oklahoma City, OK; (1); Chess Clb; Computer Clb; Drama Clb; School Play; High Hon Roll; Jr NHS; Write Poems, Short Stories; Paint; Draw; Read Books.

DYE, BOBBIE L; Tipton Jr Sr HS; Headrick, OK; (2); FHA; Spanish Clb; Bsktbl; Hon Roll; Jr NHS; Washington U.

DYE, HEATHER C; Elk City Jr HS; Elk City, OK; (1); Church Yth Grp; Band; Mrchg Band; Pep Band; Hon Roll; Sci Awd; Tchr.

DYE, JOE; Berryhill Jr HS; Tulsa, OK; (1); SADD; Bsktbl; Ftbl; Trk; Wt Lftg; Hon Roll; Prfct Atten Awd; OK ST U.

DYE, JULIE; Grace Chrn Acad; Oklahoma City, OK; (4); 7/22; Church Yth Grp; Cmnty Wkr; HOBY; Office Aide; Teachers Aide; Ed Yrbk; Pres Jr Cls; Rep Stu Cncl; Var Sec Bsktbl; Var Mgr(s); OSU; Bus Admin.

DYE, SOPHIE M; Bishop Kelley HS; Tulsa, OK; (1); Church Yth Grp; Pep Clb; Red Cross Aide; Rep Stu Cncl; French Hon Soc; High Hon Roll; Notre Dame; Mar Bio.

DYER, CRYSTAL; Binger-Orvey HS; Fort Cobb, OK; (4); 3/23; Cmnty Wkr; FHA; HOBY; Natl Beta Clb; Scholastic Bowl; Teachers Aide; Yrbk; Rep Soph Cls; Capt Bsktbl; Var Sftbl; Msnc Ldgs Stu Of Today; Redlands JC; Psych.

DYER, JASON; Wetumka Jr Sr HS; Wetumka, OK; (2); 1/56; Church Yth Grp; Key Clb; Natl FFA Org; Band; Jazz Band; Mrchg Band; JV Bsktbl; Trk; High Hon Roll; NHS; Karate; OU; Pre-Med.

DYER, MICHAEL J; Mc Loud HS; Mc Loud, OK; (2); Church Yth Grp; Church Choir; Archeology.

DYER, MICHELLE; Oaks Mission Jr Sr HS; Tahlequah, OK; (3); 10/36; Drama Clb; FHA; Yrbk; Hon Roll; Tech Ed; Bell Pow-Wow Princess; FFA Swthrt Cand; Northeastern ST Univ; Astrlgy.

DYER, PAM C; Muldrow HS; Muldrow, OK; (3); Cmnty Wkr; FHA; Red Cross Aide; Spanish Clb; Band; Mrchg Band; Orch; Pep Band; Hon Roll; Received Highest Average In Algebra II; Received High Average In Acctng.

DYER, RAYVN I; El Reno Sr HS; El Reno, OK; (1); Chorus; Intrml Vllybl; Harvard; Doctor.

DYER, ROBYN; Gracemont HS; Anadarko, OK; (1); Drama Clb; Sec Frsh Cls; Bsktbl; Mgr(s); Score Keeper; Hon Roll; Sal; Acad & Curr Conts.

DYKES, TONIA H; Covington Douglas HS; Covington, OK; (3); 5/30; Church Yth Grp; FHA; Natl FFA Org; Pres Frsh Cls; Pres Soph Cls; Bsktbl; Trk; Hon Roll; NHS; Prfct Atten Awd; Swimming; Running; Fishing; Alva; Children Psycht.

DZIALO, DEVIN; Lawton Sr HS; Lawton, OK; (2); FCA; Hosp Aide; Drill Tm; Cit Awd; High Hon Roll; Jr NHS; Kiwanis Awd; NHS; Med Explrs; Mar Bio.

EADES, STEPHANIE A; Southeast HS; Oklahoma City, OK; (1); Band; Jazz Band; Mrchg Band; Pep Band; High Hon Roll; Jr NHS; 2nd Pl OK City Regnl Sci Fair; HS Bio Tchr.

EADS, MATTHEW; Dickson HS; Ardmore, OK; (4); 23/63; Church Yth Grp; Cmnty Wkr; Pres FCA; FHA; Key Clb; Library Aide; Office Aide; Pres Spanish Clb; Ftbl; Southeastern ST U; Medcl.

EADS, MELODY N; Ft Cob-Broxton Jr Sr HS; Fort Cobb, OK; (3); 1/27; Church Yth Grp; 4-H; FHA; HOBY; Chorus; School Musical; 4-H Awd; Hon Roll; Prfct Atten Awd; Natl FFA Org; FHA Awd; Grd Mdlng Schl; Wrtr; Music.

EADS, MIRANDA; Ponca City Middle HS; Grove City, OH; (1); Var Chrldng.

EAGAN, JARED; Arapaho Schl; Arapaho, OK; (3); Natl FFA Org; Yrbk; Ofcr Bsbl; Bsktbl; Crs Cntry; Vllybl; Prfct Atten Awd; SW OK St Univ.

EAGAN, LESLIE; Jenks Tulsa Tech Cntr; Tulsa, OK; (3); Church Yth Grp; DECA; Quiz Bowl; Wt Lftg; High Hon Roll; Hon Roll; Natl Vo Tech Hnr Soc; Johnson/Wales Univ; Fshn Mrchnd.

EAGAN, SARAH; Kremlin Jr Sr HS; Enid, OK; (2); FCA; VP Soph Cls; Var Bsktbl; Var Chrldng; Capt Sftbl; Hon Roll; Bsktbl All Conf Tm; OK ST U.

EAGLE, CHER; Ponca City Sr HS; Ponca City, OK; (3); Church Yth Grp; Cmnty Wkr; DECA; Office Aide; Chorus; School Musical; High Hon Roll; Hon Roll; Oo-Kee-Hee Indian Clb Sec, VP; Ponca Tribal Yth Cncl VP; U Of OK.

EAIRHEART, JASEN R; Geronimo Jr Sr HS; Geronimo, OK; (2); Church Yth Grp; Cmnty Wkr; FCA; Speech Tm; Church Choir; Var Bsktbl; JV Trk; Cit Awd; Hon Roll; Jr NHS.

EAKES, TAMISHA N; Star Spencer HS; Oklahoma City, OK; (1); Midwest Beauty Coll; Cosmetlgst.

EAKLE, CASSIE; Quinton Jr Sr HS; Quinton, OK; (1); Church Yth Grp; FCA; Band; Bsktbl; Chrldng; Hon Roll; Schltc Meet; Sing Church.

EAKLE, EUGENE; Stigler HS; Stigler, OK; (4); Am Leg Boys St; Natl FFA Org; SADD; Teachers Aide; Band; Mrchg Band; Pep Band; Hon Roll; NHS; Prfct Atten Awd; OSU; Electrcn.

EAKLE, MATT; Quinton Jr Sr HS; Quinton, OK; (2); 6/60; Church Yth Grp; FCA; FHA; Quiz Bowl; Var Bsktbl; Var Ftbl; Var Trk; Hon Roll; All Amer Schlr; N E OK ST U; Jrnlsm.

EALEY, MISTY; Moore HS; Moore, OK; (3); JA; Spanish Clb; SADD; Swmmng; Hon Roll; Jr NHS; NHS; Peer Cnslr; U Of OK; Med.

EALOM, LESTER; Wellston Schl; Wellston, OK; (2); Church Yth Grp; FCA; Band; Chorus; Drill Tm; Mrchg Band; Pep Band; School Musical; Swing Chorus; Phtg Nwsp; Grambling; Musical Composer.

EARICKSON, KEITH; Bartlesville Sr HS; Bartlesville, OK; (3); Office Aide; Spanish Clb; Rep Jr Cls; Var L Bsbl; L Var Ftbl; JV Wrstlng; High Hon Roll; Hon Roll; Jr NHS; NHS; U Of OK; Engr.

EARLEY, DUSTIN; Kingston HS; Kingston, OK; (1); 4-H; Natl FFA Org; Spanish Clb; Star Greenhand FFA.

EARLS, KEVIN R; Edmond North HS; Edmond, OK; (2); 100/400; Math Clb; Mu Alpha Theta; Spanish Clb; Golf; Hon Roll; Jr NHS; NHS; People To People Goodwill Ambssdrs.

EARLY, KARI L; Lawton Sr HS; Lawton, OK; (3); Church Yth Grp; French Clb; Math Tm; Chorus; Church Choir; Pom Pon; High Hon Roll; Hon Roll; NHS; Pres Acad Fit Awd; OU.

EARLY, KEISHA; Okemah HS; Okemah, OK; (4); 11/49; Church Yth Grp; FHA; SADD; Band; Jazz Band; Mrchg Band; Pep Band; VP Sr Cls; Sftbl; Hon Roll; Nursing.

EARP, GREG A; Meeker HS; Chandler, OK; (1); Scholastic Bowl; Band; Jazz Band; Mrchg Band; Ftbl; Trk; Hon Roll; Pres Acad Fit Awd; St Hnr Soc.

EARP, RACHEL M; Moore HS; Moore, OK; (3); Church Yth Grp; Cmnty Wkr; Office Aide; Science Clb; Band; Church Choir; Jazz Band; Mrchg Band; Pep Band; Jr NHS; CEF & CYIA; Chrch Soloist & Youth Choir; Toddler Class Sunday Schl Tchr; UCO; Phy Thrpst; Ed.

EARWOOD, JALISA A; Tipton Jr Sr HS; Tipton, OK; (3); 3/30; Science Clb; Band; Color Guard; Mrchg Band; Yrbk; Bsktbl; High Hon Roll; NHS; Ntl Merit Ltr; Prfct Atten Awd; OK Central; Acctng/Tchng.

EASILEY, MAURENE G; B T Washington HS; Tulsa, OK; (3); 105/269; Church Yth Grp; FBLA; Church Choir; Hon Roll; Natl Voc Hnr Soc; MI ST Univ; Acctng.

EASLON, BRIAN J; Velma Alma HS; Duncan, OK; (4); 3/44; Church Yth Grp; FCA; Letterman Clb; SADD; Teachers Aide; Band; Drm Mjr(t); Jazz Band; Mrchg Band; Orch; E Central U; Pre-Med.

EASLY, JENNIFER D; Mc Lish HS; Fittstown, OK; (3); 3/15; Art Clb; 4-H; German Clb; Scholastic Bowl; Var Co-Capt Bsktbl; Var Trk; 4-H Awd; Pres Frsh Cls; Pres Soph Cls; East Cntrl Univ; Child Cnlsr.

EASON, CHRISTINA E; Velma Alma HS; Velma, OK; (2); FCA; Quiz Bowl; SADD; Church Choir; Rep Frsh Cls; Ofcr Stu Cncl; Var Chrldng; DAR Awd; Hon Roll; NHS.

EASTEP, AMY; Wellston Schl; Wellston, OK; (3); Hosp Aide; SADD; Cit Awd; Hon Roll; NHS; Psych.

EASTER, BROOKE; Perry Sr HS; Perry, OK; (2); 1/105; Church Yth Grp; FCA; Math Clb; Spanish Clb; Band; Church Choir; School Play; Yrbk; Var Golf; Jr NHS; Wake Forest; Law.

EASTER, CHRIS A; Putnam City West HS; Bethany, OK; (3); Church Yth Grp; Office Aide; Teachers Aide; Chorus; Church Choir; Rep Stu Cncl; Ofcr Bsbl; Var L Ftbl; Wt Lftg; JV Wrstlng; MO Southern St Ftbl Camp Offensive Lin MVP 96; Ed; Psych.

EASTER, JONATHAN; Midwest City HS; Oklahoma City, OK; (3); JA; ROTC; Cit Awd; High Hon Roll; Hon Roll; Jr NHS; NHS; Ntl Merit Ltr; Prfct Atten Awd; Spanish NHS; U Of MA; Comp Tech.

EASTER, SHANTELL; Weatherford HS; Weatherford, OK; (1); Band; Chorus; Mrchg Band; Pep Band; Var Chrldng; High Hon Roll; NHS; Superior Rtng Dist Solo/Esnbl Flute Duet/Cordell Band Fstvl Flute Solo; Fshn Dsgn.

EASTERBY, JENNIFER L; Owasso Sr HS; Claremore, OK; (3); Church Yth Grp; 4-H; FHA; Natl FFA Org; Teachers Aide; 4-H Awd; OK ST U; Intr Dctr.

EASTERLING, JESSICA; Plainview HS; Lone Grove, OK; (2); Church Yth Grp; FCA; Latin Clb; Natl Beta Clb; Pres Jr Cls; Intrml Bsktbl; Var Trk; Cit Awd; High Hon Roll; Hon Roll; Pdtrcs/Corp Law.

EASTERLY, BECKY D; Pond Creek-Hunter Schl; Hunter, OK; (2); Var JV Bsktbl; Var L Sftbl; Hon Roll; NHS; Prfct Atten Awd; Dr.

EASTOM, CRYSTAL C; Will Rogers HS; Tulsa, OK; (3); Church Yth Grp; Band; Chorus; Church Choir; Mrchg Band; Hon Roll.

EATON, AMBER; Thomas A Edison HS; Tulsa, OK; (3); 7/320; French Clb; HOBY; Key Clb; Science Clb; VP Frsh Cls; Pres Soph Cls; Pres Jr Cls; Rep Stu Cncl; Capt Var Chrldng; NHS; Mst Sprtd; Bst Ldr; OK ST U; Med.

EATON, BOBBIE JO; Daniel Webster HS; Tulsa, OK; (2); Church Yth Grp; Chrldng; High Hon Roll; NHS.

EATON, BROOKE E; Nathan Hale HS; Tulsa, OK; (3); Color Guard; Drill Tm; Bsktbl; Crs Cntry; Hon Roll; Volunteens; Law Enfrcmnt.

EATON, CHRISTINE E; Bartlesville Mid HS; Bartlesville, OK; (3); 208/441; Boy Scts; Church Yth Grp; FHA; Teachers Aide; L Orch; Prfct Atten Awd; Chi Alpha Chrstn Yth Group; Explorer Post Treas, Sec, Quartermaster & VP; Piano.

EATON, LEAH; Moore HS; Moore, OK; (3); 27/650; Church Yth Grp; FCA; French Clb; Library Aide; Office Aide; Rptr Lit Mag; Chorus; Ftbl; Mgr(s); Hon Roll; NHS Cnvntn Pres 96-97; Westminster Coll; Poltcl Sci.

EATON, RENISSA; Weatherford HS; Weatherford, OK; (4); 13/138; Hon Roll; FCA; FHA; DECA; Supts Hnr Roll; Southwestern OK.

EAVENSON, JOSHUA K; Norman Sr HS; Norman, OK; (4); Church Yth Grp; Spanish Clb; JV Socr; Var Tennis; Var Wrstlng; Jr NHS; U Of OK; Envrn Sci.

EAVES, JASON; Coalgate HS; Coalgate, OK; (3); 8/55; Teachers Aide; Rep Frsh Cls; Rep Soph Cls; Sec Jr Cls; Rep Stu Cncl; Ofcr Bsbl; Ftbl; Hon Roll; Jr NHS; NHS; Sthestrn OK ST U; Math.

EAVES, ROLO L; Velma Alma HS; Velma, OK; (1); Quiz Bowl; Scholastic Bowl; Band; Mrchg Band; Trk; Hon Roll; Cmptr Prgmng.

EBENHACK, CHRISTIAN; B T Washington HS; Tulsa, OK; (2); Church Yth Grp; JCL; Latin Clb; Spanish Clb; Church Choir; Vllybl; NHS; Teens Ivolved In Prblm Slvng; Meth Ministry.

EBERLE, ERINN L; Ponca City Sr HS; Ponca City, OK; (4); 57/332; Art Clb; Drama Clb; Spanish Clb; Teachers Aide; Orch; Rptr Nwsp; Hist Frsh Cls; Rep Stu Cncl; Hon Roll; Jr NHS; OK ST Univ; Civil Engr.

EBERLE, KAHLE I; Ponca City Sr HS; Ponca City, OK; (3); Church Yth Grp; Cmnty Wkr; Band; Mrchg Band; Pep Band; Ed Nwsp; High Hon Roll; Hon Roll; NHS.

EBLER, MICHELLE; Clinton HS; Clinton, OK; (4); 22/99; Church Yth Grp; FHA; SADD; Rep Key Clb; Chorus; Ed Nwsp; Rep Stu Cncl; Hon Roll; Ntl Merit Ltr; Tchr Cdts; NM ST U; Elem Ed.

EBY, ANTHONY L; Will Rogers HS; Tulsa, OK; (1); Spanish Clb; Ofcr Bsbl; Wt Lftg.

ECCLES, ERIN; Bethany HS; Bethany, OK; (2); 5/70; Church Yth Grp; Spanish Clb; Band; Mrchg Band; High Hon Roll; Hon Roll; Jr NHS; NHS; Pres Acad Fit Awd; Celestial Winds Flute Grp; ST/DIST Flute Cmptns Superior Ratings; OK Bapt Univ; Bus Admin.

ECHOLS, ANGELINA; Choctaw HS; Midwest City, OK; (3); Art Clb; Church Yth Grp; Spanish Clb; Band; Church Choir; Color Guard; Mrchg Band; Orch; Chrch Orch; Wntrguard; Music Ed.

ECHOLS, JONATHAN D; Christian Heritage Acad; Oklahoma City, OK; (2); Church Yth Grp; FCA; Letterman Clb; Church Choir; Pres Soph Cls; JV Bsktbl; Var Ftbl; L Tennis; Hon Roll; Stage Crew; Excl In Bible Awd; Baylor; Lawyer.

ECK, ROBYN M; Union Sr HS; Tulsa, OK; (4); 39/629; Cmnty Wkr; FHA; Key Clb; Nwsp; Yrbk; Jr NHS; NHS; U Tulsa; Psych.

ECK, STEPHANIE E; Broken Arrow Sr HS; Tulsa, OK; (3); Church Yth Grp; Office Aide; Church Choir; Hon Roll; NHS; Chrstn Stu Union; Natl Hnr Soc Advsry Brd.

ECKEL, DAYMON A; Parker Middle HS; Mcalester, OK; (2); Debate Tm; Speech Tm; School Play; High Hon Roll; Cngrsnl Yth Ldrshp Cncl Natl Schlr; Amer Mensa; De Molays; Author.

ECKEL, SARAH; Oklahoma Christian Schl; Edmond, OK; (2); Church Yth Grp; Drama Clb; School Play; Stage Crew; Hon Roll; Super Smmr OK Rep; Baylor Univ; Corp Law.

ECKERT, ERIN E; Claremore Sr HS; Claremore, OK; (2); Drama Clb; Library Aide; NFL; Spanish Clb; Speech Tm; Band; Drm Mjr(t); Jazz Band; Mrchg Band; Variety Show; OK ST Univ; Elem Ed/Tch.

ECKMANN, AMBER N; Newcastle HS; Newcastle, OK; (3); 1/92; FHA; Science Clb; Spanish Clb; High Hon Roll; Hon Roll; Jr NHS; NHS; Stdnt Mnth Awd; OU; Doctor.

ECKROAT, RYAN J; Bishop Mcguinness HS; Jones, OK; (3); 70/157; Am Leg Boys St; FCA; JCL; Latin Clb; Library Aide; Nwsp; Ftbl; Var Golf; Jr NHS; KAIROS Pgm; Yager Yth Ldrshp Cncl; U Of AZ; Intnl Bus & Fin.

EDDINGS, GREG; Hulbert Jr Sr HS; Hulbert, OK; (4); 1/99; Am Leg Boys St; Chess Clb; Church Yth Grp; Teachers Aide; Nwsp; Hon Roll; NHS; Val; Northwestern ST U.

EDDINGS, MARY E; Stilwell HS; Stilwell, OK; (1); Drama Clb; French Clb; FHA; Natl Beta Clb; Stage Crew; French Hon Soc; Hon Roll; Northeastern ST Univ.

EDDS, JOSHUA J; Choctaw HS; Choctaw, OK; (3); Am Leg Boys St; Church Yth Grp; Chorus; Church Choir; School Musical; Variety Show; Rep Frsh Cls; Pres Jr Cls; Pres Jr NHS; Choral Cncl Rep; Yth Ldrshp Exchng Cls I OK.

EDDY, KAREN E; Bishop Kelley HS; Tulsa, OK; (2); Church Yth Grp; Drama Clb; NFL; Speech Tm; Chorus; School Play; Stage Crew; Hon Roll; Boy Scts; Cmnty Wkr; Camp Fire Horizon; Lmp Lghtrs; SAIL; Spch, Drama Ltrs.

EDELMAN, BRYAN C; Nathan Hale HS; Tulsa, OK; (3); Cmnty Wkr; FCA; Key Clb; Ofcr Sr Cls; Ftbl; Var Swmmng; Var Trk; Var Wrstlng; High Hon Roll; Hon Roll; OK Chrstn Univ; Yth Pstr.

EDENS, JASON; Duncan HS; Duncan, OK; (3); 1/250; Church Yth Grp; Letterman Clb; Spanish Clb; VP Stu Cncl; Var L Ftbl; Hon Roll; NHS; Peer Pal Pgm; Duncan Ldrshp Pgm; Attnd OASC Basic Ldrshp Wkshp & Advanced Basic; Medicine.

EDGAR, ERIC M; B T Washington HS; Tulsa, OK; (4); 1/264; Church Yth Grp; Cmnty Wkr; French Clb; Var L Bsbl; High Hon Roll; NHS; Val; Acad Bowl Capt; Sci Bowl; Natl Merit Fnlst; U Of OK; Bio.

EDGAR, JASON; Perry Sr HS; Perry, OK; (3); FCA; German Clb; JV Bsktbl; Hon Roll; Jr NHS; NHS; U Of OK.

EDGE, HOPE; Hobart HS; Hobart, OK; (1); 6/85; Church Yth Grp; Rep Stu Cncl; Var Bsktbl; Var Golf; Var Sftbl; Var Trk; Hon Roll; NHS; OK ST U.

EDGE, JUSTIN; Hugo HS; Hugo, OK; (3); Church Yth Grp; Spanish Clb; Chorus; Church Choir; Mrchg Band; Ftbl; Wt Lftg; Hon Roll; NHS; Engrng.

EDGEMAN, NELSON S; Durant HS; Durant, OK; (2); 21/200; Church Yth Grp; Ofcr Stu Cncl; Var L Socr; Var L Tennis; High Hon Roll; Hon Roll; Noble All-Trnmt Soccer Awd; OK ST Univ.

EDGEMON, RACHEL; Little Axe Sr HS; Norman, OK; (3); Church Yth Grp; GAA; Ofcr Jr Cls; Chrldng; Trk; High Hon Roll; Hon Roll; Prfct Atten Awd; UCO; Psycht.

EDGEWORTH, APRIL M; Walters HS; Walters, OK; (1); 1/60; Art Clb; Church Yth Grp; FCA; Bsktbl; Trk; High Hon Roll; Hon Roll.

EDGEWORTH, CHAD A; Walters HS; Walters, OK; (4); 3/34; VP Art Clb; Church Yth Grp; FCA; Office Aide; Scholastic Bowl; Yrbk; Var Capt Bsbl; Var Capt Bsktbl; Var Ftbl; Trk; Acad Tm; Southwestern OK ST U; Med.

EDGMAN, BRANDON W; Bethany HS; Oklahoma City, OK; (3); Art Clb; Church Yth Grp; Key Clb; Spanish Clb; Chorus; Church Choir; Hon Roll; Jr NHS; NHS; Prfct Atten Awd; Band; Mission Trips; OBU; Sci; Bus Law; Vet.

EDGMON, LACEY; Chickasha Jr HS; Chickasha, OK; (1); VP FHA; Hon Roll; Jr NHS.

EDISON, JONATHAN M; Mt St Marys HS; Oklahoma City, OK; (3); 30/64; Church Yth Grp; FCA; JA; Key Clb; Var L Bsktbl; Hon Roll; Jr Knights Of Peter Claver Pres; U Of OK; Pre-Med; DC; MD.

EDMINSTER, MELANEY K; Hollis Jr Sr HS; Hollis, OK; (2); FHA; Pep Clb; Band; Bsktbl; Merit Awd; FHA Greenhnd Awd; Bnd Carnvl; Multi Yr Listee; Cameron Univ; Phys Thpy.

EDMONDSON, AMANDA; Pauls Valley HS; Pauls Valley, OK; (2); Church Yth Grp; Spanish Clb; Tennis; Trk; Cit Awd; High Hon Roll; Hon Roll; NHS; Prfct Atten Awd; Bsktbl.

EDMONDSON, AUTUMN B; Stillwater Sr HS; Stillwater, OK; (2); Church Yth Grp; FHA; Hosp Aide; Teachers Aide; Temple Yth Grp; Rptr Nwsp; Ed Yrbk; Dental Hygn.

EDMONDSON, LACY; Haworth Jr HS; Idabel, OK; (1); Art Clb; Dance Clb; 4-H; Natl FFA Org; Sec Frsh Cls; Bsktbl; Jr NHS; Stu Cncl Rprtr.

EDMONSON, ERIN R; Oologah HS; Oologah, OK; (2); Church Yth Grp; Drama Clb; NFL; Speech Tm; School Play; High Hon Roll; NHS; St Schlr; Sign Lang; Oologah Chrstn Flwshp Ofcr; Cntrl Bible Coll; Deaf Ministry.

EDNEY, ALECIA N; Claremore Sr HS; Claremore, OK; (3); Church Yth Grp; FHA; GAA; Bsktbl; Gym; Awd Of Hnr Alg; Athltc Excllnc Bsktbl; Rogers ST.

EDWARDS, ANDREA; Fairview HS; Fairview, OK; (3); 1/65; Church Yth Grp; FCA; Natl FFA Org; Quiz Bowl; Scholastic Bowl; School Musical; Variety Show; VP Soph Cls; Rep Jr Cls; Rep Stu Cncl; OK ST U.

EDWARDS, ANNA R; Owasso Sr HS; Owasso, OK; (3); 1/370; Church Yth Grp; Drama Clb; French Clb; NFL; Capt Quiz Bowl; Spanish Clb; Teachers Aide; Mgr Stage Crew; Hon Roll; NHS; Tulsa Fencing Clb; Chem Clb; Vanderbilt Univ.

EDWARDS, ANTHONY L; Cheyenne HS; Cheyenne, OK; (3); 20/24; Treas FBLA; Natl FFA Org; Prfct Atten Awd.

EDWARDS, AUTRY J; Calumet Schl; Calumet, OK; (2); 2/30; Church Yth Grp; VP Frsh Cls; VP Soph Cls; Bsktbl; High Hon Roll; OK Hnr Soc; OK ST U.

EDWARDS, BONNIE E; Sapulpa Sr HS; Sapulpa, OK; (3); Church Yth Grp; School Play; Nwsp; Golf; Wt Lftg; Hon Roll; U Of MI; Med.

EDWARDS, BRYANT; New Lima Jr Sr HS; Seminole, OK; (3); 4-H; Quiz Bowl; Pres Soph Cls; Rep Stu Cncl; Var Bsbl; Capt Bsktbl; Var Trk; Cit Awd; 4-H Awd; High Hon Roll; All-Conf Bsbl 2 Yrs; All-Conf Bsktbl 1 Yr; Bus Admin; Mgmt.

EDWARDS, CARLOUS D; Okmulgee HS; Okmulgee, OK; (3); Church Yth Grp; FCA; Library Aide; Office Aide; Science Clb; Spanish Clb; Var Bsktbl; Var Ftbl; Var Wt Lftg; High Hon Roll; AZ Univ; Acctg/Bus Mgmnt.

EDWARDS, CHAD E; Muldrow HS; Muldrow, OK; (1); Church Yth Grp; Natl FFA Org; Bsktbl; Ftbl; Hon Roll; Forest Mgmt Ag Profcncy Awd 96; Equine Sci Achvmnt Awd; Fish/Wldlfe Mgmt Awd; FFA Treas 96-; Welder.

EDWARDS, COLBY; Eufaula Sr HS; Eufaula, OK; (4); 3/73; Quiz Bowl; Teachers Aide; Band; Jazz Band; Mrchg Band; Rep Stu Cncl; Hon Roll; Kiwanis Awd; NHS; Pres Acad Fit Awd; All Dist Band; Alt All St Band 95; OBA Mrchng Band Chmpnshp Outstndng Trumpet Soloist; Wm Jewell Coll; Phys Thrpy.

EDWARDS, CORY L; Tahlequah Sr HS; Tahlequah, OK; (3); Church Yth Grp; Acpl Chr; Chorus; School Play; Ofcr Stu Cncl; High Hon Roll; Jr NHS; NHS; Ntl Merit Ltr; Pres Acad Fit Awd.

EDWARDS, DANIEL K; Duncan HS; Duncan, OK; (3); Boy Scts; Church Yth Grp; French Clb; Red Cross Aide; Band; Mrchg Band; Red Crss WSI & Lifeguard Instr Cert; Optometrist.

EDWARDS, EMILY D; Wagoner Sr HS; Wagoner, OK; (3); Church Yth Grp; 4-H; FBLA; FHA; Socr; Hon Roll; Fr Speaking Cmptn Awd; FFA; Prom Comm; OSU; Horse Trainer; Vet.

EDWARDS, JASON A; Duncan HS; Duncan, OK; (3); Am Leg Boys St; Boy Scts; Church Yth Grp; French Clb; Letterman Clb; Band; Mrchg Band; Pep Band; Crs Cntry; Hon Roll; OK St Univ Acad Awd; OK Univ Acad Awd; Eagle Sct Vigil Hnr Sct; OK ST Univ.

EDWARDS, JEREMIAH A; Nathan Hale HS; Tulsa, OK; (3); Science Clb; VICA; Hon Roll; OSU; Cmptr Prgrmr.

EDWARDS, JEREMIAH S; Dickson HS; Ardmore, OK; (1); Boy Scts; FCA; FHA; Band; Mrchg Band; Var Ftbl; Wt Lftg; ECU.

EDWARDS, KASSI JOE; Miami Sr HS; Miami, OK; (4); 8/132; Church Yth Grp; Yrbk; Rep Stu Cncl; Bsktbl; Chrldng; Trk; High Hon Roll; NHS; Ntl Merit SF; Pres Acad Fit Awd; Rodeo; BPW Hi-Noon Fml Of Mnth 96; All-Amer Schlr; NE OK A&M; Phy Ther.

EDWARDS, KHEVA; Clinton HS; Clinton, OK; (3); FCA; FHA; Spanish Clb; Bsktbl; Socr; Hon Roll.

EDWARDS, MELISSA G; B T Washington HS; Mannford, OK; (4); 110/264; Spanish Clb; Teachers Aide; Mrchg Band; OK ST Univ; Phys/Chem Tchr.

EDWARDS, MISTY; Mustang HS; Yukon, OK; (3); 44/397; Cmnty Wkr; Cit Awd; Hon Roll; NHS; Ntl Merit Ltr; Natl Hstry/Gobt Awd; Geomtry Acad Awd; Frnch Acad Awd; INFO Sys Mgr.

EDWARDS, SAMANTHA L; Muldrow HS; Muldrow, OK; (1); Computer Clb; FHA; Color Guard; Stat Bsktbl; Hon Roll; U Of AR; Cmptrs/Acctng.

EDWARDS, STEPHANIE A; Edmond Memorial HS; Oklahoma City, OK; (3); 231/371; Church Yth Grp; Key Clb; Library Aide; Spanish Clb; Stage Crew; Cit Awd; OU; Meterology.

EDWARDS, TAMRA D; Catoosa HS; Catoosa, OK; (4); Church Yth Grp; FHA; Teachers Aide; High Hon Roll; Hon Roll; NHS.

EDWARDS, TONY; Cheyenne HS; Cheyenne, OK; (3); Treas FBLA; Natl FFA Org; Devry Tech Schl; Comp Elec Rpr.

EDWARDS, WAYNE; Chelsea HS; Chelsea, OK; (3); 1/70; French Clb; Red Cross Aide; Spanish Clb; Band; Jazz Band; Mrchg Band; Hon Roll.

EFFENBECK, DANI; Kiowa Jr-Sr HS; Kiowa, OK; (3); Cmnty Wkr; 4-H; JA; Quiz Bowl; Yrbk; JV Bsktbl; Intrml Ftbl; Var Sftbl; Hon Roll; NHS; Nuclear Phys/Engrg.

EFURD, JARED; Eufaula Sr HS; Eufaula, OK; (2); Natl FFA Org; Rep Stu Cncl; Bsktbl; Hon Roll; NHS.

EGAN, KATHLEEN M; Bishop Kelley HS; Tulsa, OK; (2); Church Yth Grp; Latin Clb; Pep Clb; High Hon Roll; Hon Roll; 3 Yr Olds Rel Ed/Vac Bible Schl Kndgtn Tchr; Vol Day Care Ctr Hmels Chldrn; OK Univ; Med.

EGGELING, VALERIE; John Marshall HS; Oklahoma City, OK; (4); Am Leg Aux Girls St; Art Clb; Cmnty Wkr; Letterman Clb; Library Aide; Office Aide; Pep Clb; Science Clb; SADD; Teachers Aide; Camp Fire Boys & Girls Natl Yth Brd; 1st Pl St Level St Sci Fair; HIV/AIDS Peer Edctr; St Gregorys Coll; Nrs.

EGLESTON, JENNIFER; Kingfisher HS; Kingfisher, OK; (1); Church Yth Grp; Debate Tm; NFL; Speech Tm; Band; Drm Mjr(t); Jazz Band; Mrchg Band; Pep Band; Hon Roll; Southwestern OK ST; Music Ed.

EHLO, WHITNEY; Madill HS; Madill, OK; (1); FCA; FHA; SADD; Chorus; School Musical; Ofcr Stu Cncl; Sftbl; Hon Roll; TX Tech U; Physcns Asst.

EHRHART, JOHN; Dale Sr HS; Mc Loud, OK; (2); 1/55; Church Yth Grp; JA; Co-Capt Scholastic Bowl; Band; Mrchg Band; Pep Band; Var Bsbl; High Hon Roll; NHS; Pres Acad Fit Awd; Harvard; Astrnmy.

EICHINGER, BRIAN; Tomlinson Jr HS; Lawton, OK; (1); Boy Scts; Cmnty Wkr; Rep Stu Cncl; JV Socr; High Hon Roll; Jr NHS; TSA VP; Stu Of Mnth; U Of OK; Med.

EICHOR, CAREN V; B T Washington HS; Tulsa, OK; (3); Church Yth Grp; Cmnty Wkr; JA; Red Cross Aide; Spanish Clb; Varsity Clb; Yrbk; Var L Socr; NHS; Club Sccr Black Watch 79; OK ST Sccr Team; OK ST U; Vet.

EIDSON, KATIE; Sulphur HS; Sulphur, OK; (2); 1/110; HOBY; Key Clb; Chorus; School Musical; Rep Frsh Cls; Rep Soph Cls; Var Diving; Bsktbl; Chrldng; Kiwanis Awd; U Of OK; Bus.

EILERS, JUSTIN; Mooreland Jr Sr HS; Mooreland, OK; (4); 2/28; Am Leg Boys St; Church Yth Grp; Cmnty Wkr; FCA; Pres Math Clb; Natl FFA Org; Scholastic Bowl; Spanish Clb; Pres Frsh Cls; Pres Soph Cls; Naval Acad & West Point; Lt Gov Boys St; Deliver Meals Shut-Ins Bapt Church; OK ST U; Pre-Law.

EIMEN, REBECCA L; Mannford HS; Mannford, OK; (2); 1/125; Church Yth Grp; Cmnty Wkr; FCA; GAA; Spanish Clb; SADD; Rep Stu Cncl; Var Bsktbl; Var Chrldng; Var Sftbl; Summer League Sftbl ASA; MVP Sftbl Tournmnt; ST Qualifier Track; TX A&M.

EINHORN, SARA J; Newcastle HS; Newcastle, OK; (3); 33/86; Natl FFA Org; Pep Clb; Spanish Clb; VP Frsh Cls; VP Soph Cls; Pres Jr Cls; Hist Stu Cncl; Voted Cls Favorite Frosh, Soph & Jr Yr; Quantitative Analysis Summer Acad UCO; OK Univ; Pre-Law.

EISCHEN, KARA D; Okarche Jr Sr HS; Okarche, OK; (3); Am Leg Aux Girls St; Church Yth Grp; Pres FHA; Sec Treas Letterman Clb; Natl Beta Clb; Chorus; Ofcr Stu Cncl; Var Bsktbl; Sftbl; Hon Roll; Yth Adv Brd; Jr Lioness Awd; OK State Univ.

EISENHOUR, SONYA; El Reno Sr HS; El Reno, OK; (3); 1/200; Church Yth Grp; Cmnty Wkr; Rep French Clb; HOBY; Key Clb; Rep Stu Cncl; JV Var Bsktbl; Var Golf; Cit Awd; All Amer Schlr; Rnessnc; OK Hnr Soc; Med.

EISLER, CHRIS D; Newcastle HS; Newcastle, OK; (3); FBLA; Science Clb; JV Bsbl; JV Bsktbl.

ELAM, BRANNDI L; Lindsay HS; Lindsay, OK; (1); FHA; Spanish Clb; JV Bsktbl; U Of OK.

ELAM, CALLECIA D; Northeast HS; Oklahoma City, OK; (2); Latin Clb; Chorus; Church Choir; Orch; Sftbl; Hon Roll; Campus Life; Chrch Sec; Biomedical Pgm; OBU; Psych.

ELAM, MICHELE L; Oilton HS; Yale, OK; (2); Art Clb; FHA; Pep Clb; Sec Frsh Cls; Var Bsktbl; Var Chrldng; Var Sftbl; Cit Awd; Sal; Psych.

ELAND, RENEE; Jenks HS; Tulsa, OK; (4); 24/472; Art Clb; Church Yth Grp; FCA; Mu Alpha Theta; Spanish Clb; Teachers Aide; Hon Roll; NHS; Spanish NHS; Oral Roberts U; Span Ed.

ELBON, ANNE M; Wagoner Sr HS; Wagoner, OK; (3); 4-H; French Clb; Intnl Clb; Teachers Aide; Hon Roll; Eng Lit/Hum.

ELCYZYN, TIMOTHY E; Grove HS; Grove, OK; (3); 1/104; Boy Scts; FBLA; Yrbk; High Hon Roll; Hon Roll; NHS; Pres Acad Fit Awd; Gftd & Tlntd Prgm; Acad Ltr; Mck Trl.

ELDER, ANDREA; Ft Gibson HS; Fort Gibson, OK; (1); Church Yth Grp; FCA; FHA; Spanish Clb; SADD; Ofcr Frsh Cls; Ofcr Stu Cncl; Chrldng; Pom Pon; High Hon Roll; Hnrs Eng, Alg II; Tns Christ; TAGS; FHA Prlmntrn; Duke U; Orthdntcs.

ELDER, JUSTIN; Amber Pocasset Jr Sr HS; Amber, OK; (1); 1/47; Church Yth Grp; FCA; Natl FFA Org; Quiz Bowl; Scholastic Bowl; Pres Frsh Cls; Ofcr Bsbl; Bsktbl; Jr NHS; Prfct Atten Awd; Engrng.

ELDER, MIKE L; West Middle HS; Norman, OK; (2); Boy Scts; FCA; Spanish Clb; JV Socr; NHS; Pres Acad Fit Awd; Spanish NHS; Boy Sct Of Amer-Eagle Sct; Ordr Of Arrw-Vgl Hon; Memorial Presby Chrch.

ELDER, NICOLE D; Yukon Middle HS; Yukon, OK; (2); GAA; SADD; Var Bsktbl; Meteor.

ELDRIDGE, JANA L; Stilwell HS; Stilwell, OK; (2); Church Yth Grp; FHA; Office Aide; Spanish Clb; JV Powder Puff Ftbl; Hon Roll; NHS; Pres Acad Fit Awd; NSU.

ELERICK, JOE K; Harrah HS; Harrah, OK; (3); Church Yth Grp; Drama Clb; FCA; Speech Tm; Intrml Bsbl; JV Bsktbl; Var Ftbl; Var Socr; Var Tennis; Intrml Wrstlng; Gatorade NFL Punt Pass & Kick; Dallas Cowboy Champ; Player Of Wk & Mst Touchdown Passes EOC; FL ST; Commncts; Broadcasting.

ELIOT, ABBY; Union Sr HS; Tulsa, OK; (2); Church Yth Grp; Cmnty Wkr; FCA; Intnl Clb; Math Clb; Office Aide; Spanish Clb; Varsity Clb; VP Stu Cncl; JV Var Chrldng; FL ST Univ; Sports Thrpst.

ELKINS, DUSTIE R; Hobart HS; Hobart, OK; (2); Church Yth Grp; FCA; FHA; GAA; Ofcr Stu Cncl; Var Bsktbl; Var Chrldng; Var Sftbl; Hon Roll; NHS; Bus/Acctg.

ELLEDGE, BRANDI D; Westmoore HS; Oklahoma City, OK; (4); 213/610; Church Yth Grp; Cmnty Wkr; Dance Clb; FHA; Office Aide; Trk; Hon Roll; Jr NHS; Sr Cncl; Sr Trip Coordntr; Univ Of OK Academic Achvmnt Awd; OK ST Univ; Psych.

ELLEDGE, MARCUS T; West Jr HS; Oklahoma City, OK; (1); Church Yth Grp; Drama Clb; Band; Ftbl; Socr; Music.

ELLENBURG, BRANDY R; Heavener HS; Wister, OK; (1); 27/130; Church Yth Grp; GAA; Bsktbl; Sftbl; Wt Lftg; Hon Roll; TSA Mem & Pres 2 Yrs.

ELLING, JENNIFER R; Cashion HS; Cashion, OK; (2); Church Yth Grp; 4-H; FBLA; Office Aide; Pep Clb; Chorus; Yrbk; Hon Roll; U Of Cntrl OK; Motvnl Spkng.

ELLINGTON, MELISSA; Ripley HS; Stillwater, OK; (1); 1/50; Church Yth Grp; FCA; GAA; Math Clb; Science Clb; Var Bsktbl; Var Chrldng; Sftbl; High Hon Roll; FFA.

ELLINGTON, SEAN M; Putnam City HS; Oklahoma City, OK; (1); JV Ftbl; Var Wrstlng; Hon Roll.

ELLIOTT, AMANDA LEA; Antlers Sr HS; Antlers, OK; (4); 7/66; Am Leg Aux Girls St; Church Yth Grp; FBLA; SADD; Yrbk; Treas Jr Cls; Bsktbl; Chrldng; Gym; Hon Roll; S E OK St U.

ELLIOTT, ANDY PAT; Texhoma HS; Texhoma, OK; (4); 14/23; 4-H; Natl FFA Org; Teachers Aide; Phtg Yrbk; Pres Sr Cls; Var L Bsktbl; Var L Ftbl; Panhandle ST U; Ag Ed.

ELLIOTT, ANGELA D; Mc Lain Career Acad; Tulsa, OK; (2); Church Yth Grp; Computer Clb; Office Aide; ROTC; Church Choir; Hon Roll; Jr NHS; NHS; Prfct Atten Awd; Tulsa Univ; Phy Thrpst.

ELLIOTT, CASEY M; Hammon Schl; Hammon, OK; (2); 4-H; Natl FFA Org; Quiz Bowl; Hon Roll; Cls B ST Acad Bwl Chmpns 95-; OSU; Dairy Sci.

ELLIOTT, CHARLEY C; Union Intermediate HS; Broken Arrow, OK; (1); Church Yth Grp; Spanish Clb; Nwsp; Yrbk; Intrml Bsbl; JV Bsktbl; Intrml Golf; Hon Roll; Teen Mania Ministries Trip 96; U Of TX.

ELLIOTT, CODY; Hammon Schl; Hammon, OK; (3); 4-H; Pres Natl FFA Org; Quiz Bowl; Speech Tm; Hon Roll; Cls B St Acad Bowl Champs; OK ST Univ; Dairy Dutrition.

ELLIOTT, ELIZABETH A; Mustang HS; Yukon, OK; (4); 1/375; Debate Tm; FCA; VP French Clb; VP FBLA; JA; NFL; Rep Stu Cncl; VP NHS; Pres Schlr; Val; George Washington U; Intl Affrs.

ELLIOTT, JAMIE L; Yukon Middle HS; Yukon, OK; (1); Church Yth Grp; FCA; Spanish Clb; High Hon Roll; Hon Roll; Ath Trainer Sports Med Pgm; U Of AZ; Sports Medicine.

ELLIOTT, JASON; Yale Jr Sr HS; Yale, OK; (2); Natl Beta Clb; Natl FFA Org; Quiz Bowl; VP Band; Mrchg Band; Pep Band; High Hon Roll; NHS; Prfct Atten Awd; Stu/Mnth; Pblshd Anthlgy Stu Wrtng; OK ST U; Engrng.

ELLIOTT, JENNIE; Ripley HS; Ripley, OK; (4); 2/33; Church Yth Grp; FBLA; FHA; Model UN; Treas Band; NHS; Sal; Natl Voc Hnr Soc; HOSA Treas; Exec Cncl Treas; Med Lab Tech.

ELLIOTT, KRISTINA L; Sharon Mutual Jr Sr HS; Mutual, OK; (2); 10/32; Church Yth Grp; FCA; FHA; GAA; Natl FFA Org; Treas Frsh Cls; Sec Soph Cls; Var Bsktbl; Var Sftbl; Var Wt Lftg; Vet.

ELLIOTT, NANCY; Altus Sr HS; Altus, OK; (4); 47/236; Church Yth Grp; Spanish Clb; Teachers Aide; Ed Nwsp; Ofcr Stu Cncl; Swmmng; Hon Roll; Cmnty Wkr; Drama Clb; FTA; Tchr Cadet; ACTV Stff; Video Yrbk Edtr In Chf; U Of Sci & Arts Of OK; Elem Ed.

ELLIOTT, ROBYN; Ada HS; Ada, OK; (3); Church Yth Grp; FCA; French Clb; Girl Scts; Band; Church Choir; Mrchg Band; Stage Crew; High Hon Roll; NHS; FCA Huddle Ldr; Church Yth Cncl, Drama; OK Baptist U; Med.

ELLIOTT, SARAH; Glencoe Public Schl; Glencoe, OK; (2); #2 in class; French Clb; Natl FFA Org; Treas Frsh Cls; Treas Soph Cls; Var Chrldng; Var Sftbl; French Hon Soc; High Hon Roll; Hon Roll; FFA Treas.

ELLIOTT, SARAH J; Metro Christian Acad; Tulsa, OK; (2); Drama Clb; Pep Clb; Spanish Clb; Var Sftbl; OK ST Univ; Cosmetology.

ELLIOTT, SHAWN; Graham Pub Schls; Henryetta, OK; (2); 4-H; FHA; Treas Frsh Cls; VP Jr Cls; Ofcr Bsbl; Stat Bsktbl; Mgr(s); Cit Awd; 4-H Awd; Hon Roll; Life Leaders-Peer Cnslng Group.

ELLIOTT, STACI M; Charles Page HS; Sand Springs, OK; (1); Debate Tm; Hon Roll; OK ST U; Pol Sci.

ELLIOTT, TANYA; Cement Jr Sr HS; Rush Springs, OK; (3); 4-H; FHA; Natl FFA Org; Quiz Bowl; Scholastic Bowl; Teachers Aide; School Play; 4-H Awd; Hon Roll; Barrel Racer-Playdays; USAD; Vet; Dental Tech.

ELLIOTT, THOMAS S; Heavener HS; Poteau, OK; (1); Church Yth Grp; 4-H; Natl FFA Org; FFA Awd; OK ST U; Agriculture.

ELLIOTT, TIFFANY G; Mustang HS; Mustang, OK; (2); GAA; SADD; Nwsp; Var Bsktbl; Var Socr; High Hon Roll; NHS; FCA; Rnsnc; Med.

ELLIOTT, TRACY A; Edmond Memorial HS; Edmond, OK; (2); 61/408; Dance Clb; Spanish Clb; Gov Hon Prg Awd; Hon Roll; Jr NHS; NHS; Pres Acad Fit Awd; Dance Tchr Asst; Tae Kwon Do.

ELLIS, ANDREA L; Del City HS; Del City, OK; (2); Spanish Clb; Rptr Yrbk; Bsktbl; Sftbl; Hon Roll; U Of NM; Pedtrc Med.

ELLIS, HEATHER R; Sapulpa Sr HS; Sapulpa, OK; (3); 6/290; Church Yth Grp; Debate Tm; NFL; Speech Tm; Band; Jazz Band; Mrchg Band; Crs Cntry; Socr; Hon Roll; All Reg Bnd 3 Yrs; Natl Outsdng Yng German Schlr; Univ Tulsa Hnr Bnd; Music.

ELLIS, JENNIFER L; Catoosa HS; Tulsa, OK; (4); 36/136; Church Yth Grp; Sec FCA; FBLA; FHA; VP Intnl Clb; Office Aide; Pep Clb; Spanish Clb; VICA; Sec Frsh Cls; Outstdng Vo-Tech Stu, Sec; St Hnr Soc; Rogers ST Coll; Elem Ed.

ELLIS, JENNY R; Putnam City North HS; Oklahoma City, OK; (1); Church Yth Grp; Dance Clb; FCA; SADD; Stage Crew; Var Trk; 3-D Clb Don'T Do Drugs; OSCAR Mltcltrl Clb; Med.

ELLIS, JERRY; Leflore Sr HS; Wister, OK; (4); #2 in class; Church Yth Grp; Quiz Bowl; Varsity Clb; Church Choir; Co-Ed Nwsp; Rep Stu Cncl; Ofcr Bsbl; High Hon Roll; NHS; Sal; Carl Alber ST Coll.

ELLIS, JOHNATHON; Miami Sr HS; Miami, OK; (3); Am Leg Boys St; Letterman Clb; Varsity Clb; School Play; Ofcr Stu Cncl; Ftbl; Socr; Trk; Wt Lftg; High Hon Roll; Sci Tchr; Coach.

ELLIS, KIMBERLY; Hilldale HS; Muskogee, OK; (2); 5/107; Church Yth Grp; JV Sftbl; Gov Hon Prg Awd; High Hon Roll; Hon Roll.

ELLIS, KIRBY S; Strother Jr Sr HS; Seminole, OK; (4); 9/27; Church Yth Grp; 4-H; FHA; Quiz Bowl; Scholastic Bowl; Var Chrldng; Var Capt Bsktbl; Hon Roll; NHS; Prfct Atten Awd; US Army Reserve Natl Schlr Ath Awd; Seminole ST Coll.

ELLIS, KRISTI N; Ninnekah HS; Chickasha, OK; (2); Model UN; Natl FFA Org; Quiz Bowl; Spanish Clb; Treas Frsh Cls; Var Sftbl; Hon Roll; Natl FFA Legion Of Mrt Awd; OSU.

ELLIS, LAUREN E; Duncan HS; Duncan, OK; (2); Church Yth Grp; FCA; Key Clb; Letterman Clb; Rep Frsh Cls; Sec Soph Cls; Var Bsktbl; High Hon Roll; Hon Roll; AAU ST Champions Bsktbl; Natl AAU Bsktbl Trnmt.

ELLIS, SCOTT; Seminole Jr Sr HS; Seminole, OK; (1); Church Yth Grp; French Clb; Band; Mrchg Band; Tennis; High Hon Roll; Phys Thrpy.

ELLIS, TIFFANY M; Sallisaw HS; Sallisaw, OK; (2); Church Yth Grp; FHA; Spanish Clb; Band; Chorus; Church Choir; Color Guard; Flag Corp; Jazz Band; Mrchg Band; Art; NSU; Arch.

ELLIS, VALERIE J; Tecumseh HS; Tecumseh, OK; (4); FHA; NHS; U Of OK.

ELLISON, SHAMEQUA D; John Marshall HS; Oklahoma City, OK; (2); Bus Profs of Am; FHA; ROTC; Teachers Aide; High Hon Roll; Hon Roll; Lwyr; Phlsphr.

ELLSWORTH, ELIZABETH A; Cushing HS; Cushing, OK; (2); Church Yth Grp; Cmnty Wkr; Dance Clb; English Clb; FCA; GAA; Math Clb; Science Clb; Spanish Clb; Ed Yrbk.

ELMENHORST, HEIDI D; El Reno Sr HS; El Reno, OK; (3); FTA; JA; Math Clb; Science Clb; Ofcr Stu Cncl; Bsktbl; Chrldng; Cit Awd; Hon Roll; Nalt Ldrsp Awd; OK ST Univ; Elem Ed.

ELMENHORST, MANDI M; Chisholm Sr HS; Enid, OK; (2); Church Yth Grp; Spanish Clb; Band; Color Guard; Jazz Band; Mrchg Band; Pep Band; Prfct Atten Awd; Band Qn Frosh, Soph; Stu Of Month Frosh & Soph; OSU; Phy Thrpst; TV Rptr.

ELMER, JOSH; Fairland Jr Sr HS; Fairland, OK; (1); Church Yth Grp; JV Ftbl; JV Trk; High Hon Roll; NHS; Jr FFA Pres; Notre Dame.

ELMORE, ARMANDO; Hollis Jr Sr HS; Hollis, OK; (4); FBLA; Band; Jazz Band; Mrchg Band; Pep Band; Hon Roll; All Rgn, Short Grass, All Sr Hnr Bands; Western OK ST Coll; Elem Tchr.

ELMORE, CRYSTAL G; Yukon Middle HS; Yukon, OK; (1); FHA; Speech Tm; Var Socr; Hon Roll; FHA Phtgrphr; OK ST Univ; Psych.

ELMORE, TRISHA M; East Central HS; Tulsa, OK; (3); Key Clb; Science Clb; Spanish Clb; Chorus; Hon Roll; Acctng.

ELMORE, VANESSA; Seiling Schl; Seiling, OK; (2); 4/43; FCA; FBLA; FHA; Letterman Clb; Bsktbl; Trk; Wt Lftg; High Hon Roll.

ELROD, AMANDA J; Whitesboro Schl; Muse, OK; (4); 1/32; Natl FFA Org; Yrbk; Treas Soph Cls; Treas Jr Cls; Pres Sr Cls; Score Keeper; High Hon Roll; Val; Church Yth Grp; School Play; Ladn Judging, FFA Sec, VP, Sweetheart; Estrn OK ST Coll; Acctng.

ELROD, CHRISTOPHER L; Duncan HS; Marlow, OK; (2); Var Ftbl; NHS.

ELROD, JEANIE; Choctaw HS; Choctaw, OK; (4); Church Yth Grp; FCA; Key Clb; Spanish Clb; SADD; Tennis; NHS; Prfct Atten Awd; UCO; Nursng.

ELROD, JOE A; Duncan HS; Marlow, OK; (3); 47/250; FBLA; Letterman Clb; Spanish Clb; L Ftbl; Hon Roll; NHS.

ELROD, KELEE; Deer Creek HS; Guthrie, OK; (3); 34/98; Art Clb; FBLA; Teachers Aide; Hon Roll; Competitive Roller Skating; UCO; Photo.

ELWOOD, SHAWN; U S Grant HS; Oklahoma City, OK; (4); #14 in class; Am Leg Boys St; Boy Scts; Church Yth Grp; Drama Clb; FCA; Pep Clb; Service Clb; Orch; School Musical; School Play; Eagle Scout; Ordr Of Arrw; U Of OK; Arch Engrng.

EMEL, ADRIENNE N; Putnam City HS; Oklahoma City, OK; (1); Cmnty Wkr; Debate Tm; French Clb; Hosp Aide; Band; Mrchg Band; Pep Band; High Hon Roll; Hon Roll; Mock Trial Tm; Band Outstdng Frosh; Tech Ed/Hnrs Bio Outstdng Stdnt Of Yr.

EMERSON, BLAKE M; Grace Chrn Acad; Oklahoma City, OK; (3); Church Yth Grp; Hosp Aide; Rptr Nwsp; Phtg Yrbk; Var Bsbl; JV Bsktbl; Var Crs Cntry; Var Ftbl; Var Golf; Trk; Track Prep Awd; Bsebll Intnsty Awd.

EMERSON, BRANDON; Grace Chrn Acad; Oklahoma City, OK; (2); Church Yth Grp; English Clb; FHA; Letterman Clb; Scholastic Bowl; Varsity Clb; Sec Frsh Cls; VP Soph Cls; Ofcr Bsbl; Bsktbl.

EMERSON, KIMBERLY; Bartlesville Sr HS; Ochelata, OK; (3); Cmnty Wkr; FBLA; Ski Clb; Rptr Nwsp; Rep Stu Cncl; Gym; JV Tennis; French Hon Soc; Pre-Law.

EMERY, ROBYN J; South Intermediate HS; Broken Arrow, OK; (1); French Clb; Hon Roll; Prin Hnr Roll; OK Hnr Soc; Intnl Correspndance Clb; OK ST Univ; Pediatric Nrs.

EMERY, STACY D; Westmoore HS; Oklahoma City, OK; (3); French Clb; Var L Swmmng; NHS.

EMHOLTZ, RICHARD D; Bridge Creek HS; Blanchard, OK; (2); Drama Clb; Spanish Clb; Tae Kwon Do-Prpl Blt; Cmptr Prgrmr.

EMINGER, CARRIE; Cashion HS; Cashion, OK; (3); 2/27; Am Leg Aux Girls St; FCA; FBLA; Natl FFA Org; Band; Sec Frsh Cls; Var Chrldng; Var Tennis; Hon Roll; NHS; 95 Ftbl Homcmng Qn; U Of OK; Med.

EMPERT, SARA B; Brink Jr HS; Moore, OK; (1); Church Yth Grp; Debate Tm; Pep Clb; Speech Tm; Teachers Aide; Church Choir; Rptr Mgr Nwsp; Pom Pon; Jr NHS; Poetry Pub; Ed Choice Awd.

ENABNIT, LAURIE J; Bartlesville Sr HS; Ardmore, OK; (4); Church Yth Grp; FCA; Office Aide; Spanish Clb; Church Choir; JV Vllybl; High Hon Roll; Early Ed.

ENDICOTT, LAURA B; Duncan HS; Duncan, OK; (2); FBLA; Hosp Aide; Key Clb; Var Trk; Hon Roll; NHS.

ENDRES, FAITH A; Kingfisher HS; Kingfisher, OK; (1); Church Yth Grp; FCA; Natl FFA Org; Quiz Bowl; Scholastic Bowl; JV Stu Cncl; Sftbl; Hon Roll; Jr NHS; OK St U.

ENEVOLDSEN, KYLE A; Ponca City Sr HS; Ponca City, OK; (4); French Clb; Scholastic Bowl; Band; Jazz Band; Mrchg Band; Orch; Pep Band; High Hon Roll; Ntl Merit Ltr; Pres Acad Fit Awd; All St Band-Orch; OSU Regents Distngd Schlr; Colts Drum & Bugle Corps Mem; OK ST Univ; Music Ed.

ENGELMAN, BRANDON W; Turpin Schl; Turpin, OK; (4); 12/42; FCA; Letterman Clb; Office Aide; Quiz Bowl; Chorus; Var Bsktbl; Var Ftbl; Hon Roll.

ENGLAND, ELIZABETH; Bishop Mcguinness HS; Oklahoma City, OK; (4); 3/154; Cmnty Wkr; Debate Tm; FCA; French Clb; Pep Clb; Red Cross Aide; SADD; Teachers Aide; Vllybl; French Hon Soc; Hi-Lion 95-96; Red Cross Vlntr; Washington U St Louis.

ENGLAND, JEFF; Vinita HS; Vinita, OK; (4); 4/90; Am Leg Boys St; VP German Clb; Teachers Aide; Var Bsktbl; Var Trk; Hon Roll; Treas NHS; Jr Lion; Sr Rtrn; Stu Athl Trnr.

ENGLAND, PATRICIA S; Pauls Valley HS; Pauls Valley, OK; (1); FCA; Key Clb; Band; Church Choir; Mrchg Band; Hon Roll.

ENGLAND, WENDY; Idabel HS; Idabel, OK; (1); 38/135; Church Yth Grp; 4-H; FHA; Natl FFA Org; Church Choir; Rep Frsh Cls; Rep Stu Cncl; Var Chrldng; Cit Awd; 4-H Awd; Blck Blt Karate; Phy Ther.

ENGLE, MELISSA D; Sapulpa Sr HS; Sapulpa, OK; (3); Treas French Clb; Letterman Clb; Science Clb; Varsity Clb; Band; Jazz Band; Ed Nwsp; Var Chrldng; French Hon Soc; VP NHS; NHS VP; Dancing; U Of OK; Sports Phy.

ENGLE, OLIVIA A; Ponca City Sr HS; Ponca City, OK; (3); 12/320; Church Yth Grp; FCA; French Clb; Orch; Yrbk; Sec Soph Cls; Bsktbl; Trk; Jr NHS.

ENGLEBRIGHT, LOERESA L; Locust Grove HS; Locust Grove, OK; (2); Ecology; Northeastern ST Univ; Security.

ENGLES, REBECCA M; Westmoore HS; Moore, OK; (1); Church Yth Grp; SADD; OK ST Univ; Elem Tchr.

ENGLISH, CRYSTAL K; Lindsay HS; Lindsay, OK; (3); Art Clb; Church Yth Grp; FHA; Chorus; Rep Frsh Cls; Rep Soph Cls; Ultrasnd Spclst.

ENGLISH, DAVID D; Stillwater Sr HS; Stillwater, OK; (2); Natl Beta Clb; Spanish Clb; Orch; Hon Roll.

ENGLISH, JERROD; Charles Page HS; Sand Springs, OK; (4); 24/340; FCA; 4-H; FHA; Natl FFA Org; Socr; Wrstlng; Cit Awd; 4-H Awd; High Hon Roll; NHS; Vet.

ENGLISH, WHITNEY A; Christian Heritage Acad; Oklahoma City, OK; (3); Church Yth Grp; School Play; Stage Crew; Phtg Ed Yrbk; Rep Stu Cncl; Tennis; Hon Roll; Phtgrphy Edtr Yrbk; Rotary Clb Jr Ldrshp Awd; NJ Inst Tech Natl HS Arch Cntst 3rd Plc Wnnr Nation; Arch.

ENIS, BRAD C; Wilburton Sr HS; Wilburton, OK; (3); Church Yth Grp; FCA; Quiz Bowl; Chorus; Rptr Nwsp; Ofcr Bsbl; Bsktbl; Trk; Cit Awd; Hon Roll; OK ST Univ; Mech Engrng.

ENLOE, RAMONA; Will Rogers HS; Tulsa, OK; (4); 22/221; Church Yth Grp; Dance Clb; Red Cross Aide; ROTC; Band; Chorus; Drm Mjr(t); Lit Mag; Rep Jr Cls; Hon Roll; Winter Guard, Drum Line; Bibl Clb Pres; Band Chaplain; TJC; Sci Tchr.

ENRIGHT, APRIL; Liberty Acad; Shawnee, OK; (4); 4/15; Church Yth Grp; Q&S; Rptr Nwsp; Ed Yrbk; Rep Jr Cls; Ofcr Stu Cncl; Var Chrldng; High Hon Roll; Homcmng Cmmtte; OSU; Arch.

ENRIQUEZ, VICTORIA E; Panola HS; Wilburton, OK; (3); 5/22; Art Clb; Dance Clb; Drama Clb; FHA; Natl FFA Org; Pep Clb; Chorus; School Play; Stage Crew; Hon Roll; Comp, Typewriters, & 10 Keys; EOCS; RN.

ENSZ, JERENIAH D; Weatherford HS; Weatherford, OK; (3); Chorus; Swing Chorus; Chrldng; Gym; Southwestern OK ST; Bio; Med.

EPP, CONNIE R; Turpin Schl; Turpin, OK; (3); 5/30; Church Yth Grp; FCA; Letterman Clb; Band; Church Choir; Drm Mjr(t); JV Bsktbl; Var Sftbl; High Hon Roll; Eng Awd; Art Awd.

EPP, KACI D; Broken Arrow Sr HS; Broken Arrow, OK; (4); 79/921; Ofcr Sr Cls; Chrmn Stu Cncl; Bsktbl; Var Capt Socr; High Hon Roll; Jr NHS; NHS; U Of Tulsa; Mech Engr.

EPPERSON, AMANDA; Coweta HS; Coweta, OK; (4); 9/153; Church Yth Grp; FCA; SADD; Church Choir; Ed Nwsp; Ed Yrbk; Rep Sr Cls; Bsktbl; Ftbl; Pres NHS; Tulsa JC; Phys Thrpy.

EPPERSON, JENNIFER L; West Jr HS; Oklahoma City, OK; (1); Church Yth Grp; Drama Clb; French Clb; Hosp Aide; Teachers Aide; Drill Tm; School Play; Sec Frsh Cls; Trk; Cit Awd; Pom Pon Squad; Elderly Home Vol; Modeling; NY Schl Perf Arts; Actress.

EPPLER, JEFFERSON R; Classen Schl; Oklahoma City, OK; (2); 1/80; Computer Clb; Letterman Clb; VP Mu Alpha Theta; Capt Quiz Bowl; Science Clb; Spanish Clb; Acpl Chr; Chorus; Pres Soph Cls; Bsktbl; US Berkely; Physics.

EPPLIN, ALAN F; Stillwater Sr HS; Stillwater, OK; (3); 1/363; Am Leg Boys St; Church Yth Grp; French Clb; Natl Beta Clb; Church Choir; Orch; JV Bsbl; Var Bsktbl; Hon Roll; Kiwanis Awd.

EPPS, JENNIFER N; Mc Alester HS; Krebs, OK; (3); Art Clb; Church Yth Grp; FCA; 4-H; Hosp Aide; Spanish Clb; Speech Tm; Ofcr Stu Cncl; Bsktbl; Mgr(s); OK Cntrl Univ; Psychlgy.

ERASSARRET, JUSTY; Quinton Jr Sr HS; Stigler, OK; (2); Sec Natl FFA Org; Rptr Soph Cls; Ofcr Stu Cncl; Golf; Prfct Atten Awd; Rodeo; OK Jr Rodeo Assn; NHSRA Natl HS Rodeo Assn; Animal Husbandry.

ERBECK, JULIE; Claremore Sr HS; Claremore, OK; (4); 7/230; Church Yth Grp; Treas VP German Clb; Hosp Aide; Library Aide; Math Clb; Office Aide; Band; Sec Jr Cls; Ofcr Stu Cncl; NHS; OK ST U; Bio.

ERICKSON, KRISTA K; Tahlequah Sr HS; Tahlequah, OK; (2) German Clb; Girl Scts; Science Clb; Service Clb; SADD; Band; Color Guard; Yrbk; Cit Awd; Church Yth Grp; Blue Knights Drum & Bugle Corps; Black Gold Winterguard; UC-SAN Diego; Forensic Path.

ERKIE, STEVEN; Tahlequah Sr HS; Tahlequah, OK; (4); 31/243; Church Yth Grp; Cmnty Wkr; German Clb; Science Clb; Chorus; Cit Awd; Hon Roll; Office Aide; Scholastic Bowl; Teachers Aide; Sr Cls Vtd Most Ambitious Mst Dpndbl; NREC WA DC Yth Tour Essay Wnnr; Chrke Natn OK Top Intrn Awd; S W Assmely God U; Bus Admin.

ERKLE, BECKY D; Tahlequah Sr HS; Tahlequah, OK; (3); FBLA; SADD; Rep Stu Cncl; Golf; NHS; Pres Acad Fit Awd; Gftd & Tlntd Pgm; Chemical Engrng.

ERNST, HEATHER B; Westmoore HS; Oklahoma City, OK; (3); Church Yth Grp; Cmnty Wkr; FCA; French Clb; FBLA; FHA; Office Aide; Scholastic Bowl; SADD; Varsity Clb; Teens For Chrst; OK Wrld Hist Awd; Wintergrd; Acad Var, Sprst, Bnd Lttr; Frnch Awd; Acad Exc Awd.

ERWIN, CHRISTINE D; Choctaw HS; Midwest City, OK; (3); 1/3; FTA; German Clb; Key Clb; Pres Chorus; Co-Capt Color Guard; VP Frsh Cls; VP Soph Cls; VP Stu Cncl; Jr NHS; Kiwanis Awd.

ERWIN, DAVID W; Pocola HS; Pocola, OK; (2); Church Yth Grp; Ofcr Soph Cls; Bsktbl; Ftbl; Trk; Wt Lftg; Hon Roll; OK; Cmptrs.

ERWIN, MATTHEW; Piedmont HS; Piedmont, OK; (4); French Clb; Ski Clb; Band; School Play; Ofcr Bsbl; Ftbl; Wrstlng; Water & Snow Skiing; U Of OK; Dentist.

ERWIN, SHELLI; Kingston HS; Kingston, OK; (1); Church Yth Grp; FCA; FHA; Spanish Clb; Rptr Nwsp; Rep Frsh Cls; Sec Soph Cls; High Hon Roll; SEOSU; Acctng.

ERWIN, TERRON; Paoli HS; Paoli, OK; (1); Natl FFA Org; Church Choir; Chrldng; JV Bsbl; JV Bsktbl; Wt Lftg; Hon Roll; Fllwshp Chrstn Stds; Chrch Band.

ESAU, MICHAEL C; Broken Arrow Sr HS; Broken Arrow, OK; (2); German Clb; Band; Church Choir; Mrchg Band; Cit Awd; Gov Hon Prg Awd; High Hon Roll; NHS; Pres Schlr; Biochem Engrng.

ESCHBACH, KAMELA; Collinsville HS; Collinsville, OK; (3); Church Yth Grp; Chorus; Color Guard; Mrchg Band; Yrbk; Var Bsktbl; Var Sftbl; SALT Yth GrpfEMSA Explr; Tulsa U; Nrsng.

ESCOTT, ALLISON M; Cushing HS; Cushing, OK; (2); 1/180; Church Yth Grp; Cmnty Wkr; Office Aide; Pep Clb; Teachers Aide; Bsktbl; Chrldng; High Hon Roll; Hon Roll; NHS.

ESHELMAN, BRANDON C; Union Intermediate HS; Broken Arrow, OK; (2); Church Yth Grp; FCA; Spanish Clb; Rep Stu Cncl; JV Bsktbl; Var Ftbl; NHS; Prfct Atten Awd; Otstndng Eng Stu; Mon Mrng Bible Stud.

ESKANDERI, NESA; Bartlesville Sr HS; Bartlesville, OK; (3); 84/457; Church Yth Grp; Office Aide; Varsity Clb; Socr; Cit Awd; High Hon Roll; Hon Roll; NHS; K-Life; Grls Cmptv Sccr; Med.

ESKEW, JESSICA; Ardmore HS; Pooleville, OK; (3); 23/198; Church Yth Grp; Girl Scts; HOBY; JCL; Latin Clb; Mu Alpha Theta; Science Clb; Chorus; School Musical; High Hon Roll; Comp; Lbrl Arts; Frgn Lang; UCLA; Comp Prgmng.

ESLINGER, BYRON; Trinity Christian Schl; Broken Arrow, OK; (2); 1/14; Church Yth Grp; Orch; School Musical; Tennis; High Hon Roll; Photo.

ESPICH, AMBER D; Sapulpa Sr HS; Sapulpa, OK; (3); Church Yth Grp; FHA; ROTC; Band; Church Choir; Mrchg Band; Spanish NHS; Band Ltr; Tulsa Univ; Elem Tchr.

ESPINOZA, GABRIELA; Northwest Classen HS; Oklahoma City, OK; (3); Treas Church Yth Grp; FHA; High Hon Roll; Jr NHS; Southern Nazarene Univ; Rel.

ESSARY, MANDY; Porter Jr Sr HS; Porter, OK; (3); 3/38; Church Yth Grp; Quiz Bowl; Acpl Chr; Yrbk; VP Jr Cls; Rep Stu Cncl; Capt Chrldng; High Hon Roll; Jr NHS; NHS.

ESSENBERG, CARLA; Stillwater Jr HS; Stillwater, OK; (3); Church Choir; Orch; High Hon Roll; NHS; Ntl Merit Ltr; OK Summer Arts Inst 94-96.

ESSER, CHERYL L; Union Intermediate HS; Tulsa, OK; (1); FCA; German Clb; Co-Capt Drill Tm; Ofcr Stu Cncl; High Hon Roll; NHS; Amer All Str In Dnce; Gentcst.

ESSER, MATT S; Bartlesville Mid HS; Bartlesville, OK; (2); Church Yth Grp; Church Choir; Yrbk; Hon Roll; Soccer Team.

ESTELL, LAURA; Corn Bible Acad; Mustang, OK; (3); Band; Chorus; Sec Frsh Cls; VP Soph Cls; Sec Jr Cls; Ofcr Stu Cncl; Var Bsktbl; Var Chrldng; Var Vllybl; Hon Roll; Natl Hstry & Govt Awd 94-95, 95-96.

ESTEP, BRYAN J; North Intemediate HS; Broken Arrow, OK; (2); French Clb; Bsktbl; Wt Lftg; Hon Roll; OK Hnr Soc; OK ST Univ; Psych.

ESTEP, MICHELLE M; Enid Sr HS; Enid, OK; (4); Ofcr DECA; FCA; SADD; Sec Soph Cls; Sec Stu Cncl; JV Bsktbl; Var Powder Puff Ftbl; Var Sftbl; High Hon Roll; Kiwanis Awd; Environmental Clb; U Of OK; Bus.

ESTEP, REBECCA L; Putnam City West HS; Oklahoma City, OK; (4); Spanish Clb; Orch; Vllybl; Lvr String Strlling Group; OSU; Zoolgy.

ESTES, AMANDA; Mc Loud HS; Mc Loud, OK; (4); 11/103; Church Yth Grp; SADD; Thesps; School Play; Bsktbl; Mgr(s); Wrstlng; Hon Roll; Acad Ltr Jacket Recipient; Natl Engl Mrt, Ldrshp & Svc Awds; OU; Phys Thrpy.

ESTES, AMIE J; Edmond Santa Fe HS; Edmond, OK; (2); Church Yth Grp; Drama Clb; FHA; Var Sftbl; OU; Phys Thrpy.

ESTES, ANGELA M; Bartlesville Mid HS; Bartlesville, OK; (2); Church Yth Grp; Office Aide; Swmmng; Prfct Atten Awd; City Wide Sftbl; Chld Psychlgy.

ESTES, JASON; Tonkawa Jr Sr HS; Tonkawa, OK; (3); Am Leg Boys St; Church Yth Grp; FCA; Quiz Bowl; Rep Frsh Cls; Var L Bsbl; Var L Bsktbl; Var L Ftbl; High Hon Roll; NHS.

ESTES, MELISSA; Tecumseh HS; Tecumseh, OK; (4); Am Leg Aux Girls St; Church Yth Grp; French Clb; Natl Beta Clb; Teachers Aide; Band; Chorus; Jazz Band; Mrchg Band; School Musical; St Gregorys; Ed.

ESTONINA, KRISLORD; Macarthur Sr HS; Lawton, OK; (3); Church Yth Grp; Office Aide; Acpl Chr; Chorus; Orch; School Play; Ofcr Stu Cncl; Var Tennis; High Hon Roll; Hon Roll; Army Cmmnty Svcs Vol; De Paul Univ; Voice/Cmptr Engr.

ESTRADA, ISABEL; Elk City Jr HS; Elk City, OK; (1); Church Yth Grp; Latin Clb; Band; Chorus; Church Choir; Flag Corp; Mrchg Band; Pep Band; Hon Roll; Prfct Atten Awd.

ETCHISON, AMY; Indianola HS; Mcalester, OK; (4); 9/40; Church Yth Grp; Pres FBLA; Treas FHA; Teachers Aide; Var Bsktbl; Var Sftbl; Hon Roll; 4-H; Yrbk; Natl Eng Mrt Awd; Natl His & Geog Awd; Chrch Pianist; Cntrl Bapt Coll; Music.

ETCHISON, DREMIANE D; Lawton Sr HS; Lawton, OK; (4); 2/325; Church Yth Grp; Cmnty Wkr; Office Aide; Drill Tm; Trk; High Hon Roll; NHS; Pres Acad Fit Awd; Xinos Mbr; Howard Univ; Pharmacy.

ETHRIDGE, JASON; Central Mid-HS; Norman, OK; (2); School Play; Stage Crew; Variety Show; Hon Roll; Tae Kwon Do; Bass Guitar In Band; Engrng.

ETRIS, BRANDY; Cordell Sr HS; Cordell, OK; (4); Church Yth Grp; Quiz Bowl; Pres Spanish Clb; Teachers Aide; Band; Church Choir; Jazz Band; Mrchg Band; Pep Band; School Musical; 5 Yr All-Rgn Hnr Bnd; 4 Yr Shrtgrs Hnr Bnd; 95 All-Str Mrchng Bnd; Southwestern OK ST U.

ETZKORN, AMBER N; Grace Fellowship Christian Sch; Tulsa, OK; (3); Church Yth Grp; Pep Clb; Teachers Aide; Rep Soph Cls; JV Var Bsktbl; Var Crs Cntry; Var Socr; Var Trk; Hmcmng Ct 2 Yrs; OK Univ; Erly Chldhd Ed.

EUBANKS, LANCE K; Stilwell HS; Stilwell, OK; (2); FCA; 4-H; VP Frsh Cls; Sec Stu Cncl; Var Wrstlng; High Hon Roll; NHS; Sprtsmnshp Awd; 2-Time Masonic Lodge Stu Of Today Awd; OK U; Engrng.

EUPER, JARED T; Byng Sr HS; Stonewall, OK; (2); FCA; FBLA; Letterman Clb; Science Clb; Spanish Clb; Acpl Chr; Chorus; Var Bsbl; Var Wt Lftg; Hon Roll.

EVANS, ADAM; Comanche HS; Comanche, OK; (2); Art Clb; L Bsktbl; L Ftbl; Wt Lftg; Hon Roll; Jr NHS; NHS.

EVANS, AMANDA; Mannford HS; Mannford, OK; (3); Church Yth Grp; FCA; FBLA; Ofcr Soph Cls; Ofcr Jr Cls; Ofcr Stu Cncl; Bsktbl; Sftbl; Trk; Hon Roll; Evangel.

EVANS, AMANDA F; Wagoner Sr HS; Wagoner, OK; (1); Art Clb; GAA; JV Bsktbl; Var Trk; Art Awds; Bsktbl Scoring/Rebounds 2 Yrs; TX A&M; Sports Med/Vet Med.

EVANS, AMY; Timberlake Schl; Cherokee, OK; (3); 4/35; FCA; 4-H; Letterman Clb; Scholastic Bowl; Chorus; Yrbk; Ofcr Stu Cncl; High Hon Roll; NHS; OK ST U; Optmtry.

EVANS, ANNI; Bishop Mcguinness HS; Oklahoma City, OK; (4); 20/160; VP FBLA; Pep Clb; Pres Spanish Clb; SADD; Var Trk; Var Capt Vllybl; High Hon Roll; NHS; Spanish NHS; OK Grls St Dlgt 95; 100m Hrdls & Lng Jmp Schlr Record; Saint Louis U; Bus.

EVANS, ASHLEY N; Harrah HS; Harrah, OK; (1); 20/180; Church Yth Grp; FCA; FHA; JV Bsktbl; JV Var Sftbl; Var Trk; High Hon Roll; Hon Roll; Del City Chrch Of Christ Yth Group.

EVANS, BENJI A; Blackwell HS; Blackwell, OK; (1); Church Yth Grp; FCA; Pep Clb; Wt Lftg; Wrstlng; Hon Roll.

EVANS, BRANDON; Temple Jr Sr HS; Temple, OK; (4); 2/20; Church Yth Grp; FHA; HOBY; Pres Stu Cncl; Var Bsbl; Var Bsktbl; Var Trk; Cit Awd; High Hon Roll; NHS; U OK; Med.

EVANS, CHRISTA; Vinita HS; Vinita, OK; (3); Church Yth Grp; FCA; FBLA; German Clb; GAA; Math Clb; Teachers Aide; Band; Drm Mjr(t); Mrchg Band; Northeastern ST Univ; Optomtry.

EVANS, GEOFF; Coweta HS; Broken Arrow, OK; (4); 8/153; Church Yth Grp; FCA; Quiz Bowl; Scholastic Bowl; SADD; Teachers Aide; Yrbk; High Hon Roll; Jr NHS; Lbrn NHS; Stu Of Mnth; Drvrs Ed Awd; Arch.

EVANS, JENNIE J; Tonkawa Jr Sr HS; Tonkawa, OK; (2); Church Yth Grp; FCA; HOBY; Chorus; Yrbk; Pres Jr Cls; Rep Stu Cncl; JV Var Bsktbl; Var Sftbl; High Hon Roll; Extended Studies; OK ST Univ; Elem Ed.

EVANS, JESSICA R; Enid Sr HS; Enid, OK; (3); Church Yth Grp; Chorus; Socr; NHS; BYU; Bio.

EVANS, JULIE; Clinton HS; Clinton, OK; (1); Church Yth Grp; FCA; GAA; Key Clb; Chorus; Church Choir; Swing Chorus; Bsktbl; Golf; Sftbl; Phys Thrpst.

EVANS, JUSTIN; Owasso Sr HS; Owasso, OK; (4); 1/305; Am Leg Boys St; Church Yth Grp; FCA; Pres Key Clb; Teachers Aide; Church Choir; Ftbl; Trk; NHS; Val; U Of OK Acad Achvt Awd; OK ST U; Engrng.

EVANS, KARI A; Leflore Sr HS; Summerfield, OK; (3); Church Yth Grp; Speech Tm; School Musical; Ed Nwsp; Pres Jr Cls; Bsktbl; Sftbl; High Hon Roll; FFA VP 95-96 & Pres 96-97; Eastern OK ST Coll; Agri-Bus.

EVANS, KATY; Timberlake Schl; Cherokee, OK; (1); 1/35; Church Yth Grp; Cmnty Wkr; FCA; 4-H; FHA; Chorus; Sftbl; High Hon Roll; Hosp Candy-Striper Vlntr.

EVANS, KELLI; Mooreland Jr Sr HS; Mooreland, OK; (4); 8/29; Art Clb; Church Yth Grp; FCA; 4-H; FHA; Natl FFA Org; Spanish Clb; 4-H Awd; Hon Roll; Stdnt Cncl; Woodward Round-Up Club; Northwestern Jr Rodeo Assn; OSU.

EVANS, KRISTI G; Leedey Schl; Camargo, OK; (4); Rep FCA; Rep Sec 4-H; Sec FBLA; Hist FHA; Spanish Clb; Rep Jr Cls; Bsktbl; Chrldng; Sftbl; Hon Roll; Pres Acad Fitness Awd; All Amrcn Schol; OK Natl Hnr Scty; SWOSU; Med Tech.

EVANS, LEE; Marietta HS; Marietta, OK; (2); Cmnty Wkr; 4-H; Natl FFA Org; Bsktbl; Ftbl; Hon Roll; Hntng; Fshng; Cmpng; OK ST U; Med.

EVANS, M ERIC; Westmoore HS; Oklahoma City, OK; (3); 89/629; FCA; French Clb; Library Aide; Office Aide; Rep Frsh Cls; Var L Ftbl; Var Wt Lftg; Var Wrstlng; NHS; Pres Acad Fit Awd; U Of OK; Pre-Med; Orthopedics.

EVANS, MANDY C; Edmond Memorial HS; Edmond, OK; (2); 158/408; Art Clb; Church Yth Grp; Key Clb; Spanish Clb; Swing Chorus; Hon Roll; Classical Ballet & Jazz; Mission Trips; Yth Group; UCO; Pub Relations; Cnslng.

EVANS, MEGAN L; Yukon Middle HS; Yukon, OK; (1); Mgr(s); Ath Sprts Trnr 2 Yrs; Southwestern ST; Elem Tchr.

EVANS, ROBERT J; Mannford HS; Mannford, OK; (4); 1/96; Drama Clb; FCA; Science Clb; Spanish Clb; SADD; Teachers Aide; L Ftbl; L Wrstlng; Hon Roll; Val; OK ST Univ Valedictorian Schlsp; OK ST Univ.

EVANS, ROXANNA R; Owasso Sr HS; Owasso, OK; (3); FCA; French Clb; Key Clb; Office Aide; Ofcr Jr Cls; Bsktbl; Chrldng; Pom Pon; Hon Roll; NHS.

EVANS, SENE; Strother Jr Sr HS; Seminole, OK; (3); 1/29; 4-H; GAA; HOBY; Natl FFA Org; Quiz Bowl; Scholastic Bowl; Spanish Clb; Pres Frsh Cls; Pres Soph Cls; Pres Jr Cls; OK U; Biotechnlgy.

EVANS, TAMMY; Broken Arrow Sr HS; Broken Arrow, OK; (4); 7/973; Church Yth Grp; HOBY; JCL; VP Band; Quiz Bowl; VP Spanish Clb; Rep Stu Cncl; Gov Hon Prg Awd; High Hon Roll; Hon Roll.

EVANS, TAMMY E; Blair Schl; Martha, OK; (2); 4-H; HOBY; Natl Beta Clb; Speech Tm; Var Bsktbl; Var Sftbl; Var Trk; Cit Awd; Hon Roll; Voice Of Dem Spch Cntst; Lawyer.

EVANS, TORRI D; Choctaw HS; Choctaw, OK; (4); 131/298; GAA; Office Aide; Spanish Clb; Ofcr Bsbl; Var Bsktbl; Mgr(s); Sftbl; Hon Roll; Sherr Dawn Evans Schlsp; UCO; Nrsng.

EVANS, TRACI; Comanche HS; Comanche, OK; (3); FHA; Sftbl; High Hon Roll; Hon Roll; NHS; Ntl Merit Ltr; Law.

EVANS, TRICIA; Colcord Schl; Colcord, OK; (2); Church Yth Grp; FHA; Hosp Aide; Sec Frsh Cls; Sec Soph Cls; Var Bsktbl; High Hon Roll; Hon Roll; NHS; Moore Park Col; Zoolgy.

EVANS, WILLIAM; Ft Gibson HS; Fort Gibson, OK; (4); 1/140; Church Yth Grp; FCA; French Clb; Band; Ofcr Stu Cncl; Socr; High Hon Roll; NHS; Sal; Oklahoma City U; Phy Ther.

EVE, ELISE C; Carl B Albert Sr HS; Gainesville, FL; (4); 1/241; Hosp Aide; Ed Key Clb; Pep Clb; Spanish Clb; Var Tennis; High Hon Roll; Jr NHS; NHS; Pres Acad Fit Awd; Val; Chem I Hnrs Chem II Hrs Awds; U Fo Fl; Chem Eng.

EVERETT, BRYCE; Cashion HS; Piedmont, OK; (2); 9/36; Church Yth Grp; FCA; Natl FFA Org; Quiz Bowl; Band; Mrchg Band; Yrbk; JV Bsbl; Hon Roll; Prfct Atten Awd; Southern Nazarene U; Gm Wrdn.

EVERETT, MINDY L; Caddo HS; Caddo, OK; (2); Church Yth Grp; Drama Clb; FHA; Chorus; Church Choir; School Musical; School Play; Hon Roll; NHS; M-Pact; Horseback Riding; GATE; East Cntrl Univ; Music; Eqstrn.

EVERS, DEREK; Mustang HS; Yukon, OK; (3); Church Yth Grp; FCA; Var Ftbl; Wt Lftg; Wrstlng; PTSA Stdnt VP.

EVERS, REED H; Cushing HS; Yale, OK; (1); 1/100; Church Yth Grp; Band; Church Choir; Jazz Band; Mrchg Band; Pep Band; High Hon Roll; Hon Roll; NHS; St Schlr; Var Schlr; OK HS Hnr Soc; US Achvmt Acad.

EVERSON, HEATHER; Kingston HS; Kingston, OK; (3); 1/75; Church Yth Grp; FCA; FHA; Yrbk; Var Bsktbl; Trk; High Hon Roll; NHS; Pharm.

EWBANK, DREW; Fairview HS; Fairview, OK; (2); Church Yth Grp; Cmnty Wkr; Debate Tm; FCA; HOBY; Letterman Clb; NFL; Speech Tm; Varsity Clb; VICA; OK ST U; Med.

EWEN, GWEN C; Union Sr HS; Tulsa, OK; (4); 113/632; Pres Church Yth Grp; Cmnty Wkr; FCA; GAA; Key Clb; Red Cross Aide; Spanish Clb; Church Choir; Mrchg Band; School Play; OK St Univ; Anesth.

EWEN, TRAVIS; Stroad HS; Cushing, OK; (2); Var Ftbl; Hon Roll; Pres Acad Fit Awd.

EWERS, SHERRY A; Bartlesville Mid HS; Bartlesville, OK; (3); 40/441; Church Yth Grp; Spanish Clb; Teachers Aide; High Hon Roll; Hon Roll; NHS; Acad Exc Awd; Sthrn Nazareneuniv; Acctng.

EWERT, JOSH; Seminole Jr Sr HS; Seminole, OK; (3); Church Yth Grp; Math Clb; Spanish Clb; Band; Mrchg Band; Pep Band; Var Tennis; Hon Roll; NHS; Prfct Atten Awd.

EWING, JESSICA; Oologah HS; Oologah, OK; (4); 14/96; Am Leg Aux Girls St; Church Yth Grp; Cmnty Wkr; FCA; Girl Scts; Natl FFA Org; Office Aide; Red Cross Aide; Science Clb; SADD; Most Sprtd Swmmr; OK ST U; Phy Ther.

EWING, LAURETTA A; Eisenhower Sr HS; Lawton, OK; (4); 25/386; Church Yth Grp; Drama Clb; FCA; Chorus; Church Choir; School Musical; School Play; Stage Crew; High Hon Roll; NHS; Cameron Univ; Thtr Arts.

EWING JR, MICHAEL A; Eisenhower Sr HS; Lawton, OK; (3); 49/485; Boy Scts; Church Yth Grp; Drama Clb; FCA; School Musical; Stage Crew; Variety Show; High Hon Roll; Jr NHS; NHS; Tech Theater.

EWY JR, LARRY G; Blackwell HS; Blackwell, OK; (3); Church Yth Grp; FCA; Letterman Clb; Band; Mrchg Band; Ofcr Bsbl; Ftbl; Trk; Wt Lftg; Hon Roll; OK ST Univ; Ftbl Coach.

EYSTER, CRAIG A; Oklahoma Sch Of Science & Math; Guthrie, OK; (3); FBLA; Quiz Bowl; Spanish Clb; Temple Yth Grp; Rep Frsh Cls; Tennis; Cit Awd; NHS.

EZELL, ERIK L; North Intemediate HS; Broken Arrow, OK; (1); Church Yth Grp; Office Aide; Teachers Aide; Church Choir; JV Ftbl; JV Trk; JV Wt Lftg; High Hon Roll; Hon Roll; NHS; Clark Univ; Bus Admin/Math.

EZELL, VERONICA L; Durant HS; Durant, OK; (1); FHA; Hon Roll; Cmptr Sys Analyst.

EZZELL, JON W; Sayre HS; Sayre, OK; (4); Art Clb; Church Yth Grp; Pep Clb; Quiz Bowl; Scholastic Bowl; Spanish Clb; Thesps; Band; Mrchg Band; Nwsp; SWOSU; Psych.

FAGAN, JAMES E; Enid Sr HS; Enid, OK; (3); 80/400; Am Leg Boys St; Boy Scts; Chess Clb; ROTC; Band; Mrchg Band; Orch; Rptr Sr Cls; Hon Roll; NHS; U Of OK; Mtrlgy.

FAGAN, ROSEANN; Lone Grove HS; Lone Grove, OK; (2); #1 in class; FCA; Key Clb; Math Clb; Scholastic Bowl; Science Clb; Spanish Clb; Band; Chorus; Mrchg Band; Rptr Nwsp.

FAHLE, JANA; Eisenhower Sr HS; Lawton, OK; (3); Church Yth Grp; Cmnty Wkr; FCA; Girl Scts; Band; Ofcr Stu Cncl; Mgr(s); Hon Roll; Jr NHS; NHS; 1st Pl Martin Luther King Jr Wrtng Essay; Girl Sct Silver Awd; Stu Ath Trainer; OK ST; Ath Trainer; Phy Thrpst.

FAHNHOLZ, AMANDA J; Okmulgee HS; Okmulgee, OK; (2); FHA; High Hon Roll; Hon Roll; OK HS Hnr Soc.

FAILS, ROBERT B; Choctaw HS; Choctaw, OK; (4); 1/317; Am Leg Boys St; Cit Awd; High Hon Roll; NHS; Pres Acad Fit Awd; Sal; St Schlr; Val; OK U; Phy.

FAIR, CHRIS J; Westville HS; Westville, OK; (3); Pres Hist FHA; Teachers Aide; VICA; Wrstlng; Hon Roll; US Marines.

FAIRBANKS, ELAINE M; Stillwater Sr HS; Stillwater, OK; (4); 1/320; Church Yth Grp; DECA; FCA; FBLA; Girl Scts; Key Clb; Latin Clb; Sec Mu Alpha Theta; Natl Beta Clb; Spanish Clb; KS St Bus Wk; OK Rgnst Schol; Slvr And Gld Awds; OK St Univ; Mktng.

FAIRMAN, JEREMY D; Locust Grove HS; Locust Grove, OK; (2); Drama Clb; VICA; Ftbl; Wt Lftg; Hon Roll; Treas Of Locust Grove TSA Chptr; U Of OK; Law Engcnt.

FALDON, RICKEY L; Arkoma Jr Sr HS; Arkoma, OK; (2); FHA; Welding.

FANNING, JAIME D; U S Grant HS; Oklahoma City, OK; (1); Church Yth Grp; Rep Frsh Cls; Hon Roll.

FARAR, ALLISHA; Tahlequah Sr HS; Hulbert, OK; (2); Church Yth Grp; Pep Clb; SADD; Chorus; Hon Roll; Psych; Psych.

FARGUSON, KAREN; Stilwell HS; Stilwell, OK; (2); FHA; Natl Beta Clb; Var Mgr(s); High Hon Roll; Hon Roll; Pub Of Poem By Natl Lib Of Poetry; Lawyer.

FARIYIKE, SONYA S; Webster HS; Tulsa, OK; (2); Church Yth Grp; Dance Clb; Girl Scts; Bsktbl; Crs Cntry; Trk; Hon Roll; Acctng.

FARLEY, CHRIS; Deer Creek HS; Edmond, OK; (4); 29/107; Am Leg Boys St; Church Yth Grp; Science Clb; Teachers Aide; Crs Cntry; Score Keeper; Socr; Wrstlng; NHS; U Of OK; Engrng.

FARLEY, COLE J; Fletcher Jr Sr HS; Fletcher, OK; (3); Rep Stu Cncl; Ofcr Bsbl; Bsktbl; Cit Awd; Hon Roll; NHS; FFA.

FARLEY, JESSICA K; Fletcher Jr Sr HS; Fletcher, OK; (1); FCA; FHA; GAA; Pep Clb; Pep Band; Bsktbl; Chrldng; Sftbl; Cit Awd; High Hon Roll.

FARMER, ADAM W; Muskogee HS; Muskogee, OK; (1); 102/491; Church Yth Grp; JV Bsbl; Teens For Christ; Roughers Against Illegal Drugs; Casas Por Cristo; Ozark Chrstn Coll; Yth Minister.

FARMER, CHRIS; Milburn Schl; Coleman, OK; (3); 4-H; Natl FFA Org; Band; Chorus; School Play; Stage Crew; Ofcr Bsbl; Bsktbl; 4-H Awd; Natl FFA Awd; Bsbl & Bsktbl Athl Awds; FFA Greenhand Deg; Stage Band Music Awd.

FARMER, DANA L; Stringtown HS; Stringtown, OK; (4); Drama Clb; Teachers Aide; Flag Corp; Yrbk; Hon Roll; Homemaker.

FARMER, HEATHER; Moore HS; Moore, OK; (3); Drama Clb; Chorus; School Play; Hon Roll.

FARMER, JASON; Thomas A Edison HS; Tulsa, OK; (4); 42/180; Am Leg Boys St; Key Clb; Office Aide; Red Cross Aide; Spanish Clb; SADD; Crs Cntry; Socr; Swmmng; Hon Roll; Tulsa U; Engr.

FARMER, JENNIFER L; Daniel Webster HS; Tulsa, OK; (4); 10/135; Church Yth Grp; French Clb; Key Clb; VP Science Clb; Spanish Clb; Church Choir; Stage Crew; High Hon Roll; Hon Roll; NHS.

FARMER, KATIE M; Putnam City West HS; Bethany, OK; (4); 10/278; Church Yth Grp; Drama Clb; Hosp Aide; Science Clb; Sec SADD; Stage Crew; Sec Stu Cncl; Stat Bsktbl; Chrldng; Hon Roll; Southern Nazarene Univ; Pre-Med.

FARMER, KRISTINA; Oklahoma Schl Of Sci & Math; Mannford, OK; (4); Cmnty Wkr; Drama Clb; HOBY; NFL; Scholastic Bowl; Speech Tm; Band; Mrchg Band; NHS; St Schlr; Emory U.

FARMER, MITZI; Welch Jr Sr HS; Welch, OK; (3); Church Yth Grp; FBLA; FHA; Quiz Bowl; SADD; Rptr Nwsp; Hon Roll; Prfct Atten Awd; Phrmcy.

FARMER, NATHAN C; West Middle HS; Norman, OK; (2); Pres Church Yth Grp; FCA; Latin Clb; Chorus; Ofcr Stu Cncl; Mission Trip Moterrey Mexico; Paleontology.

FARMER, RICKY L; Heavener HS; Hodgen, OK; (2); 32/76; Natl FFA Org; JV Bsktbl; JV Trk; Hon Roll; Prfct Atten Awd; Won Dgrs FFA.

FARNHAM, KYLE D; Webster HS; Tulsa, OK; (1); Church Yth Grp; Scholastic Bowl; Band; Mrchg Band; Ofcr Frsh Cls; High Hon Roll; Tulsa Area United Way Outfrnt Ldrsp Pgm; Rice; Ed.

FARNSWORTH, NICHOLE R; Bethel HS; Newalla, OK; (3); Church Yth Grp; 4-H; FHA; Natl FFA Org; Office Aide; Pep Clb; Bsktbl; Hon Roll; NHS; Library Aide; Barrel Racing/Team Roping.

FARQUHAR, BETH A; Jenks HS; Tulsa, OK; (3); Church Yth Grp; Drama Clb; German Clb; Pep Clb; Thesps; Chorus; Church Choir; School Musical; Ofcr Stu Cncl; Trojans For Christ.

FARR, ERIN R; Hollis Jr Sr HS; Eldorado, OK; (3); 14/44; Church Yth Grp; 4-H; Teachers Aide; Chorus; Church Choir; Swing Chorus; Variety Show; Cit Awd; 4-H Awd; Hon Roll; Natl Solo Cmptn 1st Pl; Solo Ensble Cmptn 1st Div 1 Ratng; Girls Ensble; Acad Achvmt Awd; Pvt Voic Lessn; Southwestern OK ST U; Music.

FARR, WILLIAM T; North Intemediate HS; Broken Arrow, OK; (1); Debate Tm; Speech Tm; Rep Stu Cncl; Hon Roll; Cal-Berkeley; Genetic Engrng.

FARRAND, HEATHER N; Oklahoma Sch Of Science & Math; Fort Supply, OK; (3); Church Yth Grp; 4-H; FHA; Chorus; Yrbk; Rep Frsh Cls; Var Chrldng; High Hon Roll; Prfct Atten Awd; OK ST Univ; Math/Earth Sci.

FARRAR, BRANDI D; Putnam City North HS; Oklahoma City, OK; (3); 149/489; FCA; Spanish Clb; SADD; Rep Stu Cncl; NHS; DECA; Psych/Comm.

FARRAR, CHRISTINA D; Cameron Schl; Cameron, OK; (1); Church Yth Grp; FCA; FHA; Bsktbl; Sftbl; ST Fnlst Amer Coed Pgnt; John Casablancas Mdlng Schl; OU; Prof Bsktbl Plyr/Bio Tchr.

FARRAR, WADE; Crescent Schl; Crescent, OK; (1); Church Yth Grp; FCA; Natl FFA Org; Pep Clb; Band; Jazz Band; Mrchg Band; Orch; Pep Band; VP Frsh Cls.

FARRELL, TROY; Owasso Sr HS; Owasso, OK; (2); 2/270; Church Yth Grp; French Clb; Scholastic Bowl; Band; Chorus; Mrchg Band; School Musical; Hon Roll; Amateur Radio; Elec Eng.

FARRELL, VANESSA M; Maysville Jr Sr HS; Maysville, OK; (3); 3/26; Teachers Aide; Band; Chorus; VP FHA; Rptr Jr Cls; High Hon Roll; Hon Roll; Rep NHS; Prfct Atten Awd; Mem Parlimntry Team 3 Yrs; OK Univ; Bus Comm.

FARRIOR, MARY K; B T Washington HS; Tulsa, OK; (2); Church Yth Grp; Drama Clb; Latin Clb; Spanish Clb; Chorus; Church Choir; School Musical; NHS.

FARRIS, BRANDI; Claremore Sr HS; Claremore, OK; (3); 32/237; Dance Clb; Rep Drama Clb; FHA; Spanish Clb; Rep Temple Yth Grp; SADD; High Hon Roll; Hon Roll; NHS; Pres Schlr; Cmnty Svc Day Care; Engl Tutor; 2nd Pl Standard Oratory Speech Awd; OU; Chld Psych.

FARRIS, CINNAMON; Taloga Schl; Taloga, OK; (3); 1/13; Church Yth Grp; Rep 4-H; FHA; Rep Treas Natl FFA Org; Quiz Bowl; School Play; Mgr Yrbk; Rep Frsh Cls; Rep Jr Cls; JV Bsktbl; OK ST FFA Chorus; Tri-St Hnr Chorus, Show Choir.

FARRIS, DANI L; Claremore Sr HS; Claremore, OK; (3); 51/237; Debate Tm; Latin Clb; Spanish Clb; Variety Show; Rep Soph Cls; Ofcr Stu Cncl; High Hon Roll; NHS; Prfct Atten Awd; Cmnty Wkr; Recd Schlrshp Debate Camp 96; Recd Trophy Outstndng Delator Cmp; OK ST U; Engr.

FARRIS, JASON; Liberty Acad; Shawnee, OK; (3); Stage Crew; Rptr Nwsp; Yrbk; Lit Mag; Rep Jr Cls; Var Bsktbl; Mgr(s); Cit Awd; Ntl Merit Ltr; U Of OK; Pre-Med.

FARRIS, JASON; Holdenville HS; Holdenville, OK; (2); 8/85; Chorus; Church Choir; School Musical; NHS; Beta Clb; OK U; Medcl.

FARRIS, MELISSA L; Okeene Jr Sr HS; Isabella, OK; (2); 10/32; Church Yth Grp; Natl FFA Org; Band; Mrchg Band; Hon Roll; Kiwanis Awd; FFA Treas/Reporter; OK Salers Jr Assn Sec/Treas; Amer Salers Jr Assn; Hoberecht Awd; Star Greenhand; OSU; Ag/Bus.

FARRIS, SAMUEL; Broken Arrow Sr HS; Broken Arrow, OK; (4); 10/921; Am Leg Boys St; FCA; Pres Soph Cls; Pres VP Stu Cncl; Var Bsbl; Var Bsktbl; Var Chrldng; Cit Awd; NHS; French Clb; Johns Hopkins U Ctr Tlntd Yth; Arch Engrng.

FARROW, NATE; Eufaula Sr HS; Eufaula, OK; (2); #5 in class; Band; Ftbl; Trk.

FARTHING, JENNIFER; Newcastle HS; Newcastle, OK; (3); 1/91; Church Yth Grp; FBLA; Science Clb; Spanish Clb; Band; Chorus; Mrchg Band; Ofcr Soph Cls; Ofcr Jr Cls; Mgr(s).

FAST, PETE; Hilldale HS; Muskogee, OK; (4); 1/78; Computer Clb; FCA; Key Clb; Pres Mu Alpha Theta; Science Clb; Spanish Clb; Teachers Aide; Pres Jr Cls; Sec Stu Cncl; Var Bsbl; Primerica Stdnt Ath Of Yr; Muskogee Optmst Clb Awd Math/Sci; Stdnt Of Yr; John Brown U.

FAUCHIER, RACHEL A; Enid Sr HS; Enid, OK; (2); Girl Scts; Spanish Clb; Orch; Rptr Nwsp; Socr; Tennis; Hon Roll; Jr NHS; NHS; Pres Acad Fit Awd; Strolling Strings; Karate; Guitar; Evergreen U; Marine Biologist.

FAUDREE, WESLEY C; Christian Heritage Acad; Oklahoma City, OK; (3); Boy Scts; Church Yth Grp; Cmnty Wkr; FCA; Red Cross Aide; Color Guard; Nwsp; Phtg Yrbk; Ftbl; Wt Lftg; USNA; Comp Sci; Naval Arch.

FAULK, KARA; Sapulpa Sr HS; Sapulpa, OK; (2); FCA; School Play; L Bsktbl; L Sftbl; Gov Hon Prg Awd; Hon Roll; Jr NHS; NHS; Pres Acad Fit Awd.

FAULKENBERRY, THOMAS; Marietta HS; Marietta, OK; (4); 1/53; Debate Tm; Model UN; NFL; Quiz Bowl; Speech Tm; Teachers Aide; Variety Show; Var Bsktbl; Cit Awd; High Hon Roll; Team Ropng; Cntry Music Singr; Guitar Plyr; Southeastern OK ST U; Math.

FAULKNER, CHANNELL M; Dickson HS; Ardmore, OK; (3); French Clb; FHA; Chorus; School Musical; Hon Roll; Ntl Merit Schol; Murray ST; RN.

FAULKNER, MISTI; Luther HS; Luther, OK; (4); 16/42; Church Yth Grp; FHA; Natl FFA Org; Bsktbl; Sftbl; OK Farmers Union; Northeastern OK A&M Coll.

FAUSSETT, SUSANNE R; Blackwell HS; Blackwell, OK; (2); Church Yth Grp; Pep Clb; Band; Chorus; Church Choir; Jazz Band; Mrchg Band; Pep Band; School Musical; Tennis; OK Hnr Soc; Scndry Music Ed.

FAVER, CISSA; Westmoore HS; Oklahoma City, OK; (4); Pres Drama Clb; Rptr Thesps; Acpl Chr; School Musical; Stage Crew; Lit Mag; JV Swmmng; JV Tennis; Hon Roll; Pres Acad Fit Awd; OK ST Univ; Scndry Ed/Theatre.

FAW FAW, KRISTY; Frontier Public Schl; Red Rock, OK; (4); Church Yth Grp; 4-H; Band; Chorus; Yrbk; Ofcr Bsbl; Stu Of The Month Frosh Yr; OSU; Phy Therapy.

FEARS, BRAXTON; Bixby Sr HS; Tulsa, OK; (3); 23/209; Church Yth Grp; Cmnty Wkr; FCA; HOBY; Spanish Clb; SADD; VP Soph Cls; Sec Jr Cls; Var L Bsktbl; Var Golf; Chrch Yth Grp Stu Ldrshp Clb; Bus.

FEARS, MANDY N; Tahlequah Jr HS; Park Hill, OK; (1); Church Yth Grp; Band; Mrchg Band; Nwsp; Yrbk; Regnl His Day Cont; AAUW Mentorship Pgm.

FEARS, MARCUS E; Tahlequah Sr HS; Park Hill, OK; (3); Church Yth Grp; Band; Color Guard; Drm Mjr(t); Mrchg Band; OK All-Star Marching Band; EOP Yth Cncl.

FEATHERS, SHAWNTIA M; Ponca City Middle HS; Ponca City, OK; (1); Nwsp; Sftbl; Hon Roll; OSU; Vet.

FEAZEL, KENDRA R; Central HS; Tulsa, OK; (4); Church Yth Grp; Intnl Clb; VICA; Chorus; Hist Sr Cls; Hon Roll; Cntrl Chiefs; CNA; TJC; Sci/Nrsng.

FEDDERSEN, ASHLEY R; El Reno Sr HS; El Reno, OK; (1); Dance Clb; FHA; Natl FFA Org; Drill Tm; Pom Pon; Tennis; High Hon Roll; Jr NHS; Natl Awd Wnnr Math.

FEDICK, JULIE A; Catoosa HS; Catoosa, OK; (4); 1/135; Cmnty Wkr; FCA; Hosp Aide; Pep Clb; Spanish Clb; Speech Tm; Teachers Aide; Stage Crew; Bsktbl; Crs Cntry; Acad St Crs Cntry Chmpn 94 OK; Med.

FEIERABENAD, JERRY; Bartlesville Sr HS; Bartlesville, OK; (3); 126/458; Band; Mrchg Band; Pep Band; Actv In Chrch; Ply Recratnl Bsktbl; OK U; Bus.

FEINSTEIN, TRACY E; B T Washington HS; Tulsa, OK; (2); Pep Clb; Spanish Clb; Teachers Aide; Ed Temple Yth Grp; Rep Stu Cncl; Hon Roll; NHS; Bus.

FEISAL, JENNIFER D; Yukon Middle HS; Yukon, OK; (1); FHA; Nwsp; Gov Hon Prg Awd; Hon Roll; Excl Clmn Wrtng Awd.

FEISAL, REGINA; Putnam City West HS; Bethany, OK; (1); Church Yth Grp; Church Choir; Yrbk; Ofcr Frsh Cls; Chrldng; Numerous Piano Awds; Southern Nazarene U.

FEMAL, MATTHEW R; Memorial HS; Tulsa, OK; (2); FCA; Spanish Clb; Treas Frsh Cls; Rep Soph Cls; Var Bsbl; Var Ftbl; Hon Roll; Jr NHS; Math; Sci; Medical.

FENDLEY, CLIFTON J; Sapulpa Sr HS; Sapulpa, OK; (2); Pres Spanish Clb; Band; Mrchg Band; Rptr Nwsp; Cit Awd; Hon Roll; UCLA; Brdcst Jrnlsm/Ftbl Cmntr.

FENNELL, APRIL D; Bray-Doyle HS; Duncan, OK; (3); Church Yth Grp; FHA; Chrldng; High Hon Roll; Hon Roll; NHS; OK ST Univ; Law/Osbi.

FENTRESS, ERIC L; Sallisaw HS; Sallisaw, OK; (3); Library Aide; VP Natl FFA Org; Office Aide; Teachers Aide; School Musical; School Play; Variety Show; Bow Shooting; Rifle Shooting; Doing Mech Work On Trucks & Cars; OK ST Univ; Animal Sci.

FERGUESON, ADAM; Bennington Schl; Boswell, OK; (1); Chess Clb; 4-H; Quiz Bowl; Spanish Clb; SADD; Treas Frsh Cls; Rep Stu Cncl; Cit Awd; Hon Roll; Prfct Atten Awd; Southeastern OK ST Univ; Tchr.

FERGUESON, SHAWN; Bennington Schl; Boswell, OK; (3); 2/18; Church Yth Grp; GAA; Library Aide; Quiz Bowl; SADD; Church Choir; School Musical; School Play; Sec Frsh Cls; VP Soph Cls; OK Chrstn Univ.

FERGUSON, AARON D; Choctaw HS; Choctaw, OK; (2); Trk; Hon Roll.

FERGUSON, BECKY J; Mustang HS; Mustang, OK; (3); Church Yth Grp; FCA; French Clb; Model UN; Chorus; Church Choir; JV Socr; Var Trk; Var Vllybl; Marine Bio.

FERGUSON, CANDY L; Tuttle HS; Tuttle, OK; (3); FHA; GAA; Spanish Clb; Var Chrldng; JV Sftbl; Var Trk; Hon Roll; All-Star Chrldng; All Amer Chrldr; Rose ST Coll.

FERGUSON, CORI; Oklahoma Bible Acad; Pond Creek, OK; (2); FCA; Yrbk; Var Bsktbl; Var Sftbl; Var Trk; Var Vllybl; Hon Roll; Pres Phys Fitness Awd; Art.

FERGUSON, CORTNEY R; Madill HS; Madill, OK; (2); 16/100; Boy Scts; FCA; Science Clb; Speech Tm; SADD; Acpl Chr; Ofcr Stu Cncl; Wt Lftg; Hon Roll; Competative Acad; OK ST Univ; Vet Medicine.

FERGUSON, DANNY E; Harrah HS; Harrah, OK; (1); 1/180; Boy Scts; Church Yth Grp; FCA; Red Cross Aide; Scholastic Bowl; Ftbl; Tennis; Wrstlng; Hon Roll; Eagle Scout.

FERGUSON, DEVIN; Freedom Schl; Freedom, OK; (2); Boy Scts; FCA; 4-H; Natl FFA Org; Pres Frsh Cls; Pres Soph Cls; Var Bsktbl; Var Ftbl; Var Socr; Coll Bsktbl/Game Ranger.

FERGUSON, EMILY; Edmond North HS; Edmond, OK; (1); 111/484; FCA; Chrldng; Swmmng; Jr NHS; All City Swmmr; Chrldng Cmp Top Tm; OK U.

FERGUSON, JACOB R; Mooreland Jr Sr HS; Mooreland, OK; (1); Art Clb; Letterman Clb; Science Clb; Stage Crew; JV Bsbl; JV Bsktbl; Hon Roll; Jr NHS; Elctrncs/Mchnst.

FERGUSON, JOSH T; Catoosa HS; Catoosa, OK; (3); 18/140; Church Yth Grp; FCA; Spanish Clb; Var Bsbl; Var Ftbl; Wrstlng; High Hon Roll; NHS; Pres Acad Fit Awd.

FERGUSON, KRISTI; Comanche HS; Comanche, OK; (4); 1/61; Am Leg Aux Girls St; Church Yth Grp; Pres 4-H; HOBY; Band; Chorus; Rep Stu Cncl; High Hon Roll; Val; Farmland Yth Ldrshp Conf; SE OK ST U; Psych.

FERGUSON, ROBERT D; El Reno Sr HS; Yukon, OK; (3); Am Leg Boys St; Church Yth Grp; Cmnty Wkr; FHA; Key Clb; Quiz Bowl; Scholastic Bowl; Bsktbl; Ftbl; Sftbl; Order Of Demolay; Exec Vp Of Aero Tech Ed Cntr.

FERNALD, ADRIANNA E; Fairland Jr Sr HS; Fairland, OK; (3); 1/50; Church Yth Grp; GAA; School Play; L Trk; High Hon Roll; Pres Acad Fit Awd; KS ST Univ; Vet.

FERNALD, CALYPSO; Fairland Jr Sr HS; Fairland, OK; (4); 1/30; Church Yth Grp; Cmnty Wkr; FHA; Math Tm; Quiz Bowl; Red Cross Aide; Speech Tm; School Play; Sftbl; High Hon Roll; FHA Pres; JA Essay 1st Pl; OK Wmns Rpblcn 1st Pl St; OK U; Eng Tchr.

FEROLI, SEAN; Lone Grove HS; Ardmore, OK; (4); Am Leg Boys St; Church Yth Grp; Debate Tm; Scholastic Bowl; Speech Tm; Band; Drm Mjr(t); Pep Band; School Musical; High Hon Roll; John Philip Sousa Awd; Army & All St Bands; U Of OK; Music Educ.

FERRARA, ADAM C; Claremore Sr HS; Claremore, OK; (2); Church Yth Grp; Red Cross Aide; Mgr(s); Tennis; HS Ftbl Bsktbl Trnr; Phy Thrpst.

FERREL, MATTHEW S; Claremore Sr HS; Claremore, OK; (3); French Clb; Var Bsktbl; Golf; High Hon Roll; Hon Roll; OK ST U; Bus.

FERRELL, AMBER; Burlington Schl; Cherokee, OK; (2); 2/15; Church Yth Grp; Natl FFA Org; Scholastic Bowl; Band; School Play; Rep Frsh Cls; Var Bsktbl; High Hon Roll; OK Hnr Soc; OK ST Univ.

FERRELL, ANGELA R; Choctaw HS; Choctaw, OK; (2); Church Yth Grp; FCA; Church Choir; Sftbl; High Hon Roll; Val; Chrch Yth Grp Ldrshp Team; Sthrn Nazrene U.

FERRELL, CHARLIE; Hennessey HS; Hennessey, OK; (3); 5/65; Church Yth Grp; Natl FFA Org; VP Band; Jazz Band; Mrchg Band; Hon Roll.

FERRELL, JESSICA; Perry Sr HS; Perry, OK; (4); 8/66; Church Yth Grp; FCA; German Clb; Band; Chorus; Rep Stu Cncl; NHS; Jr Rotarn; Psych Lrng Tutorl Prog; All-Amer Schlr; Sthrn Natzrn U; Ed.

FERRELL, SHAWN E; Lone Grove HS; Lone Grove, OK; (4); 27/77; FCA; Office Aide; Chorus; Swing Chorus; Ofcr Bsbl; Ftbl; Wt Lftg; Hon Roll; Kiwanis Awd; Show Choir; Madrigals; Math Tchr/Coach.

FERRIS, AUTUMN; Wapanucka Schl; Milburn, OK; (1); 1/17; Sec 4-H; Natl FFA Org; Quiz Bowl; Scholastic Bowl; Sec Frsh Cls; Var Bsktbl; Stat Sftbl; Var Trk; Cit Awd; 4-H Awd; Horse Clb; Phys Thrpy.

FERRIS, WHITNEY; Wapanucka Schl; Milburn, OK; (2); 2/24; VP Pres 4-H; VP Natl FFA Org; Pep Clb; Quiz Bowl; Scholastic Bowl; Teachers Aide; Nwsp; Yrbk; Rep Frsh Cls; Sec Soph Cls; Top FFA Speechs & Beef Prdctn; OK ST U; Med.

FETTER JR, MICHAEL L; Central Mid-HS; Norman, OK; (2).

FEW, JEFF; Stigler HS; Quinton, OK; (4); FCA; Natl FFA Org; SADD; Yrbk; Bsktbl; Ftbl; Trk; Wt Lftg; Hon Roll; Prfct Atten Awd; Connors St Coll.

FEW, JUSTIN D; Haileyville Pub HS; Mcalester, OK; (1); Rep Frsh Cls; Rep Stu Cncl; Trk; High Hon Roll; Northeastern ST Univ; Cmptr.

FIDLER, JENNIFER R; Webster HS; Wagoner, OK; (3); Church Yth Grp; FBLA; Key Clb; Speech Tm; High Hon Roll; Hon Roll; NHS; NV-THS; Acad Ltr & Bars; Engrng.

FIEDLER, AMBER; Miami Sr HS; Miami, OK; (2); JV Chrldng; JV Gym; JV Tennis; Hon Roll; 96 Wrestling Soph Homcmng Attendant; Psychiatrist.

FIELDING, BRAD A; Wagoner Sr HS; Wagoner, OK; (3); Church Yth Grp; FBLA; Phtg Yrbk; Var Ftbl; Var Socr; Hon Roll; NHS; Okmulgee Tech; Auto Mech.

FIELDING, CHRISTI; Sulphur HS; Davis, OK; (3); Debate Tm; Drama Clb; FCA; FHA; Key Clb; Speech Tm; Chorus; School Play; Stage Crew; Yrbk; Cameron Univ; Speech; Drama.

FIELDING, JOSHUA A; Putnam City West HS; Bethany, OK; (4); Church Yth Grp; FCA; French Clb; Latin Clb; Var Bsbl; Var Wrstlng; NHS; Pres Acad Fit Awd; Latin Hnr Soc; Southwestern OK ST U; Pharmcy.

FIELDS, ANGELA R; Henryetta Sr HS; Henryetta, OK; (3); FCA; FHA; Intrml JV Bsktbl; Sftbl; High Hon Roll; Hon Roll; Secy Parlmntry Tm; Med.

FIELDS, CASEY; Walters HS; Walters, OK; (1); 14/68; Church Yth Grp; School Musical; School Play; Ofcr Bsbl; Bsktbl; Mgr(s); Yth Chr; Cameron; Comp Prgmr.

FIELDS, DAISY M; Wister Schl; Wister, OK; (4); 9/21; Debate Tm; FBLA; FHA; Library Aide; Office Aide; Quiz Bowl; Band; Chorus; Mrchg Band; Pep Band; Upwrd Bnd 3 Yrs; Carl Albert ST Coll.

FIELDS, DESTINY R; Western Heights Sr HS; Oklahoma City, OK; (3); 11/167; Church Yth Grp; FCA; Key Clb; Teachers Aide; Chorus; Church Choir; School Musical; Stage Crew; Crs Cntry; Tennis; OK Univ Acad Achvmt Awd; Outstdng Pre, AP Eng & Albegra II Stu; Northeastern ST Univ; Elem Ed.

FIELDS, ELLIOT; Walters HS; Walters, OK; (1); 10/68; Church Yth Grp; Ofcr Bsbl; Bsktbl; Mgr(s); Yth Chr Chrch; Cameron; Comp Oper.

FIELDS, EMITT T; Douglass HS; Oklahoma City, OK; (3); Church Yth Grp; Office Aide; Bsktbl; Crs Cntry; Phy Therapy.

FIELDS, GEORGE W; Blackwell HS; Blackwell, OK; (2); Boy Scts; Church Yth Grp; FCA; Band; Jazz Band; Mrchg Band; Var Bsbl; JV Bsktbl; Intrml Ftbl; Var Golf.

FIELDS, GIDGET R; Union Sr HS; Broken Arrow, OK; (3); 52/740; Church Yth Grp; Debate Tm; FCA; Hosp Aide; Key Clb; Spanish Clb; Chrldng; Trk; High Hon Roll; Jr NHS; Psych.

FIELDS, JESSICA L; Valliant HS; Millerton, OK; (1); 6/90; Church Yth Grp; 4-H; FHA; Hosp Aide; Chorus; Church Choir; Var Bsktbl; Var Chrldng; Var Powder Puff Ftbl; Var Sftbl; Super Ratings Dist Vcl Cntst; Voted Smrtst 9th Grd Cls; Crwnd Hnr Star; OU; PT.

FIELDS, JONATHAN J; Pauls Valley HS; Pauls Valley, OK; (2); Art Clb; Church Yth Grp; FCA; Bsktbl; Ftbl; Trk; Hon Roll; U Of OK.

FIELDS, LORI; Mooreland Jr Sr HS; Mooreland, OK; (1); Church Yth Grp; FCA; School Play; Stage Crew; Chrldng; Sftbl; Hon Roll; Hnr Stdnt; Piano; Southwestern ST Univ; Acctng.

FIELDS, RENEE; Putnam City HS; Oklahoma City, OK; (1); 19/487; Stat Bsbl; Chrldng; Score Keeper; Hon Roll; Pres Acad Fit Awd; U TX; Med.

FIELDS, STACEY D; Okmulgee HS; Okmulgee, OK; (2); 30/198; Church Yth Grp; Office Aide; Science Clb; Church Choir; Ofcr Stu Cncl; Var Mgr Bsktbl; Hon Roll; House Reps Pg; Nrsng.

FIELDS, TRICIA L; West Jr HS; Oklahoma City, OK; (1); Church Yth Grp; Spanish Clb; High Hon Roll; Jr NHS; Med.

FIELDS, TWYLA D; Purcell HS; Purcell, OK; (4); 6/72; Treas Key Clb; Treas Science Clb; Pres SADD; VP Band; VP Sr Cls; Capt Bsktbl; Hon Roll; Kiwanis Awd; Rptr NHS; Val; OK ST Univ; Elem Ed.

FIERRO, JOSE A; West Middle HS; El Paso, TX; (2); Spanish Clb; Stage Crew; Pres Frsh Cls; Hon Roll; Pres Awd Ed Excel; Engl II Awd.

FILBY, KYLE W; Catoosa HS; Catoosa, OK; (2); Church Yth Grp; FCA; Intrml Ftbl; Hon Roll; Prfct Atten Awd; Sprts Med.

FILCEK, AMANDA L; Choctaw HS; Nicoma Park, OK; (2); 36/387; Church Choir; School Play; Yrbk; Sec Frsh Cls; Sec Soph Cls; Hon Roll; Presdntl Ed Achvt Awd; Outstndng Stu Awd 94-95; Pre Schl Sunday Schl Tchr; OK ST U; Vet.

FILLMORE, ANDREA G; North Intemediate HS; Broken Arrow, OK; (1); Church Yth Grp; Dance Clb; Drama Clb; FHA; Teachers Aide; Band; Pep Band; Intrml Vllybl; Jr NHS; Ministry.

FILLMORE, GEOFFREY; Frontier Public Schl; Red Rock, OK; (4); 1/30; Am Leg Boys St; HOBY; Capt Scholastic Bowl; VICA; Pres Frsh Cls; VP Soph Cls; VP Jr Cls; VP Sr Cls; Rep Stu Cncl; Var Bsbl; Tech Stu Assn St Ofcr, Eastern Rgn Rep; OK ST U; Phy.

FILLMORE, KEVIN W; Frontier Public Schl; Red Rock, OK; (2); Church Yth Grp; Cmnty Wkr; Var Bsbl; Hon Roll; Prfct Atten Awd.

FILLMORE, MICHELLE; Maud HS; Maud, OK; (1); FHA; GAA; Pep Clb; Chrldng; Sftbl; Bus.

FILONOW, ANN C; Stillwater Sr HS; Stillwater, OK; (4); 10/300; Art Clb; Dance Clb; Drama Clb; Key Clb; Latin Clb; School Play; High Hon Roll; Hon Roll; NHS; Pres Acad Fit Awd; Crtve Wrtng; Macalester Coll; Neurosci.

FINCH, JENNIFER; Mustang HS; Yukon, OK; (3); 1/430; Church Yth Grp; Band; Church Choir; Mrchg Band; Hon Roll; NHS; Natl Hstry & Govt Awd; Southwestern OK ST U; Phrmcy.

FINCH, NOLAN; Bray-Doyle HS; Lindsay, OK; (2); 1/45; Church Yth Grp; FCA; Natl FFA Org; JV Var Bsbl; JV Var Bsktbl; JV Var Ftbl; Cit Awd; High Hon Roll; Hon Roll; NHS; OK Hnr Soc; Wdsmn Amer Hist Awd.

FINE, CHANCEY A; Meeker Jr Sr HS; Meeker, OK; (4); Blk Belt Tae Kwon Do; Multi Yr Listee; Master Tae Kwon Do.

FINE, ROBERT D; Locust Grove HS; Hulbert, OK; (2); Church Yth Grp; German Clb; Church Choir; High Hon Roll; Hon Roll; Schl Acad Team; OK ST Univ; Comp Engrng.

FINE JR, ROGER D; Locust Grove HS; Peggs, OK; (4); 12/90; Cmnty Wkr; German Clb; Office Aide; Spanish Clb; Bsktbl; High Hon Roll; Hon Roll; Jr NHS; NHS; Psych Clb; Sociology Clb; Vol Fireman; Northeastern ST Univ.

FINGERLIN, NANCIE; Skiatook HS; Avant, OK; (4); Am Leg Aux Girls St; Drama Clb; FCA; FHA; Natl FFA Org; Office Aide; Chorus; School Play; Nwsp; Hon Roll; OK St; Radio/TV Brdcstng.

FINLEY, BLAKE; Shawnee Sr HS; Shawnee, OK; (3); Letterman Clb; Library Aide; Pep Clb; Nwsp; Ofcr Stu Cncl; JV Bsktbl; Var L Golf; 4-H Awd; High Hon Roll; Hon Roll; AZ; Golf.

FINLEY, CHRISTOPHER P; Choctaw HS; Choctaw, OK; (2); Var Bsktbl; Var Ftbl; Var Trk; 4-H; Hon Roll; Pres Acad Fit Awd; Chrch Yth Grp; UMASS.

FINLEY, DANITA; Midwest City HS; Midwest City, OK; (3); Pres Church Yth Grp; DECA; German Clb; Band; Sec Church Choir; Mrchg Band; Var JV Mgr(s); Score Keeper; Hon Roll; Jr NHS; Southern U; Bus.

FINLEY, JACQUELYNE; Hugo HS; Hugo, OK; (2); 32/155; Church Yth Grp; Church Choir; Swing Chorus; Chrldng; Mgr(s); Sftbl; Hon Roll; NHS; Washington U St Louis; Ele Engr.

FINLEY, JAKKY; Hugo HS; Hugo, OK; (2); 24/150; Church Yth Grp; Cmnty Wkr; Girl Scts; Chorus; Swing Chorus; Chrldng; Mgr(s); Sftbl; Hon Roll; NHS; Tutor; Georgetown; Elec Engr.

FINNELL, TATE; Canute HS; Canute, OK; (4); 2/17; Math Clb; Natl FFA Org; Science Clb; Yrbk; Pres Frsh Cls; Pres Soph Cls; VP Jr Cls; VP Sr Cls; Ofcr Bsbl; Capt Bsktbl; S W OK ST U; EPA.

FINNERTY, JOHN; Muskogee HS; Muskogee, OK; (4); 22/303; Church Yth Grp; VP Computer Clb; Pres German Clb; Key Clb; Science Clb; High Hon Roll; Hon Roll; NHS; OK ST Univ; Elec Tech.

FINNEY, JEFFREY; Copan HS; Copan, OK; (3); 5/29; Pres Church Yth Grp; Pres Frsh Cls; Pres Soph Cls; Pres Jr Cls; VP Stu Cncl; Var Bsbl; Var Ftbl; Cit Awd; Hon Roll; NHS; Received Comm Awd For Fixing-Up Local Park; OK ST U.

FINSEL, BECKY; Mt St Marys HS; Oklahoma City, OK; (4); 5/62; Am Leg Aux Girls St; Pres Key Clb; Rptr Nwsp; Ed Yrbk; High Hon Roll; NHS; Jr Rtrn; REPS; Sec Ed.

FIRESTONE, BRIAN K; Velma Alma HS; Duncan, OK; (1); 1/52; Church Yth Grp; Quiz Bowl; Scholastic Bowl; Band; Jazz Band; Mrchg Band; Rep Frsh Cls; Rep Stu Cncl; Var Bsbl; Var Bsktbl; Gftd & Tlntd; Math, Sci Bwl; OBU; Cmptr Engr.

FIROR, JOSHUA N; Union Intermediate HS; Broken Arrow, OK; (1); Art Clb; Church Yth Grp; Spanish Clb; Hon Roll; Tae Kwon Do; Hockey; Guitar.

FISCHER, CINDY B; Chattanooga Schl; Chattanooga, OK; (2); 6/25; FCA; 4-H; Chorus; Rep Nwsp; Var Bsktbl; Var Sftbl; 4-H Awd; Hon Roll; Elem Ed.

FISCHER, ERICA M; Union Intermediate HS; Broken Arrow, OK; (1); Spanish Clb; Band; Var Tennis; NHS.

FISCHER, IAN T; Union Sr HS; Broken Arrow, OK; (3); 54/741; Boy Scts; Intnl Clb; Key Clb; JV Socr; Var Tennis; Jr NHS; NHS; Prfct Atten Awd; Hon Roll; Pres Schlr; Duke U Tlnt Srch St Recogntn; Teen Repblcns Sec; Laureate Pgm; TX A&M; Chem Engrng.

FISCHER, LEIGH A; Hooker Jr-Sr HS; Hooker, OK; (3); 1/42; Church Yth Grp; Natl FFA Org; Quiz Bowl; Band; Chorus; Pep Band; School Musical; High Hon Roll; NHS; Mrchg Band; OK Hnr Soc; Early Chldhd Ed.

FISCHER, SUSAN B; Chattanooga Schl; Chattanooga, OK; (4); 1/18; Sec FCA; Pres 4-H; Rep Nwsp; Yrbk; VP Jr Cls; Co-Capt Bsktbl; Sftbl; Kiwanis Awd; Val; FFA Reporter & Various Awds; Vllybl; FFA & Acad Schltc Meets; Murray ST Coll; Vet Tech.

FISCHER, TAIRA; Cache HS; Cache, OK; (3); 5/70; Church Yth Grp; Pres FCA; 4-H; GAA; Hosp Aide; Letterman Clb; Natl Beta Clb; Treas Sec Natl FFA Org; SADD; Varsity Clb; Exec Gold Card Holder; OK Hnr Soc; Dental Hygientist.

FISCHER, TINA; Grace Fellowship Christian Sch; Broken Arrow, OK; (4); 1/23; Chorus; School Play; Ed Yrbk; Rep Stu Cncl; Bsktbl; Vllybl; Hon Roll; Val; Natl Chrstn Hnr Soc; 1st Pl Sci Fair; Jrnlsm Awd; Sci Awd; Piano 11 Yrs; Oral Roberts U; Jrnlsm.

FISER, SASHA; Putnam City HS; Oklahoma City, OK; (2); Art Clb; Church Yth Grp; Ofcr Stu Cncl; Chrldng; DAR Awd; Art.

FISH, JESSICA P; Achille Schl; Achille, OK; (3); 14/45; FBLA; Chorus; School Play; Lit Mag; Var Chrldng; Var Sftbl; Hon Roll; Chrldr Of Yr 95-; Chrldng Co-Capt 96-; FSU; Marine Mammal Trng.

FISH, MONICA L; Wetumka Jr Sr HS; Wetumka, OK; (3); Art Clb; FHA; Pep Clb; Spanish Clb; Band; Mrchg Band; Ntv Amer Clb; FBLA.

FISH, VALLERY A; Guthrie Sr HS; Guthrie, OK; (1); 1/315; Church Yth Grp; Drama Clb; School Play; Hon Roll; Acad Excl Awd 96.

FISHER, AMANDA; Grove HS; Grove, OK; (1); Church Yth Grp; FCA; FHA; GAA; Ofcr Frsh Cls; Chrldng; Crs Cntry; Trk; Hon Roll; Stdnt Of Month; Mat Maid Wrstlng Team; U Of AR.

FISHER, BEN T; Owasso Sr HS; Owasso, OK; (2); Church Yth Grp; Drama Clb; FCA; School Play; Var L Ftbl; Var L Trk; Var L Wrstlng; Cmnty Wkr; Key Clb; Speech Tm; Teen Action Group; Drug Free Yth; Expressions; Bus Admin; Drama.

FISHER, BRAD J; Medford Schl; Medford, OK; (2); NHS; OK St Univ; Jrnlsm.

FISHER, BRIAN C; Tuttle HS; Tuttle, OK; (3); 1/110; Am Leg Boys St; Church Yth Grp; Var Quiz Bowl; Sec Spanish Clb; Church Choir; VP Stu Cncl; Ftbl; Trk; Hon Roll; NHS; Baush/Laumb Sci Awd; Schls Top Bio/Geog Stdnt; Teams Capt ST Wnnr; Eng.

FISHER, GRAHAM; Edmond North HS; Edmond, OK; (3); 70/400; Church Yth Grp; JA; Latin Clb; Mu Alpha Theta; Band; Mrchg Band; JV Bsbl; Var Ftbl; Var Wrstlng; NHS; Ath Trnng; Phys Thrp.

FISHER, JENNAFER; Yukon Middle HS; Yukon, OK; (1); Church Yth Grp; Quiz Bowl; Church Choir; Ofcr Frsh Cls; Rep Stu Cncl; JV Chrldng; High Hon Roll.

FISHER, JENNIFER L; North Intemediate HS; Broken Arrow, OK; (1); Band; Color Guard; Mrchg Band; Hon Roll; Chrch Orch; OK Hnr Soc.

FISHER, JENNY; Kingfisher HS; Kingfisher, OK; (1); Church Yth Grp; FCA; Rep Frsh Cls; Chrldng; Cit Awd; Hon Roll; USAA Chrldng Awd; All Amer Chrldr.

FISHER, JESSICA; Deer Creek HS; Edmond, OK; (2); #6 in class; Art Clb; Science Clb; Var Bsktbl; Var Sftbl; Hon Roll; NHS; Pres Acad Fit Awd; U OK; Pre-Med.

FISHER, KRISTA; Bartlesville Sr HS; Bartlesville, OK; (4); Church Yth Grp; Cmnty Wkr; FHA; Teachers Aide; Band; Color Guard; Flag Corp; Mrchg Band; Hon Roll; OK Univ; Nursing.

FISHER, LAUREN; Yukon HS; Yukon, OK; (3); Am Leg Aux Girls St; Hosp Aide; HOBY; Chorus; Pres VP Stu Cncl; Stat Bsbl; Mgr(s); Score Keeper; Hon Roll; NHS; Neonatal.

FISHER, MARY; Charles Page HS; Sand Springs, OK; (4); 88/388; Church Yth Grp; Cmnty Wkr; HOBY; Teachers Aide; Yrbk; Var Bsktbl; Var Crs Cntry; Var Sftbl; Var Tennis; Hon Roll; Campus Chrstn Clb; Evangel Coll; Elem Ed.

FISHER, NATHAN; Eufaula Sr HS; Eufaula, OK; (3); 3/92; Church Yth Grp; Math Clb; Natl FFA Org; Science Clb; Ofcr Stu Cncl; Ofcr Bsbl; Bsktbl; Hon Roll; NHS; Pres Acad Fit Awd; OK ST U.

FISHER, SHAWNTAE; Boynton Schl; Boynton, OK; (1); Ofcr Bsbl; Bsktbl; Chrldng; Northeastern ST Univ; RN.

FISHER, TAMI J; Chattanooga Schl; Chattanooga, OK; (2); Church Yth Grp; GAA; Chorus; Var Bsktbl; Var Sftbl; Hon Roll; NHS; Natl Sci Merit Awd; Southwestern; Pharmacist.

FISHER, TAMRA J; Enid Sr HS; Enid, OK; (2); 142/425; French Clb; Science Clb; Band; Mrchg Band; Pep Band; School Musical; School Play; Stage Crew; Rptr Nwsp; Hon Roll; Hrsbck Rdng; Perf Attndnc; Zoology.

FISK, BECKY L; Howe Public Schl; Howe, OK; (2); FBLA; FHA; Natl FFA Org; VP FFA; VP Frsh Cls; Rdng Bks; Carl Albert ST Coll; Vet.

FITCH, MARIAROSA; Cascia Hall Prep School; Tulsa, OK; (1); Church Yth Grp; Pep Clb; Spanish Clb; Var Sftbl; Hon Roll; Jr NHS; Sci Fair Reg Comp.

FITE, DARRIN D; Thomas-Fay-Custer Unified Schl; Thomas, OK; (3); Natl FFA Org; Chorus; Variety Show; Rep Stu Cncl; Ftbl; Trk; Wt Lftg.

FITE, MEGAN G; Mangum Sr HS; Mangum, OK; (2); Church Yth Grp; Sec Soph Cls; JV Bsktbl; Cit Awd; High Hon Roll; NHS.

FITTRO, AMANDA; Choctaw HS; Choctaw, OK; (3); 31/385; FBLA; Office Aide; School Musical; Variety Show; Chrldng; Wt Lftg; High Hon Roll; Hon Roll; Jr NHS; NHS; ST Hnr Soc; Rose ST; Pre Med/Bio.

FITZGERALD, AMELIA; Hilldale HS; Muskogee, OK; (2); 3/112; Yrbk; German Clb; HOBY; Key Clb; Science Clb; Church Choir; Rep Frsh Cls; VP Soph Cls; Var Bsktbl; Score Keeper.

FITZGERALD, LISA A; Union Sr HS; Tulsa, OK; (4); 33/629; Pres Church Yth Grp; Intnl Clb; Key Clb; Office Aide; Science Clb; Pres Spanish Clb; Teachers Aide; Band; Church Choir; High Hon Roll; OK U; Med.

FITZGIBBON, JACKIE; Fairland Jr Sr HS; Fairland, OK; (4); 5/40; Bus Profs of Am; Church Yth Grp; Cmnty Wkr; Debate Tm; FBLA; FHA; GAA; Band; Yrbk; Ofcr Stu Cncl; Masonic Awd; NEO A&M JC; Elem Ed.

FLADIE, JOSH A; Tahlequah Jr HS; Tahlequah, OK; (1); JV Wrstlng; Jr NHS; Prfct Atten Awd.

FLAHERTY, BECKY E; Shattuck Jr Sr HS; Shattuck, OK; (3); Church Yth Grp; FCA; FHA; Hosp Aide; Letterman Clb; Pep Clb; Red Cross Aide; Acpl Chr; Chorus; Church Choir; Certfd Red Cross Lifeguard; Northwester; Elem Ed.

FLAIM, AMANDA LEIGH; Heritage Hall Schl; Oklahoma City, OK; (3); 2/72; Am Leg Aux Girls St; Mu Alpha Theta; Hist Soph Cls; Pres Sr Cls; Fld Hcky; French Hon Soc; High Hon Roll; Jr NHS; NHS; Outstndng Heritage Hall Girl Frosh/Soph Yrs; STAR Peer Ldrshp Prgm; Rotary Yth Ldrshp Prgm; Intl Bus/Mrktng.

FLAMING, KYLE; Newcastle HS; Newcastle, OK; (3); 1/92; Boy Scts; Pres Church Yth Grp; Science Clb; Spanish Clb; Rep Stu Cncl; Ofcr Bsbl; Bsktbl; Ftbl; High Hon Roll; NHS.

FLAMING, MELISSA; Kingfisher HS; Kingfisher, OK; (2); Treas Spanish Clb; Rep Stu Cncl; JV Var Chrldng; High Hon Roll; Hon Roll; 2nd Plc At Chrldng Regnls; 3rd Plcat Chrldng St; OK St Univ; Psych.

FLAMING, MISTY M; Claremore Sr HS; Claremore, OK; (2); Church Yth Grp; Debate Tm; SADD; Chorus; Church Choir; School Musical; Hon Roll; Show Choir; Chrch Mission Trips; VBS; Pharmacists.

FLANAGAN, MISTY L; Marietta HS; Marietta, OK; (2); Art Clb; Church Yth Grp; Debate Tm; FCA; 4-H; FHA; GAA; Natl FFA Org; Speech Tm; SADD; Cmptrs; Sthestrn; Cosmtlgst/Lwyr.

FLANARY, NICK G; Wagoner Sr HS; Wagoner, OK; (3); 21/115; Am Leg Boys St; Church Yth Grp; FCA; Letterman Clb; Var L Bsbl; Capt L Ftbl; Var Wt Lftg; Hon Roll; Ntl Merit Ltr; Golf; NE ST Univ; Radio/Brdcstng.

FLANARY, SCOTT; Muskogee HS; Muskogee, OK; (4); 69/350; Am Leg Boys St; Cmnty Wkr; Latin Clb; Natl FFA Org; Ofcr Bsbl; Ftbl; Hon Roll; FFA Pres; DECA; Connors ST Coll; Wldlf Mgmt.

FLANDERS, SEAN P; Moore HS; Moore, OK; (2); Church Yth Grp; FCA; JV Var Bsktbl; Ftbl; Socr; Duke Univ.

FLANNIGAN, TARA; Miami Sr HS; Miami, OK; (3); 6/192; Church Yth Grp; NFL; Speech Tm; Band; Church Choir; Color Guard; Var Chrldng; High Hon Roll; NHS; Red Crss Lfgrd; Med.

FLATT, ELIZABETH J; Wilson HS; Wilson, OK; (4); 1/29; FCA; FHA; Natl Beta Clb; Office Aide; Sec Frsh Cls; Pres Soph Cls; Pres Jr Cls; Pres Sr Cls; Sec Stu Cncl; L Bsktbl; Bsktbl Hmcmng Queen; Tp 10 Pct; All St Fastptch Sftbl Centerfield; Southeastern OK ST U.

FLATT, SAMMY D; Carney Schl; Carney, OK; (4); Natl FFA Org; Teachers Aide; Band; JV Bsktbl.

FLEENOR, SABRINA K; Mustang HS; Mustang, OK; (3); Church Yth Grp; FCA; French Clb; Teachers Aide; Hon Roll; NHS; Wrestling Matmaid; RN.

FLEETING, AARON L; Bartlesville Sr HS; Bartlesville, OK; (4); Art Clb; German Clb; Spanish Clb; Hon Roll.

FLEETWOOD, JOSH W; Central Schl; Sallisaw, OK; (3); Pep Clb; Quiz Bowl; Stage Crew; Var L Bsbl; Var L Bsktbl; Cit Awd; Hon Roll; Prfct Atten Awd; OK HS Mock Trial Pgm Outstdng Witness 95; Bsbl Dist Champs 96; Bsbl Conf Champs 94-96.

FLELDING, CHRISTI A; Sulphur HS; Davis, OK; (3); Art Clb; Church Yth Grp; Debate Tm; Drama Clb; FCA; Key Clb; Spanish Clb; Speech Tm; Stage Crew; Yrbk; Natl Chrldr Asoc Whos Who; Cameron Univ; Psych.

FLEMING, ADAM N; Bishop Kelley HS; Tulsa, OK; (3); Varsity Clb; Var Bsktbl; Hon Roll; NHS.

FLEMING, AIMEE; Ft Towson HS; Fort Towson, OK; (4); 1/26; FCA; Pres 4-H; Quiz Bowl; SADD; Yrbk; Pres Jr Cls; Pres Stu Cncl; Capt Chrldng; Cit Awd; 4-H Awd; NEO; Phys Thrpy.

FLEMING, BRIDGETTE; Seminole Jr Sr HS; Seminole, OK; (2); FCA; French Clb; Math Clb; Chorus; Sftbl; High Hon Roll.

FLEMING, CODY L; Enid Sr HS; Enid, OK; (2); 16/425; Church Yth Grp; Cmnty Wkr; FCA; Chorus; Pres Soph Cls; Pres Stu Cncl; Var Bsbl; JV Crs Cntry; Cit Awd; NHS; OK Hon Soc; Teen Hlth Advsry Bd; Prnt/Tchr/Stu Assc Stu Pre; U Of OK; Pre Dent.

FLEMING, DENISE M; Nathan Hale HS; Tulsa, OK; (3); Var Socr; High Hon Roll; Hon Roll; Tulsa U; Psych.

FLEMING, JENNIFER; Enid Sr HS; Enid, OK; (4); 3/406; Am Leg Aux Girls St; Hosp Aide; Spanish Clb; Yrbk; Pres Soph Cls; Pres Jr Cls; Pres Sr Cls; Var Chrldng; Cit Awd; Sec NHS; OK Bapt U; Med.

FLEMING, SABRINA; Putnam City West HS; Oklahoma City, OK; (4); Treas Science Clb; Treas Spanish Clb; Orch; Phtg Yrbk; Rep Stu Cncl; Cit Awd; NHS; Yth/Govt; Med Clb; Stu-To-Stu; OK Chrstn U; Ansthslgy.

FLEMING, SARA L; Webster HS; Tulsa, OK; (3); Church Yth Grp; Cmnty Wkr; Science Clb; School Play; Var L Trk; High Hon Roll; NHS; Stck Car Rcng.

FLEMING, TANA E; Edmond North HS; Edmond, OK; (3); 69/441; Church Yth Grp; Cmnty Wkr; GAA; Mu Alpha Theta; Spanish Clb; SADD; Church Choir; Ofcr Jr Cls; Bsktbl; Jr NHS; Comm Svc Hrs Awd; UGA; Pre-Med.

FLEMING, TIM; Nathan Hale HS; Tulsa, OK; (1); JV Var Socr; Hon Roll; Clb Soccer Team Capt; Marine Bio.

FLENNIKEN, SHAWNA K; Edmond Memorial HS; Edmond, OK; (2); 213/410; Church Yth Grp; Spanish Clb; Band; Church Choir; Orch; School Musical; Variety Show; Chrch Lector & Usher; Notre Dame; Music.

FLESHMAN, AMANDA C; El Reno Sr HS; El Reno, OK; (1); Church Yth Grp; Teachers Aide; High Hon Roll; NHS.

FLESHMAN, CINDI; Merritt Schl; Elk City, OK; (2); 1/34; Rep FCA; Rptr FHA; Natl FFA Org; Rptr SADD; Pres Frsh Cls; Sec Soph Cls; Sec Stu Cncl; Capt Chrldng; Hon Roll; NHS; Piano; Taekwondo; Biochem.

FLETCHER, CHRIS; Graham Schl; Weleetka, OK; (2); 4-H; FHA; Ofcr Bsbl; Bsktbl; 4-H Awd.

FLETCHER, CRYSTAL M; Wilburton Sr HS; Wilburton, OK; (2); Church Yth Grp; FCA; GAA; Chorus; Church Choir; Ofcr Jr Cls; Bsktbl; Hon Roll; NHS; E OK St Col; Vet.

FLETCHER, ERIN; Grove HS; Grove, OK; (3); 9/140; Pres FHA; Key Clb; Rptr Spanish Clb; Band; Orch; Var Chrldng; Sec NHS; U Of AR; Music.

FLETCHER, JIMMY R; Enid Sr HS; Enid, OK; (2); Boy Scts; Quiz Bowl; Hon Roll; Jr NHS; NHS; CO Univ; Cmptr Sci/Prmng.

FLETCHER, JOSHUA; Central HS; Tulsa, OK; (1); Church Yth Grp; 4-H; Intrml Bsktbl; 4-H Awd; Hon Roll; Gld Star Achvmnt, Schlrshp, Sprtsmnshp, Ldrshp Tulsa Sprts Cmmssn & Publc Schls; OK ST U; Palntlgst.

FLETCHER, MANDY R; Meeker HS; Meeker, OK; (1); Church Yth Grp; Band; Flag Corp; Jazz Band; Mrchg Band; Hon Roll.

FLETCHER, PATRICK; Norman Sr HS; Norman, OK; (4); Am Leg Boys St; FCA; ROTC; Chorus; Swing Chorus; Ftbl; Trk; Cit Awd; Hon Roll; Jr NHS; Yng Lf; OU; Jrnlsm.

FLETCHER, RYAN; U S Grant HS; Oklahoma City, OK; (3); 5/350; Church Yth Grp; FBLA; Letterman Clb; Chorus; Church Choir; Ed Nwsp; JV Bsktbl; Var Crs Cntry; High Hon Roll; NHS; OK Bapt U.

FLETCHER, TRICIA; Mustang HS; Mustang, OK; (3); #1 in class; FHA; Key Clb; Scholastic Bowl; High Hon Roll; NHS; U Central OK; Erly Chldhd Ed.

FLEUR, NICK L; Elgin HS; Lawton, OK; (3); Boy Scts; Scholastic Bowl; Band; Mrchg Band; Socr; High Hon Roll; Hon Roll; NHS; Eagle Sct; Psychtry.

FLICK, DEBRA; Chisholm Sr HS; Enid, OK; (4); 34/67; Church Yth Grp; Cmnty Wkr; FCA; Natl FFA Org; Office Aide; Pep Clb; Spanish Clb; Speech Tm; All Amer Schlr; ST FFA Degree; Westark CC; Fin Farm Mgr.

FLOHR, RICKI; Ada HS; Ada, OK; (3); FCA; Science Clb; SADD; Var JV Bsktbl; Cit Awd; High Hon Roll; Jr NHS; NHS; Spanish NHS; Masons Stu Of Today Awd.

FLOOD, DENISE; Haworth Sr HS; Haworth, OK; (3); FHA; VP JA; Library Aide; Natl FFA Org; VP Jr Cls; Pres Sec Stu Cncl; Var Chrldng; Var Sftbl; Hon Roll; NHS.

FLORES, BARBARA S; Tipton Jr Sr HS; Tipton, OK; (3); 13/29; Church Yth Grp; FHA; Chorus; Rep Frsh Cls; Rep Soph Cls; Rep Jr Cls; Rep Stu Cncl; Var Sftbl; Hon Roll; NHS; Western OK ST Coll; Sprts Med.

FLORES, CRISSY M; Choctaw HS; Choctaw, OK; (3); Church Yth Grp; FCA; FBLA; FTA; Hosp Aide; Key Clb; Letterman Clb; Office Aide; Pep Clb; Science Clb; OK ST Univ; Vet.

FLORES, JEFF L; Del City HS; Del City, OK; (2); Boy Scts; Drama Clb; FCA; Quiz Bowl; Scholastic Bowl; Spanish Clb; SADD; Thesps; School Play; Stage Crew; Eagle Scout; OH ST; Cmmnctn.

FLORES, JESSICA; Frederick HS; Frederick, OK; (1); Church Yth Grp; Drama Clb; FCA; FHA; School Musical; Rep Stu Cncl; Var Chrldng; Hon Roll; OK Close Up; Var Choir.

FLORES, RUDY; Stilwell HS; Stilwell, OK; (2); Art Clb; Church Yth Grp; Spanish Clb; Ofcr Frsh Cls; Ofcr Soph Cls; Bsktbl; Ftbl; Trk; Hon Roll; Dist Winner Trophy/Voters Registration Poster Contest 95-; FL ST.

FLOW, CANDACE R; Hobart HS; Hobart, OK; (2); 20/80; FCA; 4-H; FHA; FTA; GAA; Ofcr Stu Cncl; Bsktbl; Chrldng; Var Sftbl; Hon Roll; H Clb; Psych/Ed.

FLOWERS, DREW; Westmoore HS; Oklahoma City, OK; (3); Boy Scts; Church Yth Grp; Cmnty Wkr; Hosp Aide; Key Clb; Teachers Aide; Band; Mrchg Band; Orch; Pep Band; Sthwstrn OK ST; Pre-Pharm.

FLOWERS, KYLE D; Meeker HS; Meeker, OK; (2); 11/70; FCA; Key Clb; Natl FFA Org; VP Soph Cls; Rep Stu Cncl; Var Bsktbl; Cit Awd; Hon Roll; Prfct Atten Awd; Meeker Octagon Clb VP; MS ST; Criminal Justice.

FLOWERS, REBECCA L; Central Mid-HS; Norman, OK; (3); Church Yth Grp; Cmnty Wkr; Hon Roll; OU; Acctnt.

FLOYD, BOBBY; Vinita HS; Vinita, OK; (4); Am Leg Boys St; FCA; Pres Math Clb; Spanish Clb; Rep Stu Cncl; Ofcr Bsbl; Bsktbl; Ftbl; OK Hwy Ptrl, Elks Ldg Cadet Lawmn; Enviro Clb VP; U Cntrl OK; Sprts Med.

FLOYD, SHIELA D; Vinita HS; Vinita, OK; (2); Church Yth Grp; FCA; FHA; Spanish Clb; Bsktbl; Cmnty Wkr; Sftbl; Trk; Hon Roll; Environmental Clb; OU; Phy Thrpst.

FLOYD, STEPHANIE; Spiro HS; Spiro, OK; (2); Drama Clb; FCA; Natl FFA Org; School Play; Yrbk; Chrldng; Hon Roll; PT.

FLUD, JACOB; Preston Schl; Preston, OK; (3); Church Yth Grp; Quiz Bowl; Scholastic Bowl; VP Jr Cls; Ofcr Bsbl; Bsktbl; High Hon Roll; NHS; Prfct Atten Awd.

FLYNN, JEFF M; Will Rogers HS; Tulsa, OK; (2); ROTC; Hon Roll; NYC Film Schl; Drctr.

FLYNN, LETISHA R; Enid Sr HS; Enid, OK; (2); VP Church Yth Grp; GAA; Letterman Clb; Spanish Clb; Church Choir; JV Var Bsktbl; Jr NHS.

FLYNT, PHILIP; Bishop Kelley HS; Tulsa, OK; (4); French Clb; Quiz Bowl; Nwsp; Yrbk; High Hon Roll; NHS; Pres Schlr; St Schlr; Acad Decathlon; St Mary Coll; Eng.

FOCHT, ERIKA; Perkins-Tryon HS; Perkins, OK; (3); Drama Clb; FHA; Intnl Clb; Pep Clb; Bsktbl; Chrldng; Gym; Hon Roll.

FOCHT, KANDYCE; Perkins-Tryon HS; Perkins, OK; (3); FHA; Intnl Clb; Yrbk; High Hon Roll; Hon Roll.

FOCHT, KENNETH R; Stillwater Jr HS; Stillwater, OK; (1); Ftbl; High Hon Roll; Hon Roll; Stillwater Police Explorers; Tae Kwon Do & Other Martial Arts; Hunting; Comps; Tools; Electronics; Lasers; OK ST U.

FOGLE, KATIE E; Choctaw HS; Choctaw, OK; (3); GAA; Office Aide; Var Bsktbl; Intrml Powder Puff Ftbl; JV Socr; JV Var Sftbl; Trk; High Hon Roll; Hon Roll; Ftbl Hmcmng Attndnt; Wrstlng Hmcmng Queen; 5a ST Fstptch Sftbl Chmp 94-95; U Of OK; Cert Ath Trnr.

FOGLE, LEIGH A; Western Heights Sr HS; Oklahoma City, OK; (3); Teachers Aide; Chorus; Poetry Wrtng; Cmptr Tech.

FOLEY, ALLISON J; Union Intermediate HS; Broken Arrow, OK; (2); 17/800; Church Yth Grp; Cmnty Wkr; Drama Clb; Hosp Aide; Key Clb; Spanish Clb; Band; Church Choir; Mrchg Band; Hon Roll; Northeastrn Band Masters HS All-Dist Hnr Band 3 Yrs; Marine Bio.

FOLEY, STEVEN M; Altus Sr HS; Altus, OK; (3); Boy Scts; ROTC; JV Ftbl; High Hon Roll; Hon Roll; Pres Acad Fit Awd; VFW Awd ROTC; Life Scout BSA; Acad Lttr; USAF Acad; Pilot.

FOLSOM, DEONNA R; Ryan Schl; Ryan, OK; (2); Church Yth Grp; 4-H; FHA; Band; Church Choir; Drm Mjr(t); Mrchg Band; Yrbk; Sftbl; 4-H Awd; Piano Cont Super Ratings; Swine Livestock Awds; East Cntrl; Spcl Ed Tchr.

FOLSOM, DEVON R; Wagoner Sr HS; Wagoner, OK; (3); 13/121; Teachers Aide; Rptr Band; Drm Mjr(t); Mrchg Band; Pep Band; Hon Roll; NHS; Prfct Atten Awd; Early Chldhd Ed.

FOLSOM, JENNIFER; Marietta HS; Marietta, OK; (1); Debate Tm; Speech Tm; Band; Mrchg Band; Pep Band; Cit Awd; Hon Roll; NHS; Pres Acad Fit Awd.

FOLSOM, JOSHUAH M; Midwest City HS; Midwest City, OK; (2); 155/488; Library Aide; Hon Roll; Prfct Atten Awd; Jrnlsm.

FOLSOM, MINDY; Perry Sr HS; Perry, OK; (3); Pres VP Church Yth Grp; Band; Jazz Band; Mrchg Band; Pep Band; Sftbl; High Hon Roll; Hon Roll; Jr NHS; NHS; All Amer Schlr; Medcl.

FOLSOM, NELLIE; Marietta HS; Marietta, OK; (3); Art Clb; Church Yth Grp; Debate Tm; 4-H; Girl Scts; Quiz Bowl; Flag Corp; Ofcr Sr Cls; Ofcr Stu Cncl; Hon Roll; Notre Dame; Psych.

FOLSOM, PEBBLES R; Morrison Public Schl; Stillwater, OK; (1); Hon Roll; Morrison Ed Assn Hon Schlr Awd; Cal U.

FOLSOM, TONY A; Mc Alester HS; Mcalester, OK; (2); Art Clb; Hon Roll; Outstdng Art Achvmt Awds.

FOLSOM, VALERIE; Clinton HS; Clinton, OK; (2); Church Yth Grp; FHA; Office Aide; Bsktbl; Golf; Hon Roll; NHS.

FONDREN, TUFFY G; Velma Alma HS; Loco, OK; (4); 8/44; Church Yth Grp; FHA; Natl FFA Org; Teachers Aide; Hon Roll; E Central U; Comp Prgrmmr.

FONT, ADIARI; Moore HS; Moore, OK; (4); French Clb; Band; Mrchg Band; Var Crs Cntry; Var Trk; Hon Roll; NHS; Acad Achvt Awd; Frnch Clb; Jr Escort; OU; Nutrition.

FOOTE, ANDREW L; Putnam City West HS; Bethany, OK; (3); 10/320; Church Yth Grp; JCL; Latin Clb; Scholastic Bowl; Orch; School Musical; L Crs Cntry; Var Capt Socr; NHS; Putnam City Slvr Strngs Schl Rep VP; Encore Strng Quartet; Slvr 7; Southern Nazarene Univ; Law/Med.

FOOTE, DANIEL E; Putnam City West HS; Bethany, OK; (1); Church Yth Grp; JCL; Latin Clb; Scholastic Bowl; Cmptr Sci; Art.

FOOTE, HOLLY C; Yukon Middle HS; Yukon, OK; (3); 1/412; Church Yth Grp; Debate Tm; Office Aide; High Hon Roll; NHS; Val; Yale Clb Awd; Med.

FOOTE, KAYLA J; Chisholm Sr HS; Enid, OK; (2); Church Yth Grp; FHA; Spanish Clb; Chorus; Church Choir; Hon Roll; NHS; OK ST Univ; Med.

FORBES, GEOFFREY L; Ponca City Sr HS; Ponca City, OK; (3); 37/371; Church Yth Grp; Band; Chorus; Church Choir; Mrchg Band; Pep Band; High Hon Roll; Hon Roll; NHS; Music Cmpstn; Painting; Gardening; OSU; Psych.

FORBES, THALIMIKA D; Webster HS; Tulsa, OK; (2); Red Cross Aide; Teachers Aide; Stage Crew; Red Cross Club VP; Indian Club VP; Peer Tutor Mltihndcpd; Photo/Jrnlst.

FORBIS, HEATHER K; Skiatook HS; Skiatook, OK; (1); Church Yth Grp; FHA; GAA; Band; Mrchg Band; Pep Band; JV Bsktbl; JV Vllybl; Hon Roll; Jr NHS; Hnrs Plaque; Dermatologist.

FORD, ADAM; Tulsa Emmanuel Christian Sch; Tulsa, OK; (3); Boy Scts; Church Yth Grp; CAP; Acpl Chr; Chorus; Church Choir; School Musical; School Play; Ed Yrbk; VP Jr Cls; Dist Chrstn HS Stu; Bus.

FORD, AMANDA; East Central HS; Tulsa, OK; (3); FCA; Key Clb; Spanish Clb; Chrldng; Hon Roll.

FORD, CAMAARA E; Millwood HS; Oklahoma City, OK; (3); FHA; JA; Sftbl; Tau Chptr Yth Group Ofcr & Sec.

FORD, CARRIE D; Durant HS; Durant, OK; (3); FBLA; JV Tennis; HOSA; CNA; Southeastern OK ST U; Pharmcy.

FORD, DARCY L; Bartlesville Mid HS; Bartlesville, OK; (2); 189/421; Church Yth Grp; Cmnty Wkr; Spanish Clb; Chorus; Stage Crew; Rep Stu Cncl; Bsktbl; Vllybl; Hon Roll; OK ST Univ; Med.

FORD, DIANA L; Charles Page HS; Sapulpa, OK; (1); Church Yth Grp; Cmnty Wkr; Natl FFA Org; Church Choir; Variety Show; Hon Roll; Prfct Atten Awd; NHS Candidate; Church Vocal Solos; Bus Mngmnt.

FORD, ERIN; Mustang HS; Yukon, OK; (2); Church Yth Grp; FCA; SADD; Teachers Aide; Church Choir; Chrldng; High Hon Roll; NHS; Schlstc Art & Writng Awds Hnrb Mntn; All-Amer Chrldr.

FORD, JACK; Bartlesville Sr HS; Bartlesville, OK; (3); 99/452; VP Spanish Clb; Var Capt Socr; Classic Cmptv Soccer; Bus.

FORD, JOHN H; Velma Alma HS; Velma, OK; (1); FCA; Quiz Bowl; Band; Jazz Band; Mrchg Band; Pep Band; Variety Show; Pres Frsh Cls; Var Golf; Jr NHS.

FORD, KATE; Gore HS; Gore, OK; (4); 10/32; Church Yth Grp; Pres FHA; Office Aide; Quiz Bowl; Teachers Aide; Band; Flag Corp; Mrchg Band; Co-Ed Nwsp; Pres Sr Cls; Connors St Col; Nrsng.

FORD, KIRK; Cement Jr Sr HS; Cement, OK; (4); 3/30; Am Leg Boys St; Boy Scts; Church Yth Grp; Cmnty Wkr; Debate Tm; Drama Clb; FCA; 4-H; JA; Natl FFA Org; SWOSU; Pre-Med.

FORD, KRISTY; Okemah HS; Okemah, OK; (4); 1/47; Am Leg Aux Girls St; Natl Beta Clb; Office Aide; Pres Jr Cls; Var Capt Bsktbl; Var Sftbl; High Hon Roll; NHS; Val; Danforth I Dare You Ldrshp Awd; U Of Cntrl OK; Pre Med/Chem.

FORD, MANDY K; Mc Loud HS; Harrah, OK; (1); 73/159; Church Yth Grp; FHA; Hon Roll; NHS; Dntl Hygnst.

FORD, NICK S; Duncan HS; Duncan, OK; (1); Church Yth Grp; Trk; Hon Roll; OK U; Med.

FORD, REGINA D; Duncan HS; Duncan, OK; (4); Church Yth Grp; Cmnty Wkr; FBLA; FHA; Key Clb; SADD; Nwsp; Yrbk; Mgr Bsktbl; Hon Roll; DECA Clb Rptr; Pepperdine Univ; Psych.

FORD, REX ANN; Watonga HS; Fay, OK; (3); 8/56; Church Yth Grp; Band; Jazz Band; Mrchg Band; Pep Band; Chrldng; Trk; High Hon Roll; Hon Roll; NHS; Hnr Band; SWOSU; Elem Ed.

FORD, STACY; Springer HS; Springer, OK; (1); Church Yth Grp; Natl FFA Org; Pres Frsh Cls; Hon Roll; OK ST Univ; Loan Ofcr.

FORD, TAYLOR A; Muskogee HS; Muskogee, OK; (3); JCL; Office Aide; SADD; School Musical; JV Var Chrldng; Gym; Hon Roll; Ecology Clb; RAID; Northeastern ST Univ.

FORD, TENESHIA N; Wagoner Sr HS; Wagoner, OK; (3); Church Yth Grp; FCA; FHA; Color Guard; Mrchg Band; Ed Yrbk; Capt Bsktbl; Var Socr; Hon Roll; Varsity Clb; Frgn Lng Clb; NSU; Med.

FORD, URENA B; Wister Schl; Wister, OK; (3); Church Yth Grp; FCA; Pep Clb; Science Clb; Teachers Aide; Nwsp; Capt Chrldng; Gym; High Hon Roll; Hon Roll; CASC; Cardiovascular Surgeon.

FORD, VANESSA; Millwood HS; Oklahoma City, OK; (2); Church Yth Grp; Library Aide; Pep Clb; ROTC; Band; Chorus; Jazz Band; Pep Band; Bsktbl; Trk.

FORD, WILLIAM P; Duncan HS; Duncan, OK; (3); Am Leg Boys St; Church Yth Grp; Key Clb; SADD; Chorus; Var JV Bsbl; Var JV Bsktbl; Var JV Ftbl; High Hon Roll; NHS; Ldrshp; OK Hnr Soc; Hlth Careers Club; U Of OK; Pre-Med.

FOREAKER, CRISTY D; Deer Creek HS; Guthrie, OK; (2); Church Yth Grp; French Clb; Science Clb; Band; Co-Capt Color Guard; Co-Capt Flag Corp; Mrchg Band; Orch; Mgr(s); 99 Prcntl Wrtn Exprsn Advncd Skills Achvmnt/Prfcncy Test; OK ST Univ; Eng Coll Prof.

FOREMAN, AMBER L; Union Intermediate HS; Tulsa, OK; (1); Church Yth Grp; Cmnty Wkr; FCA; Spanish Clb; JV Bsktbl; Hon Roll; DRY; YDA Soc Chprsn.

FOREMAN, CARA D; Harrah HS; Oklahoma City, OK; (1); Church Yth Grp; FCA; Natl FFA Org; SADD; Rptr Stu Cncl; Bsktbl; Sftbl; OK FFA; U Cntrl OK; Deaf Ed.

FOREMAN, MELISSA A; Shattuck Jr Sr HS; Shattuck, OK; (3); Rptr 4-H; FHA; Library Aide; Pep Clb; Chorus; NWOSU.

FOREMAN, ROMI; Ponce City Mid HS; Ponca City, OK; (1); Chorus; School Musical; School Play; Variety Show; Sec Stu Cncl; Var Bsktbl; Var Chrldng; Var Tennis; Hon Roll; Gymnstcs; Natl Chrldng Cmptn.

FORESEE, STACI J; Shawnee Sr HS; Shawnee, OK; (1); Church Yth Grp; Dance Clb; FCA; Spanish Clb; Church Choir; Yrbk; Sec Frsh Cls; Rep Stu Cncl.

FORESTER, AMBER L; South Intermediate HS; Broken Arrow, OK; (3); Church Yth Grp; French Clb; Intnl Clb; Church Choir; Yrbk; Piano Guild Superior; Comm Arts.

FORGIONE, TAMARA S; Macomb Schl; Macomb, OK; (2); 4/20; Natl FFA Org; Pep Clb; Sec Frsh Cls; Sec Soph Cls; Mgr(s); Hon Roll; Jr NHS; Stu Cncl Sec; Outs Stu Awd; OK Univ; Tchr.

FORMAN, MEARA; Millwood HS; Oklahoma City, OK; (2); Church Yth Grp; FHA; Office Aide; Chorus; Church Choir; Chrldng; Francs Tuttle Voc Tech Ctr; Bus.

FORREST, ZACHARY; Faith Chrstn Acad; Joplin, MO; (3); Church Yth Grp; 4-H; Band; JV Var Bsktbl; High Hon Roll; Hon Roll; Prfct Atten Awd; Poetry; Wrtng; Alternative Band Lead Singer & Lyricist; Pittsburg ST U; Eng; Music.

FORRESTER, BROOKE; Stigler HS; Stigler, OK; (3); Am Leg Aux Girls St; FHA; Speech Tm; SADD; Band; Mrchg Band; Chrldng; Hon Roll; NHS; Prfct Atten Awd; 1st Rnnr Up Jr Miss; 1st Pl RUS Essay Wnnr; Ftbl Attndnt 2 Yrs; Bnd Attndnt; FHA Offcr 3 Yrs; Northeastern OK ST Univ.

FORSBERG, EMILY; Claremore Sr HS; Claremore, OK; (2); Church Yth Grp; Hosp Aide; Quiz Bowl; Spanish Clb; Speech Tm; SADD; High Hon Roll; Prfct Atten Awd.

FORSLUND, ALICIA D; Shawnee Sr HS; Shawnee, OK; (2); Church Yth Grp; Scholastic Bowl; Spanish Clb; Chorus; Church Choir; Orch; Golf; Hon Roll; NHS; Piano.

FORSTER, JASON; Anadarko HS; Anadarko, OK; (3); Boy Scts; Church Yth Grp; French Clb; FBLA; Band; Mgr Nwsp; Mgr Yrbk; Ofcr Stu Cncl; Jr NHS; YABA.

FORSYTH, BONNIE L; Cushing HS; Cushing, OK; (4); 5/156; Cmnty Wkr; Sec Math Clb; Sec Science Clb; Spanish Clb; Stage Crew; Variety Show; Var Golf; High Hon Roll; Val; Accmpnst HS Choraliers, Church; OK ST U; Music.

FORSYTHE, ANDREA S; Charles Page HS; Sand Springs, OK; (1); Church Yth Grp; Cmnty Wkr; Debate Tm; Ed Nwsp; JV Sftbl; Hon Roll; Tulsa Yth Work Camp; Chrstn Cmps Club; OK Chrstn U Of Arts/Sci; Tchr.

FORSYTHE, HANNAH; Liberty HS; Tulsa, OK; (2); Church Yth Grp; 4-H; Pres FHA; Pres Soph Cls; Hon Roll; OK ST U; Scndry Tchr.

FORSYTHE, JEREMIAH K; Wilson HS; Wilson, OK; (2); 19/42; Letterman Clb; Var L Bsbl; Var L Bsktbl; Var L Ftbl; Hon Roll; FCA; 4-H; Natl FFA Org; Wt Lftg; FCA; Ftbl Dfnsv Plyr Of Yr 95; OU.

FORT, ANDREA; North Intemediate HS; Broken Arrow, OK; (1); Band; Orch; High Hon Roll; Jr NHS; NHS; St Schlr; Jazz Dance; Commrcl Art.

FORT, STEVE E; Hulbert Jr Sr HS; Hulbert, OK; (2); Church Yth Grp; FBLA; Var Bsbl; Var Bsktbl; JV Ftbl; Hon Roll.

FORTNER, KARA M; Deer Creek HS; Oklahoma City, OK; (2); 21/120; NFL; Science Clb; Speech Tm; School Musical; School Play; Hon Roll; NHS; Dentristy.

FOSBURY, MELISA F; Velma Alma HS; Ratliff City, OK; (3); SADD; Chorus; Rptr Nwsp; Hon Roll; NHS.

FOSHEE, ADRIENNE E; Wayne Public Schl; Wayne, OK; (2); Art Clb; FHA; Office Aide; Pep Clb; SADD; Teachers Aide; Ofcr Soph Cls; Ofcr Stu Cncl; High Hon Roll.

FOSHEE, JERI BETH; Westmoore HS; Oklahoma City, OK; (4); 22/622; Church Yth Grp; Drama Clb; French Clb; Scholastic Bowl; School Musical; School Play; Stage Crew; High Hon Roll; NHS; Val; U Of OK.

FOSSETT, CHRISTOPHER L; Wagoner Sr HS; Wagoner, OK; (2); Church Yth Grp; Math Tm; Var Ftbl; Var Trk; Var Wt Lftg; Var Wrstlng; Hon Roll; Traveling; U Of CO; Psychiatrist.

FOSTER, AMANDA B; Spiro HS; Spiro, OK; (2); Art Clb; FCA; Natl FFA Org; Band; Church Choir; Mrchg Band; Pep Band; Sftbl; Bsktbl Mgr; JC; Orthpdc Nurse.

FOSTER, ANGALA D; Mc Loud HS; Newalla, OK; (2); FHA; Hon Roll; NHS; Prfct Atten Awd.

FOSTER, ASHLEI; Valliant HS; Valliant, OK; (4); 12/86; Nwsp; Yrbk; Treas Stu Cncl; Var Bsktbl; Var Chrldng; Var Trk; Hon Roll; NHS; ECU; Ed.

FOSTER, BRAD; Claremore Sr HS; Claremore, OK; (3); Spanish Clb; Jazz Band; Ftbl; Tennis; Trk; Wt Lftg; Hon Roll; NHS; Prfct Atten Awd; Flying; USAF Acad.

FOSTER, CHRIS; Pryor Jr HS; Pryor, OK; (1); Church Yth Grp; L Band; Church Choir; Jazz Band; Mrchg Band; Var L Socr; Hon Roll; NHS; Pres Acad Fit Awd; Drama Clb; Competes Pryor Creek Track Clb USAT&F.

FOSTER, CORRIE D; Jay HS; Rose, OK; (4); 7/100; FCA; FBLA; Natl Beta Clb; Rptr Yrbk; Rep Stu Cncl; Var Bsktbl; Var Sftbl; NHS; U Of AR; Eng.

FOSTER, CRAIG H; Canton HS; Canton, OK; (2); Boy Scts; Church Yth Grp; FCA; Letterman Clb; Band; Mrchg Band; Pep Band; Ofcr Frsh Cls; Ofcr Soph Cls; Ofcr Stu Cncl; Pharmacist; Electrician.

FOSTER, D NICOLE; Claremore Sr HS; Claremore, OK; (1); Church Yth Grp; Cmnty Wkr; Phtg Yrbk; Hon Roll; Jr NHS; St Schlr; U Of OK; OT.

FOSTER, DANNY D; Owasso Sr HS; Owasso, OK; (3); Church Yth Grp; FCA; Rep Frsh Cls; Rep Soph Cls; Rep Jr Cls; Rep Sr Cls; Ofcr Stu Cncl; JV Bsbl; Var Ftbl; Wrstlng; Bus/Mktg.

FOSTER, DENNISE; Tahlequah Sr HS; Park Hill, OK; (4); 37/243; 4-H; Natl FFA Org; Cit Awd; 4-H Awd; High Hon Roll; Hon Roll; Jr NHS; NHS; Ntl Merit Ltr; Pres Acad Fit Awd; Langstn; Nrsng.

FOSTER, EMILY E; Charles Page HS; Sand Springs, OK; (1); Church Yth Grp; Band; Drm Mjr(t); Mrchg Band; Hon Roll; Lcl Libry Vol; TSA; Marine Bio.

FOSTER, FELINA M; Putnam City West HS; Oklahoma City, OK; (2); 158/385; Debate Tm; Drama Clb; Intnl Clb; NFL; Science Clb; Band; Color Guard; Flag Corp; Mrchg Band; Rep Stu Cncl; OCU; Lawyr.

FOSTER, JAKE B; Stillwater Sr HS; Stillwater, OK; (4); 46/350; Church Yth Grp; Cmnty Wkr; FCA; Key Clb; Spanish Clb; Acpl Chr; Chorus; Church Choir; School Musical; Swing Chorus; Gymnstcs Team & Chrldng Sqd Coach; U Of WA; Med.

FOSTER, JAMES D; Warner HS; Warner, OK; (4); Natl FFA Org; Office Aide; Quiz Bowl; Scholastic Bowl; Spanish Clb; SADD; Band; Co-Ed Nwsp; Ed Yrbk; Hon Roll; OK ST Univ; Elctrnc Engrng.

FOSTER, JEREMY M; West Middle HS; Norman, OK; (2); FCA; Rep Stu Cncl; Ofcr Bsbl; Ftbl; Wt Lftg; Hon Roll; Amer Legion Bsbl; Jr Olympic Bsbl Team 95.

FOSTER, JILL; Jenks HS; Tulsa, OK; (3); 20/550; Church Yth Grp; FCA; Mu Alpha Theta; Rep Chorus; School Musical; Sec Frsh Cls; Sec Soph Cls; Pres Jr Cls; VP Stu Cncl; NHS; Show Choir; Med.

FOSTER, KIM; Tahlequah Sr HS; Park Hill, OK; (3); Church Yth Grp; 4-H; Spanish Clb; SADD; Chorus; Nwsp; Ed Yrbk; 4-H Awd; NHS; OK Jr Brangus Breeders Assn Mem/Princess; Intl Jr Brangus Breeders Assn Mem; AIM Outreach Grp; Mission Work.

FOSTER, LARRY; Douglass HS; Oklahoma City, OK; (4); 1/113; Am Leg Boys St; Church Yth Grp; FBLA; Mu Alpha Theta; Church Choir; Mrchg Band; Pres Sr Cls; Capt Bsktbl; Cit Awd; SAAMP; Bus Mgmt.

FOSTER, LYNNAILE; John Marshall HS; Oklahoma City, OK; (3); Church Yth Grp; Band; Chorus; Mrchg Band; School Musical; Chrldng; High Hon Roll; Hon Roll; Jr NHS; Prfct Atten Awd; Metro Tech Nrsng I & II; Pediatrics.

FOSTER, MANDI; Westmoore HS; Oklahoma City, OK; (4); 117/610; Drama Clb; School Musical; School Play; VP Soph Cls; Rptr FTA; Rptr Sr Cls; Rep Stu Cncl; Trk; Jr NHS; NHS; Dentstry.

FOSTER, MARQUIS D; B T Washington HS; Tulsa, OK; (3); Church Yth Grp; Spanish Clb; Varsity Clb; Wt Lftg; Wrstlng; Hon Roll; U Of NE; Eng.

FOSTER, MARY; Davenport Jr Sr HS; Chandler, OK; (2); Girl Scts; Pep Clb; Quiz Bowl; Scholastic Bowl; Band; Sec Stu Cncl; St Lgsltve Page.

FOSTER, MICA; OK Schl Of Sci And Math; Clinton, OK; (3); Church Yth Grp; Cmnty Wkr; 4-H; Key Clb; Math Tm; Spanish Clb; Ofcr Stu Cncl; Golf; High Hon Roll; Hon Roll; Surgeon.

FOSTER, NATASHA S; Alva HS; Alva, OK; (4); Drama Clb; 4-H; FHA; Key Clb; NFL; Spanish Clb; Speech Tm; SADD; JV Bsktbl; 4-H Awd; Tchr Cadet; OK, Amer Kids; Occptnl Thrpst.

FOSTER, SARA; Edmond North HS; Edmond, OK; (3); 29/367; Drama Clb; HOBY; Hist Key Clb; NFL; ROTC; School Play; VP Jr Cls; Rep Stu Cncl; NHS; German Clb; Jr Rtrn Awd Ldrshp; SUN Clb.

OKLAHOMA

FOSTER, SHAWNA L; Hulbert Jr Sr HS; Hulbert, OK; (4); German Clb; Trk; High Hon Roll; Hon Roll; Pres Ed Awd, Outstdng Ed Improvement; World Geo Awd; Bacone; Dntst.

FOSTER, TONI; Wapanucka Schl; Wapanucka, OK; (2); Quiz Bowl; VP Frsh Cls; Hon Roll.

FOUNTAIN, KASSIE J; Canton HS; Southard, OK; (2); Church Yth Grp; FHA; Spanish Clb; Band; Mrchg Band; Pep Band; Hon Roll; NHS; Sthwstrn OK ST U; Chld Dev.

FOUNTAIN, STEVE; Canton HS; Southard, OK; (4); 7/45; Am Leg Boys St; Boy Scts; 4-H; Spanish Clb; Teachers Aide; Ftbl; Trk; Hon Roll; NHS; Eagle Sct; Cadet Lawmn Acad; OK ST U; Prof Art.

FOUNTAIN, STEVEN; Canton HS; Canton, OK; (4); 5/45; Am Leg Boys St; Boy Scts; 4-H; Spanish Clb; VP Stu Cncl; Trk; NHS; Cadet Lawman Acad; Close-Up; OK ST U; Commrcl Art.

FOURHORNS, NICOLE K; Canton HS; Canton, OK; (1); Pep Clb; SADD; Chorus; Drill Tm; Bsktbl; Hon Roll; NHS; Pres Acad Fit Awd; Pres Schlr; OK Univ; Law.

FOURNIER, MICHAEL P; Stillwater Sr HS; Stillwater, OK; (4); 124/340; Boy Scts; Church Yth Grp; Math Clb; JV Bsbl; Intrml JV Bsktbl; Hon Roll; Eagle Scout; Var Schlr Awd; OSU; Engr.

FOURNIER, ZEPHRA; Sapulpa Sr HS; Sapulpa, OK; (1); Church Yth Grp; SADD; Chorus; Ed Yrbk; Rep Stu Cncl; Capt Chrldng; Tennis; Hon Roll; Sapulpa Twirling Acad; AZ ST U; Envrnmntl Atty.

FOUST, CHRISTY; Thomas Jr Sr HS; Thomas, OK; (2); Church Yth Grp; FCA; FHA; Natl FFA Org; Acpl Chr; Chorus; Church Choir; School Musical; Var Chrldng; Hon Roll; St FFA Chorus; NCA Prfrmnc Tm; U Of OK; Phys Thrp.

FOUST, KOLINA D; Muskogee HS; Muskogee, OK; (3); 12/400; JCL; Latin Clb; Chorus; School Musical; Rep Jr Cls; Hon Roll; NHS; Teens For Christ; RAID Roughers Agnst Illegal Drgs; Show Choir; OSU; Mus Ed.

FOUST, ROY G; Thomas Jr Sr HS; Thomas, OK; (1); Boy Scts; Church Yth Grp; FCA; Natl FFA Org; Chorus; Church Choir; School Musical; Ftbl; Wt Lftg; OK ST U; Vet.

FOUTCH, AARON L; Stillwater Sr HS; Stillwater, OK; (2); Church Yth Grp; French Clb; Mu Alpha Theta; Natl Beta Clb; High Hon Roll; Cmptr Engrng.

FOUTS, MEGAN; Midwest City HS; Midwest City, OK; (3); 45/384; FCA; FHA; Pep Clb; Spanish Clb; SADD; Pres Soph Cls; JV Bsktbl; High Hon Roll; Hon Roll; OK Hnr Soc; OK U; Phy Asst.

FOWBLE, RYAN; Covington Douglas HS; Covington, OK; (4); Am Leg Boys St; Boy Scts; Church Yth Grp; 4-H; FHA; Spanish Clb; Varsity Clb; Band; Jazz Band; Mrchg Band; Nrthwstrn OK ST U; Pltcl Sci.

FOWLER, ANTHONY; Woodward HS; Woodward, OK; (2); Church Yth Grp; Debate Tm; German Clb; Letterman Clb; Cit Awd; High Hon Roll; Hon Roll; Kiwanis Awd; Golden W Awd; Med/Eng Sci.

FOWLER, AUTUMN N; Pauls Valley HS; Pauls Valley, OK; (3); Church Yth Grp; French Clb; FHA; Chorus; School Musical; High Hon Roll; OK St Hnr Soc; All Dist Choir.

FOWLER, BRITT D; Alva HS; Alva, OK; (3); Church Yth Grp; FCA; FHA; SADD; Chorus; Var L Bsktbl; JV Chrldng; JV Tennis; Var L Trk.

FOWLER, ERIN L; Kellyville Sr HS; Bristow, OK; (3); 1/100; Church Yth Grp; Natl FFA Org; Pres Jr Cls; Sec Stu Cncl; L Var Golf; Var L Sftbl; Hon Roll; NHS; Pres Acad Fit Awd; Sprts Med.

FOWLER, JACQUE; Hooker Jr-Sr HS; Hooker, OK; (1); 3/40; Church Yth Grp; Band; Chorus; Mrchg Band; Pep Band; Rep Stu Cncl; JV Bsktbl; Var Chrldng; Var Sftbl; Var Trk; Miss Hooker Princss Pagnt Wnnr.

FOWLER, JASON A; Ponca City Sr HS; Ponca City, OK; (3); 119/347; Boy Scts; Church Yth Grp; FCA; Spanish Clb; Teachers Aide; Church Choir; Var L Ftbl; Wt Lftg; Hon Roll; Chi Lambda Rho; OK Univ; Chiropractor.

FOWLER, JEREMY; Seminole Jr Sr HS; Seminole, OK; (4); 9/80; Am Leg Boys St; Pres Church Yth Grp; Debate Tm; FCA; Math Clb; NFL; Spanish Clb; Chorus; Church Choir; Ed Nwsp; Mck Trl Team; OSSA Comp Disc Hmnts Team St Champ; OK ST U; Engrng.

FOWLER, JERRI; Marlow HS; Marlow, OK; (4); 10/99; Am Leg Aux Girls St; FCA; Science Clb; Sec Spanish Clb; Teachers Aide; Rep Stu Cncl; Bsktbl; Capt Chrldng; Hon Roll; NHS; OK Hnr Soc Top 10 Prcnt; Mntr Mdtr; Lrnng Dsbld Tutr; U Of OK; Med.

FOWLER, KOURI C; Bixby Sr HS; Broken Arrow, OK; (1); Art Clb; Church Yth Grp; Socr; Cit Awd; High Hon Roll; Hon Roll; Jr NHS; 2nd Pl Schl Art Show.

FOWLER, MATT E; Muskogee HS; Muskogee, OK; (2); Band; Jazz Band; Mrchg Band; Orch; Pep Band; School Musical; Hon Roll; OK All ST Jazz Band 96; Estrn OK Hnr Bnd 2 Yrs; Ltrd Bnd 2 Yrs; Numrs Superior Rtngs Solo Contsts; OK ST Univ; CPA.

FOWLER, MATTHEW D; Warner HS; Porum, OK; (1); 4-H; Sec Natl FFA Org; Rep Stu Cncl; JV Bsbl; 4-H Awd; Hon Roll; Prfct Atten Awd; OK 4-H Livestock Judging Team; OK ST Univ; Vet Sci.

FOWLER, MELISSA; Seminole Jr Sr HS; Seminole, OK; (2); Church Yth Grp; Cmnty Wkr; FCA; French Clb; Library Aide; Math Clb; Science Clb; VP SADD; Acpl Chr; Chorus.

FOX, CHAD; Cameron Schl; Cameron, OK; (1); 2/40; Church Yth Grp; FCA; Quiz Bowl; Ofcr Frsh Cls; Ofcr Bsbl; Bsktbl; Wt Lftg; High Hon Roll; Hon Roll; NHS; OU.

FOX, DONNA R; Buffalo Jr Sr HS; Buffalo, OK; (2); FHA; Chrldng; Trk; Hon Roll; NHS; Pediatrician.

FOX, HAROLD G; Morris HS; Okmulgee, OK; (4); 6/72; SADD; Stage Crew; Var Bsbl; Var Trk; High Hon Roll; Hon Roll; NHS; Prfct Atten Awd; Pres Schlr; U Of AR; Phrmcy.

FOX, JAMIE M; Byng Sr HS; Ada, OK; (2); Cmnty Wkr; French Clb; FBLA; Natl Beta Clb; Office Aide; Speech Tm; Chorus; Church Choir; Stage Crew; Sec Stu Cncl; Aerobics; Play Piano; UCLA; Lawyer.

FOX, JENNIE D; Okeene Jr Sr HS; Okeene, OK; (3); #9 in class; Church Yth Grp; Cmnty Wkr; Debate Tm; Drama Clb; FCA; FHA; Library Aide; Office Aide; Pep Clb; Red Cross Aide; Northwest Hnr Bnd; Tri ST Hnr Bnd; Nrsg/Soc Wkr.

FOX, JOELEEN M; Dewey HS; Dewey, OK; (2); 10/83; Church Yth Grp; FHA; Teachers Aide; Chorus; Hon Roll; Spec Ed Coach.

FOX, JOSHUA L; Preston Schl; Preston, OK; (2); 1/40; Church Yth Grp; Red Cross Aide; Scholastic Bowl; Pres Frsh Cls; Ofcr Bsbl; Bsktbl; Hon Roll.

FOX, MEGAN L; Gore HS; Gore, OK; (2); FHA; Teachers Aide; Band; Color Guard; Mrchg Band; Ed Nwsp; Sftbl; NHS; Band Color Guard.

FOX, MELISSA D; Cashion HS; Cashion, OK; (2); Church Yth Grp; FCA; FBLA; Key Clb; Office Aide; Spanish Clb; SADD; Teachers Aide; Bsktbl; Mgr(s); Natl Yth Ldrshp Frm Law/Cnsltnt Rep; U Of OK; Bus Law.

FOX, STEVEN; Blackwell HS; Blackwell, OK; (1); Boy Scts; Church Yth Grp; Quiz Bowl; Band; Chorus; Jazz Band; Mrchg Band; Orch; Pep Band; School Musical; Plastic Model Bldg; OK Chrstn.

FOX, T BRIAN; Tipton Jr Sr HS; Tipton, OK; (2); Library Aide; Hon Roll; NHS.

FOYIL, DANIEL A; Owasso Sr HS; Owasso, OK; (2); Church Yth Grp; FCA; Ofcr Bsbl; Bsktbl; Ed.

FRAILEY, CLARK; Olive Jr Sr HS; Mannford, OK; (4); 1/25; Ed Am Leg Boys St; Debate Tm; Pres FBLA; HOBY; Scholastic Bowl; Speech Tm; Band; Mrchg Band; Ed Nwsp; St Dbtr Reg Champ; St Hmrs Intrp & Duet; FBLA St Champ & Natl Cmpttr; Hist.

FRAIRE, CARMEN; Woodward HS; Woodward, OK; (2); Art Clb; Church Yth Grp; Cmnty Wkr; FCA; FHA; FTA; Letterman Clb; Pep Clb; French Hon Soc; High Hon Roll; Arts.

FRAME, DEE J; Choctaw HS; Choctaw, OK; (4); 76/299; Church Yth Grp; JV Bsbl; NHS; HOSA; Natl Voc Tech Hnr Soc; Rose ST; Phrmcy.

FRANCIS, ASHLEY D; Hooker Jr-Sr HS; Hooker, OK; (2); Chorus; Rptr Nwsp; Var L Trk; Hon Roll; Eng Achvmt Awds; Span Hnrs; AZ ST.

FRANCIS, CYDNEY A; Stillwater Sr HS; Stillwater, OK; (2); 1/352; Church Yth Grp; FCA; Natl Beta Clb; Ofcr Stu Cncl; Swmmng; High Hon Roll; Pres Acad Fit Awd.

FRANCIS, ELVALYNN; Quinton Jr Sr HS; Quinton, OK; (2); 3/52; Scholastic Bowl; Band; Mrchg Band; Supts Hnr Stu; Dist & St Solo/Ensmble Super Ratngs Clarinet Solo; OK U; Vet Med.

FRANCIS, JUSTIN; Quinton Jr Sr HS; Quinton, OK; (2); Chess Clb; FCA; FHA; Scholastic Bowl; VICA; Ftbl; Wt Lftg; Hon Roll; Pres Acad Fit Awd.

FRANCIS, LISA; Pauls Valley HS; Pauls Valley, OK; (4); FHA; Spanish Clb; Band; Drill Tm; Flag Corp; Pep Band; Hon Roll; Math Hotline; Drug Awrns Wk; Aim High; East Central Univ; Sci/Acctng.

FRANCIS, THERESA A; Muskogee HS; Muskogee, OK; (1); Church Yth Grp; Hon Roll; Chrch Missions Walk-A-Thon; Elderly Care Provider; U Of OK; Corp Lawyer.

FRANCISCO, CODY R; East Central HS; Tulsa, OK; (2); 4/318; Church Yth Grp; FCA; Spanish Clb; JV Bsbl; Var L Ftbl; Var L Trk; High Hon Roll; Hon Roll; NHS; ASA Umpire; Spts Med Doctor.

FRANCO, CHRISTIAN; Memorial HS; Tulsa, OK; (2); French Clb; Spanish Clb.

FRANK, CASEY L; Lawton Sr HS; Lawton, OK; (3); Spanish Clb; Band; Mrchg Band; Pep Band; Nwsp; Zoology.

FRANK, CASEY M; Duncan HS; Duncan, OK; (3); 49/261; Church Yth Grp; FCA; Pres FBLA; Letterman Clb; SADD; Band; Drill Tm; Ed Yrbk; Sftbl; Hon Roll; HS Crimestoppers-VP; Bus Fin.

FRANKENFIELD, TODD; Ponca City Sr HS; Ponca City, OK; (4); Am Leg Boys St; FCA; Spanish Clb; Teachers Aide; Var Bsktbl; Var Ftbl.

FRANKLIN, BRENT K; Quinton Jr Sr HS; Quinton, OK; (3); Church Yth Grp; FCA; Rptr Nwsp; Rptr Jr Cls; Var Bsbl; Var Bsktbl; Var Ftbl; Var Trk; Hon Roll.

FRANKLIN, JACK A; Claremore Sr HS; Claremore, OK; (1); Church Yth Grp; Band; Mrchg Band; Pep Band; High Hon Roll; Mst Imprvd Novice Span Awd; Algebra II Ltr Awd.

FRANKLIN, JONATHAN R; Mangum Sr HS; Mangum, OK; (3); Drama Clb; Speech Tm; Band; School Play; Ofcr Bsbl; Bsktbl; Hon Roll; FBI.

FRANKLIN, JUSTIN W; Byng Sr HS; Ada, OK; (4); Drama Clb; FCA; French Clb; Office Aide; Teachers Aide; Ofcr Stu Cncl; Bsktbl; Trk; Cit Awd.

FRANKLIN, KATIE N; Union Sr HS; Broken Arrow, OK; (3); 107/741; FCA; FBLA; Office Aide; Spanish Clb; Chrldng; Gym; Pom Pon; Powder Puff Ftbl; Jr NHS; NHS; Outstndng Soc Stud Stu Awd; DECA VP; U Of OK.

FRANKLIN, KELLIE; Cushing HS; Cushing, OK; (3); Church Yth Grp; FCA; HOBY; Sec Frsh Cls; Sec Soph Cls; Ofcr Jr Cls; Bsktbl; Sftbl; Hon Roll; NHS; U Of OK; Meteorlgy.

FRANKLIN, LA SHONA; Madill HS; Madill, OK; (1); Cmnty Wkr; Computer Clb; FCA; GAA; Pep Clb; Spanish Clb; SADD; Teachers Aide; VP Frsh Cls; JV Bsktbl; U OK; Law.

FRANKLIN, LA TOYA; Millwood HS; Oklahoma City, OK; (4); 27/78; Church Yth Grp; FBLA; Office Aide; Chorus; Church Choir; Yrbk; Ntl Merit Ltr; UCO OK Cntrl; Sec Wrk.

FRANKLIN, MICHAEL D; Tuttle HS; Tuttle, OK; (3); 1/110; Math Tm; Quiz Bowl; Scholastic Bowl; Spanish Clb; Band; Mrchg Band; Hon Roll; NHS; St Schlr; U Of OK; Emergency Med.

FRANKLIN, NELLIE N; Inola Sr HS; Inola, OK; (3); Church Yth Grp; Pep Clb; Teachers Aide; U Of Milwaukee; Soc Wrk/Psych.

FRANKLIN, SARAH M; Union Intermediate HS; Broken Arrow, OK; (1); Church Yth Grp; FCA; Drill Tm; High Hon Roll; NHS; OK Univ; PT.

FRANKLIN, TISHA; Wilburton Sr HS; Wilburton, OK; (3); 25/79; FCA; Natl FFA Org; Chorus; School Musical; Chrldng; Hon Roll; Eastern OK ST U; Nrsng.

FRANTZ, EMILY; Aline-Cleo Jr Sr HS; Aline, OK; (2); 1/19; Church Yth Grp; FHA; Pep Clb; Quiz Bowl; Scholastic Bowl; Pres Frsh Cls; Var Bsktbl; Stat Score Keeper; Var Sftbl; High Hon Roll; OK Hnr Soc; Med.

FRASER, MARSHALL M; Bartlesville Sr HS; Bartlesville, OK; (3); Office Aide; Tennis; Cit Awd; High Hon Roll; Hon Roll; Jr NHS; NHS; Ntl Merit Ltr; Rotary Stu Of Monthy; Acad Excel Awd.

FRAZEE, KARI B; Pauls Valley HS; Pauls Valley, OK; (1); L Bsktbl; Mgr(s); Mgr Trk; Hon Roll; Prfct Atten Awd; Math I Award; English I Award; E Cntrl Univ; Sports Med.

FRAZIER, BRANDI; Apache HS; Apache, OK; (1); FHA; Natl FFA Org; Bsktbl; Chrldng; Sftbl; Hon Roll; FFA Greenhand Degree; Big Stick Awd Fast/Slow Pitch Sftbl; Star Greenhand Degree.

FRAZIER, D ANDRA A; El Reno Sr HS; El Reno, OK; (2); 1/217; Cmnty Wkr; FHA; JV Var Bsktbl; JV Crs Cntry; Mgr(s); Trk; Hon Roll; Jr NHS; Lgue Sftbl; Yth Prtcptn Grp; Crmnl Law.

FRAZIER, DE ANDREA; Millwood HS; Oklahoma City, OK; (3); Dance Clb; Debate Tm; Pep Clb; ROTC; Spanish Clb; Teachers Aide; Chorus; Hon Roll; NHS; Ntl Merit Schol; LA ST U; Corp Lwyr.

FRAZIER, GENA L; B T Washington HS; Tulsa, OK; (4); 4/264; Church Yth Grp; Cmnty Wkr; Spanish Clb; Teachers Aide; Hon Roll; NHS; 10 Yrs Piano & Dist/St Cmptns 1 Rtngs; Red Cross Clb; Attending Coll; Hendrix Coll.

FRAZIER, MIRANDA L; Spiro HS; Spiro, OK; (2); FHA; Library Aide; Office Aide; Teachers Aide; Band; Mrchg Band; Pep Band; Bsktbl; Trk; Hon Roll; Circle Trck Racing Stock Cars Dirt Trck; Westail CC.

FRECH, RACHEL; Woodward HS; Woodward, OK; (3); Art Clb; FCA; Letterman Clb; Bsktbl; Mgr(s); Tennis; Trk; High Hon Roll; Hon Roll; NHS; OK Hnr Scty; OSU Alumi Schlr; OU Slumi Schlr; OCU; Art.

FREDERICI, DAVID; Mid-Del Christian Schl; Oklahoma City, OK; (4); Pres Sr Cls; Pres Stu Cncl; Capt Var Bsktbl; L Golf; High Hon Roll; NHS.

FREDERICK, MELISSA; Canute HS; Canute, OK; (4); 1/16; Yrbk; Ofcr Stu Cncl; Bsktbl; Chrldng; Sftbl; Cit Awd; High Hon Roll; NHS; Sal; Acctng.

FREDERICK, MICHELLE; Woodward HS; Woodward, OK; (4); FCA; Letterman Clb; Pep Clb; Yrbk; Powder Puff Ftbl; High Hon Roll; NHS; Adopt-A-Hwy; Food Giveaway; Big Brothers & Big Sisters.

FREDERICK, RYAN M; Union Sr HS; Tulsa, OK; (4); 62/669; Church Yth Grp; Mu Alpha Theta; Spanish Clb; Band; Church Choir; Jazz Band; High Hon Roll; Hon Roll; Jr NHS; NHS; OK Baptist U; Bio.

FREDMAN, SHANNON L; Dale Sr HS; Mc Loud, OK; (2); FFA.

FREDRICK, RACHAEL; Oktaha Jr Sr HS; Oktaha, OK; (3); 4-H; Spanish Clb; Band; Mrchg Band; Rep Jr Cls; Chrldng; Gym; Trk; Hon Roll; NHS; OSU; Vet.

FREE, JOSH; Newkirk HS; Newkirk, OK; (4); 11/47; Am Leg Boys St; Church Yth Grp; Speech Tm; Church Choir; Var Capt Bsbl; Var Capt Ftbl; Wt Lftg; Wrstlng; Hon Roll; NHS; 2a-5 Dist MVP Ftbl 95; North OK Bsbl Coaches Assn All Star Shortstop 96; NW OK ST Univ.

FREE, MAGGIE; Newcastle HS; Newcastle, OK; (3); Teachers Aide; Sftbl; Hon Roll; Fastpitch Sftbl Little All-City Team & All-Conf Team.

FREEBERN, AUDRA; Kingfisher HS; Kingfisher, OK; (4); 1/93; Debate Tm; Drama Clb; FCA; Key Clb; NFL; Scholastic Bowl; Spanish Clb; Speech Tm; Ed Yrbk; High Hon Roll; Southwestern OK ST U; Accntng.

FREEDE, SIOBHAN V; Jay HS; Jay, OK; (3); FCA; FBLA; Rep Natl Beta Clb; Ofcr Stu Cncl; JV Var Bsktbl; Var Crs Cntry; Var Trk; Hon Roll; NHS; Law Enfrcmnt.

FREEMAN, ASHLEIGH D; Bethany HS; Oklahoma City, OK; (2); Church Yth Grp; Chorus; Hon Roll.

FREEMAN, AUDREY N; Nathan Hale HS; Tulsa, OK; (3); 84/287; Cmnty Wkr; Drama Clb; FCA; Key Clb; Library Aide; Office Aide; Teachers Aide; Band; School Play; Ofcr Stu Cncl; Demoiselles Pres; PT/LAW.

FREEMAN, BRYAN; Bartlesville Sr HS; Bartlesville, OK; (3); Church Yth Grp; OK ST U; Engr.

FREEMAN, CODY; Arnett HS; Arnett, OK; (3); 1/16; Natl Beta Clb; Natl FFA Org; School Play; Pres Jr Cls; Var Bsbl; Var Bsktbl; Ftbl; Var Golf; Hon Roll.

FREEMAN, ERICA L; Pauls Valley HS; Pauls Valley, OK; (1); Girl Scts; Rep Frsh Cls; Bsktbl; Sftbl; Hon Roll.

FREEMAN, JENNIFER L; Marlow HS; Duncan, OK; (4); 3/100; Church Yth Grp; SADD; Var Bsktbl; Var Chrldng; Var Sftbl; High Hon Roll; NHS; Sal; FTA; Library Aide; Acad All-St; Sftb All-St; U Of OK; Pre-Med.

FREEMAN, JERI D; Tishomingo HS; Ravia, OK; (3); Pres Church Yth Grp; Scholastic Bowl; Acpl Chr; Chorus; School Musical; High Hon Roll; NHS; Ntl Merit Ltr; Arts/Cmptrs.

FREEMAN, JOHN D; Amber Pocasset Jr Sr HS; Chickasha, OK; (2); Church Yth Grp; FCA; Natl FFA Org; Scholastic Bowl; Spanish Clb; Intrml JV Bsbl; Intrml JV Bsktbl; High Hon Roll; Jr NHS; Prfct Atten Awd; U Of OK; TV/RADIO Brdcstng.

FREEMAN, KARI; Tuttle HS; Tuttle, OK; (3); 37/110; Church Yth Grp; Girl Scts; Natl FFA Org; Spanish Clb; Stat Bsktbl; Score Keeper; Hon Roll; OCU; Public Rels.

FREEMAN, KENA; Tuttle HS; Tuttle, OK; (1); 25/102; Church Yth Grp; FHA; Girl Scts; Natl FFA Org; Bsktbl; Sftbl; Hon Roll; ST 3a Sftbl Team; Girl Scouts Silver Awd; Med.

FREEMAN, LA TISHA D; Picher-Cardin HS; Picher, OK; (2); 4/30; Church Yth Grp; Rptr FCA; Quiz Bowl; Science Clb; Yrbk; Sec Stu Cncl; Hon Roll; NHS; OK Hnr Soc; Engl Awd; Span Awd; Erly Chldhd Ed.

FREEMAN, LUCAS D; Dale Sr HS; Shawnee, OK; (3); 20/53; Church Yth Grp; Cmnty Wkr; Natl FFA Org; Quiz Bowl; Scholastic Bowl; Church Choir; Rep Frsh Cls; Rep Stu Cncl; JV Var Bsktbl; Jr NHS; Chrch Yth Group Cncl Rep; St Quarter Fnlst Bsktbl Team; All St Baptist Yth Choir; OK Baptist Univ; Music.

FREEMAN, MONICA B; West Middle HS; Norman, OK; (2); Church Yth Grp; FCA; Hosp Aide; Office Aide; Yth Alive; U Of OK; Tchr.

FREEMAN, RISA; Ponca City Sr HS; Ponca City, OK; (3); 42/384; Church Yth Grp; FCA; Spanish Clb; Chorus; Var Chrldng; Cit Awd; DAR Awd; High Hon Roll; Jr NHS; NHS.

FREMIN, AMY C; Ponca City Sr HS; Ponca City, OK; (2); Cmnty Wkr; Debate Tm; Drama Clb; NFL; Chorus; Bsktbl; Vllybl; Hon Roll; NHS; Lifeguard; 1st-3rd Grdrs Readng Tutor.

FREMIN, JENEFER; Eisenhower Sr HS; Lawton, OK; (1); FCA; GAA; Key Clb; Pep Clb; Var Capt Bsktbl; Var Chrldng; Powder Puff Ftbl; Var Capt Trk; High Hon Roll; Jr NHS; Work With Chldrn.

FRENCH, AMY B; Blanchard Jr Sr HS; Blanchard, OK; (3); 17/63; Sec Church Yth Grp; Treas Rptr FHA; Chrmn Pep Clb; Spanish Clb; Color Guard; Co-Ed Nwsp; Treas Frsh Cls; VP Jr Cls; Hon Roll; Jrnlsm Awd 95-; OK City Univ.

FRENCH, APRIL NICOLE; Will Rogers HS; Tulsa, OK; (2); 2/329; Treas English Clb; French Clb; Scholastic Bowl; Band; Mrchg Band; Pep Band; Lit Mag; Hon Roll; Austin Col Frgn Lang Wk 2 Super; U Of Tulsa; Math.

FRENCH, KERA L; Tecumseh HS; Tecumseh, OK; (3); FCA; Natl Beta Clb; Treas Frsh Cls; Sec Soph Cls; Treas Jr Cls; Rep Stu Cncl; Var L Tennis; NHS; Seminole ST Coll; Acctng.

FRENCH, MISTY D; Cache HS; Cache, OK; (4); Computer Clb; Science Clb; Spanish Clb; SADD; Teachers Aide; Band; Mrchg Band; Yrbk; High Hon Roll; NHS; Natl Sci Merit Awd; Natl Band Merit Awd; Natl Math Merit Awd; OK ST Univ; Med.

FRERE, JACQUELYN D; Union Intermediate HS; Broken Arrow, OK; (2); 12/800; Church Yth Grp; Key Clb; Band; Mrchg Band; Orch; Pep Band; High Hon Roll; Jr NHS; Hist NHS; Chrch Admin Bd & Nominating Cmmtte; Mech Engr.

FREY, SARAH K; Charles Page HS; Sand Springs, OK; (1); Dance Clb; Drama Clb; Thesps; Drill Tm; School Musical; Chrldng; Pom Pon; Hon Roll; NHS.

FRICK, SHELLEY R; Putnam City North HS; Oklahoma City, OK; (2); Church Yth Grp; FCA; Letterman Clb; Orch; Bsktbl; Var Capt Sftbl; High Hon Roll; Outstdng Mscn Awd; Starting First Baseman All City Tm; U Of OK; Med.

FRIDAY, JASON E; Union Sr HS; Broken Arrow, OK; (3); FCA; FBLA; Key Clb; Var Bsbl; JV Wt Lftg; High Hon Roll; Jr NHS; Pres Acad Fit Awd; OK Univ; Law Enfrcmnt.

FRIEDL, FRANK; Central HS; Tulsa, OK; (2); Church Yth Grp; ROTC; Color Guard; High Hon Roll; NHS; Stu Of Today Awd; JROTC Rifle Drill & Marksmanship Tms; Air Force Acad; Opers Research.

FRIEDL, LISA M; Union Sr HS; Tulsa, OK; (3); 2/741; Cmnty Wkr; Hosp Aide; Key Clb; Spanish Clb; Orch; Rep Jr Cls; High Hon Roll; Hon Roll; NHS; Spanish NHS.

FRIEND, CARL A; Bishop Kelley HS; Claremore, OK; (2); Boy Scts; Church Yth Grp; Cmnty Wkr; Ftbl; Golf; Wrstlng; NHS; Model Railroad Clb; Var Ltr In Wrestling; Eagle Rank In Boy Scts; Jr Scout Master; US Naval Acad; Sys Engrng.

FRIEND, CHRISSY; Bartlesville Sr HS; Bartlesville, OK; (3); 62/441; Church Yth Grp; Chorus; VP Sr Cls; Rep Stu Cncl; Var L Socr; Hon Roll; Spanish NHS; Vol Local Lit Cncl To Tutor Illiterate Children; U Of OK; Acctng.

FRIES, SILVER A; Shawnee Sr HS; Shawnee, OK; (2); Drama Clb; French Clb; Scholastic Bowl; Yrbk; Hon Roll; Corp Law.

FRIESEN, CHRISTY R; Arapaho Schl; Custer City, OK; (2); 4/30; Cmnty Wkr; Score Keeper; Hon Roll; Kiwanis Awd; NHS; SWOSU Weatherford OK.

FRIESEN, KELLY; Thomas Jr Sr HS; Thomas, OK; (1); 1/45; Church Yth Grp; FCA; FHA; Chorus; Church Choir; School Musical; Bsktbl; Chrldng; Sftbl; High Hon Roll; OK ST U; Vet.

FRIETZE, TIFFANY M; Pawnee HS; Pawnee, OK; (2); Church Yth Grp; Cmnty Wkr; FHA; Natl Beta Clb; Pep Clb; Red Cross Aide; Band; Mrchg Band; Var Chrldng; Hon Roll; NPIC; 2 Title IX Indian Ed Acad Achvmt Awds; Various Certs Of Excl Given By Tchrs; Tonkawa JC; Bio; Vet Med.

FRIEZE, JOSHUA D; Oologah HS; Oologah, OK; (4); 39/100; Church Yth Grp; Drama Clb; Speech Tm; Band; Jazz Band; Mrchg Band; Orch; Pep Band; School Musical; Rptr Nwsp; All St Bnd; All St Jazz Bnd; All Dist Bnd; NE OK A&M; Mus Ed.

FRITSCH, AMBER; Cache HS; Cache, OK; (3); 15/65; Church Yth Grp; FCA; GAA; Natl Beta Clb; Sec Frsh Cls; Sec Soph Cls; Var Bsktbl; Var Trk; Hon Roll; NHS; Univ Of AL; Corp Lwyr.

FRITTS, CLIFFORD A; Gore HS; Gore, OK; (3); Teachers Aide; Church Choir; JV Var Bsktbl; JV Var Ftbl; JV Var Wt Lftg; NE St Univ; Mus.

FRITTS, JAMIE T; Choctaw HS; Choctaw, OK; (4); Church Yth Grp; FHA; Key Clb; Chorus; Gym; School Musical; Capt Chrldng; Co-Capt Pom Pon; Powder Puff Ftbl; Miss Choctaw 96-97; Miss Congeniality 96-97; Pom Pon Squad Co-Capt; UCD.

FRITTS, SHANNON M; Cushing HS; Cushing, OK; (1); Church Yth Grp; Dance Clb; Teachers Aide; Hon Roll; Pres Acad Fit Awd; OSU; Elem Ed.

FRITZ, BRANDON M; Union Intermediate HS; Broken Arrow, OK; (2); Spanish Clb; Socr; Hon Roll; NHS; Geology.

FRITZ, CHRISTY R; Union Sr HS; Tulsa, OK; (3); Church Yth Grp; Hosp Aide; Service Clb; Jazz Band; Mrchg Band; Rep Frsh Cls; Hon Roll; NHS; USC Sec; Chrch Wrshp Tm; PT.

FRITZ, MANDY; Mountain View-Gotebo HS; Mountain View, OK; (4); 1/32; Pres FCA; Cit Awd; Gov Hon Prg Awd; High Hon Roll; Hon Roll; NHS; Ntl Merit SF; Pres Acad Fit Awd; Pres Schlr; St Schlr; FFA Pres; Masonic Lodge Stdnt Of Today Schlrshp; Valedictorian Schlrshp; OK ST Univ; Ag Comm.

FRITZ, TALLENA; Chisholm Sr HS; Enid, OK; (1); 1/86; Debate Tm; FCA; Speech Tm; Band; Jazz Band; Mrchg Band; Pep Band; Sftbl; Cit Awd; High Hon Roll; U Of OK; Law.

FRIZZELL, ADAM R; Bethel HS; Tecumseh, OK; (1); Natl FFA Org; Ofcr Bsbl; Crs Cntry; Ftbl; Trk; Prfct Atten Awd.

FRIZZELL, ALANA D; Choctaw HS; Choctaw, OK; (2); Church Yth Grp; Cmnty Wkr; Chorus; Church Choir; Wrstlng; Cit Awd; High Hon Roll; Hon Roll.

FRIZZELL, STEVEN; Miami Sr HS; Miami, OK; (4); 24/130; Band; Jazz Band; Mrchg Band; Pep Band; High Hon Roll; Hon Roll; Jr NHS; NHS; Ntl Merit Ltr; Prfct Atten Awd; U AR; Arch.

FROEHLICH, JUSTIN; Midwest City HS; Midwest City, OK; (3); 21/384; FCA; German Clb; Var Bsbl; Var Ftbl; JV Wrstlng; Hon Roll; NHS; Acad Clb.

FROGGE, ASHLEY; Collinsville HS; Collinsville, OK; (3); 8/105; Church Yth Grp; Cmnty Wkr; FCA; GAA; JA; Red Cross Aide; Scholastic Bowl; SADD; Teachers Aide; Varsity Clb; U Of OK; Pharm.

FROMM, AMY; Bluejacket Schl; Bluejacket, OK; (1); 3/22; FHA; Band; Pep Band; Sec Frsh Cls; Hon Roll; Sal; FHA Star Events; NEO A&M; Tchr.

FRY, ADAM R; Shawnee Sr HS; Shawnee, OK; (1); FCA; Office Aide; Varsity Clb; Tennis; Wt Lftg; Cit Awd; High Hon Roll; Hon Roll; NHS; Big Brothers, Big Sisters Act; OU; Med; Sci.

FRY, AMANDA J; Lone Grove HS; Lone Grove, OK; (2); Math Clb; Science Clb; Chorus; School Musical; Var Bsktbl; Powder Puff Ftbl; Hon Roll.

FRY, CHRISTY; Jenks HS; Tulsa, OK; (4); 98/519; Church Yth Grp; FCA; Math Clb; Mu Alpha Theta; Office Aide; Pep Clb; Chorus; Ofcr Stu Cncl; Powder Puff Ftbl; Hon Roll; Gamma Sigma; Abilene Chrstn U; Bus.

FRY, JAKE M; Blackwell HS; Blackwell, OK; (2); 17/138; Church Yth Grp; FCA; Letterman Clb; Spanish Clb; VP Soph Cls; VP Jr Cls; JV Var Ftbl; Var Golf; Wt Lftg; Hon Roll; OK ST U; Sprts Med.

FRY, JAMIE J; Collinsville HS; Collinsville, OK; (4); 44/96; Library Aide; Chorus; Hon Roll; NHS; HOSA; Regnl Ldrshp Conf 2nd Pl Creative Prblm Slvng; ST Ldrshp Conf 3rd Pl Creative Prblm Slvng; Tulsa JC; Nrsng.

FRY, JARROD B; Muskogee HS; Muskogee, OK; (4); 105/303; French Clb; Mu Alpha Theta; Pep Clb; Var Ftbl; Var Wt Lftg; High Hon Roll; Hon Roll; ADFPA Natl Chmpn Pwrlftr 96; ST Chmpn Pwrlftr 95-; Outstndg Lftr Awd 96; NSU.

FRY, MICAH; Central HS; Tulsa, OK; (1); Computer Clb; Orch; High Hon Roll; Hon Roll; All Dist Hnr Orch; Schl Metro Hnr Orch.

FRY, THERESA A; Vinita HS; Vinita, OK; (2); Spanish Clb; Band; Mrchg Band; Pep Band; Trk; Hon Roll; NHS; Tutoring; Tae Kwon Do; Kick Boxing; Pdtrcn.

FRYE, BYRON F; Ada HS; Ada, OK; (4); 50/356; Boy Scts; FCA; Math Clb; SADD; Church Choir; Mrchg Band; Orch; Pep Band; Bsktbl; High Hon Roll; E Central U; Enviro Sci.

FRYE, GRANT R; Nathan Hale HS; Tulsa, OK; (3); Cmnty Wkr; Science Clb; Teachers Aide; VICA; Cit Awd; Hon Roll; OSU; Automotive Technician.

FUCHS, AARON; Macomb Schl; Macomb, OK; (1); JV Var Bsbl; JV Var Bsktbl; High Hon Roll; OK Hnr Soc; OK Heritage Schlrshp.

FUCHS, BRIAN D; Stillwater Sr HS; Stillwater, OK; (3); Church Yth Grp; FCA; French Clb; Spanish Clb; Bible Bwl; Envrnmntl Clb; Psych.

FUCHS, MELISSA; Macomb Schl; Macomb, OK; (3); Pres Frsh Cls; Sec Jr Cls; Rep Stu Cncl; Chrldng; Sftbl; High Hon Roll; NHS; OK Hrtg Schlrshp; Stu Cncl.

FUENTE, JAMIE L; Union Sr HS; Tulsa, OK; (3); 80/741; DECA; FCA; Var L Bsktbl; Var L Sftbl; High Hon Roll; Jr NHS; NHS; Sftbl All Conf; Acad Ltrs; Hist/Alg I Awds; Elem Educ.

FUENTES, ALFREDO; Northeast HS; Oklahoma City, OK; (4); Church Yth Grp; Drama Clb; FBLA; Spanish Clb; Crs Cntry; Socr; Hon Roll; Pres Schlr; Rose ST Coll.

FUENTES, ANGELA M; Northeast HS; Oklahoma City, OK; (2); Spanish Clb; JV Var Vllybl; Hon Roll; Comps; Rose ST Coll; Receptionist.

FUENTEZ, AURORA; Burns Flat-Dill City Jshs; Burns Flat, OK; (4); 11/32; Church Yth Grp; FHA; German Clb; Pep Clb; Teachers Aide; Band; Chorus; Church Choir; School Musical; School Play; SW OK ST Univ; Cmrcl Art.

FUERST, PAMALA; Broken Arrow Sr HS; Broken Arrow, OK; (3); Boy Scts; Church Yth Grp; Computer Clb; Debate Tm; Drama Clb; FCA; JA; Office Aide; Church Choir; Yrbk; Explr Srch & Rsc; Mltry Stratgy Gmng Club; Ldrshp; GMI; Phy Ther.

FUGATE, ASHLEY D; Kellyville Sr HS; Sapulpa, OK; (2); HOBY; Scholastic Bowl; Pres Soph Cls; Ofcr Stu Cncl; Var L Bsktbl; L Var Sftbl; High Hon Roll; NHS; Pres Schlr; Sertoma Clb.

FUGETT, ERIC B; Muldrow HS; Muldrow, OK; (1); Natl Beta Clb; Scholastic Bowl; Spanish Clb; High Hon Roll; Hon Roll; NHS; OU; Cardiovascular Surgry.

FUKSA, ERIN; Hennessey HS; Hennessey, OK; (2); FCA; FHA; Chrldng; Hon Roll; Dance Cmptn Qualified For Natls; Pharmacy.

FULBRIGHT, DUSTIN; Warner HS; Warner, OK; (2); Band; High Hon Roll; Hon Roll; ST Hnr Soc; OK ST U; Psych/Med.

FULCO, LESLIE A; Bishop Mcguinness HS; Oklahoma City, OK; (2); 49/167; Pep Clb; Teachers Aide; Ed Lit Mag; NHS; Theater, Art & Music; Med.

FULKERSON, CHRIS; Hennessey HS; Hennessey, OK; (4); 4-H; Band; Pep Band; Var Ftbl; Var Wt Lftg; NHS; Ntl Merit Schol; U Of OK; Elec Engr.

FULKERSON, MANDY R; Muskogee HS; Muskogee, OK; (4); 40/303; Church Yth Grp; Hosp Aide; JCL; Latin Clb; School Play; High Hon Roll; NHS; Pres Schlr; St Schlr; RAID; Teens For Christ; Northeastern ST Univ.

FULLBRIGHT, BLAKE E; Dale Sr HS; Shawnee, OK; (1); Church Yth Grp; FFA.

FULLBRIGHT, JENNIFER A; Choctaw HS; Midwest City, OK; (2); Church Yth Grp; GAA; Pres Frsh Cls; Rep Jr Cls; Stat Bsbl; Stat Bsktbl; Stat Sftbl; Score Keeper; Ed.

FULLER, APRIL M; Wagoner Sr HS; Wagoner, OK; (3); 12/126; Church Yth Grp; FCA; Office Aide; Spanish Clb; Rep Frsh Cls; Stat Bsbl; Var Bsktbl; Var Chrldng; Var Socr; JV Sftbl; Pre-Med.

FULLER, DANNA L; Macarthur Sr HS; Lawton, OK; (3); Church Yth Grp; Office Aide; Band; Church Choir; Mrchg Band; Hon Roll; OU.

FULLER, JADE T; Lawton Sr HS; Lawton, OK; (3); Church Yth Grp; Treas Spanish Clb; Drill Tm; High Hon Roll; Hon Roll; Jr NHS; NHS; Phi Delta Kappa Xinos; Sepia Soc; Aerospace Acad Ldrshp Awd; Baylor; Bio.

FULLER, JOSH D; Salina HS; Pryor, OK; (1); Band; Jazz Band; Mrchg Band; Pep Band; High Hon Roll; Zoolgy.

FULLER, PAUL; Wilson Schl; Okmulgee, OK; (4); 1/17; Church Yth Grp; FBLA; Treas Natl FFA Org; Office Aide; Teachers Aide; Church Choir; Yrbk; Treas Jr Cls; Treas Sr Cls; High Hon Roll.

FULMER, AMY H; John Marshall HS; Oklahoma City, OK; (3); #12 in class; Church Yth Grp; Drama Clb; German Clb; Library Aide; Stage Crew; Tennis; High Hon Roll; Jr NHS; GAPP Club; Candidate Girls ST 96; OK Univ; PT.

FULPS, AMANDA; Union City Schl; Union City, OK; (1); 3/47; FHA; Bsktbl; Hon Roll; TCU; Drama.

FULTON, ANNETTE; Midwest City HS; Midwest City, OK; (4); 31/419; FCA; SADD; Yrbk; Var Mgr Bsbl; Var Chrldng; Var Wrstlng; NHS; Val; Karate Natl Frms Chmp 93, Natl Sparring Chmp 94; Wrstlng Hmcmng Rylty; U Of OK; Med.

FULTON, DANIEL B; Hobart HS; Hobart, OK; (2); Rptr Church Yth Grp; Rep FCA; Teachers Aide; Chorus; Church Choir; Ftbl; Wrstlng; Hobart HS Most Hnrd Choir Stu 95-; ST/REGNL Choir Contest High Score 95-; OSU; Arts.

FULTON, JEREMIAH W; Marietta HS; Marietta, OK; (2); Church Yth Grp; Computer Clb; FCA; Quiz Bowl; SADD; Ofcr Stu Cncl; Ofcr Bsbl; Bsktbl; Hon Roll; 4-H; Chrstn Club; Schlstc Shlrshp Achv Awd; OK Baptist; Smnry/Prchr.

FULTON, KRISTIN M; Stillwater Sr HS; Stillwater, OK; (3); 80/400; Rep Church Yth Grp; Drama Clb; Intnl Clb; JCL; Key Clb; Mu Alpha Theta; Natl Beta Clb; Science Clb; Spanish Clb; Chorus; Environmental Clb Parlimentarian; Key Clb Lt Governor; Ballet; Sci; Law.

FULTON, MANDY L; Del City HS; Del City, OK; (2); Library Aide; Office Aide; Teachers Aide; Rep Stu Cncl; Var L Bsktbl; Var L Sftbl; Cit Awd; NHS; US Olympic Sftbl Team 96; All Wrld Shortstop; All Wrld Trnmnt Team; Wrld Chmpn; U Of OK; Sports Med.

FULTON, ROBERT; Hollis Jr Sr HS; Hollis, OK; (4); 10/53; Am Leg Boys St; Church Yth Grp; Letterman Clb; Natl FFA Org; School Play; Var L Bsbl; Var Capt Ftbl; High Hon Roll; Hon Roll; Cmnty Wkr; Lions Clb All-Arnd Top 20 Awd; Ftbl Hmcmng Escrt; Outstndng Stu Of Mnth; U Of OK; Sprts Med.

FULTON, TINA M; Wagoner Sr HS; Wagoner, OK; (4); 4-H; FBLA; FHA; Pep Clb; 4-H Awd; Hon Roll; Lvstck Shwng; Conners ST Coll; Elem Ed.

FULTZ, JEREMY D; Wetumka Jr Sr HS; Dustin, OK; (3); 11/28; Church Yth Grp; FCA; Key Clb; Natl FFA Org; Band; Yrbk; Rep Stu Cncl; JV Bsktbl; Var Ftbl; St Lnd Jdgn Tm Wnnr; OBU; Sprt Med.

FULTZ, NATASHA M; Okmulgee HS; Okmulgee, OK; (3); 20/160; Office Aide; Pep Clb; Bsktbl; Crs Cntry; Mgr(s); Sftbl; Trk; Hon Roll; Pres Acad Fit Awd; U Of OK; Pediatrcn.

FULTZ, ZACHARY; Bishop Kelley HS; Claremore, OK; (3); 1/150; Boy Scts; JCL; Latin Clb; Quiz Bowl; High Hon Roll; NHS; Pres Acad Fit Awd; Acad Decathlon; Music; Piano; Trombone; Physics.

FUNCK, RACHAEL R; Calumet Schl; Calumet, OK; (2); Church Yth Grp; FCA; French Clb; FHA; Library Aide; Office Aide; Speech Tm; Chorus; Church Choir; School Play; Natl Yth Ldrshp Forum Law & Constitution; TAG; OSU; Law.

FUNDERBURG, GREGORY; Guymon Sr HS; Guymon, OK; (3); 23/111; Church Yth Grp; FCA; French Clb; Band; Jazz Band; Bsktbl; Hon Roll; Jr NHS; Prfct Atten Awd; Perf Attndce Awd 3 Yr; OK ST Univ; Chem Engr.

FUNDERBURGH, MANDY JO; B T Washington HS; Tulsa, OK; (3); Spanish Clb; OK U; Acctng.

FUNK, DAVID W; Union Sr HS; Broken Arrow, OK; (4); 63/692; Church Yth Grp; Key Clb; Ed Yrbk; JV Var Socr; Var Cit Awd; High Hon Roll; Hon Roll; Jr NHS; NHS; Spanish NHS; U KS.

FUNK, JESSI M; Enid Sr HS; Enid, OK; (4); Cmnty Wkr; DECA; Hosp Aide; Math Clb; Hon Roll; Jr NHS; NHS; Drama Clb; Speech Tm; Teachers Aide; Acad Letterman; Life Clb Ofcr; Awareness Big Brothers Big Sisters; Park Coll; Bio.

FUNK, NATHAN; Clinton HS; Clinton, OK; (1); Boy Scts; Band; Pep Band; JV Bsbl; Cit Awd; Hon Roll; US Air Force Acad; Pilot.

FUNKHOUSER, JED; Hobart HS; Hobart, OK; (2); Church Yth Grp; 4-H; Math Tm; Quiz Bowl; Band; Ofcr Bsbl; Bsktbl; Wt Lftg.

FUNKHOUSER, WILL; Hobart HS; Roosevelt, OK; (2); Ofcr Bsbl; Bsktbl; Hon Roll.

FUQUA, JENNIFER L; Bethel HS; Shawnee, OK; (1); 1/83; Chess Clb; Church Yth Grp; Computer Clb; Dance Clb; Quiz Bowl; Scholastic Bowl; Spanish Clb; High Hon Roll; Hon Roll; Prfct Atten Awd; Aerospace Tech & Ed Ctr; 5th Geo Bowl; 8th Span Bowl; 1st Pl Dance Cmptn; 5th At Rose St Coll-Acad Team; Astronaut.

FURLEY, WESLEY M; Capitol Hill HS; Oklahoma City, OK; (2); Ofcr Bsbl; Ftbl; Socr; Hon Roll; NHS; Highest GPA Algebra I; 13 Pl ST Spnsh I; Mammalogist/PT.

FURRY, CLINTON D; Northwest Classen HS; Oklahoma City, OK; (4); 1/190; FBLA; Library Aide; Math Clb; Mu Alpha Theta; Chorus; High Hon Roll; NHS; Ntl Merit Ltr; Pres Schlr; St Schlr; Play Guitar; Listen To Music; OK City U; Comp Sci.

FUSON, BETH; Cave Springs HS; Stilwell, OK; (4); 2/30; Am Leg Aux Girls St; French Clb; Natl FFA Org; Yrbk; Pres Soph Cls; Pres Sr Cls; Rep Stu Cncl; Bsktbl; Chrldng; Hon Roll; North Eastern ST U.

FUTRAL, STEPHANIE A; Mc Alester HS; Mcalester, OK; (3); Hosp Aide; Yrbk; High Hon Roll; Hon Roll; Pre-Med.

FUTREL, EUGENE; Millwood HS; Oklahoma City, OK; (2); Church Yth Grp; Office Aide; ROTC; Church Choir; Color Guard; Drill Tm; JV Bsktbl; JV Var Ftbl; Var Trk; Var Wt Lftg; ROTC Capt, Rifle Team; Lib Aide; OK U; Accntng.

FYE, JACEY; Comanche HS; Comanche, OK; (1); Church Yth Grp; GAA; Speech Tm; VP Frsh Cls; Bsktbl; Cit Awd; Gov Hon Prg Awd; Hon Roll; FFA Outstdng Jr Judging Livestock Cont; Outstdng Art Portfolio; Outstdng HS Stu; OSU; Photo.

GABBARD, MICHAELA; Miami Sr HS; Miami, OK; (3); 21/275; Church Yth Grp; Drama Clb; FCA; Natl Beta Clb; Speech Tm; Chorus; Church Choir; School Play; High Hon Roll; NHS; ORU; Tchr.

GABBART, AMY; Quinton Jr Sr HS; Quinton, OK; (4); 5/36; Church Yth Grp; Debate Tm; FBLA; Letterman Clb; Drill Tm; Yrbk; Sec Treas Soph Cls; Sec Treas Jr Cls; VP Stu Cncl; Bsktbl; Bacone; Med.

GABRISH, HEATHER; Moore HS; Moore, OK; (4); 33/525; Church Yth Grp; VP Mu Alpha Theta; VP Hist Band; Church Choir; Capt Color Guard; Flag Corp; Mrchg Band; Pep Band; Stage Crew; Val; JETS; OK U; Med.

GACHES JR, DARRELL E; Stilwell HS; Stilwell, OK; (2); Natl Beta Clb; Natl FFA Org; Pres Stu Cncl; Var L Bsbl; Var L Bsktbl; Var L Ftbl; Hon Roll; NHS; Bus/Ed/Sprts.

GADDIS, BILLY G; Southeast HS; Oklahoma City, OK; (2); Church Yth Grp; Band; Church Choir; Mrchg Band; Hon Roll; Mchncl Engr.

GADDIS, BLAINE H; Union Sr HS; Tulsa, OK; (4); 25/640; Boy Scts; Church Yth Grp; Cmnty Wkr; Office Aide; Ski Clb; Teachers Aide; Church Choir; Rep Sr Cls; Hon Roll; NHS; BSA Eagle Sct; Natl Sns Amer Rvltn Eagle Sct Rnnr Up, Cncl Proj Yr 93; U Of OK; Med.

GADDIS, CLAYTON T; Union Intermediate HS; Tulsa, OK; (1); Boy Scts; Cmnty Wkr; VP FCA; Ski Clb; Spanish Clb; Chorus; Church Choir; Stage Crew; Ofcr Stu Cncl; JV Bsbl; Mr Rdskn Fnlst; OK Camp Anytwn 96; Chpl Choir Cncl Boston Meth Chrch; Sprts Med.

GADDIS, WILLIAM M; Union Intermediate HS; Tulsa, OK; (2); FCA; Swmmng; High Hon Roll; Running; Phys Ftnss Workouts; Guitar.

GADDY, CHARITY; North Intemediate HS; Broken Arrow, OK; (1); Church Yth Grp; FHA; Band; Color Guard; Pep Band; JV Chrldng; North Star; Zlgst.

GAFFNEY, ROBERT; Central HS; Tulsa, OK; (2); ROTC; Stage Crew; Hon Roll; NHS; Med.

GAFREY, KIMBERLY N; Will Rogers HS; Tulsa, OK; (2); Church Yth Grp; Library Aide; Teachers Aide; Band; Church Choir; School Musical; School Play; Ofcr Frsh Cls; Ofcr Soph Cls; Rep Stu Cncl; OK ST U; Bus Admin.

GAGE, AMY R; Woodward HS; Woodward, OK; (3); Church Yth Grp; Letterman Clb; Chorus; Hon Roll; Southwestern Univ; Ped.

GAGE, ENNIKKA; U S Grant HS; Oklahoma City, OK; (1); Church Choir; Ofcr Stu Cncl; Bsktbl; Gym; Hon Roll; Morehouse Coll; Pediatrcs.

GAGE, MELINDA; Woodward HS; Woodward, OK; (1); Church Yth Grp; Letterman Clb; Chorus; High Hon Roll; 2nd Place In Writingwood Wrtng Awds For Short Story; Southwestern; Vet.

GAINES, BOBBY; Union Intermediate HS; Tulsa, OK; (2); Bio/Phys Sci II Sci Awd; Algebra I Math Awd; Elec Engrg.

GAINES, CARSON T; Bartlesville Mid HS; Bartlesville, OK; (2); Church Yth Grp; FCA; 4-H; FBLA; Library Aide; Spanish Clb; Bsktbl; Wt Lftg; 4-H Awd.

GAINES, DIANA M; Moore HS; Moore, OK; (3); Church Yth Grp; German Clb; Office Aide; Spanish Clb; SADD; Chorus; Phtg Nwsp; Phtg Yrbk; Rep Stu Cncl; NHS; FJA; Ger Clb; Nrsng.

GAITHER, BRANDI; Dewar Jr-Sr HS; Dewar, OK; (4); 2/28; 4-H; FHA; HOBY; 4-H Awd; Hon Roll; NHS; Sal; Acctng.

GAITHER, KARLI N; West Jr HS; Oklahoma City, OK; (1); School Play; Stage Crew; Rptr Nwsp; Rptr Yrbk; Intrml Sftbl; Yrbk Jrnlsm Awd; OCCC; Psych.

GALBRAITH, TANDI; Houston Homan Jr HS; Eufaula, OK; (1); 1/100; Church Yth Grp; FHA; Band; Church Choir; Mrchg Band; Capt JV Bsktbl; Var L Trk; High Hon Roll; Jr NHS; Val; Elem Tchr.

GALBREATH, APRIL D; Heavener HS; Heavener, OK; (3); 13/86; Church Yth Grp; Drama Clb; Rptr FHA; VP Spanish Clb; Band; Mrchg Band; Pep Band; School Musical; School Play; High Hon Roll; OK St Hnr Soc; Criminal Psycht.

GALDAMEZ, ERIN LYN; Markoma Bible Acad; Tahlequah, OK; (4); 1/11; Scholastic Bowl; Chorus; Pres Stu Cncl; Var Capt Bsktbl; Var Capt Vllybl; High Hon Roll; Val; US Army Rsrv Natl Schlr; All Conf Vlybl/Bsktbl; Columbia Intl Univ; Ed.

GALEGAR, CYNTHIA R; Union Intermediate HS; Tulsa, OK; (1); Church Yth Grp; FCA; Band; Church Choir; NHS; Un Stdnts Chrst; OK ST Univ.

GALES, JOSH W; Edmond North HS; Edmond, OK; (4); 86/339; Pres Art Clb; Cmnty Wkr; Mu Alpha Theta; Ntl Merit SF; OK ST U.

GALIPEAU, AMANDA D; Sapulpa Sr HS; Sapulpa, OK; (2); Art Clb; Quiz Bowl; Stage Crew; U Of Notre Dame; Law.

GALLAGHER, AMANDA; Hollis Jr Sr HS; Gould, OK; (3); 5/45; Am Leg Aux Girls St; Church Yth Grp; 4-H; Letterman Clb; School Play; Var Chrldng; Var Sftbl; St Schlr; Twirler; Jr Aeolian; OK ST U; Physiology.

GALLAGHER, CORY; Central Mid-HS; Norman, OK; (4); Drama Clb; Swmmng.

GALLANT, WENDY; Yale Jr Sr HS; Stillwater, OK; (4); 3/34; Sec Natl Beta Clb; Teachers Aide; Nwsp; Ed Yrbk; VP Sr Cls; Var Bsktbl; Var Vllybl; Cit Awd; Hon Roll; NHS; Bsktbl Bst Sprtsmnshp; Vlybl Bst Srvr; Vlybl Big Ace Awd; Lttle Drbblrs Bsktbl Coach; OSU; Acctng Tchr/Coach.

GALLANT BACON, TERESA L; Soper Schl; Soper, OK; (4); Church Yth Grp; 4-H; FHA; Chorus; Yrbk; Sec Frsh Cls; Pres Sr Cls; Hon Roll; FHA VP Sub-Dist 3, Secy; OSU; Spch Path.

GALLEGLY, JILL; Piedmont HS; Piedmont, OK; (4); 1/88; Church Yth Grp; SADD; Chorus; Sec Soph Cls; Sec Jr Cls; Rep Stu Cncl; Var Capt Chrldng; High Hon Roll; NHS; Pres Acad Fit Awd; Capt Of Var Chrldng; Natl Hon Soc Rptr; Natl Chldng Assoc All Amer Chrldr; U Of Cntrl OK; Elem Ed.

GALLION, BRANDI; Wynnewood HS; Wynnewood, OK; (2); 1/50; GAA; Hosp Aide; Letterman Clb; Var Bsktbl; High Hon Roll; Kiwanis Awd; NHS; Soph Of Yr; Sftbl; U Of OK; Pre-Med.

GALLO, KARI; North HS; Edmond, OK; (3); Church Yth Grp; Church Choir; FCA; Thesps; School Musical; Swing Chorus; Variety Show; Rep Stu Cncl; Var L Chrldng; Rep Chorus; All OMEA St Choir; KMDP Sr Co; Point Of Grace Chrstn Singing Quartet; Record; Movie Production.

GALLOP, SHARLA; Duncan HS; Duncan, OK; (2); Church Yth Grp; FHA; Red Cross Aide; Bsktbl; Socr; Swmmng; Trk; Hon Roll; NHS; Pres Acad Fit Awd; Las Reinitas Clb; Church Sftbl League; High Acad Awd Sci; OK Chrstn Univ; PT.

GALLOWAY, BEAU J; Charles Page HS; Sand Springs, OK; (1); Church Yth Grp; FCA; Ofcr Bsbl; Ftbl; Wt Lftg; High Hon Roll; Hon Roll; Pres Acad Fit Awd.

GALLOWAY, LISA J; Colcord Schl; Siloam Springs, AR; (4); 9/42; FBLA; Natl FFA Org; Teachers Aide; Ed Nwsp; Ed Yrbk; Ofcr Soph Cls; Rptr Sr Cls; Ofcr Stu Cncl; Bsktbl; Powder Puff Ftbl; Indian Clb VP; NSU; PE.

GALLOWAY, MELISSA S; Coyle Public Schl; Coyle, OK; (3); Church Yth Grp; FCA; 4-H; FHA; German Clb; Natl FFA Org; School Play; Nwsp; Yrbk; Cit Awd; Natl Engl Awd.

GALLUZZI, SARAH; Hilldale HS; Muskogee, OK; (1); 1/120; Church Yth Grp; German Clb; Band; Mrchg Band; High Hon Roll.

GAMBLE, CARRIE L; Enid Sr HS; Enid, OK; (2); GAA; Pep Clb; Spanish Clb; Bsktbl; Sftbl; NHS; Hnr Stu; OSU.

GAMBLE, ERIN; Maysville Jr Sr HS; Maysville, OK; (1); Church Yth Grp; FHA; Key Clb; Chorus; Pres Frsh Cls; High Hon Roll; Mid-Amer Voc-Tech Schltc Meet Gold Medal; OK Univ; Med Field.

GAMBLE, JACOB; Blanchard Jr Sr HS; Chickasha, OK; (2); Church Yth Grp; FCA; Letterman Clb; Spanish Clb; Bsktbl; Ftbl; Trk; Wt Lftg; Jr NHS; NHS; U Of OK; Arch.

GAMBLE, JAMIE C; Erick Jr Sr HS; Erick, OK; (1); Church Yth Grp; Natl FFA Org; Var Bsbl; Var Bsktbl; High Hon Roll; Hon Roll; Tech Stu Assn.

GAMBLE, LINDSAY S; Erick Jr Sr HS; Erick, OK; (3); Church Yth Grp; Natl FFA Org; Spanish Clb; Teachers Aide; Var Chrldng; Var Stat Mgr(s); Var Score Keeper; High Hon Roll; Tech Stu Assn.

GAMMILL, BRIAN; Putnam City North HS; Oklahoma City, OK; (4); 16/350; Am Leg Boys St; Debate Tm; German Clb; JA; Key Clb; NFL; Office Aide; Scholastic Bowl; Orch; High Hon Roll; 50th Anniversary Of D-Day Prfrmnc; Outstndng Debater 95; Philosophy.

GAMMILL, MANDI; Walters HS; Chattanooga, OK; (4); 10/33; Am Leg Aux Girls St; FCA; 4-H; FHA; HOBY; SADD; Chorus; Ofcr Stu Cncl; Chrldng; Bsktbl; Yth Ldrshp Conf Dlgt; OK ST U; Law.

GAN, TING; West Middle HS; Norman, OK; (2); Computer Clb; French Clb; Intnl Clb; Math Clb; Chorus; Tennis; Concert Pianist; U Of OK; Cmptr/Msc.

GANDHI, PUJA; Putnam City HS; Warr Acres, OK; (2); French Clb; Science Clb; Temple Yth Grp; Hist Band; Mrchg Band; Pep Band; Sec Stu Cncl; Treas NHS; Ballet Dancer With Ballet OK; Miss Jr OK Natl Teenager; John Hopkins Univ; Surgeon.

GANDY, ASHLEY S; Ringling HS; Ringling, OK; (3); 1/32; Sec Church Yth Grp; FHA; HOBY; Capt Quiz Bowl; Flag Corp; Rep Frsh Cls; Sec Jr Cls; Var Chrldng; High Hon Roll; NHS; Coll Cls; I Dare You Ldrshp Awd; Elem Stdnts Vol Tutoring; U Of OK; Physician; Microbio.

GANDY, KYLIE; Ringling HS; Ringling, OK; (2); 3/40; Church Yth Grp; Cmnty Wkr; Debate Tm; FCA; 4-H; FHA; GAA; Girl Scts; JA; Pep Clb; OU.

GANDY, SARA ASHLEY; Ringling HS; Ringling, OK; (3); 1/38; Sec Church Yth Grp; Rep FHA; HOBY; Quiz Bowl; Sec Jr Cls; Rep Stu Cncl; Var Bsktbl; Powder Puff Ftbl; High Hon Roll; Elem Stus Tutor; SWOSU Weatherford; Pharmcy.

GANDY, TIFFANY D; Jay HS; Jay, OK; (3); FCA; Natl Beta Clb; Yrbk; Ftbl; NHS; Soph Attendent Ftbl; Marine Bio/Vet.

GANN, AMANDA; Copan HS; Bowring, OK; (3); 6/26; Boy Scts; Church Yth Grp; Cmnty Wkr; Phtg Yrbk; Hon Roll; US Natl Chem Olymp; OK HS Hon Soc; SE OK St Univ; Bus.

GANN, APRIL S; South Intermediate HS; Broken Arrow, OK; (1); Church Yth Grp; Office Aide; Church Choir; Hon Roll; CSU; TJC; Psycht; Psych.

GANN, BRANDON R; Wetumka Jr Sr HS; Wetumka, OK; (2); 15/41; Key Clb; Quiz Bowl; Scholastic Bowl; Spanish Clb; Band; Hon Roll; Jrnlst.

GANN, CARLA F; Muldrow HS; Muldrow, OK; (3); Spanish Clb; Speech Tm; Band; Chorus; Mrchg Band; Pep Band; School Musical; School Play; Nwsp; Hon Roll; Intrumentlist Magzn Merit Awd; Fish/Game/Wldf Mngmt/Anml Sci.

GANN, CHEVY L; Jay HS; Jay, OK; (2); 4-H; Ofcr Bsbl; Bsktbl; Ftbl; 4-H Awd; Golf.

GANN, CHRISTINA; Soper Schl; Soper, OK; (1); 3/20; Church Yth Grp; 4-H; FHA; Chorus; Var Bsktbl; Hon Roll; NHS; Sal; Rdng; Biking; Chrch Mem; Murray ST Coll.

GANN, JACOB T; Preston Schl; Okmulgee, OK; (3); 3/40; Church Yth Grp; Quiz Bowl; Scholastic Bowl; Nwsp; High Hon Roll; Hon Roll; Karate Brown Belt; Guitar; CO Schl/Mines; Engr.

GANN, JASON E; Del City HS; Oklahoma City, OK; (3); Art Clb; Drama Clb; Quiz Bowl; Spanish Clb; School Play; Stage Crew; Hon Roll; Jr NHS; Prfct Atten Awd; Outstndng Eng II Stu; Acad Tm.

GANN, MARLA K; Muldrow HS; Muldrow, OK; (3); Spanish Clb; Speech Tm; Band; Chorus; Mrchg Band; Pep Band; School Musical; School Play; Nwsp; Hon Roll; Band Cnsl; Instrmntlst Mag Merit Awd; Westark CC; Wldlf Mngmt.

GANN, SHAWNA; Ft Towson HS; Sawyer, OK; (1); #2 in class; FCA; FHA; Yrbk; High Hon Roll; TSA Sec; Educ.

GANN, TRAVIS B; Roland Sr HS; Muldrow, OK; (3); Rptr Nwsp; JV Bsktbl; Hon Roll.

GANSAUER, RYAN M; Owasso Sr HS; Owasso, OK; (3); Natl FFA Org; Office Aide; VICA; Hon Roll; NHS; Prfct Atten Awd; T2000 Schl Wrk Pgm; Okmulgee Tech; Auto Ind.

GANT, CHARLIE; Frederick HS; Frederick, OK; (4); 1/75; Am Leg Boys St; Church Yth Grp; Cmnty Wkr; Co-Capt FCA; Letterman Clb; Spanish Clb; Teachers Aide; School Musical; Yrbk; Pres Stu Cncl; Close-Up; St Page; OSU; Med.

GANT, KENNY L; Guthrie Sr HS; Guthrie, OK; (1); 37/314; Boy Scts; Church Yth Grp; Treas FBLA; Key Clb; Spanish Clb; Band; Mrchg Band; Pep Band; U Of OK; Doc Sprts Med.

GANT, KEVIN; Senior HS; Guthrie, OK; (4); 57/177; Sec Am Leg Boys St; Boy Scts; Church Yth Grp; Pres FBLA; Key Clb; Mu Alpha Theta; Band; Yrbk; NSU; Chem Engnr.

GAO, JUDY G; Baratlesville Jr HS; Bartlesville, OK; (3); Hosp Aide; Spanish Clb; Band; Color Guard; Orch; High Hon Roll; Hon Roll; NHS; Prfct Atten Awd; Spanish NHS.

GAPPA, ERICK S; Union Intermediate HS; Tulsa, OK; (2); Physcs.

GAPPMAYER, TANYA; Panama HS; Panama, OK; (3); Girl Scts; Spanish Clb; Chrldng; Sftbl; Hon Roll; NHS; Carl Albert ST Coll.

GARBER, EMLYN; Cascia Hall Prep School; Tulsa, OK; (3); Church Yth Grp; JCL; Latin Clb; Pep Clb; Acpl Chr; Chorus; Church Choir; School Musical; School Play; Rptr Yrbk; All Amer Schlr; Wheel Throwing For Clay Dishes; Piano.

GARBER, EMMY; Cascia Hall Prep School; Tulsa, OK; (3); Church Yth Grp; JCL; Latin Clb; Pep Clb; Chorus; Church Choir; School Musical; School Play; Rptr Lit Mag; Sec Stu Cncl; All Amer Schlr; Princeton Book Clb Nom; Whos Who Awd 94-95.

GARCIA, AMY; Midwest City HS; Midwest City, OK; (3); 31/387; Church Yth Grp; Cmnty Wkr; German Clb; Key Clb; Letterman Clb; Red Cross Aide; Science Clb; SADD; Rep Soph Cls; Capt L Swmmng; Poem Pblshd In Aftr Strm; Rsrch Paper 2 Gld Mdls; Swm Tm Ldng Scorer 3xs; Lit.

GARCIA, ANITRA; Cache HS; Cache, OK; (3); #12 in class; Church Yth Grp; FCA; FHA; GAA; Natl Beta Clb; SADD; Chorus; Pres Frsh Cls; Var Stat Bsktbl; Cit Awd; Mss Cmmnctns.

GARCIA, CARLOS V; Putnam City West HS; Oklahoma City, OK; (2); Spanish Clb; JV Bsbl; Var Ftbl.

GARCIA, JOEY; Lawton Sr HS; Lawton, OK; (2); ROTC; Varsity Clb; Wt Lftg; Wrstlng; Hon Roll; Jr NHS; Cameron.

GARCIA, MATTHEW J; Putnam City North HS; Oklahoma City, OK; (2); Church Yth Grp; FCA; Spanish Clb; JV Ftbl; Wrstlng; Chiropractor.

GARD, AMANDA; Perry Sr HS; Perry, OK; (2); 1/99; Sec Church Yth Grp; Hosp Aide; Pres Spanish Clb; Band; Mrchg Band; Cit Awd; High Hon Roll; NHS; Piano Tchr; Acad Tm; US Air Force Acad.

GARDNER, CRAIG L; South Intermediate HS; Broken Arrow, OK; (2); Boy Scts; Church Yth Grp; Latin Clb; Hon Roll; MIT; Engr.

GARDNER, DUSTIN; Lone Grove HS; Lone Grove, OK; (4); 28/77; Church Yth Grp; Key Clb; Sec Pres Natl FFA Org; Rep Spanish Clb; Teachers Aide; Band; Color Guard; Jazz Band; Mrchg Band; Hon Roll; Murray ST Coll; Agronomy.

GARDNER, JAMES M; Westmoore HS; Oklahoma City, OK; (4); Art Clb; Band; Mrchg Band; OK U Recgntn Cert; U Of TX; Elec Engrng.

GARDNER, JERRY M; Lone Grove HS; Lone Grove, OK; (3); Natl Beta Clb; Varsity Clb; Chorus; Ofcr Bsbl; Hon Roll; Soph Mst Vlble Ath Bsktbl.

GARDNER, KARA; Oologah HS; Claremore, OK; (4); 3/100; Am Leg Aux Girls St; Church Yth Grp; Intnl Clb; Band; Drm Mjr(t); Jazz Band; Mrchg Band; Gov Hon Prg Awd; NHS; Sal; BYU; Music Ed.

GARDNER, KENT; Sharon Mutual Jr Sr HS; Sharon, OK; (3); 1/18; FCA; VP 4-H; HOBY; Natl FFA Org; Ed Yrbk; Pres Jr Cls; Bsktbl; Hon Roll; NHS; Natl Make It Wool, St 4-H Achvt & Elec Coop Yth Trp Wnnrs; OSU; Ag Ec.

GARDNER, MELISSA; Empire Schl; Duncan, OK; (1); 2/45; Church Yth Grp; Debate Tm; FCA; FBLA; Scholastic Bowl; Spanish Clb; SADD; Rptr Nwsp; Pom Pon.

GARDNER, SAMATHA; Silo HS; Durant, OK; (2); Church Yth Grp; Mu Alpha Theta; Church Choir; Hon Roll; NHS; Piano; Plcd 5th Murray ST Coll Curr; Brigham Young Univ; Elem Tchr.

GAREY, MATTHEW; West Middle HS; Norman, OK; (3); 233/745; Cmnty Wkr; Office Aide; Crs Cntry; Trk; Hon Roll; Pres Acad Fit Awd; Who's Who Sprts; MVP Crs Cntry 95; Hnrbl Mntn Crs Cntry All ST; DSU; Sprts Brdcstng.

GARLAND, LESLIE D; Smithville Sr HS; Watson, OK; (2); Church Yth Grp; Debate Tm; Drama Clb; NFL; Speech Tm; School Musical; School Play; High Hon Roll; Cmnty Wkr; FTA; Smithville Schltc Team Grand Champ; Family Cnslr.

GARLAND, MEREDITH A; Elgin HS; Elgin, OK; (2); 13/90; Church Yth Grp; FCA; FHA; GAA; Natl FFA Org; Ofcr Stu Cncl; JV Bsktbl; High Hon Roll; Rep Frsh Cls; Rep Soph Cls; 1st Pl ST FFA Creed Cntst; 2nd Pl ST FFA Quiz Cntst; 2 Time Frmrs Un ST Spch Qlfr; 3rd Pl ST Prl; OK ST Univ; Ag Cmmnctns/TV.

GARLAND, NATALIE A; Edmond Memorial HS; Edmond, OK; (3); 89/371; FCA; Key Clb; Spanish Clb; Var Crs Cntry; Var Trk; High Hon Roll; Hon Roll; NHS; Art Cls; U Of OK.

GARLAND, TARA; Velma Alma HS; Velma, OK; (2); Church Yth Grp; FCA; FHA; Spanish Clb; SADD; Stage Crew; Rptr Nwsp; Sftbl; Trk; Hon Roll; OSU; Bus.

GARMAN, EMILY M; Edmond Memorial HS; Edmond, OK; (4); 102/677; Church Yth Grp; Cmnty Wkr; Drama Clb; Key Clb; NFL; Spanish Clb; Speech Tm; SADD; Thesps; Acpl Chr; Cmmnty Theatre; U Of OK.

GARMAND, JEREMY D; Guthrie Sr HS; Guthrie, OK; (1); #19 in class; Boy Scts; Band; Mrchg Band; Orch; JV Bsktbl; JV Ftbl; Var Socr; Var Trk; Hon Roll; NHS; Egl Sct; St Cptl Pg.

GARNATZ, GARY; Hulbert Jr Sr HS; Hulbert, OK; (3); Computer Clb; 4-H; German Clb; Quiz Bowl; Bsktbl; Crs Cntry; Ftbl; Trk; High Hon Roll; NHS; Bowling; OK ST U; Law.

GARNER, HEATH A; Warner HS; Warner, OK; (1); FCA; JV Bsktbl; JV Trk; Smmr Leag Bsbl; FFA; Hortcltr Jdg.

GARNER, JAMIE L; Durant HS; Durant, OK; (3); Boy Scts; Church Yth Grp; FBLA; Band; Church Choir; Jazz Band; Mrchg Band; Hon Roll; U Of OK; Fin.

GARNER, JESSICA L; Colcord Schl; Colcord, OK; (3); Church Yth Grp; FHA; Ofcr Soph Cls; Treas Stu Cncl; Var Bsktbl; Hon Roll; NHS; Ntl Merit SF; OK Hnr Soc; Cong Yth Ldrshp Cncl; Ed.

GARNER, MATTHEW T; Union Intermediate HS; Tulsa, OK; (2); 86/900; Church Yth Grp; Key Clb; Orch; NHS; Pres Schlr; Pres Awd For Educl Excl.

GARNER, RANDY D; Moore HS; Oklahoma City, OK; (4); Library Aide; Ftbl; Wt Lftg; OSU Tech; Law Enforcement.

GARNER, YVONNE; Sulphur HS; Sulphur, OK; (1); FCA; GAA; Key Clb; Speech Tm; Bsktbl; Chrldng; Crs Cntry; Sftbl; High Hon Roll.

GARR, STEPHANIE N; Choctaw HS; Choctaw, OK; (2); 1/389; Church Yth Grp; JV Bsktbl; JV Sftbl; Var Trk; Prfct Atten Awd; Pres Schlr; Val; Msnc Awd; Feml Acad Athlt Awd; Obstrcn.

GARRETT, AMBER B; Moore HS; Moore, OK; (3); French Clb; JA; Library Aide; Peer Hlpr; Earth Sci/Engl III Awd.

GARRETT, AMY B; Tahlequah Sr HS; Tahlequah, OK; (2); Church Yth Grp; Science Clb; SADD; Chorus; VP Frsh Cls; Rep Stu Cncl; JV Sftbl; JV Tennis; Jr NHS; NHS; Gifted Mentorshp Prog.

GARRETT, CHARLES E; Moore HS; Moore, OK; (1); Church Yth Grp; Band; Church Choir; Jazz Band; Mrchg Band; Pep Band; Pres Acad Fit Awd; Brwn Blt Tae Kwon Do/Jiu Jitsu/Muay Thai Kickbxng; OK ST Univ; Cmptr Sci.

GARRETT, CHRISTINA M; Lone Grove HS; Lone Grove, OK; (2); Spanish Clb; Band; Color Guard; Jazz Band; Mrchg Band; Hon Roll; NHS; OK Bapt Univ.

GARRETT, HEATHER; Westmoore HS; Oklahoma City, OK; (3); Stat Ftbl; Var Socr; Jr NHS; Triathlon Races Vol; Cyclist; Duathlete; OSU; Psych.

GARRETT, JAMIE; Choctaw HS; Midwest City, OK; (4); 78/304; Cmnty Wkr; FCA; Office Aide; Ed Nwsp; Rptr Yrbk; JV Bsbl; Var Ftbl; L Trk; High Hon Roll; NHS; U OK; Jrnlst.

GARRETT, JENIFER; Tuttle HS; Tuttle, OK; (1); 1/100; Church Yth Grp; GAA; Natl FFA Org; Pres Frsh Cls; JV Var Bsktbl; Chrldng; Trk; High Hon Roll; NHS; Bible Clb Fresh Rep.

GARRETT, JERRY R; Velma Alma HS; Velma, OK; (2); Church Yth Grp; FCA; SADD; Varsity Clb; Church Choir; Rep Soph Cls; Var Bsktbl; Var Ftbl; Var Golf; Cit Awd; OU.

GARRETT, JOHN A; B T Washington HS; Tulsa, OK; (3); Church Yth Grp; JCL; Latin Clb; Hon Roll; NHS; 3.8 Cmmltv GPA; Pre-Med.

GARRETT, JONATHAN D; West Moore HS; Oklahoma City, OK; (1); Office Aide; Teachers Aide; Sec Frsh Cls; Ofcr Stu Cncl; JV Ftbl; Pres Acad Fit Awd; Notre Dame; Optometrist.

GARRETT, KARI; Wilson HS; Wilson, OK; (2); 1/41; Church Yth Grp; FCA; Natl Beta Clb; Natl FFA Org; Band; Church Choir; Var Bsktbl; Var Sftbl; Hon Roll; OK Hnr Soc; FFA Chptr Sec; OBU; Medcl.

GARRETT, KATHY M; Tahlequah Sr HS; Park Hill, OK; (2); 50/300; Church Yth Grp; Cmnty Wkr; 4-H; German Clb; Pep Clb; Service Clb; Chorus; Cit Awd; Hon Roll; Jr NHS; U Of OK; Scl Stds.

GARRETT, LACEY E; Mustang HS; Mustang, OK; (3); Church Yth Grp; French Clb; FHA; Girl Scts; Scholastic Bowl; Band; Church Choir; Var Pom Pon; High Hon Roll; NHS; Sunday Schl Tchr 2 Yrs; Ballet/Jazz Dance 10 Yrs; Dance.

GARRETT, LETICIA D; Spiro HS; Keota, OK; (1); Church Yth Grp; Band; Chorus; Church Choir; Mrchg Band; Pep Band; Cit Awd; Hon Roll; Prfct Atten Awd; Frosh Rep HS Band; 2nd Chair 1st Soprano Choir; 2nd Chair Flute HS Band; Carl Albert ST Coll; Art.

GARRETT, MICHAEL K; Putnam City HS; Oklahoma City, OK; (2); Church Yth Grp; FCA; Church Choir; OBU; Clergy.

GARRETT, NATHAN S; Midwest City HS; Choctaw, OK; (2); Acpl Chr; Band; Chorus; Church Choir; Jazz Band; Mrchg Band; Pep Band; School Musical; School Play; Calvin Smith Otsdng Jazz Stdnt; Un Jazzfst Otsdng Soloist; All ST Jazz Band; All Star Mrchng Corp; OK Univ; Music Ed/Psych.

GARRETT, NICOLE; Tuttle HS; Tuttle, OK; (2); Church Yth Grp; Natl FFA Org; Church Choir; Var Chrldng; High Hon Roll; Bible Clb Fresh Rep; Meteorolgy.

GARRETT, STACEY; Oklahoma Sch Of Science & Math; Fort Gibson, OK; (4); Debate Tm; Hosp Aide; HOBY; Math Clb; NFL; Quiz Bowl; Science Clb; Socr; Hon Roll; NHS; Churchill Schlrshp; Accptd U Of Chicago, U Of Tulsa With Schlrshp; Westminster Coll; Hstry.

GARRETT, STEPHANIE L; Welch Jr Sr HS; Welch, OK; (4); 8/24; FCA; Pres Treas FHA; Pep Clb; Nwsp; Rptr Church Yth Grp; Rep Stu Cncl; Chrldng; Score Keeper; Sftbl; Hon Roll; Craig Cty Jr Miss Poise & Apprnc Awd 96; Nrthestrn OK A&M.

GARRETT II, STEPHEN M; Inola Sr HS; Tulsa, OK; (3); 1/67; Computer Clb; Science Clb; Spanish Clb; Teachers Aide; High Hon Roll; Hon Roll; Spanish NHS; St Schlr; OK Hnr Soc; Chem I II Grd Awd; Span Awd; FBI Agent.

GARRETT, WHITNEY B; Central Mid-HS; Norman, OK; (2); Church Yth Grp; Hosp Aide; JCL; Pres Latin Clb; Mu Alpha Theta; Orch; High Hon Roll; NHS; Octgn Club Soph Rep; Clscl Ballet Acad Asstnt Dance Tchr; Page Laura Boyd Ph D; OK ST Hse Of Rep; Stanford Univ; Pre-Med.

GARRETTE, COURTNEY; Mustang HS; Yukon, OK; (3); 65/386; Church Yth Grp; FCA; Chorus; Church Choir; Var Chrldng; Powder Puff Ftbl; Var Sftbl; High Hon Roll; NHS; Pres Acad Fit Awd; Bio Awd; OBU.

GARRIS, RYAN; Oklahoma Christian Schl; Edmond, OK; (3); 4/50; Church Yth Grp; Cmnty Wkr; Computer Clb; FCA; Math Clb; Math Tm; Var Socr; Hon Roll; Prfct Atten Awd; Chemical Engrng.

GARRISON, BRANT; Elk City Jr HS; Canute, OK; (2); Church Yth Grp; Computer Clb; Science Clb; Band; Jazz Band; Rep Stu Cncl; Hon Roll; NHS; Tech Stu Assoc.

GARRISON, NAKYLA J; Mustang HS; Yukon, OK; (2); FCA; Model UN; Vllybl; Matt Maids.

GARRISON, PENNY R; Mannford HS; Sand Springs, OK; (3); Drama Clb; Sec Soph Cls; VP Jr Cls; JV Var Chrldng; Sftbl; Trk; High Hon Roll; Hon Roll; PT.

GARUIN, CHARLES; Wilson Schl; Okmulgee, OK; (1); Boy Scts; Church Yth Grp; Natl FFA Org; Varsity Clb; Treas Frsh Cls; Ofcr Bsbl; Bsktbl; High Hon Roll; Val.

GARVEY, KENIA X; Christian Heritage Acad; Del City, OK; (3); Church Yth Grp; Band; Chorus; Church Choir; Orch; Hon Roll; Prfct Atten Awd; Music.

GARZA, CARLOS; Walters HS; Walters, OK; (2); Art Clb; Church Yth Grp; FHA; Var Bsbl; Var Ftbl; Var Wt Lftg; Hon Roll; FCA; Lib Clb; Renaissance; Cameron Coll; Comp.

GARZA III, DANNY D; West Middle HS; Norman, OK; (1); Latin Clb; Cit Awd; Native American Clb; U Of OK; Biologist.

GARZA, JENNIFER; Panama HS; Panama, OK; (4); 11/59; Church Yth Grp; FCA; Hosp Aide; SADD; Sec Stu Cncl; Bsktbl; Var Capt Chrldng; Sftbl; High Hon Roll; NHS; All Area Bsktbl; Carl Albert; Phys Thrpy.

GARZA, JENNIFER J; Panama HS; Shady Point, OK; (4); 11/49; FCA; SADD; Var Bsktbl; Var Capt Chrldng; Sftbl; High Hon Roll; NHS; GAA; Hosp Aide; Letterman Clb; Stdnt Cncl Ldrshp Awd; All-Area Bsktbl; All-St Sftbl; Care Albert ST Coll; PT.

GASEM, SARAH S; Stillwater Sr HS; Stillwater, OK; (3); 88/363; French Clb; Math Clb; Math Tm; Science Clb; Hon Roll; NHS; Ntl Merit Schol; Schlrs Diploma; Var Schlr; OK ST Univ.

GASS, BYRONY; Deer Creek HS; Edmond, OK; (3); 3/110; FBLA; HOBY; Science Clb; Spanish Clb; Ofcr Stu Cncl; Chrldng; Tennis; NHS; OK ST U; Engrng.

GASSEN, JOHN; Union City Schl; Union City, OK; (4); 2/24; Church Yth Grp; FCA; FHA; Math Clb; Quiz Bowl; Scholastic Bowl; Church Choir; Pres Sr Cls; High Hon Roll; Val; OSU; Sci Ed.

GASSER, MELISSA L; Macarthur Sr HS; Lawton, OK; (3); 11/284; Church Yth Grp; Drama Clb; FCA; French Clb; German Clb; Hosp Aide; HOBY; Red Cross Aide; SADD; Band; Super Plus Rating Piano Cont; Yth Participation Convention Org Comm; Stu Dir Of One-Act Play 1st Place; Sociology Soc Worker.

GASTON, ERIC; Frederick HS; Frederick, OK; (2); 1/85; Church Yth Grp; FCA; School Musical; Rep Stu Cncl; Ftbl; Trk; Gov Hon Prg Awd; Hon Roll; NHS; TSA; TX Tech; Yth Minister.

GASTON, JIMMY F; Ardmore HS; Ardmore, OK; (3); 51/167; Church Yth Grp; Band; Church Choir; Color Guard; Jazz Band; Mrchg Band; Orch; Pep Band; JV Bsktbl; Var Ftbl; Leaves & Fishes; Ump YMCA 2 Yrs; Ref YMCA 1 Yr; City Scr 1 Yr; OK City Univ; Rlgn.

GASTON, JOLELA; Ardmore HS; Ardmore, OK; (4); 40/168; Church Yth Grp; Cmnty Wkr; FCA; Office Aide; Pep Clb; Red Cross Aide; Spanish Clb; Band; Mrchg Band; Yrbk; U Of OK; RN; Phy Assoc.

GATELEY, JOSHUA; Edmond North HS; Edmond, OK; (3); 38/348; Church Yth Grp; Cmnty Wkr; French Clb; Mu Alpha Theta; Church Choir; JV Bsbl; NHS.

GATES, CHARLES; Midwest City HS; Midwest City, OK; (4); 15/427; Am Leg Boys St; Drama Clb; FCA; Stage Crew; Ofcr Stu Cncl; Ftbl; Golf; Cit Awd; NHS; Val; Yth Vlntr Wrstlng Coach; SW OK ST U; Phrmcy.

GATES, MANDY; Bixby Sr HS; Bixby, OK; (3); FCA; German Clb; Treas Frsh Cls; Rep Jr Cls; Bsktbl; Chrldng; Mgr(s); Sftbl; Trk; Hon Roll; Neo Natal Nurse.

GATEWOOD, ADAM F; Poteau HS; Poteau, OK; (2); Math Tm; Quiz Bowl; Scholastic Bowl; Science Clb; JV Bsktbl; Mgr(s); Hon Roll; NHS; 3rd Pl OK ST Sci & Engrng Far-Math Div; 2nd Pl Carl Albert Schlstc Meet-3rd Eastern OKSC Meet; USAFA; Physics; Math; Chem.

GATHRIGHT, SHAUNA; U S Grant HS; Oklahoma City, OK; (3); 14/254; Church Yth Grp; Dance Clb; FCA; Church Choir; VP Jr Cls; Rep Stu Cncl; Var Chrldng; Gym; NHS; SHADES; U Cntrl OK; Med.

GATLIFF, JAMIE L; Lawton Sr HS; Lawton, OK; (2); French Clb; HOBY; Band; Mrchg Band; School Musical; Var Chrldng; Wt Lftg; JV Wrstlng; Hon Roll; Coed Chrldng Squd; IA St Univ; Crim.

GATZ, SONJA M; El Reno Sr HS; El Reno, OK; (1); Church Yth Grp; FCA; GAA; Bsktbl; Crs Cntry; Vllybl; Wt Lftg; Hon Roll; Bsktbl Broken Arrow All Tourn Tm 95; All Conf Tm; All Big Cty Spec Recog.

GAUGER, KRISTAL R; Ponca City Sr HS; Ponca City, OK; (2); 53/435; Church Yth Grp; Band; High Hon Roll; Hon Roll; Lettered Grds 9/10; Hanging Around With Friends; BUS/BUS Mntmnt.

GAVIN, JAMESE R; Union Intermediate HS; Tulsa, OK; (1); Spanish Clb; Cit Awd; 2 Tchr Awds; TU; Med.

GAVULA, PETER J; Bishop Mcguinness HS; Oklahoma City, OK; (2); 52/167; Boy Scts; German Clb; Ftbl; Hon Roll; Marine Sci.

GAWEY, REYNOLDS N; Edmond Memorial HS; Edmond, OK; (2); 1/450; Church Yth Grp; Key Clb; Spanish Clb; Ofcr Stu Cncl; Chrldng; Pom Pon; Powder Puff Ftbl; Gov Hon Prg Awd; Hon Roll; NHS; Med Field.

GAY, AMY; Carl Albert HS; Midwest City, OK; (4); 82/241; Art Clb; Church Yth Grp; FCA; Key Clb; Office Aide; Chorus; Church Choir; Pom Pon; Hon Roll; Shw Chr; Dnc Trp; Kiwanis Schlrshp; Rose ST Coll; Dnc Instr.

GAY, JENNIFER; Oologah-Talala HS; Talala, OK; (2); Church Yth Grp; Band; Color Guard; Flag Corp; Mrchg Band; Chrldng; Hon Roll; Prfct Atten Awd.

GAYLOR, VELDA; Roland Sr HS; Roland, OK; (2); Church Yth Grp; Quiz Bowl; Spanish Clb; Speech Tm; Nwsp; High Hon Roll; Jr NHS; NHS; Masonic Awd 95.

GAYLORD, BRYCE G; Carney Schl; Meeker, OK; (4); 3/16; Mu Alpha Theta; Natl FFA Org; Sec Jr Cls; VP Sr Cls; VP Stu Cncl; Ofcr Bsbl; Bsktbl; Cit Awd; ST FFA Degree; OK ST Univ.

GEAN, MEGGAN; Wilburton Jr HS; Wilburton, OK; (1); Band; Chrldng; Trk; Hon Roll; NHS; Estrn OK ST.

GEARY, CHRISTA; Blanchard Jr Sr HS; Blanchard, OK; (4); 9/75; Computer Clb; Pres Mu Alpha Theta; Pep Clb; Spanish Clb; Rep Soph Cls; Rep Jr Cls; Var Capt Bsktbl; Var Capt Sftbl; Hon Roll; NHS; All Amer Schlr; Bsktbl & Fast Pitch Sftbl All Conf; SWOSU; Phys Thrpy.

GEBHART, ERICA S; Claremore Sr HS; Claremore, OK; (1); VP Natl FFA Org; DAR Awd; Hon Roll; Cattle; Ride Dressage Equestrian Sprt; OSU Coll Of Vet Med; Vetrnry.

GEE, BRANDON K; Clayton Jr Sr HS; Clayton, OK; (2); Rptr Natl FFA Org; Hon Roll; Tm Roping; EOSC; Ag.

GEE, FLORENCE E; Ninnekah HS; Ninnekah, OK; (2); Church Yth Grp; Girl Scts; Scholastic Bowl; Chorus; Pep Band; School Musical; Hon Roll; Band Dirs Awd; OK HS Hnr Soc; USAO Chickasha.

GEE, MICHAEL C; Putnam City North HS; Oklahoma City, OK; (1); Chess Clb; Church Yth Grp; Drama Clb; Wt Lftg; Chrch Msn Trp Mexico.

GEE, MICHELLE L; Claremore Sr HS; Claremore, OK; (1); Natl FFA Org; Speech Tm; Hon Roll; Riding Dressage Equestrian Sprt; FFA Star Greenhand; OK ST Univ; Vet/Lg Animal.

GEIGER, ANGELA; Chelsea HS; Chelsea, OK; (3); 5/65; Model UN; Office Aide; Chorus; Ed Nwsp; Yrbk; VP Jr Cls; VP Sr Cls; Rptr Stu Cncl; Var Bsktbl; Var Chrldng; SW OK ST U; Pre-Med.

GEIGER, CHRISTA M; Nathan Hale HS; Tulsa, OK; (3); Sec Drama Clb; Thesps; School Play; Stage Crew; Tennis; High Hon Roll; NHS; Demoiselles.

GEIGER, LONNIE; Roland Sr HS; Roland, OK; (3); 11/110; Natl Beta Clb; Spanish Clb; JV Bsktbl; Var Ftbl; Var Trk; High Hon Roll.

GEIGER, MATT; Chelsea HS; Chelsea, OK; (2); FCA; Spanish Clb; Chorus; Ofcr Stu Cncl; JV Var Bsktbl; Trk; Hon Roll; Bio.

GEIS, ANDREA; Okeene Jr Sr HS; Hitchcock, OK; (3); 2/34; Church Yth Grp; 4-H; HOBY; Natl FFA Org; Bsktbl; Sftbl; Trk; 4-H Awd; NHS; Pres Acad Fit Awd; All Amer Schlr; OK ST U; Socl Work.

GEIS, CARA DAWN; Lomega HS; Kingfisher, OK; (3); 1/12; Am Leg Aux Girls St; Church Yth Grp; Pres FCA; Sec Jr Cls; Sec Stu Cncl; Var Bsktbl; High Hon Roll; NHS; Val; Dept Of Hum Svcs Vol; Southern Nazarene Univ.

GEISLER, LAURA; Deer Creek HS; Oklahoma City, OK; (2); Debate Tm; Drama Clb; 4-H; Girl Scts; Speech Tm; Child Dev.

GEIST, CHARLA; Elk City Jr HS; Elk City, OK; (3); Church Yth Grp; Natl FFA Org; Science Clb; Sec Soph Cls; Rep Stu Cncl; Var Crs Cntry; Var Golf; Cit Awd; VP NHS; Pres Acad Fit Awd; OK St Univ; Premed.

GELNAR, DANIELLE; Granite Jr Sr HS; Granite, OK; (4); Pres 4-H; VP FHA; Rep Science Clb; Church Choir; School Play; Co-Ed Yrbk; Pres Sr Cls; Var Bsktbl; Sftbl; Hon Roll; Bus.

GELNAR, JENNIFER; Granite Jr Sr HS; Granite, OK; (3); 4/20; 4-H; Natl FFA Org; Chorus; Church Choir; Var Bsktbl; Var Sftbl; 4-H Awd; Hon Roll; NHS; Sal; CPA.

GELVIN, KERI; Cache HS; Lawton, OK; (4); 13/74; Church Yth Grp; FCA; FHA; Key Clb; Natl Beta Clb; Scholastic Bowl; Science Clb; SADD; Chrldng; High Hon Roll; Punctual Attendance; OK Hnr Soc; Cert Prof Rescuer.

GEMACHLICH, T J; Clinton HS; Clinton, OK; (3); 24/122; Church Yth Grp; FBLA; Key Clb; SADD; Teachers Aide; Flag Corp; Yrbk; Var L Chrldng; Hon Roll; Kiwanis Awd; SW OK ST U; Math Tchr.

GEMINDEN, GAVIN; Chisholm Sr HS; Carrier, OK; (2); Church Yth Grp; 4-H; Natl FFA Org; SADD; Band; Jazz Band; Mrchg Band; Pep Band; Cit Awd; 4-H Awd; ST Wldlf/Fshrs 4-H Prjct Wnr; Ag.

GENIUK, PATRICIA M; South Intermediate HS; Broken Arrow, OK; (2); Church Yth Grp; Hosp Aide; Band; Mrchg Band; Pep Band; Gov Hon Prg Awd; High Hon Roll; Hon Roll; Jr NHS; NHS; Numerous Instrumental Musics Awds; Coll; Zoology; Wildlife Bio.

GENSAMER, BRAD J; Bray-Doyle HS; Marlow, OK; (2); Church Yth Grp; Cmnty Wkr; FCA; FHA; SADD; School Play; Variety Show; Rptr Frsh Cls; Rptr Soph Cls; Bsktbl; Bray Vol Fire Dept.

GENSAMER, BRIAN; Bray-Doyle HS; Marlow, OK; (4); 7/35; Am Leg Boys St; Church Yth Grp; Cmnty Wkr; FCA; FHA; SADD; Church Choir; School Play; Sprt Ed Yrbk; Var Bsbl; Stu Today; Yth Prtcptn Conf Cmmtte; Prncpls Awd Stu Mon; NEOOSU; Firefighter.

GENTRY, AMANDA M; Elmore City-Pernell Jr Sr HS; Elmore City, OK; (2); 7/47; Church Yth Grp; 4-H; FHA; Var Bsktbl; Var Sftbl; Hon Roll.

GENTRY, ANGELA S; Sapulpa Sr HS; Tulsa, OK; (3); Church Yth Grp; Sec French Clb; Letterman Clb; Science Clb; Chorus; Capt Color Guard; Ed Nwsp; DAR Awd; French Hon Soc; NHS; John Brown Univ; TV Brdcstng.

GENTRY, MOIRA; Ardmore HS; Ardmore, OK; (4); 8/140; Art Clb; Church Yth Grp; FHA; Office Aide; Quiz Bowl; Science Clb; Lit Mag; Cit Awd; NHS; Pres Acad Fit Awd; OK Bapt Univ.

GENTRY, VONI A; Howe Public Schl; Heavener, OK; (3); GAA; Teachers Aide; VP Frsh Cls; Pres Soph Cls; VP Jr Cls; Pres Sr Cls; VP Stu Cncl; Bsktbl; Sftbl; Hon Roll; Carl Albert Stcol.

GENZER, KYLE; Mt St Marys HS; Moore, OK; (1); FCA; Key Clb; Treas Frsh Cls; Bsktbl; JV Ftbl; L Trk; Reps; U Of OK.

GEORGE, ADIA G; Union Intermediate HS; Tulsa, OK; (2); 17/810; Church Yth Grp; Cmnty Wkr; Key Clb; Spanish Clb; Chorus; JV Var Pom Pon; High Hon Roll; NHS; Prfct Atten Awd; Redskin In Review; Stanford; Med.

GEORGE, ANTOINETTE M; Mc Lain Career Acad; Tulsa, OK; (3); FBLA; Office Aide; Pep Clb; Teachers Aide; Rep Jr Cls; Rep Stu Cncl; Trk; Cit Awd; High Hon Roll; Hon Roll; Grambling Univ; Acctng.

GEORGE, CHARITY B; Wright Christian Acad; Catoosa, OK; (1); Var Vllybl; High Hon Roll.

GEORGE, MONIQUE L; Chickasha HS; Chickasha, OK; (1); 4-H; French Clb; Rptr FHA; Science Clb; Hon Roll; Hrsbck Riding; Jrnlsm.

GEORGE, SALLY D; South Intermediate HS; Broken Arrow, OK; (1); Church Yth Grp; Drama Clb; Office Aide; Church Choir; Hon Roll; Ballet; OK Summer Arts Inst; Chrstn Stdnt Union.

GEORGE, SHAWN M; Wetumka Jr Sr HS; Wetumka, OK; (3); FCA; Ofcr Bsbl; Bsktbl; Ftbl; Wt Lftg; Hon Roll; OK Univ; Acctnt/Coast Guard.

GEPNER, ABRAHAM J; Central Mid-HS; Norman, OK; (2); Ofcr Bsbl; Hon Roll; Amer Legion Bsbl; Cntrl Mid-High MVP; OK St AAU Trnmt Offensive MVP; Wichita ST.

GERBER, JOHN P; Woodward HS; Woodward, OK; (4); 14/158; Art Clb; Church Yth Grp; Cmnty Wkr; Letterman Clb; Teachers Aide; Var Capt Bsktbl; Cit Awd; High Hon Roll; Hon Roll; Kiwanis Awd; Outstdng Sr; Natl Cnsrtm Acads/Sprts/Natl Coll Ath Assn Natl Stdnt Ath Day Awd; Rotary Stdnt/Month; NWOSU; Tech.

GERBER, SHANE; Lomega HS; Kingfisher, OK; (3); 6/12; FCA; HOBY; Rep Stu Cncl; Var Bsbl; Var Bsktbl; Hon Roll; FFA.

GERHARDT, SCOTT; Putnam City North HS; Oklahoma City, OK; (3); Church Yth Grp; Teachers Aide; JV Bsktbl; Var Ftbl; Wt Lftg; Hon Roll; Ftbl All-Dist, All-Conf; All Friday Team; PC Gazette & Pioneer Pie Plyr Of Week.

GERKEN, LISA M; Pioneer Jr Sr HS; Fairmont, OK; (3); Church Yth Grp; FCA; Natl FFA Org; Pres Frsh Cls; Pres Soph Cls; Pres Jr Cls; Pres Stu Cncl; Var Bsktbl; Var Sftbl; Var Trk; Numerous Schltc Meets; Outstdng Algebra & Chem Stu; Livestock Showing-Diversified Livestock Awds; OK ST U; Bio-Chem.

GERMAN, LINDSEY R; Buffalo Jr Sr HS; Buffalo, OK; (2); Church Yth Grp; FCA; Sec Frsh Cls; Rep Soph Cls; Var Bsktbl; Var Trk; Hon Roll; NHS; Chorus; Var Crs Cntry; Masonic Stu Of Today Awd; OK ST Univ; Elem Ed/Bus.

GERMANY, DALENE; Coleman Schl; Coleman, OK; (4); 1/9; Church Yth Grp; FCA; 4-H; Library Aide; Pres Pep Clb; Capt Quiz Bowl; Ski Clb; Chorus; Church Choir; Yrbk; Chem.

GEROVAC, NICHOLAS M; Jenks HS; Tulsa, OK; (4); Boy Scts; Computer Clb; Math Tm; Scholastic Bowl; Science Clb; Teachers Aide; Var L Trk; JV Wrstlng; Hon Roll; NHS; CA Inst Tech; Comp Sci.

GERSTLE, ALLIE R; Wagoner Sr HS; Wagoner, OK; (4); 5/135; FBLA; Office Aide; Teachers Aide; Stage Crew; Ed Yrbk; Hist Sr Cls; High Hon Roll; Hon Roll; NHS; Sr Exec Comm; Frgn Lang Club Pres; Northeastern ST Univ; Psych.

GESELL, ALLYSON; Edmond Memorial HS; Edmond, OK; (1); Church Yth Grp; FCA; Spanish Clb; Teachers Aide; JV Chrldng; NCA All-Amer Chrldr; U Of OK; Medcl.

GETER, TEQUETTA; Emmerson HS; Oklahoma City, OK; (4); Church Yth Grp; Cmnty Wkr; French Clb; FBLA; GAA; Quiz Bowl; ROTC; VICA; Church Choir; Color Guard.

GEYER, JESSICA; Trinity Christian Schl; Broken Arrow, OK; (2); Pep Clb; Yrbk; Pres Soph Cls; Bsktbl; Chrldng; Vllybl; Hon Roll; OK ST U; Med.

GEYER, NEIL J; Olive Jr Sr HS; Drumright, OK; (3); Church Yth Grp; Drama Clb; FBLA; Natl FFA Org; Office Aide; Quiz Bowl; Scholastic Bowl; Speech Tm; Teachers Aide; VICA; 3rd In St Comptve Spch Cont; 1st In St VICA Prncples Of Tech; Multi Yr Listee; OSU; Sci.

GHAZANFARI, TALITHA A; Edmond Memorial HS; Edmond, OK; (2); 53/440; Church Yth Grp; Mu Alpha Theta; Spanish Clb; Chorus; School Musical; Variety Show; Vllybl; NHS; Music Ministry.

GHAZIOSHARIF, TEIBA; East Central HS; Tulsa, OK; (2); Church Yth Grp; FCA; Rptr Nwsp; Phtg Yrbk; Var Sftbl; Hon Roll; NHS; Elite Hnrs Cls 2 Yrs; 3 ASA Natls; Medcl.

GHELARDUCCI, KRISTIN; Central Mid-HS; Norman, OK; (2); Boy Scts; Church Yth Grp; FCA; VP Girl Scts; Hosp Aide; JCL; Rep Latin Clb; Math Clb; Sec Mu Alpha Theta; Quiz Bowl; Latin Hon Soc; Elem Ed/Erly Chldhd.

GHOSE, DEV A; Union Intermediate HS; Tulsa, OK; (1); Boy Scts; Key Clb; Math Clb; NFL; Orch; Ofcr Stu Cncl; Capt NHS; St Sci Fair Awd; Tri-M Music Hnr Soc; Eng Or Med.

GIACOMO MURRAY, SELENA E; Mc Alester HS; Krebs, OK; (3); 24/192; Church Yth Grp; 4-H; French Clb; FHA; Quiz Bowl; Science Clb; Yrbk; Vllybl; 4-H Awd; High Hon Roll; OSU; Pre-Med.

GIBBS, CAROLINE M; Edmond North HS; Edmond, OK; (2); 1/420; Church Yth Grp; French Clb; ROTC; Color Guard; Drill Tm; Flag Corp; Rep Stu Cncl; NHS; Dghtrs Amer Clnst Mdl; Natl Essay Cont Freedoms Fdtn Wnnr; Intl Yth Ldrshp Conf Peple-People Pgm Spnsr; Rice U.

GIBBS, KIMBERLY G; Kellyville Sr HS; Sapulpa, OK; (4); 4-H; Library Aide; Natl FFA Org; Office Aide; Quiz Bowl; Scholastic Bowl; Science Clb; Ed Nwsp; Rep Stu Cncl; Bsktbl; Pub Speaking; CPA.

GIBBS, SHANNON R; Elk City Jr HS; Elk City, OK; (1); Church Yth Grp; Drama Clb; SADD; Band; Chorus; Mrchg Band; Pep Band; Hon Roll; Psych.

GIBE, JEFFREY S; Jay HS; Jay, OK; (2); Church Yth Grp; FCA; Var Bsbl; Var Bsktbl; Var Ftbl; High Hon Roll; NHS; Mr Hustle Awd Var Bsktbl 94-95; Defensive Plyr Of Yr Var Bsbl 95-; Peer Cnslr IDFY; Sports Med.

GIBONEY JR, JAMES F; Muldrow HS; Muldrow, OK; (3); Pres Band; Jazz Band; Mrchg Band; Pep Band; Young Democrats; Music Cmptn.

GIBSON, AMY; Parker Middle HS; Mcalester, OK; (3); 8/200; DECA; FHA; Spanish Clb; Ofcr Stu Cncl; Chrldng; High Hon Roll; Hon Roll; NHS; Pres Acad Fit Awd; All Amer Chrldr; Outstdng Eng; Span; His; Tchr.

GIBSON, AMY K; Mc Alester HS; Mcalester, OK; (3); 8/186; Am Leg Aux Girls St; Church Yth Grp; FCA; FBLA; FHA; Spanish Clb; Ofcr Frsh Cls; Ofcr Soph Cls; Chrldng; Gym; All Amer Chrldr; OU; Med.

GIBSON, ANDREAN; Bennington Schl; Bennington, OK; (3); 3/22; English Clb; Quiz Bowl; VP Frsh Cls; Pres Soph Cls; Sec Rep Stu Cncl; Bsktbl; Sftbl; Cit Awd; High Hon Roll; NHS; VP Upward Bound Univ SOSU Durant; Archtct.

GIBSON, CARLYE; Central Mid-HS; Norman, OK; (1); Church Yth Grp; Rep Mu Alpha Theta; Red Cross Aide; Rep Band; Orch; School Musical; Rep Frsh Cls; Ofcr Stu Cncl; Hon Roll; CODA Hnr Band & OK Yth Phlhrmnc Clarinet 4th Chair; Lk Texoma Band Cmp Symphnc Band; Psych.

GIBSON, CAROLYN L; Midwest City HS; Midwest City, OK; (2); Church Yth Grp; FCA; Hosp Aide; Key Clb; Band; Chorus; Church Choir; Mrchg Band; Pep Band; Reg Yth Cncl Dist 6 Rep; Regnl Ythcncl Sec; OBU; Choir Drctr.

GIBSON, CARRIE R; Tahlequah Sr HS; Park Hill, OK; (3); Church Yth Grp; Cmnty Wkr; GAA; Office Aide; Spanish Clb; SADD; Nwsp; Yrbk; Sftbl; Hon Roll; U Of AR; Child Psycht.

GIBSON, CORI M; Broken Arrow Sr HS; Broken Arrow, OK; (3); Church Yth Grp; Computer Clb; Pep Clb; Red Cross Aide; Spanish Clb; Teachers Aide; Ofcr Stu Cncl; Mgr(s); Hon Roll; Pres Acad Fit Awd; Northeastern ST Univ.

GIBSON, GERAD; East Central HS; Tulsa, OK; (4); Am Leg Boys St; Church Yth Grp; Debate Tm; ROTC; Spanish Clb; Drill Tm; Ed Nwsp; Rep Stu Cncl; Ftbl; Wrstlng; Law Explrs; Tstmstrs Intl; Snt Page; U Of Tulsa; Bus.

GIBSON, JESSICA; Claremore Sr HS; Claremore, OK; (2); 47/273; Church Yth Grp; French Clb; Band; Jazz Band; Mrchg Band; Pep Band; Hon Roll; Music Drctr.

GIBSON, JESSICA; Shawnee Sr HS; Shawnee, OK; (3); 13/282; Church Yth Grp; Drama Clb; FCA; Thesps; School Play; Capt Crs Cntry; Capt Trk; High Hon Roll; All-St Crss Cntry.

GIBSON, JUSTIN; Rock Creek Jr Sr HS; Caddo, OK; (2); 13/48; Church Yth Grp; Debate Tm; Drama Clb; Quiz Bowl; Scholastic Bowl; Chorus; Church Choir; School Musical; Stage Crew; Variety Show; Gifted And Talented; Southeastern OK St Univ Math Sci Prog; Law.

GIBSON, KASSI; Eakly HS; Hydro, OK; (3); Church Yth Grp; FCA; 4-H; FHA; GAA; Girl Scts; HOBY; School Play; Variety Show; Bsktbl; Star Srch Show; Bio.

GIBSON, KRISTIE M; Bixby Sr HS; Broken Arrow, OK; (1); Church Yth Grp; FCA; SADD; JV Bsktbl; JV Sftbl; JV Trk; JV Wt Lftg; Hon Roll; Pres Schlr; KS Univ.

GIBSON, KRISTIN J; Meeker HS; Meeker, OK; (1); Band; Flag Corp; Jazz Band; Var Bsktbl; Chrldng; Sftbl; Trk; Hon Roll; NHS; OBU; Acctnt.

GIBSON, LORI; Liberty Acad; Shawnee, OK; (2); Church Yth Grp; Rep Frsh Cls; Rep Soph Cls; Var Bsktbl; JV Chrldng; High Hon Roll; Art Cls.

GIBSON, MATT; Liberty Acad; Shawnee, OK; (1); Church Yth Grp; Stage Crew; Var Bsktbl; Hon Roll; 4th Pl Wrld Hstry; Chapel Club; U Of OK.

GIBSON, ROBERT R; Mid-Del Christian Schl; Midwest City, OK; (4); 6/14; Church Yth Grp; Drama Clb; Spanish Clb; Chorus; School Musical; School Play; Ofcr Bsbl; L Bsktbl; Capt Ftbl; Capt Socr; All State Ftbl; Awds For Translating Bible Into Span; OK City Univ; PT.

GIBSON, SARA D; Ardmore HS; Ardmore, OK; (3); 3/167; Am Leg Aux Girls St; Church Yth Grp; FCA; French Clb; Var Mu Alpha Theta; Chorus; Church Choir; Golf; NHS; Acctng; Cntrct Lwyr.

GIBSON, STEPHANIE; Waurika Sr HS; Waurika, OK; (3); 5/30; Drama Clb; Natl Beta Clb; Treas NFL; Spanish Clb; School Musical; Sec Frsh Cls; Sec Soph Cls; Sec Jr Cls; Ofcr Stu Cncl; Chrldng; FFA OK St Chorus; Ed; HS Eng Tchr.

GIBSON, VANCE; Hardesty Schl; Hardesty, OK; (4); 2/9; Church Yth Grp; Co-Capt FCA; Pres Natl FFA Org; Nwsp; Yrbk; Pres Frsh Cls; VP Soph Cls; Pres Sr Cls; Var L Bsbl; Var Capt Bsktbl; All-Dist Ftbl, All-Acad Dist Ftbl; OK 8 Mn All-Str Ftbl Tm W; St FFA Dgr; OK Panhandle ST U; Ag.

GIDDENS, APRIL; Idabel HS; Idabel, OK; (1); 35/135; Pep Clb; Chrldng; Sftbl; Langston U; Sec.

GIFFORD, JEREMIAH O; Locust Grove HS; Locust Grove, OK; (3); Ftbl; Wt Lftg; High Hon Roll; Acctng; Acctnt.

GIFFORD, SARAH R; Hulbert Jr Sr HS; Hulbert, OK; (2); 4-H; Rptr Yrbk; German Clb; Spanish Clb; Chorus; Cit Awd; 4-H Awd; Hon Roll; NHS; OK ST Univ.

GIGAS, DARCY; Metro Christian Acad; Tulsa, OK; (2); Church Yth Grp; Drama Clb; FCA; Key Clb; Spanish Clb; Speech Tm; Chorus; School Musical; School Play; Hist Frsh Cls; Frgn Mission Trips.

GIGLIA, CRYSTAL; Chickasha Jr HS; Chickasha, OK; (1); Church Yth Grp; FCA; Latin Clb; Sftbl; Tennis; Hon Roll; Jr NHS; NHS; Natl Jr Clscl Leag Latin Hnr Soc; OU; Law/Med.

GIL, HERMES; West Middle HS; Norman, OK; (2); Spanish Clb; Chrldng; Hon Roll; U Of OK; PT.

GILBERT, BROOKE; Sulphur HS; Sulphur, OK; (1); Church Yth Grp; FCA; GAA; School Play; Yrbk; Bsktbl; Chrldng; Crs Cntry; Trk; Hon Roll.

GILBERT, KELLY E; Bishop Kelley HS; Tulsa, OK; (3); Church Yth Grp; Cmnty Wkr; Hosp Aide; Pep Clb; Hon Roll; NHS; Pres Acad Fit Awd; OK St Univ; Psych.

GILBERT, STEPHANIE Y; Northeast HS; Oklahoma City, OK; (2); ROTC; Science Clb; Color Guard; Drill Tm; DAR Awd; Hon Roll; Jr NHS; Prfct Atten Awd; OK Univ; Cmptr Tech.

GILBERT, STEPHEN; Bixby Sr HS; Bixby, OK; (4); 1/189; Church Yth Grp; Treas French Clb; Intnl Clb; Office Aide; Quiz Bowl; Scholastic Bowl; High Hon Roll; Jr NHS; NHS; Pres Acad Fit Awd; Hist Clb VP; WA Close-Up; OK St Snt Page; U Of Tulsa; Law.

GILBREATH, MELISSA; Apache HS; Apache, OK; (4); Am Leg Aux Girls St; Church Yth Grp; FHA; Natl FFA Org; Office Aide; Teachers Aide; Church Choir; Nwsp; Yrbk; Cit Awd; Sports Med.

GILDER, WESLEY W; Muskogee HS; Muskogee, OK; (3); Church Yth Grp; Cmnty Wkr; JCL; Latin Clb; Model UN; Quiz Bowl; Chorus; Church Choir; School Play; Ofcr Frsh Cls; OK City Univ.

GILDHOUSE, NICOLE M; Newkirk HS; Ponca City, OK; (3); FCA; Sec Soph Cls; Sec Jr Cls; Stat Ftbl; Stat Wrstlng; OSU; Tchr; Law.

GILES, ERIN; Watonga HS; Watonga, OK; (2); 2/80; Bus Profs of Am; Church Yth Grp; FCA; FBLA; FHA; HOBY; VP Frsh Cls; VP Soph Cls; Var Bsktbl; Gov Hon Prg Awd; AAU Bsktbl; Southern Nazarene U; Bsktbl Cch.

GILES, JOANNA; Vian HS; Vian, OK; (2); Church Yth Grp; Spanish Clb; Band; Chorus; Color Guard; Jazz Band; Mrchg Band; Pep Band; Hon Roll.

GILES, JON JACOB; Empire Schl; Duncan, OK; (2); VP Key Clb; Hist Natl FFA Org; Rep Frsh Cls; Var Ftbl; Var Wrstlng; Prfct Atten Awd; OK ST U; Wildlife Mgmt.

GILES, KRISTIN JEAN; Putnam City West HS; Bethany, OK; (4); 59/278; Am Leg Aux Girls St; Church Yth Grp; French Clb; GAA; Chorus; Church Choir; Var Capt Vllybl; NHS; Natl Eng Mrt Awd; Vlybl All St Hnrbl Mntn; OBU; Eng Educ.

GILES, PHILIP S; Putnam City North HS; Oklahoma City, OK; (2); Church Yth Grp; Cmnty Wkr; DECA; FCA; German Clb; Office Aide; Ftbl; Hon Roll; 17th Pl Art Drawing Contest WA DC Soph Yr; Nom Red Cross Ldrshp Trng; OK ST Univ; Vet.

GILL, ADAM; Wilburton Sr HS; Wilburton, OK; (4); 34/82; Am Leg Boys St; FCA; FBLA; FHA; Letterman Clb; Office Aide; Quiz Bowl; Nwsp; Ofcr Stu Cncl; JV Bsktbl; U Of OK; FBI Agent.

GILL, JENAI; Union Intermediate HS; Broken Arrow, OK; (1); Church Yth Grp; Cmnty Wkr; FCA; 4-H; German Clb; Varsity Clb; Vllybl; Hon Roll; Jr NHS; Vllybl Frosh Awd; Home Ec Dept Awd; Young Naturalist Awd-Sci; Natl Geo Soc; Abilene Chrstn Univ.

GILL, JUSTIN W; Union Sr HS; Broken Arrow, OK; (4); 192/615; Church Yth Grp; FCA; 4-H; JV Bsbl; JV Bsktbl; JV Ftbl; 4-H Awd; Hon Roll; Jr NHS; Pres Acad Fit Awd; ACT Schlrshp NE OK A&M Coll; Citation Sen Gerald Wright; Citation Rep Don Weese; Tulsa Jr Coll.

GILL, KRISTEN E; El Reno Sr HS; El Reno, OK; (2); 54/227; Cmnty Wkr; Natl FFA Org; Cit Awd; High Hon Roll; Hon Roll; Rennaisance; Ldrs Of Tomorrow; Attnd Close-Up Washington DC 96; OU; Advrtsng/Pblcst.

GILL, TAMIESHA E; Star Spencer HS; Midwest City, OK; (1); Sec Church Yth Grp; Math Tm; Chorus; Church Choir; Mrchg Band; Rep Frsh Cls; Var Chrldng; High Hon Roll; NHS; MIT; Rsrch Scientist.

GILLESPIE, CANDACE L; Putnam City West HS; Bethany, OK; (4); 46/270; Church Yth Grp; Spanish Clb; Orch; Ofcr Stu Cncl; High Hon Roll; Jr NHS; NHS; Wrstlng Matmaid; Southern Nazarene U; Med.

GILLESPIE, JAMES C; Cushing HS; Cushing, OK; (2); Church Yth Grp; FCA; Letterman Clb; Math Clb; Spanish Clb; JV Bsbl; Var JV Ftbl; Var Wrstlng; High Hon Roll; Med.

GILLESPIE, TAYLOR; Ardmore HS; Ardmore, OK; (4); 36/220; Art Clb; Church Yth Grp; Cmnty Wkr; FCA; Latin Clb; Mu Alpha Theta; Rep Frsh Cls; Rep Soph Cls; Rep Jr Cls; Rep Sr Cls; U Of Tulsa; Eng.

GILLETTE, DARRELL W; Central Mid-HS; Norman, OK; (3); 3/22; Art Clb; Church Yth Grp; Cmnty Wkr; Teachers Aide; Ofcr Frsh Cls; Crs Cntry; Ftbl; Trk; Wt Lftg; Wrstlng; Spkng Yngr Stdnts Drgs/Othr Prblms; Schl Acts; USC; Yth Psych.

GILLEY, LAURA B; Metro Christian Acad; Tulsa, OK; (3); Church Yth Grp; Band; Jazz Band; Sec Sr Cls; Rep Stu Cncl; Hon Roll; NHS; 1st Plc ST Jazz Comp; Natl Yth Ldrshp Conf Law/Constitution.

GILLHAM, BRANDI JO; Heavener HS; Wister, OK; (2); Drama Clb; FHA; Rptr Nwsp; VP Frsh Cls; Sec Soph Cls; Hon Roll; NHS; OB/GYN.

GILLHAM, DONILEA R; Pocola HS; Pocola, OK; (3); Boy Scts; DECA; FBLA; VICA; Band; Mrchg Band; High Hon Roll; FHA; Girl Scts; Chorus; Capt Law Enfrcmnt Explorers; Natl Vo-Tech Hnr Soc; Cert Sls Person; FBI.

GILLHAM, STELLA; Burns Flat-Dill City Jshs; Burns Flat, OK; (3); 2/55; Church Yth Grp; 4-H; Rptr FHA; German Clb; HOBY; VP Frsh Cls; VP Soph Cls; Pres Jr Cls; NHS; Bsktbl; Masonic Stu Today; OSU; Med.

GILLIAM, EMIL J; Casady Schl; Edmond, OK; (4); 1/72; Pres Computer Clb; Intnl Clb; JCL; Math Clb; Spanish Clb; Orch; School Play; Lit Mag; High Hon Roll; JETS Awd; Physics Olympd Semi-Fnlst; PROMYS 95; MTNA-YAMAHA Piano Cmptn St Wnnr; Elec Engrng.

GILLIAM, HEATHER D; Bartlesville Sr HS; Bartlesville, OK; (3); Church Yth Grp; Cmnty Wkr; Chorus; Church Choir; Flag Corp; School Musical; High Hon Roll; Hon Roll; NHS; Page In OK House Of Rep; VP Chrch Yth Group; Colo Guard Mem Of The Yr; Southwestern Assemblies Of God.

GILLIAM, JASON R; Pioneer Jr Sr HS; Enid, OK; (2); #1 in class; Church Yth Grp; FCA; Natl Beta Clb; Band; Sec Soph Cls; JV Ftbl; Gov Hon Prg Awd; Hon Roll; Val.

GILLILAND, CHRISTOPHER S; Edmond Memorial HS; Edmond, OK; (2); Church Yth Grp; Key Clb; Spanish Clb; Hon Roll; NHS; Med.

GILLISPIE, MATTHEW; Claremore Sr HS; Claremore, OK; (4); 50/250; DECA; Teachers Aide; JV Socr; Hon Roll; NHS; Prfct Atten Awd; DECA Chptr Sr VP; Excl Awd Natl DECA Conf 96; Tulsa JC; Mrktg.

GILLISPIE, MISTY; Lone Grove HS; Ardmore, OK; (4); 16/72; Debate Tm; Key Clb; Model UN; Natl Beta Clb; Spanish Clb; Speech Tm; Band; Mrchg Band; High Hon Roll; NHS; OK Prin Sci Schlr; Mst Spirited Of Sr Cls; Speech Team Capt; U Of OK; Nrsng.

GILLISPIE, ROBERT J; Bishop Mcguinness HS; Edmond, OK; (3); Ftbl; Socr; NHS; Acad Awd Eng I; Chem.

GILLMAN, MIKE; Bartlesville Sr HS; Bartlesville, OK; (2); Church Yth Grp; Cmnty Wkr; FCA; JA; Office Aide; SADD; Band; Mrchg Band; School Musical; Ftbl; Chrch Puppet Mnstry; OK ST U; Naval Offcr.

GILLUM, ERIN K; Durant HS; Durant, OK; (3); Church Yth Grp; FCA; FBLA; Key Clb; Hon Roll.

GILLUM, JESSICA; Erick Jr Sr HS; Erick, OK; (4); 1/20; Church Yth Grp; Sec Treas Spanish Clb; Teachers Aide; NHS; Val; Local TSA Reporter; S W OK ST U; Elem Ed.

GILMER, ANGELA D; Wright Christian Acad; Tulsa, OK; (4); 15/36; Church Yth Grp; Spanish Clb; Teachers Aide; Var Trk; Hon Roll; NHS; Principals Awd; Oral Roberts U; Nurs.

GILMORE, JOSHUA W; Milburn Schl; Hugo, OK; (2); Mrchg Band; Trk; Vllybl; Wt Lftg; Hon Roll; Washington Univ; Art; Comic.

GILMORE, LYNDSEY R; Velma Alma HS; Velma, OK; (2); Church Yth Grp; FCA; GAA; SADD; Band; Church Choir; Mrchg Band; Pep Band; Bsktbl; Sftbl; Staticn For Ftbl & Acad Tm.

GILPIN, BECKY; Adair HS; Big Cabin, OK; (4); 9/60; Church Yth Grp; Pres Debate Tm; Drama Clb; FCA; FHA; Science Clb; Speech Tm; Teachers Aide; Chorus; Church Choir; NSU; Prof.

GILREATH, RANDALL E; Noble HS; Tinker Afb, OK; (4); 13/150; Model UN; Mu Alpha Theta; Spanish Clb; VICA; Gov Hon Prg Awd; High Hon Roll; Hon Roll; OK City CC; ASEP.

GILSTRAP, LONNIE T; Union Intermediate HS; Tulsa, OK; (2); Church Yth Grp; Pres VP FBLA; Office Aide; Spanish Clb; NHS; DFY Clb; Soc Stud Awd; Tulsa U.

GILSTRAP, TAMMIE; Coweta HS; Coweta, OK; (4); Church Yth Grp; FCA; FBLA; SADD; Jr NHS; NHS; Prfct Atten Awd; Rdlgy.

GINCHEREAU, JASON E; Oklahoma Sch Of Science & Math; Stigler, OK; (4); Boy Scts; Quiz Bowl; Band; Chorus; Mrchg Band; Orch; Ntl Merit SF; Prfct Atten Awd; Wshngtn U St Louis; Cmptr Engr.

GINCHEREAU, TRAVIS; Stigler HS; Stigler, OK; (1); Boy Scts; Church Yth Grp; Quiz Bowl; SADD; Band; Cit Awd; High Hon Roll; NHS; Tech Stdnt Assn Treas.

GINGERICH, TAMI J; Blackwell HS; Blackwell, OK; (4); 13/120; Church Yth Grp; FCA; Letterman Clb; Library Aide; Pep Clb; School Musical; Mgr Yrbk; Var Chrldng; Hon Roll; NHS; Ou Hon Stdnt; ST Hon Soc; Northern OK Coll.

GINTHER, TERI L; Panama HS; Panama, OK; (4); 16/48; Quiz Bowl; SADD; Band; Co-Capt Color Guard; Chrldng; Art Clb; NHS; Univ Of OK; Nursng.

GIPSON, CHELSEY; Owasso Sr HS; Owasso, OK; (4); 15/300; Am Leg Aux Girls St; Church Yth Grp; FCA; Ofcr Jr Cls; Ofcr Sr Cls; Rep Stu Cncl; Var Bsktbl; Var Socr; High Hon Roll; NHS; U Of OK; Geology.

GIPSON, DOMINAC J; Star Spencer HS; Midwest City, OK; (4); 42/122; Church Yth Grp; Cmnty Wkr; Hon Roll; Homecmng King 95-96; Ftbl; Rose ST Coll; Crmnl Jstc.

GIRARD, AARON M; El Reno Sr HS; El Reno, OK; (4); FCA; FTA; Natl FFA Org; Teachers Aide; VICA; Stage Crew; Cit Awd; High Hon Roll; NHS; OK Schlr; ST FFA Degree; Northwestern OK ST U; Agribus.

GIRARD, MATT; Clinton HS; Clinton, OK; (1); Ofcr Stu Cncl; Ofcr Bsbl; Ftbl; Wt Lftg; Hon Roll.

GISE, MAX E; B T Washington HS; Tulsa, OK; (3); Boy Scts; Church Yth Grp; Band; Jazz Band; Variety Show; Hon Roll; NHS; Yth & Govt VP; All City Jazz Band; IB Diploma; Psych.

GIST, JIM; Spiro HS; Spiro, OK; (4); 6/96; VP FCA; HOBY; Pres Math Clb; VP Pres Natl FFA Org; Pres Frsh Cls; Pres Soph Cls; Pres Jr Cls; Pres Sr Cls; VP Pres Stu Cncl; Var Bsktbl.

GIST, SANDY K; Spiro HS; Spiro, OK; (2); Sec FCA; Treas FHA; Rptr Natl FFA Org; Nwsp; Rep Frsh Cls; Pres Soph Cls; JV Var Chrldng; NHS.

GIULIOLI, AMY; Okmulgee HS; Okmulgee, OK; (4); 1/119; Am Leg Aux Girls St; Pres Church Yth Grp; Cmnty Wkr; French Clb; Band; Pres Jr Cls; Pres Sr Cls; Tennis; NHS; Val; 3 A & 4 A St Acad Tnns Champ Team 94 & 95; Natl Stu Cncl Cnvntn Dlgt 95; Band & Tnns Hmcmng Queen; U Of OK; Engrng.

GIVENS, CHRIS; Chandler HS; Chandler, OK; (4); 6/70; Am Leg Boys St; Church Yth Grp; Computer Clb; Letterman Clb; Math Clb; Scholastic Bowl; Var L Bsktbl; Var L Golf; Pres Acad Fit Awd; English Clb; TSA; West Pt Military Acad.

GIVENS, JOE; Verden HS; Verden, OK; (4); 1/15; Natl FFA Org; Pres Science Clb; Teachers Aide; Pres Frsh Cls; VP Soph Cls; Pres Jr Cls; Pres Sr Cls; Ofcr Bsbl; Bsktbl; Hon Roll; USAO.

GIVENS, QIANA D; Chickasha HS; Chickasha, OK; (1); Prfct Atten Awd.

GIVENS, SHERRI; Wellston Schl; Wellston, OK; (2); GAA; Treas Soph Cls; Var Bsktbl; Var Sftbl; Hon Roll; Jr NHS; NHS; Cardlgst.

GLANCE, JANELLE L; Edmond North HS; Edmond, OK; (4); 83/330; Cmnty Wkr; FHA; JA; Spanish Clb; Pres Schlr; U Of Cntrl OK; Nrsng.

GLANCEY, SHERI; Union Sr HS; Tulsa, OK; (4); Church Yth Grp; DECA; FCA; FBLA; Key Clb; Sec Frsh Cls; Var JV Chrldng; Powder Puff Ftbl; JV Trk; Hon Roll; Stu Cncl Rep; Symphny Set; Natl Chmpnshp Squad 94-95; KU; Law.

GLANCY, BRANDON K; Burns Flat-Dill City Jshs; Burns Flat, OK; (3); Am Leg Boys St; German Clb; Natl FFA Org; Sec Frsh Cls; Var Bsbl; Hon Roll; Wichita ST Univ; Law Enfrcmnt.

GLANVILLE, MATT C; Wilburton Sr HS; Wilburton, OK; (3); Church Yth Grp; FCA; FBLA; Letterman Clb; Quiz Bowl; Spanish Clb; Speech Tm; Varsity Clb; Chorus; Church Choir; Eastern OK ST Coll.

GLASMAN, JANA; Miami Sr HS; Miami, OK; (1); Ofcr Stu Cncl; Chrldng; Hon Roll; OSU; Phrmcst.

GLASMAN, JENNIE; Miami Sr HS; Miami, OK; (3); Church Yth Grp; Church Choir; Yrbk; Ofcr Stu Cncl; Chrldng; Hon Roll; NHS; OSU; Cnslr.

GLASS, AMANDA G; Stilwell HS; Stilwell, OK; (2); Indian Heritage; U Of AR; Bus.

GLASS, CRYSTAL D; Boise City HS; Boise City, OK; (1); 5/40; 4-H; Pres Frsh Cls; JV Bsktbl; Var L Trk; 4-H Awd; High Hon Roll; Hon Roll; OK St Univ; Vet.

GLASS, MICHAEL; Edmond North HS; Edmond, OK; (4); 92/420; Am Leg Boys St; Church Yth Grp; Cmnty Wkr; Pep Clb; ROTC; SADD; Band; Church Choir; Jazz Band; Mrchg Band; Outstnding Brss Ensmbl OK; Yth Deacn; Modrtr OK Presb Celebrtn; UOK.

GLAZE, RYAN; Chickasha HS; Chickasha, OK; (1); Church Yth Grp; French Clb; Letterman Clb; Chorus; Church Choir; Yrbk; JV Bsktbl; Var Tennis; Cit Awd; Jr NHS; OK Bapt U; Music Minister.

GLAZIER, FLOYD S; Lomega HS; Loyal, OK; (2); 1/15; 4-H; Natl FFA Org; Scholastic Bowl; VP Soph Cls; Var Bsbl; High Hon Roll; NHS; Trap Shooting Team.

GLEASON, MELISSA A; Cushing HS; Cushing, OK; (3); Drama Clb; FCA; Sec Math Clb; VP Spanish Clb; School Play; Sec Jr Cls; Cit Awd; High Hon Roll; Jr NHS; NHS; OK U.

GLEASON, MOLLY D; Cushing HS; Cushing, OK; (1); FCA; GAA; Spanish Clb; Pres Frsh Cls; Ofcr Stu Cncl; Bsktbl; Sftbl; High Hon Roll.

GLEAVES, TODD; U S Grant HS; Oklahoma City, OK; (2); 1/345; Boy Scts; Church Yth Grp; FCA; Ofcr Soph Cls; JV Bsbl; JV L Crs Cntry; Var Ftbl; Var L Golf; Var L Wrstlng; NHS; OK U; Hlth.

GLEICHMAN, LANI; Seminole Jr Sr HS; Seminole, OK; (2); Church Yth Grp; Math Clb; Scholastic Bowl; Band; Mrchg Band; Pep Band; Cit Awd; High Hon Roll; Hon Roll; Pres Horse Rdng Club; OSU; Vet.

GLEICHMAN, REGINA M; Wilburton Sr HS; Wilburton, OK; (3); 2/80; Am Leg Aux Girls St; Church Yth Grp; FBLA; FHA; FTA; Letterman Clb; Band; Cit Awd; High Hon Roll; NHS; OK ST Univ.

GLENN, CATHERINE M; Porter Jr Sr HS; Porter, OK; (2); 3/40; Church Yth Grp; FCA; GAA; Pres Natl FFA Org; SADD; JV Var Bsktbl; JV Var Sftbl; Hon Roll; NHS; Sal; 4-H Clb; Span Clb; Environ Law.

GLENN, CHASTITY T; Star Spencer HS; Midwest City, OK; (2); Church Yth Grp; Cmnty Wkr; Teachers Aide; Band; Var Trk; Var Vllybl; Hon Roll; Miss Soul Bazaar 1st Runner Up 96; Just Girls Pub Eassay Contest 3rd Runner Up; Law.

GLENN, JENNIFER E; Will Rogers HS; Tulsa, OK; (1); Art Clb; Church Yth Grp; English Clb; French Clb; Color Guard; Flag Corp; Mrchg Band; High Hon Roll; Hon Roll; Jr NHS; Wintergrd; CODE.

GLENNAN, MELISSA; Fairland Jr Sr HS; Fairland, OK; (3); Pres Frsh Cls; Pres Jr Cls; Var Bsktbl; Var Sftbl; Var Trk; Hon Roll; NHS; Pres Acad Fit Awd; Sprts Dr.

GLOVER, COURTNEY; B T Washington HS; Tulsa, OK; (4); 106/264; Church Yth Grp; FBLA; Teachers Aide; Band; Mrchg Band; School Musical; Rep Frsh Cls; Rep Soph Cls; Rep Jr Cls; Hist Sr Cls; AFRO Amer Soc; Alpha Kappa Xinos; Jackson ST U; Marketing.

GLOVER, DUSTIN; Elgin HS; Elgin, OK; (4); 29/74; Am Leg Boys St; VP Treas Natl FFA Org; Teachers Aide; Bsktbl; Mgr(s); 4-H Awd; Hon Roll; Cameron U; Anml Sci.

GLOVER, JOSHUA D; Ponca City Sr HS; Ponca City, OK; (2); Church Yth Grp; Office Aide; Hon Roll; Pioneer Vo-Tech; Auto Mechanic.

GLOVER, JUSTIN M; Ponca City Sr HS; Ponca City, OK; (4); 23/350; Church Yth Grp; Teachers Aide; JV Bsbl; High Hon Roll; Hon Roll; NHS; Pres Schlr; Chrch Xmas Plays; N OK Col; Bio Sci.

GLOVER, MARK B; Metro Christian Acad; Tulsa, OK; (2); 1/80; Church Yth Grp; Var L Bsbl; High Hon Roll; NHS.

GLOVER, MARY; Marlow HS; Marlow, OK; (4); 4/97; Hist FHA; Hosp Aide; Key Clb; Pep Clb; VP Spanish Clb; SADD; Pom Pon; Sftbl; Trk; High Hon Roll; OK Hnr Soc; Skpd Jr Yr; Certf Phlebotomist; U Of Tulsa; Pre Med/Bio.

GLOVER, MISTY; Mustang HS; Mustang, OK; (2); Church Yth Grp; FCA; Var Chrldng; Power Tumbling; All-Amer Chrldr; OK Univ; Sports Med.

GLOVER, MITCHELL R; Mustang HS; Yukon, OK; (1); Band; Ftbl; Trk; Hon Roll; Renaissance Hnr.

GLOVER, PATRICK M; Bishop Kelley HS; Tulsa, OK; (4); 11/150; Boy Scts; Cmnty Wkr; FCA; Spanish Clb; Ed Nwsp; Yrbk; JV Bsbl; Var Capt Ftbl; High Hon Roll; NHS; Page OK House Of Rep; Mock Trial Pgm; U Of OK; Comp Sci.

GLYNN, JOHN W; Quinton Jr Sr HS; Quinton, OK; (3); Church Yth Grp; FCA; FHA; Quiz Bowl; Band; Mrchg Band; Var Bsbl; Var Bsktbl; Var Ftbl; Var Trk.

GOAD, CRYSTAL; Mustang HS; Yukon, OK; (3); 57/386; Church Yth Grp; JA; Teachers Aide; Chorus; Church Choir; Flag Corp; Mrchg Band; Hon Roll; NHS; Yth Alive; Wntr Grd; Educ.

GOAD, JEFF D; Edmond North HS; Edmond, OK; (3); 158/348; Church Yth Grp; JV Var Bsbl.

GOAD, JENNIFER; Bartlesville Mid HS; Bartlesville, OK; (1); Church Yth Grp; School Play; Mgr Bsktbl; Mgr(s); KA U; Phys Thrpst.

GOAD, JOHN M; Midwest City HS; Del City, OK; (2); 106/480; FCA; Letterman Clb; Ftbl; Trk; Wt Lftg; Hon Roll; Prfct Atten Awd; Phys Thrpy.

GOAD, RYAN A; Edmond North HS; Edmond, OK; (3); 139/348; Church Yth Grp; JV Var Bsbl.

GOAD, STEPHANIE D; Mustang HS; Yukon, OK; (3); 1/360; Church Yth Grp; Chorus; Capt Color Guard; Capt Flag Corp; Mrchg Band; High Hon Roll; Hon Roll; NHS; Val; Youth Alive; Winterguard; Bus.

GOANS, TERRA D; Pioneer Jr Sr HS; Enid, OK; (2); 13/56; FHA; Natl Beta Clb; Sftbl; Trk; Hon Roll; NHS; OK ST U; Law.

GOBBELL, AMANDA W; Tahlequah Sr HS; Tahlequah, OK; (4); 25/250; FCA; Service Clb; SADD; Chorus; Rep Soph Cls; Rep SADD; Var Trk; NHS; Ntl Merit Ltr; Interact; Tutor; Scl Work.

GOBBLE, MATTHEW; Oilton HS; Oilton, OK; (2); Church Yth Grp; Cmnty Wkr; Church Choir; School Play; Ofcr Bsbl; Bsktbl; NE Univ; Comp.

GOBER, GREG D; Bethel HS; Shawnee, OK; (1); Art Clb; Spanish Clb; JV Ftbl; JV Trk; JV Wrstlng; Psychiatrist.

GOBIN, STEPHANIE; Henryetta Sr HS; Henryetta, OK; (2); FCA; Chorus; Var Bsktbl; Var Sftbl; Var Wt Lftg; Hon Roll; Jr NHS; Psych.

GOBLE, ALICIA L; Pauls Valley HS; Pauls Valley, OK; (2); FHA; Spanish Clb; Band; Chorus; School Musical; Hon Roll; Scndry Tchng.

GOBLE, HANNAH; Ada HS; Ada, OK; (4); 1/163; Mu Alpha Theta; NFL; Quiz Bowl; Sec Service Clb; Spanish Clb; Orch; High Hon Roll; NHS; Spanish NHS; Val; Anthology Of Poetry By Yng Amrcns; OK Yng Wrtrs Anthology; Bryn Mawr Coll.

GOCKEL, KATIE; Indianola HS; Mcalester, OK; (4); 13/40; FBLA; FHA; Teachers Aide; High Hon Roll; Hon Roll; NHS; Bus.

GODBEHERE, BROOK D; Blackwell HS; Blackwell, OK; (3); FCA; Letterman Clb; Natl FFA Org; Pep Clb; Spanish Clb; VP Jr Cls; Mgr(s); Hon Roll; FFA Sheep Proficiency Awd.

GODBENERE, KARA N; Bartlesville Mid HS; Bartlesville, OK; (2); 101/481; Church Yth Grp; FBLA; Spanish Clb; Bsktbl; Trk; Hon Roll; Jr NHS; NHS; Pol Sci/Atty.

GODDARD, TRICIA; Westmoore HS; Moore, OK; (3); Church Yth Grp; Teachers Aide; Mgr(s); Cit Awd; Hon Roll; Jr NHS; UCO; Tchr.

GODFREY, CRYSTAL; Lone Grove HS; Ardmore, OK; (2); Church Yth Grp; Speech Tm; Chorus; Hon Roll; NHS; ST Speech Cmptn 2nd Place In Humorous Duet; ST Vocal Cmptn Super Rating.

GODFREY, JENNIFER; Hobart HS; Lone Wolf, OK; (3); 8/60; Church Yth Grp; Drill Tm; School Musical; Rep Frsh Cls; Rep Soph Cls; Rep Stu Cncl; Chrldng; High Hon Roll; Hon Roll; NHS; All Star Chrldr UCA; Lifegrd; Dance; OK U; Acctng.

GODMAN, SHARON R; Cushing HS; Cushing, OK; (3); Church Yth Grp; FHA; Math Clb; Science Clb; Chorus; High Hon Roll; NHS; Prfct Atten Awd; All Amer Schlr; Chorus, Choraliers VP; Natl Hnr Rl; Tulsa JC; Dental Hygn.

GODWIN, AMY; Kerr Jr HS; Oklahoma City, OK; (2); FCA; Girl Scts; Pep Clb; Spanish Clb; Teachers Aide; Chorus; Var Pom Pon; Mgr Swmmng; Cit Awd; High Hon Roll; Psycht.

GODWIN, DOMINIC; Millwood HS; Oklahoma City, OK; (2); Bus Profs of Am; Computer Clb; Library Aide; Cit Awd; Hon Roll; Prfct Atten Awd; Southern U; Bus Comp.

GODWIN, TAMRA L; Seminole Jr Sr HS; Seminole, OK; (2); Church Yth Grp; French Clb; Math Clb; Sec Quiz Bowl; Hon Roll; Algebra I Awd; ECU; CPA.

GOEN, SANDRA D; Shawnee Sr HS; Shawnee, OK; (1); Church Yth Grp; Co-Capt Rep Drama Clb; Thesps; Stage Crew; NHS; Pres Acad Fit Awd; Speech Tm; Church Choir; School Play; Choir; Violinist; Most Prmsng Actrss Awd 96.

GOERINGER, AMANDA; Chattanooga Schl; Chattanooga, OK; (4); 9/17; Art Clb; Church Yth Grp; CAP; FBLA; Pep Clb; Chorus; Yrbk; Sec Frsh Cls; VP Jr Cls; Vllybl; Congrssnl Ldrshp Conf Delg; OK Blood Inst Donar; Cameron U; Vet Med.

GOERINGER, SARAH; Burns Flat-Dill City Schls; Foss, OK; (4); 3/33; Pres Church Yth Grp; 4-H; FHA; German Clb; GAA; Natl FFA Org; Pep Clb; School Play; Pres Frsh Cls; VP Sr Cls; OK Hwy Ptrl Cadet Lwmn; Bsktbl Hmcmng Queen; Southwestern OK ST Univ; Vet.

GOERTZ, ELISABETH A; Salina HS; Salina, OK; (2); Church Yth Grp; FTA; Quiz Bowl; Red Cross Aide.

GOERTZ, JAMES M; Salina HS; Salina, OK; (2); Church Yth Grp; Band; Jazz Band; Mrchg Band.

GOFF, JACLYN; Midwest Cty HS; Midwest City, OK; (2); 85/473; Church Yth Grp; Cmnty Wkr; FCA; German Clb; Hosp Aide; Letterman Clb; Pep Clb; Hon Roll; Jr NHS; NHS; Duke Univ; Psych.

GOFF, JILL L; Enid Sr HS; Enid, OK; (3); 184/445; Church Yth Grp; Latin Clb; Crs Cntry; Powder Puff Ftbl; Swmmng; Trk; Hon Roll; Phy Thrpst.

GOFORTH, AMY M; Union Intermediate HS; Tulsa, OK; (1); Cit Awd; Hon Roll; U Of OK; Bus.

GOFORTH, BRANDI R; Classen Schl Of Adv Stu; Oklahoma City, OK; (3); 16/63; Dance Clb; VP Drama Clb; German Clb; School Musical; School Play; Hon Roll; Jr NHS; NHS; Renaissance Acad Awd; OK Hnr Soc; Sci Fiction Clb; Bio.

GOFORTH, JOLINE M; Clayton Jr Sr HS; Clayton, OK; (2); FBLA; Pres Soph Cls; Chrldng; Sftbl; Hon Roll; Pl 2nd In Phy Sci At Curriculum Cont At Carl Albert ST Coll; Equine Vet; Comp Prgmr.

GOGGIN, KIMBERLY; Wellston Schl; Wellston, OK; (3); FHA; Bsktbl; Sftbl; Hon Roll; NHS; Vet.

GOING, JERRY E; Cushing HS; Cushing, OK; (1); Drama Clb; Spanish Clb; Band; Mrchg Band; JV Bsbl; JV Ftbl; Hon Roll; Jr NHS.

GOING, ROBYN K; Cushing HS; Cushing, OK; (4); 13/156; Church Yth Grp; Drama Clb; FHA; Hosp Aide; Math Clb; Science Clb; Spanish Clb; Teachers Aide; Chorus; Church Choir; Cushing Cmnty Theatre; Medcl Explrs; OK Hnr Soc; Var Schlr; OK ST U; Pre-Med.

GOINS, AUTUMN B; Choctaw HS; Choctaw, OK; (4); 1/302; Church Yth Grp; Key Clb; Spanish Clb; Crs Cntry; Tennis; Gov Hon Prg Awd; Jr NHS; Pres Schlr; St Schlr; Val; Oral Roberts U; Med.

GOINS, LORI; Liberty Acad; Shawnee, OK; (4); 1/15; Church Yth Grp; Teachers Aide; Stage Crew; Lit Mag; Treas Sr Cls; Treas Stu Cncl; Capt Bsktbl; Capt Chrldng; Ntl Merit Ltr; Val; All Conf Bsktbl Supts Hnr Roll; U Of OK; Poltcl Sci.

GOINS, MICHAEL; Bluejacket Schl; Bluejacket, OK; (2); 2/26; Quiz Bowl.

GOLBEK, KATHINA M; Waynoka HS; Waynoka, OK; (2); Art Clb; Church Yth Grp; FHA; Pep Clb; SADD; Teachers Aide; Rep Yrbk; L Sftbl; Hon Roll; Kids Inc Pgm Act; Rodeos; Best Of Art Show; OSU; Vet Sci.

GOLBEK, MARK R; Kingfisher HS; Kingfisher, OK; (2); Key Clb; Quiz Bowl; Scholastic Bowl; Ftbl; Wrstlng; Hon Roll.

GOLD, MILLIE; Edmond North HS; Edmond, OK; (3); Church Yth Grp; Key Clb; Mu Alpha Theta; Hist Spanish Clb; Rptr Yrbk; Sec NHS; Yth For Christ Camps Bibl Stud Grop; Outstdng Span II Stu 94-95; Stu Actn Ldrshp Team Chrch Yth Group; Pre-Med; Pediatrics.

GOLDBERG, NATALIE C; Duncan HS; Duncan, OK; (2); Hosp Aide; JV Tennis; Hon Roll; Hlth Careers Clb; Duncan Regnl Hosp Vol.

GOLDEN, CHEREA E; Western Heights Sr HS; Oklahoma City, OK; (2); Church Yth Grp; Cmnty Wkr; Service Clb; Band; Mrchg Band; Stage Crew; Hon Roll; LEAP Pgm Bd Dir/Co-Chr Cvl Comm; OK Univ; Law.

GOLDEN JR, LARRY; South Intermediate HS; Broken Arrow, OK; (1); Church Yth Grp; Library Aide; Tennis; Cit Awd; Hon Roll; OK Hnr Soc; CSU; Piano; Oro; Corp Lwyr.

GOLDEN, LETICIA; Grandfield Jr Sr HS; Grandfield, OK; (2); 5/25; HOBY; Rptr Phtg Nwsp; Rep Frsh Cls; Mgr(s); Score Keeper; Hon Roll; Cameron U Sci Acad; TSA; Acad Tm.

GOLDEN, STACI; Blackwell HS; Blackwell, OK; (1); Church Yth Grp; Hosp Aide; Band; Flag Corp; Mrchg Band; Orch; Pep Band; Golf; Hon Roll; OK ST U; Vet.

GOLDEN, TIM; Byng Sr HS; Ada, OK; (4); 6/72; Pres Church Yth Grp; Pres 4-H; Pep Clb; Quiz Bowl; Pres Band; Mrchg Band; School Musical; French Clb; Natl FFA Org; Band; E Central U; Bio.

GOLDESBE, DAVID; Cushing HS; Cushing, OK; (4); 46/156; Am Leg Boys St; Drama Clb; FCA; Natl FFA Org; Sec Frsh Cls; Sec Soph Cls; VP Jr Cls; Pres Stu Cncl; Ftbl; Trk; Tomorrows Ldrs Prog; Class Fav; Chmbr Of Cmmrc HS Rep & Stu Of Mnth; NE OK Coll; Frstry.

GOLDFARB, RACHEL L; Putnam City North HS; Oklahoma City, OK; (1); Art Clb; Temple Yth Grp; Socr; High Hon Roll.

GOLDMAN, DARLA; Stilwell HS; Stilwell, OK; (1); 2/183; Natl FFA Org; Capt Chrldng; High Hon Roll; Hon Roll; NHS; U Of AR; Ag Ed.

GOLDSBERRY, ALICE R; Panola HS; Red Oak, OK; (2); Drama Clb; Rptr FHA; Thesps; School Play; Hon Roll; Prfct Atten Awd; Cmpttve Speech; Crmnl Law.

GOLDSMITH, GREG; Pauls Valley HS; Pauls Valley, OK; (4); 1/83; Church Yth Grp; French Clb; Natl Beta Clb; Science Clb; Teachers Aide; Chorus; School Play; Var L Golf; High Hon Roll; Hon Roll; Golf 2-A St Chmpns 95; Mock Trial; Math Hotline Tutor; Pharmcy.

GOLDSMITH, JOHN M; Pauls Valley HS; Pauls Valley, OK; (1); Art Clb; Church Yth Grp; Spanish Clb; Var Golf; High Hon Roll; Med.

GOLEMAN, ERICA J; Charles Page HS; Sand Springs, OK; (1); Church Yth Grp; FCA; Chorus; Church Choir; Rptr Nwsp; Rep Stu Cncl; JV Chrldng; High Hon Roll; Hon Roll; Jr NHS; Eastrn Dist Hnr Choir 95-96-Highst Alto Score; Solo Cont, Excl At Dist, Super Tri-St; Fine Arts Fstvl.

GOLEMAN, JACQI; Norman Sr HS; Norman, OK; (3); Church Yth Grp; FBLA; Spanish Clb; Yrbk; Lit Mag; NHS; Spec Olympcs Vol; YMCA Vol; Fash Merch.

GOLIGHTLY, KAYNA; Shawnee Sr HS; Shawnee, OK; (3); 8/340; Church Yth Grp; Cmnty Wkr; FCA; Spanish Clb; VP Jr Cls; Chrldng; Crs Cntry; Tennis; Trk; High Hon Roll; Mission Trips Local/Overseas UMCOR; Salvation Army Soup Kitchen; CCYM Rep S OK City Dist/Meth Chrch; Poly Sci.

GOLL, RANDALL E; Washington Jr Sr HS; Blanchard, OK; (2); FCA; JV Var Bsbl; JV Var Ftbl; Var Wt Lftg; Cit Awd; High Hon Roll; Hon Roll; NHS; Prfct Atten Awd; U Of OK; Lawyer/Acctnt.

GOLLA, JAMEY C; Mc Alester HS; Mcalester, OK; (3); 2/194; Am Leg Aux Girls St; Church Yth Grp; FCA; Spanish Clb; Ofcr Bsbl; Ftbl; Hon Roll; NHS; Chem/Physics Club; OK Asst Univ; Pre Law.

GOLSEN, JOSHUA B; Bishop Mcguinness HS; Oklahoma City, OK; (3); Art Clb; Cmnty Wkr; German Clb; Letterman Clb; Pep Clb; SADD; VP Temple Yth Grp; Varsity Clb; Yrbk; Var L Tennis; Men's Club; Jr Cnslr; Grphc Dsgn/Cnmtgrphy.

GOLTRY, BEN; Luther HS; Luther, OK; (4); 4/41; Church Yth Grp; Letterman Clb; Teachers Aide; Band; Mrchg Band; Hon Roll.

GOMGARDNER, CHERIE A; Lawton Sr HS; Lawton, OK; (2); FHA; Hosp Aide; Pep Clb; Hon Roll; Teen Court.

GONSER, ASHLEY L; Woodward HS; Woodward, OK; (1); Church Yth Grp; Church Choir; Bsktbl/Vlybl/Sftbl/Chrch Yth Grp; NW ST; Lgl Sec.

GONSETH, AMANDA; Hilldale HS; Muskogee, OK; (3); 2/101; Church Yth Grp; Key Clb; Mu Alpha Theta; Band; School Play; Rep Stu Cncl; High Hon Roll; Treas NHS; Computer Clb; Drama Clb; Wills Guild Secy; Band Royalty Attendant; Chemist.

GONZALES, D DWIGHT; Duncan HS; Duncan, OK; (3); Boy Scts; French Clb; Key Clb; ROTC; SADD; Band; Mrchg Band; Church Yth Grp; Hon Roll; Sons Amer Rvltn; Mltry Ordr Wrld Wars; Retire Offcrs Assn; Hlth Careers Club; SAI/AI Ldrshp Awd; Pdtrc Srgn.

GONZALES, JOHN J; Cement Jr Sr HS; Cement, OK; (3); Church Yth Grp; Natl FFA Org; Nwsp; Yrbk; Ofcr Bsbl; Ftbl; Trk; Hon Roll; Dr.

GONZALES, KEVIN W; Stilwell HS; Stilwell, OK; (3); Church Yth Grp; Bsktbl; Cltrl Clb.

GONZALES, MICHAEL; Vinita HS; Vinita, OK; (2); Art Clb; FHA; Math Tm; Yrbk; Hon Roll; Ntl Merit Ltr; Prfct Atten Awd; NSU.

GONZALES, SHEILA; Capitol Hill HS; Oklahoma City, OK; (4); 3/151; Dance Clb; VP Science Clb; Pres Spanish Clb; Band; Mrchg Band; Variety Show; Co-Ed Nwsp; Hon Roll; VP NHS; Clggng Tm; Presdntl Acad Ftns Awd Pgm Awd; Nrthestrn ST U; Cmptr Prgrmng.

GONZALEZ, AALYSHA M; Union Sr HS; Broken Arrow, OK; (4); Hosp Aide; Key Clb; Office Aide; Spanish Clb; School Play; Var Socr; Trk; High Hon Roll; Jr NHS; NHS; Renssnc; Yng Dmcrts Pblcty Chrmn; Hspnc Schlrshp Fndtn; Aerntcl Engrng.

GONZALEZ, CHRISTINA D; Boise City HS; Boise City, OK; (1); Church Yth Grp; FHA; PSU; Math Tchr; Coach.

GONZALEZ, INGRID; Edmond North HS; Edmond, OK; (3); 1/430; Church Yth Grp; Mu Alpha Theta; Band; Church Choir; Mrchg Band; Orch; Ed Nwsp; Hon Roll; NHS; Brigham Young U; Pre-Med.

GONZALEZ, JOSE E; Madill HS; Madill, OK; (1).

GONZALEZ, JOSE M; Boise City HS; Boise City, OK; (3); 18/32; JV Bsktbl; Var Crs Cntry; JV Ftbl; Var Trk; Var Wt Lftg.

GONZALEZ, LEA; Hennessey HS; Hennessey, OK; (2).

GONZALEZ, ROSALINDA; Southeast HS; Oklahoma City, OK; (2); Art Clb; Socr; Sftbl; Swmmng; High Hon Roll; TX A&M; Marine Bio.

GOOCH, ALISON L; Lawton Sr HS; Lawton, OK; (2); Church Yth Grp; FCA; HOBY; Band; Var L Bsktbl; Var L Crs Cntry; Var L Socr; High Hon Roll; NHS.

GOOCH, ANGELA; Edmond Memrl HS; Edmond, OK; (2); Church Yth Grp; Key Clb; Spanish Clb; Variety Show; Rep Soph Cls; Rep Jr Cls; Rep Sr Cls; Ofcr Stu Cncl; Chrldng; Pom Pon; U Of FL; Child Psych.

GOOCH, JASON; Mulhall Orlando HS; Mulhall, OK; (4); 2/21; Church Yth Grp; FCA; Pres Sr Cls; Rep Stu Cncl; Var L Bsbl; Var L Bsktbl; NHS; Sal; German Clb; Library Aide; Lions Clb Awd; Physics By Satellite; Mst Likely To Succeed; OK ST U; Math.

GOOCH, SANDRA D; Union Sr HS; Tulsa, OK; (4); Key Clb; Powder Puff Ftbl; Var Swmmng; Hon Roll; NHS; Pres Acad Fit Awd; Natl Assn Of Stu Cncl St Guide 95; Lifegrd; Water Safty Instr; OK U; Nursng.

GOODE, ADAM; Caney Valley HS; Ramona, OK; (4); 5/44; Am Leg Boys St; Church Yth Grp; German Clb; Band; Jazz Band; Bsktbl; Trk; Gov Hon Prg Awd; Pres NHS; Prfct Atten Awd; David Lipscomb U; Bio.

GOODE, JEFF A; Grandfield Jr Sr HS; Grandfield, OK; (2); Church Yth Grp; Cmnty Wkr; Natl FFA Org; VICA; Hon Roll; FAA VP; OK St Univ; Animal Sci.

GOODE, TIMOTHY; Caney Valley HS; Ramona, OK; (4); 7/44; Am Leg Boys St; Church Yth Grp; Teachers Aide; Band; Jazz Band; Mrchg Band; Orch; Hon Roll; VP NHS; Amer Legion Bugle Corp; David Lipscomb U; Bible.

GOODEN, CRYSTAL D; Blackwell HS; Blackwell, OK; (2); Hist FHA; Church Yth Grp; Cmnty Wkr; FCA; Pep Clb; Var Bsktbl; Mgr(s); Wt Lftg; Hon Roll; Northern OK Coll; Cmptrs.

GOODEN, ERIC; Midwest City HS; Midwest City, OK; (3); FHA; Pres Stu Cncl; Var Bsktbl; Var Ftbl; Var Trk; High Hon Roll; NHS; Ftbl MVP, St Chmps; Acctnt.

GOODEN, JENNIFER; Kingfisher HS; Kingfisher, OK; (3); 1/100; Am Leg Aux Girls St; HOBY; Quiz Bowl; Scholastic Bowl; Speech Tm; Ed Nwsp; Treas Rep Stu Cncl; Chrldng; Cit Awd; NHS; Cell Bio.

GOODEN, STEFFANIE; Kingfisher HS; Kingfisher, OK; (1); 32/115; Church Yth Grp; FCA; Spanish Clb; Rptr Nwsp; Rep Frsh Cls; Ofcr Stu Cncl; Chrldng; Hon Roll; OK ST U.

GOODENOW, NATE E; Macarthur Sr HS; Lawton, OK; (3); Church Yth Grp; FCA; Science Clb; Spanish Clb; Church Choir; Ed Yrbk; Rep Stu Cncl; Tennis; High Hon Roll; NHS; OK Univ.

GOODIN, FRANCI B; Poteau HS; Poteau, OK; (3); Church Yth Grp; Drama Clb; Library Aide; Office Aide; Speech Tm; Chorus; Church Choir; Ofcr Stu Cncl; Chrldng; Hon Roll; Yth On The Rock; Med.

GOODMAN, AMBERLY; Seiling Schl; Chester, OK; (2); Church Yth Grp; FCA; HOBY; Capt Quiz Bowl; Band; Church Choir; Drm Mjr(t); Var Bsktbl; Var Trk; Hon Roll; OSU; Arch.

GOODMAN, AUDREY; Wilson Schl; Henryetta, OK; (2); Church Yth Grp; Computer Clb; Dance Clb; Drama Clb; GAA; Girl Scts; Library Aide; Pep Clb; Scholastic Bowl; Science Clb; Tmblng; OSU Stillwater; Med.

GOODMAN, AUTUMN L; Sayre HS; Sayre, OK; (2); Church Yth Grp; 4-H; GAA; Scholastic Bowl; Band; Rptr Frsh Cls; Bsktbl; 4-H Awd; Hon Roll; Math Tm; OK Crstn U Ofsci Arts; Comm.

GOODMAN, CANDRA L; Charles Page HS; Tulsa, OK; (3); 47/365; Spanish Clb; Band; Mrchg Band; Pep Band; Hon Roll; Selected All Dist Band 9th Grd; TJC/OSU; Vet.

GOODMAN, CASSEY; Sayre HS; Sayre, OK; (4); 1/40; Am Leg Aux Girls St; 4-H; Natl FFA Org; Chorus; Ed Yrbk; Rep Jr Cls; Rep Sr Cls; Stat Bsktbl; 4-H Awd; Pres Acad Fit Awd.

GOODMAN, DEBBIE; Carl Albert Jr HS; Midwest City, OK; (3); 24/233; Art Clb; Cmnty Wkr; Drama Clb; FCA; Key Clb; Letterman Clb; Library Aide; Pep Clb; Spanish Clb; Chorus; Jazz Choir; All Star Chr Sqd; Marymount Coll; Mscl Thtr.

GOODMAN, JOHN; Mannford HS; Sand Springs, OK; (3); Church Yth Grp; Drama Clb; SADD; Acpl Chr; Chorus; Church Choir; School Musical; Co-Ed Yrbk; Hon Roll; ORU; Music.

GOODMAN, JUSTIN D; Woodward HS; Woodward, OK; (1); Church Yth Grp; FCA; JV Ftbl; Var Wt Lftg; Hon Roll.

GOODMAN, MICHELLE; White Oak Jr-Sr HS; Vinita, OK; (3); Science Clb; Bsktbl; Hon Roll; NHS.

GOODMAN, WILLIAM D; Del City HS; Del City, OK; (2); Band; Mrchg Band; Pep Band; Hon Roll; Jr NHS; Pol Sci/Law Schl.

GOODNER, BRETT; Medford Schl; Medford, OK; (4); 5/25; FCA; Letterman Clb; Pep Clb; Quiz Bowl; Scholastic Bowl; Spanish Clb; Varsity Clb; Acpl Chr; Sec Band; Chorus; Engr.

GOODNER, KEELA; Medford Schl; Medford, OK; (3); 3/16; Sec Church Yth Grp; FCA; FHA; Letterman Clb; Pep Clb; Spanish Clb; Acpl Chr; Band; Pres Chorus; Church Choir; Show Choir; Phy Ther.

GOODPASTURE, AMY L; Edmond Memorial HS; Edmond, OK; (3); FBLA; Office Aide; Spanish Clb; Ldrshp Cncl Francis Tuttle Voc Tech; Natl Yth Ldrshp Cncl Invitation; Miss Amer Teen Pageants Invitatn; UCO; Acctng; Legal Secretary.

GOODRICH, GAVIN C; Skiatook HS; Skiatook, OK; (1); Boy Scts; Church Yth Grp; FBLA; Band; Chorus; Church Choir; Jazz Band; Mrchg Band; Pep Band; Jr NHS; Telecommunications.

GOODRICK, ROBERT; Midwest City HS; Midwest City, OK; (4); 26/419; Boy Scts; Church Yth Grp; Drama Clb; Chorus; School Musical; Rep Stu Cncl; NHS; 4.0 Clb; Rotry Yth Ldrshp Awd; Masonic Stu Of Today Awd; OK Chrstn U; Bus Sci.

GOODRIDGE, TED; B T Washington HS; Tulsa, OK; (3); Boy Scts; Computer Clb; Debate Tm; German Clb; NFL; ROTC; Speech Tm; Hon Roll; NHS; Pres Acad Fit Awd; Eagle Sct; Sons Amer Revolution Schlsp St Wnnr; Piano; USAF Acad; Comp Sci.

GOODSELL, HEATHER; Lawton Sr HS; Lawton, OK; (2); High Hon Roll; Hon Roll; Acctng Clss Indpndnt Stud Pgm; Gftd/Tlntd Pgm; TAP Scres 69% Or Hghr; Bus.

GOODSON, CHARLIE; Antlers Sr HS; Antlers, OK; (4); 3/65; Band; Jazz Band; Mrchg Band; Pep Band; Hon Roll; Jr NHS; NHS; Prfct Atten Awd; Supr Rating Tuba Solo St Cmptn; All Dist Band; 4 Sts Band; Southeastern OK ST U; Music.

GOODSON, JOSH G; Tecumseh HS; Earlsboro, OK; (2); Natl FFA Org; JV Bsbl; JV Var Ftbl; Var Wt Lftg; Cit Awd; Hon Roll; NHS; Chapt FFA Degree/Treas 96; Lttered Ftbl; OK ST Univ; Vet.

GOODSON, KASI; Wetumka Jr Sr HS; Wetumka, OK; (4); 3/32; FCA; Band; Flag Corp; Sec Soph Cls; Var Bsktbl; Var Chrldng; Trk; High Hon Roll; Hon Roll; NHS; East Central U; Phys Thrpy.

GOODSON, KATIE; Moyers Public Schl; Antlers, OK; (1); FCA; Sec Frsh Cls; Var Bsktbl; Var Chrldng; Var Crs Cntry; Var Trk; 3rd Pl Regnl Track Meet Hurdles; Southeastern OK ST Univ.

GOODWIN, CARRIE; Bartlesville Mid HS; Bartlesville, OK; (2); #1 in class; Church Yth Grp; Office Aide; Spanish Clb; Pom Pon; High Hon Roll; Jr NHS.

GOODWIN, CHRISTY M; Memorial HS; Tulsa, OK; (2); Church Yth Grp; German Clb; Teachers Aide; Chorus; Church Choir; School Musical; Sftbl; Hon Roll; Jr NHS; NHS; Lwyr.

GOODWIN, JASON P; Moore HS; Moore, OK; (3); Drama Clb; Pep Clb; Pres VICA; School Musical; School Play; Rptr Nwsp; Tennis; Wt Lftg; JV Wrstlng; Jr NHS; Univ Of OK.

GOODWIN, LAYNA; Stilwell HS; Stilwell, OK; (4); 9/150; Am Leg Aux Girls St; Church Yth Grp; Cmnty Wkr; Drama Clb; Hosp Aide; Natl Beta Clb; NFL; Speech Tm; Teachers Aide; Thesps; KFSM Co Anchr Teen Beat, Hstss Jrry Lws Telethon; All St/Chmp 94-95 2x; AMDA; Mscl Thtr.

GOODWIN, NICHOLAS G; Copan HS; Wann, OK; (4); 14/29; Church Yth Grp; Natl FFA Org; VP Jr Cls; L Bsbl; L Bsktbl; Sftbl; L Trk; Hon Roll; US Army Reserve; OK ST Univ; Comp Sci.

GOOSTREE, ERIC; Crowder Schl; Mcalester, OK; (2); 1/40; Var Bsbl; High Hon Roll; NHS; Ntl Merit Ltr; OK Hnr Soc.

GORBEA, ISABEL P; Bishop Kelley HS; Broken Arrow, OK; (1); Dance Clb; Ski Clb; Teachers Aide; Drill Tm; Chrldng; Gym; Mgr(s); Vllybl; Hon Roll; NHS; TSA Sec.

GORCZYCA, ALICIA M; Choctaw HS; Choctaw, OK; (2); Church Yth Grp; Cmnty Wkr; VP 4-H; Sec Natl FFA Org; Treas Spanish Clb; Band; Socr; 4-H Awd; Jr NHS; Sal; FFA Lamb Showing; OK ST U; Vet.

GORDER, BRIAN; Caney Valley HS; Ochelata, OK; (2); Church Yth Grp; German Clb; Teachers Aide; Band; Church Choir; Jazz Band; Mrchg Band; Pep Band; Cmptr Prgrmmr.

GORDIN, HEATHER; Bixby Sr HS; Bixby, OK; (3); 85/348; Church Yth Grp; Cmnty Wkr; GAA; Bsktbl; Sftbl; High Hon Roll; Hon Roll; NHS; St Gregorys; Nrsng.

GORDON, AMANDA M; Webster HS; Tulsa, OK; (3); Church Yth Grp; Drama Clb; French Clb; Speech Tm; School Play; Rep Frsh Cls; Rep Soph Cls; Rep Jr Cls; High Hon Roll; Hon Roll; Natl Eng Merit Awd; Natl Hnr Roll; Yth Ct; OSU; Pol Law.

GORDON, CANDICE; Heavener HS; Heavener, OK; (4); 1/89; Am Leg Aux Girls St; Pres FHA; Office Aide; Quiz Bowl; Scholastic Bowl; Science Clb; Band; Mrchg Band; Pres Stu Cncl; NHS; Spec Olymp Vlntr; Lions Club Flg Tour Vlntr; Jr Miss 1st R-Up Intrvw, Pres Compsr, Schlstc; Carl Albert ST Coll.

GORDON, CHRIS; Goodwell Public Schl; Goodwell, OK; (2); Library Aide; Office Aide; School Musical; School Play; JV Bsbl; JV Ftbl; JV Golf; Cit Awd; Hon Roll; Prfct Atten Awd; Prsdntl Ftnss Awd; USC; Arch.

GORDON, JANA; Oklahoma Christian Schl; Edmond, OK; (3); 11/50; Church Yth Grp; FCA; Rptr Yrbk; Stat Bsktbl; Mgr(s); Hon Roll; Acctng; Bus Mgmt.

GORDON, JILL; Comanche HS; Comanche, OK; (2); Church Yth Grp; Var Bsktbl; Sftbl; High Hon Roll; NHS; OSU.

GORDON, KYLE K; Erick Jr Sr HS; Erick, OK; (2); 1/20; Church Yth Grp; HOBY; Natl FFA Org; Quiz Bowl; Ofcr Stu Cncl; Ofcr Bsbl; Bsktbl; Mgr(s); High Hon Roll; Hon Roll; 1st Pl Chptr Tm TSA Natls; OSU; Med.

GORDON, LA CHELLE M; Haskell HS; Haskell, OK; (2); 1/70; Church Yth Grp; HOBY; Yrbk; Sec Stu Cncl; Var Chrldng; High Hon Roll; NHS; Acteens Actvtr; Missn Trp.

GORDON, LAURA B; Charles Page HS; Sand Springs, OK; (1); 1/240; VP Drama Clb; Pres FCA; Math Tm; School Play; Nwsp; Pres Frsh Cls; Capt Chrldng; Cit Awd; NHS; Pres Schlr.

GORDON, LINDSEY; Holdenville Jr HS; Holdenville, OK; (1); 5/100; Church Yth Grp; Scholastic Bowl; Band; Church Choir; Mrchg Band; Ofcr Stu Cncl; Hon Roll; Jr HS Hnr Soc.

GORDON, MINON; Poteau HS; Poteau, OK; (1); Church Yth Grp; Chorus; Church Choir; Variety Show; Bsktbl; Chrldng; Trk; High Hon Roll; Hon Roll; Jr NHS; GATE; OK ST; Brdcst Jrnlsm.

GORDON, MIRANDA L; Meeker Jr Sr HS; Meeker, OK; (4); 22/75; Church Yth Grp; FHA; Quiz Bowl; Scholastic Bowl; Teachers Aide; Chorus; Church Choir; Co-Ed Yrbk; Cit Awd; Hon Roll; NHS Mem; Outstdng Choir Ensemble & Amer Legion Awd; U Of Cntrl OK; Scndry Ed.

GORE, MELISSA D; Heavener HS; Heavener, OK; (1); Church Yth Grp; GAA; SADD; Teachers Aide; VP Frsh Cls; L Var Bsktbl; L Var Sftbl; Hon Roll; US Achvmt Acad 95 Natl Awds; Gifted/Talent Prgm.

GORE, ROSCO S; Lawton Sr HS; Lawton, OK; (2); Church Yth Grp; Cmnty Wkr; ROTC; Bsktbl; Socr; High Hon Roll; Hon Roll; NHS; St Schlr; Med.

GORMAN, CRYSTAL G; Sapulpa Sr HS; Sapulpa, OK; (3); Art Clb; Math Clb; Science Clb; Band; Mrchg Band; Dnc, Bllt Tp & Jzz 13 Yrs.

GORMAN, JODY K; Will Rogers HS; Tulsa, OK; (3); German Clb; JA; Key Clb; Rptr Nwsp; Rptr Yrbk; Var Swmmng; Var Tennis; Hon Roll; Northwood U; Mgmt Mrktng.

GORMAN, PATRICK; Holland Hall Schl; Tulsa, OK; (2); Math Tm; Jazz Band; JV Bsbl; Var Ftbl; JV Socr; High Hon Roll.

GORMAN, STACIE; Bishop Kelley HS; Broken Arrow, OK; (4); Church Yth Grp; Drama Clb; NFL; Pep Clb; Speech Tm; Teachers Aide; Chorus; Church Choir; Ed Nwsp; Ed Yrbk; Young Woman Excllnc Awd; Anchor Clb; OU; Theater.

GORNEY, JENNIFER LEA; Mannford HS; Mannford, OK; (4); 8/83; FCA; Spanish Clb; SADD; Phtg Yrbk; Sec Stu Cncl; JV Bsktbl; Co-Capt Chrldng; Var Sftbl; Trk; High Hon Roll; All St Cheer Squad Natls 3rd Pl 95; Ec Medal; OK Hnr Soc; OK ST Univ; Allied Hlth.

GORSKI, BOBBY LYNN; Laverne Jr Sr HS; Logan, OK; (1); Church Yth Grp; Dance Clb; Drama Clb; Letterman Clb; Scholastic Bowl; Church Choir; Flag Corp; Variety Show; Rptr Frsh Cls; Bsktbl; Bible Clb; ORU; Jrnlsm.

GORTON, ANGIE; Canadian Schl; Eufaula, OK; (2); 2/30; 4-H; Pres Frsh Cls; Pres Soph Cls; Sec VP Stu Cncl; Var Bsktbl; Var Sftbl; Hon Roll; Coaching.

GORTON, JANNA; Canadian Schl; Eufaula, OK; (4); 1/29; Am Leg Aux Girls St; Church Yth Grp; Yrbk; Pres Jr Cls; Pres Stu Cncl; Var Capt Bsktbl; Var Sftbl; High Hon Roll; NHS; Val; Sprts Chllng Intl Belgium Plyd Bsktbl; Natl AAU Bsktbl Tm; OK Hnr Soc; UNT; Bus.

GOSA, JULIE; Varnum Jr Sr HS; Seminole, OK; (2); 2/25; Church Yth Grp; GAA; Quiz Bowl; Church Choir; School Play; Bsktbl; Hon Roll; NHS; Spanish NHS; Wrtng Poetry; OU; Phys Thrpy.

GOSA, TRACY; Freedom Schl; Freedom, OK; (4); 2/7; VP FCA; Sec Natl FFA Org; Scholastic Bowl; Sec Sr Cls; Sec Stu Cncl; Var Capt Bsktbl; Var Capt Chrldng; Var Trk; NHS; Sal; OCU; Sprts Med.

GOSNELL, JARROD T; Lindsay HS; Lindsay, OK; (1); 12/78; Natl FFA Org; FFA Swthrt, Grnhnd Awd; Prncpls Hnr Rl; NEO; Genetics.

GOSNELL, MEGAN L; Cushing HS; Cushing, OK; (3); 1/156; Am Leg Aux Girls St; Math Clb; Science Clb; Spanish Clb; VP Jr Cls; Ofcr Stu Cncl; Bsktbl; Sftbl; Hon Roll; NHS; Optmtry.

GOSNEY, LESLI; Fairview HS; Fairview, OK; (4); 1/56; Church Yth Grp; FCA; GAA; HOBY; Treas Frsh Cls; VP Soph Cls; Pres Jr Cls; Rep Stu Cncl; Stat Bsktbl; High Hon Roll; FFA Swthrt, Clss Swthrt, Prlmntry Prcdr Tm; OK Hnr Soc; NHS Treas; John Brown U; Acctng.

GOSS, CHRISTINA; Moore HS; Moore, OK; (4); 93/549; Church Yth Grp; Cmnty Wkr; Debate Tm; Hosp Aide; NFL; Spanish Clb; Speech Tm; Rptr Nwsp; Rptr Yrbk; Rep Stu Cncl; Sthrn Nazrn U; Hstry Scndry Ed.

GOSS, JEFF D; Mustang HS; Yukon, OK; (2); 53/500; Church Yth Grp; Cmnty Wkr; FCA; Pep Clb; Chorus; School Musical; School Play; Bsktbl; Mgr(s); Score Keeper; OK Univ; Cmmnctns/Brdcstng.

GOSS, MELISSA; Tyrone Schl; Tyrone, OK; (4); 1/17; FHA; Chorus; School Musical; School Play; Pres Frsh Cls; Sec Soph Cls; Bsktbl; Chrldng; Sftbl; Trk; FCA; Wichita ST U; Jrnlsm.

GOSS, NICHOLETTE R; Hinton HS; Hinton, OK; (2); FCA; Acpl Chr; Chorus; Treas Jr Cls; Trk; Cit Awd; Gov Hon Prg Awd; NHS; Pres Acad Fit Awd; Val; Sw OK ST U; Psych.

GOSSEN, AMANDA; Cache HS; Cache, OK; (3); 1/74; Computer Clb; Natl Beta Clb; Science Clb; SADD; Band; Color Guard; Yrbk; Var Chrldng; High Hon Roll; NHS; Clogging; U Of OK; Pre-Med.

GOSSEN, CHERYL; Corn Bible Acad; Corn, OK; (1); Church Yth Grp; GAA; Band; Church Choir; Mrchg Band; Pep Band; Rep Frsh Cls; Bsktbl; Vllybl; High Hon Roll.

GOSSETT, JESSE; Moore HS; Moore, OK; (3); Church Yth Grp; FCA; French Clb; Chorus; Church Choir; Var Bsbl; Hon Roll; Jr NHS; U OK.

GOSSMAN, TERRY; Perkins-Tryon HS; Perkins, OK; (4); 9/73; FCA; Intnl Clb; Spanish Clb; Band; Jazz Band; Mrchg Band; Orch; Pep Band; VP Jr Cls; VP Sr Cls; Langston Univ; Chem.

GOTTSCHALK, SHANNON R; Mannford HS; Mannford, OK; (3); Church Yth Grp; Drama Clb; FHA; Science Clb; Spanish Clb; Band; Mrchg Band; High Hon Roll; Hon Roll; Chorus; OK ST Univ; Pre-Med.

GOUDEAU, STACIE K; Central HS; Tulsa, OK; (2); Ofcr Soph Cls; Hon Roll; Pediatrician.

GOUKER, GREG; Dale Sr HS; Shawnee, OK; (4); 4/50; Church Yth Grp; Scholastic Bowl; Spanish Clb; Rep Soph Cls; VP Sr Cls; Rep Stu Cncl; L Bsktbl; High Hon Roll; Hon Roll; Jr NHS; Acad Ltr Jacket; OK ST U; Acctng.

GOUKER, NICK M; Dale Sr HS; Shawnee, OK; (1); Church Yth Grp; Bsktbl; Golf; Hon Roll.

GOULD, ALAN C; Durant HS; Durant, OK; (1); Church Yth Grp; Cmnty Wkr; FCA; Key Clb; Chorus; Church Choir; School Musical; Ftbl; Trk; Hon Roll; Super Rating At Dist & St Level As Mem Of HS Ensemble Music Group.

GOULD, JEREMY L; Enid Sr HS; Enid, OK; (3); Am Leg Boys St; Cmnty Wkr; FCA; Letterman Clb; Varsity Clb; Var Ftbl; Trk; Wt Lftg; Sci Rsrch.

GOULDEN, CANDACE C; Ponca City Sr HS; Ponca City, OK; (3); 25/435; Debate Tm; NFL; Spanish Clb; Hon Roll; Kiwanis Awd.

GOURD, CHANCE T; Dewey HS; Bartlesville, OK; (4); 25/90; Boy Scts; Church Yth Grp; Quiz Bowl; Scholastic Bowl; Band; Church Choir; Jazz Band; Mrchg Band; Pep Band; Var L Bsktbl; Gtfd/Tlntd Music; Matthew Tyer Awd Music; All St Fnlst; OK U; Comp Analyst.

GOWAN, KARA D; Duncan HS; Duncan, OK; (4); 16/214; Church Yth Grp; FCA; FBLA; Key Clb; Letterman Clb; Office Aide; SADD; Ofcr Stu Cncl; High Hon Roll; NHS; OK ST U; Elem Ed.

GOWDY, BECKY S; Sapulpa Sr HS; Sapulpa, OK; (3); 54/300; Sec Church Yth Grp; Pres FCA; FBLA; VP Key Clb; Chorus; Ofcr Frsh Cls; Pres Soph Cls; Pres Jr Cls; Pres Sr Cls; Ofcr Stu Cncl; Prin Cncl; Drs Cd Comm; OU; Bus Admin.

GOWER, JON P; Southeast HS; Oklahoma City, OK; (3); FCA; Letterman Clb; Capt L Bsbl; NHS.

GOWER, MANDY; Tahlequah Sr HS; Tahlequah, OK; (4); 30/251; FHA; Pres SADD; Rptr Nwsp; Rptr Yrbk; Pres Sr Cls; Var Chrldng; Var Crs Cntry; Var Trk; Gov Hon Prg Awd; Hon Roll; All-Amer Schlr; NE ST U; Phys Thrpst.

GOYER, COURTNEY; Edmond Memorial HS; Edmond, OK; (2); Art Clb; Church Yth Grp; FCA; Spanish Clb; SADD; JV Capt Chrldng; U Of OK.

GRACE, LAURA; Union Intermediate HS; Tulsa, OK; (1); Church Yth Grp; FCA; Spanish Clb; SADD; JV Capt Chrldng; NHS.

GRACE, LENEA C; Edmond North HS; Edmond, OK; (2); 1/420; Sec French Clb; Mu Alpha Theta; SADD; Ed Yrbk; Var Swmmng; Trk; High Hon Roll; Hon Roll; NHS.

GRACE, MATTHEW J; Bishop Kelley HS; Tulsa, OK; (2); Key Clb; Band; Dorothy & Peggy Griffith Achvmnt Awd 93; 1st Dgr Blck Belt Tae Kwon Do Acad; 100 Comm Svc Hrs; Engr/Accntnt.

GRADY, EDWARD; Putnam City West HS; Bethany, OK; (3); 9/350; Church Yth Grp; Latin Clb; SADD; School Musical; Yrbk; Ofcr Jr Cls; Ftbl; Socr; High Hon Roll; Hon Roll; Jr Clss Pres; I Dare You Awd.

GRADY, JENNIFER E; Southeast HS; Oklahoma City, OK; (1); Art Clb; Church Yth Grp; JA; ROTC; Teachers Aide; Chorus; Ed Yrbk; Vllybl; High Hon Roll; Hon Roll; MVP Var Vlybl 95-; Frosh Ath Acad Achvmt Awd 95-; Outstdng Stdnt Awd Geometry Avg Above 100%; 4 Yr Univ.

GRAFT, AARON PAUL; Clinton HS; Clinton, OK; (4); 6/99; Church Yth Grp; Pres FCA; FBLA; Quiz Bowl; Var Bsbl; Var Ftbl; Hon Roll; NHS; Ntl Merit Schol; Mck Trl Tm, Outstndng Atty, Legal Tm Cap; Baylor U; Med.

GRAGG, CYNTHIA S; Henryetta Sr HS; Henryetta, OK; (4); 16/69; Am Leg Aux Girls St; Church Yth Grp; Cmnty Wkr; Drama Clb; FCA; FHA; Key Clb; School Play; VP Pres Stu Cncl; JV Bsktbl; Rep Natl Yth Ldrshp Conf Wash DC; Rep Key Clb Intnl; Point Loma Nazarene Coll; CPA.

GRAHAM, ALYSON; Deer Creek HS; Edmond, OK; (3); Debate Tm; Yrbk; NHS; OSU; Vet.

GRAHAM, AMANDA C; Beaver HS; Beaver, OK; (2); Drama Clb; FCA; Chorus; Stage Crew; Rptr Soph Cls; Var Sftbl; JV Tennis; Hon Roll; U Of OK; Lawyer.

GRAHAM, AMY C; Edison HS; Tulsa, OK; (3); Cmnty Wkr; SADD; Band; Mrchg Band; Orch; Pep Band; School Musical; Yrbk; JV Socr; JV Sftbl; Fleet Reserve Assn 2nd Pl Essay; OSU; Broadcast Jrnlsm.

GRAHAM, ANGELA A; Olney Schl; Coalgate, OK; (1); Church Yth Grp; Scholastic Bowl; Bsktbl; Sftbl; High Hon Roll; SE Schlstc Mt 3rd Engl I; OBU Shawnee; PT/RN.

GRAHAM, ANTHONY T; East Central HS; Tulsa, OK; (4); 8/209; Church Yth Grp; FCA; VP Math Clb; VP Mu Alpha Theta; Scholastic Bowl; VP Science Clb; Spanish Clb; Tennis; Hon Roll; NHS; Chrstns HS; Cardinals For Christ; U Of OK; Chem Engr.

GRAHAM, ASHLEY A; Muskogee HS; Muskogee, OK; (1); 60/500; Church Yth Grp; Hosp Aide; Chorus; Cit Awd; High Hon Roll; Lawyer.

GRAHAM, CARRIE; Union City Schl; Yukon, OK; (3); 2/19; FHA; Math Clb; Scholastic Bowl; Science Clb; Bsktbl; High Hon Roll; NHS; Pres Acad Fit Awd; Sal; Stu Cncl; Air Force Acad; Aviation.

GRAHAM, ERIC; Chickasha Jr HS; Chickasha, OK; (1); Church Yth Grp; Math Tm; School Play; Ofcr Bsbl; Ftbl; Wt Lftg; Cit Awd; Hon Roll; Jr NHS; Navy; Coll; Nvy Sniper/Seal.

GRAHAM, GENISHA; Midwest City HS; Oklahoma City, OK; (2); 33/500; Church Yth Grp; Letterman Clb; Pep Clb; Band; Church Choir; Drill Tm; Mrchg Band; Ofcr Stu Cncl; Score Keeper; Vllybl; A-Clb; Drama; TX Southern; Medcl.

GRAHAM, HOLLY; Perkins-Tryon HS; Perkins, OK; (3); Church Yth Grp; FHA; Intnl Clb; Chorus; Scottish Clb Of Cntrl OK; Scottish Highland Dnce; Scottish Clb Of Tulsa; Photo.

GRAHAM, JA M; Putnam City West HS; Bethany, OK; (2); Socr; Tennis; Skiing; Rollerblading; Travel.

GRAHAM, JENEVA; Victory Christian Schl; Tulsa, OK; (2); Church Yth Grp; Drama Clb; FCA; School Play; Yrbk; Ofcr Frsh Cls; Ofcr Soph Cls; Var Capt Chrldng; Var Socr; High Hon Roll; Natl Yng Ldrs Conf Schlr; Intl Frgn Lang Awd; NCA All Amer Cheerldng3 Yrs; Oral Roberts Univ; Drama.

GRAHAM, JEREMY; Healdton HS; Healdton, OK; (4); 6/51; Church Yth Grp; FCA; Chorus; School Play; Ftbl; Hon Roll.

GRAHAM, JOHN W; Yukon Middle HS; Yukon, OK; (2); Church Yth Grp; Debate Tm; FCA; NFL; Spanish Clb; Speech Tm; Acpl Chr; School Musical; School Play; NHS; Ed; Rel.

GRAHAM, KARA; Norman Sr HS; Norman, OK; (3); 175/799; Art Clb; Church Yth Grp; Cmnty Wkr; Sec French Clb; Pep Clb; SADD; Church Choir; Rep Frsh Cls; Rep Soph Cls; Ofcr Stu Cncl; Yth Group Ldrshp; FISH; U Of OK.

GRAHAM, KATHERINE; Moore HS; Moore, OK; (3); Church Yth Grp; ROTC; Drill Tm; Hon Roll; Prfct Atten Awd; Aikido Martial Arts; Reading; U Of OK; Comp Prgmr.

GRAHAM, KEITH D; Verden HS; Verden, OK; (2); Science Clb; Pres Frsh Cls; Pres Soph Cls; Var Bsbl; Var Bsktbl; Cit Awd; High Hon Roll; NHS; Prfct Atten Awd; Pres Acad Fit Awd; OK Hnr Soc; Acad Team; OK ST Univ; His.

GRAHAM, KELLI A; Jay HS; Jay, OK; (2); Church Yth Grp; FCA; FBLA; Natl Beta Clb; Science Clb; High Hon Roll; NHS; Peer Cnslr; IDFY.

GRAHAM, LAURA L; Rush Springs HS; Rush Springs, OK; (2); Spanish Clb; Yrbk; Sec Frsh Cls; Chrldng; Hon Roll; U Of OK; Psych.

GRAHAM, MATTHEW; Carl Albert HS; Midwest City, OK; (4); 25/243; Am Leg Boys St; Boy Scts; FBLA; Key Clb; Office Aide; Rptr Nwsp; Capt Crs Cntry; Trk; NHS; Val.

GRAHAM, MELISSA; Miami Sr HS; Miami, OK; (4); 29/131; Teachers Aide; Band; Capt Color Guard; Drill Tm; Capt Flag Corp; Co-Capt Pom Pon; Hon Roll; NHS; Pittsburg ST U; Phys Thrpy.

GRAHAM, PATRICK R; Edmond Memorial HS; Edmond, OK; (4); 42/346; Church Yth Grp; FCA; Spanish Clb; SADD; Teachers Aide; Var Capt Socr; Cit Awd; High Hon Roll; Hon Roll; NHS; Rotary Schol Win; Outstndg OSU Frshmn Scholar; Wood Tech Clb; OK State Univ; Geologist.

GRAHAM, ROGER L; Velma Alma HS; Ratliff City, OK; (1); Band; Mrchg Band; Crs Cntry; Trk; OU; Mtrlgy.

GRAMMER, CODY; Lone Grove HS; Ardmore, OK; (4); 35/72; Natl Beta Clb; Band; Jazz Band; Mrchg Band; Cit Awd; Hon Roll; NHS; Prfct Atten Awd; E Central Univ; Pharm.

GRAMMER, CRYSTAL L; Antlers Sr HS; Antlers, OK; (2); Church Yth Grp; FCA; 4-H; GAA; Natl FFA Org; SADD; Var JV Bsktbl; Tennis; Cit Awd; Hon Roll; Southeastern Univ.

GRAMMER, DANA; Lone Grove HS; Ardmore, OK; (2); Key Clb; Math Clb; Science Clb; Spanish Clb; Sftbl; High Hon Roll; NHS; All Amer Schl; 1st Pl Stwd 9th-12th Div Dont Lay The Trash On OK Pstr Cmptn; Spnsh I&II Awd.

GRAMOLINI, KELLY; Comanche HS; Comanche, OK; (4); 15/61; FHA; Office Aide; Pep Clb; Science Clb; Speech Tm; Teachers Aide; Sec Soph Cls; Hon Roll; NHS; Eng Outstndng Stu; OK ST U; Neonatolgy.

GRANDSTAFF, TRAVIS J; Western Heights Sr HS; Oklahoma City, OK; (2); Boy Scts; English Clb; Letterman Clb; Office Aide; Teachers Aide; Varsity Clb; Var Bsbl; Intrml Bsktbl; Var Ftbl; Hon Roll; OK U; Auto Engr.

GRANT, ERIN K; Goodwell Public Schl; Goodwell, OK; (2); Debate Tm; FCA; Letterman Clb; Speech Tm; Band; Chorus; Mrchg Band; Rep Soph Cls; Stat Bsktbl; Wt Lftg; Play Piano & Fr Horn; Panhandle ST Univ; Soc Work.

GRANT, JAMIE L; Caddo HS; Caddo, OK; (1); FHA; SADD; Chorus; School Musical; School Play; JV Bsktbl; JV Var Chrldng; JV Sftbl; JV Tennis; JV Trk; Supr Vocal Awd; SUSU; Psych.

GRANT, JUSTIN T; Central Mid-HS; Norman, OK; (2); Church Yth Grp; FCA; Natl FFA Org; Church Choir; Ofcr Bsbl; Ftbl; Trk; Wt Lftg; Wrstlng; Hon Roll; Manhatten KS; Vet.

GRANT, LA ROSA M; Wagoner Sr HS; Wagoner, OK; (4); 12/135; Church Yth Grp; FHA; Church Choir; Hon Roll; Connors ST Coll; Psychlgst.

GRANT, MARTIN L; Stillwater Sr HS; Stillwater, OK; (3); 124/363; Church Yth Grp; French Clb; Latin Clb; Mu Alpha Theta; Church Choir; Intrml Bsktbl; OK ST; Mnstry/Engr.

GRANT, MELISSA K; Durant HS; Durant, OK; (3); 4-H; FTA; Natl FFA Org; Chorus; Bsktbl; JV Var Sftbl; Hon Roll; Fmly; Frnds; Southeastern OK ST U; Tchr.

GRANTZ, LORI E; Tonkawa Jr Sr HS; Tonkawa, OK; (4); 14/38; Church Yth Grp; FCA; Letterman Clb; Teachers Aide; Chorus; Church Choir; School Musical; School Play; Var Bsktbl; Var Sftbl; Bethany Col; Ath Trng.

GRATIAS, JEREMIAH D; Ponca City Sr HS; Ponca City, OK; (3); 133/438; Church Yth Grp; Band; Church Choir; Mrchg Band; Pep Band; Hon Roll; Lettered In Band 3 Yrs; U Of Cntrl OK; Law Enforcement.

GRAUMANN, DANYELE; Mustang HS; Yukon, OK; (3); Cmnty Wkr; FBLA; GAA; JA; Letterman Clb; Teachers Aide; Varsity Clb; Var Golf; Var Sftbl; High Hon Roll; PT/ED.

GRAVENDER, LINDSAY A; Bishop Kelley HS; Tulsa, OK; (2); Church Yth Grp; Cmnty Wkr; Pep Clb; Red Cross Aide; Hon Roll; Comm Svc Extra Mile Awd; Elem Spec Ed.

GRAVES, APRIL R; Ripley HS; Ripley, OK; (2); Cmnty Wkr; FHA; Math Clb; Science Clb; Spanish Clb; High Hon Roll; NHS; OSU.

GRAVES, JOHN; Bishop Mcguinness HS; Oklahoma City, OK; (4); 34/150; Am Leg Boys St; Boy Scts; FCA; Pres French Clb; SADD; Var Bsktbl; NHS.

GRAVES, JULIE A; Laverne Jr Sr HS; Gate, OK; (4); 10/33; Church Yth Grp; Cmnty Wkr; FHA; Letterman Clb; Natl Beta Clb; Teachers Aide; School Play; VP Soph Cls; Sec Jr Cls; VP Sr Cls; MVP Bsktbl Trnmt; All Trnmt Team; Laverne Trnmt; Red Carpet All Conf; Big E Awd Sftbl & Bsktbl; Best Ath; NWOSU; Sociology; Psych.

GRAVES, NATALIE R; Union Sr HS; Tulsa, OK; (3); 47/741; Key Clb; Rep Stu Cncl; Var Bsktbl; Var Crs Cntry; Var Trk; Cit Awd; High Hon Roll; NHS; Pres Schlr; Cmnty Wkr; Stu/Yr 94-95; DFY.

GRAVLEY, ALEXANDER N; Cascia Hall Prep School; Tulsa, OK; (1); Intrml Bsktbl; Var Golf; Var Swmmng; Intrml Tennis; Hon Roll; Spanish NHS; Prof Glf.

GRAY, ADRIAN J; Walters HS; Walters, OK; (2); 6/57; Church Yth Grp; FCA; FHA; Band; Church Choir; Jazz Band; Mrchg Band; Pep Band; Hon Roll; NHS; Chrch Yth Choir, Orch; Native Amer Clb; Med.

GRAY, ALEX; Hugo HS; Hugo, OK; (2); Library Aide; Science Clb; Spanish Clb; Hon Roll; NHS; Presidential Awd Of Excl; OK Hnr Soc; Excl In Hum, World His, Lib Sci, Geog & Bio I.

GRAY, ANGELA; Piedmont HS; Piedmont, OK; (2); 4/97; Church Yth Grp; Hosp Aide; Key Clb; SADD; Band; Chorus; Church Choir; Mrchg Band; Pep Band; School Musical; Central Coll; Yth Mnstry.

GRAY, ANGELA M; Metro Christian Acad; Tulsa, OK; (3); Ofcr Church Yth Grp; FCA; Chorus; Church Choir; School Musical; Var Bsktbl; Hon Roll; Phys Thpy.

GRAY, ANGIE D; Seminole Jr Sr HS; Seminole, OK; (2); Church Yth Grp; Office Aide; Pep Clb; Scholastic Bowl; Spanish Clb; Chorus; JV Chrldng; Trk; Hon Roll; Prfct Atten Awd; Seminole JC; Cmnctn.

GRAY, BRANDI A; Muldrow HS; Muldrow, OK; (4); 7/106; Church Yth Grp; FHA; GAA; Math Clb; Natl Beta Clb; Science Clb; Bsktbl; High Hon Roll; Hon Roll; NHS; Westark CC; Indust Engr.

GRAY, CHANDRA; B T Washington HS; Tulsa, OK; (4); 116/264; Church Yth Grp; Cmnty Wkr; FBLA; Girl Scts; Office Aide; Pep Clb; Spanish Clb; Teachers Aide; Band; Church Choir; African Amer Soc; Girl Scouts Gold/Silver Awd; Alpha Kappa Xinos Yth Grp; Jack/Jill Of Amer Yth Grp; OK ST Univ; Bus Mgmt.

GRAY, CHARLES; Tomlinson Jr HS; Latty, OH; (1); Church Yth Grp; Hon Roll; Jr NHS; MI; Law.

GRAY, CHRIS J; Mustang HS; Yukon, OK; (3); Church Yth Grp; FCA; Rep Soph Cls; Rep Jr Cls; Rep Stu Cncl; Intrml Bsbl; JV Var Bsktbl; Var Ftbl; Bus Mgmnt/Intl Bus.

GRAY, CLIFTON; Moore HS; Moore, OK; (4); 5/505; Church Yth Grp; German Clb; Ski Clb; Band; Jazz Band; Mrchg Band; Orch; Pep Band; NHS; Val; U Of OK; Engrng.

GRAY, CORI; Foyil Schl; Claremore, OK; (4); 5/28; FBLA; FHA; Pep Clb; Rptr Sr Cls; Bsktbl; Chrldng; Golf; Trk; Hon Roll; Ftbl Homcmng Qn 95-96; Amer Natl Teenager Schlrshp Pgm Fnlst; Outstndng Trackstr Awd; TX Tech U; Occptnl Thry.

GRAY, DANA M; Edmond Memorial HS; Edmond, OK; (2); Art Clb; Church Yth Grp; Pep Clb; Spanish Clb; JV Socr; JV Trk; Phys Thrpst.

GRAY, ELIZABETH; Frederick HS; Frederick, OK; (1); Church Yth Grp; Drama Clb; FCA; FHA; School Play; JV Bsktbl; Chrldng; Sftbl; Hon Roll; NHS; TAG Pgm; Medcl.

GRAY, ERICA J; South Intermediate HS; Broken Arrow, OK; (1); Church Yth Grp; Chorus; Church Choir; Hon Roll; Jrnlst.

GRAY, HEATHER; Drummond Schl; Drummond, OK; (2); Natl FFA Org; Quiz Bowl; Band; Rep Soph Cls; Rep Stu Cncl; Chrldng; Hon Roll; Prfct Atten Awd; OK Hnr Soc; FFA Chptr Reptr; Psych.

GRAY, JOSH D; Noble HS; Noble, OK; (2); #1 in class; Art Clb; Church Yth Grp; Mu Alpha Theta; Scholastic Bowl; Spanish Clb; NHS; Prfct Atten Awd; U Of OK.

GRAY, JUSTIN W; Ponca City Sr HS; Ponca City, OK; (3); Church Yth Grp; Hon Roll; Jr NHS.

GRAY, KEVIN J; B T Washington HS; Tulsa, OK; (4); 40/264; Church Yth Grp; Cmnty Wkr; Debate Tm; Ofcr NFL; Scholastic Bowl; Speech Tm; Var L Golf; Hon Roll; NHS; Ntl Merit SF; U S Senate Yth Ldrshp Schlrshp Delg; Frgn Extemporaneous Speaking St Chmpn & Ntl Qlfr 95; U Of Tulsa; Hstry.

GRAY, LACEY L; Ponca City Sr HS; Ponca City, OK; (3); 15/371; Church Yth Grp; Cmnty Wkr; Chorus; High Hon Roll; OK St Univ; Acctng.

GRAY, LESLIE A; South Intermediate HS; Broken Arrow, OK; (1); Dance Clb; French Clb; Intnl Clb; Red Cross Aide; Drill Tm; Pom Pon; Gov Hon Prg Awd; Hon Roll; Jr NHS; St Schlr; Ballet; PT.

GRAY, MARIANNE; Edmond North HS; Edmond, OK; (1); Cmnty Wkr; FCA; Spanish Clb; Rep Stu Cncl; Chrldng; U Of OK.

GRAY, MATTHEW; Cleveland Sr HS; Cleveland, OK; (4); 1/100; Am Leg Boys St; FCA; HOBY; Key Clb; Quiz Bowl; Pres Spanish Clb; Capt Bsktbl; Capt Socr; NHS; Val; OK Hnr Soc; Ctzn Bee; Most Likely To Succeed; Sci/Spnsh Mst Outstndng; Enlg, Algebra, Trig Oustndng Mrt; OU; Phrmcy.

GRAY, MEGAN E; Cleveland Sr HS; Cleveland, OK; (3); #1 in class; Am Leg Aux Girls St; Sec Frsh Cls; Pres Soph Cls; Pres Jr Cls; Rep Stu Cncl; Var Bsktbl; Var Chrldng; Var Socr; NHS; Val; Kiwanis Club Stu Of Yr; OK Hnr Soc; Rep Cnvntn Page; Mst Outstndng Awds; Med.

GRAY, MICHAEL J; El Reno Sr HS; El Reno, OK; (3); 41/201; Am Leg Boys St; FCA; Key Clb; Letterman Clb; Math Clb; JV Bsbl; JV Var Bsktbl; JV Var Ftbl; JV Var Wt Lftg; Hon Roll; Redlands JC; Bus.

GRAY, MINDY L; Dale Sr HS; Shawnee, OK; (2); 9/45; Drama Clb; VP FCA; VP 4-H; Band; Chorus; Color Guard; School Musical; Rep Frsh Cls; Ofcr Stu Cncl; Var Bsktbl; OSU; Comm.

GRAY, NIKI; Wayne Public Schl; Paoli, OK; (1); Var Stu Cncl; Var Sftbl; Hon Roll; U Of TN.

GRAY, ROBYN L; John Marshall HS; Oklahoma City, OK; (1); Bsktbl; Hon Roll; Phys Thrpst.

GRAY, RUTH A; West Middle HS; Norman, OK; (2); Church Yth Grp; FCA; Hosp Aide; Mu Alpha Theta; Spanish Clb; JV Tennis; Hon Roll; NHS; SWASS; Teen Vol.

GRAY, TONY K; Muldrow HS; Muldrow, OK; (2); Natl Beta Clb; Ftbl; Hon Roll; Prfct Atten Awd.

GRAYBILL, MELISSA E; Alva HS; Alva, OK; (2); Church Yth Grp; Rptr FHA; Key Clb; Band; Chorus; Play Piano; Northwestern OK ST; Elem Ed.

GRAYSON, BRITNEY; Millwood HS; Oklahoma City, OK; (2); 10/108; Church Yth Grp; Computer Clb; Drama Clb; FHA; ROTC; Chorus; Church Choir; Drill Tm; Phtg Yrbk; Rep Soph Cls; Drwng; Bsktbll; OKU; Psych.

GRAYSON, KAPRI; Idabel HS; Idabel, OK; (2); Church Yth Grp; Church Choir; Bsktbl; Chrldng; Trk; Hon Roll.

GRAYSON, SHAWN M; Mc Loud HS; Meeker, OK; (1); 27/159; FCA; Natl FFA Org; Ftbl; Hnry Sntnl FFA; Frstry; Prin Hnr Roll; Commrcl Airline Pilot.

GREATHOUSE, DAVID; Watts HS; Westville, OK; (3); 1/17; HOBY; Math Clb; Natl Beta Clb; Natl FFA Org; Pres Soph Cls; High Hon Roll; Frstry.

GREELEY, ERICA; Dickson HS; Ardmore, OK; (3); 12/76; German Clb; Library Aide; Speech Tm; Teachers Aide; Band; Color Guard; Mrchg Band; Yrbk; Rep Stu Cncl; Hon Roll; Outstndng Bndsmn; Top 10 Prcnt Cls; SE Univ; Elem Tchr.

GREEN, ALISON; Lawton Sr HS; Lawton, OK; (4); 33/323; Church Yth Grp; Cmnty Wkr; Dance Clb; Drama Clb; FCA; GAA; Hosp Aide; JA; Key Clb; Letterman Clb; UCA All Amrcn Chrldrl; Renaissance Awd; Cameron Univ; Nrsng.

GREEN, AMBERLYN J; Wister Schl; Wister, OK; (2); Drama Clb; FHA; Quiz Bowl; Speech Tm; High Hon Roll; NHS; Pres Schlr; St Schlr; Val; OK Scndry ST Spch Trnmnt Twice; Jrnlsm.

GREEN, BRIAN; Medford Schl; Medford, OK; (2); #2 in class; FCA; Quiz Bowl; Chorus; VP Soph Cls; Var Bsbl; JV Bsktbl; Var Ftbl; Var Trk; High Hon Roll; NHS.

GREEN, CHRISTOPHER C; Christian Heritage Acad; Edmond, OK; (2); Church Yth Grp; FCA; Color Guard; Drill Tm; Flag Corp; Rptr Yrbk; Ftbl; Wt Lftg; Hon Roll; Real Est.

GREEN, CHRISTOPHER L; Duncan HS; Duncan, OK; (4); 1/210; Pres Church Yth Grp; Key Clb; Sec Rep SADD; Swing Chorus; VP Sr Cls; Cit Awd; Pres NHS; Val; Cmnty Wkr; Drama Clb; OK All St Choir; All Rgn Hnr Choir Hghst Scrng Bss 4xs; OK U Hnrs Schlr Awd; Vocal Perf.

GREEN, D. REID; Laverne Jr Sr HS; Rosston, OK; (4); FHA; Letterman Clb; Natl FFA Org; Var L Ftbl; Hon Roll; Prfct Atten Awd; OK HS Rodeo Assn; Tri ST HS Rodeo Assn TX; NW OK Jr Rodeo Org; H Rodeo Clb Rprtr Jr Yr; Pratt CC; Wldlf/Game Mgmt.

GREEN, DAVID A; Claremore Sr HS; Claremore, OK; (4); 37/231; Church Yth Grp; Band; Chorus; Jazz Band; Mrchg Band; School Musical; High Hon Roll; Hon Roll; NHS; Prfct Atten Awd; All ST Band; All ST Choir; John Phillip Sousa Awd; OK ST Univ; Music Ed.

GREEN, DUSTIN R; Stilwell HS; Stilwell, OK; (2); Drama Clb; 4-H; FBLA; Natl FFA Org; Spanish Clb; 4-H Awd; Hon Roll; OK ST Univ; Lbbyst Ag Issues.

GREEN, HAYLEE; Thomas Jr Sr HS; Thomas, OK; (4); 1/33; Church Yth Grp; Pres FCA; Sec Pres FHA; HOBY; VP Stu Cncl; Var Capt Bsktbl; Sftbl; Trk; NHS; Val; SW OK ST U; Pre-Dntstry.

GREEN, HILLARIE; Wynnewood HS; Wynnewood, OK; (2); 1/46; Church Yth Grp; FCA; FHA; Var Bsktbl; JV Chrldng; Var Golf; High Hon Roll; OK Hnr Soc; Americas Natl Teen; Karate; Sprts Med.

GREEN, J K; Caddo HS; Caddo, OK; (3); 5/32; Church Yth Grp; VP Natl FFA Org; Quiz Bowl; Var Bsbl; Var Ftbl; Cit Awd; Hon Roll; Jr NHS; NHS.

GREEN, JENNIFER; Meeker HS; Meeker, OK; (2); Church Yth Grp; Drama Clb; Acpl Chr; Chorus; Church Choir; Chrldng; Vet.

GREEN, JENNIFER; Will Rogers HS; Tulsa, OK; (4); 33/165; German Clb; Drill Tm; Cit Awd; DAR Awd; Hon Roll; NHS; Red Crss Clb; Northeastern Univ; Elem Tchr.

GREEN, JEREMY; Konawa Sr HS; Konawa, OK; (4); Am Leg Boys St; Church Yth Grp; FBLA; FHA; Natl Beta Clb; VICA; School Play; Hon Roll; Chrstn Rock Band; Elctrc Gtr; E Central U; Bio.

GREEN, JEREMY; Wellston Schl; Wellston, OK; (3); #1 in class; FCA; Var Bsbl; Var Bsktbl; Var Ftbl; Hon Roll; NHS; OK ST U; Bsbl.

GREEN, JULIE A; Guymon Sr HS; Guymon, OK; (3); FCA; Girl Scts; School Musical; Variety Show; Rptr Nwsp; Yrbk; Ofcr Stu Cncl; Lubbock Chrstn Univ; Eng/Wrtr.

GREEN, KELLY; Purcell HS; Purcell, OK; (3); Cmnty Wkr; FCA; Spanish Clb; Ofcr Frsh Cls; Pres Soph Cls; Pres Jr Cls; Pres Stu Cncl; Bsktbl; Chrldng; NHS; U Of OK; Dntstry.

GREEN, KEVIN; Valliant HS; Valliant, OK; (1); 23/89; Natl FFA Org; Ftbl; Wt Lftg; Hon Roll; NHS.

GREEN, KYLE E; Wakita Schl; Wakita, OK; (2); Band; Mrchg Band; School Play; Sec Frsh Cls; VP Soph Cls; Crs Cntry; Trk; Prfct Atten Awd; FFA Chaplin, Treas; NOC; Comp Engrng.

GREEN, LESLIE; Okemah HS; Okemah, OK; (1); 1/70; Church Yth Grp; Cmnty Wkr; Debate Tm; GAA; Math Tm; Natl Beta Clb; Quiz Bowl; Scholastic Bowl; Science Clb; SADD.

GREEN, LISA M; Lone Grove HS; Lone Grove, OK; (2); 4-H; FHA; Math Clb; Science Clb; Chorus; School Play; Hon Roll; Southeastern; Pediatrcn.

GREEN, MARIA K; Pocola HS; Pocola, OK; (2); FBLA; Acpl Chr; Band; Chorus; Drm Mjr(t); Jazz Band; Mrchg Band; Pep Band; Hon Roll; NHS; OK Hnr Soc; OK Univ; Bus Admin.

GREEN, MATTHEW P; Union Sr HS; Tulsa, OK; (3); 37/741; Church Yth Grp; Band; Chorus; Pep Band; High Hon Roll; NHS; Spanish NHS; Rnssnc Hnrs Prog; Drg Free Yth; Med.

GREEN, RACHEL D; Comanche HS; Comanche, OK; (3); Art Clb; German Clb; Bsktbl; Chrldng; Cameron Univ; PT.

GREEN, ROBERT B; Union Intermediate HS; Broken Arrow, OK; (2); Church Yth Grp; FCA; FBLA; Spanish Clb; Hon Roll; NHS; Schl Spirit Cmmtte; Frosh Ftbl; U Of OK; Law.

GREEN, ROBERT N; Yukon HS; Yukon, OK; (4); 100/400; Boy Scts; Computer Clb; Scholastic Bowl; Band; Stage Crew; Hon Roll; Explorer Post; U Of Cntrl OK; Cmptr Sci.

GREEN, ROCKY W; Stigler HS; Stigler, OK; (3); FBLA; Pep Clb; Hon Roll; Prfct Atten Awd; St Cert Bus Admin Curr; Carl Albert Coll.

GREEN, SARA; Union Intermediate HS; Broken Arrow, OK; (1); Church Yth Grp; FCA; Key Clb; Office Aide; JV Chrldng; Spec Ed Tchr.

GREEN, SHANNA; Hugo HS; Hugo, OK; (4); 13/101; Computer Clb; Office Aide; Science Clb; Spanish Clb; Teachers Aide; Flag Corp; Yrbk; Cit Awd; Hon Roll; NHS; Pre-Med.

GREEN, SHELDON; Wynnewood HS; Wynnewood, OK; (4); 7/56; Letterman Clb; Rep Frsh Cls; Pres Soph Cls; Pres Jr Cls; Pres Stu Cncl; Var Ftbl; Var Trk; Hon Roll; NHS; Ftbl All Star; Sprts Med.

GREEN, STEPHANIE; Midwest City HS; Midwest City, OK; (2); 25/500; Art Clb; Church Yth Grp; FCA; Key Clb; Library Aide; SADD; Rep Soph Cls; Jr NHS.

GREEN, SUZANNE D; Pauls Valley HS; Pauls Valley, OK; (2); Church Yth Grp; FCA; French Clb; FHA; Key Clb; Tennis; OK ST U.

GREEN, TERRY R; Enid Sr HS; Enid, OK; (2); 2/425; FCA; Rep Stu Cncl; JV Bsktbl; Var Ftbl; Cit Awd; Jr NHS; NHS; Supt Hon Rl; US Military Acad; Armd Frc Off.

GREEN, TIFFANY R; South Intermediate HS; Broken Arrow, OK; (1); Church Yth Grp; Computer Clb; Mgr(s); Socr; Hon Roll; Jr NHS; Fellowship Of Chrstn Stud; Comp Sci.

GREEN, TRINA L; Roland Sr HS; Roland, OK; (3); Spanish Clb; Speech Tm; Band; Color Guard; Mrchg Band; Hon Roll; Span Royalty 95; Westack CC; RN.

GREEN, VICTORIA ELAINE; Coweta HS; Coweta, OK; (4); 35/155; Am Leg Aux Girls St; FBLA; Girl Scts; Pres SADD; Phtg Ed Nwsp; Phtg Ed Yrbk; Pres Jr Cls; Pres Sr Cls; VP Stu Cncl; Var Sftbl; UIL Intr-Schlstc Awd; 1st Pl Photo NSU Press Day & OIPA; Oklahoma City U; Mass Comms.

GREENBURG, COURTNEY; Claremore Sr HS; Claremore, OK; (3); 2/200; Cmnty Wkr; French Clb; Hosp Aide; Spanish Clb; SADD; Teachers Aide; Ofcr Stu Cncl; JV Bsktbl; Powder Puff Ftbl; Trk.

GREENE, BRANDY; Warner HS; Warner, OK; (3); Scholastic Bowl; Spanish Clb; Mgr(s); Powder Puff Ftbl; Sftbl; Hon Roll; Connors ST Coll; Nrsng.

GREENE, MIKAEL R; Wynnewood HS; Wynnewood, OK; (3); #22 in class; FCA; Letterman Clb; Natl FFA Org; Office Aide; Ftbl; Golf; Hon Roll; East Cntrl Univ.

GREENE, TONY; Putnam City West HS; Bethany, OK; (3); 20/304; Church Yth Grp; Cmnty Wkr; Intnl Clb; JCL; Latin Clb; Letterman Clb; JV Bsktbl; Var L Ftbl; Wt Lftg; NHS; Pre-Med.

GREENFIELD, JENNIFER; Chandler HS; Chandler, OK; (2); Church Yth Grp; FCA; FHA; GAA; Rep Frsh Cls; Sec Soph Cls; Var Bsktbl; Var Chrldng; Var Sftbl; Var Trk; Southern Nazarene Univ; PE.

GREENWOOD, JANEL; Adair HS; Adair, OK; (2); Church Yth Grp; Natl FFA Org; Quiz Bowl; Science Clb; Gov Hon Prg Awd; Hon Roll; Lcl FFA Chptr Treas; Smmr Sftbl Leag; Overall Phys Sci Wnnr Sci Fair; Vet Med.

GREER, KAYONA; Douglass HS; Oklahoma City, OK; (2); Church Yth Grp; Hon Roll; Sw Med Ctr; Med Field.

GREER, MARTA; Roland Sr HS; Muldrow, OK; (3); 1/104; FCA; Natl Beta Clb; Sec Spanish Clb; Speech Tm; Band; Ed Nwsp; Yrbk; Pres Stu Cncl; Bsktbl; High Hon Roll; Page For OK House Of Reps.

GREER, ROCSANN R; Cordell Sr HS; Cordell, OK; (1); 4/60; Church Yth Grp; Cmnty Wkr; Drama Clb; FHA; Quiz Bowl; Speech Tm; Church Choir; Sec Treas Frsh Cls; Bsktbl; Mgr(s); His Image.

GREER, STEPHANIE L; Macomb Schl; Tecumseh, OK; (3); 3/20; Chrldng; Hon Roll; Acad Achiever In Ec; OK HS Hnr Soc; Stu Of The Month; Nrsng; Fshn Dsgn.

GREESON, WENDY; Sapulpa Sr HS; Sapulpa, OK; (1); Chorus; Bsktbl; Chrldng; Crs Cntry; Trk; U Of OK; Vet Med.

GREGG, CALEY; Beaver HS; Beaver, OK; (1); FCA; Chorus; Rep Frsh Cls; Bsktbl; Trk.

GREGG, CLAYTON; Beaver HS; Beaver, OK; (3); Chorus; Yrbk; Golf; Hon Roll; NHS.

GREGORY, ANDREA D; Stilwell HS; Stilwell, OK; (2); Cmnty Wkr; Drama Clb; FCA; 4-H; Natl Beta Clb; Spanish Clb; SADD; Acpl Chr; Band; Chorus; Chrs Atndnt, Rcvd Superior Ensmbl St & Dist; Bnd Atndnt, Superior St & Dist; DFY; AR U; Snd Tech.

GREGORY, CAROLYN E; Marietta HS; Marietta, OK; (3); Church Yth Grp; Cmnty Wkr; 4-H; FHA; Office Aide; Teachers Aide; Chorus; Weatherford; Pharm.

GREGORY, ELI; Cascia Hall Prep School; Muskogee, OK; (3); Church Yth Grp; Math Tm; Scholastic Bowl; Rep Sr Cls; Var L Bsktbl; Var L Ftbl; Var L Golf; Var Wt Lftg; Hon Roll; NHS; Med.

GREGORY, HEATHER D; Bethany HS; Bethany, OK; (2); Church Yth Grp; Office Aide; Chorus; OBU; Tchr.

GREGORY, JASON; Mannford HS; Tulsa, OK; (4); 9/100; Am Leg Boys St; Church Yth Grp; Cmnty Wkr; FCA; Science Clb; Spanish Clb; SADD; Bsktbl; Fld Hcky; Ice Hcky; OK U; Aviation.

GREGORY, LINDSEY; Heritage Hall Schl; Edmond, OK; (3); Cmnty Wkr; Dance Clb; FCA; GAA; Pep Clb; Spanish Clb; Varsity Clb; Yrbk; Chrldng; Fld Hcky; All Star Pom Sqd; Fashion Dsgn.

GREGORY, PYNE D; Kingston HS; Kingston, OK; (2); Art Clb; FCA; Natl FFA Org; JV Bsbl; JV Ftbl; Var Trk; Var Wt Lftg; 1st Pl Art Chr Comp 5 Times; Outstndng Artst Of Yr 95-96; Comm Art.

GREGORY, SHANNON M; West Jr HS; Oklahoma City, OK; (1); FCA; Spanish Clb; Chorus; Pres Frsh Cls; Bsktbl; Ftbl; Trk; Jr NHS; Medcl Phy.

GREGSON, JULIETTE L; Dale Sr HS; Shawnee, OK; (2); 13/50; Red Cross Aide; Mgr(s); Score Keeper; Hon Roll; Life Guides; Soc Worker.

GREIN, ANDREW; Tonkawa Jr Sr HS; Ponca City, OK; (4); 2/40; Am Leg Boys St; Church Yth Grp; FCA; Letterman Clb; Quiz Bowl; Band; Chorus; Church Choir; VP Sr Cls; Trk; St Rnnr Up High Jump 95; OK Boys St Delg.

GRELL, BRANDON; Braman Schl; Braman, OK; (4); Boy Scts; Church Yth Grp; Capt FCA; Pres Natl FFA Org; Quiz Bowl; Speech Tm; School Play; Stage Crew; Yrbk; Pres Frsh Cls; FFA & FCA Pres 2 Yrs; Connors ST Coll; Ag Ec.

GRELLE, SARAH T; Edmond Memorial HS; Edmond, OK; (3); 1/360; Church Yth Grp; German Clb; Girl Scts; Band; Treas Soph Cls; Rep Stu Cncl; JV Var Sftbl; Cit Awd; Hon Roll; NHS.

GRESH, AMANDA; Union Sr HS; Tulsa, OK; (3); 102/720; FBLA; Key Clb; Spanish Clb; Rep Frsh Cls; Rep Soph Cls; Var Capt Chrldng; Intrml Powder Puff Ftbl; NHS; All Amer Chrldr NCA Cheer Camp; 2nd Pl Natl Chrldr Cmptn Team; Bus.

GRESH, ERICA C; Union Intermediate HS; Tulsa, OK; (1); Church Yth Grp; Quiz Bowl; Speech Tm; Jazz Band; Gym; High Hon Roll; Soc Stud Awd; Outstdng Jazz Solo Awd Drury Coll 30th Annual Jazz Fstvl; Music.

GRETSINGER, JESSE E; Chattanooga Schl; Chattanooga, OK; (2); Letterman Clb; Natl FFA Org; Hon Roll; Jr NHS; NHS; Val; Var Bsbl; Var Bsktbl.

GREUEL, ALISON; Bishop Kelley HS; Tulsa, OK; (3); Church Yth Grp; HOBY; Intnl Clb; Pep Clb; Spanish Clb; Chorus; VP Soph Cls; Sec Stu Cncl; Trk; High Hon Roll; Anchr Clb Sec; Natl Hnrs Soc; Bllt; Art.

GREY, JEREMY; Midwest City HS; Choctaw, OK; (4); 11/419; Quiz Bowl; Scholastic Bowl; Mrchg Band; Golf; Gov Hon Prg Awd; High Hon Roll; Jr NHS; NHS; Pres Acad Fit Awd; Val; U Of OK; Mech Engrng.

GRIDER, AMBER L; Lexington HS; Lexington, OK; (4); 27/70; Church Yth Grp; FCA; FHA; Natl FFA Org; Ofcr Frsh Cls; Ofcr Stu Cncl; Capt Bsktbl; Capt Sftbl; L Trk; HS Heros; OPAT Prgm; All ST Fastpitch Sftbl; Connors ST Coll; Art.

GRIESEL, KEITH E; Okarche Jr-Sr HS; Okarche, OK; (4); 7/29; Church Yth Grp; Debate Tm; FHA; Letterman Clb; Natl Beta Clb; NFL; Quiz Bowl; Speech Tm; School Play; Sec Frsh Cls; OK ST Univ; Law.

GRIFFIN, AMANDA K; Choctaw HS; Choctaw, OK; (4); Church Yth Grp; Drama Clb; FCA; Teachers Aide; School Play; Rptr Nwsp; Ftbl; Mgr(s); Powder Puff Ftbl; Trk; Stu Sports Med Trainer Ftbl; Ftbl Homcmng Qn 95; Rose ST Coll; Radlgst Technen.

GRIFFIN, AMY K; Grace Chrn Acad; Oklahoma City, OK; (2); Church Yth Grp; Church Choir; Ofcr Soph Cls; Ofcr Stu Cncl; Chrldng; Cit Awd; High Hon Roll; Hon Roll; Pres Acad Fit Awd; Chrldng Ltrs; Chrch Drama Staff; Comm Svc; Natl Schlr From NYLC; OK Univ.

GRIFFIN, CANDICE R; Tahlequah Jr HS; Park Hill, OK; (1); Church Yth Grp; Band; Mrchg Band; Kiwanis Awd; Thtrcl Drama Part; DO/MD.

GRIFFIN, JENNIFER; Midwest City HS; Midwest City, OK; (3); #34 in class; Pep Clb; Spanish Clb; Socr; Swmmng; Vllybl; Hon Roll; Jr NHS; NHS; Spanish NHS; Frgn Lang.

GRIFFIN, JOHN R; Union Sr HS; Broken Arrow, OK; (3); 5/740; Key Clb; VP Math Clb; Spanish Clb; Cit Awd; Gov Hon Prg Awd; High Hon Roll; NHS; Spanish NHS; YVC; ARC; Yng Astrnts Clb Co Pres.

GRIFFIN, KELLY B; Bishop Mcguinness HS; Oklahoma City, OK; (3); Church Yth Grp; CAP; FCA; German Clb; Chorus; Church Choir; JV Bsktbl; Var Socr; JV Vllybl; All Star Yth Choir; Jr Olympc Vlybl; Chrstn Brother Univ; Crtv Wrtng.

GRIFFIN, KRYSTI L; Blair Schl; Blair, OK; (3); Natl Beta Clb; Natl FFA Org; Bsktbl; Sftbl; Hon Roll.

GRIFFIN, LANCE M; Edmond North HS; Edmond, OK; (4); 122/339; Art Clb; OSU; Art.

GRIFFIN, STEVEN; Seminole Jr Sr HS; Seminole, OK; (4); 18/82; Am Leg Boys St; Church Yth Grp; Debate Tm; FCA; Math Clb; Spanish Clb; Var Bsbl; Var Ftbl; Wt Lftg; High Hon Roll; Comp Prgmr.

GRIFFIN, TERRI M; Putnam City HS; Warr Acres, OK; (3); 90/325; Church Yth Grp; FCA; Spanish Clb; Mgr Vllybl; Stat Wrstlng; Prfct Atten Awd; Hlth Occuptns Stdnt Amer; Yth Alive; Vo-Tech Natl Hon Soc; OK City CC; Ped.

GRIFFITH, CHAD M; West Middle HS; Norman, OK; (2); FCA; Pep Clb; Spanish Clb; Stage Crew; Rep Frsh Cls; JV Bsktbl; Powder Puff Ftbl; JV Var Tennis; Hon Roll; NHS; Teen Vol; OU; Sprts Med.

GRIFFITH, HOLLY; Bray-Doyle HS; Marlow, OK; (3); 3/32; Church Yth Grp; Cmnty Wkr; FCA; VP FHA; Pep Clb; Scholastic Bowl; Church Choir; Rptr Jr Cls; Capt Chrldng; High Hon Roll; OK Hnr Soc Secy; Sci Bowl; OSU; Bus Mgmt.

GRIFFITH, JEREMY; Gans Public Schl; Gans, OK; (3); Natl FFA Org; Rep Jr Cls; Cit Awd; Hon Roll; Prfct Atten Awd; Gov Cmmndtn; Natl Voc-Tech Hnr Soc; Cherokee Nation Accomp Awd; Welder.

GRIFFITH, JERRY ELIZABETH; Yukon HS; Yukon, OK; (4); 6/420; Church Yth Grp; Cmnty Wkr; English Clb; Lit Mag; Var Tennis; High Hon Roll; NHS; 3-D Clb; Renaissance Comm Mem; Super Drug Advisory Comm; Harding; Med Missionary.

GRIFFITH, JOSHUA D; Gans Public Schl; Gans, OK; (4); 7/19; Art Clb; Spanish Clb; Teachers Aide; School Musical; Stage Crew; Nwsp; Yrbk; Cit Awd; GATE Quest; Carl Albert ST Coll; Psych.

GRIFFITH, NATASHA L; U S Grant HS; Oklahoma City, OK; (3); FHA; SADD; Gym; Mgr(s); Sftbl; Vllybl; Hon Roll; OCU; Surgeon.

GRIFFITH, SARAH; Nathan Hale HS; Tulsa, OK; (4); 41/205; Am Leg Aux Girls St; Church Yth Grp; Cmnty Wkr; Debate Tm; DECA; FCA; GAA; Key Clb; Letterman Clb; Red Cross Aide; Homcmng Qn; OSU.

GRIFFITH, TABATHA N; Madill HS; Lebanon, OK; (1); Church Yth Grp; Drama Clb; FCA; Pep Clb; Speech Tm; School Play; Vllybl; Hon Roll; Cmptv Spch Awd; TX A&M; Marine Bio.

GRIFFITH, TIFFANY N; B T Washington HS; Tulsa, OK; (2); Spanish Clb; Hon Roll; NHS; Prfct Atten Awd; I B Cand; Msnc Awd; Med.

GRIFFITTS, AMY L; Hinton HS; Hinton, OK; (2); Art Clb; Drama Clb; FHA; Bsktbl; Trk; Hon Roll.

GRIGG, BRANDI; Burns Flat/Dill City HS; Burns Flat, OK; (3); #5 in class; Church Yth Grp; FBLA; FHA; Bsktbl; Chrldng; Crs Cntry; Trk; High Hon Roll; Hon Roll; NHS; Miss Dance Of OK; Dance Intnl Australia Tour; OK Summer Arts Inst; Western OK Ballet Theater; Dance; Prof Dancer.

GRIGG, CARRIE A; South Intermediate HS; Broken Arrow, OK; (2); Band; Mrchg Band; Hon Roll; Natl Engl Merit Awd; All Amer Schlr; Lwyr.

GRIGGS, JUSTIN; Liberty Acad; Sparks, OK; (2); Church Yth Grp; High Hon Roll; Acad Tm; Engl, Sci Awds; St Gregorys Shawnee; Comp Sci.

GRIGGS, LACEY S; Harrah HS; Harrah, OK; (3); 33/153; Church Yth Grp; Cmnty Wkr; FCA; FHA; Office Aide; Scholastic Bowl; SADD; VP Teachers Aide; Chorus; Church Choir; Rose ST Coll; Kndgrtn Tchr.

GRILL, BRIAN A; Snyder HS; Snyder, OK; (3); 8/42; Ofcr Bsbl; Bsktbl; Ftbl; Trk; Wt Lftg; Hon Roll; NHS; Tchr/Coach/Sprts Med.

GRIMES, AMANDA; Ripley HS; Perkins, OK; (1); Church Yth Grp; FCA; FBLA; FHA; Math Clb; Natl FFA Org; Office Aide; Pep Clb; Science Clb; Teachers Aide; OSU; Elem Ed.

GRIMES, ANDREW; Ponca City Sr HS; Ponca City, OK; (4); Boy Scts; Pres DECA; Q&S; Spanish Clb; Band; Ed Nwsp; Sec Frsh Cls; L Ftbl; Hon Roll; Kiwanis Awd; N OK Coll.

GRIMES, ASHLY D; Guthrie Sr HS; Guthrie, OK; (1); Spanish Clb; LA ST U.

GRIMES, JEFF D; South Intermediate HS; Broken Arrow, OK; (1); Notre Dame; Dr.

GRIMES, KOREY; Newcastle HS; Tuttle, OK; (4); Art Clb; Trk; Hon Roll; OK Christian; Astronomy.

GRIMM, ANDREW RYAN; Cascia Hall Prep School; Tulsa, OK; (2); Latin Clb; Letterman Clb; Chorus; Rep Frsh Cls; Rep Soph Cls; Var Bsbl; JV Bsktbl; Var Ftbl; Hon Roll; Clvr Mltry Acad Smmr Cmp; Amer Cvl War Sprts/Law.

GRIMM, ELISSA M; Enid Sr HS; Enid, OK; (3); 34/425; Church Yth Grp; Debate Tm; Chorus; Church Choir; School Musical; Swing Chorus; Cit Awd; High Hon Roll; NHS; Pres Acad Fit Awd; NYLC Dallas; Northwestern OK ST Univ.

GRIMMETT, JEREMY L; Valliant HS; Valliant, OK; (1); 1/89; Church Yth Grp; 4-H; French Clb; School Play; VP Frsh Cls; Pres Stu Cncl; Bsktbl; Tennis; 4-H Awd; High Hon Roll; OU; Psych.

GRIMSLEY, GREGORY D; Wellston Schl; Wellston, OK; (4); FHA; Library Aide; Spanish Clb; SADD; Treas Soph Cls; Treas Sr Cls; Var Capt Bsbl; Var Capt Bsktbl; Hon Roll; All-Conf 94-96; U Of OK; Elem Ed.

GRIPE, STEVEN C; Yale Jr Sr HS; Yale, OK; (4); 7/35; FHA; Natl Beta Clb; Natl FFA Org; Bsktbl; Cit Awd; High Hon Roll; Ovrtn Brk VA Med Ctr Cert Apprctn; Acctng I, II Awds; Am Hstry Awd; OSU; Elec Engrng.

GRISHAM, TIFFANY A; Southeast HS; Oklahoma City, OK; (2); Church Yth Grp; ROTC; Drill Tm; Ofcr Soph Cls; Cit Awd; High Hon Roll; NHS; Bsktbl; Upwrd Bnd; Rose ST Coll.

GRISSO, DARCI; Shawnee Sr HS; Shawnee, OK; (4); 26/263; Church Yth Grp; Cmnty Wkr; Dance Clb; FCA; Latin Clb; Office Aide; SADD; School Play; Nwsp; VP Frsh Cls; Tri-Hi-Y Pres; Life Guides.

GRISSO, LAURA M; Norman Sr HS; Norman, OK; (4); Treas Latin Clb; Mu Alpha Theta; Office Aide; Pres Pep Clb; Quiz Bowl; Scholastic Bowl; Nwsp; Yrbk; Ofcr Stu Cncl; Hon Roll.

GRISWOLD, JENNIFER R; Rush Springs HS; Ninnekah, OK; (2); Church Yth Grp; Quiz Bowl; Scholastic Bowl; Spanish Clb; Band; Hon Roll; NHS; OK Hnr Scty; Yth Alv Pryr Grp Rprtr.

GRITTMAN, LACIE N; Yale Jr Sr HS; Yale, OK; (3); Church Yth Grp; FHA; Pep Clb; Quiz Bowl; Red Cross Aide; Acpl Chr; Chorus; Church Choir; Rep Stu Cncl; Bapt All St Yth Choir; Commercial Art.

GRIZZARD, KRISTY A; John Marshall HS; Oklahoma City, OK; (4); #17 in class; Church Yth Grp; Cmnty Wkr; Letterman Clb; Library Aide; ROTC; Spanish Clb; Teachers Aide; Church Choir; Drill Tm; Vllybl; Air Force.

GRIZZELLE, ROBERT E; El Reno Sr HS; El Reno, OK; (3); Key Clb; Natl FFA Org; Var Ftbl; Var Wt Lftg; Hon Roll; OSU.

GRIZZLE, ANDRE M; Broken Arrow Sr HS; Broken Arrow, OK; (3); Church Yth Grp; FBLA; Band; Jazz Band; Tennis; Hon Roll; Rep OK Chrch Of God Talnt Natls 3 Yrs; ST Playing Tennis Frosh Yr; Oral Roberts Univ.

GRIZZLE, DAVID R; Western Heights Sr HS; Oklahoma City, OK; (1); Var Bsbl; High Hon Roll; Hon Roll; Jr NHS; U Of OK; Bus; Law.

GROBER, CHRISTI; Muskogee HS; Muskogee, OK; (3); 3/400; Church Yth Grp; FCA; JCL; Spanish Clb; School Musical; Rep Stu Cncl; Chrldng; High Hon Roll; NHS; Ecology Club Rep.

GROEHLER, BRAD W; Lindsay HS; Lindsay, OK; (1); 19/75; 4-H; Ftbl; Wt Lftg; Hon Roll; Notre Dame; Bus.

GROFF, MEAGAN R; Will Rogers HS; Tulsa, OK; (1); GAA; Spanish Clb; Sftbl; Tennis; High Hon Roll; Hon Roll; Ntl Merit Schol.

GROOM, TIFFANY K; Stilwell HS; Stilwell, OK; (2); Church Yth Grp; Computer Clb; FBLA; GAA; Natl FFA Org; Spanish Clb; Teachers Aide; Ofcr Bsbl; Bsktbl; Mgr(s); Phy Thrpst.

GROOMS, LAMONT; El Reno Sr HS; El Reno, OK; (2); Pres Church Yth Grp; FCA; Letterman Clb; Chorus; Church Choir; Mrchg Band; Var Ftbl; Var Wt Lftg; Hon Roll; Chrstn Rapper; U Of VA; Acctng; Audit Acctnt.

GROSS, JENNIFER L; Putnam City North HS; Oklahoma City, OK; (2); Band; Mrchg Band; Southern Nazarene U; Med.

GROSS, TRINA; Wynnewood HS; Wynnewood, OK; (4); 22/56; Cmnty Wkr; Sec Hist Drama Clb; Pres 4-H; Art Clb; Natl FFA Org; Office Aide; Pep Clb; Hist SADD; Teachers Aide; Chorus; East Central U.

GROSSARDT, CRAIG R; Blackwell HS; Blackwell, OK; (2); 1/130; Boy Scts; FCA; HOBY; Quiz Bowl; Band; Mrchg Band; Pep Band; Ftbl; Wt Lftg; High Hon Roll; Bus.

GROSSMAN, JEREMY M; Weatherford HS; Weatherford, OK; (3); Church Yth Grp; Cmnty Wkr; German Clb; Band; Mrchg Band; Rep Stu Cncl; Var Ftbl; Var Socr; Wt Lftg; Gov Hon Prg Awd; CO U; Dr; Anesthesiologist.

GROSSMAN, LAURA B; Pryor Sr HS; Pryor, OK; (3); 30/200; Church Yth Grp; Cmnty Wkr; FCA; 4-H; German Clb; GAA; Quiz Bowl; JV Var Bsktbl; Intrml Sftbl; 4-H Awd.

GROTH, JOY; Mt St Marys HS; Choctaw, OK; (2); Church Yth Grp; Cmnty Wkr; Treas French Clb; Treas Jr Cls; L Chrldng; High Hon Roll; NHS; Pep Clb; Treas Soph Cls; Ofcr Stu Cncl; Explore Post Fox 25; Intl Sci/Engr Fair; Nwsanchr Mt Saint Marys Mrng Anncmnts; Brdcst/Jrnlsm.

GROTTS, ERIC J; Dibble Jr Sr HS; Blanchard, OK; (2); Chess Clb; Ftbl; Trk; Wt Lftg; Cit Awd; Natl Youth Ldrshp Forum Law.

GROUNDS, JASON L; Hooker Jr-Sr HS; Hooker, OK; (3); 3/40; Church Yth Grp; Band; Mrchg Band; Pep Band; Rptr Yrbk; Var Bsktbl; JV Golf; Intrml Wt Lftg; High Hon Roll; NHS; Msnc Stu Of Today; OK Hnr Soc.

GROVER, LANCE E; Ponca City Middle HS; Ponca City, OK; (1); Church Yth Grp; Office Aide; Stage Crew; Nwsp; Ofcr Bsbl; Tennis; Cit Awd; Band Bass/Lead Gtrs; Drftng Dsng/Music Engr.

GROVES, COBY; Edmond North HS; Edmond, OK; (4); Am Leg Aux Girls St; Church Yth Grp; FCA; French Clb; Library Aide; SADD; Ofcr Stu Cncl; Var Chrldng; Cit Awd; Hon Roll; All Amer Chrldr NCA; Girls ST Ofcr; All Star Pom; FCA Ldrshp Ofcr; All Amer Pom; Hnr Soc; Sr Ambassador; Pol Sci.

GROVES, SHAWNA G; Sapulpa Sr HS; Sapulpa, OK; (3); Dance Clb; FHA; Band; Mrchg Band; Chrldng; High Hon Roll; Hon Roll; NHS; Spanish NHS.

GROVES, WILLIAM T; Bartlesville Sr HS; Bartlesville, OK; (3); Acpl Chr; Northeastern ST Univ; His Tchr.

GRUBE, JIMMY; Durant HS; Durant, OK; (1); Intrml Bsktbl; Intrml Ftbl; Intrml Trk.

GRUNAU, NICK; Balko Public Schl; Balko, OK; (1); Church Yth Grp; Natl FFA Org; Band; Church Choir; Mrchg Band; Var Bsbl; Var Bsktbl; JV Ftbl; High Hon Roll; Hon Roll; U Of OK.

GRUNDY, DAN L; Vinita HS; Big Cabin, OK; (3); FCA; Math Clb; Office Aide; Science Clb; Spanish Clb; Var Bsktbl; Var Ftbl; Var Trk; High Hon Roll; NHS.

GRUNEWALD, GREGORY; Clinton HS; Clinton, OK; (4); 14/101; Am Leg Boys St; Church Yth Grp; FCA; Key Clb; Natl FFA Org; Quiz Bowl; Pres Stu Cncl; Bsktbl; Ftbl; NHS; OSU; Dental.

GRUVER, MANDI M; Westmoore HS; Oklahoma City, OK; (4); Office Aide; Spanish Clb; Teachers Aide; School Play; Wt Lftg; High Hon Roll; Hon Roll; NHS; Ntl Merit Ltr; High Hon Roll.

GUARA, RUDY; Bartlesville Mid HS; Bartlesville, OK; (2); VP Treas Art Clb; Church Yth Grp; Nwsp; Hon Roll; Prfct Atten Awd; Rec Soccer; Art.

GUARDIOLA, MILVET; Union Sr HS; Tulsa, OK; (4); 11/629; Am Leg Aux Girls St; DECA; FBLA; Intnl Clb; Key Clb; Rep Stu Cncl; Jr NHS; NHS; Pres Acad Fit Awd; Spanish NHS; Xerox Awd; U Of TX Austin; Advrtsng.

GUBSER, KAYLA; Hobart HS; Hobart, OK; (3); Church Yth Grp; Teachers Aide; Church Choir; School Play; Rep Frsh Cls; VP Soph Cls; Pres Jr Cls; Ofcr Stu Cncl; Var JV Bsktbl; Capt Chrldng; Med.

GUDGEL, RANDELL; Amber Pocasset Jr Sr HS; Chickasha, OK; (3); Office Aide; Science Clb; Spanish Clb; Chorus; NHS; Acad/Amer Legion Awds; Med Rsrch.

GUEDEA, ANGELICA M; John Marshall HS; Oklahoma City, OK; (3); German Clb; Library Aide; Office Aide; Teachers Aide; School Play; Stage Crew; Ofcr Frsh Cls; Cit Awd; Hon Roll; Prfct Atten Awd; DECA Clb; U Cntrl OK; Marine Bio.

GUERIN, MARIE T; Putnam City North HS; Oklahoma City, OK; (4); 50/425; Dance Clb; Debate Tm; Key Clb; School Play; Cit Awd; High Hon Roll; NHS; Ntl Merit Schol; U Of OK.

GUERRA, ERIK M; Elgin HS; Elgin, OK; (1); Ofcr Bsbl; Wrstlng; High Hon Roll; Hon Roll; NHS.

GUERRERO, LYNDA L; Inola Sr HS; Inola, OK; (3); 4-H; Office Aide; Teachers Aide; Bsktbl; Trk; Hon Roll.

GUESBY, EBONY; Tomlinson Jr HS; Lawton, OK; (1); Church Yth Grp; FCA; Church Choir; High Hon Roll; Open Doors; Langston U; Actress.

GUEST, TAMMIA L; Eisenhower Sr HS; Lawton, OK; (4); 115/386; FHA; GAA; Letterman Clb; Rep Frsh Cls; Rep Soph Cls; Rep Jr Cls; Rep Sr Cls; Rep Stu Cncl; Bsktbl; Pom Pon; 93 Hmcmng Queen; GATE; OK Univ; Chem.

GUFFEY, AMANDA L; Stilwell HS; Stilwell, OK; (1); Church Yth Grp; Cmnty Wkr; FCA; 4-H; French Clb; Natl FFA Org; SADD; Ofcr Bsbl; Bsktbl; Mgr(s); Kybrdng; U Of A; RN.

GUFFY, AMI D; Ringwood HS; Ringwood, OK; (2); 1/25; Church Yth Grp; VP FCA; HOBY; Pres Frsh Cls; Ofcr Stu Cncl; Var L Bsktbl; Var L Trk; High Hon Roll; NHS; Val; OU; Phys Therapy; Sports Medcn.

GUGLIUZZA, PAUL R; Bishop Kelley HS; Tulsa, OK; (1); Var Ice Hcky; Co-Capt Hon Roll; Mock Trial; U Of Notre Dame; Law.

GUICE, MELISSA A; U S Grant HS; Oklahoma City, OK; (3); 20/250; SADD; Thesps; Stage Crew; Rptr Yrbk; Rptr Frsh Cls; VP Sr Cls; Sftbl; Cit Awd; High Hon Roll; NHS; Teens Against Drugs; PRIDE; William Jewell; Commnctns.

GUIER, CHRISTINE N; Union Sr HS; Tulsa, OK; (4); 61/629; Church Yth Grp; FCA; Key Clb; Office Aide; Spanish Clb; Co-Capt Drill Tm; High Hon Roll; Hon Roll; NHS; Prfct Atten Awd; Renaissance Clb; Miss Union Attend 94-95; NASC Cnvntn St Guide; OU; Med.

GUILFORD, DELANEY; Frederick HS; Frederick, OK; (1); 1/85; Band; Chorus; Church Choir; Mrchg Band; School Musical; JV Golf; High Hon Roll; NHS; Top Ten; Int Dsgn.

GUILLIAMS, JAYME; Claremore Sr HS; Claremore, OK; (4); 19/261; FCA; Spanish Clb; Teachers Aide; Color Guard; Pom Pon; Cit Awd; High Hon Roll; Hon Roll; NHS; Ballet Tap, Jazz; OU; Law.

GUILLIAMS, LEZLY; Claremore Sr HS; Claremore, OK; (2); Church Yth Grp; Dance Clb; FCA; Teachers Aide; Color Guard; Drill Tm; Flag Corp; Pom Pon; Powder Puff Ftbl; Score Keeper; Taught Preschl Chldrn/Helped Bld Hm Fam Mexico; OK ST Univ; Ansthslgst.

GUILLORY, ANTOINE J; Pocola HS; Pocola, OK; (2); Quiz Bowl; Chorus; Pres Soph Cls; JV Bsktbl; Hon Roll; NHS.

GUILLORY, KELLI M; Durant HS; Durant, OK; (4); 50/149; Church Yth Grp; Debate Tm; GAA; Letterman Clb; Quiz Bowl; Spanish Clb; Varsity Clb; Tennis; Hon Roll; U Of Houston; Elec Educ.

GUILLOTT, LAURA D; Edmond North HS; Edmond, OK; (3); Church Yth Grp; Stat ROTC; SADD; NHS; Kitty Hawk Air Soc; Bartsdale Ldrshp Schl; Forestry.

GUINN, AMANDA; Moore HS; Moore, OK; (4); 22/525; French Clb; JCL; Latin Clb; Sec Treas Mu Alpha Theta; Var Swmmng; French Hon Soc; Jr NHS; NHS; Prfct Atten Awd; Val; OK Hnr Soc; Bio.

GUINN, BRANDI; Hulbert Jr Sr HS; Hulbert, OK; (2); 4-H; FBLA; Var Bsktbl; Chrldng; Var Sftbl; Trk; 4-H Awd; Hon Roll; Ofcr Jr NHS; Natl Engl Mrt Awd.

GUINN, KANDICE R; Meeker HS; Meeker, OK; (1); Church Yth Grp; Scholastic Bowl; VP Frsh Cls; Bsktbl; Var Chrldng; Gym; Sftbl; High Hon Roll; Pres Acad Fit Awd; OK Univ; Tchr.

GUINN, MALESA R; Vanoss Schl; Ada, OK; (2); FBLA; Acpl Chr; Chorus; Cit Awd; Hon Roll; Prfct Atten Awd; East Cntrl Univ Hnrs Choir Mem; East Cntrl Univ; Nrsng.

GUINN, MELISSA A; Union Intermediate HS; Tulsa, OK; (1); Cmnty Wkr; FCA; Spanish Clb; High Hon Roll; Hon Roll; Jr NHS; NHS; Young Astronauts Prgm; Acad Rsurc Cntr GATE Stu Cncl Class Rep; PT/MARINE Bio.

GUINTEBANO, MARYJEL P; Macarthur Sr HS; Lawton, OK; (3); 33/284; Church Yth Grp; Treas German Clb; Hosp Aide; HOBY; Band; Capt Mrchg Band; Ed Yrbk; Trk; Hon Roll; NHS; OK ST Univ; Biochem.

GULIKERS, JOSEPH R; Western Heights Sr HS; Oklahoma City, OK; (3); 1/167; VP FHA; Key Clb; Letterman Clb; Office Aide; VP Frsh Cls; Rep Stu Cncl; Ftbl; Socr; Hon Roll; USBEA; USNMA; OK Citation Sccer; Natl Congrsnl Yth Ldrshp Cncl Awd; DECA Exec Bd/ST Historian.

GULIKERS, PETER G; Western Heights Sr HS; Oklahoma City, OK; (3); 1/190; Am Leg Boys St; Key Clb; Letterman Clb; Chorus; Pres Frsh Cls; Pres Stu Cncl; L Var Socr; Capt Var Tennis; Hon Roll; NHS; OK St Univ; Bus.

GULIZIO, MICHELLE; Metro Christian Acad; Broken Arrow, OK; (2); Church Yth Grp; Key Clb; Spanish Clb; Phtg Rptr Yrbk; Chrmn Jr Cls; Ofcr Stu Cncl; Intrml JV Bsktbl; Golf; Tennis; Cit Awd.

GULLEDGE, JUSTIN A; Elgin HS; Elgin, OK; (2); 3/85; VP Church Yth Grp; FHA; Natl FFA Org; Office Aide; Pep Clb; Quiz Bowl; Scholastic Bowl; Spanish Clb; Church Choir; VP Frsh Cls; ST Hnr Soc; OK; Pre-Med/Peds.

GULLEY, AMBER; Braggs Schl; Braggs, OK; (4); 7/18; Church Yth Grp; FBLA; Nwsp; Yrbk; Rep Sr Cls; Bsktbl; Sftbl; Cit Awd; Hon Roll; Prfct Atten Awd; Connors ST Coll; Data Prcssng.

GULLEY, CASEY; Braggs Schl; Braggs, OK; (2); Church Yth Grp; 4-H; Church Choir; Rep Stu Cncl; Hon Roll; Connor Coll; Nrsng.

GULLEY, CHRISTOPHER; Midwest City HS; Midwest City, OK; (2); Church Yth Grp; German Clb; Quiz Bowl; Science Clb; Stage Crew; Ofcr Soph Cls; L Wt Lftg; Cit Awd; High Hon Roll; NHS; Soc.

GULLEY, MIKE W; Wagoner Sr HS; Wagoner, OK; (3); VICA; Intrml Bsktbl; Hon Roll; Atten Indian Capital Vo-Tech & Trained In Welding; AR ST; Arch; Welder.

GUNSALUS, HARDY R; Bethany HS; Oklahoma City, OK; (4); Church Yth Grp; Office Aide; Church Choir; Nwsp; Yrbk; Ofcr Bsbl; Var Bsktbl; Ftbl; Socr; Cit Awd; Med Field.

GUNTER, DOYL R; Sallisaw HS; Sallisaw, OK; (1); Chorus; Church Choir; JV Bsktbl; Cmptr Pgrmmr.

GUNTER, JEFF; Lone Grove HS; Overbrook, OK; (3); Church Yth Grp; Ftbl; Wt Lftg; Hon Roll.

GURTHET, CHARLES R; Bishop Kelley HS; Tulsa, OK; (3); VICA; JV Ftbl; Natl Voc Tech Hnr Soc; Outstdnt Stdnt Awd; OK ST Univ; Auto Tech.

GUSTAFSON, JESSICA J; Heritage Hall Schl; Oklahoma City, OK; (3); Church Yth Grp; Cmnty Wkr; Pep Clb; Spanish Clb; Chorus; Lit Mag; Fld Hcky; High Hon Roll; NHS; Spanish NHS; COPE; Peer Ldr.

GUSTAFSON, MELISSA; Tomlinson Jr HS; Lawton, OK; (1); Church Yth Grp; FHA; Hosp Aide; Office Aide; Pep Clb; Red Cross Aide; Sec Band; Yrbk; High Hon Roll; Sec Jr NHS; Northwestern St Paul; Eng.

GUTHRIE, DANIEL; Pryor Sr HS; Pryor, OK; (2); FCA; 4-H; FBLA; FHA; Bsktbl; Var Tennis; 4-H Awd; Hon Roll; NHS; Top 10 Prcnt Clss; Alg I High Grd Awd; OK ST U.

GUTHRIE, JAMIE A; Noble HS; Norman, OK; (2); Church Yth Grp; FCA; Key Clb; Spanish Clb; Socr; Hon Roll; NHS; Hnrs Eng; U Of OK.

GUTHRIE, JENNIFER M; Nathan Hale HS; Tulsa, OK; (2); Art Clb; Church Yth Grp; FCA; Girl Scts; Key Clb; Teachers Aide; Band; Church Choir; Color Guard; Mrchg Band; 3rd Pl In Sci Fair; 3rd Pl In Math Fair; OK ST Univ; Tchng; Law.

GUTHRIE, REBEKAH D; Tahlequah Sr HS; Cookson, OK; (2); Am Leg Aux Girls St; Pres Acad Fit Awd; NYU; Screen Wrtng.

GUTHRIE, VINDLE; Kansas Schl; Kansas, OK; (4); 20/72; Art Clb; Church Yth Grp; Natl FFA Org; Rep Stu Cncl; Bsktbl; Capt Ftbl; Trk; Capt Wt Lftg; Hon Roll; 5th Pl St Champ Power Lifter; OSU; Phy Ed.

GUTIEREZ, NEMUEL; Capitol Hill HS; Oklahoma City, OK; (4); 7/140; Church Yth Grp; Spanish Clb; Church Choir; Wrstlng; Hon Roll; Oklahoma City U; Nursng.

GUTIERREZ, ALISHA; Guymon Sr HS; Guymon, OK; (1); Band; Color Guard; Mrchg Band; JV Chrldng; Wt Lftg; Hon Roll; Gymnastics; Sftbl.

GUTIERREZ, BANESSA; Okay Jr Sr HS; Okay, OK; (4); 7/21; Church Yth Grp; Debate Tm; FHA; Office Aide; Spanish Clb; Ofcr Jr Cls; Ofcr Stu Cncl; Bsktbl; Chrldng; Mgr(s); Vllybll-MVP 2 Yrs; Ofnsv Plyr; Defplyr; All-Trnmnt Tm; All St Tm; Spanclb VP; Multi Yr Listee; NEO; Law.

GUTIERREZ, MANDY J; Wagoner Sr HS; Wagoner, OK; (3); 7/97; Am Leg Aux Girls St; Cmnty Wkr; Red Cross Aide; VP Frsh Cls; Treas Soph Cls; Pres Jr Cls; Rep Stu Cncl; Capt Socr; Hon Roll; NHS; Campfire; Tulsa U; Mrktg.

GUTSHALL, VANCE F; Pauls Valley HS; Pauls Valley, OK; (1); Art Clb; FCA; Natl FFA Org; Ftbl; Ice Hcky; Wt Lftg; Hon Roll; Outstdng Stdnt Awd Speech/Drama; FFA Green Hand Awd; OK ST Univ.

GUTTILLO, MICHAEL A; Stilwell HS; Stilwell, OK; (2); Natl FFA Org; Spanish Clb; Mgr(s); Wt Lftg; Hon Roll; Indian Heritage; U Of AR; Psychiatrist.

GUY, JAMIN T; El Reno Sr HS; El Reno, OK; (3); Church Yth Grp; FCA; FTA; Math Clb; Math Tm; Quiz Bowl; Scholastic Bowl; Science Clb; Spanish Clb; Rep Jr Cls; U Of OK; Comp Engrng.

GUZMAN, BRANDY; Moore HS; Moore, OK; (3); Church Yth Grp; Cmnty Wkr; Band; Church Choir; Mrchg Band; Mgr(s); Jr NHS; Awd Knwldg; OK U; Psych.

HAAG, JESSICA; Dewey HS; Dewey, OK; (4); 4/89; Church Yth Grp; Sec 4-H; Office Aide; Quiz Bowl; Spanish Clb; Treas Stu Cncl; 4-H Awd; Hon Roll; NHS; Pres Acad Fit Awd; Rgstrd NARHA Thrptc Rdng Instr; CPR First Aid Lifegrd Rgstrd Threw Red Cross; U Of NE At Kearney.

HAAR, JENNIFER I; Webster HS; Tulsa, OK; (2); Treas FBLA; Office Aide; Varsity Clb; Ofcr Frsh Cls; Treas Soph Cls; Sec Jr Cls; Ftbl; High Hon Roll; Hon Roll; Bus Mgmt; Law.

HAASE, CHEREE D; North Intemediate HS; Broken Arrow, OK; (2); Church Yth Grp; Spanish Clb; Acpl Chr; Church Choir; Jr NHS; NHS; Evangel Coll; Psych.

HABBEN JR, DARRELL; Perry Sr HS; Perry, OK; (3); Art Clb; Church Yth Grp; FHA; German Clb; Office Aide; JV Bsktbl; Var Golf; Hon Roll; Jr NHS; OK ST U; Cmptr Prgmng.

HABERLY, ELIZABETH ANN; Dewey HS; Dewey, OK; (1); 7/96; Church Yth Grp; Spanish Clb; JV Var Bsktbl; Var Trk; Hon Roll; Girls Bsktbl Outstndng Rookie Of Yr; OK ST U; Respiratory Physcn.

HABIGER, ANDREW J; Bartlesville Mid HS; Bartlesville, OK; (2); Church Yth Grp; German Clb; Letterman Clb; Intrml Bsktbl; Intrml Socr; Var L Tennis; Hon Roll; Jr NHS; NHS.

HACHEM, PAUL D; Memorial HS; Tulsa, OK; (3); French Clb; JA; Spanish Clb; Hon Roll; Jr NHS; Engrng Explorers; Church Yth Grp; Systems Anlyst.

HACK, DAWN; Valliant HS; Garvin, OK; (3); 7/79; French Clb; FHA; Pep Clb; Quiz Bowl; Science Clb; School Play; Ofcr Frsh Cls; Tennis; NHS; OK ST U; Gntc Engrg.

HACK, LEAH; Valliant HS; Garvin, OK; (4); 8/84; Cmnty Wkr; Drama Clb; French Clb; Quiz Bowl; Pres Science Clb; Rep Soph Cls; Rep Stu Cncl; Tennis; Hon Roll; OSU; Engrng.

HACKATHORN, WILLIAM DUSTY; Owasso Sr HS; Owasso, OK; (2); Church Yth Grp; JV Bsbl.

HACKER, AMANDA S; Norman Sr HS; Norman, OK; (3); Church Yth Grp; Cmnty Wkr; FBLA; Swmmng; Hon Roll; San Diego St; Marine Bio.

HACKER, ANGIE L; Wilson HS; Wilson, OK; (2); 6/46; Church Yth Grp; Sec FCA; 4-H; GAA; Letterman Clb; Sec Natl Beta Clb; Natl FFA Org; Varsity Clb; Band; Flag Corp; SOSU; Speech Pathology.

HACKETT, CLAY; Edmond North HS; Edmond, OK; (2); 167/420; Boy Scts; Church Yth Grp; Cmnty Wkr; Band; Mrchg Band; Order Of Arrow; Asst Sr Patrol Ldr BSA.

HACKLER, JOSEPH; Claremore Sr HS; Claremore, OK; (2); FCA; Quiz Bowl; Spanish Clb; JV Bsbl; Ftbl; Intrml Wrstlng; Hon Roll; Amer Leg Bsbl.

HACKLER, KELLE I; Union Intermediate HS; Broken Arrow, OK; (1); Church Yth Grp; Math Tm; Pom Pon; Hon Roll; NHS; Psychiatry.

HACKWORTH, JUSTIN E; Midwest City HS; Midwest City, OK; (2); 58/501; Church Yth Grp; ROTC; Spanish Clb; Color Guard; JV Socr; High Hon Roll; Hon Roll; Jr NHS; St Schlr; Astronaut.

HADDOCK, JAMES A; Shawnee Sr HS; Shawnee, OK; (1); Boy Scts; Church Yth Grp; Quiz Bowl; Scholastic Bowl; Spanish Clb; Ofcr Bsbl; Hon Roll; Jr NHS.

HADDOCK, SEAN; Muskogee HS; Muskogee, OK; (4); 18/303; Church Yth Grp; DECA; FBLA; VP Spanish Clb; JV Bsbl; Hon Roll; 3K Hon Soc 4 Yrs; Herbert Branan Comm Bus Awd; Teens Christ; Northeasterb ST Univ; Bus.

HADFIELD, TAMRA A; Owasso Sr HS; Owasso, OK; (2); 26/460; Church Yth Grp; Debate Tm; Office Aide; Band; Church Choir; Flag Corp; Mrchg Band; Pep Band; High Hon Roll; NHS; All St Band; Brigham Young U.

HADLEY, STEFANIE; Cascia Prep HS; Tulsa, OK; (2); Church Yth Grp; Cmnty Wkr; Drama Clb; GAA; Rep Stu Cncl; Chrldng; Gym; Cit Awd; Hon Roll; Pres Schlr.

HAEFELE, AMY I; Edmond Memorial HS; Edmond, OK; (2); 1/430; Church Yth Grp; Spanish Clb; Chorus; Rptr Nwsp; NHS; Pres Acad Fit Awd; Horseback Rdng.

HAFFNER, LANCE; Shawnee Sr HS; Shawnee, OK; (3); Church Yth Grp; French Clb; Wt Lftg; Hon Roll; Seminole JC; Lab Tech.

HAGAN, KEITH; Heritage Hall Schl; Oklahoma City, OK; (4); Am Leg Boys St; Boy Scts; Church Yth Grp; CAP; Cmnty Wkr; Debate Tm; Drama Clb; FCA; French Clb; Letterman Clb; COPE; Rssn & Engrng Clbs; SAVE; Prsdntl Comm Svc Awd.

HAGAN, LAURA L; Paoli HS; Pauls Valley, OK; (1); 4-H; Girl Scts; Pep Clb; Sec Frsh Cls; Rep Stu Cncl; Bsktbl; Wt Lftg; High Hon Roll; Pres Acad Fit Awd; Piano; Acad Team; U Of OK.

HAGEBUSCH, MATT; Chelsea HS; Chelsea, OK; (2); VP FCA; VP Natl FFA Org; Rep Soph Cls; Var Bsbl; Var Bsktbl; Capt Var Ftbl; Var Trk; Var Wt Lftg; Mock Trial; OU; Med.

HAGEMEIER, CHRISTINA; Shattuck Jr Sr HS; Shattuck, OK; (1); 3/29; FHA; Pep Clb; Quiz Bowl; Hon Roll; TSA Level II Pres; Masonics Stu Today Awd.

HAGEN, W R; Shawnee Sr HS; Shawnee, OK; (3); 8/300; Church Yth Grp; Drama Clb; NFL; Band; Jazz Band; Mrchg Band; Pep Band; High Hon Roll.

HAGER, GEOFFREY; Pawhuska HS; Pawhuska, OK; (3); 1/87; Am Leg Boys St; Church Yth Grp; FCA; Key Clb; Spanish Clb; Band; Jazz Band; Bsktbl; High Hon Roll; NHS; Engr.

HAGER, JACOB; Cherokee Jr Sr HS; Cherokee, OK; (4); 1/23; Am Leg Boys St; Boy Scts; Capt Quiz Bowl; VP Band; Pres Jr Cls; Ofcr Bsbl; Bsktbl; Ftbl; Trk; Val; Order Of Arrow Vigil Hnr; OK ST U; Pre-Dntstry.

HAGGARD, COURTNEY; Dickson HS; Ardmore, OK; (1); SADD; Bsktbl; Chrldng; Trk; High Hon Roll; Hon Roll; Natl Hstry & Govt Awd; OK U; Medcl.

HAGGARD, ERIN; Elk City Jr HS; Elk City, OK; (2); Math Clb; Science Clb; Spanish Clb; Band; Jazz Band; Mrchg Band; Sec Stu Cncl; Var Bsktbl; Sftbl; Cit Awd.

HAGGARD, LAURA; Stillwater Sr HS; Stillwater, OK; (4); 11/320; Church Yth Grp; FHA; Key Clb; Natl Beta Clb; Pep Clb; Q&S; Science Clb; Spanish Clb; Ed Yrbk; Rep Stu Cncl; Var Schlr; OK ST Univ; FRCD.

HAGGARD, MARK A; Union Intermediate HS; Tulsa, OK; (2); Boy Scts; Church Yth Grp; Hon Roll; NHS; OK Univ; PT.

HAGGARD, RYLAND J; Jay HS; Jay, OK; (3); Pres FBLA; Library Aide; Math Clb; Treas Mu Alpha Theta; Natl Beta Clb; Natl FFA Org; Hrse Jdng/5th High Inv NEO Cntst/3rd At ST; Lvstck Jdgng; Star Grn Hand Awd FFA; Hrse Prfcncy Awd; OSU; Cmptr Tech.

HAGGARD, SABRINA M; Putnam City HS; Warr Acres, OK; (2); Hosp Aide; Key Clb; Office Aide; Spanish Clb; Hon Roll; Prfct Atten Awd; U Of OK; Radlgst/Techcn.

HAGGARD, SHANNON E; Westmoore HS; Oklahoma City, OK; (3); 35/620; Am Leg Aux Girls St; Hosp Aide; JCL; Quiz Bowl; Scholastic Bowl; Chorus; Phtg Yrbk; High Hon Roll; NHS; Cmnty Wkr; Yth/Govt; UCO Edmond.

HAGUE, KIRSTEN KAY; Cherokee Jr Sr HS; Cherokee, OK; (3); 5/32; Church Yth Grp; FCA; Natl FFA Org; Co-Ed Yrbk; Var Bsktbl; Ftbl; Mgr(s); Var L Sftbl; L Var Trk; Sal; PE.

HAILE, HEIDI; Mannford HS; Mannford, OK; (4); 1/92; Am Leg Aux Girls St; Church Yth Grp; FCA; Scholastic Bowl; Spanish Clb; SADD; Chorus; Pep Band; Pres Soph Cls; Pres Jr Cls; Pre-Dntstry.

HAINES, DAVID; Mc Loud HS; Mc Loud, OK; (3); 1/140; Boy Scts; HOBY; Math Tm; NFL; Quiz Bowl; Band; Rptr Lit Mag; Ofcr Stu Cncl; Socr; NHS; OK Schl Sci, Math Fnlst 95; Am HS Math Exm Awd; Stu Mnth 95.

HAIR, CASSIE L; Liberty HS; Mounds, OK; (2); 5/30; FCA; Office Aide; Pep Clb; Band; VP Soph Cls; Bsktbl; Var Chrldng; Hon Roll; Pres Acad Fit Awd; Stdnt Cncl Treas; Law.

HAIRFIELD, JULIE A; Antlers Sr HS; Antlers, OK; (2); Speech Tm; Band; Color Guard; Drill Tm; Flag Corp; Mrchg Band; Pep Band; Chrldng; MA All Amer Flag Corp; European Mid Ages/Renaissance.

HAIRRELL, SARAH L; Clayton Jr Sr HS; Clayton, OK; (2); Church Yth Grp; 4-H; VP Natl FFA Org; Band; VP Frsh Cls; Var L Bsktbl; Var L Sftbl; 4-H Awd; High Hon Roll; Eastern OK ST Coll; Anml Sci.

HAJIMORAD, MEGHDAD; Plainview HS; Ardmore, OK; (2); Mu Alpha Theta; Cmptrs; Nuclear Chem; Genetics; Ntl Ldrshp Svc Awd; Natl Sci Merit Awd; All-Amer Schlr; Genetics.

HAKE, KERI A; Oklahoma Bible Acad; Enid, OK; (3); FHA; Band; Chorus; Mrchg Band; Pep Band; Yrbk; High Hon Roll; Hon Roll; NHS; Southwestern OK ST Univ.

HAKES, JAMIE E; Hulbert Jr Sr HS; Hulbert, OK; (2); 4-H; Hon Roll; NHS; OK ST Univ; Vet.

HAKIM, MELODY A; West Middle HS; Norman, OK; (2); Church Yth Grp; Cmnty Wkr; Dance Clb; Drama Clb; Office Aide; Orch; Cit Awd; Hon Roll; NHS; Pres Schlr; OK Bahai Yth Wrkshp Comm; OU; Psycologist.

HAKOLA, LINA S; Union Sr HS; Tulsa, OK; (3); High Hon Roll; Hon Roll; NHS; USAG Gymnstcs Lvl 10; Pre Med.

HALBROOKS, MISTY D; Macarthur Sr HS; Lawton, OK; (3); Church Yth Grp; Cmnty Wkr; FCA; Wt Lftg; High Hon Roll; Jr NHS; Nrs.

HALCOMB, MICHAEL T; Bishop Kelley HS; Tulsa, OK; (2); Hon Roll; Law.

HALDERMAN, KIMBERLY; Union Intermediate HS; Tulsa, OK; (2); Office Aide; Spanish Clb; Ofcr Soph Cls; Intrml Mgr Bsktbl; Hon Roll; Prfct Atten Awd; U Of OK; Nrs.

HALE, ANDY B; Brink Jr HS; Oklahoma City, OK; (1); Computer Clb; Phtg Ed Yrbk; High Hon Roll; Hon Roll; Jr NHS.

HALE, KRISTAN; Sapulpa Sr HS; Sapulpa, OK; (1); Church Yth Grp; Drama Clb; FHA; Speech Tm; School Musical; School Play; Chrldng; Pom Pon; Spanish NHS; Indian Ed.

HALE, LEAH M; Hominy HS; Hominy, OK; (3); Church Yth Grp; Cmnty Wkr; French Clb; FHA; GAA; Office Aide; Teachers Aide; Ed Yrbk; JV Bsktbl; JV Trk; Brdcst Jrnlsm.

HALE, MARIE B; Choctaw HS; Jones, OK; (3); Church Yth Grp; CAP; Drama Clb; Math Tm; Thesps; Band; Chorus; Drm Mjr(t); Mrchg Band; School Play; Drama Stage Crew, Asst Dir; Dance; Military.

HALE, SARAH E; Lone Grove HS; Lone Grove, OK; (3); Church Yth Grp; Spanish Clb; Teachers Aide; Acpl Chr; Chorus; Church Choir; School Musical; Variety Show; Co-Ed Nwsp; Hon Roll; All-Dist Choir; Super Dist Vocal; Super ST Vocal; UCO; Nutrition & Pharmacology.

HALE, TANYA; Collinsville HS; Collinsville, OK; (4); Office Aide; Teachers Aide; Pres Soph Cls; Hon Roll; VICA; Ldrshp Mrt Awd; Day Break Teen Vol; Peer Tutor; Ed.

HALE, VALERIE; Stilwell HS; Stilwell, OK; (3); Church Yth Grp; Natl FFA Org; Spanish Clb; Rep Stu Cncl; JV Var Bsktbl; Var Sftbl; Hon Roll; NHS; Performing Indian Sgn Lang With Grp; Physician/Nrs.

HALEY, CURTIS S; Union Sr HS; Broken Arrow, OK; (4); 43/629; Church Yth Grp; Key Clb; Math Tm; Natl FFA Org; Quiz Bowl; Scholastic Bowl; Spanish Clb; High Hon Roll; Hon Roll; NHS; OK ST U; Mechncl Engrng.

HALEY, ERIN; Mid-Del Christian Schl; Oklahoma City, OK; (4); 3/14; Hosp Aide; Yrbk; Sec Frsh Cls; Rep Soph Cls; Rep Jr Cls; Socr; Sftbl; Vllybl; High Hon Roll; Ntl Merit Ltr; OK ST U; Med.

HALEY, MELISSA; Clinton HS; Clinton, OK; (3); 9/119; Church Yth Grp; Treas FBLA; Hosp Aide; Band; Flag Corp; Mrchg Band; Var Chrldng; Hon Roll; NHS; OK U; Chem Engrng.

HALL, AMANDA; Lookeba Sickles Jr Sr HS; Lookeba, OK; (3); 4-H; Sec FHA; HOBY; Ed Nwsp; Rep Frsh Cls; Rep Soph Cls; Rep Jr Cls; Pres VP Stu Cncl; Hon Roll; NHS; OU; Bus.

HALL, AMANDA C; Shawnee Sr HS; Shawnee, OK; (2); Church Yth Grp; Drama Clb; French Clb; Thesps; School Musical; School Play; Stage Crew; Hon Roll; Theatre/Psych.

HALL, ASHLEIGH JO; Dewey HS; Bartlesville, OK; (3); FHA; Pep Clb; Spanish Clb; Chorus; Drill Tm; School Musical; Treas Frsh Cls; Treas Soph Cls; Hon Roll; NHS.

HALL, ASHLEY; Meeker HS; Sparks, OK; (2); #20 in class; Church Yth Grp; Acpl Chr; Chorus; Var Capt Chrldng; Hon Roll; Stu Of Month; Dist Solo & Ensemble Cont Super Rating 94-96; St Solo & Ensemble Cont Excl Rating 94-96; Child Psych.

HALL, BRIAN V; Union Sr HS; Tulsa, OK; (3); 66/741; Belmont; Philosphy.

HALL, BRITTANY; Quinton Jr Sr HS; Quinton, OK; (1); Quiz Bowl; Band; Color Guard; Drm Mjr(t).

HALL, CAESY; Claremore Sr HS; Claremore, OK; (2); Church Yth Grp; JV Bsbl; JV Ftbl; Var Wt Lftg; JV Wrstlng; NHS.

HALL, CASEY R; Valliant HS; Valliant, OK; (3); 28/76; Church Yth Grp; Cmnty Wkr; FCA; FHA; JA; Math Tm; Ofcr Bsbl; Bsktbl; Ftbl; Wt Lftg; Bsbl/Ftbl Awds; Math; Sci; Connors JC; PE.

HALL, CHANNA; Blackwell HS; Blackwell, OK; (2); Office Aide; Pep Clb; Band; Jazz Band; Mrchg Band; Pep Band; Hon Roll; Winter Guard; Northwestern OK ST U.

HALL, CRYSTAL; Westmoore HS; Oklahoma City, OK; (4); 119/610; Church Yth Grp; Drama Clb; JCL; Key Clb; Latin Clb; Office Aide; Science Clb; Thesps; Stage Crew; Yrbk; Magna Cum Laude Latin; U Of TX Arlington; Pre-Med.

HALL, DEBBIE K; Sapulpa Sr HS; Sapulpa, OK; (3); Art Clb; Key Clb; Math Clb; Science Clb; Spanish Clb; Color Guard; Flag Corp; Variety Show; Gov Hon Prg Awd; High Hon Roll.

HALL, DEREK; Woodward HS; Woodward, OK; (1); Mgr(s); High Hon Roll; Kiwanis Awd; NHS; Acad Ltrmn; OK Univ; Cmptr Sci.

HALL, ERICA; Douglass HS; Oklahoma City, OK; (3); Cmnty Wkr; Mrchg Band; Pep Band; Ofcr Soph Cls; Score Keeper; High Hon Roll; Hon Roll; U Of OK All Star Marching Band 95; HOSA; Phliebotomist; Surgical Tech.

HALL, JAMIE; Coweta HS; Coweta, OK; (4); Church Yth Grp; Cmnty Wkr; SADD; Band; Church Choir; Jazz Band; Mrchg Band; Orch; Pep Band; Nwsp; Dntl.

HALL, JEFFREY D; Eldorado Schl; Eldorado, OK; (1); 4-H; FHA; Natl FFA Org; Pep Clb; Rep Stu Cncl; 4-H Awd; Hon Roll; Ntl Merit Ltr; FFA Ag Prod/Ag Mech Awd/1st Pl Trctr Drvng.

HALL, JENNIFER; Moore HS; Moore, OK; (3); 121/556; Q&S; Chorus; Nwsp; Rep Stu Cncl; NHS; Future Jrnlsts Of America Secy; Bowling Green; Jrnlsm.

HALL, JENNIFER R; Midwest City HS; Midwest City, OK; (2); 162/473; Church Yth Grp; German Clb; Girl Scts; Pep Clb; Church Choir; School Play; Hon Roll; Jr NHS; Prfct Atten Awd; Choir Queen; Show Choir VP; OUTSTDNG Choir Stdnt; OK Bapt Univ; Child Psychlgst.

HALL, JESSA; Shattuck Jr Sr HS; Shattuck, OK; (3); 1/23; FHA; Pep Clb; Quiz Bowl; Teachers Aide; High Hon Roll; Hon Roll; NHS; Ntl Merit Ltr; OK Hon Soc; U Of KS; Med Tech.

HALL, JOHN; Cache HS; Lawton, OK; (1); 2/100; Church Yth Grp; Cmnty Wkr; Letterman Clb; Natl Beta Clb; Science Clb; NHS; High Hon Roll; Piano; Acad Team; Johns Hopkins; Epidermitology.

HALL, JOHN E; Mannford HS; Mannford, OK; (3); FCA; Rptr Natl FFA Org; VICA; Ftbl; Golf; Trk; Hon Roll; Prfct Atten Awd; OK St Univ; Bus.

HALL, JULIE B; Edmond North HS; Edmond, OK; (3); ROTC; JV Sftbl.

HALL, K RENEE; Meeker HS; Sparks, OK; (3); Church Yth Grp; Girl Scts; Chorus; Church Choir; Sec Soph Cls; Bsktbl; Sftbl; Trk; High Hon Roll; Hon Roll; Hnrb Mntn Slow Pitch 95-96; Hnrb Mntn Fast Pitch 94-95; Careers Awd 94.

HALL, KARIN R; Meeker HS; Sparks, OK; (3); Church Yth Grp; FCA; GAA; Chorus; Sec Soph Cls; Var Bsktbl; Var Sftbl; Var Trk; High Hon Roll; Hon Roll; Jr Indian Clb Pres; 5th Pl Reg Track Shot Put; Fast/Slow Pitch Sftbl Hnrb Mntn 94-95; OK Bapt U; Bus.

HALL, KENNY R; Amber Pocasset Jr Sr HS; Pocasset, OK; (2); Bus Profs of Am; Church Yth Grp; Computer Clb; FCA; 4-H; FHA; JA; Letterman Clb; Math Clb; Pep Clb; Hnrd With Indiv As Well As Team Awd 2nd Highest Grd In St; Acad Achvmt Awd; Super Hnr Roll; OK ST; Fire-Fighting; Parmdc.

HALL, KRYSTAL N; Southeast HS; Oklahoma City, OK; (2); Afro-Amer Clb; Coll Clb; OU.

HALL, LES A; Tahlequah Jr HS; Tahlequah, OK; (1); Church Yth Grp; Office Aide; Var Bsktbl; Trk; Chiropractor.

HALL, LINDSAY A; Ripley HS; Ripley, OK; (3); 15/35; FCA; GAA; Natl FFA Org; Pep Clb; Teachers Aide; Ed Yrbk; Var Bsktbl; Score Keeper; Var Sftbl; Var Trk; CO #5 Champ Team Penner; OK ST Univ.

HALL, LINDSAY R; Union Intermediate HS; Tulsa, OK; (2); Spanish Clb; Drill Tm; Hon Roll; Jr NHS; NHS; All Amer Dance Team Perf Austria; Psych.

HALL, LORI L; Fletcher Jr Sr HS; Fletcher, OK; (3); 2/30; Church Yth Grp; Rptr FCA; School Play; Yrbk; Rptr Soph Cls; Pres Jr Cls; Var Bsktbl; Var Chrldng; Var Sftbl; Var Vllybl; Natl Yng Ldrs Cond Alumnus; Ozark Chrstn Coll.

HALL, MARK J; Wagoner Sr HS; Wagoner, OK; (3); 4-H; Natl FFA Org; Var Capt Ftbl; Var Wt Lftg; Var Wrstlng.

HALL, MEGAN; Tahlequah Sr HS; Park Hill, OK; (3); Red Cross Aide; Science Clb; SADD; Yrbk; JV Var Bsktbl; Hon Roll; Jr NHS; NHS; Spirit Clb; Indian Hertge Clb; NSU; Premed.

HALL, MELISSA; Moore HS; Moore, OK; (3); Church Yth Grp; Hist French Clb; Science Clb; Rep Stu Cncl; Var Socr; Stu Cncl Chore Grp, St Delg & St Cmmtte Chrmn; Cmrnl Jstc.

HALL, MICHELLE R; Nathan Hale HS; Tulsa, OK; (3); 21/289; Church Yth Grp; FCA; Rep Frsh Cls; Rep Soph Cls; Rep Golf; Sftbl; Tennis; High Hon Roll; Ntl Merit Ltr; Scrkpr Wrstlng; U Of OK; Phys Thpy.

HALL, MOLLY A; Edmond North HS; Edmond, OK; (4); 82/336; Church Yth Grp; Mu Alpha Theta; Band; Lbrn Chorus; Pres Church Choir; School Musical; Variety Show; NHS; OK All-St Chorus 94-96; Music Ed.

HALL, NICOLAS A; Edmond Memorial HS; Edmond, OK; (3); Am Leg Boys St; Math Clb; Mu Alpha Theta; Ofcr Spanish Clb; SADD; Chorus; NHS; Pres Acad Fit Awd; OK Univ Hlth Sci Ctr Acad 96; Acad Ltr & Bar; OK Univ; Chem.

HALL, RACHEL L; Charles Page HS; Sand Springs, OK; (3); 94/306; Church Yth Grp; Cmnty Wkr; Drama Clb; French Clb; School Play; Hon Roll; Tulsa CC; Ed.

HALL, RUSTY M; Mc Loud HS; Mc Loud, OK; (2); Church Yth Grp; FCA; Var Bsbl; Var Bsktbl; Var Ftbl; High Hon Roll; Hon Roll; NHS; Whos Who In Sports; Natl Eng Mrt Awd; OU.

HALL, RYAN A; Union Sr HS; Tulsa, OK; (3); 154/780; Boy Scts; Church Yth Grp; Cmnty Wkr; FCA; Ofcr Bsbl; Wrstlng; High Hon Roll; Jr NHS; NHS; Prfct Atten Awd; Military.

HALL, SCOTT S; Yukon Middle HS; Yukon, OK; (2); Hon Roll; Odyssey Of Mind; U Of OK; Engrng.

HALL, STACY D; Edmond Memorial HS; Edmond, OK; (2); 1/410; Church Yth Grp; FCA; Math Clb; Mu Alpha Theta; Spanish Clb; SADD; Ofcr Stu Cncl; Capt Var Vllybl; Hon Roll; NHS; Medicine; Phy Therapy.

HALL, STEPHANIE D; Manford HS; Mannford, OK; (3); 16/108; Church Yth Grp; FCA; SADD; Bsktbl; NHS; Algebra II Schlt Medal; Schltc Ath Awd; E Cntrl; Child Psychiatrist.

HALL, SUMMAR; Crowder Schl; Mcalester, OK; (3); FHA; Natl FFA Org; JV Var Bsktbl; TSA; Marine Bio.

HALL, TARA R; B T Washington HS; Tulsa, OK; (4); 47/267; Church Yth Grp; Cmnty Wkr; French Clb; JCL; Pres Latin Clb; Red Cross Aide; Service Clb; Sec Stu Cncl; NHS; IB Diploma; Commnctns.

HALL, THERESA; Nathan Hale HS; Tulsa, OK; (1); Church Yth Grp; FCA; FBLA; Rep Frsh Cls; Rep Stu Cncl; Chrldng; High Hon Roll; Volunteens; Ldrshp; Nursng.

HALL, THOMAS; Tulsa Memorial HS; Tulsa, OK; (3); Boy Scts; HOBY; VP Key Clb; School Musical; Rptr Nwsp; Treas Frsh Cls; VP Soph Cls; Sec Stu Cncl; High Hon Roll; NHS.

HALL, VIRGINIA B; Mannford HS; Mannford, OK; (3); High Hon Roll; Hon Roll; NHS; Pres Acad Fit Awd; Pres Schlr; Acad Awd; Sci.

HALLMARK, CRYSTAL J; Tishomingo HS; Ravia, OK; (3); Church Yth Grp; Office Aide; Pres Soph Cls; Hist Jr Cls; JV Crs Cntry; JV Socr; Var Sftbl; Var Trk; Hon Roll; NHS; US Navy; Nuclear Fld.

HALLMARK, MELISSA; Moore HS; Moore, OK; (3); 94/506; Church Yth Grp; FCA; Pep Clb; SADD; Church Choir; Variety Show; Ofcr Stu Cncl; Chrldng; Powder Puff Ftbl; Hon Roll; Occupational Thrpy.

HALLSTROM, ALAN L; Macarthur Sr HS; Lawton, OK; (3); German Clb; Quiz Bowl; VICA; Band; Mrchg Band; Socr; Wt Lftg; Hon Roll; 96 Rgnl Auto Svc Tech Cntst; Auto Tech.

HALSEY, STACEY; Tupelo Jr Sr HS; Tupelo, OK; (1); Church Yth Grp; Church Choir; Hon Roll; Prfct Atten Awd; OK Bapt Univ; Physican.

HALVORSEN, LISA; Norman Sr HS; Norman, OK; (2); 1/800; Model UN; Pres Mu Alpha Theta; Red Cross Aide; Mrchg Band; Orch; Hon Roll; NHS; All St Orch; OK Yth Orch; Octagon Clb; Chem Eng.

HAM, COLBY F; Wynnewood HS; Wynnewood, OK; (3); FCA; Letterman Clb; Natl FFA Org; Teachers Aide; Varsity Clb; Yrbk; Bsktbl; Ftbl; Golf; Trk; U Of OK.

HAMAR, NICK T; Thomas Jr Sr HS; Thomas, OK; (3); Church Yth Grp; FCA; Treas Frsh Cls; Treas Soph Cls; Pres Jr Cls; Var Bsbl; Var Bsktbl; Var Ftbl; Var Trk; Cit Awd.

HAMBRICK, MAEGAN D; Westmoore HS; Oklahoma City, OK; (1); Church Yth Grp; Girl Scts; Library Aide; Chorus; Hon Roll; Jr NHS; Model Stu Awd; Pediatrician.

HAMBURG, CHARLETTE; Indianola HS; Mcalester, OK; (3); Church Yth Grp; Drama Clb; FHA; Natl Beta Clb; Thesps; School Play; Var Socr; JV Vllybl; Hon Roll; Jr NHS; Comms.

HAMBURG, DEREK; Perry Sr HS; Perry, OK; (4); Church Yth Grp; FCA; FHA; Teachers Aide; Ofcr Stu Cncl; Ftbl; Psych Of Learning Tutorial Pgm; Jr Rotarian; U Of Central OK; Tchr.

HAMBURG, DUSTIN; Perry Sr HS; Perry, OK; (2); Church Yth Grp; FCA; FHA; VP Soph Cls; Ofcr Stu Cncl; Ftbl; Cit Awd; Hon Roll; NHS; OU.

HAMER, AMY; Mc Alester HS; Mcalester, OK; (2); FHA; Spanish Clb; Speech Tm; Band; Mrchg Band; Hon Roll; NHS; OK; Bus.

HAMER, ASHLEE; Thomas Jr Sr HS; Thomas, OK; (1); 2/46; Church Yth Grp; FCA; FHA; Bsktbl; Sftbl; Trk; Cit Awd; High Hon Roll; NHS; Prfct Atten Awd.

HAMER, BLAKE M; Wapanucka Schl; Wapanucka, OK; (1); 3/14; Boy Scts; Church Yth Grp; 4-H; Scholastic Bowl; Spanish Clb; Bsktbl; Hon Roll.

HAMES, DODI D; Okmulgee HS; Okmulgee, OK; (2); Hosp Aide; Natl FFA Org; Hon Roll; Phy Thrpst.

HAMES, DUSTIN R; Bridge Creek HS; Tuttle, OK; (1); Boy Scts; Band; Jazz Band; Mrchg Band; Ftbl; Wt Lftg; Hon Roll.

HAMES, JACQUELYN; Bridge Creek HS; Tuttle, OK; (3); Church Yth Grp; Cmnty Wkr; GAA; Library Aide; Spanish Clb; SADD; Color Guard; Drm Mjr(t); Yrbk; NHS.

HAMETT, CARRIE; Newcastle HS; Oklahoma City, OK; (4); 6/71; Cmnty Wkr; FHA; Office Aide; Ed Yrbk; Hon Roll; NHS; FHA Treas; OK Math League; LEAP; OK CCC.

HAMIL, J D; Henryetta Sr HS; Henryetta, OK; (2); Band; Bsktbl; Tennis; Hon Roll; NHS; Movie Dir.

HAMILL, CECILY E; Bishop Kelley HS; Tulsa, OK; (4); 3/148; Service Clb; Teachers Aide; Church Choir; JV Vllybl; High Hon Roll; NHS; Ntl Merit SF; French Clb; Hosp Aide; Acad Dcthln; Dmstc Violnce Intrvntn Svc Vol; Chrch Ltrgcl Asst/Srvr; Med.

HAMILL, DEENA; Anadarko HS; Anadarko, OK; (4); 6/97; Church Yth Grp; Pres FCA; FBLA; GAA; Office Aide; Quiz Bowl; Teachers Aide; Varsity Clb; Ed Nwsp; Ed Yrbk; U Of Central OK; Sprts Med.

HAMILL, DUSTIN; Adair HS; Adair, OK; (3); Church Yth Grp; FCA; German Clb; HOBY; Natl FFA Org; Quiz Bowl; Science Clb; Rep Stu Cncl; High Hon Roll; Pres Acad Fit Awd.

HAMILTON, APRIL M; Moore HS; Oklahoma City, OK; (3); Church Yth Grp; Hist Drama Clb; FBLA; Church Choir; School Musical; Rep Sr Cls; Mgr(s); Tennis; Jr NHS; NHS; Jr Escort 96 Grad; OK Bapt Univ; Acctg.

HAMILTON, AUDREY; Mustang HS; Mustang, OK; (2); Church Yth Grp; FCA; Chorus; High Hon Roll; NHS; Chrch Vclst Cntmprry Chrstn Music; John Birch Soc Mem; U Of OK; PT.

HAMILTON, BRAD E; Mannford HS; Lexington, SC; (1); 33/126; FCA; Rep Frsh Cls; JV Bsbl; JV Bsktbl; L Crs Cntry; L Trk; JV Wt Lftg; Hon Roll; Pres Acad Fit Awd; Tech Stdnts Assn; Coach/Tchr.

HAMILTON, CHYANNE; Perry Sr HS; Perry, OK; (2); 24/101; Church Yth Grp; FBLA; FHA; Treas Natl FFA Org; Pep Clb; Quiz Bowl; Church Choir; Jr NHS; FFA Star Greenhand; Matmaid; OSU; Vet.

HAMILTON, JAMIE R; Mc Alester HS; Mcalester, OK; (4); 11/209; Church Yth Grp; Cmnty Wkr; FCA; Office Aide; Pres Pep Clb; Science Clb; Rep Spanish Clb; Teachers Aide; Rep Stu Cncl; NHS; OK Acad Schlr; U Cntrl OK; Early Chldhd Ed.

HAMILTON, JASON L; Edmond Memorial HS; Oklahoma City, OK; (3); JCL; Latin Clb; Office Aide; Scholastic Bowl; Bsktbl; Muslem Stu Assoc; U Of Cntrl OK; Ec.

HAMILTON, MACI; Vinita HS; Vinita, OK; (2); HOBY; Math Clb; Science Clb; Band; Sec Rep Frsh Cls; Rep Soph Cls; Rep Stu Cncl; Chrldng; High Hon Roll; NHS; Vinita Chptr VFW Money Schlrshp; Anchor Clb; FCA; Bsktbl Homcmng Attndnt 94-95; Band Featrd Twirlr; Northeastern ST U; Ed.

HAMILTON, RANDY; Pauls Valley HS; Pauls Valley, OK; (4); 1/88; Art Clb; Church Yth Grp; FCA; Key Clb; Scholastic Bowl; Science Clb; Spanish Clb; SADD; Teachers Aide; Varsity Clb; Instr Royal Ambssdr Cls Trinity Bapt Chrch; East Central U.

HAMILTON, REBECCA L; Jay HS; Jay, OK; (3); FBLA; FHA; Natl Beta Clb; NHS; Intnl Drug Free Yth; Vet.

HAMILTON, SUSAN E; West Middle HS; Norman, OK; (1); Church Yth Grp; FCA; JCL; Latin Clb; Var L Golf; Hon Roll; Pre-Law.

HAMLIN, MICHAEL; Claremore Sr HS; Claremore, OK; (4); 1/241; VP Treas Debate Tm; German Clb; NFL; Speech Tm; Teachers Aide; High Hon Roll; NHS; Blck Blt; Tae Kwn Do; Lwyr.

HAMLIN, WACO; Quinton Jr Sr HS; Quinton, OK; (3); #9 in class; Ofcr Bsbl; Bsktbl; High Hon Roll; FFA Offcr; OK Jr Rodeo Assoc Mmbr; EOSC.

HAMM, BECKY; Union Intermediate HS; Tulsa, OK; (1); Drama Clb; Speech Tm; School Play; Ofcr Frsh Cls; Chrldng; Socr; Hon Roll.

HAMM, ELAINE E; Shawnee Sr HS; Shawnee, OK; (2); Hosp Aide; Scholastic Bowl; Band; Drm Mjr(t); Jazz Band; Mrchg Band; School Musical; Natl Piano Plyng Guild; OBU Hnr Jazz Band; Music/Microbio.

HAMM, ERIN; Woodward HS; Woodward, OK; (2); Church Yth Grp; Computer Clb; FCA; Rep FTA; German Clb; Key Clb; Bsktbl; Sftbl; High Hon Roll; NHS; Delta Epsilon Phi; Whos Who Amng Yng Amer Stdnts; Acad Lttrmn; Frgn Lang.

HAMMARSTEN, ERIC; Jenks HS; Tulsa, OK; (4); 40/448; Boy Scts; Math Tm; Science Clb; Band; Mrchg Band; Orch; Hon Roll; Dstngshd Grad; Dstngshd Svc Grad; Coe Coll; Physics/Cmptr Sci.

HAMMETT, ANNETTE; Edmond North HS; Edmond, OK; (3); 26/357; Mu Alpha Theta; Band; Chorus; Church Choir; Jazz Band; Ofcr Stu Cncl; NHS; Pres Acad Fit Awd; Church Yth Grp; Cmnty Wkr; Natl Sci Merit Awd; Herbert Haupman Awd; Mdvl Clb Queen; Music Ed.

HAMMETT, BRITTNEY; Weatherford HS; Weatherford, OK; (1); Church Yth Grp; FCA; French Clb; JV Chrldng; High Hon Roll; WEDFY; LA Tech U.

HAMMOCK, STACY; Valliant HS; Valliant, OK; (2); 1/97; Drama Clb; French Clb; Library Aide; Quiz Bowl; Science Clb; Spanish Clb; School Play; Bsktbl; High Hon Roll; NHS; OK U; Marine Bio.

HAMMON, KENNY; Lone Grove HS; Lone Grove, OK; (2); Church Yth Grp; Cmnty Wkr; FCA; Math Clb; Science Clb; Nwsp; ECU.

HAMMON, TYLER; Seminole Jr Sr HS; Seminole, OK; (3); Church Yth Grp; FCA; French Clb; Ofcr Frsh Cls; Ofcr Soph Cls; Ofcr Bsbl; Ftbl; High Hon Roll; Pres Acad Fit Awd.

HAMMOND, AMANDA; Wilburton Sr HS; Wilburton, OK; (4); 5/86; Cmnty Wkr; FCA; VP FBLA; Band; Rptr Yrbk; Pres Stu Cncl; Var Golf; Kiwanis Awd; NHS; Pres Schlr; OK Acad Schlr; Golf Acad All St; Tandy Schlr; E OK St Col; Med.

HAMMOND, EMILY; Edmond Memorial HS; Edmond, OK; (1); 79/460; Church Yth Grp; Dance Clb; FCA; Church Choir; Ofcr Stu Cncl; Chrldng; Hon Roll; Tmblng; Schl Bd Alt Schdlng Cmmttee; USSCA.

HAMMONS, ALISHA D; Union Sr HS; Tulsa, OK; (4); FBLA; Key Clb; JV Bsktbl; Mgr Sftbl; Mgr Wrstlng; Pres Acad Fit Awd; Forgn Lang Clb; TJC; Acctng.

HAMMONS, APRIL D; Warner HS; Muskogee, OK; (1); Church Yth Grp; FHA; Natl FFA Org; Chrldng; High Hon Roll; Hon Roll; Green Cntry Rodeo Assn; OK Jr Rodeo Assn; Quarter Horse Assn; Sci.

HAMMONS, COURTNEY D; Madill HS; Madill, OK; (1); Art Clb; Church Yth Grp; Cmnty Wkr; Church Choir; School Musical; Stage Crew; Show Choir; Miami Univ; OB/GYN.

HAMMONS, KELLI; Stilwell HS; Stilwell, OK; (4); 20/120; VP FBLA; Natl Beta Clb; Spanish Clb; High Hon Roll; Drug Free Yth; Northeastern ST U; Elem Ed.

HAMMONS, MILLIE M; Warner HS; Muskogee, OK; (1); Church Yth Grp; 4-H; GAA; Spanish Clb; Varsity Clb; Church Choir; JV Bsktbl; JV Score Keeper; Sftbl; Trk; Rdng; Elm Grove A/G Yth Grp; Shopping; Connors Coll; Pstr/Yth Ldr/Dr.

HAMN, JEREMY D; Putnam City HS; Oklahoma City, OK; (3); Boy Scts; Church Yth Grp; Swmmng; Trk; Hon Roll; Triathlete; Lfgrd; Tch Swmmng Lssns; Exer Physlgy.

HAMON, JENNIFER G; Okmulgee HS; Okmulgee, OK; (3); Letterman Clb; Teachers Aide; Varsity Clb; Band; Mrchg Band; Pep Band; Bsktbl; Var L Sftbl; High Hon Roll; Hon Roll.

HAMPTON, ADAM; Dale Sr HS; Shawnee, OK; (4); 4/50; Church Yth Grp; Letterman Clb; Quiz Bowl; Scholastic Bowl; Spanish Clb; Teachers Aide; Band; Mrchg Band; Pep Band; Rptr Nwsp; Yng Wrtrs Awd NCTE 92, 96; Natl Yng Ldrs Conf Schlr; TDK Essay Wnnr Trp Japan; E Cntrl U; Writr.

HAMPTON, BRANDI; Hugo HS; Hugo, OK; (3); 1/103; Computer Clb; VP Math Clb; Pres Science Clb; Spanish Clb; Flag Corp; Ed Nwsp; Ofcr Stu Cncl; Treas NHS; Pres Schlr; FFA Pivot Team; Univ Of UT; Pharmacy.

HAMPTON, KATIE; Ponca City Sr HS; Ponca City, OK; (1); Church Yth Grp; Pep Clb; Ofcr Stu Cncl; Bsktbl; Chrldng; Gym; Trk; Hon Roll.

HAMPTON, SHANNA; Putnam City HS; Oklahoma City, OK; (4); 19/346; Am Leg Aux Girls St; Cmnty Wkr; Hosp Aide; Red Cross Aide; Science Clb; Spanish Clb; Yrbk; Hon Roll; Jr NHS; NHS; Jr Rotarian Rotary Club Intl; Bio/Emerg Rm Physician.

HAMRA, CINDY; Bishop Mcguinness HS; Oklahoma City, OK; (4); 15/160; Church Yth Grp; Cmnty Wkr; FCA; Pres French Clb; NFL; Pep Clb; Science Clb; SADD; Rep Sr Cls; JV Bsktbl; Tac Kown Do Grn Blt St Champ; Natlhnr Soc Tutor; Vassar Col; Med.

HAMRA, MONA C; Putnam City North HS; Oklahoma City, OK; (4); 44/451; Church Yth Grp; Pres Sec French Clb; Chrmn Key Clb; SADD; Rep Soph Cls; Rep Jr Cls; Rep Sr Cls; NHS; PALS Prog; 3-D Org; CAWS; U Of OK; Intl Bus.

HAMRICK, JAIME L; Wagoner Sr HS; Wagoner, OK; (3); FBLA; Teachers Aide; Ofcr Bsbl; JV Bsktbl; Ftbl; Wrstlng; Hon Roll; NHS; NSU; Human Hlth.

HAMRICK, RYAN E; Del City HS; Del City, OK; (3); Debate Tm; Drama Clb; German Clb; Intnl Clb; Quiz Bowl; Scholastic Bowl; Speech Tm; School Play; Yrbk; Ofcr Soph Cls; Exch Stu Germany; U Of OK; Drama.

HAMRICK, VANESSA; Turpin Schl; Turpin, OK; (4); 4/42; FCA; Letterman Clb; Quiz Bowl; SADD; Yrbk; VP Stu Cncl; Bsktbl; Chrldng; Sftbl; Trk; OK ST U.

HAMRICK, WHITNEY B; Valliant HS; Valliant, OK; (3); Church Yth Grp; Cmnty Wkr; Dance Clb; Drama Clb; 4-H; GAA; Natl FFA Org; Speech Tm; Chorus; School Play; Natl Western Lvstck Jdgng Cntst 3rd Pl; Ctznshp Washington Focus; Cty 4-H Sec/VP/PRES; Gonnors ST Coll; Ed.

HAMSHAR, RYAN J; Oklahoma Sch Of Science & Math; Claremore, OK; (4); Chess Clb; Computer Clb; English Clb; HOBY; Math Clb; Math Tm; Science Clb; High Hon Roll; Hon Roll; JETS Awd; U Of OK; Physcs.

HAN, ARUM; Edmond Memorial HS; Edmond, OK; (3); 83/383; Church Yth Grp; Cmnty Wkr; Intnl Clb; Key Clb; Math Clb; Mu Alpha Theta; Science Clb; Spanish Clb; Bsktbl; Socr; Soccer Coach; Clbs Officer; Sunday Schl Instr; U Of VA; Intl Stds.

HAN, DARA; Moore HS; Moore, OK; (4); 4/525; Church Yth Grp; French Clb; Latin Clb; Treas Chorus; High Hon Roll; Treas Jr NHS; NHS; Val; JCL; Quiz Bowl; Mltcltrl Stu Assn; Chrch Mssn Trp Mexico 95; Peer Hlpr Awd; Intnl Stud.

HAN, LIRA; Moore HS; Moore, OK; (3); 3/506; Hosp Aide; JCL; Latin Clb; Chorus; Rptr Nwsp; Yrbk; Jr NHS; NHS; Church Yth Grp; Quiz Bowl; MSA; 4.0 & Abv Plaque; Cornell; Hlth Scis.

HAN, YUJEAN; Central Mid-HS; Norman, OK; (2); JCL; Treas Latin Clb; Mu Alpha Theta; Orch; Rep Frsh Cls; Hon Roll; Pres Acad Fit Awd; Orch Cncl Pres.

HANCHEY, JESSICA R; Shawnee Sr HS; Shawnee, OK; (2); Church Yth Grp; Church Choir; Stage Crew; High Hon Roll; Jr NHS; Church Hndbl; Church Select Ensmbl.

HAND, ANDREW; Grace Fellowship Christian Sch; Broken Arrow, OK; (1); Boy Scts; Church Yth Grp; Debate Tm; Pres Frsh Cls; Var Socr; High Hon Roll; Regnl Sci Fair Soc Prof Engrs Awd 96, 2nd Pl Engrg Div 96; Schl Sci Fair 1st Pl Engrg Div 96; Aviation.

HANDING, RYAN; Southeast HS; Oklahoma City, OK; (3); FCA; Band; Ofcr Bsbl; Ftbl; Wt Lftg; Hon Roll; Univ Of OK; Chem.

HANDKINS, MELISSA; Berryhill Jr HS; Tulsa, OK; (1); Church Yth Grp; Gymnstcs Non Schl Spnsrd; OK U; Phys Trnr.

HANDLIN, CRISTIN I; Cushing HS; Cushing, OK; (3); Pres Church Yth Grp; Cmnty Wkr; Drama Clb; Hosp Aide; Math Clb; Science Clb; Service Clb; Spanish Clb; Speech Tm; Church Choir; Med.

HANDSHY, TARA A; U S Grant HS; Oklahoma City, OK; (3); Dance Clb; GAA; Natl FFA Org; Pep Clb; Spanish Clb; Rep Frsh Cls; Rep Soph Cls; Chrldng; Pom Pon; Sftbl; JA Fullerton Modeling Agency; OK City CC; PT.

HANEY, CHRISTINA R; Choctaw HS; Choctaw, OK; (3); Church Yth Grp; Computer Clb; Teachers Aide; Yrbk; Hon Roll; All Amer Schlr; Comp.

HANEY, ENOCH H; Seminole Jr Sr HS; Seminole, OK; (2); Debate Tm; Drama Clb; School Play; Stage Crew; Hon Roll; Ntl Merit Ltr; Pres Acad Fit Awd; Playing In Rock Band; Electronics; Cmptrs; Cornell Univ; Eng.

HANEY, MARK; East Central HS; Tulsa, OK; (4); 27/210; Am Leg Boys St; Church Yth Grp; Capt FCA; Pres Stu Cncl; L Capt Ftbl; L Capt Socr; High Hon Roll; NHS; L Var Trk; Hmcmng Kng; Ldr HS Bbl Stdy; Rep Tulsa Amer Frdms Fdn; Mssns.

HANGER, LISA; Perry Sr HS; Perry, OK; (2); Church Yth Grp; Dance Clb; FCA; Hist FHA; Band; Bsktbl; Pom Pon; Sftbl; Hon Roll; Jr NHS; Ped Cardiac Srgn.

HANGS, JULIA J; B T Washington HS; Tulsa, OK; (1); Church Yth Grp; Cmnty Wkr; Debate Tm; NFL; Speech Tm.

HANKE, JERRY D; Stigler HS; Stigler, OK; (3); VICA.

HANKINS, ASHLEY D; Mid-Del Christian Schl; Oklahoma City, OK; (2); 9/18; Church Yth Grp; Yrbk; Rep Soph Cls; Var Bsktbl; Var Chrldng; Var Vllybl; Hon Roll; Vllybl All St; Zoology.

HANKINS, CRYSTAL; Ripley HS; Ripley, OK; (2); 12/40; Church Yth Grp; GAA; Natl FFA Org; Spanish Clb; Var Bsktbl; Var Chrldng; Var Sftbl; Trk; Prfct Atten Awd; OSU.

HANKINS, DUANE E; Sapulpa Sr HS; Sapulpa, OK; (2); Church Yth Grp; Band; Jazz Band; Mrchg Band; Orch; School Play; Var Golf; Gym; Socr; Tennis; Music/Psychlgy.

HANKS, SHANNA M; Latta Sr HS; Ada, OK; (2); Church Yth Grp; FCA; FHA; Chorus; Church Choir; Hon Roll; Several 1 Ratngs For Ensmble, Solo & Choir; All-Dist Hnr Choir; OBU Hnr Choir; Hillsdale; Medcl.

HANLEY, SHAYNA C; Muskogee HS; Muskogee, OK; (3); Church Yth Grp; French Clb; Girl Scts; Quiz Bowl; Scholastic Bowl; Band; Church Choir; Mrchg Band; Pep Band; School Musical; U Of OK; RN.

HANNA, CRYSTAL; Salina HS; Rose, OK; (4); 1/48; Am Leg Aux Girls St; Church Yth Grp; FCA; Pres 4-H; VP Natl FFA Org; Office Aide; Quiz Bowl; School Play; Sec Soph Cls; Rptr Jr Cls; OSU; Vet.

HANNA, KENDRA M; Del City HS; Del City, OK; (3); 48/477; Cmnty Wkr; German Clb; Girl Scts; SADD; Teachers Aide; Band; Drm Mjr(t); Mrchg Band; Orch; Sftbl; Psych.

HANNA, KRISTI; Harrah HS; Harrah, OK; (4); 8/130; Church Yth Grp; Rep Debate Tm; Drama Clb; FCA; FBLA; FHA; HOBY; SADD; Teachers Aide; School Play; NHS Sec; Frgn Lang Clb Treas & Awds; St Gregory Coll; Intl Bus.

HANNA, MISTY D; Cameron Schl; Cameron, OK; (3); 1/36; FCA; FHA; Quiz Bowl; Var Bsktbl; Var Score Keeper; Var Sftbl; High Hon Roll; Hon Roll; NHS; Ntl Merit Ltr; 1st Tm All Cnty Fst Ptch Sftbll; 2nd Tm All Cnty Slw Ptch Sftbl; OSU; Vet.

HANNA, WHITSON P; Broken Arrow Sr HS; Broken Arrow, OK; (3); 268/921; Drama Clb; Acpl Chr; School Musical; School Play; Stage Crew; VP Sr Cls; Wt Lftg; Hon Roll; Church Yth Grp; Bst Frosh/Soph Actor; Film/Theatre/Directing.

HANNAGAN, MARIAH F; Anadarko HS; Anadarko, OK; (3); Drama Clb; French Clb; FBLA; FHA; Chorus; School Musical; School Play; Stage Crew; Nwsp; Nrsng.

HANNAH, BRIAR; Eisenhower Jr HS; Lawton, OK; (4); 26/386; Am Leg Aux Girls St; Church Yth Grp; VP FCA; HOBY; Chrmn Key Clb; Var Chorus; Church Choir; Stage Crew; Phtg Nwsp; Phtg Yrbk; Mst Outstndg Stu Awd 95-96; Gftd & Tlntd; U Of MN; Arch.

HANNAH, KIMBERLY D; South Intermediate HS; Broken Arrow, OK; (1); French Clb; Drill Tm; Hon Roll; Law.

HANNAH, MARSHA M; Jay HS; Jay, OK; (3); FBLA; Natl Beta Clb; Natl FFA Org; Hon Roll; Jr NHS; Hi Dey; FOMC; Prin Honor Rl; OSU; Vet.

HANNAH, NICKEYA; John Marshall HS; Oklahoma City, OK; (3); Church Yth Grp; FCA; FHA; Pep Clb; Varsity Clb; Band; Chorus; Church Choir; Flag Corp; Mrchg Band; Bears Roundtable; Perr Mediator; FHA; OK Univ; Dist Lawyer.

HANSARD, TAHSHA; Capitol Hill HS; Oklahoma City, OK; (4); 25/151; Church Yth Grp; Pres DECA; Pres FBLA; Red Cross Aide; SADD; Church Choir; Rep Stu Cncl; High Hon Roll; NHS; Prfct Atten Awd; Coll Clb; Upward Bound; Ldrshp, Intensity; Balck Heritage; US Nal Ldrshp Mrt; Langston U; Comp Prgmr.

HANSELMAN, MICHELLE R; Heavener HS; Heavener, OK; (1); FBLA; Key Clb; Chorus; Rptr Nwsp; Sec Frsh Cls; Hon Roll; Carl Albert ST Coll; Bus.

HANSEN, AMBER; Nathan Hale HS; Tulsa, OK; (4); 5/203; Church Yth Grp; English Clb; Math Tm; Quiz Bowl; Service Clb; Spanish Clb; JV Sftbl; High Hon Roll; NHS; Ntl Merit Ltr; Ecolgy Clb; U OK.

HANSEN, DE ANNA KIM; Choctaw HS; Choctaw, OK; (1); FCA; Spanish Clb; Phtg Ed Yrbk; Mgr(s); Trk; High Hon Roll; OU; Med.

HANSEN, GEOFF D; Yukon Middle HS; Yukon, OK; (1); Hon Roll; OK ST Univ.

HANSEN, JAMES T; Yukon HS; Yukon, OK; (4); Church Yth Grp; CAP; Office Aide; Red Cross Aide; Spanish Clb; Teachers Aide; High Hon Roll; Air Frce.

HANSEN, JEFF; Madill HS; Madill, OK; (3); Church Yth Grp; FCA; Band; Church Choir; Mrchg Band; School Musical; Ftbl; Trk; Wrstlng; NHS; OK ST U; Engrng.

HANSEN, KATHLYN C; B T Washington HS; Tulsa, OK; (3); Bus Profs of Am; FBLA; Pres German Clb; JCL; Latin Clb; Red Cross Aide; Ofcr Stu Cncl; Gym; High Hon Roll; Jr NHS; Voice; Piano; Lang Prz Ger, Latin; Tulsa JC.

HANSON, BRANDY M; Checotah HS; Checotah, OK; (2); 17/119; FBLA; Pep Clb; Chorus; Trk; Hon Roll; NHS; OKU; Medcl.

HANSON, KENDALL S; Pryor Sr HS; Pryor, OK; (3); Boy Scts; German Clb; Scholastic Bowl; Band; Jazz Band; Mrchg Band; Golf; Schl Cable News Prgm Editor; Comm/Tv Broadcast.

HANSON, LELAND; Miami Sr HS; Miami, OK; (4); 16/121; Am Leg Boys St; Band; Mrchg Band; Var Bsbl; Hon Roll; Jr NHS; NHS; Supr Rtng Bnd Ensmbl At St Cntst; All-Conf & All-Dist Bsbl.

HANSON, TIFFANY L; Edmond North HS; Edmond, OK; (3); 16/350; Church Yth Grp; FCA; Spanish Clb; SADD; Chorus; Church Choir; Variety Show; Var Powder Puff Ftbl; NHS; Span I Stu Awd; Eng II Stu Awd; TX Christian Univ; Intl Bus.

HANWAY, CHERYL Y; Parker Middle HS; Mcalester, OK; (3); Church Yth Grp; Red Cross Aide; Band; Chorus; Mrchg Band; School Musical; Stage Crew; Nwsp; Rep Soph Cls; Hon Roll; Rainbow Grls; Chem/Physics Clb.

HARAGAN, SANDRA; Wilson HS; Wilson, OK; (3); 2/50; Natl Beta Clb; Quiz Bowl; Band; Chorus; Rep Nwsp; Ofcr Stu Cncl; Chrldng; NHS; St Schlr; Flg Crp Capt, Rtne Chrgrphr.

HARAHAP, INDRI; Claremore Sr HS; Claremore, OK; (4); Computer Clb; English Clb; Girl Scts; Math Clb; Science Clb; Variety Show; Rptr Nwsp; Sec Stu Cncl; Var Swmmng; Hon Roll; TX A&M; Indstrl Eng.

HARDAWAY, ERIC D; Muskogee HS; Muskogee, OK; (3); FBLA; SADD; School Play; Nwsp; Ofcr Frsh Cls; Var Bsktbl; Trk; Phy Thrpst.

HARDBARGER, TIFFANIE D; Stilwell HS; Stilwell, OK; (2); Drama Clb; 4-H; FBLA; FHA; Natl Beta Clb; Spanish Clb; School Musical; School Play; Stage Crew; Powder Puff Ftbl; U Of AR.

HARDCASTLE, AUBREY; Bethany HS; Oklahoma City, OK; (2); Church Yth Grp; Office Aide; Speech Tm; SADD; Teachers Aide; Chorus; School Play; Stage Crew; Cit Awd; Hon Roll; Skipped Jr Yr; ASU; Psycht; Parapsycologist.

HARDCASTLE, JASON M; Union Sr HS; Tulsa, OK; (4); 110/741; Church Yth Grp; FCA; Math Tm; Office Aide; Spanish Clb; JV Bsktbl; Hon Roll; NHS; Pres Schlr; Hnrs Cls Stdnt; Abilene Chrstn Univ; Med.

HARDEN JR, RONALD D; Mc Lain Career Acad; Tulsa, OK; (1); Church Yth Grp; Intrml Bsktbl; Hon Roll; Georgetown Univ.

HARDER, LANCE; Shawnee Sr HS; Shawnee, OK; (3); 35/282; Spanish Clb; Rptr Nwsp; JV Tennis; Hon Roll; Shawnee Chmbr Cmmrce Stu Of Mo Feb 95; OK St U Acad Achvt Cert 96; Big Bros/Big Sisters Org.

HARDESTY, CHRIS; Sapulpa Sr HS; Sapulpa, OK; (4); 107/273; VICA; Bsktbl; Gov Hon Prg Awd; Hon Roll; Prfct Atten Awd; VICA Sec 94-95; OK ST Univ; Construction.

HARDESTY, MELISSA A; Jenks HS; Tulsa, OK; (3); Church Yth Grp; Key Clb; Ofcr Stu Cncl; Vllybl; Hon Roll; Chrch Drama; VP Mdlng Fshn Brnch Explrs; TX Tech; Psychlgst.

HARDIN, BILLY D; Bridge Creek HS; Tuttle, OK; (2); Drama Clb; FCA; Spanish Clb; School Play; Sec Soph Cls; Var L Bsbl; Var L Ftbl; Fishing; Big Bass Jr Championship Achvmt; OK Univ; Cnslng.

HARDIN, COURTNEY M; Velma Alma HS; Velma, OK; (2); Church Yth Grp; FCA; FBLA; Quiz Bowl; SADD; Band; Pres Soph Cls; Chrldng; DAR Awd; Sgn Lang; Gdnc Cnslr.

HARDIN, JEFF A; Western Heights Sr HS; Oklahoma City, OK; (3); 58/190; Cmnty Wkr; Library Aide; Office Aide; Teachers Aide; Ofcr Bsbl; Ftbl; Vllybl; Wrstlng; PE Coach.

HARDING, APRIL L; Broken Arrow Sr HS; Broken Arrow, OK; (3); VICA; Band; Mrchg Band; JV Socr; Hon Roll; Broken Arrow Scr Clb; Clsc 3 Yrs; Pol Sci/Law Enfrcmnt.

HARDWICK, AMY; Woodward HS; Woodward, OK; (2); Art Clb; Cmnty Wkr; FCA; German Clb; GAA; Pep Clb; Stage Crew; Treas Frsh Cls; Chrldng; Trk; St Chrldng Chmpn 95; Gymnstc; Lyrical Poem Wrtng Awd.

HARDY, HUMPHREY H; Ponca City Sr HS; Ponca City, OK; (3); 30/350; Church Yth Grp; Cmnty Wkr; Spanish Clb; Band; Chorus; Church Choir; Jazz Band; Mrchg Band; Orch; Pep Band; TV Broadcasting; Medicine.

HARDY, KENNETH; Harrah HS; Harrah, OK; (4); 12/128; Am Leg Boys St; Boy Scts; Church Yth Grp; FCA; Quiz Bowl; Scholastic Bowl; SADD; Rep Sr Cls; Ofcr Bsbl; Bsktbl; Rose ST Coll; Med.

HARE, CHRISTOPHER; Plainview HS; Ardmore, OK; (4); 1/85; Am Leg Boys St; Latin Clb; Mu Alpha Theta; Quiz Bowl; Scholastic Bowl; School Musical; Crs Cntry; Gov Hon Prg Awd; NHS; Val; Chickasaw Nation Stu Of Yr 94 95; CO Schl Of Mines; Engrng.

HARE, MARK; Plainview HS; Ardmore, OK; (1); Quiz Bowl; Scholastic Bowl; Chorus; School Musical; Stage Crew; Hon Roll; Prfct Atten Awd.

HARGENRADER, SABRINA; Plainview HS; Ardmore, OK; (4); 19/84; Natl Beta Clb; Quiz Bowl; SADD; Lit Mag; Mrchg Band; Band; Rep Stu Cncl; High Hon Roll; Hon Roll; NHS; E Cntrl Univ; Math Ed.

HARGIS, MARIAH D; Putnam City HS; Oklahoma City, OK; (1); Intrml Bsbl; Western Hts B-Ball & Carl Albert Invitational All Trnmt.

HARGIS, MICHAEL; Grandfield Jr Sr HS; Grandfield, OK; (4); 1/22; Church Yth Grp; Pres Natl FFA Org; VP Stu Cncl; Capt Bsbl; Capt Bsktbl; Capt Ftbl; Trk; Hon Roll; NHS; Val.

HARGRAVE, ERIC D; Mc Lain Career Acad; Tulsa, OK; (3); 2/200; Varsity Clb; Wt Lftg; Capt Wrstlng; Cit Awd; Hon Roll; Outstdng Bus Stu Awd; Acad Excl Awd; Most Valuable Wrestler; OK Univ; Acctng.

HARGRAVE, JEFF; Wewoka HS; Wewoka, OK; (4); 4/45; Am Leg Boys St; Boy Scts; Church Yth Grp; FCA; Science Clb; Yrbk; Var L Bsbl; Var L Bsktbl; Var L Ftbl; Hon Roll.

HARGRAVE, ROBERT L; Union Intermediate HS; Broken Arrow, OK; (2); FCA; Band; Var L Ftbl; Wt Lftg; Cit Awd; High Hon Roll; Hon Roll; NHS; Prfct Atten Awd; Pres Acad Fit Awd.

HARGRAVE, SUTINYA R; Union Sr HS; Broken Arrow, OK; (3); 47/708; Church Yth Grp; Office Aide; Band; Yrbk; Vllybl; Wt Lftg; Cit Awd; High Hon Roll; Hon Roll; Jr NHS; FL Inst Of Tech; Mrn Bio.

HARGROVE, BRIAN L; Midwest City HS; Midwest City, OK; (3); German Clb; Var Bsbl; Var Ftbl; Var Wrstlng; Hon Roll; PT/FBI Agnt.

HARGROVE, CHARLES J; Merritt Schl; Elk City, OK; (4); 13/36; Church Yth Grp; FCA; Natl FFA Org; SADD; Teachers Aide; Ofcr Bsbl; Ftbl; Wt Lftg; 4-H Awd; Hon Roll.

HARGROVE, CRYSTAL; Macarthur Jr HS; Lawton, OK; (1); Church Yth Grp; FCA; Var Chrldng; Score Keeper; Hon Roll; Jr NHS; VFW Ladies Aux Best Girl Awd.

HARGROVE, KASEE; Merritt Schl; Elk City, OK; (3); 2/36; Church Yth Grp; FCA; Natl FFA Org; Scholastic Bowl; Yrbk; Sec Jr Cls; Var Bsktbl; Var Chrldng; NHS; Pres Acad Fit Awd; SW OK St Univ; RN.

HARGROVE, LACY; Central Mid-HS; Norman, OK; (1); Hon Roll; OSU; Vet.

HARJO, MIRANDA; Holdenville HS; Holdenville, OK; (2); 9/85; Church Yth Grp; FHA; HOBY; Natl Beta Clb; Scholastic Bowl; Teachers Aide; Chorus; Church Choir; Ofcr Stu Cncl; High Hon Roll; HOBY Schl Rep; Hm Ec Awd; Schlstc Tm; Alg I Awd; TSA St 9th Pl; Ntv Amer Stdnt Cncl; U Of OK; Phys Thrp.

HARKEY, SCOTT; Indianola HS; Mcalester, OK; (1); 4/45; Var Bsbl; JV Bsktbl; High Hon Roll.

HARKEY, STEPHANIE; Crescent Schl; Crescent, OK; (2); Church Yth Grp; French Clb; Letterman Clb; Natl Beta Clb; Quiz Bowl; Variety Show; Sftbl; Hon Roll; Jr NHS; Prfct Atten Awd; Archtct.

HARKINS, JASON; Comanche HS; Comanche, OK; (4); 7/60; Am Leg Aux Girls St; Church Yth Grp; Library Aide; Natl FFA Org; Teachers Aide; High Hon Roll; NHS; Ntl Merit Ltr; FFA Chptr VP 94-95 & Pres 95-96; Chrch Class Tchr; NE OK A&M; Vet.

HARKINS, KATHY; Madill HS; Madill, OK; (1); Church Yth Grp; FHA; Math Clb; Quiz Bowl; Science Clb; SADD; Church Choir; High Hon Roll; Pres Acad Fit Awd.

HARKINS, MARGARET; Madill HS; Madill, OK; (3); 2/100; Natl FFA Org; Science Clb; Pres SADD; School Musical; Sec Soph Cls; VP Jr Cls; Sec Stu Cncl; Var Trk; High Hon Roll; NHS; Vet Med.

HARLAN, ASHLEY D; Wakita Schl; Wakita, OK; (1); Church Yth Grp; FCA; FHA; Rptr Band; Pep Band; School Play; Rep Frsh Cls; VP Stu Cncl; Bsktbl; Trk; OCU; Sports Med; Ath Trainer.

HARLAN, ONEY B; Hominy HS; Hominy, OK; (3); 23/64; Church Yth Grp; Drama Clb; French Clb; Speech Tm; Band; Mrchg Band; School Play; Stage Crew; Prfct Atten Awd; Psych.

HARLAND, KORI; Texhoma HS; Texhoma, OK; (2); 1/25; 4-H; Pep Clb; Bsktbl; Chrldng; TX Tech.

HARLAND, TONI M; Putnam City West HS; Oklahoma City, OK; (2); Vllybl; OK Univ; Tchr.

HARLESS, MICHAEL P; Fox Sr HS; Ratliff City, OK; (3); FCA; Natl FFA Org; Ofcr Bsbl; Bsktbl; Ftbl; Wt Lftg; 4-H Awd; Wild Life Mngmnt.

HARLESS, WESTON JACOB; Soper Schl; Soper, OK; (1); 1/22; Church Yth Grp; JA; Sec Frsh Cls; Var Bsbl; Var Bsktbl.

HARMAN, NICKY J; Calumet Schl; Calumet, OK; (2); Church Yth Grp; Sec FCA; Pres 4-H; Chorus; Rep Frsh Cls; Rep Soph Cls; Rep Jr Cls; L Bsktbl; Capt Chrldng; NHS; Baylor Univ.

HARMAN, TERRA R; Spiro HS; Spiro, OK; (4); 23/89; Rep FBLA; Rep FHA; Math Clb; Chorus; Capt Color Guard; Sec Pres Mrchg Band; School Musical; Ofcr Stu Cncl; Hon Roll; NHS; Westark CC; Acctng; CPA.

HARMON, CHRISSY L; Shawnee Sr HS; Shawnee, OK; (3); Church Yth Grp; Spanish Clb; Capt Chrldng; Var Tennis; Hon Roll; NHS; OK Univ; PT/LAB Tech.

HARMON, CHRISTIE L; Owasso Sr HS; Owasso, OK; (3); 61/387; Church Yth Grp; Cmnty Wkr; Drama Clb; Science Clb; Band; Flag Corp; Mrchg Band; Stage Crew; High Hon Roll; NHS; Teen Actn Grp; D-FY; Tulsa Univ; Nurse Prctnr.

HARMON, ELISA; Norman Sr HS; Norman, OK; (3); 67/799; Cmnty Wkr; Latin Clb; Chorus; Swing Chorus; Variety Show; Lit Mag; High Hon Roll; Ntl Merit Ltr; Pres Acad Fit Awd; OK All St Choir 95-96; Norman HS AEGIS Eng Pgm; OK Summer Arts Inst 96; Music Ed; Vocal Perfmnc.

HARMON, KASHA L; Moore HS; Moore, OK; (4); Art Clb; French Clb; Hist FBLA; Science Clb; Tennis; Trk; Hon Roll; Outstdng Engl Awd; Natl Lib Poetry Pub; Elem Ed.

HARMON, KRYSTEL D; Chickasha HS; Chickasha, OK; (4); 7/150; Church Yth Grp; SADD; Teachers Aide; Mgr(s); Hon Roll; NHS; Prfct Atten Awd; Pres Acad Fit Awd; St Schlr; Val; OK Hon Soc; Poem Plbshd In Anthlgy; OU Hnr Schol; Pres Spec Recog Awd; U Of OK; Jrnlsm.

HARMON, LISA S; Webster HS; Tulsa, OK; (3); DECA; FBLA; Office Aide; Yrbk; Hist Frsh Cls; Rep Soph Cls; Ofcr Jr Cls; Rep Stu Cncl; Hon Roll; US Engl Acad.

HARMON, STACEE; Christian Heritage Acad; Oklahoma City, OK; (4); 1/53; High Hon Roll; Hon Roll; Pres Acad Fit Awd; Val; ACSI Distgushed Chrstn HS Stu; TRUTH; 2nd Pl Physcs Rose St Coll Schlstc Mt; OK ST U; Physcs.

HARMON, TARA; Yale Jr Sr HS; Yale, OK; (4); Natl FFA Org; Office Aide; Yrbk; Pres Frsh Cls; Pres Soph Cls; Pres Jr Cls; Pres Sr Cls; Vllybl; Cit Awd; FFA Chapter Pres.

HARMS, CARA; Christian Heritage Acad; Moore, OK; (4); Church Yth Grp; Drama Clb; Speech Tm; Teachers Aide; Chorus; School Play; Bsktbl; High Hon Roll; Ntl Merit Ltr; TRUTH; Elem Ed.

HARMS, HOLLY M; Duncan HS; Duncan, OK; (4); 23/215; Church Yth Grp; Hon Roll; NHS; Prfct Atten Awd; Youth Alive; OK Bapt Univ; Scndry Math Ed.

HARMS, SABRINA D; Durant HS; Durant, OK; (2); Church Yth Grp; GAA; Varsity Clb; Acpl Chr; Chorus; Var Tennis; High Hon Roll; Hon Roll; St Schlr; OK Univ; Pharm D.

HARNAR, AARON W; Nathan Hale HS; Tulsa, OK; (3); 8/259; Church Yth Grp; FCA; French Clb; FBLA; School Play; Var Bsbl; Var Capt Ftbl; High Hon Roll; Hon Roll; Jr NHS; Med.

HARNESS, TANA; Union Sr HS; Tulsa, OK; (4); 104/615; Church Yth Grp; FHA; Key Clb; Mu Alpha Theta; Chorus; Rep Jr Cls; Rep Sr Cls; Jr NHS; NHS; Spanish NHS; Renaissance; Natl Music Hnr Soc; NSU; Elem/Music.

HAROLDS, JENNIFER L; Edmond Santa Fe HS; Edmond, OK; (3); 1/284; Cmnty Wkr; Hosp Aide; Math Clb; Pep Clb; Science Clb; Spanish Clb; SADD; Temple Yth Grp; High Hon Roll; NHS; Pre Med.

HARP, CARRIE; Jenks HS; Tulsa, OK; (3); 54/517; French Clb; FHA; Hosp Aide; Key Clb; Teachers Aide; Gov Hon Prg Awd; Hon Roll; Jr NHS; NHS; Spec Olympics Vol; Phy Thrpy.

HARP, JAMIE L; Lexington HS; Lexington, OK; (2); FHA; GAA; JV Var Bsktbl; Cit Awd; Hon Roll; OU; Dr; FBI; Archeologist.

HARPER, BRAD S; Empire Schl; Duncan, OK; (3); Chess Clb; Debate Tm; FBLA; Letterman Clb; Chorus; School Play; Ofcr Stu Cncl; Ofcr Bsbl; Bsktbl; Ftbl; OK ST U; Law.

HARPER, BRANDIE D; Spiro HS; Spiro, OK; (3); FBLA; FHA; Nwsp; Sftbl; Pocola Police Explorers; Orthodontist.

HARPER, DANIEL R; Meeker HS; Meeker, OK; (1); Church Yth Grp; FCA; Natl FFA Org; Spanish Clb; Cit Awd; Hon Roll; NHS; Pres Acad Fit Awd; Cmptrs.

HARPER, JANA S; Colcord Schl; Colcord, OK; (3); Church Yth Grp; Band; Church Choir; Mrchg Band; Pep Band; Ofcr Stu Cncl; Hon Roll; NSU; Tchr.

HARPER, JEREMY M; Bridge Creek HS; Oklahoma City, OK; (2); Spanish Clb; Ftbl; Wt Lftg; U Of OK; Civil Engr.

HARPER, JESSICA A; Tahlequah Sr HS; Tahlequah, OK; (3); Pep Clb; Teachers Aide; Mock Trl; NSU; Law.

HARPER, JON K; Edmond Memorial HS; Edmond, OK; (2); 1/408; Var Capt Debate Tm; NFL; Spanish Clb; Hon Roll; NHS; Pres Acad Fit Awd; LAW.

HARPER, JUSTIN D; Edmond Santa Fe HS; Edmond, OK; (2); 70/350; Church Yth Grp; FCA; Ftbl; Trk; Prfct Atten Awd; Stdnt Of Mnth; OK ST Univ; US Army.

HARPER, STEVI; Kellyville Sr HS; Kellyville, OK; (3); Dance Clb; Debate Tm; Model UN; Ofcr Stu Cncl; Var Chrldng; Var Pom Pon; Var Sftbl; SECA Sec; NSU; Psychology.

HARPER, TREVOR; Midwest City HS; Midwest City, OK; (3); Cmnty Wkr; DECA; Drama Clb; German Clb; Hosp Aide; Chorus; School Musical; School Play; Rptr Nwsp; Ofcr Jr Cls; Rtryn Yth Ldrshp Awd; St Ldrshp Awd; Jrnlsm.

HARPER, VANESSA M; Clayton Jr Sr HS; Tuskahoma, OK; (3); 3/25; Debate Tm; Drama Clb; FCA; FHA; NFL; School Play; Yrbk; 4-H Awd; Hon Roll.

HARRALL, CRYSTAL M; Catoosa HS; Catoosa, OK; (4); 23/167; Band; Chorus; Jazz Band; Mrchg Band; Orch; Rptr Nwsp; High Hon Roll; Hon Roll; Frnch Clb; OK U; Med.

HARRELL, GENA M; Checotah HS; Checotah, OK; (2); Cmnty Wkr; Debate Tm; Drama Clb; Natl FFA Org; Speech Tm; Jvnl Cnclr.

HARRELL, HEATH; Crescent Schl; Crescent, OK; (2); Church Yth Grp; FHA; Red Cross Aide; Band; Mrchg Band; Pep Band; JV Var Bsbl; JV Var Bsktbl; Wt Lftg; Vllybl; GA Tech.

HARRELL, JENNIFER M; Roland Sr HS; Roland, OK; (3); Church Yth Grp; FCA; Band; Mrchg Band; Yrbk; Pres Jr Cls; Var Bsktbl; Var Sftbl; Hon Roll; Prfct Atten Awd; Real Est.

HARRELL, LAUREN; Mustang HS; Yukon, OK; (2); 115/380; Church Yth Grp; Teachers Aide; Ofcr Stu Cncl; Pom Pon; Hon Roll; Ballet; Jazz.

HARRINGTON, CASEY; Frederick HS; Frederick, OK; (2); #9 in class; Church Yth Grp; FCA; Letterman Clb; Speech Tm; School Musical; Rep Stu Cncl; Var Bsbl; Var Bsktbl; Var Ftbl; Var Wt Lftg; U OK.

HARRINGTON, CHRISTOPHER L; Union Intermediate HS; Broken Arrow, OK; (2); 337/700; Boy Scts; Church Yth Grp; French Clb.

HARRINGTON, CHRISTYN J; Catoosa HS; Tulsa, OK; (1); Band; Color Guard; Mrchg Band; Chrldng; Hon Roll.

HARRINGTON, NATHAN; Watts HS; Watts, OK; (2); Math Clb; Chorus; Var Bsbl; Var Bsktbl; Cit Awd; High Hon Roll; NHS; Outdoor Rec; U Of AR; Photo.

HARRINGTON, STACY L; Colcord Schl; Colcord, OK; (4); Am Leg Aux Girls St; Church Yth Grp; Office Aide; Yrbk; Pres Frsh Cls; Sec Jr Cls; Pres Sr Cls; Rep Stu Cncl; Capt Chrldng; High Hon Roll; Hmcmng Rylty; Bst All Rnd Stu Awd; Northeastern ST U; Med.

HARRINGTON, STEPHEN; Union Intermediate HS; Broken Arrow, OK; (2); 207/800; Boy Scts; Church Yth Grp; FCA; French Clb; Rice U; Engrng.

HARRINGTON, TIFFANY R; South Intermediate HS; Broken Arrow, OK; (1); GAA; Teachers Aide; Bsktbl; Sftbl; Hon Roll.

HARRIS, AMBER; Edmond North HS; Edmond, OK; (2); 1/430; Church Yth Grp; Cmnty Wkr; Mu Alpha Theta; Spanish Clb; SADD; Orch; Hon Roll; Hist Jr NHS; NHS; Prfct Atten Awd; Jr Crtr OK City Zoo; Span I Stdnt Of Yr.

HARRIS, AMY; Bridge Creek HS; Blanchard, OK; (3); 1/50; Church Yth Grp; FCA; Science Clb; Spanish Clb; SADD; Band; Flag Corp; Yrbk; High Hon Roll; VP NHS; Engl I, Alg I & II Awds; Missn Trips; Vlntr Wrk; OK Baptist U; Relgious Ed.

HARRIS, AMY L; Canton HS; Canton, OK; (2); Church Yth Grp; FHA; GAA; Spanish Clb; SADD; Band; Drill Tm; Mrchg Band; Pep Band; Yrbk; Southwestern; Schl Tchr.

HARRIS, ANDREW C; Deer Creek HS; Edmond, OK; (3); Church Yth Grp; FBLA; Teachers Aide; School Musical; School Play; Stage Crew; Variety Show; Var L Bsktbl; JV Ftbl; Var L Golf; KFOR-TV OK City Intern; Intnl TV Assoc; NPPA; OETA St-Wide PBS Network OK City Intern; Baylor; Telecommnctn.

HARRIS, ASHLEY; Guthrie Sr HS; Guthrie, OK; (3); 17/250; Treas French Clb; Mu Alpha Theta; Science Clb; SADD; Band; Flag Corp; Mrchg Band; Sec Frsh Cls; Sec Soph Cls; Sec Stu Cncl; OK U; Med.

HARRIS, BETHANY G; Enid Sr HS; Enid, OK; (2); Church Yth Grp; Office Aide; Chorus; High Hon Roll; Hon Roll; Jr NHS; NHS.

HARRIS, BROOKE; Cement Jr Sr HS; Cement, OK; (2); Church Yth Grp; Cmnty Wkr; English Clb; Math Clb; Quiz Bowl; Science Clb; Hon Roll; OK Hnr Soc; Jr High Quiz Bowl Capt; Medicine; Pediatrics.

HARRIS, CESARE; Eisenhower Sr HS; Lawton, OK; (4); 161/386; Church Yth Grp; Cmnty Wkr; FCA; Letterman Clb; Office Aide; Varsity Clb; Band; Var Ftbl; Var Trk; Hon Roll; Cameron Univ; Eng.

HARRIS, CHEREE D; El Reno Sr HS; El Reno, OK; (1); Art Clb; Church Yth Grp; GAA; Teachers Aide; Church Choir; JV Bsktbl; JV Crs Cntry; JV Sftbl; JV Trk; High Hon Roll; OU; Jrnlst.

HARRIS, DAVID; Tonkawa Jr Sr HS; Tonkawa, OK; (4); Am Leg Boys St; Natl FFA Org; Office Aide; VICA; Var L Bsbl; Var L Ftbl; Var L Wrstlng; Hon Roll; NHS; Prfct Atten Awd; FFA Treas; Lnd Jdgng Cntst Hgh Ind Awd; Cty Lvstck Show Grnd Champ Hog.

HARRIS, DAVID A; Duncan HS; Duncan, OK; (2); Church Yth Grp; FCA; FBLA; ROTC; Yrbk; Ftbl; Hon Roll; Natl Ci Mrt Awd; Math.

HARRIS, EMILY R; Choctaw HS; Choctaw, OK; (2); Cmnty Wkr; Key Clb; Spanish Clb; Chorus; Stage Crew; Tennis; Hon Roll; Work For OK Prof Hockey Teams; Starting Right Prevention Groups Vol; TX A&M U Galveston; Marn Bio.

HARRIS, ERIC D; B T Washington HS; Tulsa, OK; (4); 115/264; Church Yth Grp; Cmnty Wkr; Teachers Aide; Church Choir; Variety Show; Ofcr Bsbl; Var L Bsktbl; Var L Ftbl; Score Keeper; Hon Roll; OK U; Engrng.

HARRIS, H MATT; Ardmore HS; Ardmore, OK; (4); 12/168; FCA; Latin Clb; Math Clb; Science Clb; Rep Stu Cncl; Ftbl; Wrstlng; Hon Roll; NHS; OK ST Univ; Pre-Med.

HARRIS, HAROLD M; Ardmore HS; Ardmore, OK; (4); 12/170; FCA; Latin Clb; Letterman Clb; Library Aide; Rep Frsh Cls; Rep Jr Cls; Rep Sr Cls; Rep Stu Cncl; Ofcr Bsbl; Var Ftbl; Explorer Post 99; OK ST Univ; Med.

HARRIS, JENNIFER; Heritage Hall Schl; Oklahoma City, OK; (1); Hosp Aide; Pep Clb; JV Bsktbl; JV Chrldng; Var Fld Hcky; Var Sftbl; Hon Roll.

HARRIS, JENNIFER M; Southeast HS; Oklahoma City, OK; (2); ROTC; Chorus; Color Guard; Drill Tm; High Hon Roll; Hon Roll; Recd Dtrs Of Fndrs & Patriots Of Amer Awd; 9 ROTC Rbbns; Trophies Drill Tm; Rose ST Coll; Law.

HARRIS, KARA L; Westmoore HS; Oklahoma City, OK; (3); French Clb; JCL; Rep Stu Cncl; Var L Golf; Rptr NHS; OK ST Univ; Biochem.

HARRIS, KIMBERLY A; Owasso Sr HS; Owasso, OK; (4); 112/296; Church Yth Grp; French Clb; Office Aide; Teachers Aide; VICA; Band; Flag Corp; Mrchg Band; Rep Stu Cncl; Hon Roll; OK ST U.

HARRIS, LA DONNA D; Milburn Schl; Milburn, OK; (3); Chorus; Hon Roll.

HARRIS, LESLI A; Glenpool HS; Glenpool, OK; (1); Church Yth Grp; FCA; Red Cross Aide; Chorus; Church Choir; Sec Frsh Cls; Ofcr Stu Cncl; Chrldng; Powder Puff Ftbl; World Changers Missions; Var Cmptn Squad; OK Univ; Corporate Psych.

HARRIS, MANDY R; Stringtown HS; Stringtown, OK; (3); 3/20; 4-H; Natl FFA Org; Chorus; School Musical; Sec Frsh Cls; Sec Soph Cls; Rep Jr Cls; Bsktbl; 4-H Awd; High Hon Roll; Southeastern OK ST Univ.

HARRIS, MARK A; Bixby Sr HS; Bixby, OK; (1); Church Yth Grp; German Clb; SADD; Ftbl; Trk; Wt Lftg; Cit Awd; Hon Roll; Jr NHS; Pres Acad Fit Awd.

HARRIS, MARLA G; Pocola HS; Pocola, OK; (3); 5/55; Church Yth Grp; FBLA; Rptr FHA; Hosp Aide; Quiz Bowl; Nwsp; Yrbk; Cit Awd; High Hon Roll; NHS; OK Hnr Soc; Comp Sci.

HARRIS, MICHAEL; Arapaho Schl; Arapaho, OK; (2); 1/22; 4-H; Ofcr Bsbl; Bsktbl; 4-H Awd; High Hon Roll; NHS; Pres Acad Fit Awd; Val; OK ST U; Wldlf Bio.

HARRIS, MICHAEL S; Will Rogers HS; Tulsa, OK; (2); Church Yth Grp; Rep Soph Cls; Hon Roll; Tulsa Univ; Field Biologist.

HARRIS, NATE E; Bixby Sr HS; Bixby, OK; (1); Church Yth Grp; FCA; SADD; Variety Show; JV Bsbl; JV Bsktbl; JV Ftbl; High Hon Roll; Jr NHS; Pres Schlr; Pres Awd For Educl Excl; OSU; Arch.

HARRIS, NYKKIA L; John Marshall HS; Oklahoma City, OK; (4); 6/160; Treas FBLA; Band; Treas Church Choir; Co-Capt Flag Corp; Orch; Treas Jr Cls; Treas Sr Cls; Treas Church Yth Grp; Scholastic Bowl; High Hon Roll; Jr Botarian; Acad Assn Intern/Tutor; Ebony Awrns Bowl Capt; FL A&M Univ; Bus.

HARRIS, QUINTON J; Perkins-Tryon HS; Stillwater, OK; (2); Church Yth Grp; FCA; 4-H; FHA; Intnl Clb; Key Clb; Letterman Clb; Ofcr Bsbl; Bsktbl; 4-H Awd.

HARRIS, RACHEL; Bixby Sr HS; Bixby, OK; (4); #1 in class; Church Yth Grp; FCA; HOBY; VP Spanish Clb; SADD; Pres Stu Cncl; High Hon Roll; VP NHS; St Schlr; Val; Acad All St; OK St Regent; Chem Engr.

HARRIS, RACHEL D; Liberty HS; Beggs, OK; (4); 2/25; Pres FCA; Rptr Yrbk; VP Frsh Cls; VP Soph Cls; VP Jr Cls; VP Sr Cls; VP Stu Cncl; Capt Bsktbl; Cit Awd; Sal; Northeastern ST U; Engl.

HARRIS, RUSSELL; Seminole Jr Sr HS; Seminole, OK; (1); Cmnty Wkr; Debate Tm; Quiz Bowl; JV Golf; High Hon Roll; NHS; Piano; Seminole JC; Math.

HARRIS, SHANON M; Roland Sr HS; Muldrow, OK; (2); Church Yth Grp; Spanish Clb; Bsktbl; Hon Roll; NHS; Hnr Clb Hnrs Model; Westark CC.

HARRIS, STEPHANIE; Sapulpa Sr HS; Sapulpa, OK; (2); Church Yth Grp; Letterman Clb; Flag Corp; Stage Crew; High Hon Roll; Spanish NHS; Flag/Acad Lttr; 1st/2nd Pl Rbbns Span Cntst; OK Univ; Peds Nrse.

HARRIS, SUSAN; East Central HS; Tulsa, OK; (4); 96/189; Church Yth Grp; Pep Clb; Yrbk; Ofcr Stu Cncl; Chrldng; Hon Roll; Pres Schlr; FCA; Library Aide; Socr; Miss East Central 95-; Northeastern ST Univ; Elem Tch.

HARRIS, SYRETA J; Haskell HS; Haskell, OK; (2); 4/48; Varsity Clb; Band; Church Choir; Ofcr Soph Cls; Bsktbl; High Hon Roll; Sports Medicine.

HARRIS, TAMEKA M; Putnam City West HS; Oklahoma City, OK; (1); Art Clb; Drama Clb; Library Aide; Teachers Aide; Ofcr Frsh Cls; Trk; Cit Awd; Hon Roll; Rdng; Wrtng; Langston.

HARRIS, TEQUILA; Capitol Hill HS; Oklahoma City, OK; (4); Church Yth Grp; FBLA; Church Choir; Chrldng; High Hon Roll; Hon Roll; Prfct Atten Awd; Natl Hnr Roll; All Amer Schlr; U Of Central OK; Accttng.

HARRIS, TERRA D; Preston Schl; Beggs, OK; (2); Church Yth Grp; FHA; GAA; Chorus; Bsktbl; Sftbl; Hon Roll; Prfct Atten Awd.

HARRIS, TERRAINIA; Lawton Sr HS; Lawton, OK; (3); Church Yth Grp; FCA; Scholastic Bowl; Spanish Clb; Band; Chorus; Drm Mjr(t); Mrchg Band; School Musical; Lit Mag; Teen Crt; Ebony Soc; All Rgn Bnd/Choir; Med Rsrchr.

HARRIS, THERESA; John Marshall HS; Oklahoma City, OK; (4); 4/182; Church Yth Grp; FCA; French Clb; HOBY; Letterman Clb; Pres Jr Cls; Sec Stu Cncl; Capt Var Socr; Capt Var Sftbl; NHS; Phys Thrpy.

HARRIS, TONI R; Rush Springs HS; Ninnekah, OK; (4); 3/44; Model UN; Spanish Clb; Band; Mrchg Band; Yrbk; High Hon Roll; Hon Roll; NHS; OK Hnr Soc 4 Yrs; Outstdng Stdnt Of Yr Art I/II/GEOMETRY/HOME Ec I/II/III/IV/ACCTG; U Of Sci/Arts OK; Acctg.

HARRIS, TOSHA D; Byng Sr HS; Ada, OK; (2); Church Yth Grp; FCA; 4-H; Natl FFA Org; Spanish Clb; Teachers Aide; Bsktbl; Crs Cntry; Sftbl; Trk; E Cntrl ST Univ; Sci; PE.

HARRIS, ZAC; Hobart HS; Hobart, OK; (1); Natl FFA Org; Ofcr Bsbl; Bsktbl; Farmer.

HARRISON, AMANDA; Whitesboro Schl; Muse, OK; (3); 1/20; Church Yth Grp; FCA; Rptr Natl FFA Org; School Play; Rptr Nwsp; High Hon Roll; Val; Treas Soph Cls; Pres Jr Cls; Msnc Ldg Stu Today Awd; FFA Star Grnhnd Awd; Estrn OK ST Coll.

HARRISON, AMANDA; Carnegie Jr HS; Carnegie, OK; (3); Church Yth Grp; Scholastic Bowl; Rptr Soph Cls; Chrldng; High Hon Roll; Hon Roll; NHS; Prfct Atten Awd; Pres Acad Fit Awd; FHA; Stu Cncl; Southwestern Weatherford; Bus.

HARRISON, ASHLEY; Beaver HS; Beaver, OK; (1); 2/34; Sec Church Yth Grp; FCA; GAA; Chorus; Var JV Bsktbl; Var Crs Cntry; Var Sftbl; Var Trk; High Hon Roll; Hon Roll.

HARRISON, ASHLEY A; Mc Alester HS; Mcalester, OK; (2); Band; Mrchg Band; Pep Band; Hon Roll; All Dist Bnd; PT.

HARRISON, BEN; Bethel Bapt Acad; Enid, OK; (3); Boy Scts; Church Yth Grp; CAP; Cmnty Wkr; Debate Tm; FCA; Quiz Bowl; Band; Jazz Band; Ofcr Frsh Cls; Air Frc Acad; Pilot/Pre-Med.

HARRISON, CRYSTAL D; Dickson HS; Ardmore, OK; (2); Rep FHA; Hosp Aide; Key Clb; SADD; High Hon Roll; Hon Roll; NHS; Prfct Atten Awd.

HARRISON, CRYSTAL L; Union Intermediate HS; Tulsa, OK; (2); 178/800; Church Yth Grp; Debate Tm; NFL; Spanish Clb; Speech Tm; Church Choir; Mrchg Band; Hon Roll; Bands Of Amer Attndnt; St Debate Qlfr; USC; OK Bapt U; Public Rels.

HARRISON, DEEANN; Ponca City Sr HS; Ponca City, OK; (2); Church Yth Grp; Office Aide; Orch; Rep Stu Cncl; Chrldng; Diving; Mgr(s); Trk; Hon Roll; All-Amer Chrldr; OSU; Sprts Med.

HARRISON, DONIELLE G; John Marshall HS; Oklahoma City, OK; (2); Dance Clb; FHA; Office Aide; ROTC; Teachers Aide; Church Choir; Rptr Yrbk; Sec Jr Cls; Pom Pon; Teen Cnslr; Spelman; Dist Atty.

HARRISON, JIL M; Edmond Memorial HS; Edmond, OK; (2); 57/408; Hon Roll; NHS; Pres Acad Fit Awd; Modlng Local Mdlng Agncy; UCO; Jrnlsm.

HARRISON, JORDANA; Indianola HS; Mcalester, OK; (2); 4-H; FBLA; Natl Beta Clb; Natl FFA Org; School Play; Yrbk; Rep Stu Cncl; 4-H Awd; Hon Roll; AJBA; OJBBA; OJBA; OK ST U; Ag Cmmnctns.

HARRISON, KELLI; Okmulgee HS; Okmulgee, OK; (4); 17/125; Church Yth Grp; Cmnty Wkr; Drama Clb; FCA; HOBY; Pep Clb; Red Cross Aide; Spanish Clb; Speech Tm; School Play; OK Stu Cncl Conv Dlgt; Indian Clb; Bst Actrss Awd 94; Meth Yth Dist VP; Cls Up; Acad Awd; DAR Gd Ctzn; OK ST U; Elem Educ.

HARRISON, LINDSEY J; Shattuck Jr Sr HS; Shattuck, OK; (3); 3/36; Rptr FHA; School Play; Pres Frsh Cls; Pres Jr Cls; Rptr Stu Cncl; Capt Bsktbl; Var L Golf; High Hon Roll; NHS; Sal; OK Hnr Soc; Golf ST Qualifier; MVP Bsktbl.

HARRISON, ROBIN R; Duncan HS; Duncan, OK; (2); Church Yth Grp; Cmnty Wkr; Mgr(s); Sftbl; Hon Roll; NHS; OK ST; Acctng.

HARRISON, SARAH; Keota Schl; Keota, OK; (4); 11/33; FHA; Sec Natl FFA Org; Pep Clb; Red Cross Aide; Teachers Aide; Rep Stu Cncl; Hon Roll; Ftbl Hmcmng Qn 96; Co-Fndr Schl Recyclng Prgm; 1st Pl Schl Sci Fair; Northeastern ST Univ.

HARROD, JENNIFER; Rock Creek Jr Sr HS; Bennington, OK; (1); FHA; Bsktbl; Cit Awd; High Hon Roll; NHS; OK ST U.

HARROLD, JOSHUA W; Oologah HS; Oologah, OK; (3); Church Yth Grp; Letterman Clb; Church Choir; JV Var Ftbl; Wt Lftg; Hon Roll; Engrng.

HARRY, BETHANY P; Putnam City North HS; Oklahoma City, OK; (4); 82/436; Art Clb; Church Yth Grp; FCA; Key Clb; Office Aide; Spanish Clb; Rep Pom Pon; Hon Roll; NHS; Comp Prmgrmmng II Stu Of Yr; OK ST; Forensic Sci.

HART, APRIL R; Edmond Santa Fe HS; Edmond, OK; (2); SADD; Wt Lftg; Art Coll; Phtgrphr/Art.

HART, J TRAVIS; Mustang HS; Mustang, OK; (4); 101/342; 4-H; JA; Key Clb; Teachers Aide; JV Ftbl; Wt Lftg; Wrstlng; Cit Awd; 4-H Awd; Hon Roll; Hall Of Fame 4-H Recipient; St Top 10 4-H Hall Of Fame Wnnr; Received 4-H Ctznshp Focus Wash DC Wnnr; Southeastern OSU; Psych.

HART, JASON A; Webster HS; Tulsa, OK; (2); Comptv Acad.

HART, JENNIFER L; Union Intermediate HS; Tulsa, OK; (2); 194/800; Church Yth Grp; Key Clb; Band; Nwsp; Yrbk; NHS; USC; Adopt-A-Grandparent; CPR Course; OK Bapt U; Child Ed.

HART, JOANNA C; Gore HS; Gore, OK; (3); Yrbk; Stat Bsktbl; NHS; Masonic Grand Lodge OK Stu Of Today Awd; 3rd Pl Cookson Hills Elec Yth Tour Essay Cont.

HART, JOHNSLYN LEVI; Wapanucka Schl; Milburn, OK; (3); Church Yth Grp; 4-H; Pep Clb; Church Choir; Treas Jr Cls; JV Bsbl; JV Bsktbl; JV Score Keeper; High Hon Roll; NHS; Murram ST Coll; Gen Ed.

HART, MELISSA; Moore HS; Moore, OK; (4); 129/505; Church Yth Grp; FCA; JCL; Treas Latin Clb; Spanish Clb; SADD; Rep Stu Cncl; Var L Chrldng; Powder Puff Ftbl; OCCC; Elem Ed.

HART, NATALEE J; Senior HS; Bowring, OK; (3); Church Yth Grp; Cmnty Wkr; Debate Tm; 4-H; FHA; Key Clb; Speech Tm; Band; Church Choir; Flag Corp; OT.

HART, SANDIE L; Ripley HS; Ripley, OK; (1); 1/50; Church Yth Grp; FHA; Math Clb; Science Clb; Sftbl; Hon Roll; OSU; Arch.

HART, SARAH B; Westmoore HS; Oklahoma City, OK; (2); Office Aide; Marine Bio.

HART, VALERIE N; Union Intermediate HS; Tulsa, OK; (2); 38/800; Church Yth Grp; Cmnty Wkr; Hosp Aide; Spanish Clb; Nwsp; Yrbk; Bsktbl; Sftbl; High Hon Roll; Sec NHS; Outstndng Achvt Awds In Eng & Bus; Med.

HARTER, SARAH A; Union Intermediate HS; Tulsa, OK; (2); 48/800; Church Yth Grp; Cmnty Wkr; Spanish Clb; Band; Mrchg Band; High Hon Roll; Jr NHS; NHS; Domestic Violnce Intervntn Svcs Vlntr; OK U; Psych.

HARTIN, MITZI; Madill HS; Madill, OK; (1); Church Yth Grp; 4-H; Natl FFA Org; Spanish Clb; 4-H Awd; Hon Roll; Prfct Atten Awd.

HARTIN, RONALD B; Madill HS; Madill, OK; (4); 27/72; 4-H; Natl FFA Org; SADD; Rep Soph Cls; Hon Roll; NHS; Pres Schlr; St FFA Degree; Star Chptr Farmer; Murray ST Coll; Wildlife Consv.

HARTING, RYAN D; Stillwater Sr HS; Stillwater, OK; (3); 115/363; Vars Schlr 2 Yrs; FFA Farm Bus Mgmnt Team; OK ST Univ; Vet.

HARTLEY, CHRISTINA N; Wagoner Sr HS; Wagoner, OK; (3); FCA; FHA; Pep Clb; Spanish Clb; Church Choir; Ofcr Jr Cls; Hon Roll; Teen For Christ; Sch Of Ozarks; Tchr Disabld Kds.

HARTLEY, MELISSA S; Choctaw HS; Choctaw, OK; (3); FCA; Sec Frsh Cls; Rep Soph Cls; JV Bsktbl; Jr NHS; NHS; Law.

HARTLEY, PAM S; Choctaw HS; Choctaw, OK; (3); 82/313; Church Yth Grp; FCA; FTA; Key Clb; Rptr Nwsp; Yrbk; JV Sftbl; Hon Roll; Jr NHS; NHS; Ed.

HARTLEY, SUMMER T; Valliant HS; Valliant, OK; (1); Church Yth Grp; Cmnty Wkr; FHA; Band; Bsktbl; Mgr(s); Sftbl; Hon Roll; Law.

HARTMAN, ASHLEY D; Marietta HS; Marietta, OK; (2); Church Yth Grp; FCA; 4-H; GAA; Natl FFA Org; Spanish Clb; Bsktbl; Chrldng; Sftbl; Trk; OK Univ; Phrmcst.

HARTMAN, MATTHEW S; Putnam City North HS; Oklahoma City, OK; (1); Church Yth Grp; Cmnty Wkr; FCA; Church Choir; JV Tennis; High Hon Roll; Hnrs Pgm; 3d; Stdnt Cncl Rep; OK Bapt Univ; Business.

HARTMAN, SHELLEY A; Union Sr HS; Broken Arrow, OK; (3); 41/741; Church Yth Grp; Rep FCA; Office Aide; Chorus; Var Co-Capt Pom Pon; High Hon Roll; Jr NHS; NHS; Pres Acad Fit Awd; Spanish NHS; Mr/Miss Union Royalty 95-96; Church Lit Dance Tm; OK ST U; Health Sci.

HARTMAN, STEPHANIE G; Claremore Sr HS; Springfield, MO; (1); Church Yth Grp; Computer Clb; Drama Clb; FHA; Band; Mrchg Band; Orch; Pep Band; Hon Roll; Evangel Coll-Springfld; Mssnry.

HARTPENCE, JASON R; Putnam City North HS; Oklahoma City, OK; (1); Boy Scts; Pres Church Yth Grp; Cmnty Wkr; FCA; Rep Frsh Cls; Rep Stu Cncl; Wt Lftg; Cit Awd; Hon Roll; Mission Work Mexico; Hot Air Ballooning; Hunting; Fishing; Law.

HARTSELL, STACEY; North Intemediate HS; Broken Arrow, OK; (1); Church Yth Grp; Math Clb; Thesps; Phtg Nwsp; Ed Yrbk; Rep Stu Cncl; Hon Roll; Jr NHS; Jazz, Tap, Ballet, Lyrical 4 Yrs; Berkley; Photo.

HARTSOCK, BENJAMIN A; Bartlesville Mid HS; Bartlesville, OK; (1); Boy Scts; FBLA; Library Aide; Math Clb; Phtg Yrbk; Bsktbl; Wt Lftg; High Hon Roll; Envir Club; BYU; Bus.

HARVEY, BECKY; Plainview HS; Ardmore, OK; (2); 3/88; Church Yth Grp; FCA; Latin Clb; Natl Beta Clb; Pres Frsh Cls; Pres Soph Cls; Var Chrldng; Var Crs Cntry; Var Trk; NHS; OK Hnr Soc.

HARVEY, BENJAMIN R; Edmond North HS; Edmond, OK; (4); 1/330; Church Yth Grp; German Clb; NFL; SADD; Ofcr Stu Cncl; Hon Roll; NHS; Ntl Merit Ltr; Pres Acad Fit Awd; U Tulsa; Chem Engr.

HARVEY, BRIAN A; Dickson HS; Ardmore, OK; (2); Art Clb; Cmnty Wkr; FCA; Intrml Bsbl; Var Bsktbl; Var Ftbl; Intrml Trk; Hon Roll; Kiwanis Awd; Southeastern ST Univ.

HARVEY, CASEY M; Eldorado Schl; Eldorado, OK; (2); Church Yth Grp; FHA; Natl FFA Org; Pep Clb; Scholastic Bowl; Band; Mrchg Band; School Play; Chrldng; Ntl Merit Ltr; WOSC.

HARVEY, CORIE; Fox Sr HS; Fox, OK; (1); 3/21; Band; Ofcr Frsh Cls; Bsktbl; Chrldng; Sftbl; Trk; Hon Roll; Pres Acad Fit Awd; US Bus Ed Awd; All Amer Schlr; Marine Bio.

HARVEY, JENNIFER L; Tahlequah Sr HS; Tahlequah, OK; (3); Jr NHS; Ntl Merit Ltr; Pres Acad Fit Awd; Northeastern ST Univ; Psychlgy.

HARVEY, LARRY R; Spiro HS; Spiro, OK; (4); 13/90; FCA; FBLA; FHA; Math Clb; SADD; Ofcr Sr Cls; Ofcr Stu Cncl; Bsktbl; Ftbl; Golf; Westark CC; Elec Eng.

HARVEY, MISTY D; Madill HS; Madill, OK; (2); Church Yth Grp; 4-H; Chorus; Church Choir; School Musical; Variety Show; 4-H Awd; Hon Roll; Dance Team; Campfire; SOSU; Attorney.

HARVEY, NINA L; Douglass HS; Oklahoma City, OK; (2); Church Yth Grp; Band; Church Choir; Mrchg Band; Pom Pon; Ntl Merit Ltr; House Of Rep Page; Upwrd Bnd; TX Tech Univ; Cmptr.

HARVEY, REBECCA; Plainview HS; Ardmore, OK; (2); 3/83; Church Yth Grp; FCA; Latin Clb; Natl Beta Clb; Pres Frsh Cls; Pres Soph Cls; Chrldng; Crs Cntry; Trk; Hon Roll.

HARWELL, CHARISSA; Central Mid-HS; Norman, OK; (1); Church Yth Grp; FCA; JCL; Latin Clb; Mu Alpha Theta; Chorus; Sec Frsh Cls; High Hon Roll; NHS; Yrbk; Awana Chldrns Ministries.

HARWELL, JOSEPH; Heavener HS; Heavener, OK; (4); 17/75; Church Yth Grp; Drama Clb; French Clb; FHA; Teachers Aide; Band; Mrchg Band; Pep Band; School Play; Stage Crew; OK ST; Music; Band Dir.

HARWI, CHRIS B; Edmond North HS; Edmond, OK; (1); 141/456; Church Yth Grp; FCA; Spanish Clb; Bsktbl; Jr NHS; U TX.

HASENMYER, HEATHER; Grandfield Jr Sr HS; Grandfield, OK; (4); 2/23; Pres 4-H; Natl FFA Org; Ofcr Frsh Cls; Rep Jr Cls; Rep Sr Cls; Rep Stu Cncl; Var Capt Bsktbl; Var Capt Sftbl; Var Trk; NHS; Miss GHS; Chem Olympd; Interschlstc Chem; Tulsa U; Sprts Med.

HASHBARGER, GENNIE; Moss Schl; Holdenville, OK; (2); 3/20; FCA; Scholastic Bowl; Sec Soph Cls; Var Bsktbl; Var Chrldng; Var Sftbl; High Hon Roll; NHS; Prfct Atten Awd; ECU; Psych.

HASHIM, ISMAEL; Bartlesville Mid HS; Bartlesville, OK; (2); Boy Scts; Church Yth Grp; Spanish Clb; Wt Lftg; Petrolum Engr.

HASKELL, JOSEPH; Stigler HS; Stigler, OK; (4); Am Leg Boys St; Church Yth Grp; FCA; JA; SADD; Sec Jr Cls; L Ftbl; Hon Roll; NHS; BSA Lf Mem, Ordr Arrow; Northeastern ST; Med.

HASKETT, SCOTT J; Midwest City HS; Midwest City, OK; (2); 146/473; Boy Scts; Church Yth Grp; German Clb; Hosp Aide; SADD; Band; Mrchg Band; Rep Jr Cls; Var L Socr; Hon Roll; Summer Mission Trips; OSU; EMT/FIREMAN.

HASSAN, SYED; Central HS; Tulsa, OK; (2); High Hon Roll; NHS; Prfct Atten Awd; U Of OK; Med.

HASSELL, SHANNON; Westmoore HS; Oklahoma City, OK; (4); 46/610; Church Yth Grp; FCA; GAA; Letterman Clb; Office Aide; Varsity Clb; Nwsp; Crs Cntry; NHS; Val; All Amer Schlr; Multi-Yr Listee; OK City Univ; Psych.

HASSEN, SOMMER R; Dale Sr HS; Mc Loud, OK; (2); Drama Clb; Spanish Clb; Band; Color Guard; Mrchg Band; Sec Soph Cls; Chrldng; Hon Roll; NHS; OU; Pediatrician.

HAST, TIMOTHY M; Edmond North HS; Edmond, OK; (3); Church Yth Grp; Key Clb; Mu Alpha Theta; Band; Jazz Band; Mrchg Band; L Wrstlng; Distinction In Natl Sci Olympiad; Medieval Clb King; Short Term Mission Peru; U Of Cntrl OK.

HASTINGS, AMANDA B; Union Sr HS; Broken Arrow, OK; (3); 97/741; FCA; Key Clb; Office Aide; Spanish Clb; Teachers Aide; Drill Tm; High Hon Roll; NHS; Spanish NHS; Rnssnc Clb.

HASTINGS, CALEB; Timberlake Schl; Nash, OK; (4); Church Yth Grp; Cmnty Wkr; Drama Clb; Office Aide; Teachers Aide; School Play; Stage Crew; Intrml Socr; Hon Roll; Pres Acad Fit Awd; Escort/Interpretor Bolivian Tchrs U OK Exchng; USAO; Comp Sci.

HASTINGS, DONNY; Watts HS; Colcord, OK; (1); Ofcr VICA; School Play; VP Frsh Cls; Hon Roll; OSU; Law.

HASTINGS, JENNA; Claremore Sr HS; Claremore, OK; (4); 1/231; Rep Church Yth Grp; Cmnty Wkr; Debate Tm; Drama Clb; FCA; Treas French Clb; Treas Math Clb; NFL; Quiz Bowl; Speech Tm; KS U; Thtr Arts.

HASTY, NICOLE; Fairview HS; Fairview, OK; (4); 1/54; Am Leg Aux Girls St; Church Yth Grp; Cmnty Wkr; Sec FCA; VP FHA; Teachers Aide; Band; VP Jr Cls; VP Stu Cncl; Var Capt Bsktbl; Psych.

HATCH, ANGELA L; Durant HS; Durant, OK; (3); Pres Church Yth Grp; Scholastic Bowl; Band; Chorus; Church Choir; Mrchg Band; Variety Show; Hon Roll; Upward Bound; Acad Team; Dist & St His Day Wnnr; BYU; Pol Sci.

HATCHER, CHANCE A; Chattanooga Schl; Chattanooga, OK; (3); Art Clb; Church Yth Grp; Natl FFA Org; Pep Clb; Scholastic Bowl; Spanish Clb; VP Soph Cls; JV Bsbl; JV Bsktbl; Hon Roll; Art Schlsp; Stu Of Month; OSU; Wildlife Mgmt.

HATCHER, JUSTIN B; Mustang HS; Mustang, OK; (2); 139/419; Band; Jazz Band; Mrchg Band; Pep Band; 2 Yrs CODA Band; NW Hnr Bnd; 2 Superior Rtngs Dist Solo/Ensmbl/Superior NW Dist/Ensmbl Rtng 1; OSU; Cmptr Sci/Music.

HATFIELD, BRYAN; Putnam City HS; Warr Acres, OK; (3); 60/370; Church Yth Grp; FCA; JCL; Latin Clb; Spanish Clb; JV Bsbl; Intrml Bsktbl; Var L Ftbl; Intrml Golf; Intrml Tennis; All-City HM Ftbl; MVP Of Wk Ftbl; PC Prep Player Of Wk Ftbl; Med/Dntstry.

HATFIELD, JUSTIN R; Stilwell HS; Stilwell, OK; (2); Church Yth Grp; Drama Clb; Natl Beta Clb; NFL; Spanish Clb; Speech Tm; Thesps; School Play; Hon Roll; OK Chrstn Univ; Brdcstng.

HATFIELD, SHAWN; Mustang HS; Mustang, OK; (3); FCA; Hosp Aide; Letterman Clb; JV Bsktbl; Var Ftbl; JV Golf; Powder Puff Ftbl; Chldrns Hosp Phys Thrp Dept Vol; NHGA; U Of OK; Phys Thrp.

HATFIELD, TIFFANY; Edmond North HS; Edmond, OK; (2); 58/420; Mu Alpha Theta; Orch; Var Golf; Jr NHS; NHS; CPA.

HATHAWAY, MELINDA LEE; Mc Loud HS; Newalla, OK; (1); Church Yth Grp; Drama Clb; Science Clb; SADD; Band; Mrchg Band; School Play; Rep Frsh Cls; Socr; Hon Roll; U Of OK.

HATHCOCK, JUSTIN R; Shawnee Sr HS; Shawnee, OK; (1); Boy Scts; Latin Clb; Math Clb; Scholastic Bowl; Var Bsktbl.

HATHORN, AUDREY; Millwood HS; Oklahoma City, OK; (4); Office Aide; L ROTC; Chorus; Pres Church Choir; Hon Roll; Ntl Merit Ltr; U Of Cntrl OK; Bus Admin.

HATLELI, RAYELLEN D; Moore HS; Moore, OK; (3); Church Yth Grp; Sec Chorus; Church Choir; School Musical; Variety Show; High Hon Roll; NHS; Received Super Ratings At Choir Dist Cont & Made St; Voted Most Outstdng Jr In Choir; Vocal Perfmnc.

HATLEY, ANGIE K; Edmond Memorial HS; Edmond, OK; (4); 21/322; Church Yth Grp; Hist FCA; Key Clb; Spanish Clb; SADD; Chorus; Church Choir; Var Chrldng; NHS; U Of Cntrl OK; Scndry Ed.

HATLEY, DANIEL A; Tecumseh HS; Shawnee, OK; (2); FCA; Bsktbl; Tennis; Cntrl Regional Trials Motorcycle Champion In Amateur Cls; Guitar In Band.

HATMAN, NATASHA N; Roland Sr HS; Roland, OK; (4); GAA; Library Aide; Spanish Clb; Teachers Aide; Yrbk; Bsktbl; Sftbl; Hon Roll; Bryon/Linda Cravens Schlrshp; Westark; Law.

HATRIDGE, TIMOTHY; Kiowa Jr-Sr HS; Wardville, OK; (4); 1/23; Am Leg Boys St; Capt Quiz Bowl; Rptr Swing Chorus; Ed Yrbk; VP Sr Cls; High Hon Roll; NHS; Prfct Atten Awd; Pres Acad Fit Awd; Val; OK ST U.

HATTAWAY, REBECCA; Claremore Sr HS; Claremore, OK; (3); Church Yth Grp; Chorus; Church Choir; School Musical; School Play; High Hon Roll; NHS; Prfct Atten Awd; All Amer Schlr; Educ.

HATTENDORF, ETHAN M; Del City HS; Oklahoma City, OK; (2); Art Clb; French Clb; Library Aide; High Hon Roll; Jr NHS; Del City Chamber Of Commerce Awd; Washington U; Art; Wrtng.

HATTER, CRYSTAL R; Wapanucka Schl; Wapanucka, OK; (3); Church Yth Grp; 4-H; Teachers Aide; Nwsp; Yrbk; Sec Frsh Cls; Rep Soph Cls; Bsktbl; Score Keeper; High Hon Roll; NHS Sec; Murray ST Univ.

HAUCK, JEFFREY A; Westmoore HS; Oklahoma City, OK; (3); German Clb; Office Aide; Scholastic Bowl; Teachers Aide; Intrml Bsbl; Intrml Ftbl; High Hon Roll; Jr NHS; NHS; Water Skng; U Of OK; Med.

HAUGHNEY, JEREMIAH; Lawton Sr HS; Lawton, OK; (4); 113/316; FHA; Natl FFA Org; Hnrs Trigonometry; Love Hockey; Play Roller Hockey; Cameron Univ; Bus Mgmnt.

HAUMPO, ANTHONY M; Geary Jr Sr HS; Greenfield, OK; (3); Art Clb; Boy Scts; Chess Clb; Computer Clb; 4-H; FHA; Natl FFA Org; Yrbk; Ofcr Stu Cncl; Ofcr Bsbl; Robotics.

HAUSER, LEIGH A; Union Intermediate HS; Broken Arrow, OK; (1); FCA; Intnl Clb; Quiz Bowl; Scholastic Bowl; Speech Tm; Ofcr Frsh Cls; High Hon Roll; NHS; Acad Lttr; Span Awd; Eng Awd; Bus Admin.

HAUSERMAN, KRYSTAL M; Union Sr HS; Broken Arrow, OK; (4); 88/649; FCA; French Clb; FHA; Intnl Clb; Drill Tm; French Hon Soc; High Hon Roll; Hon Roll; Jr NHS; NHS; U OK; Med.

HAVENER, TRISHA L; Tushka HS; Atoka, OK; (3); 13/33; Church Yth Grp; FCA; FHA; Teachers Aide; Mgr(s); Score Keeper; High Hon Roll; Hon Roll; FHA Chaplain; OK Bapt Univ; Spcl Ed.

HAVENS, ANDREW D; Muskogee HS; Muskogee, OK; (2); Church Yth Grp; Cmnty Wkr; FCA; SADD; Varsity Clb; JV Bsktbl; JV Ftbl; Var L Socr; Hon Roll; Jr NHS; PT.

HAVENS, TIMOTHY L; Eisenhower Sr HS; Lawton, OK; (3); Band; Mrchg Band; Pep Band; Socr; High Hon Roll; Jr NHS; NHS.

HAWK, AMBER R; Enid Sr HS; Enid, OK; (3); Spanish Clb; Phtg Yrbk; Mgr(s); Score Keeper; Socr; Trk; Jr NHS.

HAWK, CHRYSTAL S; Pond Creek-Hunter Schl; Pond Creek, OK; (3); 5/25; FCA; Letterman Clb; Spanish Clb; School Play; Co-Ed Yrbk; VP Frsh Cls; Sec Jr Cls; Bsktbl; Sftbl; Trk.

HAWKINS, AUSTIN K; Tecumseh HS; Tecumseh, OK; (2); 4-H; Natl FFA Org; 4-H Awd; Calf Roping; 95 Cnty 4-H Horseman Of Yr; 96 Sr 4-H Hall Of Fame; OK ST Univ; Bio.

HAWKINS, BRAD V; Edmond Santa Fe HS; Edmond, OK; (3); 23/280; Church Yth Grp; FCA; Science Clb; SADD; JV Bsktbl; JV Var Ftbl; Var Trk; Cit Awd; Gov Hon Prg Awd; NHS; Outstdng Bio Stu.

HAWKINS, CATRINA L; Memorial HS; Tulsa, OK; (2); Church Yth Grp; Cmnty Wkr; Drama Clb; Girl Scts; Hosp Aide; Spanish Clb; Speech Tm; Band; Church Choir; Mrchg Band; 1st Pl Shakespeare Cmptn Tulsa Spch Arts Fstvl; Hampton U; Pre-Med.

HAWKINS, CHAD W; Del City HS; Del City, OK; (3); 33/486; Pres Church Yth Grp; Pres FCA; JA; Spanish Clb; Varsity Clb; JV Var Bsbl; JV Var Ftbl; Hon Roll; NHS; Prfct Atten Awd; OK Bapt Univ; PT.

HAWKINS III, CHESTER; Midwest City HS; Midwest City, OK; (3); 1/390; Church Yth Grp; German Clb; SADD; Church Choir; Swing Chorus; Variety Show; Ofcr Soph Cls; Ofcr Jr Cls; Cit Awd; NHS; U Of OK.

HAWKINS, ERIN C; Weatherford HS; Weatherford, OK; (4); 11/138; Church Yth Grp; FHA; Teachers Aide; Chorus; Stage Crew; High Hon Roll; NHS; Pres Schlr; Hstry Clb; Southwestern OK ST U.

HAWKINS, JASON; Apache HS; Apache, OK; (3); 5/34; Drama Clb; Scholastic Bowl; School Play; Stage Crew; Cit Awd; Hon Roll; NHS; SW Smmr Math Sci Acad; Ldshp Trning; OK Chrstn Univ.

HAWKINS, KOURTNEY R; Millwood HS; Oklahoma City, OK; (4); Church Yth Grp; Dance Clb; Hosp Aide; ROTC; Chorus; Church Choir; Drill Tm; Hon Roll; Lincoln Essay Cntst Wnr; Blck Hist Cntst Wnr; Rose ST Coll; Brdcstng.

HAWKINS, LEAHA D; Ringling HS; Ringling, OK; (2); 4/38; Church Yth Grp; Band; Flag Corp; Mrchg Band; JV Var Bsktbl; JV Var Chrldng; Hon Roll; FHA; GAA; JV Var Powder Puff Ftbl; Eng II Awd/Bio/Art Awds.

HAWKINS, STEPHANIE J; Broken Arrow Sr HS; Broken Arrow, OK; (3); Library Aide; Office Aide; Red Cross Aide; Hon Roll; Hlth Occup Stdnts Of Amer; Natl Voc Tech Hnr Soc; Vo-Tech Class Treas; U Of OK; PT.

HAWLEY, PATRICK H; Waynoka HS; Waynoka, OK; (2); Church Yth Grp; FCA; FHA; Sec Natl FFA Org; Pep Clb; SADD; Ofcr Soph Cls; Ofcr Bsbl; Ftbl; Trk; Ranch Rodeo; 3rd Pl Wt Class 198 Lbs OK Ftbl Coaches Assn Rgnl Wtlftg Meet 96; Ranch/Farm Mgmnt.

HAWORTH, BRANDY L; Seminole Jr Sr HS; Seminole, OK; (3); FCA; GAA; Math Clb; Spanish Clb; Chorus; Var Crs Cntry; Var Trk; Hon Roll; Tchr; Coach.

HAWORTH, JON M; Enid Sr HS; Enid, OK; (3); Boy Scts; Church Yth Grp; ROTC; Band; Drm Mjr(t); Mrchg Band; Pep Band; JV Crs Cntry; JV Var Socr; NHS; AIRFORCE/MUSIC Ed.

HAWS, SUZANNE; Miami Sr HS; Miami, OK; (4); 1/121; Boy Scts; Cmnty Wkr; Debate Tm; Drama Clb; Girl Scts; NFL; Quiz Bowl; Speech Tm; Teachers Aide; Hon Roll; Mock Trial; BABES; Frnch/Engl.

HAWTHORN, CHRISTOPHER R; Cushing HS; Cushing, OK; (2); #1 in class; Church Yth Grp; 4-H; Sec Natl FFA Org; Quiz Bowl; Cit Awd; High Hon Roll; Hon Roll; NHS; Natl Chmpn Mktg Natl Polled Hereford Show; OK ST U; Embryology.

HAWTHORNE, NATALIE; Choctaw Jr HS; Choctaw, OK; (1); Church Yth Grp; VP FCA; VP Stu Cncl; Bsktbl; Sftbl; High Hon Roll; Jr NHS; OSU; Mrktng.

HAWTHORNE, WILLIAM K; Altus Sr HS; Altus, OK; (2); FCA; Natl FFA Org; Var Bsbl; JV Bsktbl; Var Crs Cntry; Hon Roll; Tchr; Coach.

HAWZIPTA, ELI; Pawhuska HS; Pawhuska, OK; (4); 1/87; Am Leg Boys St; FBLA; Key Clb; Quiz Bowl; Band; Jazz Band; Tennis; High Hon Roll; NHS; Val; OU; Elec Engr.

HAY, ADAM W; Guthrie Sr HS; Guthrie, OK; (1); Church Yth Grp; Band; Mrchg Band; Pep Band; Tennis; High Hon Roll.

HAY, ALYSSA; Guthrie Sr HS; Guthrie, OK; (3); 11/220; Church Yth Grp; FCA; Math Clb; Mu Alpha Theta; Band; Flag Corp; Ofcr Stu Cncl; Hon Roll; Jr NHS; NHS; Psychlgy.

HAYES, AMANDA; Yukon HS; Yukon, OK; (1); Church Yth Grp; Crs Cntry; Trk; Hon Roll; Jr NHS; AZ ST U; Orthdntst.

HAYES, AMANDA; Trinity Christian Schl; Broken Arrow, OK; (1); Church Yth Grp; Var Bsktbl; Hon Roll.

HAYES, AMBER; Indianola HS; Mcalester, OK; (3); Church Yth Grp; 4-H; FBLA; FHA; Natl Beta Clb; Natl FFA Org; Church Choir; Computer Clb; High Hon Roll; Carl Albert; Phys Thrpy.

HAYES, AMY; Tahlequah Sr HS; Tahlequah, OK; (4); 9/247; Church Yth Grp; German Clb; Service Clb; Chorus; Rep Stu Cncl; Hon Roll; Sec NHS; Pres Acad Fit Awd; Piano; Peer Tutor; Mntrshp; Northeastern ST U; Phys Thrpy.

HAYES, ANGELINA C; Wagoner Sr HS; Wagoner, OK; (3); Band; Mrchg Band; Pep Band; Hon Roll; Wgnr HS Most Imprvd Mrchr 94-95; FL ST; Zlgst.

HAYES, ANGELIQUE J; Claremore Sr HS; Claremore, OK; (1); Drama Clb; French Clb; Band; Chorus; Mrchg Band; School Musical; Variety Show; Harding; Law.

HAYES, CASSANDRA; Depew HS; Depew, OK; (4); 4/35; Natl FFA Org; Spanish Clb; Sec Soph Cls; VP Jr Cls; Ofcr Bsbl; Cit Awd; High Hon Roll; Prfct Atten Awd; Span Club Pres; All Conf/All Reg Bsktbl; Outstdng FFA Sr; Murray ST; PE/BUS.

HAYES, JENNIFER; Depew HS; Depew, OK; (1); Church Yth Grp; Natl FFA Org; Quiz Bowl; Spanish Clb; Band; Pep Band; Bsktbl; Cit Awd; 4-H Awd; Hon Roll.

HAYES, JEREMY L; Westmoore HS; Oklahoma City, OK; (3); Church Yth Grp; FCA; Library Aide; Spanish Clb; SADD; OK Univ; Law Enforcement.

HAYES, JILL N; Frederick HS; Frederick, OK; (4); 14/71; FCA; FHA; Office Aide; Spanish Clb; Varsity Clb; Chorus; School Musical; Yrbk; High Hon Roll; Hon Roll; OK Hnr Soc; Southwestern OK ST U; Pharmcy.

HAYES, MARK C; Wagoner Sr HS; Wagoner, OK; (3); Am Leg Boys St; Church Yth Grp; Office Aide; Teachers Aide; Hon Roll; Prfct Atten Awd; OK Hwy Patrol Cadet Lawman Acad; Boxing Club; St Archery Champion; NE OK ST U.

HAYES, MARTHA M; Wakita Schl; Wakita, OK; (2); 2/12; Drama Clb; FCA; FHA; Natl FFA Org; Band; Chorus; Jazz Band; Mrchg Band; Pep Band; School Play; Kayette Frosh Rep; Music Ed.

HAYES, MATTHEW; Sapulpa Sr HS; Tulsa, OK; (3); Boy Scts; Church Yth Grp; FBLA; Church Choir; School Play; Co-Ed Yrbk; Hon Roll; Pres Acad Fit Awd; Nrsng Home Ministry; Talent Show; OBU; Bi Voc Pastor.

HAYES, MATTHEW G; Muskogee HS; Muskogee, OK; (2); CAP; ROTC; Drill Tm; Ofcr Frsh Cls; Ofcr Soph Cls; ROTC Natl Spec Hnrs & Awds; Air Force.

HAYES, PRICE L; Star Spencer HS; Midwest City, OK; (1); Var Bsbl; Var Ftbl; JV Trk; Ftbl Offensive Player Of Yr.

HAYES, SARA J; Bartlesville Mid HS; Bartlesville, OK; (2); 178/681; FBLA; FHA; JV Chrldng; Hon Roll; Natl Yth Rodeo Assoc; OK ST Univ; Engr.

HAYES, TERESA; Kingston HS; Kingston, OK; (3); 6/65; Church Yth Grp; HOBY; Band; Yrbk; Pres Soph Cls; Pres Jr Cls; VP Stu Cncl; Var Sftbl; High Hon Roll; NHS; Freed-Hardman; Pltcs.

HAYES, WILLIE O; Elk City HS; Elk City, OK; (4); 20/130; Boy Scts; Church Yth Grp; Band; Mrchg Band; High Hon Roll; NHS; Pres Acad Fit Awd; Eagle Scout; OK ST Univ; Mech Engrng.

HAYMAKER, GRETCHEN N; Enid Sr HS; Enid, OK; (2); Drama Clb; French Clb; Q&S; Orch; School Musical; School Play; Swing Chorus; Ed Nwsp; High Hon Roll; Hon Roll; Enid Phillips Symphony; Vet Med.

HAYMAKER, SARAH E; Enid Sr HS; Enid, OK; (4); 18/400; Teachers Aide; Orch; School Musical; High Hon Roll; Hon Roll; Jr NHS; NHS; Pres Schlr; All St Orch; Enid Phillips Symph Orch; St Rgnts Wnnr; OK St Univ; Agronomy.

HAYNES, ALEX A; Hartshorne Sr HS; Hartshorne, OK; (2); FCA; Bsktbl; High Hon Roll; Hon Roll; NHS.

HAYNES, EMILY B; Kiowa Jr-Sr HS; Kiowa, OK; (2); Church Yth Grp; 4-H; HOBY; Natl FFA Org; School Play; Phtg Yrbk; Rep Stu Cncl; Var Capt Bsktbl; 4-H Awd; High Hon Roll; OSU; Optometry.

HAYNES, MELISSA; Heavener HS; Heavener, OK; (3); Church Yth Grp; FBLA; HOBY; Quiz Bowl; Spanish Clb; Band; Rep Jr Cls; Chrldng; Hon Roll; NHS; OK U; Sci.

HAYNES, MITCHEL; Woodward HS; Woodward, OK; (3); Church Yth Grp; Letterman Clb; Pep Clb; Yrbk; Ofcr Bsbl; Ftbl; Hon Roll; Natl Chmpn Amer Legion Bsbl; ST Chmpn 5a Ftbl 94.

HAYNES, SHANDA; Lone Wolf Schl; Lone Wolf, OK; (4); 10/22; Am Leg Aux Girls St; Church Yth Grp; FHA; German Clb; Natl FFA Org; Office Aide; Pep Clb; Speech Tm; School Play; Yrbk; I Dare You Ldrshp Awd; NEO A&M; Arch Drftng.

HAYNES, SUMMER D; Union Intermediate HS; Tulsa, OK; (2); 75/1000; Church Yth Grp; FCA; Office Aide; Spanish Clb; Cit Awd; Hon Roll; NHS; Pres Schlr; Level 10 Gymnast Pvt Clb; Phys Therapy.

HAYNES, TIMNA K; Clayton Jr Sr HS; Tuskahoma, OK; (2); FBLA; Scholastic Bowl; Band; Mrchg Band; Co-Ed Nwsp; Hon Roll; Pres Acad Fit Awd; OK HS Hnr Soc; Bible Tchr/Acctnt.

HAYNIE, KATHERINE E; Memorial HS; Tulsa, OK; (2); ROTC; Band; Church Choir; Drill Tm; Mrchg Band; Hon Roll; OK Amer Coed Pgnt 1st Rnr Up Tlng 96; ST Fnnlst Top Ten; Pdtrcn.

HAYS, CRYSTAL; Kellyville Sr HS; Kellyville, OK; (2); 4-H; Science Clb; VP Frsh Cls; Var L Bsktbl; Var L Chrldng; Var L Golf; Var L Sftbl; Serteen Clb Vol; Stu Cncl; LPC; OK ST Univ; Pediatric Nrs.

HAYS, DUSTIN T; Charles Page HS; Sand Springs, OK; (1); Church Yth Grp; FCA; Ftbl; High Hon Roll; U Of OK; Med/Prof Crdlgsts.

HAYS, HEATHER; Okeene Jr Sr HS; Okeene, OK; (3); 7/28; Sec Church Yth Grp; FCA; Sec FHA; GAA; Letterman Clb; Pep Clb; Scholastic Bowl; Nwsp; Sec Frsh Cls; Sec Soph Cls; 1st Pl & Hnrb Mntn Sci Fair; St Hnr Soc; Sec & VP FHA; Pronm Srvr 95-96; Southwestern U; Law.

HAYS, KELLI; Jenks HS; Tulsa, OK; (3); Church Yth Grp; Cmnty Wkr; Key Clb; Mu Alpha Theta; NFL; Pep Clb; Teachers Aide; High Hon Roll; Hon Roll; NHS; Intnl Travel; Missionary Wrk; Med.

HAYS, SHANNA J; Dewey HS; Dewey, OK; (3); #9 in class; Church Yth Grp; FCA; Spanish Clb; Band; Color Guard; Var JV Bsktbl; Hon Roll; NHS; OK U; Coaching/HS Tchng.

HAYTER, JANA J; Pioneer Jr Sr HS; Enid, OK; (3); Church Yth Grp; Pep Clb; Band; Color Guard; Mrchg Band; Pep Band; School Play; Var Sftbl; Hon Roll; Univ Of San Diego; Marine Bio.

HAYTON, JAMIE; Billings HS; Billings, OK; (3); Rptr FCA; Rptr Natl FFA Org; School Play; VP Frsh Cls; Ofcr Soph Cls; VP Jr Cls; Var Bsktbl; Sftbl; Hon Roll; Bsktbl Ofnsv Plyr Of Yr 95-; All Conf Tm 3 Yrs; OK ST Univ; Psych.

HAYWARD, KELLI; Shawnee Sr HS; Shawnee, OK; (3); Dance Clb; FCA; Library Aide; Office Aide; Spanish Clb; SADD; Nwsp; Rep Jr Cls; Rep Stu Cncl; Bsktbl; Dance; U Of OK.

HAYWARD, KRISTIN R; Bixby Sr HS; Broken Arrow, OK; (3); Church Yth Grp; FCA; French Clb; VP Pres Girl Scts; Library Aide; SADD; Teachers Aide; JV Socr; Grl Sct Gld Awd; Sci Tchr.

HAYWARD, PATRICK H; South Intermediate HS; Broken Arrow, OK; (2); Cmnty Wkr; Capt Scholastic Bowl; Orch; Var Bsktbl; Hon Roll; NHS; All Dist Orch; Acad Team Awd; De Pauw.

HAYWOOD, CHRISTOPHER; Douglass HS; Oklahoma City, OK; (3); ROTC; Chorus; Bsktbl; Ftbl; Wrstlng; Hon Roll; NHS.

HAYWOOD, JAMES C; Muldrow HS; Sallisaw, OK; (3); Church Yth Grp; Spanish Clb; Church Choir; JV Bsbl; Var L Bsktbl; Hon Roll; Pres UM Yth Flwshp; FFA.

HAZLETT, TAMMY; Liberty Acad; Shawnee, OK; (1); Hon Roll; Natl Arbr Day Fndtn; Natl Adbn Soc; Intl Wldlf Cltn Whl Adptn Proj; Prof Photo.

HAZLIP, ROBBIE M; Ripley HS; Yale, OK; (1); Natl FFA Org; JV Bsktbl; Diesel Mechanic.

HEAD, BRADLEY J; Mc Loud HS; Jones, OK; (2); Church Yth Grp; Mgr Bsktbl; Socr; Hon Roll; NHS; Prfct Atten Awd; OK ST Univ; Aerospace Engrng.

HEAD, JENNIFER; Braman Schl; Braman, OK; (2); 2/15; Church Yth Grp; FCA; GAA; Natl FFA Org; Quiz Bowl; Speech Tm; School Play; Var Bsktbl; Var Chrldng; Gym.

HEAD, KASIE L; Braman Schl; Braman, OK; (1); Church Yth Grp; Drama Clb; FCA; FHA; Quiz Bowl; Red Cross Aide; Speech Tm; Chorus; Variety Show; VP Frsh Cls; VP FCA; Grd Schl Tchr.

HEAD, MANDY L; Bixby Sr HS; Broken Arrow, OK; (4); German Clb; VICA; Variety Show; Sftbl; Hon Roll; Jr NHS; Prfct Atten Awd; Natl Voc Tech Hnr Soc; Cosmetology Stu Of Yr; Voc Ind Clubs Amer All ST; Tulsa Jr Coll.

HEAD, NEAL; Braman Schl; Braman, OK; (4); 5/12; FCA; Natl FFA Org; Quiz Bowl; Scholastic Bowl; School Play; Sec Jr Cls; Ofcr Bsbl; Bsktbl; NHS; Prfct Atten Awd; Prfct Atten 6 Yrs; OK ST U; Ag Econ.

HEAD, ZACHARY S; Mustang HS; Tyler, TX; (3); 176/493; Boy Scts; Var Ftbl; Var Trk; Hon Roll.

HEADLY, MELISSA M; South Intermediate HS; Broken Arrow, OK; (2); Church Yth Grp; Drama Clb; Library Aide; Speech Tm; Acpl Chr; Church Choir; School Musical; School Play; Mgr(s); Wt Lftg; Perfmd Theater Tulsa & Amer Theater Prdctns; Dancing, Acting, Singing Cls; Julliard Schl; Musical Theater.

HEADRICK, DUSTIN; Liberty HS; Mounds, OK; (3); Church Yth Grp; Cmnty Wkr; FCA; Rptr Nwsp; Ofcr Frsh Cls; Bsktbl; Socr; Hon Roll; Olympic Dev Prgm Sccr; Pre-Med.

HEADY, DARREN D; Oklahoma Union Schl; S Coffeyville, OK; (4); Natl FFA Org; Nwsp; Var Bsbl; Var Bsktbl; Var Wt Lftg; Hon Roll; Prfct Atten Awd; Outstndg Ofnsv Bsbl Plyr; Coffeyville CC; Athltc Trng.

HEALD, KEITH D; Harrah HS; Harrah, OK; (3); 32/169; Wt Lftg; Hon Roll; Rose ST Coll; Phy Therapy.

HEALY, PATRICIA; Enid Sr HS; Enid, OK; (4); 4/405; Am Leg Aux Girls St; Church Yth Grp; Dance Clb; Math Clb; Pep Clb; Band; Chorus; Church Choir; Rptr Nwsp; High Hon Roll; Snow Skiing; Yth Ldrshp Team; OU; Med.

HEANEY, ERIN R; Western Heights Sr HS; Oklahoma City, OK; (1); 1/215; Church Yth Grp; Chorus; Swing Chorus; Sec Frsh Cls; Socr; Jr NHS.

HEANEY, KARA K; Western Heights Sr HS; Oklahoma City, OK; (3); Am Leg Aux Girls St; Church Yth Grp; Cmnty Wkr; FCA; Key Clb; Chorus; School Musical; Swing Chorus; Sec Frsh Cls; VP Stu Cncl; OMEA All-St Choir; Commnctns.

HEARD, AMY; White Oak Jr-Sr HS; Vinita, OK; (1); 2/17; Church Yth Grp; Science Clb; Pres Frsh Cls; Ofcr Stu Cncl; Bsktbl; Sftbl; Trk; Cit Awd; High Hon Roll; Hon Roll; NE ST U; Tchr.

HEARD, TYLER M; Putnam City HS; Oklahoma City, OK; (1); Arch Dsgn.

HEARON, AUDRA; Dibble Jr Sr HS; Blanchard, OK; (1); Computer Clb; FCA; GAA; Natl FFA Org; Pep Clb; Chorus; School Musical; JV Bsktbl; JV Chrldng; Cit Awd.

HEASLET JR, JIMMY C; Crowder Schl; Mcalester, OK; (4); 1/40; Church Yth Grp; FBLA; Teachers Aide; Ed Nwsp; Ed Yrbk; Pres Soph Cls; Pres Jr Cls; Pres Sr Cls; Treas Stu Cncl; Hon Roll; TSA Pres; Upward Bnd; Native Amer Stu Assn; E Central U; Jrnlsm.

HEATH, ALLISON D; Duncan HS; Duncan, OK; (2); Church Yth Grp; Office Aide; Chorus; Var Chrldng; Hon Roll; NHS; Power Tumbling & Trampoline 2 Time Natl Jr Elite Champion.

HEATH, BRANDON D; Blackwell HS; Blackwell, OK; (2); Church Yth Grp; JV Bsktbl; Hon Roll; OK ST U; Game Ranger.

HEATH, HEATHER; Wetumka Jr Sr HS; Wetumka, OK; (2); Church Yth Grp; GAA; Band; Mrchg Band; Bsktbl; Chrldng; Trk; High Hon Roll; Hon Roll; Tulsa Univ; Lawyer.

HEATH, KAYCE; Canton HS; Canton, OK; (2); 3/40; Church Yth Grp; 4-H; FHA; Natl FFA Org; SADD; Rptr Soph Cls; High Hon Roll; NHS; L Bsktbl; L Trk; Natl Hstry Day Awd; Hstry Joseph Thoburn Awd; Acad Team.

HEATH, KOREY M; Webster HS; Tulsa, OK; (3); Church Yth Grp; Cmnty Wkr; FHA; Var Ftbl; Var Wrstlng; Cit Awd; Hon Roll; Outstndg Off Lnmn Ldrshp Awd Ftbl 95; 4 Yr Lttrmn Ftbl & Wrstlng; Ottawa U KS.

HEATH, ROBERT; Hennessey HS; Hennessey, OK; (4); 4/54; Chess Clb; Church Yth Grp; FCA; Teachers Aide; Ftbl; Trk; Vllybl; Wt Lftg; Hon Roll; NHS; OK Hnr Soc; Gftd/Tlntd Achvt Pgm; Karate; OK U; Comp Sci.

HEATH, SHELLY D; Byng Sr HS; Ada, OK; (3); 6/70; Church Yth Grp; FCA; FBLA; Office Aide; Scholastic Bowl; Spanish Clb; Teachers Aide; Church Choir; Yrbk; Rep Stu Cncl; OK Natl Hnr Scty; E Centr Univ; Ed.

HEATHERINGTON, CHARLES T; Sapulpa Sr HS; Sapulpa, OK; (2); 14/360; Letterman Clb; Math Clb; Quiz Bowl; Scholastic Bowl; Science Clb; Spanish Clb; Band; Jazz Band; Mrchg Band; Gov Hon Prg Awd; Rick; Physics/Math.

HEATHERMAN, TERRY; Cascia Hall Prep School; Tulsa, OK; (4); School Musical; Pres Stu Cncl; Var L Bsktbl; Var L Ftbl; Var L Trk; Cit Awd; Hon Roll; NHS; Cmnty Wkr; Drama Clb; Gold Medal For Ath; Cascia Medal Awded To Outstndg Overall Sr; US Naval Acad.

HEATON, AMY; Leflore Sr HS; Wister, OK; (4); 3/25; Speech Tm; School Play; Yrbk; Pres Frsh Cls; Pres Soph Cls; Pres Jr Cls; Pres Sr Cls; Rep Stu Cncl; Var Bsktbl; Var Sftbl; EOSC; Nrsng.

HEATRICE, ALEX; Midwest City HS; Oklahoma City, OK; (3); 103/500; Church Yth Grp; Cmnty Wkr; Drama Clb; FCA; Quiz Bowl; Spanish Clb; Varsity Clb; School Play; Ofcr Stu Cncl; Bsktbl; U Of OK; Med.

HEAVIN, ANDREA R; Verden HS; Verden, OK; (1); Church Yth Grp; 4-H; Scholastic Bowl; Science Clb; VP Frsh Cls; Var Bsktbl; Var Sftbl; 4-H Awd; High Hon Roll; Pres Acad Fit Awd; All Conf Bsktbl Team.

HEAVIN, MICAH L; Ninnekah HS; Ninnekah, OK; (2); Church Yth Grp; FCA; GAA; Letterman Clb; Model UN; Spanish Clb; Yrbk; Bsktbl; Crs Cntry; Sftbl; Stu Cncl Rptr; U Of Sci & Arts OK; Psych.

HEBERT, JENNIFER J; Del City HS; Del City, OK; (2); Church Yth Grp; Debate Tm; Drama Clb; Spanish Clb; School Play; Stage Crew; NHS; Mock Trial Comptn; Church Altar Server; U Of OK; Legal Prof.

HECK, BRADLEY B; Tecumseh HS; Tecumseh, OK; (4); FCA; French Clb; Natl FFA Org; Office Aide; Ftbl; High Hon Roll; Hon Roll; FFA St Farmers Degree, Beef Prodctn Awd; Amer & OK Angus Assn; Dir SE Dist Jr Angus Assn; OK ST Univ; Animal Sci.

HECK, MANDY; Sperry Brooks HS; Sperry, OK; (3); 14/87; FHA; Spanish Clb; VP Frsh Cls; VP Jr Cls; VP Sr Cls; Pres Stu Cncl; Var Chrldng; Trk; Hon Roll; Geogrphy Awd; Psych.

HECKERT, DIANNA; Lawton Sr HS; Lawton, OK; (2); Church Yth Grp; FHA; Pep Clb; Hon Roll; Prfct Atten Awd; Upward Bound; Med.

HECTOR, STEPHANIE J; Wilson HS; Lone Grove, OK; (3); 11/35; Church Yth Grp; 4-H; Natl Beta Clb; Office Aide; Spanish Clb; Teachers Aide; Band; Chorus; Ofcr Stu Cncl; Bsktbl; OK ST Univ; PT.

HEDDEN, AUDRA R; Stillwater Sr HS; Cushing, OK; (4); 149/350; Key Clb; Service Clb; Spanish Clb; Rptr Nwsp; Rep Frsh Cls; Rep Stu Cncl; Cit Awd; High Hon Roll; Hon Roll; NHS; ERASE; STEP; OK ST Univ; Intl Bus.

HEDRICK, CLINT M; Owasso Sr HS; Owasso, OK; (2); Church Yth Grp; FCA; JV Bsbl; JV Bsktbl; High Hon Roll; Hon Roll.

HEDRICK, JENNIFER M; Putnam City West HS; Bethany, OK; (4); Church Yth Grp; Cmnty Wkr; Office Aide; Teachers Aide; Band; Church Choir; Mrchg Band; School Musical; Gym; England TASIS 9-11th Grd; Chmbr Ensmbl Flute Asst Dir; Rcpnt Exec Music Awd Jr Yr; Southern Nazarene Univ; Music.

HEENEY, KRISTEN; Miami Sr HS; Miami, OK; (2); #1 in class; Church Yth Grp; Red Cross Aide; Chorus; Church Choir; Var Chrldng; Mgr(s); Hon Roll; Jr NHS; NHS; Pre-Med.

HEFLIN, AARON; Davis HS; Springer, OK; (2); Church Yth Grp; Scholastic Bowl; Band; Chorus; Church Choir; Jazz Band; Mrchg Band; Pres Soph Cls; Hon Roll; NHS.

HEFNER, AMBER RENEE; Westmoore HS; Oklahoma City, OK; (4); 36/600; Church Yth Grp; German Clb; Scholastic Bowl; Yrbk; Bsktbl; Gov Hon Prg Awd; High Hon Roll; Jr NHS; Val; Jr Escort; OSU.

HEFNER, STEPHANIE; Eufaula Sr HS; Checotah, OK; (3); #2 in class; Math Clb; Science Clb; Band; Mrchg Band; Ofcr Stu Cncl; High Hon Roll; NHS; Pres Acad Fit Awd; Pres Schlr.

HEFNER, TODD D; Westmoore HS; Oklahoma City, OK; (1); Church Yth Grp; Drama Clb; Office Aide; Bsktbl; Golf.

HEGER, RAQUEL; Hydro Jr Sr HS; Hydro, OK; (4); 9/21; Am Leg Aux Girls St; FCA; FHA; GAA; Office Aide; Teachers Aide; Yrbk; Var JV Bsktbl; Score Keeper; Wt Lftg; Southwestern U; Finance.

HEGLAND, ANDREA; Idabel HS; Idabel, OK; (1); Church Yth Grp; Chorus; Color Guard; Var Chrldng; Var Trk; Hon Roll; Vet.

HEGLIN, SCHEHERA; Laverne Jr Sr HS; Gate, OK; (2); Natl Beta Clb; Band; School Musical; Rep Frsh Cls; Ofcr Soph Cls; Rep Stu Cncl; Var Bsktbl; Chrldng; Sftbl; Trk.

HEILAMAN, AARON; Hinton HS; Hinton, OK; (4); 5/30; Church Yth Grp; FCA; SADD; Chorus; Pres Jr Cls; Pres Sr Cls; VP Stu Cncl; Capt Bsktbl; Capt Ftbl; High Hon Roll; Sthwstrn OK U; Engrng.

HEILAMAN, SHANTEL L; Mc Loud HS; Mc Loud, OK; (2); 1/150; Co-Ed Yrbk; Mgr(s); Stat Socr; OK Univ; Sys Anlyst.

HEILIGER, MARK P; Stillwater Sr HS; Stillwater, OK; (2); Church Yth Grp; Cmnty Wkr; Quiz Bowl; Orch; School Play; JV Bsbl; JV Ftbl; JV Wrstlng; Hon Roll; Elec Engrng.

HEIM, NATALIE; Yukon Middle HS; Yukon, OK; (2); Church Yth Grp; Ed Yrbk; Chrldng; Hon Roll; U Of CO; Sprts Med.

HEIMDALE, BRANDON T; Nathan Hale HS; Tulsa, OK; (1); Key Clb; Spanish Clb; JV Socr; High Hon Roll; Hon Roll; Pres Acad Fit Awd; OK ST U; Anstslgst.

HEIMDALE, ELIZABETH M; North Intemediate HS; Broken Arrow, OK; (1); French Clb; Math Clb; Science Clb; Chorus; Hon Roll; Natl Sci Found Eng Smmr Cmp; Eng.

HEINRICH, VICKI R; El Reno Sr HS; El Reno, OK; (3); 11/167; FCA; Pres Soph Cls; Pres Jr Cls; Sec Sr Cls; Var Mgr(s); Var Vllybl; NHS; Math & Sci Clb; Med.

HEITGRASS JR, MARK E; Jenks Road Christian Acad; Broken Arrow, OK; (4); #1 in class; Church Yth Grp; FCA; Teachers Aide; Yrbk; Lit Mag; Pres Soph Cls; Pres Jr Cls; Pres Sr Cls; Bsktbl; Wrstlng; OSU Okmulgee; Atmtv Svc.

HEITZKE, LEAH M; Edmond Memorial HS; Edmond, OK; (3); French Clb; Band; Color Guard; Mrchg Band; Hon Roll; NHS; Ntl Merit Ltr; Movie Dir.

HEIZER, JEREMIAH P; Enid Sr HS; Enid, OK; (3); Boy Scts; Church Yth Grp; Cmnty Wkr; FCA; Science Clb; Varsity Clb; Band; Bsktbl; Ftbl; Trk; OK ST Univ; Outdoor Ed; Firemn.

HELD, LAUREN N; Edmond Memorial HS; Edmond, OK; (3); 1/371; Cmnty Wkr; Sec FCA; French Clb; German Clb; Ofcr Stu Cncl; JV Var Pom Pon; NHS; St Schlr; Pol Sci Law.

HELFENBEIN, BRIAN K; Mc Alester HS; Mcalester, OK; (4); 51/209; Boy Scts; Natl FFA Org; Office Aide; Rep Stu Cncl; JV Var Ftbl; Var Wrstlng; Hon Roll; NE ST U; Optometry.

HELLER, BRANDAN K; Durant HS; Durant, OK; (3); Church Yth Grp; FCA; Rep Soph Cls; JV Ftbl; Var L Wrstlng; Hon Roll; RN; Phy Asst.

HELLER, CHASITY M; Noble HS; Norman, OK; (3); GAA; Pep Clb; SADD; Teachers Aide; Acpl Chr; Chorus; Church Choir; Swing Chorus; Mgr Crs Cntry; Var Trk; South Eastern; Trk Coach; His.

HELLER, JO ANN; Bishop Kelley HS; Sapulpa, OK; (2); Cmnty Wkr; Spanish Clb; SADD; Capt L Golf; Cit Awd; High Hon Roll; Duke Univ TID; Masonic Awrd Wnr; Natl Jr Cmptv Golf.

HELLER, JOHN E; Union Sr HS; Tulsa, OK; (4); 40/669; Church Yth Grp; FCA; Scholastic Bowl; High Hon Roll; Hon Roll; NHS; Geom, Typng I, Gen Bus, Bus Law, Wrld Hstry & Keybrdng Clss Awds; St Cmptn 3rd Pl Geom; U Of KS; Dentstry.

HELLINGER, KIM J; Wagoner Sr HS; Wagoner, OK; (3); Church Yth Grp; Cmnty Wkr; FBLA; Teachers Aide; Treas Frsh Cls; JV Bsktbl; Var Socr; Var Sftbl; Hon Roll; FBLA Rptr, Pres; Comp Trng; Acctng.

HELLMAN, TERRY; Harrah HS; Harrah, OK; (4); 10/130; Am Leg Boys St; Church Yth Grp; FCA; Rep Stu Cncl; Var Capt Ftbl; Wt Lftg; High Hon Roll; Pres NHS; Schlrs Club; OK Hnr Soc; Tulsa U; Engrng.

HELM, AMBER N; South Intermediate HS; Broken Arrow, OK; (1); Band; High Hon Roll; Hon Roll; OU; Dermatology.

HELM, GINA; Norman Sr HS; Norman, OK; (4); 121/677; Church Yth Grp; Cmnty Wkr; Dance Clb; JCL; Mu Alpha Theta; Service Clb; Church Choir; Ofcr Stu Cncl; High Hon Roll; NHS; Channel 29 Production Crew; BASIC Ldrshp Wkshp; Missionary Brazil & Mexico; OK ST U; Speech Pthlgy.

HELMBRIGHT, APRIL E; Putnam City North HS; Oklahoma City, OK; (2); Church Yth Grp; Girl Scts; Key Clb; Red Cross Aide; Science Clb; Acpl Chr; School Musical; Variety Show; Chorus; Hon Roll; Grl Scts Cdt Ldrshp Awd; Cdt Chlng; Drms Rlty; Slvr Awd; Rsn Club; Comm Theatre; Mdlng; Singing; Dncng; Singer/Bio Sci/Prmtlgy.

HELMER, SARA; Pawhuska HS; Pawhuska, OK; (2); 5/82; HOBY; Treas Key Clb; Band; Chorus; Church Choir; Mrchg Band; Pres Soph Cls; Treas Stu Cncl; Hon Roll; NHS; SMU; Psych.

HELMS, LISA; Plainview HS; Ardmore, OK; (3); 1/100; Am Leg Aux Girls St; Church Yth Grp; Cmnty Wkr; FCA; Math Clb; Mu Alpha Theta; Natl Beta Clb; Science Clb; SADD; Church Choir; OK Girls ST; Pre-Med.

HELORY, MIRANDA K; Stigler HS; Stigler, OK; (3); Am Leg Aux Girls St; Church Yth Grp; FCA; SADD; Nwsp; Treas Frsh Cls; Rep Soph Cls; Treas Jr Cls; Pres Stu Cncl; Bsktbl.

HELSLEY, CHERYL; Porter Jr Sr HS; Porter, OK; (3); Church Yth Grp; FCA; Letterman Clb; SADD; Church Choir; Yrbk; Pres Frsh Cls; Pres Soph Cls; Sec Stu Cncl; Var Bsktbl; Northeastern ST U.

HELT, JENNIFER; Wilburton Sr HS; Wilburton, OK; (2); FCA; Letterman Clb; Teachers Aide; Bsktbl; Chrldng; Sftbl; Hon Roll; Upward Bound Math/Sci; Nvl Acad; Nvy Pilot.

HELTON, SHANNON; Lawton Sr HS; Fort Sill, OK; (2); Church Yth Grp; Cmnty Wkr; FCA; French Clb; HOBY; Key Clb; Band; Church Choir; Pep Band; Treas Frsh Cls; Masons Stu Of Today Awd; Acad Ltr; Bldrs Clb; Baylor; Bus.

HELVY, KRISSY; Seminole Jr Sr HS; Seminole, OK; (1); Church Yth Grp; FCA; Math Clb; SADD; Chorus; Sec Frsh Cls; Var Pom Pon; Var Tennis; High Hon Roll.

HEMBREE, BRYAN C; Charles Page HS; Sand Springs, OK; (2); 27/385; Church Yth Grp; Cmnty Wkr; Debate Tm; FCA; Key Clb; Math Tm; NFL; Spanish Clb; Speech Tm; Lit Mag; 2 Yr Debate Lttrmn; 4 Yr Coll; Ec/Fin/Comm.

HEMBREE, JANA; Deer Creek-Lamont Jr Sr HS; Lamont, OK; (3); Church Yth Grp; HOBY; Natl FFA Org; Teachers Aide; Chorus; Church Choir; School Musical; School Play; Pres Frsh Cls; Hon Roll; Butler Cty CC; Bus.

HEMME, GREGORY W; Muskogee HS; Muskogee, OK; (4); 17/303; Am Leg Boys St; Boy Scts; Church Yth Grp; ROTC; Science Clb; Spanish Clb; Drill Tm; Var L Bsbl; Var L Bsktbl; Cit Awd; Eastern OK ST Coll; Phy Thrpy.

HEMPFLING, ANNA K; Enid Sr HS; Enid, OK; (2); 44/425; Church Yth Grp; Chorus; Church Choir; Hon Roll; Jr NHS; NHS; Pres Acad Fit Awd; OK St Univ.

HEMPFLING, CHRIS G; Cimarron Public Schl; Lahoma, OK; (4); 15/34; Church Yth Grp; FCA; FBLA; FHA; Letterman Clb; Natl FFA Org; Pep Clb; Science Clb; SADD; Teachers Aide; Band Pres 2 Yrs; FFA Treas 2 Yrs; OSU; Band Dir.

HEMPFLING, HAYLEY; Pioneer Jr Sr HS; Enid, OK; (1); French Clb; Band; Mrchg Band; Rep Frsh Cls; Rep Stu Cncl; Var JV Chrldng; Trk; Hon Roll.

HEMPHILL, AUTUMN A; B T Washington HS; Tulsa, OK; (4); 79/264; Church Yth Grp; Cmnty Wkr; Pep Clb; Spanish Clb; Ofcr Stu Cncl; Var Crs Cntry; Var Trk; Svc And Soc Studs Awds; Blue Ribonin Spnsh Cont; MVP Awd Grls Track; Abilene Chrstnuniv; Premed.

HENDEEN, PATRICIA A; Pawhuska HS; Pawhuska, OK; (2); Church Yth Grp; Hosp Aide; Library Aide; Office Aide; Flag Corp; Hon Roll.

HENDERSHOT, ASHLEY D; Clayton Jr Sr HS; Clayton, OK; (3); 15/30; Church Yth Grp; FBLA; FHA; Recognized As 95-96 FHA Pgm Chm; Southeastern OK ST Univ.

HENDERSON, CANDICE; Midwest City HS; Oklahoma City, OK; (4); 155/376; Sec Church Yth Grp; Ofcr DECA; FCA; Girl Scts; Pep Clb; Spanish Clb; SADD; Teachers Aide; Sec Band; Drill Tm; Phi Delta Kappa Xinos Sec; Miss Fashionetta Prtcpnt 96; Phi Delta Kappa Schlrshp Rcpnt 96; Langston U; Brdcst Jrnlsm.

HENDERSON, ERIN E; Edmond Memorial HS; Edmond, OK; (2); 154/408; Church Yth Grp; FCA; Spanish Clb; Ofcr Bsbl; Var Bsktbl; Ftbl; Stu Ath Trainer; Yth Group VP; Mst Imprvd Stu Trainer; MVP Stu Trainer; AZ ST; Elem Ed; Admin.

HENDERSON, JEFF W; Edmond North HS; Edmond, OK; (1); Band; Mem Of Medieval Clb.

HENDERSON, JULIE A; Heavener HS; Heavener, OK; (2); Church Yth Grp; Debate Tm; French Clb; FHA; Girl Scts; NFL; Speech Tm; Chorus; Hon Roll; 4-H; OK U; Law.

HENDERSON, KARA; Garber Sr HS; Garber, OK; (1); Church Yth Grp; FHA; Band; Color Guard; Mrchg Band; Pep Band; Chrldng; Sftbl; Prfct Atten Awd; Phys Thrpy.

HENDERSON, LAUREN; Nicoma Park Jr HS; Midwest City, OK; (1); 1/144; Church Yth Grp; FCA; Chrldng; Pom Pon; Tennis; Jr NHS; NHS; Pres Schlr; Val.

HENDERSON, RACHEAL; Wanette HS; Wanette, OK; (1); Natl FFA Org; Scholastic Bowl; Score Keeper; Hon Roll; ECU; Cnslr.

HENDERSON, TOBY L; Empire Schl; Comanche, OK; (3); Chess Clb; FCA; Pres Spanish Clb; Chorus; School Play; Var Bsbl; Var Capt Bsktbl; Var Ftbl; Piano Various Awds.

HENDLEY, JEFFREY TANNER; Capitol Hill HS; Oklahoma City, OK; (4); 25/151; Letterman Clb; Office Aide; Science Clb; Spanish Clb; Varsity Clb; Ofcr Bsbl; Ftbl; Wt Lftg; Hon Roll; Prfct Atten Awd; Natl Hnr Roll; All-Amer Schlr; Wrld Hist, Phy Sci & Comp Recog Awds; Northeastern ST U; Law Enf.

HENDON, FELECIA A; Madill HS; Madill, OK; (3); Church Yth Grp; FCA; FBLA; FHA; Math Clb; Spanish Clb; SADD; Teachers Aide; Variety Show; Rep Stu Cncl; Fshng; Soclzng; Swmng; Southeastern OK ST U.

HENDREN, BRUCE; Pawhuska HS; Pawhuska, OK; (4); 3/87; Am Leg Boys St; Boy Scts; Computer Clb; English Clb; FCA; FHA; Key Clb; Mu Alpha Theta; Rep Stu Cncl; Capt L Bsbl; Eagle Sctfcrss Cntry Acad St Chmpnshp Tm 95; Sprts Med.

HENDREX, JORDAN; Hilldale HS; Muskogee, OK; (2); 1/107; Church Yth Grp; Hosp Aide; Key Clb; Science Clb; Spanish Clb; Chorus; High Hon Roll; NHS; LTC; OK ST U; Med.

HENDRICKS, ALEXANDER K; Tahlequah Sr HS; Tahlequah, OK; (3); Chorus; VP Frsh Cls; Treas Stu Cncl; Capt Ftbl; Var Socr; Var Wrstlng; High Hon Roll; Hon Roll; Jr NHS; NHS; Med.

HENDRICKS, AUTUMN; Okeene Jr Sr HS; Waukomis, OK; (4); 2/26; Church Yth Grp; FCA; Natl Beta Clb; VP Sr Cls; Sec Treas Chrldng; Var Capt Bsktbl; High Hon Roll; Kiwanis Awd; NHS; Ntl Merit Ltr; OSU; Psych.

HENDRICKS, HEATHER; Duncan HS; Duncan, OK; (2); Church Yth Grp; Cmnty Wkr; Scholastic Bowl; Spanish Clb; Hon Roll; SAVE; Peer Cnslr; Outward Bnd; U Of TX Austin; Pol Sci.

HENDRICKS, JULIE; Henryetta Sr HS; Weleetka, OK; (4); 1/65; Church Yth Grp; HOBY; Office Aide; Band; Capt Color Guard; Mrchg Band; Pep Band; Yrbk; Pres Soph Cls; Var Tennis; All Dist Band; St Qlfr Solo & Ensemble Conts; Super Rtng Color Guard Solo Dist Cont; OSU; Poly Sci.

HENDRICKS, TAVIS; Trinity Christian Schl; Broken Arrow, OK; (3); Church Yth Grp; Church Choir; School Play; Rptr Nwsp; Rep Frsh Cls; Rep Soph Cls; Rep Jr Cls; Bsktbl; High Hon Roll; Hon Roll; Attnd Congressional Yth Ldrshp Jrnlsm Conf; Algebra Test Class Champion 9th Grd; Bapt Bible Coll; Missions.

HENDRICKSON, AMANDA; Okmulgee HS; Okmulgee, OK; (3); Church Yth Grp; Cmnty Wkr; Dance Clb; FCA; Hosp Aide; Office Aide; Pep Clb; Red Cross Aide; Scholastic Bowl; Band; OK St Univ; Med.

HENDRICKSON, ELIZABETH; Ada HS; Ada, OK; (4); 13/159; Drama Clb; French Clb; Science Clb; Speech Tm; Band; Mrchg Band; School Play; Ofcr Stu Cncl; High Hon Roll; NHS; E Central U; Spcl Ed.

HENDRICKSON, JEREMY B; Nathan Hale HS; Tulsa, OK; (3); 13/244; Boy Scts; Church Yth Grp; Drama Clb; French Clb; Office Aide; ROTC; High Hon Roll; NHS; Camping; Rock Climbing; ORU; Engr.

HENDRIX, CHARLES; Eufaula Sr HS; Eufaula, OK; (3); Church Yth Grp; Science Clb; Hon Roll; Ntl Merit Ltr; OSU; Animal Sci.

HENDRIX, CHRISTOPHER L; N Intermediate HS; Broken Arrow, OK; (4); 107/967; Church Yth Grp; Spanish Clb; Acpl Chr; School Musical; School Play; Bsktbl; Trk; Wt Lftg; High Hon Roll; Hon Roll; All St OMEA Chorus; Bsktbll MVP; OK Hnr Soc; U Of Tulsa; Mused.

HENDRIX, JEANNE; Olney Schl; Coalgate, OK; (4); 3/11; FBLA; FHA; Natl FFA Org; Rptr Yrbk; VP Jr Cls; VP Sr Cls; Var Capt Bsktbl; Var Chrldng; Var Sftbl; Var Trk; Murray St Col; Phys Thpy.

HENDRIX, JENNIFER; Wellston Schl; Wellston, OK; (2); 2/49; Church Yth Grp; Drama Clb; HOBY; Speech Tm; SADD; Band; School Musical; Ofcr Stu Cncl; Cit Awd; All Amer Schlr; Vet Med.

HENDRIX, JILL R; Ponca City Sr HS; Ponca City, OK; (4); Spanish Clb; Teachers Aide; Bsktbl; Vllybl; High Hon Roll; DECA; Civic Consciousness Prgm; NOC; Sonographer.

HENDRIX, MATTHEW C; Midwest City HS; Midwest City, OK; (2); 115/473; Chorus; Church Choir; Swmmng; Wt Lftg; Hon Roll.

HENDRIX, MELISHA; Piedmont HS; Piedmont, OK; (1); 1/100; SADD; Rep Stu Cncl; Var Chrldng; Gov Hon Prg Awd; High Hon Roll; Jr NHS; NHS; Pres Acad Fit Awd; OK Univ.

HENDRIX, RICKY; Foyil Schl; Claremore, OK; (3); 21/33; Church Yth Grp; HOBY; Math Clb; Rep Frsh Cls; Rep Soph Cls; Rep Jr Cls; Ofcr Bsbl; Bsktbl; Ftbl; Trk; HOBY; TSA; Math.

HENDRIX, STEPHEN K; North Intemediate HS; Broken Arrow, OK; (2); Church Yth Grp; French Clb; Acpl Chr; JV Ftbl; Wrstlng; High Hon Roll; Pres Acad Fit Awd; Competitive Clb Soccer Team.

HENDRYX, DANIELLE; Owasso Sr HS; Owasso, OK; (1); Drama Clb; FCA; School Play; Chrldng; Gym; Trk; Vllybl; High Hon Roll; Pres Acad Fit Awd; Tulsa All Star Chrldng Team; U Of OK; Pre-Med.

HENLEY, KATY D; Mustang HS; Yukon, OK; (1); Church Yth Grp; Rep French Clb; Hon Roll; Snow & Water Skiing; Children; Animals; Guitar; Piano; Art; Wrtng Poetry; OSU; Vet.

HENLEY, LANA; Mustang HS; Yukon, OK; (4); 2/347; Church Yth Grp; Debate Tm; Pres French Clb; FBLA; NFL; NHS; Sal; Var Acad Team Capt; ST Party Pro Team; OK Chrstn Univ; Acctng; Pre-Law.

HENLEY, LEE; Davis HS; Davis, OK; (3); Church Yth Grp; FCA; Math Clb; SADD; Chorus; Var Stu Cncl; Var Ftbl; L Trk; L Wt Lftg; Var Hon Roll; Shw Chr; Phys Thrpy.

HENLEY, MATT; Hammon Schl; Hammon, OK; (1); FHA; Natl FFA Org; Hon Roll; Schl Geog Champ 94 & 95.

HENNAN, LINDSEY B; Velma Alma HS; Ratliff City, OK; (1); Church Yth Grp; Ofcr FCA; SADD; JV Bsktbl; Var Trk; Hon Roll; OK U; Pediatrcs.

HENNESSEY, JEREMY L; Stillwater Sr HS; Stillwater, OK; (2); JV Golf; OK ST; Elect Engrng.

HENNIGH, CARMENCIA A; Maud HS; Tecumseh, OK; (1); Church Yth Grp; FHA; GAA; Pep Clb; SADD; Teachers Aide; Bsktbl; Chrldng; Sftbl; Trk; HS Rodeo Assn; OK Chrstn Coll; Eng.

HENNING, MARK D; Del City HS; Del City, OK; (2); JV Bsbl; Hon Roll; Jr NHS; NHS; Mr/Miss Kerr Candte; OK Univ.

HENRY, CRYSTAL G; South Coffeyville Schl; S Coffeyville, OK; (3); Church Yth Grp; Natl FFA Org; Office Aide; Chorus; Rptr Nwsp; VICA; Coffeyville CC; Chld Care Ctr.

HENRY, CRYSTAL L; Hammon Schl; Butler, OK; (3); FHA; GAA; Letterman Clb; Varsity Clb; Bsktbl; Sftbl; Hon Roll; Schlr/Ath Awd US Army Rsrvs; Bsktbl Conf All Star; Mst Rebounds/Bst Fg % Bsktbl; Southwestern OK ST Univ.

HENRY, ERIN E; Union Intermediate HS; Broken Arrow, OK; (2); Band; Mrchg Band; Rep Soph Cls; Intrml Bsktbl; JV Socr; JV Sftbl; High Hon Roll; Jr NHS; NHS; Medcl Sci.

HENRY, FELICIA R; South Intermediate HS; Broken Arrow, OK; (2); Dance Clb; French Clb; Library Aide; Office Aide; Drill Tm; Yrbk; Pom Pon; Cit Awd; Hon Roll; Prfct Atten Awd; OK ST Univ; Psych.

HENRY, JANNA; Kremlin Jr Sr HS; Kremlin, OK; (4); #6 in class; Church Yth Grp; Letterman Clb; Band; Chorus; Capt Color Guard; Phtg Nwsp; Phtg Yrbk; Capt Chrldng; Sftbl; Hon Roll; Rose ST Coll; Dntl Hygn.

HENRY, JARED K; Claremore Sr HS; Claremore, OK; (1); Church Yth Grp; Scholastic Bowl; Band; Church Choir; Mrchg Band; Pep Band; High Hon Roll; Recr Soccer League; OK ST Hnr Soc; All-Dist Bnd 1st Altrnte Alto Sax.

HENRY, LACEY J; Verden HS; Anadarko, OK; (1); Church Yth Grp; Scholastic Bowl; Speech Tm; Church Choir; Treas Frsh Cls; JV Var Bsktbl; JV Var Sftbl; High Hon Roll; Pres Acad Fit Awd; U Of OK; FBI.

HENRY, MIRANDA; Stigler HS; Stigler, OK; (3); Am Leg Aux Girls St; Church Yth Grp; FCA; SADD; Band; Rptr Nwsp; Treas Frsh Cls; Pres Stu Cncl; Bsktbl.

HENRY, NICOLE J; Byng Sr HS; Ada, OK; (2); Church Yth Grp; Computer Clb; FCA; French Clb; FBLA; Pep Clb; Science Clb; Pres Soph Cls; Rep Stu Cncl; Bsktbl; OK Hnr Soc; ECU; CPA.

HENRY, STACI L; Yukon Middle HS; Yukon, OK; (3); 15/412; FHA; GAA; Spanish Clb; Teachers Aide; Var Sftbl; High Hon Roll; NHS; OU; CPA.

HENRY, TRACEY M; Okmulgee HS; Okmulgee, OK; (1); FCA; French Clb; Bsktbl; Sftbl; Trk; Hon Roll; Southern Methodist Univ Dallas.

HENSAL, JOSH; Woodward HS; Woodward, OK; (2); Church Yth Grp; FCA; German Clb; Treas Key Clb; Quiz Bowl; Rep Stu Cncl; JV Bsktbl; Var Tennis; High Hon Roll; NHS; OK Chrstn U; Bible; Greek; Ger.

HENSLEY, CHRISTINA; Tecumseh HS; Shawnee, OK; (4); 14/130; Am Leg Aux Girls St; Church Yth Grp; Cmnty Wkr; FHA; Library Aide; Natl Beta Clb; Teachers Aide; Hon Roll; NHS; Sci.

HENSLEY, DOUGLAS E; Panola HS; Wilburton, OK; (2); 1/20; Church Yth Grp; Natl FFA Org; Quiz Bowl; Band; Chorus; Ofcr Stu Cncl; Hon Roll; Prfct Atten Awd.

HENSLEY, SARA; Sulphur HS; Sulphur, OK; (3); 9/80; Art Clb; Church Yth Grp; FCA; 4-H; FHA; Key Clb; Science Clb; Spanish Clb; Ed Yrbk; High Hon Roll; FHA Offices Rep, Sec; SE Sub-Dist Sec, Pres; Schlstc Meet Home Ec 1st Pl; Outstdng Home Ec 1st Stu; Southeastern OK; Psych.

HENSLEY, SARAH E; Union Intermediate HS; Tulsa, OK; (2); Church Yth Grp; FCA; Pep Clb; Spanish Clb; Ofcr Soph Cls; Ofcr Stu Cncl; Chrldng; High Hon Roll; NHS; Peer Mdtr; All-Amer Chrldr 94-95 & 95-96; Spec Olympcs Vol; OSU; Mrn Bio.

HENSON, C J; Watts HS; Watts, OK; (1); Ftbl; Wt Lftg; Hon Roll; Math.

HENSON, CATEASHA L; Mc Lain Career Acad; Tulsa, OK; (3); Art Clb; Church Yth Grp; FBLA; FHA; Spanish Clb; Band; Mrchg Band; Ofcr Frsh Cls; Bsktbl; Vllybl.

HENSON, CRYSTAL M; Tahlequah Sr HS; Tahlequah, OK; (2); Church Yth Grp; Cmnty Wkr; Computer Clb; Pres FBLA; Capt Quiz Bowl; ROTC; Scholastic Bowl; Color Guard; Drill Tm; Ed Rptr Nwsp; Berkley; Genetics.

HENSON, DAYA; Moore HS; Moore, OK; (2); 41/640; Sec Soph Cls; JV Chrldng; Cit Awd; Gov Hon Prg Awd; Hon Roll; Jr NHS; Office Aide; Spanish Clb; Powder Puff Ftbl; Trk; Msnc Awd.

HENSON, HEATHER; Plainview HS; Lone Grove, OK; (4); 31/81; Ed Nwsp; Yrbk; Ed Lit Mag; Band; Church Yth Grp; Cmnty Wkr; 4-H; Latin Clb; Math Clb; Science Clb; Brdcst Jrnlsm; Amer Knl Clb; OK ST Univ; Pre-Vet/Jrnlsm.

HENSON, HOLLIS J; Memorial HS; Tulsa, OK; (2); Church Yth Grp.

HENSON, JONATHON M; Muldrow HS; Muldrow, OK; (2); Boy Scts; Church Yth Grp; Cmnty Wkr; Debate Tm; Drama Clb; 4-H; Pep Clb; Spanish Clb; Speech Tm; Band; Yng Dmcrts Sequoyah Cty Treas; Grd Schl Band Tutor; OK Kids; Outstdng Mscn; OSU Stillwater.

HENSON, JUSTIN; Seminole Jr Sr HS; Seminole, OK; (4); 8/84; Church Yth Grp; Math Clb; Office Aide; Scholastic Bowl; Spanish Clb; Teachers Aide; Church Choir; Tennis; High Hon Roll; Hon Roll; U Of OK; Natural Scis.

HENSON, SHENA; Tomlinson Jr HS; Lawton, OK; (1); Church Yth Grp; Band; Church Choir; Mrchg Band; Hon Roll; Jr NHS; NHS; All Reg Band Awd; Med.

HENSON, STACEY D; Skiatook HS; Skiatook, OK; (3); #1 in class; Church Yth Grp; FCA; Band; Jazz Band; Bsktbl; Vllybl; Hon Roll; Jr NHS; NHS; Pres Acad Fit Awd.

HENSON, STACY; Paden HS; Paden, OK; (3); 2/26; Church Yth Grp; 4-H; FHA; GAA; Natl Beta Clb; Natl FFA Org; SADD; Ofcr Stu Cncl; Bsktbl; Cit Awd.

HENTGES, HEATH; Perry Sr HS; Perry, OK; (2); Church Yth Grp; Band; Jazz Band; Mrchg Band; Pep Band; JV Bsktbl; Ftbl; Trk; Hon Roll; Jr NHS; NCDA Hnr Band; OK ST U.

HERALD, GABE; Hooker Jr-Sr HS; Hooker, OK; (4); 6/39; Church Yth Grp; 4-H; Letterman Clb; Natl FFA Org; Quiz Bowl; Var Ftbl; Cit Awd; Gov Hon Prg Awd; Hon Roll; NHS; Masonic Lodge Stu Of Today; FFA Pres; Natl Modified Midget Assn 6th Natl Number; OK ST U; Agricultural Ec.

HERBER, CHRISTA; Tomlinson Jr HS; Lawton, OK; (1); Church Yth Grp; FCA; FHA; Church Choir; Yrbk; High Hon Roll; Jr NHS; Gftd/Tlntd; Marine Bio.

HERBERGER, SARA; Hinton HS; Calumet, OK; (3); FCA; Key Clb; Natl FFA Org; SADD; Yrbk; Treas Jr Cls; Rep Stu Cncl; Bsktbl; Chrldng; Crs Cntry; Advertising.

HERFORD, ANDREA; Wellston Schl; Wellston, OK; (1); 1/54; Church Yth Grp; Drama Clb; Girl Scts; Pep Clb; Spanish Clb; SADD; Band; Stage Crew; Chrldng; High Hon Roll; Piano; Sci.

HERN, KELLY; Westville HS; Westville, OK; (4); HOBY; Sec Natl FFA Org; Band; Church Choir; School Play; Sec Sr Cls; Ofcr Stu Cncl; Bsktbl; Chrldng; Vllybl; U AR; Nclr Med.

HERNANDEZ, CHRISTOPHER; Kerr Jr HS; Oklahoma City, OK; (1); Church Yth Grp; CAP; Dance Clb; Wt Lftg; High Hon Roll; Jr NHS; NHS; Ntl Merit Ltr; Prfct Atten Awd; MI ST Univ; MD.

HERNANDEZ, GINA; Plainview HS; Ardmore, OK; (3); #9 in class; Church Yth Grp; Cmnty Wkr; Dance Clb; FCA; GAA; Natl Beta Clb; School Play; Stage Crew; JV Bsktbl; Var Mgr(s).

HERNANDEZ, SONIA M; Mustang HS; Mustang, OK; (4); 72/347; Spanish Clb; Lit Mag; Hon Roll; Art Class; Univ Of OK; Visual Commnctns.

HERNDON, JAMIE L; Warner HS; Muskogee, OK; (1); 10/80; Art Clb; 4-H; Pres FHA; Natl FFA Org; Ofcr Stu Cncl; 4-H Awd; High Hon Roll; Hon Roll; CSC.

HERNDON, SADA; Oklahoma Christian Schl; Edmond, OK; (2); Church Yth Grp; Debate Tm; Drama Clb; Speech Tm; School Play; Sec Treas Frsh Cls; Sec Treas Stu Cncl; JV Bsktbl; Var Crs Cntry; Math Tm; Acapella Grps.

HERNDON, STACIE N; Duncan HS; Duncan, OK; (3); #1 in class; Church Yth Grp; Cmnty Wkr; FCA; Key Clb; Letterman Clb; Spanish Clb; Tennis; Cit Awd; Hon Roll; NHS; St Tnns Champ 94 & 96; MVTA Girls Tnns Sportsmanship Awd; Pre-Med.

HERNDON, TRICIA R; East Central HS; Tulsa, OK; (3); Church Yth Grp; Cmnty Wkr; ROTC; Church Choir; Bsktbl; Sftbl; NHS; Mission Trip To Mexico El Salvador & Guatemala; Elite Honorary Pgm; OKU; Phy.

HERRELL, BRANDI N; Putnam City North HS; Oklahoma City, OK; (2); Church Yth Grp; Church Choir; Orch; German Natl Hnr Soc; Hnr Orch; Sclgy.

HERRERA, ARIANA H; Madill HS; Madill, OK; (2); Art; Keybrdng; Cmptr Oper.

HERRERA, OLIVIA; Norman Sr HS; Norman, OK; (4); 122/677; Dance Clb; Spanish Clb; Chorus; School Musical; Cit Awd; High Hon Roll; Hon Roll; Prfct Atten Awd; Superior Ratings Vocal Music; OK Frgn Lang Tchrs Assn Awd Acad Achvmt; OK Univ; Pre-Med; Nrsng.

HERRIAN, REBEKAH; Hennessey HS; Bison, OK; (2); Church Yth Grp; FCA; FHA; Rep Soph Cls; Rep Stu Cncl; Crs Cntry; Mgr(s); Powder Puff Ftbl; Trk; High Hon Roll.

HERRIN, MANDI; Fletcher Jr Sr HS; Fletcher, OK; (4); #11 in class; Am Leg Aux Girls St; Church Yth Grp; Cmnty Wkr; FCA; FHA; GAA; Office Aide; Church Choir; Nwsp; Pres Jr Cls; Acad All Conf; Chrch Yth Cncl Pres; S W OK ST U; Legal Sec.

HERRING, BOBBY T; Henryetta Sr HS; Henryetta, OK; (4); 18/63; Church Yth Grp; FCA; Office Aide; Band; Mrchg Band; Rep Stu Cncl; JV Bsktbl; JV Var Ftbl; JV Var Golf; Var Wt Lftg; Defy; OBA Fnlsts; GATE Pgm; Golf Dist Champs; OK ST Univ.

HERRING, CHRISTIAN N; Wellston Schl; Wellston, OK; (3); 1/65; Church Yth Grp; Drama Clb; Scholastic Bowl; SADD; Chorus; School Play; Yrbk; High Hon Roll; NHS; OBU; Tchr.

HERRING, KATHRYN R; Duncan HS; Duncan, OK; (3); Church Yth Grp; Drama Clb; FBLA; GAA; SADD; Chorus; Sftbl; Trk; OSU; Bus Mngmt.

HERRING, PIA; Hartshorne Sr HS; Hartshorne, OK; (4); 3/45; Am Leg Aux Girls St; Quiz Bowl; Teachers Aide; Band; Drm Mjr(t); Mrchg Band; Pep Band; High Hon Roll; Hon Roll; Pres Acad Fit Awd; Vet Dr.

HERRINGSHAW, LYNNETTE; Boulevard Christian Schl; Muskogee, OK; (3); 1/10; Church Yth Grp; Library Aide; Office Aide; Band; JV Sftbl; Intrml Swmmng; JV Intrml Vllybl; Intrml Wt Lftg; High Hon Roll; Hon Roll; Hghst GPA Scndry Of Schl; Quality Achvmt Wrk Awd; Natural Hlprs Clb; Life Bible Coll; Rlgn Mssnry.

HERRMAN, AMANDA M; Yukon Middle HS; Yukon, OK; (4); Church Yth Grp; Debate Tm; FHA; Girl Scts; NFL; Red Cross Aide; Spanish Clb; Speech Tm; Ofcr Stu Cncl; Cit Awd; Mock Trial; LIFE; Pol Sci.

HERRMANN, BRENT; Sulphur HS; Mill Creek, OK; (4); 9/94; Am Leg Boys St; Art Clb; Church Yth Grp; FCA; Key Clb; Science Clb; Teachers Aide; L Bsbl; L Ftbl; L Wt Lftg; Hnr Grad OU Cmmnd Schlr Naval Awd; Cls 3 A All Dist Defnsv End, Ardmore All Area Team Hnrb Mntn; OK U; Pre-Med.

HERRON, SUSAN M; Thomas A Edison HS; Tulsa, OK; (3); 6/213; Cmnty Wkr; Letterman Clb; Spanish Clb; Rep Frsh Cls; Rep Soph Cls; Rep Jr Cls; High Hon Roll; Hon Roll; NHS; Academic Letterman; Principals Hnrrll; Pre-Med.

HERSHBERGER, JOE R; Jenks HS; Tulsa, OK; (3); Boy Scts; Church Yth Grp; Computer Clb; Band; Crs Cntry; Trk; Hon Roll; LA Dist Lit Rally 1st Pl; LA St Lit Rall 3rd Pl.

HESS, EMILY A; West Middle HS; Norman, OK; (2); Church Yth Grp; Cmnty Wkr; Spanish Clb; Rep Stu Cncl; Var Powder Puff Ftbl; Hon Roll; NHS; Spanish NHS; SWASS Sec & Pres; Teen Vols.

HESS, JEREMY; Newcastle HS; Newcastle, OK; (2); Math Clb; Varsity Clb; Rep Frsh Cls; Rep Soph Cls; Ofcr Bsbl; Ftbl; Wt Lftg; Hon Roll; Ntl Merit Ltr; Awded Acad Hnr Gmtry; Southwestern Coll; Pharm.

HESS, MANDY D; Pryor Sr HS; Pryor, OK; (3); Sec Church Yth Grp; German Clb; Mu Alpha Theta; Church Choir; Mrchg Band; Hon Roll; Natl Yng Ldrs Conf Nom; Bnd Cncl; RN.

HESSERT, JAMIE L; Bartlesville Mid HS; Bartlesville, OK; (2); Church Yth Grp; Cmnty Wkr; Dance Clb; FBLA; Hosp Aide; Office Aide; Pep Clb; Variety Show; Ofcr Stu Cncl; Cit Awd; Sprt Comm Awd; Trl Trs Awd Excllnc; Elem Ed.

HESTER, DUSTIN; U S Grant HS; Oklahoma City, OK; (4); 29/175; Golf; Hon Roll; Pres Schlr; League Speech & Drama; Anesthesiology.

HESTER, KATIE; Dewar Jr-Sr HS; Dewar, OK; (3); 1/25; Church Yth Grp; FCA; Office Aide; Quiz Bowl; Chorus; VP Soph Cls; Pres Stu Cncl; Var Bsktbl; Var Chrldng; Var Sftbl.

HESTER, KELLI; Frederick HS; Frederick, OK; (4); 3/75; FHA; Am Leg Aux Girls St; Church Yth Grp; FCA; HOBY; Letterman Clb; Speech Tm; Teachers Aide; Chorus; School Musical; Rtry Stu/Mnth; 96 Ms Frdrck; 95 Ftbl Hmcmng Qn; Phrmcy.

HESTER, SANDRA; Westmoore HS; Moore, OK; (3); 100/622; FCA; FBLA; JA; Spanish Clb; Var L Crs Cntry; Var L Socr; Jr NHS; NHS; All Conf Soccer; U Of OK.

HESTON, TINA E; Morris HS; Okmulgee, OK; (2); Natl FFA Org; Hon Roll; Pres Acad Fit Awd; Morris FFA Lvstck Show/Jdgng Tm; Rprtr Morris FFA Chptr; Connors ST Coll; Ag Sci.

HETHERINGTON, BROOKE; Glencoe Public Schl; Glencoe, OK; (2); 5/23; Church Yth Grp; French Clb; FHA; Natl FFA Org; Pep Clb; Speech Tm; Rep Stu Cncl; L Bsktbl; L Chrldng; L Crs Cntry; Stu Month; OSU; RN.

HETT, JAMIE; Pond Creek-Hunter Schl; Hunter, OK; (4); 1/30; English Clb; Hosp Aide; HOBY; Spanish Clb; Band; Var Chrldng; Var L Trk; High Hon Roll; NHS; Natl Beta Clb; St Hnr Soc; OSU; Molecular Bio.

HETT, JANELLE; Pond Creek-Hunter Schl; Hunter, OK; (4); 1/30; Hosp Aide; HOBY; Natl Beta Clb; Spanish Clb; Band; School Musical; Var Chrldng; Var L Trk; NHS; Val; St Hnr Soc; OSU; Chem.

HEWITT, ESTHER; Grace Fellowsip Christian HS; Broken Arrow, OK; (2); Church Yth Grp; JV Var Crs Cntry; Var Trk; Var Vllybl; High Hon Roll; NHS; Broken Arrows Girls Sftbl.

HEYEN, LANCE T; Nathan Hale HS; Tulsa, OK; (2); Golf; Hon Roll; NHS; Natl Hnr Soc; Air Force Acad.

HIATT, TRINA M; Kansas Schl; Kansas, OK; (4); Pep Clb; Teachers Aide; Nwsp; Nrs.

HIATT-FRINK, NATHAN S; Tulsa Emmanuel Christian Sch; Tulsa, OK; (2); #1 in class; Church Yth Grp; Dance Clb; Acpl Chr; Variety Show; Phtg Yrbk; VP Soph Cls; Var Bsktbl; Cit Awd; High Hon Roll.

HIBBARD, ANDREA B; Cushing HS; Cushing, OK; (3); 1/150; Treas Art Clb; Dance Clb; FCA; Math Clb; Spanish Clb; Drill Tm; School Musical; School Play; Pom Pon; NHS; U Of OK; Pre Med.

HIBBETS, BRENT C; Enid Sr HS; Enid, OK; (3); 134/445; Am Leg Boys St; Church Yth Grp; FCA; Letterman Clb; Office Aide; JV Var Bsbl; Hon Roll; Jr NHS; NHS.

HIBDON, LYNDSEY E; Putnam City North HS; Oklahoma City, OK; (1); U Of OK; Lawyer.

HIBLER, KIMBERLY L; Shawnee Sr HS; Shawnee, OK; (3); 65/288; Church Yth Grp; Drama Clb; FCA; Pep Clb; Quiz Bowl; Spanish Clb; Teachers Aide; Church Choir; School Play; Ofcr Jr Cls; OK Bapt Univ; Elem Ed/Psych.

HIBNER, TIFFANIE M; Will Rogers HS; Tulsa, OK; (1); Church Yth Grp; Spanish Clb; Swmmng; Hon Roll; Psych.

HICE, JASON; Marietta HS; Marietta, OK; (2); FCA; 4-H; Letterman Clb; Band; Mrchg Band; Bsktbl; Hon Roll; NHS; Pres Acad Fit Awd.

HICKERSON, AMBER; Victory Christian Schl; Tulsa, OK; (2); Church Yth Grp; FCA; Office Aide; Color Guard; JV Var Chrldng; Gym; Med.

HICKERSON, LYDIA; Weatherford HS; Weatherford, OK; (1); Chorus; Yrbk; Chrldng; Pre-Law.

HICKMAN, ANDY; Wilson Schl; Henryetta, OK; (1); Natl FFA Org; Quiz Bowl; Scholastic Bowl; Ofcr Bsbl; Bsktbl; Hon Roll; Interested In Tnns, Swimming & Golf.

HICKMAN, ERIKA D; Catoosa HS; Catoosa, OK; (4); 1/135; Am Leg Aux Girls St; FCA; Office Aide; Spanish Clb; Chrldng; High Hon Roll; NHS; Ntl Merit Ltr; Val; 95-96 Wrstlng Homcmng Qn; All-Amrcn Schlr; Northeastern ST U; Elem Educ.

HICKMAN, TAMARA J; Perkins-Tryon HS; Perkins, OK; (3); 10/68; Intnl Clb; Key Clb; Hon Roll; Law.

HICKS, AMANDA S; Fletcher Jr Sr HS; Fletcher, OK; (2); FHA; Chorus; Cit Awd; Hon Roll; Prfct Atten Awd; Bus.

HICKS, AMANDA S; Harrah HS; Harrah, OK; (3); FHA; Natl FFA Org; Hon Roll; Hrtcltr; Psych; Bus; OSU; Bus.

HICKS, AMBER R; Del City HS; Del City, OK; (3); Church Yth Grp; VP FCA; FHA; Library Aide; Office Aide; Pep Clb; Church Choir; Co-Ed Yrbk; Sftbl; Jr NHS; Homcmng Qn; Ed; Phy Therapy.

HICKS, ANGELA; Stratford Schl; Stratford, OK; (1); 1/50; FHA; Science Clb; Spanish Clb; Var Bsktbl; Var Trk; Hon Roll; Pres Acad Fit Awd; Prlmntry Prcdre; U Washington.

HICKS, BENJAMIN L; Liberty Acad; Meeker, OK; (1); Church Yth Grp; Scholastic Bowl; Church Choir; Stage Crew; Var Bsktbl; High Hon Roll; Jr NHS; Med.

HICKS, CORY; Odogah HS; Claremore, OK; (4); 27/100; Am Leg Boys St; FCA; SADD; Ofcr Stu Cncl; Capt Bsktbl; Var L Ftbl; Var L Trk; NHS; All St Spec Rcgntn Ftbl; All St Hnrb Mntnbsktbl; Sr Favorite; All Dist Rcvr Yr; All Conf Bsktbl; All Cty; Lindewood Coll.

HICKS II, DANIEL K; Liberty Acad; Meeker, OK; (2); Church Yth Grp; 4-H; Scholastic Bowl; Church Choir; School Musical; Variety Show; Ofcr Stu Cncl; Var Bsktbl; Golf; High Hon Roll; Aerontcl Engr.

HICKS, DUSTIE; Thackerville HS; Marietta, OK; (4); FHA; Office Aide; Pep Clb; Yrbk; Bsktbl; Chrldng; Sftbl; 4-H Awd; Hon Roll; Homcmng Royalty; All Amer Schlr 96; NCTC; Psych.

HICKS, EMILY; Guthrie Sr HS; Guthrie, OK; (3); 36/260; Sec French Clb; Mu Alpha Theta; Band; Flag Corp; Rep Frsh Cls; Rep Soph Cls; VP Stu Cncl; Hon Roll; Jr NHS; NHS; Tri-St Music Fstvl Piano, Violin Recd Supr Rtngs; Basic Ldrshp Wrkshp 95; OSU; Liberal Arts.

HICKS, HEATHER D; Brink Jr HS; Oklahoma City, OK; (1); Drill Tm; Rptr Nwsp; Hon Roll; Jr NHS; Camp Fire Boys/Girls; OK Interschlstc Press Assn Info Grphcs Awds; Alge Excl Awd; U Of OK.

HICKS, HEIDI J; Mannford HS; Mannford, OK; (3); 6/107; Drama Clb; Spanish Clb; Chrldng; Sftbl; High Hon Roll; Hon Roll; NHS; Jr Prom Comm; Med.

HICKS, JAMIE D; Blanchard Jr Sr HS; Blanchard, OK; (3); Computer Clb; FHA; Spanish Clb; Band; Mrchg Band; Pep Band; Amer Legion Ladies Auxiliary; VFW Ladies Auxiliary; Psychotherapy.

HICKS, JESSICA; Shawnee Sr HS; Shawnee, OK; (4); Church Yth Grp; Dance Clb; Drama Clb; French Clb; Sec Church Choir; Phtg Yrbk; Rep Jr Cls; Rep Stu Cncl; NHS; Prsnl Sec Immanuel Bapt Preschl; Tri-Hi-Y; Help Our Planet Earth Sec; OK Baptist U; Photo.

HICKS, N RENE; Owasso Sr HS; Owasso, OK; (4); Cmnty Wkr; French Clb; FHA; Hon Roll; Rep Stu Cncl; Tulsa JC; Chldrn Case Wrkr.

HICKS, NATHAN M; Bartlesville Sr HS; Bartlesville, OK; (3); 140/500; Church Yth Grp; Office Aide; Teachers Aide; Acpl Chr; Band; Chorus; Church Choir; Mrchg Band; Rep Frsh Cls; Rep Soph Cls; Play/Sing Chrch Praise Band; Jr Olympc Gym Regnl Team; Psych/Fmly/Mrrg Cnslng.

HICKS, REBECCA; Marietta HS; Marietta, OK; (3); Art Clb; Church Yth Grp; 4-H; Natl FFA Org; Chorus; Hon Roll.

HICKS, RENAE A; Hugo HS; Hugo, OK; (2); Church Yth Grp; FHA; Science Clb; Chorus; School Musical; Variety Show; Var Tennis; Cit Awd; Hon Roll; OSU; Arch; Teaching.

HICKS, TIFFNEY; Drummond Schl; Drummond, OK; (4); 5/22; Am Leg Aux Girls St; Natl FFA Org; VICA; Yrbk; Rep Frsh Cls; Rep Soph Cls; Pres Jr Cls; Pres Sr Cls; Rep Stu Cncl; High Hon Roll; St Tutor; Guidance Cncl; N W OK ST U; Commnctns.

HIDALGO, SHAWN W; Hooker Jr-Sr HS; Hooker, OK; (3); Natl FFA Org; Ftbl; 1st Pl Panhandle ST U Spech Cont; FFA 1st Pl Hokr Spech Cont; FFA 3rd Panhandle ST Judging Cont.

HIDLEBAUGH, COREY B; Weatherford HS; Weatherford, OK; (4); 43/165; Church Yth Grp; Drama Clb; FCA; Chorus; Church Choir; School Play; Stage Crew; Cit Awd; Hon Roll; Yth Alv Chrstn Flwshp Pres; 1st Assmbly Of God Chrch Weatherford Asst Kids Pastor; SW OK ST Univ; Pstr/Elem Tch.

HIELD, ELIZABETH A; Yukon Middle HS; Yukon, OK; (3); Church Yth Grp; Spanish Clb; Ntl Merit Ltr; Pres Acad Fit Awd; Acad Tutoring; Recreational Sftbl; Pre-Med.

HIERA, JONATHAN J; Bishop Kelley HS; Tulsa, OK; (3); Church Yth Grp; FCA; Key Clb; Var L Bsbl; JV Var Bsktbl; Var L Ftbl; Wt Lftg; Hon Roll; Wendys HS Heisman Awd Nom; Chrch Yth Grp Advy Bd.

HIGDON, EVA; Latta Sr HS; Ada, OK; (2); Church Yth Grp; 4-H; FHA; Chorus; Church Choir; School Play; Hon Roll; Puppeteers; ECU.

HIGGINBOTTOM, TIFFANY C; Westmoore HS; Oklahoma City, OK; (2); Church Yth Grp; Office Aide; Teachers Aide; Mgr(s); Wt Lftg; Hon Roll; OK Univ; Psycht.

HIGGINS, AMY R; Mc Alester HS; Mcalester, OK; (2); 7/183; Church Yth Grp; Pep Clb; Chorus; Color Guard; Gov Hon Prg Awd; High Hon Roll; All Amer Schlr.

HIGGINS, CHARLES D; Metro Christian Acad; Tulsa, OK; (3); Church Yth Grp; Teachers Aide; Pres Jr Cls; JV Bsbl; JV Ftbl; Hon Roll; OK U.

HIGGINS, JOSEPH J; Yukon HS; Yukon, OK; (3); Cmnty Wkr; Office Aide; Hon Roll; Cmpltly Rstrd A Clssc Car; Multi Yr Listing; U OK; Mech Engr.

HIGGINS, MARK S; Bishop Mcguinness HS; Oklahoma City, OK; (4); 27/153; Drama Clb; FCA; French Clb; FBLA; Science Clb; SADD; School Musical; Ed Nwsp; Rep Jr Cls; Var Swmmng; Pictrues Of Mnd Litrary Mgzn; U Of Notre Dame.

HIGGINS, WILLIAM J; Oologah HS; Claremore, OK; (4); Am Leg Boys St; FCA; Letterman Clb; Chorus; Bsktbl; Wt Lftg; High Hon Roll; OK ST U; Bus.

HIGH, TIFFANY M; Holland Hall Schl; Broken Arrow, OK; (2); Intrml Tennis; Var Trk; Intrml Wt Lftg; Sec/Treas Of Mlticltrl Awrns Comm; Dncr For San Francisco Arts Ed Fnd.

HIGHAM, RACHEL; Savanna HS; Savanna, OK; (2); Church Yth Grp; FHA; Letterman Clb; Science Clb; Band; Mrchg Band; Pep Band; Pres Soph Cls; Chrldng; Hon Roll; Estrn OK ST Coll; RN.

HIGHFIELD, BRIAN E; B T Washington HS; Tulsa, OK; (3); Computer Clb; French Clb; Jazz Band; School Musical; School Play; Stage Crew; Ofcr Stu Cncl; French Hon Soc; NHS; Japanese Clb; Acad Ltrmn; Comp Engrng.

HIGHFIELD, HOLLY; Bartlesville Mid HS; Bartlesville, OK; (3); Church Yth Grp; Cmnty Wkr; FBLA; JA; Band; Church Choir; Mrchg Band; Orch; Pep Band; High Hon Roll; OU; Bus.

HIGHLAND, RACHEL; Grace Fellowship Christian Sch; Tulsa, OK; (1); Church Yth Grp; Chorus; Ofcr Frsh Cls; Rep Stu Cncl; Var Chrldng; High Hon Roll; 1st Dist Sci Fair; 2nd Sci Fair ORVEF Natl Finals Comp; ST Sci Fair Spec Awds; Piano; Mime/Drama.

HIGHSMITH, AUTUMN; Tishomingo HS; Tishomingo, OK; (4); 3/56; Church Yth Grp; Cmnty Wkr; Office Aide; VP Quiz Bowl; Spanish Clb; Church Choir; Rptr Nwsp; High Hon Roll; 3rd Annual Chrstn Yth Ldrshp Conf; US Natl Math Awd; Natl Sci Mrt Awd; U Of OK; Chem Engr.

HIGHTOWER, ERICA; Ada HS; Ada, OK; (4); 17/170; Am Leg Aux Girls St; Cmnty Wkr; FCA; HOBY; Drm Mjr(t); Pres Sr Cls; Pres Stu Cncl; Capt Bsktbl; Score Keeper; Cit Awd; OK Miss TEEN; Gov OK Girls St, Senator Girls Nation; Cls 4a Wmns Bsktlb St Chmpn, E All St Team; Oral Roberts U; Poltcl Sci.

HIGHTOWER, LESLIE S; Byng Sr HS; Ada, OK; (2); Church Yth Grp; Band; Flag Corp; Mrchg Band; Pep Band; JV Bsktbl; Trk; Hon Roll; Prfct Atten Awd; Spanish NHS; Langston Univ; CPA.

HIGHTOWER, SHANA; Vinita HS; Vinita, OK; (3); VP Drama Clb; NFL; Science Clb; Spanish Clb; Rep Jr Cls; Capt Chrldng; Hon Roll; NHS; Environmental Clb; Anchor Clb; Lifeguard; OU; RN Pediatrics.

HIGHTOWER, STEPHANIE; Claremore Sr HS; Claremore, OK; (3); #1 in class; Church Yth Grp; Math Clb; Office Aide; Quiz Bowl; Science Clb; Spanish Clb; Tennis; High Hon Roll; NHS; OU; Phrmcy.

HIGNIGHT, KELLEY D; Broken Arrow Sr HS; Broken Arrow, OK; (3); Spanish Clb; Band; Color Guard; Flag Corp; Mrchg Band; Ofcr Jr Cls; Ofcr Stu Cncl; Trk; Hon Roll; Capt Of Winterguard 95; Capt Colorguard 96-97; Colobash Mem; OK ST Univ; Marine Bio.

HIGNITE, ANGELA M; Union Sr HS; Tulsa, OK; (3); 21/741; FBLA; Key Clb; Spanish Clb; Var Chrldng; Var Crs Cntry; Score Keeper; Var Trk; High Hon Roll; NHS; Spanish NHS; Jrnlsm.

HIGNITE, MATTHEW; Holdenville HS; Atwood, OK; (3); FCA; HOBY; Natl FFA Org; VP Soph Cls; Var JV Ftbl; Var JV Trk; Var JV Wt Lftg; High Hon Roll; NHS; Rdlgst.

HILAIRE, ERIC P; Putnam City HS; Oklahoma City, OK; (2); 109/364; JV Bsbl; Var JV Ftbl; Var Wt Lftg; 3d/Dont Do Drugs.

HILBURN, AMIE; U S Grant HS; Oklahoma City, OK; (3); 16/276; Church Yth Grp; FCA; FBLA; FHA; SADD; Band; Stage Crew; High Hon Roll; U Cntrl OK; Psych.

HILBURN, LEAH; Plainview HS; Ardmore, OK; (3); 11/83; Church Yth Grp; FCA; Mu Alpha Theta; SADD; Band; Mrchg Band; JV Var Bsktbl; Latin Clb; Natl Beta Clb; OK Indian Hon Soc; OSU Alumni Hon Soc; Nurse/Tchr/Marine Bio.

HILDABRAND, CHANDRA B; Enid Sr HS; Enid, OK; (3); Church Yth Grp; Cmnty Wkr; French Clb; Crs Cntry; Swmmng; L Trk; Hon Roll; Jr NHS; Med Field.

HILDEBRAND, ANDREA M; Union Sr HS; Broken Arrow, OK; (4); 41/629; Church Yth Grp; Drama Clb; Chorus; Church Choir; School Musical; School Play; Ofcr Sr Cls; Rep Stu Cncl; FCA; Spanish Clb; NHS; Pres Alpha Theta Chrstn Org; TX A&M.

HILDEBRAND, MARTHA C; B T Washington HS; Tulsa, OK; (3); Cmnty Wkr; Drama Clb; French Clb; Chorus; School Play; Hon Roll; NHS; Ntl Merit SF; Ecology Clb; Author Of Comparatve Analysis Late Woodland Ceramics At Evie Site In Jrnl Of Stu Resrch.

HILEMAN, ALISHA C; Shawnee Sr HS; Shawnee, OK; (1); Spanish Clb; Band; Color Guard; DAR Awd; Hon Roll; Amer Lgn Essay Awd; Big Bro/Big Sis; Acad Bwl Tm; East Cntrl Univ; Elem Ed.

HILFIGER, BEN R; Muskogee HS; Muskogee, OK; (2); Cmnty Wkr; FCA; German Clb; JCL; Latin Clb; Var Ftbl; Var Socr; Var Wrstlng; Hon Roll; U Of OK.

HILFIGER, JAMES H; Muskogee HS; Muskogee, OK; (4); 23/300; Church Yth Grp; JCL; Key Clb; Latin Clb; Science Clb; Church Choir; School Play; Ftbl; Swmmng; Tennis; U Of OK.

HILL, AMANDA; Edmond North HS; Edmond, OK; (3); Cmnty Wkr; Rep Key Clb; Mu Alpha Theta; Phtg Nwsp; Sec Stu Cncl; Var Crs Cntry; Socr; Kiwanis Awd; NHS; Pres Acad Fit Awd; Stu News Corp/Anchor KOCO Tv-Ch 5; Rcvd Mitsubishi Motors Corp Schlsp/Japan.

HILL, BRADLEY S; Davis HS; Davis, OK; (2); Boy Scts; 4-H; Band; Jazz Band; Mrchg Band; Orch; Pep Band; JV Bsbl; JV Ftbl; JV Wt Lftg; Diesel Clb; VICA; OK St Univ; Appld Sci.

HILL, CARRIE E; West Middle HS; Norman, OK; (2); Church Yth Grp; Cmnty Wkr; Sec FBLA; Spanish Clb; Rep Stu Cncl; Powder Puff Ftbl; Hon Roll; Spanish NHS; Boy Scts; FCA; SWASS; Teen Vols; OK Univ; Law.

HILL, CARRIE L; Edmond Memorial HS; Edmond, OK; (2); 52/408; Math Clb; Spanish Clb; Vllybl; Hon Roll; NHS.

HILL, COURTNEY; Ponca City Sr HS; Ponca City, OK; (4); 114/332; Am Leg Aux Girls St; Office Aide; Spanish Clb; Teachers Aide; School Play; Variety Show; Ed Yrbk; Sec Soph Cls; Rep Stu Cncl; Var Chrldng; All Amer Chrldr; All Rgn/All ST Chrldr; 8th NCB Bst Chrldr; Sr Sprltv; OK ST Univ; Therapeuter Rec.

HILL, HEATHER; Ft Gibson HS; Fort Gibson, OK; (4); 7/147; Church Yth Grp; Sec Spanish Clb; SADD; Band; Ed Nwsp; Socr; Trk; NHS; Northeastern ST U.

HILL, HEATHER M; Deer Creek-Lamont Jr Sr HS; Lamont, OK; (3); Am Leg Aux Girls St; Pres Natl FFA Org; Phtg Yrbk; Ofcr Stu Cncl; L Bsktbl; Chrldng; L Sftbl; Hon Roll; NHS; Pres Church Yth Grp; NWOLA Secr; OSU; Ag Comm.

HILL, JACINTA; Millwood HS; Oklahoma City, OK; (2); Band; Jazz Band; Mrchg Band; Orch; Cit Awd; Hon Roll; Hlth.

HILL, JASON; Hilldale HS; Muskogee, OK; (4); 11/82; Am Leg Boys St; Boy Scts; Ed HOBY; Pres SADD; Chorus; Drm Mjr(t); VP Jr Cls; Pres Stu Cncl; Drama Clb; English Clb; Chrch Pnst; OK Bapt All St Yth Choir, Orch, Ensm; OK Bapt U; Music Ed.

HILL, JEFFREY A; Balko Public Schl; Balko, OK; (2); Boy Scts; Church Yth Grp; Quiz Bowl; Red Cross Aide; Band; Chorus; Mrchg Band; Pep Band; School Play; Ftbl; Seward Cty Coll; OK Hwy Patrol.

HILL, JONNIE M; Choctaw HS; Choctaw, OK; (3); Church Yth Grp; Cmnty Wkr; FCA; FBLA; Girl Scts; Pep Clb; SADD; Acpl Chr; Chorus; Church Choir; Hnr Soc Treas 1993-94; Choir Treas 1994-95; Jazz Choir 1992-94; OK Bapt U; Acctng Clrk.

HILL, JOSH; Trinity Christian Schl; Tulsa, OK; (1); 3/20; Latin Clb; Varsity Clb; Treas Frsh Cls; Var Bsbl; JV Var Bsktbl; Var Socr; High Hon Roll; Hon Roll; Prfct Atten Awd; U Of NC.

HILL, JUSTIN; Hilldale HS; Muskogee, OK; (1); Church Yth Grp; Hosp Aide; Letterman Clb; Var Bsktbl; Var Trk; Intrml Vllybl; High Hon Roll; Comps; OK ST.

HILL, KARA S; Westville HS; Westville, OK; (2); FBLA; Natl Beta Clb; Yrbk; JV Var Sftbl; NHS; 3K ST U; Ed.

HILL, KIM; Bartlesville Mid HS; Bartlesville, OK; (1); Church Yth Grp; Chorus; Hon Roll; Prfct Atten Awd.

HILL, KRISTEN; Pryor Sr HS; Pryor, OK; (2); Church Yth Grp; FHA; GAA; Band; Jazz Band; Mrchg Band; JV Bsktbl; Var Socr; JV Sftbl; Hon Roll; Premier Soccer Club; Achvmnt Awd Engl Outstdng Work; Soccer Hustle Awd 95-.

HILL, KYLE; Stilwell HS; Stilwell, OK; (2); Drama Clb; Natl Beta Clb; NFL; Speech Tm; School Play; Rep Stu Cncl; Var Bsbl; Var Bsktbl; Var Ftbl; NHS; U AR; Engrng.

HILL, LAKISHA N; Will Rogers HS; Tulsa, OK; (2); French Clb; Hon Roll; Med; Pediatrics.

HILL, MATT W; Harrah HS; Harrah, OK; (3); Boy Scts; Var L Ftbl; Wt Lftg; Hon Roll; Guitar; Rec Reading; OK ST Univ; Forensic Sci.

HILL, MELISSA K; South Intermediate HS; Broken Arrow, OK; (1); Band; Bsktbl; High Hon Roll; Hon Roll; Jr NHS; MD.

HILL, MINDY; Okemah HS; Okemah, OK; (1); #3 in class; Quiz Bowl; Scholastic Bowl; Drill Tm; Bsktbl; Sftbl; Trk; Cit Awd; High Hon Roll; Pres Acad Fit Awd; Val; Med.

HILL, NATASHA L; Broken Bow HS; Broken Bow, OK; (4); FCA; FHA; GAA; Red Cross Aide; VICA; Prfct Atten Awd; OK Bapt U; Nrsng.

HILL, RENEE; Jenks HS; Friendswood, TX; (4); Church Yth Grp; DECA; FCA; NFL; Sec Jr Cls; Sec Sr Cls; Ofcr Stu Cncl; Powder Puff Ftbl; Capt Vllybl; Hon Roll; Ftbl/Bsktbl/Wrstlng Spirit Comms; Bsbl Spirit Comm Pres; Prom Comm Head; OK ST Univ; Mngmnt Info Syst.

HILL JR, RICKY J; Altus Sr HS; Martha, OK; (4); Math Tm; Scholastic Bowl; Spanish Clb; Teachers Aide; Var Capt Ftbl; Var Wrstlng; High Hon Roll; Church Yth Grp; Cmnty Wkr; Library Aide; Soc Crtv Anchlnsm; Gold Mdl OK Dcthln Acad; Lttr Acad; Univ Fi Sci/Arts OK; Gntc Engr.

HILL III, ROBERT D; Stillwater Sr HS; Stillwater, OK; (4); Chess Clb; Quiz Bowl; ROTC; VICA; Drill Tm; Pres Jr Cls; Pres Sr Cls; JV Bsktbl; Var Trk; Youth Dir Aid Church; Langston; Bus/Govt.

HILL, SARAH L; Durant HS; Durant, OK; (2); Art Clb; Church Yth Grp; Cmnty Wkr; French Clb; Orch; Gym; Cit Awd; High Hon Roll; Jr NHS; St Schlr; Dance Instruction; Dance Cmptns-Natl; Schl Symphonic Orch; Washington U; Animator.

HILL, TA KORYA T; Southeast HS; Oklahoma City, OK; (2); Chess Clb; Dance Clb; Model UN; Office Aide; Varsity Clb; Nwsp; Ofcr Soph Cls; Ofcr Stu Cncl; Ofcr Bsbl; Bsktbl; OK Chrstn Posse Singer; Harvard; Crmnl Jstc.

HILL, TASHA R; Western Heights Sr HS; Oklahoma City, OK; (1); Art Clb; FHA; Math Clb; Science Clb; Spanish Clb; Rep Stu Cncl; Cit Awd; Jr NHS; OK City Peace House Yth Brd Membr; Harvard; Law.

HILL, TIFFANY D; Casady Schl; Oklahoma City, OK; (2); French Clb; Letterman Clb; SADD; Ed Yrbk; Var Chrldng; Var Fld Hcky; Var Socr; High Hon Roll; NHS; Dance Clb; Comm Clb Pres And Soc Chair.

HILL, TISHA; Trinity Christian Schl; Broken Arrow, OK; (1); Church Yth Grp; Church Choir; Hon Roll; Bllt; Elem Ed.

HILL III, TONY J; Owasso Sr HS; Collinsville, OK; (3); 106/356; Office Aide; Rep Stu Cncl; Crs Cntry; Trk; Wt Lftg; Hon Roll; Bowling; 4 Yr Coll; Engr.

HILL, TRISHA; Glenpool HS; Tulsa, OK; (4); 15/121; Church Yth Grp; Cmnty Wkr; FCA; FTA; Library Aide; Office Aide; Teachers Aide; Band; Mrchg Band; JV Var Bsktbl; NHS Outstdng Mem Of Yr; OK HS Hnr Soc; All Amer Schlr; OK ST U.

HILLE, ERIN M; Edmond Memorial HS; Edmond, OK; (3); 43/350; FCA; Spanish Clb; Var Chrldng; Hon Roll; NHS; Two Time ST Champs In Chrldng; OU; Chem Engrng.

HILLEBRAND, RONNY; Stuart Sr HS; Stuart, OK; (3); 17/28; Natl FFA Org; VICA; Olkmulgee Tech; Auto Mech.

HILLHOUSE, LORI; Braman Schl; Braman, OK; (1); 2/20; Church Yth Grp; Cmnty Wkr; FCA; FHA; Hosp Aide; Letterman Clb; JV Var Bsktbl; Var Chrldng; JV Var Golf; High Hon Roll; OK ST U; Pedtrcn.

HILLIARD, JUSTIN J; Sulphur HS; Sulphur, OK; (3); Am Leg Boys St; Art Clb; Church Yth Grp; Science Clb; Spanish Clb; Band; Mrchg Band; Orch; School Musical; High Hon Roll; Summer Sci Camp OU Summer Schlrs 95 & 96; Schl Bible Stud Group Ldr; USAF Acad; Law; Politics.

HILLMAN, BRIAN E; Guyman HS; Guymon, OK; (3); FCA; Band; Chorus; JV Ftbl; Intrml Socr; Var Swmmng; Hon Roll; NHS; Pres Acad Fit Awd; OSU; Crmnl Jstc.

HILMES, STEPHEN J; John Marshall HS; Oklahoma City, OK; (3); 16/160; VP Drama Clb; Thesps; School Play; Ed Yrbk; Treas Frsh Cls; Treas Soph Cls; Treas Jr Cls; Var Capt Socr; High Hon Roll; Sec NHS; OK ST; Archtctr.

HILTON, ANGELO S; Mustang HS; Mustang, OK; (3); Art Clb; French Clb; VA ST.

HILTON, CASEY; Bowlegs Schl; Seminole, OK; (3); Drama Clb; FCA; Letterman Clb; Natl Beta Clb; Natl FFA Org; Quiz Bowl; School Play; Ofcr Stu Cncl; Var L Bsbl; Var L Bsktbl; Seminole Jr Coll.

HILTON, JESSICA; Prue Schl; Sand Springs, OK; (2); 1/40; Church Yth Grp; Drama Clb; German Clb; Letterman Clb; Pres Frsh Cls; Pres Soph Cls; Chrldng; Sftbl; High Hon Roll; NHS; Playing Piano; OSU; Acctg.

HILTON, LINDON E; Sapulpa Sr HS; Tulsa, OK; (3); 29/292; Cmnty Wkr; FCA; Scholastic Bowl; Science Clb; Spanish Clb; Band; Mrchg Band; Crs Cntry; Trk; High Hon Roll; Pilot.

HILTON, MICHELLE D; Union Intermediate HS; Tulsa, OK; (2); Church Yth Grp; FCA; German Clb; Math Tm; Church Choir; School Musical; Hon Roll; Jr NHS; NHS.

HILTON, STEPHEN M; Wilburton Sr HS; Wilburton, OK; (1); Church Yth Grp; FHA; Varsity Clb; JV Var Bsbl; Var Bsktbl; Var Ftbl; Asst T-Ball Coach; OK Univ.

HILTY II, JAMES A; Noble HS; Lexington, OK; (2); 1/150; HOBY; Mu Alpha Theta; Scholastic Bowl; Pres Frsh Cls; Pres Stu Cncl; High Hon Roll; Kiwanis Awd; NHS; Pres Acad Fit Awd; Masonic Awd.

HINDMAN, PHILIP A; Broken Arrow Sr HS; Broken Arrow, OK; (4); 14/921; Church Yth Grp; Spanish Clb; Teachers Aide; High Hon Roll; Hon Roll; Ntl Merit SF; U Of OK; Elec Engrng.

HINELINE, MAGEN F; Charles Page HS; Sand Springs, OK; (3); Math Tm; Chorus; Church Choir; High Hon Roll; Hon Roll; NHS; CMA; Premed.

HINES, BILLY J; Valliant HS; Valliant, OK; (2); FHA; JV Var Bsbl; JV Var Bsktbl; Ltr Of Achvmnt Ath; Woodshop; Marine Bio.

HINES, CHRISTEL; Hobart HS; Hobart, OK; (1); Church Yth Grp; Pep Clb; Bsktbl; Chrldng; Sftbl; Trk; Cit Awd; Hon Roll; Pres Acad Fit Awd; Sthwstrn OK ST; Phrmcy.

HINES, JARED; Wetumka Jr Sr HS; Weleetka, OK; (2); Church Yth Grp; FCA; Var Ftbl; Var Trk; Var Wt Lftg; Hon Roll.

HINES, KIM; Cordell Sr HS; Cordell, OK; (4); 1/50; Church Yth Grp; German Clb; Pep Clb; Quiz Bowl; Spanish Clb; Band; Church Choir; Jazz Band; Mrchg Band; Pep Band; Band Cncl VP; S W OK ST U; Phrmcy.

HINES, LA SHANDA J; Lindsay HS; Lindsay, OK; (3); 25/85; Art Clb; FHA; Natl FFA Org; Speech Tm; Yrbk; Cit Awd.

HINES, OZALENA A; Sallisaw HS; Sallisaw, OK; (4); 17/134; FHA; Hosp Aide; Science Clb; Spanish Clb; Hon Roll; NHS; Cherokee Nation Tribal Yth Cncl Mem; Indian Clb Sec; FHA Sub Dist Pres; Northeastern ST Univ; Pre-Med.

HININGER, JUSTIN; Woodward HS; Woodward, OK; (1); Boy Scts; Pep Clb; Rep Frsh Cls; Rep Stu Cncl; Intrml Bsbl; JV Ftbl; High Hon Roll; Kiwanis Awd; Acad Letterman; OK Hnr Soc.

HINK, JANEA N; West Jr HS; Oklahoma City, OK; (1); Church Yth Grp; Drama Clb; Office Aide; Spanish Clb; Teachers Aide; School Play; Chrldng; Golf; NHS; OU; Marriage Cnslr.

HINKLE, JASPER; Broken Arrow Sr HS; Broken Arrow, OK; (4); 84/921; Am Leg Boys St; Church Yth Grp; FCA; Treas Science Clb; Hist Spanish Clb; Varsity Clb; Rep Frsh Cls; Rep Soph Cls; Rep Sr Cls; Rep Stu Cncl; Myth; Stu Athletic Trnr; Med Clb; Tjc; Phys Thrpy.

HINKLE, JOSH; Wynnewood HS; Wynnewood, OK; (1); 1/58; Boy Scts; Church Yth Grp; Band; Jazz Band; Mrchg Band; Hon Roll.

HINKSTON, SHANNAEDI D; Del City HS; Del City, OK; (2); Cmnty Wkr; Letterman Clb; Spanish Clb; SADD; Teachers Aide; Varsity Clb; Rep Yrbk; Var Bsktbl; Var Vllybl; Cit Awd; Elem Ed.

HINMAN, ALISSA; Mustang HS; Mustang, OK; (2); 1/400; Church Yth Grp; FCA; Spanish Clb; Rep Frsh Cls; Rep Soph Cls; Treas Jr Cls; Ofcr Stu Cncl; JV Bsktbl; Hon Roll; NHS; Sci Related Field.

HINNERGARDT, NICOLE; Hugo HS; Hugo, OK; (4); Church Yth Grp; Cmnty Wkr; Computer Clb; Office Aide; Science Clb; SADD; Color Guard; Flag Corp; Hon Roll; NHS; Think Child Safety; Rotary Stu Of Month; Sthestrn OK ST U; Sprts Thrpy.

HINRICHS, KRISTIN; Tuttle HS; Tuttle, OK; (1); 1/101; Church Yth Grp; GAA; Natl FFA Org; Quiz Bowl; Scholastic Bowl; Bsktbl; Sftbl; High Hon Roll; St Schlr; Piano; OK ST U.

HINSHAW, DEANNA J; Ponca City Sr HS; Ponca City, OK; (3); Church Yth Grp; FBLA; Library Aide; Church Choir; Orch; Stage Crew; Hon Roll; Orch Sr Rep; Chrch Puppet Ministry.

HINTON, ERIN L; Empire Schl; Duncan, OK; (3); Computer Clb; FCA; Letterman Clb; Natl FFA Org; School Play; Ofcr Bsbl; Bsktbl; Ftbl; Hon Roll; Coach.

HINTON, KELLY; Empire Schl; Duncan, OK; (2); FCA; FHA; HOBY; Key Clb; SADD; Bsktbl; Chrldng; Sftbl; Hon Roll; Sports Med.

HINTON, STEPHANIE K; Hobart HS; Hobart, OK; (2); Church Yth Grp; FHA; FTA; Natl FFA Org; Teachers Aide; Rep Frsh Cls; Ofcr Stu Cncl; JV Bsktbl; JV Sftbl; Var Trk; Savings Bond Sci Fair Regnl Level; Envrmntl 4th Plc; NACE Awd; Harding Univ; Hm Ec.

HINZ JR, MICHAEL R; Hugo HS; Hugo, OK; (2); 45/142; Comm Achvmt Geog; Outstdng Achvmt Wrld His; Archaeology.

HINZ, SHANE; Forgan Schl; Forgan, OK; (3); FCA; Band; Var Bsktbl; Var Capt Ftbl; Var L Trk; High Hon Roll; NHS; Fighting Bulldog Awd 95-96; Class Favorite; Multi Yr Listing.

HIRAD, AIMEE M; B T Washington HS; Tulsa, OK; (2); Church Yth Grp; Spanish Clb; Church Choir; Var Tennis; Hon Roll; NHS; Intl Frndshp Fr; MS Walk Hlpr.

HIRE, BRANDI; Empire Schl; Duncan, OK; (2); FBLA; FHA; Chorus; Hon Roll; PT.

HIRNISEY, JUSTIN C; Edmond Memorial HS; Edmond, OK; (4); Church Yth Grp; Cmnty Wkr; DECA; German Clb; Math Clb; Science Clb; SADD; JV Var Bsktbl; Intrml Mgr Tennis; Intrml Mgr Wt Lftg; MI St Univ; Bus Admin.

HISEY, DANIEL E; Ponca City Sr HS; Ponca City, OK; (3); Boy Scts; Church Yth Grp; Eagle Sct.

HISEY, JONATHAN; Pond Creek-Hunter Schl; Hunter, OK; (2); Church Yth Grp; Quiz Bowl; Band; Mrchg Band; Pep Band; Ftbl; High Hon Roll; Hon Roll; NHS; OK Hnr Soc; OSU; Engr.

HITCHCOCK, KARRIE J; Shawnee Sr HS; Shawnee, OK; (4); 81/468; Church Yth Grp; Drama Clb; Office Aide; Red Cross Aide; Teachers Aide; Chorus; Stage Crew; Hon Roll; NHS; Stdnt Mbr Bus/Prof Wmns Club/Cmmnts Schls Advy Brd; Wife/Mother; U Of OK; Cmmnctn Sci/Dsrdrs.

HITCHCOCK, KATIE M; Chandler HS; Chandler, OK; (3); 9/80; Spanish Clb; Acpl Chr; Sec Band; Church Choir; Flag Corp; Jazz Band; Sec Soph Cls; High Hon Roll; Hon Roll; Office Aide; Schol To US Space Acad; UCA; Lwyr.

HITCHINGS, MANDY D; Boise City HS; Texhoma, OK; (3); 13/40; 4-H; Natl FFA Org; VICA; Nwsp; Yrbk; Cit Awd; 4-H Awd; Hon Roll; Drug Free Comm; Sub Dist FHA Pres; FFA Chptr Star Farmer; OSU; Commnctn.

HIX, AMY M; Tahlequah Jr HS; Tahlequah, OK; (1); 2/250; Service Clb; Chorus; Var Crs Cntry; JV Tennis; Hon Roll; Jr NHS; Pres Acad Fit Awd; Gftd/Tlntd Prgrm; All Amer Schlr; Natl Engl Mrt Wnr; PT.

HIX, BYRON C; Muskogee HS; Muskogee, OK; (3); 17/343; 4-H; JCL; Latin Clb; Treas Natl FFA Org; Service Clb; Var Socr; High Hon Roll; Jr NHS; NHS; OK Hnr Soc; Intnl Frgn Lang Awd; 3 Times OK Soccer Assoc St Champions; Wildlife Bio.

HIX, RASHELLE M; Tahlequah Sr HS; Proctor, OK; (3); Treas Am Leg Aux Girls St; German Clb; Science Clb; SADD; Teachers Aide; JV Bsktbl; Jr NHS; NHS; Pres Acad Fit Awd; Psychiatrist.

HIXON, BOBBI SUE; Apache HS; Apache, OK; (1); 10/50; Church Yth Grp; FHA; Natl FFA Org; Pres Frsh Cls; Var Bsktbl; Var Chrldng; Var Sftbl; Hon Roll; OK ST U Stillwater.

HLADIK, BECKY; Guthrie Sr HS; Crescent, OK; (4); 18/175; Treas FBLA; Key Clb; Mu Alpha Theta; Treas Spanish Clb; Treas SADD; Yrbk; Var L Bsktbl; Var L Trk; NHS; Phillips U; Engrng.

HLADIK, JOSEPH W; Kremlin Jr Sr HS; Enid, OK; (2); Boy Scts; Church Yth Grp; FCA; Letterman Clb; Band; Jazz Band; Mrchg Band; Rep Sr Cls; Var Bsbl; Var Bsktbl.

HLADIK, REGINA M; Pioneer Jr Sr HS; Douglas, OK; (3); Church Yth Grp; Cmnty Wkr; FHA; Hosp Aide; Natl Beta Clb; Pep Clb; Quiz Bowl; Band; School Play; VP Soph Cls; Nrsng.

HLADIK, STACI; Hennessey HS; Hennessey, OK; (4); 2/54; Church Yth Grp; Treas FCA; VP FHA; Yrbk; VP Frsh Cls; Rep Jr Cls; Pres Sr Cls; Rep Stu Cncl; Var Chrldng; Sal; OK ST U; Phys Thrpy.

HO, ADELENE V; Stillwater Sr HS; Stillwater, OK; (3); 1/363; Mu Alpha Theta; Natl Beta Clb; Science Clb; Spanish Clb; Varsity Clb; High Hon Roll; Hon Roll; NHS; Pres Acad Fit Awd; Orch.

HO, ERIC; Stillwater Jr HS; Stillwater, OK; (1); Natl Beta Clb; Quiz Bowl; Ed Nwsp; Ed Yrbk; Var Tennis; High Hon Roll; Pres Schlr; Super Ratngs OMTA Dist Piano Audtns; Tnns Doubles Champn Rgnl Tournmnt; Fluent In Chinese & Span; Yale Univ; Medicine.

HO, HOA; Douglass HS; Oklahoma City, OK; (1); Chorus; Hon Roll.

HO, JONATHAN N; Union Intermediate HS; Tulsa, OK; (2); 3/900; Cmnty Wkr; French Clb; Intnl Clb; Key Clb; Varsity Clb; Orch; Var Tennis; Hon Roll; Jr NHS; NHS; Stu Of Mo; Arc Gftd Pgm; City Yth Symphny; Baylor U; Med.

HOANG, LEON W; Westmoore HS; Oklahoma City, OK; (4); 130/610; Bus Profs of Am; FBLA; JA; Tennis; Hon Roll; Jr NHS; NHS; U Of OK; Comp Prgmr.

HOANG, LILI T; Mc Alester HS; Krebs, OK; (2); Church Yth Grp; FHA; Hon Roll; Cmptr Drftr.

HOANG, ROSEMARY P; Putnam City North HS; Oklahoma City, OK; (3); Church Yth Grp; Sec DECA; FCA; French Clb; Key Clb; SADD; Teachers Aide; Chorus; Rep Stu Cncl; Hon Roll; Poem Publshd Book; Bus/Law.

HOANG, TRI M; Westmoore HS; Oklahoma City, OK; (1); Art Clb; Computer Clb; 4-H; 4-H Awd; Hon Roll; Prfct Atten Awd; Martial Arts; Photo; Photographer.

HOANG, VIVIAN; Bishop Kelley HS; Tulsa, OK; (2); Sec German Clb; Hosp Aide; Key Clb; Quiz Bowl; Sec Band; High Hon Roll; Pres Acad Fit Awd; Piano; Pre-Med.

HOAR, DANIEL; Broken Arrow Sr HS; Broken Arrow, OK; (4); 10/928; Am Leg Boys St; Sec Art Clb; Church Yth Grp; German Clb; Key Clb; Varsity Clb; Rep Stu Cncl; Intrml Socr; Var Swmmng; Jr NHS; Acad Tm; Natl Mrt Commended Schlr; Adv Plcmnt Schlr; Elec Engrng.

HOBART, APRIL H; Midwest City HS; Midwest City, OK; (2); 67/501; Cmnty Wkr; Letterman Clb; Pep Clb; Spanish Clb; Band; Rptr Stu Cncl; Sftbl; Wt Lftg; Hon Roll; NHS; Harvard; Medcl.

HOBAUGH, JESSICA E; Nathan Hale HS; Tulsa, OK; (3); Church Yth Grp; FCA; Church Choir; Var Bsktbl; Ftbl; Capt Socr; High Hon Roll; Jr NHS; NHS; Pres Schlr; Outstdng Acad Achvmnt Hon OK Univ; Pre-Vet Med.

HOBBS, AMANDA; Del Crest Jr HS; Del City, OK; (2) Church Yth Grp; FCA; Spanish Clb; Band; Mrchg Band; Orch; NHS; Outstndng Dance Stu; 5 Yr Dance Awd; Boston U; Bllt Dncr.

HOBBS, BRIAN G; Bartlesville Sr HS; Bartlesville, OK; (3); Church Yth Grp; Cmnty Wkr; Hosp Aide; Spanish Clb; Band; Church Choir; Mrchg Band; Orch; Tennis; Hon Roll; Bond Sctn Ldr Trmpt; Piano Lssns 5 Yrs.

HOBBS, BRIAN M; Stillwater Sr HS; Stillwater, OK; (2); JCL; Hist Latin Clb; Natl Beta Clb; School Musical; Var Swmmng; Hon Roll; Pres Acad Fit Awd; Art.

HOBBS, CATHERINE L; Ada HS; Ada, OK; (3); 68/187; Debate Tm; Drama Clb; French Clb; NFL; SADD; Band; Capt Color Guard; Capt Flag Corp; Mrchg Band; Orch; PYAT Treas; Chrch Orch; East Central U; Music.

HOBBS, JASON D; Kellyville Sr HS; Sapulpa, OK; (2); JV Ftbl; Elctrncs.

HOBBS, JEREMIAH W; Muskogee HS; Muskogee, OK; (2); ROTC; Jr ROTC Prgm-Cdt Sr Armn-6 Rbns; Atnd Nrthsd Bapt Chrch; Rdng; Trvlng Arnd The US, Canada, DC; Mltry.

HOBBS, MICHAEL; Union Sr HS; Tulsa, OK; (3); 130/717; FCA; FBLA; Math Tm; Spanish Clb; Var Bsbl; Var Ftbl; Hon Roll; NHS; Pres Acad Fit Awd; Mr Redskin Fnlst; Hnrb Mntn All Metro Tulsa Ftbl; Selctd To All-Star Bsktbl Game; Amer Yth Summer Bsbl; Bus.

HOBBS, MOLLY; Moore HS; Moore, OK; (3); Church Yth Grp; Spanish Clb; Church Choir; VP Stu Cncl; Var Sftbl; Sftbl Natls Wnnr; Multi-Cltrl Stu Assn; OBU; Med.

HOBBS, STEPHANIE L; Union Intermediate HS; Tulsa, OK; (2); 38/800; Church Yth Grp; Band; Pres Church Choir; Mrchg Band; Pep Band; School Musical; High Hon Roll; Jr NHS; NHS; DFY; Un Stdnts Chrst; All Dist Band 2 Yrs; Elem/Music Ed.

HOBGOOD, HEATHER L; South Intermediate HS; Broken Arrow, OK; (1); Church Yth Grp; French Clb; Hosp Aide; Band; Mrchg Band; Pep Band; Hon Roll; Prfct Atten Awd; Northeast OK All-Dist Band 2 Yrs; Univ Of OK; Phy Thrpst.

HOBSON, DANA; Claremore Sr HS; Claremore, OK; (2); French Clb; Hon Roll; Ntl Merit SF; Pntng; Bus.

HOBSON, STEPHEN; Comanche HS; Comanche, OK; (3); Treas Art Clb; Chrmn Church Yth Grp; Scholastic Bowl; Science Clb; SADD; Var Bsbl; Var Wt Lftg; High Hon Roll; Hon Roll; NHS.

HODGE, AMANDA; Tulsa Emmanuel Christian Sch; Tulsa, OK; (2); Church Yth Grp; FCA; VP Frsh Cls; Pres Soph Cls; Chrldng; Cit Awd; Hon Roll; Outstndng Sci, Span Stu Awds; Pre-Med.

HODGE, AMBER N; Hammon Schl; Hammon, OK; (1); 2/25; Sec Church Yth Grp; FCA; FHA; Scholastic Bowl; Speech Tm; VP Frsh Cls; Sec Soph Cls; Var Bsktbl; Stat Score Keeper; Var Sftbl; Southwestern Interschltc Meet SWIM; Poem Pub 95-96; Art 1st In Colored Pencil, 2nd In Acrylics; OK Univ; Phy Thrpst.

HODGE, BRIAN K; Caddo HS; Caddo, OK; (1); Ofcr Stu Cncl; Ofcr Bsbl; Bsktbl; Ftbl; Trk; Wt Lftg; Hon Roll; Jr NHS; NHS; Archery.

HODGE, JACLYN C; Sayre HS; Sayre, OK; (2); 3/60; Pep Clb; Scholastic Bowl; Chorus; Church Choir; Rptr Frsh Cls; Var Bsktbl; Chrldng; Score Keeper; Capt Sftbl; High Hon Roll; Outstndng Sftbl Plyr/Vocalist; All Star Chrldr; Phrmcy.

HODGE, JOSH; Little Axe Sr HS; Norman, OK; (3); 2/120; Church Yth Grp; Ftbl; Trk; Wt Lftg; Wrstlng; Cit Awd; High Hon Roll; Hon Roll; NHS; Prfct Atten Awd.

HODGE, MIKE; Tulsa Emmanuel Christian Sch; Tulsa, OK; (4); Church Yth Grp; Computer Clb; FCA; Office Aide; Varsity Clb; Rep Stu Cncl; Bsktbl; Hon Roll; Northeastern ST Univ; Pre-Law.

HODGES, ALLISON D; Putnam City HS; Oklahoma City, OK; (1); Church Yth Grp; Key Clb; Spanish Clb; Chorus; School Musical; 3d; Church Yth Grp Svc Proj; OKC Smmr Wrk Camp; Harding Univ; Vocal Music Tchr.

HODGES, AMY L; Lexington HS; Lexington, OK; (4); 7/70; Office Aide; Teachers Aide; Rptr Soph Cls; Bsktbl; Trk; Hon Roll; NHS; Bsktbl All St Altrnt; All Conf Bsktbl All Rgnl; All Str Trck Hurdles; Rose ST Coll.

HODGES, BRANDY J; U S Grant HS; Oklahoma City, OK; (1); Hon Roll; Pediatrician.

HODGES, JAIME; Plainview HS; Ardmore, OK; (4); 8/80; Church Yth Grp; Cmnty Wkr; FCA; Natl Beta Clb; Office Aide; SADD; Varsity Clb; Nwsp; Yrbk; Lit Mag; Optimist Stdnt Of Mo; 2 OLPA Jrnslm Awds; Del Ntl Yth Ldrshp Cncl; OK ST U; Sprts Med.

HODGES, KELLI M; Shawnee Sr HS; Shawnee, OK; (1); 32/398; Church Yth Grp; Band; Mrchg Band; Hon Roll; Bnd Cncl; Tri-Hi-Y; Sister City Rep; OK Chrstn Univ; Tchr.

HODGES, KRISTA; Mustang HS; Yukon, OK; (4); Am Leg Aux Girls St; 4-H; FBLA; Sec Girl Scts; JA; Band; Mrchg Band; Pep Band; 4-H Awd; OK ST U.

HODGES, PAUL D; Owasso Sr HS; Owasso, OK; (2); 25/450; Hon Roll.

HODGES, RYAN N; Mustang HS; Yukon, OK; (2); Natl FFA Org; JV Ftbl; Wt Lftg; Hon Roll; Autombls; Mtrcycles; Welding.

HODGSON, SKYE S; Buffalo Jr Sr HS; Buffalo, OK; (2); Church Yth Grp; Cmnty Wkr; FCA; FHA; GAA; Natl FFA Org; Pep Clb; Chorus; Church Choir; School Musical; OK ST Univ; Elem Ed.

HODSON, SARAH; Oilton HS; Jennings, OK; (3); Art Clb; HOBY; Office Aide; Quiz Bowl; Spanish Clb; Nwsp; Hon Roll; Pres Acad Fit Awd; Natl Sci Bowl; Northeastern ST U; Cmmrcl Art.

HOEGH, RACHEL L; Howe Public Schl; Poteau, OK; (1); Church Yth Grp; FBLA; FHA; Natl FFA Org; Quiz Bowl; Scholastic Bowl; Church Choir; VP Frsh Cls; JV Var Bsktbl; Var Sftbl; Ltr H Awd Sftbl, Bsktbl; Elgbl GPA Rnk Salutatorn; FBLA Recmndtn Awd; Med.

HOEHNER, ANTHONY J; Edmond North HS; Edmond, OK; (2); German Clb; Mu Alpha Theta; Quiz Bowl; Scholastic Bowl; Rptr Nwsp; Hon Roll; NHS; Acad Team; Jrnlsm.

HOFEN, SCOTT; Waynoka HS; Waynoka, OK; (2); FCA; 4-H; HOBY; Pep Clb; Scholastic Bowl; Bsktbl; Ftbl; Trk; NHS; Val; HOBY; St Trnmt Of Acad Chmps; Presdntl Ftnss; FHA Rep 95-96; NW OK Dist 4-H Ofc; 200m Dash St Qualfr; Sci.

HOFFART, CARA M; Oologah HS; Claremore, OK; (3); 2/110; Am Leg Aux Girls St; Cmnty Wkr; Quiz Bowl; Scholastic Bowl; Pres SADD; Chorus; Ed Yrbk; Rep Frsh Cls; Rep Soph Cls; Ofcr Stu Cncl; OK St Univ; Med.

HOFFER, PETER M; Macarthur Sr HS; Lawton, OK; (2); French Clb; NFL; Quiz Bowl; Speech Tm; Band; School Play; Ofcr Stu Cncl; NHS; Prfct Atten Awd.

HOFFERBER, MELISSA; Hooker Jr-Sr HS; Hooker, OK; (1); Church Yth Grp; Chorus; Var Chrldng; Score Keeper; High Hon Roll; Hon Roll; Equstrn Ridng; Miss Hooker Swthrt 95.

HOFFERBER, MICHELLE L; Hooker Jr-Sr HS; Hooker, OK; (4); 1/36; FHA; Chorus; Yrbk; Pres Frsh Cls; Pres Jr Cls; Pres Sr Cls; Golf; DAR Awd; NHS; Val; OK Honor Soc; St Piano Cont; OK ST U; Phys Thrpy.

HOFFMAN, AMBER L; Muskogee HS; Muskogee, OK; (1); 119/495; Church Yth Grp; Cmnty Wkr; Computer Clb; Math Tm; Red Cross Aide; Band; Mrchg Band; Orch; Pep Band; Hon Roll; Yth Vol Corp Recvd 40 Awds; Phtgrphr.

HOFFMAN, ERIKA; Lawton Sr HS; Lawton, OK; (2); Hon Roll; NHS; Guitar & Piano; Drawng & Paintng; Poetry & Shrt Stories; Dallas Art Inst; Visual Art.

HOFFMAN, HEIDI R; Pryor Sr HS; Pryor, OK; (4); 18/180; Church Yth Grp; German Clb; Girl Scts; Mu Alpha Theta; Band; Mrchg Band; Hon Roll; NHS.

HOFFMAN, JENNIFER J; Canton HS; Watonga, OK; (1); Church Yth Grp; FCA; FHA; Scholastic Bowl; SADD; Band; Color Guard; Flag Corp; Mrchg Band; Pep Band.

HOFFMAN, JENNIFER R; South Intermediate HS; Broken Arrow, OK; (1); Church Yth Grp; JV Bsktbl; JV Var Socr; Wt Lftg; Alg I Awd.

HOFFMAN, JEREMY D; Canton HS; Watonga, OK; (2); Scholastic Bowl; Band; FFA Treas.

HOFFMAN, JULIE S; Pryor Sr HS; Pryor, OK; (3); Church Yth Grp; German Clb; Hosp Aide; Chorus; School Musical; School Play; Rptr Nwsp; Pres Frsh Cls; Rep Soph Cls; Rep Jr Cls; All Dist Sftbll; All Conf Sftbll; All Star Cheerldr; Radio.

HOFFMAN, KELLY; Mc Alester HS; Mcalester, OK; (4); 12/209; Church Yth Grp; Cmnty Wkr; FHA; Science Clb; Spanish Clb; Var Chrldng; JV Sftbl; Cit Awd; Hon Roll; NHS; OK Hnr Soc; Mercy Clinic Vol; East Cntrl Univ; Dental Hygiene.

HOFFMAN, KRISTI; Panama HS; Shady Point, OK; (4); 4/52; FCA; FHA; Pres Natl FFA Org; Speech Tm; SADD; Yrbk; Rptr Frsh Cls; Sec Sr Cls; Bsktbl; NHS; Eastern OK ST Coll; Ag Econ.

HOFFMAN, KRISTIN; Mustang HS; Yukon, OK; (1); 49/450; Church Yth Grp; FCA; Spanish Clb; Chrldng; Powder Puff Ftbl; Trk; Hon Roll; NHS; OK ST U.

HOFFMAN, MARK; Glencoe Public Schl; Glencoe, OK; (4); 2/15; Church Yth Grp; Drama Clb; Natl FFA Org; Quiz Bowl; Scholastic Bowl; Speech Tm; Rep Soph Cls; VP Sr Cls; High Hon Roll; Sal; OK ST U; Pilot.

HOFFMAN, MICHAEL C; Edmond Memorial HS; Duluth, MN; (3); JA; Ftbl; All Amer Schlr; U Of MN Duluth.

HOFFMAN, NATHAN T; Bridge Creek HS; Tuttle, OK; (3); Church Yth Grp; Natl FFA Org; Band; Church Choir; Jazz Band; Mrchg Band; Pep Band; School Musical; School Play; Swing Chorus.

HOFFMAN, SHAWN D; Pioneer Jr Sr HS; Enid, OK; (2); Var Bsbl; Var Bsktbl; Cit Awd; High Hon Roll; DECA; Free Thrw Shtr; Md Almst 40 3 Pntrs In Ssn; Md 89 Cnsctv Free Thrws In Rw; OSU; Sprts.

HOFFMAN, TRISHA; Mustang HS; Yukon, OK; (3); 113/420; Church Yth Grp; FCA; Office Aide; Chrldng; Powder Puff Ftbl; Hon Roll; OK ST U.

HOFFMASTER, ERIC J; Union Intermediate HS; Tulsa, OK; (2); French Clb; Teachers Aide; Chorus; Hon Roll; Frnch Outstndg Stu; Nex Magzne Reprtr; U Of OK; Jrnlsm.

HOGAN, ERIC; Hugo HS; Hugo, OK; (2); 2/123; FCA; Spanish Clb; Ofcr Stu Cncl; Var L Ftbl; Trk; Wt Lftg; High Hon Roll; NHS; Ntl Merit Schol; Odyssey Of The Mind St Champ Team; Leo Clb Treas; Vet; Sci.

HOGAN, JOSEPH M; Shawnee Sr HS; Shawnee, OK; (1); Stage Crew; Hon Roll.

HOGAN, LORI; Moore HS; Moore, OK; (4); Drama Clb; Latin Clb; SADD; School Musical; School Play; Stage Crew; Chrldng; VP Drama Clb; Mst Imprved In Drama; Outs Tech Iun Ddrama; Bst Drctr In Drama; Bst In Melodrama.

HOGAN, PAM; Guymon Sr HS; Guymon, OK; (3); Church Yth Grp; FCA; 4-H; Girl Scts; Band; Flag Corp; JV Var Bsktbl; Intrml Sftbl; Jr NHS; NHS; OK St Univ; Med.

HOGAN, SHAUN M; Putnam City North HS; Oklahoma City, OK; (3); Var Bsbl; Architectural Design; Mech Drawing; Washington U; Phys Therapy.

HOGG, AISHA; Midwest City HS; Midwest City, OK; (3); 40/400; Church Yth Grp; Spanish Clb; VICA; Church Choir; Vllybl; High Hon Roll; Jr NHS; NHS; Prfct Atten Awd; Multi Yr Listing; Music.

HOGG, JAREE E; Hooker Jr-Sr HS; Hooker, OK; (3); 4/38; FHA; Band; Chorus; School Musical; Pres Stu Cncl; Var Bsktbl; Powder Puff Ftbl; High Hon Roll; NHS; Letterman Clb; Own Lawn Mowng Bus; Northwestern ST U; Real Est.

HOGG, MAHKESHA; Midwest City HS; Midwest City, OK; (2); 65/510; Church Yth Grp; Church Choir; Tennis; Vllybl; NHS; Prfct Atten Awd; Art & Photo; Bass Guitar.

HOGGATT, MICKEY; Cushing HS; Cushing, OK; (4); 30/155; Am Leg Boys St; Church Yth Grp; FCA; Spanish Clb; Teachers Aide; Sprt Ed Yrbk; Var Bsbl; Var Ftbl; Hon Roll; Prfct Atten Awd; OK ST; Elem Ed.

HOGGATT, STEPHANIE; Locust Grove HS; Locust Grove, OK; (4); Church Yth Grp; Cmnty Wkr; Office Aide; Red Cross Aide; Speech Tm; Teachers Aide; Church Choir; Rptr Nwsp; Yrbk; Capt Chrldng; Tech Stu Assn Sec; All Amer Nom NCA; NASA; Northeastern ST Univ; Acctng.

HOGLE, ABBY; Hilldale HS; Muskogee, OK; (3); Church Yth Grp; Dance Clb; FCA; GAA; Key Clb; Math Clb; Pep Clb; Science Clb; Spanish Clb; SADD; Dance & Sing Won Several Overall Cmptns; All-Star Chrldr; OK Hnr Soc; NHS; OU; Med; Dr.

HOGUE, DUSTIN J; Coalgate HS; Coalgate, OK; (3); 20/48; Church Yth Grp; Drama Clb; Scholastic Bowl; Speech Tm; Band; Church Choir; Jazz Band; Mrchg Band; Pep Band; School Play; Mus.

HOGUE, JENNY L; Bluejacket Schl; Bluejacket, OK; (2); Church Yth Grp; FHA; Library Aide; Natl FFA Org; Office Aide; Pep Clb; Band; OK Bapt Univ.

HOGUE, MELISSA S; Calera HS; Calera, OK; (3); Office Aide; Spanish Clb; Chorus; Tennis; Anthropology.

HOHENSEE, HEATHER; Ponca City Sr HS; Ponca City, OK; (4); 5/358; Am Leg Aux Girls St; Church Yth Grp; Cmnty Wkr; Hosp Aide; HOBY; Spanish Clb; Teachers Aide; School Play; Nwsp; Yrbk; Yth Trffc Ct Jdg; Rtry Yth Ldr Del; Crrclr Awds Govt, Bio, Span II, Prsnl Cmptr Applctn; OK ST U; Vet Med.

HOHRMAN, DORI; Clinton HS; Clinton, OK; (3); 6/120; Church Yth Grp; DECA; FBLA; Office Aide; Hon Roll; Southwestern U; Phrmcy.

HOILE, KELLY; Blanchard Jr Sr HS; Blanchard, OK; (4); 2/73; Am Leg Aux Girls St; Computer Clb; Mu Alpha Theta; Pep Clb; Spanish Clb; School Play; Ofcr Sr Cls; Jr NHS; NHS; Sal; OK ST U; Mrn Bio.

HOKE, ERIC W; Western Heights Sr HS; Oklahoma City, OK; (2); Boy Scts; Teachers Aide; Band; Chorus; Ftbl; JV Socr; Wrstlng.

HOKE, HEATHER M; Western Heights Sr HS; Oklahoma City, OK; (4); Office Aide; Chorus; School Musical; Swing Chorus; Rptr Yrbk; Hon Roll; NHS.

HOKE, JEFFREY M; Yukon Middle HS; Yukon, OK; (2); Church Yth Grp; JV Bsbl; Var Bsktbl; Hon Roll; NHS; OK; Arch.

HOLASEK, TRACY C; Norman Sr HS; Norman, OK; (3); 266/799; Church Yth Grp; Drama Clb; FCA; Latin Clb; Pep Clb; Spanish Clb; School Play; Hon Roll; Span Clb Pres; Jobs Dghtrs; OU.

HOLBERT, LATISHA; Moore HS; Moore, OK; (2); Church Yth Grp; FBLA; Girl Scts; Mrchg Band; Spanish Clb; Band; Chorus; Mrchg Band; High Hon Roll; Intr Decorator.

HOLBROOK, LONNIE; Will Rogers HS; Tulsa, OK; (4); 23/179; Church Yth Grp; Cmnty Wkr; Debate Tm; JA; Key Clb; Library Aide; Nwsp; Yrbk; Ofcr Stu Cncl; Crs Cntry; ODP Team Sccr; Ozark Chrstn Coll.

HOLBROOK, SARA K; Stigler HS; Stigler, OK; (3); FCA; FHA; SADD; Band; Church Choir; Color Guard; Mrchg Band; Sftbl; Hon Roll; NHS; Speech Thrpy.

HOLCOMB, KYLA K; Stillwater Sr HS; Stillwater, OK; (3); 27/363; Church Yth Grp; CAP; Cmnty Wkr; FCA; Key Clb; Math Clb; Mu Alpha Theta; Natl Beta Clb; Pep Clb; Spanish Clb.

HOLCOMBE, TAMARA; Jay HS; Jay, OK; (4); 4/100; FCA; Rep FBLA; Natl Beta Clb; Rptr Natl FFA Org; Pep Clb; Rep Stu Cncl; Crs Cntry; 4-H Awd; Rep NHS; Intl Drg Free Yth; U Of AR; Educ.

HOLDBROOK, DARLA J; Temple Jr Sr HS; Temple, OK; (4); Teachers Aide; Nwsp; Hon Roll.

HOLDEH, SCOTT J; Collinsville HS; Collinsville, OK; (2); Quiz Bowl; JV Var Bsktbl; Wt Lftg; Hon Roll; OK ST Univ; Veterinary Med.

HOLDEN, DAVID L; North Intemediate HS; Broken Arrow, OK; (1); Band; Mrchg Band; Pep Band; Stage Crew; Rep Stu Cncl; Hon Roll; NHS; Auto Crssng Solo; OU; Arch.

HOLDEN, MEGHAN M; Duncan HS; Duncan, OK; (2); Church Yth Grp; FBLA; Key Clb; SADD; Tennis; High Hon Roll; NHS; Univ Of OK.

HOLDEN, SUZANNE R; Charles Page HS; Sand Springs, OK; (2); Church Yth Grp; Drama Clb; Letterman Clb; Thesps; Jazz Band; Mrchg Band; Orch; School Musical; School Play; NHS; Hosps Nrsng Homes Clowning Ministries; Music Instr; Theatre Arts.

HOLDEN, ZACH; Cookson Hills Chrn Schl; Kansas, OK; (3); 1/7; Church Yth Grp; Drama Clb; FCA; School Play; Pres Jr Cls; Pres Stu Cncl; L Bsktbl; L Co-Capt Socr; High Hon Roll; Quiz Bowl; Bible Bowl; U Of Cincinnati; Sci.

HOLDER, ASHLEI L; Warner HS; Warner, OK; (1); GAA; VP Frsh Cls; Var Bsktbl; Var Sftbl; Hon Roll; WHS Sftbl Rookie Or Yr 96; NEO.

HOLDER, BRIAN; Medford Schl; Medford, OK; (3); 7/18; FCA; FHA; Quiz Bowl; VP Stu Cncl; Var Bsbl; Var Bsktbl; Var Ftbl; Var Trk.

HOLDERBY, BETH; Timberlake Schl; Jet, OK; (1); Church Yth Grp; Dance Clb; English Clb; FCA; 4-H; FHA; GAA; Math Clb; Math Tm; Pep Clb; OSU.

HOLDERBY, STEVEN H; Ripley HS; Cushing, OK; (2); 3/45; Math Clb; Natl FFA Org; Quiz Bowl; Scholastic Bowl; Science Clb; JV Bsbl; JV Bsktbl; Var Trk; Var Wt Lftg; Hon Roll; MA Inst Of Tech; Comp Pgmng.

HOLDSCLAW, ANTHONY G; Wilburton Sr HS; Wilburton, OK; (2); 9/80; Church Yth Grp; Debate Tm; Drama Clb; FBLA; FHA; FTA; Library Aide; Math Tm; Quiz Bowl; Spanish Clb; Acad Team; EOSC; Mgmt.

HOLESKO, AMY L; Stillwater Sr HS; Stillwater, OK; (3); 79/370; DECA; FCA; Latin Clb; Mu Alpha Theta; Teachers Aide; Pom Pon; Hon Roll; NHS; OSU; Optometry.

HOLIDAY, BRANDY D; Norman Sr HS; Norman, OK; (3); 182/799; Church Yth Grp; Cit Awd; Hon Roll; Prfct Atten Awd; Orthodontist.

HOLLAN, AMY K; Heavener HS; Heavener, OK; (1); Chrldng; Hon Roll.

HOLLAN, JAMES; Afton HS; Afton, OK; (4); 6/19; FCA; Natl FFA Org; Office Aide; Quiz Bowl; SADD; Teachers Aide; Rep Frsh Cls; Rep Stu Cncl; L Bsbl; Capt Bsktbl; Ruth Norman Fnd Schlrshp; Mltpl Yr Lstng; NED A&M; Soc Stud Ed.

HOLLAND, CHRIS; Wesch Sr HS; Welch, OK; (4); 4/24; Am Leg Boys St; Church Yth Grp; FCA; FHA; Quiz Bowl; VP Soph Cls; Pres Jr Cls; Rep Sr Cls; Rep Stu Cncl; Var Bsktbl; FHA Chaplain; Acad Tm Capt; Stu Of Yr 92-95; NE OK A&M.

HOLLAND, DIXIE; Apache HS; Apache, OK; (4); Pres Drama Clb; HOBY; Capt Scholastic Bowl; Teachers Aide; Band; Drm Mjr(t); Ofcr Stu Cncl; Hon Roll; ITS Trp Pres; Bible Bwl; OK U.

HOLLAND, JARED P; Eisenhower Sr HS; Lawton, OK; (3); 107/475; Church Yth Grp; FCA; Var Bsbl; Var Bsktbl; Var Ftbl; Hon Roll; NHS; GATE; All Area Ftbl; Engr.

HOLLAND, M KENT; Snyder HS; Snyder, OK; (4); 6/40; Church Yth Grp; Treas Natl FFA Org; VP Stu Cncl; Ftbl; Wt Lftg; Wrstlng; Hon Roll; St FFA Degree; Homcmng King; FFA Star Agribusinessman; Cameron Univ; Animal Sci.

HOLLAND, M KENT; Snyder HS; Snyder, OK; (4); 6/40; Church Yth Grp; 4-H; Treas Natl FFA Org; VP Stu Cncl; Ftbl; Wt Lftg; Wrstlng; High Hon Roll; Hon Roll; Homcmng King; Parliamentarian Procedures Team Mem; St FFA Degree; Cameron Univ; Animal Sci.

HOLLAND, M RAYLEE; Westmoore HS; Oklahoma City, OK; (4); Church Yth Grp; Cmnty Wkr; Sec Treas Drama Clb; FCA; Sec French Clb; Sec Treas FHA; Hosp Aide; Office Aide; Pres Pep Clb; Thesps; Fast Pitch Sftbl Letterman-All Conf, All Dist & Hnrb Mntn All St; OCCC; Soc Worker.

HOLLAR, CANDYCE L; Coyle Public Schl; Coyle, OK; (3); Boy Scts; Quiz Bowl; Rptr Nwsp; Phtg Yrbk; Treas Jr Cls; Hon Roll; 1st Degree Black Belt Karate; Acupuncture.

HOLLARS, ANTHONY J; Douglass HS; Oklahoma City, OK; (3); FBLA; Mu Alpha Theta; ROTC; Jazz Band; Tennis; High Hon Roll; NHS; Church Yth Grp; Computer Clb; Math Clb; Supr Cadet Awd ROTC; Natl Sojourners Awd ROTC; Amer AHSME Awd; U Of Cent OK; Bus Mgnt.

HOLLE, ERIN; Garber Sr HS; Enid, OK; (2); Church Yth Grp; FHA; Scholastic Bowl; Sec Soph Cls; Sec Treas Stu Cncl; Var Chrldng; Var L Trk; High Hon Roll; NHS.

HOLLEMAN, KATY; Okmulgee HS; Okmulgee, OK; (2); Church Yth Grp; FCA; Spanish Clb; Chorus; Ofcr Stu Cncl; Chrldng; Gym; Tennis; Wt Lftg; Hon Roll; USCPA; All-Amer Schlrs; OSU; Phy Thrpst; Tchr.

HOLLEY, CARRIE; Shawnee Sr HS; Shawnee, OK; (4); #40 in class; Church Yth Grp; Sec Drama Clb; French Clb; Pres NFL; Speech Tm; Thesps; School Play; High Hon Roll; NHS; OK Bapt Univ; Spch/Drama Ed.

HOLLEY, JENNIFER; Cache HS; Cache, OK; (3); 16/76; Church Yth Grp; FCA; FHA; Key Clb; Natl Beta Clb; Church Choir; Ed Yrbk; Pres Jr Cls; Sec Stu Cncl; High Hon Roll; Ltr C Acad Awd; Supts Hnr Roll; Technlgy Ed Clss; Indian Heritage Clb; OK Baptist U.

HOLLEY, ROB R; Stillwater Sr HS; Stillwater, OK; (2); 41/400; Church Yth Grp; FCA; Natl Beta Clb; Chorus; Church Choir; JV Bsbl; JV Bsktbl; High Hon Roll; Pres Acad Fit Awd; Squires Mem & Deputy Chief.

HOLLEY, ROBYN L; Lindsay HS; Lindsay, OK; (2); 6/85; Church Yth Grp; FHA; GAA; Pep Clb; Bsktbl; Sftbl; Trk; High Hon Roll; Hon Roll; NHS; OU; Obsttrcn/RN.

HOLLEYMAN, BARY G; Putnam City North HS; Oklahoma City, OK; (3); 53/464; Church Yth Grp; FCA; Spanish Clb; Ofcr Bsbl; Bsktbl; Ftbl; Cit Awd; NHS; All-City 1st Team; Hnrb Mntn; All Conf; All Dist Ftbl; Stu Of Today; Al City & All St Hnrb Mntn Bsbl.

HOLLIDAY, AMY; Guthrie Sr HS; Guthrie, OK; (1); 132/329; Church Yth Grp; FCA; GAA; SADD; Var Chrldng; Var Sftbl; Var Trk; AZ ST; Radiology.

HOLLIDAY, KIMBERLY A; Edmond North HS; Edmond, OK; (4); 1/339; Church Yth Grp; Mu Alpha Theta; Spanish Clb; SADD; Gov Hon Prg Awd; NHS; Pres Schlr; St Schlr; Val; U Of AL; Early Chldhd Ed.

HOLLIDAY, SUMMER; Edmond North HS; Edmond, OK; (3); 1/367; Church Yth Grp; Sec Treas French Clb; Pres Mu Alpha Theta; SADD; Pres Jr Cls; Rep Stu Cncl; NHS; Prfct Atten Awd; Key Clb; Office Aide; Stu Ath Trainer For Var Trk & Ftbl; Jr Stu Of Yr Edmond Elks Clb; Pre-Med; Phy Thrpst.

HOLLIDAY, WHITNEY C; Bishop Mcguinness HS; Oklahoma City, OK; (3); 23/145; Art Clb; Church Yth Grp; Drama Clb; FCA; Pep Clb; Spanish Clb; SADD; Ofcr Stu Cncl; Crs Cntry; Sftbl; Flyfishing.

HOLLINGSHEAD, CODY A; Bartlesville Mid HS; Bartlesville, OK; (2); JA; Spanish Clb; Rep Stu Cncl; JV Bsbl; Var JV Bsktbl; Pres Acad Fit Awd; Otstndng Achvmnt Awd.

HOLLINGSHED, GARY L; Checotah HS; Checotah, OK; (4); 23/100; Ofcr Stu Cncl; Bsktbl; Hon Roll; Hnr For Outs Art Stu; Connors St Col; Tchr.

HOLLINGSWORTH, ASHLEY; Ponca City Sr HS; Ponca City, OK; (2); Church Yth Grp; Cmnty Wkr; Hosp Aide; Spanish Clb; Band; Chorus; Ofcr Frsh Cls; High Hon Roll; Prfct Atten Awd; Pres Acad Fit Awd; Ponca City Hospice Vol; Lit Cncl; Humane Soc; Jazzercise; OK Hon Soc; OK Univ; Trauma Spclst/ER.

HOLLINGSWORTH, JAMES; Fox Sr HS; Fox, OK; (3); 4/30; Computer Clb; Band; Drm Mjr(t); Mrchg Band; Var Bsbl; Chess Clb; Jazz Band; Orch; Pep Band; School Musical; USNBA; USNLMA; All-Amer Schlrs; Multi Yr Lstng; U Of OK; Arntcl Dsgn.

HOLLINGSWORTH, JAMIE S; Westmoore HS; Oklahoma City, OK; (3); 25/650; Church Yth Grp; Hosp Aide; Key Clb; Service Clb; Speech Tm; Mgr(s); Socr; Hon Roll; Jr NHS; NHS; Hlth Prof Acad; Ped.

HOLLIS, AUDRA L; Okmulgee HS; Okmulgee, OK; (4); 2/120; Cmnty Wkr; French Clb; Church Choir; Hon Roll; NHS; Closeup; OK ST Univ; Arch.

HOLLIS, GWENDOLYN M; Blackwell HS; Blackwell, OK; (1); Church Yth Grp; GAA; Letterman Clb; Speech Tm; Stage Crew; Ofcr Frsh Cls; Ofcr Bsbl; Bsktbl; Sftbl; Trk.

HOLLIS, STACEY L; Charles Page HS; Sand Springs, OK; (1); 1/200; Drama Clb; Chorus; Gov Hon Prg Awd; High Hon Roll; Jr NHS; Pres Schlr; Piano; Cmps Chrstn Clb; Bldrs Clb; OK Univ; Music/Marine Bio.

HOLLOWAY, LEAH; Stuart Sr HS; Stuart, OK; (4); 10/30; 4-H; FHA; Scholastic Bowl; VICA; Ed Rptr Nwsp; Rptr Frsh Cls; Rep Soph Cls; Rep Jr Cls; Rep Sr Cls; High Hon Roll; Kybrd; CTZN Bnd Potawatomi Trbe Crdhldr; OK ST U; Music.

HOLLOWAY, NATHAN J; Bethany HS; Bethany, OK; (2); Church Yth Grp; FCA; Band; Chorus; Mrchg Band; School Musical; Southern Nazarene Univ; Bus.

HOLLOWAY, STEPHANIE; Stuart Public Schls; Mcalester, OK; (4); 5/30; Am Leg Aux Girls St; FCA; Library Aide; Pres Natl FFA Org; Quiz Bowl; Scholastic Bowl; Teachers Aide; Rep Frsh Cls; High Hon Roll; Jr Bank Brd; Sheep Prfcncy Awd; Livestock Show Tm; OK ST U; Ag.

HOLLY, JOHN D; Guthrie Sr HS; Guthrie, OK; (1); Church Yth Grp; FCA; Ofcr Bsbl; Ftbl; Sftbl; Wt Lftg; Amer Legion Bsbl; U Of TX.

HOLMAN, JASON; Altus Sr HS; Altus, OK; (4); 3/230; Am Leg Boys St; Church Yth Grp; Quiz Bowl; School Musical; Rep Sr Cls; Rep Stu Cncl; Var L Ftbl; Var L Golf; High Hon Roll; NHS; U Of OK; Med.

HOLMAN, ROBERT; Altus Sr HS; Altus, OK; (4); 23/239; Am Leg Boys St; Church Yth Grp; Chorus; Rep Sr Cls; Rep Stu Cncl; Var L Ftbl; Var Golf; High Hon Roll; Jr NHS; NHS; U Of OK; Bus.

HOLMAN, SHAYNA S; Edmond Memorial HS; Edmond, OK; (3); 188/377; Church Yth Grp; Library Aide; Spanish Clb; Orch; Var Socr; Tchr Cadet Pgm; Ed.

HOLMBOE, LEA; Jenks HS; Tulsa, OK; (1); Church Yth Grp; FCA; Acpl Chr; Chorus; Ofcr Stu Cncl; Chrldng; Trk; High Hon Roll; Hon Roll.

HOLMES, JENNIFER; Woodward HS; Bartlett, TN; (1); 1/293; Church Yth Grp; Scholastic Bowl; Band; Mrchg Band; High Hon Roll; Hon Roll; OK Hnr Soc; Puppet Team; Acad Bowl; Sthrn Nazerene Univ.

HOLMES, JULIE M; Putnam City North HS; Oklahoma City, OK; (2); 2/488; Art Clb; Debate Tm; FCA; VP JA; Key Clb; Spanish Clb; SADD; Hon Roll; NHS; Outstdng Engl I/Art Stdnt; GATE.

HOLMES, KENDRA; Jenks HS; Tulsa, OK; (3); Church Yth Grp; Dance Clb; FCA; French Clb; Mu Alpha Theta; Red Cross Aide; JV Bsktbl; Co-Capt Var Chrldng; Powder Puff Ftbl; High Hon Roll; Medicine; Dr.

HOLMES, MICHAEL; Ponca City Sr HS; Ponca City, OK; (4); 52/387; Am Leg Boys St; Church Yth Grp; Spanish Clb; SADD; JV Bsbl; JV Ftbl; Wrstlng; High Hon Roll; Bus Mgmt.

HOLMES, STACY D; Enid Sr HS; Enid, OK; (2); Church Yth Grp; Chorus; Church Choir; School Musical; Yrbk; Ofcr Soph Cls; Hon Roll; Jr NHS; NHS; Presdntl Awd; Poems; Plays; Novels; Hiking; Camping; Fishing; Bartlesville Weslyan; Ed.

HOLMUN, LA VONNE T; Lindsay HS; Lindsay, OK; (1); Church Yth Grp; 4-H; Natl FFA Org; Pep Clb; Chrldng; Sftbl; Trk; Hon Roll.

HOLOGE, AMY E; Ft Cobb-Broxton HS; Carnegie, OK; (2); High Hon Roll; Cosmetologist; Law Enforcement.

HOLSEY, JENNIFER J; Duke Schl; Duke, OK; (3); Natl FFA Org; Quiz Bowl; VP Frsh Cls; Pres Soph Cls; Pres Jr Cls; Sftbl; High Hon Roll; OK HS Hnr Soc.

HOLSTED, ALAN; Carnegie Jr HS; Carnegie, OK; (2); Natl FFA Org; Scholastic Bowl; Hon Roll; Pres Acad Fit Awd; Tech Math Awd; Sci Fair 1st Pl; Top 10 Frshmn; OK U; Meteorlgy.

HOLSTED, KRISTI M; Mustang HS; Mustang, OK; (2); 51/405; Church Yth Grp; FCA; Key Clb; Office Aide; Teachers Aide; Mgr(s); Vllybl; High Hon Roll; Hon Roll; NHS; Yth Alive; Ice Hockey; Pathology.

HOLSTEN, JEREME; Waukomis HS; Waukomis, OK; (4); 7/29; FCA; Capt Var Bsktbl; N W OK; Math Tchr.

HOLSTEN, KERISSA B; Waukomis HS; Waukomis, OK; (1); Rptr Band; Jazz Band; Mrchg Band; Pep Band; Rptr Frsh Cls; High Hon Roll; NHS; Pres Acad Fit Awd.

HOLSTINE, KARIE A; Stringtown HS; Stringtown, OK; (2); 4-H; Natl FFA Org; Pep Clb; Quiz Bowl; Science Clb; Chorus; School Musical; School Play; Yrbk; Rep Stu Cncl; SOSU.

HOLSTINE, STEPHANIE L; Stringtown HS; Atoka, OK; (2); 4-H; Quiz Bowl; VP Frsh Cls; VP Soph Cls; Var Bsktbl; High Hon Roll; Hon Roll; PT.

HOLT, ALLISON N; Arapaho Schl; Arapaho, OK; (2); 1/28; Church Yth Grp; Cmnty Wkr; 4-H; FHA; GAA; Letterman Clb; Office Aide; Quiz Bowl; Scholastic Bowl; SADD; AAU Natl Tnmt Rep.

HOLT, ANGELA D; Muskogee HS; Muskogee, OK; (1); Church Yth Grp; Spanish Clb; Chorus; Flag Corp; School Musical; Hon Roll; Tns Chrst; RAID; Chrch Bl Chr; OU; Veterinary Med.

HOLT, BRAD; Asher Schl; Asher, OK; (1); Rptr Nwsp; Pres Frsh Cls.

HOLT, BRAD; Adair HS; Adair, OK; (4); 2/61; Church Yth Grp; FCA; Teachers Aide; Church Choir; JV Var Bsbl; JV Var Bsktbl; JV Var Ftbl; High Hon Roll; Hon Roll; NHS; Masonic Stu Yr; Cty Yth Rallies Pres; Ottawa U; Engr.

HOLT, BRANDON; Midwest City HS; Midwest City, OK; (4); 62/419; Church Yth Grp; Pres Band; Drm Mjr(t); Jazz Band; Mrchg Band; Orch; Pep Band; Gov Hon Prg Awd; NHS; Scholastic Bowl; Hnr Cncrt & Jazz Bands; U Of Cntrl OK; Psych.

HOLT, CAMERON; Stigler HS; Stigler, OK; (2); Church Yth Grp; FCA; Speech Tm; Band; Mrchg Band; School Play; Ofcr Bsbl; Bsktbl; Var Ftbl; OK ST U.

HOLT, CHRISTA; Billings HS; Garber, OK; (4); 5/15; Church Yth Grp; Drama Clb; VP 4-H; Natl FFA Org; Office Aide; Pep Clb; Spanish Clb; Varsity Clb; School Play; Pres Frsh Cls; OK ST U.

HOLT, DAVID; Putnam City North HS; Oklahoma City, OK; (3); 17/500; School Musical; School Play; Yrbk; Pres Soph Cls; VP Stu Cncl; NHS; Ntl Merit SF; Boy Scts; Drama Clb; Key Clb; BRA Pres; Clay Culver Awrd; Natl Stdnt Cncl Cnvtn Dlgt.

HOLT, ELIZABETH A; Stillwater Sr HS; Stillwater, OK; (2); Church Yth Grp; Drama Clb; Library Aide; School Musical; Stage Crew; Bsktbl; Pres Schlr; Scrpt Wrtng; Drama.

HOLT, GINGER; Hartshorne Sr HS; Mcalester, OK; (4); 4/57; Library Aide; Natl FFA Org; Sec Jr Cls; Var Chrldng; High Hon Roll; Hon Roll; NHS; E OK ST Coll; Elem Ed.

HOLT, GREGORY; North Intemediate HS; Broken Arrow, OK; (1); Latin Clb; Wt Lftg; Hon Roll; Jr NHS; Draw; Bsktbl; Med.

HOLT, JAMIE L; Deer Creek HS; Edmond, OK; (4); Church Yth Grp; Hosp Aide; Acpl Chr; Chorus; Church Choir; School Musical; School Play; Variety Show; Ofcr Sr Cls; Gym; Karate; OK U.

HOLT, JENNIFER L; Deer Creek-Lamont Jr Sr HS; Lamont, OK; (2); 1/13; Church Yth Grp; FCA; Band; Chorus; School Play; Bsktbl; Sftbl; High Hon Roll; NHS; U Of OK; Acctng.

HOLT, JERE J; West Mid HS; Norman, OK; (1); Church Yth Grp; CAP; Cmnty Wkr; Red Cross Aide; Color Guard; Intrml Mgr Trk; Hon Roll; OK Univ; USAF.

HOLT, JORDAN J; Union Intermediate HS; Tulsa, OK; (2); Boy Scts; German Clb; Var L Wrstlng; Hon Roll; NHS.

HOLT, MARIAH N; Choctaw HS; Choctaw, OK; (4); 45/303; Church Yth Grp; Drama Clb; Treas French Clb; Acpl Chr; Treas Chorus; School Musical; Swing Chorus; Variety Show; Jr NHS; Southeastern OK ST U.

HOLT, NIKI; Arapaho Schl; Arapaho, OK; (2); Church Yth Grp; Cmnty Wkr; 4-H; FHA; Library Aide; Quiz Bowl; Teachers Aide; Church Choir; Pres Frsh Cls; Pres Soph Cls; Horse Judging AJQHA Wrld Champ; 5 Cty All Conf Tm Bsktbl.

HOLT, RENE A; Catoosa HS; Catoosa, OK; (2); Church Yth Grp; FCA; French Clb; NHS; Pres Cmptr Grphcs/Sftwr Grp; Psych.

HOLT, STEPHENIE R; Ardmore HS; Ardmore, OK; (4); 85/162; Spanish Clb; Chorus; School Musical; Hon Roll; ADAPT; U Of OK; Bus.

HOLT, TIFFANY; U S Grant HS; Oklahoma City, OK; (1); Church Yth Grp; FCA; Chrldng; Gym; Mgr(s); High Hon Roll; U Of OK; Psych.

HOLTHUS, STACI; Dover Schl; Dover, OK; (1); FCA; GAA; Natl FFA Org; Chorus; Ofcr Frsh Cls; Var Bsktbl; Score Keeper; Hon Roll; Prfct Atten Awd; Ed.

HOLTON, JARED; Yukon Middle HS; Yukon, OK; (2); Church Yth Grp; Scholastic Bowl; Band; Jazz Band; Mrchg Band; Pep Band; Rep Stu Cncl; High Hon Roll; NHS; Dont Do Drugs.

HOLTON, REGAN; Midwest City HS; Midwest City, OK; (2); School Musical; School Play; Ofcr Soph Cls; Var Wt Lftg; High Hon Roll; Hon Roll; Jr NHS; NHS; Church Yth Grp; Drama Clb; Outstng 95, Art Stu, Drama, Indstrl Dsgn; Top GPA Engl, Hstry, Sci; Art Inst Of Dallas; Indstrl Sci.

HOLTZEN, SCOTT E; Pioneer Jr Sr HS; Enid, OK; (3); Am Leg Boys St; Var Bsktbl; Hon Roll.

HOLZWORTH, CORRIE S; East Central HS; Tulsa, OK; (3); Church Yth Grp; Sec FBLA; Key Clb; ROTC; Spanish Clb; Hon Roll; Bus Stu At Tulsa Tech Ctr; Tech Cls; Bus Admin; HS Tchr.

HONEA, CHRISTOPHER; Midwest City HS; Midwest City, OK; (3); 1/384; DECA; German Clb; Ftbl; Wt Lftg; Wrstlng; Gov Hon Prg Awd; High Hon Roll; Hon Roll; Prfct Atten Awd; Pres Acad Fit Awd; OK U; Med.

HONEY, KRISTIN M; Chisholm Sr HS; Enid, OK; (2); Rptr Church Yth Grp; FCA; FHA; Hosp Aide; Quiz Bowl; Scholastic Bowl; Spanish Clb; Chorus; Rep Stu Cncl; Var Chrldng.

HONEYCUTT, DANIELLE C; Roland Sr HS; Roland, OK; (2); Cmnty Wkr; 4-H; Speech Tm; Varsity Clb; JV Bsktbl; Var Score Keeper; Var Sftbl; Hon Roll; Sports Awd Mst Imprvd Sftbl Player; Northeastern ST U; Occptnl Thr.

HONEYFIELD, GERAD G; Minco HS; El Reno, OK; (3); Letterman Clb; L Ftbl; OU; Coach; Phy Thrpst.

HOOD, ANDY S; South Intermediate HS; Broken Arrow, OK; (1); Church Yth Grp; Intrml Ftbl; Trk; Cit Awd; Rnnr-Up Best Ctzn; U Of NE; Bus Mgmt.

HOOD, TRAVIS; Stuart Sr HS; Mcalester, OK; (3); 14/32; Phtg Yrbk; Hon Roll; CA ST U Fresno; Photo.

HOOD, WESLEY; Tahlequah Sr HS; Tahlequah, OK; (2); Church Yth Grp; 4-H; Natl FFA Org; Quiz Bowl; JV Bsktbl; 4-H Awd; Hon Roll; Jr NHS; NHS; St Schlr; Vet.

HOOK, BUBBA R; Tahlequah Sr HS; Tahlequah, OK; (2); Letterman Clb; Quiz Bowl; Varsity Clb; Ftbl; Wt Lftg; Hon Roll; Pres Acad Fit Awd; Air Force Acad.

HOOK, LOYD R; Tahlequah Sr HS; Tahlequah, OK; (2); Church Yth Grp; Quiz Bowl; Varsity Clb; Var Ftbl; Golf; Var Tennis; Cit Awd; Hon Roll; Jr NHS; NHS; Air Frce Acad; Bass Master.

HOOKS, JASON J; Putnam City West HS; Bethany, OK; (3); 1/320; Am Leg Boys St; Cmnty Wkr; FBLA; Spanish Clb; Rep Stu Cncl; Cit Awd; High Hon Roll; Jr NHS; NHS; Yal Clb Awd; Silow Lodge Stu Of Today; All Amer Schlr; Stanford; Comp Sci.

HOOPER, AUBREY M; Putnam City North HS; Oklahoma City, OK; (3); 63/509; Church Yth Grp; Cmnty Wkr; SADD; Chorus; Church Choir; Ofcr Sr Cls; Mgr Bsktbl; Capt Vllybl; Treas NHS; Var Mgr(s); Panther Pals VP; BRA Sec & Treas; OBU; Acctng; CPA.

HOOPER, ELIZABETH; Clinton HS; Clinton, OK; (1); Church Yth Grp; Key Clb; Band; Chorus; Mrchg Band; High Hon Roll; NHS; Math Awd; Med.

HOOPER, KRISTY; Mountain View-Gotebo HS; Mountain View, OK; (4); 3/31; Church Yth Grp; FCA; FHA; HOBY; Treas Natl FFA Org; Rep Soph Cls; VP Stu Cncl; High Hon Roll; Hon Roll; OK ST U; Ind Engrng.

HOOPER, MELANIE; Temple Jr Sr HS; Hastings, OK; (1); Church Yth Grp; Pres Frsh Cls; Bsktbl; Chrldng; Sftbl.

HOOSE, RANDY D; Warner HS; Warner, OK; (2); 4-H; FHA; Natl FFA Org; Spanish Clb; Cit Awd; 4-H Awd; Hon Roll; FHA Awd; OK ST Univ; Ag; Mech Engr.

HOOSIER, HEATHER A; Lone Grove HS; Ardmore, OK; (3); Church Yth Grp; FHA; Science Clb; Spanish Clb; Band; Jazz Band; Mrchg Band; Pep Band; Cit Awd; Hon Roll; SCOBDA; All Dist Band; Univ Of OK; OT.

HOOTEN, BECKY; Stigler HS; Eufaula, OK; (1); FHA; Pep Clb; SADD; Bsktbl; Hon Roll; Pres Acad Fit Awd.

HOOVER, AMANDA; Ada HS; Ada, OK; (3); Church Yth Grp; FCA; French Clb; Band; Mrchg Band; Sec Frsh Cls; Sec Soph Cls; VP Jr Cls; Rep Stu Cncl; Chrldng.

HOOVER, AMBER S; Depew HS; Depew, OK; (3); Church Yth Grp; Drama Clb; Natl FFA Org; Pep Clb; School Play; Stage Crew; Prfct Atten Awd; Elem Tchr.

HOOVER, JAMES; Depew HS; Depew, OK; (1); 1/52; Natl FFA Org; Quiz Bowl; Scholastic Bowl; Ski Clb; Pres Frsh Cls; Ftbl; Wt Lftg; High Hon Roll; OK U.

HOOVER, KARA; Cement Jr Sr HS; Cement, OK; (2); Church Yth Grp; FHA; HOBY; Natl FFA Org; Rep Soph Cls; Bsktbl; Trk; Vllybl; High Hon Roll; Ntl Merit Ltr; OK Hnrs Soc; Natl Stdnt Ath Day Awd; Caddo-Comancho Conf Acad All Conf.

HOOVER, LISA; Depew HS; Depew, OK; (1); 2/54; Spanish Clb; High Hon Roll; Gftd Tlntd Pgm; Acad Tm.

HOOVER, RACHEL A; Union Sr HS; Tulsa, OK; (3); 10/741; Church Yth Grp; French Clb; FBLA; Treas Key Clb; Teachers Aide; Band; Rep Stu Cncl; High Hon Roll; Hon Roll; Jr NHS; NHS; U Of OK; Med.

HOOVER, REBECCA J; Afton HS; Afton, OK; (2); Church Yth Grp; FHA; Natl FFA Org; Speech Tm; SADD; School Play; OCCP; Med.

HOOVER, SANDY; Madill HS; Madill, OK; (3); FCA; FBLA; Pres Frsh Cls; Var Bsktbl; Var Ftbl; Hon Roll; NHS.

HOOVER, SHERI L; Sapulpa Sr HS; Sapulpa, OK; (3); Church Yth Grp; French Clb; Band; Jazz Band; Mrchg Band; French Hon Soc; High Hon Roll; Ltrmn Bnd/Acad; OK HS Hon Soc; Natl Geography/Sci/Bio Olympiad; Zoology.

HOPCUS, CANDICE A; Choctaw HS; Choctaw, OK; (2); 4-H; High Hon Roll; Jr NHS; Val; Columbia; Med.

HOPE, AMANDA D; Muldrow HS; Muldrow, OK; (3); 4-H; FHA; Natl Beta Clb; Natl FFA Org; Office Aide; Mrchg Band; Var Chrldng; Cit Awd; Hon Roll; Pres Soph Cls; Homecoming Princess.

HOPE, JOSHUA R; Waynoka HS; Waynoka, OK; (2); Church Yth Grp; FCA; 4-H; FHA; Pep Clb; Pres Frsh Cls; Var L Bsbl; Var L Bsktbl; Var L Ftbl; Var Wt Lftg; FBI Agent.

HOPE, TERRY; Crooked Oak HS; Oklahoma City, OK; (4); Am Leg Boys St; Boy Scts; FCA; Office Aide; VICA; Ftbl; Trk; Wt Lftg; Hon Roll; NHS; OSU; Arch.

HOPKINS, AARON; Wellston Schl; Wellston, OK; (3); 4/58; Am Leg Boys St; Drama Clb; 4-H; Speech Tm; School Play; Ftbl; Wt Lftg; Hon Roll; NHS; Engrng.

HOPKINS, AMANDA D; Rock Creek Jr Sr HS; Bennington, OK; (2); FHA; Band; Mrchg Band; Marine Biolgst.

HOPKINS, CHEYENNE; Eufaula Sr HS; Eufaula, OK; (2); Art Clb; Church Yth Grp; FHA; Yrbk; High Hon Roll; Hon Roll; NHS; Wrtng Short Stories; OK U; Jrnlsm.

HOPKINS, CHRISTY D; Bixby Sr HS; Bixby, OK; (1); 1/260; Church Yth Grp; FCA; Spanish Clb; Ed Yrbk; Pres Stu Cncl; JV Sftbl; Stat Wrstlng; Gov Hon Prg Awd; Jr NHS; Pres Acad Fit Awd; Sprts Wrtng Awd NSU Media Day.

HOPKINS, JULIE M; Westmoore HS; Oklahoma City, OK; (3); 36/720; Church Yth Grp; FCA; Spanish Clb; Teachers Aide; Church Choir; Sec Stu Cncl; High Hon Roll; Jr NHS; NHS; Ath Trngn; Medicine.

HOPKINS, KARI; Achille Schl; Hendrix, OK; (2); 1/42; 4-H; Var Bsktbl; Var Sftbl; Hon Roll; NHS; Otstdng Wrld His Stdnt 94-95; Otstdng Eng I Stdnt 94-95; Otstdng Alg I Stdnt 94-95; SOSU.

HOPKINS, KARLA S; Bartlesville Sr HS; Barnsdall, OK; (1); 126/480; Var Crs Cntry; Var Trk; Hon Roll; NHS; AR; Jrnlst/Nws Cstr.

HOPKINS, STASHA; Eufaula Sr HS; Eufaula, OK; (2); Church Yth Grp; FHA; Ofcr Stu Cncl; JV Var Bsktbl; JV Var Chrldng; Hon Roll; Northeastern U; Neonatal Nurse.

HOPPE, KELLY J; Western Heights Sr HS; Blanchard, OK; (2); English Clb; FHA; Spanish Clb; Capt Socr; Hon Roll; Ldrshp Eng; Soccer Olympic Dev Team MVP Conf Soccer; 1st Team All City Soccer; NC.

HOPPER, MICHELLE R; Mustang HS; Yukon, OK; (4); 1/350; Church Yth Grp; 4-H; Key Clb; Spanish Clb; Cit Awd; 4-H Awd; NHS; Val; Sci Museum Vol; OK ST U; Span.

HOPPERS, JED; Madill HS; Madill, OK; (3); Church Yth Grp; FCA; Office Aide; Church Choir; Phtg Yrbk; Crs Cntry; Trk; High Hon Roll; NHS; Ntl Merit Ltr.

HOPSON, RANDY; Checotah HS; Checotah, OK; (2); Art Clb; Speech Tm; High Hon Roll; Hon Roll; OK ST Univ; Arch Engrng.

HORAN, BRIAN K; North Intemediate HS; Broken Arrow, OK; (2); Thesps; School Play; Stage Crew; Hon Roll; NY Univ; Dramatic Arts.

HORCICA, MICHELLE R; Broken Arrow Sr HS; Broken Arrow, OK; (4); FBLA; FHA; Tennis; Vllybl; NEO; Intr Dsgn.

HORGAN, COLLEEN E; Waukomis HS; Enid, OK; (3); Office Aide; Pep Clb; Spanish Clb; Var L Chrldng; Sftbl; OK ST; Acctng.

HORGAN, TARA A; Norman Sr HS; Norman, OK; (3); Spanish Clb; Teachers Aide; Chorus; Cit Awd; Hon Roll; Stu Ath Trnr; NEO; Ath Trning.

HORGES, LA TONYA; Jarman Jr HS; Oklahoma City, OK; (2); Computer Clb; Dance Clb; Letterman Clb; Pep Clb; Chorus; Swing Chorus; Chrldng; Pom Pon; High Hon Roll; Hon Roll; Dance Cmptns 1st Pl Solo Wnnr; Arts.

HORINEK, JENNY; Newkirk HS; Newkirk, OK; (4); 7/46; FCA; Band; Jazz Band; Mrchg Band; Treas Sr Cls; Ofcr Stu Cncl; Hon Roll; NHS; STEPP; UCO.

HORN, AARON D; Pocola HS; Pocola, OK; (3); 1/60; FCA; Quiz Bowl; Scholastic Bowl; Bsktbl; Gov Hon Prg Awd; Pres NHS; Westpoint Mltry Acad.

HORN, JACOB J; Mt St Marys HS; Midwest City, OK; (3); 2/80; Art Clb; Drama Clb; Key Clb; Stage Crew; Ntl Merit Ltr; Art Extracurricular Classes Taken; Math Counts; St Johns Coll; Writer; Artist.

HORN, JALYNNE E; Velma Alma HS; Duncan, OK; (1); Church Yth Grp; Band; Mrchg Band; Chrldng; Crs Cntry; Trk; Hon Roll; OK Baptist U; Psycht.

HORN, JILL; Haworth Jr HS; Haworth, OK; (1); #2 in class; Art Clb; Church Yth Grp; Natl FFA Org; Hon Roll; Jr NHS; Sal; OK Hnr Soc; OU; Med.

HORNBUCKLE, SHERROD A; Wagoner Sr HS; Wagoner, OK; (4); 4-H; Natl FFA Org; Vo Ag Tchr.

HORNBUCKLE, TONI R; Duncan HS; Duncan, OK; (3); Church Yth Grp; FBLA; Acpl Chr; Chorus; Church Choir; Orch; School Musical; School Play; Cmnty Svc; Church Compassn Clinic; Comp Repair.

HORNE, BRADLEY K; Madill HS; Madill, OK; (1); FCA; Var JV Bsbl; JV Bsktbl; JV Ftbl; Ltr M Awd Bsktbl, Bsbl, Ftbl; Cert Acad Excl JOM; U Of OK; Comp Prgmr; Meteorolgy.

HORNE, LORI A; Union Sr HS; Tulsa, OK; (3); 122/741; Church Yth Grp; Drama Clb; Spanish Clb; School Musical; School Play; Intrml JV Vllybl; Hon Roll; NHS; Pres Schlr; Spanish NHS; Northeastern ST U; Elem Ed.

HORNELL, KRISTIN M; Bartlesville Sr HS; Bartlesville, OK; (3); 35/441; Church Yth Grp; Orch; High Hon Roll; NHS; Prfct Atten Awd.

HORNER, MATTHEW J; Duncan HS; Duncan, OK; (2); Church Yth Grp; Letterman Clb; Rptr Nwsp; Var Bsbl; Var Bsktbl; L Crs Cntry; Cit Awd; DAR Awd; Hon Roll; Jr NHS; Pre-Med.

HORNER, SANDY M; Byng Sr HS; Ada, OK; (2); 24/120; Art Clb; FTA; Band; Mrchg Band; Jr NHS; Stu Missnry Belize Br Honduras 96; Geneva; Ed.

HORSTMAN, JOSEPH A; Putnam City North HS; Findlay, OH; (4); 15/430; Church Yth Grp; FHA; Math Tm; Quiz Bowl; Scholastic Bowl; Spanish Clb; SADD; Varsity Clb; Var Crs Cntry; Var Trk; CYO Bsktbl; Treas Natl Hnr Soc; U Of OK; Orthpdc Srgn.

HORSTMAN, TIMOTHY S; Whitesboro Schl; Hodgen, OK; (3); 2/17; Church Yth Grp; FCA; Letterman Clb; Natl FFA Org; Varsity Clb; Rptr Nwsp; Pres Frsh Cls; Pres Soph Cls; VP Jr Cls; Ofcr Bsbl; Sports Medicine.

HORTON, DIXIE; Victory Christian Schl; Tulsa, OK; (3); Art Clb; Church Yth Grp; Drama Clb; Intnl Clb; Speech Tm; School Musical; School Play; Yrbk; Tennis; Hon Roll; Lcl Msc; OK ST; Intl Bus.

HORTON, JOSHUA D; Wright Christian Acad; Owasso, OK; (3); 2/30; Church Yth Grp; Key Clb; School Musical; JV Bsktbl; Mgr(s); Var Capt Socr; Hon Roll; Ntl Merit SF; Natl Yng Ldrs Schlr; US Natl Math Awd Wnnr.

HORTON, KYLE L; Putnam City West HS; Bethany, OK; (2); Church Yth Grp; Debate Tm; Spanish Clb; Mrchg Band; Pep Band; Ofcr Stu Cncl; Var JV Bsktbl; Golf; Hon Roll; NHS.

HORTON, MICHAEL D; Plainview HS; Ardmore, OK; (3); Church Yth Grp; Cmnty Wkr; FCA; SADD; Var Bsktbl; Var Ftbl; Hon Roll; NHS; Prfct Atten Awd; Pres Acad Fit Awd; Ft Lewis; Bus.

HOSEK, STACY L; Bartlesville Mid HS; Bartlesville, OK; (2); 174/481; Band; Mrchg Band; Orch; Phtg Yrbk; Hon Roll; Prfct Atten Awd; All-Dist Band; Phys Thrpy.

HOSIER, ANGELA D; Mooreland Jr Sr HS; Mooreland, OK; (1); 3/35; Natl FFA Org; Hon Roll; Swmng; Pub Spkng Cmptv; Ceramics; Northwestrn OK ST U; Anml Sci.

HOSKINS, BRIAN; Perry Sr HS; Perry, OK; (4); 19/66; German Clb; Library Aide; Band; NHS; TSA; Acad Tm; OSU; Engrng.

HOSKINS, RYAN; Perry Sr HS; Perry, OK; (4); 17/66; German Clb; Library Aide; Band; Mrchg Band; TSA Pres & VP; Acad Tm Capt; Engrng.

HOUCK, APRIL L; Jay HS; Jay, OK; (3); 4-H; German Clb; Natl Beta Clb; Natl FFA Org; Pep Clb; Quiz Bowl; High Hon Roll; Hon Roll; NHS.

HOUGH, BRIAN; Goodwell Public Schl; Goodwell, OK; (2); 2/8; Church Yth Grp; FCA; Letterman Clb; Band; Mrchg Band; Pep Band; VP Soph Cls; Var Bsktbl; Var Golf; High Hon Roll.

HOUGH, ERIC E; South Intermediate HS; Broken Arrow, OK; (2); Boy Scts; Natl FFA Org; Rep Stu Cncl; Jr NHS; Acad Tm; OK ST Univ.

HOUGH, GREG; Wynona Schl; Wynona, OK; (4); 1/10; Pres Natl Beta Clb; Pres Soph Cls; Pres Jr Cls; Pres Sr Cls; Var Bsbl; Var Bsktbl; Var Golf; VP NHS; St Schlr; OSU; Mktng.

HOUGH, JAMES; Broken Arrow Sr HS; Broken Arrow, OK; (4); 1/921; Am Leg Boys St; Art Clb; Pres French Clb; JCL; Latin Clb; Crs Cntry; NHS; Ntl Merit SF; Val; Hon Stu Cncl-Offcl Artst; U Of OK; Art.

HOUGHTON, RACHEL M; Edmond North HS; Edmond, OK; (2); Church Yth Grp; Rep Stu Cncl; Hon Roll; Jr NHS; NHS; Stu Ath Trainer 2 Yrs; Rdng Tutor For Kids; AZ ST Univ; PT.

HOUK, ALISHA S; Edmond North HS; Edmond, OK; (3); French Clb; Office Aide; Band; Mrchg Band; Pep Band; Trk; High Hon Roll; Zoo.

HOURIGAN, NATALIE N; Bartlesville Sr HS; Bartlesville, OK; (2); Church Yth Grp; Cmnty Wkr; JA; Spanish Clb; Band; Church Choir; Mrchg Band; Nwsp; SPCA Work; OSU; Vetrnrn.

HOUSE, CODY R; Mooreland Jr Sr HS; Mooreland, OK; (2); 1/34; Art Clb; Scholastic Bowl; School Play; Rep Frsh Cls; High Hon Roll; Hon Roll; NHS; Pres Acad Fit Awd; Val; Mech Engr; Drafting & Design.

HOUSE, ISAAC C; Nathan Hale HS; Tulsa, OK; (3); Church Yth Grp; FCA; FBLA; Ofcr Bsbl; High Hon Roll; USA Bsbl All Star 96; U Of OK; Sprts Med.

HOUSER, MELISSA S; Catoosa HS; Catoosa, OK; (4); 1/135; Church Yth Grp; FCA; FHA; Spanish Clb; Chorus; Church Choir; High Hon Roll; NHS; Val; Pensacola Chrstn Coll; Med.

HOUSER, ROBIN A; Western Heights Sr HS; Yukon, OK; (1); 20/203; Drama Clb; Scholastic Bowl; Band; Flag Corp; School Play; Rptr Nwsp; Phtg Yrbk; Cit Awd; Gov Hon Prg Awd; High Hon Roll; Intrstd Bus Mngmt/Mrktng; Org/Ran A Recyclng Prgm At Schl; Bus Mngmt/Mrktng.

HOUSKA, NICOLE; Perry Sr HS; Perry, OK; (2); FBLA; GAA; Band; Mrchg Band; Pep Band; Nwsp; Bsktbl; Sftbl; Cit Awd; High Hon Roll; Band Cncl; Slwptch Sftl Trnmt MVP; OK ST U; Lawyer.

HOUSLEY, ADAM; Metro Christian Acad; Broken Arrow, OK; (4); 5/67; Church Yth Grp; Hist Key Clb; Mgr Teachers Aide; VP Stu Cncl; Ofcr Bsbl; NHS; Boy Of Yr; Mst Spirited; Attnd OK Assn Stu Cncl St Conv; OK ST Univ; Tchr.

HOUSLEY, HEATHER; Metro Christian Acad; Broken Arrow, OK; (2); Rep Church Yth Grp; FCA; Key Clb; Spanish Clb; Rep Stu Cncl; Capt JV Chrldng; Gym; Hon Roll; Jr NHS; NHS.

HOUSLEY, MELISSA L; Sapulpa Sr HS; Sapulpa, OK; (4); 24/279; FCA; Science Clb; Var Capt Crs Cntry; Var Capt Trk; Cit Awd; NHS; Spanish NHS; Cir/Frnds Spksprsn; U Of Tulsa; PT/BIO.

HOUSTON, HILLARY D; Mustang HS; Mustang, OK; (4); 13/350; Church Yth Grp; FCA; Church Choir; Rep Soph Cls; Rep Jr Cls; Rep Sr Cls; VP Stu Cncl; Cit Awd; NHS; Sal; OK Bapt Univ; Scndry Ed.

HOUSTON, RICHARD; Lawton Sr HS; Lawton, OK; (3); Am Leg Boys St; Drama Clb; FCA; Hosp Aide; JA; Office Aide; Speech Tm; Teachers Aide; Chorus; School Musical; All ST Choir Mem; Renaissance Acad Achvmnt Awd; Schl Ed Video Tapes Narrator; AZ ST U; Communications.

HOUSTON, ROBERT; Charles Page HS; Tulsa, OK; (4); 38/334; Am Leg Boys St; Debate Tm; French Clb; Math Tm; NFL; School Play; NHS; Yth In Govt; OK St Yth Co-Gov; Schl Clb Pres; OK Delg Natl Yth Gov Conf; Stu Advsry Cncl; Job.

HOUTZ, AMBER; Cement Jr Sr HS; Cement, OK; (3); 4-H; Natl FFA Org; Quiz Bowl; Treas Jr Cls; 4-H Awd; Hon Roll; NHS.

HOVEY, KRISTIN; Chisholm Sr HS; Enid, OK; (2); Church Yth Grp; FCA; FHA; Spanish Clb; Var Chrldng; Gym; Hon Roll; NHS.

HOVIS, MELISSA; Hobart HS; Hobart, OK; (2); 2/100; Church Yth Grp; FCA; FHA; Girl Scts; HOBY; Quiz Bowl; Speech Tm; Band; Sftbl; High Hon Roll; Wider Opportunity For Girl Scts; Girl Sct Slvr Awd; Shortgrass Hnr Band 2nd Chr; OSU; Hotel/Restaurant Mgmt.

HOWARD, ANGEL L; Pocola HS; Pocola, OK; (3); Church Yth Grp; 4-H; Teachers Aide; Band; Chorus; Jazz Band; Mrchg Band; Hon Roll; NHS.

HOWARD, BECKY R; Jay HS; Jay, OK; (4); FBLA; FHA; Library Aide; Rptr Mu Alpha Theta; Natl Beta Clb; Rptr Nwsp; Yrbk; NHS; I-D-Fy; Peer Cnslr; Bacone Coll; Lab Tech.

HOWARD, BILLY E; Moore HS; Moore, OK; (3); NHS; Prfct Atten Awd; Top 10 Soph Eng Awd; OBU Shawnee; Sci; Scndry HS Ed.

HOWARD, BRETT; Choctaw HS; Midwest City, OK; (2); Boy Scts; Chess Clb; Quiz Bowl; Scholastic Bowl; Spanish Clb; High Hon Roll; Envrnmntl Awrnss Clb; Semifnlst OK Schl Of Sci/Math; MIT; Physics.

HOWARD, CHRYSTLE; Navajo Schl; Headrick, OK; (4); 1/34; Church Yth Grp; Pres 4-H; FHA; HOBY; Letterman Clb; Pres Natl FFA Org; Pep Clb; VP Service Clb; VP Spanish Clb; Varsity Clb; OK ST U; Scndry Cnslr.

HOWARD, CRYSTAL D; Muskogee HS; Muskogee, OK; (1).

HOWARD, DEREK D; Putnam City HS; Bethany, OK; (2); French Clb; Ftbl; Hcky; OSU; Sales.

HOWARD, DINAH; Westmoore HS; Oklahoma City, OK; (3); 19/620; Church Yth Grp; Cmnty Wkr; Spanish Clb; Teachers Aide; JV Crs Cntry; Hon Roll; Jr NHS; NHS; Univ OK Field Stud In Bio, Health Scis Summer Acad; U Of OK; Chld Psych.

HOWARD, JACEY; Sayre HS; Sayre, OK; (3); 1/49; Church Yth Grp; FCA; Rep Stu Cncl; Phtg Bsbl; Var L Bsktbl; Var Chrldng; Rotry Yth Ldrshp Awd.

HOWARD, JUSTIN B; Midwest City HS; Del City, OK; (2); 84/488; Scholastic Bowl; JV Bsbl; JV Ftbl; Hon Roll; NHS; Amer Legion Bsbl; Engrng.

HOWARD, KRISTI L; Lone Grove HS; Ardmore, OK; (2); Church Yth Grp; Debate Tm; FHA; Math Clb; Science Clb; Chorus; Church Choir; Swing Chorus; Hon Roll; OK U; Anesthesiologists.

HOWARD, LISA R; Putnam City West HS; Bethany, OK; (2); 20/390; Church Yth Grp; Orch; School Musical; NHS; Geom Awd; GATE Stdnt Advy Bd Frosh/Soph Yrs; U OK Hlth Sci Acad; U Of OK; Med.

HOWARD, MARY; Moore HS; Moore, OK; (4); 42/525; Art Clb; Science Clb; Ed Nwsp; Yrbk; Swmmng; Jr NHS; NHS; Future Jrnlsts Amer; Art Awd.

HOWARD, MATTHEW T; B T Washington HS; Tulsa, OK; (4); 30/274; Pres German Clb; Girl Scts; Intnl Clb; Letterman Clb; Ski Clb; Orch; French Hon Soc; Val; AAPT; CA Polytechnic U; Tight Rope.

HOWARD, MICHAEL E; Jay HS; Jay, OK; (1); PTA Art Awd 2nd; IDFY.

HOWARD, PAM; Liberty Acad; Shawnee, OK; (1); Church Yth Grp; Bsktbl; Vllybl; Marine Bio.

HOWARD, RANDIE L; El Reno Sr HS; El Reno, OK; (2); Church Yth Grp; Drama Clb; FCA; Key Clb; Math Tm; Church Choir; Drill Tm; Swing Chorus; Chrldng; Pom Pon.

HOWARD, REBECCA D; Bishop Mcguinness HS; Oklahoma City, OK; (4); 8/157; Cmnty Wkr; FCA; Spanish Clb; SADD; JV L Bsktbl; JV Var Sftbl; NHS; Pres Schlr; Spanish NHS; St Schlr; NW OK City Rotry Clb Jr Rotarian; OK Air Space Museum Ed Pgm Asst; Truman ST Univ; Commnctn.

HOWARD, RILEY; Berryhill Jr HS; Tulsa, OK; (3); 3/80; Church Yth Grp; Cmnty Wkr; FCA; Math Tm; Mu Alpha Theta; Scholastic Bowl; Teachers Aide; Band; Church Choir; Jazz Band; FL ST U.

HOWARD, TERRELL L; Carl Albert HS; Midwest City, OK; (2); Church Yth Grp; Church Choir; Var Bsktbl; Hon Roll; NHS; St Schlr; Outstdng Alg II Stdnt; Arch Engr.

HOWE, JEREMY W; Alex Jr Sr HS; Chickasha, OK; (3); 5/40; Church Yth Grp; FCA; FBLA; Pres Frsh Cls; Rep Soph Cls; VP Jr Cls; Capt Bsbl; Capt Bsktbl; Cit Awd; FFA Pres; PT.

HOWE, JESSICA; Miami Sr HS; Miami, OK; (2); 28/168; Church Yth Grp; Cmnty Wkr; Red Cross Aide; Band; Flag Corp; Mrchg Band; Jr NHS; NHS; Cmnty Theater Play.

HOWE, KEVIN; Dale Sr HS; Mc Loud, OK; (2); 1/50; Church Yth Grp; Spanish Clb; Band; Jazz Band; Mrchg Band; Pep Band; High Hon Roll; NHS; OK; Engrng.

HOWE, MELISSA; Kingfisher HS; Kingfisher, OK; (3); Church Yth Grp; FCA; Spanish Clb; Speech Tm; Band; Church Choir; Jazz Band; Mrchg Band; Pep Band; Chrldng; Band; Schltc Meet Awds Math; Ldrshp Awds.

HOWELL, JEREMY J; Edmond Santa Fe HS; Edmond, OK; (3); Church Yth Grp; Var Golf; NHS; Bill Nicklas Mem Jr Golf Fdn Cncl.

HOWELL, LATOYA M; Mc Lain Career Acad; Tulsa, OK; (2); Church Yth Grp; Office Aide; ROTC; Teachers Aide; Church Choir; Drill Tm; School Play; Golf; Hon Roll; Med.

HOWELL, LESLIE L; Muldrow HS; Muldrow, OK; (1); FHA; Natl Beta Clb; Spanish Clb; Bsktbl; Var Sftbl; Hon Roll; Jr NHS; Pres Schlr; OK MS Hnr Soc; Vanderbilt; ER Dr.

HOWELL, MATT; Bartlesville Sr HS; Bartlesville, OK; (4); Rep Church Yth Grp; FCA; Math Clb; Band; JV Var Ftbl; JV Wrstlng; High Hon Roll; Hon Roll; Jr NHS; NHS; OK ST Univ; Arch Eng.

HOWELL, REN'NALDO S; Will Rogers HS; Tulsa, OK; (3); 38/278; Church Yth Grp; Varsity Clb; Var Bsktbl; Var Trk; Cit Awd; High Hon Roll; Hon Roll; Sci Peer Tutorng; Tchrs Asst; TX Southern; CPA.

HOWELL, RYAN; Plainview HS; Ardmore, OK; (3); 20/83; Chess Clb; FTA; Mu Alpha Theta; Quiz Bowl; Science Clb; Rep Soph Cls; Publications Video Broadcastign/Asst Ed; His Major.

HOWELL, SEAN; Chisholm Sr HS; Enid, OK; (3); Church Yth Grp; Debate Tm; Intnl Clb; Band; Mrchg Band; Yrbk; Hon Roll; NHS; Stu Mnth.

HOWELL, SKYE N; Hominy HS; Hominy, OK; (2); 4/79; Church Yth Grp; FHA; Teachers Aide; Hon Roll; St Schlr; RN.

HOWELL, WILLIAM R; Cushing HS; Cushing, OK; (1); Band; Mrchg Band; OK ST U.

HOWELLS, RENEE; Guthrie Sr HS; Edmond, OK; (3); 1/300; Church Yth Grp; FCA; FBLA; Mu Alpha Theta; SADD; Rep Soph Cls; Rep Stu Cncl; Var Chrldng; Var Tennis; High Hon Roll; Masonic Awd; Rotary Ldrshp Conf Rnnr Up; OU; Bus.

HOWELLS, THERESA; Guthrie Sr HS; Edmond, OK; (1); 20/320; Church Yth Grp; GAA; Chorus; Chrldng; Tennis; OSU; Vet.

HOWERTON, CHRIS; Nathan Hale HS; Tulsa, OK; (4); 23/206; Quiz Bowl; Ftbl; High Hon Roll; Hon Roll; NHS; DECA; OK ST U; Cnstrctn Mgmt.

HOWERTON, CLAY A; Stillwater Jr HS; Stillwater, OK; (1); Am Leg Boys St; Church Yth Grp; FCA; Office Aide; Teachers Aide; Ofcr Bsbl; Bsktbl; Ftbl; Wt Lftg; Wrstlng; Youthquake; Play Guitar; OSU.

HOWETH, MISSY E; Blanchard Jr Sr HS; Blanchard, OK; (2); Cmnty Wkr; FHA; GAA; Office Aide; Pep Band; Sec Frsh Cls; Hon Roll; Atndng Voc Tech; Csmtlgst.

HOWLINGWOLF, DENA L; Arapaho Schl; Arapaho, OK; (2); FHA; Teachers Aide; Chorus; School Musical; Var Bsktbl; Hon Roll; Southwestern OK ST Univ; Bus.

HOWSDEN, JAIME; Oklahoma Christian Schl; Edmond, OK; (1); Church Yth Grp; Cmnty Wkr; High Hon Roll; Dnc, Bllt, Pnte, Tap.

HOWZE, SHELDON S; Duke Schl; Duke, OK; (3); Church Yth Grp; FCA; JA; Natl FFA Org; Science Clb; Spanish Clb; Rptr Frsh Cls; L Bsbl; Capt L Bsktbl; L Trk; Sci Fair Awds; WOSC; Ag.

HOYLE, CLIFTON E; Pauls Valley HS; Pauls Valley, OK; (1); Church Yth Grp; Cmnty Wkr; FCA; Natl FFA Org; JV Bsbl; High Hon Roll; Hon Roll; OK St Hnr Soc; OK ST.

HOYLE, NICOLE A; Union Intermediate HS; Broken Arrow, OK; (2); 8/650; Intnl Clb; Key Clb; Band; High Hon Roll; NHS; Acad Ltr; Phy.

HOYT, AMBER M; South Intermediate HS; Broken Arrow, OK; (3); Office Aide; Teachers Aide; School Play; Rep Frsh Cls; Var Bsktbl; Var Trk; Hon Roll; Phys Thpy.

HOYT, JEROD; Grace Fellowship Christian Sch; Broken Arrow, OK; (2); Scholastic Bowl; Phtg Yrbk; Wt Lftg; Hon Roll; NHS; ORU.

HRUBIK, ANDREW; Moore HS; Moore, OK; (3); 155/525; Am Leg Boys St; Boy Scts; Church Yth Grp; CAP; French Clb; Science Clb; Band; Church Choir; Jazz Band; Mrchg Band; USAF Acad; Elec Engr.

HSU, VINCENT S; Casady Schl; Oklahoma City, OK; (3); Computer Clb; JCL; Varsity Clb; Band; Orch; JV Golf; Var Swmmng; Var Tennis; Var Vllybl; High Hon Roll; Stanford; Med.

HUANG, JOANNE; Stillwater Jr HS; Stillwater, OK; (1); Church Yth Grp; Math Tm; Natl Beta Clb; Quiz Bowl; School Play; Stage Crew; High Hon Roll; Pres Acad Fit Awd; OK Music Tchr Assn Piano Awds; Violia Lessons 8 Yrs; Piano 9 Yrs; St Cecilia Music Club Schlrshp; Harvard Univ; Med.

HUBBAND, KYLE W; Moore HS; Moore, OK; (3); Church Yth Grp; FCA; Spanish Clb; Chorus; Church Choir; Ofcr Stu Cncl; Var L Bsktbl; Hon Roll; Jr NHS; NHS; Core Grp; Engl Medal; Span/Engl/US His Awds.

HUBBARD, BRYAN; Oklahoma Christian Schl; Oklahoma City, OK; (4); 11/36; FCA; Office Aide; Speech Tm; Ofcr Bsbl; Var Co-Capt Ftbl; Trk; Wt Lftg; Hon Roll; All Dist Ftbl & Little All City; NM Military Inst; Pre-Med.

HUBBARD, JEREMY L; Enid Sr HS; Enid, OK; (2); Church Yth Grp; Hon Roll; Jr NHS; NHS; Pilot; Electronics.

HUBBARD, JOHN D; Claremore Sr HS; Chelsea, OK; (3); DECA; Drama Clb; FCA; Natl FFA Org; Rep Speech Tm; School Play; Rptr Nwsp; Hon Roll; Office Aide; Teachers Aide; Pub Spkng/ST Awds DECA; Govt/Mktg.

HUBBARD, KETITIA L; Enid Sr HS; Enid, OK; (2); Band; Mrchg Band; High Hon Roll; Hon Roll; Dr.

HUBBARD, KYLE; Moore HS; Moore, OK; (3); Church Yth Grp; FCA; Spanish Clb; Chorus; Church Choir; School Play; Rep Stu Cncl; Bsktbl; Hon Roll; Jr NHS; Law.

HUBBARD, MISSIE A; Tahlequah Sr HS; Tahlequah, OK; (3); Science Clb; SADD; Crs Cntry; Golf; Trk; Vet Med.

HUBBELL, LISA A; Beggs HS; Beggs, OK; (4); 4/49; Church Yth Grp; FCA; FHA; German Clb; GAA; Natl FFA Org; Red Cross Aide; Treas Sr Cls; Var Bsktbl; Var Sftbl; Tulsa JC; Pediatrc Nursng.

HUBBLE, LINDSEY; Perry Sr HS; Perry, OK; (2); 1/100; Church Yth Grp; FCA; German Clb; Band; Ed Nwsp; Yrbk; Golf; Pom Pon; Sftbl; High Hon Roll; Pediatrcs.

HUBER, KRISTIN S; Bishop Kelley HS; Tulsa, OK; (2); Church Yth Grp; Cmnty Wkr; French Clb; Teachers Aide; Var Golf; Hon Roll; Thrpst; Phy Thrpst.

HUCEK, TIFFANY R; El Reno Sr HS; Calumet, OK; (3); 19/195; Church Yth Grp; Cmnty Wkr; Drama Clb; Chorus; Church Choir; JV Chrldng; High Hon Roll; Jr NHS; NHS; Environmental Clb; OK Chrstn Univ; Child Psych.

HUCK, MARCUS A; Bishop Kelley HS; Tulsa, OK; (1); FCA; Ofcr Bsbl; Ftbl; Wrstlng; High Hon Roll; Duke; Bus Mngmt.

HUCKABY, STACEY J; Union Sr HS; Broken Arrow, OK; (3); Church Yth Grp; Ski Clb; Church Choir; Hon Roll; Regnl Yth Camp At Alamosa Canyon Sci Camp; OK U; Pediatric Occptnl Thrpst.

HUCKABY, WHITNEY L; Ninnekah HS; Blanchard, OK; (2); Church Yth Grp; Cmnty Wkr; FCA; FHA; Letterman Clb; Model UN; Science Clb; Spanish Clb; Teachers Aide; Varsity Clb; OK U; Sports Medicine.

HUDDLESTON, JEFF; Kingston HS; Kingston, OK; (1); Church Yth Grp; Rep Soph Cls; Hon Roll; Southeastern OK ST; Cmptr Sci.

HUDDLESTON, TRACY M; Byng Sr HS; Ada, OK; (2); Church Yth Grp; Drama Clb; FCA; FBLA; Spanish Clb; Speech Tm; School Play; Stage Crew; Mgr Bsktbl; Var Chrldng.

HUDELSON, JAMEEN; Marietta HS; Overbrook, OK; (1); Boy Scts; Debate Tm; Speech Tm; Band; Mrchg Band; School Play; Ofcr Stu Cncl; JV Sftbl; High Hon Roll; Hon Roll; Barrel Rcng; Piano; OK ST; Equine Practcnr.

HUDGENS, MANDY; Burlington Schl; Byron, OK; (3); 2/12; Sec 4-H; Natl FFA Org; Rep Band; Chorus; School Play; Pres Soph Cls; Pres Jr Cls; Bsktbl; Chrldng; Hon Roll.

HUDGEONS, TREVOR; Woodward HS; Woodward, OK; (2); Church Yth Grp; Rep Frsh Cls; Socr; Hon Roll; NHS; OK ST Univ.

HUDGINS, CHRISTA R; Duncan HS; Duncan, OK; (3); Church Yth Grp; FCA; Key Clb; SADD; Yrbk; Pres Frsh Cls; Rptr Stu Cncl; Var Chrldng; Var Tennis; High Hon Roll; OK ST Univ; PT.

HUDGINS, JAMIE D; Webster HS; Tulsa, OK; (3); Church Yth Grp; Key Clb; Office Aide; Teachers Aide; Chorus; Church Choir; Crs Cntry; Socr; Sftbl; Swmmng; Bus.

HUDGINS, JOHN D; Yale Jr Sr HS; Yale, OK; (4); 1/35; Am Leg Boys St; Church Yth Grp; Ofcr Stu Cncl; Ofcr Bsbl; Bsktbl; NHS; Val; Beta Clb Pres; Acad Tm Capt; OK ST U; Aerospace Engrng.

HUDSON, AMY; Choctaw Jr HS; Choctaw, OK; (1); Cmnty Wkr; Spanish Clb; Ed Nwsp; Ed Yrbk; U WA; Bio.

HUDSON, BRAD; Wynnewood HS; Wynnewood, OK; (3); 11/60; Church Yth Grp; Office Aide; Band; Jazz Band; Mrchg Band; Hon Roll; OK ST Contest Superior Rating; Span I Gold Medal.

HUDSON, ELIZABETH J; Tecumseh HS; Tecumseh, OK; (2); Church Yth Grp; French Clb; FHA; Natl Beta Clb; SADD; Bio-Chem.

HUDSON, ERIN; Berryhill Sr HS; Tulsa, OK; (2); 1/89; Church Yth Grp; FCA; Mu Alpha Theta; Pres Spanish Clb; Band; Jazz Band; Mrchg Band; Nwsp; NHS; Val; Med.

HUDSON, ERIN L; Edmond North HS; Edmond, OK; (1); 30/453; Bsktbl; JV Crs Cntry; Jr NHS; OK ST Univ.

HUDSON, HEATHER R; North Intemediate HS; Broken Arrow, OK; (2); Church Yth Grp; Cmnty Wkr; Latin Clb; Band; Church Choir; Color Guard; Mrchg Band; Pep Band; Hon Roll; NHS; OSU.

HUDSON, JARED; Tupelo Jr Sr HS; Coalgate, OK; (1); 2/25; Church Yth Grp; Quiz Bowl; Scholastic Bowl; Spanish Clb; Pres Frsh Cls; Pres Soph Cls; Var Bsbl; Var Bsktbl; Cit Awd; Hon Roll; Schlstc Acad Team.

HUDSON, JENNIFER; Madill HS; Madill, OK; (3); Church Yth Grp; FCA; 4-H; FHA; SADD; Nwsp; Yrbk; Ofcr Stu Cncl; Sftbl; Trk; 95 Ftbl Hmcmng Queen; Natl Eng Mrt Awd; SOSU; Phys Thrpy.

HUDSON, JENNIFER D; Byng Sr HS; Ada, OK; (2); 16/104; Sec Art Clb; Church Yth Grp; Sec 4-H; Pres FHA; Math Clb; Natl Beta Clb; Science Clb; Spanish Clb; Acpl Chr; Chorus; Offc SE Sub Dist II FHA Pres 95-; SE Sub Dist II FHA VP Elect 96-; Ponotoc Cty 4-H Sec 94-95; E Cntrl Univ; Voc Hm Ec.

HUDSON, JOE C; Pawhuska HS; Pawhuska, OK; (3); Boy Scts; Church Yth Grp; FBLA; Key Clb; Quiz Bowl; Spanish Clb; Ftbl; Trk; Wt Lftg; NHS; Hnr Roll; FCA.

HUDSON, JULIE; Kingfisher HS; Kingfisher, OK; (2); Church Yth Grp; Natl FFA Org; Quiz Bowl; Pres Spanish Clb; Pres Frsh Cls; Ofcr Stu Cncl; Bsktbl; Chrldng; Mgr(s); Hon Roll.

HUDSON, RACHELLE; Union Intermediate HS; Tulsa, OK; (2); 200/800; Spanish Clb; Rptr Nwsp; Rptr Yrbk; Rep Frsh Cls; Rep Soph Cls; JV Chrldng; Gym; Var JV Socr; Cit Awd; Hon Roll; Physically Ltd Day Camp Cnslr; ST Bars Chmpn Gymnastics; JV Chrldng Squad 3rd Natls 96; FL ST Univ; Marine Bio.

HUDSON, ROBERT L; Kellyville Sr HS; Kellyville, OK; (3); 4-H; Letterman Clb; Natl FFA Org; Ofcr Bsbl; Bsktbl; Pres Acad Fit Awd; Vo-Tech Welding; Letterman In Bsktbl & Bsbl; Navy Sea Cadets; Welder.

HUDSPETH, KELLY; Glenpool HS; Glenpool, OK; (3); 4-H; Red Cross Aide; Spanish Clb; VICA; Band; Jazz Band; Mrchg Band; Orch; Bsktbl; Powder Puff Ftbl; HOSA; TSA; Pre Med/Physcn.

HUELSMAN, SARA; Davenport Jr Sr HS; Davenport, OK; (4); 6/32; Church Yth Grp; Cmnty Wkr; FBLA; HOBY; Pep Clb; Scholastic Bowl; Teachers Aide; Phtg Yrbk; Hon Roll; Var Sftbl; Lfgds; St Gregorys Coll; Ear Chldhd Ed.

HUESING, KATHERINE M; U S Grant HS; Oklahoma City, OK; (2); Cmnty Wkr; ROTC; Hon Roll; Jr NHS; Marine Corps JROTC Outstdng Inspection Awd; MCJROTC Ribbons Civic Svc; Outstdng Acad Achvmt Ath Awd; Notre Dame Univ; Military Law.

HUESTE, MEAGHAN; Berryhill Jr HS; Tulsa, OK; (1); Church Yth Grp; FCA; FHA; Spanish Clb; Stage Crew; Yrbk; Chrldng; Gym; Powder Puff Ftbl; Sftbl; Srtns Clb; 1st Pl Srtm Hcr Essy Cntst; 2nd & 3rd Pl Grn Cntry Chrldng; OK; Anthslgy.

HUFF, DUSTIN M; Bishop Kelley HS; Tulsa, OK; (2); Var Bsbl; Hon Roll.

HUFF, HEATHER R; Choctaw HS; Choctaw, OK; (3); 98/390; Library Aide; Wt Lftg; Hon Roll; Stdnts Assisting Stdnts; Work With Mentally Retarded Yth; Small Bus.

HUFF, NAOMI; Claremore Sr HS; Claremore, OK; (2); Spanish Clb; VP Frsh Cls; High Hon Roll; NHS; Rice U.

HUFF, TALITHA J; Union Sr HS; Tulsa, OK; (4); 79/629; Church Yth Grp; FCA; FHA; German Clb; Office Aide; Pep Clb; Teachers Aide; Ofcr Soph Cls; Ofcr Sr Cls; Ofcr Stu Cncl; Rnssnc; Pepperdine; Intl Bus.

HUFFAKER, JACOB A; Norman Sr HS; Norman, OK; (3); 66/799; Boy Scts; Cmnty Wkr; Math Clb; Model UN; Mu Alpha Theta; Quiz Bowl; Spanish Clb; L Orch; Var L Tennis; Hon Roll; Sailng Clb; #1 Sngls Plyr Tnns Tm.

HUFFINE, WILLIAM B; Newcastle HS; Blanchard, OK; (3); FHA; Quiz Bowl; Scholastic Bowl.

HUFFMAN, ALANA R; Putnam City North HS; Oklahoma City, OK; (2); 95/464; Church Yth Grp; FCA; Key Clb; JV Golf; NHS; CAWS Envrmntl Club; Vol VBS; OK Univ.

HUFFMAN, REBECCA; El Reno Sr HS; El Reno, OK; (4); 17/167; Church Yth Grp; Math Clb; Science Clb; SADD; Band; Jazz Band; Mrchg Band; JV Co-Capt Vllybl; High Hon Roll; NHS; Adams ST Coll; Crmnl Jstc.

HUFFORD, CASEY; Waynoka HS; Waynoka, OK; (4); Am Leg Boys St; Church Yth Grp; FHA; Pep Clb; Pres Frsh Cls; Cert Auto Tech.

HUFFSTUTLAR, PATRISHA L; Calumet Schl; Calumet, OK; (3); 10/25; 4-H; Quiz Bowl; VP Spanish Clb; Church Choir; VP Jr Cls; Capt Chrldng; L Sftbl; Sec Frsh Cls; VP Soph Cls; L Bsktbl; Redlands; Vet.

HUGGINS, JILL; Ft Gibson HS; Fort Gibson, OK; (2); Church Yth Grp; Band; Mrchg Band; Mgr(s); Socr; High Hon Roll; NHS.

HUGGINS, JULIE; Ft Gibson HS; Fort Gibson, OK; (1); Church Yth Grp; Band; Ofcr Frsh Cls; Rptr Stu Cncl; Bsktbl; Socr; Sftbl; High Hon Roll.

HUGGINS, JUSTIN L; Stigler HS; Stigler, OK; (3); Band; Mrchg Band; Sprt Ed Nwsp; Var Capt Ftbl; Trk; Wt Lftg; Wrstlng; Wrestlng AAU St Chmpn 157 Lbs 94-95; St Trk Pole Vlt.

HUGHART, NICOLE; Braggs Schl; Braggs, OK; (2); GAA; HOBY; Quiz Bowl; Scholastic Bowl; Varsity Clb; Var Bsktbl; Var Sftbl; High Hon Roll; NHS; Sal.

HUGHES, AMANDA; New Lima Jr Sr HS; Seminole, OK; (3); Church Yth Grp; 4-H; Scholastic Bowl; School Play; Rptr Nwsp; Ofcr Jr Cls; Ofcr Stu Cncl; Chrldng; High Hon Roll; NHS.

HUGHES, ANDREA; Hennessey HS; Hennessey, OK; (2); 3/64; Church Yth Grp; FCA; FHA; Var Chrldng; High Hon Roll; NHS; OK ST U; Nrsng.

HUGHES, ANDREA; Cherokee Jr Sr HS; Corem, OK; (2); Church Yth Grp; FCA; Natl FFA Org; Spanish Clb; Speech Tm; VP Jr Cls; Bsktbl; Sftbl; Trk; Cit Awd; Intnl Order Of Rainbow For Girls; Grand Rep To CN In OK; Worthy Adv; OK Univ; Phy Thrpst.

HUGHES, ANGELA E; Del City HS; Del City, OK; (2); Church Yth Grp; Cmnty Wkr; Pep Clb; SADD; Chorus; Church Choir; Swing Chorus; Variety Show; Nwsp; Phtg Yrbk; U Of OK; Music/Mtrlgy..

HUGHES, ANGELA L; North Intemediate HS; Broken Arrow, OK; (1); Acpl Chr; Hon Roll; Law/DA.

HUGHES, ANGIE L; Wagoner Sr HS; Wagoner, OK; (2); Church Yth Grp; FBLA; FHA; Office Aide; Sftbl; Hon Roll; Stu Cncl Frosh; Northeastern ST Univ; Phy Thrp.

HUGHES, BRIAN; Ada HS; Ada, OK; (4); 13/170; Am Leg Boys St; FCA; Yrbk; Spanish Clb; Ofcr Stu Cncl; Bsktbl; Co-Capt Ftbl; Trk; NHS; Prfct Atten Awd; ECU; Mass Commcnts.

HUGHES, BRYAN G; Durant HS; Calera, OK; (3); Church Yth Grp; Debate Tm; Drama Clb; Office Aide; Pep Clb; Speech Tm; Acpl Chr; Chorus; Church Choir; School Play; Co Prdcr TV Prod FBC-TV Chnl 7; Disc Jcky; Pblc Addrss Anncr Bsktbl Gms; Tx Tech Univ; Radio/TV.

HUGHES, BRYAN S; Carl Albert HS; Midwest City, OK; (3); Church Yth Grp; CAP; Key Clb; Band; Jazz Band; Mrchg Band; Pep Band; School Play; Yrbk; Ofcr Jr Cls; Dallas Inst; Fnrl Dir.

HUGHES, DAVID; Bishop Kelley HS; Tulsa, OK; (3); Cmnty Wkr; Computer Clb; Dance Clb; Spanish Clb; Chorus; Church Choir; Hon Roll; Chrch Pianist; Comp Sftware Prog; Comp Cnsltnt.

HUGHES, FAITH; Central HS; Tulsa, OK; (3); Church Yth Grp; Hon Roll; Tulsa JC; Bus Mgmt.

HUGHES, JASON C; Haskell HS; Haskell, OK; (3); Am Leg Boys St; Church Yth Grp; Scholastic Bowl; Band; Mrchg Band; Pep Band; Var Chrldng; JV Var Ftbl; High Hon Roll; OK Hnr Soc; John Phillips Sousa Band Awd; Jr Chamber Commerce; UCA All-Star Chrldr 96; Med.

HUGHES, JOHN T; Stillwater Sr HS; Stillwater, OK; (3); Church Yth Grp; Pres VP FCA; German Clb; Letterman Clb; Office Aide; Orch; School Play; Stage Crew; Sec Soph Cls; Ofcr Stu Cncl; Repr Natl Stdnt Cncl Ldrshp Conf; Pre-Med.

HUGHES, JOHNNY W; Buffalo Jr Sr HS; Buffalo, OK; (2); 1/35; Church Yth Grp; Natl FFA Org; Band; Chorus; Church Choir; Jazz Band; Mrchg Band; Pep Band; JV Var Bsktbl; Var Trk; Masonic Lodge Stu Of Today.

HUGHES, KELVIN; Midwest City HS; Oklahoma City, OK; (3); 61/387; Art Clb; DECA; Spanish Clb; VICA; Rep Jr Cls; Trk; Hon Roll; NHS; Prfct Atten Awd; Rotary Yth Ldrshp Awd; U Of OK; Engrng.

HUGHES, KI L; Poteau HS; Poteau, OK; (2); Church Yth Grp; Stage Crew; Hon Roll; NHS; Prfct Atten Awd; Mat Maids; Hnr Soc; Spring Soccer City League; Summer Sftbl, City & Chrch Leagues; Harding Univ.

HUGHES, KRISTY; Thackerville HS; Thackerville, OK; (3); 1/17; Church Yth Grp; FHA; Math Clb; Science Clb; Phtg Yrbk; VP Jr Cls; Var Capt Chrldng; High Hon Roll; Quiz Bowl; Spanish Clb.

HUGHES, LINDSAY C; North Intemediate HS; Broken Arrow, OK; (1); Spanish Clb; Band; Color Guard; Mrchg Band; Pep Band; High Hon Roll; Pres Acad Fit Awd; OK Hon Soc; OK ST Univ; Vet.

HUGHES, REBECCA; Central HS; Tulsa, OK; (1); 2/400; Church Yth Grp; Sec Treas Frsh Cls; Capt Chrldng; Sftbl; Hon Roll; NHS.

HUGHES, REBECCA A; South Intermediate HS; Broken Arrow, OK; (1); Church Yth Grp; FCA; Office Aide; Teachers Aide; Acpl Chr; Church Choir; Rep Stu Cncl; Intrml Ftbl; Intrml Mgr(s); Intrml Wrstlng; OK Univ; Sprts Med.

HUGHES, RYAN D; Carl Albert HS; Midwest City, OK; (3); 1/250; Am Leg Boys St; Church Yth Grp; Cmnty Wkr; Key Clb; Band; Jazz Band; Mrchg Band; Gov Hon Prg Awd; High Hon Roll; Jr NHS; Rock Band; Piano; Arch.

HUGHES, STEPHANIE; Hulbert Jr Sr HS; Hulbert, OK; (3); German Clb; Spanish Clb; Hon Roll; Jr NHS; NHS.

HUGHES II, STEVEN J; Enid Sr HS; Enid, OK; (2); Hosp Aide; Orch; School Musical; High Hon Roll; Jr NHS; NHS; Show Choir; OK All-St Orch; N Cntrl Hnr Orch.

HUGHES, TRACY; Kingfisher HS; Loyal, OK; (2); Church Yth Grp; Dance Clb; Debate Tm; Drama Clb; Quiz Bowl; Spanish Clb; Stage Crew; High Hon Roll; Southwestern U; Spec Ed.

HUGHES, ZACHARY A; Mustang HS; Mustang, OK; (3); Church Yth Grp; Hon Roll; Creative Wrtng Career; Guitar; Wrtng Tchr.

HUGHEY, BROOKLYN H; El Reno Sr HS; El Reno, OK; (2); 1/225; Church Yth Grp; Rep FCA; FHA; Key Clb; VP Soph Cls; Pres Stu Cncl; Bsktbl; Golf; Vllybl; Jr NHS.

HUGO, JAKE W; Edmond North HS; Edmond, OK; (2); ROTC; Crs Cntry.

HULA, JENNIFER R; Charles Page HS; Sand Springs, OK; (1); Church Yth Grp; Drama Clb; School Musical; School Play; Rep Stu Cncl; Var Chrldng; Hon Roll; Danc; Danc Co Prodctn; 3rd Rnnr Up Teen Miss Lyricl OK Danc Mastr Cmptn 95; Sci Classrm Highst Grd.

HULL, CARINNE M; Mustang HS; Mustang, OK; (3); 1/384; FBLA; Girl Scts; Red Cross Aide; Rptr Nwsp; Vllybl; Hon Roll; NHS; French Clb; Teachers Aide; Var Trk; Natl Hist & Govt Awd; Mdlng; Dance; Psych.

HULL, JENNY; Union Intermediate HS; Broken Arrow, OK; (1); Church Yth Grp; FCA; Spanish Clb; VP Frsh Cls; Rep Stu Cncl; JV Capt Chrldng; Var L Socr; High Hon Roll; NHS; Pres Acad Fit Awd; Med.

HULL, LORA D; Meeker HS; Meeker, OK; (1); Dance Clb; GAA; Pep Clb; Scholastic Bowl; Spanish Clb; JV Bsktbl; Var Pom Pon; High Hon Roll; NHS; Pres Acad Fit Awd; OBU.

HULL, LORRY J; Marietta HS; Marietta, OK; (3); Church Yth Grp; Cmnty Wkr; Computer Clb; Debate Tm; Drama Clb; 4-H; Key Clb; Natl FFA Org; Pep Clb; Speech Tm; Outstndng Achv HS Ptry; 2nd Pl OK Yth Ptry; ST Fnl Mnghm Ptry 2nd Pl; Fnlst 96 Mid-W Amer Ptr Cntst; Southeastern ST Durant; Tchr.

HULL, OREY; Wellston Schl; Wellston, OK; (3); Cmnty Wkr; Computer Clb; Office Aide; Spanish Clb, Ofcr Bsbl, Bsktbl, Wt Lftg, Hon Roll, NHS, Connors Coll.

HULL, SARAH J; Oologah HS; Oologah, OK; (3); Natl FFA Org; Color Guard; Hon Roll; Bapt Yth Grp; MADD Essay Ovral Wnr; Art Awrd; Prin Hnr Rl.

HULLINGER, HEATHER M; Broken Arrow Sr HS; Broken Arrow, OK; (2); Church Yth Grp; Dance Clb; French Clb; Ofcr Stu Cncl; Mgr(s); Wt Lftg; High Hon Roll; Hon Roll; Jr NHS; Pres Schlr; Dent.

HULSE, ROBIN; Pawhuska HS; Pawhuska, OK; (3); 13/100; Bus Profs of Am; FBLA; Key Clb; Pep Clb; Var Tennis; High Hon Roll; Hon Roll; Real Est.

HULSEY, RE DONNA R; Maysville Jr Sr HS; Maysville, OK; (2); Chorus; Hon Roll; Wrtng Ptry 2 Publshd Pms; Med Fld.

HULTMAN, KATRIN; Chandler HS; Chandler, OK; (4); Church Yth Grp; Library Aide; Office Aide; Teachers Aide; Band; Chorus; Mrchg Band; Stat Bsktbl; Var Trk; Hon Roll; Swedish Exch Stu 95-96; Outstdng Amer His Stu 95-96; Acad Awd; Advertising.

HUMBLE, CHARLES; Putnam City West HS; Bethany, OK; (4); Am Leg Boys St; Church Yth Grp; Scholastic Bowl; Mgr Nwsp; Wrstlng; NHS; Ntl Merit SF; PTP Ambssdr; St Senate Page; Baylor; Bus Admin.

HUMBLE, CORBIN; Putnam City West HS; Bethany, OK; (4); #5 in class; Am Leg Boys St; Church Yth Grp; Math Clb; Scholastic Bowl; Teachers Aide; Mgr Nwsp; Mgr Yrbk; Ntl Merit Schol; Mock Trail; Baylor; Bus.

HUMPHREY, CHRIS D; Glenpool HS; Glenpool, OK; (4); Boy Scts; Band; Mrchg Band; Pep Band; Yrbk; Hon Roll; NHS; Stdnt Of Mnth; Quartz Mtn Summer Arts Inst 95-; 1st Pl ST/5TH Pl Natl VICA Photo Comptn 95-; CO Inst Of Art; Photo.

HUMPHREY, KAMMIE; Timberlake Schl; Jet, OK; (4); 1/24; Am Leg Aux Girls St; Church Yth Grp; FCA; Pres Frsh Cls; Pres Jr Cls; Pres Sr Cls; Bsktbl; High Hon Roll; NHS; Val; Rep 1st NTCA WA DC Yth Tour; Miss Grant Cty/Timberlak; Cherokee Strip Conf 3 Pt Chmpn/Acad All Conf; N W OK ST U; Ed.

HUMPHREY, KEELY; Turner Schl; Overbrook, OK; (2); 1/24; FHA; GAA; Rptr Natl Beta Clb; Pep Clb; Sec Frsh Cls; Bsktbl; Sftbl; High Hon Roll; NHS; Val; OK U; Psyclgst.

HUMPHREY, KENDALL; Timberlake Schl; Jet, OK; (2); 1/24; FCA; FHA; Speech Tm; Sec Frsh Cls; Pres Soph Cls; Capt Var Chrldng; High Hon Roll; NHS; Church Yth Grp; St Spch Cont 3rd Pl; Northwestern OK ST U; Educ.

HUMPHREY, KRISTY; Turner Schl; Overbrook, OK; (3); #2 in class; Sec 4-H; Spanish Clb; Yrbk; Pres Frsh Cls; Pres Soph Cls; Pres Jr Cls; Bsktbl; Sftbl; High Hon Roll; Hon Roll; Beta Sec; ECU; Ed.

HUMPHREY, MATTHEW W; Haskell HS; Haskell, OK; (4); Pres Natl FFA Org; Teachers Aide; Var Bsktbl; Capt Ftbl; JV Wt Lftg; Hon Roll; St FFA Degree; Connors ST Coll; Equine Tech.

HUMPHREY, TROY; Bethany HS; Yukon, OK; (4); 8/84; Am Leg Boys St; FCA; Sec Key Clb; Pres Chorus; Rep Jr Cls; Treas Stu Cncl; Var Bsbl; Var Bsktbl; Hon Roll; NHS; US Army Reserve Athl/Schlr Awd; Southern Nazarene U.

HUMPHREYS, BRAD; Hinton HS; Hinton, OK; (4); 12/29; Am Leg Boys St; Church Yth Grp; FCA; Chorus; Var Bsktbl; Var Ftbl; Var Trk; Hon Roll; Prfct Atten Awd; SOSU Weatherford.

HUMPHRIES, CHRISTEN; Comanche HS; Comanche, OK; (1); Art Clb; Hon Roll; Art.

HUMPHRIES, MATTHEW; Deer Creek HS; Edmond, OK; (4); 16/78; Am Leg Boys St; Rep Art Clb; French Clb; Office Aide; Pres Science Clb; SADD; JV Bsbl; Var Ftbl; JV Golf; Var Wrstlng; Futures Sci Acad; Aerospace Smmr Acad; U OK; Cvl Engrng.

HUMPHRIES, TAMMI; Yukon Mid HS; Yukon, OK; (1); FHA; Office Aide; Hon Roll; Jr NHS.

HUNLEY, JEFF R; Latta Sr HS; Ada, OK; (2); Math Tm; Scholastic Bowl; Speech Tm; Pres Frsh Cls; Intrml Bsktbl; Var Golf; Hon Roll; Geo Awd; Amer His Awd.

HUNN, SARAH B; Hobart HS; Hobart, OK; (4); FCA; FBLA; FHA; Nwsp; Yrbk; Rep Jr Cls; Rep Stu Cncl; JV Bsktbl; Hon Roll; NHS; Lifeguard; WOSC.

HUNNICUTT, JACI D; Brink Jr HS; Oklahoma City, OK; (1); Mgr Yrbk; High Hon Roll; Jr NHS; Jrnlsm Awd; Yrbk Staff; OK Univ; Accountant.

HUNSINGER, TERI E; Cushing HS; Cushing, OK; (1); Spanish Clb; JV Bsktbl; JV Sftbl; Var Trk; High Hon Roll.

HUNT, AMBER N; Wilson HS; Wilson, OK; (3); 5/35; Church Yth Grp; 4-H; Natl Beta Clb; Yrbk; Sftbl; Hon Roll; OK Hnr Soc; Southeastern; Dntl Hygnst.

HUNT, GREG A; Memorial HS; Tulsa, OK; (3); ROTC; Hon Roll; Fishing; Tulsa JC; Bus Mgmt.

HUNT, JAMES B; Central Mid-HS; Norman, OK; (2); Natl FFA Org; Hon Roll; Vo-Tech Stu; Rose ST Jr Coll; Mech.

HUNT, JESSICA; Braggs Schl; Gore, OK; (3); Church Yth Grp; FBLA; Temple Yth Grp; Church Choir; Bsktbl; Sftbl; Hon Roll; Prfct Atten Awd; Cmptr Prgrmr.

HUNT, JESSICA V; Skiatook HS; Skiatook, OK; (1); Church Yth Grp; FCA; FHA; Band; Chorus; Church Choir; Mrchg Band; Orch; School Musical; Jr NHS; OK Bapt Univ; Spec Ed.

HUNT, JOHN M; Bartlesville Sr HS; Bartlesville, OK; (2); 101/484; Spanish Clb; Ftbl; Hon Roll; Jr NHS; NHS; MD.

HUNT, KHOLTER J; Claremore Sr HS; Claremore, OK; (1); VP Church Yth Grp; Cmnty Wkr; FCA; Chorus; Church Choir; School Musical; Variety Show; Bsktbl; Ftbl; Wrstlng; Stratton Taylor OK St Sen Page; U OK; Scintst.

HUNT, KRISTINA D; Arkoma Jr Sr HS; Arkoma, OK; (2); Chorus; Church Choir; Ntl Merit Ltr; Med Doctor.

HUNT, LUCAS E; Stillwater Sr HS; Stillwater, OK; (2); Church Yth Grp; Cmnty Wkr; Computer Clb; FBLA; Latin Clb; Teachers Aide; High Hon Roll; Prfct Atten Awd; Pres Acad Fit Awd; Airline Pilot.

HUNT, MATTHEW; Henryetta Sr HS; Henryetta, OK; (3); 1/75; Boy Scts; Church Yth Grp; FCA; HOBY; Band; Var Trk; Var Wrstlng; Cit Awd; NHS; Pres Acad Fit Awd; USAF Acad; Astrnt.

HUNT, MICAH L; Norman Sr HS; Norman, OK; (3); 1/799; Mu Alpha Theta; Teachers Aide; Band; Jazz Band; Mrchg Band; JV Golf; Cit Awd; Hon Roll; NHS; OK Univ; Comp Sci.

HUNT, MICHAEL E; Wagoner Sr HS; Wagoner, OK; (3); Boy Scts; Church Yth Grp; French Clb; FBLA; Library Aide; Hon Roll; HOSA, Parliamentarian Vo-Tech; Tulsa JC; Mrktng Comp.

HUNT, REGINA; Fargo Schl; Fargo, OK; (4); 3/22; Capt FCA; Pres FHA; Pres Natl Beta Clb; Rep Natl FFA Org; Capt Quiz Bowl; VP Sr Cls; Capt Var Bsktbl; Capt Var Sftbl; NHS; Sal; Presdntl Ldrshp Awd; OK ST U Hnr Schlr; Northwest OK ST U Sr Schlr; OK ST U; Pre-Med.

HUNT, RICKY; Millwood HS; Oklahoma City, OK; (2); Church Yth Grp; FCA; FHA; Office Aide; ROTC; Band; Church Choir; Drill Tm; Mrchg Band; School Play; Bus Mgmt.

HUNT, SHANE; Covington Douglas HS; Lucien, OK; (2); 1/20; Church Yth Grp; Rptr Nwsp; Rptr Yrbk; High Hon Roll; NHS; Acad Team; St Hnr Soc; Schlrshp Prairie To Peaks Ecology Summer Acad.

HUNT, STACY; Victory Christian Schl; Broken Arrow, OK; (3); Church Yth Grp; FCA; Intnl Clb; JV Var Chrldng; Var Sftbl; Cit Awd; High Hon Roll; Hon Roll; Jr NHS; NHS; TX Chrstn Univ; Necropsyst/Vet.

HUNT, VIRGINIA R; Norman Sr HS; Norman, OK; (4); 66/677; Church Yth Grp; Hosp Aide; Mu Alpha Theta; Spanish Clb; Band; Chorus; Church Choir; Mrchg Band; Orch; NHS; OK Bapt Univ; Nrs.

HUNT-DOBBINS, KRISTI; U S Grant HS; Oklahoma City, OK; (2); Drama Clb; ROTC; Drill Tm; School Musical; School Play; Stage Crew; Rep Stu Cncl; Hon Roll; NHS; CSF; MCJROTC Rifle Team; OK U; Mrn Crps Fml Drll Instr.

HUNTER, BOBBI A; Woodward HS; Woodward, OK; (2); Drama Clb; Pep Clb; Speech Tm; Band; Mrchg Band; Pep Band; School Play; Hon Roll; Arch.

HUNTER, BRIAN C; Woodward HS; Woodward, OK; (3); 34/169; Art Clb; Church Yth Grp; Cmnty Wkr; FCA; Letterman Clb; Bsktbl; High Hon Roll; Hon Roll; NHS.

HUNTER, BRIAN M; Union Intermediate HS; Tulsa, OK; (1); Boy Scts; Spanish Clb; High Hon Roll; NHS; Outstdng Math Stu Awd Algebra I; Outstdng Span I Stu.

HUNTER, CARLOS L; B T Washington HS; Tulsa, OK; (4); 111/264; Church Yth Grp; Varsity Clb; Church Choir; Ftbl; Wt Lftg; Wrstlng; Hon Roll; NAACP; Afrcn Amrcn Scty; U Of Cent OK; CPA.

HUNTER, CHASE V; Bethany HS; Oklahoma City, OK; (2); Boy Scts; Church Yth Grp; Key Clb; Orch; Hon Roll; NHS; Eagel Sct Awd.

HUNTER, ERIC T; Woodward HS; Woodward, OK; (1); Boy Scts; Church Yth Grp; 4-H; Letterman Clb; Band; Jazz Band; Pep Band; Hon Roll; Mock Trial 2nd Pl In St Finals Cmptn; Model UN.

HUNTER, HOLLY C; Preston Schl; Okmulgee, OK; (1); 25/150; Art Clb; Church Yth Grp; 4-H; Church Choir; Bsktbl; Hon Roll; Prfct Atten Awd; Val; Swimming; Horseback Riding; Drawing; Oral Roberts U; Vet; Commrcl Art.

HUNTER, JENNIFER; U S Grant HS; Oklahoma City, OK; (1); High Hon Roll; Hon Roll.

HUNTER, JENNIFER; Woodward HS; Woodward, OK; (2); Church Yth Grp; Cmnty Wkr; German Clb; Letterman Clb; Pep Clb; Chrldng; German Exch Stu.

HUNTER, KEVIN; Grove HS; Jay, OK; (4); 21/105; Am Leg Boys St; CAP; Office Aide; Band; Jazz Band; Mrchg Band; Pep Band; Yrbk; NHS; OK ST U; Acctng.

HUNTER, LESLIE R; Woodward HS; Woodward, OK; (3); 77/169; FHA; Hon Roll.

HUNTER, MARCUS L; B T Washington HS; Tulsa, OK; (4); 92/264; Church Yth Grp; Varsity Clb; Ofcr Sr Cls; Ftbl; Wt Lftg; Wrstlng; Hon Roll; Afrcn Amercn Scty; NAACP; U Of Centr OK; Bus.

HUNTER, MLEAH; Guymon Sr HS; Guymon, OK; (2); FCA; GAA; Rep Soph Cls; Intrml Bsktbl; JV Chrldng; Gym; Pom Pon; Vllybl; Hon Roll; Prfct Atten Awd; Brdcst Jrnlsm; U Of CO; Optmlgy.

HUNTER, SAMANTHA GAIL; Jarman Jr HS; Midwest City, OK; (1); Speech Tm; Band; School Play; Yrbk; VP Stu Cncl; Var Bsktbl; Var Chrldng; Var Ftbl; Var Trk; Ntl Merit Ltr; Art-Drwng; Coach Sprts; Grp Dscssn.

HUNTER, SARAH M; Bridge Creek HS; Blanchard, OK; (1); Sec Art Clb; Church Yth Grp; Spanish Clb; Pres Frsh Cls; Ofcr Stu Cncl; Hnrs Eng I; Studio Art.

HUNTER, WILLIAM T; Coyle Public Schl; Coyle, OK; (3); Bsktbl; Ntl Merit Ltr; Congressional Yth Ldrshp Cncl; Engrng.

HUNTINGTON, BRYAN K; Central Mid-HS; Norman, OK; (2); Boy Scts; Church Yth Grp; Debate Tm; Model UN; NFL; SADD; JV Bsbl; Cit Awd.

HUNTSINGER, KEVIN S; Broken Arrow Sr HS; Broken Arrow, OK; (3); French Clb; Band; Mrchg Band; Pep Band; Hon Roll; Prfct Atten Awd; Recreational Soccer; Aerospace Camp; Engrng; Comp Sci.

HUNTZE, KATHRYN S; Cascia Hall Prep School; Tulsa, OK; (3); French Clb; Yrbk; Mgr Ftbl; Hon Roll; NHS; Scuba Dvng; Red Cross Ldrshp Camp Cnslr; Sci.

HUPFELD, KATHERINE; Bishop Mcguinness HS; Oklahoma City, OK; (3); #15 in class; Church Yth Grp; FCA; Hosp Aide; HOBY; Pres Pep Clb; VP Stu Cncl; Var Bsktbl; Var NHS; VP Spanish NHS; Red Crss Yth Ldrshp Exchng Cls 1.

HURD, DESTONY D; Oklahoma Union Schl; S Coffeyville, OK; (4); 6/45; FCA; FHA; Natl FFA Org; Teachers Aide; Yrbk; Sec Rep Stu Cncl; JV Var Bsktbl; High Hon Roll; Hon Roll; NHS; Stdnt Of Today; 1st High Individual St Ag Sales & Svc Cont; CCC; Jrnlsm.

HURLEY, MEGHAN L; Glenpool HS; Glenpool, OK; (1); Church Yth Grp; Chorus; Powder Puff Ftbl; High Hon Roll; Jr NHS; Acting Class Schlrshp; Mdl Drama; Ballet/Voice Lsns; Acting/PT.

HURRY, JENNIFER R; Union Sr HS; Broken Arrow, OK; (3); GAA; Band; Mrchg Band; Pep Band; JV Var Sftbl; High Hon Roll; Hon Roll; Jr NHS; NHS; Var Sftbl All-Frontier Conf Hnrb Mntn; OK ST U; Radiolgy.

HURRY, SARAH R; Bethany HS; Oklahoma City, OK; (2); Church Yth Grp; Office Aide; Church Choir; Hon Roll; Ltr B Awd; U Of OK.

HURST, BRANDI L; Webster HS; Oakhurst, OK; (3); Bus Profs of Am; Cmnty Wkr; FBLA; FTA; Key Clb; JV Golf; High Hon Roll; Hon Roll; Jr NHS; NHS; Treas His Amer; OK ST Univ.

HURST, JANIE; Wapanucka Schl; Bromide, OK; (3); 2/18; Church Yth Grp; 4-H; Quiz Bowl; Rptr Yrbk; Rep Soph Cls; Sec Jr Cls; VP Stu Cncl; 4-H Awd; High Hon Roll; Ntl Merit Ltr; U OK; Med.

HURST, KENNETH B; Morris HS; Okmulgee, OK; (4).

HURST, KYLA J; El Reno Sr HS; El Reno, OK; (1); Church Yth Grp; Cmnty Wkr; FCA; FHA; Natl FFA Org; Rep Frsh Cls; JV Tennis; Stat Wrstlng; Hon Roll; NHS; Leaders Of Tmrw; PT.

HURST, LACEY; Marietta HS; Marietta, OK; (4); 1/53; Am Leg Aux Girls St; HOBY; Pres NFL; Pres Sec Stu Cncl; Var Mgr Bsktbl; Var Chrldng; Val; Debate Tm; Quiz Bowl; Pres Speech Tm; All Amer Schlr; Natl Hnr Roll; OU; Phys Thrpy.

HURST, MARY; Union Sr HS; Tulsa, OK; (1); Church Yth Grp; FCA; Spanish Clb; Rptr Nwsp; Rptr Phtg Yrbk; Capt Chrldng; High Hon Roll; Jr NHS; NHS; All-Amer Schlr.

HURST, MINDI; Stigler HS; Stigler, OK; (2); FCA; GAA; Speech Tm; SADD; Sec Frsh Cls; Bsktbl; Sftbl; Hon Roll; Summer Sftbl League; Chrch Actvts; OK U; Med.

HURST, RASHAY; Carl Albert HS; Oklahoma City, OK; (1); Church Yth Grp; FCA; SADD; Chorus; VP Stu Cncl; Capt Chrldng; Hon Roll; 2 Time All Amer Chrldr; Miss Cajh & Stu Awd.

HURST, STACI L; El Reno Sr HS; El Reno, OK; (2); Cmnty Wkr; FHA; Chorus; Hon Roll; U Of GA; Crmnl Jstce.

HURT, CASEY; Midwest City HS; Midwest City, OK; (4); 39/393; Phtg Nwsp; Phtg Yrbk; Hon Roll; Kiwanis Awd; NHS; German Clb; Office Aide; VICA; Nrthestrn St U; Bus Admin.

HURT, CHRISTI L; Midwest City HS; Midwest City, OK; (2); 123/473; Church Yth Grp; French Clb; Letterman Clb; Pep Clb; Hon Roll; Jr NHS; NHS; Received Acad Ltrs Through Acad Lettering Clb; Boston Coll; Pre-Natal Nrs.

HURT, KELLY L; Colcord Schl; Colcord, OK; (1); Church Yth Grp; FHA; Var Bsktbl; Hon Roll; Homcmng Prncss Ftbl; Indian Clb; Singing Country Music.

HUSAIN, AISHA; Union Sr HS; Broken Arrow, OK; (3); French Clb; FBLA; VP Key Clb; Band; Variety Show; French Hon Soc; High Hon Roll; Hon Roll; NHS; Pres Acad Fit Awd; Acad Ltr; Outstndng Frnch Awd; U Of MI; Med.

HUSEN, A C; Ponca City Sr HS; Ponca City, OK; (4); Am Leg Boys St; Church Yth Grp; FCA; Spanish Clb; Pres Soph Cls; Capt Jr Cls; Co-Capt Sr Cls; Rptr Stu Cncl; Ftbl; Socr; Med.

HUSSAIN, SAFIA G; Union Sr HS; Tulsa, OK; (4); 28/629; French Clb; Key Clb; Nwsp; Yrbk; Var Crs Cntry; Var Trk; Hon Roll; NHS; Pres Acad Fit Awd; FCA; Big Family; Renaissance; U Of TX.

HUSTON, JEFFREY C; Union Sr HS; Tulsa, OK; (4); 76/679; Church Yth Grp; Mrchg Band; School Musical; Intrml Bsktbl; High Hon Roll; Hon Roll; NHS; Pres Acad Fit Awd; Natl Chmpn Prcssn Ensmbl; St Champ Drmline; Hstry.

HUTCHINGS, JERRY; Achille Schl; Achille, OK; (3); 1/43; 4-H; Library Aide; Natl FFA Org; Nwsp; Yrbk; Rep Stu Cncl; Hon Roll; NHS; Ntl Merit Ltr; Prfct Atten Awd; Mascot; SOSU.

HUTCHINGS, REBECCA N; Hugo HS; Hugo, OK; (3); Spanish Clb; Nwsp; Swmmng; Rdng; Psych/Law.

HUTCHINGS, WHITNEY P; Colbert Jr Sr HS; Colbert, OK; (3); Yrbk; High Hon Roll; Prfct Atten Awd; Girls Summer Sftbl Coach; Southeastern OK ST Univ.

HUTCHINS, HEATHER DE ANN; Kellyville Sr HS; Kellyville, OK; (3); French Clb; Office Aide; Pep Clb; Science Clb; Service Clb; Color Guard; Ofcr Stu Cncl; Gov Hon Prg Awd; High Hon Roll; Hon Roll; Corp Law.

HUTCHINS, LORI B; Blackwell HS; Blackwell, OK; (2); 10/138; Church Yth Grp; FCA; Hosp Aide; Letterman Clb; Pep Clb; Acpl Chr; Chorus; Mgr(s); Tennis; High Hon Roll; PRIDE; St Hnr Soc; Prom Server; U Of OK; Meteorology.

HUTCHINS, RANDA; Stuart Sr HS; Stuart, OK; (3); 5/27; Rep FHA; Key Clb; Library Aide; Pres Natl FFA Org; Scholastic Bowl; Var Capt Bsktbl; Powder Puff Ftbl; Trk; Hon Roll; Jr NHS; U Of OK; Acctng/Law.

HUTCHINSON, DONNA M; Fletcher Jr Sr HS; Fletcher, OK; (2); 7/42; Hist FHA; Pep Clb; Chorus; Hon Roll; NHS; Comp Lit, Fnd Living Awds; Tennis; Med.

HUTCHINSON, NATASHA; Foyil Schl; Claremore, OK; (1); 1/42; Pres Frsh Cls; Ofcr Stu Cncl; Var Bsktbl; Var Sftbl; Var Trk; Wt Lftg; High Hon Roll; Hon Roll; Jr NHS; NHS; Sci.

HUTCHISON, DUSTIN C; Putnam City West HS; Oklahoma City, OK; (1); Church Yth Grp; FCA; German Clb; Intnl Clb; Chorus; Rep Frsh Cls; Ofcr Stu Cncl; Bsktbl; Ftbl; JV Socr; ACU; Yth Mnstry/Fin.

HUTCHISON, JEFF; Bartlesville Sr HS; Bartlesville, OK; (4); 98/409; Boy Scts; JCL; Latin Clb; Scholastic Bowl; Spanish Clb; Teachers Aide; Rep Stu Cncl; High Hon Roll; Hon Roll; Pres Acad Fit Awd; Elec Engrng.

HUTSELL, ALISHA G; Union Sr HS; Tulsa, OK; (4); 151/615; Cmnty Wkr; FBLA; FHA; Chorus; Cit Awd; High Hon Roll; Pres Acad Fit Awd; Union Outsdng Stdnt Schlrshp; U Of Tulsa; Acctg/Bus Admin.

HUTSON, JOHNATHAN; Coweta HS; Coweta, OK; (4); 1/175; Chess Clb; Quiz Bowl; Scholastic Bowl; Science Clb; SADD; High Hon Roll; NHS; Prfct Atten Awd; St Schlr; Val; OK ST U; Cmptr Tech.

HUTSON, KRISTEN M; Chattanooga Schl; Chattanooga, OK; (1); 4/23; FCA; FBLA; GAA; Letterman Clb; Office Aide; Pep Clb; Yrbk; Bsktbl; JV Var Chrldng; Var JV Sftbl; OK ST; Comp Tech.

HUTSON, MATTHEW; Ponca City Sr HS; Ponca City, OK; (4); 128/400; Am Leg Boys St; Church Yth Grp; FCA; Office Aide; Teachers Aide; Chorus; School Musical; Rep Stu Cncl; Bsktbl; Ftbl; Vlybl City Lg; Bnch Vlybl Trnmnts; Northern OK Coll; Cmptr Anlyst.

HUTTER, CARA; Wright Christian Acad; Sand Springs, OK; (3); Church Yth Grp; Hosp Aide; HOBY; Key Clb; Chorus; School Play; Var JV Bsktbl; Var Trk; JV Vllybl; Hon Roll; Law.

HUTTON, ANGELA R; Western Heights Sr HS; Oklahoma City, OK; (1); Church Yth Grp; Bsktbl; Crs Cntry; Socr; Swmmng; Trk; O U Univ; PT/SRGN.

HUTTON, CHRIS L; U S Grant HS; Oklahoma City, OK; (1); Pep Clb; Band; Jazz Band; Mrchg Band; Pep Band; School Musical; School Play; Hon Roll; U AR; Med.

HUTTON, LAURA; Blackwell HS; Blackwell, OK; (4); #4 in class; Am Leg Aux Girls St; Church Yth Grp; Cmnty Wkr; FCA; Hosp Aide; Letterman Clb; Pep Clb; Red Cross Aide; Spanish Clb; Chorus; Peer Helper; Show Choir; Extended Stds; OK U; Med.

HUYNH, ANH T; Southeast HS; Del City, OK; (1); Computer Clb; Hon Roll; OU; Dr.

HUYNH, CAM V; Lawton Sr HS; Lawton, OK; (3); GATE Prgm; Hnr Schlr Acad Achvmnt Awd.

HUYNH, NAM V; Muskogee HS; Muskogee, OK; (2); Church Yth Grp; Computer Clb; JV Var Tennis; Hon Roll; RAID; U Of OK; Cmptr Anlyst.

HYATT, WENDY M; Cleveland Sr HS; Cleveland, OK; (4); Drama Clb; FHA; SADD; Teachers Aide; Chorus; School Musical; School Play; Hon Roll; Tulsa CC; Psych.

HYDE III, H CLARK; Casady Schl; Oklahoma City, OK; (2); 20/83; Cmnty Wkr; Spanish Clb; Band; Orch; School Musical; School Play; Variety Show; Golf; Wt Lftg; High Hon Roll; Drumming; Hiking; Comm Svc; U Of CO; Elec Engrng.

HYDE, HEATHER N; Union Sr HS; Tulsa, OK; (3); 189/673; DECA; French Clb; Teachers Aide; Hon Roll; Jr NHS; NHS; U Of OK.

HYDEN, AMANDA; Putnam City West HS; Bethany, OK; (1); Church Yth Grp; Latin Clb; Rep Stu Cncl; Chrldng; Athl Medcl Trnr; Medcl Clb; PEAK; Med.

HYDEN, JEFF C; Moore HS; Oklahoma City, OK; (3); Church Yth Grp; FCA; Office Aide; Pep Clb; SADD; Rep Stu Cncl; JV Bsbl; Ftbl; Cit Awd; Hon Roll; Am Lgn Bsbl; Dcplshp Now; OBU; Phys Ther.

HYND, ERIC; Guthrie Sr HS; Edmond, OK; (3); Art Clb; Boy Scts; Church Yth Grp; Math Clb; Mu Alpha Theta; ROTC; Science Clb; Spanish Clb; SADD; Cit Awd; Eagle Sct; Rotry Jr Ldrshp Smnr; Arch Drafting.

HYNSON, JENNIFER; Stillwater Sr HS; Stillwater, OK; (4); 63/375; Church Yth Grp; Dance Clb; FCA; Girl Scts; Hosp Aide; Key Clb; Latin Clb; Natl Beta Clb; Q&S; Spanish Clb; Girl Scout Gold & Silver Awd; Girls ST Alt; ST Essay Cont On Disabilities 1st Place; OK ST Univ; Family Relations.

IATRIDIS, ALEXIA C; Union Intermediate HS; Tulsa, OK; (2); Church Yth Grp; Dance Clb; Drama Clb; FCA; Girl Scts; Spanish Clb; Teachers Aide; Church Choir; Color Guard; Drill Tm; Chrch Choir; Winter Guard; ROTUS.

IBARRA, HUMBERTA; Douglass HS; Oklahoma City, OK; (1); Hon Roll; Awded Outstdng ESL Stdnt Awd; Nurse.

ICE, LAUREN; Central Mid-HS; Norman, OK; (1); FCA; JCL; Latin Clb; Letterman Clb; Mu Alpha Theta; Red Cross Aide; Pres Band; Orch; Rep Frsh Cls; Boy Scts.

ICE, MIRANDA N; Choctaw HS; Choctaw, OK; (3); 48/313; Church Yth Grp; Office Aide; Band; Chorus; Church Choir; Color Guard; Flag Corp; Orch; Ofcr Jr Cls; Hon Roll; OK City Univ; Music.

ICE, TODD; Thomas Jr Sr HS; Fay, OK; (2); 1/40; FCA; Natl FFA Org; VP Soph Cls; Bsktbl; Cit Awd; Gov Hon Prg Awd; High Hon Roll; Hon Roll; NHS; Ntl Merit Ltr.

ICKES, JACKIE; Kiefer Jr Sr HS; Kiefer, OK; (1); FCA; Band; Church Choir; Drm Mjr(t); Mrchg Band; Pres Frsh Cls; Var Chrldng; Hon Roll; NHS; Sal; All-Amer Schlr; Gftd & Tlntd; Phys Thrpy.

IDELL, AMBERS D; Carney Schl; Chandler, OK; (2); Church Yth Grp; FHA; Mu Alpha Theta; Quiz Bowl; Pres Frsh Cls; Ofcr Soph Cls; High Hon Roll; NHS; Cit Awd; Val; OSU; Math Tchr.

IFEKOYA, CRYSTAL L; Webster HS; Tulsa, OK; (1); Church Yth Grp; Cmnty Wkr; JA; ROTC; Teachers Aide; Church Choir; Stat Bsktbl; Mgr Mgr(s); Score Keeper; Hon Roll; Langston Univ; Cosmetology.

IGBRE, ANN; Jenks HS; Tulsa, OK; (3); 44/600; Church Yth Grp; Mu Alpha Theta; Rep Thesps; School Play; VP Sr Cls; Ofcr Stu Cncl; High Hon Roll; Hon Roll; NHS; Prfct Atten Awd; Med.

IGO, TARA D; Westville HS; Westville, OK; (1); Church Yth Grp; FHA; SADD; Intrml Bsktbl; L Var Trk; Hon Roll; Prfct Atten Awd; OK Univ.

IGOU, BRANDON; Stuart Sr HS; Stuart, OK; (3); Var L Bsbl; Hon Roll; Stuart Invitational All Trnmt Tm 96; OK ST U; Diesel Engrng.

IHRIG, CHRIS; Bristow HS; Bristow, OK; (4); 17/112; Am Leg Boys St; Church Yth Grp; FCA; Rep Stu Cncl; Bsktbl; Capt Ftbl; Golf; Cit Awd; NHS; OK ST U; Finance.

IKAVUKA, ANA P; Southeast HS; Oklahoma City, OK; (3); #2 in class; Church Yth Grp; Office Aide; Church Choir; Cit Awd; High Hon Roll; Hon Roll; Kiwanis Awd; NHS; College Clb; OU; Med.

IKER, NATALIE R; Oklahoma Sch Of Science & Math; Durant, OK; (4); Church Yth Grp; Drill Tm; Jazz Band; Ofcr Stu Cncl; Intrml Ftbl; Var Pom Pon; Intrml Socr; Intrml Swmmng; Intrml Vllybl; Cit Awd; OSU; Chemical Engr.

ILAND, TRENIKA REA DAWN; Bristow HS; Bristow, OK; (3); FHA; Office Aide; Pep Clb; Spanish Clb; Teachers Aide; Chorus; Church Choir; Drill Tm; School Play; Var Bsktbl.

ILAOA, ISAAC; Muskogee HS; Muskogee, OK; (1); Church Yth Grp; Chorus; Wrstlng; High Hon Roll; Hon Roll; Jr NHS; OK ST Univ.

ILIFF III, CHARLES E; Mannford HS; Mannford, OK; (3); 20/150; Church Yth Grp; FCA; Spanish Clb; SADD; Band; Rptr Jr Cls; Var Ftbl; JV Golf; Var Trk; Hon Roll; Ftbl Awd; Amer His Awd; Tulsa All Metro Hnrb Mntn Ftbl; OK ST.

IMEL, ZAC; Putnam City HS; Oklahoma City, OK; (3); 20/360; Church Yth Grp; Cmnty Wkr; German Clb; Service Clb; Ofcr Bsbl; High Hon Roll; Hon Roll; Jr NHS; NHS.

IMHOFF, KRISTI; Putnam City West HS; Oklahoma City, OK; (3); Pep Clb; Teachers Aide; Var Chrldng; Var Trk; NCA All Amer; SW OK ST; Pharmacy.

IMKE, LANELLE; Shattuck Jr Sr HS; Shattuck, OK; (4); 4/21; Pres FHA; HOBY; Pres Natl FFA Org; Yrbk; Capt Bsktbl; Chrldng; Sftbl; Trk; Hon Roll; NHS; North Western OK ST U; Ag.

IMMONEN, ERKKO K; Hilldale HS; Muskogee, OK; (3); Am Leg Boys St; Church Yth Grp; FHA; German Clb; Bsktbl; Hon Roll; Exch Stu Finland; Snow Boarding; Skate Boarding; Art.

INCE, KEVIN M; Lindsay HS; Lindsay, OK; (1); 27/75; Church Yth Grp; Band; Church Choir; Mrchg Band; Pep Band; School Musical; Bsktbl; Ftbl; Trk; Wt Lftg; Indian Prgm Title Ix; Indianprgm Johnson O Malley; Univ Of OK; Prfsnl Bsktbl.

INDERMILL, SETH T; Bartlesville Sr HS; Bartlesville, OK; (4); Church Yth Grp; French Clb; FBLA; Scholastic Bowl; Teachers Aide; Orch; French Hon Soc; Hon Roll; Jr NHS; NHS; U OK; Chem Engrng.

INGHAM, ELIZABETH; Preston Schl; Okmulgee, OK; (3); Church Yth Grp; NHS; Northeastern ST Univ; Tchr.

INGLE, CHRIS; Dover Schl; Dover, OK; (2); OK ST Univ.

INGLE, SARA M; Checotah HS; Checotah, OK; (2); Church Yth Grp; Chorus; Hon Roll; NHS; Phy Thrpy.

INGRAM, CHAD B; Moore HS; Moore, OK; (2); Science Clb; Spanish Clb; Var L Golf; Cit Awd; Hon Roll; Jr NHS; NHS; Dsgnd Schl T Shirt 95-; Won Awds A Avg Bio/Geometry; Stu Of Mnth Nom; 4 Yr Coll; Arch Engrng.

INGRAM, CLINT W; Elgin HS; Elgin, OK; (4); FCA; Teachers Aide; VICA; Var Bsktbl; Var Ftbl; Var Trk; Cit Awd; High Hon Roll; Cameron Univ.

INGRAM, JESSICA; Coalgate HS; Coalgate, OK; (4); 4/43; Church Yth Grp; Church Choir; High Hon Roll; Hon Roll; Jr NHS; NHS; HOSA; Stu Mo 95; Med Trmnlgy; East Central U; Med.

INGRAM, JOY; Putnam City HS; Oklahoma City, OK; (4); #131 in class; Church Yth Grp; Office Aide; Pep Clb; Service Clb; Teachers Aide; Chorus; Rep Stu Cncl; Capt Var Chrldng; Var Trk; 2 Yrs 3-D Member; 1 Yr DECA; 2 Yrs Gymnstcs Coach; Southern Nazrene U; Elem Ed.

INGRAM, KRISI; Holdenville HS; Holdenville, OK; (4); 14/75; Church Yth Grp; FCA; FHA; Science Clb; Band; Pres Acad Fit Awd; East Cntrl Univ; Pre Dentistry.

INGRAM, LAURA L; Depew HS; Depew, OK; (2); 9/35; Hon Roll; Prfct Atten Awd; Outstndg Sci Awd.

INGRAM, PATRA; Coalgate HS; Coalgate, OK; (3); 10/55; Church Yth Grp; Nwsp; Hon Roll; NHS; Nov Stu Mon 94; Engl II Outstndng Perf Medal/2nd Pl Bldg Ftr Ed Rbbn; Jrnlsm Outstndng Perf Medal; Med.

INKROTT, HILARY M; Bartlesville Mid HS; Bartlesville, OK; (2); #1 in class; Art Clb; Church Yth Grp; German Clb; Swmmng; High Hon Roll; Jr NHS.

INMAN, ASHLEE; Westmoore HS; Oklahoma City, OK; (3); 51/615; Church Yth Grp; CAP; FCA; JA; JCL; Latin Clb; Math Tm; Science Clb; Band; Mrchg Band; Southwestern OK ST U Summer Sci & Math Acad 95; WHS Eng II Excl Awd; 3rd Pl Indoor Soccer Leag; Pre-Med; Neurosurgery.

INMAN, FEATHER K; Choctaw HS; Choctaw, OK; (4); 24/304; FTA; Key Clb; Office Aide; Rptr Nwsp; Ed Yrbk; Sec Stu Cncl; Sftbl; NHS; St Hnr Soc; U Of OK; Educ.

INMAN, JENNIFER; Broken Arrow Sr HS; Broken Arrow, OK; (3); Mrchg Band; Capt Socr; Var Vllybl; Wt Lftg; Hon Roll; Intl Bus.

INMAN, JOSH; Bethany HS; Warr Acres, OK; (3); 16/70; Drama Clb; FCA; Letterman Clb; Thesps; Chorus; School Musical; School Play; Swing Chorus; Variety Show; Yrbk; U Of Cntrl OK; Enology.

INMAN, TASHA; Tonkawa Jr Sr HS; Tonkawa, OK; (3); 5/52; Church Yth Grp; Cmnty Wkr; FCA; 4-H; FHA; Library Aide; Office Aide; Pep Clb; Teachers Aide; Church Choir; Extended Stud; Childrens Reader Vol; Acad Ltr; Bus Mgmt.

INSELMAN, TRAVIS W; Enid Sr HS; Ft Smith, AR; (2); Church Yth Grp; Drama Clb; Speech Tm; Thesps; Band; Chorus; Jazz Band; Mrchg Band; Pep Band; School Musical; Roller Hockey; Theatre.

INSLEY, CHRISTIAN M; Owasso Sr HS; Owasso, OK; (4); Church Yth Grp; FCA; French Clb; Church Choir; JV Var Bsktbl; High Hon Roll; NHS; Varsity Clb; Hon Roll; WEC Essay Cntst Wnnr; Bsktbll Homecoming Crt; BYU; Elem Ed.

IRELAND, CRAIG; Stillwater Sr HS; Stillwater, OK; (3); 1/350; Am Leg Boys St; Church Yth Grp; Key Clb; Latin Clb; Mu Alpha Theta; Natl Beta Clb; Quiz Bowl; Science Clb; Band; NHS; U Of OK; Meteorlgy.

IRELAND, JEFFERY D; Hilldale HS; Muskogee, OK; (2); 22/107; German Clb; Key Clb; Hon Roll; Connors ST Coll; Engr.

IRICK, JOHN M; Strother Jr Sr HS; Seminole, OK; (2); 1/31; Church Yth Grp; 4-H; Natl FFA Org; Quiz Bowl; Scholastic Bowl; Pres Frsh Cls; JV Bsbl; JV Bsktbl; Hon Roll; Rep Stu Cncl; Commercial Airline Pilot.

IRION, LINAKA L; Buffalo Jr Sr HS; Buffalo, OK; (1); Church Yth Grp; Band; Chorus; Jazz Band; Mrchg Band; Pep Band; Var Sftbl; Prin Hnr Roll; OK ST Univ.

IRVIN, JORDON; Hobart HS; Hobart, OK; (1); Church Yth Grp; FCA; GAA; VP Frsh Cls; Ofcr Stu Cncl; Capt Bsktbl; Trk; High Hon Roll; Hon Roll; NHS.

IRVING, B DERRICK; Seiling Schl; Seiling, OK; (2); FBLA; Speech Tm; Band; Jazz Band; Mrchg Band; Pep Band; School Musical; School Play; SWOSU.

IRWIN, HOLLY M; Ponca City Sr HS; Ponca City, OK; (4); French Clb; Office Aide; Teachers Aide; High Hon Roll; Hon Roll; NHS.

IRWIN, HOLLY NICOLE; Purcell HS; Purcell, OK; (4); 1/72; Am Leg Aux Girls St; Pres FCA; Rep Spanish Clb; Chorus; Church Choir; Rep Sr Cls; Rep Stu Cncl; Capt Chrldng; Capt Crs Cntry; Var Trk; Natl Chrldng Assn All-Amer 4 Yrs; Smmr Theatr; Speech Pathlgy.

IRWIN, JIMMY T; West Middle HS; Norman, OK; (1); Church Yth Grp; 4-H; FBLA; Ofcr Bsbl; Ftbl; Wrstlng; Cit Awd; 4-H Awd; Hon Roll; Quails Unlmtd; Poetry; OK Univ; Bus Envrnmntl Sci.

ISAAC, CHRISTAL RAE; Webster HS; Tulsa, OK; (3); Am Leg Aux Girls St; Church Yth Grp; DECA; Drama Clb; Key Clb; Varsity Clb; School Play; Crs Cntry; Trk; Ntl Merit Ltr; St Spch Drma Cont; Wrld Trad Intl Contst; OK Univ; OK Univ.

ISAAC, MELISSA; Eufaula Sr HS; Eufaula, OK; (2); Church Yth Grp; Debate Tm; FHA; Spanish Clb; Hon Roll; NHS; Water Skiing; Northeastern ST; Med.

ISAAC, MONICA R; Midwest City HS; Midwest City, OK; (2); Cmnty Wkr; French Clb; German Clb; Band; Chorus; Hon Roll; NHS.

ISAACS, CHAD O; Tahlequah Sr HS; Welling, OK; (3); Church Yth Grp; German Clb; Scholastic Bowl; Science Clb; High Hon Roll; Jr NHS; NHS; Pres Acad Fit Awd; St Schlr; U Of Tulsa; Optmtry.

ISAACS, ERIC A; Charles Page HS; Sand Springs, OK; (2); 263/392; Church Yth Grp; Cmnty Wkr; FCA; Crs Cntry; Socr; Trk; Hon Roll; Prfct Atten Awd; Scuba Diving; Cmpt Soccer; Riding Dirt Bikes; Rnng 5k Charity Runs; HI Pacific Univ; Marine Collct.

ISAACSON, CLYDA; Claremore Sr HS; Chelsea, OK; (4); 12/247; Am Leg Aux Girls St; Cmnty Wkr; HOBY; Model UN; Sec Frsh Cls; Sec Soph Cls; Ofcr Stu Cncl; Intrml Gym; High Hon Roll; NHS; Mrktng Ed Chrprsn; Gymnstc Instrctr; Miss Tenn OK Schlrshp/Rcgntn Pgnt; Tulsa JC; Bus Mgmt.

ISBELL, KATY; Waukomis HS; Waukomis, OK; (4); 2/29; Pep Clb; Spanish Clb; Sec Soph Cls; Sec Jr Cls; Sec Sr Cls; Capt Bsktbl; Sftbl; High Hon Roll; NHS; Sal; FCA Pres; OK ST U; Arch.

ISBELL, LANE; Waukomis HS; Waukomis, OK; (4); 2/30; Am Leg Aux Girls St; Church Yth Grp; Quiz Bowl; Rep Frsh Cls; Sec Soph Cls; VP Jr Cls; Pres Sr Cls; VP Stu Cncl; Hon Roll; Sal; U Of Dallas; Politics.

ISBELL, VALERIE; Braggs Schl; Braggs, OK; (4); 1/18; Ed Nwsp; Yrbk; VP Frsh Cls; VP Stu Cncl; Var Chrldng; Var Sftbl; Hon Roll; Val; Phys Thrpy.

ISEMAN, AMBER D; Mc Alester HS; Mcalester, OK; (4); Art Clb; 4-H; French Clb; FHA; Natl FFA Org; Band; Hon Roll; Prfct Atten Awd; E OK St Col; Parole Ofcr.

ISENBERG, BRADLEY D; Duncan HS; Duncan, OK; (4); 28/213; Church Yth Grp; DECA; FBLA; Letterman Clb; Rptr Nwsp; JV Var Bsbl; JV Var Bsktbl; Hon Roll; NHS; Pres Acad Fit Awd; OK ST Univ; Acctng.

ISENBERG, TRISHA R; Coleman Schl; Kenefic, OK; (3); Church Yth Grp; FCA; 4-H; Pep Clb; Quiz Bowl; Ski Clb; JV Sftbl; Hon Roll; NHS; Yrbk Stff; Elem Ed.

ISENHOWER, AMANDA; Claremore Sr HS; Claremore, OK; (3); Church Yth Grp; French Clb; Math Clb; Science Clb; SADD; Chorus; Church Choir; Rep Stu Cncl; Gov Hon Prg Awd; NHS; All Dist Choir 2 Yrs; Bapt All St; SALT Tm; OU; Osteopthc Med.

ISOM, GENEVIEVE; Thomas Jr Sr HS; Thomas, OK; (1); 1/45; Church Yth Grp; 4-H; FHA; Natl FFA Org; High Hon Roll; Ntl Merit Ltr; Acad Lttr.

ISOM, JOSHUA; Apache HS; Apache, OK; (1); Church Yth Grp; Ofcr Bsbl; Ftbl; Wt Lftg; High Hon Roll; Pharmacist.

ISRAEL, ERIN; Edmond Memorial HS; Edmond, OK; (2); Debate Tm; NFL; Speech Tm; Treas Temple Yth Grp; Chorus; NHS; Medieval Clb.

ISTOOK, DIANA; Putnam City HS; Warr Acres, OK; (3); 1/502; Church Yth Grp; HOBY; Treas Key Clb; VP Spanish Clb; Rep Jr Cls; JV Stu Cncl; Cit Awd; NHS; 3 D Pres; Freedoms Fndtn Rep For OKC Chptr; BYU; Math Tchr.

ITAMI, JANET; Moore HS; Moore, OK; (2); Jr NHS; Arch.

IVEN, MAKALA; Putnam City West HS; Oklahoma City, OK; (3); Church Yth Grp; Cmnty Wkr; FCA; Ofcr Frsh Cls; Ofcr Soph Cls; Rep Jr Cls; Ofcr Stu Cncl; Var Chrldng; Hon Roll; NHS; US Ldrshp Mrt Ldrshp Awd; US Chrldr Achvt Awd; ASC Natl Chmpn Vrsty Sqd; U OK; Neontlgy.

IVERSON, MICHELLE L; Union Intermediate HS; Tulsa, OK; (2); 91/800; School Musical; Church Yth Grp; Key Clb; Chorus; Church Choir; High Hon Roll; Hon Roll; G/T Pgm Cncl; Church Musical Godspell, Yth Ldrshp Grp; Gen Contractng.

IVERY, AUDRA D; Bartlesville Mid HS; Bartlesville, OK; (2); 160/681; Church Yth Grp; FHA; Church Choir; Orch; JV Vllybl; Cit Awd; Hon Roll; Suzuki Strlng Strngs; GAWK; Northestrn ST Univ; Cmptr Sci.

IVERY, KRISHAUNDA L; Mt St Marys HS; Spencer, OK; (3); Church Yth Grp; Pep Clb; Church Choir; Variety Show; JV Bsktbl; Var L Trk; Hon Roll; Prfct Atten Awd; Acad Lttr; HS Srrty; U Of Houston; Psych.

IVES, BART F; Buffalo Jr Sr HS; Buffalo, OK; (1); Church Yth Grp; Cmnty Wkr; 4-H; Natl FFA Org; Band; Chorus; Jazz Band; Mrchg Band; Bsktbl; Trk; Southwestern OK ST Univ; Comp.

IVES, NIKKIE; Valliant HS; Valliant, OK; (2); 3/98; Church Yth Grp; Drama Clb; FHA; Girl Scts; Scholastic Bowl; Spanish Clb; School Play; Pres Soph Cls; NHS; Val; Vet.

IVEY, CHRISTOPHER W; Cimarron Public Schl; Enid, OK; (3); French Clb; Science Clb; Rptr Nwsp; High Hon Roll; Sports Announcer.

IVEY, DAVID J; Will Rogers HS; Tulsa, OK; (1); Church Yth Grp; German Clb; ROTC; Band; Church Choir; Color Guard; Drill Tm; Mrchg Band; Treas Frsh Cls; TU.

IVIE, JENNIFER L; Union Sr HS; Broken Arrow, OK; (4); 29/632; Intnl Clb; JA; Science Clb; Teachers Aide; Ed Nwsp; Ed Yrbk; Sftbl; High Hon Roll; Jr NHS; NHS; Renaissance Offcr; Math Ed.

IVIE, JODIE L; Union Intermediate HS; Broken Arrow, OK; (1); FCA; Hon Roll; NHS; Grgtwn; Eclgy.

IVINS, EMILY; Putnam City HS; Oklahoma City, OK; (1); Church Yth Grp; Drama Clb; FCA; GAA; Pep Clb; School Musical; School Play; Chrldng; PEAK.

IVINS, STACY; Yukon HS; Yukon, OK; (2); Church Yth Grp; Capt French Clb; FHA; Var Crs Cntry; Var Trk; NHS; 3-D; OK ST Univ; Vet Med.

IVY, JENNIFER N; Union Intermediate HS; Tulsa, OK; (1); Church Yth Grp; FCA; Spanish Clb; Mrchg Band; JV Vllybl; Hon Roll; Pres Acad Fit Awd; Eng Awd; U Of OK; Med; OB-GYN; Pedtrcs.

IVY, KIM D; Cleveland Sr HS; Tulsa, OK; (4); Church Yth Grp; 4-H; FHA; Library Aide; Natl FFA Org; Teachers Aide; Hon Roll; Prfct Atten Awd; FFA Chapt Sweethrt; Outs Ag Stu; Vet Med.

JACK, LANISSA S; Dustin Schl; Hanna, OK; (3); Cmnty Wkr; GAA; Natl FFA Org; Office Aide; Quiz Bowl; Spanish Clb; School Play; Var Bsktbl; Capt Sftbl; Cit Awd; Creek Nation Summer Yth 95-Outstdng Participant; Miss Muscogee Creek Nation Pageant, Spirit Women Awd; Haskell Univ; TV Broadcasting.

JACK, VICKY L; Union Sr HS; Tulsa, OK; (3); Cmnty Wkr; Key Clb; Church Choir; Nwsp; Phtg Yrbk; High Hon Roll; Jr NHS; NHS; Pres Schlr; Church Yth Grp; U Of OK; Mtrlgy.

JACKMAN, REBEKKAH; Union City Schl; Union City, OK; (2); 4-H; FHA; Girl Scts; Math Clb; Scholastic Bowl; Science Clb; Ofcr Frsh Cls; Ofcr Soph Cls; Hon Roll; Prfct Atten Awd; OK ST U; CPA.

JACKS, JEANIE; Altus Sr HS; Altus, OK; (4); 2/240; Am Leg Aux Girls St; Church Yth Grp; Quiz Bowl; Band; Chorus; Drm Mjr(t); School Musical; Cit Awd; NHS; Val; OK Chrstn; Med.

JACKS, JUSTIN; Watonga HS; Watonga, OK; (2); 6/74; Church Yth Grp; FCA; FBLA; Band; Jazz Band; Var L Ftbl; Trk; Hon Roll; NHS; Tchr.

JACKSON, AMANDA R; Caddo HS; Caddo, OK; (2); Rep Soph Cls; Sec Stu Cncl; Var Chrldng; Var Sftbl; Hist FHA; School Play; Stage Crew; Yrbk; Hon Roll; Mst Congenial Chrldr Awd; Southeastern OK ST U; Tchr.

JACKSON, AMY; Okmulgee HS; Morris, OK; (3); FCA; Math Clb; Bsktbl; High Hon Roll; Hon Roll; NHS; Ntl Merit Schol; Pres Acad Fit Awd; NE St Univ; Psych.

JACKSON, ANDREA DAWN; Charles Page HS; Sapulpa, OK; (3); 19/365; Q&S; SADD; Ed Yrbk; Ed Lit Mag; High Hon Roll; Hon Roll; Jr NHS; NHS; Broadcasting; Young Democrats Pres.

JACKSON, BENJAMIN J; Elk City Jr HS; Elk City, OK; (1); Boy Scts; Church Yth Grp; Band; Jazz Band; Mrchg Band; Pep Band; Bsktbl; Socr; Trk; Hon Roll; D.

JACKSON, BONNIE; Berryhill Sr HS; Wagoner, OK; (4); 12/51; Church Yth Grp; Computer Clb; FBLA; FHA; German Clb; JA; Spanish Clb; Hon Roll; NHS; Prfct Atten Awd; Serteens; TJC; Elem Ed.

JACKSON, BRANDI L; Midwest City HS; Midwest City, OK; (2); #162 in class; FHA; Fshn Dsgn; Interior Dsgn.

JACKSON, BRANDI M; South Intermediate HS; Broken Arrow, OK; (1); French Clb; Orch; Cit Awd; Hon Roll; OSU; Attrny.

JACKSON, BRANDON L; Booker T Washington HS; Tulsa, OK; (4); Church Yth Grp; Cmnty Wkr; Drama Clb; Office Aide; Teachers Aide; Band; Church Choir; Mrchg Band; Hon Roll; NCCJ Teen Talk Pnl; Red Rbbn Cmpgn Comm Play; Tulsa CC; Bus Admin.

JACKSON, CHARITY R; Putnam City West HS; Oklahoma City, OK; (3); Church Yth Grp; Drama Clb; FBLA; Intnl Clb; Spanish Clb; Church Choir; Vllybl; Hon Roll; NHS; Stdnt Mnth 95; Francis Tuttle Vo-Tech Suptndts Hnr Roll 95-; OK Bapt Univ; Msnry/Span.

JACKSON, DANA; Capitol Hill HS; Oklahoma City, OK; (4); 2/151; Quiz Bowl; Scholastic Bowl; SADD; Pres Band; Jazz Band; Mrchg Band; Pep Band; VP Jr Cls; Pres Treas NHS; Sal; OK City CC; Astrophyscs.

JACKSON, GARRETT Q; Del City HS; Oklahoma City, OK; (3); Church Yth Grp; FCA; Letterman Clb; Spanish Clb; Rep Stu Cncl; Golf; Cit Awd; NHS; Prfct Atten Awd; Val; Mech Engrng.

JACKSON, GRESHA; Okmulgee HS; Morris, OK; (1); GAA; JA; Rep Stu Cncl; Bsktbl; Capt Chrldng; Sftbl; Cit Awd; Hon Roll; Pres Acad Fit Awd; Sftbl Acad St Chmpns; KS U; Law.

JACKSON, HAYLEE A; Colcord Schl; Colcord, OK; (1); #1 in class; Natl FFA Org; Ofcr Stu Cncl; Bsktbl; High Hon Roll; Ntl Merit Ltr; Val.

JACKSON, JAIME L; Union Sr HS; Tulsa, OK; (3); FCA; FBLA; FHA; Key Clb; Rep Jr Cls; Rep Stu Cncl; Ofcr Bsbl; Var Chrldng; High Hon Roll; NHS.

JACKSON, JANNA B; B T Washington HS; Tulsa, OK; (4); 23/264; Church Yth Grp; Spanish Clb; Teachers Aide; Stage Crew; Sftbl; NHS; Pres Spnsh Clb, VP; U Of TX; Spansh Lit.

JACKSON, JEANA M; Davis HS; Davis, OK; (1); 10/66; Church Yth Grp; FBLA; JV Var Bsktbl; Var Sftbl; Hon Roll; Eng I Awd; OU; Dentistry.

JACKSON, JEREMY; Warner HS; Muskogee, OK; (4); 3/50; Am Leg Boys St; FCA; VP Spanish Clb; Rptr Nwsp; Ofcr Stu Cncl; Bsktbl; Ftbl; Pres NHS; Sal; Congrssnl Page; All St Ftbl Hnrb Mntn; All Conf Bsktbl & Ftbl; Med.

JACKSON, JODY C; Healdton HS; Healdton, OK; (3); Church Yth Grp; FCA; Pres 4-H; JA; Teachers Aide; Acpl Chr; Band; Chorus; Church Choir; Jazz Band; Chrstn Rock Bnd Sngr/Lead Gutrst; Sng Wrtr; U Of Central OK; PT.

JACKSON, JODY R; Thomas Jr Sr HS; Thomas, OK; (3); 11/34; Church Yth Grp; FCA; Natl FFA Org; Ofcr Bsbl; Bsktbl; Ftbl; Trk; Wt Lftg; Hon Roll; Wheatlnd All Conf; W Cntrl All St; Thomas Invit All Str Bsktbll; SWOSU.

JACKSON, JOEL B; Edmond Memorial HS; Edmond, OK; (4); 60/350; Cmnty Wkr; FCA; French Clb; Science Clb; School Play; Variety Show; Var Capt Swmmng; NHS; Ntl Merit SF; Pres Acad Fit Awd; All-St Swmmng; Church Childrns Minstry; Vlntr Wrk; Sprts Med.

JACKSON, JOHN; Midwest City HS; Midwest City, OK; (2); 28/488; Upward Bnd Pgm Rose St Coll; OK U; Med.

JACKSON, KARA L; Duncan HS; Duncan, OK; (2); Church Yth Grp; FBLA; Key Clb; Letterman Clb; SADD; Varsity Clb; Crs Cntry; Hon Roll; Rum; Ski; Time With Friends/Family; Chrstn Child Psychologist.

JACKSON, KARIS L; Muskogee HS; Muskogee, OK; (2); FCA; Ofcr Stu Cncl; Ftbl; Trk; Hon Roll; Baylor U; Pedtrcn.

JACKSON, KELLIE; Durant HS; Durant, OK; (4); Church Yth Grp; Cmnty Wkr; Key Clb; Office Aide; Variety Show; Rep Sr Cls; Rep Stu Cncl; Var Co-Capt Chrldng; Hon Roll; Southeastern OSU; Pub Reltns.

JACKSON, KEVIN; Stigler HS; Stigler, OK; (2); Pep Clb; SADD; Band; Mrchg Band; Hon Roll; TSA VP; Hnr Band.

JACKSON, KRYSTAL; Durant HS; Durant, OK; (3); Boy Scts; Church Yth Grp; Cmnty Wkr; FBLA; Pep Clb; Phtg VICA; Variety Show; Rep Frsh Cls; Rep Soph Cls; Rep Jr Cls; Jazz; Dance Lsns 7yrs; SOSU.

JACKSON, LA TOYA L; Douglass HS; Oklahoma City, OK; (2); Drama Clb; Hosp Aide; ROTC; Teachers Aide; Church Choir; School Play; Hon Roll; Prfct Atten Awd; U Of Cntrl OK; Lwyr.

JACKSON, LARISSA; Central Schl; Lawton, OK; (3); 2/30; Church Yth Grp; Pres FCA; 4-H; VP FHA; HOBY; Quiz Bowl; Scholastic Bowl; SADD; Church Choir; Ed Yrbk; Cameron U; Elem Ed.

JACKSON, MATTHEW D; Cashion HS; Cashion, OK; (2); FCA; FBLA; L JV Bsktbl; Hon Roll; Langston U; Comp Scis.

JACKSON, MEGAN A; Union Intermediate HS; Tulsa, OK; (2); Church Yth Grp; FCA; Spanish Clb; Yrbk; Sec Frsh Cls; Rep Stu Cncl; Bsktbl; JV Var Chrldng; Cit Awd; High Hon Roll; Mr & Miss Redskin Crt 95-96; NCA All Amer Chrldr 95-96; Multi Yr Listing; Phys Thrpy.

JACKSON, PATRICK R; Broken Arrow Sr HS; Broken Arrow, OK; (3); Church Yth Grp; FCA; Church Choir; Var L Ftbl; Hon Roll; Chrch Outreach Pgm; Chrch Storehouse Ministry; Bus Admin.

JACKSON, PHILLIP; Santa Fe HS; Edmond, OK; (3); FHA; Office Aide; SADD; Var Socr; OK 5a Boys Soccer St Champion 96.

JACKSON, QUIANA M; Muskogee HS; Muskogee, OK; (3); Church Yth Grp; Cmnty Wkr; Quiz Bowl; Spanish Clb; Band; Church Choir; Mrchg Band; Hon Roll; Jr NHS; NHS; Chosen Tour Europe 96; Super Rating Natl Piano Playing Auditions 96; Optimist Oratorial Cont 2nd Pl; Univ OK; Bio-Chemist.

JACKSON, RACHEL; Valliant HS; Valliant, OK; (2); 21/83; Art Clb; FHA; Chorus; Cit Awd; Frst Aide; Bio Awd; ITT; Comp Prog.

JACKSON, RONI K; Liberty HS; Beggs, OK; (3); 4/40; Teachers Aide; VP Jr Cls; Sec Stu Cncl; Chrldng; High Hon Roll; NHS; Prfct Atten Awd; NE St Univ.

JACKSON, SARAH; Grove HS; Grove, OK; (3); Church Yth Grp; Band; Church Choir; Drm Mjr(t); Jazz Band; Mrchg Band; Orch; Chrldng; NHS; Hosp Aide; OK Bapt All St Yth Choir, Orch; Child Psych.

JACKSON, SHAE L; Edmond Memorial HS; Edmond, OK; (3); 148/371; Church Yth Grp; German Clb; Key Clb; Band; Chorus; Mrchg Band; School Musical; Variety Show; L Socr; U Of OK; Erly Chldhd Ed.

JACKSON, STEPHANIE; Midwest City HS; Oklahoma City, OK; (2); 48/488; German Clb; JA; Letterman Clb; Band; Mrchg Band; Pep Band; Nwsp; Yrbk; Mgr(s); Hon Roll; Columbia U; Med.

JACKSON, STEPHANIE; Memorial HS; Tulsa, OK; (3); Drama Clb; French Clb; Hosp Aide; Pep Clb; Speech Tm; Chrldng; French Hon Soc; Hon Roll; Intl Frgn Lang Assn Frnch; Bus Mngmt.

JACKSON, SUMMER D; Waukomis HS; Waukomis, OK; (3); Church Yth Grp; FCA; FBLA; Pep Clb; SADD; Teachers Aide; Church Choir; Yrbk; Vllybl; Prfct Atten Awd; St Comptncy For Comp Arts; Bus Comp.

JACKSON, TAMEKA N; Star Spencer HS; Spencer, OK; (3); Church Yth Grp; FBLA; Girl Scts; ROTC; Teachers Aide; Band; Mrchg Band; Pep Band; Sec Soph Cls; Sec Jr Cls; Rifle Team; Env Sci Pgm; Pilot Intl Navigator; Clark Atlanta Univ; Psych.

JACKSON, TAMIKA T; Midwest City HS; Oklahoma City, OK; (2); 174/473; Art Clb; Church Yth Grp; Drama Clb; English Clb; ROTC; Church Choir; Color Guard; Orch; Treas Frsh Cls; Ofcr Stu Cncl; Sndy Schl Tchr; Bibl Trning*Instr; Air Frce; Jrnlsm.

JACKSON, TARA; Edmond North HS; Edmond, OK; (1); Dance Clb; Pep Clb; Chrldng; JETS Awd; OK U.

JACKSON, THERESE L; Yukon Middle HS; El Reno, OK; (2); FHA; Chorus; School Musical; Hon Roll; OCCC; Court Rptr.

JACKSON, TIMOTHY; Lawton Christian Schl; Lawton, OK; (4); 2/12; Letterman Clb; Ed Nwsp; Ed Yrbk; VP Stu Cncl; Var Capt Bsktbl; Cit Awd; High Hon Roll; Sal; Bsktbl All St Hnrb Mntn & Sports Chllng Intl USA Rep To Austria; Wheaton Coll; Psych.

JACOB, TONY; Yukon Middle HS; Yukon, OK; (2); Church Yth Grp; Spanish Clb; High Hon Roll; Hon Roll; Schltc Team; Renaisance Commtte; Archeology.

JACOBS, ALBERT JAMAAL; Okmulgee HS; Okmulgee, OK; (4); Am Leg Boys St; FCA; French Clb; FBLA; Math Clb; Office Aide; Science Clb; Teachers Aide; Varsity Clb; Rep Stu Cncl; U Of Tulsa; Engrng.

JACOBS, ALISHA D; Enid Sr HS; Enid, OK; (2); Teachers Aide; Chorus; JV Bsktbl; Var Trk; High Hon Roll; Hon Roll; Jr NHS; NHS.

JACOBS, BRYAN W; Edmond Memrl HS; Edmond, OK; (4); 66/350; Church Yth Grp; FCA; SADD; Var Bsbl; Intrml Bsktbl; Intrml Vllybl; High Hon Roll; Jr NHS; NHS; U Of OK; Pre-Med.

JACOBS, JULIE E; Okmulgee HS; Okmulgee, OK; (4); 42/122; French Clb; Band; Jazz Band; Mrchg Band; Pep Band; Rptr Nwsp; Hon Roll; HOSA; Close-Up; Govt; Tulsa JC; Nrsng.

JACOBS, MELISSA L; Cushing HS; Cushing, OK; (4); 1/156; Church Yth Grp; FCA; Math Clb; Spanish Clb; Band; Bsktbl; Sftbl; Trk; Hon Roll; NHS; Psych.

JACOBS, NYISHA S RODGERS; Del City HS; Oklahoma City, OK; (2); Church Yth Grp; Cmnty Wkr; Dance Clb; Library Aide; Office Aide; Pep Clb; Teachers Aide; Chorus; School Musical; School Play; Pub Spkng Teen Peer Pressure/Teen Preg Drugs/Alc Abuse; Chldrns Church Tchr Ltl Tddlrs; Air Force; Cosmptlgy.

JACOBS, SCOTT P; Sapulpa Sr HS; Sapulpa, OK; (3); 19/300; Math Clb; Scholastic Bowl; Science Clb; Spanish Clb; Chorus; Pres Acad Fit Awd; Spanish NHS; Academic Letterman 2 Years; Choir Letterman; Olympiad Finalist; Computer Engineering.

JACOBSEN, MATTHEW; Grace Fellowship Christian Sch; Broken Arrow, OK; (2); Church Yth Grp; School Play; Bsktbl; Socr; Vllybl; Hon Roll; Photo Clb; 1st Pl Sci Fair Botany; Attd Oral Roberts Educl Fllwshp; OK ST U; Arch Dsgn.

JACOBSON, DOUG; Clinton HS; Clinton, OK; (2); Church Yth Grp; English Clb; Chorus; Rep Stu Cncl; Var JV Bsbl; High Hon Roll; Hon Roll; NHS; Rapelling; U Of OK; Law.

JACOBSON, LUCAS; Pauls Valley HS; Pocasset, OK; (2); Church Yth Grp; VP Key Clb; Pres Pep Clb; Capt Scholastic Bowl; Rep Stu Cncl; Bsktbl; Ftbl; L Tennis; High Hon Roll; NHS; ST RA Pres.

JACOBSON, SHANNON L; Stillwater Sr HS; Stillwater, OK; (3); Church Yth Grp; Dance Clb; FCA; Hosp Aide; Key Clb; Math Clb; Mu Alpha Theta; Pep Clb; Spanish Clb; Teachers Aide; UDA All Star Dancer; Toe; Tap; Jazz; OSU; Phy Thrpst.

JACOBY, ERICH T; Yukon Middle HS; Yukon, OK; (3); Letterman Clb; Ftbl; Socr; Trk; Cit Awd.

JACOBY, SHANNON M; B T Washington HS; Tulsa, OK; (3); 34/269; Computer Clb; Golf; NHS; Chinese Clb; Piano; Chrch Act; Psych; Pre-Med.

JACOCKS, ERIC A; Edmond Memorial HS; Edmond, OK; (2); 85/408; Debate Tm; German Clb; Math Clb; Mu Alpha Theta; NFL; Quiz Bowl; Scholastic Bowl; JV L Swmmng; NHS; Pres Acad Fit Awd; Stu Ldrshp Day Pgm; Churchill Acad Westminster Univ; NDI-DC Debate Inst Cath Univ Amer; Duke; Sci.

JACQUES, JENNIFER R; Mustang HS; Yukon, OK; (3); Church Yth Grp; Spanish Clb; Teachers Aide; Chorus; Hon Roll; 4 Yr Univ.

JADLOW, JOANNA C; Stillwater Sr HS; Stillwater, OK; (4); 1/340; Cmnty Wkr; VP Hist French Clb; JCL; Key Clb; Hist Latin Clb; Pres VP Natl Beta Clb; Sec NHS; Pres Schlr; St Schlr; Val; Coca-Cola Schlr; Prins Ldrshp Awd; Schlstc Wrtng Awd; U Of TX At Austin; Bus/Acctng.

JAIMES, FEDERICO; Altus Sr HS; Altus, OK; (4); Quiz Bowl; Spanish Clb; L Crs Cntry; JV Socr; High Hon Roll; Hon Roll; Jr NHS; U Of OK.

JAIRAMANI, JAGAT; Central HS; Tulsa, OK; (1); Spanish Clb.

JAKUBS, KATHERINE; Midwest City HS; Midwest City, OK; (3); 1/384; French Clb; FHA; German Clb; Key Clb; Pep Clb; Quiz Bowl; Sec Soph Cls; Ofcr Jr Cls; Chrldng; High Hon Roll; Outstndng Grl Stu; Hmcmng Prncss.

JAMAR, CHAD; Ft Gibson HS; Fort Gibson, OK; (3); Church Yth Grp; FCA; French Clb; Band; Mrchg Band; Golf; Wrstlng; Hon Roll; NHS; OK Natl Hnr Soc.

JAMERSON, SUNDRIS C; Putnam City North HS; Oklahoma City, OK; (1); Church Yth Grp; Chorus; Church Choir; Orch; Rptr Yrbk; Rep Frsh Cls; Ofcr Stu Cncl; JV Sftbl; Cit Awd; Math/Sci Hnrs Prgm; AZ ST; Sci/Bio.

JAMES, AMANDA L; Mc Alester HS; Mcalester, OK; (4); 29/209; FCA; Chorus; Var Bsktbl; Var Sftbl; Var Trk; French Hon Soc; Hon Roll; All Conf, All Eastland Conf All Dist Sftbl; All Conf Hnrb Mntn Bsktbl; All Dist Choir Ensemble; Connors ST Coll; Pre-Law.

JAMES, AMY; Ketchum HS; Spavinaw, OK; (4); Art Clb; Church Yth Grp; Math Tm; Science Clb; Spanish Clb; Nwsp; Yrbk; Sec Frsh Cls; Sec Sr Cls; High Hon Roll; Roger ST Coll; RN.

JAMES, BARI M; Elgin HS; Lawton, OK; (2); Art Clb; FHA; Office Aide; Chorus; Socr; Sftbl; Hon Roll.

JAMES, DANESA; Dickson HS; Mannsville, OK; (3); 8/79; Cmnty Wkr; German Clb; Pres Key Clb; Rptr Natl FFA Org; SADD; Yrbk; Pres Treas Stu Cncl; High Hon Roll; Kiwanis Awd; NHS.

JAMES, ELIZABETH; Dale Sr HS; Shawnee, OK; (2); 16/49; FHA; SADD; Band; Mrchg Band; Var Sftbl; Jr NHS; Rec Sccr Shawnee United Chem MVP; MVP Sftbl; Connors; Sports Med.

JAMES, FELICITA; Western Heights Sr HS; Oklahoma City, OK; (1); 22/215; Girl Scts; Band; Mrchg Band; Treas Frsh Cls; Rep Stu Cncl; Bsktbl; Chrldng; Trk; Hon Roll; Jr NHS; Nrsng.

JAMES, GREGORY; Will Rogers HS; Tulsa, OK; (4); FTA; Pep Clb; ROTC; Spanish Clb; Acpl Chr; Chorus; Chrmn Frsh Cls; VP Soph Cls; Hon Roll; NHS; Circle Of Friends; Northeastern ST; Sec Spcl Ed.

JAMES, JEFF R; Tahlequah Sr HS; Welling, OK; (3); Church Yth Grp; FCA; Natl FFA Org; Quiz Bowl; Chorus; Church Choir; Stage Crew; Rep Frsh Cls; JV Var Bsktbl; Ftbl; Natl & OK St FFA Chorus 2 Yrs Each; Pol Campaign Vol; Law; Music.

JAMES, JENNELL; Bray-Doyle HS; Marlow, OK; (3); FCA; 4-H; HOBY; Speech Tm; SADD; School Play; Ed Yrbk; Rep Frsh Cls; Var Bsktbl; Var Sftbl; OK Hse Rep Page 95; SADD Vctms Impct Pnl; Pltcl Cmpgn Wrkr; Am Police Hall Fame; Georgetown U.

JAMES, JENNIFER M; Verden HS; Verden, OK; (1); GAA; Science Clb; Speech Tm; Bsktbl; Sftbl; Poem Love Publsh In Book Journey Of Mind; Marine Bio.

JAMES, JESSI L; Boise City HS; Boise City, OK; (1); 10/38; Church Yth Grp; FCA; Letterman Clb; Rep Frsh Cls; Ofcr Stu Cncl; Bsktbl; Trk; Hon Roll.

JAMES, JOSHUA; Heavener HS; Howe, OK; (1); Church Yth Grp; JV Ftbl; JV Wt Lftg; Mrn Biogst.

JAMES, KENYATTA; Valliant HS; Valliant, OK; (2); French Clb; FHA; Library Aide; Chorus; Church Choir; High Hon Roll; Hon Roll; NHS; Natl Sci Mrt Awd; All-Amer Schlrs; SE OK ST U; Med Sci.

JAMES, KIMBERLY K; Choctaw HS; Choctaw, OK; (3); Spanish Clb; Band; Color Guard; Mrchg Band; Camping; Competing In Pageants; Home Care RN.

JAMES, LEAH D; Inola Sr HS; Inola, OK; (3); Church Yth Grp; Teachers Aide; Church Choir; Hon Roll; NHS; Ntl Merit Ltr; U Of OK; Acctng.

JAMES, LINDSAY; Welch Jr Sr HS; Welch, OK; (3); FBLA; FHA; HOBY; VP Jr Cls; Sec Pres Stu Cncl; Var Bsktbl; Var Sftbl; Var Trk; NHS; Ntl Merit Schol; Msnc Stu Of Today; SW OK ST U; Phrmcst.

JAMES, MIRANDA L; Bray-Doyle HS; Duncan, OK; (3); FHA; Girl Scts; Pep Clb; SADD; Teachers Aide; School Play; Chrldng; Sftbl; 4-H Awd; Prfct Atten Awd; Cameron Univ; Daycare; Childcare.

JAMES, NATHAN N; El Reno Sr HS; El Reno, OK; (3); Church Yth Grp; FCA; Letterman Clb; Varsity Clb; Rep Soph Cls; Rep Jr Cls; Ftbl; Trk; Wrstlng; ST Wrstlng Chmp ST Chmp Dual ST Chmps 95; 3rd Wrld Team Trlr Freestyle 5th Greca; Trnr/Med.

JAMES, PRESTON; Hartshorne Sr HS; Mcalester, OK; (4); 2/42; Am Leg Boys St; Nwsp; Yrbk; Pres Frsh Cls; Pres Soph Cls; VP Jr Cls; Rptr Sr Cls; Rep Stu Cncl; Capt Bsktbl; Capt Ftbl.

JAMES, RICKY F; Sapulpa Sr HS; Sapulpa, OK; (2); Boy Scts; Church Yth Grp; Drama Clb; ROTC; Band; Mrchg Band; Rep Frsh Cls; Ofcr Bsbl; Crs Cntry; Trk; Umpire For Sapulpa Bsbl Assoc; NSU; Bsbl Player.

JAMES, WAYNE S; El Reno Sr HS; El Reno, OK; (2); Church Yth Grp; FCA; JA; Var L Wrstlng; Hon Roll; Natl Ranking For Wrstlng; Med.

JAMES, WILLIAM; Broken Bow HS; Broken Bow, OK; (4); Library Aide; Science Clb; Rep Stu Cncl; Var Golf; NHS; Prfct Atten Awd; Marines Delayed Entry Pgm; Brdcst Jrnlsm; Engrng.

JAMISON, AMY; Broken Arrow Sr HS; Broken Arrow, OK; (4); 76/971; Am Leg Aux Girls St; DECA; Ed Yrbk; Ofcr Jr Cls; Ofcr Sr Cls; Ofcr Stu Cncl; Swmmng; Cit Awd; NHS; Masonic Lodge Stu Of Today Awd; Stu Of Month; U Of OK; Pblc Rltns.

JAMISON, CINDY; Kiefer Jr Sr HS; Kiefer, OK; (2); FCA; Var Bsktbl.

JAMISON, DEREK R; Carl Albert HS; Midwest City, OK; (2); Boy Scts; Cmnty Wkr; FCA; Band; Mrchg Band; Tennis; Hon Roll.

JAMISON, ERIN E; Bartlesville Sr HS; Bartlesville, OK; (1); Church Yth Grp; Chorus; Church Choir; Hon Roll; SPCA Explorers Post; Vet.

JAMISON, LESLIE; Union Inter HS; Tulsa, OK; (1); Cmnty Wkr; Speech Tm; Ofcr Stu Cncl; JV Co-Capt Chrldng; Var Gym; High Hon Roll; Jr NHS; NHS; Pres Acad Fit Awd; All-St Gymnstcs; DFY Sec.

JAMISON, MICHELLE R; Charles Page HS; Sand Springs, OK; (3); Spanish Clb; Chrldng; Sftbl; Hon Roll; NHS.

JANDA, CHRIS; Allen HS; Allen, OK; (4); #2 in class; Church Yth Grp; HOBY; Library Aide; Var Ftbl; Trk; Var Wt Lftg; High Hon Roll; Hon Roll; Sal; OK Hnr Soc 4 Yrs; U Of OK; Med.

JANG, B J; Enid Sr HS; Enid, OK; (3); FCA; Letterman Clb; Teachers Aide; Varsity Clb; Golf; Cit Awd; Hon Roll; Jr NHS; NHS.

JANIE, VANN M; Olive Jr Sr HS; Bristow, OK; (3); 13/38; Church Yth Grp; FCA; FBLA; GAA; HOBY; Pep Clb; JV Var Bsktbl; Var Vllybl; Cntrl Vo-Tech; UCO; Bus.

JANOWSKI, BRADEN S; Nathan Hale HS; Tulsa, OK; (4); 1/203; Treas French Clb; Rep Frsh Cls; Rep Soph Cls; Rep Stu Cncl; Var L Bsbl; NHS; Val; Acad Tm Capt; Ecology Clb Pres; All Conf 1st String Pitcher; U Of OK; Elctrcl Engr/Cmptr.

JANSING, AMANDA; Moore Norman Area Voc Tech Sch; Norman, OK; (4); Service Clb; Spanish Clb; VICA; Chorus; DECA; Page St OK Capt Rep; Outstnding Acht Fine & Applied Arts; Rose St Coll; Fshn Mrchndsng.

JANSSEN, EMILY; Putnam City HS; Warr Acres, OK; (2); Church Yth Grp; Spanish Clb; Chorus; School Musical; Rep Soph Cls; Rep Stu Cncl; Var Chrldng; NHS; Piano Dist & St Auds; Chrch Sftbl; Dncng; OSU; Med.

JANTZ, JEFFREY M; Drummond Schl; Drummond, OK; (3); 4-H; Natl FFA Org; Quiz Bowl; Scholastic Bowl; Band; Ed Yrbk; 4-H Awd; Gov Hon Prg Awd; High Hon Roll; Kiwanis Awd; OK ST U; Bio Sci.

JANWAY, CHANI; Muskogee HS; Muskogee, OK; (4); 50/303; Church Yth Grp; FCA; Hist JCL; Key Clb; School Musical; Rptr Jr Cls; Treas Sr Cls; Var Chrldng; Hon Roll; NHS; Optmst Fmle Athl Yr Awd; Primericas Otstndng Athl Awd; Bsktbl Hmcmng Qn 96; OK U; Med.

JANZEN, GRANT P; Enid Sr HS; Enid, OK; (4); 9/412; Church Yth Grp; FCA; Letterman Clb; Math Clb; Math Tm; Service Clb; Spanish Clb; SADD; Varsity Clb; Orch; OK Bapt U; Chem; Orthpdc Surgn.

JANZEN, LESLIE J; Sharon Mutual Jr Sr HS; Woodward, OK; (2); Natl FFA Org; Ofcr Bsbl; Bsktbl; Hon Roll; NHS; Prfct Atten Awd; Forestry.

JANZEN, SANDRA J; Edmond Memorial HS; Edmond, OK; (4); 1/386; Church Yth Grp; Hosp Aide; Math Clb; Mu Alpha Theta; Spanish Clb; SADD; Band; Church Choir; Mrchg Band; Pep Band; Tabor Col; Med Mssnry.

JAQUES, RONNETTE; Union Sr HS; Broken Arrow, OK; (4); 213/629; Church Yth Grp; FCA; FHA; Key Clb; Office Aide; Pep Clb; Spanish Clb; Teachers Aide; Rep Frsh Cls; Ofcr Soph Cls; Trinity Vly Comm Coll; Bus Mgmt.

JARMAN, AMANDA; Vanoss Schl; Ada, OK; (1); Scholastic Bowl; Chorus; High Hon Roll; NHS.

JARNAGIN, DUSTIN L; Carnegie HS; Carnegie, OK; (3); Boy Scts; Church Yth Grp; Letterman Clb; Natl FFA Org; Church Choir; Rep Stu Cncl; L Bsbl; Bsktbl; L Ftbl; L Trk; Chrch Msns; SWOSU Weatherford; PT.

JARNAGIN, KEVIN; Elk City Jr HS; Elk City, OK; (1); Church Yth Grp; Band; Jazz Band; Mrchg Band; Pep Band; Sec Frsh Cls; Sec Stu Cncl; Var Bsktbl; Var Ftbl; Var Tennis; OK U; Med.

JARRELL, ANDREA; Cordell Sr HS; Cordell, OK; (3); 3/44; Letterman Clb; Band; Drm Mjr(t); Pep Band; Rep Jr Cls; Var Bsktbl; Var Chrldng; Var Sftbl; High Hon Roll; NHS; Stu Of 9 Wks; OK Hnr Soc; OK ST U.

JARRELL, NATALIE; Stratford Schl; Stratford, OK; (3); FCA; 4-H; FBLA; FHA; Natl FFA Org; Teachers Aide; Var Bsktbl; Var Chrldng; Var Trk; Val; OK Jr Brangus Breedrs Assn; Bus.

JARRELL, NICOLE; Stratford Schl; Stratford, OK; (3); 1/59; FCA; FBLA; FHA; Teachers Aide; Ofcr Frsh Cls; Ofcr Soph Cls; Ofcr Jr Cls; Ofcr Stu Cncl; Var Bsktbl; Var Chrldng; Hlpd Move/Sort Supplies Feed The Chldrn OK Boming; 1st Sub Dist Parlmntry Procdr Cmptn/2nd Dist; Qua; OK ST U; Bus.

JARRETT, BRANDY A; Midwest City HS; Midwest City, OK; (3); Church Yth Grp; Cmnty Wkr; Girl Scts; JA; Library Aide; Service Clb; Band; Mrchg Band; High Hon Roll; Prfct Atten Awd; Erly Chld Ed.

JARVIS, KRISTOPHER D; Union Sr HS; Broken Arrow, OK; (3); 21/741; FBLA; FHA; German Clb; Ofcr Stu Cncl; Intrml Ftbl; High Hon Roll; Jr NHS; NHS; Ntl Merit Ltr; Pres Acad Fit Awd; Ryukyu Kemp Assn; Exchng Stu; Quadrilingual.

JARVIS, NATHAN A; Rush Springs HS; Rush Springs, OK; (2); 1/40; Church Yth Grp; Scholastic Bowl; Band; Pres Soph Cls; Ofcr Stu Cncl; Var Bsktbl; Wt Lftg; High Hon Roll; NHS; OK ST U; Comp Systms Analyst.

JARVIS, PATRICIA D; Lawton Sr HS; Lawton, OK; (2); FHA; Treas Girl Scts; Key Clb; Hon Roll; Jr NHS; NHS; Art; The Univ Of Tulsa; Art.

JARVIS, RHONDA M; Putnam City North HS; Beckley, WV; (1); Church Yth Grp; Pep Clb; Chorus; Church Choir; Rep Frsh Cls; Cit Awd; Lee Coll.

JASIM, ANGELA M; East Central HS; Coweta, OK; (3); Church Yth Grp; FCA; French Clb; Key Clb; Office Aide; Hon Roll; NHS; Chrstns HS; Stu Hlpng Stu; Drug/Alchl Wk Chprsn; OSU; Early Ed.

JASZKOWIAK, ALISON; Moore HS; Moore, OK; (2); Church Yth Grp; Band; Church Choir; Jazz Band; Mrchg Band; Pep Band; Jr NHS; Piano; OK Msc Tchrs Assn Annl Fest, Awd Rbbns; Chrstn Msc Mnstry.

JAVED, NAJWA; Union Intermediate HS; Broken Arrow, OK; (1); Cmnty Wkr; Intnl Clb; Key Clb; Red Cross Aide; Spanish Clb; High Hon Roll; NHS; Spanish NHS; Natl Conf Chrstns, Jews & Mslms; Mslm Yth Grp N Amer; Mslm Yth Tulsa; Med.

JECH, SARAH; Kingfisher HS; Kingfisher, OK; (1); 1/118; Church Yth Grp; FCA; GAA; Natl FFA Org; Quiz Bowl; Church Choir; Bsktbl; Mgr Ftbl; Mgr(s); High Hon Roll.

JEDELHAUSER, RITA S; Ninnekah HS; Ninnekah, OK; (3); Spanish Clb; Teachers Aide; Band; Chorus; School Musical; Hon Roll; Ntb Lang Ger Also Spks Eng/Fr/Latin/Italian/Span; Singing Career.

JEFFERSON, JEFFREY L; Midwest City HS; Oklahoma City, OK; (2); Church Yth Grp; Church Choir; Bsktbl; Wt Lftg; Hon Roll; Yth Prgm Excptnl Svc Awd For Amer Red Crs; Moorehouse Coll.

JEFFERSON, NATALIE R; Broken Bow HS; Broken Bow, OK; (3); Rptr Church Yth Grp; Spanish Clb; Jr Miss Indian OK 96; Jr Miss Choctaw Nation Of OK; Amer Indian Ldrshhp Yth Cncl, Pub Relations; Haskell Indian Nations; Soc Wrk.

JEFFERSON, SUMMER R; Okmulgee HS; Okmulgee, OK; (4); 48/126; Natl FFA Org; Spanish Clb; Nwsp; Pom Pon; Hon Roll; NCA Dance Awds; OSU; Graphic Designer.

JEFFREY, JASON; Holdenville Jr HS; Holdenville, OK; (1); Boy Scts; Church Yth Grp; FCA; Quiz Bowl; Band; Mrchg Band; Ofcr Bsbl; Bsktbl; Ftbl; Score Keeper; Amer Legion Awd; Arch Eng.

JEFFRIES, ELISE; Ponca City Mid HS; Ponca City, OK; (1); Church Yth Grp; Pep Clb; Chorus; Church Choir; School Musical; Chrldng; Crs Cntry; Gym; Socr; High Hon Roll; CEF; All Amer Chrldng; Chrch Puppet Ministry.

JEFFRIES, JEFF T; Edmond Santa Fe HS; Edmond, OK; (2); 100/347; Church Yth Grp; FCA; SADD; VICA; JV Bsbl; JV Ftbl; Var Wrstlng; OU; Crmnl Jstc.

JEFFRIES, RACHEL; Westmoore HS; Moore, OK; (2); FCA; French Clb; Pep Clb; Chrldng; L Sftbl; Sec Jr NHS; NHS; US Chrldng Achvt Awd, All Amer Chrldr; Soph Cncl.

JEFFRIES, STACIE; Antlers Sr HS; Antlers, OK; (2); Church Yth Grp; FCA; Office Aide; SADD; Var Bsktbl; High Hon Roll; Med.

JEFFRIES, TISHA A; Blackwell HS; Ponca City, OK; (2); 20/138; Church Yth Grp; Cmnty Wkr; FCA; 4-H; GAA; Letterman Clb; Pep Clb; Red Cross Aide; Varsity Clb; Chorus; OK Univ; Intr Dsgns.

JELINEK, CHRISTOPHER; Choctaw HS; Midwest City, OK; (2); 1/389; HOBY; Key Clb; Scholastic Bowl; Pres Spanish Clb; Ed Yrbk; VP Stu Cncl; Trk; Jr NHS; Val; Publshd In HS Wrtr Natl Lit Mgzn; 2nd Hnrb Mntn Manningham Poetry Trst Awds Cont; Med.

JELINEK, JENNIFER; Bartlesville Sr HS; Bartlesville, OK; (4); Boy Scts; Church Yth Grp; FHA; German Clb; Hosp Aide; Letterman Clb; Math Clb; Pep Clb; Chorus; Church Choir; OK St Univ; Chem Eng.

JENKINS, JESSICA; Minco HS; Minco, OK; (4); 26/38; Am Leg Aux Girls St; Church Yth Grp; Cmnty Wkr; 4-H; FBLA; FHA; Library Aide; Quiz Bowl; Teachers Aide; Yrbk; Redlands JC; Nrsng.

JENKINS, KARA L; Bethany HS; Oklahoma City, OK; (3); 4/80; Church Yth Grp; Office Aide; Spanish Clb; Band; Chorus; Church Choir; Mrchg Band; Hon Roll; NHS; Letter B Awd; Big Five Awd; OK Hnr Soc; Superiors/Superior Pluses Solo Fstvl/Guild/Dist/ST/TEEN Tlnt; Nazarene Coll; Missionary.

JENNINGS, AMANDA F; Midwest City HS; Midwest City, OK; (2); 110/473; Church Yth Grp; Pep Clb; Teachers Aide; Mgr(s); Trk; Hon Roll; NHS; Prfct Atten Awd; Church Dramas/Ilstrtns; Church Msnts Grp; Wrk Chrch Nrsry; Med Field.

JENNINGS, ANGELA; Stigler HS; Stigler, OK; (3); 1/95; Drama Clb; Scholastic Bowl; Speech Tm; Band; Drill Tm; Flag Corp; Mrchg Band; School Play; VP Frsh Cls; High Hon Roll; Model Congress Rep; Mock Trials Best Witness ST Semi Finalist; OK ST Univ; Bio/Med/Chem.

JENNINGS, ARETHA; Douglass HS; Moore, OK; (4); 15/116; FHA; Teachers Aide; Ed Yrbk; Rep Stu Cncl; Hon Roll; Univ Of OK; Mrktg.

JENNINGS, CHRISTIE; Byng Sr HS; Ada, OK; (4); 19/73; Church Yth Grp; Drama Clb; Sec FCA; 4-H; Rep French Clb; Hist FBLA; Pres Natl FFA Org; Pep Clb; Church Choir; Stage Crew; Stu Cncl Vp; OK ST Univ.

JENNINGS, JULIE; Davis HS; Davis, OK; (3); Am Leg Aux Girls St; Church Yth Grp; Debate Tm; Drama Clb; FCA; 4-H; FBLA; Key Clb; Model UN; Pep Clb; Ed.

JENNINGS, KELLEY; Norman Sr HS; Norman, OK; (4); 1/677; FBLA; Office Aide; Rep Stu Cncl; Chrldng; French Hon Soc; High Hon Roll; NHS; Pres Acad Fit Awd; St Schlr; Val; U Of OK; CPA.

JENNINGS, KERRY L; El Reno Sr HS; Moore, OK; (1); Church Yth Grp; FCA; Quiz Bowl; Chorus; Variety Show; Tennis; Cit Awd; Hon Roll; Pres Acad Fit Awd; Won Super Natl Lvl Show Choir; Super 2 Solo Assmbls God Fn Arts Msc Mnstry; Stdnt Cncl Choice Awd; Southwestern Bible Coll; PT.

JENNINGS, KIP A; Velma Alma HS; Velma, OK; (3); Church Yth Grp; Cmnty Wkr; Drama Clb; FCA; SADD; Band; Jazz Band; Mrchg Band; School Play; Yrbk; Sci Tchr.

JENNINGS, MELISSA; Cement Jr Sr HS; Cement, OK; (4); 2/30; Am Leg Aux Girls St; Church Yth Grp; FCA; FHA; GAA; Scholastic Bowl; Pres Sr Cls; VP Stu Cncl; Cit Awd; High Hon Roll; USAO; Bus.

JENNINGS, NATALIE; Okmulgee HS; Okmulgee, OK; (4); 12/119; FBLA; VP Math Clb; Spanish Clb; Speech Tm; Phtg Yrbk; Capt Bsktbl; Capt Chrldng; Capt Swmmng; Capt Tennis; NHS; Hnr Roll; Stu Mon; Prncpls Ldrshp Schlrshpfnlst; U AR; Sprts Med.

JENNINGS, TABITHA R; Midwest City HS; Midwest City, OK; (2); Church Yth Grp; Teachers Aide; Church Choir; Ofcr Stu Cncl; Mgr(s); Trk; Hon Roll; NHS; Rcvc Awd Excl Female Vclsts Teen Tlnt; Chld Dev.

JENSEN, JENNIFER; Claremore Sr HS; Claremore, OK; (3); 1/300; Church Yth Grp; FCA; Spanish Clb; SADD; Var Capt Bsktbl; Var Socr; Hon Roll; NHS; Prfct Atten Awd; OK ST; Dr.

JENSEN, KRISTINA F; Union Intermediate HS; Broken Arrow, OK; (2); Yrbk; Swmmng; Hon Roll; Jr NHS; NHS; Dental.

JEON, DONG S; Union Intermediate HS; Broken Arrow, OK; (2); 8/27; Church Yth Grp; Computer Clb; Spanish Clb; Bus.

JEON, UN C; Union Sr HS; Broken Arrow, OK; (3); 79/743; Art Clb; Sec Church Yth Grp; French Clb; Intnl Clb; Key Clb; Church Choir; High Hon Roll; Hon Roll; NHS; Pres Schlr; Piano Solo-Chrch Keybrd Plyr; Hnrb Mntn PTA Rflctn Prgm 94; Mrt Cttn Natl Schl Trffc Sfty Pstr Prgm; WA U; Arch.

JERMAIN, ADAM H; West Middle HS; Norman, OK; (1); Church Yth Grp; FCA; Red Cross Aide; Spanish Clb; Band; Yrbk; Lit Mag; Socr; High Hon Roll; Prfct Atten Awd; Air Force Acad; Air Force Ofcr.

JERMAN, EMILY J; Norman North HS; Norman, OK; (2); Church Yth Grp; Cmnty Wkr; French Clb; Mu Alpha Theta; Service Clb; Band; Mrchg Band; Orch; Pep Band; French Hon Soc; Project Outreach; Piano; Band Ltr.

JERMAN, HADLEY E; Norman HS North; Norman, OK; (3); Church Yth Grp; Cmnty Wkr; French Clb; Mu Alpha Theta; Service Clb; Band; Mrchg Band; Orch; Pep Band; Gov Hon Prg Awd; Project Outreach; Piano.

JERNIGAN, JIMMY H; Heritage Hall Schl; Oklahoma City, OK; (2); Cmnty Wkr; FCA; Letterman Clb; Var L Bsktbl; Var L Ftbl; Var L Trk; Hon Roll; Stu Of Month; Heritage Hall Outstndng Soph Boy; Track ST Medalist 2 Times.

JERNIGEN, KELLY; Central Mid-HS; Norman, OK; (2); Art Clb; Drama Clb; JCL; Latin Clb; Mu Alpha Theta; School Play; Yrbk; Pres Schlr; Gymnstcs; Hlth Sci.

JERRY, MARCUS; Moore HS; Moore, OK; (3); FBLA; Spanish Clb; SADD; Pres Frsh Cls; Pres Soph Cls; Ofcr Stu Cncl; Socr; Wrstlng; Crs Cntry; Spnsh Clb; FBLA Reptr; Schl Anncr; After Prom Cmmtte Chrmn; AZ ST U; Bus Mgmt.

JESKE, JASON T; Strother Jr Sr HS; Shawnee, OK; (3); Am Leg Boys St; Natl FFA Org; Quiz Bowl; Ofcr Stu Cncl; Ofcr Bsbl; Bsktbl; High Hon Roll; NHS.

JESSEE, BRADLY J; Midwest City HS; Midwest City, OK; (3); 111/365; Church Yth Grp; FHA; Letterman Clb; Varsity Clb; Var Capt Socr; Oceanography.

JESSIE, JASON; Hulbert Jr Sr HS; Hulbert, OK; (4); 1/43; Am Leg Boys St; Office Aide; Quiz Bowl; Pres Frsh Cls; Pres Soph Cls; Bsktbl; Capt Ftbl; Trk; Pres NHS; Val; Northeastern ST U.

JESTER, GAYLA M; Yukon Middle HS; Yukon, OK; (2); Treas FHA; Quiz Bowl; Hon Roll; NHS; OK St Univ.

JESTICE, JODI; Hilldale HS; Muskogee, OK; (3); #5 in class; Church Yth Grp; Drama Clb; Key Clb; Scholastic Bowl; Science Clb; Spanish Clb; SADD; Var L Bsktbl; Intrml Powder Puff Ftbl; Var L Sftbl; Prime Amer Outstndng Stu Athl Awd 2 Yrs.

JETER, JONCIA JOI; Nathan Hale HS; Tulsa, OK; (4); Bus Profs of Am; FCA; FBLA; ROTC; Church Choir; Drill Tm; Ofcr Frsh Cls; JV Var Bsktbl; Var Chrldng; Hon Roll; NE OK A&M Col; Phy Thrpy.

JETT, ZACK E; Northwest Classen HS; Moore, OK; (4); 4/180; FBLA; Library Aide; Math Clb; Mu Alpha Theta; Office Aide; Quiz Bowl; Chorus; Stage Crew; Pres Sr Cls; Wrstlng; Natl Merit Schlr; Superior Rating Vocal Solo Dist Music Contest; OK Acad Schlr Cert Of Recog; OK City Univ; Psych.

JETTON, AMBER R; Mc Loud HS; Mc Loud, OK; (2); Drama Clb; GAA; Stage Crew; Bsktbl; Cit Awd; High Hon Roll; OU; Lawyer.

JETTON, ROBERT; Roland Sr HS; Roland, OK; (3); 5/104; Church Yth Grp; Cmnty Wkr; FCA; Natl FFA Org; Spanish Clb; Speech Tm; Church Choir; High Hon Roll; NHS; Mbr Natl Champ Pasture/Range Tm; Pres EOMBC Yth Rally; Westark CC; Bus Admin.

JEWELL, JENNIFER K; Westmoore HS; Oklahoma City, OK; (4); 13/622; Church Yth Grp; Cmnty Wkr; L Scholastic Bowl; L Band; Mrchg Band; School Musical; Rptr Nwsp; VP Jr NHS; NHS; Val; All St Bnd; CODA All Rgn Bnd; St Solo/Ensm Cont Super Rtng; OK Yth Symphny St Cont Bnd Super Rtng; U OK; Music.

JEWETT, AMY; Verden HS; Verden, OK; (3); 5/27; Church Yth Grp; FCA; FHA; HOBY; Science Clb; Spanish Clb; Nwsp; Yrbk; NHS; Natl Ldrshp Svc Awd; Natl Yth Ldrshp Conf; Cngrssnl Yth Ldrshp Conf; Med.

JILGE, CHRIS D; Choctaw HS; Choctaw, OK; (2); VICA; Acpl Chr; Chorus; Jazz Band; Swing Chorus; Variety Show; Choir Svc Awd; Auto Mechnc.

JIM, AGAR; Noble HS; Noble, OK; (3); Mu Alpha Theta; JV Var Bsktbl.

JIN, BAOZHEN; Duncan HS; Duncan, OK; (3); Math Clb; Math Tm; Mu Alpha Theta; Science Clb; Chorus; Orch; High Hon Roll; Hon Roll; Jr NHS; Made All St Orch In St Of OK; Elec Engr.

JINKENS, JASON; Canton HS; Canton, OK; (3); Boy Scts; School Play; Ofcr Stu Cncl; Var Bsktbl; Var Ftbl; Hon Roll; NHS; Acad Team; Coach.

JOBE, HEATHER; Henryetta Sr HS; Henryetta, OK; (4); 10/60; FCA; FHA; Color Guard; Mrchg Band; Pep Band; Ofcr Jr Cls; Sec Sr Cls; Rep Stu Cncl; High Hon Roll; Treas NHS; Okmulgee Tech Schlsp; Pres Schlsp; Fr Awd 2 Yrs; OSU; Psych.

JOBE, JARRETT; Westmoore HS; Oklahoma City, OK; (4); Am Leg Boys St; Church Yth Grp; FCA; HOBY; School Musical; Ofcr Stu Cncl; Ftbl; Trk; NHS; Val; U Of Cntrl OK; Scndry Ed.

JOBSON, EDWARD; Shawnee Sr HS; Shawnee, OK; (2); Boy Scts; Church Yth Grp; Cmnty Wkr; Latin Clb; SADD; Ftbl; High Hon Roll; Hon Roll; Jr NHS; NHS; U Of OK; Med.

JOHANNESSEN, ASHLEY; Plainview HS; Ardmore, OK; (2); 9/77; Natl Beta Clb; Band; Jazz Band; Mrchg Band; Hon Roll; NHS; OK Hnr Soc; Comps; Scuba Diving; MIT; Comp Engrng.

JOHN, AMANDA L; Idabel HS; Idabel, OK; (2); Cmnty Wkr; 4-H; Natl FFA Org; Science Clb; Speech Tm; Gov Hon Prg Awd; Pres Acad Fit Awd; Star Greenhand; St Speech Fnlst; NAC Pres; OK ST U; Vet.

JOHN, CASSIE; Sulphur HS; Sulphur, OK; (3); 1/80; Church Yth Grp; Key Clb; Science Clb; Spanish Clb; Yrbk; Pres Jr Cls; Ofcr Stu Cncl; Var Chrldng; High Hon Roll; NHS; G/T Pgm; SE Schlstc Meet 2nd Pl Geom; E Cntrl 5th Pl Physcs; Murray St 5th Pl Chem; OK Rep Page; U Of OK; Aerospce.

JOHN, JOHNATHAN C; Northeast HS; Oklahoma City, OK; (3); Chorus; Church Choir; School Musical; Var Bsktbl; Hon Roll; Prfct Atten Awd; Pres Acad Fit Awd; Peer Mediator; MVP Bsktbl 95-96; African Amer Cultural Soc; AAU Bsktbl; Natural Sci.

JOHN, LEEJIA M; Union Intermediate HS; Broken Arrow, OK; (2); 118/800; Cmnty Wkr; French Clb; Hosp Aide; Quiz Bowl; Spanish Clb; High Hon Roll; NHS; Acad Team; Rotary Clb; Oral Roberts U; Phrmcy.

JOHN, TAMARA; Putnam City HS; Warr Acres, OK; (4); 87/356; Church Yth Grp; Cmnty Wkr; DECA; FCA; Pep Clb; Church Choir; Nwsp; Stat Bsbl; Var Capt Chrldng; Mgr(s); TX A&M; Vet Med; Phy Thrpst.

JOHNMSON, JESSICA; Douglass HS; Oklahoma City, OK; (2); Ed Nwsp; VP Pres Frsh Cls; Bsktbl; Mgr Trk; Mgr Vllybl; Cit Awd; Jrnlsm Awd 95-96; Miss Black OK Teen USA 95-96; PRIDE; U Of Cntrl OK; Broadcst Jrnlsm.

JOHNNSON, STEFANIE B; Muldrow HS; Muldrow, OK; (1); Church Yth Grp; FCA; FHA; GAA; Natl Beta Clb; Office Aide; Chorus; Church Choir; School Musical; Swing Chorus; Elem Tchr.

JOHNS, FARLAND D; Millwood HS; Oklahoma City, OK; (1); Color Guard; Drill Tm; Hon Roll.

JOHNS, JENNIFER; Apache HS; Apache, OK; (2); Pres Church Yth Grp; VP FHA; Chrldng; Hon Roll; NHS; HOBY; US Bus Ed Awd Wnnr In Bus Ed; FFA; OU; Vet.

JOHNS, JULIE M; Drummond Schl; Drummond, OK; (4); 2/23; Cmnty Wkr; FHA; Hosp Aide; HOBY; Scholastic Bowl; SADD; Band; Drm Mjr(t); Mrchg Band; Orch; U Of OK Acad Achvt Awd; UCA All-Star Chrldr; Baptst Yth Choir & Orch, All-St; Phillips U; Med.

JOHNS, MELISSA E; Union Intermediate HS; Broken Arrow, OK; (2); Spanish Clb; Teachers Aide; Drill Tm; High Hon Roll; NHS.

JOHNSON, AIMEE; Westmoore HS; Oklahoma City, OK; (3); 15/615; Church Yth Grp; French Clb; Quiz Bowl; Scholastic Bowl; Chorus; Church Choir; School Musical; High Hon Roll; Jr NHS; NHS; ACT Awd; OK City CC Sci Acad; 5 Super Rankings Vocal Solos Regnl & St Conts; Pediatrics; Scndry Ed.

JOHNSON, ALESHA G; Yukon Middle HS; Yukon, OK; (1); Church Yth Grp; FCA; Spanish Clb; Var L Sftbl; Cit Awd; Hon Roll; Masons Ldrshp Awd.

JOHNSON, ALICIA R; Casady Schl; Edmond, OK; (2); Dance Clb; Spanish Clb; Chorus; School Musical; Var Bsktbl; Var Trk; Var Vllybl; Hon Roll; Singing; Clark Atlanta Univ.

JOHNSON, AMANDA; Shawnee Sr HS; Shawnee, OK; (3); 2/300; Dance Clb; Chrmn Drama Clb; French Clb; NFL; Speech Tm; School Play; Var Pom Pon; Hon Roll; NHS.

JOHNSON, AMANDA L; Salina HS; Salina, OK; (4); 8/42; VP FHA; Hon Roll; Rogers ST Coll; Early Chldhd.

JOHNSON, AMANDA R; South Intermediate HS; Broken Arrow, OK; (1); 199/610; Church Yth Grp; FCA; Band; Drm Mjr(t); Mrchg Band; Pep Band; Hon Roll; OK ST Univ; Band Dir.

JOHNSON, AMBER D; Bartlesville Sr HS; Bartlesville, OK; (1); 60/476; Sec Church Yth Grp; Spanish Clb; Chorus; High Hon Roll; Hon Roll; Med Explrs; 3rd Plc Brtlsvll Dist Sci Fair; BYU; Med.

JOHNSON, AMELIA C; Velma Alma HS; Loco, OK; (2); Church Yth Grp; FCA; Church Choir; Bsktbl; Crs Cntry; Trk; Hon Roll; NHS; Prfct Atten Awd; Track/Cross Cntry Runner-Up Team 94; Cross Cntry Champ Team 95; Track ST Runner-Up Team 96.

JOHNSON, ANDREA B; Del City HS; Del City, OK; (3); 23/518; Dance Clb; Drama Clb; French Clb; Girl Scts; Science Clb; Yrbk; Ofcr Stu Cncl; Jr NHS; NHS; Girl Scout Gold Awd; Wrstlg Matmaid; Univ; Bio.

JOHNSON, ANGELA J; Midwest City HS; Midwest City, OK; (2); Church Yth Grp; FCA; JA; Band; Mrchg Band; Pep Band; Bsktbl; Mgr(s); Hon Roll; Jr NHS; African Amer Alliance Clb; Getting The Pride Awd & Grand Slam Band; OBU; Vet.

JOHNSON, ASHLEY; Wetumka Jr Sr HS; Wetumka, OK; (2); 5/47; Church Yth Grp; Key Clb; Quiz Bowl; Scholastic Bowl; Band; Color Guard; Flag Corp; Mrchg Band; Pep Band; Hon Roll; St Hnr Soc; Acad Team; Law.

JOHNSON, BRAD; Hulbert Jr Sr HS; Hulbert, OK; (3); Chess Clb; German Clb; Church Choir; VP Jr Cls; Ofcr Bsbl; Bsktbl; Ftbl; Trk; Jr NHS; NHS.

JOHNSON, CALISTA C; Wright City Jr Sr HS; Garvin, OK; (4); French Clb; FHA; Natl FFA Org; Office Aide; Color Guard; Drm Mjr(t); Mrchg Band; Stage Crew; NHS; Wdshp; East TX ST Univ; Anml Sci.

JOHNSON, CARRIE B; Bishop Mcguinness HS; Oklahoma City, OK; (3); 75/134; Computer Clb; Drama Clb; FBLA; German Clb; School Play; Co-Ed Lit Mag; Rep Soph Cls.

JOHNSON, CHARLES L; Pauls Valley HS; Pauls Valley, OK; (1); Church Yth Grp; FCA; Ofcr Bsbl; Bsktbl; Ftbl; Wt Lftg; Hon Roll; Prfct Atten Awd; Prof Ftbl Player.

JOHNSON, CHESSE; Broken Arrow Sr HS; Broken Arrow, OK; (4); 491/921; Pres 4-H; Natl FFA Org; Rptr Nwsp; 4-H Awd; Living Legend Awd; Health Gold Mdl; Swine Raising; NSU; Commnctns.

JOHNSON, CHRISTINA F; Douglass HS; Oklahoma City, OK; (3); Dance Clb; Office Aide; Chorus; Church Choir; Swing Chorus; Rep Jr Cls; Cit Awd; Hon Roll; Comm.

JOHNSON, CHRISTOPHER; Chandler HS; Chandler, OK; (4); 30/80; Drama Clb; FCA; Teachers Aide; School Play; Ofcr Jr Cls; Ofcr Stu Cncl; Ftbl; Trk; Wt Lftg; Wrstlng; Stu Rotarn Of Month; Ftbl All-Star By Clss, All-Dist Defensve Linemn Of Yr; Crimnl Jstce.

JOHNSON, CHRISTOPHER S; Spiro HS; Spiro, OK; (2); Boy Scts; High Hon Roll; Eagle Scout; Elect.

JOHNSON, CRISTINA; Empire Schl; Duncan, OK; (1); Church Yth Grp; FBLA; Ofcr Natl FFA Org; Bsktbl; Sftbl; Trk; 4-H Awd; Hon Roll; Natl Hstry/Govt Awd; All-Amer Schlr.

JOHNSON, CRYSTAL; Davenport Jr Sr HS; Chandler, OK; (3); Church Yth Grp; Cmnty Wkr; 4-H; HOBY; Pep Clb; Red Cross Aide; Teachers Aide; VICA; Church Choir; Pep Band; Rose ST; Med.

JOHNSON, CRYSTAL; Douglass HS; Oklahoma City, OK; (2); Rptr Nwsp; Hon Roll; U Of OK; PT.

JOHNSON, CRYSTAL L; Jay HS; Jay, OK; (1); FHA; GAA; U Of AR.

JOHNSON, CRYSTAL M; Edmond North HS; Edmond, OK; (3); 113/348; Church Yth Grp; JA; ROTC; Color Guard; Drill Tm; Flag Corp; Military Order Of Purple Heart; UCO; Pre-Med; Pediatrics.

JOHNSON, CURTIS D; South Intermediate HS; Broken Arrow, OK; (1); 70/1000; Spanish Clb; JV Bsktbl; High Hon Roll; Tulsa U.

JOHNSON, CYNTHIA; Tahlequah Sr HS; Park Hill, OK; (4); 15/251; Sec Math Clb; Scholastic Bowl; SADD; Chorus; Hon Roll; Jr NHS; NHS; Airplane Flying; Engrng.

JOHNSON, DAN L; Parker Middle HS; Krebs, OK; (2); Band; Mrchg Band; Hon Roll; Collect Antiques; Amer Law Awd; Eastern OK Univ; Law.

JOHNSON, DANIEL L; Owasso Sr HS; Owasso, OK; (4); 53/280; Boy Scts; French Clb; Teachers Aide; Socr; Eagle Sct; Brigham Yng Univ; Cont Mgnt.

JOHNSON, DANIEL P; Deer Creek HS; Edmond, OK; (2); Cmnty Wkr; Letterman Clb; Science Clb; School Play; Stage Crew; Rep Stu Cncl; JV Ftbl; Var L Socr; Intrn/Tchr Asst Smmr Enrchmnt Prgm OK City U; Org Rcrtnl Sccr Team; Team Cptn Sccr.

JOHNSON, DANIEL T; Mounds Schl; Mounds, OK; (3); 1/58; Church Yth Grp; Natl Beta Clb; Band; Jazz Band; Mrchg Band; Pep Band; Pres Jr Cls; Bsktbl; Hon Roll; NHS; OK Band Masters Assn Outstdng Soloist Awd; Band VP; Tchng.

JOHNSON, DARCI L; Pauls Valley HS; Pauls Valley, OK; (1); Spanish Clb; Flag Corp; Sec Frsh Cls; Tennis; Hon Roll; Hnrs Eng I; Vet.

JOHNSON, DARRIEL A; Stillwater Sr HS; Stillwater, OK; (3); 91/363; Am Leg Boys St; FCA; Key Clb; Natl Beta Clb; Rptr Nwsp; Rep Stu Cncl; Var L Bsktbl; Var L Ftbl; Hon Roll; NHS; Macys Mnrties Med Schlr; Rippy Flwshp; Bio/Med.

JOHNSON, DAVID KYLE; Guymon Sr HS; Guymon, OK; (4); 1/120; Church Yth Grp; Debate Tm; Drama Clb; French Clb; NFL; Speech Tm; Teachers Aide; Band; Church Choir; Drm Mjr(t); St Champ Dramatc Interp; St Champ Tm Debate; Natl Qulfr; Natl Forensiclge; Dramatic Interp; S Nazarene Univ; Pstrl Mnstry.

JOHNSON, DAYNA M; Choctaw HS; Choctaw, OK; (4); 56/315; Church Yth Grp; 4-H; FTA; GAA; Key Clb; Variety Show; Yrbk; Bsktbl; Ftbl; Powder Puff Ftbl; Gear Grand U Ada OK; Bus.

JOHNSON, DEREK P; Macomb Schl; Tecumseh, OK; (1); 4/32; Cmnty Wkr; Natl FFA Org; Scholastic Bowl; JV Mgr(s); Cit Awd; Hon Roll; Prfct Atten Awd; FFA Greenhand/Sprtsmnshp/Wrkhrs Awds Frosh; OSU; Vet Med.

JOHNSON, DOUG M; Bixby Sr HS; Broken Arrow, OK; (2); JV Bsbl; JV Bsktbl; JV Ftbl; Hon Roll; Jr NHS; Prfct Atten Awd; Pres Acad Fit Awd; Pres Schlr; OK Univ; Engrg.

JOHNSON, EBONY L; Putnam City HS; Oklahoma City, OK; (2); 82/364; Cmnty Wkr; GAA; Hosp Aide; Key Clb; Office Aide; SADD; Teachers Aide; Sprt Ed Yrbk; Sec Frsh Cls; Sec Soph Cls; Schl/Cmnty Ldrshp; Most Outstndng Wrtr Yrbk; Clark-Atlanta; Jrnlsm Brdcstng.

JOHNSON, ELEX L; Idabel HS; Idabel, OK; (3); #17 in class; Church Yth Grp; Cmnty Wkr; Debate Tm; Drama Clb; FCA; NFL; Quiz Bowl; Speech Tm; Band; Jazz Band; St Trk Championship Team 93-94 & 94-95; OK All Star Band; Natl Field Show Champion Band Mem; U OF OK; Intnl Corporate Law.

JOHNSON, ENJOLI D; Antlers Sr HS; Snow, OK; (2); Church Yth Grp; FBLA; FHA; Var JV Sftbl; Hon Roll; Northeastern ST; Optometry.

JOHNSON, ERAINA M; Will Rogers HS; Tulsa, OK; (3); Girl Scts; Hosp Aide; Chorus; School Play; Ofcr Jr Cls; 4-H Awd.

JOHNSON, ERIC; Ft Gibson HS; Fort Gibson, OK; (2); Boy Scts; Spanish Clb; Band; Mrchg Band; Pep Band; High Hon Roll; Northeastern ST U; Cmmrcl Plt.

JOHNSON, ERIC M; Davis HS; Davis, OK; (2); Boy Scts; FCA; Band; Mrchg Band; Ofcr Bsbl; Ftbl; Wt Lftg; Prfct Atten Awd; Class 2a 1995 ST Ftbl Chmpns.

JOHNSON, ERIN B; Bethel HS; Tecumseh, OK; (2); Church Yth Grp; Library Aide; Chorus; Church Choir; Bsktbl; Mgr(s); Hon Roll; U Of OK; Elem Educ.

JOHNSON, ESTA J; Bokoshe Schl; Bokoshe, OK; (4); 4/15; Natl FFA Org; Teachers Aide; Treas Frsh Cls; VP Soph Cls; Bsktbl; Sftbl; FFA Local Chptr Sec/Reporter; Eastern OK; Vet.

JOHNSON, FLOYD A; Southeast HS; Oklahoma City, OK; (1); FCA; Chorus; Sec Frsh Cls; VP Soph Cls; Var Ftbl; High Hon Roll; Hon Roll; Prfct Atten Awd; FL ST; Jrnlsm.

JOHNSON, GINA; Bishop Mcguinness HS; Oklahoma City, OK; (4); 18/154; Church Yth Grp; Dance Clb; FCA; French Clb; Math Clb; Pep Clb; SADD; School Musical; Rep Frsh Cls; Rep Soph Cls; OU Schlr Schlrshp; Frnch I & II Awds; Rose St Acad Cont Physlgy Anat; U Of OK; Phys Thrp.

JOHNSON, GREG; Yukon Middle HS; Yukon, OK; (2); FCA; Rep Stu Cncl; Ftbl; Trk.

JOHNSON, HOLLY J; Choctaw HS; Choctaw, OK; (2); Pres VP 4-H; Treas Key Clb; Variety Show; JV Bsktbl; Chrldng; Golf; Gym; JV Sftbl; 4-H Awd.

JOHNSON, INGRID L; Edmond Memorial HS; Edmond, OK; (4); U Of OK Hlth/Sci Ctr Summer Acad Grad; Governors Commendation; U Of OK; Pre-Med.

JOHNSON, JACKI; Oologah-Talala HS; Oologah, OK; (1); 7/121; Cmnty Wkr; Dance Clb; Pres Girl Scts; Natl FFA Org; Chrldng; Wt Lftg; High Hon Roll; Hon Roll; Girl Sct Silver Awd; OSU; Biolgcl Sci.

JOHNSON, JAMES; Wetumka Jr Sr HS; Wetumka, OK; (1); 2/35; Natl FFA Org; Ftbl; Wt Lftg; 4-H Awd; Hon Roll; Jr NHS; Prfct Atten Awd; FFA Creed Cont; Cmptrs.

JOHNSON, JAMES R; Yukon Middle HS; Yukon, OK; (2); FCA; Rep Stu Cncl; Ftbl; Trk.

JOHNSON, JAMIE; Midwest City HS; Midwest City, OK; (4); 88/390; FHA; GAA; Hosp Aide; Varsity Clb; Var L Bsktbl; Var L Ftbl; Var L Golf; Var L Mgr(s); Var L Sftbl; High Hon Roll; Golf Schlrshps; All Conf, Dist 1st Team Sftbl; Southern Nazarene; Ed.

JOHNSON, JAMIE; U S Grant HS; Oklahoma City, OK; (3); 6/290; Stage Crew; Sec Frsh Cls; Ofcr Soph Cls; Rep Stu Cncl; JV Sftbl; NHS; Drury Coll; Law.

JOHNSON, JANELL; Nathan Hale HS; Tulsa, OK; (3); Cmnty Wkr; French Clb; Color Guard; High Hon Roll; Hon Roll; NHS; 30 Hr Fmn; Med.

JOHNSON, JANIE; Kingston HS; Kingston, OK; (1); Church Yth Grp; FCA; Quiz Bowl; Chorus; Rptr Nwsp; Phtg Yrbk; VP Frsh Cls; Chrldng; High Hon Roll; Southeastern Univ; PT/JRNLSM.

JOHNSON, JANIE J; Mooreland Jr Sr HS; Mooreland, OK; (1); 2/43; Church Yth Grp; FCA; FHA; Sec Frsh Cls; Var Bsktbl; Var Sftbl; High Hon Roll; NHS; Prfct Atten Awd; Sal.

JOHNSON, JEANNE; Ft Gibson HS; Fort Gibson, OK; (4); 1/110; FCA; School Musical; Ed Yrbk; Sec Frsh Cls; Rep Soph Cls; Pres Jr Cls; Capt Var Chrldng; Sec NHS; Ntl Merit Ltr; Hnrs Slct Choir; Northeastern ST Univ; Med.

JOHNSON, JENNIFER; Norman Sr HS; Norman, OK; (2); Cmnty Wkr; Computer Clb; Dance Clb; FCA; French Clb; Model UN; Mu Alpha Theta; Rep Church Yth Grp; Rep Soph Cls; Ofcr Stu Cncl; Tomorrows Ldrs; Presdntl Acad Awd; All-Star Chrldng; Pom Squad; U Of OK; Jrnlsm; Mrktg.

JOHNSON, JENNIFER; Bennington Schl; Bennington, OK; (3); 3/17; Pres 4-H; School Play; Stage Crew; Sec Jr Cls; VP Sr Cls; Pres Stu Cncl; Var Bsktbl; Var Sftbl; 4-H Awd; NHS; FFA Pres; FFA Sec.

JOHNSON, JENNIFER L; Nathan Hale HS; Tulsa, OK; (3); Rptr Nwsp; Rptr Yrbk; Rep Stu Cncl; High Hon Roll; Hon Roll; NHS; Peer Tutor; Teen Prnts As Tchrs; Tulsa Univ.

JOHNSON, JENNIFER M; Weatherford HS; Weatherford, OK; (4); 21/135; Church Yth Grp; VP DECA; FCA; Pres FTA; Library Aide; Band; Color Guard; Mrchg Band; Yrbk; Ofcr Stu Cncl; Jan Lions Stu Mon; OK ST U; Ind Engr.

JOHNSON, JERAKA E; Barnsdall Jr Sr HS; Pawhuska, OK; (2); Church Yth Grp; Flag Corp; Sec Soph Cls; L Bsktbl; Var Chrldng; L Trk; Hon Roll; Peer Hlprs.

JOHNSON, JEREMIAH D; Nathan Hale HS; Tulsa, OK; (1); Church Yth Grp; FBLA; Bsktbl; Ice Hcky; Hon Roll; Mrktg.

JOHNSON, JEREMY; Cleveland Sr HS; Cleveland, OK; (4); 15/120; Am Leg Boys St; Church Yth Grp; FCA; Key Clb; Office Aide; Science Clb; Spanish Clb; SADD; Var Socr; NHS; Sccr Def Plyr Yr 94; OK Hnr Soc; Phys Thrpy.

JOHNSON, JEREMY; Copan HS; Copan, OK; (4); 2/32; Church Yth Grp; HOBY; Scholastic Bowl; Band; Mrchg Band; Pres Stu Cncl; L Bsbl; L Bsktbl; L Ftbl; High Hon Roll; OK HS Hnr Soc; OK U; Ansthslgy.

JOHNSON, JEREMY S; Henryetta Sr HS; Henryetta, OK; (2); FCA; JV Bsktbl; Var Score Keeper; Var Trk; Var Wt Lftg; High Hon Roll; Hon Roll; Prfct Atten Awd; Art; Dentistry.

JOHNSON, JERRIS E; Enid Sr HS; Enid, OK; (2); 84/425; Boy Scts; Church Yth Grp; Speech Tm; Band; Jazz Band; Mrchg Band; Pep Band; School Play; Stage Crew; Hon Roll; Egl Sct; Outstdng Prcsnst Grd 9; Telecomm/Music.

JOHNSON, JESSICA; Carnegie HS; Carnegie, OK; (4); 3/44; Cmnty Wkr; VP Drama Clb; Quiz Bowl; Scholastic Bowl; School Play; Rep Soph Cls; Sec Jr Cls; Hon Roll; NHS; Top Ten Frshmn; Hnr Grad; U Cntrl OK; Nrsng.

JOHNSON, JESSICA A; South Intermediate HS; Broken Arrow, OK; (1); Church Yth Grp; Band; Color Guard; Hon Roll; Chrstn Stdnts Flwshp.

JOHNSON, JILL; East Central HS; Tulsa, OK; (4); 110/210; Am Leg Aux Girls St; FCA; Office Aide; Spanish Clb; VP Treas Stu Cncl; Socr; Trk; Prins Hnr Roll; Hmcmng Attndnt; Cardinal Of Month; Northeastern ST U; Med.

JOHNSON, JILL; Elk City HS; Elk City, OK; (3); Church Yth Grp; Computer Clb; Debate Tm; Drama Clb; Math Clb; Model UN; Office Aide; Pep Clb; Speech Tm; SADD; Broadcast Jrnlsm.

JOHNSON III, JIMMY G; Westmore HS; Oklahoma City, OK; (1); 86/348; Boy Scts; Church Yth Grp; Scholastic Bowl; Ftbl; Wrstlng; Jr NHS; NHS; Ftbl City/Conf Chmpnshps; Wrstlng 1st Tm Conf Chmpnshps/City Awd; Orthpdc Srgn.

JOHNSON, JOHN A; Stilwell HS; Stilwell, OK; (2); 12/161; Natl Beta Clb; Natl FFA Org; Spanish Clb; Band; Mrchg Band; Pep Band; High Hon Roll; NHS; Prfct Atten Awd; Northeastern ST Univ; Vetrnry.

JOHNSON, JOHN S; Mc Alester HS; Mcalester, OK; (3); Church Yth Grp; Cmnty Wkr; Natl Beta Clb; Spanish Clb; Nwsp; Hon Roll; OK Hon Soc.

JOHNSON, JOYCE M; Hugo HS; Hugo, OK; (2); 41/141; Outstndng Excllnc Comp I & Wrld Hstry; Cosmetology.

JOHNSON, JULIE; Midwest City HS; Midwest City, OK; (2); 99/488; Bus Profs of Am; Cmnty Wkr; Pep Clb; Ofcr Stu Cncl; Chrldng; Gym; Hon Roll; Chrldr 4 Yrs, Head; Multi Yr Listing; Accntg.

JOHNSON, KARLA L; Healdton HS; Ben Wheeler, TX; (2); 1/60; Church Yth Grp; 4-H; Quiz Bowl; Band; Jazz Band; Mrchg Band; High Hon Roll; Hon Roll; NHS; Pres Acad Fit Awd; Blue Ribbon Schlr; SCOBDA; All Dist, Super Rtng 2 Yrs; All St Final Rnd Qlfr; Tyler JC; Law.

JOHNSON, KASEY; Bray-Doyle HS; Marlow, OK; (3); FHA; SADD; School Play; Ed Yrbk; Pres Frsh Cls; Pres Soph Cls; Pres Jr Cls; Hon Roll; NHS; SADD Pres; OSU; Acctng.

JOHNSON, KATHRYN R; Edmond Memorial HS; Edmond, OK; (3); 134/371; Church Yth Grp; Cmnty Wkr; Drama Clb; Key Clb; Spanish Clb; SADD; Ofcr Frsh Cls; Ofcr Soph Cls; Ofcr Sr Cls; Ofcr Stu Cncl; OK Chrstn Univ; Nrsng.

JOHNSON, KAYLE; Yarbrough Schl; Elkhart, KS; (2); 3/16; Church Yth Grp; Pres Pep Clb; Quiz Bowl; Speech Tm; Sec Band; Sec Chorus; Church Choir; Mrchg Band; School Play; Nwsp; TX A&M Univ; Thysical Therapy.

JOHNSON, KELLI; Wyandotte Jr Sr HS; Wyandotte, OK; (3); 2/43; FCA; FTA; HOBY; Letterman Clb; Math Tm; VP Natl FFA Org; Pep Clb; Church Choir; Pres Frsh Cls; VP Soph Cls; Fresh Ldrshp, Stu Today Awds; FFA Star Greenhand; NEO; Ag.

JOHNSON, KEVIN; Deer Creek HS; Edmond, OK; (4); Am Leg Boys St; Church Yth Grp; Cmnty Wkr; FCA; Teachers Aide; School Musical; School Play; Rep Jr Cls; Pres Sr Cls; Var Bsbl.

JOHNSON, KIMBERLY T; Central Jr HS; Fort Sill, OK; (1); Key Clb; Spanish Clb; Band; School Play; Cit Awd; Hon Roll; FL Memrl Coll; Tchr; Acctnts.

JOHNSON, KINYA S; Star Spencer HS; Midwest City, OK; (1); Church Yth Grp; JA; Band; Church Choir; Mrchg Band; Cit Awd; Hon Roll; Algebra II/ADVANCED Band Awds; Internal Med/Pdtrcs.

JOHNSON, KRISTEN; Mt View-Gotebo HS; Gotebo, OK; (3); 6/32; FCA; 4-H; HOBY; Sec Natl FFA Org; Quiz Bowl; Mrchg Band; Variety Show; VP Frsh Cls; VP Soph Cls; Ofcr Jr Cls; Natl FFA Tlnt Pgm 95; Sang Natl Anthm FFA Cnvntn 95; OK ST U.

JOHNSON, KRISTIN R; Pauls Valley HS; Pauls Valley, OK; (1); 1/121; Church Yth Grp; FCA; Key Clb; Pep Clb; Pres Frsh Cls; Rep Stu Cncl; Capt Chrldng; Var Trk; High Hon Roll; NHS; Matmaids Sec.

JOHNSON, KYLE; Duncan HS; Duncan, OK; (4); 33/250; Am Leg Boys St; Church Yth Grp; Key Clb; Church Choir; Nwsp; VP Frsh Cls; VP Soph Cls; VP Jr Cls; Rep Stu Cncl; Var Ftbl; Ray A Kroc Awd; OBU; Med.

JOHNSON, LANK; Pauls Valley HS; Pauls Valley, OK; (1); Church Yth Grp; FCA; Bsktbl; Ftbl; Wt Lftg; Hon Roll; Prfct Atten Awd; Superior Wk/Attitude Eng I; Outstdng Achvmnt Study Skills; Prof Ftbl Plyr.

JOHNSON, LORI D; Midwest City HS; Midwest City, OK; (2); 60/488; Church Yth Grp; Cmnty Wkr; GAA; Pep Clb; SADD; Chrldng; Gym; High Hon Roll; NHS; Prfct Atten Awd; NHS VP; Phrmcst.

JOHNSON, LUKE A; Hinton HS; Hinton, OK; (2); FCA; SADD; Chorus; School Play; Hon Roll; OU; Cmptr Speclst.

JOHNSON, MANDI; El Reno Sr HS; El Reno, OK; (4); 12/165; FHA; Math Clb; Office Aide; Science Clb; Teachers Aide; Swing Chorus; Rptr Nwsp; Yrbk; Bsktbl; Hon Roll; USAO; Bus Admin.

JOHNSON, MATTHEW B; Putnam City North HS; Oklahoma City, OK; (2); Key Clb; Quiz Bowl; Scholastic Bowl; Ed Nwsp; Hon Roll; NHS; Dr/Metrolgst.

JOHNSON, MELISSA; Wewoka HS; Wewoka, OK; (4); 12/51; Rep Am Leg Aux Girls St; Ofcr Drama Clb; FHA; FTA; Office Aide; Quiz Bowl; Scholastic Bowl; Rptr Science Clb; SADD; Teachers Aide; Seminole Ntn Yth Cncl Bnd Rep.

JOHNSON, MELISSA A; Buffalo Jr Sr HS; Buffalo, OK; (3); 4/28; Church Yth Grp; FBLA; FHA; Band; Chorus; Pep Band; Yrbk; Sftbl; Hon Roll; NHS; U Of Central OK; Spch Path.

JOHNSON, MICHELLE; Bowlegs Schl; Bowlegs, OK; (2); 2/30; Church Yth Grp; Natl Beta Clb; Pep Clb; Quiz Bowl; Scholastic Bowl; Band; Mrchg Band; Cit Awd; High Hon Roll; Sal; Bowling; Summer League Bsbl; Outstdng Woodwind Awd; OK Hnr Soc; ECU Dist Hnr Band.

JOHNSON, MIKALA; Yarbrough Schl; Elkhart, KS; (4); 1/11; Church Yth Grp; HOBY; Pep Clb; Quiz Bowl; Teachers Aide; Band; Chorus; Bsktbl; Chrldng; NHS; Acctng.

JOHNSON, MINDY D; Newkirk HS; Newkirk, OK; (3); SADD; Teachers Aide; School Play; Yrbk; Chrldng; Sftbl; Hon Roll; Scl Wrk.

JOHNSON, NATALIE; Edmond North HS; Edmond, OK; (1); Church Yth Grp; Chrldng; Jr Olympcs Diving 91-92; US Diving 91 92; Sooner St Games Plcd St 91 92; OK U.

JOHNSON, NATALIE N; Sapulpa Sr HS; Sapulpa, OK; (4); 36/273; JA; Library Aide; Band; Mrchg Band; Hon Roll; NHS; Pres Acad Fit Awd; Spanish NHS; NAACP; Intnl Drug Free Yth Pgm; U Of OK; Acctng.

JOHNSON, NEESHA; Hartshorne Sr HS; Haileyville, OK; (2); FHA; Rep Soph Cls; Pres Stu Cncl; Var JV Chrldng; High Hon Roll; Hon Roll; NHS; Sal; Oral Roberts U; Math.

JOHNSON, NICHOLAS B; Union Intermediate HS; Tulsa, OK; (2); 207/800; Spanish Clb; Crs Cntry; Trk; Hon Roll; NHS; Prfct Atten Awd; Lnch Bible Stud; DFY; OK ST U; Bus.

JOHNSON, PIPER L; Skiatook HS; Skiatook, OK; (2); FCA; FBLA; School Play; Nwsp; Sec Frsh Cls; Pres Soph Cls; Ofcr Stu Cncl; Chrldng; Trk; NHS; OK St Bus Ed Awd; Photo; FBLA Pres; TU.

JOHNSON, QUINCY L; Northeast HS; Oklahoma City, OK; (2); Church Yth Grp; FCA; ROTC; Drill Tm; Yrbk; Rep Soph Cls; Trk; Prfct Atten Awd; ROTC Regltn Drll Tm Achvmt Cert; Army.

JOHNSON, REBECCA L; Claremore Sr HS; Claremore, OK; (2); French Clb; Band; Jazz Band; Mrchg Band; Pep Band; Hon Roll; NHS; Hygienist.

JOHNSON, ROBERT; Marlow HS; Marlow, OK; (4); 9/106; Church Yth Grp; Cmnty Wkr; FCA; 4-H; Math Tm; Office Aide; Science Clb; Teachers Aide; Church Choir; Phtg Nwsp; Bapt All-St Yth Choir & Ensemble; OK Bapt Univ; Med; Music.

JOHNSTON, ROBERT H; Choctaw HS; Choctaw, OK; (4); Boy Scts; Church Yth Grp; FCA; 4-H; FHA; ROTC; VICA; Flag Corp; Prfct Atten Awd; Auto Tech; OSU; Auto.

JOHNSON, ROBYN M; Claremore Sr HS; Claremore, OK; (3); Cmnty Wkr; Spanish Clb; SADD; Hon Roll; NHS; DECA Mem; Lawyer.

JOHNSON, SABRINA L; Buffalo Valley Schl; Talihina, OK; (3); 3/16; Church Yth Grp; FHA; GAA; Library Aide; Office Aide; Teachers Aide; Nwsp; Pres Frsh Cls; Pres Soph Cls; Pres Jr Cls; PT.

JOHNSON, SARAH R; Brink Jr HS; Moore, OK; (1); Church Yth Grp; Quiz Bowl; Scholastic Bowl; Band; Church Choir; Mrchg Band; Orch; Ed Nwsp; Cit Awd; Hon Roll; 4.0 Awd; 2nd Pl In Regnl Sci Fair; 3rd Pl At Dist PTA Reflections In Photo; Spcl Ed.

JOHNSON, SCOTT R; Alva HS; Alva, OK; (3); 20/57; Church Yth Grp; Debate Tm; Library Aide; NFL; Office Aide; Speech Tm; Thesps; School Play; Co-Ed Lit Mag; High Hon Roll; Spch Qualifier ST 5th Pl/Dist 2nd Pl; High Hnr Roll; Stdnt Of Distnctn; Bst Forensic Newcomer; U Of CT; Dramatic/Visual Arts.

JOHNSON, SHALONDA C; Idabel HS; Idabel, OK; (3); FCA; Color Guard; Ed Nwsp; Hon Roll; OK Univ; Pediatrician.

JOHNSON, SHAYE L; Stigler HS; Stigler, OK; (3); Church Yth Grp; FCA; Rptr FHA; Sec SADD; Yrbk; Var Bsktbl; Trk; High Hon Roll; NHS; Hon Roll; St Bsktbl Chmpns 95; Medcl.

JOHNSON, SHAYLA; Millwood HS; Oklahoma City, OK; (4); 15/78; Church Yth Grp; JA; Office Aide; ROTC; Band; Flag Corp; Mrchg Band; Pep Band; Hon Roll; Ntl Merit Ltr; Langston U; Nrsng.

JOHNSON, SOMER; Chisholm Sr HS; Enid, OK; (3); 1/75; Church Yth Grp; FCA; VP FHA; Math Tm; Quiz Bowl; Scholastic Bowl; Spanish Clb; Chorus; Church Choir; Rptr Nwsp; Bass Memrl Candy Stripe Vol Pgm; ROOTS Ldrshp Conf; Piano Hnrs & Awds; Ozark Chrstn Coll; Elem Ed.

JOHNSON, STANDRA N; Del City HS; Oklahoma City, OK; (4); 12/400; Pres Church Yth Grp; FCA; Spanish Clb; Pres SADD; VP Stu Cncl; L Bsktbl; Sec NHS; Pres Acad Fit Awd; Val; Multi-Cultural Clb; U Of AR; Elem Ed.

JOHNSON, STEPHANIE; Deer Creek HS; Edmond, OK; (3); 36/96; Drama Clb; Mrchg Band; Pep Band; Mgr Crs Cntry; Powder Puff Ftbl; Score Keeper; Mgr Trk; Mgr Wrstlng; Drag Racing; Wrkng On Cars; OSU; Bus Admin.

JOHNSON, SUMMER; Greater Tulsa Christian Acad; Tulsa, OK; (3); 1/7; HOBY; Sec Pres Key Clb; VP Frsh Cls; Pres Soph Cls; VP Jr Cls; Var Chrldng; Var Vllybl; High Hon Roll; NHS; Church Yth Grp.

JOHNSON, TARA I; Frontier Public Schl; Red Rock, OK; (4); FHA; Band; Yrbk; Sftbl; Wah Pe He Clb Rptr; OK ST Univ; Dietician.

JOHNSON, TASHA; Woodward HS; Woodward, OK; (2); Art Clb; German Clb; Letterman Clb; Ed Lit Mag; Rep Stu Cncl; Var Chrldng; Var Socr; High Hon Roll; Kiwanis Awd; NHS; Ger Natl Hnr Soc; Ger Amer Prtnrshp Exchng Prgm; OK Hnr Soc; Arch.

JOHNSON, TERRI; Dale Sr HS; Shawnee, OK; (4); 16/48; FHA; Natl FFA Org; Teachers Aide; Band; Mrchg Band; Nwsp; Yrbk; Hon Roll; Jr NHS; NHS; St Gregorys Coll.

JOHNSON, TICEE H; Wapanucka Schl; Wapanucka, OK; (3); Church Yth Grp; 4-H; Natl FFA Org; Nwsp; Yrbk; Var Capt Bsktbl; Var Sftbl; Var Bsktbl All Star Alt; Radiolgy.

JOHNSON, TRAVIS; Goodwell Public Schl; Goodwell, OK; (4); 1/8; Letterman Clb; Teachers Aide; Chorus; Rep Stu Cncl; Var Bsktbl; Var Ftbl; Var Trk; High Hon Roll; Hon Roll; Val; OK Panhandle ST U.

JOHNSON, TREVOR J; Deer Creek HS; Edmond, OK; (2); 17/120; FBLA; Science Clb; Stage Crew; JV Bsktbl; Var L Socr; Hon Roll; NHS; Pres Acad Fit Awd; Pilot.

JOHNSON, WENDY M; Enid Sr HS; Enid, OK; (3); 185/475; Drama Clb; Speech Tm; Teachers Aide; Band; Church Choir; Orch; Pep Band; Swing Chorus; Hon Roll; Reflctns Cont 1st Pl Lit Awd Poetry; Big Blue Band VP; Writng Poetry, Shrt Stories; OK ST U; Music Ed.

JOHNSTON, AMANDA D; Union Intermediate HS; Tulsa, OK; (2); 54/800; Sec Church Yth Grp; FCA; Spanish Clb; JV Bsktbl; JV Socr; High Hon Roll; Hon Roll; Jr NHS; NHS; Pres Acad Fit Awd; Dec Stu Mon 95; DFY; Peer Mediation; Med.

JOHNSTON, ANN MARIE; Heritage Hall Schl; Oklahoma City, OK; (2); Church Yth Grp; Cmnty Wkr; French Clb; Pep Clb; Science Clb; Chorus; Church Choir; School Musical; School Play; Chrldng; Chamber Choir, OK Chldrns Choir; Bowling; OK ST U; Vet.

JOHNSTON, ASHLEY M; Blanchard Jr Sr HS; Blanchard, OK; (3); 12/65; Computer Clb; FHA; Spanish Clb; Band; Drm Mjr(t); JV Var Bsktbl; Hon Roll; NHS; Prfct Atten Awd; Nrsng.

JOHNSTON, JENNIFER R; Muldrow HS; Muldrow, OK; (1); FHA; Natl Beta Clb; Vet.

JOHNSTON, JESSICA; Weatherford HS; Weatherford, OK; (4); 32/160; Church Yth Grp; FCA; HOBY; Spanish Clb; SADD; Teachers Aide; Chorus; Church Choir; Swing Chorus; Phtg Nwsp; Interest In Working With Early Chldhd Stus Who Are Deaf; SW OK ST U; Biological Sci.

JOHNSTON, KRYSTAL; Cimarron Public Schl; Enid, OK; (3); Church Yth Grp; FBLA; HOBY; Quiz Bowl; Science Clb; Band; Church Choir; Nwsp; Yrbk; Chrldng; OK ST U.

JOHNSTON, MARY K; Choctaw HS; Choctaw, OK; (4); 1/320; Acpl Chr; Band; Chorus; Mrchg Band; Pep Band; High Hon Roll; NHS; Prfct Atten Awd; Pres Acad Fit Awd; Val; Hi Wdwnd MIP; Wm Shkspr Awd; Chem.

JOHNSTON, SARAH K; Stillwater Sr HS; Stillwater, OK; (4); Church Yth Grp; Hosp Aide; Key Clb; Mu Alpha Theta; Spanish Clb; Band; Church Choir; Drm Mjr(t); Mrchg Band; Orch; 11th Grd Var Scholar; Computers Word Processor/Prgmng; Cmptr Sci.

JOHNSTON, SUSAN; Blackwell HS; Blackwell, OK; (3); Art Clb; Church Yth Grp; Natl FFA Org; Spanish Clb; Speech Tm; Chorus; Stage Crew; Hon Roll; Peer Helpers; Explorers; OSU; Vet.

JOLLEY, AMBER N; Central Mid-HS; Norman, OK; (2); Art Clb; Church Yth Grp; Cmnty Wkr; Drama Clb; FCA; French Clb; Gov Hon Prg Awd; Hon Roll; Variety Show; SUMMIT New Tribes Mission Org To Brazil; Nom Miss OK Chrch Of God; Acad N Awds 5 9-10th Grd; Yng Lfe; Ministry Tchr.

JONES, AMANDA; Broken Arrow South HS; Broken Arrow, OK; (3); Church Yth Grp; Cmnty Wkr; Dance Clb; Latin Clb; Spanish Clb; SADD; Drill Tm; Pom Pon; Northeastern ST U; Nrs; Dntl Hy.

JONES, AMBER; Guthrie Sr HS; Guthrie, OK; (3); 9/298; FCA; Mu Alpha Theta; Var Bsktbl; Var Sftbl; Var Tennis; High Hon Roll; Jr NHS; NHS.

JONES, ANGELA R; Mt St Marys HS; Midwest City, OK; (3); Pep Clb; Bsktbl; Hon Roll.

JONES, ANN M; Putnam City North HS; Oklahoma City, OK; (4); French Clb; JCL; Hist Latin Clb; Jr NHS; NHS; Environ Clb; OK Prncpls Sci & Math Schlrs; OK City Univ; Bio.

JONES, BERNARD M; Bishop Mcguinness HS; Oklahoma City, OK; (3); 53/134; Treas Am Leg Boys St; VP Pres Spanish Clb; SADD; Yrbk; Pres Frsh Cls; Pres Soph Cls; Ofcr Jr Cls; Pres Stu Cncl; NHS; Spanish NHS; Jr Rtrn; Stu Ment; OKC Archdioceseyth Adv Brd; Alesia Boyer Mem Schol; Crim Just.

JONES, BETHANY DENICE; Charles Page HS; Sand Springs, OK; (4); 42/340; Am Leg Aux Girls St; Church Yth Grp; FCA; French Clb; Key Clb; Hon Roll; Jr NHS; NHS; Ntl Merit Ltr; Pres Acad Fit Awd; Campus Chrstn Clb; Northeastern ST U; Frgn Lang.

JONES, BRANDI; Bowlegs Schl; Seminole, OK; (1); Church Yth Grp; Natl Beta Clb; Scholastic Bowl; Bsktbl; Chrldng; Hon Roll; NHS; Seminole Jr Coll; PT.

JONES, BRANDON; Roland Sr HS; Roland, OK; (4); 5/82; Capt Quiz Bowl; Scholastic Bowl; Spanish Clb; VP Jr Cls; Var Ftbl; Var Wt Lftg; High Hon Roll; NHS; OK Cchs All St Acad Ftbl Tm; Carl Albert ST Coll; Phys Ed.

JONES, BRIAN L; Putnam City North HS; Oklahoma City, OK; (3); Dallas Art Inst; Pro Snd Dvlp.

JONES, BRIDGET; Collinsville HS; Collinsville, OK; (4); FCA; Rep Frsh Cls; Var L Bsktbl; Var Capt Chrldng; Hon Roll; U Of OK; Dentistry.

JONES, BRYAN K; Nathan Hale HS; Tulsa, OK; (1); Edcntl Tlnt Srch.

JONES, BUCKY; Hulbert Jr Sr HS; Tahlequah, OK; (3); 3/50; Church Yth Grp; German Clb; Spanish Clb; Varsity Clb; Sec Soph Cls; Var Bsbl; Var Bsktbl; Var Ftbl; Var Trk; Var Wt Lftg; Math Awd; Best All-Around; Geom.

JONES, CANDACE; Barnsdall Jr Sr HS; Wynona, OK; (4); 1/37; Church Yth Grp; Cmnty Wkr; Drama Clb; Variety Show; Yrbk; Rep Stu Cncl; Bsktbl; Cit Awd; Pres Schlr; Val; Southeastern OK; Mrktg.

JONES, CARISSA J; Union Intermediate HS; Broken Arrow, OK; (2); 91/800; Church Yth Grp; Spanish Clb; Drill Tm; High Hon Roll; Jr NHS; NHS; Amer All Star Dance Team; Math Awd; U AR.

JONES, CARRIE L; B T Washington HS; Tulsa, OK; (3); JCL; Latin Clb; Red Cross Aide; Bsktbl; Var L Socr; NHS; Black Watch Soccer Club.

JONES, CHAD; Seminole Jr Sr HS; Seminole, OK; (2); Church Yth Grp; French Clb; Math Clb; Quiz Bowl; Rep Frsh Cls; Golf; French Hon Soc; High Hon Roll; Prfct Atten Awd.

JONES, CHERYL L; Charles Page HS; Sand Springs, OK; (3); Spanish Clb; Hon Roll; NHS; Mat Maids; HOSA; Pre Med.

JONES, CHRIS; Indiahoma Schl; Indiahoma, OK; (3); 1/11; Church Yth Grp; FCA; Letterman Clb; Pres Frsh Cls; Pres Soph Cls; Pres Jr Cls; Ofcr Stu Cncl; Capt L Bsktbl; Hon Roll; Cameron U Lawton.

JONES, CHRISTINA; Dustin Schl; Dustin, OK; (3); Church Yth Grp; GAA; Natl FFA Org; Quiz Bowl; Var Bsktbl; Var Sftbl; High Hon Roll; Jr NHS; NHS; Seminole JC; Acctng.

JONES, CHRISTINA; Calvin Public Schl; Calvin, OK; (4); 1/14; Rptr 4-H; Natl FFA Org; Spanish Clb; Teachers Aide; Treas Sr Cls; Chrldng; 4-H Awd; Hon Roll; Pres Schlr; Val; Seminole ST Coll; RN.

JONES, CHRISTOPHER C; Pauls Valley HS; Pauls Valley, OK; (3); Pep Clb; Ofcr Bsbl; Bsktbl; High Hon Roll; Hon Roll.

JONES, CODY B; Weatherford HS; Weatherford, OK; (4); 1/138; Art Clb; Church Yth Grp; Hist DECA; Rep FCA; Pres Jr Cls; Treas Sr Cls; VP Stu Cncl; Bsktbl; Kiwanis Awd; Val; Weatherford Drug Free Yth Jr Rep; Ctznsp/Schlrsp/Ldrsp Xerox Awd; Eagle Ambssdr; OK ST Univ; Mass Comm.

JONES, CORRIE; Deer Creek HS; Edmond, OK; (3); 25/110; Art Clb; Church Yth Grp; Cmnty Wkr; Science Clb; Church Choir; Rep Frsh Cls; Crs Cntry; Trk; NHS; OK ST Univ; Commercial Art.

JONES, CORY S; Shattuck Jr Sr HS; Shattuck, OK; (3); 15/38; Church Yth Grp; FCA; Letterman Clb; Library Aide; Office Aide; Teachers Aide; Varsity Clb; Pres Frsh Cls; Rep Soph Cls; Ofcr Stu Cncl; Bsbl Ptchr Schl Rcrd Jr; All Trny Tm Laverne Jr/Mooreland Frosh.

JONES, CRYSTAL L; Lindsay HS; Lindsay, OK; (2); 16/86; FHA; Hosp Aide; Natl FFA Org; Speech Tm; Yrbk; Hon Roll; Pres Schlr; St FFA Org; Local FFA Org Sec 95 & Rptr 96; Ada; RN; LPN.

JONES, DANIEL E; Mannford HS; Mannford, OK; (3); Boy Scts; FCA; Letterman Clb; SADD; Var Bsbl; Var Bsktbl; Var Chrldng; Var Crs Cntry; Hon Roll; Prfct Atten Awd; Jr Homcmng Bsktbl Attendant; NSU; Tchr; Phy Thrpst.

JONES, DANIEL F; Claremore Sr HS; Claremore, OK; (1); Church Yth Grp; JV Socr; JV Trk; High Hon Roll; St Schlr.

JONES, DAVID M; Tahlequah Sr HS; Tahlequah, OK; (4); Capt Bsbl; Capt Bsktbl; JV Ftbl; Trk; Numerous Awds & Trophies For BMX Bike Riding; Certs Of Recognition For Team Work.

JONES, DEIRDRA; John Marshall HS; Oklahoma City, OK; (4); 19/170; Am Leg Aux Girls St; FCA; FBLA; Letterman Clb; Ofcr Stu Cncl; L Bsktbl; Var Trk; Var Capt Vllybl; NHS; Church Yth Grp; Acctng.

JONES, DESIREE A; Union Intermediate HS; Tulsa, OK; (2); 128/800; Girl Scts; Letterman Clb; Teachers Aide; Band; Mrchg Band; L Swmmng; L Vllybl; High Hon Roll; NHS; Bowling High Game, Average, 1st Pl Team, High Series; Notre Dame; Comp.

JONES, DESTY D; Lindsay HS; Lindsay, OK; (3); 1/70; Art Clb; Quiz Bowl; Scholastic Bowl; Band; Mrchg Band; Pep Band; High Hon Roll; NHS; Ntl Merit Ltr; US Natl Art Awd; OK ST Univ; Physcst.

JONES, DU JUAN A; Union Intermediate HS; Tulsa, OK; (2); African Amer Soc; Georgetown Univ; Air Eng.

JONES, DUSTIN DUANE; Bixby Sr HS; Broken Arrow, OK; (3); FCA; JA; Letterman Clb; Varsity Clb; Var L Bsbl; Hon Roll; Jr NHS; Bixby Bsbll Invtnl All Tourn Tm; Tulsa Wrld All Metro Bsbll Tm; TulsaJA Bus Awd; OK St Univ; Bus Mgmt.

JONES, ELYSIA R; Catoosa HS; Claremore, OK; (2); Church Yth Grp; FCA; Band; Jazz Band; Pep Band; Var Crs Cntry; Var Trk; High Hon Roll; Hon Roll; ST Hnr Soc; ST Cross Cntry Qualfr; 9th Grd Salutatorian; Med.

JONES, ERIN B; Pauls Valley HS; Wynnewood, OK; (2); FHA; Spanish Clb; SADD; Ed Yrbk; Var Bsktbl; Var Trk; NHS; Gftd Crtv & Tlntd; Pi Phi Pi VP; OK Hnr Soc; E Cntrl U; Bus.

JONES, EVAN M; Bethany HS; Oklahoma City, OK; (3); Art Clb; Church Yth Grp; Office Aide; Varsity Clb; JV Var Bsbl; Cit Awd; High Hon Roll; Hon Roll; Pres Acad Fit Awd; U Of OK.

JONES, HAYLEY Y; Yukon Middle HS; Yukon, OK; (2); JV Bsktbl; U OK; ROTC.

JONES, HEATHER D; Stillwater Sr HS; Stillwater, OK; (2); 131/370; Church Yth Grp; Dance Clb; FCA; Latin Clb; Pep Clb; Acpl Chr; Chorus; Church Choir; Orch; Variety Show; OK ST Univ; Music Ed.

JONES, HEATHER R; Union Sr HS; Tulsa, OK; (3); 96/701; FBLA; Key Clb; Band; Flag Corp; Jazz Band; NHS; Wntrgrd; OK ST U.

JONES, JACK D; Dickson HS; Ardmore, OK; (3); Church Yth Grp; Cmnty Wkr; FCA; Key Clb; SADD; Church Choir; Pres Jr Cls; Rptr Stu Cncl; Chrch Orch; Pol; Bus.

JONES, JAMILA L; Yukon Middle HS; Yukon, OK; (2); Teachers Aide; Band; Mrchg Band; Pep Band; High Hon Roll; Hon Roll; OK ST Univ; Psychiatry.

JONES, JASON S; Stilwell HS; Stilwell, OK; (2); Church Yth Grp; Drama Clb; 4-H; Math Clb; Natl Beta Clb; Science Clb; School Play; Variety Show; Ftbl; Wt Lftg; FFA; U Of OK; Med.

JONES, JAY; Amber Pocasset Jr Sr HS; Amber, OK; (4); 1/29; Am Leg Boys St; Treas Natl FFA Org; Pres Spanish Clb; Rep Soph Cls; Var Capt Bsbl; Var Capt Bsktbl; High Hon Roll; NHS; Val; OK ST U; Acctng.

JONES, JEFFREY; Hartshorne Sr HS; Hartshorne, OK; (3); Am Leg Boys St; Natl FFA Org; Rep Soph Cls; Ftbl; Hon Roll; NHS; Pres Acad Fit Awd; OK Hon Soc; OK Indian Stu Hon Soc; Premed.

JONES, JENNIFER A; Claremore Sr HS; Foyil, OK; (2); 39/273; Art Clb; Church Yth Grp; Spanish Clb; Ed Yrbk; High Hon Roll; Hon Roll; NHS; Prfct Atten Awd; Jr Vol Doctors Hosp.

JONES, JENNIFER E; Enid Sr HS; Enid, OK; (4); 106/412; Church Yth Grp; French Clb; FHA; Church Choir; Hon Roll; NHS; U Of Cntrl OK; Psych.

JONES, JENNIFER K; Panola HS; Red Oak, OK; (3); 1/25; FHA; Chorus; School Musical; Rptr Jr Cls; Var Bsktbl; Var Sftbl; Cit Awd; Hon Roll; NHS; Prfct Atten Awd; Amer Legion Awd; Eng III, Office Procedures, Geom, Ger I & Comp Sci Awds; Eastern OSC; Speech Pathology.

JONES, JENNIFER L; Parker Middle HS; Mcalester, OK; (2); Church Yth Grp; Spanish Clb; Ofcr Frsh Cls; Ofcr Soph Cls; Sftbl; Tennis; Hon Roll; Forensic Sci.

JONES, JEREMIAH D; Southeast HS; Del City, OK; (2); Drama Clb; FCA; Thesps; School Play; Stage Crew; Ofcr Stu Cncl; Var L Bsktbl; Crs Cntry; Hnrb Mntn City All-Stars Bsktbl; OK ST Univ.

JONES, JEREMY MOOR; Jenks HS; Tulsa, OK; (4); 50/522; Church Yth Grp; Key Clb; Mu Alpha Theta; Scholastic Bowl; VP Spanish Clb; Band; School Musical; Rep Stu Cncl; High Hon Roll; Ntl Merit Schol; Phi Delta Epsilon Secy; Lamda Chi; Asian-Amer Hstrcl/Cultrl Clb; U Of OK.

JONES, JESSICA A; Kingfisher HS; Kingfisher, OK; (2); Drama Clb; Speech Tm; School Play; Stage Crew; High Hon Roll; Hon Roll.

JONES, JESSICA C; Indianola HS; Mcalester, OK; (2); Church Yth Grp; Natl FFA Org; Church Choir; Var Bsktbl; Mgr(s); Var Sftbl; CO Univ; Law Enfcmnt.

JONES, JODY; Bluejacket Schl; Bluejacket, OK; (2); Church Yth Grp; FCA; FHA; Sec Frsh Cls; Sec Treas Soph Cls; Var L Bsktbl; High Hon Roll; NEO A&M; Med.

JONES, KARA; Charles Page HS; Skiatook, OK; (4); Debate Tm; French Clb; NFL; Q&S; Speech Tm; Nwsp; Yrbk; NHS; Ntl Merit Ltr; Prfct Atten Awd; U Of Tulsa; Eng.

JONES, KEVIN M; U S Grant HS; Oklahoma City, OK; (3); Var Bsbl; NHS; Mrn Bio.

JONES, KURT R; Bridge Creek HS; Tuttle, OK; (3); Am Leg Boys St; Church Yth Grp; FCA; FBLA; Letterman Clb; Science Clb; Spanish Clb; SADD; Varsity Clb; Chorus; OK ST; Pol Sci; Pre Law.

JONES, LASHANDA L; Midwest City HS; Midwest City, OK; (2); 54/500; Church Yth Grp; Drama Clb; FCA; Pep Clb; SADD; Church Choir; Stage Crew; Stat Ftbl; JV Sftbl; High Hon Roll; OK ST U; Jrnlsm.

JONES, LAURA R; Bishop Kelley HS; Tulsa, OK; (3); Church Yth Grp; FCA; Red Cross Aide; Var Swmmng; High Hon Roll; Notre Dame.

JONES, LAURIE L; Skiatook HS; Skiatook, OK; (4); 41/110; Natl FFA Org; Band; Mrchg Band; Yrbk; Ofcr Stu Cncl; Bsktbl; Sftbl; Hon Roll; Library Aide; SADD; Horse Back Rdng; Stdnt Cncl Rep; TJC; Bus Mngmnt.

JONES, LEE; Amber Pocasset Jr Sr HS; Amber, OK; (1); FCA; 4-H; Natl FFA Org; Pres Frsh Cls; Var Bsbl; Intrml Capt Bsktbl; High Hon Roll; Jr NHS; OK ST U; Vet.

JONES, LEZLIE A; Vinita HS; Vinita, OK; (2); Natl FFA Org; NFL; Spanish Clb; Speech Tm; 4-H Awd; 4-H Qn; TX A&M; Marine Bio.

JONES, LINDSEY; Guyman HS; Guymon, OK; (1); 1/158; Debate Tm; FCA; NFL; Band; Color Guard; Mrchg Band; Yrbk; Chrldng; Cit Awd; Hon Roll; Gymnstc; Swmng; Psych.

JONES, MARY L; Hulbert Jr Sr HS; Hulbert, OK; (3); FBLA; Spanish Clb; SADD; Nwsp; Yrbk; Hon Roll; NHS; Gfted Tlnted Prog; Psych Awd; NE St Univ; Behvrl Sci.

JONES, MELANIE J; Haskell HS; Haskell, OK; (2); Church Yth Grp; FCA; Acpl Chr; Band; Chorus; Color Guard; Mrchg Band; Phtg Yrbk; Var Chrldng; Hon Roll; Prfrmng Arts.

JONES, MELINDA G; Duncan HS; Marlow, OK; (2); Cmnty Wkr; 4-H; Key Clb; Chorus; School Musical; 4-H Awd; Hon Roll; Vets Of Frgn Wars VFW Auxillary; Yth Alv Clb; Schl Tchr.

JONES, MELINDA K; Owasso Sr HS; Tulsa, OK; (3); Church Yth Grp; FHA; Hosp Aide; Red Cross Aide; VICA; HOSA Treas 2 Yrs; Blood Dr Amer Red Cross 2 Times, Vol; Tulsa JC; Phy Thrpst.

JONES, MELISSA S; Cherokee Jr Sr HS; Cherokee, OK; (3); FCA; FHA; Spanish Clb; Pres Soph Cls; Rep Jr Cls; VP Stu Cncl; Bsktbl; Trk; Hon Roll; NHS; NWDUS; Nurs.

JONES, MIA A; Douglass HS; Oklahoma City, OK; (3); Drama Clb; Mrchg Band; School Play; Mgr(s); Trk; Vllybl; Hon Roll; Eng II Awd; Majorettes Head Capt; OU Hlth & Sci Acad 96; U Of OK; Bio; Gen Dentist.

JONES, MICAH S; Tahlequah Sr HS; Tahlequah, OK; (2); Church Yth Grp; Bsktbl; Mgr(s); NHS; Pres Acad Fit Awd.

JONES, MICHAEL; Stratford Schl; Stratford, OK; (3); Church Yth Grp; FBLA; Science Clb; Spanish Clb; Teachers Aide; Gov Hon Prg Awd; High Hon Roll; Hon Roll; All Amer Schlr; OK Chrstn U; Yth Minister.

JONES, MICHAEL; Cherokee Jr Sr HS; Cherokee, OK; (4); Church Yth Grp; Debate Tm; FCA; FHA; Natl FFA Org; Spanish Clb; Speech Tm; Band; Chorus; Mrchg Band; Northwestern OK ST; Frfghtr.

JONES, MICHAEL A; Perry Sr HS; Perry, OK; (2); Church Yth Grp; Dance Clb; Drama Clb; FCA; GAA; Spanish Clb; Band; Mrchg Band; School Play; Nwsp; Wrote Article Pblshd Perry Daily Jrnl; OK ST U; Pblc Rltns.

JONES, MICHAEL E; Ponca City Sr HS; Ponca City, OK; (2); Hon Roll; Prfct Atten Awd; Northern OK Coll; Elec Engrng.

JONES, MINDY J; Shattuck Jr Sr HS; Shattuck, OK; (3); 10/34; Church Yth Grp; Sec Treas Pep Clb; Chorus; School Play; Rptr Nwsp; VP Soph Cls; VP Jr Cls; Var Trk; Hon Roll; NHS; Twirling.

JONES, MINDY S; Wakita Schl; Wakita, OK; (4); Church Yth Grp; FCA; FHA; School Play; Bsktbl; Sftbl; Hon Roll; Prfct Atten Awd; RN.

JONES, NANCY C; Grove HS; Grove, OK; (4); 16/105; Church Yth Grp; FCA; GAA; Key Clb; Var Bsktbl; Var Crs Cntry; Var Trk; Var Wt Lftg; Hon Roll; NHS; Treas Intl Drug Free Yth; Northestrn ST Univ; Sports Med.

JONES, NATHAN; Amber Pocasset Jr Sr HS; Amber, OK; (3); 5/30; Am Leg Boys St; CAP; FCA; Natl FFA Org; Pres Frsh Cls; Pres Jr Cls; Var L Bsbl; Var L Bsktbl; High Hon Roll; NHS; Billy Mitchell & Amelia Earhart Awds; FFA Chptr Rptr & Treas; FCA Huddle Rptr; OK Univ; Criminology Stud.

JONES, PHYLLIS A; Booker T Washington HS; Tulsa, OK; (2); Church Yth Grp; Debate Tm; Office Aide; Spanish Clb; Chorus; Church Choir; High Hon Roll; NHS; Spelman; Med.

JONES, PRESTON D; South Intermediate HS; Broken Arrow, OK; (1); Church Yth Grp; Debate Tm; Hosp Aide; NFL; Spanish Clb; Hon Roll; 1st Pl ST Schl Acad Team; Flmmkr.

JONES, RASHAEL; Meeker HS; Meeker, OK; (2); Dance Clb; Drama Clb; Scholastic Bowl; Speech Tm; VP Band; VP Mrchg Band; Co-Capt Pom Pon; High Hon Roll; Acad Bwl; Octgn Clb Cmmnty Svc Chrmn; Sci.

JONES, RASHEL; Hartshorne Sr HS; Mcalester, OK; (4); 1/46; HOBY; Yrbk; Rep Stu Cncl; Capt Chrldng; Cit Awd; High Hon Roll; NHS; Pres Acad Fit Awd; Val; Gftd & Tlntd; FFA Spchs & Rprtr; Acad Team; Lincoln-Douglas Dbt; St Cptl Pg; Tulsa U; Poli Sci.

JONES, RASHIDA; Douglass HS; Oklahoma City, OK; (2); Office Aide; Pep Clb; Teachers Aide; Band; Flag Corp; Mrchg Band; Yrbk; Ofcr Soph Cls; JV Bsktbl; High Hon Roll; Cmptr/Bus Tech; Tulsa U; Law.

JONES, REBEKAH; Hugo HS; Hugo, OK; (2); Natl FFA Org; Sftbl.

JONES, ROBERT J; Del City HS; Del City, OK; (2); Spanish Clb; Tennis; Jr NHS; NHS; US Natl Math Awd; OU; Psych/FBI Agent.

JONES, ROBERT W; Valliant HS; Valliant, OK; (3); Cmnty Wkr; Computer Clb; Natl FFA Org; Varsity Clb; Band; School Play; Rptr Yrbk; Sec Soph Cls; Var Bsktbl; JV Chrldng; All Dist 2nd Team; Hnrbl Mention; East TX ST Univ; Cmptr Tech.

JONES, SARAH L; Bethany HS; Bethany, OK; (3); Church Yth Grp; FCA; Key Clb; Spanish Clb; Hist Chorus; Phtg Yrbk; Hist Jr Cls; Hist Sr Cls; Ofcr Stu Cncl; Office Aide; Yth Alive; Southern Nazarene Univ.

JONES, SAVANNAH L; Claremore Sr HS; Claremore, OK; (2); Church Yth Grp; Cmnty Wkr; Dance Clb; French Clb; Hosp Aide; Office Aide; SADD; Church Choir; Hon Roll; NHS; Univ Of OK; PT.

JONES, SHANE; Midwest City HS; Midwest City, OK; (4); Hon Roll; VP VICA; Private Leagues Wrstng/Soccer/Ftbl/Bsktbl/Boxing; S OK JC; Bus.

JONES, SHANNON Y; Hulbert Jr Sr HS; Tahlequah, OK; (3); Church Yth Grp; FHA; German Clb; Spanish Clb; Rptr Nwsp; Yrbk; Bsktbl; Mgr(s); Sftbl; OSU; Nrse.

JONES, SHAUNA; Dickson HS; Gene Autry, OK; (2); 4-H; GAA; Teachers Aide; Sftbl; Hon Roll.

JONES, SHAWN; Mustang HS; Yukon, OK; (3); 21/426; Church Yth Grp; FCA; Quiz Bowl; Scholastic Bowl; Rep Jr Cls; Var Chrldng; High Hon Roll; NHS; Vol Lcl Bus Prvd Sfe Hllwn; Hlpd Org/Wrk Schlwde Toy Dr.

JONES, SHEILA A; Haskell HS; Haskell, OK; (2); Church Yth Grp; Hosp Aide; Band; Chorus; Mrchg Band; Pep Band; Nrsng.

JONES, SHENIKA L; Del City HS; Oklahoma City, OK; (2); HOBY; SADD; Church Choir; Pres Soph Cls; Bsktbl; Sftbl; Hon Roll; Miss Kett Jr HS 94-95; U Of TN; Sports Medicine.

JONES, SHERRY D; New Lima Jr Sr HS; Seminole, OK; (3); Church Yth Grp; Cmnty Wkr; 4-H; FHA; JA; Office Aide; Pep Clb; Band; Rptr Soph Cls; Rptr Jr Cls; Ballet, Jazz, Tap, Hula & Tahitian Dance; Singing; Natl Beauty & Talent Conts Wnnr; Seminole ST Coll; Bus; Dance.

JONES, STEPHANIE; Warner HS; Warner, OK; (1); FCA; FHA; Spanish Clb; Var Bsktbl; Cit Awd; High Hon Roll; Val; St Hnr Soc; Acad Team.

JONES, SUMMER K; Quinton Jr Sr HS; Quinton, OK; (3); Church Yth Grp; FCA; FHA; Yrbk; Bsktbl; Chrldng; Powder Puff Ftbl; Sftbl; Trk; Hon Roll; Connors; Law.

JONES, TANESHIA W; Will Rogers HS; Tulsa, OK; (2); Church Yth Grp; Hon Roll; OSU; PT.

JONES, TERINA; Merritt Schl; Elk City, OK; (4); 6/38; FCA; Library Aide; Pres SADD; Sprt Ed Nwsp; VP Stu Cncl; Capt Chrldng; Sftbl; Trk; NHS; Cmptr Sci.

JONES JR, THOMAS D; Bethel HS; Shawnee, OK; (4); #6 in class; Church Yth Grp; French Clb; Quiz Bowl; Band; Chorus; Church Choir; Jazz Band; Mrchg Band; Orch; Pep Band; UCO; Music Ed.

JONES, TIFFANY; Kiefer Jr Sr HS; Kiefer, OK; (3); 5/37; FCA; Teachers Aide; Pres Frsh Cls; VP Jr Cls; Var Bsktbl; Var Chrldng; Var Sftbl; Hon Roll; Ed.

JONES, TIFFANY; Douglass HS; Oklahoma City, OK; (1); Chorus; Hon Roll; NHS; Grambling Univ; Med.

JONES, TOUISSAINT L; Coyle Public Schl; Langston, OK; (3); Church Yth Grp; Cmnty Wkr; Teachers Aide; Church Choir; Variety Show; Bsktbl; Cit Awd; Prfct Atten Awd; Langston Univ.

JONES, TRACEY; Arkoma Jr Sr HS; Arkoma, OK; (2); Art Clb; FCA; GAA; Var Bsktbl; Var Chrldng; Var Sftbl; Hon Roll; Prfct Atten Awd; Gftd/Tlntd; Bsktbl Coach.

JONES, TRACI; Moore HS; Moore, OK; (2); Church Yth Grp; FCA; Rptr Nwsp; Phtg Yrbk; Rep Stu Cncl; Trk; Hon Roll; Jr NHS.

JONES, TRACY; Westmoore HS; Moore, OK; (4); 23/622; Debate Tm; Key Clb; Q&S; Hist Spanish Clb; Phtg Ed Yrbk; Rep Stu Cncl; NHS; Pres Schlr; Val; U Of OK; Industrial Engrng.

JONES, WILLIAM H; Okemah HS; Okemah, OK; (3); 17/72; Chess Clb; Quiz Bowl; Scholastic Bowl; Spanish Clb; Band; Mrchg Band; Hon Roll; 2nd Pl OK Math League; East Cntrl U Of OK; Tchr.

JOOSTEN, MELISSA A; Shawnee Sr HS; Shawnee, OK; (4); 48/259; Church Yth Grp; Cmnty Wkr; Latin Clb; Library Aide; Pep Clb; Hon Roll; Jr NHS; NHS; Prfct Atten Awd; Mat Maid Squad Co-Capt; U Of OK.

JOPLIN, DUSTIN B; Strother Jr Sr HS; Seminole, OK; (1); Church Yth Grp; FCA; Natl FFA Org; Church Choir; Ofcr Frsh Cls; Bsktbl; Hon Roll.

JOPLIN, SARAH; Skiatook HS; Skiatook, OK; (4); 30/110; Am Leg Aux Girls St; Rep FBLA; HOBY; Rep Natl FFA Org; Teachers Aide; Sec Treas Frsh Cls; Pres Soph Cls; Ofcr Stu Cncl; Powder Puff Ftbl; OK Dairy Prod Tm St Wnnr; St Dry Prod Cont 2nd Pl Hi Scrng Indvdl; OK ST U.

JORDAN, ABRA; Westmoore HS; Richardson, TX; (3); Church Yth Grp; Drama Clb; Spanish Clb; School Play; Stage Crew; Variety Show; Chrldng; Score Keeper; Hon Roll; Schl Signing Clb Mem; U Of TX-AUSTIN; Arch.

JORDAN, AMANDA; Southwest Covenant Schl; Oklahoma City, OK; (3); 1/9; Church Yth Grp; FCA; Band; Chorus; Rep Stu Cncl; Var L Bsktbl; High Hon Roll; Chld Evanglsm Fellowship Tchr; All St Bsktbl OCSAA; Dist/Solo Ensemble Flute Fnlst; Elem Ed.

JORDAN, ARIN DANIELLE; Clayton Jr Sr HS; Clayton, OK; (2); FBLA; Quiz Bowl; Treas Band; Pep Band; Rptr Nwsp; Var Bsktbl; High Hon Roll; NHS; OK Bapt U; Phy Thrpst; Oncology.

JORDAN, BILLY; Chisholm Sr HS; Carrier, OK; (2); Chess Clb; Debate Tm; Drama Clb; FCA; NFL; Quiz Bowl; Scholastic Bowl; Spanish Clb; Speech Tm; Rep Soph Cls; Natl Forensic League Spcl Distinction Awd; USC; Law; Pol.

JORDAN, CHRISSY J; Muskogee HS; Muskogee, OK; (2); Cmnty Wkr; Hon Roll; Phy Thrpy.

JORDAN, JENNIFER; Tecumseh HS; Tecumseh, OK; (4); 6/129; Art Clb; Church Yth Grp; FHA; Hosp Aide; Natl Beta Clb; School Musical; Variety Show; VP Frsh Cls; VP Sr Cls; Pres Stu Cncl; OK Baptist Univ; Nrse.

JORDAN, JENNIFER L; Alva HS; Alva, OK; (2); 5/70; FCA; FHA; Quiz Bowl; Scholastic Bowl; Spanish Clb; Acpl Chr; Chorus; Pres Frsh Cls; Pres Soph Cls; Rep Stu Cncl; OK St Univ; Comm.

JORDAN, MICHAEL; Moore HS; Moore, OK; (2); Bsktbl; Acad All-Str Sat Prog For Span; Yth In Actn Bsktbl Prog; U Of OK; Bus.

JORDAN, NATASHA; Central Mid-HS; Norman, OK; (2); Dance Clb; Scholastic Bowl; High Hon Roll; NC U; Med.

JORDAN, SANDRA RE ANNA; Owasso Sr HS; Sperry, OK; (3); 120/360; Pres Drama Clb; FCA; Rep French Clb; NFL; Capt Quiz Bowl; Chorus; School Musical; School Play; High Hon Roll; Hon Roll; Xinos Phi Delta Kappa Hnr Soc; U Of OK; Psych.

JORDAN, SARAH; Tahlequah Sr HS; Park Hill, OK; (4); #16 in class; Church Yth Grp; SADD; Band; Church Choir; Hon Roll; Jr NHS; NHS; Northeastern ST U; Vet Med.

JORDAN, SARAH; Sapulpa Sr HS; Sapulpa, OK; (3); 2/300; Church Yth Grp; Key Clb; Service Clb; Spanish Clb; Band; Mrchg Band; JV Socr; High Hon Roll; NHS; Spanish NHS; JV Capt Acad Tm.

JORDAN, SHAINE; Crescent Schl; Crescent, OK; (2); Boy Scts; Church Yth Grp; Debate Tm; Drama Clb; Letterman Clb; Natl Beta Clb; Pep Clb; Quiz Bowl; Speech Tm; SADD; Bible Club; Youth Evangelist.

JORDAN, STEPHEN; Southwest Covenant Schl; Oklahoma City, OK; (1); 10/24; Church Yth Grp; Band; Bsktbl; Crs Cntry; Cit Awd; High Hon Roll; Church Orch; Chld Evanglsm Flwshp Mnstry 2 Yr; Outstndg Band Stdnt 95-96; Med.

JORDAN, TINA; New Lima Jr Sr HS; Wewoka, OK; (4); 3/21; Bsktbl; High Hon Roll; Hon Roll; Jr NHS; NHS; Seminole JC; Acctng.

JORDAN, TONY; Midwest City HS; Midwest City, OK; (2); 1/501; German Clb; Jr NHS; Rssn Clb; Acad Tm; US Natl Math Awd.

JORGENSEN, JOSH D; Bokoshe Schl; Bokoshe, OK; (3); Ofcr Bsbl; Bsktbl; Carl Ablert ST Coll.

JOSE, MARTI; Leedey Schl; Leedey, OK; (2); 3/18; Church Yth Grp; FCA; FBLA; FHA; GAA; Spanish Clb; SADD; Rep Stu Cncl; Bsktbl; Sftbl; SW OK St Univ; Acctnt.

JOSEFY, AMANDA; Grandfield Jr Sr HS; Grandfield, OK; (2); 2/22; FHA; HOBY; Rep Stu Cncl; Hon Roll; NHS; Pres Acad Fit Awd; Acad Tm; Gftd & Tlntd Prgm; Psych.

JOSEFY, JAMIE; Grandfield Jr Sr HS; Grandfield, OK; (4); #4 in class; Am Leg Aux Girls St; Art Clb; Church Yth Grp; Church Choir; Yrbk; Bsktbl; Chrldng; High Hon Roll; Class Sacarito 11th; MIS.

JOSEFY, SHANA J; Big Pasture HS; Grandfield, OK; (4); 2/16; Church Yth Grp; Cmnty Wkr; VP 4-H; Natl FFA Org; Sec Sr Cls; Stat Mgr(s); L Trk; High Hon Roll; NHS; Sal; Midwestern ST Univ; Surgeon.

JOSEPH, MERYL; Mustang HS; Yukon, OK; (2); Church Yth Grp; Hosp Aide; Key Clb; Math Clb; Science Clb; Church Choir; NHS; Var Choir; Ana/Phy/Algbra I Acad Awds; Medicine.

JOVONA, DAVIS; Fox Sr HS; Countyline, OK; (3); Sec FHA; Pep Clb; SADD; Bsktbl; Sftbl; Hon Roll; NHS; All Amer Schlr; US Army.

JOY, JESSE Z; Putnam City West HS; Oklahoma City, OK; (3); 30/320; Church Yth Grp; FCA; Acpl Chr; Church Choir; Spanish Clb; Ofcr Stu Cncl; JV Var Bsktbl; Var Ftbl; Var Trk; NHS; Med Club; Chrstns In Action; Yng Cnsrvtvs; Baylor Univ; PT/PRE Med.

JOYCE, TOMMY; Putnam City West HS; Bethany, OK; (3); Church Yth Grp; FCA; Spanish Clb; SADD; Band; Jazz Band; Ofcr Stu Cncl; Ftbl; NHS; Prfct Atten Awd; Natl Athl Mrt; All-Amer Schlr; OSU; Chirprctr.

JUCKES, STEVE; Ponca City Sr HS; Ponca City, OK; (4); Am Leg Boys St; Boy Scts; Church Yth Grp; French Clb; Ofcr Bsbl; Ftbl; Wrstlng; Hon Roll; Kiwanis Awd; Office Aide; Cvc Clb Stu Rep; U Of Cntrl OK; Physlgy.

JUDD, AARON C; Cherokee Jr Sr HS; Cherokee, OK; (3); FHA; Natl FFA Org; Office Aide; Teachers Aide; Ofcr Bsbl; Bsktbl; Vllybl; Wt Lftg; High Hon Roll; Hon Roll; Exclnt Wdwrkng II; Wood Tech; Econ; Garden City CC; John Deere Tec.

JUDD, JOSHUA L; Muskogee HS; Muskogee, OK; (4); 9/303; Drm Mjr(t); Church Yth Grp; French Clb; Band; Jazz Band; Mrchg Band; Orch; Pep Band; School Musical; NHS; OK Hnr Soc; Cntrl Bible Col; Yth Msntry.

JUDD, STACEY J; Meeker Jr Sr HS; Meeker, OK; (4); Rep FHA; Rep Stu Cncl; NHS; Pres Acad Fit Awd; Eng II Outstndng Stu; Cade Tuition, Knights Of Columbus, Archdiocese, Archdiocese SGC Match Schlsps; St Gregorys Cath Coll; Elem Ed.

JUDD, TERESA; Del City HS; Oklahoma City, OK; (4); 31/432; Church Yth Grp; FCA; SADD; Chorus; Var Bsktbl; Capt Var Socr; Capt Var Vllybl; High Hon Roll; NHS; Pres Acad Fit Awd; OK Christian Univ Of Sci/Arts.

JUDKINS, JAMIE L; Choctaw HS; Choctaw, OK; (2); FCA; Bsktbl; JV Sftbl; Treas Tennis; Trk; High Hon Roll; Jr NHS; Pres Acad Fit Awd; Val; OK Baptist U; Med.

JUDKINS, KATRINA; Sasakwa Schl; Sasakwa, OK; (2); 2/16; FHA; Quiz Bowl; Science Clb; Speech Tm; School Play; Rptr Nwsp; Phtg Yrbk; Treas Soph Cls; Stat Bsbl; Stat Bsktbl; OU; Lawyer; Tchr.

JUERGENSON, MARI K; Memorial HS; Tulsa, OK; (2); Church Yth Grp; German Clb; Key Clb; Latin Clb; Red Cross Aide; Church Choir; Swmmng; High Hon Roll; Camp Fire Clb; Vet.

JULIAN, ANGELA A; Dickson HS; Ardmore, OK; (3); Church Yth Grp; Rptr FCA; GAA; Key Clb; Spanish Clb; Speech Tm; Treas SADD; Yrbk; Rep Stu Cncl; NHS; East Cntrl Univ; Lawyer.

JULY, DANNY R; Checotah HS; Checotah, OK; (2); 4-H; Speech Tm; Var Bsbl; JV Bsktbl; JV Ftbl; Hon Roll; Pres Schlr.

JUMPA, ASHLEY A; Colbert Jr Sr HS; Cartwright, OK; (1); Art Clb; Drama Clb; FCA; Sec Frsh Cls; Hon Roll; Karate Martial Arts; UCLA; Pre Law.

JUNGER, NICHOLAS A; Will Rogers HS; Tulsa, OK; (2); ROTC; Color Guard; Drill Tm; Var Ftbl; Var Trk; Cit Awd; Hon Roll; Prfct Atten Awd; Naval Acad; Navy Pilot.

JUNGERMANN, ANGELA S; Jay HS; Jay, OK; (2); FBLA; Math Tm; Natl Beta Clb; Science Clb; Hon Roll; NHS; Acad Bowl.

JUNKERMEIER, JOHN L; Morris HS; Morris, OK; (3); JV Bsbl; JV Bsktbl; Hon Roll; NHS.

JURCZEWSKY, MARY E; Del City HS; Oklahoma City, OK; (4); Dance Clb; SADD; Teachers Aide; Pom Pon; Score Keeper; Hon Roll; NHS; Dance Tchr; Compete In Dance Cmptns Regionally & Nationally; U Of OK.

JURGENSEN, JEREMY; Lawton Christian Schl; Lawton, OK; (1); JV Var Bsbl; JV Var Bsktbl; High Hon Roll; Epsilon Chi Honor Soc.

JURGENSEN, TIM; Lawton Christian Schl; Lawton, OK; (3); 1/6; Church Yth Grp; Teachers Aide; Yrbk; Rep Stu Cncl; Var JV Bsktbl; JV Ftbl; Cit Awd; High Hon Roll; Ntl Merit SF; Epsiolon Chi Hnr Soc; Grphc Design.

JUSTICE, A; Eisenhower Sr HS; Lawton, OK; (3); FCA; Stat Bsbl; Var Bsktbl; Capt Var Sftbl; Hon Roll; St Schlr; Bwlng Schlrshp Trnmnts; Shoot Pool; All Conf Sftbl; OU; Scndry Ed/Sftbl Coach.

JUSTICE, AMY L; Central Jr HS; Lawton, OK; (1); Church Yth Grp; Cmnty Wkr; FCA; Rep Stu Cncl; Var Chrldng; Var Sftbl; Var JV Tennis; Hon Roll; Builders Clb Pres; Postponing Sexual Involvement Teen Trainer; Cougar Qn Nom; Phy Thrpst.

JUSTICE, CHRISTY; Soper Schl; Hugo, OK; (4); 1/18; FHA; Band; Mrchg Band; Yrbk; Mgr(s); Hon Roll; NHS; Val; Prins Sci Schlr; Engl Mrt Awd; Paris JC; Medcl Transcrptnst.

JUSTICE, MICHAEL; Gore HS; Gore, OK; (3); 1/50; Church Yth Grp; FBLA; Yrbk; Pres Frsh Cls; VP Soph Cls; Treas Jr Cls; VP Stu Cncl; Var L Bsbl; Var L Bsktbl; Var L Ftbl.

JUSTICE, SARA B; Pauls Valley HS; Pauls Valley, OK; (1); Church Yth Grp; Key Clb; Math Clb; Ofcr Stu Cncl; Bsktbl; Chrldng; Trk; Hon Roll; FFA; U Of OK; Medcl.

JUSTUS, JEREMY; Collinsville HS; Collinsville, OK; (3).

JUSTUS, ROBYN Y; Western Heights Sr HS; Oklahoma City, OK; (2); 11/296; JV Bsktbl; Hon Roll; JTPA Smmr Cmp Outs Ptcpt Awd.

KACER, TODD L; Emerson Jr HS; Enid, OK; (1); Stage Crew; Ed Nwsp; High Hon Roll; Hon Roll; NHS; ACT Test 7th Grd; Dfnsv Plyr Rllr Hcky Leag.

KACHNER, MARCIA A; Ripley HS; Ripley, OK; (4); 9/32; Church Yth Grp; FCA; Sec FBLA; GAA; Office Aide; SADD; Teachers Aide; Church Choir; Rep Nwsp; Ed Yrbk; OK ST Univ; PE.

KAHLE, LINDSAY R; Putnam City North HS; Oklahoma City, OK; (3); Church Yth Grp; GAA; Bsktbl; Socr; Sftbl; Pnthr Pls; U Of OK; Arch.

KAHRS, JUSTIN H; North Intemediate HS; Broken Arrow, OK; (2); Boy Scts; Church Yth Grp; German Clb; Band; Mrchg Band; Pep Band; Egl Sct Rnk; Tulsa U; Msc.

KALINICH, KRISTI; Holdenville Jr HS; Holdenville, OK; (1); Church Yth Grp; FCA; GAA; Office Aide; Spanish Clb; Chorus; Bsktbl; Chrldng; Trk; High Hon Roll; NASC Prlmntrn; Law.

KALMBACH, KRIS; Cascia Hall Prep School; Tulsa, OK; (3); Church Yth Grp; Cmnty Wkr; JA; Letterman Clb; Spanish Clb; Chorus; School Musical; School Play; Stage Crew; Lit Mag; Eng; Jrnlsm; Drama.

KALRA, RUCHI; Westmoore HS; Oklahoma City, OK; (3); 16/673; Hosp Aide; Treas Key Clb; Math Tm; VP Soph Cls; VP Jr Cls; VP Sr Cls; Chrldng; Am Leg Boys St; NHS; Pres Acad Fit Awd; Pre-Med.

KALU, MARTINA; Lawton Sr HS; Lawton, OK; (2); ROTC; JV Bsktbl; Tennis; JV Trk; Vllybl; High Hon Roll; Hon Roll; Athl Awd; Med.

KAMMERER, NIK L; Duncan HS; Duncan, OK; (3); 39/254; Boy Scts; FBLA; Hon Roll; Eagle Scout; OK ST Univ; Elec/Cmptr Engr.

KAMP, TYLER; Laverne Jr Sr HS; Laverne, OK; (4); Letterman Clb; Natl Beta Clb; Natl FFA Org; Ftbl; Hon Roll; Pres Acad Fit Awd; ST Farmer; Northwestern OK ST U; Agribus.

KANA, ALYSSA R; Healdton HS; Healdton, OK; (3); 15/55; Church Yth Grp; FCA; FHA; GAA; Chorus; Var Bsktbl; Var Chrldng; Var Sftbl; Hon Roll; NHS; OSU; Pre-Law.

KANALY, BRENT M; Edmond Santa Fe HS; Edmond, OK; (3); 1/310; Yrbk; Ofcr Jr Cls; Bsktbl; Crs Cntry; Trk; Hon Roll; NHS; Pres Acad Fit Awd; Life Guard.

KANELAKOS, BRIAN; Ponca City Sr HS; Ponca City, OK; (3); 34/407; Am Leg Boys St; Church Yth Grp; Ofcr Stu Cncl; Var Crs Cntry; Var Socr; DAR Awd; High Hon Roll; Jr NHS; Ntl Merit Ltr; Rotary Ldrshp Awd.

KANNADY, CHRIS L; Savanna HS; Mcalester, OK; (3); 1/60; FCA; Quiz Bowl; Science Clb; Spanish Clb; Var Ftbl; Var Wt Lftg; High Hon Roll; Hon Roll; NHS; Algebra St Mt 3rd; OU; Corp Law.

KANOSKI, KATHERINE C; Bishop Mcguinness HS; Oklahoma City, OK; (3); Church Yth Grp; Pres Chorus; Rep Soph Cls; Rep Jr Cls; Stat Bsktbl; High Hon Roll; Spanish NHS; Cmnty Wkr; Dance Clb; FCA; Channel 5 Kids Who Care Fnlst; Bapt Med Ctr Sr Vol Ldrshp & Trng Rep; Voice; Outstdng Character Awd; Sci.

KANTOLA, CANDY; Yale Jr Sr HS; Yale, OK; (3); 10/50; FHA; Natl Beta Clb; Yrbk; Pres Soph Cls; VP Jr Cls; Rep Stu Cncl; Var Vllybl; Hon Roll.

KAPELLA, DARIN; Davis HS; Davis, OK; (4); 2/51; Church Yth Grp; FCA; Math Clb; Teachers Aide; Chorus; Rep Soph Cls; Pres Stu Cncl; Var Bsbl; Var Bsktbl; High Hon Roll; AR Tech U.

KAPKA, LISA L; West Middle HS; Norman, OK; (1); Church Yth Grp; FBLA; Speech Tm; Hon Roll; U Of OK; Jrnlsm.

KAPPELMAN, JESSICA L; Choctaw HS; Choctaw, OK; (2); Church Yth Grp; GAA; Girl Scts; Library Aide; Teachers Aide; Bsktbl; Score Keeper; Sftbl; Vllybl; Wt Lftg.

KARASEK, JAMIE; Grace Fellowship Christian Sch; Haskell, OK; (3); Teachers Aide; Color Guard; Socr; Vllybl; Compose Music; Piano; Write Poetry; Oral Roberts U; Linguist.

KARBER, J D; Fairview HS; Fairview, OK; (2); FCA; Band; Rep Stu Cncl; Var Ftbl; Hon Roll; NHS.

KARCH, JENNIFER; Indianola HS; Canadian, OK; (1); 1/40; Church Yth Grp; FBLA; GAA; Natl FFA Org; Ofcr Frsh Cls; L Bsktbl; L Sftbl; High Hon Roll; St Piano Cont.

KARCHER, JEFF; Perry Sr HS; Perry, OK; (3); FCA; VP Soph Cls; VP Jr Cls; Var Ftbl; Var Wt Lftg; Hon Roll; Jr NHS; NHS; OK ST U; Chem.

KARIM, TALIA S; Oklahoma Sch Of Science & Math; Norman, OK; (3); Drama Clb; Math Clb; Model UN; Mu Alpha Theta; Spanish Clb; Pres Orch; Rep Soph Cls; Hon Roll; NHS; Pres Acad Fit Awd; All St Orch, OK Summer Arts Inst Orch; Archlgy.

KARKER, CRISTAL A; Bethany HS; Bethany, OK; (2); 3/88; Church Yth Grp; Key Clb; Chorus; Yrbk; Sec Frsh Cls; Sec Soph Cls; High Hon Roll; Jr NHS; NHS; OK Hnr Soc; Southern Nazerene Univ.

KARNES, RANA M; Shattuck Jr Sr HS; Shattuck, OK; (3); 18/34; 4-H; FHA; Letterman Clb; Pep Clb; Acpl Chr; Chorus; School Play; Stage Crew; Rep Stu Cncl; Mgr(s); Farmers Union Yth; Farmers Union Awd; U Of Cntrl OK; Spech-Lang Path.

KARTOATMODJO, IZUDDIN; Central HS; Tulsa, OK; (4); 5/177; Computer Clb; Treas Intnl Clb; Key Clb; Nwsp; Yrbk; Pres Stu Cncl; Mgr Bsktbl; Capt Tennis; High Hon Roll; NHS; Son Of Amer Revolution Awd; Gold Star Awd; Svc T Awd; U Of Tulsa; Comp Info Syst.

KASINER, JINGER N; Sapulpa Sr HS; Sapulpa, OK; (4); 74/300; Church Yth Grp; Dance Clb; Drama Clb; Office Aide; Spanish Clb; Speech Tm; Teachers Aide; Tennis; Wt Lftg; Hon Roll; Pres Ed Awd For Outstdng Acad Achvmt; U Of Cntrl OK; Engrng.

KASPAR, TED W; Blackwell HS; Newkirk, OK; (2); 30/120; Spanish Clb; JV Bsktbl; Var Tennis; Hon Roll; FFA; OK Univ; Med.

KATES, ALAN; Haworth Jr HS; Haworth, OK; (1); 5/35; Natl FFA Org; Pres Frsh Cls; Ofcr Bsbl; Bsktbl; Golf; Hon Roll; Jr NHS; Sal.

KATES, RICHELL L; Eisenhower Sr HS; Lawton, OK; (3); Cmnty Wkr; FCA; Girl Scts; Natl FFA Org; Church Choir; Orch; Cit Awd; Hon Roll; Jr NHS; La Sill Octagon Clb Treas; Elem Ed/Tchng Math Jr HS.

KAUAHQUO, SARAH; Hobart HS; Hobart, OK; (3); 20/60; Church Yth Grp; FCA; FHA; FTA; GAA; Office Aide; Pep Clb; Teachers Aide; Varsity Clb; Chorus; SW OK ST Univ; Speech Thrpst.

KAUFMAN, JENNIE; Miami Sr HS; Miami, OK; (1); Church Yth Grp; FCA; Ofcr Stu Cncl; Bsktbl; Trk; High Hon Roll; Jr NHS; Tap & Ballet Dancing; Pharmacy.

KAULAITY JR, HENRY J; Mountain View-Gotebo HS; Mountain View, OK; (3); FHA; German Clb; Ftbl; Cit Awd; Hon Roll; Crmnl Jstc.

KAY, KRISTI G; Pauls Valley HS; Pauls Valley, OK; (4); 1/93; FHA; Key Clb; VP Pep Clb; Teachers Aide; Ed Yrbk; L Bsktbl; L Chrldng; Capt Golf; High Hon Roll; Val; PRIDE Awd; Lindsay Schlsp Awd; Sara Thomason Schlsp; SWOSU Distngd Schlsp; SWOSU; Phy Thrpst.

KAYS, GENA E; B T Washington HS; Tulsa, OK; (2); Quiz Bowl; ROTC; Spanish Clb; High Hon Roll; Val; Masonic Stu Of Today Awd; Explorer Post 342; SAIL Team; Camp Fire Boys & Girls Clb Treas; Med.

KEAHEY, CHANDRA; Cheyenne HS; Cheyenne, OK; (4); FBLA; Library Aide; Teachers Aide; Chorus; School Musical; Stage Crew; Bsktbl; Sftbl; Hon Roll; 4-H; FBLA Local Pres & Attnd St Ldrshp Conf 95-96; Certified Nurses Aide; SWOSU; Medcl Records.

KEARNEY II, ROBERT H; Central Jr HS; Lawton, OK; (1); Church Yth Grp; Cmnty Wkr; FCA; JA; Quiz Bowl; Spanish Clb; Var Ftbl; Var Socr; Cit Awd; Hon Roll; OK Outstdng Yth Awd; Notre Dame; Pediatrician.

KEAWPHALOUK, MICHELLE; Seminole Jr Sr HS; Seminole, OK; (3); Debate Tm; Library Aide; Math Clb; NFL; Quiz Bowl; Science Clb; High Hon Roll; NHS; Pres Acad Fit Awd; OK Math League; Pediatrcs.

KECK, PENNY; Anadarko HS; Anadarko, OK; (1); Church Yth Grp; FCA; Spanish Clb; Church Choir; Chrldng; High Hon Roll; Hon Roll; Jr NHS; Ntl Merit Ltr; FFA; U Of OK; Med.

KEE, KELLY L; Bishop Kelley HS; Bixby, OK; (1); Drama Clb; Key Clb; School Play; Stage Crew; Hon Roll; Decorative Tole Painting; Golf; Sewing.

KEECH, JOSHUA R; South Intermediate HS; Broken Arrow, OK; (1); Boy Scts; Church Yth Grp; Rep Stu Cncl; High Hon Roll; Hon Roll; OK Hnr Scty; Chrstn Stu Union.

KEEFE, JESSE M; Nathan Hale HS; Tulsa, OK; (2); Var Crs Cntry; Var Socr; Var Trk; Hon Roll; NHS.

KEEFE II, JOHN P; American Christian Acad; Oklahoma City, OK; (4); Boy Scts; Church Yth Grp; Debate Tm; Drama Clb; Library Aide; Spanish Clb; Ofcr Soph Cls; Rep Stu Cncl; Wt Lftg; Wrstlng; Invited To US Stu Ambassador To Australia Via People To People Fndtn; OK City CC; Coll Prof; Tchng.

KEEL, COURTNEY B; Edmond North HS; Edmond, OK; (2); Church Yth Grp; FCA; French Clb; HOBY; Key Clb; Mu Alpha Theta; SADD; Rep Stu Cncl; JV Pom Pon; Jr NHS; Piano 9 Yrs; Med/Pediatrician.

KEELER, CHRISTI; Ponca City Sr HS; Ponca City, OK; (4); 82/338; Natl FFA Org; Bsktbl; Hon Roll; Northern OK Coll; Veterinary.

KEELER, ELIZABETH; Coalgate HS; Coalgate, OK; (3); Flag Corp; Mrchg Band; Hon Roll; NHS; Prfct Atten Awd; ECU; Fash Mrchndsng.

KEELER, RYAN; Blanchard Jr Sr HS; Blanchard, OK; (3); Spanish Clb; Var Bsktbl; Var Trk; Var Wt Lftg; Hon Roll; Stck Mrkt Clb; Wtrs Sprts; OK U.

KEELING, C W; Kiefer Jr Sr HS; Kiefer, OK; (2); FCA; Band; Jazz Band; Mrchg Band; Pep Band; VP Soph Cls; Ftbl; Wt Lftg; Hon Roll.

KEELING, JENNIFER; Chickasha Jr HS; Chickasha, OK; (1); Church Yth Grp; Cmnty Wkr; Latin Clb; Church Choir; Phy Thrpst.

KEEN, AUDREY; Roland Sr HS; Muldrow, OK; (2); Church Yth Grp; Cmnty Wkr; Debate Tm; GAA; Quiz Bowl; Spanish Clb; Speech Tm; Nwsp; VP Soph Cls; Var Bsktbl; OU; Massage Thrpy.

KEEN, CHRISTINA L; Ponca City Sr HS; Ponca City, OK; (4); Drama Clb; Office Aide; Teachers Aide; Chorus; Orch; Hon Roll; Senatorial Page; Peer Tutor For Disabled Peers; OK ST Univ; Elem Ed.

KEEN, STACIA; Plainview HS; Ardmore, OK; (3); Church Yth Grp; Cmnty Wkr; FCA; FHA; Library Aide; Office Aide; SADD; Teachers Aide; Chorus; School Musical; UCO; Comp Prgmr.

KEENAN, KATHRYN; Plainview HS; Ardmore, OK; (2); FHA; Natl Beta Clb; Drill Tm; Rptr Nwsp; Hon Roll.

KEENAN, LARRY D; Velma Alma HS; Countyline, OK; (3); Church Yth Grp; JA; Natl FFA Org; SADD; Stage Crew; VP Frsh Cls; VP Soph Cls; Sec Jr Cls; High Hon Roll; Hon Roll; Lvstck Jdgng; OSU; Anml Sci.

KEENER, AMANDA S; Hulbert Jr Sr HS; Hulbert, OK; (2); 4-H; Chorus; Var Bsktbl; Var Sftbl; NHS.

KEENEY, SHANE C; Whitesboro Schl; Talihina, OK; (2); Church Yth Grp; FHA; Natl FFA Org; Scholastic Bowl; Spanish Clb; Hon Roll; OK ST Univ; Cmptr Prgmr.

KEESE, DANIELLE; Ft Gibson HS; Fort Gibson, OK; (1); Church Yth Grp; Band; Mrchg Band; Orch; Socr; Sftbl; Swmmng; Gov Hon Prg Awd; High Hon Roll; OK Bapt U.

KEESLING, MELANIE L; Buffalo Jr Sr HS; Buffalo, OK; (3); FBLA; FHA; Chorus; Yrbk; Ofcr Stu Cncl; Hon Roll; NHS; Show Choir; Stu Cncl Sec; FBLA Reprtr; All Amer Schlr; Southwestern OK ST; Bus.

KEETON, CHRISTINA M; Enid Sr HS; Enid, OK; (3); JV Bsktbl; JV Chrldng; JV Socr; JV Sftbl; Cit Awd; 4-H Awd; High Hon Roll; Hon Roll; NHS; Natl Yth Ldrshp Forum Law/Constutn; Crmnl Jstc.

KEETON, DUSTY G; Dickson HS; Ardmore, OK; (3); FCA; SADD; School Play; Yrbk; Bsktbl; Sftbl; Cit Awd; Whos Who In Sprts; Natl His/Govt Awd; Natl Engl Merit Awd.

KEETON, LESLIE; Clinton HS; Clinton, OK; (2); Church Yth Grp; FCA; 4-H; Spanish Clb; Band; Flag Corp; Mrchg Band; Orch; Sec Soph Cls; JV Var Bsktbl; Orthodontist.

KEETON, LORI; Lone Grove HS; Ardmore, OK; (3); Drama Clb; FHA; Math Clb; Model UN; Speech Tm; Color Guard; Mrchg Band; Hon Roll; NHS; U Of OK; Law.

KEEVER, ZACHARY C; Harrah HS; Harrah, OK; (2); 21/153; Church Yth Grp; Computer Clb; FBLA; Letterman Clb; Spanish Clb; Rep Stu Cncl; Var Ftbl; Var Socr; Cit Awd; High Hon Roll; OK U; Bus.

KEFFER, NICOLE R; U S Grant HS; Oklahoma City, OK; (1); ROTC; Color Guard; JV Chrldng; Hon Roll; NHS; Mltry Order Of World Wars Awd Of Merits; Ped Care.

KEIFFER, LOUIS J; Tecumseh HS; Tecumseh, OK; (3); Church Yth Grp; Ftbl; Cit Awd; High Hon Roll; Hon Roll; NHS; Life Guide; Chem Engrg.

KEIL, STEPHENIE; Clinton HS; Clinton, OK; (1); Church Yth Grp; Spanish Clb; Band; Chorus; Church Choir; Mrchg Band; Pep Band; All Rgn Hnr Band; Short Grass Hnr Band; All Rgn Hnr Choir; Music.

KEILHOLZ, NATHAN M; North Intermediate HS; Pryor, OK; (1); German Clb; Hon Roll; Pres Acad Fit Awd; Awd For Giving A Math Tchr The Highest Blood Pressure; Harvard Bus Coll; Bus Mrktg.

KEIM, LENICE; Coweta HS; Coweta, OK; (3); Sec FHA; HOBY; Rptr SADD; Nwsp; Yrbk; VP Frsh Cls; VP Soph Cls; Rep Stu Cncl; Var JV Bsktbl; NHS; NSU Media Day Awds; OIPA Cmptns; Schlstc Press Assn; Phys Thrpy.

KEINROTH, LEAH; Hennessey HS; Hennessey, OK; (3); 2/64; Church Yth Grp; FCA; FHA; Chorus; VP Soph Cls; VP Jr Cls; JV Bsktbl; Var JV Chrldng; Hon Roll; NHS.

KEITH, ASHLEY; Jenks HS; Tulsa, OK; (4); 113/448; DECA; Spanish Clb; Teachers Aide; Ofcr Stu Cncl; Hon Roll; Sec Spirit Comm; Acad Ltr; Northeastern ST Univ.

KEITH, DERIK K; Dibble Jr Sr HS; Blanchard, OK; (2); 4-H; Natl FFA Org; JV Bsktbl; 4-H Awd; High Hon Roll; Hon Roll; OSU; Vet/Wldlf Biolgst.

KEITH, KAREN E; B T Washington HS; Tulsa, OK; (1); Church Yth Grp; Cmnty Wkr; Chinese Clb; Acad Ltr.

KEITH, KATHY; Central HS; Tulsa, OK; (2); GAA; JA; Score Keeper; Var JV Tennis; Var JV Vllybl; Hon Roll; NHS; TU; Oceangrphy.

KEITH, RACHEL K; B T Washington HS; Tulsa, OK; (4); Church Yth Grp; Cmnty Wkr; French Clb; Science Clb; Spanish Clb; Rep Frsh Cls; NHS; Natl Art Hnr Soc; Culinary Clb Co-Fndr & Chief Of Actvts; Acad Ltr; U Of TX Austin.

KEITH JR, STANLEY; Clinton HS; Clinton, OK; (2); Band; School Play; JV Bsktbl; Var Ftbl; Trk; Wt Lftg; High Hon Roll.

KELEHER, KATY; Edmond North HS; Edmond, OK; (3); Church Yth Grp; Ofcr FCA; VP JA; Rep Stu Cncl; Var JV Chrldng; Gym; Var Trk; Hon Roll; Stu Venture Yth Ldr; Bus Mrktng.

KELIN, JOHN K; Sapulpa Sr HS; Sapulpa, OK; (3); 39/300; FBLA; Scholastic Bowl; Var Bsbl; Hon Roll; NHS; Spanish NHS; Mck Trl; Cmptr Sci.

KELLAM, DAVID; Eisenhower Sr HS; Lawton, OK; (4); Drama Clb; Intnl Clb; Letterman Clb; Model UN; Band; Mrchg Band; School Play; Nwsp; Rep Soph Cls; Hon Roll; NCTE Wrtng Achvt Awd; Acad Decath Tm; Wabash Coll; Polysci.

KELLER, KENNETH L; Putnam City West HS; Warr Acres, OK; (4); Latin Clb; Orch; High Hon Roll; Hon Roll; Frosh Ldrshp & Meinders Bus Schlsps; OCU; Bus; Comp Tech.

KELLEY, ASHLEY M; Union Intermediate HS; Tulsa, OK; (1); 71/866; Church Yth Grp; Cmnty Wkr; FCA; Spanish Clb; Drill Tm; Rep Frsh Cls; Hon Roll; Jr NHS; NHS; Amer All Star Drill Tm; Yth Grp Mission Trp Coord.

KELLEY, BRIEN T; Bishop Kelley HS; Tulsa, OK; (3); FCA; JV Var Bsbl; JV Var Bsktbl; High Hon Roll; Hon Roll; NHS; Boys ST 96; Church Yth Grp.

KELLEY, DAVA; Dewar Jr-Sr HS; Dewar, OK; (4); 1/28; FHA; Teachers Aide; Sec Sr Cls; High Hon Roll; NHS; Val; OSU; Acctng.

KELLEY, JAMIE R; Del City HS; Del City, OK; (3); Art Clb; Treas DECA; Var Vllybl; Jr NHS; Multiculture Clb Mem; OU; Pediatrics.

KELLEY, JONATHAN L; Pryor Sr HS; Pryor, OK; (2); Hon Roll; Ed Tlnt Srch.

KELLEY, KATHY; Metro Christian Acad; Tulsa, OK; (4); 1/71; Church Yth Grp; Cmnty Wkr; Drama Clb; FCA; Key Clb; Pep Clb; SADD; Teachers Aide; Varsity Clb; Chorus; Miss MCA; Girl Of Yr; Miss OK Homcmng Qn 96; U Of OK; Psych.

KELLEY, KRISTY A; Del City HS; Del City, OK; (2); French Clb; Chorus; Bsktbl Mgr; OSU; Neonatal.

KELLEY, LESLIE; Will Rogers HS; Tulsa, OK; (4); 17/179; Spanish Clb; Hon Roll; NHS; DECA; Tulsa JC; PT.

KELLEY, LISA M; West Moore HS; Oklahoma City, OK; (3); DECA; Spanish Clb; Chorus; 1st Pl St DECA Career Dev Conf; UCO; Bus.

KELLEY, MARCY R; Okmulgee HS; Okmulgee, OK; (4); Church Yth Grp; FCA; Letterman Clb; Red Cross Aide; Spanish Clb; VICA; Band; Mrchg Band; Pep Band; Yrbk; Northeastern ST Univ; Bus.

KELLEY, SETH R; Mc Alester HS; Mcalester, OK; (3); Am Leg Boys St; Office Aide; Spanish Clb; Var L Bsbl; Pol Sci.

KELLEY, SHAUN M; Putnam City West HS; Bethany, OK; (3); Art Clb; JV Bsbl; JV Golf; Hon Roll; NHS; OK ST Univ.

KELLEY, STEPHANIE A; Geronimo Jr Sr HS; Duncan, OK; (4); Church Yth Grp; 4-H; FHA; Girl Scts; Library Aide; Math Clb; Natl FFA Org; Scholastic Bowl; Science Clb; Teachers Aide; OSU.

KELLIHER, SARAH J; Bishop Kelley HS; Tulsa, OK; (3); Drama Clb; French Clb; Rptr Nwsp; Hon Roll; NHS; Frnch Awds; Piano Awds; Multi-Yr Listee; OK ST Univ; Psych/Vet Med.

KELLINGTON, DENNIS; Midwest City HS; Midwest City, OK; (4); 64/421; FCA; SADD; Church Choir; Ofcr Jr Cls; Ofcr Sr Cls; Ftbl; Hon Roll; Jr NHS; NHS; Prfct Atten Awd; Boys St Delg; FCA Pres; OK ST U; Phys Ed.

KELLOGG, JENEAL; Kiowa Jr-Sr HS; Kiowa, OK; (4); 5/23; Am Leg Aux Girls St; Rptr 4-H; Sec FHA; Office Aide; Rptr Nwsp; Pres Soph Cls; Rptr Jr Cls; Rptr Sr Cls; JV L Bsktbl; JV L Sftbl; Yth Alive; Multiple Yr Listing; Law.

KELLOGG, SONYA; Sentinel HS; Sentinel, OK; (1); 1/40; Church Yth Grp; Sec 4-H; FHA; Quiz Bowl; Chorus; Rep Stu Cncl; JV Bsktbl; High Hon Roll; Val; Cmnty Wkr; All Around Fresh Girl; Showing Livestock; Stock Market Team.

KELLY, ARON; Holdenville HS; Holdenville, OK; (3); Am Leg Boys St; VP Church Yth Grp; Debate Tm; Drama Clb; Natl Beta Clb; Quiz Bowl; Scholastic Bowl; Chorus; Church Choir; School Musical.

KELLY, DOUG B; Bartlesville Sr HS; Bartlesville, OK; (2); Boy Scts; Church Yth Grp; French Clb; Quiz Bowl; Spanish Clb; Gtr & Kybrd; Bnd.

KELLY, JEFF; Edmond North HS; Edmond, OK; (4); 23/336; Church Yth Grp; FCA; Math Clb; Mu Alpha Theta; Spanish Clb; SADD; Rep Sr Cls; Rep Stu Cncl; Var Capt Bsktbl; Jr NHS; OK Hon Soc; Acad Ltr 3 Yrs; Engrng.

KELLY, JELANI RENAULD JAMOR; Oklahoma Christian Schl; Oklahoma City, OK; (1); Drama Clb; FCA; Math Tm; Speech Tm; Ofcr Stu Cncl; JV Var Bsktbl; Swmmng; High Hon Roll; Hon Roll; NSYMCA 50 Brst Strk St Rcrd; Natl Swm Tm Qulfr; Natl AAU Bsktbl Tm; Natl Math Hnr UCLA; Duke; Math.

KELLY, RACHELLE; Moore HS; Moore, OK; (4); 58/549; JA; Ed Nwsp; Ed Yrbk; Hon Roll; Jr NHS; Recived OCCC Frosh Schlsp; OCCC; Elem Ed.

KELLY, RENEA; Moore HS; Moore, OK; (2); 41/640; Church Yth Grp; German Clb; JV Bsktbl; JV Trk; Var Cit Awd; Hon Roll; Jr NHS; Outstndg German Stu Awd; Ltr Pin; Schlstc Team 94-95; Phys Thrpy.

KELLY, SARA B; Cleveland Sr HS; Cleveland, OK; (4); 9/89; Church Yth Grp; FCA; Key Clb; Math Clb; Quiz Bowl; Spanish Clb; SADD; Yrbk; High Hon Roll; NHS; Nrthestrn ST Univ; Elem Ed.

KELLY, SHEENA; Perry Sr HS; Perry, OK; (3); 20/105; Church Yth Grp; FCA; FHA; Orch; Nwsp; Bsktbl; Crs Cntry; Trk; High Hon Roll; Jr NHS; Northern OK Coll; Med.

KELMAN, BRANDI; Comanche HS; Duncan, OK; (4); FHA; German Clb; Science Clb; Rep Stu Cncl; Var Bsktbl; High Hon Roll; Jr NHS; NHS; Val.

KELSEY, KRISLYN G; Union Sr HS; Tulsa, OK; (3); FBLA; Art Clb; Spanish Clb; Pom Pon; High Hon Roll; Jr NHS; NHS; Pres Acad Fit Awd.

KELSO, CRYSTAL; Guthrie Sr HS; Guthrie, OK; (3); #9 in class; Sec Church Yth Grp; HOBY; SADD; Pres Frsh Cls; Pres Jr Cls; Rep Stu Cncl; Capt Var Socr; Capt L Sftbl; High Hon Roll; DARE Role Model; Med.

KELSO, KIMBERLY D; West Jr HS; Oklahoma City, OK; (1); Spanish Clb; High Hon Roll; Jr NHS; Soc Studies Awd World Hstry; OU; Doctor.

KEMERLEY, JOSEPH; Bridge Creek HS; Blanchard, OK; (3); 6/56; Church Yth Grp; FCA; HOBY; Spanish Clb; Jazz Band; Mrchg Band; Orch; Var L Crs Cntry; High Hon Roll; JV Trk; Dncng Msct; U OK; Arch.

KEMP, RONALD J; Yukon Middle HS; Yukon, OK; (2); Cmnty Wkr; Band; Jazz Band; Mrchg Band; Pep Band; School Musical; School Play; Hon Roll; NHS; AT&T Poster Cont Wnnr 1st Pl; T-Ball Scorekeeper & Asst Coach Vol; Natl Anthem Trumpet Solo Grad.

KEMPER, CYNDY D; Woodward HS; Woodward, OK; (1); Drama Clb; Pep Clb; Spanish Clb; School Play; Stage Crew; Yrbk; Mgr(s); Powder Puff Ftbl; Socr; Prfct Atten Awd.

KEMPER, JASON; Woodward HS; Woodward, OK; (4); 18/146; Boy Scts; Church Yth Grp; FCA; Spanish Clb; Chorus; School Musical; Var Bsbl; High Hon Roll; NHS; Pres Schlr; Southwestern OK ST U; Phar.

KENAGA, TRACI L; Blackwell HS; Blackwell, OK; (3); Am Leg Aux Girls St; Hosp Aide; Pep Clb; Red Cross Aide; Chorus; Church Choir; Hon Roll; NHS; OSU; Ed.

KENDALL, JARROD D; East Central HS; Tulsa, OK; (2); Church Yth Grp; FCA; Office Aide; Science Clb; Service Clb; Church Choir; Nwsp; Rep Stu Cncl; Hon Roll; NHS; Soloist At Chrch; OK Bapt U; Bapt Music Minstr.

KENDALL, TRICIA A; Claremore Sr HS; Claremore, OK; (2); Church Yth Grp; Pep Clb; Band; Chorus; Church Choir; Mrchg Band; Pep Band; Hon Roll; Prfct Atten Awd; Rec Sftbl; Claremore; Comps.

KENDRICK, JENNIFER; Clinton HS; Clinton, OK; (1); FHA; Chorus; Chrldng; Hon Roll; Gymnstcs; Elem Ed.

KENDRICK, MONICA; Collinsville HS; Collinsville, OK; (4); 1/102; Church Yth Grp; Cmnty Wkr; FCA; Office Aide; Quiz Bowl; School Play; Bsktbl; Tennis; High Hon Roll; Hon Roll; Vtd Mst Likly Suceed Sr Cls; Math Awd; Intrntl Frgn Lang Awd; Crmnl Jstc.

KENNEDY, CASSIE; Guthrie Sr HS; Guthrie, OK; (3); Church Yth Grp; 4-H; Key Clb; Natl FFA Org; ROTC; Science Clb; Drill Tm; Campfire; Vlntrs; Color Guard; Oklahoma City U; Vet Med.

KENNEDY, EMILY. M; Stillwater Sr HS; Stillwater, OK; (2); 1/400; French Clb; Natl Beta Clb; Church Choir; Ed Rptr Nwsp; Yrbk; JV L Tennis; High Hon Roll; Var Schlr; 1st United Meth Yth; Builders Clb VP; Writer; Ed.

KENNEDY, ERIN E; Edmond Memorial HS; Edmond, OK; (3); 1/380; Church Yth Grp; Cmnty Wkr; Hist FCA; French Clb; VP Key Clb; SADD; Chorus; Church Choir; School Musical; School Play; Stu Of Mnth Elks Lodge; Outs Actress Edmond Mem HS Play; Bus Comm.

KENNEDY, KATIE E; Amber Pocasset Jr Sr HS; Amber, OK; (3); Church Yth Grp; FCA; 4-H; Sec Natl FFA Org; Spanish Clb; Sec Frsh Cls; Sec Soph Cls; Var Co-Capt Bsktbl; Intrml Sftbl; Prfct Atten Awd; SNU; Acctng.

KENNEDY, KIMBERLY D; Wilson HS; Ardmore, OK; (3); 3/46; FCA; FHA; JA; Natl Beta Clb; Natl FFA Org; Office Aide; Quiz Bowl; Chorus; Chrldng; High Hon Roll; U Of Cntrl OK.

KENNEDY, KYLE D; El Reno Sr HS; El Reno, OK; (2); Church Yth Grp; 4-H; Natl FFA Org; Quiz Bowl; Scholastic Bowl; 4-H Awd; High Hon Roll; OK ST U; Vet Med.

KENNEDY, LAURA L; Union Sr HS; Broken Arrow, OK; (4); 100/616; VP German Clb; Band; Color Guard; Jazz Band; Mrchg Band; Orch; Pep Band; School Musical; Sftbl; NHS; German Hnr Soc; Tri-M Music Hnr Clb Sec; 3-E Awd; OSU; Zoology.

KENNEDY, PENELOPE M; El Reno Sr HS; El Reno, OK; (3); Church Yth Grp; Drama Clb; FHA; FTA; Intnl Clb; Speech Tm; School Play; Stage Crew; Prfct Atten Awd; Photographer.

KENNEDY, TRINA M; Del City HS; Oklahoma City, OK; (3); Church Yth Grp; Cmnty Wkr; FCA; Scholastic Bowl; Spanish Clb; SADD; Teachers Aide; Church Choir; Ofcr Stu Cncl; Bsktbl; Ldrshp & Cmnty Clss; OK Baptist U; Phys Thrpy.

KENNEDY, WES D; Brink Jr HS; Oklahoma City, OK; (1); Band; Mrchg Band; Orch; Jr NHS; Prfct Atten Awd; Habitat For Hum; OK Univ; Vet.

KENNELL, CHRISTOPHER R; Ninnekah HS; Chickasha, OK; (2); FCA; Pep Clb; Var Bsbl; Var Chrldng; Wt Lftg; Ntl Merit Schol; Comp.

KENNEY, JOHN GRAHAM; Bishop Mcguinness HS; Oklahoma City, OK; (4); Church Yth Grp; Cmnty Wkr; FCA; FBLA; German Clb; Science Clb; High Hon Roll; NHS; Ntl Merit SF; Jr Rtrn; Mc Guiness Physcs Awd; FBLA Pres; Mc Guinness Engrng & Sci Soc Treas.

KENNEY, TIM; Central Mid-HS; Norman, OK; (2); Latin Clb; Mu Alpha Theta; Quiz Bowl; Chorus; Swing Chorus; Cit Awd; Gov Hon Prg Awd; Hon Roll; Masonic Stdnt; Classic Soccer; Jazz Choir; Law/CPA/MBA.

KENNY, JOHN; Cascia Hall Prep School; Tulsa, OK; (1); Cmnty Wkr; Spanish Clb; Chorus; Bsktbl; Socr; Hon Roll.

KENT, CARRIE M; Vinita HS; Big Cabin, OK; (3); Church Yth Grp; Debate Tm; Math Clb; NFL; Red Cross Aide; Science Clb; Spanish Clb; Rep Stu Cncl; High Hon Roll; Hon Roll; RYLA Camp 11th Grd; Rdlgst.

KENT, RACHEL; Bartlesville Mid HS; Bartlesville, OK; (1); Church Yth Grp; Spanish Clb; Band; Mrchg Band; Orch; Capt Chrldng; Hon Roll; Spirit Comm; Intl Frgn Lang Awd; Lwyr/Pltcn.

KERBO, TARA; Liberty Acad; Shawnee, OK; (1); Church Yth Grp; FCA; Spanish Clb; Chorus; Church Choir; Bsktbl; Chrldng; Trk; Hon Roll.

KERBY, JENNIFER; Mulhall Orlando HS; Orlando, OK; (3); 1/14; FHA; German Clb; GAA; HOBY; Office Aide; Band; Nwsp; Yrbk; Rep Frsh Cls; Pres Soph Cls; Hnrs Rcptn From OSU Alumni; OK ST U; Engrng.

KERFOOT, AMY B; Bethany HS; Oklahoma City, OK; (3); Church Yth Grp; Cmnty Wkr; Drama Clb; Key Clb; Office Aide; Spanish Clb; Speech Tm; Teachers Aide; Church Choir; School Play; Ballet & Jazz; Chrch Plays Coaching & Stage Crew; Chrch Nursery; AR ST; Soc Svcs.

KERN, EMILY C; B T Washington HS; Tulsa, OK; (2); Church Yth Grp; Sec German Clb; Church Choir; Ed Nwsp; Ofcr Frsh Cls; L Var Socr; High Hon Roll; Hon Roll; NHS.

KERN, JOI I; Western Heights Sr HS; Oklahoma City, OK; (1); #21 in class; Church Yth Grp; Cmnty Wkr; Library Aide; Office Aide; Teachers Aide; Church Choir; Hon Roll; Disabled Amer Vet Auxilary; Jr Page Dsabled Amer Vets; Pdtrc Aides/Jvnl Diabetes Fndtn; KS U; Hlth Admin.

KERN, KATIE; Edmond North HS; Edmond, OK; (2); 36/420; FCA; Spanish Clb; Sec Soph Cls; JV Chrldng; NHS; Jr Hnr Soc; Psych.

KERN, KRIS P; Putnam City West HS; Bethany, OK; (3); 26/320; Rep Frsh Cls; Ofcr Stu Cncl; Var Bsbl; Hon Roll; NHS.

KERN, MATTHEW D; Oklahoma Sch Of Science & Math; Cartwright, OK; (3); Quiz Bowl; Pres Frsh Cls; Pres Soph Cls; L Bsbl; Tech Stu Assn Natl Champ; Golden Gloves Boxing; Mech Engrng.

KERNS, AUTUMN L; Bridge Creek HS; Blanchard, OK; (1); 10/75; Spanish Clb; Lawyer.

KERNS, MICHAEL R; Mc Alester HS; Mcalester, OK; (4); Cmnty Wkr; FHA; Natl FFA Org; VICA; Gym; Wt Lftg; Wrstlng; High Hon Roll; Hon Roll; Jr NHS; Eastern OK; Cmptr Sci.

KERNS, REBECCA; Muskogee HS; Muskogee, OK; (3); Am Leg Aux Girls St; Church Yth Grp; Cmnty Wkr; FCA; French Clb; GAA; Teachers Aide; Varsity Clb; VP Frsh Cls; Var Bsktbl; Intrn House Rep Staggs 95-96; All-Dist Fst Ptch & Sccr 95-96; Wrld Trd Cmptn Fnlst; Law.

KERNTKE, ELIZABETH; Stillwater Jr HS; Stillwater, OK; (1); Natl Beta Clb; Orch; High Hon Roll; Rdng; Clscl Music; Violin Superior Rtgs; Aerospc Engr/Spc Sci.

KERNTKE, MATT H; Stillwater Sr HS; Stillwater, OK; (2); German Clb; Math Tm; Yrbk; Hon Roll; Play Guitar; Bowling; OK ST Univ; His.

KERR, APRIL L; Medford Schl; Medford, OK; (2); 4/20; Church Yth Grp; FCA; FHA; Quiz Bowl; JV Bsktbl; L Sftbl; Hon Roll; NHS; 4 Yr; Med.

KERR, JOANNA S; Morrison Public Schl; Morrison, OK; (1); 1/40; Cmnty Wkr; Letterman Clb; Spanish Clb; Nwsp; Rep Frsh Cls; Bsktbl; Chrldng; Sftbl; Trk; High Hon Roll; OK ST Univ; Med.

KERR, KASSANDRA J L; Calumet Schl; Calumet, OK; (1); Church Yth Grp; Drama Clb; Quiz Bowl; Chorus; Church Choir; School Musical; School Play; Yrbk.

KERR, REBECCA; Will Rogers HS; Tulsa, OK; (4); 1/201; Church Yth Grp; English Clb; Band; Nwsp; Yrbk; Sec Sr Cls; Treas NHS; Val; Key Clb; Scholastic Bowl; OK Indian Hnr Soc; Camp Fire Boys & Girls; Woote Lo Medallion Camp Fire Highest Awd; U Of Tulsa.

KERR, STEPHEN; Medford Schl; Medford, OK; (1); Church Yth Grp; FCA; Letterman Clb; Quiz Bowl; Band; Church Choir; School Play; L Ftbl; Wt Lftg; Hon Roll.

KERR, WHITNEY D; Clayton Jr Sr HS; Clayton, OK; (2); Church Yth Grp; Debate Tm; Drama Clb; 4-H; FHA; HOBY; Library Aide; NFL; Quiz Bowl; Speech Tm; Law.

KERSEY, JON; Asher Schl; Asher, OK; (2); Debate Tm; School Play; VP Frsh Cls; Var Bsbl; Var JV Bsktbl; Hon Roll; Ntl Merit Ltr; Sal; Med.

KERSHEN, KATHERINE S; Norman Sr HS; Norman, OK; (4); 1/700; Church Yth Grp; Cmnty Wkr; JCL; Latin Clb; Model UN; Sec Mu Alpha Theta; Orch; Rep Stu Cncl; JV Socr; Hon Roll; Tomorrows Ldrs; Octagon Clb Sec; Arts Rcgntn & Tlnt Srch Hnrb Mntn Poetry; Chem.

KESNER, JARED W; Macarthur Sr HS; Lawton, OK; (3); Hon Roll.

KESSLER, ANNA S; Charles Page HS; Sand Springs, OK; (3); 24/364; Am Leg Aux Girls St; Church Yth Grp; Cmnty Wkr; FCA; Service Clb; Spanish Clb; SADD; Acpl Chr; Church Choir; School Musical; Anchor Clb Sr Coord; Baylor U; Music; Voice.

KESTER, AMBER J; Geary Jr Sr HS; Greenfield, OK; (2); Band; Mrchg Band; JV Bsktbl; Var Chrldng; Var Sftbl; Hon Roll.

KESTER, BRANSON; Kingfisher HS; Kingfisher, OK; (2); 1/100; Computer Clb; Quiz Bowl; Scholastic Bowl; Band; Jazz Band; Mrchg Band; Pep Band; High Hon Roll; Tennis.

KETAKEA, LAHUNTA M; Mc Loud HS; Mc Loud, OK; (2); FHA; Scholastic Bowl; Hon Roll; NHS; OK Hnr Soc; UCLA; PT.

KETCHUM, KERI; Hugo HS; Hugo, OK; (4); 28/101; FHA; Office Aide; Science Clb; Spanish Clb; VICA; Yrbk; Hon Roll; OK ST Senate Page; OK Honor Soc; Kiwanis Stu Of Month; Southeastern OK ST U.

KETTER, AARON A; Westmore HS; Oklahoma City, OK; (1); L Var Socr; High Hon Roll; Jr NHS; Pres Ed Awds Prgm; Schlrshp Awd.

KETTER, CHRIS; Oklahoma Christian Schl; Edmond, OK; (4); 4/37; Cmnty Wkr; Scholastic Bowl; Ed Yrbk; Golf; High Hon Roll; Engr.

KETTER, ELLEN; Oklahoma Christian Schl; Edmond, OK; (1); Cmnty Wkr; Speech Tm; Pres Frsh Cls; High Hon Roll; Competitive Dance; 1st Pl Orgnl Oratory Speech Trnmt.

KETTER, GABRIELLE; Owasso Sr HS; Owasso, OK; (2); English Clb; Chrldng; Hon Roll; All Amer Schlrs; All Star Chdrldng; Gymnstcs Coach.

KEY, ASHLEY D; Colbert Jr Sr HS; Colbert, OK; (3); Church Yth Grp; FCA; 4-H; Office Aide; Spanish Clb; Yrbk; Treas Jr Cls; Bsktbl; Hon Roll; NHS.

KEY, BRIAN A; Union Sr HS; Tulsa, OK; (3); 87/741; Rep Stu Cncl; Var Golf; Mgr(s); High Hon Roll; High Hon Roll; NHS; Prfct Atten Awd; Pres Acad Fit Awd; Sci, Hist Awds.

KEY, CORBY W; Lone Grove HS; Lone Grove, OK; (3); #24 in class; FCA; Math Clb; Science Clb; Stage Crew; Var Bsbl; Hon Roll; NHS; Prfct Atten Awd; OSU; Physics Or Medicine.

KEY, LISA; Wellston Schl; Wellston, OK; (3); FCA; FHA; SADD; Band; Drill Tm; Stat Bsbl; Var Chrldng; Var Sftbl; NHS; Emerg Med Tech.

KEY, LISA D; Hobart HS; Hobart, OK; (2); Church Yth Grp; Cmnty Wkr; Dance Clb; FCA; FHA; FTA; GAA; Spanish Clb; Speech Tm; Teachers Aide; Shortgrass Plyhouse Little Theater; Piano; Flwshp Chrstn Ath; OK City Univ; Pre Law.

KEYES, KIMBERLEY A; Jenks HS; Tulsa, OK; (3); Mu Alpha Theta; NFL; Spanish Clb; Thesps; Stage Crew; Pre-Medicine.

KEYS, WESLEY; Kiefer Jr Sr HS; Kiefer, OK; (4); 2/40; FCA; Letterman Clb; Natl Beta Clb; Red Cross Aide; Varsity Clb; Variety Show; Rep Frsh Cls; Rep Soph Cls; VP Jr Cls; VP Sr Cls; Vo Tech Natl Hnr Soc; CPR Instr; Chiropracter.

KEYSER, KRISTEN T; Bethany HS; Bethany, OK; (2); Church Yth Grp; Spanish Clb; Ed Nwsp; Rep Stu Cncl; NHS; Wrtng; Eng.

KEYSER, KRISTIE; Collinsville HS; Collinsville, OK; (4); 32/96; Church Yth Grp; Girl Scts; Chorus; School Musical; School Play; VP Soph Cls; Rep Jr Cls; Rep Stu Cncl; Socr; Hon Roll; Super Rtngs Vocal Solo St Cmptn; Ldng Role Jr Play/Ldng Role 1995; Chorus Royalty; NSU; Sci.

KHALID, ABDALLA; Midwest City HS; Oklahoma City, OK; (3); Cmnty Wkr; Varsity Clb; Band; Mrchg Band; Orch; Fld Hcky; Golf; Capt Trk; Hon Roll; Concert Band; DECA; NC U.

KHANNA, GORAV; Duncan HS; Duncan, OK; (3); 1/250; French Clb; FBLA; Letterman Clb; Math Tm; SADD; Tennis; Hon Roll; NHS; Spanish NHS.

KHAVARI, SHAWN; Shawnee Sr HS; Shawnee, OK; (4); 2/280; Boy Scts; Church Yth Grp; Cmnty Wkr; Intnl Clb; Math Clb; Science Clb; Tennis; NHS; U OK; Med.

KHODADADIAN, SHIEDEH; Okemah HS; Okemah, OK; (1); FHA; Science Clb; Band; Mrchg Band; Pep Band; Cit Awd; Hon Roll; Prfct Atten Awd; OU; Dr.

KHORRAMDEL, KAVON; Western Heights Sr HS; Oklahoma City, OK; (4); Chess Clb; DECA; FHA; Office Aide; Ftbl; Socr; Wt Lftg; St Gregorys.

KIDD, KASEY N; Clinton HS; Clinton, OK; (3); Pres FBLA; FHA; Hosp Aide; Spanish Clb; Teachers Aide; Band; Drm Mjr(t); Mrchg Band; Var Socr; Bus.

KIDDY, CHRISTINA D; Nathan Hale HS; Tulsa, OK; (3); Drama Clb; FTA; Girl Scts; Office Aide; Teachers Aide; Thesps; School Play; High Hon Roll; Hon Roll; NHS; Phy Thrpst.

KIDWELL, JOE R; Ketchum HS; Spavinaw, OK; (3); 1/30; Am Leg Boys St; Church Yth Grp; Quiz Bowl; Scholastic Bowl; Science Clb; Rep Frsh Cls; Pres Soph Cls; Pres Jr Cls; VP Stu Cncl; Capt Bsktbl; OU; Phy Thrpst.

KIESEL, RYAN D; Seminole Jr Sr HS; Seminole, OK; (2); Debate Tm; Drama Clb; Scholastic Bowl; Thesps; School Play; Stage Crew; Hon Roll; Model Congress Senator & Best Speaker; Outstdng Sci Stu.

KIEST, TOSHA M; Central Schl; Sallisaw, OK; (3); VP Art Clb; Phtg Yrbk; Hon Roll; Hnrs Govt; Law/Vet.

KIGHT, MANDIE; Talinina HS; Talihina, OK; (4); 14/38; Office Aide; Speech Tm; Yrbk; Hon Roll; Chap FFA Rep, Jr Advsr, Degree; E OK St Col; Acctng.

KILBOURNE, MICHON R; Enid Sr HS; Enid, OK; (2); 172/431; Church Yth Grp; Cmnty Wkr; FCA; GAA; Library Aide; Office Aide; Pep Clb; Service Clb; SADD; Teachers Aide; Soloist; Dir Choir; Pres Comm Chldrns Choir; Spellman Coll; Judge.

KILBURG, SARAH K; Will Rogers HS; Tulsa, OK; (3); English Clb; French Clb; Key Clb; Drm Mjr(t); Mrchg Band; Hon Roll; Tulsa Metro Hnr Band; Selected By Tulsa Rotary Clb To Attend Camp Enterprise; OSU; Music; Vet Medicine.

KILE, CHRIS J; Union Sr HS; Tulsa, OK; (4); 49/648; Boy Scts; FCA; Letterman Clb; Service Clb; Teachers Aide; Ftbl; High Hon Roll; Hon Roll; Jr NHS; NHS; Eagle Sct; All-Dist Ftbl; Engr.

KILGORE, ADAM D; Sapulpa Sr HS; Sapulpa, OK; (2); Church Yth Grp; JV Bsbl; JV Var Tennis; Cit Awd; Hon Roll; Pres Schlr; Weightlifting; Ftbl; OU; Engrng.

KILGORE, ALAN R; Webster HS; Tulsa, OK; (3); 3/180; Var Bsbl; JV Bsktbl; Var Capt Crs Cntry; Hon Roll; NHS; Ntl Merit Ltr; U Of OK; Acctng.

KILGORE, DARLA L; Webster HS; Tulsa, OK; (1); Bsktbl; Sftbl; Hon Roll; Jr NHS; U Of OK.

KILGORE, KEVIN C; Wetumka Jr Sr HS; Wetumka, OK; (3); #6 in class; Natl FFA Org; Hon Roll; OSU; Tech.

KILGORE, KRISTI M; Westmoore HS; Oklahoma City, OK; (3); Church Yth Grp; Cmnty Wkr; Girl Scts; Swmmng; High Hon Roll; Hon Roll; Jr NHS; NHS; Close Up WA 96; Red Cross Swim Instr; Arch Engrng.

KILLGORE, CLINT W; Sallisaw HS; Sallisaw, OK; (1); Letterman Clb; Natl FFA Org; JV Ftbl; JV Trk; JV Var Wt Lftg; Cit Awd; Hon Roll; Rodeo; Pro Ftbl Plyr/Vet.

KILLIAN, TAMIKA D; B T Washington HS; Tulsa, OK; (4); 17/264; Cmnty Wkr; Debate Tm; Hosp Aide; Red Cross Aide; Sec Spanish Clb; Teachers Aide; Flag Corp; Ofcr Soph Cls; Ofcr Stu Cncl; NHS; OK ST U; Chem Engrng.

KILLINGSWORTH, CARMEN N; El Reno Sr HS; El Reno, OK; (1); 1/200; Church Yth Grp; Band; Church Choir; Jazz Band; Mrchg Band; L Chrldng; L Vllybl; High Hon Roll; OK U.

KILLINGSWORTH, TAMMY L; Westmoore HS; Oklahoma City, OK; (2); Church Yth Grp; FCA; Spanish Clb; Mgr(s); U Of OK; Bus Mrktng.

KILLMAN, DAVID N; Ponca City Sr HS; Ponca City, OK; (3); FCA; Capt Var Ftbl; Var Capt Trk; Hon Roll; Church Yth Grp; Spanish Clb; Teachers Aide; Rep Stu Cncl; Val; Explorer Post 69 Canoe Racing Team VP; Chi Lamda Rho Pres Elect; Columbia Univ; Pre-Med.

KILLPACK, BRIAN R; Edmond Santa Fe HS; Edmond, OK; (3); 83/329; Boy Scts; Church Yth Grp; Church Choir; Nwsp; Crs Cntry; Eagle Sct; Ricks Coll; Engr.

KIM, AH R; Union Intermediate HS; Tulsa, OK; (2); Church Yth Grp; Key Clb; Church Choir; Orch; NHS; Yth Grp Treas; Northeastrn OK All-Dist String Orch 94-96; Church Korean Tchr.

KIM, CHIN; Apache HS; Apache, OK; (2); 2/50; Art Clb; FHA; German Clb; Scholastic Bowl; VP Jr Cls; Ofcr Stu Cncl; Var Bsktbl; Var Wt Lftg; High Hon Roll; NHS; USAF Acad; Elec Or Comp Engrng.

KIM, MAY; Bridge Creek HS; Tuttle, OK; (3); 1/60; FCA; FBLA; Yrbk; Rep Frsh Cls; Sec Soph Cls; Pres Jr Cls; Hon Roll; NHS; U Of OK; Frgn Lang.

KIM, SALLY SUNGEWN; Bartlesville Sr HS; Bartlesville, OK; (4).

KIM, SEUNG; Moore HS; Moore, OK; (3); 50/550; Church Yth Grp; French Clb; Intnl Clb; Band; Jazz Band; Mrchg Band; Orch; JV Tennis; Jr NHS; NHS; OU; Med.

KIM, SUSIE; Apache HS; Apache, OK; (3); Art Clb; Drama Clb; Key Clb; Scholastic Bowl; Chorus; School Musical; School Play; Ofcr Stu Cncl; Hon Roll; Congressional Page; U Of OK; Medicine.

KIM, YOUNG R; Central Jr HS; Fort Sill, OK; (2); Spanish Clb; Orch; Hon Roll; Jr NHS; Prfct Atten Awd.

KIMAK, MEREDITH A; Enid Sr HS; Enid, OK; (3); 65/445; Church Yth Grp; Band; Mrchg Band; Pep Band; Rptr Nwsp; Hon Roll; NHS; Cmnty Wkr; Letterman Clb; Teachers Aide; Mock Trial; Big Bros/Big Sistrs; Psych.

KIMBALL, HOLLY M; Tahlequah Sr HS; Tahlequah, OK; (3); Church Yth Grp; FCA; Chorus; JV Var Bsktbl; JV Var Trk; Hon Roll; Jr NHS; NHS; Pres Acad Fit Awd; Phys Thpy.

KIMBALL, JASON M C; Del City HS; Del City, OK; (3); #30 in class; Cmnty Wkr; Hosp Aide; Band; Chorus; Mrchg Band; Orch; Pep Band; Swing Chorus; Jr NHS; NHS; U Of Cntrl OK; Mus Ed.

KIMBALL, KATIE L; Tishomingo HS; Tishomingo, OK; (3); Art Clb; Church Yth Grp; FHA; Yrbk; Mgr Bsbl; Hon Roll; Art Awds.

KIMBERLIN, JOSH M; Pioneer Jr Sr HS; Enid, OK; (2); Band; Okmulgee; Comp Animation.

KIMBLE, CURTIS W; Mc Alester HS; Mcalester, OK; (2); VICA; JV Var Bsktbl; Cit Awd; Prfct Atten Awd; FFA; OSU; Coach.

KIMBLE, LATONYA D; North Intemediate HS; Broken Arrow, OK; (2); Church Yth Grp; Cmnty Wkr; Dance Clb; Drama Clb; French Clb; Library Aide; Math Clb; Pep Clb; Science Clb; Teachers Aide; Interior Dsgn.

KIMBLE, SARAH; Hydro Jr Sr HS; Hydro, OK; (4); 3/18; Am Leg Aux Girls St; Treas Church Yth Grp; Cmnty Wkr; Treas FCA; Capt GAA; Pres Natl FFA Org; Office Aide; Teachers Aide; Church Choir; Pres Frsh Cls; FFA Lvstck Jdgng Team & Lvstck Shwmn; SW OK ST U; Elem Ed.

KIMBLEY, KRISTI R; Bartlesville Sr HS; Bartlesville, OK; (3); FHA; Spanish Clb; Tulsa Jr Col.

KIMBRO, CHRISSY; Bray-Doyle HS; Marlow, OK; (4); 12/33; FCA; 4-H; Natl FFA Org; Rep Sr Cls; Bsktbl; Sftbl; Cameron Univ; Elem Ed.

KIMBROUGH, AMANDA D; Del City HS; Del City, OK; (3); 226/467; Art Clb; Church Yth Grp; Cmnty Wkr; FCA; French Clb; FHA; Pep Clb; SADD; Church Choir; Var JV Socr; Awd Hgst Grade In Wrld Hist; Mat Maid; FL St Uinv; Law.

KIMES, NATHAN; Putnam City HS; Warr Acres, OK; (4); 1/345; Am Leg Boys St; German Clb; Office Aide; Spanish Clb; Var L Crs Cntry; Var Capt Socr; NHS; Ntl Merit Schol; St Schlr; U Of Tulsa.

KIMMEL, JASON; Vanoss Schl; Stratford, OK; (4); 3/48; 4-H; Pres FBLA; Office Aide; Chorus; School Play; Rptr Nwsp; Pres Jr Cls; Pres Sr Cls; Hon Roll; Pres Acad Fit Awd; OK FBLA St Sec; Mtn Plns FBLA Sec 95; E Central U; Bus Admin.

KINCADE, JESSE; White Oak Jr-Sr HS; Big Cabin, OK; (2); Elec Tech.

KINCADE, KIMBERLY; El Reno Sr HS; El Reno, OK; (3); #47 in class; Church Yth Grp; Drama Clb; FTA; Math Clb; Science Clb; Band; Color Guard; Jazz Band; Mrchg Band; Hon Roll; Bus.

KINCAID, ERIN B; Elk City HS; Elk City, OK; (3); Church Yth Grp; Drama Clb; Letterman Clb; Pep Clb; Spanish Clb; Band; School Play; Ofcr Stu Cncl; Hon Roll; Pres Acad Fit Awd; Nazarene Yth Cngrss 95; OU; Elem Ed.

KINCANNON, ERIN; Boise City HS; Boise City, OK; (2); Church Yth Grp; FCA; German Clb; Scholastic Bowl; Ofcr Stu Cncl; JV Var Bsktbl; Var Chrldng; Mgr Trk; NHS; Super Hnr Roll; OK Hnr Soc; Pianist.

KINDELL, AUDREY G; Wagoner Sr HS; Wagoner, OK; (3); 9/130; Treas FBLA; Intnl Clb; Var Scholastic Bowl; Ofcr Stu Cncl; Var Socr; NHS.

KINDER, ARIC D; Bridge Creek HS; Tuttle, OK; (1); 1/75; Church Yth Grp; Bsktbl; High Hon Roll; St Schlr.

KINDER, CHISOLM R; Chattanooga Schl; Frederick, OK; (1); 4/22; Pres Frsh Cls; Ofcr Stu Cncl; Var Bsbl; Var Bsktbl; Hon Roll; Sal; FFA Star Greenhand Awd; Mr Warrior Awd Bsktbl; Ldrshp Awd Bsbl.

KINDER, JENNIFER E; B T Washington HS; Tulsa, OK; (4); 63/264; Church Yth Grp; Cmnty Wkr; Girl Scts; Office Aide; Spanish Clb; Church Choir; Socr; Hon Roll; Jr NHS; NHS; Girl Sct Gold Awd; Acad Ltr; TX Chrstn U.

KINDER, STACY J; Deer Creek HS; Oklahoma City, OK; (2); Church Yth Grp; Cmnty Wkr; FCA; GAA; Office Aide; Science Clb; Spanish Clb; Teachers Aide; Var Mgr(s); Var Score Keeper; OK ST U.

KINDRED, BRIAN N; Blackwell HS; Blackwell, OK; (2); Boy Scts; Chorus; School Musical; Swing Chorus; Ftbl; Trk; Wt Lftg; Cit Awd; Hon Roll; Super Ratin Solo St Vocal Cont.

KINDRED, DAVID; Blackwell HS; Blackwell, OK; (4); Am Leg Boys St; FCA; Office Aide; Pep Clb; Chorus; School Musical; Var Ftbl; Var Trk; Wt Lftg; Hon Roll; Shw Chr; Rnk IV Stu Bnd Bd Dirs; Pr Hlpr.

KINDRICK, CHARISSA; Porum HS; Porum, OK; (1); 3/33; FCA; 4-H; FHA; Nwsp; JV Bsktbl; Var JV Sftbl; Hon Roll.

KINDSFATHER, JARREN N; Erick Jr Sr HS; Erick, OK; (3); 1/31; Church Yth Grp; HOBY; Quiz Bowl; Spanish Clb; Rptr Nwsp; Rep Frsh Cls; Rptr Stu Cncl; Var Bsbl; Var Bsktbl; High Hon Roll; TSA Ntl Chmpns; U Of OK; Phy Asst.

KINDSFATHER, RICKY L; Clinton HS; Clinton, OK; (4); 20/120; Am Leg Boys St; Church Yth Grp; Drama Clb; Teachers Aide; School Play; Hon Roll; NHS; Pres Acad Fit Awd; Cmptr Sci.

KING, AMY K; Drumright HS; Drumright, OK; (1); Cmnty Wkr; Scholastic Bowl; Science Clb; Spanish Clb; Sec Frsh Cls; JV Bsktbl; High Hon Roll; Prfct Atten Awd; Frosh Bsktbl Hmcmng Attdnt; Engl I Awd; OK His Awd; Algebra I Awd; Span I Awd; OSU; Pdtrcn.

KING, BRIAN J; Duncan HS; Duncan, OK; (4); 33/215; Boy Scts; FBLA; German Clb; Quiz Bowl; Scholastic Bowl; SADD; Band; Jazz Band; Mrchg Band; VP Frsh Cls; Chem Engr; Physicist.

KING, BRITNEY M; Indiahoma Schl; Indiahoma, OK; (3); 3/7; FCA; Natl FFA Org; Chorus; School Musical; Swing Chorus; Var Bsktbl; Var Chrldng; Var Sftbl; Var Vllybl; Hon Roll; Pony Clb; Lawton Rangers Rodeo Queen 96.

KING, BRYAN; Coweta HS; Coweta, OK; (4); 16/153; Am Leg Boys St; Church Yth Grp; FCA; FHA; SADD; Treas Jr Cls; Treas Sr Cls; Capt Ftbl; NHS; Pres Acad Fit Awd; OK Coaches Assoc All St All Star Ftbl; Hghst Prs Hnr Chr; Tulsa Wrld All Metro All St Ftbl Hnrb Mntn; Northeaster ST U; Pre-Med.

KING, BRYAN J; Putnam City West HS; Bethany, OK; (3); 39/337; Church Yth Grp; Spanish Clb; SADD; Varsity Clb; Rep Jr Cls; Treas Sr Cls; Rep Stu Cncl; Var L Bsbl; Var L Ftbl; L Wrstlng; Ath Of Week Twice; U Of OK Hnrs Cert; Bsbl Var Ltr; Bo Bowman All Tourny Team; All City Hnrb Mntn; Optometry.

KING, CARLINDA M; Colcord Schl; Colcord, OK; (1); Natl FFA Org; Pres Frsh Cls; Hon Roll; Lvstck Shw; Dry Jdgng; Crps Jdgng.

KING, CAYCE R; El Reno Sr HS; El Reno, OK; (3); #8 in class; Church Yth Grp; FCA; Key Clb; Math Clb; Church Choir; Pres Swing Chorus; Cit Awd; High Hon Roll; NHS; Rotry Yth Ldrshp Awd.

KING, CHERISH; Madill HS; Madill, OK; (2); Church Yth Grp; Dance Clb; Math Clb; Math Tm; Drill Tm; Pom Pon; High Hon Roll; NHS; Pres Acad Fit Awd; Med.

KING, CHRISTIE; Bartlesville Mid HS; Bartlesville, OK; (2); Pres Boy Scts; Church Yth Grp; FBLA; FHA; Spanish Clb; Ofcr Stu Cncl; Var Golf; Hon Roll; Jr NHS; NHS; OSU; Ed.

KING, CHRISTINA; Drumright HS; Drumright, OK; (3); 1/44; Computer Clb; Science Clb; Spanish Clb; JV Var Bsktbl; JV Vllybl; High Hon Roll; NHS; Woodmen Of The World Awd; Comp II Awd; Advncd Bio Awd.

KING, CHRISTINA R; Verden HS; Verden, OK; (3); Scholastic Bowl; Spanish Clb; Speech Tm; School Play; Pres Soph Cls; Pres Jr Cls; High Hon Roll; NHS; Prfct Atten Awd; Pres Acad Fit Awd.

KING, CRYSTAL N; Clayton Jr Sr HS; Clayton, OK; (1); 4-H; Natl FFA Org; Band; Rep Stu Cncl; Var Bsktbl; Var Sftbl; 4-H Awd; Hon Roll; OK ST Univ.

KING, ERIC J; Morris HS; Okmulgee, OK; (3); Band; Jazz Band; Mrchg Band; Pep Band; Yrbk; Hist Frsh Cls; Ofcr Stu Cncl; JV Bsbl; Var Ftbl; L Wt Lftg; Prom & Valentine Comm.

KING, ERIC T; Northeast HS; Midwest City, OK; (3); Hosp Aide; Chorus; School Musical; Var Bsktbl; Hon Roll; Bio Med Pgm 3 Yrs; Math/Sci Gifted Pgm; AAU Smr Bsktbl Leag St/Natls; Mech Engrng.

KING, JAMES W; Walters HS; Walters, OK; (1); Church Yth Grp; School Musical; School Play; Ofcr Bsbl; Bsktbl; Ftbl; High Hon Roll; Hon Roll; OK ST U.

KING, JAMIE; Moore HS; Moore, OK; (4); 32/505; Church Yth Grp; Library Aide; Band; Var L Bsktbl; Var Powder Puff Ftbl; Var L Sftbl; NHS; Val; S W OK ST U; Elem Ed.

KING, JAMIE L; Bixby Sr HS; Bixby, OK; (3); Church Yth Grp; FCA; Intnl Clb; Spanish Clb; SADD; Teachers Aide; Chorus; School Musical; Rep Stu Cncl; Dance Clb; His Clb Elected Stdnt Cncl Rep; Acad Lttr 95-; Jr Optimist Clb.

KING, JENNIFER; Claremore Sr HS; Claremore, OK; (3); Church Yth Grp; Girl Scts; Math Clb; Science Clb; Nwsp; High Hon Roll; NHS; Dance; TU; Comms.

KING, JENNIFER; Stratford Schl; Stratford, OK; (3); 4/46; FHA; Teachers Aide; Chorus; School Musical; Rptr Jr Cls; Cit Awd; High Hon Roll; Hon Roll; NHS; Natl Ldrshp Svc Awd; All Amer Schlr; East Cntrl U.

KING, JEREMY; Choctaw Jr HS; Choctaw, OK; (1); Church Yth Grp; Drama Clb; Intrml Bsktbl; Intrml Ftbl; Intrml Golf; Cit Awd; Jr NHS.

KING, JERMAINE A; Memorial HS; Tulsa, OK; (2); Office Aide; ROTC; Drill Tm; Trk; U MD; Military Law.

KING, JULIE; Haileyville Schl; Hartshorne, OK; (2); 3/40; FCA; Sec FBLA; Natl FFA Org; Rep Frsh Cls; VP Soph Cls; Rep Stu Cncl; Var Bsktbl; Var Chrldng; Var Sftbl; Hon Roll; OK Hnr Soc; Natl Indian Hnr Soc; Var Sftbl; Scndry Ed Tchr; Coach.

KING, KEITH E; Byng Sr HS; Ada, OK; (2); FBLA; Math Clb; Science Clb; Spanish Clb; Ofcr Bsbl; Bsktbl; Hon Roll; Jr NHS; Prfct Atten Awd; OK Univ; CPA; Stock Broker.

KING, LEAH B; Marietta HS; Burneyville, OK; (3); 4-H; Natl FFA Org; Hon Roll; Cooke Cty.

KING, LORI B; Harrah HS; Harrah, OK; (3); Band; Color Guard; Drill Tm; Flag Corp; Mrchg Band; Pep Band; Crs Cntry; Mgr(s); Sftbl; Trk; ST Trck Mt 3200m Run 8th 95-; ST Crss Cntry 95-; Lwyr/Acctnt.

KING, MATT B; Morris HS; Morris, OK; (1); JV Var Ftbl; Var Wt Lftg; OU; Sci.

KING, MATTHEW; Noble HS; Noble, OK; (3); #1 in class; Church Yth Grp; Mu Alpha Theta; Spanish Clb; Var Bsktbl; Var Socr; High Hon Roll; NHS; Pres Acad Fit Awd; FCA; Odyssey Of The Mind; Jr Arch Bearer.

KING, MISTY D; Vinita HS; Vinita, OK; (2); FHA; Science Clb; Spanish Clb; Chorus; JV Bsktbl; Hon Roll; Spanish NHS; Hnr Star Family Praise Ctr 95; NEO Nrsng Pgrm; RN.

KING, NATALIE R; Edmond Memorial HS; Edmond, OK; (3); 52/371; Church Yth Grp; FCA; GAA; Spanish Clb; SADD; Varsity Clb; Var Capt Bsktbl; Var Trk; High Hon Roll; Hon Roll; OK Hoops Top 50 Jrs Bsktbl; All Edmond Scnd Team Bsktbl; Big All Cty Spcl Rcgntn Bsktbl; Ed/Knslgy.

KING, REBECCA A; Tahlequah Sr HS; Tahlequah, OK; (2); GAA; Chorus; Church Choir; Var Bsktbl; Var Golf; Hon Roll; Jr NHS; NHS; Mentorship Pgm Through Gftd Pgm; TX A&M; Vet.

KING, ROBERT L; Choctaw HS; Midwest City, OK; (2); Art Clb; Church Yth Grp; Cmnty Wkr; High Hon Roll; Hon Roll; Art.

KING, RYAN; Chisholm Sr HS; Enid, OK; (1); Church Yth Grp; Band; Chorus; Jazz Band; Mrchg Band; Pep Band; Hon Roll; Jr NHS; NHS; Frosh Hnr Soc; Smmr Sftbl.

KING, SARAH; Grace Fellowship Christian Sch; Broken Arrow, OK; (2); 1/35; Church Yth Grp; Scholastic Bowl; Socr; High Hon Roll; Poetry Clb; Chrstn Hnr Soc Of Amer; Amer HS Math Exam Schl Wnnr; Statistics.

KING, SHAUN; Eufaula Sr HS; Eufaula, OK; (4); 8/71; FBLA; Office Aide; Yrbk; Ftbl; Hon Roll; NHS; Prfct Atten Awd; OK ST U; Comp Sci.

KINION, SARAH; Adair HS; Adair, OK; (4); 2/61; FHA; Quiz Bowl; Pres Rep Science Clb; VP Band; Chorus; Drm Mjr(t); VP Jr Cls; VP Sr Cls; NHS; Sal; Northeastern ST U.

KINKAID, KELLI; Ponca City Sr HS; Ponca City, OK; (4); FCA; French Clb; SADD; Var L Bsktbl; Var L Chrldng; Var L Socr; Var L Vllybl; Hon Roll; Nrsng.

KINMAN, C J; Prue Schl; Cleveland, OK; (3); 1/17; FCA; Letterman Clb; VP Frsh Cls; VP Soph Cls; Sec Jr Cls; Var Bsktbl; Stat Ftbl; Hon Roll; NHS; Ntl Merit Ltr; Nrsng.

KINNEY, BETHANY; Southwest Covenant Schl; Yukon, OK; (1); Church Yth Grp; FCA; Band; Chorus; Church Choir; Rep Frsh Cls; JV Vllybl; High Hon Roll; Hon Roll; Chrch Drama Tm & Stu Ldrshp Tm; Elem Ed.

KINNEY, DAVID K; Nowata HS; Nowata, OK; (4); 7/65; Am Leg Boys St; Church Yth Grp; FCA; Chorus; Sec Jr Cls; Var Bsbl; Capt Var Bsktbl; Var Ftbl; NHS; FCA Pres; NSU-TALEQUAH; Comp Sci; Acctng.

KINNEY, KYLE; Nowata HS; Nowata, OK; (4); 7/65; Am Leg Boys St; Church Yth Grp; Pres FCA; Rep Chorus; Sec Jr Cls; Var Capt Bsbl; Var Capt Bsktbl; Var Ftbl; Var Wt Lftg; NHS; OK Hnr Soc; Masonic Stu Awd; FCA Athl Of Yr; NSU; Bus.

KINNEY, RENEE E; East Central HS; Tulsa, OK; (1); Church Yth Grp; French Clb; Girl Scts; Hon Roll.

KINSEY, AUSTIN; Fairland Jr Sr HS; Fairland, OK; (4); #4 in class; Church Yth Grp; Math Tm; L Bsbl; Capt L Bsktbl; Capt L Ftbl; High Hon Roll; NHS; US Ntl Ldrshp Awd; All Am Schlr; Ntl Ldrshp/Svc Awd; Ntl Hnr Rll; All Area Bsbl; All Cnf Bskbl, Bslb, Ftb; Math.

KINSEY, LUKE; Beaver HS; Beaver, OK; (1); Church Yth Grp; FCA; Chorus; Pres Frsh Cls; Var Bsbl; Var Bsktbl; Var Ftbl; Var Trk; High Hon Roll.

KINSEY, REYNA A; Putnam City North HS; Oklahoma City, OK; (3); Church Yth Grp; Spanish Clb; Band; Church Choir; Mrchg Band; High Hon Roll; Hon Roll; Capt SE OK Nazarene Dist Bibke Qz Tm; Rcvd Spclzd Trphy Memorizing Books Of Bible; Southern Nazarene Univ; Biol.

KINSEY, ZACK; Mc Curtain HS; Mccurtain, OK; (1); 2/13; Church Yth Grp; 4-H; Quiz Bowl; Scholastic Bowl; Bsktbl; Cit Awd; High Hon Roll; NHS; Val.

KINSLER, WESLEE A; Union Sr HS; Tulsa, OK; (3); 255/673; Church Yth Grp; German Clb; Band; Mrchg Band; Hon Roll; Natl Historic Soc Mem; Antique Collector; Psych; Music Ed.

KINSLOW, AMY L; Tecumseh HS; Tecumseh, OK; (4); 19/128; Church Yth Grp; Cmnty Wkr; Pres French Clb; Natl Beta Clb; Pres SADD; Band; Jazz Band; Ed Nwsp; Cit Awd; 4-H; Tri St Jazz Bnd; St Gregory Univ; Premed.

KINZIE, KRISTOPHER D; Cushing HS; Cushing, OK; (1); 10/190; Boy Scts; Church Yth Grp; FCA; Chorus; Flag Corp; Yrbk; JV Var Ftbl; Golf; L Wt Lftg; High Hon Roll; Engrng.

KINZIE, OLIVIA; Cushing HS; Cushing, OK; (4); 27/159; Am Leg Aux Girls St; Drama Clb; FCA; HOBY; School Musical; School Play; Pres Sr Cls; Ofcr Stu Cncl; Capt Chrldng; VP NHS; U Of Sthrn CA; Film.

KIPGEN, JENNIFER L; Edmond Santa Fe HS; Edmond, OK; (3); #1 in class; Art Clb; German Clb; Hon Roll; NHS; Ntl Merit Ltr; Acad E Awd; Renaissance Schlr; Art II Excel Awd; Bio.

KIRBY, CINDY C; Olney Schl; Coalgate, OK; (4); 3/11; Church Yth Grp; Dance Clb; Quiz Bowl; VICA; Church Choir; Var Bsktbl; Var Score Keeper; Sftbl; High Hon Roll; Hon Roll; SE OK ST Univ; Pre-Law.

KIRBY, CRAIG M; Bartlesville HS; Bartlesville, OK; (4); 167/429; Pres Boy Scts; Computer Clb; Var Bsktbl; Var L Ftbl; Var L Trk; High Hon Roll; Hon Roll; FCA; Spanish Clb; Prfct Atten Awd; Prfct Attndnc Awd 13 Yrs; All Area/Class Ftbl Tm; ST Track Meet; U Of OK; MIS.

KIRBY, HOLLY M; Chickasha HS; Alex, OK; (2); Drama Clb; Science Clb; Spanish Clb; Chorus; Variety Show; Ofcr Stu Cncl; Bsktbl; Crs Cntry; Trk; Bowling Yth Ldrs Of Amer; Schlsp Hnrs Bowling; OK City CC; Interior Dsgn.

KIRBY, JESSICA; Newcastle HS; Newcastle, OK; (2); 1/87; Church Yth Grp; Bsktbl; Sftbl; Trk; Wt Lftg; NHS; Med.

KIRBY, KELLI A; Jay HS; Eucha, OK; (3); Natl Beta Clb; Natl FFA Org; Hon Roll; NHS; Ntl Merit Ltr.

KIRBY, KRISSY; Pond Creek-Hunter Schl; Lamont, OK; (2); Church Yth Grp; FCA; GAA; Pep Clb; Var L Bsktbl; Var L Sftbl; Var L Trk; Hon Roll; NHS; OK Hnr Soc Spec Hnrs & Awds; Phy Ther.

KIRBY, MELISSA; Jenks HS; Tulsa, OK; (3); 60/612; Cmnty Wkr; FCA; Key Clb; NFL; Pep Clb; Pres Service Clb; Spanish Clb; Speech Tm; Teachers Aide; School Play; Asian-Amer Cultural Soc; Envrmntl Mgmt Team; Comm/PR.

KIRBY, RANDY A; Brink Jr HS; Oklahoma City, OK; (1); Teachers Aide; Ftbl; Hon Roll; Jr NHS; OK ST Univ.

KIRBY, ROBERT J; Burns Flat-Dill City Jshs; Burns Flat, OK; (3); Boy Scts; Church Yth Grp; 4-H; German Clb; Natl FFA Org; Ofcr Bsbl; Bsktbl; 4-H Awd; High Hon Roll; NHS; OSU; Bio.

KIRBY, SANDRA; Stilwell HS; Stilwell, OK; (4); 11/124; French Clb; FBLA; JA; Natl Beta Clb; Natl FFA Org; Yrbk; Powder Puff Ftbl; High Hon Roll; NHS; Ntl Merit Ltr; Gradng Class Top Ten; Horseback Riding; Concurrent Enrollment; Connors ST Coll; Ag.

KIRCHNER, JUSTIN; Pawhuska HS; Pawhuska, OK; (2); 6/90; JV Var Bsktbl; JV Crs Cntry; JV Trk; Wt Lftg; Hon Roll; OU.

KIRCHNER, MELISSA J; Ponca City Sr HS; Ponca City, OK; (2); 219/460; Church Yth Grp; Cmnty Wkr; Hosp Aide; Ed Nwsp; Rep Stu Cncl; Hon Roll; Childrens Miracle Network Vol; U Of OK; Phy Thrpst.

KIRCKENBAUER, REBECCA D; Ponca City Sr HS; Ponca City, OK; (3); Church Yth Grp; Office Aide; Teachers Aide; Chorus; Church Choir; Orch; Cit Awd; Hon Roll; NCHO; Chrl; Orch Co Treas Sr Yr; OK Bapt Univ.

KIRK, CRYSTAL L; Salina HS; Salina, OK; (1); Natl FFA Org; Sec Frsh Cls; Var JV Bsktbl; High Hon Roll; NHS; Vet.

KIRK, JENNIFER; Sapulpa Jr HS; Sapulpa, OK; (1); French Clb; FHA; Yrbk; Ofcr Stu Cncl; Chrldng; Score Keeper; Tennis; French Hon Soc; Outstdng Soc Stdnts.

KIRK, KEVIN; Stigler HS; Stigler, OK; (1); Church Yth Grp; Band; Mrchg Band; High Hon Roll; Pres Acad Fit Awd; Acad Achvt Awd Plq.

KIRK, KRYSTAL S; Choctaw HS; Choctaw, OK; (4); 31/305; Rep Nwsp; Rep Yrbk; Hon Roll; Jr NHS; NHS; U Cntrl OK; Scndry Ed.

KIRK, NANCY M; Ripley HS; Ripley, OK; (3); 13/40; Church Yth Grp; Dance Clb; FBLA; Math Clb; Science Clb; Teachers Aide; Yrbk; Chrldng; Hon Roll; Clogging/Tap/Ballet; OK Christian; Psych.

KIRK, VALARIE V; West Middle HS; Norman, OK; (2); Church Yth Grp; Dance Clb; French Clb; Church Choir; Orch; DAR Awd; Hon Roll; Ballet Co; OK U; Jrnlsm.

KIRKENDALL, KATIE E; Stillwater Sr HS; Stillwater, OK; (3); Church Yth Grp; Cmnty Wkr; Drama Clb; FHA; Pep Clb; Spanish Clb; Teachers Aide; School Play; Yrbk; Var Swmmng; TOG; U Of Cntrl OK; Bus.

KIRKES, KIRA; Union City Schl; Mustang, OK; (2); Chess Clb; FHA; Math Clb; Quiz Bowl; Scholastic Bowl; Science Clb; Acpl Chr; Chorus; School Musical; School Play; OU; Med.

KIRKES, TABITHA A; Western Hghts HS; Oklahoma City, OK; (3); 21/167; Sec DECA; VP French Clb; Chorus; School Musical; Rep Stu Cncl; Var Chrldng; Var Crs Cntry; Var Trk; Hon Roll; NHS; LEAP; Prosecuting Attorney In OK HS Mock Trial Pgm; Natl Indian Hnr Soc Mem; OK Univ; Psychiatrist; Lawyer.

KIRKHUFF, JESSICA L; Wright Christian Acad; Tulsa, OK; (3); Church Yth Grp; Key Clb; School Play; Phtg Rptr Yrbk; Pres Soph Cls; Var Bsktbl; Score Keeper; Var Capt Socr; Var Trk; Hon Roll; Clb Sccr.

KIRKHUFF, JODI M; Wright Christian Acad; Tulsa, OK; (1); Church Yth Grp; JV Bsktbl; Var L Socr; JV Var Trk; Chrch Drama Clb.

KIRKLAND, CHRISTOPHER D; Mc Alester HS; Mcalester, OK; (2); Spanish Clb; Var Ftbl; Var Trk; Wt Lftg; Help Young Children In Sports & Flwshp; Fishing; Atv Riding; Boating; Skiing.

KIRKLAND, JON D; Bridge Creek HS; Blanchard, OK; (1); 7/75; Church Yth Grp; Spanish Clb; Bsktbl; Hon Roll; NHS; Sci Project; Frgn Lang Awd; Prins Hnr Roll.

KIRKLEY, JESSICA; Cameron Schl; Poteau, OK; (4); 1/34; Church Yth Grp; 4-H; Sec Rptr FHA; Scholastic Bowl; SADD; Co-Ed Nwsp; Yrbk; Co-Capt Chrldng; St Schlr; Val; Kids On The Block Puppeteers; Spcl Olympcs Vlntr; Mst Likeley To Succeed; Psych.

KIRKLEY, ROB M; Inola Sr HS; Inola, OK; (3); Church Yth Grp; Library Aide; Quiz Bowl; Science Clb; Speech Tm; Hon Roll.

KIRKPATRICK, AMY; Elgin HS; Elgin, OK; (4); 7/75; Am Leg Aux Girls St; Sec Natl FFA Org; Chorus; Sec Jr Cls; Ofcr Stu Cncl; JV Bsktbl; Capt Vllybl; Hon Roll; NHS; Pres Acad Fit Awd; 3rd Rnnr Up Local Pageant; OSU; Speec Pthlgy.

KIRKPATRICK, CHRISTIE; Haworth Jr HS; Haworth, OK; (1); Art Clb; Church Yth Grp; FHA; Girl Scts; Natl FFA Org; Chorus; Church Choir; Hon Roll; NHS; Mrn Bio.

KIRKPATRICK, HOLLY; Pond Creek-Hunter Schl; Pond Creek, OK; (2); Church Yth Grp; FCA; 4-H; HOBY; Pep Clb; Rep Nwsp; Yrbk; L Bsktbl; L Trk; Hon Roll; OK Hnr Soc; St Track Medlst; GATE.

KIRKPATRICK, KIM; Crescent Schl; Crescent, OK; (3); 5/40; Church Yth Grp; FCA; 4-H; Hosp Aide; Natl Beta Clb; SADD; Band; Chorus; Mrchg Band; Pep Band; Pres Awd; Schltc Awd; Chem Awd; Pre-Med.

KIRKPATRICK, MICHELLE D; Velma Alma HS; Duncan, OK; (3); 10/60; Art Clb; Natl FFA Org; Hon Roll; Horseback Riding; Ag Bus.

KIRKPATRICK, RACHEL B; Claremore Sr HS; Claremore, OK; (1); Church Yth Grp; Chorus; Church Choir; Trk; Hon Roll; NHS; Piano; Acad Bowl.

KIRSCHKE, ERIKA A; Stillwater Sr HS; Stillwater, OK; (3); 19/360; Church Yth Grp; Key Clb; Mu Alpha Theta; Natl Beta Clb; Spanish Clb; Band; Intrml Var Socr; High Hon Roll; NHS; St Schlr; Snow Ski; Water Ski; Sailing; U Of TX Austin; Stock Broker.

KIRTMAN, LYA S; Norman Sr HS; Norman, OK; (3); Latin Clb; Jazz Band; Orch; Hon Roll; Engrng.

KISLING, KIM; Burlington Schl; Burlington, OK; (3); 6/12; HOBY; Rptr Natl FFA Org; Band; Chorus; School Play; Rep Jr Cls; Ofcr Stu Cncl; Var L Bsktbl; Var Chrldng; Pres Acad Fit Awd; FFA St Spc & Rprtrs Cntst 1st Pl; Vcl Cont Vcl Solo St 1st Pl; OK ST U; Ag Comms.

KISSEE, TIFFANY; Pryor Sr HS; Pryor, OK; (3); 1/164; Am Leg Aux Girls St; Church Yth Grp; FCA; FBLA; Mu Alpha Theta; Sec Chorus; Sec Stu Cncl; Stat Bsktbl; Var Sftbl; Var Trk; All-Dist & All-Conf Sftbl 95 & 96; Miss Pryor 96.

KISTLER, BRIAN; Heritage Hall Schl; Edmond, OK; (3); Cmnty Wkr; Debate Tm; Hosp Aide; Mu Alpha Theta; Rptr Lit Mag; High Hon Roll; Hon Roll; NHS; Ntl Merit Ltr; Spanish NHS; Film Stud.

KITCHEL, ASHLEY V; Pawhuska HS; Pawhuska, OK; (3); Am Leg Boys St; English Clb; FCA; Spanish Clb; Teachers Aide; Sec Frsh Cls; Pres Soph Cls; Var Capt Bsktbl; Crs Cntry; Trk; TV Bsktbl Cmp; Five Star Bsktbl Cmp.

KITCHEN, JULIE; Moore HS; Moore, OK; (4); 44/525; FCA; Spanish Clb; Ofcr Stu Cncl; Var L Tennis; NHS; Pre-Med.

KITCHEN, LEAH; Moore HS; Moore, OK; (4); 81/525; Church Yth Grp; FCA; Spanish Clb; Rptr Stu Cncl; Powder Puff Ftbl; Var L Tennis; Jr NHS; Treas NHS; Pres Acad Fit Awd; Jr Escort; Stu Cncl St, Natl Convntn; NHS; U Of Central OK; Scndry Ed.

KITCHEN, RAE-LYN; Cimarron Public Schl; Ames, OK; (3); Church Yth Grp; FCA; FBLA; Quiz Bowl; Science Clb; SADD; VICA; Band; Pep Band; Cit Awd; Hnr Bands; Comp Aided Drafting & Dsgn; OSU; Engrng.

KITCHENS, JAY; Thomas Jr Sr HS; Thomas, OK; (2); FBLA; Quiz Bowl; Stat Frsh Cls; Sec Soph Cls; Var Bsktbl; Var Chrldng; Hon Roll; OK.

KITCHENS, JULIE A; Christian Heritage Acad; Oklahoma City, OK; (2); Church Yth Grp; Cmnty Wkr; FCA; JV Bsktbl; Intrml Chrldng; Var Tennis; Var Vllybl; Cit Awd; Hon Roll; Pres Acad Fit Awd; Chrctr Awds; City Rescue Msn; Metro Gymnstcs; OK ST Univ.

KITE, AMBER D; Parker Middle HS; Mcalester, OK; (2); Cmnty Wkr; Spanish Clb; Chrldng; Var Golf; Score Keeper; Hon Roll; House Of Rep Page; Natl His/Gov Awd; March Dimes/Spec Olympics Vol; E Centrl Univ; CPA.

KITE, CHRISTINE; Douglass HS; Oklahoma City, OK; (3); 2/125; Cmnty Wkr; Math Clb; Mu Alpha Theta; Spanish Clb; Ofcr Jr Cls; Cit Awd; High Hon Roll; Jr NHS; Kiwanis Awd; NHS; PRIDE; DARE Role Model; Teenline Crisis Hotline Vol; Oklahoma City Univ; Ed/Psych.

KITE, ERICA D; Enid Sr HS; Enid, OK; (2); Cmnty Wkr; Girl Scts; Letterman Clb; Library Aide; Varsity Clb; Band; Chorus; Bsktbl; Score Keeper; Sftbl; Chrch Nursery Vol; OU; RN.

KITTERMAN, SHAWN D; Copan HS; Copan, OK; (2); 1/31; Church Yth Grp; FHA; Band; Yrbk; Rep Soph Cls; Stat Bsktbl; High Hon Roll; NHS; Yth Crt; Eng.

KITZROW, EMILY S; Lawton Sr HS; Lawton, OK; (3); Outstdng Female Ath Of Yr Awd; Renaissance Awd; Cameron; Sports Med.

KIZER, SHANNA L; Pocola HS; Pocola, OK; (2); #2 in class; Girl Scts; Quiz Bowl; Band; Mrchg Band; Nwsp; Sftbl; High Hon Roll; Hon Roll; NHS; Bsktbl; OK Hnr Soc; OK Univ; Marine Bio.

KLEA, CHRISTINA; Choctaw HS; Harrah, OK; (4); 70/298; Church Yth Grp; Hosp Aide; Pep Clb; Hon Roll; NHS; S Nazarene Univ; Acctng.

KLEA, MICHAEL J; Choctaw HS; Harrah, OK; (2); Church Yth Grp; JV Wrstlng; High Hon Roll; Jr NHS; NHS; Pres Acad Fit Awd.

KLEIN, JOSEPH M; Bishop Kelley HS; Tulsa, OK; (1); Latin Clb; Scholastic Bowl; Hon Roll; Engr.

KLEIN, KACI N; Clinton HS; Clinton, OK; (3); 33/134; Church Yth Grp; FCA; Hist FBLA; Letterman Clb; Office Aide; Spanish Clb; Hist Stu Cncl; Capt Bsktbl; Sftbl; Hon Roll; OK St Univ; Spch Thrpy.

KLEOPFER, MICHAEL H; North Intemediate HS; Broken Arrow, OK; (2); Church Yth Grp; Library Aide; Office Aide; Spanish Clb; High Hon Roll; Hon Roll; Jr NHS; NHS; St Schlr; Christians In Action.

KLEPFER, CARL; Moore HS; Moore, OK; (4); Hosp Aide; Office Aide; Band; Jazz Band; Mrchg Band; Orch; Pep Band; 1080 Vlntr Hrs; U Of OK; Medcl.

KLETZKER, TAMARA; Grace Fellowship Christian Sch; Broken Arrow, OK; (3); Church Yth Grp; Hosp Aide; Library Aide; Chorus; Yrbk; Rep Jr Cls; Socr; Vllybl; Red Cross Swimming Instr; Photo; ORU; Nrsng.

KLIEWER, MELISSA; Corn Bible Acad; Weatherford, OK; (4); 1/12; Church Yth Grp; Band; Sec Chorus; Mrchg Band; Pep Band; School Play; Rptr Jr Cls; Pres Sr Cls; High Hon Roll; Val; Bus Admin.

KLIMKOWSKI, KRISTEN A; Seminole Jr Sr HS; Seminole, OK; (2); Church Yth Grp; FCA; French Clb; Chorus; Drill Tm; Pom Pon; Sftbl; Hon Roll; PT.

KLINE, ADAM J; Putnam City North HS; Oklahoma City, OK; (1); Church Yth Grp; JCL; Latin Clb; Ofcr Bsbl; Bsktbl; Vol Lcl Hsptl; Gftd/Tlntd Prgm; Hon Classes; Srgn.

KLINE, LYNN; Tahlequah Sr HS; Tahlequah, OK; (2); Church Yth Grp; Girl Scts; HOBY; Science Clb; SADD; Acpl Chr; Chorus; Church Choir; VP Soph Cls; High Hon Roll; HOBY; Spirit Clb; Non-Schl Sccr; OSU; Psych.

KLINE, MATT; Westmoore HS; Oklahoma City, OK; (4); 74/610; Church Yth Grp; German Clb; Quiz Bowl; Scholastic Bowl; Band; Jazz Band; Mrchg Band; School Musical; Stage Crew; JV Bsbl; OK Del To Natl Yth Sci Camp; Best Rsrch Paper In Physics, PE & St; Martial Arts; OK Chrstn Univ; Music Ed; Comp.

KLINGENBURG, PAMELA; Healdton HS; Healdton, OK; (4); 23/48; FCA; 4-H; FBLA; Band; Chorus; Church Choir; Color Guard; Ofcr Sr Cls; Trk; Hon Roll; Accounts Payable Cert; Bkkpr Cert; Spec Ed.

KLINK, JEREMY; Savanna HS; Mcalester, OK; (4); 9/50; Am Leg Boys St; Art Clb; Cmnty Wkr; Quiz Bowl; Science Clb; Band; Mrchg Band; Cit Awd; Hon Roll; NHS; Med.

KLINNERT, EMILY A; Okarche HS; Okarche, OK; (1); Church Yth Grp; FHA; Letterman Clb; Bsktbl; High Hon Roll; Hon Roll.

KLOECKLER, MATTHEW A; Sapulpa Sr HS; Sapulpa, OK; (3); Church Yth Grp; Cmnty Wkr; Letterman Clb; Scholastic Bowl; Teachers Aide; JV Bsktbl; Wt Lftg; Ntl Merit Ltr.

KLOEFKORN, AARON E; Wakita Schl; Manchester, OK; (1); Natl FFA Org; Band; Mrchg Band; Pep Band; School Play; Ofcr Bsbl; Bsktbl; Ftbl; Hon Roll; Stu Of Today; Natl Hnr Roll.

KLOPP, EVELYN M; Yukon Middle HS; Yukon, OK; (2); Church Yth Grp; FHA; Spanish Clb; School Play; Rep Soph Cls; Hon Roll; NHS; Piano Lssns 7 Yrs.

KNAPP, AMBER M; Union Intermediate HS; Tulsa, OK; (2); Church Yth Grp; FCA; JV Chrldng; Hon Roll; NHS; Tulsa Best Sr All Str Chrldng Squd; NCAA All Amer Chrldr; OK ST U; Nutrition.

KNAPP, LACEY A; Broken Arrow Sr HS; Broken Arrow, OK; (3); Vllybl; Gov Hon Prg Awd; Hon Roll; NHS; Orthpdc Srgn.

KNAUFF, SHANDA; Mustang HS; Mustang, OK; (1); 53/552; FCA; Chorus; Chrldng; Hon Roll; Renaissnce; Americas Natl Teen Schlrshp Pgm Fnlst; OK U.

KNEIB, SHARON T; Owasso Sr HS; Owasso, OK; (3); 41/356; Church Yth Grp; English Clb; Science Clb; Speech Tm; Teachers Aide; Chorus; Church Choir; High Hon Roll; Hon Roll; Prfct Atten Awd; NE ST Univ; Ed/Tchr.

KNEPPER, JULIE; Edison HS; Tulsa, OK; (3); Pres Church Yth Grp; Spanish Clb; Thesps; VICA; Band; Chorus; Pres Church Choir; Mrchg Band; Pep Band; Variety Show; Voc-Tech Hnrs Soc; The Arts.

KNIESS, JESSICA A; Yukon Middle HS; Oklahoma City, OK; (2); FHA; Library Aide; Quiz Bowl; Scholastic Bowl; Chorus; School Musical; Gov Hon Prg Awd; High Hon Roll; NHS; Pres Acad Fit Awd; Church; Karate; U Cntrl OK; Crmnlgy/Frnsc Sci.

KNIGGE, KRISTEN A; Will Rogers HS; Tulsa, OK; (1); Spanish Clb; Var Capt Socr; Hon Roll; Paleontology.

KNIGHT, AIMEE; Shawnee Sr HS; Shawnee, OK; (3); 9/320; Dance Clb; Kiwanis Awd; Pep Clb; Rptr Nwsp; Ofcr Stu Cncl; JV Chrldng; Var Pom Pon; Mgr Socr; High Hon Roll; Ldrshp Mrt Awd; OU; Med.

KNIGHT, AMBER L; Tecumseh HS; Shawnee, OK; (2); FCA; FHA; Yrbk; Rep Stu Cncl; JV Bsktbl; JV Sftbl; Hon Roll.

KNIGHT, BECKY; Yukon HS; Yukon, OK; (1); Church Yth Grp; Var Crs Cntry; Trk.

KNIGHT, J NATHAN; Ponca City Sr HS; Ponca City, OK; (3); 21/487; Am Leg Boys St; Church Yth Grp; Math Tm; Scholastic Bowl; Science Clb; Band; Mrchg Band; Pep Band; High Hon Roll; CO Schl Of Mines; Aerontcl Eng.

KNIGHT, KATIE L; Yukon Middle HS; Yukon, OK; (3); Church Yth Grp; FCA; GAA; Quiz Bowl; SADD; Varsity Clb; Chorus; Variety Show; Var Socr; NHS; Ideal Camper At Chrch Camp; Republican Conventions Page; Pre-Med; Missionary.

KNIGHT, RYAN SETH; Guthrie Sr HS; Edmond, OK; (2); 3/220; Boy Scts; Church Yth Grp; Mu Alpha Theta; SADD; Band; Mrchg Band; Rep Stu Cncl; JV Var Bsktbl; Hon Roll; NHS; AAU Bsktbl; Med.

KNIGHT, TONIKA D; Douglass HS; Oklahoma City, OK; (3); ROTC; Scholastic Bowl; Spanish Clb; Color Guard; Drill Tm; Sec Frsh Cls; Sec Soph Cls; Trk; Hon Roll; Parent As Tchrs Assn; JROTC Superior Cadet Awd 11th Grd; Langstons Univ; US Army.

KNIGHT, TY L; Mangum Sr HS; Willow, OK; (2); Art Clb; FBLA; Natl FFA Org; Variety Show; Pres Frsh Cls; Ofcr Bsbl; Bsktbl; Golf; Wt Lftg; Prfct Atten Awd; Stdnt Of Mnth; Rodeo Club.

KNIPMEYER, KELLY D; Bartlesville Mid HS; Bartlesville, OK; (2); 191/481; Church Yth Grp; Cmnty Wkr; FCA; Office Aide; L Band; L Mrchg Band; Variety Show; Phtg Yrbk; Var L Swmmng; Hon Roll; Phillips 66 Splash Clb; OSU.

KNISLEY, MICHAEL; Jarman Jr HS; Oklahoma City, OK; (1); Boy Scts; Church Yth Grp; German Clb; Band; Cit Awd; High Hon Roll; Hon Roll; Jr NHS; Outstndng Mscn & Drum Soloist.

KNOERNSCHILD, SHAUNA L; Nathan Hale HS; Tulsa, OK; (1); GAA; Girl Scts; Varsity Clb; Socr; Hon Roll; TU; Zoology; Marine Bio.

KNOLLES, BEN; Davis HS; Davis, OK; (2); Scholastic Bowl; Spanish Clb; Band; Jazz Band; Mrchg Band; Pep Band; High Hon Roll; St Schlr; OK Yth Orch; All Dist Band; All Dist Solo Cmptn; U Of OK.

KNOLLES, ERIN; Davis HS; Davis, OK; (3); 1/70; Cmnty Wkr; French Clb; Key Clb; Math Clb; Scholastic Bowl; Band; High Hon Roll; NHS; Office Aide; Quiz Bowl; Natl Yth Ldrshp Con Alumni Rep; Arbr Day Fndtn; Wrld Wldlife Fund; Amnsty Intl; Comm.

KNOP, KURT; Elk City Jr HS; Elk City, OK; (2); Pres Church Yth Grp; FCA; Key Clb; Natl FFA Org; Pep Clb; Science Clb; Pres Soph Cls; JV Var Bsbl; Var Crs Cntry; Cit Awd.

KNOPP, DEANNA R; Okeene Jr Sr HS; Okeene, OK; (3); 6/30; Am Leg Aux Girls St; Church Yth Grp; Cmnty Wkr; 4-H; FHA; JA; Natl FFA Org; Office Aide; Treas Frsh Cls; Cit Awd; APHA; OPHC; Pinto Horse Assn Of Amer; OK ST Univ; Veterinary Medicn.

KNOPP, HOLLY M; Edmond Memorial HS; Edmond, OK; (3); Church Yth Grp; Pep Clb; Spanish Clb; SADD; School Play; Variety Show; Ofcr Stu Cncl; Var Co-Capt Pom Pon; Hon Roll; NHS; Ldrshp Cncl For Sr Dnc Co; OK ST U.

KNOTT, KRISTY D; El Reno Sr HS; El Reno, OK; (2); Church Yth Grp; FCA; GAA; Library Aide; Golf; Sftbl; Hon Roll; Coll; Tchr.

KNOWLES, AMANDA L; Bethel HS; Shawnee, OK; (3); Church Yth Grp; FCA; SADD; Teachers Aide; School Play; Yrbk; VP Jr Cls; JV Var Bsktbl; Ftbl; Var Golf.

KNOWLES, RODNEY; Arnett HS; Arnett, OK; (4); 1/11; Church Yth Grp; FCA; HOBY; Natl Beta Clb; Natl FFA Org; Scholastic Bowl; Chorus; School Musical; School Play; Rptr Yrbk; OK ST U.

KNOWLES, RODNEY A; Nathan Hale HS; Tulsa, OK; (2); Church Yth Grp; Church Choir; Hon Roll; Southern Bapt Mnstr.

KNOX, KATHERINE N; Claremore Sr HS; Claremore, OK; (1); Church Yth Grp; Church Choir; High Hon Roll; Yth Cnslr For 3rd-6th Grd Chrch Camp; SALT Mem.

KOCH, KIMBERLY F; Edmond Santa Fe HS; Edmond, OK; (4); 55/209; Science Clb; Spanish Clb; SADD; Orch; Rep Soph Cls; JV Crs Cntry; Drill & Vary Dance Teams; Sr Cncl; Sr Spirit Corps; OK ST Univ; Zoology; Pre-Med.

KOCH, TIFFIANY N; Del City HS; Del City, OK; (2); Office Aide; Hon Roll; NHS; Prfct Atten Awd.

KOCSIS, JOHNNY; Dustin Schl; Dustin, OK; (2); Church Yth Grp; Treas Natl FFA Org; Ofcr Soph Cls; Var Bsbl; Prfct Atten Awd; Amer Lgn & Prfct Attndnc Awds; 4-H Pres & Treas; Mason Stu Of Today; Hnr Roll.

KOEHN, BETH; Timberlake Schl; Helena, OK; (3); 1/23; FCA; FHA; Pep Clb; Rep Frsh Cls; Pres Stu Cncl; Crs Cntry; Trk; Hon Roll; NHS; Show Choir; Wichita ST U; Occptnl Thrpst.

KOEHN, CELESTE L; Enid Sr HS; Enid, OK; (4); 22/412; French Clb; Band; Chorus; Color Guard; Mrchg Band; Orch; School Musical; School Play; Variety Show; Ed Nwsp; Yth Alive Bbl Clb Pres; Natl Hnr Soc; Cntst Spch; OK Baptist U; Music.

KOEHN, CHRIS; Chickasha HS; Chickasha, OK; (4); 6/152; Am Leg Boys St; Church Yth Grp; FCA; Rptr FBLA; Scholastic Bowl; SADD; Band; Chorus; Ed Yrbk; Rep Stu Cncl; Super Rtng Vcl Solo Solo/Ensmbl Cont; Atten OK Smmr Arts Inst Vcl Music; OK Baptist U; Religion.

KOEHN, HEIDI R; Okeene Jr Sr HS; Okeene, OK; (2); Church Yth Grp; FCA; Pres Sec Girl Scts; School Play; Rptr Nwsp; Phtg Yrbk; Var L Chrldng; Hon Roll; Kiwanis Awd; Prfct Atten Awd; Tech Stu Assn Pres, Sec; Teen Ct Jury, Baliff, Clrk, Prsctng & Defense Attorney; OCU; Law.

KOEHN, HILLARY D; Cimarron Public Schl; Enid, OK; (3); Church Yth Grp; FCA; Natl FFA Org; Band; Mrchg Band; Pep Band; School Play; Chrldng; Socr; Sftbl; Northwestern; Tchr.

KOENING, JENNIFER A; Stillwater Sr HS; Stillwater, OK; (3); Art Clb; Church Yth Grp; Dance Clb; FHA; Girl Scts; Red Cross Aide; Teachers Aide; Stage Crew; JV Crs Cntry; JV Trk; Spec Olympcs Vol; Northern OK Coll Intl Art Contest; Dntsty.

KOEPKE, KEVIN W; Choctaw HS; Choctaw, OK; (4); Church Yth Grp; Chorus; Var Ftbl; Wrstlng; Hon Roll; UCLA; Law.

KOERNER, MARCY M; Minco Jr Sr HS; Minco, OK; (4); 10/38; Church Yth Grp; 4-H; Natl FFA Org; Mrchg Band; Pep Band; Ed Yrbk; 4-H Awd; Hon Roll; Pres Schlr; OK ST FFA Dgr; Coffeyville CC; Anim Sci.

KOESTER, G ANDREW; Piedmont HS; Piedmont, OK; (4); Church Yth Grp; HOBY; Key Clb; SADD; Nwsp; Yrbk; JV Ftbl; Hon Roll; Mck Trl Pres; Hillsdale Free Will Bptst Coll.

KOETTER, PAUL; Cyril Jr Sr HS; Cyril, OK; (4); 3/28; Natl FFA Org; Var Bsbl; Var Bsktbl; Hon Roll; NHS; Acad All Conf; OK U; Med.

KOLAR, JACKIE; Union City Schl; El Reno, OK; (1); #2 in class; Church Yth Grp; Cmnty Wkr; 4-H; FHA; School Play; Bsktbl; Sftbl; Gov Hon Prg Awd; Sal; OK ST; Phys Ther.

KOLB, KANDI R; Cherokee Jr Sr HS; Cherokee, OK; (3); FCA; FHA; Office Aide; Spanish Clb; Teachers Aide; VP Frsh Cls; Sec Soph Cls; JV Var Bsktbl; Hon Roll; Northwestern; CPA.

KOLIASTASI, KIKI N; Claremore Sr HS; Claremore, OK; (3); 37/257; Am Leg Aux Girls St; Science Clb; Spanish Clb; Teachers Aide; Gym; Mgr(s); Powder Puff Ftbl; Wrstlng; Hon Roll; NHS; Tng Rpblcns; Jr Atndnt Wrstlng Hmcmng; Stdnt Impct Frst Bapt Claremore; Pre Law/Psych.

KOLIASTASIS, KIKI; Claremore Sr HS; Claremore, OK; (3); 57/237; Am Leg Aux Girls St; Cmnty Wkr; Science Clb; Spanish Clb; Church Choir; Gym; Powder Puff Ftbl; Wrstlng; High Hon Roll; NHS; MATMAID Trnr Wrestling Team; Jr Attendant For Wrestling Homcmng; Ms Amer Coed Pageant 4th Rnnr Up; U Of OK; Pre-Law; Psych.

KOLKER, TRACIE E; Choctaw HS; Choctaw, OK; (4); 22/308; French Clb; Key Clb; Office Aide; Yrbk; Hon Roll; Jr NHS; NHS; OK U; Med.

KOLP, BROOKE; Roland Sr HS; Muldrow, OK; (1); FHA; Spanish Clb; Pres Frsh Cls; Rep Stu Cncl; Chrldng; Var Sftbl; Hon Roll.

KOMAN, THEA ZOE; Mustang HS; Oklahoma City, OK; (1); Cmnty Wkr; FBLA; FHA; Vol Pre-Schl; Cncrt Choir; OK U; Judge.

KOONCE, JANA; Bridge Creek HS; Tuttle, OK; (1); Church Yth Grp; FCA; Hosp Aide; Office Aide; Spanish Clb; Chorus; Church Choir; Var Chrldng; Gym; Cit Awd; Chrldng Distngshd Awd, Acad Achvt Squad, Clss 2-A St Rnnr-Up Squad; OSU; Nursng.

KOONCE, JUSTIN; Moore HS; Moore, OK; (2); Office Aide; Ofcr Bsbl; Ftbl; Jr NHS.

KOOS, ERIN A; Classen Schl; Oklahoma City, OK; (2); Church Yth Grp; Cmnty Wkr; French Clb; GAA; Hosp Aide; Mu Alpha Theta; Rptr Nwsp; Ed Yrbk; Socr; Vllybl; Dance; Piano; Columbia Univ New York.

KOPASKA, MEGHAN; Altus Sr HS; Altus, OK; (4); 115/225; Church Yth Grp; English Clb; Math Tm; Rptr Ed Nwsp; Co-Ed Yrbk; Var L Swmmng; Cit Awd; Hon Roll; Pres Schlr; Kay Club; ACTV Prod Staff; Western OK ST Coll; Comm/Jrnl.

KOPF, MELISSA F; Skiatook HS; Skiatook, OK; (4); 21/104; Church Yth Grp; Cmnty Wkr; Drama Clb; FHA; HOBY; Quiz Bowl; Teachers Aide; Church Choir; School Play; Hon Roll; USAA Ldrshp Awd 2 Yrs, USAA Acad Awd; Multi Yr Listing; Tulsa CC; Phys Thrpy.

KOPLEMAN, JAMES; Claremore Sr HS; Claremore, OK; (3); Math Clb; Scholastic Bowl; Science Clb; Spanish Clb; Bsktbl; Var Socr; Tennis; High Hon Roll; NHS; Amateur Photo.

KORBAU, STACEY L; Piedmont HS; Piedmont, OK; (4); 11/85; Cmnty Wkr; Office Aide; Red Cross Aide; Chorus; Yrbk; VP Soph Cls; VP Stu Cncl; Stat Ftbl; High Hon Roll; Pres Acad Fit Awd; UCO; Pharmacist.

KORNBECK, KELLI S; Del City HS; Midwest City, OK; (4); Science Clb; Spanish Clb; SADD; Pres Of Ntiv Amrcn Cmmte; Vp Of HOSA; Alt Recip Of HOSA Rebecca Anderson Schol; U Of SCI Arts; Indian Stds.

KOSS, REBECCA; Edmond Santa Fe HS; Edmond, OK; (3); JCL; Latin Clb; Pep Clb; Science Clb; SADD; Band; Mrchg Band; Pep Band; Sec Soph Cls; Rep Stu Cncl; Rensselaer Medal Top Jr Stu Math & Sci; Natl Piano Guild Wnnr; Pre-Med; Bus.

KOVAC, CHRISTOPHER J; Metro Christian Acad; Tulsa, OK; (3); Chrldng; Golf; Gym; OK ST; Mech Engrng.

KOVACS, CARRIE C; B T Washington HS; Tulsa, OK; (2); JCL; Latin Clb; Spanish Clb; Hon Roll; NHS; OK St Latin Convntn Acad 1st Pl Level 1.

KOVIN, REBECCA L; Memorial HS; Tulsa, OK; (3); Church Yth Grp; Hosp Aide; Key Clb; Office Aide; Spanish Clb; Teachers Aide; Church Choir; Nwsp; Jr NHS; Cmp Fire; U Of OK; Jrnlsm.

KOWALSKI, SHANDLE L; Spiro HS; Spiro, OK; (1); Church Yth Grp; Model UN; Natl FFA Org; Quiz Bowl; Spanish Clb; Church Choir; High Hon Roll; GATE; FFA Chptr Mtng Team.

KOWIS, KENNETH; Tahlequah Sr HS; Tahlequah, OK; (4); Am Leg Boys St; Church Yth Grp; Cmnty Wkr; Science Clb; Spanish Clb; Socr; Hon Roll; Jr NHS; NHS; Pres Acad Fit Awd; All Amer Schlr 96; Schlstc Achvt Awd 96; OK ST U.

KOWNACKI, SARAH L; Bishop Kelley HS; Tulsa, OK; (3); Church Yth Grp; Pres French Clb; Pep Clb; Red Cross Aide; Nwsp; JV Ice Hcky; Var Pom Pon; French Hon Soc; High Hon Roll; NHS; Studied Blt 12 Yrs; Attnd Space Camp/Avtn Prgms Huntsville AL 5 Yrs; Intnl Bus.

KOZLOWSKI, DAVID E; Locust Grove HS; Locust Grove, OK; (2); Hon Roll; Comp; OSU; Air Force Pilot.

KRAFT, CENA; Woodward HS; Woodward, OK; (3); 1/200; Am Leg Aux Girls St; FCA; FBLA; VP FTA; HOBY; Letterman Clb; Red Cross Aide; Bsktbl; NHS; Art Clb; Mck Trl.

KRAGENBRINK, PAUL F; Deer Creek HS; Oklahoma City, OK; (3); Chess Clb; Computer Clb; Capt Debate Tm; German Clb; NFL; Quiz Bowl; ROTC; Science Clb; Speech Tm; Ntl Merit Ltr; Pre-Law.

KRAKAUSKAS, CALLIE M; Oklahoma Sch Of Science & Math; Yukon, OK; (3); Treas FHA; Math Tm; Quiz Bowl; Scholastic Bowl; High Hon Roll; NHS; Boston Univ; Marine Bio.

KRASE, MELANIE S; Union Intermediate HS; Broken Arrow, OK; (2); 15/800; Church Yth Grp; FCA; Key Clb; Office Aide; Spanish Clb; Teachers Aide; Mgr Bsktbl; High Hon Roll; NHS; Chld Psych.

KRAUSCH, CRAIG; Talihina Sr HS; Talihina, OK; (3); 1/43; Church Yth Grp; FCA; HOBY; Natl FFA Org; School Play; VP Jr Cls; Rep Stu Cncl; Var Bsbl; Var Bsktbl; Var Ftbl; Stu Of Month; Outstndng Bsktbl Plyr; All Dist Qrtrback Ftbl; E OK ST Coll.

KRAUSER, MEGAN; Adair HS; Big Cabin, OK; (3); Art Clb; Sec Church Yth Grp; Pres FCA; Pres FHA; Science Clb; Teachers Aide; Church Choir; Rep Soph Cls; Rep Jr Cls; Capt Var Chrldng; Cmp Fire Bys Grls; Piano; OSU; Phys Thrp.

KRAWCZYNSKI, LEA L; Duncan HS; Duncan, OK; (2); Church Yth Grp; SADD; Chorus; Church Choir; Hon Roll; Jr NHS; NHS.

KREBBS, EMILY C; Northwest Classen HS; Oklahoma City, OK; (3); Math Clb; Mu Alpha Theta; Scholastic Bowl; Chorus; Vllybl; High Hon Roll; NHS; All ST Choir Mem.

KREGER, JAMES D; Yukon Middle HS; Yukon, OK; (3); Letterman Clb; Var L Ftbl; L Wt Lftg; L Var Wrstlng; High Hon Roll; Hon Roll; NHS; OK Hnr Soc; Acad Ltr; OSU; Law.

KREINER, KASEY M; Claremore Sr HS; Claremore, OK; (2); Spanish Clb; Rptr Yrbk; Mgr(s); Hon Roll; UCAT; Med.

KREIZENBECK, DUSTIN; Arapaho Schl; Arapaho, OK; (2); Church Yth Grp; Letterman Clb; Teachers Aide; VP Frsh Cls; Rep Soph Cls; Var L Bsbl; Var L Bsktbl; Cit Awd; Bsktbl MVP 95-96; All Around Boy 95-96; 5 Cty Bsktbl Conf All Conf Plyr.

KREIZENBECK, TERRI; Arapaho Schl; Arapaho, OK; (3); 6/25; Am Leg Aux Girls St; 4-H; Rptr FHA; Yrbk; VP Frsh Cls; Sec Soph Cls; Sec Jr Cls; Sec Sr Cls; Pres Stu Cncl; Bsktbl; Southwestern OK ST; Pre Law.

KRENEK, SAMANTHA; Chelsea HS; Chelsea, OK; (3); FCA; FHA; HOBY; Office Aide; Chorus; Chrldng; Powder Puff Ftbl; Western TX.

KREUTZER, VERNA L; Glenpool HS; Glenpool, OK; (1); FHA; Chorus; Northeastern ST U; Acctnt.

KRICK, ALLEN; Quinton Jr Sr HS; Quinton, OK; (3); Church Yth Grp; FCA; Band; Church Choir; Mrchg Band; Orch; Pep Band; School Musical; School Play; Intrml Bsktbl; PT.

KRIEG, BRETT J; Union Sr HS; Tulsa, OK; (4); Church Yth Grp; DECA; FCA; Bsktbl; Ftbl; NHS; Pres Acad Fit Awd.

KRIEGER, LANE; Hobart HS; Hobart, OK; (4); 1/70; Church Yth Grp; FCA; Letterman Clb; Band; Sec Treas Sr Cls; Bsktbl; Ftbl; NHS; All Conf Acad Tm Capt; OK Hnr Soc; Stu Cncl; Bio.

KRIEGER, LEIGH; Hobart HS; Hobart, OK; (2); Church Yth Grp; Cmnty Wkr; FHA; Quiz Bowl; Mrchg Band; Pep Band; VP Frsh Cls; Ofcr Stu Cncl; Trk; High Hon Roll; OSU; Ed.

KRIEGER, NATALIE; Durant HS; Durant, OK; (4); 8/185; Church Yth Grp; FCA; Spanish Clb; SADD; Ed Yrbk; Rptr Stu Cncl; Bsktbl; Crs Cntry; Powder Puff Ftbl; Socr; Sthestrn OK ST U; Bio.

KRITTENBRINK, MANDI P; Wellston Schl; Wellston, OK; (3); FHA; Spanish Clb; VP Soph Cls; Rep Jr Cls; Rep Stu Cncl; Hon Roll; NHS; OSU; Photo.

KRIZ, ADAM G; Geronimo Jr Sr HS; Geronimo, OK; (2); 4-H; FHA; Math Clb; Natl FFA Org; Science Clb; Speech Tm; SADD; VICA; Ofcr Bsbl; Bsktbl; FFA Treas 95-96, VP 96-97.

KROEKER, JEANNETTE; Oklahoma Bible Acad; Enid, OK; (2); Church Yth Grp; FCA; Band; Chorus; Treas Stu Cncl; JV Var Bsktbl; Var Trk; Var Vllybl; High Hon Roll; Church Yth Ldrshp Tm.

KROUTIL, RYAN; Mustang HS; Mustang, OK; (3); 1/386; Band; Jazz Band; Mrchg Band; Bsktbl; Tennis; Hon Roll; NHS.

KRUEGER, AARON; Edmond Memorial HS; Edmond, OK; (3); 91/371; Church Yth Grp; FCA; Hosp Aide; Key Clb; Spanish Clb; SADD; Ofcr Jr Cls; Ofcr Stu Cncl; Bsktbl; NHS; Wendys HS Heisman Awd Nom; All Cty Tm Hnrbl Mntn; US Stu Cncl Awds.

KRUG, MICHELLE; Collinsville HS; Collinsville, OK; (3); Band; Color Guard; Mrchg Band; Hon Roll; NHS; Prfct Atten Awd; Bowling.

KRUMM, STEPHEN A; Skiatook HS; Skiatook, OK; (1); Church Yth Grp; FCA; Band; Chorus; Mrchg Band; School Musical; L Bsbl; Bsktbl; Hon Roll; Jr NHS; Serteens; Arch.

KRUPKA, MIKE; Guthrie Sr HS; Edmond, OK; (4); 16/178; FBLA; Key Clb; Math Clb; Mu Alpha Theta; Pres Spanish Clb; Band; Hist Mrchg Band; Pep Band; VP Jr Cls; Ofcr Stu Cncl; Grad Cum Laude; Tulsa U; Chem/Med Rsrch.

KUBILIS, ROGER; Reydon HS; Reydon, OK; (3); 1/14; Rep Jr Cls; Var Bsktbl; Var Trk; High Hon Roll; NHS; SWIM Cont 3rd Pl Chem; Math, Ecs Stu Awds; US Air Force Acad; Aero Engr.

KUCKO, LESLIE D; Western Heights Sr HS; Oklahoma City, OK; (3); Am Leg Aux Girls St; DECA; Key Clb; Chorus; School Musical; Swing Chorus; Church Yth Grp; Cmnty Wkr; FCA; FHA; I Dare You Awd; Choir Pres; Strtd Tnge Rpblcn Grp At Schl; Mock Trial Best Atty; TX Chrstn Univ; Pols/Pub Svc.

KUEHN, STEPHANIE; South Coffeyville Schl; S Coffeyville, OK; (3); 1/20; Church Yth Grp; HOBY; Natl FFA Org; Scholastic Bowl; Capt Jr Cls; Pres Stu Cncl; Var L Bsktbl; NHS; Prfct Atten Awd; OSU; Vet.

KUFAHL, HUTCHISON; Trinity Christian Schl; Broken Arrow, OK; (3); 2/9; Letterman Clb; Varsity Clb; School Play; Nwsp; Yrbk; Pres Jr Cls; Var L Bsktbl; Var L Golf; Var L Socr; Tennis; Bsktbl All-St & All-Metro Hnrbl Mntn Team; Soccer All-St 2 Yrs; Northeastern ST; Broadcasting.

KUHLMAN, JESSICA; Prague HS; Earlsboro, OK; (4); Church Yth Grp; VP FBLA; Key Clb; Library Aide; Speech Tm; Teachers Aide; Church Choir; Yrbk; VP Frsh Cls; Ofcr Stu Cncl; Yth Alv VP; Mck Trl Mem 2 Yrs; Ed Tlnt Srch 4 Yrs; Southwestern Alg U; Bus Mgmt.

KUHLMAN, LESLIE; Edmond Memorial HS; Edmond, OK; (1); Church Yth Grp; Letterman Clb; Chorus; Variety Show; JV Chrldng; Trk; Pres Acad Fit Awd.

KUHLMANN, KIRSTEN A; Union Sr HS; Tulsa, OK; (3); 39/741; Church Yth Grp; German Clb; Girl Scts; Library Aide; Treas Science Clb; Chorus; School Musical; Hon Roll; Jr NHS; Prfct Atten Awd; Teenage Republcns Treas; Acad Resrce Ctr Treas; OK All-OMEA Chorus; Law.

KULP, DAVID V; Holland Hall Schl; Tulsa, OK; (4); Boy Scts; Stage Crew; JV Bsktbl; Intrml Socr; Hon Roll; Ntl Merit SF; Eagle Sct Awd; Wlkr Fan Club; Trinity U.

KUMAR, VINOD N; Edmond North HS; Edmond, OK; (3); Cmnty Wkr; German Clb; Key Clb; Library Aide; Math Tm; Quiz Bowl; Science Clb; Var L Tennis; High Hon Roll; Hon Roll; Medicine.

KUNKEL, CHRIS M; Ryan Schl; Oscar, OK; (3); 4/23; Church Yth Grp; FCA; Letterman Clb; Natl FFA Org; Varsity Clb; Pres Frsh Cls; Pres Soph Cls; Pres Jr Cls; VP Sr Cls; Var Bsbl.

KUNTZ, AARON; Bartlesville Mid HS; Bartlesville, OK; (2); 48/450; Church Yth Grp; Spanish Clb; Bsktbl; Socr; Cit Awd; Hon Roll; Jr NHS; Soph Stdnt Of Yr.

KUNZE, JAY; Dale Sr HS; Shawnee, OK; (4); 1/50; Natl FFA Org; Office Aide; Scholastic Bowl; Spanish Clb; Teachers Aide; Band; Jazz Band; Mrchg Band; Hon Roll; NHS; FFA Star Chap Farmer, St Degree, Harley Custer Mem Schlrshp; OK ST U.

KUREY, JACOB M; Putnam City North HS; Oklahoma City, OK; (4); 82/436; German Clb; Office Aide; Quiz Bowl; Teachers Aide; Var Capt Socr; Intrml Vllybl; Hon Roll; Jr NHS; NHS; Delt Epsln Phi Hnr Soc; Spring Sports King; All-Dist, All-Conf, All-St Defnsv Plyr Socr; OK Acad Schlr; Coastal Carolina Univ; Bus.

KURSAR, KELLIE; Shawnee Sr HS; Shawnee, OK; (3); 31/331; Church Yth Grp; FCA; Pep Clb; Ofcr Stu Cncl; Chrldng; Tennis; High Hon Roll; Ntl & Intl Missions; U Of OK; Optometry.

KURTZ, KEVIN; El Reno Sr HS; El Reno, OK; (4); 9/175; FHA; FTA; Math Clb; Natl Beta Clb; Quiz Bowl; Science Clb; Yrbk; Rep Stu Cncl; Ftbl; Capt Wrstlng; Harvard Univ.

KURTZ, RYAN S; Choctaw HS; Harrah, OK; (4); 211/298; Church Yth Grp; Cmnty Wkr; FCA; SADD; Var Ftbl; Var Golf; Var Socr; Var Trk; Hon Roll; NHS; OK Chrstn Univ; Intl Bus.

KURVINK, SARAH A; Mc Alester HS; Mcalester, OK; (4); 33/209; FHA; Teachers Aide; Color Guard; Hon Roll; OK ST Univ; Elem Ed.

KURZ, ABBI; Woodward HS; Woodward, OK; (2); 26/300; FCA; Pep Clb; Socr; Hon Roll.

KUSEL, JAMIE; Ft Cobb-Broxton HS; Fort Cobb, OK; (4); 10/35; Am Leg Aux Girls St; Pres 4-H; Spanish Clb; Nwsp; Ed Yrbk; Pres Soph Cls; Pres Jr Cls; Pres Sr Cls; Pres Stu Cncl; 4-H Awd; OK Hs Rep Page; Univ Cntrl OK; Cnslr.

KUSEL, JAY B; Ft Cobb-Broxton HS; Fort Cobb, OK; (3); Church Yth Grp; Yrbk; L Bsbl; Hon Roll; FFA Sentinel Jr/Sr; OK ST Univ; Military.

KUSIK, MAREN; Hennessey HS; Hennessey, OK; (3); 1/75; FCA; Sec Frsh Cls; Ofcr Stu Cncl; Var Bsktbl; JV Chrldng; Var Crs Cntry; Var Mgr(s); High Hon Roll; NHS; Bsktbl Hmcmng Ct Jr Attndnt.

KUTCHMAN, SHARON L; Pauls Valley HS; Pauls Valley, OK; (3); 1/104; FCA; SADD; Yrbk; Sec Frsh Cls; Sec Soph Cls; VP Jr Cls; Rep Stu Cncl; Var Bsktbl; Var Trk; High Hon Roll; Phys Thrpy.

KUYKENDALL, KYLA R; Owasso Sr HS; Collinsville, OK; (2); Cmnty Wkr; FCA; Trk; Hon Roll; Non Schl Sftbl 5 Yrs; Pdtrn.

KUZMANOVIC, NIKOLA; Union Intermediate HS; Broken Arrow, OK; (2); Computer Clb; Math Clb; Var Swmmng; High Hon Roll; Hon Roll; Jr NHS; NHS; Comp Prgmng & Processing.

KWOK, THALIA A; Union Intermediate HS; Tulsa, OK; (1); Church Yth Grp; FCA; Band; Mrchg Band; High Hon Roll; Jr NHS; NHS; Drug Free Yth; Sr Auditions Piano 3rd Alt; G&T Cncl; Pediatrician.

KWON, MIRIAM; Moore HS; Moore, OK; (4); Church Yth Grp; Intnl Clb; JA; Mu Alpha Theta; Office Aide; Spanish Clb; SADD; Chorus; Church Choir; Yrbk; Outstndng Stu Awd; Natl Hnr Soc Hist; Stu Cncl Core Grp; Intl Sec; U Of OK; Pharm.

KYKER, J G; Cushing HS; Cushing, OK; (1); Church Yth Grp; Spanish Clb; Rep Frsh Cls; Rep Stu Cncl; Var Trk; Hon Roll.

KYLE, CHRISTOPHER A; Union Intermediate HS; Tulsa, OK; (2); Orch; Var Swmmng; NHS; Tulsa Yth Symphny.

KYLE, KENDEL K; Lone Grove HS; Ardmore, OK; (2); Church Yth Grp; Math Clb; Natl FFA Org; Science Clb; Bsktbl; Wt Lftg; Hon Roll.

KYLE, LATASHA; Central HS; Tulsa, OK; (2); Church Yth Grp; FBLA; Latin Clb; Church Choir; Drill Tm; Ofcr Soph Cls; Ofcr Stu Cncl; Hon Roll; NHS; Upwrd Bnd; Rghts Pssg; Frdm Fnd; Spellman; Law.

KYSAR, ASHLYN; Waynoka HS; Waynoka, OK; (2); Church Yth Grp; FCA; FHA; Pep Clb; Bsktbl; Sftbl; Trk; Hon Roll; NHS; Prfct Atten Awd; Cls Pres, Treas; Sports Med.

LA, PHUONG; Memorial HS; Tulsa, OK; (4); 62/250; Church Yth Grp; VP Intnl Clb; VP JA; Key Clb; Latin Clb; Church Choir; Rep Stu Cncl; NHS; Cmnty Wkr; Pep Clb; Gamma Sigma; Chrgrs For Christ; UOK; Pre-Med.

LABADIE, LORI; Pawhuska HS; Pawhuska, OK; (2); Church Yth Grp; FCA; Pep Clb; Sec Frsh Cls; Sec Soph Cls; L Var Bsktbl; L Var Chrldng; L Var Trk; Hon Roll; NHS.

LA BAHN, JACOB; El Reno Sr HS; El Reno, OK; (4); 1/175; Am Leg Boys St; Church Yth Grp; Cmnty Wkr; FCA; Letterman Clb; Natl FFA Org; Scholastic Bowl; Spanish Clb; Ftbl; Cit Awd; Snt Page 93; VCA MVP 95.

LABASS, LAUREN E; Okmulgee HS; Okmulgee, OK; (1); Church Yth Grp; Cmnty Wkr; FCA; Band; Church Choir; Jazz Band; Mrchg Band; Orch; Var Golf; High Hon Roll; OK Univ; Ophthalmology.

LABOUNTY, SHANE; Warner HS; Warner, OK; (4); 2/50; Am Leg Boys St; Treas FCA; Office Aide; Spanish Clb; Ed Nwsp; Sec Stu Cncl; Bsktbl; VP NHS; Sal; St Schlr; Gld Mdl Achvmnt; OSU; Dgtl Grphcs Tech.

LACEY, GIBRAN I; Southeast HS; Oklahoma City, OK; (1); Cmnty Wkr; Drama Clb; School Play; Rep Stu Cncl; High Hon Roll; Theocratic Mnstry Schl; Howard U; Engrng.

LACEY, KRISTI L; Union Sr HS; Broken Arrow, OK; (3); 30/721; FCA; FBLA; FHA; Key Clb; Spanish Clb; Capt Drill Tm; High Hon Roll; Hon Roll; Jr NHS; NHS; Dance & Prfrmng Arts; Med.

LACEY, MICHELLE M; Edmond Memorial HS; Edmond, OK; (3); #1 in class; Church Yth Grp; Drama Clb; JCL; Key Clb; Latin Clb; Chorus; School Musical; School Play; Variety Show; High Hon Roll; Supr Rtng ST Piano Cntst; Math/Scndry Ed.

LACEY, STARR; Metro Christian Acad; Sand Springs, OK; (2); Chess Clb; Church Yth Grp; Latin Clb; Band; Jazz Band; Mrchg Band; Pep Band; Chrldng; Pom Pon; Hon Roll; Latin Clb Pres; Evangelism Through The Arts Cls; OK ST U; OBGYN.

LACK, CALEB W; Mountain View-Gotebo HS; Mountain View, OK; (3); 3/40; FCA; 4-H; Natl FFA Org; Pres Frsh Cls; Pres Soph Cls; Pres Stu Cncl; Var Bsbl; Var Bsktbl; Var Capt Ftbl; Var Wt Lftg; Genetics.

LACKEY, ALECIA A; Memorial HS; Tulsa, OK; (2); Office Aide; Pep Clb; Spanish Clb; Teachers Aide; Varsity Clb; Rep Stu Cncl; Chrldng; Crs Cntry; Gym; Score Keeper; Elem Gym Coach; OK Univ; Sprtsmed.

LACKEY, AMANDA; West Middle HS; Norman, OK; (1); FCA; Ofcr Stu Cncl; JV Chrldng; Hon Roll; NCA Cheer Natls 2nd Pl 95.

LACKEY, BETH A; Charles Page HS; Sand Springs, OK; (2); 9/385; Key Clb; Spanish Clb; High Hon Roll; Jr NHS; NHS.

LACKEY, CHERYL D; Morris HS; Morris, OK; (3); Church Yth Grp; Church Choir; Hon Roll; Piano; OSU; Med Sec Tech.

LACKEY, HALEE; Plainview HS; Ardmore, OK; (3); 7/83; FCA; Natl Beta Clb; Band; Drm Mjr(t); Mrchg Band; VP Jr Cls; Rep Sr Cls; VP Stu Cncl; Bsktbl; Var Crs Cntry; Ardmore Little Theater Orch Vol; All Dist & All ST Band; All ST Crss Cntry; U Of OK; Allied Hlth Sci.

LACKEY, MONIKA; Wynnewood HS; Wynnewood, OK; (2); Church Yth Grp; JV Var Bsktbl; JV Crs Cntry; JV Trk; JV Wt Lftg; Hon Roll.

LACOURSE, JENNIFER; Midwest City HS; Midwest City, OK; (3); 21/380; Church Yth Grp; FCA; Key Clb; Office Aide; Church Choir; Var JV Socr; JV Vllybl; High Hon Roll; Hon Roll; Jr NHS; Rep SADD; Baylor U; Phys Thrpst.

LACROIX, RYAN D; Yukon HS; Yukon, OK; (3); Church Yth Grp; Rptr FCA; Spanish Clb; Church Choir; Rptr Nwsp; Intrml Bsktbl; High Hon Roll; Hon Roll; 3-D.

LACY, AMANDA M; Chattanooga Schl; Faxon, OK; (1); 7/22; Church Yth Grp; Cmnty Wkr; FHA; GAA; Letterman Clb; Var Bsktbl; Var Sftbl; Hon Roll.

LACY, AMY C; Brink Jr HS; Oklahoma City, OK; (1); Church Yth Grp; Cmnty Wkr; FCA; Hosp Aide; Office Aide; Scholastic Bowl; Teachers Aide; Church Choir; Ed Nwsp; Rep Stu Cncl; Tulsa Univ Advd Math/Sci Smr Acad; Nwspr Hghst ST Awds; Hghst Hnrs All OK Acad Swpstks; JR NHS VP; Northeastern ST U; Ophthalmlgy.

LACY, CHRISSY; Canton HS; Canton, OK; (4); 2/45; VP FHA; Natl FFA Org; Sec SADD; Band; Chorus; Drm Mjr(t); Mrchg Band; School Play; NHS; Sal; OK Hnr Socty; Blaine Cty Tn Ct; OK Panhandle ST U; Thrpy.

LACY, RACHEL; Oologah HS; Claremore, OK; (3); Phtg Yrbk; Chrldng; Gym; Hon Roll; Church Yth Grp; FCA; Hosp Aide; Pep Clb; Psych.

LADD, CHARLES; Central HS; Tulsa, OK; (1); 7/300; Church Yth Grp; FCA; Ftbl; Wt Lftg; Wrstlng; High Hon Roll; Med.

LADD, DANIEL R; East Central HS; Tulsa, OK; (3); Church Yth Grp; Cmnty Wkr; FCA; Key Clb; Letterman Clb; Spanish Clb; Wrstlng; High Hon Roll; Hon Roll; Jr NHS; Chr Camp Cnslr Vol; Nom Natl Schlstc Conf; OSU; Engr.

LADD, OLIVA L; Ponca City Sr HS; Ponca City, OK; (4); Church Yth Grp; Debate Tm; Drama Clb; Pres NFL; Q&S; Quiz Bowl; Chorus; School Play; Ed Nwsp; NHS; NCTE Wrtng Awd.

LADD, TOMMY A; Noble HS; Noble, OK; (3); Art Clb; Spanish Clb; Bsktbl; Golf; Trk; U Of OK; Engrng.

LADNER, JENNIFER L; B T Washington HS; Tulsa, OK; (1); Church Yth Grp; Var Swmmng; Hon Roll; Rookie Of Yr Swmmng.

LADWIG, JAMIE; Hennessey HS; Hennessey, OK; (1); Church Yth Grp; FHA; Quiz Bowl; Church Choir; Mrchg Band; Pep Band; JV Bsktbl; JV Chrldng; Var Crs Cntry; Var Sftbl; OSU; Ed.

LA FAVE, ROBERT D; Muskogee HS; Muskogee, OK; (2); Natl FFA Org; OK ST U; Ag.

LAFFERTY, CHAD W; Bethany HS; Oklahoma City, OK; (3); 18/88; Teachers Aide; Ed Nwsp; Var Bsbl; Hon Roll; NHS; Physics Tutor; Comp; OK Univ.

LAFFERTY, SHAWNA; Oklahoma Union Schl; Lenapah, OK; (4); 2/44; Treas FHA; Treas Spanish Clb; Teachers Aide; School Play; VP Frsh Cls; VP Soph Cls; Var Chrldng; Hon Roll; Sec NHS; Sal; Hnr Soc; Chrldr Elite All Amer; All Amer Schlr; Coffeyville CC; Bus.

LAFFOON, KRISTY; Capitol Hill HS; Oklahoma City, OK; (4); Dance Clb; Office Aide; Teachers Aide; Yrbk; Rep Stu Cncl; Chrldng; Pom Pon; Hon Roll; Dance; Rose ST; Arch.

LAGALY, SARA; Union City Schl; El Reno, OK; (4); 3/23; Treas 4-H; Math Clb; Quiz Bowl; Science Clb; Church Choir; Hon Roll; Val; Chem.

LAHR, ANNA; Woodward HS; Woodward, OK; (2); Art Clb; Church Yth Grp; Cmnty Wkr; FCA; GAA; HOBY; Letterman Clb; Pep Clb; VP Frsh Cls; Var Chrldng; Dance; Psycho Thrpst; Dancer.

LAHR, NICOLE U; Nathan Hale HS; Tulsa, OK; (1); Church Yth Grp; Drama Clb; Church Choir; High Hon Roll; Bio Chem.

LAHTI, AMANDA K; Union Intermediate HS; Tulsa, OK; (2); Church Yth Grp; FCA; Spanish Clb; Chorus; School Musical; Swmmng; Cit Awd; Hon Roll; Jr NHS; NHS; Ballet Tulsa Schl; Perf Rhythmetrn/Nutcrkr Tulsa Ballet Theatre.

LAIR, MELANIE R; Agra Schl; Cushing, OK; (3); Church Yth Grp; 4-H; Natl FFA Org; Pep Clb; School Play; Sec Jr Cls; Bsktbl; Capt Chrldng; Sftbl; Trk; Seminole ST Coll; RN.

LAIRAMORE, AMY M; Pocola HS; Pocola, OK; (4); 1/46; Church Yth Grp; VP FCA; Pres FBLA; Office Aide; Quiz Bowl; Pres Jr Cls; Pres Sr Cls; Ofcr Stu Cncl; Capt L Bsktbl; Var L Sftbl; Eng Awd; USAF Rcrtng Svc Math & Sic Awd; Army Awd; Sprts Whos Who; Westark CC; Rad.

LAIRD, COURTNEY N; Asher Schl; Asher, OK; (4); GAA; Library Aide; Natl FFA Org; Scholastic Bowl; Yrbk; Bsktbl; Hon Roll; Seminole ST Coll; Ath Trng.

LAIRD, RYAN; Bridge Creek HS; Tuttle, OK; (3); 5/75; Quiz Bowl; Scholastic Bowl; Science Clb; Spanish Clb; Var JV Ftbl; Var L Wt Lftg; High Hon Roll; Hon Roll; NHS; Ntl Merit Ltr; Prairies To Peaks Sci Camp; Sprts Med.

LAIRD, STEPHANIE J; Henryetta Sr HS; Henryetta, OK; (3); FBLA; FHA; Red Cross Aide; Spanish Clb; Pom Pon; Powder Puff Ftbl; Hon Roll; NHS; Pres Schlr; Acad Ltrmn; Med.

LAISLE, RORY; Edmond Sante Fe HS; Edmond, OK; (4); 15/209; Church Yth Grp; FCA; Treas Key Clb; Office Aide; Spanish Clb; SADD; VP Jr Cls; Treas Stu Cncl; Var L Bsktbl; Var Capt Ftbl; IN U; Bus.

LAKE, JENNIFER G; Geary Jr Sr HS; Geary, OK; (1); FHA; Natl FFA Org; Scholastic Bowl; Bsktbl; Hon Roll; U Of OK; Mech Eng.

LAKE, WARREN; Mustang HS; Yukon, OK; (3); 68/400; Church Yth Grp; Cmnty Wkr; Service Clb; VICA; Church Choir; Rep Jr Cls; High Hon Roll; NHS; Prfct Atten Awd; Sal; OK St Snt Page; Omniplex Sci Museum Apprntc; West Pt.

LAKSHMIVARAHA, BHARATHRAM; Oklahoma Sch Of Science & Math; Norman, OK; (3); Math Clb; Math Tm; Model UN; Mu Alpha Theta; Office Aide; Quiz Bowl; Scholastic Bowl; Spanish Clb; Teachers Aide; Orch; 2nd Pl Amer HS Math Exmntn; Hnrb Mntn At OK St U Math Cont; Super Ratng In Dist & St Orch Conts; Medicine.

LAKSHMIVARAHAN, BHARARTHRAM; Oklahoma Sch Of Science & Math; Norman, OK; (3); Computer Clb; Math Tm; Model UN; Mu Alpha Theta; Quiz Bowl; Scholastic Bowl; Science Clb; Spanish Clb; Orch; Rep Frsh Cls; Super Ratings Violin Solos & Ensembles At Dist & St Levels; Spllng Bee Champ; Hnrb Mntn OSU Math Cont; Medicine.

LALLI, ANGELENA M; Mc Alester HS; Mcalester, OK; (3); Spanish Clb; Band; Color Guard; Flag Corp; Mrchg Band; Capt Of Wrestling Chrldng; Univ Mgr.

LALLI, BENJAMIN; Mc Alester HS; Mcalester, OK; (4); 29/209; Am Leg Boys St; Boy Scts; Debate Tm; FCA; Office Aide; Spanish Clb; Speech Tm; Var Bsbl; Var Ftbl; Var Wt Lftg; Ftbl All Dist 5a-4, All Area Tm; Med.

LAM, JULIE K; Brink Jr HS; Oklahoma City, OK; (1); Rep Frsh Cls; NHS.

LAM, QUYNH NHU P; Westmoore HS; Oklahoma City, OK; (1); Jr NHS; NHS; OU; Phrmcst.

LAMAR, STEPHEN J; North Intemediate HS; Broken Arrow, OK; (2); Hist Debate Tm; VP French Clb; Hist NFL; Hon Roll; NHS; Pres Schlr; Best Debator; Natl Forensics League Sped Distnctn Awd; U Of MI; Psych.

LA MAR, TAMMIE; Catoosa HS; Catoosa, OK; (3); French Clb; Band; Mrchg Band; JV Var Socr; Hon Roll; Pres Acad Fit Awd; Pres Schlr; Am Leg Aux Girls St; Church Yth Grp; Library Aide; OSU Hnr Schlr; Kybrdng Awd; OK Hnr Soc; Rogers ST Coll; Vet.

LAMASTUS, TENNILLE A; Bethel HS; Shawnee, OK; (4); 38/74; Art Clb; Cmnty Wkr; 4-H; Hosp Aide; Natl FFA Org; Office Aide; Spanish Clb; Bsktbl; 4-H Awd; Rose ST Coll; RN.

LAMB, AMANDA; Panama HS; Shady Point, OK; (2); Hon Roll; Pres Jr NHS; NHS; Pharmcy.

LAMB, AUDRA; Roff HS; Roff, OK; (3); Natl Beta Clb; Scholastic Bowl; VP Jr Cls; Ofcr Stu Cncl; Cit Awd; High Hon Roll; East Central U.

LAMB, BRITTON M; Ponca City Sr HS; Ponca City, OK; (4); Boy Scts; Church Yth Grp; German Clb; SADD; Teachers Aide; Band; Mrchg Band; Orch; Pep Band; School Musical; U Of OK; Bus Mgmt.

LAMB, DEREK; Blanchard Jr Sr HS; Blanchard, OK; (3); Church Yth Grp; FCA; Scholastic Bowl; Spanish Clb; Church Choir; Ofcr Bsbl; Bsktbl; Hon Roll; Jr NHS; NHS.

LAMB, DORINDA; Stillwater Sr HS; Okeene, OK; (4); 65/351; 4-H; French Clb; FHA; Mu Alpha Theta; Natl Beta Clb; Natl FFA Org; Varsity Clb; Band; 4-H Awd; Hon Roll; OK ST Univ; PT.

LAMB, ERIN E; Union Sr HS; Tulsa, OK; (4); 56/632; Hosp Aide; Key Clb; Spanish Clb; Hon Roll; NHS; Pres Acad Fit Awd; Spanish NHS; U Tulsa; Med.

LAMB, JEREMY B; Putnam City West HS; Bethany, OK; (2); Church Yth Grp; Church Choir; Orch; Stage Crew; Ftbl; Trk; Ed/Bus.

LAMB, JEREMY L; Life Chrstn HS; Mc Loud, OK; (3); 185/230; Church Yth Grp; CAP; FCA; Capt Drill Tm; Nwsp; Ofcr Bsbl; Bsktbl; Ftbl; Tennis; Wt Lftg; Sea Cadets; Lifeguard; Army Reserves; Judge Advocate.

LAMB, KRISTIN R; Grace Fellowship Christian Sch; Broken Arrow, OK; (3); Church Yth Grp; Letterman Clb; Pep Clb; Teachers Aide; Phtg Yrbk; Ofcr Jr Cls; Score Keeper; Socr; Var Vllybl; Cit Awd; Photography Clb; Poetry Club; Character Awd; Chrstn Character Awd; Bible Awd; Current His Awd; Math Awd; Oral Roberts Univ.

LAMB, LARRY K; Asher Schl; Asher, OK; (3); Natl FFA Org; Scholastic Bowl; Pres Frsh Cls; VP Soph Cls; Ofcr Bsbl; Bsktbl; High Hon Roll; Hon Roll; Bsbl ST Chmpnshps.

LAMB, LORI; Stillwater Sr HS; Stillwater, OK; (2); Church Yth Grp; Cmnty Wkr; FCA; Hosp Aide; Natl Beta Clb; Pep Clb; Sec Stu Cncl; Capt Chrldng; Powder Puff Ftbl; Hon Roll; OSU; Tchng.

LAMB, MELISSA M; Union Sr HS; Tulsa, OK; (4); 63/616; Church Yth Grp; Band; Chorus; Church Choir; Mrchg Band; Orch; NHS; Pres Schlr; Spanish Clb; Hon Roll; Oral Roberts U Franco Autori Awd; All-St Bapt Choir; Handbells.

LAMB, MISTY D; Union Intermediate HS; Tulsa, OK; (1); Church Yth Grp; Band; Chorus; Church Choir; Mrchg Band; NHS; Pres Acad Fit Awd; Union Stu For Christ.

LAMB, TRAVIS J; Enid Sr HS; Enid, OK; (2); 3/67; Art Clb; Hosp Aide; Spanish Clb; Pep Band; School Play; Ofcr Soph Cls; Hon Roll; Jr NHS; NHS; Prfct Atten Awd; Comps; Lawyer.

LAMBERT, ACHLEY D; Blanchard Jr Sr HS; Blanchard, OK; (4); Computer Clb; FHA; Spanish Clb; Band; Mrchg Band; High Hon Roll; Aacad Tm; USAO; Mus.

LAMBERT, DANA S; Catoosa HS; Catoosa, OK; (3); 23/190; Church Yth Grp; FCA; Hist French Clb; Bsktbl; Wt Lftg; French Hon Soc; High Hon Roll; Hon Roll; NHS; Prfct Atten Awd; Yth Participation Conf; U Of OK; Sports Medicine.

LAMBERT, FRANKI L; Wakita Schl; Wakita, OK; (1); Church Yth Grp; FCA; Quiz Bowl; Band; Sec Frsh Cls; Sec Stu Cncl; Bsktbl; Sftbl; Trk; High Hon Roll; Law.

LAMBERT, GERI; Commerce HS; Commerce, OK; (1); Church Yth Grp; FCA; FHA; GAA; SADD; Rptr Frsh Cls; Bsktbl; Chrldng; Sftbl; U Of OK; Med.

LAMBERT, JEREMY W; Wakita Schl; Wakita, OK; (3); 4/14; Church Yth Grp; Debate Tm; Office Aide; Scholastic Bowl; Spanish Clb; Ed Nwsp; Bsktbl; Wt Lftg; Hon Roll; Acad Tm; Hon Acad Tm; Cptr Engr.

LAMBERT, JERRY T; Union Sr HS; Broken Arrow, OK; (3); 42/705; Church Yth Grp; Mu Alpha Theta; JV Bsktbl; Mgr(s); Score Keeper; High Hon Roll; Jr NHS; NHS.

LAMBERT, RACHAEL; Coalgate HS; Coalgate, OK; (4); 3/45; FCA; Bus Profs of Am; Sec Sr Cls; Sec Sr Cls; Capt Var Bsktbl; Capt Var Sftbl; High Hon Roll; Hon Roll; Jr NHS; NHS; Phys Thrpy.

LAMBERT, SEAN; Edmond North HS; Edmond, OK; (4); 38/336; Boy Scts; Church Yth Grp; FCA; Mu Alpha Theta; Spanish Clb; Band; JV Bsbl; Var Ftbl; Var Socr; NHS; Eagle Scout-Boy Scouts Of Amer; Brigham Young Univ; Engr/PT.

LAMBERTUS, MICHELLE P; Midwest City HS; Midwest City, OK; (2); 81/488; Boy Scts; FTA; Girl Scts; Library Aide; Pep Clb; Chorus; Church Choir; Color Guard; School Play; Hon Roll; Cdtt Sr Brd Of Girl Scts Hstrn 1 Yr/Sec 2 Yrs; Slvr Awd Girls Scts; Otstndng Soph Clrgrd; OU; Nrs.

LAMBORN, LESLEY; Jenks HS; Tulsa, OK; (4); DECA; Service Clb; Teachers Aide; Chorus; Yrbk; Rep Stu Cncl; Var Capt Chrldng; Powder Puff Ftbl; Hon Roll; St Schlr; OK Hnr Soc Acd Medal; Spirit Comm Treas; Northeastern ST U; Optometry.

LAMEBULL, KRISTIE J; El Reno Sr HS; El Reno, OK; (2); GAA; Sftbl; Ed.

LAMOREAUX, ROY; Pawhuska HS; Pawhuska, OK; (3); 1/106; Boy Scts; FBLA; Key Clb; Quiz Bowl; Spanish Clb; Yrbk; L Bsktbl; L Crs Cntry; L Tennis; L Trk; OSU.

LAMPKIN, LANETT B; Wister Schl; Wister, OK; (2); Art Clb; FHA; Speech Tm; School Play; Rptr Nwsp; High Hon Roll; NHS; Dr.

LANCASTER, AMANDA; Victory Christian Schl; Tulsa, OK; (3); Church Yth Grp; Intnl Clb; Math Clb; Office Aide; Spanish Clb; Teachers Aide; Church Choir; Socr; Sftbl; Tennis; OK Bapt Univ.

LANCASTER, DUSTIN J; Deer Creek HS; Oklahoma City, OK; (2); 16/98; Debate Tm; Drama Clb; FCA; School Musical; School Play; Stage Crew; Variety Show; Rep Frsh Cls; Rep Soph Cls; Ofcr Stu Cncl; Hnr Roll-NHS; Ftbl; Soccer; Kiwanis Awd; Prfct Attendance Awd; Drama.

LANCASTER, EMILY; Victory Christian Schl; Tulsa, OK; (1); Church Yth Grp; Church Choir; JV Chrldng; JV Sftbl; Jr NHS; Pres Acad Fit Awd; Mst Inspirational Chrldr; OBU.

LANCASTER, JAY; Hugo HS; Hugo, OK; (3); 5/79; Church Yth Grp; Spanish Clb; Variety Show; Rep Stu Cncl; Ofcr Bsbl; Bsktbl; Wt Lftg; Hon Roll; NHS; Ntl Merit Ltr; Harding U.

LANCASTER, JENNIFER N; Byng Sr HS; Ada, OK; (3); #1 in class; Am Leg Aux Girls St; Church Yth Grp; Rep Natl Beta Clb; Band; Capt Flag Corp; Rep Stu Cncl; Bsktbl; Sftbl; Rptr Jr NHS; NHS; Canadian Vly All-Conf Sftbl Tm; St Gregorys.

LANCE, SHAWNTELL R; Haskell HS; Boynton, OK; (2); Church Yth Grp; Spanish Clb; Chorus; School Musical; School Play; Bsktbl; Tennis; Vllybl; Cosmtcs.

LANCE, TASHA; Victory Christian Schl; Tulsa, OK; (2); 2/85; Sec Soph Cls; Bsktbl; Crs Cntry; Trk; High Hon Roll; NHS.

LANDEROS, MONICA; Pioneer Jr Sr HS; Enid, OK; (3); FCA; Hosp Aide; Library Aide; Natl Beta Clb; Office Aide; Pep Clb; Ofcr Stu Cncl; Chrldng; Hon Roll; Sing For Schl Pgms, Chrch, & Pol Rallies; Southwest Advntst Coll; CRNA.

LANDERS, ALICIA Y; Del City HS; Del City, OK; (3); 52/450; Church Yth Grp; FCA; Scholastic Bowl; Spanish Clb; SADD; Yrbk; Sec Stu Cncl; Jr NHS; NHS; U Of Cntrl OK; Elem Ed.

LANDERS, JOSEPH H; Okemah HS; Okemah, OK; (3); 9/80; Key Clb; Natl FFA Org; Science Clb; Bsktbl; Ftbl; Wt Lftg; Hon Roll; OK ST.

LANDERS, LIZA; Union Sr HS; Tulsa, OK; (3); 2/673; French Clb; Intnl Clb; Key Clb; Math Clb; Orch; School Musical; Rep Jr Cls; Rep Stu Cncl; High Hon Roll; Jr NHS; Tulsa Yth Symphny/96 OK All ST; Attn OK Smmr Arts Inst; Top Ten AIM-HI Math Comp ST; Tulsa Univ; Music Perf/Math Ed.

LANDERS, LYLE; Collinsville HS; Collinsville, OK; (3); FCA; Var Bsbl; Wt Lftg; Hon Roll; Ldrshp, Svc, Ldrshp Mrt, Math Awds; Cngrsnl Yth Ldrshp Cncl; OSU.

LANDERS, MARK A; Lexington HS; Lexington, OK; (3); Church Yth Grp; FCA; Natl FFA Org; Spanish Clb; Var Bsbl; Var Ftbl; Var Wrstlng; St Wrstlng Chmp & AAU All Amer; OK ST U; Math Tchr.

LANDGRAF, WESLEY B; Madill HS; Madill, OK; (3); Church Yth Grp; FCA; 4-H; NFL; Office Aide; SADD; Golf; Mgr(s); 4-H Awd; Hon Roll; OK ST Univ.

LANDIS, JOSH J; West Middle HS; Norman, OK; (1); Gymnstcs.

LANDIS, KIM; Putnam City HS; Oklahoma City, OK; (1); Church Yth Grp; Debate Tm; Latin Clb; School Musical; School Play; Chrldng; Pom Pon; Hon Roll; PEAK; Baylor Univ; Med/Anesthesiology.

LANDRITH, DONDI G; Blanchard Jr Sr HS; Blanchard, OK; (2); Art Clb; Pep Clb; City Of Blanchard Art Cont Wnnr; Day Care; Pediatrician.

LANDRRUM, APRIL L; Oklahoma Bible Acad; Waukomis, OK; (3); Church Yth Grp; Cmnty Wkr; FCA; Pep Clb; Spanish Clb; Chorus; Yrbk; Chrldng; Cit Awd; Hon Roll; Twirling; Dance; Acctng/Cmptr Sci.

LANDRUM, CHERYL A; Lawton Sr HS; Lawton, OK; (2); Church Yth Grp; Cmnty Wkr; FCA; 4-H; FHA; Key Clb; SADD; Chorus; Church Choir; School Musical; Sci Clb Mem; Chrch Nursery Vol; Vacation Bible Schl Tchr; OK ST U; Spcl Ed.

LANDRUM, VALERI; Asher Schl; Wanette, OK; (2); FBLA; Ofcr Stu Cncl; Chrldng; Sftbl; Medicine.

LANDRY, BEAU E; Bridge Creek HS; Tuttle, OK; (2); Church Yth Grp; Letterman Clb; Var L Bsktbl; Var L Ftbl; Var Wt Lftg; Hon Roll; Chrch Camp Awds; Soccer; Chrch Ldrshp; OCCC.

LANDSVERK, KARRY M; Union Intermediate HS; Tulsa, OK; (2); Church Yth Grp; Spanish Clb; Church Choir; Hon Roll; NHS; Cmnty Svc; Church Plays; Mortuary Sci.

LANE, COURTNEY L; Stigler HS; Stigler, OK; (3); Art Clb; Church Yth Grp; Cmnty Wkr; FCA; FHA; Pep Clb; SADD; Phtg Yrbk; Hon Roll; Prfct Atten Awd; U Of MN; Drama.

LANE, CRAIG S; Choctaw HS; Del City, OK; (4); 144/298; FCA; SADD; Chorus; Church Choir; Rep Stu Cncl; JV Var Bsbl; JV Bsktbl; JV Ftbl; Schlstc Achvmt; U Of OK; Acctg.

LANE, DALINA; Eufaula Sr HS; Eufaula, OK; (4); 7/73; FHA; Math Clb; Natl FFA Org; Office Aide; Science Clb; Teachers Aide; Band; Mrchg Band; JV Bsktbl; Hon Roll; FFA Pres, Secy; GT Clb; OK Hnr Soc; Estrn OK ST; Nrsng.

LANE, DONALD J; West Middle HS; Norman, OK; (1); Spanish Clb; Rep Frsh Cls; Ftbl; Trk; Wrstlng; Hon Roll; Arch/Sprts Med.

LANE, JIMMY D; Morris HS; Okmulgee, OK; (3); School Play; Stage Crew.

LANE, KANDACE R; Union Intermediate HS; Tulsa, OK; (1); Cmnty Wkr; FCA; Hosp Aide; Spanish Clb; Bsktbl; High Hon Roll; Jr NHS; NHS; Pres Acad Fit Awd; Church Yth Grp; OK ST Univ; Vet.

LANE, KIM; Seminole Jr Sr HS; Seminole, OK; (3); Church Yth Grp; Debate Tm; FCA; French Clb; Math Clb; NFL; Scholastic Bowl; Yrbk; Trk; NHS; Mck Trl; Mdl Cong; Seminole JC; Nrsng.

LANE, MARTI L; Carl Albert HS; Midwest City, OK; (4); 8/262; FCA; Key Clb; Sec Pep Clb; Var Capt Bsktbl; NHS; Val; Spanish Clb; Teachers Aide; Chorus; School Musical; Jr Rotarian; AAUW Girl Of Month; Carl Albert Hall Of Fame; GPA Clb; OK ST Univ.

LANE, MATTHEW D; Antlers Sr HS; Amity, AR; (2); Church Yth Grp; FCA; FHA; Ofcr Bsbl; Bsktbl; Ftbl; Golf; Powder Puff Ftbl; Wt Lftg; Cit Awd; OSU; Sports Med.

LANE, MISTY R; Altus Sr HS; Altus, OK; (2); Art Clb; Church Yth Grp; FCA; Acpl Chr; Chorus; Swmmng; High Hon Roll; Hon Roll; Keyboarding; Acctng.

LANE, ROBERT; Grove HS; Wyandotte, OK; (4); Boy Scts; Natl FFA Org; Band; Jazz Band; Mrchg Band; Yrbk; Ofcr Bsbl; Bsktbl; Ftbl; Wt Lftg; Indian Heritage & IDFY Clbs; FHA; Northeastern OK A&M.

LANE, RUSTY; Clinton HS; Clinton, OK; (2); Church Yth Grp; FCA; Ofcr Stu Cncl; Var L Bsbl; JV Bsktbl; JV L Ftbl; Wt Lftg; High Hon Roll; Hon Roll; NHS; Yth Bsbl Asst Coach; Yth Bsktbl Umpire; U Of OK; Dentist.

LANE, SARA; Duncan HS; Duncan, OK; (3); Church Yth Grp; Cmnty Wkr; Debate Tm; Drama Clb; 4-H; French Clb; Key Clb; NFL; School Play; Nwsp; Distruted Trees Throughout Comm; Environmental Speaker; Initiated Pilot Paper Recycling Pgms In Comm; Ecological Sci.

LANE, STEPHEN D; Depew HS; Depew, OK; (2); 11/37; Boy Scts; Church Yth Grp; HOBY; Spanish Clb; Band; Var Bsbl; Var Ftbl; Hon Roll.

LANE, TERESA M; Union Intermediate HS; Tulsa, OK; (2); 17/900; Church Yth Grp; FCA; Intnl Clb; Spanish Clb; Teachers Aide; Bsktbl; Mgr(s); Cit Awd; High Hon Roll; Jr NHS; Drg Free Yth; TX A&M.

LANE, TINA M; Miami Sr HS; Miami, OK; (4); 16/125; Church Yth Grp; Speech Tm; Band; Church Choir; Mrchg Band; Pep Band; Hon Roll; NHS; Hnr & 4 St Bands; All-St Fnlst; Sctn Ldr; Dirs Awd; Spr Rtng Dist Solo; St Excllnt Rtng; Yth Cncl Pres; Abilene Chrstn U; Msc.

LANFAIR, ELIZABETH A; Putnam City West HS; Oklahoma City, OK; (3); Church Yth Grp; Cmnty Wkr; Orch; JV Vllybl; Silver Strings Orch Chaplain; Outstdng Frosh, Soph Schl Orch; Silver 7 Ensemble.

LANG, DERRICK D; Haskell HS; Boynton, OK; (2); Church Choir; Jazz Band; School Musical; Ofcr Bsbl; Bsktbl; Ftbl; 4-H Awd; Hon Roll; NHS; Prfct Atten Awd.

LANG, EMMA; Claremore Sr HS; Claremore, OK; (1); Church Yth Grp; Cmnty Wkr; Hosp Aide; Quiz Bowl; Golf; High Hon Roll; Hon Roll; Superior Rtng ST Piano Cntst; Superior Rtng Tampa Msc Fstvl; Pre-Med/Med.

LANG, JAYMIE C; Central Mid-HS; Norman, OK; (2); Church Yth Grp; Latin Clb; Model UN; Band; Mrchg Band; Orch; Vllybl; Snw Skng.

LANG, LESLEY V; Edmond Memorial HS; Edmond, OK; (1); 1/400; Church Yth Grp; Spanish Clb; Bsktbl; Sftbl; Trk; High Hon Roll; Hon Roll; NHS; Pres Schlr; St Schlr; Orthpdc Surg.

LANG, SHARTESE S; Haskell HS; Boynton, OK; (3); Church Yth Grp; Dance Clb; FBLA; FHA; GAA; Band; Drill Tm; Jazz Band; Pep Band; School Play.

LANGFORD, AUTUMN R; Capitol Hill HS; Oklahoma City, OK; (2); Dance Clb; Pep Clb; Yrbk; Var Chrldng; Mgr(s); Hon Roll; Bus/Real Est.

LANGFORD, NATASHA R; Union Intermediate HS; Tulsa, OK; (2); Church Yth Grp; Cmnty Wkr; Drama Clb; French Clb; Church Choir; Hon Roll; DFY; TX Tech; Sclgy.

LANGHAM, DUSTY L; Rush Springs HS; Rush Springs, OK; (2); Church Yth Grp; Cmnty Wkr; FCA; Natl FFA Org; Camrron; Law Enfrcmnt.

LANGHAM, T J; Blair Schl; Blair, OK; (2); FCA; Natl Beta Clb; Quiz Bowl; Var Bsktbl; High Hon Roll; NHS; Ntl Merit Ltr; SWOSC; Envrnmnlst.

LANGLEY, BRANDON S; Deer Creek HS; Edmond, OK; (3); Church Yth Grp; Science Clb; Band; Drm Mjr(t); Mrchg Band; Pep Band; Golf; Medieval Club; OK ST U; Engrng.

LANGLEY, EMILY; Wister Schl; Wister, OK; (3); Church Yth Grp; Cmnty Wkr; FCA; FHA; Quiz Bowl; Bsktbl; Sftbl; Hon Roll.

LANGLEY, ERIC; Hugo HS; Hugo, OK; (3); 3/110; Church Yth Grp; Rep FCA; Pres Math Clb; Band; Jazz Band; Mrchg Band; Pres Frsh Cls; Ofcr Stu Cncl; Var Bsktbl; Mgr(s); 4 Sts Hnr Bnd; All Dist Hnr Bnd; All St 1st Cut; OK St U; Airline Plt.

LANGSTON, CASEY M; Muskogee HS; Muskogee, OK; (4); 51/303; Church Yth Grp; FCA; JCL; Latin Clb; SADD; Var Chrldng; Hon Roll; NHS; OK Governor Octagon Jr Optimist; Habitat For Humanity; Northeastern ST U; Bus; Pre-Law.

LANIE, EMILY K; Wakita Schl; Manchester, OK; (2); Church Yth Grp; FCA; HOBY; Scholastic Bowl; Band; Pep Band; School Play; VP Frsh Cls; Sec Soph Cls; Var Bsktbl; Stu Cncl VP.

LANIE, NICKI; Wakita Public Schls; Manchester, OK; (4); 1/15; Am Leg Aux Girls St; Church Yth Grp; Bsktbl; Crs Cntry; Trk; Gov Hon Prg Awd; High Hon Roll; NHS; Pres Acad Fit Awd; Val; Ok Bapt U; Sprts Med.

LANKFORD, JENNIFER L; Westmoore HS; Oklahoma City, OK; (3); FCA; GAA; JA; Teachers Aide; Rptr Jr Cls; Pres Sr Cls; Rep Stu Cncl; JV Bsktbl; L Mgr Ftbl; Mgr(s); DECA.

LANKFORD, MARGARET; Sapulpa Sr HS; Sapulpa, OK; (4); 26/299; Band; Mrchg Band; Cit Awd; French Hon Soc; High Hon Roll; NHS; Prfct Atten Awd; Pres Acad Fit Awd; Spanish NHS; Natl League Of Poetry; USAA Yrbk Of 94; Tulsa JC; Psych; Ed.

LANKFORD, STEPHANIE D; Choctaw HS; Choctaw, OK; (4); 27/304; Church Yth Grp; Cmnty Wkr; FCA; Chorus; Church Choir; School Musical; Variety Show; Socr; Hon Roll; NHS; Jazz, Show Choirs; Fine Arts Hnr Stdnt; Rose ST Coll; Photo.

LANKFORD, TONI CHENELL; Holdenville HS; Holdenville, OK; (2); #2 in class; Church Yth Grp; Natl FFA Org; Scholastic Bowl; Band; Flag Corp; Yrbk; VP Soph Cls; 4-H Awd; Hon Roll; NHS; Yth Cnslr.

LANMAN, DOUGLAS R; Bartlesville Mid HS; Bartlesville, OK; (2); 1/481; Computer Clb; JA; Spanish Clb; Teachers Aide; Band; Mrchg Band; Orch; High Hon Roll; NHS; Masonic Lodge Stu Of Today; 1st Place Physics OK ST Sci Fair; All Amer Schlr.

LANN, DAVID J; Norman Sr HS; Norman, OK; (3); Boy Scts; Drama Clb; Mu Alpha Theta; Spanish Clb; Thesps; School Play; Ofcr Stu Cncl; Intrml Socr; Hon Roll; Natl Yth Ldrshp Cncl Schlr.

LANNING, MELISSA S; Canton HS; Canton, OK; (3); 8/21; VP Church Yth Grp; FHA; Spanish Clb; SADD; Chorus; Rep Jr Cls; Ofcr Stu Cncl; Mgr(s); Hon Roll; Piano; Piano Tchr.

LANSDALE, CRYSTAL G; Okmulgee HS; Okmulgee, OK; (4); 41/120; French Clb; Library Aide; Band; Jazz Band; Mrchg Band; Pep Band; School Play; Stage Crew; Rptr Nwsp; Phtg Rptr Yrbk; OK Bandmasters Assn Outstdng Soloist; All St Hnr Band Alt; All Sr Hnr Band; Southeastern OK ST U; Music.

LANSFORD, ELIZABETH; U S Grant HS; Oklahoma City, OK; (2); Dance Clb; Drama Clb; School Play; Sec Soph Cls; Vllybl; High Hon Roll; NHS; OK U; Bus.

LANTZ, BRANDY S; Guthrie Sr HS; Guthrie, OK; (2); Cmnty Wkr; Drama Clb; Key Clb; Red Cross Aide; ROTC; Color Guard; Chrldng; Crs Cntry; Trk; Cit Awd.

LA PIERRE, MELISSA; Macarthur Jr HS; Elgin, OK; (1); Drill Tm; Chrldng; Pom Pon; High Hon Roll; Jr NHS; NHS; Art Work Awds; OK U.

LARA, JOEL D; Westmoore HS; Oklahoma City, OK; (2); 1/650; Cmnty Wkr; Orch; Tennis; DAR Awd; High Hon Roll; NHS; Schlstc Team; Lwyr/Pre-Law.

LARAMORE, MELISSA; Ada HS; Ada, OK; (3); Church Yth Grp; Dance Clb; FCA; Pep Clb; Spanish Clb; Band; Drill Tm; Mrchg Band; Pep Band; Sec Frsh Cls.

LARDIZABAL, TONI J; South Intermediate HS; Broken Arrow, OK; (1); 110/610; Church Yth Grp; Debate Tm; Drama Clb; FCA; School Musical; School Play; Variety Show; Sec Frsh Cls; Ofcr Stu Cncl; Hon Roll; Ballet Stu At OK Smmr Arts Inst; OK Hnr Scty; U Of OK; Fine Arts.

LARGE, ROBERT BLAKE; Durant HS; Durant, OK; (1); Church Yth Grp; FCA; JV Bsbl; Var Ftbl; Hon Roll; Stdnt Cncl; Hnrs Clss; DFY.

LARGENT, ANNE M; Catoosa HS; Tulsa, OK; (2); Church Yth Grp; Teachers Aide; Band; Chorus; Color Guard; Hon Roll; Wntrgrd; Microbio.

LARISON JR, LINDEL; Ft Cobb-Broxton HS; Anadarko, OK; (2); Church Yth Grp; Bsktbl; High Hon Roll; Prfct Atten Awd; Med.

LA ROCHE, JAMMIE; Tomlinson Jr HS; Lawton, OK; (1); Chorus; High Hon Roll; Hon Roll; Jr NHS; Ntl Merit Ltr.

LA ROCHELLE, RENEE; Midwest City HS; Midwest City, OK; (2); Church Yth Grp; Drama Clb; FCA; 4-H; German Clb; Pep Clb; Science Clb; School Musical; School Play; Rep Stu Cncl; Elem Tchr.

LARRISON, BRIAN J; Mc Loud HS; Mc Loud, OK; (1); Church Yth Grp; Optometrist.

LARSON, THOMAS; Shawnee Sr HS; Shawnee, OK; (4); Church Yth Grp; Cmnty Wkr; Latin Clb; Library Aide; Teachers Aide; Rptr Nwsp; Hon Roll; Ntl Mrt Commended Stu; Wrtng; Engl.

LARSON, TRAVIS J; Bray-Doyle HS; Foster, OK; (2); Scholastic Bowl; School Play; L Bsbl; L Bsktbl; Hon Roll; NHS; OK Hon Soc; Acad Team.

LA RUE, PRESTON W; U S Grant HS; Oklahoma City, OK; (1); Boy Scts; Ofcr Frsh Cls; Ofcr Soph Cls; Ofcr Stu Cncl; Ofcr Bsbl; Bsktbl; Hon Roll; UNC; Crtnst/Cmptr Prgrmr.

LASATER, CHRISTIE; Pawnee HS; Pawnee, OK; (3); 19/70; FHA; Hosp Aide; HOBY; Natl FFA Org; Pep Clb; Capt Vllybl; Bio.

LA SAXON, REBECCA A; Bishop Mcguinness HS; Edmond, OK; (2); 32/167; Church Yth Grp; Latin Clb; Pep Clb; NHS; Univ OK Hlth Sci Cntr 96 Summner Acad; Yth Adv Cncl Mem; St Gregorys; Med.

LASHLEY, ANDY; Oklahoma Christian Schl; Edmond, OK; (4); 2/40; Church Yth Grp; Debate Tm; Speech Tm; Yrbk; JV Bsktbl; Golf; High Hon Roll; Pres Acad Fit Awd; Pres Schlr; Sal; Stu Of Mnth; OK Chrstn U Of Sci & Arts.

LASITER, ARON; Gans Public Schl; Muldrow, OK; (2); 4-H; Rep Natl FFA Org; Spanish Clb; Band; Church Choir; School Musical; School Play; VP Frsh Cls; Pres Soph Cls; Bsktbl; Sports Challenge Belgium Bsktbl Tour 95 To Rep USA; U Of AR; Prof Bsktbl; Engrng.

LASKA, BRANDACE C; Edmond Memorial HS; Edmond, OK; (3); Church Yth Grp; Cmnty Wkr; Spanish Clb; SADD; Score Keeper; Sftbl; Prfct Atten Awd; Mission Trips To Mexico; Soc Of Plastics Engrs Essay Cont.

LASKA, KATHRYN; Edmond Memorial HS; Edmond, OK; (4); 92/335; Am Leg Aux Girls St; Church Yth Grp; Cmnty Wkr; Drama Clb; JCL; Key Clb; Latin Clb; Spanish Clb; School Play; Stage Crew; Engl.

LASSITER, JOLIE; Stigler HS; Stigler, OK; (1); Church Yth Grp; FCA; Pep Clb; SADD; Bsktbl; Chrldng; Hon Roll; Prfct Atten Awd.

LATCHAM, JEREMY R; Union Intermediate HS; Tulsa, OK; (1); Church Yth Grp; Debate Tm; NFL; Speech Tm; Ftbl; Wt Lftg; High Hon Roll; NHS; Acad Lttr Awd; Law.

LATHAM, BENJAMIN T; Broken Arrow Sr HS; Broken Arrow, OK; (4); 150/921; Boy Scts; Church Yth Grp; Debate Tm; Drama Clb; Key Clb; Speech Tm; Acpl Chr; Chorus; Church Choir; School Musical; NE St Univ; Mus.

LATHROP, ASHEAL A; Union Intermediate HS; Tulsa, OK; (2); French Clb; High Hon Roll; Hon Roll; Jr NHS; NHS; Pres Acad Fit Awd; Schlrshp To Aviation Career Acad; Astronomy.

LATIMER, CINDY; Guthrie Sr HS; Guthrie, OK; (4); 22/167; Pres Drama Clb; Hosp Aide; Intnl Clb; Pres Hist Key Clb; School Musical; School Play; Treas Sr Cls; Hon Roll; Kiwanis Awd; NHS; Intl Order Rainbow Grls St Offcr; Park Col; Mass Comm.

LATIMER, KIMBERLY D; Clayton Jr Sr HS; Clayton, OK; (3); 4/30; FHA; Nwsp; Hon Roll; Acctg.

OKLAHOMA

LAU, AMANDA; Chickasha Jr HS; Chickasha, OK; (1); Church Yth Grp; Dance Clb; Science Clb; Chorus; Church Choir; L Chrldng; Pom Pon; Hon Roll; Jr NHS; Harp; OK City U; Orthopedic Srgn.

LAU, CRYSTAL; Stroud HS; Cushing, OK; (3); Art Clb; Church Yth Grp; FCA; GAA; Spanish Clb; JV Bsktbl; JV Var Chrldng; Hon Roll; Prfct Atten Awd; St Chrldng Champ; All Conf Chrldr.

LAUBACH, CHARLES; Waukomis HS; Waukomis, OK; (1); FCA; Quiz Bowl; Rptr Yrbk; Pres Frsh Cls; High Hon Roll; Prfct Atten Awd; Stu Mnth; Span Stu Wk; Gftd/Tlntd; OK St; Engr.

LAUBACH, CHRISTY; Waukomis HS; Waukomis, OK; (3); Church Yth Grp; Drama Clb; FCA; Letterman Clb; Pep Clb; Scholastic Bowl; Bsktbl; Sftbl; High Hon Roll; Hon Roll; Southwestern ST U; Phy Ther.

LAUBERT, KRISTI L; Eisenhower Sr HS; Lawton, OK; (4); 8/386; Pres Treas Church Yth Grp; FCA; Sec Key Clb; Ofcr Stu Cncl; Var Chrldng; Cit Awd; NHS; Varsity Clb; High Hon Roll; Hon Roll; Medcl Explrs; Westminster Presbytrn Chrch Yth Delg To Session; OK ST U; Elem Ed.

LAUDERDALE, AMBER; Edmond North HS; Edmond, OK; (3); 1/391; Drama Clb; Mu Alpha Theta; Spanish Clb; NHS; Univ Of OK; Crmnl Jstc.

LAUDERDALE, JUSTIN P; Edmond North HS; Edmond, OK; (3); 47/348; Pres Drama Clb; Key Clb; NFL; Spanish Clb; Thesps; School Musical; School Play; Stage Crew; Variety Show; NHS; Theatre.

LAUFER, CHRIS; Elk City HS; Elk City, OK; (4); 12/141; Am Leg Boys St; Church Yth Grp; FCA; Letterman Clb; Model UN; Pep Clb; Band; Ftbl; Tennis; NHS; Biology.

LAUGHLIN, LINDSAY R; Deer Creek HS; Edmond, OK; (2); 12/110; Church Yth Grp; FCA; Science Clb; School Musical; School Play; Co-Ed Nwsp; Ed Yrbk; Chrldng; NHS; News 101; Jrnlsm.

LAUGHTON, B G; Freedom Schl; Freedom, OK; (2); 2/10; FCA; HOBY; Natl FFA Org; Quiz Bowl; Scholastic Bowl; Teachers Aide; Ftbl; Wt Lftg; Hon Roll; NHS.

LAUHON, LESLIE J; Union Sr HS; Tulsa, OK; (4); 117/669; Treas Church Yth Grp; Key Clb; Office Aide; Spanish Clb; Nwsp; Ed Yrbk; JV Var Sftbl; Hon Roll; NHS; Spanish NHS; Renaissance; S Nazarene Univ; Mkting.

LAUINGER, WILLIAM A; Cascia Hall Prep School; Tulsa, OK; (3); Quiz Bowl; Spanish Clb; Bsktbl; Ftbl; Tennis; High Hon Roll; NHS.

LA VALLE, ALYSSA D; West Middle HS; Norman, OK; (2); Church Yth Grp; Office Aide; Spanish Clb; Ofcr Stu Cncl; JV Sftbl; Teen Vol; U Of OK; Marriage Cnslr; Thrpst.

LAVICKY, JASON L; Enid Sr HS; Enid, OK; (4); Letterman Clb; Library Aide; Spanish Clb; Band; Jazz Band; Mrchg Band; Orch; High Hon Roll; Hon Roll; Jr NHS; Tri ST Music Fstvl Spr Rtng 93; Cameo Cntst Wnnr 94; Savannah Coll; Cartoon Art.

LA VIOLETTE, RICHARD A; Temple Jr Sr HS; Temple, OK; (2); 4-H; FHA; Letterman Clb; JV Bsbl; JV Bsktbl.

LAW, DONALD W; Union Intermediate HS; Broken Arrow, OK; (2); Boy Scts; Hon Roll; Pres Schlr; Mens Gymnstcs; Tae Kwon Do; Hntng/Cmpng/Hkng; OK ST Univ; Vet Medcn.

LAWHOH, TODD R; Blackwell HS; Blackwell, OK; (2); Natl FFA Org; Var Bsktbl; Ftbl; Wt Lftg; Hon Roll; NHS; Pep Club; FFA; Explorers; Vet.

LAWLER, ERIN K; Stillwater Sr HS; Stillwater, OK; (2); #1 in class; Spanish Clb; Rep Stu Cncl; Var L Swmmng; Hon Roll; Val.

LAWLER, JILL M; Stillwater Sr HS; Stillwater, OK; (2); Spanish Clb; Swmmng; Hon Roll; Pres Acad Fit Awd.

LAWLER, TRAVIS D; Edmond North HS; Edmond, OK; (2); German Clb; Spanish Clb; Teachers Aide; Rep Stu Cncl; Bsktbl; Socr; Hon Roll; Pres Acad Fit Awd; All Conf Bsktbl & Soccer; All Trnmnt Teams; Sports Med.

LAWLESS, CHRISTOPHER D; Sallisaw HS; Sallisaw, OK; (3); 12/132; Art Clb; Church Yth Grp; Math Clb; Spanish Clb; Phtg Yrbk; Cit Awd; Hon Roll; NHS; Prfct Atten Awd; OK St Hnr Soc; Outstndng Wrld Geog & OK Hstry Achvts.

LAWLESS, LACEY; Rattan Sr HS; Fort Towson, OK; (4); 6/33; Church Yth Grp; FCA; 4-H; French Clb; FHA; Yrbk; Sec Frsh Cls; Sec Soph Cls; Sec Jr Cls; VP Sr Cls.

LAWRENCE, BROOKE J; Bixby Sr HS; Broken Arrow, OK; (3); Church Yth Grp; Debate Tm; Drama Clb; FCA; FHA; German Clb; GAA; Speech Tm; Thesps; School Musical; Gftd & Tlntd Org; Srgn.

LAWRENCE, JENNIFER; Union Intermediate HS; Tulsa, OK; (2); Orch; Hon Roll; Bus.

LAWRENCE, KINDRA A; Warner HS; Warner, OK; (4); 6/52; Church Yth Grp; VP Pep Clb; Quiz Bowl; Scholastic Bowl; Spanish Clb; Speech Tm; Chorus; Church Choir; Color Guard; Rptr Nwsp; OK Univ; Pediatrician.

LAWRENCE, MICHAEL J; Putnam City HS; Oklahoma City, OK; (2); Church Yth Grp; FCA; Band; Pep Band; School Musical; Var Ftbl; Var Trk; Wt Lftg; TX Christian Univ; Yth Mnstry.

LAWRENCE, ROBERT O; Del City HS; Del City, OK; (3); Church Yth Grp; ROTC; Teachers Aide; Church Choir; Ofcr Stu Cncl; JV Bsktbl; Var Ftbl; Var Trk; Var Hon Roll.

LAWRENCE, SHAMESHA L; Del City HS; Oklahoma City, OK; (3); JA; Spanish Clb; SADD; Varsity Clb; Chorus; JV Var Bsktbl; Jr NHS; NHS; Prfct Atten Awd; Criminal Justice.

LAWS, JENIFER; U S Grant HS; Oklahoma City, OK; (4); 7/184; HOBY; Varsity Clb; Sec Jr Cls; Chrmn Stu Cncl; Chrldng; Gym; Kiwanis Awd; Pres Schlr; Alumni Assn Stu Yr; Med.

LAWSON, AMBER L; South Intermediate HS; Broken Arrow, OK; (2); Intnl Clb; Latin Clb; Office Aide; Rep Soph Cls; Ofcr Stu Cncl; Hon Roll; Jr NHS; NHS; Orthopedic Surgeon.

LAWSON, APRIL; Durant HS; Durant, OK; (2); 1/200; Church Yth Grp; Chorus; Church Choir; Yrbk; Pres Soph Cls; Rep Stu Cncl; Var L Chrldng; Var L Socr; High Hon Roll.

LAWSON, BRANDON; Seminole Jr Sr HS; Seminole, OK; (1); Church Yth Grp; Debate Tm; French Clb; NFL; Quiz Bowl; Band; Mrchg Band; Pep Band; High Hon Roll.

LAWSON, BRYCE D; Putnam City North HS; Oklahoma City, OK; (2); Var Bsktbl; Var Ftbl; Hon Roll; NHS.

LAWSON, CHRIS; Roland Sr HS; Roland, OK; (2); 1/110; Church Yth Grp; Math Tm; Natl FFA Org; Quiz Bowl; Scholastic Bowl; Band; Mrchg Band; Pep Band; VP Stu Cncl; Var JV Bsktbl; All Dist Bnd; Mech Engr.

LAWSON, COURTNEY G; Tecumseh HS; Tecumseh, OK; (3); 7/150; Church Yth Grp; Cmnty Wkr; FCA; GAA; Natl Beta Clb; Spanish Clb; SADD; Sec Frsh Cls; Treas Soph Cls; Var Bsktbl.

LAWSON, D COREY; Tahlequah Sr HS; Tahlequah, OK; (4); 12/251; Quiz Bowl; Pres Science Clb; Chorus; NHS; Pres Acad Fit Awd; Med.

LAWSON, DANIEL C; Union Sr HS; Tulsa, OK; (3); 35/741; German Clb; Var Ice Hcky; NHS; Ntl Merit Ltr; Pres Schlr; Tulsa Yth Hcky Assn.

LAWSON, DAVID COREY; Tahlequah Sr HS; Tahlequah, OK; (4); 9/251; Pres Science Clb; Chorus; Ftbl; Trk; Hon Roll; Jr NHS; NHS; Pres Acad Fit Awd; Music.

LAWSON, JOYCE R; Tipton Jr Sr HS; Tipton, OK; (2); Church Yth Grp; NFL; Science Clb; Band; Church Choir; Mrchg Band; Pep Band; Bsktbl; Sftbl; Vllybl; FFA Frshmn Sweethrt; Acctng.

LAWSON, L ALLISON; Sapulpa Sr HS; Sapulpa, OK; (4); 20/297; Church Yth Grp; Science Clb; Teachers Aide; Flag Corp; Nwsp; Pres Frsh Cls; Rep Soph Cls; Rep Jr Cls; Rep Sr Cls; Rep Stu Cncl; U Of OK; Ortho.

LAWSON, NICHOLAS R; Heritage Chrstn Schl; Ardmore, OK; (4); 1/8; Church Yth Grp; School Musical; School Play; L Bsktbl; Cit Awd; High Hon Roll; Val; Stu Of Yr Awd; Coaches Cup Awd; Pensacola Chrstn Coll; Cmptr.

LAWSON, VICKI J; Harrah HS; Harrah, OK; (3); 95/153; FHA; Office Aide; Band; Mrchg Band; Bsktbl; Mgr(s); Trk; Bsktbl Mgr; Technology Ed.

LAWSON, WENDY; Durant HS; Durant, OK; (4); 1/190; Am Leg Aux Girls St; HOBY; Sec Frsh Cls; Rep Soph Cls; Sec Pres Stu Cncl; Var L Bsktbl; Var L Sftbl; High Hon Roll; Kiwanis Awd; NHS; Lynda Ablott Schlr; OK Hnr Soc; Drg Free Yth; U OK; Med.

LAXAMANA, ARLENE; Glenpool HS; Glenpool, OK; (3); HOBY; Quiz Bowl; Spanish Clb; Teachers Aide; Band; Jazz Band; Mrchg Band; Sec Soph Cls; Rep Stu Cncl; NHS; Asst Drm Mjr; Pedtrcn.

LAY, ANNIE; Coweta HS; Wagoner, OK; (2); Art Clb; SADD; Yrbk; Sec Stu Cncl; Chrldng; Hon Roll; Jr NHS; NHS; Art Awd; Mst Vlbl Chrldr; Prlmntrn/Treas NJHS; U Of OK; Pre-Med.

LAY, ASHLEY J; Vinita HS; Vinita, OK; (4); 14/92; 4-H; Quiz Bowl; Science Clb; Spanish Clb; 4-H Awd; Hon Roll.

LAY, SALLY A; Midwest City HS; Midwest City, OK; (2); Drama Clb; Girl Scts; Teachers Aide; Arts 4 Smstrs.

LAYMAN, DIANA D; Vinita HS; Vinita, OK; (2); FHA; Science Clb; Spanish Clb; Band; Mrchg Band; Pep Band; Hon Roll; Northeastern ST U; Optometry.

LAYMON, TONYA; Braggs Schl; Braggs, OK; (1); 3/16; Hon Roll.

LAYTON, MATT D; Lindsay HS; Lindsay, OK; (3); 12/85; Church Yth Grp; FCA; Letterman Clb; Natl FFA Org; Acpl Chr; Chorus; Var L Ftbl; Hon Roll; NHS; Pres Acad Fit Awd; U Of OK.

LAZATIN, MELISSA S; Pauls Valley HS; Pauls Valley, OK; (3); FHA; Band; Jazz Band; Mrchg Band; Pep Band; Sftbl; Hon Roll; All Star Mrchng Bnd At All ST Ftbl Gm 95; Rodeo Bullriding; Horses; OK Univ; PT.

LE, ALICIA M; Muskogee HS; Muskogee, OK; (1); Cmnty Wkr; School Musical; Socr; Hon Roll; OK Hnr Soc.

LE, BRENDA N; Union Intermediate HS; Tulsa, OK; (1); Hosp Aide; Math Clb; Var Wt Lftg; High Hon Roll; Jr NHS; NHS; Acad Ltr Awd; Acad Team; DFY; Med.

LE, DIANA N; Westmoore HS; Oklahoma City, OK; (3); French Clb; Office Aide; Teachers Aide; NHS; OCU; Physician.

LE, HIEN N; U S Grant HS; Oklahoma City, OK; (2); Dance Clb; ROTC; Chorus; Ofcr Jr Cls; Asian Clb 95-96; OK U; Phrmcy.

LE, RICHARD T; Union Intermediate HS; Tulsa, OK; (2); 35/800; French Clb; Key Clb; Math Clb; Band; Mrchg Band; Swmmng; High Hon Roll; NHS; Acad Ltr 95; Stu Of Month Awd 94-95; All-Dist Band 1st Chair 2 Yrs; U Of Tulsa; Med.

LEACH, ERIC W; Henryetta Sr HS; Henryetta, OK; (2); Church Yth Grp; FCA; Var JV Bsbl; Var JV Bsktbl; Hon Roll; Pres Acad Fit Awd; OK Hnr Soc.

LEACHMAN, RAMEY; Seiling Schl; Vici, OK; (2); Art Clb; FCA; FHA; Swing Chorus; Ofcr Stu Cncl; Hon Roll; SW OK ST U; Acctng.

LEAF, CHRIS E; Claremore Sr HS; Claremore, OK; (1); JV Bsbl; Hon Roll; Medicine.

LEAGUE, ZACH K; Putnam City West HS; Bethany, OK; (3); Church Yth Grp; Bsktbl; Socr; Southern Nazarene Univ.

LEAMAN, JARROD A; Moore HS; Moore, OK; (1); CAP; Cmnty Wkr; French Clb; Science Clb; Color Guard; Ice Hocey Travel Team Goalie; Aikido Tae Kwon Do; Weight Trng; Soccer; US Naval Acad.

LEARMOUTH, IAN A; West Middle HS; Norman, OK; (2); Church Yth Grp; Spanish Clb; Hon Roll; Pres Schlr; St Schlr; OK N Rail Club; Cmptrs.

LEATHERMAN, SHAWN R; Blackwell HS; Blackwell, OK; (2); FCA; Letterman Clb; Pep Clb; Spanish Clb; Rep Jr Cls; Var Ftbl; Var Trk; Var Wrstlng; OK ST Univ; Med.

LEAVELL, SCOTT M; Tomlinson Jr HS; Lawton, OK; (1); 95/200; Band; Drm Mjr(t); Jazz Band; Mrchg Band; Pep Band; High Hon Roll; NHS.

LEAVITT, LUCINDA; Oaks Mission Jr Sr HS; Rose, OK; (3); 4-H; FBLA; FHA; HOBY; Chorus; 4-H Awd; Hon Roll; NHS.

LEBA, JACOB; Asher Schl; Asher, OK; (2); Natl FFA Org; Varsity Clb; Var Bsbl; Var Bsktbl; Hon Roll; OK U; Phys Thrpst.

LEBEDA, PAMELA; Medford Schl; Medford, OK; (2); 4/18; Church Yth Grp; FCA; Pep Clb; Chorus; Sec Soph Cls; Bsktbl; Sftbl; Trk; Hon Roll; Evangel; Church Ministry.

LE BLANC, KENNY; Okmulgee HS; Okmulgee, OK; (4); 5/120; Am Leg Boys St; Church Yth Grp; FCA; French Clb; FBLA; Math Clb; Yrbk; VP Jr Cls; Rep Stu Cncl; Bsktbl; OK Prncpls Sci Schlr; Northeastern ST U; Phrmcy.

LE BLANC, SAFFRON; Central Mid-HS; Norman, OK; (1); Model UN; Mu Alpha Theta; Orch; High Hon Roll; Hon Roll; Outstdng Achvmts Engl/His/Bio/Latin/Geo; Bio Chem/Eng.

LECHNER, JASON R; Haskell HS; Haskell, OK; (3); Office Aide; Yrbk; JV Bsktbl; Var L Ftbl; Var L Golf; Wt Lftg; Hon Roll; NHS; Prfct Atten Awd; Macy Schlr Awd; Sprts Med.

LEDBETTER, BRANDY N; Muskogee HS; Muskogee, OK; (1); Cmnty Wkr; Drama Clb; Hosp Aide; Hon Roll; Jr NHS; Yth Vol Corp; Spelman; Chld Psych/Mdlng.

LEDBETTER, DREW; Checotah HS; Checotah, OK; (4); 6/93; Am Leg Boys St; Church Yth Grp; Scholastic Bowl; Spanish Clb; Speech Tm; Teachers Aide; Chorus; Nwsp; Yrbk; Pres Frsh Cls; Boys Nation Delg; All St Chorus 95; 2nd Plst Voice Demcrcy Cont.

LEDBETTER, HEIDI M; Muskogee HS; Muskogee, OK; (2); Cmnty Wkr; ROTC; SADD; Color Guard; Drill Tm; Flag Corp; Mrchg Band; Rptr Nwsp; JV Bsktbl; Score Keeper; ROTC Natl Awd Daughters Of Founders/Patriots Amer; ROTC Natl Order Of Purple Heart; Hnr Flight; Grambling ST Univ; USAF.

LEDBETTER, MARK A; Pauls Valley HS; Pauls Valley, OK; (3); Art Clb; Church Yth Grp; FBLA; Chorus; School Musical; High Hon Roll; OK St Hnr Soc; All Dist Chr.

LEDDY, LAURA M; Latta Sr HS; Ada, OK; (3); FHA; Sftbl; High Hon Roll; NHS; Prfct Atten Awd; Psych.

LEDFORD, STEPHANIE M; U S Grant HS; Oklahoma City, OK; (1); Church Choir; Sec Frsh Cls; Sec Soph Cls; Gov Hon Prg Awd; Hon Roll; Peer Mediator; MIT.

LEDING, KYRSTIN; Mustang HS; Yukon, OK; (2); Church Yth Grp; FCA; Pep Clb; SADD; Varsity Clb; Var Chrldng; Var Vllybl; Hon Roll; U Cntrl OK; Nrsng/Admin/Bus.

LEDLOW, MARK; Choctaw HS; Choctaw, OK; (4); Quiz Bowl; Teachers Aide; Jr NHS; Prfct Atten Awd; Mltry.

LE DOUX, ROBIN; Metro Christian Acad; Tulsa, OK; (2); Church Yth Grp; Cmnty Wkr; Spanish Clb; Church Choir; School Musical; Chrldng; Gym; Hon Roll; Prfct Atten Awd; Tulsa's Yth Symphony; Psych.

LEE, AARON Q; Tahlequah Sr HS; Tahlequah, OK; (3); Band; Mrchg Band; U Of Ear; Cmptrprogmng.

LEE, ALLISSA A; Kansas Schl; Twin Oaks, OK; (3); 1/50; Church Yth Grp; Pres FHA; Sec Natl Beta Clb; Rptr Phtg Yrbk; Phtg Yrbk; Rptr Sr Cls; Rptr Stu Cncl; Cit Awd; Hon Roll; OK Univ; Archt.

LEE, AMANDA; Jenks HS; Tulsa, OK; (3); Church Yth Grp; JCL; Latin Clb; Teachers Aide; Chorus; Orch; School Play; Mgr(s); Swmmng; Tennis; Pgnts; Ind Sngng; OK ST U; Htl/Rest Mgmt.

LEE, ANGELA L; Okay Jr Sr HS; Okay, OK; (3); Hosp Aide; Spanish Clb; Bsktbl; Chrldng; JV Socr; Sftbl; Trk; Vllybl; Hon Roll; NSU; Child Care; Animal Care.

LEE, ANN M; Shawnee Sr HS; Shawnee, OK; (4); 20/262; Boy Scts; Hosp Aide; Spanish Clb; Band; Color Guard; Flag Corp; Mrchg Band; NHS; HOPE; OSU; Phrmcy.

LEE, BEN; Plainview HS; Ardmore, OK; (1); Church Yth Grp; JV Bsktbl; JV Ftbl; JV Wt Lftg; Hon Roll; NHS.

LEE, BRANDI E; Moore West Jr HS; Oklahoma City, OK; (1); Church Yth Grp; Spanish Clb; Variety Show; Bsktbl; Hon Roll; Jr NHS; Piano; Cert Yth Div Of Natl Bapt Congrs Chrstn Ed St Louis MO; Pres Awd Academic Achvmnt; Spellman.

LEE, CARRIE A; Dickson HS; Ardmore, OK; (3); Church Yth Grp; French Clb; GAA; Key Clb; Speech Tm; SADD; Chorus; Var Bsktbl; Var Crs Cntry; Var Trk; Bsktbl Ofnsv Plyr Yr; Phsyclgy.

LEE, DESIREE D; Union Sr HS; Tulsa, OK; (3); 127/673; Church Yth Grp; FBLA; Intnl Clb; Band; Mrchg Band; Bsktbl; Sftbl; Hon Roll; NHS; Tulsa CC; Occuptnl Thrpst Asst.

LEE, DON V; Union Intermediate HS; Tulsa, OK; (2); Church Yth Grp; Socr; Hon Roll; NHS; Car Restoration.

LEE, HANNA E; B T Washington HS; Tulsa, OK; (1); Church Yth Grp; Speech Tm; School Musical; Hon Roll; Ballet Miss Laurey's Schl Dance.

LEE, JASON C; Jenks HS; Tulsa, OK; (4); 46/522; Church Yth Grp; Model UN; VP NFL; Scholastic Bowl; Science Clb; Teachers Aide; Orch; Hon Roll; NHS; Ntl Merit SF.

LEE, JEFFREY W; El Reno Sr HS; El Reno, OK; (2); 31/224; Church Yth Grp; Cmnty Wkr; Key Clb; Sec Soph Cls; Var Bsbl; Var Bsktbl; Cit Awd; High Hon Roll; Jr NHS; NHS; Kiwanis Awd; OK ST Univ; Med.

LEE, JEREMY B; Haskell HS; Taft, OK; (2); Church Yth Grp; Cmnty Wkr; Varsity Clb; Band; Church Choir; Bsktbl; Ftbl; Golf; Socr; Swmmng; Connors.

LEE, JESSICAH R; Walters HS; Walters, OK; (4); 4/34; 4-H; FBLA; FHA; SADD; Band; Chorus; 4-H Awd; NHS; Ntl Merit Schol; Chldrns Chrch Tchr; YM; Cameron U; Medcl Tech.

LEE, JOHN; Tomlinson Jr HS; Lawton, OK; (1); Art Clb; Boy Scts; Church Yth Grp; FCA; Office Aide; School Play; Rep Frsh Cls; Golf; High Hon Roll; Jr NHS; U Of OK; Bus.

LEE, JOSH D; Vinita HS; Vinita, OK; (2); Boy Scts; Quiz Bowl; Science Clb; Spanish Clb; JV Var Bsktbl; JV Var Ftbl; JV Golf; Var Wt Lftg; Hon Roll; U Of OK; Engrng.

LEE, KENNETH W; Haskell HS; Taft, OK; (1); 28/45; Pres Church Yth Grp; Cmnty Wkr; FCA; Teachers Aide; Treas Church Choir; Co-Capt Ftbl; Hon Roll; Letterman Clb; Var Trk; L Wt Lftg; All-ST Ftbl; Black His Club; Plyr Of Yr Dist A-5 Ftbl; Northeastern ST U; Scndry Ed.

LEE, LAUREN; Lone Grove HS; Lone Grove, OK; (2); Church Yth Grp; FHA; Math Clb; Science Clb; Spanish Clb; Hon Roll; Camp Fire; Yth Alive.

LEE, LINDSEY; Edmond North HS; Edmond, OK; (1); 1/492; Church Yth Grp; FCA; Rep Stu Cncl; Chrldng; Hon Roll; Pres Acad Fit Awd; Royalty Cmmtte; Med.

LEE, LORETTA E; Emerson Jr HS; Enid, OK; (1); FHA; Chorus; Rptr Nwsp; Hon Roll; Hnr Chr; Show Chr; Nrs/Cmptr Prgr.

LEE, MELISSA A; Charles Page HS; Sand Springs, OK; (4); 21/329; Church Yth Grp; French Clb; Key Clb; Band; Hon Roll; NHS; Pres Acad Fit Awd; HOSA; Multi Yr Listee; RN.

LEE, MELISSA D; Putnam City North HS; Oklahoma City, OK; (4); 19/436; Church Yth Grp; Cmnty Wkr; French Clb; Key Clb; Office Aide; Pep Clb; Service Clb; Nwsp; Crs Cntry; Trk; Pom Pom; Mock Trial Team; Best Atty Awd 3 Times; U Of WY; Atty.

LEE, NICHOLAS E; Tecumseh HS; Shawnee, OK; (1); JV Bsbl; JV Bsktbl; High Hon Roll; Prfct Atten Awd; St Schlr; OK ST Univ.

LEE, NICHOLAS R; Hinton HS; Hinton, OK; (2); Chorus; Ofcr Jr Cls; Ofcr Bsbl; Ftbl; Wrstlng; High Hon Roll; Hon Roll.

LEE, SHALYSA N; Del City HS; Oklahoma City, OK; (3); Dance Clb; FHA; Pep Clb; Spanish Clb; Ofcr Stu Cncl; Trk; Hon Roll; Prfct Atten Awd; UCO; Ed.

LEE, SOOJIN J; Union Sr HS; Tulsa, OK; (4); 1/640; Church Yth Grp; French Clb; Intnl Clb; Key Clb; Cit Awd; High Hon Roll; Jr NHS; NHS; Pres Acad Fit Awd; Ofcr Jr Cls; Ballet; Princeton U.

LEE, STEPH; Guthrie Sr HS; Guthrie, OK; (2); 35/241; Drama Clb; FCA; Letterman Clb; Acpl Chr; Chorus; School Musical; Sec Soph Cls; Chrldng; 3rd In Nation Chrldng Squad; OU; Psych.

LEE, STEPHANIE; Newcastle HS; Tuttle, OK; (3); 1/95; VP FBLA; HOBY; Model UN; Quiz Bowl; Hist Science Clb; Spanish Clb; Ed Yrbk; Rptr Jr Cls; High Hon Roll; Rptr NHS; Med.

LEE, TATUM; Minco HS; Minco, OK; (1); Church Yth Grp; Cmnty Wkr; Hosp Aide; Math Tm; Church Choir; School Play; Chrldng; Score Keeper; Cmnty Wkr; Sftbl.

LEEBRON, DRESDEN A; Edmond North HS; Edmond, OK; (3); 61/348; VP Drama Clb; French Clb; Key Clb; Mu Alpha Theta; NFL; School Musical; School Play; Treas Soph Cls; Treas Jr Cls; Rep Stu Cncl; Stdnt Mo Frosh/Soph/Jr Yr; Nom Stdnt Yr Fnlst Soph/Jr Yr; 96 Natl Comp Forensics Leag Fyvl NC; U Of OK; Pre Law.

LEEDS, AMANDA D; Catoosa HS; Catoosa, OK; (1); FCA; Girl Scts; Color Guard; Chrldng.

LEEHAN, MARISA A; Edmond Santa Fe HS; Edmond, OK; (2); French Clb; Pep Clb; Orch; Diving; Powder Puff Ftbl; Swmmng; NHS; Soph Rep Orch Cncl; Orch & Swimming Ltrs; U Of OK.

LEEMASTER, BRETT A; Moore HS; Moore, OK; (2); Church Yth Grp; FCA; Crs Cntry; Trk; Wrstlng; OK; Med.

LEEPER, MARGIE; Agra Schl; Agra, OK; (4); 1/26; Church Yth Grp; FHA; Scholastic Bowl; Pres Frsh Cls; Pres Soph Cls; Bsktbl; NHS; Prfct Atten Awd; Val; Hmcmng Queen; OK ST U.

LEES, JULIA E; Union Sr HS; Tulsa, OK; (4); 18/629; FBLA; Band; High Hon Roll; Hon Roll; Jr NHS; NHS; Pres Acad Fit Awd; Spanish NHS; Renssnce; Acad Ltrs; Tulsa U; Mgmt Info Sys.

LEFLER, TARA J; Putnam City HS; Warr Acres, OK; (3); 1/360; VP Art Clb; VP Drama Clb; Key Clb; NFL; Science Clb; Spanish Clb; School Play; Rep Pres Stu Cncl; NHS; Ntl Merit Ltr; Siloam Lodge Stu Of Today Awd; OK St Regents Smmr Sci Acad; Biolgcl Sci.

LE FORCE, FORREST S; Oklahoma Bible Acad; Pond Creek, OK; (2); Boy Scts; Church Yth Grp; Spanish Clb; Chorus; VP Soph Cls; Socr; Trk; High Hon Roll; USAFA; Aeronautical; Astro Engr.

LE FORCE, SHELI R; Strother Jr Sr HS; Earlsboro, OK; (2); Church Yth Grp; 4-H; FHA; HOBY; Quiz Bowl; Scholastic Bowl; Var Bsktbl; Var Sftbl; Hon Roll; NHS; Piano; Osteopthlgst.

LE FORS, TALOA; Coalgate HS; Coalgate, OK; (4); 5/50; Church Yth Grp; Chorus; Church Choir; Var Chrldng; Var Trk; Jr NHS; NHS; SOSU Hnr Shw Choir; Athl Acad Awd; All Dist Choir; Oral Roberts U; Med.

LEFTWICH, LAURA; Wetumka Jr Sr HS; Wetumka, OK; (2); 4/46; FHA; Pres Key Clb; High Hon Roll; Hon Roll; FFA; E Cntrl U Ada; Anml Sci.

LE GRAND, JAMIE L; Jay HS; Eucha, OK; (2); Computer Clb; FBLA; FHA; Natl FFA Org; Bsktbl; Score Keeper; Trk; Wt Lftg; I-DFY; NSU; Ed.

LEHENBAUER, CHARITY V; Choctaw HS; Choctaw, OK; (4); 10/304; FCA; Key Clb; Spanish Clb; Stat Bsktbl; JV Crs Cntry; Mgr(s); Var JV Tennis; High Hon Roll; Jr NHS; Pres Acad Fit Awd; OK Bapt U; Psych.

LEHEW, CASEY; Comanche HS; Addington, OK; (2); Art Clb; Church Yth Grp; Science Clb; Ofcr Soph Cls; Ofcr Stu Cncl; Ofcr Bsbl; Ftbl; Wrstlng; Hon Roll; MRCA Rodeo Chmp 95 & 96; 1FYR Cntstnt MRCA; OSU; Vet Med.

LEHMAN, CARMEN J; Westmoore HS; Oklahoma City, OK; (2); Church Yth Grp; Cmnty Wkr; Office Aide; Spanish Clb; Bsktbl; Trk; Hon Roll; Jr NHS; NHS.

LEHMAN, CURTIS N; Bartlesville Sr HS; Bartlesville, OK; (1); Church Yth Grp; Chorus; Ofcr Stu Cncl; Ftbl; Var L Tennis; Wt Lftg; Hon Roll; Bass Sctn Ldr Choir; All Dist Choir; Nom Natl Yng Ldrs Conf Wash DC 96; Bus/Music.

LEHMAN, HEIDI D; Mt St Marys HS; Oklahoma City, OK; (3); Church Yth Grp; Cmnty Wkr; Key Clb; Pep Clb; Stat Bsktbl; Hon Roll.

LEHR, AMY K; Norman Sr HS; Norman, OK; (4); 1/700; Pres Cmnty Wkr; Pres French Clb; Hist Intnl Clb; Model UN; Red Cross Aide; Rep Band; Rep Orch; French Hon Soc; Ntl Merit SF; Church Yth Grp; Luth Yth Of AR & OK Pblcty Coord; OK Yth Orch; Ldrs Of Tmrrw Schlrshp; Intl Rels.

LEHRLING, SHERRI; Indianola HS; Mcalester, OK; (4); 2/40; FBLA; FHA; Pres Natl Beta Clb; VP Natl FFA Org; Pres Stu Cncl; Capt Bsktbl; Var Sftbl; High Hon Roll; Sal; Bsktbl All St; Southern Nazrene U; Sprts Mgmt.

LEIGH, EDITH; Morrison HS; Stillwater, OK; (3); Art Clb; Church Yth Grp; FCA; FBLA; HOBY; Office Aide; Pep Clb; Spanish Clb; Teachers Aide; Ed Nwsp; HOBY.

LEIGHTY, JENNA; Skiatook HS; Skiatook, OK; (4); 4/106; Church Yth Grp; FCA; Chorus; Church Choir; Var Chrldng; NHS; St Schlr; Office Aide; Teachers Aide; School Musical; Acad Bowl Team Capt; All Conf Team High Scorer; Chrstn Yth Ldrshp Awd; Serteens; U Of OK; Occptnl Therapy.

LEISY JR, TOMMY J; Westmoore HS; Oklahoma City, OK; (4); Church Yth Grp; Band; Jazz Band; Mrchg Band; Jr NHS; NHS; Multi-Yr Listee.

LELACHEUR, ERICA L; South Coffeyville Schl; S Coffeyville, OK; (2); Church Yth Grp; Chorus; Bsktbl; Chrldng; Score Keeper.

LELKES, ANNE-MARIE T; Duncan HS; Duncan, OK; (2); FBLA; DAR Awd; High Hon Roll; Hon Roll; NHS; Prfct Atten Awd; Outstdng Typing I Stdnt/Acctng I Stdnt; Cameron Univ; Acctng.

LEMKE, STENA D; Bennington Schl; Bennington, OK; (2); 3/21; Church Yth Grp; 4-H; Rep Sec Natl FFA Org; Quiz Bowl; VP Soph Cls; Bsktbl; Sftbl; Hon Roll; NHS; OK Heritage Cont Schlsp.

LE MOINE, PIPER; Jenks HS; Jenks, OK; (1); 70/479; Church Yth Grp; French Clb; Mu Alpha Theta; Quiz Bowl; Science Clb; Var L Sftbl; Hon Roll; Acad Lttr; Distngd Grad; U Of OK; Small Bus Ownrshp.

LEMON, MATTHEW W; North Intemediate HS; Broken Arrow, OK; (2); Office Aide; Band; Mrchg Band; Hon Roll; OK ST Univ; Criminology.

LEMON, RACHEL N; Muskogee HS; Muskogee, OK; (4); 11/303; Church Yth Grp; Model UN; Science Clb; Spanish Clb; SADD; Teachers Aide; Acpl Chr; Chorus; Church Choir; Stage Crew; Native Amer Stu Assn Sec; U Of AR; Pre-Med.

LEMONDS, SARA N; Edmond North HS; Edmond, OK; (2); Church Yth Grp; Natl FFA Org; Acpl Chr; Orch; Var Sftbl; Hon Roll.

LEMONS, JAMIE J; Enid Sr HS; Enid, OK; (3); Church Yth Grp; DECA; Hosp Aide; Letterman Clb; Speech Tm; Chorus; Church Choir; Swing Chorus; Swmmng; Hon Roll; Scndry Ed/Music.

LEMONS, LACY C; Hammon Schl; Hammon, OK; (1); Rptr 4-H; FHA; Chorus; School Musical; 4-H Awd; Hon Roll; Write Stories; Eng.

LEMONS, LACY L; Marietta HS; Marietta, OK; (2); FCA; 4-H; GAA; Swing Chorus; Var Bsktbl; Chrldng; Var Sftbl; 4-H Awd; Hon Roll.

LENARD, JOHNNY BUSTER; Wagoner Sr HS; Wagoner, OK; (3); Art Clb; Debate Tm; Teachers Aide; Hon Roll; Jr NHS; NHS; Art; Jr Acad Team; NSU Tahlequah; Tchng.

LENINGTON, CANDACE W; Central Schl; Sallisaw, OK; (3); Art Clb; Pep Clb; Yrbk; VP Frsh Cls; Pres Soph Cls; VP Jr Cls; Rep Stu Cncl; Var Bsktbl; Var Sftbl; Hon Roll.

LENK, CYNTHIA D; Putnam City West HS; Bethany, OK; (2); Intnl Clb; Latin Clb; Science Clb; BSA Explorers Med Post 181; Search & Rescue; 1st Responder.

LENNINGTON, CHRISTI O; Fargo Schl; Fargo, OK; (2); Church Yth Grp; FCA; 4-H; FHA; GAA; School Musical; Var Bsktbl; Var Chrldng; Var Sftbl; Var Trk; 270 Conf All Star 95-; Tchr/Coach.

LENNON, JOHN C; Casady Schl; Oklahoma City, OK; (3); 8/85; Computer Clb; Debate Tm; German Clb; Orch; Rptr Nwsp; High Hon Roll; Comp.

LENTS, ROSS; Cache HS; Indiahoma, OK; (2); FCA; Natl Beta Clb; Var Bsktbl; High Hon Roll; NHS; Prfct Atten Awd; OK Hnr Soc.

LENTZ, LYNETTE; Empire Schl; Duncan, OK; (4); 4/36; Pres Sec 4-H; HOBY; Ed Nwsp; Phtg Rptr Yrbk; Pres Frsh Cls; Sec Jr Cls; Sec Sr Cls; Sec Stu Cncl; Capt Chrldng; VP NHS; DAR Gd Ctzn Awd, Cty/Reg; 4-H Ctznshp WA Focus Trp Dlgt; Clss A St Chmp Chrldr 95; OK ST U; Educ.

LEON, JOHN; Moore HS; Oklahoma City, OK; (2); Church Yth Grp; Drama Clb; JCL; Latin Clb; Library Aide; Model UN; Quiz Bowl; Scholastic Bowl; Science Clb; School Musical; Tech Stu Assn.

LEON, LUCAS S; Yukon Middle HS; Yukon, OK; (2); Church Yth Grp; Speech Tm; Trk; Wrstlng; 3-D; U Of OK; Crmnl Jstce.

LEONARD, BRANDI; Wynnewood HS; Wynnewood, OK; (3); #6 in class; Church Yth Grp; FHA; Yrbk; Sec Frsh Cls; Rep Soph Cls; Sec Jr Cls; Sec Stu Cncl; JV Var Chrldng; Var Golf; Hon Roll.

LEONARD, CHRISTY; Trinity Christian Schl; Broken Arrow, OK; (1); Church Yth Grp; Chorus; Var Bsktbl; Var Socr; Var Vllybl; Hon Roll; Sprts Med.

LEONARD, ELIZABETH P; Lone Wolf Schl; Lone Wolf, OK; (3); 5/14; Church Yth Grp; 4-H; FHA; Pep Clb; VICA; School Play; JV Chrldng; High Hon Roll; Hon Roll; NHS; Cosmetologist.

LEONARD, JENNIFER L; Tahlequah Jr HS; Tahlequah, OK; (1); Drama Clb; Orch; JV Sftbl; High Hon Roll; Hon Roll; Jr NHS; Pres Acad Fit Awd; Mentorship Prog; Amer Leg Aux Ameressay Cntst 1st; OK Jr HS Hnr Soc; Med.

LEONARD, LAURA D; Edmond Memorial HS; Edmond, OK; (3); French Clb; Girl Scts; Speech Tm; Teachers Aide; Band; Mrchg Band; Variety Show; Hon Roll; NHS; Pres Acad Fit Awd; Yth Ldrsho Exch Mem; Designed Master Grad Pgm; Bd Mem To YLX Bd; Dance; Lang Tchr; Choreographer.

LEONARD, MIKE; Miami Sr HS; Miami, OK; (3); Am Leg Boys St; Math Tm; Chorus; Ftbl; Wt Lftg; High Hon Roll; Jr NHS; Zoology; Bio.

LEONARD, SARAH; Miami Sr HS; Miami, OK; (1); 1/150; Church Yth Grp; Chorus; Ofcr Frsh Cls; Ofcr Stu Cncl; High Hon Roll; Nrs; Stylist.

LEONARD, STORMY B; Claremore Sr HS; Claremore, OK; (2); 4-H; Natl FFA Org; Office Aide; Ftbl; Trk; Wt Lftg; Wrstlng; Hon Roll; Pres Acad Fit Awd; Panhandle ST Univ; Bus.

LEONARD, TIFFANY; Carl Albert HS; Oklahoma City, OK; (1); FCA; Pep Clb; Chorus; School Musical; Rptr Stu Cncl; Var Chrldng; High Hon Roll; NHS; Prfct Atten Awd; MAD.

LEONE, ANGELA J; Shawnee Sr HS; Shawnee, OK; (2); Church Yth Grp; Computer Clb; Dance Clb; FCA; GAA; Spanish Clb; Drill Tm; Phtg Yrbk; Bsktbl; Crs Cntry; OSU; Acctng.

LEONG, LAUREL; Stillwater Sr HS; Stillwater, OK; (3); 38/363; French Clb; Natl Beta Clb; Orch; NHS; Played Piano 7 Yrs; Chrch Pianist; Chrstn Teen Girls Mag Semifinalist For Brio; Music.

LEPAK, ADAM; Moore HS; Moore, OK; (3); Church Yth Grp; JA; Speech Tm; Stage Crew; Sktbrdng; Music Guitar; Birth Choice Vlntr; Bus Mgmt.

LEPAK, SARAH; Claremore Sr HS; Claremore, OK; (2); 1/280; Church Yth Grp; Cmnty Wkr; French Clb; FHA; Office Aide; School Musical; Ofcr Stu Cncl; Pom Pon; High Hon Roll; Hon Roll; Dance.

LERBLANCE JR, RICHARD C; Hartshorne Sr HS; Hartshorne, OK; (3); 8/60; Am Leg Boys St; Natl FFA Org; Office Aide; Quiz Bowl; Rptr Nwsp; Pres Frsh Cls; Rptr Jr Cls; Ftbl; NHS; OK Univ; Jrnlsm.

LESHER, MATT; Edmond Memorial HS; Edmond, OK; (4); 1/450; Church Yth Grp; VICA; Band; Church Choir; JV Bsbl; Jr NHS; NHS; Vo Tech Hnr Soc; Own Lawn Bus; Wrts Msc; Plays Guitar; OK ST U; Bus Ed.

LESHER, TIM C; Edmond Memorial HS; Edmond, OK; (2); Church Yth Grp; Church Choir; Hon Roll; Jr NHS; NHS; Pres Acad Fit Awd; Young Life Org VP; OBU; Comp Tech; Chrch Work.

LESLEY, SARA D; Newcastle HS; Oklahoma City, OK; (3); 14/92; Church Yth Grp; FHA; GAA; Library Aide; Teachers Aide; Chorus; School Musical; School Play; Stage Crew; Variety Show; Awds For Vcl Comps; Drama & Ppt Trps; Chldrns Chr Dir; OBU; Brdcst Jrnlsm.

LESLIE, MATT S; Collinsville HS; Collinsville, OK; (2); Boy Scts; Church Yth Grp; Jazz Band; Mrchg Band; Rep Frsh Cls; Rep Soph Cls; Rep Sr Cls; Gov Hon Prg Awd; High Hon Roll; NHS; Yth Cncl Sr HS Rep; Musical Acchvmnt Awd 2 Yrs; Animal Bhvr.

LESLIE, MELONIE; Stillwater Sr HS; Stillwater, OK; (2); #51 in class; FHA; Teachers Aide; Band; Bsktbl; Hon Roll; OK ST Univ; Vet.

LESLIE, RUSSELL; Webbers Falls Public Schls; Porum, OK; (4); 12/18; Boy Scts; HOBY; Library Aide; Natl FFA Org; Teachers Aide; Yrbk; Sec Jr Cls; Acad Team; Hstry Ed.

LESSLEY, SARAH M; Heavener HS; Heavener, OK; (2); Chorus; School Play; Pres Nwsp; Hon Roll; Chrstn Character Awd; Chrstn Singer.

LESTER, JAKE; Muskogee HS; Muskogee, OK; (2); Church Yth Grp; JCL; Latin Clb; Gov Hon Prg Awd; High Hon Roll; Jr NHS; NHS; OK U; Optometrist.

LESTER, REBECCA D; Mangum Sr HS; Mangum, OK; (3); Am Leg Aux Girls St; Church Yth Grp; FBLA; FHA; GAA; Pep Clb; Chorus; Variety Show; Phtg Yrbk; Sec Stu Cncl; OK ST U.

LETHGO, CHRISTOPHER W; Bartlesville Sr HS; Bartlesville, OK; (4); 1/400; Chess Clb; Quiz Bowl; Band; Mrchg Band; Orch; High Hon Roll; Ntl Merit SF; Tulsa Yth Symph; U Of OK; Cvl Engrng.

LETTERMAN, CHRISTINE G; Pauls Valley HS; Pauls Valley, OK; (2); FCA; 4-H; Pep Clb; Spanish Clb; Hon Roll; Pres Acad Fit Awd; Pi Phi Pi; Babystng; Shwng Lvstck; U Of OK; Biochem.

LETZIG, MATT; Pryor Jr HS; Pryor, OK; (2); Church Yth Grp; JV Bsktbl; Var Socr; High Hon Roll; NHS; Chrch Yth Grp VP.

LEU, TREVOR; Cameron Schl; Poteau, OK; (3); 3/31; Church Yth Grp; FCA; Am Leg Boys St; Office Aide; Quiz Bowl; Scholastic Bowl; Teachers Aide; Var Bsbl; Var Bsktbl; Var Ftbl; Natl Champs Bsbl Team Mid West City Outlaws AAU 17 & Under; Jr Sunbelt Bsbl Team; Med Field.

LEUCH, LINDSAY; Eisenhower Sr HS; Lawton, OK; (1); Church Yth Grp; FCA; Letterman Clb; Pep Clb; School Play; Stage Crew; Chrldng; Gym; Hon Roll; NHS; NHS Sec; Flwshp Of Chrstn Athls VP.

LEVEILLE, JOE E; Muskogee HS; Muskogee, OK; (2); Boy Scts; ROTC; Hon Roll; Auto Mech.

LEVI, JENNIE; Coweta HS; Coweta, OK; (2); Church Yth Grp; FCA; FHA; SADD; Ed Phtg Nwsp; Co-Ed Yrbk; Var L Chrldng; JV Golf; Jr NHS; NHS; OK Indian Hnr Soc/Hnr Soc/Jr Hnr Soc; PT.

LEVINGS, CAROLYN K; Hooker Jr-Sr HS; Hooker, OK; (4); #3 in class; Quiz Bowl; Teachers Aide; Band; Yrbk; High Hon Roll; NHS; OK ST U.

LEVINGS, STACY L; Tahlequah Sr HS; Hulbert, OK; (3); Church Yth Grp; German Clb; Pep Clb; Hon Roll; Jr NHS; NHS; OK Hnr Soc; Edctnl Tlnt Srch; Northeastern ST U; Acctg/Bus.

LEVINS, LESLEY S; Durant HS; Durant, OK; (4); Church Yth Grp; 4-H; Natl FFA Org; Var Bsktbl; Powder Puff Ftbl; Trk; 4-H Awd; Hon Roll; FFA Sec; Var Grls Bsktbl Lttr; FFA Awd; SE OK ST U; Law.

LEW, KATE J; Bartlesville Sr HS; Bartlesville, OK; (3); 1/481; Dance Clb; German Clb; Service Clb; High Hon Roll; NHS; All-Amer Schlr; Natl His/Govt Awd; Chem Engr.

LEWELLEN, JUSTIN T; Choctaw HS; Choctaw, OK; (3); Church Yth Grp; Office Aide; Var L Bsbl; Intrml Bsktbl; Var L Ftbl; Capt Powder Puff Ftbl; Cit Awd; Hon Roll.

LEWIN, BRANDI; Vanoss Schl; Ada, OK; (2); FCA; FBLA; Quiz Bowl; Scholastic Bowl; School Play; Cit Awd; Hon Roll; NHS; Val.

LEWIS, ADAM; Shawnee Sr HS; Shawnee, OK; (4); 10/285; Church Yth Grp; Cmnty Wkr; Hosp Aide; Band; Church Choir; Drm Mjr(t); Jazz Band; Mrchg Band; NHS; All-St Band; Music.

LEWIS, AMBER; Moore HS; Moore, OK; (4); 34/505; Am Leg Aux Girls St; Band; Color Guard; Flag Corp; Mrchg Band; Orch; Pep Band; School Musical; NHS; Val; OU; Msc.

LEWIS, ANGELA D; Ripley HS; Stillwater, OK; (2); 9/40; Dance Clb; FBLA; Natl FFA Org; Science Clb; Sec Frsh Cls; Sec Soph Cls; Mgr Bsktbl; NHS; Math & Sci Clb; STARS-N-STRIPES Clogging Team 3rd In Nation; Chiropractor.

LEWIS, BRODIE D; Woodward HS; Woodward, OK; (1); Church Yth Grp; FCA; German Clb; SADD; Ofcr Frsh Cls; Ofcr Stu Cncl; Bsktbl; Trk; Cit Awd; Hon Roll; Mech Engr.

LEWIS, BROOKLYN; Plainview HS; Ardmore, OK; (2); 1/77; Church Yth Grp; Cmnty Wkr; Natl Beta Clb; Church Choir; Drill Tm; High Hon Roll; Jr NHS; Prfct Atten Awd; OK Indian Stdnt Hnr Soc.

LEWIS, CAMERON J; Claremore Sr HS; Claremore, OK; (1); U Of WY; Psych.

LEWIS, DAVID A; Choctaw HS; Midwest City, OK; (3); Church Yth Grp; FCA; JV Bsbl; High Hon Roll; Hon Roll; NHS; Pres Acad Fit Awd; Sal.

LEWIS, DENISE M; Owasso Sr HS; Owasso, OK; (3); Church Yth Grp; Cmnty Wkr; Drama Clb; FCA; Pres FTA; Office Aide; Teachers Aide; VICA; School Play; Rep Stu Cncl; Ath Trng; Fine Arts; Pub Relations; Southwestern Assembly Of God U.

LEWIS, DERREKA L; Okmulgee HS; Okmulgee, OK; (2); FCA; FBLA; Science Clb; Var Bsktbl; Var Sftbl; Hon Roll; Ntl Merit Ltr.

LEWIS, ISAAC; Blanchard Jr Sr HS; Blanchard, OK; (3); Church Yth Grp; FCA; Office Aide; Rep CAP; Stat Bsbl; Var Bsktbl; Hon Roll.

LEWIS, JAMES R; Boswell Sr HS; Atoka, OK; (4); Church Yth Grp; Debate Tm; FCA; Key Clb; Quiz Bowl; Ed Nwsp; Yrbk; Rptr Sr Cls; Hon Roll; TSA OK St Pres; Southeastern ST U; Acctng.

LEWIS, JEANNA; Woodward HS; Woodward, OK; (1); Hon Roll; Kiwanis Awd; NHS.

LEWIS, JENNIFER; Yale Jr Sr HS; Yale, OK; (4); #2 in class; Natl Beta Clb; Var Bsktbl; Var Chrldng; Var Sftbl; Var Trk; Var Vllybl; Hon Roll; Prfct Atten Awd; Sal; OSU; Med.

LEWIS, JENNIFER M; Moore HS; Moore, OK; (3); Church Yth Grp; French Clb; Pep Clb; Scholastic Bowl; Science Clb; SADD; Rptr Nwsp; Our Green Earth; Recycling Clb; KS Univ; Psychpsychology.

LEWIS, JEREMY D; Blanchard Jr Sr HS; Blanchard, OK; (2); Church Yth Grp; FCA; Office Aide; Rep Soph Cls; Var Bsbl; JV Bsktbl; Prfct Atten Awd.

LEWIS, JEREMY M; Seminole Jr Sr HS; Maud, OK; (2); Church Yth Grp; Drama Clb; Math Clb; NFL; Speech Tm; School Play; Stage Crew; Rptr Nwsp; Hon Roll; Mock Trial; Theater.

LEWIS, JOANN M; Cashion HS; Crescent, OK; (3); Church Yth Grp; FCA; FBLA; Office Aide; Band; Chorus; Mrchg Band; Bsktbl; Sftbl; Cit Awd; Rotary Yth Ldrshp Awds Conf; OK ST Univ Ldrshp Conf; OK ST Univ; Early Chldhd Dev.

LEWIS, JONATHAN K; Hartshorne Sr HS; Hartshorne, OK; (3); Church Yth Grp; Teachers Aide; Hon Roll; FFA Horticulture I Pin Awd & Cert Recognition; Eastern OK ST Coll; Forestry.

LEWIS, KARA K; Duke Schl; Duke, OK; (2); 2/16; Church Yth Grp; Cmnty Wkr; English Clb; FCA; 4-H; GAA; Letterman Clb; Math Clb; Math Tm; Natl FFA Org; Opt.

LEWIS, KATIE V; Bishop Kelley HS; Tulsa, OK; (3); Cmnty Wkr; Hosp Aide; Key Clb; Service Clb; Spanish Clb; Rep Stu Cncl; NHS.

LEWIS, KELLI; Woodward HS; Buffalo, OK; (3); Cmnty Wkr; Sec FTA; Letterman Clb; Treas Spanish Clb; Band; Jazz Band; Mrchg Band; Pep Band; High Hon Roll; NHS; Mock Trial; Moose Intl Stdnt Congress; OK U; Scndry Schl Math Tchr.

LEWIS, KENDRA; Ponca City Sr HS; Ponca City, OK; (3); 12/347; Church Yth Grp; Cmnty Wkr; Spanish Clb; Temple Yth Grp; Band; Color Guard; Flag Corp; Mrchg Band; Orch; School Play; Brigham Young Univ.

LEWIS, LAVIDA T; Preston Schl; Okmulgee, OK; (3); GAA; Scholastic Bowl; Rptr Nwsp; Phtg Yrbk; Pres Frsh Cls; Pres Soph Cls; Pres Jr Cls; Var Bsktbl; Var Sftbl; Var Trk; OSU; Cmptrs/Bus Admn.

LEWIS, LINDA M; Moore HS; Moore, OK; (2); Art Clb; Science Clb; Spanish Clb; Teachers Aide; Cit Awd; Licensed Dog Groomer; Art Cmptns; OSU; Vet.

LEWIS, LISA; Ardmore HS; Ardmore, OK; (4); 54/162; Art Clb; Church Yth Grp; French Clb; Girl Scts; Math Clb; Mu Alpha Theta; Science Clb; Teachers Aide; Band; Mgr(s); U Of OK; Intr Dsgn.

LEWIS, LU CARRALYNN; Capitol Hill HS; Oklahoma City, OK; (4); Am Leg Aux Girls St; Church Yth Grp; FCA; SADD; Ofcr Stu Cncl; Var Bsktbl; Var Trk; Black Heritage; Grambling ST U; Phys Ed.

LEWIS, MATT B; Will Rogers HS; Tulsa, OK; (4); 30/201; Church Yth Grp; Pres DECA; Key Clb; Letterman Clb; Spanish Clb; Ofcr Stu Cncl; JV Ftbl; Capt L Socr; JV Trk; Cit Awd; Cert Merit Voc Dept 96; Co-Org Stdnt Voter Reg Drv; Nrthestrn St Univ; Intl Bus.

LEWIS, MELANIE J; Vian HS; Vian, OK; (4); 6/55; Debate Tm; Drama Clb; Quiz Bowl; Spanish Clb; Speech Tm; School Play; Stage Crew; Church Yth Grp; High Hon Roll; NHS; Native Amer Stu Assoc-Soph Rel & Treas; Johnson O Mally Prog Tutor &Annual Conf Prtcpnt; LA St Univ; Elem Ed.

LEWIS, MICAH; Clinton HS; Clinton, OK; (3); 18/150; Church Yth Grp; FCA; FHA; Spanish Clb; Chorus; School Musical; Sec Frsh Cls; Sec Soph Cls; Rep Stu Cncl; JV Var Chrldng; OK U; Spch Pthlgy.

LEWIS, NICKI L; Westmoore HS; Oklahoma City, OK; (1); Church Yth Grp; Band; Mrchg Band; Orch; Sftbl; Tennis; Hon Roll; Jr NHS; NHS; Prfct Atten Awd; Mssnts Hnr Star; OU; Algebra Tchr.

LEWIS, PAUL W; Sapulpa Sr HS; Sapulpa, OK; (3); Spanish Clb; Band; Mrchg Band; Orch; Spanish NHS; All Region & All St Bands; Music Ed.

LEWIS, RENATA L; Union Intermediate HS; Tulsa, OK; (2); Boy Scts; Cmnty Wkr; Dance Clb; FCA; Girl Scts; Pep Clb; Spanish Clb; Church Choir; Orch; Bsktbl; Spelman; Jrnlsm.

LEWIS, ROBERTA; Graham Schl; Dustin, OK; (2); 4-H; FHA; Ofcr Soph Cls; Bsktbl; Capt Sftbl; Hon Roll; NHS; Prfct Atten Awd; Sal; Law.

LEWIS, SARAH; Tahlequah Sr HS; Tahlequah, OK; (4); 3/251; HOBY; Service Clb; Rep Frsh Cls; Rep Soph Cls; Sec Jr Cls; Hist Stu Cncl; Var Tennis; Pres Jr NHS; Kiwanis Awd; NHS; Creighton U; Eng.

LEWIS, SASHA N; Del City HS; Del City, OK; (2); Church Yth Grp; Vllybl; High Hon Roll; Hon Roll; Piano; Dentistry.

LEWIS, SEAN M; Claremore Sr HS; Claremore, OK; (1); Church Yth Grp; Intrml Ftbl; JV Wt Lftg; Outstdng Offensive Lineman; OK ST Univ.

LEWIS, SETH A; Putnam City North HS; Oklahoma City, OK; (1); Boy Scts; Church Yth Grp; Drama Clb; Stage Crew.

LEWIS, SUNNIE J; Healdton HS; Healdton, OK; (2); Church Yth Grp; FHA; Teachers Aide; Stage Crew; Hon Roll; NHS; Sunday Schl Tchr; Southeastern OK ST U; Tchr.

LEWIS, TAMMY A; Stillwater Sr HS; Stillwater, OK; (2); #1 in class; Key Clb; Natl Beta Clb; Science Clb; Spanish Clb; Rptr Nwsp; Ed Yrbk; Rep Stu Cncl; JV Var Tennis; Kiwanis Awd; NHS; Var Schlr; Wrting; Pub Relations; Jrnlsm.

LEWIS, TANYA; Muskogee HS; Muskogee, OK; (3); FHA; JCL; JV Var Bsktbl; Var Trk; High Hon Roll; Hon Roll; Jr NHS; Treas NHS; OK Honor Socty:RAID; Natl Hstry Day 94; Tuskegee U; Phrmcy.

LEY, TERRENCE J; Edmond Memorial HS; Edmond, OK; (3); 110/371; Church Yth Grp; Natl FFA Org; Ftbl; Wt Lftg; Hrtlnd Srch/Rsc Dog Hndlr; Explr Scout; Coll Of Ozarks; Fish/Game Wrdn.

LEY, TYLER; Putnam City HS; Warr Acres, OK; (4); 8/346; Am Leg Boys St; Spanish Clb; Teachers Aide; Rptr Nwsp; Rptr Yrbk; Rptr Lit Mag; Rep Stu Cncl; L Bsbl; High Hon Roll; NHS; OSU; Civil Engr.

LEYBA, PATRICIA M; Choctaw HS; Choctaw, OK; (3); Hosp Aide; Red Cross Aide; Hon Roll; Jr NHS; NHS; Prfct Atten Awd; Stu Of Yr Hlth Sci Tech I; Stu Of Quarter; Nrsng.

LIBEL, AMY; Choctaw HS; Choctaw, OK; (4); Chorus; School Musical; Wt Lftg; NHS; Jazz; Music Thrpy.

LICHTENBER, JOHN; Northeast HS; Oklahoma City, OK; (4); 1/125; Am Leg Boys St; French Clb; FBLA; Scholastic Bowl; Science Clb; Orch; Swmmng; Tennis; NHS; Val; 4th Pl Intl Sci & Engrng Fair; OK Acad All-Stater; OK Orch All-St; Princeton U; Med.

LICHTENWALTER, BRIAN C; Edmond Memorial HS; Edmond, OK; (3); Church Yth Grp; Spanish Clb; NHS; Yth Actn Cncl Chrch; U Of OK; Dentistry.

LIDDELL, JOHNIE; Marietta HS; Marietta, OK; (4); 4/53; Art Clb; Model UN; Speech Tm; Chorus; Swing Chorus; Pres Frsh Cls; Pres Soph Cls; Pres Jr Cls; Pres Sr Cls; Rep Stu Cncl.

LIDDELL, LAYNIE; Heritage Hall Schl; Oklahoma City, OK; (2); Church Yth Grp; FCA; Pep Clb; Spanish Clb; Chorus; Ofcr Stu Cncl; Var Chrldng; Var Fld Hcky; Var Tennis; Hon Roll.

LIENKE, GENEVIEVE M; Bishop Mcguinness HS; Oklahoma City, OK; (3); 29/135; Cmnty Wkr; FCA; Pep Clb; Spanish Clb; SADD; Yrbk; Rep Sr Cls; Bsktbl; Sftbl; Trk; Geom Awd; Voice Lessons; Vocal Music; Medicine.

LIGA, LINDSAY M; Edmond Memorial HS; Edmond, OK; (4); 72/371; Church Yth Grp; French Clb; Band; Color Guard; Jazz Band; Mrchg Band; Orch; Pep Band; School Musical; Variety Show; U OK.

LIGARD, ARVID; Union Intermediate HS; Tulsa, OK; (2); Chess Clb; Church Yth Grp; Vllybl; ORU.

LIGHTFOOT, CHELSEA S; Mc Alester HS; Mcalester, OK; (4); 18/202; Cmnty Wkr; Drama Clb; Quiz Bowl; Science Clb; Spanish Clb; Speech Tm; Thesps; High Hon Roll; NHS; Ntl Merit Schol; Yth Bd Of Theatre OK Young Stars Pres; Chem-Physics Clb; Svc Learning; Hendrix Coll; Rel.

LIGHTFOOT, JENNIFER L; Norman Sr HS; Norman, OK; (3); Church Yth Grp; Hosp Aide; Spanish Clb; Orch; Stu Today Awd Masons; U Of OK; Socl Wrk.

LIGHTFOOT, LUKE; Oklahoma Christian Schl; Edmond, OK; (1); Church Yth Grp; Hon Roll; Music.

LIGHTFOOT, WILL; Oklahoma Christian Schl; Edmond, OK; (1); Church Yth Grp; FCA; Ofcr Frsh Cls; Ftbl; Wt Lftg; Hon Roll; Guitar.

LIGHTWINE, AARON M; Memorial HS; Tulsa, OK; (3); Library Aide; Crs Cntry; Trk; Hon Roll.

LIGON, CHARLES A; Choctaw HS; Midwest City, OK; (1); Church Yth Grp; FCA; Varsity Clb; School Play; Ftbl; Wt Lftg; Wrstlng; OK Univ; Med.

LIKES, MICHELLE D; Oklahoma Christian Schl; Edmond, OK; (4); Cmnty Wkr; Office Aide; Teachers Aide; Tennis; All Amer Schlr; Grad With Hnrs; U Of Central OK; Publ Rels.

LILE, GARY; Washington HS; Washington, OK; (2); Church Yth Grp; Ofcr Bsbl; Ftbl; Wt Lftg.

LILES, JEREMY A; Tahlequah Sr HS; Park Hill, OK; (2); Church Yth Grp.

LILES, TRACI; Anadarko HS; Anadarko, OK; (3); 8/120; FCA; 4-H; FBLA; FHA; Natl FFA Org; SADD; Pres Jr Cls; Var Chrldng; NHS; OK ST U; Bus.

LILLIE, VANESSA; Miami Sr HS; Miami, OK; (1); Church Yth Grp; Dance Clb; Drama Clb; NFL; Speech Tm; Thesps; School Play; Rep Frsh Cls; Rep Stu Cncl; Hon Roll; 2nd Pl Prose Intrptn, 3rd Pl Domestic Extemp Speech Cmptn; Deconess Bethany Chrstn Church; OK U; Commnctns.

LIN, EMILY S; Bartlesville Mid HS; Bartlesville, OK; (2); 1/481; Church Yth Grp; Dance Clb; Debate Tm; Pres French Clb; Hist FBLA; Math Tm; NFL; Service Clb; Orch; School Musical; Natl Jr Hnr Soc Pres; Masonic Lodge Stdnt Of Today Awd; V Chaney Meml Yng Artst Awd.

LIN, JOY; Oklahoma Sch Of Science & Math; Stillwater, OK; (3); Debate Tm; Spanish Clb; Ed Nwsp; Hon Roll; Ntl Merit SF; ARML; TEAMS For OK; Dartmouth Coll; Math; Comp Sci.

LINDAMOOD, MARCIE; Hugo HS; Hugo, OK; (3); 9/103; FHA; Spanish Clb; Nwsp; Yrbk; Hon Roll; NHS; OK Hnr Soc 2 Yrs; OK ST U; Dntl Hygn.

LINDBLOM, JON; Bartlesville Sr HS; Bartlesville, OK; (1); Church Yth Grp; Intrml Bsbl; High Hon Roll; Hon Roll.

LINDE, JANET L; Memorial HS; Tulsa, OK; (3); Church Yth Grp; Pep Clb; Phtg Yrbk; VP Stu Cncl; Var Capt Bsktbl; JV Tennis; JV Trk; JV Vllybl; Hon Roll; NHS; MVP Awds Bsktbl; SMS; Mrktng Ed.

LINDEN, FELIX P; Star Spencer HS; Oklahoma City, OK; (2); 3/133; Boy Scts; Bus Profs of Am; Chess Clb; Drama Clb; FBLA; HOBY; Office Aide; Quiz Bowl; Scholastic Bowl; Teachers Aide; News Room 101 Pgm; Northwestern Univ; Sports Repor.

LINDEN, JENNIFER; Muskogee HS; Muskogee, OK; (2); Church Yth Grp; JCL; Key Clb; Chorus; Church Choir; School Musical; Hon Roll; Jr NHS; Piano; OU; Music.

LINDENAU, JEREMY; Claremore Sr HS; Catoosa, OK; (4); 7/241; Math Tm; Var Bsbl; High Hon Roll; NHS; OK ST; Phys Thrpy.

LINDENBERG, KATHERINE L; South Intermediate HS; Broken Arrow, OK; (1); Church Yth Grp; Bsktbl; Vllybl; High Hon Roll; Hon Roll; Jr NHS.

LINDERS, RYAN; Westmoore HS; Oklahoma City, OK; (3); Am Leg Boys St; Church Yth Grp; Sec Treas French Clb; Chorus; Mrchg Band; Rep Stu Cncl; Ofcr Bsbl; Cit Awd; Pep Clb; Band; All Amer Mascot; NCA Smmr Camp Best Mascot; Psych/Sociology.

LINDLEY, BRIAN J; Putnam City North HS; Oklahoma City, OK; (2); Am Leg Boys St; Church Yth Grp; SADD; JV Bsbl; Intrml Golf; Intrml Trk; Hon Roll; NHS; Demolay; OK U; Pathology.

LINDLEY, BRYAN J; Hinton HS; Hinton, OK; (2); Math Clb; Natl FFA Org; Bsktbl; Ftbl; Trk; Wt Lftg; High Hon Roll; Hon Roll; Prfct Atten Awd; Sal; OK Hnr Soc; Bio Awd; Geometry Awd; Span I/II Awd; Acad Tm Awd; Alg I Awd; Hlth Awd; Various FFA Awds; OSU; Vetnrn.

LINDO, BERNADETTE; Piedmont HS; Piedmont, OK; (2); Church Yth Grp; Hosp Aide; Intnl Clb; Letterman Clb; SADD; Band; Chorus; School Musical; High Hon Roll; NHS; Tri-St Hnr Chorus 2 Yrs; Yth Ldr; Campus Life 30 Hr Famine Participant.

LINDON, MANDY; Wynona Schl; Wynona, OK; (3); 2/14; Natl Beta Clb; Pres Soph Cls; Sec Stu Cncl; Bsktbl; Sftbl; Vllybl; Hon Roll; Stu Of Today; Stu Of Yr; OCAST Recognition.

LINDSAY, GENA; Bray-Doyle HS; Duncan, OK; (3); FCA; FHA; Office Aide; Spanish Clb; SADD; Hon Roll; U Of Sci & Art Of OK.

LINDSAY, MICHELLE; Union City Schl; El Reno, OK; (2); FHA; High Hon Roll; Pres Acad Fit Awd; Publctn 12th Annual HS Poetry Anthology.

LINDSEY, CYNTHIA N; Rush Springs HS; Rush Springs, OK; (2); FCA; Scholastic Bowl; Spanish Clb; Yrbk; Pres Frsh Cls; Bsktbl; Chrldng; High Hon Roll; NHS.

LINDSEY, ERIC M; Stillwater Sr HS; Stillwater, OK; (4); 87/344; Church Yth Grp; Drama Clb; FCA; Pep Clb; Spanish Clb; Thesps; Chorus; School Musical; School Play; Variety Show; Kiwanis Chrstn Stu Awd; All-St Hnr Choir 96; U Of OK; Mscl Theatre.

LINDSEY, J MICHAEL; Sallisaw HS; Sallisaw, OK; (4); 22/147; Am Leg Boys St; Art Clb; Church Yth Grp; Math Clb; Math Tm; Quiz Bowl; Scholastic Bowl; Science Clb; Spanish Clb; School Play; Yth Alive Pres; Chrch Drama Grp; Engrng.

LINDSEY, JOSH M; Forgan Schl; Forgan, OK; (3); Church Yth Grp; FCA; SADD; Church Choir; Bsktbl; Ftbl; Wt Lftg; Hon Roll; Garden City CC; Bus Mngmnt.

LINDSEY, LARINDA; Chickasha HS; Chickasha, OK; (4); Am Leg Aux Girls St; Church Yth Grp; Drama Clb; French Clb; FHA; Band; Chorus; Mrchg Band; Pep Band; Sec Sr Cls; OK All-Star Mrchng Bnd; OK City Comm Coll Smmr Math Acad; OKU; Intr Deco.

LINDUFF, LINDSEY N; South Intermediate HS; Broken Arrow, OK; (1); Spanish Clb; Acpl Chr; Hon Roll; OSU; Eng/Prof Sngr.

LINDUFF, MARCIE B; Yukon Middle HS; Yukon, OK; (2); Debate Tm; Drama Clb; Hosp Aide; Scholastic Bowl; Spanish Clb; Speech Tm; NHS; Mock Trial; Renaissance Comm; Odyssey Of Mind; U Of OK; Med Field.

LINGENFELTER, JOHN PAUL; Claremore Sr HS; Claremore, OK; (3); Art Clb; Cmnty Wkr; Library Aide; Office Aide; Teachers Aide; Ed Yrbk; Hon Roll; Rogers U; Cmmrcl Art.

LINK, CODY A; Putnam City North HS; Oklahoma City, OK; (1); 67/539; Church Yth Grp; Bsktbl; Wt Lftg; High Hon Roll.

LINK, LINDSAY; Bartlesville Sr HS; Bartlesville, OK; (4); 158/414; Cmnty Wkr; 4-H; FBLA; FHA; Hosp Aide; Pep Clb; Red Cross Aide; Spanish Clb; Band; Chorus; U Of OK; Hlth Sci.

LINK, REBECCA J; Bishop Mcguinness HS; Oklahoma City, OK; (3); Drama Clb; Pep Clb; Spanish Clb; SADD; Thesps; School Play; Stage Crew; Crs Cntry; NHS; Spanish NHS; Piano; Sarah Lawrence; Eng.

LINKE, CHRIS N; Velma Alma HS; Velma, OK; (2); Church Yth Grp; FCA; SADD; Var Crs Cntry; Var Trk; Hon Roll; NHS; All St Crss Cntry.

LINN, ANGELA F; Bridge Creek HS; Blanchard, OK; (1); Church Yth Grp; FCA; Spanish Clb; SADD; VP Frsh Cls; JV Capt Bsktbl; Hon Roll; Ntl Merit Ltr; GAA; VP Soph Cls; Outstdng Frosh Bsktbl Plyr; OK Hon Soc; Won Soph VP 96-.

LINN, DEE J; Frontier Public Schl; Red Rock, OK; (3); 4/27; Natl FFA Org; Yrbk; Rep Stu Cncl; Mgr(s); Hon Roll; Acad Ltrmn 3 Yr; Tech Stdnts Amer; 96 OK Agrisci Stdnt Of Yr Awd; Discover Card Trib Awd Schlrshp.

LINN, GINNY G; Chandler HS; Chandler, OK; (4); 30/75; Church Yth Grp; Cmnty Wkr; FCA; FBLA; FHA; Library Aide; Spanish Clb; Thesps; School Play; Sftbl; U OK; Occptnl Thrpst.

LINNET, CHRIS; Kiefer Jr Sr HS; Sapulpa, OK; (2); Band; Jazz Band; Mrchg Band; Pep Band; Pres Soph Cls; High Hon Roll; Electrncs Repair.

LINTON, CHRISTOPHER B; Ada HS; Ada, OK; (4); FCA; French Clb; Math Clb; Mu Alpha Theta; Band; Jazz Band; Mrchg Band; Hon Roll; Engr.

LINTON, LINDSEY; Lawton Christian Schl; Lawton, OK; (2); Church Yth Grp; Cmnty Wkr; Hosp Aide; Library Aide; Office Aide; Stage Crew; Hon Roll; Jr NHS.

LINVILLE, TOMMY L; Union Sr HS; Tulsa, OK; (3); FCA; Science Clb; JV Var Ftbl; Chem Eng.

LIPHAM, AMANDA A; Canton HS; Longdale, OK; (1); Art Clb; Church Yth Grp; FHA; Plays Piano; Child Care; Elec Historian FHA 97; Southwestern; CPA.

LIPHAM, JAIME L; Moore HS; Oklahoma City, OK; (4); 86/549; Drama Clb; Latin Clb; Swmmng; Jr NHS; NHS; OK ST Univ.

LIPP, ASHLEY A; Bishop Kelley HS; Broken Arrow, OK; (2); Church Yth Grp; Cmnty Wkr; Chrldng; Hon Roll; Natl Chrldrs Assn For All Amer Chrldr Nom.

LIPPOLDT, RYAN; Yukon Middle HS; Yukon, OK; (3); Spanish Clb; Band; Mrchg Band; Pep Band; Hon Roll; OU; Comp Sci; Commnctn.

LIRA, GABRIEL J; South Intermediate HS; Broken Arrow, OK; (1); Cit Awd; Hon Roll; Utility Player On Competitive Soccer Team City Of BA OK; KS Univ; Mgmt.

LISLE, TARA A; Western Heights Sr HS; Oklahoma City, OK; (2); FHA; JV Var Sftbl; Hon Roll; OSU Upward Bound; Poem Pub; OSU; Med Field.

LIST, MARK E; Jenks HS; Tulsa, OK; (4); Boy Scts; Church Yth Grp; FCA; FHA; Key Clb; Natl FFA Org; Office Aide; Teachers Aide; Church Choir; Rptr Yrbk; Yng Life; Acad Mdl; OK HS Hnr Soc; OK ST U; Envrnmntl Sci.

LIST, PATRICK W; Claremore Sr HS; Claremore, OK; (1); Church Yth Grp; Chorus; Church Choir; School Musical; Hon Roll.

LISTER, DAWN M; Elk City HS; Elk City, OK; (4); 28/141; Church Yth Grp; Computer Clb; Debate Tm; Drama Clb; German Clb; Model UN; Office Aide; Pep Clb; Speech Tm; SADD; OK Panhandle ST U; Comp Info.

LISTER, JOHN S; Broken Arrow Sr HS; Broken Arrow, OK; (3); Boy Scts; Hon Roll; Marshall Arts; OU OK Univ; Cmptr Engr.

LISTON, JAMIE; Westmoore HS; Oklahoma City, OK; (3); 37/435; Church Yth Grp; HOBY; JCL; Latin Clb; Natl FFA Org; Cit Awd; High Hon Roll; Jr NHS; NHS; Masonic Stu Of Today; Local FFA Chptr Reprtr; OK ST U.

LITTAU, RYAN; Balko Public Schl; Balko, OK; (4); 1/19; VP Natl FFA Org; VP Chorus; Pres Frsh Cls; Pres Soph Cls; Treas Jr Cls; Pres Sr Cls; Capt Bsktbl; Capt Ftbl; NHS; Val; Mr Balko HS; All-Area Dist & Dist Acad Ftbl Teams; All-Area Bsktbl Team Hnrb Mntn; OK ST Univ; Ag; Ec; Acctng.

LITTEKEN, ANNE M; Plainview HS; Ardmore, OK; (3); 17/87; FCA; Mu Alpha Theta; Natl Beta Clb; Phtg Nwsp; Sec Stu Cncl; Var Chrldng; Ftbl; Var Trk; Hon Roll; NHS.

LITTELL, BEVERLY D; Kingston HS; Kingston, OK; (2); 4-H; Church Choir; Mrchg Band; Ofcr Bsbl; Bsktbl; Crs Cntry; Powder Puff Ftbl; Sftbl; Hon Roll; Prfct Atten Awd; Lawyer.

LITTLE, AMANDA B; Enid Sr HS; Enid, OK; (4); Spanish Clb; Nwsp; Hon Roll; Jr NHS; NHS; Ntl Merit Ltr; Pres Schlr; U Of Cntrl OK; Actuary Sci.

LITTLE, ASHLEY D; Mc Alester HS; Mcalester, OK; (2); Church Yth Grp; Spanish Clb; Diamond Dolls; Marine Bio.

LITTLE, BECKY; Liberty Acad; Tecumseh, OK; (1); Church Yth Grp; Chorus; Church Choir; School Musical; Variety Show; Var Bsktbl; Hon Roll.

LITTLE, CASEY D; Velma Alma HS; Duncan, OK; (2); 1/41; Church Yth Grp; FCA; Quiz Bowl; Ofcr Bsbl; Bsktbl; Ftbl; Cit Awd; High Hon Roll; Hon Roll.

LITTLE, HETHER DAWN; Moore HS; Moore, OK; (3); 40/625; Church Yth Grp; French Clb; Red Cross Aide; Ofcr Soph Cls; Ofcr Jr Cls; Ofcr Stu Cncl; Bsktbl; Pom Pon; Cit Awd; NHS; Psych.

LITTLE, JOSHUA D; Victory Christian Schl; Tulsa, OK; (4); Pres Chess Clb; Church Yth Grp; Science Clb; Spanish Clb; Ofcr Soph Cls; Ofcr Jr Cls; NHS; Audio & Visual Tech; Oral Roberts U; Missionary.

LITTLE, KRISTI; Woodward HS; Woodward, OK; (3); Treas FCA; FBLA; Rptr Service Clb; Varsity Clb; Rep Stu Cncl; Var Bsktbl; Cmnty Wkr; Trk; Hon Roll; Mgr Ftbl; All Dist Sccr 95/Tm Semi Fnlst/St 96; All Trnmnt Tm John Noble; 4th ST Trck Discus; Ed/Crmnl Jstc.

LITTLE, MARK C; Westmoore HS; Oklahoma City, OK; (3); 123/625; Church Yth Grp; Cmnty Wkr; FCA; Letterman Clb; Varsity Clb; Rep Stu Cncl; Var L Ftbl; Var Wt Lftg; Hon Roll; NHS.

LITTLE, MELISSA Y; Snyder HS; Snyder, OK; (3); 14/40; FHA; Pep Clb; Treas Jr Cls; Ofcr Stu Cncl; Capt Chrldng; Hon Roll; Cameron U; Dental Hygn.

LITTLEFIELD, JANET; Adair HS; Pryor, OK; (3); 1/68; Am Leg Aux Girls St; FCA; 4-H; GAA; Natl FFA Org; Office Aide; Church Choir; Bsktbl; Trk; 4-H Awd; OK Senator Page; TX A&M; Medcl Tech.

LITTLEFIELD, MELANIE; Adair HS; Vinita, OK; (4); Am Leg Aux Girls St; FCA; Math Clb; Office Aide; Chorus; Mgr(s); Prfct Atten Awd; Rogers ST Clg.

LITTLEJOHN, KEVIN W; Idabel HS; Idabel, OK; (4); Drama Clb; NFL; Chorus; Stage Crew; Hon Roll; E T Dunlap; Drama; Eng.

LITTLEPAGE, JACQUELYN; Millwood HS; Oklahoma City, OK; (4); FCA; Letterman Clb; ROTC; Scholastic Bowl; Sftbl; Trk; Hon Roll; NHS; Ntl Merit Ltr; 95-96 Homcmng Ftbl Qn; Xinos Of Phi Delta Kappa Gamma Epsilon Chptr Pres; Vogues & Esquires Pres; U Of OK; Phys Thrpy.

LITTLETON, BRAD R; Tahlequah Sr HS; Tahlequah, OK; (3); Am Leg Boys St; Church Yth Grp; FCA; SADD; Chorus; VP Frsh Cls; Pres Soph Cls; VP Jr Cls; Ofcr Stu Cncl; JV Bsktbl; Radiologist.

LITTLETON, KERRY L; Pocola HS; Pocola, OK; (4); 6/45; Church Yth Grp; Cmnty Wkr; FCA; FBLA; GAA; Hosp Aide; Office Aide; SADD; Nwsp; Yrbk; Westark Comm Coll; Nrsng.

LITWACK, ZACH D; Bishop Kelley HS; Tulsa, OK; (3); Boy Scts; Church Yth Grp; Cmnty Wkr; Key Clb; Service Clb; High Hon Roll; NHS; Eagle Sct; Creative Wrtng; Artwork; Eng Field.

LIVELY, DANIELLE; Blackwell HS; Blackwell, OK; (2); 4-H; Band; Color Guard; Flag Corp; Jazz Band; Mrchg Band; Pep Band; Bsktbl; Sftbl; Hon Roll; Trvlng Sftbl Team; OK ST U.

LIVELY, FAITH; Cordell Sr HS; Cordell, OK; (3); 1/41; Church Yth Grp; Hosp Aide; Speech Tm; Band; Jazz Band; Mrchg Band; Sec Jr Cls; Mgr Bsktbl; Var Sftbl; NHS; Rotary Ldrshp Camp; SWOSU; Pre-Med.

LIVINGSTON, BRANDI M; Bluejacket Schl; Bluejacket, OK; (2); Church Yth Grp; Hosp Aide; Sec Natl FFA Org; Hon Roll; Lvstck Judging Tm; Hrsbk Rdg; CPR/FIRST Aid Cls; NED; Med.

LIVINGSTON, CHRIS; Oologah HS; Oologah, OK; (4); 16/90; Church Yth Grp; Science Clb; Treas SADD; Teachers Aide; Chorus; Ofcr Bsbl; Ftbl; High Hon Roll; NHS; OK ST Univ; Biosys Engr.

LIVINGSTON, LEE S; Bishop Kelley HS; Tulsa, OK; (2); VP Frsh Cls; JV Var Bsktbl; JV Var Ftbl; High Hon Roll; Hon Roll; Elected Peer Helper.

LIZAMA, GORDON B; Mustang HS; Yukon, OK; (3); Church Yth Grp; Band; Church Choir; Jazz Band; Mrchg Band; Pep Band; Hon Roll; Phillips NW Hnr Band; CODA Hnr Band; Saxophone; U Of Cntrl OK; Music; Ed.

LLOYD II, JAMES R; Union Sr HS; Tulsa, OK; (4); 13/700; Am Leg Boys St; Cmnty Wkr; Spanish Clb; Orch; School Musical; Rep Stu Cncl; NHS; Ntl Merit SF; Pres Acad Fit Awd; Spanish NHS; First Dist Yng Dmcrts Pres; OK Cmnty Svc Cmmssn; Piano; KU; Law.

LLOYD, JASON M; Eisenhower Sr HS; Lawton, OK; (3); HOBY; Ed Yrbk; Rep Soph Cls; Rep Jr Cls; Rep Sr Cls; Rep Stu Cncl; High Hon Roll; NHS; Boy Scts; PTA Natl Rflctns Wrtng Cntst OK ST Wnr; PROS Stdnt Mediation Tm; Psychlgy.

LLOYD, JENNIFER A; El Reno Sr HS; El Reno, OK; (4); 83/163; Art Clb; Cmnty Wkr; Office Aide; Yrbk; Hon Roll; Prfct Atten Awd; BPW Grl Of Mnth Schol; Redlands Schol; U Of OK Acad Achvmnt; Redlands CC; Comp Bus.

LLOYD, MICKI; Leflore Sr HS; Leflore, OK; (4); 1/25; Church Yth Grp; Debate Tm; Church Choir; Treas Jr Cls; VP Sr Cls; Rep Stu Cncl; High Hon Roll; NHS; Pres Schlr; Val; Carl Albert ST Coll; Bus.

LOCH, CRISSI A; Ponca City Sr HS; Ponca City, OK; (2); Church Yth Grp; Bsktbl; Hon Roll; Rodeo-Natl HS Rodeo-Qualified In Poles 95; Goat Tying 96-8th Pl.

LOCHMANN, BRANDY N; Edmond Memorial HS; Edmond, OK; (3); 105/371; Church Yth Grp; FCA; French Clb; Red Cross Aide; Church Choir; Orch; JV Chrldng; JV Crs Cntry; Var Swmmng; JV Trk; USA Pom Pon Cmptn Squad; Chrch Orch & Ldrshp Cncl; Arch; Dsgn.

LOCKE, JOHN; Poteau HS; Poteau, OK; (4); 12/139; Am Leg Boys St; FCA; Letterman Clb; Varsity Clb; Ofcr Stu Cncl; Var Bsbl; Var Ftbl; Var Wt Lftg; Hon Roll; NHS; Amer Legion Bsbl.

LOCKE, LARRY D; U S Grant HS; Oklahoma City, OK; (2); SADD; Drill Tm; Bsktbl; Bus Mgmt.

LOCKHART, MELANIE; Stillwater Sr HS; Stillwater, OK; (4); Church Yth Grp; Dance Clb; DECA; FCA; Spanish Clb; Teachers Aide; Stage Crew; Chrldng; High Hon Roll; Hon Roll; Peer Advcte Spec Ed Stdnts; OK ST U.

LOCKLEAR, JAY; Hollis Jr Sr HS; Hollis, OK; (4); 4/54; Am Leg Boys St; 4-H; FBLA; Scholastic Bowl; Band; Mrchg Band; School Play; Capt Var Bsktbl; 4-H Awd; NHS; SW OK ST U; Chem.

LOCKLEAR, JENNIFER; Clinton HS; Clinton, OK; (1); Church Yth Grp; FHA; Band; Mrchg Band; Bsktbl; Chrldng; Trk; Hon Roll; U Of TX; Ansthslgy.

LOEBER, MATT; Oklahoma Christian Schl; Edmond, OK; (2); Hist Church Yth Grp; Debate Tm; Tennis; Cit Awd; Hon Roll; Schlstc Achvt Awds In Comp I, Cvcs & Bible; Med.

LOEFFLER, MICHAEL; Cascia Hall Prep School; Tulsa, OK; (3); Boy Scts; HOBY; JCL; Latin Clb; Ed Nwsp; Rep Stu Cncl; Jr NHS; Acad Bowl; Red Cross Vol; Gold Hnr Roll.

LOEPP, BREEAN; East Central HS; Tulsa, OK; (1); Cmnty Wkr; Pep Clb; JV Chrldng; Hon Roll; All Star Chrldng Squad.

LOFGREN, LESLIE; Piedmont HS; Piedmont, OK; (2); 16/97; Church Yth Grp; Hosp Aide; SADD; Mrchg Band; Band; Bsktbl; Hon Roll; NHS; Yth For Christ Mem; U Of OK; Meteorology.

LOFLIN, DAVID B; West Middle HS; Norman, OK; (3); FBLA; Spanish Clb; Hon Roll; Spanish NHS; Univ Of OK; Bus.

LOFTIS, ADRIENNE E; Del City HS; Del City, OK; (3); 1/518; Office Aide; Pres SADD; VP Soph Cls; VP Jr Cls; JV Vllybl; Hon Roll; Jr NHS; NHS; Prfct Atten Awd; Yth Ldrshp Exch Cls I; Peds Med.

LOFTIS, ANNA T; Jay HS; Jay, OK; (2); 8/280; Church Yth Grp; FCA; FBLA; Natl FFA Org; Office Aide; Pep Clb; High Hon Roll; Hon Roll; NHS; Comp Aided Drafting.

LOFTON, ALESHA A; Mc Lain Career Acad; Tulsa, OK; (3); #1 in class; FCA; Yrbk; Pres Jr Cls; Sec Stu Cncl; Cit Awd; High Hon Roll; Hon Roll; NHS; Bible Clb; Tulsa Univ; Tchng.

LOFTON, DIANA L; Poteau HS; Monroe, OK; (3); Church Yth Grp; Drama Clb; Library Aide; Office Aide; School Play; Ed Nwsp; Ed Yrbk; Cit Awd; Natl Yng Ldrs Conf; Upward Bound Math/Sci; Jrnlsm.

LOFTON, LAKESHIA N; Northeast HS; Oklahoma City, OK; (3); JA; ROTC; VICA; Chorus; Church Choir; Mgr(s); Pom Pon; High Hon Roll; Hon Roll; Kiwanis Awd; OK ST Univ; Nrs Asst.

LOFTON, MELVIN L; Webster HS; Tulsa, OK; (2); Ftbl; Wt Lftg; Wrstlng; OK ST U.

LOGAN, JEREMY; Choctaw HS; Choctaw, OK; (4); Church Yth Grp; Chorus; Var L Bsbl; JV Bsktbl; Hon Roll; Sthwstn OK ST U; Crmnl Jstc.

LOGAN, KRISTIN; Choctaw Jr HS; Choctaw, OK; (1); Church Yth Grp; Bsktbl; Wt Lftg; Hon Roll; Jr NHS.

LOGHRY, JOHN B; Duncan HS; Duncan, OK; (3); Am Leg Boys St; Boy Scts; VP Church Yth Grp; Pres French Clb; Band; Church Choir; Mrchg Band; Var L Crs Cntry; Jr NHS; NHS; Eagle Scout Awd BSA; Southern Nazarene Univ.

LOGUE, TANYA; Cache HS; Cache, OK; (2); Church Yth Grp; FHA; GAA; Natl Beta Clb; Band; Var Bsktbl; High Hon Roll; Hon Roll; NHS; FFA; FFA Rptr 95-; FFA Sec; PHARMICIST.

LOHMANN, JAY M; Freedom Schl; Freedom, OK; (2); 2/12; Church Yth Grp; FCA; Natl FFA Org; Scholastic Bowl; Yrbk; Pres Frsh Cls; Ofcr Soph Cls; Rep Stu Cncl; Var Bsbl; Var Bsktbl; Natl Yth Ldrshp Forum Law/Constitution; OK ST Univ; Law/Ag.

LOHMANN, LORI L; Ada HS; Ada, OK; (4); 98/166; Church Yth Grp; VP DECA; Library Aide; Spanish Clb; Band; Jazz Band; Mrchg Band; Pep Band; Hon Roll; St Band Championships; OSSAA Sweepstakes Awd; 3rd Pl Inspirational Cmptn At St DECA Conf; Seminole ST Coll.

LOK, JONATHAN Y; Union Sr HS; Tulsa, OK; (4); 34/629; Boy Scts; Intnl Clb; Key Clb; Spanish Clb; Nwsp; Var Capt Swmmng; NHS; Pres Acad Fit Awd; Spanish NHS; Renaissance; U Of OK; Elec Engrng.

LOLAR, ANISSA K; Duncan HS; Duncan, OK; (4); FBLA; Spanish Clb; Prfct Atten Awd; Rotarian Stu Awd; U Of Sci & & Art OK; Acctng.

LOLLIS, JENNIFER; Kingston HS; Kingston, OK; (1); Natl FFA Org; Spanish Clb; SADD; Bsktbl; Sftbl.

LOMAN, CORTNY L; Minco Jr Sr HS; Minco, OK; (4); 3/38; Church Yth Grp; FBLA; FHA; Office Aide; Yrbk; High Hon Roll; Hon Roll; Treas NHS; Pres Acad Fit Awd; Sal; U Of Sci & Arts Of OK; Eng.

LOMAN, LACY B; Minco Jr Sr HS; Minco, OK; (3); #5 in class; Church Yth Grp; FCA; FBLA; FHA; Jazz Band; Chrldng; Sftbl; Hon Roll; NHS; Band; Bus.

LOMANGINO, DONNA V; North Intemediate HS; Broken Arrow, OK; (1); Church Yth Grp; JV Socr; Hon Roll.

LOMANGINO, ROSANNE; North Intemediate HS; Broken Arrow, OK; (1); Church Yth Grp; JV Socr; Hon Roll; Jr NHS; OK Hnr Soc; Coll; Med Field.

LOMENICK, CARL R; Healdton HS; Healdton, OK; (3); Band; Chorus; Jazz Band; Mrchg Band; Hon Roll; NHS; All St Jazz Band; All Star All St Marching Band; All Dist Concert Band; Music.

LOMO, LETICIA; Midwest City HS; Midwest City, OK; (2); Teachers Aide; Drill Tm; Capt Bsktbl; Gym; Trk; Vllybl; Hon Roll; Prfct Atten Awd; Upward Prgm Rose ST Coll.

LONAS, TOMI; Wetumka Jr Sr HS; Wetumka, OK; (4); 5/32; Church Yth Grp; FHA; HOBY; Key Clb; Library Aide; Science Clb; Spanish Clb; Chorus; Church Choir; Sec Jr Cls; SYATP Ldr; VBS Tchr; OK Bptst U; Eng.

LONDAGIN, KENDRA D; Colcord Schl; Colcord, OK; (4); Church Yth Grp; FBLA; Office Aide; Yrbk; Intrml Bsktbl; Intrml Sftbl; Cit Awd; High Hon Roll; NHS; Ntl Merit Ltr; NSU.

LONE, APRIL D; Dewar Jr-Sr HS; Dewar, OK; (1); Church Yth Grp; Rptr FHA; Hon Roll.

LONEY, AARON C; Union Sr HS; Broken Arrow, OK; (3); 53/741; Church Yth Grp; FCA; Chorus; School Musical; Intrml JV Bsktbl; Alpha Theta; OK Chrstn U; Psych.

LONEY, DANIELLE P; Putnam City North HS; Oklahoma City, OK; (1); Church Yth Grp; Tae Kwon Do; OK ST Univ.

LONEY, KENNETH S; Bishop Kelley HS; Tulsa, OK; (3); Chorus; Lit Mag; Hon Roll; Music.

LONG, ALICIA A; Choctaw HS; Choctaw, OK; (2); Church Yth Grp; FCA; Hosp Aide; Var Bsktbl; Powder Puff Ftbl; Var Sftbl; Var Tennis; Wt Lftg; Hon Roll; Chrch Vllybl & Ldrshp Tms; SNU; Scl Work.

LONG, ANDREA L; Sapulpa Sr HS; Sapulpa, OK; (3); 78/300; Key Clb; Math Clb; Science Clb; SADD; Drill Tm; Crs Cntry; Trk; Hon Roll; NHS; Spanish NHS; U Of OK; Elem Ed.

LONG, ASHLEY D; Southeast HS; Oklahoma City, OK; (1); Art Clb; Band; Mrchg Band; Pep Band; Bsktbl; High Hon Roll.

LONG, ASHLEY L; Bixby Sr HS; Bixby, OK; (2); Church Yth Grp; German Clb; Office Aide; SADD; Sftbl; Hon Roll; Jr NHS; O U; Dntl Hygnst.

LONG, BESSIE M; Haileyville Schl; Krebs, OK; (2); FBLA; Hist FHA; Yrbk; Hon Roll; Stdnt Month; Acad Awrd Apld Bio; Wrkg Cmptrs.

LONG, CHERYL; Heritage Hall Schl; Oklahoma City, OK; (3); Church Yth Grp; Cmnty Wkr; Drama Clb; Pep Clb; Science Clb; Chorus; Church Choir; Variety Show; NHS; Amer Yth Fnd Intl Ldrshp Conf 96; I Dare You Ldrshp Awd; Msc Thtre/Dnce Prfrmnce; Law.

LONG, CHRISTOPHER; Mustang HS; Yukon, OK; (4); #21 in class; Am Leg Boys St; Pres Church Yth Grp; Debate Tm; FCA; Pres Spanish Clb; Pres Stu Cncl; Bsktbl; High Hon Roll; NHS; Pres Frsh Cls; Acad Team; OASC Basic; Mrktng.

LONG, CHRISTOPHER D; Rush Springs HS; Rush Springs, OK; (2); Church Yth Grp; Letterman Clb; Spanish Clb; Ofcr Bsbl; Bsktbl; Wt Lftg; High Hon Roll; Hon Roll; NHS; Cls Favorite; Engl Awd; OK ST U; Bus Admin.

LONG, CRYSTAL; Nowata HS; Nowata, OK; (4); 1/65; Church Yth Grp; FCA; Chorus; Pres Sec Stu Cncl; Var Capt Bsktbl; Var Capt Chrldng; Var Sftbl; NHS; St Schlr; Val; Stdnt Of Yr; Bsktbl Acdmc All-ST; Tandy Schlr; OK ST Univ; Acctng/Cmptr Sci.

LONG, DANIEL; Tipton Jr Sr HS; Tipton, OK; (3); 1/40; Church Yth Grp; Cmnty Wkr; Natl FFA Org; Scholastic Bowl; Church Choir; Ed Nwsp; Rptr Lit Mag; Ftbl; NHS; Ntl Merit Ltr; All Area Ftbl Team; 1st Pl Cameron Interschltc Meet Engl; Ust Overall Cameron U Sci Fair; Jrnlsm.

LONG, DAVID; Cache HS; Cache, OK; (4); 12/67; Natl Beta Clb; Science Clb; Rep Jr Cls; L Ftbl; L Trk; L Wrstlng; High Hon Roll; NHS; Ntl Merit Ltr; Pres Schlr.

LONG, DEANNA M; Union Intermediate HS; Tulsa, OK; (2); 188/800; Church Yth Grp; Key Clb; Spanish Clb; Church Choir; Sftbl; Swmmng; Hon Roll.

LONG, HOLLY D; Ponca City Sr HS; Ponca City, OK; (4); 38/358; Church Yth Grp; Letterman Clb; Church Choir; Orch; Yrbk; VP Stu Cncl; Mgr Bsbl; Cit Awd; Hon Roll; Kiwanis Awd; Miss Ponca City 95; RYLA Conf; OK Bapt Univ; Elem Ed.

LONG, JAMES; Guthrie Sr HS; Guthrie, OK; (3); French Clb; Mu Alpha Theta; SADD; Band; Mrchg Band; School Musical; Rep Soph Cls; NHS; OU; Law.

LONG, JANA L; Dale Sr HS; Shawnee, OK; (2); Church Yth Grp; Letterman Clb; Band; Drm Mjr(t); Ofcr Stu Cncl; Var L Bsktbl; Var L Sftbl; Hon Roll; NHS; Medicine; Pol Sci.

LONG, JASON R; Hinton HS; Hinton, OK; (2); Church Yth Grp; Drama Clb; Natl FFA Org; SADD; Acpl Chr; Chorus; School Play; JV Var Bsktbl; JV Var Ftbl; JV Var Trk; OK Univ.

LONG, JEREMY D; Guthrie Sr HS; Guthrie, OK; (3); 48/222; Am Leg Boys St; Math Clb; Mu Alpha Theta; Spanish Clb; Band; Mrchg Band; Pep Band; Socr; NHS; U Cntrl OK; Psych.

LONG, JILL; Midwest City HS; Midwest City, OK; (2); 1/501; Dance Clb; FCA; Library Aide; Pep Clb; Science Clb; Spanish Clb; SADD; Stage Crew; Rep Soph Cls; Rep Stu Cncl; People/People Stu Ambssdr Australia; Outstndng Frshmn Eng, Math Stu.

LONG, JOHN D; Heavener HS; Heavener, OK; (1); 9/110; Church Yth Grp; FCA; Letterman Clb; JV Bsktbl; JV Ftbl; Var L Trk; Hon Roll; Outsdng Frosh Boy 95-; Comm Pilot.

LONG, KEVIN; Harrah HS; Harrah, OK; (3); Drama Clb; SADD; Band; Jazz Band; Mrchg Band; Pep Band; Crs Cntry; Socr; Law Enforcement.

LONG, MICHAEL S; Claremore Sr HS; Claremore, OK; (2); Boy Scts; Chess Clb; German Clb; High Hon Roll; NHS.

LONG, MICHAELA; Antlers Sr HS; Antlers, OK; (3); Church Yth Grp; Cmnty Wkr; 4-H; Quiz Bowl; SADD; Phtg Nwsp; Phtg Yrbk; Chrldng; Tennis; Hon Roll; S E Durant; Crmnlgy.

LONG, MICHELE L; Yukon HS; Yukon, OK; (2); Church Yth Grp; Drama Clb; FBLA; FHA; Model UN; Service Clb; Thesps; School Play; Stage Crew; Sec Frsh Cls; Piano 4 Yrs; Chrch Of Chrst All My Life; Cmmnty Svc Hrs Vol Work; Law.

LONG, RAY; Clinton HS; Clinton, OK; (3); #1 in class; Scholastic Bowl; Teachers Aide; Church Choir; Var Socr; Cit Awd; High Hon Roll; Hon Roll; JETS Awd; Jr NHS; NHS; OK ST U; Engr.

LONG, REBECCA K; Western Heights Sr HS; Oklahoma City, OK; (2); Church Yth Grp; FCA; Teachers Aide; Ofcr Stu Cncl; JV Co-Capt Chrldng; High Hon Roll; NHS; Cmnty Svc Elderly; Wtrgrl Ftbl Tm; Med.

LONG, ROY; Stilwell HS; Stilwell, OK; (2); Natl FFA Org; U Of AR; Tchr.

LONG, TRAVIS L; Haskell HS; Haskell, OK; (2); 4-H; Natl FFA Org; JV Bsbl.

LONG, TRAVIS T; Byng Sr HS; Ada, OK; (2); Church Yth Grp; Drama Clb; FBLA; Natl FFA Org; Band; Chorus; Church Choir; Mrchg Band; School Play; Cit Awd.

LONGAKER, BLYTHE LEIGH; John Marshall HS; Oklahoma City, OK; (4); 10/167; Church Yth Grp; Teachers Aide; Church Choir; Yrbk; Chrldng; High Hon Roll; NHS; FCA; French Clb; Jr Class Marshall; Piano; U Of Cntrl OK; Early Chldhd.

LONGAN, BRANDY; Stillwater Sr HS; Stillwater, OK; (1); Church Yth Grp; Dance Clb; FCA; Natl Beta Clb; School Play; Stage Crew; Ofcr Stu Cncl; High Hon Roll; Pres Acad Fit Awd; OU; Surgeon; Orthopedics.

LONGHORN, STEPHANIE D; Tecumseh HS; Tecumseh, OK; (3); Spanish Clb; Rptr Ed Nwsp; Var Bsktbl; Var Crs Cntry; Var Sftbl; Var Trk; OK HS Hnr Soc; U Of NC-CHAPEL Hill; Law.

LONGLEY, J M; Edmond Memorial HS; Edmond, OK; (1); Church Yth Grp; FCA; Chorus; School Play; Tennis.

LONGLEY, SIDNEY; Edmond Memorial HS; Edmond, OK; (3); FCA; FHA; Key Clb; Spanish Clb; Var Chrldng; Hon Roll; All Star Natl Chmpn Pom Pon Squad; 2 Time St Chmpn Chrldng Squad; 3 Time All-Amer Chrldr.

LONGNECKER, TISHA M; Newcastle HS; Blanchard, OK; (3); GAA; Pep Clb; Spanish Clb; JV Sftbl; High Hon Roll; Hon Roll; OU; Comp Sci.

LONGORIA, ERNIE; Choctaw HS; Choctaw, OK; (4); 99/313; Cmnty Wkr; Key Clb; Co-Capt Quiz Bowl; ROTC; VP Science Clb; JV Var Ftbl; Pres Acad Fit Awd; JV Bsbl; JV Socr; Hon Roll; Intrmrl Rugby; Soccer Coach & Referee; U S Military Acad; Engrng.

LONIAN, HEATHER S; Heritage Hall Schl; Oklahoma City, OK; (2); Pep Clb; Science Clb; Spanish Clb; Lit Mag; JV Fld Hcky; High Hon Roll; Hon Roll; Spanish NHS.

LOONEY, CHARMALET; Midwest City HS; Oklahoma City, OK; (2); Girl Scts; JA; Spanish Clb; Ofcr Frsh Cls; Ofcr Soph Cls; Bsktbl; Crs Cntry; Trk; Wt Lftg; Hon Roll.

LOONEY III, CLIFFORD; Midwest City HS; Oklahoma City, OK; (3); Church Yth Grp; FCA; JA; Spanish Clb; Church Choir; Bsktbl; Ftbl; Trk; Jr NHS; NHS; First Bapt Chrch Green Pastures Yth Pres; 9th Grd Schl Bsktbl Player Yr; KS U; Acctng.

LOONEY, KARA L; Edmond Memorial HS; Edmond, OK; (3); 32/371; FCA; JCL; Latin Clb; Rep Stu Cncl; Var Bsktbl; Powder Puff Ftbl; Intrml Socr; Var Tennis; Intrml Vllybl; High Hon Roll; Tnns St Champ; Pblshd Poet; All-City Bsktbl & Tnns.

LOOPER, DANIELLE P; Woodward HS; Woodward, OK; (1); Church Yth Grp; School Play; Stage Crew; Variety Show; Hon Roll; NW Univ.

LOOPER, RYAN L; Hobart HS; Hobart, OK; (2); Church Yth Grp; Library Aide; Office Aide; Ftbl; Wrstlng; High Hon Roll; Hon Roll; UCO; Tchr.

LOPER, VALERIE E; Edmond Memorial HS; Edmond, OK; (2); 142/408; Church Yth Grp; Spanish Clb; Chorus; Church Choir; Orch; School Musical; Variety Show; OSU; Ed; Tchr.

LOPEZ, CAMILLE A; Muskogee HS; Muskogee, OK; (4); Library Aide; Office Aide; Ed Nwsp; Sox Gage Jrnlsm Awd For Being Ed Of Nwsp Sr Yr; Successfully Compltd Jrnlsm I, II, III & IV In HS; Virgils Beauty Coll; Cosmetolgy.

LOPEZ, CUAUHTEMOC T; Southeast HS; Oklahoma City, OK; (2); FCA; JV Bsktbl; Cit Awd; Gov Hon Prg Awd; Hnr Classes; Arch.

LOPEZ, DESIRAE R; Tuttle HS; Tuttle, OK; (3); Church Yth Grp; FCA; FHA; GAA; Church Choir; Sftbl; St Sftbl Champions; Lttrmn In Sftbl.

LOPEZ, GERARDO M; Edmond Memorial HS; Edmond, OK; (3); 1/371; Spanish Clb; SADD; Orch; Ofcr Stu Cncl; Crs Cntry; Socr; Hon Roll; NHS; All Conf Sccr; Chem.

LOPEZ, MARIA GLADIOLA LARA; Clinton HS; Clinton, OK; (3); Church Yth Grp; Key Clb; Speech Tm; Temple Yth Grp; Band; Chorus; Mrchg Band; School Play; Nwsp; Prfct Atten Awd; Sci.

LOPEZ, NAHLEEN; Yukon Middle HS; Yukon, OK; (1); JV Chrldng; Gym; NHS; Renaissance; Phys Therapist.

LO PRESTO, ANTHONY E; Putnam City West HS; Oklahoma City, OK; (3); 33/310; Treas Frsh Cls; Treas Soph Cls; Rep Stu Cncl; L Ftbl; NHS; Phrmcy.

LORENZEN, JAMES B; Liberty HS; Mounds, OK; (4); 1/25; FBLA; FHA; VICA; Yrbk; Pres Sr Cls; Treas Stu Cncl; Capt Bsktbl; Capt Ftbl; Capt Wt Lftg; High Hon Roll; Bartlesville Wesleyan.

LOSINSKE, TAMMY; Hominy HS; Hominy, OK; (3); Church Yth Grp; Drama Clb; French Clb; FHA; Speech Tm; Teachers Aide; School Play; Stage Crew; Rep Jr Cls; Ofcr Stu Cncl; TJC; Brdcstng.

LOSS, KATIE A; Canton HS; Canton, OK; (1); Church Yth Grp; FCA; FHA; Band; Chorus; Church Choir; Mrchg Band; Pep Band; School Musical; Hon Roll; S Western Wetherford OU; Lawyr.

LOTT, AMANDA; Moore HS; Newalla, OK; (4); 100/742; Church Yth Grp; Cmnty Wkr; Dance Clb; Debate Tm; Drama Clb; English Clb; JCL; Latin Clb; Q&S; Speech Tm; Archry; Non-Schl Cheer & Pom Pon; Bowling Green ST U; Jrnlsm.

LOTT, JENNIFER D; Pawhuska HS; Pawhuska, OK; (2); Church Yth Grp; Pep Clb; Band; Chorus; Color Guard; Flag Corp; Mrchg Band; Pep Band; Hon Roll; Acteens Msnry Grp For Girls; Rogers ST Coll Talent Search; OK Bapt Univ; Marine Biologist.

LOTT, MONICA; Ponca City Sr HS; Ponca City, OK; (4); Art Clb; Cmnty Wkr; DECA; Girl Scts; Teachers Aide; VP Pres Jr Cls; Ofcr Sr Cls; Hon Roll; OK U; Graphic Dsgn.

LOUCKS, LAURA A; Enid Sr HS; Enid, OK; (3); 5/475; Church Yth Grp; FCA; Spanish Clb; Teachers Aide; Chorus; Yrbk; Treas Soph Cls; Treas Stu Cncl; Crs Cntry; Stat Ftbl; Dance; Horse Showing; Aquaettes; Law.

LOUDERMILK, TERRI L; Stilwell HS; Stilwell, OK; (1); French Clb; Speech Tm; Chorus; Color Guard; Bsktbl; Chrldng; Sftbl; Trk; Hon Roll; U Of AR.

LOUGH, BRIAN K; Lindsay HS; Lindsay, OK; (2); Art Clb; Church Yth Grp; OK Chrstn U Of Sci; Art.

LOUTHAN, MACKEY; Seiling Schl; Chester, OK; (3); Church Yth Grp; FCA; FBLA; Letterman Clb; Natl FFA Org; VICA; Nwsp; Var Bsktbl; Var Ftbl; Var Wt Lftg; FFA Rptr; St Rnnr Up Ftbl Team 95; UMYF HS Rep.

LOVE, ALEX R; Stillwater Jr HS; Stillwater, OK; (1); Church Yth Grp; Cmnty Wkr; FCA; Spanish Clb; Rep Stu Cncl; Ftbl; Trk; High Hon Roll; Pres Schlr.

LOVE, CANDICE J; Idabel HS; Idabel, OK; (2); 3/137; Church Yth Grp; Band; Chorus; Church Choir; Jazz Band; Mrchg Band; Treas Soph Cls; Rep Stu Cncl; Hon Roll; NHS; U Of OK; Pre-Med.

LOVE, CAROLYN; Midwest City HS; Midwest City, OK; (4); High Hon Roll; Hon Roll; Jr NHS; Pres Acad Fit Awd; Bwlng, Cch Elem Stu; Rose ST; Bus.

LOVE, CHRIS W; Duncan HS; Duncan, OK; (4); FBLA; Rep Band; High Hon Roll; NHS; Pres Schlr; St Schlr; Jazz Band; Mrchg Band; Orch; SW OK St Univ; Comp Prog.

LOVE, DONISHA; Coweta HS; Coweta, OK; (3); French Clb; FHA; Hosp Aide; Spanish Clb; SADD; Church Choir; School Musical; Var Capt Chrldng; JV Gym; JV Trk; NSU; Bus.

LOVE, ERIN; Ponca City Sr HS; Ponca City, OK; (2); 57/600; Church Yth Grp; Band; Church Choir; Mrchg Band; Orch; Pep Band; Var Chrldng; High Hon Roll; NHS; Bible Quiz; OK ST Univ; CPA.

LOVE, JOHN H; Chattanooga Schl; Chattanooga, OK; (1); Natl FFA Org; Quiz Bowl; Art Class; FFA Grnhnd Awd; Cameron Univ.

LOVE, LINDSEY L; Midwest City HS; Midwest City, OK; (4); Cmnty Wkr; FBLA; FHA; German Clb; Library Aide; Office Aide; Teachers Aide; VICA; Sftbl; Cit Awd; Child Ed.

LOVE, PRINCESS N; Lawton Sr HS; Lawton, OK; (3); Cmnty Wkr; HOBY; Church Choir; Lit Mag; Ofcr Stu Cncl; Bsktbl; Trk; High Hon Roll; NHS; Pres Acad Fit Awd; Pre-Med.

LOVE, TRAVIS F; Hartshorne Sr HS; Hartshorne, OK; (2); Church Yth Grp; Letterman Clb; Natl FFA Org; Var Bsbl; Var Capt Bsktbl; Cit Awd; High Hon Roll; Hon Roll; Ntl Merit Ltr.

LOVELACE, CORY B; Thomas Jr Sr HS; Custer City, OK; (3); Ftbl; Wt Lftg; Vet.

LOVELACE, MELODY; Ardmore HS; Ardmore, OK; (4); 53/163; Church Yth Grp; FCA; Latin Clb; Mu Alpha Theta; Chorus; Co-Capt Chrldng; Sftbl; Hon Roll; NHS; Prfct Atten Awd.

LOVELACE, NEIL D; Sapulpa Sr HS; Sapulpa, OK; (3); 7/300; Church Yth Grp; ROTC; Band; Jazz Band; Mrchg Band; Orch; Pep Band; High Hon Roll; NHS; Prfct Atten Awd; Teens For Christ; All Regn Hnr Bnd; Ll St Bnd; OIK Univ; Compsci.

LOVELESS, ELIZABETH; Midwest City HS; Midwest City, OK; (2); 22/501; Church Yth Grp; FCA; FHA; German Clb; Office Aide; Pep Clb; SADD; Ofcr Soph Cls; Chrldng; High Hon Roll.

LOVELESS, JULI; Adair HS; Big Cabin, OK; (3); Church Yth Grp; FCA; VP FHA; Rep Frsh Cls; VP Soph Cls; VP Jr Cls; Rep Stu Cncl; Var Bsktbl; Var Trk; Hon Roll; Acctng.

LOVELESS, MICKEY D; Bethany HS; Bethany, OK; (3); Chess Clb; Church Yth Grp; Debate Tm; Key Clb; Var Bsbl; Var Ftbl; Var Wt Lftg; Hon Roll; Ntl Merit Ltr; U Of OK Smmr Schlrs Pgm 95 96; OU; Biochem.

LOVELESS, RYAN L; Noble HS; Noble, OK; (2); Spanish Clb; Ofcr Bsbl; Ftbl; Wt Lftg; Hon Roll; Bsktbl; U Of OK; Prof Ath Bsbl.

LOVELL, ADAM C; Edmond Memorial HS; Edmond, OK; (4); Boy Scts; Church Yth Grp; Cmnty Wkr; SADD; Band; Chorus; Jazz Band; Mrchg Band; Orch; Pep Band; Eagle Scout; NOAC Instruct; Northeastern State Univ; Nat Am.

LOVELL, KENDRA; Mc Curtain HS; Shady Point, OK; (4); 4-H; Girl Scts; Office Aide; Yrbk; 4-H Awd; Hon Roll; NHS; Prfct Atten Awd; Carl Albert ST Coll; Reg Nrs.

LOVELL, TALLY; Mc Curtain HS; Mccurtain, OK; (3); 1/20; Pres 4-H; HOBY; Capt Quiz Bowl; Var Bsktbl; Var Sftbl; High Hon Roll; NHS; Pres Acad Fit Awd; Val; CASC OK; Acctng.

LOVELY, ELIZABETH; Cascia Hall Prep School; Tulsa, OK; (4); German Clb; Pep Clb; Scholastic Bowl; Chorus; School Musical; Ed Yrbk; Capt Var Swmmng; High Hon Roll; NHS; Val; U Of AL.

LOVELY, JAMES; Cascia Hall Prep School; Tulsa, OK; (1); Church Yth Grp; Cmnty Wkr; Quiz Bowl; Service Clb; Chorus; Stage Crew; Tennis; Eng.

LOVES, LAKESHA N; John Marshall HS; Guthrie, OK; (2); Pep Clb; Red Cross Aide; Band; Ofcr Stu Cncl; Chrldng; Crs Cntry; Gym; Trk; Hon Roll; NHS; Natl Assn Girls & Boys Clb V Team; Med.

LOVETT, JACQUELINE D; Mc Alester HS; Mcalester, OK; (3); Church Yth Grp; French Clb; FHA; Thesps; Stage Crew; Upward Bound At ECU; Vol For Spcl Olympics; Eastern OK ST Coll; Law.

LOVETT, KIMBERLY D; Mustang HS; Mustang, OK; (3); Church Yth Grp; Pres Drama Clb; FCA; FHA; NFL; Scholastic Bowl; Spanish Clb; Speech Tm; Teachers Aide; Thesps; Bst Actrs 2 Yrs Drm; Bst All Arnd Drm; Regl Spch Trnmnt; Northeastern ST Univ; Thtr/Ed.

LOVING, CRYSTAL; Blanchard Jr Sr HS; Blanchard, OK; (2); 4/87; FHA; Pep Clb; Rep Frsh Cls; Var Bsktbl; Var Sftbl; Hon Roll; Jr NHS; NHS; ESE; OK U; Med.

LOVINGGOOD, JESSICA; Midwest City HS; Midwest City, OK; (4); Library Aide; SADD; Rep Stu Cncl; Bsktbl; Golf; Sftbl; Cit Awd; Hon Roll; Jr NHS; Val; Kiwanis Stu Of Month; Psych.

LOVITT, JOHN; Clayton Jr Sr HS; Nashoba, OK; (3); Church Yth Grp; Natl FFA Org; Quiz Bowl; Rep Frsh Cls; Rep Soph Cls; Stat Var Bsbl; JV Var Bsktbl; Intrml Ftbl; Var Socr; Intrml Sftbl; Comp Sci.

LOVITT, MELISSA; Mc Alester HS; Mcalester, OK; (2); Church Yth Grp; Dance Clb; Band; Mrchg Band; Chrldng; Tennis; High Hon Roll; Chrch Dist Wide Offc; Make Dffrnc Day; Resp Thrp.

LOVOS, ESTHER G; Central HS; Tulsa, OK; (2); Dance Clb; Gym.

LOW, ALLISON; Southwest Covenant Schl; Yukon, OK; (2); Church Yth Grp; FCA; Chorus; Mgr Yrbk; Bsktbl; Vllybl; High Hon Roll; Piano; Mssnry Trps.

LOWE, ALISON F; Bartlesville Sr HS; Bartlesville, OK; (3); Church Yth Grp; FCA; Sec French Clb; Rep Stu Cncl; JV Capt Chrldng; JV Var Pom Pon; French Hon Soc; High Hon Roll; Jr NHS; NHS; Dance Instr; UDA All-Star; Acad Excl Awd; Ed.

LOWE, ALLISON A; Mt St Marys HS; Oklahoma City, OK; (3); Pres Drama Clb; School Play; Variety Show; Rptr Nwsp; Rptr Yrbk; Hon Roll; Film; Pop Cultural Icon.

LOWE, DE LAYNA K; Meeker HS; Meeker, OK; (2); Chorus; Church Choir; Var Bsktbl; Var Chrldng; Prfct Atten Awd; Stu Of The Month; Interior Decorating.

LOWE, JACOB I; Wilburton Sr HS; Wilburton, OK; (2); Church Yth Grp; Cmnty Wkr; FCA; 4-H; Letterman Clb; Chorus; Church Choir; VP Jr Cls; Var Bsktbl; Var Fld Hcky.

LOWE, MARCUS; Perkins-Tryon HS; Perkins, OK; (1); Ofcr Frsh Cls; Hon Roll; OSU.

LOWE, MISTY; Madill HS; Madill, OK; (3); 30/85; FCA; FHA; Drill Tm; JV Bsktbl; JV Var Chrldng; Hon Roll; NHS; Southeastern ST; Law.

LOWE, RYAN N; Mustang HS; Mustang, OK; (3); 1/350; Church Yth Grp; Dance Clb; FCA; Key Clb; Math Clb; Scholastic Bowl; Spanish Clb; Church Choir; Chrldng; Pom Pon; Tulsa Univ; Med.

LOWE, SANDRA; Jenks HS; Tulsa, OK; (4); 14/500; Church Yth Grp; Service Clb; Spanish Clb; Band; Mrchg Band; High Hon Roll; Hon Roll; NHS; Sal; OK ST Univ; Acctnt; Bus.

LOWE, TIFFANY; Boynton Schl; Taft, OK; (2); Church Yth Grp; FHA; Science Clb; Church Choir; Yrbk; Ofcr Frsh Cls; Chrldng; Sftbl; Cit Awd; Hon Roll; Pres Ed Awd Ppm For Outstdng Acad; Blue & Gold Sausage Plaque For Selling Meat; OK ST U; Ag.

LOWE, WILLIAM C; Kingston HS; Kingston, OK; (2); Art Clb; Var Ftbl; Var Wt Lftg; Bio.

LOWELL, JENNIFER D; Western Heights Sr HS; Oklahoma City, OK; (4); Art Clb; Chess Clb; Church Yth Grp; Band; Flag Corp; Mrchg Band; School Musical; Crs Cntry; Cert Of Achvmt; Peer Tutor; Child Care.

LOWELL, JEREMY J; Western Heights Sr HS; Oklahoma City, OK; (2); Boy Scts; Church Yth Grp; Teachers Aide; Band; Mrchg Band; Mgr Crs Cntry; Cit Awd; Hon Roll; All Amer Schlr Awd; U Of OK; Pharmacy.

LOWERY, SARAH A; Bishop Kelley HS; Tulsa, OK; (2); Cmnty Wkr; Dance Clb; FCA; GAA; Hosp Aide; Letterman Clb; Pep Clb; Red Cross Aide; Teachers Aide; Varsity Clb; Sprtsmnshp Awd Tulsa City Tennis.

LOWERY, TERRY; Deer Creek HS; Edmond, OK; (3); Church Yth Grp; Cmnty Wkr; FCA; Science Clb; SADD; Ed Yrbk; Crs Cntry; Trk; Wt Lftg; Wrstlng; Syracuse Univ; Psych.

LOWES, JANELLE E; Edmond Memorial HS; Edmond, OK; (3); 1/400; Chrmn Am Leg Aux Girls St; Church Yth Grp; Sec French Clb; Key Clb; Mu Alpha Theta; School Musical; VP NHS; Math Clb; Quiz Bowl; Scholastic Bowl; OK All ST Choir 95; OK Summer Arts Inst Choir; OK Bapt Univ Fr Chmpn Gramer/Voc/Cltr/Cvlztn.

LOWMAN, MELISSA; Moore HS; Moore, OK; (3); Var L Swmmng; USS Regstrd; Moore Aquatic Swim Team; NM ST U; Med.

LOWMAN, TINA M; Glenpool HS; Glenpool, OK; (3); Church Yth Grp; FCA; Teachers Aide; L VP Chorus; JV Var Bsktbl; Bsktbl; Powder Puff Ftbl; Warrier Pride Awd In Bsktbl; OK Bapt Univ; Ed.

LOWRANCE, AMBER; Hobart HS; Hobart, OK; (1); 6/100; Church Yth Grp; Band; Mrchg Band; Pep Band.

LOWREY, PATRICIA; Mc Loud HS; Newalla, OK; (3); 12/127; Natl FFA Org; Sec Jr Cls; Hon Roll; NHS; OK Hnr Soc; FFA GPA Plaque; S W MO ST U; Film Edtr.

LOWRY, BRANDY R; Bartlesville Sr HS; Bartlesville, OK; (1); Pep Clb; Teachers Aide; Chorus; Chrldng; Gym; Hon Roll; Acad Excl Awd; Span Awd Strght A'S; Drm Awd For Mscl; OK Univ.

LOWRY, CODY B; Kellyville Sr HS; Bristow, OK; (3); 1/110; Church Yth Grp; Cmnty Wkr; Math Tm; Quiz Bowl; Scholastic Bowl; Ed Nwsp; Var L Bsktbl; Var L Golf; French Hon Soc; Gov Hon Prg Awd; Pre-Med.

LOWRY, DENZIL; Ada HS; Ada, OK; (3); Church Yth Grp; FCA; Office Aide; Var L Ftbl; Var Trk; High Hon Roll; NHS; U Of OK; Law.

LOWRY, JAMES D; South Intermediate HS; Broken Arrow, OK; (1); Church Yth Grp; 4-H; Acpl Chr; Band; Church Choir; Jazz Band; Mrchg Band; Pep Band; Cit Awd; Gov Hon Prg Awd; BA Med Ctr Vol; Traume Surgeon.

LOWRY, JAMES S; Edmond Memorial HS; Edmond, OK; (3); Church Yth Grp; Drama Clb; German Clb; Chorus; Church Choir; School Musical; School Play; Swing Chorus; NY U; Flm Dir.

LOWRY, JASON; Mc Alester HS; Mcalester, OK; (4); Am Leg Boys St; FCA; Spanish Clb; Var L Bsbl; JV Ftbl; Var Capt Wrstlng; Hon Roll; Arch.

LOWRY, KRISTOPHER C; Glenpool HS; Glenpool, OK; (4); FCA; Spanish Clb; Chorus; School Musical; Swing Chorus; Yrbk; Var Crs Cntry; Var Trk; Hon Roll; HOSA; Cls Rprtr; Compltd Dntl Asstng At Vo-Tech; Write Songs; Tulsa JC; Dntl Hyg.

LOWRY, REBECCA M; Glenpool HS; Glenpool, OK; (2); Church Yth Grp; FCA; Pep Clb; Spanish Clb; Chorus; Church Choir; Swing Chorus; Hon Roll; Jr NHS; FHA.

LOWRY, TRAVIS; Ada HS; Ada, OK; (3); Church Yth Grp; FCA; Var L Ftbl; Var L Golf.

LOWRY, WHEELER; Clinton HS; Clinton, OK; (4); 13/100; Boy Scts; Bus Profs of Am; Church Yth Grp; Debate Tm; FCA; FBLA; Natl FFA Org; Office Aide; Ofcr Stu Cncl; High Hon Roll.

LOY, WARREN THOMAS; Classen Schl Of Adv Studies; Oklahoma City, OK; (3); Pres Drama Clb; Pres German Clb; Thesps; Chorus; School Musical; School Play; Pres Stu Cncl; OCU; Mus Thtr.

LOYD, AARON M; Metro Christian Acad; Tulsa, OK; (4); 10/70; Key Clb; Pep Clb; Band; Chorus; School Play; Ed Yrbk; Ofcr Stu Cncl; Socr; Wt Lftg; Ntl Merit Schol; OK U.

LOYD, JEREMY E; Muskogee HS; Muskogee, OK; (1); CAP; ROTC; Drill Tm; Hon Roll; Rcvd 1st Dgre Blck Blt Amer Tae Kwon Do Assoc Cert; US Air Force Acad; Avtn.

LOYD, PAM; Stratford Schl; Stratford, OK; (1); Spanish Clb; Band; Capt Flag Corp; Jazz Band; Mrchg Band; Pep Band; Hon Roll; NHS; Harvard; Law.

LOYD, REAGAN; Putnam City West HS; Bethany, OK; (1); Church Yth Grp; Hosp Aide; Pep Clb; Church Choir; Chrldng; Sports Tchr; Chrch Plays/Musicals; Church Sftbl; Point Loma; Pre Med.

LOZANO, JENNIFER R; Norman Sr HS; Pryor, OK; (4); Cmnty Wkr; Drama Clb; 4-H; FHA; Sec FTA; GAA; Office Aide; Pep Clb; Spanish Clb; Speech Tm; Speech St Medal; Salina VFW Speech Cont Trophy & Money; Trk Medals.

LOZANO, ROBERT; Central Mid-HS; Norman, OK; (2); 1/500; Boy Scts; FCA; Math Tm; Natl FFA Org; Office Aide; Quiz Bowl; Bsktbl; Ftbl; Trk; Wt Lftg; FFA Greenhand; U Of OK; Biochem.

LU, HUONG; U S Grant HS; Oklahoma City, OK; (3); Hon Roll; NHS.

LUCAS, BRYAN E; Oklahoma Bible Acad; Enid, OK; (2); Hon Roll; Acad Tm; Asstnt YMCA Coach; Church Usher/Acolyte Ldr; Cmptr Sci.

LUCAS, CHRISTY M; Bethany HS; Bethany, OK; (2).

LUCAS, KRISTEN R; Putnam City North HS; Oklahoma City, OK; (4); 70/440; Church Yth Grp; Key Clb; Hon Roll; Jr NHS; NHS; Dance, Ballet, Pointe, Tap, Jazz & Toe-Tap; St Gregorys Coll; Ed.

LUCAS, LESLIE; Bluejacket Schl; Bluejacket, OK; (4); 3/25; Church Yth Grp; FHA; Natl FFA Org; Treas Frsh Cls; Rptr Soph Cls; Treas Jr Cls; Rptr Sr Cls; Rptr Stu Cncl; Bsktbl; Chrldng; MO Southern ST; Dntl Hygne.

LUCAS, NICOLE A; Bishop Kelley HS; Tulsa, OK; (1); Church Yth Grp; Cmnty Wkr; FCA; Bsktbl; Score Keeper; Var Trk; Vllybl; Hon Roll; Pres Schlr; Psych.

LUCAS, SUSAN; Hulbert Jr Sr HS; Proctor, OK; (2); 15/60; Computer Clb; 4-H; FHA; German Clb; GAA; Science Clb; Ofcr Soph Cls; Bsktbl; Trk; Hon Roll; Northeastern ST U; Pharmcy.

LUCERO, MICHAEL; Shawnee Sr HS; Shawnee, OK; (2); 13/325; Band; Jazz Band; Mrchg Band; High Hon Roll.

LUCHTEL, MISTIE; Morris HS; Okmulgee, OK; (3); Church Yth Grp; Cmnty Wkr; HOBY; Pres Frsh Cls; Pres Soph Cls; Pres Jr Cls; 4-H Awd; High Hon Roll; NHS; Pres Acad Fit Awd; Art; Phys Fitness; OK ST; Phys Fitness.

LUCKINBILL, JUSTIN M; Dibble Jr Sr HS; Blanchard, OK; (2); 12/48; Boy Scts; Church Yth Grp; Band; Mrchg Band; Pep Band; Bsktbl; Ftbl; Trk; Wt Lftg; Hon Roll; BYU; Sci.

LUDVICEK, TY W; Glenpool HS; Glenpool, OK; (1); Cmnty Wkr; Chorus; Bsktbl; Ftbl; Wt Lftg; Hon Roll; Jr NHS.

LUDWICK, PATRICIA L; Charles Page HS; Sand Springs, OK; (1); FCA; Natl FFA Org; Kybrdng; Rdng; Anml Care; OK Univ; Law.

LUDWIG, JEREMY M; Cleveland Sr HS; Jennings, OK; (3); Var Ftbl; Hon Roll; Prfct Atten Awd; Outs Stu Of Principles Of Tech.

LUEBCKE, ALICIA L; Ponca City Sr HS; Ponca City, OK; (4); 75/338; Church Yth Grp; Cmnty Wkr; Office Aide; Band; Chorus; Mrchg Band; Pep Band; Nwsp; JV Vllybl; Hon Roll; Northern OK Coll; Dental Hyg.

LUESADA, JARRED; Haworth Sr HS; Idabel, OK; (2); 1/60; Library Aide; Hon Roll; NHS; Prfct Atten Awd; OK HS Hnr Scty; OK St Univ.

LUFF, ERIN; Putnam City North HS; Oklahoma City, OK; (1); Rep Stu Cncl; Swmmng; Outstdng Span Stu; St Finals 4th Swimming; Bio; Zoology.

LUGO, GABRIELA A; Union Intermediate HS; Tulsa, OK; (2); French Clb; FBLA; NHS; Pres Acad Fit Awd; Stanford U; Cmptr/Eng.

LUGO, KARIM R; Altus Sr HS; Altus, OK; (2); Boy Scts; Ftbl; Trk; Wt Lftg; Wrstlng; Phy Thrpst.

LUKER, JEREMY; Stuart Sr HS; Mcalester, OK; (3); 4-H; Natl FFA Org; Quiz Bowl; Scholastic Bowl; Pres Frsh Cls; Pres Soph Cls; Rep Stu Cncl; Var L Bsktbl; 4-H Awd; High Hon Roll; Natl Sci Mrt Awd; U Of OK; Bus.

LUNA, CHRISTOPHER; Comanche HS; Comanche, OK; (4); 6/60; Am Leg Boys St; Rep Pres Frsh Cls; Rep Pres Soph Cls; Pres Jr Cls; Pres Sr Cls; Pres Stu Cncl; Var Ftbl; Cit Awd; NHS; Sal; East Cntrl U; Hist Tchr.

LUNDY, DANIEL N; Cordell Sr HS; Cordell, OK; (4); Art Clb; French Clb; Spanish Clb; Speech Tm; JV Ftbl; Var Socr; Hon Roll; Outstndg Amer Hstry Achvt; Sccr Chartr Season Hnr; Southwestern OK; Corp Law.

LUNDY, GABRIEL N; Cordell Sr HS; Cordell, OK; (3); Art Clb; Spanish Clb; Ftbl; Socr; Hon Roll; Sccr Chartr Season Hnr; Southwestern; Arch.

LUNDY, JASON; Choctaw Jr HS; Choctaw, OK; (1); Golf; Wt Lftg; High Hon Roll; Jr NHS; OK U.

LUNDY, MATT A; Choctaw HS; Choctaw, OK; (2); Church Yth Grp; FCA; JV Golf; Chrch Yth Group; OK Univ; RN.

LUNSFORD, JEREMY; Okmulgee HS; Okmulgee, OK; (2); 48/180; JV Bsbl; JV Bsktbl; Hon Roll; Wash Univ In St Louis; Engr.

LUPER, JASON R; Bethany HS; Bethany, OK; (3); 2/88; Am Leg Boys St; Chess Clb; Key Clb; JV Bsbl; Var Crs Cntry; Var Ftbl; Var Trk; Var Wt Lftg; Cit Awd; High Hon Roll; Bausch & Lomb Sci Awd; Yth Alive; His; Anatomy.

LUSK, LAURA; Sapulpa Sr HS; Sapulpa, OK; (2); Church Yth Grp; Band; Chorus; Mrchg Band; Music.

LUSSIER, KYLA M; Santa Fe HS; Edmond, OK; (2); 1/324; Hist Church Yth Grp; Science Clb; Yrbk; Mgr(s); Stat Socr; JV Vllybl; Hon Roll; NHS; Pres Acad Fit Awd; Biochemistry; Med Rsrch.

LUTER, RYAN L; Morrison Public Schl; Morrison, OK; (1); Church Yth Grp; Cmnty Wkr; 4-H; Natl FFA Org; Quiz Bowl; Spanish Clb; Speech Tm; Varsity Clb; Rptr Nwsp; Pres Frsh Cls; Hghst Clss Avg Wrld His/Span I/OK His/Alg I/Earth Sci/Eng I; 1st Cty FFA Spch Cntst/3-4th Cty Cnts; OK ST; Ag.

LUTES, JENNIFER A; Deer Creek HS; Oklahoma City, OK; (3); 28/96; Church Yth Grp; Sec FBLA; Science Clb; Yrbk; Chrldng; Var Tennis; NHS; Abilene Chrstn U; Bus.

LUTHI, JENNIFER D; Buffalo Jr Sr HS; Buffalo, OK; (2); Church Yth Grp; Band; Mrchg Band; Orch; Pep Band; VP Frsh Cls; Sec Treas Soph Cls; Hon Roll; Red Carpet Hnr Band 95-96; Tri-St Fstvl Hnr Band 95-96.

LUTHYE, JULIE; Perry Sr HS; Perry, OK; (4); 1/70; Am Leg Aux Girls St; Pres Church Yth Grp; English Clb; FCA; FBLA; Band; Jazz Band; Mrchg Band; VP Sr Cls; Stu Today Awd; Sthrn Nzrne U.

LUTHYE, PAM; Perry Sr HS; Perry, OK; (4); 5/66; Pres Church Yth Grp; Cmnty Wkr; FCA; VP FBLA; Teachers Aide; Band; NHS; Matmaids; Homcmng Attndnt; Central ST U; Speech Pathlgy.

LUTOMSKI, CANDICE D; Emerson Jr HS; Enid, OK; (1); Art Clb; Spanish Clb; Rptr Nwsp; Psycht.

LUTTON, CLAIRE E; Bartlesville Sr HS; Bartlesville, OK; (4); 49/429; Cmnty Wkr; Q&S; Band; Mrchg Band; French Hon Soc; High Hon Roll; Hon Roll; Jr NHS; NHS; Alld Arts/Hum Awd; St Edwards Univ; Fine Art Photo.

LUTTRELL, AMBER L; Claremore Sr HS; Claremore, OK; (1); Church Yth Grp; Math Tm; Scholastic Bowl; Band; Jazz Band; Mrchg Band; Pep Band; High Hon Roll; Brown Univ; Oceanogrphy/Zoology.

LUTTRELL, EVAN; Midwest City HS; Midwest City, OK; (4); 1/419; FCA; FHA; Rep Stu Cncl; Var Bsbl; Var Ftbl; NHS; Val; Letterman Clb; Office Aide; Rptr Nwsp; OK Big All-City Ftbl Tm, All-St Ftbl Tms; Mid St All Conf/All Dist Ftbl Tm.

LUTTRELL, GABRIEL; Midwest City HS; Midwest City, OK; (2); FCA; Ofcr Soph Cls; Ofcr Stu Cncl; Var Bsbl; Var Ftbl; Wt Lftg; Pres Jr NHS; NHS; Office Aide; Cntrl Conf Ftbll All-Conf Tm; Natl Jr Hnr Soc Ldrshp Conf Rep.

LUTTRELL, JENNIFER L; Anadarko HS; Anadarko, OK; (4); 9/115; Church Yth Grp; Drama Clb; French Clb; Thesps; Chorus; School Musical; Yrbk; High Hon Roll; Pres Acad Fit Awd; SADD; Dance, Jazz Ballet & Pointe; USAO; Music Ministry.

LUTTRELL, KELLY N; Charles Page HS; Sand Springs, OK; (3); Church Yth Grp; Drama Clb; Spanish Clb; Band; Church Choir; Color Guard; Mrchg Band; School Play; Hon Roll; Sec NHS; VP Music Masters; Sr Rep Band Cncl; OK Univ; Elem Ed.

LUTZ, SUSIE; Cashion HS; Cashion, OK; (4); 3/31; Am Leg Aux Girls St; Church Yth Grp; 4-H; Mrchg Band; Pres Frsh Cls; Pres Soph Cls; Sec Sr Cls; Sec Stu Cncl; Hon Roll; U Of Cntrl OK; Elem Ed.

LY, PHUNG T; Stillwater Sr HS; Stillwater, OK; (3); French Clb; Spanish Clb; NHS; OSU.

LYDE, LISA; Lawton Sr HS; Lawton, OK; (4); 60/317; Key Clb; Spanish Clb; Band; Mrchg Band; Pep Band; Stage Crew; Phtg Ed Yrbk; Rep Stu Cncl; Cit Awd; Hon Roll; Cameron Univ; Engl.

LYLE, ANNE A; Healdton HS; Healdton, OK; (2); 2/65; Church Yth Grp; 4-H; Quiz Bowl; Scholastic Bowl; Band; Jazz Band; Mrchg Band; Sec Jr Cls; Cit Awd; 4-H Awd; Acad Tutor; OK City Ldrshp Focus Trip Awd OK Congress; OK Chrstn Univ; Dietician.

LYLE, KEVIN; Seminole Jr Sr HS; Seminole, OK; (4); Am Leg Boys St; Church Yth Grp; Cmnty Wkr; Math Clb; Science Clb; Acpl Chr; Chorus; Var Bsbl; Var Ftbl; Var Tennis; Mixed Co Chorus; Ftbl St Fnslt; Tennis St Qualifr Fnlst; Rockhurst; Psych.

LYLES, ANDREW D; Union Intermediate HS; Broken Arrow, OK; (2); Church Yth Grp; FCA; JV Ftbl; Hon Roll; Bible Quizzing; Chrch Sound & Light Tech; Comp Pgm.

LYLES, LAKESHA N; Mc Lain Career Acad; Tulsa, OK; (3); Church Yth Grp; Dance Clb; Band; Chorus; Church Choir; Flag Corp; Mrchg Band; Chrldng; NHS; Langston U; Advertising Design.

LYLES, VALERIE; Berryhill Jr HS; Tulsa, OK; (2); 1/90; Church Yth Grp; FCA; FBLA; FHA; Treas Frsh Cls; Bsktbl; High Hon Roll; NHS; Prfct Atten Awd; Sal.

LYNCH, ANISSA; El Reno Sr HS; El Reno, OK; (4); 37/163; Teachers Aide; JV Bsktbl; Cit Awd; High Hon Roll; Hon Roll; Pres Acad Fit Awd; Phys Therapy; Zoology.

LYNCH, BRIAN J; South Intermediate HS; Broken Arrow, OK; (1); Church Yth Grp; Ftbl; Wt Lftg; Drum Set; Hnrb Mntn In The Reflections Cont 2-P Art; U Of OK; Meteorology.

LYNCH, CHASITY R; Oologah HS; Oologah, OK; (3); 16/112; Natl FFA Org; Chrldng; Hon Roll; NHS; Jr Wrestling Homcmng Attendent; Tulsa JC; Med; Nrsng.

LYNCH, CHRISTOPHER; Coalgate HS; Centrahoma, OK; (3); 5/55; Church Yth Grp; Quiz Bowl; Scholastic Bowl; Speech Tm; Church Choir; Color Guard; School Play; Nwsp; High Hon Roll; NHS; Stu Mo; VFW Vc Dmcrcy Dist 1st, Area 2nd Pl; Cmptr Pgrmmng.

LYNCH, CHRISTY KAY; Yukon HS; Yukon, OK; (4); 4/400; Church Yth Grp; Quiz Bowl; Scholastic Bowl; Chorus; Church Choir; School Play; NHS; Ntl Merit Ltr; St Schlr; Litry Clb Pres; Odyssey Of Mnd; Campus Life; OK City Univ; Ed.

LYNCH, DUSTIN T; Cashion HS; Cashion, OK; (2); 1/40; Quiz Bowl; Scholastic Bowl; Capt Frsh Cls; Capt Soph Cls; Hon Roll; NHS.

LYNCH, ERIN B; Bixby Sr HS; Jenks, OK; (1); Cmnty Wkr; German Clb; Hosp Aide; Chorus; Cit Awd; Hon Roll; Jr NHS; NHS; Prfct Atten Awd; Pres Awd Ed Exc; US Achvmt Acad Sci; Natl Cmmrtv Cert Sci.

LYNCH, JEREMY L; Ripley HS; Cushing, OK; (1); Church Yth Grp; FBLA; Quiz Bowl; Scholastic Bowl; Science Clb; Trk; Hon Roll; Southwestern Adventist Coll.

LYNCH, KATHRYN T; Daniel Webster HS; Tulsa, OK; (3); #4 in class; DECA; FTA; High Hon Roll; NHS; U Of Central OK; Elem Ed.

LYNCH, MORGAN V; Dewey HS; Dewey, OK; (1); 12/105; Church Yth Grp; VP Frsh Cls; Var Chrldng; Var Trk; Hon Roll; Gymnastics; Gftd & Tlntd Pgm; OK Univ; Psych.

LYNCH, SHAUN; Pryor Jr HS; Pryor, OK; (1); Art Clb; Church Yth Grp; School Play; High Hon Roll; Pres Acad Fit Awd; Bus.

LYNCH, SHAWNA; Heritage Hall Schl; Piedmont, OK; (3); Church Yth Grp; Drama Clb; HOBY; Science Clb; Spanish Clb; Chorus; Church Choir; School Musical; School Play; Stage Crew; Natl Yth Ldrshp Frm Med; Baylor U; Bio.

LYNN, AIMEE B; Bartlesville Sr HS; Bartlesville, OK; (3); Church Yth Grp; French Clb; Chorus; Orch; School Musical; Swing Chorus; Variety Show; Compttv Ice Skatng USFSA, ISIA & TFSC; Bartlesville Suzuki Strollng Strings; St Sol & Ensmbl Conts; Musical Theater.

LYNN, ANDREA L; El Reno Sr HS; El Reno, OK; (2); FHA; JV Bsktbl; JV Sftbl; Var Vllybl; Var Wt Lftg; TX A&M; Sprts Med.

LYNN, MELODY A; Choctaw HS; Oklahoma City, OK; (3); 1/317; Church Yth Grp; Chorus; School Musical; JV Socr; Hon Roll; Jr NHS; Pres Acad Fit Awd; Congrssnl Yth Ldrshp Conf Alumni Rep; Jazz Choir; Arch.

LYNN, REBEKAH S; Shawnee Sr HS; Shawnee, OK; (2); Church Yth Grp; Spanish Clb; Church Choir; Hon Roll; Yth Ldrshp Shawnee; OK Bapt Univ; Bio/Chem/Pre-Med.

LYON, JACOB W; Lindsay HS; Lindsay, OK; (4); 5/67; Church Yth Grp; Cmnty Wkr; FCA; Office Aide; Band; Chorus; Mrchg Band; Sec Sr Cls; Ofcr Stu Cncl; Var L Bsbl; Univ Of Tulsa; Mech Engr.

LYON, SARA K; Edmond North HS; Edmond, OK; (3); Church Yth Grp; JA; Mu Alpha Theta; ROTC; Color Guard; Drill Tm; Flag Corp; Dghtrs Of Confed; UOK; Intr Desgn.

LYON, SHANE D; Anadarko HS; Anadarko, OK; (3); Boy Scts; Church Yth Grp; Drama Clb; FBLA; Thesps; Yrbk; Hon Roll; NHS; Vet Med.

LYON, SUSANNAH; Oklahoma Bible Acad; Enid, OK; (2); CAP; Cmnty Wkr; HOBY; Quiz Bowl; Speech Tm; Chorus; School Play; Pres Frsh Cls; Pres Soph Cls; Var Bsktbl; AF Acad; Pilot.

LYONS, STALEENA R; Panola HS; Red Oak, OK; (4); Art Clb; Church Yth Grp; Drama Clb; FHA; German Clb; Chorus; School Musical; Yrbk; Ofcr Frsh Cls; Ofcr Soph Cls; EOSC; Med Sec.

LYSTER, COLLEEN M; Tahlequah Sr HS; Park Hill, OK; (4); Church Yth Grp; Library Aide; Office Aide; Spanish Clb; SADD; Teachers Aide; Ofcr Bsbl; Bsktbl; Chrldng; Crs Cntry; Rogers ST Coll; Attrny.

LYTLE, AMANDA A; Putnam City North HS; Oklahoma City, OK; (1); Church Yth Grp; Sftbl; Wt Lftg; 3rd Pl Drama Rgnls; Hall Deck Comm; Red Cross Cert Lfgrd.

LYTLE, JENNIFER; Lawton Sr HS; Lawton, OK; (2); Church Yth Grp; Cmnty Wkr; FCA; HOBY; Drm Mjr(t); Orch; School Play; Socr; Hon Roll; Jr NHS; Piano; Youth Rep NYC Nazarene Youth Congress 95; Southern Nazerene U; Pre-Med.

MAAG, CARISSA; Central Mid-HS; Norman, OK; (2); Art Clb; Dance Clb; FCA; French Clb; Office Aide; Teachers Aide; Rep Frsh Cls; Ofcr Soph Cls; Ofcr Stu Cncl; Bsktbl; Spec Olympcs, Nrsng Home & Scnd Chnc Vol; Comm Svc; TX Tech; Med.

MAAS, LESLIE; Wetumka Jr Sr HS; Wetumka, OK; (2); 8/47; Church Yth Grp; FCA; Key Clb; Natl FFA Org; Band; Color Guard; Mrchg Band; Treas Frsh Cls; Var Trk; Hon Roll; Duke U Tlnt Idntfctn Pgm; Sprts Med.

MAASS, SARAH; Kingfisher HS; Kingfisher, OK; (3); 4-H; Key Clb; Natl FFA Org; Quiz Bowl; Spanish Clb; Chorus; Ofcr Stu Cncl; 4-H Awd; High Hon Roll; Hon Roll; OK St U; Msc.

MABERRY, CHRISTOPHER; Edmond North HS; Edmond, OK; (3); 50/500; Boy Scts; Church Yth Grp; FCA; French Clb; JV Ftbl; Var Trk; High Hon Roll; Law.

MABRAY, HALEY L; Kiowa Jr-Sr HS; Stuart, OK; (2); Church Yth Grp; FCA; 4-H; GAA; Natl FFA Org; Church Choir; Pres Frsh Cls; VP Stu Cncl; Var Bsktbl; Var Sftbl; SNU; HS Bsktbl Coach.

MABRY, JOHN ROBERT; Muskogee HS; Muskogee, OK; (4); 27/300; Science Clb; Band; Jazz Band; Mrchg Band; Orch; Pep Band; School Musical; High Hon Roll; Hon Roll; Jr NHS; Percussion Section Ldr/Capt; Roughers Against Illegal Drugs; Pres Ed Awds Outstndng Acad Achvmnt; Northeastern ST Univ.

MABRY, LAURA M; Ponca City Sr HS; Ponca City, OK; (3); 100/347; Church Yth Grp; Chorus; Church Choir; School Musical; Phtg Yrbk; Intrml Stat Bsbl; Var L Socr; JV Var Vllybl; High Hon Roll; Hon Roll; Chrch Sftbl; Classic League Soccer; NOC; Sci; Med Field.

MAC DONALD, JEFF D; Owasso Sr HS; Owasso, OK; (2); Church Yth Grp; Hon Roll; Prfct Atten Awd; Sccr; Bsktbl; Cmptrs; Math Awd; U Of NE; Cmptr Sci.

MAC DONALD, MICHAEL I; Central Schl; Sallisaw, OK; (3); Art Clb; Boy Scts; Computer Clb; Quiz Bowl; Scholastic Bowl; Spanish Clb; Hon Roll; Prfct Atten Awd; MIT; Comp Prgmr.

MACE, LACI; Mt View-Gotebo HS; Mountain View, OK; (2); 4/29; Pres FHA; HOBY; Pep Clb; Variety Show; Pres Frsh Cls; Rep Stu Cncl; Capt Chrldng; Hon Roll; NHS; OU; Cardiology.

MACE, LEE A; B T Washington HS; Tulsa, OK; (4); 56/263; Debate Tm; Speech Tm; Teachers Aide; Chorus; School Musical; School Play; Variety Show; NHS; Biomedcl Engr.

MACEDO, AISHA A; Jenks HS; Tulsa, OK; (3); 8/517; Debate Tm; French Clb; Key Clb; Mu Alpha Theta; NFL; Rep Science Clb; Spanish Clb; Gov Hon Prg Awd; NHS; Piano; Medicine.

MAC GREGOR, TARA R; Noble HS; Noble, OK; (2); 21/169; Scholastic Bowl; Yrbk; Hon Roll; NHS; Duke Talent Id Prgm; U Of OK; Jrnlsm/Novelist.

MACHALIS, KYLE A; Bartlesville Mid HS; Bartlesville, OK; (2); Library Aide; Scholastic Bowl; Orch; School Play; Stage Crew; Cmptr Engr.

MAC INNIS, LEE-JAY; Bridge Creek HS; Blanchard, OK; (1); Intrml Bsbl; Intrml Ftbl; Intrml Wt Lftg; Hon Roll.

MACIULA, ANDREA M; Stillwater Sr HS; Stillwater, OK; (3); Church Yth Grp; Pep Clb; Teachers Aide; Acpl Chr; Chorus; Church Choir; School Musical; School Play; Hon Roll; Pres Schlr; Super Rating At St Vocal Cont; ACDA Alt 96; OK ST.

MACK II, ANTHONY W; Duncan HS; Duncan, OK; (3); Church Yth Grp; Letterman Clb; Varsity Clb; Band; Mrchg Band; Pep Band; Ftbl; Var Trk; Var Wt Lftg; Hon Roll; Excl Prgm Hon Stdnts; U Of OK; Crim Just.

MACK, TERESA; Macarthur Sr HS; Lawton, OK; (3); Church Yth Grp; FCA; Acpl Chr; Hon Roll; Prfct Atten Awd; OK ST Univ; Bus Admin.

MAC KAY, HEATHER; Perry Sr HS; Perry, OK; (2); Church Yth Grp; Ed Nwsp; Sftbl; Cit Awd; Hon Roll; Jr NHS; Church Outreach Intl; Art Inst Of Dallas; Fn Arts.

MAC KAY, MARLEY; Boswell Sr HS; Soper, OK; (3); Cmnty Wkr; 4-H; Latin Clb; Chorus; Socr; DAR Awd; 4-H Awd; NHS; Pres Acad Fit Awd; Baylor Univ; Ortho.

MACKAY, MARLEY A; Oklahoma Sch Of Science & Math; Norman, OK; (3); Cmnty Wkr; 4-H; Latin Clb; Chorus; Socr; DAR Awd; 4-H Awd; NHS; Pres Acad Fit Awd; Baylor; Orthdntst.

MACKEY, ANDRENA; Ft Cobb-Broxton HS; Fort Cobb, OK; (4); #1 in class; Church Yth Grp; Cmnty Wkr; FHA; Spanish Clb; Speech Tm; Chorus; Church Choir; Nwsp; Yrbk; Sec Jr Cls; Chrch Camp Cnslr; Lions Clb Awd; Caddo Cnty Farm Bur Awd; VFW Voice Of Dmcrcy Awd; Cmnty Masons Awd; OK Bapt Univ; Phy Asst.

MACKEY, ASHLEY; Union Sr HS; Coweta, OK; (1); Teachers Aide; Capt Chrldng; Hon Roll; OK U; Psych.

MACKEY, CHRISTOPHER; Mc Alester HS; Mcalester, OK; (4); 14/209; Am Leg Boys St; Church Yth Grp; Cmnty Wkr; Office Aide; Quiz Bowl; Band; Jazz Band; Mrchg Band; School Musical; High Hon Roll; All St Band; St Fair OK Band; Bapt All St Orch; U Cntrl OK; Sci.

MACKEY, GREG; Okemah HS; Okemah, OK; (1); 1/77; Chess Clb; FHA; Science Clb; High Hon Roll; NHS; OK ST U; Comp Sci.

MACKEY, GREG E; Oklahoma Sch Of Science & Math; Stroud, OK; (4); Church Yth Grp; Cmnty Wkr; Math Tm; Quiz Bowl; Band; Chorus; Church Choir; School Musical; Rptr Stu Cncl; Ntl Merit SF; Baylor; Music Composition.

MACKEY, KARLA; Claremore Sr HS; Claremore, OK; (3); 26/237; Chorus; Church Choir; School Musical; High Hon Roll; Hon Roll; NHS; Prfct Atten Awd; Dist Choir 3 Yrs; Dist Solo Cont I Ratng; Rogers ST; Pediatrcs.

MACKEY, KIMBERLY; Madill HS; Madill, OK; (2); Church Yth Grp; FBLA; SADD; Band; Mrchg Band; Pep Band; Hon Roll; NHS; Solo Cont Super; Jrnlsm.

MACKEY, SHERRY L; Kiowa Jr-Sr HS; Wardville, OK; (3); 5/32; Church Yth Grp; FHA; Library Aide; Yrbk; Hon Roll; TSA Treas; SOSU; Med Lab Tech.

MACON, RANDY; Kingston HS; Kingston, OK; (1); FCA; Spanish Clb; Chorus; Rep Frsh Cls; Rep Stu Cncl; Hon Roll; Southeastern OK ST U; Psych.

MAC RAE, TANYA; Lawton Sr HS; Lawton, OK; (2); HOBY; Library Aide; Office Aide; ROTC; Phtg Rptr Yrbk; High Hon Roll; Hon Roll; Jr NHS; EMT.

MAC ROBERT, MELISSA A; Byng Sr HS; Ada, OK; (2); Treas FHA; Natl FFA Org; Scholastic Bowl; Spanish Clb; SADD; Hlpng Envrnmnt; Vlybl; Rdng; Wrtng Poetry; ECU; Psychlgst/Spec Ed Tchr.

MACRORY, TASHA J; Edmond Memorial HS; Edmond, OK; (2); 126/408; Cmnty Wkr; Spanish Clb; Band; Color Guard; Jazz Band; Mrchg Band; Orch; Pep Band; School Musical; NHS; Intl Order Of Rainbow For Girls.

MADBULL, MISTY M; Antlers Sr HS; Antlers, OK; (2); Flag Corp; Church Yth Grp; Band; Color Guard; Mrchg Band; JV Var Sftbl; JV Var Tennis; RN.

MADDEN, BRANDI; Douglass HS; Oklahoma City, OK; (1); Band; Mrchg Band; Pep Band; Hon Roll; OK ST Univ.

MADDEN, JASON; Wayne Public Schl; Lindsay, OK; (4); 3/30; Church Yth Grp; FHA; Natl FFA Org; Quiz Bowl; Spanish Clb; Bsktbl; High Hon Roll; Hon Roll; NHS; Prfct Atten Awd; OK Hnr Soc; SOS; Mst Courteous; ECU; Sec Ed.

MADDEN, JENNIFER; Frederick HS; Frederick, OK; (1); 1/96; Chrmn Church Yth Grp; Chorus; Mrchg Band; Pep Band; School Musical; High Hon Roll; Acad Tm; Ped.

MADDEN, MANDY J; Washington HS; Washington, OK; (1); Pep Clb; Bsktbl; Cit Awd; Hon Roll.

MADDEN, NATALIE R; Sapulpa Sr HS; Sapulpa, OK; (2); Church Yth Grp; JV Var Bsktbl; JV Crs Cntry; Var Sftbl; JV Trk; Hon Roll; Northeastern ST Univ; Elem Ed.

MADDOX, RACHELLE; Cimarron Public Schl; Lahoma, OK; (3); Church Yth Grp; FBLA; Band; Church Choir; Var Chrldng; Cit Awd; Hon Roll; NHS; Pres Acad Fit Awd; Computer Clb; Vet Med; Piano; Vet Med.

MADDUX, AMANDA G; Del City HS; Del City, OK; (2); #120 in class; Drama Clb; FCA; Scholastic Bowl; Spanish Clb; Speech Tm; SADD; Teachers Aide; School Musical; School Play; Stage Crew; OK Univ; RN/MD.

MADDUX, CAROLYN M; Tipton Jr Sr HS; Tipton, OK; (2); 5/31; FHA; Band; Church Choir; Mrchg Band; Nwsp; Yrbk; Stat Bsktbl; Hon Roll; Jr NHS; NHS; Comp Awd; Western OK ST Coll; Sec; Comp.

MADDUX, NATALIE J; Okarche HS; Okarche, OK; (3); Church Yth Grp; FHA; JV Bsktbl; Mock Trial; OK St Univ; Optom.

MADDUX, SARAH H; Emerson Jr HS; Orange, TX; (1); Speech Tm; Band; Chorus; Mrchg Band; School Musical; School Play; Hon Roll; 3rd Pl Regl One Act Play Comp; Spr Rtngs Dist/Solo Vocal/Choir/Tri ST Music Fstvl Vocal Solo.

MADENWALD, NATHAN M; Walters HS; Walters, OK; (2); HOBY; Var JV Bsktbl; Var Trk; High Hon Roll; NHS.

MADEWELL, AMY; Midwest City HS; Midwest City, OK; (4); 65/419; Church Yth Grp; Cmnty Wkr; FHA; Pep Clb; Spanish Clb; SADD; Varsity Clb; Ed Yrbk; Rep Stu Cncl; Co-Capt Pom Pon; Spirit Cncl Exec Brd; Press Clb Secy; OU; Dietician.

MADEWELL, MINDY; Warner HS; Warner, OK; (1); Church Yth Grp; FCA; Church Choir; Sec Treas Frsh Cls; Rptr Stu Cncl; Bsktbl; Crs Cntry; Powder Puff Ftbl; Trk; Cit Awd; St Hnr Soc; Teens For Christ; Tchr; Bsktbl Coach.

MADISON, ADAM W; East Central HS; Tulsa, OK; (2); Church Yth Grp; Intnl Clb; JA; Spanish Clb; Rptr Nwsp; Chrmn Stu Cncl; Var Crs Cntry; Var Swmmng; Hon Roll; NHS; Elite Prgm 9-10th Grd; DFY 9-10th Grd; Ecology Club 9-10th Grd; Med Doctor.

MADISON, KENDRA; Hilldale HS; Muskogee, OK; (2); #5 in class; Church Yth Grp; Computer Clb; Spanish Clb; Powder Puff Ftbl; High Hon Roll; OK ST U; Pedtrcn.

MADISON, PRISCILLA E; B T Washington HS; Tulsa, OK; (3); Church Yth Grp; Office Aide; Red Cross Aide; Var Chrldng; Var Tennis; Hon Roll; Bio.

MADSEN, DALE; Chisholm Sr HS; Enid, OK; (4); Boy Scts; Church Yth Grp; Cmnty Wkr; Pep Clb; Red Cross Aide; SADD; Pres VICA; Chorus; Hon Roll; Schlsp Univ Tech Inst; Mdl Trng John Casablancas Tulsa; UTI; OSU.

MAGAR, SUNDI; Lone Wolf Schl; Lone Wolf, OK; (4); 1/22; FHA; Stage Crew; Ed Yrbk; VP Frsh Cls; VP Soph Cls; Pres Jr Cls; Pres Sr Cls; Hon Roll; NHS; Val; Cmnty Theatre; OK ST U.

MAGAR, TAMARA A; Stonewall Jr-Sr HS; Stonewall, OK; (2); Church Yth Grp; German Clb; Scholastic Bowl; Yrbk; Pres Frsh Cls; Gov Hon Prg Awd; NHS; Val; Church Choir; NCTE; OK Hon Soc; ECU Ada; Elem Schl Tchr.

MAGBY, DUSTY E; Stringtown HS; Stringtown, OK; (2); Church Yth Grp; 4-H; GAA; Natl FFA Org; Quiz Bowl; Varsity Clb; Acpl Chr; Pres Frsh Cls; Var Bsbl; Var Bsktbl; Sntnl FFA; Sec 4-H; OSU; Ag Tchr.

MAGDEBURG, J R; Cushing HS; Cushing, OK; (1); Church Yth Grp; Cmnty Wkr; FCA; Spanish Clb; Bsktbl; Golf; High Hon Roll; 95 MRCA All Around Cowboy, Rbbn Roping Chmpn; Law.

MAGEE, ROBYN N; Catoosa HS; Catoosa, OK; (4); 2/145; VP Drama Clb; FCA; Pep Clb; Rptr Spanish Clb; School Play; Var L Bsktbl; Var L Crs Cntry; Score Keeper; Var L Trk; High Hon Roll; NSU; Bus Admin.

MAGGARD, CHRISTOPHER; Thomas Jr Sr HS; Thomas, OK; (4); 5/33; Church Yth Grp; Cmnty Wkr; FBLA; Natl FFA Org; Pres Stu Cncl; Bsktbl; Ftbl; Wt Lftg; High Hon Roll; Hon Roll; Hesston Coll.

MAGNIN, KELLY; Central Mid-HS; Norman, OK; (1); JV Socr; Hon Roll; NHS.

MAGNON, PATRICK; Vinita HS; Vinita, OK; (3); Am Leg Boys St; Church Yth Grp; FCA; FHA; Math Clb; Science Clb; Spanish Clb; Var Bsktbl; Ftbl; Wt Lftg; Jr Rotarian; Sci Fair Awd; PSO Awd; NEO A&M; Med.

MAGNUS, SHANE E; Ponca City Sr HS; Ponca City, OK; (3); Boy Scts; Church Yth Grp; FCA; Natl FFA Org; SADD; VP Soph Cls; Rep Jr Cls; JV Mgr(s); JV Wt Lftg; JV Wrstlng; Boy Sct Natl Life Saving Awd; Eagle Sct.

MAGNUSEN, RITA J; B T Washington HS; Tulsa, OK; (2); Cmnty Wkr; Latin Clb; Letterman Clb; Red Cross Aide; Spanish Clb; High Hon Roll; Jr NHS; Mock Trial Tm; Young Democrats; Intl Rel.

MAGSTADT, BRYAN; Ponca City Sr HS; Ponca City, OK; (4); #2 in class; Am Leg Boys St; Treas Boy Scts; Church Yth Grp; FCA; Spanish Clb; SADD; Chorus; Variety Show; Nwsp; High Hon Roll; OK U; Phys Thrpy.

MAGUFFEE, BRENDON M; Union Intermediate HS; Broken Arrow, OK; (1); FCA; Key Clb; Spanish Clb; Golf; Swmmng; NHS; Listening To Music/Live Concerts; Internet; Surfing The Net; Stanford; Golf Prof/Cmptr Engr.

MAGUREGUI, JOHN; Altus Sr HS; Altus, OK; (3); 46/272; HOBY; Treas JV Bsbl; Bsktbl; High Hon Roll; Hon Roll; Jr NHS; U Of TX; Psych.

MAHAFFEY, MARI-ETTA; Greater Tulsa Christian Acad; Tulsa, OK; (4); 1/7; Church Yth Grp; HOBY; Pres Key Clb; Teachers Aide; VP Frsh Cls; Sec Jr Cls; Treas Sr Cls; Var Capt Bsktbl; Var Trk; Var Capt Vllybl.

MAHAR, BRIAN G; Bishop Kelley HS; Tulsa, OK; (1); Ofcr Bsbl; Ftbl; B Hon Rl Frosh Yr.

MAHIEU, LAURA; Oklahoma Bible Acad; Enid, OK; (2); Church Yth Grp; Cmnty Wkr; FCA; Spanish Clb; Band; Chorus; Pep Band; Bsktbl; Vllybl; High Hon Roll; OK ST U; Engrng.

MAHL, MARCY; Canute HS; Canute, OK; (3); 1/22; Church Yth Grp; 4-H; FHA; GAA; Ofcr Jr Cls; Ofcr Stu Cncl; Bsktbl; Sftbl; Cit Awd; 4-H Awd.

MAHON, DARBI L; Choctaw HS; Choctaw, OK; (3); Pres Frsh Cls; Jr NHS; Val; OU; Acctng.

MAI, NHU; Westmoore HS; Oklahoma City, OK; (3); 16/615; Cmnty Wkr; French Clb; FBLA; Key Clb; Jr NHS; NHS; Pres Acad Fit Awd; Stockbroker.

MAI, RICKY D; North Intermediate HS; Tulsa, OK; (1); French Clb; Ofcr Bsbl; Hon Roll; Nrs.

MAI, TAMMY H; Classen Schl; Oklahoma City, OK; (2); French Clb; Hosp Aide; Latin Clb; Mu Alpha Theta; Orch; Rptr Yrbk; Var Socr; Hon Roll; NHS.

MAIKORI, NPONANO L; Western Heights Sr HS; Oklahoma City, OK; (3); Church Yth Grp; JA; Pres Jr Cls; Rep Stu Cncl; Var L Bsktbl; Ftbl; Var Trk; Cit Awd; Hon Roll; NHS; Med.

MAINE, KIMBERLY S; El Reno Sr HS; El Reno, OK; (2); Church Yth Grp; Spanish Clb; Band; Color Guard; Mrchg Band; High Hon Roll; Prfct Atten Awd; El Reno Renaissance Acad Excel; Colorguard Capt; Pediatrician.

MAINERS, ERIN; Mc Loud HS; Mc Loud, OK; (3); FBLA; Library Aide; Church Choir; Jazz Band; Mrchg Band; Orch; Ofcr Stu Cncl; Hon Roll; Sec NHS; OK All-St Band; Psych.

MAJOR, CHRIS; Seminole Jr Sr HS; Seminole, OK; (4); 3/90; Am Leg Boys St; Church Yth Grp; Debate Tm; FCA; Math Clb; NFL; Science Clb; Spanish Clb; Nwsp; Ofcr Frsh Cls; Mock Trial; Premed.

MAJORS, NANCY L; Hinton HS; Hinton, OK; (2); Treas FCA; SADD; L Var Bsktbl; L Var Crs Cntry; L Var Trk; High Hon Roll; NHS; Val; Church Yth Grp; Band; Academic Team; GATE Prgm; OK Hnr Roll; Southwestern OK ST U; Law.

MAKASEAH, TERESA; Shawnee Sr HS; Shawnee, OK; (3); 43/282; Crs Cntry; Trk; Hon Roll; Natl Indian Hnr Soc; Cnty Chptr Hnrs Pgm; Native Amer Stu Assn.

MAKDISI, MICHAEL; Tulsa Memorial HS; Tulsa, OK; (4); 5/250; Am Leg Boys St; JCL; Key Clb; Mrchg Band; School Musical; Bsktbl; Capt L Swmmng; Cit Awd; High Hon Roll; NHS; Rnsslr Awd Math/Sci; Hnr Band All Cty; Bcyclng.

MAKER, VALERIE A; Hominy HS; Cleveland, OK; (3); French Clb; GAA; Hosp Aide; Teachers Aide; Bsktbl; Score Keeper; Sftbl; Trk; Vllybl; Kiwanis Awd; Most Veratile Sftbl Player; Tulsa JC.

MAKESCRY, ASHLEY R; Bethany HS; Bethany, OK; (3); Church Yth Grp; FCA; Key Clb; VP Jr Cls; Var L Bsktbl; Var L Trk; Wt Lftg; High Hon Roll; Hon Roll; NHS; Natl Ldrshhp Congress; Big Five.

MAKRES, DENA M; Jay HS; Disney, OK; (1); FHA; Cmptr Sci.

MALASKE, JENNY; Harrah HS; Harrah, OK; (4); 19/107; Natl FFA Org; JV Sftbl; Hon Roll; NHS; ST FFA Dgr Rcptn; Sndy Schl Tchr; Natl Jr Hort Assn Illtrtd Talk Natl Wnr; East Cntrl U; Scndry Ed/Eng.

MALCHAR, KAYLA; Shawnee Sr HS; Shawnee, OK; (4); 3/262; Church Yth Grp; Math Clb; Math Tm; Scholastic Bowl; Rep Sr Cls; Tennis; High Hon Roll; NHS; Ntl Merit Schol; U Of OK; Phys Thrpy.

MALCHER, RALPH; Yukon Middle HS; El Reno, OK; (2); Spanish Clb; OK ST Univ; Pre-Med.

MALCOLM, REBECCA L; Jenks HS; Tulsa, OK; (3); 5/600; Church Yth Grp; FCA; French Clb; Science Clb; Sec Stu Cncl; Var L Crs Cntry; Var L Trk; Hon Roll; NHS; Pres Acad Fit Awd; Hstry.

MALDONADO, ESMERELDA; Hobart HS; Hobart, OK; (1); Band; Jazz Band; Mrchg Band; Pep Band.

MALE, HEATHER J; Mt St Marys HS; Yukon, OK; (3); 1/68; Nwsp; Yrbk; Sec Jr Cls; Sec Sr Cls; JV Tennis; NHS; Pianist; Basic Ldrshp Wrkshp; Adv Ldrshp Wrkshp; St Marys Coll; Fmly Physcn.

MALES, SHAWNDA S; Choctaw HS; Choctaw, OK; (3); Church Yth Grp; GAA; Bsktbl; Trk; High Hon Roll; Hon Roll; Jr NHS; Pres Acad Fit Awd; Bus.

MALGET, MATT; Perry Sr HS; Perry, OK; (3); JV Bsbl; Var Crs Cntry; Var L Wrstlng; Hon Roll; Jr NHS; Chrch Yth Grp; Multi Yr Lstng; OK ST U; Vet.

MALIWAT, JACQUELINE DE OCAMPO; Bishop Mcguinness HS; Edmond, OK; (4); 4/158; Church Yth Grp; Cmnty Wkr; Sec Science Clb; Spanish Clb; Ed Yrbk; High Hon Roll; NHS; Pres Acad Fit Awd; Grtr OK Cty Almn Pnhllnc Conf; Piano; AP Schlr; Washington U; Biochem.

MALLAVARAPU, SANGEETHA E; Edmond Santa Fe HS; Edmond, OK; (3); 1/300; Science Clb; Spanish Clb; Band; Mrchg Band; Orch; High Hon Roll; Hon Roll; NHS; Pres Schlr; St Schlr; OK Yth Orchestra; Medicine.

MALLEY, AMBER; Mustang HS; Yukon, OK; (2); 1/406; Church Yth Grp; FCA; Quiz Bowl; Scholastic Bowl; Stat Bsktbl; Mgr(s); High Hon Roll; NHS; Boy Scouts Med Explr Pgm Exec Cncl; Acad Tm; Acad Ltrmn; Pediatrics.

MALLOY, ERIN R; Central Schl; Duncan, OK; (3); Yrbk; FCA; Library Aide; Nwsp; Yrbk; Hon Roll; Acad Tm; Cameron Univ; Pharm.

MALLOY, JENNIFER L; Walters HS; Walters, OK; (3); 5/60; FCA; FHA; Letterman Clb; SADD; Drill Tm; Yrbk; Bsktbl; Hon Roll; NHS; Phys Thrpy.

MALLOY, JOSH; Yukon Middle HS; Yukon, OK; (2); Church Yth Grp; Rptr Nwsp; JV CAP; Var Bsktbl; High Hon Roll; Hon Roll; NHS; 3d Dont Do Drugs; Rice; Sprts Med.

MALLOY, KOREY M; Muskogee HS; Muskogee, OK; (1); Boy Scts; Church Yth Grp; German Clb; JV Socr; Hon Roll; NHS.

MALONE, ANGEL L; Moore HS; Moore, OK; (3); Church Yth Grp; VICA; Intrml Bsktbl; Intrml Crs Cntry; JV Sftbl; Intrml Trk; Cit Awd; Prfct Atten Awd; YAP Grphc Arts; Nom/Acptd Trp CA Clb Jobs For Future; OKCCC; Prntng Co.

MALONE, CODY; Noble HS; Noble, OK; (4); Church Yth Grp; Model UN; Pres Acad Fit Awd; Ftbl; Whos Who HS Ath; NE St Univ.

MALONE JR, DANIEL; Piedmont HS; Yukon, OK; (4); Am Leg Boys St; Scholastic Bowl; Ftbl; Trk; High Hon Roll; Hon Roll; NHS; Army.

MALONE, JASON; Macomb Schl; Macomb, OK; (4); 3/20; Am Leg Boys St; Pres FHA; HOBY; Pres Stu Cncl; Bsktbl; Cit Awd; High Hon Roll; Hon Roll; NHS; Stu Of Yr.

MALONE, JASON P; Blanchard Jr Sr HS; Blanchard, OK; (4); Church Yth Grp; Cmnty Wkr; FCA; Scholastic Bowl; Bsktbl; Trk; Wt Lftg; Hon Roll; 4-H; Crs Cntry; Trck Otstndng Rnnr Awd 93-94; Natl Fed Of Prnts For Drug-Free Yth Lfrs Prgm Stdnt Ldr; USAO; Med.

MALONE, KASEY; Midwest City HS; Midwest City, OK; (4); FCA; French Clb; FHA; SADD; Rep Frsh Cls; Sec Soph Cls; Rep Jr Cls; Rep Sr Cls; Rep Stu Cncl; Var Capt Chrldng; Girl Mon AAUW; Concurrently Enrolld Rose St Coll; OK U; Arspc Engr.

MALONE, MANDY S; Morrison Public Schl; Stillwater, OK; (1); 3/35; Band; Jazz Band; Mrchg Band; Pep Band; VP Frsh Cls; Sftbl; Prfct Atten Awd; Outstndg Stdnt In Foundatns For Living Home Ec; Amer Musical Fdn Hnrs Awd; OK HS Hon Soc; OK ST Univ; Medical.

MALONE, VICKIE; Bennington Schl; Bennington, OK; (4); 2/25; Office Aide; Ed Yrbk; VP Frsh Cls; VP Soph Cls; Pres Jr Cls; VP Sr Cls; Rep Stu Cncl; Hon Roll; VP NHS; Sal; SE OK ST U; Nrsng.

MALONE, WILLIAM; Arapaho Schl; Arapaho, OK; (4); 4/15; Church Yth Grp; 4-H; HOBY; VP Frsh Cls; Pres Soph Cls; Pres Jr Cls; Pres Sr Cls; Ofcr Stu Cncl; 4-H Awd; St 4-H Dog Care & Trng Prjct Wnnr; St Hwy Patrol Cadet Lawmn Acad; HS Acad Tm.

MALONEY, JENNIFER; Norman Sr HS; Norman, OK; (3); 119/799; Church Yth Grp; Cmnty Wkr; Dance Clb; FCA; FBLA; Pep Clb; Spanish Clb; SADD; Varsity Clb; Drama Clb; Mst Vlbl Player FCA; Chsn Prtcpt Tomorrows Ldrs; Teen Vol Pub Rel/Pres; Berry Coll; PA.

MALONEY, THOMAS P; Cushing HS; Cushing, OK; (2); Art Clb; Church Yth Grp; Cmnty Wkr; FCA; Spanish Clb; SADD; Band; Jazz Band; Wt Lftg; High Hon Roll.

MALOY, ALICIA; Norman Sr HS; Norman, OK; (3); 1/799; Cmnty Wkr; Letterman Clb; Varsity Clb; Orch; Capt Computer Clb; High Hon Roll; Hon Roll; NHS; Pres Acad Fit Awd; Whos Who Sports; Stu Of Yr Adv Algebra & Chem; All-Conf Swimming & Diving Team.

MALOY, CHRIS; Arapaho Schl; Arapaho, OK; (3); 2/25; Am Leg Boys St; Natl FFA Org; Quiz Bowl; Pres Stu Cncl; Hon Roll; Ntl Merit Ltr; Pres Acad Fit Awd.

MALOY, CHRISTOPHER W; Mustang HS; Yukon, OK; (1); Church Yth Grp; FCA; Spanish Clb; Chorus; JV Bsbl; JV Bsktbl; Hon Roll; NHS; OK St Univ; Med.

MALOY, MICHAEL D; Arapaho Schl; Arapaho, OK; (2); Letterman Clb; Natl FFA Org; Quiz Bowl; JV Var Bsktbl; Var Crs Cntry; Hon Roll; Pres Acad Fit Awd; OK ST Univ; Firefighter.

MALTBIE, WILLIAM A; Boise City HS; Boise City, OK; (2).

MALWICK, JOSHUA B; Putnam City HS; Oklahoma City, OK; (2); JV Bsktbl; JV Golf; OK ST Univ; Commercial Pilot.

MANCHEV, CHRIS R; Moore HS; Oklahoma City, OK; (2); 30/565; Scholastic Bowl; Science Clb; Rep Stu Cncl; Hon Roll; Jr NHS; NHS; Pres Acad Fit Awd; Med Mlprctc Lwyr.

MANCINELLI, KEITH B; Union Intermediate HS; Broken Arrow, OK; (1); Boy Scts; Church Yth Grp; Hon Roll; Bst Shw Awd Un Yth Arts 96; Amer Hrt Assn Vol.

MANDELBAUM, CARYN B; Mc Alester HS; Mcalester, OK; (3); 9/230; Church Yth Grp; Spanish Clb; Band; Mrchg Band; Sec Treas Soph Cls; VP Jr Cls; Hist Stu Cncl; Chrldng; Golf; Mgr(s); Girls ST Alumni; U Of OK.

MANDERS, ABBEY; Miami Sr HS; Miami, OK; (1); 1/200; Church Yth Grp; Band; Mrchg Band; Pep Band; Rep Frsh Cls; Rep Stu Cncl; Bsktbl; Var Crs Cntry; Var Trk; High Hon Roll; Dance; Scuba Dvng; Dwnhll Skiing.

MANDERS, DUSTIN; Miami Sr HS; Miami, OK; (4); 1/121; Am Leg Boys St; Church Yth Grp; Quiz Bowl; Teachers Aide; Var L Golf; High Hon Roll; NHS; Val; OSU; Med.

MANER, MATT; Pond Creek-Hunter Schl; Pond Creek, OK; (3); 4/25; Church Yth Grp; FCA; Sec Natl FFA Org; Band; Mrchg Band; School Play; VP Stu Cncl; Var Boy Scts; Var Bsktbl; Hon Roll.

MANERING, MICHELLE; Pawhuska HS; Pawhuska, OK; (3); 1/92; Cmnty Wkr; FBLA; Key Clb; Yrbk; High Hon Roll; Hon Roll; NHS; Ntl Merit Ltr; Med.

MANESS, AMBER N; Pauls Valley HS; Pauls Valley, OK; (4); 23/81; FHA; Natl FFA Org; Teachers Aide; Cit Awd; High Hon Roll; East Cntrl Univ; RN.

MANESS, ASHLEY D; Felt Public Schl; Boise City, OK; (2); Drama Clb; Quiz Bowl; School Play; Nwsp; Yrbk; Pres Frsh Cls; Pres Soph Cls; Ofcr Stu Cncl; Bsktbl; Trk; Physical Therapy.

MANGASI, CATHERINE; Wilburton Jr HS; Wilburton, OK; (2); 1/79; FBLA; HOBY; Speech Tm; Rptr Yrbk; Pres Stu Cncl; Cit Awd; High Hon Roll; NHS; Val; Acad Tm; The U Of OK; Biomed Engrng.

MANGO, NICHOLE L; Westmoore HS; Oklahoma City, OK; (3); 150/610; Pres Church Yth Grp; French Clb; GAA; Key Clb; Speech Tm; Church Choir; Rep Jr Cls; Bsktbl; Vllybl; Yth Crisis Hotlne Cnslr; Spch Awd; Engl Awd; UCI; Pdtrcn.

MANGO, NIKKI; Westmoore HS; Oklahoma City, OK; (3); 133/636; Church Yth Grp; Drama Clb; French Clb; GAA; Key Clb; Service Clb; Speech Tm; Thesps; School Play; Ofcr Stu Cncl; Bsktbl Var Awd; Optimist Clb Speech 2nd Pl Awd; Pres Of Key Club; Med.

MANGRUM, LESLIE F; Durant HS; Durant, OK; (2); Church Yth Grp; Chorus; Church Choir; Capt Drill Tm; Mrchg Band; Swing Chorus; Variety Show; High Hon Roll; Hon Roll; ST Hon Soc; Chorus Dir.

MANGUM, CHRISTOPHER; Midwest City HS; Midwest City, OK; (2); 48/501; Band; Jazz Band; Mrchg Band; Pep Band; School Musical; Ed Yrbk; Var Bsktbl; Tennis; Hon Roll; Jr NHS; E Paul Enix Otstndng Music Stu Awd; OK ST U.

MANION, KERWIN L; Kiowa Jr-Sr HS; Kiowa, OK; (2); 4-H; FHA; Letterman Clb; Natl FFA Org; Pres Frsh Cls; Var Bsktbl; Hon Roll; St Flrcltr Jdgng Tm.

MANION, SOMMER; Madill HS; Madill, OK; (1); 7/75; Church Yth Grp; Drama Clb; FCA; FBLA; Math Clb; Science Clb; Spanish Clb; Speech Tm; SADD; Teachers Aide; Southwestern OK ST; Eng Ed.

MANLEY, BRANDON; Wilburton Jr HS; Wilburton, OK; (1); 1/80; Church Yth Grp; FBLA; Scholastic Bowl; Bsktbl; Cit Awd; High Hon Roll; NHS; Ntl Merit Ltr.

MANLEY, DE LISA L; Duncan HS; Waterford, CA; (2); Church Yth Grp; Key Clb; SADD; Hon Roll; NHS; Crimestoppers Clb; Yth Alive; Hlth Career Clb; Gen Bus Hnr; Medicine.

MANN, AMBER R; Wilson HS; Wilson, OK; (3); 1/40; Spanish Clb; Yrbk; Pres Frsh Cls; Ofcr Soph Cls; Pres Jr Cls; JV Var Bsktbl; JV Var Chrldng; JV Var Sftbl; JV Var High Hon Roll; JV Var Hon Roll; UCO.

MANN, BENJAMIN E; Union Intermediate HS; Tulsa, OK; (2); Church Yth Grp; FCA; Spanish Clb; Orch; School Musical; NHS; Young Republcns.

MANN, JENNIFER; Oklahoma Sch Of Science & Math; Pauls Valley, OK; (4); 4-H; HOBY; Key Clb; Scholastic Bowl; Rep Stu Cncl; Cit Awd; 4-H Awd; High Hon Roll; Ntl Merit Ltr; FHA; JASON Prjct Stu Argonaut; Boston U; Bio.

MANN, JOHN M; Stratford Schl; Stratford, OK; (2); FCA; Spanish Clb; Ofcr Stu Cncl; Var Bsbl; Var Bsktbl; Hon Roll; Prfct Atten Awd; OU; Optometrist.

MANN, JUSTIN; Depew HS; Depew, OK; (2); Natl FFA Org; Pres Frsh Cls; Pres Soph Cls; JV L Bsbl; Var L Bsktbl; High Hon Roll; Prfct Atten Awd; OK ST.

MANN, MATT H; Buffalo Jr Sr HS; Buffalo, OK; (1); Church Yth Grp; Natl FFA Org; Quiz Bowl; Chorus; Treas Frsh Cls; JV Bsbl; JV Bsktbl; Var Ftbl; JV Trk; High Hon Roll; OK Univ.

MANN, MATTHEW H; Checotah HS; Checotah, OK; (2); Church Yth Grp; VP Natl FFA Org; Var Bsbl.

MANN, SHAWNA; Ardmore HS; Ardmore, OK; (4); 8/168; FCA; Latin Clb; Sec Mu Alpha Theta; Sec Sr Cls; Rep Stu Cncl; Co-Capt Chrldng; Capt Sftbl; NHS; Cmnty Wkr; Drama Clb; Jr Cls Hmcmng Prncss; Hmcmng Queen Cand; Univ Of OK; Phys Asst.

MANNING, ALI M; Union Sr HS; Tulsa, OK; (3); 122/741; Church Yth Grp; FBLA; FHA; Teachers Aide; Jr NHS; NHS.

MANNING, AMANDA; Elk City Jr HS; Elk City, OK; (3); Church Yth Grp; German Clb; Science Clb; Band; Chorus; VP Frsh Cls; Chrldng; Golf; Cit Awd; Hon Roll; OK Univ; Mass Comm.

MANNING, BOBBY J; Spiro HS; Spiro, OK; (2); Church Yth Grp; FBLA; Band; Church Choir; Mrchg Band; Pep Band; Upward Bound; Psycht.

MANNING, CALEB T; El Reno Sr HS; El Reno, OK; (2); Church Yth Grp; 4-H; Rptr Natl FFA Org; JV Ftbl; Wt Lftg; Hon Roll; OK ST Univ; Vet.

MANNING, JOHN A; Bartlesville Mid HS; Bartlesville, OK; (2); Church Yth Grp; FCA; FBLA; Spanish Clb; Ofcr Stu Cncl; JV Bsbl; Bsktbl; Var Ftbl; Hon Roll; NHS.

MANNING, KEVIN M; Edmond North HS; Edmond, OK; (2); 69/420; Church Yth Grp; Var Bsktbl; Jr NHS; NHS; Soph Stdnt Of Mnth; Canidate Soph Stdnt Of Yr.

MANNING, KIMBERLY ANN; Ponca City Sr HS; Ponca City, OK; (4); 22/389; NFL; Chorus; Drill Tm; Ofcr Stu Cncl; JV Capt Chrldng; Swmmng; High Hon Roll; Kiwanis Awd; NHS; Mst Outstdng Ldr; Tulsa Univ; Mech Engrng.

MANOS, JANA; Guyman HS; Guymon, OK; (3); Church Yth Grp; FCA; Sec Frsh Cls; Sec Soph Cls; Sec Jr Cls; Sec Sr Cls; Bsktbl; Capt Chrldng; Hon Roll; Ntl Merit Schol.

MANSEL, KRISTEN R; Elgin HS; Apache, OK; (2); 8/85; Church Yth Grp; Band; Mrchg Band; Rep Frsh Cls; Rep Soph Cls; Var Bsktbl; Var Sftbl; Hon Roll; NHS; Cosglioing; Jr Optimist Local Pres; Schl Pageant; Cameron Univ; Med.

MANSELL, DANIEL; Stringtown HS; Stringtown, OK; (2); Natl FFA Org; Pres Soph Cls; Var Bsbl; JV Var Bsktbl; High Hon Roll; Hon Roll; OK ST Univ.

MANSFIELD, KATHLEEN A; South Coffeyville Schl; S Coffeyville, OK; (2); GAA; Nwsp; Yrbk; Sec Soph Cls; Var JV Bsktbl; Chrldng; Sftbl; Hon Roll; NHS; OSU; Pediatrician.

MANSFIELD, MATT A; South Intermediate HS; Broken Arrow, OK; (1); JV Socr; JV Wt Lftg; JV Var Wrstlng; St Soccer Team; OK ST Univ.

MANTINDALE, BILLY W; Howe Public Schl; Howe, OK; (3); Rep Frsh Cls; Rep Soph Cls; Ofcr Bsbl; Bsktbl; Trk; Wt Lftg; Cit Awd; High Hon Roll; Hon Roll; Carl Albert.

MANTZKE, MARC; Tomlinson Jr HS; Lawton, OK; (1); Church Yth Grp; FCA; Var Bsbl; Var Ftbl; High Hon Roll; OK U; Phrmcy.

MANUEL, MARISSA D; Newcastle HS; Newcastle, OK; (3); Church Yth Grp; Treas FHA; Pep Clb; Spanish Clb; Chorus; Church Choir; Schlstc Achvmnt Awd Clthng/Hsng Dsgn; Cert Of Hnr Bus Cmptr Applctns; U Of OK; Scis.

MANZER, DEVON; Edmond North HS; Edmond, OK; (3); 64/348; Church Yth Grp; Cmnty Wkr; Drama Clb; FCA; Mu Alpha Theta; SADD; Var Chrldng; Var Pom Pon; NHS; Rotary Yth Ldrshp Awd; Sr All Star Pom; Stdnt Of Mnth; Pre Calculus Awd.

MAPEL, MICHELLE A; Butler Jr Sr HS; Butler, OK; (3); 1/15; FCA; Girl Scts; Hosp Aide; Quiz Bowl; VP Soph Cls; VP Jr Cls; Cit Awd; Hon Roll; NHS; Sal; PT.

MAPES, R J; Edmond Santa Fe HS; Edmond, OK; (4); 1/219; Am Leg Boys St; Boy Scts; French Clb; Chorus; School Musical; Variety Show; Ftbl; Wrstlng; NHS; Val; Eagle Sct; Arch.

MAPLES, BRANDON L; Westmoore HS; Oklahoma City, OK; (3); 1/615; French Clb; Scholastic Bowl; Teachers Aide; High Hon Roll; Jr NHS; NHS; Pres Acad Fit Awd; Msnc Awd; Schlstc Ltr; St Hnr Soc; Med.

MAPLES, LA DONNA; Silo HS; Durant, OK; (1); Chess Clb; Cmnty Wkr; Math Tm; Church Choir; High Hon Roll; NHS; UALR; Pilot.

MAPLES, MELISSA A; West Jr HS; Oklahoma City, OK; (1); Church Yth Grp; French Clb; Office Aide; Teachers Aide; School Play; JV L Sftbl; Rptr Jr NHS.

MAPLES, NICHOLAS L; Broken Arrow Sr HS; Broken Arrow, OK; (3); FCA; Teachers Aide; Var Ftbl; Var Golf; Wt Lftg; Var Wrstlng; Pres Acad Fit Awd.

MARABLE, TABATHA; Battiest Jr Sr HS; Bethel, OK; (1); 2/30; Church Yth Grp; FHA; Quiz Bowl; Sec Frsh Cls; Var Bsktbl; Var Sftbl; Hon Roll; NHS.

MARABLE, TODD B; Broken Bow HS; Broken Bow, OK; (2); CAP; Natl FFA Org; Science Clb; Drill Tm; Ftbl; Hon Roll; NHS; Hunting; Fishing; Diving.

MARBLE, CHRISTOPHER M; Putnam City HS; Oklahoma City, OK; (3); 96/360; Church Yth Grp; Debate Tm; Church Choir; Hon Roll; See You At The Pole; Span; UCO; Bus.

MARCEL, MICHELLE D; Cleveland Sr HS; Cleveland, OK; (1); 49/168; Church Yth Grp; Wrtng Bks & Poems; Northeastern ST Univ; Eng.

MARCOM, JENNIFER; Frederick HS; Frederick, OK; (1); 1/80; Church Yth Grp; 4-H; Band; Chorus; Church Choir; Mrchg Band; 4-H Awd; All Reg Hnr/Symphnc Bands Bass Clarinet; Cty 4-H Meat I D/Jdgng Team 4th Pl St, Horse Clb Pres; OSU; Vet.

MARCUS, LINDSEY; Oklahoma Christian Schl; Edmond, OK; (3); 4/48; Church Yth Grp; Debate Tm; FCA; Speech Tm; Chorus; Stage Crew; Ofcr Soph Cls; Ofcr Jr Cls; Var Bsktbl; Var Powder Puff Ftbl; Bible Study.

MARCUSSEN, CARIN; Bethel HS; Shawnee, OK; (4); 1/65; Art Clb; 4-H; Scholastic Bowl; Band; Mrchg Band; Sec Sr Cls; Trk; 4-H Awd; High Hon Roll; NHS; OK HS Rodeo Queen; Natl HS Rodeo Assn; Voice Of Democracy Essay Cont; OK St Wnnr Law Day Essay; US Air Force Acad.

MARCUSSEN, TARA A; Bethel HS; Shawnee, OK; (2); 2/90; 4-H; Scholastic Bowl; Band; Mrchg Band; Sec Frsh Cls; 4-H Awd; High Hon Roll; NHS; Miss OK HS Rodeo; Amer Legion Auxillary Amer Essay St Wnnr; Law Day Essay Cont Cty Wnnr.

MARCY, TODD; Clinton HS; Clinton, OK; (4); 1/99; Pres Church Yth Grp; Key Clb; Quiz Bowl; Spanish Clb; School Play; Sec Stu Cncl; NHS; Mock Trial.

MARDEN, TYSON; Edmond Memorial HS; Edmond, OK; (4); 31/337; Am Leg Boys St; FCA; French Clb; Rep Jr Cls; Capt Var Crs Cntry; Capt Var Trk; NHS; TX A&M U; Ntrtn.

MARFURT, JESSICA A; B T Washington HS; Tulsa, OK; (3); Church Yth Grp; French Clb; Girl Scts; Jazz Band; Mrchg Band; Orch; School Musical; 4-H Awd; Hon Roll; Jr NHS; Econ.

MARICONDA, BRAD; Hardesty Schl; Hardesty, OK; (1); Church Yth Grp; FCA; Natl FFA Org; Pres Frsh Cls; Ofcr Bsbl; Bsktbl; Ftbl; Cit Awd; Hon Roll; Natl Sci, Hstry Mrt Awds; PSU; Engr.

MARICONDA, ERIC; Hardesty Schl; Hardesty, OK; (3); Church Yth Grp; FCA; Natl FFA Org; Ofcr Jr Cls; Var Bsbl; Var Bsktbl; Var Ftbl; NHS; Ntl Merit Ltr; Prfct Atten Awd; Panhandle ST; Arch Drftng.

MARINO, BRIAN; Putnam City North HS; Oklahoma City, OK; (2); 22/488; FCA; Spanish Clb; Stage Crew; Ofcr Stu Cncl; Var L Ftbl; Cit Awd; High Hon Roll; NHS; OASC Basic Ldrshp Wkshp; Panther Pals; Rice; Plastic Surgeon; Dermatolg.

MARINO, ZACHARY K; Putnam City North HS; Oklahoma City, OK; (3); 183/490; FCA; Var Bsktbl; Var Capt Ftbl; Wt Lftg; All City Ftbl; All St Hm Ftbl; All Conf, All BA-1 Dist.

MARION, MICHAEL; Classen Schl Advanced Studies; Oklahoma City, OK; (1); Boy Scts; Drama Clb; Mu Alpha Theta; Science Clb; Temple Yth Grp; School Musical; School Play; Stage Crew; High Hon Roll; NHS.

MARION, MICHAEL D; Latta Sr HS; Ada, OK; (1); FCA; Bsktbl; Golf.

MARION, SHERRY L; Muldrow HS; Muldrow, OK; (2); FHA; Chorus; High Hon Roll; Hnr Soc; Carl Albert; Math Tchr.

MARKLAND, ALICIA; Central HS; Tulsa, OK; (4); Ed Yrbk; Rptr Lit Mag; Hon Roll; U Of Tulsa; Jrnlsm.

MARKLAND, TIMOTHY; Central HS; Tulsa, OK; (2); Church Yth Grp; High Hon Roll; Hon Roll; NHS; Church Band.

MARKLEY, JOE; Mustang HS; Mustang, OK; (3); Natl FFA Org; Office Aide; Hon Roll.

MARKS, CHRIS P; Stillwater Sr HS; Stillwater, OK; (4); Teachers Aide; JV Bsbl; Var Ftbl; Hon Roll.

MARLAN, SARAH; Claremore Sr HS; Claremore, OK; (1); 1/285; Church Yth Grp; Cmnty Wkr; Spanish Clb; SADD; Chrldng; High Hon Roll; MO Southern Intl Piano Cmptn; Natl Piano Aud ; OMTA.

MARLATT, AMANDA; Oklahoma Bible Acad; Enid, OK; (2); Quiz Bowl; Scholastic Bowl; Chorus; Vllybl; High Hon Roll; JFK Rsrchr; Harvard; Law.

MARLER, CHRISTOPHER J; Del City HS; Oklahoma City, OK; (2); Art Clb; Church Yth Grp; Library Aide; ROTC; Teachers Aide; Drill Tm; Hon Roll; Aerospace Engr.

MARLEY, BRENT L; Coweta HS; Broken Arrow, OK; (3); Church Yth Grp; FCA; FHA; Letterman Clb; Varsity Clb; Ofcr Bsbl; Ftbl; Wt Lftg; Hon Roll; Pres Acad Fit Awd; Bsktbl; Crim Just.

MARLEY, CHRIS; Grace Chrn Acad; Oklahoma City, OK; (4); Church Yth Grp; FCA; Office Aide; Teachers Aide; Ofcr Bsbl; Bsktbl; Ftbl; Trk; Wt Lftg; Cit Awd.

MARLEY, LEISHA; Putnam City West HS; Bethany, OK; (4); 32/290; Am Leg Aux Girls St; DECA; SADD; Treas Jr Cls; Hist Stu Cncl; Var Chrldng; Co-Capt Pom Pon; High Hon Roll; Church Yth Grp; Dance Clb; UDA All Star Dancer; NCA Spcl Evnts Dance Team Aloha Bwl; U Of OK; Bus.

MARLOW, ANGELA L; Morrison Public Schl; Morrison, OK; (3); FBLA; FHA; Office Aide; Spanish Clb; Sprt Ed Nwsp; Yrbk; Rptr Frsh Cls; Rptr Soph Cls; Rptr Jr Cls; Bsktbl; MEA Awd; Wrtng; Jrnlsm.

MARLOW, CANDACE A; Bethel HS; Shawnee, OK; (1); Art Clb; Church Yth Grp; 4-H; Natl FFA Org; Var Bsktbl; Var Sftbl; Var Trk; Cit Awd; Hon Roll; Prfct Atten Awd.

MARLOWE, SUSAN; Moore HS; Oklahoma City, OK; (2); Church Yth Grp; Band; Mrchg Band; Hon Roll; Vlntr Nrsng Hm; Elem Ed.

MARNEY, LISA; Pryor Jr HS; Pryor, OK; (2); FHA; HOBY; Spanish Clb; Speech Tm; Yrbk; Var Sftbl; Hon Roll; NHS; Bio & Geom Awds; Med Dr; RN.

MARPLE, ERIK; Tomlinson Jr HS; Lawton, OK; (1); Church Yth Grp; Band; Drm Mjr(t); Mrchg Band; Yrbk; JV Tennis; High Hon Roll; Jr NHS; Alfl Rgn Bnd 94-96; All Rgn Awd; Bldrs Clb; Jr Key Clb; OK U; Med Sci.

MARQUARD, MEREDITH STARR; Stratford Schl; Stratford, OK; (2); Cmnty Wkr; 4-H; Rep Rptr Yrbk; Treas Frsh Cls; Treas Soph Cls; Pres Jr Cls; Rep Stu Cncl; Var Sftbl; Hon Roll; Church Yth Grp; Garvin Cty 4-H Pres; Voice Of Amer Speech Wnnr For VFW; East Cntrl U; Jrnlsm.

MARQUEZ, VICTORIA A; Owasso Sr HS; Collinsville, OK; (2); Office Aide; Stage Crew; Rep Stu Cncl; Score Keeper; Hon Roll; St Marys Coll; Tchr.

MARQUIS, JEREMY; Norman Sr HS; Norman, OK; (4); 164/677; Cmnty Wkr; FCA; Yrbk; Ofcr Stu Cncl; Bsktbl; Var Ftbl; Var Socr; High Hon Roll; Hon Roll; Pres Acad Fit Awd; Tomorrows Ldrs Hmn Rltns Bd; OHP Cadet Lawmans Acad; All ST/ALL Conf/All Dist Sccr; OU.

MARQUIS, KHARA C; Central Mid-HS; Norman, OK; (2); Cmnty Wkr; Pres French Clb; Rep Frsh Cls; Rptr Stu Cncl; JV Bsktbl; Var Sftbl; French Hon Soc; Hon Roll; Tomorrows Ldrs; Safety Town Vol; UCLA.

MARR, APRIL; Achille Schl; Durant, OK; (3); 4/43; Church Yth Grp; 4-H; FHA; VP Jr Cls; Var Bsktbl; Var Sftbl; Hon Roll; NHS; SOSU; Pre-Med.

MARR, MATT; Lone Grove HS; Ardmore, OK; (3); 7/110; Key Clb; Model UN; NFL; Speech Tm; Acpl Chr; Chorus; Swing Chorus; Hon Roll; NHS; FCA; UCA All-Star Msct; Vcl Perf.

MARR, TREY; Achille Schl; Durant, OK; (1); 4/45; Church Yth Grp; 4-H; Natl FFA Org; Rep Frsh Cls; Ofcr Stu Cncl; Var Bsbl; Var Bsktbl; Hon Roll; OK Hnr Soc; Top Stu Eng I.

MARRIOTT, CRYSTAL; Moore HS; Moore, OK; (3); French Clb; JCL; Latin Clb; Office Aide; Science Clb; Chorus; Chrldng; Pom Pon; Jr NHS; NHS; Cum Laude; Latn; Premed.

MARRIS, BILLIE DAWN; Clayton Jr Sr HS; Clayton, OK; (3); 1/35; FHA; Yrbk; Sftbl; Hon Roll; Pres Acad Fit Awd; FHA Sec 1 Yr/Pres 2 Yrs; Yrbk Layout 1 Yr/Ed 1 Yr; Choctaw Nation Upward Bnd Math/Sci Prgm; Eastern OK ST Coll; Bus Tchng.

MARROQUIN, CRAIG; Apache HS; Apache, OK; (1); 7/55; Drama Clb; German Clb; Scholastic Bowl; Thesps; Band; Orch; School Play; High Hon Roll; NHS; Pre-Med.

MARROW, BENNY H; Heavener HS; Heavener, OK; (3); 30/85; Pres Church Yth Grp; Natl FFA Org; Band; Church Choir; Mrchg Band; Pep Band; Hon Roll; Showman Awd Le Flore Cty Fair; Beef Prod Awd FFA; Breed Chmpn Angus Bull Le Flore Cty Fair; OSU; Ag Ed.

MARSALIS, VAN; Waynoka HS; Waynoka, OK; (3); 4/19; Am Leg Boys St; Church Yth Grp; Cmnty Wkr; FCA; 4-H; Natl FFA Org; Pep Clb; Scholastic Bowl; Ofcr Soph Cls; Ftbl; Woods Cty Hrs Assn; Histrcl Re-Enactmnt Clb; Northwester OK ST U; Agbus.

MARSH, AMY E; Central Mid-HS; Norman, OK; (2) Church Yth Grp; FCA; Model UN; Mu Alpha Theta; Band; Church Choir; Mrchg Band; JV Bsktbl; JV Pom Pon; Var Sftbl; Bnd Treas 95-; Fnlst Cub Prd Awd 95-.

MARSHALL, CANDIS R; Ringling HS; Ringling, OK; (2); 2/40; FCA; GAA; Natl FFA Org; JV Bsktbl; Powder Puff Ftbl; Var Sftbl; Hon Roll; OK Hnr Soc; OK ST Univ; Med.

MARSHALL, CHERYL D; Harrah HS; Harrah, OK; (2); 1/178; Natl FFA Org; SADD; Tennis; High Hon Roll; Hon Roll; Jr NHS; OK ST Univ; Bus; Mgmt.

MARSHALL, JENNIFER D; Southeast HS; Oklahoma City, OK; (1); Latin Clb; Hon Roll; OK ST Univ.

MARSHALL, JENNIFER E; Yukon Middle HS; Yukon, OK; (2); Church Yth Grp; Debate Tm; Hosp Aide; Scholastic Bowl; High Hon Roll; Jr NHS; 7th Pl Algebra II St Schltc Meet; Southwestern OK ST.

MARSHALL, JOSEPH WILLIAM; Jenks HS; Tulsa, OK; (3); Hon Roll; NHS; DECA St Champ Intnl Mrktg 95-/Natl Contestnt; Acad Lttr 95-; OK Univ; Meteorlgy.

MARSHALL, LINDSAY A; Central Mid-HS; Norman, OK; (2); OU; Comp Acctng.

MARSHALL, MICHAEL D; B T Washington HS; Tulsa, OK; (3); Church Yth Grp; Office Aide; Teachers Aide; Mrchg Band; Corp Law.

MARSHALL, RACHEL; Ninnekah HS; Ninnekah, OK; (3); 6/32; HOBY; Quiz Bowl; Scholastic Bowl; Sec VICA; Rptr Nwsp; Treas Jr Cls; Sec Stu Cncl; Var Bsktbl; Var Chrldng; Var Trk; Track 2 Mi Relay 3rd Pl Regnls & St Cmptns; 4-H Sec 2 Yrs, Reprtr, Treas; Marine Bio.

MARSHALL II, SCOTT W; Copan HS; Copan, OK; (3); #4 in class; Boy Scts; Quiz Bowl; Band; Jazz Band; Mrchg Band; Var Ftbl; Socr; Var Trk; Hon Roll; Bio.

MARSHALL, TABITHA A; Choctaw HS; Harrah, OK; (3); Spanish Clb; Band; Chorus; Church Choir; Bsktbl; Sftbl; High Hon Roll; Hon Roll; Prfct Atten Awd; FBLA; OU; Acctng; Law.

MARSHALL, TROY D; Harrah HS; Harrah, OK; (2); 25/65; Natl FFA Org; Ftbl.

MARTENS, JULIE; Kingston HS; Kingston, OK; (2); FCA; Quiz Bowl; Sec Treas Frsh Cls; VP Soph Cls; JV Stat Bsktbl; Stat Sftbl; Hon Roll; NHS; Surgeon-Stomach & Chest.

MARTENS, KASSI; Fairview HS; Fairview, OK; (1); Church Yth Grp; FCA; FHA; GAA; Band; Church Choir; Mrchg Band; Pep Band; Variety Show; Rep Frsh Cls.

MARTENS, KELSEY; Fairview HS; Fairview, OK; (3); Church Yth Grp; Cmnty Wkr; FCA; FHA; GAA; Band; Church Choir; Mrchg Band; Pep Band; School Musical; SWOSU; Phrmcy.

MARTENS, SUZANNE; Okemah HS; Okemah, OK; (4); Art Clb; Drama Clb; Spanish Clb; Bsktbl; Hon Roll; 4th Pl Seminole Jr Coll Intershltc Meet Span; Mrt Awd Span & Schl Play; Exch Stu From Holland; Graphic Dsgn.

MARTI, AMANDA; Fairview HS; Fairview, OK; (2); Church Yth Grp; FCA; NFL; Band; Ofcr Stu Cncl; Chrldng; Hon Roll; NHS; Pres Acad Fit Awd; Debate Tm.

MARTIN, AMANDA; Holland Hall Schl; Tulsa, OK; (2); Pep Clb; School Play; Rep Nwsp; Rep Frsh Cls; Rep Soph Cls; Var Bsktbl; Var Capt Chrldng; JV Fld Hcky; High Hon Roll; Jr NHS; Pre-Med.

MARTIN, AMY D; Ringling HS; Ringling, OK; (2); Church Yth Grp; FCA; Pres Frsh Cls; Pres Soph Cls; Var Bsktbl; Var Powder Puff Ftbl; JV Trk; High Hon Roll; NHS; FFA.

MARTIN, AMY R; Amber Pocasset Jr Sr HS; Chickasha, OK; (3); Drama Clb; FCA; Natl FFA Org; Pep Clb; Science Clb; Spanish Clb; School Play; Bsktbl; OK St Univ; Mgmt.

MARTIN, ANDREA D; Broken Arrow Sr HS; Broken Arrow, OK; (3); Church Yth Grp; DECA; Drama Clb; School Play; Stage Crew; Ofcr Stu Cncl; Cit Awd; NHS; Pres Acad Fit Awd; Office Aide; Comm Svc Ed Actvtes Awd; Stu Yng Author Awd 1st Plc; Natl DECA Conf Top 15; TCC; Mktng.

MARTIN, ANDREA M; Muskogee HS; Muskogee, OK; (3); Church Yth Grp; Drama Clb; FCA; Pep Clb; Spanish Clb; Chorus; Church Choir; Phtg Yrbk; Var Capt Chrldng; Hon Roll; Super In Piano St Guild; OK ST Univ.

MARTIN, ANGELA; Panama HS; Cameron, OK; (4); 20/50; FHA; Natl FFA Org; SADD; Ed Nwsp; NHS; Crl Albrt ST Coll; RN.

MARTIN, ANGELA; Noble HS; Norman, OK; (4); Church Yth Grp; FCA; Key Clb; Model UN; Spanish Clb; SADD; Chorus; Church Choir; Mgr Bsktbl; NHS; Natl His & Govt Awd; Outstndng Attorney Mock Trial; Rose ST Coll; Law; Lawyer.

MARTIN, ANGELIQUE L; Okay Jr Sr HS; Wagoner, OK; (3); 4-H; Hosp Aide; Ofcr Stu Cncl; Bsktbl; Chrldng; Northeastern ST U; Elem Tchr.

MARTIN, ANTHONY; Nathan Hale HS; Tulsa, OK; (4); 22/203; Church Yth Grp; Office Aide; Teachers Aide; Crs Cntry; Capt Socr; High Hon Roll; Hon Roll; NHS; All Dist Sccr Plyr; U Tulsa.

MARTIN, ASHLEY NICOLE; Yukon Middle HS; Yukon, OK; (4); 16/400; Church Yth Grp; FHA; Hosp Aide; Office Aide; VP Spanish Clb; VP SADD; Tennis; Hon Roll; Sec NHS; Yukon Env Soc Treas; LIFE Pro Life Org; Dont Do Drgs Org; Litry Clb; OK Chrstn Univ Of Sci; RN.

MARTIN, BENJAMIN G; Okmulgee HS; Okmulgee, OK; (1); Church Yth Grp; Quiz Bowl; Spanish Clb; Ofcr Bsbl; Cit Awd; Hon Roll; Pres Acad Fit Awd.

MARTIN, BILL; Enid Sr HS; Enid, OK; (4); 147/405; Am Leg Boys St; Church Yth Grp; FCA; Office Aide; Pep Clb; Teachers Aide; Band; Ftbl; Wt Lftg; Hon Roll; Boys St; Awrnss; VICA; UCO.

MARTIN, BLAKE D; Guthrie Sr HS; Guthrie, OK; (2); 19/304; Art Clb; Bsktbl; Golf; Hon Roll; Jr NHS.

MARTIN, CARLA B; Fargo Schl; Woodward, OK; (3); 6/14; Art Clb; Church Yth Grp; Cmnty Wkr; Debate Tm; Drama Clb; FTA; German Clb; Pep Clb; Varsity Clb; School Play; Sub Debs; Concordia Coll; Scndry Ed; Eng.

MARTIN, CHAD W; Woodward HS; Woodward, OK; (1); Debate Tm; Band; Jazz Band; Mrchg Band; Pep Band; Stage Crew; Classic Bowl Hnr Band; Red Carpet Hnr Band; Black/Gold Hnr Band; Outstdng Frosh Band Stdnt; Southwester OK ST U.

MARTIN, CHARLES H; Bishop Kelley HS; Tulsa, OK; (4); 47/147; Am Leg Boys St; Boy Scts; Cmnty Wkr; FCA; Quiz Bowl; Teachers Aide; VP Sr Cls; Rep Stu Cncl; Var Capt Ftbl; Hon Roll; Eagle Sct; Ftbl All Dist; U OK; Engrng.

MARTIN, CHRIS E; El Reno Sr HS; El Reno, OK; (2); Ofcr Bsbl; Bsktbl; Golf; Hon Roll; Scuba Diving; U Of OK; Medicine.

MARTIN, CORY; Quapaw Sr HS; Quapaw, OK; (4); 7/40; Church Yth Grp; FCA; Pep Clb; Quiz Bowl; Spanish Clb; Band; Mrchg Band; Nwsp; Yrbk; Ofcr Stu Cncl; BHSIC Ldrsp Wrkshp; Natl Assn Stu Cncl Delg; U OK Norman; Med.

MARTIN, CRYSTAL E; Durant HS; Durant, OK; (2); Art Clb; Church Yth Grp; Cmnty Wkr; Drama Clb; FTA; Natl FFA Org; Spanish Clb; Church Choir; Hon Roll; Tutor; Spcl Ed.

MARTIN, DERREK C; Canton HS; Canton, OK; (2); 4-H; Band; Mrchg Band; Pep Band; Pres Acad Fit Awd; FFA; Acad Team; Tech Ed; Law.

MARTIN, DUSTIN L; Noble HS; Noble, OK; (3); Church Yth Grp; DECA; FCA; FBLA; FHA; Spanish Clb; Yrbk; Ofcr Bsbl; Hon Roll; NHS; OK Univ; Bus; Sports Medicine.

MARTIN, EMILY L; Ponca City Sr HS; Ponca City, OK; (3); 29/406; FCA; Letterman Clb; Spanish Clb; Varsity Clb; Drill Tm; Vllybl; High Hon Roll; NHS.

MARTIN, HEATH; Smithville Sr HS; Bethel, OK; (3); 3/40; Church Yth Grp; Pres 4-H; FHA; Scholastic Bowl; Church Choir; Yrbk; Var Bsbl; Var Bsktbl; 4-H Awd; High Hon Roll; OK Hnr Soc; Awds In Typing, HE, Sci & Math; 4-H Cty Pres; Dan Forth I Dare You Awd; Cty 4-H Hall Fame.

MARTIN, HEATHER R; Mustang HS; Mustang, OK; (3); 50/420; Church Yth Grp; FCA; FBLA; SADD; Acpl Chr; Chorus; Church Choir; Var L Sftbl; Hon Roll; NHS; Cmptr Info Sys/Mngmt.

MARTIN, JANA; Chelsea HS; Chelsea, OK; (4); 4/61; Church Yth Grp; FCA; Band; Chorus; Church Choir; Drm Mjr(t); Jazz Band; Mrchg Band; Sftbl; NHS; OK Bapt All St Yth Choir/Orch; OK All Star Mrchng Band; OK Bapt U; Music.

MARTIN, JANET M; Mc Alester HS; Mcalester, OK; (2); Art Clb; FHA; GAA; Spanish Clb; Band; Mrchg Band; Vllybl; Wilburton; Animal Stud.

MARTIN, JASON; Ryan Schl; Terral, OK; (2); 4/30; FCA; 4-H; Letterman Clb; Natl Beta Clb; Natl FFA Org; Ofcr Soph Cls; JV Bsktbl; Trk; 4-H Awd; High Hon Roll.

MARTIN, JENNIFER; Stilwell HS; Stilwell, OK; (3); Church Yth Grp; FCA; Sec FBLA; Pres Natl Beta Clb; Spanish Clb; Mrchg Band; Yrbk; Ofcr Stu Cncl; High Hon Roll; NHS; Junior Board Of Directors Of People's Bank; Univ Of AR; Bus Mgmt.

MARTIN, JENNIFER J; Comanche HS; Comanche, OK; (2); Hnr Roll; Art Clb; Child Phy.

MARTIN, JENNIFER M; Tishomingo HS; Tishomingo, OK; (3); FHA; Band; Chorus; Mrchg Band; High Hon Roll; Hon Roll; SOSU Durant OK; Elem Ed.

MARTIN, JEREMY G; El Reno Sr HS; El Reno, OK; (4); 82/163; Art Clb; Boy Scts; Church Yth Grp; FCA; FTA; Office Aide; Red Cross Aide; VICA; Band; Mrchg Band; Cert Of Excllnc; Schlrshp; Redlands CC.

MARTIN, JESICA; Afton HS; Bluejacket, OK; (2); 1/32; Pres Sec 4-H; FHA; Science Clb; Bsktbl; 4-H Awd; High Hon Roll; Hon Roll; NHS; OCCP Vlntr; Vet Med.

MARTIN, JESSICA M; Union Intermediate HS; Tulsa, OK; (2); 108/800; Yrbk; High Hon Roll; Frgn Lang Clb; Piano; OU.

MARTIN, JULIE D; Christian Heritage Acad; Del City, OK; (2); Church Yth Grp; JV Vllybl; Hon Roll; Church Yth Grp, Yth Choir, Yth Girls Ensmbl.

MARTIN, JUSTIN L; El Reno Sr HS; El Reno, OK; (1); Church Yth Grp; FCA; Red Cross Aide; Ftbl; Socr; Wt Lftg; Hon Roll; Jr NHS; Pres Acad Fit Awd.

MARTIN, KELLY K; Chattanooga Schl; Faxon, OK; (2); Natl FFA Org; Chorus; Hon Roll; Med Doctor.

MARTIN, KERRY L; Dale Sr HS; Shawnee, OK; (3); 1/50; Church Yth Grp; FCA; Band; Mrchg Band; Pep Band; Var L Bsbl; Var L Bsktbl; Cit Awd; High Hon Roll; NHS.

MARTIN, KYLE R; Edmond Memorial HS; Edmond, OK; (3); Church Yth Grp; Cmnty Wkr; JCL; Key Clb; Latin Clb; Band; Mrchg Band; NHS; Pres Acad Fit Awd; Cum Laude Natl Latin Exam; OU; Phy Thrpst.

MARTIN, LESLIE; Panama HS; Panama, OK; (3); Church Yth Grp; FCA; FHA; Natl FFA Org; Variety Show; VP Frsh Cls; Pres Soph Cls; Sftbl; High Hon Roll; Hon Roll; TX A&M Galveston; Marine Bio.

MARTIN, LUKE; Blanche Thomas Jr Sr HS; Sentinel, OK; (2); Church Yth Grp; 4-H; Pres Soph Cls; Rep Stu Cncl; L Bsbl; L Bsktbl; Cit Awd; 4-H Awd; Hon Roll; 4-H Pres; Beta; Anul Royalty Soph Cls.

MARTIN, LUKE A; Mulhall Orlando HS; Mulhall, OK; (4); 13/22; Church Yth Grp; FCA; Natl FFA Org; Office Aide; Sec Rep Sr Cls; JV Var Bsbl; JV Var Bsktbl; FFA VP, Treas, Rep & Sentinal; OSU; Firefighter Field.

MARTIN, MELANIE A; Jay HS; Jay, OK; (3); FCA; FBLA; FHA; German Clb; Natl Beta Clb; Quiz Bowl; Hon Roll; NHS; MO Southern ST Coll; Parlgl.

MARTIN, MICHELLE; Eufaula Sr HS; Eufaula, OK; (2); Church Yth Grp; Math Clb; Quiz Bowl; Science Clb; Band; Jazz Band; Mrchg Band; Bsktbl; Sftbl; Trk; Hnr & All Dist Band; GATE; Scripps Inst; Marine Bio.

MARTIN, PENNY; Plainview HS; Ardmore, OK; (1); 14/100; Cmnty Wkr; GAA; JV Bsktbl; Fld Hcky; High Hon Roll; Hon Roll; Pres Acad Fit Awd; Natl Roller Hcky Lds Tm; Lwyr.

MARTIN, PHILLIP; Mc Loud HS; Newalla, OK; (3); FCA; FBLA; Ftbl; Ofcr Bsbl; Hon Roll; Ntl Merit Schol; Outstndng Athlt; All Cty Hnrb Mntn Ftbl; All Cnty Ftbl; Bus.

MARTIN, PHILLIP; Kellyville Sr HS; Kellyville, OK; (4); 4/60; Church Yth Grp; HOBY; Office Aide; Teachers Aide; Band; Jazz Band; Mrchg Band; Bsktbl; Hon Roll; NHS; OK ST U; Psych.

MARTIN, RHYS A; South Intermediate HS; Broken Arrow, OK; (1); Hon Roll; Tech Stdnts Assn.

MARTIN, S M; Owasso Sr HS; Owasso, OK; (3); GAA; Office Aide; JV Var Bsktbl; Var Sftbl; Hon Roll; Owasso ST Sftbl Championship.

MARTIN, SARAH; Spiro HS; Spiro, OK; (4); 5/91; Am Leg Aux Girls St; FCA; FBLA; Math Clb; Spanish Clb; Ed Yrbk; Chrldng; Sftbl; NHS; Westark CC; Engl Ed.

MARTIN, SARAH; Guthrie Sr HS; Guthrie, OK; (3); Church Yth Grp; 4-H; FHA; Girl Scts; Hosp Aide; Science Clb; SADD; Band; Mrchg Band; School Play; Phys Thrpy.

MARTIN, SARAH; Wynnewood HS; Wynnewood, OK; (3); 14/60; FHA; Quiz Bowl; Teachers Aide; Band; Color Guard; Drm Mjr(t); Jazz Band; Mrchg Band; Hon Roll; Aerion Awd; All-Star Marching Band.

MARTIN, SENDI; Ft Gibson HS; Fort Gibson, OK; (3); #3 in class; Art Clb; CAP; French Clb; SADD; Band; Color Guard; Mrchg Band; Pep Band; High Hon Roll; NHS; Art Ther.

MARTIN, SHANNON L; Broken Arrow Sr HS; Broken Arrow, OK; (4); 44/900; Cmnty Wkr; FTA; Intnl Clb; Key Clb; Band; Mrchg Band; Hon Roll; NHS; OK ST Univ; Elem Ed.

MARTIN, SKY; Bartlesville Sr HS; Bartlesville, OK; (4); VICA; High Hon Roll; Hon Roll; Kiwanis Awd; Prfct Atten Awd; Cosmtlgst.

MARTIN, STEPHANIE E; Choctaw HS; Choctaw, OK; (3); Church Yth Grp; Chorus; School Musical; Stage Crew; Show Choir/Girls Jazz Choir; Yth Grp Praise/Wrshp Bnd; Stdnt Hlpng Stdnts Spec Olympcs.

MARTIN, SUNNY; Wayne Public Schl; Paoli, OK; (3); Art Clb; FHA; GAA; Pep Clb; SADD; VP Soph Cls; Bsktbl; Trk; Hon Roll; NHS; PT.

MARTIN, SUZI; Choctaw HS; Midwest City, OK; (4); Am Leg Aux Girls St; Key Clb; Pres SADD; Pres Frsh Cls; VP Pres Soph Cls; Treas Jr Cls; Sec Sr Cls; Capt Pom Pon; Powder Puff Ftbl; Hon Roll; E OK Cty Acad All Star; Rose ST Coll; Scndry Ed.

MARTIN, TIM E; Wilson HS; Wilson, OK; (2); #1 in class; Boy Scts; FCA; Natl Beta Clb; Band; Mrchg Band; Pep Band; JV Var Bsktbl; High Hon Roll; Hon Roll; NHS; S Nazarene Univ; Bio.

MARTIN, TODD A; Ada HS; Ada, OK; (4); Boy Scts; Church Yth Grp; Cmnty Wkr; FCA; Varsity Clb; Yrbk; Bsktbl; Ftbl; Tennis; Hon Roll; Eagle Sct; East Cntrl Univ.

MARTINA, SHAUNTA D; Southeast HS; Oklahoma City, OK; (2); Dance Clb; FCA; Pom Pon; High Hon Roll; Rose ST Coll; RN.

MARTINDALE, JAMIE L; Sayre HS; Sayre, OK; (1); 7/67; Church Yth Grp; Sec FCA; FHA; Chorus; Church Choir; Rep Frsh Cls; Stat Bsbl; Score Keeper; Cit Awd; High Hon Roll; Cert Of Achvmt In Tech Ed, Eng I & Fndtns For Living I; Phys Therapy.

MARTINEZ, ALICIA; Kingfisher HS; Kingfisher, OK; (3); 1/98; GAA; Key Clb; Var Bsktbl; Socr; Hon Roll; NHS; All Amer Schlr; Natl Ldrshp & Svc Awd; Natl Eng Mrt Awd; UCO; Rdlgy.

MARTINEZ, CRISTOL J; Mustang HS; Yukon, OK; (3); Church Yth Grp; Cmnty Wkr; Spanish Clb; Band; Church Choir; Mrchg Band; Hon Roll; NHS; Outstdng Frosh Band Stu; Piano; Chrch Mission Projects; Bus; Music.

MARTINEZ, ELENA M; Guthrie Sr HS; Guthrie, OK; (1); 9/308; Church Yth Grp; French Clb; Stat Bsktbl; JV Var Socr; OK ST Univ; Bus.

MARTINEZ, FRANCISCA R; Altus Sr HS; Altus, OK; (2); Church Yth Grp; Cmnty Wkr; Library Aide; ROTC; Spanish Clb; Hon Roll; Prfct Atten Awd; Mayors Helping Hands; U Of OK; Elem Tchr.

MARTINEZ, JOEL E; West Middle HS; Norman, OK; (2); Band; Ftbl.

MARTINEZ JR, ROSALIO V; Bishop Kelley HS; Tulsa, OK; (1); Letterman Clb; Wrstlng; Hon Roll; Spanish NHS; Natl Span Testing Biling Category 3rd Pl.

MARTINEZ, SUMMER D; Coyle Public Schl; Shawnee, OK; (2); 6/75; Bsktbl; Hon Roll; NHS; OSU; Math/Sci Prof.

MARTINEZ, VERONICA; Stilwell HS; Stilwell, OK; (3); Boy Scts; Church Yth Grp; Drama Clb; FCA; Letterman Clb; Natl Beta Clb; Spanish Clb; Varsity Clb; L Bsktbl; Powder Puff Ftbl; Baylor; Sprts Mdcn.

MARTIRE, AMANDA; Guymon Sr HS; Guymon, OK; (4); 1/120; Debate Tm; FCA; Office Aide; Speech Tm; Band; Mgr Bsbl; Capt Chrldng; NHS; Val; OK ST U; Vet Med.

MARTIRE, MANDY; Guymon Sr HS; Guymon, OK; (4); 1/120; Debate Tm; FCA; Band; Rep Jr Cls; Rep Sr Cls; Mgr Bsbl; Capt Chrldng; Treas NHS; Val; OK ST U; Vet Med.

MARVEL, JERRY R; Wilburton Sr HS; Wilburton, OK; (3); Am Leg Boys St; FTA; Letterman Clb; Teachers Aide; Varsity Clb; Band; Mrchg Band; Orch; Pep Band; Bsktbl; Eastern OK St Coll; Biomed.

MARVEL, JILL; Wilburton Jr HS; Wilburton, OK; (1); 4-H; Office Aide; Band; Chorus; Mrchg Band; Pep Band; Var Bsktbl; Var Sftbl; Hon Roll; Prfct Atten Awd; Tchng.

MARVEL, JO; Wilburton Jr HS; Wilburton, OK; (4); 6/80; FBLA; FTA; Office Aide; Band; Chorus; Color Guard; Hon Roll; Kiwanis Awd; NHS; Pres Schlr; All Dist Bnd 5 Yrs; All Hnr Bnd 3 Yrs; Superior Flag Solo/Rifle Duet ST Comptn; E OK ST Coll; Acctg.

MARZUOLA, JEREMY L; Ponca City Sr HS; Ponca City, OK; (2); 17/500; Cmnty Wkr; Cit Awd; High Hon Roll; Pres Acad Fit Awd.

MASCHMAN, NICOLE; Wellston Schl; Wellston, OK; (2); Church Yth Grp; FHA; Band; Mrchg Band; Orch; Hon Roll; NHS; All St Band 96; U Of OK; Horn Perf.

MASHANEY, BECKY L; Del City HS; Del City, OK; (2); Church Yth Grp; Dance Clb; French Clb; SADD; Church Choir; Jr NHS; Phys Thrpy.

MASHBURN, MARIKA R; Mt St Marys HS; Norman, OK; (3); 3/75; Cmnty Wkr; Pep Clb; Sec Soph Cls; VP Jr Cls; Pres Stu Cncl; Var Capt Chrldng; Var Capt Pom Pon; High Hon Roll; Hon Roll; OK ST Hnr Soc & Sci Awd; Theatre Pgms At Boston Univ 95, Northwestern Univ 96; De Paul Univ; Theatre Arts.

MASHUNKASHEY, JULIE; Pawhuska HS; Pawhuska, OK; (4); Am Leg Aux Girls St; FCA; FBLA; FHA; Key Clb; Library Aide; Science Clb; Yrbk; Sec Frsh Cls; VP Soph Cls; NASA Sec, VP; Peer Hlprs; Northeastern ST U; Ntrtnst.

MASON, BRYAN J; Hartshorne Sr HS; Mcalester, OK; (3); Boy Scts; Church Yth Grp; Cmnty Wkr; FBLA; FHA; JA; Natl FFA Org; Acpl Chr; Chorus; School Musical; Nation Wide Score Top 10 9th Grd Writting Essays; FFA Green Hand Awd/Chptr Awd; EOSC; Law Enfrcmnt.

MASON, CHERYL R; Stillwater Sr HS; Stillwater, OK; (2); 36/355; Church Yth Grp; JCL; Latin Clb; Natl Beta Clb; Band; Church Choir; School Play; Var L Socr; Var L Swmmng; Hon Roll.

MASON, CHRISTINE; Midwest City HS; Midwest City, OK; (3); 43/384; French Clb; Hosp Aide; Band; Mrchg Band; Pep Band; Jr NHS; NHS; Pres Acad Fit Awd; Visual Arts Awd; Geom Excl; U Of OK; Med.

MASON, HEATH; Hardesty Schl; Hardesty, OK; (2); Church Yth Grp; FCA; French Clb; Natl FFA Org; Quiz Bowl; Pres Soph Cls; Var Bsktbl; Hon Roll; NHS.

MASON, JENNIFER; Moore Christian Schl; Moore, OK; (1); Stage Crew; Phtg Yrbk; Var Chrldng; Hon Roll; Top Gun Sr All Stars Pom Sqd; Amer Chmpnshp 96 Natl Champ; OK ST Univ; Vet.

MASON, JENNIFER; Eisenhower Sr HS; Lawton, OK; (2); Church Yth Grp; FCA; Key Clb; Spanish Clb; Chrldng; Gym; Powder Puff Ftbl; High Hon Roll; Hon Roll; Cameron Univ; PT/TCHR.

MASON, JENNIFER L; Memorial HS; Tulsa, OK; (4); 18/250; Church Yth Grp; Intnl Clb; Pres Pep Clb; Science Clb; Spanish Clb; Treas Sr Cls; Capt Socr; Hon Roll; NHS; Assisteens; Gamma Sigma; TX A&M Univ; Biomed.

MASON, JEREMY; Union Intermediate HS; Broken Arrow, OK; (4); 217/620; Am Leg Boys St; Boy Scts; Cmnty Wkr; Office Aide; Spanish Clb; Teachers Aide; Sec Temple Yth Grp; Hon Roll; Spanish NHS; OU.

MASON, JIMMIE J; Wister Schl; Poteau, OK; (3); Church Yth Grp; Cmnty Wkr; Debate Tm; FHA; Girl Scts; Speech Tm; SADD; Chorus; Hon Roll; Prfct Atten Awd; Carl Albert; Law.

MASON, KRISTIN L; Vinita HS; Vinita, OK; (2); Am Leg Aux Girls St; Debate Tm; Drama Clb; FHA; NFL; Speech Tm; Chorus; Golf; NHS; Spanish Clb; Envrnmntl Club; U Of OK; Med/Dr.

MASON, KRISTINA R; El Reno Sr HS; El Reno, OK; (3); Church Yth Grp; Cmnty Wkr; Drama Clb; FCA; FHA; Girl Scts; Hosp Aide; Speech Tm; SADD; Band; Comm Arts.

MASON, LACHELLE M; Brink Jr HS; Oklahoma City, OK; (1); Church Yth Grp; Quiz Bowl; Pres Science Clb; Church Choir; Ed Yrbk; Jr NHS; Band; Color Guard; Cit Awd; Fndr/Pres Poets Soc; Sci/Math Awds; Chrstn Character Awd Bible Quiz; Microbio.

MASON, LARAE; Hardesty Schl; Hardesty, OK; (1); 1/6; Church Yth Grp; Natl FFA Org; Quiz Bowl; Chorus; Pres Frsh Cls; Var Bsktbl; Var Sftbl; High Hon Roll; Ntl Merit Ltr; Val; FFA Star Grnhnd Awd; OSU.

MASON, MONICA M; Putnam City North HS; Oklahoma City, OK; (3); Church Yth Grp; German Clb; Quiz Bowl; Scholastic Bowl; Orch; NHS; Slvr Strngs; Comm Svc Cnslr Krkptrck Air & Spce Mseum; Intnl Studies.

MASON, NICHOLAS J; Coleman Schl; Coleman, OK; (3); Church Yth Grp; Cmnty Wkr; 4-H; School Play; VP Frsh Cls; VP Soph Cls; Ofcr Bsbl; Bsktbl; 4-H Awd; Hon Roll; Hunting; Fishing; Archery; Southeastern ST U.

MASON, NIKKI; Vanoss Schl; Ada, OK; (2); 5/30; Computer Clb; FBLA; Math Tm; Pres Soph Cls; JV L Bsktbl; L Sftbl; L Trk; High Hon Roll; Val; Chld Psych.

MASON II, PERRY L; Northeast HS; Oklahoma City, OK; (3); 3/107; Am Leg Boys St; VP FBLA; VP Jr Cls; Var Ftbl; Var Trk; VP Pres NHS; St Schlr; Okla City Yth Cncl; Yth Ldrshp Exch Class I; Explorer Scts Of Amer; Engr.

MASON, RHONDA; Victory Christian Schl; Broken Arrow, OK; (2); Church Yth Grp; Sec Drama Clb; Teachers Aide; Var Capt Chrldng; Gym; Vllybl; Hon Roll; Jr NHS; Pres Acad Fit Awd; All Amer Chrldr; IA ST.

MASON, RICHARD; Northwest Classen HS; Oklahoma City, OK; (4); Am Leg Boys St; Drama Clb; Letterman Clb; Pep Clb; Chorus; School Play; Nwsp; Sec Sr Cls; Sec Stu Cncl; Capt Swmmng; Homcmng Roylty; Friendshp Roylty; Oklahoma City U; Muscl Theatr.

MASON, SHERRIE D; Inola Sr HS; Inola, OK; (3); Church Yth Grp; Rptr Computer Clb; VP Pres FHA; Teachers Aide; Rep NHS; Ntl Merit Ltr; Law.

MASON, TISHA S; Coleman Schl; Coleman, OK; (2); Church Yth Grp; Cmnty Wkr; FCA; 4-H; GAA; HOBY; Quiz Bowl; SADD; School Play; Yrbk; Southeastern ST Univ.

MASSA, JESSICA; Guthrie Sr HS; Edmond, OK; (1); Hist FHA; GAA; JV Chrldng; JV Trk.

MASSEY, AMBER; Minco Jr Sr HS; Minco, OK; (3); Church Yth Grp; FCA; 4-H; GAA; Natl FFA Org; Office Aide; Spanish Clb; Sec Jr Cls; Bsktbl; Hon Roll; Csmtlgy.

MASSEY, BILLIE F; Locust Grove HS; Locust Grove, OK; (2); Natl FFA Org; Hon Roll; Prblms Of Dmcrcy; Northeastern ST U; Nrsng.

MASSEY, CORT T; Edmond Memorial HS; Edmond, OK; (3); Spanish Clb; Teachers Aide; Ofcr Frsh Cls; Ofcr Jr Cls; Ofcr Stu Cncl; Ofcr Bsbl.

MASSEY, JONATHON E; Dickson HS; Ardmore, OK; (3); Key Clb; Band; Jazz Band; Var Bsktbl; Var Crs Cntry; Var Trk; High Hon Roll; Prfct Atten Awd; 4 Time Hnr Brd 1st Chair Drums; U Of OK; Cmptr Prgrmg.

MASSEY, SARAH J; Will Rogers HS; Tulsa, OK; (1); English Clb; French Clb; High Hon Roll; Hon Roll; Jr NHS; CODE Pgm; Stdnt Today Msnc Awd; Peer Tutoring Pgm; OK ST Univ; Tchng/Cnslr.

MASSEY, VALERIE A; Lexington HS; Lexington, OK; (4); Art Clb; FHA; JA; Library Aide; Office Aide; Spanish Clb; Trk; Hon Roll; OK City CC.

MASSIE, CHRIS D; Owasso Sr HS; Owasso, OK; (2); Hon Roll; U Of OK Coll Of Geosci Smmr Cmp; U Of OK; Meteorology.

MASSIE, JOSH R; Norman Sr HS; Norman, OK; (3); Cmnty Wkr; FCA; Pep Clb; VICA; Ftbl; Trk; Natl Yth Ldrshp Forum Scurity, Dfns; Dist Spksprsn Pub Schls; Focus On Lrng Cmmtte; Law.

MASTER, PUJA G; Union Intermediate HS; Tulsa, OK; (2); Key Clb; Hon Roll; Jr NHS; NHS; Frgn Lang Clb; Soc Stud Awd; OK U; Med.

MASTER, STEWART; Broken Arrow Sr HS; Broken Arrow, OK; (4); French Clb; Key Clb; Jazz Band; Rep Sr Cls; Rep Stu Cncl; High Hon Roll; Pres NHS; Ntl Merit Ltr; Pres Acad Fit Awd; Pres Schlr; Pvt Pilots License; Space Camp Pgms; Avid Cyclist & Mountain Biker; KS U; Aerospace Engrng; Pilot.

MASTERS, MELISSA S; Westmoore HS; Oklahoma City, OK; (2); OCCC Arts Fstvl Vol 94-95; Pub Poem; Hnrbl Mntn Catch Wrtng Star Ltry Clb Cntst; OK Univ; Pschlgy.

MASTERS, MICHELLE E; Glenpool HS; Glenpool, OK; (4); 19/111; Teachers Aide; Chorus; School Musical; Co-Ed Yrbk; Mgr(s); Score Keeper; Hon Roll; Magic Music Days Disney FL; Amer Sngs Orlando 94-95; Tulsa CC; Ed.

MASTIN, SUSAN; Arkoma Jr Sr HS; Arkoma, OK; (2); 1/40; Church Yth Grp; FCA; FHA; HOBY; Sec Stu Cncl; Bsktbl; Chrldng; Sftbl; Hon Roll; St Schlr; Gftd & Tlntd Sci, Lang Arts; Westark CC.

MASTON, TOMMY V; Dibble Jr Sr HS; Alex, OK; (2); 2/48; Church Yth Grp; FCA; Natl FFA Org; Rep Stu Cncl; Var Bsbl; Var Bsktbl; Hon Roll; Pres Schlr; Letterman Clb; Scholastic Bowl; Acad Team; Var Outstdng 3-Pt Shooter 95-96; Big 8 Conf All-Star 95-96.

MATA, MAIRA; Douglass HS; Oklahoma City, OK; (3); Church Yth Grp; Cmnty Wkr; Latin Clb; ROTC; Teachers Aide; Golf; Socr; Hon Roll; Close-Up Clb Latino; Coll Clb; OK City U; Bus Admin.

MATANANE, JOSHUA J; Putnam City North HS; Oklahoma City, OK; (2); Art Clb; Intnl Clb; Latin Clb; VICA; Ofcr Jr Cls; Trk; Wrstlng; Hon Roll; Nom Run Torch 96 Olympics; OK Univ; Oceanographer; Comps.

MATHAI, PRISCILLA I; Bethany HS; Oklahoma City, OK; (3); 5/90; Church Yth Grp; Debate Tm; Sec Key Clb; High Hon Roll; NHS; Mock Trial; Yth Alive; U Of Cntrl OK; Pre-Med.

MATHEKE, HEATHER M; Eisenhower Sr HS; Lawton, OK; (3); 5/500; Cmnty Wkr; Treas FHA; Library Aide; Math Tm; High Hon Roll; Jr NHS; NHS; Aim-Hi Math Tn Plcd 1st OK; GATE Club Sec; Acad Decathln.

MATHERLY, KRISTY N; Olive Jr Sr HS; Drumright, OK; (2); Debate Tm; FBLA; Speech Tm; Hon Roll; Art Achvmt Awd.

MATHESON, BROOKE A; Ripley HS; Stillwater, OK; (2); 6/35; FCA; GAA; Math Clb; Natl FFA Org; Science Clb; Sec Frsh Cls; Sec Soph Cls; JV Bsktbl; Var Sftbl; Hon Roll; Invstgtr.

MATHESON, CHRIS J; Inola Sr HS; Inola, OK; (3); Computer Clb; Library Aide; Science Clb; Teachers Aide; Hon Roll; Prfct Atten Awd; Repair/Cnstrct Elec Dvcs.

MATHESON, SHAWN C; Perkins-Tryon HS; Tryon, OK; (2); FCA; Intnl Clb; Var Yrbk; Ofcr Bsbl; Bsktbl; Ftbl; Wt Lftg; Wrstlng; High Hon Roll; NHS; OK Hnr Soc.

MATHEW, ELIZABETH; Jenks HS; Jenks, OK; (3); Church Yth Grp; Cmnty Wkr; Mu Alpha Theta; Spanish Clb; Chorus; Church Choir; Ofcr Stu Cncl; Hon Roll; NHS; Prfct Atten Awd.

MATHEW, JOLLY P; Mustang HS; Yukon, OK; (3); 1/405; Treas Church Yth Grp; Key Clb; Band; Mrchg Band; Pep Band; Yrbk; High Hon Roll; Hon Roll; NHS; Prfct Atten Awd; Nrsng Hme Vol; Tutor; OK Cntrl Univ; Pediatrcs.

MATHEW, SANTOSH T; Mustang HS; Yukon, OK; (3); Church Yth Grp; Computer Clb; Spanish Clb; Temple Yth Grp; Band; Jazz Band; Mrchg Band; Pep Band; Stage Crew; Hon Roll; Sci Fair 3rd Pl; NW Phillips Univ Hon Band 3 Yrs; U Of OK Engrng Camp/Acad Achvmnt Awd; U Of OK; Engrng.

MATHEWS, BELINDA; New Lima Jr Sr HS; Seminole, OK; (4); 2/22; Rptr Nwsp; Rep Soph Cls; VP Jr Cls; Pres Stu Cncl; Bsktbl; Sftbl; High Hon Roll; Jr NHS; NHS; East Central U; Accntng.

MATHEWS, CARRIE S; Olive Jr Sr HS; Mannford, OK; (2); 1/35; Church Yth Grp; FBLA; HOBY; Rep Stu Cncl; Var Bsktbl; Var Trk; High Hon Roll; Congress-Bundestag Yth Exch Schlsp; Frgn Exch Stu 96-97; Pre-Med.

MATHEWS, JEREMY D; Warner HS; Webbers Falls, OK; (3); FCA; Spanish Clb; Rep Jr Cls; Var L Bsktbl; Var L Ftbl; Var L Trk; Var Wt Lftg; High Hon Roll; Teens For Christ; I Dare You Awd.

MATHEWS, MEAGAN M; Sayre HS; Sayre, OK; (1); 3/71; Church Yth Grp; FHA; Band; Chorus; Church Choir; Cit Awd; High Hon Roll; NHS; Mrchg Band; Pep Band; Otstndng Bd/Choir Mem; Red Crpt Comm Theatre; Dist/Rgnl Hnr Choir; K101 Hnr Bnd; Southwestern OK ST U; Music.

MATHEWS, PYPER L; West Middle HS; Norman, OK; (2); Church Yth Grp; Drama Clb; 4-H; Girl Scts; Hosp Aide; Library Aide; Office Aide; Red Cross Aide; Science Clb; Ski Clb; Brigham Young Univ; Govt.

MATHIAS, JACOB A; Cleveland Sr HS; Cleveland, OK; (3); Var Ftbl; JV Trk; Var Wt Lftg; OK U.

MATHIAS, WILLIAM J; Choctaw HS; Oklahoma City, OK; (3); Church Yth Grp; FCA; Spanish Clb; JV Bsbl; High Hon Roll; Hon Roll; Chrch Act; OK U.

MATHIESEN, MALISSA A; Lawton Sr HS; Lawton, OK; (3); Band; Mrchg Band; Orch; Pep Band; Stage Crew; Hon Roll; Prfct Atten Awd; Chrldr; Sftbl.

MATHIS, ATHENA; Westmoore HS; Oklahoma City, OK; (3); Library Aide; Office Aide; Rep Stu Cncl; Var Bsktbl; Var Golf; Var Sftbl; Var Trk; Hon Roll; NHS; Pres Acad Fit Awd; AAU Bsktbl Team; Var Ltr Sports; Phy Thrpst.

MATHIS, CODY S; Muldrow HS; Muldrow, OK; (4); Math Clb; Natl FFA Org; Office Aide; Band; Jazz Band; Mrchg Band; Orch; Pep Band; JV Bsbl; Hon Roll.

MATHIS, HEATHER A; Hooker Jr-Sr HS; Hooker, OK; (4); 3/36; Church Yth Grp; Pres FHA; Quiz Bowl; Teachers Aide; Band; Chorus; School Musical; Ed Yrbk; Ofcr Stu Cncl; Var Golf; Slctd To Srv On Comm Ed & Advy Cncl; Mem Of OK Hnr Soc; OK ST U.

MATHIS, JODI L; Muldrow HS; Muldrow, OK; (1); Spanish Clb; Band; Mrchg Band; Orch; Bsktbl; Trk; Hon Roll.

MATHIS, LAURA; Heritage Hall Schl; Oklahoma City, OK; (1); Church Yth Grp; FCA; French Clb; Pep Clb; Chorus; Variety Show; Chrldng; Fld Hcky; Gym.

MATHIS, RICHARD D; Heritage Hall Schl; Oklahoma City, OK; (3); Cmnty Wkr; FCA; French Clb; Letterman Clb; Wrstlng.

MATHIS, SHELLY L; Enid Sr HS; Enid, OK; (3); Letterman Clb; Math Clb; Natl Beta Clb; Quiz Bowl; Scholastic Bowl; Crs Cntry; High Hon Roll; Jr NHS; NHS; Pres Acad Fit Awd; OK ST Univ; Pre-Law.

MATHURA, SASHA; Douglass HS; Oklahoma City, OK; (3); Band; Mrchg Band; Hon Roll; NHS.

MATLI, CARINA D; Ponca City Sr HS; Ponca City, OK; (4); 28/348; Church Yth Grp; French Clb; Chorus; Flag Corp; Mrchg Band; Orch; Mgr Bsbl; High Hon Roll; NHS; Office Aide; Msc Mnstry.

MATLOCK, GREG W; Tuttle HS; Tuttle, OK; (3); Letterman Clb; Wrstlng; Cntrl ST Univ; Criminal Just.

MATLOCK, JANICE E; Catoosa HS; Tulsa, OK; (4); FCA; Office Aide; Sftbl; High Hon Roll; Hon Roll; OSU; Grphc Dsgn.

MATLOCK, KATIE A; Charles Page HS; Sand Springs, OK; (1); GAA; Bsktbl; Crs Cntry; Golf; Trk; Hon Roll; NY U; Bus.

MATLOCK, KRISTY; Silo HS; Mead, OK; (3); 4/21; Math Clb; Mu Alpha Theta; Ed Yrbk; Rep Soph Cls; Sec Jr Cls; Hon Roll.

MATLOCK, SCOTT R; Stillwater Sr HS; Stillwater, OK; (2); Boy Scts; Church Yth Grp; FCA; JCL; Key Clb; Latin Clb; Letterman Clb; Acpl Chr; Band; Chorus; OK ST Univ; Architecture.

MATLOCK, TALISA F; Bartlesville Sr HS; Bartlesville, OK; (3); 61/470; Church Yth Grp; French Clb; French Hon Soc; High Hon Roll; Hon Roll; NHS; Prfct Atten Awd; Yth Ct; Natl Fr Hnr Soc; Bus Admin.

MATON, PETRA B S; Casady Schl; Oklahoma City, OK; (4); Art Clb; Intnl Clb; Varsity Clb; School Play; Nwsp; Phtg Yrbk; Ed Lit Mag; Var L Diving; Var L Swmmng; Ntl Merit SF; Ballet; Violin; Accepted To Quartz Mtn Art Inst; Art Inst Of Chicago; Grap Dsgn.

MATOUSEK, JENNIFER; Hennessey HS; Hennessey, OK; (4); 1/54; Am Leg Aux Girls St; Church Yth Grp; Dance Clb; Pres FHA; Quiz Bowl; Scholastic Bowl; Ed Nwsp; Rep Stu Cncl; Val; FCA; Kngfshr Cty Jr Miss; Phillips U; Ophtlmlgst.

MATOUSEK, KATIE; Hennessey HS; Hennessey, OK; (2); FCA; Rep Frsh Cls; Rptr Soph Cls; Rep Stu Cncl; Var JV Bsktbl; Var Mgr(s); Var Trk; High Hon Roll; NHS; Pres Acad Fit Awd; Piano.

MATSON, BRANDY D; Durant HS; Durant, OK; (2); Church Yth Grp; Chorus; Bsktbl; Crs Cntry; Trk; Vllybl; High Hon Roll; NHS; Pres Acad Fit Awd; Val; Space Camp; Spr Rtng ST Choir Solo Cntst; All Dist Choir 9-10th Grds; Sthstrn TX A&M; Astronaut.

MATSON, CANDY J; Yukon HS; Yukon, OK; (3); 2/415; FHA; Quiz Bowl; Scholastic Bowl; Spanish Clb; NHS.

MATTHEWS, BOYD W; Durant HS; Durant, OK; (1); Church Yth Grp; FCA; Var Bsbl; Var Bsktbl; Var Ftbl; Var Ltr In Bsbl As A Frosh; Ftbl Coach.

MATTHEWS, DIANNA L; Claremore Sr HS; Claremore, OK; (1); Church Yth Grp; Chorus; Hon Roll; OSU; Vet Med.

MATTHEWS, DUSTYN R; Caney Valley HS; Broken Arrow, OK; (3); Church Yth Grp; Key Clb; Band; Chorus; Jazz Band; Mrchg Band; Bsktbl; Ftbl; Socr; Trk; Bible Mjr.

MATTHEWS, KARLENA; Fairland Jr Sr HS; Afton, OK; (4); 10/38; Church Yth Grp; Pres VP 4-H; Key Clb; Math Clb; Quiz Bowl; Red Cross Aide; Speech Tm; Teachers Aide; Lbrn Chorus; School Play; Pres Acad Achvmt Awd; CNA Nrsng Home; Gold Medal Cmptn Speech-OO Dist & Regional; ST Fair CC; Nrsng.

MATTHEWS, LEKESHA R; Purcell HS; Purcell, OK; (3); 7/90; Cmnty Wkr; GAA; Key Clb; Office Aide; Spanish Clb; Teachers Aide; Church Choir; Color Guard; Flag Corp; Ofcr Stu Cncl; OK Univ; Acctg.

MATTHEWS, MINDY; Madill HS; Madill, OK; (3); Pres Church Yth Grp; FCA; Quiz Bowl; Band; Chorus; School Musical; Sec Frsh Cls; Sec Jr Cls; Rep Stu Cncl; NHS; Ed.

MATTHEWS, RACHEL N; Purcell HS; Purcell, OK; (3); 4/97; VP FCA; Spanish Clb; Rep Stu Cncl; Var Bsktbl; Capt Chrldng; Var Golf; Var Sftbl; Var Trk; Hon Roll; NHS; Sclgy/Crmnlgy.

MATTHEWS, TERRA; Perry Sr HS; Perry, OK; (2); GAA; Spanish Clb; Band; Mrchg Band; Pep Band; Bsktbl; Powder Puff Ftbl; Hon Roll; Jr NHS; OSU; Psych.

MATTINGLY, LISA; Mustang HS; Mustang, OK; (4); 1/340; Church Yth Grp; Key Clb; Math Clb; SADD; Teachers Aide; Church Choir; School Play; NHS; Val; Drama Clb; Yth Alive Pres; OK City Univ; Bio.

MATTIX, CHANTEL M; Nathan Hale HS; Tulsa, OK; (1); Hon Roll; Damar Schl Of Drama; NSU; Nurse Or Actress.

MATTOX, SHANNON J; Drumright HS; Drumright, OK; (1); FCA; 4-H; Scholastic Bowl; Spanish Clb; Bsktbl; JV Var Sftbl; Var JV Vllybl; Hon Roll; Acctnt.

MATTS, JESSICA B; Stillwater Sr HS; Stillwater, OK; (2); 71/353; Hist German Clb; Band; Mrchg Band; Pep Band; Hon Roll; SWOSU Sci & Math Acad; Var Schlr; Sci.

MATZ, KASI; Arapaho Schl; Arapaho, OK; (2); Rep Church Yth Grp; Sec 4-H; VP FHA; Chorus; Church Choir; Co-Capt Soph Cls; 4-H Awd; Hon Roll; Pres Acad Fit Awd; Pres Schlr; Ctznshp Focus WA DC Trip 4-H; OK 1st Church Of Gov Yth Choir Priority; OK ST U; Poltcl Sci.

MAUER, SARAH J; Putnam City West HS; Bethany, OK; (1); JCL; Latin Clb; Nwsp; Var Socr; Outstandng Acad Achvt Keyboarding I; Casmeo Math Awrns Wk Tesselation Cont Sr High Level Wnnr.

MAULDIN, ANDREA L; El Reno Sr HS; Calumet, OK; (1); Church Yth Grp; Bsktbl; Crs Cntry; Golf; Hon Roll; NHS; Ldrs Of Tomorrow.

MAULDIN, ERIN; Pauls Valley HS; Pauls Valley, OK; (2); Church Yth Grp; FCA; GAA; Yrbk; Bsktbl; Tennis; Hon Roll; NHS; Prfct Atten Awd; Pi Phi Pi; OK St Hnr Soc.

MAULDIN, WILLIAM; Tahlequah Sr HS; Tahlequah, OK; (4); 26/250; Boy Scts; Pres Church Yth Grp; FCA; Rep FBLA; Mu Alpha Theta; Office Aide; Teachers Aide; L Ftbl; Hon Roll; NHS; Muskogee Dist Yth Cncl Rep OK Annual Conf; DECA; BSA Order Arrow; OCU; Bus.

MAUPIN, JOHN THOMAS; Moore HS; Moore, OK; (2); Spanish Clb; Pres Soph Cls; JV Bsbl; Bsktbl; Var Ftbl; Var Wt Lftg; Hon Roll; Jr NHS; Ntl Merit Ltr; Msnc Ldg Stu Tdy Awd.

MAURER, DOUGLAS S; Midwest City HS; Midwest City, OK; (2); French Clb; FHA; Library Aide; Band; Mrchg Band; Ofcr Bsbl; Wrstlng; U OK; Engr.

MAURER, JULIE; Midwest City HS; Midwest City, OK; (4); FHA; German Clb; Pep Clb; Band; Jazz Band; Mrchg Band; Chrldng; Hon Roll; OK ST U; Bus.

MAURER, LEANNA C; Ponca City Sr HS; Ponca City, OK; (3); Drama Clb; Spanish Clb; Color Guard; Flag Corp; Ofcr Stu Cncl; JV Sftbl; Vllybl; Hon Roll; Jr NHS; Colorguard Rookie Of Yr; Best Colorguad; Med Explorers; Miss Ponca City Pageant; PT.

MAUTE, MARIA; Afton HS; Afton, OK; (3); 2/40; Cmnty Wkr; Office Aide; Quiz Bowl; Yrbk; Var Sftbl; High Hon Roll; Hon Roll; Ntl Merit Ltr.

MAUTE, ROSS; Afton HS; Afton, OK; (1); 1/40; Cmnty Wkr; Speech Tm; Yrbk; Rep Stu Cncl; JV Bsktbl; Var Trk; Hon Roll; Ntl Merit Ltr.

MAXEY, DARRYL W; Tushka HS; Atoka, OK; (3); Natl FFA Org; Hosa; Natl Voc Hnr Soc; OU; Phy Thrpst.

MAXEY, JENNIFER N; Enid Sr HS; Enid, OK; (2); Church Yth Grp; Pep Clb; Teachers Aide; Chorus; School Play; Swing Chorus; Variety Show; High Hon Roll; Hon Roll; Jr NHS; NHS; Psych.

MAXEY, JOHN W; Yukon Middle HS; Yukon, OK; (3); Church Yth Grp; Band; Jazz Band; Mrchg Band; Orch; Pep Band; School Musical; School Play; JV Ftbl; Multi-Yr Listee; OK; Music.

MAXEY, WYNTER R; Quinton Jr Sr HS; Porum, OK; (3); 3/36; Am Leg Aux Girls St; Church Yth Grp; Debate Tm; Drama Clb; FCA; FHA; Quiz Bowl; Speech Tm; Church Choir; Sec Soph Cls; Natl Yth Ldrshp Conf Washington DC; OSU; Pre Med.

MAXSON, JENNIFER M; Ponca City Sr HS; Ponca City, OK; (4); 1/350; Church Yth Grp; Cmnty Wkr; Hosp Aide; Spanish Clb; Band; Flag Corp; Mrchg Band; Orch; NHS; Ntl Merit Ltr; OK ST U; Cvl Engrng.

MAXSON, JOSHUA; Miami Sr HS; Miami, OK; (4); 25/191; Am Leg Boys St; Church Yth Grp; FCA; Natl FFA Org; Teachers Aide; Var Bsbl; JV Ftbl; Var Wt Lftg; High Hon Roll; NHS; Northeastern A&M; Jrnlsm.

MAXWELL, HOLLIE D; Lomega HS; Omega, OK; (2); 6/15; Church Yth Grp; 4-H; Quiz Bowl; Scholastic Bowl; Yrbk; Stat Bsktbl; Mgr(s); Hon Roll.

MAXWELL, HOLLY G; Bartlesville Mid HS; Bartlesville, OK; (2); 113/481; Church Yth Grp; Library Aide; Band; Chorus; Church Choir; Color Guard; Hon Roll; Elem Ed.

MAXWELL, JASON; Metro Christian Acad; Tulsa, OK; (3); FCA; Pres Hist Key Clb; Letterman Clb; Teachers Aide; Ofcr Stu Cncl; Var L Ftbl; Wt Lftg; High Hon Roll; Sec NHS; Prfct Atten Awd; Natl Yth Ldrshp Del; 2nd Degree Blck Blt; Chem Engr/Pre-Med/Sec Ed.

MAXWELL, JEREMIAH B; Spiro HS; Keota, OK; (4); Church Yth Grp; FCA; Natl FFA Org; Ftbl; All-Dist Ftbl; All-Area SWTR Ftbl; Eufaula Ftbl Clsc All-Star; Carl Albert ST Coll.

MAY, ASHLEY; Claremore Sr HS; Claremore, OK; (3); 35/239; Church Yth Grp; Hosp Aide; Office Aide; Spanish Clb; Teachers Aide; Band; Jazz Band; Mrchg Band; Pep Band; Hon Roll; All Dist Band; OSU; Bus.

MAY, BETHANY; Bartlesville Mid HS; Bartlesville, OK; (3); 94/481; Office Aide; Rep Stu Cncl; Var Sftbl; Hon Roll; Jr NHS; K-Life Yth Grp; ASA Fastpitch Sftbl Tm Pitcher 18 Yrs; U Of OK.

MAY, CASEY; Carl Albert HS; Midwest City, OK; (4); 52/241; Art Clb; FCA; Key Clb; Pep Clb; SADD; Chorus; School Musical; Ofcr Frsh Cls; Chrldng; NHS; OK ST U.

MAY, CHANDA L; Copan HS; Copan, OK; (2); 2/32; Chess Clb; Quiz Bowl; Scholastic Bowl; Band; Jazz Band; Mrchg Band; Ofcr Stu Cncl; Mgr(s); Sftbl; Trk; Pdtrcn.

MAY, CHRIS; Clinton HS; Clinton, OK; (3); 1/150; Sec Church Yth Grp; HOBY; Rep Key Clb; Band; Chorus; Rep Stu Cncl; Diving; Socr; High Hon Roll; NHS; Astrntcl Engr.

MAY, JUSTIN; Altus Sr HS; Altus, OK; (2); Church Yth Grp; FCA; Natl FFA Org; L Bsbl; L Bsktbl; L Ftbl; Intrml Wt Lftg; High Hon Roll; Hon Roll; Prfct Atten Awd; OK Univ; PT Sprts Med.

MAY, KRISTI; Turner Schl; Leon, OK; (3); 3/19; Church Yth Grp; Natl Beta Clb; Quiz Bowl; Rptr Nwsp; Yrbk; Sec Soph Cls; High Hon Roll; NHS; Prfct Atten Awd; Med.

MAY, MICHELLE; Watonga HS; Watonga, OK; (4); 1/58; Am Leg Aux Girls St; 4-H; Pres Sec FBLA; HOBY; Sec Sr Cls; Rep Stu Cncl; Capt Bsktbl; Trk; NHS; Val; OK ST U; Bus.

MAY, RACHEL; Hominy HS; Hominy, OK; (2); Teachers Aide; Bsktbl; JV Var Sftbl; Trk; Kiwanis Awd; Prfct Atten Awd; Med Sec/Transcriber.

MAY, STACEY; Carl Albert HS; Midwest City, OK; (4); 46/241; FCA; Key Clb; Ofcr Frsh Cls; Ofcr Stu Cncl; Var Chrldng; Hon Roll; Jr NHS; Kiwanis Awd; NHS; Ntl Merit Ltr; OK ST.

MAY, STEPHANIE; Oklahoma Christian Schl; Edmond, OK; (1); Church Yth Grp; Red Cross Aide; Var Bsktbl; Var Chrldng; High Hon Roll; Sci Fair Comp Wnnr.

MAYBERRY, MELISSA M; Elmore City Jr Sr HS; Elmore City, OK; (3); 1/48; Church Yth Grp; FCA; FHA; Band; Drm Mjr(t); Mrchg Band; Treas Stu Cncl; Var Bsktbl; High Hon Roll; NHS; East Cntrl Univ; Phy Therapy.

MAYBERRY, SHAWNA R; Chickasha HS; Chickasha, OK; (1); 4-H; Girl Scts; Spanish Clb; SADD; Bsktbl; Socr; 4-H Awd; U Of AK Anchorage.

MAYDEN, DONNIE W; Blackwell HS; Blackwell, OK; (2); Boy Scts; Church Yth Grp; Math Tm; Red Cross Aide; Spanish Clb; Varsity Clb; Acpl Chr; Chorus; School Musical; JV Ftbl; Red Crss Swmmng Tchr; Natl Yth Ldrshp Forum; Law.

MAYER, ELEANOR; Stillwater Jr HS; Stillwater, OK; (1); Quiz Bowl; Church Choir; Orch; High Hon Roll; Pres Acad Fit Awd; Med/Pdtrc Onclgy.

MAYES IV, CARLOS DAYNE; Tahlequah Jr HS; Tahlequah, OK; (1); Church Yth Grp; Ftbl; Trk; Wt Lftg; Wrstlng; Pres Acad Fit Awd; Chrch Yth Group Pres; Yth Ministry.

MAYES, CHRIS; Millwood HS; Oklahoma City, OK; (3); ROTC; Mrchg Band; Var Bsbl; Var L Ftbl; Wt Lftg; Air Frc Acad; Aerospc Engrng.

MAYES, HOLLY D; Miami Sr HS; Miami, OK; (4); 10/125; Library Aide; Teachers Aide; Chorus; VP Sr Cls; High Hon Roll; Hon Roll; NHS; All Dist Slct Choir; US Natl Ldrshp Merit Awrd; Cottey Coll; Bus.

MAYES, RYAN; Northeast HS; Oklahoma City, OK; (4); 1/125; Am Leg Boys St; Chess Clb; HOBY; Scholastic Bowl; Var Tennis; NHS; Ntl Merit Schol; Val; FBLA; Mu Alpha Theta; AP Schlr; All-ST Orch; OK Yth Orch; Stanford; Music/Sci Rsrch.

MAYES, TYQUONNA D; John Marshall HS; Oklahoma City, OK; (4); Spanish Clb; Tennis; Cit Awd; High Hon Roll; Hon Roll; Cmptr Techlgy; Making The Grade; Teen Club; TX A&M; Lawyer/Cmptr Techn.

MAYFIELD, BOBBIE; Wellston Schl; Wellston, OK; (2); Drama Clb; FHA; Hon Roll; NHS.

MAYFIELD, DAWN M; South Intermediate HS; Broken Arrow, OK; (2); Church Yth Grp; Band; Color Guard; Socr; Hon Roll; Jr NHS; NHS; Club Soccer; OK HS Hnr Society 95-96.

MAYFIELD, GRACE D; Durant HS; Durant, OK; (2); Church Yth Grp; Band; Chorus; Jazz Band; Mrchg Band; Pep Band; Variety Show; OK All ST Chorus 96; Southeastern OK All Dist Symphonic Bnd 96; SOSU Curr Cntnst Eng II 1st Pl.

MAYFIELD, LEAH R; Erick Jr Sr HS; Erick, OK; (2); 1/18; Church Yth Grp; FHA; Scholastic Bowl; Teachers Aide; Rep Frsh Cls; Rptr Soph Cls; Rep Stu Cncl; Var Bsktbl; High Hon Roll; TSA Level I Rptr.

MAYHEW, MATTHEW; Midwest City HS; Midwest City, OK; (3); 28/388; German Clb; Office Aide; SADD; Ofcr Bsbl; Ftbl; Hon Roll; Jr NHS; Stu Of Yr; Outstndng Soc Stud, Math Awds.

MAYLEN, BETH A; Morris HS; Henryetta, OK; (2); Church Yth Grp; 4-H; Natl FFA Org; Office Aide; Spanish Clb; Teachers Aide; Varsity Clb; Var Bsktbl; Var Sftbl; Hon Roll; Ath Coach.

MAYNARD, DANIELLE R; Purcell HS; Purcell, OK; (3); Church Yth Grp; SADD; Rep Stu Cncl; JV Var Bsktbl; High Hon Roll; Hon Roll; Pres NHS; Cmnty Wkr; Drama Clb; Spanish Clb; U Of OK Hnrs Awd; Ltr P Awd; Coach Spec Olympcs Sftbl; OK U; Pub Rel.

MAYO, BECKY; Washington HS; Purcell, OK; (1); Pep Clb; Trk; Hon Roll; OK Univ.

MAYO, COREY E; Dewey HS; Bartlesville, OK; (3); 5/83; Church Yth Grp; Drama Clb; FCA; Pres Jr Cls; Pres Sr Cls; Bsktbl; Ftbl; Golf; Hon Roll; NHS.

MAYO, CRYSTAL; Mc Alester HS; Mcalester, OK; (3); 19/200; FCA; Spanish Clb; Band; Mrchg Band; Var Chrldng; Var Crs Cntry; Var Trk; Cit Awd; Hon Roll; All Amer Chrldr.

MAYO II, HAROLD; Sperry Sr HS; Sperry, OK; (3); #3 in class; Church Yth Grp; Scholastic Bowl; Band; Rep Stu Cncl; L Tennis; 4-H Awd; High Hon Roll; Hon Roll; NHS; OK Hnr Scty; Comp Sci.

MAYO, JAMES C; South Intermediate HS; Broken Arrow, OK; (1); Art Clb; Church Yth Grp; Band; Mrchg Band; Pep Band; Hon Roll; Tulsa Univ.

MAYO, RYAN R; Central Schl; Sallisaw, OK; (2); Var Bsbl; Var Bsktbl; Octagon Clb.

MAYS, PAUL; Newcastle HS; Newcastle, OK; (3); 7/96; Art Clb; Spanish Clb; Hon Roll; Prfct Atten Awd.

MAYS, RHONDA A; Will Rogers HS; Tulsa, OK; (2); Rep Stu Cncl; Var Bsktbl; Sociology.

MAYS, SANDRA L; Fairland Jr Sr HS; Fairland, OK; (4); Girl Scts; Speech Tm; Teachers Aide; Acpl Chr; Band; Chorus; Drm Mjr(t); Mrchg Band; Pep Band; School Musical; Masonic Acad Awd 3 Yrs; Pittsburg ST U; Music.

MAYWALD, KIMBERLY R; Altus Sr HS; Altus, OK; (3); 14/200; Church Yth Grp; Pres FHA; ROTC; Speech Tm; Church Choir; School Play; Ofcr Stu Cncl; French Hon Soc; Gov Hon Prg Awd; NHS; OK Bapt Univ; Elem Ed.

MAZAK, SHAUNA K; Macomb Schl; Macomb, OK; (1); Sec Soph Cls; Mgr Bsktbl; Mgr(s); JV Sftbl; Hon Roll; NHS; Pres Acad Fit Awd; Reading; Endangered Species; U Of OK; Acting; Drama; Vet Med.

MAZEY, PATRICIA; Tushka HS; Atoka, OK; (2); 8/24; 4-H; FHA; Bsktbl; Sftbl; Swmmng; Vllybl; Hon Roll; Prfct Atten Awd.

MAZUR, JOSH J; Blanchard Jr Sr HS; Blanchard, OK; (2); Computer Clb; Mu Alpha Theta; Spanish Clb; Band; Mrchg Band; Var Bsbl; Var Bsktbl; Var Ftbl; High Hon Roll; NHS; OK Univ; Arch Engr.

MAZZA, RAL; Guthrie Sr HS; Guthrie, OK; (3); Ofcr Stu Cncl; Tennis; Cit Awd.

MC ABEE, KEVIN P; Stillwater Sr HS; Stillwater, OK; (3); French Clb; German Clb; Spanish Clb; Band; Orch; OSU; Comp Sci.

MC ADAMS JR, FRANKIE J; Mc Alester HS; Mcalester, OK; (4); FHA; Spanish Clb; VICA; Mixed Choir.

MC ADOO, JASON G; Norman Sr HS; Norman, OK; (3); Church Yth Grp; FCA; Office Aide; Spanish Clb; Chorus; Church Choir; Ofcr Stu Cncl; Hon Roll; NHS; Jazz Choir; OK Bapt U; Yth Ministry.

MC AFEE, BRITTA; Muskogee HS; Muskogee, OK; (4); 1/303; Church Yth Grp; Model UN; VP Spanish Clb; Treas Stu Cncl; Var JV Sftbl; Var Swmmng; St Schlr; Val; French Clb; Key Clb; Ecology Clb Sgt At Arms; Yng Democrats; OU.

MC AFEE, TERRI L; Cleveland Sr HS; Cleveland, OK; (4); 39/90; Church Yth Grp; FCA; Key Clb; Spanish Clb; SADD; Teachers Aide; Chorus; School Musical; School Play; Yrbk; Girl Sct Silver & Gold Awds; Cleveland Ed Assn Schlsp; OK Bapt Univ; Elem Ed.

MC AFFREY, JENNIFER K; Mustang HS; Yukon, OK; (1); #1 in class; Art Clb; High Hon Roll; Art I/OK His/Eng I Awds; Pub Ilstrtn Schls Crtv Wrtng Anthlgy; Art/Bus.

MC ALISTER, PATRICK L; Claremore Sr HS; Claremore, OK; (2); Church Yth Grp; Church Choir; Ftbl; Trk; High Hon Roll; U Of OK; Engrng.

MC ALLISTER, JOSHUA; Duncan HS; Duncan, OK; (2); Church Yth Grp; French Clb; Hosp Aide; Quiz Bowl; SADD; Band; Jazz Band; Mrchg Band; Pep Band; Stage Crew; Chrch Hndbls; SW OK All Rgn Hnr Bnd 2 Yrs; Asst Drum Major HS Band; Med.

MC ATEER, CHRISTIE; Jenks HS; Tulsa, OK; (1); Church Yth Grp; Key Clb; Pep Clb; Ofcr Stu Cncl; JV Chrldng; Wt Lftg; Psych.

MC AVOY, MICHELLE; Yukon Middle HS; Yukon, OK; (2); 9/537; Rptr Church Yth Grp; HOBY; Capt Quiz Bowl; VP Spanish Clb; Church Choir; Ofcr Stu Cncl; High Hon Roll; St Schlr; Scholastic Bowl; Odyssey Mind Cmptn; 1st Rnnr Up Spnsh Clb.

MC BEE, BRANDON M; Putnam City North HS; Oklahoma City, OK; (2); 78/550; Church Yth Grp; JV Bsbl; JV Ftbl; Hon Roll; NHS; Engr.

MC BEE, HEATHER; Owasso Sr HS; Owasso, OK; (4); 25/296; Science Clb; Spanish Clb; Teachers Aide; Band; Color Guard; Flag Corp; Mrchg Band; Treas Soph Cls; Hon Roll; NHS; Sr Brd; Pageants; His Natl Hon Soc; Dartmouth Coll; Recstrct Surg.

MC BRIDE, JENNIFER; Wetumka Jr Sr HS; Wetumka, OK; (2); 11/48; Church Yth Grp; FCA; Natl FFA Org; Office Aide; Band; Flag Corp; Mrchg Band; Sec Frsh Cls; Sec Soph Cls; Hon Roll.

MC BRIDE, JENNIFER L; Elgin HS; Lawton, OK; (4); 17/75; Church Yth Grp; Cmnty Wkr; FCA; FHA; Natl FFA Org; Office Aide; SADD; Teachers Aide; Rep Sr Cls; Rep Stu Cncl; Cameron Univ; Elem Ed.

MC BRIDE, JESSICA; Ardmore HS; Ardmore, OK; (2); Treas DECA; Drama Clb; Sec Latin Clb; Teachers Aide; Chorus; School Musical; School Play; Hon Roll; Capt Odssy Of Mind Team; Bourbon St Plyrsdrama Grp; Ltl Thtr Prfrmr; Julliard; Thtr.

MC BRIDE, JESSICA T; Pawhuska HS; Pawhuska, OK; (1); Church Yth Grp; Cmnty Wkr; Girl Scts; Natl FFA Org; Band; Chorus; Church Choir; Jazz Band; Mrchg Band; Swing Chorus; Outstdng Soprano; Outstdnt Frosh Band Mem; Comm Theater; Music Ed/Bio.

MC BRIDE, KJERSTI J; Memorial HS; Tulsa, OK; (2); Hist Boy Scts; Cmnty Wkr; French Clb; Key Clb; Teachers Aide; Rptr Nwsp; Intrml Chrldng; Hon Roll; Jr NHS; Presdntl Yth Awd; Govrnrs Commndtn; Camp Fir Mem Ldr & Histrn; Earnd BSA Explorng Gold Awd; Peer Tutor; OU; Child Psycht.

MC BRIDE, LARRY D; Cushing HS; Cushing, OK; (1); JV Bsbl; Bsktbl; Ftbl; Wt Lftg; Hon Roll.

MC BRIDE, MARK; Newcastle HS; Newcastle, OK; (3); Natl FFA Org; Science Clb; Spanish Clb; Jr NHS; NHS; Eagle Sct.

MC BRIDE, MICHAEL CRAIG; Westmoore HS; Oklahoma City, OK; (4); 19/610; Church Yth Grp; Spanish Clb; Rptr Nwsp; Rep Stu Cncl; High Hon Roll; NHS; Val; Two Yr Acad Letterman; U Of Cntrl OK.

MC BRIDE, SHERRI L; Caney Jr Sr HS; Caney, OK; (3); 1/23; Church Yth Grp; Cmnty Wkr; FCA; 4-H; FHA; GAA; Hosp Aide; Office Aide; Scholastic Bowl; Speech Tm; Highest Grd Pnt Avrg; Dist FHA Pres; Cty 4 H Pres; Murray ST Coll; RN.

MC BROOM, BRIAN A; Fairview HS; Isabella, OK; (3); Scholastic Bowl; Band; Mrchg Band; Pep Band; School Musical; Cit Awd; High Hon Roll; NHS; Mbr Tech Stdnt Assn.

MC CABE, AMY L; Wilson HS; Healdton, OK; (3); 9/38; Am Leg Aux Girls St; Natl Beta Clb; Office Aide; Quiz Bowl; Spanish Clb; Teachers Aide; Band; Flag Corp; Mrchg Band; Hon Roll; Gifted/Talented; SE OK ST U; RN.

MC CABE, BETH; Wilburton Jr HS; Wilburton, OK; (1); 2/88; Church Yth Grp; Speech Tm; Band; Jazz Band; Mrchg Band; Pep Band; VP Stu Cncl; High Hon Roll; Acad Tm; OK ST U; Arch.

MC CABE, JENNY; Bethel HS; Shawnee, OK; (3); 6/66; Church Yth Grp; Drama Clb; FCA; French Clb; HOBY; SADD; Band; Var Trk; High Hon Roll; NHS; Lifeguides Peer Ldr; Color Guard Capt; Jazz Band; OK Bapt U; Cnslng.

MC CAGHREN, JAYE P; Union Intermediate HS; Broken Arrow, OK; (2); Spanish Clb; Teachers Aide; Band; Color Guard; Mrchg Band; Hon Roll; NHS; Jane Goodalls Roots/Shoots Pgm; Law.

MC CAHREN, JAYE P; Union Intermediate HS; Owensboro, KY; (2); 80/890; Cmnty Wkr; Dance Clb; Spanish Clb; Teachers Aide; Band; Color Guard; Mrchg Band; Swmmng; Hon Roll; Jr NHS; Natl Sr Hnr Soc; Regncy Sci Prjct Wnnr; All Dist Band.

MC CAIN, KRISTAL V; Hinton HS; Hinton, OK; (2); FHA; SADD; Band; Mrchg Band; Stage Crew; Bsktbl; Crs Cntry; Mgr(s); Trk; Hon Roll; Southwestern OK ST Univ.

MC CAIN, MARCUS; Glencoe Public Schl; Glencoe, OK; (1); 7/40; Natl FFA Org; JV Bsbl.

MC CAIN, ROYCE L; Broken Bow HS; Broken Bow, OK; (3); Church Yth Grp; Drama Clb; FHA; Speech Tm; Chorus; Stage Crew; Speech Trnmt 1st Pl; Drama Clb Twig Awd; Schl Musicals; Elem Schl Tchr.

MC CAIN, SARAH; Clinton HS; Clinton, OK; (4); 19/99; Am Leg Aux Girls St; Drama Clb; Hist FHA; VP Treas Key Clb; Science Clb; Spanish Clb; School Play; Ed Yrbk; Sec Soph Cls; Sec Jr Cls; S W OK ST U; Acctng.

MC CALIP, SHARI; Lindsay HS; Lindsay, OK; (1); Art Clb; Church Yth Grp; FHA; Pep Clb; Scholastic Bowl; JV Chrldng; JV Mgr(s).

MC CALL, ALYSA; Westmoore HS; Oklahoma City, OK; (3); GAA; JCL; Latin Clb; Sprt Ed Nwsp; Var L Bsktbl; Var L Sftbl; Hon Roll; Jr NHS; NHS; All City Slow Ptch Sftbl 95-; 3 Sprt Lttrmn 95-; 4 Pnt Acad Awd 94-95; Pre Med.

MC CALL, JENNIFER; Ardmore HS; Ardmore, OK; (4); 32/187; French Clb; Office Aide; Science Clb; Teachers Aide; High Hon Roll; Drama Clb; Speech Tm; Band; Hlth Occupations Stdnts Of Amer; Otstdng Eng Comp Stdnt; Ardmore Hghr Ed Ctr; His/Nrsng.

MC CALL, KRISTY L; Empire Schl; Duncan, OK; (3); Debate Tm; Speech Tm; Chorus; School Play; Stage Crew; Hon Roll; FFA Rptr.

MC CAMMON, ERIN; Christian Heritage Acad; Oklahoma City, OK; (3); FCA; Ofcr Frsh Cls; Ofcr Soph Cls; Ofcr Jr Cls; Var Bsktbl; Var Tennis; Var Vllybl; Cit Awd; High Hon Roll; Pres Acad Fit Awd.

MC CANDLESS, CHUCK F; Ponca City Sr HS; Burkburnett, TX; (3); Boy Scts; Church Yth Grp; Cmnty Wkr; Math Tm; SADD; Acpl Chr; Chorus; Church Choir; Hon Roll; NHS; OK All St Choir Bass II Alt; OK ST Univ; Bnkng; Fin; Psych.

MC CANN, ANDREA M; Bishop Kelley HS; Tulsa, OK; (2); Church Yth Grp; Church Choir; Hon Roll; Church Yth Ensamble; Church Bible Study Grp; Actng/Musical Theatre.

MC CANN, KRISTI E; Putnam City West HS; Bethany, OK; (3); 76/304; Church Yth Grp; Office Aide; Pep Clb; Teachers Aide; Sec Frsh Cls; Treas Soph Cls; JV Capt Chrldng; Stat Score Keeper; Var Vllybl; Hon Roll; OK ST U; Nrs.

MC CANTNEY, MELISSA J; Healdton HS; Healdton, OK; (3); Rptr FHA; Pep Clb; Chorus; Hon Roll; Pres Awd Educl Excl; HS Academician Awd.

MC CARTHICK, HEATHER; Plainview HS; Davis, OK; (3); 8/93; Church Yth Grp; FCA; Natl Beta Clb; SADD; Drill Tm; Chrldng; Hon Roll; NHS; Certfd Medcl Assist, Home Health & Nursesaide; Nrs.

MC CARTHY, ELIZABETH; Midwest City HS; Midwest City, OK; (3); Letterman Clb; Spanish Clb; Varsity Clb; Bsktbl; Sftbl; Trk; High Hon Roll; Hon Roll; NHS; Prfct Atten Awd; OK Chrstn Cage Cmp Bst Rbndr 2xs; AAU Tm Wnnr Sooner St Gms 93, 94; OK ST U; Bus Mgmt.

MC CARTHY, TODD A; Stillwater Sr HS; Stillwater, OK; (3); FCA; Spanish Clb; JV Bsktbl; Hon Roll; OK ST Univ.

MC CARTY, BLYTHE; Stillwater Sr HS; Stillwater, OK; (4); 1/320; Church Yth Grp; Cmnty Wkr; Sec Key Clb; Natl Beta Clb; Scholastic Bowl; Treas Science Clb; Ed Yrbk; NHS; St Schlr; Val; OK ST U.

MC CARTY, JENNI; East Central HS; Broken Arrow, OK; (3); French Clb; Pep Clb; Chorus; Var Chrldng; High Hon Roll; NHS; Acctng.

MC CARTY, JULIE K; Antlers Sr HS; Atoka, OK; (2); 2/100; Church Yth Grp; FCA; Treas Natl FFA Org; Quiz Bowl; Bsktbl; Hon Roll; Antlers Horse, Livestock & OJQHA Horse Judging Team; OSU.

MC CARTY, MICAH J; Lexington HS; Lexington, OK; (4); 1/67; Church Yth Grp; Pres FCA; Mu Alpha Theta; Pres Soph Cls; Pres Jr Cls; Pres Sr Cls; Ofcr Bsbl; Bsktbl; NHS; Val; Armed Forces Schlr Ath Of Yr; OK Bapt U.

MC CARTY, SARA M; Stillwater Sr HS; Stillwater, OK; (2); Church Yth Grp; Key Clb; Natl Beta Clb; Spanish Clb; Jr NHS; Var Schlrs Awd; Aerobics; OK ST Univ.

MC CARVILLE, JUSTIN J; North Intermediate HS; Broken Arrow, OK; (2); Science Clb; Cit Awd; Hon Roll; Jr NHS; NHS; Engrng.

MC CASKILL, KRISTY; Cyril Jr Sr HS; Cyril, OK; (2); 1/35; Rptr Church Yth Grp; Drama Clb; Sec 4-H; Treas FHA; Model UN; School Play; Sec Treas Frsh Cls; Rptr Pep Band; High Hon Roll; Ntl Merit Ltr; TSA Treas; Acad Team Hnrb Mntn; Most Depndbl & Most Courteous; UCLA; Chld Psych.

MC CASKILL, PRINCESS K; Central HS; Tulsa, OK; (4); Spanish Clb; Ofcr Sr Cls; Hon Roll; Spanish NHS; Acad Awd; Tulsa JC; Elem Ed.

MC CASLIN, LAURA L; Jenks HS; Tulsa, OK; (4); 151/475; DECA; FCA; Key Clb; Office Aide; Bsktbl; Mgr(s); Hon Roll; Grouped Placed 1st In DECA St Cmptn-Went On To Natls; Acad Ltr; Northeastern A&M; Elem Ed.

MC CASLIN, LISA; Jenks HS; Tulsa, OK; (4); Art Clb; DECA; FCA; FHA; Ofcr Stu Cncl; Var L Bsktbl; Powder Puff Ftbl; 3rd Pl In DECA St Finals & Went To Natls; Northeastern A&M; Brocstng.

MC CAUGHRIN, SWAIN R; Bixby Sr HS; Bixby, OK; (3); 10/210; Church Yth Grp; FCA; German Clb; SADD; School Musical; High Hon Roll; NHS; Pres Acad Fit Awd; Hist Clb Parlimentarian; Acad Team; Eng Ed.

MC CAULEY, BROOKE M; Barnsdall Jr Sr HS; Barnsdall, OK; (3); 1/40; Church Yth Grp; FCA; Office Aide; SADD; Chorus; Yrbk; Sec VP Stu Cncl; Chrldng; High Hon Roll; NHS; Jr Ftbl Homcmng Attendant; NSU; Dntl Hygienist.

MC CAULEY, CLINTON; Yukon HS; Yukon, OK; (4); 84/400; Ed Natl FFA Org; SADD; Phtg Yrbk; Hon Roll; Ntl Merit Ltr; St Schlr; Habitat For Humanity 92-96; OK Odyssey Of Mind Team 2nd Sw OK Regnl & 2nd In St; Redlands CC; Ag Engrng; Bus.

MC CAULEY, KELLY; Putnam City HS; Oklahoma City, OK; (2); 25/364; Church Yth Grp; Drama Clb; FCA; GAA; Var L Bsktbl; Mgr(s); Score Keeper; Cit Awd; Hon Roll.

MC CAULEY, LANI; Luther HS; Luther, OK; (2); Debate Tm; Drama Clb; FHA; NFL; Speech Tm; School Play; Stage Crew; Variety Show; Hon Roll; Drama Capt 96-; RN.

MC CAULEY, SUZANNE J; Catoosa HS; Tulsa, OK; (2); FCA; Bsktbl; Sftbl; Hon Roll; OU; Lawyer.

MC CAW, MARC D; Union Intermediate HS; Broken Arrow, OK; (2); 63/800; Boy Scts; Church Yth Grp; Spanish Clb; Socr; High Hon Roll; Jr NHS; NHS; FCA; Hist FBLA; Bsktbl; DFY; Young Astronauts; OK U.

MC CHURIN, MALANIE; Afton HS; Bernice, OK; (3); 3/35; Church Yth Grp; Quiz Bowl; Speech Tm; Ed Yrbk; Treas Frsh Cls; Pres Jr Cls; L Sftbl; High Hon Roll; Pres Acad Fit Awd; Ottawa Cty Comm Prtnrshp VP Jr Yr.

MC CHURIN, MELANIE B; Afton HS; Afton, OK; (3); 3/35; Church Yth Grp; Quiz Bowl; Speech Tm; Ed Yrbk; Treas Frsh Cls; Pres Jr Cls; Sftbl; NHS; Pres Acad Fit Awd; OCCP VP Jr Yr Comm Invlmnt 45 Vol Hrs Of Wrk.

MC CLAIN, ANGELA; Bartlesville Sr HS; Bartlesville, OK; (4); Cmnty Wkr; French Clb; FHA; JA; Service Clb; JV Chrldng; French Hon Soc; Hon Roll; NHS; Acad Excl Awd; Spcl Olympics Vol; Schl Bell Ringer; OK ST Univ; Ed; Bus.

MC CLAIN, ASHLEY E; Colbert Jr Sr HS; Cartwright, OK; (2); Drama Clb; School Play; Hon Roll; Prfct Atten Awd; Southeastern.

MC CLAIN, CHRISTY; Piedmont HS; Piedmont, OK; (3); 1/79; Am Leg Aux Girls St; Church Yth Grp; HOBY; Scholastic Bowl; Chorus; Pres Stu Cncl; NHS; Pres Schlr; St Schlr; FCA; Campus Lfe Fndr, Pres 2 Yrs; OK Baptist U; Scndry Ed.

MC CLAIN, JOSHUA A; Duncan HS; Duncan, OK; (3); Church Yth Grp; Cmnty Wkr; Debate Tm; Drama Clb; French Clb; NFL; Service Clb; Speech Tm; SADD; Thesps; Ldrshp Cncl; Outstdng Drama Stdnt.

MC CLAIN, VIRGINIA; Hugo HS; Soper, OK; (3); FHA; Natl FFA Org; Treas Science Clb; Hon Roll; Pres Schlr; St Schlr.

MC CLAIN, WADE G; B T Washington HS; Tulsa, OK; (2); Quiz Bowl; Scholastic Bowl; Spanish Clb; Ofcr Bsbl; NHS.

MC CLARNON, SHANNA; Blackwell HS; Blackwell, OK; (1); Church Yth Grp; FCA; FHA; Pep Clb; Spanish Clb; Rep Frsh Cls; Ofcr Stu Cncl; High Hon Roll.

MC CLARY, MANDY D; Cleveland Sr HS; Pawnee, OK; (3); Church Yth Grp; FHA; Library Aide; Band; Chorus; Color Guard; Flag Corp; Mrchg Band; Hon Roll; Tusla JC; Flight Atten.

MC CLATCHEY, KATRINA L; Mustang HS; Mustang, OK; (4); Band; Color Guard; Flag Corp; Mrchg Band; Hon Roll.

MC CLELLAN, KRISTEL; Sayre HS; Sayre, OK; (3); 6/50; Band; Chorus; Flag Corp; Mrchg Band; Pep Band; Ed Nwsp; VP Frsh Cls; VP Jr Cls; Bsktbl; Chrldng; Numerous Natl Mrt Awds; Numerous Band Awds; Lawyer; Phy Thrpst; Psych.

MC CLELLAN, MATT K; Midwest City HS; Midwest City, OK; (2); 123/473; Church Yth Grp; Drama Clb; German Clb; Library Aide; Stage Crew; JV Trk; Cit Awd; Hon Roll; Jr NHS; Prfct Atten Awd; U Of OK.

MC CLENDON, SHARLA; Blanchard Jr Sr HS; Newcastle, OK; (3); 1/63; Church Yth Grp; Computer Clb; Pres VP Mu Alpha Theta; Pep Clb; Rptr Spanish Clb; Ed Yrbk; Pres Jr Cls; Rep Stu Cncl; Jr NHS; NHS; Gftd & Tlntd; Spnsh Gftd & Tlntd; Acad Team; SWOSU; Pharmcy.

MC CLINTOCK, AMBER M; Bartlesville Sr HS; Bartlesville, OK; (3); 216/449; FCA; GAA; Girl Scts; Office Aide; Teachers Aide; Varsity Clb; Var Bsktbl; Var Sftbl; Intrml Vllybl; Prfct Atten Awd; Sftbl Hnrbl Mntn 2 Yrs; Elks Tnagr Awd; Nrsg/Jvnl Crmnl Ofcr.

MC CLOUD, CASSY; Pryor Sr HS; Pryor, OK; (4); 17/148; Am Leg Aux Girls St; Mu Alpha Theta; Spanish Clb; Sec Chorus; School Musical; Yrbk; Capt Chrldng; Hon Roll; NHS; Pres Acad Fit Awd; PSI Teen Ldr; Arts & Hmnts Soc Sec.

MC CLURE, BRANDON C; Valliant HS; Millerton, OK; (2); 23/96; Church Yth Grp; Cmnty Wkr; Computer Clb; Sec Natl FFA Org; Treas Science Clb; Phtg Nwsp; Phtg Yrbk; Ftbl; Trk; Wt Lftg; FFA, Yrbk & Math Awds; Wilburton; EMS; FFA Advisor.

MC CLURE, CHRISTEN M; Jenks HS; Tulsa, OK; (3); 25/517; Church Yth Grp; DECA; Key Clb; Chorus; Church Choir; Sec Stu Cncl; NHS; FCA; Mu Alpha Theta; Teachers Aide; Show Choir; Hyechka Clb.

MC CLURE, JACKIE A; Bethany HS; El Reno, OK; (3); Church Yth Grp; FCA; Pep Clb; Band; School Play; Chrldng; Pom Pon; High Hon Roll; Ballet Dncr; Mdl; TX Chrstn; Pre-Med.

MC CLURE, JASON S; Putnam City West HS; Bethany, OK; (1); 47/396; Church Yth Grp; Latin Clb; Chorus; Church Choir; School Musical; Rep Frsh Cls; Cit Awd; High Hon Roll; Hon Roll; Stu Of Today Awd Given By Masonic Lodge; Chrch Recreation Comm Mem; Chrch Bsktbl & Sftbl; Optimist Bsbl; OK ST U; Structural Engrng.

MC CLURE, JENNIFER R; Indiahoma Schl; Indiahoma, OK; (1); Hosp Aide; Natl FFA Org; Var Chrldng; Hon Roll; Natl FFA Beef Prdcrs Awd; OK ST Univ; Vet.

MC CLURE, JOE D; Elgin HS; Elgin, OK; (2); #1 in class; Natl FFA Org; Trk; Sal; Cameron.

MC CLURE, MEGAN E; Edmond North HS; Edmond, OK; (1); 85/456; School Play; Stage Crew; Phtg Yrbk; Rep Frsh Cls; Rep Stu Cncl; Hon Roll; U Of Cntrl OK; Interior Dsgn.

MC CLURE, SONDRA; Macarthur Sr HS; Lawton, OK; (3); Church Yth Grp; Cmnty Wkr; Drama Clb; German Clb; Acpl Chr; School Play; JV Var Socr; High Hon Roll; Jr NHS; Pres Acad Fit Awd; All Rgn Chr; Bus Mgmt.

MC CLURKIN, KELLY E; Union Intermediate HS; Broken Arrow, OK; (2); Spanish Clb; High Hon Roll; Jr NHS; NHS; Pres Schlr; TX A&M; Marine Biolgst.

MC CLYMAN, MICHELLE A; Altus Sr HS; Altus, OK; (2); Church Yth Grp; FCA; Spanish Clb; Teachers Aide; Band; Stat Wrstlng; High Hon Roll; Elem Ed.

MC COIN, MATT D; Charles Page HS; Sand Springs, OK; (3); Church Yth Grp; Cmnty Wkr; French Clb; Letterman Clb; Service Clb; Band; Mrchg Band; Pep Band; Var L Tennis; Hon Roll; All Dist Hnr Band; 2nd Pl St His Day; Commerce Dept Regional Sci Project Awd.

MC COLLOM, JOSHUA M; Hobart HS; Roosevelt, OK; (2); Church Yth Grp; FCA; Bsktbl.

MC COLLOM, WENOA R; Tishomingo HS; Tishomingo, OK; (3); Natl FFA Org; Band; Chorus; Mrchg Band; Pep Band; 95-96 Outstdng Jr Musician Awd; Speech Proficiency Awd 95-96 FFA; Murray ST; Vet.

MC COLLUM, AMY D; Bethel HS; Shawnee, OK; (2); Church Yth Grp; Drama Clb; FCA; Library Aide; Office Aide; Spanish Clb; Teachers Aide; Church Choir; L Var Chrldng; L Trk; Homcmng Attendant; Acctng.

MC COMAS, KIM; Minco Jr Sr HS; Minco, OK; (4); 17/34; Church Yth Grp; 4-H; Natl FFA Org; Teachers Aide; Bsktbl; Var Sftbl; Hon Roll; FFA ST Degree; All-Conf/Dist/Area Bsktbl; Hnrbl Men Little City Bsktbl/Fast Pitch; Coaches Awd; Western OK ST Coll; Elem Educ.

MC COMAS, MELISSA S; Chandler HS; Chandler, OK; (3); 11/75; Church Yth Grp; FCA; Natl FFA Org; Church Choir; Hon Roll; NHS; St Hnr Soc; FFA VP.

MC COMBER, LAUREN; Walters HS; Walters, OK; (4); 7/34; Art Clb; Church Yth Grp; FCA; Sec FHA; Letterman Clb; Office Aide; Sec SADD; Yrbk; Rep Stu Cncl; Co-Capt Bsktbl; Rtry Yth Ldrshp Awd; Bsktbl All Conf; Mss WHS, Mst Athltc Sr; MSU; Bus Mrktng.

MC CONATHY, ROBERT; Bridge Creek HS; Blanchard, OK; (4); 1/61; Boy Scts; Church Yth Grp; FCA; FBLA; Science Clb; Spanish Clb; Chorus; Color Guard; Pres Jr Cls; Pres Sr Cls; Eagle Sct W/Plm; FCA Pres; Med.

MC CONNELL, KIMBERLY; Union Intermediate HS; Tulsa, OK; (2); Church Yth Grp; Spanish Clb; Diving; Swmmng; NHS; Pres Schlr; Ice Skating; Poetry; Mssnry.

MC CONNELL, LARRY; Elk City HS; Elk City, OK; (4); 16/141; Am Leg Boys St; Church Yth Grp; Cmnty Wkr; FCA; Key Clb; Letterman Clb; Natl FFA Org; Office Aide; Science Clb; Ftbl; FFA Flg Dty; Mst Sprtd Stu 95; OK ST U; Vet Med.

MC CONNELL, MEGAN; Mustang HS; Yukon, OK; (2); 1/416; Church Yth Grp; Band; Drill Tm; Mrchg Band; Pep Band; Rep Frsh Cls; Rep Stu Cncl; High Hon Roll; NHS; Camp Fire; Academia Team; KWTV 9 Awd Of Excl In Math; Medicine.

MC CONNELL, SEAN M; Owasso Sr HS; Owasso, OK; (2); 76/389; Church Yth Grp; FCA; JV Var Ftbl; Var L Trk; Var L Wrstlng; High Hon Roll; Fishing/Hunting.

MC COOL, AMBER D; Edmond North HS; Edmond, OK; (4); 172/330; Treas FHA; Key Clb; Spanish Clb; SADD; Band; High Hon Roll; Stdnt/Math; Stdnt Yr; Natl W-Tech Hnr Soc; Silver Mdlst Interperson Comm/Natl Leve; OK ST Univ; Ag/Animal Sci.

MC COOL, CHRISTINA M; Putnam City West HS; Bethany, OK; (2); Hosp Aide; Spanish Clb; Teachers Aide; School Play; Stage Crew; Variety Show; Cit Awd; High Hon Roll; NHS; Elem Ed.

MC COOL, RYAN; Enid Sr HS; Enid, OK; (4); 140/405; Am Leg Boys St; Church Yth Grp; Cmnty Wkr; French Clb; Teachers Aide; Band; Mrchg Band; Pep Band; Rep Stu Cncl; Hon Roll; OSU; Music.

MC CORD, JILL; Bluejacket Schl; Bluejacket, OK; (4); 1/23; Church Yth Grp; FHA; Capt Quiz Bowl; Ed Nwsp; Ed Yrbk; Pres School Play; Var Bsktbl; Var Chrldng; High Hon Roll; Val; Ftbl Homcmng Qn; 1st Rnnr Up Jr Miss Pageant; OBU.

MC CORD, KYLE B; Heritage Hall Schl; Oklahoma City, OK; (3); Art Clb; Cmnty Wkr; FCA; Letterman Clb; Spanish Clb; Bsktbl; Ftbl; Tennis; Hon Roll; Pres Acad Fit Awd.

MC CORD, SARA; Mustang HS; Mustang, OK; (4); 53/348; Church Yth Grp; VP FHA; Hist Key Clb; School Play; Stage Crew; Foster Sister; Southwestern Assm Of God; Engl.

MC CORKLE, ELIZABETH; Bartlesville Sr HS; Bartlesville, OK; (4); Office Aide; Hon Roll; Making The Difference Awd; Attendance Aide; Acad Awd; Roger ST Coll; Elem Ed.

MC CORMACK, BRIANE; Cascia Hall Prep School; Tulsa, OK; (2); Church Yth Grp; Cmnty Wkr; Office Aide; Spanish Clb; Chrldng; Gym; Hon Roll; High Achvmt Composition & Grammer; Psych.

MC CORMICK, LACEY; Hinton HS; Hinton, OK; (2); Church Yth Grp; Drama Clb; FCA; FHA; Key Clb; Office Aide; SADD; Drill Tm; School Play; Chrldng; OU.

MC CORMICK, LAMAR J; Muskogee HS; Broken Arrow, OK; (3); Church Yth Grp; Cmnty Wkr; Pep Clb; ROTC; Teachers Aide; VICA; Ftbl; Wt Lftg; Cit Awd; YVC; OAFC; Pres Of Yth Advy Cncl; Langston Univ; Comp Pgmng.

MC CORTNEY, JILL; Ada HS; Ada, OK; (3); Am Leg Aux Girls St; Pres Spanish Clb; Ofcr Drill Tm; Sec Frsh Cls; Capt Pom Pon; DAR Awd; High Hon Roll; Pres Jr NHS; NHS; Pres Spanish NHS; U Of OK; Med.

MC COWN, RACHEL; Eisenhower Sr HS; Lawton, OK; (4); FCA; Intnl Clb; Key Clb; Yrbk; Ofcr Soph Cls; Ofcr Jr Cls; Ofcr Stu Cncl; High Hon Roll; Jr NHS; NHS.

MC COY, ATHENA L; Sallisaw HS; Marble City, OK; (3); FCA; Spanish Clb; Varsity Clb; Nwsp; Yrbk; L Var Bsktbl; Sftbl; Hon Roll; Indian Clb; OK St Class 4A St Bsktbll Champs.

MC COY, CHRISTOPHER; Mountain View-Gotebo HS; Mountain View, OK; (4); 1/31; VP Natl FFA Org; Ed Yrbk; Bsktbl; Hon Roll; Val; FCA; Quiz Bowl; VP Frsh Cls; Pres Soph Cls; Rep Stu Cncl; OK St Jr Cattleman; FFA Star Farmer OK SW Dist; Ag Exchng Stu Japan; OK ST Univ; Ag Ec/Cmpt Sci.

MC COY, CHUCK; Pond Creek-Hunter Schl; Hunter, OK; (2); 1/30; Church Yth Grp; Quiz Bowl; Scholastic Bowl; VP Frsh Cls; JV Bsbl; High Hon Roll; NHS; Prfct Atten Awd; OK Hnr Soc; OK G/T Pgm; OK ST.

MC COY, JAMI L; Poteau HS; Poteau, OK; (2); JV Bsktbl; Stat Mgr(s); Var Sftbl; Var Trk; Var Wt Lftg; High Hon Roll; Hon Roll; NHS; Northeastern ST U; Lwyr.

MC COY, JENNIFER; Quapaw Sr HS; Quapaw, OK; (4); 6/40; Church Yth Grp; Cmnty Wkr; FCA; Letterman Clb; Natl Beta Clb; Office Aide; Spanish Clb; Chorus; Pres Frsh Cls; Rep Jr Cls; Nrs.

MC COY, JENNIFER M; Blanchard Jr Sr HS; Blanchard, OK; (2); Computer Clb; Library Aide; Office Aide; Spanish Clb; Bsktbl; Hon Roll; Jr NHS; NHS; ESE; USAO.

MC COY, JEREMY K; Durant HS; Durant, OK; (2); Capt Church Yth Grp; FCA; Math Tm; Scholastic Bowl; Chorus; Church Choir; Rep Soph Cls; Var Ftbl; Var Trk; Var Wrstlng.

MC COY, KELLY; Medford Schl; Medford, OK; (4); 2/20; Am Leg Boys St; HOBY; Letterman Clb; Natl FFA Org; Spanish Clb; Chorus; Church Choir; Rep Stu Cncl; Var Bsktbl; Var Ftbl.

MC COY, KYLE; Moore HS; Moore, OK; (3); 33/535; Am Leg Boys St; Church Yth Grp; FCA; Office Aide; Spanish Clb; Rep Stu Cncl; Var Bsktbl; Var Crs Cntry; Var Ftbl; High Hon Roll; 4.0 GPA & Above Awd; CO U.

MC COY, LEILA A; Porter Jr Sr HS; Porter, OK; (2); Letterman Clb; Quiz Bowl; Scholastic Bowl; SADD; Pres Frsh Cls; Treas Stu Cncl; High Hon Roll; NHS; Prfct Atten Awd; All Conf Acad Team; ST 3rd Pl Vcblry Wnnr; Upwrd Bnd.

MC COY, LINDSAY M; Shawnee Sr HS; Shawnee, OK; (1); Office Aide; Spanish Clb; Speech Tm; Band; Color Guard; Flag Corp; Mrchg Band; Hon Roll; NHS; MA Inst Of Tech; Cmptr Pgmr.

MC COY, MONEAKEA; Capitol Hill HS; Oklahoma City, OK; (4); 9/147; Church Yth Grp; Science Clb; Spanish Clb; VICA; Chorus; Church Choir; High Hon Roll; Hon Roll; NHS; Ntl Merit Ltr; Comp Technlgy.

MC CRACKEN, AMY B; Pauls Valley HS; Pauls Valley, OK; (1); Art Clb; Church Yth Grp; FCA; 4-H; JV Bsktbl; JV Trk; 4-H Awd; Hon Roll; Pres Acad Fit Awd; Chrprctr.

MC CRACKEN, KATHERINE M; Putnam City West HS; Bethany, OK; (2); Debate Tm; Drama Clb; Intnl Clb; NFL; Spanish Clb; Band; Color Guard; Mrchg Band; Stat Bsktbl; Hon Roll; Bus Executive; Fin.

MC CRACKEN, STELL; Choctaw HS; Choctaw, OK; (4); 103/298; Natl FFA Org; JV Bsbl; Wt Lftg; Cit Awd; Hon Roll; Jr NHS; NHS; Prfct Atten Awd; I Try Awd; Allied Arts Awd; ST Farmer Awd; Murray ST Coll; Vet Tech.

MC CRARY, JASON C; Wellston Schl; Chandler, OK; (3); Church Yth Grp; Pep Clb; Band; Chorus; Church Choir; Drill Tm; Mrchg Band; Pep Band; Var Bsktbl; Var Ftbl; Yng Chrstn Ambsdrs Step Team; Miami; Bus/Cmptr Prgrm; Cmptr Pr.

MC CRAVEY, LEAH C; Edmond Memorial HS; Edmond, OK; (3); Drama Clb; FCA; FHA; GAA; Girl Scts; Spanish Clb; Thesps; School Play; JV Crs Cntry; Var Golf; Slv Awd All Edmond Golf Tm; CO School Of Mines; Engr.

MC CRAY, BOBBI DANAE; Ringwood HS; Ringwood, OK; (2); #1 in class; Rep FCA; HOBY; Var Bsktbl; Var Chrldng; Var Sftbl; High Hon Roll; NHS; Pres Acad Fit Awd; Church Yth Grp; Cmnty Wkr; Otstdng FHA Mem; Otstdng Musician-Bnd; GATE Prgm Pres; OK Univ; Med.

MC CRAY, JEANA M; Pawnee HS; Pawnee, OK; (4); 35/63; FHA; Library Aide; Ed Nwsp; Hon Roll; Prfct Atten Awd; Genrl Math, Algebra, Bio Cert; Jr Chmbr Of Cmmrce; Frshmn Fee Waiver Schlrshp; Rogers ST Coll; Writer.

MC CRAY, SEAN D; Central Mid-HS; Norman, OK; (2); JV Var Bsktbl; NC; Psych.

MC CREARY, CHRISTOPHER L; Northeast HS; Oklahoma City, OK; (2); Church Yth Grp; JV Ftbl; Hon Roll.

MC CROSKEY, CRYSTAL D; Wister Schl; Poteau, OK; (3); Spanish Clb; Acpl Chr; Chorus; Chrldng; Hon Roll; FFA; Carl Albert ST Coll; RN.

MC CUISTIAN, JAMIE L; Oologah HS; Claremore, OK; (4); 29/90; Intnl Clb; Natl FFA Org; Spanish Clb; Capt Chrldng; Hon Roll; NHS; Homcmng Attendant For Wrestling; Rogers ST Coll; Acctng.

MC CUISTON, LESLIE; Cache HS; Indiahoma, OK; (3); 10/75; Church Yth Grp; Natl Beta Clb; Natl FFA Org; Church Choir; Ofcr Frsh Cls; Sec Stu Cncl; Sftbl; Trk; High Hon Roll; NHS; Sthwstrn OK Sst; Psych Cnslr.

MC CULLAH, LUKE E; Muldrow HS; Muldrow, OK; (1); Boy Scts; Church Yth Grp; FHA; Band; Mrchg Band; Pep Band; Ftbl; Trk; Wt Lftg; Ntl Merit Ltr; Natl His/Govt/Ldrshp/All Schlstcs Awds.

MC CULLEY, AKEYAH; Dustin Schl; Dustin, OK; (4); 2/15; GAA; Natl FFA Org; Scholastic Bowl; Phtg Yrbk; VP Frsh Cls; Pres Soph Cls; Pres Jr Cls; Pres Sr Cls; Sec Stu Cncl; Var Capt Bsktbl; Comm Strtgc Plng; Estrn OK Ldrshp Prgm; Nrthestrn ST U; Radlgcl Tech.

MC CULLOH, EMILY; Plainview HS; Ardmore, OK; (4); 11/82; Church Yth Grp; FCA; GAA; Latin Clb; Mu Alpha Theta; Natl Beta Clb; SADD; Co-Ed Yrbk; Treas Sr Cls; Rep Stu Cncl; U Of OK.

MC CULLOUGH, AMY K; Durant HS; Durant, OK; (3); 9/165; Church Yth Grp; Hosp Aide; Band; Chorus; Jazz Band; Mrchg Band; Pep Band; Rep Jr Cls; Rep Sr Cls; Ofcr Stu Cncl; All Dist Choir 2 Yrs; All Dist Band 3 Yrs; Law.

MC CULLOUGH, ANGELA C; Muskogee HS; Muskogee, OK; (2); Church Yth Grp; ROTC; DAR Awd; High Hon Roll; Hon Roll; NHS; OSU; USAF.

MC CULLY, CHRISTOPHER M; Western Heights Sr HS; Oklahoma City, OK; (3); Church Yth Grp; Hosp Aide; Office Aide; Band; Mrchg Band; Intrml Wt Lftg; Hon Roll; U Of OK; Bus Mngmt.

MC CUNE, AMABER; Tonkawa Jr Sr HS; Tonkawa, OK; (3); Church Yth Grp; Natl FFA Org; NHS; N OK Coll.

MC CUNE, BETH; Luther HS; Luther, OK; (2); Debate Tm; Drama Clb; NFL; Hon Roll; Pres Acad Fit Awd; Pol Sci; Jurors Doctorate.

MC CUNE, NATALIE L; Luther HS; Luther, OK; (4); Drama Clb; French Clb; FBLA; NFL; Office Aide; School Play; Yrbk; Ofcr Stu Cncl; Hon Roll; Envrnmntl Club; Horseback Rdng; E TX ST U; Bio Oceanography.

MC CUNE, TRAYTON L; Family Of Faith Christian Schl; Stillwater, OK; (3); Church Yth Grp; Cmnty Wkr; FCA; Letterman Clb; School Musical; School Play; Pres Soph Cls; Pres Jr Cls; L Bsktbl; Hon Roll; OK ST Univ; Physician.

MC CURDY, HOLLY; Comanche HS; Comanche, OK; (1); Church Yth Grp; Debate Tm; Natl FFA Org; Speech Tm; Sec Frsh Cls; Bsktbl; Chrldng; OK HS Hnr Soc.

MC CURDY, MONICA; Grace Fellowship Christian Sch; Tulsa, OK; (3); 5/18; FCA; Rep Jr Cls; JV Var Bsktbl; Var Trk; Var Vllybl; Hon Roll; NHS; St Sci Fair; ORUEF Natl Finals Comp; OK St Univ.

MC CURRY, CARRIE; Westmoore HS; Moore, OK; (4); FTA; GAA; Teachers Aide; Sftbl; Cmptrs; UCO; Bnkng.

MC CURRY, TOM; Shawnee Sr HS; Tecumseh, OK; (4); Boy Scts; JA; Scholastic Bowl; Thesps; Stage Crew; Cmptr Systms Mgmt.

MC CUTCHEN, SARAH E; Checotah HS; Checotah, OK; (3); HOBY; Speech Tm; Chorus; VP Jr Cls; Ofcr Stu Cncl; Trk; High Hon Roll; Hon Roll; NHS; St Hnr Soc; NSU; Omptmtrst.

MC CUTCHER, AMBER; Eisenhower Sr HS; Lawton, OK; (4); Church Yth Grp; FCA; Key Clb; Pep Clb; Rep Stu Cncl; Chrldng; Gym; Trk; Hon Roll; Jr NHS; OK U; Eng Tchr.

MC DALTON, MONICA; Northeast HS; Oklahoma City, OK; (2); Church Yth Grp; Cmnty Wkr; Drama Clb; Pep Clb; Chorus; Chrldng; Trk; High Hon Roll.

MC DANIEL, ARLAINA L; Felt Public Schl; Felt, OK; (3); Church Yth Grp; Cmnty Wkr; GAA; Letterman Clb; Library Aide; Quiz Bowl; Teachers Aide; Capt Varsity Clb; School Play; Ed Rptr Nwsp; REC Yth Tr; OK St Univ; Advtsng.

MC DANIEL, BO J; Balko Public Schl; Balko, OK; (1); 1/16; Church Yth Grp; Drama Clb; Natl FFA Org; VP Frsh Cls; Var Bsbl; JV Bsktbl; JV Ftbl; High Hon Roll; Oral Roberts Univ; PT.

MC DANIEL, BRENT A; Idabel HS; Idabel, OK; (3); 13/96; Natl FFA Org; JV Var Bsbl; JV Var Ftbl; JV Var Wt Lftg; Hon Roll; OK St Univ; Vet.

MC DANIEL, BRIAN; Westmoore HS; Oklahoma City, OK; (4); 54/6310; VP JA; Library Aide; Office Aide; High Hon Roll; Hon Roll; NHS; St Schlr; Val; U Of OK.

MC DANIEL, DANA; Coleman Schl; Wapanucka, OK; (3); 1/18; Church Yth Grp; Cmnty Wkr; FCA; Pep Clb; Quiz Bowl; Ski Clb; Church Choir; School Play; Sec Soph Cls; High Hon Roll; SOSU Schlstc Mt 1st Earth/Space Sci/Ind Com Prgrmg/1st Gen Bus; Murray Schlstc 1st Com Prgmng/2d Lit; Southeastern OK ST U; Prgrmng.

MC DANIEL, MALISSA; Mc Loud HS; Midwest City, OK; (3); Pres Church Yth Grp; FCA; FBLA; Var Chrldng; Hon Roll; OK ST U Hnr Schlr Acad Achvmnt Awd; OK ST U; Elem Tchr.

MC DANIEL, RANDY; Vinita HS; Vinita, OK; (4); 2/79; Am Leg Boys St; FCA; Math Clb; Pres Frsh Cls; Ofcr Stu Cncl; Bsktbl; Ftbl; Trk; High Hon Roll; NHS; Verdigris Vly Conf & Dist Spclty Tms Plyr Of Yr Ftbl; Schl Record Fld Goals; S Nazarene U; Bus.

MC DANIEL, SHELBY L; Stigler HS; Mccurtain, OK; (3); 4-H; Band; Mrchg Band; High Hon Roll; Hon Roll; NHS; TSA Pres 3 Yrs, Natl Wnnr; St We The People; St Mock Trial.

MC DANIEL, STEPHEN L; Hulbert Jr Sr HS; Tahlequah, OK; (3); Spanish Clb; Var Bsktbl; Hon Roll; Multi Yr Listeee.

MC DANIELS, JENNY R; Dickson HS; Ardmore, OK; (2); Rep FHA; SADD; Sftbl; Eductnl Tlnt Srch; Psych.

MC DERMOTT, BRYAN; Tuttle HS; Tuttle, OK; (1); Church Yth Grp; Natl FFA Org; Bsktbl; Ftbl; Trk.

MC DERMOTT, NADINE L; Midwest City HS; Midwest City, OK; (2); 115/473; Vol At Nrsing Cntr; Med.

MC DONALD, AARON L; Mustang HS; Mustang, OK; (1); Church Yth Grp; Cmnty Wkr; FCA; Chorus; Church Choir; Stage Crew.

MC DONALD, AUDREY; Forgan Schl; Forgan, OK; (3); FCA; Pep Clb; Teachers Aide; Band; Pep Band; Sec Jr Cls; Chrldng; High Hon Roll; Hon Roll; NHS; Natl Eng Merit; OK City Univ; Nrsng.

MC DONALD, CHARNETTA J; Wellston Schl; Luther, OK; (2); Church Yth Grp; Drama Clb; FCA; Spanish Clb; Speech Tm; Band; Mrchg Band; Pep Band; School Play; Bsktbl.

MC DONALD, CLETUS P; Cashion HS; Kingfisher, OK; (1); 4/34; JV Var Bsktbl; Var Trk; Var Wt Lftg; Hon Roll; NHS; All-Amer Schlr Awd; High GPA Awd For Math; Duke Univ; Psych.

MC DONALD, CYNTHIA F; Del City HS; Del City, OK; (3); Dance Clb; Spanish Clb; Teachers Aide; Pom Pon; Cit Awd; NHS; Pres Acad Fit Awd; Interior Dsgn.

MC DONALD, JOSHUA; Blanchard Jr Sr HS; Blanchard, OK; (4); Am Leg Boys St; Computer Clb; FCA; Pep Clb; Teachers Aide; Capt Bsktbl; L Trk; L Wt Lftg; Jr NHS; NHS; Mesa ST Coll; Phy Ed.

MC DONALD, KERI B; Pryor Sr HS; Pryor, OK; (2); Church Yth Grp; JV Var Bsktbl; JV Var Sftbl; Hon Roll; NHS; Prfct Atten Awd; St Schlr; Northeastern ST U; Sprts Med.

MC DONALD, KRIS; Bartlesville Sr HS; Bartlesville, OK; (3); French Clb; FBLA; German Clb; JA; Letterman Clb; Speech Tm; JV Socr; High Hon Roll; Jr NHS; NHS; Arts Encntrs Drama; Sccr Premiere Tms; Indpndnt Fin Adv.

MC DONALD, MAGGIE R; Mustang HS; Yukon, OK; (1); 338/500; French Clb; FBLA.

MC DONALD, MARSHA; Berryhill Jr HS; Tulsa, OK; (1); Church Yth Grp; Band; Jazz Band; Mrchg Band; Pep Band; Ofcr Frsh Cls; Cit Awd; Gov Hon Prg Awd; High Hon Roll; Prfct Atten Awd; Harvard U; Law.

MC DONALD, MARY E; B T Washington HS; Tulsa, OK; (2); Red Cross Aide; Spanish Clb; Ofcr Frsh Cls; Var Socr; Hon Roll; NHS; Duke U TIP; Sprts Med.

MC DONALD, PARIS M; John Marshall HS; Oklahoma City, OK; (3); Church Yth Grp; DECA; Church Choir; Orch; JV Bsktbl; Hon Roll; OK ST Univ Stillwater.

MC DONALD, REBECCA S; Hominy HS; Osage, OK; (3); 4/62; Church Yth Grp; French Clb; Band; Mrchg Band; VP Frsh Cls; VP Jr Cls; Tennis; Hon Roll; NHS; Pres Of Tns For Chrst.

MC DONALD, TABITHA; Davis HS; Davis, OK; (2); Art Clb; Church Yth Grp; French Clb; Key Clb; Speech Tm; Chorus; Variety Show; Hon Roll; OK Hnr Soc; Acad Team; RN.

MC DONALD, TIMOTHY J; Hollis Jr Sr HS; Hollis, OK; (2); Church Yth Grp; Drama Clb; 4-H; Scholastic Bowl; Speech Tm; Band; Church Choir; Jazz Band; Mrchg Band; Sec Frsh Cls; OK Bapt Univ.

MC DONALD, TRISH K; Edmond North HS; Edmond, OK; (2); 119/420; Church Yth Grp; FCA; Church Choir; Phtg Bsbl; Trk; NHS; Belmont Univ; Music Bus.

MC DONOUGH, MARK; Central HS; Tulsa, OK; (2); 6/200; Church Yth Grp; Computer Clb; Key Clb; Quiz Bowl; Scholastic Bowl; Band; Mrchg Band; Rptr Nwsp; High Hon Roll; Hon Roll; Coll Engrng Tulsa U Summer Acad 94, Oral Roberts U Summer Math Acad 95; U Tulsa; Comp Sci.

MC DOUGAL, MATT B; Moore HS; Moore, OK; (2); Science Clb; Spanish Clb; Var Golf; Cit Awd; Hon Roll; Jr NHS; Sci, Math, Span & His Schltc Achvmt Awds; Bus; Law.

MC DOULETT, JADE T; U S Grant HS; Oklahoma City, OK; (4); Church Yth Grp; Cmnty Wkr; FCA; ROTC; SADD; Rep Stu Cncl; JV Ftbl; JV Var Wrstlng; Hon Roll; Pres Acad Fit Awd; Metro Tech; Elec.

MC DOW, MARIE; Owasso Sr HS; Owasso, OK; (3); 28/357; Church Yth Grp; Cmnty Wkr; FCA; Lbrn Chorus; Church Choir; Treas Pres Stu Cncl; High Hon Roll; Hon Roll; NHS; Art Clb; All Dist Hnr Choir 3 Yrs; Vol Spec Ed Prgm; Vol Nrsng Hm; Nrthestrn ST U; Spec Ed.

MC DOWELL, MISTY; Shawnee Sr HS; Shawnee, OK; (2); Church Yth Grp; FCA; Latin Clb; Pep Clb; Scholastic Bowl; Ofcr Stu Cncl; Chrldng; Pom Pon; Sftbl; High Hon Roll; Tri-Hi-Y; Big Brthrs/Big Sisters; OU; Acctng.

MC EACHERN, CLINT; Timberlake Schl; Jet, OK; (2); 13/25; Boy Scts; Church Yth Grp; FCA; Natl FFA Org; Pep Clb; Chorus; Bsktbl; Crs Cntry; Trk; 4-H Awd; Northwestern OK ST.

MC EACHRAN, STEPHANIE; Ada HS; Ada, OK; (3); Girl Scts; Intnl Clb; Spanish Clb; SADD; High Hon Roll; NHS; Spanish NHS; Family Crisis Vlntr; DECA; Legisltv Page.

MC ELROY, BRANDI M; Booker T Washington Mem HS; Tulsa, OK; (3); Cmnty Wkr; Dance Clb; Latin Clb; Pep Clb; Red Cross Aide; Teachers Aide; Chorus; School Musical; School Play; Rep Stu Cncl; Afro Amer Soc; Dance Line Capt; Morris Brown; Acctng.

MC ELROY, BROOKE; Davenport Jr Sr HS; Davenport, OK; (3); 3/33; Office Aide; Pep Clb; Quiz Bowl; Scholastic Bowl; Spanish Clb; Sec Soph Cls; L Chrldng; High Hon Roll; Hon Roll; NHS; OCU; Anesthesiologist.

MC ELROY, CATHERINE A; Stillwater Sr HS; Stillwater, OK; (2); Church Yth Grp; Dance Clb; French Clb; GAA; Key Clb; Natl Beta Clb; School Musical; Stage Crew; Sftbl; Trk.

MC ELROY, JONATHAN K; Oklahoma Christian Acad; Guthrie, OK; (2); 1/20; Church Yth Grp; Cmnty Wkr; Drama Clb; Speech Tm; Acpl Chr; Chorus; Variety Show; Pres Soph Cls; Rep Stu Cncl; Var L Socr; All St Soccer; TCSA Lit Mt Prose 1st Fr; Outstndng Chrstn Athl; Most Schltc Athl; Outstndng HS Chrstn; OK Chrstn U Of Sci & Arts.

MC ELROY, KEVIN; Pryor Sr HS; Pryor, OK; (4); 23/145; FBLA; Red Cross Aide; Spanish Clb; Ofcr Soph Cls; Ofcr Stu Cncl; Bsktbl; Ftbl; Golf; Tennis; Trk; U Of AR.

MC ELROY, SEAN; Tuttle HS; Tuttle, OK; (1); Church Yth Grp; Math Tm; Quiz Bowl; Scholastic Bowl; SADD; Band; Mrchg Band; High Hon Roll; JETS Awd; Prfct Atten Awd; Omniplex Sci Museum Demonstrator; Outstndng Pre-Chem & Physics Stu 95-96; OK ST U; Comp Pgm.

MC ELVANEY, AMY K; Heritage Hall Schl; Oklahoma City, OK; (4); 2/50; Church Yth Grp; FCA; Sec French Clb; Letterman Clb; Mu Alpha Theta; Pep Clb; Rep Jr Cls; Treas Sr Cls; VP Stu Cncl; Var Sftbl; Anderson Univ.

MC ELVANY, DEVYN; Moore HS; Moore, OK; (4); 11/525; Drama Clb; Latin Clb; School Musical; Rptr Jr Cls; Powder Puff Ftbl; Sftbl; Hon Roll; NHS; Prfct Atten Awd; Val; UOK; Bus.

MC ELYEA, JASON; Indianola HS; Indianola, OK; (1); Church Yth Grp; Natl FFA Org; Quiz Bowl; Hon Roll; NHS; Spanish NHS; OU; Lawyer.

MC ENTIRE, AUTUMN K; Canadian Schl; Kiowa, OK; (3); 4/25; 4-H; Math Tm; Rptr Natl FFA Org; Quiz Bowl; Spanish Clb; Speech Tm; Variety Show; Rptr Nwsp; Yrbk; Rptr Stu Cncl; Tonys Dance Studio 15 Yrs; Pub Speaking 12 Awds; FFA ST Pub Speaking Awd; Curr Contest 30 Awds; Belmont Nashville TN; Bus Mgmt.

MC ENTIRE, BRIAN; Tuttle HS; Oklahoma City, OK; (3); Church Yth Grp; Letterman Clb; Natl FFA Org; Varsity Clb; Ftbl; Wt Lftg; Hon Roll; Brown Belt Karate; OK ST U; Vet Med.

MC ENTIRE, NICOLE E; Vinita HS; Vinita, OK; (2); Spanish Clb; Band; Mrchg Band; Trk; Vllybl; Hon Roll; Comp Bus.

MC FADDEN, MICHAEL J; Altus Sr HS; Altus, OK; (4); 55/260; Church Yth Grp; FCA; Office Aide; Spanish Clb; Rep Stu Cncl; Bsktbl; Ftbl; Golf; Socr; High Hon Roll; Ftbl All Dist Tm; Soccer All Conf/Dist/ST; MO Vly Coll.

MC FADDEN, RENIKA; Douglass HS; Oklahoma City, OK; (3); Church Yth Grp; FHA; Drill Tm; Nwsp; Bsktbl; Chrldng; Trk; High Hon Roll; Hon Roll; Singing Gospel; Atlanta GA; Lawyer/Nrs.

MC FALL, BRIAN J; Bridge Creek HS; Blanchard, OK; (4); 19/57; Scholastic Bowl; Spanish Clb; Varsity Clb; JV Var Bsktbl; Var L Golf; Hon Roll; OK ST Univ; Arch Dsgn.

MC FALL, MELISSA B; Catoosa HS; Catoosa, OK; (3); Church Yth Grp; FCA; Pres FHA; Intnl Clb; Red Cross Aide; Ofcr Stu Cncl; Cit Awd; Hon Roll; Jr NHS; St Schlr; Stu Of The Month; Medicine.

MC FARLAND, ALANNA; Stilwell HS; Stilwell, OK; (3); Am Leg Aux Girls St; Church Yth Grp; 4-H; Natl Beta Clb; Band; Chorus; High Hon Roll; Hon Roll; NHS; Worlds Changers; Vet.

MC FARLAND, MICAELA A; Agra Schl; Agra, OK; (2); 1/25; Church Yth Grp; English Clb; FCA; FHA; Quiz Bowl; Science Clb; Spanish Clb; Var Bsbl; Var Bsktbl; Sftbl.

MC FARLAND, MINDY J; Bokoshe Schl; Bokoshe, OK; (3); 1/20; FHA; Pres Frsh Cls; Pres Soph Cls; Pres Jr Cls; Pres Sr Cls; Capt Bsktbl; Capt Sftbl; High Hon Roll; NHS; Val; PE.

MC FARLIN, CANDICE; Glencoe Public Schl; Glencoe, OK; (3); 2/30; Church Yth Grp; FCA; HOBY; Pres Frsh Cls; VP Soph Cls; Rep Stu Cncl; Var Bsktbl; Var Chrldng; Var Crs Cntry; Var Sftbl; Phys Thrp.

MC FERRAN, LISA; Sasakwa Schl; Sasakwa, OK; (1); 2/20; Church Yth Grp; 4-H; Girl Scts; Letterman Clb; Quiz Bowl; Teachers Aide; School Play; Sec Frsh Cls; Bsktbl; Score Keeper; Super Showmn Livestock Cmptn; Dist/Cty & Local Cattle Cmptn; OSU; Phys Thpry.

MC FERRON, ASHLEY; Miami Sr HS; Miami, OK; (1); Church Yth Grp; FCA; GAA; Rep Stu Cncl; JV Bsktbl; Var Golf; Hon Roll; Jr NHS.

MC FERRON, BRIAN; Miami Sr HS; Miami, OK; (2); 15/221; Church Yth Grp; FCA; HOBY; Rep Stu Cncl; JV Golf; High Hon Roll; NHS; Natl Hnr Roll; NHS; OK U; Med.

MC GAHA, ANNA M; Lexington HS; Lexington, OK; (3); FCA; Pres Natl FFA Org; Office Aide; JV Var Bsktbl; Var Mgr(s); High Hon Roll; Hon Roll; NHS; Hnry Jr; ECU; Spcl Ed.

MC GAHA, SAMUEL; Hobart HS; Hobart, OK; (2); 1/100; Quiz Bowl; Scholastic Bowl; Var Bsktbl; Ftbl; Hon Roll; NHS; Ftbl Tm Trnr; US Naval Acad; Navy Pilot.

MC GAHEY, MELISSA A; Dickson HS; Ardmore, OK; (1); Drama Clb; Spanish Clb; Speech Tm; SADD; School Play; Hon Roll; NHS; Phy Assoc.

MC GANN, ADAM C; Edmond Memorial HS; Edmond, OK; (2); 1/408; Spanish Clb; Band; Jazz Band; Mrchg Band; Orch; Pep Band; School Musical; Variety Show; Tennis; NHS; CODA Hnr Band; Bus.

MC GARRY, NICOLE E; Bishop Mc Guinnes HS; Oklahoma City, OK; (3); 1/140; Sec Am Leg Aux Girls St; Treas Debate Tm; FCA; French Clb; NFL; Rep Soph Cls; Pres Jr Cls; Var L Swmmng; French Hon Soc; NHS; Kairos Rtrt Yth Ldr; Northwestern U; Biomed Engrng.

MC GATH, CHRISTOPHER B; Macarthur Sr HS; Lawton, OK; (3); Cmnty Wkr; FCA; Science Clb; Variety Show; Co-Ed Yrbk; JV Socr; Wrstlng; High Hon Roll; NHS; Prfct Atten Awd; ST Sci Fair Mult Sci Awds; Org Schl Project; Lead Guitor Player Rock Band Several Concerts; Math/Med/Sci.

MC GAVOCK, JENNY; Granite Jr Sr HS; Granite, OK; (3); Am Leg Aux Girls St; Church Yth Grp; 4-H; FHA; Quiz Bowl; Science Clb; Chorus; School Play; Ed Yrbk; Pres Frsh Cls.

MC GAVOCK, MICHAEL K; Locust Grove HS; Salina, OK; (2); Church Yth Grp; FBLA; Hon Roll; TSA; Acad Bowl Team; Northeastern ST U; Comp Sys.

MC GEE, CHERYL L; Mustang HS; Mustang, OK; (3); Church Yth Grp; FCA; French Clb; Key Clb; Band; Church Choir; Mrchg Band; School Musical; Rep Frsh Cls; JV Bsktbl; OK Bapt U; Dntl.

MC GEE, JESSICA M; Antlers Sr HS; Antlers, OK; (3); Nwsp; High Hon Roll; Hon Roll; 1st Pl Lions Club Essay Cntst; Jrnlsm.

MC GEE, KAMBER D; Putnam City North HS; Oklahoma City, OK; (1); Church Yth Grp; Church Choir; Hon Roll; Peak; SW Assembly Of God; Chrstn Cnc.

MC GEE, MERREDITH D; Mc Alester HS; Mc Alester, OK; (3); 1/200; Church Yth Grp; Cmnty Wkr; Pres FHA; Spanish Clb; Band; Capt Color Guard; Cit Awd; High Hon Roll; Peer Cnslr; Yth Shelter Vol; Yth Shelter Bd Of Dir; Northeastern ST Univ; Sci; Ed.

MC GEE, SARAH E; Bishop Kelley HS; Tulsa, OK; (2); Church Yth Grp; Cmnty Wkr; Dance Clb; DECA; Drama Clb; Library Aide; Office Aide; Speech Tm; Teachers Aide; School Musical; Outstdng Speech & Drama Stu; UCLA; Theater Arts.

MC GEE, VERONICA; Lawton Sr HS; Lawton, OK; (2); FCA; Var Chrldng; Hon Roll; U Of OK.

MC GEHEE, AMY; Poteau HS; Poteau, OK; (4); 22/141; Am Leg Aux Girls St; Church Yth Grp; FCA; VP Sr Cls; Var Capt Bsktbl; Var Crs Cntry; Var Powder Puff Ftbl; Var Capt Trk; Hon Roll; NHS; S Pcl Olympcs Vol; Senate Page; Chrch Sec; Carl Albert ST Coll; Law.

MC GEHEE, BRANDI; Eufaula Sr HS; Eufaula, OK; (3); Church Yth Grp; FHA; Mrchg Band; VP Jr Cls; JV Bsktbl; Var Sftbl; Cit Awd; Hon Roll; NHS; Val; Phrmcy.

MC GEHEE, SHANNA M; Claremore Sr HS; Claremore, OK; (2); Church Yth Grp; Teachers Aide; Hon Roll; Prfct Atten Awd; Cert Trng 1st Aid, CPR Procdrs; Tchng.

MC GHEE, ADAM M; Catoosa HS; Catoosa, OK; (2); 18/180; Letterman Clb; Spanish Clb; L Crs Cntry; L Trk; Cit Awd; High Hon Roll; Hon Roll; NHS; Pres Acad Fit Awd; Tulsa Univ.

MC GILL, COURTNEY D; Owasso Sr HS; Collinsville, OK; (2); 31/432; Church Yth Grp; French Clb; Church Choir; Var Capt Swmmng; Hon Roll; Marine Bio; Marine Mammalogy.

MC GILL, JESSICA L; Claremore Sr HS; Claremore, OK; (1); Church Yth Grp; Var Bsktbl; Var Tennis; Hon Roll; NHS; Stdnt Of Mnth.

MC GILL, JOSHUA W; Altus Sr HS; Altus, OK; (3); Debate Tm; L Ftbl; L Tennis; L Wrstlng; Hon Roll; Prfct Atten Awd; Vol Local Vet Frgn Wars Post/VA Hosp; Vol Faternal Order Police With Comm Projcts; Penn ST Univ; Acctg/Psych.

MC GILL, MARK M; Bartlesville Sr HS; Bartlesville, OK; (3); Varsity Clb; JV Var Ftbl; Hon Roll; Marine Envrnmntl Sci.

MC GILL, TODD W; South Intermediate HS; Broken Arrow, OK; (1); Boy Scts; 4-H; Library Aide; Natl FFA Org; Prfct Atten Awd.

MC GINIS, SCOTT A; Cushing HS; Cushing, OK; (3); 22/148; Am Leg Boys St; Church Yth Grp; Math Clb; Natl FFA Org; Office Aide; Science Clb; Spanish Clb; Teachers Aide; Var L Bsbl; Var L Bsktbl; OK U.

MC GINLEY, TODD R; Putnam City North HS; Oklahoma City, OK; (3); Var Bsktbl; Hon Roll; Panther Pals.

MC GINNIS, JASON R; Durant HS; Durant, OK; (1); 1/200; Church Yth Grp; Church Choir; Ftbl; High Hon Roll; OK Hnr Soc; Mixed Choir; Phy Asst.

MC GINNIS, RHIANNON L; Woodward HS; Woodward, OK; (3); Dance Clb; FHA; German Clb; Key Clb; Capt Flag Corp; Mrchg Band; Nwsp; Rep Stu Cncl; Powder Puff Ftbl; Hon Roll; Frgn Exchng Stu; OK St Univ; Sociology.

MC GLOCKLIN, AGRESTA D; Milburn Schl; Milburn, OK; (4); 4/25; Sec 4-H; Teachers Aide; Rptr Yrbk; VP Sr Cls; Var Bsktbl; Var Sftbl; Cit Awd; 4-H Awd; High Hon Roll; Hon Roll; All Str In Bsktbll; Gldn Glove Recpt; Bst Off Plyr In Bsktbll; Murray St Col; Bus.

MC GOWAN, HOLLY; Haworth Jr HS; Haworth, OK; (1); 1/50; Art Clb; Church Yth Grp; 4-H; Quiz Bowl; Chorus; Rep Frsh Cls; Bsktbl; Sftbl; High Hon Roll; Val; Law.

MC GOWEN, DEANNA; Moore HS; Moore, OK; (3); 1/650; Sec Treas Debate Tm; HOBY; NFL; Spanish Clb; Sec Treas Speech Tm; Ofcr Stu Cncl; Trk; NHS; Scholastic Bowl; Pres Acad Fit Awd; Mock Trial Tm; Intl Order Of Rnbw For Grls; U Of Tulsa; Atty.

MC GOWEN, LORI; Moore HS; Moore, OK; (3); Art Clb; Capt Quiz Bowl; Science Clb; Spanish Clb; Rptr Nwsp; Rptr Yrbk; Var Capt Socr; Jr NHS; Multicltrl Stu Assn.

MC GOWEN, RA DONNA; Varnum Jr Sr HS; Seminole, OK; (4); Library Aide; Teachers Aide; Hon Roll; Blue & Gold Sausage Top Salesperson; Educl Talent Search; ETS Ldrshp; Ntl Hnr Roll; Seminole JC; Early Chldhd Ed.

MC GOWIN, BERTHA M; Dewar Jr-Sr HS; Dewar, OK; (4); 4/27; Library Aide; Co-Capt Quiz Bowl; Spanish Clb; Chorus; Sec Jr Cls; VP Sr Cls; Var Sftbl; Gov Hon Prg Awd; High Hon Roll; NHS; OSU Okmulgee; Soc Wrkr.

MC GRAW, ALISON L; Muskogee HS; Muskogee, OK; (3); 20/347; Church Yth Grp; JCL; Sec Key Clb; School Play; Treas Jr Cls; Socr; High Hon Roll; Hon Roll; Jr NHS; NHS; Octagon Clb Treas; Delphic Sec; OK Hnr Soc; OK U; Dnstry.

MC GRAW, SHANNON; Moore HS; Oklahoma City, OK; (2); Church Yth Grp; Latin Clb; Red Cross Aide; Science Clb; Band; Mrchg Band; Stage Crew; Nwsp; Yrbk; NHS; Miss OK City Jr Teen Pgnt Fnlst; OK St Sen Lgsltve Page; U OK; Med.

MC GREGOR, KATIE; Bartlesville Sr HS; Bartlesville, OK; (3); French Clb; Pep Clb; Band; Socr; Hon Roll; OK ST U Stillwater; Psych.

MC GUAR, RANI; Perry Sr HS; Perry, OK; (3); FCA; German Clb; GAA; Natl FFA Org; Band; Var Bsktbl; Var Chrldng; High Hon Roll; Hon Roll; Jr NHS; OSU; Phys Thrpy.

MC GUIRE, ADRIA; Cyril Jr Sr HS; Cyril, OK; (3); School Play; Yrbk; Bsktbl; Chrldng; Trk; High Hon Roll; Hon Roll; NHS; OU; Perf Arts.

MC GUIRE, AMANDA J; Mustang HS; Yukon, OK; (1); Church Yth Grp; Cmnty Wkr; Speech Tm; Band; Jazz Band; Mrchg Band; Pep Band; Trk; OBU; Psych/Bnd Dir.

MC GUIRE, DANIEL L; Kellyville Sr HS; Bristow, OK; (2); Church Yth Grp; Var Bsbl; FFA.

MC GUIRE, JASON E; Nathan Hale HS; Tulsa, OK; (3); 30/250; Cmnty Wkr; FCA; Key Clb; Spanish Clb; Rptr Yrbk; Ofcr Jr Cls; Var Ftbl; Var Swmmng; Natl Nmnee Wendy HS Heisman Awd; Nmntd Sr Class Pres; OK St Univ; Mech Eng.

MC GUIRE, KATIE M; Hollis Jr Sr HS; Hollis, OK; (2); Church Yth Grp; Pres Drama Clb; FHA; Quiz Bowl; Pres Speech Tm; Band; High Hon Roll; Bio Awd; Chem Awd; OK Hnr Soc; OK Chrstn Univ; Bio.

MC GUIRE, KIMBERLY D; East Central HS; Tulsa, OK; (3); Church Yth Grp; Cmnty Wkr; FCA; Hosp Aide; Band; Church Choir; Jazz Band; Mrchg Band; Orch; High Hon Roll; Church Sftbl/Vlybl/Bsktbl Team; Tulsa JC; BSN.

MC GUIRE, MARCIE; Crowder Schl; Crowder, OK; (3); Pep Clb; Nwsp; Yrbk; Rep Frsh Cls; Rep Stu Cncl; FFA VP 94-95; Paralegal.

MC GUIRE, NATHANIEL J; Del City HS; Del City, OK; (2); FCA; Var L Bsktbl; Tennis; Jr NHS; Peer Mediation; Georgetown Univ; Law.

MC GUIRE, RANDALL; Crowder Schl; Crowder, OK; (2); 4/30; Pres 4-H; Pres Soph Cls; Var Bsbl; Var Bsktbl; High Hon Roll; Hon Roll; NHS; Prfct Atten Awd; Val; Tulsa U; Comp Sci.

MC HALE, ERIN MICHELE; Bartlesville Sr HS; Bartlesville, OK; (4); 99/429; Art Clb; Church Yth Grp; Cmnty Wkr; French Clb; FBLA; FHA; Girl Scts; Hosp Aide; Science Clb; Spanish Clb; Acad Achvmt Lang Arts Cert Spcl Recognition; OK Ctr Advancement Of Sci & Tech Awd; Cottey Coll Nevada.

MC HENRY, AMANDA J; Sallisaw HS; Sallisaw, OK; (4); 9/128; Debate Tm; Drama Clb; Sec Math Clb; Office Aide; Pep Clb; Sec Science Clb; Rptr Sec Spanish Clb; VP Rptr Band; Mrchg Band; School Musical; OK Hnrs Soc; All Dist Hnr Band; Yth Fair Chance OK Rep; Westark CC; Psych.

MC HUGH, AMANDA; Moore HS; Moore, OK; (4); 19/525; JCL; Latin Clb; Mu Alpha Theta; Red Cross Aide; Rep Stu Cncl; Mgr(s); NHS; Pres Acad Fit Awd; Val; Ntl Hsty & Govt Awd; U Of MO; Brdcst Jrnlsm.

MC HUGH, CARRIE; Bishop Mcguinness HS; Edmond, OK; (4); FCA; FBLA; Pep Clb; SADD; Rep Soph Cls; Var Capt Bsktbl; Var Chrldng; Var Capt Sftbl; Homecmng Candte; Olympc Comm; U Of OK.

MC ILVAIN, MICHAEL J; Buffalo Jr Sr HS; Woodward, OK; (3); FBLA; Rep Natl FFA Org; Band; Jazz Band; Mrchg Band; Pep Band; Var Bsbl; Var Bsktbl; Hon Roll; NHS; Laverne All Trnmt Bsbl Team 95-96; Frosh Cls Favorite; Laverne All Trnmt Bsbl Team 94-95.

MC INTIRE, JARED; Durant HS; Durant, OK; (4); Church Yth Grp; Cmnty Wkr; FCA; 4-H; Natl FFA Org; VICA; Var Bsbl; Var Ftbl; FFA ST Farmer Awrd; SOSU.

MC INTIRE, JONATHAN S; Durant HS; Durant, OK; (1); Church Yth Grp; Cmnty Wkr; FCA; 4-H; Rep Stu Cncl; Ftbl; Wt Lftg; High Hon Roll; Hon Roll.

MC INTOSH, TIFFANY D; Mc Alester HS; Mcalester, OK; (4); 20/209; Church Yth Grp; Band; Color Guard; Mrchg Band; Hon Roll; NHS; OK ST Univ; Psych.

MC INTURFF, STEPHANIE; Mid-Del Christian Schl; Midwest City, OK; (1); 1/13; Church Yth Grp; Cmnty Wkr; Sec Frsh Cls; Golf; Sftbl; High Hon Roll.

MC INTYRE, ELAINE R; Edmond Memorial HS; Edmond, OK; (2); 32/408; Church Yth Grp; Key Clb; Mu Alpha Theta; Spanish Clb; Church Choir; Powder Puff Ftbl; JV Var Trk; Hon Roll; NHS; Prfct Atten Awd; Yth For Christ/Campus Life.

MC INTYRE, SEPTEMBER; Burns Flat-Dill City Jshs; Burns Flat, OK; (4); 3/34; Church Yth Grp; Pres 4-H; Pres FHA; HOBY; Chorus; School Play; Yrbk; Chrldng; 4-H Awd; NHS; OK Bapt U; Bus.

MC KAY, BRIAN M; Edmond North HS; Edmond, OK; (2); 58/420; Mu Alpha Theta; JV Bsktbl; JV Ftbl; Jr NHS; NHS; Prfct Atten Awd; OK ST Univ; Engr.

MC KAY, KARI; Choctaw HS; Choctaw, OK; (2); Key Clb; Var Crs Cntry; Var Socr; Hon Roll; OK ST U; Vet.

MC KAY, MEAGAN D; Healdton HS; Healdton, OK; (2); Church Yth Grp; Drama Clb; Band; Mrchg Band; High Hon Roll; NHS; Pres Acad Fit Awd; Traveling; U Of Cntrl OK; Psych.

MC KAY, MELISSA J; Wynnewood HS; Wynnewood, OK; (2); 10/56; Art Clb; Office Aide; Teachers Aide; Rep Jr Cls; Hon Roll; NHS; East Cntrl; Pre-Med.

MC KAY, RYAN C; Blanchard Jr Sr HS; Blanchard, OK; (2) Church Yth Grp; FCA; Var Bsbl; Var Bsktbl; Var Ftbl.

MC KEE, ERICA; Haworth Jr HS; Haworth, OK; (1); 1/60; Church Yth Grp; 4-H; Natl FFA Org; Pres Stu Cncl; Bsktbl; Hon Roll; NHS; Val; FFA Greenhand Quiz P I Dist Wnnr; OK ST U.

MC KEE, KAREN L; Putnam City West HS; Oklahoma City, OK; (1); Church Yth Grp; Chorus; Stage Crew; Nrs.

MC KEE, MAURA; Cascia Hall Prep School; Tulsa, OK; (3); Cmnty Wkr; Sec Spanish Clb; Teachers Aide; Yrbk; Lit Mag; Var Crs Cntry; Var Swmmng; High Hon Roll; NHS; Ntl Merit Ltr; Wnr Tulsa Exec Wmn Intl Schlsp Prgm; Take A Seat Invtn; Art; Pprdls; Pnt Frntr; Read; Write; 4 Yr U; Engl/Art.

MC KEE, MEG; Cascia Hall Prep School; Tulsa, OK; (1); German Clb; Chorus; School Musical; School Play; Ofcr Soph Cls; Swmmng; Hon Roll; Ballet/Tap/Jazz.

MC KEE, SCOTTIE; Hulbert Jr Sr HS; Hulbert, OK; (4); Chess Clb; Drama Clb; FBLA; Spanish Clb; Bsktbl; Ftbl; Trk; Wt Lftg; NHS; Psych.

MC KEE, TABITHA; U S Grant HS; Oklahoma City, OK; (4); 14/175; Pres Church Yth Grp; FCA; Chorus; School Musical; School Play; Rep Frsh Cls; VP Sr Cls; Ofcr Stu Cncl; Hon Roll; NHS; Pres Schlr; OK Bapt U; Ped.

MC KEE, TASHA R; Northeast HS; Oklahoma City, OK; (4); 35/126; Treas Church Yth Grp; FBLA; VICA; Rptr Nwsp; Yrbk; Treas Jr Cls; High Hon Roll; Hon Roll; St Schlr; Bus Mgmt.

MC KEE, TIFFANY A; Cordell Sr HS; Cordell, OK; (2); Church Yth Grp; FHA; Treas Spanish Clb; Band; Jazz Band; Mrchg Band; Pep Band; Hon Roll; South Western OK ST U; K Tchr.

MC KEEN, JANNA M; Checotah HS; Checotah, OK; (3); Church Yth Grp; Acpl Chr; Band; Chorus; Color Guard; Mrchg Band; Orch; Pep Band; Hon Roll; Band Sec-Treas; OK Bapt Univ; Child Psych.

MC KEEN, KIMBERLY L; Yukon HS; Yukon, OK; (2); CAP; Chorus; Hon Roll; Pres Acad Fit Awd; OK ST Univ; Vet.

MC KELLIPS, KERI R; Union Intermediate HS; Tulsa, OK; (2); Church Yth Grp; FCA; Spanish Clb; Chorus; Church Choir; Ed Yrbk; Rep Stu Cncl; Hon Roll; NHS; Southern Nazarene U; Jrnlsm; Wrt.

MC KENNA, KATIE; Bridge Creek HS; Blanchard, OK; (4); 1/56; Pres FBLA; Sec Spanish Clb; Ed Yrbk; Rep Frsh Cls; VP Jr Cls; Ofcr Stu Cncl; Chrldng; High Hon Roll; Val; Outstndgn Frosh Grl; UCO; Bus.

MC KENZIE, CASEY; Empire Schl; Duncan, OK; (2); FBLA; Ofcr Soph Cls; L Stat Bsbl; Cit Awd; Hon Roll; Ntl Merit Ltr; TX Tech; Bus Mgmt.

MC KENZIE, CHAD L; Marietta HS; Burneyville, OK; (3); Office Aide; Band; Hon Roll; Durant.

MC KENZIE, CHARITY R; Wright Christian Acad; Broken Arrow, OK; (3); 11/29; Pep Clb; School Play; Chrldng; High Hon Roll; Bus.

MC KENZIE, CONOR D; Bishop Kelley HS; Tulsa, OK; (4); Key Clb; Model UN; Office Aide; Varsity Clb; VP Frsh Cls; Pres Soph Cls; Rep Stu Cncl; JV Bsbl; Var L Ftbl; JV Wrstlng; U Of OK.

MC KENZIE, FAITH M; Wright Christian Acad; Broken Arrow, OK; (2); 4/43; Pep Clb; Chorus; School Musical; School Play; VP Frsh Cls; Var Chrldng; High Hon Roll; Piano; Chrstn Ed.

MC KIM, KELLI A; Yukon Middle HS; Yukon, OK; (1); Art Clb; Church Yth Grp; FHA; Church Choir; Elem Tchr.

MC KINLEY, ERIC W; Bridge Creek HS; Blanchard, OK; (2); Art Clb; Church Yth Grp; Library Aide; Office Aide; Spanish Clb; Band; Jazz Band; Mrchg Band; Ed Yrbk; Excl In Bio; Red Bud Classic Med Team Vol; OU; Med.

MC KINLEY, EVELYN S; Comanche HS; Comanche, OK; (2); Church Yth Grp; FHA; Teachers Aide; Church Choir; Hon Roll; TSA.

MC KINLEY, LISA M; Mannford HS; Cleveland, OK; (4); 18/83; Church Yth Grp; Drama Clb; FCA; Office Aide; Science Clb; SADD; Teachers Aide; Chorus; Church Choir; Bsktbl; Tulsa JC.

MC KINLEY, STEPHEN M; Westmoore HS; Oklahoma City, OK; (2); Church Yth Grp; Rep Soph Cls; Rep Stu Cncl; JV Bsbl; Hon Roll; NVY; Aero Eng.

MC KINNEY, DANA L; Choctaw HS; Newalla, OK; (3); Church Yth Grp; Office Aide; Chorus; Church Choir; Phtg Nwsp; Phtg Yrbk; Hon Roll; NHS; Univ Of Cntrl OK; Dntstry.

MC KINNEY, DEBBIE K; Grace Chrn Acad; Oklahoma City, OK; (4); 3/23; Teachers Aide; Phtg Yrbk; Sec Frsh Cls; Treas Jr Cls; Trk; Cit Awd; Hon Roll; Sal; Bible I, II, III Awds; Frosh Schlsp OK City Comm Coll; Algebra OK His Cert; Chrst Maturity Plaque; OK City Comm Coll.

MC KINNEY, DEON; Mc Lain Career Acad; Tulsa, OK; (1); Ofcr Frsh Cls; Ofcr Bsbl; Bsktbl.

MC KINNEY, EMILY A; Charles Page HS; Sand Springs, OK; (3); Church Yth Grp; FCA; GAA; Math Tm; Pep Clb; Spanish Clb; Varsity Clb; Yrbk; VP Frsh Cls; Pres Soph Cls; Stu Advsry Cncl; Masonic Stu Of Today Awd; Hon Grad; OK St Univ; Phys Thpy.

MC KINNEY, KORI S; Moore HS; Moore, OK; (3); 78/600; DECA; JA; Scholastic Bowl; Hon Roll; TX Tech.

MC KINNEY, LESLIE; Houston Homan Jr HS; Eufaula, OK; (1); 1/108; Band; Mrchg Band; Orch; Chrldng; Cit Awd; High Hon Roll; Jr NHS; Ntl Merit Ltr; Pres Acad Fit Awd; Val; NCA All-Amer Chrldr; U Of KS; Ortho Peds.

MC KINNEY, RACHELLE D; Edmond North HS; Edmond, OK; (2); Church Yth Grp; Rep Stu Cncl; JV Pom Pon; Jr NHS; Cmptr Engr.

MC KINNON, AMY D; Oklahoma Christian Acad; Oklahoma City, OK; (4); Church Yth Grp; Drama Clb; Acpl Chr; Chorus; Sec Jr Cls; Treas Sr Cls; Bsktbl; Chrldng; Mgr(s); Sftbl; Lead Singer In Quartet; Placed In Drama Cmptns; OK Chrstn U Of Sci & Arts; Bus.

MC KINZIE, MARY A; Indiahoma Schl; Indiahoma, OK; (1); FCA; Yrbk; Bsktbl; Sftbl; High Hon Roll; Cameron Univ; Vetrnrn.

MC KINZIE, MELISSA N; Pauls Valley HS; Pauls Valley, OK; (2); Church Yth Grp; FCA; FHA; Key Clb; Natl FFA Org; Yrbk; Mgr(s); Tennis; Hon Roll; FFA Rptr 96-; OK Hnr Scty; Med Field.

MC KINZIE, SYLVIA E; Oklahoma Bible Acad; Enid, OK; (3); Church Yth Grp; Chorus; School Musical; Hon Roll; Kids On The Block Vol; Daycare Owner.

MC KITTRICK, ADRIAN T; Union Intermediate HS; Tulsa, OK; (2); Church Choir; Ftbl; Trk; Wt Lftg; Hon Roll; African Amer Assn; TU; Forensic Sci.

MC KNIGHT, CLINT J; Tecumseh HS; Tecumseh, OK; (2); Church Yth Grp; Letterman Clb; Scholastic Bowl; Var Bsktbl; Var Trk; High Hon Roll; Hon Roll; NHS; Stdnt Mnth; Brdcstng.

MC KNIGHT, JENNIFER L; Vinita HS; Vinita, OK; (2); German Clb; Band; Chorus; Mrchg Band; Pep Band; Hon Roll; NHS; Camp Fire; MIT; Engrng.

MC KNIGHT, NATALIE D; Holland Hall Schl; Broken Arrow, OK; (2); Church Yth Grp; Band; Mrchg Band; Orch; Pep Band; JV Bsktbl; JV Trk; JV Vllybl; Hon Roll; Engrng.

MC LAIN, CRYSTAL GAIL; Buffalo Jr Sr HS; Buffalo, OK; (3); 1/25; Church Yth Grp; Band; Mrchg Band; Pep Band; Pres Soph Cls; Var L Sftbl; Hon Roll; NHS; U OK; Cmptr Sci.

MC LAIN, KURT; Dickson HS; Ardmore, OK; (2); Spanish Clb; Var Bsktbl; Var Crs Cntry; Var Golf; Trk; High Hon Roll; Hon Roll; Pres Acad Fit Awd; Water Ski.

MC LANE, VERONICA; Hinton HS; Hinton, OK; (3); 1/27; Church Yth Grp; Treas FCA; Key Clb; Chorus; School Musical; School Play; Var Chrldng; High Hon Roll; NHS; SADD; Senate Page 95; Law.

MC LAREN, JUSTIN R; Madill HS; Madill, OK; (1); Church Yth Grp; FCA; Var JV Bsbl; Intrml Bsktbl; JV Var Ftbl; Hon Roll.

MC LAUGHLIN, AMANDA M; Kellyville Sr HS; Kellyville, OK; (2); Church Yth Grp; 4-H; Natl FFA Org; Flag Corp; 4-H Awd; Hon Roll; Bus; Acctng.

MC LAUGHLIN, APRIL R; Tomlinson Jr HS; Lawton, OK; (2); Church Yth Grp; FCA; Band; Church Choir; Flag Corp; Mrchg Band; Rep Stu Cncl; Hon Roll; Chrch Puppet Team; Dr.

MC LAUGHLIN, BRANDON L; Oologah HS; Talala, OK; (2); FCA; Var Ftbl; Var Wt Lftg; Hon Roll; Woodwrkr Yr 95; NFL Ftbl.

MC LAUGHLIN, DANIEL W; Tecumseh HS; Tecumseh, OK; (3); Am Leg Boys St; Quiz Bowl; Scholastic Bowl; Science Clb; Ed Yrbk; Gov Hon Prg Awd; High Hon Roll; Hon Roll; NHS; OK ST Univ.

MC LAUGHLIN, DONITA; Anadarko HS; Anadarko, OK; (3); 17/109; Church Yth Grp; Rptr Treas 4-H; FBLA; Teachers Aide; Nwsp; Yrbk; Ofcr Stu Cncl; Hon Roll; Jr NHS; NHS; Rollerblading; Southwestern OK ST Univ; Bus.

MC LAUGHLIN, ROBERT E; Central Jr HS; Lawton, OK; (1); Church Yth Grp; Debate Tm; Drama Clb; FBLA; Intnl Clb; Key Clb; Math Tm; Ski Clb; SADD; Church Choir; Lawyer.

MC LAUGHLIN, ROSS; Woodward HS; Woodward, OK; (3); Cmnty Wkr; Computer Clb; German Clb; Key Clb; Office Aide; Pep Clb; Trk; High Hon Roll; NHS; Pres Acad Fit Awd; Ger Amer Soc.

MC LEAN, SEAN P; Stillwater Sr HS; Stillwater, OK; (2); Church Yth Grp; Cmnty Wkr; FCA; Bsktbl; Socr; Hon Roll; Pres Acad Fit Awd; Pres Schlr; OK ST Univ; Bus.

MC LEMORE, CANDACE F; Calera Jr Sr HS; Durant, OK; (4); 10/33; Church Yth Grp; Cmnty Wkr; 4-H; FHA; Math Clb; Quiz Bowl; Scholastic Bowl; Science Clb; Chorus; Church Choir; Accptd To Headlands Pgm At OU; Placed 1st & 2nd In Curriculum Cont; Southeastern OK ST; Pre-Med.

MC LEMORE, JESSICA; Midwest City HS; Midwest City, OK; (4); Church Yth Grp; Cmnty Wkr; Sec Phtg German Clb; Pres Girl Scts; Sec Science Clb; SADD; Acpl Chr; Chorus; Color Guard; Co-Capt Nwsp; Russian Clb; USAA Schlr & Bus Awd; Elem Spcl Ed.

MC LEMORE, MARCUS; Will Rogers HS; Tulsa, OK; (3); JA; Quiz Bowl; Spanish Clb; Varsity Clb; Rep Frsh Cls; Rep Stu Cncl; JV Var Bsktbl; JV Var Ftbl; NHS; Prfct Atten Awd; Lwyr.

MC LENNAN, CHAD A; Carl Albert HS; Choctaw, OK; (4); Band; Jazz Band; Mrchg Band; Pep Band; Swing Chorus; Outs Trumpet Solist; U Of Centr OK; Mus Perf.

MC LINDEN, JAMES L; Central Jr HS; Lawton, OK; (1); FCA; Spanish Clb; Hon Roll.

MC LINDEN, LEAH; Quinton Jr Sr HS; Quinton, OK; (4); 10/38; French Clb; Library Aide; Scholastic Bowl; Church Choir; Drm Mjr(t); Mrchg Band; Orch; French Hon Soc; Hon Roll; S E MS ST U; Psych.

MC MAHAN, JEANIE S; Kiowa Jr-Sr HS; Blanco, OK; (3); 3/35; 4-H; Hist VP FHA; Teachers Aide; Nwsp; Yrbk; Sec Frsh Cls; Sec Jr Cls; 4-H Awd; High Hon Roll; Hon Roll; TSA Pres; 3rd Pl Home Ec SOSU Schlstc Meet; 1st Pl Fmly Rels ECU Schlstc; 3rd Pl Home Ec St Schlstc; E Central U; Acctng.

MC MAHAN, JOY; Choctaw HS; Choctaw, OK; (4); 93/299; Church Yth Grp; Chorus; Church Choir; School Musical; Stage Crew; Swing Chorus; Hon Roll; NHS; Taekwondo; Jazz Choir.

MC MAHAN, REBECCA; Edison HS; Tulsa, OK; (4); 32/178; Drama Clb; FCA; Key Clb; Letterman Clb; Spanish Clb; SADD; Chorus; Phtg Yrbk; NHS; Church Yth Grp; Camp Fire; Metro Area Hnr Choir; Sunday Schl Tchr & Camp Cnslr; Northeastern ST Univ; Bus; Law.

MC MAINS, EMILY; Seminole Jr Sr HS; Seminole, OK; (4); 1/80; Church Yth Grp; Debate Tm; Pres VP FCA; Math Clb; Math Tm; NFL; Spanish Clb; Teachers Aide; Church Choir; Drill Tm.

MC MAINS, JEANNIE; Seminole Jr Sr HS; Seminole, OK; (2); Church Yth Grp; FCA; Math Clb; Science Clb; Spanish Clb; Church Choir; Drill Tm; Pom Pon; Tennis; High Hon Roll; OK Bapt U; Elem Ed.

MC MANAMY, AMBER D; Mulhall Orlando HS; Mulhall, OK; (4); 12/22; Library Aide; Yrbk; Var Co-Capt Bsktbl; Var Sftbl; Hon Roll; Jr NHS; NHS; Band; Nwsp; OSU Alumni; OK Chllnge; All-St Sftbl-Slowptch; UCO.

MC MARTIN, JIMMY D; Western Heights Sr HS; Oklahoma City, OK; (1); Church Yth Grp; Bsktbl.

MC MASTERS, KATY J; Sapulpa Sr HS; Sapulpa, OK; (3); 23/280; Church Yth Grp; Debate Tm; JA; NFL; Speech Tm; Acpl Chr; Band; Chorus; Church Choir; Mrchg Band; St/Reg Super Soloist Band/Choir; All-St Choir/Orch; All-Reg Band; OK Smmr Arts Inst 3 Yrs; OK U; Music Ed.

MC MASTERS, RENA M; Nathan Hale HS; Tulsa, OK; (2); ROTC; Rptr Nwsp; High Hon Roll; Hon Roll; Edtr Schl Show; Flmed In Lcl DAREVIDEO; Amrcn Lgn Awd; Vol For Proj Hope; Tulane Univ; Sci.

MC MEANS, HEATHER; Claremore Sr HS; Claremore, OK; (1); Church Yth Grp; Dance Clb; Drama Clb; French Clb; NFL; Chrldng; Golf; Score Keeper; Socr; Hon Roll; Bat Girl; Mat Maid; OK ST U; Lawyer.

MC MICHAEL, BRANDON L; Enid Sr HS; Enid, OK; (3); Cmnty Wkr; Q&S; Science Clb; Spanish Clb; Teachers Aide; Phtg Ed Yrbk; Ftbl; Trk; Hon Roll; Jr NHS; Poem Pub; Phychlgst.

MC MILLAN, KANDI M; Claremore Sr HS; Claremore, OK; (1); Dance Clb; French Clb; Girl Scts; Chorus; School Musical; High Hon Roll; Church Yth Grp; PT.

MC MILLEN, TARA; Tahlequah Sr HS; Hulbert, OK; (3); Am Leg Aux Girls St; Church Yth Grp; Cmnty Wkr; FCA; German Clb; Girl Scts; Red Cross Aide; Science Clb; Service Clb; Speech Tm; Stu Cncl Rep; OK Assoc Elect Coopyth Tour; Rotary Yth Ldrshp Awd Cmp; Brdcst Jrnlsm.

MC MILLIAN, CHRISTY; Lone Grove HS; Lone Grove, OK; (4); 1/90; Key Clb; Nwsp; VP Soph Cls; VP Sr Cls; Sec Stu Cncl; Sftbl; High Hon Roll; NHS; Prfct Atten Awd; Pres Acad Fit Awd; OK U; Med.

MC MILLIAN, MORGAN; Stillwater Sr HS; Stillwater, OK; (4); 6/350; Am Leg Aux Girls St; Hosp Aide; Key Clb; Q&S; Pres Spanish Clb; School Play; Ed Nwsp; Sec Soph Cls; Pres Stu Cncl; Hon Roll.

MC MILLIN, CALVIN; Rush Springs HS; Rush Springs, OK; (3); #1 in class; Art Clb; HOBY; Quiz Bowl; Scholastic Bowl; Spanish Clb; Rep Frsh Cls; Rep Soph Cls; Pres Jr Cls; Sec Treas Stu Cncl; Ftbl; Gftd & Tlntd; Prom Cmmtte; Ed.

MC MILLIN, KERRY E; Ft Cobb Sr HS; Fort Cobb, OK; (4); 4/36; Church Yth Grp; Rptr FHA; Spanish Clb; Chorus; Ed Nwsp; Yrbk; Chrldng; Hon Roll; Pres Acad Fit Awd; U Of Sci/Arts Of OK; Spch Pthl.

MC MILLIN, KEVIN; Ft Cobb-Broxton HS; Fort Cobb, OK; (4); 2/35; Church Yth Grp; Natl FFA Org; Nwsp; Rep Jr Cls; Rep Stu Cncl; Bsktbl; Hon Roll; NHS; Sal; U Of Sci & Arts OK; Comp Sci.

MC MULLEN, BRIAN P; Stillwater Sr HS; Stillwater, OK; (2); Church Yth Grp; FCA; Ftbl; Trk; Wt Lftg; Hon Roll; Art; Commercial Art; Law Enforcement.

MC MULLEN, MARY E; Enid Sr HS; Enid, OK; (2); 8/461; Church Yth Grp; Cmnty Wkr; Drama Clb; Spanish Clb; Speech Tm; Band; Mrchg Band; School Musical; School Play; Stage Crew; Regnls Speech Contest 1st Pl; 4 Yr U; Bus Admin/CPA.

MC MULLEN, MOLLY; Rush Springs HS; Rush Springs, OK; (4); Letterman Clb; Spanish Clb; Chorus; School Play; Stage Crew; Sftbl; Vllybl; Wt Lftg; Lfgrd; Frst Respndr; Firefghtr; Univ Of Sci/Arts; Chldhd Ed.

MC MURRAY, RYAN M; West Middle HS; Norman, OK; (1); Art Clb; Church Yth Grp; Spanish Clb; Cit Awd; High Hon Roll; Hon Roll; NHS; U OK; Arch.

MC MURRIAN, CYNDI M; Buffalo Valley Schl; Tuskahoma, OK; (2); Church Yth Grp; Debate Tm; Rep FHA; Girl Scts; Natl FFA Org; Quiz Bowl; Speech Tm; Pres Jr Cls; L Sftbl; Hon Roll; Speech & Debate Ltr; Medcn; Law Enforcmnt; Acting.

MC MURTREY, BETH; Markoma Bible Acad; Westville, OK; (4); 3/12; Church Yth Grp; Chorus; Pres Sr Cls; Capt Bsktbl; L Vllybl; High Hon Roll; Miss Markoma; Cntrl Bible Coll; Ed.

MC NABB, DONIELLE; Burns Flat-Dill City HS; Burns Flat, OK; (2); 2/28; German Clb; HOBY; Scholastic Bowl; VP Frsh Cls; VP Soph Cls; Bsktbl; Co-Capt Chrldng; High Hon Roll; NHS; Sal; OK Hnr Soc; Homecmng Qn; SWIM Medalist.

MC NAMAR, EMILY; Claremore Sr HS; Claremore, OK; (4); 24/241; Church Yth Grp; Office Aide; Scholastic Bowl; Spanish Clb; SADD; High Hon Roll; NHS; Sr Hommng Attendant; Wrestling Mat Maid; OK ST Univ Frosh Acad Schlr; OK ST Univ; Medicine.

MC NAUGHTON, RYAN A; Union Sr HS; Tulsa, OK; (3); 97/673; Am Leg Boys St; Church Yth Grp; FCA; Ofcr Stu Cncl; JV Var Bsktbl; NHS; Drug Free Yth Organ.

MC NEAL, CHAD; Owasso Sr HS; Owasso, OK; (3); Boy Scts; Chess Clb; Church Yth Grp; Computer Clb; FCA; Math Clb; Natl FFA Org; Science Clb; Teachers Aide; Varsity Clb; Jr Ldrshp Awd; Most Outstdng Stdnt Sci/Turbo Pascal; Med.

MC NEAL, CYNTHIA F; Macarthur Sr HS; Lawton, OK; (3); Church Yth Grp; Cmnty Wkr; FCA; Key Clb; ROTC; Science Clb; Color Guard; Drill Tm; JV Bsktbl; JV Sftbl; Upwrd Bnd Sec & VP; Xinos Prlmntrn & Asst Sec; Palace Ancnt Sr Prncss; Atlanta Clark U; Comms.

MC NEAL, NATALIE; Bennington Schl; Bennington, OK; (3); 1/18; Quiz Bowl; Teachers Aide; Sec Stu Cncl; Var Bsktbl; Var Trk; NHS; English Clb; 4-H; School Musical; Sec Rep Frsh Cls; Native Amer Indigenos Games; Page ST Hs Rep; ST Fnlst OK Hrtg Cntst; Ctzn Bee; Miss Bennington High.

MC NEAL, RAVEN; Ada HS; Ada, OK; (3); 1/200; Cmnty Wkr; Key Clb; Quiz Bowl; Pres Science Clb; Spanish Clb; SADD; High Hon Roll; NHS; Spanish NHS; 1st Pl OK Karate Assn 94 & 95; Hghst Scr PEC Acad Bowsl; 4th Pl St Fair Schlrs Cont; Le Cordon Bleu; Chef.

MC NEELY, KEVIN J; Fairland Jr Sr HS; Fairland, OK; (1); Church Yth Grp; FHA; High Hon Roll; Hon Roll.

MC NEELY, REBECCA; Oklahoma Christian Schl; Oklahoma City, OK; (1); School Play; Crs Cntry; Trk.

MC NEESE, MARY BETH; Ponca City Sr HS; Ponca City, OK; (1); Chorus; Rep Stu Cncl; Chrldng; Hon Roll; OU; RN.

MC NEIL, GINGER; Gans Public Schl; Muldrow, OK; (3); FHA; Spanish Clb; Hon Roll.

MC NUTT, ABBIGAIL; Lawton Sr HS; Lawton, OK; (2); FCA; Sec FHA; Key Clb; Co-Ed Yrbk; Jr NHS; NHS; OK Hnr Soc; Tenn Ct Juror/Clrk; Knwldge Mstrs; OK Univ; MD.

MC NUTT, CLINT; Elmore City-Pernell HS; Elmore City, OK; (4); 9/37; Pres VP 4-H; Band; Nwsp; Yrbk; VP Frsh Cls; VP Soph Cls; Pres Jr Cls; VP Sr Cls; Rptr Stu Cncl; Cit Awd; East Central U; Radiolgy Tech.

MC NUTT, KERRI; Wayne Public Schl; Wayne, OK; (4); 6/26; FHA; Pep Clb; Scholastic Bowl; Speech Tm; SADD; VICA; Drm Mjr(t); Jazz Band; Mrchg Band; Pep Band.

MC NUTT, MIKE; Stuart Sr HS; Haywood, OK; (3); Church Yth Grp; FCA; Treas Soph Cls; Sec Jr Cls; Var Bsbl; Var Bsktbl; Hon Roll; Natl FFA Org; Quiz Bowl; Natl Sci Mert Awd 95; Bsbl Spring All-Trnmt Team; Kenpo Karate Green Belt; Chrstn Radio Pgm DJ; ORU; Sprts Med.

MC NUTT, TERESA; Wayne Public Schl; Wayne, OK; (4); Church Yth Grp; FHA; Library Aide; Office Aide; SADD; Church Choir; School Play; Yrbk; Hon Roll; NHS.

MC PHERSON, ANDY; Anadarko HS; Anadarko, OK; (4); 23/107; Am Leg Boys St; FCA; FBLA; Pres Natl FFA Org; Sec Jr Cls; Rep Stu Cncl; Capt Ftbl; High Hon Roll; NHS; St Schlr; OSU; Ag Ed.

MC PHERSON, DANIELLE R; Southeast HS; Midwest City, OK; (2); Church Yth Grp; Cmnty Wkr; FBLA; Teachers Aide; Band; Chorus; Church Choir; Flag Corp; Jazz Band; Mrchg Band; OK Chrstn Posse; African Amer Soc; Power Chrstn Click; OK U; Comp Acctng.

MC QUEEN, KELI N; Snyder HS; Snyder, OK; (3); 15/42; Teachers Aide; Pres Soph Cls; Ofcr Stu Cncl; Hon Roll; Nrs.

MC QUEEN, MEGAN L; Stigler HS; Stigler, OK; (3); FHA; Pep Clb; Hon Roll; NHS; Recieved Natl Sci Mrt Awd, Zoology & His Awds.

MC QUIGG, HEATH; Caddo HS; Caddo, OK; (1); Church Yth Grp; English Clb; JA; Math Clb; Science Clb; JV Var Bsktbl; High Hon Roll; Hon Roll; NHS; St Schlr; Curriculum Meet Awds.

MC REYNOLDS, JOSHUA A; Pond Creek-Hunter Schl; Pond Creek, OK; (2); 6/38; FCA; VP 4-H; Letterman Clb; Ofcr Stu Cncl; Bsktbl; Ftbl; Trk; 4-H Awd; Hon Roll; NHS; OU.

MC REYNOLDS, TARYN; Sapulpa Sr HS; Sapulpa, OK; (4); 55/299; Art Clb; Cmnty Wkr; Dance Clb; VP Intnl Clb; Key Clb; Natl FFA Org; Science Clb; Service Clb; Pres Spanish Clb; SADD; Mss Tls Tn USA; Pwhsk Intl Rodeo 50th Anniv Qn; Mss OK Tn 2nd Rnnrp; Northeastern ST U; Mrktng.

MC REYNOLDS, TIFFANY A; Westville HS; Westville, OK; (3); FBLA; FHA; Hon Roll; Prfct Atten Awd; U Of AR; Opthamolgy.

MC RORIE, ANNE MARIE; Edmond North HS; Edmond, OK; (4); Church Yth Grp; Mu Alpha Theta; Spanish Clb; Chorus; Church Choir; Hon Roll; NHS; St Gregorys Coll.

MC SPADDEN, AMANDA J; Duncan HS; Duncan, OK; (4); 7/214; Church Yth Grp; Acpl Chr; Chorus; Variety Show; Yrbk; High Hon Roll; NHS; FBLA; Office Aide; Church Choir; Show Choir; Cnslrs Aide; Yth Alive Bible Stud; Cameron U; Rad & TV Brodcstng.

MC SPADEN, JAMES; Putnam City North HS; Oklahoma City, OK; (4); 28/441; Am Leg Boys St; Church Yth Grp; Key Clb; VP Latin Clb; Rptr Mu Alpha Theta; Science Clb; School Musical; School Play; Pres Swing Chorus; Rep Stu Cncl; Chrch Yth OK Conf Pres; OK St Sen Page; OU Hlth Sci Smmr Acad; Yth Mnstry.

MC SPERITT, CRYSTAL; Keota Schl; Keota, OK; (2); 1/52; Debate Tm; Drama Clb; FHA; German Clb; Natl FFA Org; NFL; Scholastic Bowl; Speech Tm; NHS; Val; OSU; Med.

MC VAY, JENIFER M; Edmond North HS; Edmond, OK; (3); Chorus; Variety Show.

MC VEY, KELLY; Chisholm Sr HS; Enid, OK; (4); 2/70; Am Leg Aux Girls St; Church Yth Grp; FCA; FHA; Natl FFA Org; Spanish Clb; Teachers Aide; Pres Frsh Cls; Pres Soph Cls; Sec VP Stu Cncl; OK ST U.

MC WATTERS, SHANE; Moore HS; Moore, OK; (4); 121/527; Am Leg Boys St; Church Yth Grp; Band; Jazz Band; Mrchg Band; Pep Band; School Musical; Variety Show; OK Yth Symphny; Bus Admin.

MC WHIRT, BRADLEY S; South Coffeyville Schl; S Coffeyville, OK; (1); 1/39; Natl FFA Org; VP Frsh Cls; Var Bsbl; Var Bsktbl; Var Ftbl; High Hon Roll.

MC WHIRTER, JIMMY S; Choctaw HS; Choctaw, OK; (2); Church Yth Grp; Cmnty Wkr; Speech Tm; School Play; Stage Crew; VP Frsh Cls; Chrldng; Sftbl; Hon Roll; Jr NHS; Stu News Pgm Main Anchor, Rptr; Columbia U; Brdcst Jrnlst.

MC WHIRTER, LISA A; Bethany HS; Bethany, OK; (2); 2/90; FCA; Letterman Clb; VP Frsh Cls; Pres Soph Cls; Pres Jr Cls; Bsktbl; Chrldng; Powder Puff Ftbl; NHS; Church Yth Grp; Yth Alive; SNU; PE.

MC WHIRTER, MARCI A; Choctaw HS; Choctaw, OK; (4); Church Yth Grp; Cmnty Wkr; FHA; Office Aide; Mgr(s); Score Keeper; Cit Awd; Hon Roll; Jr NHS; NHS; OK Chrstn U Of Sci & Arts.

MC WHIRTER, SCOTT; Choctaw HS; Choctaw, OK; (2); 37/378; Church Yth Grp; Drama Clb; Speech Tm; School Play; VP Frsh Cls; Rep Jr Cls; Var Chrldng; Cit Awd; Hon Roll; Jr NHS; Stu Broadcasting; Pepperdine; Brdcst Jrnlsm.

MC WHIRTER, THERESA L; Bethany HS; Bethany, OK; (2); FCA; Key Clb; Pep Clb; Pres Frsh Cls; Sec Jr Cls; Rep Stu Cncl; JV Var Bsktbl; Hon Roll; Jr NHS; NHS; Youth Alive; SNU; Tchr/Math.

MC WILLIAMS, AARON C; Southwest Covenant Schl; Oklahoma City, OK; (1); Church Yth Grp; FCA; Band; Chorus; Pep Band; Rep Frsh Cls; Var Bsktbl; L Ftbl; High Hon Roll.

MEACHAM, ALLISON A; Clinton HS; Clinton, OK; (4); 19/99; Art Clb; Hist DECA; FCA; Hist FHA; Spanish Clb; Ofcr Stu Cncl; Tennis; Cit Awd; Hon Roll; OK ST Univ; Fshn Merchandisng.

MEACHAM, KELLI; Claremore Sr HS; Claremore, OK; (4); Rptr Art Clb; French Clb; Hosp Aide; Science Clb; SADD; Tennis; Hon Roll; NHS; Ntl Merit Ltr; Piano; Rogers ST Coll; Psych.

MEACHAM, MELANIE; Clinton HS; Clinton, OK; (2); Church Yth Grp; FCA; 4-H; Chorus; Church Choir; Ofcr Stu Cncl; Golf; NHS; High Hon Roll; Hon Roll; Horse Shwng & Jdgng; OK ST U; Vet.

MEACHAM, MEREDITH; Clinton HS; Clinton, OK; (4); 3/99; VP FCA; Ofcr Stu Cncl; Stat Bsbl; Var Capt Bsktbl; Var JV Chrldng; Ftbl; NHS; OK Bar Assns Mck Trl Cmptn; Law.

MEACHAM, STEPHEN; Clinton HS; Clinton, OK; (4); 4/99; Church Yth Grp; Key Clb; Quiz Bowl; Science Clb; Church Choir; Sec Stu Cncl; Tennis; NHS; Library Aide; Teachers Aide; Lgl Team; Op Cnnct; Engrng.

MEAD, DAVID; Heavener HS; Heavener, OK; (3); #1 in class; Am Leg Boys St; Rep Frsh Cls; Golf; High Hon Roll; NHS; Prfct Atten Awd; OK ST Univ; Pre-Med.

MEADE, APRIL; Yukon Middle HS; Yukon, OK; (2); Church Yth Grp; Quiz Bowl; Church Choir; Bsktbl; Hon Roll; NHS; 3-D; Cmp Fire.

MEADE, LETITIA Y; Edmond Santa Fe HS; Alpharetta, GA; (3); 1/287; Church Yth Grp; Cmnty Wkr; Drama Clb; Key Clb; Pep Clb; Science Clb; Spanish Clb; SADD; Teachers Aide; Band; Rel Ortrcl Cntst 2nd Plc; Chrch Spnsrd Acad 3rd Plc; Essy Cntst Cert; GA Tech; Elect Engr.

MEADOR, AMI D; Spiro HS; Spiro, OK; (3); Church Yth Grp; Rptr FBLA; Math Clb; Spanish Clb; Teachers Aide; Band; Chorus; Ed Nwsp; Hon Roll; Mst Outstdng Musician; Westark CC; Elem Ed.

MEADORS, BRIAN L; Elgin HS; Elgin, OK; (2); Natl FFA Org; Bsktbl; Trk; Cit Awd; Hon Roll; NHS; Pres Acad Fit Awd; Acad Ltr E; Cameron.

MEADORS, SUMER D; Nathan Hale HS; Tulsa, OK; (3); 9/249; Church Yth Grp; Drama Clb; Ed Yrbk; Treas Jr Cls; Treas Sr Cls; Ofcr Stu Cncl; Sftbl; High Hon Roll; FCA; Spanish Clb; Alum Natl Yng Ldrs Conf WA DC; 3rd Rnr Up Miss OK Coed Pagnt 96; Most Promsng Modl/Acad Ach Schlsp.

MEADOWS, LAKESHA S; Bartlesville Sr HS; Bartlesville, OK; (1); Church Yth Grp; FHA; Bsktbl; Trk; Hon Roll; NHS; Work & Bus Orientation; Sec.

MEADOWS, LEESA M; Blanchard Jr Sr HS; Dibble, OK; (2); Computer Clb; FHA; Pep Clb; Teachers Aide; Rep Soph Cls; Korean Tae Kwondo; U Of WA; RN.

MEADOWS, STACY L; Empire Schl; Duncan, OK; (4); 2/36; Yrbk; Chrldng; Pom Pon; Hon Roll; NHS; Church Yth Grp; FCA; FBLA; FHA; Key Clb; Pre-Med.

MEANS, JACLYN R; Howe Public Schl; Howe, OK; (2); Church Yth Grp; FBLA; FHA; Yrbk; Chrldng; Cmptrs; Cooking; CASC; Secrtrl.

MEANS, JAROD S; Putnam City North HS; Oklahoma City, OK; (2); Art Clb; Church Yth Grp; Drama Clb; FCA; Service Clb; School Play; Stage Crew; Rep Frsh Cls; Rep Soph Cls; Ftbl.

MEANS, MICHELLE C; Ponca City Sr HS; Ponca City, OK; (3); Boy Scts; Church Yth Grp; Spanish Clb; Chorus; Ofcr Stu Cncl; Var L Tennis; High Hon Roll; NHS; Karate; Piano 2 Time Gold Cup Wnnr NFMT; Medicine.

MECHAM, ANGELA M; Talihina Sr HS; Talihina, OK; (3); Treas FBLA; Band; Mrchg Band; Pep Band; Hon Roll; Water Ed Team; OK Hnr Soc; Natl Voc Tech Hnr Soc.

MEDCALF, JOEL; Boswell Sr HS; Boswell, OK; (2); 1/32; FCA; Key Clb; Natl FFA Org; Quiz Bowl; Ofcr Stu Cncl; Bsktbl; High Hon Roll; Jr NHS; Val.

MEDGAARDEN, MATT D; Mustang HS; Mustang, OK; (1); 53/550; JV Socr; High Hon Roll; Hon Roll; NC; Arch.

MEDILL, CHERYL; Woodward HS; Woodward, OK; (1); Letterman Clb; Bsktbl; Sftbl; High Hon Roll; NHS.

MEDINA, JORGE A; Pauls Valley HS; Pauls Valley, OK; (3); Spanish Clb; Bsktbl; Golf; High Hon Roll; Hon Roll.

MEDLOCK, SHAWN; Tahlequah Sr HS; Tahlequah, OK; (4); Science Clb; Teachers Aide; Ed Yrbk; Inline Speed Skate Medals; Bus Comp Applications Awd; Bus Stu Of Month 96; NE OK ST Univ; Comp Pmgng.

MEEK, AMANDA B; Colbert Jr Sr HS; Colbert, OK; (1); Church Yth Grp; FCA; Rptr Natl FFA Org; Quiz Bowl; Treas Frsh Cls; Var Bsktbl; Var Sftbl; High Hon Roll; Prfct Atten Awd; Fstptch; Med Field.

MEEK, CRYSTAL K; Colbert Jr Sr HS; Colbert, OK; (3); Church Yth Grp; FCA; VP Rptr Natl FFA Org; VP Frsh Cls; Pres Jr Cls; Rep Stu Cncl; Var Bsktbl; Var Sftbl; NHS.

MEEK, GRANT H; Union Intermediate HS; Broken Arrow, OK; (2); Church Yth Grp; FCA; Key Clb; Varsity Clb; Ofcr Jr Cls; Ftbl; Trk; DFY Club Pres; US Air Force Acad; Psych.

MEEK, HEATHER D; Stonewall Jr-Sr HS; Stonewall, OK; (3); Natl FFA Org; Sec Frsh Cls; Var Bsktbl; Var Sftbl; Hon Roll; NHS.

MEEK, JESSICA; Wright Christian Acad; Broken Arrow, OK; (1); Church Yth Grp; GAA; Key Clb; Spanish Clb; Trk; Vllybl; High Hon Roll; OCUSA.

MEEK, TEVI K; Harrah HS; Choctaw, OK; (3); 1/168; Scholastic Bowl; SADD; Nwsp; Sec Frsh Cls; Ofcr Jr Cls; Bsktbl; Trk; High Hon Roll; Jr NHS; NHS.

MEEKER, JUSTIN; Oklahoma Union Schl; Wann, OK; (3); 1/35; FCA; HOBY; Treas Natl FFA Org; Pres Soph Cls; Pres Jr Cls; Wrstlng; High Hon Roll; NHS; IFLA; OSU; Vet.

MEEKER, SUSAN D; Union Sr HS; Tulsa, OK; (4); 123/615; Church Yth Grp; Hist DECA; FCA; FBLA; HOBY; Key Clb; Office Aide; Rptr Nwsp; Rptr Yrbk; Rep Frsh Cls; U Of OK; Bus.

MEEKS, ERIC; Braggs Schl; Braggs, OK; (2); Ofcr Stu Cncl; Bacone Coll Upwrd Bnd Pgm; GATE Pgm; Acad Tm; Engrng.

MEEKS, HEATHER; Haileyville Schl; Haileyville, OK; (3); Church Yth Grp; FCA; French Clb; Pres FHA; Chorus; Church Choir; Sec Soph Cls; Sec Jr Cls; Capt Chrldng; Sftbl; FHA Swthrt; OSU; Vet.

MEEKS, TRACY; Deer Creek HS; Edmond, OK; (2); 1/105; Cmnty Wkr; Drama Clb; Science Clb; School Play; Ofcr Stu Cncl; Bsktbl; Cit Awd; High Hon Roll; NHS; PT.

MEERS, NATALIE L; Westmoore HS; Oklahoma City, OK; (3); Church Yth Grp; FCA; School Musical; Pom Pon; Hon Roll; NHS; OK U.

MEHAGAN, STEVEN D; Olive Jr Sr HS; Mannford, OK; (2); Band; Mrchg Band; Pep Band; Sec Frsh Cls; Hon Roll; Pres Schlr.

MEHTA, DARSHNA; Idabel HS; Idabel, OK; (3); Hosp Aide; Quiz Bowl; Science Clb; Band; Mrchg Band; Rep Stu Cncl; Cit Awd; Gov Hon Prg Awd; High Hon Roll; Hon Roll; OK U; Med.

MEIER, ABBY; Oklahoma Christian Schl; Edmond, OK; (1); Church Yth Grp; Chorus; Church Choir; Sec Frsh Cls; High Hon Roll; Pres Acad Fit Awd; Super Rtng Vcl Cont.

MEIER, AUSTIN; Okeene Jr Sr HS; Hitchcock, OK; (3); 1/32; Pres Church Yth Grp; FCA; Natl FFA Org; Var Bsktbl; Var Ftbl; Var Trk; NHS; OK Hnr Soc; Dir OK Jr Angus Assn; St Wheat Kng 95; Med.

MEIER, MELODY M; Enid Sr HS; Enid, OK; (2); Church Yth Grp; Pres Frsh Cls; Rep Soph Cls; Var Diving; Var Swmmng; Var Trk; Hon Roll; Jr NHS; OK Close Up Govt Prgm; Cherokee Dist Rodeo Qn 95; OK ST Univ; Vet.

MEIER, PHILIP; Oklahoma Christian Schl; Edmond, OK; (4); 1/37; Church Yth Grp; Cmnty Wkr; Computer Clb; Ed Yrbk; Rep Sr Cls; Rep Stu Cncl; High Hon Roll; Prfct Atten Awd; Pres Acad Fit Awd.

MEINERT, JAMIE; Hobart HS; Hobart, OK; (4); 7/63; Sec FCA; Pep Clb; Ofcr Stu Cncl; Var Capt Bsktbl; Chrldng; Trk; High Hon Roll; Hon Roll; NHS; Val; Bsktbl All Area Conf Frwrd; Julie Davis Awd; Natl Hnr Soc; OK City U; Med.

MEISSNER, JOHN-DAVID; Moore HS; Moore, OK; (4); Am Leg Boys St; Church Yth Grp; FCA; Spanish Clb; Church Choir; VP NHS; Prfct Atten Awd; Val; U Cntrl OK; Elem Ed.

MELEDEO, MICHAEL; Yukon HS; Yukon, OK; (4); 1/405; Church Yth Grp; Debate Tm; French Clb; HOBY; NFL; Capt Quiz Bowl; Cit Awd; Ntl Merit SF; Val; Teenage Reps Pres; Johns Hopkins U; Bio-Med Engr.

MELENDEZ, LANI; Calvin Public Schl; Calvin, OK; (3); 1/15; FCA; HOBY; Natl FFA Org; Spanish Clb; Yrbk; Pres Frsh Cls; Pres Soph Cls; Rep Sr Cls; Sftbl; Cit Awd.

MELKER, KEITH A; Metro Christian Acad; Tulsa, OK; (2); Church Yth Grp; Spanish Clb; School Play; VP Soph Cls; Treas Stu Cncl; JV Bsktbl; Var Tennis; High Hon Roll; NHS; Pre Med.

MELROSE, LAURA; Wellston Schl; Wellston, OK; (3); 1/57; VP Church Yth Grp; Pres FCA; Pres FHA; Pres SADD; Scholastic Bowl; Pres Soph Cls; Ofcr Stu Cncl; Var Chrldng; NHS; Var Bsktbl; Vce Lssns; OK Kids Perfrmrs; Top 10 Mss Tn OK Pagnt; Bllmnt U; Sngn Cntry.

MELTON, APRIL M; Memorial HS; Tulsa, OK; (4); 39/250; Church Yth Grp; Key Clb; Pep Clb; Red Cross Aide; Spanish Clb; School Musical; Swing Chorus; Ofcr Stu Cncl; NHS; Intnl Clb; Piano Tchg; Tulsa Univ; Msc Ed.

MELTON, CHERISH N; Muldrow HS; Muldrow, OK; (1); Church Yth Grp; Cmnty Wkr; Debate Tm; Drama Clb; FHA; Natl Beta Clb; Speech Tm; School Play; Hon Roll; Tchng.

MELTON, DAWNA; Collinsville HS; Collinsville, OK; (3); Natl FFA Org; VICA; Hon Roll; Photo.

MELTON, HOLLY M; Muskogee HS; Muskogee, OK; (4); 64/300; Science Clb; Hon Roll; Connors ST Coll; Pharmacy.

MELTON, JOSEPH G; Valliant HS; Garvin, OK; (4); 37/80; Natl FFA Org; VICA; Hon Roll; NHS; Law.

MELTON, KRISTIE M; Putnam City HS; Oklahoma City, OK; (2); Drama Clb; NFL; Speech Tm; Orch; Mgr Ftbl; Mgr(s); Acctnt/Intrptr.

MELTON, LARRY D; Luther HS; Luther, OK; (3); Church Yth Grp; 4-H; Natl FFA Org; Band; Church Choir; Mrchg Band; Orch; School Musical; Var Bsbl; JV Bsktbl; OK St Univ; Cntry Singr.

MELTON, LORI R; Hulbert Jr Sr HS; Hulbert, OK; (2); Computer Clb; English Clb; German Clb; Hon Roll; NHS.

MELTON, RACHELLE A; Hydro Jr Sr HS; Hydro, OK; (2); Drama Clb; FCA; Natl FFA Org; Speech Tm; School Play; Ofcr Stu Cncl; Bsktbl; Sftbl; Hon Roll; NHS; Odyssey Of Mind 3rd Pl St Soph.

MELTON, ROBBY D; Altus Sr HS; Altus, OK; (2); Art Clb; Church Yth Grp; Cmnty Wkr; FCA; School Play; Var Bsktbl; Var Tennis; High Hon Roll; Hon Roll; Conf Tennis Champ 95; Conf Tennis Champ 96; Med/Law.

MELTON, SHAWNA; Choctaw HS; Midwest City, OK; (4); 87/313; Cmnty Wkr; FCA; GAA; Letterman Clb; Office Aide; Red Cross Aide; Teachers Aide; Varsity Clb; Var Bsktbl; Var Powder Puff Ftbl; ST Champ Bsktbl 95; ST Sftbl Champ 94; Crowder Coll; Pre Med.

MELTON, TANIA R; East Central HS; Tulsa, OK; (2); Key Clb; Spanish Clb; School Play; JV Var Sftbl; High Hon Roll; Hon Roll; NHS; Sprts Physician.

MELTZNER, JAMIE H; Edmond North HS; Edmond, OK; (3); 93/348; Drama Clb; Mu Alpha Theta; Temple Yth Grp; VP Sec Band; Mrchg Band; Sec Jr Cls; Var Capt Swmmng; Var Trk; NHS; Math Clb; Marine Bio.

MELVIN, ANYA C; Waukomis HS; Waukomis, OK; (2); Church Yth Grp; FCA; Pep Clb; Yrbk; Var Bsktbl; Capt Trk; Prfct Atten Awd; St Track Meet; Comm Svc; U Of OK.

MELVIN, MATT S; El Reno Sr HS; El Reno, OK; (1); 4-H; Natl FFA Org; High Hon Roll; Hon Roll.

MEMBRILA, MAYELI; Union Intermediate HS; Tulsa, OK; (1); NHS; OK Coll; RN.

MENDELL, CLINT A; Lomega HS; Loyal, OK; (2); Church Yth Grp; FCA; 4-H; Natl FFA Org; VP Frsh Cls; Pres Soph Cls; L Var Bsbl; L Var Bsktbl; Hon Roll; Prfct Atten Awd; Pres Local Chap FFA; Northwestern OK ST Univ.

MENDENALL, MISTY E; Plainview HS; Ardmore, OK; (4); 42/88; Dance Clb; GAA; Band; Chorus; Drill Tm; Mrchg Band; School Musical; Crs Cntry; Sftbl; Trk; OCU; Pre-Law.

MENDENHALL, CHRISTIE; Kremlin Jr Sr HS; Enid, OK; (2); Church Yth Grp; FCA; Letterman Clb; Rep Stu Cncl; Sec Bsbl; Var Bsktbl; Sec Ftbl; Mgr(s); High Hon Roll; Pres Acad Fit Awd; NW OK ST U; Coach.

MENDENHALL, JAY; Fairview HS; Fairview, OK; (1); 1/78; Church Yth Grp; Quiz Bowl; Band; Rptr Nwsp; Ofcr Bsbl; Bsktbl; Ftbl; NHS; Mrchg Band; Pep Band; 1st Pl St Engring Cntst; Amer Legn Stu Ofyr; 2 Yrs St Schlstc Chmpnshp Qualfr; OK U; Jrnlsm.

MENDENHALL, LISA S; Oilton HS; Prague, OK; (3); Church Yth Grp; FHA; Library Aide; Natl FFA Org; Cit Awd; Hon Roll; Vet.

MENDENHALL, LORI B; Muskogee HS; Muskogee, OK; (2); Church Yth Grp; SADD; Yrbk; Delphic Lit Soc; Teens For Christ; Vol Spcl Olympics; OK Bapt Univ; Soc Worker; Psych.

MENDENHALL, NATACHA A; Mustang HS; Mustang, OK; (4); 174/347; Church Yth Grp; JA; Office Aide; Spanish Clb; SADD; Teachers Aide; Chorus; Hon Roll; Street Light Outreach Ministry From Chrch; Chrch Nursery Tchr; Mid-Amer Bible Coll; Behav Sci.

MENDOZA, FRANK M; Central HS; Tulsa, OK; (1); Ofcr Bsbl.

MENEFEE, TIFFANY; Ft Towson HS; Fort Towson, OK; (2); Church Yth Grp; FCA; FHA; Church Choir; Yrbk; Sec Soph Cls; High Hon Roll; NHS; TSA; OK Baptist U; Law.

MENIFEE, TRACY A; Star Spencer HS; Spencer, OK; (3); Church Yth Grp; VICA; Sftbl; Vllybl; High Hon Roll; Hon Roll; VICA At Vo-Tech; Outsdng/Dedctd Accomplishmnts Awds; Cosmetologist.

MENNEM, LESLIE; Medford Schl; Medford, OK; (1); 4-H; Ofcr Frsh Cls; Ofcr Stu Cncl; Var Bsktbl; Var Sftbl; Var Trk; High Hon Roll; OK Hnr Soc; Gftd & Tlntd; FFA; OK ST U.

MENNIG, DESTINY J; West Middle HS; Norman, OK; (2); Church Yth Grp; FCA; Chorus; Rep Frsh Cls; Rep Soph Cls; Ofcr Stu Cncl; Trk; Feed The Children; U Of OK; Hwy Patrol.

MENNINGER, WHITNEY L; Union Sr HS; Broken Arrow, OK; (4); 52/632; Church Yth Grp; Office Aide; Color Guard; Pep Band; Hon Roll; Jr NHS; NHS; Baylor U; Med.

MENNIS, KATHY A; Mc Loud HS; Mc Loud, OK; (3); Drama Clb; Band; Color Guard; Mrchg Band; Pep Band; School Play; Jr NHS; Recreational Sccr; OK Univ; Archeologist.

MERAZ, ALMA; Vici Schl; Camargo, OK; (4); 7/27; Am Leg Aux Girls St; FBLA; FHA; Natl FFA Org; Band; Chorus; Color Guard; Drm Mjr(t); Flag Corp; Mrchg Band; Miss Vici 95-96; Ctzns Flg Allnce; Natl, St FFA Chorus 3xs; Nrthwstrn OK U; Mass Cmmnctns.

MERCADO, JIM P; Del City HS; Del City, OK; (2); Art Clb; Hghst GPA Awd Algbr; Archt.

MERCATORIS, SHAWN 5; Nathan Hale HS; Tulsa, OK; (3); FBLA; Var Capt Bsbl; Ftbl; Hon Roll; 1st Tm All Conf; Pro Bsebl.

MERCER, BOBBY; Northwest Classen HS; Oklahoma City, OK; (4); Church Yth Grp; FCA; Key Clb; Church Choir; Stage Crew; L Bsbl; Var L Crs Cntry; JV Wrstlng; High Hon Roll; OK ST U.

MERCER, CAYSIE S; Choctaw HS; Choctaw, OK; (2); School Play; Score Keeper; Trk; Hon Roll; Prfct Atten Awd; OK ST U; Med.

MERCER, CHRISTIE R; Central Schl; Marlow, OK; (4); 2/29; Rptr 4-H; FBLA; FHA; Letterman Clb; Bsktbl; 4-H Awd; High Hon Roll; Hon Roll; NHS; Sal; Acad Team; FFA; Cameron Univ; Acctng.

MERCER, HUNTER; Central Mid-HS; Norman, OK; (2); Church Yth Grp; FCA; Rptr French Clb; Bsktbl; Chrldng; Mgr(s); Mgr Wrstlng; Hon Roll; USAA In Chrldng; OK ST; Psych.

MERCHANT, WILLIAM S; Blackwell HS; Blackwell, OK; (1); Natl FFA Org; Natl FFA Org Awds; AG Mech; OK ST Tech; Diesel Mech.

MERCIER, DANIEL W; Union Intermediate HS; Tulsa, OK; (2); 82/800; Mrchg Band; NHS; Frgn Lang & Lang Arts Outstndg Achvt Awds 95; Bands America 95 Grnd Natl Chmpnshps Fnlst Marchng Band; Engrng.

MEREDITH, KACI C; Hugo HS; Hugo, OK; (2); Flag Corp; Yrbk; Var Sftbl; Var Tennis; Hon Roll; Pres Acad Fit Awd.

MERIDETH, AMY K; Putnam City West HS; Oklahoma City, OK; (3); Drama Clb; German Clb; Orch; Hon Roll; Phtgrphy/Music/Wrtng.

MERIDTH, KEVIN; Wynnewood HS; Wynnewood, OK; (1); 1/58; Boy Scts; Church Yth Grp; FCA; Letterman Clb; JV Ftbl; JV Wt Lftg; Cit Awd; Hon Roll; BSA Lifegrd; Camps; Yth Preachng; OK Baptist U; Yth Minstry.

MERITT, SKYLA; Woodward HS; Woodward, OK; (2); Art Clb; Letterman Clb; Pep Clb; Red Cross Aide; Var Chrldng; Wt Lftg; Hon Roll; Sports Physician.

MERKLE, RYAN; Guthrie Sr HS; Guthrie, OK; (3); 16/350; Am Leg Boys St; Church Yth Grp; 4-H; Math Clb; Mu Alpha Theta; Spanish Clb; Band; Church Choir; Drm Mjr(t); Mrchg Band; All Reg Hnr Band; Med.

MERKLEY, RAYNA; Woodward HS; Woodward, OK; (3); 1/150; Art Clb; Cmnty Wkr; Computer Clb; FBLA; German Clb; Hosp Aide; Key Clb; Letterman Clb; Natl Beta Clb; Pep Clb; OK ST Univ Almni Awd; Acad Exclnc Engl III AP; Central Univ; Engl Lit.

MERRELL, KIMBERLY G; Moore HS; Moore, OK; (3); 9/507; Science Clb; Spanish Clb; SADD; Chorus; Hon Roll; NHS; Val; Mltcltrl Stdnt Assn; OK City Univ; Soc Wk/Rel Ed.

MERRICK, FRANK W; West Middle HS; Norman, OK; (3); Cmnty Wkr; FCA; JA; Spanish Clb; Ofcr Stu Cncl; Cit Awd; Gov Hon Prg Awd; Hon Roll; Jr NHS; Pres Acad Fit Awd; Young Life; OK ST Soccer Chmpns Norman Celtic 80; Tulsa.

MERRILL, KURT; Stillwater Sr HS; Stillwater, OK; (4); 92/350; Am Leg Boys St; Boy Scts; Debate Tm; JCL; VP Key Clb; Latin Clb; NFL; Quiz Bowl; Var Fld Hcky; Ftbl; Yth N Govt; Mck Trl; OK ST U; Law.

MERRIMAN, KRISTA; Woodward HS; Woodward, OK; (2); Church Yth Grp; Computer Clb; FBLA; Spanish Clb; High Hon Roll; NHS; Wrtng Awds; OK Chrstn Univ; Law; Judge.

MERRITT, JENNIFER; Cheyenne HS; Crawford, OK; (4); 5/19; Am Leg Aux Girls St; Church Yth Grp; 4-H; Chorus; School Play; Rptr Nwsp; Rptr Jr Cls; Rep Stu Cncl; 4-H Awd; NHS; Oklahoma City U; Theatre.

MERRITT, MICHAEL S; Edison HS; Tulsa, OK; (3); 1/213; JCL; Key Clb; Latin Clb; Pep Clb; Ofcr Jr Cls; Ofcr Stu Cncl; High Hon Roll; NHS; Natl Latin Exam Gold/Silver Mdls; Natl Yng Ldrs Conf Yth Ldrsp Awd; Tulsa Summer Acad Math/Sci; U Of Tulsa; Appld Math.

MERRYMAN, JOSHUA K; Metro Christian Acad; Tulsa, OK; (3); Church Yth Grp; Cmnty Wkr; FCA; Spanish Clb; School Musical; School Play; Ofcr Bsbl; High Hon Roll; Mssn Work In Russia; Hmcmng Ct; Med.

MERRYMAN, RACHEL J; Heavener HS; Heavener, OK; (1); Church Yth Grp; Key Clb; Yrbk; Rep Frsh Cls; Ofcr Stu Cncl; Indian Clb; OK ST Univ; Cosmetlgst.

MESA, CHRIS; Stuart Sr HS; Stuart, OK; (3); FCA; Math Clb; Natl FFA Org; Scholastic Bowl; Science Clb; Spanish Clb; Varsity Clb; Var Bsbl; Var Bsktbl; Hon Roll; Wrld Hstry 100 Avg; Hstry, Cmptrs, Alg, Eng Spec Achvt Awds; Med.

MESKIMEN, BRIAN; Purcell HS; Purcell, OK; (3); 5/88; 4-H; HOBY; Key Clb; Natl FFA Org; Science Clb; Spanish Clb; SADD; Band; Jazz Band; Mrchg Band; OK ST U; Forestry.

MESSER, DAN; Lawton Christian Schl; Fort Sill, OK; (3); Debate Tm; School Musical; Yrbk; Treas Jr Cls; Ofcr Bsbl; Bsktbl; Golf; Socr; Cit Awd; High Hon Roll; Phys Thrpy.

MESSER, MISTY; Del City HS; Del City, OK; (3); 80/515; Chrch Act; Rose ST Coll; CPA; Acctnt.

METCALFE, WAYNE E; Pioneer Jr Sr HS; Enid, OK; (2); #8 in class; Wrstlng; Hon Roll; OK Univ; Attorney.

METEVELIS, STEPHANIE E; Union Intermediate HS; Tulsa, OK; (1); Church Yth Grp; Band; Mrchg Band; Pep Band; Ofcr Stu Cncl; Hon Roll; NHS; 1st Chair All Dist Bassoon; OK Univ; Med.

METHENY, JULIE; Putnam City North HS; Oklahoma City, OK; (2); 30/464; Church Yth Grp; FCA; Letterman Clb; Spanish Clb; SADD; Varsity Clb; Ofcr Frsh Cls; Var L Bsktbl; Var L Sftbl; High Hon Roll; Conf Nwcmr/Frdylnd Plyr Of Yr; All-State.

METHENY, SARA N; South Intermediate HS; Broken Arrow, OK; (2); Church Yth Grp; FCA; French Clb; Acpl Chr; Church Choir; Var Socr; Hon Roll; NHS.

METTRY, SHELLEY; Ada HS; Ada, OK; (4); 8/175; Church Yth Grp; Debate Tm; Drama Clb; FCA; Pep Clb; Spanish Clb; School Play; Nwsp; Yrbk; Var Chrldng; U Of OK.

METZER, MATT; Lone Grove HS; Ardmore, OK; (3); #1 in class; Am Leg Boys St; Boy Scts; Debate Tm; FCA; Model UN; Sec Stu Cncl; Ftbl; Trk; High Hon Roll; NHS; St Rnnr Up Voice Of Democracy; Bus.

MEWHORTER, AMANDA J; Del City HS; Oklahoma City, OK; (3); 67/437; Drama Clb; Letterman Clb; Vllybl.

MEYER, AMANDA; Temple Jr Sr HS; Temple, OK; (3); 3/18; FCA; Pep Clb; Teachers Aide; Bsktbl; Chrldng; Sftbl; Cit Awd; High Hon Roll; Prfct Atten Awd; Dntl.

MEYER, BOBBIE; Mulhall Orlando HS; Orlando, OK; (4); 3/21; Church Yth Grp; Library Aide; Teachers Aide; High Hon Roll; Hon Roll; Jr NHS; Prfct Atten Awd; Cert Of Literary Mrt; Outstndng Achvt Awds; Sci & Math Fair Hnrb Mntn; Cert Of Mrt; Outstndng Perf Acctg; Murray ST Coll; Vet Tech.

MEYER, CAROLEE; Okarche HS; Okarche, OK; (4); Am Leg Aux Girls St; Church Yth Grp; Sec FHA; Natl Beta Clb; Chorus; Pres Soph Cls; VP Jr Cls; Rep Sr Cls; Ofcr Stu Cncl; Var Sftbl.

MEYER, CATHERINE S; South Intermediate HS; Broken Arrow, OK; (1); Church Yth Grp; Office Aide; Church Choir; Chrmn Frsh Cls; Chrstn Stdnt Union; OK Bapt Univ; PT.

MEYER, IVY NICOLE; Stillwater Sr HS; Stillwater, OK; (4); 35/340; Key Clb; Latin Clb; Natl Beta Clb; Q&S; Spanish Clb; Phtg Nwsp; Phtg Yrbk; NHS; OK St Univ.

MEYER, JENNIFER; Stillwater Sr HS; Stillwater, OK; (2); Rptr Yrbk; Chrldng; Hon Roll.

MEYER, JENNIFER R; Preston Schl; Beggs, OK; (1); Am Leg Aux Girls St; Church Yth Grp; 4-H; Church Choir; Nwsp; Ofcr Frsh Cls; JV Bsktbl; Var Mgr(s); JV Sftbl; High Hon Roll; AQHYA; Chrch Co-Ed Sftbl Leag; OK ST Univ; PE.

MEYER, JESSICA M; South Intermediate HS; Broken Arrow, OK; (1); JV Capt Socr; High Hon Roll; Hon Roll; Jr NHS; St Schlr; U Of NC; Meteorlogist; Ped.

MEYER, MEGAN; Woodward HS; Woodward, OK; (3); Am Leg Aux Girls St; Church Yth Grp; Pres Key Clb; Quiz Bowl; Service Clb; Phtg Yrbk; Sec Stu Cncl; Mgr(s); NHS; FCA; Mock Trial Team 96 St Finalist; Outstdng Jr Girl 95-; 1st Plc Rgnl Comptn OK Citizen Bee; Architecture/Eng.

MEYER, NIKKI D; West Jr HS; Oklahoma City, OK; (1); French Clb; Red Cross Aide; JV Tennis; Pres Acad Fit Awd; House Of Reps Page 2 Yrs; Pub Relations.

MEYER, RYAN A; Ponca City Sr HS; Ponca City, OK; (2); Church Yth Grp; FCA; Office Aide; Spanish Clb; JV Bsbl; JV Bsktbl; High Hon Roll.

MEYER, SHERRI; Ponca City Sr HS; Ponca City, OK; (4); Church Yth Grp; Drama Clb; NFL; Office Aide; School Play; High Hon Roll; NHS; Band; Prfct Atten Awd; Mst Outstndg Spnsh Stu; DECA VP; Frgn Land Clb Spnsh Rep; Med.

MEYERS, CHRISTY; Canadian Schl; Canadian, OK; (2); Bsktbl; Sftbl; Hon Roll; NHS; Prfct Atten Awd; Pitt 8 Cnfrnc Trny Champ; Dist Chmps/Rgnl Rnr Ups/Area Fnlsts; Wn Hustle Awd 2 Yrs Bsktbl; TX A&M Univ; Sprts Med/Dr.

MEYERS, JENNIFER S; Liberty HS; Bixby, OK; (3); Church Yth Grp; Natl FFA Org; Chorus; Church Choir; Yrbk; Hon Roll; Chrch Msn Trips; Hrs Mgmnt; U Of Tulsa; Nrsg.

MEYERS, LAURA E; West Middle HS; Norman, OK; (2); Church Yth Grp; FCA; GAA; Pep Clb; Spanish Clb; SADD; Rep Stu Cncl; Var Trk; Hon Roll; Jr NHS; SWASS; Teen Vols; O U; PT.

MICHAELS, AMANDA; Comanche HS; Comanche, OK; (2); Church Yth Grp; Hosp Aide; Library Aide; Science Clb; SADD; Chorus; Nwsp; Yrbk; Hon Roll; Prfct Atten Awd; OSU; Pre-Law.

MICHAELSEN, MAREN; West Middle HS; Norman, OK; (1); Pres Church Yth Grp; Spanish Clb; Orch; Yrbk; Swmmng.

MICHENER, AMBER M; Claremore Sr HS; Claremore, OK; (3); Church Yth Grp; FHA; Hosp Aide; Teachers Aide; Gym; Hon Roll; Hlth Shdw Prgm; Educ Shdw Prgm; Rogers U; Nrsng.

MIDDLETON, ELIZABETH J; Okmulgee HS; Okmulgee, OK; (3); 4/130; Church Yth Grp; Cmnty Wkr; FCA; Letterman Clb; Varsity Clb; Band; Church Choir; Mrchg Band; Pep Band; Ofcr Stu Cncl; MVP Tnns; All Conf Tnns.

MIDDLETON, JULIE; Central Schl; Sallisaw, OK; (2); Pep Clb; Spanish Clb; Pres Frsh Cls; Sec Stu Cncl; Var Bsktbl; Var Chrldng; High Hon Roll; NHS.

MIDDLETON, KATHRYN W; Edmond Memorial HS; Edmond, OK; (4); 6/322; Debate Tm; Pres NFL; Speech Tm; Ofcr Stu Cncl; Cit Awd; NHS; Ntl Merit Schol; St Schlr; Val; Yng Demos Exec Cncl.

MIDDLETON, MELLISSA; Elgin HS; Elgin, OK; (3); Sec FHA; L Capt Chrldng; Bryan Career Coll; Flight Atten.

MIDDLETON, NATALIE; Bartlesville Sr HS; Bartlesville, OK; (3); Cmnty Wkr; Chorus; School Musical; Trk; High Hon Roll; Hon Roll; Prfct Atten Awd; U Of OK; Law.

MIDDLETON, TRAVIS G; Westmoore HS; Oklahoma City, OK; (2); Church Yth Grp; JV Var Ftbl; JV Wt Lftg; Ply Guitar; Outdrs; Fshng; U Of OK; Cmptr Cnsltnt.

MIERS, NATASHA R; Wetumka Jr Sr HS; Wetumka, OK; (2); 13/45; VP Pres FHA; Pres VP Key Clb; Spanish Clb; Chrldng; Hon Roll; NHS; Algebra Awd; Outstdng Hme Ec Stu Awd; Outstdng Key Clb VP Awd; ECU; Lit; Arts.

MIKETISH, JASON; Collinsville HS; Collinsville, OK; (4); Church Yth Grp; 4-H; Office Aide; Chorus; Church Choir; Ed Yrbk; L Ftbl; L Trk; 4-H Awd; Bapt Bible Coll; Mssnry.

MIKULA, TAMMY; Little Axe Sr HS; Newalla, OK; (4); 10/93; FHA; Chorus; Treas Jr Cls; Rep Stu Cncl; Chrldng; Crs Cntry; Trk; High Hon Roll; Hon Roll; Jr NHS; Phy Ther.

MILAM, HEATHER R; Miami Sr HS; Miami, OK; (3); 23/165; Am Leg Aux Girls St; Church Yth Grp; Rptr FHA; Chorus; Sec Stu Cncl; Cit Awd; Hon Roll; Jr NHS; VP NHS; Pres Acad Fit Awd; OSU; Msc Ed/Eng Ed.

MILAM, KARLA; Ft Cobb-Broxton HS; Anadarko, OK; (3); Spanish Clb; Hon Roll; Pres Schlr; OK U Norman; Early Chldhd Ed.

MILAN, TARA D; Choctaw HS; Choctaw, OK; (3); SADD; Var Bsktbl; Var Capt Chrldng; Capt Powder Puff Ftbl; Sftbl; Tennis; Hon Roll; Jr NHS; NHS; Travlng Smmr Sftbl Team; Nicoma Pk Jr HS Chrldrs Asst Coach; OK ST U; Pharmcy.

MILBURN, MARK D; Putnam City West HS; Bethany, OK; (4); 42/308; Church Yth Grp; Cmnty Wkr; French Clb; Var Bsbl; Var Bsktbl; Intrml Sftbl; High Hon Roll; NHS; Redlands CC; Acctng.

MILES, JENNIFER R; Memorial HS; Tulsa, OK; (2); German Clb; Key Clb; Socr; Hon Roll; Rainbows; OK Univ; Attorney; Law.

MILES, STACI; Norman Sr HS; Norman, OK; (4); #1 in class; JCL; Latin Clb; Mu Alpha Theta; Orch; School Musical; High Hon Roll; Hon Roll; Univ Of OK; Msc Perf.

MILEY, MARLO M; Westmoore HS; Oklahoma City, OK; (3); Cmnty Wkr; Library Aide; Office Aide; Teachers Aide; Band; Chorus; Wt Lftg; Cit Awd; Hon Roll; Tech Stu Of Amer; Southwestern Univ; Arch.

MILFORD, TISHA M; Westmoore HS; Oklahoma City, OK; (2); Church Yth Grp; Cmnty Wkr; French Clb; JA; Key Clb; Teachers Aide; Mgr(s); Cit Awd; French Hon Soc; High Hon Roll; OK ST Univ; TV Brdcstng.

MILLARD, NICHOLAS A; Wagoner Sr HS; Hulbert, OK; (3); 8/114; Am Leg Boys St; Art Clb; Church Yth Grp; FBLA; Office Aide; Teachers Aide; JV Wrstlng; Gov Hon Prg Awd; High Hon Roll; Hon Roll; Tulsa Univ; Pre-Med/Engr.

MILLBEN, MICTHEA J; Putman City HS; Oklahoma City, OK; (3); 76/360; Church Yth Grp; Cmnty Wkr; Sec Key Clb; Treas Spanish Clb; Church Choir; Sec Frsh Cls; Cit Awd; Jr NHS; Kiwanis Awd; Pres Acad Fit Awd; 3-D; Prin Ldrshp Clas; Stu To Stu; OK City Univ; Pre-Med; Span.

MILLECAN, ERIC A; Union Intermediate HS; Broken Arrow, OK; (1); 21/858; Church Yth Grp; Debate Tm; NFL; Chorus; School Musical; Intrml Ftbl; High Hon Roll; Jr NHS; NHS; Sand Vlybl; Guitar; DFY.

MILLER, AARON; Plainview HS; Ardmore, OK; (1); 12/93; Church Yth Grp; Cmnty Wkr; Band; Jazz Band; Mrchg Band; Orch; High Hon Roll; Beta Club; Ok Natl Hon Soc.

MILLER, ALICIA; B T Washington HS; Tulsa, OK; (4); 94/264; Church Yth Grp; Cmnty Wkr; GAA; Spanish Clb; Teachers Aide; Chorus; Bsktbl; Trk; Cit Awd; Hon Roll; OK Univ; PT.

MILLER, AMANDA M; West Jr HS; Oklahoma City, OK; (1); Bus Profs of Am; Church Yth Grp; Cmnty Wkr; Drama Clb; FCA; Hosp Aide; Scholastic Bowl; Teachers Aide; Thesps; Church Choir; Cook Chrch Camp; Peer Hlpr; Ftbl Trnr; Mgr Boys Bsktbl/Track; St Gregorys; Sprts Thrpst.

MILLER, AMANDA R; Allen HS; Ada, OK; (2); FBLA; Pep Clb; Spanish Clb; Pres Frsh Cls; Pres Soph Cls; Var Chrldng; Cit Awd; Hon Roll; Schlsp Awd In Eng II; ECU.

MILLER, AMBER; El Reno Sr HS; El Reno, OK; (4); Am Leg Aux Girls St; Church Yth Grp; FCA; FTA; Key Clb; Natl FFA Org; Teachers Aide; Sec Frsh Cls; Pres Soph Cls; Pres Jr Cls; Math & Sci Clb; Ranked 1 Top 10 Female Athl; S W OK St; Engl.

MILLER, ANTHONY W; Westmoore HS; Moore, OK; (3); 36/640; Boy Scts; Church Yth Grp; JCL; Mrchg Band; Hon Roll; NHS; Eagle Scout; Acad Letter; Latin; Eng.

MILLER, BECKY M; Bethany HS; Bethany, OK; (3); 5/85; Church Yth Grp; Cmnty Wkr; Hist Key Clb; Spanish Clb; Chorus; Phtg Yrbk; Sec Soph Cls; Ofcr Stu Cncl; Mgr(s); Var Trk; Pres Yth Alive Bible Group; OK Baptist Univ; Neo-Natal Nrs.

MILLER, BRETT; Ft Towson HS; Fort Towson, OK; (1); 12/35; FCA; Quiz Bowl; Varsity Clb; Rptr Nwsp; Ofcr Bsbl; Bsktbl; Hon Roll; Pres Acad Fit Awd; OK ST U; Sci.

MILLER, BRITTANY K; Stillwater Sr HS; Stillwater, OK; (4); 34/350; Church Yth Grp; FBLA; Key Clb; Natl Beta Clb; Spanish Clb; Church Choir; Ed Lit Mag; Hon Roll; NHS; Pres Acad Fit Awd; Vrsty Schlr; Outstndng Math Stu; OK ST U; Spnsh.

MILLER, CHRISTIE; Stilwell HS; Stilwell, OK; (4); 14/140; Computer Clb; French Clb; FHA; Key Clb; Library Aide; Math Clb; Natl Beta Clb; Natl FFA Org; Science Clb; Gov Hon Prg Awd; NE St Univ; Pharm.

MILLER, DANA S; Alva HS; Alva, OK; (2); Cmnty Wkr; Drama Clb; FHA; Hosp Aide; Office Aide; Speech Tm; Teachers Aide; Acpl Chr; Chorus; School Play; NWOSU; Music; Jrnlsm.

MILLER, DANETTE; Edmond North HS; Edmond, OK; (4); Mu Alpha Theta; Crs Cntry; Trk; High Hon Roll; NHS; Pres Schlr; St Schlr; U Of OK.

MILLER, DANIEL; Enid Sr HS; Enid, OK; (3); 90/450; Am Leg Boys St; Boy Scts; Church Yth Grp; DECA; Math Clb; Science Clb; Tennis; Wrstlng; NHS; Letterman Clb; Participated In ROOTS Ldrshp Conf.

MILLER, DANIELLE; Bridge Creek HS; Blanchard, OK; (4); 16/57; Church Yth Grp; FCA; FBLA; Pep Clb; Science Clb; Spanish Clb; SADD; Ed Yrbk; Rep Stu Cncl; NHS; OKC CC; Bus.

MILLER, DAVID A; Indianola HS; Indianola, OK; (2); 2/40; Church Yth Grp; 4-H; Ed Natl Beta Clb; Pres Natl FFA Org; Ofcr Stu Cncl; Ofcr Bsbl; Bsktbl; Cit Awd; 4-H Awd; High Hon Roll; Pub Speaking; FFA Star Chptr Farmer & Star Agribusinessman; OK ST U; Meteorologist.

MILLER, DAVID C; Classen Schl; Oklahoma City, OK; (3); Computer Clb; Mu Alpha Theta; Quiz Bowl; High Hon Roll; NHS.

MILLER, DENA; Midwest City HS; Midwest City, OK; (2); 23/488; Church Yth Grp; FCA; Science Clb; Spanish Clb; Band; Church Choir; Mrchg Band; Orch; NHS; Hon Roll; Outsndng Yth Awd Epsln Sgm Alph; OK Bapt U.

MILLER, DENIETRA K; Enid Sr HS; Enid, OK; (2); Teachers Aide; Ofcr Soph Cls; Trk; Hon Roll.

MILLER, DOROTHEA EAVON; Mangum Sr HS; Mangum, OK; (2); 20/55; Church Yth Grp; Drama Clb; Acpl Chr; Chorus; Church Choir; School Play; Variety Show; Pres Soph Cls; Rep Stu Cncl; Var Chrldng; Vcl Hnr Chair; Hghst GPA Spch & Drama; 3rd Pl Trck Relay Team; U Of Tulsa; Mtrlgst.

MILLER, DOUG T; Roland Sr HS; Roland, OK; (2); Band; JV Var Bsbl; High Hon Roll.

MILLER, DUSTY; Hennessey HS; Hennessey, OK; (1); Church Yth Grp; FCA; Teachers Aide; Ofcr Bsbl; Ftbl; Hon Roll; Notre Dame.

MILLER, ERIN; Mid-Del Christian Schl; Guthrie, OK; (1); 1/16; Church Yth Grp; High Hon Roll; Piano.

MILLER, GEORGE MARC; B T Washington HS; Tulsa, OK; (1); Boy Scts; Speech Tm; Hist Frsh Cls; Socr; High Hon Roll; BSA Life Rank & Sr Patrol Ldr; Chrch Acolyte; Video Production Cls; UCLA; Film Dir.

MILLER, GREGORY W; Broken Arrow Sr HS; Broken Arrow, OK; (3); Church Yth Grp; FCA; Math Clb; Math Tm; Office Aide; Science Clb; Spanish Clb; Teachers Aide; Var Wrstlng; Cit Awd; Geo/Soc Study Exclnc Awrd 94-95; Schlrshp Awrd 94-95; Prin Hnr Rl; Acad Exclnc Math/Sci; Med.

MILLER, HEATHER L; Fletcher Jr Sr HS; Fletcher, OK; (1); 1/36; Church Yth Grp; FHA; Letterman Clb; Church Choir; Bsktbl; Sftbl; Vllybl; Cit Awd; High Hon Roll; NHS.

MILLER, HEIDI; Hydro Jr Sr HS; Hydro, OK; (3); 3/25; Church Yth Grp; FCA; Hosp Aide; HOBY; Church Choir; Pres Stu Cncl; Var Bsktbl; Var Capt Chrldng; High Hon Roll; NHS.

MILLER, JAMIE J; Sallisaw HS; Gans, OK; (3); Church Yth Grp; Church Choir; Marine Bio.

MILLER, JENNIFER; Quinton Jr Sr HS; Quinton, OK; (2); Church Yth Grp; French Clb; FHA; Library Aide; Pep Clb; Church Choir; Voice Of Democracy Merit; Writing; PT.

MILLER, JENNIFER R; Frontier Public Schl; Marland, OK; (2); 1/30; HOBY; School Play; VP Frsh Cls; Sec Soph Cls; Var Bsktbl; Var Sftbl; Hon Roll; NHS; Pres Acad Fit Awd; Tech Stu Assoc; Schl Tlvsn News Cvre; Acad Tm; Coach.

MILLER, JOSH; Cascia Hall Prep School; Tulsa, OK; (1); 1/96; Church Yth Grp; Quiz Bowl; Scholastic Bowl; JV Bsbl; Bsktbl; JV Ftbl; High Hon Roll; Hnrs In Eng, Math, Sci, Frgn Lang & His; Natl Mrt Schlr; U Of OK.

MILLER, JOSH G; Lindsay HS; Lindsay, OK; (1); 7/78; Quiz Bowl; Scholastic Bowl; Hon Roll; Jr NHS; OK Univ; MD Intrnl Med.

MILLER, JULIE A; Stilwell HS; Stilwell, OK; (1); French Clb; Northeastern Univ; Pedtrcn.

MILLER, JULIE K; Howe Public Schl; Howe, OK; (2); FHA; Nwsp; Ofcr Frsh Cls; Hon Roll; Bus Mgmt.

MILLER, JUSTIN; Claremore Sr HS; Claremore, OK; (3); 12/268; Ed Nwsp; VP Frsh Cls; Var Ftbl; Var Mgr(s); Score Keeper; Trk; Hon Roll; OK Intl Publctns Assn Wnnr; St, Natl Jrnlsm Cont 1st, 2nd, 3rd; OK U; Jrnlsm.

MILLER, KARA E; Little Axe Sr HS; Newalla, OK; (4); Church Yth Grp; Teachers Aide; Acpl Chr; Chorus; Treas Jr Cls; Treas Sr Cls; Ofcr Stu Cncl; Chrldng; Crs Cntry; Trk.

MILLER, KATIE; Covington Douglas HS; Covington, OK; (3); Pres Church Yth Grp; Sec FHA; HOBY; Spanish Clb; Band; Jazz Band; Sec Stu Cncl; Var Bsktbl; Var Powder Puff Ftbl; High Hon Roll; Stu Of Today Awd Masonic Lodge; Amer Hstry Awd; Perry Elks Lodge Acad Athl 3 Yrs.

MILLER, KAYCE N; Woodward HS; Woodward, OK; (1); Art Clb; Church Yth Grp; FCA; 4-H; JV Bsktbl; JV Socr; Hon Roll; OSU; Vet.

MILLER, KELLI; Westmoore HS; Oklahoma City, OK; (3); 21/716; Church Yth Grp; Dance Clb; Drama Clb; FCA; School Musical; School Play; Stage Crew; Mgr(s); Hon Roll; NHS; Athl Trainer; First Bapt Chrch Svc Aide Awd; Puppet Ministry; OK Bapt Univ; Theater/Engl.

MILLER, KEVIN; Braman Schl; Braman, OK; (1); 2/21; Boy Scts; Church Yth Grp; FCA; Natl FFA Org; Quiz Bowl; Ofcr Bsbl; Bsktbl; High Hon Roll.

MILLER, KIMBERLY S; Rush Springs HS; Rush Springs, OK; (3); 1/40; Church Yth Grp; FCA; Scholastic Bowl; Yrbk; Pres Frsh Cls; Pres Soph Cls; VP Jr Cls; VP VP Stu Cncl; Var Sftbl; Cit Awd.

MILLER, LEANNE; Corn Bible Acad; Weatherford, OK; (2); 1/20; Band; Mrchg Band; Pep Band; Pres Frsh Cls; Var Bsktbl; Var Socr; Var Vllybl; High Hon Roll; NHS.

MILLER, LORI; Tupelo Jr Sr HS; Stonewall, OK; (2); 3/23; FHA; Natl FFA Org; Office Aide; Teachers Aide; Rep Stu Cncl; Chrldng; Hon Roll; NHS; All Amer Scholar 93; Multi-Yr Listee; E Cntrl Univ; Bus Mngmt.

MILLER, LOWELL J; Midwest City HS; Midwest City, OK; (2); Church Yth Grp; Crs Cntry; Trk; Wt Lftg; Chrch Drama Outreaches Across Metro Area; TUISAU; Psych; Broadcasting.

MILLER, MARIANNE; Leflore Sr HS; Wister, OK; (3); 4/21; Cmnty Wkr; FHA; Quiz Bowl; Scholastic Bowl; Rptr Nwsp; Hon Roll; NHS; Ntl Merit Ltr; Carl Albert Stcol.

MILLER, MARLEY R; Ponca City Sr HS; Ponca City, OK; (4); German Clb; Q&S; Band; Jazz Band; Mrchg Band; Pep Band; Nwsp; Ofcr Stu Cncl; Sftbl; Hon Roll; Outstdng Percussionist Frosh Yr.

MILLER, MATTHEW C; El Reno Sr HS; El Reno, OK; (2); 4-H; Natl FFA Org; JV Wrstlng; Hon Roll.

MILLER, MATTHEW G; Erick Jr Sr HS; Erick, OK; (1); 6/20; Church Yth Grp; Natl FFA Org; Var Bsktbl; Hon Roll; OU.

MILLER, MELINDA S; Southeast HS; Oklahoma City, OK; (2); FCA; Office Aide; Mgr(s); High Hon Roll; NHS.

MILLER, MELISSA B; Tahlequah Sr HS; Tahlequah, OK; (3); Church Yth Grp; German Clb; SADD; Chorus; Church Choir; Rep Frsh Cls; Rep Soph Cls; Rep Stu Cncl; Var Tennis; OK ST Univ; Vet.

MILLER, MELODY JOY; Jay HS; Jay, OK; (4); 1/95; Church Yth Grp; Cmnty Wkr; Drama Clb; Sec FCA; FBLA; HOBY; Capt Math Tm; Rptr Natl Beta Clb; Capt Quiz Bowl; Church Choir; Natl Hstry Day St Wnnr; Church Yth Cncl; John Brown U; Brdcstng.

MILLER, MICHAEL B; Stillwater Sr HS; Stillwater, OK; (2); 19/325; German Clb; Band; Church Choir; Mrchg Band; Pep Band; School Play; Stage Crew; Tennis; NHS; Pres Acad Fit Awd; U Of IL; Sci.

MILLER, MICHAEL D; Sallisaw HS; Sallisaw, OK; (3); Art Clb; Church Yth Grp; Spanish Clb; Band; Mrchg Band; High Hon Roll; DECA; Dallas Art Inst; Anmtr.

MILLER, MONTY W; Empire Schl; Duncan, OK; (2); FCA; Varsity Clb; Var L Bsbl; Var L Ftbl; Var L Wrstlng; Hon Roll; Whos Who In HS Sprts 95-96.

MILLER, NICKEY G; Stroud HS; Stroud, OK; (3); 1/60; Rep Am Leg Aux Girls St; VP Drama Clb; French Clb; FHA; VP Band; Jazz Band; Pres Stu Cncl; Score Keeper; Sftbl; NHS; Arion Awd Wnnr Band; Tchrs Aide Dancing; Pre-Med.

MILLER, NICOLE; Okay Jr Sr HS; Okay, OK; (3); Church Yth Grp; Rep 4-H; Office Aide; Yrbk; Var L Bsktbl; Var Chrldng; Var L Sftbl; Var L Vllybl; 4-H Awd; Hon Roll; Nrs Aide Nrsng Home Vol; Head Start Vol Awd; Connors ST Coll; Nrsng.

MILLER, NICOLE; Chickasha Jr HS; Chickasha, OK; (1); Church Yth Grp; Spanish Clb; Chorus; Intrml Sftbl; JV Tennis; Hon Roll; Jr NHS; U Of OK.

MILLER, REA S; Mustang HS; Mustang, OK; (3); 1/390; 4-H; Key Clb; Spanish Clb; Teachers Aide; Pres Jr Cls; Rep Sr Cls; Crs Cntry; Sftbl; Trk; High Hon Roll; OK ST Hlth Sci Ctr Smmr Acad; Univ Hosp Vol; Univ Of MO; Med.

MILLER, REBECCA; Plainview HS; Ardmore, OK; (2); 5/77; Church Yth Grp; Cmnty Wkr; Hosp Aide; Natl Beta Clb; Acpl Chr; Chorus; School Musical; High Hon Roll; NHS; Ntl Merit Schol; Cert Water Safety Instr; St Vocal Cont Wnnr 95-96; Tulane.

MILLER, ROBIN; Shattuck Jr Sr HS; Shattuck, OK; (3); 1/33; Church Yth Grp; Drama Clb; FCA; FHA; GAA; Letterman Clb; Natl Beta Clb; Pep Clb; Quiz Bowl; Chorus; Bsktbl Team Acad Achvmnt Awds; 1st Pl Geometry SWOSU Intersict Meet; OU.

MILLER, RUBY S; Sapulpa Sr HS; Sapulpa, OK; (2); Church Yth Grp; FHA; Chorus; Hon Roll; Spanish NHS; Chrch Clown, Mime & Puppeteer; Soloist At Chrch; Elem Ed.

MILLER, SARA M; Elk City HS; Elk City, OK; (4); 9/141; Science Clb; Band; Mrchg Band; Yrbk; Ofcr Stu Cncl; Sftbl; Trk; High Hon Roll; NHS; Pres Acad Fit Awd; U Of TX-DALLAS; Arts; Hum.

MILLER, SARAH B; Nathan Hale HS; Tulsa, OK; (3); GAA; Varsity Clb; Var Crs Cntry; Var Socr; Var Trk; Var Wt Lftg; High Hon Roll; Cmnty Wkr; Teachers Aide; Color Guard; St Johns Hosp Vol; Jr Explorer; Retirement Home Vol 2 Yrs; Jr Class Homecoming Attendant; Pre-Med.

MILLER, SARAH E; Charles Page HS; Sand Springs, OK; (2); 1/385; Church Yth Grp; Cmnty Wkr; Key Clb; Letterman Clb; Math Tm; Spanish Clb; Chorus; High Hon Roll; NHS; Prfct Atten Awd; Dance & Acad Teams.

MILLER, SERINA M; Putnam City West HS; Oklahoma City, OK; (2); 1/450; Church Yth Grp; Drama Clb; Thesps; Band; School Play; Stage Crew; Var Vllybl; High Hon Roll; NHS; FCA; All-Amer Schlr; Acctnt; CPA.

MILLER, SHANNON MARIE; Muskogee HS; Muskogee, OK; (2); Church Yth Grp; Chorus; High Hon Roll; OK Hnr Soc; RAID; Sprts Med.

MILLER, SHARON; Mustang HS; Mustang, OK; (2); 1/416; Church Yth Grp; Girl Scts; Spanish Clb; Church Choir; Mrchg Band; JV Vllybl; NHS; High Hon Roll; FCA; FBLA; Yth Alive; Mat-Maid.

MILLER, SHERRA; Midwest City HS; Midwest City, OK; (4); 18/389; Girl Scts; Hosp Aide; Letterman Clb; SADD; Stage Crew; Yrbk; Ofcr Sr Cls; Ofcr Stu Cncl; Socr; High Hon Roll; Wrstlng Mat Maid; Psych.

MILLER, STEPHANIE; Porter Jr Sr HS; Porter, OK; (3); 4-H; Quiz Bowl; Scholastic Bowl; Yrbk; Hon Roll; NHS; GATE; OSU; Scl Sci.

MILLER, STEPHANIE D; Stilwell HS; Stilwell, OK; (1); Church Yth Grp; Drama Clb; French Clb; FHA; OK U; Pre-Law.

MILLER, TARA; Mangum Jr HS; Mangum, OK; (1); 4-H; FHA; Band; Jazz Band; Mrchg Band; Pep Band; Var Chrldng; 4-H Awd; Gov Hon Prg Awd; High Hon Roll; Math & His Awd; Hnr Stu Medal; OK ST U; Dr.

MILLER, TARA D; Alva HS; Alva, OK; (1); Hosp Aide; Quiz Bowl; NWOSU; Hist/Vet Med.

MILLER, TIFFANY M; Ardmore HS; Ardmore, OK; (3); Church Yth Grp; FCA; GAA; JA; Spanish Clb; Mgr(s); Trk; Cit Awd; Hon Roll; Pres Acad Fit Awd; Delta Sigma Theta; U Of AR; Comp Tech.

MILLER, TIFFANY S; Depew HS; Depew, OK; (3); 10/35; Spanish Clb; Treas Frsh Cls; Hon Roll.

MILLER, TIM; Ada HS; Ada, OK; (3); Boy Scts; Church Yth Grp; FCA; Letterman Clb; Spanish Clb; SADD; Yrbk; Ftbl; High Hon Roll; Red Crss Lifeguard Cert; Eagle Sct; Yrbk Ed; TX A&M; Marine Bio; Oceanogphy.

MILLER, TONYA GAYLENE; Union Sr HS; Broken Arrow, OK; (4); 58/629; Pres FCA; Capt L Bsktbl; Powder Puff Ftbl; Cit Awd; High Hon Roll; NHS; Prfct Atten Awd; Trk; Spanish Clb; Church Yth Grp; Unn Soph Grl/Yr; 95 Sho-Me Clsc All-Trn Bsktbl, 96 Jnks Inv Trnm MVP Bsktbl; Sec Ed.

MILLER, TRAVIS; Lone Grove HS; Lone Grove, OK; (3); Boy Scts; Church Yth Grp; HOBY; Key Clb; Natl FFA Org; Science Clb; Spanish Clb; Speech Tm; Mrchg Band; Rep Stu Cncl; BSA Eagle Sct; OK ST U; Wldlf Bio.

MILLER, TRAVIS W; Wakita Schl; Medford, OK; (1); Pres Frsh Cls; Var Bsbl; Var Bsktbl; Var Ftbl; Var Wt Lftg; Church Yth Grp; FCA; Natl FFA Org; Hon Roll; OK ST U; Coach.

MILLER, VANESSA A; Newkirk HS; Newkirk, OK; (4); 11/46; Chorus; Church Choir; Ofcr Stu Cncl; L Stat Bsktbl; Mgr(s); Score Keeper; Hon Roll; NHS; Pres Acad Fit Awd; Office Aide; STEP Rep/Hist, Pres; OK ST U; Scndry Ed.

MILLER, WHITNEY; Weatherford HS; Weatherford, OK; (2); FCA; Bsktbl; Chrldng; Crs Cntry; Socr; Trk; Hon Roll.

MILLER, WILLIAM; Stigler HS; Stigler, OK; (2); Boy Scts; Church Yth Grp; FCA; Pep Clb; Spanish Clb; SADD; Band; Mrchg Band; JV Var Bsbl; Tennis; Med.

MILLICAN, JASON R; Putnam City HS; Oklahoma City, OK; (1); Boy Scts; Church Yth Grp; Golf; Bsktbl; Xplr Prgrm Through Bethany Hsptl; OU; Med Field.

MILLICAN, KATE E; Union Sr HS; Broken Arrow, OK; (3); 57/741; Church Yth Grp; German Clb; Key Clb; Mu Alpha Theta; Acpl Chr; Rep Stu Cncl; Jr NHS; NHS; Prfct Atten Awd; Natl Erth Smmt Rts & Shts W/Jane Goodall; Eng.

MILLICAN, LARRY H; Meeker HS; Meeker, OK; (4); Natl FFA Org; Office Aide; Teachers Aide; Ofcr Bsbl; Ftbl; Trk; Wt Lftg; Hon Roll; OSU; Ftbl Coach.

MILLICAN, MANDY L; Checotah HS; Checotah, OK; (3); Church Yth Grp; Debate Tm; Drama Clb; Spanish Clb; Speech Tm; Chorus; Church Choir; School Musical; School Play; Yrbk; NSU; Psych.

MILLIGAN, JASON D; Westmoore HS; Oklahoma City, OK; (3); Church Yth Grp; Drama Clb; Band; Chorus; Church Choir; Mrchg Band; Chrch Drama Team; Chrch Band; Comp; ORU; Comp Prgmr.

MILLIGAN, JASON M; Guthrie Sr HS; Guthrie, OK; (1); 9/307; Intrml Ftbl; Cit Awd; High Hon Roll; Jr NHS; NHS; Ntl Merit Ltr; OK Univ.

MILLIGAN, JENNIFER L; Putnam City West HS; Bethany, OK; (2); Church Yth Grp; Drama Clb; GAA; Thesps; Acpl Chr; Chorus; Church Choir; School Play; Stage Crew; Cit Awd; OK ST U; Med.

MILLIGAN, KIRK A; Putnam City North HS; Oklahoma City, OK; (2); Church Yth Grp; FCA; Letterman Clb; Spanish Clb; JV Var Bsbl; Bsktbl; JV Var Ftbl; Intrml Wt Lftg; NHS; Chrch Dcn; Coach Lil Lgue Bsbl; Engr.

MILLIGAN, LUKE B; Bartlesville Mid HS; Grove, OK; (2); French Clb; FBLA; Ofcr Bsbl; Wt Lftg; Var Wrstlng; Hon Roll; People To People Stdnt Ambsdr; Referee YMCA Yth Bsktbl; Amer Lgn Bsebl; OK ST Univ.

MILLIGAN, TIFFANY; Okmulgee HS; Okmulgee, OK; (4); 1/120; Am Leg Aux Girls St; Pres Church Yth Grp; FCA; Pres French Clb; Science Clb; Band; Church Choir; Drm Mjr(t); Jazz Band; Mrchg Band; Northeastern ST U; Music Educ.

MILLION, ANDREA J; Okemah HS; Okemah, OK; (3); Chess Clb; Computer Clb; English Clb; Math Clb; Pep Clb; Quiz Bowl; Science Clb; Spanish Clb; Band; Chorus; Nrsng.

MILLIRONS, LINDSAY; Midwest City HS; Midwest City, OK; (3); 10/386; 4-H; German Clb; Letterman Clb; Pep Clb; Yrbk; Cit Awd; 4-H Awd; High Hon Roll; Hon Roll; Jr NHS; Rssn Clb Photo; OK U; Educ.

MILLS, AMANDA; Macomb Schl; Tecumseh, OK; (2); 1/19; 4-H; Pep Clb; Quiz Bowl; Scholastic Bowl; Spanish Clb; SADD; High Hon Roll; Hon Roll; Sal; St Schlr; Notre Dame U; Med.

MILLS, APRIL A; Oilton HS; Jennings, OK; (4); 4/30; Bus Profs of Am; FBLA; Natl FFA Org; Office Aide; Pep Clb; Teachers Aide; Rptr Yrbk; Treas Frsh Cls; Sec Soph Cls; Sec Jr Cls; Miss Oilton HS; Mst Val Player Sftbll; Amer Lgn Awd For Sprts; Seminole St Univ; Elem Tchr.

MILLS, BRAD L; Lindsay HS; Lindsay, OK; (4); 4-H; Natl FFA Org; Office Aide; Teachers Aide; Var Crs Cntry; Var Golf; Cit Awd; High Hon Roll; Hon Roll; Team Crss Cntry St Champs, CC Acad St Champs 94; St Finals Crss Cntry 95; St Golf Fnlsts 94-95; Bio-Technology.

MILLS, CALEB E; Putnam City HS; Oklahoma City, OK; (2); 13/431; Church Yth Grp; FCA; JV Crs Cntry; JV Socr; NHS; Prfct Atten Awd; 3-D; Chrch Yth Choir; Med.

MILLS, JEREMY S; Hollis Jr Sr HS; Hollis, OK; (4); High Hon Roll; Hon Roll; Jr NHS; NHS; WOSC.

MILLS, JODY; Davis HS; Davis, OK; (4); 1/53; Church Yth Grp; FCA; Key Clb; Math Clb; Office Aide; Spanish Clb; Yrbk; Var Sftbl; High Hon Roll; NHS; OSU; Chem Engr.

MILLS, KEVIN; Shawnee Sr HS; Shawnee, OK; (2); Church Yth Grp; Drama Clb; NFL; Quiz Bowl; Scholastic Bowl; Speech Tm; Thesps; Band; Jazz Band; Mrchg Band; One Act Ply; Various Hnr Bands; Stanford.

MILLS, MELISSA J; Bartlesville Mid HS; Bartlesville, OK; (2); Church Yth Grp; Spanish Clb; Orch; High Hon Roll; Hon Roll; Jr NHS; Pre-Med.

MILLS, SAMANTHA A; Putnam City North HS; Oklahoma City, OK; (2); #1 in class; Pres Church Yth Grp; Cmnty Wkr; French Clb; HOBY; JA; Key Clb; Service Clb; Yrbk; Rep Frsh Cls; Rep Soph Cls; All Amer Schlr; #1 Frosh In Cls; Harvard; Medicine; Intnl Bus.

MILLS, TRAVIS; U S Grant HS; Oklahoma City, OK; (4); Church Yth Grp; FCA; ROTC; Stage Crew; Wrstlng; Hon Roll; HOSA; Fmly Practcnr.

MILLSPAUGH, MELISSA S; Oaks Mission Jr Sr HS; Rose, OK; (4); 7/16; FBLA; FHA; Office Aide; Teachers Aide; Bsktbl; Trk; Hon Roll; Johnson O'Malley Hon Stu; Johnson O'Malley Raising GPA; Northeast Vo Tech Cntr; Nrsng.

MILLSTID, CANDICE D; Putnam City West HS; Oklahoma City, OK; (4); 91/288; Art Clb; Church Yth Grp; Cmnty Wkr; Office Aide; Church Choir; Hon Roll; NHS; Nrs Aide; Tutor Eng Cls; OKCCC; Nrs.

MILNER, JASON; Duke Schl; Duke, OK; (4); 4/20; Church Yth Grp; Pres FCA; Natl FFA Org; Pres Frsh Cls; Pres Soph Cls; Pres Stu Cncl; Ofcr Bsbl; Bsktbl; Cit Awd; Hon Roll; Masonic Lodge Stu Of Today; Masonic Lodge Essay Cont Wnnr; VFW Schlsp; Northwestern OK ST U; Ag Ec.

MILNER, JASON M; Nathan Hale HS; Tulsa, OK; (1); ROTC; High Hon Roll; ROTC Highest Grd Pt Avg; Navy.

MILNER, JEREMY P; North Intemediate HS; Broken Arrow, OK; (2); Boy Scts; Church Yth Grp; Debate Tm; Latin Clb; NFL; Chorus; Church Choir; Mrchg Band; Hon Roll; Comm Play Permnc; Perform Regularly In Longest Rnng Play North Amer; Gilbert & Sullivan Soc Mem.

MILNER, KELLI A; Checotah HS; Checotah, OK; (3); Chorus; School Musical; Hon Roll; Northeastern ST U; Chld Psych.

MILSON, AMY L; Healdton HS; Ardmore, OK; (3); 4-H; Library Aide; Teachers Aide; Band; Jazz Band; Mrchg Band; Yrbk; Trk; Hon Roll; NHS; Drivers Ed Awd.

MILSON, SUMER L; Healdton HS; Ardmore, OK; (2); Church Yth Grp; Band; Mrchg Band; Hon Roll; NHS; Hldtn HS Acad Awd; Pres Ed Awds Prgm.

MILTON, AJOA; Okemah HS; Okemah, OK; (1); 13/50; Art Clb; Band; Ofcr Frsh Cls; Ofcr Bsbl; Bsktbl; Trk; Hon Roll; Med.

MILTON, MELISSA; Empire Schl; Comanche, OK; (4); 1/33; Am Leg Aux Girls St; FCA; FBLA; School Play; Sprt Ed Nwsp; Ed Yrbk; Capt Bsktbl; Capt Chrldng; NHS; Val; OK ST U; Bus Law.

MIMMS, AMANDA B; Fairland Jr Sr HS; Fairland, OK; (3); Church Yth Grp; Drama Clb; FHA; Band; Chorus; Rptr Nwsp; Rptr Jr Cls; Var Chrldng; High Hon Roll; Pres Acad Fit Awd; OK FHA NE Dist Sub-Dist 4 VP; Drama/Lit Edctr.

MIMMS, LEIGH-ANNA K; Durant HS; Durant, OK; (2); Church Yth Grp; Chorus; Church Choir; Gym; Powder Puff Ftbl; Socr; Prfct Atten Awd; Perfect Attnd; Baylor Univ; Docterite; Ed.

MIMS, RYAN; Holdenville HS; Holdenville, OK; (2); 1/85; Church Yth Grp; FCA; Letterman Clb; Natl FFA Org; Office Aide; Ofcr Bsbl; Ftbl; Wt Lftg; High Hon Roll; NHS.

MINARD, SARAH S; Edmond North HS; Edmond, OK; (3); 19/348; Church Yth Grp; Mu Alpha Theta; Chorus; School Musical; Swing Chorus; Rep Stu Cncl; Pom Pon; NHS; High Hon Roll; Cmnty Wkr; Choir Club VP; Dance Team; Mus/Theater.

MINDEMANN, JUSTIN B; Apache HS; Apache, OK; (2); Boy Scts; Church Yth Grp; 4-H; Letterman Clb; Natl FFA Org; Ftbl; Trk; Wt Lftg; Wrstlng; Hon Roll; OSU; Chem Eng.

MINER, CHASITY N; Perry Sr HS; Perry, OK; (3); Church Yth Grp; Dance Clb; FCA; FHA; German Clb; Band; Jazz Band; Mrchg Band; Pep Band; Rep Stu Cncl; U Of OK; Law.

MINER, SHAWNDA; Indianola HS; Mcalester, OK; (1); 4/35; Church Yth Grp; GAA; Natl FFA Org; Pres Frsh Cls; Bsktbl; Hon Roll; OK ST Univ.

MINGS, CRYSTAL R; Whitesboro Schl; Talihina, OK; (2); Church Yth Grp; FHA; Natl FFA Org; Church Choir; Var Sftbl; Hon Roll; Prfct Atten Awd; Cnslr.

MINICH, RACHEL L; Enid Sr HS; Enid, OK; (2); Church Yth Grp; French Clb; GAA; Speech Tm; School Musical; Var Socr; High Hon Roll; NHS; TNT Actng Trpe; Play Piano; Psych.

MINK, MARINA R; Vanoss Schl; Roff, OK; (3); FHA; Band; Hon Roll; NHS; HOSA Sec; Certfd Nrs Aide; All Amer Schlr; Murray ST Coll; RN.

MINNEY, JASON W; Mannford HS; Mannford, OK; (3); FCA; Letterman Clb; Spanish Clb; SADD; JV Var Bsbl; Var L Ftbl; Var L Trk; L Var Wrstlng; Schlr Ath 3 Yrs; USAA Natl Ftbll Awd; OSU Outstndng Acad Achvmnts Hnr; NE St Univ; Bus Mgmt.

MINNIS, MELISSA; Edmond Memorial HS; Edmond, OK; (1); #1 in class; Church Yth Grp; FCA; Key Clb; Spanish Clb; Ofcr Stu Cncl; Chrldng; Tennis; NHS.

MINOR, AARON; Comanche HS; Comanche, OK; (1); Church Yth Grp; Natl FFA Org; JV Bsbl; Var Bsktbl; JV Ftbl; Hon Roll; Lvstck Jdgn Tm; Vrs Awds Shwng Cttl & Swn; OSU.

MINTER, MICHAEL; Braggs Schl; Gore, OK; (2); Church Yth Grp; Math Tm; Teachers Aide; Pres Soph Cls; Var Bsktbl; Cit Awd; Prfct Atten Awd.

MINTER, SARA I; Madill HS; Madill, OK; (1); Church Yth Grp; FCA; Jr NHS; Pedtrcn.

MINTHORN, MARTINA R; Elgin HS; Elgin, OK; (2); Church Yth Grp; Dance Clb; Latin Clb; Library Aide; Yrbk; VP Jr Cls; Bsktbl; Cmnty Wkr; Chorus; Church Choir; Close Up Washington DC 96; Native Amer Club/Native Amer Handgame Tm; Comanche Tribe Sbstnc Abuse Cmp; OK Univ; Soc Wrk.

MINTON, SARAH; Bishop Mcguinness HS; Oklahoma City, OK; (4); 15/151; Cmnty Wkr; FCA; VP Sec French Clb; Letterman Clb; Pep Clb; SADD; Varsity Clb; Rep Frsh Cls; Capt Bsktbl; Powder Puff Ftbl; Pomona Col.

MINTON, SUSIE; Pryor Sr HS; Pryor, OK; (4); 28/145; Boy Scts; Church Yth Grp; FBLA; Rep Band; Chorus; Co-Ed Yrbk; Hon Roll; NHS; Mu Alpha Theta; Spanish Clb; Camp Fire Treas; Lmp Lghtrs Pres; Octogon Clb Treas, Secy; OK Bapt U; Chld Psych.

MINTS, REBECCA R; Duncan HS; Duncan, OK; (4); 22/214; Church Yth Grp; FCA; FBLA; Key Clb; Spanish Clb; SADD; VP Band; Church Choir; VP Mrchg Band; Pep Band; U Of OK; Occptnl Thrpst.

MINTY, BENJAMIN A; Sapulpa Sr HS; Sapulpa, OK; (3); Church Yth Grp; Debate Tm; Office Aide; Speech Tm; OK Univ.

MINYARD, JAIME L; Del City HS; Oklahoma City, OK; (2); 93/493; Church Yth Grp; FCA; Chorus; Church Choir; Mgr(s); Tennis; Cit Awd; Jr NHS; Prfct Atten Awd; Pres Acad Fit Awd; Dntl Hygne; PT.

MINYARD, MATT; Marietta HS; Marietta, OK; (4); 1/35; Quiz Bowl; Band; Jazz Band; Mrchg Band; School Musical; Hon Roll; NHS; Pres Acad Fit Awd; Val; Band Pres 93-95; OK All-St Jazz Band 96; OK All-St Band 94; Oklahoma City U; Comp Engrng.

MINYARD, NATALIE J; Yukon Middle HS; Yukon, OK; (3); 2/416; Am Leg Aux Girls St; Cmnty Wkr; Scholastic Bowl; Spanish Clb; School Musical; School Play; Acpl Chr; High Hon Roll; NHS; 3 D Dnt Do Drgs.

MIRACLE, ROBERT H; Bridge Creek HS; Blanchard, OK; (2); Art Clb; Drama Clb; School Play; Ofcr Soph Cls; Columbus Coll Of Art & Design.

MIRELES, CRISTEN S; Stillwater Sr HS; Stillwater, OK; (3); 1/383; Church Yth Grp; Treas VP 4-H; Key Clb; Mu Alpha Theta; Natl Beta Clb; Spanish Clb; Teachers Aide; 4-H Awd; High Hon Roll; NHS; Ride/Show Horses; Hum Soc Vol; OK ST Univ; Anml Sci/Pre-Vet.

MISASI, PAUL A; Cascia Hall Prep School; Tulsa, OK; (3); Art Clb; Pep Clb; Drm Mjr(t); Pep Band; Var Golf; Hon Roll; Prfct Atten Awd; Downhill Mountain Biking; Bike Mech; Hunting; Auto Mech; OSU; Arch Engrng.

MISHINA, YUKIKO; Noble HS; Noble, OK; (3); 1/186; French Clb; Sec Mu Alpha Theta; Scholastic Bowl; SADD; Band; Mrchg Band; Orch; High Hon Roll; NHS; Pres Acad Fit Awd; All-State Band/Orchestra; Pre-Med.

MITCHAEL, ANNA; Ponca City Sr HS; Ponca City, OK; (4); Am Leg Aux Girls St; NFL; Spanish Clb; Drill Tm; School Play; Yrbk; Pres Sr Cls; Var L Vllybl; High Hon Roll; NHS; Outstndng Girl; Homcmng Atten; U Of TX.

MITCHELL, ADAM L; Owasso Sr HS; Owasso, OK; (2); Boy Scts; Church Yth Grp; Drama Clb; HOBY; NFL; Quiz Bowl; School Play; Stage Crew; Rep Soph Cls; Ofcr Stu Cncl.

MITCHELL, ALICIA F; Enid Sr HS; Enid, OK; (2); FCA; 4-H; Band; Chorus; Nwsp; Sec Stu Cncl; Socr; Sftbl; High Hon Roll; Jr NHS; Environmental Engr.

MITCHELL, AMANDA L; Putnam City North HS; Oklahoma City, OK; (1).

MITCHELL, BENNETT L; Webster HS; Oklahoma City, OK; (1); Church Yth Grp; FHA; JA; Chorus; Church Choir; Hon Roll; Prfct Atten Awd; Harvard Univ; Dentist.

MITCHELL, BRANDON A; Lawton Sr HS; Lawton, OK; (3); Cmnty Wkr; Math Tm; Spanish Clb; Chorus; Var Bsktbl; Hon Roll; Pres Acad Fit Awd; U Of OK; Acctnt.

MITCHELL, CASSIE; Warner HS; Warner, OK; (1); Scholastic Bowl; Rep Stu Cncl; Bsktbl; Trk; Cit Awd; 4-H Awd; Val; 1000 Hr Awd Amer Paint Horse Assns Ride Amer Prgm; Msnc Stdnt Today Awd; Jr Rodeo Pole Bndng Chmpn 96; Enviro Engr.

MITCHELL, CHANCE P; Calumet Schl; Calumet, OK; (2); Pres Church Yth Grp; Cmnty Wkr; FCA; Quiz Bowl; Scholastic Bowl; Spanish Clb; Church Choir; School Musical; Pres Frsh Cls; VP Soph Cls; Bsktbl Coach/PT.

MITCHELL, DANIELLE; Durant HS; Durant, OK; (3); DECA; FBLA; FHA; Var Powder Puff Ftbl; Var Tennis; Hon Roll; NHS; Southeastern SOSU; Comp Sci.

MITCHELL, DARCY A; Dewey HS; Dewey, OK; (4); 13/89; Drama Clb; FHA; GAA; Chorus; School Musical; School Play; Swing Chorus; Rep Stu Cncl; Chrldng; Hon Roll; 5 ST Vocal Medals; 7 Dist Vocal Medals; Elkteen Of Mnth; Northeastern ST Univ; Ed.

MITCHELL, JAMEY; Texhoma HS; Texhoma, OK; (3); 1/15; Church Yth Grp; Natl FFA Org; Quiz Bowl; Teachers Aide; Band; School Play; Yrbk; Sec Frsh Cls; Treas Soph Cls; Pres Jr Cls; OSU.

MITCHELL, JASON; Davenport Jr Sr HS; Davenport, OK; (4); 1/33; Am Leg Boys St; Church Yth Grp; FBLA; Red Cross Aide; Scholastic Bowl; SADD; VP Stu Cncl; Capt Bsbl; Capt Bsktbl; Capt Ftbl; DARE Role Model; KOMMOTION; NE OK Univ.

MITCHELL, JESSIE; Kremlin Jr Sr HS; Kremlin, OK; (2); Church Yth Grp; FCA; Band; Drm Mjr(t); Jazz Band; Mrchg Band; Pres Soph Cls; Capt Bsktbl; Trk; Hon Roll; OK ST U.

MITCHELL, JESSIE; Perry Sr HS; Stillwater, OK; (2); FBLA; FHA; Pep Clb; Drill Tm; Hon Roll; Jr NHS; NHS; Cmpfre.

MITCHELL, JOHN; El Reno Sr HS; El Reno, OK; (4); 22/167; Am Leg Boys St; Church Yth Grp; Cmnty Wkr; Math Clb; Science Clb; Rep Sr Cls; NHS; Mock Trial Team; Natl Bus Hnr Soc; Redlands CC; Crmnl Jstc.

MITCHELL, KAREL DEAN; Piedmont HS; Piedmont, OK; (3); Church Yth Grp; Ofcr Key Clb; SADD; Pres Band; Chorus; Drm Mjr(t); Var Chrldng; Hon Roll; Kiwanis Awd; NHS.

MITCHELL, KATIE K; Owasso Sr HS; Owasso, OK; (3); Church Yth Grp; FCA; French Clb; Science Clb; VICA; Acpl Chr; Band; Church Choir; School Musical; Trk; Pharmacy.

MITCHELL, KIMBERLY D; Shattuck Jr Sr HS; Shattuck, OK; (2); 2/24; Letterman Clb; Pep Clb; Band; Mrchg Band; Pep Band; Nwsp; Ed Yrbk; Rep Frsh Cls; Rep Soph Cls; Ofcr Stu Cncl; TSA Chptr Pres Frosh & Soph Yr; NSMA Awd Frosh Yr; Clogging; Med Field.

MITCHELL, LINDSAY B; Putnam City North HS; Oklahoma City, OK; (1); Cmnty Wkr; Treas Soph Cls; Hon Roll; Arch.

MITCHELL, MICHAEL; Jarman Jr HS; Oklahoma City, OK; (1); Boy Scts; Church Yth Grp; Computer Clb; French Clb; German Clb; Letterman Clb; Math Clb; Pep Clb; Science Clb; Ofcr Frsh Cls; Mrtl Arts; Cmptrs.

MITCHELL, MIKE I; Cleveland Sr HS; Cleveland, OK; (1); Church Yth Grp; FCA; Quiz Bowl; Scholastic Bowl; Bsktbl; Wt Lftg; Hon Roll; NHS; St Schlr.

MITCHELL, NICOLE D; Guthrie Sr HS; Guthrie, OK; (1); Church Yth Grp; FBLA; FHA; Chorus; Ofcr Stu Cncl; Hon Roll; Langston Univ; Derm.

MITCHELL, OLIVIA N; Healdton HS; Healdton, OK; (2); #1 in class; Church Yth Grp; FCA; FHA; Chorus; Church Choir; Pres Frsh Cls; Pres Soph Cls; Var Bsktbl; Var Chrldng; Var Trk; Ardmrt Blue Ribbon Schlr; Outstdng Music Prtcptn; 3rd High Jum ST Class 2a 96; Georgetown; Pol Sci.

MITCHELL, RAMONA; Dale Sr HS; Shawnee, OK; (4); 2/49; VP Sec FHA; Pres Spanish Clb; SADD; Sec Soph Cls; VP Stu Cncl; Cit Awd; Hon Roll; Sec Treas Jr NHS; NHS; Sal; FL ST U; Comp Sci.

MITCHELL, SARAH JANE; Victory Christian Schl; Tulsa, OK; (2); 75/80; Chorus; Church Choir; Color Guard; High Hon Roll; NHS; Mission Trip To Thailand/Hong Kong/China; Piano; Oral Roberts Univ.

MITCHELL, SEAN; Del City HS; Oklahoma City, OK; (4); 1/400; Am Leg Boys St; Church Yth Grp; Sec FCA; Ed Nwsp; Ofcr Stu Cncl; Var L Bsbl; Var L Bsktbl; Var L Ftbl; Cit Awd; Hon Roll; 12th Grd Stfbl King; 3rd Rnnr-Up Mr Del City HS; OK St U; Acctng.

MITCHELL, SHAYLA D; Choctaw HS; Choctaw, OK; (4); 23/302; FCA; Key Clb; Math Clb; Crs Cntry; Tennis; High Hon Roll; Jr NHS; NHS; Val; OK U; Phys Thrpy.

MITCHELL, STEPHANIE J; Wakita Schl; Medford, OK; (1); Church Yth Grp; FCA; Natl FFA Org; School Play; Hon Roll; NW OK Jr Rodeo; NW OK Barrel Racers Assn; US Barrel Racer Cmptns.

MITCHELL, TERRANCE A; Claremore Sr HS; Claremore, OK; (1); Church Yth Grp; French Clb; Church Choir; JV Bsktbl; Var Crs Cntry; Var Trk; Hon Roll; U Of AR; Cmptr Sci.

MITCHELL, TESSA; Ponca City Sr HS; Ponca City, OK; (2); 128/435; Art Clb; French Clb; Nwsp; Cit Awd; Hon Roll; Prfct Atten Awd; Pres Acad Fit Awd; Dance & Art Drawing 1st & 3rd Pls; Heifer Project Intnl; Inter Schltc Schlsp Cmptn; NOC; Meteorology; Commrcl Artst.

MITCHUSSON, TONI R; Alex Jr Sr HS; Bradley, OK; (3); 3/36; Pres Hist FHA; Rep Natl FFA Org; Treas Jr Cls; Hon Roll; NHS; Acad Tm; SW OK St Univ.

MITHCELL, DARCY A; Dewey HS; Dewey, OK; (4); 14/86; Drama Clb; FHA; Red Cross Aide; Teachers Aide; Chorus; School Musical; School Play; Rep Stu Cncl; Var Chrldng; Hon Roll; Elk Teen Of Month 96; Vocal Medals 7 Dist, 5 St; Northeastern ST U; Elem Ed.

MITTELSTET, MATT K; Stillwater Sr HS; Stillwater, OK; (3); Boy Scts; Church Yth Grp; Mu Alpha Theta; Office Aide; Church Choir; JV Var Bsbl; Hon Roll; BSA Eagle Scout.

MIX, MICHAEL; Owasso Sr HS; Owasso, OK; (3); Hon Roll; Prfct Atten Awd; Boy Scts; Church Yth Grp; Debate Tm; French Clb; Teachers Aide; Dead Gnrls Scty Hstry Pres; US Mltry Academy.

MIXON, AMBER; Mustang HS; Mustang, OK; (3); 1/386; Church Yth Grp; FCA; HOBY; Rep Jr Cls; Var Crs Cntry; Var Trk; Hon Roll; NHS; Church Choir; Rep Frsh Cls; Vrsty Choir; Natl Hist Govt Awd.

MIZE, JOSH G; Liberty HS; Mounds, OK; (2); German Clb; Var Ftbl; Var Wt Lftg; Acad Team Var; Physics; Comp Sci.

MIZE, LAUREN E; Bishop Mcguinness HS; Oklahoma City, OK; (3); 2/140; Church Yth Grp; Math Tm; Science Clb; Band; Church Choir; Orch; French Hon Soc; NHS; Jr Rtrn; AHSME; AIME; OK Msc Edctrs Assn All-St Orch.

MIZER, AMBERLEY D; Sapulpa Sr HS; Sapulpa, OK; (2); 136/291; Church Yth Grp; Cmnty Wkr; Band; Chorus; Jazz Band; Mrchg Band; Hon Roll; Prfct Atten Awd; Spanish Clb; Church Choir; Karate-Goju; OBA All Star Jazz Band Lead Baritone Sax; Music; Physiology; Orch Dir.

MIZER, LYSLIE; Claremore Sr HS; Claremore, OK; (3); Cmnty Wkr; Drama Clb; French Clb; Hosp Aide; Office Aide; Yrbk; Trk; Hon Roll; NHS; OSU; Med.

MIZER, MICHELLE; South Coffeyville Schl; S Coffeyville, OK; (4); 1/22; Math Tm; Office Aide; Quiz Bowl; Spanish Clb; VICA; Rptr Nwsp; Rptr Soph Cls; Hon Roll; NHS; Val; Attnd Tri Cty Tech 11/12 Grds; 3rd Local/2nd Dist/1st ST Hairstyling Cntsts; Btcn.

MKALECH, ELIZABETH; Central HS; Tulsa, OK; (2); Computer Clb; Office Aide; Teachers Aide; High Hon Roll; Hon Roll; NHS; Freedom Fnd; Bethany; Acctng.

MLYNEK, MICHAEL; Prague HS; Prague, OK; (3); Boy Scts; Church Yth Grp; HOBY; Key Clb; Natl FFA Org; Quiz Bowl; Scholastic Bowl; Science Clb; Hon Roll; NHS; Marine Sci Awds; Schlstc Meet Awds; Quz Bwl Cptn; Advncd Scuba Dvng; TX A&M; Marine Bio.

MOBERLY, JEREMY B; Mustang HS; Yukon, OK; (3); Church Yth Grp; FCA; Teachers Aide; JV Bsktbl; Hon Roll.

MOBERLY, LAUREN; Greater Tulsa Christian Acad; Tulsa, OK; (4); 2/7; Church Yth Grp; Key Clb; School Play; Nwsp; Var L Bsktbl; Golf; Var Capt Vllybl; NHS; Sal; Cmnty Wkr; Piano; Ath Awd; Skate Boarders Of Amer; Pensacola Chrstn; Graphic Art.

MOCK, EMILY C; Memorial HS; Tulsa, OK; (2); FCA; Hosp Aide; JCL; Key Clb; Rep Latin Clb; Chorus; Swing Chorus; Co-Ed Nwsp; High Hon Roll; Hon Roll; Advanced Ballet; Clothing Industry.

MOCK, MARY KATE; Bartlesville Mid HS; Nowata, OK; (3); Cmnty Wkr; Debate Tm; Pres NFL; Speech Tm; Band; Mrchg Band; High Hon Roll; Hon Roll; Jr NHS; NHS; Tulsa Yth Symphny All Dist/Hd Jdg WA Cty Yth Ct; Eng Awd; AP Bio II/ENG; Tmbn Brtsvl Symph Mscl; Spch Pthlgy.

MODDELMOG, BRIAN; Seminole Jr Sr HS; Seminole, OK; (2); 1/105; Church Yth Grp; FCA; French Clb; Math Clb; Mu Alpha Theta; Pres Frsh Cls; Var Bsktbl; Var Ftbl; Var Golf; Cit Awd; Med.

MODEN, DARIN; Tahlequah Sr HS; Tahlequah, OK; (4); 20/300; Am Leg Boys St; Boy Scts; Church Yth Grp; Cmnty Wkr; German Clb; Math Clb; Scholastic Bowl; Teachers Aide; Chorus; Tennis; Eagle Scout; Intl Mrktng.

MOELLER, ERICA D; Oologah HS; Claremore, OK; (2); Bsktbl; Var Socr; Hon Roll; NHS; Premiere Soccer Tulsa Sheffield United; U Of OK.

MOELLER, ERIN N; Union Intermediate HS; Tulsa, OK; (1); Chorus; Jazz Band; Orch; School Musical; High Hon Roll; Jr NHS; NHS; ARC Gftd & Tlntd Pgm; Dancing; Music Ed.

MOELLER, MICHELLE M; Union Sr HS; Tulsa, OK; (4); 190/669; Speech Tm; Teachers Aide; Thesps; Acpl Chr; Chorus; School Musical; School Play; Variety Show; On Stage Yth Theater; Dance Cls; U Of Cntrl OK; Dance.

MOFFETT, TARA M; East Central HS; Tulsa, OK; (3); 20/219; Am Leg Aux Girls St; Church Yth Grp; FCA; Pres Key Clb; Spanish Clb; Ofcr Stu Cncl; Bsktbl; Sftbl; Trk; Hon Roll; Drug Free Yth; Chrstns In HS; Elem Ed.

MOHLING, AMANDA C; Putnam City West HS; Bethany, OK; (2); 2/325; Church Yth Grp; Drama Clb; FCA; Thesps; Church Choir; School Musical; School Play; Stat Crs Cntry; JV Socr; NHS; Outstndng Hnrs Chem I, Spnsh I Stu; U KS Chem Rsrch Achvt; Biochem.

MOHR, AUDREY; Luther HS; Luther, OK; (4); Natl FFA Org; Spanish Clb; Band.

MOL, TARA; Hydro Jr Sr HS; Hydro, OK; (4); 1/22; VP Pres FHA; Pres Frsh Cls; Pres Sr Cls; High Hon Roll; Jr NHS; Hist NHS; Val; Church Yth Grp; Cmnty Wkr; Drama Clb; 1st Pl Reg & 3rd Pl Dist Voice Of Dmcrcy; 1st Pl St Fnlst & Wrld Fnlst & Rep OM; Msnc Stu Of Tmrrw; SW OK ST U; Phy Ther.

MOLD, JEFFREY; Edmond Memorial HS; Edmond, OK; (3); Church Yth Grp; Cmnty Wkr; FCA; JCL; Key Clb; Latin Clb; Math Clb; Science Clb; Spanish Clb; Band; All Amer Schol; Comp Sci.

MOLES, JEFFREY; Mustang HS; Yukon, OK; (4); 1/350; FCA; Quiz Bowl; Scholastic Bowl; VP Frsh Cls; VP Soph Cls; Treas Jr Cls; VP Stu Cncl; Var Capt Bsktbl; NHS; Val; I Dare You Awd; Bsch Lmb Sci Awd.

MOLET, NATALIE R; Okmulgee HS; Okmulgee, OK; (4); #19 in class; Church Yth Grp; FCA; Spanish Clb; Rep Frsh Cls; JV Var Mgr(s); JV Sftbl; JV Var Tennis; Hon Roll; HOSA Sec; Tulsa JC.

MOLINAS, AMAR; Norman Sr HS; Norman, OK; (3); JCL; Latin Clb; Hon Roll; Quartz Mtn Arts Inst Alum Assoc; Fine Arts.

MOLLET, MAURA C; Yukon Middle HS; Bethany, OK; (3); 7/411; VP Stu Cncl; Var Bsktbl; Var Socr; Var Sftbl; NHS; Pres Acad Fit Awd; Stu Of Today; Amer Legion; 3-D; U Of MS; Pre-Med.

MOLLEUR, FAITH; Seminole Jr Sr HS; Seminole, OK; (2); FCA; French Clb; Math Clb; Yrbk; VP Soph Cls; Var L Bsktbl; Var L Sftbl; High Hon Roll; Sftbl All-Dist Fstptch 95.

MOLLOY, JAMES P; Midwest City HS; Oklahoma City, OK; (2); 142/473; Drama Clb; FCA; Spanish Clb; School Play; Var Bsbl; Var Bsktbl; Var Ftbl; Cit Awd; Hon Roll; Jr NHS; Medicine; Aerospace; Astronautic.

MOLTSAU, MICAYLA; Central Schl; Marlow, OK; (2); Church Yth Grp; FCA; Rptr Nwsp; Yrbk; Rptr Frsh Cls; Rptr Soph Cls; Var Chrldng; Var Sftbl; Hon Roll; NHS; Just Say No; Soph Yr Ftbl Homecoming; All Sports Queen/Most Attractive Frosh Yr; OK Univ; Cnslr/Missions.

MOMAN, CHRISTOPHER B; Midwest City HS; Midwest City, OK; (3); 136/473; Church Yth Grp; FCA; German Clb; Teachers Aide; School Play; JV Bsbl; JV Ftbl; Wt Lftg; Hon Roll; Jr NHS; 4 Point-O Clb; Engr.

MONACHELLA, ANDREA; Moore HS; Moore, OK; (3); French Clb; Mgr(s); JV Trk; Jr NHS; Sports Trnr.

MONAHAH, MEAGAN; Moore HS; Moore, OK; (4); Sec Pres Debate Tm; Rptr Drama Clb; JCL; Latin Clb; Model UN; NFL; Sec Pres Speech Tm; Chorus; School Musical; School Play; Supr Dstnctn Natl Frnsc League; Regl One-Act Cmptn; U Of IA; Actng.

MONDLOCH, ERIC M; Webster HS; Tulsa, OK; (4); 33/135; Key Clb; Science Clb; Band; Drm Mjr(t); Jazz Band; Mrchg Band; Pep Band; School Play; Crs Cntry; Trk; U Of Tulsa; Premed.

MONGOLD, WESLEY G; Cimarron Public Schl; Enid, OK; (1); Church Yth Grp; Math Tm; Natl FFA Org; Quiz Bowl; Scholastic Bowl; Science Clb; Band; Mrchg Band; Pep Band; Hon Roll; Roller Hockey; Law Enforcement.

MONHOLLAND, AIMEE B; Sallisaw HS; Sallisaw, OK; (4); Art Clb; Debate Tm; Drama Clb; Math Clb; Science Clb; Spanish Clb; Speech Tm; Thesps; School Musical; School Play; Cherokee Nation Awd For Excl 92 & 96; Natl Macy Schlr; Northeastern ST Univ; Psych.

MONICAL, AMY; Carl Albert HS; Midwest City, OK; (3); 23/219; FCA; JCL; Key Clb; Var Bsktbl; Var Crs Cntry; Var Sftbl; JV Trk; DAR Awd; Hon Roll; NHS; St Champs Bsktbll; St Champs All Acad Bsktbll; Eng.

MONIGOLD, MEGAN; Macarthur Sr HS; Lawton, OK; (4); 11/267; Church Yth Grp; Cmnty Wkr; FCA; French Clb; Pep Clb; Varsity Clb; Pres Frsh Cls; Var Capt Bsktbl; Chrldng; Score Keeper; Cameron Univ; Speech Pathology.

MONK, J J; Valliant HS; Garvin, OK; (1); 3/89; 4-H; Varsity Clb; Hon Roll; FFA.

MONK, LYDIA; Hooker Jr-Sr HS; Hooker, OK; (4); 16/36; Church Yth Grp; Cmnty Wkr; FHA; Teachers Aide; Chorus; Church Choir; School Musical; School Play; Chrldng; Golf; Northern OK Coll; Crimnl Justc.

MONK, TRINA; Valliant HS; Garvin, OK; (3); 1/82; Quiz Bowl; School Play; Sec Jr Cls; Rep Stu Cncl; Bsktbl; Sftbl; High Hon Roll; NHS; SOSU; Bio-Med Engrng.

MONKS, AMBER D; Quinton Jr Sr HS; Quinton, OK; (3); Church Yth Grp; FCA; FHA; Band; Color Guard; Flag Corp; Mrchg Band; Hon Roll; Law.

MONN, RACHEL D; Union Intermediate HS; Tulsa, OK; (2); 149/800; Church Yth Grp; Girl Scts; Spanish Clb; Church Choir; Mrchg Band; High Hon Roll; Jr NHS; NHS; Girl Scts Silvr Awd; HS All-Dist Band; Church Orch & Ensmbles; Jrnlsm.

MONN, SARAH L; Union Sr HS; Tulsa, OK; (4); 54/632; Church Yth Grp; FBLA; Girl Scts; Key Clb; Spanish Clb; Rep Sr Cls; Hon Roll; NHS; Pres Acad Fit Awd; Yng Dems; OK ST U; Acctng.

MONROE, DENNIS; Hobart HS; Lone Wolf, OK; (3); Church Yth Grp; FCA; HOBY; VP Natl FFA Org; School Play; Pres Frsh Cls; VP Soph Cls; VP Jr Cls; Var Bsbl; Cit Awd; Publc Speakng; Parlmntry Procdre; Livestck Judgng; OK ST U; Ag Engrng.

MONROE, EMILY; Hale HS; Tulsa, OK; (3); 37/400; Church Yth Grp; Drama Clb; FBLA; Key Clb; Teachers Aide; Thesps; VP Jr Cls; JV Chrldng; Var Capt Pom Pon; High Hon Roll; Drama Club VP; OK ST Univ; Theatre.

MONROE, ROBERT J; Frontier Public Schl; Ponca City, OK; (2); Natl FFA Org; Quiz Bowl; Chorus; Pres Frsh Cls; Treas Soph Cls; High Hon Roll; NHS; Prfct Atten Awd; Pres Acad Fit Awd; Outstnd Stdnt Awrd; Med.

MONTALVO, LAURA; Capitol Hill HS; Fort Worth, TX; (4); Drama Clb; Office Aide; ROTC; Color Guard; Flag Corp; Stage Crew; Ofcr Stu Cncl; Hon Roll; Jr NHS; Prfct Atten Awd; UT A Arlngtn TX; Tchr.

MONTALVO, MONICA C; Cherokee Jr Sr HS; Cherokee, OK; (3); Church Yth Grp; Debate Tm; Drama Clb; FCA; FHA; NFL; Office Aide; Spanish Clb; Speech Tm; Church Choir.

MONTGOMERY, ADAM I; Atoka HS; Atoka, OK; (4); Computer Clb; FBLA; Quiz Bowl; Spanish Clb; Sec VICA; Bsktbl; Wt Lftg; Hon Roll; NHS; Southeastern OK St Univ.

MONTGOMERY, ALISHA B; Boise City HS; Boise City, OK; (1); Treas Frsh Cls; Var L Bsktbl; OSU.

MONTGOMERY, ANDREA G; Union Intermediate HS; Broken Arrow, OK; (1); Church Yth Grp; Dance Clb; Drama Clb; Girl Scts; Spanish Clb; Band; Stage Crew; Bsktbl; Trk; High Hon Roll; Summer Trck; Harvard Univ; Marine Bio.

MONTGOMERY, BENJAMIN; Westmoore HS; Oklahoma City, OK; (4); 121/635; Church Yth Grp; FCA; School Musical; Variety Show; Ofcr Stu Cncl; Var Bsktbl; Var Ftbl; Var Socr; High Hon Roll; NHS; AR Tech U.

MONTGOMERY, CRYSTAL; Claremore Sr HS; Claremore, OK; (4); 1/280; Am Leg Aux Girls St; English Clb; FCA; FBLA; FHA; GAA; Hosp Aide; Math Clb; Science Clb; Spanish Clb; NHS Sec; Coca Cola Schlrshp Smfnlst; Miss Claremore Schlrshp Pgnt, J B Medcl Schlrshp/Mst Btfl Smile; OSU; Psych.

MONTGOMERY, DAWNITA M; Hobart HS; Hobart, OK; (2); Church Yth Grp; FCA; FHA; FTA; Flag Corp; Jazz Band; Mrchg Band; Stage Crew; Score Keeper; Sftbl; OK Univ; Music Ed.

MONTGOMERY, DE ANA D; Antlers Sr HS; Antlers, OK; (2); Cmnty Wkr; FHA; Girl Scts; Natl FFA Org; East TX ST; Crmnl Psych.

MONTGOMERY, JASON E; Putnam City HS; Oklahoma City, OK; (3); 25/400; Church Yth Grp; Cmnty Wkr; Band; Jazz Band; Mrchg Band; Orch; School Musical; NHS; Band All ST; U Of OK; Engr.

MONTGOMERY, LESLIE A; Wagoner Sr HS; Wagoner, OK; (3); Church Yth Grp; FHA; Library Aide; Natl FFA Org; Scholastic Bowl; Rep Stu Cncl; Hon Roll; FFA Prepared Pub Spkng Wnnr; Odd Fellow UN Pilgrimage.

MONTGOMERY, MINDY; Comanche HS; Comanche, OK; (1); Church Yth Grp; FHA; Bsktbl; High Hon Roll; TSA; Church Bible Quiz Tm.

MONTGOMERY, TREVOR L; Boise City HS; Boise City, OK; (3); Art Clb; Computer Clb; German Clb; Letterman Clb; Varsity Clb; Treas Stu Cncl; Var L Bsbl; Var L Bsktbl; Var L Ftbl; Hon Roll; OK ST Univ; Fin.

MOODY, BLAKE; Mc Loud HS; Mc Loud, OK; (3); 1/152; Church Yth Grp; FCA; Scholastic Bowl; Jazz Band; Sec Jr Cls; Ofcr Stu Cncl; Bsktbl; High Hon Roll; NHS; Church Yth Tlnt Cmptn Dist Gold Level Guitar 93-94 & 94-95; Ambassador U.

MOODY, COURTNEY; Durant HS; Durant, OK; (4); FCA; GAA; Letterman Clb; Office Aide; SADD; Varsity Clb; VICA; Var L Powder Puff Ftbl; Var L Sftbl; Hon Roll; Southeastern ST U; Elem Ed.

MOODY, JENNIFER A; Bixby Sr HS; Bixby, OK; (1); Church Yth Grp; German Clb; High Hon Roll; Jr NHS; Pres Awd Acad Excl.

MOODY, JUSTIN S; Quinton Jr Sr HS; Quinton, OK; (3); Church Yth Grp; FCA; Library Aide; Teachers Aide; Band; Church Choir; Var Bsbl; Var Co-Capt Bsktbl; Var Ftbl; Var Trk; OK ST Univ; Mech Engr.

MOODY, KRISTEN; Pryor Sr HS; Pryor, OK; (4); 14/148; Church Yth Grp; Rep FBLA; Mu Alpha Theta; Spanish Clb; Chorus; School Musical; Socr; NHS; St Hnr Soc; Top 10%; OK ST U; Elem Ed.

MOODY, KYLE G; Hartshorne Sr HS; Hartshorne, OK; (3); Church Yth Grp; FCA; Quiz Bowl; Ofcr Bsbl; Bsktbl; Ftbl; Hon Roll; Auto-Diesel.

MOOMAW, SARA; Stillwater Sr HS; Stillwater, OK; (4); 1/340; Church Yth Grp; Debate Tm; Drama Clb; German Clb; Mu Alpha Theta; Natl Beta Clb; NFL; Speech Tm; NHS; Ntl Merit Ltr; OK Acad All St Nom; Competitive Mock Trial Team Nom; U Of Richmond.

MOON, DANIELLE M; Owasso Sr HS; Collinsville, OK; (4); FCA; Chorus; Yrbk; Rep Jr Cls; Rep Sr Cls; Pres Stu Cncl; Chrldng; Crs Cntry; Tennis; NHS; Stu Of Yr; Stu Of Today; Church; Oklahoma City U; Publc Rltns.

MOON, KRISTIN; Blackwell HS; Blackwell, OK; (3); Pep Clb; Chorus; Swing Chorus; Hon Roll; OSU; Elem Ed.

MOONEY, ALEISHA ANNE; Grove HS; Grove, OK; (4); 36/104; Drama Clb; Rep FBLA; Rep FHA; Sec Natl FFA Org; Sec NFL; Speech Tm; Chorus; School Play; Capt Golf; Hon Roll; IDFY; ST FFA Deg 3rd Dist Star Frmr; Grv HS Anthlgy Crtv Wrtng Clss/Adv Layout; NEO Jr Coll; Ag Comm.

MOONEY, ANDRA; Welch Jr Sr HS; Welch, OK; (3); Sec FBLA; Sec Treas FHA; Pres Jr Cls; Rep VP Stu Cncl; Var Bsktbl; Var Sftbl; Var Trk; High Hon Roll; NHS; Prfct Atten Awd; Sftbl All Conf 2nd Tm; Trck 4x800 Rly St Mt 7th Pl; OK Hnr Soc; NEO; Occptnl Thrpy.

MOONEY, CHRISTOPHER S; Capitol Hill HS; Oklahoma City, OK; (3); Boy Scts; Band; Mrchg Band; Pep Band; VP Soph Cls; NHS.

MOONEY, JESSICA A; Owasso Sr HS; Owasso, OK; (4); 73/296; Art Clb; Pres Drama Clb; Spanish Clb; School Musical; School Play; Stage Crew; Hon Roll; Spcl Distinction In Natl Forensic League Degree; Northeastern ST Univ; Theatre.

MOONEY, KRISTEN N; Duncan HS; Duncan, OK; (1); Church Yth Grp; Key Clb; Chorus; School Musical; Variety Show; JV Chrldng; Trk; Hon Roll; Prfct Atten Awd.

MOONEY, SHAUNA C; Stillwater Sr HS; Stillwater, OK; (3); 63/346; Church Yth Grp; Drama Clb; FCA; VP Natl Beta Clb; Spanish Clb; Chorus; Rep Stu Cncl; Var Crs Cntry; Var Trk; NHS.

MOONEYHAM, SAMMY L; Lexington HS; Lexington, OK; (3); 15/68; Church Yth Grp; VP FCA; Pres JA; Natl FFA Org; Ed Yrbk; Var Crs Cntry; Var Wrstlng; High Hon Roll; Hon Roll; Prfct Atten Awd; Pharm.

MOORE, AMANDA B; Brink Jr HS; Moore, OK; (1); Computer Clb; Var Swmmng; Hon Roll; Jr NHS; Sooner ST Game 100m Btrfly Bronze Medal; Frosh Stdnt Of Month; Bobcats Basics Club Plng/Orgzn Ofcr; Med.

MOORE, AMANDA M; Midwest City HS; Midwest City, OK; (2); 67/501; Church Yth Grp; FCA; Spanish Clb; Band; Mrchg Band; Orch; Pep Band; Jr NHS; Prfct Atten Awd; CONS; OBU; Elem Schl Tchr.

MOORE, ANDREA M; Hugo HS; Hugo, OK; (3); Spanish Clb; Color Guard; Flag Corp; E TX State Univ.

MOORE, ANGELA N; Midwest City HS; Midwest City, OK; (2); 246/474; Church Yth Grp; Drama Clb; FCA; VP German Clb; Pep Clb; Science Clb; Church Choir; School Musical; Stage Crew; High Hon Roll; AZ; Jrnlsm/Marine Bio.

MOORE, APRIL D; Pocola HS; Pocola, OK; (2); #8 in class; FBLA; FHA; Band; Drm Mjr(t); Mrchg Band; Pep Band; High Hon Roll; Hon Roll; NHS; OK Hon Soc.

MOORE, ASHLEE M; South Intermediate HS; Broken Arrow, OK; (1); Church Choir; Drill Tm; Ed Yrbk; Mgr(s); Trk; Hon Roll; Spelman Univ; Med/Pediatrician.

MOORE II, BENNY A; Velma Alma HS; Ratliff City, OK; (3); Church Yth Grp; FCA; FHA; Band; Jazz Band; Mrchg Band; Nwsp; Ofcr Bsbl; Wt Lftg; Prfct Atten Awd; Multi-Yr Listee; OK Univ; Law/Music.

MOORE, BRANDI R; Enid Sr HS; Enid, OK; (2); 44/472; Church Yth Grp; FCA; Spanish Clb; Ofcr Frsh Cls; JV Var Bsktbl; Mgr(s); JV Var Sftbl; Hon Roll; Jr NHS; NHS; OK Bapt U; Chld Psch/Tch/Coach.

MOORE, BRANDI R; Charles Page HS; Sand Springs, OK; (2); French Clb; Prfct Atten Awd; Ice Hockey.

MOORE, BRENT; Mustang HS; Mustang, OK; (4); 107/343; FBLA; JA; Teachers Aide; Ofcr Bsbl; Trk; Cit Awd; Hon Roll; Northwestern OK ST Univ; Vet.

MOORE, BROCK S; Purcell HS; Purcell, OK; (3); 16/68; Church Yth Grp; Cmnty Wkr; Chorus; Color Guard; Jazz Band; Ntl Merit Ltr.

MOORE, BROOKE; Carnegie HS; Carnegie, OK; (2); FCA; Pep Clb; Teachers Aide; Chorus; School Play; VP Frsh Cls; Bsktbl; Chrldng; Score Keeper; Trk; Math Awd; OK Univ; Optmtrst.

MOORE, CARRIE; East Central HS; Tulsa, OK; (3); French Clb; Var Chrldng; Hon Roll; Northeastern ST Univ; Pre-Med.

MOORE, CASEY; Blackwell HS; Blackwell, OK; (4); 1/120; Am Leg Boys St; Church Yth Grp; FCA; Letterman Clb; Quiz Bowl; Scholastic Bowl; Spanish Clb; Chorus; Church Choir; High Hon Roll.

MOORE, CHARLES E; Tecumseh HS; Tecumseh, OK; (2); Art Clb; Church Yth Grp; Nwsp; Ofcr Stu Cncl; Hon Roll; Congress-Bundestag Schlsp; Intnl Trade.

MOORE, CHERI; Southeast HS; Oklahoma City, OK; (4); 5/64; Church Yth Grp; Dance Clb; FCA; SADD; Teachers Aide; Chorus; School Musical; JV Pom Pon; L Sftbl; Hon Roll; Coll Clb; DFYIT; OK City CC; Psych.

MOORE, CHRISTOPHER S; Comanche HS; Comanche, OK; (3); 10/61; Am Leg Boys St; Art Clb; Debate Tm; Drama Clb; German Clb; NFL; Speech Tm; Teachers Aide; Stage Crew; Hon Roll; Natl Sci Mrt Awd; Comp Applctns Outstndng Stu; Hnr Schlr Acad Achvt Awd OSU; 1st-3rd Interschlstc Cont; Law.

MOORE, CORY; Deer Creek-Lamont Jr Sr HS; Deer Creek, OK; (3); FCA; Natl FFA Org; NHS; Treas Jr Cls; Var Bsbl; Var Bsktbl; Var Ftbl; Var Wt Lftg; Local FFA Reporter; OSU; Vet.

MOORE, CRYSTAL; Bartlesville Sr HS; Bartlesville, OK; (3); Church Yth Grp; Church Choir; Hon Roll; Rollerhcky Team; Mission Trips; Missions.

MOORE, DANIEL; Panama HS; Panama, OK; (3); German Clb; Natl FFA Org; Rep Frsh Cls; Bsktbl; Hon Roll; NHS.

MOORE, DAVINA OLETA M; Porter Jr Sr HS; Tullahassee, OK; (2); Church Yth Grp; FCA; SADD; Church Choir; Bsktbl; Sftbl; Hon Roll; NHS; Comp Tech.

MOORE, DEANDRE; Millwood HS; Oklahoma City, OK; (3); 2/80; Scholastic Bowl; Varsity Clb.

MOORE, DONNA; Ringling HS; Ringling, OK; (4); 5/55; Church Yth Grp; Drama Clb; 4-H; FHA; HOBY; Quiz Bowl; School Play; Nwsp; Ed Yrbk; 4-H Awd; I Dare You; OK ST U; Art Ed.

MOORE, ELIZABETH F; Lindsay HS; Lindsay, OK; (4); 12/56; Art Clb; Church Yth Grp; FHA; Natl FFA Org; Office Aide; Hon Roll; NHS; Pres Acad Fit Awd; Upward Bound; Acad Team; Chem; His.

MOORE, HOLLY L; Yale Jr Sr HS; Yale, OK; (3); FHA; Natl Beta Clb; Office Aide; Pres Frsh Cls; Pres Soph Cls; Pres Jr Cls; Pres Sr Cls; Pres Stu Cncl; JV Bsktbl; Var Sftbl; Tulsa JC; CPA.

MOORE, JACOB; Hobart HS; Hobart, OK; (4); 2/66; Am Leg Boys St; Boy Scts; Church Yth Grp; FTA; VP Jr Cls; Rep Stu Cncl; Var Bsbl; Var Ftbl; High Hon Roll; NHS; Rotary Stu Mon; Phillips U.

MOORE, JAMIE; Del City HS; Oklahoma City, OK; (4); #1 in class; Church Yth Grp; Cmnty Wkr; FCA; Rep French Clb; Pres Frsh Cls; Rep Stu Cncl; Chrldng; Var Tennis; Val; Hon Roll; Env Club Treas; Yth For Chrst; Acad Lttrmns Jckt; OK ST; Chem Engrng.

MOORE, JAMIE; Bristow HS; Bristow, OK; (4); Teachers Aide; Pep Band; Nwsp; Yrbk; JV Bsktbl; Var Sftbl; Trk; Hon Roll; Attnd Cadet Lawman Spon By Elks & Hwy Patrol; MVP Oologah Sftbl Trnmt; Alt For All St Team; Northeaster ST U; Study Law.

MOORE, JAMIE D; Westmoore HS; Oklahoma City, OK; (2); Church Yth Grp; Drama Clb; Chorus; School Musical; Jr NHS; NHS; Trvlng On A Dist Chldrns Mnstry Tm; SW Asmblys Of God U; Chldrns M.

MOORE, JAY; Chandler HS; Chandler, OK; (3); 2/80; Am Leg Boys St; Church Yth Grp; FCA; Scholastic Bowl; Treas Spanish Clb; Rep Stu Cncl; Var Bsbl; Cit Awd; High Hon Roll; VP NHS; Acad St Champs In Bsbl 94 & 95; Attnd Mjr U; Optometry.

MOORE, JENNIFER M; Chisholm Sr HS; Enid, OK; (2); Girl Scts; Chorus; Orch; Hon Roll; NHS; Girl Scout Silver Awd; I Dist Music Omp; Tri ST Hnr Choir; Northeastern ST Univ; Cnslr.

MOORE, JEREMY D; Calumet Schl; Calumet, OK; (2); 1/30; Church Yth Grp; Spanish Clb; Pres Frsh Cls; Pres Soph Cls; Var Bsbl; Var Bsktbl; High Hon Roll.

MOORE JR, JIMMY L; John Marshall HS; Oklahoma City, OK; (3); 21/186; Am Leg Boys St; Church Yth Grp; German Clb; Quiz Bowl; Scholastic Bowl; Acpl Chr; Rptr Yrbk; Hon Roll; NHS; Acctg.

MOORE, JODY L; Warner HS; Muskogee, OK; (1); Church Yth Grp; FCA; Natl FFA Org; JV Var Bsktbl; JV Ftbl; Var Trk; Track Rookie Of Yr.

MOORE, JOSHUA C; Mustang HS; Oklahoma City, OK; (1); Ftbl; Wrstlng; High Hon Roll; Hon Roll; CO Univ.

MOORE, JULIE; Choctaw HS; Choctaw, OK; (3); Church Yth Grp; Cmnty Wkr; Hosp Aide; HOBY; Key Clb; Office Aide; Spanish Clb; Yrbk; Ofcr Stu Cncl; Var Chrldng; Med.

MOORE, JUSTIN C; Edmond Memorial HS; Edmond, OK; (4); 76/337; Drama Clb; German Clb; Chorus; Church Choir; Jazz Band; School Play; Stage Crew; Swing Chorus; Variety Show; Hon Roll; 2nd Pl St Drama Cmptn; OK Shakespeare Pk Yng Co; Medieval Clb; U Cntrl OK; Theatre.

MOORE, KARA; Timberlake Schl; Nash, OK; (2); 1/24; Church Yth Grp; FCA; FHA; Hosp Aide; Quiz Bowl; Church Choir; Rptr Soph Cls; Bsktbl; Ftbl; Gov Hon Prg Awd; Natl Engl Mrt Awd; All Amer Schlr; Accptd Oral Roberts U Smmr Math Acad.

MOORE, KEITH; Thomas Jr Sr HS; Thomas, OK; (2); Church Yth Grp; FBLA; Phtg Yrbk; Ofcr Frsh Cls; Comp; ORU.

MOORE, KELLY M; Canton HS; Canton, OK; (2); #4 in class; FCA; FHA; SADD; Band; Flag Corp; Treas Stu Cncl; Bsktbl; Crs Cntry; Trk; High Hon Roll; OK Univ.

MOORE, KENDRA L; Wynnewood HS; Wynnewood, OK; (1); Church Yth Grp; Cmnty Wkr; Drama Clb; Chorus; Church Choir; Swing Chorus; Piano; Wrtng; East Cntrl U; Legal Secy.

MOORE, KERI D; Strother Jr Sr HS; Earlsboro, OK; (4); 2/27; Office Aide; Phtg Rptr Nwsp; Phtg Yrbk; Pres Frsh Cls; Pres Soph Cls; Rep Jr Cls; Rep Sr Cls; Rep Stu Cncl; Stat Bsbl; Var Bsktbl; Page OK St Senate; Sprts Med.

MOORE, KERRY L; Yukon HS; Yukon, OK; (3); 61/385; VP Pres Band; Jazz Band; Mrchg Band; Ofcr Stu Cncl; NHS; All Star Marching Band; Natl Young Ldrs Conf DC; OK Univ.

MOORE, KEVIN; Woodward HS; Woodward, OK; (1); Church Yth Grp; JV Ftbl; Wt Lftg; Hon Roll; OK ST Univ; Chem Engr/Lawyer.

MOORE, KEVIN M; Mt St Marys HS; Oklahoma City, OK; (3); Key Clb; Regnl Sci Fair 1st Pl; St Sci Fair Cmptn.

MOORE, KYLE; Hobart HS; Hobart, OK; (1); Boy Scts; Church Yth Grp; Band; High Hon Roll.

MOORE, LA'KEYSHA; Idabel HS; Idabel, OK; (1); Church Yth Grp; Cmnty Wkr; FCA; Speech Tm; Church Choir; Ofcr Soph Cls; Bsktbl; Sftbl; Trk; Hon Roll; Duke Univ; Brdcstr/Rprtr.

MOORE, LACEY E; Claremore Sr HS; Chelsea, OK; (1); Yrbk; Hon Roll; Tap; Ballet; Jazz; OK Univ; Lwyr.

MOORE, LANA; Washington HS; Washington, OK; (4); Church Yth Grp; FCA; 4-H; FBLA; Pres Hist FHA; Pep Clb; Teachers Aide; Church Choir; Stage Crew; Phtg Yrbk; 2 Poems Pblshd Natl Lib Poetry.

MOORE, LARRY; Central HS; Tulsa, OK; (2); Art Clb; Boy Scts; Church Yth Grp; Cmnty Wkr; Office Aide; Trk; Hon Roll; St OK Cit Congratltns Art Awd Frm Sntr C R Ford; OK Spec Olympcs Awds; Tulsa Voc Trng; Truck Drvr.

MOORE, LATOYA N; Mc Lain Career Acad; Tulsa, OK; (2); Church Yth Grp; Church Choir; Hon Roll; NHS; Pedtrcn.

MOORE, LAURIE A; Panama HS; Panama, OK; (4); FHA; Quiz Bowl; Nwsp; Yrbk; CASC; Bus Adm.

MOORE, LINDSAY R; Bethany HS; Bethany, OK; (3); 6/85; Church Yth Grp; FCA; Letterman Clb; Library Aide; Office Aide; Teachers Aide; Chorus; Church Choir; School Musical; School Play; Yth Alive VP; Show Choir Secy; Yth Grp Yth Cncl; 12 Yrs Piano/10 Yrs NPG & Guild Super Rtngs; Big Five; Southern Nazarene U; Law.

MOORE, LUCAS W; Geronimo Jr Sr HS; Geronimo, OK; (4); Church Yth Grp; Var Bsbl; High Hon Roll; Hon Roll; OSU.

MOORE, MANDY; Cyril Jr Sr HS; Cyril, OK; (3); Church Yth Grp; Drama Clb; HOBY; Quiz Bowl; Scholastic Bowl; Teachers Aide; School Play; Yrbk; Sec Treas Frsh Cls; Sec Treas Soph Cls; TSA; Ed.

MOORE, MARIAH; Braggs Schl; Braggs, OK; (3); 1/16; Church Yth Grp; Quiz Bowl; Rep Nwsp; Yrbk; Sec Jr Cls; Var Sftbl; High Hon Roll; Ltr B Acad Awd; Clss Awds, Bio I, Phys Sci, Gmtry, OK Hist, Typng, Drvrs Ed & Eng; Northeastern ST U; Educ.

MOORE, MATT; Canton HS; Canton, OK; (3); FCA; Letterman Clb; Scholastic Bowl; Spanish Clb; Teachers Aide; Band; Ofcr Soph Cls; Ofcr Jr Cls; Ofcr Stu Cncl; Ftbl; SWOSU.

MOORE, MEEGAN; Purcell HS; Purcell, OK; (2); 2/105; Church Yth Grp; Rep FCA; HOBY; Scholastic Bowl; Rep Spanish Clb; Chorus; Rep Stu Cncl; Var Chrldng; NHS; Smmr Cmnty Thtre; Mock Trl; U Of OK; Occ Thrpst.

MOORE, MELVIN; Mid-Del Christian Schl; Oklahoma City, OK; (3); Church Yth Grp; School Play; JV Var Bsktbl; JV Intrml Ftbl; Sftbl; Swmmng; JV Tennis; Cit Awd; Hon Roll; Georgetown; Engr.

MOORE, MEREDITH H; North Intemediate HS; Broken Arrow, OK; (1); French Clb; Co-Capt Chrldng; Hon Roll; VP Stu Cncl 96-97; Duke.

MOORE, MICHAEL S; Lindsay HS; Lindsay, OK; (4); 16/59; Art Clb; Boy Scts; FCA; Var Bsbl; Var Ftbl; JV Golf; Var Trk; Var Wt Lftg; Hon Roll; Church Yth Grp; Page For OK House Rep; Chrtr Memb OK Jr Cattlemns Assoc; Garvin Cty Hon Schlr Awd Acad Achvmnt; OK ST Univ; Bus.

MOORE, MIKE; Tulsa Nathan Hale HS; Tulsa, OK; (4); 74/204; Am Leg Boys St; Debate Tm; Drama Clb; Key Clb; ROTC; Speech Tm; Color Guard; School Play; Co-Ed Yrbk; Pres Jr Cls; Schl TV Show Edtr; ROTC Bttln Comm; Nrsng.

MOORE, REGINALD W; Northeast HS; Oklahoma City, OK; (3); Cmnty Wkr; ROTC; Color Guard; Drill Tm; Stage Crew; Ftbl; Trk; Wt Lftg; Wrstlng; Comp Engnr.

MOORE, RYAN M; Union Sr HS; Tulsa, OK; (3); 34/741; Chorus; Church Choir; Socr; High Hon Roll; NHS; Pres Acad Fit Awd; Tri-M; Sprts Med.

MOORE, SARAH; Carl Albert HS; Midwest City, OK; (2); Art Clb; Church Yth Grp; Cmnty Wkr; VP Pres Drama Clb; FCA; Key Clb; Pep Clb; Spanish Clb; SADD; Thesps.

MOORE, SARAH R; Muskogee HS; Muskogee, OK; (3); Church Yth Grp; Office Aide; Chorus; Church Choir; School Musical; Hon Roll; 5th Ave All-Girls Choir; Teen For Christ; RAID; OK Northeast ST U; Elem Tchr.

MOORE, SHELLY; Owasso Sr HS; Collinsville, OK; (3); 8/354; Am Leg Aux Girls St; Church Yth Grp; Drama Clb; FCA; Sec French Clb; Chorus; Church Choir; School Musical; School Play; Stage Crew; Teen Actn Grp; Yth Alive Bible Study; Piano; Bus/Engrng.

MOORE, SUMNER; Clinton HS; Clinton, OK; (1); FHA; Chorus; Church Choir; Swing Chorus; Rep Stu Cncl; Golf.

MOORE, TAMARA; Midwest City HS; Midwest City, OK; (2); 7/501; Art Clb; Ofcr Soph Cls; Cit Awd; Hon Roll; Prfct Atten Awd; Pres Acad Fit Awd; Art Inst Of Dallas; Comp Grphcs.

MOORE, TAMARAH; Mc Alester HS; Mcalester, OK; (2); Church Yth Grp; FCA; Pres Frsh Cls; Rep Stu Cncl; JV Var Bsktbl; Var Chrldng; Var Trk; Hon Roll.

MOORE, TAMMY KAY; Dale Sr HS; Shawnee, OK; (3); 22/53; Dance Clb; GAA; Natl FFA Org; Band; Mrchg Band; Nwsp; Bsktbl; Cit Awd; Hon Roll; U Of OK; Pre-Med.

MOORE, THELMA O; Mannford HS; Sand Springs, OK; (1); Church Yth Grp; Girl Scts; Chorus; Hon Roll; Grl Scts 10 Yr Pin; OK ST U; Psych.

MOORE, TONIA; Kiowa Jr-Sr HS; Kiowa, OK; (2); FHA; Choctaw Natn OK Upward Bnd Pgm; E Cntrl U.

MOORE, WILLIS NATHAN; Stillwater Sr HS; Stillwater, OK; (3); 50/300; Band; Mrchg Band; Pep Band; JV Golf; Prfct Atten Awd; OK ST Univ; Cmptr Elec Engr.

MOORE, ZACHARY; Midwest City HS; Midwest City, OK; (4); 8/419; Boy Scts; Quiz Bowl; Scholastic Bowl; SADD; Band; Mrchg Band; Gov Hon Prg Awd; High Hon Roll; Hon Roll; NHS; OK St U; Chem Engrng.

MORA, TALISHA I; Union Sr HS; Tulsa, OK; (4); 115/635; DECA; Key Clb; Spanish Clb; Chorus; Rep Stu Cncl; Trk; Cit Awd; NHS; Spanish NHS; 3rd Pl ST DECA Fshn Merch Promotion Plan; Big Family Mbr; Bus/Fshn Merch.

MORALES, ALICIA A; B T Washington HS; Tulsa, OK; (2); Drama Clb; Spanish Clb; Speech Tm; Chorus; School Musical; School Play; Variety Show; Ofcr Stu Cncl; NHS; Dance/Violin Lssns; NY U; Marine Bio.

MORALES, NADIA; Putnam City West HS; Bethany, OK; (2); Church Yth Grp; FCA; Spanish Clb; Rep Stu Cncl; JV Chrldng; Gym; High Hon Roll; Hon Roll; Young Republicans; HOSA; Vanderbilt; Pediatric Oncologst.

MORAN, DAMON; Idabel HS; Idabel, OK; (4); 6/106; Am Leg Boys St; Church Yth Grp; FBLA; Office Aide; Quiz Bowl; Science Clb; Rep Stu Cncl; JV Bsktbl; Var Golf; Var Tennis; OU Outstndng Acad Achvt; Phys Sci, Geom, OK Hstry, Geog Outstndng Achvt Awds; Mlti Year Listing; U OK; Pre-Med.

MOREHEAD, MARK A; Elgin HS; Lawton, OK; (4); 5/74; FHA; Teachers Aide; Hon Roll; NHS; Cameron U; Comp Anmtr.

MOREHOUSE, JENNIFER C; Del City HS; Oklahoma City, OK; (2); Church Yth Grp; ROTC; Spanish Clb; Pr Mdtn; ROTC Ath Tm.

MORELAND, CAROLYN; Shawnee Sr HS; Shawnee, OK; (3); Spanish Clb; Band; Mrchg Band; Hon Roll; NHS; Med.

MORELAND, HEATHER A; Collinsville HS; Collinsville, OK; (2); Church Yth Grp; FCA; Var Bsktbl; Var Sftbl; High Hon Roll; NHS; Crdlgst.

MORELAND, KERRY; Bartlesville Sr HS; Bartlesville, OK; (4); 1/420; German Clb; VP Pres Math Clb; Service Clb; Rep Stu Cncl; Var Capt Socr; High Hon Roll; Kiwanis Awd; NHS; Val; OK 5A All St Soccr Tm; Ul4 Grlssccr And Bsktbll Coach; Coca Cola Reg Schol; U Of OK; Metrlgy.

MORENO, CLAYTON; Marietta HS; Marietta, OK; (2); Art Clb; Computer Clb; Quiz Bowl; Wt Lftg; SOSU; Zoology.

MORETTI, MARTIN T; Stillwater Sr HS; Stillwater, OK; (2); 1/355; Boy Scts; Church Yth Grp; Latin Clb; Natl Beta Clb; Scholastic Bowl; Chorus; Church Choir; High Hon Roll; Pres Acad Fit Awd; Biol.

MOREY, JACOB; Jarman Jr HS; Tinker Afb, OK; (1).

MOREY, JOSHUA; Frederick HS; Frederick, OK; (3); 1/85; Church Yth Grp; Drama Clb; FCA; HOBY; Letterman Clb; Quiz Bowl; Science Clb; Speech Tm; Varsity Clb; Church Choir; Page Spkr Of House Loyd Benson; OK Close Up; Medcl.

MORFORD, CATHY L; Charles Page HS; Sand Springs, OK; (3); 89/365; Church Yth Grp; Drama Clb; FCA; Chorus; Church Choir; Hon Roll; School Play; JV Var Crs Cntry; NHS; OK Bapt All St Choir; Eastern Dist Hnr Choir; Vocal Perf.

MORGAN, ADRIA L; Brink Jr HS; Oklahoma City, OK; (1); Church Yth Grp; Band; Color Guard; Var L Tennis; Hon Roll; Jr NHS; Tennis Nwcmr Yr Awd; Mssn Trp Chrch Yth Rio Bravo Mexico.

MORGAN, ALICSON; Roff HS; Roff, OK; (1); 3/33; Church Yth Grp; 4-H; Natl Beta Clb; Quiz Bowl; Pres Frsh Cls; Cit Awd; 4-H Awd; Hon Roll; Prfct Atten Awd; Val; E Central U.

MORGAN, ANDREA L; Bartlesville Mid HS; Bartlesville, OK; (2); Church Yth Grp; Office Aide; Spanish Clb; Chorus; School Musical; Crs Cntry; Swmmng; Hon Roll; All Dist Hnr Choir; All St Solo & Ensembles.

MORGAN, ANGELA D; Commerce HS; Miami, OK; (1); FHA; Science Clb; Spanish Clb; SADD; DAR Awd; Hon Roll; Jr NHS; TX A&M; Vet.

MORGAN, BILLY J; Cushing HS; Cushing, OK; (2); Church Yth Grp; Spanish Clb; Band; Jazz Band; Mrchg Band; Orch; Pep Band; School Musical; School Play; Variety Show; U Of OK; Medicine.

MORGAN, BRANDI L; Blanchard Jr Sr HS; Blanchard, OK; (3); 10/65; Computer Clb; Hist FHA; Rep Pep Clb; Sec Spanish Clb; Ed Nwsp; Sec Frsh Cls; Rep Jr Cls; Rep Stu Cncl; Var Capt Chrldng; Pres NHS; Gftd & Tlntd; ESE; U Of Cntrl OK; Spch Path.

MORGAN, BREANNA R; Caney Valley HS; Ramona, OK; (3); Church Yth Grp; FHA; Hosp Aide; Library Aide; Teachers Aide; Sec Treas Jr Cls; Var Chrldng; JV Var Trk; Hon Roll; Tulsa U; Med Rsrch.

MORGAN, CARAH M; Lone Grove HS; Lone Grove, OK; (4); 34/75; Hon Roll; NHS; Trig Awd; All Amer Schlr Awd; OU; Phy Thrpy.

MORGAN, CYNTHIA R; Enid Sr HS; Enid, OK; (2); 40/432; French Clb; Scholastic Bowl; Band; Mrchg Band; Pep Band; Hon Roll; NHS; Attnd OSU Math/Sci Summer Acad; Attend OUS Exploring Geosciences Summer Acad; Univ Of OK; Meteorology.

MORGAN, DEBBIE D; Mustang HS; Mustang, OK; (3); Art Clb; Chorus; Bus; Art; Human Nature; OU; Bus; Advertising.

MORGAN, DEBORAH R; Union Intermediate HS; Broken Arrow, OK; (1); NHS; GATE Prgm; Melee; Pshch; Phlsphy/Arts.

MORGAN, DENNY; U S Grant HS; Oklahoma City, OK; (3); 2/250; Am Leg Boys St; FCA; Rep Nwsp; Rep Stu Cncl; Var L Bsbl; High Hon Roll; NHS; Ntl Merit Ltr; RYLA; Basic Ldrshp Camp; U Of OK.

MORGAN, ERIN; Noble HS; Noble, OK; (3); Cmnty Wkr; Drama Clb; French Clb; Math Clb; Mu Alpha Theta; Hon Roll; NHS; Computer Clb; Math Tm; School Play; Poem Publ Treasured Poems Of Amer 93; CPA.

MORGAN, GINA L; Enid Sr HS; Enid, OK; (2); Church Yth Grp; FHA; Hon Roll; Jr NHS; NHS; Big Brothers & Big Sisters; Life Clb; Phy Thrpst.

MORGAN, JAMIE D; Duke Schl; Duke, OK; (3); 1/18; Pres 4-H; Sec FHA; Yrbk; Pres Frsh Cls; Rptr Jr Cls; Var Bsktbl; Capt Chrldng; Sftbl; Cit Awd; 4-H Awd; FHA STAR Evnts 2 Time Natl Gold Medal Wnnr, Parlmntry Procdre Team Pres; OK ST U; Engrng.

MORGAN, JAY I; Choctaw HS; Choctaw, OK; (2); 1/300; Quiz Bowl; Scholastic Bowl; Teachers Aide; Varsity Clb; School Play; Golf; High Hon Roll; NHS; Val; Pres NHS; All Conf Golf Tm; OK ST.

MORGAN, JAYSON; Midwest City HS; Del City, OK; (2); 25/501; Church Yth Grp; Letterman Clb; Band; Jazz Band; Mrchg Band; Hon Roll; Jr NHS; Prfct Atten Awd; Numerous Hnr Bands; OU; Arch.

MORGAN, JEFFREY S; Wilson HS; Wilson, OK; (2); 8/44; Church Yth Grp; Natl Beta Clb; Band; Jazz Band; Mrchg Band; Pep Band; Hon Roll.

MORGAN, JOHN; Vinita HS; Vinita, OK; (4); 26/76; Am Leg Boys St; FHA; Library Aide; Science Clb; Spanish Clb; Var Ftbl; Var Golf; Var Wt Lftg; OK ST U; Engrng.

MORGAN, JULIA; Hobart HS; Hobart, OK; (1); Church Yth Grp; Quiz Bowl; Band; Jazz Band; Mrchg Band; Pep Band; Hon Roll; Tech Stu Assn Hobart Chptr Pres, Sec; Nrsng Home Vol; Med.

MORGAN, KEITH; Mc Loud HS; Newalla, OK; (4); 2/103; Art Clb; Church Yth Grp; Cmnty Wkr; Letterman Clb; Math Tm; Natl Beta Clb; Scholastic Bowl; Sec Jr Cls; Pres Stu Cncl; JV Bsbl; U Of OK; Engrng.

MORGAN, KENNA; Turner Schl; Overbrook, OK; (4); 5/21; GAA; Natl Beta Clb; Pres Natl FFA Org; Pep Clb; Speech Tm; Teachers Aide; Pres Frsh Cls; VP Soph Cls; VP Jr Cls; Capt Bsktbl; Phys Ed.

MORGAN, KERI B; Duncan HS; Duncan, OK; (2); Church Yth Grp; Cmnty Wkr; Key Clb; SADD; Band; Church Choir; Drm Mjr(t); Mrchg Band; Orch; Pep Band; Band Super Ratings At Dist & St Ensemble; Band Lettered & Barred.

MORGAN, KERRY; Welch Jr Sr HS; Welch, OK; (2); 4-H; FBLA; Natl FFA Org; Quiz Bowl; Yrbk; Pres Frsh Cls; 4-H Awd; High Hon Roll; NHS; Prfct Atten Awd; Tech Stdnts Assn; Msnc Stdnt Tdy Awd; Shwng Lvstck; OSU; Vet.

MORGAN, MARIA J; Mustang HS; Oklahoma City, OK; (3); 40/370; Teachers Aide; Chorus; Hon Roll.

MORGAN, MARQUITA Y; Douglass HS; Oklahoma City, OK; (3); Church Yth Grp; Cmnty Wkr; FHA; Church Choir; Var Bsktbl; Var Trk; Var Vllybl; Hon Roll; OK Dept Of Voc & Tech Ed Cert; Law.

MORGAN, MATTHEW B; Cushing HS; Cushing, OK; (3); 18/148; Church Yth Grp; FCA; Math Clb; Teachers Aide; Sprt Ed Yrbk; Var Bsktbl; Var Golf; Hon Roll; NHS; Golf St Chmpn 95; All Amer Schlr; Bus Mgmt.

MORGAN, MISTY; Mustang HS; Yukon, OK; (4); 193/343; Church Yth Grp; Drama Clb; FCA; Spanish Clb; SADD; Teachers Aide; Church Choir; School Play; Stage Crew; Chrch Capt Vlybl Tm; Dist Vlybl Chrch Tm; In Charge Of Grds 1-6 Chldrn Chrch; Southern Nazarene U; Ed.

MORGAN, PAUL E; Enid Sr HS; Enid, OK; (3); Church Yth Grp; Cmnty Wkr; Computer Clb; Debate Tm; Drama Clb; FCA; Letterman Clb; Library Aide; Math Clb; Math Tm; Actve Yth Alive Mmbr; CBC; Pastrl Studs.

MORGAN, RHONDA M; Velma Alma HS; Duncan, OK; (1); Church Yth Grp; FCA; Quiz Bowl; Scholastic Bowl; SADD; Bsktbl; High Hon Roll; Hon Roll; NHS.

MORGAN, SHONDA L; Claremore Sr HS; Claremore, OK; (4); Teachers Aide; Band; Yrbk; Chrldng; Hon Roll; Mktg Ed; DECA Chrprsn Toastmstr Grad; Rogers ST; Psych/Soclgy.

MORGAN, TIMOTHY R; Colcord Schl; Colcord, OK; (1); Dance Clb; Sec 4-H; Hon Roll; NHS; Comp.

MORGESON, KIM A; Edmond North HS; Edmond, OK; (1); 1/456; French Clb; GAA; Key Clb; Rep Stu Cncl; Ofcr Bsbl; Bsktbl; Ftbl; Hon Roll; NHS; Ftbl/Bsktbl/Bsbl Ath Trnr.

MORICOLI, MEGAN; Norman Sr HS; Norman, OK; (4); FCA; HOBY; JCL; Latin Clb; Service Clb; VP Soph Cls; Ofcr Stu Cncl; Capt Pom Pon; Gov Hon Prg Awd; NHS; NCA All Amer Chrldr; NCA All Amer Pom; Tmrrws Ldrs; U OK; Jrnlsm.

MORLAND, NICK J; Wakita Schl; Wakita, OK; (2); Church Yth Grp; Math Tm; Natl FFA Org; Quiz Bowl; Ofcr Bsbl; Bsktbl; Ftbl; Trk; Wt Lftg; Hon Roll; OU; Acctng.

MORNHINWEG, PAUL T; Byng Sr HS; Ada, OK; (3); 3/85; Am Leg Boys St; Boy Scts; Scholastic Bowl; Band; VP Soph Cls; Cit Awd; High Hon Roll; NHS; Pres Schlr; Val; All Dist Band 4 Yrs; Hnr Band 3 Yrs; Band Rep; OK ST Univ; Ag Scientist.

MORPHEW, LINDSEY; Maysville Jr Sr HS; Maysville, OK; (1); Church Yth Grp; GAA; Pep Clb; Bsktbl; Hon Roll; E Cntrl U.

MORPHIS, MELANIE N; Northwest Classen HS; Oklahoma City, OK; (3); Church Yth Grp; Drama Clb; Mu Alpha Theta; Science Clb; Chorus; Church Choir; School Musical; School Play; High Hon Roll; NHS; PRIDE; Superior Jr Cadet Decrtn Awd; Sec/Treas Chorus; U Of Cntrl OK; PT/SOC Wrkr.

MORRELL, JACQUELYN A; Mustang HS; Mustang, OK; (3); Natl FFA Org; Teachers Aide; High Hon Roll; Hon Roll; Pres Acad Fit Awd; Natl FFA Ag Comm Awd 95/Ag Prfcncy 96-/Agri Prdctn Awd OK Univ Acad Achvmts; Tishamingo ST Coll; Vet Med.

MORRICAL, EMILY K; Comanche HS; Hastings, OK; (2); Art Clb; Computer Clb; Debate Tm; FHA; Science Clb; SADD; OK ST; Child Care:ed.

MORRIS, AMANDA; Roland Sr HS; Roland, OK; (2); Church Yth Grp; Quiz Bowl; Speech Tm; Band; Chorus; Mrchg Band; Nwsp; Ofcr Stu Cncl; Hon Roll; Natl Eng Mrt & Natl Math Awds; Westark CC; Eng.

MORRIS, AMY B; Buffalo Jr Sr HS; Buffalo, OK; (2); FBLA; Band; Chorus; Swing Chorus; Rep Stu Cncl; Var L Bsktbl; Var L Sftbl; Var L Trk; Hon Roll; NHS; St Trk Medals; All Amer Schlr; OK ST Univ.

MORRIS, BOBBIE J; Choctaw HS; Choctaw, OK; (3); 24/330; Church Yth Grp; German Clb; Band; Mrchg Band; Pep Band; High Hon Roll; Hon Roll; Jr NHS; Masnc Awd; OK Hrn Soc; UOK; Med.

MORRIS, CHESTER CURTIS; Elgin HS; Elgin, OK; (3); Cmnty Wkr; DECA; JA; Letterman Clb; Natl FFA Org; Office Aide; Teachers Aide; Varsity Clb; VICA; Band; Multi-Yr Listee; OSU; Wrestling Coach.

MORRIS, CRYSTAL; Plainview HS; Ardmore, OK; (2); Church Yth Grp; FCA; Office Aide; SADD; Teachers Aide; Church Choir; School Play; Var Chrldng; Gym; Tennis; Engrng.

MORRIS, DE ANDRE R; Okmulgee HS; Okmulgee, OK; (4); French Clb; FBLA; Math Clb; Spanish Clb; Hon Roll; OSU Okmulgee.

MORRIS, DOUG; Perry Sr HS; Perry, OK; (3); Church Yth Grp; Drama Clb; FCA; German Clb; Chorus; School Musical; Phtg Nwsp; JV Var Bsktbl; JV Var Ftbl; NHS.

MORRIS, ERICA; U S Grant HS; Oklahoma City, OK; (1); Church Yth Grp; FCA; Hosp Aide; Office Aide; SADD; Church Choir; Pres Frsh Cls; High Hon Roll; Hon Roll; Hosp Clb Explrs; Med Fld.

MORRIS, FRANCES A; Union Intermediate HS; Tulsa, OK; (1); Chld Psych.

MORRIS, HOLLY; Pauls Valley HS; Pauls Valley, OK; (4); Church Yth Grp; Cmnty Wkr; FCA; Sec French Clb; FHA; Pres Key Clb; Pep Clb; SADD; Teachers Aide; Flag Corp; Mock Trial; OK U; Jrnlsm.

MORRIS, JENNIFER G; Western Heights Sr HS; Oklahoma City, OK; (1); 1/216; Church Yth Grp; FHA; Math Clb; Scholastic Bowl; Science Clb; Cit Awd; High Hon Roll; Lawyer.

MORRIS, JENNIFER R; Whitesboro Schl; Whitesboro, OK; (3); FHA; GAA; High Hon Roll; FFA; LPN/RN.

MORRIS, JOHN R; Bixby Sr HS; Bixby, OK; (3); 51/206; Boy Scts; Church Yth Grp; Cmnty Wkr; French Clb; Variety Show; JV Ftbl; High Hon Roll; Hon Roll; Aviation Careers Acad; Explorer Group Pres; OK ST U; Avitn; Aerspc Engrng.

MORRIS, JONATHAN A; Anadarko HS; Anadarko, OK; (3); 3/110; Church Yth Grp; Cmnty Wkr; FCA; Letterman Clb; Spanish Clb; Varsity Clb; VICA; Church Choir; VP Jr Cls; Var L Bsbl; OK ST Univ; Chemical Engrng.

MORRIS, JONATHAN D; Morris HS; Okmulgee, OK; (2); 1/90; Boy Scts; Church Yth Grp; Scholastic Bowl; JV Var Bsbl; JV Var Bsktbl; High Hon Roll; OK Hon Soc.

MORRIS, KATHRYN S; Stillwater Sr HS; Stillwater, OK; (2); French Clb; Key Clb; Orch; Hon Roll; Pre Med.

MORRIS, KINDRA M; Byng Sr HS; Ada, OK; (2); Church Yth Grp; GAA; Girl Scts; Letterman Clb; Spanish Clb; Varsity Clb; Band; Church Choir; Flag Corp; Mrchg Band; Bsktbl Ll Trnmnt Tm; Trck Hgh Pnt Trphy; Trck/Fld All Stater; Sftbl Hall Fame; Southeastern; Nrsng.

MORRIS, MADELYN M; Enid Sr HS; Enid, OK; (3); 24/445; Chorus; Hon Roll; Jr NHS; NHS; ECSRC; NW OK ST U; Bus/Mngmt.

MORRIS, MELISSA; Moore HS; Moore, OK; (3); Art Clb; Church Yth Grp; Spanish Clb; Thesps; Hon Roll; Gymnstc Brt Cnnr Acad; Dnce Fab Ft; UOK; Emer Med.

MORRIS, SARAH K; Cordell Sr HS; Cordell, OK; (1); FHA; Band; Church Choir; Flag Corp; Jazz Band; Mrchg Band; Pep Band; Stat Bsktbl; Var L Sftbl; Hon Roll; Luther Leag; Southwestern OK ST U; Pharm.

MORRIS, SHAWNNA L; Bartlesville Sr HS; Bartlesville, OK; (4); 70/450; Boy Scts; Cmnty Wkr; Letterman Clb; Math Clb; Red Cross Aide; JV Stat Bsktbl; L Sftbl; High Hon Roll; NHS; Spanish NHS; U Of MO-ROLLA; Envirnmntl Engr.

MORRIS, STEPHANIE L; Spiro HS; Spiro, OK; (2); FCA; Natl FFA Org; Office Aide; Teachers Aide; Var JV Bsktbl; Var Trk; Hon Roll; Top 15 OK Yth Rodeo Assn; 4 St Brl Rcng Assn Jr Rsrv Chmpn; Leflore Cty Girls Bstkbl Chmpnshp; OK ST U; Vet.

MORRISON, AMBER H; Noble HS; Noble, OK; (3); Temple Yth Grp; Band; Hon Roll; Murry ST; Phtgrphy.

MORRISON, BRANDY; Union City Schl; Oklahoma City, OK; (4); 7/23; Math Clb; Science Clb; Teachers Aide; Yrbk; Var Bsktbl; Hon Roll; Prfct Atten Awd; U Of Cntrl OK; Engl Ed.

MORRISON, CHRIS; Hulbert Jr Sr HS; Hulbert, OK; (2); Pres Frsh Cls; Pres Soph Cls; JV Var Bsbl; Var Bsktbl; Var Ftbl; Hon Roll; Jr NHS; NHS; Ntl Merit Schol; OU.

MORRISON, DEVIN; Heavener HS; Heavener, OK; (3); FBLA; High Hon Roll; Hon Roll; NHS; Carl Albert ST Coll; Finance.

MORRISON, GARY; Ketchum HS; Langley, OK; (4); Rptr Nwsp; Ed Stat Yrbk; Ftbl; Wt Lftg; Hon Roll; Wildlife.

MORRISON, KARI A; Bartlesville Sr HS; Bartlesville, OK; (3); 4-H; Teachers Aide; Chorus; DE Pow Wow Princess 95, Operation Eagle Prncss 96; NEO A&M; Real Est.

MORRISON, SHELLY D; Latta Sr HS; Ada, OK; (4); 25/53; Debate Tm; VP Drama Clb; VP Speech Tm; Thesps; Rptr Nwsp; Rptr Yrbk; Hon Roll; FHA; Library Aide; Office Aide; All Amer Schlr Nom; OK HS Mock Trial Prgm; Intrschlstc Meets; U Of Cntrl OK; Spch/Drama/Jrnl.

MORRISON, WILLIAM H; Putnam City HS; Oklahoma City, OK; (2); Church Yth Grp; Cmnty Wkr; Math Tm; Office Aide; Orch; Nwsp; Socr; Sftbl; OK Univ; Mech Engr.

MORRISSEY, JENNIFER L; Claremore Sr HS; Claremore, OK; (2); 43/273; Church Yth Grp; Hosp Aide; Var Golf; JV Var Sftbl; High Hon Roll; Hon Roll; U Of IA; Med.

MORROW, BRENNON; Miami Sr HS; Miami, OK; (2); 15/220; FHA; Quiz Bowl; Band; Hon Roll; NHS; Biochem.

MORROW, JENNY L; Mustang HS; Mustang, OK; (1); Church Yth Grp; FCA; GAA; Bsktbl; Trk; Vllybl; Hon Roll.

MORROW, ZAC; Sapulpa Sr HS; Sapulpa, OK; (3); Church Yth Grp; Key Clb; Science Clb; Ofcr Frsh Cls; Bsktbl; Ftbl; Socr; Hon Roll; NHS.

MORSE, CAREY S; Yukon Middle HS; Yukon, OK; (3); 47/412; FHA; Var Bsktbl; High Hon Roll; Hon Roll; NHS; Pres Acad Fit Awd; OK St Univ; Med Field.

MORSE, CARRIE; Verden HS; Verden, OK; (3); 5/25; Church Yth Grp; 4-H; FHA; Science Clb; Spanish Clb; Rep Frsh Cls; Ofcr Stu Cncl; JV Bsktbl; Cit Awd; Hon Roll; USAO; Med Tech.

MORSE, TERRI L; Tahlequah Jr HS; Tahlequah, OK; (1); Church Yth Grp; Chorus; Hon Mntn Muskogee Regnl Sci Fair.

MORSETH, JEWELL P; Bokoshe Schl; Bokoshe, OK; (2); 4/30; Church Yth Grp; FHA; VP Frsh Cls; JV Bsktbl; Hon Roll; NHS; Regnl Sci Fari 1st Pl Jr Div; Yng Edison Soc; OK Schl Of Sci/Math Semifinalist; AZ Univ Tuscon; Cardiolgst/MD.

MORTENSEN, SHANNON; Ft Gibson HS; Fort Gibson, OK; (3); French Clb; Hosp Aide; Band; Mrchg Band; Var Chrldng; High Hon Roll; NHS.

MORTON, AMANDA N; Owasso Sr HS; Owasso, OK; (2); 77/400; French Clb; Band; Color Guard; Mrchg Band; Hon Roll; Modeling; OU; Phy Thrpst.

MORTON, ANGELA M; Cascia Hall Prep School; Tulsa, OK; (4); Drama Clb; Spanish Clb; Chorus; School Musical; School Play; Ed Nwsp; Ed Yrbk; Lit Mag; JV Crs Cntry; Var JV Trk; Ballet; Piano; Violin; Arch.

MORTON, JOSHUA; Grace Fellowship Christian Sch; Broken Arrow, OK; (2); Scholastic Bowl; Comp Sci.

MORTON, KIMBERLY M; Macarthur Sr HS; Lawton, OK; (4); Cmnty Wkr; German Clb; Var Capt Socr; Sftbl; Hon Roll; Soccer Team Won Sthrn Regls; TX Chrstn Univ; Crmnl Jstc.

MORTON, PHILLIP; Edmond Santa Fe HS; Edmond, OK; (3); Church Yth Grp; SADD; Var Golf; Yng Rep Mmbr; Cmptr Sci Acad Awd; Cmptr Engrng.

MORTON, SHANE L; Pioneer Jr Sr HS; Enid, OK; (3); Var Bsbl; Hon Roll; FCA; Pep Clb; Teachers Aide; Band; Mrchg Band; OK Univ.

MOSBURG, DAVID; Thomas Jr Sr HS; Custer City, OK; (3); Boy Scts; Pres Church Yth Grp; FCA; Q&S; Varsity Clb; Pres Frsh Cls; Pres Soph Cls; Pres Jr Cls; L Bsbl; L Bsktbl; FFA Pres; US Naval Acad; Pol Sci.

MOSEBY, DANIELLE; East Central HS; Tulsa, OK; (2); Church Yth Grp; FCA; Treas German Clb; Pep Clb; Church Choir; Var Chrldng; Hon Roll; NHS; DFY; Engl Tchr.

MOSELEY, MATT A; Stillwater Sr HS; Stillwater, OK; (2); 45/375; Church Yth Grp; Quiz Bowl; Science Clb; Orch; Wrstlng; Hon Roll; Pres Acad Fit Awd; Vrsty Schol; Space Cmp; NASA Spac Cmb; Water Skiing; MIT; Eng.

MOSENA, APRIL M; Morrison Public Schl; Morrison, OK; (1); Church Yth Grp; Rptr FHA; Girl Scts; Teachers Aide; Band; Drill Tm; Jazz Band; Mrchg Band; Pep Band; OSU; Acctng.

MOSER, HEATHER; Claremore Sr HS; Claremore, OK; (3); 8/268; Cmnty Wkr; FCA; Spanish Clb; Rep Soph Cls; Ofcr Stu Cncl; Capt Chrldng; Gym; High Hon Roll; NHS; Prfct Atten Awd; Fresh Stu Yr; 2xs Reg Chrldng Chmpn; Stu Mon; Psych.

MOSES, MARCY J; Union Sr HS; Broken Arrow, OK; (3); 13/741; Church Yth Grp; Cmnty Wkr; Hosp Aide; Spanish Clb; Gym; High Hon Roll; Jr NHS; NHS; Prfct Atten Awd; Spanish NHS; Spcl Olympics Coach; BYU; Deaf Ed.

OKLAHOMA

MOSES, MEGAN M; Union Intermediate HS; Broken Arrow, OK; (1); Church Yth Grp; Spanish Clb; Band; Church Choir; Hon Roll; NHS.

MOSES, MEREDITH; Norman Sr HS; Norman, OK; (4); 172/677; FBLA; Hosp Aide; Pres SADD; Hon Roll; Cmnty Wkr; Ofcr Stu Cncl; Co Chair Pub Rltns; Dance Comm; Food For Friends Vol; Spec Olympics; Univ Of OK; Pre Med.

MOSIER, CHRISTINA; Dale Sr HS; Shawnee, OK; (2); 1/48; Church Yth Grp; Drama Clb; 4-H; Band; Jazz Band; Pep Band; School Play; Mgr(s); Score Keeper; Cit Awd; NJHS VP 94-96; 4-H VP 94-96; Med.

MOSIER, SAHRA; Bridge Creek HS; Tuttle, OK; (1); GAA; Bsktbl; Chrldng.

MOSLEY, CAROLINE; Moore HS; Oklahoma City, OK; (4); Church Yth Grp; Drama Clb; German Clb; Chorus; Church Choir; School Musical; School Play; Bsktbl; Trk; NHS; 1st, 2nd Pl Track Evnts; Ltr Drama; OK U; Drama.

MOSLEY, CRYSTAL A; Claremore Sr HS; Claremore, OK; (1); 100/300; Church Yth Grp; Office Aide; Spanish Clb; Teachers Aide; Trk; High Hon Roll; Hon Roll; Phys Ftnss; U Of AR; Phys Therapy.

MOSLEY, DONYELL M; Putnam City HS; Oklahoma City, OK; (2); Church Yth Grp; Bsktbl; Socr; Campaing Aide For Local Cnsl Prsn; U Of VA; Pol Sci.

MOSLEY, KEJANA D; Midwest City HS; Midwest City, OK; (4); 141/380; VICA; Hon Roll; African Amer Alliance Clb; Dntl Hygientist.

MOSLEY, KEVIN; Northwest Classen HS; Oklahoma City, OK; (3); HOBY; Church Choir; Rep Jr Cls; Rep Stu Cncl; Bsktbl; Ftbl; Wt Lftg; Bus.

MOSLEY, MONIQUE N; Roland Sr HS; Moffett, OK; (3); Art Clb; Church Yth Grp; FCA; GAA; Letterman Clb; Spanish Clb; Var Bsktbl; Hon Roll; Math/Blue Prnt/Drftng.

MOSLEY, VALERIE; Midwest City HS; Midwest City, OK; (3); 14/387; Treas Drama Clb; Chorus; School Musical; Stage Crew; NHS; Outstndng Yth Awd; Acad Ltr.

MOSLEY, VERONICA A; Claremore Sr HS; Claremore, OK; (4); Spanish Clb; Teachers Aide; Rptr Nwsp; High Hon Roll; Hon Roll; Shdw Stdnt; Rogers ST Coll; Nrsng.

MOSS, CLAYTON G; Deer Creek HS; Oklahoma City, OK; (4); 17/68; Boy Scts; Drama Clb; FCA; Science Clb; Teachers Aide; School Musical; School Play; Stage Crew; JV Ftbl; Var Capt Socr; U OK; Atty.

MOSS II, DAVID A; Tahlequah Sr HS; Tahlequah, OK; (3); Church Yth Grp; Computer Clb; SADD; Acpl Chr; Chorus; Crs Cntry; Trk; Hon Roll; Prfct Atten Awd; 2nd Pl Regnl Sci Fair In Botony; St Sci Fair; Accomplished Pianist; AR Univ; Sports Medicine.

MOSS, DEBORAH A; Muldrow HS; Muldrow, OK; (1); Natl Beta Clb; Science Clb; Spanish Clb; Band; Drm Mjr(t); Mrchg Band; Bsktbl; Hon Roll; NHS.

MOSS, JACQUELINE E; South Intermediate HS; Broken Arrow, OK; (2); Rep Stu Cncl; Crs Cntry; Socr; Trk; Vllybl; High Hon Roll; Hon Roll; NHS; High Achvt Gmtry Awd; Var Trck; Mdld In All Trck Meets; Dntstry.

MOSS, LYNN; Panama HS; Shady Point, OK; (4); 2/52; FHA; Office Aide; Spanish Clb; SADD; Yrbk; VP Soph Cls; VP Jr Cls; High Hon Roll; NHS; Sal; Carl Albert; Nrsng.

MOSS, MYA F; B T Washington HS; Tulsa, OK; (4); 83/264; Cmnty Wkr; Hosp Aide; Spanish Clb; Teachers Aide; Band; Mrchg Band; NHS; Langston U; Cmptr Sci.

MOSS, NATALIA; Central HS; Tulsa, OK; (3); FBLA; JA; Var Chrldng; High Hon Roll; Hon Roll; MS Cntrl Qn Attndnt; Cntrl Chfs; Econ Co VP; Csmtlgy.

MOSS, SHANA; Central HS; Tulsa, OK; (4); 32/200; Church Yth Grp; FBLA; Pres JA; Church Choir; Rptr Nwsp; Pres Stu Cncl; Capt Chrldng; Hon Roll; Tulsa CC; Chld Dvlpmnt.

MOSS, STEPHANIE L; Lawton Sr HS; Lawton, OK; (3); Sec FCA; Key Clb; Office Aide; Science Clb; Spanish Clb; Sec SADD; Hon Roll; NHS; All Amer Schlr In Acad & Bus Ed; Southwestern OK ST; Crmnl Psy.

MOSSHAMMER, KATRINA M; Antlers Sr HS; Antlers, OK; (3); Church Yth Grp; Quiz Bowl; Scholastic Bowl; SADD; Band; Chorus; Drm Mjr(t); Jazz Band; Mrchg Band; Pep Band; Hnr Band/ST Solos 3 Yrs; Sthstrn OK ST Univ; Sci.

MOTE, ANGELA; Noble HS; Noble, OK; (3); 21/167; Church Yth Grp; Mu Alpha Theta; Red Cross Aide; Band; Color Guard; Drm Mjr(t); Mrchg Band; Sec Jr Cls; Rep Stu Cncl; NHS; U Of OK; Musiced.

MOTE, KARI D; Del City HS; Del City, OK; (3); French Clb; Band; Pep Band; Hon Roll; NHS; Med.

MOTEN, VERLINDA C; Muskogee HS; Muskogee, OK; (1); Band; Mrchg Band; Pep Band; Hon Roll; Cmptr Sci.

MOTLEY, JARED A; Hollis Jr Sr HS; Hollis, OK; (3); Am Leg Boys St; Church Yth Grp; 4-H; FBLA; Math Clb; Scholastic Bowl; Band; Jazz Band; School Play; Ed Yrbk.

MOTLEY, JULIE M; Hollis Jr Sr HS; Hollis, OK; (2); Pres Church Yth Grp; Treas Drama Clb; FBLA; Chess Clb; Treas Speech Tm; Pres Frsh Cls; Pres Soph Cls; Ofcr Stu Cncl; Hon Roll; NHS; OK ST U; Telecomms.

MOTT, SHAWNA LYN; Webster HS; Tulsa, OK; (2); 1/300; Church Yth Grp; Drama Clb; FCA; FBLA; HOBY; Key Clb; Speech Tm; Church Choir; Yrbk; Ofcr Frsh Cls; Bible Quiz Capt; OK Senate Page; Anytown USA Del; Tulsa Univ; Lawyer.

MOTT, TARA M; Edmond North HS; Edmond, OK; (4); Church Yth Grp; Chorus; Church Choir; Ldr Of Yth Praise Team; Mem Of 2 Chrch Praise Teams; Soloist For Many Chrstn Chrchs & Orgs; Southern Nazarene U; RN.

MOTTO, MICHAEL; Tulsa Memorial HS; Tulsa, OK; (3); 1/250; Boy Scts; Pres VP Intnl Clb; Pres VP JCL; Pres Treas Key Clb; Treas Hist Latin Clb; Quiz Bowl; Rep Stu Cncl; High Hon Roll; NHS.

MOUNGER, MATTHEW S; Bixby Sr HS; Bixby, OK; (1); Church Yth Grp; Cmnty Wkr; SADD; Yrbk; Cit Awd; Hon Roll; Jr NHS; OK Univ; Mtrlgst.

MOUNT, BRIAN R; Yukon Middle HS; Yukon, OK; (2); Church Yth Grp; Cmnty Wkr; Var JV Socr; Hon Roll.

MOUNT, JOEY B; Stillwater Sr HS; Stillwater, OK; (3); Am Leg Aux Girls St; Drama Clb; FCA; GAA; Latin Clb; Letterman Clb; Math Clb; Mu Alpha Theta; Teachers Aide; School Play; Lttr Var Bsktbl 3 Yrs; KS; PT.

MOURER, BAY; Chisholm Sr HS; Carrier, OK; (3); Natl FFA Org; FCA; HOBY; Yrbk; JV Var Bsbl; JV Ftbl; Hon Roll; NHS; Ntl Merit Ltr; Stu Cncl Sec.

MOURER, LAUREN R; Ardmore HS; Ardmore, OK; (3); Art Clb; Drama Clb; FCA; French Clb; Mu Alpha Theta; Science Clb; Drill Tm; NHS; Church Yth Grp; Library Aide; 2nd Pl Awd Freedom Essay Spon Rtry Club; Outstdng Art II Stdnt 95-; Intrr Dsgn.

MOURTON, KIMBERLY; Sapulpa Sr HS; Sapulpa, OK; (4); 10/279; FCA; Treas Spanish Clb; Var L Crs Cntry; Var Capt Ftbl; High Hon Roll; Jr NHS; Treas NHS; Pres Acad Fit Awd; Spanish NHS; Clb Scr Tulsa Sheffield Untd; U Of AR.

MOURTON, LINDSAY N; Sapulpa Sr HS; Sapulpa, OK; (4); 10/279; Pres Church Yth Grp; FCA; Science Clb; Spanish Clb; L Crs Cntry; Var L Socr; High Hon Roll; Jr NHS; Hist NHS; Pres Acad Fit Awd; Clb Scr; Chrch Yth Msn Trps Oklahoma City/WV; U Of AR.

MOWDY, AUDRA; Coalgate HS; Coalgate, OK; (4); 10/43; Church Yth Grp; FCA; FBLA; Pres FHA; Natl FFA Org; Teachers Aide; Stat Bsbl; Chrldng; Hon Roll; NHS; Ftbl Homcng; E Central U; Psych.

MOWDY, STACIE; U S Grant HS; Oklahoma City, OK; (2); Church Yth Grp; Cmnty Wkr; Dance Clb; Letterman Clb; Stage Crew; Sftbl; High Hon Roll; NHS; OK U.

MOWERY, ADAM; U S Grant HS; Oklahoma City, OK; (2); #1 in class; Church Yth Grp; Tennis; High Hon Roll.

MOYDELL, EDWARD W; Union Intermediate HS; Tulsa, OK; (2); Office Aide; High Hon Roll; Hon Roll; Pres Acad Fit Awd; Frgn Lang Clb; Interior Dsgn.

MOYDELL, MELODI; Ft Gibson HS; Fort Gibson, OK; (2); Pres SADD; Color Guard; Pres Soph Cls; JV Var Bsktbl; Var Socr; Var Sftbl; High Hon Roll; Pres Acad Fit Awd; Teens For Chrst; Psych.

MOYER, JENNIFER; Soper Schl; Soper, OK; (2); Church Yth Grp; FHA; GAA; Natl FFA Org; Bsktbl; Hon Roll; Ntl Merit Ltr; Pres Acad Fit Awd.

MOZINGO, JOETTA M; Will Rogers HS; Tulsa, OK; (3); Key Clb; Band; Flag Corp; Mrchg Band; Rptr Nwsp; Rptr Yrbk; High Hon Roll; Hon Roll; NHS; Twirler; Feature Twirler; Band Qn Attendant; Homcmng Qn Attendant; OK ST; Veterinary Medicine.

MUCK, MELISSA; Sulphur HS; Sulphur, OK; (3); Church Yth Grp; FHA; Nwsp; Rep Frsh Cls; Rep Soph Cls; Treas Jr Cls; Var JV Bsktbl; Var Chrldng; Var JV Sftbl; Hon Roll; Bsktbl Hmcmng Qn.

MUDD, LANAY; Edmond North HS; Edmond, OK; (3); 1/464; Church Yth Grp; Cmnty Wkr; Drama Clb; French Clb; Mu Alpha Theta; School Musical; NHS.

MUEGGENBORG, MANDI; Yale Jr Sr HS; Yale, OK; (4); 5/39; VP Natl FFA Org; Teachers Aide; VP Jr Cls; Var Chrldng; High Hon Roll; Hon Roll; Prfct Atten Awd; OK ST U; Vet.

MUEGGENBURG, VINCE R; Okarche HS; Okarche, OK; (4); Church Yth Grp; 4-H; FHA; Speech Tm; Stage Crew; Sec Sr Cls; Ofcr Bsbl; Bsktbl; Cit Awd; 4-H Awd; Knights Of Columbus Mem; 4-H Shooting Clb Awd; Lions Clb Awd; Redlands Coll; Ag.

MUEHLEISEN, MATT; Putnam City North HS; Oklahoma City, OK; (3); Church Yth Grp; Cmnty Wkr; Spanish Clb; Golf; Cit Awd; Hon Roll; NHS; PTSA; LDI Ldrshp Wrkshp; OK ST; Sprts Med.

MUEHLENWEG, ALAN; Choctaw Jr HS; Midwest City, OK; (1); 40/203; Church Yth Grp; Drama Clb; Quiz Bowl; School Play; Variety Show; Crs Cntry; Socr; Trk; High Hon Roll; Hon Roll; Duke U; Law.

MUELLER, ANGELA; Perry Sr HS; Stillwater, OK; (2); Church Yth Grp; FBLA; FHA; Spanish Clb; Band; Drill Tm; Drm Mjr(t); Mrchg Band; Pep Band; Sftbl; Stu/Today Awd 92 & 95; Mtrlgst.

MUELLER, RACHEL L; Mustang HS; Yukon, OK; (3); Pres Church Yth Grp; French Clb; Teachers Aide; Mgr(s); Hon Roll; Treas NHS; LYO AR/OK Synod Publ Coord; Chrch Cntrl OK Conf 2 VP; Ped.

MUHAMMAD, ELIJAH; Douglass HS; Oklahoma City, OK; (1); Church Yth Grp; Cmnty Wkr; Drama Clb; FBLA; Ed Nwsp; Ofcr Stu Cncl; Hon Roll; J C Pnnys Cldn Rl Awd Comm Svc; OCU; Tchr.

MUHAMMAD, MANSSA M; Douglass HS; Oklahoma City, OK; (3); 10/250; Chess Clb; Cmnty Wkr; Computer Clb; Math Clb; High Hon Roll; Jr Sailing Instr Com OK On Water.

MUHAMMAD, QUARANA; Douglass HS; Oklahoma City, OK; (1); #10 in class; Cmnty Wkr; Computer Clb; Dance Clb; English Clb; FBLA; Math Clb; Pep Clb; Quiz Bowl; Scholastic Bowl; Band; Spellman Coll; Ped.

MULANAX, TINA M; Meeker HS; Mc Loud, OK; (2); Church Yth Grp; Cmnty Wkr; FCA; German Clb; Letterman Clb; Natl FFA Org; Chorus; Rep Stu Cncl; Var Chrldng; Var Vllybl; Horseback Riding; Tumbling; OK ST Univ; Vet.

MULDER, ADAM P; Stillwater Sr HS; Stillwater, OK; (2); Boy Scts; Church Yth Grp; Cmnty Wkr; FCA; Ofcr Bsbl; Ftbl; Trk; Wrstlng; NHS; Pres Acad Fit Awd; OSU Enomolgy Dept; OK St Univ; Lndscpng Bus.

MULDROW, LEKISHA N; B T Washington HS; Tulsa, OK; (3); FBLA; Spanish Clb; NHS; Xinos; OK U; Med.

MULFORD, JOSH A; Putnam City West HS; Bethany, OK; (3); Church Yth Grp; Cmnty Wkr; German Clb; Rep Jr Cls; Rep Stu Cncl; Ftbl; Wt Lftg; NHS; OU; Physcs.

MULFORD, JULIE; Chandler HS; Chandler, OK; (1); Church Yth Grp; Cmnty Wkr; FCA; FHA; Chorus; School Musical; Swing Chorus; Chrldng; Hon Roll; Eng.

MULLEN, TRISHA; Oktaha Jr Sr HS; Muskogee, OK; (3); 4-H; Spanish Clb; Chorus; Pres Frsh Cls; VP Soph Cls; Pres Jr Cls; Chrldng; Cit Awd; 4-H Awd; Hon Roll; I Dare You Awd 4-H; St 4-H Swine Project Awd Wnnr 95; Washington DC Ldrshp Conf; St Ldrshp Conf OKC; Connors ST Coll; Elem Ed.

MULLENDORE, KIMBERLY A; Harrah HS; Harrah, OK; (2); GAA; Varsity Clb; Bsktbl; Trk; Hon Roll; Ntl Merit Ltr; Offnsv Plyr Of Yr; Ldng Scorer.

MULLENS, CASEY M; Pauls Valley HS; Pauls Valley, OK; (3); FCA; French Clb; FHA; Band; Drm Mjr(t); Mrchg Band; Cit Awd; Hon Roll; All Star Marching Band 95; East Cntrl All Dist Hnr Band; U Of OK; Music Ed.

MULLER, CODY; Turner Schl; Marietta, OK; (3); Am Leg Boys St; Natl FFA Org; Pep Clb; Science Clb; Speech Tm; Treas Jr Cls; OK ST Univ; DVM.

MULLIKEN, JASMINE T; Yukon HS; Yukon, OK; (3); 169/470; Art Clb; Drama Clb; Office Aide; Rep Spanish Clb; Band; Co-Capt Color Guard; Co-Capt Flag Corp; Mrchg Band; School Musical; School Play; Univ Of OK; Arch.

MULLIKIN, JODI E; Ringling HS; Ringling, OK; (4); Church Yth Grp; Cmnty Wkr; Computer Clb; FBLA; FHA; Church Choir; Yrbk; Hon Roll; Prfct Atten Awd; Outstndng Soph In FHA; Bus & Comp Cls; Murray ST Coll; Comp.

MULLINS, ASHLEY E; West Middle HS; Norman, OK; (1); Church Yth Grp; Dance Clb; Debate Tm; Drama Clb; FCA; GAA; Latin Clb; Church Choir; Orch; School Play; Mem Teen Vol; KS Univ; Phy Anesthesiologist.

MULLINS, CHASTITY M; Canton HS; Southard, OK; (1); FCA; Band; Flag Corp; Mrchg Band; Pep Band; Bsktbl; Trk; Hon Roll; Pres Acad Fit Awd; Red Carpet Hon Bnd; US Natl Bnd Awd; OK Univ; Sec/Acctng/Prlgl.

MULLINS, DAVID C; Union Sr HS; Tulsa, OK; (3); Church Yth Grp; Computer Clb; FCA; Office Aide; Teachers Aide; Band; School Musical; School Play; Stage Crew; JV Bsbl; CO At Boulder; Bus/Proprietor.

MULLINS, JAMI M; Wagoner Sr HS; Wagoner, OK; (2); FBLA; Natl FFA Org; Hon Roll; VP Of FFA Chapt; Chapln Of FBLACHAPT; Star Greenhand In FFA; TX A&M Univ; Phys Thpy.

MULLINS, JENNIFER B; Norman Sr HS; Norman, OK; (4); #1 in class; Church Yth Grp; FCA; VP Sr Cls; Sec Stu Cncl; Vllybl; High Hon Roll; NHS; Ntl Merit SF; Pres Acad Fit Awd; Val; Sr Senator; Lions Clb Stu Mon; Biomedcl Engr.

MULLINS, TYLER; Byng Sr HS; Ada, OK; (4); 1/77; Pres FCA; Pres Natl Beta Clb; VP Natl FFA Org; Capt Quiz Bowl; Pres Scholastic Bowl; School Play; Nwsp; Lit Mag; Pres Frsh Cls; VP Soph Cls; Native Amer Clb; OK Indian Hnr Soc; U Of OK; Med/Engrng.

MULVEY, CHRISTOPHER O; Stillwater Sr HS; Stillwater, OK; (4); Key Clb; Math Clb; Mu Alpha Theta; Natl Beta Clb; Science Clb; Spanish Clb; Varsity Clb; L Capt Swmmng; Hon Roll; Spanish NHS; TX A&M; Med.

MUMFORD, SHERRY; Fox Sr HS; Fox, OK; (4); 7/27; 4-H; FHA; Natl FFA Org; Pep Clb; Teachers Aide; 4-H Awd; High Hon Roll; Hon Roll; Prfct Atten Awd; U Bus Awd; Who's Who Amng Amer HS Stdnts; Spnsh Ii Awd; U Of Cntrl OK; RN.

MUNCY, MATTHEW N; Bartlesville Sr HS; Bartlesville, OK; (2); Computer Clb; Band; Mrchg Band; Phtg Yrbk; High Hon Roll; Hon Roll; Jr NHS; Chrch Band; Comp Engr.

MUNDINGER, JANA; Midwest City HS; Midwest City, OK; (4); 52/418; FCA; Band; Church Choir; Jazz Band; Mrchg Band; Pep Band; Var Bsktbl; Mgr(s); Hon Roll; Band, Outstndng Soph/Jr Awds; Chrch Yth Grp; U Of Central OK; Elem Educ.

MUNKRES, ANNE; Midwest City HS; Midwest City, OK; (4); 33/419; Hosp Aide; Capt Quiz Bowl; Scholastic Bowl; Sec Science Clb; Spanish Clb; Band; Mrchg Band; Pep Band; School Musical; Ofcr Stu Cncl; Wellesley Coll MA; Bio.

MUNN, WILLIAM A; Will Rogers HS; Tulsa, OK; (2); Hon Roll.

MUNOZ, LUTZEN M; Choctaw HS; Midwest City, OK; (3); 63/327; FCA; Key Clb; Spanish Clb; JV Intrml Crs Cntry; JV Var Socr; Hon Roll; NHS; Upwrd Bnd; OK Hlth Sci Ctr Smmr Acad; Sprts Med.

MUNSON, JODIE L; Putnam City HS; Oklahoma City, OK; (4); 141/345; Church Yth Grp; Drama Clb; Key Clb; Library Aide; VP Science Clb; Spanish Clb; Teachers Aide; Acpl Chr; Hist Chorus; Church Choir; OK All ST Choir 3 Yrs; U Of Cntrl OK; Music Ed.

MURATA, JUNKO; Shawnee Sr HS; Japan, XX; (1); 20/367; Band; Mrchg Band; Hon Roll; ECU & OBU Hnr Bands; Penmanship; Keioh Univ.

MURATA, SATOSHI S; Shawnee Sr HS; Shawnee, OK; (3); 84/254; Socr; Hon Roll.

MURDOCK, AMANDA; Felt Public Schl; Felt, OK; (3); 1/12; HOBY; Quiz Bowl; Speech Tm; School Play; Var Capt Bsktbl; Trk; Hon Roll.

MURDOCK, CRAIG D; Mt St Marys HS; Oklahoma City, OK; (3); Church Yth Grp; FCA; Key Clb; Spanish Clb; SADD; Var Bsktbl; Var Ftbl; Var Trk; Hon Roll; OK Univ; Lawyer.

MURDOCK, MELANIE T; Felt Public Schl; Felt, OK; (1); Drama Clb; Quiz Bowl; Variety Show; Sec Frsh Cls; Rep Stu Cncl; Var Bsbl; Hon Roll.

MURFIN, RORY D; Charles Page HS; Sand Springs, OK; (4); Spanish Clb; Band; Jazz Band; Mrchg Band; Pep Band; Hon Roll; Prfct Atten Awd; OK ST Univ; Mech Engr.

MURIEL, LEAH; Grace Fellowship Christian Sch; Tulsa, OK; (3); 1/18; Church Yth Grp; Quiz Bowl; Scholastic Bowl; Teachers Aide; Band; Chorus; Church Choir; Pep Band; School Musical; Socr; Summer Math Acad; EWI Schlrshp Pgm; Spcl Awd Reg Sci Fair; UT Austin; Phrmcy.

MURNAN, JUSTIN K; Noble HS; Noble, OK; (4); 1/150; Cmnty Wkr; Mu Alpha Theta; VP Natl FFA Org; Bsktbl; Ftbl; High Hon Roll; NHS; Val; Awd Hnr; Outstdng Sr Boy; OK ST U; Engr.

MURNAN, KEVIN L; Noble HS; Noble, OK; (2); Church Yth Grp; Natl FFA Org; Spanish Clb; Intrml Bsktbl; High Hon Roll; NHS; OK ST U.

MURPHY, CHARLES A; Jay HS; Jay, OK; (3); Cmnty Wkr; 4-H; Scholastic Bowl; Science Clb; Variety Show; Yrbk; Cit Awd; 4-H Awd; Gov Hon Prg Awd; High Hon Roll; Natl His Day Awd Wnnr-Outstdng Entry From OK; Medicine; Dr.

MURPHY, CODY; Glencoe Public Schl; Glencoe, OK; (3); 2/33; Church Yth Grp; FCA; French Clb; Natl FFA Org; Speech Tm; Yrbk; Pres Frsh Cls; VP Stu Cncl; Ofcr Bsbl; Bsktbl; OK ST U; Med.

MURPHY, JENNIFER F; Jenks HS; Tulsa, OK; (3); 37/517; Church Yth Grp; Dance Clb; DECA; FCA; FHA; German Clb; Pep Clb; Drill Tm; Rep Stu Cncl; Var Pom Pon; Acctng.

MURPHY, JOSHUA; Porter Jr Sr HS; Coweta, OK; (4); 2/31; Chess Clb; Church Yth Grp; FCA; Quiz Bowl; SADD; Teachers Aide; Rep Stu Cncl; Var Bsbl; Var Bsktbl; Var Wt Lftg; Missn Trips Mexico 94, MT 95; Sundy Schl Tchr; Ministry.

MURPHY, KATY; Carl Albert Jr HS; Midwest City, OK; (1); Rep FCA; Library Aide; Chorus; Rep Frsh Cls; Capt Chrldng; Hon Roll; Jr NHS; 4-H; Pep Clb; Stage Crew; Outstdng Fr Girl; FCA Rsng Star; 2 Time Acad Lttrmn.

MURPHY, KRISTIN D; Bartlesville Mid HS; Bartlesville, OK; (2); 137/481; Church Yth Grp; Chorus; Church Choir; School Musical; Hon Roll; Superior Medls ST Solo/Ensmbl Schl Chorus; Superiors TNT Yth Cmptn Asrtd Catgrs Chrch Choir Cmptns; Bartlsvl Weslyn Coll; Music Ed.

MURPHY, LA FONDA L; Will Rogers HS; Tulsa, OK; (3); 7/257; Rptr FBLA; FHA; Key Clb; Pres Spanish Clb; Ofcr Soph Cls; Ofcr Jr Cls; Tennis; High Hon Roll; NHS; CODE; Crcl Frnds; OK ST U; Bus Admin.

MURPHY, NATHAN; Guymon Sr HS; Guymon, OK; (3); Church Yth Grp; FCA; Model UN; Science Clb; Spanish Clb; Rep Jr Cls; Var L Ftbl; Var Wt Lftg; Hon Roll; NHS; Genetic Engr.

MURPHY, NICHOLE C; Norman Sr HS; Norman, OK; (3); FCA; Mu Alpha Theta; Spanish Clb; Bsktbl; JV Capt Socr; JV Var Vllybl; Cit Awd; Hon Roll; Soccer Team; United Way Vol 95-; Feed The Chldrn Vol 95; PT/PSYCH.

MURPHY, SHELLEY; Clinton HS; Clinton, OK; (4); Church Yth Grp; DECA; FCA; FBLA; FHA; Hon Roll; NHS; Natl Math, Sci & Ldrshp Mrt Awds; U Of OK; Bus.

MURPHY, TARA L; South Intermediate HS; Broken Arrow, OK; (1); Cmnty Wkr; Pep Clb; Teachers Aide; Var L Tennis; Cit Awd; Gov Hon Prg Awd; High Hon Roll; NHS; Pres Acad Fit Awd; Pres Schlr.

MURRAY, APRIL L; Claremore Sr HS; Claremore, OK; (1); Drama Clb; Hosp Aide; Stage Crew; Yrbk; Gym; Sftbl; KS ST.

MURRAY, BRIAN; Apache HS; Apache, OK; (3); 2/34; Church Yth Grp; FHA; VP Natl FFA Org; Sec Frsh Cls; Pres Soph Cls; Pres Jr Cls; Sec Stu Cncl; Var L Bsbl; Var L Ftbl; Var L Wrstlng; Southwestern OSU; Phrmcy/Ag.

MURRAY, BRYCE; Claremore Sr HS; Claremore, OK; (4); 1/241; Am Leg Boys St; Church Yth Grp; Capt Quiz Bowl; Science Clb; Pres Soph Cls; VP Treas Stu Cncl; High Hon Roll; Pres NHS; Val; Odyssy Mnd; Explrs Clb Med; Harding U; Med.

MURRAY, CODY C; Edmond Santa Fe HS; Edmond, OK; (2); FCA; JV Var Bsbl.

MURRAY, CRYSTAL L; Cashion HS; Cashion, OK; (2); Church Yth Grp; FHA; Hosp Aide; Scholastic Bowl; Spanish Clb; School Play; VP Frsh Cls; JV Bsktbl; 4-H Awd; Miss Teen Of Amer ST Pgm; Hlth Care Ctr Vol; Nurse.

MURRAY, HILLARY; Pauls Valley HS; Pauls Valley, OK; (4); 5/84; Am Leg Aux Girls St; Cmnty Wkr; FCA; French Clb; Rep Key Clb; Pres Jr Cls; Bsktbl; Chrldng; Tennis; VP Sec NHS; Hmcmng Royalty; Stu Of Mnth & Yr; OK ST U; Med.

MURRAY, KARYN; Westmoore HS; Oklahoma City, OK; (3); 2/615; Church Yth Grp; Scholastic Bowl; Hist Spanish Clb; High Hon Roll; Jr NHS; NHS; 2nd Yr Schlstc Letter; Univ Of OK; Bus Mgmnt.

MURRAY, KATI A; Cherokee Jr Sr HS; Cherokee, OK; (3); Church Yth Grp; FHA; Band; Pep Band.

MURRAY, KENDRA; Bristow HS; Bristow, OK; (4); GAA; Office Aide; Pep Clb; Ed Nwsp; Ed Yrbk; Ofcr Stu Cncl; Capt Bsktbl; Capt Sftbl; Trk; Hon Roll; Dental Career.

MURRAY, MARIAH; Pauls Valley HS; Pauls Valley, OK; (2); Art Clb; FCA; FHA; Rptr Key Clb; VP Spanish Clb; Var Golf; High Hon Roll; NHS; Hnrs Eng I Stu Of Yr 94-95; US His Stu Of Yr 95-96; OK ST Univ; Psych.

MURRAY, STEPHEN; Crescent Schl; Crescent, OK; (4); 3/35; Am Leg Boys St; Church Yth Grp; Pres FCA; Pres Natl Beta Clb; Capt Quiz Bowl; Teachers Aide; Pres Band; School Play; Nwsp; Yrbk; Qz Bwl St Champs St Beta Conv; OK St Fr Schlrs Cntst 1st Rnnr-Up 95; OK Msnc Ldg Stu/Tdy 94; Smmr Plg; OK Bapt U; Vcl Music.

MURRAY, T J; Ponca City Middle HS; Ponca City, OK; (1); Art Clb; Ski Clb; Bsktbl; Tennis; High Hon Roll.

MURRELL, J T; Comanche HS; Newcastle, OK; (2); 1/86; Church Yth Grp; FCA; German Clb; HOBY; Band; Church Choir; Drm Mjr(t); Mrchg Band; Pep Band; Var Bsktbl; OK Bapt U; Music Perf.

MURRELL, VALAUNA; Newcastle HS; Newcastle, OK; (2); Pres Church Yth Grp; FCA; Natl Beta Clb; Science Clb; SADD; Chorus; Mrchg Band; Bsktbl; High Hon Roll; NHS; Clss Rylty; Outstndnng Frosh; DOC; Ms Rnnr-Up Comanche 95; OCU; Law.

MUSE, PRISCILLA R; Glenpool HS; Glenpool, OK; (1); Letterman Clb; Teachers Aide; Varsity Clb; Flag Corp; L Var Chrldng; Intrml Powder Puff Ftbl; Var L Trk; FHA; Social Worker.

MUSE, STEVI; Stratford Schl; Pauls Valley, OK; (4); 1/47; Church Yth Grp; FCA; Pres FHA; NFL; Spanish Clb; Teachers Aide; Chorus; Yrbk; Ofcr Sr Cls; Bsktbl; East Cntrl Univ; Acctng.

MUSGROVE, HOLLY S; Wynnewood HS; Wynnewood, OK; (1); Church Yth Grp; Sec Frsh Cls; Sec Soph Cls; Ofcr Stu Cncl; Chrldng; Hon Roll; East Cntrl ST Univ; Ed.

MUSHRUSH, JEFF; Berryhill Jr HS; Tulsa, OK; (1); Rep Frsh Cls; Rep Stu Cncl; Var Ftbl; L Wt Lftg; Var Wrstlng; High Hon Roll; Hon Roll; NHS; OK Youth Participation Conf; Camp Tech 95.

MUSHRUSH, JOHN; Berryhill Sr HS; Tulsa, OK; (4); 5/51; Am Leg Boys St; Church Yth Grp; Cmnty Wkr; FCA; FBLA; Office Aide; Stage Crew; VP Jr Cls; Rep Stu Cncl; Capt Ftbl; Boys St Delg; Boy Of Month Dec; Ftbl Coaches Awd 95-96; OK ST U; Virology.

MUSHRUSH, MIKE; Berryhill Jr HS; Tulsa, OK; (4); 5/51; Am Leg Boys St; Church Yth Grp; FCA; FBLA; Office Aide; Stage Crew; VP Soph Cls; VP Jr Cls; Rep Stu Cncl; Capt Ftbl; Ftbl Cchs Awd Achvt 95; HS Boy Mo; Natl Ldrshp & Svc Awd; OK ST U; Virology.

MUSHRUSH, STACY R; Sapulpa Sr HS; Sapulpa, OK; (3); 32/340; Church Yth Grp; Key Clb; Spanish Clb; Band; Chorus; Bsktbl; Hon Roll; Jr NHS; NHS; Spanish NHS; U Of OK; PT.

MUSICK, ADRIAN E; Kingfisher HS; Kingfisher, OK; (2); #39 in class; Drama Clb; Scholastic Bowl; Speech Tm; School Play; Stage Crew; Hon Roll; Stu Cncl; Marine Bio.

MUSICK, JORDAN; Weatherford HS; Weatherford, OK; (1); 1/165; Church Yth Grp; FCA; Chorus; Church Choir; Pres Frsh Cls; Rep Stu Cncl; JV Bsktbl; Var Chrldng; Gym; Var Socr; NCA All Amer Chrldr.

MUSKRAT, SHAWNA K; Porum HS; Porum, OK; (3); FCA; Pep Clb; Rep Frsh Cls; JV Var Bsktbl; JV Var Sftbl; Hon Roll; Vice Chf Indian Clb; Mascot; Okmulgee Tech; Bus Mngmt.

MUSSER, WILL T; Turner Schl; Burneyville, OK; (3); Natl FFA Org; Quiz Bowl; Scholastic Bowl; Science Clb; JETS Awd; Prfct Atten Awd; Austin Coll; Med.

MUSSHAFEN, ED; Perry Sr HS; Perry, OK; (2); Church Yth Grp; Cmnty Wkr; FCA; Jazz Band; Bsktbl; Golf; Cit Awd; Hon Roll; Jr NHS; NHS; OSU; Prof Golf.

MUSSON, JAMIE; Noble HS; Noble, OK; (3); Church Yth Grp; Spanish Clb; Band; Mrchg Band; Hon Roll; NHS; Pharmacist.

MYATT, ANN M; Washington HS; Washington, OK; (1); 1/60; Dance Clb; 4-H; FHA; Girl Scts; Band; Mrchg Band; Orch; Pep Band; 4-H Awd; High Hon Roll; OK Historian; OK Summer Arts Institute 2 Yrs.

MYATT, RACHEL; U S Grant HS; Oklahoma City, OK; (3); Dance Clb; FHA; Swmmng; High Hon Roll; NHS; Dance Co St & Natl Wnnr.

MYERS, ALISHA; Boise City HS; Boise City, OK; (3); 3/34; Church Yth Grp; FCA; FHA; GAA; Band; Treas Jr Cls; Bsktbl; Chrldng; Wt Lftg; High Hon Roll; Phys Thrpy.

MYERS, ANDY S; Dewey HS; Dewey, OK; (1); 3/90; Church Yth Grp; FCA; Spanish Clb; JV Bsktbl; JV Ftbl; Var Trk; Hon Roll; Pres Schlr.

MYERS, ANNETTE D; Newcastle HS; Newcastle, OK; (3); Spanish Clb; Band; Mrchg Band; Pep Band; Ofcr Stu Cncl; Hon Roll; NHS; HS Band Pres 2 Yrs; U Of OK; Phy Thrpy.

MYERS, BRIAN S; Tecumseh HS; Tecumseh, OK; (3); Church Yth Grp; Band; Chorus; Mrchg Band; Swing Chorus; Variety Show; Music Ed.

MYERS, BROOKE; Berryhill Jr HS; Sapulpa, OK; (1); Church Yth Grp; FCA; GAA; Yrbk; VP Stu Cncl; JV Bsktbl; Hon Roll; Prfct Atten Awd; Sal; NSU; Phys Thrpst.

MYERS, CHRIS; Empire Schl; Duncan, OK; (1); Cmnty Wkr; FCA; Spanish Clb; SADD; Varsity Clb; Ofcr Bsbl; Bsktbl; Ice Hcky; High Hon Roll; Hon Roll; Natl Geog & Math Awds.

MYERS, CHRISTINE C; Tomlinson Jr HS; Lawton, OK; (1); #5 in class; Dance Clb; Bsktbl; Trk; Grl Track Ath Of Yr; Langston; Lwyr/Med Dr.

MYERS, CHRISTY L; Putnam City HS; Oklahoma City, OK; (2); Stat Bsbl; Stat Bsktbl; JV Sftbl; Med.

MYERS, DERRICK L; Ponca City Sr HS; Ponca City, OK; (3); 20/360; Church Yth Grp; Drama Clb; FCA; Speech Tm; JV Crs Cntry; JV Ftbl; Var Trk; Cit Awd; High Hon Roll; School Play; Fin Bus Advsr.

MYERS, HEATHER; Edmond North HS; Edmond, OK; (4); Am Leg Aux Girls St; Cmnty Wkr; HOBY; Pep Clb; Spanish Clb; SADD; Teachers Aide; Band; Ed Nwsp; Yrbk; Prof Internshp Rptr Capitol Netwrk News; Ldrshp Seminars; Jrnlsm Stu Of Yr; Jrnlsm.

MYERS, JASON; Byng Sr HS; Ada, OK; (4); 2/72; Am Leg Boys St; Church Yth Grp; Natl Beta Clb; Quiz Bowl; Band; Rep Stu Cncl; High Hon Roll; NHS; Sal; OK U; Mtrlgy.

MYERS, JODI L; Sallisaw HS; Sallisaw, OK; (4); 25/128; Rptr Art Clb; Church Yth Grp; FCA; FHA; Library Aide; Rptr Math Clb; Office Aide; Science Clb; Rptr Yrbk; Treas Sr Cls; US Chrldr Achv Awd; Unvrsl Chrldrs Assc All Star Chrldr; Spcl Olympcs Vol 4 Yrs; OK ST Univ; Pre Med.

MYERS, JOSHUA P; Lawton Sr HS; Fort Sill, OK; (4); 2/335; Red Cross Aide; Band; Mrchg Band; Co-Ed Lit Mag; JV Ftbl; High Hon Roll; Ntl Merit SF; Sal; Church Yth Grp; German Clb; Prin Awd; Hghst GPA; U Of OK; Pre-Med.

MYERS, KERRY A; Putnam City HS; Warr Acres, OK; (2); Church Yth Grp; JV Bsktbl; Var Chrldng; Score Keeper; JV Sftbl; Med Prof.

MYERS, MANDY L; Moore HS; Moore, OK; (2); Bsktbl; Mgr(s).

MYERS, MARY E; Mannford HS; Mannford, OK; (1); Church Yth Grp; FCA; Hon Roll.

MYERS, MISTY R; Stringtown HS; Stringtown, OK; (2); 4-H; Natl FFA Org; Sec Frsh Cls; Var Bsktbl; 4-H Awd; Hon Roll; Ntl Merit Ltr; Val; Chptr FFA Sec 95-; Upward Bound E Cntrl Univ.

MYERS, NADIA; Charles Page HS; Tulsa, OK; (4); Church Yth Grp; Drama Clb; FCA; Key Clb; Office Aide; Spanish Clb; School Play; Stage Crew; Rep Soph Cls; Rep Jr Cls; Deans Hnr Rl; Span Club Schlsp; Tulsa JC; Span Ed.

MYERS, NATALIE; Jenks HS; Tulsa, OK; (4); 30/540; Am Leg Aux Girls St; Cmnty Wkr; Letterman Clb; Mu Alpha Theta; Chorus; Drill Tm; School Musical; Sec Frsh Cls; Sec Soph Cls; Pres Sec Stu Cncl; Senate Page; OASC Ldrshp Wrkshps; Cmnty Theatre Productions Roles; Commnctns.

MYERS, R SCOTT; Claremore Sr HS; Claremore, OK; (3); Art Clb; Boy Scts; Church Yth Grp; Drama Clb; German Clb; Quiz Bowl; Speech Tm; School Musical; School Play; Golf; Odyssey Of Mind; Gold Key Awd Schlstc Art Cmptn; OK ST Univ; Arch.

MYERS, SAMANTHA; Ada HS; Ada, OK; (3); FCA; 4-H; GAA; Intnl Clb; Spanish Clb; Band; Ofcr Stu Cncl; Bsktbl; High Hon Roll; NHS.

MYERS, SARAH; Woodward HS; Woodward, OK; (4); 8/148; FCA; Letterman Clb; Red Cross Aide; Band; Sftbl; Tennis; High Hon Roll; NHS; Sal; Bsktbl; Who's Who In Sports; All-ST Alternate Bsktbl; OK Panhandle ST U; Sprts Chrp.

MYERS, SHANNON; Claremore Sr HS; Claremore, OK; (2); 1/273; Church Yth Grp; Cmnty Wkr; Hosp Aide; Quiz Bowl; SADD; Jazz Band; Mrchg Band; Pep Band; School Musical; BSA Explrs; Soph Band Rep; Rice U.

MYERS, SPECTRA R; Tahlequah Jr HS; Tahlequah, OK; (1); Church Yth Grp; Girl Scts; Hon Roll; Jr NHS; Pres Acad Fit Awd; Orthodontist.

MYERS, TIFFANIE; Anadarko HS; Anadarko, OK; (3); 3/120; FCA; VP FBLA; FHA; Natl FFA Org; Yrbk; Var Chrldng; High Hon Roll; NHS; VP Soph Cls; S W OK ST U; Phrmcy.

MYERS-COMPTON, SARA J; Putnam City West HS; Oklahoma City, OK; (4); 35/270; Church Yth Grp; Cmnty Wkr; NFL; Thesps; Pres Band; Pres Chorus; School Musical; School Play; Hon Roll; Drama Clb; Voice Of Dem 1 Dist/4th ST; Mcpherson; Drama.

MYLES, KIMBERLY R; Southeast HS; Oklahoma City, OK; (3); 5/100; ROTC; Band; Yrbk; VP Sr Cls; High Hon Roll; Hon Roll; NHS; Amer Lgn Schlstc Awd AFJROTC; Rtrd Ofcrs Assn Awd AFJROTC; Ordr Of The D; Nrsng/Hlth Career.

MYRES, CASSANDRA L; Catoosa HS; Tulsa, OK; (2); 9/180; Church Yth Grp; FCA; French Clb; Quiz Bowl; Band; Church Choir; Mrchg Band; Bsktbl; Crs Cntry; NHS; Trail Of Tears Awd.

MYRES, TALIA E; Catoosa HS; Tulsa, OK; (4); 12/136; Church Yth Grp; Drama Clb; FCA; French Clb; Pep Clb; Quiz Bowl; Band; Church Choir; Jazz Band; Mrchg Band; Teens To Go; OK Hnr Soc; OSU; Chld Thrpy.

MYSINGER, MINDY B; Westmoore HS; Oklahoma City, OK; (3); Church Yth Grp; Key Clb; Hon Roll; NHS; Tae Kwon Do; AAU Jr Olympics For Tae Kwon Do; Pan-Amer Games For Tae Kwon Do; OKC CC; Med Field.

MYTHEN, TIFFANY M; Putnam City HS; Oklahoma City, OK; (2); Yrbk; Socr; Law.

NABORS, AMANDA L; North Intemediate HS; Broken Arrow, OK; (1); Church Yth Grp; Drama Clb; French Clb; FHA; SADD; School Play; Chrldng; Hon Roll; NHS; Pres Acad Fit Awd; BYU; RN/PEDTRCN.

NADERI, SHAHLA J; U S Grant HS; Oklahoma City, OK; (1); Cmnty Wkr; Nwsp; Var Co-Capt Bsktbl; Hon Roll; U CT; Medicine; Law.

NADEU, AUSTIN D; Bishop Kelley HS; Tulsa, OK; (2); Boy Scts; Church Yth Grp; Ofcr Bsbl; Tennis; Schl Svc Hrs.

NADRASH, ANGELA L; B T Washington HS; Tulsa, OK; (4); 37/270; Hosp Aide; Pep Clb; Sec Spanish Clb; Teachers Aide; Var Chrldng; NHS; Acad Ltr; OK ST U; Bio.

NAEGELI, SARA J; Edmond Memorial HS; Edmond, OK; (4); 1/335; Church Yth Grp; French Clb; Band; Mrchg Band; NHS; Ntl Merit SF; Val; Piano Stu; Music.

NAEHER, MATTHEW; Bridge Creek HS; Tuttle, OK; (2); 1/85; FCA; Quiz Bowl; Scholastic Bowl; VP Frsh Cls; Pres Soph Cls; Var L Bsbl; Var L Ftbl; High Hon Roll; NHS; Prfct Atten Awd; Notre Dame; Coach.

NAEL, RAHA; Oklahoma Sch Of Science & Math; Norman, OK; (4); Cmnty Wkr; Hosp Aide; JCL; Mu Alpha Theta; Orch; Sec Frsh Cls; Rep Soph Cls; Hon Roll; NHS; Pres Acad Fit Awd; OK Hlth Sci Center Summer Acad; Spcl Olympics Vol; Super In ST Solo & Ensemble Cont; Psych.

NAFF, RICHARD A; John Marshall HS; Oklahoma City, OK; (1); Hon Roll; A Pls Acad Assn Inc.

NAFF, TIRRA; Millwood HS; Oklahoma City, OK; (4); Cmnty Wkr; Computer Clb; Office Aide; ROTC; Color Guard; Yrbk; Var JV Crs Cntry; Var Trk; U Of Cntrl OK; Bus Admin.

NAGY, JENNIFER L; Union Sr HS; Tulsa, OK; (4); Church Yth Grp; French Clb; Intnl Clb; Office Aide; High Hon Roll; Hon Roll; Jr NHS; NHS; Pres Acad Fit Awd; Marine Bio.

NAHORSKI, NICK; Oklahoma Bible Acad; Enid, OK; (3); 1/31; Church Yth Grp; Quiz Bowl; Scholastic Bowl; Chorus; Church Choir; Yrbk; Treas Jr Cls; VP Stu Cncl; Var Bsbl; JV Bsktbl; OK Hnr Soc; Rotry Yth Ldrshp Awds Conf; U Of OK Smmr Schlrs Pgm.

NAIFEH, CHARISE; Edmond Santa Fe HS; Edmond, OK; (3); Art Clb; Church Yth Grp; French Clb; SADD; Band; Jazz Band; Mrchg Band; Pep Band; Crs Cntry; NHS; U Of TX; Med.

NAIGLE, CORINNE E; Choctaw HS; Midwest City, OK; (2); Church Yth Grp; FHA; Girl Scts; Key Clb; Chorus; JV Socr; Mgr Vllybl; High Hon Roll.

NAIL, JENNIFER M; Duncan HS; Duncan, OK; (3); Church Yth Grp; FBLA; Hosp Aide; Band; Chorus; Church Choir; Jazz Band; Mrchg Band; Pep Band; Variety Show; Chrch League Sftbl; Elem Ed.

NAIL, SHELLY; Skiatook HS; Skiatook, OK; (3); Church Yth Grp; FCA; FHA; Natl FFA Org; Band; Mrchg Band; Stat Bsktbl; JV Sftbl; High Hon Roll; Hon Roll; Tulsa Univ; Nrsng.

NAKEDHEAD, JEANA R; Stilwell HS; Stilwell, OK; (1); Church Yth Grp; French Clb; Indian Heritage Clb; Elem Ed.

NALL, ETHAN; Chisholm Sr HS; Carrier, OK; (3); Church Yth Grp; FCA; Pres Natl FFA Org; Teachers Aide; Pres Jr Cls; Pres Sr Cls; Ofcr Stu Cncl; Bsktbl; Ftbl; Trk; Yth Advsry To St Gregry Parish Cncl; Sr Class Pres.

NALLEY, CORIE A; Jenks HS; Tulsa, OK; (4); 246/448; DECA; Spanish Clb; Teachers Aide; Ofcr Stu Cncl; OK ST Univ; Bus.

NANCE, JULIE M; Edmond Memorial HS; Edmond, OK; (3); 149/371; Church Yth Grp; Cmnty Wkr; FCA; Hosp Aide; Office Aide; SADD; Chorus; Socr; NHS; All Amrcn Schol; OSU; Lwyr.

NANCE, MELISSA L; Bishop Mcguinness HS; Oklahoma City, OK; (3); 62/135; Church Yth Grp; Cmnty Wkr; FCA; FBLA; Pep Clb; Red Cross Aide; Ski Clb; Spanish Clb; SADD; Teachers Aide; Pep & Span Clbs Mem At Large; Outdoor Clb; U Of CO Boulder; Vet.

NANTZ, JAMES; Broken Arrow Sr HS; Broken Arrow, OK; (4); 97/921; Church Yth Grp; HOBY; Acpl Chr; Church Choir; Rep Jr Cls; Rep Sr Cls; Rep Stu Cncl; Cit Awd; Hon Roll; NHS; OASC St Pres; OK ST U.

NAQUIN, STACIA N; Macarthur Sr HS; Lawton, OK; (3); Church Yth Grp; Cmnty Wkr; FCA; HOBY; Key Clb; Science Clb; SADD; Pres Acpl Chr; Chorus; School Play; Close-Up Govt Stud Pgm; Stu Of Month; All OMEA Choir.

NARAMOR, JASON L; Durant HS; Durant, OK; (1); Military, Weapons His; Austin Coll; Vet Med.

NASALROAD, COLLIN; Yale Jr Sr HS; Yale, OK; (2); 11/51; Church Yth Grp; Cmnty Wkr; Debate Tm; Drama Clb; English Clb; FCA; Library Aide; Natl Beta Clb; Natl FFA Org; Office Aide; Rgnl Wnnr HS Writer Litrary Awd; Northern OK Dist Music Cont Rtng Super; Family Cnslr.

NASH, DEMEKIA L; Sapulpa Sr HS; Sapulpa, OK; (3); Church Yth Grp; Drama Clb; Math Clb; Quiz Bowl; Science Clb; Chorus; Hon Roll; Spanish NHS; NAACP Club; Univ Of IA; Music Therapy.

NASH, KASANDRIA; Central HS; Tulsa, OK; (3); 12/192; Church Yth Grp; Cmnty Wkr; Dance Clb; French Clb; VP JA; Key Clb; Red Cross Aide; Science Clb; Teachers Aide; Chorus; Radiologist.

NASH, LAMARR D; Northeast HS; Oklahoma City, OK; (2); Band; Hon Roll; Bio Med Prgm; OSU; Engr.

NASH, RAUB E; Mc Loud HS; Mc Loud, OK; (2); FCA; FBLA; Scholastic Bowl; Rep Stu Cncl; Var Bsktbl; Var Socr.

NASHREDDINE, RANIA A; B T Washington HS; Tulsa, OK; (2); Debate Tm; French Clb; JA; NFL; Speech Tm; Orch; Rep Frsh Cls; Rep Soph Cls; NHS; Med.

NATH, BROOK D; Rush Springs HS; Rush Springs, OK; (2); Church Yth Grp; VP FCA; HOBY; Phtg Yrbk; Bsktbl; Gym; Score Keeper; Sftbl; Trk; Hon Roll; HOBY Ldrshp Awd; U Of OK; Soc.

NATION, SADENA R; Sapulpa Sr HS; Tulsa, OK; (3); Church Yth Grp; FCA; Key Clb; Chorus; Ofcr Jr Cls; Ofcr Sr Cls; Ofcr Stu Cncl; Sftbl; Hon Roll; Prfct Atten Awd; All ST Hnrs Choir 2 Yrs; Ed/Nrsng.

NATIONS, ELIZABETH; Ninnekah HS; Ninnekah, OK; (1); 1/48; Church Yth Grp; Rptr FHA; Girl Scts; Chorus; High Hon Roll; OK Hnr Soc; OK Bapt U; Soc Wrk.

NAUGHTON, AMY; U S Grant HS; Oklahoma City, OK; (4); 24/210; Church Yth Grp; Cmnty Wkr; Dance Clb; FCA; FBLA; FHA; Office Aide; Varsity Clb; Ofcr Stu Cncl; Chrldng; Vol Stu Tchng; 8 Yrs Gymnastics; U OK; Psych.

NAULT, LEIA M; Macarthur Sr HS; Lawton, OK; (3); Church Yth Grp; FHA; Church Choir; High Hon Roll; Hon Roll; Pensacola Chrstn Col.

NAUMANN, KIMBERLY D; Morris HS; Boynton, OK; (3); 12/71; Church Yth Grp; 4-H; FHA; Teachers Aide; Band; Mrchg Band; Pep Band; 4-H Awd; Hon Roll; NHS; I Dare You Awd; Trvlng Teen Music Grp; Ozark Chrstn Coll; Elem Tchr.

NAVA, CRYSTAL M; Walters HS; Walters, OK; (3); 1/50; Art Clb; Church Yth Grp; FCA; FHA; HOBY; Quiz Bowl; SADD; Chorus; School Musical; Yrbk; Hnr Choir All Reg; Dist St Music Cont Sups; Southern Nazarene U; Med.

NAVE, GARY B; Salina HS; Salina, OK; (2); 10/75; Math Tm; Quiz Bowl; Band; Drm Mjr(t); Jazz Band; Mrchg Band; Pep Band; Ofcr Bsbl; Wrstlng; High Hon Roll; Northeastern ST Univ; Radiolgy.

NAYERI, DINA; Edmond North HS; Edmond, OK; (3); #1 in class; Art Clb; Cmnty Wkr; French Clb; Key Clb; Treas Letterman Clb; Red Cross Aide; NHS; SADD; Sftbl; Hon Roll; Tutoring Svc Fndr/Pres; Taekwondo Trnmnt Winner; Christians On Campus Treas/Crrspndnt; Harvard; Intnl Corp Lawyer.

NAYLOR, ERIN; Union Intermediate HS; Tulsa, OK; (2); FCA; Office Aide; Chorus; School Musical; Pres Stu Cncl; Capt Chrldng; Hon Roll; NHS; Redskin In Review 95; Stu Mont 96; Ms Redskin Crt 95 96; OK U; Sec Ed.

NAYLOR, MARK I; South Intermediate HS; Broken Arrow, OK; (1); Church Yth Grp; Intrml Bsktbl; Intrml Ftbl; JV Trk; Var Cit Awd; U Of AR; Sprts Psych.

NAYLOR, NICHOLE; Grace Chrn Acad; Oklahoma City, OK; (3); 1/26; Church Yth Grp; Office Aide; Teachers Aide; Ofcr Soph Cls; Pres Jr Cls; Var Capt Bsktbl; Var Capt Vllybl; High Hon Roll; Val; Piano; Medicine.

NEAL, AMY; Midwest City HS; Midwest City, OK; (4); 29/419; Church Yth Grp; Cmnty Wkr; Drama Clb; FCA; Key Clb; Office Aide; Speech Tm; Acpl Chr; Swing Chorus; High Hon Roll; U Of Cntrl OK; Tchr.

NEAL, ASHLEY; Shawnee Sr HS; Shawnee, OK; (3); 9/280; Church Yth Grp; Cmnty Wkr; FCA; Spanish Clb; Drill Tm; Rptr Soph Cls; Rptr Jr Cls; Chrldng; Crs Cntry; Pom Pon; Tri-Hi-Y; Spirit Brigade; Big Bros/Big Sistrs; Dance 13 Yrs, Tchr.

NEAL, CASI; Quapaw Sr HS; Quapaw, OK; (3); 8/40; Church Yth Grp; FCA; 4-H; GAA; HOBY; Letterman Clb; Natl FFA Org; Pep Clb; Quiz Bowl; Teachers Aide; NEO A&M JC.

NEAL, JULIE F; Caney Jr Sr HS; Drew, MS; (2); Church Yth Grp; GAA; Speech Tm; Cit Awd; Hon Roll; Bst Schl Spirit; Mst Gnrs; Tchr Asst; Moorhead; Child Dvlpmnt.

NEAL, KENDRICK; Northwest Classen HS; Oklahoma City, OK; (4); Church Yth Grp; Computer Clb; FBLA; HOBY; Letterman Clb; Pep Clb; Spanish Clb; Varsity Clb; Acpl Chr; Band; DST Outstndng Gntlmn Awd; OK ST U.

NEAL, MELISSA; Eufaula Sr HS; Eufaula, OK; (2); Church Yth Grp; Band; Mrchg Band; Rep Stu Cncl; Jr NHS; Pres Acad Fit Awd; All Dist Band; Band Dirs Assn Hnr Band.

NEAL, STEVE D; Wilson Schl; Henryetta, OK; (4); FHA; Pres Natl FFA Org; Yrbk; Pres Frsh Cls; VP Jr Cls; Pres Sr Cls; Hon Roll.

NEAL, TED; Wilson Schl; Henryetta, OK; (3); FBLA; Natl FFA Org; Yrbk; Hon Roll; Val.

NEAL, TROY M; Putnam City North HS; Oklahoma City, OK; (2); 19/445; Church Yth Grp; Church Choir; JV Var Bsktbl; Dance Clb; Hon Roll; NHS; Siloam Lodge Stu Of Today Awd; Anatomy & Physiology Awd High Achvt.

NEASBY, MORGAN B; Bixby Sr HS; Bixby, OK; (1); Church Yth Grp; Debate Tm; FCA; Natl FFA Org; Quiz Bowl; Science Clb; Spanish Clb; Variety Show; Rep Yrbk; JV Sftbl; CUNY Brooklyn; Archaelogy.

NEATHERY, CHAD L; El Reno Sr HS; El Reno, OK; (1); Church Yth Grp; Drama Clb; FCA; Chorus; Church Choir; School Play; Rep Stu Cncl; Hon Roll; Stu Of Month; Etta Dale Jr High Hnr Soc; Ldrs Of Tomorrow.

NEDBALEK, NANCY; Midwest City HS; Midwest City, OK; (3); 69/387; Am Leg Aux Girls St; Drama Clb; German Clb; Hosp Aide; JA; SADD; Nwsp; Ofcr Stu Cncl; Hon Roll; Pres Acad Fit Awd; Univ Of OK; Dermatologist.

NEEDHAM, BILLY; Quinton Jr Sr HS; Quinton, OK; (4); 10/33; Boy Scts; Church Yth Grp; FCA; 4-H; FHA; Teachers Aide; Band; Mrchg Band; Var Bsbl; Var Bsktbl; Eastern OK ST Coll; Educ.

NEEDHAM, DUSTIN; Quinton Jr Sr HS; Quinton, OK; (4); 4/36; Office Aide; Teachers Aide; Ofcr Stu Cncl; Var Bsktbl; Var Ftbl; Hon Roll; Bacone Muskogee; Radiology.

NEEDHAM, PAULA; Perry Sr HS; Perry, OK; (2); FCA; GAA; JV Bsktbl; Var Powder Puff Ftbl; Var Sftbl; Var Trk; Cit Awd; Hon Roll; Jr NHS; NHS; U OK; Tchr.

NEEL, LARA; B T Washington HS; Tulsa, OK; (3); Debate Tm; Drama Clb; Speech Tm; School Play; Phtg Rptr Lit Mag; Swmmng; Hon Roll; Jr NHS; Ntl Merit Ltr; Intnl Bacclrt Degree Candidate; 96 Qaurtz Mountain Summer Pgm Photo; Duke U TIP Stu; Japanese Clb.

NEEL, LISA; Union Sr HS; Broken Arrow, OK; (4); 114/629; Am Leg Aux Girls St; Rep FCA; Pres VP Intnl Clb; Key Clb; Spanish Clb; Ofcr Stu Cncl; Bsktbl; Powder Puff Ftbl; Trk; NHS; Ftbl Trnr Co Capt; Renaissance; TARS; Med.

NEEL, LISA; B T Washington HS; Tulsa, OK; (3); Cmnty Wkr; Drama Clb; Speech Tm; School Musical; School Play; High Hon Roll; NHS; Ntl Merit Ltr; NFL; Service Clb; Native Amer People Sec; Japanese Clb; IB Diploma Candidate; Intnl Baccalaureate; Duke U TIP Partcpnt.

NEELAND, KENT; Hennessey HS; Bison, OK; (4); 2/54; Natl FFA Org; Rptr Nwsp; Yrbk; Treas Soph Cls; Rptr Stu Cncl; Var Ftbl; DAR Awd; NHS; OK ST U; Brdcstng.

NEELD, JESSIE; U S Grant HS; Oklahoma City, OK; (2); Stage Crew; JV Var Chrldng; JV Gym; JV Sftbl; High Hon Roll; Hon Roll; Pres Acad Fit Awd; Pres Schlr; OK Univ; Tchr; Prof.

NEELY, RYAN; Claremore Sr HS; Claremore, OK; (3); Spanish Clb; Golf; High Hon Roll; NHS; OK St Univ; Bus.

NEELY, TARA; Coleman Schl; Coleman, OK; (2); 2/10; FCA; 4-H; Sec Frsh Cls; Pres Soph Cls; Var Bsktbl; Var Sftbl; Southeastern ST Univ; Aviation.

NEEMAN, COURTNEY BROOKLYN; Metro Christian Acad; Tulsa, OK; (4); Church Yth Grp; Cmnty Wkr; Drama Clb; Key Clb; School Musical; School Play; Rep Stu Cncl; JV Var Chrldng; Var Socr; Hon Roll; U Of AR.

NEER, JILL; Sallisaw HS; Sallisaw, OK; (4); 33/134; Am Leg Aux Girls St; Art Clb; Church Yth Grp; Cmnty Wkr; FCA; FHA; Math Clb; Office Aide; Pep Clb; Science Clb; Connors ST Coll; Ed.

NEFF, JOY R; Blair Schl; Martha, OK; (3); Natl FFA Org; JV Var Gym; Hon Roll; Gymnastics Ltrs; Southwestern OK ST Univ; RN.

NEFF, JUSTIN M; Union Intermediate HS; Tulsa, OK; (1); Church Yth Grp; Spanish Clb; Band; Mrchg Band; High Hon Roll; Jr NHS; Acad Tm; Outstdng Span/Math/ARC Stdnt; All Dist Symphonic Band 2 Yrs; Pediatrcn.

NEFF, MIRANDA B; Nathan Hale HS; Tulsa, OK; (1); Church Yth Grp; Thesps; High Hon Roll; Hon Roll; Intl Music Camp Schl Of Fine Arts; Oxford; Psych/Art.

NEGELEIN, NICHOLAS; Claremore Sr HS; Claremore, OK; (4); Scholastic Bowl; Band; Ntl Merit SF; Role Playing & Comp Games; OSU; Elec Engr.

NEILL, ROBYN A; Seminole Jr Sr HS; Seminole, OK; (3); 19/91; Am Leg Aux Girls St; Church Yth Grp; FCA; GAA; Math Clb; Spanish Clb; Yrbk; Bsktbl; Golf; Tennis; Univ Of OK; Derm.

NELDON, JOSHUA D; Tahlequah Jr HS; Tahlequah, OK; (1); Boy Scts; Church Yth Grp; Scholastic Bowl; Band; Mrchg Band; Pep Band; Gov Hon Prg Awd; High Hon Roll; Jr NHS; Pres Acad Fit Awd; Duke TIP; Prof Mentor Pgm; Coll Level Tchng.

NELON, STEWART B; Midwest City HS; Midwest City, OK; (3); French Clb; Band; Chorus; Mrchg Band; Ofcr Bsbl; Ftbl; Score Keeper; WA; Musical Instr Or Tchr.

NELSON, ANGELA G; Broken Arrow Sr HS; Broken Arrow, OK; (3); Church Yth Grp; Cmnty Wkr; French Clb; Girl Scts; Pep Clb; Red Cross Aide; Church Choir; Hon Roll; Interned At Local NBC News Station; Comm Work For Chrch.

NELSON, BRANDI; Jenks HS; Jenks, OK; (1); Cmnty Wkr; Office Aide; Pep Clb; ROTC; Teachers Aide; Color Guard; Drill Tm; Rep Frsh Cls; Hon Roll; Amer Coed Pageants OK ST Hostess; Modeling Schlsp; Speed Skating Medals; OSU; Asthma Dr.

NELSON, BRIAN A; Hugo HS; Hugo, OK; (2); Service Clb; Spanish Clb; Ofcr Stu Cncl; JV Bsktbl; Var Tennis; Hon Roll; OK Univ; Cmptr Engr.

NELSON, BRIAN S; Westmoore HS; Oklahoma City, OK; (3); 3/615; Am Leg Boys St; VP Key Clb; Red Cross Aide; Scholastic Bowl; Spanish Clb; School Musical; VP NHS; Church Yth Grp; Chorus; Jr NHS; Prtcptd Univ Of OK Hlth Scis Ctr/Geoscis Summer Acads; Acad Club Treas; Pedtrcn.

NELSON, CONRAD I; Washington HS; Purcell, OK; (1); Scholastic Bowl; Jazz Band; Pep Band; Bsktbl; Hon Roll; Jr NHS.

NELSON, CRAIG S; Vanoss Schl; Ada, OK; (3); Church Yth Grp; Natl FFA Org; Ofcr Bsbl; Bsktbl; Trk; Hon Roll.

NELSON, CRYSTAL; Hennessey HS; Hennessey, OK; (3); Church Yth Grp; Sec FCA; Capt Sec FHA; Teachers Aide; Sec Pres Stu Cncl; Bsktbl; Chrldng; Score Keeper; Hon Roll.

NELSON, DUSTY L; Cando HS; Cando, ND; (1); Dance Clb; GAA; Natl FFA Org; Band; Mrchg Band; Pep Band; JV Bsktbl; Var Trk; Stat JV Vllybl; Hon Roll; Ballet/Tap/Jazz/Pointe Dancing; Modeling; Letter Winner Track/Vlybl.

NELSON, ERIC T; Owasso Sr HS; Owasso, OK; (2); 2/400; French Clb; Band; Mrchg Band; Cit Awd; High Hon Roll; NHS; Prfct Atten Awd; All Region Band 2 Yrs; 1st Band U Of AR Band Camp 2 Yrs.

NELSON, JAMES E; Union Sr HS; Broken Arrow, OK; (3); 44/750; Pres FBLA; Key Clb; Spanish Clb; Pres Nwsp; Rep Stu Cncl; Var Bsbl; Hon Roll; NHS; Spanish NHS; OK Assn Stu Cncl Pres.

NELSON, JASON J; Macarthur Sr HS; Junction City, KS; (3); Art Clb; German Clb; Band; Hon Roll.

NELSON, JEANIE L; Stratford Schl; Stratford, OK; (1); Natl FFA Org; FFA Star Grnhnd/Sm Anml Care Prfcncy Awd; OK ST Univ; Vet.

NELSON, KATIE; Southwest Covenant Schl; Yukon, OK; (2); Church Yth Grp; FCA; Ed Yrbk; Rep Frsh Cls; Var L Bsktbl; Var L Vllybl; High Hon Roll.

NELSON, KEN; Woodward HS; Woodward, OK; (3); Art Clb; Boy Scts; Hosp Aide; Letterman Clb; Red Cross Aide; Nwsp; Golf; High Hon Roll; Hon Roll; NHS.

NELSON, KRISTI B; Del City HS; Del City, OK; (3); DECA; FBLA; Office Aide; Tennis; NHS; OK Bapt Univ; Bus.

NELSON, LESLIE R; Locust Grove HS; Locust Grove, OK; (2); FBLA; German Clb; Band; Color Guard; Jazz Band; Mrchg Band; Pep Band; Hon Roll; Phy Therapy.

NELSON, RICKY J; Ponca City Sr HS; Ponca City, OK; (4); 164/338; German Clb; SADD; Hon Roll; Geometry Awd; Indstrl Ed Awd; OK ST Univ; Arch/Engr.

NELSON, SANDY; Idabel HS; Idabel, OK; (1); #14 in class; Church Yth Grp; Dance Clb; Chorus; Church Choir; Stage Crew; Yrbk; Capt Chrldng; Hon Roll; Jr NHS.

NELSON, TRISTA; Tuttle HS; Tuttle, OK; (1); VP FHA; Quiz Bowl; SADD; High Hon Roll; Tms Plcd 4th ST; Scubadvng; Explrs/Act Dir.

NEMECEK, HEATHER D; Byng Sr HS; Ada, OK; (2); 5/115; Church Yth Grp; FBLA; Natl Beta Clb; VP Frsh Cls; VP Soph Cls; Hist Rep Stu Cncl; JV Bsktbl; Hon Roll; NHS; East Cntrl Univ; Elem Ed.

NENNO, VICTORIA CHARLENA; Moore HS; Moore, OK; (4); 8/505; Am Leg Aux Girls St; JCL; Science Clb; Chorus; Ofcr Stu Cncl; Bsktbl; Mgr(s); Jr NHS; NHS; Val; OK St House Of Reps & Snt Ctatns; Med.

NERIO, CHRISTOPHER J; B T Washington HS; Tulsa, OK; (4); Boy Scts; Rep Church Yth Grp; ROTC; Spanish Clb; Church Choir; Hon Roll; NHS; School Play; Stage Crew; Prfct Atten Awd; Eagle Scout Order Of The Arrow; Anytown; LIT-ELEM Children Chrch Summer Pgms; OK ST U.

NERREN, NICK J; Charles Page HS; Sand Springs, OK; (3); 1/365; Church Yth Grp; Math Clb; Band; Chorus; Church Choir; Jazz Band; Mrchg Band; School Musical; High Hon Roll; NHS; Pipe Organ; OK; Engrng.

NESBITT, JOHNNETTA D; Northeast HS; Oklahoma City, OK; (3); 1/107; Church Yth Grp; French Clb; Pres Science Clb; Chorus; Church Choir; Cit Awd; High Hon Roll; Hon Roll; Jr NHS; OK ST Univ; Chem Engr.

NESMITH, AMANDA; Battiest Jr Sr HS; Bethel, OK; (4); 4/30; Drama Clb; FHA; German Clb; GAA; HOBY; Office Aide; Quiz Bowl; Scholastic Bowl; SADD; Ed Nwsp; Carl Albert ST Coll; Vet.

NESTER, MELISSA D; Checotah HS; Checotah, OK; (4); Drama Clb; Pep Clb; Treas Spanish Clb; Speech Tm; SADD; Teachers Aide; Color Guard; Ed Nwsp; Sftbl; Hon Roll; ST Wnnr OIPA ST Fnls 3rd Dtrs; OU; Jrnlsm.

NESTOR, JAIMIE; Jones HS; Jones, OK; (4); 4/60; FCA; Key Clb; Band; Treas Sr Cls; Bsktbl; Chrldng; Powder Puff Ftbl; Sftbl; Hon Roll; NHS; Redlands CC; Bus.

NESTOR, MELISSA E; Catoosa HS; Tulsa, OK; (2); 1/200; French Clb; HOBY; Quiz Bowl; Band; Mrchg Band; High Hon Roll; NHS; Scientific Resrch.

NETHERLAIN, SHANA; Keota Schl; Keota, OK; (4); 9/36; Teachers Aide; Band; Drm Mjr(t); Mrchg Band; Rptr Nwsp; Yrbk; Hon Roll; Pep Band; High Hon Roll; Outs Achv In Calc, Engl IV, Acctng; Acctng.

NEUGEBAUER, KEITH; Indiahoma Schl; Indiahoma, OK; (4); 1/14; HOBY; Natl FFA Org; Pres Stu Cncl; L Bsbl; L Bsktbl; Hon Roll; NHS; Val; Church Yth Grp; Acad Team Capt; Cameron U; Ag.

NEUGIN, AMANDA; Tahlequah Sr HS; Tahlequah, OK; (4); Church Yth Grp; DECA; FHA; Pep Clb; Rep Stu Cncl; JV Bsktbl; Hon Roll; Jr NHS; NHS; Prfct Atten Awd; Northeastern ST U; Bus Admin.

NEUHARTH, JENNIFER; Poteau HS; Poteau, OK; (3); 1/147; Band; Color Guard; Flag Corp; Mrchg Band; High Hon Roll; Hon Roll; NHS; Pre-Med.

NEUJAHR, TAMMY; Union City Schl; El Reno, OK; (4); 6/23; VP Art Clb; Pres Math Clb; Pres Science Clb; Teachers Aide; Sec Yrbk; VP Soph Cls; Pres Jr Cls; Sec Sr Cls; VP Stu Cncl; High Hon Roll; OK City U; Acctnt.

NEUMEYER, LEAH; Midway HS; Council Hill, OK; (4); 2/13; Church Yth Grp; Co-Capt FCA; Pres 4-H; Capt GAA; Pres Natl FFA Org; Office Aide; Teachers Aide; Church Choir; Ed Nwsp; Ed Yrbk; Connors ST Coll; Ag; Nrsng.

NEUSCHAFER, MICHAEL P; Bartlesville Sr HS; Bartlesville, OK; (3); 41/449; Church Yth Grp; German Clb; Chorus; Socr; High Hon Roll; Hon Roll; Jr NHS; NHS; Eng.

NEVILLE, KATIE; Heritage Hall Schl; Oklahoma City, OK; (3); Church Yth Grp; Cmnty Wkr; Treas French Clb; Letterman Clb; Math Clb; Mu Alpha Theta; Pep Clb; Sftbl; French Hon Soc; High Hon Roll; Math/Cmptrs.

NEVIN, HELEN H; Choctaw HS; Midwest City, OK; (3); Church Yth Grp; Band; Mrchg Band; Trk; Hon Roll.

NEVIUS, MEGAN E; Edmond Memorial HS; Edmond, OK; (4); 41/322; Church Yth Grp; Cmnty Wkr; FCA; Office Aide; Pep Clb; Spanish Clb; SADD; Mgr(s); High Hon Roll; NHS; Abilene Chrstn Univ.

NEW, JULIE C; Moore HS; Moore, OK; (4); 40/600; Church Yth Grp; Treas Acpl Chr; Church Choir; School Musical; JV Var Bsktbl; Var Vllybl; NHS; Val; UCP Gift Wrap 95; Superior Rtng For Voice Solo UCO/DUET/SOLO Dist Solo/Ensmble 96; Chem.

NEWBERRY, BRANDON; Hilldale HS; Muskogee, OK; (1); Church Yth Grp; Computer Clb; Math Clb; Science Clb; SADD; JV Bsbl; JV Bsktbl; High Hon Roll; Hon Roll; OK Bapt U; Smnry.

NEWBERRY, JOSHUA; Westmoore HS; Moore, OK; (1); Church Yth Grp; Key Clb; Acpl Chr; Band; Church Choir; Jazz Band; Mrchg Band; Trk; Musicianship Awd; OK City Univ; Music.

NEWBERRY, RICHARD; Midwest City HS; Midwest City, OK; (2); Math Tm; Spanish Clb; Teachers Aide; School Play; JV Bsbl; Hon Roll; Jr NHS; NHS.

NEWBY, BEN E; Bartlesville Sr HS; Bartlesville, OK; (2); 97/468; Church Yth Grp; Tennis; Var L Wrstlng; Hon Roll; Jr NHS; Multi-Yr Listee.

NEWBY, JEFF; Laverne Jr Sr HS; Gate, OK; (3); 5/35; Church Yth Grp; Letterman Clb; Var Bsbl; Var Bsktbl; Hon Roll; NHS; Sprts Med.

NEWBY, LORRI; Chandler HS; Meeker, OK; (3); #1 in class; Church Yth Grp; Girl Scts; Spanish Clb; Band; Church Choir; Rep Stu Cncl; JV Var Bsktbl; Var Trk; High Hon Roll; NHS; Amer Lgn Cert Schl Awd.

NEWBY, STEPHANIE; Putnam City North HS; Oklahoma City, OK; (4); 163/436; Art Clb; Cmnty Wkr; Dance Clb; Rptr Key Clb; Spanish Clb; Cit Awd; Hon Roll; Jr NHS; NHS; Fshries Bio Mntrshp Pgm; OSU Acad/Fnd Schlsps; Hrsmnshp; OK Prks/Rec Vol; OK ST Univ; Sci Rsrch.

NEWCOMB, ALYSSA; Afton HS; Afton, OK; (2); FCA; Natl FFA Org; Bsktbl; Chrldng; Sftbl; Hon Roll; Pres Acad Fit Awd.

NEWCOMB, BRENT; Clinton HS; Clinton, OK; (3); 1/120; Church Yth Grp; Chorus; Church Choir; Swing Chorus; Socr; Hon Roll; NHS; SW OK ST U; Vet.

NEWCOMB, LASHAUN; Tomlinson Jr HS; Lawton, OK; (1); Hon Roll; Jr NHS; Prfct Atten Awd; Doctor.

NEWCOMB, SHEILA; Westmoore HS; Oklahoma City, OK; (3); 42/680; Church Yth Grp; Drama Clb; French Clb; Church Choir; School Musical; School Play; Stage Crew; Variety Show; Trk; Hon Roll; Acad Excl In Advanced Acting; 4.0 Gpa Awd; Pre-Med; Drama.

NEWELL, DANIEL D; Roland Sr HS; Muldrow, OK; (3); 36/105; Church Yth Grp; Teachers Aide; Band; Church Choir; Mrchg Band; Orch; Pep Band; Hon Roll; Prfct Atten Awd; Westark Ft Smith.

NEWELL, KEISTA L; Woodward HS; Woodward, OK; (3); Hist Art Clb; Cmnty Wkr; FCA; Pep Clb; Chorus; School Musical; Rep Jr Cls; Rep Stu Cncl; Bsktbl; Powder Puff Ftbl; Jr Cls Favorite; RE DINKS; Cntry Music Singer.

NEWELL, LANTZ; Broken Arrow Sr HS; Broken Arrow, OK; (4); 108/921; Intrml Bsktbl; Intrml JV Ftbl; Intrml JV Trk; Intrml JV Wt Lftg; NHS; U Of OK; Mech Engrng.

NEWELL, SETH W; Skiatook HS; Skiatook, OK; (2); 13/140; FBLA; Varsity Clb; Band; Mrchg Band; Orch; Var L Socr; Cit Awd; High Hon Roll; NHS; OK Bus Educ Stu Awd; NSU; Sccr Coach.

NEWHOUSE, JOE; Broken Arrow Sr HS; Broken Arrow, OK; (4); 6/973; Am Leg Boys St; Cmnty Wkr; Intnl Clb; VP Jr Cls; Ofcr Stu Cncl; JV Bsktbl; Crs Cntry; High Hon Roll; NHS; Pres Acad Fit Awd; Rep Freedoms Fnd Vly Forge Ldrshp Conf; Jr Stu Mnth; Intl Bus.

NEWHOUSE, SARAH; North Intemediate HS; Broken Arrow, OK; (1); Latin Clb; Vllybl; Media Aide; Helping Hands Vol; Duke; Med.

NEWKIRK, NOLAN; Miami Sr HS; Miami, OK; (4); Am Leg Boys St; VP Art Clb; Church Yth Grp; Golf; Hon Roll; NHS; OSU; Physics.

NEWMAN, JACKIE M; Wetumka Jr Sr HS; Wetumka, OK; (2); FHA; GAA; Key Clb; Sftbl; Hon Roll; Kiwanis Awd; U Of FL; Marine Bio.

NEWMAN II, JAMES R; Putnam City HS; Oklahoma City, OK; (4); Cmnty Wkr; Debate Tm; Letterman Clb; Library Aide; NFL; Quiz Bowl; Scholastic Bowl; Science Clb; Spanish Clb; Speech Tm; Pres PC Debate; U Of AR; Eng.

NEWMAN, MATTHEW B; North Intemediate HS; Broken Arrow, OK; (2); 10/1000; French Clb; Band; Mrchg Band; Pep Band; Rep Stu Cncl; Hon Roll; Jr NHS; Arch.

NEWMAN, MICHAEL A; Ponca City Sr HS; Ponca City, OK; (3); Am Leg Boys St; Boy Scts; Yrbk; Crs Cntry; Golf; Trk; High Hon Roll; NHS; Ntl Merit SF; Frndshp Frst; Phtgrphy; Mtnrng; Anthrplgy/Med.

NEWMAN, PATRICK B; Collinsville HS; Collinsville, OK; (2); Church Yth Grp; Drama Clb; Acpl Chr; Chorus; Church Choir; School Musical; School Play; Phtg Yrbk; Treas Soph Cls; Hon Roll; All-Siar Hne Choir; Superior Vocal Ratings; Mission Trip; Southern Nazarene U; Choir Dir.

NEWMAN, SAMANTHA; Lawton Sr HS; Fort Sill, OK; (2); Church Yth Grp; Key Clb; Pep Clb; ROTC; VP Spanish Clb; Chorus; Color Guard; Drill Tm; School Musical; Cadet Of Mnth ROTC; Citation Awd Optimist Club; OH Wesleyan; RN.

NEWMAN, TONI S; Putnam City West HS; Bethany, OK; (3); 112/300; Church Yth Grp; Ofcr FCA; Teachers Aide; Band; JV Capt Bsktbl; Var Stat Golf; JV Var Sftbl; 9th Grd Ofnsv Plyr Of Yr; Dog Trng; Bsktbl Cmp Cnslr; Vet Med/PT.

NEWNAM, TERA S; Preston Schl; Okmulgee, OK; (1); Church Yth Grp; 4-H; Chorus; Var Bsktbl; Var Sftbl; Var Trk; Hon Roll; Prfct Atten Awd; 4 Yr Coll.

NEWSOM, HAYLEY B; Edmond Memorial HS; Edmond, OK; (3); 1/400; Art Clb; Church Yth Grp; Key Clb; Spanish Clb; Band; Color Guard; NHS; Pres Acad Fit Awd; Yth Impressions St Wide Art Show Excl Awd; OK City Univ Art Show Display; OK Hnr Soc; Graphic Arts; Illustration.

NEWTON, FELICIA; Lawton Sr HS; Lawton, OK; (2); Drama Clb; Key Clb; School Play; Stage Crew; Trk; Hon Roll; Spch Thpy.

NEWTON, JAMIE; Eufaula Sr HS; Eufaula, OK; (3); 15/90; Science Clb; Hon Roll; NHS; Bacone Coll; Radiology.

NEWTON, JEANESSA M; Catoosa HS; Catoosa, OK; (4); 12/136; Pres FCA; VP Spanish Clb; Chorus; Ed Yrbk; Pres Soph Cls; Sec Jr Cls; Sec Sr Cls; Ofcr Stu Cncl; Var Chrldng; Treas NHS; 4a St Acad Chmpn Crs Cntry; Mst Tlntd Sr Cls; Hmcmng Ftbl & Bsktbnl Qn; 13 Yr Clb; Ms Will Rogers; OK ST U; Vet.

NEWTON, JENNIFER; Woodward HS; Woodward, OK; (1); Church Yth Grp; Debate Tm; FCA; French Clb; Hosp Aide; Letterman Clb; Pep Clb; Red Cross Aide; Chorus; School Play; Re-Dinks.

NEWTON, JOHN W; Salina HS; Salina, OK; (1); Cmnty Wkr; 4-H; Natl FFA Org; Variety Show; Bsktbl; Wt Lftg; Wrstlng; 4-H Awd; High Hon Roll; Hon Roll; HS Rodeo Bull Rdng; FFA Shwng Sheep/Lvstck Jdgng; Wldng/Farm Mgmnt; NEO; Rnchr/Lvstck Mgmt/Blrdng.

NEWTON, MELANIE O; Edmond North HS; Edmond, OK; (1); Cmnty Wkr; Chorus; Socr; Vllybl; Calligraphy On Schl Awds; Dist, St Vocal Solo Conts Super Rating; OK Univ; Tchng; Interior Dsgn.

NEWTON, RACHAEL; Cherokee Jr Sr HS; Cherokee, OK; (3); 1/32; Church Yth Grp; 4-H; HOBY; Speech Tm; Treas Jr Cls; Var Bsktbl; Cit Awd; 4-H Awd; Hon Roll; Val; Natl Sfty Cncl Awd Hnr & AOAS Green Crss Wnnr; Spch/Debate All St 94-95; St 4-H Hlth Awd Wnnr 95; OBU; Child Psycht.

NEWTON, SARAH K; Putnam City West HS; Oklahoma City, OK; (1); Tumbling; Russian; Rdng; Cooking.

NGHIEM, HELEN M; Stillwater Sr HS; Stillwater, OK; (4); Key Clb; Science Clb; VP Spanish Clb; Ed Nwsp; Yrbk; Rep Stu Cncl; JV Var Tennis; Hon Roll; Natl Schol Wrtng Awd; Stillwater HS Vsty Schol Awd; OK St Univ.

NGO, SAM C; Westmore HS; Oklahoma City, OK; (4); 35/610; Church Yth Grp; Cmnty Wkr; French Clb; Math Tm; Scholastic Bowl; Science Clb; Teachers Aide; Bsktbl; Tennis; Cit Awd; OK Delegate Sandia Labs HS Hnrs Rsrch Prgm; OK ST Sci/Engrg Fair 1st Pl; NSF Yng Schlrs Prgm; OK ST Univ; Chem.

NGO, TRIEN; Nathan Hale HS; Tulsa, OK; (4); Church Yth Grp; Varsity Clb; Ofcr Stu Cncl; Crs Cntry; Socr; High Hon Roll; Hon Roll; NHS; Tulsa Jr Coll; Elec Engrng.

NGUYEN, AMY; Perry Sr HS; Perry, OK; (2); FBLA; FHA; Band; Mrchg Band; Pep Band; Hon Roll; OK U; Photo.

NGUYEN, AMY; Moore HS; Moore, OK; (3); 37/666; Cmnty Wkr; French Clb; Intnl Clb; Letterman Clb; Science Clb; Varsity Clb; L Mgr(s); L Tennis; Hon Roll; Treas NHS; Moore For Christmas Vol; OU.

NGUYEN, ANGIE K; Putnam City North HS; Oklahoma City, OK; (2); 2/488; French Clb; Sec Key Clb; Science Clb; SADD; Yrbk; Cit Awd; NHS; Mock Trial; Key Clubber Awd; Eastern Coll Sci Inst; Envir Sci Acad; Pre-Med.

NGUYEN, ANTHONY-QUYEN VIET; West Jr HS; Oklahoma City, OK; (1); Cmnty Wkr; French Clb; Scholastic Bowl; Rep Stu Cncl; Tennis; Hon Roll; Jr NHS; NHS; Prfct Atten Awd; Quiz Bowl; Art; Medicine.

NGUYEN, CATHY; Union Intermediate HS; Tulsa, OK; (2); Spanish Clb; Hon Roll; Prfct Atten Awd; Drug-Free Yth Clb; OK ST U; Comp Pgmng.

NGUYEN, CHRIS D; Westmoore HS; Oklahoma City, OK; (3); OK ST U; Comp Engr.

NGUYEN, DOROTHY; Union Intermediate HS; Tulsa, OK; (2); Church Yth Grp; French Clb; FBLA; Office Aide; Swmmng; Tennis; Hon Roll; Attnd Amer Coed Pageant.

NGUYEN, DZI T; Classen Schl Advance Studies; Oklahoma City, OK; (3); Church Yth Grp; Math Clb; Mu Alpha Theta; Band; Church Choir; Mrchg Band; Hon Roll; NHS; Spanish NHS; U Of OK; Comp Engrng.

NGUYEN, HONG V; East Central HS; Tulsa, OK; (4); 10/209; French Clb; NHS; Prin Hnr Roll 4 Yrs; Acad Awd 3 Yrs; Speak Fr, Eng & Vietnamese; U Of Tulsa; Pre-Med.

NGUYEN, JERRICA; Union Sr HS; Tulsa, OK; (3); Ofcr JA; Speech Tm; Temple Yth Grp; Orch; Rptr Nwsp; Phtg Yrbk; Hon Roll; Jr NHS; NHS; Pres Acad Fit Awd; Yth Crt Prsdng Jdg; Law Team; Vio Duet Cntst; Rcvd Exclnt Rtng ARC Gftd Stdnt Prgm; OK Univ; Intnl Mrktng.

NGUYEN, JIMMY; Mustang HS; Yukon, OK; (3); 1/450; French Clb; Hosp Aide; Math Clb; Scholastic Bowl; Science Clb; Church Choir; Var Tennis; High Hon Roll; Kiwanis Awd; NHS; Piano; OU; Bio.

NGUYEN, JUDY T; Westmoore HS; Oklahoma City, OK; (3); 109/615; Intnl Clb; Key Clb; Latin Clb; Spanish Clb; Hon Roll; Jr NHS; NHS; U Of TX; Med.

NGUYEN, KIM D; Union Intermediate HS; Broken Arrow, OK; (2); Church Yth Grp; Intnl Clb; Key Clb; Band; High Hon Roll; Jr NHS; NHS; Prfct Atten Awd; Pres Acad Fit Awd.

NGUYEN, KIM M; Northwest Classen HS; Oklahoma City, OK; (1); Chorus.

NGUYEN, KNANH BAO TRAN; Clinton HS; Clinton, OK; (2); Church Yth Grp; Computer Clb; Math Clb; Math Tm; Jr NHS; NHS; OSU; Elec Engr.

NGUYEN, KRISTY C; Union Sr HS; Tulsa, OK; (4); 31/629; Key Clb; Chorus; NHS; Acad Ltrs; Ntl Piano Playing Audition Awds; Candystriper; OK ST U; Comp Sci.

NGUYEN, LINDA; Midwest City HS; Midwest City, OK; (3); 92/380; Drama Clb; Scholastic Bowl; Chorus; School Musical; School Play; Variety Show; Lit Mag; Tennis; Hon Roll; Prfct Atten Awd; Several Solo Cmptn Awds Singng; Show Choir; Readng; Pediatrcs.

NGUYEN, LINDA T; Northeast HS; Oklahoma City, OK; (3); FBLA; Scholastic Bowl; High Hon Roll; NHS; Decathalon Team; OU; Pharmacist.

NGUYEN, LOAN M; John Marshall HS; Oklahoma City, OK; (4); 4/160; Computer Clb; 4-H; French Clb; FBLA; Letterman Clb; Teachers Aide; Varsity Clb; Var Tennis; 4-H Awd; High Hon Roll; OK U; Comp Sci.

NGUYEN, LUA T; Union Sr HS; Tulsa, OK; (4); 78/629; Church Yth Grp; French Clb; Church Choir; NHS; Intl Bus Mgmt.

NGUYEN, LYNN; Brink Jr HS; Oklahoma City, OK; (1); Church Yth Grp; Scholastic Bowl; Band; Color Guard; Jazz Band; Mrchg Band; Co-Ed Yrbk; Hon Roll; Jr NHS; Piano; El Rino & Sans Springs OK Music Cmptns Flute Super Ratings; OK Ctr Advncmt Of Sci & Tech Awd; Notre Dame; Law; Theology.

NGUYEN, MARY; Midwest City HS; Midwest City, OK; (2); 1/501; Pres Soph Cls; Pres Stu Cncl; Bsktbl; Ftbl; Sftbl; Hon Roll; Jr NHS; NHS; Straight A Clb; Med.

NGUYEN, MARY; Putnam City HS; Warr Acres, OK; (4); 6/345; Am Leg Aux Girls St; Church Yth Grp; Dance Clb; French Clb; Key Clb; Scholastic Bowl; Science Clb; Chorus; Variety Show; Rep Stu Cncl; Aerospce Engrng.

NGUYEN, MARY; Memorial HS; Tulsa, OK; (4); 55/250; Church Yth Grp; Cmnty Wkr; Intnl Clb; SADD; Chorus; Church Choir; Sec Sr Cls; Chrldng; High Hon Roll; Key Clb; Asst Tns Comm Svc Treas; Unity Through Dvrsty; U Of OK; Acctng.

NGUYEN, MICHAEL; Comanche HS; Comanche, OK; (4); 1/60; German Clb; Natl FFA Org; Quiz Bowl; Ofcr Jr Cls; Trk; Wt Lftg; Wrstlng; NHS; Val; OK ST U; Engrng.

NGUYEN, MICHAEL; Union Sr HS; Tulsa, OK; (4); 84/632; French Clb; NHS; U Of OK; PT/MUSICIAN.

NGUYEN, MINH K; Mustang HS; Yukon, OK; (3); French Clb; FBLA; Key Clb; Math Clb; Science Clb; SADD; Temple Yth Grp; Hon Roll; NHS; U Of OK; Optom.

NGUYEN, NGA THI; Westmoore HS; Oklahoma City, OK; (3); French Clb; Key Clb; Library Aide; Hist Rep Jr NHS; NHS; Pres Acad Fit Awd; Schltc Ltr; Asian Clb; Bus.

NGUYEN, PHUONG; Midwest City HS; Midwest City, OK; (2); 18/501; Church Yth Grp; French Clb; Quiz Bowl; Scholastic Bowl; Jr NHS.

NGUYEN, QUYNH N; Moore HS; Moore, OK; (3); 90/525; Church Yth Grp; JA; Office Aide; Spanish Clb; Yrbk; Rep Stu Cncl; Tennis; Trk; Hon Roll; Jr NHS; Piano; Mdlng; Univ Of OK; Jrnlsm Brdcstng.

NGUYEN, TAI T; Union Intermediate HS; Broken Arrow, OK; (2); Key Clb; Math Clb; Prfct Atten Awd; Yth Astronmy Clb.

NGUYEN, THANH-QUYEN; U S Grant HS; Oklahoma City, OK; (3); Hon Roll; NHS; Asian Clb; South CC.

NGUYEN, THAO; U S Grant HS; Oklahoma City, OK; (4); OK City Comm Coll; Nurse.

NGUYEN, THAO H; Union Intermediate HS; Tulsa, OK; (2); Library Aide; Spanish Clb; Temple Yth Grp; Tae Kwondo; Badmntn; TJC; Bus.

NGUYEN, THI; Westmoore HS; Oklahoma City, OK; (3); 23/615; Cmnty Wkr; FBLA; Key Clb; NHS; Schlstc Lttr; 4/Above GPA Awd; Asian Club; Bus.

NGUYEN, THUY; Broken Bow HS; Broken Bow, OK; (4); 1/150; FHA; Science Clb; Spanish Clb; Hon Roll; NHS; Prfct Atten Awd; Val; His Clb; Tns Nd Tns; Supt Stu Advy Cncl; OSU; Ed.

NGUYEN, TRAN T; Western Heights Sr HS; Oklahoma City, OK; (3); Dance Clb; FHA; Varsity Clb; Socr; Computer Clb; Office Aide; Pep Clb; Teachers Aide; Trk; Wt Lftg.

NGUYEN, TRANG C; Westmoore HS; Oklahoma City, OK; (2); Church Yth Grp; Cmnty Wkr; Computer Clb; Math Tm; Church Choir; Hon Roll; NHS; Schltc Team; Asian Clb; U Of OK; Pharmacist; Comp Prgmr.

NGUYEN, VINH; North Intermediate HS; Broken Arrow, OK; (2) Church Yth Grp; Science Clb; Trk; Wt Lftg; Hon Roll; OK ST Univ; Surgeon.

NGUYEN, VU D; Northeast HS; Oklahoma City, OK; (2); Art Clb; Drm Mjr(t); Yrbk; Ofcr Frsh Cls; Gym; Vllybl; Hon Roll.

NGUYEN, VU T; Memorial HS; Tulsa, OK; (3); Intnl Clb; VICA; Crs Cntry; Socr; Hon Roll; NHS.

NIBLETT, MILANN M; Davis HS; Davis, OK; (1); Rptr Drama Clb; 4-H; Var FBLA; Key Clb; Model UN; Rptr Natl FFA Org; Church Choir; Rptr Nwsp; 4-H Awd; High Hon Roll; ER Physcn.

NIBLOCK, LEXI L; Putnam City HS; Oklahoma City, OK; (4); 57/342; German Clb; Hosp Aide; Hist Pep Clb; Pres Band; Jazz Band; Co-Ed Yrbk; Sec Hist Stu Cncl; Cit Awd; NHS; Acad All ST Nom; Outstdng Clarinet Soloist Sand Sprgs Music Fstvl; Outstdng Yrbk Ldrshp Awd; Southwestern OK ST Univ; Vet.

NICAR, EMILY A; Union Intermediate HS; Tulsa, OK; (2); Church Yth Grp; Cmnty Wkr; Band; Hon Roll; NHS.

NICCUM, ERICA M; Colcord Schl; Colcord, OK; (3); Church Yth Grp; Pep Clb; Rptr Nwsp; Rep Jr Cls; Rep Stu Cncl; High Hon Roll; HS Schlrshp Pgm At John Brown U; John Brown U; Drama Evangelism.

NICCUM, ERIN M; Cushing HS; Cushing, OK; (4); 10/160; Church Yth Grp; FHA; Quiz Bowl; Spanish Clb; High Hon Roll; Hon Roll; NHS; OK ST Univ; Ed.

NICHOL, HEATHER N; Union Intermediate HS; Broken Arrow, OK; (2); 105/800; Church Yth Grp; FCA; French Clb; JV Var Bsktbl; Chrldng; Var Sftbl; High Hon Roll; Jr NHS; NHS.

NICHOL, MICHELLE; Union Sr HS; Broken Arrow, OK; (4); 261/669; Church Yth Grp; Cmnty Wkr; Drama Clb; FCA; Spanish Clb; Teachers Aide; Church Choir; Ofcr Jr Cls; Ofcr Sr Cls; Rep Stu Cncl; NCA Natl Champs Sqd 94-95, 1st Rnnr-Up Sqd 95-96; NCA All-Amer 95 & All-Regn 96 Chrldr; OK ST U; Sprts Brdcstng.

NICHOLAS, CINDY M; Tahlequah Sr HS; Tahlequah, OK; (3); 46/266; Church Yth Grp; German Clb; GAA; Science Clb; SADD; Chorus; Pres Yrbk; Rep Stu Cncl; Var Chrldng; Jr NHS; Northeastern ST Univ; Tchng.

NICHOLAS, CRYSTAL W; Union Intermediate HS; Tulsa, OK; (2); French Clb; Var Ftbl; Ice Hcky; Var Socr; High Hon Roll; Hon Roll; FCA; USA Hcky Assn; OK HS Hoky Var Goalie, Capt, Outstndng Goaltender Awd; TX Amatr Hcky Assn, All Star; Sprts Med.

NICHOLAS, TROY; Hugo HS; Hugo, OK; (3); Pres 4-H; Natl FFA Org; L Ftbl; Wt Lftg; 4-H Awd; NHS.

NICHOLS, ALISHA A; Hartshorne Sr HS; Wilburton, OK; (2); FHA; Natl FFA Org; Church Choir; Sftbl; Gftd & Tlntd Pgm Mem; EOSC; RN.

NICHOLS, ANITA C; John Marshall HS; Oklahoma City, OK; (3); 3/200; Cmnty Wkr; German Clb; Scholastic Bowl; Band; Mrchg Band; High Hon Roll; NHS; Acctng; Frgn Relations.

NICHOLS, BRAD; Enid Sr HS; Enid, OK; (2); 120/500; Am Leg Boys St; Cmnty Wkr; FCA; Teachers Aide; Ofcr Bsbl; Bsktbl; Ftbl; Hon Roll; Jr NHS; NHS; OK Hnr Roll Ftbl; Sports Med.

NICHOLS, BRANDY L; Heavener HS; Heavener, OK; (3); Pep Clb; Band; Color Guard; Drill Tm; Flag Corp; Mrchg Band; Var Trk; Carl Albert ST Coll; Acctnt.

NICHOLS, BRYAN A; Edmond Memorial HS; Edmond, OK; (4); Church Yth Grp; Cmnty Wkr; FCA; Office Aide; Spanish Clb; SADD; Teachers Aide; Rep Stu Cncl; Ofcr Bsbl; Ftbl; Pres Wood Sec Clb; Jr Rotarian; Northeastern ST U; Optometry.

NICHOLS, CASEY AARON; Oktaha Jr Sr HS; Oktaha, OK; (3); 2/45; Am Leg Boys St; FCA; Spanish Clb; SADD; VP Frsh Cls; VP Soph Cls; Var Bsbl; Var Bsktbl; High Hon Roll; NHS; U Of AR; Pre-Med.

NICHOLS, CORY G; Cashion HS; Cashion, OK; (3); 1/45; Am Leg Boys St; Church Yth Grp; FCA; FBLA; Scholastic Bowl; Band; Mrchg Band; Ofcr Stu Cncl; Ofcr Bsbl; Bsktbl; TSA.

NICHOLS, DIANE R; Wilson HS; Wilson, OK; (4); 11/46; FCA; 4-H; Natl Beta Clb; Band; Drm Mjr(t); Mrchg Band; Yrbk; Var Bsktbl; Var Sftbl; Hon Roll; E Cntrl Univ; Phy Therapy.

NICHOLS, JANICE; Coalgate HS; Coalgate, OK; (3); 9/55; Speech Tm; Teachers Aide; Band; Flag Corp; Mrchg Band; Variety Show; Hon Roll; Jr NHS; NHS; Chrch Bell Choir.

NICHOLS, JEREMY E; Geronimo Jr Sr HS; Geronimo, OK; (3); 1/12; Bsktbl; High Hon Roll; Hon Roll; NHS; Var Bsbl; FFA; OSU; Ag Tchr.

NICHOLS, JOE W; Clinton HS; Clinton, OK; (4); Debate Tm; FCA; Speech Tm; Teachers Aide; School Play; Variety Show; Ofcr Bsbl; Lawyer.

NICHOLS, JOSHUA P; Geronimo Jr Sr HS; Geronimo, OK; (2); 3/20; Ofcr Bsbl; Bsktbl; High Hon Roll; Hon Roll; NHS; FFA; Seminole; Sport Phys Therapy.

NICHOLS, KRISTY K; Colbert Jr Sr HS; Cartwright, OK; (3); 5/50; Church Yth Grp; FCA; Rptr Spanish Clb; Yrbk; Rep Stu Cncl; Hon Roll; NHS.

NICHOLS, MATT; Mustang HS; Mustang, OK; (3); Band; Color Guard; Jazz Band; Vllybl; Hon Roll; OK U; Med.

NICHOLS, NATALIE A; Bishop Kelley HS; Tulsa, OK; (3); Am Leg Aux Girls St; FCA; Spanish Clb; Rptr Nwsp; Yrbk; Rep Frsh Cls; Rep Jr Cls; Ofcr Stu Cncl; Var L Bsktbl; L Capt Vllybl; Nat Span Exam 3rd; Tulsa Phil Symp; Med.

NICHOLS, NICOLE L; Duncan HS; Duncan, OK; (3); Church Yth Grp; Letterman Clb; Office Aide; SADD; Chorus; Church Choir; Hon Roll; NHS; Poem Pub; OK ST Univ; Med.

NICHOLS, RENEE; Putnam City West HS; Oklahoma City, OK; (4); 40/285; Cmnty Wkr; Intnl Clb; Spanish Clb; Band; High Hon Roll; NHS; Prfct Atten Awd; Med Club/Phsiology Stdnt Of Yr; GATE; Dirs Awd Band; OSU; Pre-Med/Psych.

NICHOLS, RHONDA M; Putnam City West HS; Oklahoma City, OK; (3); 38/316; FCA; FBLA; Intnl Clb; SADD; Teachers Aide; Ed Nwsp; Rep Stu Cncl; Hon Roll; NHS; Medcl Clb; Chrstn In Action; 3-D; U Of OK; Advrtsng.

NICHOLS, RICHARD; Crescent Schl; Crescent, OK; (2); Hon Roll; Pres Acad Fit Awd.

NICHOLS JR, RICKIE G; Dale Sr HS; Dale, OK; (3); 17/55; Band; Jazz Band; Mrchg Band; Pep Band; Cit Awd; Prfct Atten Awd; 1st Pl Sci Fair; Cmptrs.

NICHOLS, SARAH D; Union Sr HS; Broken Arrow, OK; (3); 99/741; FBLA; Spanish Clb; Trk; Hon Roll; NHS; Prfct Atten Awd; Spanish NHS; Pntng; Piano; Principia.

NICHOLS, STEPHANIE B; Choctaw HS; Choctaw, OK; (3); Church Yth Grp; Quiz Bowl; Band; Color Guard; Flag Corp; Mrchg Band; Pep Band; School Musical; Hon Roll; OK Bapt U; Missionary.

NICHOLS, TAMI D; Mt St Marys HS; Oklahoma City, OK; (3); Church Yth Grp; Chorus; Church Choir; Treas Jr Cls; Treas Sr Cls; JV Vllybl; NHS; Rptr Nwsp; Yth Ldrshp Exch Cls I; Mt Evnglztn Tm/Ldrshp Bd; Cmp Fire Boys/Girls; OK Bapt Univ; Sec Math Educ.

NICHOLSON, JASON W; Marietta HS; Marietta, OK; (2); 4-H; Band; Mrchg Band; School Musical; Bsktbl; Hon Roll; NHS; Cmptr Sci.

NICHOLSON, TYLER; Westmoore HS; Oklahoma City, OK; (3); 10/615; Church Yth Grp; Scholastic Bowl; Church Choir; JV Bsbl; Jr NHS; NHS; OK Univ; Acctng.

NICHUS, BRADLEY S; Garber Sr HS; Enid, OK; (4); 1/33; Church Yth Grp; Natl FFA Org; Office Aide; Teachers Aide; Varsity Clb; School Play; Ofcr Bsbl; Bsktbl; Ftbl; Wt Lftg; OK ST U; Bus.

NICK, MICHAEL; Mc Alester HS; Mcalester, OK; (2); Spanish Clb; High Hon Roll; OK HS Hnr Soc; Outstdng Bio Stu; Outstdng Eng II Hnr Stu; OK ST U; Vet Medicine.

NICKEL, KIRK G; Stillwater Sr HS; Stillwater, OK; (2); 1/375; Church Yth Grp; FCA; Mu Alpha Theta; Natl Beta Clb; Quiz Bowl; JV Bsbl; Hon Roll; Bus Schl.

NICKEL, STACIE R; Afton HS; Afton, OK; (3); Church Yth Grp; Library Aide; Spanish Clb; Teachers Aide; Chorus; JV Chrldng; Hon Roll; Socl Wrk.

NICKELL, JOEY D; Moore HS; Moore, OK; (3); Boy Scts; Band; Ftbl; Wt Lftg; Wrstlng.

NICKELL, JOSEPH D; Moore HS; Moore, OK; (3); Boy Scts; Band; Ftbl; Wt Lftg; Wrstlng.

NICKELS, ANGELA R; Sharon Mutual Jr Sr HS; Sharon, OK; (4); 1/21; Cmnty Wkr; Pres Rptr 4-H; Sec Treas FHA; Office Aide; VP Frsh Cls; VP Soph Cls; VP Jr Cls; Rep Stu Cncl; Cit Awd; DAR Awd; Woodward Co Safety Coaltn; Safe Kids Projwrkr; U Of OK; Phys Thrpy.

NICKESON, ERICA; Fargo Schl; Fargo, OK; (4); 5/22; VP Church Yth Grp; FCA; 4-H; VP FHA; HOBY; Sec Natl FFA Org; Bsktbl; Sal; Beta Clb; Amer Legn Awd; OK ST U.

NICKLES, MACY; Caddo HS; Caddo, OK; (2); FHA; High Hon Roll.

NICKLES, MACY B; Caddo HS; Durant, OK; (2); FHA; Hon Roll; NHS; Southeastern.

NICOLOTTI, DANIEL J; Union Sr HS; Tulsa, OK; (3); 117/741; Church Yth Grp; FCA; FBLA; Key Clb; Spanish Clb; Band; Var Bsbl; Hon Roll; NHS; Ptch Dzzy Dn Sr Wrld Srs; T P Comm Crw.

NIDA, HUNTER F; Bishop Mcguinness HS; Oklahoma City, OK; (2); 58/167; Schl/Comm Svc Vol; Mens Spirit Club; Bus.

NIDA, RHONDA TAUTFEST; Tonkawa Jr Sr HS; Red Rock, OK; (3); 2/40; 4-H; FHA; Natl FFA Org; Chorus; VP Stu Cncl; Var Trk; Cit Awd; 4-H Awd; Gov Hon Prg Awd; High Hon Roll; St FFA Publc Speakng Wnnr; OK Jr Angus Qn & Pres; House Of Reps Page; OK ST U; Ag Commnctns.

NIDIFFER, ABBIE M; Dewey HS; Dewey, OK; (2); 11/215; FCA; Letterman Clb; Spanish Clb; Sftbl; High Hon Roll; NHS; Pres Acad Fit Awd; All Amer Schlr; All Dist/All Conf Sftbl; Frosh Sftbl Plyr Of Conf.

NIEDERMEYER, EMILY E; Cascia Hall Prep School; Tulsa, OK; (2); Cmnty Wkr; Hosp Aide; Chorus; JV Bsktbl; Hon Roll; OK St U Cndystrpr Ldrshp Conf 96; U Of OK; Med.

NIEHUS, BRAD; Garber Sr HS; Enid, OK; (4); 1/33; FCA; Natl FFA Org; School Play; Ofcr Bsbl; Bsktbl; Ftbl; High Hon Roll; Hon Roll; NHS; Val; OSU; Bus.

NIELSEN, ERIN; Lawton Sr HS; Lawton, OK; (4); Math Tm; Spanish Clb; Acpl Chr; Chorus; Hon Roll; Pres Acad Fit Awd; Jazz Choir; Cameron Univ; Acctng; Bus.

NIELSEN, SHASTA R; Sharon Mutual Jr Sr HS; Sharon, OK; (2); Church Yth Grp; FHA; Chorus; Stat Bsktbl; High Hon Roll; Hon Roll; Prof Nanny.

NIGHTENGALE, JASON L; Fairview HS; Isabella, OK; (2); Church Yth Grp; Cmnty Wkr; English Clb; FCA; Var Bsktbl; Var Golf; Hon Roll; OK ST U; Med Field.

NIGHTINGALE, CHAD D; Mountain View-Gotebo HS; Mountain View, OK; (3); 1/30; Church Yth Grp; Cmnty Wkr; FCA; Natl FFA Org; Pep Clb; Quiz Bowl; VICA; Variety Show; Yrbk; Rep Frsh Cls; OK ST Univ; Engr.

NIKKEL, CRYSTAL; Idabel HS; Idabel, OK; (3); 1/96; Am Leg Aux Girls St; NFL; Band; Chorus; Jazz Band; Mrchg Band; VP Stu Cncl; High Hon Roll; Pres NHS; St Schlr.

NIKKEL, KIMBRA; Corn Bible Acad; Weatherford, OK; (2); Church Yth Grp; Band; Mrchg Band; Pep Band; Ofcr Frsh Cls; Ofcr Soph Cls; Var Bsktbl; Var Sftbl; Var Vllybl; High Hon Roll.

NIKKEL, TARINA; Corn Bible Acad; Weatherford, OK; (4); 3/12; Church Yth Grp; Chorus; Church Choir; School Play; Sec Frsh Cls; Sec Soph Cls; VP Jr Cls; Sec Sr Cls; Rep Stu Cncl; Var Bsktbl; John Brown Univ; Nrs.

NILES, ZAC; Perkins-Tryon HS; Perkins, OK; (3); #11 in class; Am Leg Boys St; Church Yth Grp; FCA; FHA; Intnl Clb; Key Clb; Natl FFA Org; Pres Frsh Cls; Pres Soph Cls; VP Jr Cls.

NILL, MELINDA; Grandfield Jr Sr HS; Grandfield, OK; (2); 1/22; Church Yth Grp; FHA; HOBY; Pep Clb; Powder Puff Ftbl; Hon Roll; OU; Phrmcy.

NILSSON, CORINNE R; Stillwater Sr HS; Stillwater, OK; (3); Pres Church Yth Grp; French Clb; Girl Scts; Latin Clb; Sec Science Clb; Teachers Aide; Band; Chorus; Color Guard; High Hon Roll; Jr Cls Comm/Prom; Brigham Young Univ; Pre-Med.

NINE, JEFF; Laverne Jr Sr HS; Laverne, OK; (4); 1/33; Church Yth Grp; Drama Clb; Scholastic Bowl; Pres Sr Cls; VP Stu Cncl; Var L Ftbl; High Hon Roll; Pres Schlr; St Schlr; Val; OK ST Hnr Schlr; R G Letourneau Pres Schlr; Letourneau Univ; Mech Engr.

NINEMIRE, SANDI; Hardesty Schl; Hardesty, OK; (3); 2/6; Co-Capt FCA; Sec Natl FFA Org; Chorus; VP Jr Cls; Var Bsktbl; Var Chrldng; Var Sftbl; Hon Roll; NHS; Pres Acad Fit Awd.

NIPP, REBECCA L; Macarthur HS; Union City, TN; (4); German Clb; Library Aide; Science Clb; SADD; Band; Mrchg Band; Phtg Yrbk; High Hon Roll; Pres Acad Fit Awd; UAL; Dr.

NIPP, TRAVIS C; Turner Schl; Overbrook, OK; (2); Natl FFA Org; Quiz Bowl; Speech Tm; OK ST Univ; Ag Ed.

NIX, JENNIFER C; Glenpool HS; Glenpool, OK; (2); Church Yth Grp; FHA; Girl Scts; Chorus; Church Choir; High Hon Roll; Jr NHS; NHS; Tchr.

NIXON, JENNIFER; Stigler HS; Stigler, OK; (1); Church Yth Grp; Rep FCA; Pep Clb; Rptr SADD; Var Bsktbl; High Hon Roll; NHS; Pres Acad Fit Awd; Natl Sci Merit Awd; Pres Literary Excl Awd.

NIXON, JOSH; Stigler HS; Stigler, OK; (2); Church Yth Grp; FCA; SADD; School Play; Pres Soph Cls; Var Bsbl; Var Ftbl; Kiwanis Awd; NHS.

NOBLE, CHRISSY; Westmoore HS; Moore, OK; (4); 192/610; FCA; Latin Clb; Nwsp; Bsktbl; Jr NHS; Var Bsktbl Awd Ofnsv Plyr Yr; U Of OK; Nrsng.

NOBLE, CHRISTINA M; Kellyville Sr HS; Kellyville, OK; (3); Church Yth Grp; Cmnty Wkr; GAA; Office Aide; Red Cross Aide; Science Clb; Pres Stu Cncl; Co-Capt Bsktbl; Golf; High Hon Roll; Alpha Pi Lambda; LPC; Tulsa U; Elem Ed.

NOBLE, LACEY W; Mooreland Jr Sr HS; Mooreland, OK; (1); Church Yth Grp; FCA; FHA; GAA; Pep Clb; Spanish Clb; Church Choir; Stage Crew; VP Frsh Cls; VP Soph Cls; OK ST Univ.

NOBLE, ROBERT; Elk City Jr HS; Elk City, OK; (4); Church Yth Grp; Cmnty Wkr; Band; Church Choir; Mrchg Band; Pep Band; Tennis; OK ST U.

NOBLE, THERESA M; Bishop Kelley HS; Tulsa, OK; (1); Church Yth Grp; Vllybl; High Hon Roll; Mock Trial; Dist Attorney.

NOBLES, LACY D; Heavener HS; Heavener, OK; (3); Church Yth Grp; 4-H; Natl FFA Org; Chorus; Church Choir; 4-H Awd; Won Numerous Awd In Horse Shows; Showing Beef Cattle; Animal Sci.

NODDELMOG, BRIAN G; Seminole Jr Sr HS; Seminole, OK; (2); 1/120; FCA; French Clb; Math Clb; Pres Frsh Cls; Bsktbl; Ftbl; Golf; High Hon Roll; Kiwanis Awd; Pres Acad Fit Awd; OK Univ.

NOE, KIM; Wynnewood HS; Wynnewood, OK; (3); 2/65; Church Yth Grp; Drama Clb; Band; Church Choir; Drm Mjr(t); Jazz Band; Mrchg Band; High Hon Roll; Sec NHS; Sal; Oral Roberts U.

NOE, TYRIESHA C; Wagoner Sr HS; Wagoner, OK; (4); VICA; Chorus; Hon Roll; Prfct Atten Awd; Natl Voc Tech Hnr Soc; Nrs.

NOEL, RIKKI D; Miami Sr HS; Miami, OK; (4); Church Yth Grp; Office Aide; Band; Mrchg Band; Pep Band; Hon Roll; NHS; Hnrs Grad; Rotary Stu Of Mnth; Cheroke Vol Soc Pres; NEO A&M Col; Pharm.

NOEL, TAMMARAH L; Millwood HS; Oklahoma City, OK; (1); Church Yth Grp; ROTC; Church Choir; Drill Tm; Ofcr Frsh Cls; Cit Awd; Hon Roll; Med.

NOFIRE, TAHLINA R; Stilwell HS; Welling, OK; (2); Church Yth Grp; Drama Clb; 4-H; Natl FFA Org; NFL; Spanish Clb; School Play; Pres Soph Cls; Powder Puff Ftbl; Hon Roll; Perf Arts.

NOHELTY, LACEY; Western Heights Sr HS; Oklahoma City, OK; (3); 22/161; Computer Clb; FBLA; Letterman Clb; Scholastic Bowl; Varsity Clb; Var Bsktbl; Capt Var Chrldng; Sftbl; Trk; NHS; Supt Hnr Roll; Natl Jr Hnr Soc; Comp Sci.

NOISEY, DENNIS; Sallisaw HS; Sallisaw, OK; (4); FHA; Spanish Clb; Var L Bsbl; Bsktbl; Var L Ftbl; Wt Lftg; Hon Roll; Indian Clb Treas.

NOKES, JOSHUA A; Stillwater Sr HS; Stillwater, OK; (2); 17/400; Church Yth Grp; FCA; JV Ftbl; JV Wrstlng; Hon Roll; Beta Club.

NOLAN, BRANDY S; Westmoore HS; Oklahoma City, OK; (3); 30/615; Am Leg Aux Girls St; Church Yth Grp; Q&S; Spanish Clb; Church Choir; Co-Ed Yrbk; Rep Stu Cncl; Jr NHS; NHS; OPSS Pgm 94; MI ST U Alpha Kappa Alpha 95; Langston U Study Math/Sci Smr Pgm 96; Sci.

NOLAN, JASON A; Savanna HS; Mcalester, OK; (3); Science Clb; Spanish Clb; Var Bsbl; Var Bsktbl; Var Ftbl; Var Trk; Cit Awd; High Hon Roll; Prfct Atten Awd; Art; OSU; Commercial Art.

NOLAN, JILL N; Heavener HS; Heavener, OK; (4); 1/100; Church Yth Grp; FBLA; Ofcr Stu Cncl; Ofcr Sr Cls; Chrldng; Sftbl; Trk; Hon Roll; ST Hon Soc; Otsdng Frosh Awd.

NOLAN, ROBERT W; Claremore Sr HS; Claremore, OK; (1); Band; Jazz Band; Mrchg Band; Pep Band; Hon Roll; OK ST Univ.

NOLAND, JAMIE E; Jay HS; Jay, OK; (2); Art Clb; FHA; Natl FFA Org; Chorus; School Musical; Cosmotology.

NOLEN, JENNIFER; Eisenhower Sr HS; Lawton, OK; (1); Church Yth Grp; Drama Clb; FCA; Key Clb; School Play; Rep Treas Frsh Cls; Chrldng; Gym; Hon Roll; Jr NHS; All Amer Chrldr; U Of OK; Neurology.

NOLEN, JON S; Del City HS; Del City, OK; (2); Church Yth Grp; School Play; Ftbl; Socr; Trk; Wrstlng; Jr NHS; Pres Acad Fit Awd; Notre Dame; Sports Medicine.

NOLEN, PENNI; Vanoss Schl; Ada, OK; (4); 5/45; Art Clb; FCA; FBLA; Sec FHA; Teachers Aide; Rptr Nwsp; Yrbk; Hon Roll; NHS; Elks Stu Of Month; U S Bus Ed Awd; East Central U; Elem Ed.

NOLES, JASON K; Stillwater Sr HS; Stillwater, OK; (3); Cmnty Wkr; Office Aide; Teachers Aide; Langston; Phy Thrpst.

NOLL, DENNIS; Yukon Middle HS; Yukon, OK; (2); Boy Scts; Church Yth Grp; Band; Jazz Band; Pep Band; Cit Awd; High Hon Roll; Pres Acad Fit Awd; Tulane.

NOLLENBERGER, DUSTIN; Medford Schl; Medford, OK; (3); Church Yth Grp; FCA; HOBY; Letterman Clb; Natl FFA Org; Band; Chorus; Jazz Band; Mrchg Band; Pep Band; FFA Pres; Agribus.

NONDORF, KYLE; Heritage Hall Schl; Oklahoma City, OK; (2); FCA; Letterman Clb; Spanish Clb; Chorus; Var L Bsbl; JV Bsktbl; Var L Ftbl; Wt Lftg; Hon Roll; Newcomer Of The Yr Ftbl; Sports Med.

NOONKESTER, COLBY B; Broken Arrow Sr HS; Broken Arrow, OK; (3); VICA; Vo-Tech Elctrcl Tech; OK ST Univ; Elctrcl Engr.

NORBURY, JAKE R; Whitesboro Schl; Talihina, OK; (2); Natl FFA Org; Var Bsbl; Var Bsktbl; Eastern OK ST Coll.

NORDAHL, DAVID; Westmoore HS; Moore, OK; (4); 21/600; Boy Scts; French Clb; Scholastic Bowl; Science Clb; Band; Mrchg Band; Pep Band; High Hon Roll; Jr NHS; NHS; Tech Stdnts Assn; Eagle Sct Awd; Peer Helper; U Of OK; Geophysics.

NORDEAN, HONEY; Victory Christian Schl; Jenks, OK; (3); 1/60; Intnl Clb; Office Aide; Scholastic Bowl; Chorus; Sec Jr Cls; Mgr Bsktbl; Var Crs Cntry; Capt Var Socr; High Hon Roll; NHS; Oral Roberts Univ; Eng.

NORMAN, BRITT N; Woodward HS; Woodward, OK; (3); Church Yth Grp; Computer Clb; FBLA; FHA; Natl FFA Org; Pep Clb; Chorus; Church Choir; School Musical; School Play; Miss Woodward 96; Super Showman Awd Swine; NWOSU; Bus; Commnctn.

NORMAN, EMILY; Southwest Covenant Schl; Bethany, OK; (2); Church Yth Grp; Chorus; Church Choir; Rptr Nwsp; Ed Yrbk; Treas Stu Cncl; Var L Bsktbl; Var L Vllybl; High Hon Roll; Piano 8 Yrs.

NORMAN, JOSHUA; New Lima Jr Sr HS; Wewoka, OK; (3); 4-H; Quiz Bowl; School Play; Ed Nwsp; Treas Stu Cncl; 4-H Awd; Hon Roll; Schl Mascot; Theatre/Drama.

NORMAN, KERRI; Dale Sr HS; Shawnee, OK; (4); Pres Church Yth Grp; Spanish Clb; SADD; Sec Treas Stu Cncl; Cit Awd; Hon Roll; NHS; Lifeguides; Yth For Christ; Vet Med.

NORMAN, SHANNON BROOKE; Comanche HS; Comanche, OK; (4); 7/60; Church Yth Grp; German Clb; GAA; Scholastic Bowl; Chorus; Variety Show; Nwsp; Chrldng; Cit Awd; High Hon Roll; All St, Reg Choir; Amer Kids Inc; Bus.

NORMAN, TOMMY; Paoli HS; Paoli, OK; (2); Church Yth Grp; Teachers Aide; Ofcr Frsh Cls; Ofcr Soph Cls; Ofcr Bsbl; Bsktbl; Ftbl; Wt Lftg; Hon Roll; Pres Acad Fit Awd; U Of Cntrl OK.

NORRID, LESLIE R; Pocola HS; Pocola, OK; (3); Rptr FCA; FBLA; Pres GAA; Spanish Clb; Rptr Nwsp; Phtg Rptr Yrbk; VP Soph Cls; Pres Jr Cls; VP Stu Cncl; Capt Bsktbl; BCI Natl Chmpnshp Winner/Bsktbl; 2 Time ASA Natl Chmpnshp Winner/USSSA Wrld Runner Up Sftbl; Bsktbl Plyr.

NORRIS, CRYSTAL G; Forgan Schl; Beaver, OK; (3); Library Aide; Pep Clb; Chorus; Hon Roll; Awd Of Acad Hnr; OK HS Hon Soc; Acad Awd; Nurs.

NORRIS, MARLANA M; Okarche HS; El Reno, OK; (4); 4/36; Church Yth Grp; Sec Debate Tm; FCA; Hosp Aide; Intnl Clb; Letterman Clb; Library Aide; Model UN; Red Cross Aide; Service Clb; WHISPERS Pres; Amer Red Crss Disaster Team; 1st Aid & CPR Stu Instr; Lifeguard; Redlands CC; Paramedic Nrs.

NORRIS, MELISSA; Holdenville HS; Holdenville, OK; (2); 4/72; FHA; Natl Beta Clb; Ofcr Stu Cncl; Hon Roll; NHS; Tch Stdnt Assn VP, Rprtr; Intrschlstc Tm Cmptr Prgrmmng 2nd Pl, Cmptr Sci 2nd Pl, Span II 3rd Pl; Harvard; Law.

NORRIS, NEUDORA G; Milburn Schl; Coleman, OK; (2); Quiz Bowl; Band; School Musical; Cit Awd; High Hon Roll; Hon Roll; Prfct Atten Awd; Cosmetologist.

NORSWORTHY, TIFFANY H; Western Heights Sr HS; Oklahoma City, OK; (4); 1/152; Church Yth Grp; FCA; Key Clb; Band; Drm Mjr(t); L Crs Cntry; NHS; Pres Acad Fit Awd; Val; Ldrshp Ed Aprntcshp Prgm; U Of Cntrl OK; Elem Ed.

NORTH, JANUARY R; Strother Jr Sr HS; Seminole, OK; (2); Church Yth Grp; 4-H; GAA; Letterman Clb; Natl FFA Org; Quiz Bowl; Varsity Clb; Pres Frsh Cls; Rep Soph Cls; Var L Bsktbl; OK St U; Ag Engrng.

NORTH, KRISTI L; Blackwell HS; Blackwell, OK; (3); FCA; Letterman Clb; Pep Clb; Red Cross Aide; Varsity Clb; Chorus; Chrldng; Gym; Sftbl; High Hon Roll; Head Chrldr; Elem Ed.

NORTH, RANDY J; Seminole Jr Sr HS; Seminole, OK; (3); 12/85; Computer Clb; FCA; French Clb; JA; Math Clb; Math Tm; Varsity Clb; Bsktbl; Golf; French Hon Soc; OK ST; Mech Engr.

NORTH, RYAN G; Union Intermediate HS; Broken Arrow, OK; (2); Var Bsbl; JV Bsktbl; JV Ftbl; NHS; OK All-Stars Bsbl Team; Bsbl.

NORTHCOTT, JACK A; Seminole Jr Sr HS; Seminole, OK; (2); Church Yth Grp; FCA; Math Clb; Science Clb; Spanish Clb; Ftbl; Wt Lftg; High Hon Roll.

NORTHCUTT, JENNIFER; Ft Cobb-Broxton HS; Fort Cobb, OK; (4); 11/34; Church Yth Grp; Letterman Clb; Speech Tm; Varsity Clb; Church Choir; Nwsp; Yrbk; Bsktbl; Sftbl; Hon Roll; St Rnnr-Up Sftbl 95-96; USAO; Psych.

NORTHCUTT, MICHELLE; Frederick HS; Frederick, OK; (3); 5/61; Am Leg Aux Girls St; Church Yth Grp; Rep FHA; HOBY; Chorus; School Musical; Yrbk; VP Jr Cls; Rep Stu Cncl; NHS; OK ST U.

NORTHINGTON, LANCE; Blanchard Jr Sr HS; Blanchard, OK; (3); Church Yth Grp; Computer Clb; Spanish Clb; SADD; Ofcr Bsbl; Bsktbl; Hon Roll; Jr NHS; NHS; Prfct Atten Awd; U OK.

NORTON, AMY; Plainview HS; Ardmore, OK; (4); 11/89; FCA; HOBY; Latin Clb; Natl Beta Clb; SADD; Rep Frsh Cls; Pres Soph Cls; Pres Jr Cls; Sec Sr Cls; Sec Treas Stu Cncl; Ryonis Stu Of Month; Ftbl Homcmng Qn; U Of OK; Med.

NORTON, CLIFTON C; Choctaw HS; Midwest City, OK; (2); Church Yth Grp; Band; Church Choir; Mrchg Band; Orch; Pep Band; Stage Crew; Golf; Wt Lftg; NHS.

NORTON, JUSTIN L; Putnam City West HS; Del City, OK; (1); Boy Scts; Church Yth Grp; CAP; German Clb; Rep Frsh Cls; Hon Roll; Yale; Aviation/Cmptr Sci.

NORTON, KEITH; Velma Alma HS; Velma, OK; (3); FCA; Quiz Bowl; Ofcr Bsbl; Bsktbl; Ftbl; Trk; Wt Lftg; High Hon Roll; NHS; Pres Schlr; Northeastern ST U; Phy Thrpst.

NORTON, LANDON N; Duncan HS; Comanche, OK; (2); Church Yth Grp; Letterman Clb; Nwsp; Ftbl; Wt Lftg; High Hon Roll; Hon Roll; Jr NHS; NHS.

NORTON, ROGER K; Velma Alma HS; Velma, OK; (3); FCA; Scholastic Bowl; Nwsp; Ofcr Bsbl; Bsktbl; Ftbl; Trk; Cit Awd; Hon Roll; NHS; Southeastern OK ST U; Arch.

NORTON, SCOTT; Shawnee Sr HS; Shawnee, OK; (3); 9/360; Church Yth Grp; Cmnty Wkr; Latin Clb; Scholastic Bowl; Church Choir; Ofcr Bsbl; L Ftbl; L Wrstlng; High Hon Roll; Hon Roll.

NORTON, TANYA L; Commanche Sr HS; Comanche, OK; (3); Church Yth Grp; Office Aide; Pep Clb; Science Clb; Pres SADD; Chorus; Ed Nwsp; Phtg Rptr Yrbk; VP Frsh Cls; Hon Roll; Yng Crusaders Children Choir Dir; Elem Tchr.

NORVELL, MELISSA; Shawnee Sr HS; Shawnee, OK; (3); Debate Tm; Drama Clb; French Clb; Hosp Aide; NFL; Speech Tm; Thesps; School Musical; School Play; TX Chrstn U; Med.

NORVILL, JULIE A; Latta Sr HS; Ada, OK; (3); 4-H; Natl FFA Org; Spanish Clb; VICA; School Play; Bsktbl; Trk; Vllybl; Hon Roll; NHS; Hrsbck Rdng; 6th VICA Reg Drftng Cntsts; Schlstc Meets; OK ST U; Eng.

NORWOOD, FRANCO B; Pioneer Jr Sr HS; Enid, OK; (2); Cmnty Wkr; FCA; Pep Clb; Band; Ftbl; Wt Lftg; Bus Admin.

NOUTNY, BRANDON J; Pawnee HS; Pawnee, OK; (3); Boy Scts; Church Yth Grp; Band; Church Choir; Mrchg Band; Rep Stu Cncl; JV Var Bsbl; JV Bsktbl; Var Ftbl; JV Var Wrstlng; Trophies/Mdls In Karate/Smmr Ball Prgms; OCU Edmond; Crmnl Law.

NOVAK, JAIME K; Kellyville Sr HS; Kellyville, OK; (3); Church Yth Grp; Office Aide; Red Cross Aide; Science Clb; School Play; Rep Frsh Cls; Rep Soph Cls; Rep Jr Cls; Rep Sr Cls; Rep Stu Cncl; Stns; Astrlgy Clb; Prm Comm; Med Rsrchr.

NOVESKEY, GIANA J; Central HS; Tulsa, OK; (2); Church Yth Grp; JV Bsktbl.

NOVISKI, BILLY P; Claremore Sr HS; Claremore, OK; (3); Nwsp; Ftbl; Socr; Trk; Wrstlng; High Hon Roll; Hon Roll; Claremore Soccer Clb Yth Referee Of Yr; Bus Admin.

NOVOTNY, ANGEL D; Pauls Valley HS; Pauls Valley, OK; (1); Natl FFA Org; Chorus; Vet.

NOVOTNY, TRENT A; Pawnee HS; Pawnee, OK; (2); FBLA; Natl Beta Clb; Natl FFA Org; SADD; Ofcr Frsh Cls; Ofcr Soph Cls; Ofcr Stu Cncl; Ofcr Bsbl; Ftbl; Wt Lftg.

NOVY, ANITRA; Guthrie Sr HS; Guthrie, OK; (4); 1/176; French Clb; Mu Alpha Theta; Science Clb; Band; Flag Corp; Mrchg Band; 4-H Awd; NHS; Val; OK ST Univ; Astrophysics.

NOWAK, AMANDA D; Will Rogers HS; Tulsa, OK; (3); Church Yth Grp; Debate Tm; Service Clb; Spanish Clb; Acpl Chr; Church Choir; School Musical; Var L Swmmng; Hon Roll; NHS; Oral Roberts Univ; Elem Ed.

NOWELL, SHANEDRA D; Union Sr HS; Tulsa, OK; (3); 63/741; Church Yth Grp; DECA; Office Aide; Teachers Aide; Church Choir; Sec Frsh Cls; Hon Roll; NHS; Pres Ed Awd; Stu Tchng 3rd, 7th Grd Sci; Acad Ltr; Oral Roberts U.

NOWLIN, ASHLEY; Seiling Schl; Seiling, OK; (2); FCA; FBLA; FHA; Chorus; Sec Frsh Cls; Bsktbl; Sftbl; Trk; Hon Roll; NHS.

NOWLIN, B J; Davis HS; Davis, OK; (2); Church Yth Grp; Chorus; School Musical; Variety Show; Yrbk; Ftbl; Hon Roll.

NOWLIN, BRYAN J; Cascia Hall Prep School; Tulsa, OK; (2); Pres Debate Tm; German Clb; NFL; Scholastic Bowl; Pres Soph Cls; Pres Jr Cls; Hon Roll; Tulsa Yth Crt.

NOWLIN, KIT; Guthrie Sr HS; Edmond, OK; (4); 8/178; Boy Scts; Church Yth Grp; Debate Tm; FBLA; Key Clb; Mu Alpha Theta; SADD; Band; Mrchg Band; Yrbk; Boys St; Masonic Acad Excllnc Awd; L.

NOWLIN, PAUL; Perkins-Tryon HS; Stillwater, OK; (1); Intnl Clb; Scholastic Bowl; Hon Roll; OK ST U.

NOYES, CINDY; Dale Sr HS; Shawnee, OK; (2); 1/50; FHA; Spanish Clb; SADD; High Hon Roll; Hon Roll; Jr NHS; NHS; Ntl Merit Ltr; E Cntrl OK U; Acctng.

NUBINE, JONATHAN L; Mustang HS; Oklahoma City, OK; (1); Church Yth Grp; Letterman Clb; Varsity Clb; Church Choir; Bsktbl; AAU; BCI.

NUCKOLLS, JONATHAN; Tecumseh HS; Maud, OK; (4); 7/133; Am Leg Boys St; Church Yth Grp; Math Clb; Mu Alpha Theta; Office Aide; Church Choir; School Musical; Capt Var Bsktbl; Var Trk; High Hon Roll; 8 Clss Awds; Yth Alive; OK ST U; Math.

NUCKOLS, NATALIE J; Mustang HS; Yukon, OK; (4); 39/350; Model UN; Office Aide; Teachers Aide; Var Capt Vllybl; High Hon Roll; NHS.

NULL, JULEENA D; Amber Pocasset Jr Sr HS; Amber, OK; (4); 6/26; FHA; Spanish Clb; Teachers Aide; School Play; Rep Jr Cls; Rep Sr Cls; Capt Chrldng; Hon Roll; NHS; OK ST Univ; Elem Ed.

NULL, KELLI; Laverne Jr Sr HS; Rosston, OK; (4); 4/31; Pres Church Yth Grp; 4-H; Letterman Clb; Natl Beta Clb; Treas Pres Natl FFA Org; School Play; Rep Frsh Cls; Sec Jr Cls; Var Bsktbl; Var Crs Cntry; OK Hon Soc; U Of Cntrl OK; Pre-PT.

NUNLEY, ELIZABETH L; Mustang HS; Oklahoma City, OK; (2); 139/416; Church Yth Grp; Key Clb; Chorus; Hon Roll; Oklahoma ST Univ; Optometry.

NUNLEY, LACY; Achille Schl; Colbert, OK; (3); 1/42; FHA; Chorus; Sec Frsh Cls; Rptr Soph Cls; Pres Jr Cls; Bsktbl; Sftbl; High Hon Roll; NHS; OK Hnr Soc; Gftd & Tlntd; Southeastern OK ST U; Acctng.

NUNLEY, RANDALE E; Edmond North HS; Edmond, OK; (2); Boy Scts; Church Yth Grp; Spanish Clb; SADD; Trk; Pharmacology.

NUNLEY, SCOTT; Wynnewood HS; Wynnewood, OK; (2); 4/46; FCA; Bsktbl; Ftbl; Golf; Wt Lftg; Cit Awd; High Hon Roll; Hon Roll; NHS; Pres Schlr; All-Amer Schlr Awd.

NUNLEY, TASHOMBIA D; Capitol Hill HS; Oklahoma City, OK; (3); Church Yth Grp; Dance Clb; Teachers Aide; Church Choir; Color Guard; Trk; Cit Awd; Psych/Pre-Law.

NUNN, BRAD R; Oologah HS; Claremore, OK; (3); FCA; Teachers Aide; Ofcr Bsbl; Var Bsktbl; Intrml Ftbl; Cit Awd; Hon Roll; Outstdng Stu Of The Yr Jr Yr Art; U Of Tulsa; Art; Jrnlsm.

NUNNALLEE, ADAM R; Memorial HS; Tulsa, OK; (2); German Clb; Var L Ftbl; Var L Wt Lftg; Hon Roll.

NURNBERG, NATASHA; Washita Heights Schl; Corn, OK; (4); 2/11; Am Leg Aux Girls St; Church Yth Grp; Yrbk; VP Frsh Cls; Treas Soph Cls; Sec Jr Cls; Sec Sr Cls; Bsktbl; Chrldng; Sftbl; U Of OK.

NUSZ, JOHN C; Okeene Jr Sr HS; Okeene, OK; (2); Boy Scts; Church Yth Grp; FHA; HOBY; Speech Tm; Varsity Clb; Band; Pep Band; Var Ftbl; Var Trk; Eagle Sct; Engrng.

NUTTER, JO DENA; Waynoka HS; Waynoka, OK; (4); 6/23; Am Leg Aux Girls St; Church Yth Grp; FCA; Hist FHA; Quiz Bowl; Church Choir; Var Bsktbl; Var Sftbl; Hon Roll; Rnssnc Soc; Northwestern OK ST U; Psych.

NUTTLE, MARCI; West Middle HS; Norman, OK; (2); Church Yth Grp; Dance Clb; FCA; Mu Alpha Theta; Spanish Clb; Treas Stu Cncl; Co-Capt Chrldng; Var L Trk; High Hon Roll; NHS; All Star Pom & Cheer Squads; Tomorrows Ldrs Chmbr Of Commerce Pgm; Assisteens Comm Vol Corres Sec.

NYE, LINDSAY N; Union Intermediate HS; Tulsa, OK; (1); Church Yth Grp; Cmnty Wkr; French Clb; Office Aide; Var Gym; Vol For Vacation Bible Schl & Pub Lib; Chrch Camp; OK ST Univ.

NYEMASTER, NANCY N; Broken Arrow Sr HS; Broken Arrow, OK; (4); 235/921; Cmnty Wkr; Debate Tm; Red Cross Aide; Ofcr Jr Cls; Ofcr Sr Cls; Ofcr Stu Cncl; DECA Mrktg Natl Cmptn 2nd In ST; HOSA Cls Historian; Colabash Stu Voice Ldrshp At Schl Tchr Select; U Of OK; Mrktg.

OAKES, BARI; Aline-Cleo Jr Sr HS; Cleo Springs, OK; (3); 4/24; Church Yth Grp; FCA; FHA; Hosp Aide; HOBY; Pep Clb; School Play; Bsktbl; Sftbl; Hon Roll; Northwestern OK ST U.

OAKLEY, STEPHANIE; Fairland Jr Sr HS; Fairland, OK; (3); Church Yth Grp; FCA; Quiz Bowl; Rptr Soph Cls; JV Bsktbl; Var Chrldng; Powder Puff Ftbl; Sftbl; Trk; Pres Acad Fit Awd; St Hnr Soc; Med.

O'BREGON, CANDACE A; Ponca City Sr HS; Ponca City, OK; (4); 161/332; Debate Tm; Drama Clb; NFL; Band; Orch; School Musical; Ofcr Sr Cls; Ofcr Stu Cncl; L Bsktbl; Hon Roll; Pg OK St Cptl; OK ST U; Msc Ed.

O'BRIEN, JOHN P; Mustang HS; Mustang, OK; (1); 90/500; Boy Scts; Church Yth Grp; French Clb; Band; Hon Roll; 1st Chair Clarinet; 1st Class Boy Scout; Eye Srgry.

OCAMB, DAVID D; Carl Albert HS; Midwest City, OK; (2); 1/274; Debate Tm; Drama Clb; Key Clb; NFL; Scholastic Bowl; Yrbk; Treas Soph Cls; Ofcr Stu Cncl; Tennis; NHS; Claremont; Law; Pol Sci.

O'CONNOR, KENDRA Y; Owasso Sr HS; Owasso, OK; (3); 9/432; Var Capt Diving; High Hon Roll; NHS; Gymnstcs 10 Yrs; Art.

O'DANIEL, JASON; Maud HS; Maud, OK; (3); 1/42; Quiz Bowl; Scholastic Bowl; Yrbk; Pres Jr Cls; VP Stu Cncl; Bsktbl; Hon Roll; NHS.

O'DEA, MANDI S; Enid Sr HS; Enid, OK; (2); French Clb; Orch; High Hon Roll; Hon Roll; Jr NHS; NHS; 2nd Pl 9th Annual NW OK Stdnt Show Crafts Jr HS; Enid Strolling Strings; Cmrcl Artist.

ODELL, AMBER; Asher Schl; Byars, OK; (1); 1/12; Church Yth Grp; FHA; Church Choir; Rptr Nwsp; Sec Frsh Cls; Var Bsktbl; Var Sftbl; High Hon Roll.

O'DELL, DAISY L; Broken Arrow Sr HS; Broken Arrow, OK; (3); Art Clb; German Clb; Band; Mrchg Band; Pep Band; Capt Jr Cls; Capt Stu Cncl; Trk; High Hon Roll; Hon Roll; HOBY Fnlst; Reflxns 1st Pl City 2 Yrs, Hnrbl Mntn; Brigham Young U; Art.

ODEN, JEFFREY A; Mustang HS; Yukon, OK; (1); Cmnty Wkr; FCA; JV Bsbl; JV Ftbl; JV Wt Lftg; Hon Roll; Hnr Roll; OK Univ; Arch/Astronomy.

ODEN, SHANAY; Moore HS; Moore, OK; (4); Latin Clb; Office Aide; Ofcr Stu Cncl; Trk; Wt Lftg; Multiclltrl Stu Assoc VP; Jrnlsm.

ODGERS, CARRIE; Perry Sr HS; Perry, OK; (4); 2/66; Church Yth Grp; VP Spanish Clb; Band; Pres Jr Cls; Rptr Stu Cncl; Chrldng; Pom Pon; High Hon Roll; NHS; Spanish NHS; OK ST U; Jrnlsm.

ODMMEN, JERINE T; Mustang HS; Yukon, OK; (1); Band; Church Choir; Jazz Band; Mrchg Band; JV Tennis; Hon Roll; Bsktbl; UCO; Comp Prgmr.

ODOM, KRISTINA M; Westmoore HS; Oklahoma City, OK; (3); FBLA; FHA; Key Clb; Pep Clb; U Of OK; Phy Asst.

ODOM, MICHELLE J; Shawnee Sr HS; Shawnee, OK; (1); Church Yth Grp; FHA; High Hon Roll; HOPE; Life Guides.

ODOM, SHANNON; Kingston HS; Kingston, OK; (4); 7/54; French Clb; FHA; FTA; Spanish Clb; Teachers Aide; Nwsp; Yrbk; High Hon Roll; NHS; Frgn Lang Club/Pres; FTA VP; OK Hon Soc; Outstdng Frgn Lang Stu 3 Yrs; South Eastern OK Univ; Frgn Ln.

ODOM, SHANNON D; Tuttle HS; Tuttle, OK; (3); 16/110; Hosp Aide; Spanish Clb; Yrbk; JV Var Trk; High Hon Roll; NHS; Prfct Atten Awd; OK Hnr Soc; PT.

O'DONNELL, ERIKA L; Choctaw HS; Choctaw, OK; (2); 36/384; Church Yth Grp; Cmnty Wkr; Intnl Clb; Spanish Clb; Acpl Chr; Chorus; Church Choir; Swing Chorus; Variety Show; Nwsp; Psych.

O'DONNELL, MARTIN; Holdenville HS; Holdenville, OK; (4); 1/75; Am Leg Boys St; Library Aide; VP Natl Beta Clb; Quiz Bowl; Scholastic Bowl; Science Clb; Acpl Chr; Band; Chorus; Drm Mjr(t); All St Band; OK Chrstn U Of Sci & Arts.

O'DOR, JENNIFER; Westmoore HS; Moore, OK; (3); Hon Roll; NHS; Concert Choir; Piano; OK Univ; Child Psycht.

OEDEWALDT, SETH L; Harrah HS; Harrah, OK; (4); 13/151; Drama Clb; Spanish Clb; Speech Tm; Teachers Aide; Ed Nwsp; Rep Frsh Cls; Rep Stu Cncl; Cit Awd; High Hon Roll; Hon Roll; OK St Univ; Comp Sci.

OESTMANN, TWYLLA L; South Coffeyville Schl; S Coffeyville, OK; (2); FCA; FHA; Scholastic Bowl; School Play; JV Var Bsktbl; High Hon Roll; NHS.

OFFOLTER, KRISTIE; Dibble Jr Sr HS; Dibble, OK; (3); 3/52; Church Yth Grp; FCA; FHA; Sec Pres Natl FFA Org; Office Aide; Sec Soph Cls; Sec Jr Cls; Rep Stu Cncl; Var Bsktbl; Score Keeper; Cntrl Bapty Coll; PT.

OGAN, AARON; Mulhall Orlando HS; Guthrie, OK; (3); Church Yth Grp; Bsktbl; Socr.

OGDEN, ANGELA M; Altus Sr HS; Altus, OK; (3); #5 in class; Hosp Aide; Spanish Clb; Band; Flag Corp; Pep Band; School Musical; High Hon Roll; Jr NHS; Ntl Merit SF; Mrchg Band; Visions Of Universe Art Contest 2nd Pl 94; Piano Lessons 5 Yrs; Acad Allstar 95-; Cmptr Sci.

OGDEN, ELI; Pryor Jr HS; Pryor, OK; (2); Nwsp; JV Bsbl; Bsktbl; JV Golf; Hon Roll; NHS; Photo Clb; Arts & Hum-Film Comm; Art Awd; Photo Awd; Hnrb Mntn NE OK Area Art Show; KS Univ.

OGDEN, JENNIFER; Wright City Jr Sr HS; Broken Bow, OK; (3); Church Yth Grp; Quiz Bowl; Teachers Aide; Chorus; Sec Soph Cls; Capt Chrldng; Hon Roll; I-Stand.

OGG, ALISON; Sapulpa Sr HS; Sapulpa, OK; (2); Church Yth Grp; Debate Tm; 4-H; FHA; Natl FFA Org; Speech Tm; Chorus; Church Choir; School Musical; Variety Show.

OGG, SPARKAL; Webbers Falls Schl; Webbers Falls, OK; (3); Church Yth Grp; FCA; HOBY; Natl FFA Org; Sec Frsh Cls; Sec Soph Cls; Pres Jr Cls; Ofcr Stu Cncl; L Bsktbl; L Sftbl.

OGLE, ADAM; Fox Sr HS; Ratliff City, OK; (3); Nwsp; Yrbk; Hon Roll.

OGLE, ANGELLA; Tonkawa Jr Sr HS; Tonkawa, OK; (3); 1/60; Church Yth Grp; VP FCA; Scholastic Bowl; Band; Chorus; Mrchg Band; Pep Band; School Musical; School Play; Yrbk; RYLA; Show Choir; Phys Thrpy.

OGLE, ASHLEIGH; Moore HS; Moore, OK; (2); 42/695; Church Yth Grp; VP Frsh Cls; Jr NHS; Pres Acad Fit Awd; Top Gun Sr All Star Dance Ntl Chmpn, Sr Capts Ntl Chmpn & 2nd Pl Overall Grnd Chmpns; Med.

OGLE, BRANDY; Ninnekah HS; Chickasha, OK; (2); Church Yth Grp; FCA; Natl FFA Org; Quiz Bowl; Spanish Clb; Sec Frsh Cls; Sftbl; Hon Roll; Medcl.

OGLE, JENNIFER M; Tishomingo HS; Mannsville, OK; (3); Natl FFA Org; Yrbk; Stat Bsktbl; Hon Roll.

OGLE, JOSHUA A; Fox Sr HS; Ratliff City, OK; (4); Natl FFA Org; Nwsp; Yrbk; Hon Roll.

OGLESBY, AMANDA R; Haworth Sr HS; Haworth, OK; (2); Drama Clb; 4-H; HOBY; Natl FFA Org; Quiz Bowl; Chorus; School Musical; Sftbl; Jr NHS; NHS; Show Choir; OK Univ; Drama.

OGLESBY, MICHAEL R; Union Intermediate HS; Tulsa, OK; (2); Church Yth Grp; Hon Roll; Jr NHS; NHS; Astrnmy.

O'HANDLEY, LISA M; Woodward HS; Woodward, OK; (2); Letterman Clb; Spanish Clb; Band; Mrchg Band; Pep Band; High Hon Roll; Hon Roll; NHS; OSU; Vetrn Schl.

O'HEARON, JENNIFER M; Will Rogers HS; Tulsa, OK; (3); Boy Scts; Church Yth Grp; English Clb; German Clb; Pep Clb; ROTC; Teachers Aide; Band; Church Choir; Mrchg Band; Outfront Ldrshp Pgms; His/Elem Ed.

OHERN, PATRICK S; Pioneer Jr Sr HS; Enid, OK; (3); Pres Computer Clb; Hon Roll; OK ST Univ; Drafting.

OHLIG, MEGAN B; Union Intermediate HS; Broken Arrow, OK; (2); Church Yth Grp; Dance Clb; FCA; Office Aide; Spanish Clb; Church Choir; Drill Tm; NHS; Drill Tm Co-Capt; DFY.

OISTEN, JANICE MARIE; Choctaw HS; Spencer, OK; (3); 24/328; Church Yth Grp; Rep German Clb; Key Clb; Library Aide; Ed Yrbk; Var Bsktbl; Var Trk; Hon Roll; Jr NHS; Pres Acad Fit Awd.

OLDEN, KELVIN; Wewoka HS; Wewoka, OK; (3); HOBY; Var Bsktbl; Var Ftbl; Var Mgr(s); Var Trk; Var Wt Lftg; Hon Roll; Prfct Atten Awd; FHA Actvt Coord; Prlmntry Prcdr Tm; Vocal Music Choir Pres; OK 2 A St Bsktbl Team 95; OU; Arch.

OLDFIELD, WILLIAM; Ponca City Sr HS; Burbank, OK; (3); 5/438; Boy Scts; Church Yth Grp; HOBY; Math Tm; Spanish Clb; Orch; Sec Stu Cncl; JV Bsbl; Ftbl; High Hon Roll; Yth Trffc Ct Blff; All-St Orch 95 & 96; Engrng.

OLDHAM, JAMIE S; Harrah HS; Harrah, OK; (4); Art Clb; Church Yth Grp; FCA; FBLA; GAA; Office Aide; Pep Clb; SADD; Church Choir; Yrbk; Schlrs Clb; Eastern OK Cty Acad All Star; Herff Jones Pres Ldrsp Awd; Rose ST Coll; Scndry Ed/Math.

OLDHAM, LUKE; Sapulpa Sr HS; Sapulpa, OK; (3); FCA; Natl FFA Org; Science Clb; Spanish Clb; Trk; NHS; Rock Climbing.

OLDHAM, MICHAEL B; Sapulpa Sr HS; Sapulpa, OK; (2); 105/365; Letterman Clb; Math Clb; Science Clb; Spanish Clb; Ofcr Bsbl; Bsktbl; Hon Roll; Teens For Christ; Yth Group-Pickett Prairie Bapt Chrch; Chrch Plays; U Of OK; Anesthesiologist.

OLES, ROBIN; Mc Loud HS; Mc Loud, OK; (3); 10/145; Church Yth Grp; FCA; FBLA; Pep Clb; Rep Yrbk; Var Bsktbl; Var Sftbl; Hon Roll; NHS; OK Hnr Soc; OK ST U; Vet.

OLESON, JESSICA; Del City HS; Del City, OK; (1); GAA; Pep Clb; Teachers Aide; Rptr Frsh Cls; Rptr Stu Cncl; Bsktbl; Chrldng; Sftbl; High Hon Roll; Hon Roll; OK ST; Brdcst Jrnlsm.

OLIPHANT, CARRIE A; Putnam City West HS; Oklahoma City, OK; (1); Church Yth Grp; Church Choir; Orch; Silvr Strngs Of Putnm City; Teen Bible Quizzng; Citatn Given Gov Keating By Rep Hastings For ST OK; SNU; Music; Tchr.

OLIPHANT, JEREMY W; Skiatook HS; Skiatook, OK; (1); Scholastic Bowl; Band; Mrchg Band; Var Bsbl; Var Golf; Var Wrstlng; High Hon Roll; NBDA Hnr Bnd; MEOBDA Hnr Bnd 2 Yrs; OK Hnr Soc; PGA.

OLIVE, CRYSTAL L; Dickson HS; Ardmore, OK; (2); FHA; Key Clb; SADD; Piano.

OLIVER, ANTHONY A; Del City HS; Oklahoma City, OK; (3); Boy Scts; Cmnty Wkr; Red Cross Aide; ROTC; Teachers Aide; Drill Tm; Wt Lftg; Hon Roll; Cmndr Rifle Team; NJROTC Rifle Team Top Shooter Awd; NJROTC Admin/Comm/Records Ofcr; Air Force Acad; Aviation.

OLIVER, GWEN D; Mannford HS; Sand Springs, OK; (2); 9/104; Drama Clb; NFL; Spanish Clb; Speech Tm; SADD; Var Bsktbl; Var Crs Cntry; JV Trk; High Hon Roll; NHS; OK Hnr Soc.

OLIVER II, JOHN; Little Axe Sr HS; Norman, OK; (2); Quiz Bowl; Scholastic Bowl; JV Bsktbl; Var Co-Capt Crs Cntry; Var Trk; Hon Roll; Msns Stu Of Today.

OLIVER, SABRINA; Kingston HS; Kingston, OK; (1); Band; Jazz Band; Mrchg Band; Pep Band; Hon Roll; Zoology/Marine Bio.

OLIVEROS, AMANDA G; Sapulpa Sr HS; Sapulpa, OK; (4); 2/298; Pres Debate Tm; Pres NFL; Spanish Clb; Speech Tm; Sec Soph Cls; Pres Jr Cls; Kiwanis Awd; VP NHS; Pres Acad Fit Awd; Sal; Northeastern ST Univ; Spch.

OLMEDA, ANISSA D; Washington HS; Washington, OK; (4); 2/38; Sec FBLA; Pep Clb; Teachers Aide; NHS; Sal; HOSA Treas; U Of OK; Nrsng.

OLSEN, LINDY; Plainview HS; Ardmore, OK; (1); Ed Yrbk; Lit Mag; Hon Roll; Classical Dance Trng 10 Yrs; Eng I Hnrs Awd; OK His Awd.

OLSON, BRANDY L; Yale Jr Sr HS; Yale, OK; (3); Am Leg Aux Girls St; FBLA; FHA; Natl FFA Org; Pres Frsh Cls; VP Soph Cls; Rep Stu Cncl; JV Bsktbl; Var Vllybl; Cit Awd; Amer Lgn Axlry Jr Chptr; Phys Asst.

OLSON, JENNIFER; Tomlinson Jr HS; Lawton, OK; (1); Girl Scts; Pep Clb; Band; Chorus; Mrchg Band; Hon Roll; Jr NHS; All Region Band Flute; Harvard Medcl; Obstetrician.

OLSON, KATHY T; North Intemediate HS; Broken Arrow, OK; (2); Church Yth Grp; French Clb; School Play; Hon Roll; Six Comm Theatre; Plays/Musicals 2 Yrs; Prvt Dnc.

OLSON, MATTHEW; Mc Loud HS; Choctaw, OK; (4); 15/104; Am Leg Boys St; Art Clb; Church Yth Grp; Drama Clb; Speech Tm; Band; Mrchg Band; School Musical; School Play; Variety Show; OSU; Arch Engrng.

OLSON, MATTHEW B; Vinita HS; Vinita, OK; (1); Boy Scts; Church Yth Grp; 4-H; Natl FFA Org; 4-H Awd; Hon Roll; NHS; Eagle Sct; Eng.

OLSON, PAMELA; Stigler HS; Stigler, OK; (3); 1/121; Hosp Aide; Pep Clb; Quiz Bowl; Scholastic Bowl; Hon Roll; NHS; Prfct Atten Awd; Pres Acad Fit Awd; Scuba Diving.

OLSON, SARA A; El Reno Sr HS; El Reno, OK; (3); Church Yth Grp; FHA; Pres FTA; SADD; Yrbk; Hon Roll; Jr NHS; Lawyer.

OLSON, SHANNON M; Aline-Cleo Jr Sr HS; Aline, OK; (4); Church Yth Grp; FCA; FHA; Natl FFA Org; Pep Clb; School Play; Var Bsktbl; Var Chrldng; Var Sftbl; Hon Roll; Chrldr Awd; SW OK ST Univ; Bus Mgmt.

OLSON, SHEILA; Nathan Hale HS; Tulsa, OK; (1); Rep Frsh Cls; JV Chrldng.

OLSON, WYNTER L; Deer Creek HS; Edmond, OK; (2); Church Yth Grp; Debate Tm; NFL; Speech Tm; Church Choir; NHS; Stdnt Ambssdr N Europe; Piano/Voice Study; OK Bapt Univ; Chrst Fmly Cnslg.

OMAN, JEREMY J; Muskogee HS; Muskogee, OK; (2); CAP; ROTC; Drill Tm; NHS; OSU; Engrng; Air Force.

OMARI, MICHELLE S; Oklahoma Sch Of Science & Math; Oklahoma City, OK; (3); Church Yth Grp; Church Choir; Phtg Yrbk; Intrml Bsktbl; Intrml Vllybl; High Hon Roll; Hon Roll; Chorus; Prfct Atten Awd; Natl Macys Schlr; Fndr Akan Assn Jrs Of OK; Indian Natns Presbyn Yth Advy Gen Assmbly Del 96; Pre-Med/Ob Gyn.

O'MEALEY, RYAN T; Blackwell HS; Blackwell, OK; (3); 1/140; Am Leg Boys St; Church Yth Grp; Teachers Aide; Chorus; Church Choir; School Musical; Sec Frsh Cls; High Hon Roll; NHS; Ntl Merit Ltr; Music.

OMMART, LISA M; Yukon HS; Yukon, OK; (4); 81/400; Church Yth Grp; DECA; English Clb; FHA; Spanish Clb; Acpl Chr; Church Choir; Hon Roll; Cmps Lf; Dscpln Comm; Chmbr Chr Sctn Ldr & Stu Dir; Sthrn Nzrn U; Erly Chldhd.

O'NAN III, RALPH TREY; Canton HS; Watonga, OK; (4); Boy Scts; Church Yth Grp; FCA; Scholastic Bowl; Spanish Clb; Band; Mrchg Band; School Play; Nwsp; Bsktbl; Art Conts; OK ST U; Arch.

ONEAL, ADRIANNE; Edison HS; Tulsa, OK; (3); Cmnty Wkr; French Clb; Pep Clb; SADD; Variety Show; Sec Frsh Cls; Sec Jr Cls; Sec Sr Cls; Ofcr Stu Cncl; Chrldng; Multi-Yr Listee; U Of AR; Psych.

O'NEAL, BRANDY M; Sallisaw HS; Sallisaw, OK; (3); 1/140; Church Yth Grp; Cmnty Wkr; Math Clb; Quiz Bowl; Science Clb; Spanish Clb; Var Trk; Cit Awd; High Hon Roll; Hon Roll; Indian Clb; Indian Hnr Soc; Wrestling Homcmng Attendant; OK ST Univ; Pharmacy.

O'NEAL, DAVID; Wynnewood HS; Wynnewood, OK; (1); 12/60; Teachers Aide; Band; Chorus; Jazz Band; Mrchg Band; Orch; Pep Band; East Cntrl U; Ed.

ONEAL, DERRICK D; South Intermediate HS; Broken Arrow, OK; (1); Boy Scts; Church Yth Grp; Intnl Clb; Band; Church Choir; Mrchg Band; Pep Band; Hon Roll; All-Dist Band; Super Ratings On Trumpet Solo & Ensemble At St Cmptn.

O NEAL, EILIS A; Bishop Kelley HS; Tulsa, OK; (1); Drama Clb; NFL; Speech Tm; School Play; Hon Roll; AUTHOR.

O'NEAL, KELLY A; Union Intermediate HS; Tulsa, OK; (1); 125/1000; FCA; Teachers Aide; Drill Tm; Hon Roll.

O'NEAL, KERRI N; Comanche HS; Comanche, OK; (2); Art Clb; Church Yth Grp; Debate Tm; 4-H; FHA; German Clb; GAA; Hosp Aide; Letterman Clb; Pep Clb; Tech Stdnts Amer; West TX A&M.

O'NEAL, MATTHEW R; Lawton Sr HS; Lawton, OK; (2); Orch; School Play; Treas Soph Cls; JV Tennis; L Trk; Var Wrstlng; High Hon Roll; NHS; Pres Acad Fit Awd; Stu Of Today Awd; Engrng.

O'NEAL-BRAY, SHANEY; Clayton Jr Sr HS; Clayton, OK; (4); French Clb; Rptr Nwsp; Rep Frsh Cls; Rep Soph Cls; Rep Jr Cls; Sec Sr Cls; Sec Stu Cncl; JV Bsktbl; Hon Roll; Sooutheastern OK U; Elec Engr.

O'NEILL, ERIN; Edmond North HS; Edmond, OK; (3); 1/350; German Clb; JCL; Pres Sec Key Clb; Hist Latin Clb; Mu Alpha Theta; Service Clb; Rptr Nwsp; Golf; NHS; Ntl Merit Ltr.

ONETH, AMANDA; El Reno Sr HS; El Reno, OK; (4); Key Clb; Band; Flag Corp; Jazz Band; NHS; Elem Ed.

ONEY, AARON; Owasso Sr HS; Owasso, OK; (4); FCA; Ofcr Bsbl; Bsktbl; Hon Roll; Tulsa JC.

ONEY, TODD; Valliant HS; Valliant, OK; (3); 9/78; Red Cross Aide; School Play; Nwsp; Rep Frsh Cls; Rep Soph Cls; Treas Jr Cls; Rep Stu Cncl; Ftbl; Hon Roll; VP NHS; Drug Free Clb; U Of OK; Med.

ONKEN, JENNY R; Harrah HS; Harrah, OK; (3); Church Yth Grp; Natl FFA Org; Chorus; HOSA; Mat Maid Wrestling; Stu Of Quarter Awds; Vol Project Heartland; OK Univ; RN.

ONKEN, PRICE; Mt St Marys HS; Oklahoma City, OK; (1); 10/70; Cmnty Wkr; JV Var Bsktbl; High Hon Roll; St Schlr; OK HS Hnr Soc; Top Stdnt Acad Achvmnt Relgn 1/Span 1 Hnrs; Outstndg Achvmnt Ldrshp Medal; Wake Forest; His.

ON-THE-HILL, BRIAN; Preston Schl; Beggs, OK; (3); Church Yth Grp; Quiz Bowl; Scholastic Bowl; High Hon Roll; OK HS Hnr Soc; Comm.

ONTIVEROS, MICHELLE; Crescent Schl; Crescent, OK; (2); FCA; Band; Mrchg Band; Pep Band; Bsktbl; Sftbl; Trk; Hon Roll; Pres Acad Fit Awd; OSU; Nrsng.

OPHOFF, AMY; Victory Christian Schl; Tulsa, OK; (1); 4/75; Church Yth Grp; Band; Jazz Band; Orch; Pep Band; Chrldng; Gym; High Hon Roll; Jr NHS; Oral Roberts U; Elem Ed.

OPPEL, MARK; Lomega HS; Kingfisher, OK; (4); 1/12; Am Leg Boys St; Church Yth Grp; FCA; HOBY; Natl FFA Org; Scholastic Bowl; Phtg Rptr Yrbk; Pres Sr Cls; Sec Stu Cncl; DAR Awd; OSU; Ag Bus.

ORBAN, DANIEL T; Enid Sr HS; Enid, OK; (2); Boy Scts; Church Yth Grp; Office Aide; High Hon Roll; Hon Roll; Jr NHS; NHS; Prfct Atten Awd; Comp Sci.

ORENDORFF, KEITH; Central Schl; Gans, OK; (2); Boy Scts; Computer Clb; Pep Clb; Var Bsbl; Var Bsktbl; Hon Roll; NHS.

ORGAIN, ALLAN M; Hammon Schl; Hammon, OK; (3); Church Yth Grp; FCA; Var Bsbl; Var Bsktbl; Var Golf; High Hon Roll; NHS; Val.

OROZCO, MARIANA; U S Grant HS; Oklahoma City, OK; (1); Church Choir; Hon Roll; Cert Excllnc; OU; Psych.

ORR, AMANDA; Plainview HS; Ardmore, OK; (3); 3/83; Church Yth Grp; FCA; GAA; Mu Alpha Theta; Natl Beta Clb; SADD; Teachers Aide; Rep Stu Cncl; Var Crs Cntry; Var Trk; U Of OK; Pre-Med; Dermatologist.

ORR, AMANDA R; Choctaw HS; Choctaw, OK; (2); Church Yth Grp; FCA; Key Clb; Library Aide; Pep Clb; SADD; School Play; Bsktbl; Mgr(s); Sftbl; OU; Animal Hosp.

ORR, JENNIFER; Madill HS; Madill, OK; (3); 4-H; GAA; Natl FFA Org; SADD; Varsity Clb; VP Soph Cls; JV Var Bsktbl; JV Var Chrldng; 4-H Awd; Hon Roll; OK; Nursng.

ORR, KATHRYN E; Stillwater Sr HS; Stillwater, OK; (3); 4-H; FBLA; Sec Natl FFA Org; Teachers Aide; OK ST Univ; Vet.

ORR, MATTHEW A; Ponca City Sr HS; Ponca City, OK; (3); Church Yth Grp; 4-H; Natl FFA Org; Quiz Bowl; L Bsktbl; Hon Roll; NHS; Aero/Law Enfor.

ORR, S S; Sallisaw HS; Sallisaw, OK; (4); 6/138; Math Clb; Quiz Bowl; Science Clb; Spanish Clb; Chorus; Hon Roll; NHS; Ntl Merit SF; Vet.

ORSATTI, ANDREA R; Midwest City HS; Midwest City, OK; (2); 91/473; Flag Corp; JV Socr; Hon Roll; NHS; Russn Clb; OSU; MIS.

ORTIZ, ELISHA D; East Central HS; Tulsa, OK; (2); Spanish Clb; JV Sftbl; Hon Roll; Acctnt.

ORTLOFF, BRADLEY; Madill HS; Madill, OK; (1); Church Yth Grp; Speech Tm; School Musical; High Hon Roll; NHS; Acad Team; OK U; Physcst.

ORUM, BRENDA B; Healdton HS; Healdton, OK; (3); FHA; Teachers Aide; Nwsp; Yrbk.

ORVIS, BRANDY M; Wagoner Sr HS; Wagoner, OK; (4); English Clb; Intnl Clb; Band; Color Guard; Jazz Band; Mrchg Band; Lit Mag; Score Keeper; Var Socr; Rke Awd Bnd; Mst Imprvd Sccr; VP Frgn Lang; Hd Schl Accld; Prm Comm 95-96; TU; Geo Sci.

OSBORN, ERIN L; Little Axe Sr HS; Newalla, OK; (3); Chorus; Hon Roll; OK Univ; Dentistry.

OSBORN, KENDRA J; Union Intermediate HS; Tulsa, OK; (2); Church Yth Grp; Spanish Clb; High Hon Roll; Mission Trips El Salvador Smmr 95, Hong Kong Smmr 96; Nursng.

OSBORN, MATT L; Ardmore HS; Ardmore, OK; (4); Art Clb; Bus Profs of Am; DECA; FCA; FBLA; JA; JCL; Latin Clb; Mu Alpha Theta; Office Aide; El Chico Stu Of Month; Southeastern OK ST; Bus Mgmt.

OSBORN, MELISSA; Kingston HS; Durant, OK; (2); Church Yth Grp; Dance Clb; French Clb; FHA; Quiz Bowl; Thesps; Chorus; Sec Soph Cls; High Hon Roll; NHS; SW OK St Univ.

OSBORN, SCOTT; Bluejacket Schl; Bluejacket, OK; (1); 3/23; Church Yth Grp; Natl FFA Org; Quiz Bowl; Band; Hon Roll; Law Enfrcmnt.

OSBORN, SHARON; Comanche HS; Duncan, OK; (2); Church Yth Grp; German Clb; Girl Scts; Band; Mrchg Band; Hon Roll; Tchr.

OSBORN, SHONDA LEIGH; Norman Sr HS; Norman, OK; (4); 510/599; Church Yth Grp; Cmnty Wkr; FCA; Service Clb; Teachers Aide; Variety Show; Ofcr Sr Cls; Rep Stu Cncl; Intrml JV Chrldng; JV Var Powder Puff Ftbl; Rotry Stu Of The Month; UOK; Mrktng; Petro Land Mgmt.

OSBORN, STEPHANIE; Tonkawa Jr Sr HS; Tonkawa, OK; (3); Am Leg Aux Girls St; Church Yth Grp; FCA; Red Cross Aide; Teachers Aide; Chorus; Sec Stu Cncl; Var Bsktbl; Var Chrldng; Var Sftbl; Grls St Del; Page OK Hs Reps; 2 Time St Qulfr 100 M Dash.

OSBORNE, JENNIFER; Ft Towson HS; Fort Towson, OK; (1); 2/35; Church Yth Grp; FCA; FHA; Yrbk; Rep Stu Cncl; Cit Awd; High Hon Roll; Hon Roll; Sal; Bsktbl Camera Person; FCA Skit Team; Nrsgn Home Vol; Med.

OSBORNE, SASHA; Sasakwa Schl; Ada, OK; (1); 3/20; Church Yth Grp; Cmnty Wkr; GAA; Girl Scts; Pep Clb; SADD; Drill Tm; Pres Frsh Cls; Bsktbl; Score Keeper; East Cntrl U; Phys Thrpy.

OSBORNE, SHARELKA R; Westmoore HS; Oklahoma City, OK; (4); Cmnty Wkr; FBLA; JCL; Office Aide; Rep Stu Cncl; Tennis; Pres Acad Fit Awd; FHA; School Musical; Yth/Govt Sec; Yng Dmcrts Pres Cmpgn/Promote Awareness; Yth Ldrshp Exch; U Of OK; Eng/Atty/Judge.

OSBORNE, SUSAN M; Yukon Middle HS; Yukon, OK; (1); Spanish Clb; Trk; FFA; OK ST Univ; Anesthesiologist.

OSBURN, AUDREY; Norman Sr HS; Norman, OK; (4); 67/678; Am Leg Aux Girls St; Church Yth Grp; Socr; JCL; Latin Clb; Math Clb; Model UN; Spanish Clb; SADD; Varsity Clb; AZ ST; Accntng.

OSBURN, BOBBY L; Olive Jr Sr HS; Jennings, OK; (3); 10/36; FCA; Natl FFA Org; VICA; Var Bsktbl; Trk; Hon Roll; NHS; SW OK St Univ; Telecomm.

OSBURN, DARICE R; Tahlequah Sr HS; Tahlequah, OK; (2); Church Yth Grp; Color Guard; Drill Tm; Mrchg Band; Mgr(s); Winterguard; Tri St Hnr Bnd; OK St Univ; Mus.

OSBURN, KATIE M; Enid Sr HS; Enid, OK; (2); Dance Clb; Chorus; Hon Roll.

OSHEL, STEPHANIE; Alva HS; Aline, OK; (3); FCA; FHA; Key Clb; Spanish Clb; SADD; Bsktbl; High Hon Roll; Hon Roll; NHS; Church Yth Grp; Hnr Schlr; Nrthwstern OSU; Pre-Med.

OSMUS, BRAD; Fairview HS; Fairview, OK; (3); Church Yth Grp; Band; Mrchg Band; Ofcr Bsbl; Bsktbl; Ftbl; High Hon Roll; NHS; Prfct Atten Awd.

OSMUS, LACI; Okeene Jr Sr HS; Okeene, OK; (4); 4/30; Church Yth Grp; Speech Tm; School Play; VP Stu Cncl; Gov Hon Prg Awd; High Hon Roll; Hon Roll; Pres NHS; Prfct Atten Awd; Val; Chldrns Choir Drctr At Chrch; Tutrng Stu; Concurred Enrllmnt RedlandsCC; SW OK St Univ; Ed.

O'STEEN, EMILY; Claremore Sr HS; Claremore, OK; (2); Church Yth Grp; Cmnty Wkr; Drama Clb; Hosp Aide; NFL; Office Aide; Speech Tm; VP SADD; High Hon Roll; Jr NHS; Med.

OTERO, IVAN; Plainview HS; Ardmore, OK; (3); Quiz Bowl; ROTC; Band; Jazz Band; Mrchg Band; Pep Band; Nwsp; Lit Mag; Hon Roll; Prfct Atten Awd; Mem Of Order Of De Molay; Rep De Molay Awd; OSU; Bus; Ed.

OTERO, RANCES; Plainview HS; Ardmore, OK; (1); Quiz Bowl; Band; Jazz Band; Mrchg Band; Pep Band; Hon Roll; Intl Order De Molay; SCOBDA Concert/Jazz Bands 95-; OSU; Music.

OTEY, HILARY T; Cascia Hall Prep School; Tulsa, OK; (2); Art Clb; Pep Clb; Hon Roll; Red Cross STAY Pgm; Young Life Of TULSA; Pottery.

OTIS, MEREDITH A; Mc Alester HS; Mcalester, OK; (3); Art Clb; French Clb; Speech Tm; Drill Tm; Treas Stu Cncl; Pom Pon; Hon Roll; OK ST Univ; Eng.

O'TOOLE, ERIN E; Union Intermediate HS; Tulsa, OK; (2); Intnl Clb; Ofcr Stu Cncl; Pom Pon; Hon Roll; Jr NHS; NHS; NCA All Amer Dance Tm; Union JV Pom Co Cap; Slct Dance Trp Tm Seige.

OTT, ANGELA; Stratford Schl; Stratford, OK; (2); FCA; FHA; Var Bsktbl; Var Trk; High Hon Roll; NHS; ECU; Med.

OTT, DUSTIN L; Dibble Jr Sr HS; Blanchard, OK; (4); 7/33; FHA; Scholastic Bowl; Teachers Aide; Rep Stu Cncl; Ofcr Bsbl; Bsktbl; Hon Roll; Coca Cola Ath Schlrsp 96; Bsbl OK ST Hnrbl Mntn 96; OK Ltl All Cty Hnrble Mntn 96; Murray ST Coll; PE/COACHING.

OTT, JAMES; Central Mid-HS; Norman, OK; (2); #1 in class; Church Yth Grp; FCA; Ftbl; Wt Lftg; Cit Awd; High Hon Roll; OK U; Med.

OTT, JASON J; Dibble Jr Sr HS; Blanchard, OK; (2); Natl FFA Org; Pres Soph Cls; Rep Stu Cncl; Var Bsbl; Var Bsktbl; Hon Roll; OK All ST Hon Ment Bsbl 96; Little All Cty Hon Ment Bsbl 96; Grady Cty All Tourn Tm Bsktbl 96.

OTT, JULIE L; Cherokee Jr Sr HS; Cherokee, OK; (4); 1/23; Church Yth Grp; Debate Tm; FHA; Quiz Bowl; Speech Tm; Yrbk; Rep Jr Cls; Sec Sr Cls; Ofcr Stu Cncl; Bsktbl; OSU; Optometry.

OTT JR, LUCKY STEVE; Okemah HS; Okemah, OK; (4); 2/60; Am Leg Boys St; Boy Scts; Cmnty Wkr; Key Clb; Math Tm; Sec Natl Beta Clb; Scholastic Bowl; Science Clb; SADD; Nwsp; Mdl Cngrss Sen; Mst Lkly Scceed; Eagle Sct Awd; U OK; Bus.

OTT, MARLA; Putnam City North HS; Oklahoma City, OK; (2); Church Yth Grp; Scholastic Bowl; Spanish Clb; Orch; School Musical; Variety Show; Hon Roll; NHS; Silver Strings Of Putnam City; Chrch Orch; OSU; Vet.

OTT, MATTHEW R; Edmond North HS; Edmond, OK; (1); 141/456; Church Yth Grp; ROTC; Band; Flag Corp; Mrchg Band; Ftbl; Trk; Wrstlng; Kitty Hawk Hnr Soc.

OTTERSTROM, ABBIGAIL A; Bishop Kelley HS; Tulsa, OK; (1); Church Yth Grp; Vllybl; Hon Roll.

OTTERSTROM, SANDRA M; Bishop Kelley HS; Tulsa, OK; (2); Church Yth Grp; Pep Clb; Red Cross Aide; School Musical; Var Vllybl; Hon Roll; Right To Life Group; Tulsa Dreamcatchers, Vllybl Team Of Best Players In OK; U Of SC; Optometry; Dentistry.

OUTHIER, ALISSA; Okeene Jr Sr HS; Okeene, OK; (3); 3/30; Church Yth Grp; FHA; VP Jr Cls; Var Bsktbl; Var Chrldng; Var Sftbl; Cit Awd; High Hon Roll; Kiwanis Awd; NHS; Bus.

OVERBAY, AMY; Hennessey HS; Hennessey, OK; (3); 3/65; VP FHA; German Clb; Quiz Bowl; Pres Band; Mrchg Band; Hon Roll; NHS; Treas Frsh Cls; Rep Soph Cls; Sthwstrn OK ST U; Med.

OVERLAND, MATTHEW A; Shawnee Sr HS; Shawnee, OK; (1); Ofcr Bsbl; Ftbl; Hon Roll.

OVERTON, HEATHER R; Midwest City HS; Midwest City, OK; (2); FCA; 4-H; Band; Doctor.

OVERTON, JEFFREY A; Claremore Sr HS; Claremore, OK; (2); Boy Scts; Science Clb; Spanish Clb; Swmmng; Hon Roll; NHS; Sprts Med.

OVERTON, MATTHEW A; Midwest City HS; Midwest City, OK; (2); 177/473; Church Yth Grp; FCA; Band; Jazz Band; Mrchg Band; Pep Band; Crs Cntry; Trk; Wrstlng; Cmptr Prgmr/Engr.

OVERTURF, GINA M; Bartlesville Mid HS; Bartlesville, OK; (2); Church Yth Grp; FHA; Office Aide; Church Choir; Orch; High Hon Roll; Hon Roll.

OWEN, CHRISTINA B; Moore HS; Moore, OK; (3); Am Leg Aux Girls St; Church Yth Grp; Debate Tm; NFL; Office Aide; Spanish Clb; Speech Tm; SADD; Cit Awd; Pr Hlpr VP; Msnc Awd; U OK.

OWEN, CRYSTAL; Silo HS; Mead, OK; (3); Church Yth Grp; FHA; GAA; Pep Clb; Teachers Aide; Mrchg Band; Bsktbl; Crs Cntry; High Hon Roll; Hon Roll; Southeastern; Pre-K Tchr.

OWEN, JUSTIN; Washington HS; Norman, OK; (4); 1/40; Cmnty Wkr; Pres Natl FFA Org; Teachers Aide; Gov Hon Prg Awd; NHS; Val; OK ST Univ; Mech Engr.

OWEN, KIM; Perry Sr HS; Perry, OK; (3); FBLA; FHA; Yrbk; High Hon Roll; Jr NHS; NHS; Pres Acad Fit Awd; U Of OK; Law.

OWEN, KYLE; Tonkawa Jr Sr HS; Tonkawa, OK; (3); Church Yth Grp; FCA; Natl FFA Org; Rep Frsh Cls; Treas Stu Cncl; Var L Bsbl; Var L Bsktbl; Var L Ftbl; High Hon Roll; NHS; Bsktbl St Rnnr Up 94; Ftbl St Semi-Fnlst 95; Stu Cncl St Cnvntn Del.

OWENS, ALBERTA N; Northeast HS; Oklahoma City, OK; (2); Church Yth Grp; Cmnty Wkr; FBLA; FHA; Pep Clb; Chorus; Co-Ed Yrbk; Sec Frsh Cls; Stat Bsktbl; Hon Roll; Eta Phi Beta Yth Grp Pres Sthrn Rgn Sec; Yth Ushr Bd VP; NSBE Jr; NC A&T; Engr.

OWENS, AMBER R; Colcord Schl; Colcord, OK; (1); Natl FFA Org; Bsktbl; 4-H Awd; Hon Roll; Prfct Atten Awd; Sal; AR U; Chld Psych.

OWENS, ANN E; Broken Bow HS; Broken Bow, OK; (3); Art Clb; Cmnty Wkr; FCA; Science Clb; Spanish Clb; Variety Show; Bsktbl; Powder Puff Ftbl; Trk; Hon Roll; Comp Tech.

OWENS, CARISA NICOLE; Nowata HS; Nowata, OK; (4); FHA; Office Aide; Teachers Aide; Chorus; School Musical; School Play; Nwsp; Hon Roll.

OWENS, CHRISTINA B; Lindsay HS; Lindsay, OK; (2); 49/79; Art Clb; Church Yth Grp; FHA; Chorus; Nrsng.

OWENS, CODY M; Western Heights Sr HS; Oklahoma City, OK; (1); #1 in class; Var Bsbl; Var Bsktbl; Wt Lftg; High Hon Roll; NHS; Hunting; Fishing; OK Univ; Wldlf Bio.

OWENS, DANELLE S; Del City HS; Del City, OK; (4); 96/432; Drama Clb; High Hon Roll; Hon Roll; Prfct Atten Awd; Opthdntst.

OWENS, ELIZABETH R; Fox Sr HS; Fox, OK; (3); 11/28; Sec Church Yth Grp; FCA; 4-H; Natl FFA Org; Pres Frsh Cls; Rep Soph Cls; Sec Pres Jr Cls; Var Bsktbl; Var Sftbl; Lvstck Jdgng Tm FFA; Show Tm Lvstck FFA; Natl FFA Ldrshp Conf Ofcr Tm Rptr; Murray ST Coll; Lgl Asst.

OWENS, EMILIE; Moore HS; Moore, OK; (4); 1/525; Pres VP Church Yth Grp; FCA; English Clb; Service Clb; Band; Church Choir; Mrchg Band; Var L Swmmng; High Hon Roll; Kiwanis Awd; Valparaiso U.

OWENS, GARRETT G; Bethany HS; Bethany, OK; (3); 4/65; Church Yth Grp; Debate Tm; Drama Clb; FCA; Teachers Aide; JV Var Bsktbl; Var Trk; High Hon Roll; Hon Roll; Jr NHS; Natl Eng Merit Schlr; Southern Nazarene U; FBI/MD.

OWENS, MIKE B; Meeker HS; Meeker, OK; (1); 1/115; Scholastic Bowl; Speech Tm; School Play; JV Ftbl; Var Trk; Var Wt Lftg; NHS; Prfct Atten Awd; Pres Acad Fit Awd; St Schlr; Outstndng Geometry Stu Awd; Outstndng World His Awd; OK ST Univ; Architecture.

OWENS, MISTY D; Colcord Schl; Colcord, OK; (2); Church Yth Grp; Drama Clb; FHA; Church Choir; Nwsp; High Hon Roll; Hon Roll.

OWENS, MONICA J; Claremore Sr HS; Claremore, OK; (1); Church Yth Grp; Drama Clb; NFL; Scholastic Bowl; School Play; Stage Crew; Variety Show; Rep Stu Cncl; Hon Roll; Outstdng Nvc Drama Stdnt; Psychlgy.

OWENS, PATRICIA M; Newcastle HS; Newcastle, OK; (3); FHA; Spanish Clb; Chorus; Zoology; Zoologist.

OWENS, PAUL A; Christian Heritage Acad; Oklahoma City, OK; (2); Church Yth Grp; JV Bsktbl; Hon Roll; Prfct Atten Awd.

OWENS, ROBERT L; Spiro HS; Spiro, OK; (4); 4-H; FFA 4 Yrs; Elctrcty Tm 3 Yrs; Show Lvestck 3 Yrs; E OK ST Coll; Animal Sci.

OWENS, SARA B; Muldrow HS; Muldrow, OK; (2); Church Yth Grp; Natl Beta Clb; Science Clb; Speech Tm; Band; Mrchg Band; JV Sftbl; NHS; Pres Acad Fit Awd; His Tchr.

OWENS, SARAH M; Adair HS; Adair, OK; (3); Church Yth Grp; Debate Tm; Drama Clb; FCA; FHA; German Clb; Quiz Bowl; Science Clb; Speech Tm; Variety Show.

OWENS, SHAWN; Westmoore HS; Moore, OK; (3); Office Aide; JV L Ftbl; Pre-Law/Lawyer.

OWENS, STACIE D; Edmond Memorial HS; Edmond, OK; (2); 129/408; Church Yth Grp; Spanish Clb; Orch; NHS; Dancing; U Of OK; Psychiatry.

OWENS, TERRI D; Grove HS; Jay, OK; (2); Church Yth Grp; Girl Scts; Key Clb; Band; Jazz Band; Mrchg Band; Hon Roll; NHS; Heritage Clb.

OWENS, TINA; Putnam City HS; Bethany, OK; (4); 60/348; Church Yth Grp; Cmnty Wkr; Debate Tm; FCA; NFL; Spanish Clb; Chorus; Yrbk; Ofcr Frsh Cls; Ofcr Soph Cls; Daybreak Pres; OK Chrstn U; Engl/Law.

OWENS, TONISHIA J; B T Washington HS; Tulsa, OK; (4); 150/264; FBLA; Band; Mrchg Band; Sec Jr Cls; Jr NHS; Xino; Tutorng; Vlntr Wrk; Langston U; Biochem.

OWENS-LITTLE JIM, DEE ANN; Little Axe Sr HS; Norman, OK; (2); Church Yth Grp; Cmnty Wkr; FHA; Church Choir; Yrbk; Ofcr Bsbl; Mgr(s); Score Keeper; Cit Awd; High Hon Roll; Supt Hnr Roll; KS U; Phy.

OWL, JOSEPH B; Stilwell HS; Stilwell, OK; (2); Natl FFA Org; Hon Roll; NSU.

OWNBY, MARY; Stillwater Jr HS; Stillwater, OK; (3); 86/353; JCL; Key Clb; Latin Clb; Mu Alpha Theta; Teachers Aide; Band; Color Guard; Mrchg Band; Pep Band; Powder Puff Ftbl; Erthwtch Dig; Rode Hrses 7 Yrs; U Of AZ; Anthrplgy.

OZGUNESLILER, ONUR; Strother Jr Sr HS; Seminole, OK; (4); GAA; Library Aide; Scholastic Bowl; Band; Chorus; School Play; Rep Stu Cncl; Diving; Socr; Swmmng; Turkish, German, Spnsh Langs; Frgn Exchng Stu; OK ST U; Restrnt/Hotl Mgmt.

PACE, RHONDA R; Shawnee Sr HS; Tecumseh, OK; (4); 52/260; Library Aide; Office Aide; Spanish Clb; Band; Mrchg Band; High Hon Roll; Hon Roll; NHS; Church Yth Grp; Pep Clb; Natl His/Govt Awd; Spirit Brigade; SOS; East Cntrl Univ; Bus Mngmt/Span.

PACK, BRIANNA; Tuttle HS; Tuttle, OK; (3); Spanish Clb; Band; Mrchg Band; Hon Roll; Engl Tchr.

PACK, BRYAN; Bethany HS; Bethany, OK; (2); Church Yth Grp; Cmnty Wkr; Debate Tm; Letterman Clb; Speech Tm; Church Choir; Var Bsktbl; Var Golf; Var Trk; Var Wt Lftg; Outstdng Male Soph Ath 95-; Excl Awd Fine Arts Nal Fest 95-; KU.

PACK, CHERYL; Will Rogers HS; Tulsa, OK; (4); 32/201; Cmnty Wkr; French Clb; Key Clb; ROTC; Teachers Aide; Color Guard; Drill Tm; VP Soph Cls; Ofcr Jr Cls; VP Sr Cls; Cadet Of Month; Stdnt Of Month; Girl Of Yr; Tulsa JC; PT Asstnt.

PACK, GABRIEL J; Pauls Valley HS; Pauls Valley, OK; (2); Church Yth Grp; Cit Awd; Hon Roll; Prfct Atten Awd; Aeronautics Engr.

PACK, NACHELLE; Tuttle HS; Tuttle, OK; (1); 21/101; Church Yth Grp; GAA; Rptr Frsh Cls; Var Bsktbl; Var Chrldng; Var Wt Lftg; High Hon Roll; Hon Roll; NHS; U Of OK; Medcl.

PACK, NICOLE; Midwest City HS; Midwest City, OK; (4); 35/427; FHA; German Clb; Library Aide; Office Aide; Pep Clb; SADD; Teachers Aide; Nwsp; Ofcr Soph Cls; Ofcr Jr Cls; Rose St Jr Coll Cncrrnt Enrlmnt; OKU; Acctng.

PACZKOWSKI, CHRISTINE M; Ponca City Sr HS; Ponca City, OK; (4); #1 in class; French Clb; Math Tm; Band; Flag Corp; Mrchg Band; Orch; High Hon Roll; NHS; Ntl Merit SF; Val; Duke U; Biomed Engrng.

PADEN, BRITTANIE; Choctaw Jr HS; Choctaw, OK; (1); Church Yth Grp; FCA; Sec Treas Stu Cncl; Chrldng; Trk; Cit Awd; Hon Roll; NCA All-Amer Chrldr.

PADEN, DAWN R; Hartshorne Sr HS; Hartshorne, OK; (2); Church Yth Grp; Spanish Clb; School Play; Rptr Nwsp; Rep Frsh Cls; Var Bsktbl; Var Sftbl; Cit Awd; Hon Roll; OK Hnr Soc; Law Enforcement.

PADEN, DENICE; Hartshorne Sr HS; Hartshorne, OK; (3); Art Clb; Computer Clb; Office Aide; Rptr Nwsp; Rep Frsh Cls; VP Jr Cls; Ofcr Stu Cncl; Sftbl; NHS; Pres Acad Fit Awd; Med.

PADGETT, KYNA G; Duncan HS; Duncan, OK; (3); Church Yth Grp; Hosp Aide; SADD; Var L Bsktbl; Var L Crs Cntry; Var L Trk; NHS; OK Hnr Soc; Hlth Careers Clb; Ldrshp Duncan Cls II; OK Bapt U; Sports Med.

PADILLA, ISRAEL; Hobart HS; Hobart, OK; (2); Spanish Clb; Temple Yth Grp; Var Ftbl; Var Socr; Var Wt Lftg; 1st Pl Span SWIM; Tulsa; Eng/Arch.

PADLEY, CHRISTOPHER; Union Intermediate HS; Tulsa, OK; (2); FCA; Spanish Clb; Var Ftbl; Hon Roll; DFY; OK ST U; Bus Mgmt.

PAGE, BRYAN E; Bishop Kelley HS; Tulsa, OK; (4); Pres Church Yth Grp; Model UN; Ofcr Stu Cncl; JV Bsktbl; Hon Roll; Jr NHS; Ntl Merit SF; Pres Schlr; Yth Advsry Bd; Sr Boy Of Month; Alpha Phi Alpha Scholastic Awd; OK Univ; Engr.

PAGE, JOSHUA G; Sallisaw HS; Sallisaw, OK; (2); 1/210; Art Clb; Math Clb; Quiz Bowl; Science Clb; Spanish Clb; Yrbk; Cit Awd; Hon Roll; NHS; Prfct Atten Awd; OK His Schlr Fnlst 95; Envrnmntl Sci.

PAGE, RALPH E; Eisenhower Sr HS; Lawton, OK; (3); Art Clb; Sec Pres Intnl Clb; Hon Roll; Jr NHS; Gifted/Talented Club; Acad Ltr; Cameron; Sci Field.

PAGEL, MIKA M; Bridge Creek HS; Blanchard, OK; (3); 18/62; Acpl Chr; Chorus; Treas Sr Cls; Hon Roll; Hnrs Eng; Cshr Lngstn Wstrn Wear OK City; Essay Pckd; OK CC; Lgl Sec Tech.

PAGET, KENNETH T; Nathan Hale HS; Tulsa, OK; (3); Church Yth Grp; Cmnty Wkr; Ftbl; High Hon Roll; Hon Roll; Jr NHS; NHS; Yth Council; Fellowship Committee; Physical Therapy.

PAGET, NICKIE; Oologah Talala HS; Nowata, OK; (1); Church Yth Grp; 4-H; GAA; Varsity Clb; Ofcr Frsh Cls; Ofcr Stu Cncl; Chrldng; Gym; Sftbl; Wt Lftg; Trail Of Tears Excl Awd; Pharmacist.

PAGETT, MACHELLE; Woodward HS; Woodward, OK; (3); Church Yth Grp; Cmnty Wkr; Computer Clb; FTA; German Clb; Key Clb; Letterman Clb; Band; Color Guard; Nwsp; Re Dinks; OK ST Univ; Chrprctr.

PAIGE, AMY S; Blackwell HS; Blackwell, OK; (4); 16/117; Church Yth Grp; Pep Clb; Chorus; Church Choir; School Musical; High Hon Roll; Hon Roll; Jr NHS; NHS; St Hnr Soc; Northern OK Coll; Paralegl; Law.

PAIGE, CHERON; Midwest City HS; Oklahoma City, OK; (2); Band; Jr NHS; OK ST U.

PAINE, KRISTIN M; Edmond Memrl HS; Edmond, OK; (3); Church Yth Grp; FCA; French Clb; Latin Clb; Pep Clb; SADD; Yrbk; Var Chrldng; Powder Puff Ftbl; Trk; U Of CO; RN.

PAINTER, CLINT; Okemah HS; Okemah, OK; (1); 4-H; Key Clb; Natl FFA Org; Science Clb; SADD; Stage Crew; Var Bsbl; Var Bsktbl; Var Ftbl; Var Score Keeper; Beta Clb.

PAINTER, JUSTIN; Pauls Valley HS; Pauls Valley, OK; (3); 2/108; Am Leg Boys St; Church Yth Grp; FCA; French Clb; Pep Clb; VP Stu Cncl; Bsktbl; Golf; Cit Awd; High Hon Roll; NE OK St Univ; Optometrist.

PAINTER, TABITHA; Woodward HS; Woodward, OK; (3); Computer Clb; Debate Tm; Drama Clb; FHA; FTA; Pep Clb; Band; Drm Mjr(t); Mrchg Band; Pep Band; Sr Rep Re'Dinks; Southwestern; Tchr.

PAINTER, VANESSA A; Memorial HS; Tulsa, OK; (3); Art Clb; Red Cross Aide; High Hon Roll; Hon Roll; NHS; Art/Phtgrphy.

PALAGI, DOUGLAS J; Union Sr HS; Tulsa, OK; (3); 30/741; Church Yth Grp; Cmnty Wkr; FCA; FBLA; Spanish Clb; Teachers Aide; Varsity Clb; Ftbl; Wrstlng; Cit Awd; Aviation.

PALIDAR, SABRINA; Holdenville HS; Holdenville, OK; (4); 10/78; Church Yth Grp; Drama Clb; FCA; Natl FFA Org; Office Aide; Scholastic Bowl; Science Clb; Band; Chorus; Flag Corp; Northeastern ST U OK.

PALMER, D'YONNE R; Central HS; Tulsa, OK; (4); 74/200; Church Yth Grp; Cmnty Wkr; ROTC; Service Clb; Church Choir; School Play; Ofcr Stu Cncl; Cit Awd; Hon Roll; Prfct Atten Awd; 1st Cls Platton Ldr; St Rep Cert Of Congratulations; US Navy Naval Enlistment Pgm; Navy.

PALMER, DIRK E; Henryetta Sr HS; Checotah, OK; (3); 6/70; Church Yth Grp; Library Aide; Sec Treas Yrbk; VP Frsh Cls; Sec Treas Soph Cls; Var Bsbl; Var Bsktbl; Hon Roll; NHS; St Schlr; Hrsbck Rdng; Hunting; OK ST Univ; Cmptr Engr.

PALMER, ERIN; Kingfisher HS; Kingfisher, OK; (3); 2/100; Church Yth Grp; Key Clb; NFL; Speech Tm; Stage Crew; Tennis; Cit Awd; High Hon Roll; NHS; Drama Clb; Athl Trnr; U Of OK; Med.

PALMER, JASON M; Spiro HS; Spiro, OK; (4); Spanish Clb; Hon Roll.

PALMER, KELLY D; Claremore Sr HS; Claremore, OK; (3); 23/237; Art Clb; Church Yth Grp; Hosp Aide; Library Aide; Spanish Clb; School Play; Gym; Wrstlng; High Hon Roll; NHS; Natl Hnr Soc Treas; Wrestling Mat Maid; OK HS Hnr Soc; Natl Yth Ldrshp Med; Dr/Pre Med.

PALMER, MELAINE D; Olney Schl; Coalgate, OK; (1); Chorus; Var Sftbl; Notre Dame; CopNRS.

PALMER, MICHAEL; Chickasha Jr HS; Chickasha, OK; (1); Ofcr Bsbl; Bsktbl; Jr NHS; U Of OK.

PALMER, MICHELLE M; South Intermediate HS; Broken Arrow, OK; (2); JV Capt Socr; Phys Thpy.

PALMER, SARAH; Mc Curtain HS; Mccurtain, OK; (4); 4/11; Church Yth Grp; 4-H; Teachers Aide; Pres Sr Cls; Carl Albert ST Coll; Soc Work.

PALMER, TARA; Chickasha HS; Chickasha, OK; (3); Am Leg Aux Girls St; Cmnty Wkr; FCA; French Clb; FHA; Chorus; Ofcr Frsh Cls; Ofcr Stu Cncl; Bsktbl; Chrldng; OK U; Bus/Med.

PALMER, TYRONE V; Perkins-Tryon HS; Perkins, OK; (2); Band; Chorus; Jazz Band; Mrchg Band; Pep Band; Trk; Hon Roll; Intnl Clb; Office Aide; Bible Preaching; Comm Theatre; Austrias Millenium Musical Celebrant; Art.

PALMETER, SARAH; Shawnee Sr HS; Shawnee, OK; (3); 13/282; Church Yth Grp; Spanish Clb; Church Choir; Phtg Yrbk; High Hon Roll; Big Bros Big Sis Jr Brd; Natl Mrt Qulfr.

PALS, KENDRA; Stillwater Jr HS; Stillwater, OK; (1); Yrbk; Bsktbl; Golf; Hon Roll; Pres Ed Awds Prgm; OK ST Univ; Intnl Trvl Cnslnt.

PANACH, BECKY L; Billings HS; Billings, OK; (3); FHA; School Play; Yrbk; Nursng.

PANHEY, MAKEA C; Okmulgee HS; Okmulgee, OK; (1); Church Yth Grp; Office Aide; Chorus; Church Choir; Sec Frsh Cls; Crs Cntry; Mgr(s); Cit Awd; High Hon Roll; OK ST U; Phys Thrpy.

PANKEY, CHERISE N; Owasso Sr HS; Owasso, OK; (3); 43/357; Teachers Aide; Chorus; Rptr Nwsp; Phtg Rptr Yrbk; High Hon Roll; Prfct Atten Awd; TAG; Bus Mgmt.

PANKEY, TWYLA M; Oologah HS; Oologah, OK; (2); Debate Tm; Drama Clb; Speech Tm; Socr; NHS; OK ST Univ; Actrs/Drama Tchr.

PANKHURST, HEATHER; Lone Wolf Schl; Hobart, OK; (1); Church Yth Grp; Dance Clb; FHA; Girl Scts; Church Choir; Hon Roll; Art.

PANNELL, CRISTY; Coleman Schl; Coleman, OK; (3); 1/18; Sec Treas FCA; Quiz Bowl; Scholastic Bowl; Ski Clb; Chorus; Rptr Nwsp; Phtg Yrbk; VP Jr Cls; Var Bsktbl; NHS; Southeastern OK ST U.

PANNELL, JAMES; Coleman Schl; Coleman, OK; (1); 1/16; Church Yth Grp; Cmnty Wkr; FCA; Quiz Bowl; Scholastic Bowl; Ski Clb; Church Choir; School Play; Var Bsktbl; Cit Awd; SE OK ST; Coach.

PANNELL, JENNIFER L; Claremore Sr HS; Claremore, OK; (2); 95/270; Church Yth Grp; FCA; Natl FFA Org; Office Aide; SADD; Chorus; Church Choir; School Play; Chrldng; Pom Pon; USAA Natl Math Awd; OK ST U; Agribus.

PANTER, BEN; Stilwell HS; Stilwell, OK; (3); Church Yth Grp; FCA; Math Tm; Varsity Clb; Bsktbl; Var Ftbl; High Hon Roll; NHS.

PAPPY, RAJI; Piedmont HS; Oklahoma City, OK; (4); 2/80; Boy Scts; Church Yth Grp; Cmnty Wkr; Computer Clb; JA; Key Clb; Quiz Bowl; Scholastic Bowl; Service Clb; SADD; OK City U; Pre-Med.

PAQUE, JOEL P; Santa Fe HS; Oklahoma City, OK; (2); Church Yth Grp; VP Latin Clb; Capt Quiz Bowl; Band; Mrchg Band; Pres Jr Cls; NHS; Band Council Rep; Jrnlsm.

PAQUETT, LILY A; Edmond North HS; Edmond, OK; (4); 33/336; Art Clb; Church Yth Grp; Cmnty Wkr; JCL; Sec Latin Clb; Mu Alpha Theta; ROTC; Service Clb; Spanish Clb; Drill Tm; Amer Legion Schltc Medal; Outstdng Svc Awd Disabled Amer Vet; Masonic Stu Of Today; Lacklnd Ldrshp Schl; TX A&M Univ; Meteorology.

PARCELL, COLLEEN D; Panola HS; Wilburton, OK; (3); Church Yth Grp; Cmnty Wkr; Drama Clb; FBLA; FHA; Library Aide; Teachers Aide; Chorus; School Musical; School Play; Chld Psych.

PARDUE, HEATHER S; Edmond Memorial HS; Edmond, OK; (2); 174/408; Church Yth Grp; Key Clb; Spanish Clb; Chorus; Church Choir; Orch; Hon Roll; Church Drama Clb; Dist/St Vcl Solo/Ensmbl Contest Wnnr; Teach 3/4 Yrs Old Church Class; U Of OK; Meteorologist.

PARDUE, JERRI; Marlow HS; Duncan, OK; (3); 23/104; GAA; Teachers Aide; Chorus; Var Bsktbl; Var Sftbl; Hon Roll; Dntl Hygienist.

PARENTI, TAMMY D; Liberty HS; Mounds, OK; (3); 6/40; Church Yth Grp; German Clb; Teachers Aide; Ed Nwsp; Pres Yrbk; VP Frsh Cls; VP Soph Cls; Sec Jr Cls; Rep Stu Cncl; Var Bsktbl; Outstndng All Around Ath 95-96; Mst Vlbl Defensive Sftbl & Bsktbl Playewr 95-96; Sports Medicine.

PARHAM, ANDREA M; Bishop Kelley HS; Tulsa, OK; (3); Church Yth Grp; French Clb; Service Clb; Hon Roll; Nrsng.

PARIKH, RUCHI; Tomlinson Jr HS; Lawton, OK; (1); FCA; FHA; Hosp Aide; Ed Yrbk; Rep Stu Cncl; High Hon Roll; Hon Roll; Jr NHS; NHS; U Of MO Kansas City; Dermtlgy.

PARIKH, SHAILJA; Lawton Sr HS; Lawton, OK; (3); Cmnty Wkr; Dance Clb; Hosp Aide; HOBY; SADD; Co-Ed Yrbk; Co-Ed Lit Mag; Var Pom Pon; High Hon Roll; NHS; Ptry Pblshd Byline Mgzn; Vlly Frg Ldrshp Conf; Piano; U Of MO Kansas City; Med.

PARIS, SHAREE R; Seiling Schl; Seiling, OK; (4); Church Yth Grp; Cmnty Wkr; FCA; FBLA; FHA; GAA; Girl Scts; Letterman Clb; Library Aide; Pep Clb; FHA VP & Rptr; Cattlemans Schlrsp; SWOSA; Child Psych.

PARISH, KATHRYN B; Jenks HS; Tulsa, OK; (2); Debate Tm; Key Clb; Mu Alpha Theta; NFL; Speech Tm; Rep Frsh Cls; Rep Soph Cls; Rep Stu Cncl; L Swmmng; High Hon Roll; USS Swm Tm; Trojan Aquatio Clb Tulsa Rgn 8 Qlfr; DFY; Pre-Law/Jrnlsm.

PARIZEK, JENNIFER M; Yukon Middle HS; Yukon, OK; (2); Church Yth Grp; FHA; Spanish Clb; Hon Roll.

PARIZEK, JOE C; Yukon Middle HS; Yukon, OK; (2); Church Yth Grp; VP 4-H; Quiz Bowl; Spanish Clb; 4-H Awd; High Hon Roll; Prfct Atten Awd.

PARK, BRANDI S; Checotah HS; Checotah, OK; (2); Rptr Natl FFA Org; Sec Jr Cls; Var Bsktbl; Var Sftbl; High Hon Roll; NHS.

PARK, CHAD; Watonga HS; Watonga, OK; (3); FCA; Natl FFA Org; Office Aide; Var Bsbl; Var Ftbl; Var Vllybl; Var Wt Lftg; Ntl Merit Ltr.

PARK, DAWN; Edmond Memorial HS; Edmond, OK; (3); French Clb; Science Clb; Orch; School Musical; Hon Roll; NHS; U Of OK Hlth & Sci Smmr Acad; Allst Orch; Chem Eng.

PARK, HYON JOO; Union Intermediate HS; Tulsa, OK; (1); Treas Church Yth Grp; Key Clb; Math Clb; Orch; High Hon Roll; NHS; Frgn Lang Clb; Art Outside Of Schl; Rice Univ; Archtctr.

PARK, JUSTIN R; Edmond Santa Fe HS; Edmond, OK; (2); French Clb; Pep Clb; SADD; JV Bsbl; Var Powder Puff Ftbl; OK ST Univ.

PARK, KELI J; Hartshorne Sr HS; Hartshorne, OK; (4); Boy Scts; Church Yth Grp; English Clb; JA; Office Aide; Teachers Aide; Band; Color Guard; Flag Corp; Jazz Band; Sr Schlrshp; Amer Legn Courg Hnr Ldrshp Awd & Plag; Choctaw Natn Spec Recgntn Cert; Estrn OK ST; Spec Ed.

PARK, RON L; Choctaw HS; Choctaw, OK; (4); 28/304; Church Yth Grp; Var Bsbl; Var Ftbl; Var Wrstlng; Cit Awd; High Hon Roll; Jr NHS; NHS; Prfct Atten Awd; St Schlr; Multi Yr Listing; OU.

PARKER, BRANDI M; Putnam City HS; Oklahoma City, OK; (3); 196/401; Debate Tm; DECA; GAA; Chorus; Rep Soph Cls; Rep Jr Cls; Rep Sr Cls; Rep Stu Cncl; Stat Bsktbl; Var Sftbl; Clark Univ; Premed.

PARKER, CHANCE; Gore HS; Webbers Falls, OK; (4); 2/25; FHA; Scholastic Bowl; VP Jr Cls; Ofcr Bsbl; Bsktbl; Capt Ftbl; Wt Lftg; Hon Roll; NHS.

PARKER, CHARLES A; Choctaw HS; Midwest City, OK; (2); Chorus; Variety Show; Pres Stu Cncl; Var Socr; High Hon Roll; Jr NHS; NHS; Pres Acad Fit Awd; Coach Under-Uj Boys Sccr Team; OK St Slct Sccr Team Olympic Dev; Referee Yth Sccr Games; Sports Psych.

PARKER, ERIK J; Claremore Sr HS; Claremore, OK; (2); Art Clb; Yrbk; Cit Awd; Hon Roll; NHS; OK ST Univ; Cmptr Prgmng.

PARKER, GREGORY P; Putnam City West HS; Oklahoma City, OK; (3); Cmnty Wkr; FCA; FBLA; German Clb; Intnl Clb; Red Cross Aide; Ski Clb; Speech Tm; SADD; Prfct Atten Awd; CO Univ; Intnl Bus/Mrktng.

PARKER, JACOB C; Owasso Sr HS; Owasso, OK; (3); 13/354; Art Clb; Boy Scts; Drama Clb; Spanish Clb; Speech Tm; Teachers Aide; High Hon Roll.

PARKER, JACQUELINE; Duncan HS; Duncan, OK; (3); Church Yth Grp; Drama Clb; Office Aide; SADD; Amer Coed Pagnt; Anml Sci/Vet Med.

PARKER, JARED D; Locust Grove HS; Locust Grove, OK; (3); Am Leg Boys St; Church Yth Grp; Computer Clb; English Clb; FCA; German Clb; Math Clb; Office Aide; Red Cross Aide; Teachers Aide; Tae Kwon Do Blck Blt; USTRC Roper; Fllwshp Chrstn Stu Ldr; U Of OK; Sprtsmed.

PARKER, JENNIFER; Moore HS; Oklahoma City, OK; (3); Dance Clb; French Clb; Office Aide; Chorus; Cit Awd; Hon Roll; Jr NHS; NHS; Page PTA Convention; OK U.

PARKER, JILL J; Union Intermediate HS; Tulsa, OK; (2); 71/800; Church Yth Grp; Key Clb; Spanish Clb; Drill Tm; High Hon Roll; NHS; D-Fy-It; St Individual Dance Cmptn Fnlst.

PARKER, JUSTIN L; Allen HS; Allen, OK; (2); Church Yth Grp; FCA; Ftbl; Trk; Wt Lftg; Mustang Awd-Ftbl 95-96.

PARKER, KANDACE; Beaver HS; Elmwood, OK; (4); 1/34; Church Yth Grp; Sec FCA; Pres Sec FHA; Sec Chorus; Co-Capt Yrbk; Pres Soph Cls; Treas Sr Cls; Treas Stu Cncl; Capt Bsktbl; Chrldng; Nrsng Hm Vlntr; OK U; Nrsng.

PARKER, KELLY; Macarthur Sr HS; Lawton, OK; (4); 22/260; FCA; French Clb; Treas German Clb; Key Clb; Pep Clb; Science Clb; SADD; Var L Chrldng; Var L Socr; Var L Sftbl; Cameron U; Elem Ed.

PARKER, LA TRISHA A; Thomas Jr Sr HS; Thomas, OK; (2); 1/43; Church Yth Grp; FCA; FHA; Quiz Bowl; Rep Frsh Cls; Bsktbl; Var Score Keeper; Var Sftbl; Var Trk; High Hon Roll.

PARKER, LATRISHA; Thomas Jr Sr HS; Thomas, OK; (1); 1/45; Church Yth Grp; FCA; FHA; Letterman Clb; Pep Clb; Quiz Bowl; Band; Church Choir; Pep Band; Rep Frsh Cls.

PARKER, LISA; Western Heights Sr HS; Oklahoma City, OK; (2); Church Yth Grp; FCA; Key Clb; Letterman Clb; Chorus; Swing Chorus; Chrldng; Score Keeper.

PARKER, LISA D; Ardmore HS; Ardmore, OK; (2); 18/231; Band; Drm Mjr(t); Mrchg Band; Pep Band; JV Var Sftbl; JV Var Trk; Hon Roll.

PARKER, MACY D; Hinton HS; Hinton, OK; (2); 4-H; Key Clb; Natl FFA Org; SADD; Chorus; Rep Frsh Cls; Rep Soph Cls; Pres Jr Cls; Pres Sr Cls; Rep Stu Cncl; Masons Stu Of Today Awd; Mrktg.

PARKER, MATT B; Fairview HS; Chester, OK; (3); Am Leg Boys St; Church Yth Grp; Natl FFA Org; Band; Mrchg Band; Pep Band; School Musical; Stage Crew; Hon Roll; NHS; OSU; Vetrnrn.

PARKER, MICHELE L; Tahlequah Sr HS; Cookson, OK; (3); Church Yth Grp; Dance Clb; Pep Clb; Science Clb; SADD; Capt Var Chrldng; Gym; Var Sftbl; Var Trk; All-Star Chrldng; Orthodontist.

PARKER, MICHELLE D; Velma Alma HS; Duncan, OK; (4); Art Clb; JA; Natl FFA Org; Gov Hon Prg Awd; High Hon Roll; Hon Roll; Jr NHS; NHS; Multi-Yr Listee; OSU; Massage Thrpst.

PARKER, NANCY M; Ada HS; Ada, OK; (4); 67/159; Church Yth Grp; FCA; FHA; Band; Chorus; Church Choir; Drm Mjr(t); Mrchg Band; Orch; School Musical; Consmr Scis.

PARKER, PATIENCE; Fairview HS; Chester, OK; (2); Church Yth Grp; French Clb; FHA; Band; Color Guard; Mrchg Band; Pep Band; JV Bsktbl; JV Trk; Prfct Atten Awd; Southwestern; PT.

PARKER, ROBB L; Metro Christian Acad; Tulsa, OK; (2); Cmnty Wkr; Spanish Clb; School Musical; Swing Chorus; Bsktbl; Tennis; High Hon Roll; U Of TX.

PARKER, SABRINA M; Harrah HS; Harrah, OK; (3); 6/177; Church Yth Grp; Cmnty Wkr; FCA; FBLA; FHA; Office Aide; Scholastic Bowl; SADD; Teachers Aide; Varsity Clb; Mdcn/Sign Lang.

PARKER, SARAH J; Owasso Sr HS; Owasso, OK; (3); 24/357; Debate Tm; French Clb; NFL; Red Cross Aide; Chorus; Co-Ed Nwsp; L Socr; High Hon Roll; NHS; Bus/Law/Ec.

PARKER, SARAH KATIE; Duncan HS; Duncan, OK; (1); Church Yth Grp; Cmnty Wkr; Rptr French Clb; Sec FBLA; Church Choir; JV Golf; Hon Roll; ST FBLA Conf 6th Pl; Natl Ldrshp Conf FBLA Voting Del; Yth Day Caring For United Way; OK ST Univ; Intnl Bus.

PARKER, SHANNON; Cheyenne HS; Durham, OK; (3); Church Yth Grp; Sec Treas 4-H; Scholastic Bowl; Speech Tm; Band; School Play; Chrldng; 4-H Awd; High Hon Roll; NHS.

PARKER, SHAUNDA M; Dewar Jr-Sr HS; Henryetta, OK; (1); Church Yth Grp; FCA; FHA; GAA; Varsity Clb; Church Choir; Chrldng; Sftbl; Hon Roll.

PARKER, SOPHIA; Roland Sr HS; Roland, OK; (1); Band; Ofcr Frsh Cls; Bsktbl; Chrldng; Hon Roll.

PARKER, STUART; Rock Creek Jr Sr HS; Bokchito, OK; (1); 1/50; Natl FFA Org; Var L Bsbl; Var L Bsktbl; High Hon Roll; NHS; Currclm Tm Math, Sci, Eng.

PARKER, SUMMER; Shawnee Sr HS; Shawnee, OK; (1); Pep Clb; Spanish Clb; Ofcr Bsbl; Chrldng; Ftbl; Pom Pon; Score Keeper; Cit Awd; Hon Roll.

PARKER, TABITHA; Okemah HS; Okemah, OK; (2); Church Yth Grp; 4-H; Pres FHA; Natl FFA Org; Scholastic Bowl; Cit Awd; 4-H Awd; Hon Roll; FHA/HERO Cntrl Dist VP; OK ST U; Vet.

PARKER, TRAVIS; Cushing HS; Cushing, OK; (4); 11/160; Am Leg Boys St; Church Yth Grp; FCA; Math Clb; Science Clb; Rep Jr Cls; Var L Bsbl; Capt Var Ftbl; Hon Roll; NHS; OK U; Sprts Med.

PARKES, MATHEW D; Muskogee HS; Muskogee, OK; (1); Boy Scts; Church Yth Grp; CAP; Church Choir; Mrchg Band; Pep Band; Trk; Sr Patrl Ldr In Boy Scts; BYU; Plt.

PARKHURST, ERIC; Alva HS; Alva, OK; (4); 10/81; Am Leg Boys St; FCA; Library Aide; Office Aide; Teachers Aide; Pres Frsh Cls; Pres Soph Cls; Ofcr Stu Cncl; Var L Bsktbl; Var L Ftbl; OK Delg 95 Yth Triennium; U Of OK; Med.

PARKHURST, JESSE; Cheyenne HS; Crawford, OK; (4); Natl FFA Org; VICA; Wt Lftg; Hon Roll; Amirillo Tech; Auto Mech.

PARKHURST, MEGAN; Guymon Sr HS; Guymon, OK; (3); 12/107; French Clb; FHA; Pep Clb; Band; Chorus; Jazz Band; Mrchg Band; Pep Band; Hon Roll; NHS; Interaction Prevention Pgm; Phys Therapy; Sports Medicine.

PARKINSON, DEREK E; Blackwell HS; Blackwell, OK; (2); Natl FFA Org; Pep Clb; Ofcr Frsh Cls; Ofcr Jr Cls; JV Bsktbl; L Var Golf; Hon Roll; OK ST U; Bus Mgmt.

PARKISON, LORI; Edmond North HS; Edmond, OK; (4); 1/333; Church Yth Grp; FCA; Mu Alpha Theta; Spanish Clb; Phtg Yrbk; Stat Bsbl; Var Vllybl; Var Vllybl; NHS; Val; Tandy Tech Schlr; OSU; Pre-Med/Bus.

PARKS, BECKY; Okemah HS; Okemah, OK; (1); Church Yth Grp; SADD; School Play; Nwsp; Yrbk.

PARKS, CHAD; Pawhuska HS; Pawhuska, OK; (4); 16/87; Am Leg Boys St; Church Yth Grp; English Clb; FCA; FHA; Key Clb; Science Clb; Spanish Clb; Hon Roll; NHS; MO Vly; Scl Sci.

PARKS, MICHAELA D; Duncan HS; Duncan, OK; (2); FBLA; Key Clb; SADD; Rep Stu Cncl; Trk; Hon Roll; Natl Mrt Sci Awd; Lcky Cir Soc Clb; Scndry Ed.

PARKS, NATHAN; Skiatook HS; Skiatook, OK; (3); 12/114; Boy Scts; Church Yth Grp; FCA; HOBY; Band; Jazz Band; Mrchg Band; Bsktbl; High Hon Roll; NHS; Southwestern Bapt U; Ministry.

PARKS, PHILLIP M; Edmond Memorial HS; Edmond, OK; (3); French Clb; JV VP Drama Clb; Bsktbl.

PARMER, JUSTIN; Choctaw Jr HS; Choctaw, OK; (1); Church Yth Grp; FCA; High Hon Roll; Hon Roll; Jr NHS; Prfct Atten Awd; TSA Pres; Rllr Hcky Lg; AWANA Ldr; Rice; Engrng.

PARNACHER, LA RANDA F; Lone Grove HS; Lone Grove, OK; (4); Church Yth Grp; Key Clb; Spanish Clb; Chorus; Color Guard; Yrbk; Cit Awd; Hon Roll; NHS; Winterguard; E Central Univ; Comp Prog.

PARNELL, BREE; Blanchard Jr Sr HS; Blanchard, OK; (2); FHA; Natl FFA Org; Teachers Aide; Cit Awd; Hon Roll; Ntl Merit Ltr; Sal; U OK; Flm Cstng Dir.

PARNELL, LEAH; Hugo HS; Hugo, OK; (3); Library Aide; Spanish Clb; Teachers Aide; Flag Corp; Nwsp; Ofcr Stu Cncl; Hon Roll; NHS; SE OK ST U.

PARR, ANDREW M; Walters HS; Walters, OK; (4); 5/34; Church Yth Grp; FCA; FTA; Library Aide; Office Aide; SADD; Chorus; Church Choir; School Musical; School Play; All Amer Schlr; All Rgn Hnr Choir; Supts Hnr Roll; Best Dressed; Midwestern ST U; Acctng.

PARRET, NOEL; Dewey HS; Dewey, OK; (3); Chorus; Church Choir; Chrldng.

PARRICK, SARAH M; Depew HS; Depew, OK; (2); GAA; Rep Stu Cncl; Bsktbl; Sftbl; High Hon Roll; Prfct Atten Awd; Sftbl Ofnsv Plyr Yr.

PARRISH, AMBER R; Bethel HS; Shawnee, OK; (3); Church Yth Grp; Drama Clb; Natl FFA Org; SADD; Chorus; School Play; Natl Floriculture Cont FFA; Seminole Jr Coll Educl Talent Search; USAO; Bio Tchr; Actress.

PARRISH, JASON; Woodward HS; Woodward, OK; (3); Church Yth Grp; Cmnty Wkr; FCA; Key Clb; Letterman Clb; Socr; JV Trk; Cit Awd; High Hon Roll; Kiwanis Awd; Karate Stdnt; VP Law Enfrcmnt Explrs; 4 Yr Coll; Govt Agent.

PARRISH, SARAH J; Edmond Memorial HS; Edmond, OK; (2); 93/400; Church Yth Grp; FCA; German Clb; Sec Key Clb; Nwsp; Hon Roll; NHS; Pres Acad Fit Awd; U Of OK.

PARRISH, STEPHANIE; Pioneer Jr Sr HS; Enid, OK; (4); 2/37; Am Leg Aux Girls St; Church Yth Grp; FCA; Natl Beta Clb; Capt Quiz Bowl; Church Choir; School Play; Stage Crew; VP Stu Cncl; Capt Bsktbl; OK ST U; Acctng.

PARROTT, JOELLE; Okeene Jr Sr HS; Okeene, OK; (2); 1/35; Rep Church Yth Grp; Drama Clb; Sec Girl Scts; Speech Tm; Band; Church Choir; Mrchg Band; High Hon Roll; NHS; 95 Queen Whea-Esta Pgnt.

PARROTT, R KATHRYN; Noble HS; Noble, OK; (4); 1/147; Church Yth Grp; Mu Alpha Theta; Band; Ed Nwsp; Yrbk; Rep Stu Cncl; High Hon Roll; Pres NHS; St Schlr; Val; OK Bapt Univ; Engl.

PARROTT, RACHEL; Okeene Jr Sr HS; Okeene, OK; (4); 3/27; Sec Am Leg Aux Girls St; Pres VP FHA; Pres VP Girl Scts; Rptr Speech Tm; Pres Band; Church Choir; Mrchg Band; School Play; Sec Treas NHS; Abilene Chrstn U.

PARROTT, REBECCA K; Noble HS; Noble, OK; (4); 1/135; Church Yth Grp; Mu Alpha Theta; Band; Church Choir; Ed Nwsp; Ed Yrbk; Rep Stu Cncl; High Hon Roll; NHS; Val; OK Bapt U; Engl Ed.

PARROTT, SHAWNA L; Healdton HS; Healdton, OK; (2); FCA; Acpl Chr; Band; Chorus; Church Choir; Mrchg Band; Sftbl; Trk; Chorus Dir.

PARSONS, ALESHA A; Southeast HS; Oklahoma City, OK; (2); Bus Profs of Am; Computer Clb; Office Aide; SADD; Vllybl; Hon Roll; Nurse.

PARSONS, AMANDA S; Brink Jr HS; Oklahoma City, OK; (1); Church Yth Grp; Var Crs Cntry; Var Trk; Cit Awd; Jr NHS; NHS; OK Bapt Univ.

PARSONS, ANDI; Texhoma HS; Gruver, TX; (4); #2 in class; Church Yth Grp; Pres Pep Clb; Quiz Bowl; VP Band; VP Pres Sr Cls; L Capt Bsktbl; L Var Trk; Pres NHS; Sal; Teachers Aide; Miss Texhoma 96; I Dare You Awd; S W OK St U; Phrmcy.

PARSONS, RYAN J; East Central HS; Tulsa, OK; (2); #2 in class; Church Yth Grp; FCA; Letterman Clb; Spanish Clb; Ftbl; Var Trk; High Hon Roll; Hon Roll; NHS; Pres Acad Fit Awd; Mech Engr.

PARSONS, SUZANNE; Battiest Jr Sr HS; Broken Bow, OK; (2); 1/18; Rptr Sec 4-H; Sec Natl FFA Org; Scholastic Bowl; Rptr Stu Cncl; Sftbl; 4-H Awd; Chptr FFA Degree; Greenhand FFA Degree; Ag Sls/Svc; Grand Ch Lcl Sci Fair; 3rd Cty/Dist Sci Fair; OK ST 1.

PARSONS, TIFFANY; Del City HS; Oklahoma City, OK; (3); Teachers Aide; Chrldng; NHS; Co-Head Chrldr; Sr Class Ofcr; Stu Cncl Hm Rm Rep.

PARTIN, DEENA; Hugo HS; Hugo, OK; (3); 8/113; Church Yth Grp; Cmnty Wkr; FCA; Swing Chorus; Rep Stu Cncl; Chrldng; Gov Hon Prg Awd; NHS; Pres Acad Fit Awd; OSU.

PARTIN, MINDI R; Berryhill Sr HS; Tulsa, OK; (2); 6/98; GAA; Bsktbl; Sftbl; Trk; Wt Lftg; Hon Roll; Prfct Atten Awd; Bus.

PARTRIDGE, ERIC; Edmond North HS; Edmond, OK; (4); Am Leg Boys St; Church Yth Grp; German Clb; ROTC; Color Guard; Flag Corp; JV Crs Cntry; JV Socr; Dtrs Of Amer Colonists Natl Mdl; AFJROTC Lackland Ldrshp Schl; Cert Of Recgntn Indian Ed Pgm; Elec Engrng.

PASSLEY, JACOB N; North Intemediate HS; Broken Arrow, OK; (2); Acpl Chr; Band; Mrchg Band; Pep Band; Bsktbl; Trk; Hon Roll; OK ST Univ; Meterologist.

PASSMORE, AMY M; Oaks Mission Jr Sr HS; Rose, OK; (3); Church Yth Grp; FHA; Chorus; Wt Lftg; Hon Roll.

PATE, JESSE; Collinsville HS; Collinsville, OK; (4); Church Yth Grp; FBLA; Quiz Bowl; School Musical; School Play; Hon Roll; Natl HS Inst; Daybreak; Northwestern U; Theatre Arts.

PATE, NICOLE; Yarbrough Schl; Stratford, TX; (3); 1/10; VP Church Yth Grp; Pres Drama Clb; HOBY; Band; Chorus; Pres Stu Cncl; Var Bsktbl; Var Chrldng; NHS; Rodeo; Amer Natl Tngr Fnlst West TX Div; Fghtng Hrt Awd Bsktbl 95-; U Of AZ; Anthsst.

PATE, TAMARA; Yarbrough Schl; Stratford, TX; (3); 1/10; Church Yth Grp; HOBY; Scholastic Bowl; Speech Tm; Band; Chorus; School Musical; Pres Stu Cncl; Var Bsktbl; NHS; Stu Today Awd; Hnr Band; Mss W TX Natl Tngr; U Of AZ; Anethesist.

PATEL, AKSHAY S; Okemah HS; Okemah, OK; (3); 20/75; Boy Scts; Drama Clb; Key Clb; Math Clb; Office Aide; Science Clb; School Play; Capt Golf; Cit Awd; Hon Roll; U Of OK; Arch; Bus.

PATEL, AMISH; Moore HS; Moore, OK; (3); Science Clb; Rep Jr Cls; Var Crs Cntry; Var Trk; Jr NHS; NHS; Stu Cncl St Cnvntn Delg; U Of OK; Med.

PATEL, ANJANA M; Brink Jr HS; Oklahoma City, OK; (1); Hosp Aide; Jr NHS; Sign Lang Clb Sec; Boston Univ; Phy Therapy.

PATEL, DARSHAN G; Will Rogers HS; Tulsa, OK; (3); 8/300; English Clb; Sec FBLA; Key Clb; VP Red Cross Aide; Spanish Clb; Ofcr Bsbl; Socr; Wt Lftg; Hon Roll; NHS; Spec Olympics; U Of OK; Arch Engr.

PATEL, KRISHNA R; Enid Sr HS; Enid, OK; (3); 4/500; Spanish Clb; Band; Color Guard; Mrchg Band; Pep Band; Sec Frsh Cls; Cit Awd; High Hon Roll; NHS; Dance Clb; Winterguard; U Of OK.

PATEL, LINA R; Enid Sr HS; Enid, OK; (3); 1/475; Band; Capt Color Guard; Drill Tm; Mrchg Band; Pep Band; School Musical; School Play; Rep Stu Cncl; NHS; Dance Clb; Winterguard; U Of OK; Psych.

PATEL, NEEHA C; Norman Sr HS; Norman, OK; (3); FBLA; Mu Alpha Theta; Spanish Clb; SADD; Cit Awd; High Hon Roll; Hon Roll; Jr NHS; NHS; Pres Schlr; Funk Dancing; Recreational Sccr; Psych Clb; Mdcn.

PATEL, NEELAM; Newkirk HS; Newkirk, OK; (4); 12/47; Am Leg Boys St; FCA; Letterman Clb; Stage Crew; Treas Soph Cls; Treas Jr Cls; Treas Stu Cncl; L Bsbl; Capt Bsktbl; Hon Roll; STEPP UP Treas; OK ST U; Med.

PATEL, NINA N; Edmond Memorial HS; Edmond, OK; (2); 1/450; GAA; Key Clb; Spanish Clb; SADD; JV Trk; High Hon Roll; Hon Roll; NHS; Pres Schlr; OK Univ; Atty.

PATEL, RAKESH I; Erick Jr Sr HS; Erick, OK; (3); 1/30; Quiz Bowl; Scholastic Bowl; Spanish Clb; Varsity Clb; Pres Frsh Cls; Pres Stu Cncl; Var Bsbl; Var Bsktbl; High Hon Roll; NHS; TSA St Treas & VP; OU; Poltcl Sci.

PATEL, RICKY R; Wilburton Sr HS; Wilburton, OK; (1); FBLA; Band; Mrchg Band; Nwsp; Cit Awd; Hon Roll; Prfct Atten Awd; Acad Team; Participated In Choctaw Nation Math & Sci Pgm.

PATEL, TEJAL D; Elk City Jr HS; Elk City, OK; (1); Computer Clb; FHA; Spanish Clb; Chorus; Cit Awd; High Hon Roll; Hon Roll; Pharmacist.

PATEL, VIMAL MAGAN; Lawton Sr HS; Lawton, OK; (2); HOBY; Key Clb; Office Aide; Tennis; Wt Lftg; High Hon Roll; Hon Roll; Kiwanis Awd; Prfct Atten Awd; OU; Dental.

PATHIPVANICH, PUNN P; Putnam City North HS; Oklahoma City, OK; (4); #3 in class; German Clb; JCL; Latin Clb; Scholastic Bowl; Ftbl; Wrstlng; Hon Roll; NHS; Pres Schlr; St Schlr; OK Univ; Med.

PATMON, JOSEPH; Midwest City HS; Midwest City, OK; (4); 112/464; Var Capt Bsktbl; Cit Awd; Hon Roll; Prfct Atten Awd; AAAU Bsktbl; MVP Western Hgts; Bsktbl Blue Chip List USA Today; Mc Donalds All Amer 96; Hotel Mgmt.

PATRICK, CANDACE; Bluejacket Schl; Bluejacket, OK; (2); Church Yth Grp; Computer Clb; FCA; FHA; GAA; Math Clb; VP Soph Cls; Bsktbl; Hon Roll; Jazz, Tap & Ballet Dance; OSU Stillwater.

PATRICK, CANDACE L; Bluejacket Schl; Welch, OK; (2); Church Yth Grp; Computer Clb; FCA; FHA; GAA; Math Clb; VP Soph Cls; Bsktbl; Wt Lftg; Hon Roll; OSU.

PATRICK, ELIZABETH; Jenks HS; Tulsa, OK; (1); FHA; Spanish Clb; Chrldng; Trojans For Christ; OK ST U; Child Thrpy.

PATRICK, JASON A; Okmulgee HS; Okmulgee, OK; (3); Am Leg Boys St; Church Yth Grp; Letterman Clb; Band; Mrchg Band; Pep Band; Hon Roll; JV Var Bsktbl; Var L Tennis; Close-Up; U Of OK; Med.

PATRICK, YAHNAH; Tahlequah Sr HS; Tahlequah, OK; (4); 1/251; German Clb; SADD; Teachers Aide; Chorus; Tennis; Jr NHS; NHS; Pres Acad Fit Awd; Val; Calculus Clb VP; Acctng.

PATTEN, ASHLEY; Erick Jr Sr HS; Erick, OK; (4); 5/23; Am Leg Aux Girls St; Spanish Clb; Teachers Aide; Rep Frsh Cls; Rep Jr Cls; Rep Sr Cls; Pres Stu Cncl; Bsktbl; Chrldng; Hon Roll.

PATTERSON, CATHARINE S; Henryetta Sr HS; Henryetta, OK; (2); Church Yth Grp; FHA; Chorus; School Play; Var Bsktbl.

PATTERSON, CHRIS S; Morris HS; Henryetta, OK; (1); JV Bsbl; JV Bsktbl; Wt Lftg; Hon Roll; Pres Acad Fit Awd; OK Hnr Soc; U Of OK.

PATTERSON, DEANNA L; Choctaw HS; Choctaw, OK; (2); Church Yth Grp; Cmnty Wkr; Spanish Clb; Bsktbl; Trk; Hon Roll; Jr NHS; Marshall; Math.

PATTERSON, ELIZABETH; Stillwater Sr HS; Stilwell, OK; (3); Church Yth Grp; Pres FHA; HOBY; VP Natl Beta Clb; NFL; Pres Spanish Clb; Pres Stu Cncl; Capt Chrldng; Hon Roll; NHS; FAT St Hero Offcr; Northeastern ST U; Ed.

PATTERSON, JENNIFER; Warner HS; Porum, OK; (2); Art Clb; FHA; GAA; HOBY; Spanish Clb; Rptr Frsh Cls; VP Soph Cls; Ofcr Stu Cncl; Var Bsktbl; JV Crs Cntry; Msnc Stdnt Of Today; OK ST Hnr Scty; Sftbl Rkie Of Yr 95; Lady Eagle Sftbl Awd 96.

PATTERSON, JERID D; Woodward HS; Woodward, OK; (1); Church Yth Grp; FCA; Rep Frsh Cls; Ofcr Stu Cncl; Ftbl; Socr; Wt Lftg; Cit Awd; Art; Hunting; Fishing; OK ST U; Graphic Arts; Aquatic.

PATTERSON, JULIE M; Memorial HS; Tulsa, OK; (4); 71/250; Church Yth Grp; Pep Clb; Red Cross Aide; Spanish Clb; JV Chrldng; Powder Puff Ftbl; Cit Awd; Hon Roll; All Star Pom Natls Squad; Gamma Sigma Sec; Homeless Shelter Vol; VFW Essay Cont 1st Pl; U Of Tulsa; Psych; Elem Ed.

PATTERSON, LYNSAY L; West Middle HS; Norman, OK; (1); Drama Clb; FCA; FBLA; Office Aide; Spanish Clb; School Play; Hon Roll; Arch Engr.

PATTERSON, MATT; Collinsville HS; Collinsville, OK; (3); Church Yth Grp; FCA; Office Aide; Spanish Clb; Ofcr Bsbl; Ftbl; Trk; Wt Lftg; Wrstlng; Hon Roll; OK ST U; Const Engrng.

PATTERSON, MEGAN R; Edmond Memorial HS; Edmond, OK; (3); Church Yth Grp; 4-H; Spanish Clb; Orch; 4-H Awd; High Hon Roll; Hon Roll; NHS; Riding/Training/Showing Horse; OCU; Orthodonisty.

PATTERSON, MICAH R; Lindsay HS; Lindsay, OK; (3); 23/69; Art Clb; Church Yth Grp; FCA; FHA; Letterman Clb; Office Aide; Church Choir; Bsktbl; Ftbl; Wt Lftg; Northeastern A&M.

PATTERSON, MISTI D; Sayre HS; Sayre, OK; (3); 7/42; Church Yth Grp; FHA; Pep Clb; Band; Mrchg Band; Pep Band; Bsktbl; Trk; Hon Roll; Algebra I, Eng III & Keyboarding Awds; SWOSU; Pharmacy.

PATTERSON, SARAH M; Mc Alester HS; Mcalester, OK; (2); Church Yth Grp; Debate Tm; FHA; Red Cross Aide; School Musical; School Play; Stage Crew; Variety Show; Tennis; Hon Roll; Intl Order Of Rainbow For Grls; Firftr.

PATTERSON, SETH M; Mc Alester HS; Mcalester, OK; (2); 5/219; Boy Scts; Church Yth Grp; Cmnty Wkr; Red Cross Aide; Spanish Clb; Band; Chorus; Church Choir; Cit Awd; High Hon Roll; Lfgrd; OK Hnr Soc; Coast Guard Acad; Engr.

PATTERSON, STACY L; Chickasha HS; Chickasha, OK; (1); Church Yth Grp; Cmnty Wkr; FHA; Chorus; Church Choir; Mgr(s); Jrnlsm.

PATTERSON, TIFFANY; Fargo Schl; Fargo, OK; (3); 2/16; Church Yth Grp; 4-H; FHA; HOBY; Letterman Clb; Natl Beta Clb; Nwsp; Yrbk; Sec Soph Cls; Hon Roll; Pblctn Chrmn 4th July Fargo Fest 95; OU; Bus.

PATTERSON, VIRGINIA; Edmond North HS; Edmond, OK; (3); FCA; Chrldng; Crs Cntry; Powder Puff Ftbl; Socr; Trk; NHS; UCO; Acctng.

PATTILLO, JACLYN; Plainview HS; Ardmore, OK; (3); 12/85; FCA; Latin Clb; Natl Beta Clb; Drill Tm; School Musical; Lit Mag; Pres Frsh Cls; Pres Soph Cls; Chrldng; NHS; OK ST U; Bus.

PATTILLO, SCOTT; Skiatook HS; Skiatook, OK; (4); 50/104; Boy Scts; Bsktbl; Hon Roll; NHS; Eagle Scout Awd; FFA Sentinel Ofcr; Karate Blue Belt 6th Degree; Rogers ST Coll; Meteorology.

PATTISON, MEGAN; Jenks HS; Tulsa, OK; (3); Church Yth Grp; DECA; FCA; Sec FBLA; Key Clb; Rep Stu Cncl; Var Chrldng; Hon Roll; Symphony Set; Bus.

PATTON, AARON; Oilton HS; Oilton, OK; (4); 2/20; Am Leg Boys St; Church Yth Grp; FCA; HOBY; Pres Stu Cncl; Var Bsbl; Var Capt Bsktbl; Hon Roll; NHS; Engr.

PATTON, ANDREA; Norman Sr HS; Norman, OK; (2); 1/2000; Cmnty Wkr; Drama Clb; Intnl Clb; Mu Alpha Theta; Science Clb; Spanish Clb; Orch; Rep Frsh Cls; VP Soph Cls; Hon Roll; OK Yth Symphony; Amer Indian Clb; GATE Pgm; Chem Engrng.

PATTON, KRISTIN; Vanoss Schl; Ada, OK; (1); 1/50; Church Yth Grp; FCA; FBLA; Scholastic Bowl; Bsktbl; Hon Roll; Jr NHS; NHS; Pres Acad Fit Awd; Val; U Of OK; Med.

PATTON, LAURA D; Webster HS; Tulsa, OK; (2); Church Yth Grp; Band; Mrchg Band; High Hon Roll; NHS; Hrsbck Rdng; OK ST Univ; Vet.

PATZKOWSKI, TARA J; Deer Creek HS; Edmond, OK; (3); 15/92; Church Yth Grp; Science Clb; Color Guard; Var Golf; High Hon Roll; NHS; Cmptv Hrswmn Regnl/Natl Placings; U Of OK; Intl Bus.

PATZKOWSKY, ANDREA B; Okeen HS; Okeene, OK; (4); 16/25; Sec Church Yth Grp; Treas FHA; Teachers Aide; Hon Roll; Kiwanis Awd; Prfct Atten Awd; FBLA; FHA Outstdng Mem; Southern Nazarene Univ; Bus.

PATZKOWSKY, TYLER D; Balko Public Schl; Balko, OK; (1); 2/16; Church Yth Grp; Natl FFA Org; Speech Tm; Band; Church Choir; Pep Band; School Play; Sec Frsh Cls; Var Ftbl; Cit Awd; Univ Of OK; Attorney.

PAUL, KRISTIN K; Guthrie Sr HS; Guthrie, OK; (1); 48/350; Letterman Clb; Varsity Clb; Var Sftbl; Frosh Wrstlng Atndnt; All Conf Sftbl; OK ST Univ; Radiologist.

PAUL, MERLY N; Western Heights Sr HS; Oklahoma City, OK; (1); Flag Corp; Mrchg Band; Orch; Pep Band; Hon Roll; Chld Psych.

PAUL, MICHELE C; Guthrie Sr HS; Guthrie, OK; (1); 73/308; Church Yth Grp; Library Aide; Band; Church Choir; Mrchg Band; Pep Band; Hon Roll; Nrsng.

PAUL, MICHELLE E; Tuttle HS; Tuttle, OK; (3); 23/112; Art Clb; Church Yth Grp; Cmnty Wkr; VP FHA; GAA; Scholastic Bowl; Spanish Clb; Teachers Aide; Varsity Clb; Rep Stu Cncl; Art.

PAUL, RYAN; Collinsville HS; Collinsville, OK; (3); Church Yth Grp; FCA; Band; Var L Bsktbl; Wt Lftg; Natl Ldrshp Met Awd; People To People; Tchr.

PAULEC, JOY A; Union Sr HS; Broken Arrow, OK; (3); Church Yth Grp; FBLA; Band; Church Choir; Color Guard; Jazz Band; Mrchg Band; Orch; Pep Band; School Musical; All Dist Trumpet; All ST Jazz Band Piano; Wrtng Poetry; Pharmacy; Music.

PAULEC, MASON D; Union Intermediate HS; Broken Arrow, OK; (2); Spanish Clb; Band; Mrchg Band; Hon Roll; NHS; BSA.

PAULEY, DEVIN; Midwest City HS; Oklahoma City, OK; (2); 42/501; Spanish Clb; Band; Jazz Band; Mrchg Band; Rep Frsh Cls; Rep Soph Cls; Trk; Prfct Atten Awd; Chrch Bsktbl Team; Outstndng Band Stu; Mech Engrng.

PAULS, CYNTHIA; Corn Bible Acad; Corn, OK; (4); Church Yth Grp; Teachers Aide; Band; Chorus; Treas Sr Cls; Sec Stu Cncl; Var Capt Bsktbl; Var Vllybl; High Hon Roll; Pres Acad Fit Awd; OK Baptist U; Phys Thrpy.

PAXTON, ECERRA L; Hominy HS; Oklahoma City, OK; (3); 24/62; Cmnty Wkr; Bsktbl; Vllybl; Hon Roll; Prfct Atten Awd; VICA; TX Tech; Civil Engr/Arch.

PAXTON, JEREMY E; Yukon Middle HS; Yukon, OK; (1); Teachers Aide; Bsktbl; Fashion Dsgnr.

PAXTON, MANDY K; Ripley HS; Ripley, OK; (2); Church Yth Grp; FBLA; FHA; HOBY; Band; Church Choir; High Hon Roll; Hon Roll; NHS.

PAYNE, ABIGAIL; Beaver HS; Beaver, OK; (3); 1/32; FCA; Pres 4-H; GAA; Pres Natl FFA Org; Quiz Bowl; Acpl Chr; Band; Chorus; Church Choir; Drm Mjr(t); First Chrstn Chrch Yth Grp Ldr; 4-H St Horse Jdgng Chmpn; OK ST U; Vet.

PAYNE, ALICIA; Wellston Schl; Wellston, OK; (1); Church Yth Grp; Dance Clb; Drama Clb; FHA; Band; Chorus; Color Guard; Hon Roll; Jr NHS; Jr Lifeguard; OSU; Choregrapher.

PAYNE, ALLISON; Perry Sr HS; Perry, OK; (2); Church Yth Grp; FCA; FHA; Band; Mrchg Band; Pep Band; Sec Stu Cncl; Chrldng; Hon Roll; US Natl Math Awd; U Cntrl OK.

PAYNE, AMBER; Hugo HS; Hugo, OK; (2); 1/150; Church Yth Grp; Cmnty Wkr; HOBY; Sec Spanish Clb; Chorus; Sec Frsh Cls; VP Soph Cls; Sec Stu Cncl; Var Chrldng; Var Sftbl; OM; Leo Clb; U Of OK; Med.

PAYNE, CANDI R; Mountain View-Gotebo HS; Carnegie, OK; (4); 5/31; FHA; Natl FFA Org; Ed Yrbk; Rep Jr Cls; VP Sr Cls; Var Bsktbl; Hon Roll; Jr NHS; NHS; Natl Sci Mrt Awd; All Amer Schlr; Clss Fav Mst Attrctv; Cameron U.

PAYNE, CARMEN L; Wagoner Sr HS; Wagoner, OK; (2); FBLA; Bsktbl; Hon Roll; NHS; Best Of Show Art/Tempra/Portrait; 2nd Pastel/Scrtchbd; 3rd Graph; Northeastern ST Univ; Bus Admn.

PAYNE, CODY; Fairview HS; Fairview, OK; (2); Church Yth Grp; FCA; Letterman Clb; Natl FFA Org; Var Bsbl; Var Bsktbl; Var Ftbl; Hon Roll; NHS; Pres Acad Fit Awd.

PAYNE, JAMIE; Cushing HS; Cushing, OK; (1); Drama Clb; Spanish Clb; JV Chrldng; Hon Roll; Ntl Merit Schol; Law.

PAYNE, JAROD; Chandler HS; Chandler, OK; (3); 52/76; Am Leg Boys St; Church Yth Grp; Cmnty Wkr; FCA; Natl FFA Org; Ftbl; Golf; Wt Lftg; Prfct Atten Awd; Gordon Cooper Voctnl Tech Schl; Abilene Chrstn Univ; Jet Mech.

PAYNE, JEREMY R; Dale Sr HS; Shawnee, OK; (2); Rep Stu Cncl; JV Var Bsbl; JV Var Bsktbl; Cit Awd; Hon Roll; NHS.

PAYNE, JUSTIN K; Putnam City HS; Oklahoma City, OK; (2); Church Yth Grp; Office Aide; Spanish Clb; Church Choir; Ofcr Bsbl; Ldr Of Yth Alive; Yth Cncl Rep; OK Bapt Univ.

PAYNE, MEREDITH A; Owasso Sr HS; Owasso, OK; (3); Church Yth Grp; French Clb; Science Clb; Teachers Aide; Band; Church Choir; Color Guard; Jazz Band; Mrchg Band; Pep Band; All Reg Hnrs Bnds.

PAYNE, RACHAEL S; Lindsay HS; Lindsay, OK; (4); 8/70; Church Yth Grp; FHA; Chorus; Church Choir; Variety Show; VP Jr Cls; Ofcr Stu Cncl; Hon Roll; NHS; St Schlr; Certified Nurse Aide; Phy Thrpst.

PAYNE, RACHEL A; Charles Page HS; Sand Springs, OK; (2); 21/382; Church Yth Grp; Debate Tm; Drama Clb; Girl Scts; NFL; Speech Tm; Church Choir; School Play; Var Crs Cntry; Mgr(s); Arch.

PAYNE, RICHIE J; Velma Alma HS; Countyline, OK; (4); 4/44; Church Yth Grp; Scholastic Bowl; Teachers Aide; Band; High Hon Roll; NHS; Southwestern OK ST; Cmptr Sci.

PAYNE, SARAH; Kingfisher HS; Kingfisher, OK; (1); Treas Church Yth Grp; FCA; Spanish Clb; Speech Tm; Church Choir; High Hon Roll.

PAYNE, SHANNON; Stigler HS; Whitefield, OK; (2); Church Yth Grp; FCA; 4-H; Hosp Aide; Natl FFA Org; Pep Clb; Speech Tm; SADD; Rep Frsh Cls; Rep Soph Cls; Med.

PAYNE, SHAUN; Lone Grove HS; Lone Grove, OK; (3); Model UN; Science Clb; Yrbk; Ofcr Stu Cncl; Hon Roll; 4th Awd Intl Sci/Engr Fr; St Chmp OK Sci/Engr Fair; OU; Env Sci.

PAYNE, THOMAS; Depew HS; Stroud, OK; (2); Church Yth Grp; Natl FFA Org; Spanish Clb; VICA; Church Choir; Sec Soph Cls; JV Bsktbl; Hon Roll; Northeastern ST U Talequah.

PAYTON, HALIE; Miami Sr HS; Miami, OK; (2); Church Yth Grp; Office Aide; Chorus; Chrldng; Hon Roll; Jr NHS; Dance; Multi-Yr Listee; NEO.

PAYTON, JAMIE J; Liberty HS; Mounds, OK; (3); 3/40; FBLA; Rptr Nwsp; Phtg Yrbk; Sec Soph Cls; Treas Jr Cls; Rep Stu Cncl; Var Bsktbl; Var Sftbl; High Hon Roll; NHS; Comp Sci.

PAYTON, JESSE M; Seminole Jr Sr HS; Seminole, OK; (3); Church Yth Grp; Cmnty Wkr; Drama Clb; French Clb; School Play; Variety Show; Ofcr Bsbl; Bsktbl; Ftbl; Golf; NSU; Photo Jrnlst.

PAYTON, JESSICA; Tahlequah Sr HS; Hulbert, OK; (4); 5/251; Church Yth Grp; Cmnty Wkr; Science Clb; SADD; Band; Color Guard; Mrchg Band; NHS; Pres Acad Fit Awd; All St Bnd; U OK; Music.

PAZZO, JENNIFER; Chisholm Sr HS; Enid, OK; (2); Church Yth Grp; FCA; Band; Chorus; Mrchg Band; Pep Band; Crs Cntry; Trk; March Stu Of Month; Qualified & Attnd St Crss Cntry Championships; OK U; Elem Tchr.

PEACH, GINA; Hennessey HS; Marshall, OK; (4); 4/54; FCA; Yrbk; VP Stu Cncl; Var Bsktbl; Var Crs Cntry; Var Trk; Hon Roll; NHS; Ntl Merit Schol; OK ST Univ; Bus.

PEACH, KRISTEN P; North Intemediate HS; Broken Arrow, OK; (2); Church Yth Grp; Math Clb; Spanish Clb; High Hon Roll; Hon Roll; NHS; Pres Schlr; OK Hnr Soc; Med Field.

PEAK, CHANDRA L; Copan HS; Dewey, OK; (3); FBLA; FHA; Office Aide; Teachers Aide; Band; Drill Tm; Flag Corp; Pep Band; High Hon Roll; Hon Roll; Northeastern ST Univ; Acctng.

PEAK, JOSH E; Collinsville HS; Collinsville, OK; (3); Varsity Clb; Chorus; Ofcr Stu Cncl; Socr; Wrstlng; High Hon Roll; Hon Roll; AAU All-Amer Wrstlng 96-; Conf Champ Wrstlng 95-.

PEALOR, CANDICE; Heritage Hall Schl; Oklahoma City, OK; (2); Church Yth Grp; FCA; Letterman Clb; Mu Alpha Theta; Pep Clb; Spanish Clb; Chorus; Yrbk; Ofcr Jr Cls; Var Chrldng; NCA All Amer Chrldng; ASC All Amer Pom Pon & Edmond All Star Sqd.

PEARCE, ERIN; Marietta HS; Marietta, OK; (4); 14/53; Art Clb; Church Yth Grp; FHA; Office Aide; Teachers Aide; Chorus; Yrbk; High Hon Roll; Hon Roll; NHS; USAO Innovations Judges Choice; SOSU; Art Ed.

PEARSON, ANDREA R; Skiatook HS; Skiatook, OK; (4); 8/110; Church Yth Grp; Cmnty Wkr; FBLA; FHA; Library Aide; Office Aide; Teachers Aide; Chorus; Church Choir; School Musical; FHA Pres, Vp, Chapln; FBLA Treas, Sec; Serteens; Yth Alive Offcr; Tulsa CC; Bus.

PEARSON, CHANCE L; Edmond Memorial HS; Edmond, OK; (2); FCA; Spanish Clb; Treas Frsh Cls; Treas Soph Cls; Rep Stu Cncl; JV Bsktbl; Tennis; Cit Awd; NHS; Pres Acad Fit Awd.

PEARSON, ELIZABETH A; Deer Creek HS; Edmond, OK; (2); Church Yth Grp; FCA; Pep Clb; Science Clb; Stage Crew; Yrbk; Chrldng; Hon Roll; NHS.

PEARSON, ERIC; Stigler HS; Stigler, OK; (2); Church Yth Grp; 4-H; Natl FFA Org; Scholastic Bowl; SADD; Band; Church Choir; Mrchg Band; School Play; Hon Roll.

PEARSON, ERIN; Claremore Sr HS; Claremore, OK; (2); 31/273; Church Yth Grp; Library Aide; Spanish Clb; Var Stu Cncl; Var Chrldng; Var Mgr(s); Hon Roll; Stdnt Mnth; OK ST Hnr Soc.

PEARSON, KASEY; Tuttle HS; Tuttle, OK; (4); 6/76; FHA; Spanish Clb; SADD; Ofcr Stu Cncl; Chrldng; High Hon Roll; Hon Roll; NHS; Ntl Merit SF; Val.

PEARSON III, LINDELL E; Edmond North HS; Edmond, OK; (2); 29/420; Letterman Clb; ROTC; Color Guard; JV Bsktbl; Var L Ftbl; Hon Roll; NHS; Kitty Hawk Air Soc; Stu Of Month; Barksdale Summer Ldrshp Schl Dist Grad; Engrg.

PEARSON WHITE, HEIDI L; Fletcher Jr Sr HS; Fletcher, OK; (1); CAP; Church Choir; JV Bsktbl; JV Sftbl; Hon Roll; OK U; Chld Psych.

PEASE, ALANA C; U S Grant HS; Oklahoma City, OK; (3); Orch; Rep Sr Cls; Swmmng; High Hon Roll; NHS; Outstndng Dsktp Pblshng Stu; Bus Mgmt.

PEBLEY, JENNIFER D; Weatherford HS; Weatherford, OK; (4); 63/140; Cmnty Wkr; Drama Clb; Pres French Clb; VP German Clb; Speech Tm; Teachers Aide; School Play; Stage Crew; FHA; FTA; Vol Drs Aide; Agnes Scott Coll; Intnl Relatns.

PECE, STEPHANIE A; Owasso Sr HS; Owasso, OK; (4); Art Clb; Church Yth Grp; French Clb; Hosp Aide; Quiz Bowl; Science Clb; SADD; Teachers Aide; Chorus; Church Choir; Tulsa CC; Bus.

PECK, AARON R; Mustang HS; Mustang, OK; (1); Church Yth Grp; Band; Jazz Band; Mrchg Band; Pep Band; Hon Roll; Yth Alive; OK ST Univ.

PECK, BENJI; Oklahoma Christian Schl; Edmond, OK; (4); Church Yth Grp; FCA; Math Tm; Teachers Aide; Yrbk; Ofcr Bsbl; Ftbl; High Hon Roll; Hon Roll; Pres Schlr.

PECK, BOBBY; Bartlesville Sr HS; Bartlesville, OK; (4); 32/440; Art Clb; Church Yth Grp; FBLA; FHA; JV Bsbl; High Hon Roll; NHS; Prfct Atten Awd; Pres Acad Fit Awd; Pres Schlr; U Of OK.

PECK, DEVIN A; Enid Sr HS; Enid, OK; (2); Speech Tm; Band; Jazz Band; Mrchg Band; Pep Band; School Play; Hon Roll; Jr NHS; NHS.

PECK, JAMES; Oklahoma Christian Schl; Oklahoma City, OK; (2); 1/65; Church Yth Grp; Debate Tm; Drama Clb; Math Tm; Speech Tm; Stage Crew; Var Bsbl; High Hon Roll; Prfct Atten Awd; Boy Scts; Eagle Sct; OK U; Law.

PECK, JASON D; Westmoore HS; Oklahoma City, OK; (3); Church Yth Grp; Cmnty Wkr; French Clb; Band; Church Choir; Jazz Band; Mrchg Band; Pep Band; Jr NHS; NHS; Outstdng Mem Jr NHS; Outstdng Band Mem; OK Bapt Univ; Yth Ministry.

PECK, JAY; Oklahoma Christian Schl; Oklahoma City, OK; (2); 1/65; Pres Church Yth Grp; Debate Tm; Math Tm; Scholastic Bowl; Speech Tm; Chorus; Stage Crew; Var Bsbl; High Hon Roll; Prfct Atten Awd; Eagle Sct; Attorney.

PECK, JONATHAN D; Ponca City Sr HS; Ponca City, OK; (4); 3/338; Church Yth Grp; French Clb; SADD; Teachers Aide; Acpl Chr; Church Choir; Nwsp; High Hon Roll; NHS; Ntl Merit SF; OK Bapt U; Music.

PECK, OWEN R; Bartlesville Sr HS; Bartlesville, OK; (4); 21/460; Art Clb; Church Yth Grp; FBLA; FHA; Office Aide; JV Bsktbl; High Hon Roll; Hon Roll; NHS; Prfct Atten Awd; Cash Schlrshp Bartlesville Art Assn; Univ Of OK; Graphic Art.

PECK, REGINALD R; Edmond Santa Fe HS; Oklahoma City, OK; (3); JCL; Pres Latin Clb; JV Socr; JV Tennis; Hon Roll; Cert Of Commendation From OK Forgn Lang Tchrs Assoc; Comp Sci.

PECK, RUSSELL O; Edmond Memorial HS; Owasso, OK; (2); 56/408; Boy Scts; Debate Tm; German Clb; Mu Alpha Theta; NHS; Prfct Atten Awd; Pres Schlr; St Schlr.

PECORE, STACEY M; Bethel HS; Tecumseh, OK; (2); 15/72; FCA; GAA; Office Aide; Spanish Clb; Teachers Aide; Var Sftbl; Hon Roll; NHS; Phy Thrpst.

PEDEN, AMBER; Oklahoma Christian Schl; Edmond, OK; (4); Church Yth Grp; Cmnty Wkr; Rptr Yrbk; Sec Soph Cls; Sec Jr Cls; Pres Sr Cls; Bsktbl; Socr; Trk; High Hon Roll; OK U Of Sci & Arts; Phys Thrpy.

PEDICORD, KATIE C; Union Sr HS; Broken Arrow, OK; (3); 27/741; FCA; Hosp Aide; Spanish Clb; Ofcr Soph Cls; Ofcr Jr Cls; JV Capt Chrldng; Powder Puff Ftbl; Spanish NHS; NCA All Amrcn Tm Mem.

PEDIGO, LISA M; Putnam City West HS; Bethany, OK; (2); Church Yth Grp; Drama Clb; Chorus; Church Choir; Color Guard; Mrchg Band; CAN Vol; Chrch Acteens; U Of OK; Pediatrician.

PEEBLES, KATIE; Durant HS; Durant, OK; (4); Am Leg Aux Girls St; Chorus; Rep Stu Cncl; Sftbl; High Hon Roll; NHS; St Schlr; U S Hstry & Govt Awd; All-Amer Schlr; SE OK ST U; Hotel/Rest Mgmt.

PEEK, JERRY L; Sapulpa Sr HS; Sapulpa, OK; (2); Church Yth Grp; JV Var Bsbl; Wt Lftg; High Hon Roll; Hon Roll; Amer Lgn 2a All Star Bsbl; Prin Hon Roll; Coll.

PEELER, C STEVEN; Moore HS; Moore, OK; (3); Teachers Aide; JV Bsbl; Acctng.

PEELER, LANCE; Christian Heritage Acad; Oklahoma City, OK; (2); 1/53; Debate Tm; Band; Church Choir; School Play; Variety Show; Ftbl; Golf; Hon Roll; Ntl Merit Ltr.

PEEPER, DANNY; Chisholm Sr HS; Enid, OK; (4); 10/70; Natl FFA Org; Var Bsbl; Capt Bsktbl; Hon Roll; NHS; Wheat Capital Bsktbl All Tournament Tm; Mc Donalds Plyr Of The Game; OK ST U; Ag/Agronomy.

PEEPER, THEODORE M; Stillwater Sr HS; Stillwater, OK; (4); 1/320; Latin Clb; Math Clb; Math Tm; Mu Alpha Theta; Natl Beta Clb; NHS; St Schlr; Val; Church Yth Grp; Cmnty Wkr; 2 Gold Mdls Natl Latin Exam; Brnz Mdl Mndgms US His Comp UCD; Natl Merit Cmmnd Stdnt; OK ST Univ; Ag Ec.

PEERY, ILY; Edmond North HS; Edmond, OK; (4); 27/336; Church Yth Grp; Cmnty Wkr; Dance Clb; FTA; Math Clb; Mu Alpha Theta; ROTC; Pres Orch; School Musical; High Hon Roll; Mascot; Brigham Young U; Scndry Ed.

PEET, DAVID; Jenks HS; Tulsa, OK; (2); 1/750; Boy Scts; Church Yth Grp; DECA; FCA; French Clb; Key Clb; Math Tm; Mu Alpha Theta; Yrbk; Wt Lftg; Wtr Sfty Instr.

PEFFER, CLAYTON; El Reno Sr HS; El Reno, OK; (2); Ofcr Bsbl.

PEIL, SARAH; Woodward HS; Woodward, OK; (4); 2/154; Treas Am Leg Aux Girls St; Rep Church Yth Grp; FCA; VP German Clb; Band; Capt Color Guard; Rep Stu Cncl; NHS; Val; Intl For Lang Awd; Natl Engl Mrt Awd; Rtry Stu/Mnth; U OK.

PEITZMEIER, KAMI; Edmond North HS; Edmond, OK; (4); 153/330; Church Yth Grp; Math Clb; Mu Alpha Theta; Stage Crew; Capt Var Golf; NHS; Yth Action Cncl 95-; Outstndng Yth Of Parish Awd 96; U Of Cntrl OK; Math.

PELFERY, GINEFER M; Edmond Memrl HS; Edmond, OK; (4); 87/322; Art Clb; Hist French Clb; Edmond Arts & Hum Cncl Schlsp; Metro Chrch Nursery Tchr; Art Schlsp OK Chrstn Univ Of Sci & Arts; OK Chrstn Univ; Art.

PELKEY, KIM R; Wellston Schl; Wellston, OK; (3); Rptr Drama Clb; FCA; Rep FHA; Rep Pep Clb; Speech Tm; Pres SADD; Teachers Aide; Chorus; School Play; Nwsp; Competed In St Speech 5th Pl; St Speech 8th Pl; His Tchr.

PELL, JENNY L; Elmore City Jr Sr HS; Elmore City, OK; (3); 1/45; FCA; FHA; Pep Clb; Chorus; VP Soph Cls; Sec Jr Cls; Ofcr Stu Cncl; Bsktbl; Sftbl; NHS; Outstndng Acad Achvt Awd; Acad Meet Alg II Silver Mdl; U Of OK; Med.

PELLETIER, JAMES; Moore HS; Moore, OK; (4); #72 in class; Art Clb; NHS; Art Inst Of Dallas; Comp Anmtn.

PELTIER, NICOLE R; Norman Sr HS; Norman, OK; (3); Church Yth Grp; Latin Clb; Spanish Clb; High Hon Roll; Natl Severe Storms Lab Intern; OK Bapt Univ; Meteorologist.

PELTON, JENNIFER D; Ardmore HS; Ardmore, OK; (3); 11/200; Church Yth Grp; VP Sec DECA; Latin Clb; Mu Alpha Theta; Science Clb; Chorus; School Musical; Variety Show; High Hon Roll; Hon Roll; Msc Ed.

PEMBERTON, JENNIFER; Bethany Christian Acad; Mustang, OK; (1); Church Yth Grp; Pep Clb; Yrbk; Var L Bsktbl; High Hon Roll; Leading Scorer On Soccer Team; MVP At St Soccer Trnmt; Southern Nazarene U; Pediatrcn.

PEMBROOK, JACKIE; Fairview HS; Fairview, OK; (1); 1/77; Church Yth Grp; FCA; Natl FFA Org; Band; Church Choir; Mrchg Band; Stat Bsktbl; Hon Roll; Pep Band; Vlc Soloist; Pianist; OSU; Psych.

PENA, SHAWNA A; Wagoner Sr HS; Wagoner, OK; (2); FBLA; GAA; Band; Mrchg Band; Pep Band; VP Frsh Cls; Sftbl; NSU; Hotel Mgmnt.

PENALOSA, ANDREA; Miami Sr HS; Miami, OK; (4); Cmnty Wkr; Debate Tm; Drama Clb; NFL; Office Aide; Spanish Clb; Speech Tm; SADD; Teachers Aide; VP Soph Cls; Jr Miss Fnlst; Bowden.

PENCE, AARON; Central Mid-HS; Norman, OK; (1); Art Clb; Debate Tm; Drama Clb; Latin Clb; High Hon Roll; Hon Roll; Model Congress; Duke Univ TIP; Rice Univ; Bio Chem.

PENCE, JAMIE LYNN; Olustee Schl; Olustee, OK; (2); 4/20; Church Yth Grp; Cmnty Wkr; Dance Clb; FCA; Pres 4-H; GAA; JA; Quiz Bowl; Teachers Aide; VICA; GNHA Jr Sprtsmnshp Awd; Southwestern.

PENCE, JOEL D; Sapulpa Sr HS; Sapulpa, OK; (3); Church Yth Grp; Band; Jazz Band; Mrchg Band; Pep Band; Martial Arts Awds; Recreational Soccer; Bsktbl.

PENCE, JONSY R; Enid Sr HS; Enid, OK; (4); Hon Roll; Jr NHS; NHS; Comp Pgmng; Omnivorous Reader; Comp Sci.

PENCE, JUSTIN D; Woodward HS; Woodward, OK; (4); 4-H; Key Clb; Natl FFA Org; VICA; School Play; Stage Crew; Variety Show; Bsktbl; Golf; Wt Lftg; Round Up Clb; OHSRA, Bull Riding Competively; Kiwanis Concession Stands For Pee Wee Bsktbl; Ag; Livestock Mgmt.

PENDERGRASS, STEPHANIE; South Intermediate HS; Broken Arrow, OK; (2); Band; Color Guard; Mrchg Band; Orch; Gov Hon Prg Awd; Hon Roll; NHS; Pres Acad Fit Awd; Eqstrn; Music Prfmnc.

PENDLETON, JAQULYN R; Stillwater Jr HS; Stillwater, OK; (1); Church Yth Grp; Natl FFA Org; Office Aide; Band; Color Guard; Flag Corp; Mrchg Band; Pep Band; Pres Acad Fit Awd; Pres Schlr; OK ST Univ; Tchr.

PENINGTON, KYLE V; Southeast HS; Oklahoma City, OK; (4); Church Yth Grp; Debate Tm; Drama Clb; Office Aide; Speech Tm; Thesps; School Musical; School Play; Variety Show; Yrbk; 2 Drama Prodctns; U Cntrl OK; Theatre.

PENISTEN, JAMES R; Shawnee Sr HS; Shawnee, OK; (2); Church Yth Grp; Spanish Clb; Ofcr Bsbl; Bsktbl; Ftbl; OK ST Univ.

PENISTEN, PATRICK M; Tecumseh HS; Shawnee, OK; (2); 42/159; Church Yth Grp; Letterman Clb; Math Clb; Mu Alpha Theta; JV Bsbl; Var Bsktbl.

PENN, ALLICIA; Moore HS; Oklahoma City, OK; (2); Church Yth Grp; FBLA; GAA; Science Clb; Chorus; Church Choir; Swing Chorus; Rep Stu Cncl; Bsktbl; Trk; Band, Schl Chorus & Trk Cont Medals; Multicultrl Stu Assn Treas; TX Southern; Med.

PENN, J D; Chandler HS; Chandler, OK; (3); Natl FFA Org; Natl HS Rodeo Assn; Ag Tchr.

PENNEKAMP, DAVID; Owasso Sr HS; Owasso, OK; (3); Church Yth Grp; Office Aide; Science Clb; Spanish Clb; Band; Mrchg Band; Orch; Cit Awd; High Hon Roll; Hon Roll; Band Cncl VP; Sci Clb Pres; Band Section Ldr & Squad Ldr; U Of OK.

PENNEL, BRANDI; Paden HS; Paden, OK; (1); Church Yth Grp; 4-H; FHA; Natl Beta Clb; Bsktbl; Var Chrldng; Var Sftbl; Hon Roll.

PENNER, ERIN R; Thomas Jr Sr HS; Thomas, OK; (1); FBLA; FHA; Hon Roll; Indian Clb Sec-Treas; Hlpng Elderly/Disabled; LSU; Psych.

PENNINGTON, CHAYA; Northeast HS; Oklahoma City, OK; (3); 31/107; Church Yth Grp; FBLA; Mu Alpha Theta; Science Clb; Spanish Clb; Band; Jazz Band; Mrchg Band; Orch; Pep Band; OK ST Univ; Intl Bus.

PENNINGTON, DONNA; Comanche HS; Comanche, OK; (3); Art Clb; Church Yth Grp; FBLA; FHA; SADD; Bsktbl; Trk; Hon Roll; FFA; TSA; Cameron U; Bus.

PENNINGTON, ERIN A; Duncan HS; Duncan, OK; (2); Church Yth Grp; FBLA; Hosp Aide; Key Clb; Letterman Clb; Library Aide; SADD; Yrbk; Stat Bsktbl; Stat Tennis; OU; Phys Ther.

PENNINGTON, SHASTA R; Wapanucka Schl; Wapanucka, OK; (3); Rptr 4-H; Rptr Nwsp; Yrbk; Var Capt Bsktbl; Var Sftbl; Var Trk; 4-H Awd; Hon Roll; NHS; Murray ST Coll; Phys Therapy.

PENNINGTON, TIFFANY; Hinton HS; Hinton, OK; (3); Church Yth Grp; FCA; SADD; Chorus; Church Choir; School Musical; Sec Jr Cls; Rep Stu Cncl; High Hon Roll; Hon Roll; OK Hnr Soc; Make Up Artist.

PENRICE, JEREMI; Bartlesville Sr HS; Bartlesville, OK; (4); 200/427; Am Leg Boys St; Church Yth Grp; FCA; French Clb; Letterman Clb; Teachers Aide; Band; Jazz Band; Rep Stu Cncl; Var L Ftbl; OK ST U; Vet Med.

PENSE, STACY; Chickasha HS; Chickasha, OK; (4); 3/150; Debate Tm; NFL; Spanish Clb; Speech Tm; Rep Stu Cncl; Chrldng; Gym; Tennis; NHS; Val; OK ST U; Med.

PENWRIGHT, HEATHER K; Geronimo Jr Sr HS; Geronimo, OK; (3); Debate Tm; FCA; Girl Scts; Office Aide; Speech Tm; Teachers Aide; Var Bsktbl; Var Sftbl; Var Trk; Cit Awd; OK Chrstn Univ.

PENWRIGHT, NICOLE S; Calumet Schl; Calumet, OK; (2); 2/30; Church Yth Grp; Cmnty Wkr; GAA; Letterman Clb; Church Choir; Var Bsktbl; Var Sftbl; Var Vllybl; High Hon Roll; Hon Roll.

PEOPLES, AMANDA L; Dickson HS; Mannsville, OK; (1); Church Yth Grp; FCA; SADD; Chorus; Church Choir; Bsktbl; Trk; Cit Awd; Hon Roll; Sun Schl Tchr; Music Awds; Nrsg/Mus Tchr.

PEOPLES, CHARONNA; Mt St Marys HS; Spencer, OK; (3); 10/65; Var L Bsktbl; High Hon Roll; OK City Little All City Hnrb Mntn Team ; MSM Outstdng Ldrshp; OK SW All Trnmt Team; N All Conf Team; Bio.

PEOPLES, LISA A; Owasso Sr HS; Owasso, OK; (4); 30/296; Church Yth Grp; Spanish Clb; Band; Mrchg Band; Ofcr Jr Cls; Ofcr Sr Cls; Hon Roll; NHS; OK St Univ; Acctng.

PEOPLES, MARCIA; Lawton Sr HS; Lawton, OK; (4); Rptr FBLA; German Clb; Sec Key Clb; Office Aide; Rep Stu Cncl; High Hon Roll; Hon Roll; Jr NHS; NHS; U Of OK; Acctng.

PEOPLES, MONICA M; Star Spencer HS; Spencer, OK; (2); Nrsng.

PEOPLES JR, RICKY A; Dickson HS; Mannsville, OK; (2); Church Yth Grp; FCA; Spanish Clb; Speech Tm; SADD; Chorus; Var Bsktbl; Var Ftbl; Var Trk; Hntng; Fshng; Chrch; Ed.

PEOPLES, SUZANNE E; Woodward HS; Woodward, OK; (3); Pres Drama Clb; German Clb; Key Clb; Band; Jazz Band; Mrchg Band; Pep Band; School Play; Powder Puff Ftbl; Hon Roll; Mck Trl St Rnnr Up Tm; St Senate Pg; OK ST U; Music Ed.

PEPER, JULIE; Adair HS; Adair, OK; (2); FCA; Science Clb; Var Bsktbl; High Hon Roll; Pres Acad Fit Awd.

PERCEFUL, BRANDY E; Roland Sr HS; Roland, OK; (3); Church Yth Grp; Chorus; Church Choir; Hon Roll; His Prof.

PERCEFULL, CLINT; Choctaw Jr HS; Choctaw, OK; (1); JV Bsktbl; JV Golf; Hon Roll.

PERCELL, TRAVIS W; Drumright HS; Cushing, OK; (1); Church Yth Grp; Natl FFA Org; Science Clb; School Play; Ofcr Frsh Cls; Bsktbl; Socr; Wt Lftg; Hon Roll; Stu Of Month; OSU; Arch.

PERDUE, SARA; Oklahoma Christian Schl; Edmond, OK; (3); 1/60; Church Yth Grp; FCA; GAA; Speech Tm; Ofcr Stu Cncl; Capt Bsktbl; Var Crs Cntry; Powder Puff Ftbl; Socr; Tennis; OK Chrstn U Of Sci/Arts.

PERDUE, SHANETELLY; Yale Jr Sr HS; Yale, OK; (2); 5/51; Church Yth Grp; FCA; Natl Beta Clb; Natl FFA Org; Rep Stu Cncl; Bsktbl; Sftbl; Vllybl; Cit Awd; Hon Roll; OBU.

PEREZ, CHARLES L; Eisenhower Sr HS; Lawton, OK; (3); Church Yth Grp; Cmnty Wkr; FCA; 4-H; Key Clb; Model UN; NFL; Scholastic Bowl; Band; Mrchg Band; OSSYA Fed Certd Lic ST Soccer Coadh; Upward Bound Prgm; NCEOA Del Natl Stdnt Cngrs 96; OK Chrstn U; Biochem/Engr.

PEREZ, FRANCHESCA; Central HS; Tulsa, OK; (4); 3/190; Key Clb; ROTC; Thesps; Orch; School Musical; School Play; Yrbk; NHS; Red Cross Aide; Band; Masonic Awd; AP Engl.

PEREZ, SHEENA E; Broken Arrow Sr HS; Broken Arrow, OK; (4); English Clb; Hist Latin Clb; Spanish Clb; Acpl Chr; Church Choir; Hon Roll; Jr NHS; NHS; James E Casey Schlrshp; OK Princpls Sci/Math Schlr; Washington U; Engl.

PERIINS, LORA; Miami Sr HS; Miami, OK; (2); 33/170; Band; Mrchg Band; Pep Band; Rep Soph Cls; Rep Stu Cncl; Var Chrldng; Gym; Mgr Socr; Var Tennis; High Hon Roll; Wrstlng Hmcmng Frosh Attndnt; ACT 25; Northeastern ST U; Coll Prof.

PERINGOL, ABRAHAM K; Putnam City West HS; Bethany, OK; (4); Pres Church Yth Grp; Cmnty Wkr; Math Clb; Quiz Bowl; VP Science Clb; Spanish Clb; Rep Stu Cncl; Var L Tennis; NHS; Univ Of OK; Orthopediz Surgery.

PERKEY, BETSY; Hobart HS; Hobart, OK; (1); Church Yth Grp; Cmnty Wkr; FHA; FTA; Band; Jazz Band; Mrchg Band; Pep Band; OK Bapt Univ; Family Psych.

PERKEY, HAYLEY; Hobart HS; Hobart, OK; (2); Church Yth Grp; FCA; FHA; Teachers Aide; Church Choir; VP Frsh Cls; Ofcr Stu Cncl; Bsktbl; Chrldng; Sftbl; Piano; OK U; Med.

PERKINS, AMY; Moore HS; Oklahoma City, OK; (4); 45/525; Am Leg Aux Girls St; FCA; JCL; VP Latin Clb; Library Aide; Rep Stu Cncl; Mgr Ftbl; Mgr(s); Natl Govt & Hstry Awd Wnnr; Ftbl Homcmng Attndnt 93-94 & 94-95, Qn 95-96; Jr Escort 94-95; OK U; Law.

PERKINS, ANTHONY K; Perkins-Tryon HS; Perkins, OK; (2); Church Yth Grp; FCA; 4-H; Natl FFA Org; Band; Jazz Band; Mrchg Band; Pep Band; 4-H Awd; High Hon Roll; OSU; Pilot.

PERKINS, BARRY; Perkins HS; Perkins, OK; (4); 10/78; Am Leg Boys St; Church Yth Grp; Pres Band; Jazz Band; Mrchg Band; Var Wrstlng; High Hon Roll; NHS; FCA; US Army Rsrv Bnd; OK ST U; Frstry.

PERKINS, CARA; Elk City HS; Elk City, OK; (3); 5/150; Am Leg Aux Girls St; Church Yth Grp; FCA; German Clb; Math Clb; Scholastic Bowl; SADD; Teachers Aide; Band; Mrchg Band.

PERKINS, DAVID; Elk City Jr HS; Elk City, OK; (1); Church Yth Grp; Band; Mrchg Band; Pep Band; Socr; Tennis; Hon Roll.

PERKINS, JENNIFER; Del City HS; Del City, OK; (1); Church Yth Grp; Drama Clb; Pep Clb; Chrldng; High Hon Roll; Hon Roll; Jr NHS.

PERKINS, JEREMY; Ringling HS; Ringling, OK; (2); Church Yth Grp; Band; Mrchg Band; Bsktbl; Ftbl; Dance Clb.

PERKINS, LAURA L; Harrah HS; Harrah, OK; (1); 32/180; Natl FFA Org; Sftbl; Hon Roll; FFA Harran Chptr; Nurse/Dr.

PERKINS, LORA; Miami Sr HS; Miami, OK; (2); Pep Clb; Band; Jazz Band; Mrchg Band; Pep Band; Rep Soph Cls; Rep Stu Cncl; Var Chrldng; Var Gym; Mgr Socr; Wrstlng Homecoming Crt; NE St Univ; Ed.

PERKINS, MEGAN; Owasso Sr HS; Owasso, OK; (4); 11/296; Church Yth Grp; Math Clb; Spanish Clb; Band; Flag Corp; Mrchg Band; Pep Band; Rep Stu Cncl; NHS; FCA; World Bible Study Adlscnt Kids India; Stdnt Mnth Schlrshp Rogers Cty Bank; U Of Cntrl OK; Sclgy/Soc Wrk.

PERKINS, NICOLETTE; Sulphur HS; Sulphur, OK; (3); 5/76; Art Clb; Church Yth Grp; Drama Clb; Pres French Clb; GAA; HOBY; Key Clb; Science Clb; Speech Tm; Rptr Nwsp; OK Hnr Soc.

PERKINS, RACHEL; Perkins-Tryon HS; Carney, OK; (1); Church Yth Grp; GAA; Mgr(s); Score Keeper; Trk; Wt Lftg.

PERKINS, STEPHANIE A; Dewey HS; Bartlesville, OK; (3); 2/88; FHA; Hon Roll; NHS; Pres Acad Fit Awd; OU.

PERMENTER, JUSTIN; Spiro HS; Spiro, OK; (1); Church Yth Grp; FCA; JV Ftbl; High Hon Roll; Hon Roll; Prfct Atten Awd; OK Univ; Meteorology.

PERNG, TAMY E C; Edison HS; Tulsa, OK; (4); 1/178; Cmnty Wkr; Treas Science Clb; Treas Spanish Clb; SADD; Ofcr Jr Cls; Ofcr Sr Cls; High Hon Roll; NHS; Val; U Of OK; Biochem.

PERRIN, SARAH D; Latta Sr HS; Ada, OK; (2); Church Yth Grp; FHA; Pep Clb; Church Choir; Rptr Nwsp; Rptr Frsh Cls; VP Soph Cls; Var Chrldng; Hon Roll; Piano Lessons 5 Yrs; Early Chldhd Ed.

PERRIN, TRAVIS; Stillwater Sr HS; Stillwater, OK; (3); Pres Natl FFA Org; Speech Tm; JV Bsbl; JV Bsktbl; Hon Roll; FFA Achvt Tm Wnnr St Mt Jdgng, Natl Rnk Hgh Ind Mt Jdgng, Mr FFA Dvrsfd Crp & Fd Grn; OK ST U; Ag Ec Engr.

PERRY, BRANDON L; Charles Page HS; Sand Springs, OK; (2); Var Bsbl; Var Bsktbl; Prfct Atten Awd; Sports Medicine.

PERRY, DANIEL A; Vian HS; Sallisaw, OK; (4); 7/60; Art Clb; Boy Scts; Cmnty Wkr; Library Aide; Quiz Bowl; Spanish Clb; High Hon Roll; NHS; Ntl Merit Ltr; Nrthestrn ST U; Bus Mgmt.

PERRY, JASON R; Latta Sr HS; Ada, OK; (2); 4-H; Speech Tm; Thesps; VICA; School Play; Chrldng; 4-H Awd; Hon Roll; Drama Clb; Stage Crew; Mock Trl; Spch Trnmnt 2nd/3rd Dist 8/Th/6th ST 95-; ST Fair 5th Forestry Dsply; Murray ST Coll.

PERRY, JIMAE; Moore HS; Moore, OK; (4); 5/55; Church Yth Grp; French Clb; Q&S; Scholastic Bowl; Speech Tm; Chorus; Church Choir; Nwsp; Lit Mag; NHS; Cert Chiroproctic Asst; Bapt All St Choir Mem; OK City CC.

PERRY, KATE; Macomb Schl; Macomb, OK; (2); Art Clb; Cmnty Wkr; Computer Clb; 4-H; Natl FFA Org; Red Cross Aide; Speech Tm; Pres Frsh Cls; Pres Soph Cls; Treas Stu Cncl; OK ST U; Grnhse Mngmt.

PERRY, KIM L; Del City HS; Oklahoma City, OK; (2); FHA; OU; PT.

PERRY, LESLIE B; Choctaw HS; Choctaw, OK; (2); Church Yth Grp; Girl Scts; Office Aide; Band; Color Guard; Drm Mjr(t); Mrchg Band; Pep Band; JV Chrldng; Hon Roll.

PERRY, LISA; Heritage Hall Schl; Oklahoma City, OK; (3); Church Yth Grp; FCA; Mu Alpha Theta; Red Cross Aide; Yrbk; Ofcr Stu Cncl; Socr; Vllybl; High Hon Roll; NHS.

PERRY, MARILYN J; Indiahoma Schl; Indiahoma, OK; (1); 1/15; FCA; Yrbk; Sec Frsh Cls; JV Var Bsktbl; JV Score Keeper; JV Var Sftbl; High Hon Roll; NHS; Acad Team.

PERRY, MICHELLE; Frederick HS; Frederick, OK; (2); 5/110; Church Yth Grp; FCA; FHA; Speech Tm; Varsity Clb; School Musical; Rep Frsh Cls; Rep Stu Cncl; Hon Roll; NHS.

PERRY, SHARI; Indianola HS; Mcalester, OK; (3); Church Yth Grp; 4-H; FBLA; FHA; Natl Beta Clb; Quiz Bowl; SADD; Rep Soph Cls; 4-H Awd; Hon Roll; Choctaw Nation Upward Bound Math & Sci Ctr; OK Citizen Bee.

PERRY, STEPHANIE R; Glenpool HS; Glenpool, OK; (2); Church Yth Grp; FCA; Sec FHA; Chorus; Church Choir; Swing Chorus; Vllybl; Jr NHS; Crs Cntry; Hon Roll; Warrior Singers 2 Yrs; Vocal Cmptn 2 Yrs.

PERRY, TABETHA; Enid Sr HS; Enid, OK; (4); Church Yth Grp; French Clb; Library Aide; ROTC; Teachers Aide; Hon Roll; NHS; Elem Tchr.

PERRY, TAMMY; Vian HS; Sallisaw, OK; (4); 1/60; Library Aide; Quiz Bowl; Scholastic Bowl; Spanish Clb; SADD; Teachers Aide; Phtg Rptr Yrbk; Treas Jr Cls; High Hon Roll; NHS; Nrthestrn ST Univ.

PERRYMAN, LEANN M; Altus Sr HS; Altus, OK; (2); Church Yth Grp; FCA; Band; Chorus; Church Choir; Mrchg Band; Swmmng; High Hon Roll; Hon Roll; Jr NHS; OK U; Bio.

PERRYMAN, SHEILA M; Charles Page HS; Sand Springs, OK; (1); ST 1st Pl Wnr Natl His Day/Superior Rating Natls; Summer 96 Mission Trip Hungary.

PERSALL, LORI; Sharon Mutual Jr Sr HS; Woodward, OK; (2); Church Yth Grp; FCA; FHA; Library Aide; Natl FFA Org; VP Frsh Cls; Var Bsktbl; NHS; OK ST U; Ed.

PERTREE, COURTNEY L; Christian Heritage Acad; Oklahoma City, OK; (2); Church Yth Grp; FCA; GAA; Girl Scts; Teachers Aide; Chrldng; Gym; Hon Roll; Ntl Merit Ltr; Pres Acad Fit Awd; Participated Pagents & Won Natl Jr Miss Modeling Qn In AR; OK Univ; Phy Thrpst.

PERTREE, JAMES T; Christian Heritage Acad; Oklahoma City, OK; (3); 20/45; Church Yth Grp; FCA; Church Choir; JV Ftbl; Var L Golf; JV Tennis; JV Wt Lftg; High Hon Roll; Hon Roll; Ntl Merit Ltr; Deans List; Multi Yr Listee; Baylor; Pre-Med; Bus; Surgeon.

PESINA, ANNA; Rock Creek Jr Sr HS; Bokchito, OK; (2); 5/44; FHA; Sec Soph Cls; JV Var Bsktbl; Var Sftbl; Hon Roll; NHS; Stu Cncl; SOSU.

PETERS, AARON; Westmoore HS; Guthrie, OK; (4); Church Yth Grp; FCA; Speech Tm; School Play; Variety Show; VP Sec Stu Cncl; Bsktbl; Crs Cntry; Ftbl; Trk; Jr Cnslr BASIC ST Convent; Pres Ldrshp Schlsp; Olympic Torch Runner Selected By ST Nom; UCO; Brdcasting Sports.

PETERS, BECKY Y; Morris HS; Morris, OK; (3); 35/70; Art Clb; Debate Tm; Drama Clb; Speech Tm; Thesps; Chorus; School Musical; School Play; Variety Show; Bsktbl; Mercur Col; Drama.

PETERS, CHERYL K; Emerson Jr HS; Enid, OK; (1); Church Yth Grp; Scholastic Bowl; Teachers Aide; Band; Church Choir; Mrchg Band; Nwsp; High Hon Roll; Jr NHS; Med; Nurse.

PETERS, JEFFERY; Clinton HS; Clinton, OK; (2); Church Yth Grp; Cmnty Wkr; Debate Tm; FCA; Chorus; Swing Chorus; VP Frsh Cls; JV Diving; Var Socr; JV Bsbl; Hnr Choir; OK Chrstn U; Law.

PETERS, JOSHUA; Noble HS; Noble, OK; (4); Boy Scts; Church Yth Grp; FCA; French Clb; HOBY; Key Clb; Letterman Clb; Math Clb; Mu Alpha Theta; Spanish Clb; Eagle Sct; Page St Hs Rep.

PETERS, JULIANNA; Sapulpa Sr HS; Sapulpa, OK; (4); 8/300; Am Leg Aux Girls St; Dance Clb; Spanish Clb; Drill Tm; Hist Frsh Cls; Treas Soph Cls; Treas Jr Cls; Sec Sr Cls; Pres Stu Cncl; Var L Golf; Med.

PETERS, KEITH; Moore HS; Moore, OK; (2); Church Yth Grp; Spanish Clb; Church Choir; Rep Stu Cncl; JV Bsktbl; High Hon Roll; Hon Roll; Jr NHS; NHS; Pres Acad Fit Awd; 1st Baptist Church Yth Cncl; U Of OK; Financl Bus.

PETERS, KENNETH R; Northeast HS; Oklahoma City, OK; (2); FBLA; Hosp Aide; ROTC; Band; Church Choir; Mrchg Band; Orch; Pep Band; Mgr(s); Tennis; NSBE Jr; Sigma Beta Clb; Regulations Drill Team W/O Arms Comm; Comp.

PETERS, KRISTYN; Pawhuska HS; Pawhuska, OK; (3); 7/110; Church Yth Grp; Prfct Atten Awd; Treas Key Clb; NFL; Pep Clb; Speech Tm; Tennis; High Hon Roll; NHS; St Hnr Soc; KS U; Orthdntst.

PETERS, LARISSA N; Putnam City HS; Oklahoma City, OK; (3); 133/401; Church Yth Grp; Cmnty Wkr; Debate Tm; French Clb; Science Clb; Teachers Aide; Chrch Of God Girls Cnslr; Environmental Clb; Sr Ldrshp Cls; OK Univ; Arch; Homebuilder.

PETERS, MONICA; Watts HS; Watts, OK; (4); Math Clb; Natl Beta Clb; Natl FFA Org; Pep Clb; Teachers Aide; Nwsp; Yrbk; Hon Roll; NHS; Cmptr Sci.

PETERS, MONIQUE T; Central HS; Tulsa, OK; (2); ROTC; Band; French Hon Soc; Hon Roll; ROTC Awds; Prarie View; Dr.

PETERS, RANA; Claremore Sr HS; Claremore, OK; (2); German Clb; Hon Roll; Supts Hnr Rll; German Ltr C Awd.

PETERS, RAYNA M; Haskell HS; Haskell, OK; (3); Church Yth Grp; FCA; 4-H; Office Aide; Quiz Bowl; Speech Tm; Teachers Aide; Temple Yth Grp; Acpl Chr; Band; Piano; Saxophone; Clarinet; Sing On Tapes With A Choir; TCC; Bus.

PETERS, SABRINA; Roland Jr HS; Roland, OK; (1); Church Yth Grp; Computer Clb; Speech Tm; Band; Mrchg Band; Nwsp; Chrldng; 4-H Awd; Hon Roll; Westark; Meterologist.

PETERS, SHANNON E; Choctaw HS; Choctaw, OK; (2); Cmnty Wkr; German Clb; Girl Scts; Quiz Bowl; Chorus; Church Choir; Tennis; High Hon Roll; NHS; Prfct Atten Awd; Jazz Choir; Fresh Cls Valedictorian.

PETERS, SHANNON R; Shawnee Sr HS; Shawnee, OK; (3); 39/254; Church Yth Grp; FCA; Ofcr Stu Cncl; Bsktbl; Sftbl; Trk; High Hon Roll; NHS; Pres Acad Fit Awd; OK Bapt Univ; Sprts Med.

PETERSEN, JILL; Cleveland Sr HS; Pawnee, OK; (4); 1/90; Am Leg Aux Girls St; Key Clb; Quiz Bowl; SADD; Rptr Nwsp; Ed Yrbk; Pres Stu Cncl; Hon Roll; NHS; Val; Piano; OK ST U; Chem Engrng.

PETERSEN, T KYLE; Norman Sr HS; Norman, OK; (3); Mu Alpha Theta; Spanish Clb; Var L Socr; High Hon Roll; Hon Roll; NHS; Ntl Merit Ltr; Pres Acad Fit Awd; Spanish NHS; FCA; TOP Sccr Coach.

PETERSON, AMANDA; South Intermediate HS; Broken Arrow, OK; (1); Church Yth Grp; Acpl Chr; Chrldng; Wt Lftg; Oklahomas Cheernastics All-Star Squad; OK ST U.

PETERSON, AMANDA B; Navajo Schl; Martha, OK; (1); 5/62; Church Yth Grp; Cmnty Wkr; Drama Clb; Church Choir; Sftbl; High Hon Roll; Sal; St Schlr; Art Wrk Awds; ACU; Yth Mnstrs/Chrstn Cnclr.

PETERSON, BRENNA; Oklahoma Sch Of Science & Math; Norman, OK; (3); Math Tm; Model UN; Quiz Bowl; Red Cross Aide; Scholastic Bowl; Science Clb; Acpl Chr; School Musical; Rep Stu Cncl; JETS Awd; TEAMS Cap; MIT Rsrch Sci Inst; Biomed Rsrch.

PETERSON, HEATHER L; Roland Sr HS; Roland, OK; (3); Church Yth Grp; FCA; 4-H; GAA; Spanish Clb; Band; Church Choir; Mrchg Band; Pep Band; Rep Frsh Cls; Carl Albert ST; Tchr.

PETERSON, JEANNIE; Durant HS; Durant, OK; (3); Church Yth Grp; FHA; FTA; Teachers Aide; Ofcr Jr Cls; Gym; Hon Roll; Southeastern; Elem Ed.

PETERSON, NICOLE D; Bixby Sr HS; Bixby, OK; (4); 34/178; Pres Church Yth Grp; Cmnty Wkr; FCA; Office Aide; Spanish Clb; Nwsp; JV Bsktbl; Var Sftbl; High Hon Roll; Jr NHS; Nom Plyr Yr Smr Sftbl; Independence CC; Zoology/Tchr.

PETERSON, SHAWN T; Liberty HS; Mounds, OK; (3); Church Yth Grp; FCA; FHA; Natl FFA Org; SADD; Church Choir; Var Bsktbl; Var Stat Ftbl; Score Keeper; Socr; Bus Mgmt.

PETRASH, CHRIS L; Del City HS; Del City, OK; (2); 1/405; Church Yth Grp; French Clb; Quiz Bowl; Scholastic Bowl; Golf; French Hon Soc; Hon Roll; Jr NHS; NHS; Ntl Merit Ltr; Most Imprvd Male Stu; Upward Boundprog; OK St Univ; Eng.

PETRIK, ASHLEY; Medford Schl; Medford, OK; (1); Church Yth Grp; FCA; FHA; Chorus; Chrldng; High Hon Roll; Masonic Stu Today Awd; Med.

PETRIK, LUCRETIA; Medford Schl; Medford, OK; (3); 1/18; FBLA; Pres FHA; School Play; Rep Soph Cls; Var Chrldng; High Hon Roll; NHS; All Amer Schlr; Masonic Stu Today; Page House Rep OK; Med.

PETTICREW, ABBIE L; West Middle HS; Norman, OK; (1); Hon Roll; NHS; OK Univ.

PETTIGREW, KENDRA; Spiro HS; Spiro, OK; (3); Church Yth Grp; FCA; FBLA; Math Clb; Natl FFA Org; Church Choir; High Hon Roll; Elem Ed.

PETTIS, VANDY; Shawnee Sr HS; Shawnee, OK; (4); Am Leg Aux Girls St; Church Yth Grp; FCA; Hosp Aide; Latin Clb; Church Choir; Bsktbl; JV Crs Cntry; JV Trk; Hon Roll; TAD; Big Bros/Big Sisters Jr Brd Of Dirs; Church Prsnel & Outreach Cmmttes; OK Baptist U; Poltcl Sci.

PETTIT, COURTNEY; Lawton Sr HS; Lawton, OK; (3); FCA; HOBY; School Musical; Variety Show; Crs Cntry; NHS; Pres Acad Fit Awd; Church Yth Grp; Science Clb; Acpl Chr; March Of Dimes/Trash Bash Comm Svc; His Day 3rd Pl At Cameron U; 4th Pl Cameron Scholstc Tst Soc; OCUSA; Scndry Ed.

PETTY, CHRISTINA; Yukon Middle HS; Yukon, OK; (2); Church Yth Grp; FHA; Office Aide; Chorus; School Musical; Sftbl; Hon Roll; 3-D; Super At St Vocal Cmptn; U Of Cntrl OK; Bus Mgmt.

PETTY, JUSTIN C; Frontier Public Schl; Red Rock, OK; (2); Art Clb; Letterman Clb; Natl FFA Org; Spanish Clb; Ofcr Frsh Cls; Ofcr Soph Cls; Bsktbl; Wt Lftg; Cit Awd; High Hon Roll; OSU; Vet Med.

PETTY, LEAH; Guthrie Sr HS; Guthrie, OK; (4); 12/174; Church Yth Grp; Cmnty Wkr; Mu Alpha Theta; Band; Flag Corp; Rep Sr Cls; Bsktbl; Hon Roll; NHS; Pres Acad Fit Awd; Acctng.

PETZEL, MARIA; Norman Sr HS; Norman, OK; (4); 75/677; JCL; Sec Latin Clb; VP Mu Alpha Theta; Ed Yrbk; Rep Soph Cls; NHS; St Schlr; Tandy Tech Schlr; U Of OK; Microbio.

PETZOLD, KACY; Clinton HS; Clinton, OK; (1); FCA; Chorus; Rep Frsh Cls; Rep Stu Cncl; Mgr(s); Cit Awd; Hon Roll; OSU.

PETZOLD, KENDAL; Clinton HS; Clinton, OK; (2); 1/130; Church Yth Grp; FCA; 4-H; Spanish Clb; Chorus; Rep Stu Cncl; Bsktbl; Chrldng; Cit Awd; 4-H Awd; U OK; Acctng.

PFAFFMANN, ANNA J; Union Intermediate HS; Tulsa, OK; (2); 79/900; Office Aide; Spanish Clb; Rep Stu Cncl; JV Chrldng; Gym; Hon Roll; Jr NHS; NHS; Pres Acad Fit Awd; Peer Mediation; ARC; Mr & Mrs Redskin Crt; Washington U; Med.

PFEIL, CHARLOTTE; Moore HS; Moore, OK; (4); 43/525; FCA; JA; JCL; Latin Clb; SADD; Var Bsktbl; Var Sftbl; Var Trk; NHS; Val.

PFREHM, LESLIE M; Durant HS; Durant, OK; (2); Cmnty Wkr; Sec Key Clb; Quiz Bowl; Band; Jazz Band; Mrchg Band; Pep Band; Variety Show; Prfct Atten Awd; 5 Yr Dist/2 Yr ST Wnr Natl Hist Day; Schl Honoree Prudential Spirit Comm Awrd; SOSU Comm Bnd; Video Comm.

PHAM, DAVID N; Union Sr HS; Tulsa, OK; (3); Intnl Clb; Key Clb; Mu Alpha Theta; Temple Yth Grp; Jr NHS; NHS; Pres Acad Fit Awd; Spanish NHS; Boy Scts; Cmnty Wkr; DFY; Teen Repblcns; Med.

PHAM, JENNIFER; Western Heights Sr HS; Oklahoma City, OK; (1); Band; Flag Corp; Mrchg Band; Orch; School Musical; Hon Roll; Sheriff Upward Bound Summer Pgrm Stdnt Govt; First Chr Aband; NW Hnr Band; Ltrd; Brdcst Jrnlsm.

PHAM, NGOC T; Mustang HS; Yukon, OK; (3); 1/428; French Clb; FBLA; Key Clb; Pres Math Clb; Pres Science Clb; SADD; Temple Yth Grp; Sec NHS; Explrng Geosci Smmr Acad Univ OK/ACAD Envrnmntl Sci Rose ST Coll 94; Acad Hlth Sci Prof 95; OK ST Univ; Optmtry/Med Rsrch.

PHAM, NHUNG; U S Grant HS; Oklahoma City, OK; (4); Church Yth Grp; Hon Roll; NHS; OK Math League & Geom Acad Achvt Awds; Outstndng Acad Achvts Schl; South CC; Bus Mgmt.

PHAM, PAUL; Putnam City West HS; Bethany, OK; (1); 1/413; Chess Clb; Cmnty Wkr; Computer Clb; FBLA; JCL; Latin Clb; Boy Scts; Orch; Nwsp; VP Soph Cls; Comp Sci St Trnmt 1st Pl; Med Clb; OK Yth Philharmonia; Comp Sci.

PHAM, PHUOC V; Union Intermediate HS; Tulsa, OK; (2); TX A&M; Med.

PHAM, THUY; U S Grant HS; Oklahoma City, OK; (4); 2/183; Church Yth Grp; Hon Roll; 4-H; Ntl Merit Schol; Val; Geom & Pre-Calculus Acad Achvt Awds; OK Math League Acad Achvt Awd; OK ST U OKC; Comp Sci.

PHAN, JOHN; Westmoore HS; Oklahoma City, OK; (1); Computer Clb; Band; Jazz Band; Mrchg Band; Hon Roll; Jr NHS; NHS; MIT; Cmptr Engrng.

PHAN, LINDA; Mustang HS; Yukon, OK; (3); 1/400; Cmnty Wkr; French Clb; Hosp Aide; Key Clb; Pres Math Clb; Pres Science Clb; NHS; U Of TX-AUSTIN; Med.

PHAN, LISA L; Mustang HS; Yukon, OK; (1); 1/532; Hosp Aide; Math Clb; Science Clb; Hon Roll.

PHAN, NAM; Capitol Hill HS; Oklahoma City, OK; (4); 3/147; Cmnty Wkr; FBLA; Office Aide; Spanish Clb; JV Bsktbl; Gov Hon Prg Awd; High Hon Roll; Hon Roll; NHS; All Amer Schlr; Library Aid; VICA; OU; Phrmcy.

PHAN, TU H; Classen Schl Of Advncd Studies; Oklahoma City, OK; (3); 1/65; Art Clb; Church Yth Grp; Computer Clb; Pres French Clb; Intnl Clb; Sec Key Clb; Sec Mu Alpha Theta; Orch; Tennis; Vllybl; Acad Dcthln; 2nd Pl 2 Dlbs All Cty Tnns Trnmnt; NHS VP; Physcn.

PHARES, MARANDA D; Enid Sr HS; Enid, OK; (2); 45/411; Church Yth Grp; French Clb; Speech Tm; Chorus; School Musical; Mgr(s); Hon Roll; Jr NHS; NHS; Bio.

PHEARS, CHERIE A; Northeast HS; Oklahoma City, OK; (2); 3/160; FBLA; Hosp Aide; Pres Latin Clb; Model UN; VP Science Clb; Sec Soph Cls; Sftbl; High Hon Roll; NHS; Explorers Med Post 1889-Historian; UCA LA; Drama; Perf Arts.

PHEARS, MONIQUE R; Northeast HS; Oklahoma City, OK; (2); 6/160; FBLA; Hosp Aide; Hist Latin Clb; Model UN; Red Cross Aide; Treas Science Clb; Orch; Tennis; NHS; Explr Med Post 1889; UCLA; Pre-Med/Ped.

PHELAN, SHARON L; Gans Public Schl; Muldrow, OK; (2); 3/30; Church Yth Grp; FHA; Library Aide; Chorus; Church Choir; Pres Frsh Cls; Hon Roll; Prfct Atten Awd; Friendliest Nom Soph.

PHELPS, JASON; Santa Fe HS; Edmond, OK; (2); 1/342; Church Yth Grp; JCL; Latin Clb; SADD; NHS; St Schlr; Ltrd Acad; Renaissance Schlr; Acad Tm; Stockbroker/Lawyer.

PHELPS, KELLE; Yukon HS; Yukon, OK; (4); 89/468; Am Leg Aux Girls St; Church Yth Grp; French Clb; FHA; GAA; Hosp Aide; SADD; Ofcr Sr Cls; Sftbl; Tennis; Natl Young Ldrs Conf Yth Ldrshp Awd; BYU; Interior Dsgn.

PHELPS, LAUREN; Seminole Jr Sr HS; Seminole, OK; (2); Church Yth Grp; FCA; French Clb; Math Clb; Drill Tm; Pres Soph Cls; Ofcr Stu Cncl; Pom Pon; Tennis; High Hon Roll; Select Choir; TAD.

PHIFER, JOSHUA D; Mannford HS; Mannford, OK; (3); Church Yth Grp; Rep Soph Cls; Rep Stu Cncl; L Wrstlng; Hon Roll; Schlr Ath Awd; Prpl Prd Wrstlng Awd; Ldrshp Awd In Wrstlng; Dir Of Yth Alv; Coaching.

PHILIP, PREETHI; Yukon Middle HS; Yukon, OK; (3); Church Yth Grp; FCA; FHA; Hosp Aide; Spanish Clb; SADD; NHS; U Of OK.

PHILIPP, LESLIE A; Westmoore HS; Oklahoma City, OK; (3); JCL; Quiz Bowl; Scholastic Bowl; Science Clb; Band; Nwsp; Yrbk; Hon Roll; Jr NHS; 1st Pl Army/Air Force/Navy/Marine/NASA Sci Fair Awds; Apprentice Omniplex Sci Ctr; Southwestern OK ST Univ.

PHILIPPI, JAMIE; Owasso Sr HS; Owasso, OK; (3); 35/547; Church Yth Grp; Debate Tm; JA; Natl FFA Org; NFL; Science Clb; Temple Yth Grp; Band; Hon Roll; NHS; Tulsa Zoological Park Zoo Teens Vol Pgm; OK ST U; Pre-Veterinary Med.

PHILIPS, KATY B; Metro Christian Acad; Tulsa, OK; (2); Church Yth Grp; Dance Clb; Highest Achvmts In Royal Acad Of Dancing Exams 3 Yrs; Ballet, Jazz, Pointe & Tap Dancing; Rollerbladng; Interior Dsgn; Bus Mgmt.

PHILLIPS, AMANDA; Putnam City West HS; Oklahoma City, OK; (1); 63/436; Church Yth Grp; Drama Clb; School Play; Ofcr Stu Cncl; Chrldng; High Hon Roll; Comm Svc Prjcts Vol.

PHILLIPS, AMBER L; Will Rogers HS; Tulsa, OK; (2); Church Yth Grp; Debate Tm; English Clb; French Clb; Office Aide; Scholastic Bowl; Chorus; Lit Mag; Treas Frsh Cls; Treas Soph Cls; Vol United Way; Teddy Bear Drv/Kids/Scotland; OK Univ; Pre-Med.

PHILLIPS, BILLY W; Bridge Creek HS; Tuttle, OK; (4); 13/60; Church Yth Grp; FCA; Math Tm; Varsity Clb; Var Capt Bsbl; Var Capt Bsktbl; Var Ftbl; High Hon Roll; Hon Roll; NHS; Bronze Medal In Schltc Meet; Defensive MVP In Bsbl; Hnrb Mntn Little All-City In Bsbl & Bsktbl; OSAO; Math Ed; Coach.

PHILLIPS, BRANDY; Hulbert Jr Sr HS; Hulbert, OK; (4); 1/43; Am Leg Aux Girls St; 4-H; FBLA; German Clb; Rptr Nwsp; Ed Yrbk; Stat Ftbl; Var Trk; DAR Awd; NHS; Northeastern ST U.

PHILLIPS, BRANSON L; North Intermediate HS; Tulsa, OK; (1); French Clb; Intrml Ftbl; Var L Wrstlng; High Hon Roll; Hon Roll; Pres Acad Fit Awd; Presdntl Phy Ftnss Awd; OK Hnr Soc.

PHILLIPS, CARRIE; Owasso Sr HS; Owasso, OK; (3); Church Yth Grp; FCA; FTA; HOBY; Key Clb; Natl FFA Org; Office Aide; SADD; Rep Stu Cncl; Var JV Chrldng.

PHILLIPS, CLAUDIA S; Oklahoma Sch Of Science & Math; Wagoner, OK; (4); Drama Clb; French Clb; Girl Scts; Library Aide; Band; School Musical; Ed Yrbk; NHS; Acad Team; Tulane Univ; Engr Sci/Pysics.

PHILLIPS, CONRAD J; Choctaw HS; Nicoma Park, OK; (2); Socr; Tennis; Hon Roll; Jr NHS; NHS; Sal.

PHILLIPS, DARRELYN; Lone Grove HS; Ardmore, OK; (3); Church Yth Grp; Debate Tm; Key Clb; Math Clb; Model UN; Quiz Bowl; Scholastic Bowl; Science Clb; Spanish Clb; Speech Tm; Many Art Awds; ECU.

PHILLIPS, ELISE; Claremore Sr HS; Claremore, OK; (4); Church Yth Grp; Dance Clb; Quiz Bowl; Var Chrldng; Var Gym; Trk; Teachers Aide; Band; Mrchg Band; Rep Stu Cncl; Trd W/Dnce Crvn Smmr 93; Annl Chmbr Cmmrce Shw Chrgrphd Dnce Rtns; Oklahoma City U; Dnce.

PHILLIPS, ELIZABETH R; Skiatook HS; Skiatook, OK; (3); 1/100; Am Leg Aux Girls St; FCA; FBLA; Teachers Aide; Treas Frsh Cls; Treas Soph Cls; Treas Jr Cls; Treas Sr Cls; Ofcr Stu Cncl; Var Chrldng; Page In OK St Senate & House Of Reps; OK Baptist Univ.

PHILLIPS, ELSIE; Claremore Sr HS; Claremore, OK; (4); Church Yth Grp; Dance Clb; Quiz Bowl; Teachers Aide; Band; Mrchg Band; Rep Stu Cncl; Var Chrldng; Var Gym; Trk; Dance Caravan Tour 93; Chamber Commerce Show Dance Choreographer; OK City Univ; Dance Mgmt.

PHILLIPS, ERIC E; Shawnee Sr HS; Shawnee, OK; (3); Latin Clb; Ftbl; Wt Lftg; Ed.

PHILLIPS, ERICA L; Yukon Middle HS; Yukon, OK; (2); Treas FHA; Quiz Bowl; Spanish Clb; Hon Roll; Renssnc Commttee; OU; Bus Mgmt.

PHILLIPS, JAMES; Carl Albert HS; Midwest City, OK; (4); 17/270; Am Leg Boys St; Boy Scts; Key Clb; Letterman Clb; Quiz Bowl; Scholastic Bowl; Acpl Chr; Chorus; School Musical; Rep Frsh Cls; Rotry Yth Ldrshp Awd; OK ST U; Med.

PHILLIPS, JENNIFER; Minco HS; Minco, OK; (4); 10/38; Church Yth Grp; Ofcr 4-H; FBLA; FHA; HOBY; Natl FFA Org; Scholastic Bowl; Ofcr Band; Drm Mjr(t); Jazz Band; FFA Secr 95, VP 96; Band Secr 94, VP 95, Secr 96; Natl Hnr Soc Secr 96; OK ST U; Ag Bus.

PHILLIPS, JILL; Sharon Mutual Jr Sr HS; Sharon, OK; (2); Church Yth Grp; FCA; FHA; Natl FFA Org; Rep Frsh Cls; Rep Soph Cls; Var Bsktbl; Var Chrldng; Var Sftbl; NHS; FFA Sweetheart & Awds; SWOSU Wehterford; Elem Ed.

PHILLIPS, JOE; Talihina Sr HS; Talihina, OK; (4); 2/38; Am Leg Boys St; FCA; Rep Jr Cls; Pres Stu Cncl; Var Bsbl; Var Bsktbl; Var Ftbl; Cit Awd; High Hon Roll; Sal; Estrn OK ST Coll; Sec Ed.

PHILLIPS, JON E; Oologah HS; Claremore, OK; (2); Var Bsbl; High Hon Roll; Arch.

PHILLIPS, LEAH; Chisholm Sr HS; Enid, OK; (4); 9/69; Church Yth Grp; Pres VP Natl FFA Org; VP Treas Spanish Clb; Chorus; Church Choir; Yrbk; Ofcr Sr Cls; Rep Stu Cncl; Hon Roll; Sec NHS.

PHILLIPS, LEE ANN; Caddo HS; Caddo, OK; (2); 4/26; Drill Tm; Pres Frsh Cls; Pres Soph Cls; Var Bsktbl; Var Sftbl; High Hon Roll; Hon Roll; NHS; Sal; Southeastern ST U; Int Dsgn.

PHILLIPS, LESLIE; Seminole Jr Sr HS; Seminole, OK; (3); Cmnty Wkr; English Clb; FCA; French Clb; GAA; Varsity Clb; Var Sftbl; Hon Roll; NHS; Sftbl All Dist, All Conf; Frnch Clb Pres.

PHILLIPS, LINDSAY J; Heritage Hall Schl; Oklahoma City, OK; (2); Cmnty Wkr; Letterman Clb; Mu Alpha Theta; Pep Clb; Spanish Clb; Sftbl; Vllybl; High Hon Roll; Hon Roll; Spanish NHS; Horseback Riding; Orthopedic Surgery.

PHILLIPS, LISA; Wynnewood HS; Wynnewood, OK; (3); 3/60; Church Yth Grp; Sec FHA; Hosp Aide; Scholastic Bowl; Teachers Aide; Band; Color Guard; Hon Roll; NHS; Ntl Merit Schol; OK St U; Pre-Med.

PHILLIPS, LISA M; Putnam City West HS; Bethany, OK; (2); Church Yth Grp; Orch; School Musical; Hon Roll; NHS; Stu Athltc Trnr; Church Orch; Gftd & Tlntd Assn.

PHILLIPS, MARK; Stillwater Sr HS; Stillwater, OK; (2); Boy Scts; Key Clb; Service Clb; Acpl Chr; Band; Chorus; Jazz Band; Orch; JV Trk; Hon Roll; Stillwater Sccr Assn Clsc Leag; OK Yth Orch; OK Smmr Arts Inst-Orch 2 Yrs.

PHILLIPS, MIKAL D; Sayre HS; Sayre, OK; (3); 14/45; Church Yth Grp; GAA; Library Aide; Office Aide; Band; Chorus; Church Choir; Mrchg Band; Pep Band; Yrbk; OU; Phy Thrpst.

PHILLIPS, MIRANDA L; El Reno Sr HS; El Reno, OK; (2); 68/250; Church Yth Grp; Hon Roll; El Rino Bty Coll; Csmtlgy/Tch.

PHILLIPS, REGINA; Caddo HS; Caddo, OK; (4); FHA; SADD; Ed Nwsp; Pres Frsh Cls; Pres Soph Cls; Pres Jr Cls; Capt Bsktbl; Capt Sftbl; High Hon Roll; Hon Roll; SE OK ST U; Sec Eng Ed.

PHILLIPS, SARAH D; South Intermediate HS; Broken Arrow, OK; (1); Church Yth Grp; Cmnty Wkr; FCA; Band; Church Choir; Color Guard; Pep Band; Var Trk; High Hon Roll; Hon Roll; Painting; Drawing; Wrtng Poetry & Short Stories; OK HS Hnr Soc; Baylor U; Arch; Commercial Art.

PHILLIPS, SHANNA; Varnum Jr Sr HS; Seminole, OK; (3); Church Yth Grp; FCA; FHA; Bsktbl; Sftbl; Hon Roll; OK ST Univ.

PHILLIPS, SHAUN P; Union Intermediate HS; Tulsa, OK; (2); Hon Roll; Acctng.

PHILLIPS, SHAWNA BROOKE; Capitol Hill HS; Oklahoma City, OK; (2); Cmnty Wkr; Hosp Aide; ROTC; Chrldng; Gym; Hon Roll; OK U; Vet Med.

PHILLIPS, STEPHANIE; Lone Grove HS; Ardmore, OK; (4); 13/81; FHA; German Clb; Pres Key Clb; Math Clb; Natl Beta Clb; Science Clb; Spanish Clb; Teachers Aide; Chorus; School Musical; All Amer Schlr; Dist/Regnl Cntsts/Vocal Music Awds; Natl His/Govt Awds; U Of Cntrl OK; Dntl Hygne.

PHILLIPS, THOMAS F; Hominy HS; Hominy, OK; (3); 1/70; FCA; French Clb; Letterman Clb; Rep Frsh Cls; Rep Soph Cls; Pres Stu Cncl; Var Bsktbl; Var Ftbl; Var Wt Lftg; NHS; OK ST Univ; Acctng.

PHILLIPS, VALERIE; Paoli HS; Pauls Valley, OK; (4); 7/20; FHA; Pep Clb; Spanish Clb; Teachers Aide; Chorus; Yrbk; Pres Jr Cls; Mgr(s); Sftbl; High Hon Roll; U Cntrl OK.

PHILPOT, ALISHA M; Union Intermediate HS; Broken Arrow, OK; (1); Church Yth Grp; FCA; Spanish Clb; Capt Pom Pon; High Hon Roll; Treas NHS; Eng & Math Achvmt Awds; Duke Univ; Sports Med Dr.

PHILPOT, DANYELLE; Bray-Doyle HS; Rush Springs, OK; (3); Drama Clb; Rep Frsh Cls; Chrldng; Sftbl; High Hon Roll; Hon Roll; NHS; Ftbl Homcmng Ct Attndnt 94-95; Elem Ed.

PHILPOT, JEFF D; Sperry Sr HS; Skiatook, OK; (3); 12/75; Letterman Clb; Library Aide; Var L Bsktbl; JV L Crs Cntry; Var L Ftbl; Var L Trk; Var L Wt Lftg; Hon Roll; Sec Ed.

PHILPOTT, BRIAN J; Union Sr HS; Broken Arrow, OK; (3); 8/741; FCA; FBLA; Math Tm; Varsity Clb; Rptr Nwsp; VP Soph Cls; Ofcr Stu Cncl; Var L Bsktbl; Var L Socr; Cit Awd; Boy Of Yr 93-94; 94-95 Mr Redskin; Clb Soccer 3 Time St Chmpns; Mech Engrng.

PHIPPS, CLAYTON; Empire Schl; Duncan, OK; (2); Church Yth Grp; FCA; FHA; Letterman Clb; Natl FFA Org; Ftbl; Wt Lftg; Wrstlng.

PHIPPS, COURTNEY A; Empire Schl; Duncan, OK; (2); Church Yth Grp; FCA; FBLA; FHA; Key Clb; Letterman Clb; VP Soph Cls; Bsktbl; Chrldng; Score Keeper; Environmental Clb.

PHOLLURXA, SOUNALLY; Chickasha HS; Chickasha, OK; (3); 4/192; Church Yth Grp; French Clb; FHA; Chorus; Church Choir; Pres Soph Cls; Ofcr Stu Cncl; Gov Hon Prg Awd; High Hon Roll; NHS; OK ST Univ; Pre-Med.

PICCO, TARA M; Union Sr HS; Tulsa, OK; (3); Chrmn FBLA; Spanish Clb; Chorus; Hon Roll; Prfct Atten Awd; Tae Kwon Do Blue Belt; DECA; OK Univ; Nutritnst.

PICEK, MARESA A; West Middle HS; Norman, OK; (2); Church Yth Grp; French Clb; Band; Trk; Nrsng; Vet.

PICKENS, JENNIFER; Christian Heritage Acad; Oklahoma City, OK; (4); 1/53; Church Yth Grp; High Hon Roll; Hon Roll; Val; Pltcl Awrns VP; Baylor U; Bus.

PICKENS, JEREMY; Kingfisher HS; Kingfisher, OK; (3); 39/108; Church Yth Grp; Cmnty Wkr; Computer Clb; FCA; Key Clb; Spanish Clb; Band; Chorus; Church Choir; Drill Tm; Karate; OSU; Prchr.

PICKENS, RUSTY D; Stonewall Jr-Sr HS; Stonewall, OK; (3); 2/24; Am Leg Boys St; Church Yth Grp; FBLA; Natl FFA Org; Pep Clb; Quiz Bowl; Phtg Yrbk; Sec Frsh Cls; Rep Soph Cls; Cit Awd; St Rnnr-Up Acad Quiz Bowl Team Mem; OK ST Univ; Comp Sci; Engrng.

PICKERING, KA LYN; Kellyville Sr HS; Sapulpa, OK; (2); GAA; Letterman Clb; Varsity Clb; Var Bsktbl; Var Sftbl; High Hon Roll; Coach/Spts Med.

PICKETT, DANIEL J; Bishop Kelley HS; Tulsa, OK; (4); 4/149; Key Clb; Office Aide; Service Clb; Spanish Clb; Rep Stu Cncl; JV Bsktbl; High Hon Roll; NHS; Ntl Merit Ltr; Pres Schlr; Phillips Petroleum Schlsp 96; U Of Tulsa; Petroleum Engr.

PICKETT, KELLIE; Achille Schl; Achille, OK; (2); 3/36; HOBY; Library Aide; Pres Soph Cls; Var Bsktbl; High Hon Roll; NHS; Bryan Cty Bsktbl All Star; 3rd In Texomaland 3-Pointers; Highest Grd In Cls; SOSU.

PICKETT, MATTHEW S; Bishop Kelley HS; Tulsa, OK; (2); Cmnty Wkr; JV Ftbl; High Hon Roll; NHS.

PICKETT, WENDY W; Bishop Mcguinness HS; Oklahoma City, OK; (3); 9/134; Debate Tm; FCA; French Clb; NFL; SADD; Ed Nwsp; Tennis; French Hon Soc; NHS; Ntl Merit SF; E F Ambsdr Schlrshp 96; Lincoln Natl Bnk Essay 1st Plc OK ST; OK Friday Nwspr Stdnt Clmnst Yr 95-; Brdcst Jrnlsm/Prod.

PIDGEON, STACY J; Owasso Sr HS; Owasso, OK; (3); Church Yth Grp; FCA; Teachers Aide; Nwsp; Yrbk; Mgr(s); Socr; High Hon Roll; Hon Roll; NHS; Owasso Round Up Clb; Acctng.

PIERCE, APRIL R; Harrah HS; Harrah, OK; (1); Cmnty Wkr; Natl FFA Org; Girls Sftbl; Sr Adult Day Care Ctr Vol; OK ST Univ.

PIERCE, CHRISTOPHER; Southeast HS; Oklahoma City, OK; (2); FCA; Letterman Clb; Math Clb; ROTC; Color Guard; Drill Tm; Rep Stu Cncl; Var Ftbl; Var Golf; High Hon Roll; OU; Bus.

PIERCE, CYNTHIA; Eufaula Sr HS; Eufaula, OK; (3); FHA; Rep Stu Cncl; Bsktbl; Chrldng; NHS; Pres Acad Fit Awd; OK Hnr Soc; OU; Law.

PIERCE, JASON; Putnam City HS; Oklahoma City, OK; (4); 74/345; Church Yth Grp; German Clb; Key Clb; Model UN; Spanish Clb; Teachers Aide; Rep Nwsp; Ed Yrbk; Ed Lit Mag; Ofcr Stu Cncl; Episcopal Yth Comm; Jrnlsm Mrt Schlsp; U Of OK; Jrnlsm; Span.

PIERCE, KEESTY; Healdton HS; Healdton, OK; (2); Church Yth Grp; FCA; Chorus; School Play; Rep Jr Cls; Bsktbl; Chrldng; High Hon Roll; NHS; All Amer Mascot Awd; OK Univ; Anesth.

PIERCE, L BECKI; Watonga HS; Watonga, OK; (4); 8/59; FCA; FBLA; Spanish Clb; Band; Treas Jr Cls; Treas Sr Cls; Score Keeper; Hon Roll; NHS; Southwestern OK ST U; Elem Ed.

PIERCE, LORI; Moore HS; Moore, OK; (4); 23/530; Church Yth Grp; Scholastic Bowl; Teachers Aide; VP Frsh Cls; Rep Stu Cncl; Bsktbl; Trk; NHS; Val; U Cntrl OK; Phys Thrpy.

PIERCE, MARY K; Mc Loud HS; Newalla, OK; (1); Church Yth Grp; GAA; Bsktbl; Sftbl.

PIERCE, MATT R; Byng Sr HS; Ada, OK; (3); Church Yth Grp; FCA; FBLA; Letterman Clb; Math Clb; Science Clb; Chorus; Var Bsbl; JV Bsktbl; Hon Roll.

PIERCE, MELISSA; Chandler HS; Chandler, OK; (3); 1/80; Dance Clb; Spanish Clb; Ofcr Stu Cncl; Bsktbl; Chrldng; Golf; Sftbl; Trk; Hon Roll; NHS; OU.

PIERCE, MICHELLE R; Moore HS; Moore, OK; (3); Scholastic Bowl; Science Clb; School Musical; Stage Crew; Swing Chorus; JV Var Crs Cntry; Var Trk; High Hon Roll; NHS; Church Yth Grp; Mus.

PIERCE, STUART R; Warner HS; Warner, OK; (1); 4-H; FHA; Natl FFA Org; Ofcr Bsbl; Bsktbl; Hon Roll; Cmptrs; Fshng; Hntng.

PIERCEY, KYLEE A; Hammon Schl; Elk City, OK; (1); Art Clb; Church Yth Grp; FCA; Quiz Bowl; Speech Tm; SADD; Pres Frsh Cls; JV Bsktbl; Hon Roll; NHS; Stu Of Today; Supt Hnr Roll; Prin Hnr Roll; OK Univ; Spts Med/PT.

PIERSALL, CRYSTAL; Charles Page HS; Sand Springs, OK; (3); 41/385; Church Yth Grp; FCA; Office Aide; Pep Clb; Spanish Clb; Acpl Chr; Church Choir; Ofcr Stu Cncl; Chrldng; Crs Cntry; Rgnl, St Champs Chrldng; 3 Yr Qlfr Natl Chrldng Assn Natls; Northeastern ST U; Ansthslgst.

PIERSOL, LANCE; Coyle Public Schl; Guthrie, OK; (2); 1/25; Cmnty Wkr; Debate Tm; German Clb; Natl FFA Org; Quiz Bowl; Cit Awd; Hon Roll; NHS; Ntl Merit Schol; Logan Cty Coaltin.

PIERSON, LORETHA S; Healdton HS; Graham, OK; (2); Church Yth Grp; FCA; Band; Chorus; Flag Corp; Mrchg Band; Pep Band; Cit Awd; Hon Roll; NHS; Southern Nazarene Univ; Psych.

PIGG, MELANIE; Oklahoma Christian Schl; Edmond, OK; (3); 7/66; Church Yth Grp; Drama Clb; Office Aide; Scholastic Bowl; Thesps; Band; Pep Band; School Play; Stage Crew; Var Socr; Phy Therapy; Engrng.

PIGG, TERISA L; Broken Arrow Sr HS; Broken Arrow, OK; (3); French Clb; VP Intnl Clb; Treas Key Clb; Band; Church Choir; Ofcr Stu Cncl; Gov Hon Prg Awd; High Hon Roll; Hon Roll; VP NHS; Sci Awd; Psych.

PIKE, JENNY E; Putnam City West HS; Oklahoma City, OK; (2); Church Yth Grp; Drama Clb; FCA; Speech Tm; Orch; Score Keeper; Vllybl; Cit Awd; Slvr Strng Of Putnam City; Top Spch Stu; OCU; Tchr.

PILASK, DANA; Edmond North HS; Edmond, OK; (3); Math Tm; Mu Alpha Theta; Science Clb; Spanish Clb; Chorus; Pres NHS; Ntl Merit Ltr; Spanish NHS; St Schlr; Cmnty Wkr; Badminton JV; Chem Club Chprsn; Envrmtl; Chem Engr.

PILKINGTON, AMANDA L; Heavener HS; Heavener, OK; (3); Church Yth Grp; Natl FFA Org; Hon Roll; Carl Albert ST Coll; RN.

PILLARS, DARCI; Beaver HS; Beaver, OK; (2); Church Yth Grp; FCA; FHA; Natl FFA Org; Scholastic Bowl; Chorus; Drill Tm; Pres Frsh Cls; Pres Soph Cls; Var Bsktbl; Krt.

PILLARS, MICKI R; Soper Schl; Soper, OK; (1); 4-H; Natl FFA Org; Hon Roll; Animal Sci.

PINEDA, DINELLE M; Heritage Hall Schl; Oklahoma City, OK; (4); Cmnty Wkr; School Musical; Ed Lit Mag; L Crs Cntry; L Trk; Cit Awd; NHS; Ntl Merit Schol; Spanish NHS; Violin.

PINGLETON, CHRISTY; Mc Alester HS; Mcalester, OK; (2); Dance Clb; FHA; Pep Clb; Spanish Clb; Band; Drill Tm; Mrchg Band; Var Chrldng; Var Mgr(s); Var Pom Pon; 10 Yrs Dnc; OK U.

PINGLETON, RICHIE; Pauls Valley HS; Pauls Valley, OK; (1); Church Yth Grp; Natl FFA Org; Hon Roll; East Central.

PINIX, JESSICA A; Bishop Kelley HS; Tulsa, OK; (4); 48/150; Church Yth Grp; Pep Clb; Chorus; Rep Stu Cncl; Rep Stu Cncl; Ofcr Bsbl; Ftbl; High Hon Roll; Hon Roll; NHS; NE St Univ.

PINKERTON, BRITTNEY B; Muldrow HS; Muldrow, OK; (2); Church Yth Grp; Math Clb; Natl Beta Clb; Science Clb; Band; Church Choir; Color Guard; Sec Soph Cls; Ofcr Stu Cncl; Hon Roll; Med.

PINKERTON, JAIMIE S; Geary Jr Sr HS; Greenfield, OK; (1); Church Yth Grp; Band; Bsktbl; Tech Stu Assoc.

PINKERTON, JEFF K; Geary Jr Sr HS; Greenfield, OK; (2); Church Yth Grp; Natl Beta Clb; Band; JV Bsbl; JV Var Bsktbl; Hon Roll; TSA.

PINKERTON, MIKE P; Okarche HS; Okarche, OK; (3); Church Yth Grp; Cmnty Wkr; 4-H; FHA; Letterman Clb; Pres Frsh Cls; L Bsbl; L Bsktbl; 4-H Awd; Hon Roll; Bareback Rider 8th In ST Finals; Guitar Plyr; Southwestern Coll.

PINKERTON, ROBERT B; Muldrow HS; Muldrow, OK; (4); 3/108; Church Yth Grp; Math Tm; Natl Beta Clb; Quiz Bowl; Science Clb; Band; VP Sr Cls; Ofcr Stu Cncl; High Hon Roll; NHS; U Of AR; Elec Eng.

PINKERTON, TIFFANY; Wayne Public Schl; Paoli, OK; (1); 1/50; 4-H; SADD; Bsktbl; Sftbl; Trk; High Hon Roll; U OK; Phys Thrpy.

PINNEY, JASON A; Bartlesville Sr HS; Bartlesville, OK; (3); 139/495; Church Yth Grp; Chorus; Ofcr Stu Cncl; L Bsktbl; Var Socr; Hon Roll; Prfct Atten Awd; Eng.

PINNICK, MELISSA D; Hollis Jr Sr HS; Hollis, OK; (2); Church Yth Grp; Cmnty Wkr; Debate Tm; Drama Clb; 4-H; Speech Tm; Band; Jazz Band; Mrchg Band; Pep Band; Mem Of Natl & St NSFM Piano; Lang.

PIPES, KIM E; Edmond Memorial HS; Edmond, OK; (3); 80/380; Key Clb; Office Aide; Spanish Clb; NHS.

PIPKIN, ERIC CLIFFTON GREGORY; Yukon Middle HS; Yukon, OK; (2); Church Yth Grp; Cmnty Wkr; FCA; SADD; Chorus; Church Choir; School Musical; Bsktbl; Hon Roll; Wt Lftg; OKC Fed Bldg Bombing Vol Work; Renaissance Hnr Soc; IMPACT Comm Work Pgm Vol; OK ST Univ; Bus.

PIPPENGER, SUZI; Harrah HS; Harrah, OK; (4); 6/107; Am Leg Aux Girls St; Church Yth Grp; FCA; FBLA; Pep Clb; Spanish Clb; SADD; Teachers Aide; Varsity Clb; Rptr Nwsp; OK ST U; Phys Thrpy.

PIPPIN, JAMES L; Webster HS; Tulsa, OK; (2); Chess Clb; Stage Crew.

PIRPICH, BRADLEY G; Indianola HS; Mcalester, OK; (3); 5/35; FHA; Library Aide; Sec Frsh Cls; Sec Soph Cls; Rep Stu Cncl; Var Bsktbl; Hon Roll; Ath Trainer.

PISARRA, PAIGE A; Union Intermediate HS; Tulsa, OK; (2); 100/1000; Church Yth Grp; Cmnty Wkr; Spanish Clb; Church Choir; Color Guard; Rep Stu Cncl; High Hon Roll; Hon Roll; Jr NHS; NHS; Outstdng Fr Union Color Guard; Cttn ST Of OK/REP Thronbrugh For Svcs Rndrd; KS U; Advrtsng.

PISIO, ANNA M; Jay HS; Eucha, OK; (2); Art Clb; FBLA; FHA; Phtg Yrbk.

PITCHFORD, CARLA; Red Oak Schl; Red Oak, OK; (4); 3/19; FCA; 4-H; Pres FHA; HOBY; Natl FFA Org; Ed Yrbk; Var Capt Bsktbl; Sftbl; NHS; Hstrn; CPA.

PITCOCK, COURTNEY; Putnam City West HS; Yukon, OK; (3); 1/337; Church Yth Grp; FCA; Intnl Clb; Spanish Clb; Rep Stu Cncl; Var Chrldng; High Hon Roll; NHS; Masonci Stu Today Awd; Acctng.

PITMAN, CHARLES W; Smithville Jr Sr HS; Watson, OK; (3); Church Yth Grp; Cmnty Wkr; Debate Tm; Quiz Bowl; Scholastic Bowl; Hon Roll.

PITTMAN, BOBBY L; Madill HS; Madill, OK; (2); Ftbl; Wt Lftg; Mchnc Work.

PITTMAN, JAMES B; Broken Arrow Sr HS; Broken Arrow, OK; (3); Drama Clb; German Clb; L Golf; Hon Roll.

PITTMAN, KRISTEE; Okemah HS; Castle, OK; (2); Church Yth Grp; Scholastic Bowl; Sec FHA; Yrbk; Hon Roll; Prfct Atten Awd; OK Hnr Socty; GATE; OK Bapt U; Ed.

PITTMAN, LESLEY; Wellston Schl; Wellston, OK; (1); 3/60; FCA; SADD; Rep Stu Cncl; Bsktbl; Sftbl; Val.

PITTMAN, LISA M; Memorial HS; Tulsa, OK; (3); Church Yth Grp; French Clb; Intnl Clb; Pep Clb; Band; Mrchg Band; Var Socr; Var Swmmng; Hon Roll; Val; Intl Frgn Lang Awd; Notre Dame Univ; Med.

PITTMAN, MANDI E; Western Heights Sr HS; Yukon, OK; (3); Church Yth Grp; Cmnty Wkr; Key Clb; Red Cross Aide; Chorus; School Musical; VP Jr Cls; Rep Stu Cncl; Pres NHS; FCA; Yth Ldrshp Exchng; Show Choir; Jazz Choir; Trinity; Psych.

PITTMAN, MATTHEW R; Western Heights Sr HS; Yukon, OK; (4); 1/163; Church Yth Grp; Cmnty Wkr; FCA; HOBY; Letterman Clb; Math Tm; Scholastic Bowl; Chorus; Church Choir; School Musical; Duke.

PITTMAN, RONALD; Western Heights Sr HS; Yukon, OK; (4); 1/162; Church Yth Grp; FCA; HOBY; Key Clb; Letterman Clb; Scholastic Bowl; Spanish Clb; Varsity Clb; Chorus; Church Choir; Duke.

PITTS, ADAM S; Sapulpa Sr HS; Sapulpa, OK; (3); 3/300; Church Yth Grp; FCA; FBLA; Pres Key Clb; Spanish Clb; Band; Drm Mjr(t); Jazz Band; Mrchg Band; NHS.

PITTS, DANNY L; North Intemediate HS; Broken Arrow, OK; (2); Bsktbl; JV Ftbl; Hon Roll; Dirt Bike Rcng/Rdng; Bus Mngmt.

PITTS, EVANGULA M; Will Rogers HS; Tulsa, OK; (1); GAA; Varsity Clb; Chorus; Bsktbl; High Hon Roll; Hon Roll; Jr NHS; Grambling.

PITTS, JENNIFER L; Union Intermediate HS; Tulsa, OK; (2); FCA; Pep Clb; Spanish Clb; Drill Tm; Nwsp; Yrbk; High Hon Roll; Hon Roll; NHS; Dncr 11 Yrs; Kanakuk Kamps 4 Yrs; Drill Tm Ofcr.

PITTS, MARCUS; Warner HS; Porum, OK; (2); Church Yth Grp; Spanish Clb; Church Choir; School Play; Hon Roll; Ntl Merit Ltr; Prfct Atten Awd; Sal; Shiloh Assmbly Of God Yth Grp/Puppet Team/Drama Team Ldr; Connors ST Coll.

PITTSER, AMBER; Midwest City HS; Oklahoma City, OK; (2); 1/500; FCA; FHA; Library Aide; Rep Spanish Clb; L Capt Socr; Jr NHS; OK Hnrs Soc; Sccrs Outstndng Stu Awd.

PIWOWAREK, VICTORIA A; Bishop Kelley HS; Broken Arrow, OK; (2); Church Yth Grp; Cmnty Wkr; GAA; Hosp Aide; Letterman Clb; Pep Clb; Varsity Clb; Church Choir; Ofcr Stu Cncl; L Chrldng; Med.

PLASTER, LISA A; Metro Christian Acad; Tulsa, OK; (1); Church Yth Grp; French Clb; Red Cross Aide; Teachers Aide; Chorus; School Musical; School Play; Rptr Nwsp; Hist Soph Cls; JV Bsktbl; Ath Trainer 3 Yrs Ftbl/Bsbl/Bsktbl/Soccer; Fr Lang.

PLAYER, CANDACE; Marietta HS; Marietta, OK; (3); Church Yth Grp; FHA; Bsktbl; Trk; Hon Roll; Indoor Hockey.

PLEASANT, JULIE; Lawton Sr HS; Lawton, OK; (4); 46/318; Church Yth Grp; French Clb; FHA; Chorus; Yrbk; High Hon Roll; Hon Roll; NHS; Prfct Atten Awd; Cameron U; His.

PLETCHER, KATHRYN N; Claremore Sr HS; Claremore, OK; (3); German Clb; Chorus; Hon Roll; Mrktg Ed; Taken Trips To Dallas & NYC; OSU; Market Buying.

PLUM, HANS; OK Chrstn Schls; Edmond, OK; (2); Church Yth Grp; FCA; Letterman Clb; Office Aide; Red Cross Aide; Varsity Clb; Stage Crew; Ed Nwsp; Yrbk; Rep Frsh Cls; Dr Sprts Med.

PLUMLEE, BILLY D; Tuttle HS; Tuttle, OK; (3); 2/120; Ftbl; Wrstlng; High Hon Roll; Hon Roll; Jr NHS; NHS; Pres Acad Fit Awd; Ldrshp & Svc Natl Awd; Ftbll Natl Awd; Tuttle Wrstlng Awd And St Qualifier; Wrstlng Acad St & St Chmps; FL ST; Marine Biologist.

PLUMLEE, BRANDI; Del City HS; Oklahoma City, OK; (4); 41/352; Church Yth Grp; FCA; Sec Pep Clb; Ofcr Sr Cls; Rep Stu Cncl; Chrldng; JV Capt Socr; Jr NHS; NHS; Stu Sprts Trnr; Rotarian Mon; Tchr Cadet; OU; Phys Thrpy.

PLUMLEE, KEITHA J; Putnam City North HS; Oklahoma City, OK; (2); Art Clb; Church Yth Grp; Key Clb; Spanish Clb; NHS.

PLUMMER, ROY D; Westmoore HS; Oklahoma City, OK; (3); 178/563; German Clb; Co-Capt Swmmng; Swmmng All-America Hnrs 95, 96; Engrng.

PLYMESSER, SHELLI; Arnett HS; Arnett, OK; (2); 1/13; Church Yth Grp; Natl Beta Clb; Natl FFA Org; Yrbk; Rep Soph Cls; Bsktbl; Sftbl; High Hon Roll; Pres Acad Fit Awd; Val; U OK; Med.

PODLENA, STACY M; Putnam City HS; Bethany, OK; (3); 130/464; Church Yth Grp; Library Aide; Pep Clb; Quiz Bowl; Scholastic Bowl; Band; Flag Corp; Pom Pon; Cit Awd; NHS; Chem.

POE, AMBER; Miami Sr HS; Miami, OK; (4); 36/125; FHA; Library Aide; High Hon Roll; Hon Roll; NEO A&M Coll; RN.

POE, HEATH E; North Intemediate HS; Broken Arrow, OK; (2); Church Yth Grp; Drama Clb; Thesps; Band; Mrchg Band; School Play; JV Trk; High Hon Roll; Pres Schlr; St Schlr; Outstdng Alge Stdnt Awd; Engrng.

POE, JONATHAN; Midwest City HS; Midwest City, OK; (3); 27/435; Church Yth Grp; FCA; German Clb; Key Clb; SADD; Band; Church Choir; Jazz Band; Mrchg Band; Orch; All St Bapt Yth Choir; All Rgn Band.

POGUE, AMY S; Sapulpa Sr HS; Sapulpa, OK; (2); Band; Chorus; Mrchg Band; School Musical; School Play; Rptr Phtg Nwsp; High Hon Roll; NHS; Acad Lttr; Band Lttr.

POGUE, TINA R; Morrison Public Schl; Morrison, OK; (3); FBLA; HOBY; Natl FFA Org; Spanish Clb; Teachers Aide; JV Bsktbl; Var Sftbl; High Hon Roll; Hon Roll; NHS; Acctng.

POHLMEIER, TERRELL R; Yukon Middle HS; Yukon, OK; (3); Ftbl; Hon Roll; NHS.

POINDEXTER, KIMBERLY R; Central Schl; Sallisaw, OK; (2); Computer Clb; Spanish Clb; Bsktbl; Octagon Clb.

POLAND, LATOYA; Star Spencer HS; Oklahoma City, OK; (4); 10/122; JA; Pep Clb; VICA; Nwsp; Ofcr Stu Cncl; Sftbl; Tennis; Hon Roll; NHS; Pres Schlr; OK St Univ.

POLICH, JASON A; Owasso Sr HS; Owasso, OK; (3); 52/353; Golf; High Hon Roll; Bio/Physcl Sci.

POLISHUK, TONI R; B T Washington HS; Tulsa, OK; (3); Drama Clb; Science Clb; Speech Tm; Thesps; School Musical; School Play; Ed Nwsp; Rep Frsh Cls; Hon Roll; Jrnlsm.

POLLAK, ZACHARY G; B T Washington HS; Tulsa, OK; (2); Church Yth Grp; Jr NHS; Chinese Clb; Tusla Ldrshp Family Of Yr; Shwayder Acad Achvmnt Awd; Comp.

POLLARD, CHRISTY D; Dewar Jr-Sr HS; Henryetta, OK; (1); Church Yth Grp; Hosp Aide; Quiz Bowl; Connors ST Coll; Nrsng.

POLLARD, JAMIE; Perry Sr HS; Perry, OK; (2); FBLA; Spanish Clb; Band; Mrchg Band; Pep Band; Cit Awd; Jr NHS; NHS; Acad Team; OK ST U; Acctng.

POLLARD, JANET H; Muskogee HS; Muskogee, OK; (2); Hosp Aide; JCL; Band; Mrchg Band; Pep Band; School Musical; NHS; All-St Band; OK Schl Of Sci & Math Fnlst; Natl Latin Hnr Soc.

POLLARD, JEFFREY; Choctaw HS; Choctaw, OK; (3); 34/328; Band; Mrchg Band; Orch; Pep Band; School Musical; High Hon Roll; Hon Roll; Engrng.

POLLARD, JOHN J; Choctaw HS; Choctaw, OK; (3); 27/313; Band; Mrchg Band; Pep Band; School Musical; High Hon Roll; Hon Roll; NHS; Prfct Atten Awd; OK St Univ; Med.

POLLARD, KODI; Mt St Marys HS; Oklahoma City, OK; (3); 16/64; Am Leg Aux Girls St; Church Yth Grp; Cmnty Wkr; Var Bsktbl; Var Chrldng; Var Trk; Var Capt Vllybl; High Hon Roll; NHS; MVP Vlybl/Trck/Fld; Var Bsktbl Plyr Of Yr; PT.

POLLARD, KYLE W; Oklahoma Sch Of Science & Math; Oklahoma City, OK; (4); Cmnty Wkr; Pres Math Clb; Natl FFA Org; Capt Quiz Bowl; Hist Spanish Clb; Ed Nwsp; JV Bsktbl; JETS Awd; NHS; Ntl Merit Schol; Duke U; Biomed Engrng.

POLLARD, MATTHEW S; Union Intermediate HS; Tulsa, OK; (2); 47/800; Boy Scts; FBLA; Spanish Clb; Band; Swmmng; Hon Roll; NHS; Eagle Sct; Yng Astronauts; Troop Rifle Shooting Tm Ldr; U Of OK; Engrng.

POLLET, BRANDON C; South Coffeyville Schl; S Coffeyville, OK; (1); 1/40; Church Yth Grp; Yrbk; Bsktbl; Cit Awd; High Hon Roll; Hon Roll; Spanish NHS; Highest Grd Point Awds In Algebra, OK His & Eng; MIT; Math; Comps.

POLLIN, MICHAEL H; Pawhuska HS; Pawhuska, OK; (3); Varsity Clb; Band; Crs Cntry; Trk; Wrstlng; Hon Roll; AZ ST; Lndscp Archtctr.

POLLOCK, DAVID; Bridge Creek HS; Tuttle, OK; (4); 2/55; FCA; FBLA; Office Aide; JV Bsktbl; Trk; Cit Awd; High Hon Roll; NHS; Sal; Schlrshp Frm Soc Of OK Ptrlum Engrs; Engrng.

POLLOCK, STACIE A; Canton HS; Seiling, OK; (2); Church Yth Grp; 4-H; FHA; Natl FFA Org; Science Clb; SADD; Church Choir; Bsktbl; Trk; 4-H Awd; Natl His Day 2nd Media & 4th At St; SWOSU; Pharmacy.

POLLOCK, TONYA D; Velma Alma HS; Duncan, OK; (4); 1/44; Church Yth Grp; Pres 4-H; Pres FBLA; Hosp Aide; Natl FFA Org; Capt Quiz Bowl; SADD; Drm Mjr(t); Ed Nwsp; Pres NHS; Sprts Med.

POLMER, ANGELA L; Central Mid-HS; Norman, OK; (2); Boy Scts; French Clb; Chorus; Cit Awd; Hon Roll; Med.

POLSON, CHAD; Dustin Schl; Dustin, OK; (3); 1/17; Church Yth Grp; Quiz Bowl; Var Scholastic Bowl; Sec Jr Cls; High Hon Roll; Prfct Atten Awd.

PONDS, APRIL M; Mc Lain Career Acad; Tulsa, OK; (1); Red Cross Aide; Ofcr Frsh Cls; Bsktbl; Tennis; Hon Roll; NHS; Hlth Explrs; Med.

POOL, ANDREA L; Bishop Kelley HS; Tulsa, OK; (1); Ofcr Frsh Cls; Hon Roll.

POOL, ELIZABETH A; Shawnee Sr HS; Shawnee, OK; (3); 74/253; Church Yth Grp; Dance Clb; Pep Clb; Ofcr Stu Cncl; Hon Roll; NHS; OU; Biotech.

POOL, JASON; Clinton HS; Clinton, OK; (3); Boy Scts; Church Yth Grp; Key Clb; Natl FFA Org; JV Var Golf; Hon Roll; NHS.

POOL, MITZI A; Cimarron Public Schl; Enid, OK; (4); 121/425; Drama Clb; Pep Clb; Speech Tm; Band; Color Guard; School Play; Rep Frsh Cls; Socr; Hon Roll; NHS; Phy Thrpst.

POOL, RYAN M; Moore HS; Moore, OK; (3); FCA; Letterman Clb; Intrml Bsktbl; Var L Ftbl; Var L Trk; Mrn Bio.

POOLE, REBECCA A; Mason HS; Welty, OK; (3); FBLA; GAA; Spanish Clb; Phtg Ed Yrbk; Ofcr Stu Cncl; Var Bsktbl; Hon Roll; Comp Animation.

POPEJOY, DANIELLE D; Wynnewood HS; Wynnewood, OK; (1); 15/66; Church Yth Grp; Spanish Clb; JV Bsktbl; L Crs Cntry; L Trk; Hon Roll; Prfct Atten Awd; FHA; OU; Sec.

POPLIN, JAMES; Chisholm Sr HS; Enid, OK; (2); Letterman Clb; Natl FFA Org; Band; Jazz Band; Mrchg Band; JV L Bsbl; JV L Bsktbl; JV L Ftbl; JV L Trk; Var Wt Lftg; Frosh Yr Bullriding; OK ST Univ; PT/BSBL.

PORTER, BRIAN; Midwest City HS; Midwest City, OK; (2); 24/488; CAP; Band; Jazz Band; Mrchg Band; Yrbk; Golf; Hon Roll; Prfct Atten Awd; Chldrn Of Amer Rev; OK U; Metrlgst.

PORTER, CODY C; Edmond Memorial HS; Edmond, OK; (1); 53/437; Church Yth Grp; FCA; Spanish Clb; Rep Stu Cncl; Var Golf; Hon Roll; Pres Acad Fit Awd; Pres Schlr; Yng Life Mbr; OK ST Univ; Engr.

PORTER, DAVID W; Edmond Santa Fe HS; Edmond, OK; (2); Church Yth Grp; German Clb; JV Bsbl; JV Wrstlng; High Hon Roll; Jr NHS; Chem Explrs Post; Chemst/Cmptr Sci.

PORTER, GINA K; Owasso Sr HS; Owasso, OK; (2); 104/500; Church Yth Grp; FCA; FTA; Natl FFA Org; Office Aide; Rptr Nwsp; Phtg Yrbk; Rep Stu Cncl; JV Var Trk; Gymnastics Not Schl Spons; YET; Oral Roberts Univ; Elem Ed.

PORTER, JAMES A; Cushing HS; Cushing, OK; (3); Church Yth Grp; Drama Clb; School Play; Stage Crew; Ftbl; Wt Lftg; Wrstlng; Hon Roll; OSU; Indstrl Engr.

PORTER, JAMIE R; Broken Arrow Sr HS; Broken Arrow, OK; (4); 168/921; Church Yth Grp; Cmnty Wkr; French Clb; Band; Color Guard; Ofcr Stu Cncl; Hon Roll; Church Mission Trips; Liturgical Dance Tm; Church Yth Cncl Rep; OK ST Univ.

PORTER, JENNIFER L; Morris HS; Okmulgee, OK; (1); Church Yth Grp; FHA; Hosp Aide; Church Choir.

PORTER, JEREMY D; Morris HS; Okmulgee, OK; (3); Church Yth Grp; Natl FFA Org; Church Choir; Yrbk.

PORTER, JEREMY R; Agra Schl; Agra, OK; (1); 2/17; Church Yth Grp; Math Tm; Natl FFA Org; Quiz Bowl; Scholastic Bowl; Science Clb; Spanish Clb; Nwsp; High Hon Roll; Hon Roll; FFA Reptr; FFA Grenhand Awd; OK St Univ; Arch Drfting.

PORTER, KEITH A; Westmoore HS; Oklahoma City, OK; (4); VICA; Var L Socr; OK ST U; Elec Engrng.

PORTER, KELLI; Chisholm Sr HS; Enid, OK; (1); Scholastic Bowl; Spanish Clb; Band; Jazz Band; Mrchg Band; Pep Band; Hon Roll; Jr NHS; Prfct Atten Awd; Tech Stu Assn Rptr.

PORTER, KILEY; Chickasha HS; Chickasha, OK; (2); Church Yth Grp; FHA; SADD; Chorus; Rep Frsh Cls; Rep Soph Cls; Chrldng; Gymnstcs/Tumbling; Swimming; Chrldng Awd 95-96; OK ST U; Jrnlsm.

PORTER, LATISHA D; Enid Sr HS; Enid, OK; (3); Church Yth Grp; GAA; Church Choir; Pep Band; Bsktbl; Chrldng; Gym; Trk; Hon Roll; Jr NHS; TN Tech; Phys Ed.

PORTER, MATTHEW D; Cushing HS; Cushing, OK; (1); Church Yth Grp; Rep Stu Cncl; Intrml Ftbl; Intrml Wrstlng; High Hon Roll; Natl Sci Merit Awd.

PORTER, MATTHEW R; North Intemediate HS; Broken Arrow, OK; (2); Boy Scts; Church Yth Grp; Cmnty Wkr; German Clb; Library Aide; Band; Mrchg Band; Hon Roll; Sooner ST Games In-Line Hockey League 2nd Pl; Mission Trips Chrch.

PORTER, MICHAEL L; Shawnee Sr HS; Shawnee, OK; (2); Church Yth Grp; Var Bsktbl; High Hon Roll; Engrng.

PORTER, SUMMER; Lone Grove HS; Ardmore, OK; (4); Dance Clb; HOBY; Math Clb; Science Clb; Flag Corp; Rptr Sr Cls; Ofcr Stu Cncl; High Hon Roll; Winter Guard Capt; OK All Star Color Guard.

PORTER, TAJA T; Del City HS; Oklahoma City, OK; (2); Band; Mrchg Band; Orch; Pep Band; Var Trk; Wt Lftg; Jr NHS; Pres Acad Fit Awd; Congressional Yth Ldrshp Cncl WA DC; OK Univ; Psycht.

PORTER, WILLIAM L; Cresent Acad; Luther, OK; (3); Nwsp; Yrbk; Cmnty Wkr; School Musical; School Play; Bsktbl; Socr; Restoring 75 Buick Cnvrtbl; Elec Engr.

PORTS, KYLE; Bartlesville Sr HS; Bartlesville, OK; (2); 192/498; Boy Scts; Church Yth Grp; Church Choir; Stage Crew; Hon Roll; BSA Star Rnk; Chrch Puppt Mnstry; Chrch Sprts Bsktbl, Sftbl Lgs; OK ST U; Chld Care.

POSEY, JENNIFER L; Duncan HS; Duncan, OK; (2); Church Yth Grp; FBLA; Letterman Clb; L Trk; Hon Roll; Cameron.

POSEY, LETITIA A; Enid Sr HS; Enid, OK; (2); 48/700; Cmnty Wkr; French Clb; Speech Tm; Band; Chorus; School Musical; Crs Cntry; JV Socr; Hon Roll; NHS.

POSEY, RYAN; Chickasha Jr HS; Chickasha, OK; (1); Chorus; Drill Tm; Hon Roll; Jr NHS; Prin/Supt Hon Rl; Tutor Math; Math/Eng.

POSEY, SANDRA; Durant HS; Durant, OK; (3); Church Yth Grp; FBLA; FHA; Gym; Hon Roll; SE OK ST Univ; Bus.

POST, ANDREW R; Trinity Christian Schl; Broken Arrow, OK; (3); School Play; Treas Frsh Cls; Treas Soph Cls; Ofcr Jr Cls; Var Bsktbl; Var Socr; All St Soccer Tm 95-96; All Trnmt Bsktbl Tm 95-96; Tulsa JC; Commnctns.

POST, JAMES; Valliant HS; Millerton, OK; (2); Boy Scts; Ftbl; Wt Lftg; Hon Roll; Military.

POTTER, ADRIENNE; Fellowship Baptist Acad; Stilwell, OK; (4); 1/2; Teachers Aide; Church Choir; School Play; Phtg Co-Capt Yrbk; Stat Bsktbl; High Hon Roll; Prfct Atten Awd; Val; Chorus; JV Vllybl; Sunday Schl Tchr; Elem Schl Tutor; TX Bapt Coll; Music Ed.

POTTER, ALISON L; Wagoner Sr HS; Wagoner, OK; (3); FHA; Teachers Aide; Hon Roll; NED; Phy Thrpst.

POTTER, ALLISON; Thomas Jr Sr HS; Thomas, OK; (1); FHA; Band; Mrchg Band; Chrldng; Sftbl; Gymnastics.

POTTER, AMBER N; Calumet Schl; Yukon, OK; (3); Church Yth Grp; Varsity Clb; Bsktbl; Sftbl; Sthwstrn OK ST Univ; Pharm.

POTTER, APRIL; Moore HS; Moore, OK; (3); Debate Tm; Spanish Clb; Speech Tm; Nwsp; Yrbk; Spch Debt Tm; Law.

POTTER, CHALIENA M; Owasso Sr HS; Owasso, OK; (2); Church Yth Grp; FCA; Band; Mrchg Band; Nwsp; Yrbk; High Hon Roll; Hon Roll; English Clb; Science Clb; Drug Free Yth; Teen Action Grp; Med.

POTTER, HEATH A; Bartlesville Mid HS; Bartlesville, OK; (2); 47/681; Phtg Yrbk; French Hon Soc; Hon Roll; NHS; Cert Of Awd Lang Arts; OU Norman; Chem Engr.

POTTER, MELANIE A; Owasso Sr HS; Owasso, OK; (3); Church Yth Grp; Drama Clb; Band; Chorus; Church Choir; Mrchg Band; School Musical; School Play; Stage Crew; NHS; Ricks Coll; Nrs Practitioner.

POTTS, CHRISTY B; Union Sr HS; Broken Arrow, OK; (3); 51/741; Church Yth Grp; French Clb; Girl Scts; Key Clb; Red Cross Aide; Orch; Var Golf; NHS; GS Slvr Awd, Wkrng On Gld Awd Prjct; OK Grls Glf 5a St; Dnstry.

POTTS, JAMES L; Colbert Jr Sr HS; Colbert, OK; (1); 6/63; Math Tm; Var Bsktbl; High Hon Roll; Hon Roll; Prfct Atten Awd; Var Acad Bowl.

POTTS, JEANETTA R; Hulbert Jr Sr HS; Hulbert, OK; (2); 4-H; FBLA; FHA; German Clb; GAA; JV Bsktbl; Hon Roll; GATE Pgm; Cmptr Tech.

POTTS, MIKE J; Choctaw HS; Harrah, OK; (2); Spanish Clb; Var Bsbl; Var Ftbl; Var Wt Lftg; Hon Roll; U Of OK.

POUCHER, AMANDA A; Rush Springs HS; Chickasha, OK; (2); Church Yth Grp; FHA; Var Bsktbl; Northern OK Coll.

POUDARD, ALICIA J; Guthrie Sr HS; Guthrie, OK; (1); Nwsp; JV Bsktbl; Var Tennis; Univ Of Cntrl OK.

POWELL, ADRIAN L; Ponca City Sr HS; Ponca City, OK; (3); DECA; Nwsp; Hon Roll; Started An Environmental Awareness & Recycling Org; OK ST U.

POWELL, ALICIA A; Cordell Sr HS; Cordell, OK; (2); FHA; Hosp Aide; Sec Spanish Clb; Chorus; High Hon Roll; Hon Roll; Spec Interest Wrtng Poetry; Hom Ec/Math/Eng Awds 9th Grd; Sthwstrn OK ST U; Elem Tchr.

POWELL, ALICIA D; Woodward HS; Woodward, OK; (4); Rptr Nwsp; Powder Puff Ftbl; Hon Roll; DECA; Top 8 Natl Mrktng Comp; Srs In Action; Photo.

POWELL, AMBER L; Ardmore HS; Ardmore, OK; (3); Art Clb; Church Yth Grp; Dance Clb; Rep Math Clb; Rep Mu Alpha Theta; Science Clb; Spanish Clb; Capt Drill Tm; Rep Stu Cncl; Capt Pom Pon; Leaflets Treas; Arch/Grphc Arts.

POWELL, ASHLEE; Bridge Creek HS; Tuttle, OK; (1); Church Yth Grp; FCA; Spanish Clb; Chorus; Rep Frsh Cls; Rep Stu Cncl; Var Chrldng; Hon Roll; NHS; Ntl Merit Ltr; OK ST U.

POWELL, BANGELA; U S Grant HS; Oklahoma City, OK; (4); ROTC; Var Sftbl; Hon Roll; NHS; Wmn Mrne Assn Awd; Otstndng JROTC Prfrmnce Awd; JROTC Clr Grd Tm, Drll Tm; Am Rd Crss Vol; EMT.

POWELL, CAMILLE; Liberty Acad; Shawnee, OK; (3); 1/12; Church Yth Grp; Scholastic Bowl; Nwsp; Yrbk; Lit Mag; High Hon Roll; NHS; Natl Frat Stu Mscns; Acad Chapel Clb; OU; Law.

POWELL, CARRIE; Wilson HS; Wilson, OK; (3); 4/40; Church Yth Grp; FCA; Natl Beta Clb; Office Aide; Sec Frsh Cls; Sec Jr Cls; Var Bsktbl; Var Sftbl; Hon Roll; NHS; South OK ST U; Med.

POWELL, CASEY L; Sapulpa Sr HS; Sapulpa, OK; (2); Color Guard; Flag Corp; Rptr Nwsp; High Hon Roll; Prfct Atten Awd; Meteorologist.

POWELL, COURTNEY L; Colbert Jr Sr HS; Colbert, OK; (1); 1/60; Church Yth Grp; FCA; GAA; Pres Frsh Cls; Var Bsktbl; Var Sftbl; High Hon Roll; Jr NHS; Val; OK Chrstn Univ; Med.

POWELL, CRYSTAL J; Tecumseh HS; Tecumseh, OK; (4); 33/130; Office Aide; Spanish Clb; Teachers Aide; Ofcr Stu Cncl; Var JV Bsktbl; JV Chrldng; Mgr(s); Hon Roll; NHS; East Cntrl Univ; Eng Ed.

POWELL, ELIZABETH; Marietta HS; Thackerville, OK; (4); 8/45; 4-H; Intnl Clb; Key Clb; Speech Tm; Rep Frsh Cls; Cit Awd; 4-H Awd; High Hon Roll; Ntl Merit Ltr; Prfct Atten Awd; Mltpl Yr Lstng; East Cntrl U Ada.

POWELL, JENNIFER M; Broken Arrow Sr HS; Broken Arrow, OK; (4); 179/921; Church Yth Grp; FCA; Spanish Clb; SADD; Acpl Chr; Church Choir; School Musical; Ofcr Stu Cncl; High Hon Roll; Jr NHS; Recd Supr Rtngs Rgnl, St Vcl Cmptns; Tulsa JC; Early Ed.

POWELL, JESSE L; Bishop Kelley HS; Tulsa, OK; (1); Church Yth Grp; Cmnty Wkr; Ofcr Bsbl; Bsktbl; Wt Lftg; Hon Roll; CO ST Univ.

POWELL, KELLY D; Pioneer Jr Sr HS; Enid, OK; (3); 10/38; JV Bsbl; Wt Lftg; Hon Roll; ADDA Awd.

POWELL, MA RENDA; Savanna HS; Mcalester, OK; (4); Pres FBLA; FHA; Office Aide; Red Cross Aide; Chorus; School Play; Bsktbl; Trk; Hon Roll; Prfct Atten Awd; Top Ten In Miss OK Pageant 96; Most Recommendation Awd; Best Personality Awd; Paralegal.

POWELL, REGINA L; Haskell HS; Haskell, OK; (3); 3/73; Computer Clb; FHA; Math Tm; Scholastic Bowl; Spanish Clb; Speech Tm; High Hon Roll; Hon Roll; Jr NHS; NHS; Tlnt Search Pgm; Nrsng.

POWELL, SARA; Bartlesville Mid HS; Bartlesville, OK; (2); Boy Scts; Church Yth Grp; Cmnty Wkr; JA; Letterman Clb; Library Aide; Office Aide; Spanish Clb; Band; Color Guard; PT.

POWELL, SARAH; Lawton Sr HS; Lawton, OK; (3); Church Yth Grp; Pres FCA; 4-H; HOBY; Service Clb; Chorus; Church Choir; Ofcr Stu Cncl; Cit Awd; Hon Roll; Ldrshp Lawton 95-96; Engl Mrt Awd 95-96; Noon Optimist Ctzn Of Month; OK ST U; Spch Pthlgst.

POWELL, TODD W; Southeast HS; Oklahoma City, OK; (2); L Bsbl; Hon Roll; Outstding Stdnt Awd; Stdnt Merit Awd.

POWER, BOBBI; Kremlin Jr Sr HS; Kremlin, OK; (2); Church Yth Grp; FCA; Rep Frsh Cls; Var Bsktbl; Var Sftbl; Hon Roll; Marine Bio.

POWERS, BRETT; Ponca City Sr HS; Ponca City, OK; (4); 96/338; Hist DECA; Rptr Natl FFA Org; Band; Nwsp; Yrbk; Hon Roll; NOC.

POWERS, CHRISTOPHER L; Drumright HS; Drumright, OK; (1); 11/65; Church Yth Grp; Hon Roll; Chrch Lay Ldr; Yth Grp Pres; OK ST Univ; Mech Engrng.

POWERS, JACKIE E; Mc Alester HS; Mcalester, OK; (3); 3/200; FCA; French Clb; Var Bsktbl; Var Sftbl; Cit Awd; High Hon Roll; OK Hnr Soc; Intl For Lang Awd 2 Yrs; Nrthestrn ST U; Optmtry.

POWERS, JAMES C; Corn Bible Acad; Carnegie, OK; (3); Church Yth Grp; Quiz Bowl; Scholastic Bowl; Teachers Aide; Church Choir; Stage Crew; Nwsp; Yrbk; VP Frsh Cls; Pres Soph Cls; Geo/Govt Cls Mst Vlby Stdnt; Otsdng Svc Awd; Sthwstrn OK Sst Univ; Comm.

POWERS, JOSH; Mustang HS; Yukon, OK; (3); 78/400; Church Yth Grp; FCA; Spanish Clb; Teachers Aide; Var Bsbl; Hon Roll; NHS; Outstndng Chem Awd; Best All Around Bsbl; Chem Engr.

POWERS, KATY; Apache HS; Apache, OK; (3); 3/34; Church Yth Grp; FHA; HOBY; Natl FFA Org; Teachers Aide; Cit Awd; High Hon Roll; Hon Roll; FHA Pres; FFA Sec; Southwestern OK ST U; Elem Ed.

POWERS, P J; Reydon HS; Reydon, OK; (2); 1/12; Cmnty Wkr; Natl FFA Org; Ofcr Frsh Cls; VP Soph Cls; Var Bsbl; Var Bsktbl; Trk; High Hon Roll; Prfct Atten Awd; Val; OK Univ; Med.

POWERS, SARA M; Edmond North HS; Edmond, OK; (2); Church Yth Grp; Drama Clb; Mu Alpha Theta; Chorus; Church Choir; Variety Show; Hon Roll; Cmnty Wkr; Dance Clb; Hosp Aide; OK Kids; OK City Chorus; Chrch Mssn Trp; Rec Grp; ST Solo Cntst; U Of OK; Pedtrc Srgn.

POWLEY, KAYLAN A; Bartlesville Sr HS; Bartlesville, OK; (1); Church Yth Grp; Hon Roll; Athltc Trng.

PRAMMANASUDH, STACY L; Enid Sr HS; Enid, OK; (2); 26/431; French Clb; Pep Clb; School Play; Stage Crew; Var Golf; Hon Roll; Jr NHS; NHS; PT.

PRATER, BEVERLY R; Bixby Sr HS; Bixby, OK; (3); 12/210; Church Yth Grp; Natl Beta Clb; Spanish Clb; Teachers Aide; Chorus; Church Choir; Hon Roll; NHS; Prfct Atten Awd; Chld Choir Asst; U Of TN; Elem Ed.

PRATER, EME L; Velma Alma HS; Velma, OK; (2); Church Yth Grp; FCA; GAA; SADD; Nwsp; Sec Frsh Cls; Bsktbl; Chrldng; Trk; OK Hnr Soc; Nrs.

PRATER, KELI D; Velma Alma HS; Velma, OK; (4); 1/48; FCA; VP SADD; Var Bsktbl; Var Crs Cntry; Var Trk; Jr NHS; Sec NHS; Prfct Atten Awd; Pres Acad Fit Awd; Val; Southeastern ST U; Med.

PRATER, SHAWNA; Guymon Sr HS; Guymon, OK; (2); Church Yth Grp; Dance Clb; Speech Tm; SADD; Band; Drill Tm; Flag Corp; Mrchg Band; Rep Stu Cncl; JV Bsktbl; FCA Flwshp Chrstn Ath; Kids Inc; Guymon Comm Thtr; PT/CNSLR.

PRATER, STACIE LE ANN; Westmoore HS; Moore, OK; (4); Church Yth Grp; Cmnty Wkr; JA; Chorus; Church Choir; Jr NHS; Chrch Yth Cncl; OK Cty CC; Elem Ed.

PRATHER, LA TOSHA; Chickasha Jr HS; Chickasha, OK; (1); Church Yth Grp; Chorus; Bsktbl; Chrldng; Golf; Sftbl; High Hon Roll; Hon Roll; Jr NHS.

PRATHER, SAMANTHA J; Guthrie Sr HS; Guthrie, OK; (1); Chorus; Swing Chorus; OSU; Lawyer/Stock Broker.

PRATKA, MARRIA; Prague HS; Prague, OK; (4); 1/69; Am Leg Aux Girls St; Church Yth Grp; Pres Sec FBLA; HOBY; Pres Sec Speech Tm; School Play; Pom Pon; High Hon Roll; NHS; Val; Theatre.

PRATT, ANGELA; Yukon HS; Yukon, OK; (3); 42/420; Church Yth Grp; French Clb; FHA; Quiz Bowl; Chorus; School Play; Ice Hcky; Var Hon Roll; NHS; Cardiology.

PRATT, DAWN J; Owasso Sr HS; Owasso, OK; (2); Church Yth Grp; Cmnty Wkr; Band; Color Guard; Mrchg Band; JV Var Vllybl; High Hon Roll; Hon Roll; NHS; Pres Schlr.

PRATT, JENNIFER M; Hinton HS; Hinton, OK; (2); Church Yth Grp; FCA; SADD; Rep Soph Cls; Crs Cntry; Trk; High Hon Roll; Hon Roll; Band; Chorus; OK Chrstn; PT.

PRATT, JOSH; Bartlesville Mid HS; Bartlesville, OK; (1); Chess Clb; Church Yth Grp; Computer Clb; Spanish Clb; Orch; Nwsp; Yrbk; Tennis; High Hon Roll; NHS; Guitar.

PRATT, JOSH R; Muldrow HS; Muldrow, OK; (1); Church Yth Grp; NFL; Spanish Clb; Speech Tm; Band; Mrchg Band; School Play; Hon Roll; NHS; ST Speech Qulfr 96.

PRAY JR, STEPHEN D; Sapulpa Sr HS; Sapulpa, OK; (3); 26/299; JV Var Ftbl; Wrstlng; High Hon Roll; Pres Acad Fit Awd; FFA Outstdng Ag Prfcncy Awd 96; Acad Ltr 2 Yrs; Naval Acad; Sco/Orthpdc Med.

PREAS, TOM M; Mannford HS; Sand Springs, OK; (4); Art Clb; Church Yth Grp; Drama Clb; Quiz Bowl; Science Clb; Spanish Clb; Hon Roll; Guitarist; Tulsa CC; Arch Engr.

PREBBLE, DYLAN W; Claremore Sr HS; Claremore, OK; (1); Church Yth Grp; Church Choir; Hon Roll; Ltr C Awd Geometry/Engl I; OK Univ; Cmrcl Artst.

PREGLER, MATTHEW R; Bartlesville Mid HS; Bartlesville, OK; (3); Church Yth Grp; Cmnty Wkr; FBLA; Letterman Clb; Spanish Clb; Bsktbl; Var Tennis; High Hon Roll; NHS; Prfct Atten Awd; Bible Stud; K-Life; OK ST Univ; Bus Fin.

PRELESNCIK, DARCI; Tonkawa Jr Sr HS; Tonkawa, OK; (3); Art Clb; Church Yth Grp; Computer Clb; FCA; 4-H; FHA; GAA; Letterman Clb; Natl FFA Org; Pep Clb; Stu Cncl 3 Yrs.

PRENTICE, JYLIAN; Mountain View-Gotebo HS; Cordell, OK; (1); Church Yth Grp; FCA; FHA; Variety Show; Bsktbl; Capt Chrldng; Gym; JV Var Trk; Hon Roll.

PRENTICE, RUSSELL; Stigler HS; Stigler, OK; (3); 10/86; Am Leg Boys St; Church Yth Grp; Pres FCA; Pep Clb; Ski Clb; SADD; Band; Church Choir; Mrchg Band; Nwsp; 3rd Pl Rural Elec Coop Essay; Acad Achvt Awd; Supts Hnr Roll; Acad Awd-Sci; Estrn OK ST Coll; Bio Scis.

PRENTISS, SHANNON; Chickasha Jr HS; Chickasha, OK; (1); Var Mgr(s); Sftbl; Hon Roll; Jr NHS; NHS.

PRESCOTT, BRIAN; Indianola HS; Indianola, OK; (2); Natl FFA Org; Ofcr Bsbl; Bsktbl; Hon Roll; NHS; U Of OK; Sprts Med.

PRESLEY, AMY; Jenks HS; Tulsa, OK; (3); Church Yth Grp; FCA; Varsity Clb; Acpl Chr; Chorus; Church Choir; School Musical; Swing Chorus; Var Chrldng; Tap, Ballet; AR; Nurse.

PRESTON, RAHGNA; Millwood HS; Oklahoma City, OK; (3); Church Yth Grp; Library Aide; Quiz Bowl; Band; Chorus; Church Choir; Drm Mjr(t); Jazz Band; Mrchg Band; Orch.

PRESTON, RYAN; Union Sr HS; Tulsa, OK; (4); 248/615; DECA; FCA; FBLA; Yrbk; Ofcr Stu Cncl; JV Bsktbl; Cit Awd; Gov Hon Prg Awd; Hon Roll; Prfct Atten Awd; Vllybl Jr Olympic Team In OK; Jr Chm Of PAC Set-Up Dsgn For NASC Conf 95; OK ST Univ; Mrktg; Mgmt.

PREWETT, BRANDON K; Preston Schl; Beggs, OK; (1); Boy Scts; Church Yth Grp; Quiz Bowl; Scholastic Bowl; Color Guard; Hon Roll; Prfct Atten Awd; Art; Cars; OSU; Photo; Commercial Art.

PRICE, ADAM S; Washington HS; Washington, OK; (1); Natl FFA Org; Ofcr Bsbl; Hon Roll; U Of OK.

PRICE, ALISSA; Ft Gibson HS; Fort Gibson, OK; (3); Church Yth Grp; FCA; FHA; Spanish Clb; JV Bsktbl; Var Socr; Var Sftbl; Hon Roll; NHS; OBU; Phys Thrpy.

PRICE, BROOKE; Mid-Del Christian Schl; Oklahoma City, OK; (3); 2/19; Church Yth Grp; Speech Tm; Yrbk; Pres Soph Cls; Pres Jr Cls; Var Pres Stu Cncl; Var Bsktbl; Var Co-Capt Chrldng; Sftbl; Capt Vllybl; Natl Sci Mrt; Natl Large & Small Schl Schlr; ACSI Distngd Chrstn Stu & Ldrshp; Vllybl Tri-ST Champ; OK City U; Chem Prepharmacy.

PRICE, CHRISTOPHER J; Washington HS; Washington, OK; (2); 1/60; Quiz Bowl; Band; Mrchg Band; Bsktbl; Tennis; High Hon Roll; NHS.

PRICE, CLIFTON; Choctaw HS; Nicoma Park, OK; (3); 169/350; Church Yth Grp; Scholastic Bowl; Teachers Aide; VICA; Chorus; School Play; Ftbl; Hon Roll; Jr NHS; NHS; OSU At Okmulgee; Automtv Tech.

PRICE, CRYSTAL; Deer Creek HS; Edmond, OK; (4); 5/80; Drama Clb; French Clb; School Musical; School Play; Hon Roll; NHS; Tulsa U; Phys Thrpy.

PRICE, EMILY; Weatherford HS; Weatherford, OK; (1); Church Yth Grp; FCA; Acpl Chr; Chorus; Chrldng; Ballet Theatre Prncpl Dncr; OK Arts Inst Awd-Mdrn Dnc; 1st Pl SW OK St U Piano Cmptn.

PRICE, HEATHER; Western Heights Sr HS; Oklahoma City, OK; (2); 1/214; Church Yth Grp; Dance Clb; FCA; GAA; Chorus; Swing Chorus; Treas Soph Cls; Ofcr Stu Cncl; Bsktbl; Chrldng; Tap/Jazz/Bllt 9 Yrs.

PRICE, HOWARD J; Enid Sr HS; Enid, OK; (3); 37/445; FCA; Teachers Aide; Var Bsktbl; Var Socr; High Hon Roll; NHS; Mayor For A Day; Medicine.

PRICE, JASON W; Pawnee HS; Glencoe, OK; (3); 9/68; Natl Beta Clb; Natl FFA Org; Rptr Nwsp; Rptr Sr Cls; Rptr Stu Cncl; Var L Ftbl; Var Trk; Intrml Wt Lftg; High Hon Roll; Prfct Atten Awd; Ray Yagher Outstndng Beta Awd 96; Athl Trnr.

PRICE, JENNIFER L; South Intermediate HS; Broken Arrow, OK; (1); Church Yth Grp; Girl Scts; Intnl Clb; Church Choir; Ofcr Stu Cncl; High Hon Roll; Hon Roll; Grl Sct Slvr Awd; OK City Univ; Educl Field.

PRICE, JOHN; Hugo HS; Hugo, OK; (3); 5/103; Computer Clb; Math Clb; Natl FFA Org; VP Science Clb; Band; Jazz Band; Mrchg Band; Hon Roll; NHS; Prfct Atten Awd; U Of OK; Geophysists.

PRICE, JULIE; Dover Schl; Dover, OK; (4); 3/17; Am Leg Aux Girls St; Ed Yrbk; Pres Frsh Cls; Rep Soph Cls; Sec Jr Cls; VP Sr Cls; VP Stu Cncl; Capt Bsktbl; Capt Chrldng; NHS; Tri-St Hnr Chr 96; Bstkbl Qn; Msnc Mnth; OK ST U; Sprts Med.

PRICE, KARA L; Sayre HS; Sayre, OK; (3); FHA; Nwsp; Hon Roll; SWOSU; Ultra Sound Tchnlgy.

PRICE, KIMBERLY; Midwest City HS; Midwest City, OK; (3); 14/384; FBLA; German Clb; Pep Clb; Teachers Aide; Rptr Yrbk; VP Frsh Cls; Hon Roll; Jr NHS; NHS; Prfct Atten Awd; OU; Med.

PRICE, LA MAUR; Mc Alester HS; Mcalester, OK; (1); Am Leg Boys St; Church Yth Grp; Science Clb; Spanish Clb; Bsktbl; Crs Cntry; ASU; Psych Clb; E Cntrl Cada; Sprts Med.

PRICE, LACIE L; Guthrie Sr HS; Guthrie, OK; (1); OSU; Phys Therapy.

PRICE, LESLEY; Lone Grove HS; Lone Grove, OK; (2); Spanish Clb; Speech Tm; Nwsp; Rep Frsh Cls; Rep Soph Cls; Bsktbl; NHS; ORU; Engl Scnd Lang Tchr.

PRICE, LISA M; Pawnee HS; Pawnee, OK; (2); Hon Roll; NHS; NYLC Rep OK 96; WA Univ; Phtgrphy/Grphc Comm.

PRICE, MARHYA J; Spiro HS; Spiro, OK; (1); Church Yth Grp; Natl FFA Org; Bsktbl; Chrldng; Sftbl; High Hon Roll; Hon Roll; NHS; CASC; OK Univ; Tchng/Coaching.

PRICE, MARY BETH; Edmond North HS; Edmond, OK; (3); FCA; Office Aide; Var Chrldng.

PRICE, MATHEW; Elgin HS; Lawton, OK; (2); Art Clb; 4-H; Spanish Clb; Teachers Aide; Chorus; 4-H Awd; Hon Roll; Art/Cmptr Prgmg.

PRICE, MATT D; Union Intermediate HS; Tulsa, OK; (2); Orch; Wt Lftg; Physics.

PRICE, MATTHEW W; Stilwell HS; Stilwell, OK; (2); Church Yth Grp; Natl Beta Clb; Spanish Clb; High Hon Roll; NHS; Cmptr Prgmr.

PRICHARD, JENNIFER J; Duncan HS; Duncan, OK; (3); 7/261; Church Yth Grp; FCA; Letterman Clb; Office Aide; Intrml Bsktbl; Var Chrldng; Intrml Gym; Var Sftbl; Var Trk; Cit Awd; OK ST Track Meet 5th Plc; OK ST Univ Ldrshp Conf; Outstdng Typing Stdnt 95-; Engr.

PRICKETT, AARON; Collinsville HS; Collinsville, OK; (3); 1/120; Office Aide; JV Bsbl; Var Golf; High Hon Roll; Jr NHS; Kiwanis Awd; Hntng; Fshng; OK ST U; Gm Wldlf Mgmt.

PRIEBE, MICHELLE; Woodward HS; Woodward, OK; (2); Cit Awd; French Hon Soc; High Hon Roll; Acad Lttrmn; Writingwood Awd; Dramtc Arts.

PRIGMORE, MATT L; Norman Sr HS; Norman, OK; (4); 104/672; Church Yth Grp; Cmnty Wkr; Spanish Clb; L Socr; High Hon Roll; NHS; St Schlr; Letterman Clb; Varsity Clb; Rptr Yrbk; Outstdng Practical Arts Stu; St Champion In Drafting & Mech Arts 96; 95 OK St Champions In Soccer; Rhodes Coll Memphis; Dentistry.

PRINCE, AMANDA L; Spiro HS; Lavaca, AR; (2); Dance Clb; FCA; Drill Tm; JV Bsktbl; JV Chrldng; JV Swmmng; JV Trk; JV Vllybl; NHS; Pres Schlr; Georgetown; Fin.

PRINCE, ANGEL O; Edmond North HS; Edmond, OK; (4); 95/350; Church Yth Grp; Cmnty Wkr; Key Clb; ROTC; Spanish Clb; SADD; Ofcr Stu Cncl; High Hon Roll; Hon Roll; Jr NHS; ROTC Awd Staff Flight Supv Awd 94-96; ROTC Awd Capt E Present Awd; ROTC Trophy Group Commanders Awd; Phy Thrpst; Nrs.

PRINCE, ASHLEY; Indianola HS; Indianola, OK; (4); 12/45; Church Yth Grp; Lbrn FBLA; FHA; Natl FFA Org; Church Choir; Ed Yrbk; Ed Lit Mag; Ed Soph Cls; Var L Bsktbl; Var L Sftbl; Hnr Rl; Trnmnt Champ All Trny Tm; Swimming; E Central U.

PRINCE, CRYSTAL D; Midwest City HS; Del City, OK; (3); 75/386; Church Yth Grp; Office Aide; Pep Clb; Teachers Aide; Church Choir; Ed Yrbk; Bsktbl; Hon Roll; YES Club; Tulsa Univ; Jrnlsm.

PRINCE, JAMAR G; Duncan HS; Duncan, OK; (2); Boxing; Bus.

PRINCE, JAMIE; Miami Sr HS; Miami, OK; (3); Church Yth Grp; FCA; Yrbk; Rep Jr Cls; Var L Bsktbl; Var L Sftbl; High Hon Roll; NHS; Teachers Aide; Intrml Golf; OK HS Hnrs Soc; Elem Tchr.

PRINCE, JIMMY J; Durant HS; Durant, OK; (3); FCA; FTA; Ofcr Bsbl; Bsktbl; Prfct Atten Awd; Southeastern OK ST.

PRINCE, JOHNATHAN T; Edmond North HS; Edmond, OK; (4); Church Yth Grp; Dance Clb; Drama Clb; Acpl Chr; Chorus; Church Choir; School Play; Variety Show; Rep Sr Cls; Rep Stu Cncl; Crss Training; Movies; Arts; CUO; News Broadcaster.

PRINCE, KIMBERLY; Oklahoma Christian Schl; Edmond, OK; (3); 29/52; Church Yth Grp; Cmnty Wkr; Dance Clb; HOBY; SADD; Varsity Clb; Acpl Chr; Chorus; Stage Crew; Yrbk; Dnce Pte; Musicl Prdctn 4xs; U Cntrl OK; Fine Arts.

PRINCE, KRISTY; Cache HS; Cache, OK; (3); 9/73; Pres Sec Church Yth Grp; Computer Clb; FCA; Key Clb; Natl Beta Clb; Scholastic Bowl; Science Clb; Band; Color Guard; Drill Tm; Southwestern; Acctg.

PRINCE, MARCI N; Eakly HS; Eakly, OK; (4); 3/12; Rep FHA; Natl FFA Org; School Play; Yrbk; Rep Jr Cls; Rep Sr Cls; Var Bsktbl; Hon Roll; Outstdng Home Ec Sr; Stu Of Semester; Multi-Yr Listee; Southwestern OK ST Univ.

PRINCE, STACEY; Woodward HS; Woodward, OK; (4); 23/151; Cmnty Wkr; Hosp Aide; Key Clb; Letterman Clb; Teachers Aide; Band; Mrchg Band; High Hon Roll; Jr NHS; Sr In Action; SW OK St Univ; Poli Sci.

PRINCE, TOBY L; Bethany HS; Bethany, OK; (3); Chess Clb; School Musical; School Play; Stage Crew; Church Yth Grp; FCA; Band; Chorus; Church Choir; Jazz Band; Kngfshr Hnrs Band 10-11th Grd; Tri-State Hnrs Band 11th Grd; Superior Rtngs Brass Ensmble ST/REGNL; Rhema Bible Trng Ctr; Minister.

PRINGLE, JOSH R; Catoosa HS; Catoosa, OK; (2); Church Yth Grp; FCA; French Clb; Band; Mrchg Band; Pep Band; Hon Roll; OU; Anesthlgy.

PRITCHARD, CORBI H; Owasso Sr HS; Owasso, OK; (3); 27/357; Art Clb; Church Yth Grp; English Clb; FCA; French Clb; FTA; Chorus; Church Choir; Hon Roll; NHS; Dist Solo/Ensemble Contest Superior Ratings; All Dist Hnr Choir; Choice Bible Study.

PRITCHARD, LESLIE; Seminole Jr Sr HS; Seminole, OK; (1); 1/110; FCA; VP Frsh Cls; Rep Stu Cncl; Var Bsktbl; Var Chrldng; Var Trk; Cit Awd; High Hon Roll; Kiwanis Awd; Pres Acad Fit Awd.

PRITCHETT, KRISTI; Deer Creek-Lamont Jr Sr HS; Lamont, OK; (4); 5/13; Church Yth Grp; FCA; Rep FHA; Quiz Bowl; Ed Yrbk; Rptr Frsh Cls; Rep Jr Cls; Co-Capt Sr Cls; Capt Var Bsktbl; Trk; 95 Ftbl Homcmng Qn; 96 Bsktbl Homcmng Qn; OK St Senate Page; U Cntrl OK; Chld Psych.

PRITCHETT, LISA; Hulbert Jr Sr HS; Hulbert, OK; (3); Church Yth Grp; Spanish Clb; Chorus; Church Choir; Bsktbl; Hon Roll; NHS; Optomerist.

PRIVETTE, SAMANTHA; Guthrie Sr HS; Guthrie, OK; (1); 19/309; Church Yth Grp; VP FHA; Var JV Bsktbl; Var Chrldng; Var Crs Cntry; Var Socr; Var Tennis; Jr NHS; All City Hnrb Mntn & St Runner-Up Crss Cntry; 3rd Pl Small Co-Ed NCA Ntls; OK U; EMT.

PROCHASKA, JENNIFER; Westmoore HS; Oklahoma City, OK; (1); Sec Stu Cncl; Chrldng; High Hon Roll; NHS; Cmptn Dance; Phys Thrpy.

PROCK, JENNIFER; Garber Sr HS; Garber, OK; (2); Church Yth Grp; FCA; FHA; Ofcr Stu Cncl; Bsktbl; Chrldng; Sftbl; Hon Roll; NHS; Ntl Merit Ltr.

PROCTOR, CODY; Lone Grove HS; Lone Grove, OK; (4); 3/80; Church Yth Grp; Key Clb; Library Aide; Natl Beta Clb; Spanish Clb; Teachers Aide; Chorus; School Musical; School Play; Pres Stu Cncl; OK Christian U; Elem Ed.

PROCTOR, DANIEL W; Choctaw HS; Choctaw, OK; (3); 171/390; Church Yth Grp; Natl FFA Org; Hon Roll; OK Chrstn Univ; Tchr.

PROCTOR, JENNIFER; Wetumka Jr Sr HS; Wetumka, OK; (4); 2/32; FHA; Key Clb; Natl FFA Org; Spanish Clb; Band; Drm Mjr(t); High Hon Roll; Hon Roll; NHS; Sal; Seminole JC; Acctng.

PROSSER, JENNIFER J; Union Intermediate HS; Tulsa, OK; (2); Cmnty Wkr; Debate Tm; Drama Clb; Girl Scts; Speech Tm; School Play; Var Swmmng; NHS; Red Cross Aide; Hon Roll; Silver Awd Girl Scouts; ROTUS; Juilliard Schl; Drama.

PROUGH, CRYSTAL R; Macomb Schl; Macomb, OK; (1); 2/30; Church Yth Grp; Treas FHA; School Play; Rep Stu Cncl; High Hon Roll; NHS; Dance Clb; Stu Of The Yr; Natl His & Govt Awd; Tchr.

PROVENCE, KERRIE A; Valliant HS; Valliant, OK; (1); 5/81; Bsktbl; Chrldng; Powder Puff Ftbl; Trk; Hon Roll.

PROVINCE, NATASHA J; Claremore Sr HS; Claremore, OK; (1); Church Yth Grp; Hosp Aide; Teachers Aide; Cit Awd; Hon Roll; Ped.

PROVINE, JOE; Oklahoma Bible Acad; Pond Creek, OK; (2); 1/40; Chess Clb; Church Yth Grp; Quiz Bowl; Scholastic Bowl; Sec Soph Cls; High Hon Roll; Jr NHS; NHS.

PRUCHNICKI, JENNIFER A; Lawton Sr HS; Fort Sill, OK; (4); 22/317; VP FCA; Ed Nwsp; Sec Frsh Cls; Mgr Bsbl; Sftbl; Cit Awd; High Hon Roll; Sec NHS; Prfct Atten Awd; Acad Team; U Of OK; Jrnlsm.

PRUDOM III, WESLEY J; Booker J Washington HS; Tulsa, OK; (3); Church Yth Grp; JA; Church Choir; Jazz Band; Dpty Grnd Knght Of Jr Knghts St Peter Claver; Acctng.

PRUETT, BETHANY N; Choctaw HS; Harrah, OK; (2); GAA; Scholastic Bowl; Var Mgr(s); JV Sftbl; Var Trk; Hon Roll; Jr NHS; NHS; Arch Engr.

PRUETT, GREG D; Enid Sr HS; Enid, OK; (2); Church Yth Grp; Band; Church Choir; Mrchg Band; Pep Band; Rep Stu Cncl; Hon Roll; NHS; Missionary To Mexico 95 & 96; Chrch Drama Team; Outstdng Bible Quizzer.

PRUITT, ALICIA; Rock Creek Jr Sr HS; Bokchito, OK; (4); 4/39; Church Yth Grp; FCA; FHA; Teachers Aide; Chorus; School Play; Nwsp; Yrbk; Ofcr Stu Cncl; Var Bsktbl; Princpls Ldrshp, Lady Mustang Awds; Acad Achvrs; S E OK ST U; Engl.

PRUITT, ALLISON L; Putnam City North HS; Oklahoma City, OK; (2); Church Yth Grp; Drama Clb; Key Clb; Spanish Clb; Rptr Yrbk; Stat Score Keeper.

PRUITT, JENNIFER A; Nathan Hale HS; Tulsa, OK; (4); Art Clb; Yrbk; Hon Roll; Cars; Charcoal Sketch; Race Cars; Tulsa JC; Brdcstng/Med.

PRUITT, LYNNETTE J; Buffalo Jr Sr HS; Buffalo, OK; (3); Church Yth Grp; Pres DECA; FBLA; Natl FFA Org; Quiz Bowl; Chorus; Pres Frsh Cls; Chrldng; Sftbl; NHS; 2 Yr Mrktng Prgm:actng; Comm Svc; OSU; Drama/Fshn Mrktg.

PRY, JENNIFER A; Tahlequah Sr HS; Tahlequah, OK; (2); Band; Color Guard; Mrchg Band; Crs Cntry; Trk; NHS.

PRY, RAGEN R; Vinita HS; Vinita, OK; (4); #5 in class; German Clb; Math Clb; Science Clb; Band; Mrchg Band; Pep Band; Hon Roll; NHS; Top Schlr; Environmental Clb; Northeastern ST Univ; Paralegl.

PRYOR, AMY; Stillwater Jr HS; Stillwater, OK; (1); Church Yth Grp; FCA; Teachers Aide; Ofcr Stu Cncl; Chrldng; Hon Roll; Dancing; OK ST U.

PRYOR, BRANDON; Western Heights Sr HS; Oklahoma City, OK; (3); Art Clb; Church Yth Grp; Cmnty Wkr; English Clb; Varsity Clb; Bsktbl; Swmmng; Hon Roll; Prfct Atten Awd; Natl Yth Ldrshp Forum Law/Cnstn; OK Univ; Attrny/Bsktbl.

PRYOR, DANYELLE; Antlers Sr HS; Antlers, OK; (4); 2/66; FBLA; Band; Color Guard; Bsktbl; Sftbl; Tennis; High Hon Roll; NHS; Prfct Atten Awd; Grls ST Altrnt; All Amer Schlr; US Natl Ldrshp Awd; E Cntrl U Of OK.

PRYOR, DAVID E; Union Intermediate HS; Broken Arrow, OK; (2); 63/800; Drama Clb; Key Clb; Spanish Clb; School Musical; School Play; Rep Stu Cncl; High Hon Roll; Jr NHS; Kiwanis Awd; NHS; D-Fy The High; ARC Pgm Cncl; LA ST U.

PRYOR, KENDALL; Seminole Jr Sr HS; Seminole, OK; (2); Drama Clb; FCA; French Clb; Math Clb; NFL; Sec Frsh Cls; Co-Capt Var Chrldng; Tennis; High Hon Roll; Hon Roll; CO Univ.

PUAKETT, CHAD L; Healdton HS; Healdton, OK; (3); Pres Frsh Cls; Pres Soph Cls; Hon Roll; Pres Acad Fit Awd; Curriculum.

PUCKET, AMY M; Charles Page HS; Sand Springs, OK; (3); French Clb; FTA; Band; Chorus; Church Choir; Mrchg Band; Pep Band; School Musical; Hon Roll; Prfct Atten Awd; All Dist Band 3 Yrs; All St Bapt Choir/Orch 2 Yrs; Erly Chldhd Ed.

PUCKET, JONATHAN D; Charles Page HS; Sand Springs, OK; (1); Yrbk; Chorus; High Hon Roll; Hon Roll; Prfct Atten Awd; Otsdng Art Stdnt 9th Grd; OK ST Univ; Arch Engr.

PUCKETT, AMY; Jenks HS; Jenks, OK; (4); FCA; Key Clb; Teachers Aide; Acpl Chr; Chorus; School Musical; Swing Chorus; VP Frsh Cls; Pres Soph Cls; Pres Jr Cls; OK ST U; Pub Rel.

PUCKETT, HILARY; Bartlesville Sr HS; Bartlesville, OK; (3); Church Yth Grp; Chorus; Socr.

PUCKETT III, WALTER; Muskogee HS; Muskogee, OK; (2); 71/481; Ofcr ROTC; Color Guard; Drill Tm; Hon Roll.

PUGH, CHRISTINA; Moore HS; Oklahoma City, OK; (4); Pres Art Clb; Rptr DECA; Nwsp; Rep Stu Cncl; Intrml Powder Puff Ftbl; JV Tennis; High Hon Roll; Hon Roll; Jr NHS; MAAHC Art Cntst 1st Pl, Bst Shw; Exhbt Art Hlsy Gllry OCU; OKU.

PUGH, CLINT D; West Jr HS; Oklahoma City, OK; (1); Church Yth Grp; Math Clb; Quiz Bowl; Science Clb; Chorus; School Musical; School Play; Ftbl; Gov Hon Prg Awd; Hon Roll; Univ Of OK; Psych.

PUGH, JOANN D; Eisenhower Sr HS; Lawton, OK; (3); 28/485; Church Yth Grp; FCA; Var Chrldng; JV Var Tennis; High Hon Roll; Hon Roll; Jr NHS; NHS; Natl His/Govt Awd Wnr; Acad Ltr 3 Yrs; OK Univ; Dr.

PUGH II, RICHARD; Caney Jr Sr HS; Caney, OK; (3); Church Yth Grp; Cmnty Wkr; Natl FFA Org; SADD; Church Choir; Fishing; Hunting; Farming; Southeastern OK.

PUGH, TAMARA J; Douglass HS; Oklahoma City, OK; (2); Church Yth Grp; Cmnty Wkr; ROTC; Drill Tm; Rptr Nwsp; Sec Soph Cls; Pres Jr Cls; Chrldng; Golf; Tennis; Supr Cadet Decrtn Awd; Sociolgy.

PUGSLEY, SARAH; Edmond North HS; Edmond, OK; (2); Church Yth Grp; FCA; Spanish Clb; Chrldng; Pom Pon; Hon Roll.

PULIS, DENISE; Anadarko HS; Anadarko, OK; (3); 1/109; Am Leg Aux Girls St; 4-H; FBLA; Natl FFA Org; SADD; Chorus; School Play; Ed Nwsp; Sec Stu Cncl; 4-H Awd; Ped.

PULLEY, JOSHUA M; Bridge Creek HS; Tuttle, OK; (2); Church Yth Grp; Math Clb; Spanish Clb; Var Ftbl; Var Trk; Var Wt Lftg; Cit Awd; Hon Roll; U Of OK; Airplane Pilot.

PUNCHES, CRYSTAL; Pawhuska HS; Pawhuska, OK; (3); 5/95; Church Yth Grp; FCA; FBLA; Key Clb; SADD; Jazz Band; Mrchg Band; Sftbl; NHS.

PURDY, STEVEN; Classen Schl Advanced Studies; Oklahoma City, OK; (2); 2/90; Boy Scts; German Clb; HOBY; Math Clb; Mu Alpha Theta; Quiz Bowl; Scholastic Bowl; High Hon Roll; NHS; Engr.

PURI, PUJA K; Oklahoma Sch Of Science & Math; Edmond, OK; (3); Sec Debate Tm; Sec French Clb; Key Clb; Sec NFL; Pres Science Clb; Chorus; Variety Show; Yrbk; NHS; Indian Stdnt Soc; Bio/Dr.

PURKAPLE, LISHA R; Ponca City Sr HS; Ponca City, OK; (4); 18/334; Church Yth Grp; Library Aide; Church Choir; Orch; High Hon Roll; Hon Roll; Kiwanis Awd; NHS; OK All-St Orch; Natl Schl Orch Awd; Hardin-Simmons Univ; Math Tchr.

PURSCELLEY, STEPHANY L; Commerce HS; Miami, OK; (1); Church Yth Grp; FCA; FHA; GAA; Ofcr Frsh Cls; Bsktbl; Sftbl; Hon Roll; Gftd/Tlntd Cls; Sprts Med.

PURSER, APRIL; Woodward HS; Woodward, OK; (1); 10/200; Church Yth Grp; Hosp Aide; Intnl Clb; Pep Clb; Chorus; Church Choir; School Musical; Trk; High Hon Roll; Mentor Dels Peer Cnslng; Mythlgy /Wrting Wood Awds; Prdctn Asst Comm Thtr.

PUTMAN, ELIZABETH; Cascia Hall Prep School; Tulsa, OK; (4); Church Yth Grp; Cmnty Wkr; Library Aide; Pep Clb; Scholastic Bowl; Spanish Clb; School Play; Nwsp; Ed Yrbk; Lit Mag; Boston Col.

PYATT, RUSTY; Woodward HS; Woodward, OK; (3); Ofcr Bsbl; Wt Lftg; Hon Roll.

PYLE, KEVIN D; Anadarko HS; Anadarko, OK; (3); 17/119; FCA; FBLA; Spanish Clb; Var Bsbl; Var Ftbl; Intrml Score Keeper; Hon Roll; Jr NHS; NHS; Sports Medicine Dr; Phy Ther.

PYLE, MATTHEW A; Bridge Creek HS; Blanchard, OK; (3); Church Yth Grp; Cmnty Wkr; FCA; Spanish Clb; JV Ftbl; High Hon Roll; NHS.

PYLE, RYNDA L; Depew HS; Depew, OK; (2); 8/45; Church Yth Grp; GAA; Letterman Clb; Pep Clb; Spanish Clb; Rep Soph Cls; Rep Stu Cncl; Var L Bsktbl; Hon Roll; East Cntrl Univ.

PYLE, TANA E; Yukon Middle HS; Yukon, OK; (2); FHA; Mgr(s); Hon Roll; NHS; Sports Medicine Stu Trainer; OU; Sports Medicine; Phy Thrpst.

PYRON, JOSH L; Seminole Jr Sr HS; Seminole, OK; (3); FCA; Ftbl; Golf; Wt Lftg; Hon Roll; OK Univ; Law.

PYRON, STEVEN W; South Intermediate HS; Broken Arrow, OK; (1); Church Yth Grp; High Hon Roll; Hon Roll; Jr NHS.

QUACKENBUSH, JEANA; Luther HS; Luther, OK; (1); Church Yth Grp; Cmnty Wkr; Drama Clb; FHA; Prfct Atten Awd; Farmers Union Yth Summer Camp; Connors ST Coll; Phy Thrpst.

QUADEER, ERUM A; Memorial HS; Tulsa, OK; (2); 1/275; Hosp Aide; Intnl Clb; JCL; Rep Key Clb; Hist Rep Latin Clb; Treas Science Clb; Pres Acad Fit Awd; Prin Hon Roll; Summa Cum Laude On Natl Latin Exam/4th Plc Overall Latin 2 In ST; Acad Team; Pre Med/Engr.

QUAID, SHERRI; Durant HS; Durant, OK; (3); Church Yth Grp; Debate Tm; Pres Drama Clb; Treas Sec Key Clb; Speech Tm; Chorus; School Play; Stage Crew; Rptr Nwsp; High Hon Roll.

QUALLS, CHERYL L; Muldrow HS; Muldrow, OK; (2); Church Yth Grp; Band; Church Choir; Mrchg Band; High Hon Roll; Hon Roll; Bob Jones; Vet.

QUALLS, HEATH; Stratford Schl; Stratford, OK; (2); FCA; Sec Natl FFA Org; Yrbk; Pres Frsh Cls; Pres Soph Cls; Ofcr Stu Cncl; Bsktbl; Ftbl; Trk; Hon Roll; OSU; Vet.

QUALLS, JAMES T; Haskell HS; Haskell, OK; (2); Church Yth Grp; FCA; Church Choir; Pres Frsh Cls; Bsktbl; Chrldng; High Hon Roll; Hon Roll; OK Masonic Lodge Stu Of Today Awd; Tulsa Univ Engrng Camp.

QUALLS, JASON W; Tahlequah Sr HS; Tahlequah, OK; (4); Natl FFA Org; NHS; NSU.

QUALLS, JULIE A; Gore HS; Gore, OK; (3); FHA; Capt Quiz Bowl; SADD; Ed Nwsp; Rep Stu Cncl; Capt Bsktbl; L Sftbl; High Hon Roll; Hon Roll; NHS; Comp Sci.

QUALLS, MISSOURI L; Mustang HS; Yukon, OK; (2); 1/417; High Hon Roll; NHS.

QUIBLE, CHRIS; Stillwater Sr HS; Stillwater, OK; (4); 27/350; Am Leg Boys St; Boy Scts; Church Yth Grp; Cmnty Wkr; JCL; Key Clb; Latin Clb; Mu Alpha Theta; Natl Beta Clb; Science Clb; Rippy Fellow; Hosp Intern; Sister Cities Cncl & Travel To Japan; CPR Instr; Bio.

QUICK, CHERMEL; Carl Albert HS; Midwest City, OK; (2); FCA; Hosp Aide; Key Clb; Pep Clb; SADD; Chorus; Church Choir; Variety Show; Var Chrldng; Socr; Howard Univ; Obstetrician.

QUICK, ROWENA; Quinton Jr Sr HS; Quinton, OK; (3); Church Yth Grp; FCA; Teachers Aide; JV Bsktbl; Var Sftbl; Var Trk; Pre-Med.

QUIGLEY, JENNIFER S; Kingfisher HS; Kingfisher, OK; (4); 29/88; Key Clb; Spanish Clb; Band; Chorus; Mrchg Band; School Musical; Rptr Nwsp; High Hon Roll; Hon Roll; NHS; Redlands CC; Nrsng.

QUINN, APRIL J; Pocola HS; Pocola, OK; (2); Girl Scts; Quiz Bowl; Band; Jazz Band; Mrchg Band; Pep Band; Hon Roll; Prfct Atten Awd; OK Hon Soc; Gftd/Tlntd Prgm; Eductl Talent Search; Tchr.

QUINTIN, MICHELE R; Macarthur Sr HS; Lawton, OK; (2); 9/350; German Clb; Speech Tm; Chorus; School Play; High Hon Roll; Jr NHS; Pres Acad Fit Awd; Mock Trail; Vol Nrsng Hm.

QUINTON, ELIZABETH A; Sapulpa Sr HS; Sapulpa, OK; (3); 31/292; Church Yth Grp; Letterman Clb; Band; Chorus; Church Choir; Jazz Band; Mrchg Band; High Hon Roll; NHS; All ST Band 95-; All Rgn Bnd 4 Yrs; Teens For Christ; Math.

QUINTON, JENNIFER L; Sapulpa Sr HS; Sapulpa, OK; (3); Band; Mrchg Band; Stage Crew; Piano; Attorney.

QUINTON, NATALIE; Hulbert Jr Sr HS; Hulbert, OK; (2); 4-H; German Clb; Bsktbl; Chrldng; Sftbl; Trk; Hon Roll; Jr NHS; NHS; Val; OK ST U; Phys Thrpy.

QUIREY, MATT; Blackwell HS; Blackwell, OK; (1); 1/138; Boy Scts; Quiz Bowl; Band; Jazz Band; School Musical; School Play; Ofcr Bsbl; Bsktbl; High Hon Roll.

QUIREY, RUSSELL; Blackwell HS; Blackwell, OK; (3); 13/124; Boy Scts; Church Yth Grp; HOBY; Office Aide; Quiz Bowl; Scholastic Bowl; Band; Chorus; Hon Roll; NHS.

QUIRK JR, ALLEN A; Mc Loud HS; Mc Loud, OK; (2); #1 in class; Natl FFA Org; Ftbl; Wt Lftg; Hon Roll; NHS; Electronics.

QUISENBERRY, ERIC T; Caney Valley HS; Ramona, OK; (2); Natl FFA Org; Ofcr Frsh Cls; Ofcr Bsbl; Ftbl; Wt Lftg; Cit Awd; High Hon Roll; NHS; Show Cattle/Hogs; OK ST; Strctrl Engr.

QUOSS, STEVEN; Claremore Sr HS; Claremore, OK; (4); 22/325; Church Yth Grp; Cmnty Wkr; German Clb; Red Cross Aide; Var Socr; High Hon Roll; Hon Roll; NHS; Prfct Atten Awd; Rogers U.

RAAB, DESRA E; Arapaho Schl; Arapaho, OK; (3); Rep Church Yth Grp; 4-H; FHA; Teachers Aide; Church Choir; JV L Bsktbl; L Chrldng; 4-H Awd; Mid Amer Bible Coll.

RABE, BRIDGETT; Putnam City West HS; Bethany, OK; (3); 67/300; Art Clb; JV Bsktbl; JV Var Sftbl; JV Trk; NHS; Dallas Art Inst; Comp Anmtn Art.

RABOLD, CHRIS S; Enid Sr HS; Enid, OK; (2); 58/431; Cmnty Wkr; JV Var Tennis; Hon Roll; Jr NHS; NHS; PTSA 94-; US Natl Art Awd Nom; USTA.

RACHAL, SHANNON; Midwest City HS; Midwest City, OK; (4); Cmnty Wkr; French Clb; German Clb; Office Aide; Pep Clb; Science Clb; Service Clb; Chorus; NHS; Val; Jr Rtry Clb; Med.

RACHEL, TARA; Byng Sr HS; Ada, OK; (4); 8/71; Church Yth Grp; Drama Clb; French Clb; FBLA; Chorus; School Play; Ofcr Stu Cncl; Var Chrldng; Hon Roll; NHS; ECU.

RACKLEY, CRAIG R; Savanna HS; Savanna, OK; (3); Church Yth Grp; FCA; 4-H; Natl FFA Org; Quiz Bowl; Science Clb; Spanish Clb; Yrbk; Sec Frsh Cls; Sec Soph Cls; Cornell U; Biologist.

RADCLIFF, TIMOTHY; El Reno Sr HS; El Reno, OK; (4); 61/167; Am Leg Boys St; Natl FFA Org; L Bsbl; Hon Roll; Frank Myers Mem Schlrshp; OK Hwy Ptrl Cadet Lawman Acad; All Amer Schlr; Rnssnc Hnr Roll; Redlands; Vet.

RADEMEYER, KAREN; Jenks HS; Tulsa, OK; (3); 32/650; Church Yth Grp; Ofcr FCA; Ofcr French Clb; Math Clb; Mu Alpha Theta; Teachers Aide; Varsity Clb; Nwsp; Ofcr Stu Cncl; Capt Gym; Gymnstcs 2 Time ST Chmpn/1 Time Rnnr Up; Trck/ST Rnnr Up High Jmp; 5a ST Team Chmps; Hmcmng Nom.

RADER, AMANDA M; Woodward HS; Woodward, OK; (4); 53/150; Church Yth Grp; FCA; FTA; Hosp Aide; Key Clb; Spanish Clb; Acpl Chr; Chorus; Church Choir; Variety Show; Writng Wood 1st Pl; SWOSU; Sci/Span.

RADIN, CYNTHIA L; Union Intermediate HS; Broken Arrow, OK; (2); Stat Bsbl; Bsktbl; High Hon Roll; NHS; Suprt Grp; Pr Mediation.

RAEFIELD, SHERI L; Okmulgee HS; Okmulgee, OK; (3); Church Yth Grp; FCA; FBLA; Spanish Clb; Band; Church Choir; Ofcr Stu Cncl; Golf; Hon Roll; NHS; Bus Mngmt.

RAFI, NADIA; B T Washington HS; Tulsa, OK; (2); Latin Clb; Spanish Clb; Orch; NHS; Intl Baccalaureate; Muslima Yth Of Tulsa; Pedtrcn.

RAGAN, CHASITY; Hugo HS; Hugo, OK; (3); 4-H; FHA; Sec Science Clb; Spanish Clb; Yrbk; Stat Bsktbl; Var Sftbl; High Hon Roll; NHS; U OK; Med.

RAGAN, KRISTA; Indianola HS; Mcalester, OK; (4); 10/40; Church Yth Grp; 4-H; FBLA; FHA; Natl Beta Clb; VP Stu Cncl; Var Bsktbl; Hon Roll; Sprts Mgmt.

RAGLE, AMANDA D; Olive Jr Sr HS; Mannford, OK; (2); Church Yth Grp; Speech Tm; Chorus; Sec Frsh Cls; Elem Tchr.

RAGSDALE, JAMIE E; Weatherford HS; Weatherford, OK; (3); Spanish Clb; Chorus; Sftbl; High Hon Roll; Hon Roll; His Cl; Physician.

RAHLF, KATHRYN; Mc Loud HS; Mc Loud, OK; (1); 1/150; Church Yth Grp; Band; Color Guard; Mrchg Band; Pep Band; Prfct Atten Awd; OK Hnr Soc; Gftd & Tlntd.

RAHLF, RYAN; Mc Loud HS; Mc Loud, OK; (3); 14/129; Boy Scts; Church Yth Grp; Band; Jazz Band; Mrchg Band; Pep Band; High Hon Roll; Hon Roll; NHS; OK Hnr Soc; Hnr Schlr-Acad Achvt Awd.

RAHMAN, NAZIA; Bartlesville Mid HS; Bartlesville, OK; (1); 1/476; Hosp Aide; Spanish Clb; Orch; High Hon Roll; OK HS Hnr Soc; Rel Act; Med Explorers Post 911; Sci Explorers Post 007; Medicine.

RAHMANZADEH, RAHD; Mustang HS; Yukon, OK; (2); 107/400; Bsktbl; Golf; Hon Roll; OK Univ.

RAILEY, LEISA A; Sharon Mutual Jr Sr HS; Woodward, OK; (2); Church Yth Grp; 4-H; FHA; Chorus; Church Choir; School Musical; Hon Roll; NHS; Camp Cnslr; Union Col; Art Ed; Spcl Ed.

RAINES, KIM; Adair HS; Adair, OK; (3); Art Clb; FCA; Science Clb; Band; Flag Corp; Mrchg Band; Nwsp; Bsktbl; Trk; Hon Roll; NSU.

RAINES, ROBERT G; Sharon Mutual Jr Sr HS; Woodward, OK; (2); 1/33; Var L Ftbl; Var Trk; Var Wt Lftg; High Hon Roll; NHS; Prfct Atten Awd; OSU; Med Fld.

RAINES, TASHA; Idabel HS; Idabel, OK; (1); Cit Awd; Jr NHS; Prfct Atten Awd; Participant In Chowtaw Nation Upward Bound Math & Sci; Acctng.

RAINEY, JAMES M; Memorial HS; Broken Arrow, OK; (2); FCA; Key Clb; Bsktbl; High Hon Roll; NHS; Ec/Bus.

RAINS, VALERIE L; Moore HS; Oklahoma City, OK; (3); 2/550; Art Clb; Church Yth Grp; French Clb; Treas Science Clb; Chorus; Jr NHS; NHS; Ntl Merit Ltr; Jr Escort At Commencement.

RAINWATER, CARRIE A; Whitesboro Schl; Whitesboro, OK; (2); FHA; Natl FFA Org; Treas Soph Cls; Hon Roll.

RAKOWSKI, KIMBERLY M; Union Sr HS; Broken Arrow, OK; (3); 112/705; Church Yth Grp; Cmnty Wkr; Debate Tm; Drama Clb; Intnl Clb; Spanish Clb; Speech Tm; Swmmng; High Hon Roll; Hon Roll; Korean Martial Arts.

RALEY, SARAH M; Memorial HS; Tulsa, OK; (2); Church Yth Grp; Cmnty Wkr; German Clb; GAA; Hosp Aide; Pep Clb; Teachers Aide; Var Chrldng; Var Golf; Var Trk; Chemical Engr; Lab Sci.

RALPH, STEVEN J; Edmond Memorial HS; Edmond, OK; (3); Boy Scts; Math Clb; Mu Alpha Theta; Science Clb; Spanish Clb; High Hon Roll; Ntl Merit SF; Prfct Atten Awd; Greater San Diego Sci Fair 2nd Pl; Golden St Exam Bio High Hnrs; All-Amer Schlsp; OH ST; Engrng.

RALSTON, ALISHA K; Clayton Jr Sr HS; Clayton, OK; (2); Cmnty Wkr; FHA; Natl FFA Org; Yrbk; Eastern OK ST Coll.

RAMACHANDRA, KOMALA; Stillwater Jr HS; Stillwater, OK; (1); Boy Scts; Dance Clb; Hosp Aide; Math Tm; Natl Beta Clb; Quiz Bowl; Orch; High Hon Roll; Pres Schlr; OEF Engrng Fair 1st Pl 96; Rose St Coll Statwd Acad Cmptn 2nd Pl In Span; Outstdng Sci & Span Stu Awd.

RAMBO, SHANA B; Memorial HS; Tulsa, OK; (2); Church Yth Grp; Cmnty Wkr; French Clb; Pep Clb; Capt Pom Pon; Hon Roll; Capt Fresh Pom Pom Sqd; 2nd Yr Mem Var; Miss Congnlty 95-; Co Jazz Dance.

RAMEY, RICKIE; Afton HS; Vinita, OK; (3); 6/36; Am Leg Boys St; Church Yth Grp; FCA; Natl FFA Org; Quiz Bowl; School Play; Rep Jr Cls; Rep Sr Cls; L Var Bsbl; L Var Bsktbl; Northeastern A&M; Aero Maint.

RAMIREZ, ALFREDO; Lawton Sr HS; Lawton, OK; (4); 15/323; Church Yth Grp; Debate Tm; Capt FCA; School Play; Lit Mag; Rep Stu Cncl; JV Bsbl; JV Var Tennis; High Hon Roll; Jr NHS; Tchr Cadets Pgm Mem; Sgt-At-Arms For Tech Stu Assn; Jr Cnslr For Intnl Order Of Demolay; Cameron U; Comp Sci.

RAMM, SELENA; Claremore Sr HS; Claremore, OK; (4); 28/276; Church Yth Grp; FCA; Natl FFA Org; Spanish Clb; Ofcr Stu Cncl; Var Bsktbl; Var Socr; JV Trk; 4-H Awd; Optmst Clb; Yth Bsktbl, Sccr Coach; Natl Yth Coaches Assn; OK ST U; Ag Cmmnctns.

RAMON, JULIE D; Turner Schl; Burneyville, OK; (2); 3/25; Ofcr Natl Beta Clb; Church Yth Grp; 4-H; FHA; Pep Clb; Quiz Bowl; Scholastic Bowl; Var Bsktbl; Var Chrldng; Var Sftbl; Accntng.

RAMOS, YOLANDA M; Temple Jr Sr HS; Temple, OK; (3); Church Yth Grp; Debate Tm; FHA; GAA; Teachers Aide; Rptr Nwsp; Phtg Yrbk; Ofcr Bsbl; Bsktbl; Chrldng; Bus Tech; Cotton Elec Essay Cont Fnlst; Bus.

RAMPEY, CHRIS L; Webster HS; Tulsa, OK; (3); 14/144; Am Leg Boys St; Boy Scts; Church Yth Grp; FBLA; Ofcr Soph Cls; Ofcr Jr Cls; Var Ftbl; Wrstlng; Cit Awd; Hon Roll; Natl Hon Rl; Natl Eng Merit Awd; Eagle Scout; Yth Mnstry/Bus.

RAMSEY, AMY; Edmond Memorial HS; Edmond, OK; (3); 66/408; Hosp Aide; Art Awds; Pres Ed Awds Pgm; FIDM; Fshn Dsgn.

RAMSEY, JOSHUA D; Choctaw HS; Choctaw, OK; (4); 1/313; Am Leg Boys St; FCA; HOBY; Ofcr Key Clb; Capt Quiz Bowl; Pres Soph Cls; Pres Jr Cls; Pres Sr Cls; Var Capt Crs Cntry; Val; Soph Yr OK/TX Kiwanis; Sci Stu Yr; Stu Today Masons; Chem Engr.

RAMSEY, LORI L; Muldrow HS; Muldrow, OK; (1); Church Yth Grp; Debate Tm; Drama Clb; Natl Beta Clb; NFL; Science Clb; Spanish Clb; Speech Tm; Band; High Hon Roll; Speech Team Best Nwcmr/Speech Hon Roll 96; OU; Broadcst Jrnlsm.

RAMSEY, NIKKI; Westmoore HS; Oklahoma City, OK; (3); FCA; Office Aide; Spanish Clb; Rep Stu Cncl; Var Pom Pon; 2 Yr St Champion Pom Pons; 2nd Pl Natls; UCO; Cardio Pump Tech.

RAMSEY, SADIE; Woodward HS; Woodward, OK; (2); Cmnty Wkr; High Hon Roll; Kiwanis Awd; NHS; Microbiology.

RAMSEY, STORMY E; Wetumka Jr Sr HS; Wetumka, OK; (3); Church Yth Grp; FCA; FHA; Spanish Clb; Band; Mrchg Band; Pep Band; Bsktbl; Mgr(s); Sftbl; Ridng Horses/Mules; Cadet Lawman Green Platoon; Seminole ST Coll.

RAMSEY, TERRA M; Sapulpa Sr HS; Sapulpa, OK; (3); Church Yth Grp; FBLA; FHA; Key Clb; Science Clb; Spanish Clb; Teachers Aide; Band; Church Choir; Mrchg Band; OK ST Univ; Elem Ed.

RAMSEY, ZACK J; Shawnee Sr HS; Shawnee, OK; (3); Church Yth Grp; Band; Jazz Band; Mrchg Band; Pep Band; NHS; OK St Univ; Brdcst.

RANALLO, ASHLEY M; Mc Alester HS; Junction City, KS; (4); 4/209; FCA; Science Clb; Spanish Clb; Band; Var Capt Bsktbl; High Hon Roll; NHS; Chem & Physcs Clb; Sr Srns Treas; SOK Hnr Soc; Cloud Cty CC; Bio.

RANDALL, BROC A; Mc Alester HS; Mcalester, OK; (2); #35 in class; Art Clb; Church Yth Grp; Cmnty Wkr; FCA; Letterman Clb; Varsity Clb; Ofcr Bsbl; Hon Roll; U Of OK; Mech Eng.

RANDALL, KEVIN; Tonkawa Jr Sr HS; Tonkawa, OK; (3); 10/49; Church Yth Grp; FCA; Letterman Clb; Natl FFA Org; Teachers Aide; Treas Stu Cncl; Var L Bsbl; Var L Ftbl; Var Trk; Intrml Wt Lftg.

RANDALL, NANCY; Holdenville Jr HS; Holdenville, OK; (1); Scholastic Bowl; Chorus; Intrml Bsktbl; L Sftbl; Hon Roll; Jr NHS; GATE.

RANDALL, NICHOLE B; Choctaw HS; Choctaw, OK; (2); Scholastic Bowl; Treas Soph Cls; Bsktbl; Crs Cntry; Socr; Tennis; Hon Roll; Prfct Atten Awd; Pres Ed Awds Pgm Outstdng Acad Achvmt.

RANDALL, ROCHELLE; Bartlesville Sr HS; Dewey, OK; (2); Church Yth Grp; Model UN; Office Aide; Teachers Aide; Band; Chorus; Bsktbl; Chrldng; Trk; Hon Roll; Grls Clb; Grl Scts; Boys, Grls Clbs; OK ST U; Ped.

RANDALL, SARA; Ada HS; Ada, OK; (3); Church Yth Grp; French Clb; Pep Clb; SADD; Church Choir; Co-Ed Yrbk; High Hon Roll; Jr NHS; NHS; E Central U; Child Psych.

RANDOL, JIMMY; Wayne Public Schl; Purcell, OK; (3); 2/25; Natl FFA Org; Office Aide; Scholastic Bowl; VP Frsh Cls; Var Bsbl; Var Bsktbl; High Hon Roll; Hon Roll; NHS; MI.

RANDOLPH, SHANE J; Cushing HS; Cushing, OK; (1); #1 in class; Science Clb; Speech Tm; Chorus; School Musical; Nwsp; Cit Awd; Hon Roll; Pres Schlr; OK ST U; Engrng.

RANEY, LISA; Eisenhower Jr HS; Lawton, OK; (1); Rep Stu Cncl; Var Chrldng; Hon Roll; Pwr Rumbling Power Twistarts Tm Regnl/ST Champ; AZ ST; RN.

RANEY, MARY E; Muldrow HS; Sallisaw, OK; (2); HOBY; Math Clb; Natl Beta Clb; NFL; Quiz Bowl; Science Clb; Spanish Clb; Band; Var Chrldng; Hon Roll.

RANGE, CARMEN; Plainview HS; Ardmore, OK; (1); 1/93; Sec Frsh Cls; Rep Stu Cncl; Var Trk; High Hon Roll; Hon Roll; Prfct Atten Awd; OK HS Hnr Soc.

RANGEL, SAMMY; Clinton HS; Clinton, OK; (1); Church Yth Grp; FCA; FHA; Letterman Clb; Varsity Clb; JV Bsktbl; JV Ftbl; Var Socr; Var Tennis; High Hon Roll.

RANK, MARINN; Chisholm Sr HS; Enid, OK; (1); Debate Tm; FHA; Pep Clb; Speech Tm; Band; Mrchg Band; Pep Band; JV Bsktbl; High Hon Roll; Hon Roll; Stu Of Month; Vet.

RANKIN, APRIL A; Freedom Schl; Freedom, OK; (3); Nwsp; Intrml Bsktbl; High Hon Roll; Hon Roll; NHS; Ntl Merit Schol; Sal; FFA; Pep Clb; NWOSU; Pre-Med; Bus.

RANKIN, BECKIE A; Okarche HS; El Reno, OK; (2); Church Yth Grp; Natl Beta Clb; NFL; Speech Tm; Chorus; Church Choir; School Musical; School Play; NHS; Hon Roll; All St Chorus; Western OK Hnr Choir; All-St Cast In Drama; OK City U; Med Field.

RANKIN, MATTHEW A; Sapulpa Sr HS; Sapulpa, OK; (4); Church Yth Grp; Cmnty Wkr; Band; Mrchg Band; JV Bsktbl; Var Socr; Wt Lftg; Hon Roll; NHS; Pres Acad Fit Awd; Circle Of Friends; Bartlesville Wesleyan Coll; Bus.

RANKIN, RENEE; El Reno Sr HS; El Reno, OK; (3); Church Yth Grp; FHA; Speech Tm; Band; Chorus; Church Choir; Mrchg Band; Orch; School Musical; Var Sftbl; Nrsng.

RANO, PATRICK R; OK Schl Of Sci & Math; Yale, OK; (3); Pres Church Yth Grp; CAP; Natl Beta Clb; Quiz Bowl; Scholastic Bowl; Drill Tm; Ed Lit Mag.

RANSOM, DUSTY L; Wakita Schl; Wakita, OK; (1); Church Yth Grp; FCA; Natl FFA Org; School Play; Pres Stu Cncl; Var Bsbl; Var Bsktbl; Var Ftbl; Wt Lftg; High Hon Roll; HS Sci Fair; Plcd 4-5th Schlstc Meets Physcl Sci; IA Bsc Skls Tst 98 Prcnt.

RAO, ROHINI M; Edmond Memorial HS; Edmond, OK; (4); French Clb; Key Clb; Science Clb; SADD; Orch; Prfct Atten Awd; Dance; U Of Cntrl OK; Child Psych.

RAPIER, CELESTA; Ringling HS; Ringling, OK; (3); Church Yth Grp; 4-H; FHA; Var Bsktbl; Chrldng; Powder Puff Ftbl; Hon Roll; Southeastern; Pharm.

RAPP, ERIN C; Wakita Schl; Wakita, OK; (1); 1/22; Church Yth Grp; FCA; FHA; GAA; Pep Clb; Band; Church Choir; Pep Band; Var Bsktbl; Var Chrldng; Dar Awd Band; St Champ In 3200m Relay; Cls B Bsktbl St Semi-Fnlsts; U Of OK; Pediatrician.

RAPP, JENNY L; East Central HS; Tulsa, OK; (3); Am Leg Aux Girls St; Church Yth Grp; FCA; French Clb; Key Clb; Band; Tennis; Hon Roll; NHS; High Hon Roll; Drug Free Yth; Stu Hlpng Stu; Metrohnr Bnd.

RAPSON, BRIAN M; Del City HS; Oklahoma City, OK; (4); 23/495; Cmnty Wkr; Band; Jazz Band; Mrchg Band; Orch; Pep Band; NHS; Ntl Merit Ltr; Val; Class 5a ST Jazz Band Champ 2 Yrs; Del City HS Drum Line 10th At OSAAA; U Of Central OK; Engrng.

RAPSON, MEI LI; Glenpool HS; Glenpool, OK; (3); Art Clb; HOBY; Math Tm; Quiz Bowl; Chorus; Hon Roll; NHS; Natl Art Hnr Soc; Select Womens Chorus; Gftd & Tlntd Pgm; Long Island U; Commercial Art.

RASMUSSEN, D KADE; Okmulgee HS; Okmulgee, OK; (2); Boy Scts; Church Yth Grp; French Clb; Hosp Aide; Var Ftbl; Wt Lftg; High Hon Roll; Ntl Merit Ltr; Medcl.

RASMUSSEN, TIMOTHY DAVID; Jones HS; Jones, OK; (4); 28/51; VP FBLA; VP FHA; Sec Key Clb; Pres SADD; Pres Thesps; Band; VP Stu Cncl; Cit Awd; Hon Roll; NHS; Stu Of Yr Nom; Recipient Of Natl Peer Ed Stu Body Awd N FHA; 2nd Pl Job Interview At STAR Events; U Of Cntrl OK; Hotel Mgmt.

RASOLKHANI, KAYVAN K; West Middle HS; Norman, OK; (1); Boy Scts; Debate Tm; 4-H; FBLA; Office Aide; Service Clb; Spanish Clb; Hon Roll; Prfct Atten Awd; Spanish NHS; Yale; Doctor.

RASOR, MERIDETH; Cascia Hall Prep School; Tulsa, OK; (1); Quiz Bowl; Spanish Clb; Chorus; Var Chrldng; JV Vllybl; Hon Roll; Young Life; MIT; Gen Surgeon.

RASPOTNIK, PENNY; Wilburton Sr HS; Hartshorne, OK; (4); 1/83; Pres FBLA; HOBY; Natl FFA Org; Capt Quiz Bowl; Speech Tm; School Play; Sec Sr Cls; NHS; Pres Acad Fit Awd; Val; 1st Pl Gen Bus OK Trnmnt Chmpns Schlstc Cont; USA Outstndng Envrmntl Sci Prjct, Estrn OK Reg Sci Fr; Estrn OK ST Coll; Ag Ec.

RATERMAN, NICKOLAS S; Union Intermediate HS; Broken Arrow, OK; (2); Debate Tm; Letterman Clb; NFL; Speech Tm; Bsktbl; Ftbl; High Hon Roll; NHS; Law.

RATHBUN, JASON E; Rush Springs HS; Rush Springs, OK; (3); Church Yth Grp; Cmnty Wkr; 4-H; Church Choir; Rptr Nwsp; Var L Bsbl; Stat Bsktbl; Var L Ftbl; 4-H Awd; Hon Roll; OK ST Univ; Eng.

RATHBURN, RACHEL; Claremore Sr HS; Claremore, OK; (4); 21/231; Natl Beta Clb; VP Spanish Clb; Yrbk; VP Frsh Cls; Crs Cntry; Powder Puff Ftbl; Trk; High Hon Roll; VP NHS; Pres Acad Fit Awd; OK St Univ.

RATLIFF, REBECCA N; Ft Cobb-Broxton HS; Fort Cobb, OK; (4); 8/36; Church Yth Grp; Pres Sec FHA; Pres Spanish Clb; Speech Tm; Chorus; Church Choir; Nwsp; Phtg Yrbk; Sec Treas Soph Cls; VP Jr Cls; Piano; HS Whos Who Wittiest; Sr & Jr Cls Favorite; Southwestern OK ST Univ; Ed.

RATLIFF, ROSLYN; Chickasha Jr HS; Chickasha, OK; (1); Church Yth Grp; Science Clb; Spanish Clb; Church Choir; JV Bsktbl; JV Sftbl; JV Tennis; High Hon Roll; Hon Roll; NHS; OK U; Advrtsng.

RATLIFF, SHANAE D; Mc Alester HS; Mcalester, OK; (4); 8/209; Church Yth Grp; Cmnty Wkr; FCA; GAA; Math Clb; Office Aide; Pep Clb; Science Clb; Spanish Clb; Church Choir; OK Natl Indian Hnr Soc; OUPRES Ldrshp Class Scholar; U Of OK; Pharmacy.

RATLIFF, TANA; Norman Sr HS; Norman, OK; (3); Church Yth Grp; French Clb; FBLA; Chorus; Ofcr Stu Cncl; Var Chrldng; French Hon Soc; High Hon Roll; NHS; Val; Sprts Med.

RATOWT, SYLVESTER; Ada HS; Ada, OK; (3); Church Yth Grp; Sec Mu Alpha Theta; Quiz Bowl; Scholastic Bowl; Science Clb; Var Trk; High Hon Roll; NHS; Spanish NHS; 1st Pl Schlstc Mts Physcs, Gentcs, Alg II; Physcs.

RAUH, BARBARA; Okeene Jr Sr HS; Okeene, OK; (2); 5/35; Church Yth Grp; FCA; Natl FFA Org; Treas FBLA; Rep Soph Cls; Var Bsktbl; Var Sftbl; High Hon Roll; NHS; 4-H; Msnc Stdnt Of Today; OSU; PT.

RAUH, JUSTIN; Canton HS; Canton, OK; (3); 1/25; FCA; HOBY; Model UN; Pres Frsh Cls; Sec Jr Cls; Ofcr Stu Cncl; Var Bsktbl; Var Ftbl; High Hon Roll; OSU; Med.

RAUH, MANDI L; Lomega HS; Hitchcock, OK; (1); FCA; 4-H; GAA; Varsity Clb; VP Frsh Cls; Var Bsktbl; High Hon Roll; Hon Roll; Jr NHS; OK ST Univ; Pediatrician.

RAULSTON, BECKY A; Mangum Sr HS; Mangum, OK; (2); Church Yth Grp; FHA; Band; Chorus; Flag Corp; Jazz Band; Mrchg Band; Pep Band; Hon Roll; Jr NHS; Vocal Music; Nrsng.

RAUPE, BRANDON M; Kingfisher HS; Okarche, OK; (3); 10/95; Am Leg Boys St; Church Yth Grp; Cmnty Wkr; 4-H; Letterman Clb; Varsity Clb; Ofcr Bsbl; Bsktbl; Wt Lftg; Cit Awd; Wgt Lftng; Redlands JC; PT/SPRTS Trnr.

RAWDON, JOSEPH C; Shattuck Jr Sr HS; Shattuck, OK; (2); 3/25; HOBY; Letterman Clb; Scholastic Bowl; Band; School Play; NHS; Sec Church Yth Grp; Chorus; Jazz Band; Orch; John Philip Sousa Band Awd; Pediatrician.

RAWDON, LORI B; Shattuck Jr Sr HS; Shattuck, OK; (3); 5/35; Am Leg Aux Girls St; Church Yth Grp; Cmnty Wkr; FCA; GAA; Letterman Clb; Pep Clb; Quiz Bowl; Scholastic Bowl; Teachers Aide; Comm Musical; OK ST Univ; Poly Sci.

RAWLINGS, ANGELA M; Henryetta Sr HS; Henryetta, OK; (2); Church Yth Grp; FCA; FHA; Chorus; School Musical; School Play; Var Chrldng; Hon Roll; U Of OK; Psych.

RAY, AMANDA; Braman Schl; Braman, OK; (2); 1/14; Red Cross Aide; Speech Tm; Band; Color Guard; Jazz Band; School Musical; School Play; Stat Bsktbl; Trk; Hon Roll; Arts Adventure Camp; NOC & NCDA Hnr Bands; OK ST U; Music Ed.

RAY, ANDREA; Claremore Sr HS; Claremore, OK; (2); Spanish Clb; Trk; High Hon Roll.

RAY, CHRIS; Dale Sr HS; Mc Loud, OK; (4); 12/49; Office Aide; SADD; Band; Church Choir; Drm Mjr(t); Jazz Band; Mrchg Band; VP Jr Cls; Pres Stu Cncl; Hon Roll; Life Guides Peer Hlpr; DARE Rl Mdl; Prin Ldrshp Awd; OK Bapt U; Clncl Psych.

RAY, CHRISTY J; Pauls Valley HS; Pauls Valley, OK; (1); OK Univ; Nrse/Mid-Wife.

RAY, JESSIE L; Deer Creek HS; Edmond, OK; (2); Church Yth Grp; GAA; School Play; Stage Crew; Var L Socr; U Of WA; PT.

RAY, JOSEPH; Deer Creek HS; Edmond, OK; (3); 15/100; Science Clb; Stage Crew; Crs Cntry; Ftbl; Wt Lftg; High Hon Roll; NHS; Prfct Atten Awd; Pres Acad Fit Awd; Sal; OK ST U; Dentistry.

RAY, JOSH A; Bartlesville Mid HS; Bartlesville, OK; (1); Church Yth Grp; Hon Roll; Indoor Archery; Natl Field Archery Assn Trnmt Yth Champion; Rodeo Bull Riding.

RAY, KATHY L; Edmond Santa Fe HS; Edmond, OK; (2); FHA; Hosp Aide; Pep Clb; Chorus; School Musical; Stage Crew; Swing Chorus; Variety Show; NHS; Tchng.

RAY, KAYCEE M; B T Washington HS; Tulsa, OK; (2); Cmnty Wkr; French Clb; Spanish Clb; Capt Gym; Cit Awd; NHS; Elem Frgn Lang Ed.

RAY, KRYSTAL; Mc Lish HS; Ada, OK; (3); 2/13; 4-H; Scholastic Bowl; Yrbk; Rep Soph Cls; Rep Jr Cls; Capt Bsktbl; Capt Sftbl; Hon Roll; Ntl Merit Ltr; Prfct Atten Awd; Natl Ldrshp & Svc Awd; Eng Mrt Awd; Stu Mo; Lcl Nwsppr & Msnc Ldg Awd; CPA.

RAY, LINDSEY M; Heritage Hall Schl; Oklahoma City, OK; (2); Church Yth Grp; Cmnty Wkr; FCA; French Clb; Pep Clb; Var Bsktbl; Var Fld Hcky; Var Tennis; Hon Roll.

RAY, LYNDSEY N; South Intermediate HS; Porter, OK; (1); Hosp Aide; Spanish Clb; Band; Intrml Vllybl; Hon Roll; Jr NHS; Pres Acad Fit Awd.

RAY, RYAN D; Henryetta Sr HS; Henryetta, OK; (2); 62/110; Church Yth Grp; Scholastic Bowl; Spanish Clb; Band; Mrchg Band; Hon Roll; Pres Acad Fit Awd.

RAY, WILLIAM; Charles Page HS; Sand Springs, OK; (3); 8/365; Am Leg Boys St; Boy Scts; Church Yth Grp; Cmnty Wkr; FCA; French Clb; Letterman Clb; Band; Mrchg Band; Orch; Engrng.

RAYBURN, AMANDA; Wetumka Jr Sr HS; Wetumka, OK; (4); 1/32; Church Yth Grp; FHA; Key Clb; Natl FFA Org; Science Clb; Spanish Clb; Band; Flag Corp; Sec Frsh Cls; Chrldng.

RAYBURN, MONIQUE D; Putnam City North HS; Oklahoma City, OK; (3); 100/500; Cit Awd; High Hon Roll; Jr NHS; NHS; HOSA; Stu Of Yr Hlth Sci Tech; OK Univ Hlth Sci Summer Acad; Phy Thrpst.

RAYBURN, PAUL D; Southeast HS; Oklahoma City, OK; (2); CAP; ROTC; Band; Drill Tm; Mrchg Band; Hon Roll; Electronics.

RAYBURN, RACHEL E; Wright Christian Acad; Tulsa, OK; (1); Church Yth Grp; Key Clb; Sec Frsh Cls; JV Bsktbl; JV Var Mgr(s); Stat Vllybl; High Hon Roll; Stdnt Athl Awd; Law.

RAYL, BARBARA L; B T Washington HS; Tulsa, OK; (2); Debate Tm; German Clb; NFL; Speech Tm; Rep Frsh Cls; Rep Soph Cls; Var Swmmng; Var Tennis; NHS; Debate 2 Yrs/Semi-Fnlst Harvard Tourn/1st Alt Natl; Pol Sci.

RAYMER, SHANNON P; Edmond Memorial HS; Edmond, OK; (3); 51/371; Church Yth Grp; Cmnty Wkr; Hosp Aide; Spanish Clb; SADD; Sftbl; Swmmng; Tennis; Hon Roll; NHS; Mission Work Vol.

RAYNER, MATTHEW T; Wakita Schl; Nash, OK; (3); Church Yth Grp; FCA; Natl FFA Org; Ed Frsh Cls; Var Capt Bsbl; Var Capt Bsktbl; Var Capt Ftbl; Var Capt Trk; Capt Wt Lftg; Hon Roll; John Wood CC; Agriculture.

RAZOOK, JOHN; Stillwater Sr HS; Stillwater, OK; (4); Am Leg Boys St; Church Yth Grp; FCA; Natl Beta Clb; Acpl Chr; Chorus; Church Choir; School Musical; School Play; Var Ftbl; OK ST.

READE, JESSICA; Oklahoma Sch Of Science & Math; Seminole, OK; (3); Debate Tm; French Clb; Library Aide; Math Clb; NFL; Quiz Bowl; Scholastic Bowl; Band; Jazz Band; Mrchg Band; Bio; Comp Pgmng.

REAGAN, LILLIE A; Cushing HS; Cushing, OK; (4); 53/156; Church Yth Grp; Cmnty Wkr; FHA; Hosp Aide; Red Cross Aide; Spanish Clb; Teachers Aide; Band; Mrchg Band; Nwsp; OK ST Univ; Acctng.

REAL, LEOTA; Panama HS; Shady Point, OK; (3); 8/44; Ofcr Spanish Clb; Yrbk; Bsktbl; High Hon Roll; Hon Roll; JETS Awd; NHS; Ntl Merit Ltr; Northeastern.

REALE, LATONYA L; Sapulpa Sr HS; Sapulpa, OK; (4); 51/273; Art Clb; Church Yth Grp; French Clb; FHA; Science Clb; SADD; JV Crs Cntry; JV Trk; French Hon Soc; Hon Roll; USAO; Art.

REASNOR, JOSHUA P; Mangum Sr HS; Mangum, OK; (3); Art Clb; Band; Mrchg Band; Pep Band; Jr NHS; NHS; OK Bapt Univ.

REASONOR, JENNIFER; Deer Creek HS; Edmond, OK; (4); 17/75; Art Clb; Church Yth Grp; French Clb; FBLA; Science Clb; SADD; Teachers Aide; Chorus; NHS; OK ST U; Bus.

REAVIS, DUSTIN; Woodward HS; Woodward, OK; (4); 27/153; Am Leg Boys St; Boy Scts; Letterman Clb; Model UN; Scholastic Bowl; Band; Tennis; High Hon Roll; VP NHS; German Clb; VFW Voice Democrcy Awd; Ldrshp High; W Clb; OK ST U; Aeronautics.

REBARCHIK, FRANK E; Christian Heritage Acad; Harrah, OK; (2); Church Yth Grp; FCA; Church Choir; Socr; Hon Roll.

REBER, CASSIE M; Northeast HS; Oklahoma City, OK; (2); Church Yth Grp; Cmnty Wkr; Drama Clb; French Clb; Hosp Aide; Intnl Clb; Office Aide; Pep Clb; ROTC; Speech Tm; Med Dr.

RECORD, SHARLA R; Putnam City West HS; Oklahoma City, OK; (3); Church Yth Grp; Church Choir; Mu Alpha Theta; Dance Club; Span Club; OU; Bus/Cmptrs.

RECTOR, BRYAN D; Capitol Hill HS; Oklahoma City, OK; (4); 35/150; Drama Clb; Library Aide; Chorus; Church Choir; School Musical; Bsktbl; Ftbl; Wt Lftg; Hon Roll; DECA; Prntng Ed; Coll Clb; Intnsty; East Cntrl; Psychlgy.

RECTOR, DARRELL R; Miami Sr HS; Miami, OK; (2); Church Yth Grp; Hon Roll; NHS; Environmental Clb; Bio.

RECTOR, KERRY L; Stringtown HS; Lane, OK; (2); Drama Clb; FHA; GAA; Teachers Aide; Chorus; Sec Soph Cls; Var JV Bsktbl; Hon Roll.

RECTOR, TIFFANY; Hilldale HS; Muskogee, OK; (2); 8/208; Church Yth Grp; Drama Clb; Hosp Aide; Key Clb; Spanish Clb; Rep Soph Cls; Ofcr Stu Cncl; Intrml Bsktbl; High Hon Roll; Hon Roll; Tulsa U; Law.

RED ELK, ASHLEY; Empire Schl; Duncan, OK; (1); Church Yth Grp; FCA; Natl FFA Org; Pep Clb; SADD; JV Bsktbl; Var Sftbl; JV Trk; Hon Roll; Marine Bio.

REDFEARN, ROBBIE; Collinsville HS; Talala, OK; (3); Pres Natl FFA Org; Pres Jr Cls; Ftbl; Wt Lftg; High Hon Roll; NHS; Chem Engrng.

REDFEARN, STEPHANIE R; Jay HS; Jay, OK; (1); Chrldng; NSU; Archlgy.

REDING, LINDSAY R; Wilburton Sr HS; Wilburton, OK; (3); Church Yth Grp; Cmnty Wkr; Computer Clb; FCA; FBLA; FHA; GAA; Letterman Clb; Office Aide; Pep Clb; Stu Cncl Pres; Okmulgee Tech; Legal Asst.

REDMON, ABBY R; Edmond Santa Fe HS; Edmond, OK; (3); 168/500; Church Yth Grp; Debate Tm; Drama Clb; HOBY; Science Clb; Chorus; School Musical; School Play; Stage Crew; Swing Chorus; Baylor; Psych; Choir Tchr.

REDNOUR, AMANDA; Valmeyer HS; Columbia, IL; (3); Church Yth Grp; FHA; FTA; Pep Clb; Quiz Bowl; Stage Crew; Var Capt Chrldng; Hon Roll; TREND; FHA Subdist Ofcr; Stu Cncl Rep FNA & Pep Clb; Mc Kendree; Tchr.

REDWAY, JAMIE; Grandfield Jr Sr HS; Grandfield, OK; (1); 2/25; Church Yth Grp; FCA; 4-H; Natl FFA Org; Pep Clb; Quiz Bowl; VP Frsh Cls; Cit Awd; Hon Roll; Kiwanis Awd; OK Jr Brahman Breedrs Assn; OK ST U; Nursng.

REDWINE, KATIE; Kingfisher HS; Kingfisher, OK; (1); Church Yth Grp; GAA; Chorus; Bsktbl; Hon Roll; Pres Acad Fit Awd; Tri-St Music Fest Super Ratng Piano; Frosh Clss Qn; Phys Thrpy.

REECE, JAMIE; Yale Jr Sr HS; Yale, OK; (4); 10/35; JV Var Vllybl; Church Yth Grp; FCA; Rptr FHA; HOBY; Natl Beta Clb; Teachers Aide; Rep Stu Cncl; JV Bsktbl; Cit Awd; OK ST U.

REECE, JAMIE; Hilldale HS; Muskogee, OK; (4); 9/110; Art Clb; Church Yth Grp; Cmnty Wkr; Drama Clb; Key Clb; Mu Alpha Theta; Spanish Clb; Ed Yrbk; High Hon Roll; Hon Roll; Connors ST Coll; Nrsng.

REED, AMBER M; Turner Schl; Burneyville, OK; (3); 6/17; 4-H; FHA; Natl Beta Clb; Office Aide; Spanish Clb; Rptr Yrbk; Bsktbl; Sftbl; Hon Roll; 2nd Pl ECU Schltc Meet In Bus Math.

REED, JESSICA; Roff HS; Roff, OK; (1); Math Clb; Natl Beta Clb; Quiz Bowl; Scholastic Bowl; Chorus; VP Frsh Cls; Var Chrldng; High Hon Roll; Val; Intrschlstc Mdls; OK U; Med.

REED, JOANNE M; Charles Page HS; Sand Springs, OK; (3); Church Yth Grp; Treas Key Clb; Office Aide; Spanish Clb; Band; Mrchg Band; Hon Roll; NHS; Pres Acad Fit Awd; Young Life; OK Univ; Wildlife Mngmt.

REED, JORDAN; Claremore Sr HS; Claremore, OK; (2); French Clb; Quiz Bowl; Scholastic Bowl; Pres Frsh Cls; Pres Soph Cls; JV Bsbl; Var Ftbl; Hon Roll; Prfct Atten Awd.

REED, JOSH D; Skiatook HS; Sperry, OK; (2); Boy Scts; Church Yth Grp; Sec 4-H; SADD; JV Var Ftbl; JV Var Wt Lftg; Var JV Wrstlng; 4-H Awd; Hon Roll; Prfct Atten Awd; Sea Explr Commdrs Awd Advnc Slrs; NRA Smlbr Rfl Pro Marksman Jr Olmpc Prgm; Cdt Mrn Mltry Acad; Bio Chemst.

REED, KEISHA; Roff HS; Roff, OK; (4); 3/21; Library Aide; Natl Beta Clb; Spanish Clb; Chorus; Yrbk; VP Jr Cls; Capt Chrldng; High Hon Roll; Cmptr Sci.

REED, KENNETH G; Edmond North HS; Edmond, OK; (3); Hist Drama Clb; NFL; School Musical; School Play; Stage Crew; Variety Show; Drma Stdnt Of Yr; Mst Creative In Drama Clss; Bst Cameo Awd; U Of Cntrl OK; Acting/Theater.

REED, LACY; Comanche HS; Comanche, OK; (1); 1/99; Church Yth Grp; Cmnty Wkr; Quiz Bowl; SADD; Band; Chorus; Church Choir; Drm Mjr(t); Mrchg Band; NHS; Band Cncl; Med.

REED, MARISA; Miami Sr HS; Miami, OK; (3); 50/250; Church Yth Grp; FCA; Teachers Aide; Var Capt Chrldng; Gym; Sftbl; Hon Roll; Jr NHS; NHS; Ntl Merit Ltr; NE A&M Univ; RN.

REED, MELANIE E; Sallisaw HS; Sallisaw, OK; (3); Art Clb; Church Yth Grp; Cmnty Wkr; Rep Stu Cncl; Chrldng; Score Keeper; Cit Awd; Hon Roll; NHS; HSH/HOSP Comm Svc Spk Ot Agnst Smoking; HS Sci Fair 2nd Pl/On To Reg On Sm/King; Comm Svc Nrsg Hm.

REED, MELISSA K; Southeast HS; Oklahoma City, OK; (1); Church Yth Grp; Computer Clb; FBLA; ROTC; Spanish Clb; Drill Tm; Nwsp; Yrbk; Hon Roll; NHS; Grnd Ofcr Intl Ordr Rnbw Grls OK.

REED, MELISSA K; South Intermediate HS; Broken Arrow, OK; (2); French Clb; Teachers Aide; U Of Denver; Psych.

REED, MIKKI; Central HS; Tulsa, OK; (2); Church Yth Grp; Cmnty Wkr; Office Aide; Church Choir; Chrldng; High Hon Roll; Hon Roll; NHS; Prfct Atten Awd; Band; Mck Trls; Tlsa Yth Ct; U Of TN; Obstrcs.

REED, RACHEL R; Nathan Hale HS; Tulsa, OK; (3); Cmnty Wkr; Scholastic Bowl; Spanish Clb; Teachers Aide; Cit Awd; Hon Roll; NHS; Salvtn Army Boys & Girls Clb Vol; Outstdng Acctng Stu Awd; Outstdng Acad Achvmt Awd From Tulsa World; Soc Svcs.

REED, REBECCA L; Liberty HS; Mounds, OK; (3); 3/45; Cmnty Wkr; FHA; Hosp Aide; Capt Chrldng; Nwsp; Phtg Yrbk; Score Keeper; Hon Roll; NHS; Var Acad Team; Pharmacy.

REED, ROBERT S; Owasso Sr HS; Owasso, OK; (2); Church Yth Grp; FCA; Spanish Clb; Var Bsbl; Hon Roll; Dr.

REED, SAMANTHA; Woodward HS; Woodward, OK; (4); 12/152; Am Leg Aux Girls St; Church Yth Grp; Cmnty Wkr; FCA; Sec German Clb; GAA; HOBY; Key Clb; Pep Clb; Service Clb; Page US Rep; Mock Trial; Miss Congnlty Miss Woodward Pgnt 95-96; Chrstn Ldrshp Awd Chrch Camp; OK Chrstn U; Erly Chldhd Dev.

REED, SHELLY D; Enid Sr HS; Enid, OK; (2); #23 in class; Orch; Var Crs Cntry; Var Trk; High Hon Roll; Jr NHS; NHS; Pres Acad Fit Awd; Wrtng/Ptry 8 Natl Awds; 19 Poems Pub.

REED, SHERRY L; Will Rogers HS; Tulsa, OK; (3); English Clb; Sec German Clb; ROTC; Color Guard; Var Tennis; Hon Roll; CODE Hnrs Clss; CU.

REED, SUSIE R; Deer Creek HS; Edmond, OK; (2); 5/105; Cmnty Wkr; 4-H; Science Clb; Spanish Clb; Teachers Aide; Band; Mrchg Band; Pep Band; 4-H Awd; High Hon Roll; Horseback Riding/Showing; Vet Med/Zlgy.

REED, SYLINA M; Panola HS; Red Oak, OK; (4); 9/16; Church Yth Grp; FHA; German Clb; Band; Chorus; Yrbk; Ofcr Stu Cncl; Hon Roll; FFA Sweetheart 96-97; EOSC; Baking; Culinary Arts.

REEDY, AMANDA; Union Sr HS; Tulsa, OK; (4); Church Yth Grp; Key Clb; Library Aide; Office Aide; Teachers Aide; Band; Chorus; Mrchg Band; Pep Band; School Musical; Renaissance; Tri-M; OK ST Univ; Engl.

REEDY, LAURA B; Union Intermediate HS; Tulsa, OK; (1); Spanish Clb; Orch; Jr NHS; NHS; Prfct Atten Awd; All Dist Orchestra; Explorer Post.

REEDY, WALTER A; Union Sr HS; Tulsa, OK; (3); 14/741; Boy Scts; German Clb; High Hon Roll; NHS; Acad Tm; Eagle Sct; Yng Repblcns; Explorers; Acturial Sci.

REES, LAURA D; Elgin HS; Elgin, OK; (2); 5/85; Cmnty Wkr; FHA; Scholastic Bowl; Teachers Aide; Chorus; Cit Awd; High Hon Roll; Hon Roll; NHS; Pres Acad Fit Awd; Spec Achvmnt Awds Biol/Zoology/Algebra/Span/Engl/His; Vet.

REESE, NAOMI; Eufaula Sr HS; Eufaula, OK; (3); Chorus; Hon Roll; NHS; Prfct Atten Awd; OK U; Med.

REESE, NATHAN B; Mannford HS; Mannford, OK; (2); Trk; Hon Roll; Stu Of Month; Athl & Engl Awds; OSU; Phys Thrpy.

REESE, NATHAN D; Blackwell HS; Nardin, OK; (2); 26/123; Boy Scts; Chess Clb; Church Yth Grp; FCA; Letterman Clb; Pep Clb; Spanish Clb; Nwsp; Rep Soph Cls; Rep Stu Cncl; OK ST Ag & Sci Seminar; Northern OK Coll Acad Cmptn; Concoco Stu Day; Spcl Investigator.

REESE, RENEE; Garber Sr HS; Lamont, OK; (3); Church Yth Grp; FCA; Sec Treas FHA; GAA; Office Aide; Pep Clb; Quiz Bowl; Scholastic Bowl; Teachers Aide; Chorus; OK ST U.

REESE, RYAN; Duncan HS; Duncan, OK; (4); 1/210; Am Leg Boys St; Boy Scts; Debate Tm; Key Clb; Quiz Bowl; SADD; Band; Ed Lit Mag; Var L Crs Cntry; NHS; Eagle Sct, Patroll Ldr; Ldrshp Pgm; Studied Scanning Tunneling Microscopy OU Smmr Schlrs Pgm; W Point Military Acad; Chem Eng.

REEVES, AARON C; Stillwater Sr HS; Stillwater, OK; (3); Church Yth Grp; Cmnty Wkr; FCA; Natl Beta Clb; Office Aide; Spanish Clb; Teachers Aide; Var Bsbl; Hon Roll; OK ST Univ; Bus.

REEVES, AMANDA; Pond Creek-Hunter Schl; Pond Creek, OK; (2); Church Yth Grp; FCA; 4-H; Yrbk; Rep Soph Cls; Var Chrldng; Var Crs Cntry; Var Sftbl; Hon Roll; NHS; Poem Pub/Yng Amer; Drama/Dance/Music/Wrtng/Frgn Clturs/Ftnss/Trvlng; Rec Sup Rtng NWOSU Curr Cntst; OK Univ; Ntrtnl Psych; Jrnlsm.

REEVES, BRIAN D; Collinsville HS; Collinsville, OK; (2); Var JV Ftbl; Var JV Trk; Var JV Wrstlng; Cit Awd; High Hon Roll; Jr NHS; NHS; Ntl Merit Ltr; Pres Acad Fit Awd; Geometry Hnrs; Scuba Diving Clb; Congrssnl Yth Ldrshp Cncl Candidate; Marine Biolgst.

REEVES, ERICA L; Roland Sr HS; Roland, OK; (3); Rptr Church Yth Grp; Rptr FHA; Teachers Aide; Pres Chorus; Church Choir; Rptr Nwsp; Hon Roll; Most Outstdng Chrl Stdnt; Vocal Solo Cntst Supr Rtng All Dist; Soloist Prfmr.

REEVES, J M; Glencoe Public Schl; Glencoe, OK; (2); 2/26; Church Yth Grp; FCA; French Clb; Rep Stu Cncl; Var Bsbl; Var Bsktbl; High Hon Roll; NHS; Prfct Atten Awd; OK ST U.

REEVES, JENNIFER J; Little Axe Sr HS; Newalla, OK; (4); 7/90; Chorus; Ed Yrbk; VP Sr Cls; Ofcr Stu Cncl; Hon Roll; Jr NHS; NHS; Intl Order Of Jobs Daughtrs; Orderof Eastern Star; Grad With Hnrs Diplma; U Of MT; Publcrltns.

REEVES, KRISTA; Maysville Jr Sr HS; Maysville, OK; (2); 1/34; FHA; HOBY; Key Clb; Yrbk; Ofcr Soph Cls; Mgr(s); High Hon Roll; Kiwanis Awd; Prfct Atten Awd.

REEVES, MARIE; Dale Sr HS; Shawnee, OK; (1); 5/49; Cmnty Wkr; Treas FHA; Band; Mrchg Band; Hon Roll; OBIMR Theraptc Hrsbck Riding Vol; St Gregory's Coll; Bus.

REEVES, ROBIN S; Bartlesville Mid HS; Bartlesville, OK; (2); German Clb; Explorer Post Medieval His; Acad Bowl; Ind Games Ger 5th Pl In ST Of OK.

REEVES, WHITNEY; Chisholm Sr HS; Carrier, OK; (4); 14/68; Church Yth Grp; Cmnty Wkr; FCA; FHA; Scholastic Bowl; Speech Tm; Band; Chorus; Jazz Band; Mrchg Band; Hnrs Band; NE ST Univ; Speech Pathology.

REGIER, AMANDA; Oklahoma Bible Acad; Enid, OK; (2); Church Yth Grp; Scholastic Bowl; Band; Pep Band; Yrbk; Mgr(s); JV Vllybl; High Hon Roll; Hon Roll; OK Hstrcl Cty Schlrshp Wnr; 6th Grd Pres Awd; Masonic Awd; Bus/Eng.

REGIER, JENNIFER J; Turpin Schl; Turpin, OK; (3); 3/27; Church Yth Grp; FCA; Band; Chorus; Drm Mjr(t); Var Bsktbl; Var Sftbl; Hon Roll; NHS; FHA; Accmplshd Pianist.

REGNIER, JOSHUA L; Frontier Public Schl; Marland, OK; (3); Church Yth Grp; Capt Frsh Cls; Capt Soph Cls; Ofcr Stu Cncl; Var Bsbl; Var Bsktbl; Hon Roll; Pres Acad Fit Awd; TSA.

REGNIER, SHELLY; Balko Public Schl; Balko, OK; (2); 1/19; Church Yth Grp; Drama Clb; Natl FFA Org; Pep Clb; Scholastic Bowl; Band; Mrchg Band; Pep Band; School Play; Pres Soph Cls.

REICH, BRIAN G; Bartlesville Sr HS; Bartlesville, OK; (3); 80/441; Boy Scts; Teachers Aide; Band; Mrchg Band; Pep Band; Hon Roll; Jr NHS; NHS; Optmtry.

REICH, JAMI; Ft Towson HS; Fort Towson, OK; (2); Church Yth Grp; FCA; FHA; Church Choir; Yrbk; Rep Stu Cncl; Stat Bsktbl; Score Keeper; High Hon Roll; NHS; TSA Sec, Prepared Speech 1st Pl Level 2, 1st Pl Level 2 Chptr Team Cmptn; FCA Skit Team; East Central U Ada OK.

REICH, MELODIE L; Valliant HS; Millerton, OK; (2); 21/78; Church Yth Grp; Cmnty Wkr; French Clb; FHA; Chorus; Color Guard; Hon Roll; Upwrd Bnd Math & Sci; Med.

REICHARDT, JULIE; Edmond Memorial HS; Edmond, OK; (2); Letterman Clb; Pep Clb; Spanish Clb; Varsity Clb; Var JV Chrldng; High Hon Roll; Hon Roll; NHS; Pres Acad Fit Awd; All Star Pom Chrs/More Trng Ctr; Bost Pom Dancer ASC Regnls 95; JV & Fresh Chr Capt; Psych.

REICHER, LENA M; Northeast HS; Oklahoma City, OK; (2); Dance Clb; Drama Clb; FHA; Library Aide; Office Aide; Chorus; School Play; Nwsp; Ofcr Soph Cls; Pom Pon.

REICHERT, STACIE; Roland Sr HS; Roland, OK; (3); 8/110; Sec Church Yth Grp; Cmnty Wkr; FCA; Spanish Clb; Band; Nwsp; Yrbk; Chrldng; Hon Roll; Prfct Atten Awd; Hnrs Clb; OK All Star Band 95; Bus.

REICHMAN, CLARINA E; Preston Schl; Okmulgee, OK; (1); Quiz Bowl; Scholastic Bowl; High Hon Roll; NHS; Tnmt Of Champs For Home Ec; Gentc Eng.

REICHMAN, NATHANAEL W; Clayton Jr Sr HS; Tulsa, OK; (1); 1/46; Boy Scts; Church Yth Grp; 4-H; Natl FFA Org; Quiz Bowl; Band; Church Choir; Var Bsktbl; Gov Hon Prg Awd; Eagle Scout; U Of Ar; Lawyer.

REICHMAN, RENEE; Stillwater Sr HS; Stillwater, OK; (3); Church Yth Grp; French Clb; FBLA; Hosp Aide; Key Clb; Mu Alpha Theta; Pep Clb; Var Chrldng; Var Tennis; JV Trk; OK U.

REID, CODY; Frederick HS; Frederick, OK; (1); Church Yth Grp; JV Bsbl; JV Bsktbl; JV Ftbl; High Hon Roll; Hon Roll; NHS.

REID, JAIMEE L; Bishop Kelley HS; Tulsa, OK; (1); Church Yth Grp; Cmnty Wkr; Vllybl; Hon Roll.

REID, JEOY R; Cleveland Sr HS; Cleveland, OK; (4); Church Yth Grp; FHA; SADD; Bsktbl; Ftbl; Socr; Trk; Wt Lftg; Hon Roll; All-Dist Soccer; FHA VP; NSU; Psych.

REID, LARRY L; Midwest City HS; Midwest City, OK; (2); Bsktbl; Georgetown; Engrng.

REID, SHARON; Bartlesville Mid HS; Bartlesville, OK; (2); Church Yth Grp; Cmnty Wkr; Acpl Chr; Church Choir; Hon Roll; Brigham Young U.

REID, TRICIA B; Cushing HS; Cushing, OK; (4); 1/156; FHA; Pres JA; Math Clb; Pres Science Clb; Drill Tm; Sec Stu Cncl; High Hon Roll; NHS; Val; OK ST U; Microbio.

REIER, KIMBERLY K; Choctaw HS; Choctaw, OK; (3); Office Aide; Nwsp; Yrbk; Rep Frsh Cls; Ofcr Stu Cncl; Stat Bsbl; Stat Bsktbl; Stat Ftbl; Mgr(s); Score Keeper; Rose ST U; Educ.

REIFSTECK, LYNDEE F; Muskogee HS; Muskogee, OK; (3); Church Yth Grp; Computer Clb; Debate Tm; French Clb; Drill Tm; Flag Corp; Yrbk; Ofcr Soph Cls; Ofcr Jr Cls; Ofcr Sr Cls; Natl Yth Ldrshp Forum On Law 96; OK ST Univ.

REIGH, EMILY V; Chickosha HS; Chickasha, OK; (3); 2/200; Am Leg Aux Girls St; Church Yth Grp; FCA; 4-H; French Clb; VP Girl Scts; Quiz Bowl; Scholastic Bowl; Band; Chorus; Natl Jr Acad Sci Delg; Bausch & Lomb Sci Awd; 1st Pl Natl Dance Cmptn Fnls W/Schl Dance Art Sr Co; Chem.

REIGH, MARSHALL C; Yale Jr Sr HS; Yale, OK; (3); Art Clb; Church Yth Grp; FHA; Natl FFA Org; JV Bsktbl; Hon Roll.

REIM, DANIEL; Thomas Jr Sr HS; Thomas, OK; (2); Boy Scts; Natl FFA Org; Band; Mrchg Band; Ftbl; Wt Lftg; High Hon Roll; Mtrcycle Rdng; Hntng; Engr.

REIM, NATHAN; Thomas Jr Sr HS; Thomas, OK; (2); Boy Scts; Natl FFA Org; Band; Ftbl; Wt Lftg; High Hon Roll; Engrng.

REIMAN, MARTA; Central HS; Tulsa, OK; (4); Church Yth Grp; Drama Clb; Thesps; Church Choir; School Play; Pres Frsh Cls; Var Chrldng; High Hon Roll; Dance; Mss Cntrl Hmcmng Attndnt.

REIMER, AMY; Holdenville HS; Holdenville, OK; (3); 15/80; Natl Beta Clb; Quiz Bowl; Scholastic Bowl; School Play; Ed Yrbk; Hon Roll; Jr NHS; NHS; Pres Acad Fit Awd; Chorus; Tech Stu Assn Pres & Treas.

REIMER, PORSCHE; Ponca City Sr HS; Ponca City, OK; (4); Debate Tm; Pres DECA; Drama Clb; Sec NFL; Quiz Bowl; Speech Tm; School Play; Hon Roll; Child Psych.

REINART, ROBIN; Clinton HS; Clinton, OK; (2); 1/138; FCA; FBLA; FHA; Spanish Clb; Chorus; Treas Soph Cls; Ofcr Stu Cncl; NHS; Jazz & Show Choir; OU; Med.

REINERT, HEATHER R; Jenks HS; Tulsa, OK; (4); 106/475; DECA; Teachers Aide; Chorus; Hon Roll; DECA 3rd Pl At St Cmptn In Food Mrktg Rsrch; TCC; Bus.

REININGER, DARYL; Ada HS; Ada, OK; (3); Church Yth Grp; FCA; Spanish Clb; Ftbl; Trk; Fac Hnr Roll; ST Ftbl ST Champn 3 Times; OK Bapt Univ; Uth Mnstr.

REININGER, LAURA J; Fairview HS; Chester, OK; (2); Church Yth Grp; Cmnty Wkr; Dance Clb; FCA; French Clb; Intrml Ofcr FHA; Letterman Clb; Pep Clb; Varsity Clb; 6th Plc UCA Chrldng Natls; OSU; Optmtrst.

REINSCHMIEDT, BRYAN; Hennessey HS; Hennessey, OK; (2); 3/68; VP Hist Natl FFA Org; Band; Mrchg Band; VP Frsh Cls; Treas Stu Cncl; L Crs Cntry; High Hon Roll; NHS.

REIST, LAURA; Bartlesville Mid HS; Bartlesville, OK; (2); 22/481; Church Yth Grp; FBLA; Spanish Clb; Chorus; Church Choir; High Hon Roll; Hon Roll; NHS; Pt/Nrsng.

REIST, MIRANDA S; Bartlesville Sr HS; Bartlesville, OK; (4); 41/429; Church Yth Grp; Chorus; Church Choir; Capt Chrldng; High Hon Roll; NHS; Spanish NHS; U Of OK.

REMER, JOSHUA A; Okmulgee HS; Okmulgee, OK; (1); Church Yth Grp; Red Cross Aide; Scholastic Bowl; Mrchg Band; Pep Band; Band; Ofcr Bsbl; Wt Lftg; Hon Roll; Pres Acad Fit Awd; Acad Team; Red Cross Blood Drive Comm; OU; Med.

REMINGTON, CHRISTY L; B T Washington HS; Tulsa, OK; (2); Church Yth Grp; Cmnty Wkr; Computer Clb; Drama Clb; Library Aide; Red Cross Aide; Spanish Clb; Var JV Socr; Hon Roll; NHS; BOTM 204 Sec.

REMPE, JENNIFER E; West Middle HS; Norman, OK; (1); Spanish Clb; Hon Roll.

REMUS, ANNMARIE L; Union Sr HS; Broken Arrow, OK; (3); #51 in class; Church Yth Grp; German Clb; Hosp Aide; School Play; Stage Crew; JV Var Vllybl; Hon Roll; NHS; Renaisnnce; Alpha Theta; Phys Thrpy.

REMUS, KATIE J; Union Intermediate HS; Broken Arrow, OK; (2); Church Yth Grp; FCA; Spanish Clb; Church Choir; Nwsp; Yrbk; Vllybl; Hon Roll; Jr NHS; NHS; Eng Awd; Sci Awd; Geo Awd; Union Stdnts For Christ; ROTUS; Northern ST Univ; Chrstn Psych.

REMY, SEAN E; Southeast HS; Oklahoma City, OK; (2); FCA; Letterman Clb; Ofcr Bsbl; Bsktbl; Ftbl; Trk; Wt Lftg; Wrstlng; Hon Roll; City Wd Sci Fair; Schl Wide Hstry Fair; Spec Olympcs Vol; Nrs/Ansthlgy.

RENEGAR, ANDY; Shawnee Sr HS; Shawnee, OK; (3); 32/280; Church Yth Grp; FCA; JA; Letterman Clb; Library Aide; Office Aide; Quiz Bowl; Spanish Clb; Var L Ftbl; Wt Lftg; OK U; Engrng.

RENES, RACHEL; Christian Heritage Acad; Edmond, OK; (3); 1/50; Church Yth Grp; Chorus; Ed Nwsp; Stat Bsktbl; High Hon Roll; Hon Roll; Ntl Merit Ltr; FEW; Piano Tchr; U Of OK; Nrsng.

RENFRO, ANDY; Thackerville HS; Thackerville, OK; (4); 4-H; Natl FFA Org; VICA; Var Capt Bsktbl; Var Capt Ftbl; 4-H Awd; Hon Roll; Prfct Atten Awd; Hussle Awd Bsktbl 2 Yrs; OSU; Const.

RENFRO, CORINNE; Mannford HS; Mannford, OK; (3); 2/120; Drama Clb; HOBY; Quiz Bowl; Speech Tm; SADD; Sal; Church Yth Grp; Cmnty Wkr; FCA; Alg I, Engl I Adv, Amer Hstry, Psych, Lstr Rhds Hstry Awds; St Altrnt Mnlg; Drama Clb Treas; OK U; Medcl Fld.

RENFRO, TRISHA; Central HS; Tulsa, OK; (1); Church Yth Grp; Cmnty Wkr; Teachers Aide; Jazz Band; Mrchg Band; Orch; Rep Frsh Cls; EMT.

RENFROE, CYNTHIA A; Union Sr HS; Tulsa, OK; (3); 231/673; French Clb; GAA; Hosp Aide; Orch; Intrml Bsktbl; Var Sftbl; NHS; Renaissance Clb; Amature Sftbl Assoc; Meteorology Internship KJRH TV-2 Tulsa; Meteorology.

RENFROW, ELIZABETH; Stigler HS; Stigler, OK; (4); 1/78; Am Leg Aux Girls St; Church Yth Grp; Hosp Aide; HOBY; Pres Natl FFA Org; Speech Tm; Sec Frsh Cls; Rep Soph Cls; Treas Jr Cls; Pres Stu Cncl; Estrn OK ST U; Elem Ed.

RENFROW, GARTH; Stigler HS; Stigler, OK; (4); 1/73; Am Leg Boys St; Church Yth Grp; Rep FCA; Office Aide; Pep Clb; VP Jr Cls; VP Sr Cls; Ofcr Stu Cncl; Var Bsktbl; Var Ftbl; Northwestern ST U; Phy.

RENFROW, KAY; Stigler HS; Stigler, OK; (4); 1/78; Am Leg Aux Girls St; HOBY; Pres Natl FFA Org; Speech Tm; Rep Frsh Cls; Sec Soph Cls; Pres Stu Cncl; Cit Awd; Hon Roll; Hosp Aide.

RENFROW, LAKAYA; Southeast HS; Oklahoma City, OK; (2); VP FCA; Model UN; Chorus; Flag Corp; Ed Nwsp; VP Soph Cls; Sec Stu Cncl; Mgr(s); Pom Pon; Cit Awd; Ldrshp Cls; Arspc Acad 9th Grd, Aviation I10th Grd; Write Short Stories; Dance; Commnctns.

RENFROW, MELANIE L; Dewey HS; Ochelata, OK; (3); 12/95; Church Yth Grp; GAA; Spanish Clb; Band; Jazz Band; Mrchg Band; Hon Roll; NHS; Pres Acad Fit Awd; Drm Mjr(t); Matthew Tyer Awd; U Of AR; Safety; Engrng.

RENFROW, SCOTT; Wetumka Jr Sr HS; Wetumka, OK; (2); 1/46; FCA; German Clb; Natl FFA Org; Band; VP Soph Cls; Bsktbl; Ftbl; Trk; Hon Roll; NHS; FFA Land Jdgn; Page St Sen; Med.

RENIERS, MELANIE A; Putnam City North HS; Oklahoma City, OK; (2); 129/464; FCA; Capt L Bsktbl; JV Sftbl; Hon Roll; AAU B Bl 4th Plc 96; OU; Bus.

RENO, JEREMY L; Jay HS; Jay, OK; (4); 7/95; FCA; Natl FFA Org; Ofcr Stu Cncl; Ofcr Bsbl; Bsktbl; Ftbl; Hon Roll; Jr NHS; NHS; Ag Bus.

RENOLLET, JR G; Stillwater Sr HS; Stillwater, OK; (2); Church Yth Grp; Teachers Aide; High Hon Roll; Pres Acad Fit Awd; Tae Kwon Do.

RENYER, CHRIS O; Duncan HS; Duncan, OK; (1); Church Yth Grp; Ftbl; Trk; Hon Roll; OK Univ; Dermatlgy.

REPASS, JEFF; Southwest Covenant Schl; Oklahoma City, OK; (4); Church Yth Grp; Cmnty Wkr; Ofcr FCA; Office Aide; Church Choir; Yrbk; Rep Jr Cls; Rep Sr Cls; Ofcr Stu Cncl; Bsktbl; U Cntrl OK.

REPASS, JULIE; Southwest Covenant Schl; Oklahoma City, OK; (2); Church Yth Grp; Rep FCA; Chorus; Church Choir; Rep Stu Cncl; Var Capt Chrldng; High Hon Roll; School Musical; Variety Show; Tennis; Msn Trp Guatemala; OK Bapt U; Music.

REPLOGLE, JENNIFER J; Owasso Sr HS; Owasso, OK; (3); Church Yth Grp; FCA; FTA; Office Aide; Science Clb; Varsity Clb; Rep Stu Cncl; Var Bsktbl; Var Trk; Hon Roll.

REPP, JAMIE; Ft Cobb-Broxton HS; Fort Cobb, OK; (2); 1/35; VP Soph Cls; Bsktbl; Sftbl; High Hon Roll; NHS; Prfct Atten Awd; Pres Acad Fit Awd; Horse Riding; Singing.

RESENOIZ, JOSE P; Southeast HS; Oklahoma City, OK; (2); Church Yth Grp; FCA; FBLA; Spanish Clb; Chorus; Socr; NHS; Soccer Clb.

RETTIG, CHRIS; Bishop Mcguinness HS; Oklahoma City, OK; (4); 1/153; Am Leg Boys St; FCA; Pres German Clb; Ofcr Stu Cncl; Var L Ftbl; Var L Socr; Var L Tennis; VP NHS; Ntl Merit SF; Val; Yale Book Top Stu Awd; Jr HS Bsktbl & Elem Sccr Coach; Med.

REUDY, KATHERINE; Claremore Sr HS; Claremore, OK; (4); 9/241; High Hon Roll; Hon Roll; NHS; Ntl Merit Ltr.

REUST, DEREK K; Tahlequah Jr HS; Tahlequah, OK; (1); Church Yth Grp; Band; Mrchg Band; Pep Band; Var Ftbl; Var Wrstlng; Hon Roll; Jr NHS.

REUTER, A K; El Reno Sr HS; El Reno, OK; (4); 5/175; FCA; Letterman Clb; Quiz Bowl; Scholastic Bowl; Ftbl; Wt Lftg; High Hon Roll; NHS; OK City U; Law Enforcement.

REUTER, F BLAKE; El Reno Sr HS; El Reno, OK; (3); 1/190; Am Leg Boys St; Church Yth Grp; FCA; Scholastic Bowl; Sec Jr Cls; Bsktbl; JV Ftbl; Hon Roll; NHS; Chambr Of Comm Ldrshp Cls; Stu Of The Month; All Amer Schlr; Bio; Pre-Med.

REUTLINGER, DAWN D; Owasso Sr HS; Owasso, OK; (3); 78/323; Church Yth Grp; FCA; Girl Scts; Band; Color Guard; Flag Corp; Mrchg Band; High Hon Roll; Hon Roll; Prfct Atten Awd; Elem Tchr.

REVIS, TAMARA N; Sapulpa Sr HS; Sapulpa, OK; (4); Church Yth Grp; Math Clb; Science Clb; Band; Jazz Band; Trk; Hon Roll; Jr NHS; NHS; Pres Acad Fit Awd.

REXROAT, AMBER D; Ft Cobb-Broxton HS; Fort Cobb, OK; (3); Cmnty Wkr; GAA; Pep Clb; Spanish Clb; VICA; Chorus; Var L Bsktbl; Var Crs Cntry; Var L Sftbl; Hon Roll; Redland's CC; Law Enforcement.

REXWINKLE, JOSH; Elk City HS; Elk City, OK; (3); 1/120; Boy Scts; Church Yth Grp; Computer Clb; HOBY; Math Clb; Rep Jr Cls; JV Bsktbl; Cit Awd; NHS; Val; Engrng.

REXWINKLE, KENNETH J; South Coffeyville Schl; S Coffeyville, OK; (3); Boy Scts; Church Yth Grp; Cmnty Wkr; FCA; Service Clb; Teachers Aide; Ofcr Bsbl; Bsktbl; Ftbl; Trk; Drury Col; Elec Eng.

REXWINKLE, KIMBERLY; Oklahoma Union Schl; S Coffeyville, OK; (4); FCA; Pres FBLA; FHA; Sec Natl FFA Org; Speech Tm; Teachers Aide; Rptr Nwsp; 4-H Awd; Sec Frsh Cls; Sec Sr Cls; OK ST Univ.

REYES, BRENDA; El Reno Sr HS; El Reno, OK; (4); 27/167; Cmnty Wkr; GAA; Key Clb; Math Clb; Scholastic Bowl; Science Clb; SADD; Teachers Aide; Rep Stu Cncl; Tennis; Narl Bus Hnr Soc; Redlands; Mass Commnctns.

REYNOLDS, BRANDY L; Checotah HS; Checotah, OK; (3); 12/98; Spanish Clb; Sec Treas Frsh Cls; Sec Treas Soph Cls; Hist Stu Cncl; Capt Bsktbl; Trk; NHS; NE St Univ; Acctng.

REYNOLDS, CARRIE; Little Axe Sr HS; Newalla, OK; (2); FHA; Hosp Aide; Var Trk; Cit Awd; Hon Roll; Jr NHS; NHS; U OK; Sprts Med.

REYNOLDS, CRAIG; Oklahoma Union Schl; Coffeyville, KS; (4); 1/50; FCA; VP Spanish Clb; Ed Nwsp; Var Capt Ftbl; Var L Trk; Var Capt Wrstlng; High Hon Roll; Treas NHS; St Schlr; Val; NROTC Schlsp; U Of Notre Dame; Comp Sci.

REYNOLDS, ELIZABETH; Christian Heritage Acad; Oklahoma City, OK; (2); Church Yth Grp; FCA; Office Aide; Chorus; Church Choir; Bsktbl; Trk; High Hon Roll; Hon Roll; TX A&M.

REYNOLDS, GLADYS M; Wynnewood HS; Wynnewood, OK; (2); FHA; Office Aide; Teachers Aide; E Cntrl U; Nrsng.

REYNOLDS III, JOHN HAYNES; Muskogee HS; Muskogee, OK; (4); 50/305; VP DECA; Pres JCL; Capt Letterman Clb; VP Frsh Cls; Ofcr Soph Cls; Ofcr Jr Cls; Pres Sr Cls; Ofcr Stu Cncl; L Bsktbl; Var L Ftbl; Math, Sci Eng Hnrs Pgm; Reg Sci Fr Cont 1st Pl; St Sen OK Pg; U Of OK; Bus.

REYNOLDS, JOSEPH D; Stilwell HS; Stilwell, OK; (2); 4-H; French Clb; FBLA; Math Clb; Math Tm; Science Clb; Nwsp; 4-H Awd; Hon Roll; Ntl Merit Schol.

REYNOLDS, KELLIE; Wyandotte Jr Sr HS; Fairland, OK; (4); 8/37; Am Leg Aux Girls St; Church Yth Grp; FCA; FHA; Pres FTA; Red Cross Aide; Rptr Nwsp; Capt Sftbl; Hon Roll; NHS; OK ST U; Elem Ed.

REYNOLDS, KORTNEY K; Nathan Hale HS; Tulsa, OK; (3); Drama Clb; Rptr FBLA; Color Guard; Var Crs Cntry; Var Trk; Vo-Tech Stdnt Of Yr Cmptr Tech; Tulsa Jr Coll; Cmptr Prgrmmr.

REYNOLDS, RENADA; Central HS; Tulsa, OK; (1); Church Yth Grp; Office Aide; Church Choir; Hon Roll.

REYNOLDS, SPENCE T; Ryan Schl; Ryan, OK; (3); Church Yth Grp; Letterman Clb; Natl FFA Org; SADD; Chorus; Church Choir; School Musical; Pres Jr Cls; Var Bsktbl; Var Gym; Stu Of Today; Midwestern; Archaeologist.

REYNOLDS, WANETTE; Nathan Hale HS; Tulsa, OK; (3); Art Clb; English Clb; French Clb; Rptr Nwsp; NHS; Lib Shelver.

RHEA, SHAWN; Wynnewood HS; Wynnewood, OK; (2); 8/48; Church Yth Grp; Letterman Clb; Scholastic Bowl; Church Choir; Pres Frsh Cls; Pres Soph Cls; Var Bsktbl; Hon Roll; NHS.

RHINEHART, ROBERT L; Wetumka Jr Sr HS; Wetumka, OK; (4); Ofcr Bsbl; Bsktbl; Ftbl; Trk; Wt Lftg; Acctng.

RHOADES, ANDREA; Frontier Public Schl; Marland, OK; (4); 4/30; Am Leg Aux Girls St; FBLA; GAA; Scholastic Bowl; Band; School Play; Treas Stu Cncl; Stat Bsktbl; High Hon Roll; Pres Acad Fit Awd; Tech Educ Stu Assn; Mstng Media Prdctn; Northern OK Coll; Mass Comms.

RHOADS, BRAD A; Ada HS; Ada, OK; (4); 40/160; DECA; FCA; Letterman Clb; Spanish Clb; Varsity Clb; Var Capt Ftbl; High Hon Roll; Pres Schlr; Pale Ryders Schl Pep Clb; East Central.

RHODES, CHRISTINA; Bartlesville Mid HS; Bartlesville, OK; (2); 99/481; Church Yth Grp; French Clb; Band; Chorus; Church Choir; Mrchg Band; School Musical; Variety Show; Hon Roll; NHS; 96 OK All ST Choir; OSU; Music Ed.

RHODES, COURTNEY; Central HS; Tulsa, OK; (3); 1/195; HOBY; Key Clb; Yrbk; Pres Jr Cls; Var Chrldng; Var Socr; Var Capt Swmmng; Treas NHS; Natl Engl & Math Merit Awds; Pediatrcs.

RHODES, JACQUELINE; Pryor Sr HS; Chouteau, OK; (3); 1/195; Church Yth Grp; Cmnty Wkr; Debate Tm; Pres FBLA; Pres German Clb; HOBY; Mu Alpha Theta; Red Cross Aide; Speech Tm; Church Choir; PSI; Optimist Clb High Five Awd; 9 Yrs Piano.

RHODES, JAMIE L; Deer Creek HS; Oklahoma City, OK; (3); Church Yth Grp; GAA; Science Clb; Spanish Clb; SADD; School Musical; School Play; Intrml JV Bsktbl; JV Powder Puff Ftbl; Var L Sftbl; Piano 12 Yrs; Bus/Music/Phtgrphy.

RHODES, KELLI M; Moore HS; Moore, OK; (3); French Clb; Office Aide; Science Clb; Chorus; Jr NHS; NHS; 96 Teen Miss DEA Regl; U Of OK Yth Modern/Ballet Schlrshps 93-95; 95 Dance Mstrs OK Ballet Schlrsp; Dance.

RHODES, MICHELLE L; Yukon Middle HS; Yukon, OK; (2); Art Clb; Church Yth Grp; Drama Clb; Quiz Bowl; Spanish Clb; Chorus; Southern Nazarene Univ; Psych.

RHODES, NITA M; Tahlequah Sr HS; Tahlequah, OK; (3); Church Yth Grp; Spanish Clb; Chorus; Rep Frsh Cls; High Hon Roll; Hon Roll; Jr NHS; NSU; Law.

RHODES, RACHEL K; Catoosa HS; Catoosa, OK; (4); 10/140; Church Yth Grp; FHA; Spanish Clb; Teachers Aide; Church Choir; High Hon Roll; NHS; Tulsa JC; Bus.

RHOTON, TRAVIS L; Dale Sr HS; Shawnee, OK; (1); 5/46; Boy Scts; Church Yth Grp; Band; Jazz Band; Mrchg Band; Pep Band.

RIALS, JAY H; Carl Albert HS; Midwest City, OK; (4); Art Clb; Church Yth Grp; FCA; Key Clb; Var Crs Cntry; Var Ftbl; Capt Var Socr; Var Trk; St Georges Col; Acctng.

RICCARDI, ELISABETH; Union Intermediate HS; Tulsa, OK; (2); 17/800; Cmnty Wkr; German Clb; Key Clb; Orch; Hon Roll; Jr NHS; NHS; Medcl Explorers Clb.

RICE, ANDREW W; Walters HS; Walters, OK; (3); 2/49; Church Yth Grp; HOBY; Quiz Bowl; Scholastic Bowl; Spanish Clb; Band; Chorus; Mrchg Band; Pep Band; School Musical; OK Chrstn U; Pre-Med.

RICE, APRIL R; Salina HS; Salina, OK; (1); Church Yth Grp; FCA; FTA; Rep Frsh Cls; Hon Roll; NHS.

RICE, BARRY; Coweta HS; Coweta, OK; (4); Chess Clb; FBLA; Science Clb; Nwsp; Hon Roll; Jr NHS; NHS; Stock Market Tm; U Of OK; Film Dir.

RICE, BECKY; Kingfisher HS; Kingfisher, OK; (4); 2/110; Key Clb; Natl FFA Org; Red Cross Aide; Sec Soph Cls; Var Bsktbl; Cit Awd; High Hon Roll; NHS; Sal; 2nd Pl Ntl Parlimentary Prdcdr Tm 95; 1st Pl St Trnmt Of Chmpns Extmrns Speaking 95; 3rd St Pblc Spkng; TCU; Sci.

RICE, HEATHER M; Heritage Hall Schl; Oklahoma City, OK; (2); Cmnty Wkr; FCA; Letterman Clb; Mu Alpha Theta; Pep Clb; Red Cross Aide; Var Bsktbl; Var Fld Hcky; Var Sftbl; High Hon Roll; Outstdng Frosh & Soph Girl; Stu Of Month; MVP Received At OK Chrstn Cage Camp For Bsktbl; Orthopedic Surgeon.

RICE, JEREMY M; Westmoore HS; Oklahoma City, OK; (1); FCA; JA; Teachers Aide; Ftbl; Cit Awd; Hon Roll; Jr NHS; OK U; Sprts Med.

RICE, JESSI; Guymon Sr HS; Guymon, OK; (3); 1/100; Church Yth Grp; NFL; School Musical; Rptr Phtg Yrbk; Pres Jr Cls; Rep Stu Cncl; Capt Chrldng; NHS; Pres Acad Fit Awd; FCA; Peer Hope Dlgtn; Sept Grl Of Mnth; City Lge Vllybll And Swm Tm; U Of KS; Sprtsmed.

RICE, JESSICA; Kingfisher HS; Kingfisher, OK; (4); 3/93; Drama Clb; NFL; Speech Tm; School Play; Nwsp; Ofcr Sr Cls; Ofcr Stu Cncl; High Hon Roll; NHS; Kingfisher Civic Clb; OK ST U; Psych.

RICE, JOSH; Merritt Schl; Elk City, OK; (3); 1/35; Church Yth Grp; Pres FHA; VP SADD; Chorus; Rptr Nwsp; Treas Soph Cls; Treas Stu Cncl; High Hon Roll; Prfct Atten Awd; FCA; Acad Team; Animator.

RICE, JULEE M; Bridge Creek HS; Tuttle, OK; (1); Church Yth Grp; Drama Clb; FCA; GAA; SADD; School Play; JV Capt Bsktbl; Var Sftbl; Ltr In Sftbl.

RICE, JUSTIN W; Webster HS; Tulsa, OK; (1); 10/150; Boy Scts; Church Yth Grp; Band; Church Choir; Mrchg Band; High Hon Roll; Jr NHS; Bible Qzzng; Church Ensmbl; Harvard; Lwyr.

RICE, KEVIN R; Choctaw HS; Midwest City, OK; (3); 49/314; Am Leg Boys St; Church Yth Grp; Var L Bsktbl; Var L Socr; Hon Roll; NHS; His Acad Comp 9th; Bio Acad Comp 10th; PT.

RICE, MATT; Kingfisher HS; Kingfisher, OK; (1); Boy Scts; Church Yth Grp; Speech Tm; Bsktbl; Ftbl; Golf; Hon Roll.

RICE, PETER; Walters HS; Walters, OK; (1); 1/70; Church Yth Grp; Quiz Bowl; Scholastic Bowl; Band; Jazz Band; Mrchg Band; Rep Stu Cncl; Intrml Trk; Intrml Wt Lftg; High Hon Roll.

RICE, RENA; Claremore Sr HS; Claremore, OK; (4); 12/271; Library Aide; Quiz Bowl; Science Clb; Spanish Clb; Teachers Aide; Band; Mrchg Band; Pep Band; Yrbk; Hon Roll; OK Indn Hnr Soc; Clrmr Intr-Trbl Yth Cncl Pres.

RICE, RMENDA A; Ketchum HS; Langley, OK; (3); FBLA; FHA; Hosp Aide; Ed Yrbk; Comp; Kids Summer Rdng Pgm; Commnctns.

RICE, RONALD M; Wagoner Sr HS; Wagoner, OK; (3); 5/125; FBLA; Red Cross Aide; Spanish Clb; Yrbk; Rep Stu Cncl; Hon Roll; NHS; Am Leg Boys St; Church Yth Grp; FBLA OK St Parlmntrn 95-96; FBLA St Sec 96-97; OK St Parlmntry Procdr Team 95-97; Piano Lessons; U Of Tulsa; Intnl Bus; Mrktg.

RICE, RYAN; Westmoore HS; Oklahoma City, OK; (1); Boy Scts; Church Yth Grp; FCA; Chorus; Church Choir; Nwsp; Bsktbl; Crs Cntry; Hon Roll; OK ST Univ; Musician.

RICE, SHANNA M; Rush Springs HS; Rush Springs, OK; (3); 1/40; Church Yth Grp; Scholastic Bowl; Spanish Clb; Band; Church Choir; VP Soph Cls; Chrldng; High Hon Roll; NHS; Yrbk; Yth Alv Clb Pres 10th Grd/VP 11th Grd; HS Math Tchr.

RICH, BRANDON L; Woodward HS; Woodward, OK; (1); Hon Roll; Bldg/Drvng Hi Tec Remote Controlled Cars; Woodworking; TX A&M; Engr.

RICH, KRISTY A; Stilwell HS; Stilwell, OK; (2); Church Yth Grp; FHA; Var Trk; Wrld Chgrs Intl Cmp Cnslr; NE ST Univ; Elem Schl Tchr.

RICHARD, AMANDA J; Edmond Memorial HS; Edmond, OK; (2); Church Yth Grp; Key Clb; Spanish Clb; Orch; School Musical; NHS; Pres Acad Fit Awd; North Cntrl OK Hnrs Orch Mem; OK All ST Orch; Superior Rating Solo/Ensmbl Dist/ST Contests.

RICHARD, BRODERICK; Capitol Hill HS; Oklahoma City, OK; (4); 20/150; French Clb; Chorus; Ftbl; Hon Roll; U Of Tulsa; Mech Engrng.

RICHARDS, DESTRY W; Grandfield Jr Sr HS; Grandfield, OK; (3); 9/24; FBLA; Yrbk; Hon Roll; OK ST Univ; Cmptr App.

RICHARDS, JOSH T; Bethel HS; Shawnee, OK; (2); Art Clb; Church Yth Grp; Spanish Clb; Teachers Aide; VP Soph Cls; Var Bsbl; Var Bsktbl; High Hon Roll; NHS; Pres Acad Fit Awd.

RICHARDS, LESLIE; Kremlin Jr Sr HS; Enid, OK; (2); Church Yth Grp; FCA; Letterman Clb; Math Tm; Band; Mrchg Band; Pep Band; Chrldng; Sftbl; Hon Roll; OSU Stillwater; Phys Thrp.

RICHARDS, MARK M; Altus Sr HS; Altus, OK; (2); ROTC; Var Bsktbl; High Hon Roll; Hon Roll; OK ST U.

RICHARDS, MATTHEW C; Bishop Kelley HS; Tulsa, OK; (2); German Clb; Ofcr Bsbl; Bsktbl; Ftbl; Wt Lftg; Hon Roll.

RICHARDS, MICHAEL D; Roland Sr HS; Roland, OK; (2); Cmnty Wkr; FCA; Natl FFA Org; Band; Mrchg Band; Pep Band; Ftbl; Wt Lftg; Hon Roll; Prfct Atten Awd; Natl Chmpns Roland FFA Prstre/Rnge 96.

RICHARDS, TARA; Crescent Schl; Crescent, OK; (3); 9/40; Natl Beta Clb; Chorus; School Play; JV Stu Cncl; Mgr Bsbl; Var Bsktbl; Var Crs Cntry; Var Sftbl; Hmcmng Ct; OK ST U; Nrsng.

RICHARDSON, AMANDA I; Broken Arrow Sr HS; Tulsa, OK; (4); 111/921; Church Yth Grp; Key Clb; Spanish Clb; Teachers Aide; Acpl Chr; Church Choir; High Hon Roll; NHS; OK Hnr Soc; Tulsa JC; Anthropology.

RICHARDSON, ARLANDO M; Del City HS; Del City, OK; (2); Church Yth Grp; Intrml Bsktbl; Intrml Ftbl; Hon Roll; Jr NHS; OK Univ; Sports Medicine.

RICHARDSON, BILLY R; Guthrie Sr HS; Guthrie, OK; (1); Band; Mrchg Band; Pep Band; Girl Scts; JV Crs Cntry; Jr NHS; OK ST Univ.

RICHARDSON, BRANDY; Catoosa HS; Catoosa, OK; (3); Church Yth Grp; FCA; Treas French Clb; Chorus; Church Choir; School Play; Ofcr Stu Cncl; Chrldng; Socr; Sec NHS; OK Hstry Awd; Bio Awd; Acctng.

RICHARDSON, DANA J; Claremore Sr HS; Claremore, OK; (2); Drama Clb; FHA; Girl Scts; Library Aide; Natl FFA Org; Rptr Yrbk; Hon Roll; Eastern OK ST Coll.

RICHARDSON, ELIZABETH P; South Intermediate HS; Broken Arrow, OK; (1); Church Yth Grp; Band; Mrchg Band; Pep Band; Hon Roll; Chrstn Stdnt Union; Univ Of Tulsa; Bus.

RICHARDSON, HEATHER A; Oologah HS; Talala, OK; (2); Church Yth Grp; Intnl Clb; SADD; Band; Mrchg Band; Pep Band; High Hon Roll; Tulsa JC; Comp.

RICHARDSON, ISAAC; Arapaho Schl; Arapaho, OK; (2); 5/27; Church Yth Grp; Pres Rptr 4-H; VP Natl FFA Org; Quiz Bowl; Teachers Aide; Cit Awd; 4-H Awd; Hon Roll; Pres Acad Fit Awd; Horse Jdng Tm; AJQHA Wrld Chmpn Tm; Lvstck Jdng Tm; 4-H Horse Clb; OK ST U; Vet.

RICHARDSON, JERAMEY L; Velma Alma HS; Velma, OK; (3); FCA; Letterman Clb; Orch; SADD; Chorus; Ftbl; Trk; Wt Lftg; High Hon Roll; NHS; S E OK ST U; Sci Tchr.

RICHARDSON, KEVIN; Watonga HS; Watonga, OK; (4); Church Yth Grp; Dance Clb; FCA; Rptr FBLA; Office Aide; Pep Clb; Teachers Aide; Band; Drill Tm; Pres Frsh Cls; Bstkbl Al Conf; Stdnt Cncl Lngr Lnch Cmte Chm, Hmcmng Chm, Assmbly Chm; Sr Fav; U Of Central OK; Bus.

RICHARDSON, KILY; Amber Pocasset Jr Sr HS; Amber, OK; (1); Church Yth Grp; FCA; FHA; Math Clb; Natl FFA Org; Speech Tm; Treas Frsh Cls; Rep Stu Cncl; Bsktbl; Sftbl; YABA St Chmpnshp, Schlrshp & Natl Cmptn; Duke U; Mrn Bio.

RICHARDSON, LAURA M; Christian Heritage Acad; Norman, OK; (4); Church Yth Grp; FCA; Teachers Aide; Church Choir; Var L Bsktbl; Hon Roll; OK ST U; Comp Sci.

RICHARDSON, MICHELLE; Watonga HS; Watonga, OK; (4); 21/58; Natl FFA Org; Band; Ofcr Jr Cls; Ofcr Sr Cls; Chrldng; Hon Roll; Southwestern OK ST; Soc Work.

RICHARDSON, NICK; Cascia Hall Prep School; Tulsa, OK; (1); Boy Scts; Church Yth Grp; Debate Tm; Scholastic Bowl; Spanish Clb; Bsktbl; Trk; Hon Roll; Notre Dame.

RICHARDSON, PORSHA; Boley HS; Prague, OK; (1); 4-H; Girl Scts; Natl FFA Org; Band; Bsktbl; Sftbl; High Hon Roll; Hon Roll.

RICHARDSON, SHANE; Dickson HS; Ardmore, OK; (4); 4/63; Church Yth Grp; Cmnty Wkr; FCA; Letterman Clb; Spanish Clb; SADD; Teachers Aide; VP Frsh Cls; VP Sr Cls; Rep Stu Cncl; Cls 3a-1 All Dist Lineman & Offensive Player Of Yr Ftbl 96; SE OK ST; Chem; Bio.

RICHARDSON, SHANE A; Sallisaw HS; Sallisaw, OK; (2); FCA; Math Clb; Science Clb; Spanish Clb; Stat Bsktbl; Mgr Ftbl; Score Keeper; Mgr Wt Lftg; High Hon Roll; Hon Roll; Ftbl Letterman; Phys Sci Awd; Octagon Clb; Ftbl Coach.

RICHARDSON, ZAC; Seminole Jr Sr HS; Seminole, OK; (3); 6/90; Church Yth Grp; French Clb; Math Clb; Math Tm; Science Clb; Ofcr Bsbl; Var Ftbl; High Hon Roll; NHS.

RICHERSON, MATHA; Braggs Schl; Muskogee, OK; (4); 6/18; VP FBLA; Rptr Nwsp; Ed Yrbk; Sec Soph Cls; Sec Jr Cls; Hon Roll; Natl Voc Hnr Soc; Baeone Coll; Radiology.

RICHEY, CLAY; Moore HS; Moore, OK; (2); Church Yth Grp; FCA; Intnl Clb; Scholastic Bowl; Spanish Clb; Band; Ofcr Stu Cncl; High Hon Roll; Jr NHS; NHS; Page OK House Reps; U Of OK; Arch.

RICHEY, DAVID W; Union Intermediate HS; Tulsa, OK; (1); Bus Mgmt.

RICHEY, MANDI D; Inola Sr HS; Inola, OK; (3); Church Yth Grp; FCA; Library Aide; Pep Clb; Science Clb; Teachers Aide; Church Choir; Drill Tm; School Play; JV Bsktbl; Chosen UCA All-Star Chrldr 95; Eng Awd; UCLA; Sports Medicine.

RICHEY, TORI D; Bethany HS; Oklahoma City, OK; (2); Hosp Aide; Office Aide; Chorus; Bus Mgmt.

RICHISON, MICHELLE L; Del City HS; Oklahoma City, OK; (2); Debate Tm; FHA; Pep Clb; SADD; Church Choir; Rep Soph Cls; Var Mgr(s); Hon Roll; OK Univ; Defense Attorney.

RICHMOND, KORI L; Oklahoma Sch Of Science & Math; Holdenville, OK; (3); Church Yth Grp; Key Clb; Natl FFA Org; Band; Chrldng; Trk; High Hon Roll; Hon Roll; NHS; Prfct Atten Awd; Kiwanis Clb Soph Of Yr Awd; OK Schl Of Sci & Math Cls 97; U Of TX-AUSTIN; Biochemistry.

RICHMOND, TIFFANY M; Blackwell HS; Blackwell, OK; (2); Pep Clb; Chorus; Chrldng; Tennis; High Hon Roll; Hon Roll; NHS; Prfct Atten Awd.

RICHTER, LUCAS D; Mustang HS; Mustang, OK; (3); Church Yth Grp; Red Cross Aide; Chorus; Swing Chorus; Vllybl; OK City Univ Perf Arts Acad; OK Smmr Arts Inst; All ST 95- Tenor I; OK City Univ; Music.

RICKETTS, JOHN; Daniel Webster HS; Tulsa, OK; (4); Am Leg Boys St; Church Yth Grp; Cmnty Wkr; VP FBLA; Key Clb; Chorus; Rep Stu Cncl; JV Bsbl; JV Bsktbl; Hon Roll; Tusla Metro Honor Choir; Acctng.

RICKS, CHERYL RAE; Putnam City North HS; Oklahoma City, OK; (4); 19/453; Key Clb; Service Clb; Spanish Clb; SADD; Flag Corp; NHS; Ntl Merit Schol; Pres Schlr; Intl Order Of Jobs Daughters; U Of OK; Pharm.

RICO, CHRISTINA M; Latta Sr HS; Ada, OK; (3); FCA; FHA; Pep Clb; Teachers Aide; Sec Frsh Cls; Sec Soph Cls; Sec Jr Cls; Var L Chrldng; Hon Roll; NHS; HS Math Tchr.

RIDDEL, RYAN J; Mc Alester HS; Mcalester, OK; (2); Church Yth Grp; French Clb; Band; Chorus; Church Choir; Jazz Band; Mrchg Band; School Musical; Swing Chorus; High Hon Roll.

RIDDLE, ANJI; Putnam City West HS; Bethany, OK; (1); Office Aide; Chrldng; Hon Roll; DECA Calendar Model; Ed.

RIDDLE, BRIAN; Anadarko HS; Anadarko, OK; (4); 1/100; Am Leg Boys St; Church Yth Grp; FCA; FBLA; Spanish Clb; Chorus; School Musical; Ofcr Stu Cncl; High Hon Roll; NHS; Page OK Hs Of Rep; 1st Pl Comp Concepts OK FBLA Cnvntn.

RIDDLE, JEREMY T; Byng Sr HS; Ada, OK; (4); 39/76; Church Yth Grp; Teachers Aide; Capt Crs Cntry; Capt Trk; Hnrbl Mntn All ST Crs Cntry; All ST Crs Cntry; East Cntrl Univ; Bus Mgmnt.

RIDDLE, KANDLE; Turpin Schl; Turpin, OK; (4); 7/42; Church Yth Grp; FCA; Speech Tm; SADD; Chorus; School Musical; Ed Yrbk; Bsktbl; Chrldng; Golf; Jr Clss Fav; Supts Hnr Roll; Prncpls Hnr Roll; U Of North TX; Phys Thrp.

RIDDLE, MEGAN L; Union Sr HS; Broken Arrow, OK; (3); 69/741; Church Yth Grp; Key Clb; Spanish Clb; Ofcr Frsh Cls; Capt L Crs Cntry; L Trk; Hon Roll; NHS; Pres Schlr; Spanish NHS; Med.

RIDDLES, AMANDA L; Rush Springs HS; Rush Springs, OK; (4); Church Yth Grp; Scholastic Bowl; Spanish Clb; Sec Treas Band; Mrchg Band; Hon Roll; NHS; OK Hnr Soc; Cameron Univ.

RIDDLES, DARREN C; Mustang HS; Mustang, OK; (3); Church Yth Grp; Ftbl; Trk; Wt Lftg; Hon Roll; OK Univ Acad Achvmt Hnr.

RIDEN, MICHAEL; Putnam City West HS; Oklahoma City, OK; (4); 9/278; Am Leg Boys St; Art Clb; Church Yth Grp; Cmnty Wkr; FCA; German Clb; Scholastic Bowl; Stat Bsktbl; Ftbl; Trk; Creative Wrtng Think Ink Short Story Awds; Lfgrd; Amer Lgn Boys St 95; U Of OK; Pre-Med.

RIDENER, JUSTIN E; Charles Page HS; Sand Springs, OK; (1); Am Leg Boys St; FCA; Letterman Clb; Intrml Bsbl; Intrml Bsktbl; Intrml Ftbl; High Hon Roll; NHS; Acad Ltr; PE; Bsbl Coach.

RIDER, BLAINE; John Marshall HS; Oklahoma City, OK; (4); 8/180; Am Leg Boys St; Church Yth Grp; FCA; Letterman Clb; Scholastic Bowl; Thesps; Pres Stu Cncl; L Socr; High Hon Roll; VP NHS; OK ST U.

RIDER, TRAVIS; Holdenville HS; Holdenville, OK; (4); 9/80; Am Leg Boys St; Church Yth Grp; FCA; Scholastic Bowl; Ofcr Soph Cls; Ftbl; Wt Lftg; High Hon Roll; NHS; Pres Acad Fit Awd; Natl Athltc Strngth Assn Recrd Holdr; FL Inst Of Tech; Comp Engrng.

RIDGE, JEREMY A; Seminole Jr Sr HS; Seminole, OK; (3); 11/120; Quiz Bowl; Teachers Aide; Pres Frsh Cls; Var Bsktbl; High Hon Roll; Hon Roll; NHS; GATE Pgm; Acctng.

RIDGE, PAMELA J; North Intemediate HS; Broken Arrow, OK; (1); Band; Mrchg Band; Pep Band; Hon Roll; Rec Scr; 4 Yr Coll; Tchr/Cnslr.

RIDGWAY, AMERY D; Caney Jr Sr HS; Caney, OK; (3); 5/21; Church Yth Grp; Computer Clb; Dance Clb; FCA; GAA; Spanish Clb; Church Choir; Yrbk; Pres Jr Cls; Var Bsktbl.

RIDGWAY, BRINA; Caney Jr Sr HS; Caddo, OK; (2); Church Yth Grp; FCA; GAA; Church Choir; Yrbk; Ofcr Stu Cncl; Bsktbl; Hon Roll; Prfct Atten Awd; Sal; Southeastern ST Univ; Tchr.

RIDGWAY, LAURA A; Putnam City West HS; Oklahoma City, OK; (4); 40/270; French Clb; Office Aide; Ofcr Stu Cncl; Bsktbl; Golf; Trk; NHS; Med Clb; Wrtng Clb; U Of Cntrl OK; Bus.

RIDLEY, EMILY D; Haskell HS; Haskell, OK; (2); 4-H; Rptr Natl FFA Org; Bsktbl; Var Sftbl.

RIDLEY, JAY C; Deer Creek HS; Edmond, OK; (2); 40/150; Church Yth Grp; Drama Clb; FCA; French Clb; Letterman Clb; Pep Clb; Science Clb; Service Clb; SADD; Varsity Clb; Bellmont Coll; Msc/Cntry Sngr.

RIEDL, MELISSA J; Woodward HS; Woodward, OK; (4); 45/154; Cmnty Wkr; Computer Clb; Ofcr FBLA; Ofcr FHA; German Clb; Key Clb; Pep Clb; Band; Mrchg Band; Rep Jr Cls; Big Bros/Sisters; Phi Beta Lambda; Ftr Bus Ldrs/Tmrrw; Northwestern OK ST Univ.

RIEGER, LISA; Cherokee Jr Sr HS; Cherokee, OK; (3); 1/32; Church Yth Grp; NFL; Spanish Clb; Speech Tm; Yrbk; Bsktbl; Trk; High Hon Roll; OK Hnr Soc.

RIEMER, BRADFORD S; Lawton Sr HS; Lawton, OK; (3); Church Yth Grp; FCA; Spanish Clb; Chorus; JV Var Bsbl; Wt Lftg; Hon Roll; Cameron; Archtctl Engr.

RIERA, VERONICA I; Union Intermediate HS; Tulsa, OK; (2); 91/800; Art Clb; Church Yth Grp; Science Clb; Spanish Clb; Band; Mrchg Band; Pep Band; High Hon Roll; Jr NHS; NHS; 2-1st Pl Ribbons For Frgn Lang Art Prjcts; All-Dist Band Plyr Qualifyng For All-St Band; Chem.

RIGGINS, RANDY R; Mannford HS; Terlton, OK; (3); 18/106; Art Clb; Church Yth Grp; Drama Clb; FCA; Letterman Clb; Spanish Clb; Varsity Clb; Bsktbl; Crs Cntry; Cit Awd.

RIGGLE, PATRICIA; Asher Schl; Asher, OK; (3); 3/22; FHA; Rep Frsh Cls; VP Soph Cls; VP Jr Cls; Rep Stu Cncl; Bsktbl; Hon Roll; Ntl Merit Ltr; Cameron U; Med.

RIGGS, ANDY D; North Intemediate HS; Broken Arrow, OK; (1); Church Yth Grp; Teachers Aide; Wt Lftg; Hon Roll.

RIGGS, ANGEL; Wellston Schl; Wellston, OK; (2); 4/42; FHA; Band; Drm Mjr(t); Rptr Frsh Cls; Rptr Soph Cls; Hon Roll; Jr NHS; NHS; Music.

RIGGS, BARRY M; Pocola HS; Pocola, OK; (2); Var Bsbl.

RIGGS, BETTY J; Roland Sr HS; Roland, OK; (2); 1/110; FHA; Quiz Bowl; Speech Tm; Band; Ed Nwsp; Rep Frsh Cls; Rep Soph Cls; Hon Roll; NHS; Ntl Merit Ltr; Med.

RIGGS, DANIEL A; Ardmore HS; Ardmore, OK; (3); Am Leg Boys St; Church Yth Grp; FCA; Key Clb; Spanish Clb; Teachers Aide; Stage Crew; Yrbk; JV Var Bsbl; JV Var Ftbl; OK Univ; Sports Medicine.

RIGGS, DAYLIN B; Claremore Sr HS; Claremore, OK; (1); Hon Roll; Skateboarding.

RIGGS, JANEAN; El Reno Sr HS; El Reno, OK; (4); 8/167; Am Leg Aux Girls St; Church Yth Grp; VP FTA; Girl Scts; Key Clb; Speech Tm; Teachers Aide; Ed Nwsp; Ed Yrbk; VP NHS; Phys Thrp.

RIGGS, STACEY A; Westmoore HS; Oklahoma City, OK; (3); Church Yth Grp; Cmnty Wkr; Office Aide; Teachers Aide; Crs Cntry; Sftbl; Wt Lftg; Jr NHS; NHS; 2nd Pl Awrd Catgry Essay Wrtg Cntst 95; OK City CC; Psych.

RIGHTMER, BRETT E; Eisenhower Sr HS; Lawton, OK; (4); 32/436; Cmnty Wkr; FCA; Key Clb; Office Aide; Var Chrldng; High Hon Roll; NHS; Lawton Com Theater; Ecology Comm Chprsn; Cameron Univ; Bio; Pre-Med.

RIGHTMER, NATHAN; Tomlinson Jr HS; Lawton, OK; (1); FCA; Chorus; School Musical; School Play; Rep Stu Cncl; Var Tennis; Cit Awd; Jr NHS; NHS; Lawton Comm Theatre; Arch.

RIGNEY, TRACI; Mc Loud HS; Mc Loud, OK; (4); 4/107; FBLA; FHA; Office Aide; Ed Yrbk; Sec Sr Cls; Stat Bsktbl; JV Chrldng; Mgr(s); High Hon Roll; NHS.

RIGSBY, AUDREY M; Putnam City West HS; Bethany, OK; (3); 17/271; Cmnty Wkr; Computer Clb; FCA; FBLA; Key Clb; Office Aide; Science Clb; Spanish Clb; Rep Frsh Cls; Rep Soph Cls; OK Univ; Dermtlgst.

RILEY, AMY L; Enid Sr HS; Enid, OK; (4); VICA; Ed Yrbk; Ofcr Stu Cncl; NHS; U Of OK.

RILEY, CHARLES A; Okmulgee HS; Okmulgee, OK; (1); Church Yth Grp; FCA; Hon Roll.

RILEY, DANNABETH; Coalgate HS; Coalgate, OK; (3); Quiz Bowl; Band; High Hon Roll; NHS; E Central U; Tchr.

RILEY, DEZMONT D; Bishop Kelley HS; Tulsa, OK; (2); Church Yth Grp; Cmnty Wkr; JV Var Bsktbl; Hon Roll; Prfct Atten Awd.

RILEY, EMILY C; Enid Sr HS; Enid, OK; (2); Church Yth Grp; French Clb; Hosp Aide; Office Aide; Teachers Aide; School Play; Yrbk; NHS.

RILEY, JENNIFER A; Shawnee Sr HS; Shawnee, OK; (3); DECA; SADD; Chorus; Cit Awd; Hon Roll; NHS; Doctor.

RILEY, JOSH; Roff HS; Fitzhugh, OK; (2); Church Yth Grp; Natl Beta Clb; Quiz Bowl; Scholastic Bowl; Spanish Clb; Chorus; Nwsp; High Hon Roll; OK Hnr Soc; Phys Thrp.

RILEY, KAYLA; Watonga HS; Watonga, OK; (3); 11/60; FHA; Hon Roll; NHS; Mem Of Eco Clb 2 Yrs; Chprsn Of Decrtng Comm For 96 Prm; Southwestern U.

RILEY, LESA G; Del City HS; Del City, OK; (2); Art Clb; Church Yth Grp; FHA; Pep Clb; Science Clb; Spanish Clb; SADD; Teachers Aide; Wt Lftg; Maitmaid; OK U; Sprts Med.

RILEY, MEGHAN R; Bartlesville Mid HS; Bartlesville, OK; (2); 146/428; Church Yth Grp; Ofcr Soph Cls; Bsktbl; Sftbl; High Hon Roll; Hon Roll; Jr NHS; Prfct Atten Awd; Sftbl Schlsp; His; Eng.

RILEY, MICHAEL; Panama HS; Shady Point, OK; (2); 1/59; Natl FFA Org; Capt Quiz Bowl; Pres Soph Cls; Cit Awd; Gov Hon Prg Awd; High Hon Roll; NHS; Ntl Merit Ltr; Pres Acad Fit Awd; Art; OK ST U; Arch.

RILEY, PAUL C; West Middle HS; Norman, OK; (2); 1/650; Church Yth Grp; Cmnty Wkr; FCA; Library Aide; SADD; Stage Crew; Cit Awd; Gov Hon Prg Awd; NHS; Pres Acad Fit Awd; U Of OK; Elec Engr.

RILEY, SARAH J; Mannford HS; Mannford, OK; (2); Church Yth Grp; Cmnty Wkr; FCA; Science Clb; SADD; Yrbk; VP Frsh Cls; Rep Jr Cls; Rep Stu Cncl; High Hon Roll; Hmlss Shltr Srvr; Pdtrc Orthndtst.

RILEY, SUSAN E; Mustang HS; Yukon, OK; (1); Church Yth Grp; Cmnty Wkr; Key Clb; SADD; Chorus; Church Choir; Lit Mag; Rep Frsh Cls; Ofcr Stu Cncl; Hon Roll.

RILLO, MARIA T; Union Sr HS; Broken Arrow, OK; (4); 82/700; Church Yth Grp; VP Intnl Clb; Key Clb; Mu Alpha Theta; Band; Mrchg Band; Jr NHS; NHS; Pres Acad Fit Awd; Spanish NHS; Rnnsnc Clb; All-Dist Bnd 2 Yrs; All-Amrcn Schlr Awd 95-96; Bio Sci.

RIMMER, DARCI R; Newcastle HS; Newcastle, OK; (4); Art Clb; Pep Clb; Hist Spanish Clb; Chrldng; Poetry; UCO; Phsycology.

RINDERER, CHRISTINA; Bridge Creek HS; Blanchard, OK; (2); Spanish Clb; Chorus; Church Choir; Hon Roll; OK Hnr Soc; U Of OK; Archeologist.

RINEHART, RUSTI A; Western Heights Sr HS; Oklahoma City, OK; (3); 17/168; Church Yth Grp; Cmnty Wkr; French Clb; Key Clb; Scholastic Bowl; Chorus; School Musical; Rep Frsh Cls; Rep Soph Cls; Rep Jr Cls; Ldrshp Clb; DECA; Show Choir; Mock Trial; Bus Ed Awd; Comp Awds; Dancer At Top Hat Talent Studio; OK City Univ; Veterinary Med.

RINEHART, STACEY; Geary Jr Sr HS; Geary, OK; (3); Church Yth Grp; HOBY; Natl Beta Clb; Treas Natl FFA Org; Band; Mrchg Band; Pep Band; Rep Stu Cncl; Cit Awd; High Hon Roll; Cindy Sharry Meml Awd.

RINGEISEN, TOBIE L; Bartlesville Sr HS; Bartlesville, OK; (4); FHA; Service Clb; VP Sr Cls; Ofcr Stu Cncl; Ath Trng; K-Life; Med Explr Grp; U Of OK; Ath Trng.

RINGGOLD, JENNIFER M; Cleveland Sr HS; Cleveland, OK; (4); 1/89; Pres FCA; Pres Sr Cls; Capt Chrldng; Score Keeper; Kiwanis Awd; VP NHS; St Schlr; Val; Sftbl; OK ST Univ; Pre-Med.

RINGWALD, LISA M; Heritage Hall Schl; Oklahoma City, OK; (3); 2/62; Church Yth Grp; Cmnty Wkr; FCA; Letterman Clb; Mu Alpha Theta; Pep Clb; Yrbk; Sec Soph Cls; Sec Jr Cls; Sec Sr Cls; Star Peer Ldr Intrvwd/Slctd; Infant Crisis Svc Smmr Vol; SMU.

RINRODT, TARA L; Deer Creek HS; Edmond, OK; (2); 1/102; Church Yth Grp; FCA; FBLA; GAA; Science Clb; School Musical; School Play; Fld Hcky; Sftbl; NHS.

RIOS, MONICA; U S Grant HS; Oklahoma City, OK; (3).

RIPLEY, ELVIS A; Union Intermediate HS; Tulsa, OK; (2); FCA; French Clb; Teachers Aide; NHS; Cosmetology.

RIPLEY, JOHN P; Mustang HS; Mustang, OK; (3); 116/386; Military Officer.

RISENHOOVER, CRYSTAL D; Quinton Jr Sr HS; Stigler, OK; (2); Dance Clb; FHA; Library Aide; JV Bsktbl; JV Capt Chrldng; Hon Roll; FHA Officer; FCA; OK Univ; Pediatrician.

RISEWICK, SARAH; Prue Schl; Prue, OK; (1); #2 in class; Church Yth Grp; FCA; 4-H; FHA; Letterman Clb; Red Cross Aide; SADD; Varsity Clb; Var Bsktbl; Ftbl.

RISHER, BRIANNE G; Del City HS; Del City, OK; (2); Church Yth Grp; Band; Jazz Band; Mrchg Band; Pep Band; Bsktbl; Hon Roll; Jr NHS; Fnlst In N Amer Open Poetry Cont 95; 30 Hr Famine For World Vision 95; Bible Quiz Team Capt 95; Arch.

RISHI, ANJALI; Shawnee Sr HS; Shawnee, OK; (3); Cmnty Wkr; GAA; Spanish Clb; Var Tennis; High Hon Roll; Pres Acad Fit Awd.

RISI, NICK J; Putnam City West HS; Oklahoma City, OK; (1); Church Yth Grp; Drama Clb; Church Choir; Orch; School Musical; Socr; Silver Strings Strolling Orch.

RISING SUN BRADEN, ROBERT L; Locust Grove HS; Locust Grove, OK; (3); Computer Clb; Library Aide; High Hon Roll; Hon Roll; Jr NHS; NHS; Foundr Of Comptr Clb; Comp.

RISLEY, DEBORAH L; Prague HS; Prague, OK; (3); 11/78; Church Yth Grp; FBLA; GAA; Key Clb; Science Clb; Band; Mrchg Band; Pep Band; JV Var Bsktbl; Var Sftbl; Acad Team; Mock Trial; OU; Medicine.

RISLEY, NICKOLAS O; Boise City HS; Boise City, OK; (1); Boy Scts; Church Yth Grp; 4-H; Treas Natl FFA Org; 4-H Awd; 4-H Vp; OK St Univmed.

RISNER, CASSIE R; Union Intermediate HS; Tulsa, OK; (2); Boy Scts; Church Yth Grp; Hosp Aide; Drill Tm; Cit Awd; High Hon Roll; NHS; Pres Acad Fit Awd; 13 Yrs Dance; Sci Outstndng Achvt; Soph Semi Formal Cmmtte.

RITCHEY, JOSHUA D; Nathan Hale HS; Tulsa, OK; (2); Church Yth Grp; FCA; Rep Soph Cls; Var Bsktbl; Var Golf; High Hon Roll; Jr NHS; NHS; Del-OK Assoc Of Stu Cncls Summer 95; Natl Yth Ldrshp Forum On Law & The Constitution 96.

RITCHIE, STEPHEN K; Yukon Middle HS; Yukon, OK; (1); TX A&M.

RITTER, BRYAN J; Ripley HS; Stillwater, OK; (4); 1/32; Church Yth Grp; Library Aide; Math Clb; Model UN; Capt Quiz Bowl; Spanish Clb; Church Choir; Yrbk; Cit Awd; High Hon Roll; OK ST Univ; Mnstr.

RITTER, DAVID; Elgin HS; Elgin, OK; (3); FCA; Natl FFA Org; SADD; Varsity Clb; Band; Rep Jr Cls; Rep Sr Cls; Ftbl; Trk; Wt Lftg; OK St Univ; Chem Eng.

RITTER, KEVIN S; Union Intermediate HS; Tulsa, OK; (2); 38/800; FCA; JV Bsbl; Var L Bsktbl; High Hon Roll; Jr NHS; NHS; Prfct Atten Awd; Stu Of Month; FCA; Tchr/Coach.

RITTER III, ROBERT J; Union Intermediate HS; Tulsa, OK; (2); 108/800; FBLA; German Clb; Band; NHS; DFY; ARC Cncl; Bus Law.

RITTER, SHAWN D; Stilwell HS; Stilwell, OK; (2); Science Clb; 4-H; Natl FFA Org; SADD; School Play; Yrbk; Ftbl; Wrstlng; 4-H Awd; Sci.

RITTER, STUART; Cascia Hall Prep School; Jenks, OK; (2); Boy Scts; Church Yth Grp; Debate Tm; Drama Clb; German Clb; Chorus; School Musical; School Play; Swmmng; Acting.

RITZE, AMITY E; Trinity Christian Schl; Broken Arrow, OK; (2); 4-H; Pep Clb; School Play; Sec Treas Soph Cls; Var Chrldng; Capt Var Socr; 4-H Awd; Hon Roll; Church Yth Grp; FCA; Spch Comptns; Summer Camp Newspaper Asst Ed/Rep; John Birch Soc; OSU; Sports Med.

RITZHAUPT, AMBER; Tahlequah Sr HS; Tahlequah, OK; (4); 3/244; Office Aide; Quiz Bowl; SADD; Treas Chorus; Rep Stu Cncl; Var Var Bsktbl; Hon Roll; NHS; Pres Acad Fit Awd; OK ST; Med.

RIVERA, JENNY M; Tomlinson Jr HS; Lawton, OK; (2); Church Yth Grp; Dance Clb; ROTC; Spanish Clb; JV Vllybl; Trinity Univ; Nursing.

RIVERS, AMANDA C; Cordell Sr HS; Cordell, OK; (2); Church Yth Grp; Rptr Drama Clb; Spanish Clb; Rptr SADD; School Play; High Hon Roll; NHS; Span II/SOCIOLOGY/ENG I II/ALGEBRA I/Govt Ec/Bio Awds; OK Hnr Soc; Speech Clb; SLASH; Southwestern OK ST U; Phrmcy.

RIZZO, CARYN B; Putnam City North HS; Oklahoma City, OK; (2); Drama Clb; JA; Spanish Clb; Hon Roll; Nrsng.

RO, SUSAN; Stillwater Sr HS; Stillwater, OK; (4); Am Leg Aux Girls St; FCA; Hosp Aide; Treas Intnl Clb; VP Mu Alpha Theta; Band; Chorus; Sec Stu Cncl; Var Tennis; NHS; Yth & Govt Jdcl VP & Pres; Coca-Cola Schlr Semi-Fnlst; Hollins Coll; Env Sci.

ROACH, DILLON J; Stillwater Sr HS; Stillwater, OK; (2); Church Yth Grp; Cmnty Wkr; FCA; Ofcr Bsbl; Bsktbl; Ftbl; Hon Roll; Pres Acad Fit Awd; Rising Star In FCA; Boy Scts Epxlorer Pgm Med Mem; Dr; Sport Medicine.

ROACH, GLEN M; Okeene Jr Sr HS; Hitchcock, OK; (2); 6/36; Letterman Clb; Natl FFA Org; Ofcr Bsbl; Wt Lftg; Hon Roll; Prfct Atten Awd; Lawyer.

ROACH, JACKIE C; Weatherford HS; Weatherford, OK; (4); Church Yth Grp; DECA; FHA; Band; Sftbl; Hon Roll; NHS; Pres Schlr; Dist Schol; Germn Amer Ptnshp Prog; SW OK St Univ; Sec Ed.

ROACH, JARROD; Watonga HS; Watonga, OK; (1); FCA; FBLA; Rep Stu Cncl; JV Bsktbl; L Ftbl; Var Trk; Hon Roll.

ROACH, JENNIFER; Union Sr HS; Tulsa, OK; (4); 118/636; Church Yth Grp; Mgr Dance Clb; FCA; French Clb; Treas FBLA; Key Clb; Office Aide; Pep Clb; Service Clb; Teachers Aide; U Of OK; Pre-Med.

ROACH, KEVIN T; Cushing HS; Cushing, OK; (2); 20/159; Church Yth Grp; Quiz Bowl; Band; Jazz Band; Mrchg Band; Pep Band; Cit Awd; High Hon Roll; Hon Roll; OSU; Comp Pgmng.

ROACH, PRINCESS; Stigler HS; Stigler, OK; (2); Girl Scts; Hosp Aide; Math Tm; Band; Mrchg Band; Pep Band; Hon Roll; NHS; Pres Acad Fit Awd; OU U; Med Fld.

ROADS, ELOUISE; Kremlin Jr Sr HS; Enid, OK; (1); 1/13; Church Yth Grp; FCA; Letterman Clb; Scholastic Bowl; Spanish Clb; Band; Rep Stu Cncl; Var Bsktbl; Hon Roll; Pres Schlr; OU; Sprts Med.

ROARK, WHITNEY L; Ryan Schl; Ryan, OK; (3); Church Yth Grp; FCA; FHA; Letterman Clb; Natl Beta Clb; Natl FFA Org; Pep Clb; Chorus; Church Choir; School Musical; PT/ATH Trnr.

ROBB, REBECCA E; Bishop Kelley HS; Tulsa, OK; (1); Church Choir; Trk; Vllybl; High Hon Roll; Hon Roll; Med.

ROBBEN, CHRISTINE; Clinton HS; Clinton, OK; (4); 9/99; Pres Church Yth Grp; FHA; Sec Key Clb; Sec Science Clb; Treas Spanish Clb; Rptr Yrbk; Treas Jr Cls; Ofcr Stu Cncl; Hon Roll; NHS; Natl Yng Ldrshp Conf; SW OK ST U; Optmtry.

ROBBEN, KRISTIE A; Choctaw HS; Choctaw, OK; (4); 1/305; Church Yth Grp; Key Clb; Office Aide; SADD; Crs Cntry; Trk; High Hon Roll; NHS; Val; OK ST U; Chem Engrng.

ROBBINS, BRENDA; Wanette HS; Wanette, OK; (4); 2/20; Pres FHA; Quiz Bowl; Yrbk; Ofcr Stu Cncl; Capt Bsktbl; Var Sftbl; 4-H Awd; High Hon Roll; Treas NHS; Sal; East Central U; CPA.

ROBBINS, BRENT R; Broken Arrow Sr HS; Broken Arrow, OK; (3); Am Leg Boys St; CAP; Cmnty Wkr; JA; Band; Mrchg Band; Wt Lftg; High Hon Roll; Jr NHS; NHS; RC Airplane Pilot; USAF Acad; Fighter Pilot.

ROBBINS, DEBORAH; Duncan HS; Duncan, OK; (3); 19/260; Church Yth Grp; Cmnty Wkr; Key Clb; Spanish Clb; SADD; Chorus; Church Choir; Swing Chorus; Hon Roll; NHS; All OMEA Chorus; Selected To OK All-ST Chorus; Liberty Univ; Chrstn Ministry.

ROBBINS, JESSICA; Crowder Schl; Crowder, OK; (4); 18/40; Am Leg Aux Girls St; Art Clb; Church Yth Grp; FHA; Office Aide; Teachers Aide; Orch; School Musical; Nwsp; Yrbk; E OK ST Coll; Art Ed.

ROBBINS, KARI E; Union Intermediate HS; Tulsa, OK; (2); 9/850; Church Yth Grp; Cmnty Wkr; Spanish Clb; Band; Mrchg Band; Hon Roll; Jr NHS; NHS; Pres Acad Fit Awd.

ROBBINS, KELLI; Marietta HS; Marietta, OK; (1); Church Yth Grp; Debate Tm; Drama Clb; Speech Tm; Band; Mrchg Band; School Play; Hon Roll; Piano & Dance.

ROBBINS, MAGGIE; Hammon Schl; Hammon, OK; (3); Church Yth Grp; FCA; FHA; Letterman Clb; Pep Clb; SADD; L Bsktbl; Capt Chrldng; L Sftbl; Hon Roll.

ROBBINS, MATT; Christian Heritage Acad; Midwest City, OK; (3); 1/50; Church Yth Grp; Var L Tennis; High Hon Roll.

ROBBINS, RACHEL; Grace Chrn Acad; Oklahoma City, OK; (4); 1/23; Office Aide; Capt Scholastic Bowl; Band; VP Sr Cls; Stat Bsktbl; Mgr Ftbl; L Mgr(s); High Hon Roll; Val; OK City CC; Acctg.

ROBBINS, SARAH E; Union Sr HS; Tulsa, OK; (4); 12/629; Church Yth Grp; French Clb; Key Clb; Office Aide; Church Choir; Hon Roll; Jr NHS; NHS; Pres Acad Fit Awd.

ROBBINS, SHEILA; Medford Schl; Medford, OK; (4); 13/22; Church Yth Grp; FCA; FHA; Teachers Aide; Chorus; School Play; Ed Yrbk; VP Jr Cls; Var Sr Cls; Hon Roll; Sthwstrn OK St U; Sprts Med.

ROBBINS, STEPHANIE; Sallisaw HS; Sallisaw, OK; (4); Am Leg Aux Girls St; Church Yth Grp; Pres FCA; HOBY; Math Clb; Pep Clb; Science Clb; Spanish Clb; Chorus; Church Choir; 95-96 Ftbl Homcmng Qn; Clss Bst All-Arnd Girl 95-96; Octagon Clb Pres; OSU.

ROBBINS, TAMARA; Marietta HS; Marietta, OK; (3); Computer Clb; Debate Tm; HOBY; NFL; Speech Tm; Band; Drm Mjr(t); High Hon Roll; NHS; Pres Acad Fit Awd; Dance & Piano; Stu Helper Dance.

ROBBINS, TARA; Tonkawa Jr Sr HS; Tonkawa, OK; (3); Church Yth Grp; Band; Yrbk; Hon Roll; NHS; Bus.

ROBBINS, TONY; Clinton HS; Clinton, OK; (1); Key Clb; Quiz Bowl; Scholastic Bowl; Ofcr Stu Cncl; Golf; High Hon Roll; NHS; Pre-Med.

ROBERDS, MANDY; Preston Schl; Preston, OK; (3); Church Yth Grp; 4-H; Church Choir; Rep Frsh Cls; Sec Soph Cls; Var Bsktbl; Var Sftbl; Var Trk; Hon Roll; Pryr Ldr; 2nd Plc At Natl Free Wl Bapt Phtgrphy Cntst; Mrn Bio.

ROBERSHAW, STEFANI JOY; Lawton Sr HS; Lawton, OK; (4); 72/263; Debate Tm; Drama Clb; Natl FFA Org; NFL; Spanish Clb; Speech Tm; Chorus; Church Choir; Stage Crew; Hon Roll; Debate Ltr; NFL Historian & Sec; Cameron Univ; Child Psych.

ROBERSON, B J; Seminole Jr Sr HS; Seminole, OK; (3); Church Yth Grp; Debate Tm; FCA; Math Clb; NFL; Rptr Stu Cncl; Var JV Ftbl; Var Wt Lftg; High Hon Roll; NHS.

ROBERSON, CHIQUIA; Christian Heritage Acad; Oklahoma City, OK; (4); 8/53; Church Yth Grp; Letterman Clb; Band; Var Bsktbl; Var L Tennis; Cit Awd; High Hon Roll; Hon Roll; Prfct Atten Awd; Multi Yr Listing; Washington U St Louis; Law.

ROBERSON, CODY; Woodward HS; Woodward, OK; (3); Church Yth Grp; Cmnty Wkr; FCA; Quiz Bowl; Teachers Aide; JV Bsbl; Intrml Bsktbl; High Hon Roll; Hon Roll; NHS; OSU Alumni Schlr; Writingwood Awd; Engrng.

ROBERSON, LESLIE D; Lexington HS; Lexington, OK; (4); 23/62; Church Yth Grp; Drama Clb; FCA; FHA; VP Frsh Cls; Treas Jr Cls; JV Var Bsktbl; Var Chrldng; Var Sftbl; Var Hon Roll; Bid Stick; Defense, Offence Awd Sftbl; All Star Fast Ptch Sftbl; All St Slow Ptch Sftbl; Rose ST; Dntl Hygn.

ROBERSON, RACHEL L; Spiro HS; Spiro, OK; (4); 14/89; FBLA; Math Clb; Spanish Clb; Bsktbl; Cit Awd; High Hon Roll; Hon Roll; Jr NHS; NHS; FBLA; Cert Of Exc; NAACP Cert Of Awd; Carl Albert Univ; Acctng.

ROBERT, ADAM; Independence Acad; Oklahoma City, OK; (2); Var Bsbl; High Hon Roll; Univ Of OK Paleontology Preparators 96; Pale OK VP; ST Sci Fair Phys Sci 1st Pl.

ROBERTS, ALLISON; Ardmore HS; Ardmore, OK; (4); 20/176; Am Leg Aux Girls St; Church Yth Grp; Cmnty Wkr; FCA; French Clb; Math Clb; Mu Alpha Theta; Office Aide; Science Clb; Bsktbl; Rtry Stu Of Mnth.

ROBERTS, AMBER; Nowata HS; Nowata, OK; (3); Art Clb; FHA; Art Clb Pres; FHA Historian; Art Awds; Rogers ST Coll; Art; Tchr.

ROBERTS, AMY A; Dickson HS; Ardmore, OK; (2); 1/74; Church Yth Grp; FCA; Sec 4-H; Sec FHA; Sec Spanish Clb; SADD; Rep Frsh Cls; Rep Soph Cls; JV Bsktbl; Co-Ed Chrldng.

ROBERTS, BARRY J; Charles Page HS; Sand Springs, OK; (2); 35/385; Church Yth Grp; FCA; Key Clb; Chorus; Church Choir; Var Socr; High Hon Roll; NHS; Hon Roll; Premier Soccr Team Co-Capt; Stage Choir Auditn.

ROBERTS, BOYD J; Ringling HS; Ringling, OK; (4); 1/36; Church Yth Grp; Cmnty Wkr; Church Choir; Rep Stu Cncl; DAR Awd; High Hon Roll; NHS; Ntl Merit Ltr; Val; OK Hnr Soc; 24 Cls Awds; Perfect Attend Trophy 2 Yrs; USAO Chickasha; Cmptr Sci.

ROBERTS, BRIAN J; Duncan HS; Duncan, OK; (3); Key Clb; Var Bsktbl; DAR Awd; NHS; OK ST U; Civil Engr.

OKLAHOMA

ROBERTS, CHERYL; Foyil Schl; Claremore, OK; (4); 3/25; Am Leg Aux Girls St; Church Yth Grp; Drama Clb; HOBY; Church Choir; Nwsp; Yrbk; Sec Jr Cls; VP Sr Cls; Sec Stu Cncl; Sterling Coll; Sec Ed.

ROBERTS, CLINT W; Checotah HS; Checotah, OK; (2); 1/125; Debate Tm; Speech Tm; JV Bsktbl; High Hon Roll; Kiwanis Awd; NHS; Tech Stu Assn Clb Pres; Kiwanis Of Yr.

ROBERTS, CODY; Piedmont HS; Piedmont, OK; (2); 30/97; Church Yth Grp; SADD; Band; Mrchg Band; Pres Frsh Cls; VP Soph Cls; Ofcr Stu Cncl; Chrldng; Mgr(s); Sftbl; OK ST Univ.

ROBERTS, CODY; Latta Sr HS; Ada, OK; (3); Am Leg Boys St; Boy Scts; Church Yth Grp; FCA; Pres 4-H; HOBY; Letterman Clb; VP Natl FFA Org; Office Aide; Varsity Clb; East Cntrl Univ; Cmptr Bus.

ROBERTS, DUSTY L; Enid Sr HS; Enid, OK; (1); Church Yth Grp; CAP; 4-H; Chorus; Golf; Prfct Atten Awd; Mechanics.

ROBERTS, ELEXA; Chandler HS; Chandler, OK; (3); 14/75; Church Yth Grp; Dance Clb; Drama Clb; Spanish Clb; Thesps; Chorus; Rep Jr Cls; Ofcr Stu Cncl; Chrldng; Hon Roll; Perf Arts.

ROBERTS, EMILY; Union Intermediate HS; Broken Arrow, OK; (1); 52/866; Cmnty Wkr; Hosp Aide; Intnl Clb; Math Clb; Spanish Clb; Band; High Hon Roll; NHS; Forgn Lang Clb.

ROBERTS, GARRETT J; Byng Sr HS; Ada, OK; (3); French Clb; Office Aide; Chorus; U Of OK; Dr.

ROBERTS, HEATHER; Edmond Memorial HS; Edmond, OK; (4); Spanish Clb; Teachers Aide; Var Capt Chrldng; Var Capt Pom Pon; Prfct Atten Awd; Tap, Jazz, Ballet & Lyrical Dance 16 Yrs; OSU Oklahoma City; Psych.

ROBERTS, HOLLY D; Charles Page HS; Sand Springs, OK; (1); Drama Clb; Pres Chorus; Sec Frsh Cls; Ofcr Stu Cncl; Chrldng; High Hon Roll; Hon Roll; Pres Acad Fit Awd; Piano 8 Yrs; Bldrs Club.

ROBERTS, JAMES A; Liberty HS; Mounds, OK; (2); FCA; Spanish Clb; Treas Soph Cls; JV Bsktbl; Hon Roll; 2 Natl Math Awds; Natl Acad Awd; Natl Ldrshp Awd; OK ST Univ; Dr.

ROBERTS, JARED; Timberlake Schl; Helena, OK; (4); 2/24; Church Yth Grp; FHA; German Clb; Co-Ed Nwsp; High Hon Roll; NHS; Prfct Atten Awd; Sal; NW OK ST U; Acctng.

ROBERTS, JEFF; Blair Schl; Blair, OK; (4); Am Leg Boys St; Church Yth Grp; FCA; Natl FFA Org; Quiz Bowl; Intrml Bsbl; Intrml Score Keeper; Intrml Wt Lftg; Cit Awd; Hon Roll; Umpire; Chem.

ROBERTS, JEFF B; Boise City HS; Kenton, OK; (1); Church Yth Grp; Ftbl; Wt Lftg; Hon Roll; ACCTNT/MECH Engr.

ROBERTS, JEFF T; Ardmore HS; Ardmore, OK; (3); 26/200; Church Yth Grp; FCA; Mu Alpha Theta; Tennis; High Hon Roll; Hon Roll; Jr NHS; U Of OK; Med.

ROBERTS, JENNIFER; Charles Page HS; Tulsa, OK; (3); 54/381; Church Yth Grp; FTA; Letterman Clb; Office Aide; Q&S; Spanish Clb; Church Choir; Ed Yrbk; Gov Hon Prg Awd; Hon Roll; HS Rodeo Assn; Intnl Pro Rodeo Assn; Tulsa U; Elem Ed.

ROBERTS, JENNIFER C; Choctaw HS; Newalla, OK; (4); 12/313; Church Yth Grp; Cmnty Wkr; Chorus; School Musical; Rep Sr Cls; Mgr Var Bsktbl; Jr NHS; Var Sftbl; Gov Hon Prg Awd; NHS; 3 Yr All-St Chr; All-Amer Schlr; Grl Mnth Sr Clss; U OK; Musc Ed.

ROBERTS, JIMMY R; Claremore Sr HS; Claremore, OK; (2); Natl FFA Org; Hon Roll; Horses; Motorcycles; Hunting/Fishing.

ROBERTS, JOHN D; Del City HS; Oklahoma City, OK; (3); Am Leg Boys St; Church Yth Grp; German Clb; Church Choir; Ed Yrbk; Ofcr Frsh Cls; Rep Stu Cncl; Cit Awd; Licensed To Preach Gospel Of Jesus Christ; 6 Yrs Prophets Cls; OK Bapt Univ; Preacher.

ROBERTS, JONNITA; Vanoss Schl; Ada, OK; (3); Am Leg Aux Girls St; Church Yth Grp; FCA; Sec 4-H; FBLA; FHA; HOBY; Natl FFA Org; Chrldng; East Central U.

ROBERTS, K J; Weleetka Sr HS; Weleetka, OK; (4); Art Clb; Scholastic Bowl; Science Clb; Spanish Clb; School Play; Sec Sr Cls; Sec Stu Cncl; Bsktbl; Ftbl; Trk; US Army Rsrv Natl Schlr/Ath Awd; Natv Amer Clb VP; Seminole JC; Tribal Lwyr.

ROBERTS, KATERA P; Owasso Sr HS; Owasso, OK; (4); 22/296; Church Yth Grp; Sec Drama Clb; French Clb; FHA; Speech Tm; High Hon Roll; Hon Roll; NHS; Teen Action Grp; Tulsa Univ; Drama/Psych.

ROBERTS, KATINA R; El Reno Sr HS; El Reno, OK; (1); Cmnty Wkr; Girl Scts; Hon Roll; NHS; FHA; Marine Bio.

ROBERTS, KIM; Owasso Sr HS; Sperry, OK; (3); Church Yth Grp; FCA; FTA; SADD; Ed Nwsp; Rptr Yrbk; Rep Soph Cls; Rep Jr Cls; Rep Stu Cncl; Stat Bsktbl; Pharmacy Field.

ROBERTS, LINDA T; Eisenhower Sr HS; Lawton, OK; (4); 128/386; Church Yth Grp; Computer Clb; Natl FFA Org; Band; Flag Corp; Pep Band; Ofcr Stu Cncl; USAA Mrt Schlr Sci; Mst Imprvd Stu 96; Eagle Pride Person Of Month; OU; Nrsng.

ROBERTS, MELISSA; Cement Jr Sr HS; Cement, OK; (2); FHA; GAA; Math Clb; Quiz Bowl; Spanish Clb; Bsktbl; Trk; Vllybl; High Hon Roll; NHS; U OK; Comp.

ROBERTS, MELISSA L; Edmond North HS; Edmond, OK; (2); 136/420; Church Yth Grp; Cmnty Wkr; Chorus; Church Choir; Hon Roll; Leadville Mission Team; OK Chrstn U Of Sci & Arts.

ROBERTS, MISTY; Glencoe Public Schl; Glencoe, OK; (1); FHA; High Hon Roll; OSU.

ROBERTS, REGAN M; Muldrow HS; Muldrow, OK; (3); 3/225; Church Yth Grp; FHA; Math Clb; Natl Beta Clb; Science Clb; Spanish Clb; Church Choir; Var Capt Chrldng; High Hon Roll; NHS; Amer Govt Awd; IDFY; Span Awd; 2nd Pl Sci Fair; MLK Awd Cmnty Svc; Bio Awd; Piano; Clarinet; Xavier U; Phys.

ROBERTS, RONICA R; Valliant HS; Valliant, OK; (2); 23/90; Church Yth Grp; 4-H; FHA; GAA; SADD; Church Choir; Sec Frsh Cls; JV Bsktbl; Var Chrldng; Var Powder Puff Ftbl; Ms VHS Pgtn 2nd Pl 96; RN.

ROBERTS, RYAN; Union Sr HS; Broken Arrow, OK; (4); 20/629; Am Leg Boys St; Church Yth Grp; FCA; Office Aide; Quiz Bowl; Spanish Clb; Teachers Aide; Varsity Clb; Var Bsbl; JV Bsktbl; OK ST U; Mech Engrng.

ROBERTS, SHANNON R; Oklaha HS; Oktaha, OK; (4); 18/46; Office Aide; Spanish Clb; SADD; Teachers Aide; Band; Drm Mjr(t); Jazz Band; Mrchg Band; Yrbk; Hon Roll; John Philips Sousa Band Awd; Span Excl Awd; Connors ST Coll; Ed; Psych.

ROBERTS, TAMMY; Colbert HS; Cartwright, OK; (4); 8/29; Drama Clb; FHA; Sec VICA; Chorus; Sftbl; High Hon Roll; Prfct Atten Awd; Southeastern OK ST U; Drama.

ROBERTS, TIFFANY; Skiatook HS; Skiatook, OK; (3); Drama Clb; FBLA; Pep Clb; Teachers Aide; VICA; Chorus; Drill Tm; School Play; Stage Crew; Yrbk; Med.

ROBERTS, TRACY M; Union Intermediate HS; Tulsa, OK; (2); 38/800; L Swmmng; High Hon Roll; Pres NHS; Cmpfr; Lib Vol; SAIL; For Lang Clb; Med.

ROBERTS, ZACH; Chandler HS; Chandler, OK; (4); 2/80; Am Leg Boys St; FCA; Chorus; Yrbk; Pres Frsh Cls; Pres Soph Cls; Pres Sr Cls; Var L Ftbl; Var L Wrstlng; Pres NHS; Tae Kwon Do.

ROBERTSON, ANGELA C; South Coffeyville Schl; South Coffeyville, OK; (1); Church Yth Grp; Pres Sec 4-H; Cit Awd; 4-H Awd; Hon Roll; AZ ST Univ; Arch.

ROBERTSON, ANTHONY R; Checotah HS; Checotah, OK; (2); Speech Tm; Chorus; VP Stu Cncl; Bsktbl; Ftbl; Trk; Pres Acad Fit Awd.

ROBERTSON, BENJAMIN W; Dustin Schl; Dustin, OK; (4); Cmnty Wkr; Natl FFA Org; Quiz Bowl; Ofcr Bsbl; Bsktbl; All Star Bsktbl/Bsbl; All Conf Bsktbl/Bsbl; All Trnmnt Bsktbl.

ROBERTSON, CARRIE; Eisenhower Sr HS; Lawton, OK; (3); 49/485; CAP; ROTC; Science Clb; Color Guard; Drill Tm; Rptr Nwsp; Ofcr Sr Cls; NHS; High Hon Roll; Jr NHS; Young Rep Clb; SAVE; Med Explorers; OK Univ; Aviation:pilot.

ROBERTSON, ELLIOTT; Konawa Sr HS; Konawa, OK; (2); 2/70; FBLA; Library Aide; Natl Beta Clb; Teachers Aide; Band; Mrchg Band; Stage Crew; NHS; Ada Schlstc Mt 1st Pl Cmptr/2nd Pl Math; 2nd ST FBLA Cmptr Tech; 3rd Pl Cmptr Fndmntls Murray ST; E Cntrl ST; Mltmd Tech Cnsltnt.

ROBERTSON, GABRIEL L; Del City HS; Del City, OK; (2); VP Church Yth Grp; Cmnty Wkr; Chorus; Church Choir; School Musical; Jr NHS; NHS; Merit Awd 95; Pres Awd For Educl Excl 95; OK Hse Of Rep Page 95; Music Ed.

ROBERTSON, HEATHER; Blanchard Jr Sr HS; Blanchard, OK; (1); Church Yth Grp; FCA; Pep Clb; Church Choir; Var Bsktbl; Chrldng; Wt Lftg; Ftbl Homecoming Attendant.

ROBERTSON, JOE; Blanchard Jr Sr HS; Blanchard, OK; (4); Am Leg Boys St; Church Yth Grp; Computer Clb; Spanish Clb; Teachers Aide; Var Capt Bsbl; Var Capt Bsktbl; Hon Roll; Stu Mo.

ROBERTSON, JUSTIN D; Newcastle HS; Blanchard, OK; (3); 16/100; Church Yth Grp; Scholastic Bowl; Science Clb; Spanish Clb; Church Choir; Intrml Bsktbl; Cit Awd; Gov Hon Prg Awd; Hon Roll; NHS; U OF OK; Soundrec Eng.

ROBERTSON, KAMI J; Minco Jr Sr HS; Minco, OK; (3); 7/30; Church Yth Grp; FCA; FHA; Band; Church Choir; Mrchg Band; Pep Band; VP Jr Cls; JV Bsktbl; JV Chrldng; U Of Cntrl OK.

ROBERTSON, KELLIE; Del City HS; Del City, OK; (4); 42/374; Am Leg Aux Girls St; Church Yth Grp; Cmnty Wkr; French Clb; Red Cross Aide; Church Choir; Ed Nwsp; Yrbk; Var L Swmmng; High Hon Roll; Spcl Cooresprndt Lcl Nwsp; Frgn Lang Clb; Spirit Squad Pblcty Chrprsn; Knox Coll; Popltcl Sci.

ROBERTSON, KYLIE; Carl Albert Jr HS; Oklahoma City, OK; (2); 1/300; Church Yth Grp; FCA; Key Clb; Chorus; VP Soph Cls; Sec Stu Cncl; Chrldng; Golf; High Hon Roll; NHS; Natl Champion Chrldng Squad 94-95; Yth For Christ Clb; OK ST Univ; Photographer.

ROBERTSON, LAKESHA R; Star Spencer HS; Spencer, OK; (2); Church Yth Grp; Pep Clb; Spanish Clb; Band; Church Choir; Mrchg Band; Pep Band; School Musical; Tennis; Cit Awd; TX A&M; Lwyr/Nurse/Bus Mngmt.

ROBERTSON, RASHELLE J; Checotah HS; Checotah, OK; (2); FHA; Girl Scts; Library Aide; Office Aide; Pep Clb; Hon Roll; NHS; Irs Invstgtr.

ROBERTSON, SCOTT B; South Intermediate HS; Broken Arrow, OK; (1); Church Yth Grp; Band; Mrchg Band; Orch; Soccer; Winter Drum Line; Wind Ensemble Concert Band.

ROBERTSON, STEPHANIE M; Wilburton Sr HS; Wilburton, OK; (1); #6 in class; Church Yth Grp; FBLA; Chorus; Nwsp; Ofcr Soph Cls; JV Var Chrldng; Var Sftbl; Hon Roll; NHS; Eastern OK ST Coll.

ROBINETT, ALISHA R; Dibble Jr Sr HS; Blanchard, OK; (4); FCA; 4-H; GAA; Hosp Aide; Natl FFA Org; Red Cross Aide; SADD; Var Bsktbl; Hon Roll; VICA; HOSA Chptr Rprtr.

ROBINETT, DWAYNE A; Noble HS; Noble, OK; (3); 29/167; Art Clb; Church Yth Grp; Key Clb; Model UN; Mu Alpha Theta; U Of OK.

ROBINETTE, RICHARD L; Union Sr HS; Tulsa, OK; (4); 36/632; Boy Scts; Church Yth Grp; FBLA; Ofcr Sr Cls; High Hon Roll; NHS; Pres Acad Fit Awd; Stage Crew; Alpha Theta; Stu Bible Study, Prayer Grp; Teenage Prblcns; Renaissance Acad Achvt; Bus Mgmt.

ROBINOWITZ, BETH H; B T Washington HS; Tulsa, OK; (3); Art Clb; Cmnty Wkr; Computer Clb; Spanish Clb; School Play; Var Crs Cntry; NHS; Debate Tm; Intnl Clb; ROTC; Ecology Clb VP; ECCO; Engrng.

ROBINSON, AARON; Boswell Sr HS; Boswell, OK; (1); Church Yth Grp; Natl FFA Org; Band; High Hon Roll; Hon Roll; NHS; West Point; Pilot.

ROBINSON, ADAM; Bishop Kelley HS; Claremore, OK; (4); Am Leg Boys St; FCA; Service Clb; Band; Jazz Band; Var Capt Bsktbl; Var Capt Socr; Cit Awd; High Hon Roll; NHS; Med.

ROBINSON, ALAN C; Hollis Jr Sr HS; Hollis, OK; (3); 4/50; Church Yth Grp; FBLA; Quiz Bowl; Band; Church Choir; Mrchg Band; School Play; Hon Roll; OK Hnr Soc; Southwestern OK ST U; Pharmcy.

ROBINSON, ANTHONY C; West Middle HS; Norman, OK; (2); Cmnty Wkr; Spanish Clb; Teachers Aide; Band; Jazz Band; Mrchg Band; Orch; OK Univ; Jrnlsm/Brdcstng.

ROBINSON, ASHLEY A; B T Washington HS; Tulsa, OK; (1); Church Yth Grp; Church Choir.

ROBINSON, BRADLEY J; Claremore Sr HS; Claremore, OK; (2); Cmnty Wkr; Natl FFA Org; Office Aide; Hon Roll; CYBA.

ROBINSON, CASSANDRA; Stigler HS; Stigler, OK; (4); 1/73; Am Leg Aux Girls St; Church Yth Grp; Rep Sec FHA; Hosp Aide; SADD; Band; Color Guard; Hon Roll; NHS; Prfct Atten Awd; Child Psych.

ROBINSON, EXCELL D; Del City HS; Oklahoma City, OK; (4); Art Clb; FBLA; Church Choir; Ofcr Sr Cls; Ofcr Bsbl; Bsktbl; Wt Lftg; KS Univ; Bus.

ROBINSON, GENICE Y; Del City HS; Oklahoma City, OK; (2); Church Yth Grp; Spanish Clb; Church Choir; Drill Tm; Hon Roll; Langston; Phslgst.

ROBINSON, HEIDI; Moore HS; Moore, OK; (4); Art Clb; Church Yth Grp; VP JA; Library Aide; Rptr Chorus; Church Choir; Jr NHS.

ROBINSON, JADE; Holdenville Jr HS; Holdenville, OK; (1); Church Yth Grp; FCA; Intrml Bsktbl; Intrml Wt Lftg; Hon Roll.

ROBINSON, JAMIE M; Altus Sr HS; El Paso, TX; (4); 30/230; Sec Church Yth Grp; Cmnty Wkr; Letterman Clb; Quiz Bowl; Chorus; Church Choir; School Musical; School Play; Ed Nwsp; Ed Yrbk; Var Choir Sec, Memorial Awd For Music; Purdue Univ; Speech Pathology.

ROBINSON, JARED W; Hollis Jr Sr HS; Hollis, OK; (3); Am Leg Boys St; Church Yth Grp; Letterman Clb; Natl FFA Org; School Play; Var Bsbl; Var Ftbl; Wt Lftg; Hon Roll; FFA Grnhand And Star Grnhnd.

ROBINSON, JAY; Hollis Jr Sr HS; Hollis, OK; (4); 16/56; Am Leg Boys St; Cmnty Wkr; FBLA; Letterman Clb; Teachers Aide; Varsity Clb; School Play; Nwsp; Pres Soph Cls; Pres Jr Cls; Sprts Med.

ROBINSON, JON; Cheyenne HS; Cheyenne, OK; (3); Natl FFA Org; Band; Chorus; Jazz Band; Stage Crew; Phtg Yrbk; Cit Awd; High Hon Roll; NHS.

ROBINSON, JOY M; Del City HS; Del City, OK; (3); Pres Drama Clb; FBLA; Hist SADD; Thesps; School Musical; School Play; Stage Crew; Jr NHS; NHS; Elem Ed/Theatre.

ROBINSON, KAREN E; Oklahoma Sch Of Science & Math; Shawnee, OK; (3); NFL; Scholastic Bowl; Spanish Clb; Thesps; School Play; Yrbk; High Hon Roll; Jr NHS; Ntl Merit Ltr; Shawnee Sister Cities Cncl.

ROBINSON, KEITH G; Durant HS; Durant, OK; (4); Mrchg Band; Orch; SOSU Bnd Schol; SOSU; Elect Eng.

ROBINSON, KIERA; Miami Sr HS; Miami, OK; (3); 8/180; Church Yth Grp; GAA; Letterman Clb; Teachers Aide; Lit Mag; Var Capt Bsktbl; Golf; High Hon Roll; Hon Roll; Jr NHS; Regnl/Natl/Intnl Arabian Horse Assn Shows; All Conf Bsktbl Tm; Agri Co Classic Bsktbl Tourn; U Of Tulsa; Vetrnrn.

ROBINSON, LALISSIA A; Westmoore HS; Oklahoma City, OK; (4); JCL; Latin Clb; Pep Clb; Band; Mrchg Band; Ed Yrbk; Bsktbl; Hon Roll; Future Jrnlst Of Amer; Langston; Phy Thrpst.

ROBINSON, LAURA D; Carl Albert HS; Palm Harbor, FL; (4); Art Clb; Church Yth Grp; French Clb; Girl Scts; Science Clb; Pres Band; Church Choir; Color Guard; Flag Corp; Mrchg Band; Super Rtng Solo & Emsbl St Cont 3 Yrs; FL Tech; Marine Bio.

ROBINSON, LESLIE A; Durant HS; Durant, OK; (1); Tennis; Cooking; Art.

ROBINSON, MATT; Stillwater Jr HS; Stillwater, OK; (1); Boy Scts; Church Yth Grp; Cmnty Wkr; Library Aide; High Hon Roll; Pres Schlr; Acad Bowl Tm; Schl Rep State Wide Engrng Fair; Northern OK Coll Acad Swpstks Awd Jr HS Div; Astronaut.

ROBINSON, MAYA L; Northeast HS; Oklahoma City, OK; (2); Church Yth Grp; Chorus; Church Choir; Rep Soph Cls; High Hon Roll; NHS; Pres Acad Fit Awd; OK City Univ; Fash Desgn.

ROBINSON, PATRICK W; Durant HS; Durant, OK; (4); OK Arts Inst Smmr Cmp; SOSU; Art.

ROBINSON, RANDY; Yukon Middle HS; Yukon, OK; (1); JV Socr; DARE.

ROBINSON, ROY; Sapulpa Sr HS; Sand Springs, OK; (3); 157/299; Church Yth Grp; FCA; Pres Natl FFA Org; VP VICA; Socr; Hon Roll; Prfct Atten Awd; Soil & Water Cnsrvtn Bd VP; OK ST U; Frfghtr.

ROBINSON, SARAH; Senior HS; Edmond, OK; (1); FCA; Spanish Clb; Drill Tm; Yrbk; Chrldng; Cit Awd; High Hon Roll; Hon Roll; NHS; Comp Pom Pn Sqd Natl Champs; U OK.

ROBINSON, SHANA E; Caddo HS; Caddo, OK; (1); 4-H; FHA; Pep Clb; SADD; Chorus; School Musical; School Play; Var JV Bsktbl; JV Chrldng; Var Sftbl; FHA Historian; Acad Achiever; Southeastern OK ST U.

ROBINSON, SHENELL L; Stillwater Jr HS; Stillwater, OK; (1); Church Yth Grp; FCA; Church Choir; Bsktbl; Hon Roll; Pres Acad Fit Awd; Pres Awd Ed Imprvmnt; Awd Rose ST Coll Schlstc Prtcpnt; Acctng.

ROBINSON, TENEISHA D; Midwest City HS; Midwest City, OK; (2); 66/488; ROTC; Mgr(s); Trk; NHS; Langston U; Psych.

ROBINSON, WHITNEY; Chickasha Jr HS; Chickasha, OK; (1); Church Yth Grp; Library Aide; Science Clb; Band; Church Choir; Mrchg Band; Orch; Pep Band; Ofcr Stu Cncl; High Hon Roll; Band Qn.

ROBISON, AMBER; Cushing HS; Cushing, OK; (1); Church Yth Grp; Spanish Clb; Ed Yrbk; VP Frsh Cls; VP Stu Cncl; Bsktbl; Chrldng; Wt Lftg; Hon Roll; Piano; OK U.

ROBISON, DANIEL L; Durant HS; Durant, OK; (2); Wt Lftg; Hon Roll; Hunting; Fishing; Swimming; Skiing; Southeastern OK ST Univ.

ROBISON, DARENDA; Elk City HS; Elk City, OK; (4); 6/141; Church Yth Grp; Rptr FBLA; Key Clb; Letterman Clb; Math Clb; Pep Clb; Sec Science Clb; Spanish Clb; Band; Mrchg Band; SW OK ST Univ; Pharmacy.

ROBISON, RACHEL D; Altus Sr HS; Altus, OK; (3); German Clb; Band; Chorus; Mrchg Band; Pep Band; School Musical; School Play; Hon Roll; Cir The ST; SW Reg Hnr Choir; SW Rgnl Hnr Band; Dctrt/Dhrl Mscl Ed.

ROBLYER, KRISTIN R; Guthrie Sr HS; Guthrie, OK; (3); 3/250; Am Leg Aux Girls St; French Clb; Mu Alpha Theta; SADD; Band; Flag Corp; Mrchg Band; School Musical; Rep Jr Cls; NHS; Mst Outstndg Woodwind Plyr 94-95, 95-96; All-St Band 2 Yrs.

ROBNETT, RANDY C; Putnam City West HS; Bethany, OK; (2); 20/380; Church Yth Grp; Cmnty Wkr; FCA; Spanish Clb; SADD; Acpl Chr; Chorus; Church Choir; School Musical; Pres Soph Cls; Southern Nazarene U; Pre-Med.

ROBSON, BRENT S; Edmond Santa Fe HS; Oklahoma City, OK; (3); Church Yth Grp; Pres Treas Latin Clb; Orch; Yrbk; Sec Jr Cls; Pres Stu Cncl; JV Crs Cntry; Cit Awd; Hon Roll; NHS; Orch Cncl Pres; Yale Club Awd; Natl Yng Ldrs Conf; Bus.

ROBUCK, CHALYN; Tipton Jr Sr HS; Tipton, OK; (2); Natl FFA Org; Science Clb; Var L Bsbl; Var L Bsktbl; Var L Ftbl; Var Wt Lftg; Hon Roll; Spanish NHS; Cntrl OK; Coach/Mechnc.

ROCK, GREGORY F; Mc Alester HS; Mcalester, OK; (3); Am Leg Boys St; Church Yth Grp; Debate Tm; Speech Tm; Church Choir; Rptr Nwsp; Var Capt Bsktbl; Hon Roll; Natl Yth Ldrs Conf Washington D C; ST Rep Lloyd Fields Page 2 Yrs; Pre Law.

ROCKEY, APRIL; Stuart Sr HS; Mcalester, OK; (3); 2/23; 4-H; VP FHA; Quiz Bowl; Teachers Aide; Nwsp; Var Sftbl; Hon Roll; U OK; Bus.

ROCKOW, KIM; Choctaw Jr HS; Choctaw, OK; (1); Church Yth Grp; Spanish Clb; Rep Stu Cncl; Hon Roll; Auburn U; Law.

ROCKWELL, AUDREY D; Choctaw HS; Choctaw, OK; (2); 36/384; Church Yth Grp; Cmnty Wkr; Girl Scts; Key Clb; Spanish Clb; School Play; Stage Crew; Sec Treas Yrbk; Hon Roll; Jr NHS; Girl Scts Silvr Awd; Senators Page.

ROCKWELL, CYNTHIA R; Northeast HS; Oklahoma City, OK; (3); Church Yth Grp; Cmnty Wkr; FBLA; FHA; Pep Clb; Chorus; Church Choir; Drill Tm; Ofcr Jr Cls; Hon Roll; OK Univ; Acctng.

ROCKWOOD, KATHY M; Bixby Sr HS; Bixby, OK; (1); SADD; Drill Tm; Var L Crs Cntry; Var L Trk.

RODGERS, JENNIFER L; Shawnee Sr HS; Shawnee, OK; (3); 54/254; 4-H; Hosp Aide; Office Aide; Quiz Bowl; 4-H Awd; High Hon Roll; Jr NHS; NHS; Prfct Atten Awd; Rose ST; Med Field.

RODGERS, KATIE M; Jenks HS; Tulsa, OK; (3); 72/517; Dance Clb; Debate Tm; Hosp Aide; Office Aide; Treas Pep Clb; Treas Stu Cncl; Capt Chrldng; JV Socr; High Hon Roll; Stu Ambsdr; U Of KS.

RODGERS, KRISTEN L; Durant HS; Durant, OK; (2); Pres Frsh Cls; Sec Soph Cls; Rep Stu Cncl; L Chrldng; Church Yth Grp; FBLA; Powder Puff Ftbl; Hon Roll; Drug Free Yth; PT.

RODGERS, MELISSA; Durant HS; Durant, OK; (4); #49 in class; Am Leg Aux Girls St; Church Yth Grp; FBLA; Rep Frsh Cls; Rep Soph Cls; Rep Jr Cls; Sec Stu Cncl; Var Chrldng; Powder Puff Ftbl; Hon Roll; 4 Yr Drg Free Yth Mem; U OK; Optmtry.

RODGERS, MICHELE D; Poteau HS; Poteau, OK; (3); Art Clb; CAP; Drama Clb; 4-H; French Clb; VICA; Chorus; School Musical; School Play; Stage Crew; FL Inst Of Tech; Psych.

RODKIN, BUCKY RAY; Tahlequah Sr HS; Tahlequah, OK; (4); Church Yth Grp; Math Clb; Quiz Bowl; Scholastic Bowl; Science Clb; Spanish Clb; Band; Mrchg Band; Pep Band; Sprt Ed Nwsp; All Trnmnt Team Connors ST Coll Brain Bowl; 2nd Pl Sprts Wrtng NSU Media Pay; NE ST U; Jrnlsm.

RODMAN, LEIGHA; Guymon Sr HS; Guymon, OK; (2); Church Yth Grp; French Clb; SADD; Sec Soph Cls; Bsktbl; Chrldng; Wt Lftg; Hon Roll; PHD; Class Rep; UCO.

RODMAN, MORGAN; Claremore Sr HS; Claremore, OK; (2); 1/270; Debate Tm; Office Aide; Quiz Bowl; Science Clb; Treas Soph Cls; Ofcr Stu Cncl; High Hon Roll; Parliamentarian Claremore Intertrbl Yth Cncl; Rep Of Rogers Cty Cherokee Natl Yth Cncl; Stu Mnth 94; Dartmouth.

RODOLPH, STEPHANIE; Clinton HS; Clinton, OK; (1); Church Yth Grp; FCA; FHA; Chorus; Swing Chorus; JV Chrldng; Var Golf; Hon Roll; UCA All Star Chrldr; Showchoir; U Of OK.

RODRIGUEZ, COURTNEY; Durant HS; Durant, OK; (4); 16/190; Church Yth Grp; SADD; VICA; Rep Soph Cls; Rep Sr Cls; Rep Stu Cncl; Var L Chrldng; Var L Socr; Var L Sftbl; High Hon Roll; HOSA Sec, Rprtr; Phrmcy.

RODRIGUEZ, JASON; Victory Christian Schl; Tulsa, OK; (3); Church Yth Grp; Quiz Bowl; Jazz Band; Pep Band; Var Socr; Var Trk; High Hon Roll; NHS; Ntl Merit Ltr; Oral Roberts Univ; Comp Grphcs.

RODRIGUEZ, MICHELLE; Plainview HS; Ardmore, OK; (1); 25/93; Var Bsktbl; Var Chrldng; OK U.

RODRIGUEZ, NANCY; Kingfisher HS; Kingfisher, OK; (1); Debate Tm; Speech Tm; Chorus; School Musical; Cit Awd; Hon Roll; Prfct Atten Awd.

RODRIGUEZ, NORMA E; Texhoma HS; Texhoma, OK; (4); 12/23; Church Yth Grp; Pep Clb; Teachers Aide; Band; Drill Tm; Mrchg Band; Yrbk; OK Panhandle ST Univ; Comp Sy.

RODRIGUEZ, OLIVIA; Clinton HS; Clinton, OK; (2); 1/138; Church Yth Grp; FCA; FBLA; FHA; Chorus; Pres Rep Stu Cncl; High Hon Roll; Hon Roll; NHS; Math Awd; All Amer Schlr; Evangel Coll; Law.

RODRIGUEZ, TARA M; Westmoore HS; Oklahoma City, OK; (3); Church Yth Grp; Hosp Aide; Band; Church Choir; Mrchg Band; JV Bsktbl; Jr NHS; NHS; Stu Ath Trainer; Sports Medicine; Tchr.

RODRIGUEZ, TIFFANY M; Cordell Sr HS; Cordell, OK; (4); Church Yth Grp; FHA; Teachers Aide; Chorus; School Play; Swing Chorus; Variety Show; Pres Jr Cls; Ofcr Sr Cls; Ofcr Stu Cncl; SWOSU Weatherford; Poltcl Sci.

ROE, CHARISSA; Newcastle HS; Newcastle, OK; (3); 19/92; FCA; Spanish Clb; JV Var Bsktbl; JV Var Sftbl; JV Trk; Intrml Wt Lftg; Cit Awd; Hon Roll; NHS; Natl Hnr Roll; All Amer Schlr; Natl Yth Ldrshp Frm Med 96; U Of OK; Bus/PT.

ROE, JEFF; Tulsa Emmanuel Christian Sch; Tulsa, OK; (2); Church Yth Grp; Ed Nwsp; Treas Frsh Cls; Rep Soph Cls; Hon Roll; Comp Programming; Comp Repair.

ROE, SHANE C; Roland Sr HS; Muldrow, OK; (2); Natl FFA Org; JV Bsktbl; Hon Roll.

ROEBUCK, HOLLY; Nowata HS; Nowata, OK; (4); 2/60; Am Leg Aux Girls St; FCA; Pres FHA; HOBY; Chorus; Rep Stu Cncl; Var L Golf; Var L Sftbl; High Hon Roll; VP NHS; U Of Tulsa; Spch Pthlgy.

ROEHL, BRYAN C; Ada HS; Ada, OK; (3); Am Leg Boys St; Church Yth Grp; French Clb; Rptr Yrbk; Tennis; High Hon Roll; NHS; East Cntrl Univ; Doctor.

ROEHR, MICHAEL S; Lawton Sr HS; Fort Sill, OK; (3); Computer Clb; Key Clb; Science Clb; High Hon Roll; Hon Roll; Pres Acad Fit Awd; Early Grad; Univ Of S FL; Cmptr Sci.

ROENSENER, KATRINA; Hardesty Schl; Hardesty, OK; (1); 3/6; Church Yth Grp; FCA; Quiz Bowl; Bsktbl; Hon Roll.

ROESENER, PIPER; Hardesty Schl; Hardesty, OK; (4); #1 in class; Church Yth Grp; FCA; HOBY; Natl FFA Org; Quiz Bowl; Bsktbl; Chrldng; DAR Awd; High Hon Roll; Pres Acad Fit Awd.

ROGERS, AARON J; Stillwater Sr HS; Stillwater, OK; (2); Boy Scts; Natl Beta Clb; Band; Church Choir; Mrchg Band; Pep Band; High Hon Roll; Envrmntl Clb; Var Schlr Awd; Vet Sci.

ROGERS, ABIGAIL; Central HS; Tulsa, OK; (2); Church Yth Grp; Quiz Bowl; Red Cross Aide; Tennis; Cit Awd; High Hon Roll; Hon Roll; NHS; Frdm Found; Artwk Dsply Glcrs Museum; Pst Awd; NSU; Med.

ROGERS, AIMEE; Noble HS; Norman, OK; (3); 1/168; French Clb; Hosp Aide; Library Aide; Mu Alpha Theta; SADD; Hon Roll; NHS; Intnl Bus.

ROGERS, APRIL N; Warner HS; Warner, OK; (1); Church Yth Grp; Cmnty Wkr; FCA; Pep Clb; Spanish Clb; Varsity Clb; Church Choir; School Play; Variety Show; Rep Frsh Cls; Frosh Ftbl Attndt 95-; Crs Cntry ST Acad Chmps; Crs Cntry/Track ST Qlfr; Northeastern OK; Chldrns Thrpy.

ROGERS, CORTNI; Ponca HS; Ponca City, OK; (1); Pep Clb; Chorus; Drill Tm; Chrldng; Gym; Pom Pon; Hon Roll; Dncng; Span; Sci; Psych.

ROGERS, FELICIA D; Shattuck Jr Sr HS; Shattuck, OK; (3); 10/31; 4-H; FHA; Pep Clb; Band; Chorus; Jazz Band; School Play; Chrldng; Hon Roll; NHS; Outstdng Stu; Northwestern OK ST Univ; Med.

ROGERS, JA MEISHA; Bartlesville Sr HS; Bartlesville, OK; (4); Drama Clb; French Clb; FBLA; JA; Best PM Stdnt Awd 94-95; Most Spprtv Drama Stdnt Awd; CEBSF Schlsp; Prairie View A&M; Bus/Law.

ROGERS, JAMIE; Ponca City Sr HS; Ponca City, OK; (4); 7/380; Church Yth Grp; Cmnty Wkr; Library Aide; Ofcr Stu Cncl; Tennis; High Hon Roll; NHS; Ntl Merit Schol; Pres Schlr; St Schlr; OK ST U; Comp Sci.

ROGERS, JARROD; Seiling Schl; Fairview, OK; (3); 2/35; Church Yth Grp; Natl FFA Org; Band; School Play; VP Frsh Cls; Rep Stu Cncl; Ftbl; Wt Lftg; High Hon Roll; Hon Roll.

ROGERS, JOHN; Moore HS; Moore, OK; (4); 6/505; Ski Clb; Pres Band; Drm Mjr(t); Jazz Band; Mrchg Band; Pep Band; L Crs Cntry; L Trk; NHS; Val; U Of OK; Msc Ed.

ROGERS, JUSTIN K; Dickson HS; Ardmore, OK; (3); 1/70; Spanish Clb; Speech Tm; School Play; Hon Roll; NHS; St Schlr.

ROGERS, KALE; Thomas Jr Sr HS; Thomas, OK; (2); Church Yth Grp; Letterman Clb; Natl FFA Org; Sec Frsh Cls; Rep Soph Cls; Var Bsktbl; Var Ftbl; Wt Lftg; High Hon Roll.

ROGERS, KELLY; Crowder Schl; Mcalester, OK; (4); 1/40; FBLA; FHA; HOBY; VP Frsh Cls; VP Jr Cls; VP Stu Cncl; Var Bsktbl; High Hon Roll; NHS; Lrshp Mrt Awd.

ROGERS, KELLY; Indianola HS; Indianola, OK; (3); 2/32; FBLA; VP Natl Beta Clb; Natl FFA Org; Spanish Clb; Pres Frsh Cls; Treas Jr Cls; Treas Stu Cncl; Var Bsktbl; Var Sftbl; High Hon Roll; Sprts Med.

ROGERS, KYLE; Choctaw Jr HS; Choctaw, OK; (1); 74/210; Church Yth Grp; FCA; Office Aide; Var Ftbl; Wt Lftg; High Hon Roll; Hon Roll; Pres Acad Fit Awd; Black Belt Tae Kwon Do; FL ST; Corp Law.

ROGERS, LEA ANNE; Medford Schl; Medford, OK; (3); FCA; School Play; Yrbk; Pres Jr Cls; Var Bsktbl; Var Sftbl; Var Trk; Hon Roll; NHS; St Discus Fnlst; OK ST U; Elem Tchr.

ROGERS, MELISSA D; Midwest City HS; Midwest City, OK; (2); 115/480; Church Yth Grp; Band; Mrchg Band; Pep Band; Hon Roll; Jr NHS; NHS; Prfct Atten Awd; Rose ST Univ; Ed.

ROGERS, MICHELLE; Noble HS; Norman, OK; (3); 1/169; Mu Alpha Theta; Spanish Clb; SADD; Chorus; Cit Awd; High Hon Roll; NHS; Pres Acad Fit Awd; OK ST U; Dr.

ROGERS, NEIL G; Union Intermediate HS; Broken Arrow, OK; (1); German Clb; Hon Roll; Extracurricular Soccer TSC 81 Goalkeeper.

ROGERS, PHILLIP; Pawhuska HS; Pawhuska, OK; (2); 1/95; Church Yth Grp; FCA; Bsktbl; Crs Cntry; Trk; Cit Awd; High Hon Roll; NHS; Prfct Atten Awd.

ROGERS, QWENDA; Wagoner Sr HS; Wagoner, OK; (3); Sec VICA; Chorus; Hist Soph Cls; Intrml Bsktbl; Intrml Chrldng; High Hon Roll; North Central Dist Sec OK VICA; Csmtlgy 2nd Yr Stdnt Indn Cptl Vo-Tech; All Schl Sec VICA 95-; Nrs.

ROGERS, REID T; Oklahoma Christian Schl; Oklahoma City, OK; (4); Cmnty Wkr; FCA; Library Aide; Office Aide; Teachers Aide; JV Var Ftbl; Wt Lftg; JV Wrstlng; Hon Roll; Baylor U; Bus/Finance.

ROGERS, SHAWN W; Savanna HS; Mcalester, OK; (3); Church Yth Grp; Drama Clb; Natl FFA Org; Teachers Aide; Ftbl; Hon Roll; Works With Handicapped Children.

ROGERS, SHELLEY; Luther HS; Luther, OK; (4); 18/42; FHA; Natl FFA Org; Office Aide; Teachers Aide; Hon Roll; Prfct Atten Awd; ST/CHPTR FFA Orgs Sec 95-; Northeastern A&M Coll; Ag Ed.

ROGERS, SUNNIE; Wetumka Jr Sr HS; Wetumka, OK; (3); HOBY; Key Clb; Spanish Clb; Rep Jr Cls; Var Sftbl; Hon Roll; Tulsa U; Jrnlst.

ROGERS, TOM; Mid-Del Christian Schl; Oklahoma City, OK; (4); Church Yth Grp; Rptr Yrbk; Ofcr Stu Cncl; High Hon Roll; Ntl Merit Ltr; Distngshd Chrstn HS Stu Acad; Central Bible Coll; Pastoral.

ROGERS JR, TOMMY M; Charles Page HS; Sapulpa, OK; (4); 52/329; Church Yth Grp; Cmnty Wkr; Red Cross Aide; VICA; Band; Mrchg Band; Hon Roll; NHS; Prfct Atten Awd; VICA Prntng Cmptn 95; Prin Hnr Rl; Yrbk Hall Of Fame; Sandite Awd For Outstdng Eng Stdnt; U Of Tulsa; Cmptr Sci/Elctrl En.

ROGGOW, SHEILA; Perkins-Tryon HS; Perkins, OK; (2); 1/110; Church Yth Grp; FHA; Girl Scts; Intnl Clb; Treas Key Clb; High Hon Roll; NHS; Prod Awd FFA/TREAS; Slvr Awd Girl Scts; Wrld His Eng III Outstndng Stu Awd; OK ST Univ.

ROGNAS, ERIC L; Edmond Memorial HS; Edmond, OK; (2); Church Yth Grp; FCA; Ofcr Bsbl; AMBUCS.

ROLAND, AMANDA D; Charles Page HS; Sand Springs, OK; (2); 34/378; Church Yth Grp; FCA; GAA; Key Clb; Spanish Clb; Ofcr Stu Cncl; Var JV Bsktbl; JV Sftbl; Hon Roll; Jr NHS; Native Amer Stu Assn; U Of AZ; Sports Medicine.

ROLAND, JASON I; Moore HS; Moore, OK; (3); Am Leg Boys St; French Clb; L Ftbl; Var L Trk; Jr NHS; NHS.

ROLAND, LATICIA; Enid Sr HS; Enid, OK; (2); 199/431; Church Yth Grp; FCA; Varsity Clb; Church Choir; Swing Chorus; Rep Stu Cncl; Var Chrldng; Var Trk; Cit Awd; Hon Roll; Langston U; Scl Wrk.

ROLL, DELLA K; Stillwater Sr HS; Stillwater, OK; (3); Church Yth Grp; Hosp Aide; Sec Key Clb; Natl Beta Clb; Spanish Clb; Band; Mrchg Band; Orch; Var L Crs Cntry; Var L Trk; Var Schlr; Environmental Clb; Rice; Bio.

ROLLER, MARCI D; Union Sr HS; Broken Arrow, OK; (3); 69/875; Cmnty Wkr; FCA; FBLA; Key Clb; Rep Jr Cls; Treas Stu Cncl; Var Chrldng; Hon Roll; NHS; Spanish NHS; 2nd Pl Natl Chrldng Sqd Var Div; Miss Union Fnlst; OU.

ROLLINS, ELIZABETH A; Altus Sr HS; Altus, OK; (2); Sec Boy Scts; Cmnty Wkr; German Clb; Swmmng; Hon Roll; Schl Achvmnt Ger; Intnl Order Rainbow Girls; Karate Black Belt; Prestl Sports Fitness Awd.

ROMBERG, DEREK J; Shawnee Sr HS; Shawnee, OK; (4); 56/265; Library Aide; Spanish Clb; Teachers Aide; Nwsp; Golf; Ice Hcky; Socr; Tennis; Hon Roll; NHS; Big Brothers & Big Sisters; OK Univ; Pharmacy; Bus.

ROMERO, BILLIE J; Pauls Valley HS; Pauls Valley, OK; (2); Church Yth Grp; Spanish Clb; Rptr Yrbk; Sftbl; TX Tech U; Nrsng.

ROMERO, JASON N; Broken Arrow Sr HS; Broken Arrow, OK; (3); Church Yth Grp; JA; Office Aide; VICA; Var Stu Cncl; Wt Lftg; OK Univ.

ROMERO, MICHAEL; Norman Sr HS; Norman, OK; (3); FCA; Mu Alpha Theta; Spanish Clb; Acpl Chr; Chorus; Church Choir; School Musical; Variety Show; Swing Chorus; NHS.

ROMERO, NICK J; Chandler HS; Port Arthur, TX; (3); Art Clb; Teachers Aide; VICA; Band; Mrchg Band; Rep Frsh Cls; Rep Soph Cls; Ofcr Stu Cncl; Hon Roll; Art Stu; Attnd & Entered Art Shows; Attnd Tech Schl; Guiatr; MIT; Comp Prgmr-Tech.

ROMIGH, MELISSA M; Union Intermediate HS; Tulsa, OK; (2); 3/800; Church Yth Grp; FCA; German Clb; Girl Scts; Sec Soph Cls; Socr; Hon Roll; Jr NHS; NHS; Key Clb; USC; DFY; GSA Slvr Awd; Marine Bio.

ROMINE, CHARLA M; East Central HS; Tulsa, OK; (3); 18/345; Church Yth Grp; Cmnty Wkr; Hosp Aide; Spanish Clb; Chorus; Ed Yrbk; Rep Jr Cls; Hon Roll; NHS; Rep Soph Cls; Stu Adv Cncl Sec; Rogers ST Coll; Pre-Medicine.

ROMINES, TIFFANY; Dustin Schl; Dustin, OK; (1); 1/15; Church Yth Grp; English Clb; FCA; Scholastic Bowl; Science Clb; Spanish Clb; Church Choir; Score Keeper; Sftbl; High Hon Roll; OK Bapt U; Sci.

ROMO, DANIEL; Plainview HS; Ardmore, OK; (4); 17/81; Am Leg Boys St; Natl Beta Clb; Quiz Bowl; Teachers Aide; Rptr Sr Cls; Rep Stu Cncl; Bsktbl; Crs Cntry; Trk; Hon Roll; U OK; Archtctr.

ROMSA, LAURA; Claremore Sr HS; Claremore, OK; (2); 1/273; Sec Church Yth Grp; Phtg Rptr Yrbk; Hon Roll; NHS; Med.

RONEY, MATT; Edmond North HS; Edmond, OK; (2); 92/420; FCA; SADD; Ofcr Bsbl; Ftbl; Jr NHS; NHS.

RONEY, MELISSA; Edmond North HS; Edmond, OK; (4); 41/330; Cmnty Wkr; FCA; Key Clb; Mu Alpha Theta; Office Aide; Spanish Clb; SADD; Variety Show; Rep Stu Cncl; Var Chrldng; Ftbll & Wrstlng Homecoming Queen Cand; Var Cheer/Pom; OK St Univ; Vet.

RONNOW, ANDREW C; Union Intermediate HS; Tulsa, OK; (2); Church Yth Grp; Band; Church Choir; Orch; Union Soccer Clb; Masters Coll.

ROOF, JESSICA B; Morrison Public Schl; Morrison, OK; (3); 4/30; Am Leg Aux Girls St; Church Yth Grp; FCA; FBLA; FHA; Spanish Clb; Teachers Aide; Sprt Ed Nwsp; Ed Nwsp; Var Bsktbl; OK Univ; PT.

ROOKER, JASON; Tuttle HS; Tuttle, OK; (3); Natl FFA Org; Hon Roll; SW OK ST Univ; Pharmacy.

ROOKER, JOSH; Mc Loud HS; Mc Loud, OK; (3); 9/129; Church Yth Grp; FCA; Letterman Clb; Pep Clb; Pres Jr Cls; Rep Stu Cncl; Var Bsbl; Capt Var Bsktbl; High Hon Roll; NHS; FFA; Stu Wk & Mo; OBU; Med.

ROOKS, JENNIFER; Valliant HS; Valliant, OK; (4); 4/86; Church Yth Grp; SADD; Teachers Aide; Band; Drm Mjr(t); Mrchg Band; Pep Band; High Hon Roll; NHS; SE OK ST U; Bus.

ROOKS, WHITNEY; Prue Schl; Prue, OK; (2); FCA; Letterman Clb; Sec Frsh Cls; Sec Soph Cls; Var Bsktbl; Socr; High Hon Roll; Hon Roll; Yth Sccr Coach/Ref; Northeastern ST Univ; Med.

ROONEY, ALLYSSA R; Moore HS; Moore, OK; (3); Pres Rep Church Yth Grp; Cmnty Wkr; French Clb; Hosp Aide; Science Clb; SADD; Teachers Aide; Chorus; Jr NHS; NHS; Channel 5 Kids Who Care Awd April 96; Jr Escort For Grad; Vol Childrens Miracle Network Telethon; Pediatric Oncology Nrs.

ROPER, AMBER; Varnum Jr Sr HS; Seminole, OK; (3); 1/15; HOBY; Pres Soph Cls; Pres Jr Cls; Var Bsktbl; Capt Chrldng; Var Sftbl; Hon Roll; NHS; SW OK ST U; Pharmacy.

ROPER, EMILY; Chickasha HS; Chickasha, OK; (2); Church Yth Grp; Cmnty Wkr; FCA; Chorus; Var Chrldng; Var Socr; Hon Roll; Sec Jr NHS; Office Aide; Church Choir; Grls Sccr Acad St Chmpns 95; Med.

ROPP, JEREMY; Bartlesville Sr HS; Bartlesville, OK; (3); Church Yth Grp; FCA; Trk; NHS.

ROPP, SHELLY R; Bartlesville Mid HS; Bartlesville, OK; (4); 103/447; Church Yth Grp; Bsktbl; Chrldng; Sftbl; High Hon Roll; Hon Roll; Prfct Atten Awd; Acad Awd; All St Sftbl; All Star Chrldr; Pittsburg ST Univ; Orthopedic.

ROSAS, LORIANN; Boise City HS; Boise City, OK; (2); Church Yth Grp; Band; Pep Band; Hon Roll; OU; Dev Pedtrcs.

ROSBACH, BETH; Putnam City HS; Warr Acres, OK; (4); 7/344; Church Yth Grp; German Clb; Teachers Aide; Pres Orch; School Musical; Var L Crs Cntry; Var L Trk; Hon Roll; Jr NHS; NHS; OK Yth Symphony; Chrch Music Group; OK All ST Orch; U Of OK; Genetic Researcher.

ROSE, BUDI; Plainview HS; Ardmore, OK; (1); GAA; Chorus; School Musical; Nwsp; Capt Chrldng; Trk; High Hon Roll; U Of OK; Nrs.

ROSE, CHIVON M; John Marshall HS; Oklahoma City, OK; (2); Church Yth Grp; Cmnty Wkr; Varsity Clb; Church Choir; Rep Stu Cncl; Bsktbl; Scholastic Bowl; Spanish Clb; Chorus; School Musical; Y Teen Club; Encore; FL ST Univ.

ROSE, CHRIS; Hartshorne Sr HS; Mcalester, OK; (4); 5/48; Am Leg Boys St; Boy Scts; Church Yth Grp; FHA; Scholastic Bowl; Teachers Aide; VP Frsh Cls; VP Soph Cls; Pres Jr Cls; Pres Sr Cls; Natl & OK Hnr Soc; Phys Ed.

ROSE, CHRISTOPHER; Midwest City HS; Midwest City, OK; (4); 21/419; Boy Scts; Church Yth Grp; Math Tm; ROTC; Scholastic Bowl; Spanish Clb; Band; Jazz Band; Mrchg Band; School Musical; Harvey Mudd; Engrng.

ROSE, GARRETT T; Valliant HS; Valliant, OK; (1); Natl FFA Org; Ftbl; Trk; Wt Lftg; Arspc Engr.

ROSE, JAYDON G; Tahlequah Sr HS; Tahlequah, OK; (3); Church Yth Grp; VICA; Acpl Chr; Chorus; Church Choir; Wt Lftg; High Hon Roll; Hon Roll; Jr NHS; Pres Acad Fit Awd; NVTHS; GATE; OSU; Auto Mechanic; Bdy Repair.

ROSE, JENNIFER E; Muldrow HS; Muldrow, OK; (2); Chess Clb; Office Aide; Quiz Bowl; Spanish Clb; Band; Jazz Band; Mrchg Band; Hon Roll; Jr NHS; Pres Acad Fit Awd; RAP Schl Suprt Grp; GATE; OK ST Univ; Vet.

ROSE, JOSHUA; Stringtown HS; Stringtown, OK; (4); 1/21; 4-H; Natl FFA Org; Quiz Bowl; Chorus; Church Choir; Ed Nwsp; Rep Sr Cls; Var Bsbl; Var Bsktbl; Pres Schlr; SE OK St Univ.

ROSE, KENDRA; Keyes HS; Keyes, OK; (3); 3/9; Church Yth Grp; FCA; FHA; Quiz Bowl; Nwsp; Var Bsktbl; Var Chrldng; High Hon Roll; NHS; Sthrn Nazerene U.

ROSE, KENNY; Luther HS; Luther, OK; (3); 5/50; Band; Mrchg Band; Pep Band; School Play; Var Ftbl; Var Trk; Wt Lftg; Hon Roll; NHS; Prfct Atten Awd; Envrnmntl Club; Arch Engr.

ROSE, KERRI L; Kiowa Jr-Sr HS; Stuart, OK; (2); Drama Clb; 4-H; FHA; School Play; Bsktbl; Sftbl; 4-H Awd; Ada E Centrl Univ; Erly Ed.

ROSE, KRISTINA; Edmond North HS; Edmond, OK; (3); Church Yth Grp; Hosp Aide; Mu Alpha Theta; Spanish Clb; NHS; Chrstns On Campus; Univ Of Cntrl OK; Chiropractic.

ROSE, LOTTIE M; Hulbert Jr Sr HS; Hulbert, OK; (1); GAA; JV Bsktbl; JV Wt Lftg; High Hon Roll; Hon Roll; Jr NHS; Med Field; Nrs.

ROSE, MICHELLE I; Union Intermediate HS; Tulsa, OK; (4); Color Guard; Ed Nwsp; Ed Yrbk; Gym; Wt Lftg; High Hon Roll; NHS; Pres Schlr; St Schlr; Play/Tch Piano; Dance; DFY.

ROSE, RICHARD; Woodward HS; Woodward, OK; (4); Boy Scts; Pres Church Yth Grp; Letterman Clb; Nwsp; Mgr Bsktbl; High Hon Roll; NHS; Bus Stdnt Of Yr 95-; Who's Who Multi Yr Listee; Southwestern OK ST U; Acctng.

ROSENFELT, JENNIFER L; Noble HS; Noble, OK; (2); 16/180; Church Yth Grp; Spanish Clb; Church Choir; Hon Roll; NHS; Elem/Scndry Educ.

ROSS, ADRIANNE I; Northeast HS; Oklahoma City, OK; (3); Am Leg Aux Girls St; Computer Clb; FBLA; Hosp Aide; Science Clb; Teachers Aide; Band; Church Choir; Mrchg Band; High Hon Roll; Jr Class Prom Comm; College Clb; Campus Life; Southern Meth Univ; Pre-Med.

ROSS, AMBER; Durant HS; Durant, OK; (4); 3/185; Church Yth Grp; FCA; Church Choir; Ofcr Stu Cncl; Chrldng; Socr; High Hon Roll; Hon Roll; Kiwanis Awd; NHS; Kiwanis Sr Mo; Southeastern OK ST U.

ROSS, CASEY R; U S Grant HS; Oklahoma City, OK; (3); 30/254; Church Yth Grp; Pres Drama Clb; School Musical; School Play; Stage Crew; Rep Frsh Cls; Rep Soph Cls; Mgr(s); Score Keeper; Sftbl; OU; Chem.

ROSS, CHELCY S; Edmond Horth HS; Edmond, OK; (4); 128/336; Church Yth Grp; GAA; Pep Clb; ROTC; SADD; Rptr Yrbk; Ofcr Stu Cncl; Sftbl; TX Tech Univ; Cmptr Sci Engr.

ROSS, CHRISSI; Warner HS; Checotah, OK; (2); Church Yth Grp; VP Pres FHA; Hosp Aide; Rep Soph Cls; Ofcr Stu Cncl; Var Sftbl; High Hon Roll; Hon Roll; Sal; Val; ST Hnr Soc; GATE Pgm.

ROSS, CHRISTIE M; Durant HS; Durant, OK; (4); Church Yth Grp; FBLA; Hosp Aide; Band; Mrchg Band; Tennis; Hon Roll; SOSU; PT.

ROSS, CHRISTOPHER; Tulsa Memorial HS; Tulsa, OK; (4); 42/250; French Clb; Pep Clb; Band; Drm Mjr(t); Jazz Band; Mrchg Band; School Musical; Capt Trk; High Hon Roll; NHS; Supr St Slst; Chrgrs For Chrst; FCA; Oral Roberts U; Msc Tech.

ROSS, JAYME; Waynoka HS; Dacoma, OK; (2); 1/21; Church Yth Grp; FCA; VP Pep Clb; Quiz Bowl; VP Soph Cls; Var Bsbl; Var Bsktbl; Var Ftbl; High Hon Roll; U Of OK; Arch.

ROSS, JEFF A; Okay Jr Sr HS; Wagoner, OK; (2); 2/34; Spanish Clb; Rep Stu Cncl; Var Bsbl; Var Bsktbl; Hon Roll; NHS; Ntl Merit Ltr; VP Soph Cls.

ROSS, JEREMY; Texhoma HS; Texhoma, OK; (3); Church Yth Grp; Quiz Bowl; Sec Frsh Cls; VP Soph Cls; Treas Jr Cls; Var Bsktbl; Var Ftbl; Var Wt Lftg; High Hon Roll; NHS; TX Tech; Envrnmntl Engrng.

ROSS, JUSTIN; Oklahoma Christian Schl; Oklahoma City, OK; (3); 7/50; Am Leg Boys St; Church Yth Grp; Debate Tm; Drama Clb; FCA; Speech Tm; Teachers Aide; School Musical; School Play; Stage Crew; OK Christian U; Engl.

ROSS, KELLY; Bartlesville Sr HS; Bartlesville, OK; (4); Drama Clb; Pep Clb; Chorus; Hon Roll; Acad Awd; NE St Univ; Optom.

ROSS, LINDSEY E; Lawton Sr HS; Lawton, OK; (3); Dance Clb; FCA; FHA; HOBY; Ofcr Drill Tm; Powder Puff Ftbl; Hon Roll; Gftd/Tlntd Prgm; Sr Smnr Ed Cls 96-; U Of OK.

ROSS, MARGIE; Stuart Sr HS; Mcalester, OK; (4); 1/29; Church Yth Grp; 4-H; FHA; Quiz Bowl; Scholastic Bowl; Teachers Aide; High Hon Roll; Hon Roll; Educ.

ROSS, MELANI G; Union Intermediate HS; Tulsa, OK; (1); Church Yth Grp; FCA; GAA; Church Choir; Intrml Bsktbl; Hon Roll; Jr NHS; Drug Free Yth Pgm; Mission Trip To MO.

ROSS, MELISSA; Stilwell HS; Stilwell, OK; (4); 6/114; Sec Treas Cmnty Wkr; Treas FBLA; Sftbl; Vllybl; Gov Hon Prg Awd; High Hon Roll; Ntl Merit Ltr; St Schlr; Library Aide; Indian Hrtge Clb Prncss.

ROSS, TERAH; Claremore Sr HS; Claremore, OK; (2); French Clb; Cmnty Wkr; SADD; Band; Mrchg Band; Orch; Pep Band; Gov Hon Prg Awd; High Hon Roll; Hon Roll; UCLA; Med.

ROSSANDER, MANDY; Glencoe Public Schl; Glencoe, OK; (3); 4/28; Church Yth Grp; FCA; Natl FFA Org; VP Frsh Cls; Pres Soph Cls; Rep Stu Cncl; Var Bsktbl; Var Sftbl; Hon Roll; NHS; Pres FFA; OSU; Ag Sci.

ROSSON, CHRISTI L; Kellyville Sr HS; Kellyville, OK; (3); Church Yth Grp; Computer Clb; Library Aide; Office Aide; Hon Roll; Pres Acad Fit Awd.

ROSSON, DANIEL S; Checotah HS; Checotah, OK; (4); 4/89; Cmnty Wkr; Debate Tm; Speech Tm; Teachers Aide; High Hon Roll; Hon Roll; NHS; Pres Schlr; OK Honor Soc; Mayors Hnr Awd; NHS Treas; Top 10% Awd; Connor ST Coll; Med.

ROSSON, TRACEY D; Bishop Kelley HS; Broken Arrow, OK; (1); High Hon Roll; Ftbl Trnr; Ballet/Jazz Dance.

ROTH, HEATHER R; Ponca City Sr HS; Ponca City, OK; (3); 4/400; Am Leg Aux Girls St; Cmnty Wkr; GAA; Letterman Clb; Spanish Clb; Teachers Aide; Varsity Clb; Variety Show; Yrbk; VP Sr Cls; All-Conf V-Ball; OSU; Pre-Med; Dr.

ROTH, LESLIE; Perry Sr HS; Perry, OK; (3); #1 in class; Church Yth Grp; FCA; German Clb; Band; School Musical; Ed Nwsp; Sec Stu Cncl; Pom Pon; NHS; Co Pres Trig Club; Math Stu Of Yr; Back Door Tn Cmmtte; Med.

ROTH, ROBIN; Washington HS; Purcell, OK; (4); 8/43; Natl FFA Org; Scholastic Bowl; Teachers Aide; VICA; Bsktbl; Hon Roll; NHS; U OK.

ROTHER, RORY W; Okarche HS; Okarche, OK; (1); Church Yth Grp; Computer Clb; English Clb; Math Tm; Scholastic Bowl; Science Clb; JV Bsktbl; Cit Awd; Gov Hon Prg Awd; High Hon Roll.

ROTHERMEL, LORI; Mulhall Orlando HS; Orlando, OK; (4); 4/22; German Clb; GAA; Office Aide; Speech Tm; SADD; Phtg Nwsp; Rptr Yrbk; VP Jr Cls; Pres Stu Cncl; Var L Bsktbl; OK Chllng; OK ST U; Phys Thrpy.

ROTHERMEL, LORI; Mulhall Orlando HS; Mulhall, OK; (4); 4/21; German Clb; Office Aide; Speech Tm; Yrbk; VP Jr Cls; Rep Pres Stu Cncl; Bsktbl; Score Keeper; Var Sftbl; Hon Roll; OK St Univ; Hlth.

ROTHLEIN, MEGAN M; Bishop Kelley HS; Tulsa, OK; (2); Cmnty Wkr; Service Clb; Rep Soph Cls; Hon Roll; Stu Cncl; OK St Univ; Vet.

ROTT, MICHAELA R; Oologah HS; Oologah, OK; (2); 4-H; Natl FFA Org; Sftbl; Hon Roll; Vet Schl.

ROUGHFACE, SARAH J; Ponca City Sr HS; Ponca City, OK; (4); Intnl Clb; Office Aide; Varsity Clb; Var Capt Bsktbl; Capt Var Sftbl; Hon Roll; Ath Of Yr; All Conf Hnrbl Mntn Bsktbl & Sftbl; Bacone JC; Comp Sci.

ROUNTREE, ANGELIN M; Skiatook HS; Skiatook, OK; (3); Church Yth Grp; Band; Church Choir; Mrchg Band; Hon Roll; Jr NHS; NHS; Ntl Merit Ltr; Prfct Atten Awd; Karate.

ROUNTREE, CARY M; Lexington HS; Lexington, OK; (4); 15/65; Chess Clb; Cmnty Wkr; Hosp Aide; JA; Scholastic Bowl; Science Clb; Spanish Clb; Teachers Aide; L Golf; Hon Roll; Ldrshp Awd; Acad Team; Murray ST Coll; Comp Sci.

ROUNTREE, TROY M; North Intermediate HS; Broken Arrow, OK; (2); JCL; Latin Clb; Office Aide; Service Clb; Co-Ed Nwsp; Yrbk; Cit Awd; High Hon Roll; Jr NHS; NHS.

ROUSE, BRANT; Vian HS; Vian, OK; (4); 3/50; Library Aide; Pep Clb; Quiz Bowl; Scholastic Bowl; Band; Jazz Band; Mrchg Band; Pep Band; Variety Show; Ofcr Bsbl; OK Univ; Dntstry.

ROUSE, KIM; Claremore Sr HS; Claremore, OK; (2); 1/273; Church Yth Grp; Var JV Socr; Trk; Hon Roll; NHS.

ROUSEY, DONNA L; Warner HS; Muskogee, OK; (1); FHA; Hosp Aide; Spanish Clb; Chorus; OK U.

ROUSH, ELIZABETH J; Westmoore HS; Oklahoma City, OK; (3); 51/625; Rep Stu Cncl; JV Var Crs Cntry; NHS; U Of OK; Pharm.

ROUSH, JAMI LORINDA; South Intermediate HS; Broken Arrow, OK; (3); Church Yth Grp; Drama Clb; Intnl Clb; VICA; Acpl Chr; School Musical; School Play; Hon Roll; Natl Voc Tech Hnr Soc; Cosmetologist; Presch Tchr.

ROUSSEL, COREY M; Ponca City Sr HS; Ponca City, OK; (3); 1/400; Church Yth Grp; Cmnty Wkr; Debate Tm; French Clb; Math Tm; Scholastic Bowl; Orch; Pres Stu Cncl; Crs Cntry; Tennis.

ROUTHIER, TRISH; Gans Public Schl; Muldrow, OK; (4); 6/18; FHA; Sec Treas Spanish Clb; Teachers Aide; VP Chorus; School Play; Stage Crew; Rptr Nwsp; Cit Awd; High Hon Roll; Hon Roll.

ROVICK, JONATHAN R; Stillwater Sr HS; Stillwater, OK; (2); Debate Tm; Mu Alpha Theta; Natl Beta Clb; Temple Yth Grp; Mrchg Band; Rep Stu Cncl; JV Golf; Hon Roll; Pres Schlr; Key Clb; Teen Advy Brd VP; U Of MI; Engr.

ROVIG, MEGHAN J; Stillwater Sr HS; Stillwater, OK; (2); Church Yth Grp; FCA; French Clb; Letterman Clb; Stage Crew; Nwsp; Yrbk; Ofcr Stu Cncl; Diving; Swmmng; Parks & Recreation Sftbl; Episcopal Diocese Of OK Yth Bd; U Of TX Austin; Phys Therapy.

ROWAN, CHARISSA; Owasso Sr HS; Owasso, OK; (2); Church Yth Grp; FCA; Natl FFA Org; Red Cross Aide; JV Chrldng; Pres Acad Fit Awd; Lifegrd; Cch Chrldng; Show Pig; OSU; Tchr.

ROWAN, SETH S; South Intermediate HS; Broken Arrow, OK; (1); Church Yth Grp; Cmnty Wkr; Latin Clb; Church Choir; High Hon Roll; Jr NHS; Acad Tm Lttrd; Tulsa Univ; Cmptr Engrng.

ROWBOTHAM, BRANDY M; Catoosa HS; Tulsa, OK; (2); Church Yth Grp; FCA; Spanish Clb; JV Socr; NHS.

ROWE, AMANDA N; Del City HS; Midwest City, OK; (2); Church Yth Grp; Drama Clb; FCA; School Play; Stage Crew; Rep Stu Cncl; Stat Mgr(s); Stat Score Keeper; Yth Show Choir Church; Hstry Awd; Drama Awd; NESU; Elem Educ.

ROWE, CHERON; Plainview HS; Ardmore, OK; (1); 1/93; JA; Bsktbl; Chrldng; Hon Roll; Jr NHS; Pres Acad Fit Awd; U Of OK; Med.

ROWE, JENNIFER L; Union Intermediate HS; Broken Arrow, OK; (3); Church Yth Grp; French Clb; Key Clb; Chorus; Church Choir; Rep Frsh Cls; High Hon Roll; NHS; Dance.

ROWE, REGINA KAY; Vanoss Schl; Stratford, OK; (3); 1/45; Cmnty Wkr; 4-H; FBLA; Letterman Clb; Pres Jr Cls; Rep Stu Cncl; Capt Bsktbl; NHS; Pres Acad Fit Awd; Val; Vet Med.

ROWELL, MARY M; Mc Alester HS; Mcalester, OK; (3); 16/194; Drama Clb; FHA; Spanish Clb; Speech Tm; Thesps; Hon Roll; Prfct Atten Awd; OK Univ; Law.

ROWELL, MICHAEL N; Douglass HS; Oklahoma City, OK; (2); Intrml Golf; Hon Roll; Bsktbl; OK Univ; RN.

ROWLAND, APRIL; Stilwell HS; Stilwell, OK; (1); Church Yth Grp; Sec Drama Clb; FBLA; Natl Beta Clb; NFL; Ofcr Stu Cncl; Chrldng; Trk; NHS; FHA; Acad Tm; Ole Miss; Pharmacy.

ROWLAND, ASHLEY; B T Washington HS; Tulsa, OK; (2); JCL; Latin Clb; Pep Clb; Band; Chorus; Flag Corp; Socr; Sr Ctzns Ctr Vol.

ROWLAND, CALVIN; Silo HS; Mead, OK; (4); 2/40; Am Leg Boys St; Church Yth Grp; HOBY; Natl FFA Org; Quiz Bowl; Teachers Aide; Mgr Yrbk; Pres Frsh Cls; Pres Soph Cls; Pres Jr Cls; EOSC; Ag Econ.

ROWLAND, CODY W; Colbert Jr Sr HS; Colbert, OK; (4); 5/30; Am Leg Boys St; FCA; Natl FFA Org; Sec Jr Cls; VP Sr Cls; Ofcr Bsbl; Bsktbl; Hon Roll; NHS; Murray ST Coll; Engrng.

ROWLAND, DAVID; Heavener HS; Heavener, OK; (2); Church Yth Grp; Debate Tm; FCA; Key Clb; Chorus; Church Choir; Var Bsbl; JV Bsktbl; Var Ftbl; Var Golf; Fllswhp Chrstn Stus; HS Amer Indian Clb.

ROWLETT, BETHNEY J; Claremore Sr HS; Claremore, OK; (2); Church Yth Grp; French Clb; Hon Roll; Prfct Atten Awd; Meml Hghts Bapt Church Yth Grp; OK Bapt Univ; Meterology.

ROWLETT, KEVIN; Muskogee HS; Muskogee, OK; (4); Church Yth Grp; Cmnty Wkr; Hist DECA; Pres Natl FFA Org; Spanish Clb; Intrml Ftbl; Hon Roll; Muskogee Bowhntrs Assn; Bass Anglers Sprtsmn Soc; Fish/Wildlf Ecology.

ROY, BRANDI; Navajo Schl; Blair, OK; (3); Pres FHA; HOBY; Sec Stu Cncl; L Var Bsktbl; L Var Sftbl; High Hon Roll; Hon Roll; VP NHS; Ntl Merit Ltr; Pres Acad Fit Awd; Tech Stu Assn VP; U Of KY.

ROY, JACOB T; Newkirk HS; Newkirk, OK; (3); 3/40; Am Leg Boys St; Boy Scts; Church Yth Grp; Quiz Bowl; Band; High Hon Roll; Hon Roll; NHS; Ntl Merit Ltr; Pres Acad Fit Awd.

ROYE, BRANDON; Jenks HS; Jenks, OK; (2); Ofcr Natl FFA Org; Church Yth Grp; Ftbl; OSU; Biotech.

ROYE, GEORGEANN; Miami Sr HS; Miami, OK; (3); 1/180; Church Yth Grp; School Play; Rep Jr Cls; Trk; Hon Roll; Kiwanis Awd; NHS; St Schlr; Val; Equestrn Studies; Creatv Wrtng ST Awds; Writer.

ROYE, KIMARIE J; Stigler HS; Lequire, OK; (3); FCA; 4-H; Pep Clb; SADD; Band; Mrchg Band; JV Bsktbl; L Chrldng; Hon Roll; Prfct Atten Awd; Singing; Vllybl; Sftbl; Estrn OK ST Coll; Law.

ROYE, ROSS H; Stilwell HS; Stilwell, OK; (2); Church Yth Grp; Cmnty Wkr; FCA; 4-H; Letterman Clb; Math Clb; Natl Beta Clb; Science Clb; SADD; Varsity Clb; AR Univ; Acctng.

ROYO, KRISTIN; Jenks HS; Tulsa, OK; (4); DECA; FCA; Office Aide; Chrldng; High Hon Roll; Hon Roll; U AR.

ROZANOVA, ALLA; Tonkawa Jr Sr HS; Tonkawa, OK; (4); Dance Clb; English Clb; FCA; GAA; Library Aide; School Play; Pres Soph Cls; Rep Stu Cncl; JV Bsktbl; Var Sftbl; Spk Eng, Rssn & Ger; Northern OK Acad Cont Math; Northern OK Coll; Bus.

ROZELL, JENNIFER M; Will Rogers HS; Tulsa, OK; (3); Teachers Aide; Socr; Hon Roll; YABA Bowling League; Tchr.

RUARK, COURTNEY; Kingfisher HS; Kingfisher, OK; (1); Debate Tm; FCA; Key Clb; Quiz Bowl; Spanish Clb; Speech Tm; Treas Frsh Cls; Hon Roll; All Amer Schlr.

RUBIO, DANA C; Jenks HS; Tulsa, OK; (3); 76/530; Cmnty Wkr; Drama Clb; VP Treas Key Clb; Mu Alpha Theta; Office Aide; Quiz Bowl; Red Cross Aide; Service Clb; Spanish Clb; High Hon Roll; Naval Acad.

RUBIO, DENA; Guthrie Sr HS; Guthrie, OK; (3); 32/230; FHA; Hosp Aide; Mu Alpha Theta; Natl FFA Org; Spanish Clb; Mgr(s); Score Keeper; Hon Roll; Jr NHS; NHS; Sftbl; Rose ST Univ; Crmnl Jstc.

RUBIO, LINDA; Chickasha Jr HS; Chickasha, OK; (1); JCL; Latin Clb; Science Clb; Phtg Yrbk; Jr NHS; Intnl Bus.

RUBLE, AMBERLY; Guthrie Sr HS; Guthrie, OK; (3); Math Clb; Mu Alpha Theta; Spanish Clb; Rptr Yrbk; Treas Jr Cls; Score Keeper; Jr NHS; OU; Hlth.

RUBY, STEVEN; Enid Sr HS; Enid, OK; (3); Am Leg Boys St; Church Yth Grp; FCA; Teachers Aide; Varsity Clb; Var Bsbl; JV Crs Cntry; Hon Roll; Jr NHS; NHS; Med.

RUCKER, AMANDA A; Union Intermediate HS; Tulsa, OK; (1); 71/870; FCA; JV Bsktbl; JV Socr; NHS; Medicine.

RUCKER, JAMES M; Hugo HS; Hugo, OK; (2); Spanish Clb; Var Bsbl; Var Bsktbl; Wt Lftg; Prfct Atten Awd.

RUCKER, KIM; Newcastle HS; Newcastle, OK; (3); FBLA; Science Clb; Spanish Clb; Cit Awd; High Hon Roll; Hon Roll; Pres Jr NHS; NHS; OK ST U; Vet Medicine; Hsbndry.

RUCKER, MEREDITH M; Tahlequah Jr HS; Tahlequah, OK; (1); Rep Stu Cncl; Chrldng; Hon Roll; Jr NHS; Ntl Merit Ltr; Pres Acad Fit Awd; Dance.

RUCKER, NICOLE; Putnam City West HS; Oklahoma City, OK; (1); Church Yth Grp; Hosp Aide; Ofcr Stu Cncl; Chrldng; Gym; Hon Roll; U Of OK; Med.

RUCKER, SARAH; Pawhuska HS; Pawhuska, OK; (2); Church Yth Grp; Hosp Aide; Band; Sec Chorus; Jazz Band; Mrchg Band; Pep Band; Stage Crew; High Hon Roll; St Vocal Cont 2 Yrs; Med.

RUCKMAN, GARY W; Roland Sr HS; Muldrow, OK; (3); 8/104; Library Aide; Ofcr Natl FFA Org; Teachers Aide; Band; Mrchg Band; Rptr Stu Cncl; Hon Roll; NHS; Prfct Atten Awd; Play Guitar In Blue Grass Group & At Chrch; Several Ag Ribbons For Raising Chickens.

RUDD, CRYSTAL L; Lone Grove HS; Lone Grove, OK; (3); Church Yth Grp; Natl FFA Org; Spanish Clb; Chorus.

RUDD, KRISTI L; Memorial HS; Tulsa, OK; (3); Intnl Clb; Key Clb; Red Cross Aide; Spanish Clb; Teachers Aide; Vllybl; Hon Roll; NHS; Gamma Sigma; OCU; Phys Thrpy.

RUDICK, CRISSY D; Jay HS; Jay, OK; (4); Church Yth Grp; FCA; Sec Treas Natl Beta Clb; Natl FFA Org; Ed Yrbk; Capt Chrldng; Hon Roll; NHS; Peer Cnslr; IDFY Pres; U Of AR.

RUDICK, MICHEAL C; Jay HS; Jay, OK; (2); Church Yth Grp; FCA; Natl FFA Org; Var Bsbl; Var Bsktbl; Var Ftbl; Hon Roll; NHS.

RUDROW, CHRISTINA S; Hugo HS; Hugo, OK; (2); Church Yth Grp; GAA; Spanish Clb; Socr; Sftbl; Outstndng Achvmts In Geog; Outstndng Achvmt In Typing; Var Ltr In Sftbl.

RUEB, KEVIN M; South Intermediate HS; Broken Arrow, OK; (1); FCA; Intrml Bsbl; JV Ftbl; JV Wt Lftg; Gov Hon Prg Awd; Most Imprvd Acads; OK; Bus Mgmt/Cmptrs.

RUFFIN, TAISHA R; John Marshall HS; Oklahoma City, OK; (4); 45/160; Treas FBLA; Band; Church Choir; Mrchg Band; Pep Band; Ofcr Stu Cncl; High Hon Roll; Hon Roll; Langston Univ; Comp Sci.

RUHL, KAREN; Watonga HS; Greenfield, OK; (1); Church Yth Grp; 4-H; Natl FFA Org; Quiz Bowl; Bsktbl; 4-H Awd; Gov Hon Prg Awd; High Hon Roll; Pres Acad Fit Awd; OSU; Bio.

RUIZ, LISA; Mt St Marys HS; Oklahoma City, OK; (3); Pep Clb; Spanish Clb; Nwsp; Yrbk; Hon Roll; Optometry.

RUKES, BRIAN; Geary Jr Sr HS; Geary, OK; (3); 1/30; Natl Beta Clb; Office Aide; Quiz Bowl; Scholastic Bowl; Nwsp; Yrbk; Rptr Lit Mag; High Hon Roll; Hon Roll; NHS; Acad Awd; RYLA Awd; Antique Tractor Clb Newsltr Edtr; Historian Clb Rptr/Secy; Registry Starter Tractor; OK ST U; Industrial Engrng.

RULE, MELISSA E; Edmond Memorial HS; Edmond, OK; (2); 76/408; Pres Intnl Clb; Key Clb; Spanish Clb; Acpl Chr; Chorus; Hon Roll; NHS; Pres Acad Fit Awd; U Of Cntrl OK; Ed.

RUMLEY, ANNE; Jenks HS; Jenks, OK; (3); 111/517; CAP; FHA; VICA; Hon Roll; Jr NHS; HOSA; Vo-Tech Cls VP; Tulsa JC; Occptnl Therapy.

RUMLEY, JERROD P; Jenks HS; Tulsa, OK; (3); Church Yth Grp; Ofcr FCA; Pres Stu Cncl; JV Bsktbl; Var Capt Socr; Hon Roll; NHS; Schl Mascot; Yng Life.

RUMSEY, ALLYSON E; Shawnee Sr HS; Shawnee, OK; (4); 55/268; FCA; Library Aide; Office Aide; Spanish Clb; Nwsp; JV Bsktbl; Sftbl; Trk; Hon Roll; Jr NHS; Rose ST Coll; Dntl Hygnst.

RUMSEY, JOSH W; Western Heights Sr HS; Oklahoma City, OK; (1); Cmnty Wkr; Band; Mrchg Band; Ftbl; Wt Lftg; NHS; Pres Schlr; Southwstrn OK ST Univ Tools For Trd Smr Acad 96; NW Hnr Bnd 95-; CODA Hnr Bnd 95-; OK ST Univ.

RUNNELS, NIKKI; Thomas Jr Sr HS; Thomas, OK; (1); 13/45; Church Yth Grp; FCA; FBLA; Band; L Bsktbl; L Chrldng; L Sftbl; L Trk; Hon Roll; Acad Lttrmn.

RUNYON, AMBER R; Eufaula Sr HS; Eufaula, OK; (2); 9/90; Church Yth Grp; Debate Tm; Speech Tm; Chorus; Church Choir; High Hon Roll; Hon Roll; Jr NHS; NHS; Dist Vocal Comp 95-.

RUNYON, STACY L; Macarthur Sr HS; Lawton, OK; (3); Cmnty Wkr; FCA; Intnl Clb; Office Aide; Science Clb; SADD; Band; Flag Corp; Mrchg Band; Pep Band; Lawton-Ft Sill Jr Bowling Assoc VP & Secc; Cameron U; Tchng; Elem Ed.

RUPE, BRANDON; Poteau HS; Shady Point, OK; (4); 40/142; Am Leg Boys St; Church Yth Grp; Natl FFA Org; Sec Stu Cncl; Var Ftbl; Var Wrstlng; Hon Roll; AAU Freestyle Wrstlng Ntl Chmpn 95; Phys Thrpy.

RUPP, STACIE; Perry Sr HS; Perry, OK; (4); 14/66; VP Drama Clb; FCA; Pres Spanish Clb; Band; Rep Stu Cncl; Chrldng; NHS; Church Yth Grp; FBLA; FHA; Mat Maid; All Amer Schlrs; DARE Role Mdl; U Of Central OK; Speech Path.

RUSH, BRANDON D; Central Mid-HS; Norman, OK; (2); Church Yth Grp; FCA; French Clb; Scholastic Bowl; Variety Show; JV Ftbl; JV Wt Lftg; Finished 11th ST French Contest; Jrnlsm.

RUSH, JASON R; Ripley HS; Ripley, OK; (2); #2 in class; FBLA; FHA; Math Clb; Natl FFA Org; Science Clb; Varsity Clb; Ofcr Frsh Cls; Ofcr Soph Cls; Bsktbl; Cit Awd; Track; High Hnr Rl; Hnr Rl; Langston Univ; PT.

RUSH, KENDALL G; Mc Loud HS; Newalla, OK; (1); Church Yth Grp; Science Clb; Band; Color Guard; Jazz Band; Mrchg Band; Ofcr Stu Cncl; Hon Roll; OSU; Engr.

RUSHING, AMANDA D; Davis HS; Davis, OK; (2); Key Clb; Quiz Bowl; Scholastic Bowl; Spanish Clb; Band; Color Guard; Flag Corp; Jazz Band; Mrchg Band; Pep Band; Phys Thrpst.

RUSHING, DENVER; Madill HS; Kingston, OK; (2); Church Yth Grp; 4-H; Band; Jazz Band; Mrchg Band; School Musical; 4-H Awd; High Hon Roll; Hon Roll; Prfct Atten Awd; OK U; Pharmctcl.

RUSHING, TARA; El Reno Sr HS; El Reno, OK; (3); Church Yth Grp; Cmnty Wkr; 4-H; Key Clb; Math Clb; Science Clb; Rptr Nwsp; Rptr Yrbk; Cit Awd; 4-H Awd; Redlnds Co Coll.

RUSSELL, ANGELA S; B T Washington HS; Tulsa, OK; (3); Computer Clb; JCL; Latin Clb; Red Cross Aide; Sftbl; Sftbl MVP 95-; Sftbl Capt 95-; Ntv Amer Stdnt Hnr Roll; Arch Drftng Club; Ed/Eng.

RUSSELL, APRIL M; Roland Sr HS; Roland, OK; (3); Church Yth Grp; FHA; Library Aide; Office Aide; Chorus; Church Choir; Nwsp; Hon Roll; Northeastern ST U; Jrnlsm/Wrtg.

RUSSELL, ASHLEY S; Oologah HS; Claremore, OK; (2); FCA; 4-H; FHA; GAA; Hosp Aide; SADD; Yrbk; Treas Frsh Cls; Var Bsktbl; Cit Awd; Lions Clb; Tulsa Univ; Med Fld.

RUSSELL, BRENT A; Westmoore HS; Oklahoma City, OK; (3); Church Yth Grp; Rep Band; Jazz Band; Mrchg Band; Orch; Pep Band; School Musical; Lit Mag; NHS; All St Fnlst Piccolo Flute; All Dist CODA Flute; Prin Flute Piccoloist In Chrch Orch; OK City U; Flute; Music Ed.

RUSSELL, BRIAN L; Quinton Jr Sr HS; Quinton, OK; (3); Church Yth Grp; Cmnty Wkr; FCA; FHA; Scholastic Bowl; Church Choir; Sec Jr Cls; Pres Sr Cls; Ofcr Stu Cncl; L Bsbl; Play Guitar & Sing In Chrch Yth Band; Yth Ministry.

RUSSELL, CHARLES S; Putnam City North HS; Oklahoma City, OK; (2); 4th Pl ST Autocad Drafting Cmptn; Chrch Ldrshp Team; Civil Eng.

RUSSELL, CHRISSY J; Wilson HS; Wilson, OK; (2); 1/45; FCA; HOBY; Natl Beta Clb; Sec Frsh Cls; Treas Soph Cls; Bsktbl; Sftbl; Cit Awd; High Hon Roll; NHS.

RUSSELL, EMILY C; Stillwater Sr HS; Stillwater, OK; (3); 63/363; Church Yth Grp; Cmnty Wkr; FCA; Hosp Aide; Latin Clb; Mu Alpha Theta; Service Clb; Teachers Aide; Chorus; School Play; Med Fld.

RUSSELL IV, GEORGE; Little Axe Sr HS; Newalla, OK; (2); Quiz Bowl; Scholastic Bowl; Sec Soph Cls; JV Crs Cntry; Var Trk; High Hon Roll; Jr NHS; Pres Acad Fit Awd; Indoor Track V; Scntfc Engr.

RUSSELL, GRAHAM R; Enid Sr HS; Enid, OK; (3); 160/419; Cmnty Wkr; Letterman Clb; Quiz Bowl; Science Clb; Band; Mrchg Band; Pep Band; Rep Stu Cncl; Tennis; NHS; OK Heritage Assn Schlsp 95.

RUSSELL, JAMES; Quinton Jr Sr HS; Quinton, OK; (4); Church Yth Grp; FCA; FHA; Rep Soph Cls; VP Jr Cls; Ofcr Stu Cncl; Var L Bsktbl; Var L Ftbl; Var L Trk; Var Wt Lftg; Trk St Chmpn 4-40, Reg Chmp 3200 Rly; Reg Chmps; Dist Off Bck Of Yr; Tulsa All-St HM & All-St Def Bck.

RUSSELL JR, JAMES C; Union Sr HS; Broken Arrow, OK; (3); 87/741; Church Yth Grp; Var JV Bsktbl; JV Ftbl; Mgr(s); Score Keeper; High Hon Roll; Hon Roll; Jr NHS; NHS; Pres Acad Fit Awd.

RUSSELL, JENNIFER L; Mc Alester HS; Mcalester, OK; (2); Debate Tm; Speech Tm; Thesps; Band; Mrchg Band; School Play; Sec Frsh Cls; Chrldng; High Hon Roll; NHS; 1st Pl Writers Guild Cont; All-Dist Bank; OK Univ.

RUSSELL, JENNIFER S; Hartshorne Sr HS; Hartshorne, OK; (3); Church Yth Grp; FHA; Library Aide; Hon Roll; Legal Asst.

RUSSELL, JENNY J; Hobart HS; Hobart, OK; (2); 4-H; FHA; Pep Clb; Chorus; Swing Chorus; Rep Frsh Cls; JV Bsktbl; JV Vllybl; Hon Roll; Prfct Atten Awd; Jazz Choir; Spirit Choir; Wmns Show Choir; OU; Legal Asst.

RUSSELL, JOY; Bartlesville Mid HS; Bartlesville, OK; (1); Church Yth Grp; Non-Schl Spnsrd Swimming Team; Osteopathic Coll.

RUSSELL, JULIE S; Velma Alma HS; Velma, OK; (3); 1/50; FCA; SADD; Rptr Nwsp; Sec Frsh Cls; Bsktbl; Chrldng; Sftbl; Trk; High Hon Roll; NHS; OK U; Pre-Med.

RUSSELL, LE ANNE R; Okay Jr Sr HS; Muskogee, OK; (3); Church Yth Grp; Acpl Chr; Yrbk; Ofcr Stu Cncl; Bsktbl; Sftbl; Vllybl; Hon Roll; NHS; Library Aide; LTC Awd; Homcmng Jr Attendant; Northeastern ST Univ.

RUSSELL, PATRICE; Mid-Del Christian Schl; Oklahoma City, OK; (1); Girl Scts; Teachers Aide; Church Choir; VP Frsh Cls; Bsktbl; Tennis; Trk; Vllybl; High Hon Roll; Hon Roll; Acctng.

RUSSELL, PATTY S; Northwest Classen HS; Oklahoma City, OK; (1); Girl Scts; Chorus; High Hon Roll; OK Univ; Pharm.

RUSSELL, ROBERT; Gans Public Schl; Gans, OK; (4); 1/24; HOBY; Pres Natl FFA Org; Pres Frsh Cls; Cit Awd; High Hon Roll; NHS; Val; Spanish Clb; Rep Stu Cncl; Srvyng Tm; EMT Lfstr 1st Rspndrs Crs; U Of OK Norman; Med.

RUSSELL, SHAWNA; Okemah HS; Okemah, OK; (4); 6/49; Thesps; School Play; Yrbk; Chrldng; Sftbl; DAR Awd; NHS; Beta Clb; OK Hnr Soc; U Of Cntrl OK; Ultrasnd Tech.

RUSSELL, STACY; Quinton Jr Sr HS; Quinton, OK; (1); Church Yth Grp; FCA; FHA; Band; Church Choir; Mrchg Band; VP Frsh Cls; Bsktbl; Capt Chrldng; Trk.

RUSSELL, STEPHANIE D; Wilson HS; Wilson, OK; (3); 18/44; Yrbk; Var Trk; Wt Lftg; Nrs.

RUSSELL, STEVEN T; Putnam City HS; Oklahoma City, OK; (3); 67/297; Church Yth Grp; FCA; Spanish Clb; Var L Ftbl; Var L Wt Lftg; Hon Roll; Jr NHS; NHS; OK Bapt Univ; Med.

RUSSELL, THOMAS; Kiefer Jr Sr HS; Sapulpa, OK; (3); Boy Scts; Church Yth Grp; FCA; French Clb; Temple Yth Grp; VP Soph Cls; Bsktbl; Ftbl; Golf; Trk; BYU.

RUST, BREA; Poteau HS; Poteau, OK; (1); Church Yth Grp; GAA; Pres Frsh Cls; Bsktbl; Var Chrldng; Powder Puff Ftbl; Trk; Cit Awd; Hon Roll; Church Cncl Rep; True Love Waits; CASC; Med.

RUSTIN, BROCK A; Durant HS; Durant, OK; (2); VP Key Clb; Band; Hon Roll; Guitar; Vol Humane Soc.

RUTH, RYAN E; Sapulpa Sr HS; Sapulpa, OK; (4); Cmnty Wkr; Quiz Bowl; Scholastic Bowl; VICA; Cit Awd; Natl Voc-Tech Hnr Soc; Amer VICA Degree; OK VICA Statesman Awd Wnnr; TJL; Forensic Scientist.

RUTHERFORD, CHRISTINA; B T Washington HS; Tulsa, OK; (2); Church Yth Grp; French Clb; Science Clb; Ofcr Stu Cncl; Sftbl; Hon Roll; Prom Comm; African Amer Soc Act; FL ST Univ; Marie Bio.

RUTHERFORD, CONNIE A; Putnam City North HS; Oklahoma City, OK; (3); 94/489; Hosp Aide; Intnl Clb; Spanish Clb; Flag Corp; Variety Show; Hon Roll; NHS; DECA; Band; Color Guard; Hlth Occup Stdnts Of Amer; 3D; Prtcpnt Of Univ Of OK Hlth Sci Smmr Acad; Ntlgist.

RUTHERFORD, JILL; Shawnee Sr HS; Shawnee, OK; (3); 34/282; Church Yth Grp; Cmnty Wkr; Hosp Aide; Spanish Clb; Yrbk; Hon Roll; NHS; Pres Acad Fit Awd; Stu Of Month; Yrbk Edtr.

RUTHERFORD, JONATHAN L; Midwest City HS; Midwest City, OK; (3); Church Yth Grp; FCA; German Clb; Stage Crew; Intrml Bsktbl; Var L Ftbl; Wt Lftg; Prfct Atten Awd.

RUTLAND, PATRICK; Depew HS; Depew, OK; (3); 1/40; Natl FFA Org; VICA; High Hon Roll; NHS; Pres Acad Fit Awd; OSU; Arch Engr.

RUTLEDGE, ANGELA D; Stilwell HS; Stilwell, OK; (2); Drama Clb; FBLA; Spanish Clb; Speech Tm; Chorus; School Musical; School Play; Stage Crew; Hon Roll; Prfrmng Arts.

RUTLEDGE, LINDSAY; Nicoma Park Jr HS; Choctaw, OK; (1); Chrldng; Gov Hon Prg Awd; High Hon Roll; Jr NHS; Prfct Atten Awd; Pres Acad Fit Awd; Val; Head Chrldr; Span Acad Awd; Outstdng Frosh Of Yr 96/Nicoma Park Kiwanis Club.

RUTLEDGE, MATTHEW W; Choctaw HS; Choctaw, OK; (3); 79/313; Var Bsbl; NHS; Guthrie HS All Tourn Bsbl Tm 96; All Eastern OK Cty Bsbl Tm 96; Sunblt Clsc Jr All Stars Bsbl Tm 96.

RUTTMAN, REBECCA; Moore HS; Moore, OK; (3); German Clb; Band; Mrchg Band; Pep Band; Cit Awd; Solo/Ensmble Cont 1 Ratng; OK U; Law Enfrcmt.

RUYLE, AMANDA M; Nathan Hale HS; Tulsa, OK; (3); Church Yth Grp; Cmnty Wkr; Pres Drama Clb; FCA; Thesps; School Play; Ed Yrbk; VP Sr Cls; Rep Stu Cncl; Hon Roll; Photography; Natl Yng Ldrs Conf WA DC; U Of Tulsa.

RUYLE, MONICA; Clinton HS; Clinton, OK; (1); 1/140; Church Yth Grp; 4-H; Band; Chorus; Church Choir; Mrchg Band; Pep Band; Cit Awd; High Hon Roll; NHS.

RYALS, JEREMY; Tahlequah Sr HS; Tahlequah, OK; (4); Am Leg Boys St; Church Yth Grp; Letterman Clb; Teachers Aide; Var L Ftbl; Var Capt Socr; Trk; Pres Acad Fit Awd; Sccr All Dist Tm 94-96; Northeastern St U; Law Enfrcmnt.

RYAN, ADAM M; Jenks HS; Tulsa, OK; (3); VP Church Yth Grp; FCA; French Clb; Mu Alpha Theta; VP Church Choir; Rep Frsh Cls; Rep Jr Cls; JV Crs Cntry; JV Tennis; Hon Roll.

RYAN, CASEY; Wynnewood HS; Wynnewood, OK; (3); Cmnty Wkr; FCA; FHA; Letterman Clb; Rptr Natl FFA Org; Office Aide; Teachers Aide; Rptr Phtg Yrbk; Var Bsktbl; Var Ftbl; East Cntrl Univ; PT.

RYAN, CHRISTIE L; Choctaw HS; Harrah, OK; (2); Church Yth Grp; Spanish Clb; Cit Awd; High Hon Roll; Hon Roll; Jr NHS; Prfct Atten Awd; Val; Masonic Yth Awd; All Amer Schlr; Ntl Ldrshp & Svc Awd; U Of OK; Chem.

RYAN, CHRISTINA L; Prague HS; Prague, OK; (4); 1/69; Church Yth Grp; FCA; Key Clb; Library Aide; Science Clb; JV Chrldng; Var Crs Cntry; Var Pom Pon; Powder Puff Ftbl; Var Trk; Escrt Rnnr Olympc Trch Relay 96; US Mrn Crps Dstngshd Athl Awd; OK Bptst U; Sprts Med.

RYAN, DARLA J; Mc Alester HS; Mcalester, OK; (2); Church Yth Grp; FHA; Spanish Clb; Band; Mrchg Band; Stat Bsktbl; Var Mgr(s); Var Sftbl; Hon Roll; NHS.

RYAN, DAWN M; Choctaw HS; Harrah, OK; (2); Church Yth Grp; Cmnty Wkr; Hosp Aide; Gov Hon Prg Awd; High Hon Roll; NHS; Prfct Atten Awd; Outstndng Yth Awd; OCU; Med.

RYAN, EUGENE C; Lawton Sr HS; Lawton, OK; (2); FHA; Bsktbl; Ftbl; Wrstlng; MI; Prof Bktsbl Plyr.

RYAN, IAN M; Woodward HS; Woodward, OK; (2); Debate Tm; School Play; Ftbl; Var Wrstlng; Hon Roll; Explorer; His Day.

RYAN, JONATHAN; Wister Schl; Wister, OK; (2); Rptr Natl FFA Org; Scholastic Bowl; Speech Tm; Hon Roll; Stock Shows; Eastern OK ST Coll; Vo-Ag Tch.

RYAN, KARI; Oktaha Jr Sr HS; Oktaha, OK; (4); 16/43; Office Aide; Spanish Clb; Speech Tm; Teachers Aide; Rptr Nwsp; Phtg Yrbk; Hon Roll; NHS; Connors ST Coll; Math/Span.

RYAN, KARLA D; Mc Alester HS; Mcalester, OK; (2); Church Yth Grp; Spanish Clb; Band; Color Guard; Jazz Band; Mrchg Band; Rep Stu Cncl; JV Var Bsktbl; JV Var Sftbl; Hon Roll; Eastern OK ST Coll; Med.

RYAN, KELLI L; Canton HS; Canton, OK; (3); Letterman Clb; Band; Flag Corp; Mrchg Band; Pep Band; Rep Frsh Cls; Rep Soph Cls; Rptr Jr Cls; Ofcr Stu Cncl; Hon Roll; TSA Clb; Med Fld.

RYAN, LINDSAY A; Ada HS; Ada, OK; (3); Church Yth Grp; FHA; Spanish Clb; Teachers Aide; Color Guard; Interact Clb Pres; PYAT; ECU.

RYAN, REBEKAH S; Yukon Middle HS; Yukon, OK; (2); Church Yth Grp; FCA; FHA; Hosp Aide; Church Choir; Ofcr Stu Cncl; Mgr(s); High Hon Roll; NHS; Ntl Merit Ltr; Pre-Med; Pediatrics.

RYAN, SHAWN M; Choctaw HS; Harrah, OK; (4); 214/298; Cmnty Wkr; Science Clb; Band; Pep Band; Intrml Bsbl; Intrml Bsktbl; Prfct Atten Awd; Enlisted In US Air Force; Teen Vol; Multi Yr Listee; Bus Admin.

RYAN, SLOANE R; Holland Hall Schl; Tulsa, OK; (4); Church Yth Grp; Cmnty Wkr; Acpl Chr; Chorus; Church Choir; School Musical; School Play; Pres Frsh Cls; Var Crs Cntry; JV Fld Hcky; Dtch Chrst Pres; Yng Lf; TX A&M U; Bioengrng.

RYBA, TANNER M; El Reno Sr HS; El Reno, OK; (3); Hon Roll; Ntl Merit Schol; Ldrshp & Svc Awd; All Amer Schlr; Comp.

RYBURN, MELISSA S; Checotah HS; Porum, OK; (3); Art Clb; Cmnty Wkr; Computer Clb; FTA; GAA; Natl FFA Org; Office Aide; Pep Clb; Teachers Aide; Nwsp.

RYEL, CRYSTAL; Aline-Cleo Jr Sr HS; Aline, OK; (1); 2/15; FCA; FHA; Natl FFA Org; Pep Clb; Var Bsktbl; Var Sftbl; 4-H Awd; Hon Roll; Jr NHS.

RYEL, JEFF; Timberlake Schl; Aline, OK; (1); Church Yth Grp; FCA; JV Ftbl; Cit Awd.

RYKER, JARED D; Sapulpa Sr HS; Sapulpa, OK; (3); Church Yth Grp; Key Clb; Office Aide; Hon Roll; NHS; Pres Acad Fit Awd; Engrng.

RYKER, JASON W; Dewey HS; Bartlesville, OK; (1); Yrbk; Bsktbl; Trk; High Hon Roll; NHS; Pres Acad Fit Awd.

RYLANT, MIRANDA M; Elk City Jr HS; Elk City, OK; (1); Quiz Bowl; Hon Roll; Tech Stdnt Assn VP; Elk City Round Up Club Princess.

RYMER, NICK H; Thomas Jr Sr HS; Thomas, OK; (1); Band; Mrchg Band; Pep Band.

RYSER, JULIA L; Owasso Sr HS; Owasso, OK; (3); #100 in class; Church Yth Grp; FCA; FTA; Intnl Clb; Office Aide; Teachers Aide; Church Choir; Bsktbl; Tennis; Prfct Atten Awd; Prmry Ed.

RYSER, SARA A; Blackwell HS; Blackwell, OK; (2); 1/138; Church Yth Grp; FCA; Letterman Clb; Pep Clb; Quiz Bowl; Stat Bsbl; JV Var Bsktbl; JV Var Sftbl; Var L Trk; High Hon Roll; Peer Hlpr; OK City Univ; Biochem.

SABLOTNE, CHRISTOPHER M; Ponca City Sr HS; Ponca City, OK; (4); Church Yth Grp; Cmnty Wkr; French Clb; SADD; Teachers Aide; Band; Rep Soph Cls; Rep Jr Cls; Rep Sr Cls; Trk; U Of OK; Psych.

SACK, OLIVIA; Pawhuska HS; Pawhuska, OK; (4); 2/88; FBLA; HOBY; Key Clb; Mu Alpha Theta; Pres Jr Cls; Rep Stu Cncl; Var Bsktbl; Capt Tennis; NHS; Sal; Acad Excl Awd; Elks Stu Of Month; Lions Clb Alg Stu Of Yr; U Of CO Boulder; Intl Affrs.

SACZYNSKI, MARK A; South Intermediate HS; Wyoming, MI; (1); OK ST U; Mech Engrng.

SADLER, BROOKE; Edmond Meml HS; Edmond, OK; (1); Church Yth Grp; FCA; Chrldng; Powder Puff Ftbl; Trk; High Hon Roll; Hon Roll; Pres Schlr.

SADLER, MARKA; Cheyenne HS; Cheyenne, OK; (3); Church Yth Grp; 4-H; Speech Tm; Chorus; Rep Jr Cls; Rep Stu Cncl; Bsktbl; Chrldng; Sftbl; 4-H Awd; OK Baptist U; Mnstry.

SADLER, MICHELLE L; Ripley HS; Stillwater, OK; (3); Treas FBLA; Math Clb; Natl FFA Org; Science Clb; Yrbk; L Sftbl; Hon Roll; NHS.

SAGER, LORI; Kellyville Sr HS; Sapulpa, OK; (3); Church Yth Grp; Cmnty Wkr; 4-H; GAA; Letterman Clb; Natl FFA Org; Pep Clb; Science Clb; Ofcr Stu Cncl; JV Var Bsktbl; Northeastern ST U; Psych.

SAGONDA, JILL B; Edmond North HS; Edmond, OK; (2); 1/420; Church Yth Grp; Mu Alpha Theta; Var Pom Pon; Jr NHS; NHS; Spanish NHS; Optometrist; Radiologist.

SAHAI, RENU K; Oklahoma Sch Of Science & Math; Ponca City, OK; (3); Hosp Aide; Intnl Clb; Scholastic Bowl; Spanish Clb; Orch; School Play; High Hon Roll; Ntl Merit Ltr; TSA Pres; Natl Fed Msc Clbs; Dr.

SAHAI, SUNIL K; Oklahoma Sch Of Science & Math; Ponca City, OK; (4); Intnl Clb; Capt Math Tm; Scholastic Bowl; Orch; Rptr Nwsp; Tennis; High Hon Roll; Spanish Clb; School Play; Socr; Paderewski Gold Medalist; 3 Xs All St Orch Violin; AP Schlr Awd; Southern Methodist U; Med.

SAINT, BRIDGET N; Blackwell HS; Blackwell, OK; (4); Drama Clb; FHA; GAA; Pep Clb; School Musical; Stage Crew; Ofcr Stu Cncl; Hon Roll; Yth Cnslr.

SAKELARIS, NICHOLAS; Union Intermediate HS; Broken Arrow, OK; (2); 244/800; Hon Roll; Mech Engrng.

SALAMON, NICOLE D; Union Intermediate HS; Tulsa, OK; (2); 48/800; Spanish Clb; Band; Mrchg Band; Pep Band; School Musical; High Hon Roll; NHS; Bio.

SALAS, MARTIN; Marietta HS; Marietta, OK; (2); Bsktbl; Crs Cntry; Ftbl; Trk; Wt Lftg; Cit Awd; Hon Roll; Pres Schlr.

SALAS, RHONDA; Tomlinson Jr HS; Lawton, OK; (1); FCA; Tennis; High Hon Roll; Hon Roll; NHS; Marine Bio.

SALATHE, STACY L; Wagoner Sr HS; Wagoner, OK; (2); Key Clb; X-Ray Tech.

SALDANA, ADRIANA; Union Sr HS; Tulsa, OK; (3); 115/741; Church Yth Grp; FBLA; Rep Intnl Clb; Key Clb; Letterman Clb; Pep Clb; Variety Show; Rep Stu Cncl; JV Capt Vllybl; High Hon Roll; Renaissance & Drug Free Yth Clbs; Miss Fiesta Tulsa Hispnc Schlrshp Fndtn; U Of Tulsa; Acctng/Bus Admin.

SALDANA, MIGUEL A; Union Intermediate HS; Tulsa, OK; (1); Church Yth Grp; FCA; Rep Stu Cncl; JV Var Ice Hcky; High Hon Roll; NHS; In-Line Hockey; Natl Math League; DFY; Med.

SALDIVAR, ANA L; Will Rogers HS; Tulsa, OK; (4); 45/179; Boy Scts; Latin Clb; Office Aide; VICA; Nwsp; Rep Stu Cncl; Cit Awd; Gov Hon Prg Awd; Hon Roll; Peer Tutor; TSC; Interior Dsgn.

SALISBURY, DARCI; Arnett HS; Harmon, OK; (3); HOBY; Natl Beta Clb; Natl FFA Org; School Play; Rep Frsh Cls; VP Soph Cls; Sec Jr Cls; Var Bsktbl; Var Chrldng; Hon Roll; Bus Admin.

SALISBURY, RANDA; Beaver HS; Beaver, OK; (3); #5 in class; Pres Church Yth Grp; FCA; Sec Jr Cls; Sec Stu Cncl; Var Capt Bsktbl; Var Sftbl; Var Tennis; Hon Roll; Jr NHS; NHS; OK U.

SALLASKA, JO REL DA'RIE; Oklahoma Sch Of Science & Math; Corn, OK; (3); Church Yth Grp; Quiz Bowl; Scholastic Bowl; Science Clb; Chorus; Yrbk; Var L Bsktbl; High Hon Roll; Hon Roll; Pres Acad Fit Awd.

SALLASKA, JOREL D; Oklahoma Sch Of Science & Math; Corn, OK; (3); Church Yth Grp; Library Aide; Quiz Bowl; Scholastic Bowl; Science Clb; Chorus; Church Choir; Ed Yrbk; Bsktbl; Sftbl; Natl Mrt High-Scorer; Sci; Psychiatry.

SALLAVAN, BRIANA; Carnegie Jr HS; Carnegie, OK; (2); Church Yth Grp; Pres Frsh Cls; Pres Soph Cls; Sec Stu Cncl; Var Bsktbl; Sftbl; Var Trk; Hon Roll; NHS; Pres Acad Fit Awd; OK U; Dntl Hygnst.

SALLEE, AMY C; Charles Page HS; Sand Springs, OK; (2); 1/385; Church Yth Grp; Key Clb; Spanish Clb; Cit Awd; Hon Roll; NHS; Ntl Merit Ltr; Prfct Atten Awd; Chrstn Cmps/Anchr Clubs; Bldrs Club Pres.

SALLIS, KACEY R; Muskogee HS; Muskogee, OK; (1); Cmnty Wkr; Band; Mrchg Band; Orch; Pep Band; OK Hnr Soc; Band Attendent; RAID.

SALLLADAY, JACKIE; Yukon HS; Yukon, OK; (2); FHA; Varsity Clb; Yrbk; Var Chrldng; Gym; Powder Puff Ftbl; Trk; UCA All-Star; Cheers Sr All-Star Natl Champions 96; OK U; Mass Commnctn.

SALMON, JAKE I; Locust Grove HS; Salina, OK; (2); Computer Clb; JV Bsktbl; Hon Roll; Tech Stu Assn Team Took 6th In Control Tech Natl Cmptn; NSU; Comp Sys Analysis.

SALMON, JOSHUA I; Locust Grove HS; Salina, OK; (2); Computer Clb; Natl FFA Org; Var Bsktbl; Hon Roll; TSA 6th Pl St & Natl Comp; Cmptr Engr.

SALMON, MANDIE; Antlers Sr HS; Antlers, OK; (3); FBLA; BAD; Write Poems/Short Stories; Prlgl.

SALSMAN, AMY M; El Reno Sr HS; El Reno, OK; (1); Church Yth Grp; 4-H; FHA; Office Aide; Teachers Aide; Band; Mrchg Band; Pep Band; Sftbl; Cit Awd; OK ST U; Tchr.

SALTER, LISA; Westmoore HS; Oklahoma City, OK; (3); 8/610; Sec Church Yth Grp; Key Clb; Q&S; Ed Nwsp; Sec Jr NHS; NHS; Lit Clb Mem; Stdnts For A Cleaner Environment Mem; Future Jrnlsts Of Amer Mem.

SALTER, SARA; Shawnee Sr HS; Shawnee, OK; (4); 22/267; Church Yth Grp; FCA; Latin Clb; Library Aide; Pep Clb; Nwsp; Sec Jr Cls; Hist Sr Cls; Var Capt Bsktbl; Var Tennis; OSU; Dental Hygn.

SAM, ANNIE; Mustang HS; Yukon, OK; (3); 1/350; Church Yth Grp; Key Clb; Spanish Clb; SADD; High Hon Roll; NHS.

SAM, TACEY D; Wilburton Sr HS; Hartshorne, OK; (1); Church Yth Grp; High Hon Roll; NHS.

SAM, TERESA; Wilburton Sr HS; Hartshorne, OK; (3); Church Yth Grp; FHA; Spanish Clb; Chorus; Hon Roll; NHS; Pres Acad Fit Awd; Elem Ed.

SAMARRIPAS, NICHOLAS J; Sayre HS; Sayre, OK; (2); 15/58; Church Yth Grp; Band; Rep Frsh Cls; Var Bsbl; Var Bsktbl; Var Golf; Hon Roll; Prfct Atten Awd; Sci.

SAMPLE, JOHNATHON; Bennington Schl; Bennington, OK; (4); 1/28; Chess Clb; Drama Clb; 4-H; Capt Natl Beta Clb; Speech Tm; School Play; Yrbk; Pres Frsh Cls; Pres Soph Cls; Pres Stu Cncl; SE OK ST Univ; Comp Sci; Math.

SAMPSON, CARTER; Edmond North HS; Edmond, OK; (2); Drama Clb; FCA; NFL; Thesps; School Musical; School Play; Variety Show; Yrbk; Chrldng; Stu Of Month; Guitar; Acting, Singing; Juilliard; Perfmng Arts.

SAMSON, HOLLY I; Bartlesville Mid HS; Bartlesville, OK; (3); 52/468; Art Clb; Church Yth Grp; Drama Clb; Library Aide; Chorus; Orch; School Play; Variety Show; Chrldng; High Hon Roll; Show Choir; Music Or Art.

SAMUEL III, LEONARD W; Midwest City HS; Oklahoma City, OK; (2); Church Yth Grp; Debate Tm; Quiz Bowl; Scholastic Bowl; Band; Church Choir; Drm Mjr(t); Jazz Band; Mrchg Band; School Musical; 96 MA Camp Grnd Chmpn Drum Mjr; Natnly Renownd Saxophnst Of Church Of Living God; Southern U LA; Comp Pgmng.

SAMUELSON, LORI; Hobart HS; Hobart, OK; (1); 1/100; 4-H; Girl Scts; Band; Mrchg Band; Pep Band; Hon Roll; NHS; Grl Sct Slvr Awd.

SAMWEL, PETER; Mc Loud HS; Mc Loud, OK; (4); 1/120; Am Leg Boys St; Church Yth Grp; FCA; FBLA; Office Aide; Scholastic Bowl; Science Clb; Varsity Clb; Variety Show; Yrbk.

SANCHEZ, NOHEMI; Marietta HS; Marietta, OK; (2); Church Yth Grp; Cmnty Wkr; FHA; Acpl Chr; Band; Mrchg Band; School Musical; Hon Roll; Prfct Atten Awd; Accptd To SOSU Upwrd Bound Math & Sci; Vllybl; Math; Southeastern; Elem Tchr.

SANDEFUR, LAURA C; Union Intermediate HS; Tulsa, OK; (2); 387/900; Church Yth Grp; FCA; FBLA; German Clb; GAA; Key Clb; JV Socr; JV Swmmng; Hon Roll; Ath Awd Sccr; FBLA Awd Outstdng Initiative/Ldrshp Skills; Tchr/Law Enfrcmnt.

SANDEFUR, SUMMER L; Madill HS; Madill, OK; (3); Church Yth Grp; FCA; FHA; Office Aide; SADD; Band; Color Guard; Mrchg Band; Pep Band; Ofcr Stu Cncl; Chickasaw Stdnt Cncl Sec; Impact; Southern Nazarene Coll; Psych.

SANDER, BONNI; Seiling Schl; Fairview, OK; (2); Church Yth Grp; FCA; FBLA; FHA; Speech Tm; School Musical; School Play; DAR Awd; Hon Roll; Jr NHS; HS Acad Tm; OSU; Comp Prgmr.

SANDER, KRISTY; Seiling Schl; Seiling, OK; (3); 12/36; Sec Art Clb; Sec Church Yth Grp; FHA; Rep Frsh Cls; Hon Roll; Phy Ed; NW OK ST U; Elem Ed.

SANDERS, CINDY; Porter Jr Sr HS; Porter, OK; (3); Letterman Clb; Scholastic Bowl; SADD; Band; Nwsp; Yrbk; JV Var Bsktbl; High Hon Roll; NHS; Quiz Bowl; Acad Cntst Wnnr; 6th Pl Acad Chllng 95; Med.

SANDERS, CODY W; Duncan HS; Duncan, OK; (3); Church Yth Grp; High Hon Roll; Hon Roll; Jr NHS; NHS.

SANDERS, DE LEASSA; Elk City Jr HS; Elk City, OK; (2); Church Yth Grp; Science Clb; Spanish Clb; Band; Chorus; Church Choir; Yrbk; Rep Soph Cls; High Hon Roll; Hon Roll; Southwestern Assembly Of God.

SANDERS, HEATHER R; Mc Alester HS; Mcalester, OK; (2); Church Yth Grp; FHA; Quiz Bowl; Band; Jazz Band; Yrbk; Cit Awd; Percussion Ensmbl; OK Hon Soc; Math.

SANDERS, JACKIE; Roland Sr HS; Roland, OK; (1); Church Yth Grp; Band; Chorus; Mrchg Band; Ofcr Frsh Cls; Chrldng; Hon Roll; Sftbl; Westark CC.

SANDERS, JAESEN; Seminole Jr Sr HS; Seminole, OK; (3); 4/95; Math Clb; Math Tm; Science Clb; Spanish Clb; Variety Show; Yrbk; Treas Soph Cls; Sec Jr Cls; Sec Stu Cncl; Bsktbl; Outstndng Geom Stu; Gftd & Tlntd Pgm; Hnrs Pgm; OK ST U; Engrng.

SANDERS, JAIME M; Choctaw HS; Nicoma Park, OK; (2); Church Yth Grp; Chorus; Church Choir; Hon Roll; U Of OK.

SANDERS, JARROD; Claremore Sr HS; Claremore, OK; (2); Math Clb; Ofcr Bsbl; Bsktbl; Ftbl; High Hon Roll.

SANDERS, JASON R; Putnam City North HS; Oklahoma City, OK; (1); Church Yth Grp; Rptr Nwsp; Hon Roll; OIPA Wnnr For Sports Feature, Critical Review & Sports Stories; Sports Rptr; Jrnlsm.

SANDERS, JENNIFER L; Wynnewood HS; Wynnewood, OK; (1); #6 in class; Church Yth Grp; FHA; Church Choir; Hon Roll; Phy Thrpst.

SANDERS, JEREMY; Bridge Creek HS; Blanchard, OK; (4); 24/60; Varsity Clb; Ofcr Bsbl; Ftbl; Ltl All City Pitcher Hnrb Mntn 95-96, All Dist Receiver 96; All St Pitcher Hnrb Mntn 96; U Of OK; Sci & Arts.

SANDERS, JERRY M; Tulsa Emmanuel Christian Sch; Bixby, OK; (1); Church Yth Grp; Office Aide; Pres Frsh Cls; Bsktbl; Hon Roll; NC; Sprts Trnr/Anncr.

SANDERS, KAMILAH; Union Sr HS; Tulsa, OK; (4); Church Yth Grp; DECA; FBLA; Key Clb; Mu Alpha Theta; Chorus; Intrml Bsktbl; Hon Roll; NHS; Law Tm; 5th St DECA St Cmptn; U Of FL; Mrktng.

SANDERS, MARRELL E; Del City HS; Del City, OK; (3); 151/315; Church Yth Grp; FCA; Quiz Bowl; ROTC; Church Choir; Color Guard; Drill Tm; Jazz Band; Mrchg Band; Orch; John Philip Sousa Awd; Cmptr Tech.

SANDERS, MARTIN; Frontier Public Schl; Red Rock, OK; (2); Art Clb; Church Yth Grp; Cmnty Wkr; 4-H; Natl FFA Org; Quiz Bowl; Ofcr Frsh Cls; Ofcr Soph Cls; Ofcr Jr Cls; Ofcr Bsbl; Stu Of Today-Masonic Grand Lodge; Presdntl Acad Ftnss Awds Pgm; OSU; Drafting; Engrng.

SANDERS, MATT; Amber Pocasset Jr Sr HS; Amber, OK; (1); Church Yth Grp; FCA; Natl FFA Org; Scholastic Bowl; Church Choir; Var Bsktbl; Golf; High Hon Roll; Hon Roll; Prfct Atten Awd.

SANDERS, MATT; Tulsa Emmanuel Christian Sch; Bixby, OK; (1); Church Yth Grp; Office Aide; Pres Frsh Cls; Bsktbl; Hon Roll; Sports Trnr/Ancr.

SANDERS, MICHEL R; Del City HS; Del City, OK; (4); Church Yth Grp; SADD; VICA; Rep Frsh Cls; VP Soph Cls; VP Jr Cls; Rep Sr Cls; Rep Stu Cncl; Cit Awd; Kiwanis Awd; VICA Awds, Outstndng Stu Awds, Music Awd; Multi Yr Listing; U OK; Bus Mgmt.

SANDERS, RICHARD K; Olive Jr Sr HS; Mannford, OK; (2); FFA; Universal Tech Inst; Diesel Mch.

SANDERS, ROBIN S; Elgin HS; Elgin, OK; (2); Church Yth Grp; Drama Clb; FCA; Hosp Aide; Letterman Clb; Office Aide; Speech Tm; Band; Mrchg Band; JV Var Bsktbl; Pediatrics Physician.

SANDERS, SAMMI; Wilson Schl; Okmulgee, OK; (2); 1/22; Letterman Clb; Math Tm; Scholastic Bowl; Var Bsktbl; High Hon Roll; Northeastern ST Univ.

SANDERS, SARA; Carl Albert HS; Oklahoma City, OK; (3); 114/224; Church Yth Grp; Pep Clb; Chorus; Capt Chrldng; Gym; Mgr Trk; Hon Roll; OK Christian U; Psych.

SANDERS, SARA C; Washington HS; Washington, OK; (1); Rep Church Yth Grp; Rep FHA; Band; Mrchg Band; The Areel M Gibson Stu Historian Awd; Marine Mammals; OK Univ; Marine Bio.

SANDERS, SHELLEY L; Charles Page HS; Tulsa, OK; (3); 68/422; Church Yth Grp; FCA; French Clb; JA; Key Clb; Office Aide; Church Choir; Rptr Yrbk; Rep Stu Cncl; Var Tennis; Hiking; OK Bapt Univ; Ed.

SANDERS, STEVE; Stratford Schl; Stratford, OK; (2); Natl FFA Org; High Hon Roll; Hon Roll; TSA; OK ST Univ; Vetinerian.

SANDERS, STUART A; South Intermediate HS; Broken Arrow, OK; (2); French Clb; Var Ice Hcky; JV Socr; Geog Awd.

SANDERS, SUZANNA K; Howe Public Schl; Poteau, OK; (1); GAA; Chorus; Bsktbl.

SANDERS, TARA L; Lexington HS; Lexington, OK; (3); Art Clb; Church Yth Grp; Computer Clb; FCA; GAA; Girl Scts; Library Aide; Office Aide; Pep Clb; Spanish Clb; Sprts Med.

SANDERS, TATUM; Westmoore HS; Oklahoma City, OK; (2); Office Aide; Pep Clb; School Play; Variety Show; VP Rep Stu Cncl; Chrldng; Golf; Gym; NHS; All Amer Chrldr; OK U; Coaching.

SANDERS, TOSHA N; Union Sr HS; Broken Arrow, OK; (3); 61/741; Spanish Clb; NHS; Spanish NHS; Zoology.

SANDERSFIELD, MARK A; Moore HS; Moore, OK; (3); Am Leg Boys St; Church Yth Grp; German Clb; Science Clb; Band; Jazz Band; Mrchg Band; Chemical Engrng.

SANDOVAL, SILVIA; Anadarko HS; Anadarko, OK; (4); 4/108; Drama Clb; 4-H; French Clb; FBLA; FHA; Girl Scts; Math Clb; SADD; Chorus; Rep Stu Cncl; OK Hnr Soc; Natl Sci Awd; Natl Eng Mrt Awd; OU-NORMAN; Medicine.

SANDY, CRYSTAL; Holdenville Jr HS; Holdenville, OK; (1); Church Yth Grp; Teachers Aide; Band; Chorus; Mrchg Band; Rep Stu Cncl; Bsktbl; High Hon Roll; Hon Roll; Piano; OK U; Pedtrcn.

SANFORD, DEREK; Pauls Valley HS; Pauls Valley, OK; (2); Church Yth Grp; FCA; Ofcr Bsbl; Ftbl; Trk; Wt Lftg; Wrstlng; Prfct Attendance.

SANGER, COLEMAN D; Lawton Sr HS; Lawton, OK; (3); FCA; Spanish Clb; School Play; Ofcr Jr Cls; Intrml Tennis; Internal Med.

SANKEY, LORENDA F; Canton HS; Canton, OK; (2); 13/48; FHA; Science Clb; Spanish Clb; Band; Pep Band; Hon Roll; Indian Yth Clb; Upward Bound; Southwestern OK ST Univ.

SANTEE, SARAH E; Bishop Kelley HS; Tulsa, OK; (3); Cmnty Wkr; Quiz Bowl; Scholastic Bowl; Rep Stu Cncl; JV L Crs Cntry; Var L Tennis; Hon Roll; NHS; Ntl Merit Ltr.

SANTIAGO, JOEY A; Union Intermediate HS; Tulsa, OK; (2); 115/800; Drama Clb; FCA; Intnl Clb; Math Tm; Spanish Clb; Teachers Aide; JV Bsktbl; Hon Roll; Acctnt.

SANTIAGO, MARTA M; Eisenhower Sr HS; Lawton, OK; (4); Church Yth Grp; Intnl Clb; Key Clb; Church Choir; Ofcr Stu Cncl; Tennis; Hon Roll; OK Univ; Lawyer.

SANTINO, SHAUN L; Mc Alester HS; Krebs, OK; (4); 16/209; Church Yth Grp; Debate Tm; Science Clb; Chorus; Church Choir; School Musical; School Play; Ofcr Stu Cncl; NHS; U Of OK; Poli Sci.

SANTOS, FABIO S; Northeast HS; Spencer, OK; (3); Chess Clb; Intrml Socr; High Hon Roll; Hon Roll; NHS; U Of OK.

SAO, ARMANNWAH; Millwood HS; Oklahoma City, OK; (3); Church Yth Grp; ROTC; Chorus; Church Choir; Hon Roll; Sci.

SARCOXIE, SHELLEY A; Bartlesville Mid HS; Bartlesville, OK; (2); 137/481; Church Yth Grp; French Clb; Chorus; High Hon Roll; Hon Roll; Cnslr Aide; U Of OK; Scndry Ed Tchr.

SARTIN, CYNTHIA L; Putnam City North HS; Oklahoma City, OK; (1); Church Yth Grp; FCA; Chorus; Church Choir; Swing Chorus; VP Frsh Cls; VP Soph Cls; Rep Stu Cncl; JV Socr; Dist Nazarene Cncl; Southern Nazarene U; Med Fld.

SARTIN, TYLER M; Deer Creek HS; Edmond, OK; (1); 1/95; Cmnty Wkr; Letterman Clb; Red Cross Aide; Spanish Clb; Nwsp; Var L Tennis; High Hon Roll; NHS; Var Tennis Ltr Frosh Yr; Orthpdc Srgn.

SARTIN, ZACHARY M; Deer Creek HS; Edmond, OK; (3); Art Clb; Cmnty Wkr; Debate Tm; French Clb; FBLA; Letterman Clb; Science Clb; Speech Tm; Ftbl; Golf; Aviation; Dntstry.

SASSER, AMANDA L; Webster HS; Tulsa, OK; (3); 2/172; Church Yth Grp; Cmnty Wkr; FBLA; Hosp Aide; Key Clb; Teachers Aide; Church Choir; Ofcr Frsh Cls; Pres Soph Cls; Treas Jr Cls; Tusla St Fair Grand Prize & 1st Pl Jr Div Fine Arts; Tulsa Univ.

SASSER, SAMANTHA; Carnegie HS; Apache, OK; (3); Church Yth Grp; FHA; Pep Clb; Teachers Aide; Chorus; Church Choir; Var Chrldng; Bilingl Ed.

SASSER, SHANNON; Carnegie HS; Apache, OK; (4); FCA; FHA; Teachers Aide; VICA; Chorus; Chrldng; Hon Roll; Redlands CC; Comp Bus.

SASSER, SHAWN A; Sapulpa Sr HS; Tulsa, OK; (2); Var JV Bsktbl; Phys Ed.

SATORIS, KAYLA J; Wilburton Sr HS; Gowen, OK; (2); Church Yth Grp; Drama Clb; FHA; Speech Tm; Teachers Aide; Band; Color Guard; Stage Crew; Dir/Acting Schl.

SATTERFIELD, AMANDA; Hugo HS; Hugo, OK; (2); Band; Science Clb; Mrchg Band; Pep Band; NHS; Collect Pencils; OSU.

SATTERFIELD, BENJAMIN G; Edmond Santa Fe HS; Edmond, OK; (4); Art Clb; Church Yth Grp; SADD; Var Ftbl; Var Socr; Var Trk; Mosnic Awd; OKC Bombing Vol; Coll Of Charleston; Bus Admin.

SATTERFIELD, TARA; Indianola HS; Quinton, OK; (3); 1/32; FBLA; Library Aide; Natl Beta Clb; VP Jr Cls; Rep Stu Cncl; Var Bsktbl; Var Sftbl; High Hon Roll; Bus.

SATTERLEE, CASEY; Edmond North HS; Oklahoma City, OK; (3); Church Yth Grp; Mu Alpha Theta; Spanish Clb; Band; Church Choir; Mrchg Band; Church Orch; OK ST U.

SATTRE, HEATHER C; Ponca City Sr HS; Ponca City, OK; (4); 29/332; FCA; Hosp Aide; Spanish Clb; SADD; Var Bsktbl; High Hon Roll; NHS; Office Aide; Teachers Aide; Chorus; Camp Fire Inc; Natl Vo Tech Hon Soc; HOSA Pres; U Of Cntrl OK; RN.

SATTRE, MINDY M; Ponca City Middle HS; Ponca City, OK; (1); 96/455; Hosp Aide; Hon Roll; Fashion.

SATWALEKAR, JASON S; Edmond Santa Fe HS; Edmond, OK; (3); 1/285; Debate Tm; Science Clb; Spanish Clb; SADD; VP Stu Cncl; Crs Cntry; Trk; High Hon Roll; NHS; Spanish NHS; Bus.

SAUCEDA, JENNIFER L; Will Rogers HS; Tulsa, OK; (3); 10/200; Church Yth Grp; JA; Key Clb; Spanish Clb; Ofcr Stu Cncl; Tennis; Hon Roll; NHS; OK ST U; Scl Sci.

SAUER, NICOLE; Beaver HS; Beaver, OK; (2); Church Yth Grp; FCA; HOBY; Quiz Bowl; Chorus; Sec Soph Cls; L Crs Cntry; High Hon Roll.

SAULER, JOHN M; Edmond Santa Fe HS; Edmond, OK; (3); French Clb; Pep Clb; Red Cross Aide; Science Clb; SADD; Chorus; School Musical; School Play; Stage Crew; Swing Chorus; Choir Mem Of Yr; Outstdng Crew Mem Of Yr; Sound Engr Schl Productions; Rose ST Coll; Soung Engr/Prdcr.

SAULS, PATIENCE; Eldorado Schl; Quanah, TX; (4); #1 in class; Church Yth Grp; FHA; Natl FFA Org; Pep Clb; Sec Sr Cls; Bsktbl; Score Keeper; Hon Roll; Ntl Merit Ltr; Western OK ST Coll.

SAULSBERRY, ROBERT Z; Shawnee Sr HS; Shawnee, OK; (3); Church Yth Grp; Pep Clb; Rep Stu Cncl; JV Var Bsbl; Intrml JV Bsktbl; Vllybl; Hon Roll; Prfct Atten Awd; Pres Acad Fit Awd; Stdnt Ath Spprtrs.

SAUM, RYAN T; Marietta HS; Marietta, OK; (3); Church Yth Grp; FCA; 4-H; 4-H Awd; Hon Roll; Var Bsbl; Var Ftbl; Var Golf; Var Wt Lftg; U Of OK; Sprts Med/Coach.

SAUTER, DANIEL; Will Rogers HS; Tulsa, OK; (2); Church Yth Grp; ROTC; Church Choir; Drill Tm; Crs Cntry; Ftbl; Trk; Hon Roll; Church Drama Tm; Karate.

SAUTER, JENNIE; Fairview HS; Fairview, OK; (4); Church Yth Grp; FCA; FHA; Church Choir; Rep Jr Cls; L Bsktbl; L Trk; Hon Roll; Rep NHS; Outstndng All Arnd Track; U Of Cntrl OK; Elem Educ.

SAVAGE, RAYNA S; Lindsay HS; Lindsay, OK; (4); Church Yth Grp; FCA; FHA; Library Aide; Office Aide; Spanish Clb; Stage Crew; Yrbk; JV Sftbl; High Hon Roll; OK Univ; Bus.

SAVILLE, STEFANI N; Velma Alma HS; Velma, OK; (3); 1/60; FCA; Quiz Bowl; Sec SADD; School Play; Nwsp; Pres Frsh Cls; Sec Stu Cncl; Chrldng; Crs Cntry; Trk; UCA All-Star Chrldr; OK U; Psych.

SAWATZKY, FAYNE A; Arapaho Schl; Arapaho, OK; (2); Treas Rptr Natl FFA Org; Quiz Bowl; Yrbk; Bsktbl; Crs Cntry; Hon Roll; Pres Acad Fit Awd; Martial Arts; Southwestern OK ST.

SAWATZKY, HEATHER J; Hooker Jr-Sr HS; Hooker, OK; (3); Church Yth Grp; Rptr Natl FFA Org; Chorus; Church Choir; Hon Roll; NHS; OK Panhandle ST U; Elem Tchr.

SAWATZKY, HEIDI J; Hooker Jr-Sr HS; Hooker, OK; (3); Church Yth Grp; Natl FFA Org; Chorus; Church Choir; High Hon Roll; NHS; Show Steers FFA; OK Panhandle ST U.

SAWATZKY, HOLLY J; Hooker Jr-Sr HS; Hooker, OK; (3); Church Yth Grp; Natl FFA Org; Chorus; Church Choir; Hon Roll; NHS; OK Panhandle ST U.

SAWATZKY, WAYNE; Arapaho Schl; Arapaho, OK; (3); Natl FFA Org; Quiz Bowl; Bsktbl; Crs Cntry; Hon Roll; Karate; Southwestern ST Univ.

SAWYER, MIKE; Edmond Memorial HS; Edmond, OK; (4); 107/322; OK Chrstn Univ.

SAWYERS, JACKLYN D; Ponca City Middle HS; Ponca City, OK; (1); Office Aide; Chorus; School Musical; Ofcr Frsh Cls; Hon Roll.

SAYLOR, DESIREE M; Webster HS; Tulsa, OK; (1); Church Yth Grp; Drama Clb; Lawyer.

SAYLOR, MATTHEW; Midwest City HS; Oklahoma City, OK; (4); 128/419; FCA; FHA; German Clb; L Ftbl; Socr; Wrstlng; OK U.

SAYRE, KRISTY D; Seminole Jr Sr HS; Seminole, OK; (3); Church Yth Grp; FCA; French Clb; Math Clb; SADD; Teachers Aide; Chorus; Rep Sec Stu Cncl; Var Bsktbl; Var Chrldng; Ftbl & Bsktbl Homcmng Attendent; Northeastern.

SBONG, MARDY; Putnam City HS; Oklahoma City, OK; (1); Church Yth Grp; German Clb; Socr.

SCAHRDT, SARAH G; Eufaula Sr HS; Eufaula, OK; (2); Church Yth Grp; FHA; HOBY; Drum Tm; Natl FFA Org; Science Clb; Pres Soph Cls; Rep Stu Cncl; Sftbl; Ophthalmology.

SCALES, ANDREA M; Clinton HS; Clinton, OK; (3); 24/111; Church Yth Grp; FCA; GAA; Office Aide; Varsity Clb; Chorus; Var Bsktbl; Var Chrldng; Var Socr; Var Tennis.

SCANTLEN, MARTY R; Oklahoma Sch Of Science & Math; Thackerville, OK; (3); Church Yth Grp; Cmnty Wkr; FHA; Math Clb; Scholastic Bowl; Science Clb; Teachers Aide; Church Choir; Nwsp; Ofcr Frsh Cls; Amer Indian Heritage Clb; Arch Engr.

SCARBERRY, ERIN E; Shawnee Sr HS; Shawnee, OK; (2); Debate Tm; Drama Clb; Latin Clb; NFL; Speech Tm; Thesps; Orch; School Play; Stage Crew; Cit Awd; Intl Thspn Soc; Big Brthrs/Big Sstrs Prgm; Theatre/His.

SCARBERRY, FARON W; Carnegie HS; Carnegie, OK; (3); Church Yth Grp; Natl FFA Org; Band; Church Choir; Jazz Band; Mrchg Band; Pep Band; Ofcr Bsbl; Ftbl; Wt Lftg; Mst Dedicated Band 91-92; Outstndng Solist 94-95; Dir Awd Band; Math Awd 94; FFA Deg; Ltr C Athltc Awd; Panhandle ST U; Ag Bus.

SCARBERRY, KRISTY; Warner HS; Warner, OK; (4); 11/50; Church Yth Grp; FCA; GAA; Rptr Spanish Clb; Teachers Aide; Rptr Yrbk; Powder Puff Ftbl; High Hon Roll; NHS; St Schlr; Teens For Christ; Acctng Awd; Connors St Coll Regeants Schlsp; Connors ST Coll; Acctng.

SCHACHLE, JAYME; Cordell Sr HS; Cordell, OK; (4); 11/48; Rptr FHA; Spanish Clb; Teachers Aide; Band; Flag Corp; Jazz Band; Mrchg Band; Pep Band; Yrbk; High Hon Roll; SW OK U; Acctng/Bus Ed.

SCHADE, MICHAEL ANTHONY; Norman Sr HS; Norman, OK; (4); 1/766; JCL; Latin Clb; Math Clb; Mu Alpha Theta; Science Clb; SADD; Orch; Rep Frsh Cls; Rep Soph Cls; Rep Jr Cls; Violin; U Of OK; Microbiology/Bio-Chem.

SCHAEF, TOBY; Boswell Sr HS; Boswell, OK; (1); Church Yth Grp; FCA; 4-H; Bsktbl; 4-H Awd; High Hon Roll; Hon Roll; NHS.

SCHAEFER, MATT; Edmond North HS; Edmond, OK; (2); Mu Alpha Theta; Orch; JV Tennis; Jr NHS; School Musical; Span I Awd; All-ST Orch; OK ST Orch; N Cntrl Hnrs Orch; Acadmc Ltr.

SCHAEFER, TIMOTHY; Garber Sr HS; Garber, OK; (3); Am Leg Boys St; Church Yth Grp; FCA; Letterman Clb; Natl FFA Org; Quiz Bowl; Teachers Aide; School Play; VP Soph Cls; VP Jr Cls; OK ST U.

SCHALLNER, JEREMY; Fairview HS; Fairview, OK; (1); 1/77; Church Yth Grp; Quiz Bowl; Scholastic Bowl; Band; Mrchg Band; Pep Band; Ofcr Bsbl; Bsktbl; Ftbl; Hon Roll.

SCHANK, BOBBY; Moore HS; Norman, OK; (4); 65/525; Rep Frsh Cls; Var L Ftbl; U Of OK.

SCHATZ, ZACK B; Stillwater Sr HS; Stillwater, OK; (3); Hon Roll; NHS; Pres Acad Fit Awd; 2 Yr Var Schlr; Acad Achvt Awd; Tae Kwon Do Blue Belt; Law Enfrcmt.

SCHAUB, LYNDSAY L; Heritage Hall Schl; Edmond, OK; (3); Cmnty Wkr; Debate Tm; FCA; NFL; Pep Clb; Spanish Clb; Chorus; Nwsp; Ed Yrbk; Lit Mag; Outstdng Novice Debator; Jrnlsm.

SCHECHTER, JENNIFER; Perry Sr HS; Perry, OK; (3); Church Yth Grp; FBLA; German Clb; Quiz Bowl; Sec Frsh Cls; Hon Roll; NHS; Bible Bapt Coll; Acctnt.

SCHEETZ, MELISSA S; Pryor Sr HS; Pryor, OK; (3); Church Yth Grp; German Clb; Chorus; Yrbk; Hon Roll; UCO; Nrsng.

SCHEFFLER, LESLEY; Lomega HS; Hitchcock, OK; (2); 3/15; FCA; 4-H; Yrbk; Var Bsktbl; High Hon Roll; NHS.

SCHEID, PAIGE; Nathan Hale HS; Tulsa, OK; (4); 62/203; Hosp Aide; Office Aide; Capt Chrldng; Hon Roll; NHS; DECA Sec; Fire Fghtrs Aux Mmbr; Schl Svc; OK St Univ; Spch Path.

SCHEIDEMANTEL, MARIE; Corn Bible Acad; Elk City, OK; (1); Church Yth Grp; FCA; Quiz Bowl; Scholastic Bowl; Band; Chorus; Bsktbl; Chrldng; Vllybl; High Hon Roll; U Of OK; Med.

SCHELERN, KRISTA B; Putnam City West HS; Bethany, OK; (3); 1/400; Church Yth Grp; FBLA; Scholastic Bowl; Spanish Clb; SADD; Ed Yrbk; Jr NHS; NHS; Bible Quizzing; Chrch Orch; Chrch Childrens Worker; Southern Nazarene U; Scndry Ed.

SCHERDT, DANIEL; Edmond North HS; Edmond, OK; (4); 41/339; Am Leg Boys St; Pres Church Yth Grp; ROTC; Spanish Clb; Color Guard; Flag Corp; Var Socr; NHS; Elec Engr.

SCHIBER, JOHN M; Okarche HS; Okarche, OK; (3); Am Leg Boys St; Church Yth Grp; FCA; 4-H; Letterman Clb; Ofcr Stu Cncl; Ofcr Bsbl; Bsktbl; Prfct Atten Awd; OK ST U.

SCHICK, DOUG R; Putnam City North HS; Oklahoma City, OK; (1); Church Yth Grp; Hon Roll; Optomist Bsbl; Sports Medicine.

SCHIFFMAN, AUDREY L; Calumet Schl; Calumet, OK; (1); Church Yth Grp; 4-H; Spanish Clb; Church Choir; Regis Univ; Arch.

SCHILDE, ADAM; Dover Schl; Dover, OK; (4); 6/17; FCA; Natl FFA Org; Teachers Aide; Yrbk; Rep Stu Cncl; Var L Bsktbl; Cit Awd; Hon Roll; FFA Pres & Washigton DC Ldrshp Conf Delg; Redlands JC; Crmnl Law.

SCHILLING, ALYSSA; Shattuck Jr Sr HS; Shattuck, OK; (3); 1/35; Church Yth Grp; FCA; HOBY; Pep Clb; Quiz Bowl; Nwsp; Ed Yrbk; Lit Mag; Var Bsktbl; Var Hist Sftbl; U Of TX Austin.

SCHILLING, KATRIN I; Owasso Sr HS; Owasso, OK; (4); Church Yth Grp; Dance Clb; French Clb; Intnl Clb; Latin Clb; Ski Clb; Chorus; School Musical; JV Var Swmmng; Var Vllybl; Germany Col; Tour Ind.

SCHILLING, SUSAN R; Haskell HS; Haskell, OK; (3); Church Yth Grp; Hosp Aide; Library Aide; Band; Mrchg Band; Chrldng; Hon Roll; Acteens; Pre-Med Peds.

SCHIMMEL, EMILY; Clinton HS; Clinton, OK; (3); FCA; Pres FHA; Hist Chorus; VP Frsh Cls; VP Soph Cls; VP Jr Cls; Var Chrldng; Hon Roll; US Natl Ldrshp Mrt Awd; Show, Jazz Choir; OK ST U; Nrsng.

SCHIMMEL, MELINDA; Arapaho Schl; Arapaho, OK; (4); 1/15; Cmnty Wkr; 4-H; FHA; GAA; Letterman Clb; Spanish Clb; Yrbk; Sec Treas Stu Cncl; Bsktbl; Chrldng; OK ST Hnr Soc; All Star Acad Athlt Awd; Sthwstrn OK ST Univ; Soc Sci.

SCHINNERER, CHRIS W; Edmond Memorial HS; Edmond, OK; (2); 93/408; Church Yth Grp; Mu Alpha Theta; Quiz Bowl; Science Clb; High Hon Roll; NHS; Prfct Atten Awd; Presl Acad Awd; Acad Lttr; Natl Schlr.

SCHLECHT, BENJAMIN L; Owasso Sr HS; Owasso, OK; (2); 17/450; Church Yth Grp; Science Clb; Teachers Aide; Var Socr; High Hon Roll; Hon Roll; Part Clb Soccer; Cmptd Odyssey Of Mind.

SCHLESSELMAN, ANNE M; Idabel HS; Idabel, OK; (2); Church Yth Grp; FCA; Red Cross Aide; Band; Chorus; Drm Mjr(t); Jazz Band; Mrchg Band; Stage Crew; Chrldng; FSU.

SCHLIEMANN, MATTHEW L; Altus Sr HS; Altus, OK; (4); Art Clb; Boy Scts; Church Yth Grp; Cmnty Wkr; Model UN; Office Aide; Spanish Clb; Lit Mag; High Hon Roll; Hon Roll; Tech Stu Assn; Art Inst Of Seattle; Art.

SCHLOTTHAUER, HEATHER; Purcell HS; Purcell, OK; (2); 1/100; Scholastic Bowl; Spanish Clb; Chorus; VP Frsh Cls; Sec Soph Cls; JV Bsktbl; Var Chrldng; Var Tennis; High Hon Roll; St Schlr; Math; U Of OK; Math Prof.

SCHLUMBOHM, CARRIE A; Geronimo Jr Sr HS; Geronimo, OK; (2); Bus Profs of Am; FBLA; FHA; Natl FFA Org; Chorus; Orch; School Musical; Hon Roll; Voc Tech Schls; Hlth Sci; Pediatrician.

SCHMALBACH, ERIC C; Metro Christian Acad; Tulsa, OK; (3); Cmnty Wkr; Treas Key Clb; Band; Ed Yrbk; Rep Stu Cncl; JV Bsbl; Var Bsktbl; Var Socr; High Hon Roll; Pres NHS; Mem Of De Molay; Play Guitar; Sci.

SCHMEDT, LINDY; Plainview HS; Ardmore, OK; (2); 1/85; Natl Beta Clb; Quiz Bowl; School Musical; Sec Frsh Cls; Sec Soph Cls; Chrldng; High Hon Roll; NHS; Pres Acad Fit Awd.

SCHMEH, JON A; Edmond Memorial HS; Edmond, OK; (2); Spanish Clb; Ofcr Bsbl; JV Var Bsktbl; Ftbl; Pres Acad Fit Awd; Pol Sci/Bus.

SCHMID, JULIE M; Union Intermediate HS; Tulsa, OK; (1); 319/866; Church Yth Grp; FCA; Key Clb; Library Aide; Office Aide; JV Socr; Var Vllybl; Hon Roll; DFY.

SCHMIDT, ERIN; Union Intermediate HS; Broken Arrow, OK; (1); FCA; Pom Pon; NHS.

SCHMIDT, JACOB F; Drummond Schl; Enid, OK; (2); Church Yth Grp; FHA; Var Bsbl; Var Bsktbl; Var Score Keeper; Hon Roll.

SCHMIDT, JENNY; Edmond North HS; Edmond, OK; (2); 15/420; Church Yth Grp; Cmnty Wkr; FCA; Key Clb; Mu Alpha Theta; Rep Stu Cncl; Var Bsktbl; Var Vllybl; Jr NHS; NHS; Acad Excl Awd; Mu Alpha Theta; Wrkd Spec Ed Kids 9th Grd; Duke.

SCHMIDT, KAPRYCE; Seiling Schl; Seiling, OK; (4); 12/34; VP Church Yth Grp; FCA; Sec FBLA; FHA; GAA; Letterman Clb; Band; Ed Phtg Yrbk; Sec Soph Cls; Hon Roll; S W OK ST U; Dietician.

SCHMIDT, RYAN M; Memorial HS; Tulsa, OK; (2); Cmnty Wkr; ROTC; Spanish Clb; Teachers Aide; School Play; Rep Frsh Cls; Cit Awd; High Hon Roll; Hon Roll; Tulsa Yth Ct; SBI Prep Schl; Lwyr.

SCHMIT, KRISTIN M; Putnam City North HS; Oklahoma City, OK; (4); 97/436; Church Yth Grp; Drama Clb; French Clb; Rep Stu Cncl; Var Pom Pon; Var Socr; Var Vllybl; NHS; Sr Cncl; Mock Trial Tm; U Of GA; Law.

SCHMITT, ANTHONY; Mt St Marys HS; Oklahoma City, OK; (3); 8/64; Key Clb; Var Bsbl; Var Bsktbl; High Hon Roll; NHS; Comp Sci.

SCHMITT, HEATHER; Western Heights Sr HS; Oklahoma City, OK; (3); 49/190; FCA; FHA; Key Clb; Letterman Clb; Chorus; JV Chrldng; Var Crs Cntry; Var Socr; Var Trk; Hon Roll; OK U; Phys Thrpst.

SCHMITZ, HEATHER I; Bartlesville Sr HS; Bartlesville, OK; (4); German Clb; Hosp Aide; Math Clb; Pep Clb; Chorus; School Musical; Capt Chrldng; Hon Roll; Jr NHS; NHS; 8th Grd Tutor; Tch Gymnastics; OK Univ; Med Rsrchr.

SCHMITZ, JASON A; Union Sr HS; Broken Arrow, OK; (3); 73/741; JV Bsktbl; High Hon Roll; NHS; Outstndng Alg I, Frgn Lang & Scl Stds Stu Awds; Pres Outstndng Acad Achvt; U Of Tulsa; Med.

SCHNAKENBERG, GENIE; Miami Sr HS; Miami, OK; (2); Bsktbl; Golf; Hon Roll; NHS; Stdnt Cncl; Rdlgst Tech.

SCHNEIDER, AMANDA; Owasso Sr HS; Owasso, OK; (4); Drama Clb; FCA; Mrchg Band; Rptr Ed Nwsp; Rptr Ed Yrbk; Rep Hist Stu Cncl; Chrldng; Trk; Hon Roll; Pres Acad Fit Awd; NCA & All Amer Chrldr; All Star Chrldng 3rd Pl Natls 95 & 96; Area Co-Ed Chrldng Squad Mem; OK ST Univ; Broadcst Jrnlsm.

SCHNEIDER, AMY M; North Intemediate HS; Broken Arrow, OK; (2); Cmnty Wkr; Math Clb; Orch; High Hon Roll; Hon Roll; NHS; Soph Lit Awd; Engrng.

SCHNEIDER, DANYL L; Noble HS; Noble, OK; (2); 4-H; FHA; Office Aide; Teachers Aide; Chorus; Var Socr; Cit Awd; High Hon Roll; Hon Roll; NHS; Friend Of Spe Ed Awd; Eng Awd; His Awd; Neuro Surgeon.

SCHNEIDER, JOHN HAMILTON; Deer Creek HS; Edmond, OK; (3); FBLA; Science Clb; Sec Jr Cls; Ftbl; Trk; NHS; Pres Acad Fit Awd; VMI; Military.

SCHNEIDER, LINDSEY; Stillwater Sr HS; Stillwater, OK; (3); Spanish Clb; Thesps; Acpl Chr; Chorus; Swing Chorus; Chrldng; Trk; High Hon Roll; OK Summer Arts Inst Chorus 96; Ldrshp Of Tomorrow Pgm; Town & Gowns Prdctn West Side Story.

SCHNEIDER, MATT; Fargo Schl; Fargo, OK; (2); 4/22; Church Yth Grp; FCA; Natl Beta Clb; Natl FFA Org; Quiz Bowl; Ofcr Stu Cncl; Ofcr Bsbl; Bsktbl; High Hon Roll.

SCHNEITER, KURT; Shawnee Sr HS; Shawnee, OK; (3); Church Yth Grp; Cmnty Wkr; Spanish Clb; Pres Soph Cls; Ofcr Jr Cls; Ofcr Stu Cncl; Var JV Tennis; High Hon Roll; Hon Roll; NHS.

SCHNELL, JEREMIAH D; Owasso Sr HS; Owasso, OK; (3); Church Yth Grp; Drama Clb; Chorus; School Musical; School Play; Yrbk; Harding Univ; Bible.

SCHNELL, PAMELA; Oologah-Talala HS; Oologah, OK; (1); School Play; Chrldng.

SCHNIEDERJAN, JORIE; Westmoore HS; Oklahoma City, OK; (4); FCA; Office Aide; Rep Stu Cncl; Var L Ftbl; Var L Sftbl; NHS; Minority Achvmnt Schlrshp From OSU; OK ST Univ; Pre Med.

SCHNORRENBERG, RACHEL; Marietta HS; Marietta, OK; (4); Art Clb; Church Yth Grp; FHA; GAA; Speech Tm; Band; Mrchg Band; VP Frsh Cls; JV Var Bsktbl; Var Sftbl; OU; MIS.

SCHOELEN, MARGARET N; Okarche HS; Okarche, OK; (2); Church Yth Grp; Letterman Clb; Natl Beta Clb; NFL; Speech Tm; School Play; JV Var Bsktbl; Var Sftbl; High Hon Roll; NHS; OK Univ; PT.

SCHOELING, DOUGLAS D; Okarche HS; Okarche, OK; (3); Church Yth Grp; Cit Awd; 4-H Awd; Hon Roll.

SCHOELING, RYAN C; Pond Creek-Hunter Schl; Hunter, OK; (3); Am Leg Boys St; FCA; Natl FFA Org; Spanish Clb; Var L Bsbl; Var Bsktbl; JV Ftbl; Cit Awd; Prfct Atten Awd; FFA Treas; Ag.

SCHOENHALS, KRISTIN D; Shattuck Jr Sr HS; Shattuck, OK; (3); Cmnty Wkr; Sec FHA; Pep Clb; Chorus; Rep Stu Cncl; Var Chrldng; Hon Roll; NHS; St Schlr; U Of OK; Pt.

SCHOFIELD, GRANT; Bishop Mc Guinnes HS; Oklahoma City, OK; (3); 11/205; Debate Tm; Drama Clb; FCA; German Clb; NFL; Quiz Bowl; Scholastic Bowl; Speech Tm; Lit Mag; Socr; Phlsphy.

SCHOLLENBARGER, ROBERT M; Cordell Sr HS; Cordell, OK; (2); Band; Jazz Band; Mrchg Band; Orch; Pep Band; Prfct Atten Awd; Crmnlgy.

SCHONDELMAYER, SHONNA; Owasso Sr HS; Owasso, OK; (3); FCA; Natl FFA Org; VICA; Band; Rep Stu Cncl; Var Chrldng; Var Crs Cntry; Powder Puff Ftbl; Sftbl; Var JV Trk; All Star Chrldng Awd; Hmcmng Attndnt; OK ST U; Med.

SCHONRANK, KARA; Jarman Jr HS; Oklahoma City, OK; (1); Pres Spanish Clb; Pres Band; Pep Band; Tennis; Jr NHS; Acad Ltr; Marine Bio.

SCHONS, MICHAEL; Mc Alester HS; Mcalester, OK; (4); 20/216; Am Leg Boys St; Boy Scts; Church Yth Grp; Band; Mrchg Band; JV Var Bsbl; Var Crs Cntry; Var Trk; High Hon Roll; NHS; Eagle Scout; All-Dist & All-St Bands; ECU; Acctng.

SCHONS, MICHELLE; Parker Middle HS; Mcalester, OK; (3); 29/194; Church Yth Grp; FCA; Spanish Clb; Band; Mrchg Band; VP Soph Cls; Sec Jr Cls; Rep Stu Cncl; Chrldng; Trk; Dntl Hygenist.

SCHOONVELD, MEGAN; Bartlesville Mid HS; Bartlesville, OK; (3); 69/481; Church Yth Grp; Cmnty Wkr; FBLA; Letterman Clb; Spanish Clb; Rep Stu Cncl; JV Var Bsktbl; Var Trk; JV Var Vllybl; Hon Roll.

SCHOUTEN, STEPHANIE L; Owasso Sr HS; Owasso, OK; (4); 12/300; Church Yth Grp; Drama Clb; FCA; FTA; Spanish Clb; Co-Ed Nwsp; Rep Jr Cls; Rep Sr Cls; JV Trk; High Hon Roll; Dance Cls; Tulsa JC; Comp Sci.

SCHOVANEC, SHELLIE; Garber Sr HS; Hunter, OK; (4); 1/33; FHA; Office Aide; Pres Stu Cncl; Capt Bsktbl; High Hon Roll; Pres NHS; Ntl Merit Schol; Val; Rotary Ldrshp Awd; Elks Ldrshp Awd; OK ST U; Pre-Med.

SCHRACK, STEPHANIE A; Jenks HS; Keller, TX; (4); Church Yth Grp; DECA; FCA; FHA; Pep Clb; Teachers Aide; Ofcr Stu Cncl; Var Chrldng; Distngd Svc Grad; Diamon Dolls VP; DFY; Bus Mrktg; Elem Ed.

SCHRADER, LISA; East Central HS; Tulsa, OK; (1); Church Yth Grp; Cmnty Wkr; Drama Clb; Key Clb; Pep Clb; Spanish Clb; School Play; Rep Frsh Cls; Sec Jr Cls; Var Chrldng; Vol 2 Days Wk Lttle Lght House Pre-Schl Spec Need Chldrn; Lawyer.

SCHRADER, SHARI L; East Central HS; Tulsa, OK; (3); Sec Jr Cls; Gym; Cit Awd; French Hon Soc; High Hon Roll; NHS; Pres Acad Fit Awd; Lil Light Hous Vol; Crdnls For Christ; Cmpttve Gymnst Level 8; Pdtrcn.

SCHREIBER, KIMBERLYH; Antlers Sr HS; Antlers, OK; (1); FCA; GAA; JV Bsktbl; Var Sftbl; DAR Awd; High Hon Roll; NHS; Cmptv Acad.

SCHREINER, DUSTIN; Duncan HS; Duncan, OK; (3); Am Leg Boys St; Church Yth Grp; FCA; 4-H; Key Clb; Letterman Clb; Var L Bsbl; Var L Ftbl; High Hon Roll; Hon Roll; Chem.

SCHREMMER, MELISSA L; Bartlesville Mid HS; Bartlesville, OK; (2); 1/481; Church Yth Grp; FBLA; Hosp Aide; Spanish Clb; Ofcr Stu Cncl; JV Bsktbl; Var Sftbl; Var Vllybl; High Hon Roll; Jr Natl Hon Soc Sec.

SCHRODER, CHRISTOPHER K; Okarche HS; Okarche, OK; (3); Church Yth Grp; FHA; Treas Letterman Clb; VP Jr Cls; Ofcr Bsbl; Bsktbl; High Hon Roll; Hon Roll; NHS; Prfct Atten Awd; U Of OK.

SCHROEDER, CHAD; Chisholm Sr HS; Enid, OK; (4); 7/70; Church Yth Grp; FCA; Letterman Clb; Library Aide; Natl FFA Org; Speech Tm; School Play; Yrbk; Pres Stu Cncl; Capt Var Bsbl; Mc Donalds Stu Awd; OK ST U.

SCHROEDER, JEREMY J; Okarche HS; Okarche, OK; (3); Church Yth Grp; 4-H; Natl Beta Clb; NFL; Speech Tm; Treas Soph Cls; Ofcr Bsbl; Hon Roll; NHS; Prfct Atten Awd; OK ST Univ.

SCHROEDER, JESSE; Freedom Schl; Freedom, OK; (1); FCA; Quiz Bowl; Teachers Aide; School Play; Var Bsktbl; Hon Roll; Val; FFA; OK Hse Of Reps Page; Pediatrcs.

SCHROEDER, KLINT; Kingfisher HS; Okarche, OK; (3); 16/95; FCA; Key Clb; Natl FFA Org; Spanish Clb; Hon Roll.

SCHRUPP, JONATHAN F; Choctaw HS; Choctaw, OK; (4); 43/303; Boy Scts; Computer Clb; German Clb; Teachers Aide; Nwsp; Yrbk; Ftbl; Cit Awd; Gov Hon Prg Awd; High Hon Roll; Hstry.

SCHUBERT, DEREK; Central Mid-HS; Norman, OK; (1); Cmnty Wkr; Orch; High Hon Roll; Hon Roll; Prfct Atten Awd.

SCHUBERT, HILLARY; Crescent Schl; Crescent, OK; (4); Cmnty Wkr; FCA; 4-H; GAA; Key Clb; Natl FFA Org; Office Aide; SADD; Teachers Aide; Varsity Clb; Homcng Ftbl Qn 95-96; All Trnmt Bsktbl Team Luther & Cimarron Tourney; OSU Stillwater; Phys Thrpy.

SCHUCHARDT, CARRIE; Ft Towson HS; Sawyer, OK; (1); #1 in class; FCA; FHA; Cit Awd; High Hon Roll; Hon Roll; Kiwanis Awd; NHS; Pres Acad Fit Awd; Val.

SCHUERMANN, ERICA D; Pond Creek-Hunter Schl; Lamont, OK; (2); FCA; Pres Rptr Natl FFA Org; Pep Clb; Sftbl; Trk; Hon Roll; NHS; Cls Favorite; Ag.

SCHUHMACHER, JACLYN; Lawton Sr HS; Lawton, OK; (2); FCA; Key Clb; Pep Clb; Ofcr Stu Cncl; Chrldng; Hon Roll; NHS; TX A&M; Tchr.

SCHULER, REBECCA A; Westmoore HS; Oklahoma City, OK; (4); Church Yth Grp; Cmnty Wkr; Drama Clb; Scholastic Bowl; Spanish Clb; Band; Mrchg Band; Piano Natl Guild Assn Awd, Cameron U Schlstc Trnmt 3rd Pl; St Solo/Ensmble I Ratng; U Of OK; Nursng.

SCHULKE, GREGORY N; Edmond Memorial HS; Edmond, OK; (3); 48/386; Boy Scts; Church Yth Grp; German Clb; Math Clb; Mu Alpha Theta; Quiz Bowl; Science Clb; SADD; Chorus; School Musical; Eagle Scout; Mission Wrk Mexico.

SCHULTE, TARA N; Edmond North HS; Edmond, OK; (2); 87/420; Church Yth Grp; Var Golf; Hon Roll; Jr NHS; Bowlng; OK ST U.

SCHULTHEIS, CHRIS L; Union Sr HS; Tulsa, OK; (3); 166/673; Church Yth Grp; FCA; Spanish Clb; Church Choir; Var L Ftbl; Var L Trk; Pres Acad Fit Awd; Bus Admin.

SCHULTZ, AMANDA; Stillwater Sr HS; Stillwater, OK; (3); Church Yth Grp; FBLA; Pep Clb; Spanish Clb; Teachers Aide; School Musical; Hon Roll; TOG Sorority; Friends Clb; Math Tutor; OSU.

SCHULTZ, DUSTY; Wagoner Sr HS; Wagoner, OK; (4); 11/136; Pres Church Yth Grp; FHA; Intnl Clb; Office Aide; Pep Clb; Teachers Aide; Chorus; School Musical; School Play; Rep Stu Cncl; Hllsdle Free Wll Bptst Col; Mus.

SCHULZ, ISAAC E; Chisholm Sr HS; Enid, OK; (2); FCA; Natl FFA Org; Bsktbl; Wt Lftg.

SCHULZ, LACY; Ft Gibson HS; Fort Gibson, OK; (2); VP Soph Cls; Var Bsktbl; Var Socr; Var Sftbl; Var Trk; Hon Roll.

SCHUMACHER, JEFF; Lone Grove HS; Lone Grove, OK; (3); 5/98; Boy Scts; Church Yth Grp; Ftbl; Wt Lftg; High Hon Roll; NHS; Prfct Atten Awd; Pres Acad Fit Awd; Fish.

SCHUMACHER, JULIE; Lone Grove HS; Lone Grove, OK; (2); 9/106; Church Yth Grp; Math Clb; Science Clb; Spanish Clb; Speech Tm; Band; Hon Roll; NHS; Prfct Atten Awd; OSU; Vet.

SCHUMACHER, TRAVIS L; Bixby Sr HS; Bixby, OK; (1); Var Chrldng; Ftbl; Var Golf; Wrstlng; High Hon Roll; Jr NHS; Art Clb; Stdnt Of Yr 95-; Pres Awd Eductl Excl; OU.

SCHUMAN, CHRISTOPHER J; Edmond North HS; Edmond, OK; (4); 135/330; FCA; Capt L Bsbl; U Cntrl OK; Rest Mgmt.

SCHUSTER, JONATHAN B; Edmond Memorial HS; Edmond, OK; (1); Church Yth Grp; FCA; Letterman Clb; Sec Spanish Clb; Ofcr Bsbl; Bsktbl; Ftbl; Pres Acad Fit Awd; U Of OK.

SCHUSTER, MYCHAL B; East Central HS; Tulsa, OK; (3); 37/243; Spanish Clb; Band; Jazz Band; Mrchg Band; Pep Band; Hon Roll; NHS; Pres Acad Fit Awd; Stdnt Advy Comm VP; Franco Autori Schlsp Awd; Univ Of Tulsa; Law.

SCHUSTER, SARAH N; Edmond Memorial HS; Edmond, OK; (2); Church Yth Grp; Spanish Clb; Mgr Ftbl; OK ST Univ.

SCHWAB, TORY; Broken Arrow Sr HS; Broken Arrow, OK; (4); 418/921; Spanish Clb; SADD; Rep Frsh Cls; Rep Soph Cls; Rep Jr Cls; Rep Sr Cls; Rep Stu Cncl; Intrml Chrldng; Intrml Mgr(s); Intrml Jr NHS; U Of Cntrl OK.

SCHWARTZ, STACY MICHELLE; Carl Albert HS; Oklahoma City, OK; (3); Art Clb; Church Yth Grp; FCA; Key Clb; SADD; Chorus; JV Var Chrldng; Gym; Library Aide; Office Aide; All Amer Chrldr Nom; Brdcstng Rprtr CA TV; Rose ST Jr Coll; PT.

SCHWARZKOPF, JENNIFER K; Union Sr HS; Tulsa, OK; (3); 40/741; VP Church Yth Grp; Band; Rep Frsh Cls; Rep Soph Cls; Rep Stu Cncl; High Hon Roll; Sec NHS; Pres Acad Fit Awd; Spanish NHS; DFY; Super Chrch St Fine Arts Fstvl; USC; Bus.

SCHWEIKHARD, JEANA; Shawnee Sr HS; Shawnee, OK; (3); Church Yth Grp; JV Var Bsktbl; High Hon Roll; Pres Big Brothers, Big Sisters Jr Bd; Ed.

SCHWEIKHARD, KIMBERLY; Shawnee Sr HS; Shawnee, OK; (4); 12/282; Church Yth Grp; Spanish Clb; Tennis; Hon Roll; NHS; Stu Of Month; Piano; Harding U; Law.

SCHWEIKHART, AMBER K; Brink Jr HS; Oklahoma City, OK; (1); Church Yth Grp; Drama Clb; St Gregorys Coll; Law.

SCHWEIZER, BEN; Valliant HS; Valliant, OK; (4); 6/86; Am Leg Boys St; Church Yth Grp; FCA; HOBY; Library Aide; Pep Clb; Quiz Bowl; Teachers Aide; Band; Mrchg Band; Paris JC; Nrsng.

SCHWEMLEY, BECKY S; Kingspark Baptist Acad; Oklahoma City, OK; (4); Hosp Aide; Teachers Aide; Yrbk; High Hon Roll; Hon Roll; Prfct Atten Awd; Early Grad; Supvrs & Monitors Awds; Reading.

SCHWENK, LEAH A; Catoosa HS; Tulsa, OK; (4); 20/136; Church Yth Grp; FCA; Hosp Aide; Spanish Clb; Ofcr Sr Cls; Ofcr Stu Cncl; Bsktbl; Socr; Hon Roll; NHS; Northeastern ST U; Nrs.

SCHWERDTFEGER, ERIC; Burlington Schl; Capron, OK; (1); 1/10; Church Yth Grp; Natl FFA Org; Quiz Bowl; Scholastic Bowl; Band; Rptr Frsh Cls; High Hon Roll; NHS; OSU.

SCHWINN, ERICH M; Union Intermediate HS; Bixby, OK; (2); 54/800; Church Yth Grp; FCA; German Clb; Math Tm; Church Choir; High Hon Roll; NHS; Pres Schlr; Outstdng Math Stu; Drug Free Yth Pgm; Bus Mgmt.

SCIFRES, BUCK A; Velma Alma HS; Velma, OK; (3); FCA; SADD; School Play; Nwsp; Sec Jr Cls; Rep Stu Cncl; Var Bsbl; Var Bsktbl; Var Ftbl; Var Wt Lftg.

SCIFRES, HEATHER D; Ringling HS; Ringling, OK; (2); 7/40; Church Yth Grp; Cmnty Wkr; VP 4-H; FHA; Band; Flag Corp; Phtg Yrbk; Hon Roll; Video Yrbk Photo.

SCIVALLY, DANIEL B; Marietta HS; Marietta, OK; (2); Church Yth Grp; Natl FFA Org; JV Bsbl; JV Bsktbl; Hon Roll; Vol Chrstn Buildrs.

SCOFF, REBECCA S; Westmoore HS; Oklahoma City, OK; (2); Church Yth Grp; Chorus; Church Choir; JV Trk; JV Vllybl; High Hon Roll; Hon Roll; OK Univ; Arch.

SCOGGINS, MONICA D; Douglass HS; Oklahoma City, OK; (3); Art Clb; 4-H; French Clb; FBLA; Rptr Nwsp; Rep Stu Cncl; Intrml Sftbl; Mkng Grd; Rcvd Svngs Bonds; Nwsrm 101; Prtcptd Miss Black OK USA Mtrplx Pgnt Syst; Lbrl Arts/Ed.

SCONZO, MICHAEL; Classen Schl Of Advncd Studies; Oklahoma City, OK; (3); Art Clb; Letterman Clb; Varsity Clb; Stage Crew; Rep Stu Cncl; Var Socr; Var Wrstlng; High Hon Roll; OK Smmr Arts Inst; OCU Norick Art Ctr Awd; Odyssey Of Mind ST Champn.

SCOTT, AMANDA; Stratford Schl; Byars, OK; (2); Natl FFA Org; Speech Tm; Chorus; Yrbk; High Hon Roll; NHS; OK St U; Vet Med.

SCOTT, AMANDA; Plainview HS; Ardmore, OK; (1); 14/93; Church Yth Grp; Chorus; Church Choir; School Musical; School Play; Swing Chorus; Hon Roll.

SCOTT, AMY; U S Grant HS; Oklahoma City, OK; (2); Church Yth Grp; Drama Clb; FCA; Acpl Chr; Chorus; School Musical; School Play; Swing Chorus; Treas Soph Cls; Cit Awd; Sweet Adelines Reg Cmptn Wnnr, 11th Pl Natls; A1 Solo & Ensemble; OK U; Singer.

SCOTT, BRANDON A; Muldrow HS; Muldrow, OK; (2); 3/120; Math Clb; Natl Beta Clb; Science Clb; Spanish Clb; Ftbl; Wt Lftg; Hon Roll; NHS; Supt Hnr Rll; Law.

SCOTT, BRANDON J; Catoosa HS; Catoosa, OK; (2); Church Yth Grp; FCA; Spanish Clb; Var Bsktbl; Var Socr; High Hon Roll; NHS; St Hnr Scty; Tulsa Univ.

SCOTT, DAVID; Canton HS; Canton, OK; (4); 1/46; Am Leg Boys St; HOBY; Pres Frsh Cls; VP Pres Soph Cls; Pres Jr Cls; Pres Sr Cls; Treas Pres Stu Cncl; Capt Ftbl; Cit Awd; Val; Boy Scts; Bsktbl; Trck; NHS; U Of OK; Pre-Med.

SCOTT, DAVID A; Yukon HS; Yukon, OK; (4); 67/417; JV L Bsktbl; Var Capt Socr; High Hon Roll; NHS; All Conf/Dist/City/ST Goalkeeper Soccer; 4 Yrs ODP/3 Yrs ODP Regnl Camp; Univ Of Cntrl AR; Grphc Dsgn.

SCOTT, DONNIE; El Reno Sr HS; El Reno, OK; (3); Church Yth Grp; Natl FFA Org; Band; Church Choir; Jazz Band; Mrchg Band; Hon Roll; Redlands CC; Music Mnstr.

SCOTT, ELIZABETH; Corn Bible Acad; Carnegie, OK; (3); 5/20; Church Yth Grp; Band; Chorus; School Play; VP Jr Cls; Var Bsktbl; Var Vllybl; High Hon Roll; Pres Acad Fit Awd; Tri-St All-Conf Vlybl; Comm.

SCOTT, HEAVEN S; Tahlequah Sr HS; Hulbert, OK; (4); 61/222; Church Yth Grp; Science Clb; Band; Color Guard; Mrchg Band; Winter Guard; Outstdng Colorguard Mem 95-96; Safeguard & Sabre Capt 95-96; NE ST Univ; Cellular Bio.

SCOTT, JAI; Berryhill Jr HS; Tulsa, OK; (2); #10 in class; Church Yth Grp; GAA; JV Bsktbl; Var Crs Cntry; Trk; High Hon Roll; Oil Painting; Fine Arts.

SCOTT, JENNIFER; Byng Sr HS; Ada, OK; (4); 5/77; Cmnty Wkr; Computer Clb; French Clb; FBLA; Natl Beta Clb; Office Aide; Science Clb; Chorus; High Hon Roll; Pres Acad Fit Awd; Beta Clb; U Of OK; Phrmcy.

SCOTT, JENNIFER; Madill HS; Madill, OK; (1); Church Yth Grp; FCA; FBLA; Band; Flag Corp; Mrchg Band; Orch; School Musical; Chrldng; Hon Roll; OK U.

SCOTT, JENNIFER; Norman Sr HS; Norman, OK; (4); 1/677; JCL; Latin Clb; Mu Alpha Theta; Rep Stu Cncl; Capt Chrldng; Hon Roll; NHS; St Schlr; Val; U Of OK.

SCOTT, JENNIFER R; Western Hts HS; Oklahoma City, OK; (3); 18/167; Church Yth Grp; DECA; FCA; Key Clb; Chorus; Stage Crew; Ofcr Stu Cncl; Tennis; Hon Roll; NHS; Ldshp Ed Apprntcshp Prog.

SCOTT, JERRON D; Okmulgee HS; Okmulgee, OK; (2); Drama Clb; Library Aide; Red Cross Aide; Speech Tm; School Play; Stage Crew; Lit Mag; Pres Frsh Cls; Hon Roll; Comm Dstr Drill; Art; Music; OSU; Grphc Arts/Bus.

SCOTT, JULIE L; Heritage Hall Schl; Oklahoma City, OK; (2); Church Yth Grp; FCA; Mu Alpha Theta; Spanish Clb; Chorus; Church Choir; Variety Show; Lit Mag; Fld Hcky; High Hon Roll; Church Ldrshp; Vocal Comp; OK Bapt Univ; Coll Lit Prof.

SCOTT, KEIANN; Wagoner Sr HS; Wagoner, OK; (4); 25/100; Church Yth Grp; Pres FCA; Office Aide; Chorus; Rep Stu Cncl; Chrldng; Vllybl; Hon Roll; Tour Of Champ Jr Yr; Nom All Amer Chldr; VP Pres Of Teens For Christ; John Brown Univ; Music Mnstries.

SCOTT, LA SHAUNA; Fox Sr HS; Tatums, OK; (4); 14/30; Am Leg Aux Girls St; FCA; FHA; Office Aide; Pep Clb; Teachers Aide; Yrbk; Trk; Hon Roll; Prfct Atten Awd; FHA Stu Cncl Rep, Tres, Soc Dir, Rep; Multi Yrs Lstd; Cameron U; Law.

SCOTT, LEE G; Perkins-Tryon HS; Stillwater, OK; (4); 1/72; Church Yth Grp; FHA; Office Aide; Church Choir; Yrbk; Rep Stu Cncl; Var L Bsktbl; Var Capt Trk; NHS; Val; OK St Univ.

SCOTT, LEON B; Bray-Doyle HS; Marlow, OK; (2); Cmnty Wkr; 4-H; FHA; Math Tm; Natl FFA Org; Scholastic Bowl; SADD; Band; Chorus; School Musical.

SCOTT, LESLIE M; Blair Schl; Martha, OK; (2); Speech Tm; Bsktbl; Sftbl; Pres HOSA; WOSC.

SCOTT, LINDSEY L; Heavener HS; Heavener, OK; (1); Church Yth Grp; Band; Bsktbl; Chrldng; Sftbl; Hon Roll; GATE Ldrshp/Chrldng; Carl Albert Jr Coll.

SCOTT, LIZ E; Clinton HS; Clinton, OK; (3); Church Yth Grp; FCA; FHA; Pep Clb; Chorus; Rptr Nwsp; Rptr Frsh Cls; Var Bsktbl; Stat Sftbl; Var Trk; All Conf & All Area Bsktbl Team; All Amer Schlr Awd.

SCOTT, MELISSA; Holdenville HS; Holdenville, OK; (2); 11/85; Church Yth Grp; FCA; German Clb; Girl Scts; Natl Beta Clb; Band; Church Choir; Flag Corp; School Musical; Rep Stu Cncl; Chrch Mission Trips; OK ST U; Teen Cnslr.

SCOTT, MELISSA; Bartlesville Sr HS; Bartlesville, OK; (3); 1/460; Church Yth Grp; French Clb; Hist FBLA; Co-Ed JV Chrldng; French Hon Soc; High Hon Roll; Jr NHS; NHS.

SCOTT, NATALIE; Madill HS; Madill, OK; (3); FCA; FBLA; Math Clb; Quiz Bowl; Science Clb; SADD; Teachers Aide; Band; Drm Mjr(t); Rptr Nwsp; OK Hnr Soc; All Amer Schlr; Educ.

SCOTT, RACHEL A; Bixby Sr HS; Bixby, OK; (1); Band; Mrchg Band; Pep Band; Soccer; Pres Awd For Educl Excl; Rdng; U Of Tulsa; Lawyer; Bus Owner.

SCOTT, RIANN L; Putnam City HS; Oklahoma City, OK; (2); 19/490; GAA; Key Clb; Red Cross Aide; Var Bsktbl; JV Var Socr; Var JV Sftbl; High Hon Roll; Southwestern ST Univ; Pharmst.

SCOTT JR, RICHARD L; Yale Jr Sr HS; Yale, OK; (3); 2/42; Church Yth Grp; Cmnty Wkr; Natl Beta Clb; Natl FFA Org; Science Clb; Teachers Aide; School Play; Stage Crew; Variety Show; Nwsp; U Of OK; Outs Acad Achv; Rep To Rtry Yth Ldshp Awd Conf; Gftd And Tlnted Org; OK St Univ; Psych.

SCOTT, ROBERT; Ardmore HS; Ardmore, OK; (3); Church Yth Grp; Cmnty Wkr; FCA; Office Aide; Spanish Clb; Speech Tm; Teachers Aide; Church Choir; School Play; Nwsp; OK ST Univ; Psych.

SCOTT, ROBIN RENAE; Thackerville HS; Thackerville, OK; (4); 13/17; Church Yth Grp; Computer Clb; FCA; 4-H; FHA; Library Aide; Math Clb; Pep Clb; Science Clb; Spanish Clb; N Cntrl TX Col; Bus Admin.

SCOTT, ROSIE L; Hulbert Jr Sr HS; Hulbert, OK; (1); Church Yth Grp; Chorus; Church Choir; Hon Roll; Jr NHS; Prfct Atten Awd; OK Bapt U.

SCOTT, STACIE M; Drummond Schl; Enid, OK; (2); 1/27; FHA; GAA; Quiz Bowl; Scholastic Bowl; SADD; Rep Soph Cls; Var Bsktbl; Var Sftbl; Var Trk; High Hon Roll.

SCOTT, STEPHANIE; Bowlegs Schl; Bowlegs, OK; (4); Church Yth Grp; Natl Beta Clb; Pep Clb; Teachers Aide; Band; Church Choir; Mrchg Band; Nwsp; Yrbk; VP Stu Cncl; Nursng.

OKLAHOMA

SCOTT, TIM; Clinton HS; Clinton, OK; (4); Am Leg Boys St; Church Yth Grp; FCA; Var Bsktbl; Capt Ftbl; Capt Socr; High Hon Roll; NHS; OK Chrstn.

SCOTT, WILLIAM B; Claremone HS; Vinita, OK; (1); CAP; Nwsp; Yrbk; High Hon Roll; Hon Roll; His/Sci Tchr.

SCOUTEN, MICHAEL T; Elgin HS; Elgin, OK; (1); Church Yth Grp; Natl FFA Org; Chorus; JV Wrstlng; Hon Roll; Zoolgy.

SCRIBNER, DANA; Guthrie Sr HS; Guthrie, OK; (3); 1/300; Church Yth Grp; Cmnty Wkr; Mu Alpha Theta; SADD; Band; Flag Corp; NHS; JA; Math Clb; Pep Band; St Page; Sunday Schl Tchr; Masons Acad Achvt Awd; Bus.

SCROGGINS, KIM A; Byng Sr HS; Ada, OK; (3); Church Yth Grp; FCA; FBLA; Teachers Aide; VP Frsh Cls; Rep Stu Cncl; Var Bsktbl; Cit Awd; High Hon Roll; Sec NHS; OK ST Univ; Interior Dsgnr.

SCRUGGS, JEREMY; Mc Loud HS; Mc Loud, OK; (4); 12/105; Am Leg Boys St; Letterman Clb; Office Aide; Science Clb; Teachers Aide; Varsity Clb; Var L Bsbl; Var L Ftbl; High Hon Roll; Hon Roll; Phys Ed.

SCUTTLER, KIMBERLY J; B T Washington HS; Tulsa, OK; (3); French Clb; German Clb; Teachers Aide; Rep Stu Cncl; NHS; U Of KS; Psych.

SEABOLT, SHANNON; Chelsea HS; Chelsea, OK; (3); 1/70; Church Yth Grp; FCA; Office Aide; Chorus; Pres Frsh Cls; Pres Soph Cls; Pres Jr Cls; Ofcr Stu Cncl; High Hon Roll; Hon Roll; FCA Sec; OU; Med.

SEABORN, ANDREA D; Mc Loud HS; Mc Loud, OK; (2); Church Yth Grp; FTA; Band; Church Choir; Color Guard; Mrchg Band; Yrbk; Hon Roll; NHS; Prfct Atten Awd; OK Bapt Univ; Photo.

SEAGER, KYLE J; Norman Sr HS; Norman, OK; (3); Church Yth Grp; Cmnty Wkr; FCA; Spanish Clb; SADD; Hon Roll; Optimist Clb; Chrch Group Ldrshp Cncl; Optimist Clb Soccer; Multi-Yr Listee; Southern Nazarene U; Math; Bus.

SEAGRAVE, MEGAN; Ardmore HS; Ardmore, OK; (2); Church Yth Grp; French Clb; Latin Clb; Mu Alpha Theta; Science Clb; Co-Capt Chrldng; Mgr(s); Trk; Hon Roll; Jr NHS; Camp Fire; Free Medcl Ctr Vol; OK ST U; Medcl Assist.

SEAL, MIKE; Ada HS; Ada, OK; (3); SADD; Rptr Nwsp; High Hon Roll; NHS; Mass Media; Jrnlsm.

SEALS, ADAM B; Enid Sr HS; Enid, OK; (3); 7/450; Church Yth Grp; Cmnty Wkr; FCA; Spanish Clb; JV Bsktbl; Var Crs Cntry; Var Socr; High Hon Roll; Hon Roll; Jr NHS.

SEALS, JENTRI J; Union Intermediate HS; Tulsa, OK; (2); Key Clb; Spanish Clb; Ice Hcky; Mgr(s); Jr NHS; Tulsa Oilers Booster Clb; OK U; Pediatrcs.

SEAMAN, STACEY L; Poteau HS; Poteau, OK; (2); Art Clb; Hon Roll; Art.

SEARCY, LAKESHA G; Douglass HS; Oklahoma City, OK; (2); Drama Clb; Hon Roll; Surgn.

SEARLES, DANIEL J; Lawton Sr HS; Fort Sill, OK; (2); CAP; FCA; German Clb; HOBY; Library Aide; Color Guard; Golf; Socr; Hon Roll; Best In Schl Basic Lifeskills, Food Prep; USAC; Airforce Ofcr.

SEARS, JAMI S; Salina HS; Adair, OK; (2); Church Yth Grp; Drama Clb; FCA; 4-H; Hosp Aide; Natl FFA Org; Quiz Bowl; Speech Tm; School Play; Stage Crew; Best Beginner Welder; RN; Orthodontist.

SEARS, JEFFREY; El Reno Sr HS; El Reno, OK; (4); 7/180; Am Leg Boys St; FCA; Key Clb; Math Clb; Scholastic Bowl; Science Clb; High Hon Roll; NHS; Ntl Merit Ltr; St Schlr; Engrng.

SEARS, KRISTY D; Healdton HS; Healdton, OK; (2); Hon Roll; NHS; Pres Acad Fit Awd; Pharm.

SEARS, KURTIS; Nowata HS; Nowata, OK; (3); 7/68; Am Leg Boys St; Natl FFA Org; Hon Roll; NHS; FFA Chapt.

SEATON, AMY; Paden HS; Paden, OK; (4); 2/19; Church Yth Grp; 4-H; Sec Natl Beta Clb; Speech Tm; JV Bsktbl; Capt Chrldng; 4-H Awd; High Hon Roll; Pres Acad Fit Awd; Sal; Poem Publshd; OK ST U; Vet Med.

SEATON, TIFFANY; Midwest City HS; Midwest City, OK; (2); 1/501; FHA; GAA; Girl Scts; Pep Clb; Var Socr; Cit Awd; High Hon Roll; Hon Roll; Jr NHS; NHS; John Casablancas Schl Of Mdlng & Careers; Rainbow Grls Of The Estrn Star Assn; FL ST; Mrn Bio.

SEAWRIGHT, SHAWNA; Butner Schl; Wewoka, OK; (2); Natl FFA Org; Hon Roll; NHS.

SEAY, DUSTIN; Harrah HS; Harrah, OK; (4); 10/104; Am Leg Boys St; Band; Drm Mjr(t); Jazz Band; Mrchg Band; Orch; School Musical; Tennis; Cit Awd; NHS; 2 Yr OK Arts Inst Alumni, Orch; Sprir Rtng At St Solo Cntst; John Philip Sousa Awd, Otstndng Mscn; OK City U; Msc.

SEBA, KRISTI C; Glenpool HS; Glenpool, OK; (3); Church Yth Grp; Drama Clb; Spanish Clb; Chorus; Church Choir; School Musical; School Play; Intrml Bsktbl; JV Vllybl; Hon Roll; Planet Earth Clb; St Page At CapitalOK City; Tulsa JC; Bus.

SEBA, LORI D; Del City HS; Oklahoma City, OK; (3); Church Yth Grp; FCA; Library Aide; SADD; Teachers Aide; Chorus; Sftbl; U Of OK; Army; Pediatrician.

SEBERT, PAUL A; Bishop Kelley HS; Tulsa, OK; (3); Church Yth Grp; Var L Bsbl; Hon Roll; Church Acolyte; Hnrbl Mntn 96 Al Metro Bsbl Team; OK ST Univ; Arch/Physics Engr.

SEBESTA, APRIL; Adair HS; Adair, OK; (4); 10/61; Computer Clb; Drama Clb; German Clb; Math Clb; Natl FFA Org; Science Clb; Stage Crew; Hon Roll; OK St FFA Degree; Mem Of St Winning FFA Ag Ec Team & 3rd High Ind At 96 St Ag Ec Cont; NEO A&M; Ag Ec.

SECORY, JOSEPH; Will Rogers HS; Tulsa, OK; (2); Church Yth Grp; Drama Clb; Variety Show; Tennis; Evan Bible Coll; Mnstr.

SECREST, CARRIE; Ardmore HS; Ardmore, OK; (3); Science Clb; Teachers Aide; Var Chrldng; Hon Roll.

SECREST, SCOTT R; Jenks HS; Tulsa, OK; (3); DECA; Mu Alpha Theta; Spanish Clb; Ofcr Stu Cncl; Pres, VP Youth Grp; Edtr Church Nesltr; Baylor; Bus Admin.

SECREST, TRAVIS; Seiling Schl; Seiling, OK; (4); 10/34; Pres Church Yth Grp; Pres FCA; FBLA; Letterman Clb; Natl FFA Org; School Musical; Yrbk; Ftbl; Wt Lftg; Hon Roll; OSU; Engrng.

SEEFELDT, RAGAN C; Stillwater Sr HS; Stillwater, OK; (4); 54/340; Church Yth Grp; Cmnty Wkr; FCA; Hosp Aide; Letterman Clb; Natl Beta Clb; Q&S; Spanish Clb; Chorus; Church Choir; Frntr Rtry Stdnt Mnth; Sec Yth N Govt; Wngs Rtry Ambssdr Japan; Univ OK; Nrsng.

SEEFELDT, REBECCA M; Union Intermediate HS; Tulsa, OK; (2); 115/800; Church Yth Grp; GAA; Spanish Clb; JV Sftbl; Hon Roll; Jr NHS; NHS.

SEELEY, JENNIFER; Moore HS; Moore, OK; (2); 67/640; Office Aide; Science Clb; Ofcr Stu Cncl; JV Chrldng; Var L Mgr(s); High Hon Roll; Jr NHS; NHS; Pres Acad Fit Awd; U Of OK; Med.

SEELY, JAMIE M; El Reno Sr HS; El Reno, OK; (1); Dance Clb; Natl FFA Org; Pep Clb; Drill Tm; Rep Soph Cls; JV Chrldng; Pom Pon; Sftbl; Engl/Basic Bus/Span/FFA Grnhnd/OK His/Wrld His/Sic Awds 9th Grd; Chrldng; O U; Psych/Spclst Dctr.

SEGALL, LORNA E; Stillwater Sr HS; Stillwater, OK; (4); Church Yth Grp; FCA; Hosp Aide; Key Clb; Latin Clb; Teachers Aide; Chorus; Church Choir; School Musical; Variety Show; OK Smmr Arts Inst; ACDA Hnr Choir; Vrsty Schlr; OK ST U.

SEGER, JARED A; Bartlesville Sr HS; Bartlesville, OK; (3); 146/449; Church Yth Grp; Bsktbl; Ftbl; Hon Roll; Prfct Atten Awd; Northwestern; Law Enfrcmnt.

SEGNER, THOMAS; Bixby Sr HS; Bixby, OK; (2); 1/210; Church Yth Grp; FCA; German Clb; Spanish Clb; Capt Socr; Wt Lftg; Hon Roll; Jr NHS; Pres Acad Fit Awd; Intntl Bus.

SEGURA, CHRISTINA; Guthrie Sr HS; Guthrie, OK; (4); 12/178; Cmnty Wkr; Pres FHA; Phtg Key Clb; Mu Alpha Theta; Natl FFA Org; Dance Clb; Science Clb; Spanish Clb; SADD; Yrbk; Vlntrs Of Amer; Scl Wrkr.

SEGURA, RICKY A; Guthrie Sr HS; Guthrie, OK; (1); Cmnty Wkr; Key Clb; Spanish Clb; SADD; Hon Roll; Jr NHS; Kiwanis Awd; Silver Vly Neighborhood Assn; OK Chrstn Univ; Vet.

SEIBER, TANYA N; East Central HS; Tulsa, OK; (3); SADD; Ofcr Jr Cls; Ofcr Sr Cls; High Hon Roll; Hon Roll; NHS; Stdnts Hlpng Stdnts; Per Mediation; Tulsa Univ; Cmptr Arts.

SEIBOLD, MICHAEL W; Edison HS; Tulsa, OK; (2); JCL; Latin Clb; Band; Mrchg Band; Orch; Var Socr; High Hon Roll; NHS.

SEIBOLD, SARAH; Cache HS; Lawton, OK; (4); 5/67; Church Yth Grp; Computer Clb; VP FBLA; Natl Beta Clb; VP Science Clb; SADD; Yrbk; Cit Awd; High Hon Roll; NHS; Cameron U; Elem Ed.

SEIDEL, TIFFANY H; Central Jr HS; Lawton, OK; (1); Var Chrldng; Hon Roll; Kiwanis Awd; Builders Clb-A Comm Svc Clb VP; Post-Poning Sexual Involvmnt Teen Trnr; Acctnt.

SEIDL, AMANDA; Garber Sr HS; Garber, OK; (1); 4-H; Natl FFA Org; Band; Mrchg Band; Pep Band; 4-H Awd; Hon Roll; Sal; Hnr Bands; 4-H/FFA Local, Cty, Dist, St Levels Shwmnshp Cont Chmpn; Band Dir.

SEIGARS, JASON A; Enid Sr HS; Enid, OK; (4); 3/415; Pres Spanish Clb; School Play; VP Jr Cls; Rep Stu Cncl; High Hon Roll; Pres NHS; Pres Acad Fit Awd; US Senate Yth Pgm; Amer Acad Of Achvmt Hnr Stu; We The People Citizen & Constitution Cmptn Natl Awd; OK ST U; Bus.

SEIM, RYAN; Enid Sr HS; Enid, OK; (4); 21/403; Am Leg Boys St; Boy Scts; Church Yth Grp; Letterman Clb; Office Aide; Quiz Bowl; Spanish Clb; Teachers Aide; Band; Jazz Band; Eagle Scout; We The People Cnstitutn Team St Champs; Engrng.

SEITZ, MARC A; Putnam City North HS; Franklin, TN; (1); 118/541; Church Yth Grp; Band; Mrchg Band; Rep Stu Cncl; Golf; Crestwood Animal Hosp Vol; Vet/Marine Bio.

SELF, AMY; Stringtown HS; Stringtown, OK; (3); 1/18; Church Yth Grp; 4-H; Natl FFA Org; Quiz Bowl; Scholastic Bowl; Chorus; Church Choir; School Musical; Variety Show; 4-H Awd; FFA Local Chptr Org VP 95-97; Stu Cncl 93-96; Acctnt.

SELF, ANITA L; Arkoma Jr Sr HS; Arkoma, OK; (2); FHA; Hosp Aide; Pep Clb; Scholastic Bowl; Chorus; School Play; Yrbk; High Hon Roll; Hon Roll; 9th Gde Histrn; 1st Pl In Alg II At CAJC; Carl Albert ST Coll; Med.

SELF, LEAH; Madill HS; Madill, OK; (2); Church Yth Grp; FCA; FBLA; FHA; SADD; Var Sftbl; Hon Roll; NHS; OCU; Tchr.

SELF, PAUL; Edmond North HS; Edmond, OK; (2); 1/473; Boy Scts; Church Yth Grp; Mu Alpha Theta; Orch; JV Crs Cntry; Hon Roll; NHS; Prfct Atten Awd; N Cntrl Hnr Orch; Eagle Sct; Music Tchr.

SELF, PHILLIP; Kiowa Jr-Sr HS; Stringtown, OK; (4); 4/22; Am Leg Boys St; 4-H; HOBY; Natl FFA Org; Quiz Bowl; Science Clb; VP Frsh Cls; L Bsbl; Hon Roll; Prfct Atten Awd; Intl Sci & Engrng Fair; Amer Assn Advancemnt Of Sci & Ntl Sci/Humanities Symposium Presenter; OU; Bus.

SELF, SHALYNN R; Maysville Jr Sr HS; Maysville, OK; (3); Art Clb; FHA; Varsity Clb; School Play; Yrbk; Var Bsktbl; Var Trk; Hon Roll; NHS; US Airfrc Acad; Lwyr.

SELF, STEVE; Westmoore HS; Oklahoma City, OK; (2); Boy Scts; Church Yth Grp; Cmnty Wkr; FCA; Band; Mrchg Band; Orch; Hon Roll; Jr NHS; NHS; U OK; Sci Tchr.

SELFRIDGE, HEATHER J; Shawnee Sr HS; Shawnee, OK; (1); 1/400; Dance Clb; Debate Tm; French Clb; NFL; Speech Tm; Church Choir; Rptr Frsh Cls; Church Yth Grp; Drama Clb; School Play; Red League Scr; OBU Voice Lsns/Superior Rtng; Model J C Penny'S; Pres Rcgntn Acad Top 3%.

SELL, AMBRA L; Pawhuska HS; Pawhuska, OK; (3); FCA; FHA; Teachers Aide; Ofcr Jr Cls; Ofcr Stu Cncl; Sftbl; Hon Roll; Dntstry.

SELLARS, JASON; Mustang HS; Mustang, OK; (3); 78/386; Am Leg Boys St; FCA; Spanish Clb; Acpl Chr; Pres Stu Cncl; Var Bsktbl; Var Socr; NHS; Church Yth Grp; SADD; Magpies Soccer Team 94-96; OK ST Soccer Chmpns 93; Local Chrch Sermon Yth Sunday 94-95.

SELLERS, JENNIFER; Braggs Schl; Braggs, OK; (2); Church Yth Grp; Quiz Bowl; Sec Soph Cls; Bsktbl; Sftbl; Hon Roll; Northeastern ST U; Tchr.

SELLERS, KARMEN; Tupelo Jr Sr HS; Allen, OK; (2); 3/20; Church Yth Grp; Computer Clb; Quiz Bowl; Scholastic Bowl; Band; Church Choir; Rep Frsh Cls; Cit Awd; High Hon Roll; Sal; Poems Pub Two Different Bks; ECU; Lwyr.

SELLS, ZACH; Hulbert Jr Sr HS; Hulbert, OK; (1); 4-H; FHA; Quiz Bowl; Scholastic Bowl; Varsity Clb; Nwsp; Var Bsktbl; Var Crs Cntry; Var Ftbl; Var Trk; Plntlgy.

SELLY, CORINA; Oklahoma Union Schl; Delaware, OK; (3); Cmnty Wkr; Pres FBLA; Pres FHA; HOBY; VP Soph Cls; High Hon Roll; Hon Roll; Ntl Merit Ltr; Prfct Atten Awd; OK Hnr Soc; Military.

SELMAN, SCOTT L; Bishop Kelley HS; Tulsa, OK; (2); Church Yth Grp; Cmnty Wkr; FCA; French Clb; Key Clb; Variety Show; Rep Frsh Cls; VP Soph Cls; Rep Stu Cncl; JV Bsktbl; Natl Yth Ldrshp Forum Nom; Bus; Law.

SELPH, ASHLEY D; Heritage Hall Schl; Oklahoma City, OK; (2); FCA; Chorus; VP Frsh Cls; VP Soph Cls; Var Fld Hcky; High Hon Roll; Spanish NHS; Hosp Aide; Letterman Clb; Pep Clb; Outstdng Frosh; Outstdng Soph; Pep Club Offcr.

SELSOR, NICK R; Cresent Acad; Oklahoma City, OK; (3); Drama Clb; Bsktbl.

SELVEY, LINDY S; Stillwater Sr HS; Stillwater, OK; (3); Church Yth Grp; Key Clb; Spanish Clb; Var L Socr; Hon Roll; Chrch Hnr Star; Var Schlr; OSU; Optometry.

SEMESKI, ANDI; Hartshorne Sr HS; Hartshorne, OK; (2); Church Yth Grp; FCA; Bsktbl; Chrldng; Gym; Sftbl; NHS; NCA All-Amer 2 Yrs.

SEMMEL, JASON C; Woodward HS; Woodward, OK; (4); 58/150; Church Yth Grp; Natl FFA Org; Hon Roll; FFA ST Frmr Dgree; Northwestern OK ST U; Ag Bus.

SEMMEL, STEVEN LANCE; Woodward HS; Woodward, OK; (1); Church Yth Grp; Natl FFA Org; Hon Roll; FFA Star Greenhand; His Awd; Ag.

SEMRAD, BRICE W; Guthrie Sr HS; Guthrie, OK; (2); Church Yth Grp; Drama Clb; FBLA; ROTC; Chorus; Ofcr Soph Cls; Ofcr Bsbl; Cit Awd; Hon Roll; Show Choir; OSU.

SEMTNER, ANDREA; Shawnee Sr HS; Shawnee, OK; (3); 37/290; Church Yth Grp; Hosp Aide; Spanish Clb; Sec Lbrn Chorus; Church Choir; School Musical; School Play; Ofcr Jr Cls; High Hon Roll; Prfct Atten Awd; Math Lab Hlpr; Lib Vlntr; Cmnty Musical; Elem Ed.

SEMTNER, LORI E; Mustang HS; Oklahoma City, OK; (3); 94/403; Church Yth Grp; FCA; FHA; Spanish Clb; SADD; Treas Soph Cls; Hist Stu Cncl; Vllybl; NHS; Stu Ath Trainer; St Gregorys; Sports Medicine.

SEN, ANITA; B T Washington HS; Tulsa, OK; (4); 73/264; Cmnty Wkr; Hosp Aide; NFL; Red Cross Aide; Pres Science Clb; Service Clb; Speech Tm; Orch; Swmmng; NHS; Tulsa Yth Symphny Concrtmstr; Japanese Clb Actvty Dir; 3rd Pl Best Violinst OK All St Orch; St Louis U; Med.

SERATTE, RAYNA; Comanche HS; Comanche, OK; (1); Church Yth Grp; SADD; Band; Chorus; Church Choir; Mrchg Band; Orch; Pep Band; Hon Roll; Cnslr.

SERFOSS, KYLE; Clinton HS; Clinton, OK; (3); Am Leg Boys St; Church Yth Grp; FCA; FBLA; FHA; Natl FFA Org; Office Aide; Teachers Aide; Church Choir; Var Bsbl; U OK; Dnstry.

SERNA, MICHAEL J; Boise City HS; Boise City, OK; (1); Spanish Clb; SADD; Teachers Aide; Temple Yth Grp; Bsktbl; Crs Cntry; Ftbl; Trk; Wt Lftg.

SERRANO, JASON; Cache HS; Cache, OK; (3); Church Yth Grp; Band; Hon Roll; Fnshd CNA Crs Vo-Tech; Med.

SESSION, TAMARA; Broken Arrow Sr HS; Broken Arrow, OK; (3); Church Yth Grp; Debate Tm; Key Clb; NFL; Speech Tm; Teachers Aide; Yrbk; Ofcr Stu Cncl; Hon Roll; Prfct Atten Awd; Soc Work.

SESSUMS, ANDI D; Marlow HS; Marlow, OK; (4); 33/96; Teachers Aide; Chorus; Drill Tm; Yrbk; Chrldng; Hon Roll; Tchr Cadet; Mentor, Mediator Pgm; U Of Sci & Arts OK; Scndry Ed.

SETH, RAHUL; Union Intermediate HS; Tulsa, OK; (2); 1/800; Hosp Aide; Key Clb; Spanish Clb; High Hon Roll; JETS Awd; NHS; Pres Acad Fit Awd; Gftd Pgm Cncl Govt Pres; Pre-Med.

SETH, RISHI; Union Intermediate HS; Tulsa, OK; (1); 1/1000; Hosp Aide; Key Clb; Math Clb; Quiz Bowl; Spanish Clb; Intrml Bsktbl; JV Tennis; Cit Awd; High Hon Roll; NHS; Johns Hopkins; Neuro Surg.

SETTLE, KIM; Moore HS; Moore, OK; (4); 106/525; FCA; French Clb; SADD; Varsity Clb; Mrchg Band; Orch; Var L Crs Cntry; Var L Trk; NHS; Pres Acad Fit Awd; Chrch Aim Mission Trip & Orch; Hosp Vlntr; Baylor U; Envrnmntl Sci.

SETTLE, RUTH; Bartlesville Sr HS; Bartlesville, OK; (3); Church Yth Grp; French Clb; FBLA; Nwsp; Chrldng; Pom Pon; High Hon Roll; Hon Roll; Jr NHS; NHS.

SETZER, BRANDY T; Valliant HS; Garvin, OK; (3); 4-H; FHA; Chorus; Yrbk; Chrldng; Bus Mgmt.

SETZER, JILL M; Ft Cobb-Broxton HS; Apache, OK; (2); FHA; VP Frsh Cls; Rep Stu Cncl; Bsktbl; Hon Roll; Lifeguard; OSU; Dentist.

SEVENOAKS, AUDREY; Cascia Hall Prep School; Tulsa, OK; (1); Spanish Clb; Chorus; JV Bsktbl; JV Var Sftbl; Hon Roll; OMTA Awds In Violin 4 Yrs; TAMTA Awds In Violin 5 Yrs.

SEVERE, MELISSA; Stillwater Sr HS; Stillwater, OK; (3); Church Yth Grp; VP FBLA; HOBY; Key Clb; Natl Beta Clb; Spanish Clb; School Play; Hist Stu Cncl; Pom Pon; Cit Awd; Msnc Ldg Stu Of Today Awd; Rtry Clb Stu Of Mnth.

SEVIER, KYLE R; Mustang HS; Mustang, OK; (3); 51/400; FCA; Teachers Aide; Bsktbl; Hon Roll; NHS; Cert Hnr Outstdng Acad Achvmt HS OU 96; Natl Yth Ldrshp Frm Washington D C 96; Stckbrkr.

SEWARD, JAMIE M; Edmond Memorial HS; Edmond, OK; (4); Spanish Clb; Ed Nwsp; Capt Bsktbl; JV Vllybl; NHS; U Of NE.

SEWARD, MONA; Wagoner Sr HS; Wagoner, OK; (4); Church Yth Grp; FBLA; Math Clb; Office Aide; Spanish Clb; High Hon Roll; NHS; Prfct Atten Awd; St Schlr; Notre Dame.

SEWELL, AMANDA; U S Grant HS; Oklahoma City, OK; (3); 6/230; Church Yth Grp; Drama Clb; FCA; Orch; Mgr(s); Score Keeper; Swmmng; High Hon Roll; NHS; OK Yth Symphony; Ad Design.

SEWELL, ANDREA; Blackwell HS; Blackwell, OK; (2); Church Yth Grp; FHA; Pep Clb; Spanish Clb; Rep Soph Cls; Treas Stu Cncl; Var Chrldng; Hon Roll; Prfct Atten Awd; St Hnr Soc.

SEWELL, ANGELA; Noble HS; Norman, OK; (3); Mu Alpha Theta; Spanish Clb; Chorus; Hon Roll; Jr NHS; Ntl Merit Ltr; Deca; OK Univ; Human Resources.

SEXSON, CHARLES; Jenks HS; Tulsa, OK; (4); FCA; Pres Key Clb; NFL; Rep Sr Cls; Rep Stu Cncl; Hon Roll; Kiwanis Awd; Church Yth Grp; Office Aide; Jr ST Pres; Sandy Nininger Awd; Video Prod Team; IN Univ.

SEXTON, ALICIA; Grandfield Jr Sr HS; Grandfield, OK; (1); 6/22; Church Yth Grp; FHA; Pep Clb; Pres Frsh Cls; Chrldng; Powder Puff Ftbl; Hon Roll; Vet.

SEXTON, BRANDI; Shawnee Sr HS; Shawnee, OK; (2); GAA; Latin Clb; Bsktbl; Sftbl; United Minorities Dev Clb; Med.

SEXTON, JAMIE; Broken Bow HS; Broken Bow, OK; (4); 7/150; Drama Clb; Quiz Bowl; Science Clb; Band; Mrchg Band; School Musical; Nwsp; Hon Roll; Spanish Clb; All Dist Band; OK ST U; Brdcst Jrnlsm.

SEXTON, JAMY; Thomas Jr Sr HS; Thomas, OK; (3); 1/40; Church Yth Grp; Sec FCA; FHA; GAA; Varsity Clb; Var Bsktbl; Var Trk; High Hon Roll; Hon Roll; NHS.

SEXTON, MATTHEW R; Eisenhower Sr HS; Lawton, OK; (2); CAP; Band; Jazz Band; Mrchg Band; Orch; Pep Band; High Hon Roll; Hon Roll; Jr NHS; NHS; U Of OK; Music.

SEYBOLD, SARAH L; Weatherford HS; Weatherford, OK; (4); 27/134; FCA; FHA; FTA; Flag Corp; Swing Chorus; Stat Bsktbl; High Hon Roll; NHS; Church Yth Grp; Cmnty Wkr; Weatherford DFY VP; Eagle Ambssdrs Clss Coordntr; Southwestern OK ST U; Music.

SEYMOUR, NATALIE K; Edmond Memorial HS; Edmond, OK; (4); 39/325; Church Yth Grp; Cmnty Wkr; FCA; Key Clb; Latin Clb; Rep Yrbk; Rep Stu Cncl; JV Chrldng; Var Pom Pon; Powder Puff Ftbl; U Of KS; Bio Chem.

SEYMOUR, PHILIP J; Enid Sr HS; Enid, OK; (3); Church Yth Grp; Drama Clb; Teachers Aide; Band; Chorus; Mrchg Band; School Musical; School Play; Variety Show; Hon Roll; Show Choir; Thtre/Drama.

SHACKELFORD, MEGHAN R; Cushing HS; Cushing, OK; (2); 1/150; Church Yth Grp; FCA; Letterman Clb; Math Clb; Science Clb; Spanish Clb; VP Frsh Cls; Sec Soph Cls; Var Bsktbl; Var Trk; OK Bapt Yth Chr; Ars Nova Msc Stdo; Natl Yth Ldrshp Conf WA DC; SW Bapt U; Rlgs Music.

SHACKLE, KENNETH M; Edison HS; Tulsa, OK; (4); 14/178; Church Yth Grp; Cmnty Wkr; Latin Clb; Library Aide; Jr NHS; NHS; Comp Clb; Engl Explr Post; U Of Tulsa; Comp Eng.

SHADDAY, SYDNEY V; Bishop Kelley HS; Tulsa, OK; (2); Cmnty Wkr; Hon Roll; Stdnt Cncl; Photography/Painting.

SHADID, JEROD R; Oklahoma Christian Schl; Edmond, OK; (4); Church Yth Grp; Office Aide; Ski Clb; Teachers Aide; Stage Crew; Yrbk; Prfct Atten Awd; Co-Chr Randel Shadid For Mayor Edmond Comm; Space Camp; OK Chrstn Univ Of Sci/Arts.

SHAFER, ALISHA; Central Mid-HS; Norman, OK; (2); Cmnty Wkr; Latin Clb; Band; Mrchg Band; Orch; Hon Roll; Ifla Awd; Octgn Club; U Of OK; PT.

SHAFER, AMY; Collinsville HS; Collinsville, OK; (4); GAA; Spanish Clb; Ofcr Sr Cls; Crs Cntry; Socr; Trk; High Hon Roll; Ntl Merit Ltr; Coll Crdt Clss; Rogers ST Coll; Med.

SHAFER, ANDREA L; Alva HS; Alva, OK; (2); FCA; Hist FHA; Chorus; Treas Frsh Cls; Var Bsktbl; Var Sftbl; Var Tennis; Hon Roll; NHS; OK Hnr Soc; Medicine.

SHAFER, DIANA; Chattanoogo HS; Faxon, OK; (4); 5/18; Am Leg Aux Girls St; Pres FBLA; Natl FFA Org; High Hon Roll; Prfct Atten Awd; Pres Acad Fit Awd; Sal; Cameron U; Comm.

SHAFER, RACHEL; Kingfisher HS; Kingfisher, OK; (4); 1/92; Cmnty Wkr; FCA; GAA; Key Clb; Spanish Clb; Rep Sr Cls; Ofcr Stu Cncl; Hon Roll; NHS; Val; Natl Hnr Roll; US Math & All-Amer Schlr Awds; Sthrn Nazarene U; Chld Psych.

SHAFER, STACEY; Putnam City West HS; Oklahoma City, OK; (3); Church Yth Grp; Cmnty Wkr; FCA; French Clb; FBLA; Intnl Clb; Key Clb; SADD; French Hon Soc; Hon Roll; Natl Forum On Law & The Constitution; Think Ink 1st Place; Art Inst; Dsgnr.

SHAFER, STACY A; Ponca City Sr HS; Ponca City, OK; (4); Church Yth Grp; Cmnty Wkr; Teachers Aide; Trk; Vllybl; Wt Lftg; Cit Awd; DAR Awd; Hon Roll; OK ST U.

SHAFFER, DEVIN; Chisholm Sr HS; Enid, OK; (3); Am Leg Boys St; Church Yth Grp; Debate Tm; Pres NFL; Quiz Bowl; Scholastic Bowl; Speech Tm; Pres Stu Cncl; NHS; Envrnmntl Engrng.

SHAH, DAR B; Oklahoma Sch Of Science & Math; Mooore, OK; (3); Cmnty Wkr; French Clb; FBLA; Red Cross Aide; Science Clb; Hon Roll; Kiwanis Awd.

SHAH, NEAL D; Edmond Memorial HS; Edmond, OK; (3); Computer Clb; French Clb; Hosp Aide; Math Clb; Science Clb; Temple Yth Grp; JV Tennis; High Hon Roll; Ntl Merit Ltr.

SHAH, SONALI N; Putnam City HS; Oklahoma City, OK; (1); 1/750; Quiz Bowl; Scholastic Bowl; Cit Awd; Hon Roll; Outstdng Bio/Eng Stdnt 9th Grd; 1st Pl Think Ink Competition Personal Narrative; OCU; Cardiologist.

SHAHAN, KARI L; Westmoore HS; Oklahoma City, OK; (2); Computer Clb; Office Aide; Teachers Aide; Jr NHS; Cnslr Aide; U Of OK; Elem Tchr.

SHAHAN, KELLI C; Union Sr HS; Broken Arrow, OK; (3); 12/741; Church Yth Grp; FCA; FBLA; Drill Tm; Cit Awd; DAR Awd; High Hon Roll; Jr NHS; NHS; Mary Lee Nemic Highst Score Awd; Teach Yngr Drill Team; Non-Schl Dance; Bus Mgmt.

SHAHAN, REGINA; Lawton Sr HS; Lawton, OK; (2); Band; Mrchg Band; Pep Band; Rep Frsh Cls; Hon Roll; Jr NHS; NHS; Med.

SHAKLEE, JADE; Cimarron Public Schl; Lahoma, OK; (4); 2/35; Am Leg Boys St; Church Yth Grp; Cmnty Wkr; HOBY; Capt Quiz Bowl; Band; School Play; Rep Sr Cls; Pres Stu Cncl; Trk; Frgn Exchng Stu Frnce Summr 95; USA Today Teen Panel; Chem.

SHAKLEE, KY L; Cimarron Public Schl; Lahoma, OK; (2); FCA; FHA; GAA; Letterman Clb; Natl FFA Org; Band; Bsktbl; Sftbl; Trk; Cit Awd; OSU; Bus.

SHAMBLES III, JOHN A; Barnsdall Jr Sr HS; Bartlesville, OK; (3); 3/54; Am Leg Boys St; VP Pres Jr Cls; Var L Bsktbl; Var L Trk; High Hon Roll; Hon Roll; Prfct Atten Awd; OSU; Electr Engr.

SHANAHAN, RACHEL S; Union Sr HS; Tulsa, OK; (4); 56/629; Church Yth Grp; DECA; Key Clb; Teachers Aide; Chorus; Church Choir; Orch; School Musical; NHS; Spanish NHS; OK Baptist U; Spnsh.

SHANDY, JASON M; Mangum Sr HS; Mangum, OK; (2); Boy Scts; FHA; Scholastic Bowl; Stage Crew; Variety Show; Ofcr Soph Cls; Ofcr Bsbl; Ftbl; Mgr(s); Score Keeper; OK ST Univ.

SHANE, AMANDA K; Buffalo Jr Sr HS; Buffalo, OK; (2); 2/35; Church Yth Grp; FCA; Chorus; Var Bsktbl; Var Crs Cntry; Var Sftbl; Var Trk; Cit Awd; Hon Roll; NHS; All Amer Schlr; All Trnmnt Team Bsktbl; Conf All Star; Dly Oklhmn All ST Spec Recgnt Fr/Soph; OK ST Univ.

SHANKLE, AMANDA; Westmoore HS; Oklahoma City, OK; (2); 22/700; Quiz Bowl; ROTC; Scholastic Bowl; Band; Mrchg Band; NHS; Lettered Schlstcs 95-; Westmoores Mock Trial Team; OK UMCA Yth/Gov Prgm.

SHANKLE, AMBER; Enid Sr HS; Enid, OK; (4); 15/386; Am Leg Aux Girls St; Cmnty Wkr; Dance Clb; French Clb; Math Clb; Science Clb; Service Clb; Band; Drill Tm; Mrchg Band; Camp Fire Wo-He-Lo Awd, Camp Fire Brd Dir Yth Member; OK All Star Band; U OK; Astronaut.

SHANKLE, KENNETH K; Hulbert Jr Sr HS; Hulbert, OK; (2); Art Clb; Church Yth Grp; Computer Clb; 4-H; FBLA; Pres Frsh Cls; JV Var Bsbl; JV Capt Ftbl; Mgr(s); Wt Lftg; Regnl Sci Fair Awds; Cls Awds; NSU; Dntl; Sport Medicine.

SHANKLE, RACHEL; Hulbert Jr Sr HS; Hulbert, OK; (2); Church Yth Grp; 4-H; VP Soph Cls; Var Bsktbl; Var Sftbl; Hon Roll; NHS; AR U.

SHANKLES, AMIE; Marietta HS; Marietta, OK; (3); FCA; Yrbk; Ofcr Stu Cncl; Var Bsktbl; Crs Cntry; Sftbl; Trk; Vllybl; High Hon Roll; Hon Roll; Phys Thrpst.

SHANKS, CHRISTIAN R; Central Jr HS; Lawton, OK; (1); FCA; Spanish Clb; Golf; Hon Roll; High Hon Roll; Jr NHS; OSU; Medicine.

SHANNON, AMANDA; Victory Christian Schl; Tulsa, OK; (2); Church Yth Grp; Pep Clb; Color Guard; Chrldng; High Hon Roll; Hon Roll; Jr NHS; Kiwanis Awd; Trvld Paraguqy Smmr 94; Phys Thrpy.

SHANNON, ERICA; Collinsville HS; Collinsville, OK; (4); Church Yth Grp; FBLA; Girl Scts; Band; Color Guard; Hon Roll; Prfct Atten Awd; Natl Voc Tech Hnr Socty; Voc Stu Org; Child Psych.

SHANNON, JACOB A; Union Intermediate HS; Broken Arrow, OK; (2); FCA; FBLA; Key Clb; Office Aide; Stage Crew; Ed Nwsp; Ed Yrbk; Rptr Lit Mag; Rep Stu Cncl; Hon Roll; Most Outstdng In Jrnlsm; OU Univ; Mass Media/Comm.

SHANNON, RYAN M; Edmond Memorial HS; Edmond, OK; (3); Art Clb; FCA; Var Tennis; Rec Sand Vllybl, Snow Ski; Music.

SHANS, MISTY; Lone Grove HS; Lone Grove, OK; (3); FHA; Pres Spanish Clb; Rptr Nwsp; High Hon Roll; NHS; Vo-Tech Med Asst Stu.

SHANTA, SABRINA L; Broken Arrow Sr HS; Broken Arrow, OK; (3); Church Yth Grp; VP FCA; Var Capt Bsktbl; Hon Roll.

SHAPARD, JESSICA; Heritage Hall Schl; Oklahoma City, OK; (3); Mu Alpha Theta; Ofcr Pep Clb; Ed Yrbk; Rep Stu Cncl; Var Bsktbl; Var Tennis; Var Vllybl; High Hon Roll; NHS; Spanish NHS; Jrnlsm.

SHAPPIE, REBECCA; Mid-Del Christian Schl; Oklahoma City, OK; (1); Church Yth Grp; Girl Scts; Church Choir; Pres Frsh Cls; Tennis; Hon Roll; OK Chrstn U; Psych.

SHARBER, CASEY; Sapulpa Sr HS; Sapulpa, OK; (2); 6/365; Church Yth Grp; French Clb; Natl FFA Org; Science Clb; Cit Awd; French Hon Soc; 4-H Awd; Hon Roll; Jr NHS; NHS; St Floriculture Awd Wnnr FFA 96-Natls Fall 96.

SHARMA, PRIYAM; Bartlesville Sr HS; Bartlesville, OK; (4); 23/412; Hosp Aide; Quiz Bowl; Pres Science Clb; Rep Spanish Clb; Orch; Ofcr Stu Cncl; Cit Awd; High Hon Roll; NHS; St Schlr; Nom To Attend 95 Yth Ldrshp Forum On Medicine; Univ Of OK Hnr Schlr; Dirs Awd In Orch; U Of OK; Zoology; Psych; Med.

SHARP, ASHLEY N; Edmond North HS; Edmond, OK; (1); 39/456; Church Yth Grp; Chorus; Hon Roll; Yth Alive; Yth For Christ.

SHARP, BECKY R; Webster HS; Tulsa, OK; (3); Art Clb; FCA; Letterman Clb; Yrbk; Bsktbl; Sftbl; High Hon Roll; Hon Roll; NHS; Cmmrcl Artst.

SHARP, BRANDY L; Midwest City HS; Midwest City, OK; (3); 204/364; Art Clb; Cmnty Wkr; FCA; Girl Scts; Red Cross Aide; Teachers Aide; OK ST; Lab Tech Analysis.

SHARP, CHARLES; Little Axe Sr HS; Newalla, OK; (3); 3/90; Scholastic Bowl; Chorus; Nwsp; Sec Frsh Cls; Rep Soph Cls; Rep Stu Cncl; Var Bsbl; JV Bsktbl; Var Crs Cntry; NHS; Public Admin.

SHARP, DEBRA A; Owasso Sr HS; Claremore, OK; (3); 4-H; FBLA; FBLA; Acupressure.

SHARP, DESI L; Arapaho Schl; Arapaho, OK; (2); Church Yth Grp; Cmnty Wkr; Pres 4-H; FHA; Model UN; Scholastic Bowl; Teachers Aide; Band; Chorus; Church Choir; Psychiatrist; Psychiatry.

SHARP, KELLIE L; Clayton Jr Sr HS; Clayton, OK; (1); Church Yth Grp; 4-H; Chorus; Sec Frsh Cls; Var JV Bsktbl; 4-H Awd.

SHARP, KRISTA; Kremlin Jr Sr HS; Enid, OK; (2); Church Yth Grp; Band; Sftbl; Hon Roll; Cirricular Conts; OSU; Arch.

SHARP, TINA; Hobart HS; Hobart, OK; (3); 3/60; Church Yth Grp; FCA; FHA; FTA; Stage Crew; Rptr Jr Cls; Rep Stu Cncl; Var Bsktbl; Golf; NHS; Soph Cls Favorite; OK Hnr Soc; OK ST U; Psych.

SHARP, TRACEY A; Spiro HS; Spiro, OK; (2); 3/100; FBLA; Math Clb; Spanish Clb; Color Guard; Mrchg Band; Sftbl; Vllybl; Hon Roll; Jr NHS; Ntl Merit Ltr.

SHAUN, BONNIE J; Preston Schl; Okmulgee, OK; (1); Church Yth Grp; Chorus; School Musical; Var Bsktbl; Var Chrldng; Var Sftbl; Var Trk; High Hon Roll; Hon Roll; Ftnss Instr.

SHAVER, CLARK D; Locust Grove HS; Locust Grove, OK; (3); Church Yth Grp; VICA; Church Choir; Var Bsbl; Wrstlng; High Hon Roll; Hon Roll; 1st Pl OK VICA Cmptn/7th Pl Nation; Amatuer Radio Operator; Brigham Yng Univ; Elec Engr.

SHAVER, MANDI; Eufaula Sr HS; Eufaula, OK; (4); #4 in class; Debate Tm; Drama Clb; Math Clb; Science Clb; Speech Tm; Chorus; School Play; High Hon Roll; NHS; Pres Acad Fit Awd; Pedtrcn.

SHAW, AARON; Bartlesville Sr HS; Bartlesville, OK; (4); 38/420; FCA; Ftbl; Wt Lftg; High Hon Roll; Hon Roll; St Schlr; Geneva Coll; Bus Admin.

SHAW, AMY F; Norman Sr HS; Norman, OK; (3); 92/799; Cmnty Wkr; Spanish Clb; Hon Roll; NHS; OU; Vet.

SHAW, BRIGETTA; Midwest City HS; Oklahoma City, OK; (3); Hosp Aide; Bio.

SHAW, CARA B; Carney Schl; Carney, OK; (2); Church Yth Grp; FHA; Mu Alpha Theta; Quiz Bowl; Var Bsktbl; Var Sftbl; Hon Roll; NHS.

SHAW, CASEY R; Woodward HS; Woodward, OK; (1); Natl FFA Org; Hon Roll; NHS; Writingwood Wordsworth Awd 96.

SHAW, JENNIFER; Duncan HS; Duncan, OK; (2); 2/360; Church Yth Grp; Cmnty Wkr; Dance Clb; GAA; Key Clb; Letterman Clb; Red Cross Aide; SADD; Varsity Clb; JV Var Bsktbl.

SHAW, JON M; Ripley HS; Ripley, OK; (4); 1/50; Church Yth Grp; FCA; FHA; Math Clb; Quiz Bowl; Science Clb; Spanish Clb; Band; Mrchg Band; Pep Band; Msnc Ldrshp Awd; OK ST U; Vet.

SHAW, JUSTIN; Dickson HS; Ardmore, OK; (3); Church Yth Grp; Computer Clb; Key Clb; Pep Clb; SADD; Teachers Aide; JV Bsbl; Var Bsktbl; Capt Golf; Var Mgr(s); Eng Awd; CPR Cert; Reg Golf Mdlst; Murray ST.

SHAW, KATY D; Union Intermediate HS; Broken Arrow, OK; (2); Church Yth Grp; Dance Clb; FCA; French Clb; FBLA; Teachers Aide; Church Choir; School Musical; Powder Puff Ftbl; DFY; USC; Voice Lessons; Dance; Musical Theater.

SHAW, KELLI; Westmoore HS; Oklahoma City, OK; (4); 40/610; Church Yth Grp; FBLA; Latin Clb; Teachers Aide; Church Choir; Chrldng; Wt Lftg; Cit Awd; Chrldng 5a St Chmpnshp & Awds; Top Gun Sr Dance Ntl Chmpnshp; 3rd Pl Sci Fair; Prin Awd; OCCC; Acctnt.

SHAW, MARY L; Western Heights Sr HS; Oklahoma City, OK; (2); 1/211; Church Yth Grp; FCA; Letterman Clb; Quiz Bowl; Scholastic Bowl; Spanish Clb; Teachers Aide; Var Crs Cntry; Var Trk; Cit Awd; OK Indian Hnr Soc.

SHAW, REBECCA; Blanchard Jr Sr HS; Blanchard, OK; (2); 3/88; Computer Clb; Mu Alpha Theta; Spanish Clb; Church Choir; Yrbk; High Hon Roll; NHS; FHA; Blanchard Pblc Lib Vol; U OK; Law.

SHAY, ROBERT J; North Intemediate HS; Tulsa, OK; (2); Boy Scts; Church Yth Grp; Computer Clb; Teachers Aide; Rptr Nwsp; Yrbk; Hon Roll; NHS; U OF CT; Bus Mgnt.

SHAY, SARAH K; Bethany HS; Oklahoma City, OK; (4); 1/80; Church Yth Grp; Sec Spanish Clb; Chorus; School Musical; Rep Stu Cncl; Var L Trk; High Hon Roll; Hon Roll; NHS; Val; Southern Nazarene Univ; Arch.

SHEA, LAURA A; Edmond Memorial HS; Edmond, OK; (2); FCA; Spanish Clb; Chrldng; OK ST Univ.

SHEARER, CHRISTY D; Stillwater Sr HS; Stillwater, OK; (4); 72/320; FBLA; German Clb; Latin Clb; Band; Mrchg Band; Pep Band; Hon Roll; Pres Acad Fit Awd; Schlsp Achvmt; Var Schlr; OSU; Bus.

SHEARER, SUZANNE; Southwest Covenant Schl; Mustang, OK; (2); Church Yth Grp; FCA; Band; Chorus; Rep Soph Cls; Bsktbl; Vllybl; Gov Hon Prg Awd; High Hon Roll; Prfct Atten Awd; Bst Bsktbl Dfnsv Plyr.

SHEEHAN, ELIZABETH; Grace Fellowship Christian Sch; Tulsa, OK; (1); Church Yth Grp; Dance Clb; Drama Clb; Church Choir; Rep Stu Cncl; Var Vllybl; Hon Roll; Mission Trps; Chdrns Chrch; Piano.

SHEEHAN III, ROBERT D; Holland Hall Schl; Tulsa, OK; (2); 1/90; Drama Clb; Capt Golf; French Hon Soc; High Hon Roll; French Clb; Letterman Clb; Math Tm; School Play; Nwsp; Intrml Bsktbl; Duke Univ Grand Math Awd; Stanford Univ Law & Ldrshp; 1st In US In Kumon Math.

SHEETS, JENNY; Altus Sr HS; Altus, OK; (4); Am Leg Aux Girls St; Church Yth Grp; Model UN; Spanish Clb; Chorus; Ed Nwsp; Sec Soph Cls; Rep Stu Cncl; Swmmng; NHS; Tchr Cadet; Harding U; Elem Ed.

SHEETS, LESLIE C; Tahlequah Jr HS; Tahlequah, OK; (1); Church Yth Grp; Service Clb; Pres Stu Cncl; JV Bsktbl; Jr NHS; OETA St Wnnr For Short Story Wrtng; OK ST Univ; Phy Thrpst.

SHEETS, MISTY DAWN; Soper Schl; Hugo, OK; (4); 3/17; 4-H; Treas FHA; Yrbk; VP Frsh Cls; Var Bsktbl; Crs Cntry; 4-H Awd; Prfct Atten Awd; All Around Sr; Cert Of Completion Schl Of Bus-Southeastern U; Bsktbl Qn; Typing I Awd; Paris JC; Legal Sec.

SHEETS, SUSAN L; Tipton Jr Sr HS; Tipton, OK; (3); Quiz Bowl; Band; Var Bsktbl; Var Chrldng; High Hon Roll; NHS; Prfct Atten Awd; Ed.

SHEFFIELD, JANUARY T; Afton HS; Bernice, OK; (2); Church Yth Grp; FCA; 4-H; FHA; GAA; Pres Frsh Cls; Var Bsktbl; Var Chrldng; Var Trk; Bsktbl Coach.

SHEFFIELD, RACHAEL; Ft Gibson HS; Fort Gibson, OK; (2); 1/161; Church Yth Grp; High Hon Roll; FCA; HOBY; SADD; Drm Mjr(t); School Musical; Sec Stu Cncl; Chrldng; High Hon Roll; Hmcmng Ct; Yth Mssnry; Lfgrd; All-Amer Chrldr; All-Amer Schlr; OK Bptst U; Psych.

SHEIK, AARON R; Cimarron Public Schl; Lahoma, OK; (3); Church Yth Grp; Computer Clb; French Clb; JA; Band; Mrchg Band; Pep Band; School Musical; Ofcr Bsbl; Wt Lftg; Northwestern; Math.

SHEKARESTAN, SIYMACK; Putnam City North HS; Oklahoma City, OK; (1); SADD; Ofcr Stu Cncl; Tennis; Hon Roll; 3d; Hall Decorations; UCLA.

SHELBY, CHRIS; Comanche HS; Comanche, OK; (4); 10/55; Am Leg Boys St; Church Yth Grp; FHA; Natl FFA Org; Science Clb; Teachers Aide; Var Golf; Wrstlng; High Hon Roll; NHS; SW OK ST U; Phrmcy.

SHELBY, SONDRA R; Choctaw HS; Choctaw, OK; (3); 63/313; Church Yth Grp; Key Clb; Spanish Clb; Pres Treas Band; Jazz Band; Mrchg Band; Pep Band; School Musical; Hon Roll; NHS; Show Choir Combo; Awd Mst Imprvd High Brass 95; Awd Highest Grd Prnt Adv Rdng 1 Schl Yr; OK ST Univ; Vet.

SHELBY, TIMOTHY; Comanche HS; Comanche, OK; (1); German Clb; Var Bsktbl; Hon Roll; Air Force; Aerontcl Engr.

SHELDON, MARIE L; Westmoore HS; Oklahoma City, OK; (4); Rep Soph Cls; Rep Jr Cls; Rep Sr Cls; NHS; Chm Citizenship Comm; Child Dev.

SHELITE, SHANNON C; Aline-Cleo Jr Sr HS; Aline, OK; (2); CAP; Hosp Aide; JV Bsktbl; JV Sftbl; JV Trk; JV Vllybl; Hon Roll; Sci Tchr; Helicpoter Rescue.

SHELKETT, AMBER M; Lawton Sr HS; Lawton, OK; (3); Dance Clb; Spanish Clb; Var Chrldng; Var Pom Pon; High Hon Roll; Hon Roll; Jr NHS; NHS; Pres Acad Fit Awd; Amer Natl Teenager Fnlst; All Amer Schl 94; OK HS Hnr Soc; Cameron Univ; Med.

SHELTON, ADAM; Claremore Sr HS; Claremore, OK; (3); 44/237; Boy Scts; Church Yth Grp; FCA; Teachers Aide; JV Var Bsbl; Ftbl; Trk; High Hon Roll; Hon Roll; NHS; OK ST U; Arch Engr.

SHELTON, ALISHA; Heritage Hall Schl; Oklahoma City, OK; (3); Cmnty Wkr; GAA; Letterman Clb; Pep Clb; Service Clb; Spanish Clb; Chorus; Variety Show; Yrbk; VP Frsh Cls; NCA Chrldng Camp All Amer; UCA Chrldng Camp All Star; Peer Ldrshp Pgm; U Of OK.

SHELTON, ALLISON; Lawton Sr HS; Lawton, OK; (2); FCA; Chorus; Church Choir; Orch; School Musical; School Play; Variety Show; High Hon Roll; Hon Roll; Jr NHS; Boise ST U; Nursng.

SHELTON, AMBER D; Wilburton Sr HS; Kinta, OK; (3); 15/80; FCA; FBLA; Office Aide; Red Cross Aide; Chorus; Phtg Nwsp; Yrbk; Rep Frsh Cls; Rep Jr Cls; Rep Sr Cls; Piano Accmpnst Chorus; Northeastern ST U; Optmtry.

SHELTON, AUTUMN M; South Intermediate HS; Broken Arrow, OK; (1); Church Yth Grp; Acpl Chr; Gov Hon Prg Awd; High Hon Roll; Hon Roll.

SHELTON, BRANDON C; Yukon HS; Yukon, OK; (4); 92/404; Band; Jazz Band; Mrchg Band; Pep Band; Hon Roll; OM Crtvty Cmptn-Wrld Cmptn 93; Hlpng Hnd 95-96; Rnssnc Prog; U Cntrl OK; Msc Ed.

SHELTON, CASSIE M; Brink Jr HS; Oklahoma City, OK; (1); Church Yth Grp; FCA; Church Choir; Gtr; Chrstn Rck Bnd; Wrtng Music; OK Bapt Univ; Rck Bnd.

SHELTON, CHAD; Sapulpa Sr HS; Sapulpa, OK; (4); 2/400; Church Yth Grp; Key Clb; Office Aide; Spanish Clb; High Hon Roll; Val; Teens For Chirst; Multiple Art Awds; 1st Pl Intnl; Rock Climbing; Rappelling; Assembly Pep Team; Art; Bus.

SHELTON, HAZEL; Bray-Doyle HS; Marlow, OK; (2); 4-H; FHA; Chorus; VP Frsh Cls; VP Soph Cls; Bsktbl; Cit Awd; Murry ST.

SHELTON, JAMES M; Lindsay HS; Lindsay, OK; (3); 12/69; Church Yth Grp; FCA; Natl Beta Clb; Office Aide; Teachers Aide; Ofcr Soph Cls; Bsktbl; Ftbl; Trk; Cit Awd; OK ST U.

SHELTON, JOHN B; Glenpool HS; Glenpool, OK; (3); Chess Clb; Church Yth Grp; FCA; Math Tm; Capt Scholastic Bowl; Acpl Chr; Chorus; Ofcr Stu Cncl; High Hon Roll; NHS; Tri-ST/DIST Hnrs Choirs; Chrch Drama Troupe; Habitat For Hum; Oral Roberts Univ; Pol Sci.

SHELTON, KIMBERLY C; Durant HS; Durant, OK; (3); Drama Clb; French Clb; FTA; Chorus; School Play; Hon Roll; Shksprn Fstvl 8 Yrs; Psych.

SHELTON, LAURIE; Cushing HS; Cushing, OK; (4); 10/156; Church Yth Grp; Cmnty Wkr; Pres FBLA; VP Math Clb; Drill Tm; Pom Pon; Tennis; High Hon Roll; NHS; Pres Schlr; Proj Self Estm; VBS Tchr; Var Schlr; Pscyh/Fmly Cntr.

SHELTON, PAUL T; Union Sr HS; Tulsa, OK; (3); Church Yth Grp; JCL; Latin Clb; Orch; Hon Roll; OK Baptist Univ; Math.

SHELTON, SCOTT A; Western Heights Sr HS; Oklahoma City, OK; (4); 55/135; Chess Clb; Band; Jazz Band; Mrchg Band; Orch; Pep Band; School Musical; JV Bsbl; Var JV Crs Cntry; Band Schlsp SOSU; Southeastern OK ST; Music Ed.

SHELTON, TIFFANY R; Morris HS; Okmulgee, OK; (2); Teachers Aide; Treas Frsh Cls; Treas Soph Cls; Ofcr Stu Cncl; Hon Roll; Prfct Atten Awd; Fha/Sub-Dist Pres/Lcl Treas 95-; Acad Team 94-; Brain Bowl Team 94-.

SHEN, STEPHEN; Jenks HS; Tulsa, OK; (4); 22/540; Pres FBLA; Mu Alpha Theta; NFL; Science Clb; Service Clb; Hon Roll; NHS; Debate Tm; Model UN; Speech Tm; Tulsa City-Cty Lib Literacy Vol; Theatre Tulsa Vol; Distngd Grad; U Of IL Urbana; Acctng.

SHENOLD, CHAD; Anadarko HS; Anadarko, OK; (3); 1/124; Church Yth Grp; FCA; FBLA; Quiz Bowl; Scholastic Bowl; Spanish Clb; Varsity Clb; Bsktbl; Hon Roll; NHS.

SHEPARD, AARON P; Geronimo Jr Sr HS; Geronimo, OK; (1); 1/25; 4-H; Math Clb; Pres Science Clb; Pres Soph Cls; 4-H Awd; High Hon Roll; Hon Roll; Val; St FFA Drummer; OSU.

SHEPARD, BRANDON R; Mc Alester HS; Mcalester, OK; (3); VICA; Rptr Nwsp; Hon Roll; Architectural Skills; OSU; Arch.

SHEPARD, KEITH; Newcastle HS; Newcastle, OK; (4); 7/72; Church Yth Grp; FCA; FBLA; Office Aide; Scholastic Bowl; Hon Roll; Ntl Merit Ltr; FBLA Cmptns; OK Hnr Soc; OU; Bus.

SHEPARD, MATTHEW S; Moore HS; Moore, OK; (3); FCA; Rep Stu Cncl; Var Socr; Clb Soccer; Golf; Tnns; U Of KS; Psych.

SHEPHARD, BRANDIE L; Lexington HS; Purcell, OK; (4); Art Clb; Church Yth Grp; Sec FCA; Natl FFA Org; Rep SADD; Band; Ofcr Bsbl; Mgr Ftbl; Var Sftbl; Hon Roll; Academic Team 1 Yr; St Gregorys; Comm Art.

SHEPHERD, ANGELA D; Hammon Schl; Hammon, OK; (1); Acpl Chr; Chorus; Rep Nwsp; Rep Frsh Cls; High Hon Roll; WOCDA; Tulsa Univ.

SHEPHERD, CHRISTINA; Clinton HS; Clinton, OK; (3); 1/118; Church Yth Grp; FCA; Pres VP 4-H; Sec Natl FFA Org; Chorus; Ofcr Stu Cncl; 4-H Awd; Hon Roll; NHS; OK St U; Vet Med.

SHEPHERD, DAVID; Enid Sr HS; Enid, OK; (4); 28/405; Am Leg Boys St; Office Aide; Band; Var L Golf; Hon Roll; NHS; U OK; Med.

SHEPHERD, GARY E; Eisenhower Sr HS; Lawton, OK; (3); 21/486; Intnl Clb; Yrbk; Rep Stu Cncl; Var Bsktbl; Var Tennis; High Hon Roll; Jr NHS; NHS; Pres Acad Fit Awd; SAVE Treas; Peer Mediator; Gifted/Talented.

SHEPHERD, JEREMY W; Arapaho Schl; Arapaho, OK; (3); Computer Clb; Sec Natl FFA Org; Yrbk; Mgr(s).

SHEPHERD, JESSE H; North Intemediate HS; Broken Arrow, OK; (1); Teachers Aide; Wt Lftg; Hon Roll; Jr NHS; Soccer 9 Yrs; Tulsa Univ; Vet.

SHEPHERD, JOHNATHON L; Catoosa HS; Catoosa, OK; (4); 16/148; Church Yth Grp; FCA; FBLA; Intnl Clb; Pres Stu Cncl; Var Ftbl; Var Trk; Var Wt Lftg; Var Wrstlng; Hon Roll; FCA Ath Of Yr Awd 95-96; Wrestling Dist Champ & St Qualifier; BASIC; MOI; GMI; Elec Engrng; Mech Engrng.

SHEPHERD, JONATHAN; Shawnee Sr HS; Shawnee, OK; (2); Var JV Golf; JV Tennis; High Hon Roll; Sci Awd; Dist & St Piano Perf Awds.

SHEPHERD, KRISTEN; Blackwell HS; Blackwell, OK; (1); Church Yth Grp; Cmnty Wkr; FCA; FHA; Letterman Clb; Office Aide; Pep Clb; Red Cross Aide; Teachers Aide; Acpl Chr; OK Kids Inc; Actv Gymnst; Solos Chrch Act; OK ST U; Pdtrcn.

SHEPHERD, LARISSA; Bartlesville Mid HS; Bartlesville, OK; (1); 123/476; Church Yth Grp; Var Bsktbl; Var Sftbl; Hon Roll.

SHEPHERD, THOMAS E; South Intermediate HS; Broken Arrow, OK; (3); Church Yth Grp; DECA; Letterman Clb; Varsity Clb; Golf; Bus.

SHEPPARD, AMY; Sallisaw HS; Sallisaw, OK; (3); 33/120; Church Yth Grp; Drama Clb; FHA; Library Aide; Math Clb; Office Aide; Pep Clb; Science Clb; Spanish Clb; Speech Tm; NOC Blackwell OK; Bus.

SHEPPARD, HEATHER K; Arapaho Schl; Arapaho, OK; (2); Var Bsktbl; Hon Roll.

SHEPPARD, JIMI; Wynona Schl; Pawhuska, OK; (3); 1/14; Am Leg Boys St; VP Natl Beta Clb; Co-Capt Quiz Bowl; Pres Spanish Clb; VP Frsh Cls; Pres Soph Cls; Pres Jr Cls; Var Capt Bsktbl; Cit Awd; Hon Roll; OK ST Univ; Acctng/Pre Law.

SHEPPARD, SEAN; Lawton Sr HS; Lawton, OK; (3); Church Yth Grp; SADD; Church Choir; Var Ftbl; High Hon Roll; Hon Roll; Jr NHS; Ntl Merit Ltr; TAP; Ebny Soc.

SHERFIELD, CORY E; Dickson HS; Ardmore, OK; (2); Church Yth Grp; Office Aide; JV Var Bsktbl; JV Var Crs Cntry; Var Trk; High Hon Roll; Hon Roll.

SHERFIELD, REGINA J; Whitesboro Schl; Hodgen, OK; (4); 6/31; Church Yth Grp; FCA; Sec FHA; Library Aide; Office Aide; Quiz Bowl; Speech Tm; SADD; School Play; Nwsp; Carl Albert ST Coll; Bus Admin.

SHERMAN, CARRIE R; Pryor Sr HS; Pryor, OK; (2); Church Yth Grp; FCA; Chorus; Pres Soph Cls; Ofcr Stu Cncl; Bsktbl; Chrldng; Golf; Pom Pon; Hon Roll; Teen Ldr Pstpng Sxl Invlvmnt Pgm.

SHERMAN, DARIN; Chandler HS; Chandler, OK; (4); 6/69; Am Leg Boys St; Church Yth Grp; Cmnty Wkr; FCA; Natl FFA Org; Sec Jr Cls; Sec Sr Cls; Var Bsbl; Var Ftbl; NHS; All St Acad Bsbl Tm 94-95; Outstndng Span I Stu 93; Sr Capt Ftbl Tm 95.

SHERMAN, HEATHER D; Charles Page HS; Sand Springs, OK; (2); Church Yth Grp; Cmnty Wkr; FCA; Key Clb; Spanish Clb; Band; Church Choir; Mrchg Band; Pep Band; Hon Roll; Yth In Govt; Psych.

SHERMAN, MATTHEW; Grace Fellowship Christian Sch; Tulsa, OK; (2); Church Yth Grp; Teachers Aide; Band; Orch; School Play; Ofcr Frsh Cls; Ofcr Stu Cncl; Wrstlng; Hon Roll; Film Maker.

SHERMAN, REBECCA; Westmoore HS; Oklahoma City, OK; (4); 8/622; Cmnty Wkr; Key Clb; Spanish Clb; Ed Nwsp; NHS; Val; Acad Ltr; Sndy Schl Tchr; Lib Vol; U Of OK; Elem Educ.

SHERMAN, TRACY L; Pryor Sr HS; Pryor, OK; (3); 7/200; Church Yth Grp; FCA; VP Soph Cls; VP Jr Cls; Ofcr Stu Cncl; Var Bsktbl; Var Chrldng; Var Golf; High Hon Roll; PSI Teen Ldr; Phillips U; Elem Ed.

SHERRARD, GINNY R; Ponca City Sr HS; Ponca City, OK; (3); 58/371; Church Yth Grp; FCA; Natl FFA Org; Office Aide; Treas Pep Clb; SADD; Church Choir; Ftbl; Mgr(s); Wrstlng; Frgn Lang Clb; Schl Chorale; OK ST Univ; Phy, Sports Thrpy.

SHERRARD, KIM R; Moore HS; Moore, OK; (3); Church Yth Grp; Drama Clb; FCA; Teachers Aide; Acpl Chr; Chorus; Church Choir; School Play; Stage Crew; Jr NHS; Play Piano For 9 Yrs; Beach Vllybl; OK Bapt Univ; Womens Hlth; Ed.

SHERRARD, NICK; Miami Sr HS; Miami, OK; (3); Church Yth Grp; NFL; Quiz Bowl; Scholastic Bowl; Speech Tm; Band; Jazz Band; Mrchg Band; Hon Roll; Med Field/Crmnl Psych.

SHERRELL, JOSEPH N; Webster HS; Tulsa, OK; (2); Boy Scts; Church Yth Grp; Letterman Clb; Quiz Bowl; Var Ftbl; Var Golf; Var Wt Lftg; High Hon Roll; Hon Roll; Jr NHS; OK ST Univ; Fire Protection.

SHERRER, JOHN; Central Mid-HS; Norman, OK; (1); Church Yth Grp; FCA; JCL; Latin Clb; Mu Alpha Theta; Treas Frsh Cls; Ofcr Stu Cncl; Co-Capt Bsktbl; High Hon Roll; Spec Olympcs Vol.

SHERRICK, CANDICE; Edmond Santa Fe HS; Edmond, OK; (2); Pep Clb; SADD; Rep Frsh Cls; Ofcr Soph Cls; Ofcr Stu Cncl; JV Var Chrldng; Powder Puff Ftbl; NHS; Hrsbck Rdng.

SHERWOOD, CORTNE; Jones HS; Jones, OK; (4); 3/64; Pres Church Yth Grp; GAA; Band; Jazz Band; Mrchg Band; Bsktbl; Powder Puff Ftbl; Trk; Pres NHS; Val; Ricks Col.

SHETTY, ANUP S; Shawnee Sr HS; Shawnee, OK; (1); 1/350; Quiz Bowl; Spanish Clb; Tennis; Piano.

SHETZ, JAMIE; Nathan Hale HS; Tulsa, OK; (3); Church Yth Grp; Cmnty Wkr; FCA; L Vllybl; Hon Roll; Elem Ed.

SHEWMAKE, DOROTHY; Whitesboro Schl; Muse, OK; (3); 5/20; Church Yth Grp; FHA; HOBY; Library Aide; NFL; Chorus; School Musical; School Play; Nwsp; Hon Roll; Crmnl Jstc.

SHIELDS, AMY; Pioneer Pleasant Vale HS; Enid, OK; (3); 7/45; Church Yth Grp; Cmnty Wkr; FCA; 4-H; FHA; HOBY; Natl Beta Clb; Church Choir; Mrchg Band; Orch; Intl Cmptvt Twrlr, Pom Pon Squad; OK St 4-H Ambsdr; Law.

SHIELDS, MARY K; Charles Page HS; Sand Springs, OK; (1); Church Yth Grp; Cmnty Wkr; Drama Clb; School Musical; School Play; Stage Crew; Ed Nwsp; Yrbk; Ofcr Stu Cncl; Hon Roll; Tulsa Wrk Cmp; Crntn 96 Rep Nwsppr Org; Chrstn Cmps Club; OK Univ; Elem Ed Tchr.

SHIELDS, VALERIE J; Mc Alester HS; Mcalester, OK; (4); 7/208; Church Yth Grp; Cmnty Wkr; Thesps; Chorus; Church Choir; School Musical; School Play; High Hon Roll; NHS; St Schlr; Yth In Rel Awd; Chrch Choir Pres; OK Bapt Univ; Voice Perfmnc.

SHIERS, NICHOLAS; Jarman Jr HS; Del City, OK; (1); Library Aide; Spanish Clb; Band; Jr NHS; Acad Tm; Schlstc Lttrng Clb.

SHIEVER, JUSTIN; Morrison Public Schl; Morrison, OK; (4); 1/40; Am Leg Boys St; Natl FFA Org; Jazz Band; Pres Frsh Cls; Treas Jr Cls; VP Sr Cls; Pres Stu Cncl; Bsktbl; Ftbl; NHS; OK ST U; Vet.

SHIEVER, LINDSEY L; Morrison Public Schl; Morrison, OK; (2); Church Yth Grp; Natl FFA Org; Sec Frsh Cls; Sec Soph Cls; L Bsktbl; L Chrldng; L Sftbl; L Trk; Wt Lftg; High Hon Roll; AAU Bsktbl.

SHIFF, JOSEPH D; Choctaw HS; Choctaw, OK; (3); FCA; Letterman Clb; Spanish Clb; Ofcr Bsbl; Score Keeper; Tennis; Hon Roll; Prfct Atten Awd; OK JC; Law Enforcement.

SHIKHNAN, JULIA; Putnam City HS; Oklahoma City, OK; (1); 4/458; Cmnty Wkr; Dance Clb; Hosp Aide; High Hon Roll; AIU Ldrshp Camp; UCLA; Neonatal Srgn.

SHILLING, JULIE; Moore HS; Moore, OK; (4); 11/505; Spanish Clb; Phtg Yrbk; Ed Lit Mag; Jr NHS; NHS; Prfct Atten Awd; Pres Acad Fit Awd; Spanish NHS; Val; Cmnty Wkr; Lion Lit League Hstrn; Future Jrnlst Amer; OU.

SHINE, TONYA; Bartlesville Sr HS; Bartlesville, OK; (4); 26/470; Church Yth Grp; French Clb; Girl Scts; Band; Mrchg Band; Pep Band; French Hon Soc; High Hon Roll; Hon Roll; Jr NHS; Northeastern ST U; Scndry Math.

SHINN, DARCY; Welch Jr Sr HS; Welch, OK; (3); Drama Clb; FBLA; Speech Tm; School Play; Trk; Hon Roll; Speech Tm St Chmpns; 5th Pl High Jump St; NSU.

SHINNEN, HOLLY N; Sapulpa Sr HS; Sapulpa, OK; (3); 43/292; Am Leg Aux Girls St; Church Yth Grp; Red Cross Aide; Ofcr Bsbl; Ftbl; Wrstlng; NHS; Pres Acad Fit Awd; Spanish NHS; Cmnty Wkr; Miss Sapulpa Fest 95; Hd Var Ath Trnr 96; Sprts Med.

SHIPLEY, JEREMY R; Del City HS; Oklahoma City, OK; (2); U Of OK.

SHIPLEY, JULIE L; Wynnewood HS; Elmore City, OK; (2); Teachers Aide; Hon Roll; GATE; Art; Jrnlsm; U Of OK; Graphic Design Artist.

SHIPLEY, LACI A; Morris HS; Okmulgee, OK; (3); Church Yth Grp; FCA; Rptr FHA; GAA; SADD; Varsity Clb; Ed Nwsp; Hist Soph Cls; Hist Jr Cls; Ofcr Stu Cncl; Sftbl All Conf 93-94; OK ST Hnr Soc; Tchr/Coach.

SHIPMAN, DAVID S; Cleveland Sr HS; Cleveland, OK; (2); Church Yth Grp; FCA; SADD; L Ftbl; Var L Trk; Hon Roll; NHS; Fshng; Hntng; Archery; Tulsa Jr Coll; Elctrl Eng/Pilot.

SHIPMAN, JEFF L; Oologah HS; Claremore, OK; (3); 5/107; Church Yth Grp; FCA; Var Bsbl; High Hon Roll; NHS; 4a Bsbl ST Chmpns 96; Sports Med/Pharm.

SHIPMAN, JENNI N; Wagoner Sr HS; Wagoner, OK; (3); Cmnty Wkr; FBLA; High Hon Roll; Hon Roll; Jr NHS; NHS; Prfct Atten Awd; OK Cntrl U; Mortuary Sci.

SHIPMAN, JEREMY; Durant HS; Durant, OK; (3); 3/175; Debate Tm; FBLA; HOBY; VP Frsh Cls; Pres Soph Cls; Rep Stu Cncl; Ftbl; Socr; High Hon Roll; NHS; Drug Free Yth; Presdntl Clsrm Delg; Bus Mgmt.

SHIPMAN, LEANNDA M; Howe Public Schl; Howe, OK; (1); 4-H; FBLA; Natl FFA Org; Rep Frsh Cls; Ofcr Bsbl; Bsktbl; Sftbl; 4-H Awd; High Hon Roll; Hon Roll; TX A&M Univ.

SHIRAZI, JASON A; Putnam City North HS; Oklahoma City, OK; (2); Spanish Clb; Cit Awd; USU; Med.

SHIREMAN, JENNIFER; Perry Sr HS; Perry, OK; (2); Cmnty Wkr; FCA; FHA; Spanish Clb; Band; Mrchg Band; Pep Band; Rep Soph Cls; VP Stu Cncl; Var Bsktbl.

SHIRES, TERRI I; Harrah HS; Harrah, OK; (3); 19/169; Art Clb; Church Yth Grp; Computer Clb; SADD; High Hon Roll; Hon Roll; Jr NHS; NHS.

SHIRES, TIFFANY A; Webster HS; Tulsa, OK; (4); FBLA; Spanish Clb; Yrbk; Var Golf; Hon Roll; Art; Traveling; Phys Therapy.

SHIREY, JESSICA R; Putnam City West HS; Bethany, OK; (3); Latin Clb; Sftbl; High Hon Roll; NHS; Latin Hnr Soc; People To People Stdnt Ambass Pgrm.

SHIRLEY, BECKY D; Moore HS; Moore, OK; (4); Drama Clb; ROTC; Deca Clb; OK Cty CC; Law.

SHIRLEY, MICHAEL; Berryhill Jr HS; Tulsa, OK; (3); Church Yth Grp; Teachers Aide; VP Band; Church Choir; Jazz Band; Mrchg Band; Orch; High Hon Roll; NHS; All St Jzz Ensmbl; Yth Hndbll Choir; Prfrm Lvng Chrstms Tree Orch Frst Bapt Tlsa; Tulsa U; Music.

SHIRLEY, RACHEL G; Stillwater Sr HS; Stillwater, OK; (3); Church Yth Grp; FCA; Hosp Aide; Spanish Clb; Teachers Aide; Chorus; School Musical; School Play; Trk; Hon Roll; Madrical Show Choir; Prv Vcl Lsn; Berkley Coll Of Music; Vocal.

SHIRLEY, TAMMY; Mounds Schl; Morris, OK; (3); Library Aide; Natl Beta Clb; Office Aide; Band; Chorus; High Hon Roll; Med.

SHIRLEY, TIM; Woodward HS; Woodward, OK; (4); 19/141; Bus Profs of Am; FCA; FBLA; Letterman Clb; Varsity Clb; Var Bsktbl; High Hon Roll; Hon Roll; Snrs In Actn; United Way; NW OK ST; Bus.

SHIVERS, ANGELA; Kingston HS; Kingston, OK; (2); Church Yth Grp; Jazz Band; Mrchg Band; Rep Frsh Cls; Hon Roll; NHS; Curr Engl II/ALGEBRA II; OU; Corp Lwyr.

SHOCKLEY, DENISE; Northeast HS; Oklahoma City, OK; (2); Church Yth Grp; Hosp Aide; Pep Clb; Band; Chorus; Church Choir; Mrchg Band; Pep Band; School Musical; Sec Frsh Cls; UCLA.

SHOEMAKE, CORY L; Edmond Memorial HS; Edmond, OK; (4); Church Yth Grp; VP Computer Clb; FCA; JCL; Key Clb; Latin Clb; Mu Alpha Theta; Science Clb; Ofcr Spanish Clb; SADD; Supr Fns; Md Cws Sccr Tm; Jared; U OK; Med.

SHOEMAKE, MANDY; Pawhuska HS; Pawhuska, OK; (4); 27/87; Am Leg Aux Girls St; Church Yth Grp; Debate Tm; Drama Clb; FCA; FBLA; FHA; Hosp Aide; JA; Key Clb; Wrstlng Hmcmng Qn 95-96; Spch St Chmpnshp Hmrs Duet Rnnr Up 95; Spch St Chmpnshp W/Drmtc Duet 4th Pl.

SHOEMAKER, BENJAMIN; Union Intermediate HS; Tulsa, OK; (2); 3/700; Church Yth Grp; Cmnty Wkr; Church Choir; JV Socr; JV Wt Lftg; Hon Roll; Jr NHS; NHS.

SHOEMAKER, CODY; Drummond Schl; Enid, OK; (1); Church Yth Grp; FHA; Quiz Bowl; Scholastic Bowl; Teachers Aide; Church Choir; Cit Awd; High Hon Roll; Hon Roll; NHS; Phys Ther.

SHOEMAKER, COLBERT; Wagoner Sr HS; Wagoner, OK; (4); Am Leg Boys St; Church Yth Grp; FCA; French Clb; Hosp Aide; Letterman Clb; Varsity Clb; Ftbl; Trk; Wt Lftg; Math Tchr.

SHOOK, BRANDYE; Medford Schl; Medford, OK; (3); Art Clb; Drama Clb; FCA; Letterman Clb; Pep Clb; Spanish Clb; Chorus; School Play; Sec Treas Frsh Cls; JV Bsktbl; All-Amer Schlr; Natl Hnr Roll; OK U; Med.

SHOOK, CURT; Seiling Schl; Seiling, OK; (3); 3/36; Church Yth Grp; FCA; FBLA; Ofcr Soph Cls; Ofcr Bsbl; Bsktbl; Ftbl; Wt Lftg; High Hon Roll; Hon Roll; Stu Of Today Awd.

SHOOK, NATALIE; Bartlesville Sr HS; Bartlesville, OK; (3); German Clb; Office Aide; Band; Mrchg Band; High Hon Roll; NHS; Psych.

SHOOK, ROBBYN R; Putnam City West HS; Bethany, OK; (4); 18/281; Church Yth Grp; Sec FBLA; Intnl Clb; SADD; Orch; Ofcr Stu Cncl; Hon Roll; Treas NHS; Slvr Strings Of PC Chapln; OK St Univ; Elem Ed.

SHOPE, LAURA; Charles Page HS; Sand Springs, OK; (3); 19/380; Am Leg Aux Girls St; Cmnty Wkr; Pres French Clb; Q&S; School Play; Ed Nwsp; Pres Frsh Cls; Pres Sr Cls; Pres Stu Cncl; Pres Acad Fit Awd; NHS Pres; OK Intrschlstc Press Assn Pres; Grls Nation Sntr; George Washington U; Intl Bus.

SHORE, ANNIE; Weatherford HS; Weatherford, OK; (1); Church Yth Grp; FCA; Chorus; Bsktbl; Chrldng; Mgr(s); Trk; Hon Roll; SW OK St Univ.

SHORE, KRISTIN; Crescent Schl; Crescent, OK; (3); Church Yth Grp; Dance Clb; FHA; Natl Beta Clb; SADD; Chorus; Church Choir; School Musical; Rptr Nwsp; Prfct Atten Awd; Pblshd Poet; 4th Pl Dist FHA Cmptn; U Of Cntrl OK; Jrnlsm.

SHORES, R T; Edmond North HS; Edmond, OK; (4); 32/330; Am Leg Boys St; Church Yth Grp; FCA; JCL; Latin Clb; Mu Alpha Theta; SADD; VP Stu Cncl; Var Capt Socr; NHS; Vanderbilt; Poltcs.

SHORT, EMILY C; Union Sr HS; Tulsa, OK; (3); 62/673; Church Yth Grp; Math Clb; Band; Mrchg Band; Pep Band; School Musical; Ed Nwsp; Hon Roll; School Play; British Band Exch; Fr Exch; Civic Theater; Pub Relations.

SHORT, MARTIN; Ada HS; Ada, OK; (3); Boy Scts; Church Yth Grp; Band; Mrchg Band; Orch; Wrstlng; Hon Roll; Young Adult Bd Mem Archdiocese Of OKC; ECOS; Comp Sci; Sys Analysts.

SHORT, MOLLY; Putnam City North HS; Oklahoma City, OK; (4); 116/451; Art Clb; FCA; GAA; Office Aide; Spanish Clb; Rep Sr Cls; Bsktbl; Vllybl; High Hon Roll; NHS; OK ST Univ.

SHORT, SHELLY D; John Marshall HS; Oklahoma City, OK; (1); FHA; Natl FFA Org; ROTC; Hon Roll; Y Club Inte Club Cncl; OK ST Univ.

SHORT, STACIE; Bethany HS; Oklahoma City, OK; (2); Church Yth Grp; Church Choir; High Hon Roll; Hon Roll; NHS; OK Hon Soc.

SHORTT, DORI; Bluejacket Schl; Bluejacket, OK; (3); Church Yth Grp; FHA; GAA; Math Clb; Quiz Bowl; Yrbk; VP Jr Cls; Bsktbl; Chrldng; Trk; Law.

SHOTT, SHEILA; Macarthur Sr HS; Lawton, OK; (4); 41/261; Cmnty Wkr; Dance Clb; Drama Clb; FCA; French Clb; FHA; German Clb; HOBY; Key Clb; Library Aide; Cameron Univ; Acctng.

SHOULTZ, CASSANDRA R; Dewey HS; Dewey, OK; (1); 1/97; Church Yth Grp; FCA; Band; Mrchg Band; Bsktbl; Mgr Trk; High Hon Roll; Pres Acad Fit Awd; OK Hnr Soc Awd.

SHOUN, MYSTI D; Pauls Valley HS; Pauls Valley, OK; (3); FHA; Spanish Clb; Hon Roll; Csmtlgy/Mid-Amer Vo-Tech; Csmtlgy.

SHOUSE, JENNIFER; Morrison Public Schl; Morrison, OK; (3); Church Yth Grp; FCA; FBLA; FHA; Spanish Clb; Ed Nwsp; VP Frsh Cls; Var JV Bsktbl; Var Chrldng; Var Sftbl; FCA Pres; Merit Awds; Player Of Week; OK ST U; Speech Pathologist.

SHOUSE, KRISTINA M; Kellyville Sr HS; Kellyville, OK; (3); Art Clb; Church Yth Grp; French Clb; Pep Clb; Chorus; Hon Roll; Med.

SHRADER, OLIVIA A; Blanchard Jr Sr HS; Blanchard, OK; (2); Church Yth Grp; Computer Clb; FBLA; FHA; Pep Clb; Var Intrml Chrldng; Hon Roll; NHS; Westark Of Ft Smith; Arch.

SHREFFLER, BRANDON L; Berryhill Sr HS; Sand Springs, OK; (1); FCA; OK Univ; Metrlgy.

SHREVE, ASHLEY; Wynnewood HS; Pauls Valley, OK; (3); FHA; Chorus; Yrbk; Psych.

SHREWSBURY, NATHAN K; Booker T Washington HS; Tulsa, OK; (4); 64/267; Computer Clb; Chorus; School Musical; VP Stu Cncl; L Wrstlng; Ntl Merit Schol; State Sci Bowl Champs.

SHROFF, PURVI L; Union Intermediate HS; Tulsa, OK; (2); 37/800; French Clb; Key Clb; Natl Beta Clb; Band; Hon Roll; Pres Acad Fit Awd; RAD; DFY; Class Musician MIP 95; Frnch Icont 1st Pl; Math.

SHROYER, AUSTIN M; Pauls Valley HS; Paoli, OK; (1); Church Yth Grp; FCA; Scholastic Bowl; Spanish Clb; JV Bsbl; JV Ftbl; High Hon Roll; St Schlr; Pi Phi Pi Comm Svc Grp; OK St Hnr Soc; OSU; Vet Med.

SHROYER, TRAVIS; Tuttle HS; Tuttle, OK; (4); 35/77; Church Yth Grp; Natl FFA Org; Capt Var Ftbl; Wt Lftg.

SHUFELDT, STEPHANIE; Ft Towson HS; Fort Towson, OK; (1); #3 in class; Church Yth Grp; FCA; VP Frsh Cls; Var Bsktbl; Hon Roll.

SHULLER, MARY A; Choctaw Jr HS; Choctaw, OK; (1); Quiz Bowl; Scholastic Bowl; Band; Orch; CODA Hnr Bnd.

SHULTS, ANDREA L; Duncan HS; Duncan, OK; (4); 68/214; Church Yth Grp; Pres FBLA; Sec FHA; Teachers Aide; Crimestoppers Sec; Yth Alive Chstnclb Comm Membr; SW Assembliesof God Univ; Ed.

SHULTS, BRANDI A; Vinita HS; Vinita, OK; (3); Church Yth Grp; Hosp Aide; Science Clb; Spanish Clb; Band; Mrchg Band; Pep Band; Rogers ST; Mrktng.

SHULTS, REBEKAH; Midwest City HS; Oklahoma City, OK; (3); 30/386; Library Aide; Church Choir; Hon Roll; Bible Quiz St Chmpns; Church Drama Org; Christian Bible Coll; Yth Mnstr.

SHULTZ, PETER A; Ponca City Sr HS; Ponca City, OK; (3); #2 in class; Math Tm; Acpl Chr; Band; Jazz Band; Mrchg Band; Orch; Pep Band; Co-Capt Swmmng; High Hon Roll; NHS.

SHULTZ, TARA; Yukon HS; Oklahoma City, OK; (4); Church Yth Grp; Spanish Clb; Ed Yrbk; High Hon Roll; Hon Roll; OK Intrschl Press Assn Stu Life Awd; Univ Of Cntrl OK; Spch Pthlgy.

SHUMATE, MELISSA; Stigler HS; Stigler, OK; (2); Church Yth Grp; Pep Clb; Quiz Bowl; SADD; Band; Mrchg Band; Treas Soph Cls; High Hon Roll; Engl I & Typing Mdls; Freed-Hardeman U; Music Ed.

SHUPERT, SHEENA M; Clayton Jr Sr HS; Clayton, OK; (1); Church Yth Grp; English Clb; 4-H; GAA; Math Clb; Office Aide; Science Clb; SADD; Chorus; Church Choir; 2nd Runner Up Chamber Beauty Pgnt; Cnty And Dist Share The Fun; OSU; Med.

SHUTTERLY, CASSIDY L; Westmoore HS; Oklahoma City, OK; (1); Church Yth Grp; Pep Clb; Spanish Clb; School Play; Rep Stu Cncl; JV Chrldng; Var Pom Pon; Gov Hon Prg Awd; High Hon Roll; Hon Roll; Pedtrcn.

SHY, KAMILAH N; Del City HS; Oklahoma City, OK; (3); 1/500; Rep Am Leg Aux Girls St; Art Clb; Spanish Clb; Sec SADD; Jr NHS; NHS; Pres Acad Fit Awd; Medicine.

SHYR, JENNIFER; Casady Schl; Oklahoma City, OK; (4); Art Clb; Cmnty Wkr; Computer Clb; Letterman Clb; Pep Clb; Quiz Bowl; Scholastic Bowl; Spanish Clb; Varsity Clb; Orch; Carnegie Mellon U; Indstrl Mgmt.

SIDES, ASHLEY M; Drumright HS; Drumright, OK; (4); 1/42; Pres Computer Clb; Capt Quiz Bowl; Pres Science Clb; Chorus; School Musical; School Play; Pres Stu Cncl; JV Var Bsktbl; Ntl Merit SF; Prfct Atten Awd.

SIDES, CARSON; Reydon HS; Reydon, OK; (4); 2/9; Pres Natl FFA Org; Speech Tm; School Play; Yrbk; Ofcr Stu Cncl; Hon Roll; Sal; Reydon FFA Chapter Stu Yr; S W OK ST U; Phrmcy.

SIDES, JARROD; Empire Schl; Duncan, OK; (1); FCA; Key Clb; Bsktbl; Ftbl.

SIDES, KATIE M; Empire Schl; Duncan, OK; (2); FBLA; Nwsp; Sec Soph Cls; Var Bsktbl; Hon Roll; Kiwanis Awd; Val.

SIDES, OLAN R; Drumright HS; Drumright, OK; (1); Church Yth Grp; Cmnty Wkr; Drama Clb; German Clb; Quiz Bowl; Scholastic Bowl; Science Clb; School Musical; School Play; JV Bsktbl; U Of OK.

SIDWELL, BAMBI; Timberlake Schl; Goltry, OK; (1); Church Yth Grp; FCA; VP 4-H; FHA; Natl FFA Org; VP Frsh Cls; JV Var Bsktbl; Var Chrldng; Var Sftbl; 4-H Awd; Homecmng Ftbl; Piano; Cls Favorite; OSU.

SIEBERT, JASON L; Choctaw HS; Choctaw, OK; (2); 1/387; Church Yth Grp; French Clb; Quiz Bowl; Scholastic Bowl; JV Bsbl; JV Bsktbl; Var L Ftbl; French Hon Soc; High Hon Roll; Jr NHS; Msnc Awd.

SIEMENS, JEFF P; Bartlesville Mid HS; Bartlesville, OK; (2); Art Clb; Church Yth Grp; Hon Roll; Prfct Atten Awd.

SIEMENS, WENDY M; Del City HS; Del City, OK; (3); 1/450; Cmnty Wkr; Hosp Aide; SADD; Jr NHS; NHS; Pres Acad Fit Awd; Mat Maid/Wrestling; WA Univ; Arch/Eng.

SIERAKOWSKI, SAMANTHIA M; B T Washington HS; Tulsa, OK; (3); Church Yth Grp; Cmnty Wkr; Drama Clb; VP German Clb; Rep NFL; High Hon Roll; NHS; VP Soph Cls; Ofcr Jr Cls; VP Sr Cls; Yth And Govt; Mock Trial; Jrnlsm.

SIGLER, LEIA; Perry Sr HS; Perry, OK; (3); Church Yth Grp; Drama Clb; Hosp Aide; Treas Natl FFA Org; Speech Tm; Band; Mrchg Band; School Musical; School Play; Chrldng; Chosen To Attend Natl Schlr At NYLC; U Of FL; Acting & Directing.

SIKES, ASHLEY M; Bartlesville Sr HS; Bartlesville, OK; (3); JV Bsktbl; Var Socr; Var Sftbl; Hon Roll; All Dist Soccer Rnnr Up, Hustle Awd; Hnrb Mntn All Conf Sftbl; Phy Thrpy.

SIKES, BROOKE; Nathan Hale HS; Tulsa, OK; (4); 10/207; Cmnty Wkr; Key Clb; Ed Yrbk; Ofcr Sr Cls; Rep Stu Cncl; Var L Chrldng; Var Sftbl; Var L Trk; High Hon Roll; NHS; Yth Vol Corps Of Tulsa; Stu Ath Of The Week; U Of OK; Zoology; Plastic Surgn.

SIKES, EMILY B; Nathan Hale HS; Tulsa, OK; (4); 10/203; Cmnty Wkr; Key Clb; Ed Yrbk; Ofcr Sr Cls; Ofcr Stu Cncl; Var L Chrldng; Var L Sftbl; Var L Trk; High Hon Roll; St Schlr; Yth Vol Corps Tulsa; U Of OK; Pre-Dentistry.

SIKES, WENDY; Kingston HS; Kingston, OK; (2); Church Yth Grp; FCA; Band; Church Choir; Jazz Band; Mrchg Band; Var Bsktbl; Var Chrldng; NHS; Chrch Sec & Sng Ldr; Phys Ther.

SIKKA, SEEMA R; Oklahoma Sch Of Science & Math; Tulsa, OK; (3); Hosp Aide; Science Clb; Spanish Clb; Yrbk; Hon Roll; Piano; Drama; Art; Med Research.

SILER, JESSICA L; El Reno Sr HS; Okarche, OK; (3); FTA; Math Clb; Science Clb; Chrldng; Crs Cntry; Trk; High Hon Roll; Hon Roll; NHS.

SILL, J DAVINA; Okemah HS; Clearview, OK; (3); 1/67; Church Yth Grp; Natl Beta Clb; Science Clb; SADD; Ed Yrbk; High Hon Roll; NHS.

SILL, SCOTT; Miami Sr HS; Miami, OK; (4); 16/127; Church Yth Grp; Cmnty Wkr; FCA; Pres Stu Cncl; L Bsktbl; Capt L Socr; High Hon Roll; NHS; Rotary Stu Of Month; MO Southern ST Coll; Acctng.

SILLINGS, LAURA A; Bethany HS; Bethany, OK; (3); Church Yth Grp; Key Clb; Spanish Clb; Teachers Aide; Jr NHS; NHS; Big 5 Awd 3 Yrs; Southern Nazarene U; Nrs.

SILVA, ARACELI N; Capitol Hill HS; Oklahoma City, OK; (3); Dance Clb; Girl Scts; Latin Clb; Socr; Hon Roll; NHS; Algebra I; Bio.

SILVA, HEATHER M; Charles Page HS; Sand Springs, OK; (3); Church Yth Grp; Drama Clb; French Clb; Chorus; School Musical; School Play; Rep Stu Cncl; Anchr Club; Sandite Spirit Squad; Super Rating All Dist/All ST Solos.

SILVERS, SARAH N; Cushing HS; Cushing, OK; (1); Church Yth Grp; Band; Mrchg Band; Hon Roll.

SILVESTRE, DIVINA GRACE C; Charles Page HS; Sand Springs, OK; (1); Hon Roll; U Of Tulsa; Acctng.

SIMARD, KYLENE; Pioneer Jr Sr HS; Enid, OK; (2); VP 4-H; Hist FHA; Pep Clb; Band; Flag Corp; Var Chrldng; Trk; Cit Awd; Kiwanis Awd; Rotatory Ldrshp Awd; Nrthwstrn OK ST U; Chld Wlfr.

SIMARD, TRACIE R; Pioneer Jr Sr HS; Enid, OK; (3); 1/40; Rptr 4-H; Sec FHA; Key Clb; Natl Beta Clb; Band; Co-Capt Flag Corp; School Play; Ofcr Stu Cncl; Kiwanis Awd; NHS; Phy Or Recreational Therapy.

SIMIC, BRIAN; Garber Sr HS; Garber, OK; (2); Church Yth Grp; Debate Tm; FCA; Treas Natl FFA Org; Quiz Bowl; Scholastic Bowl; Gov Hon Prg Awd; High Hon Roll; NHS; Ntl Merit Ltr.

SIMIC, PRESTON; Garber Sr HS; Garber, OK; (4); 4/39; Am Leg Boys St; Church Yth Grp; FCA; Natl FFA Org; Scholastic Bowl; School Play; Ofcr Stu Cncl; Var Ftbl; Var Trk; NHS; OSU; Bus.

SIMMONS, AMBER N; Caddo HS; Caddo, OK; (2); Church Yth Grp; FHA; Chorus; Church Choir; School Play; Rep Frsh Cls; Sec Soph Cls; Hon Roll; NHS; Southeastern OK ST U; Jrnlsm.

SIMMONS, ASHLEY BROOKE; Bixby Sr HS; Bixby, OK; (3); 26/206; Church Yth Grp; FCA; Spanish Clb; SADD; Church Choir; Ed Nwsp; VP Stu Cncl; Capt Var Chrldng; Treas Jr NHS; Treas NHS; U Of OK; Med; Bus.

SIMMONS, BRIAN; Waukomis HS; Waukomis, OK; (4); 6/29; Am Leg Boys St; Church Yth Grp; FCA; Quiz Bowl; Scholastic Bowl; Var Ftbl; Var Trk; Var Wt Lftg; Hon Roll; NHS; 145 Lb Class B St Pwrlftng Champ 95; Oklahoma City U; Med.

SIMMONS, CHRIS; Waukomis HS; Waukomis, OK; (1); 1/40; Church Yth Grp; FCA; Quiz Bowl; Scholastic Bowl; VP Frsh Cls; Var Bsktbl; Var Ftbl; Var Wt Lftg; High Hon Roll; NHS; OU.

SIMMONS, DANIELLE R; Putnam City North HS; Oklahoma City, OK; (3); Jr NHS.

SIMMONS, JEANNE L; Mc Alester HS; Krebs, OK; (4); 88/193; Church Yth Grp; DECA; Natl FFA Org; Band; Jazz Band; Mrchg Band; Orch; Rptr Nwsp; Ofcr Stu Cncl; Prfct Atten Awd; Food Mrktng Mgmt Levl Cmptn 8th Pl St; Children Chrch & Sunday Schl As Tchr Aid; Eastern OK ST; Art Ed.

SIMMONS, JEFF; Caddo HS; Caddo, OK; (4); 2/26; Cmnty Wkr; Natl FFA Org; Scholastic Bowl; Pres Sr Cls; Rep Stu Cncl; Var Bsbl; Capt Bsktbl; Capt Ftbl; High Hon Roll; Sal.

SIMMONS, JENNIFER L; Geronimo Jr Sr HS; Geronimo, OK; (2); Pres Church Yth Grp; Drama Clb; Capt FCA; FHA; Hosp Aide; HOBY; VP Soph Cls; Sftbl; Hon Roll; Church Choir; 2nd Place Class 1a Dramatic Duet SWOSU; 3rd Place Class 1a Dramatic Interptn SWOSU; Slwpitch MVP; Radiologist.

SIMMONS, JEREMY J; Kellyville Sr HS; Sapulpa, OK; (2); Var Ftbl; JV Golf; Hon Roll; Pres Awd For Edcul Excl.

SIMMONS, JESSICA; Elk City Jr HS; Elk City, OK; (1); 4-H; Band; OU.

SIMMONS, JESSICA D; Caddo HS; Caddo, OK; (1); Church Yth Grp; Cmnty Wkr; Dance Clb; 4-H; Pep Clb; SADD; Chorus; Church Choir; Drill Tm; Ofcr Frsh Cls; Drll Tm Awds; Murray; Nursng.

SIMMONS, JOHN G; Hartshorne Sr HS; Hartshorne, OK; (2); Hon Roll.

SIMMONS, LA TISHA; Cement Jr Sr HS; Cement, OK; (2); Church Yth Grp; FHA; School Play; Pres Soph Cls; Rep Stu Cncl; Var Bsktbl; Var Vllybl; High Hon Roll; Prfct Atten Awd; OK Univ; Bus.

SIMMONS, LESLYE A; Vinita HS; Vinita, OK; (2); Art Clb; Church Yth Grp; Hon Roll; Acads In Art Awd; Art Achvmt Cert; US Hnr Roll.

SIMMONS, NATE W; Claremore Sr HS; Claremore, OK; (2); Hon Roll; Ride Motorcycles; Work On Motorcyle Frames & Engines; Comp; Comp Sci.

SIMMS, JAMES A; Tahlequah Jr HS; Tahlequah, OK; (1); Boy Scts; Quiz Bowl; Band; Mrchg Band; Pep Band; High Hon Roll; Jr NHS; Pres Acad Fit Awd; Pres Schlr; NSU Nwsp Mentorship Under Ed; Attnd NSU Sci Acad 96.

SIMMS, SHONDA R; Capitol Hill HS; Oklahoma City, OK; (2); Church Yth Grp; Cmnty Wkr; French Clb; FHA; ROTC; Teachers Aide; JV Bsktbl; JV Trk; Photo; Wrld Hstry; OK U; Registere.

SIMODYNES, KENT R; Edmond Memorial HS; Edmond, OK; (2); 47/408; FCA; Spanish Clb; Rep Stu Cncl; JV Bsbl; JV Bsktbl; Var Ftbl; Var Trk; High Hon Roll; Hon Roll; NHS.

SIMON, SHANA E; Southeast HS; Oklahoma City, OK; (2); FCA; Chorus; Chrldng; Sftbl; High Hon Roll; Outstdng Stu Awd Art; Natl Consortium For Acads & Sports Awd; UCO; Ed.

SIMON, SHERRI; Shawnee Sr HS; Shawnee, OK; (4); Church Yth Grp; Drama Clb; Sec French Clb; Thesps; Band; Church Choir; Co-Capt Color Guard; Jazz Band; School Musical; High Hon Roll; U Of OK; Psych.

SIMON, STEPHANIE; Clinton HS; Clinton, OK; (1); FCA; FHA; JA; Ofcr Stu Cncl; Var Bsktbl; JV Chrldng; Var Tennis; St Schlr; UCA All-Star Chrldr.

SIMONS, ANGELINA; Kerr Jr HS; Del City, OK; (1); FCA; Speech Tm; Hist Stu Cncl; Var Chrldng; Gym; Hon Roll; Jr NHS; NCA All-Amer Chrldg Team; Wrestlng Homcmng Qn 95-96; Wrestlng Mgr 95-96; FSU; Phys Thrpy.

SIMONS, CASSANDRA A; B T Washington HS; Tulsa, OK; (3); Spanish Clb; Teachers Aide; Rep Frsh Cls; OK Ctr Advncmt Sci, Tech Awd; 2 1st Pl, 1 2nd Pl Austin Coll Spnsh Cmptn; Fort Lewis; Soc Sci.

SIMONS, JULIA M; Mustang HS; Mustang, OK; (1); Cmnty Wkr; Ed Key Clb; Library Aide; Scholastic Bowl; Service Clb; Spanish Clb; Hist SADD; Chorus; Hon Roll; Paramedic.

SIMONS, NICOLE; Coalgate HS; Coalgate, OK; (1); #3 in class; FBLA; Quiz Bowl; Scholastic Bowl; Var Chrldng; High Hon Roll; Hon Roll; Jr NHS; NHS; Masons Awd; Acad Achvt; OSU.

SIMONS, REGENA R; Marietta HS; Marietta, OK; (3); Pres Church Yth Grp; Treas FHA; Office Aide; Chorus; Mrchg Band; Sec Jr Cls; Rep Stu Cncl; Hon Roll; St Schlr; Chapter Treas/Chaplain; Southeastern; Psych.

SIMPLER, JENNIFER M; Dickson HS; Ardmore, OK; (3); 30/72; FCA; 4-H; Girl Scts; Library Aide; Natl FFA Org; SADD; Teachers Aide; L Bsktbl; L Sftbl; L Trk; Murray ST.

SIMPSON, AMANDA K; Midwest City HS; Midwest City, OK; (2); 79/473; FCA; FHA; German Clb; Stage Crew; Bsktbl; Trk; Jr NHS; OK Univ; Tchr; Bsktbl Coach.

SIMPSON, CHRIS J; Mc Loud HS; Mc Loud, OK; (2); Scholastic Bowl; Chorus; In Band; U Of OK; Crnr.

SIMPSON, DANETTA F; Hulbert Jr Sr HS; Hulbert, OK; (2); FBLA; Conner ST Coll; RN.

SIMPSON, DANIELLE; Wesoka HS; Wewoka, OK; (4); Pres FTA; VP Science Clb; Band; Color Guard; Pep Band; Yrbk; Sec Frsh Cls; VP Soph Cls; Rep Stu Cncl; Capt Chrldng; All Star Chrldr; Acad All St Chrldng Awd; Sci Fair Best Ctgry, Photo, Qlfd Reg & St; OU; Phys Thrpy.

SIMPSON, ERICKA D; Macarthur Sr HS; Lawton, OK; (3); Cmnty Wkr; Speech Tm; Rep Jr Cls; JV Sftbl; Hon Roll; Mst Competive Speech Team; Acad Ltr; Cross Exam Lawyer Mock Trial; OSU Hnr Schlr; Delta Sigma Theta; Clark Univ; Eng; Law.

SIMPSON, GERRIT L; Oologah HS; Claremore, OK; (2); Science Clb; Var Bsbl; Var Bsktbl; High Hon Roll; Bsbl St Champion 96; OSU.

SIMPSON, GLEN E; Ponca City Sr HS; Ponca City, OK; (3); 6/347; Boy Scts; Church Yth Grp; Scholastic Bowl; Spanish Clb; Church Choir; Orch; High Hon Roll.

SIMPSON, JOSA L; Bartlesville Mid HS; Bartlesville, OK; (2); Church Yth Grp; FHA; Library Aide; Church Choir; School Play; Hon Roll; Jury Trl Judge; Mktg.

SIMPSON, JULIANNA E; Checotah HS; Porum, OK; (3); FBLA; Chorus.

SIMPSON, KYLE D; Putnam City North HS; Oklahoma City, OK; (3); 37/464; Art Clb; Church Yth Grp; Band; Church Choir; Mrchg Band; Orch; Pep Band; Nwsp; NHS; Chess Clb; PEAK; Odyssey Of Mind; Nmrs 1st Plart & Schol Awds; U Of OK; Comp Sci.

SIMPSON, LEA J; Bishop Kelley HS; Tulsa, OK; (2); Church Yth Grp; Cmnty Wkr; Letterman Clb; Varsity Clb; JV Sftbl; Var L Tennis; Hon Roll; Multi-Yr Listee; U Of AR; Scndry Ed; Span.

SIMPSON, MANDY S; Preston Schl; Okmulgee, OK; (2); Library Aide; Office Aide; Teachers Aide; Chorus; Yrbk; JV Chrldng; JV Tennis; Hon Roll; NHS; Prfct Atten Awd.

SIMPSON, MATTHEW C; Meeker HS; Meeker, OK; (2); 6/74; Church Yth Grp; Natl FFA Org; Pres Frsh Cls; Pres Soph Cls; VP Stu Cncl; Var Bsbl; Var Bsktbl; Var Ftbl; Var Wt Lftg; Hon Roll; Ortho.

SIMPSON, RICHARD D; Catoosa HS; Catoosa, OK; (2); Spanish Clb; Band; Jazz Band; Mrchg Band; Pep Band; High Hon Roll; Hon Roll; NHS; All Dist Concert Band; Dist & St Instrumental Solo -1 Or Superior Rating; U Of Tulsa; Musician; Tchr.

SIMPSON II, ROBERT D; Agra Schl; Cushing, OK; (3); 2/12; Natl FFA Org; VICA; Pres Frsh Cls; Pres Soph Cls; VP Jr Cls; L Bsbl; L Bsktbl; Numerous FFA Awds; Ag Sci.

SIMPSON, RYAN P; South Intermediate HS; Broken Arrow, OK; (1); Ftbl; Wt Lftg; Univ Of OK; Dr Med.

SIMPSON, TERRI A; Durant HS; Durant, OK; (2); Church Yth Grp; Cmnty Wkr; FCA; FBLA; Pep Clb; Chorus; Church Choir; Swing Chorus; Variety Show; Ofcr Stu Cncl; Chorus Natl Fnlst; Mssnry Wrk; ST Bible Quiz Fnlst; CO ST Univ; Mntl Hlth Thrpst.

SIMS, EVA; Oklahoma Bible Acad; Enid, OK; (3); Church Yth Grp; FCA; Hosp Aide; Chorus; Church Choir; VP Jr Cls; Bsktbl; Trk; High Hon Roll; OSU; Music.

SIMS, HANNAH G; Nathan Hale HS; Tulsa, OK; (3); Church Yth Grp; Cmnty Wkr; Debate Tm; Library Aide; Office Aide; Teachers Aide; Acpl Chr; Church Choir; Ed Yrbk; Cit Awd; Essay Cont Wnnr; Chrch Pianist; Missionary Work; Tulsa Univ; K-12 Tchr.

SIMS, JEREMIAH M; Putnam City West HS; Bethany, OK; (1); Church Yth Grp; Drama Clb; FCA; Thesps; School Play; Nwsp; Yrbk; Ftbl; Wt Lftg; Hon Roll.

SIMS, MIGNON; Cyril Jr Sr HS; Cyril, OK; (1); Church Yth Grp; Natl FFA Org; Quiz Bowl; Band; Rptr Nwsp; Hon Roll; Lawyer.

SIMUNEK, REBECCA; Waukomis HS; Waukomis, OK; (1); 3/48; Church Yth Grp; FCA; 4-H; Natl FFA Org; Pep Clb; Teachers Aide; Band; Bsktbl; Sftbl; Trk; Acctng.

SINCALIR, CORY D; Coweta HS; Coweta, OK; (2); 14/158; Church Yth Grp; Hon Roll; Jr NHS; NHS; Tech Stdnt Assn Sec.

SINCLAIR, SALLY; Bishop Mcguinness HS; Oklahoma City, OK; (2); Church Yth Grp; FCA; Pep Clb; Spanish Clb; Rep Frsh Cls; Rep Soph Cls; Chrldng; Hon Roll; NHS.

SINGER, ANDREA; Miami Sr HS; Miami, OK; (2); #1 in class; Church Yth Grp; Band; Yrbk; Ofcr Stu Cncl; Mgr(s); High Hon Roll; Jr NHS; NHS.

SINGLER, BRIDGET D; Muskogee HS; Muskogee, OK; (3); 7/443; Church Yth Grp; FHA; Hosp Aide; Rptr Natl FFA Org; Spanish Clb; High Hon Roll; Jr NHS; NHS; Acctng.

SINGLETON, ERIC W; Lawton Sr HS; Fort Sill, OK; (3); Church Yth Grp; FCA; HOBY; ROTC; Var Ftbl; Var Trk; Hon Roll; NHS; Pres Acad Fit Awd; Kudos; Ebony Soc; PT.

SINGLETON, JOCK B; Broken Bow HS; Broken Bow, OK; (3); Church Yth Grp; FCA; Spanish Clb; Ofcr Stu Cncl; Ofcr Bsbl; Bsktbl; Hon Roll; OK ST Univ; Elec Engrng.

SINK, JAMES; Jenks HS; Tulsa, OK; (4); 40/550; Am Leg Boys St; FCA; Spanish Clb; Pres Frsh Cls; Treas Soph Cls; Treas Jr Cls; Treas Sr Cls; Var Capt Ftbl; Wrstlng; Sec NHS; PDE Pres; West Point; Polysci.

SINKS, MICHAEL; Bartlesville Sr HS; Barnsdall, OK; (4); 106/456; Am Leg Boys St; Boy Scts; Church Yth Grp; Cmnty Wkr; Computer Clb; Debate Tm; FBLA; JA; Quiz Bowl; Red Cross Aide; Eagle Sct, Order Arrow; KU; Comp Engr.

SINNES, TARA C; Stillwater Jr HS; Stillwater, OK; (1); Church Yth Grp; Key Clb; Rep Frsh Cls; Hon Roll; Pres Schlr; Dance Tap/Ponte/Jazz.

SINOR, ALLISON MARIE; Broken Arrow Sr HS; Broken Arrow, OK; (4); 65/921; Church Yth Grp; French Clb; FTA; Intnl Clb; Key Clb; Scholastic Bowl; Cit Awd; Gov Hon Prg Awd; Hon Roll; Jr NHS; Intnl Yth Forum; Street Law Stu Of Yr; Street Law II Stu Of Yr; U Of Tulsa; Scndry Ed.

SINOR, BRADLEY R; Durant HS; Durant, OK; (2); Var Socr; JV Tennis; High Hon Roll; Hon Roll.

SIPES, RAY; Western Heights Sr HS; Oklahoma City, OK; (1); 1/205; English Clb; FHA; Science Clb; Spanish Clb; JV Bsbl; Cit Awd; Gov Hon Prg Awd; High Hon Roll; Jr NHS; Pres Acad Fit Awd; OK.

SIPPY, MELINDA B; Bartlesville Sr HS; Bartlesville, OK; (1); Church Yth Grp; Dance Clb; Church Choir; JV Pom Pon; High Hon Roll.

SIRMANS, JAYNA; Hartshorne Sr HS; Hartshorne, OK; (4); 8/46; FHA; Office Aide; Teachers Aide; Co-Ed Yrbk; Rep Stu Cncl; Var Chrldng; Hon Roll; NHS; VFW Dist Awd; Estrn OK ST U.

SIRMANS, MANDY; Hartshorne Sr HS; Hartshorne, OK; (3); 1/60; Am Leg Aux Girls St; Pres Frsh Cls; Rep Soph Cls; Rep Jr Cls; Rep Stu Cncl; Var Bsktbl; Capt Chrldng; Hon Roll; Jr NHS; Sal; Red Cross Swmmng Instr, Lifeguard; U Of OK; Medcl.

SIRMONS, AMANDA L; Shattuck Jr Sr HS; Fargo, OK; (2); 1/25; FHA; Chorus; Orch; Nwsp; Rptr Soph Cls; Chrldng; Hon Roll; Jr NHS; NHS; UT Arlington.

SIRMONS, MANDY; Shattuck Jr Sr HS; Fargo, OK; (2); 1/25; FHA; Chorus; Orch; Stage Crew; Yrbk; Rptr Soph Cls; Chrldng; Hon Roll; Jr NHS; NHS; UT Arlington.

SISCO, MARIYA D; Roland Sr HS; Roland, OK; (2); Cmnty Wkr; Drama Clb; FHA; ROTC; Teachers Aide; Pres Chorus; Color Guard; School Musical; School Play; High Hon Roll; Westark CC Part Time Stu; Attend Marvin Altman Fitness Cntr; Frgn Lang.

SISEMORE, SUMMER; Owasso Sr HS; Owasso, OK; (4); Church Yth Grp; Office Aide; Science Clb; Spanish Clb; Teachers Aide; Ofcr Jr Cls; Ofcr Stu Cncl; Chrldng; Capt Pom Pon; U Of Tulsa; Nrsng.

SISK, CHARLOTTE E; Buffalo Valley Schl; Talihina, OK; (2); Church Yth Grp; Sec FHA; VP Frsh Cls; Rep Soph Cls; Rep Jr Cls; Rep Stu Cncl; Var Bsktbl; Var Sftbl; Hon Roll, OK HS Hnr Soc 94-95; Masonic Stdnt Of Today Awd 94-95.

SISK, WAYNE; Guthrie Sr HS; Guthrie, OK; (3); 24/250; Mu Alpha Theta; VICA; NHS; Tech Stu Assn; Foreman Of Wood Tech Assn; OSU; Arch; Engr.

SISSON, KEVIN; Empire Schl; Comanche, OK; (2); Boy Scts; Church Yth Grp; Natl FFA Org; Eagle Sct Awd; OSU; Vet.

SISSONS, WENDI D; Empire Schl; Comanche, OK; (2); Church Yth Grp; Girl Scts; Chorus.

SITZMAN, CHRISTOPHER M; South Intermediate HS; Broken Arrow, OK; (2); Tulsa Police Explorer Post; Cmptv Bsbl Broken Arrow Yth Bsbl; U Of Tulsa; Police Sci.

SIVLEY, ROY A; Union Intermediate HS; Broken Arrow, OK; (2); 2/800; Boy Scts; Office Aide; Spanish Clb; Band; Eagle Scout.

SIXKILLER, BRYAN; Claremore Sr HS; Claremore, OK; (2); Church Yth Grp; Library Aide; Spanish Clb; JV Bsbl; JV Bsktbl; Hon Roll; NHS; Post Ofce.

SIXKILLER, MICHAEL; Tahlequah Sr HS; Tahlequah, OK; (4); 22/243; Computer Clb; FBLA; Teachers Aide; Traveling Acad Team; Comp Sci.

SIZEMORE, ABIGAIL; Barnsdall Jr Sr HS; Barnsdall, OK; (4); #3 in class; Chorus; School Play; Rep Soph Cls; JV Var Bsktbl; Gov Hon Prg Awd; Hon Roll; NHS; Pres Acad Fit Awd; OK Hnr Soc; OK Indian Hnr Soc; SW Bapt Univ; Med.

SKAGGS, BRENDA K; Beaver HS; Beaver, OK; (3); 6/32; FCA; FHA; Chorus; Rep Frsh Cls; Sec Soph Cls; Bsktbl; Chrldng; Crs Cntry; Trk; NHS; KS ST U; Math.

SKAGGS, KELLY; West Middle HS; Norman, OK; (1); FCA; Spanish Clb; Chrldng; High Hon Roll; Teen Vol; HS Heroes.

SKAGGS, MATTHEW R; Charles Page HS; Sand Springs, OK; (3); 10/320; Church Yth Grp; Cmnty Wkr; FCA; FBLA; Service Clb; Spanish Clb; Varsity Clb; Rep Sr Cls; Var Capt Wrstlng; Cit Awd; 1st Pl Regnl Sci Fair Qualified For St; 4th Pl In 5a Regnls Qualified For St; Wrestling; OK ST Univ; Pre-Law.

SKAGGS, RYAN R; Deer Creek-Lamont Jr Sr HS; Lamont, OK; (2); Boy Scts; Church Yth Grp; FCA; Natl FFA Org; Chorus; School Musical; Sec Soph Cls; Ftbl; Wt Lftg; Hon Roll.

SKAGGS, SUZANNE; Indianola HS; Indianola, OK; (3); 3/32; FBLA; FHA; GAA; Natl Beta Clb; Natl FFA Org; Ed Yrbk; VP Frsh Cls; Bsktbl; High Hon Roll; Hon Roll; NHS; Tulsa U; Medcl.

SKAGGS, TONYA; Roland Sr HS; Muldrow, OK; (2); Cmnty Wkr; GAA; Spanish Clb; Speech Tm; Nwsp; Rep Stu Cncl; JV Bsktbl; Var Sftbl; Wt Lftg; Hon Roll; OU; Med.

SKELLY, MIKE A; Choctaw HS; Choctaw, OK; (2); Office Aide; Ofcr Bsbl; Hon Roll; Jr NHS; Golden Glove Awd Basbl; Mst Vlbl Hitter Bsbl.

SKELTON, MERANDA; Valliant HS; Valliant, OK; (3); #6 in class; Cmnty Wkr; FHA; HOBY; Natl FFA Org; Pep Clb; Red Cross Aide; Science Clb; High Hon Roll; NHS; St Schlr; OK ST U; Vet.

SKELTON, ROCKY; Panama HS; Panama, OK; (2); Ofcr Bsbl; Ftbl; Hon Roll.

SKELTON, STEPHANIE; Elk City Jr HS; Elk City, OK; (1); Church Yth Grp; FCA; GAA; Band; Church Choir; Jazz Band; Mrchg Band; Pep Band; Rep Frsh Cls; Bsktbl.

SKINNER, AMANDA A; Hartshorne Sr HS; Hartshorne, OK; (2); #1 in class; Church Yth Grp; FCA; HOBY; Natl FFA Org; School Play; High Hon Roll; Val; FFA Speech Contest/Livestock Showing; OSU; Vet/Ag Tchr.

SKINNER, LATOSHA C; Nathan Hale HS; Tulsa, OK; (3); VP Church Yth Grp; FBLA; Spanish Clb; VICA; Band; Chorus; Pres Church Choir; School Play; Cit Awd; Hon Roll; OK ST Univ; Comp.

SKINNER, MATTHEW E; Durant HS; Durant, OK; (2); Church Yth Grp; FCA; Spanish Clb; VICA; JV Bsbl; Var Ftbl; Var Wt Lftg; U Of OK; Med Surgeon.

SKINNER, MIKE C; Tahlequah Sr HS; Tahlequah, OK; (2); Church Yth Grp; Rep Frsh Cls; Rep Soph Cls; Rep Jr Cls; Rep Stu Cncl; Bsktbl; Ftbl; Trk; High Hon Roll; Hon Roll.

SKINNER, MISTY D; Chisholm Sr HS; Enid, OK; (2); Church Yth Grp; FCA; FHA; GAA; Pep Clb; Chorus; Var Bsktbl; Var Chrldng; Gym; Var Sftbl.

SKOCH, JENNIFER L; Stillwater Sr HS; Stillwater, OK; (3); Church Yth Grp; Cmnty Wkr; Dance Clb; Natl Beta Clb; Spanish Clb; Teachers Aide; Ed Yrbk; High Hon Roll; NHS; U Of Cntr OH; Sec Ed.

SKOKOWSKI, ADAM; Jarman Jr HS; Midwest City, OK; (1); Quiz Bowl; School Play; Ofcr Bsbl; Ftbl; Mgr(s); Score Keeper; High Hon Roll; Hon Roll; Pres Acad Fit Awd; FL ST U; Math.

SLABAUGH, GINA; Wright City Jr Sr HS; Wright City, OK; (4); #1 in class; FHA; Natl FFA Org; Quiz Bowl; School Musical; Yrbk; VP Soph Cls; Ofcr Sr Cls; Capt Chrldng; Pres Acad Fit Awd; Val; Carl Albert Stcol; Bio.

SLAGLE, CHRISTINA D; Sr HS; Newalla, OK; (3); CAP; 4-H; Drill Tm; Singing.

SLAJER, AIMEE; Noble HS; Noble, OK; (3); 1/128; Sec 4-H; HOBY; Treas Mu Alpha Theta; Spanish Clb; Band; Mrchg Band; Orch; Crs Cntry; Hon Roll; Rptr NHS; Art.

SLAKTER, DAVID A; Woodward HS; Woodward, OK; (2); German Clb; Model UN; Chorus; Hon Roll; Guitar; Pitt Univ; Law; His; Music.

SLATON, ARTHEA G; Hugo HS; Hugo, OK; (2); 31/141; Church Yth Grp; Sec FHA; Ofcr Stu Cncl; Southeastern ST U; Law.

SLATON, JASON; Perry Sr HS; Perry, OK; (3); 8/120; Church Yth Grp; FBLA; Quiz Bowl; Spanish Clb; Rep Stu Cncl; Ftbl; Wrstlng; High Hon Roll; Jr NHS; NHS.

SLATON, KATERRA I; North Intemediate HS; Broken Arrow, OK; (1); Church Yth Grp; Acpl Chr; Orch; Trk; Hon Roll; Jr NHS; Chrch Drama Pgm; Solo Cntsts; OSU; Fshn Merch.

SLATON, TERRA; North Intemediate HS; Broken Arrow, OK; (1); Church Yth Grp; Acpl Chr; Orch; Hon Roll; Harding U; Pharm.

SLAUGHTER, CORY M; Meeker HS; Shawnee, OK; (4); 7/74; Church Yth Grp; VP French Clb; Service Clb; High Hon Roll; Hon Roll; NHS; Pres Acad Fit Awd; TSA Hist, Vp Schol Wnnr; Rding Tutr; OSU Schol; OK St Univ; Bio Systm Eng.

SLAVENS, HEATHER A; Union Sr HS; Tulsa, OK; (3); Key Clb; Hon Roll; Jr NHS; NHS; Pres Acad Fit Awd; Nrsng.

SLEDGE, PATRICK; Mc Alester HS; Mcalester, OK; (4); 7/209; Art Clb; Boy Scts; Church Yth Grp; French Clb; Library Aide; Band; Mrchg Band; Ed Yrbk; High Hon Roll; Hon Roll; U Of OK; (4); Pol Sci.

SLEMP, TIFFANY; Yukon HS; Yukon, OK; (4); 42/400; Church Yth Grp; Natl FFA Org; NHS; All Amer Schlr; Natl Ldrshp & Svcs Awd; Rodeo; OK ST Univ; Equine Medicine.

SLIFER, PAMELA; Duncan HS; Duncan, OK; (3); Church Yth Grp; FBLA; Hosp Aide; Key Clb; SADD; Trk; Hon Roll; NHS; Prfct Atten Awd; Las Reinitas Soc Club Sec.

SLIGAR, JONATHON C; Ardmore HS; Ardmore, OK; (3); 7/235; Church Yth Grp; Science Clb; Spanish Clb; Band; Mrchg Band; Tennis; High Hon Roll; Jr NHS; OK ST Hnr Soc; Ardmoreite Blue Ribbon Schlr; Schlr Ath Awd.

SLIGER, HEATHER; Turner Schl; Burneyville, OK; (4); 1/21; 4-H; Rptr Natl Beta Clb; VP Natl FFA Org; Quiz Bowl; Rptr Nwsp; Pres Jr Cls; Bsktbl; High Hon Roll; Val; FFA Speech Tm; Murray ST Coll; Ag Comms.

SLOAN, APRIL L; Duke Schl; Duke, OK; (3); 4-H; Natl FFA Org; Spanish Clb; Bsktbl; Co-Capt Chrldng; Sftbl; Trk; Hon Roll; HOSA; Head Start Vol; Western OSC; Child Psych.

SLOAN, BRANDON; Amber Pocasset Jr Sr HS; Amber, OK; (2); JA; Ofcr Bsbl; Bsktbl; High Hon Roll; Jr NHS; NHS; Ntl Merit Ltr; Prfct Atten Awd.

SLOAN, MISTI; Shattuck Jr Sr HS; Shattuck, OK; (4); 11/23; FCA; Letterman Clb; Natl FFA Org; Ed Yrbk; Sec Treas Jr Cls; Sec Treas Sr Cls; Sec Stu Cncl; Var Capt Sftbl; Hon Roll; Rptr Soph Cls; OK FFA ST Farmer Rcpnt; VP Pres FFA Jr/Sr Yrs; NWOSU; Agribus.

SLOAN, SHANNON M; Union Intermediate HS; Broken Arrow, OK; (2); Church Yth Grp; FCA; Spanish Clb; Treas Soph Cls; JV Chrldng; Hon Roll; Rnkd 3rd In Ntn-Tulsas Bst All-Str Chrldng Sqd; All-Amer Chrldr; Sprts Med.

SLONE, TRICIA M; Charles Page HS; Tulsa, OK; (3); Church Yth Grp; Natl FFA Org; Spanish Clb; VICA; Flag Corp; Bsktbl; Trk; Hon Roll; Dance Clb; Prfct Atten Awd; Purple Belt In Karate.

SLOTT, SARAH B; Putnam City HS; Oklahoma City, OK; (2); Church Yth Grp; German Clb; Church Choir; Orch; L Var Swmmng; Trk; 3d Clb; Putnam City Silver Strings; OBU; Phys Thrpy.

SMALL, LANCE H; Oologah HS; Claremore, OK; (2); Church Yth Grp; Cmnty Wkr; FCA; Science Clb; Ofcr Stu Cncl; Var Bsbl; JV Bsktbl; Ftbl; Hon Roll.

SMALL, NICOLE E; Wright Christian Acad; Tulsa, OK; (3); Church Yth Grp; Key Clb; Chorus; Church Choir; JV Crs Cntry.

SMALL, THOMAS R; Harrah HS; Harrah, OK; (2); 11/173; Church Yth Grp; Drama Clb; Scholastic Bowl; Band; Mrchg Band; School Musical; School Play; JV Bsbl; High Hon Roll; Hon Roll.

SMALLEY, PAIGE J; Broken Arrow Sr HS; Tulsa, OK; (4); 189/921; Spanish Clb; Chorus; Rep Stu Cncl; Hon Roll; Horseback Riding; Nutrition Advy Cncl; OK ST Univ; Acctnt.

SMALLING, JUSTIN K; Hugo HS; Hugo, OK; (2); 2/140; Church Yth Grp; Natl FFA Org; Scholastic Bowl; Ofcr Stu Cncl; Trk; Hon Roll; NHS; Pres Acad Fit Awd; Leo Clb VP; Engrng.

SMALLWOOD, SHANNON J; Kingston HS; Kingston, OK; (2); Cmnty Wkr; Var Bsktbl; Var Sftbl; OK ST Univ; Sftbl Coach.

SMART, STEPHANIE; Berryhill Jr HS; Claremore, OK; (2); FCA; Band; Jazz Band; Mrchg Band; Pep Band; Sftbl; Gov Hon Prg Awd; Hon Roll; Ntl Merit Schol; Pres Acad Fit Awd; U Of Tulsa.

SMARTT, RACHEL L; Ardmore HS; Ardmore, OK; (3); Art Clb; Church Yth Grp; Mu Alpha Theta; Church Choir; Drill Tm; School Musical; Swing Chorus; Hon Roll; Jr NHS; NHS; Lflts Study Club Sec.

SMEDLEY, SEAN; Choctaw HS; Choctaw, OK; (2); Key Clb; Spanish Clb; JV Crs Cntry; JV Socr; Var Tennis; Wt Lftg; High Hon Roll; Prfct Atten Awd; All Amer Schlr; Prin Choice Awd; Penn ST; Engr.

SMETTE, RACHEL; Edmond North HS; Edmond, OK; (4); 17/330; Pres Church Yth Grp; Cmnty Wkr; Mu Alpha Theta; Spanish Clb; Band; Mrchg Band; JV Crs Cntry; Gov Hon Prg Awd; NHS; Pres Acad Fit Awd; Coll; Bio.

SMIDDY, JENNIFER; Fairview HS; Fairview, OK; (3); Church Yth Grp; FCA; FHA; GAA; Spanish Clb; Band; Rptr Yrbk; Pres Frsh Cls; Rep Stu Cncl; Hon Roll; OSU.

SMILEY, BECKY L; Waynoka HS; Waynoka, OK; (2); Church Yth Grp; FCA; FHA; Pep Clb; Rep Soph Cls; Var Bsktbl; Var Chrldng; Var Sftbl; Hon Roll; FHA Chptr Sec; Marine Bio.

SMILEY, JEROMY J; Hominy HS; Hominy, OK; (3); Church Yth Grp; Spanish Clb; Teachers Aide; Ftbl; Wt Lftg; Hon Roll.

SMITH, ADAM; Berryhill Jr HS; Tulsa, OK; (3); 2/90; Church Yth Grp; FCA; Mu Alpha Theta; Office Aide; Nwsp; Ofcr Stu Cncl; Bsktbl; Socr; Hon Roll; NHS; Freedom Fnd Ldrshp Conf PA; Page House Of Reg OK; OSU; Med.

SMITH, ADAM; Woodward HS; Woodward, OK; (2); Boy Scts; Church Yth Grp; FCA; German Clb; Letterman Clb; Bsktbl; Ftbl; High Hon Roll; NHS; Outstdng Fr Bo/Soph Boy; Soph Clss Fvrte; Brigham Young U.

SMITH, ADRIENNE; Tahlequah Sr HS; Tahlequah, OK; (3); FHA; Pep Clb; Var JV Bsktbl; Var JV Sftbl; Trail Of Tears Awd; FHA Sec; Home Ec Awd; U Of AR; FBI.

SMITH, ALEXIS; Ft Gibson HS; Fort Gibson, OK; (2); 1/194; FCA; Math Clb; Spanish Clb; SADD; Chorus; School Musical; Var Chrldng; High Hon Roll; Pres Acad Fit Awd.

SMITH, ALFRED; Heritage Hall Schl; Oklahoma City, OK; (4); 2/48; Cmnty Wkr; Letterman Clb; Mu Alpha Theta; Spanish Clb; Chorus; Pres Jr Cls; Rep Stu Cncl; Tennis; NHS; OK Yth Achvrs Awd 95; U OK Outstndng Acad Achvt Awd; Jr Rtry Clb; Physics.

SMITH, ALLISON; Putnam City West HS; Oklahoma City, OK; (2); Church Yth Grp; Cmnty Wkr; FCA; Hosp Aide; Chorus; Church Choir; Orch; Score Keeper.

SMITH, AMBER; Indianola HS; Indianola, OK; (2); 4-H; FBLA; Natl FFA Org; Speech Tm; Church Choir; School Play; Ofcr Stu Cncl; Bsktbl; 4-H Awd; Hon Roll; East Central U; Psych.

SMITH, AMBER; Checotah HS; Checotah, OK; (4); 12/91; FCA; FHA; HOBY; Spanish Clb; Chorus; Rptr Nwsp; Stat Bsbl; Var Co-Capt Chrldng; Var Trk; NHS; Nrthestrn ST U; Phys Thrpst.

SMITH, AMBER D; Weatherford HS; Weatherford, OK; (3); FHA; Model UN; Band; Mrchg Band; Mock Trial; Southwestern OK ST U; Crmnlgy.

SMITH, AMIE L; New Lima Jr Sr HS; Wewoka, OK; (4); Church Yth Grp; 4-H; FHA; Sec Frsh Cls; Sec Soph Cls; VP Jr Cls; High Hon Roll; Hon Roll; Seminole Jr Coll Schltc Meet 4th Pl In Bookkeeping; Seminole ST Coll; Acctng.

SMITH, AMY; Piedmont HS; Piedmont, OK; (4); 9/79; Church Yth Grp; Office Aide; Scholastic Bowl; Nwsp; Ed Yrbk; Hon Roll; NHS; Pres Acad Fit Awd; SW OK ST U.

SMITH, AMY; Stratford Schl; Stratford, OK; (3); FHA; Science Clb; Spanish Clb; Pres Sr Cls; Rep Stu Cncl; Var Chrldng; Var Sftbl; Hon Roll; NHS; Natl Young Ldr Conf Washington DC Natl Schlr Nom; ECU; Rsrch Bio.

SMITH, ANDREA A; Frederick HS; Loveland, OK; (4); 13/70; Church Yth Grp; FBLA; Natl FFA Org; Speech Tm; Teachers Aide; Thesps; Band; Drm Mjr(t); Mrchg Band; Trk; Cameron Univ; Phys Thpy.

SMITH, ANDREANA T; Mc Loud HS; Newalla, OK; (4); Church Yth Grp; FHA; Mgr(s); Hon Roll; U Of OK.

SMITH, ANNE; Clayton Jr Sr HS; Clayton, OK; (3); Church Yth Grp; FCA; German Clb; HOBY; Quiz Bowl; Scholastic Bowl; Science Clb; Speech Tm; SADD; Varsity Clb; Most Points Awd Schltc Meets; 3rd Pl Dont Lay That Trash On OK Art Cont; OSU; Bio Engrng.

SMITH, ANNETTE; Luther HS; Jones, OK; (2); Sec Treas 4-H; Natl FFA Org; Band; Mrchg Band; Pep Band; 4-H Awd; High Hon Roll; Hon Roll; Prfct Atten Awd; U Of Cntrl OK; Bus.

SMITH, ASHLEY B; Perkins-Tryon HS; Cushing, OK; (3); FHA; Intnl Clb; Natl FFA Org; High Hon Roll; Hon Roll; NHS; Pres Acad Fit Awd; Chrprtc Care/PT.

SMITH, AUSTIN L; South Intermediate HS; Broken Arrow, OK; (2); Intrml Wt Lftg; Intrml Wrstlng.

SMITH, AVADELLE K; Enid Sr HS; Enid, OK; (3); Church Yth Grp; Office Aide; Spanish Clb; Band; Color Guard; Bsktbl; Sftbl; Hon Roll; NHS.

SMITH, BARRY S; Wilson HS; Wilson, OK; (3); FFA; Hunt; Fish; Ardmore Higher Ed Ctr; Law Enfr.

SMITH, BEAU D; Depew HS; Depew, OK; (2); 1/45; Church Yth Grp; Cmnty Wkr; FCA; Math Tm; Natl FFA Org; Spanish Clb; Pres Frsh Cls; Rep Soph Cls; Rep Stu Cncl; JV Var Bsbl; All Conf Bsktbl; Bsktbl Escort; DARE Role Model; Gftd & Tlntd Team Captain; Natl Yth Ldrshp Forum Law; OK U; Pre-Law.

SMITH, BEN D; Memorial HS; Tulsa, OK; (2); HOBY; Key Clb; Latin Clb; Scholastic Bowl; Science Clb; Var Swmmng; JV Tennis; High Hon Roll.

SMITH, BETH; Cache HS; Cache, OK; (3); 3/65; Church Yth Grp; FCA; Pres Natl Beta Clb; Pres Rptr Natl FFA Org; SADD; Bsktbl; Sftbl; High Hon Roll; NHS; Cameron Univ; Pub Rltns.

SMITH, BETH A; Tipton Jr Sr HS; Tipton, OK; (4); 1/17; 4-H; FHA; Natl FFA Org; Band; Yrbk; Chrldng; 4-H Awd; Hon Roll; NHS; Val.

SMITH, BOBBI; Eufaula Sr HS; Eufaula, OK; (3); #15 in class; NHS; Tchr.

SMITH, BRANDI L; Cherokee Jr Sr HS; Cherokee, OK; (4); 8/22; French Clb; FHA; Office Aide; Speech Tm; Teachers Aide; Chorus; High Hon Roll; Hon Roll; Sal; Northwestern OK ST; Bus Admin.

SMITH, BRANDI N; John Marshall HS; Oklahoma City, OK; (3); Church Yth Grp; FBLA; Spanish Clb; Mrchg Band; Hon Roll; NACC; NABC; Northeastern ST Univ; Nutrtnst.

SMITH, BRANDON; Hobart HS; Hobart, OK; (1); 14/93; Church Yth Grp; Ofcr Bsbl; Trk; Capt Wrstlng; Hon Roll; Bio.

SMITH, BRANDY; Perry Sr HS; Perry, OK; (3); FBLA; FHA; Spanish Clb; Band; Mrchg Band; Pep Band; All Amer Schol; Intl Forgn Lang Awd; Spansh I Awd; N OK Col; Nurs.

SMITH, BRIAN; Valliant HS; Valliant, OK; (3); 1/88; Quiz Bowl; Band; Mrchg Band; School Play; Ed Nwsp; Ofcr Stu Cncl; High Hon Roll; NHS; Prfct Atten Awd; OK U; Brdcst Jrnlsm.

SMITH, BRIAN E; Mustang HS; Yukon, OK; (3); Church Yth Grp; Teachers Aide; Hon Roll; Cmptr Prgmmng.

SMITH, BRUCE A; Checotah HS; Checotah, OK; (3); Ftbl; Hon C Wrld His; Tns Chrst; Arkansas.

SMITH, CALE T; Del City HS; Oklahoma City, OK; (2); JV Bsbl; JV Ftbl; Cit Awd; Jr NHS; Pres Acad Fit Awd; OK ST Univ; Sprts Med/PE Tch.

SMITH, CANDRA; Temple Jr Sr HS; Temple, OK; (4); 5/21; FHA; Teachers Aide; Yrbk; Capt Bsktbl; Chrldng; Sftbl; Trk; High Hon Roll; Prfct Atten Awd; Pres Acad Fit Awd; Natl Young Ldrs Conf Alumni; U Of OK; Pre-Med.

SMITH, CHAD; Mc Alester HS; Krebs, OK; (3); 16/194; Church Yth Grp; FCA; HOBY; Red Cross Aide; Var L Bsbl; Var L Ftbl; Hon Roll; OK Heritage Day Essay Wnnr; OU; Sports Med.

SMITH, CHANCIE L; Rush Springs HS; Rush Springs, OK; (2); Spanish Clb; Sftbl; Trk; Hon Roll.

SMITH, CHARITY E; Westmoore HS; Oklahoma City, OK; (3); Church Yth Grp; Pep Clb; Acpl Chr; Chorus; Church Choir; School Musical; Variety Show; Youth Alive; Sweet Adelines Intl; Ed.

SMITH, CHARLOTTE; Nathan Hale HS; Tulsa, OK; (4); 12/209; Am Leg Aux Girls St; Church Yth Grp; FCA; Pres Frsh Cls; Pres Soph Cls; VP Stu Cncl; Var Bsktbl; Var Capt Socr; Var Capt Sftbl; Var Tennis; WA St Chmpnshps Bsktbl & Sftbl; All-St Sftbl; Sec Ed.

SMITH, CHRANDRA D; Geronimo Jr Sr HS; Geronimo, OK; (4); 1/26; Debate Tm; FHA; Math Clb; Scholastic Bowl; Science Clb; Speech Tm; Teachers Aide; Hon Roll; St Schlr; Val; U Of OK; Anthropology.

SMITH, CHRIS; Hartshorne Sr HS; Mcalester, OK; (4); 13/45; Am Leg Boys St; Boy Scts; Church Yth Grp; Cmnty Wkr; FHA; Library Aide; Natl FFA Org; Nwsp; Yrbk; Hon Roll.

SMITH, CHRIS; Mustang HS; Mustang, OK; (3); 40/400; Church Yth Grp; FCA; Office Aide; Ftbl; Trk; Hon Roll; NHS; OK U.

SMITH, CHRIS; Vanoss Schl; Ada, OK; (3); 1/40; Am Leg Boys St; Church Yth Grp; VP FCA; FBLA; Office Aide; Pep Clb; Quiz Bowl; Chorus; Rep Frsh Cls; VP Jr Cls; PR.

SMITH, CHRISTINE J; Stillwater Sr HS; Stillwater, OK; (3); 112/360; Art Clb; Church Yth Grp; Cmnty Wkr; Latin Clb; Natl Beta Clb; Science Clb; Spanish Clb; School Play; High Hon Roll; Environ Clb; Var Schlr; Fash Brd; OK St Univ; Vet Med.

SMITH, CHRISTOPHER K; Midwest City HS; Midwest City, OK; (3); French Clb; Library Aide; Rep Stu Cncl; Ftbl; Wt Lftg; Cit Awd; Hon Roll.

SMITH, CHRISTY; Werst Mid HS; Norman, OK; (2); Church Yth Grp; FCA; Spanish Clb; JV Var Chrldng; JV Trk; Hon Roll; NHS; Yng Life.

SMITH, CLAUDIA K; Charles Page HS; Skiatook, OK; (4); Sec Rep French Clb; NFL; Speech Tm; Acpl Chr; Chorus; Cit Awd; French Hon Soc; High Hon Roll; Hon Roll; NHS; U Of IA.

SMITH, CLIFF L; Edmond Santa Fe HS; Edmond, OK; (2); Church Yth Grp; French Clb; Scholastic Bowl; JV Tennis; Hon Roll.

SMITH, CRYSTAL D; Southeast HS; Oklahoma City, OK; (3); 4/140; Drama Clb; FCA; Office Aide; Thesps; Stage Crew; Pres Jr Cls; High Hon Roll; Jr NHS; NHS; Pr Mdtr; Grls St; NHS VP; OK City U; Elem Ed.

SMITH, CRYSTAL R; Valliant HS; Garvin, OK; (1); Church Yth Grp; FHA; Chorus; Swing Chorus; Var Bsktbl; Powder Puff Ftbl; Hon Roll; PT.

SMITH, CYLIE; Clinton HS; Clinton, OK; (1); Church Yth Grp; FCA; FHA; Chorus; Swing Chorus; Ofcr Stu Cncl; Chrldng; Score Keeper; NHS; Chld Psych.

SMITH, DANA; Braggs Schl; Braggs, OK; (1); 1/16; Church Yth Grp; Scholastic Bowl; Church Choir; Sec Frsh Cls; High Hon Roll; NHS; Val; NSU; Pharm.

SMITH, DANA; Yale Jr Sr HS; Yale, OK; (2); 21/51; Church Yth Grp; Sec Natl FFA Org; Pres Frsh Cls; Pres Soph Cls; Stat Bsktbl; Chrldng; Mgr(s); Sftbl; OK St Univ.

SMITH, DANA L; Coleman Schl; Kenefic, OK; (4); 1/12; Church Yth Grp; Cmnty Wkr; Sec FCA; 4-H; Key Clb; Pep Clb; Quiz Bowl; Scholastic Bowl; Church Choir; Nwsp; 4-H OK ST Ambsdr.

SMITH, DANNY; Edmond Memorial HS; Edmond, OK; (2); 152/408; School Play; Ftbl; Trk; Var Trk As Frosh; Var Running Back As Soph.

SMITH, DAVID; U S Grant HS; Oklahoma City, OK; (2); High Hon Roll; NHS; U OK.

SMITH, DAVID C; Henryetta Sr HS; Henryetta, OK; (2); 1/125; Cmnty Wkr; FCA; Chorus; School Musical; School Play; Stage Crew; Var L Bsktbl; Intrml Wt Lftg; High Hon Roll; NHS; PT/MED.

SMITH, DAVID S; Fargo Schl; Fargo, OK; (2); Church Yth Grp; Pres Frsh Cls; VP Soph Cls; Bsktbl; Hon Roll; FFA; Schlstc Meets; Rdlgy.

SMITH, DEIDRA T; Choctaw HS; Midwest City, OK; (2); Cmnty Wkr; Quiz Bowl; Band; Chorus; Church Choir; Orch; School Play; Swing Chorus; Yrbk; Ofcr Jr Cls; Envir Club; Future Doctors Amer; Psych.

SMITH, DUSTIN; Kingston HS; Kingston, OK; (2); Hon Roll; Cmptr Sci.

SMITH, DUSTIN J; Pawnee HS; Glencoe, OK; (3); 4/68; Natl Beta Clb; VP Sr Cls; Ofcr Stu Cncl; Var Bsktbl; Var L Ftbl; Var L Golf; OK Hnr Soc; U OK; Scndry Ed.

SMITH, ELIOT D; Barnsdall Jr Sr HS; Barnsdall, OK; (3); 4/40; VP Pres Yrbk; Rep Jr Cls; Ofcr Stu Cncl; Var L Bsbl; Var L Bsktbl; Var L Ftbl; Wt Lftg; High Hon Roll; NHS; Stu Of Yr; Masonic Ldg Awd; OK Hwyptrl Cadet Lawman Awd; OK Pandhandlest Univ; Ed.

SMITH, ELIZABETH J; Union Intermediate HS; Tulsa, OK; (1); Church Yth Grp; Spanish Clb; High Hon Roll; NHS; OK ST Univ; Comm.

SMITH, GINA; Ada HS; Ada, OK; (4); 15/130; Treas DECA; Math Clb; Spanish Clb; Color Guard; Flag Corp; Mrchg Band; Ed Nwsp; Ed Yrbk; NHS; Spanish NHS; Rotry Stu Of Mnth; Baylor U; Law.

SMITH, GINA M; Lone Grove HS; Ardmore, OK; (2); Math Clb; Science Clb; Spanish Clb; Yrbk; Hon Roll; NHS; Law/Pre-Med.

SMITH, HANNAH R; Buffalo Jr Sr HS; Buffalo, OK; (2); Band; Chorus; Mrchg Band; Pep Band; Hon Roll; NHS; Northwestern; Acctng.

SMITH, HAROLD D; Star Spencer HS; Spencer, OK; (3); Var Bsktbl; Var Ftbl; Var Trk; Hon Roll; All City Ftbl/Track Tm; High Jump 2nd In ST; Elctrl Engrng.

SMITH, HOLLY E; Erick Jr Sr HS; Erick, OK; (1); 1/23; Church Yth Grp; Natl FFA Org; Var JV Bsktbl; Hon Roll; NHS; Technlgy Stu Assn; OK ST U.

SMITH II, JACK R; Deer Creek HS; Edmond, OK; (1); 12/100; Church Yth Grp; Rep FBLA; L Capt Quiz Bowl; Red Cross Aide; Church Choir; Intrml Bsktbl; JV Ftbl; Hon Roll; Cmnty Wkr; Pres Ecology Club; Camerman News 101; U Of TX; Cmptr Tech/Span.

SMITH, JACLYN A; Colcord Schl; Colcord, OK; (1); Church Yth Grp; Computer Clb; Natl FFA Org; Pep Clb; Var Bsktbl; Hon Roll; Bus.

SMITH, JAMES L; Morris HS; Okmulgee, OK; (3); French Clb; Band; Church Choir; Jazz Band; Mrchg Band; JV Var Bsktbl; Wt Lftg; NHS; Pres Acad Fit Awd; Physcl Thrpy.

SMITH, JAMES R; Pawnee HS; Pawnee, OK; (3); 25/75; Church Yth Grp; FCA; 4-H; Yrbk; Rep Stu Cncl; L Ftbl; L Golf; L Trk; Cit Awd; Hon Roll; Cvl Engrng.

SMITH, JAMIE; Arapaho Schl; Arapaho, OK; (3); 1/25; FCA; FHA; Pres Frsh Cls; VP Soph Cls; VP Jr Cls; Var Bsktbl; Capt Chrldng; High Hon Roll; Val.

SMITH, JAMIE; Savanna HS; Mcalester, OK; (3); FBLA; Scholastic Bowl; Science Clb; Teachers Aide; Band; Mrchg Band; Bsktbl; Chrldng; Trk; Hon Roll; Eastern OK ST.

SMITH, JAMIE L; Choctaw HS; Midwest City, OK; (4); Church Yth Grp; Chorus; Church Choir; Variety Show; Hon Roll; Jr NHS; NHS; Jazz/Mdrgl & Show Choirs; U Of Cntrl OK; Early Chldhd Ed.

SMITH, JAMIE L; Okeene Jr Sr HS; Okeene, OK; (3); Church Yth Grp; Drama Clb; Girl Scts; Speech Tm; Bsktbl; Chrldng; Gym; Hon Roll; Silver Awds Girl Scouts; OK ST Univ; PT.

SMITH, JARED; Woodward HS; Woodward, OK; (4); 20/150; Am Leg Boys St; Boy Scts; Church Yth Grp; FCA; Key Clb; Letterman Clb; Model UN; Service Clb; Teachers Aide; Church Choir; All-St & All-Dist Ftbl; OK ST U.

SMITH, JARED; Midwest City HS; Midwest City, OK; (2); #1 in class; Pres French Clb; FHA; HOBY; Key Clb; Library Aide; Chorus; School Musical; School Play; Rep Stu Cncl; Jr NHS; Intl Bus.

SMITH, JASON; Drummond Schl; Enid, OK; (4); 5/23; Am Leg Boys St; Church Yth Grp; Natl FFA Org; Quiz Bowl; Phtg Yrbk; Var Stat Bsktbl; Hon Roll; Ed.

SMITH, JASON K; Weatherford HS; Weatherford, OK; (3); Ftbl; Trk; Acctng.

SMITH, JASON P; Duncan HS; Duncan, OK; (2); Church Yth Grp; FCA; Key Clb; Letterman Clb; Office Aide; Varsity Clb; Church Choir; Var Crs Cntry; Var Golf; Hon Roll; OSU.

SMITH, JEFF; Mc Loud HS; Mc Loud, OK; (3); 1/140; Church Yth Grp; FCA; FBLA; Var Bsktbl; Var Socr; High Hon Roll; NHS; Prfct Atten Awd; Wdmn Wrld Amer Hstry; Stu Mnth; FBLA Stu Mnth 95; OBU; Bus.

SMITH, JENNIFER C; Temple Jr Sr HS; Temple, OK; (2); Church Yth Grp; FHA; Bsktbl; Sftbl; Hon Roll; Mdwstrn St Univ; Dent Hyg.

SMITH, JENNIFER G; Claremore Sr HS; Claremore, OK; (2); Church Yth Grp; German Clb; Hosp Aide; Speech Tm; Chorus; Orch; School Musical; High Hon Roll; Hon Roll; NHS; Dist Hon Choir; Dental Recptnst Claremore Indian Hosp NE Job Trng; Outstndng String Player; Northeastern ST U; Forgn Lang.

SMITH, JENNIFER L; Elgin HS; Elgin, OK; (3); 3/80; Band; Chorus; VP Jr Cls; Rep Stu Cncl; Var Chrldng; DAR Awd; High Hon Roll; NHS; Pres Acad Fit Awd; Sal; Piano; Taekwondo; Dentistry.

SMITH, JENNIFER R; Snyder HS; Mountain Park, OK; (2); 3/38; Church Yth Grp; Rptr FHA; VP Soph Cls; Ofcr Stu Cncl; JV Bsktbl; Sftbl; Hon Roll; NHS; GATE; ST Hon Soc; FL ST Univ; Ocngrphy.

SMITH, JENNY; Edmond North HS; Edmond, OK; (3); 24/348; Church Yth Grp; Cmnty Wkr; Sec Key Clb; Mu Alpha Theta; Spanish Clb; SADD; Band; Mrchg Band; Hon Roll; NHS; Natl Piano Guild.

SMITH, JENNY; Ponca City Sr HS; Ponca City, OK; (4); Church Yth Grp; DECA; French Clb; Hosp Aide; Teachers Aide; Church Choir; Yrbk; High Hon Roll; Hon Roll; NHS; Yth Alive; Bible Clb Sec/Treas; OK Bapt Univ; Mktg/Buyer.

SMITH, JEREMIAH; Clinton HS; Clinton, OK; (3); Boy Scts; Church Yth Grp; DECA; Cit Awd; Hon Roll.

SMITH, JEREMIAH; Elgin HS; Elgin, OK; (2); Chorus; Crs Cntry; Trk; Hon Roll; Coll; Marine Bio.

SMITH, JEREMY; Cheyenne HS; Cheyenne, OK; (4); 3/19; Church Yth Grp; HOBY; Pres Natl FFA Org; Speech Tm; Band; Chorus; Church Choir; Jazz Band; Mrchg Band; School Play; OK Bapt U; Youth Mnstry.

SMITH, JEREMY; Vici Schl; Vici, OK; (3); 2/25; Church Yth Grp; FCA; HOBY; Pres Jr Cls; Pres Stu Cncl; Ofcr Bsbl; Wt Lftg; High Hon Roll; NHS; Pres Acad Fit Awd; Phys Thrpy.

SMITH, JEREMY; Valliant HS; Valliant, OK; (3); 10/75; Natl FFA Org; JV Ftbl; Score Keeper; Wt Lftg; Hon Roll.

SMITH, JILL; U S Grant HS; Oklahoma City, OK; (1); Church Yth Grp; Chrldng.

SMITH, JODIE N; Wister Schl; Wister, OK; (3); 1/30; Art Clb; English Clb; FHA; GAA; Hosp Aide; Office Aide; Science Clb; Ofcr Frsh Cls; Pres Jr Cls; Sec Stu Cncl; Homcmng Frosh Attnd, Bsktbl; Jr Attnd Bsktbl; Carl Albert ST Coll.

SMITH, JOSHUA C; Keota Schl; Keota, OK; (3); 5/30; Am Leg Boys St; Church Yth Grp; Computer Clb; Debate Tm; Drama Clb; German Clb; JA; NFL; Science Clb; Band; Sr Escort; Multi-Yr Listee; Frosh Historian; Math/Sci Hnr Classes; Carl Albert ST Coll; Cmptr.

SMITH, JOSHUA D; Westmoore HS; Oklahoma City, OK; (2); 6/700; Church Yth Grp; FCA; Office Aide; Pres Frsh Cls; Rep Soph Cls; Rep Stu Cncl; Bsktbl; Var Ftbl; Var Trk; Cit Awd; Masonic Stu Today Awd; Law.

SMITH, JOVAN; Del City HS; Oklahoma City, OK; (4); 1/410; Am Leg Boys St; Church Yth Grp; FCA; FHA; Church Choir; Bsktbl; Var Ftbl; Mgr(s); Socr; Wt Lftg; Dfnsv Plyr Yr 95-95, Mid Del Plyr Wk; All Dist & Mid St Conf; Bus.

SMITH, JULIE; Elk City HS; Elk City, OK; (4); 15/126; Am Leg Aux Girls St; HOBY; Pres Math Clb; Natl FFA Org; School Play; Pres Sr Cls; Rep Stu Cncl; Chrldng; High Hon Roll; NHS; Rotary Ldrshp Awd; Stu Cncl & Rotary Stu Of Mnth; OK U; Med.

SMITH, JULIE A; Heavener HS; Heavener, OK; (2); Drama Clb; FBLA; FHA; Spanish Clb; Chorus; School Play; Hon Roll; NHS.

SMITH, JUSTIN D; Putnam City HS; Oklahoma City, OK; (2); Church Yth Grp; PEAR.

SMITH, KARI; Cyril Jr Sr HS; Cyril, OK; (3); VP Frsh Cls; High Hon Roll; NHS; U Cntrl OK; Bus.

SMITH, KARLYN L; Sallisaw HS; Sallisaw, OK; (2); Church Yth Grp; Drama Clb; Spanish Clb; Speech Tm; Band; Sec Soph Cls; Cit Awd; Hon Roll; NHS; St Schlr; 1st Pl Sci Fair Awd; Ttrl Pstn Frosh Yr; Octagon Club Spcl Olympcs; PT.

SMITH, KATIE A; Bartlesville Mid HS; Bartlesville, OK; (2); 135/450; Church Yth Grp; Ofcr French Clb; Pep Clb; Acpl Chr; Chorus; Church Choir; School Play; Variety Show; French Hon Soc; Fr/Eng Strght A'S; Hon Mnt Schl/Dist Sci Fair; Spr Dist/ST Solo/Ensmbl Cntst; UT ST Univ.

SMITH, KELLY; Edmond North HS; Edmond, OK; (4); Church Yth Grp; FCA; Mu Alpha Theta; SADD; Church Choir; Socr; NHS; Office Aide; Mem Jr Diaconate; Edmond Soccer Club; Presdntl Awd Ed Excl 96; OK ST U At Stillwater; Arch.

SMITH, KENYATTA K; Edmond North HS; Edmond, OK; (3); Spanish Clb; NHS; African Amer Clb; Neurology.

SMITH, KERI; Putnam City West HS; Bethany, OK; (4); 52/314; FCA; French Clb; Science Clb; Teachers Aide; Sec Jr Cls; VP Sr Cls; Var Capt Chrldng; Tennis; NHS; Ntl Merit Ltr; Ftbl Homcmng Qn 95; ICF, NCA, ASC All-Amer Chrldr; U Of OK.

SMITH, KEVIN J; Woodward HS; Woodward, OK; (2); Boy Scts; Church Yth Grp; 4-H; French Clb; Key Clb; 4-H Awd; High Hon Roll; Hon Roll; NHS; Eagle Scout; Astronautical Engr.

SMITH, KIYONTE A; Del City HS; Oklahoma City, OK; (3); 79/465; Bsktbl; Trk; Hon Roll; NHS; Spanish NHS; Lgn Of Yr; Xavier U; Engrng.

SMITH, KIZZI N; Boise City HS; Boise City, OK; (2); 18/36; Church Yth Grp; 4-H; FHA; GAA; Teachers Aide; JV Var Bsktbl; Var L Trk; Hon Roll; OK ST Univ.

SMITH, KORY P; Star Spencer HS; Midwest City, OK; (2); Church Yth Grp; Dance Clb; Natl Beta Clb; ROTC; Mrchg Band; Pep Band; Ofcr Soph Cls; Ofcr Stu Cncl; Golf; Hon Roll; OK Univ; Electronics Engr.

SMITH, KRISTAL; Cherokee Jr Sr HS; Cherokee, OK; (2); Church Yth Grp; Drama Clb; FHA; Letterman Clb; NFL; Pep Clb; Spanish Clb; Speech Tm; SADD; Chorus; OSU.

SMITH, KRISTI; Depew HS; Depew, OK; (4); 1/34; Natl FFA Org; Spanish Clb; Sec Jr Cls; Rep Stu Cncl; Var Bsktbl; Var Chrldng; Var Sftbl; Var Trk; NHS; Val; Comm Bank Of Bristow Stu Bd Of Dirs; OK ST U; Med Tech.

SMITH, KRISTINA A; Catoosa Sr HS; Tulsa, OK; (4); Church Yth Grp; Drama Clb; Band; Chorus; Church Choir; Mrchg Band; School Musical; Swing Chorus; Hon Roll; Rogers ST; Cnslr; Sec.

SMITH, KRISTY; Bray-Doyle HS; Marlow, OK; (3); Pres Church Yth Grp; Cmnty Wkr; Pres FHA; Hosp Aide; Chorus; Church Choir; School Play; Nwsp; Yrbk; Sec Frsh Cls; Page OK ST Senate; RN.

SMITH, LA RENA; Thomas Jr Sr HS; Thomas, OK; (3); 1/38; Church Yth Grp; Natl FFA Org; Chorus; Var Bsktbl; Cit Awd; High Hon Roll; Jr NHS; NHS; Val; Exhbt/Raise Reg Polled Hereford Cattle; ST Wnrs Preprd Pub Spkg; Orange Belt Karate; Med/AG Law.

SMITH, LACI; Stillwater Jr HS; Stillwater, OK; (1); Church Yth Grp; FCA; Chrldng; Hon Roll; Frosh Chrldng Sqd NCA Natl Fnlsts 11th Pl, All Amer Prfrmnc Tm; OK ST U; Dietician.

SMITH, LACY G; South Intermediate HS; Broken Arrow, OK; (1); Church Yth Grp; Drama Clb; Natl FFA Org; Sftbl; Hon Roll; Pres Acad Fit Awd; Vet.

SMITH, LANCE T; Mc Loud HS; Harrah, OK; (1); Hon Roll; NHS; Bdy Bldng; Karate; Biochmst.

SMITH, LARRY; Atoka HS; Atoka, OK; (4); 5/89; Am Leg Boys St; Chess Clb; Drama Clb; FBLA; Spanish Clb; VICA; Hon Roll; Jr NHS; NHS; Vo-Tech Natl Hnr Soc & Stu Of Mnth; U Of OK; Aerospc Engrng.

SMITH, LASHAUN; Coyle Public Schl; Edmond, OK; (2); Cmnty Wkr; FHA; Pep Clb; Rptr Nwsp; Rptr Yrbk; Hon Roll; Dist Mem Of Natl Piano Guild; Natl Ldrshp & Svc Awd; All Amer Schlr; Eng Schlr; Veterinary Sci.

SMITH, LAURA; Byng Sr HS; Francis, OK; (3); Church Yth Grp; VP Drama Clb; VP 4-H; Math Clb; Science Clb; Band; Church Choir; Pres Soph Cls; Ofcr Stu Cncl; Cit Awd; NJAS.

SMITH, LAURA D; Salina HS; Salina, OK; (3); Church Yth Grp; Pep Clb; Red Cross Aide; Chorus; Church Choir; Yrbk; Powder Puff Ftbl; Stu Of Mnth Awd.

SMITH, LAURIE A; Owasso Sr HS; Collinsville, OK; (2); #51 in class; Church Yth Grp; FHA; Science Clb; Hon Roll; NHS; Piano; Anmls; Bio/Music.

SMITH, LEIA; Claremore Sr HS; Claremore, OK; (2); Tennis; Hon Roll; Soph Math Awd.

SMITH, LEIGH; Valliant HS; Valliant, OK; (4); 5/86; Pres VP Church Yth Grp; Pres Sec FHA; Co-Ed Yrbk; Pres Frsh Cls; Pres Soph Cls; Pres Jr Cls; Pres Sr Cls; VP Sec Stu Cncl; High Hon Roll; Sec NHS; E Cntrl OK U; Chem.

SMITH, LENA J; Mustang HS; Mustang, OK; (2); Church Yth Grp; Teachers Aide; Band; Mrchg Band; School Musical; Cntrl OK Dir Assn Hnr Band; OK U; Microgenetics.

SMITH, LORI; Ft Cobb-Broxton HS; Fort Cobb, OK; (3); 1/30; Church Yth Grp; Treas FHA; HOBY; Spanish Clb; Treas Stu Cncl; Bsktbl; Sftbl; High Hon Roll; NHS.

SMITH, LORI A; North Intemediate HS; Broken Arrow, OK; (2); Band; Mrchg Band; JV Bsktbl; JV Sftbl; Hon Roll; Jr NHS; NHS; OSU; Sales/Sports Med.

SMITH, LUNA; Hominy HS; Hominy, OK; (2); Church Yth Grp; English Clb; FHA; GAA; Girl Scts; Quiz Bowl; Spanish Clb; Teachers Aide; Band; Church Choir; Tulsa Jr Col; RN.

SMITH, MARION; Seminole Jr Sr HS; Seminole, OK; (1); FCA; French Clb; Scholastic Bowl; Chorus; Drill Tm; Sec Frsh Cls; Rep Stu Cncl; Trk; High Hon Roll; TAD.

SMITH, MARISA; Mustang HS; Yukon, OK; (3); Church Yth Grp; Spanish Clb; Chorus; Color Guard; Flag Corp; Hon Roll; NHS; Var Choir; Winterguard; Yth Alive; Tchng.

SMITH, MARK R; Claremore Sr HS; Claremore, OK; (2); Bsktbl; JV Tennis; High Hon Roll; Hon Roll; Prfct Atten Awd.

SMITH, MASIE J; Hinton HS; Hinton, OK; (2); Church Yth Grp; Natl FFA Org; Band; Chorus; Jazz Band; Mrchg Band; Orch; Ofcr Soph Cls; Hon Roll; Write Poetry, Songs & Short Stories; Keyboard Composition; Western; Inter Decorate, Dsgn.

SMITH, MATT; Hinton HS; Hinton, OK; (3); 1/26; Church Yth Grp; FCA; Office Aide; Quiz Bowl; Scholastic Bowl; SADD; Teachers Aide; Pres Jr Cls; Rep Stu Cncl; Capt Bsbl; OK U; Psych.

SMITH, MATT W; Broken Arrow Sr HS; Broken Arrow, OK; (3); Church Yth Grp; Cmnty Wkr; Computer Clb; Key Clb; Office Aide; Band; Chorus; Church Choir; School Play; Ed Yrbk; Tulsa Univ; Psych.

SMITH, MC KENNA; Sallisaw HS; Sallisaw, OK; (3); Drama Clb; 4-H; HOBY; Quiz Bowl; Scholastic Bowl; Science Clb; Speech Tm; Chorus; Church Choir; School Musical; Lfgrd; 1st Responder Med Provider; OK ST U; Performing Arts.

SMITH, MELISSA; Okeene Jr Sr HS; Okeene, OK; (3); 4/27; Church Yth Grp; Letterman Clb; Band; Rep Frsh Cls; Pres Soph Cls; Pres Jr Cls; Var L Bsktbl; Var L Chrldng; Var L Sftbl; High Hon Roll; Blaine Cty Teen Ct Attorney; William & Mary; Law.

SMITH, MELISSA A; Okay Jr Sr HS; Okay, OK; (2); 4-H; Spanish Clb; Chorus; Bsktbl; Chrldng; Hon Roll.

SMITH, MICHAEL; Kingfisher HS; Kingfisher, OK; (4); 12/96; Church Yth Grp; FCA; Office Aide; Church Choir; Ofcr Stu Cncl; Ftbl; Trk; Wt Lftg; Wrstlng; High Hon Roll; Bys St Del; Jr Lion; UOK; Hlth Sci Fld.

SMITH, MICHAEL A; Okmulgee HS; Okmulgee, OK; (2); 7/170; FCA; Spanish Clb; Var Bsbl; Intrml Wt Lftg; Hon Roll; Ntl Merit Schol; Pres Acad Fit Awd; U Of OK.

SMITH, MICHELLE; Ada HS; Ada, OK; (4); Church Yth Grp; Computer Clb; Math Clb; Mu Alpha Theta; Office Aide; Color Guard; Flag Corp; Mrchg Band; Hon Roll; NHS; Rifle Crps; Acctng Clb; E Cntrl U; Acctng.

SMITH, MINDY M; Western Heights Sr HS; Oklahoma City, OK; (2); Rose ST Coll; RN.

SMITH, MISTY D; Spiro HS; Spiro, OK; (2); Church Yth Grp; Cmnty Wkr; FCA; FHA; Natl FFA Org; Quiz Bowl; Teachers Aide; School Play; Yrbk; Gym; OSU; Tchng.

SMITH, MONTRELL; Midwest City HS; Oklahoma City, OK; (2); 13/507; Church Yth Grp; Red Cross Aide; Church Choir; Hon Roll; Prfct Atten Awd; Pres Acad Fit Awd; Chrch Yth Fllwshp Dpt Prs, Ryl Ambssdrs, Bsktbl, Ushr; Rd Crss Hmntrn Awd; OK St Sntr Mnsn Page; Morehouse Coll; Acctng.

SMITH, NATASHA L; Harrah HS; Luther, OK; (1); Church Yth Grp; FCA; 4-H; Hosp Aide; Natl FFA Org; Chrldng; Tennis; 4-H Awd; FFA Star Grnhnd Awd/Rprtr 96-; OU; Neonatal RN.

SMITH, NATHAN P; Elgin HS; Elgin, OK; (2); FCA; Ofcr Soph Cls; Ftbl; Trk; Wt Lftg; Wrstlng; Hon Roll; Wrestling All Conf Team.

SMITH, NATONYA M; John Marshall HS; Oklahoma City, OK; (3); 17/200; Church Yth Grp; FBLA; Office Aide; Teachers Aide; Church Choir; School Play; VP Jr Cls; Var Chrldng; Cit Awd; High Hon Roll; Serenity Bapt Chrch Yth Dept Pres; OK ST U; Engr.

SMITH, NICHOLE C; Elk City Jr HS; Elk City, OK; (1); Church Yth Grp; Pep Clb; SADD; Band; Chorus; Church Choir; Color Guard; Flag Corp; Mrchg Band; Pep Band; Southwestern; Mscn.

SMITH, NICOLE; Ada HS; Ada, OK; (4); 2/165; Pres Church Yth Grp; Cmnty Wkr; FCA; Mu Alpha Theta; VP Science Clb; Chorus; Rep Stu Cncl; L Capt Bsktbl; NHS; Spanish NHS; Austin Coll; Phys Thrpst.

SMITH, OLIVER L; East Central HS; Tulsa, OK; (3); Cmnty Wkr; Chess Clb; Science Clb; Spanish Clb; High Hon Roll; NHS; Chrstns HS.

SMITH, PAM; Cordell Jr HS; Cordell, OK; (3); 2/43; Am Leg Aux Girls St; Church Yth Grp; Cmnty Wkr; FHA; Letterman Clb; VP Spanish Clb; Sec Rep Stu Cncl; Var Bsktbl; Var Sftbl; High Hon Roll; Kiwash Elect Coop Yth Tour; Stdnt Yr; Gld Piano; Southwestern OK ST U; Pharm.

SMITH, PARKER; Aline-Cleo Jr Sr HS; Ringwood, OK; (4); 3/25; Am Leg Boys St; FHA; Pep Clb; Quiz Bowl; Scholastic Bowl; School Play; Rep Sr Cls; Var Bsbl; Capt Bsktbl; High Hon Roll; OK ST U; Bus Admin.

SMITH, RAYNA L; B T Washington HS; Tulsa, OK; (3); Art Clb; Dance Clb; Drama Clb; Thesps; School Musical; School Play; Hon Roll; NHS; Church Yth Grp; Cmnty Wkr; Miss Dance Of OK 94; Voice; Spotlight Theatre Vlntr; Cmnty Theatre; Martial Arts; Theatre.

SMITH, REBA S; Stilwell HS; Stilwell, OK; (2); Drama Clb; FHA; Speech Tm; Gov Hon Prg Awd; High Hon Roll; Hon Roll; NHS; Pres Acad Fit Awd; Indian Heritage Club.

SMITH, RICKY A; Mustang HS; Yukon, OK; (2); French Clb; Key Clb; Math Clb; Science Clb; Tennis; Hon Roll; Arch.

SMITH, RONALD; Mc Loud HS; Harrah, OK; (3); 14/160; Church Yth Grp; FCA; FBLA; Bsktbl; Socr; Cit Awd; High Hon Roll; Hon Roll; NHS; Prfct Atten Awd; OK ST U; Engrng.

SMITH, RYAN J; Colbert Jr Sr HS; Colbert, OK; (2); Church Yth Grp; Math Tm; Rptr Nwsp; High Hon Roll; St Schlr; Micro Bio.

SMITH, SALLY; Moore HS; Moore, OK; (2); Church Yth Grp; Cmnty Wkr; GAA; Science Clb; Band; Church Choir; Mrchg Band; Pep Band; School Musical; School Play; Med.

SMITH, SAMANTHA; Wynnewood HS; Wynnewood, OK; (4); 3/70; Church Yth Grp; FHA; Yrbk; Rep Sr Cls; High Hon Roll; St Schlr; OK Hnr Soc; FHA VP; Acad Tm; East Cntrl U Ada; Cytotechnolgy.

SMITH, SANDINA M; Allen HS; Allen, OK; (2); Nrsg.

SMITH, SARA; Elk City HS; Elk City, OK; (2); 10/130; German Clb; Letterman Clb; Pep Clb; Science Clb; Church Choir; VP Stu Cncl; Sftbl; Hon Roll; NHS; Comm Svc Work For Local Meals On Wheels; U Of AZ; Coach; His Instr.

SMITH, SARA K; Mustang HS; Mustang, OK; (3); Church Yth Grp; Dance Clb; FHA; Spanish Clb; Chorus; Lit Mag; Hon Roll; Jr NHS.

SMITH, SARAH; Midwest City HS; Midwest City, OK; (2); 21/488; Church Yth Grp; FCA; French Clb; FHA; Pep Clb; Church Choir; Ofcr Soph Cls; Var Chrldng; Var Trk; Hon Roll; NCA All-Amer Chrldr; Chrch Vcl Ensmbl.

SMITH, SARAH; Enid Sr HS; Enid, OK; (1); Sec Church Yth Grp; Drama Clb; Speech Tm; Band; Color Guard; Mrchg Band; School Play; Stage Crew; JV Var Swmmng; Hon Roll; Jr Olympic Sftbl; City Swim Team; Chrch Acolyte; Yth Group; HS Math Tchr.

SMITH, SARAH J; Arkoma Jr Sr HS; Arkoma, OK; (4); 3/27; Sec FCA; Teachers Aide; Capt Bsktbl; Sftbl; Gov Hon Prg Awd; Hon Roll; Hist NHS; Historian; Gftd & Tltd; Carl Albert ST Coll; Legal Sec.

SMITH, SCOTT; South Intermediate HS; Broken Arrow, OK; (2); 4-H; Natl FFA Org; Teachers Aide; Ofcr Soph Cls; Ftbl; Wt Lftg; Cit Awd; 4-H Awd.

SMITH, SENECA; Okemah HS; Okemah, OK; (4); 21/48; Am Leg Boys St; Church Yth Grp; Debate Tm; HOBY; Red Cross Aide; SADD; School Play; Ofcr Bsbl; Ftbl; Hon Roll; Bys St Del; OK TX Kiwanas Awd; Soph Yr; Johnson O'Malley Ldrshp Del; Southwestern; Phrmcy.

SMITH, SHAMICA L; Midwest City HS; Tinker Afb, OK; (2); 128/473; Red Cross Aide; Bsktbl; Mgr(s); Score Keeper; Ntl Merit Ltr; PT.

SMITH, SHANDA; Goodwell Public Schl; Goodwell, OK; (1); 2/15; Girl Scts; Library Aide; Band; Pres Frsh Cls; Var Chrldng; Hon Roll; Ballet; West TX A&M; Dance.

SMITH, SHANNON M; Norman Sr HS; Norman, OK; (3); 1/799; JCL; Latin Clb; Model UN; Mu Alpha Theta; Service Clb; High Hon Roll; Hon Roll; NHS; Hlth Sci Acad Univ Of OK; OK HS Hon Soc; Natl Jr Clsscl Leag Latin Hon Soc; Physcn.

SMITH, SHAUN E; East Central HS; Tulsa, OK; (4); Church Yth Grp; Var Bsbl; High Hon Roll; NHS; Church Sftbl Tm; Acctg.

SMITH, SHAWNDA M; Northwest Classen HS; Oklahoma City, OK; (2); Church Yth Grp; Teachers Aide; Chorus; Church Choir.

SMITH, SHEA; Rattan Sr HS; Antlers, OK; (2); 1/45; Church Yth Grp; FCA; Pres 4-H; Sec French Clb; FHA; Quiz Bowl; Yrbk; Pres Frsh Cls; VP Soph Cls; Var Bsktbl; Ctznshp WA Fcs Trp Del; 1st Pl Frnch I Comp Curr Cntst & St 4-H Spch Cntst.

SMITH, STACEY; Shawnee Sr HS; Shawnee, OK; (4); 34/259; Church Yth Grp; FCA; Library Aide; Office Aide; Spanish Clb; High Hon Roll; NHS; Prfct Atten Awd; St Gregorys Coll; Optmtry.

SMITH, STACY D; Yukon Middle HS; Yukon, OK; (2); Church Yth Grp; FHA; Spanish Clb; Hon Roll; Cert Lfgrd; Phys Thpy.

SMITH, STEPHANIE J; Clayton Jr Sr HS; Clayton, OK; (1); 4-H; Bsktbl; Sftbl; 4-H Awd; High Hon Roll; Hon Roll.

SMITH, TABITHA; Porter Jr Sr HS; Porter, OK; (4); 1/30; Church Yth Grp; FHA; SADD; Yrbk; Chrldng; Cit Awd; High Hon Roll; Hon Roll; NHS; Val; 1st Rnr Up Ms Peach Pgnt; Jr Atndnt Ftbl Hmcmng; Sr Atndnt Ftbl Hmcmng; Northeastern ST U Of OK; Bus.

SMITH, TAMRA K; Tecumseh HS; Tecumseh, OK; (3); 4/125; Church Yth Grp; Natl FFA Org; Scholastic Bowl; Mrchg Band; NHS; Dist Prprd Pub Spkng Qlfr; Acad Ltr Jckt; Yth Alive; OK ST Univ; Biotech.

SMITH, TASHA; Thomas Jr Sr HS; Thomas, OK; (3); 9/36; GAA; Natl FFA Org; Band; Chorus; Flag Corp; Mrchg Band; Treas Jr Cls; Treas Stu Cncl; Bsktbl; Trk; FFA Sec; Red Lands JC; Phy Thrpst.

SMITH, TIFFANY; Newcastle HS; Tuttle, OK; (4); #9 in class; Office Aide; Spanish Clb; JV Var Bsktbl; Var Trk; High Hon Roll; Hon Roll; NHS.

SMITH, TIMOTHY A; Putnam City West HS; Bethany, OK; (1); Church Yth Grp; Red Cross Aide; Ftbl; Trk; Wrstlng; Amateur Radio Operator Assisted With Logistics In OK City Bombing Through Red Crss; OK U.

SMITH, TRACI L; Liberty HS; Beggs, OK; (3); 3/35; Pres FHA; Var Capt Scholastic Bowl; Teachers Aide; Band; Chorus; Flag Corp; Ed Nwsp; Hon Roll; NHS; Prfct Atten Awd; Rockhurst; Pediatrics; Neo-Natal.

SMITH, TRACY; Westmoore HS; Oklahoma City, OK; (4); 34/610; Church Yth Grp; Sec Key Clb; School Musical; Rep Stu Cncl; High Hon Roll; Kiwanis Awd; Chrmn NHS; St Schlr; Val; Drama Clb; Cmptv Dnc Trp; ST Summer Sci Acad; Sea Wrld Careers Camp; U Of OK; Marine Bio.

SMITH, TRACY E; B T Washington HS; Tulsa, OK; (2); Church Yth Grp; Cmnty Wkr; Debate Tm; Intnl Clb; NFL; Spanish Clb; Speech Tm; SADD; Ballet; Intl Baccalaureate Degree Pgm Early Admissions; Japanese Clb Publcty Dir; Intl Stud.

SMITH, TRAVIS B; Putnam City North HS; Oklahoma City, OK; (3); JCL; Latin Clb; Orch; School Musical; School Play; High Hon Roll; Hon Roll; Music; Bus.

SMITH, TWANA; Douglass HS; Oklahoma City, OK; (1); ROTC; High Hon Roll; Movie Actor.

SMITH, TYQUCONDRA K; Midwest City HS; Oklahoma City, OK; (2); 64/488; Rep Stu Cncl; Bsktbl; High Hon Roll; Hon Roll; Church; Trvlng; Exercising; Morehouse; Engrng/Math.

SMITH, VAREE S; Jones HS; Jones, OK; (2); Drama Clb; GAA; VP Mu Alpha Theta; Quiz Bowl; Scholastic Bowl; Spanish Clb; Treas SADD; Thesps; Var Powder Puff Ftbl; Var Sftbl; Academic Team; Planet Earth; Obgyn.

SMITH, WES; Hinton HS; Hinton, OK; (2); Church Yth Grp; Natl FFA Org; SADD; Band; Jazz Band; Mrchg Band; Pep Band; School Musical; Variety Show; Ofcr Soph Cls; SWOSU; Pharmacy.

SMITH, WILLIAM; Moore HS; Oklahoma City, OK; (3); Boy Scts; Var Bsbl; U OK; Sprts Med.

SMITH, ZACHARY D; Warner HS; Muskogee, OK; (1); Church Yth Grp; Varsity Clb; Var Bsbl; Var Bsktbl; JV Trk; Hon Roll; Connors; Sci.

SMITH, ZACHARY S; Ryan Schl; Oscar, OK; (3); Boy Scts; 4-H; JA; Natl FFA Org; Pep Clb; Cit Awd; 4-H Awd; Cert Achvmt; Eng Mst Imrpvd; Natl Eng Mrt Awd; Chptr Farmer Degree; Jet Ski Racer; Multi-Yr Listee; OSU.

SMITHEY, JODIE D; Elk City Jr HS; Elk City, OK; (3); Drama Clb; Model UN; Pep Clb; Science Clb; Chorus; School Musical; School Play; Swing Chorus; High Hon Roll; NHS; ST/NATL Swing Choir Cmpttns; Piano 13 Yrs; Sngng 7 Yrs; Write Ptry/Entrd Cntsts; U Of OK.

SMOTHERMAN, CHRISSY M; Skiatook HS; Skiatook, OK; (4); 32/104; Hon Roll; Schol For Acad Achv To Rogers Univ; Rogers Univ; Bio.

SMOTHERS, JENNIFFER D; Skiatook HS; Owasso, OK; (4); 63/125; Office Aide; Teachers Aide; Band; Mrchg Band; Pep Band; JV Tennis; Skiatook Serteen Sertoma.

SNAPP, CASSONDRA; Carney Schl; Chandler, OK; (4); 1/16; Church Yth Grp; FHA; Mu Alpha Theta; Quiz Bowl; Score Keeper; Hon Roll; Val; VP Soph Cls; Rep Stu Cncl; Stat Bsbl; St Gregorys Coll; CPA.

SNAVELY, BRENDA L; Harrah HS; Harrah, OK; (2); Church Yth Grp; FHA; Girl Scts; Library Aide; Chorus; Church Choir; Cit Awd; High Hon Roll; Jr NHS; NHS; Scnd In Acctng II Rose ST Coll Schlstc Meet; OK Bapt Univ.

SNIDER, CHRIS L; Del City HS; Oklahoma City, OK; (3); 47/515; Church Yth Grp; FCA; Red Cross Aide; Spanish Clb; Var L Socr; Hon Roll; NHS; Yth For Christ; Spirit Cncl; Arch.

SNIDER, HEATHER D; Mustang HS; Mustang, OK; (2); 101/403; Cmnty Wkr; Debate Tm; HOBY; Var Rep Frsh Cls; Var Rep Soph Cls; Var Rep Jr Cls; Co-Capt Pom Pon; NHS; Yth Ldrshp Exch; U Of OK.

SNIDER, JASON; Bixby Sr HS; Bixby, OK; (4); 87/178; Church Yth Grp; CAP; Cmnty Wkr; FCA; Letterman Clb; Rptr Natl FFA Org; Spanish Clb; SADD; Varsity Clb; Var Bsbl; Awded Hnrbl Mntn Sr Yr Outstndng Ftbl Perf; Invlvd Bthphg Mssn Cncl Help Hdncp Chldrn; Bethany Coll; Bio/Envrmntl Sci.

SNIDER, MICAH; Clinton HS; Clinton, OK; (3); Art Clb; Church Yth Grp; FCA; FHA; Spanish Clb; Church Choir; Var L Socr; Hon Roll; Natl Sci Mrt Awd; OK Bptst U; Art Ed.

SNIDER, RICHARD J; Roland Sr HS; Roland, OK; (3); JV Ftbl; Hon Roll; U Of AR; Cmptrs.

SNIPES, ASHLEY; Oklahoma Christian Schl; Oklahoma City, OK; (4); 15/35; FCA; Letterman Clb; Service Clb; Treas Soph Cls; Ofcr Sr Cls; Rep Stu Cncl; Fld Hcky; Socr; Sftbl; Tennis; OU; Phys Thrpy.

SNODDY, REGINALD B; B T Washington HS; Tulsa, OK; (3); Church Yth Grp; Church Choir; Hon Roll; Jr NHS; OMTA Sup Rtngs; TAMTA; OK U; Mtrlgy.

SNODGRASS, JACOB D; Cimarron Public Schl; Ames, OK; (2); Pres Natl FFA Org; Science Clb; School Play; Pres Frsh Cls; Pres Soph Cls; Var Bsbl; Cit Awd; Hon Roll; Prfct Atten Awd; Stu Cncl Mem.

SNOOK, WILLIAM D; Union Sr HS; Tulsa, OK; (3); 18/741; Cmnty Wkr; Band; Church Choir; NHS.

SNOVEL, SHAUN P; Chandler HS; Chandler, OK; (2); CAP; FCA; Spanish Clb; Color Guard; Var Bsbl; Var Ftbl; Var Wrstlng; Hon Roll; Var 4a Bsbl St Rnnr Up Champnshps; OK Kids Chandlr Prep Bsbl Champns; Civil Air Patrol Color Guard; OK Univ; Airline/Fighter Pilot.

SNOW, DANIEL; Christian Heritage Acad; Oklahoma City, OK; (3); Church Yth Grp; Scholastic Bowl; Church Choir; Stage Crew; JV Var Ftbl; Cit Awd; High Hon Roll; OK Baptist U.

SNOW, DERICK E; Webster HS; Tulsa, OK; (2); Drama Clb; NFL; Speech Tm; Thesps; School Play; Ofcr Jr Cls; Hon Roll; Jr NHS; Coll Of Ozarks; Actor.

SNOW, LINDSAY; Seminole Jr Sr HS; Seminole, OK; (2); 1/110; Church Yth Grp; FCA; French Clb; GAA; HOBY; Math Clb; Var Bsktbl; Var Chrldng; Var Trk; Pres Acad Fit Awd; Ftbl, Bsktbl Soph Attndnt Hmcmng; OC.

SNOW, LYNN F; Pioneer Jr Sr HS; Enid, OK; (2); 4/35; Sec Rep 4-H; Office Aide; Teachers Aide; Band; Mrchg Band; Rep Frsh Cls; Rep Soph Cls; Var Bsktbl; Var Sftbl; Hon Roll; OK ST; Lwyr/Jdg.

SNOW, PAUL E; Bartlesville Mid HS; Bartlesville, OK; (2); Boy Scts; Church Yth Grp; Drama Clb; Phtg Yrbk; Wt Lftg; Hon Roll; Jr NHS; Prfct Atten Awd; Star Wars Clb.

SNOWDEN, PAUL; Lomega HS; Omega, OK; (3); 1/12; FCA; Rptr Nwsp; Pres Frsh Cls; VP Jr Cls; VP Stu Cncl; Var Bsktbl; NHS; Southwestern OK ST U Schltc Geog Meet 1st Place; All Conf Acad Team; Outstdng Chem Lab Stu Awd; Southwestern OK ST U; Pre-Opt.

SNYDER, AMELIA J; Putnam City West HS; Oklahoma City, OK; (3); Church Yth Grp; Office Aide; Teachers Aide; Yrbk; Ntl Merit Ltr; OU; Sec Ed.

SNYDER, GREG K; Central Mid-HS; Norman, OK; (2); Cmnty Wkr; Band; Jazz Band; Orch; Hon Roll; Prfct Atten Awd; CODL Regnl Hnr Band 1st Chair; OK Univ; Mech Engr.

SNYDER, HEATHER A; Choctaw HS; Choctaw, OK; (2); Church Yth Grp; FTA; Color Guard; Winterguard ST Contest; Drama; Psych.

SNYDER, JENNIFER; Wapanucka Schl; Wapanucka, OK; (1); 6/16; GAA; Bsktbl; Dentist Asst.

SNYDER, MATT T; Mt St Marys HS; Oklahoma City, OK; (3); Church Yth Grp; FCA; Letterman Clb; Scholastic Bowl; Service Clb; Var Bsktbl; OK ST Univ; Arch.

SNYDER, MONICA; Mt St Marys HS; Oklahoma City, OK; (2); Church Yth Grp; VP French Clb; Pep Clb; Rptr Nwsp; Pres Soph Cls; Capt Chrldng; Co-Capt Pom Pon; Gov Hon Prg Awd; Hon Roll; NHS; REPS; OK Univ.

SNYDER, RUSSELL B; West Jr HS; Oklahoma City, OK; (1); Boy Scts.

SNYDER, SAMUEL C; Muskogee HS; Muskogee, OK; (1); Church Yth Grp; ROTC; Band; Mrchg Band; Pep Band.

SNYDER, STACIE; Tonkawa Jr Sr HS; Tonkawa, OK; (4); 4/38; Am Leg Aux Girls St; Ed Yrbk; Rep Sr Cls; Var L Bsktbl; High Hon Roll; NHS; Pres Schlr; St Schlr; Church Yth Grp; Cmnty Wkr; Rotary Youth Ldrshp Awd; Natl Young Ldrs Conf; Ms Tonkawa Princess; Southwestern Winfield; Ed.

SOBER, HEATHER J; Union Sr HS; Tulsa, OK; (3); 73/741; Church Yth Grp; French Clb; Band; Chorus; Color Guard; Mrchg Band; Jr NHS; NHS.

SODERSTROM, MARK E; Union Intermediate HS; Tulsa, OK; (1); Church Yth Grp; Cmnty Wkr; Pres Math Clb; Spanish Clb; Intrml Bsktbl; JV Tennis; High Hon Roll; NHS; Prfct Atten Awd; Pres Acad Fit Awd; DFY; Acad Team; Peer Mdtn Prgm; OK ST Univ; Acctng.

SOLENBERGER, MATT W; Bartlesville Mid HS; Bartlesville, OK; (1); #61 in class; Church Yth Grp; Office Aide; Pep Clb; Ofcr Bsbl; Wt Lftg; Hon Roll; OK Univ; Sci/Bus.

SOLES, SARAH; Midwest City HS; Oklahoma City, OK; (3); 36/386; Am Leg Aux Girls St; Science Clb; Band; Jazz Band; Mrchg Band; Ofcr Jr Cls; NHS; Ntl Merit SF; Drama Clb; Letterman Clb; Bst Band Girl Awd 3 Yrs; 6 Solo/Ensmble Medals; Drama Cont 1st Pl Prose, 2nd Pl Monologue; Acad Team; Harvard; Music.

SOLINGER, LISA M; Mc Loud HS; Newalla, OK; (2); Cmnty Wkr; FCA; Acpl Chr; Chorus; Church Choir; Variety Show.

SOLIS, CALIXTO; Capitol Hill HS; Oklahoma City, OK; (4); 1/151; Am Leg Boys St; FBLA; High Hon Roll; Hon Roll; NHS; Val; Mntrs Prgm; Hspnc & Latino Clubs; Oklahoma City CC; Bus Admin.

SOLIS, LUIS; U S Grant HS; Oklahoma City, OK; (2); Church Yth Grp; JV Crs Cntry; Var Socr; High Hon Roll; Prfct Atten Awd; KXY/TWISTER Radio Brdcstng Explorer Grp; OK U.

SOLIS, MICHAEL R; North Intemediate HS; Broken Arrow, OK; (1); Church Yth Grp; Science Clb; Spanish Clb; Band; Mrchg Band; Pep Band; Trk; Hon Roll; Jr NHS; U Of TX; Pediatrician.

SOLIZ, LINDSEY; Grace Chrn Acad; Oklahoma City, OK; (2); Church Yth Grp; English Clb; GAA; HOBY; Letterman Clb; Spanish Clb; Bsktbl; Powder Puff Ftbl; Sftbl; Swmmng; Certfd Lifeguard With YMCA Staff; Hnrs Eng; Schltcs Team Mem; Applied Arts.

SOLOMAN, STEPHANIE J; Union Sr HS; Tulsa, OK; (3); 100/750; Treas FBLA; Ofcr Pom Pon; Frgn Lang Clb; Acad Lttr; Pres Ed Awd; Sprts Med.

SOLOMON, JIMMIE; Del City HS; Oklahoma City, OK; (4); 18/374; HOBY; Quiz Bowl; Pres SADD; Phtg Yrbk; Pres Soph Cls; NHS; JA; Office Aide; Wt Lftg; Cit Awd; HOBY Jr Cnslr, Ambssdr; ACT Score 32; TX War Drgs Cmp Smmr 95; U Sci Arts OK.

SOMERS, RAYNA L; Pauls Valley HS; Pauls Valley, OK; (2); Church Yth Grp; FCA; FHA; GAA; Key Clb; Tennis; High Hon Roll; Hon Roll; St Schlr; Phi Pi Phi; Cmnty Svc For Bombing Victims; U Of OK; Phys Thrpy.

SOMERVILLE, AMANDA; Westmoore HS; Moore, OK; (3); 11/615; Am Leg Aux Girls St; Scholastic Bowl; Hon Roll; Ofcr NHS; Ofcr Soph Cls; Ofcr Jr Cls; Bsktbl; Peer Helping; Acad Excl Span III; Acad Excl Comm Styles; Drake U; Acturial Scis.

SOMERVILLE, VANESSA; Union Intermediate HS; Tulsa, OK; (2); Orch; School Play; High Hon Roll; Hon Roll; Jr NHS; NHS; Pres Schlr; All Dist Hnrs Orch; Dist, St Solo/Ensm Supr Rtng; Prfmng Arts.

SOMMERS, AMBER; Nathan Hale HS; Tulsa, OK; (3); #16 in class; Church Yth Grp; DECA; FTA; VP Soph Cls; Rep Jr Cls; Treas VP Stu Cncl; JV Bsktbl; Var Golf; JV Sftbl; NHS.

SON, MICHAEL C; Memorial HS; Tulsa, OK; (3); Church Yth Grp; German Clb; Intnl Clb; ROTC; Spanish Clb; Acpl Chr; School Musical; Swing Chorus; NHS; Ntl Merit Ltr.

SON, REGAN N; Bridge Creek HS; Tuttle, OK; (1); Art Clb; Church Yth Grp; Spanish Clb; Sec Frsh Cls; Bsktbl; Sftbl; Cit Awd; Hon Roll; Ntl Merit Ltr.

SONDERGELD, AMY J; Union Sr HS; Broken Arrow, OK; (4); 10/629; Cmnty Wkr; Key Clb; Spanish Clb; High Hon Roll; Jr NHS; NHS; Pres Acad Fit Awd; Spanish NHS; Bio.

SONG, ANGELA; Edmond Memorial HS; Edmond, OK; (4); 51/322; German Clb; Key Clb; Spanish Clb; Science Clb; Chrch Intl Ministry; U Of Cntrl OK; Acctng.

SONHEIM, SARAH F; Bethany HS; Bethany, OK; (4); 27/80; Church Yth Grp; Chorus; Acad Ltr B Awd; U Cntrl OK; Bus Admin.

SONNENBERG, JOE L; North Intemediate HS; Broken Arrow, OK; (1); Band; Hon Roll; Bsbl, Bsktbl.

SORG, RACHELLE; Eisenhower Sr HS; Lawton, OK; (3); #1 in class; Cmnty Wkr; HOBY; Key Clb; Quiz Bowl; Ofcr Jr Cls; Art Clb; Socr; NHS; Acad Tm; Young Republicans; Johns Hopkins; Pre-Med.

SORRELL, RYAN; Durant HS; Colbert, OK; (3); 4-H; FTA; Natl FFA Org; Rep Jr Cls; VP Stu Cncl; Var Ftbl; L Trk; L Wrstlng; 4-H Awd; Hon Roll; SE Dist VP 4-H; Durant FFA Pres; OK ST Univ; Ag Ed.

SORRELLS, JESSICA L; Bixby Sr HS; Bixby, OK; (1); FCA; SADD; Ed Yrbk; Rep Stu Cncl; Var Bsktbl; Var L Chrldng; Var L Trk; Var Wt Lftg; Pres Jr NHS; Pres Acad Fit Awd; All Amer Schlr; Frosh Stu Of Yr; Optmtrst.

SORRELLS, MATT P; Bixby Sr HS; Bixby, OK; (3); 58/208; Phys Thrpy.

SOSSAMON, JILL M; Choctaw HS; Midwest City, OK; (4); 16/308; Church Yth Grp; Cmnty Wkr; FCA; Key Clb; Office Aide; SADD; Yrbk; Pres Frsh Cls; JV Bsktbl; NHS; U Of OK; Med.

SOUKIEH, STEVE A; Metro Christian Acad; Tulsa, OK; (2); Hon Roll.

SOULEK, AMY; Perry Sr HS; Perry, OK; (3); 12/93; Church Yth Grp; FCA; FHA; German Clb; Band; Color Guard; Drill Tm; Flag Corp; Mrchg Band; Pep Band; NOC Hnr Bnd 2xs; U Cntrl OK; Bus Finance.

SOURIE, CA SHAWNA; Muskogee HS; Muskogee, OK; (3); French Clb; Bsktbl; Creative Wrtng; Jrnlsm.

SOURIE, CASHAWNA; Muskogee HS; Muskogee, OK; (3); Church Yth Grp; French Clb; Bsktbl; OK St Univ; TV Brdcstng.

SOUTEE, ERIN; Wynnewood HS; Wynnewood, OK; (2); 7/46; Church Yth Grp; Hosp Aide; Band; Color Guard; Jazz Band; Mrchg Band; Var L Bsktbl; Hon Roll; NHS; Twrlr; Hlth Careers.

SOUTH, BRIAN E; Mc Alester HS; Mcalester, OK; (3); 1/200; Quiz Bowl; Spanish Clb; Church Choir; Cit Awd; High Hon Roll; U Of OK.

SOUTH, DANA; Ardmore HS; Ardmore, OK; (2); Art Clb; Church Yth Grp; FCA; Ofcr Latin Clb; Science Clb; Teachers Aide; Rep Frsh Cls; Chrldng; Hon Roll; GAA; Cmp Fire Grls Assn; Pharm.

SOUTH, TRACI; Lawton Sr HS; Lawton, OK; (3); Spanish Clb; Chorus; High Hon Roll; Jr NHS; NHS; Pres Acad Fit Awd; Occptnl Thrpst.

SOUTHERLAND, NICK W; Tahlequah Sr HS; Tahlequah, OK; (2); Bsktbl; Ftbl; Trk; Wrstlng; NHS; Dentist.

SOUTHERN, AMY D; Charles Page HS; Sand Springs, OK; (4); Church Yth Grp; FCA; FBLA; JA; Key Clb; Spanish Clb; Chorus; Color Guard; Stage Crew; Hon Roll; Tulsa CC; Compprog.

SOUTHERN, AMY L; Pawnee HS; Pawnee, OK; (4); 16/60; Church Yth Grp; FBLA; FHA; Pep Clb; Church Choir; Ed Nwsp; Chrldng; High Hon Roll; OK Bapt Allstar Yth Choir; Church Puppet, Drama Grp; OK Bapt U; Chrstn Cnslr.

SOWEKA, SHABON; Graham Schl; Henryetta, OK; (3); Rptr 4-H; FHA; Var Bsktbl; Var Sftbl; Hon Roll; Life Ldr; Connors; Nrsng; Law Enforcement.

SOWELLS, HEATHER; Claremore Sr HS; Claremore, OK; (4); 60/273; Cmnty Wkr; Teachers Aide; Chrldng; Gym; Powder Puff Ftbl; Tennis; Hon Roll; Homcmng Atten; Natl Chrldng Chmpn; Homcmng Qn; U Of AR; Pre-Dntl.

SOWERS, JILINDA K; Bartlesville Jr HS; Bartlesville, OK; (3); Church Yth Grp; FBLA; Yrbk; Rep Stu Cncl; Var Capt Pom Pon; High Hon Roll; Hon Roll; NHS.

SPAETH, NEIL A; Putnam City West HS; Bethany, OK; (3); 67/303; Cmnty Wkr; French Clb; FBLA; Phtg Nwsp; Phtg Yrbk; Cit Awd; St Newspapr Cont St Champ Sprts Actn Photo; St PTA Reflectns Conts.

SPAHR, DAVID G; Edmond North HS; Edmond, OK; (4); 71/330; Mu Alpha Theta; ROTC; NHS; Embry-Riddle Aeronutcl; Aerospc.

SPAIN, LINDSEY E; Edmond North HS; Edmond, OK; (2); 130/420; Drama Clb; Spanish Clb; Band; Mrchg Band; Pep Band; Chrldng; Socr; Jr NHS; NHS; KC Msc Clb; KC Chmbr Msc Soc; Dist Natl Piano Plyng Auditions; Tulane; Med/Span.

SPAIN, LISA A; Choctaw HS; Choctaw, OK; (3); 58/250; FHA; Girl Scts; Cit Awd; High Hon Roll; NHS; Pres Acad Fit Awd; Rose ST Univ; Cop.

SPALDING, THAN M; Soper Schl; Antlers, OK; (4); 2/20; Church Yth Grp; 4-H; Natl FFA Org; Church Choir; Treas Sr Cls; 4-H Awd; Hon Roll; Sal; Estrn OK ST Coll; Ag Ed.

SPANGENBERG, ERICA R; Westmoore HS; Oklahoma City, OK; (3); 64/615; German Clb; Scholastic Bowl; Bsktbl; JV Socr; Jr NHS; NHS; Ger & OK HS Hnr Soc Awds; U Of OK.

SPANNAGEL, DAVID; Apache HS; Apache, OK; (3); #1 in class; Drama Clb; Quiz Bowl; Thesps; Rptr Stu Cncl; High Hon Roll; Pres Acad Fit Awd; TSA VP; Jrnlsm.

SPARKMAN, CHAD M; Lexington HS; Lexington, OK; (4); Church Yth Grp; FCA; 4-H; Library Aide; Math Clb; Mu Alpha Theta; Office Aide; Spanish Clb; Teachers Aide; OKU.

SPARKMAN, CHANCE; Shawnee Sr HS; Tecumseh, OK; (2); 1/350; Church Yth Grp; FCA; Latin Clb; Varsity Clb; Bsktbl; Ftbl; Tennis; High Hon Roll; OK U.

SPARKMAN, JENNY; Idabel HS; Idabel, OK; (4); 1/107; Am Leg Aux Girls St; Church Yth Grp; Band; Chorus; VP Jr Cls; Rep Stu Cncl; NHS; Val; Regents Schlr; OK ST U; Chem/Bio.

SPARKMAN, SKYE; Guymon Sr HS; Guymon, OK; (2); Band; Chorus; School Musical; JV Bsktbl; Hon Roll; Ntl Merit Ltr; SW OK ST U; Phy Thrpst.

SPARKS, ANTHONY L; Choctaw HS; Jones, OK; (3); Var Ftbl; Var Wt Lftg; Hon Roll; Phys Thrp.

SPARKS, BRANDI J; Ponca City Middle HS; Ponca City, OK; (1); Church Yth Grp; English Clb; GAA; Letterman Clb; Mrchg Band; Pep Band; Swmmng; Cit Awd; High Hon Roll; Hon Roll; NOC Acad Achvt Testng Top 50 Score; Med.

SPARKS, CRYSTAL; Edmond Santa Fe HS; Edmond, OK; (4); 18/209; Science Clb; SADD; Chorus; Swing Chorus; Variety Show; Var Chrldng; Gov Hon Prg Awd; High Hon Roll; NHS; Pres Schlr; Chr Mem/Yr; Northeastern ST U; Optmlgy.

SPARKS, JENNIFER C; Porter Jr Sr HS; Porter, OK; (3); Church Yth Grp; Cmnty Wkr; Hosp Aide; SADD; Hon Roll; NHS; Acad Team; OK HS Hnr Scty; Math/Sci/Gntcs.

SPARKS JR, JOE R; Wetumka Jr Sr HS; Wetumka, OK; (2); Church Yth Grp; FCA; Natl FFA Org; Band; Mrchg Band; Var Bsbl; Var Bsktbl; Var Ftbl; Trk; Hon Roll; Hnrb Mntn Bsktbl; 12th In St For Stolen Bases Bsbl; Natl Land Judging Team FFA.

SPARKS, MELISA; Westmoore HS; Oklahoma City, OK; (3); Church Yth Grp; Hosp Aide; Library Aide; Band; Chorus; Color Guard; Drill Tm; Mrchg Band.

SPARKS, SUMMER L; Putnam City West HS; Oklahoma City, OK; (3); 39/300; Church Yth Grp; Cmnty Wkr; Drama Clb; FCA; GAA; Letterman Clb; Spanish Clb; Teachers Aide; Band; Church Choir; Band Qn Attendant; US Vllybl Team; Childrens Camp Sponsor; S Nazarene U; Elem Tchr.

SPARKS, TONY L; Choctaw HS; Jones, OK; (3); 21/317; Office Aide; Var Ftbl; Powder Puff Ftbl; Wt Lftg; High Hon Roll; NHS; Phys Thrpy.

SPARLING, DAVID P; Bishop Mcguinness HS; Oklahoma City, OK; (3); 8/134; VP Drama Clb; Science Clb; SADD; School Musical; School Play; Stage Crew; Pres NHS; Ntl Merit Ltr; Yale Clb Of Western OK 96.

SPAULDING, HEATHER L; Elgin HS; Elgin, OK; (2); 18/70; Church Yth Grp; Dance Clb; FCA; Letterman Clb; Office Aide; Treas Soph Cls; Treas Jr Cls; Bsktbl; Chrldng; Crs Cntry; Dance Tap/Jazz/Ballet 9 Yrs; Schl Pgnt 2 Yrs; Chrldng Camp Cnslr; Southwestern OK ST Univ.

SPEAKER, JESS; Mc Loud HS; Mc Loud, OK; (3); Pres Church Yth Grp; FBLA; Sec FTA; Jazz Band; Mrchg Band; Rep Stu Cncl; Hon Roll; Eagle Sct; Cmnty Theatre; Life Guide; Theatre.

SPEAR, B J; Edmond North HS; Edmond, OK; (2); Church Yth Grp; JV Crs Cntry; Mgr(s); Chrch Day Care Vol; Comp Engr.

SPEAR, BROOKE M; Mannford HS; Mannford, OK; (3); 9/113; Church Yth Grp; Drama Clb; Girl Scts; NFL; Speech Tm; School Play; Hon Roll; Reg Spch Champ; St Spch Champ; Chrch Yth Drama; Psych.

SPEAR, JACK; Hanna Public Schl; Hanna, OK; (1); 2/11; Quiz Bowl; Bsktbl; Cit Awd; Hon Roll; Interschlstc Meet; OHLAP Stu; OU.

SPEAR, KIM L; Yukon Middle HS; Yukon, OK; (1); Church Yth Grp; FHA; Chorus; Church Choir; Variety Show; Hon Roll; Southern Norarene Univ.

SPEAR, WADE O; Central Mid-HS; Norman, OK; (2); FCA; Mu Alpha Theta; Spanish Clb; Ofcr Stu Cncl; Ofcr Bsbl; Ftbl; Hon Roll; House Of Rep Page; Univ Of OK.

SPEARS, DEIDRA A; Jay HS; Eucha, OK; (3); Church Yth Grp; 4-H; FHA; Girl Scts; Cit Awd; 4-H Awd; Hon Roll; Girl Sct Silver & Gold Awds; Feather Of Many Colors.

SPEARS, MONICA; Tahlequah Sr HS; Tahlequah, OK; (4); Office Aide; High Hon Roll; Jr NHS; NHS; Pres Acad Fit Awd; Rotary Intl Schlr; Natl Hnr Roll; All Amer Schlr; Northeastern ST U; Spec Ed.

SPEARS, ROBERT L; Pawnee HS; Pawnee, OK; (3); Boy Scts; Church Yth Grp; Natl Beta Clb; Band; Jazz Band; Mrchg Band; Ftbl; Hon Roll; Prfct Atten Awd.

SPEARS, STEPHANIE J; Union Sr HS; Broken Arrow, OK; (3); 187/689; Church Yth Grp; Computer Clb; DECA; Girl Scts; Intnl Clb; Key Clb; Band; Yrbk; Hon Roll; NHS; Young Republicans; Young Astronauts; Northeastern ST U; Frgn Ed.

SPECKETER, BRANDON M; Putnam City North HS; Oklahoma City, OK; (1); Church Yth Grp; Bsktbl; Ftbl; Cit Awd; PC North Clay Culver Awd Of Excl; OK Univ; Arch.

SPECTOR, SHANA A; B T Washington HS; Tulsa, OK; (3); Temple Yth Grp; Stage Crew; Hon Roll; Jr NHS; NHS; Eco Clb Pres; Clnry Clb; Rabbi Rsnthl Awd.

SPEEGLE, ASHLEY B; Duncan HS; Duncan, OK; (1); Key Clb; Chorus; Trk; High Hon Roll; Hon Roll; NHS; Pres Schlr; OK Univ; Law Schl.

SPEER, AUSTIN K; Putnam City North HS; Oklahoma City, OK; (2); Boy Scts; Church Yth Grp; Church Choir; Orch; Eagle Sct Awd; OK Yth Symphny 95-; OK Yth Orch 96-; Clsc Rock Bnd Evolution; Untd Meth Chr Srvnt Orch; Engr/Music.

SPEER, EMMA; Seminole Jr Sr HS; Seminole, OK; (2); Drama Clb; FCA; French Clb; Math Clb; Thesps; Chorus; School Play; Rptr Nwsp; High Hon Roll; Hon Roll; Mock Trl; St One Act Play; Hstry Awd; UNLV.

SPEERS, ALLAIRE GUILIA; Putnam City North HS; Oklahoma City, OK; (1); Church Yth Grp; Cmnty Wkr; Drama Clb; French Clb; Key Clb; Chorus; Stage Crew; Rep Stu Cncl; Cit Awd.

SPEIR, SCOTT A; Wagoner Sr HS; Wagoner, OK; (3); Church Yth Grp; 4-H; Natl FFA Org; Ftbl; Wt Lftg; Wrstlng; Hon Roll; Prfct Atten Awd; Toppers Vlntr Fire Dept; Connors JC; Ag Tchr.

SPENCE, CHRIS E; Webster HS; Tulsa, OK; (3); Office Aide; Teachers Aide; Band; Var Crs Cntry; Trk; 2 Yrs Span; Ntve Amer Achvmnt Awd; Chem/Physcs Asst; Elec Engr.

SPENCE, CHRISTINA M; Mustang HS; Mustang, OK; (3); 1/380; Ofcr FHA; Key Clb; Scholastic Bowl; Teachers Aide; Nwsp; Gov Hon Prg Awd; NHS; Rnssnc Prog; 1st Pl Team Projs Schl Sci Fair 95; Med.

SPENCE, HEATHER; Meeker HS; Meeker, OK; (4); 11/74; Church Yth Grp; FBLA; Chorus; Church Choir; Hon Roll; NHS; Pres Acad Fit Awd; Natl Voc Tech Hnr Soc; , Th Pl Intro Bus FBLA St Spring Conf; Outstdng Stu Bus Office Tech; U Of Cntrl OK; Psych.

SPENCE, RUTH; Fairview HS; Fairview, OK; (1); 1/82; Church Yth Grp; FCA; Natl FFA Org; Scholastic Bowl; Band; Bsktbl; Sftbl; High Hon Roll; Radiology.

SPENCER, AMANDA A; Heavener HS; Heavener, OK; (1); Drama Clb; Band; Mrchg Band; School Play; Hon Roll; NHS; Child Psych.

SPENCER, BECKY S; Dewey HS; Dewey, OK; (1); 8/97; Church Yth Grp; Hon Roll; Pres Acad Fit Awd; Sngs Cntry Gspl Band; OK Bapt Univ; Nrs/Peds.

SPENCER, CALEAB; Heavener HS; Heavener, OK; (4); 30/90; Stage Crew; Rep Frsh Cls; Pres Sr Cls; Rep Stu Cncl; Capt Ftbl; Var Trk; Var Wt Lftg; Hon Roll; OK Natl Grd PFC; Murry ST Coll; Nursng.

SPENCER, CAROLYN S; Christian Heritage Acad; Oklahoma City, OK; (4); 1/50; Church Yth Grp; Cmnty Wkr; Chorus; School Play; Nwsp; Ofcr Jr Cls; VP Stu Cncl; Cit Awd; Pres Acad Fit Awd; Val; TX A&M; Eng; His.

SPENCER, CHERISH; Metro Christian Acad; Tulsa, OK; (1); Church Yth Grp; Chrldng; High Hon Roll; Prfct Atten Awd; Piano.

SPENCER, JENNIFER G; Jay HS; Eucha, OK; (3); Natl Beta Clb; Science Clb; Ed Nwsp; Rptr Jr Cls; Hon Roll; NHS; Clncl Psych.

SPENCER, KELLY V; Bartlesville Mid HS; Bartlesville, OK; (2); Drama Clb; French Clb; Chorus; School Play; Hon Roll; Mst Otstndng Chr Stu; Drama Tm; 3rd Pl In Natl Fr Exm; All St Chr; Dist Hnrs Chr; Cvtn Stu Of Mnth; Mscl Thtr.

SPENCER, MANDY; Central Schl; Lawton, OK; (3); FCA; FHA; Yrbk; VP Jr Cls; Var Bsktbl; Var Chrldng; Var Sftbl; Hon Roll; Cameron U; Acctng.

SPENCER, MARY; Welch Jr Sr HS; Welch, OK; (3); Church Yth Grp; FBLA; Quiz Bowl; SADD; Band; Chorus; Sec Stu Cncl; Chrldng; Hon Roll; Ntl Merit Ltr; Msns Stu Today Awd; Educ.

SPENCER, MELISSA R; Central HS; Tulsa, OK; (4); 9/177; Cmnty Wkr; FBLA; JA; Teachers Aide; Mrchg Band; Ofcr Sr Cls; Swmmng; High Hon Roll; NHS; OK St Univ; Bus Mgmt.

SPENCER, MICHAEL; Moore HS; Moore, OK; (2); JA; Red Cross Aide; Science Clb; Spanish Clb; Speech Tm; Temple Yth Grp; Socr; Hon Roll; NHS; U Of OK; Med.

SPENCER, ROBIN L; Lawton Sr HS; Lawton, OK; (2); Church Yth Grp; Natl FFA Org; Chorus; Church Choir; Chrch Yth Mission Team; OK Bapt U; Nrs.

SPENCER, ROSSLYN; Chickasha HS; Chickasha, OK; (3); Am Leg Aux Girls St; Church Yth Grp; Cmnty Wkr; 4-H; HOBY; Natl FFA Org; Quiz Bowl; Scholastic Bowl; Spanish Clb; Band; Natl Cath Yth Conf Gst Spkr 95; Notre Dame; Law.

SPENCER, SUZANNE; Christian Heritage Acad; Oklahoma City, OK; (4); 1/53; Cmnty Wkr; Scholastic Bowl; Chorus; Church Choir; School Play; Nwsp; Ofcr Jr Cls; Ofcr Stu Cncl; Cit Awd; Val; Ballet; TX A&M; Engl.

SPENCER, TRISHA; Midwest City HS; Midwest City, OK; (4); Drama Clb; FHA; Office Aide; Spanish Clb; Varsity Clb; School Play; Yrbk; Chrldng; Gym; All-Amer Chrldr; Rose ST; Phy Ther.

SPEZIO, TIFFANY; Southeast HS; Oklahoma City, OK; (4); 13/70; Church Yth Grp; Key Clb; Office Aide; ROTC; Spanish Clb; Band; Chorus; Color Guard; Drill Tm; Orch; Air Force Assn Awd; OK Air Force Assn Cadet Of Yr 95; Tchr Cadet Clss; U Of OK Norman; Psych.

SPICER, CHRISTINA; Sperry Sr HS; Sperry, OK; (4); 33/76; Church Yth Grp; Drama Clb; Spanish Clb; Band; Chorus; Church Choir; Mrchg Band; School Play; Chrldng; Key Clb; Color Gd Cap; TJC; Med.

SPIDLE, CRYSTAL L; Westmoore HS; Oklahoma City, OK; (2); Church Yth Grp; Cmnty Wkr; Office Aide; Church Choir; Hon Roll; Soc Wrkr.

SPIEGLE, JOSHUA R; West Middle HS; Norman, OK; (2); Computer Clb; Letterman Clb; Spanish Clb; Thesps; Band; Jazz Band; Mrchg Band; Orch; Pep Band; Ltrd Bnd; Publshd Wrtr; Notre Dame; Zoology.

SPIGNER JR, KENNY; Fox Sr HS; Ratliff City, OK; (4); 2/27; Church Yth Grp; VP Frsh Cls; VP Soph Cls; Pres Jr Cls; Pres Sr Cls; Var Capt Bsktbl; Var Capt Ftbl; NHS; Sal; Outstndng African Amer Teen; 3 Xs All Amer Schlr; Mr Schl; UCO; Acctng.

SPIKES, VIRGINIA D; Stratford Schl; Stratford, OK; (2); Hon Roll; Cndtns For Lvng II 10th Grd; Highest Grd Awd; Frosh Class Queen; OK Schl Photo; Mdlng/Actng.

SPINDLER, REBECCA D; Putnam City North HS; Oklahoma City, OK; (1); 3-D; Natl Lib Of Poetry Mem; Daycare Vol; U Of OK; Child Psych.

SPINKS, JESSICA D; Mc Loud HS; Mc Loud, OK; (2); Church Yth Grp; FCA; FBLA; Pep Clb; VP Jr Cls; Sec Stu Cncl; JV Var Bsktbl; Hon Roll; NHS; Prfct Atten Awd; Life Guides Peer Helpers; Chrldng Vol Coach; OK Univ; Child Care.

SPINNER, BRAD; Guthrie Sr HS; Edmond, OK; (4); 1/175; Am Leg Boys St; Church Yth Grp; Cmnty Wkr; Math Clb; Mu Alpha Theta; Quiz Bowl; Spanish Clb; SADD; Rep Jr Cls; Rep Sr Cls; Masonic Acad Excllnc Awd; Lions Clb Stu Of Month; OK ST U; Math.

SPIRLOCK, LINDSAY D; Hilldale HS; Muskogee, OK; (3); Church Yth Grp; Cmnty Wkr; FCA; VP Key Clb; Mu Alpha Theta; Church Choir; Rep Treas Stu Cncl; Var Chrldng; Var Trk; High Hon Roll; Rotary Yth Ldrshp Awd Camp; Northeastern ST Univ.

SPIRLOCK, TYLER A; Sapulpa Sr HS; Sapulpa, OK; (3); Church Yth Grp; Cmnty Wkr; FCA; Letterman Clb; Var L Ftbl; Var L Socr; Var Wt Lftg; Hon Roll; NHS; Mission Wk Tour.

SPITZ, EMILY; Fairview HS; Fairview, OK; (1); Church Yth Grp; FHA; Var Sftbl; Hon Roll; Piano; U Of OK; Mtrlgy.

SPLINTER, DAVID; Classen Schl; Oklahoma City, OK; (2); 1/120; Letterman Clb; Math Tm; Model UN; Socr; Wrstlng; High Hon Roll; NHS; Val; Spanish Clb; Band; Aikido; Clscl Quitar; Stdnt Of Yr Awd; Chem.

SPOMER, STEPHANIE R; Thomas Jr Sr HS; Thomas, OK; (2); Chorus; High Hon Roll; Hon Roll.

SPOMER, TAMRA L; Thomas Jr Sr HS; Thomas, OK; (1); 17/50; FBLA; FHA; Hon Roll.

SPORES, MISTY; Carl Albert HS; Midwest City, OK; (4); 41/259; FCA; Key Clb; Sec Pep Clb; Chorus; Nwsp; Ed Yrbk; Var Sftbl; High Hon Roll; Jr NHS; NHS; U Of OK; Broadcasting; Jrnlsm.

SPRADLIN, ANGELA B; Grandfield Jr Sr HS; Grandfield, OK; (3); 4/25; Church Yth Grp; Quiz Bowl; Yrbk; Treas Jr Cls; Var Bsktbl; Var Sftbl; Var Trk; Hon Roll; NHS; Nom To Natl Yng Ldr Conf; All Amerschol; Class Fvt; OK St Univ.

SPRADLIN, BRIAN; Grandfield Jr Sr HS; Grandfield, OK; (1); 1/22; Church Yth Grp; FCA; VICA; Rep Stu Cncl; Var Bsbl; Var Bsktbl; Var Ftbl; JV Wt Lftg; Hon Roll; TSA Pres & Tchnlgy Bowl; OK U; Law.

SPRADLIN, CHARLES A; Porum HS; Porum, OK; (3); FCA; Natl FFA Org; Office Aide; Var L Bsbl; Var L Bsktbl; Cit Awd; Hon Roll; Pres Acad Fit Awd; Connors ST Coll.

SPRADLIN, JEREMY W; Asher Schl; Asher, OK; (2); Church Yth Grp; FHA; Natl FFA Org; Var Bsktbl; Hon Roll; Fish/Game Warden.

SPRADLIN, TERRI; Miami Sr HS; Miami, OK; (4); 2/110; Debate Tm; Drama Clb; Pres Science Clb; Quiz Bowl; Mrchg Band; Tennis; Hon Roll; NHS; St Schlr; Church Actvts; OK ST U; Cell/Moleculr Bio.

SPRADLING, LAURA HEATH; Bishop Kelley HS; Tulsa, OK; (2); Art Clb; Socr; Hon Roll; Earth Clb Pres; U Of VA.

SPRAY, TIMOTHY; Eisenhower Sr HS; Lawton, OK; (3); Ofcr Bsbl; Sftbl; Wt Lftg; Hon Roll; Jr NHS; NHS; U Of NC; Acctng; Math.

SPRIGGS, CHERYL L; Choctaw HS; Choctaw, OK; (3); Acctng.

SPRING, JESSICA; Deer Creek HS; Edmond, OK; (3); 11/110; Cmnty Wkr; FCA; Science Clb; Yrbk; Chrldng; Powder Puff Ftbl; Score Keeper; Socr; High Hon Roll; NHS; CO Schl Of Mines; Dntl.

SPRING, NATALIE; Deer Creek HS; Edmond, OK; (2); Church Yth Grp; FCA; FBLA; Science Clb; School Play; Stage Crew; VP Frsh Cls; Var L Bsktbl; Var L Chrldng; Trk; Engr; Lawyer.

SPRINGER, CHARISSA; Midwest City HS; Midwest City, OK; (4); 36/419; Church Yth Grp; Cmnty Wkr; FCA; FHA; Spanish Clb; SADD; Nwsp; Stat Bsktbl; Stat Ftbl; High Hon Roll; Senate Page; Schlstc Stu Of Month; Jr Rotarian; OK ST U; Phys Thrpy.

SPROUL, JAMI; Fairview HS; Fairview, OK; (3); 1/60; Natl FFA Org; Sec Jr Cls; High Hon Roll; NHS; OSU.

SPROUL, JESSE; Fairview HS; Fairview, OK; (3); 1/60; VP Natl FFA Org; Pres Jr Cls; High Hon Roll; NHS; HS Acad Bwl Team; Ust Pl St FFA Jr Parlmntry Prdcr Team; 3rd Pl FFA Ag-Sci Spch Wnnr; OK ST U.

SPROUL, SCOTT; Fairview HS; Isabella, OK; (4); 28/55; Church Yth Grp; FBLA; Teachers Aide; Hon Roll; FFA Prlmnty Procedure Team; FFA Sentinel; FFA Prlmntrn; Chptr FFA ST Degree; Stu Of Month; OK ST Univ; Animal Sci.

SPROUL, STACY L; Fairview HS; Isabella, OK; (2); Church Yth Grp; FCA; Natl FFA Org; Var Bsktbl; Hon Roll; Prfct Atten Awd; OK Jr Brangus Breeders VP; Southwestern OK ST Univ.

SPROUSE, KAROLYN E; Okmulgee HS; Okmulgee, OK; (4); Cmnty Wkr; FBLA; FHA; Office Aide; Spanish Clb; Color Guard; Drill Tm; Drm Mjr(t); Hon Roll; Tulsa Comm Coll; Bus.

SPRUILL, ERIC L; Tecumseh HS; Tecumseh, OK; (2); Church Yth Grp; Var Ftbl; Var Trk; Hon Roll; U Of OK; Broadcast Jrnlsm.

SPRUILL, JEFF R; Moore HS; Moore, OK; (3); Am Leg Boys St; Boy Scts; Church Yth Grp; Pres Drama Clb; Band; Chorus; Mrchg Band; School Musical; School Play; U Of OK.

SPRUILL, KANDICE; Moore HS; Moore, OK; (2); Art Clb; Church Yth Grp; Dance Clb; Drama Clb; Natl FFA Org; Pep Clb; Science Clb; Speech Tm; School Play; 4-H Awd; OK ST U.

SPRUNGER, HEATHER; Canton HS; Canton, OK; (4); 10/46; Church Yth Grp; Rep FCA; Pres FHA; SADD; Flag Corp; Pres Soph Cls; VP Jr Cls; Capt L Bsktbl; Var Chrldng; Capt L Trk; NW OK St Univ; Elem Ed.

SPURGEON, BOBBIE; Alva HS; Hopeton, OK; (4); 6/72; Church Yth Grp; FCA; 4-H; GAA; Key Clb; NFL; Band; Yrbk; Sftbl; High Hon Roll; N W Sr Schlr; RYLA Delg; Northwestern; Sprts Thrpy.

SPURLIN, ASPEN; Reydon HS; Reydon, OK; (1); 1/20; FHA; Girl Scts; Chorus; Bsktbl; High Hon Roll.

SPURLIN, STEFANIE; Edmond North HS; Edmond, OK; (4); 1/336; Am Leg Aux Girls St; Church Yth Grp; Cmnty Wkr; FCA; Treas VP French Clb; Pres Sr Cls; Var L Tennis; NHS; Val; Im 3rd Awd 92 & 93; Chmbr Of Cmmrc Ldrshp Awd; Wake Forest U; Immnlgst.

SQUIRE, AMANDA F; Kansas Schl; Colcord, OK; (4); 2/29; FHA; Letterman Clb; Band; Flag Corp; Sal.

SQUIRE, RYAN N; Northeast HS; Del City, OK; (3); FBLA; Science Clb; Church Choir; Pres Stu Cncl; Var Capt Bsbl; Var Golf; Cit Awd; NHS; High Hon Roll; Hon Roll; Rotry Yth Ldrshp Awd; Close-Up Washington; Dist Stu Cncl Pres; Southwestern OK ST U; Med.

SRAMEK, PETR; Southeast HS; Del City, OK; (4); Boy Scts; Church Yth Grp; FCA; Model UN; Varsity Clb; Crs Cntry; Socr; Swmmng; Trk; Hon Roll; U OK; Arch.

SREAVES, AMBER; Grove HS; Grove, OK; (4); 1/105; Church Yth Grp; Computer Clb; FCA; GAA; Letterman Clb; Spanish Clb; SADD; Teachers Aide; Varsity Clb; Ofcr Bsbl; MO Southern ST Coll; Cmptr Sc.

SRUM, JAMIE; Blanchard Jr Sr HS; Blanchard, OK; (4); 1/72; Church Yth Grp; Computer Clb; Mu Alpha Theta; Spanish Clb; SADD; Band; Mrchg Band; NHS; Val; Natl Cmptr Clb Prlmntrn; Bible Schl Tchr; Mltpl Yr Lstng; Southwestern OK ST; Math.

STAATS, MEGAN; Macarthur Jr HS; Lawton, OK; (1); Church Yth Grp; FCA; Pep Clb; Science Clb; Pres Acpl Chr; Rep Stu Cncl; Capt Chrldng; Trk; VP Jr NHS; Mst Ath; Psych.

STACEY, DANIEL E; Norman Sr HS; Norman, OK; (4); Church Yth Grp; L JV Bsbl; Hon Roll; Army Rsrve.

STACEY, MARYBETH; Ft Gibson HS; Fort Gibson, OK; (1); Church Yth Grp; Spanish Clb; Band; High Hon Roll; NHS; Pres Acad Fit Awd.

STACH, CHARRI L; Warner HS; Warner, OK; (1); Art Clb; Cmnty Wkr; English Clb; Math Clb; Math Tm; Science Clb; Powder Puff Ftbl; Sftbl; Hon Roll; OK Parent & Tchrs Assn Babysitter; Conners ST Coll; Pediatrics.

STACKLER, JULIA M; Bishop Kelley HS; Tulsa, OK; (1); Church Yth Grp; Cmnty Wkr; Hosp Aide; Spanish Clb; Bsktbl; Vllybl; High Hon Roll.

STACY, JAMES S; Heavener HS; Heavener, OK; (1); 21/101; Natl FFA Org; Ftbl; Golf; Trk; Wt Lftg; Hon Roll.

STACY, JANET; Tahlequah Sr HS; Tahlequah, OK; (4); 21/251; Library Aide; Science Clb; Sec SADD; VP Band; Mrchg Band; Rptr Nwsp; Yrbk; Hon Roll; NHS; Pres Acad Fit Awd; Lib Sci.

STAFFORD, AIMEE M; Putnam City HS; Oklahoma City, OK; (2); Church Yth Grp; Cmnty Wkr; Drama Clb; French Clb; Office Aide; Chorus; Church Choir; School Musical; Stage Crew; Rep Soph Cls; Tchr.

STAFFORD, ASHLEY; Edmond North HS; Edmond, OK; (4); Church Yth Grp; Cmnty Wkr; FCA; Pres JA; Ofcr Stu Cncl; Chrldng; Pom Pon; Art Clb; FHA; Key Clb; OK City Jr Rotarian; Edmond Exch Yth Of Month; Edmond Masonica Lodge Schlrsp; OK ST Univ; Elem Ed.

STAFFORD, CASSANDRA; Wetumka Jr Sr HS; Wetumka, OK; (3); FCA; Pep Clb; Band; Mrchg Band; Yrbk; Bsktbl; Chrldng; Sftbl; Trk; Hon Roll; Acad Team; OK Univ; Phy Thrpst.

STAFFORD, DEDRA; Moore HS; Oklahoma City, OK; (4); JCL; Latin Clb; SADD; Chorus; Jr NHS; NHS; Pres Acad Fit Awd; U Of OK; Premed.

STAFFORD, GREGORY R; Dewey HS; Dewey, OK; (3); Band; Jazz Band; Mrchg Band; Pep Band; Co-Ed Yrbk; Hon Roll; NHS; Quiz Bowl; 4th Chair Alto Sax 96 OK Bapt All ST; 2nd Chair Baritone Sax 95 Mideast Hon Bnd.

STAFFORD, RUSSELL E; Edmond North HS; Edmond, OK; (1); 192/460; Church Yth Grp; JV Tennis; OK ST.

STAFFORD, SALLY E; Bishop Kelley HS; Tulsa, OK; (4); 33/148; Cmnty Wkr; Drama Clb; French Clb; Hosp Aide; Red Cross Aide; Service Clb; Rptr Nwsp; Yrbk; Lit Mag; French Hon Soc; Drms & Prcssn Instrmnts; Fr Lnc Mgzns; Tls Bnd Cltn; Ncl Intl Exchng Stu; Fren St Trnmnt Awds; UT At Austin; Coll Prof.

STAGGS, SARAH; Sapulpa Sr HS; Sapulpa, OK; (3); 43/300; Church Yth Grp; Hosp Aide; Science Clb; Ed Nwsp; Mgr(s); JV Stat Socr; Hon Roll; NHS; Prfct Atten Awd; Pres Acad Fit Awd; Aviation/Aerospace; Astronomy; Ftbl-Soccer Trnr; Aerospace Engrng.

STAGNER, CARA; Christian Heritage Acad; Norman, OK; (4); 1/53; Church Yth Grp; Chorus; School Play; Sec Treas Stu Cncl; Hon Roll; Ntl Merit Ltr; Val; Talent Review; TRUTH Secy & Treas; U Of OK; Engrng.

STAHLMAN, LESLIE R; Bartlesville Sr HS; Bartlesville, OK; (3); Church Yth Grp; FCA; 4-H; FHA; Letterman Clb; Natl FFA Org; Pep Clb; Chorus; Stage Crew; Rep Soph Cls; Ftbl Game Flmr.

STAHLMAN, TECIA; Fargo Schl; Fargo, OK; (2); 4/15; FHA; HOBY; Natl Beta Clb; Church Choir; School Play; Bsktbl; Sftbl; Cit Awd; DAR Awd; Hon Roll.

STAHRE, MANDY A; Altus Sr HS; Altus, OK; (4); Art Clb; Band; Jazz Band; Mrchg Band; School Musical; JETS Awd; Jr NHS; NHS; U North TX.

STAKE, PAUL R; Amber Pocasset Jr Sr HS; Blanchard, OK; (2); Church Yth Grp; Spanish Clb; OU; Acctng.

STAKEM, TIMMY D; Casady Schl; Oklahoma City, OK; (2); FCA; German Clb; Letterman Clb; SADD; Varsity Clb; Sprt Ed Nwsp; JV Var Bsbl; JV Var Bsktbl; Var Crs Cntry; High Hon Roll; Comm Club Soc Chm; Thomas T Tongue Schlrshp 95.

STALCUP, CAYDEE; Ponca City Sr HS; Ponca City, OK; (1); Church Yth Grp; Pep Clb; Chorus; Variety Show; Var Chrldng; High Hon Roll; Hon Roll; Kiwanis Awd; Stdnt Cncl Pres 95-; Abilene Chrstn U; Drmtlgst.

STALCUP, KATIE A; Sapulpa Sr HS; Sapulpa, OK; (3); 3/299; Church Yth Grp; Cmnty Wkr; Band; Mrchg Band; Hon Roll; NHS; Ntl Merit Ltr; Spanish NHS.

STALCUP, SAM R; Ponca City Sr HS; Ponca City, OK; (3); Am Leg Boys St; Boy Scts; Church Yth Grp; Cmnty Wkr; FCA; Yrbk; Pres Soph Cls; Sec Jr Cls; Rep Stu Cncl; L Crs Cntry; Acad St Champ C Cntry; Olymp Trch Brer; Pres Natl Hnr Soc.

STALEY, HEATHER T; Glenpool HS; Mounds, OK; (2); Spanish Clb; Bsktbl; Mgr(s); Powder Puff Ftbl; Score Keeper; Vllybl; Wt Lftg; TJC; Police.

STALEY, JANET S; Maysville Jr Sr HS; Maysville, OK; (2); Church Yth Grp; VP FHA; Band; Chorus; Mrchg Band; Hon Roll; Soph Cls Qn; East Cntrl Univ; Adv/Music.

STALEY, MAUTRA L; Ardmore HS; Ardmore, OK; (3); Latin Clb; Math Clb; Mu Alpha Theta; Science Clb; Drill Tm; Co-Ed Yrbk; Ofcr Stu Cncl; Hon Roll; NHS; Hon Schlr Acad Achvmnt Awd OSU Alumni Assn; Pre Med.

STALL, KARA G; Owasso Sr HS; Claremore, OK; (3); 84/357; FCA; Spanish Clb; Rep Stu Cncl; Var Crs Cntry; Var Trk; High Hon Roll; Hon Roll; TAG DFY.

STALLCUP, SHERAH Z; Stonewall Jr-Sr HS; Stonewall, OK; (1); 4/21; 4-H; Scholastic Bowl; School Play; Bsktbl; Sftbl; 4-H Awd; Hon Roll; Plcd 2nd Alg I/Reg Schlstc Cmptn.

STALLINGS, JOSH; Glencoe Public Schl; Glencoe, OK; (4); 3/15; Church Yth Grp; FCA; Office Aide; Pep Clb; School Play; Pres Yrbk; Var Bsbl; JV Bsktbl; Hon Roll; Prfct Atten Awd; Rtry Yth Ldrshp Awd; Phys Thrpy.

STALLINGS, LINDSAY P; Jay HS; Jay, OK; (3); FBLA; Girl Scts; HOBY; Natl Beta Clb; VP Band; Jazz Band; Rptr Nwsp; Sec Treas Jr Cls; VP Stu Cncl; Rep NHS.

STALLINGS, MICHAEL; Tishomingo HS; Tishomingo, OK; (4); 10/56; Church Yth Grp; Quiz Bowl; Teachers Aide; Band; Drm Mjr(t); Pres Sr Cls; Bsktbl; Crs Cntry; Trk; Hon Roll; ECU.

STALLINGS, TABITHA; Glencoe Public Schl; Glencoe, OK; (2); 2/26; Church Yth Grp; FCA; French Clb; Rep Stu Cncl; Var Bsktbl; Var Chrldng; Var Sftbl; High Hon Roll; NHS; Prfct Atten Awd; OK ST U; Lawyer.

STALSBY, REBECCA; El Reno Sr HS; El Reno, OK; (3); Drama Clb; FTA; Girl Scts; Math Clb; Band; Mrchg Band; Hon Roll; Environmental Clb; Upward Bound; Drama Clb; Comp Sci.

STALSBY, SARAH; El Reno Sr HS; El Reno, OK; (3); 23/196; Drama Clb; Girl Scts; Math Clb; SADD; Band; Mrchg Band; High Hon Roll; Jr NHS; NHS; Envrnmntl Clb; Upward Bnd; Bio.

STALZER, ROBERT; Stillwater Jr HS; Stillwater, OK; (1); Band; Mrchg Band; Pep Band; High Hon Roll; Pres Ed Awd.

STALZER, THOMAS; Stillwater Jr HS; Stillwater, OK; (1); Band; Mrchg Band; Pep Band; High Hon Roll; Pres Ed Awd Prgm/Outstdng Acad Achvmnt.

STAMETZ, TIFFANY J; Hooker Jr-Sr HS; Aurora, CO; (4); 5/36; Teachers Aide; Var Sftbl; High Hon Roll; Hon Roll; NHS; Outstanding Sci Awd; CO ST U; Comp Sci.

STAMPER, DUSTIN; Indiahoma Schl; Indiahoma, OK; (3); #2 in class; Church Yth Grp; HOBY; Natl FFA Org; Rptr Nwsp; Rep Jr Cls; High Hon Roll; Okmulgee Tech; Chef.

STAMPS, BRANDON J; Okay Jr Sr HS; Wagoner, OK; (1); Church Yth Grp; Pres 4-H; Band; Mrchg Band; 4-H Livstck Judgng Team; 4-H Ambssdr & 1st Pl Intrmdt St Tractr Drivng Skills; Natl Jr Angus Assn.

STAMPS, KRISTY R; Sapulpa Sr HS; Sapulpa, OK; (2); Hon Roll; Bus Mgmt.

STANBERRY, JANETTE; Bowlegs Schl; Maud, OK; (4); 1/25; FBLA; FHA; Natl Beta Clb; Quiz Bowl; Band; Nwsp; Yrbk; High Hon Roll; NHS; Val; St FBLA Conf Cmptr Applctns 1st Pl; Smnl JC Intrschlstc Mt Eng Essays 1st Pl, Gmtry 5th Pl; Seminole JC; Cmptr Sci.

STANBERRY, MELISSA; Bowlegs Schl; Maud, OK; (1); FBLA; FHA; Natl Beta Clb; Pep Clb; Quiz Bowl; Band; Mrchg Band; Orch; Pep Band; Cit Awd; Seminole ST Coll; Comp Sci.

STANDEFER, JULIE D; Putnam City North HS; Oklahoma City, OK; (3); 52/474; Hosp Aide; Red Cross Aide; Sec Science Clb; Spanish Clb; Orch; NHS; Hosp Vol; Pre-Med; Nrsng.

STANDIFER, CARLA L; Duncan HS; Duncan, OK; (3); Church Yth Grp; Computer Clb; Hosp Aide; Chorus; Church Choir; School Musical; School Play; Swing Chorus; Variety Show; Ofcr Stu Cncl; Chorale; Rflctns Show Choir; Lttrwmn; Ls Rnts Scl Clb; Karate; SS Tchr; U Central OK; Reg Nrs.

STANDINGWATER, JAMIE G; Salina HS; Salina, OK; (1); JV Bsktbl; Var Sftbl; Gov Hon Prg Awd; High Hon Roll; Bio I, Govt, Span I & OK His Hnr Pins; Handcppd Childrn Phy Thrpst.

STANDRICH, ANTHONY J; Noble HS; Norman, OK; (3); Church Yth Grp; Mu Alpha Theta; Scholastic Bowl; Science Clb; Spanish Clb; SADD; Church Choir; Hon Roll; NHS; Ntl Merit Ltr; Amer Legion Cert Of Schl Awd.

STANDRICH, JENNIFER; Putnam City West HS; Adrmore, OK; (4); 13/298; Church Yth Grp; Spanish Clb; Ed Nwsp; Pres Jr NHS; NHS; Natl Mrt Commended Stu; Hnr Grad; U Of Cntrl OK; Missionary.

STANDRIDGE, KIM; Little Axe Sr HS; Newalla, OK; (3); Art Clb; Dance Clb; Acpl Chr; Chorus; Drill Tm; Powder Puff Ftbl; Sftbl; Trk; High Hon Roll; NHS; East Central; Vet.

STANDRIDGE, SUZANEE; Blair Schl; Blair, OK; (3); Natl Beta Clb; Speech Tm; Sec Frsh Cls; Var Bsktbl; Var Sftbl; Var Trk; High Hon Roll; Jr NHS; NHS; Ntl Merit Schol.

STANFIELD, KARA L; Edmond Memorial HS; Edmond, OK; (3); 1/400; Church Yth Grp; Debate Tm; Key Clb; Mu Alpha Theta; NFL; Spanish Clb; Sec NHS; Acad Lttr; OK St Univ; Vet.

STANFORD, AMANDA R; Panola HS; Red Oak, OK; (2); Sec 4-H; Natl FFA Org; Treas Frsh Cls; Treas Soph Cls; Var Bsktbl; Var Sftbl; Hon Roll; Prfct Atten Awd; FFA Spch Tm; FFA Livestock Shw Tm; E OK St Col; Animal Sci.

STANFORD, CANDI; Oologah-Talala Schl; Talala, OK; (1); Church Yth Grp; GAA; Pep Clb; Varsity Clb; Chrldng; Diving; Powder Puff Ftbl; Score Keeper; Sftbl; Swmmng; Natl Chrldr Assn All Amer Chrldr Frosh Yr; Alg I Awd Frosh Yr; Tchr/Gymnastics Coach.

STANFORD, CHELLE A; Yukon HS; Yukon, OK; (3); 124/409; French Clb; FHA; SADD; Socr; Trk; Hon Roll; OK Univ.

STANGE, JOSH; Mustang HS; Mustang, OK; (3); Church Yth Grp; Band; L Bsbl; L Ftbl; Phillips Univ Hnr Bnd; Bnd Ltr; Acctg/Sprts Med.

STANGL, MELISSA; Clinton HS; Clinton, OK; (2); 12/165; Church Yth Grp; Sec Key Clb; Spanish Clb; Band; Sprt Ed Nwsp; Rep Soph Cls; Chrldng; High Hon Roll; Hon Roll; Kiwanis Awd; TX-OK Dist Ed Of Key Clb Intnl 96-97, Lt Governor 95-96; Boston Univ; Jrnlsm; Commnctn.

STANGLE, NICOLE; Owasso Sr HS; Owasso, OK; (3); 18/357; Drama Clb; French Clb; Key Clb; School Play; Stage Crew; Ofcr Jr Cls; High Hon Roll; Hon Roll; NHS; Chorus; TAG; U Of OK; Pre-Med.

STANGLIN, AMY I; Colbert Jr Sr HS; Colbert, OK; (2); 16/55; Drama Clb; FHA; Chorus; Ofcr Stu Cncl; Span Clb; Show Chr; Southeastern; Elem Tchr.

STANHOUSE, KYLE O; Heritage Hall Schl; Oklahoma City, OK; (2); Cmnty Wkr; Hosp Aide; Letterman Clb; Mu Alpha Theta; Spanish Clb; Rptr Nwsp; Var Bsbl; Var Bsktbl; High Hon Roll; Hon Roll.

STANLEY, BRANDY R; Henryetta Sr HS; Henryetta, OK; (4); Church Yth Grp; Cmnty Wkr; English Clb; FCA; FHA; Girl Scts; Library Aide; Scholastic Bowl; Spanish Clb; Teachers Aide; Hnrs Cls; GATE; All Dist Band; OK ST U; Bus Admin.

STANLEY, DANIELLE L; Mc Lain Career Acad; Tulsa, OK; (4); Dance Clb; Pep Clb; ROTC; Chorus; Church Choir; Nwsp; Ofcr Stu Cncl; Cit Awd; Hon Roll; NHS; MS St; RN.

STANLEY, ERIN; Bartlesville Sr HS; Bartlesville, OK; (3); 1/441; Church Yth Grp; Cmnty Wkr; Dance Clb; FCA; FBLA; Red Cross Aide; Teachers Aide; Yrbk; Pom Pon; High Hon Roll.

STANLEY, ERIN N; Putnam City West HS; Bethany, OK; (2); Church Yth Grp; Intnl Clb; Spanish Clb; Band; Jazz Band; Mrchg Band; Orch; Pep Band; JV Swmmng; Gov Hon Prg Awd; Super & Excl Ratings At Dist & St Music Cont; Silver Strings Of Putnam City; Chrch Mission Trips & Orc; U Of TX; Archaeology; Music.

STANLEY, GREG B; Mid-Del Christian Schl; Oklahoma City, OK; (4); CAP; Chorus; Yrbk; VP Jr Cls; VP Sr Cls; High Hon Roll; Ntl Merit Ltr; Eastern OK Acad Schlsp; Rose ST; Petroleum Engrng.

STANLEY, KARI; Tomlinson Jr HS; Lawton, OK; (1); 49/318; FHA; Flag Corp; Rep Stu Cncl; Var Pom Pon; Var Tennis; Hon Roll; Jr NHS; Pres Acad Fit Awd; Math SW Interschlstc Meet; U Corpus Christi; Marine Bio.

STANLEY, MELISSA K; Hooker Jr-Sr HS; Hooker, OK; (3); 6/45; Church Yth Grp; FCA; FHA; Chorus; Church Choir; School Musical; Stage Crew; Yrbk; Rep Frsh Cls; Rep Jr Cls; OK Bapt All-ST Yth Choir/Orch; OK Bapt Univ.

STANLEY, SAMANTHA D; Mustang HS; Yukon, OK; (1); Girl Scts; Office Aide; Woodworking Blue Ribbon St Cmptn; U Of OK.

STANLEY, SARAH; Dale Sr HS; Shawnee, OK; (3); 4/55; HOBY; Sec Spanish Clb; SADD; Band; Flag Corp; Rep Soph Cls; Capt Bsktbl; Sec NHS; Phys Ed.

STAPLES, RYAN P; Mannford HS; Mannford, OK; (2); Bus Profs of Am; FCA; FBLA; Science Clb; Spanish Clb; Pres Soph Cls; Pres Jr Cls; Chrldng; Ftbl; Golf; Plastic Surgeon.

STAPLETON, ELICIA; Oklahoma Union Schl; Wann, OK; (4); 7/42; Rep FBLA; VP FHA; Sec Spanish Clb; Nwsp; Yrbk; Stat Ftbl; Mgr Wrstlng; High Hon Roll; NHS; Chorus; Wrestling Homcmng Qn; Coffeyville CC; Horticulture.

STAPLETON, SHARI; Moore HS; Moore, OK; (2); Church Yth Grp; Latin Clb; Model UN; Scholastic Bowl; Science Clb; Chorus; Stage Crew; Ed Nwsp; Ed Phtg Yrbk; JV Computer Clb; Piano, Reading & Fishing; OSU; Med.

STAPP, CHANCE D; Westmoore HS; Oklahoma City, OK; (3); Church Yth Grp; Letterman Clb; Var L Wrstlng; Jr NHS; NHS; Wtrskiing; OK ST U; Vet Sci.

STAPP, KELLY D; Shawnee Sr HS; Shawnee, OK; (2); Church Yth Grp; FCA; Pep Clb; Spanish Clb; JV Fld Hcky; Pom Pon; Tennis; Comptv Dncng; Spirit Brigade; SOS; Mrktg/Early Chldhd Dev.

STARK, AMY; Stigler HS; Whitefield, OK; (3); Church Yth Grp; FCA; Pep Clb; SADD; Chorus; Church Choir; Rptr Nwsp; Hon Roll; Church Youth Cmmtte; Eastern OK ST Coll; Phrmcy.

STARK, JULIE D; Lexington HS; Lexington, OK; (4); Church Yth Grp; FHA; Office Aide; Spanish Clb; Teachers Aide; Hon Roll; FHA Soph Rep, Prtr & Sec; Sr Cls Favorite; East Cntrl Univ.

STARK, SHANNON; North Intermediate HS; Broken Arrow, OK; (1); Church Yth Grp; FCA; Latin Clb; Science Clb; Chrldng; Hon Roll; CIA.

STARKS, KENDRA L; Stillwater Sr HS; Stillwater, OK; (3); 96/353; Am Leg Aux Girls St; Church Yth Grp; Dance Clb; DECA; FCA; FBLA; Key Clb; Latin Clb; Natl Beta Clb; Pep Clb; Ldrshp Tomorrow Cls IV; Soph Ftbl Hmncmng Qn Attend; Universal Dance Assn All Star; OK ST U.

STARKS, LEAMETRIA E; Star Spencer HS; Midwest City, OK; (2); Church Yth Grp; Hosp Aide; Band; Church Choir; Mrchg Band; Bsktbl; Tennis; Vllybl; Hon Roll; Voice Of Democracy St Cmptn 1st Pl Essay; OK Univ; Law Enforcement.

STARKS, MANDY; Vinita HS; Vinita, OK; (2); Church Yth Grp; FCA; GAA; Science Clb; Spanish Clb; Teachers Aide; School Play; Bsktbl; Chrldng; Trk; Envir Clb; OK U; Med.

STARKS, SHAUNA M; Cushing HS; Cushing, OK; (2); 8/181; Church Yth Grp; Math Clb; Science Clb; Spanish Clb; Teachers Aide; Ed Yrbk; Tennis; High Hon Roll; NHS; Sprts Med.

STARKS, SYNEL M; Union Intermediate HS; Tulsa, OK; (2); 271/881; French Clb; Trk; Hon Roll; Crdc Srgn.

STARKUS, ALBERT A; Silo HS; Durant, OK; (4); #6 in class; Church Yth Grp; Cmnty Wkr; Library Aide; Math Clb; Mu Alpha Theta; Quiz Bowl; Teachers Aide; Lit Mag; Var Bsbl; Hon Roll; Curriculum Conts Medals; Sci.

STARKUS, ASHLEY; Silo HS; Durant, OK; (3); Church Yth Grp; Cmnty Wkr; Drama Clb; 4-H; Pres Rptr FHA; Hosp Aide; Quiz Bowl; Rptr Nwsp; Sec Frsh Cls; Sftbl; Rnnr Up SOSU Ctznshp Bee St Level; SOSU; Anesthesiologist.

STARLING, GREGORY A; Mustang HS; Oklahoma City, OK; (2); Church Yth Grp; FCA; Letterman Clb; Varsity Clb; Rep Frsh Cls; Rep Soph Cls; Rep Jr Cls; Var Bsktbl; Var Crs Cntry; JV Capt Socr; 4 Time ST Fine Arts Chmpn; Natl Merit Awd Short Story; Sprts Ed Chrch Yth Nwsltr; Mech Engr/Literature.

STARNES, BENNETT P; B T Washington HS; Tulsa, OK; (4); 57/264; Boy Scts; Pres Church Yth Grp; Pres French Clb; German Clb; NFL; Scholastic Bowl; School Musical; School Play; VP Pres Sr Cls; Golf.

STARR, ASHLEY D; Bartlesville Mid HS; Bartlesville, OK; (2); Church Yth Grp; FBLA; Spanish Clb; Rep Stu Cncl; JV Pom Pon; Hon Roll.

STARR, BROOKE; Westmoore HS; Oklahoma City, OK; (4); Church Yth Grp; Chorus; Church Choir; OSU OKC; His Tchr.

STARR, MICAH S; Porum HS; Porum, OK; (4); Teachers Aide; Hon Roll; ST Comptn 3rd Pl Acctng; Carl Albert ST Coll Schlstc Mt 1st Pl Psych/2nd Pl Acctng.

STARR, RYAN A; Bartlesville Sr HS; Bartlesville, OK; (1); 1/475; Church Yth Grp; Dance Clb; Orch; L Var Crs Cntry; L Var Swmmng; L Var Trk; High Hon Roll; Pres Acad Fit Awd; All Amer AAU Natls & All St Crss Cntry; Competitive Soccer Clb.

STARR, TARA; Altus Sr HS; Altus, OK; (4); #35 in class; Am Leg Aux Girls St; Church Yth Grp; Cmnty Wkr; Spanish Clb; Chorus; Nwsp; Var Chrldng; Powder Puff Ftbl; High Hon Roll; NHS; Acad All Star Awd; OSU; Bus.

STASKAL, ELIZABETH; Union Intermediate HS; Broken Arrow, OK; (2); Church Yth Grp; Cmnty Wkr; FCA; Church Choir; Pub Svc Anncmnts Drugs/Alcohol/Union Stdnts For Christ; Drug Free Yth; OK U; Vet Medcn.

STASSER, TALIA J; Kingfisher HS; Kingfisher, OK; (2); Church Yth Grp; FCA; Spanish Clb; Band; Chorus; Church Choir; Swing Chorus; Rep Stu Cncl; Bsktbl; Mgr(s); Vocal Music Pres; OK ST Univ.

STATON, CANDICE A; Pocola HS; Pocola, OK; (2); FHA; Color Guard; Flag Corp; Var Sftbl; Hon Roll; NHS; St Schlr; GATE; Whitewater Rafting; Westark CC.

STATON, KEVIN; Achille Schl; Hendrix, OK; (4); Church Yth Grp; FHA; Natl FFA Org; School Musical; Ofcr Stu Cncl; Hon Roll; VP NHS; 1st Plc In Consrvtn At SOSU; Luthrn Yth Gathering; SOSA; Consvtn.

STATON, MISTY S; Duke Schl; Mangum, OK; (1); 1/20; Church Yth Grp; FHA; Quiz Bowl; Yrbk; Sec Frsh Cls; Bsktbl; High Hon Roll; Pres Acad Fit Awd; Val.

STATON, REBECCA; Hugo HS; Hugo, OK; (2); Natl FFA Org; Science Clb; Band; Color Guard; Mrchg Band; Pep Band; VP Soph Cls; Hon Roll; NHS; OK ST Univ; Pre-Med.

STATON, WENDY BELLE; Duke Schl; Mangum, OK; (4); 1/20; Church Yth Grp; FCA; FHA; Yrbk; VP Soph Cls; Pres Jr Cls; Pres Sr Cls; Var Bsktbl; Pres Acad Fit Awd; Val; ST/NATL Winnr FHA Speeches; Western OK ST Coll; Elem Ed.

STAUDT, MICHELLE; Guthrie Sr HS; Guthrie, OK; (4); 8/176; Key Clb; Mu Alpha Theta; Red Cross Aide; SADD; Rep Jr Cls; VP Sr Cls; Ofcr Stu Cncl; Sftbl; NHS; 95 HS Hiesman Natl Nom; Prtcptd 95 ASA Jr Olympc 18-Undr Natl Sftbl Trnmnt; Cleveland ST Univ; Chem Eng.

STAUFFER, KARL; Midwest City HS; Oklahoma City, OK; (2); 32/501; Boy Scts; German Clb; Library Aide; Var L Socr; Hon Roll; Jr NHS.

STAUSS, DAVID M; Hulbert Jr Sr HS; Hulbert, OK; (2); Church Yth Grp; Computer Clb; FCA; 4-H; FBLA; Science Clb; Spanish Clb; Varsity Clb; Var Frsh Cls; Rep Soph Cls; Washington U St Louis; Med.

STAUTER, SARAH M; Edmond Memorial HS; Edmond, OK; (3); Church Yth Grp; FCA; French Clb; Phtg Yrbk; Jr NHS; Dance; Pom Pon; OK Univ.

STAWITZ, KATHERINE M; Union Sr HS; Broken Arrow, OK; (4); 73/629; Church Yth Grp; Treas French Clb; FBLA; Hosp Aide; Chrmn Key Clb; Mu Alpha Theta; Church Choir; Rep Stu Cncl; Jr NHS; NHS; Piano; Church Mssn Trps; Acctng.

STEARMAN, SHARILYN S; Putnam City West HS; Bethany, OK; (2); Church Yth Grp; FCA; French Clb; Office Aide; Rep Stu Cncl; Tennis; Vllybl; NHS; Southern Nazarene U.

STEARNS, KIMBERLY R; Wilson HS; Wilson, OK; (3); Church Yth Grp; FCA; Var Sftbl; Hon Roll; UCO.

STEBENS, J R; Freedom Schl; Freedom, OK; (1); 4/13; FCA; FTA; Nwsp; Yrbk; Ofcr Bsbl; Bsktbl; Ftbl; Golf; Socr; Hon Roll.

STEELE, AARON; Okmulgee HS; Okmulgee, OK; (4); Am Leg Boys St; Boy Scts; Church Yth Grp; Spanish Clb; Golf; Hon Roll; Sthestrn OK U; Psych.

STEELE, ANDREA; Westmoore HS; Moore, OK; (3); Hist DECA; Intnl Clb; Office Aide; Red Cross Aide; Gov Hon Prg Awd; DECA St Champn; DECA Natl Contstnt; Spok At Govrnrs Convntn At U Of Cntrl OK As Guest Speaker; OSU; Fashion Merchandising.

STEELE, BRAD; Putnam City North HS; Oklahoma City, OK; (2); FCA; Key Clb; SADD; JV Ftbl; L Wrstlng; Ldrshp Dev Inst; BASIC; PEAK; OK ST Univ; Bus.

STEELE, STACY; Kremlin Jr Sr HS; Enid, OK; (1); FCA; Quiz Bowl; VP Frsh Cls; Bsktbl; Sftbl; Swmmng; Hon Roll; Sal.

STEELE, TRAVIS; Catoosa HS; Tulsa, OK; (4); Am Leg Boys St; FCA; FBLA; Office Aide; Teachers Aide; VICA; Bsktbl; Trk; Hon Roll; Technlgy Stu Assn.

STEELMAN, TABITHA; Heavener HS; Heavener, OK; (3); Church Yth Grp; FBLA; VP FHA; Spanish Clb; Band; Chorus; Drm Mjr(t); School Play; Chrldng; NHS; Indian Club; Drug Free Club Secy; Eastern OK ST Coll; Music.

STEEN, WHITNEY L; Union Intermediate HS; Tulsa, OK; (2); Girl Scts; Band; Chorus; School Musical; Hon Roll; Jr NHS; NHS; All-Dist Pianst 95; Ballet 10 Yrs; Jazz 2 Yrs; Church Altar Servr; Dance.

STEFFANI, KIMBERLY; Guthrie Sr HS; Guthrie, OK; (4); 22/167; Dance Clb; Drama Clb; Mu Alpha Theta; Office Aide; Spanish Clb; SADD; Rep Frsh Cls; Ofcr Stu Cncl; Hon Roll; Kiwanis Awd; OK City CC; Bus.

STEFFANS, BRANDON; Choctaw HS; Newalla, OK; (4); 70/350; Church Yth Grp; Bsktbl; Cit Awd; High Hon Roll; Hon Roll; Jr NHS; Masonic Stu Of Today; Rose; Bio Sci.

STEGER, JILL; Seminole Jr Sr HS; Seminole, OK; (2); Church Yth Grp; Cmnty Wkr; Dance Clb; Debate Tm; Drama Clb; FCA; Math Clb; NFL; Pep Clb; Quiz Bowl; Knowldge Mastr Open; Natl Fornsic League Sec; St Debate/Drama Qualifier; St 1-Act Play Qualifier 2 Yrs; Poltcl Sci.

STEHR, AMANDA; Mangum Jr HS; Willow, OK; (1); Church Yth Grp; 4-H; FHA; NFL; Bsktbl; Var Sftbl; High Hon Roll; Jr NHS; NHS; Tri-St HS Rodeo Assoc; FFA Greenhand Awd, Several FFA Project Awds; NW OK Rodeo Assoc; OSU; Vet.

STEHR, JARETTA; Clinton HS; Clinton, OK; (2); 4/110; Art Clb; Church Yth Grp; Pres VP 4-H; Spanish Clb; Pres Band; Color Guard; Mrchg Band; Pep Band; 4-H Awd; High Hon Roll; OK ST U; Comm Art.

STEICHEN, MARK A; B T Washington HS; Tulsa, OK; (3); VP Spanish Clb; Orch; Rep Jr Cls; Var Swmmng; NHS.

STEIMAN, KRISTEN M; Westmore HS; Moore, OK; (1); Church Yth Grp; Hosp Aide; Chorus; Church Choir; Hon Roll; Jr NHS; Med.

STEIN, EDWARD; Stillwater Sr HS; Stillwater, OK; (1); Boy Scts; CAP; Cmnty Wkr; Math Tm; Hon Roll; Pres Acad Fit Awd; Tae Kwon Do Black Belt; Moro Visayan Tribal Arts; Soc Creative Anachronism; Comps; Kinesiology; Martial Arts Instr.

STEIN, JASON L; Cherokee Jr Sr HS; Cherokee, OK; (3); Church Yth Grp; Debate Tm; FCA; French Clb; NFL; Speech Tm; Church Choir; School Play; Trk; All ST Yth Choir; U Of OK.

STEIN, MADELAINE S; Central Jr HS; Lawton, OK; (2); Church Yth Grp; Cmnty Wkr; FCA; FHA; Speech Tm; Tennis; Hon Roll; NHS; Bldrs Clb; Postponing Sexual Invlvmnt Teen Trnr; 1 Tm Pub Poet; Crmnl Jstce.

STEINBRUCK, KRISTIN; El Reno Sr HS; El Reno, OK; (3); Church Yth Grp; 4-H; Key Clb; Speech Tm; School Play; Variety Show; 4-H Awd; Hon Roll; Jr NHS; Ntl Merit Ltr; Mck Trl Tm; Enviro Clb; Pre-Law.

STEINER, ELLIOT S; Mustang HS; Yukon, OK; (3); 1/400; Am Leg Boys St; Quiz Bowl; Spanish Clb; Pres Soph Cls; Rep Stu Cncl; Var L Crs Cntry; Var L Socr; Var L Trk; High Hon Roll; NHS; Westpoint; Engr.

STEINER, JACOB; Jenks HS; Tulsa, OK; (3); Key Clb; DECA; Kiwanis Clb; OK ST U; Bus & Personal Fin.

STEINER, KEVIN C; Byng Sr HS; Ada, OK; (2); Art Clb; Church Yth Grp; FHA; Spanish Clb; SE Sub-Dist 2 FHA Sec 96-97; SE Sub-Dist 2 FHA VP 95-96; FHA Chptr VP; AZ ST; Arch.

STEINERT, SCOTT; Garber Sr HS; Enid, OK; (1); Church Yth Grp; 4-H; Letterman Clb; Natl FFA Org; Pep Clb; Ofcr Bsbl; Bsktbl; Ftbl; Hon Roll; Sal.

STEINKE, JEFFREY A; North Intemediate HS; Broken Arrow, OK; (2); Office Aide; Science Clb; NHS; Pres Acad Fit Awd; Tulsa Univ; Comp Sci.

STEINKOGLER, SHEA; Guymon Sr HS; Guymon, OK; (3); 12/94; Church Yth Grp; FCA; FBLA; SADD; Sec Frsh Cls; Var Capt Chrldng; High Hon Roll; NHS; NCA All Amer Chrldr; U Of OK; Nrsng.

STEINLE, ALAN M; B T Washington HS; Tulsa, OK; (4); 8/264; Computer Clb; German Clb; Var Crs Cntry; JV Socr; Intrml Vllybl; NHS; Ntl Merit SF; Sci Bowl; Mchncl Engrng.

STEINMAN, KAPRINA K; West Middle HS; Norman, OK; (2); Drama Clb; FBLA; Spanish Clb; Ofcr Stu Cncl; Hon Roll; Teen Vols Clb; OU.

STEINMETZ, STEFFANY B; Cascia Hall Prep School; Tulsa, OK; (1); Cmnty Wkr; Spanish Clb; Chorus; Bsktbl; Socr; Jr NHS; Jr Cnslr Rsnc Camp For Girls; Nrsng Home Vol.

STENGLE, JENNIFER B; Yukon Middle HS; Oklahoma City, OK; (3); 5/400; FHA; Spanish Clb; Ed Yrbk; Mgr(s); Cit Awd; High Hon Roll; NHS.

STENSETH, TRAVIS; Wilson HS; Ringling, OK; (4); 8/32; Church Yth Grp; FCA; Natl Beta Clb; Office Aide; Quiz Bowl; Chorus; Church Choir; Var Bsbl; Var Bsktbl; Ntl Merit SF; East Central U; Bus.

STEPHEN, CORRIN ANN; Bartlesville Sr HS; Bartlesville, OK; (3); 1/433; FBLA; Red Cross Aide; Ed Yrbk; Rep Soph Cls; Rep Jr Cls; JV Chrldng; Sftbl; High Hon Roll; Pres Jr NHS; Pres NHS; Publc Rltns; Bus.

STEPHENS, ANDREW K; Union Intermediate HS; Tulsa, OK; (2); 207/881; Church Yth Grp; FCA; JV Bsktbl; Tennis; Hon Roll; Jr NHS; DFY.

STEPHENS, ANGEL T; Star Spencer HS; Oklahoma City, OK; (2); ROTC; Church Choir; JV Bsktbl; Sftbl; Hon Roll; Langston Univ; Law; Bus Owner.

STEPHENS, ASHLEY; Tahlequah Jr HS; Tahlequah, OK; (2); Church Yth Grp; SADD; Church Choir; Ftbl; Wt Lftg; 4-H Awd; High Hon Roll; Hon Roll; Jr NHS; NHS.

STEPHENS, ASHLEY; Metro Christian Acad; Tulsa, OK; (2); Church Yth Grp; Key Clb; Spanish Clb; Pres Frsh Cls; Var Bsktbl; Var Trk; High Hon Roll; NHS; Yth Group Ldrshp Team.

STEPHENS, CHRISTOPH R; Comm Chrstn Schl; Moore, OK; (3); Church Yth Grp; Debate Tm; FCA; Speech Tm; Varsity Clb; Church Choir; VP Soph Cls; Ofcr Sr Cls; Ofcr Stu Cncl; Var Bsbl; Schlr Ath Of The Yr; Tri St Golf Champion 94-96; Pastor.

STEPHENS, CYDNEY J; West Middle HS; Norman, OK; (1); Church Yth Grp; FCA; Office Aide; Spanish Clb; Hon Roll; HS Heroes Clb; Teen Vol Clb; OK Univ.

STEPHENS, ELANE E; Duke Schl; Gould, OK; (1); Church Yth Grp; Cmnty Wkr; GAA; Letterman Clb; Natl FFA Org; Pep Clb; School Play; Var Bsbl; JV Bsktbl; JV Chrldng; All Conf Team Var Sftbl; Wstrn OK ST Coll; PT.

STEPHENS, JACLYN; Ft Gibson HS; Tahlequah, OK; (4); 8/132; FHA; Math Clb; Natl FFA Org; Science Clb; High Hon Roll; NHS; Ntl Merit Ltr; Rodeo; NEO; Vet.

STEPHENS, JENNIFER M; Del City HS; Oklahoma City, OK; (2); Computer Clb; Drama Clb; Sec FCA; 4-H; Pres German Clb; Letterman Clb; Math Clb; Pep Clb; Scholastic Bowl; VP Science Clb; Help Coach Cheer Squad; Modelng; Trvl; OCU Sci Dept Smmr Rsrch; Speak Frosh Grad; Med Schl/Field.

STEPHENS, JEREMY C; Midwest City HS; Midwest City, OK; (3); Science Clb; Band; Church Choir; Jazz Band; Mrchg Band; Pep Band; Tennis; Jr NHS; Prfct Atten Awd; U Of OK; Engr.

STEPHENS, JESSICA; Medford Schl; Medford, OK; (2); Church Yth Grp; FCA; Natl FFA Org; Band; Chorus; Var L Bsktbl; Var L Sftbl; Hon Roll; NHS; St Schlr.

STEPHENS, JESSICA D; Woodward HS; Woodward, OK; (1); German Clb; Trk; Arts.

STEPHENS, JIMMY D; Skiatook HS; Skiatook, OK; (3); Var Wrstlng; Hon Roll; Jr NHS.

STEPHENS, JOLENA; Skiatook HS; Skiatook, OK; (4); 3/110; Church Yth Grp; FBLA; Sec Natl FFA Org; Socr; Cit Awd; High Hon Roll; NHS; Pres Acad Fit Awd; Sal; Chrstn Yth Ldrshp Awd; St Champion Dairy Products Judger; Natl Dairy Products Cont 9th High Ind; OK ST Univ; Food Sci.

STEPHENS, LEAH M; Stroud HS; Stroud, OK; (4); 6/34; Church Yth Grp; FHA; Spanish Clb; Chorus; Color Guard; Rep Stu Cncl; Hon Roll; NHS; Pres Acad Fit Awd; OK St Univ.

STEPHENS, MARLO J; Sapulpa Sr HS; Sapulpa, OK; (3); Church Yth Grp; FHA; Teachers Aide; Flag Corp; Sec Sr Cls; Crs Cntry; Trk; VP French Hon Soc; Hon Roll; NHS.

STEPHENS, MICHAEL; Collinsville HS; Collinsville, OK; (3); Church Yth Grp; FCA; Band; Church Choir; Mrchg Band; Orch; Bsktbl; Ftbl; Tennis; Trk; OK Baptist U; Ed.

STEPHENS, ROBERT; Moore HS; Moore, OK; (4); Am Leg Boys St; Church Yth Grp; CAP; German Clb; Model UN; Office Aide; ROTC; Band; Mrchg Band; AFJROTC Cadet Humanitarian Awd; U Of OK; Poltcl Sci.

STEPHENS, SAM; Wynnewood HS; Wynnewood, OK; (1); 1/60; Church Yth Grp; FCA; Scholastic Bowl; Rep Frsh Cls; JV Bsktbl; Var Ftbl; JV Trk; JV Wt Lftg; High Hon Roll; Sports Med.

STEPHENS, SASHA; Guymon Sr HS; Guymon, OK; (3); Church Yth Grp; Dance Clb; FCA; French Clb; NFL; SADD; Drill Tm; Jr NHS; NHS; Pres Acad Fit Awd; OSU.

STEPHENSON, BROOKE N; Clinton HS; Clinton, OK; (4); 36/99; DECA; FCA; French Clb; FBLA; FHA; GAA; Bsktbl; Chrldng; Trk; Hon Roll; Schlmstrs Of Custer Cty Schlrshp; Rotary Schlsp; ESA Schlsp; Sthwstrn OK ST U; Fshn Mrchnd.

STEPHENSON, CHAD A; Charles Page HS; Sand Springs, OK; (3); 29/365; FCA; French Clb; Math Tm; Band; Mrchg Band; Pep Band; Tennis; High Hon Roll; Hon Roll; NHS; Music Masters; Cmptr Engrng.

STEPHENSON, JASON R; Alex Jr Sr HS; Alex, OK; (3); Church Yth Grp; Cmnty Wkr; Natl FFA Org; Office Aide; Teachers Aide; VICA; Chorus; Church Choir; L Bsbl; JV Var Bsktbl; Crop Jdgng Tm Star Frmr Grnhnd; Lvstck Shwng Chmpn Limousine/Simmental; OK Poetry Cntst; OSU; Ag.

STEPHENSON, JERRED; Midwest City HS; Midwest City, OK; (4); Drama Clb; FCA; Letterman Clb; Service Clb; Teachers Aide; School Musical; School Play; Stage Crew; Bsktbl; Ftbl; Voted Mst Dramatic By Sr Cls; Sr Ath Trnr; Best Male Actor Sr Yr; Drama Clb VP; Jr Rotarian; OK ST Univ; Drama; Actor.

STEPHENSON JR, JON; Ada HS; Ada, OK; (4); 6/159; Am Leg Boys St; FCA; Ofcr Stu Cncl; Var Bsbl; Var Capt Ftbl; NHS; Church Yth Grp; Cmnty Wkr; Math Clb; All Amer Schlr; OK Coaches Assn All St Tm Ftbl; OK U.

STEPHENSON, JOSHUA; Muskogee HS; Muskogee, OK; (4); 14/309; Church Yth Grp; Debate Tm; JCL; NFL; Capt Quiz Bowl; Church Choir; High Hon Roll; NHS.

STEPHENSON, TIMOTHY L; Muskogee HS; Muskogee, OK; (2); Church Yth Grp; Computer Clb; Quiz Bowl; Church Choir; Ftbl; Hon Roll; Elec Engr.

STEPP, ARLENA; Savanna HS; Kiowa, OK; (1); Church Yth Grp; FCA; FHA; Science Clb; Band; Church Choir; Mrchg Band; Pep Band; Bsktbl; Chrldng; Perfmnc As Mascot In Hula Bowl In HI; All Amer & Best Mascot Awds.

STEPP, HEATHER D; Yukon Middle HS; Yukon, OK; (2); FHA; Spanish Clb; High Hon Roll; NHS; 3-D; Bio Outstndg Achvmnt Awd; FHA Outstndg Achvmnt Awd.

STERLING, DARBI; Alva HS; Alva, OK; (1); Church Yth Grp; FCA; FHA; Key Clb; Chorus; Swing Chorus; Var Chrldng; Var Golf; High Hon Roll; Speech Tm; Rainbow For Girls; Le Clb.

STEUART, ADAM M; Woodward HS; Woodward, OK; (1); Boy Scts; Church Yth Grp; Letterman Clb; Band; Jazz Band; Mrchg Band; Pep Band; Classic Bwl Band; Southwestern OK ST U; Music.

STEUART, JERAN; Woodward HS; Woodward, OK; (3); 1/220; FCA; FBLA; VP Key Clb; Letterman Clb; Rep Stu Cncl; Bsktbl; Ftbl; Capt Socr; Trk; NHS.

STEVENER, KYLE D; El Reno Sr HS; El Reno, OK; (3); Am Leg Boys St; Church Yth Grp; FBLA; Pres Frsh Cls; Var Ftbl; Var Golf; Wt Lftg; 4-H Awd; Hon Roll; NHS; Ldrs Of Tom Morgan Boys ST; Comm Ldrshp; City Of El Reno Stdnt Advsry; Bank/Fin.

STEVENS, ANDREA; Waller Jr HS; Enid, OK; (1); Pep Clb; Var Chrldng; Var Swmmng; High Hon Roll; NHS; HS Swimming St Freestyle Champion & Ltr 96.

STEVENS, ASHLI; Stigler HS; Stigler, OK; (1); Church Yth Grp; Drama Clb; FCA; FHA; SADD; Hon Roll; SADD Fr Rep; Tech Stu Assn; Oral Roberts U; Child Psych.

STEVENS, DAINA S; Agra Schl; Delta, CO; (1); 1/18; VP Church Yth Grp; FHA; Natl FFA Org; VP Pep Clb; Sec Frsh Cls; JV Var Bsktbl; Var Sftbl; High Hon Roll.

STEVENS, HEATH; Plainview HS; Ardmore, OK; (4); Natl Beta Clb; Quiz Bowl; Lit Mag; Hon Roll; NHS; St Schlr; U Of OK; Cmptr Sci/Physcs.

STEVENS, JENNY; Woodward HS; Woodward, OK; (2); Church Yth Grp; Drama Clb; German Clb; Letterman Clb; Pep Clb; Mgr(s); Trk; High Hon Roll; Kiwanis Awd; NHS; Yth Alive Sec; Ballet Neet Crckr; Cltr Exchng Sec; Southern Nazarene Univ; Rlgn.

STEVENS, KACI; Frederick HS; Frederick, OK; (3); 8/80; FHA; HOBY; Chorus; Stage Crew; Yrbk; Var L Bsktbl; Var L Sftbl; Var L Trk; Hon Roll; NHS; Midwstrn U; Elem Ed.

STEVENS, KASSIE; Broken Arrow Sr HS; Broken Arrow, OK; (2); DECA; Drama Clb; Office Aide; Thesps; Varsity Clb; Stage Crew; Var JV Chrldng; Cit Awd; Hon Roll; Pres Acad Fit Awd; Forum Gifted Prgm; OSU; Mrktng/Acctng.

STEVENS, LUZ A; Southeast HS; Oklahoma City, OK; (4); 3/70; Am Leg Aux Girls St; Cmnty Wkr; FCA; French Clb; German Clb; Office Aide; Pep Clb; Spanish Clb; Chorus; Ed Yrbk; Engrng Cont HS Div 2nd Pl; U Of OK Hnrs Acad Achvt; U Of OK; Intl Bus.

STEVENS, MICHAEL S; Alva HS; Alva, OK; (2); Church Yth Grp; FCA; Letterman Clb; SADD; Teachers Aide; Chorus; Variety Show; VP Frsh Cls; Rep Soph Cls; Var L Bsktbl; Player Of Week Ftbl; Defense/Offense Player Of Game; Coaching.

STEVENS, MISTY; Woodward HS; Woodward, OK; (4); #16 in class; Intnl Clb; Letterman Clb; Band; School Play; Bsktbl; L Crs Cntry; Ftbl; L Trk; NHS; Pres Schlr; Yth Alive Bible Club; Southern Nazarene Univ; Pre-PT.

STEVENS, NECHELLE F; Midwest City HS; Midwest City, OK; (3); 44/384; Science Clb; Spanish Clb; Band; Color Guard; Mrchg Band; School Musical; Hon Roll; Jr NHS; Color Guard Capt; Southwestern OK ST Univ/Phry.

STEVENS, PENNY D; Varnum Jr Sr HS; Seminole, OK; (3); 4-H; FHA; VP Soph Cls; VP Jr Cls; VP Stu Cncl; Var Chrldng; Var Sftbl; Hon Roll; Gordon Cooper Vo-Tech; Nursng.

STEVENS, TIM A; Western Heights Sr HS; Oklahoma City, OK; (4); #1 in class; Boy Scts; Church Yth Grp; Computer Clb; FCA; FBLA; Band; Ofcr Stu Cncl; Cit Awd; NHS; Val; U Of OK; Optom.

STEVENS, TRAVIS L; Owasso Sr HS; Owasso, OK; (2); Church Yth Grp; FCA; Spanish Clb; Ofcr Stu Cncl; Ftbl; Trk; Wrstlng; Odyssey Of Mind.

STEVENSEN, JERROD; Douglass HS; Spencer, OK; (1); Church Yth Grp; Cmnty Wkr; Drama Clb; Color Guard; Drill Tm; School Play; Hon Roll; Prince ROTC Ball.

STEVENSON, AMBER M; Skiatook HS; Skiatook, OK; (3); OK Univ; Med.

STEVENSON, COREY; Tonkawa Jr Sr HS; Tonkawa, OK; (3); Letterman Clb; SADD; Varsity Clb; Var L Ftbl; Var L Trk; Var L Wt Lftg; Var L Wrstlng; Ed.

STEVENSON, JAROD T; Lone Grove HS; Ardmore, OK; (4); 50/78; Chorus; School Musical; Nwsp; Var L Bsktbl; Var L Ftbl; Var L Trk; SE OK St Univ; Psych.

STEVENSON, JARROD; Lawton Sr HS; Lawton, OK; (3); Debate Tm; Sal; FCA; HOBY; Key Clb; NFL; Speech Tm; Hon Roll; NHS; Church Yth Grp; Close-Up; U Of OK; Chem.

STEVENSON, JEFFREY; Douglass HS; Spencer, OK; (1); Church Yth Grp; Drama Clb; Band; Church Choir; Drill Tm; Mrchg Band; Stage Crew; Bsktbl; Crs Cntry; Trk.

STEVENSON JR, LARRY; Mt St Marys HS; Spencer, OK; (4); 13/68; Am Leg Boys St; Church Yth Grp; Cmnty Wkr; JA; Key Clb; Scholastic Bowl; Science Clb; Band; Church Choir; Drill Tm; Jr Rtrn; Rgnl & St Sci & Engrng Fairs; Fisk U; Elec Engrng.

STEVESON, AMANDA; Millwood HS; Oklahoma City, OK; (3); Teachers Aide; VICA; Band; Chorus; Church Choir; Mrchg Band; School Musical; Hon Roll; Prof Dev Prog Trnee Deg; Cstmlgy; Pauls Beauty Coll; Cstmlgst.

STEVESON, KRISTEN; Grace Fellowship Christian Sch; Broken Arrow, OK; (4); 8/22; Church Yth Grp; Cmnty Wkr; Drama Clb; Chorus; School Musical; School Play; Ofcr Jr Cls; Ofcr Sr Cls; Ofcr Stu Cncl; NHS; Ms Brkn Arrw; Oral Roberts U; Vcl Perf.

STEWARD, NICHOLAS TODD; Tecumseh HS; Shawnee, OK; (1); 4-H; Natl FFA Org; Bsktbl; Ftbl; Trk; NHS; Farming.

STEWARD, RANDECCA C; Muskogee HS; Muskogee, OK; (2); Church Yth Grp; Spanish Clb; Church Choir; Pediatrician.

STEWART, AMY M; Ninnekah HS; Ninnekah, OK; (2); FCA; VP FHA; GAA; Letterman Clb; Model UN; Nwsp; Bsktbl; Chrldng; Crs Cntry; Sftbl; Math Prof.

STEWART, ANDREW C; Ponca City Sr HS; Ponca City, OK; (3); 11/371; Church Yth Grp; Acpl Chr; Band; Church Choir; Drm Mjr(t); Mrchg Band; Orch; High Hon Roll; NHS; Cmnty Wkr; All-St Choir; All-Dist Band; Chrch Piano Accompanist; Medicine.

STEWART, APRIL; Ninnekah HS; Ninnekah, OK; (2); FCA; FHA; Letterman Clb; Spanish Clb; Pres Soph Cls; Var L Bsktbl; Var Crs Cntry; Var L Sftbl; High Hon Roll; Val; OK Hnr Soc; Bsktbl All Conf 95-96.

STEWART, CARL D; Brink Jr HS; Oklahoma City, OK; (1); Ofcr Bsbl.

STEWART, CRYSTAL; Kiefer Jr Sr HS; Kiefer, OK; (2); Var Chrldng; Stat Score Keeper; High Hon Roll; NHS; Outstndg Stu Of Quartr.

STEWART, CRYSTAL L; Elmore City Jr Sr HS; Elmore City, OK; (3); 27/47; Teachers Aide; Bsktbl; Score Keeper; Hon Roll.

STEWART, CRYSTAL L; Idabel HS; Idabel, OK; (2); Art Clb; Church Yth Grp; Dance Clb; FCA; GAA; Office Aide; Pep Clb; Science Clb; Teachers Aide; Sec Frsh Cls; Outstdng Artst Awd; U Cntrl AR Conway.

STEWART, EMILY; Woodward HS; Woodward, OK; (1); School Play; Variety Show; Hon Roll; Var Schlr; Violin.

STEWART, JENNIFER N; Yukon Middle HS; Yukon, OK; (2); FCA; GAA; Varsity Clb; Var Sftbl; Hon Roll; Big All City Plyr Yr 95; Newcmr Yr 94; Var Ltr Sftbl Frosh/Soph Yrs.

STEWART, JOHN D; Mountain View-Gotebo HS; Mountain View, OK; (3); 1/32; Am Leg Boys St; Boy Scts; FCA; Quiz Bowl; Var Bsbl; Var Bsktbl; Var Ftbl; Var Wt Lftg; Cit Awd; High Hon Roll; Tech Stdnt Assn Ofcr; His/Law.

STEWART, JOSEPH R; Cordell Sr HS; Cordell, OK; (3); Teachers Aide; Band; Jazz Band; Mrchg Band; Pep Band; Hon Roll; Prfct Atten Awd; OK ST U.

STEWART, JYMME; Lone Grove HS; Ardmore, OK; (3); 5/100; Natl Beta Clb; Quiz Bowl; Science Clb; Spanish Clb; Chorus; Color Guard; School Musical; Sftbl; High Hon Roll; NHS; U Of OK; Phys Thrpy.

STEWART, LA WAYNE N; Duke Schl; Duke, OK; (4); Art Clb; Computer Clb; Natl FFA Org; Band; Bsktbl; Chrldng; Crs Cntry; Sftbl; Trk; Hon Roll.

STEWART, MEGAN; Deer Creek HS; Edmond, OK; (3); Church Yth Grp; Cmnty Wkr; French Clb; Science Clb; Stat Socr; Var Sftbl; High Hon Roll; NHS; Page At St Captl; Adpt Hwy Pgrm; OK Bapt U.

STEWART, NATALIE N; Mustang HS; Yukon, OK; (3); 4-H; JV Sftbl; JV Trk; 4-H Awd; CCCC; PT.

STEWART, ROBBI I; Stillwater Sr HS; Stillwater, OK; (2); German Clb; Latin Clb; Orch; Kndgtn Tchr.

STEWART, SHAWNA; Woodward HS; Woodward, OK; (3); FTA; Nwsp; Hon Roll; Vol Work; Bus.

STEWART, STEPHANEE S; Woodward HS; Woodward, OK; (2); Church Yth Grp; 4-H; German Clb; Intnl Clb; Hon Roll; Art; Photo; Music; OK ST Univ; Fshn Dsgn; Acting.

STEWART, STEPHANIE D; Edmond Memrl HS; Edmond, OK; (2); Church Yth Grp; Drama Clb; Girl Scts; Spanish Clb; Acpl Chr; Chorus; Church Choir; School Musical; School Play; Stage Crew; OK Hnrs Soc; Competetive Drama Team; Pre-Med.

STEWART, WESLEY M; Warner HS; Muskogee, OK; (1); FCA; Spanish Clb; Sec Frsh Cls; Rep Stu Cncl; JV Var Bsbl; JV Var Bsktbl; JV Trk; Hon Roll; Sal; Trl Of Tears Achvmnt Acad; Hnor Soc; Stu Cncl; OK Hstry Achvmnt Cert; OSU; Eng.

STICKNEY, KRISTIN D; Union Sr HS; Tulsa, OK; (3); 66/741; FBLA; Spanish Clb; Treas Soph Cls; Treas Jr Cls; Rep Stu Cncl; Mgr(s); Hon Roll; NHS; Pres Acad Fit Awd; OK U; Psych.

STIDHAM, MELISSA J; Panola HS; Wilburton, OK; (2); FHA; Chorus; School Musical; Bsktbl; Sftbl; High Hon Roll; Hon Roll; OU; Pre Med.

STIDHAM, SCOTT; Checotah HS; Checotah, OK; (4); #13 in class; Am Leg Boys St; Pres Church Yth Grp; Kiwanis Awd; Spanish Clb; Chorus; Ofcr Stu Cncl; L Bsktbl; L Ftbl; L Golf; NHS; U Of AR; Med.

STIERWALT, DANNY W; Bartlesville Mid HS; Dewey, OK; (2); 88/488; High Hon Roll.

STILES, JEFF T; Mannford HS; Mannford, OK; (3); 6/106; FCA; SADD; Ftbl; Trk; Cit Awd; High Hon Roll; NHS; St Schlr; US Coast Guard Acad; Meterolgy.

STILES, JEREMY G; Bixby Sr HS; Broken Arrow, OK; (4); Church Yth Grp; Spanish Clb; Teachers Aide; Ftbl; Pres Schlr.

STILL, TONYA M; Tahlequah Sr HS; Tahlequah, OK; (3); Band; Chorus; Mrchg Band; Orch; Stage Crew; Outstdng Band Stu; All Dist; Solos/Ensembles Superior Rating; Northeastern ST Univ; History.

STILLWAGEN, KIMBERLY D; Enid Sr HS; Enid, OK; (3); Church Yth Grp; Hosp Aide; Service Clb; Spanish Clb; Speech Tm; Chorus; Mrchg Band; School Musical; School Play; Swing Chorus.

STILWEL, SCOTT A; Seminole Jr Sr HS; Seminole, OK; (3); Church Yth Grp; FCA; Math Clb; Science Clb; Chorus; Swing Chorus; Var Ftbl; Var Wt Lftg; High Hon Roll; Kiwanis Awd; U Of OK; Dentist.

STILWELL, MICHELLE; Tuttle HS; Tuttle, OK; (1); 41/101; Church Yth Grp; Cmnty Wkr; GAA; Girl Scts; Natl FFA Org; Bsktbl; Sftbl; Cit Awd; Hon Roll; Girl Scts Silver Awd; Sftbl Team 3a Fastpitch Chmpnshp 95-96; Hosted 1st Open House Gov Mansion; Med.

STILWELL II, RANDY E; Henryetta Sr HS; Henryetta, OK; (2); FCA; Var Ftbl; Var Wt Lftg; Var Wrstlng; High Hon Roll; Hon Roll; Prfct Atten Awd; Math.

STIMSON, STEPHANIE N; Claremore Sr HS; Claremore, OK; (2); Church Yth Grp; Cmnty Wkr; Cit Awd; High Hon Roll; Prfct Atten Awd.

STINNETT, CANDACE L; Bray-Doyle HS; Marlow, OK; (3); Natl FFA Org; Bsktbl; Sftbl; High Hon Roll; Hon Roll; NHS; OK Hnr Soc; Med.

STINNETT, DONNA; Ft Towson HS; Fort Towson, OK; (1); 5/35; Church Yth Grp; 4-H; FHA; GAA; Ofcr Stu Cncl; Bsktbl; Sftbl; 4-H Awd; High Hon Roll; OSU; Phys Thrpy.

STINSON, AARON D; Del City HS; Oklahoma City, OK; (4); Bsktbl; Var Crs Cntry; Ftbl; Var Trk; Rose St Univ; Phys Thpy.

STINSON, BLAKE; Thomas Jr Sr HS; Fay, OK; (3); FCA; Natl FFA Org; Band; Ftbl; Wt Lftg; Wgtlftng Clb; Acad Lttrmn; Coaching; Sprts Med Thrpy.

STINSON, LESLIE B; Thomas Jr Sr HS; Fay, OK; (3); FCA; Natl FFA Org; Band; Ofcr Frsh Cls; Ftbl; Wt Lftg; Wghtlftng Clb; Acad Ltrmn; Coaching/Sports Med.

STINSON II, MARION D; Salina HS; Salina, OK; (2); JV Bsbl; JV Bsktbl; JV Ftbl; Cit Awd; Hon Roll; U Of OK; Prof Bsbll.

STINSON, SARAH; Woodward HS; Woodward, OK; (1); Art Clb; Church Yth Grp; Spanish Clb; Trk; Hon Roll; NHS; Acctnt.

STINSON, VICKI; Woodward HS; Woodward, OK; (3); FCA; FBLA; Letterman Clb; Var Bsktbl; Var Socr; High Hon Roll; Tech Stdnt Assn; All Dist Socr Tm; Law.

STIRLING, LAURA LEIGH; Olustee Schl; Olustee, OK; (2); 4-H; Chorus; Stage Crew; Bsktbl; Chrldng; Sftbl; Tennis; Hon Roll; Hnrs Cls; Comp Lit Awd; Bio Awd; UCLA; Comp Applicator.

STITES, JENNIFER D; Preston Schl; Okmulgee, OK; (1); VP Frsh Cls; Hon Roll; NHS; Top Stdnt World His; Esmonds Vet Clinic Vol; OK ST Univ; Vet Med.

STITH, MELISSA; Caney Valley HS; Ramona, OK; (4); 4/47; Am Leg Aux Girls St; German Clb; Scholastic Bowl; Teachers Aide; VP Rep Stu Cncl; Var Capt Bsktbl; Hon Roll; NHS; Acad Tm St Chmps 94/St Rnnr Up 95; Hist Clb Estblshd Museum; MO Southern ST Coll; Educ.

STITT, BRADLY G; Dover Schl; Dover, OK; (3); 3/13; Am Leg Boys St; Church Yth Grp; FCA; Church Choir; Orch; Pres Jr Cls; Var L Bsbl; Var L Bsktbl; Hon Roll; NHS; Multi Yr Listee.

STOCK, CURTIS; Kingfisher HS; Kingfisher, OK; (2); Scholastic Bowl; Bsktbl; Golf; Hon Roll; NHS; Ntl Merit Ltr; St Schlr; OK ST U.

STOCKDALE, AMBER D; Harrah HS; Harrah, OK; (3); 21/153; Church Yth Grp; FHA; Girl Scts; Band; Flag Corp; Mrchg Band; Socr; Hon Roll; Jr NHS.

STOCKLEY, RACHEL L; B T Washington HS; Tulsa, OK; (4); 32/250; Church Yth Grp; Drama Clb; French Clb; Red Cross Aide; Service Clb; Church Choir; School Musical; School Play; Treas Frsh Cls; Rptr Soph Cls; Tulsa Crew Team; Knox Coll; Psych.

STOCKSEN, LEE A; Bridge Creek HS; Tuttle, OK; (1); Spanish Clb; Treas Stu Cncl; Bsktbl; Chrldng; Cit Awd; Hon Roll; Jr NHS; Pres Schlr; Amer Natl Teengr Pgnt; OK Hnr Soc; Prin Hnr Roll; OK U; Marine Bio.

STOCKTON, ADRIENNE; Moore HS; Moore, OK; (4); 8/505; Art Clb; Church Yth Grp; FCA; FBLA; Spanish Clb; VP Frsh Cls; Sec Jr Cls; Rep Stu Cncl; NHS; Val; Southeastern OK ST U; Accntng.

STOCKTON, MARISSA; Blair Schl; Blair, OK; (2); Church Yth Grp; Natl Beta Clb; Church Choir; Bsktbl; High Hon Roll; NHS; Val.

STOCKWELL, LORI; Victory Christian Schl; Mounds, OK; (4); 3/60; Intnl Clb; Library Aide; Teachers Aide; Yrbk; Rep Frsh Cls; Rep Soph Cls; Bsktbl; Socr; High Hon Roll; NHS; US Ldrshp Merit Awd; All Amer Scholar; US Achvmnt Acad; Oral Roberts U; Elem Ed.

STODDARD, LAVEENA L; Webster HS; Oakhurst, OK; (3); Church Yth Grp; Science Clb; Var JV Bsktbl; Score Keeper; Sftbl; Hon Roll; NHS; Heart Surgeon; Dntst.

STOECKLEY, HEIDI N; Ponca City Sr HS; Ponca City, OK; (3); 1/500; Cmnty Wkr; Dance Clb; Math Tm; Band; Chorus; Mrchg Band; Orch; High Hon Roll; NHS; Dance/Peds.

STOELZING, STEPHANIE; Welch Jr Sr HS; Welch, OK; (2); 1/26; Debate Tm; Drama Clb; FBLA; FHA; Quiz Bowl; Speech Tm; Rep Soph Cls; Rep Stu Cncl; Hon Roll; Scholastic Bowl; Psych.

STOGSDILL, GENEVA K; Catoosa HS; Catoosa, OK; (4); 30/140; Church Yth Grp; FCA; FBLA; FHA; Intnl Clb; Library Aide; Pep Clb; School Play; Ofcr Stu Cncl; Hon Roll; Mst Schl Spirited Cls 96; Abilene Chrstn U; Psych.

STOKES, LEEANNA M; Mc Alester HS; Mcalester, OK; (3); Spanish Clb; Band; Mrchg Band; Pep Band; School Musical; Hon Roll; Natl Sci Olympd Bio Distnctn; Multi-Yr Listee; KCAI/ART.

STOKES, NATHAN; Stratford Schl; Stratford, OK; (1); 1/40; Spanish Clb; Band; Jazz Band; Mrchg Band; Pep Band; Variety Show; Rep Stu Cncl; Gov Hon Prg Awd; High Hon Roll; Pres Acad Fit Awd; St Cmptn Super Percssn Ensmble; All-Dist Band 3 Yrs; Interschlstc Meets; SW OK St U Band Camp; SWOSU Weatherford; Pharmclgy.

STOKES, NICOLE; Western Heights Sr HS; Oklahoma City, OK; (2); 1/215; Rep Stu Cncl; High Hon Roll; Hon Roll; U Of AR-FAYETTEVILLE.

STOKKE, KAREN E; Ponca City Sr HS; Ponca City, OK; (4); 5/360; NFL; Speech Tm; Sec Treas Chorus; Pres Orch; School Play; Nwsp; Cit Awd; High Hon Roll; Kiwanis Awd; NHS; NCTE Achvt Awd Wrtng 95; OK All-St Orch; Acad Team; Msc.

STONE, ADAM; Putnam City HS; Oklahoma City, OK; (4); Am Leg Boys St; Church Yth Grp; Debate Tm; Drama Clb; JCL; NFL; Mrchg Band; School Play; Stage Crew; NHS; Page OK House Rep; U Cntrl OK; Radio/TV/FILM.

STONE, ALISON L; Bixby Sr HS; Bixby, OK; (1); Church Yth Grp; FCA; Ofcr Frsh Cls; Bsktbl; Gov Hon Prg Awd; Hon Roll; JETS Awd; Jr NHS; Art.

STONE, ANGIE; Freedom Schl; Freedom, OK; (1); Cmnty Wkr; FCA; Rep Natl FFA Org; VP Frsh Cls; Var Bsktbl; Var Chrldng; Var Trk; OSU; Acctng.

STONE, ASHLEY N; Memorial HS; Tulsa, OK; (2); German Clb; Band; Flag Corp; Jazz Band; Mrchg Band; Pep Band; Stage Crew; Rep Stu Cncl; Hon Roll; TX A&M Galvaston; Marine Bio.

STONE, DAVID G; Latta Sr HS; Ada, OK; (3); Debate Tm; Drama Clb; Quiz Bowl; Scholastic Bowl; Speech Tm; Thesps; School Play; Stage Crew.

STONE, HEATHER M; Blackwell HS; Blackwell, OK; (3); 13/105; FCA; Letterman Clb; Pep Clb; Chorus; Bsktbl; Sftbl; Trk; Hon Roll; NHS; Prfct Atten Awd; Physical Therapy.

STONE, JACEY; Clinton HS; Clinton, OK; (4); 6/94; Church Yth Grp; FCA; 4-H; Spanish Clb; SADD; Chorus; Church Choir; Swing Chorus; VP Frsh Cls; VP Soph Cls; OU; Nrsng.

STONE, JACOB; Chandler HS; Chandler, OK; (2); Church Yth Grp; VP 4-H; Scholastic Bowl; Spanish Clb; 4-H Awd; High Hon Roll; Hon Roll; NHS; Tech Stu Assn Sgt At Arms; Aerontcl Engrng.

STONE, JAKE; Clinton HS; Clinton, OK; (2); Church Yth Grp; FCA; 4-H; Chorus; Church Choir; Swing Chorus; Pres Frsh Cls; Ofcr Stu Cncl; Bsktbl; Golf; OU; Rdlgy.

STONE, JAMIE; Blackwell HS; Blackwell, OK; (4); 14/118; Church Yth Grp; Cmnty Wkr; HOBY; Pep Clb; Red Cross Aide; Teachers Aide; Band; Church Choir; Color Guard; Drm Mjr(t); Gold Card Pgm; Extended Stds Pgm; Prom Server; NOC Hnr Band; Chrch Yth Grp/Repr Liturgy Cmmtte; OSU; Scndry Ed.

STONE, JENNY; Liberty Acad; Shawnee, OK; (4); 3/15; Teachers Aide; School Play; Rptr Nwsp; Yrbk; VP Sr Cls; VP Stu Cncl; Chrldng; Hon Roll; Natl Sci Mrt Awd; All Amer Schlr; U Of Cntrl OK; Nrs.

STONE, JEREMY; Berryhill Jr HS; Tulsa, OK; (4); 1/51; Church Yth Grp; Computer Clb; Mu Alpha Theta; Office Aide; Quiz Bowl; Service Clb; Sec Spanish Clb; Church Choir; School Play; Ed Nwsp; Bbl Qz Tm Cap/St Chmps 4x; OK Interschlstc Pss Assn Wrtng Awds; Tulsa U.

STONE, JOANNA C; Guymon Sr HS; Guymon, OK; (4); 26/120; Church Yth Grp; Cmnty Wkr; Drama Clb; NFL; Speech Tm; School Musical; School Play; Kiwanis Awd; NHS; FHA; Speech & Debate One-Act All-St Cast; OK ST U; Humn Envrnmntl Sci.

STONE, KAELIN; Poteau HS; Poteau, OK; (1); Church Yth Grp; FCA; Chorus; Church Choir; Chrldng; Powder Puff Ftbl; Var Trk; Wt Lftg; Hon Roll; Carnegie Hall Choir; Adopt-A-Block; Columbia; Law.

STONE, LESLEE; Woodward HS; Woodward, OK; (1); German Clb; Intnl Clb; Quiz Bowl; Scholastic Bowl; Chorus; High Hon Roll; Kiwanis Awd; NHS; OK Univ; Marine Bio; Zoology.

STONE, MICHELLE; Jenks HS; Tulsa, OK; (3); Church Yth Grp; Dance Clb; FHA; Key Clb; Math Clb; Mu Alpha Theta; Teachers Aide; Drill Tm; Var Capt Pom Pon; Hon Roll; Gamma Sigma; Chrysalis; Early Chldhd Ed.

STONE, PHILLIP B; Nowata HS; Nowata, OK; (4); 13/62; Boy Scts; Church Yth Grp; Math Tm; Teachers Aide; Band; Jazz Band; Mrchg Band; Pep Band; Ftbl; Golf; E Cntrl Univ; Comp Sci.

STONE, SARAH N; Ponca City Middle HS; Ponca City, OK; (1); Nwsp; Psych.

STONE, SHELLEY; Coweta HS; Coweta, OK; (4); 1/153; FCA; Treas FHA; SADD; Nwsp; Yrbk; VP Jr Cls; Pres Stu Cncl; VP NHS; Val; OU; Bus Admin.

STONER, JAMILYN B; Bixby Sr HS; Bixby, OK; (3); Cmnty Wkr; FCA; French Clb; FHA; GAA; Teachers Aide; Var Bsktbl; Var Trk; Var Wt Lftg; Hon Roll; OSU; Acctng.

STONER, KIRK A; Central HS; Tulsa, OK; (2); Church Yth Grp; Drama Clb; Thesps; School Play; Socr; Swmmng; Kyokushin-Kia Karate 1st Pl Fighting US Karate Championships 96; OSU; Karate Tchr.

STONER, STEPHANIE; Bluejacket Schl; Bluejacket, OK; (4); Church Yth Grp; FHA; Quiz Bowl; VICA; Nwsp; Yrbk; Sec Treas Frsh Cls; Rep Jr Cls; Capt Bsktbl; Prfct Atten Awd.

STOPP, MICHAEL; Tahlequah Sr HS; Tahlequah, OK; (3); Church Yth Grp; HOBY; ROTC; SADD; Chorus; Color Guard; Drill Tm; Rep Soph Cls; VP Pres Stu Cncl; Var Ftbl; Masonic Awd; OK Jr Acad Sci; Chrch Yth Cncl; US Mil Acad; Mil.

STOREY, ERIC B; Northeast HS; Spencer, OK; (3); 2/125; High Hon Roll; NHS; St Schlr; Xerox Awd Wnnr; Biomedical Pgm; Biomed Stu Of Month; Eng & Microbiology Awds.

STOREY, SCOTT S; Haworth Sr HS; Haworth, OK; (3); 1/50; 4-H; Natl FFA Org; Ofcr Stu Cncl; 4-H Awd; Hon Roll; NHS; Val; FFA Treas, Pres; Estrn OK ST; Ag.

STORJOHANN, REBECCA; Midwest City HS; Oklahoma City, OK; (2); 18/501; Church Yth Grp; Pres FCA; Church Choir; Drm Mjr(t); Mrchg Band; Ofcr Stu Cncl; Hon Roll; NHS; Amer Leg Awd; 5th Pl HS Schlstc Trnmnt.

STORM, TAMMY D; Granite Jr Sr HS; Granite, OK; (2); FCA; 4-H; FHA; Office Aide; Pep Clb; Science Clb; Spanish Clb; Teachers Aide; Nwsp; Yrbk; OK ST Univ.

STORMS, AMANDA M; Will Rogers HS; Tulsa, OK; (1); Boy Scts; Girl Scts; Quiz Bowl; Orch; School Musical; Hon Roll; Sing, Dance & Act; Outdoor Act; Psychiatrist.

STORMS, BRYAN; Chickasha HS; Chickasha, OK; (4); 4/152; Am Leg Boys St; Pres Church Yth Grp; HOBY; VP Pres Stu Cncl; Var Ftbl; Var Capt Socr; DAR Awd; NHS; Val; Capt FCA; Kanakuk & Kanakomo Kmps Chf Chctws 2nd Trm 96; Bus.

STORMS, LINDSAY; Pryor Sr HS; Pryor, OK; (3); Church Yth Grp; FCA; FBLA; Band; Chorus; School Musical; Yrbk; Ofcr Stu Cncl; High Hon Roll; NHS; RN.

STORY, BARBIE L; Muldrow HS; Muldrow, OK; (1); Church Yth Grp; FHA; Natl FFA Org; Chorus; Raise Rabbits; Hrsebck Rdng; OK ST Univ; Vet.

STORY, CHRISTINA; Comanche HS; Comanche, OK; (2); Art Clb; Church Yth Grp; Debate Tm; JA; Library Aide; Spanish Clb.

STOTT, SARAH; Jenks HS; Jenks, OK; (1); Church Yth Grp; Dance Clb; Chrldng; NHS; Miss Studio Star Of Amer Pgnt 4th Rnr Up; Daybreak Dynamics Drug Rehab Vol; Visit Retrmnt Ctr; OK ST U; Commctns.

STOTTS, JIMMY R; Mc Loud HS; Mc Loud, OK; (2); Natl FFA Org; Bsktbl; Prfct Atten Awd.

STOTTS, JOHN C; Mc Loud HS; Mc Loud, OK; (3); Natl FFA Org; Mrchg Band; NHS; OK St Univ; Agri.

STOUGH, CHAD A; Union Intermediate HS; Tulsa, OK; (2); Church Yth Grp; FCA; Spanish Clb; JV Bsbl; Intrml Bsktbl; JV Wt Lftg; Hon Roll.

STOUGH, JAMIE L; Duncan HS; Duncan, OK; (4); Church Yth Grp; FHA; Hosp Aide; Key Clb; Office Aide; SADD; Trk; DECA; Ldrshp Schlrshp Awd; Faulkner U; Psych.

STOULIL, MATTHEW J; Bishop Kelley HS; Tulsa, OK; (3); Key Clb; Nwsp; Yrbk; Rep Frsh Cls; Pres Soph Cls; Pres Jr Cls; Treas Sr Cls; Treas Stu Cncl; French Hon Soc; High Hon Roll; Peer Hlprs; Kairos/Srch Retrts; Guitar.

STOUT, AMANDA L; Clayton Jr Sr HS; Daisy, OK; (2); FHA; Natl FFA Org; Band; Mrchg Band; Pep Band; Cit Awd; High Hon Roll; Hon Roll.

STOUT, AMBER D; El Reno Sr HS; El Reno, OK; (3); Art Clb; Church Yth Grp; FHA; Chorus; Rptr Nwsp; Phtg Yrbk; Cit Awd; Hon Roll; Panhandle ST; Jrnlst; Rptr.

STOUT, CANDI L; Meeker HS; Shawnee, OK; (2); Hon Roll; Pres Acad Fit Awd; Psych.

STOUT, CODY; Guthrie Sr HS; Guthrie, OK; (1); Red Cross Aide; Spanish Clb; Band; Ofcr Bsbl; Ftbl; Socr; Swmmng; Wt Lftg; Wrstlng; On Only 14 & Undr Bsbl Team For Dist Conf; Wrstlng Team 1st Win At Harrah; OK Univ; Tech.

STOUT, KELLY; Roland Sr HS; Roland, OK; (3); 10/110; FCA; Speech Tm; Band; Mrchg Band; Nwsp; Yrbk; Var Stat Bsktbl; Var Chrldng; Mgr(s); Hon Roll; OK All Star Mrchng & All Dist Bands.

STOUT, LAURA; Frederick HS; Frederick, OK; (2); #3 in class; 4-H; Natl FFA Org; Scholastic Bowl; School Musical; Co-Capt Rep Frsh Cls; Cit Awd; 4-H Awd; Hon Roll; NHS; Pres Acad Fit Awd; OK ST; Vet Med.

STOUT, LAURIE; Panama HS; Panama, OK; (4); FHA; German Clb; Quiz Bowl; SADD; Nwsp; Yrbk; Bus Admin.

STOUT, LESLIE A; Will Rogers HS; Tulsa, OK; (1); French Clb; VP Frsh Cls; Ofcr Stu Cncl; JV Sftbl; Hon Roll; Advncd Choir; 10th Yr Cmpfr; Tulsa Univ; Psych.

STOUT, MATT; Wagoner Sr HS; Wagoner, OK; (3); Boy Scts; Church Yth Grp; Hon Roll; NHS; Indn Cptl Vo-Tech.

STOUT, ZACHARY K; Guthrie Sr HS; Guthrie, OK; (1); Art Clb; Church Yth Grp; Ofcr Bsbl; Ftbl; Hon Roll.

STOVALL, COURTNEY; Miami Sr HS; Miami, OK; (3); 26/179; Church Yth Grp; FCA; NFL; Red Cross Aide; Speech Tm; Thesps; Drill Tm; Chrldng; NHS; OK ST Univ; Spch Lang Pthlgy.

STOVALL, PEYTON; Clinton HS; Clinton, OK; (1); Church Yth Grp; FCA; FHA; Teachers Aide; Chorus; Yrbk; VP Frsh Cls; Ofcr Stu Cncl; Bsktbl; Chrldng; Show Choir; Chrch Yth Grp Cmnty Svc; Rec Sccr; OU; Med.

STOVALL, STEPHANIE; Putnam City West HS; Bethany, OK; (3); Var Bsktbl; Var Golf; Var Sftbl; All Tnmt Tm; Hon Mntn In GA HS Bsktbll In Dist.

STOVER, AARON; Stillwater Sr HS; Stillwater, OK; (3); FCA; Spanish Clb; Teachers Aide; JV Bsbl; Intrml Bsktbl; Hon Roll; NHS.

STOVER, DAVID J; Metro Christian Acad; Tulsa, OK; (2); Church Yth Grp; Band; Church Choir; Jazz Band; Var Socr; Var Tennis; High Hon Roll; JV Bsbl; Hon Roll; Pep Band; Intl Kart Fed Rd Race 94/KART Rd Race 95 Grnd Matl Chmpn; Wrld Karting Assn Wrld Enduro Chmpn 95; Baylor; Engr.

STOVER, MARY E; Claremore Sr HS; Claremore, OK; (1); Church Yth Grp; French Clb; Hon Roll; Med.

STOWE, DIANE; Central Mid-HS; Norman, OK; (2); Church Yth Grp; Pres FCA; Pres Chorus; VP Stu Cncl; JV Bsktbl; JV Sftbl; JV Vllybl; NHS; Jzz Choir Outstdng Soph Hnr; Meml Svc Awd; Masonic Stdnt Today; Chmbr Comm Tomrrws Ldrs; Fcm Ath Yr 95.

STOWE, KEISHA; Moore HS; Moore, OK; (2); FCA; Pres Science Clb; Intrml Var Chrldng; High Hon Roll; Jr NHS.

STOWERS, JENNIFER K; Rush Springs HS; Rush Springs, OK; (4); 22/43; Art Clb; Letterman Clb; Spanish Clb; Speech Tm; Pres Band; Drm Mjr(t); Mrchg Band; Pep Band; School Play; Hon Roll; Swosu Hnr Band; Superior Rating South Cntrl Contest; Outstdng Band Stu; OK City CC; Travel Mgmt.

STRACEY, DAWN N; Claremore Sr HS; Claremore, OK; (2); Church Yth Grp; Teachers Aide; L Socr; Hon Roll; Soccer ST Champions 96; FL ST; Med.

STRACK, CASEY; Bartlesville Mid HS; Bartlesville, OK; (1); 1/500; Debate Tm; Letterman Clb; School Play; Diving; Cit Awd; High Hon Roll; Kiwanis Awd; NHS; Prfct Atten Awd; Pres Acad Fit Awd; Natl Frnsc Leag Stan Oratory ST Qlfr; Adelphi Univ; Prof Actor.

STRADER, TAWNY R; Pauls Valley HS; Pauls Valley, OK; (3); Church Yth Grp; French Clb; FHA; Chorus; Phtg Rptr Yrbk; High Hon Roll; Careers Stu Yr; Elem Ed.

STRAHAN, SARA; Coweta HS; Coweta, OK; (4); 15/153; Rptr Art Clb; FHA; SADD; Band; Mrchg Band; Ed Nwsp; Ed Yrbk; High Hon Roll; NHS; Pres Hnr Roll Tulsa JC; Mass Commnctns.

STRAIN, ANGELA; Glencoe Public Schl; Glencoe, OK; (4); 1/15; Sec French Clb; Office Aide; Ed Nwsp; VP Jr Cls; Pres Sr Cls; Var Crs Cntry; Var Trk; French Hon Soc; NHS; Val; MI Columbia; Med.

STRAIN, BECKY L; Goodwell Public Schl; Goodwell, OK; (4); 5/12; Church Yth Grp; Letterman Clb; Library Aide; Teachers Aide; Yrbk; Rep Jr Cls; VP Stu Cncl; Var Bsktbl; Var Golf; Hon Roll; Tri St HS Rodeo Assoc; OK Panhandle St Univ; Acctng.

STRAIN, KYLIA N; Quinton Jr Sr HS; Quinton, OK; (3); Art Clb; Dance Clb; Debate Tm; Natl FFA Org; Drill Tm; L Pom Pon; L Sftbl; Hon Roll; Prfct Atten Awd; Swmmng; Hrsbck Rdng; Soccer; Cmptr Tech.

STRAKA, KIMBERLY; Union City Schl; Union City, OK; (2); Church Yth Grp; Pres 4-H; Math Clb; Quiz Bowl; Scholastic Bowl; Science Clb; High Hon Roll; Hon Roll.

STRANGE, AMY; Meeker HS; Meeker, OK; (4); 10/74; Church Yth Grp; Treas FCA; Teachers Aide; Band; Pres Chorus; Pres Jazz Band; Mrchg Band; Orch; VP Jr Cls; Ofcr Stu Cncl.

STRANGE, CHRISTOPHER M; Western Heights Sr HS; Oklahoma City, OK; (1); #22 in class; Var Bsbl; Var Wrstlng; OSU; Vet.

STRANGE, JENNIFER K; Westmoore HS; Oklahoma City, OK; (4); 51/610; Church Yth Grp; NFL; Speech Tm; Band; Church Choir; Rep Stu Cncl; Hon Roll; Jr NHS; NHS; Val; Southwestern OK ST; Pharmacy.

STRANGE, MELISSA J; Muldrow HS; Muldrow, OK; (1); Church Yth Grp; Natl Beta Clb; Science Clb; Speech Tm; Band; Mrchg Band; High Hon Roll; Hon Roll; NHS; MIT.

STRANGE, TRAMERA L; Savanna HS; Mcalester, OK; (3); Church Yth Grp; 4-H; FHA; GAA; Girl Scts; Office Aide; Bsktbl; Sftbl; 4-H Awd; Hon Roll; Pushmatdga Fd Prsntn Awd Grnd Chmpn 92; FHA Sr Crd Spkng Awd 94-95; Kiamich Vly Conf Hon Mntn 92-93; Eastern OK ST Coll; Cmptr/Bus.

STRANGE, TYSON J; Meeker HS; Meeker, OK; (1); Church Yth Grp; Chorus; Bsktbl.

STRASIA, LINDSAY; Boise City HS; Boise City, OK; (2); 4/36; Church Yth Grp; GAA; Letterman Clb; Red Cross Aide; SADD; Varsity Clb; VP Frsh Cls; VP Soph Cls; Bsktbl; Chrldng; SWOSU; Dermatology.

STRASIA, RHYS P; Boise City HS; Boise City, OK; (4); Church Yth Grp; Letterman Clb; SADD; Ftbl; Wt Lftg; High Hon Roll; Jr NHS; Pres Acad Fit Awd; U Of OK; Chem Engrng.

STRATTON, DAVID; Claremore Sr HS; Claremore, OK; (3); 1/268; Church Yth Grp; Pres FCA; HOBY; Science Clb; VP Stu Cncl; Var L Ftbl; Var L Trk; High Hon Roll; NHS; St Schlr; Msnc Stu/Tdy; Mxco Mssn Trp 2 Yrs; Bst Ovrl Stu; OK U; Orth Dr.

STRATTON, H D; Chisholm Sr HS; Enid, OK; (1); FCA; Letterman Clb; Quiz Bowl; Band; Jazz Band; Pep Band; Ofcr Bsbl; Bsktbl; Crs Cntry; Cit Awd; OU.

STRAUGHN, JONATHAN R; Putnam City North HS; Oklahoma City, OK; (3); Church Yth Grp; FCA; SADD; Ofcr Bsbl; Bsktbl; High Hon Roll; Clss Hall Dcrtn Comm; OK Univ.

STRAWN, SHANNAN; Valliant HS; Valliant, OK; (2); 6/86; Drama Clb; School Play; Stage Crew; Var Sftbl; Hon Roll; NHS; Southeastern; Scndry Math Ed.

STREBER, NATHAN; Tuttle HS; Tuttle, OK; (1); Church Yth Grp; FCA; 4-H; Natl FFA Org; Church Choir; Rep Stu Cncl; Golf; Score Keeper; Wt Lftg; 4-H Awd; Ministry.

STREBER, SUMMER; Tuttle HS; Tuttle, OK; (3); 6/115; Am Leg Aux Girls St; Church Yth Grp; Cmnty Wkr; FCA; GAA; Natl FFA Org; Chorus; Church Choir; VP Frsh Cls; VP Soph Cls; OK ST Univ; Pharmacy.

STREET, DEANNE R; Noble HS; Norman, OK; (4); 1/143; Church Yth Grp; Mu Alpha Theta; SADD; Chorus; Church Choir; Color Guard; NHS; Val; Show Choir; U Of OK; Phy Assoc.

STREET, TIFFANY A; Broken Arrow Sr HS; Broken Arrow, OK; (3); Church Yth Grp; Hon Roll; Natl Vo-Tech Hnr Soc; HERO; Culinary Inst Of Amer; Chef.

STREET, WILAINIA K; Carter Schl; Carter, OK; (3); Treas FHA; VP Natl FFA Org; Treas Jr Cls; Rep Stu Cncl; Var Bsktbl; Var Sftbl; Cit Awd; Hon Roll; Spanish NHS; Val; Piano; U Of OK; PT.

STREETER, TIFFANY; Claremore Sr HS; Claremore, OK; (1); Church Yth Grp; GAA; Chrldng; Tennis; High Hon Roll.

STREETMAN, KYLE M; Putnam City North HS; Oklahoma City, OK; (4); 32/436; Church Yth Grp; FCA; Key Clb; Spanish Clb; Bsktbl; Hon Roll; NHS; OK Univ.

STREETS, AMBER D; West Middle HS; Norman, OK; (3); 122/799; Math Clb; Spanish Clb; Ofcr Soph Cls; Ofcr Stu Cncl; Hon Roll; Jr NHS; NHS; OU; Anthro.

STRETCH, JESSICA R; Warner HS; Warner, OK; (1); Cmnty Wkr; 4-H; Pep Clb; JV Bsktbl; JV Crs Cntry; Powder Puff Ftbl; Trk; 4-H Awd; OSU.

STRETESKY, KELLI; Plainview HS; Ardmore, OK; (2); Cmnty Wkr; FCA; Natl Beta Clb; Rep Frsh Cls; Rep Soph Cls; Rep Jr Cls; Rep Stu Cncl; Chrldng; Crs Cntry; Trk.

STRICKLAND, ALISA M; Davis HS; Davis, OK; (2); Art Clb; French Clb; FBLA; Bsktbl; Mgr(s); Powder Puff Ftbl; Score Keeper; Sftbl; Trk; Hon Roll; E Central Univ; Vet Lab Tech.

STRICKLAND, DEVON; Newcastle HS; Newcastle, OK; (2); Boy Scts; Church Yth Grp; Debate Tm; Math Clb; Quiz Bowl; Scholastic Bowl; Science Clb; Band; Jazz Band; Mrchg Band; Band Clb Offcr; OK U; Engrng.

STRICKLAND, HOLLI J; Balko Public Schl; Turpin, OK; (2); 9/19; 4-H; FHA; Natl FFA Org; Pep Clb; Yrbk; Pres Frsh Cls; VP Soph Cls; JV Var Bsktbl; Var Chrldng; Var Trk; Earth Clb; TES; 4-H Cnty & Lcl Ofcs; FFA Proficiency Awd; Paralegal Sec.

STRICKLAND, MARK T; Moore HS; Oklahoma City, OK; (2); Church Yth Grp; Library Aide; Natl FFA Org; Quiz Bowl; Scholastic Bowl; Science Clb; Band; Jazz Band; Mrchg Band; Ofcr Bsbl; OK ST Univ; Electrology.

STRICKLAND, SEAN C; Heritage Hall Schl; Oklahoma City, OK; (3); Am Leg Boys St; FCA; Letterman Clb; Mu Alpha Theta; VP Jr Cls; Ofcr Stu Cncl; Var Bsktbl; Var Crs Cntry; Var Trk; NHS.

STRICKLIN, BRIANNE D; Strother Jr Sr HS; Paden, OK; (2); 1/28; Church Yth Grp; 4-H; GAA; Natl FFA Org; Quiz Bowl; Scholastic Bowl; Rep Soph Cls; Rep Stu Cncl; Var Bsktbl; Var Sftbl; Sci & Math Acads; All Conf Bsktbl; OK ST U; Ag Engr.

STRICKLIN, ERICK G; Stigler HS; Keota, OK; (3); Achvt Awd Hustle Ftbl.

STRICKLIN, MANDY R; Keota Schl; Keota, OK; (2); FHA; Natl FFA Org; Pep Clb; Sec Frsh Cls; Rep Soph Cls; Bsktbl; Sftbl; Stdnt Cncl; PT.

STRIMPLE, IAN A; Enid Sr HS; Enid, OK; (2); 97/531; Boy Scts; Church Yth Grp; Dance Clb; Drama Clb; FCA; Pep Clb; Speech Tm; Teachers Aide; Varsity Clb; Band.

STRIMPLE, JENNY L; North Intemediate HS; Broken Arrow, OK; (2); GAA; Ofcr Soph Cls; JV Bsktbl; JV Vllybl; High Hon Roll; Hon Roll; Jr NHS; NHS.

STRINGER, CARL A; Velma Alma HS; Duncan, OK; (1); Church Yth Grp; FCA; Quiz Bowl; Band; Jazz Band; Mrchg Band; Trk; Trmbne Solo; SCOBDA Hnr Bnd; USAO; Bnd Dir.

STROBEL, ANDREA M; Liberty HS; Mounds, OK; (4); 7/25; Church Yth Grp; VP FCA; Office Aide; Teachers Aide; Yrbk; Sec Jr Cls; Sec Sr Cls; Sec Pres Stu Cncl; Bsktbl; Sftbl; OSU Tech.

STRONG, AMANDA; Shawnee Sr HS; Shawnee, OK; (4); Boy Scts; Church Yth Grp; Hosp Aide; Latin Clb; Band; Church Choir; Mrchg Band; Pep Band; Hon Roll; NHS; All Amer Schlr; ECU/OBU Hnr Bands; BB/BS Jr Brd Dir; OK Bapt U; Optometry.

STRONG, EMILY; Shawnee Sr HS; Shawnee, OK; (2); Pres Church Yth Grp; Drama Clb; Scholastic Bowl; Spanish Clb; Chorus; Church Choir; School Musical; High Hon Roll; Chmbr Of Commrce Stu Of Month; OSSAA St Solo/Ensmble Super Solo Ratng; OMTA St Piano Super Ratng; Music Ed.

STRONG, EMILY J; Will Rogers HS; Tulsa, OK; (3); Church Yth Grp; GAA; Letterman Clb; Teachers Aide; Varsity Clb; Rep Stu Cncl; Ofcr Bsbl; Bsktbl; Var L Vllybl; High Hon Roll; Tchng HS Math/Coach Bskbl.

STRONG, SCOTT; Oaks Mission Jr Sr HS; Tahlequah, OK; (4); 1/18; Pres Natl FFA Org; Rep Stu Cncl; Var Bsbl; Capt Var Bsktbl; Capt Var Ftbl; Hon Roll; St Schlr; Val; St FFA Degree; Eastern OK ST Coll; Ag Ec.

STRONG, STEPHANIE R; Weatherford HS; Weatherford, OK; (4); Art Clb; Church Yth Grp; Cmnty Wkr; FHA; Band; Chorus; Mrchg Band; Pep Band; Score Keeper; W Tech Coll; Med Records Tech.

STROPE, MARY E; Spiro HS; Warner, OK; (2); Church Yth Grp; FCA; GAA; Spanish Clb; Teachers Aide; Bsktbl; Powder Puff Ftbl; Sftbl; OK ST Univ; Eng; Math.

STROTHMANN, AMALIA E; South Intermediate HS; Broken Arrow, OK; (1); Band; Color Guard; Drm Mjr(t); Mrchg Band; High Hon Roll; NHS; Pres Acad Fit Awd; French Clb; Intnl Clb; Pep Band; Acad Team Capn; Acad Ltr; Chrstn Stu Union; Frosh Schlr Of Yr; U Of Notre Dame; Nvlst.

STROUD, DONNA C; Tahlequah Sr HS; Tahlequah, OK; (2); Office Aide; Pep Clb; Var JV Tennis; Stat Wrstlng; Ntl Merit Ltr.

STROUD, SHELLEY; Moore HS; Moore, OK; (4); 6/549; Church Yth Grp; Pres Drama Clb; French Clb; Chorus; School Musical; School Play; Rep Stu Cncl; Hon Roll; NHS; Val; SWOSU; Psych.

STRUNK, AMY K; Chickasha HS; Chickasha, OK; (3); 4/200; Sec Church Yth Grp; Pres FCA; French Clb; Quiz Bowl; Band; Color Guard; Var L Socr; Var L Swmmng; NHS; Natl FFA Org; All St Band.

STUART, BILLY K; Latta Sr HS; Ada, OK; (2); 2/60; Church Yth Grp; FCA; 4-H; Natl FFA Org; Varsity Clb; Ofcr Soph Cls; Bsktbl; Hon Roll; NHS; Pres Acad Fit Awd; OK Hnr Scty; OK Univ; Dntl Mjr.

STUART, CLAY L; Shattuck Jr Sr HS; Shattuck, OK; (4); 3/23; FCA; Quiz Bowl; School Play; Pres Jr Cls; Pres Sr Cls; Pres Stu Cncl; Capt Bsbl; Capt Bsktbl; Capt Ftbl; DAR Awd; OK ST Univ; Coaching/Bnkng.

STUART, JEFF D; Deer Creek HS; Edmond, OK; (3); Am Leg Boys St; French Clb; FBLA; Science Clb; School Musical; School Play; Var Bsbl; Var Ftbl; Var Tennis; NHS; Eagle Scout; Pre-Med Anesthlgst.

STUBBLEFIELD, CRYSTAL L; Stigler HS; Stigler, OK; (3); Model UN; Natl FFA Org; SADD; Var Bsktbl; Var Sftbl; Hon Roll; Mock Trials Voted Best Lawyer; Conners ST; Law.

STUBBLEFIELD, JUSTIN; Collinsville HS; Collinsville, OK; (4); FCA; Office Aide; Chorus; Rep Sr Cls; Ofcr Bsbl; Var Ftbl; Var Trk; Wt Lftg; Hon Roll; OK ST U; Scndry Ed.

STUBBS, COREY; Grace Fellowship Christian Sch; Broken Arrow, OK; (4); 7/22; Church Yth Grp; Teachers Aide; Ofcr Soph Cls; Ofcr Sr Cls; Ofcr Stu Cncl; Var Bsbl; Var Capt Bsktbl; Crs Cntry; Vllybl; High Hon Roll.

STUBBS, KARA R; Durant HS; Durant, OK; (1); Church Yth Grp; Dance Clb; Chorus; Church Choir; Drill Tm; Variety Show; Yrbk; Rep Frsh Cls; Pom Pon; High Hon Roll; Yth Quest A Chrch Talent Pgm; Southeastern.

STUCK, JACK W; Haskell HS; Haskell, OK; (4); JV Bsbl; Var Ftbl; High Hon Roll; Hon Roll; Spartan Schl Arntcs; Arcrft Mec.

STUCKER, RANDALL W; Arapaho Schl; Arapaho, OK; (2); Church Yth Grp; Natl FFA Org; Scholastic Bowl; Ofcr Bsbl; Bsktbl; Crs Cntry; 4-H Awd; Gov Hon Prg Awd; Hon Roll; NHS; South Western OK ST; Ag Engr.

STUCKEY, CAREYLYN; Arnett HS; Arnett, OK; (4); 4/11; Am Leg Aux Girls St; Cmnty Wkr; FCA; GAA; Pres Natl Beta Clb; Sec Natl FFA Org; Teachers Aide; Chorus; School Musical; School Play; Page To Sntr Williams; Dist & St Msc Cntsts; OK Kids Prfrmng Grp; Gftd & Tlntd; Lfgrd; Ms Arnett; SW OK ST U; Med.

STUCKEY, CHRYSTAL G; Tahlequah Sr HS; Tahlequah, OK; (2); Church Yth Grp; Chorus; Church Choir; Yth Drama; Central Bible Coll; Yth Mnstry.

STUCKEY, JEFF; Wetumka Jr Sr HS; Wetumka, OK; (1); 2/36; Church Yth Grp; Band; Mrchg Band; Bsktbl; Hon Roll; Pres Acad Fit Awd; FFA; OU.

STUDEBAKER, JENNIFER D; Byng Sr HS; Ada, OK; (2); 1/110; Church Yth Grp; Math Clb; Natl Beta Clb; Quiz Bowl; Scholastic Bowl; Science Clb; Spanish Clb; Chorus; Pres Stu Cncl; Cit Awd; Masonic Ldg Stdnt Today Awd; East Cntrl Univ; Math Ed.

STUEMKY, MATTHEW D; Ponca City Sr HS; Ponca City, OK; (3); Church Yth Grp; Acpl Chr; Chorus; School Musical; School Play; Variety Show; Rep Stu Cncl; Bsktbl; Ftbl; Tennis.

STUESSY, RENEE L; Broken Arrow Sr HS; Broken Arrow, OK; (4); 249/921; Church Yth Grp; Girl Scts; Library Aide; Teachers Aide; Band; Mrchg Band; Orch; Pep Band; Hon Roll; Dir Awd Outstdng Mscl Achvmt; Made All ST Bnd 93-95; Tulsa Jr Coll; Dental Hygnst.

STUEVE, LUCINDA; Perry Sr HS; Perry, OK; (2); 10/98; Church Yth Grp; 4-H; FBLA; GAA; Natl FFA Org; Pep Clb; Red Cross Aide; Church Choir; Ed Nwsp; Var Bsktbl; Rodeo; Song Ldr Bapt Church; KS ST U; Elem Ed.

STUEVER, ANGELA D; Blackwell HS; Blackwell, OK; (4); Cmnty Wkr; FHA; Hosp Aide; Pep Clb; Red Cross Aide; Spanish Clb; Chorus; Hon Roll; NOC.

STUEVER, JUSTIN P; Blackwell HS; Blackwell, OK; (2); 17/120; FCA; Spanish Clb; Var Bsktbl; Ftbl; Hon Roll; St Hnr Soc.

STUMBAUGH, TALARA DAWN; Central Schl; Sallisaw, OK; (3); Computer Clb; 4-H; Pep Clb; Scholastic Bowl; Phtg Yrbk; Var Sftbl; Hon Roll; Veterinary Practices; Stu Of Today Awd; Emu Ranching; OK ST Univ; Vet.

STUMP, RYAN L; Yukon Middle HS; Yukon, OK; (3); Church Yth Grp; Spanish Clb; Church Choir; Hon Roll; Harding Univ; Bus.

STUMPE, JAYLEEN; Caney Valley HS; Ochelata, OK; (3); 10/64; German Clb; HOBY; Teachers Aide; Ed Nwsp; Ed Yrbk; Pres Frsh Cls; VP Jr Cls; Co-Capt Var Chrldng; Var Trk; Hon Roll; Ballet; Hstry Clb; Soph Homcmng Crt; CU; Phys Thrpy.

STUMPE, JESSICA M; Putnam City North HS; Oklahoma City, OK; (4); 51/464; Sec Treas Church Yth Grp; Drama Clb; Sec Spanish Clb; JV Chrldng; Jr NHS; NHS; OK St Univ; Vet.

STUPAK, CHRISTIE; Moore HS; Moore, OK; (4); Band; Mrchg Band; Jr NHS; OK City CC; Ad.

STURCH, ERIN; Moore HS; Oklahoma City, OK; (4); 78/525; FCA; HOBY; Office Aide; VP Sr Cls; Rep Stu Cncl; Golf; Powder Puff Ftbl; NHS; OK ST U; Phtgrphy.

STURGEON, MICHAEL; Copan HS; Copan, OK; (4); 3/30; Am Leg Boys St; Chess Clb; Quiz Bowl; Scholastic Bowl; Pres Frsh Cls; Pres Soph Cls; Pres Sr Cls; Ofcr Stu Cncl; L Bsbl; L Bsktbl; OK ST U; Sprts Med.

STURGEON, PAULA; Braggs Schl; Braggs, OK; (1); High Hon Roll; Hon Roll.

STURGEON, SCOTT; Cordell Sr HS; Cordell, OK; (4); 4/48; Pres 4-H; Pres Natl FFA Org; Lit Mag; 4-H Awd; High Hon Roll; Kiwanis Awd; Prfct Atten Awd; Office Aide; Teachers Aide; Cit Awd; OK Club Calf Assoc Pres; Tulsa ST Fair Res Grd Champion Steer 95; OK ST Univ; Agribus.

STURGIS, KYLE; Chisholm Sr HS; Enid, OK; (1); Church Yth Grp; Spanish Clb; Chorus; Hon Roll; Jr NHS; Elctrncs Engr.

STURM, COLIN D; Moore HS; Moore, OK; (3); 18/566; Am Leg Boys St; Science Clb; Hist Spanish Clb; VP NHS; Math & Sci Tutor; Medicine.

STUTEVILLE, JENNIFER; Kingfisher HS; Kingfisher, OK; (1); 1/100; Church Yth Grp; FCA; Key Clb; Natl FFA Org; Quiz Bowl; Pres Frsh Cls; Ofcr Stu Cncl; Bsktbl; Chrldng; Hon Roll.

STUTEVILLE, KATHY; Seiling Schl; Seiling, OK; (3); 8/34; Art Clb; Church Yth Grp; FCA; 4-H; FBLA; GAA; HOBY; Key Clb; Letterman Clb; Teachers Aide; 4-H Hall Of Fame; IORG St Offcr; Govs Awdintl Postmarking Awd; Historical Soc; Masonic Stu Of Today Awd; OU; Med.

STUTZMAN, AMY; Adair HS; Pryor, OK; (3); Pres Sec Art Clb; Church Yth Grp; FCA; Sec FHA; Sec Jr Cls; Var Chrldng; High Hon Roll; Hon Roll; Pres Acad Fit Awd; Science Clb; Accntng.

STUTZMAN, MANDY S; Weatherford HS; Weatherford, OK; (3); Church Yth Grp; Chorus; Hon Roll; Southwestern OK ST U.

STYERS, FRANSIS G; Shawnee Sr HS; Shawnee, OK; (3); Latin Clb; Teachers Aide; Orch; Cit Awd; Hon Roll; ER; Cancer Treatment.

SUBIA, JULIE P; Depew HS; Bristow, OK; (2); Church Yth Grp; FCA; GAA; Pep Clb; Quiz Bowl; Spanish Clb; Ofcr Frsh Cls; Ofcr Stu Cncl; Bsktbl; Sftbl; Outstdng Achvmt Awd; Natl Eng Merit Awd; OK ST Univ; Law.

SUGGS, ANGI B; Calumet Schl; Calumet, OK; (1); 2/40; Church Yth Grp; FCA; Pep Clb; Quiz Bowl; Scholastic Bowl; Spanish Clb; Var Bsktbl; Var Chrldng; Gov Hon Prg Awd; High Hon Roll; TX A&M; CPA.

SUGGS, CRYSTAL M; Ponca City Sr HS; Ponca City, OK; (3); Church Yth Grp; Chorus; Church Choir; Gym; Vllybl; Hon Roll; Worksite Lrng; Chorale.

SUITER, CORI S; Edmond Memorial HS; Edmond, OK; (1); 87/437; JV Pom Pon; Hon Roll; U Of OK.

SUITER, DIANE J; Duncan HS; Duncan, OK; (3); 10/235; Am Leg Aux Girls St; Church Yth Grp; Hosp Aide; Key Clb; Letterman Clb; Quiz Bowl; Sec Spanish Clb; Tennis; NHS; Pres Acad Fit Awd; Delg Natl Yth Ldrshp Cncl; Yth Advy Cncl Peer Pal Prgm; Boston Univ; Intl Rltns.

SUITER, ROBERT; Duncan HS; Duncan, OK; (4); 32/214; Am Leg Boys St; French Clb; Letterman Clb; Quiz Bowl; Ofcr Stu Cncl; Var Bsktbl; Socr; Var Trk; Hon Roll; Jr NHS; Frgn Exch Stu To Blgm 95; Yng Dems/Yng Reps Sgt At Arms.

SUKOW, JILL K; Bartlesville Mid HS; Bartlesville, OK; (2); Church Yth Grp; French Clb; Library Aide; Chorus; Church Choir; French Hon Soc; Hon Roll.

SULLAWAY, STACY M; Edmond Memorial HS; Edmond, OK; (2); Church Yth Grp; Spanish Clb; Chorus; School Musical; School Play; Stage Crew; Variety Show; Hon Roll; Pres Acad Fit Awd; Mus.

SULLINS, TRISHA; Checotah HS; Checotah, OK; (2); #33 in class; FHA; Chorus; Jom Tutor Jr HS Stdnts; Med Dr.

SULLIVAN, BETH S; Fletcher Jr Sr HS; Elgin, OK; (4); FHA; Sec Soph Cls; Sec Jr Cls; Rep Sr Cls; Sec Stu Cncl; Bsktbl; Sftbl; Cit Awd; Hon Roll; Prfct Atten Awd; Msc Bus.

SULLIVAN, JAIME; Midwest City HS; Midwest City, OK; (2); 58/501; Spanish Clb; Teachers Aide; Ed Yrbk; Cit Awd; Gov Hon Prg Awd; NHS; Prfct Atten Awd.

SULLIVAN, JULIE; Durant HS; Durant, OK; (4); Church Yth Grp; Dance Clb; VICA; Chorus; Church Choir; Sec Jr Cls; Sec Sr Cls; Rep Stu Cncl; Capt Chrldng; High Hon Roll; Southeastern OK ST U; Bus Mgm.

SULLIVAN, LIONEL C; Durant HS; Durant, OK; (4); Church Yth Grp; Computer Clb; DECA; Quiz Bowl; Scholastic Bowl; Chorus; Rptr Nwsp; L Golf; Hon Roll; NHS; His Awd; Bus/Info Systms.

SULLIVAN, MEAGAN B; Charles Page HS; Sand Springs, OK; (1); Church Yth Grp; Debate Tm; NFL; Hon Roll; Kempo Karate; Pvt Voice Lssns; Vocal Music.

SULLIVAN, MITCHELL A; Will Rogers HS; Tulsa, OK; (1); Church Yth Grp; ROTC; Hon Roll; Amer Bus Acad; Cmptr Technlgy; Fndmntl Bus Technlgy; Chiropractor.

SULLIVAN, RENEE; Oklahoma Bible Acad; Nash, OK; (4); Church Yth Grp; FCA; Chorus; Treas Jr Cls; Var Capt Bsktbl; Var L Trk; High Hon Roll; NHS; Val; OK ST U; Scndry Ed.

SULLIVAN, RYAN; Vian HS; Vian, OK; (3); 2/50; Art Clb; FCA; Science Clb; Pres Frsh Cls; Ofcr Soph Cls; Sec Jr Cls; Pres Sr Cls; Var Bsbl; Var Bsktbl; Var Ftbl; U Of OK; Pre Med.

SULLIVAN, RYAN G; Grove HS; Grove, OK; (3); Natl FFA Org; Ed Nwsp; Phtg Yrbk; JV Var Ftbl; Var Golf; Var Mgr(s); Score Keeper; Wt Lftg; Hon Roll; Show Lvstck Lcl Prgms/ST Wd; Ft Lewis U; Bus/Agric.

SULLIVAN, SHANNEY L; Anadarko HS; Anadarko, OK; (3); Church Yth Grp; FCA; Chorus; Church Choir; Rep Stu Cncl; Bsktbl; Powder Puff Ftbl; Trk; Hon Roll; NHS; U Of Sci & Arts Of OK; Bus.

SULLIVAN, STEVEN R; Hydro Jr Sr HS; Weatherford, OK; (3); 4/30; English Clb; FHA; Natl FFA Org; Quiz Bowl; School Play; Rep Soph Cls; Intrml Bsbl; Hon Roll; SWOSU; Pharm.

SULLIVAN, TARA; Anadarko HS; Anadarko, OK; (2); 1/120; Pres Church Yth Grp; Cmnty Wkr; VP FBLA; SADD; Sec Thesps; Chorus; Pres Frsh Cls; Pres Soph Cls; Treas Stu Cncl; NHS; Brigham Young U; Theatre.

SUMMERS, ASHLEY D; Catoosa HS; Catoosa, OK; (4); 20/250; Church Yth Grp; HOBY; Pep Clb; Spanish Clb; Teachers Aide; Ed Yrbk; Pres Frsh Cls; VP Soph Cls; Ofcr Sr Cls; Pres Stu Cncl; Tulsa U; Psych.

SUMMERS, JASON W; Okmulgee HS; Okmulgee, OK; (2); Church Yth Grp; Hon Roll.

SUMMERS, JONATHAN Z; Roff HS; Roff, OK; (3); Natl Beta Clb; Natl FFA Org; Pres Frsh Cls; Var Bsktbl; Upward Bound Math/Sci; Comp Sci.

SUMMERS, JULIE; Locust Grove HS; Locust Grove, OK; (2); 1/100; Church Yth Grp; German Clb; Speech Tm; Co-Capt Chrldng; Hon Roll; NHS.

SUMMERS JR, MAURICE C; Midwest City HS; Midwest City, OK; (3); 67/387; Drama Clb; ROTC; VICA; Wt Lftg; Cit Awd; Jr NHS; Rcvd Schltc Ltr; Bus; Tchr.

SUMMERS, MELISSA; Shawnee Sr HS; Shawnee, OK; (4); Pres DECA; French Clb; Hosp Aide; HOBY; Church Choir; Ofcr Frsh Cls; Ofcr Soph Cls; JV Tennis; NHS; U Of Central OK; Accntng.

SUMMERS, ROBERT L; Valliant HS; Valliant, OK; (4); Church Yth Grp; Natl FFA Org; Teachers Aide; Chorus; Mgr Yrbk; JV Bsktbl; Var Ftbl; Var Tennis; Ntl Merit Ltr; Tech Stu Assn Rep; Southwestern A/G Univ; Minstr.

SUMMERS, ROBERT R; Dustin Schl; Dustin, OK; (3); 4/17; Cmnty Wkr; VP Rptr Natl FFA Org; Quiz Bowl; FFA Spch Cntst; Livestck Exhibtr.

SUMMERS, TODD; Shawnee Sr HS; Shawnee, OK; (2); Quiz Bowl; Scholastic Bowl; Bsktbl; Socr; Wt Lftg; High Hon Roll; U NC; Engr.

SUMMERS, TONYA L; Ft Cobb-Broxton HS; Fort Cobb, OK; (2); Church Yth Grp; FHA; Ofcr Stu Cncl; Chrldng; Hon Roll; Upward Bound Pgm Southwestern; Amer His Awd; Southwestern; Pediatrician.

SUMMY, ERICA; Moss Schl; Wetumka, OK; (4); 1/16; Church Yth Grp; Pres FCA; Ed Nwsp; Ed Yrbk; VP Frsh Cls; Sec Soph Cls; VP Jr Cls; Var Chrldng; Var Sftbl; Hon Roll; Woodmen Of The World Amer His Awd; Outstndng Young Schlr In Ger; Tandy Corp Outstdng Stu Awd; East Cntrl Univ; Jrnlsm.

SUMNER, CRISTI; Wellston Schl; Wellston, OK; (4); 1/42; Church Yth Grp; Hist FHA; Office Aide; Var Capt Bsktbl; Var Capt Sftbl; Hon Roll; NHS; Val; FCA; VP Pep Clb; Bsktbl Homcmng Qn 96; 66 Conf All Acad Team Bsktbl, Sftbl 95-96; OK Bapt Univ; Math Ed.

SUMPTER, BRANDY; Wister Schl; Fanshawe, OK; (2); Church Yth Grp; Cmnty Wkr; FCA; FHA; Nwsp; High Hon Roll; NHS; Val; Typng; Carl Albert ST Coll.

SUMPTER, DIANNA L; Broken Arrow Sr HS; Broken Arrow, OK; (3); VP Drama Clb; NFL; Thesps; School Musical; School Play; Stage Crew; Phtg Ed Nwsp; Phtg Ed Yrbk; Treas Stu Cncl; Socr; Taekwondo; Stu Cncl Person Of Yr; Commnctn; Theatre; Pub Relations.

SUMPTER, LORA A; Colcord Schl; Colcord, OK; (4); FBLA; FHA; Office Aide; Band; Yrbk; Hon Roll; Ntl Merit Schol; NSU; Nrsng.

SUMRAL, DERRICK E; U S Grant HS; Oklahoma City, OK; (3); Church Yth Grp; JV Bsktbl; JV Crs Cntry; Hon Roll; Three Star Gen Awd Soc Stud 95-96.

SUMRALL, LORI; Midwest City HS; Midwest City, OK; (4); 7/419; Rptr French Clb; Key Clb; SADD; Ed Yrbk; Ofcr Jr Cls; Ofcr Sr Cls; Vllybl; NHS; Prfct Atten Awd; Val; U Cntrl OK; Elem Ed.

SUNDERLAND, CHAD R; Union Sr HS; Broken Arrow, OK; (3); 27/705; Cmnty Wkr; Spanish Clb; Var L Swmmng; Cit Awd; High Hon Roll; Hon Roll; Jr NHS; NHS; Pres Acad Fit Awd; Spanish NHS; All St Swimming Team; 1st Rnnr Up HS St 100 Breaststoke; DFY.

SUNSTRUM, BRANDEE W; Putnam City North HS; Oklahoma City, OK; (3); JV Chrldng; Hon Roll; Gymnstcs; CO.

SURRATT, AMY; Moore HS; Moore, OK; (4); 92/550; Spanish Clb; Rep Stu Cncl; Mgr Ftbl; L Pom Pon; Powder Puff Ftbl; Mgr Wrstlng; Hon Roll; Jr NHS; NHS; Future Phy Tomorrow; Jr Ftbl Attendant; Sr Wrestling Qn; Oil Bowl Qn Candidate; TX OK All-Star Game; OK Univ; Phy Thrpy.

SURRATT, DAVID A; Union Intermediate HS; Tulsa, OK; (2); 356/800; Am Leg Boys St; Church Yth Grp; Spanish Clb; JV Bsbl; Hon Roll; Peer Mediatr; ARC Stu; Tae Kwon Do; KS U; Bio.

SURRATT, WENDY; Valliant HS; Valliant, OK; (3); 8/76; VP FHA; Library Aide; Pep Clb; Quiz Bowl; Science Clb; JV Bsktbl; Trk; NHS; Spanish Clb; Mst Imprvd Track; 1st Pl Creed Speaking & Interpretation Jr Div; KMO; U Of OK; Law.

SUTER, JOY L; Ponca City Sr HS; Kaw, OK; (3); 147/356; Church Yth Grp; Crs Cntry; Mgr(s); Score Keeper; Trk; Hon Roll; Yth Alive Bible Clb; Retirement Ctr Vol.

SUTHERLAND, DENVER R; Agra Schl; Agra, OK; (2); Church Yth Grp; FHA; Natl FFA Org; Quiz Bowl; Scholastic Bowl; School Play; Treas Soph Cls; JV Var Bsbl; JV Var Bsktbl; JV Ftbl.

SUTHERLAND, LISA; Chickasha Jr HS; Chickasha, OK; (1); Church Yth Grp; French Clb; Girl Scts; Quiz Bowl; Band; Mrchg Band; Var Swmmng; Hon Roll.

SUTHERLIN, CHRISTINA M; El Reno Sr HS; El Reno, OK; (2); Church Yth Grp; FTA; Band; Color Guard; Drm Mjr(t); Mrchg Band; High Hon Roll; Jr NHS; Show Choir; OK Close Up; Leaders Of Tomorrow; OK Univ; Medicine; OB-GYN; Ped.

SUTMILLER, GREGORY; Heavener HS; Heavener, OK; (2); Church Yth Grp; Quiz Bowl; Band; Chorus; Church Choir; Mrchg Band; Hon Roll; Math.

SUTTER, BETHANY; Macarthur Jr HS; Lawton, OK; (1); Art Clb; Church Yth Grp; FCA; Girl Scts; Church Choir; Chrldng; Gym; Hon Roll; NHS; Seat Belt, Belt Safety Art Cont 1st Pl; Arts For All Art Cont 2nd Pl; Top Schl Artist; Chrldng Squad; Cal-Art; Anomator.

SUTTON, ANDREA; Woodward HS; Woodward, OK; (3); Church Yth Grp; Letterman Clb; Model UN; Pep Clb; Bsktbl; Powder Puff Ftbl; High Hon Roll; Hon Roll; Kiwanis Awd; NHS; OK Hnr Soc; U Of OK; Psych.

SUTTON, DANA R; Velma Alma HS; Loco, OK; (2); Church Yth Grp; FCA; Var Bsktbl; Var Crs Cntry; Var Trk; Hon Roll; Ntl Merit Ltr; Prfct Atten Awd; Hist Awd; OK Hnr Soc; 4th Pl OK Hist Schlstc Meet; Sprts Med.

SUTTON, ELINOR C; Cascia Hall Prep School; Tulsa, OK; (2); Church Yth Grp; HOBY; Service Clb; Teachers Aide; Chorus; Var Tennis; High Hon Roll; Jr NHS; Cmnty Wkr; French Clb; Ballet; Piano; Soccer.

SUTTON, JARED J; Seminole Jr Sr HS; Seminole, OK; (4); 25/110; Church Yth Grp; FCA; Math Clb; Spanish Clb; Chorus; Church Choir; VP Frsh Cls; Pres Soph Cls; VP Jr Cls; VP Sr Cls; Scored Super Scores At Dist Regional & St Vocal Solo; Natl Champs-Free Will Bapt Vocal Solo 2 Times; Phy Thrpst; Sports Medicine.

SUVAK, MIRANDA G; B T Washington HS; Tulsa, OK; (3); Spanish Clb; Teachers Aide; High Hon Roll; Hon Roll; NHS; Yount Adult Advy Bd; Tn Tm Vol; U Of OK; Envrnmntl Sci.

SWAFFORD, CARISSA P; Union Sr HS; Tulsa, OK; (4); Cmnty Wkr; FCA; Red Cross Aide; Ed Yrbk; Capt Chrldng; Capt Pom Pon; Powder Puff Ftbl; Hon Roll; Pres Acad Fit Awd; Intnl Clb; Lt Gov Div 15 E Key Clb; Best Capt NCA Dance Camp; Symph Set; U Of OK.

SWAGERTY, ADAM L; Fletcher Jr Sr HS; Fletcher, OK; (4); 10/32; Church Yth Grp; Office Aide; Scholastic Bowl; Teachers Aide; Yrbk; JV Bsktbl; Hon Roll; Pres Acad Fit Awd; Gftd & Tlntd Pgm; Stu Of Month 93 & 96; Cameron U; Accntg.

SWAIM, AMY D; El Reno Sr HS; El Reno, OK; (2); 28/230; Church Yth Grp; Spanish Clb; Band; Church Choir; Mrchg Band; JV Bsktbl; Crs Cntry; Cit Awd; High Hon Roll.

SWAIM, MARIA; Charles Page HS; Sand Springs, OK; (4); 19/342; Church Yth Grp; French Clb; HOBY; Speech Tm; Color Guard; VP Soph Cls; Sec Jr Cls; Chrldng; Pom Pon; NHS; Ballet; U Of OK; Dsgn.

SWAIN, JESSICA N; Union Intermediate HS; Tulsa, OK; (2); 53/800; Cmnty Wkr; Dance Clb; FBLA; Key Clb; Office Aide; Spanish Clb; Gov Hon Prg Awd; Hon Roll; Jr NHS; NHS; DFY VP; Child Dev.

SWAIN, MICHAEL E; Colcord Schl; Colcord, OK; (4); 5/42; Cmnty Wkr; English Clb; Letterman Clb; Library Aide; Office Aide; Q&S; Scholastic Bowl; Spanish Clb; Varsity Clb; School Play; Pub Poetry Natl Authologies; Poets Guild Mbr; Goddard Coll; Creative Wrtng.

SWANDA, AMY E; Putnam City HS; Oklahoma City, OK; (3); 137/407; Cmnty Wkr; Girl Scts; Spanish Clb; Stage Crew; Variety Show; Mock Trial Prgm 3 Yrs; TSA Cngrssnl Dgree; Architecture.

SWANEGAN, KAREN; Kingfisher HS; Kingfisher, OK; (2); Debate Tm; Drama Clb; NFL; VP Spanish Clb; Speech Tm; Thesps; Band; School Play; Treas Soph Cls; Hon Roll; Clss Fav 94-95; All-St Speech 94-95; HS Yng Black Amer Qn 95-96; Spelman Coll; Neurolgy.

SWANSON, ANNIE R; Swanson Home Schl; Guthrie, OK; (1); 1/1; Cmnty Wkr; Computer Clb; Debate Tm; Library Aide; Office Aide; Red Cross Aide; Teachers Aide; School Play; Pres Frsh Cls; God Lovers Bible Study.

SWANSON, CARA F; Stillwater Jr HS; Stillwater, OK; (1); Church Yth Grp; Office Aide; Band; Color Guard; Mrchg Band; Pep Band; Mgr(s); Pres Acad Fit Awd; Girls Smmr Sftbl League; BYU; Paralegal; Photo.

SWANSON, JOHNNIE L; Douglass HS; Midwest City, OK; (2); Office Aide; Chorus; Church Choir; School Musical; Ftbl; Socr; Tennis; Trk; Wrstlng; Hon Roll; Grambling; Phy Thrpst.

SWANSON, LESLEY; Putnam City North HS; Oklahoma City, OK; (3); HOBY; School Musical; School Play; Pres Frsh Cls; Rep Soph Cls; Ofcr Jr Cls; Ofcr Stu Cncl; Pom Pon; Cit Awd; Amer Legion Stu Today; Commnctns.

SWANSON, MEGAN A; Stillwater Sr HS; Stillwater, OK; (2); Church Yth Grp; Girl Scts; Teachers Aide; Orch; Var Socr; Cit Awd; Hon Roll; Pres Acad Fit Awd; Langston Univ; Phy Thrpst.

SWANSON, MISTY M; Warner HS; Webbers Falls, OK; (4); 20/50; FCA; Pres VP 4-H; Pres FHA; Spanish Clb; Phtg Nwsp; Ofcr Stu Cncl; Var Bsktbl; JV Crs Cntry; Var Sftbl; Cit Awd; Yth Ctznshp Awd Wnnr Schlsp Presntd By Sorptmst; St Projct Wnnr In Are Of Shep Prodctn Schlsp; Connors ST Coll; Medicine.

SWARB, STACEE; Carl Albert HS; Midwest City, OK; (1); 46/310; Church Yth Grp; Cmnty Wkr; FCA; Library Aide; Pep Clb; Chorus; Var Chrldng; Trk; High Hon Roll; Jr NHS; Natl Chmpnshp Chrldng Sqd Rnnr-Up; Motivated Against Drugs; All Amer Chrldr NCA; OK Chrstn U.

SWARER, CORBI R; Locust Grove HS; Locust Grove, OK; (2); German Clb; Ecology Club; Law.

SWART, RYAN P; Cimarron Public Schl; Ames, OK; (4); 3/33; French Clb; Natl FFA Org; Teachers Aide; Band; Mrchg Band; Pep Band; JV Bsbl; NHS; Pres Acad Fit Awd; St FFA Degree; OSU; Diesel Tech.

SWARTWOOD, KARA; Cheyenne HS; Cheyenne, OK; (3); 1/24; Church Yth Grp; HOBY; Chorus; Rep Soph Cls; Rep Jr Cls; Wt Lftg; Jr NHS; NHS; Math & Sci Acad; SW OK ST U; Pharmacy.

SWEARENGIN, HEATHER D; Gore HS; Gore, OK; (3); German Clb; JV Var Bsktbl; Hon Roll; Connors St Col; Bus.

SWEAT, RENATA D; Harrah HS; Harrah, OK; (1); 37/175; Church Yth Grp; Chorus; School Musical; School Play; Hon Roll; Modeling Cls.

SWEDLUND, STACY M; Macarthur Sr HS; Lawton, OK; (4); 56/260; Church Yth Grp; Pres FBLA; Science Clb; Spanish Clb; Score Keeper; High Hon Roll; Prfct Atten Awd; Pres Acad Fit Awd; Cmnty Wkr; Scholastic Bowl; Great Plains Area Vo-Tech Employabilty Awd; Great Plains Area Vo-Tech Natl Henos Soc Mem; Cameron Univ; Fin.

SWEENEY, CHRISTINA R; Latta Sr HS; Ada, OK; (2); FHA; Quiz Bowl; Rep Soph Cls; Rep Stu Cncl; JV Var Bsktbl; Var L Sftbl; Hon Roll; NHS; Masonic Awd 94-95; Nrsng.

SWEENY, REBECCA R; Ripley HS; Stillwater, OK; (2); 2/40; FBLA; FHA; Math Clb; Natl FFA Org; Science Clb; Var Bsktbl; Trk; High Hon Roll; Val.

SWEET, BRIAN; Edmond Memorial HS; Edmond, OK; (4); 61/329; JV Ftbl; Wt Lftg; High Hon Roll; Hon Roll; Jr NHS; NHS; Pres Acad Fit Awd; St Schlr; U Of OK; Aerospce Eng.

SWEET, JOSHUA T; Choctaw HS; Choctaw, OK; (2); Church Yth Grp; FCA; Golf; UCO; Rsrvs.

SWEETIN, HILLARY; Pittsburg Schl; Blanco, OK; (2); #1 in class; Var Bsktbl; Var Sftbl; High Hon Roll; Hon Roll.

SWENN, MISTIE S; Woodward HS; Gage, OK; (4); 64/154; Church Yth Grp; Computer Clb; Key Clb; Natl FFA Org; Pep Clb; Spanish Clb; Teachers Aide; Powder Puff Ftbl; Hon Roll; Rodeo Clb; NW St Univ; Elem Ed.

SWENSON, SONDRA L; Jenks HS; Tulsa, OK; (3); Boy Scts; DECA; French Clb; Key Clb; Teachers Aide; Ed Yrbk; Rep Stu Cncl; Chrldng; Pom Pon; Hon Roll; DECA 1st Pl St Cmptn; Dance Co Jazz & Pointe; Lbrl Arts.

SWEPSTON, SHANNON; Tahlequah Sr HS; Tahlequah, OK; (4); 22/351; Church Yth Grp; Pres DECA; Pep Clb; Spanish Clb; SADD; Var Crs Cntry; Var Trk; Cit Awd; Jr NHS; NHS; Mrktng Intrnshp; Northeastern ST U; Bus Dvlpmnt.

SWEZEY, NICK D; Bartlesville Sr HS; Bartlesville, OK; (3); 186/485; Boy Scts; Church Yth Grp; Computer Clb; Science Clb; Spanish Clb; Hon Roll; NHS; Prfct Atten Awd; Spanish NHS.

SWIFT, JENNIFER; Hugo HS; Hugo, OK; (2); Church Yth Grp; Band; Jazz Band; NHS; OK ST Univ; Vet Med.

SWIFT, JENNIFER M; Antlers Sr HS; Antlers, OK; (2); Chorus; Ofcr Jr Cls; Bsktbl; Vllybl; Ntl Merit Ltr; Choctaw Nation Coll; Home Dcrtr.

SWIFT, STEPHANNIE N; Stilwell HS; Stilwell, OK; (2); Drama Clb; 4-H; Girl Scts; NFL; Spanish Clb; Varsity Clb; Sec Frsh Cls; VP Soph Cls; Var L Bsktbl; Powder Puff Ftbl; Soph Bsktbl Attndnt; Frosh Sec D-Fy; NSU; Pedtrcn.

SWIGART, JEFFREY; Woodward HS; Woodward, OK; (2); Church Yth Grp; Computer Clb; Treas High German Clb; Rep Key Clb; Model UN; Church Choir; NHS; Art Clb; FBLA; Letterman Clb; TSA Pres/Sgt At Arms; Mock Trial Outstdng Lwyr.

SWIGER, BRETT; Enid Sr HS; Enid, OK; (4); 55/420; Am Leg Boys St; CAP; Debate Tm; Math Clb; ROTC; School Play; VP Stu Cncl; L Crs Cntry; NHS; Church Yth Grp; Teens Need Teens Drm Trp; US Air Frc Acad; Pilot.

SWIGERT, SUSAN L; Mounds Schl; Mounds, OK; (3); Church Yth Grp; FHA; Band; Chorus; Church Choir; Jazz Band; Mrchg Band; Pep Band; Hon Roll; Prfct Atten Awd; Csmtlgst.

SWINDELL, DUSTIN; Wellston Schl; Wellston, OK; (4); 3/51; Church Yth Grp; FCA; FHA; Math Tm; Scholastic Bowl; SADD; Teachers Aide; Var Bsktbl; Var Ftbl; High Hon Roll; OK ST U; Engrng.

SWINDLES, LUCAS; Westmoore HS; Oklahoma City, OK; (4); 247/610; German Clb; JA; Library Aide; Office Aide; Scholastic Bowl; Jr Achvmnt Del Co Mstrs Prgm; Stdnt For Cleaner Envrnmnt; Spec Recog Awd Appld Ec; OSU; Forestry.

SWINFORD, LESLEE; Wynnewood HS; Wynnewood, OK; (2); 1/47; Hosp Aide; HOBY; Band; Flag Corp; Jazz Band; VP Soph Cls; High Hon Roll; NHS; OK Hnr Soc; ECU, OBU & SCOBDA Hnr Bands; OK ST U; Orthdntst.

SWINK, JOEY; Stigler HS; Stigler, OK; (1); Art Clb; Hon Roll; Rdo.

SWISHER, BRENDON; Bartlesville Mid HS; Bartlesville, OK; (2); Letterman Clb; Varsity Clb; JV Var Bsktbl; JV Var Ftbl; Var Trk; Wt Lftg; Cit Awd; High Hon Roll; Masonic & Civitan Awds.

SWYDEN, KATY J; Heritage Hall Schl; Edmond, OK; (4); Art Clb; Cmnty Wkr; Pep Clb; Spanish Clb; Chorus; Stat Sftbl; Hon Roll; Tumbling Gymnastics; Piano, Voice Lssns; OSO; Bus.

SYKES, ANREA L; Mc Lain Career Acad; Tulsa, OK; (3); Church Yth Grp; Cmnty Wkr; Key Clb; ROTC; Ofcr Stu Cncl; Bsktbl; High Hon Roll; Hon Roll; Jr NHS; NHS; TX A&M; Nrsng.

SYKORA, KARA; Edmond Meml HS; Edmond, OK; (3); 49/371; Church Yth Grp; Cmnty Wkr; FHA; Spanish Clb; SADD; NHS.

SYLVESTER, JASON D; Perry Sr HS; Perry, OK; (3); FBLA; Natl FFA Org; Bsktbl; Golf; Jr NHS; Pres Acad Fit Awd; OK St Univ.

SZELA, BEN R; Union Sr HS; Tulsa, OK; (3); Chorus; Jr NHS; NHS; ARC Giftd Prog; Eng.

TABBERER, CHRISTOPHER A; Broken Arrow Sr HS; Broken Arrow, OK; (4); 327/921; Boy Scts; Church Yth Grp; Cmnty Wkr; Teachers Aide; Acpl Chr; Ofcr Soph Cls; Ofcr Sr Cls; Ofcr Stu Cncl; Hon Roll; Pres Acad Fit Awd; Schl D J; Tulsa CC; Pub Rltns Spclst.

TABER, RETHA L; Mc Loud HS; Newalla, OK; (1); Church Yth Grp; FHA; Natl FFA Org; Ofcr Stu Cncl; Sftbl.

TABOR, AMY L; Muldrow HS; Muldrow, OK; (1); Natl Beta Clb; Science Clb; Spanish Clb; Var Chrldng; Hon Roll.

TABOR, KELLY D; Roland Sr HS; Muldrow, OK; (4); Church Yth Grp; Speech Tm; Band; Color Guard; Sec Soph Cls; Rep Jr Cls; Rep Sr Cls; Rep Stu Cncl; Var L Bsktbl; Var L Chrldng; Homecoming Queen; Westark CC.

TABOR, TEDDY W; Antlers Sr HS; Antlers, OK; (3); Natl FFA Org; Ofcr Bsbl; Ftbl; Hon Roll; OK Yth Rodeo Assn; Yth Bullriders Assn.

TAC, SINGI; Northeast HS; Oklahoma City, OK; (3); 14/125; FBLA; Office Aide; Science Clb; Spanish Clb; JV Vllybl; High Hon Roll; Hon Roll; Natl Acad Decatholon; Coll Clb; Yth Ct; Hnr Soc; U Of CA Irvine; Sci.

TACKER, JUSTIN; Pauls Valley HS; Pauls Valley, OK; (2); 13/257; High Hon Roll; OK Hnr Soc 95-; E Cntrl Univ; Busn Mngmt.

TACKER, TRAVIS L; Mountain View-Gotebo HS; Mountain View, OK; (3); Am Leg Boys St; Church Yth Grp; Cmnty Wkr; FCA; 4-H; Natl FFA Org; Quiz Bowl; Pres Jr Cls; Pres Sr Cls; Sec Stu Cncl; OK FFA Prfcncy Awd; Local FFA Pres; Pre Dntstry.

TACKETT, BRANDON; Wagoner Sr HS; Wagoner, OK; (4); 10/137; Am Leg Boys St; Church Yth Grp; Cmnty Wkr; FCA; 4-H; FBLA; Letterman Clb; Pres Sr Cls; Rep Stu Cncl; L Ftbl; Danforth I Dare You Awd; Top 10%; All Dist Ftbl; OU; Med.

TACKETT, LISA; Panama HS; Bokoshe, OK; (4); 1/53; HOBY; Yrbk; Ofcr Soph Cls; Rptr Jr Cls; Pres Stu Cncl; Bsktbl; Chrldng; Sftbl; NHS; Val; OSU.

TACKETT, SARA E; Edmond Santa Fe HS; Edmond, OK; (2); 61/343; FCA; Pep Clb; SADD; Chorus; JV Var Chrldng; JV Trk; NHS; Ldrshp Trng Wrkshp; Tri-M Msc Hnr Soc; OK ST U; PT.

TADLOCK, KELLI A; Kiowa Jr-Sr HS; Mcalester, OK; (3); 4-H; Girl Scts; Quiz Bowl; SADD; Church Choir; Nwsp; Yrbk; 4-H Awd; Hon Roll; Yth Alive.

TAFOYA, DUGAN J; Western Heights Sr HS; Oklahoma City, OK; (3); 43/165; Church Yth Grp; Cmnty Wkr; FCA; Church Choir; Ftbl; Golf; Wt Lftg; Wrstlng; Hon Roll; NHS; LEAP Engl I/II; OSU; Forestry/Game Mgmnt.

TAGGART, KENDRA; Gracemont HS; Gracemont, OK; (4); 1/16; Am Leg Aux Girls St; 4-H; HOBY; Ed Nwsp; Ed Yrbk; Rep Frsh Cls; Rep Soph Cls; Rep Jr Cls; Rep Sr Cls; Var L Bsktbl; Show Angus Heifers; OK ST U; Ag Ec.

TAGGART, KENDRA; Gracemont HS; Fort Cobb, OK; (4); 1/16; Am Leg Aux Girls St; HOBY; Ed Nwsp; Ed Yrbk; Rep Frsh Cls; Rep Soph Cls; Rep Jr Cls; Rep Sr Cls; Var L Bsktbl; Var L Sftbl; Show Angus Heifers; OK ST U; Ag Ec.

TAGGART, LAUREN PAIGE; Thomas A Edison HS; Tulsa, OK; (3); Church Yth Grp; VP Sec Key Clb; Church Choir; Sprt Ed Yrbk; Ofcr Jr Cls; Hon Roll; NHS; French Clb; Camp Fire Hrzn Club; SAIL Explr Pres; Boy Scout Gold Awd; OK ST Univ; Bus Mgmt.

TAGGART, LIBBY; Putnam City North HS; Oklahoma City, OK; (3); Church Yth Grp; DECA; Treas JCL; Rep Key Clb; Chorus; School Play; Crs Cntry; DECA Chpln 2 Yrs/ST/NATL Career Dvlpmnt Conf/3rd Plc Retail Mrchndsng; U Of Cntrl OK; Mrktg.

TAI, JOYCE; Jenks HS; Tulsa, OK; (4); 8/540; Sec Art Clb; German Clb; Key Clb; Treas Mu Alpha Theta; Chorus; Yrbk; Kiwanis Awd; NHS; Pres Schlr; Val; OK Acad Schlr; Pres Ed Awd; Tandy Tech Schlr; U Of OK; Vsl Comm/Bus.

TAKACH, MELISSA J; Memorial HS; Tulsa, OK; (4); 27/250; Cmnty Wkr; Spanish Clb; Chorus; Jazz Band; School Musical; Swing Chorus; Gov Hon Prg Awd; NHS; Intnl Clb; High Hon Roll; Camp Fr; Intl Frgn Lang Awd; Intl Yth Coalition Sec, Treas; U Of Tulsa; Music.

TAKES-HORSE, ADAM C; Colbert Jr Sr HS; Colbert, OK; (3); Church Yth Grp; Library Aide; JV Var Bsktbl; Hon Roll; Amer Indian Stu Assn Pres; Chickasaw Nation Soph Stu Of The Yr; Chickasaw Soph Ath & Jr Ath Of The Yr.

TALBOTT, FRANKIE D; Bartlesville Jr HS; Bartlesville, OK; (3); 64/445; Church Yth Grp; Library Aide; Band; Mrchg Band; High Hon Roll.

TALBOTT, TIMOTHY B; Mc Loud HS; Mc Loud, OK; (2); Church Yth Grp; Cmnty Wkr; FCA; Letterman Clb; Natl FFA Org; Bsktbl; Ftbl; Score Keeper; Wt Lftg; Hon Roll; FFA Greenhand Sec; U Of OK; HS Tchr/Ftbl Coach.

TALIAFERRO, TARA; Lone Grove HS; Ardmore, OK; (4); FHA; Sec Key Clb; Math Clb; Science Clb; Pres Chorus; School Musical; Sec Treas NHS; Untd Cmmrcl Trvlrs Stu Of Mnth; Natl Eng Mrt, Natl Hist & Govt Awds; U Of Cntrl OK; Vcl Msc Ed.

TALKINGTON, DEREK; Newcastle HS; Newcastle, OK; (2); #7 in class; VP FBLA; Sec Soph Cls; JV Bsktbl; FCA; HOBY; Hon Roll; NHS; Air Force Acad.

TALKINGTON, KAILEE J; Dickson HS; Ardmore, OK; (2); Church Yth Grp; FHA; German Clb; Key Clb; Office Aide; SADD; Teachers Aide; Chorus; Yrbk; Hon Roll; Chrch Yth Choir; SOSU; Sprts Med.

TALLANT, RICHARD H; Owasso Sr HS; Owasso, OK; (2); 1/451; FCA; JV Var Bsktbl; L Var Ftbl; L Var Socr; High Hon Roll; NHS; Odyssey Mind; Olympc Dev Pgm.

TALLBEAR, NECOLE E; Hartshorne Sr HS; Asher, OK; (4); 1/20; FBLA; FHA; Natl Beta Clb; Bsktbl; Var Crs Cntry; Trk; Hon Roll; NHS; Ntl Merit Ltr; Val; OK Hnr Soc; OK Indian Hnr Soc; 95 Kateri Hnr Dance Princess; Northeastern ST Univ; Pediatrn.

TALLENT, BREMEN; Victory Christian Schl; Sand Springs, OK; (1); Church Yth Grp; Color Guard; JV Chrldng; Gym; Hon Roll; Homcmng Attendant; OK Jr Rodeo Assn, Natl Barrel Horse Assn; Tchr.

TALLENT, KYLE C; Verden HS; Anadarko, OK; (4); 9/27; Church Yth Grp; FHA; Letterman Clb; Natl FFA Org; Science Clb; Rep Frsh Cls; VP Jr Cls; Ofcr Bsbl; Bsktbl; Hon Roll.

TALLEY, CHEVONNE L; Westmoore HS; Oklahoma City, OK; (3); Cmnty Wkr; FCA; Math Tm; Office Aide; Spanish Clb; Teachers Aide; Sec Frsh Cls; Var Bsktbl; Chrldng; Sftbl; Var Bsktbl Tm Courage Awd; Trck/Fld Jaguar Pride Awd; Med.

TALLEY, JENNIFER; Deer Creek HS; Oklahoma City, OK; (3); #5 in class; Church Yth Grp; FBLA; Science Clb; School Play; Powder Puff Ftbl; Var L Sftbl; Var L Tennis; NHS; News 101; OK ST Univ; Engrng.

TALLEY, KENNY L; Star Spencer HS; Spencer, OK; (4); 32/122; Church Yth Grp; Computer Clb; FBLA; Yrbk; Ofcr Frsh Cls; Pres Soph Cls; Ofcr Jr Cls; Ofcr Sr Cls; Bsktbl; Crs Cntry; Murray ST Coll; Cmptr Sci.

TALLEY, MATTHEW D; Okeene Jr Sr HS; Okeene, OK; (2); Boy Scts; Church Yth Grp; Hon Roll; Prfct Atten Awd; Tech Stdnt Assoc; Regnl Sci Fair Math/Engrng 1st Plc; Cdtrl Tech ST Tech 4th Plc; Stdnt Assoc ST Con.

TALLEY, NATALIE; Lawton Sr HS; Lawton, OK; (2); FCA; French Clb; Chrmn Key Clb; SADD; Chorus; School Musical; School Play; High Hon Roll; Hon Roll; Ntl Hnr Roll; All Amer Schlr; Presdntl Awd; Acctng.

TALLEY, VINCENT R; Union Intermediate HS; Broken Arrow, OK; (1); JV Bsktbl; JV Socr; High Hon Roll; NHS.

TAM, RONNIE O; Holland HS; Broken Arrow, OK; (3); Treas Sec French Clb; Orch; JV Crs Cntry; Var L Tennis; French Hon Soc; High Hon Roll; Bausch/Lomb Hnry Sci Awd; Perfect Score Natl Latin Exam Summa Cum Laude Awd; Cum Laude Hnr Soc; Physician.

TAMPLEN, ANNIE C; Schulter Schl; Schulter, OK; (2); 2/14; Cmnty Wkr; Pres Soph Cls; Var Bsktbl; Hon Roll; Acad Meets 1st Pl Alg II; OK Schl Of Sci & Math; U Of OK; DVM.

TAMPLEN, KATINA M; Schulter Schl; Schulter, OK; (4); 6/17; Office Aide; Speech Tm; Teachers Aide; Sec Frsh Cls; Sec Soph Cls; Pres Jr Cls; Sec Sr Cls; Bsktbl; Hon Roll; Prfct Atten Awd; OSU.

TANKERSLEY, MATTHEW V; Mustang HS; Mustang, OK; (1); JV Bsbl; JV Bsktbl.

TANKSLEY, STEVEN; Bridge Creek HS; Blanchard, OK; (2); Spanish Clb; Chorus; JV Bsktbl; Var Ftbl; JV Wt Lftg; Hon Roll; NHS; Prfct Atten Awd; OK Hnr Soc; OU.

TANNEHILL, AMBERLIN; Heritage Hall Schl; Oklahoma City, OK; (2); Cmnty Wkr; Debate Tm; French Clb; NFL; Pep Clb; Speech Tm; JV Sftbl; Hon Roll; Prfct Atten Awd; Mgr Fld Hcky; Ronald Mc Donald Hse/OK Aerospace Msum Charity Wrk; Debate Trnmnt Awd; Debate Sec; 6LD Rep; Sprts Mgmnt.

TANNEHILL, CODY; Hulbert Jr Sr HS; Tahlequah, OK; (1); 4-H; Var Bsktbl; Var Ftbl; Var Trk; Hon Roll; Jr NHS; Stu Of Month.

TANNER, BILLY K; Okemah HS; Okemah, OK; (4); 32/47; Am Leg Boys St; FHA; Key Clb; Natl FFA Org; Red Cross Aide; VICA; Golf; Cit Awd; Hon Roll; Pres Acad Fit Awd; FFA Star Greenhand; Glen Johnson & Dick Wilkerson Citation; FFA Proficiency Awd; OK ST Univ; Mrktg; Race Cars.

TANNER, JULIE R; Cushing HS; Cushing, OK; (1); Church Yth Grp; Spanish Clb; Bsktbl; Golf; Hon Roll; NHS; Pres Acad Fit Awd; OK Hnr Soc.

TANNER, NIC; Westmoore HS; Oklahoma City, OK; (4); Cmnty Wkr; FCA; Library Aide; Office Aide; Spanish Clb; Rep Stu Cncl; Ofcr Bsbl; Bsktbl; Ftbl; All ST Trnr ST OK; Peer Hlpr Cnslrs HS; U Of Cntrl OK; Ed/Med.

TAPLIN, ROSHONDA L; Mid-Del Christian Schl; Oklahoma City, OK; (4); 3/14; Cmnty Wkr; Hosp Aide; Acpl Chr; Chorus; Church Choir; School Musical; Hist Stu Cncl; Cit Awd; High Hon Roll; Hon Roll; OU; Law.

TAPP, DACIA; Owasso Sr HS; Owasso, OK; (2); FCA; FTA; Pep Clb; SADD; Nwsp; Yrbk; Chrldng; Trk; Hon Roll; VICA; OK ST U.

TAPP, KYLE P; Felt Public Schl; Boise City, OK; (2); Quiz Bowl; VP Frsh Cls; Rep Soph Cls; Var Bsktbl; Var Trk; High Hon Roll; Prfct Atten Awd.

TARDY, HEATHER D; Edmond North HS; Edmond, OK; (4); 125/336; French Clb; Band; Chorus; Ed Yrbk; Ofcr Stu Cncl; Capt Swmmng; Top 16 St Swimmer; OK ST Univ.

TARMAN, LYNDA M; Will Rogers HS; Tulsa, OK; (1); Church Yth Grp; Key Clb; Spanish Clb; Hon Roll; Oral Roberts Univ.

TARPELY, SARAH; Cyril Jr Sr HS; Cyril, OK; (2); 1/28; Church Yth Grp; FHA; GAA; Letterman Clb; Math Clb; Varsity Clb; Pres Frsh Cls; VP Soph Cls; Var L Bsktbl; Var L Sftbl; Cty Acad All Conf Tm; Amer Lgn Awd; FHA Rptr.

TARRANCE, MELISSA A; Whitesboro Schl; Whitesboro, OK; (2); Church Yth Grp; 4-H; Natl FFA Org; Quiz Bowl; Rptr Nwsp; Yrbk; Hon Roll; Prfct Atten Awd; OK Hnr Soc; Carl Albert; Pediatrician.

TARRANT, SARAH D; West Middle HS; Norman, OK; (1); Spanish Clb; JV Bsktbl; High Hon Roll; Wst Md Hgh Ldrshp Acad.

TARYOLE, VALERIE; Okmulgee HS; Okmulgee, OK; (2); 36/198; Intrml Vllybl; Hon Roll; Indian Club Sec; Otstndng Schlrsp Awd Algr I; Ntv Amer-Crk Trb.

TARZWELL, SYDNEY A; Casady Schl; Oklahoma City, OK; (4); Art Clb; Letterman Clb; Nwsp; Ed Yrbk; Ed Lit Mag; Pres Stu Cncl; JV Crs Cntry; Var L Sftbl; High Hon Roll; Ntl Merit Schol; Improv Tm; Cum Laude Soc; Yng Tlnt Prtfl; Princeton.

TASKER, ANDY P; Bartlesville Mid HS; Bartlesville, OK; (2); Church Yth Grp; JV Bsbl.

TATE, ANDREA D; Oklahoma Christian Schl; Yukon, OK; (4); Art Clb; Cmnty Wkr; Computer Clb; Debate Tm; FCA; French Clb; GAA; Latin Clb; Library Aide; Office Aide; Heartlnds Awd; Hnr Roll; Sftbl MVP 94-; OK Chrstn Coll; Psychiatry.

TATE, ASHLEY; Mustang HS; Yukon, OK; (2); FCA; Teachers Aide; Chrldng; Powder Puff Ftbl; High Hon Roll; NHS; Alg Ii Anatmy Awds; Mmbr Schl Renaissance Prog.

TATE, DEMETA R; Shawnee Sr HS; Shawnee, OK; (2); 69/375; Cmnty Wkr; HOBY; Mgr(s); Score Keeper; Trk; Wt Lftg; Hon Roll; NHS; Prfct Atten Awd; Attend Aide; LA ST U; Coach.

TATE, DESSIE; Plainview HS; Ardmore, OK; (1); Church Yth Grp; GAA; Natl Beta Clb; Bsktbl; Hon Roll; NHS; UCO.

TATE, HEATHER M; Drumright HS; Drumright, OK; (1); Church Yth Grp; 4-H; FHA; Chorus; Ofcr Soph Cls; Bsktbl; Chrldng; Score Keeper; Sftbl; Swmmng.

TATE, JALINDA L; Durant HS; Durant, OK; (3); Chorus; Ed Yrbk; Powder Puff Ftbl; Hon Roll; Southeastern OK ST Univ; PT.

TATE, MANDI S; Alex Jr Sr HS; Ninnekah, OK; (3); Church Yth Grp; Hist Rep FHA; Natl FFA Org; Church Choir; Var Sftbl; Var Trk; Hon Roll; Farmland Indstrs Yth Ldrshp Camp; Natl Ftr Hmkrs Amer Cnvntn Washington DC; Psych.

TATE, MOLLIE JEAN; Liberty HS; Mounds, OK; (3); FCA; FHA; GAA; Teachers Aide; Sec Frsh Cls; Sec Soph Cls; Ofcr Stu Cncl; JV Var Bsktbl; Stat Ftbl; Score Keeper; Sftbl Offnse MVP; Natl Young Ldrs Conf, Dc; Ed.

TATE, SHELLEY D; Durant HS; Durant, OK; (2); Debate Tm; Sec Treas Drama Clb; Speech Tm; Yrbk; Cit Awd; Hon Roll; NHS; Outstdng Art Stdnt 96; 2 Sec Pl/1 Thrd Pl Ribbon Art Show; 4th Pl Ribbon Art Show; SOSU; Comm Art.

TATE, SUSAN; Hugo HS; Hugo, OK; (3); 3/102; Church Yth Grp; Cmnty Wkr; Sec Computer Clb; Sec Math Clb; VP Science Clb; Spanish Clb; Church Choir; Ed Nwsp; Phtg Yrbk; Rep Stu Cncl; Cmptr Prgmmng.

TATUM, REBECCA; Midwest City HS; Midwest City, OK; (4); 1/448; Church Yth Grp; French Clb; Key Clb; Band; Jazz Band; High Hon Roll; NHS; Val; SADD; Pres Acad Fit Awd; CODA Band 94-95; All-St Band 95-96; Band VP & Prncss; Oklahoma City U; Acctng.

TAYLOR, AARON; Frederick HS; Frederick, OK; (3); #2 in class; Am Leg Boys St; Debate Tm; HOBY; Scholastic Bowl; Speech Tm; Ftbl; Golf; Wt Lftg; Hon Roll; NHS.

TAYLOR, ALANNA R; Panola HS; Red Oak, OK; (3); FHA; Letterman Clb; Natl FFA Org; Quiz Bowl; Ofcr Soph Cls; Ofcr Jr Cls; Ofcr Stu Cncl; Bsktbl; Sftbl; High Hon Roll.

TAYLOR, ALISON; Cascia Hall Prep School; Tulsa, OK; (4); Sec Church Yth Grp; Hosp Aide; HOBY; Chorus; School Musical; Var L Crs Cntry; Var L Sftbl; Hon Roll; NHS; Sal; Elem Ed.

TAYLOR, AMANDA K; Bishop Mcguinness HS; Oklahoma City, OK; (3); 67/145; Cmnty Wkr; FCA; Girl Scts; HOBY; Latin Clb; NFL; Pep Clb; Red Cross Aide; Spanish Clb; SADD; Infant Crisis Ctr Vol; Span Hnr Soc VP; Basic Geom Awd; Southeastern OSU; Pilot.

TAYLOR, AMANDA M; Meeker HS; Meeker, OK; (4); 17/77; Church Yth Grp; Cmnty Wkr; 4-H; Teachers Aide; Band; Flag Corp; Cit Awd; 4-H Awd; Hon Roll; SWOSU; Bus Mgmt.

TAYLOR, ANGELA; Perry Sr HS; Perry, OK; (4); 1/67; Church Yth Grp; Drama Clb; German Clb; Hosp Aide; Band; Jazz Band; High Hon Roll; NHS; TSA Sec, Rprtr, Sgt Armsflit Discussion Grp; OSU; Sci.

TAYLOR, ANYA A; Union Sr HS; Broken Arrow, OK; (4); 49/629; German Clb; Intnl Clb; Ofcr Bsbl; Ftbl; Wrstlng; Hon Roll; Jr NHS; NHS; Pres Acad Fit Awd; Drama Clb; Renaissance Chm; TX Chrstn U; Athl Trng.

TAYLOR, ASHLEE; Berryhill Jr HS; Tulsa, OK; (3); Mu Alpha Theta; Spanish Clb; Yrbk; Ofcr Stu Cncl; Var Capt Bsktbl; Var Trk; Hon Roll; NHS.

TAYLOR, AUBREY; Perkins-Tryon HS; Perkins, OK; (3); 3/75; Church Yth Grp; FCA; French Clb; HOBY; Scholastic Bowl; Band; Chorus; Church Choir; Color Guard; Jazz Band; Choir, Bnd All St; Sthwstrn Div Amer Chrl Dirs Assn Hnr Choir; Musicl Theatre.

TAYLOR, BETH; Frederick HS; Frederick, OK; (1); Church Yth Grp; FCA; FHA; School Musical; Rep Stu Cncl; Bsktbl; Sftbl; Hon Roll; NHS; OK ST U; Phys Thrpy.

TAYLOR, BRAD; Madill HS; Madill, OK; (3); FCA; Treas Frsh Cls; Treas Soph Cls; Treas Jr Cls; JV Bsbl; High Hon Roll; Hon Roll; Ntl Merit Ltr; Mech Engr.

TAYLOR, BRIAN; Perry Sr HS; Perry, OK; (3); Church Yth Grp; German Clb; Band; Jazz Band; Mrchg Band; Orch; High Hon Roll; Hon Roll; Jr NHS; NHS; OSU.

TAYLOR, BRYAN J; Southwest Covenant Schl; Hinton, OK; (3); Church Yth Grp; CAP; Pres FCA; Chorus; Rep Jr Cls; Var Bsktbl; Var L Crs Cntry; Var L Ftbl; Var L Golf; Hon Roll; Le Tourneau Univ; Elec Eng.

TAYLOR, CARIE; Eufaula Sr HS; Eufaula, OK; (3); Church Yth Grp; FHA; Band; Capt Color Guard; Mrchg Band; School Musical; Cit Awd; High Hon Roll; NHS; Pres Acad Fit Awd; Conners ST Coll; Nrsng.

TAYLOR, CARL D; Spiro HS; Spiro, OK; (1); Intrml Bsktbl; Intrml Ftbl; Wt Lftg; Cit Awd.

TAYLOR, CHRYSTI D; Bridge Creek HS; Newcastle, OK; (1); Church Yth Grp; Cmnty Wkr; FCA; Hosp Aide; Letterman Clb; Acpl Chr; Yrbk; JV Bsktbl; L Sftbl; High Hon Roll.

TAYLOR, CLINT; Sayre HS; Sayre, OK; (4); 13/42; Am Leg Boys St; Church Yth Grp; Spanish Clb; Chorus; Sec Frsh Cls; Capt Bsktbl; Capt Ftbl; Var Wt Lftg; Hon Roll; Ftbl All-St Hnrbl Mntl; Presl Acad Achvt Awd; Cert CPR & 1st Aid; Boys St; SWOSU; Athl Trnr.

TAYLOR, CORY; Carl Albert HS; Oklahoma City, OK; (4); 1/241; Church Yth Grp; FCA; HOBY; Key Clb; SADD; Chorus; School Musical; VP Treas Stu Cncl; Var L Bsbl; Capt Crs Cntry; Acad St Crs Cnty Chmpn, All City Tm; Jr Rotarian; Trinity U; Engr.

TAYLOR, CRISTOPHER B; Edmond Memorial HS; Edmond, OK; (4); 60/322; Church Yth Grp; FCA; Office Aide; Spanish Clb; SADD; Yrbk; Var Bsbl; NHS; Wood Tech Club; Sci/Tech Awd 96; Indstrl Arts/Tech Ed St Cmptn 1st Pl Project.

TAYLOR, CRYSTAL; Prue Schl; Prue, OK; (3); Ofcr Soph Cls; Ofcr Jr Cls; Wt Lftg; High Hon Roll; Hon Roll; Russn Clb; Hnr Soc; Tulsa Jr Col; Pedtrc Nurs.

TAYLOR, CYNTHIA D; Bridge Creek HS; Newcastle, OK; (3); 3/64; Church Yth Grp; Drama Clb; FCA; GAA; Spanish Clb; SADD; Thesps; School Play; Var Bsktbl; Var Sftbl; Fast Pitch Sftbl; OK ST Univ; Zoologist.

TAYLOR, DESTINY L; Spiro HS; Spiro, OK; (2); FCA; Math Clb; Natl FFA Org; Office Aide; Teachers Aide; JV Bsktbl; Var Trk; Cit Awd; Hon Roll; Ntl Merit Ltr; TSA; Westark; Zoologist; Phy Thrpst.

TAYLOR, DUSTIN; Welch Jr Sr HS; Welch, OK; (1); Church Yth Grp; FHA; Speech Tm; Chorus; School Play; Chrldng; Hon Roll; Gymnst; Spch Mdls 1st, 2nd & 3rd; One Act Ply St 1st Pl; Bus.

TAYLOR, ERIC R; Pauls Valley HS; Pauls Valley, OK; (3); VP Church Yth Grp; Cmnty Wkr; FCA; Key Clb; Math Tm; Quiz Bowl; Scholastic Bowl; Band; Chorus; Mrchg Band; GATE Pgm; Chrch Missions Outreach Work; Mechncl Engr.

TAYLOR, ERNIE; Hugo HS; Hugo, OK; (4); FCA; Yrbk; Pres Frsh Cls; Pres Soph Cls; Ofcr Stu Cncl; JV Ftbl; Var Golf; NHS; Church Yth Grp; OK ST U; Engrng.

TAYLOR, JENNIFER; Sweetwater Public Schl; Sweetwater, OK; (4); Am Leg Aux Girls St; NFL; Church Choir; School Play; Nwsp; Yrbk; Cit Awd; Hon Roll; NHS; Ntl Merit Schol; SW OK ST U; Child Psych.

TAYLOR, JENNIFER L; Caney Jr Sr HS; Caney, OK; (3); Church Yth Grp; Cmnty Wkr; VP 4-H; Rptr Natl FFA Org; Church Choir; 4-H Awd; Hon Roll; Ch Pianist; Sunday School Tchr; Southern OK ST Univ/Accnt.

TAYLOR, JEREMY R; Walters HS; Walters, OK; (2); Church Yth Grp; FCA; Natl FFA Org; Church Choir; Ftbl; Trk; Wt Lftg; High Hon Roll; Hon Roll.

TAYLOR, JERI L; Charles Page HS; Sand Springs, OK; (4); Church Yth Grp; Cmnty Wkr; Drama Clb; Pep Clb; Chorus; School Play; Variety Show; Cit Awd; Outstndng Vclst Tri St Msc Fstvl 92, 93, 95; Stdyng Prvt Vcl Instrctn; Broadway Mscls, Rcrdng; U Cntrl OK; Singer.

TAYLOR, JIM; Pawhuska HS; Pawhuska, OK; (4); Am Leg Boys St; Church Yth Grp; FCA; FHA; Key Clb; Library Aide; Math Clb; Quiz Bowl; Science Clb; Hon Roll; Wynona Roundup Clb; 1st Chrstn Church; Northwestern OK ST U; Vet Med.

TAYLOR, JOSHUA; Wilburton Sr HS; Wilburton, OK; (4); Am Leg Boys St; Debate Tm; FCA; Letterman Clb; Speech Tm; L Bsbl; L Bsktbl; Stat Ftbl; Ftbl; Prfct Atten Awd.

TAYLOR, KANDI L; Haskell HS; Haskell, OK; (2); Church Yth Grp; Spanish Clb; Band; Mrchg Band; Pep Band; Nwsp; Yrbk; Sec Soph Cls; Honor Bnd; Northeastern ST U; Jrnlsm.

TAYLOR, KATTIE L; Del City HS; Oklahoma City, OK; (2); Church Yth Grp; FCA; Pres Church Choir; Rptr Yrbk; Stat Var Bsbl; Stat Var Bsktbl; Var Mgr(s); Var L Socr; Rptr Jr NHS; NHS; OK ST Univ.

TAYLOR, KELLI B; Lindsay HS; Lindsay, OK; (3); 1/70; Pres Art Clb; FCA; Office Aide; Sec Jr Cls; High Hon Roll; NHS; St Schlr; OSU; Pre Med/Physcs.

TAYLOR, LATEISHA; Tulsa East Cntrl HS; Tulsa, OK; (1); Church Yth Grp; Key Clb; ROTC; SADD; Church Choir; Sec Frsh Cls; Rep Stu Cncl; Var Co-Capt Chrldng; Wt Lftg; Prfct Atten Awd; Vlnc Intrvntn Prvntn; Red Cross; DFY; OK ST U; Crmnl Jstc.

TAYLOR, LEAH N; Hugo HS; Hugo, OK; (2); Library Aide; Hon Roll; Most Imprvd Algb I; Outstndt Achvmnt Wld His; Bus Woman.

TAYLOR, LOY DUSTIN; Meeker HS; Meeker, OK; (1); Church Yth Grp; JV Ftbl; Var Wt Lftg; Hon Roll; FFA; Weatherford; Pharmacy.

TAYLOR, MEGAN E; North Intemediate HS; Broken Arrow, OK; (2); Drama Clb; French Clb; Band; Mrchg Band; Pep Band; Vllybl; Comm Sftbl; Marine Biologist.

TAYLOR, NALENA D; Star Spencer HS; Spencer, OK; (1); Chorus; School Musical; Hon Roll; Ntl Merit SF; Langston U; Tchr.

TAYLOR, NATALIE J; Union Sr HS; Tulsa, OK; (3); 23/705; Church Yth Grp; Drama Clb; Key Clb; Spanish Clb; School Play; Stage Crew; Swmmng; Cit Awd; Gov Hon Prg Awd; Hon Roll; Excllnt Achvt Engl & Sci; Missn Trip Mexico; OBU; Nursng.

TAYLOR, NIKOLE; Ada HS; Ada, OK; (4); 3/174; Pres Church Yth Grp; Ofcr FCA; Pres Mu Alpha Theta; Pres Spanish Clb; Pres Church Choir; Rep Stu Cncl; Var Chrldng; Var Sftbl; NHS; Spanish NHS; FCA All-St Fml Athl Of Yr; Elks Ldg Stu Of Mnth; OK Bptst U; Math.

TAYLOR, RACHEL; Newcastle HS; Norman, OK; (4); Church Yth Grp; FBLA; Scholastic Bowl; Church Choir; High Hon Roll; Hon Roll; NHS; Ntl Merit Ltr; Val; Stu Of Month 94-95; John Brown U; Spcl Ed Tchr.

TAYLOR, REBEKAH; Metro Christian Acad; Tulsa, OK; (4); Church Yth Grp; Cmnty Wkr; Dance Clb; FCA; Key Clb; Office Aide; Pep Clb; SADD; Teachers Aide; Varsity Clb; Star Srch; OK Univ; Phys Thpy.

TAYLOR, RENEE L; Beaver HS; Beaver, OK; (2); Church Yth Grp; Drama Clb; Rptr FCA; FHA; GAA; Scholastic Bowl; Chorus; Church Choir; Var Sftbl; Var Tennis; OK Hnr Scty; OK Baptist Univ.

TAYLOR, ROBERT C; Mustang HS; Yukon, OK; (3); Boy Scts; Church Yth Grp; Teachers Aide; Band; Jazz Band; Hon Roll; Jr NHS; Won Lcl/Regnl Sci Fairs; ST Sci Fair Prtcpnt; Wdwrkng Fair Two Tm ST Champn.

TAYLOR, RYAN B; Putnam City North HS; Oklahoma City, OK; (1); Hon Roll; Prfct Atten Awd.

TAYLOR, SARAH; Berryhill Jr HS; Tulsa, OK; (2); Church Yth Grp; Intnl Clb; Chorus; Church Choir; Hon Roll; Jr NHS; Assmb God Fn Arts Fest, Sprr Rtng, Fml Vcl Solo Natl; Ed.

TAYLOR, SARAH V; Bishop Kelley HS; Tulsa, OK; (1); Church Yth Grp; Cmnty Wkr; Hon Roll; Interest In Enviormental Issues.

TAYLOR, SHAMIKA; B T Washington HS; Tulsa, OK; (3); Church Yth Grp; Cmnty Wkr; Band; Mrchg Band; Stage Crew; Ofcr Frsh Cls; Ofcr Soph Cls; Ofcr Jr Cls; Tennis; Jr NHS; Comm Vol; U Of Tulsa.

TAYLOR, SHANNON D; Midwest City HS; Midwest City, OK; (2); Teachers Aide; Band; Jazz Band; Mrchg Band; Ofcr Bsbl; Hon Roll; Prfct Atten Awd.

TAYLOR, STEPHANIE; Bartlesville Mid HS; Bartlesville, OK; (2); Church Yth Grp; Spanish Clb; Acpl Chr; Chorus; High Hon Roll; Hon Roll; Jr NHS; Prfct Atten Awd.

TAYLOR, SUSAN P; Del City HS; Del City, OK; (3); Church Yth Grp; Band; Jazz Band; Mrchg Band; Orch; Pep Band; NHS.

TAYLOR, TARA T; Lindsay HS; Lindsay, OK; (1); 1/65; Church Yth Grp; FCA; Band; Chorus; Color Guard; Mrchg Band; Pep Band; Pres Soph Cls; Chrldng; High Hon Roll; OCUSA; Med.

TAYLOR, TERRI J; Temple Jr Sr HS; Temple, OK; (3); 1/20; FHA; Teachers Aide; Band; Drm Mjr(t); Mrchg Band; Rep Frsh Cls; Rep Soph Cls; Rep Jr Cls; Ofcr Stu Cncl; Cit Awd; John Philip Sousa Band Awd.

TAYLOR, TIFFANY A; Northeast HS; Oklahoma City, OK; (2); Church Yth Grp; Cmnty Wkr; Office Aide; Red Cross Aide; Chorus; Church Choir; OK Univ; Hlth Careers.

TAYLOR, TRACY; Madill HS; Madill, OK; (3); Math Clb; Quiz Bowl; Science Clb; SADD; Chorus; School Musical; School Play; Stage Crew; Hon Roll; NHS; DEVRY Univ; Tech Eng.

TAYLOR, TRENNA; Big Pasture HS; Randlett, OK; (4); 1/16; Am Leg Aux Girls St; HOBY; Natl FFA Org; Pres Soph Cls; VP Jr Cls; Pres Stu Cncl; Bsktbl; NHS; Pres Acad Fit Awd; Val; FFA Pres 95-96; Sen Page Dist 51 Sen Sam Helton; DARE Rle Mdl; OK ST U; Anml Sci.

TEA, LEANG H; Lawton Sr HS; Lawton, OK; (2); FCA; HOBY; Letterman Clb; Spanish Clb; Crs Cntry; Var L Socr; Wt Lftg; Hon Roll; NHS; Intl Scr Slct Team; OK Hon Soc; U Of VA; Scr/Psych.

TEAGARDEN, KATHRYN LYNN; Jenks HS; Broken Arrow, OK; (3); FHA; German Clb; Pep Clb; High Hon Roll; Hon Roll; Rec Sccr & YMCA Cchng; Cmptr Sci.

TEAGUE, AUDRIE A; Empire Schl; Duncan, OK; (3); Sec FCA; FBLA; Key Clb; Rep Stu Cncl; Var Bsktbl; Var Chrldng; Var Sftbl; Var Trk; OK U; Acctng.

TEAGUE, BRIAN; Westmoore HS; Oklahoma City, OK; (4); 122/610; Church Yth Grp; English Clb; FBLA; German Clb; Office Aide; Chorus; School Musical; Lit Mag; Wt Lftg; Wrstlng; Wrtng Awd; Norwich Univ; Aerosp, Civil Eng.

TEAGUE, CHRIS; Hulbert Jr Sr HS; Hulbert, OK; (1); Church Yth Grp; FBLA; FHA; Church Choir; Bsktbl; JV Ftbl; Hon Roll; Jr NHS; 4-H; Trk; Acad Team; TSA; GATE.

TEAGUE, ELIZABETH J; Deer Creek HS; Edmond, OK; (2); Church Yth Grp; GAA; Science Clb; SADD; Band; Color Guard; Mrchg Band; Trk; Hon Roll; NHS; OK Christian Univ; Med.

TEAL, MELANIE; Miami Sr HS; Miami, OK; (1); Church Yth Grp; FCA; Spanish Clb; Church Choir; VP Frsh Cls; Ofcr Stu Cncl; Chrldng; Gym; Tennis; Trk; UCLA; Pharm.

TEAL, SARAH M; B T Washington HS; Tulsa, OK; (4); 12/264; Drama Clb; Latin Clb; Thesps; School Musical; School Play; VP Soph Cls; Sec Jr Cls; High Hon Roll; NHS; Chinese Clb; Yng Dems; Yth & Govt; Washington U St Louis; Bio.

TEAPE, CHRISTEN; West Norman Mid HS; Norman, OK; (2); Church Yth Grp; FCA; Latin Clb; Pep Clb; Church Choir; Ofcr Stu Cncl; JV Bsktbl; Cit Awd; High Hon Roll; Jr NHS; Tri Hi Y; Harvard U; Phys Thrpy.

TEASLEY, GRETCHEN G; Weatherford HS; Weatherford, OK; (3); Church Yth Grp; FCA; Sec Soph Cls; Sec Jr Cls; Sec Sr Cls; Var Bsbl; JV Bsktbl; Var Sftbl; High Hon Roll; Hon Roll; Mthrs Study Club Awd; OU; Ed/Psych.

TEBOW, BROOKE; Deer Creek-Lamont Jr Sr HS; Lamont, OK; (2); 1/17; Church Yth Grp; Sec FCA; 4-H; Treas Natl FFA Org; Chorus; Drm Mjr(t); Rep Frsh Cls; L Var Bsktbl; L Var Crs Cntry; L Var Trk; 4-H Sr Hall Of Fame; St Qulfr Track; MVP C Cntry; OK St Univ; Law.

TEBOW, HEATH; Deer Creek-Lamont Jr Sr HS; Lamont, OK; (4); 1/13; Am Leg Boys St; Church Yth Grp; Pres FCA; HOBY; VP Natl FFA Org; Capt Quiz Bowl; Var L Bsbl; Capt Bsktbl; Capt Ftbl; Pres NHS; Natl Fnl Coca Cola Schlrs Prog; Washington DC Yth Tour Wnnr; OK ST U; Dntstry.

TEBOW, KELLI; Waller Jr HS; Enid, OK; (1); Dance Clb; FCA; Spanish Clb; Chrldng; Swmmng; High Hon Roll; Jr NHS; Prfct Atten Awd; OK ST U; Sprts Med.

TEDDER, RYAN B; Deer Creek HS; Oklahoma City, OK; (3); Church Yth Grp; Cmnty Wkr; FCA; FBLA; Science Clb; School Play; Variety Show; Rep Frsh Cls; JV Var Bsktbl; Socr; Mission Trip Prague, Inner City London & Inner City OKC Bus Ministry; Lead Role In Various Plays; Baylor.

TEDLOCK, JENNIFER; Graham Schl; Weleetka, OK; (1); 1/18; Church Yth Grp; Sec 4-H; FHA; Chorus; Bsktbl; 4-H Awd; Hon Roll; NHS; Optimist Clb Essay Awd; Parlimentary Procedure Team.

TEDLOCK, MEGAN; Graham Schl; Weleetka, OK; (3); 2/17; Church Yth Grp; Pres 4-H; Pres FHA; Chorus; Rptr Nwsp; Sec Frsh Cls; Sec Soph Cls; Rep Jr Cls; Var Bsktbl; 4-H Awd; Life Ldr; 1st In Music His At Schltc Meet; ECU; Criminal Law.

TEEHEE, ANDREW R; Nathan Hale HS; Tulsa, OK; (2); Church Yth Grp; Cmnty Wkr; FCA; Library Aide; SADD; VP Frsh Cls; JV Var Bsbl; High Hon Roll; Hon Roll; NHS; Multi Yr Listee; Wnnr Reg Bsebll Title; Psych.

TEEL, SHANE; Cement Jr Sr HS; Ninnekah, OK; (4); 4/22; Natl FFA Org; Nwsp; Yrbk; Var Bsbl; Var Bsktbl; High Hon Roll; Competitive 3-D Archery; FFA St Farmer Degree; Cameron Univ.

TEEPLES, DAVID; Ft Gibson HS; Fort Gibson, OK; (2); Band; School Musical; Var Golf; Hon Roll; Pres Acad Fit Awd; 9 Yrs Piano.

TEETER, JIM; Lawton Christian Schl; Lawton, OK; (1); Sec Stu Cncl; JV Bsktbl; Hon Roll; NHS; CO ST; Law.

TEHRANI, KENDRA; Hugo HS; Hugo, OK; (2); Church Yth Grp; Drama Clb; Science Clb; Spanish Clb; Band; Color Guard; Mrchg Band; Stage Crew; Yrbk; Chrldng; Hnr Soc; Southeastern OK.

TEMPEST, JESSICA M; Union Intermediate HS; Broken Arrow, OK; (2); Key Clb; Color Guard; Yrbk; High Hon Roll; Jr NHS; NHS; Pres Acad Fit Awd; Wntr Grd; Stu Mo; Lang Arts Awd; Elem Ed.

TEMPLE, CHRISTOPHER L; Madill HS; Madill, OK; (3); Church Yth Grp; Drama Clb; Band; Chorus; Mrchg Band; School Musical; Cit Awd; Prfct Atten Awd; Greenville Civic Chorus; ROPES; OCUSA; Musican Vocal.

TEMPLES, SHERRI; Valliant HS; Valliant, OK; (4); 2/86; Church Yth Grp; Cmnty Wkr; FHA; Hosp Aide; Teachers Aide; Band; Drm Mjr(t); Mrchg Band; NHS; Sal; Hosp & Americorps Vlntr; ECU; Med.

TEMPLETON, KURT W; Edmond North HS; Edmond, OK; (3); 1/365; Art Clb; Church Yth Grp; FCA; HOBY; Quiz Bowl; Scholastic Bowl; Yrbk; Rep Frsh Cls; Rep Soph Cls; Bsktbl; Capt Of Acad Bowl Team, Finished In Top 20 At Natls; OK ST Univ; Architecture.

TEMPLIN, JASON D; Wakita Schl; Wakita, OK; (2); Natl FFA Org; Hon Roll; Prfct Atten Awd; 1st Pl Sci Fair Phy Sci; 2nd Pl Indv Land Jdg Cntst Soils Cons Fair; FFA Turf/Lndscp Mgmt Awds 95-.

TENNELL, LISA; Bartlesville Sr HS; Bartlesville, OK; (4); 62/429; Church Yth Grp; Cmnty Wkr; Teachers Aide; Ed Nwsp; Bsktbl; High Hon Roll; NHS; Tulsa Jr Col; Elem Ed.

TENNYSON, TAMARA; Foyil Schl; Claremore, OK; (2); VP Drama Clb; Ballet; Writer.

TENZYTHOFF, ANNA; Cascia Hall Prep School; Tulsa, OK; (3); Church Yth Grp; Drama Clb; French Clb; Pep Clb; Chorus; Church Choir; School Musical; School Play; Powder Puff Ftbl; Var Capt Socr; Pre-Med/Bus Admin.

TEOLI, JOSEPH F; Putnam City North HS; Oklahoma City, OK; (4); Church Yth Grp; FCA; Spanish Clb; SADD; Hon Roll; NHS; OK Univ; PT.

TEPEL, KELEIGH K; Norman Sr HS; Norman, OK; (4); Cmnty Wkr; Hosp Aide; SADD; Chorus; School Play; Lit Mag; Var Fld Hcky; Var Lcrss; Var JV Swmmng; Var Trk; Global Routes Cmnty Work; Certfd CPR, WSI, Liefguard; George Washington U; Bio Rsrch.

TERRELL, HEATHER M; Varnum Jr Sr HS; Seminole, OK; (3); Chess Clb; Drama Clb; 4-H; Key Clb; ROTC; SADD; Color Guard; Drill Tm; Ed Nwsp; Socr; Read; Help Othrs; MO Rolla; Engr.

TERRELL, JARAE M; Lindsay HS; Lindsay, OK; (1); Art Clb; Red Cross Aide; Ofcr Soph Cls; Art; USAO.

TERRELL, JEFFREY; Kingfisher HS; Dover, OK; (2); 1/100; Church Yth Grp; HOBY; Natl FFA Org; VP Frsh Cls; Rep Stu Cncl; Var L Bsbl; Var L Bsktbl; Var L Ftbl; High Hon Roll.

TERRELL, JENNIFER; West Middle HS; Norman, OK; (3); Church Yth Grp; Math Clb; Mu Alpha Theta; Red Cross Aide; Chrldng; Hon Roll; Explorer Post 901 Clb; Physician Asst.

TERRILL, MC KINZIE D; Stillwater Sr HS; Stillwater, OK; (3); 115/386; CAP; Cmnty Wkr; FCA; Key Clb; Natl Beta Clb; Pres Spanish Clb; Chorus; Yrbk; Capt Swmmng; Hon Roll; Footbl; Diving Capt; Track.

TERRONEZ, BRANDY L; Glenpool HS; Glenpool, OK; (2); FHA; GAA; Spanish Clb; Teachers Aide; Chorus; School Musical; Variety Show; Hon Roll; Prfct Atten Awd; Baylor Univ; Bus.

TERRY, CLINT; Moore HS; Moore, OK; (2); Science Clb; Spanish Clb; OSU; Auto Dsgnr.

TERRY, ELIZABETH E; Union Sr HS; Springdale, AR; (3); School Musical; School Play; Stage Crew; Yrbk; Crs Cntry; Hon Roll; NHS; Twc Bn Slctd Otstndng Prfrmnc In One Act; U Of AR; Drama.

TERRY, MATT L; Midwest City HS; Midwest City, OK; (2); 190/450; Church Yth Grp; Office Aide; Band; Jazz Band; Mrchg Band; Pep Band; Yrbk.

TERRY, MICHELLE; Edmond North HS; Edmond, OK; (3); 29/367; Church Yth Grp; FCA; Key Clb; Pep Clb; Spanish Clb; Mrchg Band; School Play; Var L Chrldng; Jr NHS; NHS; Piano Cmptns Super Rtngs; Acad Ltr; All Dist Flute; U OK.

TERRY, NIKKI; Ponca City Sr HS; Ponca City, OK; (2); Church Yth Grp; Chorus; Nwsp; Ofcr Soph Cls; Trk; Hon Roll; Chrldng; Jr Miss Dance Of OK; Teen Miss Dance Of OK; Sr Miss Dance Of OK; Singing.

TERRY, RANDY H; Amber Pocasset Jr Sr HS; Amber, OK; (2); Church Yth Grp; FCA; Science Clb; Spanish Clb; Church Choir; School Play; Variety Show; Var Bsktbl; Hon Roll; Military.

TESSMANN, KIMBERLY; Stroud HS; Blackwell, OK; (2); Church Yth Grp; FCA; FHA; Band; Pres Frsh Cls; Pres Soph Cls; Stat Bsbl; JV Var Chrldng; High Hon Roll; NHS; OK ST U.

TESTER, KELLY; Southwest Covenant Schl; El Reno, OK; (1); Church Yth Grp; Sec FCA; Chorus; Church Choir; Nwsp; Phtg Yrbk; Var Bsktbl; Var L Tennis; Hon Roll; Hd Stdnt Asst Chldrn Chrch Crfts.

TESTERMAN, AMY; Hugo HS; Hugo, OK; (4); 14/94; Church Yth Grp; Computer Clb; FCA; Natl FFA Org; Science Clb; Spanish Clb; Nwsp; Sec Soph Cls; Sec Jr Cls; Pres Stu Cncl; Soph Server; E T Dunlap; Bus Admin.

TESTERMAN, JENNIFER; Hollis Jr Sr HS; Hollis, OK; (4); 3/53; Am Leg Aux Girls St; Pres 4-H; Natl FFA Org; Band; School Play; Bsktbl; Chrldng; Sftbl; Trk; 4-H Awd; OK Hse Rep Page; OK Sen Page; Top 5 Hnr Stu; OSU; Ag Ecs.

TESTERMAN, LINDSEY B; Cushing HS; Cushing, OK; (4); 7/156; Drama Clb; 4-H; Math Clb; Natl FFA Org; Office Aide; Science Clb; Spanish Clb; Teachers Aide; Varsity Clb; School Play; ST/LOCAL/NATL FFA Awds; Num C Awds; Wrestling Homecoming Queen/Attendent; Northern OK Coll; Horticltre.

TETTEH, MACK N; Edmond Santa Fe HS; Edmond, OK; (3); French Clb; Office Aide; SADD; Var Bsktbl; NHS; Outstdng Amer His Stu; Outstdng Fr 2 Stu; Pharmacology.

TETTER, SHELBY L; Dewey HS; Bartlesville, OK; (2); Church Yth Grp; Cmnty Wkr; FHA; Office Aide; Spanish Clb; Chorus; Ofcr Stu Cncl; Swmmng; Cit Awd; Hon Roll; UCLA; Oceanographer; Environmen.

THACKER, AMBER N; Velma Alma HS; Ratliff City, OK; (1); Church Yth Grp; FCA; FBLA; GAA; Church Choir; Bsktbl; Crs Cntry; Trk; Cit Awd; High Hon Roll; OK Bapt U.

THACKER, MELISSA G; Velma Alma HS; Ratliff City, OK; (2); FCA; Quiz Bowl; SADD; Band; Drm Mjr(t); Var Bsktbl; Var Crs Cntry; Var Trk; Hon Roll; NHS.

THAI, VU; Westmoore HS; Oklahoma City, OK; (4); 5/610; Math Tm; Scholastic Bowl; Science Clb; Lit Mag; Tennis; NHS; Val; Taekwondo; Whittier Coll; Bio Chem; Math.

THANKACHAN, JIMMY P; Putnam City Original HS; Oklahoma City, OK; (2); 16/216; Art Clb; Church Yth Grp; Computer Clb; Debate Tm; FBLA; HOBY; Yrbk; Tennis; High Hon Roll; Jr NHS; CPA.

THARP, AARON C; Choctaw HS; Choctaw, OK; (3); 79/327; Church Yth Grp; Cmnty Wkr; Drama Clb; FCA; Library Aide; Quiz Bowl; Speech Tm; Teachers Aide; Band; School Musical; Mst Imprvd Awd For Ftbl; Character Acting Awd For Drama Wnnr; Schls First Live News Team Awd; OK ST Univ; Psych.

THARP, CHRISTY K; Delaware Public Schl; Delaware, OK; (2); 1/11; Church Yth Grp; VP FHA; Office Aide; Church Choir; Ed Yrbk; Rep Stu Cncl; Var Bsktbl; Trk; Hon Roll; Masonic Stdnt Today Awd; PT.

THAYER, ASHLEY A; Putnam City West HS; Bethany, OK; (2); Church Yth Grp; Cmnty Wkr; Drama Clb; Spanish Clb; Teachers Aide; Chorus; Church Choir; School Musical; School Play; Stage Crew; Shekinah-Singing Group Of 4 Girls That Tour; Worked With Multi-Handicapped Child; Baylor; Medicine.

THAYER, JEREMY; Okay Jr Sr HS; Wagoner, OK; (4); 4/22; Spanish Clb; Teachers Aide; Rep Frsh Cls; Sec Soph Cls; Rep Jr Cls; Pres Sr Cls; Rep Stu Cncl; Capt Bsbl; Capt Bsktbl; High Hon Roll; Natl Hnr Soc; OK Hnr Soc; Natl Voc Hnr Soc; Northeasten ST Univ; Med.

THEMER, TRACI; Kingfisher HS; Kingfisher, OK; (3); 16/98; Church Yth Grp; Computer Clb; Tennis; Hon Roll; NHS.

THENMADATHIL, ASHLEY V; Putnam City North HS; Oklahoma City, OK; (3); 33/497; Spanish Clb; Hon Roll; NHS; Acctng; OK Univ; Comp Eng.

THETFORD, LESLEY; Holdenville HS; Holdenville, OK; (2); 1/85; FCA; Rptr FBLA; Natl Beta Clb; Natl FFA Org; Scholastic Bowl; Science Clb; Yrbk; 4-H; TX A&M; Lg Anml Vet.

THIELE, ROBERT; Pawhuska HS; Pawhuska, OK; (3); 7/90; Art Clb; Church Yth Grp; FCA; Science Clb; Teachers Aide; Var Trk; Var Wt Lftg; Var Wrstlng; High Hon Roll; NHS; U Houston.

THIESSEN, AARON; Corn Bible Acad; Weatherford, OK; (1); 1/24; Church Yth Grp; Scholastic Bowl; Band; Mrchg Band; Pep Band; JV Bsktbl; Var Socr; High Hon Roll; Prfct Atten Awd; Pres Acad Fit Awd.

THIESSEN, JOHN; Ft Gibson HS; Park Hill, OK; (2); 5/161; Church Yth Grp; Spanish Clb; SADD; Band; Mrchg Band; Ftbl; High Hon Roll; Jr NHS.

THIESSEN, MATTHEW; Corn Bible Acad; Corn, OK; (1); Church Yth Grp; Quiz Bowl; Band; Mrchg Band; Pep Band; Bsktbl; Hon Roll.

THIGPEN, AMY G; Putnam City North HS; Oklahoma City, OK; (1); Church Yth Grp; Rep Frsh Cls; Cit Awd; Arch.

THIYAGARAJAN, VENKATESH; Bartlesville Sr HS; Bartlesville, OK; (3); 34/540; JA; Spanish Clb; Orch; Tennis; High Hon Roll; Hon Roll; Jr NHS; NHS; Spanish NHS; Eng.

THOMAS, ADAM D; Morris HS; Morris, OK; (3); Church Yth Grp; Quiz Bowl; Scholastic Bowl; Band; Jazz Band; Mrchg Band; Pep Band; Var Ftbl; High Hon Roll; NHS.

THOMAS, AIMEE L; Chattanooga Schl; Chattanooga, OK; (1); 1/21; Church Yth Grp; Cmnty Wkr; 4-H; FHA; Library Aide; Teachers Aide; Var Bsktbl; Hon Roll; Ntl Merit Ltr; Val; St Beauty Fnlst; VA Tech; Radiology.

THOMAS, ALAINA D; Union Intermediate HS; Tulsa, OK; (1); Church Yth Grp; French Clb; Stage Crew; Jr NHS; NHS; Explrs; Lang Art Awd.

THOMAS, AMANDA; New Lima Jr Sr HS; Wewoka, OK; (1); Chess Clb; 4-H; Hon Roll; Art; Piano; Ptry; Vet.

THOMAS, ANITA; Coweta HS; Coweta, OK; (3); Church Yth Grp; Hosp Aide; SADD; Band; Jazz Band; Mrchg Band; Pep Band; Yrbk; Chrldng; Gym; Northeastern ST Univ; Music.

THOMAS, BRANDI J; Ardmore HS; Springer, OK; (3); 194/300; Church Yth Grp; FCA; French Clb; Math Clb; Quiz Bowl; ROTC; Church Choir; Yrbk; JV Var Bsktbl; JV Crs Cntry; Piano Awd SE OK St U; Essay Cont Wnnr; Chrch Missn Trips; OK St Bsktbl Camp Awd; Ms Blk Ardmr Rnnr-Up; Med Field.

THOMAS, BRANDI S; Bixby Sr HS; Broken Arrow, OK; (4); 104/198; Rep Drama Clb; Pres French Clb; NFL; Scholastic Bowl; Teachers Aide; Thesps; Chorus; School Musical; School Play; Stage Crew; United Way Out Front Pgm; U Of Tampa; Commnctn.

THOMAS, CHRISTI D; Choctaw HS; Choctaw, OK; (2); FCA; GAA; JV Bsktbl; JV Sftbl; Var Tennis; Cit Awd; High Hon Roll; Jr NHS; Pres Acad Fit Awd; Hntng; Cmpng; OBU; Vet.

THOMAS, DAWN M; U S Grant HS; Oklahoma City, OK; (1); Hosp Aide; Model UN; Spanish Clb; Teachers Aide; Acpl Chr; Chorus; Yrbk.

THOMAS, DEDRECK; B T Washington HS; Tulsa, OK; (4); Church Yth Grp; Cmnty Wkr; NFL; Office Aide; Speech Tm; Varsity Clb; Church Choir; Capt Bsktbl; Hon Roll; Pres Acad Fit Awd; 1st Pl Frnsc Lgue Dist Spch Fnls 96; Mr Hrbt For BT Washington All Amer Boys Bsktbl Team 96; Syracuse U; Psych.

THOMAS, ELIZABETH H; Mc Alester HS; Mcalester, OK; (2); Church Yth Grp; Debate Tm; Drama Clb; Speech Tm; Chorus; Drill Tm; School Musical; Yrbk; Pom Pon; Hon Roll; OCU; Ballet.

THOMAS, EVANGELA; Lone Grove HS; Ardmore, OK; (4); FCA; German Clb; Math Clb; Natl Beta Clb; Science Clb; Chorus; Bsktbl; Chrldng; High Hon Roll; NHS; U Of Cntrl OK; Bus Admin.

THOMAS, JASON; Millwood HS; Oklahoma City, OK; (3); Art Clb; Church Yth Grp; Hosp Aide; VICA; Church Choir; Howard U; Art.

THOMAS, JENI; Miami Sr HS; Miami, OK; (2); 10/150; Church Yth Grp; Dance Clb; FCA; Chorus; Church Choir; JV Bsktbl; Chrldng; Mgr Socr; Hon Roll; NHS; Red Cross Lfgrd/Adult/Child/Infant CPR/FIRST Aid; FL ST U; Commercial Artist.

THOMAS, JENNIFER; Del City HS; Oklahoma City, OK; (2); Church Yth Grp; FCA; Spanish Clb; SADD; Rep Stu Cncl; Chrldng; Pom Pon; Jr NHS; NHS; Natl Eng Mrt Awd; Pres Awd For Educl Excl.

THOMAS, JENNIFER C; Memorial HS; Tulsa, OK; (2); Church Yth Grp; FCA; FHA; Key Clb; Pep Clb; Teachers Aide; Chorus; Church Choir; School Musical; School Play; Stu Dir Of All-Schl Musical 96; Ozark Chrstn Coll.

THOMAS, JESSE R; Colcord Schl; Colcord, OK; (1); Natl FFA Org; JV Ftbl; JV Wt Lftg; OU; Ag.

THOMAS, JULIE K; Edmond Memorial HS; Edmond, OK; (1); 170/437; Church Yth Grp; Ofcr Frsh Cls; Bsktbl; Var Sftbl; Hon Roll; AAU Bsktbl 5th Pl ST OK; OK Chrstn.

THOMAS, JUSTIN; Star Spencer HS; Spencer, OK; (1); Church Yth Grp; Band; VP Frsh Cls; JV Bsktbl; Var Ftbl; JV Trk; Hon Roll.

THOMAS, KAREN M; Bishop Kelley HS; Tulsa, OK; (1); Church Yth Grp; Latin Clb; School Musical; Hon Roll.

THOMAS, KEIANA; Douglass HS; Oklahoma City, OK; (1); Bsktbl; Pom Pon; Cit Awd; Hon Roll; Phys Sci/Hon Eng I/Ec Acad Awds; Scientfc Rsrch Dctr.

THOMAS, KELLI G; Nw Classen HS; Oklahoma City, OK; (4); 7/198; Church Yth Grp; Computer Clb; English Clb; FBLA; FTA; Hosp Aide; VP Chorus; Church Choir; School Musical; Cit Awd; Trch Schlrshp; OKC Pnhllnc Assn, Fclty, Hrld, Bnnr Prsdntl Acad & FBLA Awds; OK Acad Schlr; Piano; U Cntrl OK; Ed.

THOMAS, LA DONNA M; Bartlesville Sr HS; Bartlesville, OK; (3); FCA; GAA; Teachers Aide; Varsity Clb; Phtg Yrbk; Var Capt Vllybl; Hon Roll; NHS; Prfct Atten Awd; OK ST; Law.

THOMAS, LANA; Moore HS; Moore, OK; (2); Science Clb; Spanish Clb; Teachers Aide; Chrldng; Gym; U Of OK; Prmry Ed Tchr.

THOMAS, LESLEY; Millwood HS; Oklahoma City, OK; (3); Church Yth Grp; ROTC; Mrchg Band; Var Ftbl; Trk; Wt Lftg; Hon Roll; Teachers Aide; Church Choir; Mst Outstndng, VP Bnd; KUDOS; Phys Thrpy.

THOMAS, LISA; Mustang HS; Yukon, OK; (3); Church Yth Grp; Cmnty Wkr; Hosp Aide; Key Clb; Spanish Clb; SADD; Trk; Cit Awd; NHS; Baylor U; Med.

THOMAS, LONNIE; Liberty HS; Mounds, OK; (2); Church Yth Grp; FCA; Natl FFA Org; Band; Ofcr Stu Cncl; Var Bsbl; Var Bsktbl; Var Ftbl; High Hon Roll; Prfct Atten Awd; OK ST U.

THOMAS, MANDY; El Reno Sr HS; El Reno, OK; (4); Cmnty Wkr; 4-H; Key Clb; Office Aide; Quiz Bowl; Speech Tm; Teachers Aide; Cit Awd; 4-H Awd; High Hon Roll; FFA Offcr; Lvstck Jdgng Tm; Stdnt Yr Awd; Connors ST Coll; Ag Comms.

THOMAS, MATHEW C; Mt St Marys HS; Oklahoma City, OK; (3); #4 in class; FCA; Key Clb; Varsity Clb; Bsktbl; Gov Hon Prg Awd; High Hon Roll; Hon Roll; Comp Engrng.

THOMAS, MELVIN; Yukon Middle HS; Yukon, OK; (2); Church Yth Grp; FHA; Quiz Bowl; Spanish Clb; Church Choir; Hon Roll; 3-D; Hosp Vlntr; U Of OK; Medcl.

THOMAS, MICHAEL; Collinsville HS; Collinsville, OK; (4); FCA; Ofcr Bsbl; Capt Var Ftbl; Wt Lftg; Friends U; Bus Admin.

THOMAS, MICHAEL A; Midwest City HS; Midwest City, OK; (3); Spanish Clb; Rep Soph Cls; Var Bsktbl; Wt Lftg; Hon Roll; Prfct Atten Awd; Northwestern U; Bus Commnctn.

THOMAS, NICOLAS; Lawton Christian Schl; Indiahoma, OK; (3); 2/6; VP Jr Cls; Var L Bsbl; Var L Bsktbl; Var Capt Golf; Socr; Hon Roll; Pres Acad Fit Awd; Coach Mini Bsktbl Grls Team; Instr Jr Golf Clnc; Chmst.

THOMAS, RAECHEL; Clinton HS; Clinton, OK; (2); 14/156; Church Yth Grp; FTA; GAA; Office Aide; Teachers Aide; Bsktbl; Sftbl; Trk; Hon Roll; NHS; Legal Team; Med.

THOMAS, RAVEN V; Pauls Valley HS; Pauls Valley, OK; (2); FCA; Sec FHA; Sec FTA; Key Clb; Color Guard; Flag Corp; Rep Stu Cncl; Hon Roll; NHS; Pep Clb; Mat Md 1 Yr; Wrstlng Hmcmng Cndt Frosh Yr; Huston-Tilloson Univ; OB/GYN.

THOMAS, ROBERT M; Elgin HS; Lawton, OK; (2); Speech Tm; Ofcr Stu Cncl; Hon Roll; Jr NHS; NHS; Pres Acad Fit Awd; Pres Schlr; FFA Spch Events 1st/2nd/3rd Pl; Chiroprctr.

THOMAS, ROBYN; B T Washington HS; Tulsa, OK; (4); 97/264; Church Yth Grp; Spanish Clb; School Musical; Swing Chorus; Variety Show; Chrldng; Gym; Socr; U Of Tulsa; Scndry Tchr.

THOMAS, SAMMI; Claremore Sr HS; Claremore, OK; (1); JV Chrldng; Sftbl; Hon Roll.

THOMAS, SETH M; Indianola HS; Mcalester, OK; (2); 4-H; Natl FFA Org; Quiz Bowl; Sec Frsh Cls; Var Bsbl; High Hon Roll; NHS; Greenhand & Chptr FFA Degree Awd; U Of OK; Meteorologist.

THOMAS, SHANNON L; Mannford HS; Mannford, OK; (4); 6/92; Cmnty Wkr; Drama Clb; FCA; Library Aide; Science Clb; Spanish Clb; SADD; High Hon Roll; NHS; OK Hnr Soc; OK St Univ; Acctng.

THOMAS, SHAWN D; Woodward HS; Woodward, OK; (1); Cit Awd; Comps; Models; Hunting.

THOMAS, STEPHANIE; Bixby Sr HS; Bixby, OK; (4); 17/185; Cmnty Wkr; Drama Clb; German Clb; Teachers Aide; Thesps; School Play; Chrldng; Socr; NHS; Pres Acad Fit Awd; NSU; Chem.

THOMAS, STEVEN C; Colcord Schl; Colcord, OK; (3); FHA; Treas Natl FFA Org; Rep Jr Cls; Var Ftbl; Var Trk; Var Wt Lftg; Cit Awd; Hon Roll; NHS; Prfct Atten Awd; Northeastern ST; Animal Sci.

THOMAS, TARA D; Midwest City HS; Midwest City, OK; (2); #138 in class; Dance Clb; FCA; FHA; Pep Clb; SADD; Teachers Aide; Chorus; Swing Chorus; Rep Soph Cls; Var Pom Pon; SADD; OK Univ; Crmnl Justice.

THOMAS, TERRA; Dewey HS; Dewey, OK; (3); FCA; Spanish Clb; Phtg Ed Yrbk; Ofcr Stu Cncl; JV Var Bsktbl; Var Sftbl; JV Var Trk; Vllybl; Hon Roll; NHS; 3a Sftbll St Champ; Tchr.

THOMAS, VANCE; Claremore Sr HS; Claremore, OK; (4); #17 in class; FCA; L Capt Ftbl; L Capt Wrstlng; High Hon Roll; Jr NHS; NHS; Mgr Am Leg Boys St; Quiz Bowl; Sprts Med.

THOMAS, XAVIERA L; Webster HS; Tulsa, OK; (2); Cmnty Wkr; Science Clb; Var Bsktbl; High Hon Roll; Hon Roll; NHS; Indian Clb Pres; Summer Yth Pgm & Spon By OK Tribal; Outstdng Achvmnt In Indian Ed Asst Pgm; CPA.

THOMASON, CHEVY; Asher Schl; Shawnee, OK; (3); Church Yth Grp; FCA; Letterman Clb; Scholastic Bowl; Ofcr Bsbl; Bsktbl; Ftbl; Hon Roll; Jr NHS; NHS; Ntl Merit Ltr.

THOMASON, CHRISTY M; Warner HS; Warner, OK; (4); 5/49; Church Yth Grp; FCA; Office Aide; Spanish Clb; Band; Rptr Yrbk; VP Jr Cls; Ofcr Stu Cncl; Hon Roll; NHS; Northeastern ST Univ; Pre Med.

THOMASON, JENNIFER L; Will Rogers HS; Tulsa, OK; (1); Sec German Clb; JV Bsktbl; Var Cit Awd; Hon Roll; Med.

THOMASON, RUSSELL; Dickson HS; Ardmore, OK; (3); 2/84; FCA; HOBY; Key Clb; VP Natl FFA Org; Pres Spanish Clb; VP Church Choir; Pres Frsh Cls; Pres Soph Cls; VP Jr Cls; VP Stu Cncl; 1st Pl Natl Wstrn Shp Shw 96; US Stu Cncl & Natl Eng Mrt Awds; OK U; Dntstry.

THOMASON, SCOTT; Perry Sr HS; Perry, OK; (2); 1/100; Church Yth Grp; FCA; Natl FFA Org; Quiz Bowl; Band; Mrchg Band; Pep Band; Bsktbl; Ftbl; Cit Awd.

THOMASSON, ASHLEY; Ketchum HS; Disney, OK; (4); 1/31; Church Yth Grp; Rep FHA; HOBY; SADD; VP Stu Cncl; Bsktbl; Chrldng; Mgr(s); Powder Puff Ftbl; Sftbl; Trl Trs Aws Excel; Nrthestrn ST U; Ed.

THOMPSON, ANNA E; Union Sr HS; Tulsa, OK; (3); 87/741; Church Yth Grp; Key Clb; Spanish Clb; Yrbk; Swmmng; NHS; Orace Fllwshp Chldrns Chrch Wrkr.

THOMPSON, BETH A; Stroud HS; Stroud, OK; (4); 4/37; Sec Church Yth Grp; Pres DECA; Treas Drama Clb; Treas Band; Jazz Band; School Musical; NHS; Pres Acad Fit Awd; Natl Voc Tech Hnr Soc; Bus & Prof Women Girl Of The Month; Hnr Band; U Of Cntrl OK; Theatre.

THOMPSON, BETHANY; Weatherford HS; Weatherford, OK; (1); FCA; FHA; GAA; Chorus; Ofcr Stu Cncl; Bsktbl; Golf; Trk; Hon Roll; U Of OK; Dr Dntl Srgry.

THOMPSON, BLAIR N; Memorial HS; Tulsa, OK; (2); Church Yth Grp; Drama Clb; FCA; Key Clb; Pep Clb; Red Cross Aide; Chorus; Church Choir; Var Sftbl; Hon Roll; Sprts Med.

THOMPSON, BRANDY; El Reno Sr HS; El Reno, OK; (2); 43/225; Church Yth Grp; FCA; FTA; JA; L Chrldng; High Hon Roll; Natl Yth Ldrsp Forum; OK ST Univ.

THOMPSON, BRETT A; Mustang HS; Yukon, OK; (1); Church Yth Grp; Cmnty Wkr; Band; Jazz Band; Mrchg Band; Hon Roll; Outstdng Awd Indstrl Art Fair; OK U; Arch/Eng.

THOMPSON, BRIAN M; Brink Jr HS; Oklahoma City, OK; (1); Computer Clb; Office Aide; Phtg Yrbk; Hon Roll; NHS.

THOMPSON, CHRIS; Blair Schl; Hobart, OK; (2); Natl Beta Clb; Quiz Bowl; Var Bsktbl; Cit Awd; High Hon Roll; Hon Roll; Val; Comp Tech.

THOMPSON, CHRISTINA; Shawnee Sr HS; Shawnee, OK; (3); Church Yth Grp; FCA; Pep Clb; Spanish Clb; Chrldng; Hon Roll; Med.

THOMPSON, CORRIE; Broken Arrow Sr HS; Broken Arrow, OK; (4); 69/921; Church Yth Grp; Cmnty Wkr; French Clb; Hosp Aide; Church Choir; Hon Roll; NHS; Prfct Atten Awd; Office Aide; Temple Yth Grp; Yng Wmnhd Rcgntn Awd; Ballet; Jazz; Brigham Young Univ.

THOMPSON, CRIS; Cache HS; Cache, OK; (2); 1/112; Church Yth Grp; HOBY; Natl Beta Clb; Band; Jazz Band; Yrbk; NHS; Mrchg Band; Cit Awd; High Hon Roll; Hnr Jazz Band; All Region Band; OK Hnr Soc; FL ST Univ; Anesthesiologist.

THOMPSON, CRYSTAL D; Western Heights Sr HS; Oklahoma City, OK; (4); FHA; Office Aide; Teachers Aide; Stu Of Month Francis Tuttle Voc-Tech; HOSA 95-96; OKC CC; Nrsng.

THOMPSON, CRYSTAL L; Preston Schl; Okmulgee, OK; (1); Church Yth Grp; Hosp Aide; Scholastic Bowl; Church Choir; Ofcr Frsh Cls; Plcd 4th ST Gen Bus/Trnmnt Chmpns; Plcd 1st Art E Cntrl U; OK HS Hnr Soc; PT.

THOMPSON, CYNTHIA; Panama HS; Panama, OK; (3); Church Yth Grp; FHA; German Clb; Band; Chorus; Yrbk; Bsktbl; Mgr(s); Sftbl; Hon Roll.

THOMPSON, DARIN; Stillwater Sr HS; Stillwater, OK; (4); Boy Scts; Church Yth Grp; Key Clb; Mu Alpha Theta; Natl Beta Clb; Q&S; Spanish Clb; Acpl Chr; Chorus; Church Choir; OK ST Univ; Bus.

THOMPSON, DARIN S; Del City HS; Del City, OK; (2); Church Yth Grp; Drama Clb; VP FCA; Chorus; School Play; Stage Crew; Phtg Yrbk; Var Bsbl; Tennis; NHS; Arch.

THOMPSON, DAVID; Madill HS; Madill, OK; (3); JV Var Bsbl; JV Var Bsktbl; JV Var Ftbl; Var Golf; Var Trk; JV Var Hon Roll; OBU.

THOMPSON, DUSTIN E; Owasso Sr HS; Owasso, OK; (2); Spanish Clb; High Hon Roll; Rice Univ.

THOMPSON, ELIJAH B; Wetumka Jr Sr HS; Wetumka, OK; (2); Church Yth Grp; FCA; German Clb; Band; Mrchg Band; Pep Band; Bsktbl; Hon Roll; OK ST U; Play Bsktbl.

THOMPSON, ELISABETH A; South Intermediate HS; Broken Arrow, OK; (1); Church Yth Grp; Cmnty Wkr; Library Aide; Band; Mrchg Band; Pep Band; Hon Roll; Pres Schlr; Stu Ambassador To England, Ireland, Scotland & Wales Spon Thru People To People; All Dist Band Mem; Pensacola Chrstn Coll; Psycht.

THOMPSON, ERIN N; Boise City HS; Boise City, OK; (3); 2/35; Church Yth Grp; Rep Chrmn FHA; German Clb; Band; High Hon Roll; NHS; Sal; OK Hon Soc; CO St Univ; Archl.

THOMPSON, GRETCHEN; Lone Grove HS; Lone Grove, OK; (2); Church Yth Grp; Yrbk.

THOMPSON, JACOB; Shawnee Sr HS; Shawnee, OK; (4); 17/262; Am Leg Boys St; Church Yth Grp; Treas FCA; Spanish Clb; Ftbl; Golf; Wt Lftg; High Hon Roll; NHS; OK Indn Hnr Soc; Bst Lkng Sr Boy; Baylor U.

THOMPSON, JACQUELYN; Cyril Jr Sr HS; Cyril, OK; (4); 1/28; Church Yth Grp; Pres Math Clb; Capt Quiz Bowl; Spanish Clb; Church Choir; Ed Yrbk; Treas Sr Cls; Rep Stu Cncl; Var L Bsktbl; Var L Chrldng; Interschlstc Team; Amer Legion Awd; Fresh & Sr Stu Yr; USAO; Med.

THOMPSON, JAMIE L; Pauls Valley HS; Pauls Valley, OK; (1); Church Yth Grp; FCA; GAA; Key Clb; Natl Beta Clb; Pep Clb; Spanish Clb; Mgr Bsktbl; Mgr(s); Tennis; Acctng.

THOMPSON, JASON; East Central HS; Tulsa, OK; (4); 8/209; Am Leg Boys St; Church Yth Grp; FCA; French Clb; Key Clb; Office Aide; Red Cross Aide; Science Clb; Var L Bsbl; High Hon Roll; OK U HS Stus Hnrs Awd; Bus Mgmt.

THOMPSON, JENNIFER; Choctaw HS; Choctaw, OK; (4); FCA; Key Clb; Scholastic Bowl; VP Stu Cncl; Socr; High Hon Roll; Jr NHS; NHS; Sal; OK U; Med.

THOMPSON, JERI; Okemah HS; Okemah, OK; (1); 7/76; Church Yth Grp; Natl Beta Clb; Science Clb; SADD; Ofcr Stu Cncl; Bsktbl; Chrldng; Golf; High Hon Roll; OSU; Phys Thrpst.

THOMPSON, JOE; Collinsville HS; Collinsville, OK; (3); Boy Scts; Band; Mrchg Band; High Hon Roll; Hon Roll; Ntl Merit Ltr; Prfct Atten Awd; Pres Acad Fit Awd; OK ST U.

THOMPSON, JOEL; Metro Christian Acad; Tulsa, OK; (3); 1/54; Chess Clb; Church Yth Grp; FCA; Latin Clb; VP Frsh Cls; Treas Soph Cls; Treas Jr Cls; Rep Stu Cncl; Var L Bsktbl; Var L Ftbl; Premed.

THOMPSON, JULIE; Stillwater Sr HS; Stillwater, OK; (2); Church Yth Grp; DECA; FCA; Church Choir; School Musical; School Play; Chrldng; OSU.

THOMPSON, JULIE M; B T Washington HS; Tulsa, OK; (3); Spanish Clb; Jazz Band; Chrldng; DAR Awd; Hon Roll; NHS; Med.

THOMPSON, KATHRYN M; Ringling HS; Ringling, OK; (3); 2/39; FHA; Spanish Clb; Ofcr Soph Cls; Bsktbl; Powder Puff Ftbl; Trk; High Hon Roll; GATE; Acad Team; Pediatrics.

THOMPSON, KRISTEN; Putnam City HS; Oklahoma City, OK; (3); Church Yth Grp; Cmnty Wkr; Office Aide; Teachers Aide; Chorus; Rep Stu Cncl; Stat Bsbl; Score Keeper; Ldrshp Cls; DECA; OSU.

THOMPSON, KRISTI R; El Reno Sr HS; El Reno, OK; (1); JV Bsktbl; JV Crs Cntry; JV Tennis; Hon Roll; NHS; Math/Eng Hnrs; Bus.

THOMPSON, KYMBERLY; Bray-Doyle HS; Marlow, OK; (4); 1/35; VP FCA; FHA; HOBY; Sec SADD; Pres Sr Cls; High Hon Roll; NHS; Pres Church Yth Grp; Cmnty Wkr; Teachers Aide; Sci Tm; OK Hnr Soc; SADD Tres, Sec; OU; Med.

THOMPSON, LANDIS L; Henryetta Sr HS; Henryetta, OK; (2); Acpl Chr; Band; School Musical; School Play; Cit Awd; Hon Roll; Solo Exclnt Rating ST.

THOMPSON, LAUREN M; Mc Alester HS; Mcalester, OK; (2); FHA; Red Cross Aide; Spanish Clb; Rep Frsh Cls; Sec Soph Cls; Rep Stu Cncl; Cit Awd; High Hon Roll; NHS; Univ Of Cntrl OK; Pharm.

THOMPSON, LAUREN N; Bishop Mcguinness HS; Oklahoma City, OK; (3); 52/157; Church Yth Grp; Sec Treas FCA; French Clb; GAA; HOBY; Pep Clb; Red Cross Aide; SADD; Rep Frsh Cls; Rep Soph Cls; Frosh Class Mentor; Jr Hmcmng Cand.

THOMPSON, LEANN; Graham Schl; Henryetta, OK; (3); 4-H; FHA; Scholastic Bowl; Ed Nwsp; VP Frsh Cls; Var Bsktbl; 4-H Awd; Graham Speech Awd 95-96; Stu Of The Month; VOD Local 1st Pl, Dist 2nd Pl; Haskell Indian Natns U; Amer In.

THOMPSON, MELISSA A; Dover Schl; Dover, OK; (1); Chorus; Elem Ed.

THOMPSON, MICHAEL; Noble HS; Noble, OK; (2); Church Yth Grp; Mu Alpha Theta; Natl FFA Org; Hon Roll; NHS; OK ST U; Ag Ed.

THOMPSON, PAUL E; Charles Page HS; Sand Springs, OK; (2); JV Bsbl; Bsktbl; FL St Univ; Bus.

THOMPSON, RACHEL; Braman Schl; Braman, OK; (1); 2/21; FCA; FHA; Quiz Bowl; Scholastic Bowl; Speech Tm; Bsktbl; Chrldng; High Hon Roll; NHS; St Schlr; 1st Pl In Humorous Metro/Monologue; 3rd Pl In Prose; Bus Awd; OK ST U; RN.

THOMPSON, REGINA M; Classen Schl; Oklahoma City, OK; (2); Cmnty Wkr; Hosp Aide; Sec Letterman Clb; Rptr Mu Alpha Theta; Orch; Var Chrldng; JV Socr; JV Trk; Hon Roll; Bus.

THOMPSON, ROBERT R; Olive Jr Sr HS; Drumright, OK; (2); FBLA; Teachers Aide; Band; Chorus; Mrchg Band; Pep Band; U Of CA Los Angeles; Cmptr Anm.

THOMPSON, SABRINA J; Noble HS; Noble, OK; (3); Pres French Clb; Key Clb; Mu Alpha Theta; Pep Clb; Ofcr Stu Cncl; Var Bsktbl; Hon Roll; NHS; DECA.

THOMPSON, SARAH A; Pauls Valley HS; Pauls Valley, OK; (3); Church Yth Grp; FCA; FHA; Key Clb; Pep Clb; Spanish Clb; Teachers Aide; Yrbk; Var JV Chrldng; JV Tennis; Psych.

THOMPSON, SARAH S; Deer Creek HS; Edmond, OK; (2); FCA; Spanish Clb; School Play; Sftbl; Hon Roll; NHS.

THOMPSON, SHANA; Hollis Jr Sr HS; Hollis, OK; (4); 19/65; Cmnty Wkr; GAA; Capt Bsktbl; Chrldng; Sftbl; Trk; NHS; 4-H; FTA; Letterman Clb; St Acad Awd Bsktbl, Sftbl & Chrldng; All-St, All Conf Bsktbl Nom; All St & NCA Chrldr Nom; Clarendon Coll; Occptnl Thrpst.

THOMPSON, STEPHEN L; Ponca City Sr HS; Ponca City, OK; (2); Church Yth Grp; Hon Roll.

THOMPSON, TAYLA; Putnam City West HS; Bethany, OK; (1); Church Yth Grp; GAA; Sec Frsh Cls; Sec Soph Cls; JV Var Chrldng; Competitive Girls Fast Pitch Sftbl; Outstndng Hnrs Eng Stu Awd; Med Clb.

THOMPSON, TIFFANY; Watts HS; Watts, OK; (1); Church Yth Grp; Natl Beta Clb; Natl FFA Org; Nwsp; Yrbk; Sftbl; Hon Roll; Med.

THOMPSON, TORREY; Daniel Webster HS; Tulsa, OK; (4); 27/140; FBLA; Key Clb; Ofcr Soph Cls; Ofcr Jr Cls; Ofcr Sr Cls; Ofcr Stu Cncl; JV Bsktbl; Var Ftbl; Var Capt Trk; Cit Awd; Summea Trck/Field; OK ST; Engrng/Bus Admin.

THOMPSON, TRAVIS S; Blackwell HS; Blackwell, OK; (2); Church Yth Grp; FCA; Pep Clb; JV Var Bsbl; JV Var Bsktbl; Ftbl; Trk; Hon Roll; Bsktbl Royalty.

THOMPSON, VALERIE D; Pawnee HS; Pawnee, OK; (3); 7/75; Natl Beta Clb; Pres Frsh Cls; Pres Soph Cls; Rep Jr Cls; Var Bsktbl; Capt Chrldng; Var Sftbl; Var Trk; Hon Roll; FHA; All Sprts Attndnt; Attnd YLC; OK ST Univ; Comm.

THOMPSON, WILLIAM B; Union Intermediate HS; Tulsa, OK; (2); Church Yth Grp; Drama Clb; School Musical; School Play; Stage Crew; Intrml Bsktbl; Capt Socr; Hon Roll; Jr NHS; NHS; Theatre.

THOMPSON, ZAVIER V; Northeast HS; Oklahoma City, OK; (3); 12/175; Church Yth Grp; French Clb; FBLA; Science Clb; Church Choir; Yrbk; Pres Acad Fit Awd; Rotary Club; Young Explrers Club; Fisk Univ; Med.

THOMSON, MANDY; Pauls Valley HS; Pauls Valley, OK; (2); Church Yth Grp; FCA; French Clb; Key Clb; Natl Beta Clb; Sec Frsh Cls; VP Soph Cls; Rep Stu Cncl; JV Var Chrldng; JV Mgr(s); Play Piano; OK Univ; Pre Med/Radiologist.

THOMSON, TRACY N; Pauls Valley HS; Pauls Valley, OK; (3); Am Leg Aux Girls St; Church Yth Grp; FCA; French Clb; FHA; Key Clb; Natl Beta Clb; Spanish Clb; Teachers Aide; VP Frsh Cls; Univ OK Schl Dance; OK Summer Arts Inst Dance; U Of OK; Dance/Pre-Med.

THORNE, KAREN A; Choctaw HS; Choctaw, OK; (3); 69/317; FCA; Library Aide; Pres VICA; Mgr Bsktbl; Elem Tchr.

THORNELL, KRISTY S; Sallisaw HS; Muldrow, OK; (4); Spanish Clb.

THORNLEY, KELLY E; Morris HS; Morris, OK; (3); Church Yth Grp; Cmnty Wkr; 4-H; Pres FHA; Sec Natl FFA Org; Teachers Aide; Phtg Yrbk; Mgr Bsktbl; Score Keeper; Mgr Sftbl; U Of Central OK; Nrsng.

THORNTON, CONNIE G; Chouteau HS; Chouteau, OK; (3); Church Yth Grp; FHA; Chorus; Church Choir; Hon Roll; Tri St Hnr Choir; Bus.

THORNTON, LAKISHA M; John Marshall HS; Oklahoma City, OK; (3); Art Clb; Pres Church Yth Grp; Cmnty Wkr; Treas DECA; FCA; Quiz Bowl; ROTC; Spanish Clb; Stage Crew; Yrbk; OKC Afterschl Optns Tchr; Mero Tech Voc Schl Hlth Sci Tech Recvd Svrl Awds; OK ST Univ; HS Tchr.

THORNTON, SARAH; Haileyville Schl; Hartshorne, OK; (2); FCA; FBLA; Var Bsktbl; Var Chrldng; Var Sftbl; Hon Roll; FFA; NCA.

THORP JR, MICHAEL L; Garber Sr HS; Garber, OK; (2); Boy Scts; Church Yth Grp; Band; Mrchg Band; Orch; Pep Band; High Hon Roll; Hon Roll; NHS; Prfct Atten Awd.

THORPE, BENJAMIN D; Sapulpa Sr HS; Sapulpa, OK; (4); 19/298; Church Yth Grp; Band; Mrchg Band; Ftbl; Jr NHS; NHS; Pres Acad Fit Awd; Comp Prog; Savannah Col Of Art; Comp Art.

THORPE, JOHN A; Sapulpa Sr HS; Sapulpa, OK; (4); 11/298; Church Yth Grp; Band; Jazz Band; Mrchg Band; Var L Ftbl; Cit Awd; DAR Awd; Kiwanis Awd; NHS; Ntl Merit SF; Tns For Christ; Intl Drug Free Youth; Oral Roberts U.

THORSON, JULIE; Temple Chrstn Acad; Bethany, OK; (4); Church Yth Grp; Pep Clb; Band; Chorus; Bsktbl; Intrml Socr; Var Vllybl; High Hon Roll; Prfct Atten Awd; Val; IM Kickball; OK Bapt Coll; Missions.

THORTON, SHARON; Central HS; Tulsa, OK; (3); FBLA; Church Choir; JV Var Bsktbl; Hon Roll; NHS; MI ST; Bus.

THRALL, TRAVIS L; Boise City HS; Felt, OK; (3); 14/38; Church Yth Grp; FCA; Letterman Clb; VP Natl FFA Org; Var Ftbl; Var Wt Lftg; Hon Roll; Pres Acad Fit Awd; OK Hwy Ptrl Cdt Lwmn; FFA Lvstck Jdg Team; FFA Chptr Star Frmr Awd 95-96; W TX ST U; Crmnl Jstc.

THRALLS, ANGIE; Billings HS; Billings, OK; (1); Church Yth Grp; FCA; 4-H; Natl FFA Org; Pep Clb; Band; Nwsp; Ofcr Frsh Cls; Bsktbl; Sftbl; FFA, Algegbra & Sci Awds; OK ST Univ; Bus.

THRASH, CHANTRI S; Felt Public Schl; Felt, OK; (3); 1/10; Quiz Bowl; Chorus; Rptr Nwsp; Ed Yrbk; Pres Jr Cls; VP Stu Cncl; Var Bsktbl; Trk; High Hon Roll; NHS; W TX A&M U; Bus.

THRASH, DUSTIN B; Felt Public Schl; Felt, OK; (4); 1/5; Church Yth Grp; Cmnty Wkr; Quiz Bowl; Scholastic Bowl; Teachers Aide; School Play; Pres Frsh Cls; Pres Soph Cls; Pres Jr Cls; Pres Sr Cls; U Of OK; Microbio.

THRASH, MINDI; Moore HS; Moore, OK; (2); Chorus; Jr NHS; Multicltrl Stu Assn.

THRASHER, ANGEL; Central Mid-HS; Norman, OK; (2); FCA; Mu Alpha Theta; Chorus; Church Choir; Swmmng; Hon Roll; NHS; Green Stripe Tae Kwon Do; Pre-Law/Law Schl.

THRASHER, GABE; Laverne Jr Sr HS; Buffalo, OK; (4); 6/32; Pres 4-H; Letterman Clb; Pres Natl Beta Clb; Scholastic Bowl; Chorus; VP Stu Cncl; Capt Bsktbl; Capt Crs Cntry; Capt Golf; NHS; Natl Frmrs Union Schol; Farnland Yth Ldrshp Conf; Oral Roberts Univ; Intl Bus.

THRASHER, KATHRYN NOEL; Midwest City HS; Midwest City, OK; (4); 66/419; Church Yth Grp; Spanish Clb; Pres SADD; Variety Show; Nwsp; Rep Stu Cncl; Var Chrldng; Var Pom Pon; Tennis; NHS; All-Amer Pom 95-96; U Of OK; Bus Mgmt.

THRELKELD, JENNIFER; Capitol Hill HS; Oklahoma City, OK; (2); Art Clb; Pep Clb; Chorus; Hon Roll; Prfct Atten Awd; Sci.

THROWER, MICHAEL; Deer Creek HS; Edmond, OK; (3); 1/92; Boy Scts; French Clb; FBLA; Science Clb; Band; JV Bsbl; JV Crs Cntry; JV Ftbl; Wrstlng; Med.

THROWER, PATRICIA A; Deer Creek HS; Edmond, OK; (1); Church Yth Grp; Spanish Clb; Hon Roll; Ntl Merit Ltr; Phtgrphy; Hons Stdnt; Psychlgst.

THULIN, MATTHEW D; Glenpool HS; Sand Springs, OK; (3); Church Yth Grp; FBLA; Office Aide; Spanish Clb; Chorus; Tulsa Tech Ctr.

THURMAN, AMANDA B; Walters HS; Walters, OK; (3); FCA; HOBY; SADD; Chorus; Sec Soph Cls; Sec Jr Cls; Chrldng; High Hon Roll; Kiwanis Awd; NHS; Miss Walters 96; Hnr Choir; Midwestern ST U; Dntl Hygn.

THURMAN, JACOB; Liberty Acad; Shawnee, OK; (2); Church Yth Grp; Var Bsktbl; Var Golf; High Hon Roll; Hon Roll.

THURMAN, KIRSTEN; Valliant HS; Valliant, OK; (4); 3/86; Church Yth Grp; FCA; FHA; Quiz Bowl; Ed Nwsp; Rep Frsh Cls; Rep Stu Cncl; Chrldng; NHS; Miss Valliant HS; Ftbl Hmecmg Attend; U Of OK; Ed.

THURMAN, KRISTINA; Heavener HS; Howe, OK; (4); Am Leg Aux Girls St; Drama Clb; FHA; Hosp Aide; Natl FFA Org; Office Aide; Hon Roll; NHS; Natl Vo-Tech Hnr Soc; HOSA Pres; Carl Albert Coll; Reg Nrs.

THURMOND, STACY M; Edmond Memorial HS; Edmond, OK; (3); 1/371; Church Yth Grp; Spanish Clb; Band; Color Guard; Mrchg Band; Hon Roll; NHS; Pres Acad Fit Awd; D-Fy-It; OK Hnr Soc; Nom For Jr Ofmnth; OK St Univ; Pharm.

THUSTON, TREVER J; Jenks HS; Tulsa, OK; (4); 38/522; Church Yth Grp; Cmnty Wkr; Math Tm; Band; JV Bsktbl; Capt Socr; NHS; Ntl Merit SF; DECA; German Clb; Natl Mrt Commended Schlr; Premier Clb Soc.

TICE, MANDY E; Duke Schl; Duke, OK; (3); 8/17; Treas 4-H; FHA; Natl FFA Org; Science Clb; Var Bsktbl; Var Chrldng; Var Sftbl; 4-H Awd; Hon Roll; Prfct Atten Awd; DU Engrng Summer Acad; Recycled Cardboard-Duke Project For FFA; Comm Svc For Elderly; Southwestern OK ST U; Comp.

TICE, VANESSA; Kingston HS; Kingston, OK; (1); Church Yth Grp; FCA; FHA; GAA; Var Bsktbl; Var Sftbl; Hon Roll; NHS; 1st Dist/2nd ST/1ST Sub-Dist Jr Job Intrvw; Denison Herald Necomer Of Yr; MVP/SOSU/CARTER Cty.

TIDMORE, STEPHANIE A; East Central HS; Tulsa, OK; (2); FBLA; Rep Stu Cncl; High Hon Roll; NHS; Envrmntl Clb; Explorerers; Tulsa Wrld Awd Acad Excel; Radiologist.

TIDWELL, BRENT D; Checotah HS; Checotah, OK; (2); Natl FFA Org.

TIDWELL, DEVON S; Stilwell HS; Stilwell, OK; (2); Drama Clb; Spanish Clb; Drug Free Yth; Indian Heritage Clb Cncl Mem; OK ST Univ; Anthropology.

TIDWELL, HEATHER; Dewar Jr-Sr HS; Henryetta, OK; (3); FCA; GAA; HOBY; Office Aide; Pep Clb; Scholastic Bowl; Teachers Aide; Varsity Clb; Band; Chorus; Phys Thrpy.

TIDWELL, JENNIFER J; Cheyenne HS; Cheyenne, OK; (3); 10/24; Church Yth Grp; FHA; Natl FFA Org; Chorus; Church Choir; Hon Roll; Prfct Atten Awd; Stdnt Yr Hlth Sci Tech Prgm; Prfct Attndnc Yr Wstrn Tech Ctr; 1st Pl Natl Poem Cntst; PT.

TIDWELL, NATALIE; Westmoore HS; Oklahoma City, OK; (4); 50/622; Am Leg Aux Girls St; Church Yth Grp; Dance Clb; VP Drama Clb; FCA; School Musical; Rep Stu Cncl; High Hon Roll; NHS; Val; U Of Tulsa; Pre-Med.

TIDWELL, NICHOLAS; Jarman Jr HS; Tinker AFB, OK; (1); Church Yth Grp; Cmnty Wkr; French Clb; Varsity Clb; Var Capt Bsbl; Var Bsktbl; Wt Lftg; High Hon Roll; Hon Roll; Jr NHS; Comm Chrch Vol Bsktbl Ref; Psych.

TIELKE, MYRANDA; Perry Sr HS; Perry, OK; (3); FHA; German Clb; Nwsp; Jr NHS; NHS; OSU; Phys Thrpy.

TIGER, ANGELA M; Mounds Schl; Mounds, OK; (3); Church Yth Grp; Natl Beta Clb; Band; Mrchg Band; JV Bsktbl; Hon Roll; Jr NHS; NHS; Auto Mech.

TIGER, JOSH; Chickasha Jr HS; Chickasha, OK; (1); Art Clb; Hon Roll; NHS.

TIGER, TALITHA RENEE; Skiatook HS; Skiatook, OK; (4); 41/112; Church Yth Grp; Office Aide; Teachers Aide; Var Stat Bsktbl; Var Mgr(s); JV Var Score Keeper; JV L Trk; Var L Vllybl; Hon Roll; Top Art Stu; All Amer Schol; Ultrasound Tech.

TIGGEMAN, SHELLY M; Stillwater Sr HS; Stillwater, OK; (2); Church Yth Grp; Drama Clb; FCA; Key Clb; Spanish Clb; Teachers Aide; Chorus; Church Choir; School Musical; School Play; Taletn Show 9th 1st Plc; Supr UIL Compt Singng 4 Yrs; Singng; Tourng Europe Singng Grp; Chrstn Cnslng/Music.

TIGNOR, JENNI; Rock Creek Jr Sr HS; Bokchito, OK; (1); Church Yth Grp; Cmnty Wkr; FCA; FHA; Yrbk; Bsktbl; Hon Roll; NHS; Cmnty Hospice Vlntr; SEOSU; Ed.

TILLER, ANDREA L; Afton HS; Afton, OK; (2); 4/34; Cmnty Wkr; Natl FFA Org; Office Aide; Spanish Clb; Pres Soph Cls; Score Keeper; Hon Roll; Pres Acad Fit Awd.

TILLER, DANIEL; Choctaw HS; Choctaw, OK; (3); 21/320; Drama Clb; German Clb; Key Clb; Math Tm; Scholastic Bowl; School Play; JV Socr; High Hon Roll; Jr NHS; Rptr Nwsp; 7th Pl 5th Annl OSU HS Math Cnst 1995; U Of OK; Mech Engnr.

TILLER, JEFF; Afton HS; Afton, OK; (1); 2/34; FCA; Var L Bsbl; Var L Bsktbl; High Hon Roll; NHS; Bsktbl, Bsbl Ltrs; OK ST U; Comp Engr.

TILLER, KELLI D; Union Intermediate HS; Broken Arrow, OK; (1); 71/800; Church Yth Grp; FCA; Church Choir; Nwsp; Yrbk; High Hon Roll; Jr NHS; NHS; Union Stus For Christ; 5 Yrs Piano; OK U; Deaf Interpreter.

TILLER, KIMBERLY D; Union Sr HS; Broken Arrow, OK; (4); 62/632; Church Yth Grp; Key Clb; Acpl Chr; Yrbk; Ofcr Sr Cls; Ofcr Stu Cncl; NHS; FCA; FHA; Spanish Clb; OK Bapt All St Yth Choir; Union HS Ldrshp Cls; Alpha Theta & Union Stu For Christ; Northeastern ST U; Elem Educ.

TILLERY, AMBER N; Woodward HS; Woodward, OK; (4); 50/148; Church Yth Grp; Debate Tm; Pres FBLA; FHA; Sec Key Clb; Pep Clb; SADD; Rep Frsh Cls; VP Soph Cls; JV Var Bsktbl; U Of Cntrl OK; Bus Admin/Fin.

TILLERY, JADE ELLEN M; Union Intermediate HS; Tulsa, OK; (1); Sec Church Yth Grp; Girl Scts; Intnl Clb; Sec Math Clb; Band; Church Choir; Hon Roll; Jr NHS; NHS; Girl Sct Cadette Silver Awd; Piano Stdnt 8 Yrs; ARC; Gifted/Tlntd Prgm; BYU HI; Oceanographer.

TILLEY, BRANDON L; Byng Sr HS; Ada, OK; (2); 3/120; Church Yth Grp; Drama Clb; FCA; FBLA; Natl Beta Clb; Speech Tm; Var Bsbl; Var Bsktbl; High Hon Roll; NHS.

TILLEY, CARRIE; Comanche HS; Comanche, OK; (1); Church Yth Grp; Cmnty Wkr; Debate Tm; Drama Clb; German Clb; NFL; Speech Tm; Hon Roll; Cameron U; Eng Tchr.

TILLMAN, TYSON J; Hollis Jr Sr HS; Vinson, OK; (2); 20/75; 4-H; FBLA; Ofcr Bsbl; Bsktbl; Ftbl; Wt Lftg.

TIMBERLAKE, MICHELLE L; Star Spencer HS; Spencer, OK; (1); Church Yth Grp; Pres Frsh Cls; Clctng Stamps/Trolls/Clwns; OK City Univ; Scientst.

TIMBS, MELINDA D; Lawton Sr HS; Lawton, OK; (2); Girl Scts; Key Clb; Band; Mrchg Band; Jr NHS; NHS; OK Hnr Soc; Acad Team; Vet; Zoologist.

TIMMONS, ANGELA; North Intemediate HS; Broken Arrow, OK; (1); Spanish Clb; Chrldng; Frnds; OK St Hnr Soc; Law.

TIMMONS, JEDEDIAH; Mc Alester HS; Mcalester, OK; (4); Am Leg Boys St; French Clb; Capt Quiz Bowl; Band; Drm Mjr(t); Jazz Band; Mrchg Band; Pep Band; Bsktbl; Hon Roll; Indn Clb; Cngrssnl Acad.

TIMMONS, JOSHUA DAN; Mc Alester HS; Mcalester, OK; (3); 7/200; Am Leg Boys St; Quiz Bowl; Science Clb; Spanish Clb; Band; Jazz Band; Mrchg Band; Pep Band; Golf; High Hon Roll; U Of OK; Med Field.

TIMMS, AMANDA; Grandfield Jr Sr HS; Grandfield, OK; (2); 3/24; FHA; Ofcr Frsh Cls; Hon Roll; HOBY; CLEW; Meterologist.

TINDALL, JAMIE M; Mt St Marys HS; Yukon, OK; (3); Church Yth Grp; Cmnty Wkr; French Clb; Girl Scts; Key Clb; Church Choir; Stat Bsbl; JV Bsktbl; Mgr(s); Sftbl; Northeastern ST U; Comp Prgmr.

TINER, AMY L; Healdton HS; Wilson, OK; (2); FCA; FHA; Ofcr Stu Cncl; Bsktbl; Chrldng; NHS; Pres Acad Fit Awd; ST Acad Chrldng Awd; ST Chrldng Qualifer; Supt Hnr Roll; OSU; Acctng; Math.

TINER, COREY D; Healdton HS; Wilson, OK; (3); Treas Stu Cncl; Bsktbl; NHS; Eagle Scout; Ag Adventure Awd; Prin Hnr Roll; All Conf Bsktbl; V A All Tourney Tm; Cert Scuba Diver; Souteastern OK ST U; Engrg Ag.

TINKER, NATASHA L; Eisenhower Sr HS; Lawton, OK; (3); Cmnty Wkr; French Clb; Library Aide; Cit Awd; Prfct Atten Awd; U Cntrl OK.

TINNELL, TASHA N; Savanna HS; Mcalester, OK; (3); 4/60; FHA; Red Cross Aide; Science Clb; Teachers Aide; Sec Treas Jr Cls; Trk; Hon Roll; Prfct Atten Awd; Sub-Dist VP FHA; Vet Medicine.

TINNEY, MELISSA R; Duncan HS; Duncan, OK; (3); Church Yth Grp; FBLA; Chorus; Church Choir; Hon Roll; Elem Ed.

TINNIN, CHAD A; Wynnewood HS; Wynnewood, OK; (2); 13/48; Office Aide; Rep Frsh Cls; Rep Jr Cls; Bsktbl; Crs Cntry; Hon Roll.

TINNIN, LAURA; Hulbert Jr Sr HS; Hulbert, OK; (1); FHA; GAA; Pep Clb; SADD; School Play; Ofcr Frsh Cls; Bsktbl; Cit Awd; High Hon Roll; Jr NHS; NHS; Beacon; Med.

TINSLEY, JESSICA M; Yukon Middle HS; Yukon, OK; (3); 19/400; Church Yth Grp; FCA; Rep Spanish Clb; SADD; Church Choir; Bsktbl; Hon Roll; NHS; OBU; Eng Tchr.

TINSLEY, NATASHA A; Central Jr HS; Lawton, OK; (1); Math Tm; Spanish Clb; Ofcr Frsh Cls; High Hon Roll; Hon Roll; ITT Tec H; Novelist.

TIPPETT, NATASHA L; Edmond Memorial HS; Edmond, OK; (4); 186/322; FHA; Hosp Aide; JCL; Latin Clb; Office Aide; Spanish Clb; Teachers Aide; VICA; Wt Lftg; Hon Roll; Natl Vo-Tech Hnr Soc; Piraxis Col; Mass Thrpy.

TIPPIT, KATIE; Commerce HS; Commerce, OK; (2); 1/47; Church Yth Grp; Sec FCA; HOBY; SADD; Pres Soph Cls; Sec Stu Cncl; Bsktbl; Chrldng; Hon Roll; NHS; NCA All-Amer Chrldr; OK ST Univ; MD.

TIPPIT, STEPHEN; Keota Schl; Keota, OK; (2); German Clb; Natl FFA Org; Ftbl; Wt Lftg; High Hon Roll; NHS.

TIPPS, RICKY K; Westmoore HS; Oklahoma City, OK; (1); Library Aide; Office Aide; Spanish Clb; Teachers Aide; Ofcr Stu Cncl; Intrml Bsbl; Intrml Bsktbl; Intrml Ftbl; Intrml Trk; High Hon Roll.

TIPTON, BRANDON; Prague HS; Prague, OK; (4); 1/69; Am Leg Boys St; Church Yth Grp; Key Clb; Speech Tm; Sec Sr Cls; Ftbl; Trk; Hon Roll; NHS; Val; Jr Stu Yr; U Cntrl OK; Psych.

TIPTON, LIA M; Claremore Sr HS; Claremore, OK; (3); 49/237; Natl FFA Org; Spanish Clb; Intrml JV Bsktbl; Intrml JV Tennis; High Hon Roll; NHS; Prfct Atten Awd; ST FFA Nusery Operations Proficiency Awd 2nd Place; OK ST Univ; Horticulture.

TIPTON, LINDSY; Chandler HS; Chandler, OK; (3); #1 in class; Church Yth Grp; FHA; Girl Scts; Scholastic Bowl; Band; Jazz Band; Var Bsktbl; Var Sftbl; High Hon Roll; NHS; U Of OK; Psych.

TIPTON, MATT; Afton HS; Afton, OK; (2); 8/34; FCA; Yrbk; Rep Stu Cncl; L Bsbl; L Bsktbl; L Ftbl; L Trk; Hon Roll; Stu Of Month; Plyr Of Week; FFA Treas; Northeastern A&M; Sprts Med.

TIPTON, MATT; Mc Loud HS; Shawnee, OK; (1); FBLA; Band; Jazz Band; Mrchg Band; Pep Band; Hon Roll; All Dist Hnr Bnd; All Star Jazz Bnd; OBU Hnr Bnd; St Solo Ensmbl Cntst Superior; OBU Algebra Awd.

TIPTON, ROCHELLE; Hobart HS; Hobart, OK; (2); Church Yth Grp; Band; Flag Corp; Mrchg Band; Pep Band; Ofcr Stu Cncl; U Of OK; Med.

TISCARENO, CELIA; Woodward HS; Woodward, OK; (1); Art Clb; FCA; Hosp Aide; Pep Clb; Yrbk; Socr; Cit Awd; High Hon Roll; Hon Roll; Kiwanis Awd; Photography.

TISDALE, AARON; Apache HS; Apache, OK; (1); 2/60; Scholastic Bowl; Band; Mrchg Band; High Hon Roll; Hon Roll; Short Grass Hnr Bnd; SW Interschol Meet; U Of Sci And Arts Of OK Intschol Meet; OK HS Hnr Soc.

TISDALE, RUSTI; Midwest City HS; Midwest City, OK; (3); HOBY; Letterman Clb; Pres Pep Clb; Treas Jr Cls; Rep Stu Cncl; Var Sftbl; Var Swmmng; Cit Awd; Hon Roll; Jr NHS; Citywde Art Cont 1st Pl; Arch Engr.

TITSWORTH, JEREMY R; Okmulgee HS; Okmulgee, OK; (1); Church Yth Grp; Band; Church Choir; Mrchg Band; Pep Band; Hon Roll; Pres Acad Fit Awd; OK Bapt All ST Yth Choir; Marine Bio.

TITSWORTH, JONATHAN; Okmulgee HS; Okmulgee, OK; (4); 22/120; Am Leg Boys St; Office Aide; Spanish Clb; Band; Jazz Band; Mrchg Band; Pep Band; School Play; Hon Roll; Church Choir; Acad Bwl; U OK; Music.

TITSWORTH, TERESA E; Okmulgee HS; Okmulgee, OK; (2); Church Yth Grp; Band; Church Choir; Flag Corp; Mrchg Band; Pep Band; Hon Roll; Lib Yth Advy Cncl; OK Bapt All St Yth Choir; U Of OK; Meteorology.

TITTERUD, ERI P; Bishop Kelley HS; Tulsa, OK; (3); Model UN; Quiz Bowl; Scholastic Bowl; Nwsp; Yrbk; Stat Ice Hcky; Score Keeper; Hon Roll; NHS; Ntl Merit Ltr; Mock Trial; Pol Dbt Club; Guitar; Psych/Prof.

TITUS, DERRICK D; Madill HS; Madill, OK; (3); FCA; Band; Church Choir; Mrchg Band; Var Bsktbl; Stat Score Keeper; JV Trk; Mech Engrng.

TO, MICHAEL V; Brink Jr HS; Oklahoma City, OK; (1); Computer Clb; Quiz Bowl; Scholastic Bowl; VP Science Clb; Variety Show; Ed Nwsp; Rep Stu Cncl; Cit Awd; DAR Awd; Hon Roll; Peer Hlpr; Masonic Awd; Martial Art; U Of OK; Biomedcl Tech.

TOBEY, ANGELA G; Westmoore HS; Moore, OK; (3); Church Yth Grp; Jr NHS; NHS; OK Hnr Star 94; OK U.

TOBEY, HAYDEN H; Edmond Memorial HS; Edmond, OK; (2); Dance Clb; FCA; Spanish Clb; SADD; Pom Pon; Powder Puff Ftbl; NHS; Pres Schlr; All Amer Pom Pon; Dsgnd Schl Muriel.

TOBEY, TANNER HOWELL; Edmond Memorial HS; Edmond, OK; (3); FCA; Letterman Clb; Spanish Clb; SADD; Ftbl; Wrstlng; Cit Awd; NHS; All Amer Schlr; Stu Of Month; HS Hero; OK Univ.

TOBJY, VERONICA; Victory Christian Schl; Tulsa, OK; (4); Dance Clb; Intnl Clb; Teachers Aide; Orch; High Hon Roll; NHS; Piano; Violin.

TOBLER, APRIL D; Spiro HS; Spiro, OK; (1); FHA; Lawyer.

TOBUREN, ANDREA L; Union Intermediate HS; Tulsa, OK; (1); Church Yth Grp; FCA; Spanish Clb; JV Bsktbl; High Hon Roll; Jr NHS; NHS; Stu Of Month; Acad Ltr; Ballet/Jazz.

TOBY, RYAN; Mt St Marys HS; Oklahoma City, OK; (3); 3/75; Am Leg Boys St; Boy Scts; Ftbl; Wt Lftg; Gov Hon Prg Awd; High Hon Roll; Hon Roll; NHS; Hnting; Archery; Guns; Wldlf Field.

TODD, AMANDA D; Bethel HS; Mc Loud, OK; (3); #10 in class; 4-H; FHA; Natl FFA Org; Teachers Aide; NHS; Sfty Chm Bethel FFA; Multi-Yr Listee; Seminol JC; Med Schl/Srgn.

TODD, ANDREA; Collinsville HS; Collinsville, OK; (2); Church Yth Grp; 4-H; FHA; Band; Mrchg Band; 4-H Awd; Twirlng; Missionettes; Coop Jb Hr; Chld Care.

TODD, BRENT M; West Middle HS; Norman, OK; (2); Church Yth Grp; Cmnty Wkr; 4-H; Hon Roll; Pres Acad Fit Awd; OK CC; Cert Mchnc.

TODD, COURTNEY M; East Central HS; Tulsa, OK; (2); 3/301; Cmnty Wkr; Spanish Clb; Band; Jazz Band; Mrchg Band; Pep Band; High Hon Roll; Hon Roll; NHS; DFV Brd; Supr Band Rtng Dist, St, Tri-St Solo & Ensmbl Cntst; Tchr.

TODD, GALADRIEL; Talihina Sr HS; Talihina, OK; (4); 7/39; Am Leg Aux Girls St; Church Yth Grp; Debate Tm; NFL; Quiz Bowl; Science Clb; School Play; VP Jr Cls; JV Bsktbl; Tennis; 95 Tulsa U Summer Math & Sci Acad; Baylor U; Med.

TODD, KARA B; El Reno Sr HS; El Reno, OK; (2); Church Yth Grp; Natl FFA Org; SADD; Rep Frsh Cls; Rep Soph Cls; Rep Jr Cls; Ofcr Stu Cncl; Score Keeper; Sftbl; Cit Awd; Renaissance; Ldrs Of Tomorrow; Southwestern OK ST U; Vet Med.

TODD, KERRI; Sulphur HS; Sulphur, OK; (3); 5/93; Art Clb; FCA; Spanish Clb; VP Frsh Cls; VP Soph Cls; VP Jr Cls; Var Bsktbl; Var Chrldng; Var Crs Cntry; Var Trk; OK Hnrs Soc; Ftbl Homcmng Qn 94-95; East Central U; Ed.

TODD, MICHAEL A; Putnam City North HS; Oklahoma City, OK; (4); Pres VP Art Clb; Pres VP Drama Clb; NFL; Capt Quiz Bowl; Spanish Clb; Speech Tm; Chorus; School Musical; School Play; Stage Crew; Multi-Yr Listee; U Of OK; Musiccal Theatre.

TOEPEL, MARCY; Enid Sr HS; Kremlin, OK; (4); 83/412; Am Leg Aux Girls St; Church Yth Grp; Cmnty Wkr; Science Clb; Service Clb; Teachers Aide; Band; Mrchg Band; Orch; Pep Band; OK Otstndng Cth Yth Awd Rgn 7; NW OK St U Rgnl Sci Fr 2nd Pl; OK Sci Fr Excl; Tn Age Rep Pres; U OK Nrmn; Med.

TOEWS, GINGER; Chisholm Sr HS; Enid, OK; (3); 3/75; FHA; Hosp Aide; Natl FFA Org; Band; Rep Stu Cncl; Sftbl; High Hon Roll; NHS; Southwestern OK ST U; Phrmcy.

TOEWS, LACY R; Cimarron Public Schl; Meno, OK; (1); 1/30; GAA; Letterman Clb; Natl FFA Org; Pep Clb; Quiz Bowl; Scholastic Bowl; Science Clb; Band; Mrchg Band; Pep Band; NW OK ST U; Acctng.

TOLAND, CARISSA A; Cushing HS; Cushing, OK; (4); Church Yth Grp; Sec VICA; Chorus; Mgr Bsktbl; Var JV Sftbl; High Hon Roll; Hon Roll; NHS; Var Schlr 2 Yrs; Central Vo-Tech Offset Printng 2 Yrs, Prfct Atten 2 Yrs, Outstndg Stu 95-96; OSU Okmulgee; Desk-Top Publsh.

TOLAND, TIFFANY; Garber Sr HS; Garber, OK; (3); 5/40; Art Clb; Pres Church Yth Grp; FCA; FHA; HOBY; Pep Clb; Chorus; Church Choir; Bsktbl; Sftbl; Chrch Enid Dist Yth Pres; OK City U; Fmly Thrp.

TOLBERT, BOB O; Maysville Jr Sr HS; Pauls Valley, OK; (1); 4-H; Natl FFA Org; Ftbl; Trk; Wt Lftg; Pres Acad Fit Awd; OK ST U.

TOLENTINO, AMANDA C; Bishop Mcguinness HS; Oklahoma City, OK; (3); 27/143; Church Yth Grp; Hosp Aide; Pep Clb; Spanish Clb; SADD; Hon Roll; Jr NHS; NHS; Spanish NHS; Med.

TOLES, AMBER R; Ripley HS; Ripley, OK; (3); 9/34; FCA; GAA; Math Clb; Natl FFA Org; Science Clb; Spanish Clb; Teachers Aide; Band; Rep Frsh Cls; Rep Soph Cls; Trck-V; Langston U; PT.

TOLES, ANDY C; Ripley HS; Ripley, OK; (1); 7/50; FCA; Ofcr Stu Cncl; Var Bsbl; Var Bsktbl; Hon Roll.

TOLLE, TAMMY S; Shattuck Jr Sr HS; Shattuck, OK; (3); 23/38; Pres FHA; Pep Clb; SADD; Band; Chorus; Mrchg Band; Pep Band; Sayer JC; Radiology.

TOMAJAN, KATIE L; Brink Jr HS; Oklahoma City, OK; (1); Church Yth Grp; Debate Tm; Drama Clb; Speech Tm; Tennis; Vllybl; Gov Hon Prg Awd; High Hon Roll; Jr NHS; NHS; Teach Bible Schl At Chrch; Notre Dame; Jrnlsm; Broadcasting.

TOMAJAN, REBECCA; Midwest City HS; Moore, OK; (3); Church Yth Grp; Drama Clb; Band; Mrchg Band; School Musical; VP Stu Cncl; Swmmng; Tennis; Gov Hon Prg Awd; High Hon Roll; DECA; Phy Ther.

TOMAR, SHALINI B; B T Washington HS; Tulsa, OK; (2); Spanish Clb; Orch; High Hon Roll; Hon Roll; NHS; Clb Soccer Team.

TOMBERLIN, KATY; Seiling Schl; Mooreland, OK; (3); Art Clb; Church Yth Grp; FCA; FHA; Band; Drm Mjr(t); Mrchg Band; Hon Roll.

TOMBLIN, KELLI A; Tahlequah Sr HS; Hulbert, OK; (2); Chorus; Bsktbl; Trk; Jr NHS; NHS; Pres Schlr; Church Head Pianist; Northeastern ST Univ; Med.

TOMLIN, WENDY M; El Reno Sr HS; El Reno, OK; (1); Spanish Clb; Chorus; Tennis; High Hon Roll; Hon Roll; FHA Parlimentarian; Vocal, Family & Consumer Sci, Pre-Algebra, Sci & World His Ltrs; OSU.

TOMLINSON, CLAY; Guyman HS; Guymon, OK; (3); 4/130; Co-Capt FCA; HOBY; Letterman Clb; VP Science Clb; Band; Church Choir; Jazz Band; Mrchg Band; Pep Band; Pres Stu Cncl; ORU; Med.

TOMLINSON, KARA S; Westmoore HS; Oklahoma City, OK; (2); Dance.

TOMLINSON, TRENT C; Union Intermediate HS; Tulsa, OK; (2); Library Aide; Band; Orch; Photo; Visual Arts; Hnrb Mntn Reflections 95; Advertising Field.

TOMPKINS, KASEY; Tomlinson Jr HS; Lawton, OK; (1); FCA; FHA; Speech Tm; Var Chrldng; High Hon Roll; Jr NHS; Jr Natl Hnr Soc Rep; All Amer Schlr; Astronaut.

TOMPKINS, SARA; Medford Schl; Medford, OK; (2); Church Yth Grp; FCA; FHA; Pep Clb; School Play; Sec Frsh Cls; Var Bsktbl; Var Sftbl; Var Trk; Hon Roll; KS U.

TONEY, AMBER N; Okmulgee HS; Okmulgee, OK; (3); 28/150; FBLA; FHA; Science Clb; Spanish Clb; Hon Roll; Jr NHS; NHS; Curtural Heritage Awd; Comp Tech.

TONEY, LESLIE A; Wapanucka Schl; Bromide, OK; (2); Pres 4-H; HOBY; Natl FFA Org; Pres Frsh Cls; Pres Soph Cls; Ofcr Bsbl; 4-H Awd.

TONEY, LINDY S; Bartlesville Mid HS; Bartlesville, OK; (2); 114/489; VP Church Yth Grp; Orch; Hon Roll; Rodeo; Horsetrainer/Tchr.

TONUBBEE, SAMANTHA L; Union Sr HS; Tulsa, OK; (3); 130/730; French Clb; Math Clb; Band; Mrchg Band; Orch; Pep Band; Intrml Sftbl; NHS; All Dist Band; Hendrix; Pre-Med.

TOOHEY, LAURA J; Alva HS; Alva, OK; (2); Cmnty Wkr; FCA; Library Aide; Office Aide; SADD; Crs Cntry; Tennis; Wt Lftg; Littl Leg T-Bll Coach; U Of MI; Law.

TOOLEY, CARMEN S; Boise City HS; Boise City, OK; (3); Church Yth Grp; FCA; FHA; Letterman Clb; Office Aide; Red Cross Aide; Sec Cmnty Wkr; Var L Bsktbl; High Hon Roll; NHS; TX Tech U; Med Records Admin.

TOOLEY, KAYL; Asher Schl; Asher, OK; (3); 1/23; Church Yth Grp; FHA; GAA; Church Choir; Pres Jr Cls; Bsktbl; Sftbl; High Hon Roll; Math.

TOOLEY, MAHAYLA B; Boise City HS; Boise City, OK; (1); 6/37; Church Yth Grp; FCA; GAA; Letterman Clb; Varsity Clb; VP Frsh Cls; JV Var Bsktbl; Chrldng; Gym; Var Trk.

TOOLEY, TIFFANY D; Boise City HS; Boise City, OK; (2).

TOOMBS, ANGELA; Achille Schl; Achille, OK; (1).

TOPE, SCOTT; Perry Sr HS; Perry, OK; (2); FBLA; FHA; NHS; Natl Ldrshp, Svc Awd; All Amer Schlr; U Of CA Berkley; Chem.

TORRALBA, TAVIA; Carnegie HS; Carnegie, OK; (4); Art Clb; Church Yth Grp; Cmnty Wkr; Drama Clb; FCA; HOBY; Letterman Clb; NFL; Quiz Bowl; Speech Tm; Amer Indian Heritage Clb; OK Odyssey Of Mind Reg, St Qlfr; OK Indian Stu Ortry Reg Chmpn; OK ST U; Psych.

TORRENCE, KIRSTIN E; South Intermediate HS; Broken Arrow, OK; (1); Church Yth Grp; Cmnty Wkr; Letterman Clb; Ofcr Stu Cncl; Tennis; Cit Awd; Hon Roll; Chrstn Stu Union; OU.

TORRES, JOANNA; Lawton Sr HS; Fort Sill, OK; (3); HOBY; Intnl Clb; Spanish Clb; Chorus; School Musical; Hon Roll; NHS; All Region Chorus 9th-11th Grd; All ST Chorus 10th Grd; Psych/Music.

TORRES, MELISA; Lawton Sr HS; Lawton, OK; (2); Spanish Clb; Hon Roll; TIVY Math Cmptn; Northwestern; Med.

TORRES, MICHAEL S; Choctaw HS; Choctaw, OK; (2); German Clb.

TORRES, REBECCA R; Stilwell HS; Stilwell, OK; (2); Church Yth Grp; 4-H; French Clb; FHA; Library Aide; Teachers Aide; School Play; High Hon Roll; Hon Roll; Northeastern ST Univ; Tchr.

TORRES FLORES, YOLANDA V; Central Jr HS; Fort Sill, OK; (1); Band; Mrchg Band; Pep Band; Hon Roll; Jr NHS; Sci.

TORREZ, ELISA L; Blair Schl; Blair, OK; (2); Hosp Aide; Quiz Bowl; Chorus; Pres Soph Cls; High Hon Roll; Hon Roll; NHS; 3K ST Univ; Dr.

TOSO, DONG; Tomlinson Jr HS; Lawton, OK; (1); Golf.

TOTTE, DENNIS; Tomlinson Jr HS; Lawton, OK; (1); FCA; Letterman Clb; Office Aide; Teachers Aide; Rptr Nwsp; Var Bsbl; Var Ftbl; Gov Hon Prg Awd; High Hon Roll; Hon Roll; OK U; Med.

TOTTEN, BETHANY J; Edmond Memorial HS; Edmond, OK; (2); Church Yth Grp; Cmnty Wkr; French Clb; GAA; Orch; Rep Stu Cncl; OK Yth Symph; Edmond Mem HS Chamber Orch; Chem.

TOTTRESS, JEREMIAH; Boynton Schl; Boynton, OK; (4); 3/10; Church Yth Grp; FHA; Teachers Aide; Nwsp; Sec Sr Cls; Var Bsktbl; Chrldng; Hon Roll; U Of OK Hnrs Acad Achvmnts.

TOWERY, CRAIG A; Noble HS; Norman, OK; (4); 9/147; Church Yth Grp; Cmnty Wkr; FCA; Mu Alpha Theta; Spanish Clb; Yrbk; Bsktbl; High Hon Roll; NHS; Pres Acad Fit Awd; OK Bapt Univ; Pastor.

TOWLER, CRAIG; Lindsay HS; Lindsay, OK; (2); 1/85; FCA; Varsity Clb; Pres Frsh Cls; Var Ftbl; Hon Roll; NHS; Pres Acad Fit Awd.

TOWLER, KENNITH D; Blanchard Jr Sr HS; Blanchard, OK; (3); Computer Clb; Natl FFA Org; Spanish Clb; Ftbl; Trk; Wt Lftg; NHS.

TOWLER, MICHELLE R; Capitol Hill HS; Oklahoma City, OK; (4); DECA; Library Aide; Spanish Clb; JV Var Bsktbl; JV Var Sftbl; Hon Roll; NHS.

TOWNER, KRISTINE A; B T Washington HS; Tulsa, OK; (4); 31/264; Church Yth Grp; Intnl Clb; Latin Clb; Pep Clb; Teachers Aide; Varsity Clb; Ofcr Stu Cncl; Crs Cntry; Socr; High Hon Roll; Japanese Club; Sunday Schl Tchr; Centennary; Pre-Med.

TOWNLEY, AMY; Amber Pocasset Jr Sr HS; Amber, OK; (2); 1/46; Church Yth Grp; FCA; Pres FHA; Scholastic Bowl; Church Choir; VP Soph Cls; Var Chrldng; Hon Roll; Jr NHS; Ntl Merit Ltr.

TOWNLEY, PETER; Heritage Hall Schl; Oklahoma City, OK; (4); 7/49; HOBY; Letterman Clb; Mu Alpha Theta; School Play; Var L Ftbl; Var L Trk; NHS; Spanish NHS; Spanish Clb; School Musical; COPE; STAR; Phy Ther.

TOWNSEND, ASHLEY B; Muldrow HS; Muldrow, OK; (2); Church Yth Grp; Debate Tm; Natl Beta Clb; NFL; Science Clb; Spanish Clb; Band; Chrldng; High Hon Roll; USAA Chdrlng, Band, Ldrshp, Eng, Govt & His Awds; Criminal Law.

TOWNSEND, DUSTY; Carney Schl; Carney, OK; (3); Church Yth Grp; FCA; Letterman Clb; Math Tm; Natl FFA Org; Teachers Aide; Var JV Bsbl; Var JV Bsktbl; 4-H Awd; High Hon Roll; FFA Star Greenhand, St Meats Tm, St Farmer, Swine Prdctn Awds, Wildlf Mgmt Awds & Dvrsfd Livestck Awds.

TOWNSEND, MARSHA L; Madill HS; Madill, OK; (1); Color Guard; Drill Tm; Flag Corp; Pres Frsh Cls; Trk; SOSU; Med.

TOWNSEND, MATT; Amber Pocasset Jr Sr HS; Amber, OK; (4); 1/29; Church Yth Grp; FCA; Scholastic Bowl; Science Clb; Spanish Clb; Teachers Aide; Ed Yrbk; Ofcr Soph Cls; Mgr Bsktbl; High Hon Roll; All Amer Schlr; U Cntrl OK; Comp Prgmr.

TOWNSEND, MELANIE; Altus Sr HS; Altus, OK; (3); Church Yth Grp; FCA; FHA; Office Aide; Service Clb; Spanish Clb; Church Choir; Mgr(s); Swmmng; Hon Roll; Msn Wrk.

TOWNSEND, SARAH; Amber Pocasset Jr Sr HS; Amber, OK; (1); 1/47; Church Yth Grp; FCA; FHA; Girl Scts; Scholastic Bowl; Chrldng; High Hon Roll.

TOWNSEND, TABITHA J; Wynnewood HS; Wynnewood, OK; (1); Church Yth Grp; Drama Clb; Girl Scts; Chorus; Church Choir; Swing Chorus; East Central Univ; Drmtlgst.

TOWNSEND, TIM; Tecumseh HS; Tecumseh, OK; (4); 1/128; Church Yth Grp; FCA; Pres Mu Alpha Theta; Natl Beta Clb; Natl FFA Org; Science Clb; Ofcr Stu Cncl; Ftbl; Wt Lftg; Wrstlng; Natl Ftbl Fdn; Coll Hl/Fm Otsdng Stdnt Ath Fnlst; Lttl All Cty Ftbl/Wrstlng Otsdng Stdnt/Ath Nom; U Of OK; Elec Engr.

TRACY, AMY C; Choctaw HS; Choctaw, OK; (4); Church Yth Grp; FHA; GAA; Key Clb; Pres Spanish Clb; Rptr Nwsp; Phtg Yrbk; Sec Stu Cncl; Ofcr Bsbl; Mgr Ftbl; OK U; Bus.

TRACY, BRETT; Mt St Marys HS; Oklahoma City, OK; (4); 6/63; Church Yth Grp; Cmnty Wkr; FCA; HOBY; JA; Pres Key Clb; Letterman Clb; Pres Frsh Cls; Pres Soph Cls; Rep Stu Cncl; Outstndg Stu Ldr Awds 4 Yrs; Acad Achvt 4 Yrs; Sci/Engrg Fair Navy Sci Awd; Jr Rotrn; MET; Vlntr Wrk; Saint Gregorys Coll; Psych.

TRACY, CHRIS; Maysville Jr Sr HS; Maysville, OK; (1); 4-H; JV Bsktbl; JV Ftbl; JV Trk; JV Wt Lftg; 4-H Awd; Prfct Atten Awd; FFA Treas; 4-H VP.

TRACY, CHRISTOPHER; Ada HS; Ada, OK; (4); 39/159; FCA; Pres Jr Cls; VP Pres Sr Cls; Pres Stu Cncl; Ftbl; Cit Awd; High Hon Roll; Boy Scts; Church Yth Grp; Cmnty Wkr; Schl TV Anchrmn; Pres Ldrshp Cls At OK Univ; Stu Of Today Awd; OK Univ; Optom.

TRACY, DANNY; Maysville Jr Sr HS; Maysville, OK; (4); 1/55; 4-H; FHA; Key Clb; Rep Frsh Cls; Rep Stu Cncl; Cit Awd; 4-H Awd; High Hon Roll; Jr NHS; U Of OK; Botany.

TRACY, JENNIFER L; Glenpool HS; Glenpool, OK; (2); Sec Church Yth Grp; Chorus; Chrldng; Hon Roll; Jr NHS; NHS; OU; PT.

TRACY, LINDY; Madill HS; Madill, OK; (2); Church Yth Grp; SADD; Band; Chorus; Mrchg Band; Pep Band; Stage Crew; Cit Awd; 1st, 2nd Pl Marshall Cty Fr, Reserve Chmpn Wnnr; Show Choir; Cert Acad Excllnc Awd; Band/Music Ltr; Murray ST Coll; Nrs.

TRADII, CAROLINE M; Mustang HS; Yukon, OK; (2); Church Yth Grp; Debate Tm; FHA; Hon Roll; NHS; Dance Co; Hair Designer; Psychiatrist.

TRAIL, KARA; Lone Grove HS; Springer, OK; (2); Math Clb; Science Clb; Spanish Clb; Yrbk; Powder Puff Ftbl; High Hon Roll; NHS; U Of OK; Medcl Lab Tech.

TRAMMEL, CRYSTAL R; Tahlequah Sr HS; Moodys, OK; (4); 13/251; Computer Clb; Office Aide; Red Cross Aide; Spanish Clb; Bsktbl; High Hon Roll; Jr NHS; NHS; Ntl Merit Ltr; OK Indian Hnr Soc; Rotary Clb Awd; Northeastern ST U; Prof Hlth.

TRAMMELL, ELLEN M; Tecumseh HS; Tecumseh, OK; (2); Natl FFA Org; Ofcr Soph Cls; JV Var Bsktbl; Var Trk; High Hon Roll; NHS.

TRAMMELL, HEATHER D; Pauls Valley HS; Pauls Valley, OK; (1); Church Yth Grp; 4-H; Library Aide; Pep Clb; Band; Flag Corp; Tennis; Hon Roll; Horse Back Riding; OK ST U; Csmtlgst.

TRAMMELL, LORA; Leflore Sr HS; Wister, OK; (1); Speech Tm.

TRAMMELL, TELIA; Leflore Sr HS; Wister, OK; (3); HOBY; Quiz Bowl; Speech Tm; Hon Roll; NHS; Upward Bnd CASC; OSU; Vet.

TRAMMELL, TILIA; Leflore Sr HS; Wister, OK; (2); 8/21; Church Yth Grp; FHA; Speech Tm; Chorus; High Hon Roll; Hon Roll; NHS; OSU; Phys Thrpst.

TRAMMELL, VIC H; Bishop Kelley HS; Broken Arrow, OK; (2); Key Clb; Var Bsbl; Var Ftbl; Hon Roll; KS; Orthpdc Surgeon.

TRAN, CUONG V; Moore HS; Moore, OK; (3); Med.

TRAN, DAVID H; Union Intermediate HS; Broken Arrow, OK; (2); Church Yth Grp; Cmnty Wkr; French Clb; FBLA; Intnl Clb; Key Clb; Math Clb; Quiz Bowl; Service Clb; Orch; Taekwondo; OK ST Univ; Cmptr Sci.

TRAN, HUY; U S Grant HS; Oklahoma City, OK; (4); 3/183; Val; Mayors Awd Smmr Yth Emplymnt & Trng Prgm; Excllnc In Math Awd; Chem Engrng.

TRAN, LE; Northwest Classen HS; Oklahoma City, OK; (3); French Clb; Key Clb; Socr.

TRAN, MAI; Macomb Schl; Macomb, OK; (1); 4-H; Chrldng; Sftbl; Acad Tm; Gftd & Tlntd; Friends U.

TRAN, NAM; Mustang HS; Yukon, OK; (3); 1/400; FCA; HOBY; Spanish Clb; Teachers Aide; Ofcr Soph Cls; Ofcr Jr Cls; Ofcr Stu Cncl; Hon Roll; NHS; Duke; Pre-Med.

TRAN, PATTY C; North Intemediate HS; Broken Arrow, OK; (1); Church Yth Grp; English Clb; Latin Clb; Teachers Aide; Church Choir; Rep Frsh Cls; Trk; Wt Lftg; Gov Hon Prg Awd; NHS; OK Hon Soc; Med.

TRAN, PHUOC LIEN THI; Webster HS; Tulsa, OK; (4); Temple Yth Grp; Hon Roll; TJC; Pharmacy/Med.

TRAN, RICHARD; Union Sr HS; Tulsa, OK; (3); 61/740; NHS.

TRAN, SI SI; John Marshall HS; Oklahoma City, OK; (4); 2/180; Drama Clb; French Clb; German Clb; Quiz Bowl; Scholastic Bowl; Teachers Aide; Band; Mrchg Band; School Play; Stage Crew; Piano; Martial Arts; U Of OK; Pre-Med.

TRAN, SISI; John Marshall HS; Oklahoma City, OK; (4); 2/180; Drama Clb; French Clb; German Clb; JA; Quiz Bowl; Scholastic Bowl; Teachers Aide; Thesps; Band; Mrchg Band; U Of OK; Med.

TRAN, THAO; Mc Loud HS; Newalla, OK; (4); FHA; Office Aide; Ed Yrbk; VP Jr Cls; VP Sr Cls; Rep Stu Cncl; Mgr Bsktbl; Mgr Ftbl; Hon Roll; NHS.

TRAN, TINA C; North Intemediate HS; Broken Arrow, OK; (2); Church Yth Grp; Debate Tm; FCA; JCL; Latin Clb; NFL; Speech Tm; Hon Roll; St Schlr; Natl His Day; Comm.

TRAN, TRANG T; Union Intermediate HS; Tulsa, OK; (2); Math Clb; NHS; OK ST U; Banking.

TRAN, VU H; Union Intermediate HS; Tulsa, OK; (2); Math Clb; OSU; Auto Mech.

TRANG, MAI Q; Union Sr HS; Tulsa, OK; (3); Church Yth Grp; Drama Clb; FCA; FBLA; Office Aide; Chorus; School Musical; School Play; Stage Crew; Variety Show; Voice Cntst Super.

TRANN, TRAM; Westmoore HS; Moore, OK; (3); Spanish Clb; NHS; OK Univ; Pharmacy.

TRANTHAM, JENNIFER M; Durant HS; Durant, OK; (3); Band; Chorus; Mrchg Band; Hon Roll; Natl Lib Of Poetry Cont Fnlst; Southeastern ST Univ; Tchr.

TRAUE, CHRISTI; Jarman Jr HS; Midwest City, OK; (1); Church Yth Grp; FCA; Spanish Clb; Rep Stu Cncl; Bsktbl; Vllybl; Cit Awd; High Hon Roll; Hon Roll; Pres Jr NHS.

TRAUGOTT, SHAILA D; Stillwater Sr HS; Stillwater, OK; (3); 1/363; DECA; JCL; Key Clb; Latin Clb; Library Aide; Mu Alpha Theta; Natl Beta Clb; Office Aide; Teachers Aide; Chorus; RAP; Envrmntl Clb VP; Piano Awds 8 Yrs.

TRAUT, MELINDA; Indianola HS; Mcalester, OK; (2); 1/45; Church Yth Grp; FBLA; FHA; Natl Beta Clb; High Hon Roll; Prfct Atten Awd; OK Hnr Soc; OK ST.

TRAVIS, EMILY; Thomas Jr Sr HS; Thomas, OK; (4); 2/33; FBLA; FHA; Natl FFA Org; Chorus; Church Choir; Flag Corp; Yrbk; Hon Roll; Pres Acad Fit Awd; Sal; Sthwstrn Wthrfrd OK.

TRAVIS, LATOYA L; B T Washington HS; Tulsa, OK; (4); Cmnty Wkr; Hist FBLA; Teachers Aide; Chorus; High Hon Roll; Hon Roll; Try-Angles Yth Org; Bus Comp Tech Intern BCTI Stu; African Amer Soc; Deans Hnr Roll Tulsa JR Coll; Tulsa JC; Nrsng; RN.

TRAVIS, REESE; Carl Albert HS; Midwest City, OK; (4); 27/265; Am Leg Boys St; Church Yth Grp; FCA; Key Clb; Bsktbl; Ftbl; Trk; Wrstlng; High Hon Roll; NHS; 4.0 Clb; NEO A&M JC.

TRAVIS, SHANTELL M; Putnam City North HS; Oklahoma City, OK; (2); FCA; SADD; Chrldng; Golf; Trk; NHS.

TRAWEEK, VICKY J; Choctaw HS; Choctaw, OK; (2); JV Bsktbl; Score Keeper; JV Socr; Mgr Sftbl; Mgr Trk; Hon Roll; Jr NHS; Pres Acad Fit Awd; Acad Team.

TRAYLOR, CHRISTOPHER A; Central Mid-HS; Norman, OK; (2); Cmnty Wkr; FCA; French Clb; Letterman Clb; Varsity Clb; JV Ftbl; Var Trk; Var Wt Lftg; Var Wrstlng; ASB Friend Grp; Cntrl Mid-Hi Stopm Dance Grp; FSU; Law.

TRAYLOR, CORY D; Heritage Hall Schl; Oklahoma City, OK; (2); Spanish Clb; Varsity Clb; Var L Bsbl; JV L Bsktbl; Var L Ftbl; Var L Socr; Hon Roll; Mech Engrng.

TRAYLOR, PERTRICEE; Luther HS; Luther, OK; (4); 8/42; Treas Church Yth Grp; Dance Clb; Pres Debate Tm; VP FHA; NFL; Speech Tm; Chorus; Sec Jr Cls; VP Stu Cncl; Hon Roll; Greater OK City Alumnae Panhellenic Awd; Outstdng Debater; UCO; Bio; Orthopedic Surgeon.

TREADAWAY, ERIN; Woodward HS; Woodward, OK; (2); Church Yth Grp; Computer Clb; German Clb; Letterman Clb; Quiz Bowl; Scholastic Bowl; High Hon Roll; NHS; Mock Trial Best Witness Awd.

TREADWELL, CARLA M; Gore HS; Gore, OK; (4); 9/26; Church Yth Grp; FHA; Hosp Aide; Office Aide; Pres SADD; Sftbl; Connor St Col; RN.

TREADWELL, NATALIE; Holdenville HS; Holdenville, OK; (3); Am Leg Aux Girls St; Church Yth Grp; FCA; 4-H; Natl Beta Clb; Natl FFA Org; Office Aide; VP Soph Cls; Treas Jr Cls; Ofcr Stu Cncl; St Champ Relays 95; St Qulfr Dash 95; Class 2 A Dist Regl, St Champ 95; St Qulfr Crss Cntry 93, 94; OK ST U; Phys Thrpy.

TREASE, KARA; Fairland Jr Sr HS; Fairland, OK; (3); FHA; Sec Frsh Cls; Sec Soph Cls; VP Jr Cls; Var Bsktbl; Var Sftbl; Var Trk; Hon Roll; Ntl Merit Ltr; Pres Acad Fit Awd; Med.

TREAT, CLINTON W; Dale Sr HS; Shawnee, OK; (1); Natl FFA Org; Ofcr Bsbl; Bsktbl; Ftbl; Bus.

TREAT, GREGORY L; Catoosa HS; Catoosa, OK; (4); 9/150; Am Leg Boys St; Library Aide; Spanish Clb; Ofcr Sr Cls; Bsktbl; Socr; High Hon Roll; Hon Roll; NHS; Cngrssnl Yth Ldrshp Cnsl.

TREAT, LORI L; Muldrow HS; Muldrow, OK; (1); Church Yth Grp; Natl Beta Clb; Natl FFA Org; Science Clb; Spanish Clb; Band; Mrchg Band; Swing Chorus; JV Chrldng; High Hon Roll; Piano; Dentist.

TREECE, T J; Waynoka HS; Waynoka, OK; (3); 2/2; Church Yth Grp; FCA; FHA; Pep Clb; Scholastic Bowl; VP Soph Cls; Var Bsbl; Var Bsktbl; Var Ftbl; Hon Roll.

TREECE, TRACY; Sharon Mutual Jr Sr HS; Woodward, OK; (3); Church Yth Grp; FCA; FHA; Ofcr Frsh Cls; Pres Soph Cls; Var Bsktbl; Var Chrldng; Var Sftbl; Hon Roll; NHS.

TRENNEPOHL, ADRIENNE A; Stillwater Sr HS; Stillwater, OK; (2); Church Yth Grp; Debate Tm; FCA; Key Clb; SADD; Church Choir; Phtg Nwsp; Phtg Yrbk; Powder Puff Ftbl; Tennis; Nurses Aid; OSU; Hotel Mgmt.

TRENT, COURTNEY A; Bartlesville Mid-High Schl; Bartlesville, OK; (3); Band; Mrchg Band; Hon Roll; NHS; Ath Trnr; Med.

TRENT, HEATHER; Westmoore HS; Oklahoma City, OK; (4); 68/610; Church Yth Grp; DECA; Band; Mrchg Band; Schltc Testing Team; Acad Letterman; Bapt All St Yth Choir; OK ST Univ; Scndry Ed; Soc Stu.

TRENT, JAIMIE L; Bartlesville Mid HS; Bartlesville, OK; (2); Pep Clb; Teachers Aide; JV Capt Chrldng; Hon Roll; Jr NHS; Csmtlgy.

TRENT, JOSH; Cordell Sr HS; Cordell, OK; (4); 15/47; Church Yth Grp; Yrbk; Var Bsbl; Co-Capt Bsktbl; Co-Capt Ftbl; Hon Roll; JETS Awd; Prfct Atten Awd; Art Clb; Letterman Clb; 10th Grd Stdnt Yr; All Star Bsktbl; Stndt 9 Wk 12th Grd; All Dist Back Sr Ftbl; Alt 8-Mn All Star Gm; OK Panhandle St Univ; Coach.

TRENT, MACK; Kingston HS; Kingston, OK; (4); 2/57; FCA; French Clb; Natl FFA Org; Quiz Bowl; Spanish Clb; Nwsp; Treas Jr Cls; Pres Sr Cls; Rep Stu Cncl; Var Bsktbl; SOSU; Pharm.

TRENT, SALLY M; Western Heights Sr HS; Oklahoma City, OK; (4); 1/171; Key Clb; Chorus; School Musical; Ofcr Sr Cls; Rep Stu Cncl; Bsktbl; Capt Var Sftbl; NHS; St Schlr; Val; All ST Sftbl/Choir; Miss Wstrn Hghts; Outstdng Sr Grl Awd; Army Schlr; Ath Awd; Exch Clb Yth Mnth; Southern Nazarene Univ; PT.

TRENTHAM, CARRIE L; Balko Public Schl; Balko, OK; (2); Church Yth Grp; Pres 4-H; FHA; Natl FFA Org; Scholastic Bowl; Band; Mrchg Band; Pep Band; High Hon Roll; NHS.

TREPAGNIER, ANGELIQUE M; Putnam City HS; Warr Acres, OK; (3); German Clb; Office Aide; Teachers Aide; Yrbk; Outstndng German II Stu/Photoftrvlng Singapore/Australia; OK U; Photo.

TRETTER, MICHELLE D; Elgin HS; Elgin, OK; (2); Church Yth Grp; FHA; Hosp Aide; Natl FFA Org; Office Aide; Teachers Aide; Church Choir; Mgr(s); Hon Roll; GAA; Hosp Vol Cncr Patients; Vol Vet; U Of OK; PT.

TRIBBEY, MOLLY; Sulphur HS; Sulphur, OK; (3); Church Yth Grp; FCA; GAA; Speech Tm; Varsity Clb; Rep Soph Cls; Rep Jr Cls; Ofcr Stu Cncl; JV Var Bsktbl; Var Chrldng; Bsktbl Hmcmng Queen 96; OSU; Dntl Hyg.

TRICKEY, SARAH; Clinton HS; Clinton, OK; (3); Church Yth Grp; FBLA; FHA; Band; Mrchg Band; Hon Roll; NHS.

TRIM, DELAYNNA; Liberty Acad; Shawnee, OK; (4); 1/15; Church Yth Grp; Hosp Aide; Model UN; Scholastic Bowl; Teachers Aide; Church Choir; School Play; Ed Nwsp; Ed Yrbk; Ed Lit Mag; OK Baptist U; Archaeolgy.

TRIMBLE, MARY E; Edmond Santa Fe HS; Edmond, OK; (3); 47/327; Church Yth Grp; JCL; Natl FFA Org; SADD; NHS; OK ST Univ; Biotechnology.

TRIMMER, REBEKAH; Tonkawa Jr Sr HS; Tonkawa, OK; (4); 1/40; Am Leg Aux Girls St; FCA; FHA; Letterman Clb; Quiz Bowl; Teachers Aide; Band; Chorus; Drm Mjr(t); Jazz Band; OK Bapt U.

TRIPLETT, AMBER M; Broken Arrow Sr HS; Broken Arrow, OK; (3); Sec Church Yth Grp; French Clb; FBLA; Teachers Aide; Band; Mrchg Band; Nwsp; Ofcr Frsh Cls; Ofcr Soph Cls; Ofcr Jr Cls; MYTH; Baylor; Mrktg/Bus Jrnlsm.

TRIPLETT, JAMES; Crescent Schl; Crescent, OK; (3); Church Yth Grp; Band; Church Choir; Yrbk; Auto Tech.

TRIPP, CHARLES A; Claremore Sr HS; Claremore, OK; (3); Am Leg Boys St; Church Yth Grp; FCA; Stage Crew; Ofcr Stu Cncl; Var Ftbl; Var Socr; Var Wt Lftg; NHS; Metro Lks Tourn Soccr MVP; OK Univ.

TRIPP, SHANA; Anadarko HS; Anadarko, OK; (2); 6/141; Church Yth Grp; FHA; Spanish Clb; Band; Color Guard; High Hon Roll; Jr NHS; NHS; Prfct Atten Awd; Spanish NHS; Yth Fllwshp.

TRIPP, TIMOTHY; Midwest City HS; Midwest City, OK; (2); Church Yth Grp; Letterman Clb; Teachers Aide; Band; Mrchg Band; Hon Roll; NHS.

TRIPP, VINCENT R; Okarche HS; Okarche, OK; (4); Wt Lftg; High Hon Roll; Hon Roll; Prfct Atten Awd; OSU.

TRIPPETT, DANIEL A; Nathan Hale HS; Tulsa, OK; (3); Art Clb; Church Yth Grp; English Clb; Teachers Aide; Nwsp; High Hon Roll; NHS; U Of Tulsa.

TRISCIANI JR, WILLIAM A; Lone Grove HS; Lone Grove, OK; (2); FCA; Acpl Chr; Ofcr Bsbl; Bsktbl; Ftbl; Cit Awd; Hon Roll; Univ Of Southern CA; Ath Coach.

TROGLIN, CRISTIE; New Lima Jr Sr HS; Seminole, OK; (4); 1/23; Chess Clb; Pep Clb; Quiz Bowl; School Play; Phtg Rptr Nwsp; VP Stu Cncl; L Bsktbl; L Sftbl; High Hon Roll; Hon Roll; VICA Gordon Cooper Appld Wldng Tech; Seminole JC; OB Nrs.

TROGLIN, RONDA; New Lima Jr Sr HS; Wewoka, OK; (4); 3/22; Sec FHA; Natl Beta Clb; Pep Clb; Quiz Bowl; School Play; Nwsp; Sec Soph Cls; VP Jr Cls; VP Sr Cls; Var Capt Bsktbl; Seminole St Col; Nrsng.

TROJAN, TIM; Oklahoma Bible Acad; Enid, OK; (3); Boy Scts; Rep Church Yth Grp; Band; Pres Soph Cls; Pres Jr Cls; VP Stu Cncl; L Bsbl; L Socr; High Hon Roll; NHS.

TROJANOWSKI, RACHEL E; Tecumseh HS; Tecumseh, OK; (2); FHA; High Hon Roll; NHS; Spnd Time With Fmly/Close Frnds; Cmptrs; Bible Knowledge; Seminole ST Coll; Dietitian.

TROLLINGER, BRANDY; Watts HS; Watts, OK; (4); 6/33; GAA; Math Clb; Natl Beta Clb; Natl FFA Org; Teachers Aide; Nwsp; Yrbk; Var Capt Bsktbl; Var Sftbl; High Hon Roll; Bsktbl Homcmng Qn; Bsktbl Atten; Northeastern ST; Elem Ed.

TROOK, BENJAMIN M; South Intermediate HS; Broken Arrow, OK; (3); Boy Scts; Church Yth Grp; Pres FCA; Spanish Clb; Band; Mrchg Band; Pep Band; Ftbl; Wt Lftg; Cit Awd; Ldrshp Cls; OK ST Univ; Sales/Mrktg.

TROSKY, JENNIFER E; Inola Sr HS; Inola, OK; (2); Quiz Bowl; Spanish Clb; Band; Color Guard; Mrchg Band; OU; Bio-Chem; Molecular Bio.

TROTTER, CRISTALLE B; Piedmont HS; Piedmont, OK; (3); French Clb; Key Clb; Scholastic Bowl; Pres SADD; Chorus; School Play; Phtg Rptr Nwsp; Yrbk; Comp Sci Awd Of Mrt; Tri-St Attendee; U Of OK; Psych.

TROTTER, KIMBERLY; Shawnee Sr HS; Shawnee, OK; (4); 1/342; Pres French Clb; Church Choir; NHS; Val; HOPE Pres; Psychbio.

TROTTER, LAURA; Elk City HS; Elk City, OK; (2); Pep Clb; Science Clb; Band; Mrchg Band; Sec Frsh Cls; Rep Soph Cls; Var Sftbl; High Hon Roll; Hon Roll; NHS; Frgn Lang Clb; Church Yth Grp; Law.

TROTTER, STEPHANIE; Silo HS; Durant, OK; (3); FHA; Math Clb; Mu Alpha Theta; Quiz Bowl; Teachers Aide; Chorus; School Musical; School Play; Bsktbl; Score Keeper; Piano; SOSU; Pharm.

TROUT, BRANDY; Liberty Acad; Shawnee, OK; (3); Chorus; School Play; Nwsp; Yrbk; Lit Mag; Ofcr Frsh Cls; Chrldng; High Hon Roll; NHS; Church Yth Grp; Chapel Clb; Rose ST Coll; Nrsng.

TROUT, MICHAEL D; Wagoner Sr HS; Wagoner, OK; (3); Church Yth Grp; FCA; 4-H; FBLA; Letterman Clb; Lit Mag; Socr; Wrstlng; Var Letterman In Soccer; Green Cty Soccer Assn; Tulsa Philharmonic Symphony Set; Ducks Unltd Sportsman; Northeastern.

TROWBRIDGE, BRANDI R; Salina HS; Salina, OK; (4); 6/48; Church Yth Grp; FCA; 4-H; FTA; GAA; Letterman Clb; Spanish Clb; School Play; Yrbk; Ofcr Sr Cls; Connors ST Coll; Tech Ed.

TROWBRIDGE, TAMMY K; Salina HS; Salina, OK; (1); FCA; 4-H; FTA; GAA; Girl Scts; Pres Frsh Cls; JV Bsktbl; Var Sftbl; NHS.

TROXEL, COURTNEY D; Velma Alma HS; Ratliff, OK; (4); 12/46; FCA; FBLA; SADD; Teachers Aide; School Musical; Var Bsktbl; Var Crs Cntry; Var Trk; High Hon Roll; Hon Roll; Ada OK; Nrsng.

TROXEL JR, RICKY D; Moore HS; Moore, OK; (3); Scholastic Bowl; Hon Roll; NHS; Prfct Atten Awd; Received 3 Medals In Eng III, Comp Programming & Span IV; OU; Tchr.

TROXELL, KRISTA L; Memorial HS; Tulsa, OK; (2); Church Yth Grp; FCA; Hosp Aide; JCL; Chorus; Church Choir; School Musical; High Hon Roll; Hon Roll; Latin Clb; Piano; Southern Nazarene Univ.

TROYER, STEPHANIE; Adair HS; Adair, OK; (2); Church Yth Grp; FCA; Math Clb; Natl FFA Org; Science Clb; Church Choir; Pres Frsh Cls; Rptr Stu Cncl; Var Bsktbl; Var Sftbl; 3rd Bsmn St 3 A Sftbl; FFA VP; OSU; Vet.

TRUEL, MELISSA A; Moore HS; Moore, OK; (4); 62/549; Church Yth Grp; French Clb; Natl FFA Org; Hon Roll; Jr NHS; NHS; FFA Intrschlstc ST Chmpns/3rd Indiv; Jr Escort; OSU; Horticulture.

TRUELOCK, RICHARD L; Sulphur HS; Sulphur, OK; (3); Art Clb; Band; Mrchg Band; Rptr Nwsp; Acad Team.

TRUITT, SHANA D; Velma Alma HS; Velma, OK; (3); Church Yth Grp; Ofcr FCA; SADD; Band; School Play; Nwsp; Rep Stu Cncl; Chrldng; Sftbl; NHS; Jhn Phlp Sousa Awd; S Cntrl OK Hnr Bnd; Sthwstrn OK Hnr Bnd; Mss Vlma Alma Mss Cngnlty, 1st Rnnr Up; OK Bapt U.

TRUJILLO, MICHAEL; Edmond North HS; Edmond, OK; (2); Boy Scts; Church Yth Grp; Mu Alpha Theta; Quiz Bowl; Band; Jazz Band; Mrchg Band; Pep Band; Rptr Nwsp; JV Socr; Eagle Sct Awd; OJ Cmptr Acad Grad.

TRUMBLY, ALAN; Bridge Creek HS; Blanchard, OK; (4); #4 in class; Church Yth Grp; FCA; FBLA; Spanish Clb; SADD; Chorus; Bsktbl; NHS; Val; Math Tm; Sccr, USYSA-OSA Cch; OK Sccr Assn West Sd Pl 95; OK City U; Bus.

TRUMBLY, KYLE; Westmoore HS; Oklahoma City, OK; (4); 140/610; Debate Tm; FCA; School Musical; VP Jr Cls; Ofcr Stu Cncl; Capt Ftbl; NHS; Church Yth Grp; Cmnty Wkr; Office Aide; Coaches Assn All Conf Player, High/All Dist 6A-2 Linebacker; All Acad Hnr Roll; OK Assn Stu Cncl Sec; OU; Bus.

TRUONG, DANH C; Oklahoma Sch Of Science & Math; Oklahoma City, OK; (4); French Clb; Math Tm; Scholastic Bowl; Temple Yth Grp; Rep Stu Cncl; Intrml Mgr Socr; JETS Awd; NHS; WA Univ; Bio.

TRUONG, HENRY Q; Putnam City West HS; Oklahoma City, OK; (2); Boy Scts; Intnl Clb; Math Clb; Math Tm; Spanish Clb; Orch; Hon Roll; NHS; HOSA; U Of OK; Phy; Comp Sci.

TRUONG, MINH; Classen Schl; Oklahoma City, OK; (3); 2/60; Mu Alpha Theta; Scholastic Bowl; Tennis; High Hon Roll; JETS Awd; NHS; Ntl Merit Ltr; Spanish NHS; U Of OK; Pre-Medicine.

TRUONG, NHI T; Del City HS; Del City, OK; (2); Spanish Clb; Jr NHS.

TRZEBIATOWSKI, SARAH; Waynoka HS; Carmen, OK; (2); Church Yth Grp; FCA; 4-H; FHA; Pep Clb; Sec Frsh Cls; JV Bsktbl; Hon Roll; All Amer Schlr; Acad Tm; OK ST U; Caterer.

TUBBS, MYKA L; Sallisaw HS; Sallisaw, OK; (2); Church Yth Grp; Cmnty Wkr; FCA; GAA; Letterman Clb; Office Aide; Spanish Clb; Band; Nwsp; Yrbk; Dent.

TUCK, ANGELA M; Heavener HS; Howe, OK; (2); Girl Scts; Key Clb; Chorus; Church Choir; Variety Show; Hon Roll; Internet II Hnrs; Natl Schlr; Cmnty Invlvmnt; OU; Phy.

TUCKER, AMBER; Ft Towson HS; Fort Towson, OK; (3); FHA; Var Chrldng; Hon Roll; NHS; Clss Favs 96; Schl Brain 96; Multi Yr Listing; Accntng.

TUCKER, ANGIE; Collinsville HS; Collinsville, OK; (2); Church Yth Grp; FCA; Chorus; Chrldng; Score Keeper; Sftbl; Trk; Secrtrl.

TUCKER, ASHLEY B; Central Mid-HS; Norman, OK; (2); Pres Church Yth Grp; FCA; Mu Alpha Theta; Sec Chorus; Church Choir; Rep Stu Cncl; Stat Ftbl; Mgr Wrstlng; NHS; Pres Schlr; Southern Nazarene U; Nentl Nrs.

TUCKER, BRITTANY K; Woodward HS; Woodward, OK; (2); Church Yth Grp; Debate Tm; Natl FFA Org; Band; Mrchg Band; Southern Nazarene Univ; Acctnt.

TUCKER, CHET B; Davis HS; Davis, OK; (3); Art Clb; Church Yth Grp; FCA; Ftbl; Wt Lftg; 2-A St Ftbl Champions 95-96; FFA Vo Ag Clb; Rebuilt & Show 67 Mustang; Art Awd 95-96; Okmulgee Tech.

TUCKER, JAMES T; Ardmore HS; Ardmore, OK; (3); Art Clb; Boy Scts; Church Yth Grp; FHA; Teachers Aide; Acpl Chr; Color Guard; School Play; Ftbl; Hon Roll.

TUCKER, JENNIFER; Hulbert Jr Sr HS; Fort Gibson, OK; (2); Art Clb; Computer Clb; FBLA; German Clb; Rptr Phtg Yrbk; JV Bsktbl; Hon Roll; NHS; Pres Schlr; U Of OK; Comp.

TUCKER, JENNIFER LEIGH; Yukon HS; Yukon, OK; (4); 58/400; Cmnty Wkr; Natl FFA Org; Speech Tm; Yrbk; Bsktbl; Mgr(s); Trk; Cit Awd; Gov Hon Prg Awd; High Hon Roll; Amer Bus Womens Schlrshp; Amer Legion Awd; Renaissnce Cmmtte VP; U MO Columbia; Hotl/Rest Mgmt.

TUCKER, JOEY; Collinsville HS; Collinsville, OK; (3); Church Yth Grp; FCA; VICA; Var Bsbl; Var Ftbl; Var Wt Lftg; Var Wrstlng; Prfct Atten Awd.

TUCKER, JULIE; Schulter Schl; Henryetta, OK; (2); 4-H; Spanish Clb; Speech Tm; Rptr Nwsp; Rptr Soph Cls; Var Chrldng; 4-H Awd; High Hon Roll; NHS; Dance Lessons; OU; Med.

TUCKER, LAUREN D; Broken Arrow Sr HS; Broken Arrow, OK; (3); Church Yth Grp; FCA; GAA; Spanish Clb; Var L Bsktbl; Var L Sftbl; Hon Roll; Prfct Atten Awd; Pres Acad Fit Awd; Med.

TUCKER, LINDA E; Guthrie Sr HS; Guthrie, OK; (1); 144/271; Band; Mrchg Band; Pep Band.

TUCKER, MARC; Seiling Schl; Seiling, OK; (2); Church Yth Grp; FCA; Letterman Clb; Band; Chorus; Church Choir; Jazz Band; Mrchg Band; Orch; Pep Band.

TUCKER, MATTHEW; Shawnee Sr HS; Shawnee, OK; (4); 37/250; Latin Clb; Letterman Clb; Office Aide; Nwsp; Var Bsbl; Var Ftbl; High Hon Roll; NHS; U Of OK.

TUCKER, RACHEL K; Oklahoma Bible Acad; Jet, OK; (4); Church Yth Grp; Pep Clb; Var Bsktbl; Var Vllybl; High Hon Roll; Hon Roll; NHS; School Play; Church Pianist; Oil Painting; Awd Chrctr/Cmtmnt; Baylor Univ.

TUCKER, SCOTT; Antlers Sr HS; Antlers, OK; (3); Var Bsbl; Var Bsktbl; Var Ftbl; High Hon Roll; Hon Roll; NHS; Acctng.

TUCKER, STEVE; Turner Schl; Overbrook, OK; (4); VP Sr Cls; Hon Roll; Am Leg Boys St; 4-H; Pep Clb; Teachers Aide; Var Capt Bsbl; Var Bsktbl; Southeastern; Ed.

TUCKER, SYDNEY S; B T Washington HS; Tulsa, OK; (2); Sec German Clb; Ed Nwsp; NHS; Rcvd Acad Ltr Frshmn Yr; Mem Eclgy Clb & Yng Dems; Ply Bss Gtr; CO U At Boulder; Jrnlsm.

TUCKER, TOISHA A; B T Washington HS; Tulsa, OK; (2); Band; Mrchg Band; Pep Band; NHS; Macy Schlr; Intnl Bcclrte Cand; Med.

TUCKER, TREY; Comanche HS; Comanche, OK; (1); Church Yth Grp; VICA; Ofcr Soph Cls; Ofcr Bsbl; Bsktbl; UCLA.

TUGGLE, KRYSTAL L; Catoosa HS; Tulsa, OK; (2); Drama Clb; FCA; French Clb; FBLA; FHA; Intnl Clb; Nwsp; Hon Roll; Intl Order Rainbow Girls; St Hnr Soc; Psych.

TULL, AMY; Yale Jr Sr HS; Jennings, OK; (2); 4/51; Pres 4-H; Natl Beta Clb; Natl FFA Org; Var Bsktbl; Var Sftbl; Var Vllybl; Cit Awd; 4-H Awd; High Hon Roll; Hon Roll; FFA, Dry Cttl Jdgng Cont 2nd Pl Indvdl; Grls Bsktbl Hstl Awd; Top Alg I, Phys Sci Awd; OK ST U; Med.

TULL, BRANDI D; Newkirk HS; Newkirk, OK; (4); 14/47; FCA; SADD; Teachers Aide; Band; Mrchg Band; Pep Band; Co-Ed Yrbk; JV Sftbl; Hon Roll; N OK Coll; Jrnlsm.

TULLOS, KRISTA; Temple Jr Sr HS; Temple, OK; (4); Church Yth Grp; Nwsp; Yrbk; Sec Rep Stu Cncl; Capt Chrldng; Hon Roll; Sal; FHA; Pep Clb; Cameron U; Crmnl Law.

TULLY, RYAN E; Christian Heritage Acad; Oklahoma City, OK; (4); 21/56; Church Yth Grp; FCA; Rptr Nwsp; Var Capt Chrldng; Cit Awd; Gov Hon Prg Awd; High Hon Roll; Pres Schlr; Cmnty Wkr; Chrstn Intnl Sports Fed All Amer & Natl Ath Of Yr Awd 96; Ctr For Chrstn Cnslng Chrstn Ldrshp Awd 96; U Of Cntrl OK; Jrnlsm.

TULLY, TONIA L; Sulphur HS; Sulphur, OK; (2); Church Yth Grp; 4-H; Band; Color Guard; Mrchg Band; Hon Roll; Vet Tech.

TUMA, JACLYN; Waukomis HS; Waukomis, OK; (3); 1/37; Band; Mrchg Band; Pep Band; Trk; High Hon Roll; Hon Roll; Prfct Atten Awd.

TUNDER, JENNIFER L; Buffalo Jr Sr HS; Buffalo, OK; (3); 6/27; Cmnty Wkr; 4-H; FBLA; Key Clb; Band; Chorus; 4-H Awd; Hon Roll; NHS; Pep Band; OK ST 4-H Ambsdr; Pol Wrkr.

TUNE, ANGELA R; East Central HS; Tulsa, OK; (4); 34/209; Church Yth Grp; Office Aide; ROTC; Chorus; Color Guard; Drill Tm; Hon Roll; NHS; Cmnty Wkr; Daughters Of Founders And Patriots Of Amrca; Suprs In Tri St Chorus; U Of OK; Jrnlst.

TUNE, JENNIFER B; Waynoka HS; Waynoka, OK; (1); FCA; FHA; Pep Clb; VP Frsh Cls; Bsktbl; Chrldng; Score Keeper; Sftbl; Trk; Wt Lftg; Hmcmng Cand 95-; OK Univ; Cmptr Tech.

TUNE, JESICA L; Vinita HS; Vinita, OK; (3); Pres Debate Tm; Pres Drama Clb; GAA; Library Aide; Science Clb; Spanish Clb; Pres Speech Tm; Ed Yrbk; Bsktbl; Score Keeper; Law.

TUNE, JILL; Norman Sr HS; Norman, OK; (3); Church Yth Grp; FCA; Pep Clb; SADD; Yrbk; Ofcr Soph Cls; Hist Stu Cncl; Capt Pom Pon; Hon Roll; Jr NHS; Page House/Senate At Capitol; Pres Awd Acad Excl; Young Life; U Of OK; Brdcst Jrnlsm.

TUNNELL, AMANDA; Miami Sr HS; Miami, OK; (2); 1/255; Sec Church Yth Grp; Sec FHA; Band; Mrchg Band; DAR Awd; Hon Roll; NHS; Dance; OU; Psycht.

TUNNELL, TIFFANY M; Mustang HS; Yukon, OK; (3); 35/359; Church Yth Grp; FCA; Spanish Clb; Var JV Bsktbl; Intrml Sftbl; Var Trk; Hon Roll; NHS; Work At Zios Italian Kitchen As A Hostess; Renaissance; Pre-Med; Cardio-Vascular Surgn.

TUNNELL, TIMOTHY G; Choctaw HS; Newalla, OK; (3); 18/330; Church Yth Grp; Key Clb; Spanish Clb; Band; Mrchg Band; Pep Band; School Musical; School Play; Stage Crew; High Hon Roll.

TURINETTI, AMBER M; Bartlesville Jr HS; Bartlesville, OK; (3); FBLA; Spanish Clb; JV Chrldng; Hon Roll; English Awd; OSU; Social Work.

TURK, HEATHER; Hulbert Jr Sr HS; Tahlequah, OK; (4); Spanish Clb; Yrbk; High Hon Roll; Jr NHS; NHS; Indn Hnr Soc; Northeastern ST U.

TURLEY, KRISTI; Henryetta Sr HS; Henryetta, OK; (4); 3/75; Red Cross Aide; SADD; Yrbk; Pres Sr Cls; Rep VP Stu Cncl; Bsktbl; Sftbl; Trk; Cit Awd; DAR Awd; OK Bapt Univ; Sports Medicine.

TURNBOUGH, TERRY; White Oak Jr-Sr HS; Vinita, OK; (1); 1/17; Cit Awd; High Hon Roll; Hon Roll; NHS; Val; Northeastern ST U; Tchr.

TURNBULL, BECCA; Warner HS; Muskogee, OK; (3); 2/55; Rep Church Yth Grp; Treas FCA; HOBY; Spanish Clb; Variety Show; VP Frsh Cls; VP Pres Stu Cncl; Var Bsktbl; Var Crs Cntry; Powder Puff Ftbl; Rd Crs Vol; Fml Trc Ath Of Yr; Northeastern ST U; Pub Rel.

TURNBULL, JACE; Warner HS; Muskogee, OK; (4); 1/55; Am Leg Boys St; Church Yth Grp; VP FCA; HOBY; VP Sr Cls; Pres Stu Cncl; Capt Bsktbl; Crs Cntry; Trk; NHS; Engrng Mgmt Technlgy.

TURNBULL, MILEY; Warner HS; Muskogee, OK; (1); 1/80; Church Yth Grp; FCA; Spanish Clb; Variety Show; Ofcr Stu Cncl; JV Bsktbl; Var Crs Cntry; Powder Puff Ftbl; Var Trk; High Hon Roll; Tns For Christ; Wnnr Of Mile/Two Mile ST Trck Meet; Crss Cntry Acad ST Chmpnshp Tm/Regnl Wnnr; OSU; Lndscpe Archtct.

TURNER, ABBY; Cimarron Public Schl; Ames, OK; (3); 10/48; Am Leg Aux Girls St; Church Yth Grp; Computer Clb; Drama Clb; 4-H; French Clb; Hosp Aide; Math Clb; Office Aide; Pep Clb; OK ST U; RN.

TURNER, APRIL J; Choctaw HS; Choctaw, OK; (3); Church Yth Grp; HOSA; Rose ST; LPN.

TURNER, AUSTIN L; Tahlequah Sr HS; Tahlequah, OK; (4); 6/250; Math Clb; Science Clb; Spanish Clb; Band; Chorus; Mrchg Band; School Play; High Hon Roll; NHS; Bahai Fiath; Musician & Artist; Fighting Equality Pres; OU; Hstry.

TURNER, AVIS E; Del City HS; Del City, OK; (3); GAA; ROTC; Band; Church Choir; Mrchg Band; Bsktbl; Trk; Cit Awd; Hon Roll; Prfct Atten Awd; OK Univ.

TURNER, B J; Velma Alma HS; Fox, OK; (3); FCA; Office Aide; SADD; Teachers Aide; Nwsp; Yrbk; Ofcr Frsh Cls; Ofcr Soph Cls; Ofcr Jr Cls; Bsktbl; Ada Coll; Sports Medicine.

TURNER, BROOKLYN; Amber Pocasset Jr Sr HS; Amber, OK; (2); 1/46; Cmnty Wkr; Natl FFA Org; Quiz Bowl; Spanish Clb; Cit Awd; 4-H Awd; High Hon Roll; Parliamntry Procdre Team; Livestck Judgng Team; Publc Speakr; OK ST U; Pediatrcs.

TURNER, BRYANT W; John Marshall HS; Oklahoma City, OK; (3); Spanish Clb; Tennis.

TURNER, CARMEN D; Duncan HS; Duncan, OK; (3); Letterman Clb; SADD; Stat Mgr Bsktbl; Var Sftbl; Hon Roll; SAVE; Acctnt.

TURNER, CHRISTINA M; Bridge Creek HS; Blanchard, OK; (1); 10/75; FHA; Band; Flag Corp; Mrchg Band; Hon Roll; Ntl Merit Ltr; OK Univ.

TURNER, DETRIECH; Dewar Jr-Sr HS; Dewar, OK; (2); 1/24; Church Yth Grp; FCA; Girl Scts; HOBY; Chorus; Sec Treas Frsh Cls; Treas Soph Cls; Chrldng; Pom Pon; Sftbl; Estrn Dist Hnr Choir 95 & 96.

TURNER, ERIC A; Wilburton Sr HS; Wilburton, OK; (3); Boy Scts; Church Yth Grp; FCA; 4-H; French Clb; Letterman Clb; Library Aide; Natl FFA Org; Office Aide; Teachers Aide; Lvstck Jdg Tm; 1st Plc Crd Cntst; Chmpn Ag Mech; Rsrv Crs Chmp; Lvstck Shwmn; Crs Chmpn Rsrv Brd Slfk; OSU; Vet Sci.

TURNER, GENEVIEVE; Ft Gibson HS; Fort Gibson, OK; (2); 3/194; FCA; Spanish Clb; SADD; Band; Mrchg Band; Ofcr Soph Cls; Ofcr Stu Cncl; Socr; Hon Roll; Pres Acad Fit Awd; Teens For Chrst.

TURNER, HEATHER D; Bartlesville Sr HS; Bartlesville, OK; (3); Church Yth Grp; German Clb; Quiz Bowl; Band; Church Choir; Mrchg Band; Hon Roll; OK Bapt Univ; Elem Ed.

TURNER, JEREMY; Lone Grove HS; Ardmore, OK; (4); 10/78; FCA; Letterman Clb; Natl Beta Clb; Natl FFA Org; Ed Yrbk; Pres Sr Cls; Var Bsbl; Var Ftbl; High Hon Roll; NHS; Stu Of Mnth; NTA Awd; Wldlf Bio.

TURNER, JONATHAN; Oklahoma Christian Schl; Edmond, OK; (4); 2/36; Church Yth Grp; FBLA; Ed Yrbk; High Hon Roll; NHS; Prfct Atten Awd; Sal; Plc Explr Pgm; OK Chrstn.

TURNER, JOSHUA; Edmond North HS; Edmond, OK; (4); Boy Scts; Mu Alpha Theta; Hon Roll; OK Bicycle Soc; OK ST Univ; Chemical Engrng.

TURNER, JOSHUA G; Harrah HS; Harrah, OK; (3); 33/175; Boy Scts; Church Yth Grp; Band; Jazz Band; Mrchg Band; Socr; Cit Awd; Hon Roll; NHS; HS Band Dirs Awd; OK Chrstn Univ Of Sci & Arts.

TURNER, KRYSTAL; Bray-Doyle HS; Marlow, OK; (3); 2/34; FCA; Natl FFA Org; SADD; Teachers Aide; Capt Bsktbl; High Hon Roll; Hon Roll; NHS; Weatherford; Ed.

TURNER, LESLEY D; Edmond Memorial HS; Edmond, OK; (4); 36/335; FCA; FTA; Key Clb; Math Clb; Science Clb; Spanish Clb; SADD; Variety Show; Powder Puff Ftbl; NHS; Young Life; U Of OK.

TURNER, MEGAN L; Edmond Memorial HS; Edmond, OK; (3); 83/371; FCA; FHA; Key Clb; Letterman Clb; Spanish Clb; Hon Roll; Yng Life; OK Univ; Pharm.

TURNER, MEGAN R; Westmoore HS; Oklahoma City, OK; (3); French Clb; Key Clb; Rptr Nwsp; Lit Mag; JV Var Swmmng; Hon Roll; NHS; U Of OK; Pre-Med.

TURNER, RAE D; Maysville Jr Sr HS; Maysville, OK; (3); Rptr FHA; Rptr Key Clb; Teachers Aide; Yrbk; Rptr Stu Cncl; Var Bsktbl; Var Trk; Hon Roll; NHS; Jrnlsm.

TURNER, ROBY L; El Reno Sr HS; El Reno, OK; (3); Church Yth Grp; Key Clb; Math Clb; Science Clb; Band; Jazz Band; Mrchg Band; Hon Roll; NHS; Natl Bus Hnr Soc; SW All-Reg Hnr Band 4 Yrs; OCU; Law Enfrcmt.

TURNER, SHARMAINE L; Tishomingo HS; Tishomingo, OK; (2); Art Clb; Santa Barbara City Coll.

TURNER, THOMAS; Chickasha Jr HS; Chickasha, OK; (1); High Hon Roll; Hon Roll; Acad Team; Commercial Artist.

TURNEY, BRADLEY K; Charles Page HS; Sand Springs, OK; (3); 38/420; Am Leg Boys St; Church Yth Grp; FCA; FBLA; Letterman Clb; Office Aide; Spanish Clb; Varsity Clb; Ofcr Bsbl; Cit Awd; OK ST U; Eng.

TURNEY, DANA; Perry Sr HS; Perry, OK; (2); 1/100; Church Yth Grp; FCA; German Clb; VP Frsh Cls; Pres Soph Cls; Pres Stu Cncl; Var Chrldng; Hon Roll; FHA; NJHS VP; SMART; OK ST U; Law.

TURNHAM, MICHELLE D; Kellyville Sr HS; Sapulpa, OK; (4); 2/53; Church Yth Grp; Scholastic Bowl; Science Clb; Band; Chorus; Drm Mjr(t); NHS; Pres Acad Fit Awd; Sal; St Schlr; Smpr Fdls Awd; Baccalaureate Rgnts Schlrshp USAO; Spr Rtng Choir Solo ST Comp 94/96; U Of Sci/Arts OK; Sec Eng Ed.

TURRENTINE, JEFFREY L; Roland Sr HS; Roland, OK; (2); Church Yth Grp; Band; Mrchg Band; Pep Band; Var Bsbl; JV Bsktbl; Wt Lftg; Hon Roll; Prfct Atten Awd; MI Univ; Mech Engr.

TURRENTINE, JULIE; Stigler HS; Stigler, OK; (2); Debate Tm; Quiz Bowl; Speech Tm; Gov Hon Prg Awd; High Hon Roll; NHS; Ntl Merit Ltr; Pres Acad Fit Awd; Model Congrss.

TURTLE, BRANDI R; Oaks Mission Jr Sr HS; Oaks, OK; (3); Rptr FHA; Color Guard; Yrbk; Hon Roll; NHS; Indian Hertge Clb Pres; NE St Univ; Soc Wrk.

TURVEY, KRISTINE; Oklahoma Sch Of Science & Math; Braman, OK; (4); Church Yth Grp; Pres Sec FHA; Pres Hosp Aide; Capt Quiz Bowl; Speech Tm; Pres Soph Cls; Ofcr Stu Cncl; Var Intrml Bsktbl; NHS; Ntl Merit SF; Chem Engrng.

TUTTLE, JACOB L; Cushing HS; Cushing, OK; (3); 16/148; Cmnty Wkr; FCA; Math Clb; Pres Frsh Cls; Pres Jr Cls; Rep Stu Cncl; Var Bsbl; Var Bsktbl; Var Ftbl; Var Wt Lftg; All Amer Schlr; OK ST U; Med.

TUTTLE, TRISTA; Kellyville Sr HS; Kellyville, OK; (1); Church Yth Grp; 4-H; JA; Pres Frsh Cls; Ofcr Stu Cncl; Var L Bsktbl; Co-Capt Chrldng; Var L Sftbl; Hon Roll; Frosh Girl Cls Favorite; OK ST Univ.

TUTWILER, JACLYN; Thomas Jr Sr HS; Custer City, OK; (3); 1/32; Letterman Clb; Natl FFA Org; Chorus; Flag Corp; School Musical; Variety Show; Cit Awd; High Hon Roll; Hon Roll; Jr NHS; Masonic Stu Of Today Awd; Southwestern ST U; Pre-Med.

TWYMAN, MATT; Bartlesville Mid HS; Bartlesville, OK; (2); Boy Scts; Church Yth Grp; FBLA; Office Aide; Spanish Clb; Varsity Clb; Bsktbl; Ftbl; Hon Roll; Prfct Atten Awd; AR.

TWYMAN, NATHAN W; Boise City HS; Boise City, OK; (2); Boy Scts; Church Yth Grp; FCA; HOBY; Band; Mrchg Band; Pep Band; JV Bsktbl; Var Crs Cntry; Var Trk; Ordr Arrow.

TYCKER, JAQUITA M; Cimarron Public Schl; Enid, OK; (2); Drama Clb; FHA; Natl FFA Org; Ofcr Soph Cls; Hon Roll.

TYE, DONNA R; Choctaw HS; Nicoma Park, OK; (2); 157/359; Church Yth Grp; Key Clb; Chorus; Church Choir; Mgr Socr; Wrstlng; Baylor Univ; Spec Ed Chldrn.

TYLER, JOY L; Putnam City North HS; Oklahoma City, OK; (2); Church Yth Grp; Orch; Slvr Strngs Of Putnam City Vet; Brk Trgh Yth Mnstrs; Yth For Yth; Rn.

TYLER II, KARL; Ada HS; Ada, OK; (4); 34/133; Am Leg Boys St; Church Yth Grp; Pres DECA; Intnl Clb; Science Clb; SADD; Band; Rptr Chorus; Jazz Band; Mrchg Band; Mass Comm Dept Prod; E Cntrl Univ; Hist Prof.

TYLER, MICHAEL A; Mc Alester HS; Mcalester, OK; (3); 9/200; Am Leg Boys St; Church Yth Grp; Spanish Clb; Var Wrstlng.

TYLER, STACY L; El Reno Sr HS; El Reno, OK; (1); 1/180; Church Yth Grp; Cmnty Wkr; FCA; Quiz Bowl; Red Cross Aide; L Bsktbl; L Crs Cntry; Stat Mgr(s); Stat Score Keeper; L Trk; Southern Nazarene Univ; PT.

TYLER, TONY N; Yukon Middle HS; Yukon, OK; (2); Church Yth Grp; Spanish Clb; Church Choir; Stage Crew; VP Stu Cncl; High Hon Roll; NHS; 3-D.

TYNER, TEDDY J; Del City HS; Del City, OK; (3); 276/515; Cmnty Wkr; Letterman Clb; Chorus; Rep Frsh Cls; Var L Bsbl; Var L Ftbl; Var L Wrstlng; Outstdng Ath; OK Pigskin Preview; Page For OK St Senate; His & Or Eng Tchr.

TYNES, KERRI; Turner Schl; Burneyville, OK; (4); 7/22; Church Yth Grp; FHA; Natl Beta Clb; Pep Clb; Yrbk; Sec Frsh Cls; Sec Soph Cls; Sec Jr Cls; Sec Sr Cls; Var Capt Bsktbl; Miss THS 95; U Of OK.

TYNES, SHAWN M; Velma Alma HS; Velma, OK; (3); Church Yth Grp; SADD; Ftbl; Wt Lftg.

TYREE, JENNIFER; Hinton HS; Calumet, OK; (4); 6/32; Church Yth Grp; Cmnty Wkr; Drama Clb; FCA; Key Clb; SADD; Teachers Aide; Band; Chorus; Church Choir.

TYRRELL, BETH M; Putnam City West HS; Oklahoma City, OK; (3); FCA; Latin Clb; VICA; Sftbl; NHS; Cmptr Sys Anlyst.

TYRRELL, WILLIAM D; Muskogee HS; Muskogee, OK; (4); 4/303; Boy Scts; Treas Church Yth Grp; Computer Clb; VP FBLA; Treas German Clb; Science Clb; Var Crs Cntry; JV Tennis; NHS; Hon Roll; U Of MO Rolla; Chem Engr.

UEKERMANN, KRISTEN; Cascia Hall Prep School; Tulsa, OK; (4); Am Leg Aux Girls St; Cmnty Wkr; Pep Clb; Rptr Nwsp; Var L Sftbl; Var L Swmmng; Hon Roll; NHS; Church Yth Grp; Drama Clb; Rlgs Rtrt Ldr; Vol Work; Lfgrd; U Of OK; Med.

UHLENHAKE, BRAD A; Lomega HS; Loyal, OK; (4); 6/11; Natl FFA Org; VP Frsh Cls; VP Soph Cls; Ofcr Stu Cncl; Capt Bsktbl; Hon Roll; NHS; Prfct Atten Awd; St FFA Degree; Relands CC; Tele-Commnctn.

ULMER, AMANDA Y; Muldrow HS; Muldrow, OK; (1); Church Yth Grp; FHA; Hon Roll.

ULRICH, DAVID W; Muldrow HS; Muldrow, OK; (1); Church Yth Grp; Cmnty Wkr; Computer Clb; FBLA; Varsity Clb; Ftbl; Trk; Wt Lftg; Hon Roll; OK Univ; Mech Engr.

ULRICH, KATHY; Plainview HS; Overbrook, OK; (3); 10/83; Church Yth Grp; Mu Alpha Theta; Natl Beta Clb; Chorus; Church Choir; School Musical; Ed Yrbk; High Hon Roll; NHS; Bio.

ULRICH, LEALA R; El Reno Sr HS; El Reno, OK; (2); 13/250; Band; Mrchg Band; Hon Roll; All Amer Schlr; El Reno Rnsnc Awd.

ULSAKER, DANIELLE; Kingfisher HS; Kingfisher, OK; (1); Key Clb; Rep Stu Cncl; Mgr(s); Hon Roll; KU; Phys Thrpy.

UMSTED, LESLIE M; Caney Jr Sr HS; Caney, OK; (2); Church Yth Grp; FCA; 4-H; FHA; GAA; Natl FFA Org; Var Bsktbl; Var Sftbl; 4-H Awd; Hon Roll; OK ST; Phrmcst/Marine Biol.

UNDERHILL, BRANDY D; Checotah HS; Checotah, OK; (4); Art Clb; Church Yth Grp; FHA; Letterman Clb; Office Aide; Yrbk; Var Bsbl; Var Ftbl; Score Keeper; Coach.

UNDERHILL, STEPHANIE; Central HS; Tulsa, OK; (3); Pres FTA; Girl Scts; Sec Key Clb; Band; Mrchg Band; Orch; VP Jr Cls; Hon Roll; NHS; Native Amer Stu Assn Pres; NSU; Ed.

UNDERWOOD, CANDY L; Muskogee HS; Muskogee, OK; (1); Concert Choir; Baccne; RN/PEDIATRCN.

UNDERWOOD, GEOFFREY S; Lawton Christian Schl; Lawton, OK; (2); French Clb; Pres Soph Cls; Bsktbl; High Hon Roll; Pres Schlr; Natl Hnr Roll; Stanford; Medicine.

UNDERWOOD, JAMIE M; Geary Jr Sr HS; Greenfield, OK; (2); 1/25; Church Yth Grp; FHA; Natl Beta Clb; SADD; Church Choir; Sftbl; Cit Awd; High Hon Roll; Hon Roll; NHS; Cindy Sherry Austin Awd; Tn Ct; OK ST U; Psycht.

UNDERWOOD, LEA A; Western Heights Sr HS; Oklahoma City, OK; (2); Church Yth Grp; Cmnty Wkr; Band; Drm Mjr(t); Jazz Band; Mrchg Band; School Musical; Var Socr; Hon Roll; LEAP Eng; Ed; Kndgtn Tchr.

UNDERWOOD, STEPHEN; Spiro HS; Spiro, OK; (3); FCA; VP FBLA; Math Clb; Spanish Clb; Teachers Aide; Sec Soph Cls; VP Jr Cls; Var Bsbl; L Bsktbl; L Ftbl; Pre-Law.

UNDERWOOD, TARA L; Warner HS; Stigler, OK; (3); Spanish Clb; Bsktbl; Crs Cntry; Sftbl; Hon Roll.

UNREIN, STEPHANIE M; Claremore Sr HS; Claremore, OK; (1); Hon Roll; Phys Therapy.

UNRUH, BRIAN J; Okeene Jr Sr HS; Hitchcock, OK; (2); Church Yth Grp; FCA; 4-H; JA; Natl FFA Org; SADD; Rep Frsh Cls; Treas Soph Cls; L Bsbl; L Bsktbl; 4-H Hall Of Fame; Phy Therapy.

UNRUH, JAMEY; Chisholm Sr HS; Enid, OK; (4); 1/69; Church Yth Grp; FCA; Quiz Bowl; Spanish Clb; Var Bsktbl; Co-Capt Var Crs Cntry; Var Trk; NHS; Val; TSA Sgt-At-Arms; OK ST U.

UNRUH, JESSICA D; Mustang HS; Mustang, OK; (1); FBLA; Spanish Clb.

UNRUH, KASSIE L; Okmulgee HS; Okmulgee, OK; (2); Band; Jazz Band; Mrchg Band; Pep Band; Golf; All Dist Hnr Band; All St Band 2nd Rnds; Stdnt Mo; Music.

UNRUH, RICHARD A; Choctaw HS; Harrah, OK; (3); Pres FBLA; JV Socr; Rose ST Coll; Bus; Acctng.

UNRUH, SHAYNA M; Oklahoma Bible Acad; Enid, OK; (3); Church Yth Grp; Cmnty Wkr; FCA; Band; Chorus; Pep Band; School Play; L Bsktbl; L Sftbl; L Vllybl.

UNTERKIRCHER, DAVID; Okemah HS; Okemah, OK; (3); 6/65; Key Clb; Natl FFA Org; Hon Roll; Raise & Show Sheep; Show Hogs; OK ST U.

UPDIKE, GARRETT; Broken Arrow Sr HS; Broken Arrow, OK; (4); 67/984; Boy Scts; Church Yth Grp; Drama Clb; Service Clb; Thesps; Acpl Chr; School Musical; School Play; Stage Crew; Variety Show; Brigham Young Univ; Sports Med.

UPSHAW, JADEE; Shawnee Sr HS; Shawnee, OK; (3); 11/282; Church Yth Grp; French Clb; Pres Latin Clb; JV Bsktbl; JV Crs Cntry; JV Trk; High Hon Roll; Jr NHS; Math Clb; Science Clb; Sea Scts VP; Piano Natl & Intl Guild; Genetic Engrng.

UPSHAW, TOMMY W; Velma Alma HS; Velma, OK; (1); Church Yth Grp; FCA; Letterman Clb; Quiz Bowl; SADD; Var Bsbl; Var Bsktbl; Var Ftbl; Wt Lftg; Cit Awd; OK Hnr Soc; Cll Antqs, Fshng Lrs; Sprts Med.

UPTON, AMY; Seminole Jr Sr HS; Seminole, OK; (1); Debate Tm; Drama Clb; French Clb; NFL; Speech Tm; Thesps; School Play; High Hon Roll; Pres Acad Fit Awd.

UPTON, APRIL D; Dewar Jr-Sr HS; Schulter, OK; (2); Ofcr Soph Cls; High Hon Roll; Vet.

UPTON, JEFFERY O; Stigler HS; Stigler, OK; (3); 96/119; FCA; 4-H; Pep Clb; SADD; VICA; Ofcr Jr Cls; Bsktbl; Trk; Cit Awd; FFA; Emporia ST Coll; His Prof.

URASAKI, JULIE N; Owasso Sr HS; Owasso, OK; (3); FBLA; VICA; JV Sftbl; Hon Roll; Prfct Atten Awd; Comp Software; Data Processing; Graphics; Comp Applications.

URBAN, NATHAN L; Lindsay HS; Lindsay, OK; (3); 5/80; Art Clb; Boy Scts; Hon Roll; NHS; Eagle Scout; Frosh/Jr Class Schlr; Rlbldg/Rock Clmbg; OK Univ; Med Field.

URDANETA, CHRISTINA H; Union Intermediate HS; Broken Arrow, OK; (2); Spanish Clb; Hon Roll; Ballet Dncr & Stu Tchr; Bstn Smmr Dnc & NC Schl Of Arts Progs; Ballet Dncr.

URIAS, DANIEL; Southeast HS; Odessa, TX; (1); Var Bsktbl; Hon Roll.

URWIN, JASON; Goodwell Public Schl; Guymon, OK; (4); Boy Scts; German Clb; Ofcr Soph Cls; Ofcr Sr Cls; Ofcr Bsbl; Hon Roll; PSU; Drftng.

USHER, COLENE M; Snyder HS; Snyder, OK; (4); 7/42; Church Yth Grp; FHA; Natl FFA Org; Teachers Aide; Band; Mrchg Band; Ed Yrbk; Sftbl; High Hon Roll; Hon Roll; Yth Alv; SWOSU; Spch Pthlgy.

USHER, GARY; Snyder HS; Snyder, OK; (4); 23/40; Pres Church Yth Grp; FCA; FHA; Natl FFA Org; Office Aide; L Church Choir; Cntrl Bible Coll; Chrch Plantng.

UTLEY, JASON; Chickasha Jr HS; Chickasha, OK; (1); Church Yth Grp; Science Clb; Spanish Clb; Socr; Wrstlng; High Hon Roll; Jr NHS; NHS; Prfct Atten Awd; Pres Acad Fit Awd; OK ST U.

UTZ, MEGAN E; Bishop Kelley HS; Tulsa, OK; (1); FCA; Hosp Aide; JV Bsktbl; Var Socr; Hon Roll; OK ST Slct Soccer Tm 95-; Soccer Tm Capt.

VACLAVICEK, MELISSA J; Metro Christian Acad; Tulsa, OK; (4); 7/65; Church Yth Grp; FCA; Girl Scts; Key Clb; Pep Clb; Teachers Aide; Chorus; School Musical; School Play; Treas Soph Cls; Brunswick Found Schol; U Of Tulsa; Mused.

VADEN, KATI D; Cushing HS; Cushing, OK; (1); Church Yth Grp; Natl FFA Org; Hon Roll; NHS; Dncng; Prlmntry Prcdr Team.

VAILE, VALERIE; Lone Grove HS; Lone Grove, OK; (3); 10/95; FCA; Mrchg Band; Yrbk; Chrldng; Sftbl; Cit Awd; High Hon Roll; NHS; Pres Acad Fit Awd; Amer Legn Awd; Blue Rbbn Schlr; OK Hnr Schlr; Pharmcy.

VAILS, CONNIE; Wilson HS; Wilson, OK; (4); 6/29; Am Leg Aux Girls St; FCA; German Clb; Natl Beta Clb; Spanish Clb; Phtg Yrbk; L Bsktbl; L Chrldng; Hon Roll; Ntl Merit Ltr; Ntl Hnr Roll; Phys Thrpy.

VALANEJAD, KAMRAN A; Choctaw HS; Midwest City, OK; (3); 1/376; Var Bsktbl; Var Crs Cntry; Var Tennis; High Hon Roll; Jr NHS; Ntl Merit Ltr; Pres Acad Fit Awd; Val; Prdcr/Drctr Schl TV Pgm; Head Snd Engr Schl Vcl Jazz, Choir; U Of Southern CA; Music Prdcr.

VALANEJAD, KARMAN A; Choctaw HS; Midwest City, OK; (3); 1/317; Am Leg Boys St; Pres Sr Cls; Var Bsktbl; Var Crs Cntry; Var Tennis; NHS; Val; Sound Engr; Producer & Dir Of Schl Tv Show; U Of Southern CA; Musc Recrdng.

VALDEZ, CHE M; Broken Bow HS; Broken Bow, OK; (3); Drama Clb; Quiz Bowl; Science Clb; Spanish Clb; Speech Tm; Var L Ftbl; Var Golf; Hon Roll; NHS.

VALDEZ, JASON; Waynoka HS; Waynoka, OK; (3); 2/18; FCA; Natl FFA Org; ROTC; Sec Frsh Cls; Ofcr Bsbl; Ftbl; Wt Lftg; High Hon Roll; Hon Roll; OSU.

VALENTIN, VANESSA; Mustang HS; Mustang, OK; (4); 99/350; Church Yth Grp; FCA; FBLA; Office Aide; Scholastic Bowl; Spanish Clb; Teachers Aide; Crs Cntry; Powder Puff Ftbl; Socr; OK ST Univ; Bus.

VALENTINE, KATIE A; Metro Christian Acad; Tulsa, OK; (2); Church Yth Grp; FCA; Spanish Clb; Church Choir; Stage Crew; Bsktbl; Mgr(s); Hon Roll; Recreational Sports; FL ST; Speech Pathology.

VALENTINE, NATHAN I; Oklahoma Sch Of Science & Math; Tulsa, OK; (3); Ofcr Stu Cncl; Bio Capt; Natl Comp Fnlst Tm 96; Tst Engrng Aptd, Math, & Sci; Psycht.

VALENTINE, SHAWNNA; Thomas Fay Custer Public HS; Custer City, OK; (2); 30/45; Church Yth Grp; CAP; 4-H; FBLA; FHA; Natl FFA Org; Drill Tm; Ofcr Soph Cls; Bsktbl; Sftbl; Outstndng FHA Stu; FFA Greenhand.

VALERIUS, KERRI; Gracemont HS; Gracemont, OK; (4); 2/14; 4-H; NHS; Sal; Letterman Clb; Scholastic Bowl; Yrbk; Sec Jr Cls; Sec Sr Cls; Var Bsktbl; USAO; Bus.

VALLASTER, LINDSAY; Bartlesville Sr HS; Bartlesville, OK; (3); #51 in class; Church Yth Grp; Dance Clb; FBLA; Yrbk; Pom Pon; High Hon Roll; Jr NHS; Kiwanis Awd; NHS.

VALLEY, JAMIE; Stillwater Sr HS; Stillwater, OK; (3); Church Yth Grp; Cmnty Wkr; German Clb; Intnl Clb; Mu Alpha Theta; Natl Beta Clb; Teachers Aide; Orch; High Hon Roll; NHS.

VALLIERE, JAMMI M; Union Intermediate HS; Tulsa, OK; (2); Dance Clb; French Clb; Girl Scts; Orch; Hon Roll; Girl Sct Silver Awd; OU; RN.

VALOIS, MATTHEW P; South Intermediate HS; Broken Arrow, OK; (1); Sec Church Yth Grp; Cmnty Wkr; Acpl Chr; Band; Church Choir; Jazz Band; Mrchg Band; Gov Hon Prg Awd; High Hon Roll; Hon Roll; Chrch Hndbls; Schl Chrstn Stdnt Union; Sngr/Keybrds Rock Bnd; Music.

VANARSDEL, TIFFANY D; Edmond Santa Fe HS; Edmond, OK; (3); Church Yth Grp; Drama Clb; FCA; JCL; Key Clb; Latin Clb; Math Clb; Science Clb; SADD; Church Choir; 3 Yrs Hnrs Eng; Hnrs Bio, Chem & Algebra II; Tnns Regnls; 3rd Pl St Tnns Tnrmt; OU; Nuclear Engrng.

VAN BUSKIRK, MELINDA M; Lone Grove HS; Ardmore, OK; (3); Church Yth Grp; Math Clb; Quiz Bowl; Science Clb; High Hon Roll; NHS; Ntl Merit Schol; St Schlr; Sci Fair; OSU Hnrs Schlr; Multi-Yr Listee; OB-GYN.

VANCE, KIMBERLY M; Mannford HS; Mannford, OK; (3); FCA; FBLA; Var Chrldng; Hon Roll; Prfct Atten Awd; OSU; Bus Mgmt.

VANCE, LINDSAY C; Union Intermediate HS; Tulsa, OK; (2); Treas Key Clb; Crs Cntry; Mgr(s); Trk; High Hon Roll; Jr NHS; NHS; Fin.

VANCE, MONICA L; Turner Schl; Burneyville, OK; (3); Debate Tm; Natl FFA Org; Quiz Bowl; Speech Tm; Phtg Yrbk; Sec Soph Cls; Rep Jr Cls; JV Var Bsktbl; Sftbl; Prfct Atten Awd; Soph FFA Treas; Murray ST Coll; RN.

VAN CLEAVE, TERA; Mustang HS; Mustang, OK; (3); Sec Debate Tm; JA; NFL; Spanish Clb; Teachers Aide; Band; High Hon Roll; Hon Roll; NHS; Alg I Acad Awd; OK Mock Trial Pgm Cmptn.

VANDE, DONALD; Westmoore HS; Oklahoma City, OK; (1); FCA; Teachers Aide; Bsktbl; Ftbl; Trk; Guard On OK Magic 16 & Under St Bsktbl Champs; Awded All Conf Ftbl-Quarterback Awd.

VAN DEN BORN, JOHN W; Henryetta Sr HS; Henryetta, OK; (3); 3/75; Am Leg Boys St; FCA; Library Aide; Chorus; School Musical; Stage Crew; VP Frsh Cls; Var L Bsktbl; Var L Ftbl; Var L Golf.

VAN DENBOS, JAY S; Tahlequah Sr HS; Tahlequah, OK; (3); Am Leg Boys St; Church Yth Grp; ROTC; Science Clb; SADD; Chorus; Color Guard; Drill Tm; Rep Soph Cls; High Hon Roll; Hendrix; Sci.

VANDERBURG, JENNY; Noble HS; Noble, OK; (4); Art Clb; Church Yth Grp; DECA; FHA; Spanish Clb; Chorus; Church Choir; Yrbk; Var Sftbl; Hon Roll; Rose ST; Intr Dcrtng/Arch.

VANDERBURG, JORDANA; Hugo HS; Hugo, OK; (3); 6/96; Computer Clb; FCA; Science Clb; Flag Corp; Nwsp; Yrbk; Pres Soph Cls; Pres Jr Cls; Tennis; NHS; Jrnlsm.

VANDER HAAR, ZACHARY L; Yukon HS; Yukon, OK; (4); 135/420; FHA; Spanish Clb; Speech Tm; Yrbk; Var L Socr; Hon Roll; W TX AM; Sprts Med.

VANDERHEYDEN, JAMIE M; Midwest City HS; Midwest City, OK; (2); 84/473; FHA; Swing Chorus; Ofcr Soph Cls; Ofcr Jr Cls; Psych.

VANDERHOOF, DUSTIN J; Stroud HS; Stroud, OK; (2); 3/70; French Clb; Band; JV Stat Bsktbl; Var L Ftbl; Var Golf; High Hon Roll; Hon Roll; NHS; OK St Hnr Soc; Bio Chem.

VANDERLINDE, MEGAN; Luther HS; Luther, OK; (4); 1/42; Church Yth Grp; Drama Clb; FCA; HOBY; NFL; Scholastic Bowl; Pres Stu Cncl; Capt Bsktbl; NHS; Val; E Cntrl Univ; Pre Med.

VANDERSLICE, JARROD J; Mason HS; Welty, OK; (2); Church Yth Grp; Quiz Bowl; Ofcr Bsbl; Bsktbl; Mgr(s); Cit Awd; Mid-America Bible Coll OK.

VANDEVEER, CHARLIE R; South Intermediate HS; Broken Arrow, OK; (1); Church Yth Grp; Cmnty Wkr; GAA; Socr; Wt Lftg; Hon Roll; Ft Lewis Coll; Phys Therapy.

VANDEVER, JEFFERY W; El Reno Sr HS; El Reno, OK; (3); 125/200; Church Yth Grp; FCA; SADD; Church Choir; Bsktbl; Ftbl; High Hon Roll.

VAN DOORN, KRISTINA; Oologah HS; Claremore, OK; (4); 7/101; Science Clb; Pres SADD; Var Capt Socr; Wt Lftg; Hon Roll; NHS; IA St Univ; Premed.

VAN DORN, BRENDAN M; Shattuck Jr Sr HS; Shattuck, OK; (3); Church Yth Grp; FCA; Letterman Clb; Natl FFA Org; Band; Jazz Band; Pep Band; Ofcr Bsbl; Bsktbl; Ftbl; OK ST Univ.

VAN DORN, LINDSAY; Buffalo Jr Sr HS; Buffalo, OK; (4); 12/30; Church Yth Grp; FBLA; Hosp Aide; Intnl Clb; Red Cross Aide; Church Choir; Cit Awd; High Hon Roll; Jr NHS; Letterman Clb; Tech Stu Assn; Dodge City CC; Child Dev.

VAN DUSER, TIM; Meeker HS; Meeker, OK; (2); Ofcr Bsbl; Bsktbl; Ftbl; Hon Roll; Jr NHS; Pres Acad Fit Awd; OK ST Univ; Ath Dir.

VAN DUYN, VALERIE M; Edmond Memorial HS; Edmond, OK; (2); 57/440; Spanish Clb; Var Trk; Var Vllybl; Hon Roll; USVBA Club Ball 96.

VAN EATON, DAVID S; Union Intermediate HS; Tulsa, OK; (1); Boy Scts; Church Yth Grp; Cmnty Wkr; FCA; Band; Church Choir; High Hon Roll; NHS; Stus For Christ; Natl Respecteen Yth Forum OK Delg; Oral Roberts U.

VAN EVERY, MATTHEW F; Putnam City North HS; Oklahoma City, OK; (3); German Clb; Quiz Bowl; Scholastic Bowl; School Play; Rep Stu Cncl; JV Ftbl; Var Tennis; Wt Lftg; Hon Roll; CAWS; Bus.

VAN GORDON, PHILLIP G; Choctaw HS; Harrah, OK; (4); 36/326; Boy Scts; High Hon Roll; NHS; Natl Yth Ldrshp Forum; U Of OK; Pre-Med.

VAN GUNDY, CYNTHIA; El Reno Sr HS; El Reno, OK; (2); 87/227; Church Yth Grp; Drama Clb; Speech Tm; Thesps; School Play; Variety Show; Hon Roll; Placed In Regnl Cont For Speech In Prose; Peer Ldrs; Redlands CC; Law.

VAN HOESEN, MANDY; Perry Sr HS; Perry, OK; (4); 9/66; Church Yth Grp; Cmnty Wkr; Drama Clb; FCA; Pres German Clb; Hosp Aide; HOBY; Speech Tm; Teachers Aide; Chorus.

VAN METER, COURTNEY M; Choctaw HS; Choctaw, OK; (3); Church Yth Grp; Chorus; Church Choir; Swing Chorus; Variety Show; Yrbk; Bsktbl; Powder Puff Ftbl; Sftbl; Tennis; Marine Bio.

VANN, BETH M; Oaks Mission Jr Sr HS; Oaks, OK; (3); Treas FBLA; VP FHA; GAA; Sec Natl FFA Org; Yrbk; Pres Soph Cls; Pres Jr Cls; Rep Stu Cncl; Var L Bsktbl; Var L Sftbl; Cherokee Natn Tribal Yth Cncl Mmbr; NE St Univ; Dent.

VANN, TRACY L; Locust Grove HS; Locust Grove, OK; (3); FCA; Office Aide; Pep Clb; Spanish Clb; SADD; Chrldng; Socr; Trk; Wt Lftg; Prfct Atten Awd; Class Queen Grd 9; Homecoming Queen Grd 10; NSU; Pediatric Cardiologist.

VAN NOSTRAND, ABBIE; Woodward HS; Woodward, OK; (3); Art Clb; Hosp Aide; Letterman Clb; Pep Clb; Bsktbl; Hon Roll; Kiwanis Awd; NHS; SWOSU.

VAN OSDOL, KACY; Edmond Memorial HS; Edmond, OK; (4); 15/336; Church Yth Grp; Spanish Clb; SADD; VP Church Choir; NHS; Sal; U Of Cntrl OK; Arcch.

VAN SCHUYVER, TIFFANY A; Byng Sr HS; Ada, OK; (2); 1/104; Treas Art Clb; Natl Beta Clb; Spanish Clb; Band; Mrchg Band; High Hon Roll; Jr NHS; NHS; Prfct Atten Awd; All Dist Band; Schlstc Mts; OK ST Univ; Vet.

VAN SCODER, KARA; Anadarko HS; Anadarko, OK; (2); 21/150; Church Yth Grp; Drama Clb; FBLA; FHA; Spanish Clb; SADD; Chorus; Church Choir; School Musical; School Play; Miss Warrior Cand; Psych.

VANSCOY, VANESSA; East Central HS; Tulsa, OK; (2); FCA; Red Cross Aide; Science Clb; Sec Spanish Clb; Rep Soph Cls; Var Chrldng; Univ Of OK.

VAN VORMER, BECKY; Trinity Christian Schl; Broken Arrow, OK; (2); 3/12; Church Yth Grp; Pep Clb; School Play; Sec Frsh Cls; VP Soph Cls; Var L Chrldng; Vllybl; Hon Roll; NSU.

VAN WOERKOM, LINDSEY; Choctaw Jr HS; Oklahoma City, OK; (1); Chorus; Church Choir; Jr NHS; VP Jr NSH; Weber ST U; Vet.

VAN WORMER, AMY; Trinity Christian Schl; Broken Arrow, OK; (4); 2/7; Pep Clb; School Play; Nwsp; Yrbk; VP Jr Cls; Pres Sr Cls; Var L Chrldng; Co-Capt Vllybl; High Hon Roll; Sal; Northeastern ST Univ; Acctng.

VANZANDT, JENNIFER N; Muldrow HS; Muldrow, OK; (1); Church Yth Grp; Drama Clb; Natl Beta Clb; Spanish Clb; Speech Tm; Band; Mrchg Band; Pep Band; School Play; OSU; Vet.

VAN ZANDT, NATHAN; Seiling Schl; Seiling, OK; (4); 11/34; Church Yth Grp; VP FCA; Ofcr FBLA; Letterman Clb; VP Natl FFA Org; Spanish Clb; Teachers Aide; Pres Jr Cls; Rep Stu Cncl; Var L Bsbl; 11th Pl Cls 2 A Bsbl Batting Avg 95; A-2 All Dist Ctr, Cls A St Rnnr Up Ftbl Tm 95; OKC Sprg Stck Shw; Northwstrn OK ST U; Anml Sci.

VAP, APRIL D; Frontier Public Schl; Newkirk, OK; (3); Church Yth Grp; Sec Jr Cls; Sec Stu Cncl; Var Co-Capt Bsktbl; Var Co-Capt Sftbl; Hon Roll; NHS; Sports Med.

VARBEL, MICHELLE; Olney Schl; Coalgate, OK; (4); 1/12; HOBY; Library Aide; Scholastic Bowl; Rptr Nwsp; Rptr Jr Cls; Rptr Sr Cls; L Bsktbl; High Hon Roll; Val; SOSU; Med.

VARDEY, SHEELA; Union Intermediate HS; Tulsa, OK; (1); French Clb; Hosp Aide; Key Clb; Math Clb; Var Vllybl; High Hon Roll; NHS.

VARGHESE, JAISON; Putnam City HS; Oklahoma City, OK; (3); 8/327; Art Clb; Church Yth Grp; Cmnty Wkr; French Clb; Library Aide; Science Clb; Service Clb; Hon Roll; Jr NHS; NHS; U Of OK; Phy Therapy.

VARLEY, KRISTY; Chickasha Jr HS; Chickasha, OK; (1); Church Yth Grp; Spanish Clb; Chorus; Church Choir; Tennis; Hon Roll; Jr NHS; NHS; Dance Competition; Univ Of OK; Pre Med.

VARNELL, KENNDA L; Weatherford HS; Weatherford, OK; (4); Art Clb; Cmnty Wkr; FHA; Model UN; Teachers Aide; Band; Mrchg Band; Pep Band; Hon Roll; Southwestern OK St Univ; Sp Ed.

VARNELL, LYNSEY D; Stillwater Sr HS; Stillwater, OK; (4); 93/320; Church Yth Grp; Cmnty Wkr; FCA; Natl Beta Clb; Office Aide; Spanish Clb; Rep Soph Cls; Rep Jr Cls; Rep Sr Cls; Ofcr Stu Cncl; OK State Univ; Medicine.

VARNER, KARA L; Mannford HS; Mannford, OK; (2); 16/113; Church Yth Grp; Cmnty Wkr; Drama Clb; FCA; GAA; NFL; Science Clb; Spanish Clb; Speech Tm; SADD.

VARUGHESE, CHRISTINA; Victory Christian Schl; Broken Arrow, OK; (3); Cmnty Wkr; Debate Tm; Intnl Clb; Speech Tm; Chorus; Nwsp; High Hon Roll; Jr NHS; NHS; Span Clb; Cmptr Engrng.

VARUGHESE, JIBY; Mustang HS; Yukon, OK; (1); Church Choir; High Hon Roll; Hon Roll; Prfct Atten Awd; Comp Sci.

VARUGHESE, MANJU; Yukon Middle HS; Yukon, OK; (2); Church Yth Grp; Sec FHA; Hosp Aide; Spanish Clb; Hon Roll; NHS; US Natl Math Awd; OU.

VASCELLARO, MARIA S; Yukon Middle HS; Yukon, OK; (3); 24/427; Trk; Hon Roll; NHS; HS Rcrd Hldr Trpl Long Jmp; Dist & St Piano Awds; Med.

VASQUEZ, AMANDA; Anadarko HS; Anadarko, OK; (1); Church Yth Grp; 4-H; Chorus; School Musical; Treas Frsh Cls; Chrldng; FFA Chrs.

VASQUEZ, JAMIE L; Latta Sr HS; Ada, OK; (3); FHA; Hosp Aide; Acpl Chr; Chorus; Rptr Nwsp; Hon Roll; Admin Asst Skills Cert.

VASQUEZ, SYLVIA; Hollis Jr Sr HS; Hollis, OK; (2); Pres Church Yth Grp; FHA; Letterman Clb; Math Clb; Speech Tm; Band; JV Var Bsktbl; Trk; Hon Roll; Ntl Merit Ltr; Home Ec, Rdng & Lang Awds; Adopt-A-Hwy Pgm; Gftd & Tlntd Pgm; Nrsng Home Vol; Chrch Act; Wrtng Poetry; Dr; Lawyer.

VASS, MEGAN; Midwest City HS; Midwest City, OK; (4); 6/419; Church Yth Grp; Cmnty Wkr; Drama Clb; FCA; Hosp Aide; Office Aide; Pep Clb; Spanish Clb; SADD; School Musical; Outstndng Math Achvt; Midwest City Jr Rotarian; 4.0 Clb; OSU; Math.

VASSAR, KENDALL; Woodward HS; Woodward, OK; (2); Church Yth Grp; Cmnty Wkr; FCA; JV Bsktbl; Hon Roll; Kiwanis Awd; NHS; Acad Ltr; OK Coll.

VASSAR, MANDY; Woodward HS; Woodward, OK; (2); Hon Roll.

VASSILAKOS, ROB N; West Middle HS; Norman, OK; (1); Cmnty Wkr; FCA; Hon Roll; Prfct Atten Awd.

VASSO, RICHARD L; Cushing HS; Cushing, OK; (1); Church Yth Grp; Band; Mrchg Band; Ofcr Bsbl; Ftbl; Wt Lftg; Dr.

VAUGHAN, ASHLEY; Macarthur Sr HS; Lawton, OK; (2); Church Yth Grp; FCA; HOBY; Science Clb; Phtg Yrbk; Capt Chrldng; Tennis; High Hon Roll; Hon Roll; Jr NHS; 4 Tm NCA All Amer Chlrdr; OK Baptst Univ.

VAUGHAN, BRAD G; Putnam City HS; Oklahoma City, OK; (3); U Of Central OK; Aerospc Engr.

VAUGHAN, JAMIE A; Antlers Sr HS; Antlers, OK; (3); Drama Clb; Sec FHA; Hosp Aide; School Play; Stage Crew; Hon Roll; Prfct Atten Awd; BAD; Paris Jr Coll; RN.

VAUGHAN, MARIAH; Noble HS; Noble, OK; (3); 12/146; Church Yth Grp; FCA; French Clb; Mu Alpha Theta; Chorus; Sec Jr Cls; Treas Stu Cncl; Socr; Hon Roll; NHS; OK U; Vet.

VAUGHAN, MARK L; Cheyenne HS; Cheyenne, OK; (4); Art Clb; Church Yth Grp; Library Aide; VICA; Chorus; Rptr Sr Cls; Ntl Merit SF; Prfct Atten Awd; FHA; FHA Pres & King; Amarillo Tech; Brdcstng.

VAUGHAN, SHAWNA; Atoka HS; Atoka, OK; (4); 3/87; Church Yth Grp; Drama Clb; FBLA; FHA; Math Clb; Pres Natl FFA Org; Office Aide; Science Clb; Spanish Clb; Speech Tm; Mock Trl Tm Dfns Atty; ST FFA Degree; Star Chptr Farmr; Cty/Dist/ST/NATL Lvstck Exhbts; Murray ST Coll; Pre-Vet Med.

VAUGHN, BASILIO D; Choctaw HS; Choctaw, OK; (3); Church Yth Grp; Acpl Chr; Chorus; Church Choir; School Musical; School Play; Swing Chorus; Variety Show; Pres Frsh Cls; Bsktbl; All OMEA Hnr Choir; Outstdng Jr Guy; Stdnt Of Month; Choctaw Acaad Hnr Stdnt Spec Parking Permit; U Of Northern CO; Music Ed.

VAUGHN, CARRIE; Washington HS; Purcell, OK; (4); 1/38; Am Leg Aux Girls St; Church Yth Grp; FCA; Var Capt Bsktbl; Var Capt Chrldng; Var Capt Sftbl; Var Trk; High Hon Roll; NHS; Val; Southeastern OK ST.

VAUGHN, CHRISTINA M; Tahlequah Sr HS; Tahlequah, OK; (3); Cmnty Wkr; Girl Scts; Pep Clb; Service Clb; Pres Spanish Clb; Treas SADD; Chorus; School Musical; Golf; Gov Hon Prg Awd; All ST Choir.

VAUGHN, ERIN K; Stillwater Sr HS; Stillwater, OK; (2); Cmnty Wkr; Girl Scts; Key Clb; Diving; High Hon Roll; Arch.

VAUGHN, JAMES W; Washington HS; Purcell, OK; (1); Church Yth Grp; FCA; Pres Frsh Cls; JV Var Bsbl; Var Ftbl; Var Trk; High Hon Roll; Prfct Atten Awd; Sthestrn OK ST Univ; Bsbl.

VAUGHN, JARROD; Lindsay HS; Lindsay, OK; (2); 5/84; Art Clb; Debate Tm; Math Clb; Quiz Bowl; Scholastic Bowl; Teachers Aide; Mrchg Band; Cit Awd; Hon Roll; Pres Acad Fit Awd; FFA Greenhand Quiz To ST.

VAUGHN, MELISSA; Perry Sr HS; Perry, OK; (2); FHA; Band; Mrchg Band; Rep Stu Cncl; Hon Roll; Jr NHS; NHS; Pep Clb; Mat Maids; All Amer Schlr; Ldrshp & Svc Awd; OU; Acctng.

VAUGHN, MIRANDA; Hobart HS; Hobart, OK; (4); 1/59; Am Leg Aux Girls St; Church Yth Grp; Pres FHA; Ed Nwsp; Ed Yrbk; VP Sr Cls; Pres Stu Cncl; NHS; FCA; Pres FTA; Hmcmng Queen; Miss HHS; Mst Lkly To Sccd; U Of OK.

VAUGHN, NICK D; Edmond North HS; Edmond, OK; (2); Church Yth Grp; Cmnty Wkr; FCA; Spanish Clb; L Bsbl; L Bsktbl; Cit Awd; Hon Roll; Prfct Atten Awd.

VAUGHN, SHONTESA D; Northeast HS; Spencer, OK; (2); Chorus; Color Guard; OCAST; Meritorious Edctl Achvmt Awd; Howard Univ; Law/Psych.

VAVRICKA, TIM; Ada HS; Ada, OK; (3); 2/175; FCA; Mu Alpha Theta; Science Clb; Mrchg Band; Orch; Var Bsbl; Var Ftbl; NHS; Ntl Merit Schol; OK U; Med.

VAY, CHRIS S; Meeker HS; Meeker, OK; (2); Boy Scts; Cmnty Wkr; Spanish Clb; High Hon Roll; NHS; Pres Acad Fit Awd.

VAZQUEZ, JAY W; Vinita HS; Welch, OK; (3); Math Tm; Quiz Bowl; Hon Roll; NHS; Moto-Cross Rcng; Miami OK.

VAZQUEZ, ROBERT E; Lawton Sr HS; Lawton, OK; (2); Hon Roll; Elem Schl Stdnts 10th Grd Play; U Of Miami; Math/Sci.

VCULEK, JAN; Waukomis HS; Waukomis, OK; (4); 1/30; School Play; Quiz Bowl; Spanish Clb; Yrbk; VP Frsh Cls; Pres Jr Cls; VP Sr Cls; Pres Stu Cncl; Stat Bsktbl; Val; Vlntr Horn Of Plenty; St Senate Page; Reg Cmmtte OK St Tchr Of Yr; U Of Dallas; Poltcl Sci.

VEACH, GINNY; Norman Sr HS; Norman, OK; (4); 1/596; Church Yth Grp; Debate Tm; Hosp Aide; JCL; Latin Clb; Model UN; Mu Alpha Theta; NFL; NHS; Val; VP Of Med Explr Post 901; U Of OK; Microbio.

VEACH, MICHAEL W; West Middle HS; Norman, OK; (1); Church Yth Grp; U Of OK.

VEAL, REBECCA A; Central Mid-HS; Norman, OK; (2); Church Yth Grp; VP French Clb; Mu Alpha Theta; Church Choir; DAR Awd; French Hon Soc; Hon Roll; NHS; Hope Lovelace Meml Awd Outstdng Svc/Dedication Fr 96; U Of OK; Archlgy.

VEALES, TAMARA L; Pauls Valley HS; Pauls Valley, OK; (1); FCA; Key Clb; Pep Clb; Chorus; Flag Corp; Ed Yrbk; Sec Frsh Cls; JV Bsktbl; JV Sftbl; Cit Awd; OK ST U; Phys Thrpy.

VEAZEY, LAURA A; Putnam City North HS; Oklahoma City, OK; (4); 56/436; Church Yth Grp; Pres Drama Clb; FCA; JCL; Latin Clb; Math Clb; Office Aide; Red Cross Aide; Teachers Aide; Band; U Of OK; Premed.

VEGA, MARYANN. C; Stillwater Sr HS; Stillwater, OK; (3); FHA; Natl FFA Org; JV Gym; Hon Roll; Vrsty Schlr 2 Yrs; OSU; His/Tch HS.

VELASCO, GLORIA; Choctaw Jr HS; Choctaw, OK; (1); High Hon Roll.

VENABLE, ASHLEY; Anadarko HS; Anadarko, OK; (1); Church Yth Grp; 4-H; FBLA; Natl FFA Org; Speech Tm; Golf; Tennis; 4-H Awd; High Hon Roll; NHS; OK Jr Chianina Assn; OK Jr Cattlemens Assn; OK ST U; Med.

VENABLE, C PRESTON; Edmond North HS; Edmond, OK; (2); Church Yth Grp; Cmnty Wkr; FCA; Letterman Clb; Mu Alpha Theta; ROTC; Ofcr Bsbl; Wrstlng; Hon Roll; Jr NHS; Water Skiing.

VENEMA, AMANDA R; North Intemediate HS; Broken Arrow, OK; (1); Church Yth Grp; FHA; Latin Clb; Thesps; Hon Roll.

VERA, CONNIE; Blair Schl; Blair, OK; (3); Cmnty Wkr; Debate Tm; Drama Clb; FCA; HOBY; Natl FFA Org; Spanish Clb; Speech Tm; Chorus; School Play; Marriage Cnslr.

VERBAL, DERRICK; Douglass HS; Oklahoma City, OK; (1); French Clb; ROTC; Var Bsbl; JV Bsktbl; Var Ftbl; Var Trk; Wt Lftg; Var Wrstlng; Hon Roll; Prfct Atten Awd; MI Univ; Acctg.

VERITY, MARY A; Heritage Hall Schl; Oklahoma City, OK; (2); Cmnty Wkr; FCA; Pep Clb; Spanish Clb; Chorus; L Bsktbl; L Fld Hcky; L Trk; Ed.

VERMEDAHL, MATTHEW TODD; Duncan HS; Duncan, OK; (4); 5/214; Church Yth Grp; VP Key Clb; Rep SADD; Swing Chorus; Cit Awd; High Hon Roll; Rptr NHS; Cmnty Wkr; FCA; Spanish Clb; 4 Pt Stdnt; Jari Askins House Rep Page; ST Supt Awd Exclnc Fine Arts/Vocal Music; OK City Univ; Vocal Performnc.

VERMILLION, AMY; Catoosa HS; Catoosa, OK; (2); Church Yth Grp; French Clb; Band; Color Guard; Mrchg Band; Orch; Sftbl; Hon Roll; Univ Of OK; Med.

VERMILLION, JENNIFER N; Elk City Jr HS; Elk City, OK; (1); 9/168; Church Yth Grp; Ed Yrbk; Ofcr Frsh Cls; Ofcr Stu Cncl; Bsktbl; Crs Cntry; Golf; Sftbl; High Hon Roll; NHS.

VERMILLION, JULIA A; Nathan Hale HS; Tulsa, OK; (2); Red Cross Aide; Band; Mrchg Band; High Hon Roll; NHS; All Dist Hnr Band; St HS Hnr Soc; Medicine.

VERMILLION, WALTER D; Valliant HS; Valliant, OK; (2); Church Yth Grp; Natl FFA Org; Varsity Clb; JV Var Bsktbl; JV Trk.

VERNON, BEVILL E C; Pauls Valley HS; Pauls Valley, OK; (3); 4/150; FCA; Key Clb; Math Clb; Science Clb; Spanish Clb; Ftbl; Golf; Cit Awd; Gov Hon Prg Awd; Hon Roll; Univ Of OK; Golf Prfsnl.

VERNON, ERIN L; Davis HS; Davis, OK; (4); 10/47; Church Yth Grp; FHA; Key Clb; Spanish Clb; SADD; Chorus; Variety Show; Hon Roll; NHS; Dntl Hygiene.

VERNON, JODI C; Wilson HS; Wilson, OK; (4); 2/29; Church Yth Grp; FHA; German Clb; Natl Beta Clb; Natl FFA Org; Quiz Bowl; Teachers Aide; Band; Yrbk; Chrldng; FFA Pres, Rptr; Cls Rptr; Southeastern ST Coll; Elem Ed.

VERNON, PAMELA KIM; Davis HS; Davis, OK; (3); French Clb; FBLA; FHA; Key Clb; SADD; Chorus; School Musical; Powder Puff Ftbl; Hon Roll; Key Clbbr Of Month; Chem Awd; Multi-Cultural His Awd; East Cntrl Univ; Commnctn.

VERTREES, RICHARD; Lone Grove HS; Lone Grove, OK; (3); FCA; VP Natl FFA Org; Science Clb; Ofcr Bsbl; Bsktbl; L Ftbl; L Trk; Wt Lftg; NHS.

VERVILLE, TIMOTHY D; Putnam City West HS; Oklahoma City, OK; (2); Church Yth Grp; Orch; Sprt Ed Phtg Yrbk; OK Yth Philharmonia 9th Grd; OK Yth Orch 10th Grd; North Cntrl Hnrs Orch 9-10th Grd; Music/Photo.

VESANEN, ANJA; Jenks HS; Tulsa, OK; (4); 4/522; Am Leg Aux Girls St; Church Yth Grp; Mu Alpha Theta; Science Clb; Spanish Clb; Band; Mrchg Band; Hon Roll; NHS; Meteorology.

VICK, JOHN W; Star Spencer HS; Spencer, OK; (1); Band; Mrchg Band; Rep Frsh Cls; JV Ftbl; Wt Lftg; Wrstlng; High Hon Roll; FL ST; Ftbl/PT.

VICK, MEREDITH R; Prague HS; Paden, OK; (3); Church Yth Grp; Cmnty Wkr; Drama Clb; FBLA; Key Clb; Speech Tm; Var Bsktbl; Var Chrldng; Hon Roll; U Of OK; Rsrntmgnt.

VICTORY, ANGELA; Chelsea HS; Chelsea, OK; (4); Pres FHA; Pres Spanish Clb; Speech Tm; Teachers Aide; Hon Roll; NHS; U Of Cntrl OK; Fnrl Svc.

VIDACAK, JOEY; Muskogee HS; Muskogee, OK; (2); Church Yth Grp; FCA; HOBY; JCL; Latin Clb; Church Choir; School Play; Stage Crew; VP Frsh Cls; Pres Soph Cls; JCL Pres; OK Hnr Soc; OK U; Med Schl.

VIDAL, PAULINA; Putnam City HS; Oklahoma City, OK; (2); Church Yth Grp; German Clb; Girl Scts; Intnl Clb; Band; Mrchg Band; Socr; Sftbl; Trk; Vllybl; Super Rtng OSSAA Msc Cntst ST; Music Flute/Ballet/Jazz; Lang Trnsltn/Music.

VIERLING, JEREMY A; Okmulgee HS; Okmulgee, OK; (2); Quiz Bowl; Science Clb; Prfct Atten Awd; OSU; Comp Arch Designer.

VIEUX, LACY; Stuart Sr HS; Stuart, OK; (3); 9/28; FHA; Teachers Aide; Rptr Nwsp; Rptr Yrbk; Rptr Jr Cls; Hon Roll; ECU.

VIEUX, STACY; Stuart Sr HS; Stuart, OK; (3); 10/28; Rptr FHA; Library Aide; Teachers Aide; Rptr Nwsp; Treas Jr Cls; Prncpls Hnr Roll.

VIGNAL, DEIDRA L; Sayre HS; Sayre, OK; (2); 4/55; Lubbock Chrstn Univ; Radio.

VIK, ROXY; Bartlesville Sr HS; Bartlesville, OK; (4); Ed Church Yth Grp; Cmnty Wkr; Hosp Aide; Math Clb; Office Aide; Red Cross Aide; Service Clb; Band; Chorus; Color Guard; Specl Olympc Vlntr; J Baird Soc; Harding U; Phys Thrpy.

VILLANUEVA, ENRIQUE; Clinton HS; Clinton, OK; (2); 1/138; Church Yth Grp; FHA; Key Clb; Hon Roll; NHS; Acad Excl Awd; N Cntrl Imprvmnt Pln Cmmttee; Rennsnce Gld.

VILLINES, TOSHA; Weatherford HS; Weatherford, OK; (3); Church Yth Grp; DECA; FCA; FHA; FTA; Teachers Aide; Varsity Clb; VP Frsh Cls; VP Soph Cls; Ofcr Stu Cncl; Lfgrd; U OK; Crdlgy.

VINCENT, BRANDON R; North Intemediate HS; Broken Arrow, OK; (1); Church Yth Grp; Intrml Ftbl; JV Wt Lftg; Hon Roll; Pres Acad Fit Awd; Chrstn; KS ST; Chiro/Physc.

VINCENT, LAURA E; Macarthur Sr HS; Lawton, OK; (4); 6/256; Church Yth Grp; Cmnty Wkr; FCA; VP FHA; Hosp Aide; Pres Acpl Chr; Church Choir; Ofcr Stu Cncl; Wrstlng; NHS; OK City Univ; Music Ed.

VINCENT, MELISSA L; Christian Heritage Acad; Oklahoma City, OK; (3); Church Yth Grp; School Play; High Hon Roll; Hon Roll; Martial Arts; Piano; PT.

VINCENT, NAN; Shawnee Sr HS; Shawnee, OK; (1); 1/400; Church Yth Grp; Latin Clb; DAR Awd; High Hon Roll; Jr NHS; Tmblng/Trmpln; Piano.

VINCENT, RICKIE R; Shawnee Sr HS; Shawnee, OK; (1); JA; High Hon Roll; Hon Roll; Kiwanis Awd; Prfct Atten Awd; East Cntrl Univ.

VINCENT, SARAH L; Stillwater Sr HS; Stillwater, OK; (3); 88/380; Chorus; Church Choir; School Musical; School Play; Stage Crew; Rptr Nwsp; Sec Stu Cncl; Tennis; Yth & Govt Treas; St Piano Auditions; Broadcasting; Commnctn.

VINCENT, SCHYLA; Shawnee Sr HS; Shawnee, OK; (2); Latin Clb; High Hon Roll; Hon Roll; Natl Hnr Roll; OU; Mrktng.

VINSON, HOLLY; Noble HS; Noble, OK; (3); Church Yth Grp; Mu Alpha Theta; Spanish Clb; Teachers Aide; Chorus; JV Sftbl; Hon Roll.

VINSON, JOI L; B T Washington HS; Tulsa, OK; (3); Church Yth Grp; Cmnty Wkr; FBLA; Spanish Clb; Var Sftbl; High Hon Roll; Hon Roll; African Amrcn Scty; Dftng Clb; U Of OK; Premed.

VINSON, PENNY; Westmoore HS; Oklahoma City, OK; (3); 120/625; Dance Clb; FCA; Rep Frsh Cls; Rep Soph Cls; Rep Jr Cls; Pom Pon; Hon Roll; NHS; Pres Acad Fit Awd; Sr Miss Dance Of OK 95; NCA Natl Soloist Champ 95-; Jr Wrstlng Homecmng Attndnt 96; Univ Of OK.

VINYARD, CODY; Choctaw Jr HS; Choctaw, OK; (1); 10/150; Church Yth Grp; FCA; SADD; Ofcr Bsbl; Ftbl; Gym; Trk; Wt Lftg; Cit Awd; High Hon Roll; Notre Dame U; Bus.

VINYARD, MARTIN C; Harrah HS; Harrah, OK; (3); 17/165; Drama Clb; FCA; Letterman Clb; Varsity Clb; Rep Frsh Cls; Bsktbl; Ftbl; Tennis; Trk; Hon Roll; NC; Pre-Med.

VIRDEN, DOTTIE; Moore HS; Moore, OK; (2); 12/500; Capt Scholastic Bowl; Pres Church Choir; French Clb; NFL; Science Clb; Speech Tm; SADD; Socr; Jr NHS; NHS; Harvard; Bus.

VIRDEN, JEREMY; Moore HS; Moore, OK; (4); Am Leg Boys St; Debate Tm; Latin Clb; NFL; Speech Tm; Band; OKU; Law.

VIVAR, ALISA D; Wister Schl; Wister, OK; (1); Art Clb; Church Yth Grp; FHA; Ofcr Frsh Cls.

VIVAS, OLIVIA; Mt St Marys HS; Norman, OK; (3); Church Yth Grp; Cmnty Wkr; Hosp Aide; Model UN; Pep Clb; Speech Tm; Rep Frsh Cls; Treas Sr Cls; Ofcr Stu Cncl; Mgr Ftbl; Rel Retreat Ldr; Peer Hlpr Spprt Grp Ldr; Smmr Yth Prgm Wrk Rcgntn Awd; Psych/PT.

VIVONA, EMILIA B; Deer Creek HS; Edmond, OK; (3); Pres Art Clb; Church Yth Grp; VP FCA; Office Aide; Science Clb; School Musical; School Play; Phtg Nwsp; Rep Frsh Cls; Rep Sr Cls; Art; Dsgn.

VIVONA, NATALIE A; Deer Creek HS; Edmond, OK; (2); Church Yth Grp; FCA; Science Clb; School Musical; School Play; Yrbk; Sec Frsh Cls; Sec Jr Cls; Mgr(s); Early Chldhd Dev; Publishing.

VIZCAYA, JUAN M; Union Intermediate HS; Tulsa, OK; (2); JV Bsbl; Pres Schlr; Chem Eng.

VO, ALICIA HONG; Union Intermediate HS; Tulsa, OK; (2); 30/800; Cmnty Wkr; Key Clb; Letterman Clb; Math Clb; Spanish Clb; Cit Awd; Hon Roll; Jr NHS; NHS; Ntl Merit Ltr; Peer Mediation; Yth Vol Corp; Gatesway Fdn Intl Balloon Festvl.

VO, BRIAN H; Union Sr HS; Tulsa, OK; (4); 1/616; French Clb; Key Clb; Math Tm; Tennis; Jr NHS; NHS; Ntl Merit Ltr; Prfct Atten Awd; Pres Acad Fit Awd; Yng Dems Treas; 2nd Deg Blck Blt Tae Kwon Do; Cmptr Chllng 94; U Of OK; Med.

VO, MARGRETTE N; Union Sr HS; Tulsa, OK; (3); 49/741; French Clb; Key Clb; Mu Alpha Theta; Office Aide; Spanish Clb; VP Orch; Rep Stu Cncl; Jr NHS; NHS; Pres Acad Fit Awd; DFY; Renssnce Clb; Jr Brd; Washington U; Bio.

VO, TAM; Nw Classen HS; Oklahoma City, OK; (4); Art Clb; Church Yth Grp; French Clb; FBLA; Church Choir; Hon Roll; PRIDE; Rnssnc Awd; Herald Awd; Univ Of Cntrl OK; Ed K Tchr.

VO, THUONG X; Daniel Webster HS; Tulsa, OK; (4); 11/135; Cmnty Wkr; Science Clb; Temple Yth Grp; Hon Roll; NHS; Outstndng Acad Achvt; Cert Of Achvt Color/Dsgn; Acad Ltr Awd; U Of OK; Nrsng.

VOEGELI, JASON; Seiling Schl; Seiling, OK; (4); 3/32; Pres Church Yth Grp; FCA; FBLA; Natl FFA Org; VICA; Var Bsbl; Var Ftbl; Wt Lftg; Hon Roll.

VOGEL, AMANDA E; Jenks HS; Tulsa, OK; (4); 34/540; Hist Drama Clb; Office Aide; Hist Thesps; Stage Crew; Ofcr Stu Cncl; High Hon Roll; Cultrl Clb; Schl Of Amer Ballet Smmr 94 & 95; Pro Ballet Dancer.

VOGLER, BRIEANNE; Putnam City West HS; Oklahoma City, OK; (3); 40/400; Church Yth Grp; FCA; French Clb; Hosp Aide; Intnl Clb; Math Clb; Pep Clb; Science Clb; Varsity Clb; Var L Chrldng; Medcl Clb; HOSA; Rice U; Med.

VOGLER, JEREMY W; Westmoore HS; Moore, OK; (4); 27/610; Church Yth Grp; Church Choir; JV Bsktbl; Var Ftbl; High Hon Roll; Val; Cntrl Bapt Coll; Math; Engr.

VOGT, BRANDON; Byng Sr HS; Ada, OK; (4); Drama Clb; 4-H; French Clb; FBLA; Natl FFA Org; Quiz Bowl; Scholastic Bowl; Speech Tm; Teachers Aide; Rep Stu Cncl.

VOGT, GRETCHEN A; Sequoyah Claremore HS; Claremore, OK; (1); CAP; FCA; Quiz Bowl; Band; Mrchg Band; Pep Band; Sftbl; Var Trk; Swimming; Trk Natls In Trk & Field; Diving; OU; Tchr.

VOGT, KIM N; Checotah HS; Checotah, OK; (2); Church Yth Grp; Debate Tm; FBLA; Speech Tm; SADD; Teachers Aide; Acpl Chr; Chorus; Church Choir; Rep Frsh Cls; Kiwanis Awd; OK Bapt Univ; Ed.

VOGT, MICHAEL; Okarche HS; Okarche, OK; (4); Am Leg Boys St; Letterman Clb; Natl Beta Clb; Quiz Bowl; Pres Sr Cls; Var Bsktbl; NHS; Pres Acad Fit Awd; Church Yth Grp; Natl Yng Ldrs Conf Wshngtn DC; OK U; Metrlgy.

VOGT, RACHEL E; Sequoyah Claremore HS; Claremore, OK; (2); 1/110; CAP; FCA; FBLA; Quiz Bowl; Mrchg Band; Rep Soph Cls; Rep Stu Cncl; Var Trk; High Hon Roll; NHS; Courage Awd; Toured Nationally With Prof Dance Co; Enrolled In Hnr Classes; USAF Acad; Math; Prof Pilot.

VOGT, WILLIAM R; Okarche HS; Okarche, OK; (3); Church Yth Grp; Cmnty Wkr; Letterman Clb; Natl Beta Clb; Quiz Bowl; Scholastic Bowl; School Musical; Bsktbl; High Hon Roll; NHS; Red Headed League; Field Marshal; OK ST; Civil Engr.

VOLBERDING, BETH M; Union Intermediate HS; Tulsa, OK; (2); Church Yth Grp; Cmnty Wkr; Red Cross Aide; Band; Mrchg Band; Orch; Swmmng; High Hon Roll; Jr NHS; NHS; All Dist Band Cncrt.

VOLKMANN, RONY; Binger-Oney HS; Fort Cobb, OK; (4); 1/24; Church Yth Grp; 4-H; Pres Natl Beta Clb; Rptr Natl FFA Org; Pep Clb; Capt Scholastic Bowl; Yrbk; High Hon Roll; NHS; Pres Schlr; Concurrent Enrollment; OK ST U; Biochem.

VOLLAN, LISA; Panama HS; Bokoshe, OK; (3); 16/60; HOSA Treas; Upwrd Bnd Math Sci Pgm; OK ST U; Vet.

VOLLBRECHT, JESSICA L; Edmond North HS; Edmond, OK; (2); 202/420; Church Yth Grp; Dance Clb; Drama Clb; FCA; Key Clb; Office Aide; Spanish Clb; SADD; Variety Show; Rep Frsh Cls; Musical Thtr Grp Encore 4 Yrs; Dance 6 Yrs; Outside Of Schl Tnns/Bsktbl/Sftbl/Swmmng; Washington & Lee.

VOLLIN, MELISSA; Fargo Schl; Fargo, OK; (3); FCA; FHA; Ofcr Jr Cls; Ofcr Stu Cncl; Bsktbl; Chrldng; Sftbl; Cit Awd; Hon Roll; NHS; Hnrs Wrtng Clsses; Inst Chldrns Lit; Quartz Mtn Arts Inst; OK ST Univ; Chld Psychtry.

VOLLMER, AARON; Mustang HS; Mustang, OK; (2); 69/403; Church Yth Grp; Church Choir; JV Bsbl; Hon Roll; NHS.

VOLLMER, RICHARD A; Mustang HS; Mustang, OK; (2); 69/403; Church Yth Grp; JV Bsbl; High Hon Roll; NHS.

VONMOSS, AMY N; Miami Sr HS; Miami, OK; (3); Church Yth Grp; Cmnty Wkr; FHA; Band; Drm Mjr(t); Mrchg Band; Pep Band; Hon Roll; Jr NHS; NHS; NEO; Bus.

VON RAESFELD, TIMOTHY J; Eldorado Schl; Eldorado, OK; (1); Rep Church Yth Grp; 4-H; FHA; Pep Clb; Quiz Bowl; Chorus; School Play; Pres Frsh Cls; Var Bsbl; Var Bsktbl.

VON TUNGELN, CHAD S; Putnam City West HS; Bethany, OK; (3); Church Yth Grp; Cmnty Wkr; DECA; FCA; Letterman Clb; Spanish Clb; Rep Stu Cncl; Var Bsbl; JV Bsktbl; Var Ftbl; PEAK-GATE; Security-St Stu Cncl Convention Voted Best Of West; Attnd Ldrshp Retreats; US Marshall.

VORDERLANDWEHR, ANN M; Kingfisher HS; Kingfisher, OK; (2); Church Yth Grp; Computer Clb; Drama Clb; 4-H; Girl Scts; Spanish Clb; Speech Tm; Church Choir; School Play; Stage Crew; SW OK St Univ; Comp.

VORONOV, ROMAN S; West Middle HS; Norman, OK; (2); English Clb; Var JV Swmmng; Hon Roll; Princeton; Engrng.

VOSS, LINDSAY; Chisholm Sr HS; Goltry, OK; (2); 1/90; Church Yth Grp; HOBY; Spanish Clb; Chorus; Crs Cntry; Sftbl; Trk; High Hon Roll; Hon Roll; NHS; OK ST U; Vet.

VOTH, DANIEL; Kremlin Jr Sr HS; Kremlin, OK; (3); 1/19; Church Yth Grp; FCA; Quiz Bowl; Band; Jazz Band; Pep Band; Var Bsktbl; High Hon Roll; NHS; Val; OK U; Med.

VOTH, HOLLIE; Fairview HS; Orienta, OK; (3); Church Yth Grp; FCA; Natl FFA Org; Band; Church Choir; Color Guard; Mrchg Band; Pep Band; Rptr Jr Cls; Ofcr Stu Cncl; John Brown U; Med.

VOYLES, CHRISTINE A; Tahlequah Sr HS; Tahlequah, OK; (2); German Clb; Acpl Chr; Chorus; Var Chrldng; Var Golf; High Hon Roll; Hon Roll; NHS; OU; Sport Medication; Phy Thrpy.

VREELAND, RICHARD; Butner Schl; Wewoka, OK; (4); 1/22; Am Leg Boys St; Church Yth Grp; Teachers Aide; Phtg Yrbk; Pres Frsh Cls; Rep Soph Cls; Rep Jr Cls; Pres Sr Cls; Pres Stu Cncl; Pres NHS; OK ST U.

VROOME, KYLE M; Union Intermediate HS; Tulsa, OK; (1); 42/866; Church Yth Grp; German Clb; Swmmng; High Hon Roll; Jr NHS; NHS; Prfct Atten Awd; Wrkd W/Chldrn Smmr Camp; Lfgrd YWCA; Redskins Aqdc Allnc Swmmng Team Out Of Schl Team; Harvard Univ; Pre-Med.

VU, TRUONG D; Mustang HS; Yukon, OK; (2); Key Clb; Math Clb; Science Clb; SADD; Hon Roll.

WACKERLY, BRANDON A; Edmond Memorial HS; Edmond, OK; (3); Church Yth Grp; Debate Tm; FCA; Office Aide; Spanish Clb; Church Choir; Var Golf; NM ST U; Prof Golf Mgmt.

WADDELL, CASSIE; Deer Creek-Lamont Jr Sr HS; Lamont, OK; (4); 3/15; Am Leg Aux Girls St; Church Yth Grp; Cmnty Wkr; FCA; 4-H; Chorus; School Play; Sec Sr Cls; Sftbl; NHS; Amer Legion Aux; Hosp Vlntr 4 Yrs; Mission Trip Costa Rica; Northern OK Coll; Phys Thrpy.

WADDELL, CHRISTOPHER R; Empire Schl; Sayre, OK; (4); 8/35; Cmnty Wkr; FBLA; Office Aide; Spanish Clb; School Musical; Phtg Yrbk; Pres Sr Cls; Rep Stu Cncl; Hon Roll; Ntl Merit Ltr; UCO Mind Games Edmond; Career Dev Mon Brochure; Arch.

WADDLE, DYLAN; Westmoore HS; Oklahoma City, OK; (4); 129/610; Church Yth Grp; FBLA; Ftbl; Tennis; Wt Lftg; Cit Awd; ST FBLA Ec 1st Pl; Oklahoma City Univ; Corp Atty.

WADDLE, MYNDE; Coweta HS; Coweta, OK; (4); 18/152; Cmnty Wkr; FCA; FBLA; SADD; Nwsp; Mgr Yrbk; Rep Sr Cls; Rep Stu Cncl; Golf; Cit Awd; All Conf Golf 94; Stu Of Month 92 & 95; USBEA; U Of OK; Bus/Acctng.

WADE, AMBER M; B T Washington HS; Tulsa, OK; (2); Cmnty Wkr; French Clb; Chorus; Drm Mjr(t); Swing Chorus; NHS; Pre-Med.

WADE JR, BOBBY; Fox Sr HS; Tussy, OK; (2); Chess Clb; FCA; FHA; VICA; Ofcr Bsbl; Ftbl; Mgr(s); Score Keeper; Trk; Wt Lftg; Auto Mechanic.

WADE, BRANDON S; Ringling HS; Ringling, OK; (2); Church Yth Grp; FCA; Treas Natl FFA Org; Ofcr Bsbl; Bsktbl; Ftbl.

WADE, BRIAN T; Empire Schl; Duncan, OK; (1); Church Yth Grp; FCA; Key Clb; Letterman Clb; Bsktbl; Trk; Gov Hon Prg Awd; Hon Roll; Pres Acad Fit Awd; USAF Acad; Pilot.

WADE, CARISSA; Fox Sr HS; Tussy, OK; (3); FCA; FHA; Natl FFA Org; Pep Clb; Color Guard; Flag Corp; Rep Stu Cncl; Sftbl; High Hon Roll; Hon Roll.

WADE, CRAIG A; Washington HS; Washington, OK; (3); Church Yth Grp; Cmnty Wkr; FCA; Spanish Clb; JV Var Bsbl.

WADE, ERIC R; B T Washington HS; Tulsa, OK; (4); 19/264; French Clb; Rep Stu Cncl; NHS; Ntl Merit SF; Acad Team; Sooner St Judo Games Silver Medal; All St Judo Games Silver Medal; MIT; Elec Engr.

WADE, ERICA N; Muskogee HS; Muskogee, OK; (2); Cmnty Wkr; Computer Clb; GAA; Hosp Aide; SADD; Nwsp; Hon Roll; Jr NHS; NHS; TX A&M; Obsttrcn/Cmptr Sci.

WADE, JAMES; Westmoore HS; Oklahoma City, OK; (4); 85/610; Church Yth Grp; VP FCA; Pres JA; JCL; Latin Clb; Yrbk; Rep Frsh Cls; Rep Soph Cls; Rep Sr Cls; Rep Stu Cncl; OK ST U; Bus.

WADE IV, JOHNNIE M; Webster HS; Tulsa, OK; (1); Church Yth Grp; Bsktbl; Wt Lftg; High Hon Roll; Hon Roll; CO Univ.

WADE, LIZ; Elk City HS; Elk City, OK; (4); 1/141; Am Leg Aux Girls St; VP Computer Clb; Model UN; Capt Scholastic Bowl; Pres SADD; Pres NHS; Val; OK All St Orch 1st Chr Oboist 2xs; U OK; Engrng.

WADE, NEIL A; B T Washington HS; Tulsa, OK; (2); Spanish Clb; Ofcr Soph Cls; Swmmng; Trk; High Hon Roll; Jr NHS; NHS; AK Chap Kudos; Saxophone; Arch Engrng.

WADE, TORI; Ringling HS; Ringling, OK; (3); 9/37; Church Yth Grp; FCA; GAA; Varsity Clb; Band; Color Guard; Flag Corp; Mrchg Band; Rep Frsh Cls; Rep Soph Cls; SOSU; Nursng.

WADLEY, KRISTA; Mc Alester HS; Mcalester, OK; (3); 5/215; Am Leg Aux Girls St; Church Yth Grp; French Clb; Sec Stu Cncl; Var Chrldng; JV Sftbl; High Hon Roll; Hon Roll; All Amer Chrldr.

WADLEY, MICHAEL; Sapulpa Sr HS; Sapulpa, OK; (3); Boy Scts; Church Yth Grp; German Clb; ROTC; Band; Jazz Band; Mrchg Band; Hon Roll; NHS; Tns For Christ; Music.

WADLEY, NEAL D; Edmond Memorial HS; Edmond, OK; (3); 1/371; Church Yth Grp; FCA; Ofcr Stu Cncl; Ftbl; Trk; NHS; Pres Acad Fit Awd; Artst; Art.

WADLEY, RANCE; Paoli HS; Paoli, OK; (3); 1/25; VP Natl FFA Org; Pres Frsh Cls; Pres Soph Cls; Pres Jr Cls; Sec Stu Cncl; Var L Bsktbl; Var L Ftbl; High Hon Roll; NHS; Pres Acad Fit Awd; Bsktbl All-Trnmt Team; Phys Thrpy.

WADSWORTH, LESLI D; Union Intermediate HS; Tulsa, OK; (2); Church Yth Grp; Drama Clb; Spanish Clb; School Play; Stage Crew; Wt Lftg; Bus Ed Awd; Psychtry.

WADSWORTH, MELISSA; Fargo Schl; Fargo, OK; (2); Church Yth Grp; FCA; FHA; Ofcr Soph Cls; Ofcr Stu Cncl; Bsktbl; Chrldng; Sftbl; Cit Awd; DAR Awd; Amer Legion; Inst Childrens Lit Nom; Quartz Mtn Wrtng Schl; OK ST Univ; Psych/Psychlgy.

WAEGER, MISHELLE; Kingfisher HS; Kingfisher, OK; (4); 33/96; Church Yth Grp; Drama Clb; FCA; Rep Soph Cls; Pres Jr Cls; Ofcr Stu Cncl; Chrldng; Tennis; Cit Awd; Hon Roll; Univ Of Cntrl OK; Elem Ed.

WAFFORD, TERI S; Wilburton Sr HS; Wilburton, OK; (1); 10/90; Church Yth Grp; GAA; Bsktbl; Chrldng; Sftbl; Trk; High Hon Roll; Office Aide; Varsity Clb; Chorus; Masonic Lodge Awd.

WAGEMAN, AMANDA D; Pauls Valley HS; Pauls Valley, OK; (3); Art Clb; Scholastic Bowl; Spanish Clb; Chorus; Church Choir; School Musical; Phtg Yrbk; JV Capt Chrldng; High Hon Roll; Hon Roll; Photo Jrnlsm.

WAGENSELLER, JAMIE; Turpin Schl; Turpin, OK; (4); 4/43; VP Pres FHA; Band; Pep Band; Ed Nwsp; Golf; Sftbl; NHS; Prfct Atten Awd; OK Hnrs Scty; SW OK St Univ; Comp Sci.

WAGER, DAVID; Ft Cobb-Broxton HS; Anadarko, OK; (2); Boy Scts; FHA; Bsktbl; Prfct Atten Awd.

WAGGONER, DUSTIN V; Blackwell HS; Ponca City, OK; (2); 4-H; JV Bsbl; JV Ftbl; Blackwell FFA; Northern OK Coll.

WAGGONER, EMILY R; Sapulpa Sr HS; Sapulpa, OK; (3); Church Yth Grp; FCA; Teachers Aide; Band; Chorus; Jazz Band; Mrchg Band; Hon Roll; NHS; Music.

WAGGONER, ROBERT L; Chisholm Sr HS; Cherokee, OK; (1); Church Yth Grp; Natl FFA Org; Spanish Clb; Var Bsbl; Var Bsktbl; Var Ftbl; 4-H Awd; OK U; Law.

WAGGONER, SUE A; Pocola HS; Pocola, OK; (3); Boy Scts; Quiz Bowl; Chorus; Sftbl; NSU; Phy Thrpst.

WAGNER, ALICIA; Claremore Sr HS; Claremore, OK; (2); 1/273; Church Yth Grp; French Clb; Chorus; Church Choir; School Musical; JV Var Socr; High Hon Roll; NHS; Congrssnl Yth Ldshp Cncl Natl Schol.

WAGNER, AMY; Westmoore HS; Moore, OK; (3); 17/615; Church Yth Grp; English Clb; Office Aide; School Musical; Hon Roll; Jr NHS; NHS; 8 Yr Troupe Mem At Connies Schl Of Dance.

WAGNER, DENISE; Panama HS; Cameron, OK; (3); German Clb; GAA; Quiz Bowl; SADD; Pres Frsh Cls; VP Jr Cls; Bsktbl; Sftbl; High Hon Roll; NHS.

WAGNER, IDASHLA K; Stillwater Sr HS; Stillwater, OK; (2); Boy Scts; CAP; Latin Clb; Natl Beta Clb; Quiz Bowl; Scholastic Bowl; Socr; High Hon Roll; Pres Acad Fit Awd; Washington U; Medicine.

WAGNER, JENNIFER; Carl Albert HS; Oklahoma City, OK; (4); 1/10; Am Leg Aux Girls St; Key Clb; Scholastic Bowl; Chorus; School Musical; Chorus; School Musical; Pres Sec Stu Cncl; Chrldng; Socr; Channel 5 Ldr Tomorrow; Natl Jr High/St Cheer Chmpns; OSU; Pblc Rltns.

WAGNER, JOSEPH; Nathan Hale HS; Tulsa, OK; (4); 4/203; English Clb; French Clb; Quiz Bowl; Capt Scholastic Bowl; Science Clb; Varsity Clb; Ftbl; Var Tennis; High Hon Roll; Hon Roll; Eclgy Club VP; U Of OK; Elec Engr.

WAGNER, JULIA S; Bartlesville Mid HS; Bartlesville, OK; (2); Church Yth Grp; Girl Scts; Hosp Aide; Service Clb; Teachers Aide; Varsity Clb; Church Choir; JV Bsktbl; JV Var Socr.

WAGNER, KATIE; Bishop Kelley HS; Tulsa, OK; (1); Church Yth Grp; FCA; Pep Clb; Service Clb; Crs Cntry; Trk; High Hon Roll; Jr NHS.

WAGNER, KRISTEN; Edmond North HS; Edmond, OK; (3); 67/367; Church Yth Grp; VP French Clb; Mu Alpha Theta; SADD; Band; NHS; HS Mascot; Stu Ath Trainer; Ed.

WAGNER, LAURA; Muskogee HS; Muskogee, OK; (3); 13/375; Church Yth Grp; Cmnty Wkr; FCA; JCL; Latin Clb; Pep Clb; Ofcr Stu Cncl; Chrldng; Socr; Tennis; U Of OK; Dntl.

WAGNER, MICHELE R; Stillwater Jr HS; Stillwater, OK; (1); Church Yth Grp; FCA; Bsktbl; Hon Roll; RAP; PT/ATH Trainer.

WAGNER, ROB D; Duncan HS; Duncan, OK; (3); Church Yth Grp; French Clb; Red Cross Aide; Band; Jazz Band; Mrchg Band; Pep Band; Stage Crew; Swing Chorus; Pres Sr Cls; Songwriter; Copyright On 2 Original Compositions; OU; Music; Yth Minister.

WAGNER, SELENA M; Moore HS; Moore, OK; (4); 59/500; FBLA; Office Aide; Rptr Nwsp; Rptr Yrbk; Rep Stu Cncl; NHS; Jr Escort; U Of Cntrl OK; Bus.

WAGNER, TAMARA A; B T Washington HS; Tulsa, OK; (4); 96/264; Church Yth Grp; Cmnty Wkr; Debate Tm; French Clb; Latin Clb; Letterman Clb; Red Cross Aide; Speech Tm; Teachers Aide; Varsity Clb; Var Ltrmn; Tm Capt; Vol Wrk; All St Soccer All Dist, MVP, Most Val Defndr; Soccer Schlrshp; William Wood U; Sprts Med.

WAGNON, BRIAN M; Tahlequah Sr HS; Hulbert, OK; (3); Church Yth Grp; Quiz Bowl; Chorus; Church Choir; Ofcr Stu Cncl; High Hon Roll; Jr NHS; NHS; Pres Acad Fit Awd; Northeastern ST U; Wldlf Mgmnt.

WAGON, JOSHUA L; Allen HS; Allen, OK; (2); Church Yth Grp; Ofcr Stu Cncl; Ftbl; Animal Sci.

WAGONER, LACY; Broken Arrow Sr HS; Broken Arrow, OK; (2); Church Yth Grp; German Clb; GAA; Office Aide; Sftbl; Hon Roll; Jr NHS; Cmptr Prgmng; NSU; Cmptr Prgmng/Anlyst.

WAGONER, LAURA R; Madill HS; Madill, OK; (2); Church Yth Grp; FCA; 4-H; FBLA; FHA; SADD; Var Bsktbl; JV Var Trk; Hon Roll; Phy Thrpst.

WAGONER, NANCI; Guthrie Sr HS; Guthrie, OK; (2); Chorus; Var Chrldng; Bus.

WAHEM, CAROLYN; Stillwater Sr HS; Stillwater, OK; (3); Am Leg Aux Girls St; Debate Tm; Mu Alpha Theta; Natl Beta Clb; NFL; Nwsp; Tennis; NHS; Drama Clb; Key Clb; Var Schlr.

WAHL, BRIAN; Fairview HS; Fairview, OK; (2); Church Yth Grp; Cmnty Wkr; FCA; Letterman Clb; Natl FFA Org; Varsity Clb; Band; Chorus; Mrchg Band; Pep Band; Fresh & Soph Stu Mon.

WAHLGREN, LUKE L; Oklahoma Bible Acad; Enid, OK; (3); 8/35; Church Yth Grp; Cmnty Wkr; FCA; 4-H; Scholastic Bowl; Chorus; School Musical; L Trk; Cit Awd; 4-H Awd; Xerox Awd; Acad Tm; Odessey Of Mind; Bus Admin.

WAHPEKECHE, RION D; Stillwater Sr HS; Stillwater, OK; (2); 150/350; Spanish Clb; Socr; Wt Lftg; Hon Roll; Pres Acad Fit Awd; Stdnt Rep 95-Indian Ed Title IX; Sjpec Olympcs Vol; Wrtng; Art; Rdng; Marine Bio.

WAHWEAH, ANNA L; El Reno Sr HS; El Reno, OK; (4); 43/167; FCA; FHA; Math Clb; Science Clb; Teachers Aide; VICA; Chrldng; Tennis; Cit Awd; Hon Roll; OK ST U; Mrktng.

WAIBEL, DACIA; Chisholm Sr HS; Enid, OK; (3); Church Yth Grp; Cmnty Wkr; French Clb; FHA; GAA; Scholastic Bowl; Spanish Clb; Band; Church Choir; Color Guard; Chrch Choir; All-Amer Music Fstvl 1st Pl.

WAID, ASHLEY BROOKE; Skiatook HS; Skiatook, OK; (2); Church Yth Grp; Cmnty Wkr; FCA; Key Clb; Drill Tm; School Play; Chrldng; Score Keeper; Hon Roll; NHS; OU; Bus/Csmtlgy.

WAINGANKAR, NEERA; Shawnee Sr HS; Shawnee, OK; (4); 3/262; Hosp Aide; Pep Clb; Treas Frsh Cls; Treas Jr Cls; Treas Sr Cls; Ofcr Stu Cncl; Var Tennis; VP NHS; Big Brothers, Big Sisters Jr Brd; SHOCK Co Chrmn.

WAINGANKAR, NIKHIL; Shawnee Sr HS; Shawnee, OK; (1); Hosp Aide; Quiz Bowl; Scholastic Bowl; Spanish Clb; JV Bsktbl; Var Tennis; High Hon Roll; Med Field.

WAITS, JUSTIN; Bartlesville Mid HS; Bartlesville, OK; (2); 42/481; Boy Scts; Church Yth Grp; French Clb; Spanish Clb; Band; Mrchg Band; Phtg Yrbk; High Hon Roll; Hon Roll; Jr NHS; Vlntr With Habitat For Hmnty.

WAKEFIELD, TERRANCE; Edmond North HS; Edmond, OK; (3); Church Yth Grp; FCA; Office Aide; SADD; Church Choir; Rep Stu Cncl; Var Bsktbl; Var Trk; Cntrl Rgn Teen Treas; 4 Time All ST Track; 2 Time ST Chmpn Class 5a Track.

WAKELEE, MEGANN; Choctaw HS; Midwest City, OK; (4); 34/305; Cmnty Wkr; Key Clb; Library Aide; Quiz Bowl; Scholastic Bowl; Yrbk; Tennis; High Hon Roll; Hon Roll; Jr NHS; Natl Schlr.

WAKLEY, BRIAN; Carney Schl; Chandler, OK; (2); Chess Clb; Church Yth Grp; Math Clb; Math Tm; Mu Alpha Theta; Natl FFA Org; Pres Jr Cls; Pres Stu Cncl; Bsktbl; Hon Roll.

WALCUTT, TIFFANY; Hilldale HS; Muskogee, OK; (1); German Clb; Hosp Aide; Band; Mrchg Band; Hon Roll; OK ST U; Med.

WALDEN, GINGER; Choctaw Jr HS; Choctaw, OK; (1); FCA; Quiz Bowl; Band; NHS; Prfct Atten Awd; Val.

WALDEN, JON W; Muskogee HS; Muskogee, OK; (4); 35/303; JCL; Key Clb; Latin Clb; Office Aide; Science Clb; Band; Jazz Band; Mrchg Band; Pep Band; Stage Crew; OK Hn Soc; Dist Hnr Band; Cum Laude Boston Russell Jazz Awd; Purdue Univ; Pre Vet/Engr.

WALDEN, MELISSIA; Blanchard Jr Sr HS; Blanchard, OK; (4); 8/73; Computer Clb; FHA; Mu Alpha Theta; Pep Clb; Spanish Clb; Rptr Sr Cls; Hon Roll; NHS; Pres Acad Fit Awd; FHA Homcmng Sweethrt, Ofcr; Clss Ofcr 95-96; U Of OK; Finance.

WALDO, JENNIFER L; Stillwater Sr HS; Stillwater, OK; (2); Church Yth Grp; FCA; Latin Clb; JV Bsktbl; Hon Roll; EEC; Native Amer Clb Sec; OSU; Law; Math.

WALDRON, JENIFER R; Parker Mid HS; Mcalester, OK; (3); Art Clb; Church Yth Grp; DECA; Drama Clb; FCA; French Clb; Pep Clb; SADD; Acpl Chr; Chorus; Natl Sci Merit Awd; SE OK St Col; RN.

WALDROOP, COREY; Watts HS; Watts, OK; (1); Natl FFA Org; Hon Roll; U AR.

WALDROOP, MICAH B; Tahlequah Sr HS; Tahlequah, OK; (4); Boy Scts; Church Yth Grp; Acpl Chr; Chorus; Hon Roll; Harding Univ.

WALDROP, MATTHEW; Shawnee Sr HS; Shawnee, OK; (2); 20/325; Church Yth Grp; Hon Roll; NHS; Guitar; Law.

WALKER, AARON K; Deer Creek HS; Edmond, OK; (3); 22/96; Church Yth Grp; FCA; FBLA; Science Clb; Spanish Clb; Treas Jr Cls; Var Bsktbl; Var Golf; Hon Roll; NHS; OK Ctr For Advancement Of Sci & Tech Awd; OK ST.

WALKER, AJA; Little Axe Sr HS; Newalla, OK; (3); 1/100; HOBY; Quiz Bowl; Scholastic Bowl; Band; Rep Frsh Cls; VP Soph Cls; VP Stu Cncl; JV Crs Cntry; Var Ftbl; Var Trk; Comp Prog.

WALKER, ALYSSA; Freedom Schl; Freedom, OK; (3); 1/6; FCA; HOBY; Natl FFA Org; Yrbk; VP Jr Cls; Var Capt Bsktbl; Var Capt Chrldng; High Hon Roll; Prfct Atten Awd; Val; OK ST U; Pediatrics.

WALKER, AMY; Chickasha Jr HS; Chickasha, OK; (1); Church Yth Grp; FCA; Spanish Clb; Church Choir; JV Bsktbl; Var Crs Cntry; Intrml Sftbl; JV Vllybl; Gov Hon Prg Awd; Jr NHS; BYU.

WALKER, ANNE; Central HS; Tulsa, OK; (2); ROTC; Drill Tm; Ofcr Soph Cls; Hon Roll; NHS.

WALKER, BECKY; Panola HS; Red Oak, OK; (3); 2/20; Natl FFA Org; Speech Tm; Sftbl; Hon Roll; NHS; Church Yth Grp; 4-H; Chorus; Yrbk; Pres Frsh Cls; ST FFA Proficency Awd; Eastern OK ST Coll; Ag Comm.

WALKER, BETH A; Union Intermediate HS; Tulsa, OK; (2); 63/800; Band; Church Choir; Mrchg Band; High Hon Roll; NHS; Music.

WALKER, BILLY; Central HS; Tulsa, OK; (3); 19/175; Hon Roll; NHS; Med.

WALKER, BRANDI A; Oklahoma Sch Of Science & Math; Madill, OK; (4); Church Yth Grp; Treas Girl Scts; Speech Tm; Chorus; Mrchg Band; Orch; NHS; Ntl Merit SF; Pres Schlr; OK Yth Advsry Brd Cath Chrch; Sthrn Methdst U; Bio-Chem.

WALKER, CARLEE; Freedom Schl; Freedom, OK; (2); Church Yth Grp; FCA; GAA; Natl FFA Org; Pep Clb; VP Frsh Cls; Sec Soph Cls; Bsktbl; Chrldng; Hon Roll; OK ST U; Ed.

WALKER, CARRIE; Fox Sr HS; Fox, OK; (2); 1/27; Natl FFA Org; Ofcr Stu Cncl; Bsktbl; Hon Roll; Ntl Merit Ltr; FFA Lvstck Jdng Tm; Prlmntry Offc; Natl Hnr Roll; Frshmn Grad Bndctn.

WALKER, CARY; White Oak Jr-Sr HS; Vinita, OK; (4); 1/23; Cmnty Wkr; Math Tm; Quiz Bowl; Red Cross Aide; Ed Nwsp; Phtg Yrbk; Rep Stu Cncl; Intrml Mgr(s); High Hon Roll; OK Hnr Roll Soc; IA Testing Schl Wd Top Scorer; Enrlld Rogers ST Coll; Northeastern ST U; Acctng.

WALKER, CASEY; Hilldale HS; Muskogee, OK; (2); 4/125; Hist Stu Cncl; Bsktbl; Powder Puff Ftbl; Sftbl; High Hon Roll; All Conf Bsktbl, Plyr Of Yr 96; All Conf Fast Pitch Sftbl.

WALKER, CASEY E; Bartlesville Sr HS; Bartlesville, OK; (4); Church Yth Grp; Cmnty Wkr; Crs Cntry; Socr; Camping; Rock Climbing In OK & UT; OK ST Univ; Engrng; Chem.

WALKER, CASI J; Crescent Schl; Crescent, OK; (1); Natl FFA Org; Band; School Play; Pres Frsh Cls; Chrldng; Sftbl; Trk; Hon Roll; NHS; Prfct Atten Awd; OK ST U; Brdcstng.

WALKER, COREY; Millwood HS; Oklahoma City, OK; (4); Church Yth Grp; ROTC; Band; Jazz Band; Mrchg Band; Pep Band; School Play; Cit Awd; Prfct Atten Awd; Cntrl OK; Bus Mgmt.

WALKER, CRAIG T; Del City HS; Del City, OK; (3); 58/518; Cmnty Wkr; French Clb; Library Aide; Scholastic Bowl; SADD; Treas Jr Cls; Swmmng; Cit Awd; Jr NHS; NHS; Knox Coll; Bio.

WALKER, DANIEL J; Union Sr HS; Tulsa, OK; (4); 5/669; Key Clb; Band; Mrchg Band; School Musical; High Hon Roll; NHS; Pres Acad Fit Awd; Grmn Hnr Soc; Natl Cmmnd Schlr; Bnd Cncl; U OK; Elect Engrng.

WALKER, DUSTIN C; Putnam City North HS; Oklahoma City, OK; (3); 31/464; Letterman Clb; Spanish Clb; SADD; Orch; JV Bsbl; Var L Ftbl; Var Wrstlng; Cit Awd; High Hon Roll; Jr NHS; Whos Who HS Sports 94-96; Outstdng Wrestler; Aeronautical Or Chem Engrng.

WALKER, EDITH; Fox Sr HS; Wilson, OK; (4); 1/29; Pres Sec Natl FFA Org; Quiz Bowl; Pres Frsh Cls; Rep Soph Cls; Sec Jr Cls; Sec Sr Cls; Treas Stu Cncl; Trk; NHS; Val; Murray ST Coll; Ag.

WALKER, FARA D; Mc Alester HS; Krebs, OK; (4); 15/212; Pep Clb; Science Clb; Spanish Clb; Ofcr Stu Cncl; Sftbl; Tennis; Hon Roll; NHS; U Of OK; Pre Med.

WALKER, GLEN; Welch Jr Sr HS; Welch, OK; (3); Am Leg Boys St; Church Yth Grp; FCA; Natl FFA Org; Quiz Bowl; Scholastic Bowl; Speech Tm; VICA; Rep Stu Cncl; JV Bsktbl; 1st Pl NEO Sci Bwl Regl; 2nd Pl Regl Sci Fair; 1st Pl Regl Tech Prblm Solvng Awd; Mech Engrng.

WALKER, JACK D; Boynton Schl; Boynton, OK; (3); Boy Scts; Church Yth Grp; Cmnty Wkr; 4-H; FHA; JA; Natl FFA Org; Science Clb; Band; Church Choir; Northeastern ST U; Ftbl/Cmp Op.

WALKER, JAMIE; Midwest City HS; Midwest City, OK; (3); 67/384; Church Yth Grp; Cmnty Wkr; Drama Clb; Key Clb; Band; Chorus; Church Choir; Mrchg Band; School Musical; Nwsp; Prss Clb VP; U OK; Jrnlsm.

WALKER, JAMIE L; Newcastle HS; Newcastle, OK; (2); 4/90; Natl FFA Org; Treas Soph Cls; Hon Roll; NHS; OK St Univ; Equine Med.

WALKER, JANUARY B; Duncan HS; Duncan, OK; (1); Church Yth Grp; GAA; Letterman Clb; SADD; Teachers Aide; Chorus; Variety Show; Var Chrldng; Score Keeper; JV Tennis; Frosh Ftbl Hmecmng Queen Canidate; Jolly Jills Soc Club; OK Hnr Soc; U Of FL; Child Psychlgst.

WALKER, JASON; Vanoss Schl; Ada, OK; (3); 1/40; Church Yth Grp; FCA; FBLA; Office Aide; Quiz Bowl; Scholastic Bowl; Pres Frsh Cls; Treas Soph Cls; Treas Jr Cls; Rep Stu Cncl; OK U; FBI.

WALKER, JASON W; Harrah HS; Harrah, OK; (2); 41/153; Bsktbl; Hon Roll; Yth In Action Bsktbl; AAU Bsktbl; Guitar; OSU; CPA.

WALKER, JENNIFER J; Putnam City North HS; Oklahoma City, OK; (4); Church Yth Grp; French Clb; JCL; Latin Clb; Office Aide; Science Clb; SADD; Teachers Aide; Hon Roll; Envrmntl Club; 3-D; U Of OK; Bio/Pre Med.

WALKER, JENNIFER K; Mc Alester HS; Durant, OK; (3); Church Yth Grp; Spanish Clb; Chorus; Church Choir.

WALKER, JESSIE L; Boise City HS; Kenton, OK; (1); Letterman Clb; Band; JV Ftbl; L Trk; Hon Roll; Univ Of CA; Nuclear Engrng.

WALKER, JONATHAN B; Oklahoma Christian Schl; Edmond, OK; (2); 2/50; Church Yth Grp; Speech Tm; Hon Roll; OK Chrstn U; Med.

WALKER, JUSTIN S; Muskogee HS; Muskogee, OK; (4); 78/303; Pres Computer Clb; French Clb; Office Aide; SADD; Temple Yth Grp; Hon Roll; Southwestern Assembly God; Cnsl.

WALKER, KATHRYN V; Union Intermediate HS; Broken Arrow, OK; (2); Trk; Hon Roll; Perf Arts.

WALKER, KORRYN M; Westmoore HS; Oklahoma City, OK; (1); Church Yth Grp; Cmnty Wkr; Girl Scts; Teachers Aide; Rep Frsh Cls; Rep Stu Cncl; Mgr(s); Tennis; Lib Rdr Ldr; Morgan ST U.

WALKER, KRYSTAL; Okemah HS; Henryetta, OK; (3); 10/68; Am Leg Aux Girls St; Natl Beta Clb; Science Clb; SADD; Nwsp; Yrbk; Ofcr Stu Cncl; Chrldng; Trk; NHS; OK Univ.

WALKER, LAWRESSE N; John Marshall HS; Oklahoma City, OK; (4); #11 in class; Cmnty Wkr; FBLA; HOBY; Spanish Clb; Teachers Aide; School Play; Trk; Jr NHS; NHS; Ntl Merit Ltr; Miss Talented Teen OK 94-95; Miss Jr Miss 94-95; Frosh Ftbl Homcmng Qn; OK City Univ; Corporate Commnc.

WALKER, LE ANN; Kingston HS; Kingston, OK; (2); Band; JV Bsktbl; Hon Roll; East Cntrl; Psych.

WALKER, MAC KENZIE B; Central Jr HS; Lawton, OK; (1); JA; Pep Clb; Chorus; Rep Stu Cncl; Ofcr Bsbl; Var Bsktbl; Var Sftbl; Var Tennis; Var Vllybl; Hon Roll; Engrng Camp Nom; Super Hosp Vol; Stu Of The Week & Month Several Times; UCLA.

WALKER, MISTI D; Durnat HS; Durant, OK; (2); Church Yth Grp; Drama Clb; Key Clb; Tennis; Trk; High Hon Roll; Hon Roll; OK ST On Soc.

WALKER, OZ; B T Washington HS; Tulsa, OK; (4); 160/264; Cmnty Wkr; ROTC; Teachers Aide; Color Guard; Drill Tm; Pep Band; Ftbl; Powder Puff Ftbl; Score Keeper; Wt Lftg; Vet Of Foreign War Awd; Hampton Univ; Physician Therapy.

WALKER, SHELLEY; Wanette HS; Wanette, OK; (4); 3/20; Sec FHA; Quiz Bowl; Teachers Aide; Phtg Yrbk; Ofcr Jr Cls; Rptr Stu Cncl; Capt Bsktbl; Var Sftbl; Hon Roll; Pres NHS; Pres Schol; All-Star Bsktbll; East Central Univ.

WALKER, SHELLY; Stratford Schl; Stratford, OK; (4); Church Yth Grp; FHA; HOBY; Rptr Ofcr Natl FFA Org; Spanish Clb; Chorus; Yrbk; Hon Roll; FBLA; Fd Chldrn Aftr OK City Bmbmng Vol; Wrkhrs Awd; Lndscpng.

WALKER, SHILOH L; Stillwater Sr HS; Stillwater, OK; (2); Boy Scts; Church Yth Grp; Latin Clb; High Hon Roll; Hon Roll; Arch.

WALKER, STEPHANIE L; Bishop Kelley HS; Tulsa, OK; (2); Cmnty Wkr; Hosp Aide; Pep Clb; Hon Roll; Anchor Clb; Med.

WALKER, TAMMI M; B T Washington HS; Tulsa, OK; (4); 8/264; Church Yth Grp; Cmnty Wkr; Drama Clb; Hosp Aide; Spanish Clb; Teachers Aide; School Musical; High Hon Roll; Hon Roll; NHS; Assist Dir Chrch Drama Troupe; Oral Roberts U; Med.

WALKER, TIMOTHY A; Union Sr HS; Tulsa, OK; (3); 103/741; Key Clb; Math Clb; Spanish Clb; Ed Nwsp; Ofcr Stu Cncl; Crs Cntry; Trk; NHS; Prfct Atten Awd; Pres Schlr; Harvard; Natl Scrty Cncl.

WALKER, WESLEY; Stigler HS; Stigler, OK; (2); Bsktbl; Ftbl; Wt Lftg; Hon Roll; Fishing; Camping.

WALKER, WILLIAM; Comanche HS; Comanche, OK; (2); Scholastic Bowl; SADD; Teachers Aide; Band; Chorus; Church Choir; Jazz Band; Mrchg Band; Ofcr Frsh Cls; NHS; Super Ratngs At St Cont For Instrumntl & Vocl Sols; All-Regn Chor; All-Regn Band; IAJA Awd Pin Perfmnc; Southeastern OK ST U; Musc Ed.

WALKINGSTICK, SARA; Shawnee Sr HS; Shawnee, OK; (4); Church Yth Grp; Drama Clb; Office Aide; Band; Church Choir; Mrchg Band; Orch; School Play; Chrldng; Ftbl; E Cntrl U; Ath Trng.

WALKUP, MATTHEW; Hilldale HS; Muskogee, OK; (2); Church Yth Grp; Spanish Clb; Band; Mrchg Band; NHS; Ryl Rngrs; Northeastern ST U; Vet.

WALL, BECKIE M; Nathan Hale HS; Tulsa, OK; (3); Chorus; Hon Roll; Psych.

WALL, BRYAN; Keota Schl; Keota, OK; (4); 18/36; Am Leg Boys St; Debate Tm; NFL; Quiz Bowl; Speech Tm; Teachers Aide; School Play; Rptr Nwsp; Ed Yrbk; French Hon Soc; U OK; Jrnlsm.

WALL, JENNIFER J; John Marshall HS; Oklahoma City, OK; (3); 1/160; Church Yth Grp; Cmnty Wkr; German Clb; Office Aide; Swmmng; High Hon Roll; VP NHS; OSU; Eng.

WALL, LISA; Plainview HS; Ardmore, OK; (3); 5/86; Am Leg Aux Girls St; FCA; Girl Scts; Hosp Aide; Mu Alpha Theta; VP SADD; Rptr Jr Cls; Var Capt Chrldng; Trk; NHS; Teenage Crimestoppers Pres; Occptnl Thrpy.

WALL, NATHAN L; Enid Sr HS; Enid, OK; (4); Hon Roll; U Of OK; Chemistry.

WALL, RITA M; Dover Schl; Dover, OK; (1); GAA; Scholastic Bowl; SADD; Acpl Chr; Chorus; Rep Frsh Cls; Rep Stu Cncl; Var Bsktbl; Var Sftbl; High Hon Roll; OK Hnr Soc; Marine Bio.

WALLA, CHRISTOPHER; Mc Alester HS; Mcalester, OK; (4); 13/216; Am Leg Boys St; FCA; French Clb; Office Aide; Science Clb; Capt Bsbl; Bsktbl; Ftbl; French Hon Soc; High Hon Roll; Good Citizen Month; Med.

WALLACE, AMANDA; Yale Jr Sr HS; Jennings, OK; (2); 1/51; Natl Beta Clb; Sec Spanish Clb; Lit Mag; Cit Awd; High Hon Roll; Jr NHS; Gftd & Tlntd Pgm.

WALLACE, AMY; Tahlequah Sr HS; Tahlequah, OK; (4); 33/251; Am Leg Aux Girls St; Church Yth Grp; FCA; SADD; Chorus; L Var Crs Cntry; Var L Trk; Hon Roll; Jr NHS; Ntl Merit Ltr.

WALLACE, ASHLEY N; El Reno Sr HS; El Reno, OK; (2); 1/240; Church Yth Grp; Dance Clb; FCA; FHA; Rep Soph Cls; Pom Pon; High Hon Roll; Rnsnc Clb.

WALLACE, BRENDA; U S Grant HS; Oklahoma City, OK; (1); 4/418; Girl Scts; Office Aide; Pep Clb; ROTC; Acpl Chr; Church Choir.

WALLACE, CHRIS; Marietta HS; Marietta, OK; (2); Quiz Bowl; Ftbl; Hon Roll; Pres Acad Fit Awd; OSU; Cmptr Pgrmng.

WALLACE JR, GARY A; Moore HS; Oklahoma City, OK; (3); Am Leg Boys St; Boy Scts; CAP; Drama Clb; Band; Mrchg Band; School Musical; Air Force Acad.

WALLACE, JENNY; Jones HS; Jones, OK; (4); 19/51; Cmnty Wkr; FCA; GAA; Key Clb; Spanish Clb; Band; Mrchg Band; Yrbk; Lit Mag; Bsktbl; All-Amer Schlr; Southwestern OK ST Univ; Law.

WALLACE, LEIA M; Calumet Schl; Calumet, OK; (1); 1/43; Page OK ST Capitol; Acad Bowl Team Point Team Ldr.

WALLACE, RYAN A; Union Intermediate HS; Tulsa, OK; (2); CAP; Var L Swmmng; Ldrshp Citation; Military Order Of The Purple Heart; OK Wing Commanders Citation CAP; Pararescue; USAF Acad; Us Military.

WALLACE, SHAWN M; Union Sr HS; Broken Arrow, OK; (3); 20/769; Church Yth Grp; Spanish Clb; Band; Church Choir; Mrchg Band; Pep Band; High Hon Roll; Jr NHS; NHS; Spanish NHS; Optmst Clb Ortrcl Cont St Fnlst; Sccr; Trmpt Choir.

WALLACE, STACI; Cache HS; Cache, OK; (2); FCA; GAA; Hosp Aide; Natl Beta Clb; Scholastic Bowl; SADD; Teachers Aide; Band; Mrchg Band; JV Bsktbl; Med Explorers; Exec Gold Card; OK Hnr Soc; Medicine.

WALLACE, SUNNY N; B T Washington HS; Tulsa, OK; (3); Cmnty Wkr; French Clb; Pep Clb; Jazz Band; Orch; School Musical; Stage Crew; Ofcr Frsh Cls; Ofcr Soph Cls; Ofcr Jr Cls; Horseback Riding; 14 Yrs Dance; 12 Yrs Piano; Jrnlsm.

WALLACE, SUSAN M; Ada HS; Atwood, OK; (3); Church Yth Grp; FCA; Spanish Clb; Band; Mrchg Band.

WALLACE, TRACI L; Caney Jr Sr HS; Caddo, OK; (2); Church Yth Grp; FHA; Spanish Clb; Church Choir; Rptr Nwsp; Rptr Yrbk; Hon Roll; SOSU Upward Bound; Church Bell Choir; SOSU; Lab Tech/Phrmcst.

WALLACE, TRAVIS; Ada HS; Ada, OK; (3); 4/200; Church Yth Grp; FCA; French Clb; Band; Mrchg Band; Rep Stu Cncl; Capt Ftbl; Wt Lftg; High Hon Roll; Jr NHS.

WALLACE, WENDY; Heritage Hall Schl; Oklahoma City, OK; (4); Church Yth Grp; Cmnty Wkr; Letterman Clb; Pep Clb; Ed Lit Mag; Var L Fld Hcky; High Hon Roll; NHS; Ntl Merit Ltr; Spanish NHS; RYLA; NCTE Wrtng Awd; OU; Engl.

WALLEN, SAMANTHA; Wilburton Jr HS; Wilburton, OK; (1); Chorus; High Hon Roll; NHS.

WALLENBERG, GRANT M; Brink Jr HS; Oklahoma City, OK; (1); Hist Computer Clb; Office Aide; Ofcr Bsbl; High Hon Roll; Jr NHS; Cit Awd; Duzzy Dean Bsbl OK ST Championship Team Pitcher; Sci.

WALLENBERG, STACIE; Westmoore HS; Oklahoma City, OK; (4); French Clb; Library Aide; Chrldng; Hon Roll; Jr NHS; NHS; 4 Yr NCA All Amer Chrldr, St Chmpn Chrldng Squad; U OK; Zoology.

WALLER, BECKY; Shawnee Sr HS; Shawnee, OK; (4); 53/252; Hosp Aide; Latin Clb; Library Aide; Office Aide; Nwsp; High Hon Roll; NHS; Prfct Atten Awd; Tri-Hi-Y VP; Big Brthrs/Sisters Jr Brd Pres; OSU.

WALLER, COURTNEY D; Davis HS; Hennepin, OK; (1); FBLA; FHA; Spanish Clb; JV Chrldng; U Of OK; Law.

WALLER, TRISHA N; Putnam City HS; Warr Acres, OK; (2); NFL; Speech Tm; Stdnt To Stdnt; Explrs Pres; OU; Psych.

WALLING, KENNY R; Webster HS; Tulsa, OK; (3); 6/300; Boy Scts; Church Yth Grp; Quiz Bowl; Stage Crew; JV Bsktbl; Var Golf; High Hon Roll; Hon Roll; Jr NHS; NHS; Engrng.

WALLINGER, TAMARA L; Choctaw HS; Choctaw, OK; (3); 29/330; Treas Church Yth Grp; Treas German Clb; Band; Mrchg Band; Pep Band; School Musical; Var Tennis; Hon Roll; Jr NHS; Ltl Leag Score Kpr Bsktbl; Piano; OK ST; Engrng.

WALLIS, JENNIFER R; Warner HS; Warner, OK; (2); Spanish Clb; Church Choir; JV Sftbl; Warner Photo Clb; Warner United Meth Youth Pres.

WALLIS III, ROBERT A; Webbers Falls Schl; Webbers Falls, OK; (4); Natl FFA Org; Quiz Bowl; Scholastic Bowl; Teachers Aide; Bsktbl; Ftbl; Wt Lftg; High Hon Roll; Hon Roll; Ntl Merit Ltr; OK HS Hnr Scty; Connors St Col.

WALLIS, SARA R; Shawnee Sr HS; Shawnee, OK; (1); Church Yth Grp; FHA; Red Cross Aide; High Hon Roll; Hon Roll; OK Univ; Med.

WALLRAVEN, MISTI R; Guthrie Sr HS; Guthrie, OK; (2); Natl FFA Org; Spanish Clb; SADD; Socr; Hon Roll; Jr NHS; Prfct Atten Awd; OK ST Univ; Vet.

WALLS, ANDREA; Owasso 9th Grade Ctr; Owasso, OK; (1); FCA; School Play; Chrldng; Amer All-Star Dance Team Intl Goodwill Perfrmnce At Eurodisney; OK ST U; Fashn Dsgn.

WALLS, LISA; Plainview HS; Ardmore, OK; (3); 5/83; Am Leg Aux Girls St; Church Yth Grp; FCA; Girl Scts; Hosp Aide; Mu Alpha Theta; Natl Beta Clb; SADD; Rptr Jr Cls; Rep Stu Cncl; Pres Teenage Crime Stoppers; U Of Cntrl OK; OT/PT.

WALLS, LORIE; Panama HS; Panama, OK; (3); FHA; German Clb; Sec Jr Cls; Var Bsktbl; Var Sftbl; Hon Roll; NHS; Gftd & Tlntd; Carl Albert ST Coll.

WALLS, MISTY; Roff HS; Roff, OK; (4); 2/23; Art Clb; Natl Beta Clb; Scholastic Bowl; Yrbk; Rep Frsh Cls; Ofcr Stu Cncl; Bsktbl; Sftbl; High Hon Roll; NHS; East Cntrl U; Phys Ed.

WALSH, STEPHANIE; Mid-Del Christian Schl; Oklahoma City, OK; (4); 2/14; Church Yth Grp; Red Cross Aide; Spanish Clb; Ed Yrbk; Pres Frsh Cls; Pres Soph Cls; Pres Jr Cls; Pres Sr Cls; Sec Stu Cncl; Capt Var Bsktbl; Natl Engl Mrt Awd; US Stu Cncl Awd; Natl Ldrshp & Svc Awd; OK U; Sports Med.

WALSH III, THOMAS P; Will Rogers HS; Tulsa, OK; (1); Am Leg Boys St; Varsity Clb; Cit Awd; League Bsbl Tchr.

WALTA, RACHEL; Hennessey HS; Hennessey, OK; (1); Hosp Aide; Quiz Bowl; Band; Mrchg Band; Pep Band; Hon Roll; Relay For Life Cncr Walk-A-Thon; OSU; Bio.

WALTER, KRISTI K; Guthrie Sr HS; Guthrie, OK; (3); 32/220; Art Clb; Drama Clb; FBLA; Mu Alpha Theta; SADD; Rep Sr Cls; Rep Stu Cncl; Bsktbl; Chrldng; Golf; UCO; Bus.

WALTER, SUE A; B T Washington HS; Tulsa, OK; (3); Spanish Clb; Teachers Aide; NHS; Ntl Merit Ltr; OK ST U; Med.

WALTERS, ANNA M; Claremore Sr HS; Claremore, OK; (4); 21/235; Church Yth Grp; GAA; Teachers Aide; Stage Crew; JV Bsktbl; JV Crs Cntry; JV Var Sftbl; JV Trk; JV Vllybl; High Hon Roll; Roger ST Coll; Horse Trainer.

WALTERS, BONNIE; Tahlequah Jr HS; Tahlequah, OK; (2); Quiz Bowl; Science Clb; Rep Stu Cncl; Hon Roll; Native Amer Heritage Clb; Engrng.

WALTERS, HOLLIE; Kingston HS; Kingston, OK; (1); Band; Jazz Band; Mrchg Band; Pep Band; Hon Roll; Prfct Atten Awd; Music.

WALTERS, JUSTIN; Edmond Santa Fe HS; Edmond, OK; (2); FCA; JCL; Ofcr Bsbl; Var Ftbl; Golf; Wt Lftg; Med/Law.

WALTERS, KATHRYN R; Putnam City HS; Oklahoma City, OK; (3); Cmnty Wkr; DECA; Pep Clb; Quiz Bowl; Orch; Rep Stu Cncl; Chrldng; Pom Pon; Trk; Tchr.

WALTERS, LESLIE R; Morris HS; Morris, OK; (1); 4-H; Var Bsktbl; JV Sftbl; Hon Roll.

WALTERS, MARY S; Claremore Sr HS; Claremore, OK; (1); Church Yth Grp; Chorus; Stage Crew; Var Socr; Sftbl; Hon Roll; Tulsa Univ; Art.

WALTERS, RACHEL L; Muskogee HS; Muskogee, OK; (3); Am Leg Aux Girls St; Church Yth Grp; DECA; French Clb; Acpl Chr; Chorus; School Musical; School Play; Hon Roll; Teens/Christ; RAID; Norhteastern OK ST Univ.

WALTERS, RISA; West Middle HS; Norman, OK; (1); Church Yth Grp; Spanish Clb; Rep Stu Cncl; JV Chrldng; Pres Acad Fit Awd; Octagon Clb; Dance; Power Tumbling; Pediatric Medicine.

WALTERS, RONNIE A; Coleman Schl; Wapanucka, OK; (4); Church Yth Grp; FCA; Church Choir; Rep Frsh Cls; VP Soph Cls; VP Sr Cls; VP Stu Cncl; Capt Var Bsbl; Capt Var Bsktbl; Boy Scts; Natl Scholar Ath Awd; SOSU.

WALTERS, SHERI; Coleman Schl; Wapanucka, OK; (3); 1/18; FCA; Quiz Bowl; Ski Clb; Yrbk; Rptr Jr Cls; Bsktbl; Sftbl; 4-H Awd; Hon Roll; Bstkbl All Star.

WALTON, CRYSTAL D; Antlers Sr HS; Antlers, OK; (4); Church Yth Grp; FCA; 4-H; FBLA; SADD; Church Choir; Var Bsktbl; Powder Puff Ftbl; Score Keeper; Hon Roll; E Central Univ; Med.

WALTON, JAMI R; Bishop Kelley HS; Tulsa, OK; (2); Var JV Sftbl; High Hon Roll; Comm Svc; Pre-Med.

WALTON, LEIGH; Lone Grove HS; Wilson, OK; (3); 3/100; Church Yth Grp; Debate Tm; Model UN; Speech Tm; Capt Color Guard; High Hon Roll; NHS; Ntl Merit Ltr.

WALTON, SUSANNE M; Union Sr HS; Tulsa, OK; (3); 166/741; FBLA; Intnl Clb; Spanish Clb; Chorus; JV Swmmng; Hon Roll; NHS; Prfct Atten Awd; Spanish NHS; OK ST Univ; Ed.

WALTRIP, LESLI A; Sapulpa Sr HS; Sapulpa, OK; (3); Sec Church Yth Grp; Key Clb; Science Clb; Spanish Clb; Band; Church Choir; Mrchg Band; Hon Roll; NHS; Spanish NHS; Free Will Bapt Yth Conf; Chfs In Actn Clb; Teens For Chrst Clb; Northeastern ST Univ; Bus.

WAMBLE, JABARI; Oklahoma Christian Schl; Edmond, OK; (3); 19/48; Church Yth Grp; Debate Tm; FCA; Office Aide; Speech Tm; Varsity Clb; VP Frsh Cls; Var Bsktbl; Trk; Hon Roll; OK ST U.

WANER, JEFF B; Edmond Memorial HS; Edmond, OK; (3); 104/371; French Clb; Var Crs Cntry; Var Socr.

WARD, AMBER; Duman HS; Duncan, OK; (4); Church Yth Grp; Girl Scts; Key Clb; ROTC; Spanish Clb; Chorus; Church Choir; Color Guard; School Musical; Variety Show; Show Choir; Girl Scout Silver Awd; Stdnts Against Vandelism Of Envir; Southwestern OK ST U; Nrsng.

WARD, BRANDIE D; Olney Schl; Coalgate, OK; (1); Church Choir; Ofcr Soph Cls; Bsktbl; Score Keeper; Sftbl; Grphc Artst.

WARD, BRONC W; Foyil Schl; Claremore, OK; (2); 18/42; FBLA; Math Tm; School Play; Phtg Yrbk; Var Bsbl; Var Capt Bsktbl; Var Capt Ftbl; Var Trk; Wt Lftg; Hon Roll; Haskell Indianntns Univ.

WARD, BRYAN D; Yukon Middle HS; Yukon, OK; (1); Wrstlng; Hon Roll; Pres Acad Fit Awd; OK ST Univ; Bus.

WARD, CANDACE PATRICE; Idabel HS; Idabel, OK; (2); FCA; Bsktbl; Hon Roll.

WARD, CARI A; El Reno Sr HS; El Reno, OK; (2); Church Yth Grp; Drama Clb; FCA; Key Clb; Rep Frsh Cls; Rep Soph Cls; Ofcr Stu Cncl; Var Pom Pon; Tennis; Cit Awd; Chamber Of Commerce Ldrshp Cls 95; OK ST; Commnctns.

WARD, CHARLETA; Douglass HS; Oklahoma City, OK; (3); 1/11; Art Clb; Church Yth Grp; Cmnty Wkr; French Clb; Chorus; Cmmnctn Comm; Sabbath Schl Asst; OSU; Arch.

WARD, CRYSTAL; Copan HS; Copan, OK; (3); 1/30; Church Yth Grp; FHA; HOBY; Quiz Bowl; Band; Drm Mjr(t); Treas Stu Cncl; Bsktbl; Chrldng; Val.

WARD, DANIEL; Stigler HS; Stigler, OK; (1); Boy Scts; Church Yth Grp; FCA; Band; Mrchg Band; Pres Frsh Cls; Ofcr Bsbl; Bsktbl; High Hon Roll.

WARD, EARL H; Durant HS; Durant, OK; (2); 4-H; Natl FFA Org; JV Var Wrstlng; 4-H Awd; OK ST Univ; Vet.

WARD, ELI C; Mannford HS; Mannford, OK; (3); Speech Tm; SADD; Teachers Aide; Rptr Nwsp; Var Bsbl; JV Ftbl; Var Wrstlng; Cit Awd; JETS Awd; Prfct Atten Awd; NSU.

WARD, ELIZABETH A; Memorial HS; Tulsa, OK; (2); Church Yth Grp; Cmnty Wkr; German Clb; Treas Key Clb; Pep Clb; VP Red Cross Aide; Varsity Clb; Var L Swmmng; High Hon Roll.

WARD, ERICA; Hennessey HS; Hennessey, OK; (2); FCA; Quiz Bowl; Band; Color Guard; Mrchg Band; Var Chrldng; Var Crs Cntry; Var L Trk; High Hon Roll; NHS.

WARD, ERIN R; Stigler HS; Stigler, OK; (4); 1/80; Church Yth Grp; FHA; SADD; Band; Chorus; Drm Mjr(t); Sec Soph Cls; Hon Roll; NHS; Pres Acad Fit Awd; BYU; Mus.

WARD, GREG; Hennessey HS; Hennessey, OK; (4); 1/5; FCA; Quiz Bowl; SADD; Band; Var L Bsbl; Var L Bsktbl; Var L Ftbl; Var L Trk; High Hon Roll; NHS; OK ST U; Acctng.

WARD, JENNIFER; Oklahoma Sch Of Science & Math; Tuttle, OK; (4); Church Yth Grp; Rptr FHA; Math Tm; Scholastic Bowl; Church Choir; Yrbk; Ofcr Stu Cncl; High Hon Roll; NHS; Dept Of Energy Summer Sci Hnrs Pgm; Eagle Of The Cross Awd; U MO Rolla; Chem Engrng.

WARD, JENNIFER L; Mangum Sr HS; Mangum, OK; (2); Wrestling Mgr; Ftbl Mgr; OK ST Univ.

WARD, JUSTIN A; Stillwater Sr HS; Stillwater, OK; (2); Church Yth Grp; Church Choir; Rep Frsh Cls; Hon Roll; Pres Acad Fit Awd; Chrtr Mmbr Brsn Of Stllwtr; Sqrs Jr Knghts Of Clmbs; CCD Coord Ofce Asst; Soph Var Schlr; Archlgy/Anthrplgy/His.

WARD, KATIE; Crowder Schl; Mcalester, OK; (3); 1/40; FHA; VP Pep Clb; Rptr Yrbk; Sec Frsh Cls; VP Soph Cls; Pres Jr Cls; VP Stu Cncl; Capt Bsktbl; Var Sftbl; High Hon Roll; OK Hnr Soc; Dntl.

WARD, KYLE S; Haskell HS; Haskell, OK; (3); Var Bsbl; Var Ftbl; Hon Roll; Coll; Coach.

WARD, LAURA E; Memorial HS; Tulsa, OK; (2); Key Clb; Red Cross Aide; High Hon Roll; Ballet; U Of Tulsa.

WARD, LAURA J; Sperry Sr HS; Sperry, OK; (3); Church Yth Grp; Treas FHA; Key Clb; Pep Clb; Spanish Clb; Chorus; Rep Sr Cls; Rep Stu Cncl; JV Tennis; Cit Awd; NSU; Ed.

WARD, MARK; Will Roger HS; Big Cabin, OK; (4); 11/236; Am Leg Boys St; Key Clb; Model UN; Scholastic Bowl; Rptr Nwsp; Phtg Yrbk; Treas Stu Cncl; Capt Var Swmmng; Cit Awd; NHS; U Of OK; Med.

WARD, MATTHEW J; Salina HS; Salina, OK; (1); 4-H; Natl FFA Org; Hon Roll; Salina TSA; Won Crtv Wrtng Esy Cntst Mdrn Woodmen Amer; Frosh Stu Of Mnth.

WARD, MATTHEW N; Midwest City HS; Oklahoma City, OK; (3); Spanish Clb; Var Ftbl; Mgr Socr; OK Univ.

WARD, MICHAL M; Blackwell HS; Blackwell, OK; (2); 8/138; Sec Church Yth Grp; FCA; Hosp Aide; Letterman Clb; Rep Pep Clb; Red Cross Aide; Spanish Clb; Nwsp; Sec Frsh Cls; Sec Soph Cls; Peer Hlprs; ST Hnr Soc; Soph Ftbl Attendant.

WARD, ROBERT C; Mc Alester HS; Mcalester, OK; (2); Boy Scts; Church Yth Grp; Acpl Chr; Chorus; Church Choir; School Musical; Swing Chorus; Ofcr Bsbl; Ftbl; Cit Awd; Yth Elder 1st Presbyn Chrch; Handbell Choir; Music Perf/Ed.

WARDE, MELISSA J; Union Intermediate HS; Tulsa, OK; (2); Cmnty Wkr; Chorus; School Musical; Wrt Short Stories/Poems/Essays; Psychtrst.

WARDEN, BECCA S; Claremore Sr HS; Claremore, OK; (3); 46/273; Cmnty Wkr; Office Aide; Teachers Aide; High Hon Roll; Hon Roll; Vol Time Towards Spcl Olympics; U OK; Phy Thrpst.

WARDEN, JEANNA; Chickasha Jr HS; Chickasha, OK; (1); Church Yth Grp; 4-H; Math Tm; Science Clb; Chorus; Church Choir; 4-H Awd; Hon Roll; Jr NHS; NHS.

WARDEN, JEFF D; Henryetta Sr HS; Henryetta, OK; (2); 1/110; Church Yth Grp; FCA; Letterman Clb; Scholastic Bowl; Var Bsktbl; L Tennis; High Hon Roll; Hon Roll; Pres Acad Fit Awd; OK Hnr Soc; Gftd & Tlntd.

WARDRIP, DANIELLE R; Thackerville HS; Thackerville, OK; (4); Drama Clb; 4-H; FHA; Science Clb; Spanish Clb; Hon Roll; Natl Sci Merit Awd; All Am Schlr; NLSA; X-Ray Tech.

WARE, CARRIE; Broken Bow HS; Broken Bow, OK; (3); Art Clb; Church Yth Grp; FCA; GAA; Bsktbl; Sftbl; Trk; Hon Roll; NHS.

WARE, DARLISHA A; Capitol Hill HS; Oklahoma City, OK; (2); Church Yth Grp; Chorus; Hon Roll; NHS; Pediatrician.

WARE, KIMBERLEE; Sequoyah HS; Claremore, OK; (4); 6/75; English Clb; FCA; FBLA; FHA; Office Aide; Teachers Aide; Ed Yrbk; VP Pres Stu Cncl; Chrldng; High Hon Roll; Tulsa Jr Col; Erly Chldhd Devlp.

WARE, TERRY L; Ft Cobb-Broxton HS; Fort Cobb, OK; (2); 4-H; FHA; Rep Stu Cncl; Hon Roll; Pres Acad Fit Awd; Acad Team; Mineral Ed Pgm For Young Schlrs; FFA; Broadcast Jrnlsm.

WAREHIME, AMANDA; Dewey HS; Dewey, OK; (1); 2/97; Church Yth Grp; Scholastic Bowl; Spanish Clb; Band; Color Guard; Chrldng; Hon Roll; Pres Acad Fit Awd; St Schlr; Tap/Jazz/Ballet Dance.

WARFIELD, KARIN; Chisholm Sr HS; Enid, OK; (3); 1/75; Church Yth Grp; Pres FHA; Office Aide; Spanish Clb; Chorus; Nwsp; Ed Yrbk; High Hon Roll; Hon Roll; Jr NHS; Cook, Exercise, Sew; TX A&M; Dietics.

WARING, BRANDON C; Westville HS; Westville, OK; (2); FHA; ABS OK; Radio Disc Jockey.

WARING, MARIN B; Putnam City North HS; Oklahoma City, OK; (3); Church Yth Grp; Office Aide; Spanish Clb; Variety Show; Ofcr Sr Cls; Ofcr Stu Cncl; Var Tennis; Dance Trng; Tap Tchr; Sunday Schl Vol Tchr; Scndry Ed.

WARMA, LAURA D; Catoosa HS; Catoosa, OK; (4); French Clb; JA; Library Aide; Ofcr Sr Cls; Bsktbl; French Hon Soc; High Hon Roll; Jr NHS; NHS; Ntl Merit Schol; Tulsa JC; Psych.

WARN, DAVID; Tomlinson Jr HS; Lawton, OK; (1); Drama Clb; Model UN; Spanish Clb; High Hon Roll; Jr NHS; Prfct Atten Awd; Amer Sign Lang Interpreter; FRIENDS; Deaf Ed.

WARNER, AMBER; Felt Public Schl; Boise City, OK; (3); Teachers Aide; Chorus; School Play; Nwsp; Rptr Yrbk; Ofcr Stu Cncl; Var Capt Bsktbl; Trk; Hon Roll; Treas NHS; All Conf Tm Bsktbll; All Tnmt Tm; Bst Engl Stu; WTA.

WARNER, BLAKE; Macarthur Sr HS; Lawton, OK; (4); Church Yth Grp; Cmnty Wkr; Drama Clb; FCA; FHA; Spanish Clb; Speech Tm; School Play; Girl Scts; Ftbl; Med Explorers; Pre-Med.

WARNS, NICOLE M; Lomega HS; Kingfisher, OK; (2); 4/16; JA; Math Tm; Rep Soph Cls; Rep Stu Cncl; Var Bsktbl; JV Sftbl; High Hon Roll; Hon Roll; NHS; Ntl Merit Schol; KS Univ; Arch Engrng.

WARREN, ALLEN BERNHARDT; Tahlequah Sr HS; Tahlequah, OK; (4); #95 in class; Am Leg Boys St; Church Yth Grp; Office Aide; Science Clb; Acpl Chr; Band; Chorus; Church Choir; Mrchg Band; Ice Hcky Team Capt; All-St Chorus; SMU; Med.

WARREN, ALYCIA RENEA; Yukon HS; Yukon, OK; (4); 43/400; Band; Jazz Band; Mrchg Band; Orch; Pep Band; NHS; OK Cty Univ; Entrmnt Bus.

WARREN, BRANDEN L; Midwest City HS; Midwest City, OK; (3); 43/850; Ofcr Bsbl; Ftbl; Swmmng; Wt Lftg; High Hon Roll; Hon Roll; NHS; Prfct Atten Awd; OK U; Frfghtr.

WARREN, EMILY A; Union Sr HS; Broken Arrow, OK; (4); 71/669; DECA; FCA; Office Aide; Co-Capt Bsktbl; Powder Puff Ftbl; Co-Capt Socr; Hon Roll; Jr NHS; NHS; Stdnt Ath Wk; Bsktbl All Conf Tm; Hmcmng Qn; U Of Tulsa.

WARREN, ERIC; Trinity Christian Schl; Coweta, OK; (1); 1/20; Chess Clb; Socr; Hon Roll; Engrng.

WARREN, JENNIFER C; Union Intermediate HS; Tulsa, OK; (2); Church Yth Grp; FCA; Spanish Clb; Rep Frsh Cls; Rep Soph Cls; Treas Stu Cncl; Var Chrldng; Hon Roll; Jr NHS; NHS; All Amer Chrldr, Only Soph V Chrldng; DFY; Phys Ther.

WARREN, JUSTIN R; Harrah HS; Harrah, OK; (3); Boy Scts; 4-H; FHA; JA; Natl FFA Org; 4-H Awd; Hon Roll; 1st OK St FFA Entrepreneurship & Placement Forage Production; Harrah FFA Pres Local Chptr; OK ST Tech Coll; Disl Mechncs.

WARREN, KIM A; Liberty HS; Mounds, OK; (3); Church Yth Grp; FCA; Rptr Nwsp; Bsktbl; Tulsa JC.

WARREN, MARK K; B T Washington HS; Tulsa, OK; (2); Church Yth Grp; ROTC; Socr; Chinese Clb.

WARREN, SARAH; Claremore Sr HS; Claremore, OK; (4); 2/241; Jazz Band; Pres Jr Cls; Ofcr Stu Cncl; Pom Pon; Socr; High Hon Roll; NHS; Pres Acad Fit Awd; Val; Ldrshp Mrt Awd 95-96; All Amer Schlr Awd; OK U; Bus.

WARREN, SARAH R; Tahlequah Sr HS; Tahlequah, OK; (2); Church Yth Grp; Acpl Chr; Band; Chorus; Mrchg Band; Pep Band; Music Solos & Ensembles; Short Stories; Music.

WARREN, WES; Coweta HS; Coweta, OK; (4); 1/130; FCA; SADD; Var Bsktbl; Ntl Merit Ltr; Val; OK ST U; Mechncl Engrng.

WARRIOR, HARLAND; Midwest City HS; Oklahoma City, OK; (4); 74/419; Cmnty Wkr; FHA; Quiz Bowl; Teachers Aide; Variety Show;,Var Bsktbl; Ftbl; Wt Lftg; High Hon Roll; NHS; NE OK ST U; Clssrm Tchr.

WARRIOR, MICHAEL; Millwood HS; Oklahoma City, OK; (3); Church Yth Grp; Speech Tm; Church Choir; VP Frsh Cls; JV Var Bsktbl; Hon Roll; Prfct Atten Awd; Sigma Beta Clb; Bus Adm.

WARRIOR, ROBERT A; Ponca City Sr HS; Ponca City, OK; (3); Church Yth Grp; Ofcr Bsbl; Bsktbl; Ftbl; Trk; Wt Lftg; Hon Roll; OK U; Med.

WARTLUFT, KRISTA M; Broken Arrow Sr HS; Broken Arrow, OK; (3); FCA; French Clb; Library Aide; Natl FFA Org; Teachers Aide; JV Vllybl; Scrkpr Var Wrstlng; Scrkpr Var Bsbl; Var Ftbl Wrestling Bsbl Ath Trainer; Future Med Prof; Sports Med.

WARUSZEWSKI, JULIE; Bishop Kelley HS; Tulsa, OK; (3); Church Yth Grp; Cmnty Wkr; Dance Clb; Hon Roll.

WASHBURN, BOBBI L; Waukomis HS; Enid, OK; (3); Computer Clb; FCA; Letterman Clb; Math Tm; Pep Clb; Spanish Clb; Varsity Clb; Pep Band; Var Bsktbl; Var Sftbl; Horse Breaking; Barrel Racing; Sports Medicine; Comp Bus.

WASHBURN, CORY; Alva HS; Alva, OK; (3); Church Yth Grp; Debate Tm; Drama Clb; HOBY; Key Clb; NFL; Spanish Clb; Speech Tm; Teachers Aide; Thesps; Exchng Stu Australia W/AIYSEP.

WASHBURN, KYLE A; Shawnee Sr HS; Shawnee, OK; (2); Church Yth Grp; Band; Jazz Band; Mrchg Band; Pep Band; High Hon Roll; Hon Roll; GA Tech; Engr.

WASHINGTON, CANDICE R; Okmulgee HS; Okmulgee, OK; (1); Church Yth Grp; FBLA; Yrbk; Ofcr Stu Cncl; Bsktbl; Mgr(s); Score Keeper; Trk; Cit Awd; High Hon Roll; Gramvbling ST Univ; Acctng.

WASHINGTON, KELLY; Berryhill Jr HS; Tulsa, OK; (1); Office Aide; Teachers Aide; Ftbl; Wt Lftg; Hon Roll; Wrstlng Mgr.

WASHINGTON, LAKISHA Y; Putnam City HS; Oklahoma City, OK; (3); 87/396; Teachers Aide; Chorus; Rep Stu Cncl; Stat Bsktbl; Mgr(s); Sftbl; Bus.

WASHINGTON, LATRINA; Will Rogers HS; Tulsa, OK; (4); 19/179; Church Yth Grp; Pres FBLA; Treas JA; Treas Key Clb; Latin Clb; Pep Clb; Spanish Clb; Teachers Aide; Rptr Nwsp; Rptr Yrbk; Stu Of Month; Homcmng Attndnt 95-96; Tulsa JC; Accntng.

WASHINGTON, MECOLE C; Mc Lain Career Acad; Tulsa, OK; (3); Church Yth Grp; 4-H; GAA; JA; Pep Clb; SADD; Teachers Aide; Chorus; Church Choir; Yrbk; 7th Pl In Mc Lain Schlsp Pageant; Most Spirited Person; OSU; Phys Therapy.

WASHINGTON, RASHOD; Boley HS; Boley, OK; (4); 1/9; Am Leg Boys St; Boy Scts; Church Yth Grp; 4-H; FBLA; Natl FFA Org; Scholastic Bowl; Band; Mrchg Band; School Musical; Eagle Sct; Stu Of Yr Chrch; Langston U; Bus Mgmt.

WASHINGTON, SCOTT; Mulhall Orlando HS; Orlando, OK; (4); 9/20; VP FBLA; Church Choir; Ed Nwsp; Yrbk; Jr NHS; NHS; Prfct Atten Awd; FBLA St Cntst 2nd Pl Cmptr Appl; 95 Nrthrn OK Coll 1st Pl Wrd Prcsng; Ed Orlandochrstn Chrch Nwsltr; OK ST U; Mrktng.

WASSERBECK, LIBBY; Newcastle HS; Newcastle, OK; (3); 1/91; Church Yth Grp; FBLA; Science Clb; Spanish Clb; Rptr Sec Chorus; Church Choir; High Hon Roll; NHS; OK Natl Hnr Soc; Stu Of Month 95; OK Bapt U; Chrstn Ministry.

WASSERLEBEN, KARRIE; Carl Albert HS; Oklahoma City, OK; (3); Drama Clb; Key Clb; Library Aide; Band; School Play; Sftbl; Hon Roll; Jr NHS; Pres Acad Fit Awd; 4.0 Cert; U Of OK; Engrng.

WASSON, LINDSEY; Tomlinson Jr HS; Lawton, OK; (1); Church Yth Grp; FCA; FHA; Var Chorus; Sec Frsh Cls; Co-Capt Chrldng; Var Golf; Cit Awd; Gov Hon Prg Awd; High Hon Roll; U Of OK; Phy.

WATASHE, SHEILA R; Caney Valley HS; Talala, OK; (3); Am Leg Aux Girls St; Church Yth Grp; German Clb; Teachers Aide; Band; Church Choir; Drm Mjr(t); Capt L Bsktbl; Var Mgr(s); Var L Trk; Natl Macy Mnrties In Med Schol; E OK St Col; Nrsing.

WATERMAN, CHRISTY; Liberty Acad; Shawnee, OK; (4); 2/15; Church Yth Grp; Hosp Aide; Teachers Aide; Church Choir; School Play; Stage Crew; Co-Ed Nwsp; Co-Ed Yrbk; Lit Mag; NHS; Acad Chapel Clb; OK ST U; Pre-Vet.

WATERS, NICHOLAS A; Wynnewood HS; Wynnewood, OK; (1); 10/66; Church Yth Grp; Cmnty Wkr; Natl FFA Org; Church Choir; Ftbl; Trk; Wt Lftg; Hon Roll; Grad Of Dale Carnegie Course; OASC; Several FFA Awds; Univ.

WATERS, TREY R; Stillwater Sr HS; Stillwater, OK; (2); 20/350; Church Yth Grp; Mu Alpha Theta; Sprt Ed Yrbk; Var L Bsbl; Var L Bsktbl; Var L Ftbl; High Hon Roll; Kiwanis Awd; Pres Acad Fit Awd; 2 Time Ath Of Wk; KS Univ; Pre-Med.

WATKINS, BETTY S; Muldrow HS; Muldrow, OK; (1).

WATKINS, BRYAN C; Jenks HS; Tulsa, OK; (4); 73/448; Boy Scts; DECA; FCA; Ed Yrbk; Ofcr Stu Cncl; L Crs Cntry; High Hon Roll; Pres Schlr; St Schlr; Trk; Natl Mrt Commended Stu; St Regents Schlr; Phi Delta Epsilon Ofcr; U Of OK.

WATKINS, COLIN M; Mc Alester HS; Mcalester, OK; (2); Art Clb; FCA; Letterman Clb; Spanish Clb; Var Bsbl; High Hon Roll; U Of OK; Graphic Artist.

WATKINS, DONALD; Charles Page HS; Sand Springs, OK; (4); 16/340; Am Leg Boys St; Church Yth Grp; Debate Tm; Pres Band; Jazz Band; Hon Roll; NHS; Prfct Atten Awd; Music Mastrs; Natve Amer Stu Assn; OK Chrstn U; Comp Sci.

WATKINS, GREG; Arapaho Schl; Arapaho, OK; (4); 6/18; Church Yth Grp; Letterman Clb; Natl FFA Org; Varsity Clb; Yrbk; Sec Sr Cls; Var Capt Bsbl; Var Capt Bsktbl; Intrml Capt Vllybl; Prfct Atten Awd; Driver Ed, Woodshop & Advanced Woodshop , Algebra II, Stu Of Month Awds; OK ST Univ; Construction Tech.

WATKINS, JERRY R; Oologah HS; Claremore, OK; (2); Boy Scts; Band; Jazz Band; Mrchg Band; Pep Band; Rptr Nwsp; Swmmng; High Hon Roll; Hon Roll; OK U; Mscn.

WATKINS, JONATHON; Preston Schl; Okmulgee, OK; (4); 3/30; Church Yth Grp; VP 4-H; Yrbk; Var L Bsktbl; Cit Awd; High Hon Roll; NHS; Prfct Atten Awd; St Schlr; U Of OK; Engrng.

WATKINS, KERI L; Enid Sr HS; Enid, OK; (4); DECA; FCA; Teachers Aide; VICA; Band; Color Guard; Drill Tm; Mrchg Band; Var Pom Pon; Hon Roll; Parent Tchr Stu Assn; Autry Tech.

WATKINS, KLINT L; Pryor Sr HS; Pryor, OK; (3); Church Yth Grp; FCA; FBLA; German Clb; Mu Alpha Theta; Yrbk; High Hon Roll; NHS; St Hnr Soc; PSI; Schl News Brdcst; TX Christian U; Meteorlgy.

WATKINS, KRISTIN; Fellowship Baptist Acad; Stilwell, OK; (4); Church Yth Grp; Teachers Aide; Chorus; Church Choir; Ed Yrbk; Var Bsktbl; Var Vllybl; Hon Roll; Prfct Atten Awd; Home Ec & Music Awds; Piano Duet & Sciripture Memory Acclrtd Chrstn Ed Cnvtn Medals; Nrs.

WATKINS, RICHARD; Heavener HS; Heavener, OK; (4); 11/86; Chess Clb; Church Yth Grp; FCA; FBLA; FHA; Key Clb; Spanish Clb; Teachers Aide; Pres Jr Cls; Bsktbl; Wendys HS Heiseman Awd; OSU-OKC; Fire Prtctn.

WATKINS, RICKY G; Kellyville Sr HS; Sapulpa, OK; (2); Church Yth Grp; Debate Tm; Letterman Clb; Speech Tm; VP Soph Cls; JV Bsbl; JV Bsktbl; JV Var Ftbl; High Hon Roll; NHS.

WATKINS, SANDRA; Fox Sr HS; Healdton, OK; (3); Murry ST; Medicine; RN; Dr.

WATKINS, SELENA M; Oaks Mission Jr Sr HS; Tahlequah, OK; (3); Drama Clb; Chorus; School Play; Var Chrldng; Sftbl; Hon Roll; NHS; Val; 2 Rating St Choral Cont.

WATKINS, SHAMITRA D; Midwest City HS; Oklahoma City, OK; (2); Church Yth Grp; FHA; ROTC; Scholastic Bowl; Band; Church Choir; Mrchg Band; Bsktbl.

WATKINS, TANNER L; Ardmore HS; Ardmore, OK; (3); 16/195; Church Yth Grp; FCA; French Clb; Mu Alpha Theta; Science Clb; Golf; High Hon Roll; Hon Roll; Jr NHS; NHS.

WATKINS, TARA B; Union Intermediate HS; Tulsa, OK; (2); 11/950; Church Yth Grp; Drama Clb; Teachers Aide; School Play; Bsktbl; Hon Roll; Jr NHS; NHS; Pres Schlr; Most Outstdng Lit Stu 95-; Theatre/Lit.

WATLEY, CATHY M; Elgin HS; Elgin, OK; (2); 19/90; Church Yth Grp; FCA; Band; Mrchg Band; Ofcr Bsbl; Bsktbl; Sftbl; Trk; Hon Roll; NHS; Chrch Yth Grp; OK Baptst Univ; Sprts Med.

WATSEK, ANDREW; Medford Schl; Medford, OK; (2); Treas Church Yth Grp; FHA; Library Aide; Quiz Bowl; Chorus; Var Bsktbl; Var Ftbl; Trk; Wt Lftg; FFA Treas; UO.

WATSON, ALICIA; Okemah HS; Okemah, OK; (2); 4-H; Natl Beta Clb; Natl FFA Org; SADD; Yrbk; Var Chrldng; Var Golf; Cit Awd; Hon Roll; NHS; OK ST U.

WATSON, AMIE C; Healdton HS; Healdton, OK; (4); 14/48; Teachers Aide; Sec VICA; Chorus; Hon Roll; NHS; Natl All Amer Schlr; Natl Schlstc Ldrshp Assn; Prncpl Hnr Rll; OSU Okmulgee; Photo.

WATSON, BRANDI D; Commanche Sr HS; Comanche, OK; (2); Church Yth Grp; Debate Tm; GAA; NFL; Quiz Bowl; VP Frsh Cls; Pres Soph Cls; Bsktbl; Chrldng; Powder Puff Ftbl; Pres Of Tech Class; N TX Univ; Med.

WATSON, BRANDON; Ponca City Middle HS; Ponca City, OK; (1); Chorus; Hon Roll; CML Awd; OSU; Comp Prog.

WATSON, CHRISTY; Stuart Sr HS; Stuart, OK; (3); Church Yth Grp; FHA; Office Aide; Quiz Bowl; Teachers Aide; School Play; Phtg Yrbk; Stat Bsktbl; Cit Awd; Pres Acad Fit Awd; Natl Guard; Dr.

WATSON, CLIFF; Okemah HS; Okemah, OK; (4); 4/47; Am Leg Boys St; Quiz Bowl; Scholastic Bowl; Spanish Clb; Yrbk; VP Frsh Cls; VP Soph Cls; VP Jr Cls; Sec Sr Cls; Pres VP Stu Cncl; U Of OK; Med.

WATSON, EMEKA D; Will Rogers HS; Tulsa, OK; (4); Pres Church Yth Grp; Rptr FBLA; Letterman Clb; Varsity Clb; Church Choir; Lit Mag; JV Var Ftbl; Var Wt Lftg; Hon Roll; Prfct Atten Awd; Central ST Univ; Comp Sci.

WATSON, ERIN; Shawnee Sr HS; Shawnee, OK; (4); 3/282; Cmnty Wkr; French Clb; Math Tm; Scholastic Bowl; Orch; Rep Frsh Cls; Rep Soph Cls; NHS; Discover Card Tribute Schlrshp; String Quartet; Music Jrnlsm.

WATSON, HEATHER A; Bridge Creek HS; Tuttle, OK; (4); School Play; Clothing; U Of Sci & Arts; Bus.

WATSON, JENNIFER; U S Grant HS; Oklahoma City, OK; (3); #15 in class; Church Yth Grp; Drama Clb; Thesps; Church Choir; School Play; Swmmng; NHS; St Super Rtng Vocal; OK Bapt U.

WATSON, LANCE; Grandfield Jr Sr HS; Grandfield, OK; (3); 1/28; Church Yth Grp; Natl FFA Org; Quiz Bowl; Pres Soph Cls; Pres Jr Cls; Var Bsbl; Var Bsktbl; Var Ftbl; NHS.

WATSON, LORI; U S Grant HS; Oklahoma City, OK; (4); 5/170; Am Leg Aux Girls St; Pres Service Clb; SADD; Pres Band; Mrchg Band; Pep Band; Yrbk; Ofcr Jr Cls; Sec Stu Cncl; Sftbl; OK U; Govt.

WATSON, LUCAS; Central Mid-HS; Norman, OK; (1); Boy Scts; Latin Clb; Band; Jazz Band; Musician.

WATSON, MICHAEL D; Duncan HS; Duncan, OK; (3); Jr NHS; DECA; Karate Brown Belt; Comp Scis.

WATSON, MICHAEL L; Grandfield Jr Sr HS; Grandfield, OK; (3); 1/25; Church Yth Grp; Quiz Bowl; Scholastic Bowl; Church Choir; Pres Soph Cls; Pres Jr Cls; Ofcr Bsbl; Bsktbl; Ftbl; NHS.

WATSON, MICHELLE L; Broken Arrow Sr HS; Broken Arrow, OK; (4); 38/921; French Clb; Key Clb; Spanish Clb; Socr; Hon Roll; NHS; All-Amer Schlr; William Woods Univ; Sprts Med.

WATSON, TYSON; Guymon Sr HS; Guymon, OK; (3); FCA; Science Clb; Bsktbl; High Hon Roll; Hon Roll; Prfct Atten Awd.

WATSON, ZAMANTHA; Webbers Falls Schl; Webbers Falls, OK; (3); 1/29; FCA; Pres VP 4-H; Pres Frsh Cls; Sec Soph Cls; VP Jr Cls; VP Pres Stu Cncl; Var L Bsktbl; High Hon Roll; Sec NHS; Val; Johnson Omalley Outstndng Stu Awd; Class A St Bsktbl Champs 95-96; Outstndng Stu Awds In Svl Classes; Zoology.

WATT, SCARLETT K; Owasso Sr HS; Owasso, OK; (4); 32/296; Church Yth Grp; FCA; Bsktbl; Socr; Hon Roll; NHS; OSU; Child Dev Pre-Prof.

WATT, TYLER C; Owasso Sr HS; Owasso, OK; (2); 38/389; Church Yth Grp; Drama Clb; FCA; JV Var Bsbl; Var Wrstlng; Hon Roll; NHS; Pharmacy.

WATTERS, ELIZABETH M; Pawnee HS; Maramec, OK; (2); Church Yth Grp; Pep Clb; Scholastic Bowl; Teachers Aide; Band; Powder Puff Ftbl; Hon Roll; Algbr I Awd; Cert Of Excl; Geom Awd & Medl; Cert Of Excl; High Recgntn For Cls; OSU; Math Tchr; Bus.

WATTERS, JENNIFER; Dewar Jr-Sr HS; Henryetta, OK; (3); 2/28; Teachers Aide; Ofcr Stu Cncl; Var Bsktbl; Var Sftbl; NHS.

WATTERS, MANDY L; Keota Schl; Keota, OK; (2); FHA; Pep Clb; Chorus; Variety Show; Chrldng; Hon Roll; Cosmo.

WATTIE, STACI E; Westmoore HS; Oklahoma City, OK; (1); Office Aide; Bsktbl; Sftbl; Cit Awd; Hon Roll; Jr NHS.

WATTMAN, FRANCES M; B T Washington HS; Tulsa, OK; (1); Church Yth Grp; Speech Tm; Yrbk; Ballet 12 Yrs; 2nd Pl Speech Trnmnt; Prof Ballet Perfrmnc.

WATTS, ANNA; Rock Creek Jr Sr HS; Bokchito, OK; (2); 1/44; Church Yth Grp; FHA; Quiz Bowl; Chorus; School Musical; High Hon Roll; NHS; Southwestern Assemblies Of God.

WATTS, DESIREE D; Tahlequah Jr HS; Park Hill, OK; (1); Church Yth Grp; Service Clb; Rptr Stu Cncl; Var JV Bsktbl; Var Sftbl; High Hon Roll; Jr NHS.

WATTS, KATRINA; Boley HS; Boley, OK; (4); 2/9; Church Yth Grp; 4-H; FHA; Girl Scts; Natl FFA Org; Teachers Aide; Church Choir; Nwsp; Ofcr Jr Cls; Ofcr Sr Cls; FFA, Schl & Chrch Awds; Seminole JC; Acctng.

WATTS, SANDI L; Drumright HS; Drumright, OK; (2); Hon Roll.

WATTS, SETH; Rock Creek Jr Sr HS; Bokchito, OK; (4); 2/38; Am Leg Boys St; Church Yth Grp; Capt Scholastic Bowl; Teachers Aide; Pres Frsh Cls; VP Jr Cls; Ofcr Stu Cncl; Var Capt Bsktbl; VP NHS; Sal; Dnfrth I Dare You Awd; Drnt Yth Apprntcshp Prog; SE OK ST U; Bnkng.

WAUGH, CHARLES; Buffalo Jr Sr HS; Buffalo, OK; (4); 2/30; HOBY; Capt Quiz Bowl; Band; Chorus; Ed Yrbk; Ofcr Bsbl; Ftbl; DAR Awd; NHS; Val; Southwestern OK ST U; Phrmcy.

WAUGH III, W SCOTT; Edmond North HS; Edmond, OK; (4); 1/330; Am Leg Boys St; Pres Church Yth Grp; FCA; Key Clb; Mu Alpha Theta; ROTC; Spanish Clb; SADD; Church Choir; Variety Show; Pilot Lic; AFJROTC Aerospc Hnr Soc Pres; Masonic Stu Of Today Awd; Orthpdc Srgn.

WAYMAN, SCOTT; Vinita HS; Vinita, OK; (4); Am Leg Boys St; FCA; Math Clb; Spanish Clb; Teachers Aide; Var Bsbl; Var Ftbl; Var Trk; Var Wt Lftg; Hon Roll; OK St U; Finance.

WEABE, SHELLY; Collinsville HS; Collinsville, OK; (4); 1/105; Office Aide; Quiz Bowl; Pres Frsh Cls; Pres Soph Cls; JV Var Bsktbl; Sftbl; Tennis; High Hon Roll; Sec NHS; Val; Med.

WEATHERINGTON, NIKI; Guthrie Sr HS; Guthrie, OK; (1); Dance Clb; Girl Scts; Band; Church Choir; Mrchg Band; School Musical; Bsktbl; Chrldng; Trk; Head Chrldr.

WEATHERLEY, DAVID D; Tecumseh HS; Tecumseh, OK; (3); Band; Mrchg Band; Var Ftbl; Var Wt Lftg; Hon Roll.

WEATHERLEY, JAMIE D; Tecumseh HS; Tecumseh, OK; (1); Church Yth Grp; Mu Alpha Theta; SADD; Rep Frsh Cls; Var Pom Pon; High Hon Roll; NHS; ECO; OK Hnr Soc; Outstdng Stdnt/Ath; U Of OK; Pedtrcn.

WEATHERLY, ERIN; Jenks HS; Tulsa, OK; (1); Church Yth Grp; Pep Clb; Ofcr Stu Cncl; Capt Chrldng; High Hon Roll; Hon Roll; NCA All-Amer Chrldr; Squad 4th Pl Natn 95-96; Tulsas Bst Allstar Squad, 3rd Pl Natn.

WEATHERS, SHAWNNA J; Great Plains Avt-Comanche; Lawton, OK; (4); 32/72; FBLA; Teachers Aide; Varsity Clb; Band; Chorus; Rptr Nwsp; Var Bsktbl; Wrstlng; High Hon Roll; Hon Roll; Voice Of Democracy Awd; Cameron Univ; RN.

WEAVER, ALENA J; Choctaw HS; Choctaw, OK; (2); Art Clb; Cmnty Wkr; Library Aide; Hon Roll; OK Univ; Atty.

WEAVER, AMANDA R; Okay Jr Sr HS; Muskogee, OK; (2); Spanish Clb; Hon Roll; Acad Tm; CPA.

WEAVER, BEN D; Edmond Memorial HS; Edmond, OK; (3); Church Yth Grp; FCA; VP German Clb; Spanish Clb; SADD; Ofcr Stu Cncl; NHS; Bass Fishing; Snow Skiing.

WEAVER, DAVID M; Muldrow HS; Uniontown, AR; (1); High Hon Roll; Rsrch Lost City Atlantis/Bermuda Triangle.

WEAVER, DON O; Wagoner Sr HS; Wagoner, OK; (3); 33/133; Church Yth Grp; FCA; ROTC; JV Bsktbl; Hon Roll; Northeastern ST U; Tchng.

WEAVER, JENNIE; Kingfisher HS; Kingfisher, OK; (3); FHA; Key Clb; Scholastic Bowl; Spanish Clb; Hon Roll; OSU; Bus.

WEAVER, JENNIFER; White Oak Jr-Sr HS; Vinita, OK; (3); 1/15; Church Yth Grp; 4-H; Science Clb; Pres Frsh Cls; Pres Soph Cls; Pres Jr Cls; Var Bsktbl; Hon Roll; NHS; Southwestern ST; Phrmcy.

WEAVER, JERROD; Mason HS; Welty, OK; (2); 3/23; Church Yth Grp; Bsktbl; Hon Roll; NHS; OK Hnr Soc.

WEAVER, LEE; Antlers Sr HS; Antlers, OK; (4); 11/66; Am Leg Aux Girls St; Church Yth Grp; FBLA; Office Aide; Band; Flag Corp; Hon Roll; Jr NHS; NHS; Southeastern OK ST U; Law.

WEAVER, LORI D; Noble HS; Noble, OK; (2); 1/203; Church Yth Grp; FCA; French Clb; GAA; Church Choir; Bsktbl; Chrldng; Crs Cntry; Sftbl; Trk; Music; Creative Wrtng; Water Sports.

WEAVER, MASON A; Putnam City North HS; Oklahoma City, OK; (1); Cmnty Wkr; Drama Clb; English Clb; French Clb; Quiz Bowl; Scholastic Bowl; Speech Tm; Jazz Band; Orch; School Play; U Of TX; Flm Schl.

WEAVER, RYAN; Hugo HS; Hugo, OK; (4); 5/108; Church Yth Grp; Cmnty Wkr; Computer Clb; English Clb; Library Aide; Math Clb; Scholastic Bowl; Rep Stu Cncl; Intrml Bsktbl; Intrml Ftbl; Child Sfty Instr; OK Hnr Soc; OK ST U; Comp Sci.

WEAVER, SARA B; Bishop Kelley HS; Tulsa, OK; (4); Church Yth Grp; Debate Tm; Drama Clb; NFL; Red Cross Aide; Speech Tm; Thesps; Rep Sr Cls; High Hon Roll; Hon Roll; Ldng Rlgus Rtrts For Peers; 300 Hrs Vol Svc; Trinity Univ; Physics.

WEAVER, SHALYN B; El Reno Sr HS; El Reno, OK; (3); Church Yth Grp; Pres Drama Clb; Pres 4-H; VP Natl FFA Org; Speech Tm; 4-H Awd; Hon Roll; Natl HS Rodeo Assn; Appaloosa Horse Clb; El Reno Rodeo Qn; OK ST; Vet Med.

WEAVER, SHAWNA; Del City HS; Del City, OK; (4); 20/460; Church Yth Grp; VP FCA; Rep SADD; Chorus; Mgr Bsbl; Wrstlng; NHS; Prfct Atten Awd; Val; Miss Wrestling; PT/SPRTS Med.

WEAVER, SHELLY E; South Intermediate HS; Broken Arrow, OK; (1); Church Yth Grp; FCA; Acpl Chr; Rep Stu Cncl; Hon Roll; Pres Schlr; U Of Tulsa; Bus Admin.

WEAVER, TRACI; Guthrie Sr HS; Guthrie, OK; (3); 2/229; Church Yth Grp; Mu Alpha Theta; Rptr VP Natl FFA Org; Spanish Clb; High Hon Roll; Jr NHS; NHS; Intnl Ordr Rnbw For Girls Drll Ldr/Grnd Rep Jpn Mem Team; Pol Sci/Intnl Ag.

WEBB, ABBY C; Elgin HS; Lawton, OK; (2); Natl FFA Org; Spanish Clb; Teachers Aide; Chrldng; Sftbl; Hon Roll; OK ST Univ; Med.

WEBB, ALEXANDER; Durant HS; Durant, OK; (3); #2 in class; FBLA; Key Clb; Co-Capt Quiz Bowl; Ed Nwsp; High Hon Roll; Hon Roll; NHS; Prfct Atten Awd; Pres Acad Fit Awd; Mensa Sierra Club; Pres Pituitary Club; Film Making.

WEBB, ALLISON M; Bixby Sr HS; Bixby, OK; (1); Church Yth Grp; GAA; Girl Scts; Spanish Clb; SADD; Ofcr Frsh Cls; Ofcr Stu Cncl; Bsktbl; Sftbl; Trk; Pres Ed Awds Pgrm 96.

WEBB, ANDREA D; Broken Arrow Sr HS; Broken Arrow, OK; (3); Church Yth Grp; FCA; Hosp Aide; Intnl Clb; Band; Church Choir; Hon Roll; Cls Rep For Concert Band; Chrstn Schl Union Sec; OBU; Kndgtn Tchr.

WEBB, APRIL; Perry Sr HS; Perry, OK; (2); FHA; Drill Tm; Hon Roll; Jr NHS; Cmpfr Boys & Grls; OSU; Eng Tchr.

WEBB, APRIL M; Fox Sr HS; Ratliff City, OK; (2); Church Yth Grp; Spanish Clb; SADD; Band; Chorus; Mrchg Band; Pep Band; Hon Roll; Carmen OK; Music.

WEBB, ASHLEY R; Union Sr HS; Tulsa, OK; (4); 8/645; Church Yth Grp; Band; School Musical; Ofcr Jr Cls; Ofcr Sr Cls; VP Stu Cncl; Capt Tennis; Hist NHS; FCA; German Clb; Mr Dance Of OK; Mr Prsnlty; Natl Mrt Fnlst; Grmn Hnr Soc; Mr Un 1st Runnr Up; Vp Yng Rpblcns; Law.

WEBB, CHRIS; Moore HS; Moore, OK; (2); JV Bsbl; Cit Awd; NHS.

WEBB, DAVID J; Pocola HS; Pocola, OK; (4); 3/48; Church Yth Grp; Quiz Bowl; Teachers Aide; Band; Jazz Band; Nwsp; Yrbk; Ofcr Stu Cncl; NHS; Pres Acad Fit Awd; TS St Wnnr; Natl Fnslt; Sci Fair 3rd Plc In St Cont; Westark CC; Cvl Eng.

WEBB, ERIC; Sulphur HS; Sulphur, OK; (4); 25/95; Pres Art Clb; Quiz Bowl; Scholastic Bowl; Stage Crew; Variety Show; Ed Nwsp; Ofcr Stu Cncl; Hon Roll; Schlstc Team 4 Yrs; 1st Pl Art His 3 Yrs; 1st Pl Drwng 3 Yrs; 1st Pl Sclpture 2 Yrs; Bst Show 2 Yrs; KS City Art Inst; Cmmrcl Arts.

WEBB, JEANETTE; Agra Schl; Tryon, OK; (4); 6/27; Church Yth Grp; FHA; Natl FFA Org; Scholastic Bowl; Teachers Aide; School Play; Capt Bsktbl; Chrldng; Capt Sftbl; Hon Roll; U Of Cntrl OK; Elem Ed.

WEBB, JENNIFER S; Strother Jr Sr HS; Earlsboro, OK; (1); 1/30; FHA; Rep Frsh Cls; Rep Stu Cncl; Mgr(s); High Hon Roll; OK U.

WEBB, JULIE A; Edmond Santa Fe HS; Edmond, OK; (3); 33/279; Art Clb; Pres German Clb; Science Clb; SADD; Band; Mrchg Band; Pep Band; Hon Roll; NHS; Pres Acad Fit Awd; Poetry Publshd Natl Libry Of Poetry; Creative Arts; Advrtsng.

WEBB, KEITH; Southwest Covenant Schl; Oklahoma City, OK; (1); Church Yth Grp; FCA; Band; Chorus; VP Stu Cncl; Var L Bsktbl; Var L Ftbl; High Hon Roll.

WEBB, MICHELLE L; Tahlequah Jr HS; Tahlequah, OK; (1); JV Sftbl; High Hon Roll; U Of TX; Pediatrician.

WEBB, NATHAN G; Guthrie Sr HS; Guthrie, OK; (1); 9/317; Am Leg Boys St; Church Yth Grp; Intrml Bsbl; High Hon Roll; Schlrs Banquet Honoring Acad Achvmt Participant; U Of OK; Chiropractor.

WEBB, PAULA F; Mountain View-Gotebo HS; Mountain View, OK; (3); 7/32; FHA; Hosp Aide; Hon Roll; NHS; Southwestern OK ST Univ.

WEBB, TINA; Turner Schl; Overbrook, OK; (3); 3/18; Church Yth Grp; Capt Debate Tm; FHA; Natl Beta Clb; Sec Pep Clb; Rptr Yrbk; VP Frsh Cls; Sec Soph Cls; Sec Jr Cls; High Hon Roll; OU.

WEBBER, JENNIFER; Oologah-Talala HS; Oologah, OK; (1); Ofcr Stu Cncl; JV Var Bsktbl; JV Chrldng; JV Var Sftbl; JV Var Trk; Wt Lftg; High Hon Roll; Hon Roll.

WEBBER, KASEY JO; Yukon Middle HS; Yukon, OK; (2); Church Yth Grp; FCA; FHA; Church Choir; Ofcr Stu Cncl; Mgr(s); Hon Roll; NHS; Mid-Amer Bible Coll; Phy Ther.

WEBER, GIFFORD; Valliant HS; Valliant, OK; (2); 2/86; Quiz Bowl; Ofcr Bsbl; NHS.

WEBER, JASON W; Okeene Jr Sr HS; Okeene, OK; (3); Cmnty Wkr; Drama Clb; Speech Tm; Ofcr Stu Cncl; Hon Roll; Electrncs.

WEBER, JILL; Okeene Jr Sr HS; Okeene, OK; (2); Art Clb; Church Yth Grp; FHA; Girl Scts; Speech Tm; School Play; Stage Crew; Rptr Nwsp; Phtg Yrbk; Rep Frsh Cls.

WEBER, NATHAN; Deer Creek HS; Edmond, OK; (3); French Clb; FBLA; Science Clb; SADD; Band; Crs Cntry; Gym; Tennis; High Hon Roll; NHS; Tae Kwon Do; U Tulsa; Elec Engr.

WEBER, ROBERT L; Weatherford HS; Weatherford, OK; (1); CAP; Band; Mrchg Band; Pep Band; Bsktbl; Crs Cntry; Trk; Wt Lftg; High Hon Roll; Pharmacy.

WEBER, SHAUNNA M; Olustee Schl; Olustee, OK; (3); Church Yth Grp; Science Clb; School Play; Rep Frsh Cls; Rep Soph Cls; Sec Jr Cls; Bsktbl; 4-H Awd; High Hon Roll; Hon Roll; OK Bapt Univ; Marine Biologist.

WEBSTER, AMY; Pryor Jr HS; Pryor, OK; (1); Church Yth Grp; Spanish Clb; Band; Jazz Band; Mrchg Band; School Play; Tennis; Hon Roll; NHS; Photo Clb; Bus.

WEBSTER, CINDI M; Putnam City North HS; Oklahoma City, OK; (3); 67/490; Church Yth Grp; Cmnty Wkr; Hosp Aide; Spanish Clb; Teachers Aide; Sec Sr Cls; Rep Stu Cncl; JV Bsktbl; Capt Golf; NHS; All-Conf Team Slctn Golf 94-; Physc Asst.

WEBSTER, JARED; Oktaha Jr Sr HS; Oktaha, OK; (4); 1/48; Am Leg Boys St; HOBY; Pres Spanish Clb; Pres SADD; Sprt Ed Nwsp; Pres Stu Cncl; Capt Bsbl; Capt Bsktbl; Pres NHS; Val.

WEBSTER, JESSICA; Oktaha Jr Sr HS; Oktaha, OK; (3); 1/49; 4-H; HOBY; Spanish Clb; Speech Tm; SADD; Yrbk; Sec Stu Cncl; Var Stat Bsktbl; Cit Awd; NHS; 4-H St Clthng Proj Wnnr, Cty Hll Fm; Fash Dsgn.

WEBSTER, KATHLEEN B; Enid Sr HS; Fridley, MN; (2); Church Yth Grp; Pep Clb; Band; Chorus; Mrchg Band; Pep Band; Swmmng; Hon Roll; NHS; Hnr Band Red Crpt/Tri-ST; Med Sci.

WEBSTER, MELISSA D; Harrah HS; Harrah, OK; (1); 1/180; FHA; Spanish Clb; JV Var Socr; High Hon Roll; Hon Roll; Pres Acad Fit Awd; Jujitsu; UCO; Art Dir; Photo.

WEBSTER, SARINA R; Kansas Schl; Kansas, OK; (4); Church Yth Grp; FCA; FBLA; GAA; Natl Beta Clb; Natl FFA Org; Office Aide; Nwsp; Yrbk; Bsktbl; Best All Around Girl; Northeastern ST Univ.

WECHSLER, R BRADLEY; Edmond Memorial HS; Jones, OK; (2); Church Yth Grp; FCA; Spanish Clb; Rep Soph Cls; Ofcr Jr Cls; JV Bsbl; Gov Hon Prg Awd; Hon Roll; NHS; Soph Stuco Rep Of Yr 95-.

WEDEL, KIM; Moore HS; Moore, OK; (4); Church Yth Grp; FCA; SADD; Var L Bsbl; NHS; Elem Ed.

WEDEL, SHANNON; Bridge Creek HS; Tuttle, OK; (4); 1/60; Cmnty Wkr; 4-H; HOBY; Key Clb; SADD; Ed Yrbk; Sec Rep Stu Cncl; Cit Awd; NHS; Art Clb; Grdy Co 4-H Hll Fm; Friends Chldrn St Awd; St Govs Ldrshp Awd; OK ST U; Vet Med.

WEDEL, TODD; Oklahoma Sch Of Science & Math; Hillsdale, OK; (4); Chess Clb; HOBY; Quiz Bowl; Orch; Ofcr Stu Cncl; High Hon Roll; JETS Awd; NHS; Ntl Merit SF; U OK; Arch.

WEED, RUSSELL W; Western Heights Sr HS; Oklahoma City, OK; (1); Boy Scts; Computer Clb; FBLA; Band; Jazz Band; Mrchg Band; Pep Band; High Hon Roll; Hon Roll; Supt Hon Rl; OK City Univ; Cmptr Sftwr Engr.

WEEDEN, RYAN; Elk City Jr HS; Elk City, OK; (1); Church Yth Grp; Natl FFA Org; Band; Jazz Band; Mrchg Band; Pep Band; Ofcr Bsbl; Golf; Tennis; High Hon Roll; FFA; OK U; Med.

WEEHUNT, VE RONICA R; Mc Alester HS; Mcalester, OK; (4); Church Yth Grp; DECA; French Clb; FHA; Science Clb; Speech Tm; Drill Tm; Flag Corp; Mgr Rptr Nwsp; Hon Roll; Poetry Pub By Natl Lib Of Congress; Schlsp For East Cntrl U In Ada; East Cntrl U; Pharmacy.

WEEKER, DAWN; Owasso Sr HS; Owasso, OK; (3); Church Yth Grp; FCA; Office Aide; Spanish Clb; Var Chrldng; Hon Roll; U Of OK.

WEEKS, AMY; Oolagah-Talala HS; Oologah, OK; (1); 20/121; Var Chrldng; Hon Roll; Co-Capt Chrldng; Comp Dance Troupe; Ped Phys Thrpy.

WEEKS, AMY R; Putnam City HS; Oklahoma City, OK; (1); Church Yth Grp; Cmnty Wkr; Chorus; Church Choir; School Musical; Lee Coll; Music; Choir.

WEEKS, ANGELA; Wynnewood HS; Wynnewood, OK; (3); 7/64; Cmnty Wkr; 4-H; FHA; Sec Natl FFA Org; Office Aide; Teachers Aide; Rep Soph Cls; Chrldng; Golf; NHS; OK ST Univ; Optometry.

WEEKS, BONNY L; Oklahoma Christian Acad; Edmond, OK; (3); Church Yth Grp; School Musical; School Play; Stage Crew; Rptr Nwsp; Yrbk; VP Soph Cls; Ofcr Bsbl; Bsktbl; Chrldng; Publctn Of Two Poems Through Natlsoc Of Poets; Jrnlsm.

WEEKS, LACEY; Edmond Memorial HS; Edmond, OK; (3); Church Yth Grp; Cmnty Wkr; French Clb; Office Aide; SADD; Varsity Clb; Chrldng; Capt Var Pom Pon; Cit Awd; Hon Roll; Natl Chmpn ASC Top Dncr Pom Pon; Capt Yar Pom Pon Sqd; AZ ST; Psych.

WEESE, DUSTIN L; Wagoner Sr HS; Wagoner, OK; (4); Bus Profs of Am; DECA; FCA; FBLA; FHA; Red Cross Aide; Teachers Aide; Rep Frsh Cls; Rep Soph Cls; Rep Jr Cls; Dist Ftbl Dfnsv End Of Yr; Lions Clb/Muskogee Pheonix All Star Tm; Rotary Stdnt Of Mnth; Tchr/Coach.

WEESE, JAMIE L; Union Intermediate HS; Broken Arrow, OK; (1); Church Yth Grp; Cmnty Wkr; FCA; GAA; JV Sftbl; High Hon Roll; Hon Roll; NHS; Tng Rep Sec; Pg St Leg; OK ST U; Elem Tchr.

WEESE, JONI; Shattuck Jr Sr HS; Shattuck, OK; (1); 2/36; Band; VP Chorus; Rep Nwsp; Pres Frsh Cls; Rep Stu Cncl; L Bsktbl; L Chrldng; Hon Roll; Southern Nazarene U; Poltcl Sci.

WEGLEY, BRIAN; Preston Schl; Preston, OK; (4); 2/29; Boy Scts; Church Yth Grp; Quiz Bowl; Scholastic Bowl; Nwsp; Yrbk; JV Bsktbl; Trk; High Hon Roll; NHS; OK St Univ; Chem Eng.

WEGNER, LORI A; Broken Arrow Sr HS; Broken Arrow, OK; (3); German Clb; Quiz Bowl; Chorus; Hon Roll; Jr NHS; Pres Acad Fit Awd; Explr Sct Post Sec; Engl.

WEHMEYER, JAMIE R; Union Intermediate HS; Tulsa, OK; (2); Church Yth Grp; Spanish Clb; High Hon Roll; Jr NHS; Taekwondo Blk Blt; Law.

WEIBLING, SARAH; Caddo HS; Caddo, OK; (2); 1/28; Church Yth Grp; FHA; HOBY; Capt Drill Tm; VP Frsh Cls; VP Soph Cls; Ofcr Stu Cncl; Var Bsbl; Var Bsktbl; Var Sftbl; Southeastrn OK St Currclm Meet Engl II, Vcblry, Alg I; Murray St Currclm Meet Vcblry, Engl I, Wrtng; SOSU; Jrnlsm.

WEIBLING, STEVEN; Caddo HS; Caddo, OK; (3); 2/30; Cmnty Wkr; Natl FFA Org; VP Soph Cls; Pres Jr Cls; Ftbl; Wt Lftg; High Hon Roll; Hon Roll; NHS; Prfct Atten Awd; Ftbl All-Dist Awd 95-96, Hnrb Mntn All-Dist Awd 94-95; OU; Ag.

WEICHBRODT, AUSTIN; Norman Sr HS; Norman, OK; (4); 1/650; FCA; Chorus; School Musical; Swing Chorus; Pres Frsh Cls; Ofcr Stu Cncl; Var Capt Bsktbl; Ftbl; JV Var Socr; Gov Hon Prg Awd; OK Baptist Univ; Pre-Med; Span.

WEICHBRODT, JOBE; Norman Sr HS; Norman, OK; (3); FCA; Var Bsktbl.

WEIDENMAIER, AMBER D; Ft Cobb Jr Sr HS; Fort Cobb, OK; (3); 5/29; Church Yth Grp; Cmnty Wkr; Pep Clb; Spanish Clb; Pres Soph Cls; Pres Jr Cls; Rep Stu Cncl; Bsktbl; Chrldng; Sftbl.

WEIGANT, JAMES; Pawhuska HS; Pawhuska, OK; (3); Boy Scts; Church Yth Grp; FCA; FBLA; Key Clb; Mu Alpha Theta; Quiz Bowl; Yrbk; Var Ftbl; High Hon Roll; St Gregory.

WEIKLE, JASON A; Guymon Sr HS; Guymon, OK; (4); 15/112; Church Yth Grp; Teachers Aide; Rep Stu Cncl; Var L Ftbl; Hon Roll; Jr NHS; NHS; Pres Acad Fit Awd; TX Tech Univ; Tchr & Coaching.

WEIL, LATASHA N; Clinton HS; Clinton, OK; (3); 43/129; Church Yth Grp; FHA; Hosp Aide; Yrbk; Rodeo Clb; Nrsng.

WEINGARTNER, HEATHER; Paoli HS; Pauls Valley, OK; (2); FHA; Office Aide; Teachers Aide; Rptr Nwsp; VP Soph Cls; Rep Stu Cncl; Hon Roll; Playng Guitar; Writng Poetry & Music.

WEINKAUF, BOBI; Perry Sr HS; Perry, OK; (3); Church Yth Grp; Drama Clb; German Clb; Chorus; School Musical; Hon Roll; Jr NHS; NHS; Poetry Awds; Vocal Perf.

WEIS, BEN; Edmond North HS; Edmond, OK; (4); 55/336; Cmnty Wkr; Math Clb; Mu Alpha Theta; Spanish Clb; SADD; High Hon Roll; Hon Roll; Jr NHS; NHS; Pres Acad Fit Awd; OK ST Univ; Engrg.

WEISS, ALEXANDRA D; B T Washington HS; Tulsa, OK; (3); VP Art Clb; Red Cross Aide; Spanish Clb; Ofcr Frsh Cls; Rep Soph Cls; Ofcr Jr Cls; Crs Cntry; Hon Roll; NHS; Med.

WEISSINGER, LYNN; Goodwell Public Schl; Goodwell, OK; (1); 1/16; Girl Scts; Library Aide; Band; Chorus; Rep Frsh Cls; Rep Stu Cncl; Hon Roll; Peer Hlprs.

WEISSINGER, MICHELLE; Guymon Sr HS; Guymon, OK; (3); Debate Tm; FCA; Band; VP Frsh Cls; Rep Soph Cls; Rep Jr Cls; Pres Sr Cls; Rep Stu Cncl; NHS.

WEISZ, KERRY A; B T Washington HS; Tulsa, OK; (2); Spanish Clb; Ed Nwsp; Rep Frsh Cls; Rep Stu Cncl; Var L Swmmng; NHS; Acad Ltr 94-95; Auto Clb; Vet Med.

WELCH, BARBARA E; Owasso Sr HS; Tulsa, OK; (2); Cmnty Wkr; Natl Beta Clb; Quiz Bowl; Science Clb; Rep Frsh Cls; Rep Soph Cls; Rep Stu Cncl; Hon Roll; Ntl Merit Ltr; Pres Acad Fit Awd; Harvard; Virologist.

WELCH, DIANA E; Westmoore HS; Oklahoma City, OK; (4); 14/610; French Clb; JA; Band; Color Guard; High Hon Roll; NHS; Val; Schlstc Tm; Oklahome City U; Acntng.

WELCH, DUSTIN; Hobart HS; Hobart, OK; (2); Church Yth Grp; Ofcr Bsbl; Bsktbl; Ftbl; Hon Roll; OK ST Univ; Bus.

WELCH, ERIC; Claremore Sr HS; Claremore, OK; (3); Library Aide; Teachers Aide; Ed Yrbk; Var Bsktbl; Socr; Cit Awd; High Hon Roll; Hon Roll; NHS; Prfct Atten Awd; KS U; Med.

WELCH, ERICA E; Waynoka HS; Waynoka, OK; (4); 5/25; Ed Yrbk; High Hon Roll; Hon Roll; NHS; Natl Voc Tech Hnr Soc Hlth Sci; Home Hlth.

WELCH, JOSEPH S; Ponca City Sr HS; Ponca City, OK; (3); Boy Scts; Church Yth Grp; Office Aide; Spanish Clb; Band; Mrchg Band; Rep Stu Cncl; Crs Cntry; Tennis; Hon Roll; St Gregories.

WELCH, KRISTI L; Byng Sr HS; Ada, OK; (2); Art Clb; VP FHA; Spanish Clb; Hon Roll; East Central Univ.

WELCH, MARTHA J; Putnam City North HS; Oklahoma City, OK; (4); 107/436; Church Yth Grp; Key Clb; SADD; Hon Roll; Jr NHS; NHS; OK ST Univ.

WELCHEL, DAWN; Mc Lish HS; Fittstown, OK; (3); 1/14; German Clb; VP Quiz Bowl; Rep Frsh Cls; Rep Soph Cls; Rep Jr Cls; High Hon Roll; Kiwanis Awd; NHS; Ntl Merit Ltr; Prfct Atten Awd; Stu Of Mnth; SOSU; CPA.

WELCHEL, REBEKAH; Bridge Creek HS; Blanchard, OK; (2); Art Clb; Church Yth Grp; FCA; SADD; Chorus; NHS; Ntl Merit Ltr.

WELD, VIRGINIA; Union City Schl; Mustang, OK; (2); Church Yth Grp; FHA; Girl Scts; Pep Clb; Chorus; Church Choir; School Musical; Sec Soph Cls; High Hon Roll; Hon Roll; Girl Scts Silver Awd; OK Bapt U; Bus.

WELDON, KAYCE M; Mangum Sr HS; Mangum, OK; (4); 10/46; FBLA; Natl FFA Org; Office Aide; SADD; Nwsp; Yrbk; Ofcr Frsh Cls; Ofcr Soph Cls; Ofcr Jr Cls; Ofcr Sr Cls; All St Spcl Recognition; All Conf; Altus Times All Area Hnrb Mntn; Western OK ST Coll; Bus Admin.

WELDON, KYLE C; Enid Sr HS; Enid, OK; (2); Church Yth Grp; Cmnty Wkr; Golf; Wt Lftg; Show Choir; Arch.

WELDON, MISTY; Eldorado Schl; Eldorado, OK; (4); #2 in class; FHA; Pep Clb; Pres Frsh Cls; Pres Jr Cls; Rptr Sr Cls; High Hon Roll; NHS; Pres Acad Fit Awd; Sal; Masonic Stu Of Today; W OK ST Coll; Nrsng.

WELKER, ALLISON S; Spiro HS; Spiro, OK; (3); Church Yth Grp; FHA; Natl FFA Org; Spanish Clb; Teachers Aide; Church Choir; Hon Roll; Carl Albert ST Coll; Tchr.

WELKER III, JOHN D; Putnam City North HS; Oklahoma City, OK; (4); 79/451; Church Yth Grp; Spanish Clb; SADD; Rep Bsktbl; Var Capt Tennis; Treas Jr NHS; NHS; Gftd & Tlntd Pgm; Friday Nwsp Pioneer Pies Ath Of The Week 4 Times; All-City Team 1 & 2 Doubles; OK Chrstn Univ; Engrng.

WELLES, JESSICA; Moore HS; Moore, OK; (4); 28/505; Art Clb; Church Yth Grp; French Clb; Math Clb; Math Tm; Mu Alpha Theta; Office Aide; Science Clb; Ski Clb; SADD; Waterpolo; OU; Engr.

WELLHAUSEN, MISTY L; North Intemediate HS; Broken Arrow, OK; (1); Art Clb; GAA; Band; Color Guard; Mrchg Band; Crs Cntry; Trk; Hon Roll; Jr NHS; Law.

WELLS, ASHLEY D; West Jr HS; Oklahoma City, OK; (1); French Clb; GAA; Rep Stu Cncl; Var L Socr; JV Trk; Hon Roll; NHS; Mmbr Classic Scr Team-Cptl City Elite 80.

WELLS, AZURE D; Putnam City North HS; Oklahoma City, OK; (3); German Clb; Socr; Trk; Jr NHS; NHS; Bio.

WELLS, BECKI R; Bray-Doyle HS; Foster, OK; (2); VP FHA; Speech Tm; SADD; Chorus; Sec Frsh Cls; L Bsktbl; OK Bapt Univ.

WELLS, CANDICE; Putnam City West HS; Bethany, OK; (2); Church Yth Grp; FCA; Latin Clb; Chrldng; Soccer Mgr; CIA; OSU; Intnl Bus.

WELLS, CHRIS; Plainview HS; Ardmore, OK; (1); Church Yth Grp; FHA; Church Choir; High Hon Roll; Intnl Ord De Moley.

WELLS, CINDI; Stoud HS; Stroud, OK; (4); 2/32; Am Leg Aux Girls St; Church Yth Grp; FCA; HOBY; Chorus; School Musical; Yrbk; Rep Stu Cncl; Sal; Msct; U Of Cntrl OK; Phy Ther.

WELLS, ERIC; Deer Creek HS; Edmond, OK; (4); 6/68; Art Clb; Church Yth Grp; FCA; Office Aide; Science Clb; Teachers Aide; Var L Bsbl; Var Ftbl; NHS; Jr HS Dscplshp Ldr; Art Clb Pres; Hbt Hmnty Cmnty Svc Wk; U Of Cntrl OK; Art Ed.

WELLS, G MICHELLE; Washington HS; Washington, OK; (2); 9/48; Church Yth Grp; FCA; 4-H; FBLA; FHA; Sftbl; NHS; Frosh Rep, Treas, Pres & Pub Relations Sub Dist; FHA Sr Talk Cont; Gold Sash Kung-Fu; Law.

WELLS, GRACE; Bixby Sr HS; Bixby, OK; (2); Cmnty Wkr; Drama Clb; German Clb; Office Aide; SADD; Thesps; School Play; Hist Frsh Cls; High Hon Roll; Jr NHS; Cornell Univ; Wrtng.

WELLS, JAMES T; Union Intermediate HS; Tulsa, OK; (2); Mrchg Band; Diving; High Hon Roll; Hon Roll; Pres Schlr; Spanish NHS; Swmmng; Presidential Schlr; USS Diving Jr Olympic; Frontier Conf; All Star Ath; Whos Who In Sports.

WELLS, JENNIFER L; Tahlequah Sr HS; Tahlequah, OK; (2); Band; Drm Mjr(t); Mst Otsdng Soph Female HI Band; All Dist Hnr Band/Tri ST Hnr Band 95-; Superior Rtngs Dist/ST Solo; Pharm.

WELLS, KENDALL; Berryhill Jr HS; Tulsa, OK; (3); 2/95; FCA; Mu Alpha Theta; Office Aide; Spanish Clb; Teachers Aide; Rptr Stu Cncl; L Ftbl; Var Wt Lftg; High Hon Roll; NHS; Chrch Yth Grp; Big Bro/Sis; Srteens; OK ST U; Med.

WELLS, KRISTINA M; Carl Albert HS; Choctaw, OK; (3); 53/219; Chorus; JV Tennis; High Hon Roll; Hon Roll; NHS; Publctns In Schl Dist Editorial; Law.

WELLS, LEANNA M; Dibble Jr Sr HS; Dibble, OK; (2); GAA; Bsktbl; Sftbl; Vllybl; CPA; Acctng; Comps.

WELLS, MELISSA L; Bartlesville Sr HS; Bartlesville, OK; (1); Dance Clb; Office Aide; Hon Roll; Pres Acad Fit Awd; OK ST Univ.

WELLS, MICHAEL; Roff HS; Fitzhugh, OK; (2); Church Yth Grp; Cmnty Wkr; Natl FFA Org; Hon Roll; FFA Cls Ofcr 95-97; Vol Firefighter; FFA Speech Team; OSU; Paramedic; Firefighter.

WELLS, RACHEL; Yukon Middle HS; Yukon, OK; (3); 219/409; FHA; Pom Pon; Multi-Yr Listee; OK Univ; Commnctns.

WELLS, RICKY; Broken Bow HS; Broken Bow, OK; (4); 2/150; Am Leg Boys St; FCA; Capt Quiz Bowl; Science Clb; Spanish Clb; Var L Ftbl; High Hon Roll; Hon Roll; NHS.

WELLS, RUSSELL R; Lindsay HS; Lindsay, OK; (3); 5/70; Natl FFA Org; Scholastic Bowl; Varsity Clb; Bsktbl; Cit Awd; Hon Roll; NHS; Rodeo OK HS; Ag; Bus.

WELLS, TAMMY; Salina HS; Salina, OK; (2); Color Guard; Jazz Band; VP Mrchg Band; Pep Band; Hon Roll; Bnd Ldrsp Awd; Clr Grd Ldrsp Awd; Marine Bio.

WELLS, TEKISHA; Central HS; Tulsa, OK; (4); 13/176; Church Yth Grp; Intnl Clb; Ofcr Stu Cncl; High Hon Roll; Hon Roll; NHS; Prfct Atten Awd; HOSA VP 94-95; Tulsa JC; Med.

WELLS, TRISHA D; Bartlesville Mid HS; Bartlesville, OK; (2); 81/481; Church Yth Grp; French Clb; Pep Clb; Chorus; School Musical; Hon Roll; Prfct Atten Awd; OK ST Univ.

WELTER, LISA K; South Intermediate HS; Broken Arrow, OK; (1); Church Yth Grp; Cmnty Wkr; French Clb; Band; Mrchg Band; Pep Band; Hon Roll; Jr NHS; Pres Acad Fit Awd; Brigham Young U; Elem Ed.

WELTY, SARAH; Elmore City-Pernell HS; Wynnewood, OK; (1); 16/67; 4-H; Chorus; Pep Band; School Musical; Bsktbl; Chrldng; Trk; 4-H Awd; Cty 4-H Hll Fm; Prk Cncl Assn; OK ST U.

WENDLANDT, BRIAN; Stigler HS; Stigler, OK; (4); Am Leg Boys St; Boy Scts; Church Yth Grp; Natl FFA Org; Teachers Aide; Band; Church Choir; Mrchg Band; Pep Band; Ofcr Stu Cncl; Conners St Coll; Ag.

WENDT, JENNIFER; Lone Grove HS; Lone Grove, OK; (2); 2/107; Church Yth Grp; FCA; Yrbk; Sftbl; High Hon Roll; NHS; Pres Acad Fit Awd; 1st Tm All Area Sftbl; U Of OK; Meteorology.

WENDTE, JEREMY; Empire Schl; Duncan, OK; (2); Cmnty Wkr; FCA; Key Clb; Science Clb; Spanish Clb; Pres Frsh Cls; Ftbl; Cit Awd; Kiwanis Awd; Eagle Scout 94.

WENRICH, JOHN; Eufaula Sr HS; Eufaula, OK; (2); Hon Roll; VA Military Inst; Arspc.

WERHAN, CHRISTY D; Velma Alma HS; Velma, OK; (4); Church Yth Grp; Cmnty Wkr; 4-H; Girl Scts; Key Clb; NFL; Pep Clb; Scholastic Bowl; Speech Tm; Teachers Aide; Southwestern OK St Univ Bus.

WERMY, KRISTOPHER KIAS; Clinton HS; Clinton, OK; (1); Boy Scts; Church Yth Grp; Cmnty Wkr; FCA; Letterman Clb; Spanish Clb; Ofcr Stu Cncl; Ofcr Bsbl; Bsktbl; Ftbl; Eagle Sct.

WERMY, MARIA D; Cache HS; Cache, OK; (3); Church Yth Grp; Key Clb; Acpl Chr; Chorus; Church Choir; School Musical; Hon Roll; Punctual Attendance Awd; Cameron; Vet Medicine.

WERNER, KEVIN; Broken Arrow Sr HS; Broken Arrow, OK; (4); 9/921; Am Leg Boys St; Boy Scts; Church Yth Grp; FCA; Band; Ofcr Sr Cls; Ftbl; Cit Awd; VP NHS; St Schlr; Oral Roberts U; Comp Sci.

WERNER, REGINA; Roff HS; Roff, OK; (3); 2/25; Am Leg Aux Girls St; Natl Beta Clb; Scholastic Bowl; Teachers Aide; Rptr Nwsp; Sec Frsh Cls; Rep Soph Cls; Rep Jr Cls; Capt Chrldng; NHS; Wdmn Of Wrld Awd OK His.

WERT, HEATHER; Moore HS; Moore, OK; (4); 137/549; Sec Treas Science Clb; SADD; Band; Capt Color Guard; Mrchg Band; Wntrgrd; Bnd Cncl Hstrn; U Of OK; Ed.

WESCOATT, BENJAMIN M; Guymon Sr HS; Guymon, OK; (4); 1/120; Church Yth Grp; Band; Chorus; School Musical; Bsktbl; Kiwanis Awd; Pres NHS; Val; Rotary Stu Of Month; OK ST U; Civil Engrng.

WESLEY, HOLLY; Rattan Sr HS; Ft Towson, OK; (3); 3/41; Church Yth Grp; FCA; 4-H; HOBY; Quiz Bowl; Sec Jr Cls; High Hon Roll; NHS; Ntl Merit Ltr; East Central U; Nursng.

WESLEY, JONATHON I; Mc Alester HS; Mcalester, OK; (2); FCA; JV Var Ftbl; Hon Roll; Military.

WESLEY, SIAH; Holdnville HS; Holdenville, OK; (4); 27/75; Am Leg Boys St; FBLA; Natl Beta Clb; Office Aide; Yrbk; Var Bsbl; Var Bsktbl; Var Ftbl; Var Wt Lftg; Hon Roll; Upwrd Bound; Weightlftng 3rd Pl St; Murray St Comp Pgmng 2nd Pl 95; East Central U; Envrnmntl Sci.

WESSEL, KRISTIN N; Claremore Sr HS; Claremore, OK; (1); Church Yth Grp; Treas German Clb; Quiz Bowl; Socr; Hon Roll; Ntl Merit Ltr; US Natl Math Awd; Yale; Arch.

WESSEL, MATTHEW R; Ripley HS; Stillwater, OK; (1); Church Yth Grp; Natl FFA Org; Quiz Bowl; Var Bsbl; JV Bsktbl; Trk; Hon Roll; OK ST U; Law Enfrcmnt.

WEST, AMBER N; Putnam City North HS; Oklahoma City, OK; (1); Church Yth Grp; Cmnty Wkr; FCA; JA; Key Clb; Office Aide; Quiz Bowl; Scholastic Bowl; Chorus; Church Choir; Cause Clb; OSU; Psych/Cnslr.

WEST, ASHLEE E; Edmond North HS; Edmond, OK; (3); 98/347; Church Yth Grp; Mu Alpha Theta; Spanish Clb; Phy Thrpst.

WEST, ELIZABETH; Haileyville Schl; Mc Alester, OK; (3); 6/35; FBLA; Natl FFA Org; Var Bsktbl; Var Sftbl; Hon Roll; NHS; OK Hnr Soc; Indian Hnr Soc; Stu Of The Month Dec; VP FFA Org; Dntst.

WEST, JAMES B; Mill Creek Schl; Mill Creek, OK; (2); 1/14; Church Yth Grp; Ofcr Soph Cls; Ofcr Bsbl; Bsktbl; Hon Roll; Elec Engr.

WEST IV, JOHN; Moore HS; Moore, OK; (4); 271/505; Am Leg Boys St; Art Clb; Church Yth Grp; Drama Clb; JCL; Latin Clb; Science Clb; Acpl Chr; Band; Jazz Band; Cert Recog Chrstn Ldrshp; 1st Pl OJCL Pncl Inks; Hndbll Chr; Chrch Bnd; U Cntrl OK; Vsul Perfrmng Arts.

WEST, LORI M; Catoosa HS; Tulsa, OK; (4); 5/135; Church Yth Grp; FCA; FHA; Intnl Clb; Spanish Clb; Chorus; Church Choir; Color Guard; Chrldng; NHS; OK Bptst U.

WEST, RAY B; Central Schl; Muldrow, OK; (2); Church Yth Grp; Quiz Bowl; Var Bsktbl; Var Wt Lftg; NHS; Octagon Clb Rptr; OK Bapt Univ; Tchng; Broadcstng.

WEST, RYAN L; Western Heights Sr HS; Oklahoma City, OK; (4); 21/138; Boy Scts; VP Chess Clb; Pres Cmnty Wkr; Pres French Clb; VP FBLA; Co-Capt Math Tm; Co-Capt Quiz Bowl; Pres Science Clb; Teachers Aide; Rep Sr Cls; U Of OK; Civil Engrng.

WESTBERRY, JILL; Moore HS; Moore, OK; (2); Church Yth Grp; Chorus; Church Choir; Rptr Nwsp; Ed Yrbk; Bsktbl; Tennis; Cit Awd; Jr NHS.

WESTBROOK, FORREST L; Edmond Memorial HS; Edmond, OK; (3); 92/371; Band; Mrchg Band; Pep Band; OK ST U; Chem.

WESTBROOK, JANA L; Putnam City North HS; Oklahoma City, OK; (1); Church Yth Grp; 4-H; Band; Church Choir; Mrchg Band; Pep Band; Cit Awd; 4-H Awd; Modeling; Marching Band Section Ldr; Elem Grd Tchr.

WESTBROOK, JENA; Broken Bow HS; Broken Bow, OK; (4); 15/150; Drama Clb; Science Clb; Speech Tm; Pres Chorus; Church Choir; School Musical; School Play; Stage Crew; NHS; St Supts Art Excllnc Awd; Natl Miss Teen Of Amer Pgnt Vocal Talent Awd; Northwestern ST U; Vocal Perf.

WESTER, ALISA L; Guymon Sr HS; Guymon, OK; (4); 1/111; Church Yth Grp; Model UN; Teachers Aide; Band; Mrchg Band; Treas Stu Cncl; Hon Roll; NHS; Val; FHA; Peer Hope Delgation; OK ST U; Bus.

WESTERN, CHARITY; Bartlesville Sr HS; Bartlesville, OK; (4); Science Clb; Spanish Clb; Chorus; Church Choir; School Musical; Vllybl; High Hon Roll; Hon Roll; Spanish NHS; SPCA Post Mem; Sci Clb VP; Med Post Mem; Northeastern ST U; Pre-Pharmcy.

WESTERVELT, ABBIE; Guthrie Sr HS; Meridian, OK; (3); Hosp Aide; Key Clb; Mu Alpha Theta; Science Clb; Spanish Clb; SADD; School Play; Variety Show; Nwsp; JV Var Crs Cntry; Tchr.

WESTERVELT, DUSTON R; Calumet Schl; Calumet, OK; (2); School Musical; School Play; Ofcr Bsbl; Bsktbl.

WESTMORELAND, BROOKE; Cushing HS; Cushing, OK; (3); Church Yth Grp; Math Clb; Science Clb; Spanish Clb; Band; Drm Mjr(t); Mrchg Band; Ed Yrbk; Rep Stu Cncl; Tennis; Rotry Yth Ldrshp Awd; PSE; Stu Rotarian Of Week; OU; Psych.

WESTON, DANYALE; Wilburton Jr HS; Wilburton, OK; (1); 11/96; Church Yth Grp; Spanish Clb; Nwsp; Bsktbl; Cit Awd; NHS; Pres Acad Fit Awd; Tennis.

WESTON, JANNA D; Wilburton Sr HS; Wilburton, OK; (1); 10/96; Church Yth Grp; Spanish Clb; Nwsp; Var Bsktbl; Cit Awd; Hon Roll; NHS; Pres Acad Fit Awd; Tnns; Roller Blading; Swimming; Sftbl.

WESTON, TIM; Carl Albert HS; Midwest City, OK; (4); 19/239; Am Leg Boys St; FCA; Key Clb; Office Aide; Pep Clb; Jazz Band; Rep Stu Cncl; Ftbl; Val; Acad Ltr Jacket; OK ST U; Mech Engr.

WESTPHAL, ANNICA B; Union Intermediate HS; Tulsa, OK; (2); Church Yth Grp; Swmmng; Hon Roll; NHS; Frgn Lang Clb 95-96; Childrns Church Tchr 2 Yrs; Oral Roberts U; Bus.

WETMORE, JENNIFER L; Broken Arrow Sr HS; Broken Arrow, OK; (3); Pres Church Yth Grp; Debate Tm; NFL; Mgr(s); NHS; Nutrition Advy Cncl Pres.

WETMORE, MATTHEW A; Union Sr HS; Tulsa, OK; (3); Debate Tm; Scholastic Bowl; Speech Tm; Acad Rsrc Ctr; Natl Frnscs Lg Spec Dstnctn; Yng Rpblcns; Drg Free Yth; U Of OK; Polysci.

WETMORE, MISTY; Macarthur Sr HS; Lawton, OK; (3); 1/200; Am Leg Aux Girls St; Church Yth Grp; HOBY; Acpl Chr; Chorus; Church Choir; Rep Frsh Cls; Rep Soph Cls; Rep Jr Cls; High Hon Roll; Keywanettes Clb VP.

WETZ, MARCUS; Midwest City HS; Midwest City, OK; (3); 10/384; Art Clb; Debate Tm; Hosp Aide; Letterman Clb; Treas Frsh Cls; Var L Golf; High Hon Roll; Hon Roll; Jr NHS; NHS; Intl Bus.

WETZEL, SHAYLA D; Jay HS; Jay, OK; (4); Church Yth Grp; FCA; FBLA; Natl Beta Clb; Ofcr Stu Cncl; Bsktbl; Powder Puff Ftbl; Sftbl; Hon Roll; NHS; NSU.

WETZLER, KIM; North Intemediate HS; Broken Arrow, OK; (1); Church Yth Grp; Spanish Clb; Band; Pep Band; JV Chrldng; Gym; High Hon Roll; NHS; Kneebrdng/Water Skiing; Snow Skiing & Swmmng.

WEWELL, STEPHANIE M; Woodward HS; Woodward, OK; (1); Art Clb; Church Yth Grp; Cmnty Wkr; Dance Clb; Debate Tm; FCA; German Clb; Girl Scts; Speech Tm; Church Choir; Speech Clb; Southwestern OK U; Child Psych.

WHALEY, CHARISSA M; Moore HS; Moore, OK; (3); 18/600; Church Yth Grp; Cmnty Wkr; FBLA; Model UN; Band; Chorus; French Hon Soc; NHS; Pres Acad Fit Awd; French Clb; Mock Trl; Harding U.

WHALLON, KRISTY J; Westville HS; Westville, OK; (3); Church Yth Grp; FHA; Chorus; Church Choir; Cert Prtcptn 95 OK Stck Mrkt Gm; 4 Tm Spr Slst Cert Awd Northeastern OK A&M Coll Msc Fstvl.

WHANG, TIMOTHY; Western Heights Sr HS; Oklahoma City, OK; (3); 1/215; Church Yth Grp; Letterman Clb; Varsity Clb; Sec Soph Cls; Rep Stu Cncl; JV L Bsktbl; Cit Awd; High Hon Roll; NHS; Prfct Atten Awd; Pre-Med; Sports Med.

WHATLEY, LA DONNA; Dickson HS; Ardmore, OK; (1); Church Yth Grp; FHA; Spanish Clb; SADD; JV Chrldng; NHS; Natl His/Govt Awd; Obstrcn.

WHAYLEN, ALLISON; Blackwell HS; Blackwell, OK; (3); Church Yth Grp; Hosp Aide; Letterman Clb; Pep Clb; Spanish Clb; Band; Tennis; High Hon Roll; NHS; St Schlr; Bnd Stu Mnth; Grls St; Phrmcy.

WHEAT, ANGELA; Bartlesville Sr HS; Bartlesville, OK; (4); Church Yth Grp; FHA; Chorus; School Musical; Sftbl; Trk; Cit Awd; High Hon Roll; Hon Roll; Jr NHS; U Of OK; PT.

WHEELER, AMY; Victory Christian Schl; Broken Arrow, OK; (1); Church Yth Grp; Band; Jazz Band; Pep Band; Chrldng; High Hon Roll; Jr NHS; Nursng.

WHEELER, BRIAN S; Milburn Schl; Milburn, OK; (4); 4/24; Am Leg Boys St; Cmnty Wkr; Capt Debate Tm; VP Pres 4-H; Natl FFA Org; Quiz Bowl; Scholastic Bowl; Varsity Clb; Rep Jr Cls; VP Sr Cls; Top 3 With 4-H St Record Bk; Natl Congress 4-H Wnnr; Ctznshp Focus 4-H Wnnr; Murray ST Coll; Chem Eng.

WHEELER, CHRIS A; Putnam City North HS; Oklahoma City, OK; (3); Church Yth Grp; Key Clb; Spanish Clb; Church Choir; Stage Crew; Ofcr Stu Cncl; Var L Crs Cntry; Var L Trk; Cit Awd; Hon Roll; TX A&M; Law Enforcement; Music.

WHEELER, CHRISTOPHER A; Union Sr HS; Tulsa, OK; (3); 30/741; School Musical; Rep Stu Cncl; High Hon Roll; NHS; Prfct Atten Awd; Pres Schlr; Church Yth Grp; Chorus; Outstndng Soph Boy 94-95; Mr Union Rylty 95-96; Tri-M; Tee-Pee Crw; Baylor U; Chrstn Mnstry.

WHEELER, JOHN S; Muskogee HS; Muskogee, OK; (3); Drama Clb; FCA; Math Clb; Office Aide; Varsity Clb; Stage Crew; Var Ftbl; JV Wrstlng; Hon Roll; Jr NHS; Senate Page; OK Univ; Bus Admin.

WHEELER, JOSHUA; Crescent Schl; Crescent, OK; (2); 2/53; FCA; Band; Pep Band; L Bsbl; L Ftbl; L Wt Lftg; High Hon Roll; FFA; OSU.

WHEELER, KRISTOPHER RYAN; Deer Creek HS; Edmond, OK; (3); Phtg Yrbk; Var L Bsbl; Capt L Ftbl; Ice Hcky; Bus Profs of Am; Church Yth Grp; Cmnty Wkr; Computer Clb; Drama Clb; FCA; His Clb; Ecology; Clemson; Bus.

WHEELER, LINDSAY B; West Jr HS; Oklahoma City, OK; (1); Church Yth Grp; Spanish Clb; Chorus; Mgr Bsktbl; Hon Roll; Jr NHS; Med.

WHEELER, LISA M; Muskogee HS; Muskogee, OK; (1); Church Yth Grp; Chorus; Church Choir; Treas Frsh Cls; JV Chrldng; Hon Roll; RAID; Teens For Christ; NE ST U; Med Dr.

WHEELER, MITZI; Chandler HS; Chandler, OK; (4); 7/69; Am Leg Aux Girls St; Church Yth Grp; Pres FHA; HOBY; Chorus; Rep Frsh Cls; Rep Stu Cncl; High Hon Roll; NHS; Lifeguides Peer Helper; Office Aide; Rotarian Mon; Elem Ed.

WHEELER, NATALIE L; Douglass HS; Oklahoma City, OK; (4); 36/116; Chorus; Var Chrldng; Crs Cntry; Capt Pom Pon; Hon Roll; PRIDE; Coll Clb; Northeastern ST U; Elem Ed/Jrn.

WHEELER III, ROGER XM; B T Washington HS; Tulsa, OK; (1); Boy Scts; Golf; Intnl Baccalaureate Stdnt; Engr.

WHEELER, RUSTY; Valliant HS; Valliant, OK; (2); 3/86; Drama Clb; FHA; Quiz Bowl; Spanish Clb; Speech Tm; Rep Stu Cncl; Hon Roll; NHS.

WHEELER, STEPHANIE L; Westmoore HS; Oklahoma City, OK; (4); 220/610; FCA; Pres Stu Cncl; Var Bsktbl; Var Mgr(s); Var Sftbl; Bsktbl Queen; All ST Sftbl; Sftbl Plyr Yr; OK ST Univ; Mktg.

WHEELER, YASMIN ALEXANDRA; Cascia Hall Prep School; Tulsa, OK; (3); 10/80; Church Yth Grp; Cmnty Wkr; Latin Clb; Chorus; School Musical; Ed Yrbk; Var L Trk; Hon Roll; NHS; Prfct Atten Awd; Magna Cum Laude Natl Latin Exam; William & Mary; Envirnmntl Stu.

WHELCHEL, DAWN; Mc Lish HS; Pontotoc, OK; (3); 1/14; German Clb; Quiz Bowl; Scholastic Bowl; Rep Frsh Cls; Rep Soph Cls; Rep Jr Cls; High Hon Roll; NHS; Ntl Merit Ltr; Prfct Atten Awd; ECU; Pre-Med.

WHERLEY, JAMIE; North Intermediate HS; Broken Arrow, OK; (1); Natl FFA Org; Quiz Bowl; Rep Stu Cncl; Chrldng; Cit Awd; Hon Roll; Jr NHS; OSU; Bus Mgmt.

WHETSTINE, TAMRA M; Blackwell HS; Blackwell, OK; (3); Art Clb; Church Yth Grp; Library Aide; Artist Of Yr Awd Nom; Elem Ed.

WHETSTONE, AARON LLOYD; Trinity Christian Schl; Broken Arrow, OK; (4); Church Yth Grp; Chorus; Church Choir; School Play; Nwsp; Var Bsktbl; Var Socr; Hon Roll; Prfct Atten Awd; Sports Med.

WHETSTONE, RACHEL L; Trinity Christian Schl; Broken Arrow, OK; (2); Church Yth Grp; Pep Clb; Chorus; Church Choir; School Play; Chrldng; Vllybl; Hon Roll; Msc/Missions.

WHINERY, BRAD; Sayre HS; Sayre, OK; (4); 5/42; Am Leg Boys St; Church Yth Grp; FCA; Letterman Clb; Scholastic Bowl; Band; Jazz Band; Mrchg Band; OU; Med.

WHISENANT, BECKY; Hollis Jr Sr HS; Hollis, OK; (4); 5/53; Am Leg Aux Girls St; FBLA; Library Aide; Nwsp; Yrbk; NHS; Jr Aeolian Pres; SW OK ST U.

WHISENHUNT, AMBER; Oklahoma Sch Of Science & Math; Broken Arrow, OK; (3); CAP; Cmnty Wkr; Dance Clb; Latin Clb; Bsktbl; Sftbl; Wt Lftg; High Hon Roll; Jr NHS; NHS; Billy Mitchell Awd; Masonic Stu Today Awd; U Of OK; Engrng.

WHISENHUNT, AMY K; Enid Sr HS; Enid, OK; (4); 18/412; Library Aide; Q&S; Ofcr Science Clb; Teachers Aide; Chorus; High Hon Roll; Jr NHS; NHS; Pres Acad Fit Awd; St Schlr; Big Brother/Big Sisters; Hnrs Grad; Acad Ltrmn; Northwestern OSU; Medcl.

WHISENHUNT, ANTHONY R; Wilburton Sr HS; Wilburton, OK; (1); FCA; Ftbl; Trk; Wt Lftg; Pres Acad Fit Awd; Conners Univ.

WHISENHUNT, JEREMY W; Bridge Creek HS; Tuttle, OK; (2); Church Yth Grp; Cmnty Wkr; Spanish Clb; Band; Jazz Band; Mrchg Band; Orch; Bsktbl; Prfct Atten Awd; Flyng Lsns.

WHITAKER, LEANDA S; Colbert Jr Sr HS; Cartwright, OK; (1); FCA; Hosp Aide; MIT; Pediatrician.

WHITAKER, LINDSAY C; Deer Creek HS; Edmond, OK; (1); Church Yth Grp; Band; Church Choir; Mrchg Band; High Hon Roll; Hon Roll; NHS; OK All ST Bapt Yth Choir; ST Level In Band; Church Yth Actvts; OK Bapt Univ.

WHITCOMB, COURTNEY; Woodward HS; Woodward, OK; (1); Church Yth Grp; FCA; GAA; Pep Clb; Yrbk; Bsktbl; Chrldng; Trk; High Hon Roll; 4 Yr Coll.

WHITE, AMANDA E; Union Intermediate HS; Tulsa, OK; (1); Church Yth Grp; FCA; Chorus; Church Choir; High Hon Roll; NHS; Union Stdnts For Christ; ROTUS Bible Study.

WHITE, AMBER; Varnum Jr Sr HS; Seminole, OK; (2); 1/26; Church Yth Grp; FCA; 4-H; FHA; HOBY; Rep Frsh Cls; Bsktbl; Sftbl; High Hon Roll; NHS.

WHITE, AMY E; Stillwater Sr HS; Stillwater, OK; (3); 47/350; Church Yth Grp; JCL; Key Clb; Mu Alpha Theta; Natl Beta Clb; Band; Chorus; Orch; NHS; Kiwanis Awd; Key Clb Lt Govnr; OK St Univ; Mus.

WHITE, APRIL D; Warner HS; Muskogee, OK; (4); 23/51; 4-H; FBLA; FHA; 4-H Awd; Hon Roll; Social Day Awd; 4-H Qn; OSU-OKMULGEE Schlsps; OSU; Med Secy.

WHITE, BILL; Paoli HS; Paoli, OK; (2); 1/22; Church Yth Grp; HOBY; Natl FFA Org; Quiz Bowl; Scholastic Bowl; Pres Soph Cls; Var Bsbl; Var JV Bsktbl; Var Ftbl; Hon Roll; Male Stu Yr 94-95; Cmptr Prgmmng.

WHITE, BRAD A; Cushing HS; Cushing, OK; (1); Church Yth Grp; FCA; 4-H; Natl FFA Org; Scholastic Bowl; JV Bsbl; JV Ftbl; JV Wt Lftg; High Hon Roll; Hon Roll.

WHITE, BRENDA; Putnam City HS; Oklahoma City, OK; (3); 30/327; Church Yth Grp; French Clb; Orch; Rep Stu Cncl; Mgr Ftbl; Hon Roll; NHS; Art Clb; FCA; Library Aide; Silver Strings Of Putnam City; Stdnt St Stdnt; OK Bapt Symphny; Music/Pre Med.

WHITE, BRET W; Cushing HS; Cushing, OK; (2); Church Yth Grp; FCA; 4-H; Natl FFA Org; Office Aide; Teachers Aide; JV Bsbl; JV Ftbl; JV Wt Lftg; High Hon Roll.

WHITE, BRIAN D; B T Washington HS; Tulsa, OK; (1); Church Yth Grp; French Clb; JCL; Latin Clb; Scholastic Bowl; Church Choir; Ofcr Bsbl; High Hon Roll; Acad Bowl.

WHITE, CARL; Hilldale HS; Muskogee, OK; (4); 3/92; Am Leg Boys St; FCA; Key Clb; Mu Alpha Theta; Science Clb; Ftbl; Vllybl; Wt Lftg; High Hon Roll; NHS; Defensve Plyr Of Yr 95; Ftbl All-Star All-Area 96; Optmst Clb Mr Teen 96; OK ST U; Comp Engrng.

WHITE, CARMEN; Woodward HS; Woodward, OK; (1); Church Yth Grp; Cmnty Wkr; FCA; Letterman Clb; Spanish Clb; Bsktbl; Mgr(s); Trk; High Hon Roll; NHS; PT.

WHITE, CARRIE; Woodward HS; Woodward, OK; (1); Church Yth Grp; Cmnty Wkr; FCA; Letterman Clb; Pep Clb; Bsktbl; Mgr(s); Trk; Hon Roll.

WHITE, CHAD; Crowder Schl; Crowder, OK; (2); Natl FFA Org; Varsity Clb; Ofcr Bsbl; Bsktbl; Hon Roll; Archry Trnmnts; Bllrdng.

WHITE JR, CHARLES L; North Intemediate HS; Broken Arrow, OK; (2); Church Yth Grp; Debate Tm; FCA; Hosp Aide; Scholastic Bowl; Rptr Nwsp; Hon Roll; Jr NHS; Pres Acad Fit Awd; Tulsa Zoo Teen Vol; Nutrtnl Adsry Cncl; West Point; Law/Pol.

WHITE, CHAZ A; Yukon Middle HS; Yukon, OK; (2); JV Bsbl; JV Ftbl; Intrml Wrstlng; Hon Roll; Rylty Kng.

WHITE, CHERYL; Moore HS; Moore, OK; (3); Church Yth Grp; Drama Clb; Spanish Clb; Bsktbl; Tennis; Wt Lftg; OK U; Dentstry.

WHITE, CORENA; Mc Alester HS; Mcalester, OK; (4); 28/216; Am Leg Aux Girls St; Church Yth Grp; Science Clb; Spanish Clb; Church Choir; Yrbk; Var Bsktbl; Sec Mgr(s); Cit Awd; Afro Stu Union Sec; DECA Rprtr; Langston U; Phys Thrpy.

WHITE, COURTNEY D; Durant HS; Durant, OK; (1); Church Yth Grp; FCA; Pres Frsh Cls; Ofcr Stu Cncl; Bsktbl; Crs Cntry; Powder Puff Ftbl; Trk; Cit Awd; Hon Roll; Cub Awd; Masons Achvmt Awd; Ath Awd; Dr.

WHITE, CURTIS L; Lindsay HS; Lindsay, OK; (1); Church Yth Grp; Ofcr Bsbl; Bsktbl; MVP Awd Bsebl Tourn; OK Univ.

WHITE, DANIEL O; B T Washington HS; Tulsa, OK; (1); ROTC; Natl Eagle Sct Assn.

WHITE, ERIN; Yukon HS; Yukon, OK; (3); Church Yth Grp; FCA; SADD; Nwsp; Pres Jr Cls; Ofcr Stu Cncl; NHS; Stdnt Ath Trnr Ftbl/Bsktbl/Bsbl; Art/Comm/Med.

WHITE, GENESIS L; Duncan HS; Duncan, OK; (3); Church Yth Grp; Cmnty Wkr; Debate Tm; FCA; Letterman Clb; NFL; SADD; JV Bsktbl; Var Trk; Hon Roll; OK ST U; Pre-Med.

WHITE, GINA M; Coyle Public Schl; Coyle, OK; (3); #8 in class; Cmnty Wkr; FCA; FHA; Ed Nwsp; Yrbk; Var Bsktbl; Cit Awd; Hon Roll; German Clb; Pep Clb; Amer Pride; Natl Yng Ldrs Conf; Church; Langston Univ; Acctng/Bkkpng.

WHITE, GRETCHEN; Okeene Jr Sr HS; Ames, OK; (4); 6/26; Church Yth Grp; FHA; HOBY; Letterman Clb; Speech Tm; Stage Crew; Nwsp; Yrbk; Pres Frsh Cls; Rep Soph Cls; Natl Yng Ldrs Conf; OU.

WHITE, HEATHER L; Plainview HS; Ardmore, OK; (2); Church Yth Grp; Cmnty Wkr; Drama Clb; Math Clb; Mu Alpha Theta; Office Aide; Chorus; Church Choir; School Musical; School Play; Pre-Law/Psych.

WHITE, HOLLY M; Muskogee HS; Muskogee, OK; (2); German Clb; Cit Awd; Hon Roll; U Of OK; Meteorology.

WHITE, IVAN L; Coyle Public Schl; Coyle, OK; (4); FHA; German Clb; Ofcr Bsbl; Bsktbl; High Hon Roll; Hon Roll; Langston Univ; Cmptr Sci.

WHITE, JACOB D; U S Grant HS; Oklahoma City, OK; (2); ROTC; Color Guard; Drill Tm; Ofcr Bsbl; Cit Awd; Hon Roll; Mrksmnshp Team; Drill Team W/Arms; US Military Acad.

WHITE, JENNIFER L; Del City HS; Del City, OK; (2); Church Yth Grp; FCA; Office Aide; Nwsp; Yrbk; Chrch Daycare Tchr; U Of Cntrl OK; Ed; Medicine.

WHITE, JENNIFER LEE ANN; Rock Creek Jr Sr HS; Bokchito, OK; (3); 1/29; VP 4-H; Rptr Phtg FHA; Chorus; Church Choir; Var Chrldng; 4-H Awd; High Hon Roll; Hon Roll; NHS; St Schlr; Music Ensmble Awds; Miss Rock Crk Pagnt 1st Rnnr Up 1996; Piano; Southeastern OK ST U; Elem Ed.

WHITE, JESSICA; Chickasha Jr HS; Chickasha, OK; (1); Church Yth Grp; Science Clb; Chorus; Ofcr Frsh Cls; Chrldng; Hon Roll; Jr NHS; OK Univ; Therapist.

WHITE, JESSICA; Choctaw HS; Midwest City, OK; (3); Drama Clb; Key Clb; Spanish Clb; Band; Church Choir; Mrchg Band; School Play; Stage Crew; Rep Soph Cls; NHS.

WHITE, JO D; Oologah HS; Talala, OK; (2); Science Clb; Bsktbl; Chrldng; Trk; Hon Roll; Barrel Rcng; Rogers ST Coll; Prmry Ed.

WHITE, JOHN B; Lawton Sr HS; Lawton, OK; (2); Band; Mrchg Band; Pep Band; School Musical; School Play; Stage Crew; Hon Roll; Jr NHS; Marine Bio/Zoology.

WHITE, JORDANA; Okeene Jr Sr HS; Ames, OK; (2); Church Yth Grp; FHA; Letterman Clb; Office Aide; SADD; Var Bsktbl; Var Sftbl; Hon Roll; Kiwanis Awd; NHS.

WHITE, JOSEPH; Walters HS; Walters, OK; (4); 18/36; Art Clb; Church Yth Grp; Letterman Clb; Natl FFA Org; Red Cross Aide; Teachers Aide; School Musical; Ofcr Stu Cncl; Diving; Ftbl; Cameron; Ath Trng; Phy Thrpst.

WHITE, JOSH M; Mc Loud HS; Mc Loud, OK; (2); Church Yth Grp; FCA; Var L Bsbl; Var L Bsktbl; Var L Ftbl; Cit Awd; Hon Roll; Bsktbl Acad ST Champ; Bsbl ST Tourmnt.

WHITE, KATIE L; North Intemediate HS; Broken Arrow, OK; (1); Church Yth Grp; Office Aide; Science Clb; Spanish Clb; Band; Color Guard; Ofcr Stu Cncl; JV Bsktbl; JV Trk; Hon Roll; Oral Roberts U; Sprts.

WHITE, KELLIE; Indianola HS; Mcalester, OK; (4); Church Yth Grp; FHA; Library Aide; Office Aide; Hon Roll; Ntl Merit Ltr; Outstndng Stu FHA; Mst Dedicated ADAPT Pgm; Eastern OK ST U; Acctng.

WHITE, KERRI; Ponca City Sr HS; Ponca City, OK; (3); 2/346; Sec Am Leg Aux Girls St; Church Yth Grp; Math Tm; Capt Scholastic Bowl; Church Choir; Ed Yrbk; Rep Stu Cncl; High Hon Roll; NHS; Ntl Merit Ltr; Yth Alive Bible Club Pres; OK Bapt Univ; Church Yth Mnstr.

WHITE, KIMBERLY; Ft Supply Schl; Fort Supply, OK; (3); 1/12; HOBY; VP Natl FFA Org; Pres Frsh Cls; Pres Jr Cls; VP Stu Cncl; Var Bsktbl; Var Chrldng; Hon Roll; NHS; OK ST U; Law.

WHITE, KRISTOPHER F; Edmond Memorial HS; Edmond, OK; (3); FBLA; Spanish Clb; NHS; Mdvl Club; Cmptr Grphc Dsgn.

WHITE, LA DONNA L; John Marshall HS; Oklahoma City, OK; (3); Art Clb; Natl FFA Org; Science Clb; Spanish Clb; Teachers Aide; Nwsp; Yrbk; Pom Pon; High Hon Roll; Hon Roll; OK U; Prof.

WHITE, LA'DONNA L; John Marshall HS; Oklahoma City, OK; (3); Art Clb; Natl FFA Org; Science Clb; Spanish Clb; Nwsp; Yrbk; Pom Pon; High Hon Roll; Hon Roll.

WHITE, LEE ANN; Rock Creek Jr Sr HS; Bokchito, OK; (3); 1/36; Church Yth Grp; French Clb; Ofcr FHA; Chorus; Var Chrldng; 4-H Awd; High Hon Roll; NHS; St Schlr; Hstry Clb; Upward Bnd; Piano; SE OK ST U; Elem Ed.

WHITE, LINDSAY C; B T Washington HS; Tulsa, OK; (3); 18/300; Church Yth Grp; French Clb; Red Cross Aide; Chrldng; NHS; Bio.

WHITE, LIZ; Alva HS; Alva, OK; (3); Church Yth Grp; Drama Clb; FCA; FHA; Key Clb; NFL; Speech Tm; Yrbk; Rep Stu Cncl; Var Chrldng; Northwestern OK ST U.

WHITE, MANDY F; Caddo HS; Caddo, OK; (2); FCA; FHA; Drill Tm; Ofcr Stu Cncl; Bsktbl; Sftbl; Hon Roll; NHS; SOSU.

WHITE, MELANIE; Mc Loud HS; Newalla, OK; (3); Church Yth Grp; Band; Drm Mjr(t); Mrchg Band; Pep Band; Hon Roll; NHS; Supr Ratng ST Solo Ensembl Bnd, Flute; Radlgy.

WHITE, MIKA; Watonga HS; Fay, OK; (3); Church Yth Grp; FBLA; Quiz Bowl; Scholastic Bowl; Band; Mrchg Band; Pep Band; Ofcr Stu Cncl; Hon Roll; NHS; Lions Clb Awd; OK Hnr Soc; Ecology Clb Pres.

WHITE, MISTY D; Ft Cobb-Broxton HS; Fort Cobb, OK; (4); Church Yth Grp; Cmnty Wkr; Drama Clb; FHA; Natl FFA Org; Spanish Clb; Speech Tm; Chorus; Church Choir; School Musical; Vlybl/Sftbl; Hnrd Awrd High Avrgs Cls; Radiology.

WHITE, MONIQUE R; Putnam City West HS; Oklahoma City, OK; (2); Orch; Ofcr Stu Cncl; NHS; Blck Hist Mnth Recog Plnnr & Org; CO U; Law.

WHITE, SAMANTHA D; Blanche Thomas Jr Sr HS; Sentinel, OK; (3); Church Yth Grp; School Play; Hon Roll; History.

WHITE, SHAWNA R; Blackwell HS; Blackwell, OK; (4); 9/118; Am Leg Aux Girls St; Church Yth Grp; FCA; Office Aide; Pep Clb; Chorus; Ed Yrbk; Rep Soph Cls; Rep Jr Cls; Bsktbl; Participant Of RYLA Conf; OK City U; Acctng.

WHITE, TERRILL E; Tahlequah Sr HS; Tahlequah, OK; (4); 100/225; Church Yth Grp; Drama Clb; 4-H; Science Clb; Speech Tm; SADD; Acpl Chr; Chorus; Church Choir; School Play; Suprior Solo Rating; Suprior Ensble Rtng; Lions Clb Spch Cntst Smifnlst; Nthestrn St Univ; Music Ed.

WHITE, TIANA; B T Washington HS; Tulsa, OK; (4); 65/264; Drama Clb; Latin Clb; Teachers Aide; School Musical; High Hon Roll; NHS; Tulsa World Acad Ltr; Chinese Clb Pres VP; B T Washington Childrens Theatre Choreographer; Dance Tchr; Hamilton Coll.

WHITE, TYLER R; Byng Sr HS; Ada, OK; (2); 1/120; Church Yth Grp; FCA; Pres FBLA; HOBY; Math Clb; Natl Beta Clb; Quiz Bowl; Scholastic Bowl; Science Clb; Chorus; OK Heritage Cont 1st Pl & Schlsp; Top Geometry Stu; Tulsa Univ.

WHITE, TYRELL A; Woodward HS; Woodward, OK; (2); Letterman Clb; Natl FFA Org; Golf; Hon Roll.

WHITED, AMY; Hominy HS; Hominy, OK; (3); Church Yth Grp; French Clb; FHA; Teachers Aide; Yrbk; Pres Frsh Cls; Bsktbl; Var Capt Chrldng; Tennis; Gov Hon Prg Awd; All Amer Chrldr; Elem Ed.

WHITEFIELD, APRIL N; Mustang HS; Yukon, OK; (2); Church Yth Grp; FCA; Spanish Clb; Varsity Clb; Chorus; Church Choir; Variety Show; Hon Roll; NHS; Yth Alive; OK Univ; Nrsng/Law.

WHITEFIELD, KELLI J; Tecumseh HS; Earlsboro, OK; (3); FHA; Natl FFA Org; High Hon Roll; Hon Roll; NHS; Acad Ltr Jacket; Yth Alive; Med Sec; Bus Office Tech.

WHITEHEAD, AMBER M; Muldrow HS; Muldrow, OK; (3); Cmnty Wkr; Drama Clb; Hosp Aide; NFL; Speech Tm; Band; Jazz Band; Mrchg Band; High Hon Roll; Church Choir; IDFY; Carl Albert ST Coll.

WHITEHEAD, CHRISTIE; Nathan Hale HS; Tulsa, OK; (2); Key Clb; Office Aide; Stage Crew; Rep Frsh Cls; Sec Soph Cls; Treas Jr Cls; JV Var Chrldng; Wt Lftg; High Hon Roll; Hon Roll; Kiwanis Club; Southwestern; Phy Ther.

WHITEHEAD, JESSE H; Union Sr HS; Tulsa, OK; (3); 310/800; Boy Scts; Church Yth Grp; Key Clb; Office Aide; SADD; Band; Orch; Golf; Wt Lftg; Cit Awd; OK Univ; Wthr Sci.

WHITEHEAD, TASHA D; Arkoma Jr Sr HS; Arkoma, OK; (3); Church Yth Grp; Sec FCA; FHA; Rep Stu Cncl; Var Bsktbl; Hon Roll; Hist NHS; Sal; Msnc Awd; CASC; Physcns Asst.

WHITEHOUSE, MARCY M; Jay HS; Jay, OK; (4); Natl Beta Clb; Science Clb; Band; Drm Mjr(t); Jazz Band; Mrchg Band; Hon Roll; NHS; Rcvd John Philip Souse Awd; All ST Mrchng Band; All Dist Hmr Band Drum Mjr; Rogers ST Coll; Ed.

WHITELEY, ERICK W; Choctaw HS; Nicoma Park, OK; (2); Am Leg Boys St; Church Yth Grp; Cmnty Wkr; FCA; FHA; German Clb; Teachers Aide; Chorus; Church Choir; Var Bsbl; NCU; Math.

WHITELEY, SHANNON L; Choctaw HS; Nicoma Park, OK; (4); Church Yth Grp; Cmnty Wkr; FCA; French Clb; FHA; GAA; Hosp Aide; Office Aide; Pep Clb; Teachers Aide; Soccer Trainer; Rose ST Coll; Nrsng.

WHITENECK, SARAH K; Woodward HS; Woodward, OK; (2); Art Clb; Church Yth Grp; GAA; Pep Clb; Ofcr Stu Cncl; Trk; High Hon Roll; Hon Roll; OK Chrstn; Med.

WHITFIELD, JED; Crowder Schl; Indianola, OK; (3); Cmnty Wkr; Quiz Bowl; Teachers Aide; Chorus; Sec Treas Jr Cls; Hon Roll; NHS; Natl Indian Hnr Soc; Hnr Choir; Tech Stu Assn Rprtr; Air Frce Acad; Tech Engrng.

WHITFIELD, PATRICIA; Vinita HS; Vinita, OK; (3); DECA; German Clb; Math Clb; Science Clb; Spanish Clb; Chrldng; Dist 9 Rep Cherokee Nation Trbl Yth Cncl; Anchor Clb; Cherokee Nation Rep UNITY Cncl; NSU; Ed.

WHITFIELD, ZENNA Y; Comanche HS; Loco, OK; (3); Debate Tm; German Clb; NFL; Speech Tm; SADD; Midwestern ST Univ; Bus.

WHITLEY, DANIEL R; Union Intermediate HS; Broken Arrow, OK; (2); Church Yth Grp; Math Clb; VICA; Band; Jazz Band; Wt Lftg; Math Awd Outstdng Achvmnt; PE Awd; BMX Bike Rcng Trphs/Awds; Drums Car Audio Equip Instlr; Tech/Elec Engr.

WHITLEY, STACI; Stillwater Sr HS; Stillwater, OK; (4); Church Yth Grp; Key Clb; Office Aide; Q&S; Band; Color Guard; Flag Corp; Jazz Band; Yrbk; Yth/Govt; OK Chrstn Univ; PT.

WHITLOCK, JIMMY; Seminole Jr Sr HS; Seminole, OK; (1); Church Yth Grp; JV Bsbl; JV Ftbl; Var Wt Lftg; Hon Roll; U Of OK; Tchng.

WHITLOW, RONALD K; Hugo HS; Hugo, OK; (2); ROTC; Ftbl; USU Okmulgee.

WHITMAN, JONI; Porum HS; Porum, OK; (3); Church Yth Grp; FCA; 4-H; Sec FHA; Yrbk; Ofcr Stu Cncl; Var Bsktbl; Sec Frsh Cls; Rep Soph Cls; On Ballot ST FHA HERO Pres.

WHITMARSH, STACEY L; Union Sr HS; Tulsa, OK; (4); 84/670; FCA; Rep Stu Cncl; Var Chrldng; Hon Roll; Jr NHS; NHS; Ntl Merit Ltr; Pres Acad Fit Awd; NCA Natl Chmpn; OU.

WHITNERY, ROYAL B; Sayre HS; Sayre, OK; (4); 5/48; Am Leg Boys St; Church Yth Grp; Letterman Clb; Scholastic Bowl; Band; Jazz Band; Mrchg Band; Pres Frsh Cls; Pres Sr Cls; Bsktbl; Harding Univ; Pre Med.

WHITNEY, AMY D; Asher Schl; Lindsay, OK; (2); 4/22; GAA; Natl FFA Org; Scholastic Bowl; Sec Frsh Cls; Var Bsktbl; Var Sftbl; 4-H Awd; Hon Roll; NHS; Ntl Merit Ltr; Central ST Edmond OK.

WHITNEY, APRIL; Eufaula Sr HS; Eufaula, OK; (3); Church Yth Grp; Band; Mrchg Band; Pep Band; School Play; Stage Crew; Prfct Atten Awd; Hstry.

WHITNEY, JASON W; Bishop Kelley HS; Tulsa, OK; (4); 1/149; Church Yth Grp; French Clb; Chorus; Church Choir; Hon Roll; NHS; Ntl Merit SF; Val; Acad Decathlon; Pro Life Clb; Engr.

WHITNEY, JEREMY D; Bishop Kelley HS; Tulsa, OK; (2); Church Yth Grp; Church Choir; School Musical; Socr; Hon Roll.

WHITNEY, MATTHEW S; Ponca City Sr HS; Ponca City, OK; (3); Boy Scts; VP Church Yth Grp; Spanish Clb; School Play; Stat Bsktbl; JV Var Mgr(s); Hon Roll; Pre-Med/Pre-Dntl.

WHITSITT, TAMMY; Roland Sr HS; Roland, OK; (1); Church Yth Grp; Natl Beta Clb; Chorus; Rptr Frsh Cls; Bsktbl; Chrldng; Sftbl; Hon Roll; Prfct Atten Awd.

WHITT, NICOLE; Putnam City West HS; Bethany, OK; (4); 60/282; Varsity Clb; Ofcr Stu Cncl; Var Chrldng; High Hon Roll; NHS; Tulsa U; Poli Sci.

WHITTEN, JEREMIAH; Empire Schl; Duncan, OK; (2); FCA; FBLA; SADD; Band; Yrbk; Ofcr Bsbl; Ftbl; Tennis; Wrstlng; Hon Roll; Engrng.

WHITTET, MICHAEL J; Macomb Schl; Macomb, OK; (1); Bsktbl; Hon Roll; NHS; Prfct Atten Awd.

WHITTINGTON, KENDALL D; Grandfield Jr Sr HS; Grandfield, OK; (2); 6/21; Church Yth Grp; Natl FFA Org; Quiz Bowl; VP Soph Cls; Ofcr Bsbl; Bsktbl; Capt Ftbl; Wt Lftg; Cit Awd; Hon Roll.

WHITTLESEY, JENNY E; Owasso Sr HS; Owasso, OK; (3); Drama Clb; French Clb; Thesps; Chorus; School Play; Stage Crew; Rep Stu Cncl; Commrcl Plt.

WHITTMORE, DAVID W; Tahlequah Sr HS; Tahlequah, OK; (3); Church Yth Grp; Office Aide; Spanish Clb; SADD; Church Choir; Trk; Northeastern ST.

WHITWORTH, JACK R; Caney Valley Middle Sr HS; Ochelata, OK; (3); Church Yth Grp; German Clb; Teachers Aide; Rep Soph Cls; Var Ftbl; Var Wt Lftg; Hon Roll; His Clb; NSU; Sports Dr.

WHITWORTH, KACEY; Newkirk HS; Newkirk, OK; (4); 1/47; Am Leg Aux Girls St; Church Yth Grp; FCA; Quiz Bowl; Teachers Aide; School Play; Sec Frsh Cls; Pres Soph Cls; VP Jr Cls; Rep Sr Cls; SHEPP; Sprts Med.

WHORTON, AMANDA K; Caddo HS; Caddo, OK; (2); Church Yth Grp; FHA; Bsktbl; Sftbl; Hon Roll; NHS; Southeastern ST Univ; Bus.

WHORTON, DARLA; Garber Sr HS; Fairmont, OK; (4); 3/34; Am Leg Aux Girls St; Cmnty Wkr; Rptr Natl FFA Org; Quiz Bowl; Ed Nwsp; Rptr Soph Cls; Rep Jr Cls; Rptr Sr Cls; Rptr Stu Cncl; Var Mgr(s); OK ST U; Vet Med.

WHORTON, JOSHUA; Hollis Jr Sr HS; Hollis, OK; (4); Am Leg Boys St; Boy Scts; Church Yth Grp; Cmnty Wkr; FCA; 4-H; Pres Natl FFA Org; Quiz Bowl; Varsity Clb; Church Choir.

WHORTON, SHARON; Midwest City HS; Midwest City, OK; (3); 63/384; Rptr German Clb; Hosp Aide; SADD; Yrbk; Var L Bsktbl; L Trk; Jr NHS; NHS; 4-H; Letterman Clb; Billy Branum Schlr Awd; Law.

WHORTON, TIFFANY S; Colcord Schl; Colcord, OK; (1); Church Yth Grp; FHA; VP Frsh Cls; Hon Roll; NHS; Sal; Piano; Comptrs; Law.

WICHERT, KAYLEEN; Fairview HS; Fairview, OK; (4); 1/55; Church Yth Grp; VP FCA; FHA; Teachers Aide; Band; Church Choir; Color Guard; Capt Var Bsktbl; Hon Roll; Pres NHS.

WICKER, BRIAN; Macomb Schl; Macomb, OK; (3); FHA; Var Bsktbl; Hon Roll; NHS; Bsktbl Homcmng King.

WICKERSHAM, JAMES P; Putnam City West HS; Bethany, OK; (3); 20/400; Church Yth Grp; German Clb; Quiz Bowl; Scholastic Bowl; Church Choir; Mrchg Band; Orch; School Musical; Hon Roll; NHS; Soccer Referee; Strolling Strings Orch Ofcr; Chrch Orch; Engrng.

WICKERSHAM, JODY; Newcastle HS; Newcastle, OK; (4); 1/71; Church Yth Grp; FCA; FBLA; Model UN; Scholastic Bowl; Pres Science Clb; Rep Sr Cls; Rep Stu Cncl; Capt Bsktbl; Hon Roll; Natl Hnr Soc Sr Prlmntrn; GT 4 Yrs; Supts Hnr Rll 4 Yr.

WICKWARE, ARIC C; Marietta HS; Marietta, OK; (2); Drama Clb; German Clb; Thesps; Chorus; School Play; Ftbl; Trk; High Hon Roll; Hon Roll; Kenpo Karate; St Bsktbl; Navy.

WIDEMAN, JODI K; Broken Arrow Sr HS; Broken Arrow, OK; (4); 81/921; Church Yth Grp; French Clb; Speech Tm; Acpl Chr; Church Choir; School Musical; School Play; High Hon Roll; NHS; Chrstn Union Sec; Intl Thspn Scty; OK Bptst Univ; Telecomm.

WIDOWSKI, BRANDI; Shawnee Sr HS; Tecumseh, OK; (4); 17/262; Am Leg Aux Girls St; Church Yth Grp; FCA; Latin Clb; Office Aide; Pep Clb; Rptr Nwsp; Trk; High Hon Roll; NHS; Cmptv Gymnstcs; Acad Lttr Jckt; U Of OK.

WIEDENMANN, CASIE R; Yukon Middle HS; Yukon, OK; (1); Church Yth Grp; Quiz Bowl; Hon Roll; NHS; ST Comptn Blue Ribbn/Gold Pin Piano Plyng; Chrch Vlybl; All Amer Tm Plyr Slctn; Southern Nazarene Univ; Brdcstg.

WIEDERKEHR, DANIEL; Oklahoma Bible Acad; Enid, OK; (2); Boy Scts; Church Yth Grp; Varsity Clb; Chorus; Var Bsktbl; L Socr; Var Trk; High Hon Roll; Finance.

WIEDERSTEIN, ZACH; Shattuck Jr Sr HS; Shattuck, OK; (1); 6/31; Band; Jazz Band; Mrchg Band; Pep Band; Ofcr Frsh Cls; Ofcr Stu Cncl; Ofcr Bsbl; Bsktbl; Ftbl; U Of OK; Mtrlgst/Pro-Athltcs.

WIENS, KATIE D; Sulphur HS; Sulphur, OK; (3); Church Yth Grp; Cmnty Wkr; FCA; Sec Treas French Clb; FHA; Key Clb; Teachers Aide; Rptr Nwsp; Intrml JV Bsktbl; Intrml JV Trk.

WIER, JEREMY D; Duncan HS; Duncan, OK; (3); 17/260; FBLA; Key Clb; Letterman Clb; JV Var Golf; High Hon Roll; Hon Roll; NHS; OK St Univ.

WIERSIG, KEVIN D; Alva HS; Alva, OK; (2); Church Yth Grp; Band; Mrchg Band; Orch; Pep Band; Hon Roll; NHS; Act I Comm Theater Drummer; Acad Team.

WIGGER, ERIC F; Mustang HS; Mustang, OK; (3); Band; Drm Mjr(t); Mrchg Band; Pep Band; JV Capt Socr; High Hon Roll; Hon Roll; ST Chmpn Bwlng Chmpn Sngls; 2 Tm ST Chmpn Schl Tm Bwlng Chmpn; Chem Engr.

WIGGINS, CHERYL D; Velma Alma HS; Velma, OK; (2); Church Yth Grp; Girl Scts; Teachers Aide; Band; Mrchg Band; Hon Roll; Prfct Atten Awd.

WIGGS, RICHARD R; Stillwater Sr HS; Stillwater, OK; (4); 2/350; Church Yth Grp; Debate Tm; Drama Clb; JCL; Latin Clb; NFL; Quiz Bowl; NHS; Ntl Merit SF; Arch.

WIGHT, AVERY J; Byng Sr HS; Ada, OK; (2); Boy Scts; Church Yth Grp; Drama Clb; Natl Beta Clb; Speech Tm; Band; School Musical; School Play; Prfct Atten Awd; Debate Tm; Beta Alpha Phi; Perf Arts/Comm.

WIGHT, JEANETTE M; Edmond Memorial HS; Edmond, OK; (3); 1/400; Hosp Aide; JCL; Pres Key Clb; Variety Show; Hon Roll; NHS; Prfct Atten Awd; Chrch Yth Grp; Acteens; Phys Thpy.

WIGINTON, JENNIFER A; Drumright HS; Drumright, OK; (1); FCA; 4-H; Science Clb; Rep Frsh Cls; Intrml Bsktbl; 4-H Awd; Hon Roll; Pres Acad Fit Awd; 4h Cnty Rptr; Frosh Ftbl Hmcmng Attndt; Spts Med.

WIGLEY, HOLLY; Christian Heritage Acad; Oklahoma City, OK; (2); Church Yth Grp; Office Aide; Chorus; Hon Roll; Bob Jones; Creatv Wrtng.

WILBER, BECKY; Cherokee Jr Sr HS; Cherokee, OK; (4); 5/24; Am Leg Aux Girls St; Church Yth Grp; FCA; FHA; Girl Scts; Treas Natl FFA Org; Office Aide; Pres Spanish Clb; Band; Mrchg Band; OK Hwy Ptrl Cadet Lawman Acad; Page St Rep; Girls St Delg; Northwestern OK ST; Phy Thrpy.

WILBURN, JENNIFER; Fox Sr HS; Ratliff City, OK; (3); 1/25; Sec FCA; HOBY; Quiz Bowl; Band; Var Bsktbl; Var Chrldng; Var Sftbl; Var Trk; High Hon Roll; NHS; FFA; Physcn.

WILBURN, JOLINE M; Central HS; Tulsa, OK; (3); Pep Clb; ROTC; Chorus; Color Guard; Drill Tm; Swing Chorus; Ofcr Jr Cls; Mgr(s); Sftbl; Mgr Wrstlng; Colorguard Comm; Platoon Ldr; Operation Officer; Law.

WILBURN, NICK T; Haskell HS; Haskell, OK; (3); Art Clb; Church Yth Grp; FCA; VICA; Hon Roll; NHS; Excls In Art; Engrng; Drafting.

WILBURN, TAMARA; Fox Sr HS; Ratliff City, OK; (4); 3/27; Church Yth Grp; VP FCA; FHA; Capt Quiz Bowl; Teachers Aide; Pres Band; Pres Stu Cncl; Bsktbl; Chrldng; Sftbl; OK St Univ; Chld Psych.

WILCOX, FREDDA M; Cement Jr Sr HS; Cement, OK; (4); 7/22; Church Yth Grp; 4-H; FHA; Office Aide; Quiz Bowl; Teachers Aide; School Musical; School Play; Var Mgr(s); 4-H Awd; FHA Subdist VP, Natl Cnvntn Vtng Del; Southwestern OK ST U; Elem Ed.

WILCOX, SUSAN; Mustang HS; Yukon, OK; (4); 1/310; Math Clb; Co-Capt Scholastic Bowl; Science Clb; VP Spanish Clb; SADD; Var Sftbl; High Hon Roll; NHS; St Schlr; OK Fndtn For Excl Acad All St; OK St Regents Schlr; Univ Of OK Awd Of Excl; U Of OK; Span; Pre Med.

WILCOX, TRISHA; Cement Jr Sr HS; Cement, OK; (1); Church Yth Grp; Scholastic Bowl; Church Choir; Sec Frsh Cls; Ofcr Soph Cls; Ofcr Stu Cncl; Var Bsktbl; Intrml Trk; Var Vllybl; Hon Roll.

WILCZEK, JOSHUA A; Lomega HS; Kingfisher, OK; (1); 4-H; Quiz Bowl; Scholastic Bowl; Pres Frsh Cls; JV Var Bsbl; JV Var Bsktbl; High Hon Roll; Hon Roll; Jr NHS; Prfct Atten Awd; Jr HS Acad All Conf; Elks Essay Winner; OSU.

WILD, ROBBIE C; Edmond Memorial HS; Edmond, OK; (3); Church Yth Grp; FCA; French Clb; Key Clb; SADD; Stage Crew; JV Crs Cntry; JV Trk; JV Wrstlng; NHS.

WILDER, JENNIFER L; Charles Page HS; Sand Springs, OK; (2); 9/386; VP Sec Church Yth Grp; Key Clb; Band; Drm Mjr(t); Mrchg Band; High Hon Roll; NHS; Prfct Atten Awd; Pres Acad Fit Awd; Girl Scts; Music Mstrs Reptr; OK City U; Psych/Cnslng.

WILDRIX, AIMEE; Fairview HS; Fairview, OK; (2); Natl FFA Org; Scholastic Bowl; High Hon Roll; NHS; Math Ed.

WILDS, JARED A; El Reno Sr HS; Yukon, OK; (1); Church Yth Grp; FCA; Natl FFA Org; L Golf; High Hon Roll; Hon Roll; Kiwanis Awd; NHS; OK His Awd; Sci Awd; Univ Of OK; Meteorologist.

WILEY, ALEXA K; Memorial HS; Tulsa, OK; (2); Var Bsktbl; Var Vllybl; Childrens Med Ctr Vol; U Of TX-AUSTIN; Psychiatry.

WILEY, CARA; Ardmore HS; Ardmore, OK; (3); 2/282; Church Yth Grp; Drama Clb; FCA; French Clb; Mu Alpha Theta; Chorus; School Musical; Chrldng; High Hon Roll; NHS; NCA All Amer Chrldr; All Amer Schlr; Leaflets Std Clb; Law.

WILEY, CHENOA D; Claremore Sr HS; Claremore, OK; (2); Natl FFA Org; Crs Cntry; Trk; Hon Roll; OK U In Stillwater.

WILEY, KENDALL R; South Coffeyville Schl; South Coffeyville, OK; (1); Var L Bsbl; Var Capt Ftbl; Coffeyville Wrestling Clb Mem.

WILEY, LINDSAY; Union Sr HS; Tulsa, OK; (2); Debate Tm; FCA; Spanish Clb; JV Chrldng; Hon Roll; JV Chrldng Squad 3rd Pl NCA Natls In Dallas; U Of OK; Psych.

WILEY, MELISSA; Claremore Sr HS; Claremore, OK; (3); Treas Natl FFA Org; Teachers Aide; School Play; Stage Crew; Vllybl; Cit Awd; High Hon Roll; Hon Roll; Prfct Atten Awd; C Awd Engl II; U Of Tulsa; Criminal Investgtn.

WILHITE, CHRISTINA; Yukon HS; Yukon, OK; (3); 7/412; Church Yth Grp; Service Clb; Spanish Clb; SADD; Varsity Clb; Ofcr Stu Cncl; Crs Cntry; Trk; High Hon Roll; NHS; Intl Bus.

WILHITE, LAURA A; Tahlequah Jr HS; Tahlequah, OK; (1); Sec Chorus; Orch; Crs Cntry; Tennis; Hon Roll; Jr NHS; Pres Acad Fit Awd; Piano Stu.

WILHITE, SARA; Tonkawa Jr Sr HS; Tonkawa, OK; (4); 7/40; Am Leg Aux Girls St; Pres Frsh Cls; Sec Treas Soph Cls; Pres Jr Cls; Pres Stu Cncl; Var Bsktbl; Capt Chrldng; Var Trk; Cit Awd; DAR Awd; Hmcmng Queen; OK ST U; Intl Bus.

WILHITE, TANYA; Canton HS; Canton, OK; (4); 9/46; Church Yth Grp; Rptr FHA; Model UN; Pres SADD; Flag Corp; Rptr Sr Cls; Chrldng; NHS; Pres Acad Fit Awd; FCA; Teen Ct; OK Pnhndl ST U; Law.

WILK, DANIEL J; Elgin HS; Elgin, OK; (2); Hon Roll; Tae Kwon Do Blue Belt; OK U; Bnkng.

WILKERSON, CHRIS; Mustang HS; Yukon, OK; (3); 46/650; Church Yth Grp; FCA; Band; Mrchg Band; JV Crs Cntry; JV Socr; Hon Roll; NHS; U Of OK; Med.

WILKERSON, JERRY S; Pauls Valley HS; Pauls Valley, OK; (1); Var Church Yth Grp; FCA; Ofcr Bsbl; Bsktbl; Ftbl; Wt Lftg; Cit Awd; Hon Roll; Prfct Atten Awd; Pres Acad Fit Awd; Pi Phi Pi; U Of OK; Coach.

WILKERSON, RIKKI; Union City Schl; Union City, OK; (4); 5/24; Church Yth Grp; FHA; Hosp Aide; Chorus; Church Choir; Yrbk; Rptr Sr Cls; Rep Stu Cncl; Hon Roll; Sal; Southwestern OK ST U; Nursng.

WILKERSON, SARAH L; Ripley HS; Ripley, OK; (1); Church Yth Grp; Cmnty Wkr; FHA; Teachers Aide; Band; Hon Roll; FNA Reporter; Engl Fundrsng Comm; Home Ec Class Sec; OK Bapt Univ; Ped Asst/Elm Tch.

WILKES, DONIELLE; Oologah HS; Oologah, OK; (4); Drama Clb; FCA; SADD; Teachers Aide; Var Capt Chrldng; Hon Roll; Ntl Merit Ltr; Rogers ST Coll; Elem Ed.

WILKES, MELISSA; Will Rogers HS; Tulsa, OK; (4); 1/180; Spanish Clb; Teachers Aide; Pres Stu Cncl; Hon Roll; Pres NHS; Pres Acad Fit Awd; Val; Future Ldrs Advy Group Of Stdnts; TJC; Med.

WILKETT, KELLEY D; Mc Alester HS; Mcalester, OK; (4); 42/209; Art Clb; Church Yth Grp; Cmnty Wkr; Hosp Aide; Science Clb; Spanish Clb; Band; Drill Tm; Mrchg Band; Chrldng; Natl Yth Ldrshp Forum On Medicine; SOSU Math & Sci Acad; EOSC; Med.

WILKINS, DAVID; Sulphur HS; Sulphur, OK; (1); Key Clb; Band; Mrchg Band; School Musical; ST Band 2 Yrs; Upward Bound; Bible Schl; Oasis.

WILKINS, TYRUS D; Bixby Sr HS; Tulsa, OK; (1); Church Yth Grp; FCA; Bsktbl; High Hon Roll; Jr NHS; Pres Schlr; Grphc Arts.

WILKINSON, JENNIFER; Central Mid-HS; Norman, OK; (1); Church Yth Grp; Chorus; Cit Awd; Hon Roll; NHS.

WILKINSON, JENNIFER; Putnam City North HS; Oklahoma City, OK; (3); Church Yth Grp; Dance Clb; FCA; Spanish Clb; SADD; Yrbk; Rep Stu Cncl; Var Golf; Mgr(s); Hon Roll; OK ST; Mar Biolgst.

WILKINSON, KRISTIN L; Stillwater Sr HS; Stillwater, OK; (2); #1 in class; Church Yth Grp; FCA; Natl Beta Clb; Spanish Clb; Church Choir; School Musical; L Var Crs Cntry; Var Swmmng; L Var Trk; Hon Roll; Baylor; Phys Therapy; Bus.

WILKINSON, MARNIE J; Yukon Middle HS; Yukon, OK; (1); Church Yth Grp; Band; NHS; Lwyr.

WILKINSON, SCOTT; Stroud HS; Stroud, OK; (4); 13/37; Am Leg Boys St; FHA; Natl FFA Org; Chorus; VP Frsh Cls; VP Soph Cls; Rep Jr Cls; Ofcr Stu Cncl; Var Capt Ftbl; Var Trk; All Stater Track; Mst Vlbl Track, Ftbl Plyr.

WILLAIMS, TIA; Ponca City Mid HS; Ponca City, OK; (1); Church Yth Grp; Dance Clb; Office Aide; Church Choir; Bsktbl; Chrldng; Trk; Hon Roll.

WILLARD, KAY DEE; Ripley HS; Ripley, OK; (1); 10/52; Church Yth Grp; FCA; Band; Var Bsktbl; Var Chrldng; NEO JC; Elem-Spcl Ed.

WILLARD, MATT; Cordell Sr HS; Cordell, OK; (4); 20/50; Natl FFA Org; Teachers Aide; VP Jr Cls; VP Sr Cls; Capt Soph Cls; Capt Wrstlng; Hon Roll; Kiwanis Awd; All Dist Ftbll; All Conf, Reg Champ, St Rnnr Up, All St Tm Wrstlng; Ftbll Schol Panhandle St Univ; Panhandle St Univ; Coach.

WILLETT, DAVID; Claremore Sr HS; Claremore, OK; (3); 3/237; Am Leg Boys St; FCA; Letterman Clb; Quiz Bowl; Spanish Clb; Ftbl; Golf; Wt Lftg; NHS; Prfct Atten Awd; Westminster; Psych.

WILLEY, AMY; Owasso Sr HS; Owasso, OK; (3); Church Yth Grp; FCA; JA; Office Aide; Ofcr Stu Cncl; Var JV Chrldng; Sftbl; Trk; Hon Roll; NHS; Tulsa Univ; Pre-Med.

WILLEY, MELISSA S; Owasso Sr HS; Owasso, OK; (4); FHA; FTA; SADD; Band; Mrchg Band; Rptr Nwsp; Powder Puff Ftbl; Sftbl; Hon Roll; Prfct Atten Awd; Church Yth Grp; Tp Stu Sci, His Merit Awds; OK ST U.

WILLHIGHT, KRISTIAN D; Mangum Sr HS; Mangum, OK; (4); 11/47; Am Leg Boys St; FBLA; Scholastic Bowl; Band; Drm Mjr(t); Jazz Band; Pep Band; Nwsp; Yrbk; NHS; U WA; Bus.

WILLHITE, JANICE R; Duncan HS; Duncan, OK; (2); FBLA; Hon Roll; NHS; OK HS Hnr Soc; ECU; Elem Tchr.

WILLIAMS, AALIYAH N; Union Intermediate HS; Tulsa, OK; (2); 3/800; French Clb; Key Clb; Chorus; Rep Soph Cls; High Hon Roll; Pres NHS; Pres Schlr; Rep Frsh Cls; Rep Stu Cncl; Jr Sttsmn Amer; Johns Hopkins U Smmr Pre Coll Pgm; Macy Schlr; Med.

WILLIAMS, ADAM E; Moore HS; Oklahoma City, OK; (3); 17/566; Am Leg Boys St; Pep Clb; Spanish Clb; Band; Mrchg Band; Bsktbl; Jr NHS; NHS; Pres Acad Fit Awd; USAF Acad; Aviation.

WILLIAMS, ALAN F; Metro Christian Acad; Tulsa, OK; (2) Church Yth Grp; FCA; Pep Clb; Spanish Clb; Teachers Aide; Jazz Band; Stage Crew; JV Bsktbl; Var Ftbl; Var Tennis; FL ST Univ; Pre-Law.

WILLIAMS, AMANDA; Houston Homan Jr HS; Eufaula, OK; (1); Church Yth Grp; Computer Clb; FHA; JV Bsktbl; L Trk; High Hon Roll; Hon Roll; Jr NHS.

WILLIAMS, AMY; Clinton HS; Clinton, OK; (1); Key Clb.

WILLIAMS, AMY B; Empire Schl; Duncan, OK; (4); 4/34; FCA; Treas FBLA; Key Clb; Nwsp; Yrbk; Treas Sr Cls; Rptr Stu Cncl; Chrldng; Trk; Sec NHS; U Of Cntrl OK.

WILLIAMS, ANGIE D; North Intemediate HS; Broken Arrow, OK; (1); Acpl Chr; Hampton Univ; Elec Eng/Singer.

WILLIAMS, ANNETTE; Piedmont HS; Piedmont, OK; (1); SADD; Band; Chorus; Flag Corp; Mrchg Band; Tri-ST Hnr Choir; Southern Nazarene U; Elem Tchr.

WILLIAMS, APRIL; Metro Christian Acad; Tulsa, OK; (1); 5/90; Church Yth Grp; Drama Clb; FCA; Teachers Aide; Band; Pep Band; School Play; Stage Crew; JV Chrldng; Hon Roll; OK U; Med.

WILLIAMS, APRIL R; El Reno Sr HS; El Reno, OK; (3); Church Yth Grp; FTA; Girl Scts; Key Clb; Math Clb; SADD; Band; Mrchg Band; High Hon Roll; Jr NHS; Mock Trial; Upwrd Bnd; Oklahoma City Univ; Ed.

WILLIAMS, ASHLEA R; Washington HS; Washington, OK; (4); 1/38; Church Yth Grp; FCA; Pres VP Band; Var Chrldng; Var Sftbl; High Hon Roll; Hist NHS; Val; Sec Sr Cls; Commended Stdnt Natl Merit Prg; OK Baptist Univ.

WILLIAMS, ASHLEY; Hilldale HS; Muskogee, OK; (3); 3/101; German Clb; Key Clb; Math Clb; Red Cross Aide; Science Clb; Church Choir; School Play; Yrbk; Pres Soph Cls; Rep Jr Cls; Tap, Ballet; Chrch Yth Grp.

WILLIAMS, AVA J; Hartshorne Sr HS; Mcalester, OK; (3); Natl FFA Org; Yrbk; Sec Frsh Cls; Sec Soph Cls; Hon Roll; NHS; All Amrcn Schol; Hortcltre Tm; Art Hstry.

WILLIAMS, BARRY; Wapanucka Schl; Atoka, OK; (3); 1/18; Drama Clb; Quiz Bowl; School Play; Rptr Nwsp; Rptr Yrbk; VP Frsh Cls; Pres Soph Cls; Pres Jr Cls; High Hon Roll; Ntl Merit Ltr.

WILLIAMS, BENJAMIN C; Claremore Sr HS; Claremore, OK; (1); Church Yth Grp; Science Clb; Bsktbl; Golf; Cit Awd; High Hon Roll; Pres Acad Fit Awd; Masonic Lodge Stdnt Of Today Awd; Battle Of Bks Champ; Prof Degree.

WILLIAMS, BRENNA K; East Central HS; Tulsa, OK; (3); Band; Mrchg Band; Pep Band; Diving; Swmmng; Hon Roll; Pres Acad Fit Awd; Pres Schlr; SAC For Band; Ltr In Band; Swim Team Capt; Swimming Ltr.

WILLIAMS, BRIAN; Butner Schl; Okemah, OK; (1); Pres Frsh Cls; Bsktbl; Hon Roll; Stu Cncl.

WILLIAMS, BRIAN D; Sallisaw HS; Sallisaw, OK; (2); Art Clb; Office Aide; Band; Ftbl; Wrstlng; Hon Roll; Guitar; Comp.

WILLIAMS, BROOKE; Thomas Jr Sr HS; Thomas, OK; (1); 1/48; Church Yth Grp; FHA; Band; Chorus; Church Choir; Mrchg Band; Pep Band; Sec Frsh Cls; High Hon Roll; Ntl Merit Ltr; SWOSU.

WILLIAMS, BROOKE L; Midwest City HS; Midwest City, OK; (2); 51/488; Drama Clb; FCA; Yrbk; VP Frsh Cls; VP Stu Cncl; Bsktbl; High Hon Roll; Hon Roll; Jr NHS; NHS; Acad Ltrmn 2 Yrs; Dntl.

WILLIAMS, CASEY L; Indianola HS; Mcalester, OK; (2); FBLA; GAA; SADD; Yrbk; JV Var Bsktbl; Var Sftbl; VP Frsh Cls; Natl FFA Org; OSU; Tchr; Coach; Comps.

WILLIAMS, CASSIE; Clinton HS; Clinton, OK; (2); FHA; Girl Scts; Key Clb; Spanish Clb; Band; Mrchg Band; Hon Roll; NHS; Acad Excllnc Awd; Yth Alive; Rep Key Clb; OK U; Cardiologist.

WILLIAMS, CHARESSA; Maud HS; Maud, OK; (2); 4/25; Church Yth Grp; FHA; Chorus; Church Choir; Sec Frsh Cls; Rep Stu Cncl; Bsktbl; Chrldng; Trk; Wt Lftg.

WILLIAMS, CHARLA M; Walters HS; Walters, OK; (4); 8/36; Church Yth Grp; FCA; 4-H; Band; Chorus; Church Choir; Mrchg Band; 4-H Awd; Hon Roll; NHS; OK Bptst U; Elem Ed.

WILLIAMS, CHASSIDY M; Star Spencer HS; Oklahoma City, OK; (2); Church Yth Grp; Band; Church Choir; Mrchg Band; Pep Band; School Musical; Hon Roll; UCO; Bus.

WILLIAMS, CHRIS L; Bixby Sr HS; Bixby, OK; (1); Church Yth Grp; Intrml Bsbl; Intrml Ftbl; Gov Hon Prg Awd; Jr NHS; Pres Acad Fit Awd.

WILLIAMS, CHRISTINE; Bennington Schl; Bennington, OK; (1); 4-H; JV Bsktbl; Cit Awd; High Hon Roll; Hon Roll; Val; Attend Cornerstone Bapt Chrch In Bennington; Bsktbl; Nrsng.

WILLIAMS, CHRYSTAL; Stuart Sr HS; Stuart, OK; (3); 18/28; Church Yth Grp; 4-H; FHA; GAA; Varsity Clb; Pres Frsh Cls; Ofcr Stu Cncl; Capt Bsktbl; Sftbl; Hon Roll; All Trnmnt, All Conf Plyr Bsktbl 94-96; All Conf Plyr Sftbl 94-96; Southeastern OK ST U; Elem Ed.

WILLIAMS, CHYANNA; Noble HS; Noble, OK; (3); 1/186; Mu Alpha Theta; Spanish Clb; SADD; Yrbk; Cit Awd; High Hon Roll; Jr NHS; NHS; Prfct Atten Awd; Pres Acad Fit Awd; Outstdng Soph Girl; Jr Arch Bearer; Pre-Med.

WILLIAMS, CLINT; Hobart HS; Hobart, OK; (1); Band; Jazz Band; Mrchg Band; Pep Band; Hon Roll; TSA Pres; Class Fav.

WILLIAMS, CRYSTAL; Guthrie Sr HS; Guthrie, OK; (4); 1/178; Am Leg Aux Girls St; FBLA; Hist Key Clb; Mu Alpha Theta; Science Clb; Spanish Clb; Trk; High Hon Roll; Kiwanis Awd; Val; Berkeley U; Cmptr Sci.

WILLIAMS, CRYSTAL; Norman Sr HS; Norman, OK; (2); Church Yth Grp; FBLA; Latin Clb; Mu Alpha Theta; Spanish Clb; Bsktbl; Trk; Cit Awd; Hon Roll; NHS; HS HEROES; Chrch Usher; Nrsng.

WILLIAMS, CRYSTAL D; Haskell HS; Haskell, OK; (3); Rep Stu Cncl; Hon Roll; Numerous Subject Awds; Tchng; Cnslr.

WILLIAMS, CURTIS B; Midwest City HS; Midwest City, OK; (3); 28/400; Cmnty Wkr; German Clb; JA; Library Aide; Band; Jazz Band; Mrchg Band; Pep Band; School Musical; Ofcr Bsbl; Outstdng Frosh; SW OK Univ; Pharmiceutical.

WILLIAMS, DALE; Sperry Sr HS; Sperry, OK; (4); 2/78; Am Leg Boys St; Boy Scts; Church Yth Grp; HOBY; Capt Quiz Bowl; Pres Band; Rep Stu Cncl; Var Capt Wrstlng; NHS; Sal; Eagle Sct; Gftd/Tlntd; Enrll Tulsa JC; Tulsa U; Med.

WILLIAMS, DANIKA; Will Rogers HS; Wagoner, OK; (4); 12/179; French Clb; Pep Clb; Teachers Aide; Ed Nwsp; Rep Frsh Cls; Rep Soph Cls; Rep Jr Cls; Rep Sr Cls; Wrstlng; High Hon Roll; OK St; Ed.

WILLIAMS, DAVID M; Memorial HS; Sand Springs, OK; (2); Pres Art Clb; Church Yth Grp; FCA; French Clb; Key Clb; Natl Beta Clb; JV Swmmng; Hon Roll; Royal Rangers; Jr Ldrs Svc Awd; Humane Soc Vol; Oral Roberts; Commercial Art.

WILLIAMS, DAWN; Wellston Schl; Wellston, OK; (1); Rep Frsh Cls; Treas Stu Cncl; JV Var Bsktbl; JV Var Sftbl; High Hon Roll; Pres Jr NHS.

WILLIAMS, DIANNA B; Thomas Jr Sr HS; Thomas, OK; (1); Church Yth Grp; FHA; Band; Chorus; Church Choir; Mrchg Band; Pep Band; Sec Frsh Cls; High Hon Roll; Southwestern OK ST Univ.

WILLIAMS, DIEDRA D; Davis HS; Hennepin, OK; (1); FBLA; FHA; Hon Roll; Swmmng; Bsktbl; Drwng; Langston U.

WILLIAMS, DIXON; Bishop Mcguinness HS; Edmond, OK; (4); Am Leg Boys St; Art Clb; Church Yth Grp; Drama Clb; FCA; Letterman Clb; SADD; Var L Ftbl; Wt Lftg; High Hon Roll; All-Dist Ftbl; Gavula Ftbl Awd; Jr Rotrn; Med.

WILLIAMS, DIXY E; Bishop Kelley HS; Tulsa, OK; (2); Church Yth Grp; Pep Clb; JV Crs Cntry; High Hon Roll; SPCA Vol; VBS Vol; Choices Teen Advy Cncl Mem; Biola Univ; Bio.

WILLIAMS, ELIZABETH; Dickson HS; Ardmore, OK; (1); FHA; Pep Clb; SADD; Band; Chrldng; Hon Roll; OK ST U; Vet.

WILLIAMS, ELIZABETH A; Hulbert Jr Sr HS; Hulbert, OK; (2); Pres FHA; Hon Roll; FHA Awd Bst Wrkng Stuff; Bst Prsn Excd; NSU; Nurse.

WILLIAMS, EMILY R; Muskogee HS; Muskogee, OK; (2); Church Yth Grp; JCL; Key Clb; Quiz Bowl; Church Choir; Jazz Band; School Musical; Var Crs Cntry; JV Tennis; High Hon Roll; Intl Ordr Or Rainbow Grls; RAID; Biochem.

WILLIAMS, ERIK T; Cashion HS; Cashion, OK; (1); Church Yth Grp; FCA; Quiz Bowl; Scholastic Bowl; VP Frsh Cls; Pres Soph Cls; Var Bsktbl; Var Ftbl; Var Wt Lftg; High Hon Roll; U Of OK; Arch Engr.

WILLIAMS, ERIN; Prue Schl; Prue, OK; (3); 3/17; Church Yth Grp; Drama Clb; FCA; FHA; German Clb; GAA; Letterman Clb; Varsity Clb; School Play; Stage Crew; Tulsa JC; His Tchr; Coach.

WILLIAMS, GENA K; Hollis Jr Sr HS; Hollis, OK; (2); 4/60; Church Yth Grp; FBLA; Letterman Clb; Natl FFA Org; Var Bsktbl; Var Sftbl; NHS; FFA Explorer Pgm To Costa Rica; Natl Schlr To Attend The Congressional Yth Ldrshp Cncl; OK ST Univ; Vet.

WILLIAMS, HALEY; Medford Schl; Medford, OK; (1); Church Yth Grp; FCA; FHA; Natl FFA Org; School Play; Bsktbl; Chrldng; Sftbl; High Hon Roll; Stu Of Today; Southern Nazarene U; Phy.

WILLIAMS, JAMES; Yale Jr Sr HS; Yale, OK; (2); 4/70; Natl Beta Clb; Quiz Bowl; Sec Soph Cls; Rep Stu Cncl; Ofcr Bsbl; Bsktbl; Cit Awd; NHS; Pres Acad Fit Awd; Masonic Stu Of Today.

WILLIAMS, JANNA G; Boise City HS; Boise City, OK; (3); 1/35; FCA; 4-H; Library Aide; Office Aide; Scholastic Bowl; Var Trk; High Hon Roll; NHS; OK Hon Soc; Gfted Tlnted Prog.

WILLIAMS, JASON; Butner Schl; Seminole, OK; (1); Computer Clb; 4-H; JA; Quiz Bowl; Scholastic Bowl; Bsktbl; Ftbl; Mgr(s); Wt Lftg; High Hon Roll; OU; Xray Tech.

WILLIAMS, JENIFER K; Choctaw HS; Choctaw, OK; (4); 53/299; FCA; HOBY; Var Bsktbl; Powder Puff Ftbl; Var Sftbl; Trk; High Hon Roll; Hon Roll; Jr NHS; NHS; Nicoma Park/Choctaw Bus Womens Clb Calender Girl; U NE; Med.

WILLIAMS, JENNIFER; Waukomis HS; Waukomis, OK; (2); 1/40; Quiz Bowl; Scholastic Bowl; High Hon Roll; Sal.

WILLIAMS, JENNIFER; Sterling Jr Sr HS; Lawton, OK; (3); Natl FFA Org; Office Aide; Quiz Bowl; School Play; Yrbk; Rep Soph Cls; Rep Stu Cncl; Hon Roll; Pres Acad Fit Awd; NBHA Natl Barrel Horse Assoc; Mar Jr Qtr Horse Assoc; Natl Montadale Assoc; OK ST Univ; Phy Thrpst.

WILLIAMS, JEREMY; Grace Fellowship Christian Sch; Broken Arrow, OK; (3); 4/18; Chess Clb; Church Yth Grp; Quiz Bowl; Scholastic Bowl; Teachers Aide; Rptr Yrbk; VP Jr Cls; Var Bsbl; JV Bsktbl; Var Socr; Phy Ed & Fthfl Srvnt Awds; Mission Trip Mexico; OK ST U; Sprts Med.

WILLIAMS, JERONE T; Roland Sr HS; Roland, OK; (4); Church Yth Grp; FHA; Ofcr Bsbl; Bsktbl; Ftbl; Mgr(s); Trk; High Hon Roll; Hon Roll.

WILLIAMS, JESSICA; Clinton HS; Clinton, OK; (4); 12/99; Drama Clb; Girl Scts; Pres Key Clb; Sec Math Clb; Sec Science Clb; Pres Spanish Clb; Chorus; School Play; Ed Yrbk; Hon Roll; Congrssnl Yth Ldrshp Awd; Southwestern OK ST U; Engl.

WILLIAMS, JESSICA; Oologah-Talala HS; Claremore, OK; (1); Church Yth Grp; Cmnty Wkr; Quiz Bowl; Scholastic Bowl; Rep Frsh Cls; Rep Stu Cncl; Stat Bsktbl; Capt Chrldng; Gym; Score Keeper; Duke U Tlnt Srch; Spec Olympcs Vol; St Hnrs Soc; U Of Tulsa.

WILLIAMS, JESSICA; Blackwell HS; Blackwell, OK; (2); FTA; Pep Clb; Chrldng; Hon Roll.

WILLIAMS, JORDAN A; Memorial HS; Tulsa, OK; (2); Church Yth Grp; JCL; Key Clb; Latin Clb; Nwsp; Hon Roll; Jr NHS; Pres Acad Fit Awd; Pres Schlr; Soccer Referee; Law.

WILLIAMS, JOSH; Newcastle HS; Newcastle, OK; (4); 1/70; Sec Treas FBLA; Model UN; Quiz Bowl; Science Clb; Sec Sr Cls; Capt Var Bsktbl; Hon Roll; Val; Natl Hnr Soc Pres; Schlstc Tm; Qz Bwl All Conf; Southwestern OK ST U.

WILLIAMS, JULIE; Shattuck Jr Sr HS; Shattuck, OK; (4); Am Leg Aux Girls St; Church Yth Grp; FCA; Pep Clb; Chorus; Var Bsktbl; High Hon Roll; Hon Roll; NHS; Sal; Chorus Pres.

WILLIAMS, JULIE R; Jay HS; Jay, OK; (2); Church Yth Grp; FCA; FBLA; Math Tm; Natl FFA Org; Church Choir; VP Frsh Cls; Var Co-Capt Chrldng; 4-H Awd; High Hon Roll.

WILLIAMS, KEETRA N; Putnam City HS; Oklahoma City, OK; (2); 89/364; Drama Clb; NFL; Chorus; School Musical; Ofcr Stu Cncl; Pom Pon; Var L Trk; Howard Univ; Mrktng/Pub Rltns.

WILLIAMS, KELLI N; Duncan HS; Duncan, OK; (3); Church Yth Grp; FBLA; Key Clb; Letterman Clb; SADD; Var Sftbl; High Hon Roll; OK St U; Acctng.

WILLIAMS, KENNETH A; Inola Sr HS; Inola, OK; (3); FHA; Letterman Clb; Library Aide; Science Clb; Teachers Aide; Ftbl; Wt Lftg; Prfct Atten Awd; 2nd Pl St TSA Meet; Spartan Schl Of Aeronautics.

WILLIAMS, KIMBERLEE M; Warner HS; Checotah, OK; (1); Church Yth Grp; Dance Clb; FCA; Pep Clb; Spanish Clb; Chrldng; Conners ST; Phy Thrpst.

WILLIAMS, KIMBERLY D; Broken Arrow Sr HS; Broken Arrow, OK; (4); Treas Art Clb; Drama Clb; Hist German Clb; Office Aide; Band; Mrchg Band; Pep Band; School Play; Stage Crew; Hon Roll; African Hand Drumming; U Of OK; Art.

WILLIAMS, KRISTY; Midwest City HS; Midwest City, OK; (4); 8/419; Church Yth Grp; Sec German Clb; Key Clb; Quiz Bowl; ROTC; Mrchg Band; Ofcr Soph Cls; L Var Socr; NHS; Val; U Of OK; Mech Engrng.

WILLIAMS, KYLIE A; Eisenhower Sr HS; Lawton, OK; (3); FHA; Math Tm; Pep Clb; Yrbk; High Hon Roll; Jr NHS; NHS; Whos Who In Math; Acad Awds; U Of OK Outstdng Acad Achvmt; OK ST Univ; Pre-Vet Med.

WILLIAMS, LE KESHA; Midwest City HS; Midwest City, OK; (1); Cmnty Wkr; Drama Clb; FCA; Speech Tm; Band; Mrchg Band; Pep Band; School Musical; School Play; Stage Crew; Feml Ath Of Yr; Chrch Bsktbl MVP; Prks/Rec Vol.

WILLIAMS, LORI A; Noble HS; Noble, OK; (3); DECA; FHA; Key Clb; Mu Alpha Theta; Spanish Clb; Socr; U Of OK; Bus.

WILLIAMS, LYDELL K; Southeast HS; Oklahoma City, OK; (4); 13/65; Office Aide; L Capt Bsktbl; Crs Cntry; Hon Roll; Antl Sut-Ath Day Awd; All Star Bsktbll Tm; All City, All Conf Bsktbll; All Amer Schlr; S Nazarene Univ; Elec Eng.

WILLIAMS, MARIE A; Muldrow HS; Muldrow, OK; (1); Cmnty Wkr; FHA; Natl FFA Org; Spanish Clb; Speech Tm; Hon Roll; Vol Lcl Vet Clnc; Art; Hrptlgy.

WILLIAMS, MARLENE R; John Marshall HS; Oklahoma City, OK; (2); Office Aide; ROTC; Chorus; Drill Tm; Crs Cntry; Sftbl; Trk; Vllybl; Hon Roll; OK ST U; Math.

WILLIAMS, MARY H; Canton HS; Longdale, OK; (4); FHA; Intnl Clb; Band; Mrchg Band; Pep Band; Yrbk; Rep Stu Cncl; Chrldng; Cit Awd; Native Amer Hnr Perf Arts; Pale Moon Trdtnl/Ctzn Awds; Southwestern OK ST Univ; Cmpr.

WILLIAMS, MEGHAN M; Carl Albert HS; Oklahoma City, OK; (4); 11/243; Church Yth Grp; Drama Clb; Hosp Aide; Key Clb; Teachers Aide; Church Choir; Nwsp; NHS; Ntl Merit SF; Chorus; Brown U; Bichem.

WILLIAMS, MELANIE R; Kiowa Jr-Sr HS; Wardville, OK; (3); 1/30; 4-H; FHA; Library Aide; Yrbk; High Hon Roll; TSA VP, Reprtr; SOSU; Psych.

WILLIAMS, MELIKA; Capitol Hill HS; Oklahoma City, OK; (4); 14/146; FBLA; Science Clb; Chorus; Church Choir; Flag Corp; School Musical; Ofcr Soph Cls; Sftbl; Trk; Vllybl; Hmcmng Qn; Acctng.

WILLIAMS, MELISSA D; Henryetta Sr HS; Henryetta, OK; (2); 2/95; Church Yth Grp; Cmnty Wkr; FCA; French Clb; FHA; GAA; Letterman Clb; Office Aide; Spanish Clb; Chorus; GATE; Nazarene Yth Cncl Bd; DARE; Connors ST Coll; Phy Thprst.

WILLIAMS, MELISSA L; Cameron Schl; Cameron, OK; (3); FHA; Quiz Bowl; SADD; Yrbk; Hon Roll; Pres Acad Fit Awd; St Schlr; Med.

WILLIAMS, MELISSA S; Minco HS; Minco, OK; (2); Church Yth Grp; FCA; FHA; Scholastic Bowl; Teachers Aide; Band; Church Choir; Jazz Band; Mrchg Band; Pep Band; Legal Sec.

WILLIAMS, MELONI; Crescent Schl; Crescent, OK; (2); FHA; Natl Beta Clb; Band; Mrchg Band; Pep Band; Mgr Stat Bsbl; Hon Roll; Med.

WILLIAMS, MICHAEL J; Temple Jr Sr HS; Temple, OK; (2); Natl FFA Org; Band; Jazz Band; Mrchg Band; Pep Band; Wt Lftg; Hon Roll; Cmptr Prgmg; Cmptr Prgmg.

WILLIAMS, MICHELLE E; Perkins-Tryon HS; Perkins, OK; (1); Church Yth Grp; Band; Chorus; Jazz Band; Mrchg Band; Pep Band; Hon Roll; Engl II Acad Achv Awd; Fine Arts Acad Achv Awd; Fund Raiser For Bnd Trip; OSU.

WILLIAMS, MICHELLE M; Walters HS; Walters, OK; (2); Latin Clb; Sec Band; Rptr Nwsp; Pres Frsh Cls; Var Swmmng; Var Trk; Hon Roll; NHS; MA Inst Of Tech; Arch Engrng.

WILLIAMS, MINDY; Frontier Public Schl; Red Rock, OK; (3); 4/28; Church Yth Grp; Cmnty Wkr; 4-H; HOBY; Natl FFA Org; Stage Crew; Pres Jr Cls; Capt Var Bsktbl; Var Sftbl; Cit Awd; Phys Ed.

WILLIAMS, MISTY K; Duncan HS; Duncan, OK; (2); Church Yth Grp; FBLA; Hosp Aide; SADD; Chorus; School Musical; Hon Roll; 4-H; Cameron Univ; Psych.

WILLIAMS, NATHAN J; John Marshall HS; Oklahoma City, OK; (4); 75/160; Church Yth Grp; Drama Clb; Church Choir; Stage Crew; Golf; Hon Roll; OK ST Univ; Arch.

WILLIAMS, NICHOLAS; B T Washington HS; Tulsa, OK; (2); JV Bsktbl; JV Var Ftbl; Wt Lftg; Wrstlng; Hon Roll; Prfct Atten Awd; Knights Of Pythagerus Master Knight; FL.

WILLIAMS, NICOLE; Perry Sr HS; Perry, OK; (3); Church Yth Grp; FCA; HOBY; Band; Jazz Band; Ed Yrbk; Treas Stu Cncl; Pom Pon; NHS; Mat Maid; OK City U.

WILLIAMS, PAMELA; Yarbrough Schl; Goodwell, OK; (3); 3/12; Quiz Bowl; Band; Chorus; Pep Band; School Musical; School Play; Ed Nwsp; Var Bsktbl; Var Chrldng; Var Trk; Speech Clb; OK ST U; Bus Admin.

WILLIAMS, PATRICK; Douglass HS; Oklahoma City, OK; (3); Am Leg Boys St; FBLA; Math Clb; Mu Alpha Theta; Spanish Clb; Ofcr Bsbl; High Hon Roll; NHS; U Of OK; Elect Eng.

WILLIAMS, PATRICK A; Mt St Marys HS; Oklahoma City, OK; (3); Church Yth Grp; FCA; Sec Key Clb; Var Bsktbl; Var L Ftbl; Var L Trk; Jr Knights Of Peter Claver.

WILLIAMS, PATRICK N; Bridge Creek HS; Blanchard, OK; (4); 15/61; Church Yth Grp; FCA; Office Aide; Spanish Clb; Bsktbl; Trk; Hon Roll; U Of MD Baltimore Cty; Pre-Med.

WILLIAMS III, PHILLIP E; Oklahoma Christian Acad; Arcadia, OK; (2); Mgr Stage Crew; Treas Soph Cls; High Hon Roll; Otstdng Stdnt Awd Eng/Hlth/Mus/Art; ST Tae Kwon Do Chmpn Gld Mdls; Jr Olym Nat Tae Kwon Do; Piano; Physics/Cmptr Sci.

WILLIAMS, PRESTON J; Putnam City HS; Warr Acres, OK; (1); Church Yth Grp; Orch; Socr; Belong To Silver Strings Of OK Prof Strings Group; Altar Server At Chrch.

WILLIAMS, PRESTON M; Cashion HS; Cashion, OK; (3); Church Yth Grp; FCA; Teachers Aide; Rep Frsh Cls; VP Soph Cls; Rep Jr Cls; Rep Sr Cls; VP Stu Cncl; Var Bsbl; Var Bsktbl; TSA; Constr Engr/Bus Mgr/Hse Bldr.

WILLIAMS, ROBIN S; Elgin HS; Lawton, OK; (3); 17/89; Church Yth Grp; Office Aide; Sec Sr Cls; VP Stu Cncl; Hon Roll; Native Amer Clb; OU; Med.

WILLIAMS, ROCKELL E; Capitol Hill HS; Oklahoma City, OK; (4); 73/121; Dance Clb; Ofcr Soph Cls; Ofcr Bsbl; Var Trk; High Hon Roll; Prfct Atten Awd; OK City CC; Electronics.

WILLIAMS, ROSS; Hobart HS; Hobart, OK; (3); Church Yth Grp; Quiz Bowl; Scholastic Bowl; Teachers Aide; High Hon Roll; NHS; OK ST U.

WILLIAMS, RUSSELL; Prue Schl; Sand Springs, OK; (2); Drama Clb; School Play; Hon Roll; OK ST Coll; Automtv Engr.

WILLIAMS, RYAN B; Ardmore HS; Ardmore, OK; (3); 95/202; Art Clb; Church Yth Grp; French Clb; Letterman Clb; JV Bsktbl; JV Ftbl; Var Tennis; ECU; Ag.

WILLIAMS, SCOTT; Commerce HS; Commerce, OK; (1); Church Yth Grp; FCA; Letterman Clb; Quiz Bowl; Science Clb; SADD; Band; Pres Frsh Cls; Ofcr Bsbl; Bsktbl; Optometry.

WILLIAMS, SCOTT M; Arkoma Jr Sr HS; Arkoma, OK; (3); FCA; Var Bsbl; Capt Bsktbl; High Hon Roll; Hon Roll; HS All Area Bsktbl Team; All St Hnrb Mn Tn; All Cty Bsktbl Team; Baylor U; Bsktbl Coach.

WILLIAMS, SHANNON L; Washington HS; Washington, OK; (1); Pep Clb; JV Var Sftbl.

WILLIAMS, SHAUNDONA C; Jones HS; Jones, OK; (3); Church Yth Grp; Rptr FBLA; Key Clb; Pres Mu Alpha Theta; Thesps; Chorus; Rep Stu Cncl; Powder Puff Ftbl; FCA; FHA; Jones Agnst Drgs; Planet Earth Club; Prin Advy Bd; Soc Work.

WILLIAMS, SHEILA; Crowder Schl; Mcalester, OK; (2); 5/43; Church Yth Grp; FHA; Sec Soph Cls; Var Bsktbl; Var Sftbl; Hon Roll; Prfct Atten Awd; OK Hnr Soc; Hnr Rll; Murray ST Coll; Dntl Hygnst.

WILLIAMS, SHYLA D; Mc Loud HS; Mc Loud, OK; (1); Church Yth Grp; FHA; Hosp Aide; Pep Clb; Ofcr Frsh Cls; Chrldng; Hon Roll; Prfct Atten Awd; La Danse Vivante Dncr; OK Univ; Med Field.

WILLIAMS, STACY J; Stillwater Jr HS; Stillwater, OK; (1); Church Yth Grp; Dance Clb; Orch; Nwsp; Ed Yrbk; Hist Frsh Cls; Ofcr Stu Cncl; Tennis; High Hon Roll; Pres Schlr; OK Interschlastic Pres Assn 2nd Pl St Cont; Model; 2nd Pl Runway Cont; HS Chamber Orch; Violin.

WILLIAMS, STEPHANE R; Edmond North HS; Edmond, OK; (1); 219/456; JV Bsktbl; JV Crs Cntry; Var Socr; PR/SPRTS Med.

WILLIAMS, STEPHANIE M; Bishop Kelley HS; Tulsa, OK; (1); Hon Roll; Karate; ARF Vol.

WILLIAMS, STEWART; Pryor Sr HS; Pryor, OK; (4); 1/148; FBLA; VP Math Clb; VP Mu Alpha Theta; Spanish Clb; Teachers Aide; VP Jr Cls; Pres Stu Cncl; Ofcr Bsbl; NHS; Val; OK ST Univ; Bus.

WILLIAMS, TAMMI E; Hugo HS; Hugo, OK; (3); Natl FFA Org; Chorus; School Musical; School Play; Swing Chorus; Lit Mag; Upward Bound Pgm.

WILLIAMS, TENEKA; Choctaw HS; Oklahoma City, OK; (4); Bsktbl; Trk; Hon Roll; NHS; Bus.

WILLIAMS, THOMAS; Douglass HS; Oklahoma City, OK; (4); 3/116; Church Yth Grp; FBLA; Mu Alpha Theta; Office Aide; Ofcr Bsbl; High Hon Roll; NHS; Pres Schlr; Pre-AP/AP Calculus Awds; U Of OK; Cmptr Sci.

WILLIAMS, TRINA L; Tishomingo HS; Tishomingo, OK; (3); Church Yth Grp; FHA; Band; Chorus; Church Choir; Jazz Band; Mrchg Band; Pep Band; Hon Roll; Prfct Atten Awd; Singing Cont Supr & Excl Ratings; Fine Arts Fstvl Super Rating & Going To Natls; Murray ST Coll; Nrsng.

WILLIAMS, VA NESSA; Wynnewood HS; Wynnewood, OK; (4); 3/60; Church Yth Grp; Cmnty Wkr; FCA; GAA; HOBY; Letterman Clb; Office Aide; Scholastic Bowl; Teachers Aide; Varsity Clb; Bsktbl Homcmng Qn; Ftbl Homcmng Qn; Southern Nazarene U; Pre-Med.

WILLIAMS, VANESSA; Wynnewood HS; Wynnewood, OK; (4); 3/60; Church Yth Grp; Cmnty Wkr; HOBY; Band; VP Frsh Cls; VP Soph Cls; VP Jr Cls; VP Stu Cncl; Var Capt Bsktbl; Var L Crs Cntry; All St Track; Natl Yth Forum Sci; Med.

WILLIAMS, WESLEY H; Leflore Sr HS; Heavener, OK; (3); Quiz Bowl; Speech Tm; High Hon Roll; Hon Roll; Rptr Nwsp; Rep Frsh Cls; Pres Soph Cls; VP Jr Cls; Carl Albert ST Coll; Tchng.

WILLIAMS, WINDY; Perry Sr HS; Perry, OK; (2); Church Yth Grp; Band; Mrchg Band; Pep Band; Cit Awd; Hon Roll; NHS; TSA; Pilot.

WILLIAMS, ZACKERY R; Stillwater Sr HS; Stillwater, OK; (2); 1/263; Latin Clb; Spanish Clb; Beta Clb; OSU; Meteorology.

WILLIAMSON, AUBURN; Tonkawa Jr Sr HS; Tonkawa, OK; (1); Church Yth Grp; FCA; 4-H; FHA; Acpl Chr; Chorus; School Musical; Ofcr Frsh Cls; Ofcr Stu Cncl; Chrldng; Northern OK Coll.

WILLIAMSON, BRANDI; Panama HS; Panama, OK; (3); FCA; FHA; German Clb; GAA; Natl FFA Org; SADD; Ofcr Frsh Cls; Ofcr Soph Cls; Rptr Jr Cls; Var Bsktbl; Westark; Nrs.

WILLIAMSON, DANA J; Ada HS; Ada, OK; (3); Art Clb; Church Yth Grp; Hosp Aide; Key Clb; Chorus; Bsktbl; Hon Roll; Inter Tribal Cncl Clb; Johnson O Malley Stu Of Yr; High Acad Awd; U Of OK; Mrktng; Advertising.

WILLIAMSON, EMILY; Shawnee Sr HS; Shawnee, OK; (4); 22/162; Church Yth Grp; FCA; Latin Clb; Library Aide; Var Crs Cntry; Var Trk; High Hon Roll; NHS; Ntl Merit Ltr; Natl Ldrshp Merit Awd; Wrstlng Hmcmng Princess; Tri-H-Y Secy; U Of OK.

WILLIAMSON, HEATHER R; Frontier Public Schl; Red Rock, OK; (2); Church Yth Grp; Cmnty Wkr; 4-H; FHA; GAA; Chorus; Northern OK Coll.

WILLIAMSON, JENNIFER; Panama HS; Panama, OK; (3); FHA; SADD; Rep Soph Cls; Bsktbl; Chrldng; Hon Roll; NHS; Gftd & Tlntd; FCA; E Cntrl U; Pre-Law.

WILLIAMSON, JENNIFER L; Lawton Sr HS; Lawton, OK; (2); Hon Roll; Ed.

WILLIAMSON, JENNY A; Newkirk HS; Newkirk, OK; (3); Band; Mrchg Band; Phtg Yrbk; Pres Frsh Cls; VP Soph Cls; Pres Jr Cls; Pres Stu Cncl; Cit Awd; NHS; FCA; STEPP Pres.

WILLIAMSON, JOSHUA; Elk City Jr HS; Elk City, OK; (2); Band; Mrchg Band; Var Socr; Hon Roll.

WILLIAMSON, KATIE; Shawnee Sr HS; Shawnee, OK; (2); 1/350; Church Yth Grp; FCA; Scholastic Bowl; Pres Frsh Cls; Pres Soph Cls; Ofcr Stu Cncl; Var Chrldng; Var L Crs Cntry; Mgr(s); High Hon Roll; Bsktbl Hmcmng Ct; Chrldr; Tri-Hi-Y; Arch.

WILLIAMSON, MELEIA; Choctaw HS; Oklahoma City, OK; (2); Key Clb; Office Aide; Swing Chorus; Var Chrldng; Gym; Tennis; Cit Awd; High Hon Roll; Hon Roll; Prfct Atten Awd; Pom Squad Danz Natls Perfmnc; NCA Finals Dallas 4th Pl; OK Univ.

WILLIAMSON, ROBERT C; Jay HS; Jay, OK; (3); Chess Clb; Church Yth Grp; Cmnty Wkr; FCA; Letterman Clb; Pep Clb; Quiz Bowl; Scholastic Bowl; Science Clb; SADD; US Mrshl.

WILLIAMSON, SHANNON L; Alex Jr Sr HS; Alex, OK; (3); Church Yth Grp; Computer Clb; FCA; FBLA; FHA; Natl FFA Org; Pep Clb; Teachers Aide; Chorus; Church Choir; USAO; RN.

WILLIANS, LINDSAY; Moore HS; Moore, OK; (2); Church Yth Grp; FCA; Variety Show; Var Chrldng; Var JV Trk; Hon Roll; Jr NHS; NHS.

WILLINGHAM, ALICIA D; Sapulpa Sr HS; Sapulpa, OK; (3); Key Clb; Letterman Clb; Math Clb; Science Clb; Mgr Ftbl; L Stat Wrstlng; Hon Roll; Jr NHS; NHS; Pres Acad Fit Awd; U Of Cntrl OK; Pre-Med.

WILLINGHAM, DAVID H; El Reno Sr HS; El Reno, OK; (4); 12/167; Art Clb; Church Yth Grp; FCA; Math Clb; Crs Cntry; Socr; High Hon Roll; NHS; Concordia Univ; DCE.

WILLINGHAM, DEAH; Lone Grove HS; Ardmore, OK; (3); 15/100; Church Yth Grp; FCA; Natl FFA Org; Rep Spanish Clb; Yrbk; Sftbl; High Hon Roll; Hon Roll; NHS; Pres Acad Fit Awd; Dntl Hygnst.

WILLINGHAM, MARIAH; Okmulgee HS; Okmulgee, OK; (3); Church Yth Grp; Girl Scts; Science Clb; Band; Jazz Band; Mrchg Band; Ofcr Stu Cncl; Mgr(s); Hon Roll; NHS; All Dist Bnd; Bio.

WILLINGHAM, RAE A; Lone Grove HS; Lone Grove, OK; (3); Math Clb; Natl Beta Clb; NFL; Science Clb; Speech Tm; Chorus; School Musical; High Hon Roll; NHS; Show Choir; All Dist Chorus; 3rd Pl Spnsh I Schlstc Meet; Se OK ST U; Psych.

WILLINGHAM, STEPHANIE; Union Intermediate HS; Tulsa, OK; (2); 58/850; Church Yth Grp; FCA; Hosp Aide; Spanish Clb; Church Choir; Drill Tm; High Hon Roll; NHS; Drug Free Yth Pres.

WILLINGHAM, VALORIE L; Mooreland Jr Sr HS; Mooreland, OK; (1); Art Clb; Church Yth Grp; FCA; FHA; Bsktbl; Hon Roll; TSA; Northwestern ST U; CPA.

WILLIS, CLARA D; Hulbert Jr Sr HS; Hulbert, OK; (1); Cit Awd; Northeastern ST U.

WILLIS, EVA E; Madill HS; Madill, OK; (2); FCA; Ofcr 4-H; SADD; Band; Mrchg Band; Orch; 4-H Awd; Hon Roll; Speech Tm; Pep Band; Dance Tm; St Jude Bike-A-Thon Coord; SE Univ; Comp.

WILLIS, GRACELYN S; Marietta HS; Marietta, OK; (2); Church Yth Grp; FCA; Band; Mrchg Band; Bsktbl; Crs Cntry; Sftbl; Trk; Vllybl; Hon Roll; Weatherford; Phrmcst.

WILLIS, HEATHER; Moore HS; Moore, OK; (4); Church Yth Grp; FCA; GAA; Band; Mrchg Band; JV Bsktbl; JV Chrldng; Var Swmmng; Var Trk; High Hon Roll; Drumline Band.

WILLIS, HOLLIE; Madill HS; Ardmore, OK; (2); FCA; GAA; Var Bsktbl; Var Sftbl; Sftbl; Phys Thrpst.

WILLIS, JOHN; Moore HS; Oklahoma City, OK; (2); FBLA; Spanish Clb; Golf; Bus.

WILLIS, LORA E; Wellston Schl; Wellston, OK; (3); Church Yth Grp; Drama Clb; FHA; Pep Clb; SADD; Chorus; Church Choir; Stage Crew; Cit Awd; Citation Of Appreciation By Senator Leftwich For Yth Force Work; Soc Work.

WILLIS, MELISSA R; Union Intermediate HS; Broken Arrow, OK; (2); 221/800; French Clb; Key Clb; Chorus; School Musical; Pres Schlr; U Of OK; Psych/Med.

WILLIS, MIKHAEL L; Marietta HS; Marietta, OK; (2); Church Yth Grp; Cmnty Wkr; GAA; Speech Tm; Mrchg Band; Ofcr Bsbl; Chrldng; Sftbl; Vllybl; Hon Roll; St Speech.

WILLIS, ROBBIE; Hobart HS; Hobart, OK; (3); 1/64; Church Yth Grp; FCA; FTA; Letterman Clb; Quiz Bowl; Scholastic Bowl; Rep Stu Cncl; L Bsbl; L Bsktbl; L Ftbl; U Of OK; Meteorology.

OKLAHOMA

WILLIS, TRENT; Tuttle HS; Tuttle, OK; (1); Church Yth Grp; Cmnty Wkr; FCA; 4-H; Natl FFA Org; Var JV Ftbl; JV Wt Lftg; Cit Awd; 4-H Awd; High Hon Roll; 3 Xs Breed Chmpn Natl OK City Spring Livestock Show; SWOSU; Phrmcy.

WILLISTON, DIANA R; Idabel HS; Idabel, OK; (3); 15/115; Hosp Aide; Science Clb; Jazz Band; Mrchg Band; Hon Roll; Jr NHS; NHS; Band; Ofcr Stu Cncl; Native Amer Club Rprtr/Pres; Hon Mntn 94 OK ST Univ ST Math Cntst; Bnd Plcd 1st 3a Orlando Musfst; Bio.

WILLISTON, LANCE A; Idabel HS; Idabel, OK; (2); CAP; FCA; Band; Mrchg Band; Ofcr Bsbl; Ftbl; Hon Roll; USMC.

WILLOUGHBY, KRISTY N; Meeker Jr Sr HS; Meeker, OK; (4); 17/76; Cmnty Wkr; Computer Clb; English Clb; FCA; GAA; Math Clb; Pep Clb; Science Clb; Spanish Clb; Teachers Aide; OK HS Rodeo Assoc; OK Baptist Univ; Ed.

WILLOUGHBY, SARAH C; Pauls Valley HS; Pauls Valley, OK; (2); FHA; Key Clb; Spanish Clb; Chorus; School Musical; School Play; High Hon Roll; NHS; OK Hnr Soc; Pi Phi Pi; OK U; Hlth.

WILLS, AMY; Grace Fellowship Christian Sch; Tulsa, OK; (3); Church Yth Grp; Rep Soph Cls; Pres Jr Cls; Rep Stu Cncl; Var Capt Chrldng.

WILLSON, JOHN W; Crescent Schl; Crescent, OK; (2); Cmnty Wkr; Letterman Clb; Natl FFA Org; Band; Mrchg Band; Pep Band; Ofcr Bsbl; Bsktbl; Gov Hon Prg Awd; Hon Roll; OK ST Univ; Bus Adm.

WILLY, MANDYE R; Vinita HS; Vinita, OK; (3); 12/98; DECA; FCA; FHA; German Clb; Math Clb; Office Aide; Red Cross Aide; Science Clb; Spanish Clb; Teachers Aide; OK ST Univ; Comm Design/Mktng.

WILMETH, LYDIA A; West Middle HS; Norman, OK; (1); Spanish Clb; Lit Mag; Rep Stu Cncl; Cit Awd; Gov Hon Prg Awd; High Hon Roll; Hon Roll; Admin Asst Teletraining Inst; Harvard U; Poltcl Sci.

WILMORE, CHERALYN; Moore HS; Moore, OK; (4); Church Yth Grp; DECA; Spanish Clb; SADD; Church Choir; U Cntrl OK; Math Educ.

WILMOTH, MISTY; Fairland Jr Sr HS; Fairland, OK; (3); Teachers Aide; Pres Frsh Cls; Treas Soph Cls; Bsktbl; Powder Puff Ftbl; Sftbl; Trk; Hon Roll; Prfct Atten Awd; Med.

WILSACK, PETER R; Del City HS; Del City, OK; (2); 77/493; Art Clb; Boy Scts; Church Yth Grp; Jr NHS; NHS; Rcrtnl Scr; Rice Univ; Cmptr Prgrmng.

WILSEY, KRISTIN; Heritage Hall Schl; Oklahoma City, OK; (3); 2/55; Cmnty Wkr; Mu Alpha Theta; Pep Clb; Chorus; Yrbk; Sec Jr Cls; High Hon Roll; NHS; Spanish NHS; Girls All-ST Rnnr Up.

WILSIE, JASON D; Edmond North HS; Edmond, OK; (3); Church Yth Grp; FCA; Letterman Clb; Spanish Clb; Church Choir; Var JV Bsbl; Var JV Bsktbl; Prfct Atten Awd; Bsktbl Camps Coach; Coaching Awd Named In My Hnr; Coaching; Sports Casting.

WILSON, AMANDA D; Soper Schl; Soper, OK; (1); 2/23; Church Yth Grp; 4-H; FHA; Church Choir; Hon Roll; OK Bptst Yth Choir; OK Bptst U; Msc Fld.

WILSON, AMY; Smithville Sr HS; Smithville, OK; (4); 1/20; Church Yth Grp; Drama Clb; Quiz Bowl; Scholastic Bowl; Church Choir; Nwsp; Co-Ed Yrbk; NHS; Val; Debate Tm; CYIA; Carl Albert ST Coll; Bus Admn.

WILSON, AMY C; Clayton Jr Sr HS; Nashoba, OK; (2); 8/60; 4-H; Rptr Natl FFA Org; Quiz Bowl; JV Bsktbl; High Hon Roll; Hon Roll; Pub Spkng; Livestock Judging; Stock Shows; OK ST Univ; Vet Med.

WILSON, AMY D; Yukon HS; Yukon, OK; (3); 30/420; Church Yth Grp; FHA; Spanish Clb; VP Jr Cls; Hist Stu Cncl; Bsktbl; Hon Roll; NHS; Pres Acad Fit Awd; 3-D; S Nazarene U; Psycht.

WILSON, AMY L; Duncan HS; Duncan, OK; (2); Church Yth Grp; Cmnty Wkr; GAA; Key Clb; Letterman Clb; Chorus; Church Choir; School Musical; Crs Cntry; Trk; Elem Ed; Music.

WILSON, ANDREA; Stilwell HS; Stilwell, OK; (3); Church Yth Grp; 4-H; Hosp Aide; Natl Beta Clb; Red Cross Aide; Chorus; Rep Soph Cls; Chrldng; Hon Roll; Piano; Westark CC; Med.

WILSON, ANGELEE M; Drumright HS; Drumright, OK; (1); Church Yth Grp; FCA; Spanish Clb; JV Bsktbl; Var Sftbl; Hon Roll; NHS.

WILSON, BECKY; Varnum Jr Sr HS; Seminole, OK; (4); 1/15; Pres FHA; Library Aide; Yrbk; VP Frsh Cls; Pres Soph Cls; Pres Jr Cls; Treas Stu Cncl; Hon Roll; Val; Seminole ST Coll.

WILSON, BRAD A; Putnam City West HS; Bethany, OK; (1); Church Yth Grp; Stage Crew; Bsktbl; High Hon Roll; Southern Nazarene Univ.

WILSON, BRETT; Carney Schl; Carney, OK; (1); 1/16; Natl FFA Org; Rptr Stu Cncl; Ofcr Bsbl; High Hon Roll.

WILSON, BROOKE; Spiro HS; Spiro, OK; (3); 15/95; Church Yth Grp; FCA; FHA; Red Cross Aide; Spanish Clb; SADD; Band; Yrbk; Ofcr Stu Cncl; Chrldng.

WILSON, CARLA D; Okmulgee HS; Okmulgee, OK; (2); 4-H; Natl FFA Org; Office Aide; Teachers Aide; Church Choir; Sociology; Psych; Spelman; Comp Engr.

WILSON, CHRIS B; Muskogee HS; Muskogee, OK; (3); Boy Scts; SADD; VICA; Band; Mrchg Band; Pep Band; OK ST Tech Okmulgee; Drftng.

WILSON, CHRISTOPHER J; Edmond Santa Fe HS; Edmond, OK; (4); 88/209; French Clb; Ofcr Stu Cncl; Var Socr; U Of Cntrl OK; Sprts Med.

WILSON, COLLEEN; Cyril Jr Sr HS; Cyril, OK; (3); School Play; Ofcr Frsh Cls; Rep Soph Cls; Rep Jr Cls; Var Bsktbl; Var Chrldng; Var Trk; High Hon Roll; NHS; Ntl Merit Schol; U Of OK; Med.

WILSON, COREY; Midwest City HS; Midwest City, OK; (3); 1/389; German Clb; Band; Jazz Band; Ofcr Soph Cls; Ofcr Jr Cls; Var L Tennis; Cit Awd; High Hon Roll; NHS; Pres Acad Fit Awd; Msnc Stu Today; OK St Lgsltr Page; All St Jazz; Coda Hnr Bnds; Outstndng Solst Awds; U OK; Music Arts.

WILSON, COURTNEY D; Afton HS; Afton, OK; (2); Church Yth Grp; FCA; 4-H; FHA; GAA; Natl FFA Org; Rep Stu Cncl; Var Bsktbl; Chrch Yth Grp; NEO; PT.

WILSON, CRYSTAL; Roland Sr HS; Roland, OK; (3); Church Yth Grp; Cmnty Wkr; Band; Mrchg Band; Pep Band; Pres Stu Cncl; Var Bsktbl; High Hon Roll; Hon Roll; FCA; U AR; Bus.

WILSON, CYNTHIA J; B T Washington HS; Tulsa, OK; (4); 44/264; Spanish Clb; School Musical; School Play; Stage Crew; Var L Socr; Hon Roll; NHS; U Of OK; Phys Thrpy.

WILSON, DESIREE M; Quapaw Sr HS; Quapaw, OK; (3); 12/36; Quiz Bowl; Spanish Clb; Teachers Aide; Band; Chorus; Co-Ed Nwsp; Ed Yrbk; Hon Roll; Marine Bio.

WILSON, DEVON M; Cushing HS; Cushing, OK; (1); 19/194; Church Yth Grp; Math Clb; Science Clb; Color Guard; Phtg Yrbk; Intrml JV Bsktbl; Var JV Ftbl; Var JV Golf; Intrml Sftbl; High Hon Roll; OK Bapt U; Orthodonics.

WILSON, DINAH L; Drumright HS; Drumright, OK; (1); Church Yth Grp; FCA; Spanish Clb; JV Bsktbl; Var Sftbl; Hon Roll; NHS.

WILSON, DUSTIN M; Christian Heritage Acad; Oklahoma City, OK; (2); Church Yth Grp; FCA; Church Choir; JV Bsktbl; JV Var Ftbl; Var L Tennis; Var Wt Lftg; Var Hon Roll; Natl Leag Jr Catilian Tchr; Sports Nutrition.

WILSON, ELIZABETH; Tahlequah Sr HS; Tahlequah, OK; (4); 3/251; Church Yth Grp; German Clb; Math Clb; SADD; Chorus; Tennis; Hon Roll; NHS; Pres Acad Fit Awd; Indian Hrtge Clb; NSU; Law.

WILSON, FELICIA; Stuart Sr HS; Stuart, OK; (3); 7/29; Am Leg Aux Girls St; 4-H; Spanish Clb; Teachers Aide; Yrbk; Cit Awd; 4-H Awd; Hon Roll; Pres Acad Fit Awd; Sal; NEO; Comm/PR.

WILSON, GALEN; Perry Sr HS; Perry, OK; (4); Teachers Aide; VICA; Cit Awd; DAR Awd; Hon Roll; Pres Acad Fit Awd; TSA; NOC.

WILSON, GINNIFER M; Moore HS; Moore, OK; (3); 99/566; Church Yth Grp; FCA; Chorus; Rep Stu Cncl; Var L Chrldng; Hon Roll; NHS; Office Aide; Variety Show; Show Choir; NCA All Amer Chrldr; All Amer Schlr; Rainbows; Camp Fire; OU; Interior Decorater.

WILSON, GLENN P; Perry Sr HS; Perry, OK; (3); Art Clb; Church Yth Grp; Band; Mrchg Band; OCC; Electronic Engr.

WILSON, GREGORY; B T Washington HS; Tulsa, OK; (1); Church Yth Grp; JV Var Bsktbl; Swmmng; Wt Lftg; NC; Bus.

WILSON, JAKE; Jenks HS; Jenks, OK; (4); 60/540; Church Yth Grp; Debate Tm; FCA; Math Clb; Mu Alpha Theta; NFL; Quiz Bowl; Science Clb; Speech Tm; Teachers Aide; De Mola Delta Chptr Spon By Jenks Masonic Lodge 741; Univ Of OK; Cardovasclr Srgn.

WILSON, JANEY L; Lone Grove HS; Lone Grove, OK; (3); 23/98; Church Yth Grp; Debate Tm; Model UN; NFL; Speech Tm; Chorus; Hon Roll; Early Childhd; Scndry Ed.

WILSON, JEFFREY L; Savanna HS; Mcalester, OK; (3); 5/65; FCA; Quiz Bowl; Science Clb; Pres Soph Cls; Ofcr Bsbl; Bsktbl; Ftbl; Cit Awd; High Hon Roll; Aerospace Engrng.

WILSON, JENNIFER; Cimarron Christian Acad; Oilton, OK; (2); Am Leg Aux Girls St; Church Yth Grp; GAA; Office Aide; Pep Clb; Teachers Aide; Chorus; Orch; School Play; Yrbk.

WILSON, JENNIFER H; North Intermediate HS; Broken Arrow, OK; (1); Church Yth Grp; CAP; FCA; Spanish Clb; Band; Chorus; Church Choir; Mrchg Band; Pep Band; Nutritional Advy Cncl Sec; Mt Biking; Climbing; Hiking; Cnslng.

WILSON, JEREMY; Guthrie Sr HS; Guthrie, OK; (4); Church Yth Grp; FCA; French Clb; Letterman Clb; Mu Alpha Theta; Varsity Clb; Rep Stu Cncl; Capt Wrstlng; Demolay; Tchng.

WILSON, JESSICA D; Ponca City Sr HS; Ponca City, OK; (3); 26/435; Cmnty Wkr; Hosp Aide; Spanish Clb; Flag Corp; Mrchg Band; Orch; Swmmng; High Hon Roll; Pre-Med; Music.

WILSON, JONI; Inola Sr HS; Inola, OK; (3); Church Yth Grp; FCA; FHA; Rep Science Clb; Rep Nwsp; Rep Yrbk; Sec Jr Cls; Treas Stu Cncl; Var L Bsktbl; Var Sftbl; Rogers ST; Pre PT.

WILSON, JULIE; Muskogee HS; Muskogee, OK; (4); 19/300; Am Leg Aux Girls St; DECA; Sec FHA; JCL; Latin Clb; Chrldng; Rep Stu Cncl; High Hon Roll; NHS; 95 Washngtn Jrnlsm Conf; Ecol Clb; Nrthestrn; Orthdntst.

WILSON, JUSTIN; Elgin HS; Elgin, OK; (2); Natl FFA Org; FFA Rprtr; Show Sheep/Compete Frm Shp Tm; Connors ST Colld.

WILSON, KARRI; Perkins-Tryon HS; Perkins, OK; (2); 1/110; Intnl Clb; Natl FFA Org; Cit Awd; High Hon Roll; Pres Schlr; Acad Tm; Vol Bible Ed Wk; OK Hon Soc.

WILSON, KELLI J; Skiatook HS; Skiatook, OK; (1); Church Yth Grp; Band; Jazz Band; Mrchg Band; Bsktbl; Sftbl; Hon Roll.

WILSON, KINDA; Chelsea HS; Chelsea, OK; (2); Drama Clb; FCA; 4-H; Model UN; Rep Natl FFA Org; Quiz Bowl; Spanish Clb; Rptr Soph Cls; NHS; Mock Trial.

WILSON, KIRK; Frederick HS; Frederick, OK; (4); 10/72; Debate Tm; Letterman Clb; Office Aide; Scholastic Bowl; Speech Tm; Varsity Clb; School Musical; Ftbl; Wt Lftg; NHS; Cameron Univ; Commnctn.

WILSON, KRISTINA; Blanchard Jr Sr HS; Blanchard, OK; (3); Church Yth Grp; Computer Clb; Pep Clb; Spanish Clb; Hon Roll; NHS; Span Gftd & Tlntd; All Amer Schlr Awd; OK Univ; Phy Therapy.

WILSON, LANA; Balko Public Schl; Balko, OK; (4); 6/19; Pep Clb; Band; Chorus; Drm Mjr(t); Mrchg Band; Pep Band; Chrldng; Trk; Hon Roll; FHA; Author Pblshd Poetry; Western OK Hnr Choir; K101 Marching Band; Seward Cty CC; Cnslr.

WILSON, LATRECIA K; Stilwell HS; Stilwell, OK; (2); Pres 4-H; GAA; Sec Natl Beta Clb; Treas Rep Natl FFA Org; Spanish Clb; Var Bsktbl; Capt Powder Puff Ftbl; 4-H Awd; Hon Roll.

WILSON, LINDSAY; Oklahoma Christian Schl; Edmond, OK; (2); Sec Soph Cls; Capt Var Bsktbl; Mgr(s); Var Socr; Prfct Atten Awd.

WILSON, MADELINA; Drumright HS; Drumright, OK; (2); 4/50; Cmnty Wkr; FCA; HOBY; Science Clb; Spanish Clb; School Musical; School Play; JV Var Bsktbl; Var L Chrldng; Var L Golf; Cngrsnl Yth Ldrshp Conf; Anesthesiolgst/Pedtrn.

WILSON, MELEA; Ninnekah HS; Chickasha, OK; (1); Church Yth Grp; FCA; FHA; VP Frsh Cls; Var Bsktbl; High Hon Roll; OK Hnr Soc; Stu Mo; Piano; U Of OK; Med.

WILSON, MELISSA F; Mustang HS; Mustang, OK; (3); Church Yth Grp; FCA; Spanish Clb; SADD; Teachers Aide; Bsktbl; Golf; Vllybl; Hon Roll; Holland With Yth Understndng Intl Trade; Sprts Med.

WILSON, MICHAEL; Empire Schl; Duncan, OK; (2); Band; Var Bsktbl; Var Ftbl; Wt Lftg.

WILSON, MICHAEL A; Mc Alester HS; Mcalester, OK; (3); Southeastern; Drafting.

WILSON, MICHAEL L; South Intermediate HS; Broken Arrow, OK; (1); Church Yth Grp; Band; Mrchg Band; TX A&M.

WILSON, MIKE; Central Schl; Lawton, OK; (4); 7/29; Am Leg Boys St; Church Yth Grp; FCA; Yrbk; VP Sr Cls; Pres Stu Cncl; Ofcr Bsbl; Bsktbl; Ftbl; Golf; Natl Rcrd Hldr Ftbl Career Extra Pt Kcks; Natl Rcrd Hldr Bsbl RBIS In A Season; AR U; Phy Ther.

WILSON, MINDY; Bethany HS; Oklahoma City, OK; (3); Church Yth Grp; FCA; Pres Jr Cls; Rep Stu Cncl; Bsktbl; Chrldng; Sftbl; High Hon Roll; NHS; GAA; Female Athl Of Yr; OK Hnr Soc; Yth Alive.

WILSON, NICHOLAS O; Parker Middle HS; Mcalester, OK; (2); French Clb; Natl FFA Org; Hon Roll.

WILSON, RACHELLE; Haileyville Schl; Haileyville, OK; (2); Var Bsktbl; Var Chrldng; Var Sftbl; Hghst Grd Hmnts Avg 104; Cert Mntng A Eng Clss; JOM Cert Hnr Rll; Nrthstn ST Coll; Med.

WILSON, ROB W; Davis HS; Davis, OK; (4); 1/51; Computer Clb; Debate Tm; FBLA; German Clb; Key Clb; Latin Clb; Math Clb; Natl Beta Clb; Natl FFA Org; Quiz Bowl; OK Univ; Medicine.

WILSON, ROMEO M; Tahlequah Sr HS; Tahlequah, OK; (2); JV Bsktbl; Hon Roll; Prfct Atten Awd; Native Amer Stu Clb; U Of AR.

WILSON, RUSSTINA D; Roff HS; Roff, OK; (3); Chorus; Hon Roll; Murray ST; Vet Tech.

WILSON, SAMUEL A; Mc Lain Career Acad; Tulsa, OK; (3); Church Yth Grp; English Clb; Math Tm; SADD; Yrbk; Ofcr Jr Cls; Ofcr Bsbl; Bsktbl; High Hon Roll; NHS; Elec Engr; Criminal Justice.

WILSON, SARA E; Edmond Memorial HS; Edmond, OK; (4); 124/350; Church Yth Grp; FCA; Key Clb; Spanish Clb; SADD; Chorus; School Musical; Variety Show; VP Hist Stu Cncl; Pom Pon; Yng Lfe; Cmmnty Svc; Muli Yr Listee; HPERD Majr Schol; USSA Awd; U Of Centr OK; Hlth.

WILSON, SARAH E; North Intemediate HS; Broken Arrow, OK; (1); Church Yth Grp; French Clb; Vllybl; Hon Roll.

WILSON, SHARONDA; Northeast HS; Oklahoma City, OK; (3); Cmnty Wkr; Chorus; Church Choir; Chrldng; Gym; Hon Roll; Prairie View A&M U; Bus Mgmt.

WILSON, SHELDON M; Empire Schl; Duncan, OK; (2); Letterman Clb; Band; Bsktbl; Ftbl; OK ST Univ.

WILSON, STACY; Perkins-Tryon HS; Perkins, OK; (3); 4/72; Cmnty Wkr; Intnl Clb; VICA; High Hon Roll; Hon Roll; NHS; St Schlr; Gftd Tlntd Clb; Lcl Area Vo Tech Wldng Cmptn 1st Pl; OK ST U; Engrng.

WILSON, STEPHANIE; Coalgate HS; Coalgate, OK; (2); 1/58; Computer Clb; FBLA; Pep Clb; Scholastic Bowl; VP Soph Cls; Var JV Bsktbl; Var Chrldng; Sftbl; High Hon Roll; NHS; 94 & 95 Ftbl Homcmgn Attend; Acad Athl Awd.

WILSON, TARA M; West Jr HS; Oklahoma City, OK; (1); Dance Clb; Jr NHS.

WILSON, WHITNEY A; Cushing HS; Cushing, OK; (3); Church Yth Grp; Hosp Aide; Math Clb; Office Aide; Science Clb; Spanish Clb; NHS; Tomorrows Ldrs Pgm; OK ST U.

WIMBERLY, JENNIFER; Stuart Sr HS; Stuart, OK; (4); 11/30; Church Yth Grp; FCA; 4-H; Hist FHA; Teachers Aide; Yrbk; JV Bsktbl; JV Sftbl; Hon Roll; East Cntrl U; Med.

WIMBISH, AMANDA G; Preston Schl; Beggs, OK; (1); Church Yth Grp; Bus Math Plq 3rd Pl; OSU Okm Ulgee Smmr Acad; OSU; Sec.

WIMBISH, MITCHELL B; Union Sr HS; Tulsa, OK; (3); German Clb; Rep Stu Cncl; Hon Roll; NHS; E2 Awd German II.

WINBURN, MEGAN H; Metro Christian Acad; Tulsa, OK; (3); 5/52; Church Yth Grp; Teachers Aide; Yrbk; VP Soph Cls; Ofcr Jr Cls; Rep Stu Cncl; Var Bsktbl; Hon Roll; NHS; Prfct Atten Awd; Tchr.

WINBURN, PAIGE E; Union Intermediate HS; Tulsa, OK; (2); 91/800; FCA; Spanish Clb; Ofcr Frsh Cls; Rep Soph Cls; Hist Stu Cncl; High Hon Roll; Hon Roll; Jr NHS; NHS; Capt JV Chrldng; NCA All Amer Chrldr 2 Yrs; 3rd Pl Nation NCA Natls JV Squad; Genetics.

WINCHESTER, MANDI; Gracemont HS; Gracemont, OK; (2); 1/15; Drama Clb; 4-H; GAA; Scholastic Bowl; Pres Frsh Cls; Treas Soph Cls; Var Bsktbl; Var Sftbl; Hon Roll; Prfct Atten Awd.

WINCHESTER, MENDI; Texhoma HS; Texhoma, OK; (4); 1/25; Church Yth Grp; Quiz Bowl; Scholastic Bowl; School Play; Ed Yrbk; Capt Bsktbl; Chrldng; Gov Hon Prg Awd; NHS; Val; OSU; Phmcy.

WIND, APRIL R; Okmulgee HS; Okmulgee, OK; (2); Scholastic Bowl; Spanish Clb; Speech Tm; Rptr Nwsp; Lit Mag; High Hon Roll; NHS; Indian Clb; OSU; Drama.

WINDERS, MICHAEL R; Arkoma Jr Sr HS; Arkoma, OK; (2).

WINDHOLZ, ANGELA; Woodward HS; Woodward, OK; (2); Pep Clb; Chorus; Orch; JV Chrldng; Ushrtte Miss Grdn City Pgnt 95; Vol Work; Job Olympcs At GCCC 95; Vol Wrstlng Trnmnts; K ST; Child Psych.

WINDSOR, CHANDA; Blanchard Jr Sr HS; Blanchard, OK; (4); 10/66; Computer Clb; FHA; Library Aide; Office Aide; Spanish Clb; Chorus; Hon Roll; NHS; Pres Acad Fit Awd; Intnl Soc Of Poets; Misfits Fiend Clb; USAO; Mortician.

WINFORD, CHRISTY R; Nathan Hale HS; Tulsa, OK; (3); Office Aide; Teachers Aide; High Hon Roll; Hon Roll; Prncpls Hnr Roll; Hnr Sci.

WINFREY, JOSH D; Metro Christian Acad; Tulsa, OK; (3); 6/75; Var L Bsbl; Var L Ftbl; High Hon Roll; Sec NHS.

WINFREY, KESHET; Victory Christian Schl; Tulsa, OK; (1); 2/65; Church Yth Grp; Cmnty Wkr; Color Guard; Sec Frsh Cls; JV Var Chrldng; High Hon Roll; Jr NHS; NCA All Amer Chrldr; Toured With Young Continentals Vocal Grp.

WING, DUSTIN; Guymon Sr HS; Guymon, OK; (4); Am Leg Boys St; Boy Scts; Church Yth Grp; Debate Tm; NFL; Science Clb; Speech Tm; Teachers Aide; Band; Mrchg Band; Private Pilots License; Five Sts Hnr Band; St Citation Speech & Debate; Bus Law.

WINGFIELD, CHRISTINE E; Claremore Sr HS; Claremore, OK; (3); Church Yth Grp; Debate Tm; Drama Clb; NFL; Speech Tm; School Play; Stage Crew; Rptr Phtg Yrbk; Hon Roll; VFW Voice Of Dmcrcy Essay Cntst 1st Pl; DECA Mrktng Ed; Shadow Intrn Bus RLCB Bank; Cmptr Sci/Brdcst Jrnlsm.

WINGO, ASHLEY; Mc Loud HS; Harrah, OK; (1); Cit Awd; Hon Roll; Jr NHS; Life Guides; Bus.

WINGO, BRANDY; Holdenville HS; Holdenville, OK; (4); 1/82; Am Leg Aux Girls St; VP FBLA; Natl Beta Clb; Natl FFA Org; Science Clb; Band; Color Guard; Mrchg Band; Pres Frsh Cls; Treas Sr Cls.

WINGO, JOEL; Hartshorne Sr HS; Hartshorne, OK; (3); Church Yth Grp; FCA; Band; Chorus; Church Choir; Mrchg Band; Ofcr Bsbl; Ftbl; Cit Awd; Hon Roll; Cntrl Bible Coll; Ministry.

WINIGER, REBEKAH A; Brink Jr HS; Oklahoma City, OK; (1); Church Yth Grp; FCA; Chorus; Church Choir; Socr; High Hon Roll; Jr NHS.

WININGER, EMILY; Duncan HS; Duncan, OK; (4); 13/215; Am Leg Aux Girls St; Church Yth Grp; Cmnty Wkr; FCA; Hosp Aide; HOBY; Sec Key Clb; Letterman Clb; Service Clb; SADD; Yth Ldrshp Cls; Yth Rpe Dale Carnegie Course; Yng Rpblcns, Yng Democrats Clb; U Of OK; Med.

WINKELER, ROSE M; Mt St Marys HS; Bethany, OK; (3); 2/64; Yrbk; Mgr(s); Var Sftbl; Hon Roll; NHS; Natl Yth Ldrshp Forum DC 96; Bio.

WINKELMAN, JIM; Shawnee Sr HS; Shawnee, OK; (4); 169/352; Church Yth Grp; DECA; Quiz Bowl; Teachers Aide; Varsity Clb; Ftbl; Hon Roll; DECA VP, Pres & OK St Chaplain; U Of Cntrl OK; Mrktng Ed.

WINKLEMAN, ALYSSA M; Enid Sr HS; Enid, OK; (3); Church Yth Grp; Hosp Aide; Speech Tm; Teachers Aide; Band; Church Choir; School Musical; Hon Roll; Jr NHS; NHS; Big Bros/Sis; Northwestern OK ST Univ; RN.

WINKLER, BRIAN; Westmoore HS; Oklahoma City, OK; (4); 3/610; FBLA; Scholastic Bowl; Var Bsktbl; Jr NHS; NHS; Val; U Of OK; Acctng.

WINKLER, JULIA; Tuttle HS; Tuttle, OK; (3); Church Yth Grp; FHA; Spanish Clb; Rep Stu Cncl; Var Chrldng; High Hon Roll; Hon Roll; U Of Central OK.

WINKLER, KIMI; West Middle HS; Norman, OK; (1); Dance Clb; Drama Clb; Chrldng; Var Tennis; Adv Drama Clss; Top Gun Chrldng Natl Chmp & All Amer; Cmptv Acting Clss; U Of OK; Drama.

WINKLER, LEESA; Tuttle HS; Tuttle, OK; (4); 13/79; Church Yth Grp; FHA; Office Aide; Spanish Clb; SADD; Rep Soph Cls; Chrldng; Cnslr Church Camp; Chrldng Squad St Title 3 Yrs; Acad St Awd; Rose ST Coll; Dntl Hygn.

WINKLER, MIKE P; West Jr HS; Oklahoma City, OK; (1); 1/313; Cmnty Wkr; FCA; Spanish Clb; Bsktbl; Golf; High Hon Roll; Hon Roll; Jr NHS; Pres Acad Fit Awd; Pres Schlr; U Of OK; Attorney.

WINN, ABBY M; Stillwater Jr HS; Stillwater, OK; (2); Church Yth Grp; Band; Color Guard; Mrchg Band; Pep Band; School Play.

WINN, DAVY; Verden HS; Anadarko, OK; (2); Church Yth Grp; HOBY; Science Clb; SADD; Rep Stu Cncl; Bsktbl; Cit Awd; Hon Roll; NHS; Pres Acad Fit Awd; OK Chrstn Univ; Ed.

WINN, DOUGLAS R; Mannford HS; Mannford, OK; (4); Drama Clb; FCA; Letterman Clb; Office Aide; Teachers Aide; Varsity Clb; Var Capt Ftbl; Var L Trk; Var L Wrstlng; Hon Roll; Hnrb Mntn All St Ftbl; All Metro Ftbl; SW Coll Of KS.

WINN, JOSHUA; Depew HS; Bristow, OK; (2); Cmnty Wkr; Drama Clb; Natl FFA Org; School Play; VP Soph Cls; Var Ftbl; Var Trk; High Hon Roll; Hon Roll; Track MVP; OK ST; Coach.

WINN, LA KEYLA; Northwest Classen HS; Oklahoma City, OK; (4); 44/180; Church Yth Grp; Cmnty Wkr; Teachers Aide; VICA; Church Choir; Stat Bsktbl; Var Mgr(s); JV Tennis; Cit Awd; Hon Roll; Ms OK Tn USA Pgnt Dlgt 95; Jst Grls Pub 96 Esy Cntst 2nd Pl; Tn Advct ORFUM Mnstrs; U Of Cntrl OK; Cmptr Sci.

WINN, SHAWN H; Bishop Mcguinness HS; Oklahoma City, OK; (2); 9/167; Cmnty Wkr; FCA; German Clb; Letterman Clb; SADD; Varsity Clb; Rep Jr Cls; Bsktbl; Var L Tennis; NHS; Natl Ger Hnr Soc; OK His Hnrb Mntn Awd; Qualified For St Tnns Trnmt As Soph; Architecture.

WINN, TAMARA L; Shawnee Sr HS; Shawnee, OK; (2); Church Yth Grp; Spanish Clb; Band; Mrchg Band; School Musical; School Play; Hon Roll; Bnd Cncl Hist; Big Sisters; OK Crstn Univof Sci; Engl.

WINNARD, LORI D; Putnam City West HS; Bethany, OK; (3); Church Yth Grp; Cmnty Wkr; Pep Clb; SADD; Pom Pon; L Trk; Dance Clb; FCA; GAA; Office Aide; Stdnt Cncl Comm Hd; JV Co-Hd/Hd/Let; UCO; Envrmntl Sci/Ed.

WINNEBECK, JASON P; North Intemediate HS; Broken Arrow, OK; (1); Boy Scts; Hon Roll; Prfct Atten Awd; Top Hnrs Cmptrs; OK Hnr Soc; 3rd Pl TJC Cmptr Chllng; Cmptr Sci/Systms Anlyst.

WINNINGHAM, BRAD; Wilburton Sr HS; Wilburton, OK; (2); Natl FFA Org; Teachers Aide; Chorus; Hon Roll; NHS.

WINNINGHAM, TRAVIS M; Hominy HS; Hominy, OK; (4); French Clb; Letterman Clb; Office Aide; Teachers Aide; Varsity Clb; Band; Mrchg Band; Orch; Pep Band; Ofcr Sr Cls; 2 Yr Jr Coll.

WINSETT, JAKE; Altus Sr HS; Elmer, OK; (4); 10/250; Am Leg Boys St; Pres Church Yth Grp; Cmnty Wkr; Office Aide; Quiz Bowl; Science Clb; Service Clb; Spanish Clb; Chorus; Church Choir; OK Hstry Exam St Top 20; OK Senate Hnr Page; Missn Trip Costa Rica; OK ST U; Bnkng/Finance.

WINSTON, KIMBERLY D; Edmond Memorial HS; Edmond, OK; (4); 1/329; Church Yth Grp; FCA; German Clb; Hosp Aide; Treas Key Clb; Mu Alpha Theta; Chorus; Co-Capt Golf; NHS; Val; OK Acad Schlr; Tndy Tech Schlr; U OK; Spch Pthlgy.

WINSTON, LATEEF N; Choctaw HS; Midwest City, OK; (4); Church Yth Grp; Letterman Clb; Library Aide; Scholastic Bowl; Varsity Clb; Church Choir; Bsktbl; Trk; Hon Roll; Jr NHS; Upwrd Bnd; Concrrnt Enrllmnt; NC A&T; Bus Adm.

WINTER, BEN; Mustang HS; Yukon, OK; (3); Church Yth Grp; FCA; Bsktbl; Crs Cntry; Trk; High Hon Roll; NHS.

WINTER, KRYSTAL L; Pond Creek-Hunter Schl; Pond Creek, OK; (4); Church Yth Grp; Pep Clb; Yrbk; Sec Frsh Cls; Rep Sr Cls; Bsktbl; Sftbl; Cit Awd; High Hon Roll; Hon Roll; Pep Clb Reptr; Tchr Aide; Vo Tech Univ; Tchr.

WINTER, LISA Y; Stringtown HS; Stringtown, OK; (3); 4-H; Natl FFA Org; Ofcr Jr Cls; Ofcr Stu Cncl; Bsktbl; Mgr(s); 4-H Awd; High Hon Roll; NHS; PT.

WINTERHALTER JR, JERRY D; Stillwater Sr HS; Stillwater, OK; (2); Wrstlng; Var Schlrs Cert; OSU; Cmptr/Med.

WINTERS, ANGELA L; Douglass HS; Oklahoma City, OK; (3); Church Yth Grp; Model UN; Band; Church Choir; Ofcr Stu Cncl; Hon Roll; Jackson ST U; Bus Mgmt.

WINTERS, ASHLEY; Guymon Sr HS; Guymon, OK; (1); Church Yth Grp; Dance Clb; FCA; JV Bsktbl; Var Chrldng; Sftbl; Hon Roll; Jr NHS; Bsbl Trnr; Hrsbck Rdng.

WINTERS, CARA J; Mooreland Jr Sr HS; Mooreland, OK; (1); 4/38; Church Yth Grp; Rep FCA; Rep FHA; Pres Frsh Cls; Bsktbl; Chrldng; Hon Roll; TSA Jr HS Pres; St Of AL.

WINTERS, CHERYLL; Cache HS; Cache, OK; (2); 2/110; Church Yth Grp; FCA; Natl Beta Clb; Yrbk; Chrldng; Trk; High Hon Roll; NHS; Ntl Merit Schol; Prfct Atten Awd; Yale Univ; Law.

WINTERS, DUSTY; Heavener HS; Heavener, OK; (2); Key Clb; Treas Natl FFA Org; Color Guard; Drill Tm; Flag Corp; Pres Soph Cls; Bsktbl; Hon Roll; Vet.

WINTERS, JOHN J; Harrah HS; Harrah, OK; (3); 5/165; Am Leg Boys St; FCA; SADD; Ofcr Bsbl; Bsktbl; Ftbl; High Hon Roll; Kiwanis Awd; NHS; Church Yth Grp; Med Dr.

WINTERS, MARIAH D; Bethany HS; Yukon, OK; (3); Church Yth Grp; FCA; Key Clb; Letterman Clb; Spanish Clb; Chorus; Yrbk; VP Frsh Cls; Hist Soph Cls; Hist Jr Cls; UCO.

WINTERS, TAMMY; Woodward HS; Woodward, OK; (2); Church Yth Grp; Cmnty Wkr; FCA; Pep Clb; SADD; Ofcr Stu Cncl; Chrldng; Gym; Hon Roll; Debate Tm; OSU; Premed.

WINTERS, TRACY; Woodward HS; Woodward, OK; (1); Church Yth Grp; FCA; Pep Clb; Bsktbl; Chrldng; Gym; Socr; Hon Roll; NHS.

WINTERS, TYLER; Wynnewood HS; Wynnewood, OK; (1); 1/58; Church Yth Grp; FCA; Letterman Clb; Varsity Clb; L Bsktbl; L Ftbl; L Golf; L Trk; Wt Lftg; Hon Roll; OK Hnr Soc.

WINTERS, WILEY; Wynnewood HS; Wynnewood, OK; (3); 16/56; Church Yth Grp; Band; Jazz Band; Mrchg Band; Hon Roll.

WINTERSCHEID, JEREMY; Foyil Schl; Claremore, OK; (3); 2/38; 4-H; Quiz Bowl; Speech Tm; Var Ftbl; High Hon Roll; OSU; Ag Sci.

WINTON, KENDALL L; Skiatook HS; Skiatook, OK; (2); Church Yth Grp; VICA; Band; Mrchg Band; NSU; Elem Ed.

WINZENBURG, DENISE M; Charles Page HS; Sand Springs, OK; (3); 92/375; Church Yth Grp; Cmnty Wkr; Pep Clb; Spanish Clb; Bsktbl; Socr; Cit Awd; Hon Roll; Prfct Atten Awd; FCA; Girls Var Soccer 3 Yr Ltr; PT.

WINZENBURG, SARAH D; Claremore Sr HS; Claremore, OK; (1); Girl Scts; Stage Crew; High Hon Roll; NHS; Slver Awd Grl Scts; Hgh GPA Awd Bio I; Dance Cls Ballet, Jazz, Clggng; OSU; Wldlife Mgmt.

WIPF, DEBORAH N; Owasso Sr HS; Owasso, OK; (3); FCA; Band; Mrchg Band; High Hon Roll; Hon Roll; NHS; Teen Mania Ministries Mission Trips; Frgn Bus Mngmt.

WIRTH, ANDY D; Putnam City West HS; Oklahoma City, OK; (3); Spanish Clb; Golf; Ice Hcky; Southwestern OK ST Univ.

WISE, AMANDA; Woodward HS; Woodward, OK; (1); Church Yth Grp; FCA; Letterman Clb; Pep Clb; Yrbk; JV Chrldng; Var Socr; High Hon Roll; Pharmacist.

WISE, BRANDON T; Heavener HS; Poteau, OK; (2); Church Yth Grp; FCA; FBLA; Nwsp; Rep Frsh Cls; Rep Soph Cls; Rep Stu Cncl; Var Bsbl; Var Ftbl; High Hon Roll.

WISE, JESSICA D; Vinita HS; Vinita, OK; (2); Church Yth Grp; Math Tm; Spanish Clb; Band; Mrchg Band; Orch; Pep Band; Hon Roll; NHS; Chrch Schl Tchr; Camp Fire; OK ST Univ; Child Ed Tchr.

WISE, SEAN; Clinton HS; Clinton, OK; (3); 15/118; Church Yth Grp; Drama Clb; FBLA; Key Clb; Spanish Clb; Chorus; Rptr Nwsp; Socr; Jazz Choir; Clinton Dist Cncl Cmmtte On Yth Minstries Rep; Clinton Family Dev Assn; Medcl.

WISEMAN, JEFFERSON C; West Middle HS; Norman, OK; (1); 1/474; Boy Scts; Model UN; Quiz Bowl; Band; Church Choir; Mrchg Band; Hon Roll; Pres Acad Fit Awd; St Schlr; Hons In Band/Suprs At Contest; Brazil Miss Trip With Church Choir/Yth 96; U Of OK; Music/Scndry Ed/Law.

WISEMAN, JOHN W; Bishop Kelley HS; Tulsa, OK; (2); Boy Scts; Church Yth Grp; Drama Clb; Letterman Clb; Speech Tm; School Play; Ftbl.

WISEMAN, SHVADA M; Lawton Sr HS; Fort Sill, OK; (2); Office Aide; Hon Roll; Rnsnc Acad Achvmt Awd; WA Univ; Lib Arts.

WISEMAN, TRISHA; Midwest City HS; Oklahoma City, OK; (4); 9/419; Am Leg Aux Girls St; Pres Church Yth Grp; FCA; Key Clb; SADD; VP Stu Cncl; Var Capt Bsktbl; NHS; Spanish NHS; Val; OK ST U; Ed.

WISSEN, LACEY B; Owasso Sr HS; Owasso, OK; (3); Art Clb; Church Yth Grp; Girl Scts; NFL; Spanish Clb; Teachers Aide; Orch; Rep Jr Cls; Rep VP Stu Cncl; Powder Puff Ftbl; Natl Epscpln Yth Conv Rep; Grl Sctslvr Awd; Episcopal Diocese Yth Brd; U Of OK; Med.

WITHAM, JERRI B; Okemah HS; Okemah, OK; (1); Church Yth Grp; Natl FFA Org; SADD; Hon Roll; Okemah Round-Up Clb Prncss 94; Barrel Racing; Vet.

WITHERS, SHERMEKA S; U S Grant HS; Oklahoma City, OK; (2); Cmnty Wkr; Dance Clb; Variety Show; Cit Awd; Hon Roll; Kiwanis Awd; Coll Clb; PT.

WITHIAM, SAMUEL B; Cushing HS; Cushing, OK; (3); 12/148; Art Clb; Church Yth Grp; Math Clb; Spanish Clb; SADD; Band; School Play; Hon Roll; NHS; Var Schlr; Prjct Slf-Estm.

WITT, JOSEPH D; Holland Hall Schl; Tulsa, OK; (4); Rep Church Yth Grp; Drama Clb; Acpl Chr; Chorus; Church Choir; School Musical; School Play; Stage Crew; JV Socr; Tennis; S W Reg Yth/Adult Chrch Cmmtte Scl Action Chr; Scl Sci.

WITTEN, TERESA J; Milburn Schl; Milburn, OK; (2); 4/16; FHA; Hosp Aide; Pep Clb; SADD; Teachers Aide; Band; Mrchg Band; Sftbl; OK Univ; PT.

WITWER, AMY; South Coffeyville Schl; S Coffeyville, OK; (4); FCA; Teachers Aide; Nwsp; Sec Treas Sr Cls; Rptr Stu Cncl; Capt Bsktbl; Capt Chrldng; Sftbl; Hon Roll; NHS; Coffeyville CC.

WITZEL, ROSS A; Putnam City HS; Oklahoma City, OK; (2); Church Yth Grp; Math Clb; Intrml Bsbl; Intrml Bsktbl; Intrml Ftbl; Prfct Atten Awd; OU; Rgstrd PT.

WODRASKA, BRANDON L; Westmoore HS; Oklahoma City, OK; (3); French Clb; Scholastic Bowl; Science Clb; Spanish Clb; Jr NHS; NHS; Regnl Sci Fair; St OJAS; STUCO Rep.

WOFFORD, AMBER; Jay HS; Jay, OK; (2); FCA; Natl Beta Clb; Pep Clb; Nwsp; Bsktbl; Sftbl; Trk; Hon Roll; OSU.

WOFFORD, JEAN A; Velma Alma HS; Velma, OK; (2); FCA; GAA; SADD; Var Bsktbl; Var Sftbl; Var Trk; His; Coach.

WOFFORD, TIMOTHY D; Walters HS; Walters, OK; (2); Church Yth Grp; FCA; SADD; Band; Jazz Band; Mrchg Band; Pep Band; Nwsp; Hon Roll; SCOBDA HS Hnr Band; SCOBDA Hnr Jazz Band; Southwestern OK ST U.

WOLERY, BENJAMIN; Union Intermediate HS; Tulsa, OK; (2); 40/800; French Clb; Math Tm; French Hon Soc; High Hon Roll; NHS; Pres Acad Fit Awd; Psych.

WOLF, CATHERINE L; Moore HS; Moore, OK; (3); FBLA; JCL; Latin Clb; OU; Anthropology.

WOLF, CHRIS T; Yukon Middle HS; Yukon, OK; (1); Church Yth Grp; FHA; Socr; U Of VA; Pro Soccer Player.

WOLF, ERIC; Ponca City Sr HS; Ponca City, OK; (4); 9/350; Am Leg Boys St; Church Yth Grp; Teachers Aide; Church Choir; Jazz Band; Orch; Intrml Vllybl; NHS; Ntl Merit Ltr; SADD; Spec Olympcs Vol; U Of OK.

WOLF, JOSEPH R; Durant HS; Durant, OK; (2); Art Clb; Spanish Clb; SADD; Chorus; JV Bsktbl; Cit Awd; 3rd Pl Yth Art Show 96 Red River Arts Cncl; Meterolgst.

WOLF, SEAN A; Union Sr HS; Tulsa, OK; (3); 113/670; FBLA; Key Clb; Spanish Clb; Band; High Hon Roll; NHS; Ntl Merit Ltr; Renaissance Club.

WOLFE, CHERI; Union Intermediate HS; Broken Arrow, OK; (1); Church Yth Grp; Cmnty Wkr; FCA; Office Aide; Spanish Clb; Sec Frsh Cls; Capt Chrldng; Trk; High Hon Roll; NHS; Sing; Wrtng; Work With Children; OSU; Psych.

WOLFE, CODY R; Vinita HS; Vinita, OK; (3); Natl FFA Org; Golf; Hon Roll; Rodeo-Team Rpng; NEO A&M.

WOLFE, DIANA; Madill HS; Madill, OK; (3); 1/66; FCA; FHA; VP Science Clb; Treas SADD; Band; School Play; High Hon Roll; NHS; Church Yth Grp; Math Clb; Acad Team; Native Amer Clb Treas; Southwestern OK ST U; Phrmcy.

WOLFE, EVA; Hobart HS; Hobart, OK; (2); 1/85; Church Yth Grp; Cmnty Wkr; FHA; Pres Soph Cls; Sftbl; Trk; High Hon Roll; Hon Roll; NHS; OK HS Hnr, OK Assn FHA Awds; OU; Med.

WOLFE, LINDSEY; Hugo HS; Hugo, OK; (3); Church Yth Grp; FCA; Church Choir; Swing Chorus; Ofcr Stu Cncl; Chrldng; Hon Roll; NHS; OK Bapt All St Yth Choir 94-95, 95-96; Yth Choir Ensemble; OSU.

WOLFE, ROBERT; Watonga HS; Watonga, OK; (1); Natl FFA Org; Spanish Clb; Hon Roll.

WOLLISON, DELLA N; Pond Creek-Hunter Schl; Pond Creek, OK; (3); 1/24; Am Leg Aux Girls St; Church Yth Grp; Pep Clb; Quiz Bowl; Band; School Musical; Bsktbl; Sftbl; NHS; Mrchg Band; OK Hon Soc; Pre-Med.

WOLLISON, NICKI; Pond Creek-Hunter Schl; Pond Creek, OK; (3); #1 in class; Church Yth Grp; Pep Clb; Scholastic Bowl; Spanish Clb; Band; School Play; Bsktbl; Sftbl; NHS; Med.

WOLOWICZ, BRIAN; Edmond North HS; Edmond, OK; (3); 35/348; Boy Scts; Mu Alpha Theta; Band; Drm Mjr(t); Jazz Band; Mrchg Band; Cit Awd; Kiwanis Awd; NHS; Church Yth Grp; Eagle Scout With Bronze Palm; Ad Altare Dei/Parvuli Dei Relgs Scouts Awds; Explr Post 77 Pres; Cmptr Anmtn/Art.

WOLSEY, JESSE; Watonga HS; Watonga, OK; (3); #1 in class; Church Yth Grp; FBLA; Quiz Bowl; Spanish Clb; Rep Frsh Cls; Pres Stu Cncl; Hon Roll; NHS; Spanish NHS; Gnrl Bus & Span Awds; Intl Bus.

WOLTER, HEATHER; Wright Christian Acad; Broken Arrow, OK; (3); Church Yth Grp; Key Clb; Chorus; Pres Frsh Cls; Pres Soph Cls; Sec Jr Cls; Var Bsktbl; Var Crs Cntry; Var Trk; Hon Roll; Med PT.

WOMACK, AMBER N; Velma Alma HS; Velma, OK; (3); Church Yth Grp; FCA; FHA; SADD; VICA; Ed Nwsp; Pres Jr Cls; Hon Roll; NHS; Southeastern; Landscp Arch.

WOMACK, DAVID J; Stillwater Sr HS; Stillwater, OK; (2); FCA; Var Bsbl; JV Intrml Bsktbl; Var Ftbl; Var Wt Lftg; JV Var Hon Roll; Pres Acad Fit Awd; Amer Legion Bsbl; OSU.

WOMACK, DEBBIE A; Duncan HS; Duncan, OK; (3); 1/260; Pres French Clb; VP FHA; Key Clb; SADD; Treas Jr Cls; Var Crs Cntry; Var Tennis; NHS; Bus.

WOMACK, JOHN M; Valliant HS; Garvin, OK; (2); Cmnty Wkr; 4-H; Natl FFA Org; Red Cross Aide; Chorus; Nwsp; Ofcr Bsbl; Bsktbl; Ftbl; Mgr(s); FFA; Bsbll, Bsktbll, Ftbll Mgr; Sngng Awds; Durant; Hwy Ptrl.

WOMACK, MARY ELIZABETH; Stillwater Jr HS; Stillwater, OK; (1); Drama Clb; School Play; Stage Crew; Ofcr Stu Cncl; High Hon Roll; Pres Acad Fit Awd; Centennial Rotry Clb Stu Of Month; Recreation Sftbl 9 Yrs; Vacation Bible Schl Vol.

WONDERLY, RYAN; Putnam City West HS; Bethany, OK; (4); 52/285; Rep Church Yth Grp; Cmnty Wkr; Teachers Aide; Church Choir; Sec Orch; School Musical; Rep Stu Cncl; Hon Roll; Jr NHS; NHS; OK Yth Orch; Silver Strings Sec, VP & Stu Conductor; Southern Nazarene U; Music Ed.

WONG, PHILIP D; Putnam City North HS; Oklahoma City, OK; (3); 25/494; Church Yth Grp; Pres German Clb; Key Clb; Office Aide; Scholastic Bowl; Spanish Clb; Var Socr; Cit Awd; Hon Roll; NHS; Masonic Stu Of Today; Putnam City North Stu Of The Month; Bus; Medicine.

WONG-SICK-HONG, CHRISTIAN S; Muskogee HS; Muskogee, OK; (2); Debate Tm; French Clb; Band; Jazz Band; Mrchg Band; Orch; Pep Band; High Hon Roll; OK Hnr Soc; Comp Prgmr.

WOOD, APRIL R; Yukon Middle HS; Yukon, OK; (2); Church Yth Grp; Treas Girl Scts; Band; Church Choir; Jazz Band; Mrchg Band; Pep Band; School Musical; High Hon Roll; NHS; Trinity U; DVM.

WOOD, BRANDON T; Brink Jr HS; Oklahoma City, OK; (1); Boy Scts; Roller Hcky.

WOOD, CHRIS; Stratford Schl; Stratford, OK; (3); Church Yth Grp; FCA; Var Bsktbl; Pres FBLA; FHA; HOBY; Natl FFA Org; Pep Clb; Spanish Clb; Teachers Aide; EMT.

WOOD, DERIKA; Liberty Acad; Shawnee, OK; (1); Cmnty Wkr; Drama Clb; Church Choir; Stage Crew; Bsktbl; Vllybl; Hon Roll; Ntl Merit Ltr; Nrs.

WOOD, DIANNE; Stratford Schl; Stratford, OK; (4); 1/47; Church Yth Grp; FBLA; FHA; Office Aide; Yrbk; Sec Jr Cls; Sec Pres Stu Cncl; Bsktbl; Chrldng; Hon Roll; Outstndng Dancer Cntrl OK Dance Ctr; Tremaine Dancer Cnvntn & Show Biz & Starlight Dance Cmptns; East Cntrl U; Acctnt.

WOOD, ERIC A; Locust Grove HS; Locust Grove, OK; (2); Church Yth Grp; Cmnty Wkr; Drama Clb; Speech Tm; Church Choir; Variety Show; Rep Soph Cls; Var Bsktbl; High Hon Roll; NHS; Bsktbl.

WOOD, JAMES P; Wapanucka Schl; Wapanucka, OK; (2); 1/21; Quiz Bowl; Mrchg Band; Ofcr Stu Cncl; Bsktbl; Trk; High Hon Roll; Hon Roll; NHS; Arch.

WOOD, JAYME; Stratford Schl; Stratford, OK; (3); 8/55; Church Yth Grp; FCA; FBLA; FHA; Pep Clb; Spanish Clb; Teachers Aide; Sec Sr Cls; Ofcr Stu Cncl; Var Bsktbl; Masonic Lodge Stdnt Of Today Awd; Bsktbl Bulldog Awd; Outstdng Girl Track Awd; OBU.

WOOD, JENNIFER A; Mc Loud HS; Mc Loud, OK; (3); Natl FFA Org; Chorus; Army.

WOOD, JENNY; Ninnekah HS; Chickasha, OK; (1); Bsktbl; Sftbl; Hon Roll; Art & Drftng.

WOOD, JOSHUA; Holdenville HS; Holdenville, OK; (3); Am Leg Boys St; Boy Scts; Church Yth Grp; Cmnty Wkr; FCA; Natl Beta Clb; Natl FFA Org; Quiz Bowl; Scholastic Bowl; Science Clb; Dist Math Counts Awd; Amer Legion Awd; OK U; Pharmcy.

WOOD, KAREN; Tomlinson Jr HS; Lawton, OK; (1); FHA; High Hon Roll; Jr NHS; Ntl Merit Ltr; Med.

WOOD, KATIE J; Yukon HS; Yukon, OK; (3); 87/409; Church Yth Grp; Phy Thpry.

WOOD, KELLY L; Mt St Mary HS; Oklahoma City, OK; (4); 8/62; Drama Clb; French Clb; Science Clb; Service Clb; School Play; High Hon Roll; Kiwanis Awd; NHS; Pres Schlr; Keywanettes Lt Governor For OK; Ldr Of Ldrs Awd; Fred & Dottie Seals Awd; 2nd Place ST Paper Cont; Southwestern Coll; Marine Bio.

WOOD, MATT; Latta Sr HS; Ada, OK; (2); 12/55; Church Yth Grp; 4-H; Chorus; Rep Frsh Cls; Var Bsbl; Var Bsktbl; Prfct Atten Awd; Pres Acad Fit Awd; Plt.

WOOD, MATTHEW D; Muskogee HS; Muskogee, OK; (3); Church Yth Grp; FCA; JCL; Key Clb; Latin Clb; Var Bsbl; Var Bsktbl; High Hon Roll; Jr NHS; NHS; 3 Yr Ltrmn Bsebl; 2 Yr Ltrmn Bsktbl.

WOOD, MELISSA K; Kansas Schl; Kansas, OK; (4); 10/29; 4-H; FHA; German Clb; Library Aide; Natl FFA Org; SADD; Band; Mrchg Band; The John Philip Sousa Band Awd; Comp Tech.

WOOD, MICHAEL L; Hartshorne Sr HS; Hartshorne, OK; (2); FHA; Spanish Clb; Hon Roll; NHS; Amer Legion Awd.

WOOD, MICHELLE L; Union Intermediate HS; Tulsa, OK; (2); Church Yth Grp; FCA; Spanish Clb; Teachers Aide; Ofcr Stu Cncl; Chrldng; Socr; High Hon Roll; NHS; U Of Tulsa; Sprts Med.

WOOD, OLIN J; Union Sr HS; Tulsa, OK; (3); Intnl Clb; Key Clb; Math Tm; Spanish Clb; Intrml Ftbl; Var Socr; High Hon Roll; NHS; Spanish NHS; Aim Hi Math Cont St Fnlst; Outstndng Spnsh Stu; Outstndng Excllnc Acad Achvt Chem 95.

WOOD, PHILLIP; Wapanucka Schl; Wapanucka, OK; (2); 1/22; Math Tm; Natl FFA Org; Quiz Bowl; Scholastic Bowl; Mrchg Band; School Play; Rep Stu Cncl; Bsktbl; Trk; Hon Roll; Arch.

WOOD, RHIANNON; Moore HS; Moore, OK; (3); Church Yth Grp; DECA; German Clb; Variety Show; Pom Pon; Jr NHS; Mem Of Top Gun All Star Sr Dance Team; OK Univ; Med.

WOOD, SHANNON; Moore HS; Moore, OK; (3); Church Yth Grp; DECA; German Clb; Variety Show; Pom Pon; Jr NHS; Mem Of Top Gun All Star Sr Dance Team; OK Univ; Med.

WOOD, TIFFANY L; South Intermediate HS; Broken Arrow, OK; (1); Church Yth Grp; 4-H; Spanish Clb; Teachers Aide; Varsity Clb; Var Tennis; 4-H Awd; Hon Roll; UT; Scndry Ed/Span/Eng.

WOODALL, ANGELA M; Snyder HS; Mountain Park, OK; (3); 4/40; Church Yth Grp; FCA; Scholastic Bowl; Band; Church Choir; Mrchg Band; Hon Roll; NHS; All ST Hnr Band; All Regn Hnr Band; Shortgrass Hnr Band; U Of Cntrl OK Edmond; Music Ed.

WOODARD, AMANDA R; Muldrow HS; Muldrow, OK; (4); 21/100; Church Yth Grp; Debate Tm; Drama Clb; 4-H; Model UN; NFL; Quiz Bowl; Spanish Clb; Speech Tm; Band; Northeastern; Mass Commnctn.

WOODARD, BRANDI; Guthrie Sr HS; Guthrie, OK; (3); 1/220; Am Leg Aux Girls St; Church Yth Grp; FCA; Mu Alpha Theta; Red Cross Aide; Spanish Clb; Crs Cntry; Trk; DAR Awd; NHS; Sports Medicine.

WOODARD, MISTY D; Westmoore HS; Oklahoma City, OK; (1); Computer Clb; Drama Clb; French Clb; Quiz Bowl; Scholastic Bowl; School Play; High Hon Roll; Jr NHS; Pres Acad Fit Awd; Reflections Lit; U Of OK; Microbiology.

WOODARD, SARA A; Mannford HS; Mannford, OK; (3); Cmnty Wkr; Math Tm; SADD; Band; Mrchg Band; Pres Soph Cls; Pres Jr Cls; Var JV Chrldng; Hon Roll; NHS; Schlr Ath Awd; Prom Comm; U Of OK; Psych.

WOODARD, STACY; Claremore Sr HS; Claremore, OK; (3); 1/268; Pres Art Clb; Sec FHA; Nwsp; High Hon Roll; NHS; Ntl Merit Ltr; Pres Acad Fit Awd; Val; Quiz Bowl; Chorus; Mst Outstndng Chr Stu 94 Awd; Ltr C Awds Vrs Clsses; Art.

WOODARD, TERRA; B T Washington HS; Tulsa, OK; (2); Church Yth Grp; Pep Clb; Spanish Clb; Band; Mrchg Band; Pep Band; NHS; Tutor Elem Stu; IB Diploma; Plastic Srgn.

WOODIE, ANGELA D; Grace Chrn Acad; Oklahoma City, OK; (3); Church Yth Grp; Ed Yrbk; High Hon Roll; Spanish NHS; Chrch Yth Cncl.

WOODIN, ERIC P; Owasso Sr HS; Owasso, OK; (3); FCA; JV Bsbl; Var Ftbl; Var Trk; Chem Engrng.

WOODRUFF, REBECCA A; Ringling HS; Ringling, OK; (2); 1/44; Church Yth Grp; FCA; Natl FFA Org; Quiz Bowl; Band; JV Bsktbl; Var Powder Puff Ftbl; Var Sftbl; Hon Roll; Jr NHS; Natr Sci.

WOODRUFF, TYLER W; Woodward HS; Woodward, OK; (2); Art Clb; Church Yth Grp; Cmnty Wkr; Sec Treas Computer Clb; Rptr FBLA; Sec FHA; Key Clb; Model UN; Pep Clb; Red Cross Aide; Daily Seminary Sec; Ldrshp High.

WOODRUM, JENNIFER; Battiest Jr Sr HS; Bethel, OK; (4); 2/23; FHA; Quiz Bowl; Nwsp; Yrbk; Pres Soph Cls; Rep Sr Cls; Rep Stu Cncl; Var Bsktbl; Var Sftbl; Hon Roll; PANDA; Bsktbl All Conf; Schlstc Tm; Eastern OK ST Coll; Drftng.

WOODS, AMBER; Fairview HS; Fairview, OK; (2); Church Yth Grp; FHA; Band; Mrchg Band; Treas Frsh Cls; Bsktbl; Crs Cntry; Trk; High Hon Roll; NHS.

WOODS, ANGELA; Yale Jr Sr HS; Yale, OK; (2); 5/58; Church Yth Grp; Natl Beta Clb; Band; Mrchg Band; Pep Band; L Vllybl; Hon Roll; GATE; OSU; Arspc Engr.

WOODS, CHANDRA N; Mc Alester HS; Mcalester, OK; (3); Am Leg Aux Girls St; Church Yth Grp; FCA; Spanish Clb; Bsktbl; Golf; Sftbl; High Hon Roll; Jr NHS; Pres Acad Fit Awd; Pharmacy.

WOODS, CHRIS; Owasso Sr HS; Owasso, OK; (3) Church Yth Grp; FCA; JV Ftbl; Wt Lftg; Hon Roll.

WOODS, CORY; Holdenville HS; Holdenville, OK; (2); 18/82; Boy Scts; FCA; Natl FFA Org; Scholastic Bowl; Ofcr Stu Cncl; Ofcr Bsbl; Ftbl; Wt Lftg; Hon Roll; NHS; OK ST U; Animal Sci.

WOODS, JAMIE T; Deer Creek-Lamont Jr Sr HS; Lamont, OK; (3); FCA; Natl FFA Org; School Play; Yrbk; Sec Jr Cls; Var Chrldng; Var Crs Cntry; Var Sftbl; Hon Roll; NHS.

WOODS, JOHN P; Panola HS; Wilburton, OK; (2); Church Yth Grp; 4-H; Natl FFA Org; Band; Var Bsbl; Var Bsktbl; 4-H Awd; Hon Roll; Eastern OK ST Univ; Math.

WOODS, JOHN S; Cherokee Jr Sr HS; Cherokee, OK; (4); Boy Scts; Church Yth Grp; FCA; FHA; Office Aide; Band; Mrchg Band; Var Bsbl; Var Bsktbl; Var Trk; U CENTRAL OK; Arch.

WOODS, JULIE D; Chattanooga Schl; Faxon, OK; (2); FCA; Chorus; VP Soph Cls; Var Bsktbl; Var Vllybl; Hon Roll; Lawyer.

WOODS, LARONDA A; Haworth Sr HS; Haworth, OK; (1); Art Clb; Chorus; Hon Roll; NHS; Prfct Atten Awd; Splng Bee Wnnr; Ped.

WOODS, LAURA E; Edmond Memorial HS; Edmond, OK; (4); Church Yth Grp; Hosp Aide; Spanish Clb; SADD; Band; Church Choir; Jazz Band; Mrchg Band; Orch; Pep Band; Church Handbell Choir/Musicals/Covenant Grp; 4 Mission Trips; U Of OK.

WOODS, SANDY M; El Reno Sr HS; El Reno, OK; (2); FHA; Key Clb; Prfct Attendance; Renaissance.

WOODS, SUSAN; Lawton Sr HS; Lawton, OK; (2); Spanish Clb; Belmont U; Cncrt Sls.

WOODS, TANIESHA; Midwest City HS; Oklahoma City, OK; (4); 46/419; Church Yth Grp; Cmnty Wkr; DECA; FHA; Library Aide; Red Cross Aide; Spanish Clb; Band; Score Keeper; Socr; OU Hlth Sci Smmr Acad; OK U; Pre-Med.

WOODS, TRACY; Holdenville HS; Holdenville, OK; (4); 22/75; Boy Scts; Church Yth Grp; Pres FCA; Natl FFA Org; Rep Stu Cncl; Var Capt Bsbl; Var Capt Ftbl; Var Capt Wt Lftg; Science Clb; Hon Roll; OK ST U; Anml Sci.

WOODS, VIOLET R; Bixby Sr HS; Bixby, OK; (4); 13/189; Drama Clb; VP German Clb; Pres SADD; Band; Chorus; Rptr Stu Cncl; Pres NHS; Sal; Gftd & Tlntd Org; Jr Optmst Clb Pres; Vanderbilt U; Elem Ed.

WOODS, WHITNEY E; Duncan HS; Duncan, OK; (1); Church Yth Grp; Cmnty Wkr; Chorus; Church Choir; Variety Show; Sec Frsh Cls; Ofcr Stu Cncl; Chrldng; Trk; Hon Roll; Frosh Wrstlng Hmcmg Ct; OK Univ; Radiologst.

WOODS, WILLIAM H; Hominy HS; Hominy, OK; (3); 25/70; Spanish Clb; Teachers Aide; Ofcr Frsh Cls; Ofcr Soph Cls; Ofcr Bsbl; Bsktbl; Ftbl; Trk; Wt Lftg; Hon Roll; Osage All Star Tm Ftbl; Clue Chip Ftbl; Tulsa; Ed.

WOODS-BURROWS, TIFFANY; Yukon HS; Yukon, OK; (4); 19/420; Church Yth Grp; Library Aide; Pres Spanish Clb; Hist SADD; Chorus; Ed Nwsp; Ed Yrbk; Mgr(s); NHS; Pres Schlr; OK Chrstn Univ Of Sci & Arts.

WOODSIDE, SARAH; Panama HS; Panama, OK; (2); FHA; Spanish Clb; NHS; Ntl Merit Ltr; Carol Albert ST Coll; Nrsng.

WOODSON, BRANDI K; B T Washington HS; Tulsa, OK; (3); Art Clb; Church Yth Grp; Cmnty Wkr; Dance Clb; GAA; Girl Scts; Service Clb; Spanish Clb; Ed Yrbk; Swmmng; Psych.

WOODSON, JESSICA L; Lawton Christian Schl; Lawton, OK; (3); Church Yth Grp; Letterman Clb; Yrbk; Ofcr Soph Cls; Bsktbl; Score Keeper; Hon Roll.

WOODSON, JESSICA N; Cameron Schl; Cameron, OK; (1); FCA; 4-H; FHA; GAA; Bsktbl; Sftbl; Pres Schlr; Horseback Riding; Vllybl; Elem Tchr.

WOODWARD, BRANDON K; Carnegie HS; Carnegie, OK; (3); Am Leg Boys St; Ofcr Bsbl; Golf; Lcrss; Hon Roll; Prfct Atten Awd; OK Univ; Bus.

WOODWARD, KRISTIN; Putnam City West HS; Oklahoma City, OK; (3); 20/304; Intnl Clb; Orch; School Musical; NHS; Silver Strings; Fnatl Engl Merit Awd Wnnr; Psychology.

WOODWARD, WHITNEY; Christian Heritage Acad; Oklahoma City, OK; (3); 2/44; Church Yth Grp; FCA; Rptr Nwsp; Var Bsktbl; Var Chrldng; High Hon Roll.

WOODWORTH, C JAMES; Minco Jr Sr HS; Minco, OK; (3); #4 in class; Church Yth Grp; FCA; Pres FBLA; Mrchg Band; Pep Band; Yrbk; Bsktbl; Ftbl; High Hon Roll; Hon Roll; Attnd Natl Yng Ldrs Conf; ST Hnr Soc; OK ST Univ; Arch.

WOODY, AMANDA D; Sallisaw HS; Sallisaw, OK; (3); FHA; Office Aide; Science Clb; Spanish Clb; Chorus; Treas Frsh Cls; Treas Soph Cls; Sec Jr Cls; Hon Roll; Octagon Clb; Indian Clb; Spcl Olympcs Vlntr; U Of AR; Pediatrc Nursng.

WOODY, MELISSA K; Del City HS; Del City, OK; (2); GAA; Girl Scts; Pep Clb; Spanish Clb; Teachers Aide; Band; Yrbk; Ofcr Bsbl; Ftbl; Mgr(s); Pitcher For League Sftbl Took St 1st Pl, 2nd Pl Natl; Mr & Miss Kerr Bsbl Qn; OU; Fashion Dsgnr; Intr Decrtng.

WOODY, SILVER; Midwest City HS; Midwest City, OK; (4); Science Clb; Band; Jazz Band; Mrchg Band; Orch; Pep Band; U OK; Med.

WOOLARD, SHILOH R; Oologah HS; Claremore, OK; (3); Art Clb; Drama Clb; Science Clb; Acpl Chr; Chorus; Ofcr Stu Cncl; L Var Socr; L JV Sftbl; Wt Lftg; High Hon Roll; Clinical Psych.

WOOLDRIDGE, APRIL B; Yukon Middle HS; Yukon, OK; (1); Church Yth Grp; FHA; Chorus; Hon Roll; Alge Awd; Vcl Solo Cntst 3 Supr Ratngs; Music Ed.

WOOLERY, SCOTT R; Putnam City HS; Warr Acres, OK; (1); Church Yth Grp; Spanish Clb; Golf; Hon Roll; Prin Hnr Roll; Drama Awd; Law Enforcement.

WOOLEVER, RACHEL S; B T Washington HS; Tulsa, OK; (3); Church Yth Grp; Office Aide; Spanish Clb; Teachers Aide; Rptr Soph Cls; Rep Jr Cls; Rep Sr Cls; Rep Stu Cncl; JV Bsktbl; New Tribes Missions Brazil 96; Masters Coll CA; Ed.

WOOLFOLK, ERIKA N; Northeast HS; Spencer, OK; (2); Church Yth Grp; Latin Clb; ROTC; Color Guard; Drill Tm; Orch; Stat Bsktbl; Mgr(s); Score Keeper; Hon Roll; Bio Med Sci Pgm Mem; Natl Macy Schlr; Natl Yth Forum On Law & Constitution Nom; Pre-Med; Neo-Natal Surgery.

WOOLVERTON, MIKE W; Christian Heritage Acad; Del City, OK; (2); Boy Scts; Church Yth Grp; Band; Orch; Golf.

WOOMACK, LAURA N; Checotah HS; Checotah, OK; (3); FBLA; Natl FFA Org; Speech Tm; Chorus; Hon Roll; HOSA Rprtr; Dallas Inst/Fnrl Svcs; Dir.

WOOSTER, CARSON R; Edmond North HS; Edmond, OK; (2); 62/420; Church Yth Grp; Cmnty Wkr; FCA; JV Bsbl; Var Socr; Jr NHS; NHS; Fishing; Hunting.

WOOSTER, SHANNON; Kingfisher HS; Kingfisher, OK; (4); 6/96; FCA; Key Clb; VP Chorus; Ed Nwsp; Ed Yrbk; Treas Stu Cncl; Var Chrldng; NHS; Pres Schlr; U Of OK; Jrnlsm.

WOOTEN, VALERIE; Duncan HS; Comanche, OK; (4); 49/215; Church Yth Grp; Cmnty Wkr; FCA; FHA; Natl FFA Org; Office Aide; Sftbl; NHS; Civil War Rennactment; SE OK ST U; Cnslng Teens.

WOOTERS, CHRISTOPHER; Elk City Jr HS; Elk City, OK; (2); Church Yth Grp; Computer Clb; Pep Clb; Science Clb; Band; Church Choir; Jazz Band; Mrchg Band; Pep Band; Var Ftbl; Engrng.

WOOTON, STARLA; Watonga HS; Fay, OK; (1); FHA; Quiz Bowl; High Hon Roll; FFA.

WORDEN, AMY E; Edmond Memorial HS; Edmond, OK; (4); Church Yth Grp; Red Cross Aide; Band; Color Guard; Mrchg Band; Band Awd; UCO; Elem Tchr.

WORDEN, LA DONNA M; Harrah HS; Harrah, OK; (3); 1/165; Am Leg Aux Girls St; Sec Cmnty Wkr; FCA; SADD; School Play; Rptr Nwsp; Rep Stu Cncl; Sor; Cit Awd; Art Clb; Sec/Indian Club; Sccr Ref; Scndry Ed.

WORDEN, SAMANTHA; Hennessey HS; Hennessey, OK; (4); 2/54; FCA; Teachers Aide; Band; Color Guard; Yrbk; Treas Sr Cls; Chrldng; High Hon Roll; NHS; Sal; 95 OK All Star Marching Band; German By Satellite Awd; OSU Hnr Schlr; Phillips U; Med.

WORKMAN, ELIZABETH A; Catoosa HS; Claremore, OK; (2); FCA; French Clb; Library Aide; JV Crs Cntry; Var Trk; Hon Roll; NHS; St Schlr; OK Hon Soc; OK ST Univ; Tchr.

WORKMAN, MATTHEW A; Muldrow HS; Muldrow, OK; (2); Math Clb; Spanish Clb; JV Var Ftbl; Hon Roll; NHS; OK Univ.

WORKMAN, PHILLIP B; Ninnekah HS; Ninnekah, OK; (2); FCA; Var Bsktbl; Hon Roll; Prfct Atten Awd.

WORKMAN, SUNNIE R; Allen HS; Allen, OK; (2); 4-H; Pep Clb; Quiz Bowl; Band; Chorus; Nwsp; Hon Roll; Eng II Schlrshp Awd; JH ILO GATE; East Cntrl Univ.

WORKMAN, TESSA A; Claremore Sr HS; Claremore, OK; (2); Church Yth Grp; Dance Clb; DECA; Drama Clb; Hosp Aide; Speech Tm; SADD; Teachers Aide; High Hon Roll; Hon Roll; Dance Instr; Rogers Univ; Elem Ed.

WORNOM, JASON; Perry Sr HS; Perry, OK; (2); Boy Scts; Pres Church Yth Grp; Band; Jazz Band; Mrchg Band; Pep Band; Golf; High Hon Roll; Hon Roll; JETS Awd; Stu Of Mnth; TSA; BSA God & Cntry; Pilot.

WORSHAM, LACEY; Lone Grove HS; Lone Grove, OK; (2); FCA; Math Clb; Science Clb; Rptr Nwsp; Hon Roll; NHS; Pres Acad Fit Awd; Intl Sci Fair Alt; Dermatlgy.

WORSTELL, AMANDA; Collinsville HS; Collinsville, OK; (3); Church Yth Grp; 4-H; Band; Mrchg Band; Ed Yrbk; Var Tennis; 4-H Awd; Hon Roll; Danforth I Dare You Awd; Marine Bio.

WORTHINGTON, AMY J; Rush Springs HS; Rush Springs, OK; (3); 4/37; Church Yth Grp; German Clb; Spanish Clb; Bsktbl; Sftbl; High Hon Roll; NHS; Prfct Atten Awd; Southwestern OK ST; Commnctns.

WORTHINGTON, CARISA D; Cushing HS; Cushing, OK; (2); #10 in class; Church Yth Grp; Dance Clb; FCA; HOBY; Spanish Clb; Varsity Clb; Pres Frsh Cls; Rep Stu Cncl; High Hon Roll; NHS; Natl Dance Tm.

WORTHY, TIM; Hugo HS; Hugo, OK; (4); 21/110; Am Leg Boys St; Church Yth Grp; FCA; Natl FFA Org; Office Aide; Science Clb; Spanish Clb; Ofcr Bsbl; Wt Lftg; Hon Roll.

WOSEL, ADREINNE; Bartlesville Mid HS; Bartlesville, OK; (2); 150/500; Church Yth Grp; FBLA; GAA; Girl Scts; Spanish Clb; Socr; High Hon Roll; Hon Roll; Jr NHS; NHS; KS Univ; Child Psych.

WRAY, ANDREW K; Guthrie Sr HS; Guthrie, OK; (1); 47/308; Church Yth Grp; ROTC; Cit Awd.

WREN, LAURA B; Ft Towson HS; Fort Towson, OK; (1); FCA; 4-H; Varsity Clb; Pres Frsh Cls; Chrldng; 4-H Awd; Val; Stu Cncl; Tech Stu Assn Level 1 Pres; Missionary.

WRIDE, JARRED M; Pauls Valley HS; Pauls Valley, OK; (3); Hon Roll; NHS; Prfct Atten Awd; U Of Cntrl OK; Genetic Engnr.

WRIGHT, ALAINA D; Clayton Jr Sr HS; Nashoba, OK; (2); Church Yth Grp; FCA; French Clb; Scholastic Bowl; VP Soph Cls; Var Bsktbl; High Hon Roll; NHS; Masonic Awd; Southeastern OK ST U; Acctg.

WRIGHT, ALISHA; Broken Bow HS; Golden, OK; (4); 6/145; Drama Clb; Scholastic Bowl; Science Clb; Sec Sr Cls; Sec Stu Cncl; High Hon Roll; Hon Roll; Kiwanis Awd; NHS; Hstry Clb Pres; Carl Albert ST Coll; Envrnmtl.

WRIGHT, ANNETTE; Watts HS; Watts, OK; (1); Church Yth Grp; Natl Beta Clb; Natl FFA Org; Bsktbl; Sftbl; Natl Hnr Rl; FL ST; Coaching.

WRIGHT, CHARLOTTE; Vian HS; Vian, OK; (4); 5/59; 4-H; Pres Natl FFA Org; Co-Capt Quiz Bowl; VP Soph Cls; VP Stu Cncl; Var Capt Bsktbl; Var Trk; DAR Awd; High Hon Roll; Pres Acad Fit Awd; Rodeo; Natl Eng Merit Awd; Masonic Lodge Stdnt Today; OK Panhandle ST U; Agri.

WRIGHT, DANAE A; Putnam City West HS; Oklahoma City, OK; (2); 72/354; Church Yth Grp; Cmnty Wkr; DECA; Drama Clb; FCA; Red Cross Aide; SADD; Hist Acpl Chr; Church Choir; School Musical; Mat Maid; BASIC; 4 Bible Stud Groups; Southern Nazarene Univ; Psych.

WRIGHT, ELIZABETH; Prague HS; Prague, OK; (4); 14/71; Am Leg Aux Girls St; Church Yth Grp; FBLA; Rptr Key Clb; Teachers Aide; Pres Band; Drm Mjr(t); Ofcr Jr Cls; Sec NHS; Ntl Merit Ltr; SW OK ST U; Msc Ed.

WRIGHT, ELIZABETH; Heritage Hall Schl; Oklahoma City, OK; (2); 25/65; Church Yth Grp; FCA; GAA; Mu Alpha Theta; Pep Clb; Service Clb; Spanish Clb; Chorus; Variety Show; Ofcr Stu Cncl; Outstdng Soph Stu Awd; Var Letterman; Bsktbl Awd For Mst Imprvd.

WRIGHT, ERIN L; Stillwater Sr HS; Stillwater, OK; (2); Church Yth Grp; French Clb; Girl Scts; Key Clb; Latin Clb; Natl Beta Clb; Band; Var Swmmng; Hon Roll; Pres Acad Fit Awd; Amer Guild/Orgnsts; Dermtlgy.

WRIGHT, GEORGE; Shawnee Sr HS; Shawnee, OK; (2); 2/300; Church Yth Grp; FCA; Latin Clb; Scholastic Bowl; Var Crs Cntry; Var Trk; High Hon Roll; St Chmpn Acad Bwl.

WRIGHT, HOLLY; Seminole Jr Sr HS; Seminole, OK; (2); 1/120; Church Yth Grp; FCA; GAA; Math Clb; Scholastic Bowl; Church Choir; Drill Tm; Pom Pon; Var Tennis; High Hon Roll.

WRIGHT, JENNIFER L; Edmond Santa Fe HS; Edmond, OK; (2); FCA; FHA; SADD; Rptr Nwsp; Var Sftbl; Var Trk; STAR Evnts FHA/HERO Comp Job Intrvwng Sklls 4th Pl; OK ST Univ; Jrnlsm.

WRIGHT, KAREN; Victory Christian Schl; Broken Arrow, OK; (2); Church Yth Grp; Band; Color Guard; Jazz Band; Chrldng; Tennis; Hon Roll; Oral Roberts Univ.

WRIGHT, KENNETH R; Altus Sr HS; Altus, OK; (2); ROTC; Ftbl; Wt Lftg; Hon Roll; Bus.

WRIGHT, KRISTI; Hilldale HS; Muskogee, OK; (3); 6/101; Church Yth Grp; German Clb; Key Clb; Nwsp; Yrbk; Sec Jr Cls; Rep Stu Cncl; Stat Bsbl; Co-Capt Chrldng; High Hon Roll; Stdnt Of Month Feb 96/Mar 95; JOM; NSU; PT.

WRIGHT, KRISTINA M; Northeast HS; Oklahoma City, OK; (3); Art Clb; Cmnty Wkr; FBLA; Science Clb; Spanish Clb; Sftbl; High Hon Roll; U OK; Environmental Engr.

WRIGHT, MATT; Jenks HS; Tulsa, OK; (4); 16/500; Church Yth Grp; Cmnty Wkr; Key Clb; Church Choir; Rep Stu Cncl; Var L Swmmng; NHS; Pres Schlr; Sal; St Schlr; Water Polo; St & Local Piano Cmptns; Hyechka-Oldest & Mst Respected Music Soc In OK, By Audition; U Of Tulsa; Music Composition.

WRIGHT, MIA I; B T Washington HS; Tulsa, OK; (3); Drama Clb; Rep Red Cross Aide; Teachers Aide; Rep Stu Cncl; Hon Roll; Poetry Soc Hnr 95; Poetry Clb Pres; OK Ctr Adv Sci/Tech 96 Hnr; Eng Prof/Nvlst.

WRIGHT, MICHAEL R; Stillwater Sr HS; Stillwater, OK; (4); Art Clb; French Clb; Q&S; Phtg Nwsp; Phtg Yrbk; Golf; High Hon Roll; Hon Roll; Jr NHS; NHS; Rtry Stu Of Mnth; Natl Rnnr-Up Photo PTA Rflctns; Natl Fnlst Coll Photo Cmptn; Kansas City Art Inst; Photo.

WRIGHT, MINDI L; Velma Alma HS; Ratliff City, OK; (3); FBLA; FHA; HOBY; Scholastic Bowl; Teachers Aide; Chorus; School Play; Ed Nwsp; Hon Roll; NHS; U Of OK; Law.

WRIGHT, MONICA P; Healdton HS; Healdton, OK; (2); Cmnty Wkr; FCA; GAA; Pep Clb; Chorus; Sec Soph Cls; Bsktbl; Sftbl; NHS; Pres Acad Fit Awd; OSU.

WRIGHT, NATASHIA D; Mc Alester HS; Mcalester, OK; (4); 38/193; FCA; Hosp Aide; Office Aide; Spanish Clb; JV Bsktbl; JV Sftbl; Hon Roll; East Cntrl Univ; Pre-Med.

WRIGHT, RANDIN D; Sapulpa Sr HS; Tulsa, OK; (2); 17/365; French Clb; Letterman Clb; Scholastic Bowl; Var Bsbl; JV Ftbl; JV Wrstlng; High Hon Roll; Jr NHS; NHS; Pres Schlr.

WRIGHT, ROBERT L; Edmond North HS; Edmond, OK; (1); Church Yth Grp; FCA; Nwsp; Capt Wrstlng; Blk Belt Tae Kwon Do/ST Chmpn; Fwlshp Chrstn Ath; Univ Of OK; Artist/Crtnst.

WRIGHT, SABRINA M; Stonewall Jr-Sr HS; Stonewall, OK; (1); 2/20; School Play; Sftbl; High Hon Roll; Hon Roll; GATE Pgm; OK ST Univ; Lawyer.

WRIGHT, SAMANTHA D; Hobart HS; Hobart, OK; (4); 13/56; Cmnty Wkr; Ofcr FHA; Hist FTA; Library Aide; Office Aide; Teachers Aide; Chorus; Yrbk; Rep Stu Cncl; JV Bsktbl; Rotary Clb Schlrshp; Future Tchrs Amer Schlrshp; Earl/Agnes Eberhart Schlrshp; Southwestern OK ST U; Psych.

WRIGHT, STACEY L; Weatherford HS; Weatherford, OK; (4); 33/136; FTA; Teachers Aide; Band; Drm Mjr(t); Swing Chorus; Ofcr Stu Cncl; Score Keeper; High Hon Roll; NHS; Prfct Atten Awd; SW OK ST Univ; Nrsng.

WRIGHT, TARA J; Velma Alma HS; Duncan, OK; (2); Church Yth Grp; FCA; FBLA; FHA; Natl FFA Org; Office Aide; Scholastic Bowl; SADD; Band; Church Choir; Lawyer.

WRIGHT, THOMAS; Muskogee HS; Muskogee, OK; (4); 103/303; Am Leg Boys St; Pres Church Yth Grp; Key Clb; Model UN; Office Aide; Service Clb; Pres Spanish Clb; Pres Stu Cncl; Hon Roll; Rptr Jr Cls; Mr Teenager Optimist Clb Awd; RYLA Ldrshp Smmr Camp; Cnslr YMCA Camp Takatoka 2 Yrs; U Of OK.

WRIGHT, TIFFANY; Muskogee HS; Muskogee, OK; (2); St Schlr; RAID; OK Hnr Soc; Teens For Christ.

WRIGHT, TODD B; Hinton HS; Hinton, OK; (2); Church Yth Grp; Acpl Chr; Chorus; School Musical; Ofcr Bsbl; Ftbl; Wrstlng; Hon Roll; Kybrdng; Osu; Phrmcst.

WRIGHT, TRACI; Madill HS; Madill, OK; (2); Church Yth Grp; FCA; FHA; Natl FFA Org; JV Var Bsktbl; High Hon Roll; Hon Roll; NHS.

WULF, COURTNEY L; Union Intermediate HS; Broken Arrow, OK; (2); 38/800; Church Yth Grp; FBLA; Spanish Clb; Drill Tm; Hon Roll; Jr NHS; OK St Chldrns Hunter Riding Champ; Acctng.

WYATT, ERICK; Del City HS; Oklahoma City, OK; (3); FCA; Letterman Clb; SADD; Church Choir; Var Socr; Var Trk; Chrch Yth Group Pres; Mem Of Yth For Christ; Elem Wrestling Coach Vol; His; Pre-Law.

WYATT, KELLY D; Midwest City HS; Midwest City, OK; (1); Church Yth Grp; FCA; French Clb; Pep Clb; Rptr Nwsp; Co-Ed Yrbk; Var Bsktbl; Var Vllybl; Hon Roll; Jr NHS; Var Bsktbl Plyr Of Yr; Ftbl Hmcmng Royalty/Fresh Sweetheart Royalty; MI U.

WYCKOFF, CAMMIE; Frontier Public Schl; Marland, OK; (4); 4/27; Church Yth Grp; 4-H; Treas French Clb; Pres FHA; Natl FFA Org; SADD; Band; Stage Crew; Yrbk; Rep Jr Cls; Concurrent Enrollment At Northern OK Coll; Northern OK Coll; Nrsng.

WYCKOFF, DANIEL; Mustang HS; Mustang, OK; (3); Church Yth Grp; FCA; Var L Tennis; Yth Alive Offcr; Sthwstrn Assmbls God U; Mnstry.

WYCKOFF II, RICHARD; Seiling Schl; Chester, OK; (4); 3/34; Art Clb; Church Yth Grp; FBLA; Natl Beta Clb; Band; Mrchg Band; High Hon Roll; NHS; Yth Alv; Sld Rck Yth Grp; OK ST U; Bus.

WYLIE, CHRIS; Marietta HS; Marietta, OK; (3); FCA; Treas Band; Mrchg Band; School Musical; Rep Stu Cncl; Ftbl; Trk; Wt Lftg; Hon Roll; NHS.

WYLIE, MICAH A; Memorial HS; Tulsa, OK; (2); Drama Clb; German Clb; Latin Clb; Speech Tm; Band; Chorus; Mrchg Band; School Musical; School Play; Hon Roll; Pvt Vocal Instr From Laven Sowell; Super Rating At St Solo Cont Vocal Solo; Broadway Actor.

WYMAN, SAMUEL K; Enid Sr HS; Enid, OK; (3); Library Aide; Teachers Aide; Band; Jazz Band; Mrchg Band; Wt Lftg; EPSIN Mem & Organizer; Amarillo Coll; Comp Engrng.

WYMORE, TIM J; South Intermediate HS; Broken Arrow, OK; (1); Poem Published In Echoes From Silnce.

WYNN, JASON W; Elk City Jr HS; Elk City, OK; (1); Church Yth Grp; Ofcr Bsbl; Bsktbl; Wt Lftg; Hon Roll; Southwestern ST Univ.

WYNN, JENNY; Frederick HS; Frederick, OK; (4); Church Yth Grp; HOBY; Speech Tm; School Play; Ed Yrbk; Rep Soph Cls; Sec Jr Cls; Sec Sr Cls; Hon Roll; NHS; Med.

WYNN, JEREMY; Mc Loud HS; Mc Loud, OK; (3); 12/140; Church Yth Grp; FCA; Bsktbl; High Hon Roll; Hon Roll; NHS; Gftd & Tlntd; OK U.

WYNN, MICHAEL; Mc Alester HS; Mcalester, OK; (3); Am Leg Boys St; Spanish Clb; Var Golf; Var Capt Wrstlng; Cit Awd; U Of OK.

WYNN, TIMOTHY T; Putnam City North HS; Oklahoma City, OK; (4); 200/450; Church Yth Grp; Cmnty Wkr; FCA; Library Aide; Office Aide; Teachers Aide; Church Choir; Variety Show; Ftbl; Multi Cultural Awareness Group; NEO A&M Coll; Vocal Perfmnc.

WYRICK, BRANDY R; Okemah HS; Okemah, OK; (2); Art Clb; Church Yth Grp; Computer Clb; Debate Tm; Key Clb; Natl FFA Org; Quiz Bowl; Scholastic Bowl; Science Clb; Spanish Clb; Mdl Cngrs; GATE; Tulsa JC; Crmnl Jstc.

WYRICK, CHERYL K; Barnsdall Jr Sr HS; Barnsdall, OK; (1); 1/35; Church Yth Grp; FCA; 4-H; FHA; Letterman Clb; Scholastic Bowl; Varsity Clb; L Bsktbl; L Sftbl; Cit Awd; Sftbl MVP, All Dist & ASA; Eng Awd; HI Pacific.

WYRICK, KRISTINA L; Star Spencer HS; Midwest City, OK; (1); ROTC; Chorus; School Musical; Ofcr Stu Cncl; High Hon Roll; Grambling; Csmtlgy.

YAEGER, RACHAEL M; Norman Sr HS; Norman, OK; (4); Church Yth Grp; Cmnty Wkr; Model UN; Red Cross Aide; Ski Clb; Teachers Aide.

YAFFE, STACY; Westmoore HS; Oklahoma City, OK; (3); 130/615; Church Yth Grp; Spanish Clb; Temple Yth Grp; VP Frsh Cls; Pres Soph Cls; VP Stu Cncl; Bsktbl; JV Socr; DAR Awd; NHS; Masonic Awd.

YANCEY, MELISSA S; Bridge Creek HS; Blanchard, OK; (2); Girl Scts; Library Aide; Office Aide; Scholastic Bowl; Spanish Clb; SADD; Acpl Chr; Chorus; School Musical; Bus/Cmptr Tech.

YANCY, RODNEY T; Owasso Sr HS; Owasso, OK; (2); Church Yth Grp; Drama Clb; English Clb; FCA; Science Clb; Pres Soph Cls; JV L Bsbl; JV L Ftbl; Var L Wrstlng; High Hon Roll.

YANDA, ANTON V; Yukon Middle HS; Yukon, OK; (2); Church Yth Grp; Ofcr Bsbl; Bsktbl; Ftbl; Wt Lftg; Amer Legion Bsbl; OK ST U.

YANDELL, DREW D; Durant HS; Durant, OK; (1); Letterman Clb; Var Bsbl; Hon Roll.

YANDELL, LESLIE M; Oklahoma Sch Of Science & Math; Gage, OK; (3); Church Yth Grp; Quiz Bowl; Chorus; Church Choir; Var Bsktbl; Var Intrml Sftbl; Var Trk; NHS; FCA; Scholastic Bowl; Masonic Stu Today; Red Carpet All Conf Team 94; OK ST U; Vet.

YANDLE, KRYSTAL S; Henryetta Sr HS; Henryetta, OK; (3); Art Clb; Church Yth Grp; Girl Scts; Spanish Clb; Speech Tm; High Hon Roll; Hon Roll; Rec Essy Cont Wnnr; U Of Chicago; Media Cmmnctns.

YANG, BAO; Union Intermediate HS; Tulsa, OK; (2); 118/800; Church Yth Grp; Church Choir; Cit Awd; Hon Roll; NHS; Ntl Merit Ltr; Prfct Atten Awd; Pres Acad Fit Awd; Frgn Lang Clb; Chrch Yth Grp Sec; Design.

YANOSIK, JOHN S; Union Sr HS; Tulsa, OK; (4); 4/629; Boy Scts; Church Yth Grp; Key Clb; Capt Var Swmmng; Hon Roll; NHS; Pres Acad Fit Awd; Spanish NHS; Eagle Sct; Water Polo; Rice U; Elec Engr.

YANOSIK, JUSTIN E; Union Intermediate HS; Tulsa, OK; (1); Boy Scts; Church Yth Grp; Cmnty Wkr; Band; Swmmng; High Hon Roll; Jr NHS; Pres Acad Fit Awd; Acad Team.

YARBROGH, MATT; Chouteau HS; Chouteau, OK; (4); 6/58; Am Leg Boys St; Church Yth Grp; Office Aide; Teachers Aide; Rptr Nwsp; Yrbk; Rep Stu Cncl; Var Bsbl; Hon Roll; NHS; NSU; Bus.

YARBROUGH, DEIDRE A; Mc Loud HS; Mc Loud, OK; (2); Scholastic Bowl; Bsktbl; Sftbl; Hon Roll; NHS; Prfct Atten Awd; Bus.

YARBROUGH, JASON T; Shawnee Sr HS; Meeker, OK; (1); Church Yth Grp; Band; Mrchg Band; Pep Band; Bsktbl; Hon Roll.

YARBROUGH, LAURENA; Kingfisher HS; Kingfisher, OK; (3); 14/80; Church Yth Grp; Spanish Clb; Bsktbl; Wt Lftg; Cit Awd; NHS; All-Amer Schlr; Oklahoma City U; Law.

YARNELL, LAYNA B; Foyil Schl; Claremore, OK; (2); Drama Clb; Math Tm; Speech Tm; School Play; Stage Crew; Vets Frgn Wars US Voice Democracy Awrd; Dncg/Swim/Water Ski; Upward Bnd; Rogers Univ; PT.

YASSER, ELIZABETH J; Bishop Kelley HS; Tulsa, OK; (2); 2/240; Cmnty Wkr; Pep Clb; Ofcr Frsh Cls; Rep Soph Cls; Var L Bsktbl; Var L Tennis; High Hon Roll.

YAZDANIPANAH, VANESSA A; West Middle HS; Norman, OK; (2); Drama Clb; Office Aide; Speech Tm; Hon Roll; NHS; Med Explorers Post Act; OK Univ; Med.

YEAHQUO, AMBER M; Carnegie HS; Carnegie, OK; (3); FCA; FHA; Office Aide; Pep Clb; Chorus; Yrbk; Rep Jr Cls; Rep Sr Cls; Hon Roll; School Musical; Heritage Clb Rprtr, Pres; 5th Pl Swim Meet; Ec Prncpls Hnr Roll; OK U; Med.

YEAHQUO, ELIZABETH R; Carnegie HS; Carnegie, OK; (2); Art Clb; Cmnty Wkr; Library Aide; Office Aide; Teachers Aide; Drill Tm; School Musical; School Play; Ofcr Stu Cncl; Bsktbl; Publication In Bk; Won Poetry Cntst; Wrte Poetry/Shrt Stories; Law/Psych.

YEARGAIN, JEREMY S; Harrah HS; Harrah, OK; (3); 5/168; FCA; JV Bsbl; JV Bsktbl; Tennis; Trk; Cit Awd; Hon Roll; Jr NHS; NHS; Pres Acad Fit Awd.

YEE, CHRIS; Tulsa Emmanuel Christian Sch; Broken Arrow, OK; (3); Art Clb; Acpl Chr; Yrbk; Pres Frsh Cls; Pres Soph Cls; Pres Jr Cls; Ofcr Bsbl; Bsktbl; JETS Awd; All-St Bsktbl; Sci Engrng Challenge Awds 1st Pl; MVP Bsktbl Conf; Oral Roberts Univ.

YELL, CINDY A; South Coffeyville Schl; South Coffeyville, OK; (2); Chorus; Ed Phtg Yrbk; Hon Roll; NHS; Celtic/Medieval His; Wrtng Short Stories/Poetry; O U.

YENTER, KRISTA; Glenpool HS; Glenpool, OK; (4); 6/120; Pres 4-H; HOBY; Spanish Clb; Chorus; Swing Chorus; Yrbk; Hon Roll; NHS; Ntl Merit Ltr; OK Eastern Dist Hnr Choir; Dist Cmptn Super Ratng Vocal Music; Select Womens Vocal Grp; Weber ST U; Scndry Ed.

YERBY, JAMIE B; Vanoss Schl; Ada, OK; (3); Art Clb; FHA; VICA; Hon Roll; NHS; Ntl Merit Ltr; HOSA VP; All Amer Schlr Awd; OCU; Nrsng; RN.

YI, MIKIE; Moore HS; Moore, OK; (4); 133/527; Latin Clb; Library Aide; Office Aide; Rep Stu Cncl; Var Mgr Ftbl; Mgr(s); Trk; Wrstlng; MSA Clb Scl Coord; U Of OK; Ed.

YINGLING, CHARLES; Deer Creek HS; Edmond, OK; (3); 13/100; FCA; FBLA; Science Clb; Yrbk; Ofcr Bsbl; Bsktbl; Ftbl; NHS; Pres Acad Fit Awd.

YINGLING, JESSICA; Deer Creek HS; Edmond, OK; (3); Science Clb; Ed Yrbk; Sec Frsh Cls; Rep Soph Cls; VP Jr Cls; VP Stu Cncl; Var Capt Chrldng; NHS; All-Star Pom & Chrldng Squads; OU.

YINGLING, SAMUEL; Deer Creek HS; Edmond, OK; (3); FCA; FBLA; Science Clb; Ofcr Bsbl; Bsktbl; Ftbl; High Hon Roll; NHS; Pres Acad Fit Awd.

YIRSA, STEPH; Grove HS; Grove, OK; (2); 7/115; Drama Clb; 4-H; HOBY; Key Clb; Speech Tm; Band; Var Chrldng; 4-H Awd; Hon Roll; NHS; Soph Of The Yr; IDFY; FNA Sub-Dist Pres; OSU; Meterology; Jrnlsm.

YOAKUM, WESLEY H; Edmond North HS; Edmond, OK; (2); Church Yth Grp; JV Bsbl; Var Wrstlng; TX A&M; Mech Engr.

YOCHAM, TERENA M; Vinita HS; Afton, OK; (4); 34/72; Church Yth Grp; German Clb; Natl FFA Org; Band; Mrchg Band; Bsktbl; Tennis; HOSA Hsrtn/Pres; Neo A&M Coll; RN.

YODER, BRAD; Piedmont HS; Piedmont, OK; (4); Am Leg Boys St; Boy Scts; FCA; Rep Frsh Cls; Var JV Bsbl; Var Socr; Var Wrstlng; High Hon Roll; NHS; U Of OK; Elec Engrng.

YOHANNAN, SUJI A; Yukon Middle HS; Yukon, OK; (4); OU; Med Dr.

YOON, JIHYE; Del City HS; Del City, OK; (2); Church Yth Grp; Hosp Aide; Quiz Bowl; Spanish Clb; SADD; Band; Color Guard; Drm Mjr(t); Jr NHS; NHS; OU; Med/Hlth Care.

YORK, ANGIE; Mangum Jr HS; Mangum, OK; (1); Church Yth Grp; Pres 4-H; FHA; Band; Jazz Band; Pep Band; Hon Roll; Jr NHS; SWOBDA All Region Band; Shortgrass Band.

YORK, BRYAN J; Choctaw HS; Choctaw, OK; (2); Church Yth Grp; Intrml Golf; NHS; Snow Skiing.

YORK, DEREK; Midwest City HS; Midwest City, OK; (3); Boy Scts; Cmnty Wkr; VP Pres German Clb; Quiz Bowl; Science Clb; SADD; High Hon Roll; NHS; Pol Expl Major 4 Yrs; Northeastern ST U; Bio.

YORK, JARED D; Westmoore HS; Oklahoma City, OK; (3); 33/610; Church Yth Grp; FCA; French Clb; JV Var Ftbl; Var L Socr; NHS; Ntl Merit SF; Val; Amer Red Crss HS Yth Cncl; Acad Excl Awd; Phy Thrpst.

YORK, TONYA R; Checotah HS; Checotah, OK; (3); 3/100; Church Yth Grp; Cmnty Wkr; Debate Tm; Drama Clb; Pres Natl FFA Org; NFL; Speech Tm; Pres Soph Cls; VP Stu Cncl; Mgr(s).

YORK, TORIE M; Southeast HS; Oklahoma City, OK; (1); FCA; Mgr(s); Swmmng; Vllybl; Cit Awd; High Hon Roll; Hon Roll; Prfct Atten Awd; OK U; Psych.

YORMAN, KARI; Owasso Sr HS; Owasso, OK; (3); 24/350; Am Leg Aux Girls St; Church Yth Grp; Spanish Clb; Teachers Aide; Band; Drm Mjr(t); Flag Corp; Mrchg Band; Var Socr; Hon Roll; NHS Pres; Band Cncl Sec; Mech Engrng.

YOSHIDA, GARCEY T; Edmond North HS; Edmond, OK; (2); Math Clb; Math Tm; Science Clb; SADD; Teachers Aide; Band; Ofcr Stu Cncl; Cit Awd; High Hon Roll; Hon Roll; Cmptrs; Sci; Math; Mus; Berkeley; Med Sci.

YOST, GLORIA A; Kingfisher HS; Kingfisher, OK; (2); Church Yth Grp; Spanish Clb; Speech Tm; Band; Church Choir; Mrchg Band; Hon Roll.

YOST III, HARVEY; Perry Sr HS; Perry, OK; (4); 21/66; Am Leg Boys St; Church Yth Grp; Cmnty Wkr; FCA; German Clb; Hosp Aide; Office Aide; Spanish Clb; Band; Chorus; Rtry Amb To Japan; Prncpls Adv Comm; Chrch Altr Boy; Mrktng.

YOST, LAUREN B; Norman Sr HS; Norman, OK; (3); Church Yth Grp; FCA; Spanish Clb; SADD; OU.

YOST, SHELLI; Kingfisher HS; Kingfisher, OK; (2); Church Yth Grp; Debate Tm; Drama Clb; FHA; GAA; NFL; Spanish Clb; Tennis; Cit Awd; Hon Roll; SWOSU; Phrmcst.

YOST, TREY; Perry Sr HS; Perry, OK; (4); 21/66; Am Leg Boys St; Cmnty Wkr; FCA; German Clb; Office Aide; Spanish Clb; Band; Chorus; Mrchg Band; Pep Band; Princpls Advsry Cmmtte; Rotry Intl Ambssdr To Japan; St Marks Episcopal Altar Boy; Mrktng.

YOUNG, ALISHA D; Westmoore HS; Newcastle, OK; (3); Art Clb; Spanish Clb.

YOUNG, BRIAN P; Del City HS; Del City, OK; (4); 46/374; Debate Tm; French Clb; Scholastic Bowl; Speech Tm; School Play; Ed Yrbk; VP Sr Cls; Ofcr Stu Cncl; NHS; Ntl Merit SF; Natl Merit Fnlst; U Of OK; Poltcl Sci.

YOUNG, BRYAN; Putnam City West HS; Bethany, OK; (3); 2/350; Church Yth Grp; JCL; Latin Clb; Orch; School Musical; Rep Stu Cncl; NHS; All St Orch; Silver Strings Of Putnam City Pres 96-97; Southern Nazarene Univ; Med.

YOUNG, CARRIE; Miami Sr HS; Miami, OK; (4); 12/132; Cmnty Wkr; FCA; Teachers Aide; Church Choir; Yrbk; Rep Stu Cncl; JV Mgr(s); Var Capt Chrldng; Sftbl; Trk; U Of OK.

YOUNG, CHAD; Elk City Jr HS; Elk City, OK; (1); Church Yth Grp; Natl FFA Org; Rep Stu Cncl; Ftbl; Golf; Tennis; High Hon Roll; Hon Roll; Tech Stdnts Assn.

YOUNG, CHRISTIN; Weatherford HS; Weatherford, OK; (2); Church Yth Grp; Spanish Clb; Bsktbl; Chrldng; Powder Puff Ftbl; Sftbl; Hon Roll.

YOUNG, DANNY R; Bartlesville Mid HS; Bartlesville, OK; (1); 244/543; Church Yth Grp; Chorus; School Musical; Bsktbl; Ftbl; Wt Lftg; Prfct Atten Awd; OSU; Ag.

YOUNG, DEAYN L; Skiatook HS; Skiatook, OK; (4); 14/104; FCA; GAA; Library Aide; Office Aide; Speech Tm; Teachers Aide; Varsity Clb; Yrbk; Bsktbl; High Hon Roll; Class Awd; Tulsa CC; Elemed.

YOUNG, DOUGLAS; Bristow HS; Bristow, OK; (4); 30/98; Am Leg Boys St; Church Yth Grp; FCA; Ftbl; Wt Lftg; Wrstlng; Cit Awd; High Hon Roll; Hon Roll; Prfct Atten Awd; U Cntrl OK; Scndry Math.

YOUNG, ISAAC M; Glenpool HS; Glenpool, OK; (1); Boy Scts; Chorus; Color Guard; Rptr Nwsp; Ofcr Bsbl; Crs Cntry; Ftbl; Mgr(s); Trk; Wt Lftg; Brigham Young U; Bus.

YOUNG, JACKIE; Aline-Cleo Jr Sr HS; Aline, OK; (2); 1/23; Church Yth Grp; FCA; Natl FFA Org; Pep Clb; Bsktbl; High Hon Roll; NHS; Pres Acad Fit Awd; Val; NW OK ST Univ; Sci Field.

YOUNG, JARED G; Christian Heritage Acad; Oklahoma City, OK; (4); 13/49; Church Yth Grp; Pres Chorus; Rep Soph Cls; Pres Stu Cncl; Var Capt Ftbl; Cit Awd; Hon Roll; Var L Bsbl; JV Bsktbl; Var L Golf; Mexico Missn Trip; Intensity Awd In Ftbl; Crusader Awd In Bsbl; All-St & Littl All-City Hrnb Mntn Bsbl; Bob Jones Univ; Bus Admin.

YOUNG, JASON; Eldorado Schl; Eldorado, OK; (3); Church Yth Grp; FHA; Pep Clb; Scholastic Bowl; Chorus; Church Choir; School Play; Rptr Nwsp; Yrbk; Pres Frsh Cls; TX Tech; Geolgst/Prof Paleonty.

YOUNG, JASON P; Union Intermediate HS; Tulsa, OK; (2); Band; Mrchg Band; Pep Band; NHS; Music.

YOUNG, JEFFREY B; Vinita HS; Vinita, OK; (2); Church Yth Grp; DECA; Spanish Clb; School Musical; Quitar; Drums; Pencil Sketch Drawing.

YOUNG, JEFFREY C; Claremore Sr HS; Claremore, OK; (2); Bsktbl; Golf; Hon Roll; OK ST U.

YOUNG, JEFFREY D; Norman Sr HS; Norman, OK; (3); Boy Scts; Computer Clb; Library Aide; High Hon Roll; Hon Roll; Shell Clb; Scuba Diving; Marine Bio.

YOUNG, JESSICA E; Westmoore HS; Oklahoma City, OK; (1); Church Yth Grp; Hosp Aide; Office Aide.

YOUNG, JO A; Arkoma Jr Sr HS; Arkoma, OK; (3); 4/40; FCA; FHA; Office Aide; VP Jr Cls; Pres Stu Cncl; Capt Bsktbl; Capt Sftbl; High Hon Roll; Sec NHS; GATE; Westark; Tchr/Coach.

YOUNG, JODIE; Thackerville HS; Thackerville, OK; (3); 1/15; Pres 4-H; FHA; Math Clb; Treas Natl FFA Org; Science Clb; VP Soph Cls; Pres Jr Cls; Rep Stu Cncl; Bsktbl; Cit Awd.

YOUNG, JOSHUA A; Yukon Middle HS; Yukon, OK; (2); Vet.

YOUNG, JULIE; Hulbert Jr Sr HS; Hulbert, OK; (4); 4/42; FBLA; FHA; Office Aide; Quiz Bowl; Pres Jr Cls; Pres Sr Cls; Var Capt Bsktbl; Var Capt Trk; Hon Roll; NHS; S Clb Pres, Treas; Homcmng Qn; NSU; Med.

YOUNG, KARA; Western Heights Sr HS; Oklahoma City, OK; (3); 12/200; FCA; Key Clb; Teachers Aide; Chorus; School Musical; Treas Jr Cls; Ofcr Stu Cncl; Var Bsktbl; Hon Roll; NHS; OK All ST Choir; OK Bapt Univ; Music/PT.

YOUNG, KEISHA; Northeast HS; Oklahoma City, OK; (4); 29/150; Cmnty Wkr; Dance Clb; Band; Chorus; Church Choir; Color Guard; Flag Corp; Mrchg Band; Orch; Stat Bsbl; Langston Univ; Law.

YOUNG, KERRY D; Tecumseh HS; Tecumseh, OK; (4); 1/165; Am Leg Aux Girls St; Cmnty Wkr; Natl Beta Clb; VP Spanish Clb; VP Frsh Cls; VP Soph Cls; Pres Jr Cls; Sec Stu Cncl; Chrldng; NHS; Pres Yth Svc Awd; Frosh Ftbl Attendant; House Of Reps Page; OK City Univ; Mass Commnctn.

YOUNG, KIMBERLY; Deer Creek HS; Edmond, OK; (4); 2/66; Church Yth Grp; FCA; Science Clb; SADD; Teachers Aide; Mgr(s); NHS; Pres Acad Fit Awd; Sal; OK Bapt U.

YOUNG, KIMBERLY A; Warner HS; Warner, OK; (2); Art Clb; Teachers Aide; Mgr(s); Trk; Gen Bus; Psych; Drawing; Northeastern ST Univ; Med.

YOUNG, KRISTEN; Newcastle HS; Newcastle, OK; (2); Art Clb; FBLA; Hosp Aide; Science Clb; Spanish Clb; Chrldng; Hon Roll; NHS.

YOUNG, LEE D; Nathan Hale HS; Tulsa, OK; (1); FCA; JV Var Bsktbl; Var Ftbl; Hon Roll; Ntl Merit Ltr; Natl Math Awd; Natl Schlstc Mrt Awd; Acctng.

YOUNG, LESLEY; Victory Christian Schl; Tulsa, OK; (4); 15/65; Church Yth Grp; Cmnty Wkr; Intnl Clb; Teachers Aide; Yrbk; Socr; High Hon Roll; NHS; Sftbl; Oral Roberts U.

YOUNG, LINDSAY; Putnam City West HS; Newcastle, OK; (4); 33/304; Church Yth Grp; Pres VP FBLA; HOBY; Model UN; Band; Drm Mjr(t); Mrchg Band; Rep Stu Cncl; High Hon Roll; NHS; Band Cncl Rep & VP; Stu To Stu; 3-D; OK Chrstn U Sci Arts; Music.

YOUNG, MARSHA L; Tahlequah Sr HS; Park Hill, OK; (3); Church Yth Grp; SADD; Teachers Aide; Northeastern ST U.

YOUNG, MATT; Chelsea HS; Chelsea, OK; (4); 1/60; Church Yth Grp; FCA; Model UN; Quiz Bowl; Band; Jazz Band; Mrchg Band; Yrbk; Pres Sr Cls; High Hon Roll; All-St Band; OBU; Instrumntl Music Ed.

YOUNG, MISSY; Comanche HS; Duncan, OK; (1); Church Yth Grp; Computer Clb; Hon Roll; Sun Schl Tchr; Frosh Hmcmng Queen; Tech Stdnt Assn; Algebra Highest Achvr; Cameron Univ; Math Tchr.

YOUNG, SARAH; Clayton Jr Sr HS; Nashoba, OK; (3); Church Yth Grp; Debate Tm; Drama Clb; VP 4-H; HOBY; Rep NFL; Speech Tm; Var Bsktbl; Var Sftbl; 4-H Awd; Upward Bound; Pblc Spkng & Engl Mrt Awds; U Tulsa; Pblc Rltns.

YOUNG, SARAH; Timberlake Schl; Helena, OK; (3); 6/23; FHA; Natl FFA Org; Pep Clb; Ofcr Frsh Cls; Ofcr Soph Cls; Ofcr Jr Cls; Ofcr Bsbl; Bsktbl; Hon Roll; Jr NHS; St Star Events Wnnr Creed Spkng; FFA Sweetheart, Rptr; FFA Farmers Union Speech Cont Wnnr; NWOSU; Elem Ed.

YOUNG, SARAH B; Tomlinson Jr HS; Lawton, OK; (1); Church Yth Grp; FCA; FHA; Pep Clb; Chrldng; NHS; Tchr.

YOUNG, SCOTT A; Midwest City HS; Midwest City, OK; (3); JA; Quiz Bowl; Scholastic Bowl; Spanish Clb; SADD; Band; Drm Mjr(t); Jazz Band; Mrchg Band; Orch; VW Collector; Music Ed.

YOUNG, SOPHIA; Battiest Jr Sr HS; Pickens, OK; (2); Church Yth Grp; 4-H; FHA; HOBY; Natl FFA Org; School Musical; Nwsp; Pres Soph Cls; Ofcr Stu Cncl; Sftbl; Miss Battiest High 95-96; Ctzn Washington Focus 96; 4-H All-Around.

YOUNG, STEPHANIE; Glenpool HS; Glenpool, OK; (4); Pres Church Yth Grp; Pres Chorus; Pres Frsh Cls; Rep Soph Cls; Sec Stu Cncl; Capt Vllybl; High Hon Roll; NHS; Ntl Merit Ltr; Musical Rdrs Thtr Pianist/Vocalist; Brigham Young Univ; Bus.

YOUNG, TIFFANY A; Enid Sr HS; Enid, OK; (3); Office Aide; Pep Clb; Speech Tm; Teachers Aide; Acpl Chr; Chorus; Stage Crew; High Hon Roll; Hon Roll; Jr NHS; Autry Vo-Tech; Acctng.

YOUNG, TOMEKA C; Stillwater Sr HS; Stillwater, OK; (2); #11 in class; FCA; Church Choir; Drill Tm; Bsktbl; Trk; Wt Lftg; Hon Roll; Seek Clb; Lit.

YOUNG, TRISTAN; Woodward HS; Woodward, OK; (2); Boy Scts; Quiz Bowl; Wrstlng; NHS; MIT.

YOUNGBLOOD, ALEXA L; Catoosa HS; Catoosa, OK; (4); Intnl Clb; Spanish Clb; Teachers Aide; Band; Flag Corp; Mrchg Band; Ofcr Stu Cncl; Hon Roll; Pres Ed Awds Pgm; OK St Hnr Soc.

YOUNGBLOOD, AMY M; Guthrie Sr HS; Guthrie, OK; (1); Hon Roll; Cntrl ST Univ; Lawyer.

YOUNGBLOOD, HOLLI; Kremlin Jr Sr HS; Enid, OK; (4); 1/26; Am Leg Aux Girls St; Church Yth Grp; FCA; Red Cross Aide; Band; Drm Mjr(t); Jazz Band; Mrchg Band; Pep Band; School Musical; Plts Licns; Bsktbl, All Conf Tm, Trny MVP; Trk, St Meet Rnnr Up 100m & 200m; OK ST U; Med.

YOUNGBLOOD, JOEY P; Webbers Falls Schl; Webbers Falls, OK; (3); 15/29; Am Leg Boys St; Math Tm; Teachers Aide; Ofcr Sr Cls; Ofcr Bsbl; Ftbl; Hon Roll; Prfct Atten Awd.

YOUNGBLOOD, STEPHANIE; Broken Arrow Sr HS; Broken Arrow, OK; (4); 3/920; Am Leg Aux Girls St; Treas Church Yth Grp; French Clb; HOBY; Band; JV Sftbl; Pres NHS; Ntl Merit SF; Pres Schlr; Val; OK U; Law.

YOUNT, KRISTY L; Pawhuska HS; Pawhuska, OK; (3); 4-H; Office Aide; Science Clb; Teachers Aide; JV Bsktbl; Var Trk; Sec 4-H Awd; Hon Roll; Jr NHS; OSU; Vet Schl.

YOW, ERIC J; Elk City HS; Elk City, OK; (3); Boy Scts; Church Yth Grp; Computer Clb; Science Clb; Band; Jazz Band; Cit Awd; Hon Roll.

YU, RAYMOND; Union Sr HS; Tulsa, OK; (4); 4/669; Pres French Clb; Key Clb; Scholastic Bowl; Band; Mrchg Band; Pep Band; Var Tennis; High Hon Roll; NHS; Pres Acad Fit Awd; Tulsa Engrng Chllng 1st Pl; U Of OK Engrng Fr 1st Pl; OK Art/Poster Cont 1st Pl; U Of TX Austin; Mech Engrng.

YU, SIMON; Pryor Jr HS; Pryor, OK; (1); Quiz Bowl; Spanish Clb; Band; Jazz Band; Mrchg Band; Orch; School Play; High Hon Roll; Prfct Atten Awd.

ZACCARELLO, CASSANDRA N; Sapulpa Sr HS; Sapulpa, OK; (4); 11/311; Cmnty Wkr; JA; Key Clb; Letterman Clb; Office Aide; Science Clb; Spanish Clb; SADD; Teachers Aide; Chorus; Elks Tngr Yr; Dupree Dnc Top Awd Schlrshp; Mck Trl Tm Outstndng Atty; OK U; Law.

ZACHARIAE, KRISTA; Nathan Hale HS; Tulsa, OK; (3); FCA; HOBY; VP Key Clb; Pres Frsh Cls; Pres Soph Cls; Sec Stu Cncl; Crs Cntry; Mgr(s); Pom Pon; NHS; Natl Yng Ldrs Conf Wshngtn DC; Org Yth Crsde-Gnrtn X Vol; Otfrnt I Untd Way Prjct; OSU; Hmn Rsrcs.

ZACHARY, MISTY O; Midwest City HS; Midwest City, OK; (2); Art Clb; Church Yth Grp; German Clb; Letterman Clb; Pep Clb; Rptr Nwsp; Rptr Yrbk; JV Bsktbl; JV Sftbl; Var Trk; Most Improved Sftbl Awd; Bsktbl Acad Letter; Homecoming Attendent 9th Grd; Competency Cert; OK Univ; Animal Sci.

ZACKERY II, JOHN W; Eisenhower Sr HS; Lawton, OK; (2); Boy Scts; Church Yth Grp; Cmnty Wkr; 4-H; Intnl Clb; JA; Church Choir; Orch; School Musical; School Play; Piano Sr Dist/Sr Wnr St; Wnr OK Chrl Msc Schlsp; OK Math/Sci Schlsp Wnnr OSU; Med.

ZAHIR, AMINA P; Union Intermediate HS; Tulsa, OK; (1); Church Yth Grp; Key Clb; High Hon Roll; NHS; Med.

ZALONKA, NOELLE F; Drumright HS; Cushing, OK; (2); FHA; School Play; Bsktbl; Hon Roll; Stillwater; Anml Behvrst.

ZAMOR, RICH M; Owasso Sr HS; Owasso, OK; (2); #9 in class; Church Yth Grp; Drama Clb; FCA; Rep Soph Cls; JV Var Ftbl; Var Trk; Var Wrstlng; High Hon Roll; VP NHS; Zoologist.

ZAREMBA, ELISABETH; South Intermediate HS; Broken Arrow, OK; (3); Treas Drama Clb; NFL; Speech Tm; Thesps; Acpl Chr; Church Choir; School Musical; School Play; Mgr Stage Crew; Variety Show; Taught Musical Theatre; Regnl Play Asst Dir; Asisted The Kids W/Heart Benefit In NYC Benefited FACES; OK City Univ; Musical Theatre.

ZARRABI, LAYLA; Stillwater Sr HS; Stillwater, OK; (3); 1/500; Debate Tm; French Clb; Pres Natl Beta Clb; Sec NFL; Ed Nwsp; NHS; Pres Acad Fit Awd; Girl Scts; Key Clb; Quiz Bowl; Del Natl Young Ldrs Conf In Wash DC; Page For OK House Of Reps; Silver Awd Girl Scts.

ZAVODNY, CLINT; Perry Sr HS; Red Rock, OK; (3); Church Yth Grp; German Clb; Stage Crew; Nwsp; Ofcr Stu Cncl; Wrstlng; High Hon Roll; NHS; All-Amer Schlr; Multi Yr Lstng; Berkley; Law.

ZAVY, KRISTIN; El Reno Sr HS; El Reno, OK; (3); Cmnty Wkr; DECA; 4-H; Key Clb; School Play; Stage Crew; Variety Show; Cit Awd; 4-H Awd; Hon Roll.

ZEIEN, APRIL L; Choctaw HS; Midwest City, OK; (2); Library Aide; Quiz Bowl; Spanish Clb; Teachers Aide; Band; SAS; OK Univ; Law.

ZEIGLER, CRYSTAL R; Claremore Sr HS; Claremore, OK; (2); Church Yth Grp; Girl Scts; Hosp Aide; Chorus; School Musical; Hon Roll; Select Choir; Spcl Ed.

ZELLER, CHRIS; Macarthur Sr HS; Lawton, OK; (3); Art Clb; Computer Clb; L Bsbl; L Ftbl; L Socr; Fishing & Hunting; AZ ST; Phys Thrpy.

ZELLNER, LESLEY K; Tahlequah Sr HS; Tahlequah, OK; (3); Am Leg Aux Girls St; Spanish Clb; SADD; Chorus; Rep Stu Cncl; High Hon Roll; Jr NHS; NHS; Ntl Merit Ltr; Pres Acad Fit Awd.

ZENNER, ROBERT A; Christian Heritage Acad; Midwest City, OK; (2); Drama Clb; German Clb; Band; Chorus; Yrbk; Var Bsbl; Stat Bsktbl; L Tennis; Jr NHS; Natl Leag Jr Cotlns 95-; Southwstrn OK ST Univ Smr Sci/Math Acad 96; Math/Sci.

ZEPF, ERIN LYNNE; Jenks HS; Tulsa, OK; (3); Church Yth Grp; Mu Alpha Theta; Science Clb; Service Clb; Chorus; School Musical; Ofcr Stu Cncl; Gov Hon Prg Awd; High Hon Roll; NHS.

ZERR, BRENT; Perry Sr HS; Perry, OK; (3); Church Yth Grp; FCA; Math Clb; Sec Frsh Cls; Treas Soph Cls; Sec Jr Cls; Rep Stu Cncl; Var Bsktbl; Hon Roll; NHS; OK ST U; Acctng.

ZICKEFOOSE, SOMMER; Charles Page HS; Sand Springs, OK; (4); 107/329; Cmnty Wkr; FCA; French Clb; Library Aide; VP Pep Clb; VP Frsh Cls; VP Sr Cls; VP Stu Cncl; Var Capt Chrldng; Sr Of Mnth; Sandite Queen; All ST Chrldr; All Reg Chrldr; NCA All Amer; OK Univ; Pre-Med.

ZIEGLER, CAMERON M; Okmulgee HS; Okmulgee, OK; (3); Letterman Clb; Rep Jr Cls; Rep Stu Cncl; Var Ftbl; Var Wt Lftg; High Hon Roll; Hon Roll; NHS; St Schlr.

ZIELNY, LISA; Hennessey HS; Hennessey, OK; (2); FHA; Chrldng; Crs Cntry; Trk; High Hon Roll; NHS.

ZIMMER, JEREMY M; Union Intermediate HS; Tulsa, OK; (2); Church Yth Grp; Cmnty Wkr; Debate Tm; German Clb; Band; Var Swmmng; Hon Roll; Jr NHS; NHS; Tae Kwon Do; Vet.

ZIMMERMAN, DEREK; Marlow HS; Duncan, OK; (4); Am Leg Boys St; Art Clb; Church Yth Grp; Cmnty Wkr; Debate Tm; Drama Clb; 4-H; Chorus; Yrbk; JV Trk; Dncn Fllfst 1st Tnagr Chr; 4-H Cmdy Shr Fn Conts Grnd Chmpn 9xs; Elec; Wdwrkng; Photo; Ckng; Sng; Rckts.

ZIMMERMAN, JON; Moore HS; Moore, OK; (2); Quiz Bowl; Scholastic Bowl; Science Clb; Band; Mrchg Band; Pep Band; Socr; High Hon Roll; Hon Roll; Jr NHS; Bands Of Amer SE Rgnl Band Cntst Fnlst; 3 Intl Sccr Trnmnts In Europe; Elec Engrng.

ZIMMERMAN, MATTHEW; Meeker HS; Meeker, OK; (3); 2/69; Church Yth Grp; Debate Tm; Pres FCA; HOBY; Pres Speech Tm; School Play; Stage Crew; Pres Soph Cls; Ftbl; Am Leg Boys St; Tech Stu Ass Natl Treas; US Naval Acad; Pltcs.

ZIMMERMAN, TRACY M; Duncan HS; Duncan, OK; (2); 4-H; Red Cross Aide; Hon Roll; Deaf Ed.

ZINK, MELISSA S; Agra Schl; Tryon, OK; (2); 1/20; Church Yth Grp; FCA; Natl FFA Org; Var Bsktbl; Var Sftbl; Cit Awd; 4-H Awd; High Hon Roll; Hon Roll; Jr NHS; UCO; Elem Ed.

ZINKE, ARIN; Bishop Kelley HS; Tulsa, OK; (1); Debate Tm; FCA; Bsktbl; Wt Lftg; Cit Awd; Jr NHS.

ZINN, WILLIAM C; Putnam City West HS; Bethany, OK; (1); Ftbl; Wt Lftg; OH ST Univ.

ZMEK, STEPHEN J; Guthrie Sr HS; Guthrie, OK; (1); Am Leg Boys St; Ofcr Bsbl; Ftbl; OK U.

ZMIJSKI, ROBIN M; Brink Jr HS; Oklahoma City, OK; (1); Church Yth Grp; Rep Stu Cncl; Trk; High Hon Roll; Paging At ST Capital.

ZODROW IV, JOSEPH; Skiatook HS; Skiatook, OK; (4); Am Leg Boys St; Church Yth Grp; FCA; Speech Tm; Teachers Aide; Thesps; Chorus; Church Choir; School Musical; School Play; Natl Engl Mrt Schlr; OK Allstar Team Belgium Bsktbl; Bsktbl Ministries Intl; OK Bapt U; Educ.

ZOLBE, MAKARIA A; Casady Schl; Oklahoma City, OK; (2); Drama Clb; School Play; Interested In Creative Wrtng & Acting; Psych.

ZOLLINGER, BEN T; Buffalo Jr Sr HS; Buffalo, OK; (2); 2/33; Cmnty Wkr; Band; Chorus; Jazz Band; Mrchg Band; Pep Band; Swing Chorus; Rep Stu Cncl; Var L Bsbl; Var L Bsktbl; Brad Mc Vicker Awd; All Amer Schlr; Hnr Chorus Tri St Music Fstvl; OK ST U.

ZORGER, RONA L; Duke Schl; Duke, OK; (1); 2/17; Church Yth Grp; FHA; Natl FFA Org; Teachers Aide; Yrbk; Ofcr Stu Cncl; Var Bsktbl; High Hon Roll; Hon Roll; NHS; Masonics Stdnt Today; Southwestern OK ST U; Phrmcy.

ZUEGE, GAIL; Berryhill Jr HS; Tulsa, OK; (1); Church Yth Grp; FHA; Girl Scts; Bsktbl; Chrldng; Hon Roll; Prfct Atten Awd.

ZUHDI, ZACK; Heritage Hall Schl; Oklahoma City, OK; (2); Cmnty Wkr; Science Clb; Spanish Clb; Chorus; School Musical; Variety Show; Pres Soph Cls; Golf; Cit Awd; High Hon Roll; Med/Transplant Surgeon.

ZUMWALT, BRANDI N; Kellyville Sr HS; Kellyville, OK; (3); 4-H; Natl FFA Org; Office Aide; Teachers Aide; Acpl Chr; Chorus; Ofcr Stu Cncl; 4-H Awd; Hon Roll; Licensed Poney Rider ST OK; OK Jr Rodeo Assn Barrel Racers; Serteens Comm Base Grp Kellyville; Tulsa Jr Coll; Para Legal/Law.

ZUNIGA, ELZORA; Piedmont HS; Piedmont, OK; (1); 1/95; Math Tm; Chorus; High Hon Roll; Hon Roll; Pres Acad Fit Awd.

ZUNIGHA, TONYA; Southwest Covenant Schl; El Reno, OK; (1); Church Yth Grp; FCA; Chorus; Rep Nwsp; Yrbk; Rep Stu Cncl; Var L Bsktbl; Stat Ftbl; Var Tennis; Var L Vllybl.

ARKANSAS

Aaron, Tabitha M
Spring Hill HS
Hope, AR

Abercrombie, Billy
Bauxite Jr Sr HS
Benton, AR

Ables, Daniel
Norphlet HS
Calion, AR

Abson, Alison L
Parkview
Arts-Science HS
Mabelvale, AR

Adams, Ashley L
Bryant Sr HS
Alexander, AR

Adams, Ben
England HS
Tucker, AR

Adams, Nathan
Bentonville Sr HS
Bentonville, AR

Adams, Sean
Kirby HS
Amity, AR

Adams, Tawny S
England HS
England, AR

Adamson, Devon
Northside HS
Fort Smith, AR

Adcock, Jeremy S
Horatio HS
De Queen, AR

Adcock, Laura
Drew Central Jr Sr HS
Monticello, AR

Agee, Mary
Prairie Grove HS
Prairie Grove, AR

Ahart, Eric A
Bryant Sr HS
Alexander, AR

Akbar, Nadeem A
Russellville Sr HS
Russellville, AR

Akbar, Safdar
Arkansas Schl Math &
Science
Russellville, AR

Akers, Amber R
Cabot HS
Cabot, AR

Akins, Emily S
Foreman Jr Sr HS
Foreman, AR

Albertson Jr, James R
Jessieville HS
Hot Springs Villa, AR

Albertson, Myrriah L
Jessieville HS
Hot Springs Natio, AR

Albright, Jessica J
Oden Schl
Sims, AR

Alexander, Beckah
Bentonville Sr HS
Bentonville, AR

Alexander, Celeste
Pine Bluff HS
Pine Bluff, AR

Alexander, Jason W
North Little Rock
Hs-West
North Little Rock, AR

Alexander, Paige
Arkansas Sr HS
Texarkana, AR

Allen, Adam D
Greenwood Sr HS
Greenwood, AR

Allen, Ashley L
Greenwood Sr HS
Greenwood, AR

Allen, Bryan O
Blytheville Sr HS
Blytheville, AR

Allen, Jennifer L
Southside HS
Fort Smith, AR

Allinder, Melissa D
Conway Sr HS
Conway, AR

Allison, Amber
Hackett Schl
Hackett, AR

Allison, Jennifer
Morrilton Sr HS
Morrilton, AR

Allmon, John
Brinkley HS
Brinkley, AR

Allspach, Steven D
Mansfield Jr Sr HS
Booneville, AR

Alton, Toni M
West Fork HS
West Fork, AR

Alvarado, Angelica L
Benton Cty Christian
School
Springdale, AR

Alverson, Zack
Humphrey Schl
Humphrey, AR

Alvis, Harry G
Southside HS
Batesville, AR

Ambro, Amber
Augusta HS
Augusta, AR

Amerson, Greg
Mt Ida Jr Sr HS
Mount Ida, AR

Ammons, Kristi
Gosnell Jr Sr HS
Blytheville, AR

Anderson, Amanda K
Lake Hamilton Sr HS
Pearcy, AR

Anderson, Amy
Van Buren Sr HS
Fort Smith, AR

Anderson II, Dennis L
Lake Hamilton Sr HS
Pearcy, AR

Anderson, Julie E
Central Sr HS
Little Rock, AR

Anderson, Millicent D
Mills HS
Little Rock, AR

Anderson, Ryan Collin
Monticello HS
Monticello, AR

Anderson, Shelly N
Van Buren Sr HS
Alma, AR

Anderson, Torez L
Hope HS
Hope, AR

Andrepont, Veronica
Greenwood Sr HS
Greenwood, AR

Anglin, Trenton C
Dollarway HS
Pine Bluff, AR

Anthony, Alisha L
Forrest City HS
Forrest City, AR

Archer, Jennifer L
Springdale Sr HS
Springdale, AR

Arnold, Amanda B
Trumann HS
Harrisburg, AR

Arnold, Brooke
Jonesboro HS
Jonesboro, AR

Arnold, Crissa
Fayetteville Sr HS
Fayetteville, AR

Arnold, Daniel
Cabot HS
Austin, AR

Aronhalt, Kevin E
Russellville Sr HS
Russellville, AR

Arrington, Dorothy E
Cabot HS
Lonoke, AR

Arterbury, Mark W
Hope HS
Hope, AR

Asfahl, Erica R
Fayetteville Sr HS
Fayetteville, AR

Ashley, E Jennifer
Lee Acad
Aubrey, AR

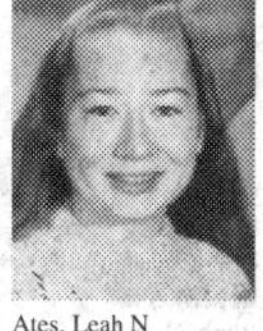

Ates, Leah N
Arkansas Sr HS
Texarkana, AR

Atkins, Henry J
Mc Crory Jr Sr HS
Mc Crory, AR

Atkinson, Christina
Conway Sr HS
Conway, AR

Aubrey, Aaron
Emerson HS
Emerson, AR

Aud, Shanae S
Rison HS
Rison, AR

Ausburn, William J
Bryant HS
Benton, AR

Austin, Ronda L
Gravette HS
Gravette, AR

ARKANSAS

Austin, Shane M
Star City HS
Star City, AR

Avery, Jered L
Valley Springs Schl
Harrison, AR

Avilez, Gershun
Mills HS
Jacksonville, AR

Baggett, Jacy
Charleston HS
Charleston, AR

Baggett, Jheri D
North Little Rock
Hs-East
North Little Rock, AR

Bailey, Amy M
Fayetteville Sr HS
Fayetteville, AR

Bailey, Anthony E
Horatio HS
Horatio, AR

Bailey, Mary A
Lake Hamilton Sr HS
Hot Springs, AR

Bailey, Sherrhonda
John L Mcclellan
Magnet HS
Little Rock, AR

Baird, Heather A
Evening Shade Schl
Sidney, AR

Baker, Jeri A
Mountain Home HS
Mountain Home, AR

Baker, Kratina N
John L Mcclellan
Magnet HS
Little Rock, AR

Baker, Rachel B
Pine Bluff HS
Pine Bluff, AR

Ball, Shanna M
Mc Gehee HS
Mc Gehee, AR

Banks, Heather
Mills HS
Little Rock, AR

Barenberg, Kathryn
El Dorado Sr HS
El Dorado, AR

Barham, Teah J
Southside HS
Desha, AR

Barnard, Spencer R
Valley Springs Schl
Harrison, AR

Barnes, Beckie L
Valley Springs Schl
Harrison, AR

Barnett, Angela D
J A Fair Sr HS
Little Rock, AR

Barnett, Brandy E
Van Buren Sr HS
Van Buren, AR

Barrett, Raegan B
Mc Gehee HS
Mc Gehee, AR

Bartholomew,
Samantha L
Russellville Sr HS
Russellville, AR

Bartlett, Jessica R
Marvell Acad
Marvell, AR

Barton, Jeri E
Alma HS
Alma, AR

Bass, Mandy
Eureka Springs Jr
Sr HS
Eureka Springs, AR

Bass, Stephanie
J A Fair Sr HS
Little Rock, AR

Bates, Ashley S
Star City HS
Star City, AR

Bates, Haley M
Conway Sr HS
Conway, AR

Bates, Jill
Robinson HS
Little Rock, AR

Bates, Michelle R
Lake Hamilton Sr HS
Pearcy, AR

Battisto, Alycia A
Sheridan Sr HS
Mabelvale, AR

Battles, Carletter
Sylvan Hills Jr HS
North Little Rock, AR

Baxter, Kevin R
Valley View HS
Jonesboro, AR

Baxter, Kristy M
Dumas HS
Watson, AR

Beale, Latoya S
Wynne HS
Wynne, AR

Beam, Amanda
Van Buren Sr HS
Van Buren, AR

Beam, Sara N
Southside HS
Fort Smith, AR

Beard, Meghan
Arkansas Bapt Schl
Little Rock, AR

Beard, Shawnn
Monticello HS
Monticello, AR

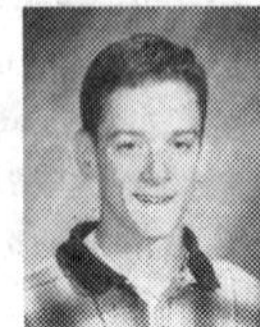
Beasley, Andrew D
Rogers HS
Rogers, AR

Beasley, J Kyle
Springdale Sr HS
Springdale, AR

Becker, Amy M
Southside HS
Fort Smith, AR

Beckham, Jon Regan
Hope HS
Hope, AR

Beene, Amy S
Magnolia HS
Magnolia, AR

Bei, Shihong
Arkansas Schl Math &
Science
Rego Park, NY

Belcher, Amy D
Oden Schl
Oden, AR

Belcher, Steffany D
Marvell Acad
Brinkley, AR

Bell II, Edward Becton
Rivercrest HS
Wilson, AR

Bell, Jennifer
Delight HS
Delight, AR

Bell, Lori
Delight HS
Murfreesboro, AR

Bell, Tonya
Morrilton Sr HS
Perry, AR

Belotti, Leah M
Central Sr HS
North Little Rock, AR

Bender, Joshua
Lake Hamilton Jr HS
Hot Springs, AR

Bennett, J R
Mammoth Spring HS
Thayer, MO

Bennett, Kevin D
Rivercrest HS
Dyess, AR

Bennett, William K
Fountain Lake Jr Sr HS
Hot Springs, AR

Bercher, Courtney
Northside HS
Barling, AR

Berger, Allison M
Jacksonville HS
Sherwood, AR

Bergman, Diana L
North Little Rock
Hs-East
North Little Rock, AR

Bernard, Steven
Mills HS
North Little Rock, AR

Berry, Brandy M
Fordyce HS
Fordyce, AR

Berumen, Michael
Southside HS
Fort Smith, AR

Bethany, Ashley
Smackover HS
Smackover, AR

Bettis, Amy
Arkansas Bapt Schl
Little Rock, AR

Bible, Cindy
Bradford Jr Sr HS
Bradford, AR

Biggs, Cody L
England HS
Scott, AR

Biler, Jessica L
Conway Sr HS
Conway, AR

Biley, Margaret L
Pine Bluff HS
Pine Bluff, AR

Billingsley, Michelle D
Lavaca Jr Sr HS
Lavaca, AR

Billingsley Jr, Rickey A
Newport HS
Newport, AR

Binam, Linda
Springdale HS
Fayetteville, AR

Binns, Amanda L
Russellville Sr HS
Russellville, AR

Bird, Latisha
Pangburn Jr Sr HS
Searcy, AR

Bisbee, Christina
Mayflower HS
Mayflower, AR

Bishop, Jamie R
Ridgecrest HS
Paragould, AR

Bishop, Kevin D
Trumann HS
Trumann, AR

Bishop, Lisa
Southside HS
Fort Smith, AR

Bivens, Ronniesha R
Parkview
Arts-Science HS
Little Rock, AR

Black, Benjamin A
Morrilton Sr HS
Plumerville, AR

Black, Dane T
Hot Springs HS
Hot Springs, AR

Black, Kristi L
Dewitt HS
De Witt, AR

Black, Laura D
Stuttgart Sr HS
Humphrey, AR

Blackshear, Emily K
Ridgecrest HS
Paragould, AR

Blackwell, La Quandria D
Jacksonville HS
Sherwood, AR

Blackwood, Emily R
Greenwood Sr HS
Greenwood, AR

Blair, Ramonda
Crossett Sr HS
Crossett, AR

Blake, Melissa A
Sheridan Sr HS
Hensley, AR

Blakely, Timiko
Lakeside HS
Montrose, AR

Bland, Mark L
Rivercrest HS
Joiner, AR

Blankenship, Courtney D
Corning HS
Corning, AR

Blankenship, Jamie L
Ridgecrest HS
Paragould, AR

Bleau, Nick R
Russellville Sr HS
Russellville, AR

Blevins, Sarah R
Lake Hamilton Sr HS
Hot Springs Natio, AR

Blevins, Shane
Bradford Jr Sr HS
Bradford, AR

Blocker, Lenard T
Russellville Sr HS
Russellville, AR

Bobo, Crystal
Blevins HS
Hope, AR

Boddie, Natasha R
Russellville Sr HS
Russellville, AR

Boeckmann, Ashley
Wynne HS
Wynne, AR

Boerner, Carey D
Northside HS
Fort Smith, AR

Boettger, Lindsay
Lake Hamilton Jr HS
Hot Springs, AR

Bogan, Tiffany N
Mills HS
Jacksonville, AR

Bogy, Nick
Humphrey Schl
Wabbaseka, AR

Bohannan, David S
Huntsville HS
Huntsville, AR

Bolding, Allison Blake
Woodlawn Schl
Monticello, AR

Bollinger, Sara
Re Wells Jr HS
Greenwood, AR

Bolner, Jennifer C
Springdale Sr HS
Springdale, AR

Bolner, Tonya T
Springdale Sr HS
Springdale, AR

Bond, April
Lee Sr HS
Marianna, AR

Bonds, Nicole E
White Co Central Schl
Judsonia, AR

Booher, Kelly A
Mt St Mary Acad
Memphis, TN

Book, Andee L
Piggott HS
Saint Francis, AR

Booker, John Russell
Marvell Acad
Clarendon, AR

Boone, Melissa A
Searcy HS
Searcy, AR

Booth, Robert P
West Side HS
Weiner, AR

Borden, Jaime L
Lonoke Jr HS
Jacksonville, AR

Borders, Tracey
Arkansas Schl Math & Science
North Little Rock, AR

Boren, James D
Goza Jr HS
Arkadelphia, AR

Bosch, Chris L
Mena HS
Mena, AR

Bost, Aaron A
Salem HS
Salem, AR

Bottoms, Heather J
Cty Line HS
Ratcliff, AR

Bousquet, Mikia
Central Sr HS
Little Rock, AR

Boward, Travis J
Weiner HS
Weiner, AR

Bowdler, Jennifer A
Rivercrest HS
Luxora, AR

Bowdler, Steven
Rivercrest HS
Luxora, AR

Bowers, Eric
Arkansas Schl Math & Science
Kirby, AR

Bowers, Shiloh
Springdale Sr HS
Springdale, AR

Bowers, Trey R
Corning HS
Corning, AR

Bowman, Emily
Mc Gehee HS
Mc Gehee, AR

Bowser, Hailey M
Ridgecrest HS
Paragould, AR

Box, David
Trumann HS
Trumann, AR

Box, Ginger
Abundant Life Schls
Jacksonville, AR

Box, Trish L
Abundant Life Schools
Jacksonville, AR

Boxnick, Stephen S
Russellville Sr HS
London, AR

Boyd, Stephen
Hoxie Schl
Hoxie, AR

Boykin, Vickie
Crawfordsville HS
Crawfordsville, AR

Brackett, Montana L
Concord Jr Sr HS
Drasco, AR

Bradberry, Ashley
Concord Jr Sr HS
Concord, AR

Bradford, Arthur
Magnolia HS
Magnolia, AR

Bradford, James Casey
Springdale Sr HS
Springdale, AR

Bradley, Jason
Rison HS
Rison, AR

Bradley, Tiffany L
Mills HS
Mabelvale, AR

Bradshaw, Jody A
Ozark HS
Ozark, AR

Brady, Ginger D
North Little Rock
Hs-West
North Little Rock, AR

Brady, Nicole M
Russellville Sr HS
Russellville, AR

Bramlett, Heather R
Russellville Sr HS
Russellville, AR

Brand, Tonya R
North Little Rock
Hs-East
North Little Rock, AR

Brandebura,
Matthew E
Southside HS
Fort Smith, AR

Brannan, Shallan
Coleman Jr HS
Van Buren, AR

Branscum, Bryan J
Southside HS
Batesville, AR

Branscum, Devan R
North Pulaski HS
Jacksonville, AR

Branson, Naaron E
Southside HS
Fort Smith, AR

Branton, Christy R
Mills HS
Jacksonville, AR

Branton, Mary K
Mills HS
Jacksonville, AR

Brassfield, Adam H
Gosnell Jr Sr HS
Blytheville, AR

Bratton, Elizabeth A
Cabot HS
Austin, AR

Brawley, John R
Bismarck Jr-Sr HS
Bismarck, AR

Brawner, Begina
Wynne HS
Wynne, AR

Bray, Michael
West Memphis
Christian Schl
West Memphis, AR

Brazile, Kristi M
Sylvan Hills HS
Sherwood, AR

Brent, Cody
Genoa Cntrl HS
Fouke, AR

Brewer, Brandy S
Jacksonville HS
Jacksonville, AR

Brewer, Denise
Rural Special Schl
Mountain View, AR

Brewer, Dustin D
Stamps HS
Stamps, AR

Brewer, Heather A
Van Buren Sr HS
Van Buren, AR

Brewer, Kindra D
North Little Rock
Hs-West
North Little Rock, AR

Brewer, Ricky S
Glenwood Jr Sr HS
Amity, AR

Brewer, Sherry M
Lake Hamilton Sr HS
Pearcy, AR

Bridges, Michael A
Lonoke Jr HS
Lonoke, AR

Bright, Zachary M
Oak Grove HS
Maumelle, AR

Brim, Angie C
Mountain Home HS
Mountain Home, AR

Brinegar, Jennifer
Lake Hamilton Sr HS
Hot Springs, AR

Britt, Ayrelle
Nashville HS
Nashville, AR

Britting, Stuart M
Greenwood Sr HS
Fort Smith, AR

Broadway, Jayme
Black Rock Jr Sr HS
Portia, AR

Broadway, Jennifer
Brinkley HS
Brinkley, AR

Brock, Britney M
Southside HS
Batesville, AR

Brock, Kelly
Atkins Schl
Atkins, AR

Brooks, Benjamin D
Crossett Sr HS
Crossett, AR

Brooks, Crystal
Bryant Sr HS
Benton, AR

Brooks, Edmund D
Dollarway HS
Pine Bluff, AR

Brooks, Yolanda P
Maynard Jr Sr HS
Maynard, AR

Brown, Amanda
Charleston HS
Charleston, AR

Brown, Billy D
Mills HS
Little Rock, AR

Brown, Brandon C
Arkansas Sr HS
Texarkana, AR

Brown, Bridget A
Central Sr HS
Little Rock, AR

Brown, Carleton H
Forrest City HS
Forrest City, AR

Brown, Jessica N
Mena HS
Mena, AR

Brown, Jody D
Crossett Sr HS
Crossett, AR

Brown, John L
Russellville Sr HS
Russellville, AR

Brown, Joshua B
Booneville Jr Sr HS
Booneville, AR

Brown, Misti L
Marked Tree Jr Sr HS
Marked Tree, AR

Brown, Natasha R
Northside HS
Fort Smith, AR

Brown, Nicholas A
Catholic HS
Little Rock, AR

Brown, Nikki D
Springdale Sr HS
Springdale, AR

Brown, Samantha A
Russellville Sr HS
Russellville, AR

Brown, Scott
Woodlawn Schl
Star City, AR

Brownfield, Brandi J
Greenwood Sr HS
Greenwood, AR

Bruce, Bonnie
Southside HS
Fort Smith, AR

Bruce, Chris D
Dierks HS
Dierks, AR

Brune, Trisha D
Bryant Sr HS
Alexander, AR

Bryant, Belinda A
Mills HS
Jacksonville, AR

Bryant, Clint D
Fountain Lake Jr Sr HS
Hot Springs Natio, AR

Bryant, Jacque
Crossett Sr HS
N Crossett, AR

Bryson, Erin L
Russellville Sr HS
London, AR

Buck, John
Rogers HS
Rogers, AR

Buckmaster,
Sonje Anne
Clarksville HS
Clarksville, AR

Buckner, Trintiy M
Crossett Sr HS
Crossett, AR

Buford, Kendra
Lee Sr HS
Lexa, AR

Bui, Ben
Southside HS
Fort Smith, AR

Buie, Amy R
Russellville Sr HS
Russellville, AR

Bulice, Jonathan R
Rose Bud Jr Sr HS
Rose Bud, AR

Bulloch, Chris
Central Sr HS
Little Rock, AR

Bump, Bart O
Lake Hamilton Sr HS
Royal, AR

Bumpers, Melodie P
Mc Crory Jr Sr HS
Mc Crory, AR

Burke, Casey L
Westside HS
Coal Hill, AR

Burkes, Andrea L
Southside HS
Fort Smith, AR

Burkhart, Amy L
Alma HS
Rudy, AR

Burkheart, Derick A
Corning HS
Corning, AR

Burks, Jaime L
Magnet Cove HS
Malvern, AR

Burnett, Brandt J
Mills HS
North Little Rock, AR

Burnett, Christie
West Side HS
Higden, AR

Burnett, Katrina D
Central Sr HS
Little Rock, AR

Burns, Krystal
Dewitt HS
De Witt, AR

Burns, Latoya L
Dumas HS
Dumas, AR

Burns, Marie D
Russellville Sr HS
Russellville, AR

Burnworth, Brandi M
Malvern Sr HS
Malvern, AR

Burrow, Tara
Calico Rock HS
Calico Rock, AR

Bussey, Shannan H
Berryville HS
Berryville, AR

Butcher, Justin
Lake Hamilton Jr HS
Hot Springs, AR

Butler, Ayana K
Hot Springs HS
Hot Springs, AR

Butler, Erika L
Sheridan Sr HS
Pine Bluff, AR

Butler, Gary
John L Mcclellan
Magnet HS
Little Rock, AR

Butler, Jennifer M
Springdale Sr HS
Springdale, AR

Butler, Tonikka S
Arkansas Sr HS
Texarkana, AR

Butterfield, Lori J
Yellville Summit HS
Yellville, AR

Buttrum, Kimberly M
Mountain Pine Jr
Sr HS
Mountain Pine, AR

Buzik, Alex
Rogers HS
Rogers, AR

Byington, Crystal D
Bryant Sr HS
Bryant, AR

Byrd, Mark
Nettleton HS
Jonesboro, AR

Cagle, Monica A
Clarksville HS
Clarksville, AR

Caldwell, Jake A
Junction City HS
Junction City, AR

Caldwell, Tanya M
Poyen Schl
Leola, AR

Caldwell, Trever
Hackett Schl
Fort Smith, AR

Calhoun, Leslie A
Jonesboro HS
Jonesboro, AR

Callaway, Susan G
Dierks HS
Dierks, AR

Camarillo, Diana E
Dequeen HS
De Queen, AR

Campbell, Annette M
Benton Sr HS
Benton, AR

Campbell, Jennifer
Bismarck Jr-Sr HS
Bismarck, AR

Campbell, Jordan T
Fountain Lake Jr Sr HS
Hot Springs Natl, AR

Campbell, Julie
Sylvan Hills HS
Sherwood, AR

Campbell, Robby
Bergman Schl
Harrison, AR

Camper, Nathaniel
Brinkley HS
Brinkley, AR

Canada, Tashanda
Pine Bluff HS
Pine Bluff, AR

Canard, Natalie
Mtn View HS
Mountain View, AR

Carbonero, Louis M
Monticello HS
Monticello, AR

Carden, De Wayne
East End Jr Sr HS
Bigelow, AR

Cardwell, Lauren A
Southside HS
Fort Smith, AR

Carey, Nicole J
Mills HS
Little Rock, AR

Cargile, Jamie
Nashville HS
Nashville, AR

Carle, Laura T
El Dorado Sr HS
El Dorado, AR

Carney, Penny
Hermitage Jr Sr HS
Warren, AR

Carroll, Alindria
Pine Bluff HS
Pine Bluff, AR

Carroll, Gina
Murfreesboro HS
Murfreesboro, AR

Carruth, Felicia Y
J A Fair Sr HS
Little Rock, AR

Carter, Almeita
Kimberly
Searcy HS
Searcy, AR

Carter, Amy A
Crossett Sr HS
Crossett, AR

Carter, Heather L
De Soto Schl
West Helena, AR

Carter, Jefferson C
Russellville Sr HS
Russellville, AR

Carter, Kimberly S
Parkview
Arts-Science HS
North Little Rock, AR

Carter, Kristy
North Little Rock
Hs-West
North Little Rock, AR

Carter, Troy A
Fairview HS
Camden, AR

Casteel, Amie L
Huntsville HS
Huntsville, AR

Casteel, Brandi
Bauxite Jr Sr HS
Bauxite, AR

Casteel, Keisha
Lee Acad
Marianna, AR

Caststeel, Johnny
Cotter Jr Sr HS
Gassville, AR

Cater, Kathleen E
Siloam Springs Sr HS
Siloam Springs, AR

Cates, Heather L
Bergman Schl
Harrison, AR

Cathcart, Nancy G
Greenwood Sr HS
Greenwood, AR

Cathey, Michelle
Warren Jr HS
Warren, AR

Catlett, Brandy L
Booneville Jr Sr HS
Booneville, AR

Cazzell, Jeff
Ft Smith Christian Schl
Fort Smith, AR

Chaffey, Travis P
Southside HS
Fort Smith, AR

Chamberlin, James A
Mena HS
Mena, AR

Chamberlin, Kristen L
Mena HS
Mena, AR

Chambers, Micah
Harmony Grove Jr
Sr HS
Camden, AR

Charleston, Angela L
Beebe Sr HS
Beebe, AR

Charlton, Jason K
Greenwood Sr HS
Greenwood, AR

Chatham, Emily R
Greenwood Sr HS
Fort Smith, AR

Chavarria, Trisha C
Fountain Lake Jr Sr HS
Hot Springs Natio, AR

Chavez, Amber C
Piggott HS
Piggott, AR

Cheatham, Lynsi
Hope HS
Hope, AR

Cheek, Leslee T
Dewitt HS
De Witt, AR

Chia, Anne M
Piggott HS
Piggott, AR

Chilcoat, Jason D
Ashdown Sr HS
Ashdown, AR

Childers, Elizabeth
Greenwood Sr HS
Greenwood, AR

Childers, Garrett
North Little Rock
Hs-East
North Little Rock, AR

Childress, Rocky A
Fouke Jr Sr HS
Fouke, AR

Choi, Sam Y
North Little Rock
Hs-West
North Little Rock, AR

Chrisp, Randy R
Rogers HS
Rogers, AR

Christenson, Jennifer
Harrison Sr HS
Harrison, AR

Christian, Jessica L
Southside HS
Fort Smith, AR

Christie, Sara J
Booneville Jr Sr HS
Booneville, AR

Christopher, Aaron
Cabot HS
Ward, AR

Christopher, Bronica L
John L Mcclellan
Magnet HS
Little Rock, AR

Christy, Nathan D
Springdale Sr HS
Springdale, AR

Chronister, Megen
Southside HS
Fort Smith, AR

Cingolani, Misty M
Mc Gehee HS
Mcgehee, AR

Claret, Roger A
Sheridan Sr HS
Pine Bluff, AR

Clark, Ashley
Walnut Ridge HS
Walnut Ridge, AR

Clark, Candace L
Mansfield Jr Sr HS
Booneville, AR

Clark, Erika P
Nettleton HS
Jonesboro, AR

Clark, Jeb S
Clarksville HS
Clarksville, AR

Clark, Kristy
Hackett Schl
Hackett, AR

Clark, Mandy M
Rogers HS
Rogers, AR

Clark, Michael J
Nettleton HS
Jonesboro, AR

Clark, Nikyia
Jonesboro HS
Jonesboro, AR

Clark, Shannon
Sulphur Rock Schl
Batesville, AR

Clark, Shannon N
Central Sr HS
Sherwood, AR

Clark, Summer
Paron Schl
Paron, AR

Clausing, Cameron P
Rogers HS
Rogers, AR

Clay, Billy J
Bryant Sr HS
Benton, AR

Clay, Kara D
Searcy HS
Searcy, AR

Clay, Renaldo
West Memphis Sr HS
Proctor, AR

Clay, Shavonda M
North Little Rock
Hs-East
Little Rock, AR

Cleghorn, Bridgett L
Horatio HS
Eagletown, OK

Clement, Casey
Rogers HS
Rogers, AR

Clement, Erin N
Jacksonville HS
Cabot, AR

Clement, Matt S
Lake Hamilton Sr HS
Pearcy, AR

Clement, Meghan J
Russellville Sr HS
Dardanelle, AR

Clements, Mark
Central Ark
Christian Schl
Sherwood, AR

Clemons, Andy C
Hope HS
Hope, AR

Clinkingbeard, Tami M
Russellville Sr HS
Russellville, AR

Clinton, Robert
Walnut Ridge HS
Walnut Ridge, AR

Closson, Jessica R
Dewitt HS
Crocketts Bluff, AR

Cloud, Brandy L
Harmony Grove Jr
Sr HS
Benton, AR

Cobb, Leslie
North Little Rock HS
N Little Rock, AR

Coble, Aaron K
Springdale Sr HS
Springdale, AR

Coburn, Shannon R
Mc Crory Jr Sr HS
Mc Crory, AR

Cochran, Amber Leann
Bryant Sr HS
Benton, AR

Cochran, Ashlea M
Russellville Sr HS
Russellville, AR

Cody, Ramanda F
Valley Springs Schl
Harrison, AR

Coe, Nicholas C
Cave City HS
Batesville, AR

Coffee, Jason D
Arkansas Sr HS
Texarkana, AR

Cogburn, Misty
Amity Jr Sr HS
Amity, AR

Coggins, Jeremy D
El Dorado Sr HS
El Dorado, AR

Cogshell, Kimberly J
J A Fair Sr HS
Little Rock, AR

Coker, Tracy
Pocahontas HS
Pocahontas, AR

Colbert, Jennifer R
Searcy HS
Searcy, AR

Cole, J Michael
Springdale Sr HS
Springdale, AR

Coleman, Jennifer
Mountainburg Jr Sr HS
Mountainburg, AR

Collie, Chris
Bismarck Jr-Sr HS
Donaldson, AR

Collie, Stephanie L
Malvern Sr HS
Malvern, AR

Collins, Jennifer L
Star City HS
Star City, AR

Collins, Julia G
Fayetteville Sr HS
Fayetteville, AR

Coltrane Jr, Ronald Douglas
Cabot HS
Ward, AR

Combs, Courtney
Mc Rae Schl
Searcy, AR

Combs, Jeramy
Bismarck Jr-Sr HS
Bismarck, AR

Condrey, Rachel A
John L Mcclellan Magnet HS
Little Rock, AR

Conley, Shaun P
England HS
Scott, AR

Connell, Casey
Batesville Sr HS
Batesville, AR

Connelly, Siobhan E
Ashdown Sr HS
Ashdown, AR

Contratto, Christy
Magnolia HS
Magnolia, AR

Conway, Kimberly L
White Hall Sr HS
Pine Bluff, AR

Cook, Brandy
Butterfield Jr HS
Van Buren, AR

Cook, David
Rogers HS
Conway, MO

Cook, Dianna M
Mena HS
Mena, AR

Cook, Katrina A
Oak Grove HS
North Little Rock, AR

Cook, Kyle L
Valley View HS
Jonesboro, AR

Cook, Misty
Southside HS
Fort Smith, AR

Cook, Rachel B
Sylvan Hills HS
Sherwood, AR

Cook, Rusell E
Arkansas Sr HS
Texarkana, AR

Cook, Stephanie
Sylvan Hills HS
Sherwood, AR

Cook, Wesley M
Magnolia HS
Fouke, AR

Cooksey, Samantha E
Springdale Sr HS
Springdale, AR

Coombe, Travis M
Bald Knob HS
Bald Knob, AR

Coonts, Cynthia N
Valley Springs Schl
Harrison, AR

Cooper, Brett A
Southside HS
Fort Smith, AR

Cooper, Camelia
Gurdon HS
Gurdon, AR

Cooper, Erica L
Dollarway HS
Pine Bluff, AR

Cooper, Jonathan D
Ridgecrest HS
Paragould, AR

Cooper, Lisa A
Springdale Sr HS
Springdale, AR

Cooper, Nicholas L
Van Buren Sr HS
Van Buren, AR

Cooper, Scotty E
Siloam Springs Sr HS
Siloam Springs, AR

Cooper, Terroy D
Sheridan Sr HS
Prattsville, AR

Cope, Leah R
Bergman Schl
Bergman, AR

Copelin, Priscilla G
Dumas HS
Dumas, AR

Corbell, Michael S
Ashdown Sr HS
Ben Lomond, AR

Cordell, Stacie L
Lake Hamilton Sr HS
Hot Springs, AR

Corley, Waylon T
Glen Rose HS
Malvern, AR

Cornelius, Misty C
Arkansas Sr HS
Texarkana, AR

Costner, Matt
Southside HS
Fort Smith, AR

Cotton, Joseph A
Arkansas Sr HS
Texarkana, AR

Couch, Jason
Van Buren Sr HS
Van Buren, AR

Courson, Amanda R
Crossett Sr HS
Crossett, AR

Courson, Jill D
Magnolia HS
Magnolia, AR

Covington, Katherine M
Cabot HS
Ward, AR

Cowan, Fredreca D
Palestine-Wheatley HS
Palestine, AR

Cowdery, Josh
Sylvan Hills HS
Sherwood, AR

Cowell, Jared
Lamar HS
Lamar, AR

Cowger, Scarlet L
Russellville Sr HS
Russellville, AR

Cox, Amanda B
Mt St Mary Acad
Maumelle, AR

Cox, Amy R
Bald Knob HS
Bald Knob, AR

Cox, Blair
Walnut Ridge HS
Walnut Ridge, AR

Cox, Bryen G
Beebe Sr HS
Mc Rae, AR

Cox, Christy C
Russellville Sr HS
Russellville, AR

Cox, Jolee R
Bald Knob HS
Bald Knob, AR

Cox, Kathy J
Corning HS
Corning, AR

Cox, Kristopher M
Alma HS
Alma, AR

Cox, Stephanie D
Bald Knob HS
Bald Knob, AR

Cox, Stephanie J
North Little Rock Hs-East
North Little Rock, AR

Cox, Teresea
Delight HS
Lexington, SC

Coyle, Camista D
Piggott HS
Piggott, AR

Crabtree, R K
Ridgecrest HS
Paragould, AR

Craft, Casey
Glenwood Jr Sr HS
Glenwood, AR

Crain, Benjamin J
Rogers HS
Rogers, AR

Crain, Katherine
Camden Fairview HS
Camden, AR

Crain, Rosalyn M
El Dorado Sr HS
El Dorado, AR

Crandell, Jenny
Pleasant View Schl
Mulberry, AR

Crane, Rebecca I
Southside HS
Fort Smith, AR

ARKANSAS

Cranford, Priscila G
Horatio HS
Horatio, AR

Crawford, Joshua
Fayetteville
Christian Schl
Lincoln, AR

Creacy, Tonya A
Watson Chapel Sr HS
Pine Bluff, AR

Creed, Phillip
West Side
Christian Schl
Magnolia, AR

Creekmore, Jamie C
Southside HS
Fort Smith, AR

Crenshaw, Angela D
Parkview
Arts-Science HS
Little Rock, AR

Crenshaw, Jeff D
Booneville Jr Sr HS
Magazine, AR

Crill, Morris
Humphrey Schl
Humphrey, AR

Critton, Myra
Magnolia HS
Magnolia, AR

Cross, Richie
Southside HS
Fort Smith, AR

Crow, Monica N
Sloan Hendrix HS
Pocahontas, AR

Crowell, Casey M
Van Buren Sr HS
Van Buren, AR

Crumley, Casandra
Forrest City HS
Forrest City, AR

Cullen, Mike J
Flippin Jr Sr HS
Flippin, AR

Cullins, Jane C
Jonesboro HS
Jonesboro, AR

Culpepper, Autumn
Lake Hamilton Jr HS
Hot Springs, AR

Culpepper, Daniel A
Arkansas Schl Math &
Science
Alexander, AR

Culpepper, Jason A
North Little Rock HS
Sherwood, AR

Cummings, Amanda C
Nevada Schl
Emmet, AR

Cummings, Kcristii
Rison HS
Rison, AR

Curbo, James R
Mc Crory Jr Sr HS
Mc Crory, AR

Cursh, Keisha
Arkansas Sr HS
Texarkana, AR

Curtis, Amber R
Lee Acad
Marianna, AR

Dailey, J Patrick
Marked Tree Jr Sr HS
Marked Tree, AR

Daniel, Allison
West Memphis
Christian Schl
West Memphis, AR

Daniel, Edwin E
Pine Bluff HS
Pine Bluff, AR

Daniel, Luke
Fairview HS
Camden, AR

Daniels, Darah L
Cutter Morning
Star HS
Hot Springs, AR

Daniels, Matt L
Harrison Sr HS
Harrison, AR

Darby, Jamie
Arkansas City Schl
Arkansas City, AR

Davenport, Dena
Dewitt HS
De Witt, AR

David, Cori
Pea Ridge HS
Pea Ridge, AR

Davidson, Corey M
Conway Sr HS
Conway, AR

Davis, Amanda
Dollarway HS
Pine Bluff, AR

Davis, Angela
West Memphis Sr HS
West Memphis, AR

Davis, Daniel C
Arkansas Sr HS
Texarkana, AR

Davis, Elecia D
Poyen Schl
Leola, AR

Davis, Erin M
West Memphis
Christian Schl
Memphis, TN

Davis, James O
Batesville Sr HS
Batesville, AR

Davis, Jason
Nashville HS
Nashville, AR

Davis, Jed
Beebe Jr HS
Beebe, AR

Davis, Jenifer
Pleasant View Schl
Ozark, AR

Davis, K Wesley
Paris HS
Paris, AR

Davis, Kara
Ft Smith Christian Schl
Fort Smith, AR

Davis, Kara A
El Dorado Sr HS
El Dorado, AR

Davis, Keith L
Gravette HS
Gravette, AR

Davis, Keri N
Crowleys Ridge Acad
Walnut Ridge, AR

Davis, Kristin L
Gosnell Jr Sr HS
Blytheville, AR

Davis, Laketra L
Crossett Sr HS
Crossett, AR

Davis, Mackenzie L
Ridgecrest HS
Paragould, AR

Davis, Stephanie
Crowleys Ridge Acad
Walnut Ridge, AR

Davis, Wesley
Wynne HS
Wynne, AR

Dawson, Gina M
Fountain Lake Jr Sr HS
Benton, AR

Day, Alicia
Perryville Jr Sr HS
Perryville, AR

Day, Chris L
Magnet Cove HS
Malvern, AR

Dayberry, Jenn
Springdale Sr HS
Springdale, AR

Deacon, Jennifer L
West Memphis Sr HS
West Memphis, AR

De Chaine, Jacob A
Siloam Springs Sr HS
Siloam Springs, AR

Deckard, Sarah
Lake Hamilton Jr HS
Pearcy, AR

Decker, Mary
Yellville Summit HS
Yellville, AR

De Clerk, Shea
Pocahontas HS
Pocahontas, AR

Dedmon, Nikki
R E Wells Jr HS
Greenwood, AR

De Laughter, Trinity K
Parkview
Arts-Science HS
Jacksonville, AR

Delee, Adam N
Lake Hamilton Sr HS
Hot Springs, AR

Denman, Monica
Little Rock Cntrl HS
Little Rock, AR

Dent, Angela
Jonesboro HS
Jonesboro, AR

Denton, Amanda L
Clarksville HS
Clarksville, AR

Denton, Regina A
Bentonville Sr HS
Bentonville, AR

Dever, Devron J
Cutter Morning Star Jr
Sr HS
Hot Springs, AR

Dewey, Russell J
Mountain Home HS
Mountain Home, AR

Dicker, Shandra L
Central Sr HS
Little Rock, AR

Dickerson, Chris
Oark HS
Oark, AR

Dickerson, Crystal
Mulberry HS
Mulberry, AR

Dickey, Jill
Central Ark
Christian Schl
North Little Rock, AR

Dickey, Ketrina
West Memphis Sr HS
West Memphis, AR

Dickey, Kimberley D
Highland HS
Ash Flat, AR

Dickey, Kinsey R
Fayetteville
Christian Schl
Fayetteville, AR

Diest, Lisa
Kirby HS
Glenwood, AR

Dietz, Nicole N
Piggott HS
Piggott, AR

Diggs, Trina D
Parkview
Arts-Science HS
Little Rock, AR

Dildine Jr, Ricky
Wynne HS
Wynne, AR

Dillion, Kevin L
Dewitt HS
De Witt, AR

Dingler, Audrey
Ouachita Jr Sr HS
Malvern, AR

Disel, Jamaica D
Decatur HS
Decatur, AR

Disney, Lianna O
Fayetteville
Christian Schl
Fayetteville, AR

Disterdick, Mindi
North Little Rock
Hs-West
North Little Rock, AR

Dixon, Denisha R
Strong Jr Sr HS
Strong, AR

Dixon, Rachel A
Arkansas Schl Math &
Science
Morristown, NJ

Do, Stacy
Hot Springs HS
Hot Springs, AR

Dobbs, Tracy
Dumas HS
Dumas, AR

Dodd, R Adam
Southside HS
Fort Smith, AR

Dodd, Regina A
Crossett Sr HS
Crossett, AR

Dollar Jr, Dow
Russellville Sr HS
Russellville, AR

Donelson, Shaylan A
Arkansas Sr HS
Texarkana, AR

Donham, Douglas C
Central Sr HS
North Little Rock, AR

Donovan, Shawn M
Searcy HS
Searcy, AR

Dorethy, Kelly A
Springdale Sr HS
Springdale, AR

Dorman, Casey
Prairie Grove HS
Prairie Grove, AR

Dorsey, Ashley
Berryville HS
Berryville, AR

Douglas, Bobby E
Lavaca Jr Sr HS
Lavaca, AR

Douglas, Brian L
Lavaca Jr Sr HS
Lavaca, AR

Dowdy, Kelly J
Southside HS
Batesville, AR

Downes, Rochelle M
Cabot HS
Cabot, AR

Drake, Chrislyn
Rogers HS
Rogers, AR

Drake, Sandra Lynn
Mountain Home HS
Mountain Home, AR

Draper III, Donald D
Booneville Jr Sr HS
Booneville, AR

Draughon, Meghan
Forest Heights Jr HS
Little Rock, AR

Driggs, Brandy
Bentonville Sr HS
Bentonville, AR

Ducker, Courtney N
Riverview HS
Searcy, AR

Duckworth, Staci R
Hot Springs HS
Hot Springs Natio, AR

Duggin, Gene K
Elkins Jr Sr HS
Fayetteville, AR

Duke, Matthew D
Monticello HS
Monticello, AR

Dunas, Rachiel A
J A Fair Sr HS
Little Rock, AR

Dunaway, Lane
Hughes Jr-Sr HS
Forrest City, AR

Duncan, Chris
Morrilton Sr HS
Morrilton, AR

Duncan, Faith E
Lake Hamilton Sr HS
Royal, AR

Duncan, Ginger
Lee Acad
Marianna, AR

Dunham, Curtis W
Scotland Schl
Scotland, AR

Dunkum, Angela C
Pine Bluff HS
Pine Bluff, AR

Dunlap, Vincent K
Conway Sr HS
Conway, AR

Dunn, Ashley D
Lavaca Jr Sr HS
Lavaca, AR

Dunn, Leslie
Bradford Jr Sr HS
Bradford, AR

Dupuy, Joshua C
Bald Knob HS
Bald Knob, AR

Dupuy, Robert W
Mann Magnet Jr HS
Maumelle, AR

Durham, Diana
Bradford Jr Sr HS
Bradford, AR

Durham, Lori M
Lake Hamilton Sr HS
Hot Springs, AR

Durham, Zachary M
Springdale Sr HS
Springdale, AR

Dussex, Elizabeth
Sheridan Sr HS
Sheridan, AR

Earleywine, Ashley
Little Rock Cntrl HS
Little Rock, AR

Eason, Drew
Walker Schl
Magnolia, AR

Easter, Floyd J
Bryant Sr HS
Mabelvale, AR

Easterling, Larae
Huntsville HS
Huntsville, AR

Echols, Susan M
Southside HS
Fort Smith, AR

Eckels, Maria A
Springdale Sr HS
Springdale, AR

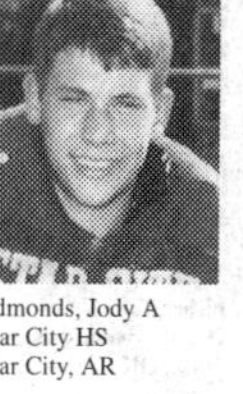
Edmonds, Jody A
Star City HS
Star City, AR

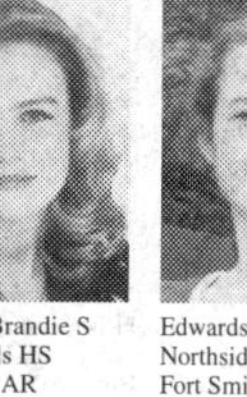
Edwards, Brandie S
Sylvan Hills HS
Sherwood, AR

Edwards, Brooke A
Northside HS
Fort Smith, AR

Edwards, Crandall D
Pine Bluff HS
Pine Bluff, AR

Edwards, Jemeca D
Pine Bluff HS
Pine Bluff, AR

Edwards, Jill
Northside HS
Fort Smith, AR

ARKANSAS

Edwards, Lauren L
Bald Knob HS
Bald Knob, AR

Edwards, Michael P
Valley Springs Schl
Harrison, AR

Edwards, Shelly
Poyen Schl
Poyen, AR

Efird, Allison E
Mc Gehee HS
Mc Gehee, AR

Eggert, Christina M
Mountain Home HS
Mountain Home, AR

Egleston, Ashlea J
Bauxite Jr Sr HS
Bauxite, AR

Egloff, Aimee
Van Buren Sr HS
Van Buren, AR

Eichelberger, Misty
Lamar HS
Knoxville, AR

Eifert, Kelly
Fayetteville Sr HS
Tontitown, AR

Eilbott, Lee E
Pine Bluff HS
Pine Bluff, AR

Elam, Amanda
Amity Jr Sr HS
Amity, AR

Elia, Ashur E
Mc Clellan HS
Little Rock, AR

Elkins, Renae L
Clarksville HS
Clarksville, AR

Elledge, Chris L
Pulaski Acad
Roland, AR

Ellery, Kerri
Northside HS
Fort Smith, AR

Ellis, Christi M
Smackover HS
El Dorado, AR

Ellison, Augustus G
Fairview HS
Camden, AR

Ellison, Patrick B
Mansfield Jr Sr HS
Huntington, AR

Elrod, Natalie G
North Little Rock
Hs-West
North Little Rock, AR

Elzey, Amanda C
West Memphis
Christian Schl
West Memphis, AR

Embry, Benjamin P
Atkins Schl
Atkins, AR

Emery, Amber
Newport HS
Newport, AR

Emmick, Michelle
Mountain Home HS
Mountain Home, AR

England, Kellie J
Searcy HS
Searcy, AR

Engle, James
Norphlet HS
Norphlet, AR

Engledowl, Christy
Genoa Cntrl HS
Fouke, AR

English, Christopher E
El Dorado Sr HS
El Dorado, AR

English, Jason W
Clarksville HS
Clarksville, AR

Ennis, Olivia C
Monticello HS
Monticello, AR

Ephlin, Beth
Rivercrest HS
Luxora, AR

Erwin, Michelle
Bergman Schl
Harrison, AR

Estep, Casey L
Van Buren Sr HS
Van Buren, AR

Estes, Cherrie
Calico Rock HS
Calico Rock, AR

Estes, Kelli D
Oden Schl
Sims, AR

Estes White, Tonya L
Drew Central Jr Sr HS
Wilmar, AR

Estoker, Chris
Sheridan Sr HS
Little Rock, AR

Ethridge, Billy
Bright Star Schl
Doddridge, AR

Eubanks, Andee
Hamburg HS
Hamburg, AR

Evans, Ellie
Prairie Grove HS
Prairie Grove, AR

Evans, Julie
North Little Rock
Hs-East
North Little Rock, AR

Evans, Syard G
Cty Line HS
Charleston, AR

Evans, Timothy Lloyd
El Dorado Sr HS
El Dorado, AR

Evans-Morgan, Randy
Southside HS
Fort Smith, AR

Everett, Roy P
Mena HS
Mena, AR

Ewbank, Christopher P
Rogers HS
Lowell, AR

Ezell, Darriel L
Searcy HS
Searcy, AR

Fagala, Phil
Crowleys Ridge Acad
Jonesboro, AR

Fagan, Talitha
Heber Springs HS
Drasco, AR

Fairless, Jodie L
Mena HS
Hatfield, AR

Fairley, Mariah T
El Dorado Sr HS
El Dorado, AR

Fannin, Jarrod R
Dierks HS
Dierks, AR

Fannon, Eric
Altus Denning HS
Altus, AR

Farmer, Kelly J
Booneville Jr Sr HS
Booneville, AR

Farmer,
Kimberly Dawn
Booneville Jr Sr HS
Booneville, AR

Feldman, Iris Jaynell
West Side
Christian Schl
El Dorado, AR

Fellows, Ryan
Bergman Schl
Harrison, AR

Ferguson III, Robert L
Booneville Jr Sr HS
Booneville, AR

Ferrari, Connie M
Bergman Schl
Harrison, AR

Fetz, Breihan
Sheridan Sr HS
Lewisville, TX

Finch, Lisa R
Beebe Sr HS
Beebe, AR

Fincher, Christie D
Springdale Sr HS
Springdale, AR

Finster, Carla M
Batesville Sr HS
Batesville, AR

Fischer, Kimberly A
Sheridan Sr HS
Hensley, AR

Fisher, Betsy
Wynne HS
Wynne, AR

Fisher, Justin
Spring Hill HS
Hope, AR

Fisher, Lori C
Ozark Adventist Acad
Tulsa, OK

Flemens, Angela C
Dierks HS
Newhope, AR

Fletcher, Kami L
Pine Bluff HS
Pine Bluff, AR

Floden, Loralei
Morrilton Sr HS
Plumerville, AR

Flory, Tiffany L
Russellville Sr HS
Russellville, AR

Floyd, Melanie V
Cabot HS
Cabot, AR

Floyd, Will
Hoxie Schl
Walnut Ridge, AR

Fluhart, Jonathan T
West Side
Christian Schl
El Dorado, AR

Foley, Heather
Gosnell Jr HS
Blytheville, AR

Folk, Michael A
Bald Knob HS
Bald Knob, AR

Foote, Jennifer
Winslow Schl
Winslow, AR

Forbes, Matthew L
Farmington Jr Sr HS
Farmington, AR

Ford, Brandi A
Russellville Sr HS
Russellville, AR

Foreman, Angela H
Bryant Sr HS
Benton, AR

Forsberg, Chaila R
Southside Schl
Damascus, AR

Foshee, Jayme E
Jessieville HS
Hot Springs Natio, AR

Foster, Charla
Central Ark
Christian Schl
North Little Rock, AR

Foster, Priscilla
Hope HS
Hope, AR

Foust, Sonya D
Ridgecrest HS
Paragould, AR

Fowler, Christie
Arkansas Schl Math &
Science
Atkins, AR

Fowler, Jennifer
Corning HS
Corning, AR

Fowler, Jon
Beebe Sr HS
Beebe, AR

Fox, Joel M
Jessieville Jr-Sr HS
Hot Springs, AR

Frady, Jonathan S
Horatio HS
Winthrop, AR

Fraley, Kandace L
Valley Springs Schl
Harrison, AR

France, Lena C
Alma HS
Mountainburg, AR

Francis, Jinger C
Trumann HS
Trumann, AR

Francis, Julie
Blytheville Sr HS
Blytheville, AR

Franks, Sandra N
Vilonia HS
Conway, AR

Frasher, Stephen Keith
Hartford Schl
Midland, AR

Frauenthal, Julie A
Springdale Sr HS
Fayetteville, AR

Frazer, Nicholas
Gosnell Jr Sr HS
Blytheville, AR

Frazier, Rodney
Fairview HS
Louann, AR

Frazier, Shannon M
Riverview HS
Floral, AR

Freeman, Brandi D
Oak Grove HS
N Little Rock, AR

Freeman, Melinda A
Russellville Sr HS
Russellville, AR

French, Lauri M
Mayflower HS
Mayflower, AR

French, Nick R
St Paul Schl
Combs, AR

Frix, Katie M
Russellville Sr HS
Russellville, AR

Frizzell, Jeff D
Clarksville HS
Clarksville, AR

Frizzell, Josalyn D
Dover HS
Vilonia, AR

Frost, Joshua L
Lee Acad
Marianna, AR

Fry, Kristin L
Nevada Schl
Emmet, AR

Fryar, Christina M
Rogers HS
Rogers, AR

Fryer, Jerry D
Ozark HS
Ozark, AR

Fuller, Michelle
Atkins Schl
Atkins, AR

Fuller, Octavia S
Mills HS
Maumelle, AR

Fults, Amy
Redfield Jr HS
Redfield, AR

Fureigh, Amanda K
Russellville Sr HS
London, AR

Furlow, Lindsay
Beebe Sr HS
Beebe, AR

Gabriel, Brandon J
Sylvan Hills HS
Sherwood, AR

Gabriel, William
Parkview
Arts-Science HS
North Little Rock, AR

Galgani, Samantha
Lakeside HS
Hot Springs, AR

Gallegly, Jason C
North Little Rock
Hs-West
North Little Rock, AR

Gallegos, Lydia
Hall Sr HS
Little Rock, AR

Gallegos, Tina M
Jacksonville HS
Jacksonville, AR

Galloway, Annie
Southside HS
Fort Smith, AR

Gammage, Damon H
Nevada Schl
Prescott, AR

Gann, Amanda
Beebe Sr HS
Beebe, AR

Garcia, Julie
Lake Hamilton Sr HS
Royal, AR

Gardner, Misha
Van Buren Sr HS
Van Buren, AR

Garland, Sara D
Corning HS
Corning, AR

Garrett, Anthony D
Alma HS
Alma, AR

Garrett, Grant W
Siloam Springs Sr HS
Siloam Springs, AR

Garris, Jared J
Mountain Home HS
Lakeview, AR

Gaskins, Jean Ann
Izard Co Cons Jr Sr HS
Horseshoe Bend, AR

Gatewood, Felicia R
Piggott HS
Piggott, AR

Gee, Kristyn M
John L Mcclellan
Magnet HS
Mabelvale, AR

Geisler, Amber K
Marvell Acad
Brinkley, AR

Gentry, Cristin M
Arkansas Sr HS
Texarkana, AR

Gentry, Gabe S
Searcy HS
Searcy, AR

George, Brandon
Butterfield Jr HS
Van Buren, AR

Gerber, Jennifer S
Lake Hamilton Sr HS
Hot Springs, AR

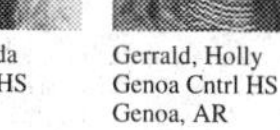
Gerrald, Amanda
Genoa Central HS
Genoa, AR

Gerrald, Holly
Genoa Cntrl HS
Genoa, AR

ARKANSAS

Gibby, Tessica C
Morrilton Sr HS
Morrilton, AR

Gibson, Jennifer L
Wynne HS
Wynne, AR

Gibson, Robert B
Monticello HS
Monticello, AR

Gifford, Shawna L
Crossett Sr HS
Crossett, AR

Gilbert, Nikki
Wynne HS
Wynne, AR

Gilbert, Stephanie
Southwest
Christian Acad
Mabelvale, AR

Giles, Chris
Lavaca Jr Sr HS
Lavaca, AR

Gill, Bobby
Bradley Jr Sr HS
Bradley, AR

Gilley, Lori
Yellville Summit HS
Yellville, AR

Gilliam, Brandi
Gosnell Jr HS
Blytheville, AR

Gilliam, Jenny
Gosnell Jr HS
Blytheville, AR

Gillis, Lori B
Jonesboro HS
Jonesboro, AR

Gillman, Julie A
Lake Hamilton Sr HS
Hot Springs, AR

Gillming, Dennis G
Gravette HS
Gravette, AR

Gilmore, Travis
Van Buren Sr HS
Van Buren, AR

Gilpin, Miranda B
Southside HS
Batesville, AR

Giurbino, Gina L
Springdale Sr HS
Springdale, AR

Givens, Eve L
Sheridan Sr HS
Sheridan, AR

Glandon,
Chavaughn M
Pangburn Jr Sr HS
Pangburn, AR

Glenn, Diane L
Rogers HS
Rogers, AR

Glenn, Stacy
Jonesboro HS
Jonesboro, AR

Glidewell, Bethany
Booneville Jr Sr HS
Booneville, AR

Glover, David Jason
North Little Rock
Hs-East
North Little Rock, AR

Glover, Sonya
Stephens Jr Sr HS
Stephens, AR

Goad, Angela
Nettleton HS
Jonesboro, AR

Gocke, Leighanne
Bryant Sr HS
Alexander, AR

Goddard, Felicia
Mansfield Jr Sr HS
Mansfield, AR

Godfrey, Aaron K
Springdale Sr HS
Springdale, AR

Godfrey, Travis L
Sylvan Hills HS
Sherwood, AR

Godwin, Gary L
Jessieville HS
Jessieville, AR

Goff, Bonnie I
Armorel HS
Armorel, AR

Goff, Jessica A
North Little Rock
Hs-West
North Little Rock, AR

Goffeney, David A
Lake Hamilton Sr HS
Hot Springs Natio, AR

Goforth, Justin
Mountain Home HS
Gamaliel, AR

Goines, Shawna
Oak Grove HS
Maumelle, AR

Goins, Randall T
Southside HS
Fort Smith, AR

Golden, Tara A
Lake Hamilton Sr HS
Hot Springs Natio, AR

Golightly, Holly
Norfork Jr Sr HS
Norfork, AR

Golston, Avery
Saratoga Schl
Washington, AR

Gonzales, Michael
East Poinsett Sr HS
Lepanto, AR

Goodman, Michael W
Lonoke Sr HS
Jacksonville, AR

Goodsell, Jane
Warren Sr HS
Warren, AR

Goodsell, Sally
Warren Jr HS
Warren, AR

Goodson, Kelly L
Robinson HS
Little Rock, AR

Goodwin, Amanda
Bradford Jr Sr HS
Newark, AR

Goodwin, Ronald J
North Little Rock
Hs-West
Sherwood, AR

Gosnell, Amber P
Russellville Sr HS
Russellville, AR

Goss, Samantha A
Mountain Home HS
Mountain Home, AR

Gottsponer, Erin M
St Joseph HS
North Little Rock, AR

Graddy, Erica L
Valley Springs Schl
Harrison, AR

Graddy, Josh B
Valley Springs Schl
Harrison, AR

Gragg, Adrianna K
Monticello HS
Monticello, AR

Graham, Jenny L
El Dorado Sr HS
El Dorado, AR

Grant, Perry C
Fairview HS
Camden, AR

Graves, Bethany K
Dewitt HS
De Witt, AR

Graves, Melinda D
Mc Crory Jr Sr HS
Mc Crory, AR

Gray, Brad L
Ridgecrest HS
Paragould, AR

Gray, Karen B
Southside HS
Batesville, AR

Gray, Mary Beth E
North Little Rock
Hs-East
North Little Rock, AR

Grayson, John A
Bald Knob HS
Bald Knob, AR

Green, Brittani
Malvern Jr HS
Malvern, AR

Green, Felicia Nacole
Gosnell Jr Sr HS
Gosnell, AR

Green, Holly
Jessieville HS
Hot Springs, AR

Green, Katadra D
Parkview
Arts-Science HS
Little Rock, AR

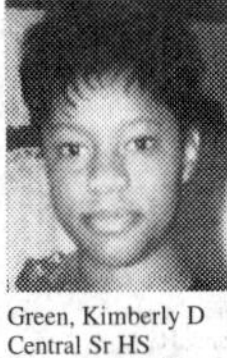
Green, Kimberly D
Central Sr HS
Little Rock, AR

Green, Roderick N
El Dorado Sr HS
El Dorado, AR

Greene, Heather M
Arkansas Sr HS
Texarkana, AR

Greene, Randall H
Arkansas Sr HS
Texarkana, AR

Greer, Jamie E
Russellville Sr HS
Russellville, AR

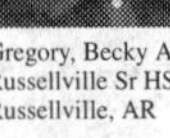
Gregory, Becky A
Russellville Sr HS
Russellville, AR

Gregory, Laura K
Sylvan Hills HS
Sherwood, AR

Gresham, Nancy M
Crossett Sr HS
Crossett, AR

Griffin, Melinda A
Lavaca Jr Sr HS
Lavaca, AR

Griffin, Troy V
Taylor HS
Stamps, AR

Griffis, Lindsay L
White Co Central Schl
Judsonia, AR

Griffith, Griff M
De Soto Schl
Elaine, AR

Grisham, Alisha R
Alpena Schl
Alpena, AR

Gross, Kristin
Marion HS
Marion, AR

Groves, Regina
Omaha Schl
Omaha, AR

Groves, Tracy C
Highland HS
Hardy, AR

Grubbs, Mary F
De Soto Schl
West Helena, AR

Grundy, Alfreda
Arkansas City Schl
Arkansas City, AR

Gryka, Bryan J
Catholic HS
Little Rock, AR

Gubanski, Laura A
Oak Grove HS
North Little Rock, AR

Gudgeon, Rebecca A
Mountainburg Jr Sr HS
Mountainburg, AR

Guenther, Arline
Oark HS
Oark, AR

Guist, Jered M
Prairie Grove HS
Prairie Grove, AR

Gulley, Shea L
Melbourne HS
Melbourne, AR

Gunnells, Tomika D
Conway Sr HS
Bigelow, AR

Gunnels, Rebecca J
Cabot HS
Cabot, AR

Haddox, Carrie
Glen Rose HS
Benton, AR

Haga, Kimberly A
Booneville Jr Sr HS
Booneville, AR

Hagler, Latisha D
Berryville HS
Berryville, AR

Haile, Jennifer L
Heber Springs HS
Heber Springs, AR

Halferty, Victoria
North Little Rock
Hs-East
North Little Rock, AR

Hall, Ashley D
Corning HS
Peach Orchard, AR

Hall, Courtney L
Sylvan Hills HS
North Little Rock, AR

Hall, Karen Le Ann
Morrilton Sr HS
Plumerville, AR

Hall, Rachel
Prairie Grove HS
Prairie Grove, AR

Hall, Sean C
Hall Sr HS
Little Rock, AR

Hall, Sheri Michelle
Sylvan Hills HS
North Little Rock, AR

Haller, Jennifer R
Mazazine HS
Booneville, AR

Hallman, Charity
Dermott HS
Dermott, AR

Halpine, Michael R
Bryant Sr HS
Alexander, AR

Ham, David G
Dewitt HS
De Witt, AR

Hamby, Jennifer L
Mountain Home HS
Mountain Home, AR

Hamilton, Amanda S
Cutter Morning
Star HS
Hot Springs, AR

Hamilton, Jamie E
Crossett Sr HS
Crossett, AR

Hammer, Justin C
Fayetteville Sr HS
Fayetteville, AR

Hammons, Austin
Abundant Life Schools
North Little Rock, AR

Hampton, Deszama D
El Dorado Sr HS
El Dorado, AR

Hampton, Shawna R
Biggers-Reyno HS
Biggers, AR

Hanaway, Christen R
Sloan Hendrix HS
Poughkeepsie, AR

Handley, Africa
Dermott HS
Dermott, AR

Handley, Charley
Shane
Bryant Sr HS
Benton, AR

Hanley, Beth
Calico Rock HS
Pineville, AR

Hansen, Amanda
Cave City HS
Cave City, AR

Hardcastle, Brandon
Oak Grove HS
Maumelle, AR

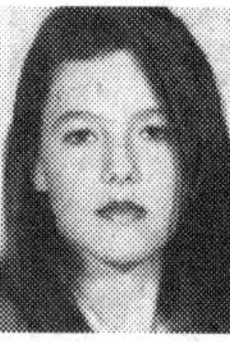
Hardin, Cynthia R
Northside HS
Barling, AR

Harelson, Kristen
Russellville Sr HS
Russellville, AR

Hargett, Kristin
Arkansas Bapt Schl
Little Rock, AR

Harmon, J C
Caddo Hills Jr Sr HS
Bonnerdale, AR

Harmon, Lori M
Hope HS
Hope, AR

Harp, Sarah
Brookland Jr Sr HS
Jonesboro, AR

Harper, Sandra K
Star City HS
Star City, AR

Harrell, Leah S
El Dorado Sr HS
El Dorado, AR

Harrelson, Patrick
Warren Jr HS
Warren, AR

Harris, Cami
Marion HS
Marion, AR

Harris, Cecil W
Searcy HS
Searcy, AR

Harris, Corie L
Magnolia HS
Magnolia, AR

Harris, Kristy R
Pea Ridge HS
Pea Ridge, AR

Harris, Mandy
Dumas Jr HS
Dumas, AR

Harris, Mary A
Rogers HS
Rogers, AR

Harris, Natosha T
Lake Hamilton Sr HS
Royal, AR

Harrison, Amber N
Bauxite Jr Sr HS
Bauxite, AR

Harrison, Bethany
Alma HS
Alma, AR

Harrison, Juanita
Pine Bluff HS
Pine Bluff, AR

Harrison, M Stephen
Lakeside HS
Hot Springs, AR

Hart, Christie L
Morrilton Sr HS
Morrilton, AR

Hart, John
Watson Chapel Sr HS
Pine Bluff, AR

ARKANSAS

Hart, Michael A
Corning Jr Sr HS
Success, AR

Hart, Tamara S
Springdale Sr HS
Fayetteville, AR

Hart, Tara L
Greenwood Sr HS
Greenwood, AR

Hartman, Ben
Greenbrier HS
Greenbrier, AR

Harvey, David C
Highland HS
Cherokee Village, AR

Harvill, Tonya
Humphrey Schl
Humphrey, AR

Harwood, Leigh E
Huntsville HS
Huntsville, AR

Haslip, Mary K
Beebe Sr HS
Beebe, AR

Hastings, Cody
Nevada Schl
Rosston, AR

Hatch, Michael
Gosnell Jr Sr HS
Gosnell, AR

Hatfield, Joseph M
Catholic HS
Little Rock, AR

Hatfield, Kristy R
Huntsville HS
Huntsville, AR

Hatfield, Wendy
Prairie Grove HS
Prairie Grove, AR

Hathcoat, Melissa
Mansfield Jr Sr HS
Mansfield, AR

Hawkins, Joseph A
Pine Bluff HS
Pine Bluff, AR

Hawkins, Talesia
Camden-Fairview HS
Camden, AR

Hawley, Tia M
Trumann HS
Trumann, AR

Hayes, Kitina
North Pulaski HS
Jacksonville, AR

Hayes, Sara E
Crossett Sr HS
Crossett, AR

Hayes, Stacy
Monticello HS
Monticello, AR

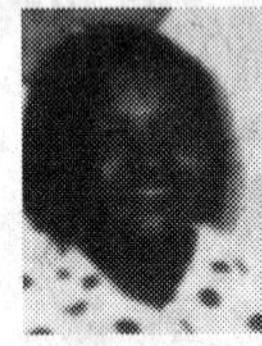
Haynes, Latonya
Newport HS
Newport, AR

Haynes, Tosh I
Alma Sr HS
Park Hill, OK

Hays, Angela M
Central Sr HS
Little Rock, AR

Hazlewood, Quiara M
Westside HS
Bono, AR

Heagwood, Tiffany L
De Soto Schl
Helena, AR

Heard, Cassey
Lake Hamilton Sr HS
Hot Springs, AR

Heard, Jefferson R
Mills HS
Sherwood, AR

Heard, Karla G
Greenwood Sr HS
Greenwood, AR

Hearne, Amanda
Atkins Schl
Atkins, AR

Hearnsberger, Jan
Arkansas Bapt Schl
Little Rock, AR

Hecke, Geoffrey Scott
Malvern Sr HS
Malvern, AR

Hefner, Justine C
Lake Hamilton Sr HS
Pearcy, AR

Heisler, Lauri
Wynne HS
Wynne, AR

Helmick, Robert W
Blevins HS
Prescott, AR

Helms, Cynthia N
White Co Central Schl
Judsonia, AR

Helms, Sharee N
Mansfield Jr Sr HS
Mansfield, AR

Helton, Mellena G
Magazine Jr Sr HS
Magazine, AR

Henderson, Allison
Central Ark
Christian Schl
Little Rock, AR

Henderson, Zack
Fayetteville Sr HS
Fayetteville, AR

Hendricks, Amy D
Stuttgart Sr HS
Stuttgart, AR

Hendricks, William L
Russellville Sr HS
Russellville, AR

Hendrix, Amy J
Bergman Schl
Harrison, AR

Hendrix, Clay
Bergman Schl
Harrison, AR

Hendrix, Joshua T
Russellville Sr HS
Russellville, AR

Henry, Brett
Southside HS
Fort Smith, AR

Henry, Kirsten
Pulaski Acad
Little Rock, AR

Hensley, Brandy N
Rivercrest HS
Wilson, AR

Henson, Heather D
Central HS
West Helena, AR

Herrin, Jason
Fayetteville Sr HS
Fayetteville, AR

Herrington, Orenda M
Star City HS
Star City, AR

Herrmann, Shannon R
Southside HS
Fort Smith, AR

Herron, Daniel
Lee Acad
Marianna, AR

Hertenstein, Stefanie
Greenbrier HS
Greenbrier, AR

Hess, Daniel P
Heber Springs HS
Heber Springs, AR

Hess, Joel
Sheridan Sr HS
Sheridan, AR

Hester, Woody A
Hartford Schl
Hartford, AR

Hewett, Marisha
Henderson Magnet
Jr HS
Little Rock, AR

Heydenreich, Stacy L
Mansfield Jr Sr HS
Mansfield, AR

Hickam, Jordan
Lake Hamilton Jr HS
Hot Springs, AR

Hickerson, Amber L
Piggott HS
Piggott, AR

Hickerson, Shanda
Humphrey Schl
Humphrey, AR

Hicks, Marisa
Greenwood Sr HS
Fort Smith, AR

Hicks, Stephany K
Sheridan Sr HS
Little Rock, AR

Hicks, Tricia S
Parkview Arts/Sci
Magnet HS
North Little Rock, AR

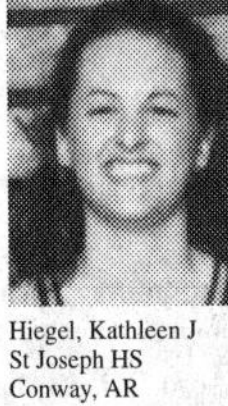
Hiegel, Kathleen J
St Joseph HS
Conway, AR

Higginbotham, Leslie J
Cabot HS
Cabot, AR

Highsmith, Terrye A
Fairview HS
Camden, AR

Hill, Amber J
Eureka Springs Jr
Sr HS
Eureka Springs, AR

Hill, Christopher D
Central Arkansas
Christian HS
Jacksonville, AR

Hill, Dustin J
Dierks HS
Newhope, AR

Hill, Jason
Brinkley HS
Brinkley, AR

Hill, Jeremy D
Valley Springs Schl
Valley Springs, AR

Hill, Lynn
Arkansas Bapt Schl
Little Rock, AR

Hill, Stephanie R
Morrilton Sr HS
Morrilton, AR

Hill, Virginia E
Central Ark
Christian Schl
Jacksonville, AR

Hill, Wesley A
Trumann HS
Trumann, AR

Hillhouse, Alissa
Taylor HS
Taylor, AR

Hilton, Brandi
Bradley Jr Sr HS
Bradley, AR

Hines, Amanda M
Taylor HS
Taylor, AR

Hinsley, Jill M
Jacksonville HS
Jacksonville, AR

Hinterthuer, Adam M
Harrison Sr HS
Harrison, AR

Hippler, Alisha
Bryant Sr HS
Bryant, AR

Hitchcock, Shay
Gosnell Jr Sr HS
Blytheville, AR

Hobbs, Sally K
Alma HS
Alma, AR

Hobby, Pamela R
Benton Sr HS
Benton, AR

Hobby, Patricia A
Sheridan Sr HS
Mabelvale, AR

Hodge, Tabitha L
Lead Hill Schl
Lead Hill, AR

Hoffman, Lisa
Southside HS
Fort Smith, AR

Hogan, Erin
Gosnell Jr Sr HS
Blytheville, AR

Hogan, Nathan M
Trumann HS
Trumann, AR

Hogner, Melody
Farmington Jr Sr HS
Farmington, AR

Hogue, Mary K
Southside HS
Fort Smith, AR

Hoke, Tracy L
Springdale Sr HS
Springdale, AR

Holladay, Meggan
Sheridan Sr HS
Sheridan, AR

Holland, Brandi N
North Little Rock
Hs-West
North Little Rock, AR

Holland, Emily A
Springdale Sr HS
Springdale, AR

Holland Jr, Jimmie
Wayne
Benton Sr HS
Benton, AR

Holland, Matthew G
Cty Line HS
Branch, AR

Holleman, Brandi
Nicole
Sheridan Sr HS
Hensley, AR

Holloway, Amanda M
Star City HS
Star City, AR

Holloway, Christina J
Bryant Sr HS
Benton, AR

Holman, Jeff A
Springdale Sr HS
Springdale, AR

Holmes, Amy S
Harrison Sr HS
Harrison, AR

Holmes, Jennifer N
Dewitt HS
De Witt, AR

Holt, Amber C
Mc Gehee HS
Mcgehee, AR

Holthoff, Jay
Dumas HS
Dumas, AR

Honnoll, Bethany
Valley View HS
Jonesboro, AR

Hooker, Tara E
Trumann HS
Trumann, AR

Hooper, Jessica R
Southside HS
Batesville, AR

Hoover, Amanda C
Berryville HS
Berryville, AR

Hooves, Jill
J A Fair Sr HS
Little Rock, AR

Hopkins, Jennifer E
Sheridan Sr HS
Sheridan, AR

Hopkins Jr, Jesse
Rogers HS
Rogers, AR

Hopkins, John
Coleman Jr HS
Van Buren, AR

Hopkins, Kim
Van Buren Sr HS
Van Buren, AR

Hoppe, Justin L
Crowleys Ridge Acad
Paragould, AR

Hoppe, Richard
Catholic HS
Little Rock, AR

Hopper, Lindsay
Southside HS
Fort Smith, AR

Hopson, Amy Ann
Star City HS
Star City, AR

Horine, Lyndell
Cheston
Springdale Sr HS
Springdale, AR

Horn, Jennifer E
Russellville Sr HS
Russellville, AR

Horn, Ramsey M
Southside HS
Fort Smith, AR

Horne, Gena
Prairie Grove HS
Prairie Grove, AR

Horton, Rachael
Mena HS
Mena, AR

Hoseason, Charles
Watson Chapel Sr HS
Pine Bluff, AR

Hosey, Bonnie K
Marvell Acad
Marvell, AR

Hosman, Josh A
Quitman Jr Sr HS
Quitman, AR

Houchins, Tara L
Jacksonville HS
Jacksonville, AR

House, Jenny L
Mt St Mary Acad
Little Rock, AR

Houser, Dedra N
England HS
England, AR

Howard, Ami M
Northside HS
Fort Smith, AR

Howard, Angela
Blytheville Sr HS
Blytheville, AR

Howell, Brandy S
Magnolia HS
Magnolia, AR

Howell III, John Carl
Conway Sr HS
Conway, AR

Hubertus, Rachel
Strong Jr Sr HS
Strong, AR

Huckleberry, Tina
Marie
Rogers HS
Rogers, AR

Huddleston, Lisa
White Hall Sr HS
Pine Bluff, AR

Hudlow, Andrea M
Russellville Sr HS
Russellville, AR

Hudson, Aaron D
Drew Central Jr Sr HS
Monticello, AR

Hudson, Heather
Nettleton HS
Jonesboro, AR

Hudson, Matt S
Springdale Sr HS
Springdale, AR

Hudson, Megan J
Southside HS
Fort Smith, AR

Hudson, Michael A
Delaplaine Schl
O Kean, AR

Hudson, Nina
Greenland Jr Sr HS
Fayetteville, AR

Hudson, Shane
Rivercrest HS
Osceola, AR

Huett, Leanne N
Morrilton Sr HS
Morrilton, AR

Huff Jr, Matthew
Mammoth Spring HS
Mammoth Spring, AR

Huffman, Ashley N
Southside HS
Fort Smith, AR

Huffstutter, Elizabeth M
West Memphis Christian Schl
West Memphis, AR

Huffstutter, Paul J
West Memphis Christian Schl
West Memphis, AR

Huffstuttler, Mollie
Calvary Christian Schl
Colt, AR

Hughey, Lance
Gosnell Jr Sr HS
Blytheville, AR

Hull, Chessica
Bryant Sr HS
Benton, AR

Hunt, Adam S
Corning HS
Corning, AR

Hunt, Marcus D
Ridgecrest HS
Paragould, AR

Hussain, Raza
Pine Bluff HS
Pine Bluff, AR

Hutson, Melissa
Mammoth Spring HS
Mammoth Spring, AR

Huynh, An T
Central Sr HS
Little Rock, AR

Huynh, Anna N
Marked Tree Jr Sr HS
Marked Tree, AR

Hyde, Amie
Ridgecrest HS
Paragould, AR

Infalt, April
Hackett Schl
Hackett, AR

Ingold, Amy
Lee Sr HS
Marianna, AR

Inman, Briana D
Alma HS
Alma, AR

Inman, Geoffrey R
Searcy HS
Kohler, WI

Irwin, Jill S
Central Sr HS
Little Rock, AR

Isacksen, Katie R
St Joe Public Schl
Saint Joe, AR

Isom, Heather M
Jonesboro HS
Jonesboro, AR

Ivey, Mary
Warren Jr HS
Warren, AR

Ivy, Christie K
Weiner HS
Weiner, AR

Iwatsuru, Nikki J
Bismarck Jr-Sr HS
Amity, AR

Jack, Madalyn
Bradley Jr Sr HS
Bradley, AR

Jacks, Ashley
Jack Robey Jr HS
Pine Bluff, AR

Jackson, Benjamin E
Mansfield Jr Sr HS
Booneville, AR

Jackson, Chicketta L
Conway Sr HS
Conway, AR

Jackson II, Dennis D
Parkview HS
Jacksonville, AR

Jackson, Heather M
Benton Cty Christian School
Pineville, MO

Jackson, Jamie
Nashville HS
Nashville, AR

Jackson, Mary Ann
Mt St Mary Acad
Little Rock, AR

Jackson, Melanie D
Mills HS
Little Rock, AR

Jackson, Tiffany P
Hope HS
Hope, AR

Jackson, Tonya A
Mc Crory Jr Sr HS
Mc Crory, AR

Jakus, Christina H
Sheridan Sr HS
Sheridan, AR

James, Amanda J
Bryant HS
Benton, AR

James, Carrie R
Pulaski Acad
Little Rock, AR

James, Christina M
Sylvan Hills HS
North Little Rock, AR

James, David W
Huntsville HS
Huntsville, AR

James, Jason D
Mt Ida Jr Sr HS
Story, AR

James, Renee D
Dequeen HS
De Queen, AR

Jansen, John A
Greenwood Sr HS
Fort Smith, AR

Jansen, Michael R
Catholic HS
Sherwood, AR

Jarrell, Christopher S
Oak Grove HS
Maumelle, AR

Jasmin, Aubrey N
Mena HS
Mena, AR

Jeffrey, Carma
Newark Jr Sr HS
Newark, AR

Jenkins, Amanda
Calico Rock HS
Calico Rock, AR

Jenkins, Elizabeth D
Central Sr HS
Little Rock, AR

Jenkins, Jeff B
Central Ark Christian Schl
Little Rock, AR

Jennings, Chrissy L
Mills HS
North Little Rock, AR

Jennings, Christopher S
Van Buren Sr HS
Van Buren, AR

Jeter, Joshua D
Bismarck Jr-Sr HS
Malvern, AR

Jeter, W Brandon
Crossett Sr HS
Crossett, AR

Jewell, Jeremy
Arkansas Schl Math & Science
Benton, AR

Jobe, Temple L
Lake Hamilton Sr HS
Royal, AR

Johns, Christian J
Springdale Sr HS
Springdale, AR

Johnson, Amanda
Cabot HS
Cabot, AR

Johnson, Amanda D
Biggers-Reyno HS
Corning, AR

Johnson, Chris S
Mena HS
Mena, AR

Johnson, Daniel P
Russellville Sr HS
Russellville, AR

Johnson, Frances K
Cty Line HS
Ozark, AR

Johnson, Halie J
Calvary Christian Schl
Forrest City, AR

Johnson, Holly
Jessieville HS
Mountain Pine, AR

Johnson, Ja Juan S
Osceola HS
Osceola, AR

Johnson, Jamie
West Side
Christian Schl
El Dorado, AR

Johnson, Jennifer J
St Paul Schl
Witter, AR

Johnson, Kristy
Southside HS
Fort Smith, AR

Johnson, Matthew S
Magnolia HS
Magnolia, AR

Johnson, Melissa J
Pine Bluff HS
Pine Bluff, AR

Johnson, Michael
Mountainburg Jr Sr HS
Mountainburg, AR

Johnson, Mindy
Ashdown Jr HS
Ashdown, AR

Johnson, Natalie N
North Little Rock
Hs-East
Little Rock, AR

Johnson, Natalie S
Piggott HS
Piggott, AR

Johnson, Nicholas S
Magnolia HS
Magnolia, AR

Johnson, Patrice R
Booneville Jr Sr HS
Booneville, AR

Johnson, Ryan L
Searcy HS
Searcy, AR

Johnson, Tabitha S
Holly Grove HS
Holly Grove, AR

Johnson, Taj A
Elkins Jr Sr HS
Fayetteville, AR

Johnson Jr, Wallace L
Magnolia HS
Magnolia, AR

Johnsons, Felicia L
Fountain Lake Jr Sr HS
Hot Springs Natio, AR

Johnston, Chris H
Searcy HS
Rose Bud, AR

Johnston, Christian D
Atkins Schl
Atkins, AR

Johnston, Laura L
Robinson HS
Little Rock, AR

Johnston, Stephanie
Lakeside HS
Hot Springs, AR

Johnston, Timothy J
Oak Grove HS
Maumelle, AR

Jones, Ashley L
Forrest City HS
Forrest City, AR

Jones, Brandon
Lee Acad
Palestine, AR

Jones, Cindy
Southside HS
Fort Smith, AR

Jones, Crystal
Central HS
West Helena, AR

Jones, David L
Beebe Sr HS
Beebe, AR

Jones, Deon
Dumas HS
Dumas, AR

Jones, Holly R
De Soto Schl
Helena, AR

Jones, Jerrod M
Hope HS
Hope, AR

Jones, Joanelle L
John L Mcclellan
Magnet HS
Little Rock, AR

Jones, Joshua E
Jessieville HS
Mountain Pine, AR

Jones, Karen M
Russellville Sr HS
London, AR

Jones, Kristi J
Crossett Sr HS
Crossett, AR

Jones, Lakesha
Hope HS
Hope, AR

Jones, Melissa D
Russellville Sr HS
Russellville, AR

Jones, Nathan A
Jessieville HS
Hot Springs Natio, AR

Jones, Nick
Southwest
Christian Acad
Mabelvale, AR

Jones, Taneadra
Lee Sr HS
Marianna, AR

Jones, Tasha D
Biggers-Reyno HS
Biggers, AR

Jones, Teya M
Alma HS
Alma, AR

Jordan, Stacie D
Fordyce HS
Fordyce, AR

Joyce, David T
Van Buren Sr HS
Alma, AR

Kaney, Melissa L
Fountain Lake Jr Sr HS
Hot Springs, AR

Karn, Tiffany M
Cutter Morning
Star HS
Hot Springs, AR

Karnes, James E
Trumann HS
Trumann, AR

Karr, Jared K
Dequeen HS
De Queen, AR

Karschner, Jennifer
Newport HS
Newport, AR

Karwoski, Melinda B
Russellville Sr HS
Russellville, AR

Kassees, Natalie
Sylvan Hills HS
Sherwood, AR

Kaulfurst, Michael A
Gosnell Jr Sr HS
Blytheville, AR

Kee, Amanda R
Clarendon Jr Sr HS
Monroe, AR

Keeling, Amanda Gail
Rogers HS
Rogers, AR

Keen, Kristie D
Springdale Sr HS
Springdale, AR

Keener, Tiffaney
North Little Rock
Hs-East
North Little Rock, AR

Keeter, Eric T
Lavaca Jr Sr HS
Lavaca, AR

Keeter, Jessica J
Valley Springs Schl
Harrison, AR

Keithly, Sabrina
Omaha Schl
Omaha, AR

Keller, Justin P
Russellville Sr HS
Russellville, AR

Kemp, Audra L
Mountain Home HS
Mountain Home, AR

Kersh, William G
Valley Springs Schl
Harrison, AR

Ketchum, April B
Russellville Sr HS
Russellville, AR

Ketron, Nikki
Calico Rock HS
Calico Rock, AR

Khamis, Rommy M
John L Mcclellan
Magnet HS
Little Rock, AR

Kilbreath, Marcus G
Corning HS
Mc Dougal, AR

Kilburn, Justin
Dumas HS
Dumas, AR

Kilgore, Jason
Jasper HS
Jasper, AR

Killian, Candina D
Mena HS
Kirby, AR

Kimbrell, Karen
Morion HS
West Memphis, AR

Kimery, Todd
Murfreesboro HS
Murfreesboro, AR

ARKANSAS

King, Alisha
Delta Special Schl
Tillar, AR

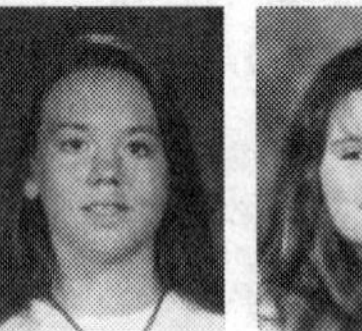
King, Arwen
Beebe Jr HS
Beebe, AR

King, Dorrie L
Russellville Sr HS
Russellville, AR

King, Dustin
De Soto Schl
West Helena, AR

King V, James B
Parkers Chapel Schl
El Dorado, AR

King, James L
Central HS
Helena, AR

King, Jeff S
Harrison Sr HS
Harrison, AR

King, Jon D
Arkansas Schl Math & Science
Wynne, AR

King, Kyla A
Clarksville HS
Clarksville, AR

King, Laura L
Ft Smith Christian Schl
Van Buren, AR

King, Yolanda R
Central HS
Helena, AR

Kinney, Kimberly A
Arkansas Sr HS
Texarkana, AR

Kirby, Angela K
Cty Line HS
Barling, AR

Kirk, Colin W
Sloan Hendrix HS
Ravenden, AR

Kirk, David P
Springdale Sr HS
Springdale, AR

Kirk, Mary Amanda
Morrilton Sr HS
Morrilton, AR

Kirtley, Jennifer
Oak Grove HS
North Little Rock, AR

Kitchens, James
Lewisville HS
Lewisville, AR

Kivell, William D
Catholic HS
Little Rock, AR

Kizer, Angela A
Southside HS
Fort Smith, AR

Kizer, Tara J
Southside HS
Fort Smith, AR

Kleinmenz, Sarah
Hot Springs HS
Hot Springs, AR

Knight, Danielle L
Dardanelle HS
Dardanelle, AR

Knighton, Terrance M
North Little Rock Hs-East
North Little Rock, AR

Knipscheer, Christine E
Conway Sr HS
Conway, AR

Knobloch, Jason
Southside HS
Fort Smith, AR

Koch, Joylyn D
Heritage Christian Schl
Little Rock, AR

Koehler, Tammy C
North Little Rock Hs-West
North Little Rock, AR

Kondo, Shinji
Pine Bluff HS
Pine Bluff, AR

Kourakis, Jason R
Cave City HS
Cave City, AR

Kramer, Ashley L
Southside HS
Rosie, AR

Kratochvil, Joey
Calico Rock HS
Pineville, AR

Kretz, Jeremy D
Nevada Schl
Rosston, AR

Krisanits, Rey
Green Forest Jr Sr HS
Green Forest, AR

Krouse, Tara J
Van Cove HS
Cove, AR

Krout, Phillip T
Russellville Sr HS
Russellville, AR

Kumpuris, Frank
Pulaski Acad
Little Rock, AR

Kuznechenkova, Maria V
Prairie Grove HS
Prairie Grove, AR

Kyukendall, Trena
Southside HS
Fort Smith, AR

Lacaze, Terry J
Fountain Lake Jr Sr HS
Hot Springs Natio, AR

Lacefield, Angie
Pea Ridge HS
Pea Ridge, AR

Lacy, Katrina
Gordon HS
Gurdon, AR

Lamb, Heath
Nettleton HS
Jonesboro, AR

Lamberson, Beth B
Bay Jr Sr HS
Bay, AR

Lamberson, Nikki N
Highland HS
Ash Flat, AR

Lambert, Hollie M
Arkansas Sr HS
Texarkana, AR

Lamberth, Josie N
Fountain Lake Jr Sr HS
Hot Springs Natio, AR

Lambeth, Jennifer K
Dequeen HS
De Queen, AR

Lamoureux, Lisa
Dover HS
Dover, AR

Lampkin, Ahmad J
Malvern Sr HS
Malvern, AR

Lancaster, April R
Mountain View Jr Sr HS
Mountain View, AR

Lancaster, Brent M
Melbourne HS
Melbourne, AR

Landers, Peter L
Valley Springs Schl
Harrison, AR

Landry, Euphraise L
Nevada Schl
Rosston, AR

Lane, Birch D
Springdale Sr HS
Springdale, AR

Lane, Rebecca D
Springdale Sr HS
Springdale, AR

Lang, Erin L
Greenwood Sr HS
Greenwood, AR

Langdon, Kenya
Deer Jr Sr HS
Ozone, AR

Langley, Jasen
Valley View HS
Jonesboro, AR

Lankford, Lakisha
West Memphis Sr HS
West Memphis, AR

Larkin Jr, Randy P
Pea Ridge HS
Jay, OK

Larmoyeux, Christophe
Central Arkansas Chrstn HS
Little Rock, AR

Larry, La Sonya
Bright Star Schl
Doddridge, AR

Latta, Larissa M
Morrow Valley Christian Acad
Canehill, AR

Lausten, Ryan
Pine Bluff HS
Pine Bluff, AR

La Voice, Allison
Foreman Jr Sr HS
Foreman, AR

Law, Lindsay
Hamburg Jr HS
Hamburg, AR

Lawrence, Elisabeth A
Conway Sr HS
Conway, AR

Lawrence, Heather S
Abundant Life Schools
Sherwood, AR

Lawson, Byron
Lonoke Jr HS
Scott, AR

Lawson, Heather D
Bentonville Sr HS
Bentonville, AR

Lawson, Jeremy
Sheridan Sr HS
Leola, AR

Layrock, Tony K
Searcy HS
Searcy, AR

Layton, Billy J
Oden Schl
Oden, AR

Layton, Jermaine
Arkansas Sr HS
Texarkana, AR

Lazenby, Jamie N
North Little Rock
Hs-West
North Little Rock, AR

Lee, Angel
Parkview
Arts-Science HS
North Little Rock, AR

Lee, Chelli
Dover HS
Dover, AR

Lee, Tonya Sue
Devalls Bluff Jr Sr HS
De Valls Bluff, AR

Leisure, Brandy D
Ridgecrest HS
Paragould, AR

Lemle II, James E
Catholic HS
Little Rock, AR

Lemley, Kevin
Conway Sr HS
Conway, AR

Lemon, Teresa A
Fayetteville Sr HS
Fayetteville, AR

Leslie, Carrie A
Mt Holly Schl
Mount Holly, AR

Lessel, Geoffrey P
Pulaski Acad
Little Rock, AR

Lessenberry,
Courtney A
Robinson HS
Little Rock, AR

Lewellyn, Amber M
Lonoke Jr HS
Lonoke, AR

Lewis, Calandra F
Harmony Grove Jr
Sr HS
Camden, AR

Lewis, Crystal
Lake Hamilton Jr HS
Royal, AR

Lewis, Marc A
Forrest City HS
Forrest City, AR

Liles, Paige
Huntsville HS
Huntsville, AR

Limgo, Kim Anne B
Russellville Sr HS
Russellville, AR

Linder, Sarah
Malvern Sr HS
Malvern, AR

Lindsey, Jerry R
Midland HS
Pleasant Plains, AR

Lingenfelter, Shonia J
Mayflower HS
Mayflower, AR

Lingo, Monica S
Northside HS
Barling, AR

Linson, Karen
Southside HS
Barling, AR

Little, Jamie D
Springdale Sr HS
Springdale, AR

Littrell, Brian F
Huntsville HS
Huntsville, AR

Lively, Daniel B
Southside HS
Fort Smith, AR

Livingston, Toney
Bismarck Jr-Sr HS
Bismarck, AR

Lloyd, Leah M
Arkadelphia Sr HS
Arkadelphia, AR

Lockwood, Jennifer E
Southside HS
Fort Smith, AR

Loftis, Mary A
North Little Rock HS
Jacksonville, AR

Lofton, Artis T
North Little Rock
Hs-East
North Little Rock, AR

Lofton, Kadesha C
Arkansas Sr HS
Texarkana, AR

Long, Matthew K
Mountain View Jr
Sr HS
Mountain View, AR

Long, Ryan S
Nettleton HS
Jonesboro, AR

Loretz Jr, Danny
Carlisle Jr Sr HS
Carlisle, AR

Lovelace, Kurt
Bergman Schl
Harrison, AR

Lovett, Amanda L
Waldron HS
Waldron, AR

Lowery, Jayson
Kirby HS
Glenwood, AR

Lowery, John W
Junction City HS
El Dorado, AR

Loy, Ktrina A
Lake Hamilton Sr HS
Hot Springs, AR

Lusby, Danyelle
Ft Smith Christian Schl
Fort Smith, AR

Luster, Amber N
Trumann HS
Trumann, AR

Luster, Eboni C
Trumann HS
Trumann, AR

Luther, Greta E
Mountain Home HS
Mountain Home, AR

Lybrand, Jeffrey N
Sheridan Sr HS
Grapevine, AR

Lynch, Kiley
Southside HS
Fort Smith, AR

Lynch, Kristen L
Atkins Schl
Russellville, AR

Lynn, Philip M
Catholic HS
Little Rock, AR

Lynn, Shelley
Mt St Mary Acad
Little Rock, AR

Lyons, Veronica E
Wynne HS
Wynne, AR

Madar, Ben M
Carlisle Jr Sr HS
Carlisle, AR

Magdaleno, Jennifer L
Cabot HS
Cabot, AR

Mahar, Laura
Conway Sr HS
Conway, AR

Mainer, Kara L
Southside HS
Fort Smith, AR

Malik, Nathan R
Mills HS
Little Rock, AR

Mallard, Ben
Coleman Jr HS
Van Buren, AR

Malloy, Joe
Farmington Jr Sr HS
Farmington, AR

Malloy, Nick
Farmington Jr Sr HS
Farmington, AR

Malone, Angie M
Rivercrest HS
Dyess, AR

Maloney, Alandra
Fayetteville
Christian Schl
Fayetteville, AR

Mangrum, Christy D
Nettleton HS
Jonesboro, AR

Many, Julie
Clinton HS
Clinton, AR

Marks, Donna
Hackett Schl
Hackett, AR

Marks, Jason
Arkansas Bapt Schl
Little Rock, AR

Marlowe, Stephanie L
Mc Crory Jr Sr HS
Mc Crory, AR

Marsh, Mary
Pulaski Acad
Little Rock, AR

Marshall, Jeff D
Pottsville Schl
Atkins, AR

Marshall, Tifany M
Bryant Sr HS
Benton, AR

Martin, Andrea R
Arkansas Sr HS
Texarkana, AR

Martin, April
Wynne HS
Wynne, AR

Martin, Brad A
Dequeen HS
Green Forest, AR

Martin, Carol
Stuttgart Sr HS
Stuttgart, AR

Martin, Caroline R
Searcy HS
Searcy, AR

Martin, Charles E
Southside HS
Fort Smith, AR

Martin, Kendra K
Jonesboro HS
Jonesboro, AR

Martin, Michele
Marion HS
West Memphis, AR

Martin, Michelle J
Sheridan Sr HS
Hensley, AR

Martin, Rebecca C
White Co Central Schl
Judsonia, AR

Martin, Richard
Calico Rock HS
Wideman, AR

Martin, Russ W
Pulaski Acad
Little Rock, AR

Martin, Sarah
Southside HS
Fort Smith, AR

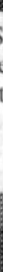

Martin, Sonya
J A Fair Sr HS
Little Rock, AR

Martin, Tomeka S
North Little Rock
Hs-West
North Little Rock, AR

Martindale,
Samantha D
Bryant Sr HS
Alexander, AR

Martinez, Shantan B
Scotland Schl
Scotland, AR

Mascoe, Ryan M
Mills HS
North Little Rock, AR

Mason, Jaclyn B
Russellville Sr HS
Russellville, AR

Massardo, James R
Valley Springs Schl
Valley Springs, AR

Massey, Gregory L
Conway Sr HS
Conway, AR

Massey, Jeremy M
Bryant Sr HS
Benton, AR

Massey, Kris J
Highland HS
Ash Flat, AR

Massey, Ollie
Lee Sr HS
Marianna, AR

Masters, Sara A
Oak Grove HS
Maumelle, AR

Matheny, Matthew R
Batesville Sr HS
Batesville, AR

Mathews, Eric C
Pulaski Acad
Little Rock, AR

Matias, Eugenia R
Batesville Sr HS
Batesville, AR

Matthews, Aaron W
Southside HS
Fort Smith, AR

Matthews, Carmen M
Fouke Jr Sr HS
Fouke, AR

Matthews, Grant J
Cabot HS
Cabot, AR

Matthews, Sarah E
Oak Grove HS
N Little Rock, AR

Mauney, Crystal R
Norphlet HS
Norphlet, AR

Mauppins, Dana
Wynne HS
Wynne, AR

Mauppins, Desiree
Wynne HS
Wynne, AR

May, Kristi M
Pulaski Acad
Maumelle, AR

May, Micah
Magnet Cove HS
Malvern, AR

May, Sarah E
North Pulaski HS
Sherwood, AR

Mayhan, Cynthia R
Oak Grove HS
N Little Rock, AR

Maynard, Roark
Augusta HS
Augusta, AR

Mayo, Robert
Sublac Acad
Magazine, AR

Mc Afee, Jason D
Harrison Sr HS
Harrison, AR

Mc Allister, Ashley
Van Buren Sr HS
Van Buren, AR

Mc Anally, Sara E
Beebe Sr HS
Beebe, AR

Mc Bride, Jared
Nashville HS
Nashville, AR

Mc Bride, Laci L
Sheridan Sr HS
Little Rock, AR

Mc Candless, C
Michelle
Springdale Sr HS
Springdale, AR

Mc Candless, Lessa
Van Cove HS
Cove, AR

Mc Carroll, Nathan
Cabot HS
Cabot, AR

Mc Carty, Elizabeth
Southside HS
Fort Smith, AR

Mc Cauley, Jason
Van Buren Sr HS
Van Buren, AR

Mc Clain, Heather R
North Little Rock
Hs-West
North Little Rock, AR

Mc Clendon, James M
Hartford Schl
Hackett, AR

Mc Cluskey,
Katala Rose
Fayetteville Sr HS
Fayetteville, AR

Mc Collum, Brittany
Lake Hamilton Jr HS
Hot Springs, AR

Mc Cool, Mary E
Russellville Sr HS
Russellville, AR

Mc Cormick III,
Charley G
Conway Sr HS
Conway, AR

Mc Coy, Amber
Forrest City HS
Forrest City, AR

Mc Coy, Angela
Lakeside HS
Eudora, AR

Mc Coy, Craig A
Sloan Hendrix HS
Imboden, AR

Mc Creery, Crystal
Bright Star Schl
Doddridge, AR

Mc Cutchen, Brennan
Mountain Home HS
Mountain Home, AR

Mc Dade, Josh
Lakeside HS
Hot Springs, AR

Mc Daniel, Alison N
Arkansas Sr HS
Texarkana, AR

Mc Donald, Greg L
Beebe Sr HS
El Paso, AR

Mc Donald, Jami
Hamburg HS
Hamburg, AR

Mc Donald, Kris
Mammoth Spring HS
Mammoth Spring, AR

Mc Donald, Kristin L
Beebe Sr HS
El Paso, AR

Mc Donald, Michael E
Marion HS
West Memphis, AR

Mc Donald, Shyla
Mammoth Spring HS
Mammoth Spring, AR

Mc Elroy, Amanda D
Sheridan Sr HS
Sheridan, AR

Mc Elroy, Laura A
Hazen Jr Sr HS
Hazen, AR

Mc Elroy, Ryan M
Jacksonville HS
Jacksonville, AR

Mc Farland, Aaron M
Cabot HS
Lonoke, AR

Mc Farland, Julie A
Southside HS
Fort Smith, AR

Mc Fee, Crystal L
Huntsville HS
Huntsville, AR

Mc Garrah, Rebecca A
Bergman Schl
Harrison, AR

Mc Gee, Krisha
Gentry HS
Gentry, AR

Mc Gehee, Amy
Ozark Adventist Acad
Inola, OK

Mc Ghee, Shamond L
Dollarway HS
Pine Bluff, AR

Mc Googan, Michael Brian
Russellville Sr HS
Russellville, AR

Mc Gough, Melinda
Prescott HS
Prescott, AR

Mc Grew, Melissa
Butterfield Jr HS
Van Buren, AR

Mc Intosh, Chris M
Alma HS
Rudy, AR

Mc Intyre, Laura M
Central Sr HS
Little Rock, AR

Mc Kamie, Wesley A
Nevada Schl
Rosston, AR

Mc Kav, Tiffanie K
Dewitt HS
De Witt, AR

Mc Kee, Christopher K
Wynne HS
Wynne, AR

Mc Kinney, Laurie M
Russellville Sr HS
Russellville, AR

Mc Kinney, Tara
Northside HS
Fort Smith, AR

Mc Kinzie, Scott D
Conway Sr HS
Conway, AR

Mc Knight, Jason B
Bald Knob HS
Bald Knob, AR

Mc Koin, Rachel A
Mt St Mary Acad
Little Rock, AR

Mc Lean, Matt
Lake Hamilton Sr HS
Pearcy, AR

Mc Lelland, Leah B
Rogers HS
Rogers, AR

Mc Mahan, Tara
Ouachita Jr Sr HS
Donaldson, AR

Mc Million, Michelle
Brinkley HS
Brinkley, AR

Mc Nair, Matt
Marion Co Rural Schl
Bruno, AR

Mc Neill, Joyce M
North Little Rock Hs-West
North Little Rock, AR

Mc Pherson, Douglas P
Magnolia HS
Magnolia, AR

Mc Williams, Jeffrey G
Emerson HS
Emerson, AR

Medford, Brandon
Brinkley HS
Brinkley, AR

Medina, Jose A
Lavaca Jr Sr HS
Lavaca, AR

Meeker, Tommy H
Siloam Springs Sr HS
Siloam Springs, AR

Meeks, Kristin L
Southside HS
Fort Smith, AR

Menke, Amanda J
Hartford Schl
Hackett, AR

Meredith, Kurt
Lakeside HS
Hot Springs, AR

Meredith, Mandy
Rogers HS
Rogers, AR

Meredith, Mark
Lake Hamilton Jr HS
Hot Springs, AR

Merry, Bryan C
Southside HS
Fort Smith, AR

Messmer, Dana M
Springdale Sr HS
Springdale, AR

Metcalf, April M
Bradford Jr Sr HS
Bradford, AR

Metcalf, Bob E
Crowleys Ridge Acad
Jonesboro, AR

Metheny, Ryan
Hughes Jr-Sr HS
Hughes, AR

Methvin, Bryan
Bergman Schl
Harrison, AR

Methvin, Justin M
Lead Hill Schl
Lead Hill, AR

Metzner, Brandy
Morrilton Sr HS
Morrilton, AR

Meyers, Ryan P
Northside HS
Fort Smith, AR

Mickels, Kathryn
West Side HS
Higden, AR

Middlecamp, Matthew A
Southside HS
Batesville, AR

Miesner, Andrea
River Valley HS
Strawberry, AR

Mikles, Katherine L
Lavaca Jr Sr HS
Central City, AR

Miles, Amber M
Lake Hamilton Sr HS
Hot Springs, AR

Miller, Allison
Arkansas Bapt Schl
Maumelle, AR

Miller, Andrea M
Parkview Arts-Science HS
Little Rock, AR

Miller, Ashley M
Harrison Sr HS
Harrison, AR

Miller, Corinne R
Russellville Sr HS
London, AR

Miller, Eddie D
El Dorado Sr HS
El Dorado, AR

Miller, Jenny
Izard County HS
Horseshoe Bend, AR

Miller, Larry
Piggott HS
Pollard, AR

Miller, Leslie A
Bergman Schl
Harrison, AR

Miller, Mandy M
White Co Central Schl
Judsonia, AR

Miller, Melissa
Elaine Jr Sr HS
Elaine, AR

Miller, Miranda
Farmington Jr Sr HS
Farmington, AR

Miller, Paul T
Catholic HS
Sherwood, AR

Miller, Wendy G
Mills HS
Little Rock, AR

Milligan, Steven O
Tuckerman HS
Tuckerman, AR

Milligan, Tiffany
Bryant Sr HS
Alexander, AR

ARKANSAS

Mills, Cassie M
Arkansas Sr HS
Texarkana, AR

Mills, Kristi L
Harrisburg HS
Harrisburg, AR

Mills, Lamont
Hermitage Jr Sr HS
Warren, AR

Mills, Melissa
Sulphur Rock Schl
Batesville, AR

Mills, Shannon
Lake Hamilton Jr HS
Pearcy, AR

Mills, Tammy L
West Fork HS
West Fork, AR

Mincer, Tony M
Valley Springs Schl
Harrison, AR

Miner, Rhonda M
Ozark HS
Alix, AR

Minor, Rebekah M
Heritage Christian Schl
Little Rock, AR

Minton, Christopher L
Russellville Sr HS
Russellville, AR

Minton, Melissa M
Bryant Sr HS
Alexander, AR

Mitchell, Ashley R
Pine Bluff HS
Pine Bluff, AR

Mitchell, Aubrey D
Mountain Pine Jr
Sr HS
Mountain Pine, AR

Mitchell, Jennifer R
Osceola HS
Osceola, AR

Mitchell, Kellee
Lee Sr HS
Marianna, AR

Mitchell, Lori A
Sheridan Sr HS
Hensley, AR

Mitchell, Myranda L
Ozark HS
Ozark, AR

Mitchell, Trayce
J A Fair Sr HS
Little Rock, AR

Mitchusson, Kelli M
Mississippi Co
Christian Acad
Luxora, AR

Mixon, Randall
Crossett Sr HS
Crossett, AR

Moe, Marin A
Rogers HS
Rogers, AR

Moellers, Chrissie M
Ft Smith Christian Schl
Van Buren, AR

Mohn, Aaron
Southside HS
Fort Smith, AR

Moix, Amanda M
St Joseph HS
Conway, AR

Money, Crystal G
Bradford Jr Sr HS
Bradford, AR

Montag, Reeca R
Alma HS
Rudy, AR

Montague, Robert L
Cabot HS
Ward, AR

Montgomery, Brad
East Poinsett Sr HS
Lepanto, AR

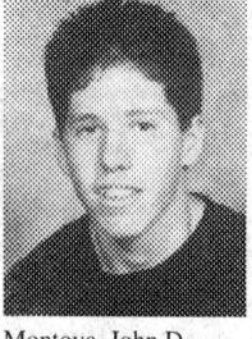
Montoya, John D
Hartford Schl
Midland, AR

Moody, Brent D
Riverview HS
Searcy, AR

Moody, Jessica L
Riverview HS
Searcy, AR

Moody, Joshua D
Blytheville Sr HS
Blytheville, AR

Moody, Lucas B
Russellville Sr HS
Russellville, AR

Mooneyhan,
Christopher E
Arkansas Sr HS
Texarkana, AR

Moore, Alan
Wynne HS
Wynne, AR

Moore, Alexis R
Tuckerman HS
Tuckerman, AR

Moore, Amanda R
Dierks HS
Dierks, AR

Moore, Anthony
Saratoga Schl
Washington, AR

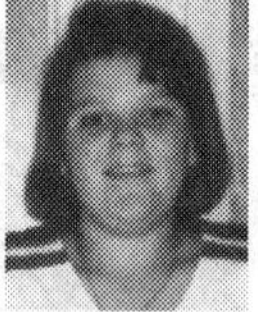
Moore, April L
Midland HS
Concord, AR

Moore, Benjamin
Hackett Schl
Hackett, AR

Moore, Dusty J
Atkins Schl
Atkins, AR

Moore, Jennifer M
Lonoke Jr HS
Lonoke, AR

Moore, Katina T
Taylor HS
Taylor, AR

Moore, Lashonda
Cross Co Jr Sr HS
Wynne, AR

Moore, Michelle P
Nettleton HS
Jonesboro, AR

Moore, Nicole
Pangburn Jr Sr HS
Searcy, AR

Moore, Summer L
Lake Hamilton Sr HS
Hot Springs, AR

Moragne, Curtis L
Parkview
Arts-Science HS
North Little Rock, AR

Moren, Bobbye
J A Fair Sr HS
Little Rock, AR

Morgan, Allison Beth
Forrest City HS
Forrest City, AR

Morgan, Debra R
Gosnell Jr Sr HS
Blytheville, AR

Morgan Jr, Perry A
Parkview
Arts-Science HS
Mabelvale, AR

Morgan, Ronika J
Northside HS
Fort Smith, AR

Morgan, Sarah
Elizabeth
Southside HS
Fort Smith, AR

Morphis, Christy
Lakeside HS
Lake Village, AR

Morrell, Brooke N
Alma HS
Alma, AR

Morris, Bret P
Rogers HS
Rogers, AR

Morris, Dekara
Crawfordsville HS
Crawfordsville, AR

Morris, Devin
Lake Hamilton Sr HS
Hot Springs, AR

Morrison, Courtney E
Bismarck Jr-Sr HS
Bismarck, AR

Morrison, Heather S
Hot Springs HS
Hot Springs Natio, AR

Morrison, Michael
Cabot HS
Cabot, AR

Morton, Ashley O
Mt St Mary Acad
Little Rock, AR

Morton, Dominik D
John L Mcclellan
Magnet HS
Little Rock, AR

Moseley, Joseph Salem
Warren Jr HS
New Edinburg, AR

Moser, Leslie G
North Little Rock
Hs-East
North Little Rock, AR

Moser, Melanie A
Cushman Schl
Batesville, AR

Moses, Brandie N
Booneville Jr Sr HS
Booneville, AR

Moses, Greg
Southside HS
Fort Smith, AR

Mosher, Samantha
Lake Hamilton Sr HS
Hot Springs, AR

Moss, Elonda Y
Lewisville HS
Lewisville, AR

Mudd, Mindy
Rogers HS
Rogers, AR

Muldrew, Durand C
Saratoga Schl
Ozan, AR

Mull, Joni
Little Rock Acad
Little Rock, AR

Mulligan, Holly L
Sheridan Sr HS
Sheridan, AR

Munroe, Jennifer
Highland HS
Ash Flat, AR

Murphy, Alysha M
Cabot HS
Cabot, AR

Murphy, Bobby
Russellville Sr HS
Russellville, AR

Murphy, Jamae
Westside Jr Sr HS
Bono, AR

Murphy, Joseph P
Bryant Sr HS
Alexander, AR

Muse, Shannon
Hazen Jr Sr HS
Hazen, AR

Myers, Brittney A
Southside HS
Fort Smith, AR

Myers, Jemecia S
Dollarway HS
Pine Bluff, AR

Myers, Sharel E
Rogers HS
Rogers, AR

Myers, Stephanie
Van Buren Sr HS
Van Buren, AR

Myles, Creshun A
Lakeside HS
Lake Village, AR

Nall, Shaun F
Corning HS
Corning, AR

Napier, David J
North Little Rock
Hs-West
North Little Rock, AR

Narens, Jessica A
Arkansas Sr HS
Texarkana, AR

Narveson, Nicole R
Russellville Sr HS
Russellville, AR

Nash, Tesha A
Abundant Life Schools
Conway, AR

Neal, Jamie L
Gosnell Jr Sr HS
Gosnell, AR

Neel, Patrick Henry
Trumann HS
Trumann, AR

Neighbors, Jennifer
Joe T Robinson HS
Little Rock, AR

Neighbors, Shanna
Bradford Jr Sr HS
Bradford, AR

Nelms, Andrea
Brookland Jr Sr HS
Brookland, AR

Nelson, Jennifer L
Smackover HS
Smackover, AR

Nelson, Parren D
Pine Bluff HS
Pine Bluff, AR

Netherton, Kellie A
Springdale Sr HS
Springdale, AR

Newberry, Jerritt D
Springdale Sr HS
Springdale, AR

Newell, Kathy Y
Sheridan Sr HS
Mabelvale, AR

Newman, Crissy M
Mansfield Jr Sr HS
Mansfield, AR

Newman, Jennifer M
Lavaca Jr Sr HS
Lavaca, AR

Newton, Crystal L
Star City HS
Star City, AR

Newton, Lucy
Southside HS
Fort Smith, AR

Nguyen, Kevin L
Southside HS
Batesville, AR

Nguyen, Van T
Rogers HS
Rogers, AR

Nichols, Jason W
North Pulaski HS
North Little Ro, AR

Nichols, Jillian
Pocahontas HS
Pocahontas, AR

Nichols, Rachel
Van Buren Sr HS
Van Buren, AR

Nicholson, Rusty E
Vilonia HS
Conway, AR

Nickolson, Sarah
Delta Special Schl
Tillar, AR

Nimmo, Wayne
Crossett Sr HS
Crossett, AR

Nivens, James
Blevins HS
Prescott, AR

Nix, Ginger K
Central Sr HS
Little Rock, AR

Nix, Krissy
Wynne HS
Wynne, AR

Nixon, Jamie
Bismarck Jr-Sr HS
Bismarck, AR

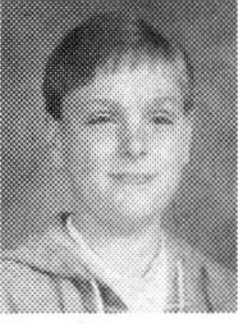
Nixon, Jeremy
Bismarck Jr-Sr HS
Bismarck, AR

Nobles, C Elizabeth
El Dorado Sr HS
El Dorado, AR

Noblin, Elizabeth R
Cabot HS
Cabot, AR

Norcross, Sarah A
Mountain Home HS
Mountain Home, AR

Nunally, Jennifer D
Black Rock Jr Sr HS
Black Rock, AR

Nye, Brad
Abundant Life Schools
Sherwood, AR

O'Bier, Autumn M
Lake Hamilton Sr HS
Hot Springs Natio, AR

O'Daniel, Becky
Southside HS
Fort Smith, AR

O'Daniel, Ginger
Mills HS
North Little Rock, AR

O Dell, David M
Arkansas Bapt Schl
Bryant, AR

Odle, Chris
Hackett Schl
Fort Smith, AR

Odle, Meredith M
Lamar HS
Knoxville, AR

Ogden III, Earl
Prairie Grove HS
Prairie Grove, AR

Ogden, Nathan Loren
Prairie Grove HS
Prairie Grove, AR

Oglesby, Demesia L
Pine Bluff HS
Pine Bluff, AR

O'Keefe, Brent W
Blytheville Sr HS
Blytheville, AR

O'Keefe, Lori B
Nevada Schl
Rosston, AR

Okuwoash, Omeetra V
North Little Rock
Hs-West
North Little Rock, AR

Olbricht, Theodore
Mammoth Spring HS
Mammoth Spring, AR

Olguin, Rhiannon L
Harmony Grove Jr
Sr HS
East Camden, AR

Oliver, Kendra J
Rivercrest HS
Wilson, AR

Olson, Asia
Deer Jr Sr HS
Jasper, AR

Olson, Megan B
Lake Hamilton Sr HS
Hot Springs, AR

ARKANSAS

Olson, Melissa P
Lake Hamilton Sr HS
Hot Springs, AR

O'Mell, Buckley
Lee Acad
Marianna, AR

O'Mell, Lewis B
Lee Acad
Marianna, AR

Opela, Melissa D
Fayetteville Sr HS
Fayetteville, AR

Opitz, Jonathan C
Benton Sr HS
Benton, AR

Orlansky, Allison L
Marvell Acad
Holly Grove, AR

Orr, Amanda
Mann Magnet Jr HS
Little Rock, AR

Orr, Brandi N
Highland HS
Ash Flat, AR

Osborn, Amanda
Atkins Schl
Atkins, AR

Osborne, Billie J
Booneville Jr Sr HS
Booneville, AR

Osburn, April
Lake Hamilton Jr HS
Hot Springs, AR

Otis, Cynthia
Hughes Jr-Sr HS
Hughes, AR

Ottinger, Jennifer K
Hot Springs HS
Hot Springs Natio, AR

Otts, Angela
Little Rock Acad
Mabelvale, AR

Overton, Amber L
England HS
England, AR

Owen, Anthony A
Star City HS
Star City, AR

Owen, Brooke
Van Buren Sr HS
Van Buren, AR

Owen, Nate
Fayetteville Sr HS
Fayetteville, AR

Owens, Christopher S
Benton Sr HS
Benton, AR

Owens, Claudia L
Springdale Sr HS
Springdale, AR

Owens, Debra R
Ozark HS
Ozark, AR

Owens, Kodi L
Pine Bluff HS
Pine Bluff, AR

Pace, Adrienne L
Hope HS
Hope, AR

Packard, Clay P
Central Sr HS
Little Rock, AR

Page, Daniel
Harrisburg HS
Harrisburg, AR

Pair, Angela D
Greenwood Sr HS
Fort Smith, AR

Palmer, Shevonda N
North Little Rock
Hs-East
Little Rock, AR

Pan, Daniel C
Central Sr HS
Little Rock, AR

Pannell, Natalie A
Osceola HS
Osceola, AR

Parish, Jason K
Gosnell Jr Sr HS
Blytheville, AR

Park, Robert
Arkansas Sr HS
Texarkana, AR

Parke, Laura E
Southside HS
Fort Smith, AR

Parker, Christy M
Rison HS
Rison, AR

Parker, David K
Crossett Sr HS
Crossett, AR

Parker, Erica Lynn
Mt St Mary Acad
Little Rock, AR

Parker, Erin
North Little Rock
Hs-West
N Little Rock, AR

Parker, Melissa D
Arkansas Sr HS
Texarkana, AR

Parker, Michael S
Dollarway HS
Pine Bluff, AR

Parker, Rachel
Carlisle Jr Sr HS
Carlisle, AR

Parks, Alicia P
John L Mcclellan
Magnet HS
Little Rock, AR

Parks, Amanda L
Hartford Schl
Hackett, AR

Parks, Charles
Cross Co Jr Sr HS
Wynne, AR

Parks, Kristen
Sylvan Hills HS
Sherwood, AR

Parrish, Tommie A
Marvell Acad
Holly Grove, AR

Parsons, James
Brandon
Jonesboro HS
Jonesboro, AR

Pasley, Carlie N
Searcy HS
Searcy, AR

Pasley, Melanie
Lake Hamilton Jr HS
Hot Springs, AR

Pate, Amber
Alpena Schl
Alpena, AR

Patel, Heena G
Jonesboro HS
Jonesboro, AR

Patrick, Brandy N
Timbo Schl
Timbo, AR

Patrick, Lindsay B
Bergman Schl
Bergman, AR

Patrick, Spencer A
Watson Chapel Sr HS
Pine Bluff, AR

Pattie, Jody A
Harrison Sr HS
Harrison, AR

Patton, Justin B
Wynne HS
Wynne, AR

Peacock, Craig
Central Ark
Christian Schl
North Little Rock, AR

Peak, Chandra D
Marion HS
West Memphis, AR

Pearce, Leslie A
Newport HS
Newport, AR

Pease, Amy K
Southside HS
Batesville, AR

Peaster, Michael J
Valley View HS
Jonesboro, AR

Peck, Allison
Black Rock Jr Sr HS
Black Rock, AR

Pederson, T J
Springdale Sr HS
Springdale, AR

Pemmaraju, Naveen
Arkansas Schl Math &
Science
Hot Springs, AR

Pendleton, Antonio S
Forrest City HS
Madison, AR

Pendleton, Michael A
Fayetteville Sr HS
Fayetteville, AR

Pennington, April L
Dumas HS
Dumas, AR

Penningtron, April
Dumas HS
Dumas, AR

Peoples, Jennfier M
Springdale Sr HS
Lowell, AR

Perez, Angelica
Dequeen HS
De Queen, AR

Perkey, Beth M
Evening Shade Schl
Evening Shade, AR

Perry, Britney Y
Lake Hamilton Sr HS
Pearcy, AR

Perry, Gina K
Malvern Sr HS
Malvern, AR

Perry, Su-Lauren E
Central Sr HS
Little Rock, AR

Perry, Tia Quanda S
J A Fair Sr HS
Little Rock, AR

Peters, Brandon K
Alma HS
Alma, AR

Peters, Jason M
Cabot HS
Cabot, AR

Peters, Ryan G
Catholic HS
Maumelle, AR

Petersen, Casey
Crossett Sr HS
Crossett, AR

Peterson, Anthony R
Jacksonville HS
Jacksonville, AR

Peterson, Michelle L
Rogers HS
Garfield, AR

Peterson, Rana N
Bentonville Sr HS
Rogers, AR

Peterson, Tia N
Smackover HS
Louann, AR

Pettz, Suzanne R
Huntsville HS
Huntsville, AR

Pevey, Lisa M
Star City HS
Pine Bluff, AR

Pharis, Billy
Butterfield Jr HS
Van Buren, AR

Phelan, Kim
Mills HS
Little Rock, AR

Phillips, Amy
Jasper HS
Jasper, AR

Phillips, Bryan D
Bentonville Sr HS
Bentonville, AR

Phillips, Megan B
Rogers HS
Rogers, AR

Phillips, Michael W
Mayflower HS
Conway, AR

Phillips, Ryan M
Russellville Sr HS
Russellville, AR

Phillips, Susan
Sylvan Hills HS
Sherwood, AR

Pickett, Brandy
J A Fair Sr HS
Mabelvale, AR

Pickings, Benjear M
Magnolia HS
Magnolia, AR

Piechocki, Jon P
Catholic HS
Sherwood, AR

Pierce, Andrew W
Pine Bluff HS
Pine Bluff, AR

Pierce, Derek R
Pine Bluff HS
Pine Bluff, AR

Pierce, Lisa M
Rose Bud Jr Sr HS
Rose Bud, AR

Pierce, Melissa C
Ft Smith Christian Schl
Fort Smith, AR

Pierce, Mona J
Stamps HS
Buckner, AR

Pierce, Wrona R
Pulaski Acad
Little Rock, AR

Pilkington, Paige L
Sheridan Sr HS
Sheridan, AR

Pirani, Anthony J
Central HS
West Helena, AR

Pirani, Rachel J
Marion HS
Marion, AR

Pitchford, Landon H
Mountain Home HS
Mountain Home, AR

Pitts, Erica
Charleston HS
Charleston, AR

Platt, Jessica
Central Ark
Christian Schl
Little Rock, AR

Plumle, Nancy J
Arkansas Sr HS
Texarkana, AR

Plumlee, Ruth L
Marvell Acad
Clarendon, AR

Plummer, Chris O
Northside HS
Fort Smith, AR

Poff, Amanda G
Southside HS
Desha, AR

Poindexter, Jessica
Ridgecrest HS
Paragould, AR

Polk, Renee E
Marvell Acad
Marvell, AR

Pollard, Emily H
Pulaski Acad
Little Rock, AR

Pollock, Melissa
Ridgecrest HS
Paragould, AR

Pool, Jennifer
West Memphis Sr HS
West Memphis, AR

Porta, Becky
Kimmons Jr HS
Fort Smith, AR

Porter, Kara
Cntrl Arkansas
Chrstn Schl
Mabelvale, AR

Porter, Lawanda P
Hope HS
Hope, AR

Pottorff, Daryld
Pea Ridge HS
Pea Ridge, AR

Powell, Jason
Butterfield Jr HS
Van Buren, AR

Powell, John
Mc Gehee HS
Mc Gehee, AR

Powell, Kristi L
Nevada Schl
Rosston, AR

Powell, Larry W
North Little Rock
Hs-East
North Little Rock, AR

Powell, Melissa
Harding Acad
Beebe, AR

Powell, Steven W
Mc Gehee HS
Mcgehee, AR

Power, Jenny
Nashville HS
Nashville, AR

Pratt, Holly R
Riverview HS
Judsonia, AR

Prescott, Robert S
Highland HS
Ravenden, AR

Pressler, Donna L
Brinkley HS
Brinkley, AR

Prim, Yavonda A
Fairview HS
Camden, AR

Privett, Jonathan S
Parkview Arts
Magnet Schl
Little Rock, AR

Pryor, Crystal J
Southside HS
Fort Smith, AR

Pullins, Gena D
Cushman Schl
Cushman, AR

Qualls, Amanda
Pottsville Schl
Pottsville, AR

Query, Desma J
Flippin Jr Sr HS
Flippin, AR

Quillin, Amanda R
Spring Hill HS
Hope, AR

Quinn, Jana K
De Soto Schl
Elaine, AR

Quinton, Reid
Rivercrest HS
Luxora, AR

Rabideau, Brooks
Southside HS
Fort Smith, AR

Ragan, Crystal D
Marshall HS
Marshall, AR

ARKANSAS

Ragar, Heather N
Cabot HS
Cabot, AR

Ragsdale, Suzanne
Ozark Adventist Acad
Benton, AR

Raible, Sherry
Van Buren Sr HS
Alma, AR

Rains, Brandon R
Atkins Schl
Atkins, AR

Ralston, Stephen S
Nettleton HS
Jonesboro, AR

Ramsey, Amy
Cabot HS
Cabot, AR

Rand, Ginger L
Ozark Adventist Acad
Fort Smith, AR

Raney III, Robert
William
Pulaski Acad
Little Rock, AR

Ranz, Jamie L
Mansfield Jr Sr HS
Mansfield, AR

Rash, Ginger K
Vilonia HS
Vilonia, AR

Rateliff, Kristin
Oak Grove HS
Maumelle, AR

Rath Jr, Russell
Concord Public Schls
Concord, AR

Ratliff, Stephanie D
North Little Rock
Hs-West
North Little Rock, AR

Rawls, Amanda N
Crossett Sr HS
Crossett, AR

Ray, Jamie S
Lavaca Jr Sr HS
Lavaca, AR

Ray, Jimmy T
Strawberry Jr Sr HS
Strawberry, AR

Ray, Stephanie A
Lavaca Jr Sr HS
Lavaca, AR

Raymond, Mark
Southside HS
Fort Smith, AR

Reading, Jeremy M
Springdale Sr HS
Springdale, AR

Reaves, Steven R
Mc Gehee HS
Mc Gehee, AR

Reece, Shannon L
Jonesboro HS
Jonesboro, AR

Reed, Alisha M
Sheridan Sr HS
Sheridan, AR

Reed, Amy M
Smackover HS
Smackover, AR

Reed, David
Central Ark
Christian Schl
Sherwood, AR

Reed, Eric L
Dierks HS
Dierks, AR

Reed, Lori
Bryant Sr HS
Bryant, AR

Reeder, Rachael A
Mountain Home HS
Mountain Home, AR

Reese, Kaylee
Ozark Adventist Acad
Claremore, OK

Rendel, Stephanie L
Jacksonville HS
Jacksonville, AR

Renfroe, Cara
Harrison Sr HS
Harrison, AR

Rettig, Charley D
Beebe Sr HS
Beebe, AR

Revelle, Allen
Humphrey Schl
Humphrey, AR

Revels, Gary Thomas
Lockesburgh HS
Lockesburg, AR

Reynolds, Kimberly S
Pine Bluff HS
Pine Bluff, AR

Reynolds, Marilyn M
Stuttgart Sr HS
Stuttgart, AR

Reynolds, Timothy M
Pulaski Acad
North Little Rock, AR

Rheome, Amanda M
Lonoke Jr HS
Lonoke, AR

Rhew, Tamara D
Midland HS
Pleasant Plains, AR

Ribbing, Jason J
Cabot HS
Cabot, AR

Rice, Brittney A
Riverview HS
Judsonia, AR

Rice, Shannon
Arkansas Bapt Schl
Little Rock, AR

Richardson, Brandon J
Midland HS
Batesville, AR

Richardson, Matthew
Greene Co Tech HS
Bono, AR

Richey, Christine
Pleasant View Schl
Mulberry, AR

Richison, Marie
Southside HS
Fort Smith, AR

Richison, Sarah L
Southside HS
Fort Smith, AR

Ridge, Melissa
West Memphis Sr HS
Proctor, AR

Rietzke, Heather N
Conway Sr HS
Conway, AR

Riggs, Charissa
Gosnell Jr Sr HS
Blytheville, AR

Riggs, Derek
Coleman Jr HS
Van Buren, AR

Riley, Thomas M
Jonesboro HS
Jonesboro, AR

Rimmer, Angela
Guy Perkins Schl
Greenbrier, AR

Rink, Chris L
Booneville Jr Sr HS
Booneville, AR

Rippy, Mark
Searcy HS
Searcy, AR

Rivaldo, Jayme
Northside HS
Van Buren, AR

Rivas, Shannon D
Hot Springs HS
Hot Springs, AR

Robbins, Chris
Hackett Schl
Hackett, AR

Roberts, Angela D
Trumann HS
Trumann, AR

Roberts, Brandi
Rogers HS
Rogers, AR

Roberts, Galicia W
Valley Springs Schl
Harrison, AR

Roberts, Stacia J
Arkansas Sr HS
Texarkana, AR

Roberts, Tabitha
Bergman Schl
Harrison, AR

Robertson, Kendra
Green Forest Jr Sr HS
Green Forest, AR

Robertson, Mandi J
Taylor HS
Taylor, AR

Robertson, Samantha L
Rivercrest HS
Bassett, AR

Robinson, Corey B
Amity Jr Sr HS
Amity, AR

Robinson, Jennifer
Arkansas City Schl
Arkansas City, AR

Robinson, La Pria
Mayflower HS
Mayflower, AR

Robinson, Sha
Neisha E
Star City HS
Star City, AR

Robinson, Tiffany L
Southside HS
Batesville, AR

Robinson, Tony W
Fouke Jr Sr HS
Fouke, AR

Rocole, Tracy A
Deer Jr Sr HS
Deer, AR

Rodgers, Amber C
Crossett Sr HS
Crossett, AR

Rodgers, Michael W
West Memphis
Christian Schl
Earle, AR

Roe, Regina
Green Forest Jr Sr HS
Green Forest, AR

Rogers, Alan M
Abundant Life Schools
Jacksonville, AR

Rogers, Brian Jared
Greene Co Tech HS
Paragould, AR

Rogers, Carrie L
Springdale Sr HS
Springdale, AR

Rogers, Christopher
Sprindale HS
Springdale, AR

Rogers, Christopher P
Des Arc Jr Sr HS
Des Arc, AR

Rogers, Elizabeth L
Southside HS
Batesville, AR

Rogers, Jennifer M
Taylor HS
Taylor, AR

Rogers, Michael
Lead Hill Schl
Yellville, AR

Rogne, Lisa
Southside HS
Fort Smith, AR

Romine, Jacqueline N
Vilonia HS
Vilonia, AR

Rooney, Thomas P
Catholic HS
North Little Rock, AR

Rorie, Jennifer D
Fountain Lake Jr Sr HS
Hot Springs Natio, AR

Rose, Roger W
Ashdown Sr HS
Ashdown, AR

Ross, Charnelle
J A Fair Sr HS
Little Rock, AR

Ross, Gary L
Russellville Sr HS
Russellville, AR

Ross, Philip
Arkadelphia Sr HS
Arkadelphia, AR

Ross, Susan
Springdale Sr HS
Springdale, AR

Rossworn, Tamara L
Parkview
Arts-Science HS
North Little Rock, AR

Rostan, Amanda Y
Fountain Lake Jr Sr HS
Hot Springs Natio, AR

Rounds, Gary S
Southside HS
Batesville, AR

Rouse, Erick S
Gosnell Jr Sr HS
Blytheville, AR

Rowland, Jeana S
Heritage Christian Schl
Benton, AR

Rowland, Jessica R
Booneville Jr Sr HS
Booneville, AR

Rowland, Tricia
J A Fair Sr HS
Little Rock, AR

Rowlett, Amanda M
Mt Vernon-Enola HS
Prim, AR

Rowton, Holly
Clay Co Central Jr
Sr HS
Rector, AR

Roy, Christy Lynn
Rogers HS
Pea Ridge, AR

Rudder, Matt
Atkins Schl
Atkins, AR

Rudder, Melissa Patton
Central Sr HS
Little Rock, AR

Rudolph, Sherese D
Huntsville HS
Fayetteville, AR

Ruestow, Michele M
Northside HS
Fort Smith, AR

Runnells, Rhonda L
Bryant Sr HS
Alexander, AR

Rushing, Jennifer
Cabot HS
Cabot, AR

Russell, Becky D
Huntsville HS
Huntsville, AR

Russell, Laura A
Oak Grove HS
Maumelle, AR

Rutschke, Mica C
Sylvan Hills HS
Sherwood, AR

Rydell, Karen A
Waldron HS
Mena, AR

Ryder, Stuart
Russellville Sr HS
Russellville, AR

Ryken, Geoffrey R
Conway Sr HS
Conway, AR

Sairls, Nicole
Brookland Jr Sr HS
Brookland, AR

Salmon, Angey C
Southside HS
Fort Smith, AR

Salsbury, Suzanne
Van Buren Sr HS
Alma, AR

Saltmarsh, Jamie
North Little Rock
Hs-East
North Little Rock, AR

Samples, Donny R
Glen Rose HS
Benton, AR

Sanders, Kristi N
Lake Hamilton Sr HS
Hot Springs Natio, AR

Sanders, Russell
Hermitage Jr Sr HS
Hermitage, AR

Sanders, Shawnda
Southside HS
Fort Smith, AR

Sansing, Sandy Allen
Mills HS
Jacksonville, AR

Santiago, Luisa M
Mills HS
Cabot, AR

Sartain, Nick
Sylvan Hills HS
Sherwood, AR

Satterfield, Mary M
Conway Sr HS
Conway, AR

Saul, Abigail
Devalls Bluff Jr Sr HS
De Valls Bluff, AR

Saunders, Scott A
Searcy HS
Searcy, AR

Savacool, Adam
Harmony Grove Jr
Sr HS
Camden, AR

Sawyer, Kurt
Gosnell Jr Sr HS
Blytheville, AR

Sayasone, Souvanny
Victoria
Northside HS
Fort Smith, AR

Scales, Shannon
Fordyce HS
New Edinburg, AR

Schaal, George
Mineral Springs Schl
Mineral Springs, AR

Schaal, Henry
Mineral Springs Schl
Mineral Springs, AR

Schaefer, Courtnie L
North Little Rock
Hs-East
North Little Rock, AR

Schaefer, David
Benton Sr HS
Benton, AR

Schaffer, Michelle K
Harrison Sr HS
Harrison, AR

Schaffhauser, Michael
Marvell HS
West Helena, AR

Scherer, Erin M
Pulaski Acad
Little Rock, AR

Scherrey Jr, Thomas J
Southside HS
Fort Smith, AR

Schlenker, Aaron Kyle
Trumann HS
Trumann, AR

Schmidt, Brooke E
Conway Sr HS
Conway, AR

Schrader, Russ L
Rogers HS
Rogers, AR

Schultz, Casey C
Ridgecrest HS
Paragould, AR

Schulz, Jamie L
Springdale Sr HS
Springdale, AR

Scopa, Rebecca K
Fayetteville Sr HS
Fayetteville, AR

Scott, Angela M
Mountain Home HS
Mountain Home, AR

Scott, Dustin L
Lonoke Jr HS
Lonoke, AR

Scott, Leah B
Marvell Acad
Clarendon, AR

Scott, Mandy
Van Buren Sr HS
Van Buren, AR

Scott, Margaret
Lincoln HS
Morrow, AR

Scott, Ngozi O
Central Sr HS
Little Rock, AR

Scott, Rolanda D
Forrest City HS
Forrest City, AR

Scott, Trisha
Harrison Sr HS
Harrison, AR

Scrape, Jennifer A
Trumann HS
Trumann, AR

Seal, Kristen J
Newport HS
Newport, AR

Seamans, Faith R
Sloan Hendrix HS
Imboden, AR

Sebren, Leslie
Benton Sr HS
Benton, AR

Seeger, Leigh Ann
Batesville Sr HS
Batesville, AR

Seelen, Jonathan
Southside HS
Fort Smith, AR

Seelen, Raedonna C
Southside HS
Fort Smith, AR

Selby, Kristen
Butterfield Jr HS
Van Buren, AR

Sellers, Brandy L
Searcy HS
Searcy, AR

Serrano, Leslie M
Springdale HS
Lowell, AR

Sewell, Kristi
Bright Star Schl
Doddridge, AR

Sexton, Marc R
Jonesboro HS
Jonesboro, AR

Seydel, Mariah J
Jonesboro HS
Jonesboro, AR

Shackelford, Scott Oliver
Shiloh Christian Schools
Springdale, AR

Shaddock, Melissa
Oak Grove HS
Maumelle, AR

Shahbandar, Oubai M
Mann Magnet Jr HS
Little Rock, AR

Shannon, Christie A
Huntsville HS
Huntsville, AR

Shannon, Joshua P
Rogers HS
Bentonville, AR

Sharp, Curtis
Magnolia HS
Magnolia, AR

Sharp, Jodie L
Valley Springs Schl
Harrison, AR

Sharp, Toni M
Valley Springs Schl
Harrison, AR

Shatswell, Brandon K
Harrison Sr HS
Harrison, AR

Shaw, Leanne
Yellville Summit HS
Yellville, AR

Shea, Brian M
Springdale Sr HS
Springdale, AR

Sheets, Chad A
Vilonia HS
Conway, AR

Shelley, Brooke
Farmington Jr Sr HS
Farmington, AR

Shelton, Brandon J
Yellville Summit HS
Flippin, AR

Shepherd, Elizabeth
Gurdon HS
Gurdon, AR

Shepherd, Holly C
Mountainburg Jr Sr HS
Mountainburg, AR

Shepherd, Tracie D
Huntsville HS
Huntsville, AR

Sheppard, Andrea
Central Ark Christian Schl
Maumelle, AR

Sheppard, Julius
El Dorado Sr HS
El Droado, AR

Sherrill, Amber
Central Ark Christian Schl
Sherwood, AR

Shinn, Jocelyn B
Huntsville HS
Huntsville, AR

Shipley, Josh A
Arkansas Schl Math & Science
Marion, AR

Shipman, James D
Bald Knob HS
Bald Knob, AR

Shipman, Jonathan E
Yellville Summit HS
Yellville, AR

Shirley, Melanie D
Ridgecrest HS
Paragould, AR

Shirley, Zach R
West Memphis Christian Schl
Crawfordsville, AR

Shirron, Melissa D
Sheridan Sr HS
Hensley, AR

Shoemake, Jennifer L
Oak Grove HS
Maumelle, AR

Shofner, Marisa M
Rogers HS
Rogers, AR

Shoppach, Jonthan M
Harmony Grove Jr Sr HS
Benton, AR

Shores, Brian R
Alma HS
Alma, AR

Shourd, Andrea N
Searcy HS
Searcy, AR

Shryock, Sydney M
Malvern Sr HS
Malvern, AR

Shurr, Allison
Southside HS
Fort Smith, AR

Sibley, Rahshanda K
Central Sr HS
Little Rock, AR

Siharath, Chansouphaphon
Southside HS
Fort Smith, AR

Sikes, April D
Conway Sr HS
Conway, AR

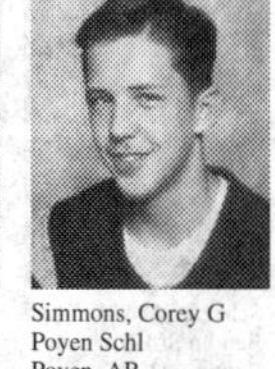
Simmons, Corey G
Poyen Schl
Poyen, AR

Simon, Morten
Nettleton HS
Jonesboro, AR

Simpson, David
Eudora HS
Little Rock, AR

Simpson, Levi S
Ozark HS
Ozark, AR

Simpson, Veronica A
Malvern Sr HS
Malvern, AR

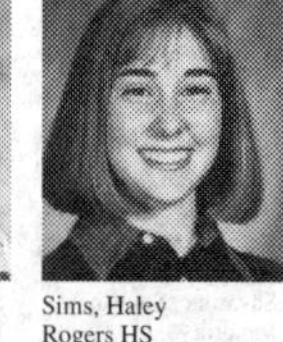
Sims, Haley
Rogers HS
Lowell, AR

Sims, Jerry
Southside HS
Barling, AR

Sims, Katherine A
North Little Rock
Hs-West
North Little Rock, AR

Sipes, Kimberly S
Crossett Sr HS
Crossett, AR

Sisco, Chasity
Harrison Sr HS
Harrison, AR

Skaggs, Michelle L
Osceola HS
Osceola, AR

Skates, Jennifer M
Hot Springs HS
Hot Springs, AR

Skinner, Ashlie J
Gravette HS
Gravette, AR

Skinner, Jillian C
Gravette HS
Gravette, AR

Slayton, Josh L
Nettleton HS
Jonesboro, AR

Small, Becky
Lake Hamilton Sr HS
Hot Springs, AR

Smelko, John Paul
Hall Sr HS
Little Rock, AR

Smith, Alison L
Benton Sr HS
Benton, AR

Smith, Anna
Nettleton Jr HS
Jonesboro, AR

Smith, Ashley
Parkers Chapel Schl
El Dorado, AR

Smith, Ashley A
Southside HS
Fort Smith, AR

Smith, Brad
Blevins HS
Mc Caskill, AR

Smith, Brandi K
Sylvan Hills HS
Sherwood, AR

Smith, Brian A
Northside HS
Fort Smith, AR

Smith, Christal Brandi
Marshall HS
Marshall, AR

Smith, Christopher L
Newport HS
Newport, AR

Smith, Counts
Wynne HS
Wynne, AR

Smith, Danielle S
Mena HS
Mena, AR

Smith, Dorothy A
Pea Ridge HS
Pea Ridge, AR

Smith, Grayson
Charleston HS
Charleston, AR

Smith, Heather L
Fouke Jr Sr HS
Fouke, AR

Smith, Jana D
Springdale Sr HS
Springdale, AR

Smith, Jason A
Van Buren Sr HS
Van Buren, AR

Smith, Johnelle
Mills HS
Little Rock, AR

Smith, Jonathan B
Mills HS
North Little Rock, AR

Smith, Joy
Ft Smith Christian Schl
Alma, AR

Smith, Kashana J
Strong Jr Sr HS
Strong, AR

Smith, Laura
Maynard Jr Sr HS
Maynard, AR

Smith, Laura B
Crowleys Ridge Acad
Paragould, AR

Smith, Lisa
Sylvan Hills HS
North Little Rock, AR

Smith, Mandy E
Clarendon Jr Sr HS
Monroe, AR

Smith, Michelle E
Jonesboro HS
Jonesboro, AR

Smith, Mikel
East Poinsett Sr HS
Lepanto, AR

Smith, Natasha V
Hope HS
Fulton, AR

Smith, R Dustin
Lonoke Jr HS
Lonoke, AR

Smith, Sabrina L
Mc Gehee HS
Mc Gehee, AR

Smith, Sarah
Southside HS
Fort Smith, AR

Smith, Shakita R
Emerson HS
Emerson, AR

Smith, Sharon E
Bentonville Sr HS
Bentonville, AR

Smith, Stacy L
El Dorado Sr HS
El Dorado, AR

Smith, Stevie M
Lake Hamilton Sr HS
Hot Springs, AR

Smith, Terrance A
Watson Chapel Sr HS
Pine Bluff, AR

Smith, Thomas J
Southside HS
Fort Smith, AR

Smith, Tiffany
Lake Hamilton Jr HS
Royal, AR

Smithwick,
Elizabeth M
Pine Bluff HS
Pine Bluff, AR

Sonnier, Anna M
Southside HS
Fort Smith, AR

Spack, Steven M
Russellville Sr HS
London, AR

Spangler, Kris
Farmington Jr Sr HS
Farmington, AR

Spann, Jason C
Pine Bluff HS
Pine Bluff, AR

Spencer, Jason P
Sheridan Sr HS
Little Rock, AR

Spillers, Chivonne L
Fouke Jr Sr HS
Fouke, AR

Spilman, Anna K
Southside HS
Fort Smith, AR

Spurlin, Candyce L
Pangburn Jr Sr HS
Judsonia, AR

Squires, David A
Mills HS
Little Rock, AR

Stacey, Heath
Bergman Schl
Harrison, AR

Stafford, Gregory L
North Little Rock
Hs-West
North Little Rock, AR

Staley, Kyla
J A Fair Sr HS
Little Rock, AR

Standridge, Alisha
Mt Ida Jr Sr HS
Mount Ida, AR

Standridge, Summer F
Parkview
Arts-Science HS
Scott, AR

Stanick, Jennifer
Greenwood Sr HS
Greenwood, AR

Stanley, Chad M
Nashville HS
Ozan, AR

Stanley, Tabitha A
Stuttgart Sr HS
Stuttgart, AR

Staples, Kelli M
North Little Rock
Hs-West
North Little Rock, AR

Starks, Stephanie A
John L Mcclellan
Magnet HS
Little Rock, AR

Stellmon, Melissa E
Fayetteville Sr HS
Fayetteville, AR

Stephens, Karla
Bradley Jr Sr HS
Taylor, AR

ARKANSAS

Stephens, Linda
Emmet Schl
Emmet, AR

Stevens, Amy R
Searcy HS
Searcy, AR

Stevens, Andrea
Central Ark
Christian Schl
Little Rock, AR

Stevens, Christopher R
Southside HS
Batesville, AR

Stevens, Melissa
Leslie Schl
Leslie, AR

Stevens, Scotty W
Rural Special Schl
Prim, AR

Stevens, Shannon
West Side
Christian Schl
El Dorado, AR

Stevenson, Amber
Cross Co Jr Sr HS
Hickory Ridge, AR

Stevenson, Misty M
Cave City HS
Batesville, AR

Steward, Ashley
Augusta HS
Augusta, AR

Steward, Jeremy R
West Memphis
Christian Schl
West Memphis, AR

Steward, Josh R
West Memphis
Christian Schl
West Memphis, AR

Stewart, Amber
Dollarway HS
Pine Bluff, AR

Stewart, Jeremy W
Harmony Grove Jr
Sr HS
Benton, AR

Stewart, Jill S
Arkansas Bapt Schl
Little Rock, AR

Stewart, Robert A
Hampton Jr Sr HS
Hampton, AR

Stiers, Ashley L
Cabot HS
Cabot, AR

Stokes, Laura
Cross Co Jr Sr HS
Hickory Ridge, AR

Stolarik, Rick
Mountain Home HS
Mountain Home, AR

Stottman, Heather L
Russellville Sr HS
Russellville, AR

Stout, Randy
Hermitage Jr Sr HS
Warren, AR

Stout, Tina M
Armorel HS
Blytheville, AR

Stover, Melissa D
Casa Schl
Casa, AR

Stracener, Amanda
North Little Rock
HS East
North Little Rock, AR

Stracener, Carrie A
Midland HS
Pleasant Plains, AR

Strack, Bridget A
St Joseph HS
Conway, AR

Strasner, Sam S
Russellville Sr HS
Dover, AR

Stratton, Stephanie D
Harrison Sr HS
Harrison, AR

Strawn, Todd
Atkins Schl
Atkins, AR

Strickland, John
Ozark Adventist Acad
Gentry, AR

Stricklin, Kimberly
Watson Chapel Schl
Pine Bluff, AR

Stroud, Thomas J
Maynard Jr Sr HS
Maynard, AR

Stuart, Ginger M
Carlisle Jr Sr HS
Carlisle, AR

Stuckey, Anna
Van Buren Sr HS
Van Buren, AR

Stucky, Susan C
Arkansas Sr HS
Texarkana, AR

Sullivan, Michael F
Trumann HS
Trumann, AR

Summerhill, Andrea B
Beebe Sr HS
Beebe, AR

Summerhill, Kelly S
Searcy HS
Searcy, AR

Summers, Matthew S
Bryant Sr HS
Bryant, AR

Sutliff, Dianna R
White Hall Sr HS
Pine Bluff, AR

Sutton, Mitzi
Southside HS
Fort Smith, AR

Swan, Michelle
Rogers HS
Rogers, AR

Sweat, Emily
Blevins HS
Mc Caskill, AR

Sweat, Kyla
Blevins HS
Mc Caskill, AR

Sweet, Brandy R
Siloam Springs Sr HS
Siloam Springs, AR

Swift, Brian C
Booneville Jr Sr HS
Booneville, AR

Tabor, Malina A
Mc Gehee HS
Mcgehee, AR

Tackett, Michael B
Harmony Grove Jr
Sr HS
Benton, AR

Taksakulvith, Mit
Jacksonville HS
Jacksonville, AR

Tanner, Lawrence
Robert
Booneville Jr Sr HS
Booneville, AR

Tanner, Sarah R
Booneville Jr Sr HS
Booneville, AR

Tappan, Charles
De Soto Schl
Helena, AR

Tarrant, Andy H
Southside HS
Fort Smith, AR

Tarver, Kristie A
Stuttgart Sr HS
Stuttgart, AR

Tatum, Victoria
Crossett Sr HS
Crossett, AR

Taylor, Amy
Trumann HS
Trumann, AR

Taylor, Amy C
Dumas HS
Dumas, AR

Taylor, Christy
Walnut Ridge HS
Walnut Ridge, AR

Taylor, Erick T
Pine Bluff HS
Pine Bluff, AR

Taylor, Felicia
AR Math &
Science Schl
Bauxite, AR

Taylor, Jennifer H
Beebe Sr HS
Beebe, AR

Taylor, Joseph A
Ridgecrest HS
Paragould, AR

Taylor, Julia
Bradley Jr Sr HS
Bradley, AR

Taylor, Karli R
Dequeen HS
De Queen, AR

Taylor, Kreston A
Hazen Jr Sr HS
Hazen, AR

Taylor, Lori L
Greenwood Sr HS
Fort Smith, AR

Taylor, Nancy C
Harrison Sr HS
Harrison, AR

Taylor, Patrick B
Alma HS
Alma, AR

Taylor, Sarah
North Little Rock
Hs-East
North Little Rock, AR

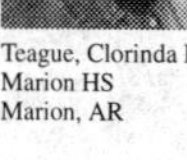

Teague, Clorinda L
Marion HS
Marion, AR

Teague, James D
Gillett Jr Sr HS
Gillett, AR

Teague, John T
Lake Hamilton Sr HS
Hot Springs, AR

Teater, Mandie
Victory Christian Schl
Hampton, AR

Tedder, Lacy S
Dierks HS
Newhope, AR

Tempelmeyer, Darla M
Lakeside HS
Hot Springs, AR

Temple, Tabitha L
Hermitage Jr Sr HS
Warren, AR

Templeton, Ashley A
El Dorado Sr HS
El Dorado, AR

Tenbensel, Amanda K
Bentonville Sr HS
Bentonville, AR

Terrell, Joy
Hermitage Jr Sr HS
Hermitage, AR

Terrell, Nichole
Brinkley HS
Brinkley, AR

Thach, Haeen
Northside HS
Fort Smith, AR

Thilmont, Ashley A
Mountain Home HS
Mountain Home, AR

Thomas, Angela
Central HS
West Helena, AR

Thomas, Jestin Z
Pine Bluff HS
Pine Bluff, AR

Thomas, Nicole
Southside HS
Fort Smith, AR

Thomas, Rebekah
Ridgecrest HS
Paragould, AR

Thomas, Shawn N
Southside HS
Batesville, AR

Thomas, Tara O
Central Sr HS
Little Rock, AR

Thomas, Terri L
Marvell Acad
Poplar Grove, AR

Thomas, Tia S
Arkadelphia Sr HS
Arkadelphia, AR

Thomas, Tonya
Nashville HS
Nashville, AR

Thomason, John W
Rivercrest HS
Lynnville, TN

Thompson, Candis L
Smackover HS
Smackover, AR

Thompson, Chris P
Rogers HS
Rogers, AR

Thompson, Jenny
Wynne HS
Wynne, AR

Thompson, Kassie
Ridgecrest HS
Paragould, AR

Thompson, Tiffany D
Newport HS
Newport, AR

Thompson, Valeri A
North Pulaski HS
Jacksonville, AR

Thorn, Shirhonda D
Forrest City HS
Colt, AR

Thornburg, Klint K
Southside HS
Fort Smith, AR

Thornton, Brandon
Calvary Christian Schl
Forrest City, AR

Thorpe, Jennifer N
Bentonville Sr HS
Bella Vista, AR

Throckmorton, Joshua
Mountain View Jr
Sr HS
Mountain View, AR

Throgmartin,
Amanda C
Ridgecrest HS
Paragould, AR

Thurman, Taylor
Danville HS
Danville, AR

Tipton, Corey A
Dierks HS
Dierks, AR

Tobias, Eric M
Mountain Home HS
Mountain Home, AR

Todd, Jason L
Huntsville HS
Hindsville, AR

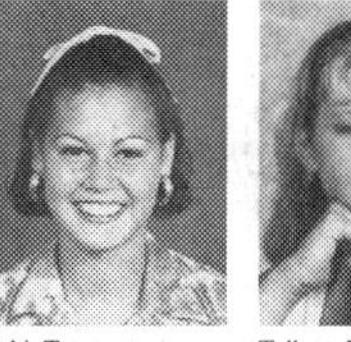
Toki, Tammy
Mc Clellan HS
Mabelvale, AR

Tolbert, Melinda R
Ozark HS
Ozark, AR

Tomlin, Samantha P
El Dorado Sr HS
El Dorado, AR

Tomlinson, Julie A
Springdale Sr HS
Springdale, AR

Tomlinson, Laura N
Springdale Sr HS
Springdale, AR

Toombs, Sabrina R
Jacksonville HS
Jacksonville, AR

Toomer, Rosalynd J
Dollarway HS
Pine Bluff, AR

Toston, Steven
Dermott HS
Dermott, AR

Totty, Michael
East Poinsett Sr HS
Marked Tree, AR

Townsend, Dusty D
Arkansas Sr HS
Texarkana, AR

Townsend, Raven N
Arkansas Sr HS
Texarkana, AR

Townsend, Terri T
Robinson HS
Little Rock, AR

Townson, Monty W
Rivercrest HS
Dyess, AR

Trammel, Chandra E
Springdale Sr HS
Springdale, AR

Trammell, Dena F
Timbo Schl
Mountain View, AR

Tran, Mary
Southside HS
Fort Smith, AR

Travis, Susanna
Ft Smith Christian Schl
Fort Smith, AR

Treadway, Ryan G
Hartford Schl
Hartford, AR

Treat, Sara
Central Ark
Christian Schl
North Little Rock, AR

Treece, Christa
Marion HS
Marion, AR

Treece, Jason
Sylvan Hills HS
Sherwood, AR

Trice, Cicely
Pine Bluff HS
Pine Bluff, AR

Trimble, Ryan
North Little Rock
Hs-West
North Little Rock, AR

Trotter II, Steven
Arkansas Schl Math &
Science
Hot Springs Natio, AR

Tucken, Lisa M
Fairview HS
Camden, AR

Tucker, Dottie
Beebe Sr HS
El Paso, AR

Tucker, Everett C
Central Sr HS
Little Rock, AR

Tuckfield, K Melissa
Russellville Sr HS
Russellville, AR

Tullos, Stephanie N
Central Ark
Christian Schl
North Little Rock, AR

Tunner, Alesia L
Cave City HS
Sulphur Rock, AR

Turneg, Amanda
Russellville Sr HS
Russellville, AR

Turner, Breanne L
Pea Ridge HS
Pea Ridge, AR

Turner, Dawn M
Northside HS
Fort Smith, AR

Turner, Katrina
Pea Ridge HS
Garfield, AR

Turner, Lanita L
Cabot HS
Cabot, AR

Turner, Tami
Sheridan Sr HS
Sheridan, AR

Turner, Thomas S
Hamburg HS
Crossett, AR

Turner, Troy E
Barton HS
Lexa, AR

Twilley, Dionne
Murfreesboro HS
Murfreesboro, AR

Tyler, Sarah L
Quitman Jr Sr HS
Quitman, AR

Tyner, Mike F
Cty Line HS
Charleston, AR

Tyree, Mary M
Bauxite Jr Sr HS
Bauxite, AR

Umerah, Catherine U
Parkview
Arts-Science HS
North Little Rock, AR

Umphress, Megan A
Conway Sr HS
Conway, AR

Underwood, Kerri L
Arkansas Sr HS
Texarkana, AR

Urbanek, Joey
Mountain Home HS
Mountain Home, AR

Vaden, Danika B
Beebe Sr HS
Mc Rae, AR

Valbracht, Gary W
Jacksonville HS
Cabot, AR

Valentine, Vicky
Crawfordsville HS
Crawfordsville, AR

Valenzvela, Chantal A
Springdale Sr HS
Springdale, AR

Van Amburg, Chris B
Cord-Charlotte Schl
Charlotte, AR

Vanderleest, Christopher R
Russellville Sr HS
Russellville, AR

Vassol, La Shonda M
Dumas HS
Dumas, AR

Vaughan, Kristen R
Hampton Jr Sr HS
Hampton, AR

Vaughn, Kerry L
Waldron HS
Waldron, AR

Vaught, Jake
Amity Jr Sr HS
Amity, AR

Veeder, Courtney B
Southside HS
Batesville, AR

Verrett, Sandy R
Parkers Chapel Schl
El Dorado, AR

Vest, Gina M
Mountain Home HS
Mountain Home, AR

Vickery, Alyson
Pulaski Acad
Little Rock, AR

Villines, Heather L
Harrison Sr HS
Compton, AR

Vines, Amy L
Jonesboro HS
Jonesboro, AR

Vinson, Shannon
Batesville Sr HS
Batesville, AR

Vizena, Val
Jasper HS
Dogpatch, AR

Voigt, Amber L
Bergman Schl
Harrison, AR

Vondran, Stephanie D
Searcy HS
Searcy, AR

Voytko, Donna R
Cabot HS
Cabot, AR

Wade, Dawn E
Van-Cove HS
Vandervoort, AR

Wadley, Randy A
Tuckerman HS
Tuckerman, AR

Wafford, Lisa D
Sheridan Sr HS
Pine Bluff, AR

Waggle, Lisa K
Rose Bud Jr Sr HS
Rose Bud, AR

Wagner, Erin C
Cabot HS
Cabot, AR

Wagner, Sarah
Northside HS
Fort Smith, AR

Wagner, Stacie D
Pulaski Acad
Little Rock, AR

Waits, Brandi S
Northside HS
Fort Smith, AR

Waldrup, Derrick
Dermott HS
Dermott, AR

Walker, Amy B
Mills HS
Jacksonville, AR

Walker, Candie M
Alma HS
Alma, AR

Walker, Delores J
Holly Grove HS
Pine Bluff, AR

Walker, Dustin H
Cotter Jr Sr HS
Gassville, AR

Walker, Jennifer J
Southside HS
Fort Smith, AR

Walker, Liesl F
Fayetteville
Christian Schl
Fayetteville, AR

Walker, Sarah E
Booneville Jr Sr HS
Booneville, AR

Walker, Sarah E
Springdale Sr HS
Springdale, AR

Walker, Sherita
Saratoga Schl
Ozan, AR

Walker, Waynita L
Arkansas Sr HS
Texarkana, AR

Wallace, Kendra D
Pine Bluff HS
Pine Bluff, AR

Wallis, Keith W
Drew Central Jr Sr HS
Monticello, AR

Wallrath, Jennifer D
Mountain Home HS
Mountain Home, AR

Walls, Brittany S
Booneville Jr Sr HS
Clinton, AR

Walls, Bryan
Butterfield Jr HS
Van Buren, AR

Walsh, Brad J
Crossett Sr HS
Crossett, AR

Walters, Courtney L
Lake Hamilton Sr HS
Royal, AR

Walters, Todd D
Southside HS
Fort Smith, AR

Ward, Aimee K
Southside HS
Fort Smith, AR

Ward, Jason W
Osceola HS
Osceola, AR

Ward, Joshua
Murfreesboro HS
Murfreesboro, AR

Ward, Julie N
Southside Schl
Damascus, AR

Ward, Melanie A
Junction City HS
Junction City, AR

Ward, Timothy J
Ridgecrest HS
Paragould, AR

Warnick, Jason E
Jonesboro HS
Jonesboro, AR

Warntjes, Melissa S
Springdale Sr HS
Springdale, AR

Warr, Stephanie K
Cabot HS
Cabot, AR

Warren, Jason K
Bryant Sr HS
Alexander, AR

Warren, Roberta
St Paul Schl
Witter, AR

Warrick, Matthew D
Booneville Jr Sr HS
Booneville, AR

Washington, Alisha
Lashun
Ashdown Sr HS
Ashdown, AR

Washington, Ericka
Ashdown Sr HS
Ashdown, AR

Waters, James R
Mc Rae Schl
Beebe, AR

Waters, Leah A
Hoxie Schl
Sedgwick, AR

Watkins, Amanda
Central Ark
Christian Schl
Little Rock, AR

Watkins, Brandi
Brinkley HS
Brinkley, AR

Watkins, Christophe
Greenland Jr Sr HS
Fayetteville, AR

Watkins, Deanna
Van Buren Sr HS
Van Buren, AR

Watkins, Edward P
Nettleton HS
Jonesboro, AR

Watkins, Summer
Augusta HS
Augusta, AR

Watkins, Traci J
Van Buren Sr HS
Van Buren, AR

Waymack, Emily
Cabot HS
Austin, AR

Wear, Jaime L
Southside HS
Fort Smith, AR

Weatherford, Tammy L
Des Arc Jr Sr HS
Des Arc, AR

Weaver, Justin
Van Buren Sr HS
Van Buren, AR

Weaver, Kimberly
Jessieville HS
Jessieville, AR

Weaver, Michael E
Booneville Jr Sr HS
Booneville, AR

Weaver, Mollie E
Lavaca Jr Sr HS
Lavaca, AR

Weaver, Nathan L
Vilonia HS
Vilonia, AR

Webb, Athena M
Parkview
Arts-Science HS
Little Rock, AR

Webb, Courtney
Lee Acad
Marianna, AR

Webb, Crystal D
Fayetteville Sr HS
Elkins, AR

Weddington, Keri
Lee Acad
Forrest City, AR

Wedgworth, Vickie
Augusta HS
Augusta, AR

Weeks, April L
Star City HS
Star City, AR

Weeks, Mckale S
Northside HS
Fort Smith, AR

Weems, Kristy L
Stamps HS
Buckner, AR

Weems, Latana
Holly Grove HS
Holly Grove, AR

Weens, Kristy L
Stamps HS
Buckner, AR

Weinsinger, Emily
Northside HS
Van Buren, AR

Welch, Tiffany M
Vilonia HS
Conway, AR

Wells, Kiley J
Clay Co Central Jr
Sr HS
Greenway, AR

Wells, Melissa A
Fayetteville Sr HS
Fayetteville, AR

Werschky, Aimee S
Greenwood Sr HS
Fort Smith, AR

Wesley, Kameelah
Parkview
Arts-Science HS
Little Rock, AR

West, Amanda M
Russellville Sr HS
Russellville, AR

West, Ashley
El Dorado Sr HS
El Dorado, AR

West, Joedi D
Concord Jr Sr HS
Drasco, AR

West, Josh S
Lavaca Jr Sr HS
Lavaca, AR

Westerman, Amber L
Harmony Grove Jr
Sr HS
Benton, AR

Weston, William D
Atkins Schl
Atkins, AR

Whalin, Cory M
Cabot HS
Cabot, AR

Whatley Jr,
Stephen Lee
Lakeside HS
Hot Springs, AR

Wheeler, Adam E
Corning HS
Corning, AR

Wheeler, Amanda A
Rivercrest HS
Dyess, AR

Wheeler, Britton Ross
Fayetteville Sr HS
Fayetteville, AR

Wheeler, Paul D
Marshall HS
Marshall, AR

Wheeler, William
Wayne
Lake Hamilton Sr HS
Hot Springs, AR

Wheeley, Stephanie M
Central HS
West Helena, AR

Whetsel, Angela M
Buffalo Island
Central HS
Monette, AR

Whitaker, Marcy P
West Memphis
Christian Schl
West Memphis, AR

White II, Claud Daniel
Abundant Life Schools
Sherwood, AR

White, Crystal A
Hughes Jr-Sr HS
Heth, AR

White, John R
Lake Hamilton Jr HS
Royal, AR

White, Kristina M
Greene Co Tech HS
Paragould, AR

White, Melissa R
Magnolia HS
Magnolia, AR

White, Shannon
Hartford Schl
Hartford, AR

Whitehead, A W
Lee Acad
Marianna, AR

Whitehead, Dylana
Morrilton Sr HS
Morrilton, AR

Whitehurst, Stephen C
Monticello HS
Monticello, AR

Whitley, Staci
Coleman Jr HS
Van Buren, AR

Whitney, Cameron W
Bergman Schl
Harrison, AR

Whitney, Dena L
Southside HS
Fort Smith, AR

Whittaker, Amber
Northside HS
Barling, AR

Whittemore, John D
Central Ark
Christian Schl
Little Rock, AR

Whittington, William
Northside HS
Fort Smith, AR

Wickard, Jennifer
J A Fair Sr HS
Little Rock, AR

Wiedemann, Heather A
Rogers HS
Rogers, AR

Wiedower, Elizabeth
Sacred Heart Schl
Morrilton, AR

Wiemann, Tiffany L
Lake Hamilton Sr HS
Pearcy, AR

Wilcox, Nathan W
Mulberry HS
Mulberry, AR

Wildhagen, Rachel
Clinton HS
Shirley, AR

Wiles, Jennifer
Highland HS
Ash Flat, AR

Wiles, John E
Highland HS
Hardy, AR

Wilkerson, Koquese S
Ozark HS
Ozark, AR

Wilkerson, Rebecca P
Parkview
Arts-Science HS
Little Rock, AR

Wilkerson, Susan K
Bryant Sr HS
Benton, AR

Wilkes, Byron N
Cave City HS
Cave City, AR

Wilkie, Ashley
Calvary Christian Schl
Forrest City, AR

Wilkinson, Amanda J
Dollarway HS
Pine Bluff, AR

Willams, Mary A
Southside HS
Rosie, AR

Willcutt, Brandy E
Morrilton Sr HS
Morrilton, AR

Willcutt, Daniel H
Atkins Schl
Atkins, AR

Williams, Amanda K
Lavaca Jr Sr HS
Lavaca, AR

Williams, Ashlee A
Central Sr HS
Little Rock, AR

Williams, Brad
Southwest
Christian Acad
Little Rock, AR

Williams, Brian G
Rogers HS
Rogers, AR

Williams, Carnita S
Oak Grove HS
North Little Rock, AR

Williams, Elizabeth L
Henderson Magnet
Jr HS
Little Rock, AR

Williams, Erin
Rivercrest HS
Wilson, AR

Williams, Irvette S
John L Mcclellan
Magnet HS
Little Rock, AR

Williams, Jackie E
Nettleton HS
Jonesboro, AR

Williams Jr, James R
Rogers HS
Lowell, AR

Williams, Jeffrey
Southside HS
Fort Smith, AR

Williams, Kim D
Lonoke Jr HS
Lonoke, AR

Williams, Kissa
Southside HS
Fort Smith, AR

Williams, Leodis
Forrest City HS
Forrest City, AR

Williams, Lindsay
Van Buren Sr HS
Van Buren, AR

Williams, Mendy
Bearden HS
Bearden, AR

Williams, Regina
Mc Gehee HS
Tillar, AR

Williams, Sara M
Clarksville HS
Clarksville, AR

Williams, Sarah
Lake Hamilton Sr HS
Hot Springs, AR

Williams, Stephanie D
Arkansas Sr HS
Texarkana, AR

Williams, Tracie
Dumas HS
Dumas, AR

Williams, Yolanda D
Mc Gehee HS
Mc Gehee, AR

Williford, Courtney B
Sheridan Sr HS
Sheridan, AR

Willis, Ericka R
Hot Springs HS
Hot Springs, AR

Willis, Vincent D
Jacksonville HS
Jacksonville, AR

Wilson, Bridget R
Harrison Sr HS
Harrison, AR

Wilson, Chris
Strong Jr Sr HS
Strong, AR

Wilson, Donna
Marion HS
Marion, AR

Wilson, Jamie L
Abundant Life Schools
Jacksonville, AR

Wilson, Jason C
Dewitt HS
De Witt, AR

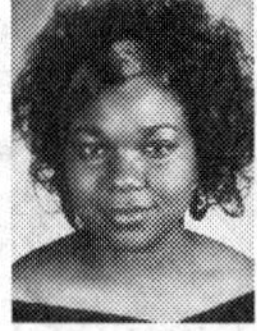
Wilson, Latonya S
John L Mcclellan
Magnet HS
Little Rock, AR

Wilson, Lori
Malvern Sr HS
Malvern, AR

Wilson, Melissa A
Lake Hamilton Sr HS
Hot Springs Natio, AR

Wilson, Shane
Nashville HS
Nashville, AR

Wilson, Stacey
Gould HS
Gould, AR

Winfrey, Jo D
Searcy HS
Searcy, AR

Winston, Rachel A
Sheridan Sr HS
Sheridan, AR

Winters, Matthew R
Russellville Sr HS
Russellville, AR

Wirges, Kevin C
Catholic HS
North Little Rock, AR

Wise, Heather
West Side
Christian Schl
El Dorado, AR

Wisler, Angie
Greenbrier HS
Greenbrier, AR

Witcher, Shu'Mia L
Magnolia HS
Waldo, AR

Witherspoon, Krystal
Yerger Jr HS
Hope, AR

Witherspoon, Nick K
Bryant Sr HS
Bryant, AR

Witt, Nathan L
Pine Bluff HS
Pine Bluff, AR

Wolfe, April
Mt Pleasant Jr Sr HS
Sage, AR

Wolken, Daniel J
Lakeside HS
Hot Springs, AR

Womack, Trisha J
Huttig Schl
Huttig, AR

Wood, Michael B
Cushman Schl
Cushman, AR

Wood, Tyler H
Van Buren Sr HS
Van Buren, AR

Woodard, Elizabeth K
Conway Sr HS
Conway, AR

Woodard, Jeremy S
Corning HS
Success, AR

Woodmansee, Summer
Watson Chapel Sr HS
Pine Bluff, AR

Woodruff, Amy G
Lavaca Jr Sr HS
Lavaca, AR

Woods, Courtney J
Arkansas Schl Math & Science
Hot Springs Natio, AR

Woods, Whitney
Prairie Grove HS
Prairie Grove, AR

Wooten, Dale
Genoa Central HS
Texarkana, AR

Workman, Cristy L
Cty Line HS
Paris, AR

Wright, Crenisha M
Forrest City HS
Forrest City, AR

Wright, Drew
Central Ark Christian Schl
Little Rock, AR

Wright, Jennifer G
Sloan Hendrix HS
Imboden, AR

Wright, Josh
Calico Rock HS
Calico Rock, AR

Wright, Rita C
Smackover HS
Smackover, AR

Wroten, Amy
East Poinsett Sr HS
Dyess, AR

Wunder, Laurie
Robinson HS
Roland, AR

Wyatt, Michael A
Southside HS
Batesville, AR

Wyles, Eric
Lamar HS
Lamar, AR

Wyles, Lea A
Lamar HS
Lamar, AR

Wynne, Kristi M
Forrest City HS
Forrest City, AR

Wynne, Wesley G
Ozark Adventist Acad
Waskom, TX

Wyss, Virginia E
Clay Co Central Jr Sr HS
Greenway, AR

Yager, Scott T
Oak Grove HS
Maumelle, AR

Yang, Cindy
Fayetteville East HS
Fayetteville, AR

Yarbrough, Elaina D
Lake Hamilton Sr HS
Hot Springs Natio, AR

Yarbrough, Van
Van Buren Sr HS
Van Buren, AR

Yates, Eddie
Cabot HS
Austin, AR

Yates, Kellie A
Fayetteville Christian Schl
Springdale, AR

Yeager, Tiffany M
Arkansas Sr HS
Texarkana, AR

York, Brandy
Blytheville Sr HS
Blytheville, AR

York, Reggie D
Star City HS
Star City, AR

Young, Daniel R
Rogers HS
Rogers, AR

Young, Jeremy
Lincoln HS
Summers, AR

Young, Laura
Jessieville HS
Hot Springs Natio, AR

Young, Lee
Booneville Jr Sr HS
Booneville, AR

Young, Sarah A
Lake Hamilton Sr HS
Hot Springs Natio, AR

Youngman, Robert M
Hoxie Schl
Hoxie, AR

Zarate, Juanita
Dequeen HS
De Queen, AR

Zerr, Julie A
Harrison Sr HS
Harrison, AR

KANSAS

Abernethy, Lindsay
Bishop Miege HS
Leawood, KS

Abernethy, Stacy A
St Thomas Aquinas HS
Leawood, KS

Abner, Nathan S
Riley Cty HS
Manhattan, KS

Abplanalp, Allison L
Washburn Rural HS
Topeka, KS

Abrahamson, Ty J
Olathe South Sr HS
Olathe, KS

Abu-Yousif, Adnan
Blue Valley Northwest HS
Overland Park, KS

Acheson, Saprina M
Russell HS
Russell, KS

Achterberg, Elliott
F L Schlagle HS
Kansas City, KS

Ackerman, Shawn L
Sabetha HS
Sabetha, KS

Adam, Nathan
Pittsburg HS
Pittsburg, KS

Adams, Laurie
Riley Cty HS
Manhattan, KS

Adams, Raushanah
Wichita West HS
Wichita, KS

Adams, Sarah J
Anderson Cty Jr Sr HS
Garnett, KS

Admire, Christina
Arkansas City HS
Arkansas City, KS

Adorante, Ashley B
Shawnee Mission S Sr HS
Overland Park, KS

Aduddell, Jerald R
Haven HS
Haven, KS

Agustin, Angela
Kapaun-Mt Carmel HS
Wichita, KS

Ahlvers, Jennifer
Waconda East HS
Glen Elder, KS

Albertson, Aaron L
Shawnee Mission N HS
Shawnee, KS

Albino, Maria L
Leavenworth HS
Gatesville, TX

Albino, Rosin L
Leavenworth HS
Fort Leavenworth, KS

Alcala, Donna
Ulysses HS
Ulysses, KS

Alcantar, Melissa A
Topeka West HS
Topeka, KS

Alexander, Shelly P
Campus HS
Haysville, KS

Aliani, Stephanie
Caney Valley Jr Sr HS
Caney, KS

Allen, Brad T
Burlington HS
Burlington, KS

Allen, Quentin T
Valley Falls HS
Valley Falls, KS

Allen, Teiah
Stafford Jr Sr HS
Stafford, KS

Aller, Taryn
Hiawatha HS
Hiawatha, KS

Alley, Joshua D
Blue Valley Northwest HS
Overland Park, KS

Allison, Tara R
Wichita West HS
Wichita, KS

Allmon, Deana
Ellsworth HS
Ellsworth, KS

Alloway, Robyn J
Labette Co HS
Parsons, KS

Allsup, Kelly
Sterling HS
Sterling, KS

KANSAS

Alonzo, Stacy M
Topeka HS
Topeka, KS

Alwin, Marc S
Colby Sr HS
Colby, KS

Amaro, John A
Olathe East Sr HS
Olathe, KS

Amaya, Isabel
Pierson Jr HS
Kansas City, KS

Ammar, Alex S
Wichita East HS
Wichita, KS

Anderson, Bryce A
Wichita Northwest HS
Wichita, KS

Anderson, Cristy R
Berean Acad
Valley Center, KS

Anderson, Jason P
Wichita East HS
Wichita, KS

Anderson, Kandis
Goodland HS
Goodland, KS

Anderson, Katie M
Basehor Linwood HS
Basehor, KS

Anderson, Rachael E
Shawnee Mission E
Sr HS
Prairie Village, KS

Anderson, Scott
Manhattan HS
Manhattan, KS

Anderson, Scott C
Bishop Miege HS
Kansas City, MO

Anderson, Shannon R
Pierson Jr HS
Kansas City, KS

Anderson, Verne Y
Sumner Acad Of Arts
& Science
Kansas City, KS

Andrews, Sarah
Spring Hill HS
Olathe, KS

Anduss, Mindy
Peabody-Burns Jr
Sr HS
Peabody, KS

Aneja, Tia
Wichita East HS
Wichita, KS

Angelo, Tom J
Kapaun-Mt Carmel HS
Wichita, KS

Anschutz, Carl E
Great Bend Sr HS
Great Bend, KS

Anschutz, Cynthia D
Great Bend Sr HS
Great Bend, KS

Anschutz, Joshua B
Great Bend Sr HS
Great Bend, KS

Anschutz, Melissa
Hays HS
Hays, KS

Anspaugh, Jodie
Washburn Rural HS
Topeka, KS

Anthony, Dana M
Shawnee Mission W
Sr HS
Shawnee Mission, KS

Anthony, Tiffany
Summer Acad
Kansas City, KS

Appier, Eric
Frontenac Jr Sr HS
Frontenac, KS

Apple, Allison D
Louisburg HS
Louisburg, KS

Applebaum, Jeremy
Blue Valley
Northwest HS
Overland Park, KS

Archer, Erin J
Anderson Cty Jr Sr HS
Garnett, KS

Ard, Kevin L
Maize HS
Maize, KS

Ardery, Rustin
South Gray HS
Copeland, KS

Arellano, Chris
Hugoton HS
Hugoton, KS

Arendt, Kathleen J
Colby Sr HS
Colby, KS

Arias, Jose
Great Bend Sr HS
Great Bend, KS

Armijo, Phillip A
El Dorado HS
El Dorado, KS

Armstrong, Allison B
Wichita Heights HS
Wichita, KS

Armstrong,
Christine M
Dodge City HS
Dodge City, KS

Armstrong, Matt
Campus HS
Haysville, KS

Arnhold, Leah
Miltonvale HS
Marion, KS

Arnold, Audra A
Maize HS
Wichita, KS

Arnold, Emily S
Baldwin HS
Baldwin City, KS

Artman, Beth A
El Dorado HS
El Dorado, KS

Arzate, Mercedes
Emporia HS
Emporia, KS

Ashby, Jennifer L
Southeast HS
Wichita, KS

Ashcraft, Leanna
Field Kindley Mem
Sr HS
Coffeyville, KS

Asher, Jana
Turner HS
Kansas City, KS

Asquith, Aaron R
Olathe South Sr HS
Olathe, KS

Ast, Juliette
Wichita East HS
Wichita, KS

Atlas, Jonathan B
Shawnee Mission E
Sr HS
Shawnee Mission, KS

Augustine, Rachelle
Buhler HS
Hutchinson, KS

Austin, Jeremy C
Parsons HS
Parsons, KS

Avila, Jose E
Wichita East HS
Wichita, KS

Baber, Phillip
Central Christian Schl
Hutchinson, KS

Baca, Suzanne
St John Jr Sr HS
Saint John, KS

Bach, Huyen N
Newton Sr HS
Newton, KS

Backes, Thomas D
Kapaun-Mt Carmel HS
Wichita, KS

Bacon, Anne
Topeka HS
Topeka, KS

Baer, Julie
Manhattan HS
Manhattan, KS

Bagby, Darren
Frederic
Remington HS
Wichita, KS

Bahl, Brandon K
Ulysses HS
Ulysses, KS

Bailey, Amber M
Galena HS
Galena, KS

Bailey, Devon L
Galena HS
Galena, KS

Bailey, Gabriel K
Ellsworth HS
Ellsworth, KS

Bailey, Owen R
Osawatomie HS
Osawatomie, KS

Bailey, Wendy L
Otis Bison HS
Otis, KS

Bailey, William
St Thomas Aquinas HS
Lenexa, KS

Baker, Amy C
Maize HS
Wichita, KS

Baker, Barbara L
Junction City HS
Junction City, KS

Baker, Daniel
Arkansas City HS
Arkansas City, KS

Baker, Michael L
Iola Sr HS
Iola, KS

Baker, Rusty A
Liberal HS
Liberal, KS

Baker, Tyler
Maize HS
Wichita, KS

Balch, Andrea D
El Dorado HS
El Dorado, KS

Baldwin, Adam S
Inman Jr Sr HS
Mc Pherson, KS

Baldwin, Greg S
Olathe East Sr HS
Olathe, KS

Baldwin, Mark A
Santa Fe Trail Jr HS
Olathe, KS

Bales, Brian J
Shawnee Mission W
Sr HS
Overland Park, KS

Bales, Christopher A
Olathe East Sr HS
Overland Park, KS

Bales, Nicole M
Washburn Rural HS
Topeka, KS

Ball, Jessica A
Blue Valley
Northwest HS
Overland Park, KS

Balsly, Eden M
Blue Valley
Northwest HS
Overland Park, KS

Balzano, Laura K
St Thomas Aquinas HS
Overland Park, KS

Banks, Kristy L
Eureka Jr Sr HS
Toronto, KS

Banks, Paul
Washburn Rural HS
Topeka, KS

Barber, Judith
Burrton Schl
Burrton, KS

Barclay, Heidi
Arkansas City HS
Arkansas City, KS

Barlow, Minisa R
Wichita HS SE
Wichita, KS

Barnes, Carinda
Sumner Acad Of Arts
& Science
Kansas City, KS

Barnes, Jason
Louisburg HS
Louisburg, KS

Barnes, Sonia J
Elkhart HS
Elkhart, KS

Barnes, Travis
Newton Sr HS
Newton, KS

Barnett, Jeff R
Maur Hill Prep Schl
Lawrence, KS

Barnett, Jeni
El Dorado HS
El Dorado, KS

Barnett, Sasha N
Garden City Sr HS
Garden City, KS

Barr, Brandon
Lebo Schl
Lebo, KS

Barr, Emily
St Thomas Aquinas HS
Overland Park, KS

Barrett, Debbie
Deerfield HS
Deerfield, KS

Barta, Amber D
Ellsworth HS
Wilson, KS

Bartelli, Brad
Parsons HS
Parsons, KS

Barthelman, Eli D
Maize HS
Wichita, KS

Bartz, Nicole
El Dorado HS
El Dorado, KS

Basel II, Wendell R
Lawrence HS
Lawrence, KS

Basinski, Brian A
Louisburg HS
Louisburg, KS

Bass, Camille
Sumner Acad Of Arts
& Science
Kansas City, KS

Bassell, Candice M
Wichita
Collegiate Schl
Wichita, KS

Bates, Derrick D
Seaman Sr HS
Topeka, KS

Bathurst, Neeley R
Chapman HS
Abilene, KS

Bauer, Luke D
Buhler HS
Hutchinson, KS

Baus, Leigh A
Pratt HS
Pratt, KS

Bays, Aimee N
Topeka West HS
Topeka, KS

Beam, Kristen L
Washburn Rural HS
Topeka, KS

Bean, Broderick G
Onaga HS
Onaga, KS

Beard, Shannon R
Kapaun-Mt Carmel HS
Wichita, KS

Beashore, Ryan P
Shawnee Mission
N HS
Shawnee Mission, KS

Beatson, Brandi M
Olathe East Sr HS
Olathe, KS

Bechard, Dayna A
Tescott HS
Culver, KS

Bechtelheimer, Jessica
Bishop Carroll
Catholic HS
Wichita, KS

Beck, Naomi
Clay Ctr Cmty HS
Clay Center, KS

Becker, Kent R
Hayden HS
Topeka, KS

Becker, Shane A
Great Bend Sr HS
Great Bend, KS

Beckham, R Jason
Piper HS
Kansas City, KS

Beckmon, Nathan
Crest HS
Kincaid, KS

Beeghly-Hills,
Jennifer L
Burlington HS
Burlington, KS

Beery, Heath C
Cimarron HS
Kalvesta, KS

Belcher, Brandi
Maranatha Acad
Olathe, KS

Bell, Brandee D
Shawnee Mission W
Sr HS
Overland Park, KS

Bell, Cassandra M
Wichita South HS
Wichita, KS

Bell, Ja Meya L
Wichita North HS
Wichita, KS

Bell, Stuart K
Bishop Miege HS
Kansas City, KS

Belles, Duwayne N
Beloit Jr Sr HS
Beloit, KS

Belt, Aimee C
Paola HS
Paola, KS

Bencomo, Sonia
Ulysses HS
Ulysses, KS

Bender, Joshua M
Wichita East HS
Wichita, KS

Benefield, Joshua
St Mary's Colgan HS
Pittsburg, KS

Benfer, Sarah L
Salina HS Central
Salina, KS

Bennefeld, Joy
Olathe East Sr HS
Olathe, KS

Bennett, Angela D
Girard HS
Girard, KS

Bennett, Arvilla
Winfield HS
Winfield, KS

Bennett, Matthew E
Santa Fe Trail Jr HS
Olathe, KS

Bennett, Molly W
Shawnee Mission
N HS
Shawnee Mission, KS

Bennington, Scott G
El Dorado HS
El Dorado, KS

Benson, Eric F
Sumner Acad Of Arts
& Science
Kansas City, KS

Benteman, Annette L
Yates Ctr HS
Yates Center, KS

Berenbom, Anne
Shawnee Mission E
Sr HS
Shawnee Mission, KS

Berg, Brian D
Robert E Clark Jr HS
Bonner Springs, KS

Berg, Kim
Lyndon HS
Vassar, KS

Berger, Erin R
Horton HS
Everest, KS

Bergkamp, Lori
Sedgwick HS
Valley Center, KS

Bergman, Jami
Smith Ctr Jr Sr HS
Lebanon, KS

Berry, Krista
Holcomb HS
Holcomb, KS

Berry, Matthew A
Emporia HS
Emporia, KS

Berry, Shawnda R
Maize HS
Wichita, KS

Berryman, Jacob W
Ashland HS
Ashland, KS

Bever, James F
Campus HS
Wichita, KS

Beyah, Khajriyyah N
Northeast Magnet HS
Wichita, KS

Beyer, Jason E
Santa Fe Trail Jr HS
Olathe, KS

Beynon, Matt S
St John's Military Schl
Wichita, KS

Billinger, Dawn M
Thomas More
Prep-Marion HS
Hays, KS

Billings, Richard P
Bishop Ward HS
Kansas City, KS

Billingsley,
Samantha A
Sumner Acad
Kansas City, KS

Bilyk, Tyler
Sedan HS
Pawhuska, OK

Bingaman, Rachelle J
Wichita
Collegiate Schl
Wichita, KS

Bird, Jeff A
Deerfield HS
Deerfield, KS

Bird, Tari A
Topeka West HS
Topeka, KS

Birk, Mandy L
Burlington HS
Burlington, KS

Bishop, Carmaletta C
Washington HS
Kansas City, KS

Bishop, Jessica M
Lawrence HS
Lawrence, KS

Black, Charlene M
El Dorado HS
El Dorado, KS

Black, Keely R
Ottawa HS
Ottawa, KS

Blackburn, Amanda M
Labette Co HS
Parsons, KS

Blackerby, Shaila A
Maize HS
Wichita, KS

Blackford, Beau
Buhler HS
Hutchinson, KS

Blake, Charlene M
Topeka HS
Topeka, KS

Blakesley, Stacy
Garden City Sr HS
Garden City, KS

Blanton, April
Cheney Jr Sr HS
Murdock, KS

Blasi, Nathan
Goddar HS
Wichita, KS

Blasing, Jeremy
Washburn Rural HS
Topeka, KS

Blass, Kenda D
Hayden HS
Fort Worth, TX

Blattner, Barton
Atchison Sr HS
Atchison, KS

Blattner, Eric
Atchison Sr HS
Atchison, KS

Blazic, Adam
Girard HS
Girard, KS

Bliss, Maureen E
Colby Sr HS
Colby, KS

Bloesing, G Jared
Wichita South HS
Wichita, KS

Blomquist, Jennifer
Salina HS Central
Salina, KS

Bloom, Ginny
Andover HS
Wichita, KS

Blosser, Tara
Shawnee Mission
South HS
Overland Park, KS

Blubaugh, Stephanie K
Labette Co HS
Parsons, KS

Boaz, Rebecca L
Troy HS
Troy, KS

Bobbitt, Jodi R
Hoisington HS
Hoisington, KS

Bodine, Toni L
Rock Creek Jr Sr HS
Manhattan, KS

Bogenhagen, Nicole
Wallace Cty HS
Wallace, KS

Boggs, Tiffany L
Campus HS
Haysville, KS

Bogle, Tracette M
Winfield HS
Winfield, KS

Bogner, Cheryl
Spearville Jr Sr HS
Wright, KS

Bohannon, Christophe
Blue Valley
Northwest HS
Overland Park, KS

Bohi, Jennifer A
Olathe East Sr HS
Olathe, KS

Bohme, Brooke
Goodland HS
Goodland, KS

Bolden, Cristal A
F L Schlagle HS
Kansas City, KS

Boles, John
Emporia HS
Emporia, KS

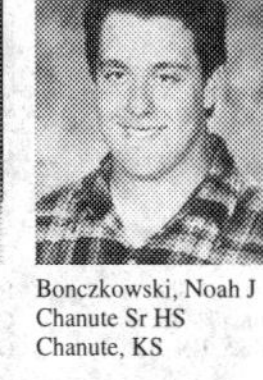

Bolling, Melanie
Ft Scott HS
Fort Scott, KS

Bolmer, Steffani
Dodge City HS
Dodge City, KS

Bolton, Kari
Marysville HS
Marysville, KS

Bolyard, Tabitha J
Trinity Catholic HS
South Hutchinson, KS

Bonczkowski, Noah J
Chanute Sr HS
Chanute, KS

Bonewitz, Ryan
Newton Sr HS
Newton, KS

Bonnell, Stephanie
Goddard HS
Wichita, KS

Boor, Richard Todd
Hoisington HS
Hoisington, KS

Bosse, Brian K
Independence HS
Independence, KS

Bowden, Amanda R
Morland Jr Sr HS
Hill City, KS

Bowden, Ashley
Louisburg HS
Bucyrus, KS

Bowell, Lindsay
Abilene HS
Abilene, KS

Bowen, Desiree D
Kapaun-Mt Carmel HS
Wichita, KS

Bowen, Jennifer L
Shawnee Mission W
Sr HS
Lenexa, KS

Bowen, Richard W
Blue Valley HS
Lawton, OK

Bowling, Kim M
Leavenworth HS
Leavenworth, KS

Bowman, Heather
Prairie View Jr Sr HS
La Cygne, KS

Boxberger, Stephanie
Mc Pherson HS
Mc Pherson, KS

Boyce, Brandilyn
Spring Hill HS
Olathe, KS

Boyd, Cheryl
Turner HS
Kansas City, KS

Boyd, Deena
Shawnee Mission W
Sr HS
Lenexa, KS

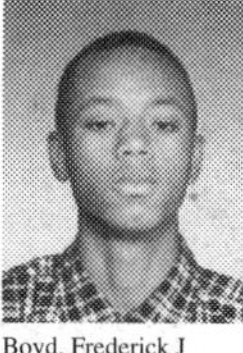
Boyd, Frederick J
Wyandotte HS
Kansas City, KS

Boyd, Melissa J
Shawnee Mission E
Sr HS
Shawnee Mission, KS

Boyko, Megan A
Olathe East Sr HS
Olathe, KS

Boyles, Deidra M
White Rock HS
Superior, NE

Bradstreet, Eric C
Hutchinson HS
Hutchinson, KS

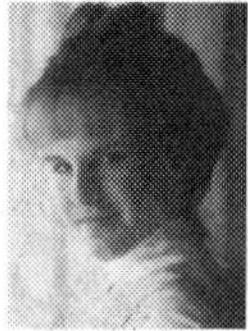
Brandt, Kristen N
Andover HS
Andover, KS

Branick, Misty D
Russell HS
Russell, KS

Brant, Charles E
Arkansas City HS
Arkansas City, KS

Brazier, Carrie A
Southeast HS
Wichita, KS

Bredfeldt, Nichole
Dodge City HS
Dodge City, KS

Brees, Jessica
Goddard HS
Wichita, KS

Brenn, Brooks
Colby Sr HS
Colby, KS

Brennan, Sean
Leavenworth HS
Fort Leavenworth, KS

Breuer, Shannon L
Atchison Sr HS
Atchison, KS

Brewer, Dane A
Kapaun-Mt Carmel HS
Andover, KS

Brewer, Elizabeth C
Coldwater Jr Sr HS
Coldwater, KS

Brewer, William A
Washington HS
Kansas City, KS

Brewington, Joshua D
Blue Valley HS
Olathe, KS

Bridges, Jessica
Shawnee Mission
South HS
Overland Park, KS

Briggeman, Steven M
Pratt HS
Iuka, KS

Briggs, Joss E
Dighton HS
Gove, KS

Brigham, Jon R
Iola Sr HS
Iola, KS

Brim, Heather L
Basehor Linwood HS
Basehor, KS

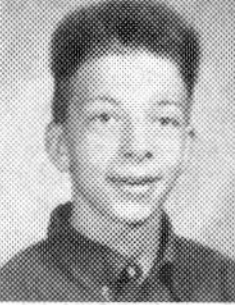
Bringham, Darin A
Meade HS
Meade, KS

Brink, Lisa D
Ft Scott HS
Fort Scott, KS

Bristow, Mike K
Immaculata HS
Leavenworth, KS

Brittian, Rebecca A
Downtown Law
Magnet HS
Wichita, KS

Brizendine, Kristen A
Blue Valley HS
Overland Park, KS

Brobst, Jeremy N
Scott Comm HS
Scott City, KS

Brock, Dustin R
Derby HS
Derby, KS

Brodersen, Catherine
Junction City HS
Fort Leavenworth, KS

Brooks, Catherine
St Thomas Aquinas HS
Lenexa, KS

Brooks, Laura
Atchison Sr HS
Atchison, KS

Brower, Julie
Olathe South Sr HS
Olathe, KS

Brown, Arianne M
Colby Sr HS
Colby, KS

Brown, Chanda R
Colby Sr HS
Colby, KS

Brown, Dustin P
Washburn Rural HS
Auburn, KS

Brown III, George L
Sedan HS
Sedan, KS

Brown, Jennifer
St Mary's Colgan HS
Pittsburg, KS

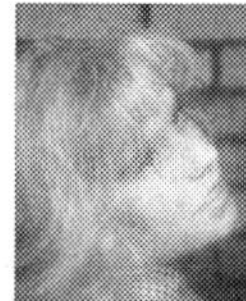
Brown, Jennifer
Atwood HS
Atwood, KS

Brown, Kristy J
Ft Scott HS
Fulton, KS

Brown, Ronnie
Syracuse Jr Sr HS
Coolidge, KS

Brown, Shameka D
Washington HS
Kansas City, KS

Brown, Stacey M
Blue Valley
Northwest HS
Overland Park, KS

Brown, Tamara L
Wallace Cty HS
Wallace, KS

Brown, Trey
Kansas City Area Voc
Tech Sch
Leavenworth, KS

Brown, Wade D
Central Heights Sr HS
Richmond, KS

Brownewell, Tiffany J
Parsons HS
Parsons, KS

Browning, Michael
Winfield HS
Winfield, KS

Browning, Tarrah
Shawnee Mission S
Sr HS
Overland Park, KS

Bruce, Brad T
Shawnee Mission
N HS
Roeland Park, KS

Bruce, Hope
St Thomas Aquinas HS
Shawnee Mission, KS

Bruggeman, Nicole
Golden Plains HS
Rexford, KS

Brumback, Jeana M
Arkansas City HS
Arkansas City, KS

Brumback, Jessica
Columbus HS
Columbus, KS

Brumwell, Sean C
Shawnee Mission E
Sr HS
Shawnee Mission, KS

Brune, Daniel K
Olathe South Sr HS
Olathe, KS

Bruner, Jeremy E
Augusta Sr HS
Augusta, KS

Brungardt, Amanda L
Victoria HS
Gorham, KS

Brunhoeber, Amy C
Wichita Southeast HS
Wichita, KS

Brunk, Jamie A
Berean Acad
Wichita, KS

Brunn, Danielle
Rossville HS
Rossville, KS

Bryan, Janna L
Blue Valley HS
Overland Park, KS

Bryant, Chrissy
Atwood HS
Atwood, KS

Bryant, Kendra M
Liberal HS
Liberal, KS

Bryant, Mc Clain E
Sumner Acad Of Arts & Science
Kansas City, KS

Bryant, Michael
South Gray HS
Copeland, KS

Buchanan, Bryce W
Minneola Schl
Minneola, KS

Buchheister, Mendy D
Manhattan HS
Manhattan, KS

Buchmueller, Daniel J
Pratt HS
Pratt, KS

Buczinski, Erica M
Goddard HS
Wichita, KS

Budig, Heather J
Great Bend Sr HS
Great Bend, KS

Buehler, Jana
North Central HS
Haddam, KS

Bueno, Renee G
Garden City Sr HS
Garden City, KS

Bullock, Kelli A
Olathe East Sr HS
Olathe, KS

Bumgarner, Jennifer
Field Kindley Mem Sr HS
Coffeyville, KS

Bunker, Leslie J
Olathe East Sr HS
Olathe, KS

Burch, Wendee
Holcomb HS
Holcomb, KS

Burchett, Jennifer
Wakefield Schl
Longford, KS

Burchett IV, Lawrence R
St Thomas Aquinas HS
Overland Park, KS

Burdick, Amy
Andover HS
Andover, KS

Burgess, Justin
Ulysses HS
Ulysses, KS

Burgey, Dawn R
Fairfield HS
Sylvia, KS

Burkdoll, Jeffrey S
Marais Des Cygnes Valley HS
Melvern, KS

Burke, Daniel
Maur Hill Prep Schl
Atchison, KS

Burke, Heather E
Wichita West HS
Wichita, KS

Burke, Samantha R
Chanute Sr HS
Walnut, KS

Burkhart, Hollie J
Hayden HS
Topeka, KS

Burnor, Amie S
Independence HS
Cherryvale, KS

Burns, Bethany D
Newton Sr HS
Newton, KS

Burns, Tammy
Prairie View Jr Sr HS
Osawatomie, KS

Burress, Jessica
Erie HS
Erie, KS

Burroughs, Chad D
Great Bend Sr HS
Great Bend, KS

Burrows, Brandi R
Rolla HS
Rolla, KS

Burton, Benjamin
Enterprise Sda Acad
Manhattan, KS

Burton, Brian
Enterprise Sda Acad
Wichita, KS

Burton, Lu Juana M
Topeka HS
Topeka, KS

Busch, Angeline
Dodge City HS
Dodge City, KS

Busch, Noah
Marysville HS
Home, KS

Busick, Misty
Parsons HS
Parsons, KS

Busse, Andrea
Cheylin West Jr Sr HS
Bird City, KS

Butler, Angie K
Great Bend Sr HS
Great Bend, KS

Butts, Dacia R
Derby HS
Wichita, KS

Byerly, Allen E
Pratt HS
Pratt, KS

Byers, David P
Blue Valley HS
Overland Park, KS

Cadek, Jason L
Wellington Sr HS
Howard, OH

Cady, Stephen M
Olathe South Sr HS
Olathe, KS

Cahow, Leslie E
Blue Valley Northwest HS
Overland Park, KS

Cain, Patrick
Hayden HS
Topeka, KS

Callier, Sarah B
Bishop Miege HS
Overland Park, KS

Calovich, Jenny D
Piper HS
Kansas City, KS

Cameron, Lakisha Y
Highland Park HS
Topeka, KS

Campbell, Melissa S
Blue Valley HS
Overland Park, KS

Canady, Kristina R
Washburn Rural HS
Topeka, KS

Cansler, Jessica
Turner HS
Kansas City, KS

Cantrall, Seth
Greensburg HS
Greensburg, KS

Carey, Lisa K
Washburn Rural HS
Topeka, KS

Carey, Stephanie M
Leavenworth HS
Leavenworth, KS

Carlin, Mike
Manhattan HS
Manhattan, KS

Carlson, Brandon C
Lyons HS
Lyons, KS

Carlson, Brent
Pike Valley HS
Courtland, KS

Carlton, Robert S
Hiawatha HS
Hiawatha, KS

Carnal, Nathan
Parsons HS
Parsons, KS

Carnao, Carol L
Bishop Miege HS
Kansas City, MO

Carpenter, Travis A
Blue Valley HS
Stilwell, KS

Carpentier, Jamie
Elwood Schl
Elwood, KS

Carr, Alicia D
Augusta Sr HS
Augusta, KS

Carr, Melissa A
Maize HS
Wichita, KS

Carrico, Sherri A
Basehor Linwood HS
Bonner Springs, KS

Carrithers, Sara E
Wichita North HS
Wichita, KS

Carroll, James T
Burlingame HS
Burlingame, KS

Carson, Jennifer L
Labette Co HS
Parsons, KS

Carter, Eric
Santa Fe Trail HS
Overbrook, KS

Carthen, Warnell D
Wichita East HS
Wichita, KS

Cartwright, Chris
Arkansas City HS
Arkansas City, KS

Carty, Elizabeth B
Blue Valley
Northwest HS
Shawnee Mission, KS

Casey, Tracie
Olathe North Sr HS
Olathe, KS

Casey, Trina
South Gray HS
Copeland, KS

Casher, Nichol R
Derby HS
Wichita, KS

Casteel, Corey
Abilene HS
Abilene, KS

Cauble, Justin R
Riverton Schl
Baxter Springs, KS

Caulkins, Angela L
Field Kindley Mem
Sr HS
Coffeyville, KS

Caywood, Brad W
Sterling HS
Sterling, KS

Chacey, Michael D
Derby HS
Derby, KS

Chairs, Brittni F
Wichita North HS
Wichita, KS

Chambers, Carrie L
Yates Ctr HS
Yates Center, KS

Champlin, David G
Blue Valley
Northwest HS
Overland Park, KS

Chance, Raymond D
Cheney Jr Sr HS
Cheney, KS

Chandler, Carly
Shawnee Mission
Northwest HS
Shawnee Mission, KS

Chang, Albert M
Blue Valley HS
Overland Park, KS

Chang, Jesse
Olathe East Sr HS
Overland Park, KS

Charboneau, Angela T
Derby Christian Schl
Haysville, KS

Charpentier, Nicole
Shawnee Mission Nw
Sr HS
Lenexa, KS

Chase, Heather S
St Thomas Aquinas HS
Shawnee Mission, KS

Chastain, Jackie L
El Dorado HS
El Dorado, KS

Cheatum, Travis
Syracuse Jr Sr HS
Syracuse, KS

Chee, Bernard A
Derby HS
Wichita, KS

Cheney, Jenny
Syracuse Jr Sr HS
Syracuse, KS

Chowning, Joey D
Turner HS
Kansas City, KS

Christman, Lindsay
Wichita
Collegiate Schl
Wichita, KS

Chronister, Levi
Pittsburg HS
Pittsburg, KS

Church, Becky
Emporia HS
Emporia, KS

Clacher, Raylyn A
Maize HS
Wichita, KS

Clare, Jessica L
Jefferson West HS
Meriden, KS

Clark, Annessa D
Newton Sr HS
Newton, KS

Clark, Brittany A
Chanute Sr HS
Chanute, KS

Clark, Heather
Atchison Co Cmty HS
Lancaster, KS

Clark, Jennifer J
Junction City HS
Junction City, KS

Clark, Justin W
Garden City Sr HS
Garden City, KS

Clark, Karrie
Burlington HS
Burlington, KS

Clark, Nicole R
Shawnee Mission E
Sr HS
Roeland Park, KS

Clarke, Catherine L
Desoto HS
Shawnee, KS

Clarkson, Eric
Cimarron HS
Cimarron, KS

Clawson, Stephanie
Springa Hill HS
Olathe, KS

Clay, Sandra A
Gardner-Edgerton HS
Gardner, KS

Clements, Andy L
Northwest HS Wichita
Wichita, KS

Click, Tim
Great Bend Sr HS
Great Bend, KS

Cline, Shea R
Berean Acad
Valley Center, KS

Cliver, Irona Marcella
Wichita South HS
Wichita, KS

Coats, Jason E
Shawnee Mission
N HS
Shawnee Mission, KS

Cobb, Michelle L
Russell HS
Russell, KS

Coble, Abby C
Salina HS Central
Salina, KS

Coburn, Katharine
Arkansas City HS
Arkansas City, KS

Coffey, Ben J
Louisburg HS
Paola, KS

Coffie, Trudy C
Topeka HS
Topeka, KS

Colbert, Taylor
Manhattan HS
Manhattan, KS

Colclausure,
Stephanie C
Olathe North Sr HS
Olathe, KS

Cole, Aaron O
Olpe Schl
Emporia, KS

Cole, Angie
Hays HS
Hays, KS

Cole, Jason E
Olpe Schl
Emporia, KS

Cole, Michael A
Washington HS
Kansas City, KS

Cole, Nicholas
Olathe East Sr HS
Olathe, KS

Coles, Kristy
Olathe South HS
Cabot, AR

Collier, Tracey D
Washburn Rural HS
Topeka, KS

Collins, Amber M
Parsons HS
Parsons, KS

Collins, Brooke
Wichita North HS
Wichita, KS

Collins, Dorothy E
Northeast HS
Arma, KS

Collins, Gregory L
F L Schlagle HS
Kansas City, KS

Collins, Matthew
Northwest HS Wichita
Wichita, KS

KANSAS

Collins, Rebecca
Manhattan HS
Manhattan, KS

Collman, Candice L
Washburn Rural HS
Topeka, KS

Collmann, Julie L
Belleville HS
Cuba, KS

Colson, Jason L
Goodland HS
Goodland, KS

Combes, Loretta D
Humboldt HS
Humboldt, KS

Combs, Jeremy
Wichita West HS
Wichita, KS

Comstock, Jennifer L
Wichita Heights HS
Wichita, KS

Conard, Danielle L
Central Christian Schl
Hutchinson, KS

Condon, Travis A
Labette Co HS
Altamont, KS

Conklin, Blake
Topeka HS
Topeka, KS

Conn, Jason M
Downs HS
Harlan, KS

Connell, Jeff
Olathe North Sr HS
Olathe, KS

Connor, David
Wichita West HS
Wichita, KS

Conrad, Kimberly L
Field Kindley Mem
Sr HS
Coffeyville, KS

Conrad, Michael W
Field Kindley Mem
Sr HS
Coffeyville, KS

Consiglio, David N
Shawnee Mission
Northwest HS
Shawnee Mission, KS

Conway IV, Lawrence
Leavenworth HS
Fort Leavenworth, KS

Cook, Bethany L
Lawrence HS
Lawrence, KS

Cook, Chris G
Ft Scott HS
Fort Scott, KS

Cook, Crystal M
Riverton Schl
Riverton, KS

Cook, Julie A
Eudora HS
Eudora, KS

Coomes, Heather L
St Paul HS
Saint Paul, KS

Coonfield, Brandon J
Coldwater Jr Sr HS
Coldwater, KS

Cooper,
Elizabeth Anne
Wichita East HS
Wichita, KS

Cooper, Jacob A
Circle HS
El Dorado, KS

Cop, Carrie
Shawnee Mission
N HS
Merriam, KS

Copp, Erika
Oskaloosa HS
Ozawkie, KS

Corbett, Kendra Renee
Salina HS South
Salina, KS

Corby, Victoria M
Salina HS Central
Salina, KS

Corcoran, Mary K
Lawrence HS
Lawrence, KS

Corcoran, Matthew
St Thomas Aquinas HS
Lenexa, KS

Corke, Eric
Goodland HS
Goodland, KS

Corle Jr, Aldon E
Independence HS
Independence, KS

Cornett, J Ryan
Garden City Sr HS
Garden City, KS

Cornett, Steven R
Fredonia HS
Fall River, KS

Cornwell, Lesley B
Wichita East HS
Wichita, KS

Corporon, Jay A
Topeka West HS
Topeka, KS

Costello, Stacy G
Dodge City HS
Dodge City, KS

Coulter, Chris
Mulvane Sr HS
Mulvane, KS

Coulter, Lea B
Colby Sr HS
Colby, KS

Courtway, Edgar N
Ft Scott HS
Fort Scott, KS

Cox, Benjamin R
Salina HS South
Salina, KS

Cox, Brent D
Beloit Jr Sr HS
Beloit, KS

Coyle, Maria L
Wyandotte HS
Kansas City, KS

Crable, Cory H
Olathe North Sr HS
Olathe, KS

Craft, Shaun R
Marion HS
Marion, KS

Craig, Kimberly A
Great Bend Sr HS
Great Bend, KS

Craig, Nathan G
Goodland HS
Goodland, KS

Cramer, Aleeta L
Leavenworth HS
Leavenworth, KS

Crandall, Jessica
Little River Jr Sr HS
Little River, KS

Crane, Breann
Ottawa HS
Ottawa, KS

Cranmer, Chandra R
Maize HS
Wichita, KS

Cranston, Jake J
Colby Sr HS
Colby, KS

Crawford, Amanda R
Hartford HS
Neosho Rapids, KS

Creed, Annie
North HS
Wichita, KS

Creekmore, Daniel L
Campus HS
Wichita, KS

Criser, Angie E
Wichita East HS
Wichita, KS

Cross, Brian S
Skyline Schl
Pratt, KS

Cross, Gina S
Wichita East HS
Wichita, KS

Crow, Christy E
Shawnee Heights
Sr HS
Tecumseh, KS

Crowder, Jason
Spring Hill HS
Spring Hill, KS

Crowder, Jeanette M
Spring Hill HS
Spring Hill, KS

Crowe, Kerstan L
Maize HS
Wichita, KS

Crowe, Melinda M
Maize HS
Wichita, KS

Crubel, Robert
St Marys HS
Saint Marys, KS

Crumb, Laurie
Mission Valley HS
Burlingame, KS

Cruz, Rainier T
St Xavier's HS
Ft Riley, KS

Culbertson, Ashley K
El Dorado HS
El Dorado, KS

Culp, Terri A
Chanute Sr HS
Walnut, KS

Cumming, Sariah
Garden City Sr HS
Garden City, KS

Cummins, Erin
Wichita North HS
Wichita, KS

Cummins, Tara
Wichita North HS
Wichita, KS

Cunningham,
Andrea M
Sumner Acad Of Arts
& Science
Kansas City, KS

Cunningham, La
Tisha D
Hays HS
Hays, KS

Curnutt, Carri L
El Dorado HS
El Dorado, KS

Currey, Christina
Manhattan HS
Manhattan, KS

Curry, Patrick
Nathaniel
Southeast KS Spec
Ed Coop
Galena, KS

Dalbom, Christophr
Shawnee Mission
Northwest HS
Shawnee Mission, KS

Dale, Ryan T
Great Bend Sr HS
Great Bend, KS

Dalke, Denai
Wichita North HS
Wichita, KS

Dalke, Justin D
Moundridge HS
Moundridge, KS

Dalton, Stephanie L
Northeast HS
Pittsburg, KS

Daly, Megan
Olathe East Sr HS
Olathe, KS

Daniel, Matthew
Great Bend Sr HS
Great Bend, KS

Danielson, Matt A
Lenora HS
Lenora, KS

Dardenne, Elissa
Galena HS
Galena, KS

Da Silva, Heather
Immaculata HS
Leavenworth, KS

Daugherty, Brandi
Shawnee Mission
N HS
Merriam, KS

Dauphin, Quinn
Washburn Rural HS
Topeka, KS

Davied, Susan L
Lyndon HS
Lyndon, KS

Davis, Alicia
Wichita South HS
Wichita, KS

Davis, Alison
Oak Grove
Baptist Schl
Mission, KS

Davis, Brian S
Northwest HS
Wichita, KS

Davis, Erin
Wichita East HS
Wichita, KS

Davis, Jaime L
Chapman HS
Enterprise, KS

Davis, Jason R
Manhattan HS
Manhattan, KS

Davis, Jonathan W
Newton Sr HS
Newton, KS

Davis, Kesia M
Olathe East Sr HS
Olathe, KS

Davis, Lacey
Newton Sr HS
Newton, KS

Davis, Matt
Salina HS Central
Salina, KS

Davis, Rachael M
Hillsboro HS
Hillsboro, KS

Dawson, Serena
Northwest HS
Wichita, KS

Day, Lisa
Council Grove HS
Council Grove, KS

Day, Melissa
Shawnee Heights
Sr HS
Topeka, KS

Day, Tina J
Elwood Schl
Elwood, KS

Dealy, Nolan J
Halstead HS
Halstead, KS

Dean, Molly R
Louisburg HS
Bucyrus, KS

Dearinger, Steven
South Gray HS
Montezuma, KS

Dechant, Linzie E
Larned HS
Larned, KS

Dechant, Ryan
Sacred Heart HS
Salina, KS

Dechant, Tammy R
Dodge City HS
Dodge City, KS

De Donder,
Kimberly L
Lebo Schl
Reading, KS

Dee, Jessica K
Acad Of Mt St
Scholastica
Lawrence, KS

Dees, Michelle
Paola HS
Paola, KS

De Filippo, Kristen L
Derby HS
Derby, KS

De Graftenreed,
Leanda M
Washington HS
Kansas City, KS

Degruson, Debra
Wichita Heights HS
Kechi, KS

Dehner, Michelle
Atchison Sr HS
Atchison, KS

Deibert, Renelle D
Great Bend Sr HS
Great Bend, KS

Deichert, Alison
Mulvane Sr HS
Mulvane, KS

Deidra, Boyles
White Rock HS
Superior, NE

Deines, Erin E
Chapman HS
Chapman, KS

Deines, Nathan A
Chapman HS
Chapman, KS

Deines, Sally R
Trego Comm HS
Wa Keeney, KS

Delladio, Heather N
Bonner Springs HS
Bonner Springs, KS

Delmez, Shannon M
Olathe East Sr HS
Olathe, KS

Del Percio, Marlo
Sumner Acad Of Arts
& Science
Kansas City, KS

Demby-Pennington,
Danielle D
Lawrence HS
Lawrence, KS

Demel, Dustin M
Hoisington HS
Hoisington, KS

Demel, Melissa R
Great Bend Sr HS
Great Bend, KS

Demott, Susie I
Baldwin HS
Baldwin City, KS

Demuth, Shannon
Hays HS
Hays, KS

Denton, Ashley R
Dodge City HS
Dodge City, KS

Depenbusch, Carrie
Columbus HS
Columbus, KS

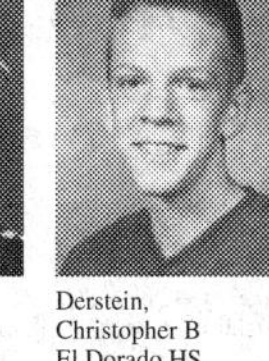

Derstein,
Christopher B
El Dorado HS
El Dorado, KS

De Ruyscher, Simon O
Immaculata HS
Leavenworth, KS

Detrixhe, Alan J
Clifton-Clyde HS
Concordia, KS

Detrixhe, Monica
Concordia Jr Sr HS
Concordia, KS

Deuvall, Kristine L
Olathe North Sr HS
Olathe, KS

De Wald, Jessica Marie
Trego Comm HS
Wa Keeney, KS

De Wald, Shane R
Otis Bison HS
Otis, KS

Dexter, Brandon L
Ness City HS
Ness City, KS

Dibble, Sara A
Santa Fe Trail HS
Scranton, KS

Dice, Jennifer S
Blue Valley HS
Stilwell, KS

Dick, Melissa
Rossville HS
Rossville, KS

Dick, Pamela D
Russell HS
Russell, KS

Dick, Tanya M
Blue Valley HS
Stanley, KS

Dickens, Blossom M
Labette Co HS
Cherryvale, KS

Dickinson, Sharon E
Leavenworth HS
Leavenworth, KS

Dickson, Kari
Newton Sr HS
Newton, KS

Diepenbrock, Stephanie L
Wichita East HS
Wichita, KS

Dill, Megan M
Hartford HS
Hartford, KS

Dillinger, Camilla L
Altoona Midway HS
Buffalo, KS

Dillon, David N
Northeast Magnet HS
Wichita, KS

Dilts, Brad
Wichita Collegiate Schl
Sedgwick, KS

Dishman, Sara
Goddard HS
Wichita, KS

Diskin, Monica A
St Paul HS
Walnut, KS

Disrud, Ginger A
Blue Valley HS
Olathe, KS

Dixon, Erika J
Halstead HS
Sedgwick, KS

Dixon, Melissa R
Berean Acad
Wichita, KS

Djajich, Mike T
Olathe East Sr HS
Olathe, KS

Doeblin, Melissa R
Wichita Collegiate Schl
Wichita, KS

Doherty, Andrew D
Ft Scott HS
Fort Scott, KS

Doile, Tracy
El Dorado HS
El Dorado, KS

Dolsky, Ron A
Wichita Southeast HS
Wichita, KS

Dominguez, Heather R
Oak Grove Baptist Schl
Kansas City, KS

Donley, Jenny L
Ellsworth HS
Lincoln, KS

Donley, Martha
Crest HS
Colony, KS

Donnell, Maria
Sumner Acad Of Arts And Sci
Kansas City, KS

Donnelly, Chris L
Olathe East Sr HS
Olathe, KS

Donnelly, Kristen
Washington HS
Kansas City, KS

Donnelly, Kyle
Manhattan HS
Manhattan, KS

Dooley, Ryan Michael
Maur Hill Prep Schl
Atchison, KS

Dort, Rachel L
Washington HS
Kansas City, KS

Dorzweiler, Eric
Ellis HS
Ellis, KS

Dorzweiler, Richard
Hays HS
Catharine, KS

Dotson, Brandi A
Wichita Heights HS
Wichita, KS

Dotzour, Melanie L
Wichita Southeast HS
Wichita, KS

Douglas, Aaron J
Lansing HS
Lansing, KS

Douthart, Heather C
Washburn Rural HS
Auburn, KS

Dover, Jamey A
Newton Sr HS
Newton, KS

Dowling, Tammie
Protection Schl
Protection, KS

Dowling, Tanner
Minneola Schl
Dodge City, KS

Dowling, Thomas
Thomas More Prep-Marion HS
Hays, KS

Dragoo, Vanessa R
Northeast Magnet HS
Wichita, KS

Drake, Adam D
Bishop Miege HS
Leawood, KS

Drake, Angela
Kansas City Christian Schl
Leawood, KS

Drake, Damon
Eureka Jr Sr HS
Eureka, KS

Drake, Daphne L
South Barber HS
Kiowa, KS

Drake, Nicholas J
Pleasanton HS
Pleasanton, KS

Draper, Crystal H
Turner HS
Kansas City, KS

Dray, Melissa L
Lawrence HS
Lawrence, KS

Dreher, Jennifer A
El Dorado HS
El Dorado, KS

Dressler, Deanna
Shawnee Mission N HS
Shawnee Mission, KS

Dressler, Michael J
Manhattan HS
Manhattan, KS

Drietz, Ragan P
Liberal HS
Liberal, KS

Droge, Justin Leon
Shawnee Heights Sr HS
Tecumseh, KS

Drown, Eli J
Basehor Linwood HS
Tonganoxie, KS

Dryden, Jaime
St John Jr Sr HS
Saint John, KS

Dubin, Joseph
Blue Valley North HS
Leawood, KS

Dubin, William J
Santa Fe Trail Jr HS
Olathe, KS

Duffy, Colleen
Eureka Jr Sr HS
Eureka, KS

Dunaway, Candi F
Buhler HS
Hutchinson, KS

Dunback, Christopher Deane
Belleville HS
Belleville, KS

Duncan, Jennifer M
Buhler HS
Buhler, KS

Duncan, Jeremiah J
Hutchinson HS
Hutchinson, KS

Duncan, Maranatha J
Manhattan HS
Dupont, WA

Dungey, Amber N
Maize HS
Wichita, KS

Dunham, Marcy E
Great Bend Sr HS
Great Bend, KS

Dunmire, Elly
Bern Schl
Bern, KS

Dunn, Alexandria S
Holton HS
Holton, KS

Dunn, Cortland R
St John's Military Schl
Englewood, CO

Dunn, Katie
Paola HS
Paola, KS

Durham, Benjamin J
Oak Grove
Baptist Schl
Kansas City, KS

Dusil II, Antone L
Sumner Acad Of Arts
& Science
Kansas City, KS

Dutcher, Sarah L
El Dorado HS
Augusta, KS

Early, Allison
Shawnee Mission E
Sr HS
Shawnee Mission, KS

Earnhart, Melanie D
Blue Valley HS
Olathe, KS

Eastes, Beau
Pratt HS
Pratt, KS

Eastwood, James J
Ft Scott HS
Fort Scott, KS

Ebaben, Andre
Centre Jr Sr HS
Lincolnville, KS

Ebeling, Pamela
Dodge City HS
Dodge City, KS

Eckhardt, Amanda
Columbus HS
Columbus, KS

Eden, Jessica
Peabody-Burns Jr
Sr HS
Peabody, KS

Edington, Amanda D
Chase Co HS
Emporia, KS

Edmonds, Katherine A
Great Bend Sr HS
Great Bend, KS

Edwards, Daniel J
Bishop Miege HS
Kansas City, MO

Edwards, Jason
Meade HS
Fowler, KS

Edwards, Nicole E
Colby Sr HS
Colby, KS

Edwards, Peter M
Independence HS
Independence, KS

Edwards, Rebecca L
Independence HS
Independence, KS

Eichelberger, Jeanne
Marie
Wichita East HS
Wichita, KS

Eilrich, Steven
Mc Pherson HS
Mc Pherson, KS

Elliot, Steven
Hays HS
Hays, KS

Elliott, Cody L
Great Bend Sr HS
Great Bend, KS

Elliott, Katie
Kapaun-Mt Carmel HS
Wichita, KS

Elliott, Laura
St Thomas Aquinas HS
Paola, KS

Elliott, Rodney R
Haven HS
Mount Hope, KS

Ellis, Chad
Independence HS
Independence, KS

Ellis, Kody J
St John Jr Sr HS
Saint John, KS

Elliss, Denita K
Anderson Cty Jr Sr HS
Westphalia, KS

Elmore, Andi
Sedgwick HS
Valley Center, KS

Elmore, Jerry
Argonia Jr Sr HS
Argonia, KS

Elrod, Bree
Topeka HS
Topeka, KS

Elsten, Eric
Baxter Springs HS
Baxter Springs, KS

Emmert, Terrye L
Riverton Schl
Riverton, KS

Engebretson, Megan
Lansing HS
Lansing, KS

Engelkemier, Monte
Blue Valley HS
Overland Park, KS

Engels, Jeremy D
Wichita Northwest HS
Wichita, KS

Engle, Ryan
Madison Jr Sr HS
Madison, KS

Engstrom, Nicholas J
Wamego HS
Wamego, KS

Enlee, Brooke
Atchison Sr HS
Atchison, KS

Enlow, Kristie
Dodge City HS
Dodge City, KS

Ensley, Jill Rae Anne
Seaman Sr HS
Topeka, KS

Entwistle, Anika
Shawnee Mission E
Sr HS
Leawood, KS

Enz, Nicholas J
Newton Sr HS
Newton, KS

Epperson, Joshua
Peabody-Burns Jr
Sr HS
Peabody, KS

Eppler, Beth A
Blue Valley North HS
Leawood, KS

Epps, Colby
Topeka West HS
Topeka, KS

Erickson, Geneva J
Smoky Valley HS
Lindsborg, KS

Ericson, Mynon M
Mission Valley HS
Maple Hill, KS

Eschke, Stacy
Riley Cty HS
Riley, KS

Espinosa, Rachel I
Dodge City HS
Dodge City, KS

Essman, Russell F
Oskaloosa HS
Oskaloosa, KS

Etling, Tina M
Cimarron HS
Ensign, KS

Eubank, Robin
Protection Schl
Protection, KS

Evans, Amanda L
El Dorado HS
El Dorado, KS

Evans, Desiree R
Washington HS
Kansas City, KS

Evans, Ryan W
Great Bend Sr HS
Great Bend, KS

Every, Adam D
Parsons HS
Parsons, KS

Every, Jason C
Wichita South HS
Wichita, KS

Ewell, Jordan Alicia
Washburn Rural HS
Topeka, KS

Ewing, Kelly M
Turner HS
Kansas City, KS

Ewing, Shannon
Erie HS
Erie, KS

Ezell, Jeremy H
Galena HS
Galena, KS

Ezell, Nathan A
Galena HS
Galena, KS

Ezell, Sammie
Galena HS
Galena, KS

Fabrizius, Jenny
Solomon Jr Sr HS
Solomon, KS

Falk, Jeanne S
Atchison Co Cmty HS
Atchison, KS

Fanska, Joe
Spring Hill HS
Spring Hill, KS

KANSAS

Farber, Mandie
Hoxie HS
Hoxie, KS

Farber, Rachel R
Hoxie HS
Hoxie, KS

Farkes, Helen M
Shawnee Mission S Sr HS
Overland Park, KS

Farmer, Crystal D
Anderson Cty Jr Sr HS
Welda, KS

Farmer, Rachel S
Blue Valley HS
Overland Park, KS

Farney, Christopher J
Shawnee Mission N HS
Merriam, KS

Farris, Matt
Goddard HS
Goddard, KS

Farris, Pat H
St John's Military Schl
Oklahoma City, OK

Faudel, Lorry A
Halstead HS
Halstead, KS

Feaster, Rachel L
Hays HS
Kansas City, MO

Fee, Lawrence
Turner HS
Kansas City, KS

Fehr, Tammy
Emporia HS
Emporia, KS

Fenner, Michael J
Goodland HS
Goodland, KS

Ferguson, Olivia P
Kensington Jr Sr HS
Kensington, KS

Ferman, Chris
Mulvane Sr HS
Mulvane, KS

Fernando, Harendra N
Larned HS
Larned, KS

Fernkopf, Lura D
Holton HS
Holton, KS

Ferrell, Jeffrey W
Shawnee Mission S Sr HS
Shawnee Mission, KS

Ferris, Jennifer L
Maize HS
Christiansburg, VA

Fields, Nikki S
Olathe East Sr HS
Overland Park, KS

Fife, Kate
Spring Hill HS
Spring Hill, KS

Figgins, Jennifer R
Mankato Jr Sr HS
Mankato, KS

Filsinger, Stacie
Spring Hill HS
Spring Hill, KS

Fincham, Rachel E
Leavenworth HS
Leavenworth, KS

Findley, Leah
Ulysses HS
Ulysses, KS

Finley, Jason A
Goodland HS
Goodland, KS

Finley, Jennifer L
Basehor Linwood HS
Kansas City, KS

Finley, Zachary A
Shawnee Mission West HS
Lenexa, KS

Finnigin, Kevin
Lansing HS
Leavenworth, KS

Fischer, Brooke R
Hutchinson HS
Hutchinson, KS

Fischer, Carisa L
Hutchinson HS
Hutchinson, KS

Fischer, Heidi E
Hutchinson HS
Hutchinson, KS

Fischer, Helen
Arkansas City HS
Arkansas City, KS

Fischer, Renee L
Salina HS South
Salina, KS

Fisher, Kathy S
Shawnee Mission Nw Sr HS
Shawnee, KS

Fitts, Carissa C
Sumner Acad Of Arts & Science
Kansas City, KS

Fitzgerrel, Kelvie Ann
Ransom Jr Sr HS
Ransom, KS

Fitzgibbon, Travis W
Topeka HS
Topeka, KS

Fitzmaurice, Stephanie J
Olathe East Sr HS
Olathe, KS

Fletcher, Jennifer L
Shawnee Mission W Sr HS
Overland Park, KS

Flohrschutz, Willie R
Holton HS
Denison, KS

Florence Jr, Sarah
West HS
Wichita, KS

Florquist, Lane
Syracuse Jr Sr HS
Syracuse, KS

Flynn, Breanna
Gardner-Edgerton HS
Gardner, KS

Fogelberg, Stacie
Hoisington HS
Great Bend, KS

Folck, Lindsay A
Lyons HS
Lyons, KS

Foley, Ross G
Cheney Jr Sr HS
Cheney, KS

Follmer, Holly
Washburn Rural HS
Topeka, KS

Folsom, Rebecca P
Osawatomie HS
Osawatomie, KS

Foos, Jendee
Lacrosse HS
La Crosse, KS

Ford, Melissa R
Wichita North HS
Wichita, KS

Ford, Miranda S
Campus HS
Haysville, KS

Forman, Kimberly E
Jefferson West HS
Meriden, KS

Forsythe Jr, Steven A
Highland Park HS
Topeka, KS

Fose, Jayme
Trego Comm HS
Wa Keeney, KS

Foskuhl, Jason
Dodge City HS
Dodge City, KS

Foster, Brandon A
Great Bend Sr HS
Great Bend, KS

Foster, Gregory A
Labette Co HS
Oswego, KS

Foster, Theresa M
Walnut Creek HS
Eskridge, KS

Fotovich, Brian
Piper HS
Kansas City, KS

Fountaine, Elizabeth A
Arkansas City HS
Arkansas City, KS

Fouraker, Sarah L
Maranatha Acad
Shawnee, KS

Fouts, Keith
Ottawa HS
Ottawa, KS

Fox, Carolee
Waverly HS
Waverly, KS

Foxx, Marianne
Wakefield HS
Milford, KS

Francis, Lindy
Garden City Sr HS
Garden City, KS

Frank, Shannon
Shawnee Mission S Sr HS
Shawnee Mission, KS

Frankel, Leslie M
Blue Valley Northwest HS
Overland Park, KS

Franken, Andrew W
Troy HS
Troy, KS

Franklin, Patricia A
Girard HS
Hepler, KS

Franklin, Tara
Arkansas City HS
Arkansas City, KS

Franz, Karl N
Olathe East Sr HS
Overland Park, KS

Franz, Natasha
Wichita Southeast HS
Tulsa, OK

Frederking, Matthew D
Beloit Jr Sr HS
Beloit, KS

Freeman, Aubrey
Pratt HS
Pratt, KS

Freeman, Dani
Lansing HS
Lansing, KS

French, John M
Buhler HS
Hutchinson, KS

French, Lance M
Trego Comm HS
Wa Keeney, KS

Frese, Amy L
Council Grove HS
Alta Vista, KS

Frey, Kenny
Inman Jr Sr HS
Mc Pherson, KS

Fridy, Melinda K
Liberal HS
Liberal, KS

Friedly, Dawn R
Phillipsburg HS
Phillipsburg, KS

Frierson, Sedric T
Wyandotte HS
Kansas City, KS

Friesen, Christopher D
Hesston HS
Hesston, KS

Friesen, Kelly
Hutchinson HS
Hutchinson, KS

Friesen, Kim A
Hutchinson HS
Hutchinson, KS

Friesen, Tracy D
Berean Acad
Galva, KS

Frisbie, Meghan
Herington HS
Herington, KS

Fry, Jamie A
El Dorado HS
El Dorado, KS

Fry, Toby J
Bishop Ward HS
Kansas City, KS

Frye, Jenny
Wallace Cty HS
Sharon Springs, KS

Fryman, Lynnlea
Garden City Sr HS
Garden City, KS

Fuchs, Kim
Shawnee Mission
N HS
Shawnee Mission, KS

Fukunaga, Edwin T
Blue Valley
Northwest HS
Overland Park, KS

Funk, Corey D
Maize HS
Wichita, KS

Funk, Cory
Russell HS
Russell, KS

Furst, Kara
St Thomas Aquinas HS
Overland Park, KS

Fye, Sunshine C
Summer Acad Of Arts
& Sci
Kansas City, KS

Fyler, Jeremy
Otis Bison HS
Olmitz, KS

Fyock, Summer L
Jayhawk-Linn HS
Prescott, KS

Gable, William
Wichita West HS
Wichita, KS

Gafford, Kris
Nemaha Valley HS
Seneca, KS

Gaines, Ronald
James Rj
El Dorado HS
Cassoday, KS

Gallardo, Justin C
Wichita North HS
Wichita, KS

Gamalo, Santipong
Northeast Magnet HS
Wichita, KS

Gantz, Bryan L
Sterling HS
Sterling, KS

Gaona, Jaime J
Shawnee Mission
N HS
Mission, KS

Garard, Dana
Erie HS
Erie, KS

Garcia, Carla M
Yates Ctr HS
Yates Center, KS

Garner, Christopher M
Dodge City HS
Victoria, VA

Garrett, Brandon M
Great Bend Sr HS
Great Bend, KS

Garrett, Terry M
Prairie View Jr Sr HS
La Cygne, KS

Garrison, Heather L
Derby HS
Derby, KS

Garrison, Jared D
Wichita South HS
Wichita, KS

Gary, John D
Junction City HS
Junction City, KS

Gasper, Julie
Lawrence HS
Lawrence, KS

Gast, Amelia L
Leavenworth HS
Leavenworth, KS

Gaston, Amanda L
Baxter Springs HS
Baxter Springs, KS

Gatewood, Amber D
Columbus HS
Columbus, KS

Gattshall, Travis
Goodland HS
Goodland, KS

Gaughan, Amy
Spring Hill HS
Spring Hill, KS

Gaunt, Staci L
Great Bend Sr HS
Great Bend, KS

Gavin, Sean M
Leavenworth HS
Leavenworth, KS

Gayley, Scott A
Bishop Miege HS
Prairie Village, KS

Gebhart, Whitney E
Salina HS Central
Salina, KS

Gee, Jodi
Ulysses HS
Ulysses, KS

Gentry, Shana
Rossville HS
Rossville, KS

George, Jamie D
Wichita East HS
Wichita, KS

George, Lyndsay N
Goodland HS
Goodland, KS

Gerken, Scott
Paola HS
Paola, KS

German, Sara D
Yates Ctr HS
Neosho Falls, KS

Gerstner, Nicole L
Trego Comm HS
Collyer, KS

Gettler, Toby
Independence HS
Independence, KS

Geurian, Brienna B
Hutchinson HS
Hutchinson, KS

Gibson, Rodney
Turner HS
Kansas City, KS

Gier, Kristi N
Shawnee Mission E
Sr HS
Leawood, KS

Gier, Tina M
Girard HS
Hepler, KS

Giesick, Melissa
Buhler HS
Buhler, KS

Giessel, Andrew J
Larned HS
Larned, KS

Gilbert, Janelle
Clay Ctr Cmty HS
Morganville, KS

KANSAS

Gilbert, Rebecca A
Shawnee Mission
Northwest HS
Kansas City, KS

Gilchrist, Carrie C
Salina HS South
Salina, KS

Gilchrist, Nicholas
Valley Ctr HS
Valley Center, KS

Gillikin, Angela
Olathe East Sr HS
Overland Park, KS

Gillispie, Jennifer
Maize HS
Wichita, KS

Gilreath, Kristi A
Salina HS South
Salina, KS

Ginie, Ryan
Olathe South Sr HS
Olathe, KS

Ginter, Angie
Shawnee Heights
Sr HS
Topeka, KS

Gish, Sam L
Washburn Rural HS
Topeka, KS

Gisler, Jennifer
Shawnee Mission
East HS
Shawnee Mission, KS

Glass, Shana M
Blue Valley
Northwest HS
Overland Park, KS

Gleason, Ryan
Garden City Sr HS
Garden City, KS

Glennie, Amber S
Wichita East HS
Wichita, KS

Goddard, Jason D
Beloit Jr Sr HS
Glasco, KS

Godfrey III, James R
Salina HS South
Salina, KS

Godfrey, Jana M
Labette Co HS
Parsons, KS

Godfrey, Vanessa
St John Jr Sr HS
Saint John, KS

Godown, Casey
Maize HS
Maize, KS

Godsil, Josh T
Dodge City HS
Dodge City, KS

Goering, Kathryn F
Lawrence HS
Lawrence, KS

Goertzen, William
Hillsboro HS
Hillsboro, KS

Goetz, Astrid R
Russell HS
Russell, KS

Goetz, Jennifer J
Thomas More
Prep-Marion HS
Hays, KS

Goetz, Tammy
Cunningham HS
Zenda, KS

Goetz, Tiffany
Cunningham HS
Zenda, KS

Goins, Adrian D
Independence
Bible Schl
Thayer, KS

Goldstein, David K
Blue Valley North HS
Leawood, KS

Goltra, Sarah L
Ft Scott HS
Fort Scott, KS

Gonzalez, Jennifer L
Shawnee Heights HS
Topeka, KS

Good, Laura
Blue Valley HS
Olsburg, KS

Goodno, Jamie
St John Jr Sr HS
Seward, KS

Gordee, Hollie D
Great Bend Sr HS
Great Bend, KS

Gordon, Cheryl K
Rossville HS
Rossville, KS

Gordon, Varee
Rock Creek Jr Sr HS
Westmoreland, KS

Gordy, Jenny
Cair
Paravel-Latin Schl
Topeka, KS

Gorup, Geoff
Maize HS
Wichita, KS

Goss, Danielle R
Leavenworth HS
Leavenworth, KS

Goth, Amanda
Waconda East HS
Beloit, KS

Gottschalk, Ryan C
Thomas More
Prep-Marian HS
Hays, KS

Gough, Erin L
Newton Sr HS
Newton, KS

Graber, Jennifer L
Kingman HS
Kingman, KS

Graber, Karen H
Kingman HS
Kingman, KS

Grace, Lee Anne R
Beloit Jr Sr HS
Beloit, KS

Grafos, Gina L
Wichita East HS
Wichita, KS

Grant, Adam J
Liberal HS
Liberal, KS

Grant, Eric C
Larned HS
Larned, KS

Graue, Christine E
Blue Valley HS
Overland Park, KS

Graves, Joe D
Labette Co HS
Bartlett, KS

Gray, Kristiane
Shawnee Mission
Northeast HS
Lenexa, KS

Green, Chris
Hutchinson HS
Hutchinson, KS

Green, Jana M
Emporia HS
Emporia, KS

Green, Toby
Dodge City HS
Dodge City, KS

Greenbaum, Stacy L
Blue Valley HS
Overland Park, KS

Greenwald, Jesse R
El Dorado HS
El Dorado, KS

Griffeth, Erin C N
Lawrence HS
Lawrence, KS

Griffin, Lila G
J C Harmon HS
Kansas City, KS

Griffiths, Tonya R
Abilene HS
Abilene, KS

Grimes, Steve S
Wichita Northwest HS
Wichita, KS

Grimsley, Tricia D
Maize HS
Wichita, KS

Grishom, Sharee S
Junction City HS
Junction City, KS

Groening, Jenny
Marion HS
Marion, KS

Groff, Michael R
Manhattan HS
Manhattan, KS

Gross, Marshall A
Shawnee Mission
South Ctr
Overland Park, KS

Grossardt, Amber L
Claflin Jr Sr HS
Claflin, KS

Grother, Laura
Northern Heights HS
Americus, KS

Gruenbaum, Michael
Immaculata HS
Leavenworth, KS

Gruwell, Sarah
Waconda East HS
Glen Elder, KS

Guess, Deneika
Washington HS
Kansas City, KS

Guinn, Kevan K
Maize HS
Wichita, KS

Gullino, Alycee M
J C Harmon HS
Kansas City, KS

Guyer, Donna B
Highland Park HS
Topeka, KS

Haag, Eric
Leavenworth HS
Leavenworth, KS

Haag, Michael R
Leavenworth HS
Leavenworth, KS

Haase, Micah
Galena HS
Galena, KS

Hackley, Marlena L
Wichita East HS
Wichita, KS

Hagar, Kellie L
Wellington Sr HS
Wellington, KS

Hagedorn, Amy E
Robert E Clark Jr HS
Bonner Springs, KS

Hagedorn, Scott
Bonner Spgs HS
Bonner Springs, KS

Hageman, Sherri
Kingman HS
Spivey, KS

Hageman, Steve
Kingman HS
Spivey, KS

Hager, Jennifer M
Gardner-Edgerton HS
Edgerton, KS

Hager, Megan
Gardner-Edgerton HS
Edgerton, KS

Hague, Michael
Peabody-Burns Jr Sr HS
Peabody, KS

Haines, Brian T
Olathe South Sr HS
Olathe, KS

Hake, Katie B
Buhler HS
Hutchinson, KS

Halderson, Bjorn
Cunningham HS
Cunningham, KS

Haley, Crystal K
El Dorado HS
El Dorado, KS

Hall, Andi
Campus HS
Wichita, KS

Hall, Stephanie L
Atchison Co Cmty HS
Effingham, KS

Hall, Tiffany L
Atchison Co Cmty HS
Effingham, KS

Halliburton, Brandi L
Field Kindley Mem Sr HS
Coffeyville, KS

Halterman, Kelly
Shawnee Mission Northwest HS
Shawnee Mission, KS

Hamel, Erin J
South Haven Schl
South Haven, KS

Hamlin, Jason
Newton Sr HS
Newton, KS

Hamm, Faye L
Goddard HS
Goddard, KS

Hammes, Shaun D
Nemaha Valley HS
Seneca, KS

Hampton, Carol
Lansing HS
Colorado Springs, CO

Hampton, Shaun M
Independence HS
Independence, KS

Handy, Shawn E
Shawnee Mission N HS
Shawnee Mission, KS

Hanes, Jared S
Eastern Heights Jr Sr HS
Republican City, NE

Hansen, Philip C
Independence HS
Independence, KS

Hanson, Kale W
Blue Valley HS
Stilwell, KS

Hardcastle, Michelle
Shawnee Mission S Sr HS
Lenexa, KS

Harding, Amy
Louisburg HS
Louisburg, KS

Harding, Jessica A
Holton HS
Mayetta, KS

Hardy, Erika V
Salina HS South
Salina, KS

Hargis, Teri A
Field Kindley Mem Sr HS
Coffeyville, KS

Harkins, Dawn M
Central Heights Sr HS
Richmond, KS

Harlin Jr, William R
Wyandotte HS
Kansas City, KS

Harlow, Kolissa
White City HS
Herington, KS

Harma, Trisha
Derby HS
Derby, KS

Harms, Greg
Ulysses HS
Ulysses, KS

Harper, Shawn J
J C Harmon HS
Kansas City, KS

Harrington, Katherine
Olathe South Sr HS
Olathe, KS

Harris, Jodi L
Emporia HS
Augusta, KS

Harris, Matt
Valley Ctr HS
Valley Center, KS

Harris, Michael E
St John's Military Schl
Mayer, AZ

Harris, Nicole
Hugoton HS
Liberal, KS

Harris, Stephen Welsh
Shawnee Mission E Sr HS
Fairway, KS

Harris, Tanyon R
Lawrence HS
Lawrence, KS

Harris, William
Great Bend Sr HS
Great Bend, KS

Harrison, Lisa
St John Jr Sr HS
Saint John, KS

Harrison, Tabitha
Olathe North Sr HS
Olathe, KS

Harrity, Bryan J
Sumner Acad Of Arts & Science
Kansas City, KS

Harrity, Shannon M
Sumner Acad Of Arts & Science
Kansas City, KS

Harshman, Burton L
Chase Co HS
Cedar Point, KS

Hart, Betsey C
Olathe East Sr HS
Shawnee Mission, KS

Hart, Meredith C
Galena HS
Galena, KS

Hart, Niki
Nickerson HS
Nickerson, KS

Harte Mitchell, Tim J
Blue Valley HS
Overland Park, KS

Hartig, Timothy B
Sumner Acad Of Arts & Science
Kansas City, KS

Harting, Matthew H
Derby HS
Derby, KS

Hartman, Brooke Tamarron
Wichita Northwest HS
Wichita, KS

Hartsell, Meggin E
Great Bend Sr HS
Great Bend, KS

Hartwick, Kacie D
Dodge City HS
Dodge City, KS

Harvey, Chad
Pratt HS
Pratt, KS

Hasan, Heather L
Halstead HS
Newton, KS

Hash, Nicole
Louisburg HS
Louisburg, KS

Hashmi, Michelle C
Emporia HS
Emporia, KS

Haslett, Cassi
Syracuse Jr Sr HS
Syracuse, KS

Hasselle, Suzanne M
Lawrence HS
Lawrence, KS

Hasty, Herndon S
Blue Valley
Northwest HS
Overland Park, KS

Hathaway, Keisha N
Derby HS
Derby, KS

Hatridge, Jill
Olathe South Sr HS
Olathe, KS

Haug, Susan J
Frankft HS
Frankfort, KS

Hauschild, Heidi
Sterling HS
Sterling, KS

Hawkins, Andy
West Elk Jr Sr HS
Grenola, KS

Hawkins, Scott M
Washburn Rural HS
Topeka, KS

Hawthorne, Nicole
Goddard HS
Goddard, KS

Hay, Brandon N
Bishop Carroll
Catholic HS
Wichita, KS

Haynie, Nicole
Goddard HS
Goddard, KS

Hays, Jamie A
Pratt HS
Pratt, KS

Head, Sara
Yates Ctr HS
Yates Center, KS

Headings, Andrea
Central Christian Schl
Hutchinson, KS

Headley, Matt
Hutchinson HS
Hutchinson, KS

Heaton, Danniell A
Russell HS
Russell, KS

Heavey, Brandon A
Blue Valley
Northwest HS
Overland Park, KS

Heim, Ryan M
Shawnee Mission
N HS
Roeland Park, KS

Hein, Carmen
Hillsboro HS
Hillsboro, KS

Heinen, Glenn
Nemaha Valley HS
Seneca, KS

Heinen, Jennifer J
Axtell Schl
Axtell, KS

Heiniger, Leslie J
Bern Schl
Bern, KS

Heinitz, Katina
Ulysses HS
Ulysses, KS

Heiskell, Sarah M
Derby HS
Derby, KS

Heitz, Christin H
Maize HS
Wichita, KS

Heller, Jessica R
Sylvan Unified HS
Hunter, KS

Helm, Amber
Kingman HS
Kingman, KS

Helm, Kristina A
Turner HS
Kansas City, KS

Helm, Rebecca D
Pierson Jr HS
Kansas City, KS

Helmers, Shawna M
Campus HS
Haysville, KS

Helstrom, Clark A
Maize HS
Wichita, KS

Helton, Josh J
Syracuse Jr Sr HS
Syracuse, KS

Hembree, Derek F
Ness City HS
Ness City, KS

Hembree, Jennifer S
Ness City HS
Ness City, KS

Henderson, Amy C
Shawnee Mission
West HS
Lenexa, KS

Henderson, Heath W
Yates Ctr HS
Yates Center, KS

Henderson, Kristi L
Topeka West HS
Topeka, KS

Henderson, Todd
Washington HS
Kansas City, KS

Hendrickson, Cassy
Paola HS
Paola, KS

Henley, Annie L
Bishop Miege HS
Prairie Village, KS

Henley, Jason D
J C Harmon HS
Kansas City, KS

Henne, Marla
Quirira Heights HS
Holyrood, KS

Hennig, Jason S
Chanute Sr HS
Chanute, KS

Hennigh, David Shane
Ulysses HS
Ulysses, KS

Hentzen, Jamie C
Bishop Carroll
Catholic HS
Wichita, KS

Herbert, Toni L
Maize HS
Wichita, KS

Herl, Clinton
Victoria HS
Victoria, KS

Herlein, Jamie M
Ottawa HS
Ottawa, KS

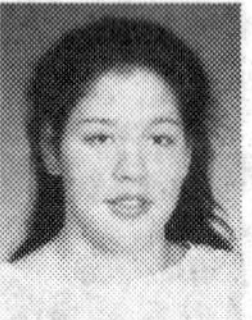

Hernandez, Dawn V
Sumner Acad Of Arts
& Science
Kansas City, KS

Hernandez, Marissa M
Bishop Miege HS
Kansas City, KS

Herndon, Katy L
Goddard HS
Goddard, KS

Herr, Poung
J C Harmon HS
Kansas City, KS

Herrmann, Tonya
Kinsley HS
Kinsley, KS

Hertel, Lyn
Cheylin HS
Bird City, KS

Hertzler, Julie L
Southeast HS
Wichita, KS

Hess, Michael B
Baldwin HS
Baldwin City, KS

Hesseltine, Travis S
Lyndon HS
Vassar, KS

Hestehave, Josh R
St John's Military Schl
Upland, CA

Heston, Michelle
Louisburg HS
Louisburg, KS

Heuertz, Thomas E
Valley Falls HS
Valley Falls, KS

Hiatt, Daniel V
Bishop Miege HS
Prairie Village, KS

Hiatt, Lisa A
Bishop Miege HS
Prairie Village, KS

Hickey, Angel
Liberal HS
Liberal, KS

Hickmon, Jazmin
Sumner Acad Of Arts
& Science
Kansas City, KS

Hicks, Mindy
Horton HS
Everest, KS

Hiebert, Karen
Goddard HS
Goddard, KS

Higley, Candice G
Troy HS
Cummings, KS

Hilbish, Beth
Shawnee Heights HS
Tecumseh, KS

Hildebrand, Jessica
Maize HS
Wichita, KS

Hildreth, Brandy E
Perry Lecompton HS
Grantville, KS

Hill, Brooke L
Osage City HS
Osage City, KS

Hill, Christie M
Pierson Jr HS
Kansas City, KS

Hill, Donna L
Labette Co HS
Altamont, KS

Hill, Garrett
Liberal HS
Liberal, KS

Hill, Heather F
Wallace Cty HS
Sharon Springs, KS

Hill, Hyda-James
Manhattan HS
Manhattan, KS

Hill, Mandi J
Campus HS
Wichita, KS

Hill, Nathan L
Topeka HS
Topeka, KS

Hilleary, Alisha
Derby HS
Wichita, KS

Hilley, Amanda
Stafford Jr Sr HS
Stafford, KS

Hillman, Cassie
Norton Comm HS
Norton, KS

Hillman, Christina
Frankft HS
Frankfort, KS

Hills, Amanda Lynn
Ulysses HS
Ulysses, KS

Hills, Andrew J
Parsons HS
Parsons, KS

Hills, Jason W
Oxford HS
Geuda Springs, KS

Hinds, William W
Derby HS
Wichita, KS

Hinkley, Jennifer R
Spring Hill HS
Spring Hill, KS

Hirt, Andrew J
St Thomas Aquinas HS
Lenexa, KS

Hittle, Kane
Winfield HS
Winfield, KS

Hixon, Jennifer
Girard HS
Pittsburg, KS

Hockman, Elizabeth D
Muncie Christian Schl
Bonner Springs, KS

Hodgson, Dan L
Olathe East Sr HS
Overland Park, KS

Hodgson, Jon
Little River Jr Sr HS
Little River, KS

Hoeting, Crystal E
Hill City HS
Hill City, KS

Hoffman, Amanda
North Central HS
Haddam, KS

Hoffman, Jason A
Bishop Carroll
Catholic HS
Wichita, KS

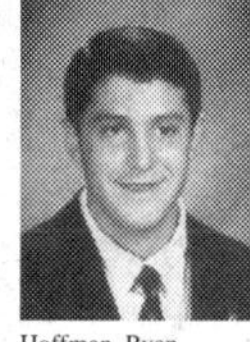
Hoffman, Ryan
Thomas More
Prep-Marion HS
Hays, KS

Hoffman, Trisha S
Northeast HS
Mulberry, KS

Hogan, Brian
Skyline Schl
Pratt, KS

Hogan, Kathryn R
Shawnee Mission
N HS
Merriam, KS

Hogue, Candace M
Blue Valley
Northwest HS
Overland Park, KS

Holcomb, April
Flinthills HS
Rosalia, KS

Hole, P Aaron
Erie HS
Erie, KS

Holland, Amanda J
Immaculata HS
Leavenworth, KS

Holland, Tara A
Arkansas City HS
Arkansas City, KS

Holliday, Adam B
Stanton Co HS
Johnson, KS

Holliger, Joyce F
Mc Louth Schl
Mc Louth, KS

Hollingsworth, Barbie
Shawnee Mission
N HS
Overland Park, KS

Holloway, Cara
Greensburg HS
Greensburg, KS

Holmes, Nicholas R
Washburn Rural HS
Topeka, KS

Holmes, Niki
Louisburg HS
Bucyrus, KS

Holste, Jared
Atwood HS
Ludell, KS

Holt, Gretchen M
Shawnee Mission
West HS
Lenexa, KS

Holt, Keila L
Derby Christian Schl
Wichita, KS

Holtwick, Jennifer
Colby Sr HS
Colby, KS

Homolka, Lora
Ellsworth HS
Ellsworth, KS

Hook, Tiffany
Olathe South Sr HS
Olathe, KS

Hooker, Kevin J
Shawnee Mission
N HS
Shawnee Mission, KS

Hoover, Catherine J
Shawnee Mission S
Sr HS
Shawnee Mission, KS

Hoover, Erica
Independence HS
Independence, KS

Hoover, Tisha
Wichita South HS
Wichita, KS

Horan, Robin
Abilene HS
Abilene, KS

Horner, Kristan E
Smoky Valley HS
Lindsborg, KS

Hornung, Pete T
Ottawa HS
Ottawa, KS

Horton, Chris
Pittsburg HS
Pittsburg, KS

Horton, Stacie
Elkhart HS
Elkhart, KS

Hoskinson, Kevin
Garden City Sr HS
Garden City, KS

Hough, Scarlett E
Field Kindley HS
Coffeyville, KS

Housholder, Heidi
Syracuse Jr Sr HS
Coolidge, KS

Housholder, Holly
Halstead HS
Halstead, KS

Housman, Larae
Jetmore HS
Jetmore, KS

Hovel, Sarah
Shawnee Mission E
Sr HS
Prairie Village, KS

Howard, Chelsie
Atchison Co Cmty HS
Lancaster, KS

Howard, Stephanie
Hiawatha HS
Hiawatha, KS

Howell, Darla L
Southeast HS
Mc Cune, KS

Howell, Scott
Shawnee Mission S
Sr HS
Shawnee Mission, KS

Hubbard, Michelle
Smith Ctr Jr Sr HS
Smith Center, KS

Huber, Sarah B
Wichita South HS
Wichita, KS

Hueber, Sarah R
Robert E Clark Jr HS
Bonner Springs, KS

Hufferd, Nicole
Field Kinley HS
Coffeyville, KS

Huffman, Cheryl
Faith Christian Schl
Osawatomie, KS

Hufford, John M
Wyandotte HS
Kansas City, KS

Hughes, Curtrina
Sumner Acad
Kansas City, KS

Hughes, Jamie D
Scott Comm HS
Scott City, KS

Hughes, Melissa M
Olathe East Sr HS
Overland Park, KS

Hullum, Dionna
Sumner Acad Of Arts
& Science
Kansas City, KS

Humbard, Amanda
Pittsburg HS
Pittsburg, KS

Humble, Tiffany
Goddard HS
Wichita, KS

Humphreys, Alicia
Emporia HS
Emporia, KS

Hundley, Shelly L
Holton HS
Holton, KS

Hunsaker, Heather
Highland HS
Highland, KS

Hunsucker, Mary
Central Jr Sr HS
Burden, KS

Hunt, Jay
Tonganoxie HS
Lansing, KS

Hunt, Jerusha
Olathe North Sr HS
Olathe, KS

Hunt, Michelle
Olathe East Sr HS
Lenexa, KS

Hunter, Alyssa R
Scott Comm HS
Scott City, KS

Hunter, Tammy
Turner HS
Kansas City, KS

Hupp, Carmen M
Immaculata HS
Leavenworth, KS

Hurst, Kendall M
Wichita North HS
Wichita, KS

Hurst, Stacey L
Blue Valley North HS
Leawood, KS

Hustead, Lori M
Topeka West HS
Topeka, KS

Huston, Natalie
Garden City Sr HS
Garden City, KS

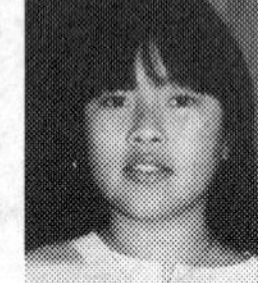
Huynh, Sang K
Wichita South HS
Wichita, KS

Huynh, Thaihoa Thi
Wichita Southeast HS
Wichita, KS

Huyser, Becky
Blue Valley
Northwest HS
Lenexa, KS

Ice, Heather
St Marys HS
Saint Marys, KS

Ihnow, Geoffrey K
Blue Valley North HS
Overland Park, KS

Imakawa, Akiko
Blue Valley
Northwest HS
Overland Park, KS

Ingram, Jessica M
Washburn Rural HS
Topeka, KS

Ingram, Liz
Shawnee Mission S
Sr HS
Overland Park, KS

Irby, Chris M
Wichita
Collegiate Schl
Wichita, KS

Irsik, Max
Dodge City HS
Dodge City, KS

Irwin, Kendall D
Russell HS
Bunker Hill, KS

Isaacs, Melissa K
Topeka HS
Topeka, KS

Isabell, Paul J
Bishop Ward HS
Kansas City, KS

Ivey, Courtney
Syracuse Jr Sr HS
Syracuse, KS

Jackson, Amiee D
Wichita South HS
Wichita, KS

Jackson, Deona
J C Harmon HS
Kansas City, KS

Jackson, Kara M
Maize HS
Wichita, KS

Jackson, Kirstin D
Clifton-Clyde HS
Clifton, KS

Jackson, La Renda D
F L Schlagle HS
Kansas City, KS

Jackson, Tera
Ft Scott HS
Fort Scott, KS

Jacob, Nicholas E
Emporia HS
Emporia, KS

Jacobs, Jacky
Wichita North HS
Wichita, KS

Jacobs, Joe B
Blue Valley
Northwest HS
Overland Park, KS

Jahr, Cara
Mc Louth Schl
Mc Louth, KS

James, Kerry A
Dighton HS
Shields, KS

James, Kevin M
Emporia HS
Emporia, KS

James, Lindsay D
Dighton HS
Shields, KS

James, Luke
Dighton HS
Dighton, KS

Jamvold, Kirk
Troy HS
Troy, KS

Janis, Michael E
Shawnee Mission S
Sr HS
Lenexa, KS

January, Amanda M
Gardner-Edgerton HS
Edgerton, KS

January, Ryan J
Lyons HS
Lyons, KS

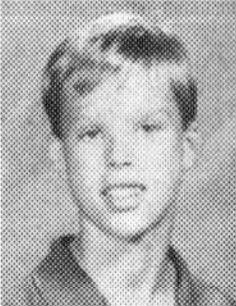
January, Travis
Hutchinson HS
Hutchinson, KS

Janzen, Dustin T
Scott Comm HS
Scott City, KS

Jarratt, Clay M
Turner HS
Kansas City, KS

Jay, David
Beloit Jr Sr HS
Beloit, KS

Jefferson, Cory
Wyandotte HS
Kansas City, KS

Jegen, Danielle
Blue Valley HS
Stilwell, KS

Jenkins, Erica L
Dodge City HS
Dodge City, KS

Jenkins, Travis D
Troy HS
Troy, KS

Jenkinson, Kelli L
Great Bend Sr HS
Great Bend, KS

Jennings, Amy M
Clearwater HS
Clearwater, KS

Jennings, Brandy M
Bishop Miege HS
Kansas City, KS

Jennings, Jennifer L
Washburn Rural HS
Topeka, KS

Jennings, Scott K
Olathe South Sr HS
Olathe, KS

Jensen, G Dailey
Olpe Schl
Olpe, KS

Jezmir, Alla
Blue Valley North HS
Overland Park, KS

Jindra, Brian N
Manhattan HS
Manhattan, KS

Joe III, Darnell
F L Schlagle HS
Kansas City, KS

Johnson, Adam
Blue Valley HS
Olsburg, KS

Johnson, Bianca L
Washington HS
Kansas City, KS

Johnson, Chad
Iola Sr HS
Iola, KS

Johnson, Gena
Buhler HS
Hutchinson, KS

Johnson, James C
Minneola Schl
Minneola, KS

Johnson, Jasmine B
Leavenworth HS
Newport News, VA

Johnson, Jennifer
Campus HS
Wichita, KS

Johnson, Kelley
Solomon Jr Sr HS
New Cambria, KS

Johnson, Lacey
Columbus HS
Columbus, KS

Johnson, Mandy
Ellsworth HS
Ellsworth, KS

Johnson, Melinda
Little River Jr Sr HS
Little River, KS

Johnson, Ryan
Colby Sr HS
Colby, KS

Johnson, Stacy L
Olathe North Sr HS
Olathe, KS

Johnson, Tamara
Baldwin HS
Baldwin City, KS

Johnson, Tracy E
Tescott HS
Culver, KS

Johnson, Vivienne P
Bishop Ward HS
Kansas City, KS

Johnston, Jeremy D
Garden City Sr HS
Garden City, KS

Johnston, Shawn
Elwood USD 486
Saint Joseph, MO

Johnstone, Jeremy S
Wichita Southeast HS
Wichita, KS

Jones, Adam R
Smoky Valley HS
Marquette, KS

Jones, Adrian
Wyandotte HS
Kansas City, KS

Jones, Aimee L
Shawnee Heights
Sr HS
Berryton, KS

Jones, Amie D
Derby HS
Derby, KS

Jones, Diana L
Pleasant Ridge HS
Easton, KS

Jones, Jeffrey R
Bishop Miege HS
Merriam, KS

Jones, Jenna
Olathe South Sr HS
Olathe, KS

Jones, Jeremy
Campus HS
Wichita, KS

Jones, Josh
Northwest HS
Wichita, KS

Jones, Keisha
Wichita
Collegiate Schl
Wichita, KS

Jones, Mandy R
Piper HS
Kansas City, KS

Jones, Nikia M
Junction City HS
Fort Riley, KS

Jones, Randee L
Chase Co HS
Cottonwood Falls, KS

Jones, Tempress N
Northeast Magnet HS
Wichita, KS

Jones, Trent
Lebo Schl
Lebo, KS

Journagan, Rebecca
Goddard HS
Wichita, KS

Joyce, Jason T
Washburn Rural HS
Topeka, KS

Joyner, Mackale R
Sumner Acad
Kansas City, KS

Juarez, Kristina R
Shawnee Mission
Northwest HS
Shawnee Mission, KS

Julian, Nicole D
Yates Ctr HS
Yates Center, KS

Jungel, Scott L
Solomon Jr Sr HS
New Cambria, KS

Kahle, Linda
Buhler HS
Hutchinson, KS

Kahrs, Stacy
Clay Ctr Cmty HS
Clay Center, KS

Kaiser, Aaron P
Great Bend Sr HS
Great Bend, KS

Kaiser, Ryan J
Great Bend Sr HS
Great Bend, KS

Kallenberger, Lora
Wichita Heights HS
Kechi, KS

Kaltenbach, Erin L
Ashland HS
Ashland, KS

Kalusha, Jana L
Olathe East Sr HS
Overland Park, KS

Kanarek, Steven T
Blue Valley
Northwest HS
Overland Park, KS

Kane, Brian D
Dodge City HS
Dodge City, KS

Kane, Candace
Atchison Sr HS
Atchison, KS

Karber, Kayla
Southeast Saline Schl
Gypsum, KS

Karleskint, Joseph D
Ft Scott HS
Fort Scott, KS

Karst, Jessica
Shawnee Heights HS
Topeka, KS

Katcher, Jennifer S
Shawnee Mission S
Sr HS
Shawnee Mission, KS

Kauten, Jennifer R
Liberal HS
Liberal, KS

Kay, Pete
Ottaws HS
Ottawa, KS

Kearn, Brendan D
Salina HS South
Salina, KS

Kearns, Kelly A
Shawnee Mission W
Sr HS
Lenexa, KS

Kearns, Kelly J
Shawnee Heights HS
Wakarusa, KS

Keck, Elizabeth A
Shawnee Mission E
Sr HS
Prairie Village, KS

Keearns, Deborah L
Halstead HS
Halstead, KS

Keeler, Kristy L
Salina HS South
Salina, KS

Keil, David M
Russell HS
Russell, KS

Keiser, Kevin
Juan Padilla Acad HS
Wichita, KS

Keith, Sarah A
Buhler HS
Buhler, KS

Keller, Janice L
Chase Co HS
Cottonwood Falls, KS

Kellerman, Josh A
Norton Comm HS
Norton, KS

Kelley, Carolyn
Trinity Catholic HS
Hutchinson, KS

Kelley, Courtney L
Santa Fe Trail Jr HS
Olathe, KS

KANSAS

Kelley, Lewis
Rossville HS
Rossville, KS

Kelley, Michael E
Atchison Sr HS
Atchison, KS

Kelty, Marti
Wamego HS
Wamego, KS

Kemmis, Rachel M
Skyline Schl
Pratt, KS

Kemp, Kara
Arkansas City HS
Arkansas City, KS

Kemp, Tracy D
Blue Valley HS
Overland Park, KS

Kems, Briana N
Ottawa HS
Ottawa, KS

Kendrick, Melissa
Jackson Heights HS
Whiting, KS

Kendrick, Peter M
Parsons HS
Parsons, KS

Kenemore, Kevin L
Wellington Sr HS
Wellington, KS

Kennedy, Donald J
Chanute Sr HS
Chanute, KS

Kenney, Tara C
Hayden HS
Topeka, KS

Kennyhertz, Johnny C
Shawnee Mission Nw
Sr HS
Lenexa, KS

Kent, Katrina K
Riverton Schl
Galena, KS

Kepka, Jennifer A
Buhler HS
Hutchinson, KS

Kernal, Sophia N
Sumner Acad Of Arts
& Science
Kansas City, KS

Kershner, Elise T
Shawnee Mission W
Sr HS
Lenexa, KS

Ketter, Staci D
Washburn Rural HS
Topeka, KS

Ketterl, Sarah B
Herndon Schl
Herndon, KS

Key, Audra
Campus HS
Wichita, KS

Khan, Tara
Blue Valley
Northwest HS
Overland Park, KS

Kidder, Beth A
Goodland HS
Goodland, KS

Kilmer, Julie L
Campus HS
Haysville, KS

Kimball, Amy B
Manhattan HS
Manhattan, KS

Kimball, Jennifer S
Manhattan HS
Manhattan, KS

Kimberlin, Nikole J
Madison Jr Sr HS
Madison, KS

Kimbrel, Ryan
Dodge City HS
Dodge City, KS

Kimmel, Rebecca D
Leavenworth HS
Leavenworth, KS

Kindscher, Lauren R
Beloit Jr Sr HS
Beloit, KS

King, Dulcinea D
Council Grove HS
Council Grove, KS

King, Jennifer
El Dorado HS
El Dorado, KS

King, Jennifer E
Hays HS
Hays, KS

King, Mari
Rose Hill HS
Derby, KS

King, Merideth L
Shawnee Mission S
Sr HS
Overland Park, KS

King, Tamara
Campus HS
Haysville, KS

Kippes, Jennifer A
Blue Valley HS
Overland Park, KS

Kirkendoll, Bridget D
Olathe East Sr HS
Overland Park, KS

Kirkland, Jennifer
Marysville HS
Marysville, KS

Kirkpatrick, Kellee Jo
Ellinwood Jr Sr HS
Great Bend, KS

Kissel, Jennifer A
Blue Valley HS
Stilwell, KS

Kistner, Angie
Waverly HS
Waverly, KS

Kivett, Lisa
Kinsley HS
Kinsley, KS

Klapmeyer, Ryan R
Blue Valley HS
Stilwell, KS

Klaus, Jennifer
Holcomb HS
Holcomb, KS

Klaus, Sayre
Hays HS
Hays, KS

Klein, Jason R
Newton Sr HS
Newton, KS

Kliethermes, Angela D
Wichita Northwest HS
Wichita, KS

Kliewer, John P
Hesston HS
Halstead, KS

Klima, Cynthia K
Great Bend Sr HS
Great Bend, KS

Kline, Mindy J
Medicine Lodge HS
Medicine Lodge, KS

Kline, Season C
Sumner Acad Of Arts
& Science
Kansas City, KS

Klingele, Julianne
Leavenworth HS
Leavenworth, KS

Knape, Kim A
Ottawa HS
Ottawa, KS

Knapp, Mckensy
Shawnee Mission
Northwest HS
Shawnee Mission, KS

Knecht, Joe E
Paola HS
Paola, KS

Kniep, Jay
Colby Sr HS
Colby, KS

Knoche, Brent
Stafford Jr Sr HS
Stafford, KS

Knopp, Shane Austin
Olathe North Sr HS
Lenexa, KS

Knott, Crystal
Maize HS
Wichita, KS

Kobiskie, Kelly
Manhattan HS
Manhattan, KS

Koch, Amanda
Mulvane Sr HS
Wichita, KS

Koehler, Alison M
Wellington Sr HS
Wellington, KS

Koehn, Karen
Protection Schl
Protection, KS

Koelling, Shanna
Quivira Heights HS
Holyrood, KS

Koerner, Kevin W
Ness City HS
Ness City, KS

Kohler, John P
Olathe East Sr HS
Overland Park, KS

Konen, Kelsey M
Maize HS
Maize, KS

Kongmanychanh, Orn
Wichita East HS
Wichita, KS

Konrade, Traci
Dodge City HS
Dodge City, KS

Koon, Lacey
Bucklin Schl
Bucklin, KS

Korb, Katrina
Tonganoxiw HS
Tonganoxie, KS

Koster, Chris J
Great Bend Sr HS
Great Bend, KS

Kostman, Corey
Troy HS
Troy, KS

Kraemer, Kristin L
Ottawa HS
Ottawa, KS

Kraft, Leah E
Olathe East Sr HS
Overland Park, KS

Kramer, Dawn
Jefferson West HS
Meriden, KS

Kramer, Kristine
Elk Valley Jr Sr HS
Longton, KS

Kreeger, Jennifer
Columbus HS
Galena, KS

Kreller, Chris
Victoria HS
Victoria, KS

Kriley, Isaac
Ulysses HS
Ulysses, KS

Krouse, Karyl E
Great Bend Sr HS
Great Bend, KS

Krstulic, Annie
Shawnee Mission
Northwest HS
Shawnee Mission, KS

Kruger, Jonathan
Midland Sda Schl
Overland Park, KS

Kruleski, Bryan
Garden City Sr HS
Garden City, KS

Kuchment, Olga
Wichita East HS
Wichita, KS

Kueker, Ryan
Concordia Jr Sr HS
Concordia, KS

Kuhlman, Les
Manhattan HS
Manhattan, KS

Kuhlmann, Valerie D
Olpe Schl
Emporia, KS

Kujawa, Suzanne
Atchison Sr HS
Atchison, KS

Kunantaeva, Naila A
Hillsboro HS
Hillsboro, KS

Kunshek, Scott
Frontenac Jr Sr HS
Frontenac, KS

Kuntz, Emma E
Topeka HS
Topeka, KS

Kuntz, Rudi P
Topeka HS
Topeka, KS

Kwon, Soon You
Wichita East HS
Wichita, KS

Lacio, Derec
Kingman HS
Kingman, KS

La Fay, Kelsey L
Stanton Co HS
Johnson, KS

La Flash, Maria J
Junction City HS
Junction City, KS

Laforge, Chris R
El Dorado HS
El Dorado, KS

Lall, Jonathan D
Blue Valley North HS
Overland Park, KS

Lamb, Angela
Pittsburg HS
Pittsburg, KS

Lamb, Christina
Rock Creek Jr Sr HS
Westmoreland, KS

Lamb, Michael
Seton Home
Study Schl
Halstead, KS

Lamb, Rachel
Seton Home
Study Schl
Halstead, KS

Lamb III, Robert
Seton Home
Study Schl
Halstead, KS

Lambert, Elise K
Manhattan HS
Manhattan, KS

Lamme, Amy E
Horton HS
Horton, KS

Land, Jennifer C
Topeka West HS
Topeka, KS

Lane, Callie A
Basehor Linwood HS
Linwood, KS

Lane, Jacob M
Garden City Sr HS
Garden City, KS

Lang, Catherine L
Hill City HS
Hill City, KS

Lang, Kyle
Seaman Sr HS
Topeka, KS

Lange, Jocelyn
Miltonvale HS
Miltonvale, KS

Langerot, Nathan
Mulvane Sr HS
Mulvane, KS

Langley, Erica E
Blue Valley North HS
Leawood, KS

Langston, Jared P
Quivira Heights HS
Holyrood, KS

Lara, David J
Buhler HS
Buhler, KS

Larkin, Earnie G
Goddard HS
Wichita, KS

Larsen, Harmonee
Lincoln Jr Sr HS
Lincoln, KS

Larsen, Heather D
Lincoln Jr Sr HS
Lincoln, KS

Larsen, Shawna
Spring Hill HS
Spring Hill, KS

Larson, Brooke L
Smoky Valley HS
Lindsborg, KS

Larson, Kristi M
Iola Sr HS
Iola, KS

Larson, Sarah E
Cunningham HS
Cunningham, KS

La Salle, Robert J
Halstead HS
Mc Pherson, KS

Lashinski II,
Anthony F
Derby HS
Derby, KS

Lasiter, Marie G
Mulvane Sr HS
Wichita, KS

Latham, Steven
Wyandotte HS
Kansas City, KS

Lathrop, Amanda L
Shawnee Mission
N HS
Shawnee Mission, KS

Lathrop, Angela N
Great Bend Sr HS
Ellinwood, KS

Latta, Krista M
Bishop Carroll
Catholic HS
Wichita, KS

Lattimer, James
Newton Sr HS
Newton, KS

Latty, David I
Caldwell Jr Sr HS
Caldwell, KS

Lauffer, Laci
Protection Schl
Protection, KS

Lauffer, October D
Wichita Heights HS
Wichita, KS

Lawson, Carrie
Blue Valley HS
Stilwell, KS

Lay, Jana E
Neodesha Jr Sr HS
Neodesha, KS

Leach, Mimi M
Ft Scott HS
Fort Scott, KS

Leach, Rebecca E
Desoto HS
De Soto, KS

Ledford, Trina L
Ashland HS
Ashland, KS

Le Dou, Jay
Colby Sr HS
Colby, KS

Le Duc, Jessica A
Clifton-Clyde HS
Clyde, KS

Lee, Brittany L
Derby HS
Derby, KS

Lee, Donald
Manhattan HS
Manhattan, KS

Lee, La'Tosha N
Wichita Southeast HS
Wichita, KS

Lee, Rickenia A
Field Kindley Mem
Sr HS
Liberty, KS

Lee, Stephanie E
Bishop Miege HS
Shawnee Mission, KS

Lee, Tatum
Ness City HS
Ness City, KS

Lee, Travis T
Field Kindley Mem
Sr HS
Liberty, KS

Leeper, Katie
Columbus HS
Columbus, KS

Lefler, Brian
Lansing HS
Lansing, KS

Legg, Lori
Olathe South Sr HS
Olathe, KS

Lehman, Josh P
Topeka West HS
Topeka, KS

Leichliter, Stacey
Decatur Cmty Jr Sr HS
Clayton, KS

Leichtman,
Alexandra M
Washburn Rural HS
Topeka, KS

Leidy, Michelle R
Derby Christian Schl
Wichita, KS

Leikam, Sarah
Victoria HS
Victoria, KS

Leitnaker, Mandy
Ottawa HS
Ottawa, KS

Leitner, Denise G
Blue Valley North HS
Leawood, KS

Lemley, Tabitha
Weskan Schl
Arapahoe, CO

Lennington, Krissie S
Lakin HS
Lakin, KS

Lenz, Erica R
Maize HS
Maize, KS

Leonard, Kelly
Shawnee Mission W
Sr HS
Lenexa, KS

Leroy, Bill T
Smoky Valley HS
Lindsborg, KS

Lewis, Josh
Blue Valley North HS
Leawood, KS

Lickteig, Angela
Udall HS
Udall, KS

Lickteig, Brad
Udall HS
Udall, KS

Liezert III, John W
Topeka West HS
Topeka, KS

Lightcap, Justin D
Buhler HS
Hutchinson, KS

Ligon, Nina
Wichita South HS
Wichita, KS

Likely, Tommi
Prairie View Jr Sr HS
Parker, KS

Liles, Joshua
Trinity Catholic HS
Hutchinson, KS

Lillich, Justin
Turner HS
Kansas City, KS

Limaye, Rupali
Olathe East Sr HS
Olathe, KS

Lind, Mike
Chanute Sr HS
Chanute, KS

Lindblad, Tamme
Hugoton HS
Hugoton, KS

Lindenberger, Kreg
Inman Jr Sr HS
Inman, KS

Linder, Amy M
Highland Park HS
Topeka, KS

Linkous, Jamie
Wichita Heights HS
Wichita, KS

Lippold, Miranda
Hiawatha HS
Hiawatha, KS

Lister, David C
Blue Valley North HS
Leawood, KS

Littleford, James A
Field Kindley Mem
Sr HS
Coffeyville, KS

Liverman, Chris
Shawnee Mission E
Sr HS
Fairway, KS

Lix, Karen
Dodge City HS
Wright, KS

Llanes, Tony D
Chase HS
Chase, KS

Llorente, Rafael A
St John's Military Schl
Walnut, CA

Lock, Amber N
Hesston HS
Hesston, KS

Locke, Garratt A
Arkansas City HS
Arkansas City, KS

Lockhart, Adam D
Atchison Co Cmty HS
Effingham, KS

Lockwood, Johnee
Arkansas City HS
Arkansas City, KS

Lohman, Erin M
Leavenworth HS
Leavenworth, KS

Lohrding, Brian
Protection Schl
Coldwater, KS

Lollis, Tyrice L
Wichita Southeast HS
Wichita, KS

Long, Brandie J
Kensington Jr Sr HS
Kensington, KS

Long, Charlie D
Midland Sda Schl
Kansas City, KS

Long, Kelly E
Independence HS
Independence, KS

Long, Nathan
East HS
Wichita, KS

Long, Nikki L
Washington HS
Kansas City, KS

Looney, Amber J
Wichita West HS
Wichita, KS

Lopez, Loree
Ulysses HS
Ulysses, KS

Loren, Danny P
Hyman Brand
Hebrew Acad
Shawnee Mission, KS

Loroff, Mandie
Troy HS
Troy, KS

Louderback, Miriam L
Andover HS
Wichita, KS

Lourentzos, Anne E
Lansing HS
Lansing, KS

Love, Betsy
Lebo Schl
Lebo, KS

Lovell, Michelle
Olathe East Sr HS
Olathe, KS

Lovesee, Joel
Kinsley HS
Kinsley, KS

Lovett, Jennifer I
Salina HS South
Salina, KS

Lucas, Heather M
Clearwater HS
Clearwater, KS

Lucas, Michael R
Liberal HS
Liberal, KS

Lucas Swingle, Mary
El Dorado HS
El Dorado, KS

Luckeroth, Acacia L
Holton HS
Holton, KS

Luedke, Linda
Michelle
Crest HS
Colony, KS

Lutz, Chris
Eureka Jr Sr HS
Eureka, KS

Lynch, Kaytee A
Council Grove HS
Alta Vista, KS

Lynd, Brooke
Trego Comm HS
Ellis, KS

Lynn, Ryan
El Dorado HS
El Dorado, KS

Lynnes, Ryan
Piper HS
Kansas City, KS

Lyon, Ashley N
Emporia HS
Emporia, KS

Lyons, Daniel P
Shawnee Mission W
Sr HS
Overland Park, KS

Machtley, Brian J
Blue Valley
Northwest HS
Shawnee Mission, KS

Macias, Nancy
Wabaunsee HS
Alma, KS

Macken, Jared G
Maize HS
Wichita, KS

Mackie, Deidra D
Sumner Acad Of Arts
& Science
Kansas City, KS

Madden, Curtis M
Wellsville Jr Sr HS
Ottawa, KS

Madden, Deborah
Liberal HS
Liberal, KS

Madden, Robby J
Washington HS
Kansas City, KS

Mader, Lisa M
Kapaun-Mt Carmel HS
Wichita, KS

Madison, Adam C A
Horton HS
Everest, KS

Madison, Arthur R
Olathe East Sr HS
Olathe, KS

Madlock, Summer M
Sumner Acad
Kansas City, KS

Magee, D Amber
Junction City HS
Ft Knox, KY

Magette, Amanda N
Claflin Jr Sr HS
Claflin, KS

Maginley, Amber
Wabaunsee HS
Paxico, KS

Magwire, Lanie
Wallace Cty HS
Sharon Springs, KS

Mah, Chris
Wichita North HS
Wichita, KS

Mahoney, Curtis
Russell HS
Russell, KS

Malaknov, Michael
Blue Valley
Northwest HS
Overland Park, KS

Malan, Denise N
Oswego HS
Pittsburg, KS

Malek, Devin
Northern Valley HS
Long Island, KS

Malkin, Blaire
Wichita
Collegiate Schl
Wichita, KS

Malthesen, Nolan S
Lyons HS
Lyons, KS

Mangelsdorf,
Kathryn A
Shawnee Mission
Northwest HS
Lenexa, KS

Manning, De Andre N
Sumner Acad Of Arts
& Science
Kansas City, KS

Manns, Jodi K
Pittsburg HS
Pittsburg, KS

Manor, Michael E
Garden City Sr HS
Garden City, KS

Manwarren, Cortney G
Great Bend Sr HS
Great Bend, KS

Mapes, Mindy J
Northeast HS
Arma, KS

Marcum, Lisa M
Washburn Rural HS
Topeka, KS

Marden, Michael
Musil
Olathe East Sr HS
Olathe, KS

Marglin, Nicholaus J
Blue Valley HS
Overland Park, KS

Mark, Lacie J
Maize HS
Maize, KS

Markley, Melinda
Shawnee Mission
N HS
Merriam, KS

Markus, Aubrey
Raelynne
Hutchinson HS
Hutchinson, KS

Marnett, Jason
Goddard Jr HS
Goddard, KS

Marron, George L
Bishop Ward HS
Kansas City, KS

Martens, Stacy
Winfield HS
Winfield, KS

Martin, Adrian L
Derby HS
Derby, KS

Martin, Brandi J
Galena HS
Galena, KS

Martin, Brandon T
Protection Schl
Protection, KS

Martin, Eren Nalani
Goddard HS
Goddard, KS

Martin, Erin M
Andale HS
Andale, KS

Martin, Jennalee L
Russell HS
Russell, KS

Martin, Kimberly
Shawnee Mission
Northwest HS
Lenexa, KS

Martin, Shannon
Shawnee Heights HS
Topeka, KS

Martin, Shatoja
Sumner Acad Of Arts
& Science
Kansas City, KS

Martino, Louis
Anthony
Pittsburg HS
Pittsburg, KS

Mason, Julie
Hugoton HS
Hugoton, KS

Mason, La Donna C
Wichita West HS
Wichita, KS

Massey, Rebecca J
Campus HS
Wichita, KS

Massoth, Rebekah L
Cimarron HS
Cimarron, KS

Masterson, Parc W
Olathe East Sr HS
Overland Park, KS

Masud, Farihah M
Wichita East HS
Wichita, KS

Matas, Tim P
Chapman HS
Abilene, KS

Mathes, Andrew R
Dodge City HS
Dodge City, KS

Mathew, Selia
Wichita Northwest HS
Tulsa, OK

Mathews, Stephanie D
Campus HS
Haysville, KS

Matlack, Justin
Burrton Schl
Burrton, KS

Matney, Dennis L
Turner HS
Kansas City, KS

Matson, Daniel R
Centralia Schl
Vermillion, KS

Matthews, Bryan R
Liberal HS
Liberal, KS

Mattocks, Shelley M
Great Bend Sr HS
Great Bend, KS

Mauch, Julie A
Smoky Valley HS
Lindsborg, KS

Mauk, Adam W
Douglass HS
Rose Hill, KS

Max, Josh B
Blue Valley
Northwest HS
Overland Park, KS

Maxwell, Lakeisha S
Washington HS
Kansas City, KS

May, April M
Halstead HS
Newton, KS

May, Dustin L
Larned HS
Pawnee Rock, KS

May, Jeremy R
Wellington Sr HS
Wellington, KS

May, Tricia L
Topeka West HS
Topeka, KS

Mc Anulla, Kevin M
Great Bend Sr HS
Great Bend, KS

Mc Cabe, Austin E
Olathe North Sr HS
Olathe, KS

Mc Cabe, Sarah H
Salina HS South
Salina, KS

Mc Callop, Nicole R
Sumner Acad Of Arts
& Science
Kansas City, KS

Mc Caskey, Jennifer
Mulvane Sr HS
Mulvane, KS

Mc Christian, Jackie
Arkansas City HS
Arkansas City, KS

Mc Clintick, Chad
Eureka Jr Sr HS
Eureka, KS

Mc Clure, Jody
Nickerson HS
Hutchinson, KS

Mc Clure, Joshua P
Goddard HS
Clearwater, KS

Mc Connell, Rory W
Bonner Springs HS
Edwardsville, KS

Mc Cormack, Amy L
El Dorado HS
El Dorado, KS

Mc Cormick, Cali D
Osawatomie HS
Osawatomie, KS

Mc Cormick, Kelly D
Pittsburg HS
Pittsburg, KS

Mc Cormick, Wyndi
Sante Fe Trail HS
Carbondale, KS

Mc Coskey, Desire M
Great Bend Sr HS
Great Bend, KS

Mc Coy, Amy Liane
Blue Valley North HS
Leawood, KS

Mc Coy, Christine M
Augusta Sr HS
Augusta, KS

Mc Cracken,
Christopher
Ness City HS
Ness City, KS

Mc Crary, Ginny
Goddard HS
Goddard, KS

Mc Cullough, Anna T
Washburn Rural HS
Topeka, KS

Mc Cullough,
Ashley L
Wichita Southeast HS
Wichita, KS

Mc Cullough, Carrie L
Desoto HS
Shawnee, KS

Mc Cullough,
Cindee D
Iola Sr HS
La Harpe, KS

Mc Cullough, Kirk
St Thomas Aquinas HS
Leawood, KS

Mc Cullum, Tina A
Great Bend Sr HS
Great Bend, KS

Mc Cune, Staci A
Flinthills HS
Cassoday, KS

Mc Curry, Sara S
Great Bend Sr HS
Great Bend, KS

Mc Daniel,
Benjamin R
Newton Sr HS
Newton, KS

Mc Daniel, Kristi
Pretty Prairie HS
Pretty Prairie, KS

Mc Daniel, Steve
Wichita Northwest HS
Spokane, WA

Mc Diffett, Jody
Wamego HS
Wamego, KS

Mc Dill, Briana L
Junction City HS
Fort Riley, KS

Mc Donald, Jennifer
Osage City HS
Osage City, KS

Mc Donald, Mary
Elizabaeth
Holton HS
Holton, KS

Mc Donald, Miki L
Rolla HS
Rolla, KS

Mc Dowell, Alicia D
Gardner-Edgerton HS
Gardner, KS

Mc Dowell, Jeremy M
Basehor Linwood HS
Linwood, KS

Mc Dowell, Nicki J
Basehor Linwood HS
Linwood, KS

Mc Echron, Ronald
Turner HS
Kansas City, KS

Mc Elheny, Stacy D
Hutchinson HS
Hutchinson, KS

Mc Gehee, Kristen M
Field Kindley Mem
Sr HS
Coffeyville, KS

Mc Ginnis, Nicole M
Basehor Linwood HS
Linwood, KS

Mc Ginnis, Randy M
Beloit Jr Sr HS
Beloit, KS

Mc Granahan, Jennifer
St Marys HS
Saint Marys, KS

Mc Graw, Jesse L
Olathe South Sr HS
Olathe, KS

Mc Keithan, Ryan A
Jefferson West HS
Ozawkie, KS

Mc Kibbin, Rochelle
Thomas More
Prep-Marion HS
Hays, KS

Mc Kindra, Traci K
Sumner Acad
Kansas City, KS

Mc Kinley, Noel
Olathe North Sr HS
Olathe, KS

Mc Kinney, Jernale D
Leavenworth HS
Leavenworth, KS

Mc Millian,
Nicholas D
Basehor Linwood HS
Basehor, KS

Mc Mullen, Brant W
Lawrence HS
Lawrence, KS

Mc Mullen, Heather D
El Dorado HS
El Dorado, KS

Mc Nally, Matthew T
St Mary's Colgan HS
Pittsburg, KS

Mc Nolty, Leslie A
Newton Sr HS
Newton, KS

Mc Nown,
Christopher W
Shawnee Heights
Sr HS
Topeka, KS

Mc Partlin, Molly
St Thomas Aquinas HS
Overland Park, KS

Mc Queen, Megan
Wabaunsee HS
Alma, KS

Mc Quilkin, Lisa M
Hayden HS
Topeka, KS

Mc Quiller, Amber K
Leavenworth HS
Leavenworth, KS

Mc Reynolds,
Angela D
Ottawa HS
Ottawa, KS

Mc Vicker, Kelly
Buhler HS
Hutchinson, KS

Mc Williams, Brent J
Washington HS
Kansas City, KS

Mc Williams, Justin A
Central Heights Sr HS
Richmond, KS

Mead, Ben D
Northwest HS Wichita
Largo, FL

Mechnig, Dustin C
Anderson Cty Jr Sr HS
Westphalia, KS

Mecom, Josh B
Field Kindley Mem
Sr HS
Coffeyville, KS

Meder, Renee S
Victoria HS
Pfeifer, KS

Medlock, Ben
Dodge City HS
Dodge City, KS

Medrano, Johnnie A
Maize HS
Wichita, KS

Meek, Mark
Spring Hill HS
Bucyrus, KS

Mehl, Kristen A
Blue Valley
Northwest HS
Shawnee Mission, KS

Meier, Augustine G
Washburn Rural HS
Topeka, KS

Meier, Kendra
Ulysses HS
Ulysses, KS

Meier, Liz
Shawnee Mission
Northwest HS
Lenexa, KS

Meier, Stephanie D
Lincoln Jr Sr HS
Lincoln, KS

Meis, James
Hays HS
Catharine, KS

Meisel, Jeffrey A
Lakin HS
Lakin, KS

Mellegaard, Shelli R
Olathe East Sr HS
Overland Park, KS

Mellon, Brandy M
North East HS
Arcadia, KS

Melton, Drusilla E
Wichita Heights HS
Wichita, KS

Melvin, Jason E
Northeast HS
Arma, KS

Mendoza, J R
Shawnee Heights
Sr HS
Topeka, KS

Menning, Tony
Lawrence HS
Lawrence, KS

Merrell, Russel
Waverly HS
Waverly, KS

Merrick, Livia
Macksville HS
Belpre, KS

Merrill, Tonya G
Concordia Jr Sr HS
Concordia, KS

Merriman, Victoria L
Field Kindley Mem
Sr HS
Coffeyville, KS

Merryman, Erik D
Bishop Miege HS
Kansas City, MO

Mertens, Lance
South Gray HS
Montezuma, KS

Mesplay, Tracy T
Northeast HS
Arma, KS

Messer, Jennifer
Olathe North Sr HS
Olathe, KS

Messing, Jeremy
Wellington Sr HS
Wellington, KS

Meyer, Jason
Smith Ctr Jr Sr HS
Smith Center, KS

Meyerhoff, Melissa
Linn Schl
Palmer, KS

Michael, Cale E
Washburn Rural HS
Topeka, KS

Michel, Cesar
Liberal HS
Liberal, KS

Milfeld, Tyler
Wichita
Collegiate Schl
Wichita, KS

Millard, Jennifer
Ulysses HS
Ulysses, KS

Miller, Benjamin G
Robert E Clark Jr HS
Bonner Springs, KS

Miller, Charles J
Plainville HS
Plainville, KS

Miller, Cory J
Arkansas City HS
Arkansas City, KS

Miller, Glenn
Campus HS
Haysville, KS

Miller, Jessica
Royal Valley HS
Mayetta, KS

Miller, Joie R
St Xavier's HS
Fort Riley, KS

Miller, Jordan L
Anderson Cty Jr Sr HS
Greeley, KS

Miller, Laura J
Independence HS
Neodesha, KS

Miller, Mindy A
Ottawa HS
Ottawa, KS

Miller, Morgan
Downs HS
Downs, KS

Miller, Sara E
Buhler HS
Hutchinson, KS

Miller, Sarah
Rossville HS
Topeka, KS

Miller, Sarah E
Mankato Jr Sr HS
Mankato, KS

Mills, Carrie
Cunningham HS
Cunningham, KS

Mills, Jennifer L
Clearwater HS
Clearwater, KS

Mills, Kristina
Columbus HS
Weir, KS

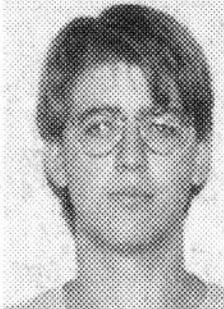
Millsap, Kyle
Wichita East HS
Wichita, KS

Miner, Andy R
Beloit Jr Sr HS
Beloit, KS

Minor, Melanie M
Wichita Southeast HS
Wichita, KS

Mirsafian, Sudaben
Wichita East HS
Wichita, KS

Mitchell, David
Hays HS
Hays, KS

Mitchell, Erin
Shawnee Mission
N HS
Leawood, KS

Mitchell, Holly
Emporia HS
Emporia, KS

Mitchell, Jay
Wellington Sr HS
Wellington, KS

Mitchell, Melissa A
Louisburg HS
Paola, KS

Moats, Ashley S
Blue Valley HS
Stilwell, KS

Moats, Orin
Blue Valley HS
Stilwell, KS

Modich, Michael R
Independence HS
Independence, KS

Modrow, Justin A
Ellsworth HS
Kanopolis, KS

Mogle, Brandy
Basehor Linwood HS
Basehor, KS

Mohlman, Claire
White Rock HS
Esbon, KS

Molz, Philene
St Thomas Aquinas HS
Overland Park, KS

Montgomery, Danny J
Hays HS
Hays, KS

Moody, Erik B
Protection Schl
Protection, KS

Mooney, Jennifer J
Washington HS
Kansas City, KS

Moore, Andrea V
Hartford HS
Neosho Rapids, KS

Moore, Astasia L
Olathe East Sr HS
Olathe, KS

Moore, Aubree L
Great Bend Sr HS
Great Bend, KS

Moore, Brent N
Olathe South Sr HS
Olathe, KS

Moore II, Clinton W
Cherryvale HS
Independence, KS

Moore, Dawn M
Baldwin HS
Baldwin City, KS

Moore, Javen D
Sedan HS
Chautauqua, KS

Moore, Kinsey M
Manhattan HS
Manhattan, KS

Moore, Malia
Hope HS
Woodbine, KS

Moore, Nick
Central Christian Schl
Hutchinson, KS

Moore, Philip J
Ashland HS
Ashland, KS

Moore, Sara N
Halstead HS
Halstead, KS

Moorhous, Jaclyn A
Wheatland Middle
Sr HS
Grainfield, KS

Morel, Lindy A
Oakley HS
Oakley, KS

Moreno, Jason
Garden City Sr HS
Garden City, KS

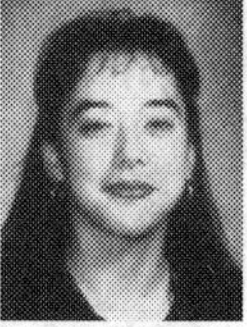
Moreno, Yanet
Scott Comm HS
Scott City, KS

Morgan, Brian J
Blue Valley North HS
Leawood, KS

Morgan, Jacob
Olathe South Sr HS
Olathe, KS

Morgan, Jared M
Hope HS
Hope, KS

Morgan, Stephen M
Blue Valley HS
Overland Park, KS

Moriarty, Corinne
Trinity Catholic HS
Hutchinson, KS

Morris, Jessica
Topeka HS
Topeka, KS

Morris, Joshua P
Salina HS South
Salina, KS

Morris, Lisa
Leavenworth HS
Leavenworth, KS

Morris, Lisa M
Blue Valley
Northwest HS
Overland Park, KS

Morris, Rosalynn
Plainville HS
Plainville, KS

Morrison, Jessica L
Washington HS
Kansas City, KS

Morrison, Mary E
Louisburg HS
Louisburg, KS

Morrou, Matthew S
Olathe East Sr HS
Olathe, KS

Morse, Brandon J
Newton Sr HS
Newton, KS

Morse, Jenni
Wichita
Collegiate Schl
Wichita, KS

Morter, Matthew R
Ft Scott HS
Fort Scott, KS

Morton, Kevin
Ottawa HS
Ottawa, KS

Mosher, Joseph D
Glasco HS
Glasco, KS

Mosier, Karla M
Buhler HS
Hutchinson, KS

Moskalew, Michelle N
Kinsley HS
Kinsley, KS

Mott, Dustin D
Independence HS
Independence, KS

Mott, Dwayne A
Enterprise Sda Acad
Kansas City, MO

Mottin, Angela
Miltonvale HS
Miltonvale, KS

Mountain, Seth
Garden Plain Jr Sr HS
Viola, KS

Mourning, Josh B
Ottawa HS
Ottawa, KS

Mowery, Kayla
Northern Heights HS
Americus, KS

Moyer, Stacy
Shawnee Mission Nw
Sr HS
Shawnee Mission, KS

Mueller, Jodie L
Shawnee Mission W
Sr HS
Lenexa, KS

Mueller, John Robert
Olathe North Sr HS
Olathe, KS

Mueller, Ryan
Hanover Schl
Hanover, KS

Mulcahy, Marty
Olathe South Sr HS
Olathe, KS

Mulder, Jeffery J
Eastern Heights Jr
Sr HS
Phillipsburg, KS

Muldrew, Melissa A
Garden City Sr HS
Garden City, KS

Mull, Brian J
Maize HS
Maize, KS

Mullikin, Annette M
Osawatomie HS
Osawatomie, KS

Multhaup, Karen
Wichita
Collegiate Schl
Goddard, KS

Munoz, Regina M
Hayden HS
Topeka, KS

Murdock, Jada
Spring Hill HS
Spring Hill, KS

Murphree, Rebekah S
Dexter Jr Sr HS
Dexter, KS

Murray, Cody L
Mankato Jr Sr HS
Mankato, KS

Murrell, Teresa
Apostolic Acad
Junction City, KS

Murry, Carmen R
Great Bend Sr HS
Great Bend, KS

Musson, Micah
Arkansas City HS
Arkansas City, KS

Muthukrishman,
Aravind
Manhattan HS
Manhattan, KS

Myers, Brady
Washburn Rural HS
Topeka, KS

Myers, Dusty K
Topeka HS
Topeka, KS

Myers, Erik V
Great Bend Sr HS
Great Bend, KS

Naasz, Melanie R
Wichita East HS
Wichita, KS

Napier, Brad C
Oswego HS
Oswego, KS

Narino, Julian
Mc Pherson HS
Mc Pherson, KS

Nash, Chad M
Field Kindley Mem
Sr HS
Coffeyville, KS

Nash, Joseph J
Olathe East Sr HS
Olathe, KS

Nash, Tammy
Garden City Sr HS
Garden City, KS

Nash, Trevor
Garden City Sr HS
Garden City, KS

Nau, Kimberly N
Spearville Jr Sr HS
Spearville, KS

Nau, Terri D
Spearville Jr Sr HS
Spearville, KS

Navinsky, Brandon J
Basehor Linwood HS
Basehor, KS

Naylor, Laticia
Leavenworth HS
Fort Leavenworth, KS

Nead, Amy
Pierson Jr HS
Kansas City, KS

Nech, James R
Norton Comm HS
Norton, KS

Needham, Kelsey D
Jayhawk-Linn HS
Mound City, KS

Negrete, Angelina C
Olathe East Sr HS
Olathe, KS

Nelson, Janelle
Little River Jr Sr HS
Marquette, KS

Nelson, Samantha K
Olathe North Sr HS
Lenexa, KS

Nelson, Sandi A
Troy HS
Troy, KS

Nelzen, John A
Hesston HS
Hesston, KS

Nesmith, Alaina D
Dodge City HS
Dodge City, KS

Neve, Jennifer
Lansing HS
Lansing, KS

Nevels, Brandi
Dodge City HS
Dodge City, KS

Neves, Brandi A
Olathe South Sr HS
Olathe, KS

Newcomb, Rachel E
Wichita Southeast HS
Wichita, KS

Newcomer, Craig K
Trego Comm HS
Ogallah, KS

Newman, Misty S
Rock Creek Jr Sr HS
Saint George, KS

Newton, Amy D
Independence HS
Independence, KS

Ney, Jessica L
Hoisington HS
Hoisington, KS

Nguon, Le M
Garden City Sr HS
Garden City, KS

Nguyen, Lan T
Wichita North HS
Wichita, KS

Nichol, Jana M
Salina HS South
Salina, KS

Nicholl, Kate A
Liberal HS
Liberal, KS

Nichols, Julie L
Olathe East Sr HS
Olathe, KS

Nichols, Ryan
Osborne HS
Alton, KS

Nicholson, Sarah J
Bishop Miege HS
Fairway, KS

Nickel, Lori
Olathe North Sr HS
Olathe, KS

Nickell, Richard Dean
Lawrence HS
Lawrence, KS

Nickerson, Janelle L
Highland Park HS
Topeka, KS

Nicolay, Jason M
Buhler HS
Hutchinson, KS

Nightengale, Natasha
South Gray HS
Sublette, KS

Nix, Holly N
Moscow HS
Hugoton, KS

Nolan, Spencer
Maur Hill Prep Schl
Atchison, KS

Noll, Jesse
Jefferson Co North HS
Nortonville, KS

Norez, Rodolfo
Lyons HS
Lyons, KS

Norman, Tamika R
J C Harmon HS
Kansas City, KS

Norris, Michele R
Kensington Jr Sr HS
Kensington, KS

Norris, Niki
Wichita East HS
Wichita, KS

North, Tyler J
Ellis HS
Ellis, KS

Northrip, David F
Bishop Miege HS
Shawnee Mission, KS

Norton, Gwayain
F L Schlagle HS
Kansas City, KS

Norwood, Carl A
Ottawa HS
Ottawa, KS

Novak, Abby
Belleville HS
Belleville, KS

Nowak, Christina S
Abilene Baptist Acad
Salina, KS

Nowak, Jessica A
Blue Valley
Northwest HS
Overland Park, KS

Nunley, Tiffany
Summer Acad Of
Arts/Science
Kansas City, KS

Nussbaum, Tim A
Wichita North HS
Wichita, KS

Nutz, Andrew
Derby HS
Derby, KS

Nystrom, Jared
Maize HS
Wichita, KS

Oakleaf, Greg J
Atchison Co Cmty HS
Effingham, KS

Obermeyer, Lori A
Garden City Sr HS
Garden City, KS

Oberzan, Meghan E
Lawrence HS
Lawrence, KS

Oborny, Erica
Derby HS
Derby, KS

Oborny, Josiah D
Larned HS
Larned, KS

Oborny, Nathan J
Great Bend Sr HS
Larned, KS

O'Bryant, Carie A
Shawnee Mission
N HS
Shawnee Mission, KS

Ochs, Stephanie A
Triplains Schl
Russell Springs, KS

Ocker, Travis A
Hutchinson HS
Hutchinson, KS

O'Connor, Christine
Olathe South Sr HS
Olathe, KS

O'Donnell, Annie
Blue Valley HS
Overland Park, KS

Oehmke, Jessica A
Wichita
Collegiate Schl
Derby, KS

Oetinger, Cathryn J
Hesston HS
Hesston, KS

Offutt, Traci L
Coldwater Jr Sr HS
Coldwater, KS

Okeson, Kendall
Winfield HS
Winfield, KS

Oleson, Patricia J
Maize HS
Wichita, KS

Olmos, Sonia K
Leavenworth HS
Leavenworth, KS

Olsen, Jeremie M
Lyndon HS
Lyndon, KS

Olson, Andrew
Maranatha Acad
Kansas City, MO

Olson, Ingrid
Hays HS
Hays, KS

Olson, Skyler M
Greeley Co Schl
Tribune, KS

Olson, Tamara K
Washburn Rural HS
Auburn, KS

O'Neill, Brandon
Spearville Jr Sr HS
Spearville, KS

O'Neill, Tiffany
Dodge City HS
Spearville, KS

Oplothik, Amber
Columbus HS
Baxter Springs, KS

Oplothik, Ashley
Columbus HS
Baxter Springs, KS

Oppliger, Becky
Lakin HS
Deerfield, KS

Ornopia, Daisy L
Midland Sda Schl
Olathe, KS

Ortman, Sarah I
Mankato Jr Sr HS
Mankato, KS

Osborn, Shannon
Dodge City HS
Dodge City, KS

Osenbaugh, Jeff
Hutchinson HS
Hutchinson, KS

Osgood, Lauren N
Maize HS
Wichita, KS

O'Shea, Winter
Blue Valley HS
Blaine, KS

Otto, Ann
Manhattan HS
Manhattan, KS

Ouderkirk, Theresa
Washburn Rural HS
Topeka, KS

Overman, Morgan
Columbus HS
Columbus, KS

Owen, Nick
Concordia Jr Sr HS
Concordia, KS

Owens, Danielle
Wichita West HS
Wichita, KS

Owens, Justin
Caney Valley Jr Sr HS
Tyro, KS

Owens, Miranda
Quivira Heights HS
Bushton, KS

Owensby, Crystal D
Shawnee Mission S
Sr HS
Overland Park, KS

Oxler, Jason P
Blue Valley
Northwest HS
Shawnee Mission, KS

Padavic, Michael
Shawnee Mission
Northwest HS
Shawnee Mission, KS

Paden, Aron
Faith Christian Schl
Osawatomie, KS

Page, Kristi
Girard HS
Girard, KS

Pagenkopf, Cambry L
Skyline Schl
Pratt, KS

Paine, Alison M
Olathe East Sr HS
Olathe, KS

Palkowitsh, Carrie A
Garden City Sr HS
Garden City, KS

Palmer, Gary A
Ft Scott HS
Fort Scott, KS

Palmer, Travis
Maize HS
Maize, KS

Pantazis, Alethia H
Blue Valley North HS
Leawood, KS

Panter, Cindy
Derby HS
Derby, KS

Papes, Latricia
Marysville HS
Marysville, KS

Parcells, Shawn L
Topeka West HS
Topeka, KS

Parish, Graham R
Sumner Acad Of Arts
& Science
Kansas City, KS

Parker, Brad
Olathe North Sr HS
Olathe, KS

Parker, Brandy B
Sumner Acad Of Arts
& Science
Kansas City, KS

Parker, Jessica M
Olathe East Sr HS
Olathe, KS

Parker, John M
Buhler HS
Hutchinson, KS

Parks, Ashley
Emporia HS
Emporia, KS

Parks, Candy
El Dorado HS
El Dorado, KS

Parks, Jory D
Wallace Cty HS
Sharon Springs, KS

Parman, Staci
Seaman Sr HS
Topeka, KS

Parrott, Jessica L
Buhler HS
Hutchinson, KS

Parsons, Becky A
Russell HS
Russell, KS

Parsons, Tom D
Quivira Heights HS
Holyrood, KS

Pasek, Michele
Russel HS
Russell, KS

Pastor, Aaron
Blue Valley HS
Stilwell, KS

Patrick, Heather L
Blue Valley
Northwest HS
West Palm Bch, FL

Patterson, Lisa
Olathe North Sr HS
Olathe, KS

Patterson, Sara
Olathe North Sr HS
Olathe, KS

Patterson, Valerie J
Blue Valley HS
Leawood, KS

Paugh, Robert R
Olathe North Sr HS
Olathe, KS

Paxson, Ashley
Columbus HS
Columbus, KS

Payne, Amanda D
Labette Co HS
Oswego, KS

Payne, Danielle R
Hays HS
Hays, KS

Payne, Eric
Salina HS Central
Salina, KS

Payne, Tausha M
Wyandotte HS
Kansas City, KS

Pearon, Janelle
Valley Ctr HS
Valley Center, KS

Pearse, Michelle J
Eureka Jr Sr HS
Eureka, KS

Peck, Crystal L
Sedan HS
Peru, KS

Peck, David S
Great Bend Sr HS
Great Bend, KS

Peckham, Amber M
Canton-Galva HS
Galva, KS

Peed, Brandy L
Turner HS
Kansas City, KS

Peek, Zach
Waverly HS
Williamsburg, KS

Peine, Marilyn A
Anderson Cty Jr Sr HS
Greeley, KS

Peirano, Candi L
Maize HS
Wichita, KS

Pellegrini, Andrea
Udall HS
Udall, KS

Penner, Chad Allen
Labette Co HS
Edna, KS

Penner, Robyn P
Berean Acad
Whitewater, KS

Peoples, Christopher S
Santa Fe Trail Jr HS
Olathe, KS

Pepple, William D
Lawrence HS
Lawrence, KS

Perkins, Keli
F L Schlagle HS
Kansas City, KS

Perkins, Kristin E
Maize HS
Wichita, KS

Perry, Matt D
Salina HS South
Salina, KS

Perry, Suzanne
St Mary's Colgan HS
Pittsburg, KS

Pershin, Neke N
Neodesha Jr Sr HS
Neodesha, KS

Peschka, Ryan J
Ellsworth HS
Ellsworth, KS

Peterman, Kasie D
Maize HS
Maize, KS

Peters, Mandy
Emporia HS
Emporia, KS

Petersen, Sarah K
Bishop Miege HS
Roeland Park, KS

Petersilie, Jared
Ness City HS
Ness City, KS

Peterson, Colette
Blue Valley HS
Overland Park, KS

Peterson, Danielle L
Wichita Southeast HS
Wichita, KS

Peterson, John J
Rose Hill HS
Rose Hill, KS

Peterson, Matthew D
Ft Scott HS
Fort Scott, KS

Peterson, Sallyann
Spring Hill HS
Spring Hill, KS

Pfannenstiel, Amanda M
Ness City HS
Ness City, KS

Pfannenstiel, Lisa
Ellis HS
Hays, KS

Pfeifer, Mandy
Hays HS
Hays, KS

Pfeifley, Kristin
Manhattan HS
Manhattan, KS

Pham, Huy Q
F L Schlagle HS
Kansas City, KS

Phelps, Natacha
Junction City HS
Junction City, KS

Phillips, Betty T
Wichita West HS
Wichita, KS

Phillips, Jenny
Kingman HS
Cheney, KS

Phillips, Jerrod D
Goodland HS
Goodland, KS

Phillips, Nicole
Otis Bison HS
Albert, KS

Pickett, Jenny L
Goodland HS
Goodland, KS

Pickman, Michael C
Maur Hill Prep Schl
Atchison, KS

Picolet, Angela M
Council Grove HS
Dwight, KS

Picow, David H
Shawnee Mission E Sr HS
Shawnee Mission, KS

Pinkham, Candice
Maryville HS
Marysville, KS

Pintar, Adam L
Northeast HS
Arcadia, KS

Pitner, Tionna
Atwood HS
Atwood, KS

Pittman, Brande J
Turner HS
Kansas City, KS

Pivonka, Jeremy C
Great Bend Sr HS
Great Bend, KS

Plante, Tabitha
Hill City HS
Hill City, KS

Plumb, Kelly A
Olathe North Sr HS
Olathe, KS

Polston, Leslie A
Pittsburg HS
Pittsburg, KS

Poore, Jenny
Stockton HS
Woodston, KS

Pope, Amanda L
Southeast HS
Wichita, KS

Popelka, Aaron
Belleville HS
Munden, KS

Popp, Miranda
Ness City HS
Utica, KS

Poppelreiter, Heidi
St Marys HS
Maple Hill, KS

Popperlreiter, Heidi M
St Marys HS
Maple Hill, KS

Porter, Elizabeth
Columbus HS
Galena, KS

Porter, James R
Goodland HS
Goodland, KS

Post, Jennifer L
Wichita East HS
Wichita, KS

Potter, Travis W
Labette Co HS
Coffeyville, KS

Poulson, Bobbie D
Muncie Christian Schl
Kansas City, KS

Powell, Bubba J
Shawnee Mission W Sr HS
Overland Park, KS

Powell, Cody E
Minneola Schl
Minneola, KS

Powell, Larissa
Eureka Jr Sr HS
Eureka, KS

Powell, Myca J
Shawnee Mission W Sr HS
Overland Park, KS

Powers, Rachelle R
Labette Co HS
Altamont, KS

Pownell, Jessica L
Newton Sr HS
Newton, KS

Pratt, Amanda E
Turner HS
Kansas City, KS

Pressgrove, Cindy L
Topeka West HS
Topeka, KS

Prewo, Paul E
Thomas More Prep-Marion HS
Hays, KS

Price, Josh
Seaman Sr HS
Topeka, KS

Prieb, Trevin S
Canton-Galva HS
Canton, KS

Prince, Jeff E
Pittsburg HS
Pittsburg, KS

Prochaska, Kelly A
Blue Valley Northwest HS
Overland Park, KS

Proctor, Amber A
Washburn Rural HS
Auburn, KS

Proctor, Eric A
Goddard HS
Goddard, KS

Profitt, Aaron
Kansas City Bible Clg High
Overland Park, KS

Prosser, Elesa J
Pratt HS
Pratt, KS

Pruner, Courtney A
Central Heights Sr HS
Princeton, KS

Puchosic, Sarah
Mc Pherson HS
Mc Pherson, KS

Pulliam, Christina
Olathe South Sr HS
Olathe, KS

Pyle, Heather
Pittsburg HS
Pittsburg, KS

Quackenbush, Kim
Olathe North Sr HS
Olathe, KS

Quandt, Alexia L
Valley Ctr HS
Valley Center, KS

Quigley, Kari
Cherryvale HS
Cherryvale, KS

Raab, Nichole
Pierson Jr HS
Kansas City, KS

Radenberg, Katrina D
Hoisington HS
Hoisington, KS

Ragain, Heather L
Columbus HS
Columbus, KS

Raghavan, Amit
Wichita
Collegiate Schl
Wichita, KS

Raiburn, Paula J
Campus HS
Wichita, KS

Rains, Shiloh
Wellington Sr HS
Wellington, KS

Ramaglia, Rebecca D
Olathe South Sr HS
Olathe, KS

Ramchandani, Anjali
Ulysses HS
Ulysses, KS

Ramirez, Mikki L
Wichita South HS
Wichita, KS

Ramsey, Chad D
Jewell HS
Randall, KS

Randall, Millicent
Olathe North Sr HS
Olathe, KS

Randel, Betsy J
Baldwin HS
Baldwin City, KS

Raney, Lori J
Pratt HS
Iuka, KS

Rapp, Rebekah K
Northeast HS
Arma, KS

Rapson, Hillary A
Gardner-Edgerton HS
Gardner, KS

Rasmussen, Erika N
Independence HS
Independence, KS

Rassette, Matthew
Abilene HS
Abilene, KS

Rathbun, Tiffani D
Great Bend Sr HS
Great Bend, KS

Ravis, Lori N
Blue Valley
Northwest HS
Overland Park, KS

Ray, Danica E
Maize HS
Wichita, KS

Ray, Diana L
Medicine Lodge HS
Lake City, KS

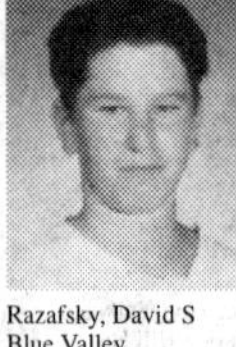
Razafsky, David S
Blue Valley
Northwest HS
Overland Park, KS

Rebeck, Nicholas
Bishop Ward HS
Kansas City, KS

Reddig, Robert T
Bishop Miege HS
Kansas City, MO

Reed, Alicia M
Great Bend Sr HS
Great Bend, KS

Reed, Heather D
Lawrence HS
Lawrence, KS

Reed, Katie M
Erie HS
Erie, KS

Reed, Mischelle M
Goddard HS
Wichita, KS

Reed, Raymond J
Shawnee Mission
Northwest HS
Shawnee, KS

Reed, Shaune C
Galena HS
Galena, KS

Reese, Christopher
Reagan
St John's Military Schl
Prior Lake, MN

Reichel, Christina M
Shawnee Mission
N HS
Overland Park, KS

Reid, Erin N
Leavenworth HS
Leavenworth, KS

Reilly, Diane Carleen
Leavenworth HS
Leavenworth, KS

Reimer, Brooke
Cimarron HS
Cimarron, KS

Reimer, Karissa
Wichita West HS
Wichita, KS

Reimer, Tyler G
Sedgwick HS
Sedgwick, KS

Reinert, Carrie
Herington HS
Herington, KS

Reinert, Jeffery J
Dodge City HS
Ensign, KS

Reinert, Tara
Wabaunsee HS
Ness City, KS

Renfro, Courtney
Mulvane Sr HS
Derby, KS

Renne, Frances A
Wyandotte HS
Kansas City, KS

Reno, Joshua D
Maranatha Acad
Linwood, KS

Reser, Benjamin
Topeka HS
Topeka, KS

Rewerts, Shannon C
Stafford Jr Sr HS
Stafford, KS

Reyes, Christina M
Bishop Miege HS
Kansas City, MO

Reynolds, Julie
Columbus HS
Columbus, KS

Reynolds, Kristy L
Emporia HS
Emporia, KS

Reynolds, Lisa M
Wellington Sr HS
Wellington, KS

Reynolds, Salena M
El Dorado HS
El Dorado, KS

Rheem, Amy
Wichita
Collegiate Schl
Wichita, KS

Rhodes, Bethanie I
Northeast HS
Arma, KS

Rhodes, Erin M
Louisburg HS
Louisburg, KS

Rhodes, Jennifer R
Turner HS
Kansas City, KS

Rhodes, Laura J
Lawrence HS
Lawrence, KS

Rhynerson, Arica
Prairie View Jr Sr HS
La Cygne, KS

Rice, Brandon L
Maize HS
Wichita, KS

Rice, Janet M
Washburn Rural HS
Topeka, KS

Rice, Karen J
Washburn Rural HS
Topeka, KS

Rice, Scott A
Marais Des Cygnes
Valley HS
Melvern, KS

Richard, Rebecca
St John's HS
Beloit, KS

Richards, Eric L
Trego Comm HS
Wa Keeney, KS

Richardson, Toni
Dexter Jr Sr HS
Dexter, KS

Ricke, Benjamin J
Nickerson HS
Hutchinson, KS

Ricke, David A
Great Bend Sr HS
Great Bend, KS

Ricklefs, Trenton
Manhattan HS
Manhattan, KS

Ricks, Kizzie T
Lawrence HS
Lawrence, KS

Rider, Tyler
Ness City HS
Ness City, KS

Riebel, Bradley W
Iola Sr HS
La Harpe, KS

Riedesel, Amy
Shawnee Heights HS
Berryton, KS

Riegel, Amy
St John Jr Sr HS
Saint John, KS

Riggs, Jason L
Desoto HS
De Soto, KS

Riggs, Sheila
Clearwater HS
Clearwater, KS

Riley, Amanda R
Blue Valley
Northwest HS
Overland Park, KS

Riley, Erin J
Hartford HS
Emporia, KS

Riley, Heather S
Bishop Ward HS
Kansas City, KS

Riley, Jacob
South Gray HS
Montezuma, KS

Riley, Marian L
Wichita Co HS
Leoti, KS

Ringwald, Amy
Iola Sr HS
Iola, KS

Ripley, Matt R
Minneola Schl
Dodge City, KS

Ritter, Misti K
Junction City HS
Fort Bragg, NC

Robben, Jackie
Mc Pherson HS
Mc Pherson, KS

Roben, Melanie
Ellsworth HS
Ellsworth, KS

Roberts, Brian
Newton Sr HS
Newton, KS

Roberts, Joel M
Palco HS
Palco, KS

Roberts, Melanie M
Lawrence HS
Lawrence, KS

Roberts, Strother E
Manhattan HS
Manhattan, KS

Robertson, Kimberly C
Shawnee Mission W
Sr HS
Lenexa, KS

Robertson, Michelle L
Independence HS
Elk City, KS

Robinson, Amber N
Independence HS
Independence, KS

Robinson, Betsy
Valley Ctr HS
Valley Center, KS

Robinson, Cynthia L
Sumner Acad Of Arts
& Science
Kansas City, KS

Robinson, Jill D
Dodge City HS
Dodge City, KS

Robinson, Justin R
Washburn Rural HS
Melvern, KS

Robinson, Kirsten J
Gardner-Edgerton HS
Edgerton, KS

Robinson, Natasha L
Oswego HS
Oswego, KS

Robison, Michaela J
Colby Sr HS
Colby, KS

Robson, Stephanie M
Wichita East HS
Wichita, KS

Rodgers, Misty
Hugoton HS
Hugoton, KS

Roemisch, Larisa E
Andover HS
Andover, KS

Roenne, Rita K
Downtown Law
Magnet HS
Wichita, KS

Rogers, Amber D
Wichita North HS
Wichita, KS

Rogers, Andrea
Wichita Heights HS
Wichita, KS

Rogers, Nate
Blue Valley HS
Overland Park, KS

Rogers, Tara J
Pratt HS
Dodge City, KS

Rogers, Trisha M
Maize HS
Wichita, KS

Rohling, Megan L
Norton Comm HS
Prairie View, KS

Rohling, Ryan M
Northern Valley HS
Prairie View, KS

Rohlmeier, Jesusita A
Washburn Rural HS
Topeka, KS

Rohlmeier, Micheal R
Washburn Rural HS
Topeka, KS

Rolo, Stacy
Ness City HS
Ness City, KS

Rolph, Jonathan D
Wichita
Collegiate Schl
Wichita, KS

Rose, Benjamin W
Salina HS Central
Salina, KS

Rose, Brian
Jefferson West HS
Meriden, KS

Rosel, Angela
Washburn Rural HS
Topeka, KS

Rosel, Paul D
Washburn Rural HS
Topeka, KS

Ross, Haley
Dodge City HS
Dodge City, KS

Rossi, Adrian
Northwest HS
Wichita, KS

Roth, Justin R
Blue Valley
Northwest HS
Overland Park, KS

Rothchild, Erin
St John's HS
Beloit, KS

Roush, Kelly
Stafford Jr Sr HS
Stafford, KS

Roush, T J
Wichita
Collegiate Schl
Wichita, KS

Rowe, Wayne Douglas
Midland Sda Schl
Belton, MO

Rowland, John K
Sumner Acad Of Arts
& Science
Kansas City, KS

Ruble, Jeff P
Great Bend Sr HS
Great Bend, KS

Rude, Dezerae
Burlington HS
Burlington, KS

Ruder, Cori L
Thomas More
Prep-Marion HS
Hays, KS

Ruff, Charliss L
Hanston Jr Sr HS
Hanston, KS

Rugg, Sandra A
Anderson Cty Jr Sr HS
Garnett, KS

Ruggiero, Mary J
Smoky Valley HS
Lindsborg, KS

Rullman, Laura
Wathena Schl
Wathena, KS

Rumisek, Jay D
Wichita
Collegiate Schl
Wichita, KS

Rundle, Anne C
St Thomas Aquinas HS
Shawnee Mission, KS

Runnion, Sabastin J
El Dorado HS
El Dorado, KS

Russell, Emily D
Junction City HS
Junction City, KS

Russell, Jennifer J
Basehor Linwood HS
Bonner Springs, KS

Russell, Rebecca L
Derby HS
Derby, KS

Rutherford, Dusty D
Labette Co HS
Edna, KS

Rutherford, Michele
Campus HS
Haysville, KS

Ryan, Katie
Kapaun-Mt Carmel HS
Wichita, KS

Rys, Tomek P
Manhattan HS
Manhattan, KS

Salazar, Nicoles D
Maize HS
Wichita, KS

Saliger, Christina
Chaparral HS
Harper, KS

Salisbury, Jenny M
Augusta Sr HS
Augusta, KS

Salmans Jr, Gary
El Dorado HS
El Dorado, KS

Salmon, Patricia J
Olathe North Sr HS
Olathe, KS

Salmon, Tara J
Santa Fe Trail Jr HS
Olathe, KS

Salof, Suzanne M
Shawnee Mission W
Sr HS
Lenexa, KS

Saloga, Teri
Skyline Schl
Coats, KS

Samples, Shauntelle L
Topeka HS
Topeka, KS

Sanchez, Elisa M
Bishop Ward HS
Kansas City, KS

Sander, Lora L
Great Bend Sr HS
Great Bend, KS

Sanderholm, Eric
Olathe North Sr HS
Olathe, KS

Sanderson, Jay L
Douglass HS
Douglass, KS

Sanko, Cassie L
Spearville Jr Sr HS
Spearville, KS

Sanneman, Lindsay
Clay Ctr Cmty HS
Clay Center, KS

Sannes, Matthew R
Blue Valley HS
Overland Park, KS

Sanson, Tanya L
Blue Valley HS
Overland Park, KS

Santiago, Marisol
Wichita Northwest HS
Wichita, KS

Sare, Justin E
Osawatomie HS
Rantoul, KS

Satterfield, Shawna M
Great Bend Sr HS
Great Bend, KS

Sauber, Tammie
Southwestern Hgts HS
Liberal, KS

Sauber, Teresa
Southwestern
Heights HS
Liberal, KS

Saunders, Lori L
Olathe East Sr HS
Olathe, KS

Savage, Megan L
Blue Valley
Northwest HS
Overland Park, KS

Saville, Tabitha
Olathe North Sr HS
Olathe, KS

Scanlon, Luke C
El Dorado HS
El Dorado, KS

Schaefer, Lindsey R
Wichita South HS
Wichita, KS

Schake, Dawn M
El Dorado HS
El Dorado, KS

Schamber, John J
Palco HS
Damar, KS

Schantz, Wendy
Shawnee Mission
North Schl
Shawnee Mission, KS

Schaub, Jeana L
Northeast HS
Arcadia, KS

Scheopner, Kendra D
Goodland HS
Goodland, KS

Scherer, Angela
Lansing HS
Lansing, KS

Scherer, Michael H
Atchison Co Cmty HS
Atchison, KS

Scherer, Rebecca R
Atchison Co Cmty HS
Lancaster, KS

Scheuerman, Andrea L
Maize HS
Wichita, KS

Schindler, John M
Colby Sr HS
Colby, KS

Schippert, David
Great Bend Sr HS
Great Bend, KS

Schlepp, Jessica
Salina HS South
Salina, KS

Schloemer, Brandon
Ulysses HS
Ulysses, KS

Schmanke, Keith S
Wabaunsee HS
Alma, KS

Schmersey, Kelly L
Shawnee Heights
Sr HS
Berryton, KS

Schmidt, Brandon P
Mc Pherson HS
Mc Pherson, KS

Schmidt, Carissa S
Blue Valley HS
Overland Park, KS

Schmidt, Jackie
Victoria HS
Victoria, KS

Schmidt, Justa L
Shawnee Heights HS
Berryton, KS

Schmidt, Kendra L
Haven HS
Haven, KS

Schmidt, Kevin C
Shawnee Mission
N HS
Shawnee, KS

Schmidt, Samantha M
Lawrence HS
Lawrence, KS

Schmieding, Thomas B
Turner HS
Kansas City, KS

Schmitz, Mikayla
St John's HS
Beloit, KS

Schmotzer, Tai A
Burlington HS
Burlington, KS

Schnee, Lee
Washburn Rural HS
Topeka, KS

Schneider, Daniel
Blue Valley
Northwest HS
Overland Park, KS

Schneider, Jeff D
Trego Comm HS
Wa Keeney, KS

Schneider, Julie M
Andale HS
Goddard, KS

Schnepp, Jessica
Olathe East Sr HS
Olathe, KS

Schneweis, Rachel L
Lawrence HS
Lawrence, KS

Schoen, Charles W
Moundridge HS
Moundridge, KS

Scholssesr, Dani
Goodland HS
Goodland, KS

Schoonover, Bradley P
Santa Fe Trail Jr HS
Olathe, KS

Schratter, Amanda
Schlagle HS
Kansas City, KS

Schreiber, Burt D
St Thomas Aquinas HS
Overland Park, KS

Schreiber, Julee
Claflin Jr Sr HS
Beaver, KS

Schroeder, Bonnie
Central Christian Schl
Buhler, KS

Schuler, Jacob J
Goddard HS
Wichita, KS

Schultz, Melissa D
Great Bend Sr HS
Great Bend, KS

Schulz, Katie
Holton HS
Holton, KS

Schumacher Jr, Daniel J
Manhattan HS
Manhattan, KS

Schwartz, Audrey A
Dighton HS
Alamota, KS

Schwartz, Mary
Blue Valley North HS
Leawood, KS

Schwenn, Steven J
Emporia HS
Emporia, KS

Schwerdtfeger, Ryan D
Wellington Sr HS
Wellington, KS

Schwerman, Aaron
St John's HS
Beloit, KS

Schwertfeger, Jennifer
Mc Pherson HS
Mc Pherson, KS

Schwieterman, Lucie
Garden City Sr HS
Garden City, KS

Schwindt, Joel D
Smoky Valley HS
Lindsborg, KS

Scott, Chantry C
Stanton Co HS
Johnson, KS

Scott, Jimmica M
Bishop Ward HS
Kansas City, KS

Scott, Mike P
Shawnee Mission W Sr HS
Overland Park, KS

Scroggins, Marlisha Y
Washington HS
Kansas City, KS

Seacat, Michelle
Dodge City HS
Dodge City, KS

Searle, Shelly D
Lyons HS
Lyons, KS

Sears, Sarah
Olathe South Sr HS
Olathe, KS

Seastrom, David W
Burlingame HS
Burlingame, KS

Segrist, Sarah
Shawnee Heights HS
Berryton, KS

Seib, Kristin J
Ness City HS
Ness City, KS

Sekavec, Daniel A
Ness City HS
Ness City, KS

Selk, Lou Anna
Wellington Sr HS
Wellington, KS

Semmel, Kim L
Lyons HS
Lyons, KS

Serven, Jeffrey W
Shawnee Mission S Sr HS
Lenexa, KS

Setzkorn, Ryan H
Udall HS
Rock, KS

Shah, Rajvee M
Shawnee Mission E Sr HS
Lenexa, KS

Shahan, Tennille
Udall HS
Udall, KS

Shain, Kari Ann
Buhler HS
Buhler, KS

Sharon, Richard H
Wichita East HS
Wichita, KS

Shaw, Kelly
Ashland HS
Ashland, KS

Shaw, Linn
Wellington Sr HS
Wellington, KS

Shaw, Tasha
Golden Plains HS
Selden, KS

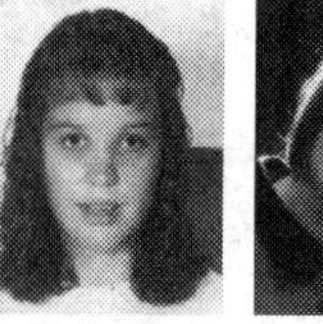
Sheaffer, Katy L
Central Heights Sr HS
Richmond, KS

Shear, Lisa
Hesston HS
Hesston, KS

Shelton, Michael J
Lawrence HS
Lawrence, KS

Shepherd, Jennifer I
Maize HS
Wichita, KS

Shepherd, Joseph
Ellis HS
Ellis, KS

Shepherd, Michael
Ellis HS
Ellis, KS

Shields, Brad M
Smoky Valley HS
Lindsborg, KS

Shields, Tyler
Labette Co HS
Oswego, KS

Shindley, Leslie D
Dighton HS
Dighton, KS

Shipley, Marileigh M
Dodge City HS
Dodge City, KS

Shirk, Abby M
Great Bend Sr HS
Great Bend, KS

Shockey, Tavi L
Leavenworth HS
Leavenworth, KS

Shoemaker, Danelle
St John's HS
Beloit, KS

Shoemaker, Garrett
Lebo Schl
Lebo, KS

Shoup, Joshua D
Larned HS
Larned, KS

Showalter, Kate
Shawnee Mission West HS
Lenexa, KS

Shriner, Brian P
Shawnee Mission W Sr HS
Overland Park, KS

Shroyer, Ashley
Sterling HS
Sterling, KS

Shroyer, Jason D
Wichita North HS
Wichita, KS

Shum, Justin
Marysville HS
Marysville, KS

Shurtz, Lindsey A
Ness City HS
Ness City, KS

Siebert, Elizabeth A
Hoisington HS
Hoisington, KS

Siebert, Wes
Salina HS Central
Salina, KS

Siegele, Cam S
Shawnee Mission W Sr HS
Overland Park, KS

Simmons, Brandie M
Great Bend Sr HS
Great Bend, KS

Simmons, Labrial T
Wyandotte HS
Kansas City, KS

Simon, Jeremy R
Leavenworth HS
Leavenworth, KS

Simoneau, Carrie L
Concordia Jr Sr HS
Concordia, KS

Simonich, Jackson L
Lawrence HS
Lawrence, KS

Simpson, Courtney A
Blue Valley HS
Stanley, KS

Simpson, Katherine
Garden City Sr HS
Garden City, KS

Simpson, Summer
Stafford Jr Sr HS
Stafford, KS

KANSAS

Sims, Angela J
Sumner Acad Of Arts & Science
Kansas City, KS

Sims, Benjamin J
Salina HS South
Salina, KS

Sims, Jeffrey L
Sumner Acad Of Arts & Science
Kansas City, KS

Sims, Laurel R
Buhler HS
Buhler, KS

Sims, Parks
Pierson Jr HS
Kansas City, KS

Sims, Robynn M
Buhler HS
Buhler, KS

Sipp, Stephanie C
Emporia HS
Emporia, KS

Sisk, Cheryl Ann
Campus HS
Haysville, KS

Sisney, Brock G
Ft Scott HS
Arcadia, KS

Sisson, Adam F
Spearville Jr Sr HS
Spearville, KS

Sisson, Kenneth E
Derby HS
Derby, KS

Sivils, Tyson J
Oxford HS
Geuda Springs, KS

Skaggs, Cara
Derby HS
Derby, KS

Skea, Matt
Faith Christian Schl
Ottawa, KS

Skinner, William E
Wichita East HS
Wichita, KS

Skolaut, Angela C
Great Bend Sr HS
Great Bend, KS

Slack, Amanda K
Rose Hill HS
Rose Hill, KS

Slack, Melissa B
Pittsburg HS
Pittsburg, KS

Slattery, Alesha M
Dodge City HS
Dodge City, KS

Slaughter, Casey
Maize HS
Wichita, KS

Slaven Jr, Ronald D
Arkansas City HS
Arkansas City, KS

Slepicka, Kevin R
Santa Fe Trail Jr HS
Olathe, KS

Sloan, Emily A
Blue Valley North HS
Leawood, KS

Slous, Jason D
Hoisington HS
Hoisington, KS

Small, Dustin A
Chapman HS
Junction City, KS

Smalley, Cary S
St Thomas Aquinas HS
Leawood, KS

Smarsh, Sarah
Kingman HS
Murdock, KS

Smith, Amanda
Shawnee Mission Northwest HS
Shawnee Mission, KS

Smith, April E
Campus HS
Haysville, KS

Smith, Audrey L
Kingman HS
Kingman, KS

Smith, Becky A
Lawrence HS
Lawrence, KS

Smith, Bradley H
Smoky Valley HS
Lindsborg, KS

Smith, Chris S
Maize HS
Wichita, KS

Smith, Christopher M
Shawnee Mission W Sr HS
Overland Park, KS

Smith, Cynthia
Mulvane Sr HS
Mulvane, KS

Smith, Jaclyn R
Bishop Miege HS
Kansas City, MO

Smith, James L
Sumner Acad Of Arts & Science
Basehor, KS

Smith, Jennifer L
Wellington Sr HS
Wellington, KS

Smith, Jeremi A
Erie HS
Erie, KS

Smith, Keisha
Liberal HS
Liberal, KS

Smith, Kye
Washburn Rural HS
Topeka, KS

Smith, Kylie J
Dighton HS
Dighton, KS

Smith, Matt
Protection Schl
Protection, KS

Smith, Meghan E
Blue Valley North HS
Leawood, KS

Smith, Melanie
Pittsburg HS
Pittsburg, KS

Smith, Melody J
Olathe South Sr HS
Olathe, KS

Smith, Miranda M
Maize HS
Wichita, KS

Smith, Nicholas
Junction City HS
Fort Riley, KS

Smith, Richard B
Kapaun-Mt Carmel HS
Wichita, KS

Smith, Sandra K
Douglass HS
Douglass, KS

Smith, Schoen
Shawnee Mission S Sr HS
Overland Park, KS

Smith, Segen
Manhattan HS
Manhattan, KS

Smith, Seth
Wichita Southeast HS
Rose Hill, KS

Smith, Shane
Jetmore HS
Jetmore, KS

Smith, Sherrie M
Wichita West HS
Wichita, KS

Smith, Stephanie Ellen
Mulvane Sr HS
Mulvane, KS

Smitha, Erin
Mission Valley HS
Harveyville, KS

Sneller, Kelly
Atchison Sr HS
Atchison, KS

Snodgrass, April D
Shawnee Mission W Sr HS
Olathe, KS

Snyder, Erin L
Ft Scott HS
Fort Scott, KS

Snyder, Zachary R
Lawrence HS
Lawrence, KS

Soctt, Carmen
Louisburg HS
Louisburg, KS

Sohm, Vicki L
Great Bend Sr HS
Great Bend, KS

Sojka, Candice
Wichita West HS
Wichita, KS

Solko, Kristal Elaine
Herndon Schl
Herndon, KS

Solly, Clare
Pittsburg HS
Pittsburg, KS

Solomon, Casey
Wichita West HS
Wichita, KS

Soukup, Laura
Lakin HS
Lakin, KS

Southerland, Levi
Gardner-Edgerton HS
Gardner, KS

Southerlnad, Stacey
Campus HS
Haysville, KS

Sova, Becky L
Andale HS
Maize, KS

Sowers, Rebecca
Salina HS South
Salina, KS

Spaeny, Ryan
Hutchinson HS
Hutchinson, KS

Spangenberg, Melissa
St John Jr Sr HS
Hudson, KS

Spanier, Jill
Garden City Sr HS
Garden City, KS

Spaulding, Che Tiana
Hayden HS
Topeka, KS

Speer, Alissa L
Maize HS
Overbrook, KS

Speer, Kasey L
Dodge City HS
Dodge City, KS

Speer, Sonya
Atchison Co Cmty HS
Horton, KS

Spitzengel, Jeannie
Career Opportunity
Center
Kansas City, KS

Spohn, Darlene R
Liberal HS
Liberal, KS

Spooner, Jerald
Turner HS
Kansas City, KS

Sprague, Rebecca M
Yates Ctr HS
Yates Center, KS

Sramek, Paula
Shawnee Mission W
Sr HS
Overland Park, KS

Staats, Shaleah L
Greensburg HS
Greensburg, KS

Stacy, Kevin C
Arkansas City HS
Arkansas City, KS

Stafford, Courtney A
Blue Valley
Northwest HS
Overland Park, KS

Stafford, Matthew W
Parsons HS
Parsons, KS

Stallbaumer,
Melissa Sue
Paola HS
Paola, KS

Stamm, Jennifer L
Cair
Paravel-Latin Schl
Tecumseh, KS

Stanfield, Melissa L
Topeka HS
Topeka, KS

Stanley, David
Augusta Sr HS
Augusta, KS

Stanley, Garret B
Dodge City HS
Dodge City, KS

Stanley, Joseph B
Field Kindley Mem
Sr HS
Coffeyville, KS

Stansbury, Daniel K
Northeast HS
Mulberry, KS

Stapp, Trevor
Holcomb HS
Holcomb, KS

Stark, Levi J
Campus HS
Wichita, KS

Staudacher, Vickie S
Wichita North HS
Wichita, KS

Steffen, Tyson M
Pawnee Heights
East HS
Burdett, KS

Stein, Michael W
Halstead HS
Halstead, KS

Stein, Phillip
Olathe East Sr HS
Overland Park, KS

Steinke, Cory
Olpe Schl
Olpe, KS

Steinmetz, Deanna M
Immaculata HS
Bonner Springs, KS

Stelljes, Spencer H
Derby HS
Derby, KS

Stephens, Emelia M
Lawrence HS
Lawrence, KS

Stephens, Lyne
Ashland HS
Ashland, KS

Stephens, Starr R
St Mary's Colgan HS
Arcadia, KS

Stephens, Susan L
Field Kindley Mem
Sr HS
Coffeyville, KS

Stephens, Timothy
Lawrence HS
Lawrence, KS

Stephenson, Charles D
Central Heights Sr HS
Rantoul, KS

Stevens, Curtis L
Scott Comm HS
Scott City, KS

Stevens, Jennifer D
Lacrosse HS
La Crosse, KS

Stevens, Jonelle
Ashland HS
Ashland, KS

Stevens, Kendra
Oxford HS
Oxford, KS

Stewart, Brian R
Uniontown HS
Bronson, KS

Stewart, Mandi
Hutchinson HS
Hutchinson, KS

Stinemetz, Deanna
Garden City Sr HS
Garden City, KS

Stinemetz, Jennifer R
Pawnee Heights
East HS
Burdett, KS

Stinnett, John
Arkansas City HS
Arkansas City, KS

Stith, Brianne L
Blue Valley
Northwest HS
Overland Park, KS

Stockton, Amy K
Shawnee Mission Nw
Sr HS
Shawnee Mission, KS

Stockwell, Jim R
Ness City HS
Ness City, KS

Stockwell, Sarah
Burlington HS
Burlington, KS

Stoffer, Jennifer
Chapman HS
Abilene, KS

Stohs, Amber
Marysville HS
Marysville, KS

Stoker, Matt
Olathe North Sr HS
Olathe, KS

Stone, Ben E
Emporia HS
Emporia, KS

Stone, Kelli L
F L Schlagle HS
Kansas City, KS

Stoppel, Christopher
Sublette HS
Sublette, KS

Stos, Danah L
Hoisington HS
Hoisington, KS

Stotler, Dan W
Iola Sr HS
Iola, KS

Stoutenborough,
James W
Louisburg HS
Louisburg, KS

Strader, Meridith A
Wellington Sr HS
Wellington, KS

Strait, Jennifer
Kingman HS
Kingman, KS

Straley, Mike
Spring Hill HS
Spring Hill, KS

Stremel, Kara
Thomas More
Prep-Marion HS
Hays, KS

Strickland, Tandi J
Hoisington HS
Hoisington, KS

Strohm, Daniel
Augusta Sr HS
Augusta, KS

Stroud, Brad
Frontenac Jr Sr HS
Frontenac, KS

Stroup Jr, Raymond L
Wabaunsee HS
Mc Farland, KS

KANSAS

Stryker, Travis E
Topeka HS
Topeka, KS

Stuart, Lisa M
Washington HS
Kansas City, KS

Stuby, Monica
Seaman Sr HS
Topeka, KS

Stucky, Shelese
Hesston HS
Moundridge, KS

Stumps, Austin T
Derby HS
Derby, KS

Sturgis, Amanda K
Riverton Schl
Columbus, KS

Subelka, Adam
Mc Louth Schl
Mc Louth, KS

Sullivan, Anna M
Field Kindley Mem
Sr HS
Coffeyville, KS

Sullivan, Grant
Ulysses HS
Ulysses, KS

Sultzer, Erik M
Hays HS
Hays, KS

Summers, Traci J
Great Bend Sr HS
Great Bend, KS

Summerson,
Courtney D
St Thomas Aquinas HS
Overland Park, KS

Surmeier, Darrell P
Colby Sr HS
Colby, KS

Sutherland, Misty
Belle Plaine HS
Peck, KS

Sutter, Carrie
Pratt HS
Pratt, KS

Sutton, Aaron M
South Haven Schl
South Haven, KS

Swaffar, Mitzi N
Blue Valley
Northwest HS
Overland Park, KS

Swafford, Michelle
Sumner Acad Of Arts
& Science
Kansas City, KS

Swanwick, Daniel L
Ft Scott HS
Fort Scott, KS

Swart, Steven C
Wichita West HS
Wichita, KS

Swartz, Rebekah
Wellington Sr HS
Wellington, KS

Swearengin, Leigh M
Parsons HS
Parsons, KS

Swenson, Jennifer
Beloit Jr Sr HS
Beloit, KS

Swick, Christopher E
Mc Pherson HS
Mc Pherson, KS

Swift, Brooks D
Shawnee Heights HS
Topeka, KS

Swindall, Andy D
Shawnee Heights
Sr HS
Tecumseh, KS

Swingle, Marnie L
Blue Valley
Northwest HS
Plano, TX

Swingle, Marta L
Blue Valley
Northwest HS
Overland Park, KS

Swisher, Keir G
Smoky Valley HS
Lindsborg, KS

Tabin, Patrick
Junction City HS
Fort Riley, KS

Tackling, Sebastian M
Manhattan HS
Manhattan, KS

Taddiken, Tawnya
Clay Ctr Cmty HS
Clifton, KS

Tadlock, Brian D
Cimmaron Jr Sr HS
Cimarron, KS

Talbott, Mark D
Smoky Valley HS
Lindsborg, KS

Talbott, Traci L
Smoky Valley HS
Lindsborg, KS

Tannini, Eddie P
Chapman HS
Chapman, KS

Tate, Andrea
Central USD 462
Latham, KS

Tate, Shanae N
Acad Of Mt St
Scholastica
Atchison, KS

Taul, Kelly K
Baldwin HS
Baldwin City, KS

Taylor, Curtis R
Olathe South Sr HS
Olathe, KS

Taylor, Johnna K
Louisburg HS
Louisburg, KS

Taylor, Michelle
Newton Sr HS
Newton, KS

Taylor, Rochelle M
Immaculata HS
Orlando, FL

Taylor, Russell J
Desoto HS
Shawnee Mission, KS

Taylor, Tara N
Neodesha Jr Sr HS
El Dorado, KS

Templeton, Alisha
Olathe South Sr HS
Olathe, KS

Terhune, Michael D
Conway Springs HS
Conway Springs, KS

Terronez, Stephanie D
Campus HS
Haysville, KS

Thalmann, Damian D
Hoisington HS
Hoisington, KS

Tharp, Amy
Indian Trail Jr HS
Olathe, KS

Thayer, Kelly R
Wichita East HS
Wichita, KS

Thieme, Justina M
Kingman HS
Zenda, KS

Thirakul, Katrina V
Garden City Sr HS
Garden City, KS

Thomas, Drew A
Hays HS
Hays, KS

Thomas, Jennifer
Augusta Sr HS
Augusta, KS

Thomas, Julie L
Bishop Miege HS
Overland Park, KS

Thomas, Matthew
Leavenworth HS
Leavenworth, KS

Thomas, Michael
Leavenworth HS
Leavenworth, KS

Thompson, Annette C
Goddard HS
Goddard, KS

Thompson, Chandra F
Newton Sr HS
Newton, KS

Thompson, Erin E
Blue Valley HS
Overland Park, KS

Thompson, Jasmine E
Wichita East HS
Wichita, KS

Thompson, Jessica L
Olathe East Sr HS
Overland Park, KS

Thompson, Jessica L
Wichita East HS
Wichita, KS

Thompson, Kara A
Newton Sr HS
Newton, KS

Thompson, Kym R
Leavenworth HS
Leavenworth, KS

Thompson, Tammy M
Shawnee Heights HS
Tecumseh, KS

Thompson, Thomas A
Protection Schl
Protection, KS

Thomson, Elizabeth C
Pittsburg HS
Pittsburg, KS

Thornburg, Eric
Ulysses HS
Ulysses, KS

Thornbury, Michelle
Spring Hill HS
Olathe, KS

Thornton, Brandi A
Meade HS
Meade, KS

Thornton, Mickey
Oakley HS
Oakley, KS

Tiemann, Cheryl
Chanute Sr HS
Chanute, KS

Tiesmeyer, Lacey
Kingman HS
Kingman, KS

Tilford, Eva J
F L Schlagle HS
Kansas City, KS

Tillery, Kacy M
Piper HS
Kansas City, KS

Tilley, Joseph R
Frankft HS
Frankfort, KS

Tillotson, Tiffany
Wichita Northwest HS
Wichita, KS

Timberlake, Emily A
Shawnee Mission
N HS
Shawnee Mission, KS

Tims, Jessica S
Northeast HS
Arma, KS

Tindal, Darrell
Northwest HS
Wichita, KS

Tindle, Beth M
Blue Valley
Northwest HS
Overland Park, KS

Tinkler, Sandra M
Smoky Valley HS
Lindsborg, KS

Tobias, Aaron
Lyons HS
Lyons, KS

Todd, Patrick N
El Dorado HS
El Dorado, KS

Tollett, Barbie J
Hartford HS
Hartford, KS

Tomasich, Nick
Shawnee Mission
Northwest HS
Shawnee, KS

Tonn, Ramee
Wichita West HS
Wichita, KS

Toombs, Jerome A
Sumner Acad Of Arts
& Science
Kansas City, KS

Tosh, Kristi A
Field Kindley Mem
Sr HS
Coffeyville, KS

Toth, Jennifer M
Turner HS
Overland Park, KS

Tovar, Melissa
Augusta Sr HS
Augusta, KS

Townsend, Craig
Goodland HS
Goodland, KS

Trammell, Brent
Olathe East Sr HS
Olathe, KS

Tran, Vinhan H
Garden City Sr HS
Garden City, KS

Trapp, Andrew
Hoisington HS
Susank, KS

Treder, Stephen L
Dodge City HS
Dodge City, KS

Treece, Akya R
Field Kindley Mem
Sr HS
Coffeyville, KS

Trent, Jessica A
Wichita East HS
Wichita, KS

Tretheway, Angela J
Derby HS
Derby, KS

Trevino, Crystal H
Garden City Sr HS
Garden City, KS

Triebel, Justin A
Labette Co HS
Coffeyville, KS

Trimmell, Holly M
Wichita West HS
Wichita, KS

Trombold, John M
Blue Valley North HS
Leawood, KS

Trotter, Tera R
Wichita East HS
Wichita, KS

Trowbridge, Julie A
Wichita West HS
Wichita, KS

Truta, Bryan A
Bishop Miege HS
Overland Park, KS

Tucker, Heidi M
Salina HS South
Salina, KS

Tucker, Jordan T
Kingman HS
Kingman, KS

Tucker, Julia E
Blue Valley
Northwest HS
Overland Park, KS

Tucker, Sabrina N
Scott Comm HS
Scott City, KS

Tucker, Tammy L
Washburn Rural HS
Topeka, KS

Tunnell, Russ R
Riverton Schl
Baxter Springs, KS

Turley, Sharnell R
Scott Comm HS
Marienthal, KS

Turnbow, Stuart D
Ellsworth HS
Geneseo, KS

Turner, Brandi N
Labette Co HS
Hallowell, KS

Turner, Dena R
Wyandotte HS
Kansas City, KS

Turner, Jerri L
Valley Ctr HS
Valley Center, KS

Turner, Roland D
Eureka Jr Sr HS
Eureka, KS

Turney, Ross D
Basehor Linwood HS
Bonner Springs, KS

Tuttle, Eletha J
Washington HS
Kansas City, KS

Twaddle, Kelly
Desoto HS
Olathe, KS

Tyner, Hayley
Topeka HS
Topeka, KS

Uhl, Katherine E
Garden City Sr HS
Garden City, KS

Ukena, Jamie K
Rock Creek Jr Sr HS
Saint George, KS

Ulbrich, Lisa
Sedgwick HS
Valley Center, KS

Ulbrich, Tenessa
Sedgwick HS
Valley Center, KS

Ulsh, Amber L
Olathe East Sr HS
Olathe, KS

Ummel, Staci D
Great Bend Sr HS
Great Bend, KS

Umstead, Randy
Olathe South Sr HS
Olathe, KS

Underwood, Melissa
Ft Scott HS
Garland, KS

Ung, Nelson
Wichita Heights HS
Wichita, KS

Unrein, Chad W
Maize HS
Wichita, KS

Unrein, Shane W
Maize HS
Wichita, KS

Unruh, Anthony
Field Kindley Mem
Sr HS
Coffeyville, KS

Unruh, Jamie L
UPN HS
Weskan, KS

Unruh, Matt
Burrton Schl
Burrton, KS

Urczyk, Kylie F
Olathe East Sr HS
Olathe, KS

Vachal, Jane A
Garden City Sr HS
Garden City, KS

KANSAS

Vaille, Mandy J
Blue Valley
Northwest HS
Overland Park, KS

Valdez, Matt
Thomas More
Prep-Marion HS
Hays, KS

Valkenaar, Jill
Augusta Sr HS
Augusta, KS

Vallejos, Cesar Daniel
Shawnee Mission E
Sr HS
Prairie Village, KS

Van Blaricum, Jay P
Pratt HS
Pratt, KS

Vandecreek, Rob
Chapman HS
Enterprise, KS

Van Denabeele, Matt E
Gardner-Edgerton HS
Kansas City, KS

Vanderbogart, Lee A
Lawrence HS
Lawrence, KS

Vanek, Jennifer Ann
Thomas More
Prep-Marian HS
Hays, KS

Vanek, Jessica M
Thomas More
Prep-Marion HS
Hays, KS

Van Sickle, Amy R
Emporia HS
Emporia, KS

Vantuyl, Shanna
Perry Lecompton HS
Perry, KS

Van Winkle,
Christine N
Field Kindley Mem
Sr HS
Coffeyville, KS

Varney, Amy
Shawnee Heights HS
Tecumseh, KS

Varney, Brent R
Shawnee Hgts HS
Tecumseh, KS

Vasquez, Chrissy M
Blue Valley North HS
Leawood, KS

Vaughn, Eric
Waverly HS
Waverly, KS

Vaughn, Jennifer L
Lawrence HS
Jefferson City, MO

Vavricka, Chris V
Ness City HS
Ness City, KS

Vazquez, Felicita
Junction City HS
Fort Riley, KS

Vazquez, James P
Sumner Acad Of Arts
And Sci
Kansas City, KS

Venerable, Jennifer
Sumner Acad
Kansas City, KS

Venkatesh, Nina
Blue Valley
Northwest HS
Leawood, KS

Vering, Kendra
St John's HS
Beloit, KS

Vetter, Gerica L
Beloit Jr Sr HS
Beloit, KS

Vicknair, Ashley
Derby HS
Derby, KS

Viergets, Aaron
Goodland HS
Goodland, KS

Viescas, Renee L
Claflin Jr Sr HS
Ellsworth, KS

Vieux, Alexander N
Garden City Sr HS
Garden City, KS

Vignery, Curtis J
Desoto HS
De Soto, KS

Villarreal, Sallie A
Thomas More
Prep-Marion HS
Grand Prairie, TX

Vineyard, Amy
Independence HS
Independence, KS

Vinsonhaler, Jason S
Seaman Sr HS
Topeka, KS

Vix, Karie L
Olathe East Sr HS
Olathe, KS

Vogel, Adrian L
Cimarron HS
Cimarron, KS

Vogel, Alicia D
Cimarron HS
Cimarron, KS

Vogel, Lindsay
Manhattan HS
Manhattan, KS

Volmer, Monica D
Field Kindley Mem
Sr HS
Coffeyville, KS

Von Knorring, Angie
Spring Hill HS
Spring Hill, KS

Von Schriltz,
Amanda E
Washburn Rural HS
Topeka, KS

Voorhees, Amanda J
Maize HS
Maize, KS

Voth, Amandad
Independence HS
Independence, KS

Voth, Kristina L
Arkansas City HS
Arkansas City, KS

Vyzourek, Joe
Atwood HS
Atwood, KS

Wade, Amber R
Galena HS
Galena, KS

Wade, Isaac I
Galena HS
Galena, KS

Waggoner, Ashley
Shawnee Mission E
Sr HS
Leawood, KS

Wagner, Becky M
El Dorado HS
El Dorado, KS

Wagner, Jill M
Larned HS
Garfield, KS

Wagoner, Bobby L
Quinter Jr Sr HS
Quinter, KS

Wagstaff, Jeffrey S
St John's Military Schl
Granada Hills, CA

Wahlmeier, Joshua A
Trego Comm HS
Wa Keeney, KS

Wait, Ali
Sublette HS
Sublette, KS

Walker, Damian
Wellington Sr HS
Wellington, KS

Walker, Danielle D
Turner HS
Kansas City, KS

Walker, Felicia
Jefferson West HS
Meriden, KS

Walker, Stacee
Wyandotte HS
Kansas City, KS

Walker, Tracee M
Wyandotte HS
Kansas City, KS

Wallace, Beau R
Chase Co HS
Cottonwood Fall, KS

Wallace, Lindsay R
Garden City Sr HS
Garden City, KS

Wallace, Melanie D
Anderson Cty Jr Sr HS
Garnett, KS

Wallace, Michael P
Olathe South Sr HS
Olathe, KS

Wallace, Wendy A
Douglass HS
Douglass, KS

Wallgren, Mandy
Phillipsburg HS
Phillipsburg, KS

Walling, Caroline
Wichita
Collegiate Schl
Wichita, KS

Walsh, Andria
Bishop Carroll
Catholic HS
Wichita, KS

Walshire, Jason M
Shawnee Heights
Sr HS
Topeka, KS

Walter, Andrew
Hays HS
Catharine, KS

Walter, Elizabeth
Mc Pherson HS
Mc Pherson, KS

Walters, Blake N
Centralia Schl
Centralia, KS

Walters, Heather
Olathe East Sr HS
Olathe, KS

Walton, Donovan
Mankato Jr Sr HS
Mankato, KS

Walton, Jennifer L
Humboldt HS
Humboldt, KS

Wang, Joline
St Xavier's HS
Junction City, KS

Wanklyn, Kevin
Lakin HS
Lakin, KS

Wapelhorst, Joseph P
Great Bend Sr HS
Great Bend, KS

Ward, Amanda R
Shawnee Heights HS
Topeka, KS

Ward, Joseph
Wilson Jr Sr HS
Wilson, KS

Ward, Joshua
Mulvane Sr HS
Mulvane, KS

Ward, Stephanie E
Bishop Ward HS
Kansas City, KS

Warinner, Tina G
St Thomas Aquinas HS
Overland Park, KS

Warner, Brandon K
Otis Bison HS
Bison, KS

Warnken, Erik J
Great Bend Sr HS
Great Bend, KS

Warren, Clinton S
Blue Valley HS
Overland Park, KS

Warren, Svonne
Leavenworth HS
Leavenworth, KS

Washington, Beonca
Wichita Heights HS
Kechi, KS

Wasinger, Nick P
Wichita East HS
Wichita, KS

Wassinger, Suzann N
Ness City HS
Ness City, KS

Waters, Andrew
Blue Valley
Northwest HS
Overland Park, KS

Waters, Jocelyn Nicci
Campus HS
Haysville, KS

Waters, Steven J
Salina HS South
Salina, KS

Watkins, Casse
Ellinwood Jr Sr HS
Ellinwood, KS

Watkins, Misty
Columbus HS
Columbus, KS

Watkins, Tracy L
Galena HS
Galena, KS

Watson, Candace M
Northeast Magnet HS
Peck, KS

Watson, Christy L
El Dorado HS
El Dorado, KS

Watson, Michael
Kansas Schl For
The Deaf
Topeka, KS

Watson, Naudia T
Washington HS
Kansas City, KS

Watson, Shawn M
Clearwater HS
Peck, KS

Watson III, Virgil
Arkansas City HS
Arkansas City, KS

Watts, Dana
Syracuse Jr Sr HS
Syracuse, KS

Watts, Kari
Syracuse Jr Sr HS
Syracuse, KS

Waugh, Christina
Dighton HS
Dighton, KS

Way, Adrian N
Topeka HS
Topeka, KS

Way, Kristen N
Maize HS
Wichita, KS

Waymaster, Troy L
Russell HS
Bunker Hill, KS

Weaver, David
Shawnee Mission
East HS
Prairie Village, KS

Weaver, Doug
Wichita North HS
Wichita, KS

Webb, Jeffery A
Muncie Christian Schl
Kansas City, KS

Webb, Justus
Leavenworth HS
Leavenworth, KS

Weber, Annette L
Yates Ctr HS
Yates Center, KS

Weber, Dustin
Wathena Schl
Wathena, KS

Webster, Brity
Winfield HS
Winfield, KS

Wedel, Angie
Lyons HS
Lyons, KS

Weeks, Alisa
Burlington HS
Strawn, KS

Weeks, Cortney P
Salina HS South
Salina, KS

Wegeng, Courtney A
Kapaun-Mt Carmel HS
Wichita, KS

Wegner, Erin M
Beloit Jr Sr HS
Beloit, KS

Wegner, Leah
Desoto HS
De Soto, KS

Weible, Stacy
Valley Ctr HS
Wichita, KS

Weide, Steven W
Arkansas City HS
Arkansas City, KS

Weigant, David
Campus HS
Haysville, KS

Weigel, April M
Russell HS
Gorham, KS

Weigel, Jennifer A
Bishop Miege HS
Kansas City, KS

Weisbrod, Kristen J
Manhattan HS
Manhattan, KS

Weller, Tiffany
Arkansas City HS
Arkansas City, KS

Weltmer, Melody R
Plainville HS
Plainville, KS

Welton, Melanee B
Caney Valley Jr Sr HS
Caney, KS

Wendell, Amanda
St John's HS
Beloit, KS

Wendt, Melissa L
Salina HS South
Salina, KS

Wendt, Shanna A
Derby HS
Derby, KS

Werring, Andrew
Maur Hill Prep Schl
Atchison, KS

Wesley, Daniel S
Turner HS
Kansas City, KS

Wesley, Rachel A
Elyria Christian Schl
Mc Pherson, KS

Wesley, Toni M
Medicine Lodge HS
Lake City, KS

Wessel, Michelle E
Marion HS
Marion, KS

Wessel, Patricia
Holton HS
Holton, KS

Westfahl, Nicholas A
Maize HS
Wichita, KS

Westfahl, Tim J
Maize HS
Wichita, KS

Westhoff, Brandon
Arkansas City HS
Arkansas City, KS

Westmark, Keri L
Shawnee Mission
South HS
Overland Park, KS

Wetmore, Trent
Neodesha Jr Sr HS
Neodesha, KS

Wetschensky, Tracy L
Piper HS
Kansas City, KS

Wheat, Rosann
Hamilton HS
Eureka, KS

Whetstone, Shaun E
Labette Co HS
Parsons, KS

Whiles, Tiffany D
Shawnee Mission E
Sr HS
Fairway, KS

Whisler, Cheryl D
Washington HS
Kansas City, KS

Whitaker, Jolyn D
Dodge City HS
Dodge City, KS

White, Brian C
Argonia Jr Sr HS
Argonia, KS

White, Donje E
Hayden HS
Topeka, KS

White, Stephanie
Argonia Jr Sr HS
Argonia, KS

White, Venessa
Peabody-Burns Jr
Sr HS
Peabody, KS

Whitehill, Jordan L
Maize HS
Wichita, KS

Whiteside, S S
Wichita
Collegiate Schl
Wichita, KS

Whittredge,
Benjamin L
Buhler HS
Hutchinson, KS

Wichmann, John-Paul
Shawnee Mission Nw
Sr HS
Shawnee, KS

Wiedower, Sarah
Wellington Sr HS
Wellington, KS

Wieland, Coleena M
Colby Sr HS
Colby, KS

Wieland, Karen E
Colby Sr HS
Colby, KS

Wiesner, Rebecca A
Salina HS Central
Salina, KS

Wigner, Jaime
Garden City Sr HS
Garden City, KS

Wigner, Lori A
Garden City Sr HS
Garden City, KS

Wilbur, Jennifer A
Wichita Co HS
Leoti, KS

Wiley, David
Independence HS
Independence, KS

Wilfong, Michael J
Douglass HS
Douglass, KS

Wilhite, Julie A
Baldwin HS
Baldwin City, KS

Wilhite, Vanessa A
Wichita Hghts HS
Wichita, KS

Wilkens, Adena
Linn Schl
Clifton, KS

Wilkinson, Stephanie
Wichita East HS
Wichita, KS

Will, Jamin D
Burlingame HS
Burlingame, KS

Will, Jennifer L
Burlingame HS
Burlingame, KS

Williams, Amos D
Bluestem HS
El Dorado, KS

Williams, Brandis A
Turner HS
Kansas City, KS

Williams, Cynthia
Turner HS
Kansas City, KS

Williams, Jessica E
Wichita North HS
Wichita, KS

Williams, Jonathan
Manhattan HS
Manhattan, KS

Williams, Kathy L
Rolla HS
Rolla, KS

Williams, Kelley
Derby HS
Derby, KS

Williams, Kristen
Shawnee Mission E
Sr HS
Shawnee Mission, KS

Williams, Linda
Girard HS
Girard, KS

Williams, Marianne C
Maize HS
Wichita, KS

Williams, Pamela D
Salina HS South
Salina, KS

Williams, Quanita
Jewell HS
Jewell, KS

Williams, Renee A
Caldwell Jr Sr HS
Caldwell, KS

Williams II,
Roderick M
Derby HS
Derby, KS

Williams, Samantha A
Colby Sr HS
Colby, KS

Williams, Tiffany H
Shawnee Heights
Sr HS
Topeka, KS

Williamson, Jenni L
Meade HS
Meade, KS

Williamson, Matt K
Blue Valley
Northwest HS
Overland Park, KS

Willingham, Robert D
Washington HS
Kansas City, KS

Willis, Michelle
Olathe North Sr HS
Olathe, KS

Willson, Jennifer
Udall HS
Udall, KS

Wilson, Andrea D
Kansas City
Chrstn Acad
Overland Park, KS

Wilson, Ashley
Salina HS Central
Salina, KS

Wilson, Heather D
Maize HS
Wichita, KS

Wilson, Jimmie E
Burlingame HS
Carbondale, KS

Wilson, Justin
Waconda East HS
Cawker City, KS

Wilson, Matt
Olathe South Sr HS
Olathe, KS

Wilson, Rochelle
Anderson Cty Jr Sr HS
Garnett, KS

Wilson, Ryan D
Marysville HS
Marysville, KS

Wilson, Sara
Olathe North Sr HS
Olathe, KS

Wiltse, Amy L
Ft Scott HS
Fort Scott, KS

Winans, Christie
Olathe East Sr HS
Olathe, KS

Windholz, Sarah J
Trego Comm HS
Ogallah, KS

Windler, Jennifer D
Shawnee Mission S
Sr HS
Shawnee Mission, KS

Wineinger, Nicole E
Holcomb HS
Holcomb, KS

Wines, Clark A
Liberal HS
Liberal, KS

Wingert, Emily
Shawnee Mission
N HS
Mission, KS

Winright, Kyle
Lakin HS
Lakin, KS

Winter, Kristen A
Shawnee Mission
West HS
Lenexa, KS

Winter-Foss, Melissa A
Trinity Catholic HS
Nickerson, KS

Wise, Jessi M
Ellsworth HS
Ellsworth, KS

Wise, Stephen R
Wichita North HS
Wichita, KS

Wiske, Jolinda
Medicine Lodge HS
Medicine Lodge, KS

Wissink, Jeremy R
Garden City Sr HS
Garden City, KS

Wissler, Kellie
Lawrence HS
Lawrence, KS

Withroder, Elizabeth A
Halstead HS
Halstead, KS

Witt, Kari
Junction City HS
Junction City, KS

Witte, Amber L
Andale HS
Colwich, KS

Wittluhn, Brent
Halstead HS
Sedgwick, KS

Wohlfort-Barnes, Alexa
South East Of Saline HS
Assaria, KS

Wohlgemuth, Bryan
Lansing HS
Leavenworth, KS

Wohlgemuth, Derek
Atchison Sr HS
Atchison, KS

Wojtkiewicz, Nathan E
Shawnee Mission N HS
Overland Park, KS

Wolff, Brandon M
Maize HS
Wichita, KS

Wolters, Dayna R
Turner HS
Leavenworth, KS

Wondra, Tracie R
Great Bend Sr HS
Great Bend, KS

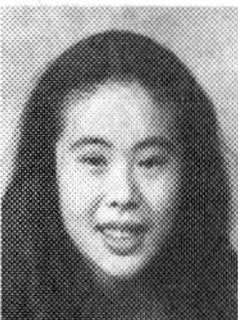
Woo, Jamie
Wichita North HS
Wichita, KS

Wood, Katy S
Turner HS
Kansas City, KS

Wood, Marietta
Troy HS
Atchison, KS

Woodford, Jennifer
Manhattan HS
Manhattan, KS

Woods, Camille
Mulvane Sr HS
Mulvane, KS

Woods, Derek W
Manhattan HS
Manhattan, KS

Woods, Tesa
Cimarron HS
Cimarron, KS

Woody, Nathan R
El Dorado HS
El Dorado, KS

Woolard, Josh D
Lewis Schl
Lewis, KS

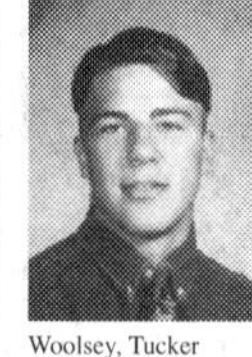
Woolsey, Tucker
Decatur Cmty Jr Sr HS
Oberlin, KS

Woolsoncroft, Tiara D
Salina HS South
Salina, KS

Worrall, Casey M
Lansing HS
Leavenworth, KS

Wortham, Tamarir M
J C Harmon HS
Kansas City, KS

Worthen, Jennifer A
Campus HS
Wichita, KS

Woydziak, Amber
Lyons HS
Lyons, KS

Wren, Sabrina M
Turner HS
Kansas City, KS

Wright, Deborah A
Canton-Galva HS
Canton, KS

Wright, Jeremy W
Manhattan HS
Manhattan, KS

Wright, Stacey L
Maize HS
Maize, KS

Wyatt, Jayme L
Topeka HS
Topeka, KS

Wycoff, Laura
Wichita West HS
Wichita, KS

Wyer, Brandi D
Maize HS
Wichita, KS

Wynn, Clint P
Sumner Acad Of Arts & Science
Kansas City, KS

Yambot, Jove F
Olathe East Sr HS
Olathe, KS

Yasuhara, Kelli D
Shawnee Mission S Sr HS
Shawnee Mission, KS

Yeager, Anna
Rock Creek Jr Sr HS
Saint George, KS

Yeingst, Feather A
Great Bend Sr HS
Great Bend, KS

Yerke, Shannon M
Sacred Heart HS
Salina, KS

Yoachim, Collin D
Arkansas City HS
Arkansas City, KS

Yoachim, Marye E
Arkansas City HS
Arkansas City, KS

Yockey, Jennifer
Campus HS
Haysville, KS

Yoder, Andrew L
Nickerson HS
South Hutchinson, KS

York, Christopher
St Thomas Aquinas HS
Overland Park, KS

Young, Abby
Kingman HS
Kingman, KS

Young, Erin
Olathe East Sr HS
Olathe, KS

Young, Holly
Atchison Co Cmty HS
Effingham, KS

Young, Jennifer
Kansas City Bible Clg High
Shawnee Mission, KS

Young, Joni L
Haven HS
Burrton, KS

Young, Katherine E
Topeka HS
Topeka, KS

Young, Malissa A
Olathe North Sr HS
Olathe, KS

Young, Michael
Lawrence HS
Lawrence, KS

Younger, Casey L
Basehor Linwood HS
Tonganoxie, KS

Yust, Richard D
Haven HS
Haven, KS

Yutzy, Carrie N
Haven HS
Haven, KS

Zarter, C Ryan
Shawnee Mission Nw Sr HS
Shawnee, KS

Zebell-Mann, Savannah R
Derby Christian Schl
Wichita, KS

Zehneder, Sarah B
Smoky Valley HS
Lindsborg, KS

Zehner, Jennifer L
Gardner-Edgerton HS
Edgerton, KS

Zeller, Margie
Desoto HS
Shawnee Mission, KS

Zimmerman, Heather A
Protection Schl
Protection, KS

Zimmerman, Melissa
Arkansas City HS
Arkansas City, KS

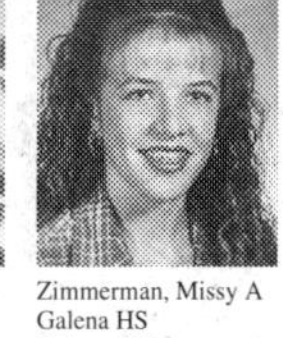
Zimmerman, Missy A
Galena HS
Galena, KS

Zink, Sarah M
Great Bend Sr HS
Great Bend, KS

OKLAHOMA

Abdullah, Ibn Z
Spiro HS
Spiro, OK

Abel, Aaron J
B T Washington HS
Tulsa, OK

Abel, Angela D
Wagoner Sr HS
Wagoner, OK

Abercrombie, Brian M
Edmond North HS
Edmond, OK

Ables, Hiedi B
Walters HS
Walters, OK

Abramian, Jared R
Ponca City Sr HS
Ponca City, OK

Abrams, Jessica L
Pawhuska HS
Pawhuska, OK

Acre, Amy L
Canton HS
Canton, OK

Adair, Bobbie J
Okmulgee HS
Okmulgee, OK

Adair, Matt D
Western Heights Sr HS
Oklahoma City, OK

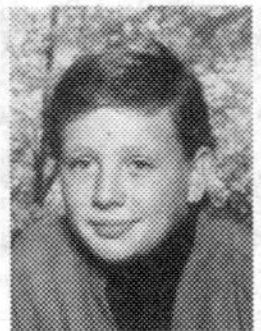
Adams, Allen D
Madill HS
Madill, OK

Adams, Ashley M
Putnam City North HS
Oklahoma City, OK

Adams, Danielle
Comanche HS
Hastings, OK

Adams, Karen D
Sapulpa Sr HS
Tulsa, OK

Adams, Nina
Mustang HS
Yukon, OK

Adams, Stacey C
Jenks HS
Tulsa, OK

Adams, T'Nika
Millwood HS
Oklahoma City, OK

Adams Halvorso, Jennifer
Harrah HS
Harrah, OK

Adesina, Ore-Ofe O
West Middle HS
Norman, OK

Adkins, Rachel
Okeene Jr Sr HS
Okeene, OK

Aebischer, Chad E
Westmore HS
Oklahoma City, OK

Agnew, Huling W
Caney Valley HS
Ramona, OK

Agnew, Nicole C
Pauls Valley HS
Pauls Valley, OK

Aguilera, Alene
Shawnee Sr HS
Shawnee, OK

Aguilera, Andrea
Shawnee Sr HS
Shawnee, OK

Ahlefeld, Kelsea
Mustang HS
Yukon, OK

Ahmad, Nabeel
Western Heights Sr HS
Oklahoma City, OK

Ahmad, Tariq
Western Heights Sr HS
Oklahoma City, OK

Ahmed, Natasha R
Owasso Sr HS
Owasso, OK

Ahrend, T S
Ada HS
Ada, OK

Ainooson, Jeff
Jarman Jr HS
Oklahoma City, OK

Ainooson, Richard
Midwest City HS
Oklahoma City, OK

Airington, Ashley R
Central Mid-HS
Norman, OK

Aishman, Samantha
Spiro HS
Spiro, OK

Alarcon, Maricela H
Northeast HS
Oklahoma City, OK

Alarid, Joseph C
U S Grant HS
Oklahoma City, OK

Albee, Ryan D
Choctaw HS
Choctaw, OK

Alcantara, Raquel
Moore HS
Moore, OK

Aldrich, Amber K
Luther HS
Luther, OK

Aldrich, Jason
Fargo Schl
Gage, OK

Aldridge, Stephen
Wakita Schl
Manchester, OK

Alene, Kelli
Westmoore HS
Oklahoma City, OK

Alexander, Ashley K
Union Intermediate HS
Tulsa, OK

Alexander Jr, Barry C
Life Christian HS
Norman, OK

Alexander, Beau D
North Intermediate HS
Broken Arrow, OK

Alexander, Ben C
Bartlesville Sr HS
Bartlesville, OK

Alexander, Jennifer M
Byng Sr HS
Ada, OK

Alexander, Jeremy L
Union Intermediate HS
Tulsa, OK

Alexander, Nicole
Woodward HS
Woodward, OK

Alexander, Shane H
Byng Sr HS
Ada, OK

Alfers, Keri E
Catoosa HS
Catoosa, OK

Allen, Amber D
El Reno Sr HS
El Reno, OK

Allen, Angela L
Pona City HS
Ponca City, OK

Allen, Daniel
Perry Sr HS
Perry, OK

Allen, Dustin J
Bishop Kelley HS
Broken Arrow, OK

Allen, Jaclyn
Moore HS
Norman, OK

Allen, Jeremy D
Yukon Middle HS
Yukon, OK

Allen, Jonathan A
B T Washington HS
Tulsa, OK

Allen, Kelsey J
Spiro HS
Spiro, OK

Allen, Nicole J
Midwest City HS
Midwest City, OK

Allen, Ryan
Enid Sr HS
Enid, OK

Allen, Scott E
North Intemediate HS
Broken Arrow, OK

Allen, Stefanie
Owasso Sr HS
Collinsville, OK

Allen, Zachary S
Choctaw HS
Oklahoma City, OK

Alles Jr, Rodney Neal
Mc Alester HS
Mcalester, OK

Allison, April D
Bartlesville Sr HS
Bartlesville, OK

Allison, Melissa
Midwest City HS
Midwest City, OK

Allison, Susan L
Cushing HS
Cushing, OK

Alta, Steven A
West Mid HS
Norman, OK

Amen, Lacy M
Putnam City West HS
Oklahoma City, OK

Amey, Brooke L
Ripley HS
Stillwater, OK

Anderson, Amanda
Hilldale HS
Muskogee, OK

Anderson, Andre L
Mc Alester HS
Krebs, OK

Anderson, Donde R
Oklahoma Sch Of Science & Math
Broken Arrow, OK

Anderson, Erica J
Jenks HS
Jenks, OK

Anderson, Ira B
Choctaw HS
Choctaw, OK

Anderson, Keith A
Bartlesville Mid HS
Bartlesville, OK

Anderson, Kellie
Ponca City Sr HS
Ponca City, OK

Anderson, Romi L
Sayre HS
Sayre, OK

Anderson, Russell C
Moore HS
Moore, OK

Anderson, Sonja J
Edmond Memorial HS
Edmond, OK

Anderson, Zachary D
Cushing HS
Cushing, OK

Andrews, Bradley
Muldrow HS
Muldrow, OK

Andrews, Melissa
Claremore Sr HS
Claremore, OK

Angala, Jenifer
Midwest City HS
Midwest City, OK

Anglen, Bobbie A
Muldrow HS
Muldrow, OK

Anthony, Shellie
Norman Sr HS
Norman, OK

Aragon, Trina
Turpin Schl
Turpin, OK

Arambula, Eliana M
Southeast HS
Oklahoma City, OK

Arambula, Teasha D
Moore HS
Oklahoma City, OK

Archuleta, Melisha G
Hartshorne Sr HS
San Juan Pueblo, NM

Ardle, Jackie
Owasso Sr HS
Owasso, OK

Argo, Jimmy
Hollis Jr Sr HS
Hollis, OK

Armstrong, Jeremy
Ada HS
Ada, OK

Armstrong, Lindsey
Holdenville Jr HS
Holdenville, OK

Armstrong, Sarah R
Bishop Kelley HS
Tulsa, OK

Arney, Ayla
Moore HS
Oklahoma City, OK

Arnold, April D
Charles Page HS
Sand Springs, OK

Arnold, Sherry
Kingston HS
Kingston, OK

Arnold, Tomi-Lynn
Tishomingo HS
Milburn, OK

Arpelar, Eric R
Mc Alester HS
Mcalester, OK

Arroika, C W B
Indianola HS
Mcalester, OK

Arroyave, Claudia
Claremore Sr HS
Claremore, OK

Arstingstall, Craig E
Midwest City HS
Midwest City, OK

Arvizo III, Teodoro
Oklahoma Schl Of Science
Stillwater, OK

Aryiku, Rhoda A
Westmoore HS
Oklahoma City, OK

Ash, Misty D
Catoosa HS
Tulsa, OK

Ashford, Bobbi Jean
Kiefer Jr Sr HS
Kiefer, OK

Ashworth, Amber M
Union Sr HS
Broken Arrow, OK

Askins, Lindsey B
Westmoore HS
Oklahoma City, OK

Aston, Jo E
Woodland HS
Fairfax, OK

Atchison, Melanie
Mustang HS
Yukon, OK

Atkins, Casey L
Woodward HS
Woodward, OK

Atwood, Brian B
Union Intermediate HS
Broken Arrow, OK

Atwood, Nick C
Shawnee Sr HS
Shawnee, OK

Auld, April L
Shawnee Sr HS
Shawnee, OK

Austin, Angela R
Muskogee HS
Muskogee, OK

Austin, Drew A
Choctaw HS
Choctaw, OK

Austin, Rachel M
Choctaw HS
Choctaw, OK

Austin, Stacey J
Mustang HS
Mustang, OK

Austin, William A
Choctaw HS
Choctaw, OK

Avery, Aerial A
Eisenhower Sr HS
Lawton, OK

Avington, Corneshia
Central HS
Tulsa, OK

Axsom, Andrew G
Bishop Kelley HS
Broken Arrow, OK

Axsom, Caleb J
South Intermediate HS
Broken Arrow, OK

Axsom, Monica L
Bishop Kelley HS
Broken Arrow, OK

Ayers, Ken
Wilson HS
Wilson, OK

Ayers, Sara
North Intemediate HS
Broken Arrow, OK

Ayres, Ashley
Madill HS
Madill, OK

Babione, Molly B
Altus Sr HS
Altus, OK

Babonjo, Sia N
Southeast HS
Oklahoma City, OK

Bacon, Holly M
Claremore Sr HS
Claremore, OK

Baeriswy, Pamela J
Wilson HS
Ardmore, OK

Baggitt, Charles E
Enid Sr HS
Enid, OK

Bagwell, Jessica C
Union Sr HS
Broken Arrow, OK

Bahlinger, Erin E
Bishop Kelley HS
Tulsa, OK

Bailey, Kendric
Coweta HS
Coweta, OK

Baker, Audrey
Chelsea HS
Chelsea, OK

Baker, Autumn
Keifer Public Schl
Sapulpa, OK

Baker, Bethany
Cimarron
Christian Acad
Mannford, OK

Baker, Brooke
Victory Christian Schl
Jenks, OK

Baker, Celena R
Putnam City West HS
Oklahoma City, OK

Baker, James E
Purcell HS
Purcell, OK

Baker, Jay
Sapulpa Sr HS
Sapulpa, OK

Baker, Julie D
Moore HS
Norman, OK

Baker, Kelley D
Cashion HS
Cashion, OK

Baker, Kyle
Bartlesville Sr HS
Bartlesville, OK

Baker, Misty D
Tishomingo HS
Denver, CO

Baker, Summer
Reydon HS
Durham, OK

Baker, Wren J
Valliant HS
Valliant, OK

Bakewell, Daniel J
Lindsay HS
Lindsay, OK

Baldridge, Jason
White Oak Jr-Sr HS
Vinita, OK

Baldridge, Roy
White Oak Jr-Sr HS
Vinita, OK

Baldwin, Kathy S
Owasso Sr HS
Owasso, OK

Baldwin, Kiana
Mc Lain Career Acad
Tulsa, OK

Bales, Thomas B
Ponca City Middle HS
Ponca City, OK

Ball, Michael H
Putnam City North HS
Oklahoma City, OK

Ballard, Michelle R
Muskogee HS
Muskogee, OK

Ballew, Jaime
Collinsville HS
Collinsville, OK

Ballew, Ricky J
Western Heights Sr HS
Oklahoma City, OK

Bandy, Lindsey B
Verden HS
Anadarko, OK

Banis, Mary C
Claremore Sr HS
Claremore, OK

Banks, Chantry S
Hammon Schl
Hammon, OK

Banning, Laurisa A
Stillwater Sr HS
Stillwater, OK

Barber, Jennifer A
Yukon Middle HS
Yukon, OK

Barby, Ashlea
Laverne Jr Sr HS
Laverne, OK

Barentine, Dustin L
Pocola HS
Pocola, OK

Bargas, Kevin E
Mc Alester HS
Mcalester, OK

Barker, Matt
Yukon HS
Yukon, OK

Barnes, Brooke
Jenks HS
Tulsa, OK

Barnes, Jeremy O
Panola HS
Red Oak, OK

Barnes, Kanita L
Classen Schl
Oklahoma City, OK

Barnes, Lindsay J
Southeast HS
Oklahoma City, OK

Barnes, Michael G
Ada HS
Ada, OK

Barnes, Missy
Memorial HS
Edmond, OK

Barnes, Noah
Porter Jr Sr HS
Porter, OK

Barnes, Rachel
Stigler HS
Stigler, OK

Barnes, Steven L
Sallisaw HS
Sallisaw, OK

Barnes Jr, Thomas
Mc Loud HS
Mc Loud, OK

Barnett, Amber R
Duncan HS
Marlow, OK

Barnett, Hayley
Durant HS
Durant, OK

Barnett, Kim
Roland Sr HS
Roland, OK

Barney, Lisa
Pauls Valley HS
Pauls Valley, OK

Barnhart, Marlo A
South Coffeyville Schl
S Coffeyville, OK

Barr, Nikkia N
Southeast HS
Oklahoma City, OK

Barrett, Erin
Coweta HS
Coweta, OK

Barrett, Jamie
Owasso Sr HS
Owasso, OK

Barrett, Leann R
Mannford HS
Mannford, OK

Barrett, Sherita
Star Spencer HS
Oklahoma City, OK

Barrett, Teresa A
Claremore Sr HS
Claremore, OK

Barron, Amanda
Canadian Schl
Eufaula, OK

Barron, Timothy N
Bishop Kelley HS
Tulsa, OK

Barter, Jennifer I
Muldrow HS
Muldrow, OK

Bartlett, Jonathan L
Union Sr HS
Tulsa, OK

Bartmann, Jessica
Cascia Hall Prep
School
Tulsa, OK

Bass, Emily
Oklahoma
Christian Schl
Edmond, OK

Bass, Kim
Vinita HS
Vinita, OK

Bassett, F Scott
Union Sr HS
Tulsa, OK

Batchelor, Chad E
Valliant HS
Broken Bow, OK

Batdorf, Rick
Pawhuska HS
Pawhuska, OK

Bateman, Paula K
Will Rogers HS
Tulsa, OK

Bates, Crystal A
Byng Sr HS
Ada, OK

Bates, Emily
Edmond North HS
Edmond, OK

Bathe, Christie L
Midwest City HS
Midwest City, OK

Battese, Tamara
Apache HS
Apache, OK

Battle, Mindy E
Claremore Sr HS
Claremore, OK

Bauer, Katie R
Putnam City North HS
Oklahoma City, OK

Baxter, Robby J
Caddo HS
Caddo, OK

Bays, Emily E
Alva HS
Alva, OK

Beach, Carissa
Muskogee HS
Muskogee, OK

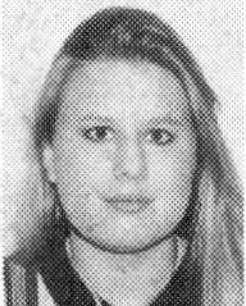
Beall, Kristin J
North Intemediate HS
Broken Arrow, OK

Beam, Katheran
Broken Arrow Sr HS
Broken Arrow, OK

Beam, Sharon K
Harrah HS
Harrah, OK

Bean, Andie
Dickson HS
Ardmore, OK

Bean, Jessi R
Madill HS
Madill, OK

Bearden, Michelle
Kingston HS
Kingston, OK

Beaven, Monica D
Catoosa HS
Claremore, OK

Beaver, Dustin L
Washington HS
Washington, OK

Beaver, Jason
Bethany HS
Bethany, OK

Beavers, Daniel C
Putnam City North HS
Oklahoma City, OK

Becerra, Fabian A
Southeast HS
Oklahoma City, OK

Beck, Jennifer
Holdenville HS
Atwood, OK

Beck, Kenneth A
Atoka HS
Stringtown, OK

Becker, Crystal
Okeene Jr Sr HS
Isabella, OK

Becker, John R
Enid Sr HS
Enid, OK

Beda, Stephanie N
Weatherford HS
Weatherford, OK

Beesley, Lacy J
Minco HS
Minco, OK

Beeson, Jaime
Edmond Memorial HS
Edmond, OK

Beeson, Jedd E
Duncan HS
Duncan, OK

Beisley, Dustin
Dewey HS
Dewey, OK

Beittenmiller,
Nathan C
Ardmore HS
Ardmore, OK

Belk, Denise M
Sapulpa Sr HS
Sapulpa, OK

Bell, Frederick
Central HS
Tulsa, OK

Bell, Lori
Catoosa HS
Catoosa, OK

Bell, Priscilla M
El Reno Sr HS
El Reno, OK

Bellamy, Heather C
Yukon Middle HS
Yukon, OK

Belton, Kesha L
Boynton Schl
Boynton, OK

Ben, Moe M
Clayton Jr Sr HS
Clayton, OK

Bender, Emily D
Putnam City North HS
Oklahoma City, OK

Benjamin, Loretta J
Checotah HS
Council Hill, OK

Bennett, Alecia M
Will Rogers HS
Tulsa, OK

Bennett, Chris D
Shawnee Sr HS
Shawnee, OK

Bennett, Cody L
Shawnee Sr HS
Shawnee, OK

Bennett, Matthew
Poteau HS
Poteau, OK

Bennett, T J
Mustang HS
Yukon, OK

Bennett, Timia J
Union Sr HS
Tulsa, OK

Bensch, Rhonda
Seiling Schl
Chester, OK

Bentley, Julia
Edmond Memorial HS
Edmond, OK

Bentley, Melissa D
Altus Sr HS
Altus, OK

Benton, Tony
Jarman Jr HS
Tinker Afb, OK

Berg, Sabrina
Timberlake Schl
Helena, OK

Berkowitz, Aaron M
B T Washington HS
Tulsa, OK

Bertolasio, Leslie M
Yukon HS
Yukon, OK

Best, Becky J
Putnam City West HS
Oklahoma City, OK

Best, James A
Plainview HS
Ardmore, OK

Betancourt, Raul C
Ardmore HS
Ardmore, OK

Bezdek, Amber N
West Jr HS
Oklahoma City, OK

Bhatti, Edmond S
El Reno Sr HS
El Reno, OK

Bible, Michelle D
Miami Sr HS
Miami, OK

Bible, Moran A
Frontier Public Schl
Red Rock, OK

Bielli, Jennifer L
North Intemediate HS
Broken Arrow, OK

Biggs, Patrick
Perry Sr HS
Perry, OK

Bigham, Cindi A
Durant HS
Durant, OK

Bigpond, Amy
Mounds Schl
Sapulpa, OK

Bilbrey, Amanda
Putnam City North HS
Oklahoma City, OK

Billings, Sommer A
East Central HS
Tulsa, OK

Billingslea, Crystal
Westmoore HS
Oklahoma City, OK

Bilyeu, Jason N
Union Intermediate HS
Tulsa, OK

Bingham, Nick G
Edmond Memorial HS
Edmond, OK

Bingham, Warren D
Westmoore HS
Oklahoma City, OK

Bingman, Annie E
Sapulpa Sr HS
Sapulpa, OK

Birdshead, Jennfer
Apache HS
Apache, OK

Birdwell, Ashley
Stillwater Sr HS
Stillwater, OK

Biscoe, Brandi P
Putnam City North HS
Oklahoma City, OK

Bishop, Emma J
Putnam City HS
Oklahoma City, OK

Bishop, Thomas C
Broken Arrow Sr HS
Broken Arrow, OK

Blachly, Melanie D
Ft Gibson HS
Fort Gibson, OK

Black, Jamie L
North Intemediate HS
Broken Arrow, OK

Black, Jason R
Mustang HS
Mustang, OK

Black, Luke L
Locust Grove HS
Locust Grove, OK

Blackham, Ashley N
Durant HS
Durant, OK

Blackman, Cara
Cascia Hall Prep School
Tulsa, OK

Blair, Carissa M
Moore HS
Norman, OK

Blair, Eric
East Central HS
Tulsa, OK

Blair, Lisa
Kingfisher HS
Kingfisher, OK

Blair, Michelle
Moore HS
Moore, OK

Blair, Mikelyn S
Muldrow HS
Muldrow, OK

Blakley, Abbey V
Pioneer Jr Sr HS
Douglas, OK

Blalock, Daniel E
Will Rogers HS
Tulsa, OK

Blanche, Josh
Tuttle HS
Chickasha, OK

Blanchett Jr, John O
Rush Springs HS
Rush Springs, OK

Bland, Frances J
Mannford HS
Mannford, OK

Blanton, Jenny
Oklahoma Bible Acad
Enid, OK

Blanton, Kimber
Edmond North HS
Edmond, OK

Blaschke, Emily
Heritage Hall Schl
Oklahoma City, OK

Blaylock, Erin S
Poteau HS
Howe, OK

Blizzard, April L
Fairland Jr Sr HS
Fairland, OK

Blouch, Jayson Patrick
Will Rogers HS
Tulsa, OK

Bloxham, Cindi L
Spiro HS
Spiro, OK

Blunt, Codi
Millwood HS
Oklahoma City, OK

Boardman, Mary Frances
Stillwater Sr HS
Stillwater, OK

Boatman, Alicia A
Muldrow HS
Muldrow, OK

Bocock, Darla A
Boise City HS
Boise City, OK

Bodine, Adam
Ada HS
Ada, OK

Boeckman, Andrew
Okeene Jr Sr HS
Hitchcock, OK

Boeckman, Kim
Woodward HS
Woodward, OK

Boeckman, Shelly C
Enid Sr HS
Enid, OK

Bogie, Lauren
Jenks HS
Tulsa, OK

Bohannon, Chrystal R
Charles Page HS
Sand Springs, OK

Bolay, Robyn
Perry Sr HS
Perry, OK

Bolding, Tiya
Blanchard Jr Sr HS
Blanchard, OK

Bolin, Melissa
Vian HS
Vian, OK

Bolt, Matt T
Edmond Memorial HS
Edmond, OK

Bolton, Krystal
Grandfield Jr Sr HS
Grandfield, OK

Bombach, Roger
Beaver HS
Beaver, OK

Bomhoff, Louie G
El Reno Sr HS
El Reno, OK

Bond, Mary E
Stillwater Sr HS
Stillwater, OK

Bond, Mike
Broken Bow HS
Broken Bow, OK

Bone, Amy
Turner Schl
Marietta, OK

Bone, Cory M
Wilson HS
Wilson, OK

Bonham, Amanda G
Ponca City Middle HS
Ponca City, OK

Boone, Keri
Merritt Schl
Elk City, OK

Bostian, Laura B
Bixby Sr HS
Bixby, OK

Bostick, Robert Neil
Broken Bow HS
Broken Bow, OK

Bottom, Brian
Cordell Jr HS
Cordell, OK

Bottom, Brooke R
Altus Sr HS
Altus, OK

Bowden, Leah F
Claremore Sr HS
Claremore, OK

Bowen, Barbara M
Mc Lain Career Acad
Tulsa, OK

Bowen, Nancy
Drumright HS
Drumright, OK

Bowers, Billy
Canton HS
Longdale, OK

Bowers, Colby J
Duncan HS
Duncan, OK

Bowers, Shawn L
Blanchard Jr Sr HS
Blanchard, OK

Bowie, Jessica R
Shawnee Sr HS
Shawnee, OK

Bowles, Amanda L
Union Intermediate HS
Tulsa, OK

Box, Jamie
Keota Schl
Keota, OK

Boyattia, Tiffany S
Muskogee HS
Muskogee, OK

Boyce, J Wilford H
Bartlesville Sr HS
Bartlesville, OK

Boyd, Barry B
Midwest City HS
Oklahoma City, OK

Boyd, Kimberly D
Fairland Jr Sr HS
Miami, OK

Bozone, Sheri J
Webster HS
Tulsa, OK

Braden, Chris D
El Reno Sr HS
El Reno, OK

Bradford, Joseph I
Waynoka HS
Waynoka, OK

Bradford, Katy
Edmond Memorial HS
Edmond, OK

Bradford, Keri
Sperry Sr HS
Sperry, OK

Bradford, Matthew D
Waynoka HS
Waynoka, OK

Bradley, Gwendolyn D
Dickson HS
Ardmore, OK

Bradshaw, Monica K
Westmoore HS
Oklahoma City, OK

Brady, Jennifer L
Durant HS
Durant, OK

Bragg, Jonathan P
Deer Creek HS
Edmond, OK

Brakhage, Jason G
Edmond Santa Fe HS
Edmond, OK

Brame, Lori A
Christian
Heritage Acad
Del City, OK

Bramlett, Eric
Jenks HS
Jenks, OK

Brammer, David A
Macarthur Sr HS
Lawton, OK

Branscum, Larra
Seminole Jr Sr HS
Seminole, OK

Branscum, Marshall
Seminole Jr Sr HS
Seminole, OK

Brashear, Carl W
Stilwell HS
Stilwell, OK

Brasher, Stacy
Edmond North HS
Edmond, OK

Brashers, Kevin
Wyandotte Jr Sr HS
Miami, OK

Breding, Nichole
Katherine
Westmoore HS
Oklahoma City, OK

Breedlove, Nicole
Roland Sr HS
Roland, OK

Brenner, Rachel M
Midwest City HS
Midwest City, OK

Brewer, Carissa D
Muldrow HS
Muldrow, OK

Brewer, Da Cole
Nichelle
Del City HS
Oklahoma City, OK

Briant, Crystal L
Cresent Acad
Edmond, OK

Brice, Sarah
Little Axe Sr HS
Newalla, OK

Bridenstine, Chris A
Madill HS
Kingston, OK

Bridges, Brandon K
Roland Sr HS
Roland, OK

Bridges, Christopher K
Chandler HS
Chandler, OK

Briggs, Angela M
Tecumseh HS
Tecumseh, OK

Brijalba, Cathy
Cache HS
Cache, OK

Brilliant, Carolyn R
Coweta HS
Porter, OK

Brissey, Rodney G
Union Intermediate HS
Tulsa, OK

Bristle, Melanie L
Owasso Sr HS
Owasso, OK

Broadfoot, Becky
Heritage Hall Schl
Oklahoma City, OK

Brock, Julie L
Heritage Hall Schl
Oklahoma City, OK

Brock, Melody L
Crescent Schl
Crescent, OK

Brock, Samantha Y
El Reno Sr HS
El Reno, OK

Brookfelt, Kimberly R
Wister Schl
Wister, OK

Brooks, Aisha L
John Marshall HS
Oklahoma City, OK

Brooks, Erika
Muskogee HS
Muskogee, OK

Brooks, Jackie
Wetumka Jr Sr HS
Wetumka, OK

Brooks, Jason E
Sayre HS
Sayre, OK

Brooks, Kristi K
Sayre HS
Sayre, OK

Brooks, Lisa
Goodwell Public Schl
Goodwell, OK

Brookshire, Jennifer
Hinton HS
Hinton, OK

Brookshire, Kelli
Oklahoma
Christian Schl
Oklahoma City, OK

Broughton, Amanda L
Ardmore HS
Ardmore, OK

Brown, Alee E
Heritage Hall Schl
Oklahoma City, OK

Brown, Amanda
Stilwell HS
Bunch, OK

Brown, Amber D
Altus Sr HS
Altus, OK

Brown, Beth
Houston Homan Jr HS
Eufaula, OK

Brown, Bravis S
Tahlequah Sr HS
Tahlequah, OK

Brown, Carli
Sayre HS
Sayre, OK

Brown, Carmell L
Muskogee HS
Muskogee, OK

Brown, Charles
Norman Sr HS
Norman, OK

Brown, Ciara Kaisha
Union Sr HS
Tulsa, OK

Brown, Heather R
Claremore Sr HS
Claremore, OK

Brown, Jennifer R
Putnam City West HS
Oklahoma City, OK

Brown, Jessica M
Perkins-Tryon HS
Perkins, OK

Brown, Jill R
Putnam City North HS
Oklahoma City, OK

Brown, Joey J
Union Intermediate HS
Tulsa, OK

Brown, Kelli
Bixby Sr HS
Bixby, OK

Brown, Kristen
Cordell Sr HS
Cordell, OK

Brown, Lester M
Midwest City HS
Midwest City, OK

Brown, Lisa
Putnam City HS
Oklahoma City, OK

Brown, Lori R
Mustang HS
Oklahoma City, OK

Brown, Mark L
West Middle HS
Norman, OK

Brown, Matthew
Western Area Voc
Tech Schl
Oklahoma City, OK

Brown, Nicholas W
Elgin HS
Elgin, OK

Brown, Phoebe
Charles Page HS
Tulsa, OK

Brown, Rachel
U S Grant HS
Oklahoma City, OK

Brown, Rachel J
Deer Creek HS
Oklahoma City, OK

Brown, Ricki Lea
Putnam City West HS
Oklahoma City, OK

Brown, Ronnie A
Velma Alma HS
Ratliff City, OK

Brown, Ryan
Edmond North HS
Edmond, OK

Brown, Shelly
Lawton Sr HS
Lawton, OK

Brown, Stephen
Douglass HS
Oklahoma City, OK

Brown, Tiffany
Northeast HS
Oklahoma City, OK

Brown, Traci R
Bixby Sr HS
Bixby, OK

OKLAHOMA

Brown, Tyra
Del City HS
Oklahoma City, OK

Brownlee, Melissa R
Ardmore HS
Ardmore, OK

Broyles, Kati
Newkirk HS
Newkirk, OK

Brumley, Heather
Jenks HS
Jenks, OK

Brundidge, Ashley
Latta Sr HS
Ada, OK

Brungardt, Carrie
Edmond North HS
Edmond, OK

Brunk Jr, Roger D
Roland Sr HS
Roland, OK

Brunken, Jennifer
Midwest City HS
Midwest City, OK

Bruton, Harold P
Sapulpa Sr HS
Sapulpa, OK

Bryan, Jennifer
Holdenville HS
Holdenville, OK

Bryan, John S
Edmond Santa Fe HS
Edmond, OK

Bryant, Anna M
Bridge Creek HS
Blanchard, OK

Bryant, Beau
Okemah HS
Okemah, OK

Bryant, Brandon E
Southeast HS
Choctaw, OK

Bryant, Kenzi L
Putnam City West HS
Bethany, OK

Bryant, Krystal M
Stigler HS
Stigler, OK

Bryant, Nicole L
Charles Page HS
Sand Springs, OK

Bryce, Stacey D
Owasso Sr HS
Owasso, OK

Bryer, Amanda M
Woodward HS
Woodward, OK

Buchanan, Christy L
Sapulpa Sr HS
Sapulpa, OK

Buchanan, Jennifer J
Glenpool HS
Glenpool, OK

Buchanan, Jeri Dawn
Clayton Jr Sr HS
Clayton, OK

Buchanan, Merrick A
Union Intermediate HS
Tulsa, OK

Buck, Karen
Eufaula Sr HS
Eufaula, OK

Buckner, Michelle
Okeene Jr Sr HS
Okeene, OK

Budde, Annika
Westmoore HS
Oklahoma City, OK

Bufton, Angelia M
Ponca City Sr HS
Ponca City, OK

Bulleigh, Adam L
South Intermediate HS
Broken Arrow, OK

Bumgarner, Bradley
Will Rogers HS
Tulsa, OK

Bumpers, Amber
Stigler HS
Stigler, OK

Bunch, Amanda J
Lindsay HS
Lindsay, OK

Bunch, Stephanie M
Ardmore HS
Wilson, OK

Burau, M Scott
Union Intermediate HS
Tulsa, OK

Burch, Ashley D
Catoosa HS
Tulsa, OK

Burch, Felicia
Sperry Sr HS
Sperry, OK

Burch, Laura J
Enid Sr HS
Enid, OK

Burch, Micah
Blanchard Jr Sr HS
Blanchard, OK

Burcham, Patrick
Mangum Jr HS
Mangum, OK

Burd, Jamie
Texhoma HS
Texhoma, OK

Burdett, Mariah N
Moore HS
Moore, OK

Burgess, Jessica D
Antlers Sr HS
Antlers, OK

Burgess, Stacey
East Central HS
Tulsa, OK

Burgess, Tammy L
Caddo HS
Durant, OK

Burke, Amanda
Edmond North HS
Edmond, OK

Burke, Christina L
Wilson HS
Wilson, OK

Burkett, Bridget A
East Central HS
Tulsa, OK

Burkett, Nicholas C
Edmond Memorial HS
Edmond, OK

Burkhart, David M
Del City HS
Oklahoma City, OK

Burkhart, Wendy M
Choctaw HS
Choctaw, OK

Burks, Kelea T
Enid Sr HS
Enid, OK

Burleson, Jordon L
Edmond Santa Fe HS
Edmond, OK

Burlie, Justin A
Wakita Schl
Wakita, OK

Burness, Jessie C
Bartlesville Sr HS
Bartlesville, OK

Burnett, Kathryn S
B T Washington HS
Tulsa, OK

Burnett, Robyn M
Claremore Sr HS
Claremore, OK

Burney, Brian
Moore HS
Moore, OK

Burnham, J Russell
Stillwater Jr HS
Stillwater, OK

Burns, Carrie E
Calvin Public Schl
Calvin, OK

Burpo, Laci
Kingfisher HS
Kingfisher, OK

Burris, Lori
Plainview HS
Ardmore, OK

Burrow, Justin
Mustang HS
Oklahoma City, OK

Burt, Brandon W
Christian
Heritage Acad
Oklahoma City, OK

Burton, Kristy
Shawnee Sr HS
Shawnee, OK

Burton, Nathan K
South Intermediate HS
Broken Arrow, OK

Bush, Brian
Altus Sr HS
Altus, OK

Butcher, Lindsay J
West Middle HS
Norman, OK

Butcher, Scott L
Vinita HS
Vinita, OK

Butler, Chevonne
Chisholm Sr HS
Enid, OK

Butler Jr, Evertt A
Wilson HS
Wilson, OK

Butler, Gil T
Elgin HS
Cyril, OK

Butler, Kristen
Nathan Hale HS
Tulsa, OK

Butler, Melody B
Stigler HS
Stigler, OK

Butler, Scott B
Oklahoma Sch Of
Science & Math
Tonkawa, OK

Buttress, Amanda J
Tahlequah Jr HS
Tahlequah, OK

Butts, Adam
Union Intermediate HS
Tulsa, OK

Butts, Ryan Kirk
Edmond North HS
Edmond, OK

Byer, Melissa L
Edmond Memorial HS
Edmond, OK

Byerley, Ashlee J
Edmond North HS
Edmond, OK

Byerly, Alisha
Holdenville HS
Holdenville, OK

Byers, Kaycie
Roff HS
Roff, OK

Byford, Lori
Stratford Schl
Stratford, OK

Bynum, Jason E
Latta Sr HS
Ada, OK

Bynum, Robyn L
Union Intermediate HS
Tulsa, OK

Cable, Matthew G
Pauls Valley HS
Pauls Valley, OK

Cadion, Amanda S
Bishop Kelley HS
Tulsa, OK

Caffey, Brent
Spiro HS
Keota, OK

Cahlik, Lindsay A
Westmoore HS
Oklahoma City, OK

Cain, Cassie D
Duncan HS
Duncan, OK

Caine, Nichole D
Ponca City Sr HS
Ponca City, OK

Calahan, Amie
Eufaula Sr HS
Eufaula, OK

Caldwell, Brandi C
Preston Schl
Okmulgee, OK

Caldwell, Cindi L
Deer Creek HS
Edmond, OK

Caldwell, Jamie D
Yukon Middle HS
Yukon, OK

Caldwell, Jason
Pawhuska HS
Pawhuska, OK

Caldwell, Terra J
Union Intermediate HS
Tulsa, OK

Caley, Angela
Mangum Sr HS
Mangum, OK

Calhoun, Misty C
Okay Jr Sr HS
Lawton, OK

Calhoun, Tammy
Broken Bow HS
Broken Bow, OK

Calico, Amanda E
Union Intermediate HS
Broken Arrow, OK

Call, Joshua C
Edison HS
Tulsa, OK

Callahan, Crystal M
Anadarko HS
Anadarko, OK

Callan, Susan M
Choctaw HS
Choctaw, OK

Callies, Marti
Little Axe Sr HS
Norman, OK

Calvert, Derrick
Kiefer Jr Sr HS
Sapulpa, OK

Camacho, Elizabeth
Midwest City HS
Midwest City, OK

Camp, Krissie A
Morris HS
Okmulgee, OK

Camp, Trenton A
Okeene Jr Sr HS
Okeene, OK

Campbell, Breanna
Stillwater Jr HS
Joplin, MO

Campbell, Brock
Perry Sr HS
Perry, OK

Campbell, Crystal Z
West Middle HS
Norman, OK

Campbell, Heather
Putnam City West HS
Oklahoma City, OK

Campbell, Holley J
Sapulpa Sr HS
Sapulpa, OK

Campbell, Jaime L
Latta Sr HS
Ada, OK

Campbell, Jennifer
Clinton HS
Clinton, OK

Campbell, Judd
Kingfisher HS
Kingfisher, OK

Campbell, Markus D
Cordell Sr HS
Cordell, OK

Campbell, Melanie
Del City HS
Del City, OK

Campbell, Melinda
Lawton Sr HS
Lawton, OK

Campos, Marcus S
Central HS
Tulsa, OK

Canada, Sabrina A
Dickson HS
Ardmore, OK

Canady, Crystal M
Webster HS
Tulsa, OK

Canning, Jeremy
Guthrie Sr HS
Guthrie, OK

Cannon, Alicia
Cordell Sr HS
Cordell, OK

Cantrell, Allison M
Stillwater Sr HS
Stillwater, OK

Cantu, David Isaac
Bartlesville Sr HS
Bartlesville, OK

Capezza, Rick A
Owasso Sr HS
Owasso, OK

Capps, Jina
Valliant HS
Millerton, OK

Cardenas, Lucia
Capitol Hill HS
Oklahoma City, OK

Carey, Jo Beth
Eufaula Sr HS
Stidham, OK

Carey, Michael
Mid-Del Christian Schl
Del City, OK

Cariker, Ami L
Central Schl
Sallisaw, OK

Carlile, Michael C
Tahlequah Sr HS
Tahlequah, OK

Carlock, Ashley G
Putnam City West HS
Oklahoma City, OK

Carlson, Gregory
Claremore Sr HS
Claremore, OK

Carmichael, Robert E
Oklahoma Bible Acad
Enid, OK

Carnagey, Kara
Ft Gibson HS
Fort Gibson, OK

Carothers, Shannon
Midwest City HS
Midwest City, OK

Carpenter, Catherine E
Guthrie Sr HS
Guthrie, OK

Carpenter, David G
Owasso Sr HS
Owasso, OK

Carpenter, Rachelle D
Christian
Heritage Acad
Oklahoma City, OK

OKLAHOMA

Carr, Jamie L
Harrah HS
Harrah, OK

Carr, Justin G
Colcord Schl
Colcord, OK

Carrell, Danieal G
Dickson HS
Ardmore, OK

Carr-Lalli, Benjamin D
Mc Alester HS
Mcalester, OK

Carroll, Christopher S
Cashion HS
Cashion, OK

Carroll, Jamie
B T Washington HS
Tulsa, OK

Carroll, Jayme
Miami Sr HS
Miami, OK

Carroll, Jennifer
Cashion HS
Cashion, OK

Carson, Christi B
Fargo Schl
Fargo, OK

Carson, Christopher C
Heritage Hall Schl
Edmond, OK

Carson, Shenna C
Union Intermediate HS
Tulsa, OK

Carson, Thomas J
Ada HS
Ada, OK

Carter, Brittany
Moore HS
Moore, OK

Carter, Christi L
Meeker HS
Chandler, OK

Carter, Jeremy
Broken Arrow Sr HS
Broken Arrow, OK

Carter, Jeremy L
Central Schl
Sallisaw, OK

Carter, Jerry L
Mustang HS
Yukon, OK

Carter, Josh L
Butler Jr Sr HS
Hammon, OK

Carter, Nick W
Choctaw HS
Midwest City, OK

Casburn, Elizabeth A
Edmond North HS
Edmond, OK

Case, Brad
Midwest City HS
Midwest City, OK

Case, Carrie
Seiling Schl
Fairview, OK

Case, David J
Clayton Jr Sr HS
Clayton, OK

Case, Jeremy D
Union Intermediate HS
Tulsa, OK

Cash, Kevin M
Union Intermediate HS
Tulsa, OK

Casillas, Ricky D
Skiatook HS
Avant, OK

Casper, Eric D
Edmond North HS
Edmond, OK

Cassavaugh, Felicia
Asher Schl
Byars, OK

Castillo, Amy E
Frontier Public Schl
Red Rock, OK

Castle, Brook
Clinton HS
Crawford, OK

Castner, Christy L
Mustang HS
Yukon, OK

Castro, Amy
Mt St Marys HS
Norman, OK

Caswell, Joseph F
Macarthur Sr HS
Lawton, OK

Cates, Lesley
Stuart Sr HS
Haywood, OK

Cates, Will
Beaver HS
Beaver, OK

Catlett, Michelle A
Claremore Sr HS
Claremore, OK

Caughman, Jerry W
Sallisaw HS
Sallisaw, OK

Cauthon, Cary L
Ponca City Sr HS
Ponca City, OK

Cavalli, Cirilo A
Bishop Kelley HS
Tulsa, OK

Cavin, Ashley
Tonkawa Jr Sr HS
Tonkawa, OK

Cayton, Latonia F
Boise City HS
Boise City, OK

Caywood,
Christopher A
Mid-Del Christian Schl
Del City, OK

Cazzelle, Heather
Ripley HS
Stillwater, OK

Cederblom, Jason L
Afton HS
Afton, OK

Cerda, Aaron M
Del City HS
Oklahoma City, OK

Chaffin, David P
Davis HS
Davis, OK

Chalakee, Sheila K
Eufaula Sr HS
Eufaula, OK

Challis, Trisha L
Ponca City Sr HS
Ponca City, OK

Chaloupek, Amber L
Owasso Sr HS
Owasso, OK

Chamberlain, Brook L
South Intermediate HS
Broken Arrow, OK

Chambers, Deena
Ripley HS
Ripley, OK

Chambers, Gregory S
West Middle HS
Norman, OK

Chambers, Mandi
Achille Schl
Achille, OK

Champlain, Tamarkia
Ponca City Sr HS
Ponca City, OK

Chance, Shawna L
Billings HS
Billings, OK

Chancellor, Evan G
Shawnee Sr HS
Shawnee, OK

Chancellor, Ruby
Apache HS
Tishomingo, OK

Chang, Bill
Edmond North HS
Edmond, OK

Chansombath,
Soutsakho S
Westmoore HS
Oklahoma City, OK

Chappell, Bradley P
Metro Christian Acad
Tulsa, OK

Charbeneau, Kelly
Mt St Marys HS
Oklahoma City, OK

Charles, Jarrod
Sequoyah HS
Claremore, OK

Chastain, Brian
Wetumka Jr Sr HS
Wetumka, OK

Chastain, Mindy S
Coalgate HS
Coalgate, OK

Chaves, Eileen A
Union Intermediate HS
Broken Arrow, OK

Chavez, Tiffany G
Noble HS
Noble, OK

Cheek, Lisa Brittany
Tahlequah Jr HS
Tahlequah, OK

Cheek, Tiffany K
Jenks HS
Tulsa, OK

Chelenza, Nicole A
Eisenhower Sr HS
Lawton, OK

Chen, Best
Edmond North HS
Edmond, OK

Chen, Chih-Wei
Putnam City West HS
Oklahoma City, OK

Chennault, Rashell
Comanche HS
Comanche, OK

Chenoweth, Aaron
Okemah HS
Okemah, OK

Chesney, Robert B
Central HS
Tulsa, OK

Chesser, Nicole M
Altus Sr HS
Altus, OK

Chestnut, Shane A
Cushing HS
Cushing, OK

Chew, Kelli N
Bishop Kelley HS
Tulsa, OK

Cheynet, Renay
Edmond Memorial HS
Edmond, OK

Childs, Derek M
Bishop Kelley HS
Broken Arrow, OK

Childs, Shelly M
Edmond North HS
Edmond, OK

Choate, Lance
Battiest Jr Sr HS
Pickens, OK

Chown, Benjamin
Enid Sr HS
Enid, OK

Chrisman, Johnathan W
Putnam City HS
Oklahoma City, OK

Chrismon, Sybil
Cyril Jr Sr HS
Cyril, OK

Christensen, Cara
Muskogee HS
Muskogee, OK

Christensen, Kathryn M
Bartlesville Mid HS
Bartlesville, OK

Christian, Caleb M
Stonewall Jr-Sr HS
Stonewall, OK

Christian, Derrick G
Enid Sr HS
Enid, OK

Christian, Joshua
Stonewall Jr-Sr HS
Stonewall, OK

Christian, Robert A
Morris HS
Okmulgee, OK

Christian, Tiffany B
Byng Sr HS
Ada, OK

Christie, Rachel L
Lindsay HS
Lindsay, OK

Christine, Kimberly J
Edmond North HS
Edmond, OK

Christman, Brandy
Kiowa Jr-Sr HS
Pittsburg, OK

Christman, Stacey L
Eisenhower Sr HS
Lawton, OK

Chronister, Randy L
Charles Page HS
Sapulpa, OK

Chubbee, Frank C
Hugo HS
Hugo, OK

Chung, Tony Ngoc
Union Intermediate HS
Tulsa, OK

Church II, Joel D
Anadarko HS
Anadarko, OK

Cisco, Jamie
Ft Cobb-Broxton HS
Ft Cobb, OK

Ciskowski, Amanda M
Bishop Kelley HS
Tulsa, OK

Claflin, Cory
Burlington Public Schls
Byron, OK

Clampitt, Rachel M
Wynnewood HS
Wynnewood, OK

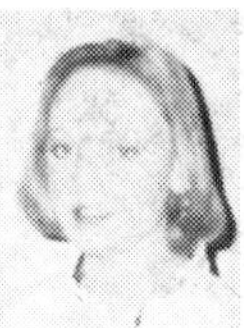
Clardy, Dustin A
Valliant HS
Idabel, OK

Clark, Ginny
Sapulpa Sr HS
Sapulpa, OK

Clark, Jill
Family Of Faith HS
Shawnee, OK

Clark, Joshua A
Wright Christian Acad
Tulsa, OK

Clark, Kari A
Shattuck Jr Sr HS
Shattuck, OK

Clark, Kirsten
Morris HS
Okmulgee, OK

Clark, Marie
Poteau HS
Poteau, OK

Clark, Michael C
Claremore Sr HS
Chouteau, OK

Clark, Michael S
Midwest City HS
Midwest City, OK

Clark, Ryan K
Claremore Sr HS
Claremore, OK

Clark, Sarah
Woodward HS
Woodward, OK

Clark, Tracy L
Claremore Sr HS
Chouteau, OK

Clark-Gillum, Sharla
Panama HS
Spiro, OK

Clarkson, Rachel B
South Intermediate HS
Broken Arrow, OK

Claunch, Andrea L
South Intermediate HS
Broken Arrow, OK

Claxton, Tara M
Union Intermediate HS
Tulsa, OK

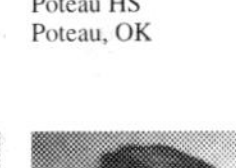
Clayburn, Timothy R
Poteau HS
Poteau, OK

Clayton, Kaylee D
Dale Sr HS
Shawnee, OK

Clement, Sandy L
Noble HS
Noble, OK

Clements, April S
Heavener HS
Heavener, OK

Clements, Obie
Apache HS
Apache, OK

Clemons, Aaron K
Will Rogers HS
Tulsa, OK

Cleveland, Dustin
Metro Christian Acad
Tulsa, OK

Cleveland, Hylary L
Sapulpa Sr HS
Sapulpa, OK

Cline, Amber C
Jenks HS
Tulsa, OK

Clonce, Christopher
Choctaw HS
Choctaw, OK

Cloud, Keri L
Edmond North HS
Edmond, OK

Clouse, Matthew
Grove HS
Grove, OK

Clouse, Matthew A
Muskogee HS
Muskogee, OK

Clover, Nikki
Wakita Schl
Wakita, OK

Clubb, Brian N
Norman Sr HS
Norman, OK

Clytus, Mark
Douglass HS
Oklahoma City, OK

Coates, Michael P
Owasso Sr HS
Owasso, OK

Coats, Dena R
Ponca City Sr HS
Ponca City, OK

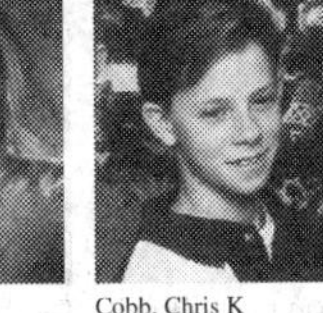
Cobb, Chris K
Nathan Hale HS
Tulsa, OK

Cobb, Patricia
Victory Christian Schl
Tulsa, OK

Cobb, Samuel A
Nathan Hale HS
Tulsa, OK

OKLAHOMA

Coble, Angela
Sapulpa Sr HS
Sapulpa, OK

Cobourn, Teri
Claremore Sr HS
Claremore, OK

Cochran, Hillary
Little Axe Sr HS
Norman, OK

Cochran, Katy D
East Central HS
Tulsa, OK

Cochrane, Shasta D
Pocola HS
Pocola, OK

Cockerham, Charlina E
Dibble HS
Blanchard, OK

Cockrell, Amber D
Colcord Schl
Colcord, OK

Coffman, Kim D
Metro Christian Acad
Tulsa, OK

Coffman, Ronna M
Mc Loud HS
Mc Loud, OK

Cogburn, Amanda R
Edmond Memorial HS
Edmond, OK

Cohea, Jamie
Edmond North HS
Edmond, OK

Colbert, Casey J
Mustang HS
Yukon, OK

Coldwater, Lafe
Forgan Schl
Forgan, OK

Coldwell, Kathryn J
B T Washington HS
Tulsa, OK

Cole, Carisa R
Locust Grove HS
Rose, OK

Cole, Cecil L
Star Spencer HS
Midwest City, OK

Cole, Danielle E
Preston Schl
Okmulgee, OK

Cole, Kenneth C
Union Intermediate HS
Tulsa, OK

Cole, Kenny
Claremore Sr HS
Claremore, OK

Cole, Leandra Berry
Edmond North HS
Edmond, OK

Cole, Rachel D
Haileyville Schl
Alderson, OK

Cole, Ron C
Del City HS
Del City, OK

Cole, Ryan
Silo HS
Durant, OK

Cole, Shirlette T
Haskell HS
Haskell, OK

Coleman, Matthew D
Mustang HS
Mustang, OK

Coleman, Stacey M
Lawton Sr HS
Lawton, OK

Coleman, Stacia R
Union Sr HS
Tulsa, OK

Coles, Jamie L
Luther HS
Luther, OK

Collins, Billy J
Muldrow HS
Muldrow, OK

Collins, Camisha N
Star Spencer HS
Spencer, OK

Collins, Cindy S
Brink Jr HS
Oklahoma City, OK

Collins, Julie
Holdenville Jr HS
Holdenville, OK

Collins, Karen R
Mannford HS
Sand Springs, OK

Collins, Krystal
Boynton Schl
Boynton, OK

Collum, Clayton D
Shawnee Sr HS
Shawnee, OK

Collyar, Janie L
Brink Jr HS
Moore, OK

Colman, Skyler D
Central Jr HS
Lawton, OK

Colombin, Shavlin A
Claremore Sr HS
Claremore, OK

Combs, Joshua T
Charles Page HS
Sand Springs, OK

Compton, Brian R
Deer Creek HS
Guthrie, OK

Conard, Casey L
Oologah HS
Talala, OK

Conatser, Mindy A
North Intemediate HS
Broken Arrow, OK

Cone, Sharla
Tahlequah Sr HS
Park Hill, OK

Connelly, Jeremy L
Del City HS
Del City, OK

Conner, Byron
Newkirk HS
Newkirk, OK

Conrad, Amanda D
Pocola HS
Pocola, OK

Conway, Deanna L
Stillwater Sr HS
Stillwater, OK

Cook, Alexandra B
Bartlesville Mid HS
Bartlesville, OK

Cook, Amy S
Westmoore HS
Oklahoma City, OK

Cook, Candice L
Cordell Sr HS
Cordell, OK

Cook,
Christopher Ryan
Putnam City North HS
Oklahoma City, OK

Cook, Colleen M
Putnam City West HS
Bethany, OK

Cook, Crystal
Cordell Sr HS
Cordell, OK

Cook, Princetta D
Northwest Classen HS
Tulsa, OK

Cooks, Melanie J
John Marshall HS
Oklahoma City, OK

Coons, Justin A
Catoosa HS
Tulsa, OK

Cooper, Courtney E
Union Intermediate HS
Broken Arrow, OK

Cooper, Kendra L
Frontier Public Schl
Marland, OK

Cooper, Nicholas
Nathan Hale HS
Tulsa, OK

Cope, Jaime L
North Intermediate HS
Broken Arrow, OK

Copeland,
Angela Dawn
Moore HS
Moore, OK

Copeland, Roxanna J
Choctaw HS
Choctaw, OK

Coppenberger, Heidi B
Davis HS
Davis, OK

Cormany, April M
Wayne Public Schl
Wayne, OK

Cornejo, Cameron M
Woodward HS
Woodward, OK

Costello, Dena L
Del City HS
Oklahoma City, OK

Costephens, Chanda
Midwest City HS
Del City, OK

Cotton, Gina
Yukon Mid HS
Yukon, OK

Cotton, Heather E
Union Intermediate HS
Broken Arrow, OK

Cotton, M'Kayla D
Westmoore HS
Oklahoma City, OK

Courouleau, Trevor P
Putnam City HS
Oklahoma City, OK

Covel, Deana
Westmoore HS
Moore, OK

Cowan, Jamie R
Muskogee HS
Muskogee, OK

Coward, Teresa
Tahlequah Sr HS
Tahlequah, OK

Cowger, Deana
Edmond North HS
Edmond, OK

Cowley, Phillip D
Morrison Public Schl
Morrison, OK

Cowling, James D
Choctaw HS
Choctaw, OK

Cox, Brian E
Madill HS
Madill, OK

Cox, Curtis R
Northeast HS
Oklahoma City, OK

Cox, Jared J
Bartlesville Mid HS
Bartlesville, OK

Cox, Jason
Elk City Jr HS
Elk City, OK

Cox, Jennifer L
Madill HS
Madill, OK

Cox, Jonathan G
Woodward HS
Woodward, OK

Cox, Julie
Putnam City North HS
Oklahoma City, OK

Cox, Kesha
Newcastle HS
Newcastle, OK

Cox, Matthew R
Bixby Sr HS
Bixby, OK

Cox, Tammy
Choctaw Jr HS
Midwest City, OK

Cox, Willie D
Valliant HS
Valliant, OK

Crabtree, Michele R
Mustang HS
Yukon, OK

Craddock, Chris A
Union Intermediate HS
Tulsa, OK

Craft, Carlie D
Henryetta Sr HS
Henryetta, OK

Craig, Harold D
Northeast HS
Oklahoma City, OK

Craig, Jerry Paul
Duncan HS
Duncan, OK

Crain, Christopher
Union Sr HS
Broken Arrow, OK

Cram, Ananda S
Tishomingo HS
Tishomingo, OK

Crank, Erin E
Sperry Sr HS
Sperry, OK

Cranke, Angela M
Jenks HS
Tulsa, OK

Crawford, Angela
B T Washington HS
Tulsa, OK

Crawford, Chesney
Woodward HS
Woodward, OK

Crawford, Crystal D
Claremore Sr HS
Claremore, OK

Crawford, Jason I
Thomas Jr Sr HS
Custer City, OK

Crawford, Katia
Charles Page HS
Sand Springs, OK

Crawford, Marshall E
Locust Grove HS
Locust Grove, OK

Crelly, Marti J
Fairview HS
Isabella, OK

Cricks, Christel
Macarthur Sr HS
Lawton, OK

Criesforribs, Desiree L
Ponca City Middle HS
Ponca City, OK

Crim, Summer C
Putnam City North HS
Oklahoma City, OK

Crisp, Adam D
Charles Page HS
Sand Springs, OK

Crispin-Stevens, Luz-Amor
Southeast HS
Oklahoma City, OK

Crissup, Landon G
Norman Sr HS
Norman, OK

Cronch, Lindsay E
Edmond North HS
Edmond, OK

Cronister, Benjamin D
Crescent Schl
Crescent, OK

Crooks, Justin R
Putnam City North HS
Oklahoma City, OK

Croslin, Jennifer A
Midwest City HS
Midwest City, OK

Cross, Justin E
Stillwater Sr HS
Stillwater, OK

Crosse, Cheryl A
Lawton Sr HS
Lawton, OK

Crossland, Michael D
Grandfield Jr Sr HS
Grandfield, OK

Crosswy, Kara K
Bixby Sr HS
Bixby, OK

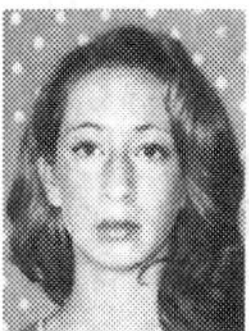
Crouch, Susan B
Heritage Chrstn
Home Schl
Tecumseh, OK

Crow, Andrea
Marlow HS
Marlow, OK

Crow, Gretchen
Stilwell HS
Stilwell, OK

Crowdis, Casey E
Duncan HS
Duncan, OK

Crowdis, Natalie A
Duncan HS
Duncan, OK

Crowell, Heather
Union Sr HS
Tulsa, OK

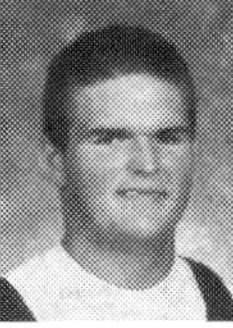
Crump, David D
Putnam City West HS
Bethany, OK

Crump, Melissa G
Putnam City West HS
Bethany, OK

Crutcher, Charmaine R
Eisenhower Sr HS
Lawton, OK

Culley, Tarsha
Holdenville HS
Holdenville, OK

Cullom, Erica
Union Intermediate HS
Tulsa, OK

Cummings, Carrie E
Sapulpa Sr HS
Sapulpa, OK

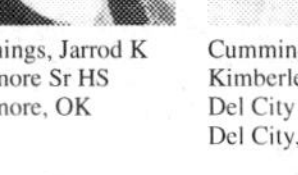
Cummings, Jarrod K
Claremore Sr HS
Claremore, OK

Cummings, Kimberley R
Del City HS
Del City, OK

Cummins, Amanda S
Colbert Jr Sr HS
Colbert, OK

Cummins, Bobby A
Bartlesville Mid HS
Bartlesville, OK

Cummins, Mary E
West Middle HS
Norman, OK

Curran, Laura
Midwest City HS
Oklahoma City, OK

Curry, Jennifer
Lawton Sr HS
Lawton, OK

Curry, Karrie D
Norman Sr HS
Norman, OK

Curry, Sammi B
Jay HS
Jay, OK

Curtis, Austin M
Muskogee HS
Muskogee, OK

OKLAHOMA

Custer, J W
Cushing HS
Cushing, OK

Cynthia, Taylor V
Muldrow HS
Muldrow, OK

Cypert, Jackie
Putnam City HS
Warr Acres, OK

Cypert, Kelsie
South Intermediate HS
Broken Arrow, OK

Dafforn, Robin L
East Central HS
Tulsa, OK

Dahr, Mona
Heritage Hall Schl
Oklahoma City, OK

Daily, Mindi J
Newcastle HS
Norman, OK

Dale, Jonathan
Webster HS
Tulsa, OK

Dale, Missy A
Western Heights Sr HS
Oklahoma City, OK

Dallal, Monique
Bishop Mcguinness HS
Oklahoma City, OK

Daly, Jennifer
Blackwell HS
Blackwell, OK

Damron, Kristi L
Durant HS
Durant, OK

Dan, Derrick A
Checotah HS
Checotah, OK

Dancy, Jonathan B
Christian
Heritage Acad
Oklahoma City, OK

Dangott, Laura
Henryetta Sr HS
Henryetta, OK

Daniel, Brooke
Claremore Sr HS
Claremore, OK

Daniel, Duane
Stonewall Jr-Sr HS
Stonewall, OK

Daniel, Lisa
Talihina Sr HS
Albion, OK

Daniels, Amy
Edmond Santa Fe HS
Edmond, OK

Daniels, Robert G
Enid Sr HS
Enid, OK

Danker, Adam W
Edmond North HS
Edmond, OK

Dao, David T
Oklahoma Sch Of
Science & Math
Yukon, OK

Darby, Sabrina P
B T Washington HS
Tulsa, OK

Darling, Kennah A
Velma Alma HS
Velma, OK

Darneal, Fanci
Panama HS
Panama, OK

Davidson, Gregory C
Olney Schl
Coalgate, OK

Davidson, Krystal
Perry Sr HS
Perry, OK

Davidson, Kylie
Choctaw HS
Choctaw, OK

Davidson, Tammy
Westmoore HS
Oklahoma City, OK

Davidson, Will
Merritt Schl
Carter, OK

Davis, Amber L
Charles Page HS
Sand Springs, OK

Davis, Ashley M
Metro Christian Acad
Broken Arrow, OK

Davis, Brandon S
Edmond North HS
Edmond, OK

Davis, Brandy L
Enid Sr HS
Enid, OK

Davis, Catherine L
Will Rogers HS
Tulsa, OK

Davis, Christina D
Great Plains
Avt-Comanche
Lawton, OK

Davis, Devin
Strother Jr Sr HS
Seminole, OK

Davis, Eric
Edmond North HS
Edmond, OK

Davis, Heath T
Webster HS
Tulsa, OK

Davis, Jason
Lawton Sr HS
Lawton, OK

Davis, Kathryn M
Putnam City
Original HS
Oklahoma City, OK

Davis, Kenya
Will Rogers HS
Tulsa, OK

Davis, Kevin
Westmoore HS
Oklahoma City, OK

Davis, Lesley
Dale Sr HS
Shawnee, OK

Davis, Leslie T
Tahlequah Sr HS
Tahlequah, OK

Davis, Nathan
Dewey HS
Dewey, OK

Davis, Rachel R
Snyder HS
Mountain Park, OK

Davis, Staci
Marietta HS
Marietta, OK

Davis, Stephanie A
Hulbert Jr Sr HS
Hulbert, OK

Davis, Steven E
Claremore Sr HS
Claremore, OK

Davis, Tiffany
East Central HS
Tulsa, OK

Davis, Tiffany M
Catoosa HS
Catoosa, OK

Davis, Tressa K
South Coffeyville Schl
S Coffeyville, OK

Dawes, Travis W
Stillwater Jr HS
Stillwater, OK

Dawson, Marisha
Douglass HS
Oklahoma City, OK

Day, Jaime
Elmore
City-Pernell HS
Elmore City, OK

Day, Jenice L
Union Sr HS
Coweta, OK

Day, Jennifer C
Plainview HS
Ardmore, OK

Day, Melissa R
Wagoner Sr HS
Wagoner, OK

Deal, Emily
Midwest City HS
Oklahoma City, OK

Dean, Anthony
Morrison Public Schl
Morrison, OK

Dean, Jennifer D
North Intemediate HS
Frankston, TX

Dean, Stephanie
Hilldale HS
Muskogee, OK

Deans, Angela M
Cushing HS
Cushing, OK

Deason, Hannah R
Wright Christian Acad
Sand Springs, OK

Deason, Michael J
Okay Jr Sr HS
Okay, OK

Deaton, Brandy L
Pauls Valley HS
Pauls Valley, OK

De Baud III, Joseph E
U S Grant HS
Oklahoma City, OK

De Boer, Melinda R
Stillwater Jr HS
Stillwater, OK

De Bose, Andrea D
Mc Lain Career Acad
Tulsa, OK

Debouse, Paul
Star Spencer HS
Spencer, OK

De Busk II, Ronald Craig
Inola Sr HS
Broken Arrow, OK

De Deyne, Jamie L
Bishop Kelley HS
Tulsa, OK

Deen, Carl A
Choctaw HS
Choctaw, OK

De Gase, Kim
Daniel Webster HS
Tulsa, OK

De Graffenreid, Jaime
Del City HS
Oklahoma City, OK

De Graffenreid II, Michael T
Del City HS
Oklahoma City, OK

Deibler, Shannon R
Norman Sr HS
Norman, OK

Delay, Trisha
Turpin Schl
Liberal, KS

Delphine, Le Rol
Choctaw HS
Midwest City, OK

Delucca, Jorge A
Midwest City HS
Midwest City, OK

Demaree, Bruce A
Bluejacket Schl
Vinita, OK

Dempsey, Tiece
Northeast HS
Oklahoma City, OK

Denham, Shelly D
Lone Grove HS
Lone Grove, OK

Dennis, Christopher D
Pauls Valley HS
Pauls Valley, OK

Dennis, Jeremy P
Del City HS
Del City, OK

Dennis, Libby A
Oologah HS
Claremore, OK

Dennis, Matthew C
Nathan Hale HS
Tulsa, OK

Dent, Richard J
Bishop Kelley HS
Tulsa, OK

Denton, Christy L
Nathan Hale HS
Tulsa, OK

Depasse, Eugina
Coalgate HS
Coalgate, OK

De Paulo, Nathan G
Olive Jr Sr HS
Jennings, OK

De Priest, Lelia
U S Grant HS
Oklahoma City, OK

Derryberry, Paige
Westmoore HS
Oklahoma City, OK

De Spain, Jennifer
Edmond North HS
Edmond, OK

Despain, Steve M
Stilwell HS
Stilwell, OK

Devine, Beth S
Woodward HS
Woodward, OK

Devlin, Shala
Perry Sr HS
Perry, OK

Dewberry, Katie L
Metro Christian Acad
Tulsa, OK

De Witt, Amanda L
Pocola HS
Pocola, OK

Dick, Deidra L
Cordell Sr HS
Bessie, OK

Dickey, Rennetta P
Alva HS
Alva, OK

Dickinson, Ann Marie
Jenks HS
Jenks, OK

Diehl, Allyson L
Mustang HS
Mustang, OK

Dietz, Amanda
Bartlesville Mid HS
Bartlesville, OK

Dilbeck, Ann Marie
Jay HS
Jay, OK

Dillon, Steven D
Warner HS
Warner, OK

Dinkins, Lamar E
B T Washington HS
Tulsa, OK

Dischinger, Lori M
Elgin HS
Elgin, OK

Dittfuth, Ryan W
Union Intermediate HS
Broken Arrow, OK

Ditto, Laurie N
Ardmore HS
Ardmore, OK

Divine, Ashley
Shawnee Sr HS
Shawnee, OK

Dixon, Carrie E
Duncan HS
Duncan, OK

Dixon, Jason B
West Middle HS
Norman, OK

Dixon, La Toisha D
Mc Lain Career Acad
Tulsa, OK

Dixon, Wes
Dewey HS
Bartlesville, OK

Dobbs, Matthew H
Bridge Creek HS
Blanchard, OK

Dodge, Jennifer
Henryetta Sr HS
Henryetta, OK

Dodson, Amy
Dickson HS
Ardmore, OK

Dodson, Marshell
Elgin HS
Medicine Park, OK

Dodson, Ryan
Washingtn HS
Washington, OK

Doern, Johna
Edmond North HS
Edmond, OK

Donaldson, Celeste
Mustang HS
Mustang, OK

Doney, Misty A
Drummond Schl
Enid, OK

Donnelly, Ryan Patrick
Elgin HS
Elgin, OK

Donovan, Beth
Perkins-Tryon HS
Wellston, OK

Dorn, Ricki J
Will Rogers HS
Tulsa, OK

Doroteo, Angelica M
Capitol Hill HS
Oklahoma City, OK

Dorr, Lori J
Tahlequah Sr HS
Tahlequah, OK

Dorris, Kris
Chickasha Jr HS
Chickasha, OK

Dorton, Angela M
Carl Albert HS
Tinker Afb, OK

Dorton, David
Grandfield Jr Sr HS
Grandfield, OK

Doss, Carissa A
Putnam City North HS
Oklahoma City, OK

Doss, Erin R
Putnam City North HS
Oklahoma City, OK

Dotson, Emily L
Choctaw HS
Midwest City, OK

Dotson, Wesley
Broken Arrow Sr HS
Broken Arrow, OK

Dotter, Kathryn
Clinton HS
Clinton, OK

Doty, Garrett
Lone Grove HS
Ardmore, OK

Douget, Michael C
Union Intermediate HS
Tulsa, OK

Douglas, Chaquise
U S Grant HS
Oklahoma City, OK

Douglass, Sara
Broken Arrow Sr HS
Broken Arrow, OK

Douthit, Alan R
Union Sr HS
Broken Arrow, OK

Douthit, Shawna D
Owasso Sr HS
Collinsville, OK

Dowell, Jessica
Claremore Sr HS
Claremore, OK

Dowling, Melissa K
Westmoore HS
Oklahoma City, OK

Downing, Brian A
Yukon HS
Yukon, OK

Downs, Charlotte
Durant HS
Durant, OK

Downs, Kasi S
Collinsville HS
Collinsville, OK

Drake, Corie L
Ponca City Sr HS
Ponca City, OK

Drake, Tammy L
East Central HS
Tulsa, OK

Draper, Jenny
Central Mid-HS
Norman, OK

Drawbaugh, Tina R
Byng Sr HS
Ada, OK

Drennan, Matthew P
Velma Alma Jr Sr HS
Lindsay, OK

Dresher, Matthew J
Union Sr HS
Tulsa, OK

Dressel, Nakia C
Jay HS
Jay, OK

Dressen, Amy S
Ponca City Middle HS
Ponca City, OK

Dressler, Brent A
Union Intermediate HS
Broken Arrow, OK

Driggers, Ryan A
Mustang HS
Yukon, OK

Driver, Lakeissa M
Macarthur Sr HS
Lawton, OK

Dryden, Nicole L
Walters HS
Walters, OK

Du, Hai T
Westmoore HS
Oklahoma City, OK

Dubberly, Jesse L
Norman Sr HS
Norman, OK

Dubie, Christina
Booker T
Washington HS
Tulsa, OK

Duck, Stefanie M
Union Intermediate HS
Tulsa, OK

Duff, Sarah R
Nathan Hale HS
Tulsa, OK

Dugger, Ashley
Canton HS
Canton, OK

Duke, Corbyn
Yukon Middle HS
Yukon, OK

Dumler, Eric
Texhoma HS
Texhoma, OK

Duncan, Brandi
Cameron Schl
Cameron, OK

Duncan, Denise A
Altus Sr HS
Altus, OK

Duncan, Shanna D
Eufaula Sr HS
Eufaula, OK

Dungy, Dan A
Oklahoma
Christian Schl
Oklahoma City, OK

Dunham, Jeremy
Okmulgee HS
Okmulgee, OK

Dunn, Bruce L
Cushing HS
Cushing, OK

Dunn, John S
Union Sr HS
Broken Arrow, OK

Dupree, Patricia J
Colbert Jr Sr HS
Colbert, OK

Durant, William B
Putnam City HS
Warr Acres, OK

Durant, Zack D
Eisenhower Sr HS
Lawton, OK

Durbin, Nikki J
Central Jr HS
Lawton, OK

Durgin, Dana
Tomlinson Jr HS
Lawton, OK

Durham, Cara G
Enid Sr HS
Enid, OK

Dusenberry, Brooke N
Mc Alester HS
Mcalester, OK

Dutton, Rebecca
Okmulgee HS
Okmulgee, OK

Dutton, Tiffany L
Union Intermediate HS
Tulsa, OK

Dye, Julie
Grace Chrn Acad
Oklahoma City, OK

Dyer, Pam C
Muldrow HS
Muldrow, OK

Dzialo, Devin
Lawton Sr HS
Lawton, OK

Eads, Melody N
Ft Cob-Broxton Jr
Sr HS
Fort Cobb, OK

Eads, Miranda
Ponca City Middle HS
Grove City, OH

Eairheart, Jasen R
Geronimo Jr Sr HS
Geronimo, OK

Earls, Kevin R
Edmond North HS
Edmond, OK

Earp, Rachel M
Moore HS
Moore, OK

Easiley, Maurene G
B T Washington HS
Tulsa, OK

Easter, Chris A
Putnam City West HS
Bethany, OK

Easter, Shantell
Weatherford HS
Weatherford, OK

Eastom, Crystal C
Will Rogers HS
Tulsa, OK

Eaton, Amber
Thomas A Edison HS
Tulsa, OK

Eaton, Christine E
Bartlesville Mid HS
Bartlesville, OK

Ebenhack, Christian
B T Washington HS
Tulsa, OK

Eccles, Erin
Bethany HS
Bethany, OK

Echols, Jonathan D
Christian
Heritage Acad
Oklahoma City, OK

Eckert, Erin E
Claremore Sr HS
Claremore, OK

Eddy, Karen E
Bishop Kelley HS
Tulsa, OK

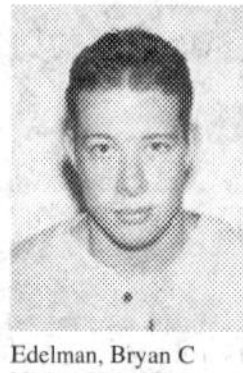
Edelman, Bryan C
Nathan Hale HS
Tulsa, OK

Edens, Jason
Duncan HS
Duncan, OK

Edgeman, Nelson S
Durant HS
Durant, OK

Edney, Alecia N
Claremore Sr HS
Claremore, OK

Edwards, Carlous D
Okmulgee HS
Okmulgee, OK

Edwards, Chad E
Muldrow HS
Muldrow, OK

Edwards, Daniel K
Duncan HS
Duncan, OK

Edwards, Jason A
Duncan HS
Duncan, OK

Edwards, Samantha L
Muldrow HS
Muldrow, OK

Egan, Kathleen M
Bishop Kelley HS
Tulsa, OK

Eichor, Caren V
B T Washington HS
Tulsa, OK

Eidson, Katie
Sulphur HS
Sulphur, OK

Eilers, Justin
Mooreland Jr Sr HS
Mooreland, OK

Elam, Callecia D
Northeast HS
Oklahoma City, OK

Eldridge, Jana L
Stilwell HS
Stilwell, OK

Elerick, Joe K
Harrah HS
Harrah, OK

Elledge, Brandi D
Westmoore HS
Oklahoma City, OK

Ellenburg, Brandy R
Heavener HS
Wister, OK

Ellington, Melissa
Ripley HS
Stillwater, OK

Elliott, Charley C
Union Intermediate HS
Broken Arrow, OK

Elliott, Jamie L
Yukon Middle HS
Yukon, OK

Elliott, Kristina L
Sharon Mutual Jr Sr HS
Mutual, OK

Elliott, Nancy
Altus Sr HS
Altus, OK

Elliott, Sarah J
Metro Christian Acad
Tulsa, OK

Ellis, Heather R
Sapulpa Sr HS
Sapulpa, OK

Ellis, Jenny R
Putnam City North HS
Oklahoma City, OK

Ellis, Johnathon
Miami Sr HS
Miami, OK

Elmenhorst, Heidi D
El Reno Sr HS
El Reno, OK

Elmore, Crystal G
Yukon Middle HS
Yukon, OK

Emerson, Kimberly
Bartlesville Sr HS
Ochelata, OK

Enabnit, Laurie J
Bartlesville Sr HS
Ardmore, OK

Endicott, Laura B
Duncan HS
Duncan, OK

Endres, Faith A
Kingfisher HS
Kingfisher, OK

Engelman, Brandon W
Turpin Schl
Turpin, OK

Engle, Melissa D
Sapulpa Sr HS
Sapulpa, OK

English, Jerrod
Charles Page HS
Sand Springs, OK

English, Whitney A
Christian Heritage Acad
Oklahoma City, OK

Enright, April
Liberty Acad
Shawnee, OK

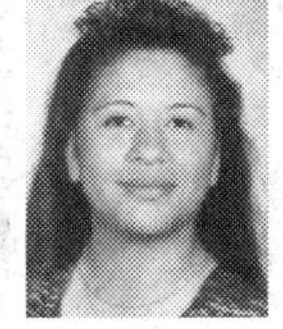
Enriquez, Victoria E
Panola HS
Wilburton, OK

Epp, Connie R
Turpin Schl
Turpin, OK

Epp, Kaci D
Broken Arrow Sr HS
Broken Arrow, OK

Epperson, Jennifer L
West Jr HS
Oklahoma City, OK

Erbeck, Julie
Claremore Sr HS
Claremore, OK

Erickson, Krista K
Tahlequah Sr HS
Tahlequah, OK

Erwin, Shelli
Kingston HS
Kingston, OK

Eskew, Jessica
Ardmore HS
Pooleville, OK

Espich, Amber D
Sapulpa Sr HS
Sapulpa, OK

Estrada, Isabel
Elk City Jr HS
Elk City, OK

Etchison, Amy
Indianola HS
Mcalester, OK

Etchison, Dremiane D
Lawton Sr HS
Lawton, OK

Ethridge, Jason
Central Mid-HS
Norman, OK

Evans, Amanda
Mannford HS
Mannford, OK

Evans, Ashley N
Harrah HS
Harrah, OK

Evans, Geoff
Coweta HS
Broken Arrow, OK

Evans, Lee
Marietta HS
Marietta, OK

Evans, Megan L
Yukon Middle HS
Yukon, OK

Evans, Robert J
Mannford HS
Mannford, OK

Ezell, Erik L
North Intemediate HS
Broken Arrow, OK

Ezell, Veronica L
Durant HS
Durant, OK

Fahle, Jana
Eisenhower Sr HS
Lawton, OK

Fahnholz, Amanda J
Okmulgee HS
Okmulgee, OK

Fanning, Jaime D
U S Grant HS
Oklahoma City, OK

Farley, Chris
Deer Creek HS
Edmond, OK

Farmer, Jason
Thomas A Edison HS
Tulsa, OK

Farr, Erin R
Hollis Jr Sr HS
Eldorado, OK

Farrar, Brandi D
Putnam City North HS
Oklahoma City, OK

Farrar, Christina D
Cameron Schl
Cameron, OK

Farrior, Mary K
B T Washington HS
Tulsa, OK

Farris, Brandi
Claremore Sr HS
Claremore, OK

Farris, Jason
Liberty Acad
Shawnee, OK

Farris, Melissa L
Okeene Jr Sr HS
Isabella, OK

Faulk, Kara
Sapulpa Sr HS
Sapulpa, OK

Faulkner, Channell M
Dickson HS
Ardmore, OK

Faulkner, Misti
Luther HS
Luther, OK

Fears, Braxton
Bixby Sr HS
Tulsa, OK

Fears, Mandy N
Tahlequah Jr HS
Park Hill, OK

Fears, Marcus E
Tahlequah Sr HS
Park Hill, OK

Feazel, Kendra R
Central HS
Tulsa, OK

Fendley, Clifton J
Sapulpa Sr HS
Sapulpa, OK

Ferguson, Candy L
Tuttle HS
Tuttle, OK

Ferguson, Emily
Edmond North HS
Edmond, OK

Ferrell, Charlie
Hennessey HS
Hennessey, OK

Ferrell, Jessica
Perry Sr HS
Perry, OK

Ferris, Autumn
Wapanucka Schl
Milburn, OK

Fetter Jr, Michael L
Central Mid-HS
Norman, OK

Fiedler, Amber
Miami Sr HS
Miami, OK

Fielding, Joshua A
Putnam City West HS
Bethany, OK

Fields, Daisy M
Wister Schl
Wister, OK

Fields, Lori
Mooreland Jr Sr HS
Mooreland, OK

Fields, Renee
Putnam City HS
Oklahoma City, OK

Finch, Jennifer
Mustang HS
Yukon, OK

Fine, Chancey A
Meeker Jr Sr HS
Meeker, OK

Finley, Danita
Midwest City HS
Midwest City, OK

Finnell, Tate
Canute HS
Canute, OK

Firestone, Brian K
Velma Alma HS
Duncan, OK

Fischer, Ian T
Union Sr HS
Broken Arrow, OK

Fish, Jessica P
Achille Schl
Achille, OK

Fisher, Ben T
Owasso Sr HS
Owasso, OK

Fisher, Jessica
Deer Creek HS
Edmond, OK

Fisher, Tami J
Chattanooga Schl
Chattanooga, OK

Fitzgibbon, Jackie
Fairland Jr Sr HS
Fairland, OK

Flaherty, Becky E
Shattuck Jr Sr HS
Shattuck, OK

Flanagan, Misty L
Marietta HS
Marietta, OK

Flanders, Sean P
Moore HS
Moore, OK

Fleenor, Sabrina K
Mustang HS
Mustang, OK

Fleetwood, Josh W
Central Schl
Sallisaw, OK

Fleming, Denise M
Nathan Hale HS
Tulsa, OK

Fleming, Sabrina
Putnam City West HS
Oklahoma City, OK

Fleming, Sara L
Webster HS
Tulsa, OK

Fleming, Tim
Nathan Hale HS
Tulsa, OK

Fletcher, Chris
Graham Schl
Weleetka, OK

Flick, Debra
Chisholm Sr HS
Enid, OK

Flohr, Ricki
Ada HS
Ada, OK

Flores, Rudy
Stilwell HS
Stilwell, OK

Flowers, Kyle D
Meeker HS
Meeker, OK

Floyd, Bobby
Vinita HS
Vinita, OK

Floyd, Shiela D
Vinita HS
Vinita, OK

Focht, Kenneth R
Stillwater Jr HS
Stillwater, OK

Foley, Steven M
Altus Sr HS
Altus, OK

Folsom, Devon R
Wagoner Sr HS
Wagoner, OK

Folsom, Joshuah M
Midwest City HS
Midwest City, OK

Folsom, Mindy
Perry Sr HS
Perry, OK

Forbis, Heather K
Skiatook HS
Skiatook, OK

Ford, Carrie D
Durant HS
Durant, OK

Ford, Darcy L
Bartlesville Mid HS
Bartlesville, OK

Ford, Diana L
Charles Page HS
Sapulpa, OK

Ford, Mandy K
Mc Loud HS
Harrah, OK

Ford, Urena B
Wister Schl
Wister, OK

Ford, Vanessa
Millwood HS
Oklahoma City, OK

Ford, William P
Duncan HS
Duncan, OK

Forster, Jason
Anadarko HS
Anadarko, OK

Forsythe, Jeremiah K
Wilson HS
Wilson, OK

Foshee, Jeri Beth
Westmoore HS
Oklahoma City, OK

Fossett, Christopher L
Wagoner Sr HS
Wagoner, OK

Foster, Amanda B
Spiro HS
Spiro, OK

Foster, Corrie D
Jay HS
Rose, OK

Foster, Jake B
Stillwater Sr HS
Stillwater, OK

Foster, James D
Warner HS
Warner, OK

Foster, Jeremy M
West Middle HS
Norman, OK

Foster, Jill
Jenks HS
Tulsa, OK

Foster, Kim
Tahlequah Sr HS
Park Hill, OK

Foster, Natasha S
Alva HS
Alva, OK

Foster, Sara
Edmond North HS
Edmond, OK

Fowler, Matt E
Muskogee HS
Muskogee, OK

Fox, Melissa D
Cashion HS
Cashion, OK

Foyil, Daniel A
Owasso Sr HS
Owasso, OK

Frame, Dee J
Choctaw HS
Choctaw, OK

Francis, Theresa A
Muskogee HS
Muskogee, OK

Francisco, Cody R
East Central HS
Tulsa, OK

Frankenfield, Todd
Ponca City Sr HS
Ponca City, OK

Franklin, Katie N
Union Sr HS
Broken Arrow, OK

Franklin, La Shona
Madill HS
Madill, OK

Fraser, Marshall M
Bartlesville Sr HS
Bartlesville, OK

Frazier, D Andra A
El Reno Sr HS
El Reno, OK

Frederick, Ryan M
Union Sr HS
Tulsa, OK

Fredman, Shannon L
Dale Sr HS
Mc Loud, OK

Fredrick, Rachael
Oktaha Jr Sr HS
Oktaha, OK

Free, Maggie
Newcastle HS
Newcastle, OK

Freeman, Audrey N
Nathan Hale HS
Tulsa, OK

Freeman, Bryan
Bartlesville Sr HS
Bartlesville, OK

Freeman, Erica L
Pauls Valley HS
Pauls Valley, OK

Freeman, Jennifer L
Marlow HS
Duncan, OK

Freeman, Jeri D
Tishomingo HS
Ravia, OK

Fremin, Amy C
Ponca City Sr HS
Ponca City, OK

French, Misty D
Cache HS
Cache, OK

Frere, Jacquelyn D
Union Intermediate HS
Broken Arrow, OK

Friend, Carl A
Bishop Kelley HS
Claremore, OK

Frietze, Tiffany M
Pawnee HS
Pawnee, OK

Frogge, Ashley
Collinsville HS
Collinsville, OK

Fromm, Amy
Bluejacket Schl
Bluejacket, OK

Fry, Jamie J
Collinsville HS
Collinsville, OK

Fry, Jarrod B
Muskogee HS
Muskogee, OK

Fry, Micah
Central HS
Tulsa, OK

Frye, Byron F
Ada HS
Ada, OK

Fuentez, Aurora
Burns Flat-Dill
City Jshs
Burns Flat, OK

Fugett, Eric B
Muldrow HS
Muldrow, OK

Fullbright, Jennifer A
Choctaw HS
Midwest City, OK

Fuller, Jade T
Lawton Sr HS
Lawton, OK

Fulton, Annette
Midwest City HS
Midwest City, OK

Fulton, Daniel B
Hobart HS
Hobart, OK

Fulton, Mandy L
Del City HS
Del City, OK

Fulton, Robert
Hollis Jr Sr HS
Hollis, OK

Fultz, Jeremy D
Wetumka Jr Sr HS
Dustin, OK

Funderburg, Gregory
Guymon Sr HS
Guymon, OK

Funderburgh,
Mandy Jo
B T Washington HS
Tulsa, OK

Furry, Clinton D
Northwest Classen HS
Oklahoma City, OK

Gaches Jr, Darrell E
Stilwell HS
Stilwell, OK

Gaddis, Clayton T
Union Intermediate HS
Tulsa, OK

Gaddy, Charity
North Intemediate HS
Broken Arrow, OK

Gaffney, Robert
Central HS
Tulsa, OK

Galdamez, Erin Lyn
Markoma Bible Acad
Tahlequah, OK

Gallion, Brandi
Wynnewood HS
Wynnewood, OK

Gallo, Kari
North HS
Edmond, OK

Galloway, Beau J
Charles Page HS
Sand Springs, OK

Galloway, Lisa J
Colcord Schl
Siloam Springs, AR

Gamble, Carrie L
Enid Sr HS
Enid, OK

Gann, Brandon R
Wetumka Jr Sr HS
Wetumka, OK

Gann, Çarla F
Muldrow HS
Muldrow, OK

Gann, Marla K
Muldrow HS
Muldrow, OK

Gant, Kenny L
Guthrie Sr HS
Guthrie, OK

Garcia, Amy
Midwest City HS
Midwest City, OK

Garcia, Carlos V
Putnam City West HS
Oklahoma City, OK

Gard, Amanda
Perry Sr HS
Perry, OK

Garey, Matthew
West Middle HS
Norman, OK

Garland, Meredith A
Elgin HS
Elgin, OK

Garland, Tara
Velma Alma HS
Velma, OK

Garner, Heath A
Warner HS
Warner, OK

Garner, Randy D
Moore HS
Oklahoma City, OK

Garr, Stephanie N
Choctaw HS
Choctaw, OK

Garrett, Charles E
Moore HS
Moore, OK

Garrett, Christina M
Lone Grove HS
Lone Grove, OK

Garrett, Jenifer
Tuttle HS
Tuttle, OK

Garrett, Jonathan D
West Moore HS
Oklahoma City, OK

Garrett, Leticia D
Spiro HS
Keota, OK

Garrett, Nathan S
Midwest City HS
Choctaw, OK

Garrett, Nicole
Tuttle HS
Tuttle, OK

Garrett II, Stephen M
Inola Sr HS
Tulsa, OK

Garrett, Whitney B
Central Mid-HS
Norman, OK

Garrison, Brant
Elk City Jr HS
Canute, OK

Garrison, Nakyla J
Mustang HS
Yukon, OK

Garrison, Penny R
Mannford HS
Sand Springs, OK

Garza, Carlos
Walters HS
Walters, OK

Garza III, Danny D
West Middle HS
Norman, OK

Gasem, Sarah S
Stillwater Sr HS
Stillwater, OK

Gateley, Joshua
Edmond North HS
Edmond, OK

Gauger, Kristal R
Ponca City Sr HS
Ponca City, OK

Gaylor, Velda
Roland Sr HS
Roland, OK

Gebhart, Erica S
Claremore Sr HS
Claremore, OK

Gee, Michael C
Putnam City North HS
Oklahoma City, OK

Gentry, Moira
Ardmore HS
Ardmore, OK

Genzer, Kyle
Mt St Marys HS
Moore, OK

George, Charity B
Wright Christian Acad
Catoosa, OK

George, Monique L
Chickasha HS
Chickasha, OK

Gesell, Allyson
Edmond Memorial HS
Edmond, OK

Giboney Jr, James F
Muldrow HS
Muldrow, OK

Gibson, Amy
Parker Middle HS
Mcalester, OK

Gibson, Cori M
Broken Arrow Sr HS
Broken Arrow, OK

Gibson, Kassi
Eakly HS
Hydro, OK

Gibson, Robert R
Mid-Del Christian Schl
Midwest City, OK

Gibson, Sara D
Ardmore HS
Ardmore, OK

Gifford, Sarah R
Hulbert Jr Sr HS
Hulbert, OK

Giglia, Crystal
Chickasha Jr HS
Chickasha, OK

Gilbert, Stephen
Bixby Sr HS
Bixby, OK

Gildhouse, Nicole M
Newkirk HS
Ponca City, OK

Giles, Erin
Watonga HS
Watonga, OK

Giles, Kristin Jean
Putnam City West HS
Bethany, OK

Giles, Philip S
Putnam City North HS
Oklahoma City, OK

Gill, Adam
Wilburton Sr HS
Wilburton, OK

Gill, Jenai
Union Intermediate HS
Broken Arrow, OK

Gill, Justin W
Union Sr HS
Broken Arrow, OK

Gill, Kristen E
El Reno Sr HS
El Reno, OK

Gillham, Donilea R
Pocola HS
Pocola, OK

Gilliland,
Christopher S
Edmond Memorial HS
Edmond, OK

Gilpin, Becky
Adair HS
Big Cabin, OK

Gilstrap, Lonnie T
Union Intermediate HS
Tulsa, OK

Gilstrap, Tammie
Coweta HS
Coweta, OK

Gipson, Dominac J
Star Spencer HS
Midwest City, OK

Girard, Aaron M
El Reno Sr HS
El Reno, OK

Gise, Max E
B T Washington HS
Tulsa, OK

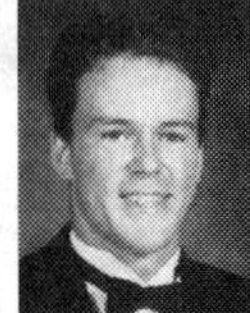
Gist, Jim
Spiro HS
Spiro, OK

Gist, Sandy K
Spiro HS
Spiro, OK

Givens, Qiana D
Chickasha HS
Chickasha, OK

Glancy, Brandon K
Burns Flat-Dill
City Jshs
Burns Flat, OK

Glass, Amanda G
Stilwell HS
Stilwell, OK

Glass, Michael
Edmond North HS
Edmond, OK

Glaze, Ryan
Chickasha HS
Chickasha, OK

Glenn, Chastity T
Star Spencer HS
Midwest City, OK

Glover, Mary
Marlow HS
Marlow, OK

Glover, Mitchell R
Mustang HS
Yukon, OK

Goad, Crystal
Mustang HS
Yukon, OK

Gober, Greg D
Bethel HS
Shawnee, OK

Godbenere, Kara N
Bartlesville Mid HS
Bartlesville, OK

Goeringer, Amanda
Chattanooga Schl
Chattanooga, OK

Goforth, Brandi R
Classen Schl Of
Adv Stu
Oklahoma City, OK

Golbek, Kathina M
Waynoka HS
Waynoka, OK

Golden, Cherea E
Western Heights Sr HS
Oklahoma City, OK

Golden Jr, Larry
South Intermediate HS
Broken Arrow, OK

Golden, Staci
Blackwell HS
Blackwell, OK

Golden, Tim
Byng Sr HS
Ada, OK

Goldesbe, David
Cushing HS
Cushing, OK

Goll, Randall E
Washington Jr Sr HS
Blanchard, OK

Golsen, Joshua B
Bishop Mcguinness HS
Oklahoma City, OK

Gonser, Ashley L
Woodward HS
Woodward, OK

Gonzales, John J
Cement Jr Sr HS
Cement, OK

Gonzalez, Aalysha M
Union Sr HS
Broken Arrow, OK

Goodman, Candra L
Charles Page HS
Tulsa, OK

Goodson, Josh G
Tecumseh HS
Earlsboro, OK

Goodson, Katie
Moyers Public Schl
Antlers, OK

Goodwin, Christy M
Memorial HS
Tulsa, OK

Goostree, Eric
Crowder Schl
Mcalester, OK

Gorbea, Isabel P
Bishop Kelley HS
Broken Arrow, OK

Gordin, Heather
Bixby Sr HS
Bixby, OK

Gordon, Jana
Oklahoma
Christian Schl
Edmond, OK

Gordon, Laura B
Charles Page HS
Sand Springs, OK

Gordon, Minon
Poteau HS
Poteau, OK

Gordon, Miranda L
Meeker Jr Sr HS
Meeker, OK

Gore, Rosco S
Lawton Sr HS
Lawton, OK

Gorman, Patrick
Holland Hall Schl
Tulsa, OK

Gorman, Stacie
Bishop Kelley HS
Broken Arrow, OK

Gorney, Jennifer Lea
Mannford HS
Mannford, OK

Gossett, Jesse
Moore HS
Moore, OK

Gould, Jeremy L
Enid Sr HS
Enid, OK

Gourd, Chance T
Dewey HS
Bartlesville, OK

Goyer, Courtney
Edmond Memorial HS
Edmond, OK

Grady, Edward
Putnam City West HS
Bethany, OK

Graft, Aaron Paul
Clinton HS
Clinton, OK

Graham, Ashley A
Muskogee HS
Muskogee, OK

Graham, Eric
Chickasha Jr HS
Chickasha, OK

Graham, Ja M
Putnam City West HS
Bethany, OK

Graham, Kara
Norman Sr HS
Norman, OK

Graham, Roger L
Velma Alma HS
Ratliff City, OK

Grant, Melissa K
Durant HS
Durant, OK

Gratias, Jeremiah D
Ponca City Sr HS
Ponca City, OK

Graves, April R
Ripley HS
Ripley, OK

Gray, Chandra
B T Washington HS
Tulsa, OK

Gray, Chris J
Mustang HS
Yukon, OK

Gray, Erica J
South Intermediate HS
Broken Arrow, OK

Gray, Justin W
Ponca City Sr HS
Ponca City, OK

Gray, Kevin J
B T Washington HS
Tulsa, OK

Gray, Leslie A
South Intermediate HS
Broken Arrow, OK

Gray, Niki
Wayne Public Schl
Paoli, OK

Grayson, Shawn M
Mc Loud HS
Meeker, OK

Green, D. Reid
Laverne Jr Sr HS
Rosston, OK

Green, Dustin R
Stilwell HS
Stilwell, OK

Green, Julie A
Guymon Sr HS
Guymon, OK

Green, Kyle E
Wakita Schl
Wakita, OK

Green, Maria K
Pocola HS
Pocola, OK

Green, Robert B
Union Intermediate HS
Broken Arrow, OK

Green, Terry R
Enid Sr HS
Enid, OK

Green, Trina L
Roland Sr HS
Roland, OK

Green, Victoria Elaine
Coweta HS
Coweta, OK

Greene, Tony
Putnam City West HS
Bethany, OK

Gregory, Andrea D
Stilwell HS
Stilwell, OK

Gregory, Eli
Cascia Hall Prep
School
Muskogee, OK

Gregory, Heather D
Bethany HS
Bethany, OK

Gregory, Lindsey
Heritage Hall Schl
Edmond, OK

Gresh, Amanda
Union Sr HS
Tulsa, OK

Gretsinger, Jesse E
Chattanooga Schl
Chattanooga, OK

Griffin, Amy K
Grace Chrn Acad
Oklahoma City, OK

Griffith, Jerry
Elizabeth
Yukon HS
Yukon, OK

Grigg, Brandi
Burns Flat/Dill
City HS
Burns Flat, OK

Grigg, Carrie A
South Intermediate HS
Broken Arrow, OK

Griggs, Justin
Liberty Acad
Sparks, OK

Griggs, Lacey S
Harrah HS
Harrah, OK

Grimm, Andrew Ryan
Cascia Hall Prep
School
Tulsa, OK

Grimm, Elissa M
Enid Sr HS
Enid, OK

Grizzard, Kristy A
John Marshall HS
Oklahoma City, OK

Grizzle, Andre M
Broken Arrow Sr HS
Broken Arrow, OK

Grizzle, David R
Western Heights Sr HS
Oklahoma City, OK

Groehler, Brad W
Lindsay HS
Lindsay, OK

Groves, Coby
Edmond North HS
Edmond, OK

Guier, Christine N
Union Sr HS
Tulsa, OK

Guinn, Melissa A
Union Intermediate HS
Tulsa, OK

Guintebano, Maryjel P
Macarthur Sr HS
Lawton, OK

Gulledge, Justin A
Elgin HS
Elgin, OK

Gulley, Christopher
Midwest City HS
Midwest City, OK

Gustafson, Jessica J
Heritage Hall Schl
Oklahoma City, OK

Guthrie, Vindle
Kansas Schl
Kansas, OK

Habben Jr, Darrell
Perry Sr HS
Perry, OK

Haberly, Elizabeth Ann
Dewey HS
Dewey, OK

Hackathorn, William Dusty
Owasso Sr HS
Owasso, OK

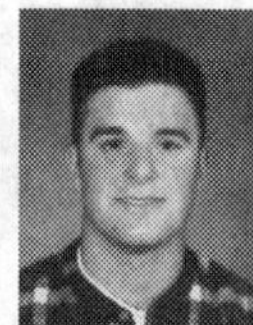
Hackler, Joseph
Claremore Sr HS
Claremore, OK

Hackworth, Justin E
Midwest City HS
Midwest City, OK

Haggard, Mark A
Union Intermediate HS
Tulsa, OK

Haggard, Sabrina M
Putnam City HS
Warr Acres, OK

Hague, Kirsten Kay
Cherokee Jr Sr HS
Cherokee, OK

Haile, Heidi
Mannford HS
Mannford, OK

Hakim, Melody A
West Middle HS
Norman, OK

Hakola, Lina S
Union Sr HS
Tulsa, OK

Halderman, Kimberly
Union Intermediate HS
Tulsa, OK

Haley, Erin
Mid-Del Christian Schl
Oklahoma City, OK

Hall, Amanda C
Shawnee Sr HS
Shawnee, OK

Hall, Debbie K
Sapulpa Sr HS
Sapulpa, OK

Hall, Erica
Douglass HS
Oklahoma City, OK

Hall, Jeffrey D
Eldorado Schl
Eldorado, OK

Hall, John
Cache HS
Lawton, OK

Hall, K Renee
Meeker HS
Sparks, OK

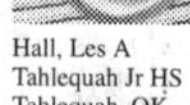
Hall, Les A
Tahlequah Jr HS
Tahlequah, OK

Hall, Lindsay A
Ripley HS
Ripley, OK

Hall, Lindsay R
Union Intermediate HS
Tulsa, OK

Hall, Melissa
Moore HS
Moore, OK

Hall, Stephanie D
Manford HS
Mannford, OK

Hall, Theresa
Nathan Hale HS
Tulsa, OK

Hames, Dodi D
Okmulgee HS
Okmulgee, OK

Hamill, Cecily E
Bishop Kelley HS
Tulsa, OK

Hamilton, April M
Moore HS
Oklahoma City, OK

Hamilton, Maci
Vinita HS
Vinita, OK

Hamm, Becky
Union Intermediate HS
Tulsa, OK

Hammarsten, Eric
Jenks HS
Tulsa, OK

Hampton, Adam
Dale Sr HS
Shawnee, OK

Hampton, Brandi
Hugo HS
Hugo, OK

Hampton, Shanna
Putnam City HS
Oklahoma City, OK

Hamrick, Ryan E
Del City HS
Del City, OK

Hamrick, Whitney B
Valliant HS
Valliant, OK

Han, Dara
Moore HS
Moore, OK

Han, Lira
Moore HS
Moore, OK

Hand, Andrew
Grace Fellowship Christian Sch
Broken Arrow, OK

Handshy, Tara A
U S Grant HS
Oklahoma City, OK

Haney, Christina R
Choctaw HS
Choctaw, OK

Haney, Mark
East Central HS
Tulsa, OK

Hanna, Kendra M
Del City HS
Del City, OK

Hanselman, Michelle R
Heavener HS
Heavener, OK

Hansen, De Anna Kim
Choctaw Jr HS
Choctaw, OK

Haragan, Sandra
Wilson HS
Wilson, OK

Harden Jr, Ronald D
Mc Lain Career Acad
Tulsa, OK

Hardin, Billy D
Bridge Creek HS
Tuttle, OK

Harding, April L
Broken Arrow Sr HS
Broken Arrow, OK

Hardy, Humphrey H
Ponca City Sr HS
Ponca City, OK

Hardy, Kenneth
Harrah HS
Harrah, OK

Hargrave, Robert L
Union Intermediate HS
Broken Arrow, OK

Hargrave, Sutinya R
Union Sr HS
Broken Arrow, OK

Hargrove, Brian L
Midwest City HS
Midwest City, OK

Harman, Terra R
Spiro HS
Spiro, OK

Harmon, Chrissy L
Shawnee Sr HS
Shawnee, OK

Harms, Cara
Christian Heritage Acad
Moore, OK

Harolds, Jennifer L
Edmond Santa Fe HS
Edmond, OK

Harper, Jana S
Colcord Schl
Colcord, OK

Harper, Jeremy M
Bridge Creek HS
Oklahoma City, OK

Harper, Stevi
Kellyville Sr HS
Kellyville, OK

Harper, Trevor
Midwest City HS
Midwest City, OK

Harrall, Crystal M
Catoosa HS
Catoosa, OK

Harrell, Heath
Crescent Schl
Crescent, OK

Harrington, Stacy L
Colcord Schl
Colcord, OK

Harris, Andrew C
Deer Creek HS
Edmond, OK

Harris, David
Tonkawa Jr Sr HS
Tonkawa, OK

Harris, Emily R
Choctaw HS
Choctaw, OK

Harris, Eric D
B T Washington HS
Tulsa, OK

Harris, Jennifer M
Southeast HS
Oklahoma City, OK

Harris, Lesli A
Glenpool HS
Glenpool, OK

Harris, Mark A
Bixby Sr HS
Bixby, OK

Harris, Michael S
Will Rogers HS
Tulsa, OK

Harris, Nykkia L
John Marshall HS
Oklahoma City, OK

Harris, Stephanie
Sapulpa Sr HS
Sapulpa, OK

Harris, Syreta J
Haskell HS
Haskell, OK

Harris, Theresa
John Marshall HS
Oklahoma City, OK

Harris, Tosha D
Byng Sr HS
Ada, OK

Harrison, Ashley
Beaver HS
Beaver, OK

Harrison, Ashley A
Mc Alester HS
Mcalester, OK

Harrison, Ben
Bethel Bapt Acad
Enid, OK

Harrison, Crystal L
Union Intermediate HS
Tulsa, OK

Harrison, Deeann
Ponca City Sr HS
Ponca City, OK

Harrison, Kelli
Okmulgee HS
Okmulgee, OK

Hart, J Travis
Mustang HS
Mustang, OK

Hart, Jennifer L
Union Intermediate HS
Tulsa, OK

Hart, Valerie N
Union Intermediate HS
Tulsa, OK

Hartin, Ronald B
Madill HS
Madill, OK

Harting, Ryan D
Stillwater Sr HS
Stillwater, OK

Hartley, Christina N
Wagoner Sr HS
Wagoner, OK

Hartley, Melissa S
Choctaw HS
Choctaw, OK

Hartman, Ashley D
Marietta HS
Marietta, OK

Hartman, Matthew S
Putnam City North HS
Oklahoma City, OK

Harvey, Nina L
Douglass HS
Oklahoma City, OK

Hashim, Ismael
Bartlesville Mid HS
Bartlesville, OK

Haskell, Joseph
Stigler HS
Stigler, OK

Haskett, Scott J
Midwest City HS
Midwest City, OK

Hast, Timothy M
Edmond North HS
Edmond, OK

Hastings, Amanda B
Union Sr HS
Broken Arrow, OK

Hatch, Angela L
Durant HS
Durant, OK

Hatcher, Justin B
Mustang HS
Mustang, OK

Hatfield, Shawn
Mustang HS
Mustang, OK

Hatfield, Tiffany
Edmond North HS
Edmond, OK

Hathaway,
Melinda Lee
Mc Loud HS
Newalla, OK

Hatley, Daniel A
Tecumseh HS
Shawnee, OK

Hauck, Jeffrey A
Westmoore HS
Oklahoma City, OK

Hawkins, Brad V
Edmond Santa Fe HS
Edmond, OK

Hawkins, Kourtney R
Millwood HS
Oklahoma City, OK

Hawkins, Leaha D
Ringling HS
Ringling, OK

Hawkins, Stephanie J
Broken Arrow Sr HS
Broken Arrow, OK

Hawley, Patrick H
Waynoka HS
Waynoka, OK

Haworth, Brandy L
Seminole Jr Sr HS
Seminole, OK

Haworth, Jon M
Enid Sr HS
Enid, OK

Hawthorne, William K
Altus Sr HS
Altus, OK

Hayes, Angelina C
Wagoner Sr HS
Wagoner, OK

Hayes, Matthew
Sapulpa Sr HS
Tulsa, OK

Hayes, Willie O
Elk City HS
Elk City, OK

Hays, Dustin T
Charles Page HS
Sand Springs, OK

Hayward, Patrick H
South Intermediate HS
Broken Arrow, OK

Hazlett, Tammy
Liberty Acad
Shawnee, OK

Head, Kasie L
Braman Schl
Braman, OK

Head, Mandy L
Bixby Sr HS
Broken Arrow, OK

Heald, Keith D
Harrah HS
Harrah, OK

Heard, Tyler M
Putnam City HS
Oklahoma City, OK

Heath, Korey M
Webster HS
Tulsa, OK

Heatherington,
Charles T
Sapulpa Sr HS
Sapulpa, OK

Heatherman, Terry
Cascia Hall Prep
School
Tulsa, OK

Heatrice, Alex
Midwest City HS
Oklahoma City, OK

Hebert, Jennifer J
Del City HS
Del City, OK

Heck, Bradley B
Tecumseh HS
Tecumseh, OK

Hedden, Audra R
Stillwater Sr HS
Cushing, OK

Heimdale, Brandon T
Nathan Hale HS
Tulsa, OK

Heitgrass Jr, Mark E
Jenks Road
Christian Acad
Broken Arrow, OK

Helfenbein, Brian K
Mc Alester HS
Mcalester, OK

Heller, Jo Ann
Bishop Kelley HS
Sapulpa, OK

Hellinger, Kim J
Wagoner Sr HS
Wagoner, OK

Helmbright, April E
Putnam City North HS
Oklahoma City, OK

Helms, Lisa
Plainview HS
Ardmore, OK

Hembree, Bryan C
Charles Page HS
Sand Springs, OK

OKLAHOMA

Hemme, Gregory W
Muskogee HS
Muskogee, OK

Hempfling, Chris G
Cimarron Public Schl
Lahoma, OK

Hendershot, Ashley D
Clayton Jr Sr HS
Clayton, OK

Henderson, Julie A
Heavener HS
Heavener, OK

Henderson, Lauren
Nicoma Park Jr HS
Midwest City, OK

Hendricks, Heather
Duncan HS
Duncan, OK

Hendrix, Jill R
Ponca City Sr HS
Ponca City, OK

Hendrix, Ricky
Foyil Schl
Claremore, OK

Hendryx, Danielle
Owasso Sr HS
Owasso, OK

Henley, Katy D
Mustang HS
Yukon, OK

Henley, Lana
Mustang HS
Yukon, OK

Hennigh, Carmencia A
Maud HS
Tecumseh, OK

Henning, Mark D
Del City HS
Del City, OK

Henry, Crystal G
South Coffeyville Schl
S Coffeyville, OK

Henry, Crystal L
Hammon Schl
Butler, OK

Henry, Erin E
Union Intermediate HS
Broken Arrow, OK

Henry, Staci L
Yukon Middle HS
Yukon, OK

Hensley, Sara
Sulphur HS
Sulphur, OK

Hensley, Sarah E
Union Intermediate HS
Tulsa, OK

Henson, C J
Watts HS
Watts, OK

Henson, Daya
Moore HS
Moore, OK

Henson, Jonathon M
Muldrow HS
Muldrow, OK

Hern, Kelly
Westville HS
Westville, OK

Hernandez, Gina
Plainview HS
Ardmore, OK

Hernandez, Sonia M
Mustang HS
Mustang, OK

Herndon, Sada
Oklahoma
Christian Schl
Edmond, OK

Herndon, Tricia R
East Central HS
Tulsa, OK

Herrera, Olivia
Norman Sr HS
Norman, OK

Herring, Bobby T
Henryetta Sr HS
Henryetta, OK

Herring, Kathryn R
Duncan HS
Duncan, OK

Hess, Emily A
West Middle HS
Norman, OK

Hester, Sandra
Westmoore HS
Moore, OK

Hiatt, Trina M
Kansas Schl
Kansas, OK

Hiatt-Frink, Nathan S
Tulsa Emmanuel
Christian Sch
Tulsa, OK

Hicks, Angela
Stratford Schl
Stratford, OK

Hicks, Cory
Odogah HS
Claremore, OK

Hicks, Heather D
Brink Jr HS
Oklahoma City, OK

Hicks, Heidi J
Mannford HS
Mannford, OK

Hicks, Jamie D
Blanchard Jr Sr HS
Blanchard, OK

Hicks, Jessica
Shawnee Sr HS
Shawnee, OK

Hiera, Jonathan J
Bishop Kelley HS
Tulsa, OK

Higgins, Joseph J
Yukon HS
Yukon, OK

Highsmith, Autumn
Tishomingo HS
Tishomingo, OK

Hightower, Leslie S
Byng Sr HS
Ada, OK

Hightower, Shana
Vinita HS
Vinita, OK

Hignite, Angela M
Union Sr HS
Tulsa, OK

Hignite, Matthew
Holdenville HS
Atwood, OK

Hilaire, Eric P
Putnam City HS
Oklahoma City, OK

Hilburn, Leah
Plainview HS
Ardmore, OK

Hileman, Alisha C
Shawnee Sr HS
Shawnee, OK

Hill, Amanda
Edmond North HS
Edmond, OK

Hill, Bradley S
Davis HS
Davis, OK

Hill, Carrie E
West Middle HS
Norman, OK

Hill, Courtney
Ponca City Sr HS
Ponca City, OK

Hill, Jacinta
Millwood HS
Oklahoma City, OK

Hill, Jeffrey A
Balko Public Schl
Balko, OK

Hill, Kristen
Pryor Sr HS
Pryor, OK

Hill, Kyle
Stilwell HS
Stilwell, OK

Hill III, Tony J
Owasso Sr HS
Collinsville, OK

Hill, Trisha
Glenpool HS
Tulsa, OK

Hillebrand, Ronny
Stuart Sr HS
Stuart, OK

Hilliard, Justin J
Sulphur HS
Sulphur, OK

Hilton, Stephen M
Wilburton Sr HS
Wilburton, OK

Hines, Billy J
Valliant HS
Valliant, OK

Hines, La Shanda J
Lindsay HS
Lindsay, OK

Hininger, Justin
Woodward HS
Woodward, OK

Hinkston, Shannaedi D
Del City HS
Del City, OK

Hinman, Alissa
Mustang HS
Mustang, OK

Hinshaw, Deanna J
Ponca City Sr HS
Ponca City, OK

Hitchings, Mandy D
Boise City HS
Texhoma, OK

Hixon, Bobbi Sue
Apache HS
Apache, OK

Ho, Eric
Stillwater Jr HS
Stillwater, OK

Hoang, Rosemary P
Putnam City North HS
Oklahoma City, OK

Hoang, Vivian
Bishop Kelley HS
Tulsa, OK

Hobaugh, Jessica E
Nathan Hale HS
Tulsa, OK

Hobbs, Amanda
Del Crest Jr HS
Del City, OK

Hodge, Amanda
Tulsa Emmanuel
Christian Sch
Tulsa, OK

Hodge, Amber N
Hammon Schl
Hammon, OK

Hodge, Brian K
Caddo HS
Caddo, OK

Hodge, Mike
Tulsa Emmanuel
Christian Sch
Tulsa, OK

Hodges, Allison D
Putnam City HS
Oklahoma City, OK

Hodges, Ryan N
Mustang HS
Yukon, OK

Hodgson, Skye S
Buffalo Jr Sr HS
Buffalo, OK

Hofen, Scott
Waynoka HS
Waynoka, OK

Hofferber, Melissa
Hooker Jr-Sr HS
Hooker, OK

Hoffman, Kelly
Mc Alester HS
Mcalester, OK

Hoffman, Michael C
Edmond Memorial HS
Duluth, MN

Hogle, Abby
Hilldale HS
Muskogee, OK

Hoke, Eric W
Western Heights Sr HS
Oklahoma City, OK

Hoke, Jeffrey M
Yukon Middle HS
Yukon, OK

Holden, Meghan M
Duncan HS
Duncan, OK

Holland, M Kent
Snyder HS
Snyder, OK

Holland, M Raylee
Westmoore HS
Oklahoma City, OK

Holleman, Katy
Okmulgee HS
Okmulgee, OK

Holliday, Amy
Guthrie Sr HS
Guthrie, OK

Hollingsworth, Ashley
Ponca City Sr HS
Ponca City, OK

Hollis, Gwendolyn M
Blackwell HS
Blackwell, OK

Hollis, Stacey L
Charles Page HS
Sand Springs, OK

Holloway, Nathan J
Bethany HS
Bethany, OK

Holloway, Stephanie
Stuart Public Schls
Mcalester, OK

Holman, Jason
Altus Sr HS
Altus, OK

Holman, Robert
Altus Sr HS
Altus, OK

Holmes, Kendra
Jenks HS
Tulsa, OK

Hologe, Amy E
Ft Cobb-Broxton HS
Carnegie, OK

Holsted, Kristi M
Mustang HS
Mustang, OK

Holstine, Stephanie L
Stringtown HS
Atoka, OK

Holt, Brandon
Midwest City HS
Midwest City, OK

Holt, Jordan J
Union Intermediate HS
Tulsa, OK

Honea, Christopher
Midwest City HS
Midwest City, OK

Honeycutt, Danielle C
Roland Sr HS
Roland, OK

Honeyfield, Gerad G
Minco HS
El Reno, OK

Hood, Andy S
South Intermediate HS
Broken Arrow, OK

Hooper, Aubrey M
Putnam City North HS
Oklahoma City, OK

Hoose, Randy D
Warner HS
Warner, OK

Hoosier, Heather A
Lone Grove HS
Ardmore, OK

Hoover, Rachel A
Union Sr HS
Tulsa, OK

Hopcus, Candice A
Choctaw HS
Choctaw, OK

Hopkins, Amanda D
Rock Creek Jr Sr HS
Bennington, OK

Hopkins, Cheyenne
Eufaula Sr HS
Eufaula, OK

Hopper, Michelle R
Mustang HS
Yukon, OK

Horan, Brian K
North Intemediate HS
Broken Arrow, OK

Horgan, Colleen E
Waukomis HS
Enid, OK

Horges, La Tonya
Jarman Jr HS
Oklahoma City, OK

Horn, Jill
Haworth Jr HS
Haworth, OK

Horne, Bradley K
Madill HS
Madill, OK

Horner, Sandy M
Byng Sr HS
Ada, OK

Horstman, Timothy S
Whitesboro Schl
Hodgen, OK

Horton, Joshua D
Wright Christian Acad
Owasso, OK

Houck, April L
Jay HS
Jay, OK

Hough, Eric E
South Intermediate HS
Broken Arrow, OK

Hough, James
Broken Arrow Sr HS
Broken Arrow, OK

Houghton, Rachel M
Edmond North HS
Edmond, OK

Hourigan, Natalie N
Bartlesville Sr HS
Bartlesville, OK

House, Isaac C
Nathan Hale HS
Tulsa, OK

Houser, Robin A
Western Heights Sr HS
Yukon, OK

Housley, Adam
Metro Christian Acad
Broken Arrow, OK

Housley, Heather
Metro Christian Acad
Broken Arrow, OK

Housley, Melissa L
Sapulpa Sr HS
Sapulpa, OK

Houston, Hillary D
Mustang HS
Mustang, OK

Houston, Richard
Lawton Sr HS
Lawton, OK

OKLAHOMA

Howard, Brett
Choctaw HS
Midwest City, OK

Howard, Crystal D
Muskogee HS
Muskogee, OK

Howard, Justin B
Midwest City HS
Del City, OK

Howard, Mary
Moore HS
Moore, OK

Howard, Pam
Liberty Acad
Shawnee, OK

Howard, Terrell L
Carl Albert HS
Midwest City, OK

Howe, Jessica
Miami Sr HS
Miami, OK

Howell, Jeremy J
Edmond Santa Fe HS
Edmond, OK

Howell, Leslie L
Muldrow HS
Muldrow, OK

Howell, Ren'Naldo S
Will Rogers HS
Tulsa, OK

Howell, Skye N
Hominy HS
Hominy, OK

Howerton, Clay A
Stillwater Jr HS
Stillwater, OK

Howlingwolf, Dena L
Arapaho Schl
Arapaho, OK

Howsden, Jaime
Oklahoma
Christian Schl
Edmond, OK

Howze, Sheldon S
Duke Schl
Duke, OK

Hoyle, Clifton E
Pauls Valley HS
Pauls Valley, OK

Hrubik, Andrew
Moore HS
Moore, OK

Hubbard, Jeremy L
Enid Sr HS
Enid, OK

Hubbard, John D
Claremore Sr HS
Chelsea, OK

Huckaby, Whitney L
Ninnekah HS
Blanchard, OK

Huddleston, Jeff
Kingston HS
Kingston, OK

Hudson, Heather R
North Intemediate HS
Broken Arrow, OK

Hudson, Rachelle
Union Intermediate HS
Tulsa, OK

Hueste, Meaghan
Berryhill Jr HS
Tulsa, OK

Huff, Talitha J
Union Sr HS
Tulsa, OK

Huffman, Alana R
Putnam City North HS
Oklahoma City, OK

Huffstutlar, Patrisha L
Calumet Schl
Calumet, OK

Hughes, Kelvin
Midwest City HS
Oklahoma City, OK

Hughes, Lindsay C
North Intemediate HS
Broken Arrow, OK

Hughes, Rebecca A
South Intermediate HS
Broken Arrow, OK

Hula, Jennifer R
Charles Page HS
Sand Springs, OK

Hull, Carinne M
Mustang HS
Mustang, OK

Hultman, Katrin
Chandler HS
Chandler, OK

Humphreys, Brad
Hinton HS
Hinton, OK

Humphries, Tammi
Yukon Mid HS
Yukon, OK

Hunnicutt, Jaci D
Brink Jr HS
Oklahoma City, OK

Hunt, Greg A
Memorial HS
Tulsa, OK

Hunt, Kholter J
Claremore Sr HS
Claremore, OK

Hunt, Micah L
Norman Sr HS
Norman, OK

Hunt, Michael E
Wagoner Sr HS
Wagoner, OK

Hunter, Chase V
Bethany HS
Oklahoma City, OK

Hunter, Leslie R
Woodward HS
Woodward, OK

Huntsinger, Kevin S
Broken Arrow Sr HS
Broken Arrow, OK

Hurry, Jennifer R
Union Sr HS
Broken Arrow, OK

Hurst, Brandi L
Webster HS
Oakhurst, OK

Hurst, Rashay
Carl Albert HS
Oklahoma City, OK

Hurst, Staci L
El Reno Sr HS
El Reno, OK

Hurt, Christi L
Midwest City HS
Midwest City, OK

Husain, Aisha
Union Sr HS
Broken Arrow, OK

Hutchison, Jeff
Bartlesville Sr HS
Bartlesville, OK

Hutsell, Alisha G
Union Sr HS
Tulsa, OK

Hutson, Johnathan
Coweta HS
Coweta, OK

Hutson, Kristen M
Chattanooga Schl
Chattanooga, OK

Hutson, Matthew
Ponca City Sr HS
Ponca City, OK

Hyde III, H Clark
Casady Schl
Oklahoma City, OK

Hyden, Jeff C
Moore HS
Oklahoma City, OK

Hynd, Eric
Guthrie Sr HS
Edmond, OK

Ibarra, Humberta
Douglass HS
Oklahoma City, OK

Igbre, Ann
Jenks HS
Tulsa, OK

Iliff III, Charles E
Mannford HS
Mannford, OK

Immonen, Erkko K
Hilldale HS
Muskogee, OK

Indermill, Seth T
Bartlesville Sr HS
Bartlesville, OK

Ingram, Chad B
Moore HS
Moore, OK

Ingram, Joy
Putnam City HS
Oklahoma City, OK

Inman, Josh
Bethany HS
Warr Acres, OK

Ireland, Craig
Stillwater Sr HS
Stillwater, OK

Irick, John M
Strother Jr Sr HS
Seminole, OK

Irwin, Holly M
Ponca City Sr HS
Ponca City, OK

Irwin, Holly Nicole
Purcell HS
Purcell, OK

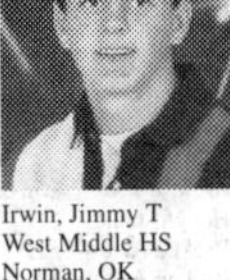
Irwin, Jimmy T
West Middle HS
Norman, OK

OKLAHOMA

Isaac, Melissa
Eufaula Sr HS
Eufaula, OK

Isaacs, Eric A
Charles Page HS
Sand Springs, OK

Ivery, Audra D
Bartlesville Mid HS
Bartlesville, OK

Ivery, Krishaunda L
Mt St Marys HS
Spencer, OK

Ives, Bart F
Buffalo Jr Sr HS
Buffalo, OK

Ivey, Christopher W
Cimarron Public Schl
Enid, OK

Ivy, Jennifer N
Union Intermediate HS
Tulsa, OK

Jack, Lanissa S
Dustin Schl
Hanna, OK

Jacks, Jeanie
Altus Sr HS
Altus, OK

Jackson, Andrea Dawn
Charles Page HS
Sapulpa, OK

Jackson, Benjamin J
Elk City Jr HS
Elk City, OK

Jackson, Jeana M
Davis HS
Davis, OK

Jackson, Kara L
Duncan HS
Duncan, OK

Jackson, Patrick R
Broken Arrow Sr HS
Broken Arrow, OK

Jackson, Quiana M
Muskogee HS
Muskogee, OK

Jackson, Tameka N
Star Spencer HS
Spencer, OK

Jackson, Tara
Edmond North HS
Edmond, OK

Jacobs, Albert Jamaal
Okmulgee HS
Okmulgee, OK

Jacobs, Julie E
Okmulgee HS
Okmulgee, OK

Jacobs, Nyisha S
Rodgers
Del City HS
Oklahoma City, OK

Jacobson, Doug
Clinton HS
Clinton, OK

Jacobson, Lucas
Pauls Valley HS
Pocasset, OK

Jacoby, Erich T
Yukon Middle HS
Yukon, OK

Jacoby, Shannon M
B T Washington HS
Tulsa, OK

Jacocks, Eric A
Edmond Memorial HS
Edmond, OK

Jadlow, Joanna C
Stillwater Sr HS
Stillwater, OK

Jamar, Chad
Ft Gibson HS
Fort Gibson, OK

Jamerson, Sundris C
Putnam City North HS
Oklahoma City, OK

James, Amanda L
Mc Alester HS
Mcalester, OK

James, Danesa
Dickson HS
Mannsville, OK

James, Elizabeth
Dale Sr HS
Shawnee, OK

James, Jennell
Bray-Doyle HS
Marlow, OK

James, Jessi L
Boise City HS
Boise City, OK

James, Nathan N
El Reno Sr HS
El Reno, OK

James, Ricky F
Sapulpa Sr HS
Sapulpa, OK

James, Wayne S
El Reno Sr HS
El Reno, OK

Jamison, Amy
Broken Arrow Sr HS
Broken Arrow, OK

Janssen, Emily
Putnam City HS
Warr Acres, OK

Jarnagin, Dustin L
Carnegie HS
Carnegie, OK

Jarrell, Andrea
Cordell Sr HS
Cordell, OK

Jarvis, Kristopher D
Union Sr HS
Broken Arrow, OK

Jasim, Angela M
East Central HS
Coweta, OK

Jaszkowiak, Alison
Moore HS
Moore, OK

Javed, Najwa
Union Intermediate HS
Broken Arrow, OK

Jedelhauser, Rita S
Ninnekah HS
Ninnekah, OK

Jefferson, Jeffrey L
Midwest City HS
Oklahoma City, OK

Jefferson, Natalie R
Broken Bow HS
Broken Bow, OK

Jeffries, Elise
Ponca City Mid HS
Ponca City, OK

Jeffries, Tisha A
Blackwell HS
Ponca City, OK

Jelinek, Christopher
Choctaw HS
Midwest City, OK

Jenkins, Kara L
Bethany HS
Oklahoma City, OK

Jennings, Angela
Stigler HS
Stigler, OK

Jennings, Kerry L
El Reno Sr HS
Moore, OK

Jeon, Dong S
Union Intermediate HS
Broken Arrow, OK

Jernigan, Jimmy H
Heritage Hall Schl
Oklahoma City, OK

Jerry, Marcus
Moore HS
Moore, OK

Jetton, Robert
Roland Sr HS
Roland, OK

Jewell, Jennifer K
Westmoore HS
Oklahoma City, OK

Jewett, Amy
Verden HS
Verden, OK

Johannessen, Ashley
Plainview HS
Ardmore, OK

Johnson, Aimee
Westmoore HS
Oklahoma City, OK

Johnson, Alesha G
Yukon Middle HS
Yukon, OK

Johnson, Amelia C
Velma Alma HS
Loco, OK

Johnson, Calista C
Wright City Jr Sr HS
Garvin, OK

Johnson, Chesse
Broken Arrow Sr HS
Broken Arrow, OK

Johnson, Dan L
Parker Middle HS
Krebs, OK

Johnson, Doug M
Bixby Sr HS
Broken Arrow, OK

Johnson, Eraina M
Will Rogers HS
Tulsa, OK

Johnson, Eric M
Davis HS
Davis, OK

Johnson, Floyd A
Southeast HS
Oklahoma City, OK

OKLAHOMA

Johnson, Ingrid L
Edmond Memorial HS
Edmond, OK

Johnson, James
Wetumka Jr Sr HS
Wetumka, OK

Johnson, Jamie
U S Grant HS
Oklahoma City, OK

Johnson, Janie J
Mooreland Jr Sr HS
Mooreland, OK

Johnson, Jeremiah D
Nathan Hale HS
Tulsa, OK

Johnson, Jessica A
South Intermediate HS
Broken Arrow, OK

Johnson III, Jimmy G
Westmore HS
Oklahoma City, OK

Johnson, John A
Stilwell HS
Stilwell, OK

Johnson, Julie
Midwest City HS
Midwest City, OK

Johnson, Kimberly T
Central Jr HS
Fort Sill, OK

Johnson, Matthew B
Putnam City North HS
Oklahoma City, OK

Johnson, Michelle
Bowlegs Schl
Bowlegs, OK

Johnson, Natalie
Edmond North HS
Edmond, OK

Johnson, Neesha
Hartshorne Sr HS
Haileyville, OK

Johnson, Quincy L
Northeast HS
Oklahoma City, OK

Johnson, Rebecca L
Claremore Sr HS
Claremore, OK

Johnson, Scott R
Alva HS
Alva, OK

Johnson, Shalonda C
Idabel HS
Idabel, OK

Johnson, Stephanie
Deer Creek HS
Edmond, OK

Johnson, Tara I
Frontier Public Schl
Red Rock, OK

Johnston, Amanda D
Union Intermediate HS
Tulsa, OK

Johnston, Ann Marie
Heritage Hall Schl
Oklahoma City, OK

Johnston, Susan
Blackwell HS
Blackwell, OK

Jolley, Amber N
Central Mid-HS
Norman, OK

Jones, Amanda
Broken Arrow
South HS
Broken Arrow, OK

Jones, Amber
Guthrie Sr HS
Guthrie, OK

Jones, Angela R
Mt St Marys HS
Midwest City, OK

Jones, Bethany Denice
Charles Page HS
Sand Springs, OK

Jones, Candace
Barnsdall Jr Sr HS
Wynona, OK

Jones, Carissa J
Union Intermediate HS
Broken Arrow, OK

Jones, David M
Tahlequah Sr HS
Tahlequah, OK

Jones, Desiree A
Union Intermediate HS
Tulsa, OK

Jones, Desty D
Lindsay HS
Lindsay, OK

Jones, Jennifer E
Enid Sr HS
Enid, OK

Jones, Kara
Charles Page HS
Skiatook, OK

Jones, Lezlie A
Vinita HS
Vinita, OK

Jones, Lindsey
Guyman HS
Guymon, OK

Jones, Michael
Stratford Schl
Stratford, OK

Jones, Mindy J
Shattuck Jr Sr HS
Shattuck, OK

Jones, Nancy C
Grove HS
Grove, OK

Jones, Preston D
South Intermediate HS
Broken Arrow, OK

Jones, Rashael
Meeker HS
Meeker, OK

Jones, Savannah L
Claremore Sr HS
Claremore, OK

Jones, Sheila A
Haskell HS
Haskell, OK

Jones, Terina
Merritt Schl
Elk City, OK

Jones, Tiffany
Douglass HS
Oklahoma City, OK

Jones, Touissaint L
Coyle Public Schl
Langston, OK

Jones, Tracey
Arkoma Jr Sr HS
Arkoma, OK

Jones, Tracy
Westmoore HS
Moore, OK

Jordan, Michael
Moore HS
Moore, OK

Jordan, Sandra
Re Anna
Owasso Sr HS
Sperry, OK

Jordan, Tony
Midwest City HS
Midwest City, OK

Josefy, Shana J
Big Pasture HS
Grandfield, OK

Joy, Jesse Z
Putnam City West HS
Oklahoma City, OK

Juckes, Steve
Ponca City Sr HS
Ponca City, OK

Juergenson, Mari K
Memorial HS
Tulsa, OK

July, Danny R
Checotah HS
Checotah, OK

Jumpa, Ashley A
Colbert Jr Sr HS
Cartwright, OK

Junger, Nicholas A
Will Rogers HS
Tulsa, OK

Justice, A
Eisenhower Sr HS
Lawton, OK

Kalinich, Kristi
Holdenville Jr HS
Holdenville, OK

Kalmbach, Kris
Cascia Hall Prep
School
Tulsa, OK

Kana, Alyssa R
Healdton HS
Healdton, OK

Kappelman, Jessica L
Choctaw HS
Choctaw, OK

Karber, J D
Fairview HS
Fairview, OK

Karnes, Rana M
Shattuck Jr Sr HS
Shattuck, OK

Kasiner, Jinger N
Sapulpa Sr HS
Sapulpa, OK

Kaulaity Jr, Henry J
Mountain
View-Gotebo HS
Mountain View, OK

Kays, Gena E
B T Washington HS
Tulsa, OK

Kearney II, Robert H
Central Jr HS
Lawton, OK

Keefe II, John P
American
Christian Acad
Oklahoma City, OK

Keel, Courtney B
Edmond North HS
Edmond, OK

Keen, Christina L
Ponca City Sr HS
Ponca City, OK

Keeton, Christina M
Enid Sr HS
Enid, OK

Keffer, Nicole R
U S Grant HS
Oklahoma City, OK

Keim, Lenice
Coweta HS
Coweta, OK

Keith, Ashley
Jenks HS
Tulsa, OK

Keleher, Katy
Edmond North HS
Edmond, OK

Keller, Kenneth L
Putnam City West HS
Warr Acres, OK

Kelley, Jamie R
Del City HS
Del City, OK

Kelley, Kristy A
Del City HS
Del City, OK

Kelley, Stephanie A
Geronimo Jr Sr HS
Duncan, OK

Kelliher, Sarah J
Bishop Kelley HS
Tulsa, OK

Kelly, Aron
Holdenville HS
Holdenville, OK

Kelly, Doug B
Bartlesville Sr HS
Bartlesville, OK

Kelly, Jeff
Edmond North HS
Edmond, OK

Kelly, Jelani Renauld
Jamor
Oklahoma
Christian Schl
Oklahoma City, OK

Kelso, Crystal
Guthrie Sr HS
Guthrie, OK

Kelso, Kimberly D
West Jr HS
Oklahoma City, OK

Kemper, Cyndy D
Woodward HS
Woodward, OK

Kemper, Jason
Woodward HS
Woodward, OK

Kendall, Jarrod D
East Central HS
Tulsa, OK

Kennedy, Cassie
Guthrie Sr HS
Guthrie, OK

Kennedy, Penelope M
El Reno Sr HS
El Reno, OK

Kennedy, Trina M
Del City HS
Oklahoma City, OK

Kennedy, Wes D
Brink Jr HS
Oklahoma City, OK

Kennell, Christopher R
Ninnekah HS
Chickasha, OK

Kenney, John Graham
Bishop Mcguinness HS
Oklahoma City, OK

Kern, Joi I
Western Heights Sr HS
Oklahoma City, OK

Kerr, Kassandra J L
Calumet Schl
Calumet, OK

Kessler, Anna S
Charles Page HS
Sand Springs, OK

Key, Brian A
Union Sr HS
Tulsa, OK

Keyser, Kristie
Collinsville HS
Collinsville, OK

Kiddy, Christina D
Nathan Hale HS
Tulsa, OK

Kilburg, Sarah K
Will Rogers HS
Tulsa, OK

Killgore, Clint W
Sallisaw HS
Sallisaw, OK

Killingsworth,
Carmen N
El Reno Sr HS
El Reno, OK

Killman, David N
Ponca City Sr HS
Ponca City, OK

Kincannon, Erin
Boise City HS
Boise City, OK

Kinder, Jennifer E
B T Washington HS
Tulsa, OK

Kindsfather, Ricky L
Clinton HS
Clinton, OK

King, Britney M
Indiahoma Schl
Indiahoma, OK

King, Bryan
Coweta HS
Coweta, OK

King, Bryan J
Putnam City West HS
Bethany, OK

King, Cherish
Madill HS
Madill, OK

King, Christie
Bartlesville Mid HS
Bartlesville, OK

King, Eric T
Northeast HS
Midwest City, OK

King, Jamie
Moore HS
Moore, OK

King, Jamie L
Bixby Sr HS
Bixby, OK

King, Jennifer
Stratford Schl
Stratford, OK

King, Rebecca A
Tahlequah Sr HS
Tahlequah, OK

Kinkaid, Kelli
Ponca City Sr HS
Ponca City, OK

Kinsey, Austin
Fairland Jr Sr HS
Fairland, OK

Kinzie, Kristopher D
Cushing HS
Cushing, OK

Kinzie, Olivia
Cushing HS
Cushing, OK

Kirby, Craig M
Barltesville HS
Bartlesville, OK

Kirby, Jessica
Newcastle HS
Newcastle, OK

Kirby, Melissa
Jenks HS
Tulsa, OK

Kirby, Sandra
Stilwell HS
Stilwell, OK

Kirchner, Justin
Pawhuska HS
Pawhuska, OK

Kirchner, Melissa J
Ponca City Sr HS
Ponca City, OK

Kirkland,
Christopher D
Mc Alester HS
Mcalester, OK

Kirkpatrick, Holly
Pond
Creek-Hunter Schl
Pond Creek, OK

Kitchel, Ashley V
Pawhuska HS
Pawhuska, OK

Kitchens, Julie A
Christian
Heritage Acad
Oklahoma City, OK

Kite, Amber D
Parker Middle HS
Mcalester, OK

Kite, Christine
Douglass HS
Oklahoma City, OK

Kite, Erica D
Enid Sr HS
Enid, OK

Kitzrow, Emily S
Lawton Sr HS
Lawton, OK

Kizer, Shanna L
Pocola HS
Pocola, OK

OKLAHOMA

Kleopfer, Michael H
North Intemediate HS
Broken Arrow, OK

Kletzker, Tamara
Grace Fellowship
Christian Sch
Broken Arrow, OK

Knapp, Amber M
Union Intermediate HS
Tulsa, OK

Knigge, Kristen A
Will Rogers HS
Tulsa, OK

Knight, Aimee
Shawnee Sr HS
Shawnee, OK

Knight, Ryan Seth
Guthrie Sr HS
Edmond, OK

Knopp, Deanna R
Okeene Jr Sr HS
Okeene, OK

Knowles, Rodney A
Nathan Hale HS
Tulsa, OK

Koch, Kimberly F
Edmond Santa Fe HS
Edmond, OK

Koester, G Andrew
Piedmont HS
Piedmont, OK

Kolker, Tracie E
Choctaw HS
Choctaw, OK

Koman, Thea Zoe
Mustang HS
Oklahoma City, OK

Koos, Erin A
Classen Schl
Oklahoma City, OK

Kopleman, James
Claremore Sr HS
Claremore, OK

Kownacki, Sarah L
Bishop Kelley HS
Tulsa, OK

Kraft, Cena
Woodward HS
Woodward, OK

Kreutzer, Verna L
Glenpool HS
Glenpool, OK

Krittenbrink, Mandi P
Wellston Schl
Wellston, OK

Kriz, Adam G
Geronimo Jr Sr HS
Geronimo, OK

Kroutil, Ryan
Mustang HS
Mustang, OK

Krumm, Stephen A
Skiatook HS
Skiatook, OK

Kubilis, Roger
Reydon HS
Reydon, OK

Kucko, Leslie D
Western Heights Sr HS
Oklahoma City, OK

Kuhlman, Leslie
Edmond Memorial HS
Edmond, OK

Kulp, David V
Holland Hall Schl
Tulsa, OK

Kunze, Jay
Dale Sr HS
Shawnee, OK

Kursar, Kellie
Shawnee Sr HS
Shawnee, OK

Kusel, Jamie
Ft Cobb-Broxton HS
Fort Cobb, OK

Kyle, Kendel K
Lone Grove HS
Ardmore, OK

Kyle, Latasha
Central HS
Tulsa, OK

Labass, Lauren E
Okmulgee HS
Okmulgee, OK

Lacey, Gibran I
Southeast HS
Oklahoma City, OK

Lacey, Kristi L
Union Sr HS
Broken Arrow, OK

Lacey, Starr
Metro Christian Acad
Sand Springs, OK

Lacourse, Jennifer
Midwest City HS
Midwest City, OK

Ladner, Jennifer L
B T Washington HS
Tulsa, OK

Lafferty, Chad W
Bethany HS
Oklahoma City, OK

Lake, Warren
Mustang HS
Yukon, OK

Lalli, Angelena M
Mc Alester HS
Mcalester, OK

Lam, Julie K
Brink Jr HS
Oklahoma City, OK

Lamar, Stephen J
North Intemediate HS
Broken Arrow, OK

Lamb, Jeremy L
Life Chrstn HS
Mc Loud, OK

Lamb, Larry K
Asher Schl
Asher, OK

Lamb, Lori
Stillwater Sr HS
Stillwater, OK

Lamb, Misty D
Union Intermediate HS
Tulsa, OK

Lambertus, Michelle P
Midwest City HS
Midwest City, OK

Lamebull, Kristie J
El Reno Sr HS
El Reno, OK

Lampkin, Lanett B
Wister Schl
Wister, OK

Landers, Lyle
Collinsville HS
Collinsville, OK

Landis, Kim
Putnam City HS
Oklahoma City, OK

Landrrum, April L
Oklahoma Bible Acad
Waukomis, OK

Landsverk, Karry M
Union Intermediate HS
Tulsa, OK

Lane, Craig S
Choctaw HS
Del City, OK

Lane, Donald J
West Middle HS
Norman, OK

Lane, Misty R
Altus Sr HS
Altus, OK

Lane, Sara
Duncan HS
Duncan, OK

Lang, Lesley V
Edmond Memorial HS
Edmond, OK

Langham, Dusty L
Rush Springs HS
Rush Springs, OK

Langley, Eric
Hugo HS
Hugo, OK

Langston, Casey M
Muskogee HS
Muskogee, OK

Lann, David J
Norman Sr HS
Norman, OK

Lansford, Elizabeth
U S Grant HS
Oklahoma City, OK

La Pierre, Melissa
Macarthur Jr HS
Elgin, OK

Large, Robert Blake
Durant HS
Durant, OK

Larrison, Brian J
Mc Loud HS
Mc Loud, OK

La Rue, Preston W
U S Grant HS
Oklahoma City, OK

Lasiter, Aron
Gans Public Schl
Muldrow, OK

Lassiter, Jolie
Stigler HS
Stigler, OK

Lau, Crystal
Stroud HS
Cushing, OK

Laufer, Chris
Elk City HS
Elk City, OK

Lawrence, Shamesha L
Del City HS
Oklahoma City, OK

Lawson, Amber L
South Intermediate HS
Broken Arrow, OK

Lawson, April
Durant HS
Durant, OK

Lawson, Nicholas R
Heritage Chrstn Schl
Ardmore, OK

Lawson, Wendy
Durant HS
Durant, OK

Layman, Diana D
Vinita HS
Vinita, OK

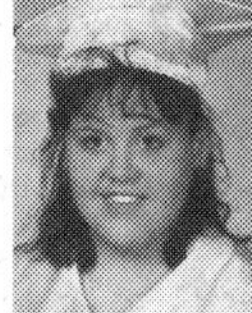
Laymon, Tonya
Braggs Schl
Braggs, OK

Layton, Matt D
Lindsay HS
Lindsay, OK

Le, Diana N
Westmoore HS
Oklahoma City, OK

Leaman, Jarrod A
Moore HS
Moore, OK

Ledbetter, Drew
Checotah HS
Checotah, OK

Lee, Amanda
Jenks HS
Tulsa, OK

Lee, Angela L
Okay Jr Sr HS
Okay, OK

Lee, Ann M
Shawnee Sr HS
Shawnee, OK

Lee, Ben
Plainview HS
Ardmore, OK

Lee, Brandi E
Moore West Jr HS
Oklahoma City, OK

Lee, Desiree D
Union Sr HS
Tulsa, OK

Lee, Jeffrey W
El Reno Sr HS
El Reno, OK

Lee, Jeremy B
Haskell HS
Taft, OK

Lee, Josh D
Vinita HS
Vinita, OK

Lee, Kenneth W
Haskell HS
Taft, OK

Lee, Lindsey
Edmond North HS
Edmond, OK

Lee, Loretta E
Emerson Jr HS
Enid, OK

Lee, Nicholas E
Tecumseh HS
Shawnee, OK

Lee, Steph
Guthrie Sr HS
Guthrie, OK

Leebron, Dresden A
Edmond North HS
Edmond, OK

Le Grand, Jamie L
Jay HS
Eucha, OK

Lehman, Curtis N
Bartlesville Sr HS
Bartlesville, OK

Leisy Jr, Tommy J
Westmoore HS
Oklahoma City, OK

Lelkes, Anne-Marie T
Duncan HS
Duncan, OK

Le Moine, Piper
Jenks HS
Jenks, OK

Lenard, Johnny Buster
Wagoner Sr HS
Wagoner, OK

Lenk, Cynthia D
Putnam City West HS
Bethany, OK

Lentz, Lynette
Empire Schl
Duncan, OK

Leon, John
Moore HS
Oklahoma City, OK

Leonard, Stormy B
Claremore Sr HS
Claremore, OK

Lepak, Adam
Moore HS
Moore, OK

Levings, Stacy L
Tahlequah Sr HS
Hulbert, OK

Levins, Lesley S
Durant HS
Durant, OK

Lewellen, Justin T
Choctaw HS
Choctaw, OK

Lewis, Amber
Moore HS
Moore, OK

Lewis, Angela D
Ripley HS
Stillwater, OK

Lewis, Brodie D
Woodward HS
Woodward, OK

Lewis, Brooklyn
Plainview HS
Ardmore, OK

Lewis, David A
Choctaw HS
Midwest City, OK

Lewis, Denise M
Owasso Sr HS
Owasso, OK

Lewis, James R
Boswell Sr HS
Atoka, OK

Lewis, Jennifer
Yale Jr Sr HS
Yale, OK

Lewis, Matt B
Will Rogers HS
Tulsa, OK

Lewis, Micah
Clinton HS
Clinton, OK

Lewis, Nicki L
Westmoore HS
Oklahoma City, OK

Lewis, Sean M
Claremore Sr HS
Claremore, OK

Lewis, Seth A
Putnam City North HS
Oklahoma City, OK

Lienke, Genevieve M
Bishop Mcguinness HS
Oklahoma City, OK

Lightfoot, Jennifer L
Norman Sr HS
Norman, OK

Lightfoot, Luke
Oklahoma
Christian Schl
Edmond, OK

Lightfoot, Will
Oklahoma
Christian Schl
Edmond, OK

Lillie, Vanessa
Miami Sr HS
Miami, OK

Lindenberg,
Katherine L
South Intermediate HS
Broken Arrow, OK

Lindley, Bryan J
Hinton HS
Hinton, OK

Lindsay, Michelle
Union City Schl
El Reno, OK

Lindsey, Eric M
Stillwater Sr HS
Stillwater, OK

Lindsey, Josh M
Forgan Schl
Forgan, OK

Linduff, Lindsey N
South Intermediate HS
Broken Arrow, OK

Linduff, Marcie B
Yukon Middle HS
Yukon, OK

Linn, Dee J
Frontier Public Schl
Red Rock, OK

Linn, Ginny G
Chandler HS
Chandler, OK

Lipham, Amanda A
Canton HS
Longdale, OK

Lira, Gabriel J
South Intermediate HS
Broken Arrow, OK

Lister, Dawn M
Elk City HS
Elk City, OK

Littlefield, Melanie
Adair HS
Vinita, OK

Littlejohn, Kevin W
Idabel HS
Idabel, OK

Littleton, Brad R
Tahlequah Sr HS
Tahlequah, OK

Lively, Danielle
Blackwell HS
Blackwell, OK

Livingston, Brandi M
Bluejacket Schl
Bluejacket, OK

Livingston, Chris
Oologah HS
Oologah, OK

Lloyd, Micki
Leflore Sr HS
Leflore, OK

Loch, Crissi A
Ponca City Sr HS
Ponca City, OK

Locke, John
Poteau HS
Poteau, OK

Lockhart, Melanie
Stillwater Sr HS
Stillwater, OK

Locklear, Jennifer
Clinton HS
Clinton, OK

Loeber, Matt
Oklahoma
Christian Schl
Edmond, OK

Lofgren, Leslie
Piedmont HS
Piedmont, OK

Loftis, Adrienne E
Del City HS
Del City, OK

Loftis, Anna T
Jay HS
Jay, OK

Lofton, Diana L
Poteau HS
Monroe, OK

Lofton, Lakeshia N
Northeast HS
Oklahoma City, OK

Lofton, Melvin L
Webster HS
Tulsa, OK

Loney, Kenneth S
Bishop Kelley HS
Tulsa, OK

Long, Andrea L
Sapulpa Sr HS
Sapulpa, OK

Long, Ashley L
Bixby Sr HS
Bixby, OK

Long, Bessie M
Haileyville Schl
Krebs, OK

Long, Cheryl
Heritage Hall Schl
Oklahoma City, OK

Long, John D
Heavener HS
Heavener, OK

Long, Roy
Stilwell HS
Stilwell, OK

Longaker, Blythe
Leigh
John Marshall HS
Oklahoma City, OK

Longan, Brandy
Stillwater Sr HS
Stillwater, OK

Longoria, Ernie
Choctaw HS
Choctaw, OK

Looney, Charmalet
Midwest City HS
Oklahoma City, OK

Lopez, Camille A
Muskogee HS
Muskogee, OK

Lopez, Desirae R
Tuttle HS
Tuttle, OK

Love, Candice J
Idabel HS
Idabel, OK

Love, Lindsey L
Midwest City HS
Midwest City, OK

Lovett, Kimberly D
Mustang HS
Mustang, OK

Lovinggood, Jessica
Midwest City HS
Midwest City, OK

Low, Allison
Southwest
Covenant Schl
Yukon, OK

Lowe, Alison F
Bartlesville Sr HS
Bartlesville, OK

Lowe, De Layna K
Meeker HS
Meeker, OK

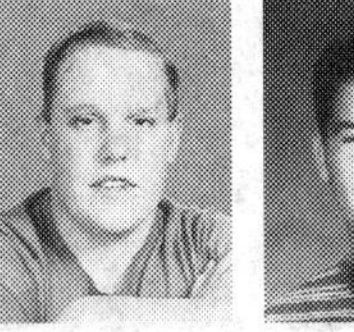

Lowe, William C
Kingston HS
Kingston, OK

Lowell, Jeremy J
Western Heights Sr HS
Oklahoma City, OK

Lowery, Terry
Deer Creek HS
Edmond, OK

Lowry, Brandy R
Bartlesville Sr HS
Bartlesville, OK

Lozano, Jennifer R
Norman Sr HS
Pryor, OK

Lucas, Nicole A
Bishop Kelley HS
Tulsa, OK

Luckinbill, Justin M
Dibble Jr Sr HS
Blanchard, OK

Lundy, Daniel N
Cordell Sr HS
Cordell, OK

Lundy, Gabriel N
Cordell Sr HS
Cordell, OK

Lundy, Jason
Choctaw Jr HS
Choctaw, OK

Lundy, Matt A
Choctaw HS
Choctaw, OK

Lunsford, Jeremy
Okmulgee HS
Okmulgee, OK

Luthye, Pam
Perry Sr HS
Perry, OK

Lutton, Claire E
Bartlesville Sr HS
Bartlesville, OK

Luttrell, Jennifer L
Anadarko HS
Anadarko, OK

Luttrell, Kelly N
Charles Page HS
Sand Springs, OK

Ly, Phung T
Stillwater Sr HS
Stillwater, OK

Lyles, Lakesha N
Mc Lain Career Acad
Tulsa, OK

Lynch, Erin B
Bixby Sr HS
Jenks, OK

Lynch, Shawna
Heritage Hall Schl
Piedmont, OK

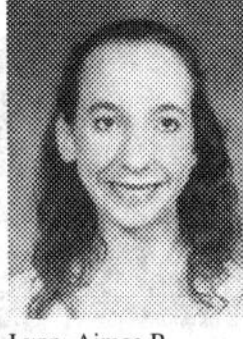

Lynn, Aimee B
Bartlesville Sr HS
Bartlesville, OK

Lyon, Jacob W
Lindsay HS
Lindsay, OK

Lytle, Jennifer
Lawton Sr HS
Lawton, OK

Maass, Sarah
Kingfisher HS
Kingfisher, OK

Mabry, John Robert
Muskogee HS
Muskogee, OK

Mabry, Laura M
Ponca City Sr HS
Ponca City, OK

Mac Donald, Jeff D
Owasso Sr HS
Owasso, OK

Mack II, Anthony W
Duncan HS
Duncan, OK

Mac Rae, Tanya
Lawton Sr HS
Lawton, OK

Madbull, Misty M
Antlers Sr HS
Antlers, OK

Madden, Brandi
Douglass HS
Oklahoma City, OK

Maddux, Sarah H
Emerson Jr HS
Orange, TX

Madewell, Mindy
Warner HS
Warner, OK

Madison, Adam W
East Central HS
Tulsa, OK

Madsen, Dale
Chisholm Sr HS
Enid, OK

Magar, Tamara A
Stonewall Jr-Sr HS
Stonewall, OK

Magby, Dusty E
Stringtown HS
Stringtown, OK

Magnus, Shane E
Ponca City Sr HS
Ponca City, OK

Magnusen, Rita J
B T Washington HS
Tulsa, OK

Maguregui, John
Altus Sr HS
Altus, OK

Maine, Kimberly S
El Reno Sr HS
El Reno, OK

Majors, Nancy L
Hinton HS
Hinton, OK

Makaseah, Teresa
Shawnee Sr HS
Shawnee, OK

Maker, Valerie A
Hominy HS
Cleveland, OK

Malaske, Jenny
Harrah HS
Harrah, OK

Malget, Matt
Perry Sr HS
Perry, OK

Malley, Amber
Mustang HS
Yukon, OK

Malone, Angel L
Moore HS
Moore, OK

Malone, Kasey
Midwest City HS
Midwest City, OK

Malone, Mandy S
Morrison Public Schl
Stillwater, OK

Maloney, Jennifer
Norman Sr HS
Norman, OK

Maloney, Thomas P
Cushing HS
Cushing, OK

Manders, Abbey
Miami Sr HS
Miami, OK

Maness, Amber N
Pauls Valley HS
Pauls Valley, OK

Mangum, Christopher
Midwest City HS
Midwest City, OK

Mann, Benjamin E
Union Intermediate HS
Tulsa, OK

Mann, Matt H
Buffalo Jr Sr HS
Buffalo, OK

Manning, Bobby J
Spiro HS
Spiro, OK

Manning, Kevin M
Edmond North HS
Edmond, OK

Manning,
Kimberly Ann
Ponca City Sr HS
Ponca City, OK

Manos, Jana
Guyman HS
Guymon, OK

Mansel, Kristen R
Elgin HS
Apache, OK

Mansfield, Matt A
South Intermediate HS
Broken Arrow, OK

Manzer, Devon
Edmond North HS
Edmond, OK

Maples, Melissa A
West Jr HS
Oklahoma City, OK

Marable, Tabatha
Battiest Jr Sr HS
Bethel, OK

Marble, Christopher M
Putnam City HS
Oklahoma City, OK

Marion, Michael D
Latta Sr HS
Ada, OK

Marley, Leisha
Putnam City West HS
Bethany, OK

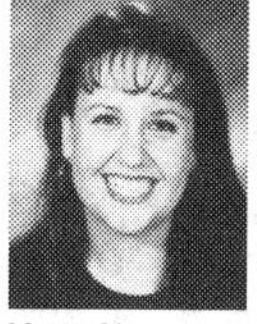
Marney, Lisa
Pryor Jr HS
Pryor, OK

Marple, Erik
Tomlinson Jr HS
Lawton, OK

Marquard, Meredith
Starr
Stratford Schl
Stratford, OK

Marquis, Jeremy
Norman Sr HS
Norman, OK

Marquis, Khara C
Central Mid-HS
Norman, OK

Marr, April
Achille Schl
Durant, OK

Marr, Trey
Achille Schl
Durant, OK

Marris, Billie Dawn
Clayton Jr Sr HS
Clayton, OK

Marsh, Amy E
Central Mid-HS
Norman, OK

Marshall, Lindsay A
Central Mid-HS
Norman, OK

Marshall, Tabitha A
Choctaw HS
Harrah, OK

Martens, Suzanne
Okemah HS
Okemah, OK

Martin, Chad W
Woodward HS
Woodward, OK

Martin, Charles H
Bishop Kelley HS
Tulsa, OK

Martin, Dustin L
Noble HS
Noble, OK

Martin, Jason
Ryan Schl
Terral, OK

Martin, Jennifer M
Tishomingo HS
Tishomingo, OK

Martin, Jessica M
Union Intermediate HS
Tulsa, OK

Martin, Justin L
El Reno Sr HS
El Reno, OK

Martin, Kyle R
Edmond Memorial HS
Edmond, OK

Martin, Luke A
Mulhall Orlando HS
Mulhall, OK

Martin, Melanie A
Jay HS
Jay, OK

Martin, Phillip
Mc Loud HS
Newalla, OK

Martin, Rhys A
South Intermediate HS
Broken Arrow, OK

Martin, Shannon L
Broken Arrow Sr HS
Broken Arrow, OK

Martin, Todd A
Ada HS
Ada, OK

Martinez Jr, Rosalio V
Bishop Kelley HS
Tulsa, OK

Mashburn, Marika R
Mt St Marys HS
Norman, OK

Mashunkashey, Julie
Pawhuska HS
Pawhuska, OK

Mason, Bryan J
Hartshorne Sr HS
Mcalester, OK

Mason, Cheryl R
Stillwater Sr HS
Stillwater, OK

Mason, Christine
Midwest City HS
Midwest City, OK

Mason, Jennifer
Moore Christian Schl
Moore, OK

Mason, Nicholas J
Coleman Schl
Coleman, OK

Mason II, Perry L
Northeast HS
Oklahoma City, OK

Mason, Rhonda
Victory Christian Schl
Broken Arrow, OK

Mason, Richard
Northwest Classen HS
Oklahoma City, OK

Mason, Tisha S
Coleman Schl
Coleman, OK

Massey, Billie F
Locust Grove HS
Locust Grove, OK

Massey, Sarah J
Will Rogers HS
Tulsa, OK

Massie, Chris D
Owasso Sr HS
Owasso, OK

Mastin, Susan
Arkoma Jr Sr HS
Arkoma, OK

Mata, Maira
Douglass HS
Oklahoma City, OK

Matanane, Joshua J
Putnam City North HS
Oklahoma City, OK

Matheke, Heather M
Eisenhower Sr HS
Lawton, OK

Matherly, Kristy N
Olive Jr Sr HS
Drumright, OK

Mathew, Santosh T
Mustang HS
Yukon, OK

Mathews, Meagan M
Sayre HS
Sayre, OK

Mathias, Jacob A
Cleveland Sr HS
Cleveland, OK

Mathis, Athena
Westmoore HS
Oklahoma City, OK

Mathis, Cody S
Muldrow HS
Muldrow, OK

Mathis, Jodi L
Muldrow HS
Muldrow, OK

Mathis, Laura
Heritage Hall Schl
Oklahoma City, OK

Mathis, Richard D
Heritage Hall Schl
Oklahoma City, OK

Matlock, Katie A
Charles Page HS
Sand Springs, OK

Matlock, Scott R
Stillwater Sr HS
Stillwater, OK

Maton, Petra B S
Casady Schl
Oklahoma City, OK

Matthews, Boyd W
Durant HS
Durant, OK

Matthews, Dustyn R
Caney Valley HS
Broken Arrow, OK

Matz, Kasi
Arapaho Schl
Arapaho, OK

Maupin, John Thomas
Moore HS
Moore, OK

Maurer, Leanna C
Ponca City Sr HS
Ponca City, OK

Maxey, Darryl W
Tushka HS
Atoka, OK

Maxson, Joshua
Miami Sr HS
Miami, OK

Maxwell, Jason
Metro Christian Acad
Tulsa, OK

Maxwell, Jeremiah B
Spiro HS
Keota, OK

May, Ashley
Claremore Sr HS
Claremore, OK

May, Chris
Clinton HS
Clinton, OK

May, Stephanie
Oklahoma
Christian Schl
Edmond, OK

Mayberry, Shawna R
Chickasha HS
Chickasha, OK

Mayhew, Matthew
Midwest City HS
Midwest City, OK

Maynard, Danielle R
Purcell HS
Purcell, OK

Mayo, Ryan R
Central Schl
Sallisaw, OK

Mazak, Shauna K
Macomb Schl
Macomb, OK

Mazey, Patricia
Tushka HS
Atoka, OK

Mc Adoo, Jason G
Norman Sr HS
Norman, OK

Mc Affrey, Jennifer K
Mustang HS
Yukon, OK

Mc Ateer, Christie
Jenks HS
Tulsa, OK

Mc Bride, Kjersti J
Memorial HS
Tulsa, OK

Mc Bride, Michael
Craig
Westmoore HS
Oklahoma City, OK

Mc Call, Jennifer
Ardmore HS
Ardmore, OK

Mc Cammon, Erin
Christian
Heritage Acad
Oklahoma City, OK

Mc Cann, Andrea M
Bishop Kelley HS
Tulsa, OK

Mc Cantney, Melissa J
Healdton HS
Healdton, OK

Mc Carthy, Todd A
Stillwater Sr HS
Stillwater, OK

Mc Carty, Julie K
Antlers Sr HS
Atoka, OK

Mc Carville, Justin J
North Intermediate HS
Broken Arrow, OK

Mc Caslin, Laura L
Jenks HS
Tulsa, OK

Mc Caslin, Lisa
Jenks HS
Tulsa, OK

Mc Cauley, Clinton
Yukon HS
Yukon, OK

Mc Caw, Marc D
Union Intermediate HS
Broken Arrow, OK

Mc Clain, Angela
Bartlesville Sr HS
Bartlesville, OK

Mc Clarnon, Shanna
Blackwell HS
Blackwell, OK

Mc Clellan, Matt K
Midwest City HS
Midwest City, OK

Mc Clintock,
Amber M
Bartlesville Sr HS
Bartlesville, OK

Mc Clure, Jason S
Putnam City West HS
Bethany, OK

Mc Clure, Jennifer R
Indiahoma Schl
Indiahoma, OK

Mc Clyman,
Michelle A
Altus Sr HS
Altus, OK

Mc Coin, Matt D
Charles Page HS
Sand Springs, OK

Mc Collom, Wenoa R
Tishomingo HS
Tishomingo, OK

Mc Comas, Kim
Minco Jr Sr HS
Minco, OK

Mc Connell, Kimberly
Union Intermediate HS
Tulsa, OK

Mc Connell, Sean M
Owasso Sr HS
Owasso, OK

Mc Cool, Amber D
Edmond North HS
Edmond, OK

Mc Corkle, Elizabeth
Bartlesville Sr HS
Bartlesville, OK

Mc Coy, Chuck
Pond
Creek-Hunter Schl
Hunter, OK

Mc Crary, Jason C
Wellston Schl
Chandler, OK

Mc Cray, Bobbi Danae
Ringwood HS
Ringwood, OK

Mc Cray, Sean D
Central Mid-HS
Norman, OK

Mc Creary,
Christopher L
Northeast HS
Oklahoma City, OK

Mc Croskey, Crystal D
Wister Schl
Poteau, OK

Mc Cullah, Luke E
Muldrow HS
Muldrow, OK

Mc Culley, Akeyah
Dustin Schl
Dustin, OK

Mc Culloh, Emily
Plainview HS
Ardmore, OK

Mc Cune, Trayton L
Family Of Faith
Christian Schl
Stillwater, OK

Mc Daniel, Bo J
Balko Public Schl
Balko, OK

Mc Daniel, Brian
Westmoore HS
Oklahoma City, OK

Mc Donald,
Charnetta J
Wellston Schl
Luther, OK

Mc Donald, Cletus P
Cashion HS
Kingfisher, OK

Mc Donald, Joshua
Blanchard Jr Sr HS
Blanchard, OK

Mc Donald, Mary E
B T Washington HS
Tulsa, OK

Mc Elroy, Brandi M
Booker T Washington
Mem HS
Tulsa, OK

Mc Entire, Autumn K
Canadian Schl
Kiowa, OK

Mc Entire, Brian
Tuttle HS
Oklahoma City, OK

Mc Fadden, Michael J
Altus Sr HS
Altus, OK

Mc Fall, Brian J
Bridge Creek HS
Blanchard, OK

Mc Gaha, Samuel
Hobart HS
Hobart, OK

Mc Gahey, Melissa A
Dickson HS
Ardmore, OK

Mc Gath,
Christopher B
Macarthur Sr HS
Lawton, OK

Mc Gee, Kamber D
Putnam City North HS
Oklahoma City, OK

Mc Gee, Merredith D
Mc Alester HS
Mc Alester, OK

Mc Gee, Sarah E
Bishop Kelley HS
Tulsa, OK

Mc Gehee, Amy
Poteau HS
Poteau, OK

Mc Gill, Joshua W
Altus Sr HS
Altus, OK

Mc Ginley, Todd R
Putnam City North HS
Oklahoma City, OK

Mc Gowen, Deanna
Moore HS
Moore, OK

Mc Gowen, Lori
Moore HS
Moore, OK

Mc Graw, Alison L
Muskogee HS
Muskogee, OK

Mc Graw, Shannon
Moore HS
Oklahoma City, OK

Mc Guire, Daniel L
Kellyville Sr HS
Bristow, OK

Mc Guire, Nathaniel J
Del City HS
Del City, OK

Mc Hale, Erin Michele
Bartlesville Sr HS
Bartlesville, OK

Mc Ilvain, Michael J
Buffalo Jr Sr HS
Woodward, OK

Mc Intire, Jared
Durant HS
Durant, OK

Mc Intire, Jonathan S
Durant HS
Durant, OK

Mc Intosh, Tiffany D
Mc Alester HS
Mcalester, OK

Mc Intyre, Elaine R
Edmond Memorial HS
Edmond, OK

Mc Kay, Brian M
Edmond North HS
Edmond, OK

Mc Keen, Kimberly L
Yukon HS
Yukon, OK

Mc Kinley, Lisa M
Mannford HS
Cleveland, OK

Mc Kinney, Debbie K
Grace Chrn Acad
Oklahoma City, OK

Mc Kinney,
Rachelle D
Edmond North HS
Edmond, OK

Mc Kinzie, Melissa N
Pauls Valley HS
Pauls Valley, OK

Mc Laren, Justin R
Madill HS
Madill, OK

Mc Laughlin,
Amanda M
Kellyville Sr HS
Kellyville, OK

Mc Laughlin,
Brandon L
Oologah HS
Talala, OK

Mc Lemore,
Candace F
Calera Jr Sr HS
Durant, OK

Mc Lemore, Jessica
Midwest City HS
Midwest City, OK

Mc Millan, Kandi M
Claremore Sr HS
Claremore, OK

Mc Millin, Kevin
Ft Cobb-Broxton HS
Fort Cobb, OK

Mc Mullen, Brian P
Stillwater Sr HS
Stillwater, OK

Mc Mullen, Molly
Rush Springs HS
Rush Springs, OK

Mc Murray, Ryan M
West Middle HS
Norman, OK

Mc Murrian, Cyndi M
Buffalo Valley Schl
Tuskahoma, OK

Mc Namar, Emily
Claremore Sr HS
Claremore, OK

Mc Neal, Cynthia F
Macarthur Sr HS
Lawton, OK

Mc Neese, Mary Beth
Ponca City Sr HS
Ponca City, OK

Mc Nutt, Abbigail
Lawton Sr HS
Lawton, OK

Mc Nutt, Mike
Stuart Sr HS
Haywood, OK

Mc Pherson, Andy
Anadarko HS
Anadarko, OK

Mc Pherson,
Danielle R
Southeast HS
Midwest City, OK

Mc Queen, Megan L
Stigler HS
Stigler, OK

Mc Reynolds, Taryn
Sapulpa Sr HS
Sapulpa, OK

Mc Spaden, James
Putnam City North HS
Oklahoma City, OK

Mc Vay, Jenifer M
Edmond North HS
Edmond, OK

Meacham, Allison A
Clinton HS
Clinton, OK

Meacham, Melanie
Clinton HS
Clinton, OK

Meacham, Stephen
Clinton HS
Clinton, OK

Meade, Letitia Y
Edmond Santa Fe HS
Alpharetta, GA

Meadors, Sumer D
Nathan Hale HS
Tulsa, OK

Meadows, Stacy L
Empire Schl
Duncan, OK

Means, Jarod S
Putnam City North HS
Oklahoma City, OK

Means, Michelle C
Ponca City Sr HS
Ponca City, OK

Medcalf, Joel
Boswell Sr HS
Boswell, OK

Medgaarden, Matt D
Mustang HS
Mustang, OK

Medlock, Shawn
Tahlequah Sr HS
Tahlequah, OK

Meeks, Eric
Braggs Schl
Braggs, OK

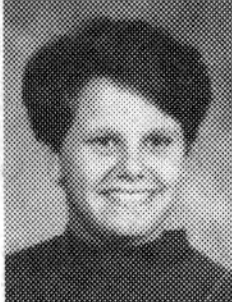
Meeks, Heather
Haileyville Schl
Haileyville, OK

Meers, Natalie L
Westmoore HS
Oklahoma City, OK

Meier, Austin
Okeene Jr Sr HS
Hitchcock, OK

Meissner, John-David
Moore HS
Moore, OK

Melton, April M
Memorial HS
Tulsa, OK

Melton, Dawna
Collinsville HS
Collinsville, OK

Melton, Joseph G
Valliant HS
Garvin, OK

Melton, Kristie M
Putnam City HS
Oklahoma City, OK

Mendenall, Misty E
Plainview HS
Ardmore, OK

Mercer, Christie R
Central Schl
Marlow, OK

Meredith, Kaci C
Hugo HS
Hugo, OK

Merideth, Amy K
Putnam City West HS
Oklahoma City, OK

Meritt, Skyla
Woodward HS
Woodward, OK

Merrell, Kimberly G
Moore HS
Moore, OK

Merrick, Frank W
West Middle HS
Norman, OK

Merrill, Kurt
Stillwater Sr HS
Stillwater, OK

Merritt, Michael S
Edison HS
Tulsa, OK

Merryman, Joshua K
Metro Christian Acad
Tulsa, OK

Mesa, Chris
Stuart Sr HS
Stuart, OK

Metcalfe, Wayne E
Pioneer Jr Sr HS
Enid, OK

Mettry, Shelley
Ada HS
Ada, OK

Meyer, Jennifer R
Preston Schl
Beggs, OK

Meyers, Jennifer S
Liberty HS
Bixby, OK

Middleton, Elizabeth J
Okmulgee HS
Okmulgee, OK

Middleton, Travis G
Westmoore HS
Oklahoma City, OK

Miers, Natasha R
Wetumka Jr Sr HS
Wetumka, OK

Miley, Marlo M
Westmoore HS
Oklahoma City, OK

Milford, Tisha M
Westmoore HS
Oklahoma City, OK

Millben, Micthea J
Putman City HS
Oklahoma City, OK

Miller, Alicia
B T Washington HS
Tulsa, OK

Miller, Amanda R
Allen HS
Ada, OK

Miller, Anthony W
Westmoore HS
Moore, OK

Miller, Brittany K
Stillwater Sr HS
Stillwater, OK

Miller, Danette
Edmond North HS
Edmond, OK

Miller, Dorothea
Eavon
Mangum Sr HS
Mangum, OK

Miller, Dusty
Hennessey HS
Hennessey, OK

Miller, George Marc
B T Washington HS
Tulsa, OK

Miller, Josh G
Lindsay HS
Lindsay, OK

Miller, Kelli
Westmoore HS
Oklahoma City, OK

Miller, Lori
Tupelo Jr Sr HS
Stonewall, OK

Miller, Marley R
Ponca City Sr HS
Ponca City, OK

Miller, Melody Joy
Jay HS
Jay, OK

Miller, Nickey G
Stroud HS
Stroud, OK

Miller, Nicole
Okay Jr Sr HS
Okay, OK

Miller, Sarah B
Nathan Hale HS
Tulsa, OK

Miller, Sarah E
Charles Page HS
Sand Springs, OK

Miller, Serina M
Putnam City West HS
Oklahoma City, OK

Miller, Shannon Marie
Muskogee HS
Muskogee, OK

Miller, Sherra
Midwest City HS
Midwest City, OK

Miller, Stephanie D
Stilwell HS
Stilwell, OK

Miller, Tara
Mangum Jr HS
Mangum, OK

Miller, Tim
Ada HS
Ada, OK

Miller, Tonya Gaylene
Union Sr HS
Broken Arrow, OK

Miller, Whitney
Weatherford HS
Weatherford, OK

Milligan, Luke B
Bartlesville Mid HS
Grove, OK

Mills, Brad L
Lindsay HS
Lindsay, OK

Mills, Caleb E
Putnam City HS
Oklahoma City, OK

Mills, Kevin
Shawnee Sr HS
Shawnee, OK

Mills, Samantha A
Putnam City North HS
Oklahoma City, OK

Millspaugh, Melissa S
Oaks Mission Jr Sr HS
Rose, OK

Milner, Jeremy P
North Intemediate HS
Broken Arrow, OK

Mimms, Amanda B
Fairland Jr Sr HS
Fairland, OK

Mimms, Leigh-Anna K
Durant HS
Durant, OK

Minard, Sarah S
Edmond North HS
Edmond, OK

Miner, Shawnda
Indianola HS
Mcalester, OK

Mings, Crystal R
Whitesboro Schl
Talihina, OK

Mink, Marina R
Vanoss Schl
Roff, OK

Minthorn, Martina R
Elgin HS
Elgin, OK

Minty, Benjamin A
Sapulpa Sr HS
Sapulpa, OK

Minyard, Jaime L
Del City HS
Oklahoma City, OK

Minyard, Matt
Marietta HS
Marietta, OK

Misasi, Paul A
Cascia Hall Prep School
Tulsa, OK

Mitchell, Alicia F
Enid Sr HS
Enid, OK

Mitchell, Cassie
Warner HS
Warner, OK

Mitchell, John
El Reno Sr HS
El Reno, OK

Mitchell, Stephanie J
Wakita Schl
Medford, OK

Mittelstet, Matt K
Stillwater Sr HS
Stillwater, OK

Mix, Michael
Owasso Sr HS
Owasso, OK

Mixon, Amber
Mustang HS
Mustang, OK

Mizer, Amberley D
Sapulpa Sr HS
Sapulpa, OK

Mizer, Lyslie
Claremore Sr HS
Claremore, OK

Mlynek, Michael
Prague HS
Prague, OK

Monachella, Andrea
Moore HS
Moore, OK

Monk, J J
Valliant HS
Garvin, OK

Monn, Sarah L
Union Sr HS
Tulsa, OK

Monroe, Robert J
Frontier Public Schl
Ponca City, OK

Montgomery, Alisha B
Boise City HS
Boise City, OK

Montgomery, Benjamin
Westmoore HS
Oklahoma City, OK

Montgomery, Crystal
Claremore Sr HS
Claremore, OK

Montgomery, Dawnita M
Hobart HS
Hobart, OK

Montgomery, Trevor L
Boise City HS
Boise City, OK

Moody, Blake
Mc Loud HS
Mc Loud, OK

Moomaw, Sara
Stillwater Sr HS
Stillwater, OK

Mooney, Kristen N
Duncan HS
Duncan, OK

Mooneyham, Sammy L
Lexington HS
Lexington, OK

Moore, Amanda B
Brink Jr HS
Moore, OK

Moore, Amanda M
Midwest City HS
Midwest City, OK

Moore, April D
Pocola HS
Pocola, OK

Moore, Ashlee M
South Intermediate HS
Broken Arrow, OK

Moore, Brandi R
Enid Sr HS
Enid, OK

Moore, Brent
Mustang HS
Mustang, OK

Moore, Carrie
East Central HS
Tulsa, OK

Moore, Charles E
Tecumseh HS
Tecumseh, OK

Moore, Holly L
Yale Jr Sr HS
Yale, OK

Moore Jr, Jimmy L
John Marshall HS
Oklahoma City, OK

Moore, Lacey E
Claremore Sr HS
Chelsea, OK

Moore, Michael S
Lindsay HS
Lindsay, OK

Moore, Reginald W
Northeast HS
Oklahoma City, OK

Moore, Thelma O
Mannford HS
Sand Springs, OK

Moore, Zachary
Midwest City HS
Midwest City, OK

Morford, Cathy L
Charles Page HS
Sand Springs, OK

Morgan, Adria L
Brink Jr HS
Oklahoma City, OK

Morgan, Erin
Noble HS
Noble, OK

Morgan, Gina L
Enid Sr HS
Enid, OK

Morgan, Jamie D
Duke Schl
Duke, OK

Morgan, Jay I
Choctaw HS
Choctaw, OK

Morgan, John
Vinita HS
Vinita, OK

Morgan, Keri B
Duncan HS
Duncan, OK

Morgan, Timothy R
Colcord Schl
Colcord, OK

Morgeson, Kim A
Edmond North HS
Edmond, OK

Morland, Nick J
Wakita Schl
Wakita, OK

Mornhinweg, Paul T
Byng Sr HS
Ada, OK

Morphew, Lindsey
Maysville Jr Sr HS
Maysville, OK

Morphis, Melanie N
Northwest Classen HS
Oklahoma City, OK

Morrell, Jacquelyn A
Mustang HS
Mustang, OK

Morris, Amanda
Roland Sr HS
Roland, OK

Morris, Amy B
Buffalo Jr Sr HS
Buffalo, OK

Morris, Chester Curtis
Elgin HS
Elgin, OK

Morris, Crystal
Plainview HS
Ardmore, OK

Morris, Holly
Pauls Valley HS
Pauls Valley, OK

Morris, Kindra M
Byng Sr HS
Ada, OK

Morris, Melissa
Moore HS
Moore, OK

Morris, Shawnna L
Bartlesville Sr HS
Bartlesville, OK

Morris, Stephanie L
Spiro HS
Spiro, OK

Morse, Carrie
Verden HS
Verden, OK

Morse, Terri L
Tahlequah Jr HS
Tahlequah, OK

Moseby, Danielle
East Central HS
Tulsa, OK

Moses, Meredith
Norman Sr HS
Norman, OK

Mosley, Crystal A
Claremore Sr HS
Claremore, OK

Mosley, Kevin
Northwest Classen HS
Oklahoma City, OK

Mosley, Valerie
Midwest City HS
Midwest City, OK

Moss, Clayton G
Deer Creek HS
Oklahoma City, OK

Moss, Mya F
B T Washington HS
Tulsa, OK

Mott, Shawna Lyn
Webster HS
Tulsa, OK

Mott, Tara M
Edmond North HS
Edmond, OK

Motto, Michael
Tulsa Memorial HS
Tulsa, OK

Mount, Brian R
Yukon Middle HS
Yukon, OK

Mowdy, Stacie
U S Grant HS
Oklahoma City, OK

Moydell, Edward W
Union Intermediate HS
Tulsa, OK

Mozingo, Joetta M
Will Rogers HS
Tulsa, OK

Muck, Melissa
Sulphur HS
Sulphur, OK

Mueggenborg, Mandi
Yale Jr Sr HS
Yale, OK

Mueggenburg, Vince R
Okarche HS
Okarche, OK

Mundinger, Jana
Midwest City HS
Midwest City, OK

Murata, Junko
Shawnee Sr HS
Japan, XX

Murfin, Rory D
Charles Page HS
Sand Springs, OK

Murphy, Joshua
Porter Jr Sr HS
Coweta, OK

Murphy, Kristin D
Bartlesville Mid HS
Bartlesville, OK

Murphy, Nichole C
Norman Sr HS
Norman, OK

Murphy, Tara L
South Intermediate HS
Broken Arrow, OK

Murray, Crystal L
Cashion HS
Cashion, OK

Murray, Karyn
Westmoore HS
Oklahoma City, OK

Murray, Stephen
Crescent Schl
Crescent, OK

Murrell, J T
Comanche HS
Newcastle, OK

Murrell, Valauna
Newcastle HS
Newcastle, OK

Mushrush, Stacy R
Sapulpa Sr HS
Sapulpa, OK

Muskrat, Shawna K
Porum HS
Porum, OK

Myatt, Ann M
Washington HS
Washington, OK

Myatt, Rachel
U S Grant HS
Oklahoma City, OK

Myers, Christine C
Tomlinson Jr HS
Lawton, OK

Myers, Christy L
Putnam City HS
Oklahoma City, OK

Myers, Jason
Byng Sr HS
Ada, OK

Myers, Kerry A
Putnam City HS
Warr Acres, OK

Myers, Nadia
Charles Page HS
Tulsa, OK

Myers-Compton, Sara J
Putnam City West HS
Oklahoma City, OK

Naff, Richard A
John Marshall HS
Oklahoma City, OK

Naff, Tirra
Millwood HS
Oklahoma City, OK

Naigle, Corinne E
Choctaw HS
Midwest City, OK

Nail, Jennifer M
Duncan HS
Duncan, OK

Nakedhead, Jeana R
Stilwell HS
Stilwell, OK

Nance, Melissa L
Bishop Mcguinness HS
Oklahoma City, OK

Nasalroad, Collin
Yale Jr Sr HS
Yale, OK

Nash, Kasandria
Central HS
Tulsa, OK

Nashreddine, Rania A
B T Washington HS
Tulsa, OK

Naumann, Kimberly D
Morris HS
Boynton, OK

Nayeri, Dina
Edmond North HS
Edmond, OK

Naylor, Erin
Union Intermediate HS
Tulsa, OK

Naylor, Mark I
South Intermediate HS
Broken Arrow, OK

Neathery, Chad L
El Reno Sr HS
El Reno, OK

Nedbalek, Nancy
Midwest City HS
Midwest City, OK

Needham, Paula
Perry Sr HS
Perry, OK

Neeland, Kent
Hennessey HS
Bison, OK

Neff, Justin M
Union Intermediate HS
Tulsa, OK

Nelon, Stewart B
Midwest City HS
Midwest City, OK

Nelson, Brian A
Hugo HS
Hugo, OK

Nelson, Brian S
Westmoore HS
Oklahoma City, OK

Nelson, Conrad I
Washington HS
Purcell, OK

Nelson, Dusty L
Cando HS
Cando, ND

Nelson, Jeanie L
Stratford Schl
Stratford, OK

Nelson, Katie
Southwest
Covenant Schl
Yukon, OK

Nelson, Leslie R
Locust Grove HS
Locust Grove, OK

Nelson, Ricky J
Ponca City Sr HS
Ponca City, OK

Nemecek, Heather D
Byng Sr HS
Ada, OK

Nenno, Victoria
Charlena
Moore HS
Moore, OK

Nerren, Nick J
Charles Page HS
Sand Springs, OK

Nester, Melissa D
Checotah HS
Checotah, OK

Neville, Katie
Heritage Hall Schl
Oklahoma City, OK

Newberry, Brandon
Hilldale HS
Muskogee, OK

Newberry, Joshua
Westmoore HS
Moore, OK

Newberry, Richard
Midwest City HS
Midwest City, OK

Newby, Stephanie
Putnam City North HS
Oklahoma City, OK

Newell, Daniel D
Roland Sr HS
Muldrow, OK

Newell, Keista L
Woodward HS
Woodward, OK

Newman, Patrick B
Collinsville HS
Collinsville, OK

Newman, Samantha
Lawton Sr HS
Fort Sill, OK

Newman, Toni S
Putnam City West HS
Bethany, OK

Newnam, Tera S
Preston Schl
Okmulgee, OK

Newton, Jennifer
Woodward HS
Woodward, OK

Newton, Sarah K
Putnam City West HS
Oklahoma City, OK

Nguyen, Angie K
Putnam City North HS
Oklahoma City, OK

Nguyen, Dorothy
Union Intermediate HS
Tulsa, OK

Nguyen, Jerrica
Union Sr HS
Tulsa, OK

Nguyen, Jimmy
Mustang HS
Yukon, OK

Nguyen, Knanh
Bao Tran
Clinton HS
Clinton, OK

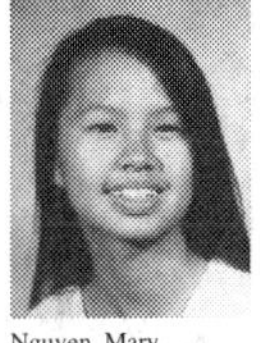

Nguyen, Mary
Midwest City HS
Midwest City, OK

Nguyen, Quynh N
Moore HS
Moore, OK

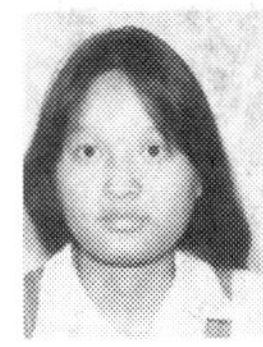

Nguyen, Trang C
Westmoore HS
Oklahoma City, OK

Niblett, Milann M
Davis HS
Davis, OK

Niblock, Lexi L
Putnam City HS
Oklahoma City, OK

Nichol, Heather N
Union Intermediate HS
Broken Arrow, OK

Nichol, Michelle
Union Sr HS
Broken Arrow, OK

Nicholas, Cindy M
Tahlequah Sr HS
Tahlequah, OK

Nicholas, Crystal W
Union Intermediate HS
Tulsa, OK

Nichols, Alisha A
Hartshorne Sr HS
Wilburton, OK

Nichols, Anita C
John Marshall HS
Oklahoma City, OK

Nichols, Brad
Enid Sr HS
Enid, OK

Nichols, Brandy L
Heavener HS
Heavener, OK

Nichols, Casey Aaron
Oktaha Jr Sr HS
Oktaha, OK

Nichols, Renee
Putnam City West HS
Oklahoma City, OK

Nichols Jr, Rickie G
Dale Sr HS
Dale, OK

Nicholson, Jason W
Marietta HS
Marietta, OK

Nicolotti, Daniel J
Union Sr HS
Tulsa, OK

Nida, Hunter F
Bishop Mcguinness HS
Oklahoma City, OK

Nida, Rhonda Tautfest
Tonkawa Jr Sr HS
Red Rock, OK

Nidiffer, Abbie M
Dewey HS
Dewey, OK

Nilsson, Corinne R
Stillwater Sr HS
Stillwater, OK

Nipp, Travis C
Turner Schl
Overbrook, OK

Noble, Theresa M
Bishop Kelley HS
Tulsa, OK

Nohelty, Lacey
Western Heights Sr HS
Oklahoma City, OK

Nolan, Jason A
Savanna HS
Mcalester, OK

Nolen, Jon S
Del City HS
Del City, OK

Norman, Britt N
Woodward HS
Woodward, OK

Norrid, Leslie R
Pocola HS
Pocola, OK

Northcutt, Michelle
Frederick HS
Frederick, OK

Norvell, Melissa
Shawnee Sr HS
Shawnee, OK

Noviski, Billy P
Claremore Sr HS
Claremore, OK

Nowak, Amanda D
Will Rogers HS
Tulsa, OK

Nowlin, Ashley
Seiling Schl
Seiling, OK

Nowlin, Bryan J
Cascia Hall Prep
School
Tulsa, OK

Nubine, Jonathan L
Mustang HS
Oklahoma City, OK

Nunley, Elizabeth L
Mustang HS
Oklahoma City, OK

Nunley, Lacy
Achille Schl
Colbert, OK

Nunn, Brad R
Oologah HS
Claremore, OK

Nurnberg, Natasha
Washita Heights Schl
Corn, OK

Nye, Lindsay N
Union Intermediate HS
Tulsa, OK

Nyemaster, Nancy N
Broken Arrow Sr HS
Broken Arrow, OK

OKLAHOMA

Ocamb, David D
Carl Albert HS
Midwest City, OK

Oden, Shanay
Moore HS
Moore, OK

Odom, Shannon
Kingston HS
Kingston, OK

O'Donnell, Erika L
Choctaw HS
Choctaw, OK

Ogan, Aaron
Mulhall Orlando HS
Guthrie, OK

Ogden, Angela M
Altus Sr HS
Altus, OK

Ogle, Jennifer M
Tishomingo HS
Mannsville, OK

Oglesby, Michael R
Union Intermediate HS
Tulsa, OK

O'Hearon, Jennifer M
Will Rogers HS
Tulsa, OK

Oldham, Michael B
Sapulpa Sr HS
Sapulpa, OK

Oliver, Anthony A
Del City HS
Oklahoma City, OK

Oliver, Sabrina
Kingston HS
Kingston, OK

Olson, Sheila
Nathan Hale HS
Tulsa, OK

Oman, Jeremy J
Muskogee HS
Muskogee, OK

Oneal, Adrianne
Edison HS
Tulsa, OK

O'Neal, Kelly A
Union Intermediate HS
Tulsa, OK

Oney, Aaron
Owasso Sr HS
Owasso, OK

Onken, Jenny R
Harrah HS
Harrah, OK

On-The-Hill, Brian
Preston Schl
Beggs, OK

Orban, Daniel T
Enid Sr HS
Enid, OK

Orr, Amanda R
Choctaw HS
Choctaw, OK

Orr, Kathryn E
Stillwater Sr HS
Stillwater, OK

Orsatti, Andrea R
Midwest City HS
Midwest City, OK

Osborn, Scott
Bluejacket Schl
Bluejacket, OK

Osborn, Stephanie
Tonkawa Jr Sr HS
Tonkawa, OK

Osborne, Sasha
Sasakwa Schl
Ada, OK

Oshel, Stephanie
Alva HS
Aline, OK

O'Steen, Emily
Claremore Sr HS
Claremore, OK

Ott, Dustin L
Dibble Jr Sr HS
Blanchard, OK

Ott, Jason J
Dibble Jr Sr HS
Blanchard, OK

Ott Jr, Lucky Steve
Okemah HS
Okemah, OK

Ott, Matthew R
Edmond North HS
Edmond, OK

Otterstrom, Abbigail A
Bishop Kelley HS
Tulsa, OK

Otterstrom, Sandra M
Bishop Kelley HS
Tulsa, OK

Owen, Christina B
Moore HS
Moore, OK

Owens, Alberta N
Northeast HS
Oklahoma City, OK

Owens, Ann E
Broken Bow HS
Broken Bow, OK

Owens, Mike B
Meeker HS
Meeker, OK

Owens, Sara B
Muldrow HS
Muldrow, OK

Owens, Shawn
Westmoore HS
Moore, OK

Owens, Tonishia J
B T Washington HS
Tulsa, OK

Owens-Little Jim, Dee Ann
Little Axe Sr HS
Norman, OK

Pack, Bryan
Bethany HS
Bethany, OK

Paden, Brittanie
Choctaw Jr HS
Choctaw, OK

Padilla, Israel
Hobart HS
Hobart, OK

Padley, Christopher
Union Intermediate HS
Tulsa, OK

Page, Bryan E
Bishop Kelley HS
Tulsa, OK

Paget, Nickie
Oologah Talala HS
Nowata, OK

Paige, Amy S
Blackwell HS
Blackwell, OK

Paige, Cheron
Midwest City HS
Oklahoma City, OK

Palmer, Kelly D
Claremore Sr HS
Claremore, OK

Palmer, Tara
Chickasha HS
Chickasha, OK

Pals, Kendra
Stillwater Jr HS
Stillwater, OK

Paquett, Lily A
Edmond North HS
Edmond, OK

Pardue, Heather S
Edmond Memorial HS
Edmond, OK

Parikh, Ruchi
Tomlinson Jr HS
Lawton, OK

Parikh, Shailja
Lawton Sr HS
Lawton, OK

Parish, Kathryn B
Jenks HS
Tulsa, OK

Park, Ron L
Choctaw HS
Choctaw, OK

Parker, Chance
Gore HS
Webbers Falls, OK

Parker, Charles A
Choctaw HS
Midwest City, OK

Parker, Gregory P
Putnam City West HS
Oklahoma City, OK

Parker, Jill J
Union Intermediate HS
Tulsa, OK

Parker, Lisa
Western Heights Sr HS
Oklahoma City, OK

Parker, Matt B
Fairview HS
Chester, OK

Parker, Michele L
Tahlequah Sr HS
Cookson, OK

Parker, Patience
Fairview HS
Chester, OK

Parker, Sophia
Roland Sr HS
Roland, OK

Parkhurst, Megan
Guymon Sr HS
Guymon, OK

Parmer, Justin
Choctaw Jr HS
Choctaw, OK

Parnell, Bree
Blanchard Jr Sr HS
Blanchard, OK

Parrish, Amber R
Bethel HS
Shawnee, OK

Parrish, Jason
Woodward HS
Woodward, OK

Parsons, Ryan J
East Central HS
Tulsa, OK

Patrick, Elizabeth
Jenks HS
Tulsa, OK

Patterson, Chris S
Morris HS
Henryetta, OK

Patterson, Jennifer
Warner HS
Porum, OK

Patterson, Jerid D
Woodward HS
Woodward, OK

Patterson, Julie M
Memorial HS
Tulsa, OK

Patterson, Matt
Collinsville HS
Collinsville, OK

Patterson, Micah R
Lindsay HS
Lindsay, OK

Patterson, Misti D
Sayre HS
Sayre, OK

Pattillo, Scott
Skiatook HS
Skiatook, OK

Patzkowski, Tara J
Deer Creek HS
Edmond, OK

Patzkowsky, Andrea B
Okeen HS
Okeene, OK

Paul, Kristin K
Guthrie Sr HS
Guthrie, OK

Paul, Ryan
Collinsville HS
Collinsville, OK

Paulec, Joy A
Union Sr HS
Broken Arrow, OK

Paulec, Mason D
Union Intermediate HS
Broken Arrow, OK

Pauley, Devin
Midwest City HS
Oklahoma City, OK

Paxton, Ecerra L
Hominy HS
Oklahoma City, OK

Paxton, Jeremy E
Yukon Middle HS
Yukon, OK

Payne, Abigail
Beaver HS
Beaver, OK

Payne, Allison
Perry Sr HS
Perry, OK

Payne, Cody
Fairview HS
Fairview, OK

Payne, Jamie
Cushing HS
Cushing, OK

Payne, Jarod
Chandler HS
Chandler, OK

Payne, Rachael S
Lindsay HS
Lindsay, OK

Payton, Halie
Miami Sr HS
Miami, OK

Peach, Kristen P
North Intemediate HS
Broken Arrow, OK

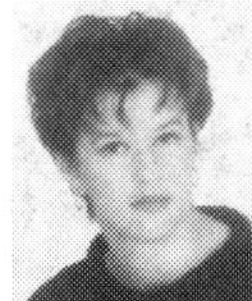
Pearce, Erin
Marietta HS
Marietta, OK

Pearson, Chance L
Edmond Memorial HS
Edmond, OK

Pearson, Elizabeth A
Deer Creek HS
Edmond, OK

Pearson III, Lindell E
Edmond North HS
Edmond, OK

Pearson White,
Heidi L
Fletcher Jr Sr HS
Fletcher, OK

Pease, Alana C
U S Grant HS
Oklahoma City, OK

Peck, Benji
Oklahoma
Christian Schl
Edmond, OK

Peck, Jonathan D
Ponca City Sr HS
Ponca City, OK

Pedigo, Lisa M
Putnam City West HS
Bethany, OK

Peebles, Katie
Durant HS
Durant, OK

Peek, Jerry L
Sapulpa Sr HS
Sapulpa, OK

Pelton, Jennifer D
Ardmore HS
Ardmore, OK

Pemberton, Jennifer
Bethany
Christian Acad
Mustang, OK

Pendleton, Jaqulyn R
Stillwater Jr HS
Stillwater, OK

Penisten, James R
Shawnee Sr HS
Shawnee, OK

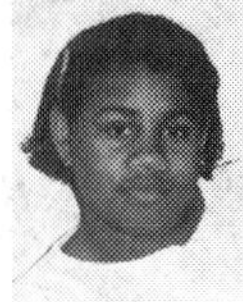
Pennington, Chaya
Northeast HS
Oklahoma City, OK

Pennington, Erin A
Duncan HS
Duncan, OK

Peoples Jr, Ricky A
Dickson HS
Mannsville, OK

Peper, Julie
Adair HS
Adair, OK

Perceful, Brandy E
Roland Sr HS
Roland, OK

Perez, Charles L
Eisenhower Sr HS
Lawton, OK

Peringol, Abraham K
Putnam City West HS
Bethany, OK

Perkins, Nicolette
Sulphur HS
Sulphur, OK

Permenter, Justin
Spiro HS
Spiro, OK

Perrin, Travis
Stillwater Sr HS
Stillwater, OK

Perry, Brandon L
Charles Page HS
Sand Springs, OK

Pertree, Courtney L
Christian
Heritage Acad
Oklahoma City, OK

Pertree, James T
Christian
Heritage Acad
Oklahoma City, OK

Peters, Julianna
Sapulpa Sr HS
Sapulpa, OK

Peters, Kenneth R
Northeast HS
Oklahoma City, OK

Peters, Monica
Watts HS
Watts, OK

Peters, Shannon R
Shawnee Sr HS
Shawnee, OK

Peterson, Amanda
South Intermediate HS
Broken Arrow, OK

Pettit, Courtney
Lawton Sr HS
Lawton, OK

Phan, John
Westmoore HS
Oklahoma City, OK

Phelps, Jason
Santa Fe HS
Edmond, OK

Philipp, Leslie A
Westmoore HS
Oklahoma City, OK

Phillips, Amber L
Will Rogers HS
Tulsa, OK

Phillips, Branson L
North Intermediate HS
Tulsa, OK

Phillips, Eric E
Shawnee Sr HS
Shawnee, OK

Phillips, Shanna
Varnum Jr Sr HS
Seminole, OK

Phillips, Shawna
Brooke
Capitol Hill HS
Oklahoma City, OK

Philpot, Alisha M
Union Intermediate HS
Broken Arrow, OK

Phipps, Clayton
Empire Schl
Duncan, OK

Phipps, Courtney A
Empire Schl
Duncan, OK

Phollurxa, Sounally
Chickasha HS
Chickasha, OK

Picco, Tara M
Union Sr HS
Tulsa, OK

Pickens, Rusty D
Stonewall Jr-Sr HS
Stonewall, OK

Pickett, Wendy W
Bishop Mcguinness HS
Oklahoma City, OK

Pierce, Jason
Putnam City HS
Oklahoma City, OK

Pierce, Stuart R
Warner HS
Warner, OK

Pierson, Loretha S
Healdton HS
Graham, OK

Pingleton, Christy
Mc Alester HS
Mcalester, OK

Pingleton, Richie
Pauls Valley HS
Pauls Valley, OK

Pipkin, Eric Cliffton
Gregory
Yukon Middle HS
Yukon, OK

Pirpich, Bradley G
Indianola HS
Mcalester, OK

Pitchford, Carla
Red Oak Schl
Red Oak, OK

Pitts, Adam S
Sapulpa Sr HS
Sapulpa, OK

Pitts, Danny L
North Intemediate HS
Broken Arrow, OK

Pitts, Evangula M
Will Rogers HS
Tulsa, OK

Plumlee, Billy D
Tuttle HS
Tuttle, OK

Plumlee, Brandi
Del City HS
Oklahoma City, OK

Plumlee, Keitha J
Putnam City North HS
Oklahoma City, OK

Poe, Amber
Miami Sr HS
Miami, OK

Poe, Heath E
North Intemediate HS
Broken Arrow, OK

Pollard, Kodi
Mt St Marys HS
Oklahoma City, OK

Pollet, Brandon C
South Coffeyville Schl
S Coffeyville, OK

Polson, Chad
Dustin Schl
Dustin, OK

Pool, Ryan M
Moore HS
Moore, OK

Porter, Brian
Midwest City HS
Midwest City, OK

Porter, David W
Edmond Santa Fe HS
Edmond, OK

Porter, Gina K
Owasso Sr HS
Owasso, OK

Porter, Kiley
Chickasha HS
Chickasha, OK

Posey, Jennifer L
Duncan HS
Duncan, OK

Potter, Adrienne
Fellowship
Baptist Acad
Stilwell, OK

Potter, Chaliena M
Owasso Sr HS
Owasso, OK

Potts, Christy B
Union Sr HS
Broken Arrow, OK

Potts, Mike J
Choctaw HS
Harrah, OK

Poudard, Alicia J
Guthrie Sr HS
Guthrie, OK

Powell, Alicia A
Cordell Sr HS
Cordell, OK

Powell, Ashlee
Bridge Creek HS
Tuttle, OK

Powell, Jennifer M
Broken Arrow Sr HS
Broken Arrow, OK

Powell, Sarah
Lawton Sr HS
Lawton, OK

Powers, Brett
Ponca City Sr HS
Ponca City, OK

Powers, Christopher L
Drumright HS
Drumright, OK

Powers, Josh
Mustang HS
Yukon, OK

Powers, Sara M
Edmond North HS
Edmond, OK

Prater, Shawna
Guymon Sr HS
Guymon, OK

Pratt, Jennifer M
Hinton HS
Hinton, OK

Pratt, Josh
Bartlesville Mid HS
Bartlesville, OK

Preas, Tom M
Mannford HS
Sand Springs, OK

Prebble, Dylan W
Claremore Sr HS
Claremore, OK

Presley, Amy
Jenks HS
Tulsa, OK

Prewett, Brandon K
Preston Schl
Beggs, OK

Price, Brooke
Mid-Del Christian Schl
Oklahoma City, OK

Price, Julie
Dover Schl
Dover, OK

Price, Kara L
Sayre HS
Sayre, OK

Price, Marhya J
Spiro HS
Spiro, OK

Price, Mary Beth
Edmond North HS
Edmond, OK

Prichard, Jennifer J
Duncan HS
Duncan, OK

Prickett, Aaron
Collinsville HS
Collinsville, OK

Prigmore, Matt L
Norman Sr HS
Norman, OK

Prince, Amanda L
Spiro HS
Lavaca, AR

Prince, Angel O
Edmond North HS
Edmond, OK

Prince, Ashley
Indianola HS
Indianola, OK

Prince, Crystal D
Midwest City HS
Del City, OK

Prince, Jamie
Miami Sr HS
Miami, OK

Prince, Marci N
Eakly HS
Eakly, OK

Prince, Toby L
Bethany HS
Bethany, OK

Pritchard, Corbi H
Owasso Sr HS
Owasso, OK

Privette, Samantha
Guthrie Sr HS
Guthrie, OK

Prochaska, Jennifer
Westmoore HS
Oklahoma City, OK

Prosser, Jennifer J
Union Intermediate HS
Tulsa, OK

Prudom III, Wesley J
Booker J
Washington HS
Tulsa, OK

Pruett, Greg D
Enid Sr HS
Enid, OK

Pruitt, Allison L
Putnam City North HS
Oklahoma City, OK

Pryor, David E
Union Intermediate HS
Broken Arrow, OK

Pucket, Jonathan D
Charles Page HS
Sand Springs, OK

Pugh II, Richard
Caney Jr Sr HS
Caney, OK

Quackenbush, Jeana
Luther HS
Luther, OK

Qualls, James T
Haskell HS
Haskell, OK

Quible, Chris
Stillwater Sr HS
Stillwater, OK

Quinton, Elizabeth A
Sapulpa Sr HS
Sapulpa, OK

Quinton, Jennifer L
Sapulpa Sr HS
Sapulpa, OK

Quisenberry, Eric T
Caney Valley HS
Ramona, OK

Rachel, Tara
Byng Sr HS
Ada, OK

Radcliff, Timothy
El Reno Sr HS
El Reno, OK

Rader, Amanda M
Woodward HS
Woodward, OK

Ragle, Amanda D
Olive Jr Sr HS
Mannford, OK

Railey, Leisa A
Sharon Mutual Jr
Sr HS
Woodward, OK

Raines, Robert G
Sharon Mutual Jr
Sr HS
Woodward, OK

Rainey, James M
Memorial HS
Broken Arrow, OK

Rambo, Shana B
Memorial HS
Tulsa, OK

Ramey, Rickie
Afton HS
Vinita, OK

Ramirez, Alfredo
Lawton Sr HS
Lawton, OK

Ramsey, Nikki
Westmoore HS
Oklahoma City, OK

Randall, Kevin
Tonkawa Jr Sr HS
Tonkawa, OK

Randolph, Shane J
Cushing HS
Cushing, OK

Raney, Mary E
Muldrow HS
Sallisaw, OK

Rankin, Matthew A
Sapulpa Sr HS
Sapulpa, OK

Rano, Patrick R
OK Schl Of Sci
& Math
Yale, OK

Ransom, Dusty L
Wakita Schl
Wakita, OK

Rapson, Brian M
Del City HS
Oklahoma City, OK

Rasmussen, Timothy
David
Jones HS
Jones, OK

Rasor, Merideth
Cascia Hall Prep
School
Tulsa, OK

Ray, Amanda
Braman Schl
Braman, OK

Ray, Christy J
Pauls Valley HS
Pauls Valley, OK

Ray, Kaycee M
B T Washington HS
Tulsa, OK

Ray, Krystal
Mc Lish HS
Ada, OK

Ray, Lindsey M
Heritage Hall Schl
Oklahoma City, OK

Ray, William
Charles Page HS
Sand Springs, OK

Rayburn, Monique D
Putnam City North HS
Oklahoma City, OK

Rayburn, Rachel E
Wright Christian Acad
Tulsa, OK

Reagan, Lillie A
Cushing HS
Cushing, OK

Rector, Darrell R
Miami Sr HS
Miami, OK

Red Elk, Ashley
Empire Schl
Duncan, OK

Redway, Jamie
Grandfield Jr Sr HS
Grandfield, OK

Reed, Jessica
Roff HS
Roff, OK

Reed, Kenneth G
Edmond North HS
Edmond, OK

Reed, Lacy
Comanche HS
Comanche, OK

Reed, Melanie E
Sallisaw HS
Sallisaw, OK

Reed, Rachel R
Nathan Hale HS
Tulsa, OK

Reed, Sylina M
Panola HS
Red Oak, OK

Reedy, Laura B
Union Intermediate HS
Tulsa, OK

Reedy, Walter A
Union Sr HS
Tulsa, OK

Reeves, Erica L
Roland Sr HS
Roland, OK

Reeves, Krista
Maysville Jr Sr HS
Maysville, OK

Reeves, Marie
Dale Sr HS
Shawnee, OK

Reeves, Robin S
Bartlesville Mid HS
Bartlesville, OK

Regier, Amanda
Oklahoma Bible Acad
Enid, OK

Reich, Jami
Ft Towson HS
Fort Towson, OK

Reichert, Stacie
Roland Sr HS
Roland, OK

Reichman,
Nathanael W
Clayton Jr Sr HS
Tulsa, OK

Reichman, Renee
Stillwater Sr HS
Stillwater, OK

Reimer, Amy
Holdenville HS
Holdenville, OK

Reininger, Daryl
Ada HS
Ada, OK

Reininger, Laura J
Fairview HS
Chester, OK

Remer, Joshua A
Okmulgee HS
Okmulgee, OK

Renfroe, Cynthia A
Union Sr HS
Tulsa, OK

Renfrow, Melanie L
Dewey HS
Ochelata, OK

OKLAHOMA

Reniers, Melanie A
Putnam City North HS
Oklahoma City, OK

Renyer, Chris O
Duncan HS
Duncan, OK

Reuter, F Blake
El Reno Sr HS
El Reno, OK

Revis, Tamara N
Sapulpa Sr HS
Sapulpa, OK

Reynolds, Craig
Oklahoma Union Schl
Coffeyville, KS

Reynolds III, John
Haynes
Muskogee HS
Muskogee, OK

Reynolds, Kortney K
Nathan Hale HS
Tulsa, OK

Rhea, Shawn
Wynnewood HS
Wynnewood, OK

Rhoads, Brad A
Ada HS
Ada, OK

Rhodes, Jamie L
Deer Creek HS
Oklahoma City, OK

Rhodes, Nita M
Tahlequah Sr HS
Tahlequah, OK

Rice, Barry
Coweta HS
Coweta, OK

Rice, Justin W
Webster HS
Tulsa, OK

Rice, Ryan
Westmoore HS
Oklahoma City, OK

Richards, Matthew C
Bishop Kelley HS
Tulsa, OK

Richardson, Amanda I
Broken Arrow Sr HS
Tulsa, OK

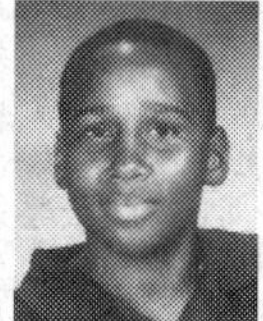
Richardson,
Arlando M
Del City HS
Del City, OK

Richardson, Brandy
Catoosa HS
Catoosa, OK

Richardson, Dana J
Claremore Sr HS
Claremore, OK

Richardson, Kily
Amber Pocasset Jr
Sr HS
Amber, OK

Richardson, Laura M
Christian
Heritage Acad
Norman, OK

Richardson, Nick
Cascia Hall Prep
School
Tulsa, OK

Richey, Mandi D
Inola Sr HS
Inola, OK

Richison, Michelle L
Del City HS
Oklahoma City, OK

Richmond, Kori L
Oklahoma Sch Of
Science & Math
Holdenville, OK

Riddel, Ryan J
Mc Alester HS
Mcalester, OK

Riddle, Megan L
Union Sr HS
Broken Arrow, OK

Riddles, Amanda L
Rush Springs HS
Rush Springs, OK

Riddles, Darren C
Mustang HS
Mustang, OK

Ridener, Justin E
Charles Page HS
Sand Springs, OK

Ridgway, Amery D
Caney Jr Sr HS
Caney, OK

Riedl, Melissa J
Woodward HS
Woodward, OK

Riemer, Bradford S
Lawton Sr HS
Lawton, OK

Riggs, Barry M
Pocola HS
Pocola, OK

Riggs, Daniel A
Ardmore HS
Ardmore, OK

Rightmer, Nathan
Tomlinson Jr HS
Lawton, OK

Riley, Amy L
Enid Sr HS
Enid, OK

Riley, Dezmont D
Bishop Kelley HS
Tulsa, OK

Riley, Emily C
Enid Sr HS
Enid, OK

Riley, Jennifer A
Shawnee Sr HS
Shawnee, OK

Riley, Josh
Roff HS
Fitzhugh, OK

Riley, Sarah J
Mannford HS
Mannford, OK

Riley, Susan E
Mustang HS
Yukon, OK

Rimmer, Darci R
Newcastle HS
Newcastle, OK

Rinderer, Christina
Bridge Creek HS
Blanchard, OK

Rinehart, Rusti A
Western Heights Sr HS
Oklahoma City, OK

Ringgold, Jennifer M
Cleveland Sr HS
Cleveland, OK

Ringwald, Lisa M
Heritage Hall Schl
Oklahoma City, OK

Risher, Brianne G
Del City HS
Del City, OK

Risley, Deborah L
Prague HS
Prague, OK

Risner, Cassie R
Union Intermediate HS
Tulsa, OK

Ritter, Kevin S
Union Intermediate HS
Tulsa, OK

Ritter, Shawn D
Stilwell HS
Stilwell, OK

Rivers, Amanda C
Cordell Sr HS
Cordell, OK

Rizzo, Caryn B
Putnam City North HS
Oklahoma City, OK

Robbins, Jessica
Crowder Schl
Crowder, OK

Robbins, Kelli
Marietta HS
Marietta, OK

Robbins, Rachel
Grace Chrn Acad
Oklahoma City, OK

Robbins, Sheila
Medford Schl
Medford, OK

Robbins, Tamara
Marietta HS
Marietta, OK

Robbins, Tara
Tonkawa Jr Sr HS
Tonkawa, OK

Roberds, Mandy
Preston Schl
Preston, OK

Roberts, Cheryl
Foyil Schl
Claremore, OK

Roberts, John D
Del City HS
Oklahoma City, OK

Roberts, K J
Weleetka Sr HS
Weleetka, OK

Roberts, Katera P
Owasso Sr HS
Owasso, OK

Roberts, Regan M
Muldrow HS
Muldrow, OK

Roberts, Tammy
Colbert HS
Cartwright, OK

Robertson, Anthony R
Checotah HS
Checotah, OK

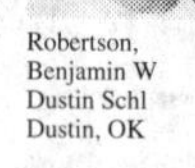
Robertson,
Benjamin W
Dustin Schl
Dustin, OK

Robertson, Carrie
Eisenhower Sr HS
Lawton, OK

Robertson, Elliott
Konawa Sr HS
Konawa, OK

Robertson, Gabriel L
Del City HS
Del City, OK

Robertson, Joe
Blanchard Jr Sr HS
Blanchard, OK

Robertson, Lakesha R
Star Spencer HS
Spencer, OK

Robinette, Richard L
Union Sr HS
Tulsa, OK

Robinson, Alan C
Hollis Jr Sr HS
Hollis, OK

Robinson, Anthony C
West Middle HS
Norman, OK

Robinson, Genice Y
Del City HS
Oklahoma City, OK

Robinson, Matt
Stillwater Jr HS
Stillwater, OK

Robinson, Roy
Sapulpa Sr HS
Sand Springs, OK

Robinson, Shenell L
Stillwater Jr HS
Stillwater, OK

Robinson, Whitney
Chickasha Jr HS
Chickasha, OK

Robison, Amber
Cushing HS
Cushing, OK

Rock, Gregory F
Mc Alester HS
Mcalester, OK

Rockwood, Kathy M
Bixby Sr HS
Bixby, OK

Rodgers, Jennifer L
Shawnee Sr HS
Shawnee, OK

Rodgers, Kristen L
Durant HS
Durant, OK

Rodgers, Melissa
Durant HS
Durant, OK

Rodgers, Michele D
Poteau HS
Poteau, OK

Rodriguez, Courtney
Durant HS
Durant, OK

Rodriguez, Michelle
Plainview HS
Ardmore, OK

Rodriguez, Tara M
Westmoore HS
Oklahoma City, OK

Roe, Jeff
Tulsa Emmanuel
Christian Sch
Tulsa, OK

Roehr, Michael S
Lawton Sr HS
Fort Sill, OK

Rogers, Aaron J
Stillwater Sr HS
Stillwater, OK

Rogers, Felicia D
Shattuck Jr Sr HS
Shattuck, OK

Rogers, Lea Anne
Medford Schl
Medford, OK

Rogers, Melissa D
Midwest City HS
Midwest City, OK

Rogers Jr, Tommy M
Charles Page HS
Sapulpa, OK

Rognas, Eric L
Edmond Memorial HS
Edmond, OK

Roland, Amanda D
Charles Page HS
Sand Springs, OK

Roland, Laticia
Enid Sr HS
Enid, OK

Roll, Della K
Stillwater Sr HS
Stillwater, OK

Roller, Marci D
Union Sr HS
Broken Arrow, OK

Romberg, Derek J
Shawnee Sr HS
Shawnee, OK

Romero, Jason N
Broken Arrow Sr HS
Broken Arrow, OK

Romero, Nick J
Chandler HS
Port Arthur, TX

Romine, Charla M
East Central HS
Tulsa, OK

Roney, Matt
Edmond North HS
Edmond, OK

Rooker, Jason
Tuttle HS
Tuttle, OK

Rooker, Josh
Mc Loud HS
Mc Loud, OK

Roper, Amber
Varnum Jr Sr HS
Seminole, OK

Rose, Chivon M
John Marshall HS
Oklahoma City, OK

Rose, Richard
Woodward HS
Woodward, OK

Ross, Adrianne I
Northeast HS
Oklahoma City, OK

Ross, Casey R
U S Grant HS
Oklahoma City, OK

Ross, Lindsey E
Lawton Sr HS
Lawton, OK

Rother, Rory W
Okarche HS
Okarche, OK

Rountree, Cary M
Lexington HS
Lexington, OK

Rovig, Meghan J
Stillwater Sr HS
Stillwater, OK

Rowe, Cheron
Plainview HS
Ardmore, OK

Rowell, Mary M
Mc Alester HS
Mcalester, OK

Roy, Brandi
Navajo Schl
Blair, OK

Roye, Brandon
Jenks HS
Jenks, OK

Rozanova, Alla
Tonkawa Jr Sr HS
Tonkawa, OK

Ruark, Courtney
Kingfisher HS
Kingfisher, OK

Ruby, Steven
Enid Sr HS
Enid, OK

Rucker, Meredith M
Tahlequah Jr HS
Tahlequah, OK

Rucker, Nicole
Putnam City West HS
Oklahoma City, OK

Ruhl, Karen
Watonga HS
Greenfield, OK

Rule, Melissa E
Edmond Memorial HS
Edmond, OK

Rumley, Anne
Jenks HS
Jenks, OK

Rumsey, Josh W
Western Heights Sr HS
Oklahoma City, OK

Runnels, Nikki
Thomas Jr Sr HS
Thomas, OK

Runyon, Stacy L
Macarthur Sr HS
Lawton, OK

Rupe, Brandon
Poteau HS
Shady Point, OK

Rush, Brandon D
Central Mid-HS
Norman, OK

Russell, April M
Roland Sr HS
Roland, OK

Russell, Brent A
Westmoore HS
Oklahoma City, OK

OKLAHOMA

Russell, Charles S
Putnam City North HS
Oklahoma City, OK

Russell, Le Anne R
Okay Jr Sr HS
Muskogee, OK

Russell, Steven T
Putnam City HS
Oklahoma City, OK

Russell, Thomas
Kiefer Jr Sr HS
Sapulpa, OK

Rust, Brea
Poteau HS
Poteau, OK

Ruth, Ryan E
Sapulpa Sr HS
Sapulpa, OK

Rutherford, Connie A
Putnam City North HS
Oklahoma City, OK

Rutledge, Lindsay
Nicoma Park Jr HS
Choctaw, OK

Rutledge, Matthew W
Choctaw HS
Choctaw, OK

Ruyle, Amanda M
Nathan Hale HS
Tulsa, OK

Ryan, Adam M
Jenks HS
Tulsa, OK

Ryan, Casey
Wynnewood HS
Wynnewood, OK

Ryan, Dawn M
Choctaw HS
Harrah, OK

Ryan, Rebekah S
Yukon Middle HS
Yukon, OK

Ryan, Shawn M
Choctaw HS
Harrah, OK

Ryba, Tanner M
El Reno Sr HS
El Reno, OK

Ryel, Jeff
Timberlake Schl
Aline, OK

Rylant, Miranda M
Elk City Jr HS
Elk City, OK

Sadler, Marka
Cheyenne HS
Cheyenne, OK

Sager, Lori
Kellyville Sr HS
Sapulpa, OK

Salamon, Nicole D
Union Intermediate HS
Tulsa, OK

Saldana, Adriana
Union Sr HS
Tulsa, OK

Saldana, Miguel A
Union Intermediate HS
Tulsa, OK

Sallee, Amy C
Charles Page HS
Sand Springs, OK

Sallis, Kacey R
Muskogee HS
Muskogee, OK

Sallladay, Jackie
Yukon HS
Yukon, OK

Salmon, Jake I
Locust Grove HS
Salina, OK

Salmon, Mandie
Antlers Sr HS
Antlers, OK

Sanchez, Nohemi
Marietta HS
Marietta, OK

Sandefur, Laura C
Union Intermediate HS
Tulsa, OK

Sander, Kristy
Seiling Schl
Seiling, OK

Sanders, Jason R
Putnam City North HS
Oklahoma City, OK

Sanders, Michel R
Del City HS
Del City, OK

Sanders, Sara
Carl Albert HS
Oklahoma City, OK

Sanders, Shelley L
Charles Page HS
Tulsa, OK

Sanders, Tara L
Lexington HS
Lexington, OK

Sanders, Tatum
Westmoore HS
Oklahoma City, OK

Sandy, Crystal
Holdenville Jr HS
Holdenville, OK

Sanford, Derek
Pauls Valley HS
Pauls Valley, OK

Santee, Sarah E
Bishop Kelley HS
Tulsa, OK

Satoris, Kayla J
Wilburton Sr HS
Gowen, OK

Sauler, John M
Edmond Santa Fe HS
Edmond, OK

Saulsberry, Robert Z
Shawnee Sr HS
Shawnee, OK

Saum, Ryan T
Marietta HS
Marietta, OK

Savage, Rayna S
Lindsay HS
Lindsay, OK

Saylor, Desiree M
Webster HS
Tulsa, OK

Sayre, Kristy D
Seminole Jr Sr HS
Seminole, OK

Scarberry, Faron W
Carnegie HS
Carnegie, OK

Scarberry, Kristy
Warner HS
Warner, OK

Schachle, Jayme
Cordell Sr HS
Cordell, OK

Schaefer, Matt
Edmond North HS
Edmond, OK

Schallner, Jeremy
Fairview HS
Fairview, OK

Schatz, Zack B
Stillwater Sr HS
Stillwater, OK

Schaub, Lyndsay L
Heritage Hall Schl
Edmond, OK

Schilde, Adam
Dover Schl
Dover, OK

Schliemann,
Matthew L
Altus Sr HS
Altus, OK

Schmidt, Jenny
Edmond North HS
Edmond, OK

Schmitt, Heather
Western Heights Sr HS
Oklahoma City, OK

Schmitz, Heather I
Bartlesville Sr HS
Bartlesville, OK

Schneider, Amanda
Owasso Sr HS
Owasso, OK

Schniederjan, Jorie
Westmoore HS
Oklahoma City, OK

Schnorrenberg, Rachel
Marietta HS
Marietta, OK

Schoeling, Ryan C
Pond
Creek-Hunter Schl
Hunter, OK

Schrack, Stephanie A
Jenks HS
Keller, TX

Schreiner, Dustin
Duncan HS
Duncan, OK

Schuermann, Erica D
Pond
Creek-Hunter Schl
Lamont, OK

Schultz, Amanda
Stillwater Sr HS
Stillwater, OK

Schumacher, Travis L
Bixby Sr HS
Bixby, OK

Schuster, Jonathan B
Edmond Memorial HS
Edmond, OK

Schuster, Sarah N
Edmond Memorial HS
Edmond, OK

Schwemley, Becky S
Kingspark
Baptist Acad
Oklahoma City, OK

Sconzo, Michael
Classen Schl Of
Advncd Studies
Oklahoma City, OK

Scott, Elizabeth
Corn Bible Acad
Carnegie, OK

Scott, Heaven S
Tahlequah Sr HS
Hulbert, OK

Scott, Jerron D
Okmulgee HS
Okmulgee, OK

Scott, Lindsey L
Heavener HS
Heavener, OK

Scott, Riann L
Putnam City HS
Oklahoma City, OK

Scroggins, Kim A
Byng Sr HS
Ada, OK

Seager, Kyle J
Norman Sr HS
Norman, OK

Sears, Jami S
Salina HS
Adair, OK

Sears, Kristy D
Healdton HS
Healdton, OK

Seaton, Tiffany
Midwest City HS
Midwest City, OK

Seba, Kristi C
Glenpool HS
Glenpool, OK

Sebesta, April
Adair HS
Adair, OK

Secrest, Travis
Seiling Schl
Seiling, OK

Seeley, Jennifer
Moore HS
Moore, OK

Seely, Jamie M
El Reno Sr HS
El Reno, OK

Seiber, Tanya N
East Central HS
Tulsa, OK

Seibold, Michael W
Edison HS
Tulsa, OK

Seidel, Tiffany H
Central Jr HS
Lawton, OK

Seitz, Marc A
Putnam City North HS
Franklin, TN

Self, Paul
Edmond North HS
Edmond, OK

Self, Phillip
Kiowa Jr-Sr HS
Stringtown, OK

Selfridge, Heather J
Shawnee Sr HS
Shawnee, OK

Sellars, Jason
Mustang HS
Mustang, OK

Sells, Zach
Hulbert Jr Sr HS
Hulbert, OK

Selman, Scott L
Bishop Kelley HS
Tulsa, OK

Selph, Ashley D
Heritage Hall Schl
Oklahoma City, OK

Selsor, Nick R
Cresent Acad
Oklahoma City, OK

Session, Tamara
Broken Arrow Sr HS
Broken Arrow, OK

Sevier, Kyle R
Mustang HS
Mustang, OK

Sexson, Charles
Jenks HS
Tulsa, OK

Sexton, Brandi
Shawnee Sr HS
Shawnee, OK

Seymour, Natalie K
Edmond Memorial HS
Edmond, OK

Shafer, Stacey
Putnam City West HS
Oklahoma City, OK

Shafer, Stacy A
Ponca City Sr HS
Ponca City, OK

Shahan, Kelli C
Union Sr HS
Broken Arrow, OK

Shahan, Regina
Lawton Sr HS
Lawton, OK

Shannon, Amanda
Victory Christian Schl
Tulsa, OK

Shannon, Jacob A
Union Intermediate HS
Broken Arrow, OK

Shapard, Jessica
Heritage Hall Schl
Oklahoma City, OK

Sharp, Brandy L
Midwest City HS
Midwest City, OK

Sharp, Tracey A
Spiro HS
Spiro, OK

Shaver, Mandi
Eufaula Sr HS
Eufaula, OK

Shaw, Justin
Dickson HS
Ardmore, OK

Shaw, Katy D
Union Intermediate HS
Broken Arrow, OK

Shaw, Kelli
Westmoore HS
Oklahoma City, OK

Shaw, Rebecca
Blanchard Jr Sr HS
Blanchard, OK

Shea, Laura A
Edmond Memorial HS
Edmond, OK

Sheehan, Elizabeth
Grace Fellowship
Christian Sch
Tulsa, OK

Sheehan III, Robert D
Holland Hall Schl
Tulsa, OK

Sheets, Jenny
Altus Sr HS
Altus, OK

Sheets, Misty Dawn
Soper Schl
Hugo, OK

Sheffield, January T
Afton HS
Bernice, OK

Shelkett, Amber M
Lawton Sr HS
Lawton, OK

Shelton, Amber D
Wilburton Sr HS
Kinta, OK

Shelton, Autumn M
South Intermediate HS
Broken Arrow, OK

Shelton, Cassie M
Brink Jr HS
Oklahoma City, OK

Shelton, James M
Lindsay HS
Lindsay, OK

Shelton, Tiffany R
Morris HS
Okmulgee, OK

Shenold, Chad
Anadarko HS
Anadarko, OK

Shephard, Brandie L
Lexington HS
Purcell, OK

Shepherd, Jesse H
North Intermediate HS
Broken Arrow, OK

Shepherd, Johnathon L
Catoosa HS
Catoosa, OK

Sherfield, Regina J
Whitesboro Schl
Hodgen, OK

Sherman, Heather D
Charles Page HS
Sand Springs, OK

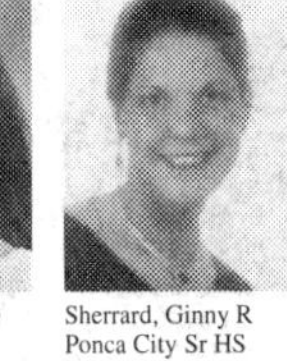
Sherrard, Ginny R
Ponca City Sr HS
Ponca City, OK

Sherrard, Kim R
Moore HS
Moore, OK

Sherrell, Joseph N
Webster HS
Tulsa, OK

Shields, Amy
Pioneer Pleasant
Vale HS
Enid, OK

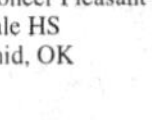

OKLAHOMA

Shields, Mary K
Charles Page HS
Sand Springs, OK

Shinnen, Holly N
Sapulpa Sr HS
Sapulpa, OK

Shipley, Laci A
Morris HS
Okmulgee, OK

Shipman, Jeff L
Oologah HS
Claremore, OK

Shipman, Jeremy
Durant HS
Durant, OK

Shirley, Rachel G
Stillwater Sr HS
Stillwater, OK

Shockley, Denise
Northeast HS
Oklahoma City, OK

Shoemake, Cory L
Edmond Memorial HS
Edmond, OK

Shore, Kristin
Crescent Schl
Crescent, OK

Short, Shelly D
John Marshall HS
Oklahoma City, OK

Short, Stacie
Bethany HS
Oklahoma City, OK

Shortt, Dori
Bluejacket Schl
Bluejacket, OK

Shouse, Jennifer
Morrison Public Schl
Morrison, OK

Shroyer, Travis
Tuttle HS
Tuttle, OK

Shutterly, Cassidy L
Westmoore HS
Oklahoma City, OK

Siebert, Jason L
Choctaw HS
Choctaw, OK

Siemens, Wendy M
Del City HS
Del City, OK

Sikes, Ashley M
Bartlesville Sr HS
Bartlesville, OK

Sikes, Brooke
Nathan Hale HS
Tulsa, OK

Sikes, Emily B
Nathan Hale HS
Tulsa, OK

Sikka, Seema R
Oklahoma Sch Of
Science & Math
Tulsa, OK

Silva, Heather M
Charles Page HS
Sand Springs, OK

Silvestre, Divina
Grace C
Charles Page HS
Sand Springs, OK

Simard, Kylene
Pioneer Jr Sr HS
Enid, OK

Simard, Tracie R
Pioneer Jr Sr HS
Enid, OK

Simic, Preston
Garber Sr HS
Garber, OK

Simmons, Ashley
Brooke
Bixby Sr HS
Bixby, OK

Simmons, Brian
Waukomis HS
Waukomis, OK

Simmons, Nate W
Claremore Sr HS
Claremore, OK

Simpler, Jennifer M
Dickson HS
Ardmore, OK

Simpson, Lea J
Bishop Kelley HS
Tulsa, OK

Simpson II, Robert D
Agra Schl
Cushing, OK

Simpson, Ryan P
South Intermediate HS
Broken Arrow, OK

Sincalir, Cory D
Coweta HS
Coweta, OK

Singleton, Eric W
Lawton Sr HS
Fort Sill, OK

Sink, James
Jenks HS
Tulsa, OK

Sinnes, Tara C
Stillwater Jr HS
Stillwater, OK

Sinor, Allison Marie
Broken Arrow Sr HS
Broken Arrow, OK

Sisco, Mariya D
Roland Sr HS
Roland, OK

Sisk, Charlotte E
Buffalo Valley Schl
Talihina, OK

Sisson, Kevin
Empire Schl
Comanche, OK

Sissons, Wendi D
Empire Schl
Comanche, OK

Sitzman,
Christopher M
South Intermediate HS
Broken Arrow, OK

Sivley, Roy A
Union Intermediate HS
Broken Arrow, OK

Skaggs, Matthew R
Charles Page HS
Sand Springs, OK

Skaggs, Tonya
Roland Sr HS
Muldrow, OK

Skinner, Matthew E
Durant HS
Durant, OK

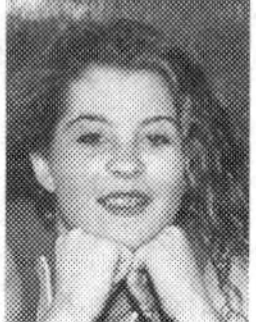
Skinner, Misty D
Chisholm Sr HS
Enid, OK

Slaton, Arthea G
Hugo HS
Hugo, OK

Slaton, Jason
Perry Sr HS
Perry, OK

Slavens, Heather A
Union Sr HS
Tulsa, OK

Sloan, Misti
Shattuck Jr Sr HS
Shattuck, OK

Smedley, Sean
Choctaw HS
Choctaw, OK

Smith, Adrienne
Tahlequah Sr HS
Tahlequah, OK

Smith, Amber
Checotah HS
Checotah, OK

Smith, Avadelle K
Enid Sr HS
Enid, OK

Smith, Barry S
Wilson HS
Wilson, OK

Smith, Ben D
Memorial HS
Tulsa, OK

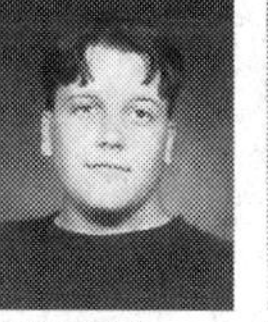
Smith, Brian E
Mustang HS
Yukon, OK

Smith, Chad
Mc Alester HS
Krebs, OK

Smith, Charlotte
Nathan Hale HS
Tulsa, OK

Smith, Christy
Werst Mid HS
Norman, OK

Smith, Crystal R
Valliant HS
Garvin, OK

Smith, Dana L
Coleman Schl
Kenefic, OK

Smith, Elizabeth J
Union Intermediate HS
Tulsa, OK

Smith II, Jack R
Deer Creek HS
Edmond, OK

Smith, Jamie
Savanna HS
Mcalester, OK

Smith, Jamie L
Choctaw HS
Midwest City, OK

Smith, Jeff
Mc Loud HS
Mc Loud, OK

Smith, Jennifer G
Claremore Sr HS
Claremore, OK

Smith, Jeremy
Cheyenne HS
Cheyenne, OK

Smith, Jill
U S Grant HS
Oklahoma City, OK

Smith, Karlyn L
Sallisaw HS
Sallisaw, OK

Smith, Kelly
Edmond North HS
Edmond, OK

Smith, Kizzi N
Boise City HS
Boise City, OK

Smith, Kristina A
Catoosa Sr HS
Tulsa, OK

Smith, Laci
Stillwater Jr HS
Stillwater, OK

Smith, Laura
Byng Sr HS
Francis, OK

Smith, Lori A
North Intemediate HS
Broken Arrow, OK

Smith, Mc Kenna
Sallisaw HS
Sallisaw, OK

Smith, Melissa
Okeene Jr Sr HS
Okeene, OK

Smith, Natasha L
Harrah HS
Luther, OK

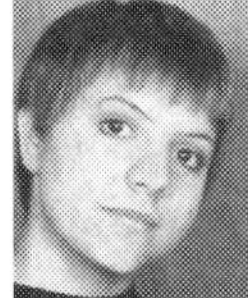
Smith, Rayna L
B T Washington HS
Tulsa, OK

Smith, Sandina M
Allen HS
Allen, OK

Smith, Sara
Elk City HS
Elk City, OK

Smith, Sarah
Midwest City HS
Midwest City, OK

Smith, Sarah
Enid Sr HS
Enid, OK

Smith, Shamica L
Midwest City HS
Tinker Afb, OK

Smith, Shannon M
Norman Sr HS
Norman, OK

Smith, Tabitha
Porter Jr Sr HS
Porter, OK

Smith, Traci L
Liberty HS
Beggs, OK

Smith, Tracy
Westmoore HS
Oklahoma City, OK

Smith, Tracy E
B T Washington HS
Tulsa, OK

Smith, Twana
Douglass HS
Oklahoma City, OK

Smith, Zachary D
Warner HS
Muskogee, OK

Smothers, Jenniffer D
Skiatook HS
Owasso, OK

Snider, Jason
Bixby Sr HS
Bixby, OK

Snoddy, Reginald B
B T Washington HS
Tulsa, OK

Snovel, Shaun P
Chandler HS
Chandler, OK

Snow, Derick E
Webster HS
Tulsa, OK

Snyder, Amelia J
Putnam City West HS
Oklahoma City, OK

Snyder, Samuel C
Muskogee HS
Muskogee, OK

Somers, Rayna L
Pauls Valley HS
Pauls Valley, OK

Somerville, Amanda
Westmoore HS
Moore, OK

Sommers, Amber
Nathan Hale HS
Tulsa, OK

Sonnenberg, Joe L
North Intemediate HS
Broken Arrow, OK

Sparkman, Skye
Guymon Sr HS
Guymon, OK

Sparks, Crystal
Edmond Santa Fe HS
Edmond, OK

Sparks, Melisa
Westmoore HS
Oklahoma City, OK

Sparks, Summer L
Putnam City West HS
Oklahoma City, OK

Speaker, Jess
Mc Loud HS
Mc Loud, OK

Spear, Jack
Hanna Public Schl
Hanna, OK

Spear, Wade O
Central Mid-HS
Norman, OK

Spears, Stephanie J
Union Sr HS
Broken Arrow, OK

Spence, Heather
Meeker HS
Meeker, OK

Spencer, Trisha
Midwest City HS
Midwest City, OK

Spirlock, Lindsay D
Hilldale HS
Muskogee, OK

Spradling, Laura Heath
Bishop Kelley HS
Tulsa, OK

Spray, Timothy
Eisenhower Sr HS
Lawton, OK

Sproul, Scott
Fairview HS
Isabella, OK

Sproul, Stacy L
Fairview HS
Isabella, OK

Spurlin, Stefanie
Edmond North HS
Edmond, OK

Stach, Charri L
Warner HS
Warner, OK

Stafford, Ashley
Edmond North HS
Edmond, OK

Stafford, Cassandra
Wetumka Jr Sr HS
Wetumka, OK

Staley, Mautra L
Ardmore HS
Ardmore, OK

Stallcup, Sherah Z
Stonewall Jr-Sr HS
Stonewall, OK

Stalsby, Rebecca
El Reno Sr HS
El Reno, OK

Stalsby, Sarah
El Reno Sr HS
El Reno, OK

Stanberry, Janette
Bowlegs Schl
Maud, OK

Standefer, Julie D
Putnam City North HS
Oklahoma City, OK

Stangle, Nicole
Owasso Sr HS
Owasso, OK

Stanley, Greg B
Mid-Del Christian Schl
Oklahoma City, OK

Stapleton, Elicia
Oklahoma Union Schl
Wann, OK

Stapp, Kelly D
Shawnee Sr HS
Shawnee, OK

Starr, Micah S
Porum HS
Porum, OK

Starr, Tara
Altus Sr HS
Altus, OK

Stasser, Talia J
Kingfisher HS
Kingfisher, OK

Staton, Candice A
Pocola HS
Pocola, OK

Staton, Misty S
Duke Schl
Mangum, OK

OKLAHOMA

Staton, Wendy Belle
Duke Schl
Mangum, OK

Stauss, David M
Hulbert Jr Sr HS
Hulbert, OK

Steele, Andrea
Westmoore HS
Moore, OK

Steele, Brad
Putnam City North HS
Oklahoma City, OK

Steele, Travis
Catoosa HS
Tulsa, OK

Stein, Edward
Stillwater Sr HS
Stillwater, OK

Steiner, Kevin C
Byng Sr HS
Ada, OK

Stephens, Elane E
Duke Schl
Gould, OK

Stephens, Jennifer M
Del City HS
Oklahoma City, OK

Stephens, Jeremy C
Midwest City HS
Midwest City, OK

Stephens, Jolena
Skiatook HS
Skiatook, OK

Stephens, Sasha
Guymon Sr HS
Guymon, OK

Stephenson, Brooke N
Clinton HS
Clinton, OK

Stephenson, Jason R
Alex Jr Sr HS
Alex, OK

Stepp, Heather D
Yukon Middle HS
Yukon, OK

Sterling, Darbi
Alva HS
Alva, OK

Stevener, Kyle D
El Reno Sr HS
El Reno, OK

Stevens, Ashli
Stigler HS
Stigler, OK

Stevens, Kaci
Frederick HS
Frederick, OK

Stevens, Nechelle F
Midwest City HS
Midwest City, OK

Stewart, Crystal L
Idabel HS
Idabel, OK

Stewart, Emily
Woodward HS
Woodward, OK

Stewart, Joseph R
Cordell Sr HS
Cordell, OK

Stewart, Natalie N
Mustang HS
Yukon, OK

Stewart, Stephanee S
Woodward HS
Woodward, OK

Stilwell, Michelle
Tuttle HS
Tuttle, OK

Stimson, Stephanie N
Claremore Sr HS
Claremore, OK

Stockdale, Amber D
Harrah HS
Harrah, OK

Stocksen, Lee A
Bridge Creek HS
Tuttle, OK

Stockwell, Lori
Victory Christian Schl
Mounds, OK

Stogsdill, Geneva K
Catoosa HS
Catoosa, OK

Stokes, Nathan
Stratford Schl
Stratford, OK

Stone, Ashley N
Memorial HS
Tulsa, OK

Stoner, Kirk A
Central HS
Tulsa, OK

Stoner, Stephanie
Bluejacket Schl
Bluejacket, OK

Storey, Eric B
Northeast HS
Spencer, OK

Storms, Bryan
Chickasha HS
Chickasha, OK

Story, Barbie L
Muldrow HS
Muldrow, OK

Stott, Sarah
Jenks HS
Jenks, OK

Stout, Candi L
Meeker HS
Shawnee, OK

Stout, Cody
Guthrie Sr HS
Guthrie, OK

Stout, Leslie A
Will Rogers HS
Tulsa, OK

Stovall, Peyton
Clinton HS
Clinton, OK

Stover, David J
Metro Christian Acad
Tulsa, OK

Stowers, Jennifer K
Rush Springs HS
Rush Springs, OK

Stracey, Dawn N
Claremore Sr HS
Claremore, OK

Strain, Kylia N
Quinton Jr Sr HS
Quinton, OK

Strange, Jennifer K
Westmoore HS
Oklahoma City, OK

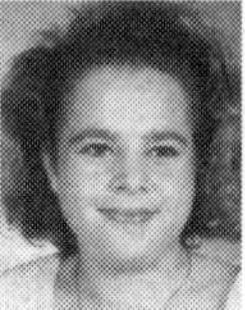
Strange, Tramera L
Savanna HS
Mcalester, OK

Straughn, Jonathan R
Putnam City North HS
Oklahoma City, OK

Strawn, Shannan
Valliant HS
Valliant, OK

Street, Tiffany A
Broken Arrow Sr HS
Broken Arrow, OK

Strickland, Alisa M
Davis HS
Davis, OK

Strickland, Sean C
Heritage Hall Schl
Oklahoma City, OK

Strong, Scott
Oaks Mission Jr Sr HS
Tahlequah, OK

Strope, Mary E
Spiro HS
Warner, OK

Stubbs, Kara R
Durant HS
Durant, OK

Stuckey, Jeff
Wetumka Jr Sr HS
Wetumka, OK

Stuessy, Renee L
Broken Arrow Sr HS
Broken Arrow, OK

Sturch, Erin
Moore HS
Oklahoma City, OK

Sturgeon, Scott
Cordell Sr HS
Cordell, OK

Sturm, Colin D
Moore HS
Moore, OK

Sukow, Jill K
Bartlesville Mid HS
Bartlesville, OK

Sullins, Trisha
Checotah HS
Checotah, OK

Sullivan, Jaime
Midwest City HS
Midwest City, OK

Sullivan, Mitchell A
Will Rogers HS
Tulsa, OK

Surratt, Amy
Moore HS
Moore, OK

Suter, Joy L
Ponca City Sr HS
Kaw, OK

Sutton, Jared J
Seminole Jr Sr HS
Seminole, OK

Suvak, Miranda G
B T Washington HS
Tulsa, OK

Swain, Jessica N
Union Intermediate HS
Tulsa, OK

Swanda, Amy E
Putnam City HS
Oklahoma City, OK

Swanson, Cara F
Stillwater Jr HS
Stillwater, OK

Swanson, Johnnie L
Douglass HS
Midwest City, OK

Swanson, Megan A
Stillwater Sr HS
Stillwater, OK

Swedlund, Stacy M
Macarthur Sr HS
Lawton, OK

Sweeney, Christina R
Latta Sr HS
Ada, OK

Swenson, Sondra L
Jenks HS
Tulsa, OK

Swepston, Shannon
Tahlequah Sr HS
Tahlequah, OK

Swift, Stephannie N
Stilwell HS
Stilwell, OK

Swindell, Dustin
Wellston Schl
Wellston, OK

Tabor, Teddy W
Antlers Sr HS
Antlers, OK

Tac, Singi
Northeast HS
Oklahoma City, OK

Tacker, Justin
Pauls Valley HS
Pauls Valley, OK

Tackett, Sara E
Edmond Santa Fe HS
Edmond, OK

Tadlock, Kelli A
Kiowa Jr-Sr HS
Mcalester, OK

Tafoya, Dugan J
Western Heights Sr HS
Oklahoma City, OK

Takes-Horse, Adam C
Colbert Jr Sr HS
Colbert, OK

Tallent, Bremen
Victory Christian Schl
Sand Springs, OK

Talley, Chevonne L
Westmoore HS
Oklahoma City, OK

Talley, Matthew D
Okeene Jr Sr HS
Okeene, OK

Talley, Natalie
Lawton Sr HS
Lawton, OK

Tanksley, Steven
Bridge Creek HS
Blanchard, OK

Tannehill, Amberlin
Heritage Hall Schl
Oklahoma City, OK

Tanner, Billy K
Okemah HS
Okemah, OK

Tanner, Nic
Westmoore HS
Oklahoma City, OK

Taryole, Valerie
Okmulgee HS
Okmulgee, OK

Tate, Andrea D
Oklahoma
Christian Schl
Yukon, OK

Tate, Jalinda L
Durant HS
Durant, OK

Tate, Mandi S
Alex Jr Sr HS
Ninnekah, OK

Tatum, Rebecca
Midwest City HS
Midwest City, OK

Taylor, Alison
Cascia Hall Prep
School
Tulsa, OK

Taylor, Amanda M
Meeker HS
Meeker, OK

Taylor, Anya A
Union Sr HS
Broken Arrow, OK

Taylor, Bryan J
Southwest
Covenant Schl
Hinton, OK

Taylor, Carie
Eufaula Sr HS
Eufaula, OK

Taylor, Carl D
Spiro HS
Spiro, OK

Taylor, Cristopher B
Edmond Memorial HS
Edmond, OK

Taylor, Destiny L
Spiro HS
Spiro, OK

Taylor, Jennifer
Sweetwater
Public Schl
Sweetwater, OK

Taylor, Jeremy R
Walters HS
Walters, OK

Taylor, Jeri L
Charles Page HS
Sand Springs, OK

Taylor, Jim
Pawhuska HS
Pawhuska, OK

Taylor, Kattie L
Del City HS
Oklahoma City, OK

Taylor, Leah N
Hugo HS
Hugo, OK

Taylor, Loy Dustin
Meeker HS
Meeker, OK

Taylor, Nikole
Ada HS
Ada, OK

Taylor, Robert C
Mustang HS
Yukon, OK

Taylor, Shamika
B T Washington HS
Tulsa, OK

Taylor, Tiffany A
Northeast HS
Oklahoma City, OK

Teagarden,
Kathryn Lynn
Jenks HS
Broken Arrow, OK

Teague, Audrie A
Empire Schl
Duncan, OK

Teague, Brian
Westmoore HS
Oklahoma City, OK

Tedder, Ryan B
Deer Creek HS
Oklahoma City, OK

Temple, Christopher L
Madill HS
Madill, OK

Templin, Jason D
Wakita Schl
Wakita, OK

Teoli, Joseph F
Putnam City North HS
Oklahoma City, OK

Terrell, Jarae M
Lindsay HS
Lindsay, OK

Terrell, Jeffrey
Kingfisher HS
Dover, OK

Terronez, Brandy L
Glenpool HS
Glenpool, OK

Terry, Michelle
Edmond North HS
Edmond, OK

Tessmann, Kimberly
Stroud HS
Blackwell, OK

Tester, Kelly
Southwest
Covenant Schl
El Reno, OK

Thomas, Adam D
Morris HS
Morris, OK

Thomas, Alaina D
Union Intermediate HS
Tulsa, OK

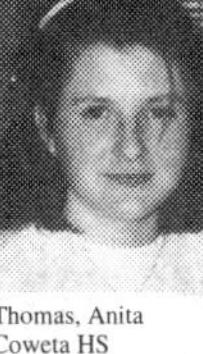
Thomas, Anita
Coweta HS
Coweta, OK

Thomas, Brandi J
Ardmore HS
Springer, OK

Thomas, Christi D
Choctaw HS
Choctaw, OK

Thomas, Dawn M
U S Grant HS
Oklahoma City, OK

Thomas, Dedreck
B T Washington HS
Tulsa, OK

Thomas, Elizabeth H
Mc Alester HS
Mcalester, OK

Thomas, Jason
Millwood HS
Oklahoma City, OK

Thomas, Keiana
Douglass HS
Oklahoma City, OK

Thomas, La Donna M
Bartlesville Sr HS
Bartlesville, OK

Thomas, Lonnie
Liberty HS
Mounds, OK

Thomas, Michael A
Midwest City HS
Midwest City, OK

Thomas, Nicolas
Lawton Christian Schl
Indiahoma, OK

Thomas, Raechel
Clinton HS
Clinton, OK

Thomas, Raven V
Pauls Valley HS
Pauls Valley, OK

Thomas, Robert M
Elgin HS
Lawton, OK

Thomas, Tara D
Midwest City HS
Midwest City, OK

Thomason, Christy M
Warner HS
Warner, OK

Thomason, Russell
Dickson HS
Ardmore, OK

Thomasson, Ashley
Ketchum HS
Disney, OK

Thompson, Beth A
Stround HS
Stroud, OK

Thompson, Bethany
Weatherford HS
Weatherford, OK

Thompson, Brandy
El Reno Sr HS
El Reno, OK

Thompson, Brett A
Mustang HS
Yukon, OK

Thompson, Brian M
Brink Jr HS
Oklahoma City, OK

Thompson, Cris
Cache HS
Cache, OK

Thompson, Crystal D
Western Heights Sr HS
Oklahoma City, OK

Thompson, Crystal L
Preston Schl
Okmulgee, OK

Thompson, Darin S
Del City HS
Del City, OK

Thompson, Elijah B
Wetumka Jr Sr HS
Wetumka, OK

Thompson,
Elisabeth A
South Intermediate HS
Broken Arrow, OK

Thompson, Julie M
B T Washington HS
Tulsa, OK

Thompson, Kristen
Putnam City HS
Oklahoma City, OK

Thompson, Lauren N
Bishop Mcguinness HS
Oklahoma City, OK

Thompson, Rachel
Braman Schl
Braman, OK

Thompson, Sabrina J
Noble HS
Noble, OK

Thompson, Shana
Hollis Jr Sr HS
Hollis, OK

Thompson, Tayla
Putnam City West HS
Bethany, OK

Thompson, Valerie D
Pawnee HS
Pawnee, OK

Thompson, William B
Union Intermediate HS
Tulsa, OK

Thorson, Julie
Temple Chrstn Acad
Bethany, OK

Thrall, Travis L
Boise City HS
Felt, OK

Thrasher, Angel
Central Mid-HS
Norman, OK

Thrasher,
Kathryn Noel
Midwest City HS
Midwest City, OK

Tidmore, Stephanie A
East Central HS
Tulsa, OK

Tidwell, Natalie
Westmoore HS
Oklahoma City, OK

Tiggeman, Shelly M
Stillwater Sr HS
Stillwater, OK

Tignor, Jenni
Rock Creek Jr Sr HS
Bokchito, OK

Tiller, Daniel
Choctaw HS
Choctaw, OK

Tiller, Kelli D
Union Intermediate HS
Broken Arrow, OK

Tiller, Kimberly D
Union Sr HS
Broken Arrow, OK

Timmons, Jedediah
Mc Alester HS
Mcalester, OK

Tindall, Jamie M
Mt St Marys HS
Yukon, OK

Tiner, Amy L
Healdton HS
Wilson, OK

Tiner, Corey D
Healdton HS
Wilson, OK

Tippit, Stephen
Keota Schl
Keota, OK

Tipton, Lindsy
Chandler HS
Chandler, OK

Tipton, Matt
Mc Loud HS
Shawnee, OK

Tipton, Rochelle
Hobart HS
Hobart, OK

Tisdale, Rusti
Midwest City HS
Midwest City, OK

Titsworth, Jeremy R
Okmulgee HS
Okmulgee, OK

Titsworth, Jonathan
Okmulgee HS
Okmulgee, OK

Titsworth, Teresa E
Okmulgee HS
Okmulgee, OK

To, Michael V
Brink Jr HS
Oklahoma City, OK

Tobey, Hayden H
Edmond Memorial HS
Edmond, OK

Tobey, Tanner Howell
Edmond Memorial HS
Edmond, OK

Tobler, April D
Spiro HS
Spiro, OK

Todd, Andrea
Collinsville HS
Collinsville, OK

Todd, Michael A
Putnam City North HS
Oklahoma City, OK

Toews, Lacy R
Cimarron Public Schl
Meno, OK

Toland, Tiffany
Garber Sr HS
Garber, OK

Townley, Peter
Heritage Hall Schl
Oklahoma City, OK

Townsend, Melanie
Altus Sr HS
Altus, OK

Trail, Kara
Lone Grove HS
Springer, OK

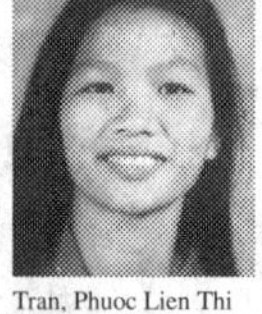
Tran, Phuoc Lien Thi
Webster HS
Tulsa, OK

Tran, Tina C
North Intemediate HS
Broken Arrow, OK

Travis, Latoya L
B T Washington HS
Tulsa, OK

Traweek, Vicky J
Choctaw HS
Choctaw, OK

Traylor, Pertricee
Luther HS
Luther, OK

Treadwell, Natalie
Holdenville HS
Holdenville, OK

Treece, Tracy
Sharon Mutual Jr
Sr HS
Woodward, OK

Tretter, Michelle D
Elgin HS
Elgin, OK

Tribbey, Molly
Sulphur HS
Sulphur, OK

Tripp, Shana
Anadarko HS
Anadarko, OK

Trisciani Jr, William A
Lone Grove HS
Lone Grove, OK

Trout, Michael D
Wagoner Sr HS
Wagoner, OK

Trowbridge, Brandi R
Salina HS
Salina, OK

Trowbridge, Tammy K
Salina HS
Salina, OK

Trujillo, Michael
Edmond North HS
Edmond, OK

Trumbly, Alan
Bridge Creek HS
Blanchard, OK

Trumbly, Kyle
Westmoore HS
Oklahoma City, OK

Tucker, Chet B
Davis HS
Davis, OK

Tucker, Marc
Seiling Schl
Seiling, OK

Tucker, Scott
Antlers Sr HS
Antlers, OK

Tucker, Sydney S
B T Washington HS
Tulsa, OK

Tull, Amy
Yale Jr Sr HS
Jennings, OK

Tull, Brandi D
Newkirk HS
Newkirk, OK

Tune, Jill
Norman Sr HS
Norman, OK

Turk, Heather
Hulbert Jr Sr HS
Tahlequah, OK

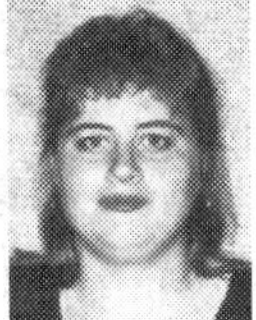
Turner, April J
Choctaw HS
Choctaw, OK

Turner, Eric A
Wilburton Sr HS
Wilburton, OK

Turner, Heather D
Bartlesville Sr HS
Bartlesville, OK

Turner, Jonathan
Oklahoma
Christian Schl
Edmond, OK

Turner, Joshua G
Harrah HS
Harrah, OK

Turney, Bradley K
Charles Page HS
Sand Springs, OK

Tuttle, Trista
Kellyville Sr HS
Kellyville, OK

Tyner, Teddy J
Del City HS
Del City, OK

Tyrrell, Beth M
Putnam City West HS
Oklahoma City, OK

Uekermann, Kristen
Cascia Hall Prep
School
Tulsa, OK

Ulrich, David W
Muldrow HS
Muldrow, OK

Umsted, Leslie M
Caney Jr Sr HS
Caney, OK

Underwood, Candy L
Muskogee HS
Muskogee, OK

Underwood, Stephen
Spiro HS
Spiro, OK

Upshaw, Tommy W
Velma Alma HS
Velma, OK

Urban, Nathan L
Lindsay HS
Lindsay, OK

Vaden, Kati D
Cushing HS
Cushing, OK

Vaile, Valerie
Lone Grove HS
Lone Grove, OK

Vanarsdel, Tiffany D
Edmond Santa Fe HS
Edmond, OK

Van Buskirk,
Melinda M
Lone Grove HS
Ardmore, OK

Vance, Monica L
Turner Schl
Burneyville, OK

Van Cleave, Tera
Mustang HS
Mustang, OK

Vande, Donald
Westmoore HS
Oklahoma City, OK

Van Every, Matthew F
Putnam City North HS
Oklahoma City, OK

Van Gundy, Cynthia
El Reno Sr HS
El Reno, OK

Van Schuyver,
Tiffany A
Byng Sr HS
Ada, OK

Varughese, Christina
Victory Christian Schl
Broken Arrow, OK

Vaughan, Jamie A
Antlers Sr HS
Antlers, OK

Vaughn, Basilio D
Choctaw HS
Choctaw, OK

Vaughn, Erin K
Stillwater Sr HS
Stillwater, OK

Vaughn, Miranda
Hobart HS
Hobart, OK

Vaughn, Nick D
Edmond North HS
Edmond, OK

Vaughn, Shontesa D
Northeast HS
Spencer, OK

Veal, Rebecca A
Central Mid-HS
Norman, OK

Vega, Maryann. C
Stillwater Sr HS
Stillwater, OK

Venema, Amanda R
North Intemediate HS
Broken Arrow, OK

Verville, Timothy D
Putnam City West HS
Oklahoma City, OK

Vick, John W
Star Spencer HS
Spencer, OK

Vidal, Paulina
Putnam City HS
Oklahoma City, OK

Vignal, Deidra L
Sayre HS
Sayre, OK

Villanueva, Enrique
Clinton HS
Clinton, OK

Villines, Tosha
Weatherford HS
Weatherford, OK

Vincent, Brandon R
North Intermediate HS
Broken Arrow, OK

Vinson, Penny
Westmoore HS
Oklahoma City, OK

Vivas, Olivia
Mt St Marys HS
Norman, OK

Vo, Margrette N
Union Sr HS
Tulsa, OK

Voegeli, Jason
Seiling Schl
Seiling, OK

Vogt, Gretchen A
Sequoyah
Claremore HS
Claremore, OK

Vogt, Rachel E
Sequoyah
Claremore HS
Claremore, OK

Vollbrecht, Jessica L
Edmond North HS
Edmond, OK

Vroome, Kyle M
Union Intermediate HS
Tulsa, OK

Waddell, Cassie
Deer Creek-Lamont Jr Sr HS
Lamont, OK

Waddle, Dylan
Westmoore HS
Oklahoma City, OK

Waddle, Mynde
Coweta HS
Coweta, OK

Wade, Brandon S
Ringling HS
Ringling, OK

Wade, Brian T
Empire Schl
Duncan, OK

Wade, Erica N
Muskogee HS
Muskogee, OK

Wade IV, Johnnie M
Webster HS
Tulsa, OK

Wade, Liz
Elk City HS
Elk City, OK

Wade, Neil A
B T Washington HS
Tulsa, OK

Wadley, Krista
Mc Alester HS
Mcalester, OK

Wadley, Michael
Sapulpa Sr HS
Sapulpa, OK

Wadley, Neal D
Edmond Memorial HS
Edmond, OK

Wadsworth, Lesli D
Union Intermediate HS
Tulsa, OK

Wagner, Kristen
Edmond North HS
Edmond, OK

Wagner, Michele R
Stillwater Jr HS
Stillwater, OK

Wagner, Selena M
Moore HS
Moore, OK

Wagner, Tamara A
B T Washington HS
Tulsa, OK

Wagoner, Lacy
Broken Arrow Sr HS
Broken Arrow, OK

Wagoner, Laura R
Madill HS
Madill, OK

Wahpekeche, Rion D
Stillwater Sr HS
Stillwater, OK

Walden, Jon W
Muskogee HS
Muskogee, OK

Waldo, Jennifer L
Stillwater Sr HS
Stillwater, OK

Walker, Casey E
Bartlesville Sr HS
Bartlesville, OK

Walker, Craig T
Del City HS
Del City, OK

Walker, Dustin C
Putnam City North HS
Oklahoma City, OK

Walker, Glen
Welch Jr Sr HS
Welch, OK

Walker, Jack D
Boynton Schl
Boynton, OK

Walker, Jamie
Midwest City HS
Midwest City, OK

Walker, January B
Duncan HS
Duncan, OK

Walker, Jason W
Harrah HS
Harrah, OK

Walker, Jennifer J
Putnam City North HS
Oklahoma City, OK

Walker, Jennifer K
Mc Alester HS
Durant, OK

Walker, Jessie L
Boise City HS
Kenton, OK

Walker, Justin S
Muskogee HS
Muskogee, OK

Walker, Korryn M
Westmoore HS
Oklahoma City, OK

Walker, Mac Kenzie B
Central Jr HS
Lawton, OK

Walker, Stephanie L
Bishop Kelley HS
Tulsa, OK

Walker, Timothy A
Union Sr HS
Tulsa, OK

Walker, Wesley
Stigler HS
Stigler, OK

Wall, Beckie M
Nathan Hale HS
Tulsa, OK

Wall, Bryan
Keota Schl
Keota, OK

Wallace, Ashley N
El Reno Sr HS
El Reno, OK

Wallace, Leia M
Calumet Schl
Calumet, OK

Wallace, Ryan A
Union Intermediate HS
Tulsa, OK

Wallenberg, Grant M
Brink Jr HS
Oklahoma City, OK

Waller, Trisha N
Putnam City HS
Warr Acres, OK

Walls, Andrea
Owasso 9th Grade Ctr
Owasso, OK

Walsh, Stephanie
Mid-Del Christian Schl
Oklahoma City, OK

Walters, Rachel L
Muskogee HS
Muskogee, OK

Walters, Ronnie A
Coleman Schl
Wapanucka, OK

Walton, Jami R
Bishop Kelley HS
Tulsa, OK

Waltrip, Lesli A
Sapulpa Sr HS
Sapulpa, OK

Wamble, Jabari
Oklahoma
Christian Schl
Edmond, OK

Ward, Amber
Duman HS
Duncan, OK

Ward, Bryan D
Yukon Middle HS
Yukon, OK

Ward, Charleta
Douglass HS
Oklahoma City, OK

Ward, Erica
Hennessey HS
Hennessey, OK

Ward, Greg
Hennessey HS
Hennessey, OK

Ward, Jennifer L
Mangum Sr HS
Mangum, OK

Ward, Laura E
Memorial HS
Tulsa, OK

Warden, Becca S
Claremore Sr HS
Claremore, OK

Wardrip, Danielle R
Thackerville HS
Thackerville, OK

Ware, Terry L
Ft Cobb-Broxton HS
Fort Cobb, OK

Warehime, Amanda
Dewey HS
Dewey, OK

Waring, Marin B
Putnam City North HS
Oklahoma City, OK

Warren, Allen
Bernhardt
Tahlequah Sr HS
Tahlequah, OK

Warren, Justin R
Harrah HS
Harrah, OK

Wartluft, Krista M
Broken Arrow Sr HS
Broken Arrow, OK

Washington, Candice R
Okmulgee HS
Okmulgee, OK

Washington, Latrina
Will Rogers HS
Tulsa, OK

Wasserleben, Karrie
Carl Albert HS
Oklahoma City, OK

Waters, Nicholas A
Wynnewood HS
Wynnewood, OK

Watkins, Bryan C
Jenks HS
Tulsa, OK

Watkins, Colin M
Mc Alester HS
Mcalester, OK

Watkins, Donald
Charles Page HS
Sand Springs, OK

Watkins, Keri L
Enid Sr HS
Enid, OK

Watkins, Kristin
Fellowship Baptist Acad
Stilwell, OK

Watson, Emeka D
Will Rogers HS
Tulsa, OK

Watson, Heather A
Bridge Creek HS
Tuttle, OK

Watson, Tyson
Guymon Sr HS
Guymon, OK

Waugh, Charles
Buffalo Jr Sr HS
Buffalo, OK

Waugh III, W Scott
Edmond North HS
Edmond, OK

Weatherly, Erin
Jenks HS
Tulsa, OK

Weathers, Shawnna J
Great Plains Avt-Comanche
Lawton, OK

Weaver, Amanda R
Okay Jr Sr HS
Muskogee, OK

Weaver, David M
Muldrow HS
Uniontown, AR

Weaver, Jennie
Kingfisher HS
Kingfisher, OK

Weaver, Jennifer
White Oak Jr-Sr HS
Vinita, OK

Weaver, Shawna
Del City HS
Del City, OK

Weaver, Shelly E
South Intermediate HS
Broken Arrow, OK

Webb, Andrea D
Broken Arrow Sr HS
Broken Arrow, OK

Webb, Ashley R
Union Sr HS
Tulsa, OK

Webb, Eric
Sulphur HS
Sulphur, OK

Webb, Michelle L
Tahlequah Jr HS
Tahlequah, OK

Webster, Amy
Pryor Jr HS
Pryor, OK

Webster, Cindi M
Putnam City North HS
Oklahoma City, OK

Webster, Kathleen B
Enid Sr HS
Fridley, MN

Wechsler, R Bradley
Edmond Memorial HS
Jones, OK

Weeks, Lacey
Edmond Memorial HS
Edmond, OK

Weese, Dustin L
Wagoner Sr HS
Wagoner, OK

Weese, Jamie L
Union Intermediate HS
Broken Arrow, OK

Wehmeyer, Jamie R
Union Intermediate HS
Tulsa, OK

Weidenmaier, Amber D
Ft Cobb Jr Sr HS
Fort Cobb, OK

Weis, Ben
Edmond North HS
Edmond, OK

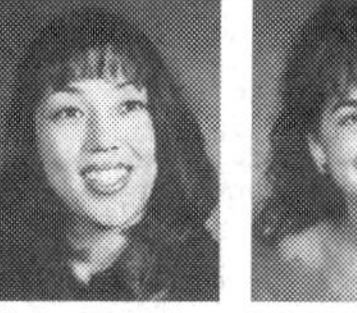
Weissinger, Michelle
Guymon Sr HS
Guymon, OK

Welch, Diana E
Westmoore HS
Oklahoma City, OK

Welch, Joseph S
Ponca City Sr HS
Ponca City, OK

Welch, Martha J
Putnam City North HS
Oklahoma City, OK

Welker, Allison S
Spiro HS
Spiro, OK

Welker III, John D
Putnam City North HS
Oklahoma City, OK

Wellhausen, Misty L
North Intemediate HS
Broken Arrow, OK

Wells, Candice
Putnam City West HS
Bethany, OK

Wells, G Michelle
Washington HS
Washington, OK

Wells, Kristina M
Carl Albert HS
Choctaw, OK

Wells, Leanna M
Dibble Jr Sr HS
Dibble, OK

Wells, Rachel
Yukon Middle HS
Yukon, OK

Wells, Tammy
Salina HS
Salina, OK

Welter, Lisa K
South Intermediate HS
Broken Arrow, OK

Welty, Sarah
Elmore City-Pernell HS
Wynnewood, OK

Wendt, Jennifer
Lone Grove HS
Lone Grove, OK

Wendte, Jeremy
Empire Schl
Duncan, OK

Wermy, Kristopher Kias
Clinton HS
Clinton, OK

Wermy, Maria D
Cache HS
Cache, OK

Wert, Heather
Moore HS
Moore, OK

Wessel, Kristin N
Claremore Sr HS
Claremore, OK

West, Amber N
Putnam City North HS
Oklahoma City, OK

West, Ashlee E
Edmond North HS
Edmond, OK

West, Ryan L
Western Heights Sr HS
Oklahoma City, OK

Westberry, Jill
Moore HS
Moore, OK

Westbrook, Jana L
Putnam City North HS
Oklahoma City, OK

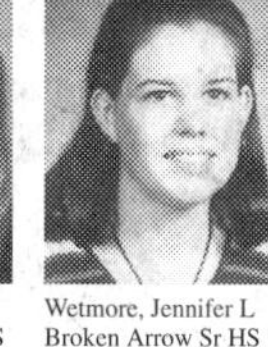

Wetmore, Jennifer L
Broken Arrow Sr HS
Broken Arrow, OK

Wetzler, Kim
North Intemediate HS
Broken Arrow, OK

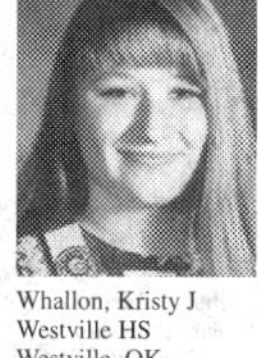
Whallon, Kristy J
Westville HS
Westville, OK

Whatley, La Donna
Dickson HS
Ardmore, OK

Wheat, Angela
Bartlesville Sr HS
Bartlesville, OK

Wheeler, Chris A
Putnam City North HS
Oklahoma City, OK

OKLAHOMA

Wheeler,
Christopher A
Union Sr HS
Tulsa, OK

Wheeler,
Kristopher Ryan
Deer Creek HS
Edmond, OK

Wheeler, Stephanie L
Westmoore HS
Oklahoma City, OK

Wheeler, Yasmin
Alexandra
Cascia Hall Prep
School
Tulsa, OK

Wherley, Jamie
North Intermediate HS
Broken Arrow, OK

Whisenhunt, Amber
Oklahoma Sch Of
Science & Math
Broken Arrow, OK

Whitaker, Leanda S
Colbert Jr Sr HS
Cartwright, OK

Whitaker, Lindsay C
Deer Creek HS
Edmond, OK

White, Brenda
Putnam City HS
Oklahoma City, OK

White, Carl
Hilldale HS
Muskogee, OK

White Jr, Charles L
North Intemediate HS
Broken Arrow, OK

White, Courtney D
Durant HS
Durant, OK

White, Holly M
Muskogee HS
Muskogee, OK

White, Jacob D
U S Grant HS
Oklahoma City, OK

White, Jo D
Oologah HS
Talala, OK

White, Jordana
Okeene Jr Sr HS
Ames, OK

White, Josh M
Mc Loud HS
Mc Loud, OK

White, Kellie
Indianola HS
Mcalester, OK

White, Kimberly
Ft Supply Schl
Fort Supply, OK

White, Kristopher F
Edmond Memorial HS
Edmond, OK

White, Lindsay C
B T Washington HS
Tulsa, OK

White, Tyler R
Byng Sr HS
Ada, OK

Whitefield, April N
Mustang HS
Yukon, OK

Whitehead, Amber M
Muldrow HS
Muldrow, OK

Whitehouse, Marcy M
Jay HS
Jay, OK

Whitfield, Patricia
Vinita HS
Vinita, OK

Whitley, Daniel R
Union Intermediate HS
Broken Arrow, OK

Whitlock, Jimmy
Seminole Jr Sr HS
Seminole, OK

Whitney, Matthew S
Ponca City Sr HS
Ponca City, OK

Whitt, Nicole
Putnam City West HS
Bethany, OK

Whitworth, Jack R
Caney Valley Middle
Sr HS
Ochelata, OK

Whitworth, Kacey
Newkirk HS
Newkirk, OK

Whorton, Sharon
Midwest City HS
Midwest City, OK

Whorton, Tiffany S
Colcord Schl
Colcord, OK

Wiedenmann, Casie R
Yukon Middle HS
Yukon, OK

Wilber, Becky
Cherokee Jr Sr HS
Cherokee, OK

Wilcox, Susan
Mustang HS
Yukon, OK

Wilds, Jared A
El Reno Sr HS
Yukon, OK

Wiley, Alexa K
Memorial HS
Tulsa, OK

Wiley, Kendall R
South Coffeyville Schl
South Coffeyville, OK

Wiley, Lindsay
Union Sr HS
Tulsa, OK

Wilhite, Sara
Tonkawa Jr Sr HS
Tonkawa, OK

Wilkerson, Chris
Mustang HS
Yukon, OK

Wilkerson, Jerry S
Pauls Valley HS
Pauls Valley, OK

Wilkett, Kelley D
Mc Alester HS
Mcalester, OK

Wilkinson, Jennifer
Putnam City North HS
Oklahoma City, OK

Willaims, Tia
Ponca City Mid HS
Ponca City, OK

Willey, Melissa S
Owasso Sr HS
Owasso, OK

Willhite, Janice R
Duncan HS
Duncan, OK

Williams, Aaliyah N
Union Intermediate HS
Tulsa, OK

Williams, Amy B
Empire Schl
Duncan, OK

Williams, Barry
Wapanucka Schl
Atoka, OK

Williams, Brenna K
East Central HS
Tulsa, OK

Williams, Brooke L
Midwest City HS
Midwest City, OK

Williams, Casey L
Indianola HS
Mcalester, OK

Williams, Chassidy M
Star Spencer HS
Oklahoma City, OK

Williams, Christine
Bennington Schl
Bennington, OK

Williams, Crystal
Norman Sr HS
Norman, OK

Williams, Curtis B
Midwest City HS
Midwest City, OK

Williams, Dawn
Wellston Schl
Wellston, OK

Williams, Dixon
Bishop Mcguinness HS
Edmond, OK

Williams, Elizabeth
Dickson HS
Ardmore, OK

Williams, Jennifer
Sterling Jr Sr HS
Lawton, OK

Williams, Jeremy
Grace Fellowship
Christian Sch
Broken Arrow, OK

Williams, Jessica
Oologah-Talala HS
Claremore, OK

Williams, Keetra N
Putnam City HS
Oklahoma City, OK

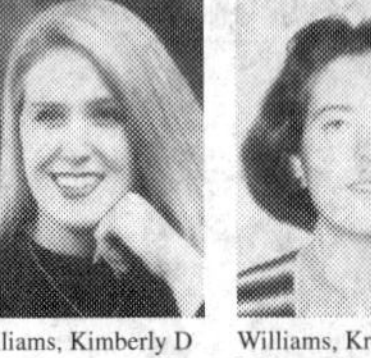

Williams, Kimberly D
Broken Arrow Sr HS
Broken Arrow, OK

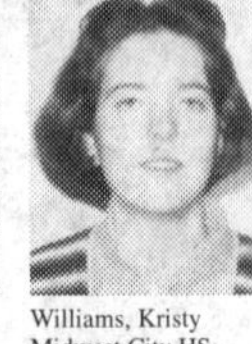

Williams, Kristy
Midwest City HS
Midwest City, OK

Williams, Kylie A
Eisenhower Sr HS
Lawton, OK

Williams, Marie A
Muldrow HS
Muldrow, OK

Williams, Marlene R
John Marshall HS
Oklahoma City, OK

Williams, Mary H
Canton HS
Longdale, OK

Williams, Melika
Capitol Hill HS
Oklahoma City, OK

Williams, Nathan J
John Marshall HS
Oklahoma City, OK

Williams, Pamela
Yarbrough Schl
Goodwell, OK

Williams, Patrick
Douglass HS
Oklahoma City, OK

Williams, Patrick A
Mt St Marys HS
Oklahoma City, OK

Williams, Preston J
Putnam City HS
Warr Acres, OK

Williams, Ross
Hobart HS
Hobart, OK

Williams,
Shaundona C
Jones HS
Jones, OK

Williams, Stacy J
Stillwater Jr HS
Stillwater, OK

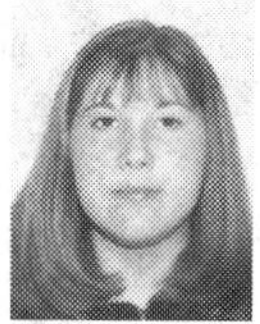
Williams, Stephanie M
Bishop Kelley HS
Tulsa, OK

Williams, Thomas
Douglass HS
Oklahoma City, OK

Williamson, Dana J
Ada HS
Ada, OK

Williamson, Meleia
Choctaw HS
Oklahoma City, OK

Willingham, Stephanie
Union Intermediate HS
Tulsa, OK

Willis, John
Moore HS
Oklahoma City, OK

Willis, Lora E
Wellston Schl
Wellston, OK

Willis, Mikhael L
Marietta HS
Marietta, OK

Williston, Diana R
Idabel HS
Idabel, OK

Willy, Mandye R
Vinita HS
Vinita, OK

Wilsie, Jason D
Edmond North HS
Edmond, OK

Wilson, Brooke
Spiro HS
Spiro, OK

Wilson, Dustin M
Christian
Heritage Acad
Oklahoma City, OK

Wilson, Galen
Perry Sr HS
Perry, OK

Wilson, Ginnifer M
Moore HS
Moore, OK

Wilson, Glenn P
Perry Sr HS
Perry, OK

Wilson, Jake
Jenks HS
Jenks, OK

Wilson, Kelli J
Skiatook HS
Skiatook, OK

Wilson, Madelina
Drumright HS
Drumright, OK

Wilson, Melea
Ninnekah HS
Chickasha, OK

Wilson, Melissa F
Mustang HS
Mustang, OK

Wilson, Michael A
Mc Alester HS
Mcalester, OK

Wilson, Nicholas O
Parker Middle HS
Mcalester, OK

Wilson, Romeo M
Tahlequah Sr HS
Tahlequah, OK

Wilson, Stephanie
Coalgate HS
Coalgate, OK

Wilson, Whitney A
Cushing HS
Cushing, OK

Winburn, Megan H
Metro Christian Acad
Tulsa, OK

Winburn, Paige E
Union Intermediate HS
Tulsa, OK

Winfrey, Keshet
Victory Christian Schl
Tulsa, OK

Wingfield, Christine E
Claremore Sr HS
Claremore, OK

Wininger, Emily
Duncan HS
Duncan, OK

Winkler, Brian
Westmoore HS
Oklahoma City, OK

Winkler, Kimi
West Middle HS
Norman, OK

Winkler, Mike P
West Jr HS
Oklahoma City, OK

Winn, La Keyla
Northwest Classen HS
Oklahoma City, OK

Winn, Shawn H
Bishop Mcguinness HS
Oklahoma City, OK

Winnebeck, Jason P
North Intermediate HS
Broken Arrow, OK

Winsett, Jake
Altus Sr HS
Elmer, OK

Winston, Kimberly D
Edmond Memorial HS
Edmond, OK

Winterhalter Jr, Jerry D
Stillwater Sr HS
Stillwater, OK

Winters, Ashley
Guymon Sr HS
Guymon, OK

Winters, Tyler
Wynnewood HS
Wynnewood, OK

Wipf, Deborah N
Owasso Sr HS
Owasso, OK

Wise, Jessica D
Vinita HS
Vinita, OK

Wiseman, Jefferson C
West Middle HS
Norman, OK

Wiseman, Shvada M
Lawton Sr HS
Fort Sill, OK

Wiseman, Trisha
Midwest City HS
Oklahoma City, OK

Witwer, Amy
South Coffeyville Schl
S Coffeyville, OK

Witzel, Ross A
Putnam City HS
Oklahoma City, OK

Wodraska, Brandon L
Westmoore HS
Oklahoma City, OK

Wofford, Timothy D
Walters HS
Walters, OK

Wolf, Eric
Ponca City Sr HS
Ponca City, OK

Wolf, Sean A
Union Sr HS
Tulsa, OK

Wolowicz, Brian
Edmond North HS
Edmond, OK

Wolter, Heather
Wright Christian Acad
Broken Arrow, OK

Womack, David J
Stillwater Sr HS
Stillwater, OK

Womack, Debbie A
Duncan HS
Duncan, OK

Wonderly, Ryan
Putnam City West HS
Bethany, OK

Wong, Philip D
Putnam City North HS
Oklahoma City, OK

OKLAHOMA

Wood, Derika
Liberty Acad
Shawnee, OK

Wood, Dianne
Stratford Schl
Stratford, OK

Wood, Kelly L
Mt St Mary HS
Oklahoma City, OK

Wood, Olin J
Union Sr HS
Tulsa, OK

Wood, Rhiannon
Moore HS
Moore, OK

Wood, Shannon
Moore HS
Moore, OK

Woodard, Sara A
Mannford HS
Mannford, OK

Woodin, Eric P
Owasso Sr HS
Owasso, OK

Woods, Julie D
Chattanooga Schl
Faxon, OK

Woods, Sandy M
El Reno Sr HS
El Reno, OK

Woods, Whitney E
Duncan HS
Duncan, OK

Woodson, Jessica L
Lawton Christian Schl
Lawton, OK

Woodward, Kristin
Putnam City West HS
Oklahoma City, OK

Woody, Melissa K
Del City HS
Del City, OK

Wooldridge, April B
Yukon Middle HS
Yukon, OK

Woolery, Scott R
Putnam City HS
Warr Acres, OK

Woolever, Rachel S
B T Washington HS
Tulsa, OK

Wooster, Carson R
Edmond North HS
Edmond, OK

Worden, La Donna M
Harrah HS
Harrah, OK

Workman, Elizabeth A
Catoosa HS
Claremore, OK

Workman, Tessa A
Claremore Sr HS
Claremore, OK

Worsham, Lacey
Lone Grove HS
Lone Grove, OK

Wosel, Adreinne
Bartlesville Mid HS
Bartlesville, OK

Wright, Danae A
Putnam City West HS
Oklahoma City, OK

Wright, Elizabeth
Heritage Hall Schl
Oklahoma City, OK

Wright, Jennifer L
Edmond Santa Fe HS
Edmond, OK

Wright, Kristi
Hilldale HS
Muskogee, OK

Wright, Matt
Jenks HS
Tulsa, OK

Wright, Mia I
B T Washington HS
Tulsa, OK

Wright, Natashia D
Mc Alester HS
Mcalester, OK

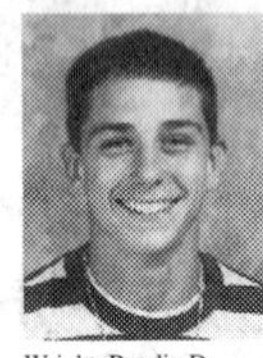
Wright, Randin D
Sapulpa Sr HS
Tulsa, OK

Wright, Robert L
Edmond North HS
Edmond, OK

Wulf, Courtney L
Union Intermediate HS
Broken Arrow, OK

Wyatt, Kelly D
Midwest City HS
Midwest City, OK

Wyckoff, Daniel
Mustang HS
Mustang, OK

Wynn, Michael
Mc Alester HS
Mcalester, OK

Yancey, Melissa S
Bridge Creek HS
Blanchard, OK

Yanda, Anton V
Yukon Middle HS
Yukon, OK

Yarnell, Layna B
Foyil Schl
Claremore, OK

Yeahquo, Elizabeth R
Carnegie HS
Carnegie, OK

Yenter, Krista
Glenpool HS
Glenpool, OK

Yerby, Jamie B
Vanoss Schl
Ada, OK

Yirsa, Steph
Grove HS
Grove, OK

Yoon, Jihye
Del City HS
Del City, OK

York, Jared D
Westmoore HS
Oklahoma City, OK

Young, Jared G
Christian
Heritage Acad
Oklahoma City, OK

Young, Kara
Western Heights Sr HS
Oklahoma City, OK

Young, Kimberly A
Warner HS
Warner, OK

Young, Missy
Comanche HS
Duncan, OK

Young, Tomeka C
Stillwater Sr HS
Stillwater, OK

Youngblood, Stephanie
Broken Arrow Sr HS
Broken Arrow, OK

Zaccarello,
Cassandra N
Sapulpa Sr HS
Sapulpa, OK

Zachariae, Krista
Nathan Hale HS
Tulsa, OK

Zachary, Misty O
Midwest City HS
Midwest City, OK

Zaremba, Elisabeth
South Intermediate HS
Broken Arrow, OK

Zeien, April L
Choctaw HS
Midwest City, OK

Zenner, Robert A
Christian
Heritage Acad
Midwest City, OK

Zickefoose, Sommer
Charles Page HS
Sand Springs, OK

Zimmer, Jeremy M
Union Intermediate HS
Tulsa, OK

Zimmerman, Derek
Marlow HS
Duncan, OK

Zmijski, Robin M
Brink Jr HS
Oklahoma City, OK

Zolbe, Makaria A
Casady Schl
Oklahoma City, OK

Zuhdi, Zack
Heritage Hall Schl
Oklahoma City, OK

Zumwalt, Brandi N
Kellyville Sr HS
Kellyville, OK